Who's Who in American Law

Biographical Titles Currently Published by Marquis Who's Who

Who's Who in America
   Who's Who in America supplements:
      Geographic/Professional Area Index
      Supplement to Who's Who in America
      Who's Who in America Classroom Project Book
Who Was Who in America
   Historical Volume (1607–1896)
   Volume I (1897–1942)
   Volume II (1943–1950)
   Volume III (1951–1960)
   Volume IV (1961–1968)
   Volume V (1969–1973)
   Volume VI (1974–1976)
   Volume VII (1977–1981)
   Volume VIII (1982–1985)
   Index Volume (1607–1985)
Who's Who in the World
Who's Who in the East
Who's Who in the Midwest
Who's Who in the South and Southwest
Who's Who in the West
Who's Who in American Law
Who's Who of American Women
Who's Who of Emerging Leaders in America
Who's Who in Finance and Industry
Index to Who's Who Books
Directory of Medical Specialists

Who's Who in American Law®

5th edition
1987-1988

MARQUIS
Who's Who

Macmillan Directory Division
3002 Glenview Road
Wilmette, Illinois 60091 U.S.A.

Library of Congress Catalog Card Number 77-79896
International Standard Book Number 0-8379-3505-9
Product Code Number 030460

Distributed in Asia by
United Publishers Services Ltd.
Kenkyu-Sha Bldg.
9, Kanda Surugadai 2-Chome
Chiyoda-Ku, Tokyo, Japan

Manufactured in the United States of America

Table of Contents

Preface

The fifth edition of *Who's Who in American Law* provides biographical information on approximately 24,000 lawyers and professionals in law-related areas including, among others, judges, legal educators, law librarians, legal historians, and social scientists.

The biographical sketches include such information as education, vital statistics, career history, awards, publications, memberships, address(es), and more. In addition, each sketch includes the fields of legal practice or interest designated by the biographee. For enhanced reference usefulness, the "Index: Fields of Practice or Interest" enables *Who's Who in American Law* users to access biographees geographically by state within each of these fields. Example fields include judicial administration, antitrust, federal civil litigation, corporate, state civil litigation, taxation, criminal, and approximately forty other fields of law.

The descriptions of fields came from lawyers themselves and represent current perceptions of areas of practice within the legal profession. The list was derived from three main sources, beginning with the specialty categories described by the American Bar Association Standing Committee on Specialization. Further information was supplied by state committees and boards on specialization, outlining the specific specialties recognized or certified within the respective states. These lists reflect the varying degrees of specialty certification from state to state. Finally, an acknowledged expert on specialization in the legal profession provided valuable information and recommendations for a comprehensive list of recognized areas of law.

The resulting list was sent to each biographee, who was asked to select up to three fields that reflected personal practice or interest. Thus, the Index, as well as the sketches, contains multiple entries for most biographees in *Who's Who in American Law*. Individualized fields not encompassed in the list and newly emerging areas with relatively few practitioners are listed by biographee name at the end of the Index under the category "Other."

The Index provides the reference user additional access points to the sketch information beyond biographee name. The user can find legal professionals in specific fields and geographic areas. The multiple listings allow comprehensive coverage of Who's Who names for each area of practice or interest.

As in all Marquis Who's Who biographical volumes, the principle of current reference value determines selection of biographees. Reference interest is based either on position of responsibility or noteworthy achievement. To supplement the efforts of Marquis researchers, and to assure comprehensive coverage of important legal professionals, members of the distinguished Board of Advisors nominated outstanding individuals in their own geographic regions or fields of practice for inclusion in this volume.

In most instances the biographees furnished their own data. They reviewed proofs of the sketches to assure accurate, current information. In some cases where individuals failed to supply information, Marquis staff members compiled the data through independent research. Each sketch composed in this manner is denoted by an asterisk. Brief key information is provided in the sketches of selected individuals who did not submit data.

Marquis Who's Who editors exercise diligent care in preparing each biographical sketch for publication. Despite all precautions, errors do occasionally occur. Users of this directory are asked to report such errors to the publisher so that corrections can be made in a later edition.

Board of Advisors

Marquis Who's Who gratefully acknowledges the following distinguished individuals who have made themselves available for review, evaluation, and general comment with regard to the publication of the fifth edition of *Who's Who in American Law*. The advisors have enhanced the reference value of this edition by the nomination of outstanding individuals for inclusion. However, the Board of Advisors, either collectively or individually, is in no way responsible for the final selection of names appearing in this volume, nor does the Board of Advisors bear responsibility for the accuracy or comprehensiveness of the biographical information or other material contained herein.

Clinton R. Ashford
Senior Partner
Ashford & Wriston
Honolulu, Hawaii

Lewis T. Booker
Hunton & Williams
Richmond, Virginia

Charles N. Brower
Deputy Special Counsellor to the President
Washington, D.C.

John Crump
Executive Director
National Bar Association

Barbara Curran
Associate Executive Director
American Bar Foundation

Joseph A. DeGrandi
Beveridge, DeGrandi & Weilacher
Washington, D.C.

John P. Heinz
Professor of Law and Sociology
Northwestern University
Distinguished Research Fellow
American Bar Foundation

James W. Hewitt
Attorney-at-Law
Lincoln, Nebraska

David L. Hirsch
Vice President and Senior Counsel
NI Industries, Inc.

Joseph H. Johnson, Jr.
Partner
Johnson & Thorington
Birmingham, Alabama

Stanley N. Katz
President
American Council of Learned Societies

Arthur L. Liman
Paul, Weiss, Rifkind, Wharton & Garrison
New York, New York

Terrance Sandalow
Professor
University of Michigan Law School

Forrest L. Tozer
Lord, Bissell & Brook
Chicago, Illinois

George H. Williams
Past Executive Vice President
American Judicature Society

Standards of Admission

Selection of biographees for *Who's Who in American Law* is determined by reference interest. Such reference value is based on either of two factors: (1) incumbency in a defined position of responsibility or (2) attainment of a significant level of achievement.

Admission based on position includes the following examples:

Justices of the U.S. Supreme Court

Judges of the U.S. Court of Appeals

Judges of the U.S. District Court

Attorney General of the United States and other high-ranking federal executive attorneys

Chief counsels of congressional committees

Justices of state and territorial courts of the highest appellate jurisdiction

State and territorial attorneys general

Chief judges of selected county courts, based on population

Deans and professors at leading law schools

General counsels of major corporations and labor unions as defined by quantitative criteria

Officials of the American Bar Association and specialized bar groups

Officials of state and territorial bar associations

Officials of selected county and city bar associations, based on population

Editors of important legal journals

Admission by the factor of significant achievement is based on objective criteria for measuring accomplishments within the legal profession.

Key to Information

❶ WATTS, BENJAMIN GREENE, ❷ lawyer; **❸** b. May 21, 1935; **❹** s. George Oliver and Sarah Jane (Carson) W.; **❺** m. Ellen Louise Spencer, Sept. 12, 1960; **❻** children: John Allen, Lucy Anne. **❼** BS, Northwestern U., 1956; JD, U. Chgo., 1965. **❽** Bar: Ill. 1965, U.S. Supreme Ct. 1980. **❾** Mem. legal dept. Standard Publs. Corp., Chgo., 1965-73, asst. counsel, 1973-81, counsel, 1981-83; ptnr. Watts, Clayborn, Johnson & Miller, Oak Brook, Ill., 1983-85, sr. ptnr., 1985—; lectr. Coll. of DuPage, 1970—. **❿** Author: Legal Aspects of Educational Publishing, 1975, Copyright Legalities, 1986. **⓫** Chmn. Downers Grove (Ill.) chpt. ARC, 1982-83; active DuPage council Boy Scouts Am.; trustee Elmhurst (Ill.) Hist. Mus., 1972—. **⓬** Served to lt. USAF, 1959-61. **⓭** Recipient Outstanding Alumnus award Northwestern U., 1971. **⓮** Mem. ABA, Ill. Bar Assn., Chgo. Bar Assn., Am. Mgmt. Assn., Phi Delta Phi. **⓯** Democrat. **⓰** Lutheran. **⓱** Clubs: Caxton, Tavern (Chgo.). **⓲** Lodge: Masons. **⓳** Avocations: golf, antique collecting. **⓴** General practice, Trademark and copyright, General corporate. **㉑** Home: 543 Farwell Ave Elmhurst IL 60126 **㉒** Office: Watts Clayborn Johnson & Miller 1428 Industrial Ct Oak Brook IL 60521

KEY

- ❶ Name
- ❷ Occupation
- ❸ Vital statistics
- ❹ Parents
- ❺ Marriage
- ❻ Children
- ❼ Education
- ❽ Certifications
- ❾ Career
- ❿ Writings and creative works
- ⓫ Civic and political activities
- ⓬ Military record
- ⓭ Awards and fellowships
- ⓮ Professional and association memberships
- ⓯ Political affiliation
- ⓰ Religion
- ⓱ Clubs
- ⓲ Lodges
- ⓳ Avocations
- ⓴ Fields of legal practice or interest
- ㉑ Home address
- ㉒ Office address

Table of Abbreviations

The following abbreviations and symbols are frequently used in this book.

*An asterisk following a sketch indicates that it was researched by the Marquis Who's Who editorial staff and has not been verified by the biographee.

AA, A.A. Associate in Arts
AAAL American Academy of Arts and Letters
AAAS American Association for the Advancement of Science
AAHPER Alliance for Health, Physical Education and Recreation
AAU Amateur Athletic Union
AAUP American Association of University Professors
AAUW American Association of University Women
AB, A.B. Arts, Bachelor of
AB Alberta
ABA American Bar Association
ABC American Broadcasting Company
AC Air Corps
acad. academy, academic
acct. accountant
acctg. accounting
ACDA Arms Control and Disarmament Agency
ACLU American Civil Liberties Union
ACP American College of Physicians
ACS American College of Surgeons
ADA American Dental Association
a.d.c. aide–de–camp
adj. adjunct, adjutant
adj. gen. adjutant general
adm. admiral
adminstr. administrator
adminstrn. administration
adminstrv. administrative
ADP Automatic Data Processing
adv. advocate, advisory
advt. advertising
AE, A.E. Agricultural Engineer
A.E. and P. Ambassador Extraordinary and Plenipotentiary
AEC Atomic Energy Commission
aero. aeronautical, aeronautic
aerodyn. aerodynamic
AFB Air Force Base
AFL–CIO American Federation of Labor and Congress of Industrial Organizations
AFTRA American Federation of TV and Radio Artists
agr. agriculture
agrl. agricultural
agt. agent
AGVA American Guild of Variety Artists
agy. agency
A&I Agricultural and Industrial
AIA American Institute of Architects

AIAA American Institute of Aeronautics and Astronautics
AID Agency for International Development
AIEE American Institute of Electrical Engineers
AIM American Institute of Management
AIME American Institute of Mining, Metallurgy, and Petroleum Engineers
AK Alaska
AL Alabama
ALA American Library Association
Ala. Alabama
alt. alternate
Alta. Alberta
A&M Agricultural and Mechanical
AM, A.M. Arts, Master of
Am. American, America
AMA American Medical Association
A.M.E. African Methodist Episcopal
Amtrak National Railroad Passenger Corporation
AMVETS American Veterans of World War II, Korea, Vietnam
anat. anatomical
ann. annual
ANTA American National Theatre and Academy
anthrop. anthropological
AP Associated Press
APO Army Post Office
apptd. appointed
Apr. April
apt. apartment
AR Arkansas
ARC American Red Cross
archeol. archeological
archtl. architectural
Ariz. Arizona
Ark. Arkansas
ArtsD, ArtsD. Arts, Doctor of
arty. artillery
AS American Samoa
AS Associate in Science
ASCAP American Society of Composers, Authors and Publishers
ASCE American Society of Civil Engineers
ASHRAE American Society of Heating, Refrigeration, and Air Conditioning Engineers
ASME American Society of Mechanical Engineers
assn. association
assoc. associate
asst. assistant
ASTM American Society for Testing and Materials
astron. astronomical
astrophys. astrophysical
ATSC Air Technical Service Command

AT&T American Telephone & Telegraph Company
atty. attorney
Aug. August
AUS Army of the United States
aux. auxiliary
Ave. Avenue
AVMA American Veterinary Medical Association
AZ Arizona

B. Bachelor
b. born
BA, B.A. Bachelor of Arts
BAgr, B.Agr. Bachelor of Agriculture
Balt. Baltimore
Bapt. Baptist
BArch, B.Arch. Bachelor of Architecture
BAS, B.A.S. Bachelor of Agricultural Science
BBA, B.B.A. Bachelor of Business Administration
BBC British Broadcasting Corporation
BC, B.C. British Columbia
BCE, B.C.E. Bachelor of Civil Engineering
BChir, B.Chir. Bachelor of Surgery
BCL, B.C.L. Bachelor of Civil Law
BCS, B.C.S. Bachelor of Commercial Science
BD, B.D. Bachelor of Divinity
bd. board
BE, B.E. Bachelor of Education
BEE, B.E.E. Bachelor of Electrical Engineering
BFA, B.F.A. Bachelor of Fine Arts
bibl. biblical
bibliog. bibliographical
biog. biographical
biol. biological
BJ, B.J. Bachelor of Journalism
Bklyn. Brooklyn
BL, B.L. Bachelor of Letters
bldg. building
BLS, B.L.S. Bachelor of Library Science
Blvd. Boulevard
bn. battalion
B.&O.R.R. Baltimore & Ohio Railroad
bot. botanical
BPE, B.P.E. Bachelor of Physical Education
BPhil, B.Phil. Bachelor of Philosophy
br. branch
BRE, B.R.E. Bachelor of Religious Education
brig. gen. brigadier general
Brit. British, Brittanica
Bros. Brothers
BS, B.S. Bachelor of Science
BSA, B.S.A. Bachelor of Agricultural Science
BSD, B.S.D. Bachelor of Didactic Science

BST, B.S.T. Bachelor of Sacred Theology
BTh, B.Th. Bachelor of Theology
bull. bulletin
bur. bureau
bus. business
B.W.I. British West Indies

CA California
CAA Civil Aeronautics Administration
CAB Civil Aeronautics Board
Calif. California
C.Am. Central America
Can. Canada, Canadian
CAP Civil Air Patrol
capt. captain
CARE Cooperative American Relief
  Everywhere
Cath. Catholic
cav. cavalry
CBC Canadian Broadcasting Company
CBI China, Burma, India Theatre of
  Operations
CBS Columbia Broadcasting System
CCC Commodity Credit Corporation
CCNY City College of New York
CCU Cardiac Care Unit
CD Civil Defense
CE, C.E. Corps of Engineers, Civil Engineer
cen. central
CENTO Central Treaty Organization
CERN European Organization of
  Nuclear Research
cert. certificate, certification, certified
CETA Comprehensive Employment
  Training Act
CFL Canadian Football League
ch. church
ChD, Ch.D. Doctor of Chemistry
chem. chemical
ChemE, Chem.E. Chemical Engineer
Chgo. Chicago
chirurg. chirurgical
chmn. chairman
chpt. chapter
CIA Central Intelligence Agency
CIC Counter Intelligence Corps
Cin. Cincinnati
cir. circuit
Cleve. Cleveland
climatol. climatological
clin. clinical
clk. clerk
C.L.U. Chartered Life Underwriter
CM, C.M. Master in Surgery
CM Northern Mariana Islands
C.&N.W.Ry. Chicago & North Western
  Railway
CO Colorado
Co. Company
COF Catholic Order of Foresters
C. of C. Chamber of Commerce
col. colonel

coll. college
Colo. Colorado
com. committee
comd. commanded
comdg. commanding
comdr. commander
comdt. commandant
commd. commissioned
comml. commercial
commn. commission
commr. commissioner
condr. conductor
Conf. Conference
Congl. Congregational, Congressional
Conglist. Congregationalist
Conn. Connecticut
cons. consultant, consulting
consol. consolidated
constl. constitutional
constn. constitution
constrn. construction
contbd. contributed
contbg. contributing
contbn. contribution
contbr. contributor
Conv. Convention
coop. cooperative
CORDS Civil Operations and
  Revolutionary Development Support
CORE Congress of Racial Equality
corp. corporation, corporate
corr. correspondent, corresponding,
  correspondence
C.&O.Ry. Chesapeake & Ohio Railway
CPA, C.P.A. Certified Public Accountant
C.P.C.U. Chartered Property and
  Casualty Underwriter
CPH, C.P.H. Certificate of Public Health
cpl. corporal
C.P.R. Cardio-Pulmonary Resuscitation
C.P.Ry. Canadian Pacific Railway
C.S. Christian Science
CSB, C.S.B. Bachelor of Christian Science
C.S.C. Civil Service Commission
CSD, C.S.D. Doctor of Christian Science
CT Connecticut
ct. court
ctr. center
CWS Chemical Warfare Service
C.Z. Canal Zone

D. Doctor
d. daughter
DAgr, D.Agr. Doctor of Agriculture
DAR Daughters of the American
  Revolution
dau. daughter
DAV Disabled American Veterans
DC, D.C. District of Columbia
DCL, D.C.L. Doctor of Civil Law
DCS, D.C.S. Doctor of Commercial Science
DD, D.D. Doctor of Divinity

DDS, D.D.S. Doctor of Dental Surgery
DE Delaware
Dec. December
dec. deceased
def. defense
Del. Delaware
del. delegate, delegation
Dem. Democrat, Democratic
DEng, D.Eng. Doctor of Engineering
denom. denomination, denominational
dep. deputy
dept. department
dermatol. dermatological
desc. descendant
devel. development, developmental
DFA, D.F.A. Doctor of Fine Arts
D.F.C. Distinguished Flying Cross
DHL, D.H.L. Doctor of Hebrew Literature
dir. director
dist. district
distbg. distributing
distbn. distribution
distbr. distributor
disting. distinguished
div. division, divinity, divorce
DLitt, D.Litt. Doctor of Literature
DMD, D.M.D. Doctor of Medical Dentistry
DMS, D.M.S. Doctor of Medical Science
DO, D.O. Doctor of Osteopathy
DPH, D.P.H. Diploma in Public Health
DPhil, D.Phil. Doctor of Philosophy
D.R. Daughters of the Revolution
Dr. Drive, Doctor
DRE, D.R.E. Doctor of Religious Education
DrPH, Dr.P.H. Doctor of Public Health,
  Doctor of Public Hygiene
D.S.C. Distinguished Service Cross
DSc, D.Sc. Doctor of Science
D.S.M. Distinguished Service Medal
DST, D.S.T. Doctor of Sacred Theology
DTM, D.T.M. Doctor of Tropical Medicine
DVM, D.V.M. Doctor of Veterinary
  Medicine
DVS, D.V.S. Doctor of Veterinary Surgery

E. East
ea. eastern
E. and P. Extraordinary and Plenipotentiary
Eccles. Ecclesiastical
ecol. ecological
econ. economic
ECOSOC Economic and Social Council
  (of the UN)
ED, E.D. Doctor of Engineering
ed. educated
EdB, Ed.B. Bachelor of Education
EdD, Ed.D. Doctor of Education
edit. edition
EdM, Ed.M. Master of Education
edn. education
ednl. educational

EDP Electronic Data Processing
EdS, Ed.S. Specialist in Education
EE, E.E. Electrical Engineer
E.E. and M.P. Envoy Extraordinary and Minister Plenipotentiary
EEC European Economic Community
EEG Electroencephalogram
EEO Equal Employment Opportunity
EEOC Equal Employment Opportunity Commission
E.Ger. German Democratic Republic
EKG Electrocardiogram
elec. electrical
electrochem. electrochemical
electrophys. electrophysical
elem. elementary
EM, E.M. Engineer of Mines
ency. encyclopedia
Eng. England
engr. engineer
engring. engineering
entomol. entomological
environ. environmental
EPA Environmental Protection Agency
epidemiol. epidemiological
Episc. Episcopalian
ERA Equal Rights Amendment
ERDA Energy Research and Development Administration
ESEA Elementary and Secondary Education Act
ESL English as Second Language
ESSA Environmental Science Services Administration
ethnol. ethnological
ETO European Theatre of Operations
Evang. Evangelical
exam. examination, examining
exec. executive
exhbn. exhibition
expdn. expedition
expn. exposition
expt. experiment
exptl. experimental

F.A. Field Artillery
FAA Federal Aviation Administration
FAO Food and Agriculture Organization (of the UN)
FBI Federal Bureau of Investigation
FCA Farm Credit Administration
FCC Federal Communications Commission
FCDA Federal Civil Defense Administration
FDA Food and Drug Administration
FDIA Federal Deposit Insurance Administration
FDIC Federal Deposit Insurance Corporation
FE, F.E. Forest Engineer
FEA Federal Energy Administration

Feb. February
fed. federal
fedn. federation
FERC Federal Energy Regulatory Commission
fgn. foreign
FHA Federal Housing Administration
fin. financial, finance
FL Florida
Fla. Florida
FMC Federal Maritime Commission
FOA Foreign Operations Administration
found. foundation
FPC Federal Power Commission
FPO Fleet Post Office
frat. fraternity
FRS Federal Reserve System
FSA Federal Security Agency
Ft. Fort
FTC Federal Trade Commission

G-1 (or other number) Division of General Staff
GA, Ga. Georgia
GAO General Accounting Office
gastroent. gastroenterological
GATT General Agreement of Tariff and Trades
gen. general
geneal. genealogical
geod. geodetic
geog. geographic, geographical
geol. geological
geophys. geophysical
gerontol. gerontological
G.H.Q. General Headquarters
G.N. Ry. Great Northern Railway
gov. governor
govt. government
govtl. governmental
GPO Government Printing Office
grad. graduate, graduated
GSA General Services Administration
Gt. Great
GU Guam
gynecol. gynecological

hdqrs. headquarters
HEW Department of Health, Education and Welfare
HHD, H.H.D. Doctor of Humanities
HHFA Housing and Home Finance Agency
HHS Department of Health and Human Services
HI Hawaii
hist. historical, historic
HM, H.M. Master of Humanics
homeo. homeopathic
hon. honorary, honorable
Ho. of Dels. House of Delegates
Ho. of Reps. House of Representatives

hort. horticultural
hosp. hospital
HUD Department of Housing and Urban Development
Hwy. Highway
hydrog. hydrographic

IA Iowa
IAEA International Atomic Energy Agency
IBM International Business Machines Corporation
IBRD International Bank for Reconstruction and Development
ICA International Cooperation Administration
ICC Interstate Commerce Commission
ICU Intensive Care Unit
ID Idaho
IEEE Institute of Electrical and Electronics Engineers
IFC International Finance Corporation
IGY International Geophysical Year
IL Illinois
Ill. Illinois
illus. illustrated
ILO International Labor Organization
IMF International Monetary Fund
IN Indiana
Inc. Incorporated
Ind. Indiana
ind. independent
Indpls. Indianapolis
indsl. industrial
inf. infantry
info. information
ins. insurance
insp. inspector
insp. gen. inspector general
inst. institute
instl. institutional
instn. institution
instr. instructor
instrn. instruction
intern. international
intro. introduction
IRE Institute of Radio Engineers
IRS Internal Revenue Service
ITT International Telephone & Telegraph Corporation

JAG Judge Advocate General
JAGC Judge Advocate General Corps
Jan. January
Jaycees Junior Chamber of Commerce
JB, J.B. Jurum Baccalaureus
JCB, J.C.B. Juris Canoni Baccalaureus
JCD, J.C.D. Juris Canonici Doctor, Juris Civilis Doctor
JCL, J.C.L. Juris Canonici Licentiatus
JD, J.D. Juris Doctor
jg. junior grade

jour. journal
jr. junior
JSD, J.S.D. Juris Scientiae Doctor
JUD, J.U.D. Juris Utriusque Doctor
jud. judicial

Kans. Kansas
K.C. Knights of Columbus
K.P. Knights of Pythias
KS Kansas
K.T. Knight Templar
KY, Ky. Kentucky

LA, La. Louisiana
lab. laboratory
lang. language
laryngol. laryngological
LB Labrador
lectr. lecturer
legis. legislation, legislative
LHD, L.H.D. Doctor of Humane Letters
L.I. Long Island
lic. licensed, license
L.I.R.R. Long Island Railroad
lit. literary, literature
LittB, Litt.B. Bachelor of Letters
LittD, Litt.D. Doctor of Letters
LLB, LL.B. Bachelor of Laws
LLD, LL.D. Doctor of Laws
LLM, LL.M. Master of Laws
Ln. Lane
L.&N.R.R. Louisville & Nashville Railroad
LS, L.S. Library Science (in degree)
lt. lieutenant
Ltd. Limited
Luth. Lutheran
LWV League of Women Voters

M. Master
m. married
MA, M.A. Master of Arts
MA Massachusetts
mag. magazine
MAgr, M.Agr. Master of Agriculture
maj. major
Man. Manitoba
Mar. March
MArch, M.Arch. Master in Architecture
Mass. Massachusetts
math. mathematics, mathematical
MATS Military Air Transport Service
MB, M.B. Bachelor of Medicine
MB Manitoba
MBA, M.B.A. Master of Business
Administration
MBS Mutual Broadcasting System
M.C. Medical Corps
MCE, M.C.E. Master of Civil Engineering
mcht. merchant
mcpl. municipal
MCS, M.C.S. Master of Commercial Science
MD, M.D. Doctor of Medicine

MD, Md. Maryland
MDip, M.Dip. Master in Diplomacy
mdse. merchandise
MDV, M.D.V. Doctor of Veterinary Medicine
ME, M.E. Mechanical Engineer
ME Maine
M.E.Ch. Methodist Episcopal Church
mech. mechanical
MEd, M.Ed. Master of Education
med. medical
MEE, M.E.E. Master of Electrical
Engineering
mem. member
meml. memorial
merc. mercantile
met. metropolitan
metall. metallurgical
MetE, Met.E. Metallurgical Engineer
meteorol. meteorological
Meth. Methodist
Mex. Mexico
MF, M.F. Master of Forestry
MFA, M.F.A. Master of Fine Arts
mfg. manufacturing
mfr. manufacturer
mgmt. management
mgr. manager
MHA, M.H.A. Master of Hospital
Administration
M.I. Military Intelligence
MI Michigan
Mich. Michigan
micros. microscopic, microscopical
mid. middle
mil. military
Milw. Milwaukee
mineral. mineralogical
Minn. Minnesota
Miss. Mississippi
MIT Massachusetts Institute of
Technology
mktg. marketing
ML, M.L. Master of Laws
MLA Modern Language Association
M.L.D. Magister Legnum Diplomatic
MLitt, M.Litt. Master of Literature
MLS, M.L.S. Master of Library Science
MME, M.M.E. Master of Mechanical
Engineering
MN Minnesota
mng. managing
MO, Mo. Missouri
moblzn. mobilization
Mont. Montana
M.P. Member of Parliament
MPE, M.P.E. Master of Physical Education
MPH, M.P.H. Master of Public Health
MPhil, M.Phil. Master of Philosophy
MPL, M.P.L. Master of Patent Law
Mpls. Minneapolis
MRE, M.R.E. Master of Religious Education

MS, M.S. Master of Science
MS, Ms. Mississippi
MSc, M.Sc. Master of Science
MSF, M.S.F. Master of Science of Forestry
MST, M.S.T. Master of Sacred Theology
MSW, M.S.W. Master of Social Work
MT Montana
Mt. Mount
MTO Mediterranean Theatre of
Operations
mus. museum, musical
MusB, Mus.B. Bachelor of Music
MusD, Mus.D. Doctor of Music
MusM, Mus.M. Master of Music
mut. mutual
mycol. mycological

N. North
NAACP National Association for the
Advancement of Colored People
NACA National Advisory Committee for
Aeronautics
NAD National Academy of Design
N.Am. North America
NAM National Association of Manufacturers
NAPA National Association of
Performing Artists
NAREB National Association of Real
Estate Boards
NARS National Archives and Record
Service
NASA National Aeronautics and Space
Administration
nat. national
NATO North Atlantic Treaty Organization
NATOUSA North African Theatre of
Operations
nav. navigation
NB, N.B. New Brunswick
NBC National Broadcasting Company
NC, N.C. North Carolina
NCCJ National Conference of Christians
and Jews
ND, N.D. North Dakota
NDEA National Defense Education Act
NE Nebraska
NE Northeast
NEA National Education Association
Nebr. Nebraska
NEH National Endowment for Humanities
neurol. neurological
Nev. Nevada
NF Newfoundland
NFL National Football League
Nfld. Newfoundland
NG National Guard
NH, N.H. New Hampshire
NHL National Hockey League
NIH National Institutes of Health
NIMH National Institute of Mental Health
NJ, N.J. New Jersey
NLRB National Labor Relations Board

NM New Mexico
N. Mex. New Mexico
No. Northern
NOAA National Oceanographic and Atmospheric Administration
NORAD North America Air Defense
Nov. November
NOW National Organization for Women
N.P.Ry. Northern Pacific Railway
nr. near
NRC National Research Council
NS, N.S. Nova Scotia
NSC National Security Council
NSF National Science Foundation
N.T. New Testament
NT Northwest Territories
numis. numismatic
NV Nevada
NW Northwest
N.W.T. Northwest Territories
NY, N.Y. New York
N.Y.C. New York City
NYU New York University
N.Z. New Zealand

OAS Organization of American States
ob–gyn obstetrics–gynecology
obs. observatory
obstet. obstetrical
Oct. October
OD, O.D. Doctor of Optometry
OECD Organization of European Cooperation and Development
OEEC Organization of European Economic Cooperation
OEO Office of Economic Opportunity
ofcl. official
OH Ohio
OK Oklahoma
Okla. Oklahoma
ON Ontario
Ont. Ontario
ophthal. ophthalmological
ops. operations
OR Oregon
orch. orchestra
Oreg. Oregon
orgn. organization
ornithol. ornithological
OSHA Occupational Safety and Health Administration
OSRD Office of Scientific Research and Development
OSS Office of Strategic Services
csteo. osteopathic
otol. otological
otolaryn. otolaryngological

PA, Pa. Pennsylvania
P.A. Professional Association
paleontol. paleontological
path. pathological

P.C. Professional Corporation
PE Prince Edward Island
P.E.I. Prince Edward Island (text only)
PEN Poets, Playwrights, Editors, Essayists and Novelists (international association)
penol. penological
P.E.O. women's organization (full name not disclosed)
pfc. private first class
PHA Public Housing Administration
pharm. pharmaceutical
PharmD, Pharm.D. Doctor of Pharmacy
PharmM, Pharm.M. Master of Pharmacy
PhB, Ph.B. Bachelor of Philosophy
PhD, Ph.D. Doctor of Philosophy
PhM, Ph.M. Master of Philosophy
Phila. Philadelphia
philharm. philharmonic
philol. philological
philos. philosophical
photog. photographic
phys. physical
physiol. physiological
Pitts. Pittsburgh
Pkwy. Parkway
Pl. Place
P.&L.E.R.R. Pittsburgh & Lake Erie Railroad
P.O. Post Office
PO Box Post Office Box
polit. political
poly. polytechnic, polytechnical
PQ Province of Quebec
PR, P.R. Puerto Rico
prep. preparatory
pres. president
Presbyn. Presbyterian
presdl. presidential
prin. principal
proc. proceedings
prod. produced (play production)
prodn. production
prof. professor
profl. professional
prog. progressive
propr. proprietor
pros. atty. prosecuting attorney
pro tem pro tempore
PSRO Professional Services Review Organization
psychiat. psychiatric
psychol. psychological
PTA Parent–Teachers Association
ptnr. partner
PTO Pacific Theatre of Operations, Parent Teacher Organization
pub. publisher, publishing, published
pub. public
publ. publication
pvt. private

quar. quarterly

qm. quartermaster
Q.M.C. Quartermaster Corps
Que. Quebec

radiol. radiological
RAF Royal Air Force
RCA Radio Corporation of America
RCAF Royal Canadian Air Force
RD Rural Delivery
Rd. Road
REA Rural Electrification Administration
rec. recording
ref. reformed
regt. regiment
regtl. regimental
rehab. rehabilitation
Rep. Republican
rep. representative
Res. Reserve
ret. retired
rev. review, revised
RFC Reconstruction Finance Corporation
RFD Rural Free Delivery
rhinol. rhinological
RI, R.I. Rhode Island
RN, R.N. Registered Nurse
roentgenol. roentgenological
ROTC Reserve Officers Training Corps
R.R. Railroad
Ry. Railway

S. South
s. son
SAC Strategic Air Command
SALT Strategic Arms Limitation Talks
S.Am. South America
san. sanitary
SAR Sons of the American Revolution
Sask. Saskatchewan
savs. savings
SB, S.B. Bachelor of Science
SBA Small Business Administration
SC, S.C. South Carolina
SCAP Supreme Command Allies Pacific
ScB, Sc.B. Bachelor of Science
SCD, S.C.D. Doctor of Commercial Science
ScD, Sc.D. Doctor of Science
sch. school
sci. science, scientific
SCLC Southern Christian Leadership Conference
SCV Sons of Confederate Veterans
SD, S.D. South Dakota
SE Southeast
SEATO Southeast Asia Treaty Organization
SEC Securities and Exchange Commission
sec. secretary
sect. section
seismol. seismological

sem. seminary
Sept. September
s.g. senior grade
sgt. sergeant
SHAEF Supreme Headquarters Allied Expeditionary Forces
SHAPE Supreme Headquarters Allied Powers in Europe
S.I. Staten Island
S.J. Society of Jesus (Jesuit)
SJD Scientiae Juridicae Doctor
SK Saskatchewan
SM, S.M. Master of Science
So. Southern
soc. society
sociol. sociological
S.P. Co. Southern Pacific Company
spl. special
splty. specialty
Sq. Square
S.R. Sons of the Revolution
sr. senior
SS Steamship
SSS Selective Service System
St. Saint, Street
sta. station
stats. statistics
statis. statistical
STB, S.T.B. Bachelor of Sacred Theology
stblzn. stabilization
STD, STD Doctor of Sacred Theology
subs. subsidiary
SUNY State University of New York
supr. supervisor
supt. superintendent
surg. surgical
SW Southwest

TAPPI Technical Association of the Pulp and Paper Industry
Tb Tuberculosis
tchr. teacher
tech. technical, technology
technol. technological
Tel.&Tel. Telephone & Telegraph
temp. temporary
Tenn. Tennessee
Ter. Territory
Terr. Terrace
Tex. Texas
ThD, Th.D. Doctor of Theology
theol. theological
ThM, Th.M. Master of Theology
TN Tennessee
tng. training
topog. topographical
trans. transaction, transferred
transl. translation, translated
transp. transportation
treas. treasurer
TT Trust Territory

TV television
TVA Tennessee Valley Authority
twp. township
TX Texas
typog. typographical

U. University
UAW United Auto Workers
UCLA University of California at Los Angeles
UDC United Daughters of the Confederacy
U.K. United Kingdom
UN United Nations
UNESCO United Nations Educational, Scientific and Cultural Organization
UNICEF United Nations International Children's Emergency Fund
univ. university
UNRRA United Nations Relief and Rehabilitation Administration
UPI United Press International
U.P.R.R. United Pacific Railroad
urol. urological
U.S. United States
U.S.A. United States of America
USAAF United States Army Air Force
USAF United States Air Force
USAFR United States Air Force Reserve
USAR United States Army Reserve
USCG United States Coast Guard
USCGR United States Coast Guard Reserve
USES United States Employment Service
USIA United States Information Agency
USMC United States Marine Corps
USMCR United States Marine Corps Reserve
USN United States Navy
USNG United States National Guard
USNR United States Naval Reserve
USO United Service Organizations
USPHS United States Public Health Service
USS United States Ship
USSR Union of the Soviet Socialist Republics
USV United States Volunteers
UT Utah

VA Veterans' Administration
VA, Va. Virginia
vet. veteran, veterinary
VFW Veterans of Foreign Wars
VI, V.I. Virgin Islands
vice pres. vice president
vis. visiting
VISTA Volunteers in Service to America
VITA Volunteers in Technical Service
vocat. vocational
vol. volunteer, volume
v.p. vice president

vs. versus
VT, Vt. Vermont

W. West
WA Washington (state)
WAC Women's Army Corps
Wash. Washington (state)
WAVES Women's Reserve, US Naval Reserve
WCTU Women's Christian Temperance Union
we. western
W.Ger. Germany, Federal Republic of
WHO World Health Organization
WI Wisconsin
W.I. West Indies
Wis. Wisconsin
WSB Wage Stabilization Board
WV West Virginia
W.Va. West Virginia
WY Wyoming
Wyo. Wyoming

YK Yukon Territory
YMCA Young Men's Christian Association
YMHA Young Men's Hebrew Association
YM & YWHA Young Men's and Young Women's Hebrew Association
yr. year
YT, Y.T. Yukon Territory
YWCA Young Women's Christian Association

zool. zoological

Alphabetical Practices

Names are arranged alphabetically according to the surnames, and under identical surnames according to the first given name. If both surname and first given name are identical, names are arranged alphabetically according to the second given name. Where full names are identical, they are arranged in order of age—with the elder listed first.

Surnames beginning with De, Des, Du, however capitalized or spaced, are recorded with the prefix preceding the surname and arranged alphabetically under the letter D.

Surnames beginning with Mac and Mc are arranged alphabetically under M.

Surnames beginning with Saint or St. appear after names that begin Sains, are arranged according to the second part of the name, e.g. St. Clair before Saint Dennis.

Surnames beginning with Van, Von or von are arranged alphabetically under letter V.

Compound hyphenated surnames are arranged according to the first member of the compound. Compound unhyphenated surnames are treated as hyphenated names.

Parentheses used in connection with a name indicate which part of the full name is usually deleted in common usage. Hence Abbott, W(illiam) Lewis indicates that the usual form of the given name is W. Lewis. In such a case, the parentheses are ignored in alphabetizing. However, if the name is recorded Abbott, (William) Lewis, signifying that the entire name William is not commonly used, the alphabetizing would be arranged as though the name were Abbott, Lewis.

Who's Who in American Law

AADALEN, DAVID KEVIN, lawyer; b. Hamilton, Calif., Dec. 23, 1953; s. Arlie Vernon and Irma Jean (Willig) A.; m. Rhonda Kay Kramer, May 29, 1976; children: Luke David, Amy Johanna. Student U. Kans., 1971; BA, Washburn U., 1975, JD, 1979. Bar: Kans. 1980, U.S. Dist. Ct. Kans. 1980. Sole practice, Topeka, 1980—. Deacon Topeka Bible Ch., 1981—. Named Outstanding Young Man in Am., U.S. Jaycees, 1982. Mem. Kans. Bar Assn., Topeka Bar Assn. (probate com.), Christian Legal Soc. Republican. Probate, Real property, General practice. Home: 1031 SW Parkview Topeka KS 66604 Office: 1108 Bank IV Tower Topeka KS 66603

AARON, ALLEN HAROLD, lawyer; b. Mpls., June 19, 1932; s. Theodore and Marian (Bassin) A.; m. Barbara L. Perlman, Nov. 16, 1954; children—Deborah, Cynthia; m. Ruth H. Litwak, Oct. 7, 1979. Student, Harvard U., 1950-51; B.S., U. Minn., 1953, LL.B., 1955. Bar: Minn. 1955, U.S. Dist. Ct. Minn. 1955. Spl. asst. atty. gen. State of Minn., St. Paul, 1955-56; mem. Silver, Goff, Ryan, Cochrane & Aaron, St. Paul, 1956-63, Shanedling, Phillips, Gross & Aaron, Mpls., 1963-79, Phillips, Gross & Aaron, Mpls., 1979—; guest panelist Quiz Kids nat. broadcast radio program, 1949; instr. law U. Minn., 1960, 63. Bd. dirs. Pillsbury House Alumni Assn., 1966—, pres., 1968-70, 82-85; trustee Temple Israel, Mpls., 1970-79, v.p., 1975-77. Recipient 1st Pl. award Multi-state World Affairs Contest Mpls. Star and Tribune, 1949. Mem. Minn. Bar Assn., Hennepin County Bar Assn., Assn. Trial Lawyers Am., Am. Arbitration Assn. (arbitrator), Order of Coif, Phi Delta Pni. Lodge: B'nai B'rith. Personal injury, Family and matrimonial, Business litigation. Home: 4715 Wedgewood Dr Minnetonka MN 55345 Office: Phillips Gross & Aaron 700 Norwest Midland Bldg Minneapolis MN 55401

AARON, MARCUS, II, lawyer; b. Pitts., Oct. 24, 1929; s. Marcus Lester and Maxine (Goldmark) A.; m. Barbara Goldman, Feb. 6, 1955; children: Susan, Judith, Barbara. AB, Princeton U., 1950; JD, Harvard U., 1953. Bar: Pa. 1953, D.C. 1953, U.S. Dist. Ct. (we. dist.) Pa. 1956, U.S. Supreme Ct. 1969, U.S. Ct. Appeals (3d cir.) 1971. Assoc. Glick, Berkman & Engel, Pitts., 1956-64; ptnr. Berkman, Ruslander, Pohl, Lieber & Engel, Pitts., 1965—; asst. solicitor City of Pitts., 1957-67; bd. dirs. Homer Laughlin China Co., Newell, W.Va., v.p., sec., 1967—; bd. dirs. Centre Engring. Inc., State College, Pa. Pres. Western Pa. Sch. for Blind Children, Pitts., 1984—; bd. dirs., sec. Blue Cross of Western Pa., Pitts., 1972-86. Served with U.S. Army, 1953-55. Mem. ABA, Pa. Bar Assn., Allegheny County Bar Assn., Acad. Hosp. Attys., Nat. Health Lawyers Assn. Democrat. Jewish. Clubs: Concordia, Rivers, Harvard-Yale-Princeton (Pitts.). General corporate, Health. Home: 1925 Wightman St Pittsburgh PA 15217-1537 Office: Berkman Ruslander et al 1 Oxford Ctr 40th Floor Pittsburgh PA 15219-6498

AARONSON, DAVID ERNEST, lawyer, educator; b. Washington, Sept. 19, 1940; s. Edward Allan and May (Rosett) A. B.A. in Econs, George Washington U., 1961, M.A., 1964, Ph.D., 1970; LL.B., Harvard U., 1964; LL.M. (E. Barrett Prettyman fellow), Georgetown U., 1965. Bar: D.C. bar 1965, Md. bar 1975, U.S. Supreme Ct. bar 1969. Research asst. Office of Commr., Bur. Labor Stats., U.S. Dept. Labor, Washington, 1961; staff atty. legal intern program Georgetown Grad. Law Center, Washington, 1964-65; research asso. patent research project dept. econs. George Washington U., Washington, 1966; asso. firm Aaronson and Aaronson, Washington, 1965-67; partner Aaronson and Aaronson, 1967-70; mem. faculty Am. U. Law Sch., Washington, 1970—; prof. Sch. Justice, Coll. Public and Internat. Affairs, 1981—; dep. dir. Law and Policy Inst. abroad in, Jerusalem, Israel, summer, 1978; interim dir. clin. programs Md. Criminal Justice Clinic, 1971-73, founder prosecutor criminal litigation clinic, 1972, co-dir. trial practice litigation program, 1982—; vis. prof. Law Sch. of Hebrew U., Jerusalem, summer, 1978; trustee Montgomery-Prince George's Continuing Legal Edn. Inst., 1983—. Author: Maryland Criminal Jury Instructions and Commentary, 1975, (with N.N. Kittrie and D. Saari) Alternatives to Conventional Criminal Adjudication: Guidebook for Planners and Practitioners, 1977, (with B. Hoff, P. Jaszi, N.N. Kittrie and D. Saari) The New Justice: Alternatives to Conventional Criminal Adjudication, 1977, (with C.T. Dienes and M.C. Musheno) Decriminalization of Public Drunkenness: Tracing the Implementation of a Public Policy, 1981, Public Policy and Police Discretion: Processes of Decriminalization, 1984; contbr. articles to legal and public policy jours. Mem. council Friendship Heights Village Council, 1979. Recipient Outstanding Community Service award, 1980; Outstanding Tchr. award Am. U. Law Sch., 1978, 81; Pauline Ruyle Moore scholar in Pub. Law, 1983. Mem. Am. Bar Assn., D.C. Bar Assn. (chmn. criminal code rev. com. 1971-73), Md. State Bar Assn., (criminal law sect. council 1984—), Montgomery County (Md.) Bar Assn., Am. Law Inst., Phi Beta Kappa. Legal education. Office: American Univ Law School Myers Hall Room 205 Mass and Nebraska Ave NW Washington DC 20016

AARONSON, MARK N., lawyer; b. Phila., Apr. 25, 1944; s. Lester H. and Esther Sara (Plaskow) A.; m. Marjorie Gelb, Dec. 28, 1969; children: Johanna Aaronson-Gelb, Marisa Aaronson-Gelb. AB, U. Calif., Berkeley, 1965, MA in Polit. Sci., 1966, PhD in Polit. Sci., 1975; JD, U. Chgo., 1969. Bar: Calif. 1970, Conn. 1970, U.S. Dist. Ct. (no. and cen. dists.) Calif., U.S. Dist. Ct. Conn., U.S. Ct. Appeals (2d and 9th cirs.), U.S. Supreme Ct. Atty. Mandel Legal Aid Soc., Chgo., 1969-70, Hartford (Conn.) Neighborhood Legal Services, 1970-71; asst. prof. or lectr. CCNY and U. Calif., Davis and Berkeley, 1975-77; exec. dir. San Francisco Lawyers Com. For Urban Affairs, 1977—. Mem. Calif. Bar Assn. (chmn. exec. com. legal services sect.), Phi Beta Kappa. Democrat. Jewish. Civil rights, Poverty Law. Office: San Francisco Lawyers Com For Urban Affairs 301 Mission #400 San Francisco CA 94105

ABADY, SAMUEL AARON, lawyer; b. Richmond, Va., Dec. 7, 1954; s. Abraham Aaron and Nina (Friedman) A. BA, Colgate U., 1977; JD, U. Pa., 1981. Bar: N.Y. 1982, U.S. Dist. Ct. (so. and ea. dists.) N.Y. 1982, U.S. Ct. Appeals (2d cir.) 1984. Assoc. Finley, Kumble, Wagner, Heine, Underberg & Casey, N.Y.C., 1981-82, Sage, Grey, Todd & Sims, N.Y.C., 1982-83; ptnr. Abady & Jaffe, N.Y.C., 1983—. Democrat. Jewish. Federal civil litigation, State civil litigation, Criminal. Home: 1315 3d Ave Apt 2B New York NY 10021 Office: Abady & Jaffe 342 Madison Ave New York NY 10173

ABATE, ERNEST NICHOLAS, state legislator; b. New Haven, Aug. 10, 1943; s. Nicholas Anthony and Rose Marie (Virgulto) A.; m. Barbara Zempel, June 16, 1966; children: Charles Porter, Edward Stockton. B.S. in Polit. Sci, Villanova (Pa.) U., 1965; LL.B., J.D., Notre Dame U., 1968. Bar: Conn. bar 1969. With firm Abate & Fox, Stamford, Conn., 1972—; mem. Conn. Ho. of Reps., 1974—, chmn. judiciary com., 1977-78, speaker of house, 1979-83; mem. Conn. Law Revision Commn., 1983-85. City committeeman City of Stamford, 1974-77; bd. dirs. Fed. Health Systems Agy., Inc., 1975-78, Community Return, Inc., Touch, Inc., Aid for the Retarded, Inc.; incorporator Stamford Hosp. Corp.; trustee Conn. Pub. TV and Radio.; bd. dirs. Alcoholism Council, Inc.; del. Dem. Nat. Conv., 1980. Served to capt. USMC, 1969-72. Named Young Man of Yr. and; recipient Disting. Service award Stamford Jaycees, 1976, Navy Achievement medal. Mem. ABA, Conn. Bar Assn., Stamford Bar Assn. Real property, Estate planning, Contracts commercial. Home: 69 Old North Stamford Rd Stamford CT 06905 Office: 607 Bedford St Stamford CT 06901

ABBATE, PAUL J., judge; b. N.Y.C., Mar. 28, 1919; s. Salvatore and Mary (Clemente) A.; married, Sept. 8, 1946; children: Michael, Paul, Greg (dec.), Maria. B.S., U.S. Mcht. Marine Acad., 1943; LL.B., St. Johns U., 1949; LL.M., Bklyn. Law Sch., 1952. Bar: U.S. Supreme Ct. bar 1956. Practiced law N.Y.C., 1952-66; atty. gen. Guam, Agana, 1966-68; judge Island Ct., 1968-74; presiding judge Superior Ct. of Guam, 1974—; prof. law Coll. Guam; chmn. Jud. Council, 1979—, Bd. Law Examiners, 1979—. Ordained deacon Roman Catholic Ch. Served with USN. Decorated Bronze Star, Purple Heart. Office: Presiding Judge Superior Ct of Guam Judiciary Bldg Agana GU 96910 *

ABBOTT, BARRY A., lawyer; b. New Haven, Aug. 20, 1950; s. Harold and Norma (Kaufman) A.; m. Marcia Ann Stewart, June 19, 1976; 1 child, Anne Stewart. AB, Dartmouth Coll., 1972; JD, U. Fla., 1975; MBA, Stanford U., 1977. Bar: Fla. 1975, Calif. 1976, U.S. Dist. Ct. (so. dist.) Fla. 1976, U.S. Dist. Ct. (no. dist.) Calif. 1976, U.S. Ct. Appeals (9th cir.) 1976, U.S. Supreme Ct. 1979, D.C. 1985, N.Y. 1986. Assoc. Morrison & Foerster, San Francisco, 1977-83, ptnr., 1983—; lectr. on corp., comml. and fin. inst. law various orgns. Co-author: Truth in Lending: A Comprehensive Guide, 1985; contbr. articles to profl. jours. Named one of Outstanding Young Men of Am., U.S. Jaycees, 1980. Fellow Royal Soc. Arts (Silver medal 1972); mem. ABA (chmn. fin. inst. regulation and consumer fin. subcom. 1985—, active various coms.), Calif. Bar Assn., D.C. Bar Assn., Fla. Bar Assn., San Francisco Bar Assn. (chmn. membership com. 1984—, bd. dirs. 1982, 87—, Award of Merit 1985), Am. Arbitration Assn. (panelist), Barristers Club (bd. dirs. 1981-83, treas., pres. 1982), Order of Coif, Phi Beta Kappa, Phi Kappa Phi. Democrat. Clubs: World Trade (San Francisco), Commonwealth (Calif.). Banking, General corporate, Consumer commercial. Office: Morrison & Foerster 345 California St San Francisco CA 94104-2105

ABBOTT, CHARLES FAVOUR, JR., lawyer; b. Sedro-Woolley, Wash., Oct. 12, 1937; s. Charles Favour and Violette Doris (Boulter) A.; m. Oranee Harward Sept. 19, 1958; children: Patricia, Stephen, Nelson, Cynthia, Lisa, Alyson. BA in Econs., U. Wash., 1959, JD, 1962. Bar: Calif. 1962, Utah 1981. Law clk. Judge M. Oliver Koelsch, U.S. Ct. Appeals (9th cir.), San Francisco, 1963; assoc. Jones, Hatfield & Abbott, Escondido, Calif., 1964; sole practice, Escondido, 1964-77; of counsel Meuller & Abbott, Escondido, 1977—; ptnr. Abbott, Thorn & Hill, Provo, Utah, 1981-83; sole practice, Provo, Utah, 1983—. Mem. Utah Bar Assn., Calif. Bar Assn., Assn. Trial Lawyers Am. Mem. Ch. of Jesus Christ of Latter Day Saints. Editorial bd. Wash. Law Rev. and State Bar Assn. Jour., 1961-62; author: How to Do Your Own Legal Work, 1976, 2d edit., 1981, How to Win in Small Claims Court, 1981, How to be Free of Debt in 24 Hours, 1981, How to Hire the Best Lawyer at the Lowest Fee, 1981, The Lawyers' Inside Method of Making Money, 1979, The Millionaire Mindset, 1987; contbr. articles to profl. jours. Marketing law. Home: 3737 Foothill Dr Provo UT 84604

ABBOTT, CHARLES WARREN, lawyer; b. Miami, Fla., Jan. 16, 1930; s. Voyle E. and Katherine (Paschall) A.; m. Betty Jo Eckholdt, Sept. 27, 1936; children—Brenda Jean, Katherine Louise, Abigail Jill. B.S. in Bus. Adminstrn., U. Fla., 1951, J.D., 1953. Bar: Fla. 1953, U.S. Dist. Ct. (so. dist.) Fla. 1955, U.S. Dist. Ct. (mid. dist.) Fla., U.S. Supreme Ct. 1960, U.S. Ct. Appeals (11th cir.) 1981, U.S. Dist. Ct. (no. dist.) Fla. 1981. Assoc. firm Maguire, Voorhis & Wells, P.A., Orlando, Fla., 1955-59, ptnr., 1959-68, dir., 1968—, v.p., 1980-84. Chmn. Goldenrod Fire Control Dist., 1966-79. Served with JAGC, USAF, 1953-55; served to capt. USAFR, 1951-62. Fellow Am. Coll. Trial Lawyers; mem. ABA, Fla. Bar, Orange County Bar Assn., Fla. Def. Lawyers Assn. (sec.-treas. 1983, pres. elect 1984, pres. 1985), Def. Research Inst. (state chmn. 1981-85, so. regional v.p. 1986—), Fedn. Ins. Counsel, Internat. Assn. Ins., Phi Delta Phi. Democrat. Methodist. Clubs: University, Citrus. State civil litigation, Personal injury, Insurance. Address: 2 S Orange Plaza Orlando FL 32802

ABBOTT, JACQUELYN MENG, lawyer; b. Sandusky, Ohio, Oct. 9, 1951; d. Donald Elroy and Frances Blanche (Meilink) Meng; m. James Thomas Abbott, Oct. 6, 1979; children: James Scott, Elizabeth Ruth. Student, Oberlin Coll., 1970-71; BA with honors, Bowling Green State U., 1974; JD, Ohio State U., 1977. Bar: Ind. 1977, Ohio 1977, U.S. Dist. Ct. (so. dist.) Ind. 1977, U.S. Dist. Ct. (no. dist.) Ind. 1983. Atty. Lincoln Nat. Life, Ft. Wayne, Ind., 1977-79; asst. counsel Lincoln Nat. Corp., Ft. Wayne, Ind., 1979-81, assoc. counsel, 1981-83, asst. gen. counsel, 1983—; bd. dirs. polit. action com. Lincoln Nat. Corp., Ft. Wayne. Bd. dirs. Ft. Wayne Philharm. Womens Com., 1983-84. Mem. ABA, Ind. Bar Assn., Allen County Bar Assn. (vice chmn. tax sect. 1985-87), Am. Council Life Ins. (pension com. fid. task force 1980—, risk classification com. 1985-87, pension com. plan asset reversion task force 1987—), Am. Corp. Counsel Assn. (program chmn. Ind. chpt. 1986—), Phi Delta Phi (outstanding mem. award 1977). Avocation: children. Pension, profit-sharing, and employee benefits, Health. Home: 4004 Nottingham Dr Fort Wayne IN 46815 Office: Lincoln Nat Corp 1300 S Clinton St PO Box 1110 Fort Wayne IN 46801

ABBOTT, KEITH EUGENE, lawyer, consultant; b. Wichita, Kans., Feb. 11, 1949; s. Robert E. Abbott and Dorothy E. (Thompson) McDermott; m. Amy L. Bachman, Nov. 26, 1977; children: Jessica Jeanne, Dana Jeanne, Kellie Jeanne. AA, Aims Coll., 1975; BA, U. No. Colo., 1978; JD, Ohio No. U., 1980. Bar: Colo. 1982, U.S. Dist. Ct. Colo. 1982. Freelance landman oil and gas Greeley, Colo., 1981-83; atty. JRC Oil, Greeley, 1981-83; pres. RA Resourses, Inc., Greeley, 1983—, also bd. dirs.; bd. dirs. First No. Savs. & Loan, Greeley, 1984—. Rep. precinct chmn., Greeley, 1985—. Served with USN, 1967-70, Vietnam.p. Mem. ABA, Colo. Bar Assn., Weld County Bar Assn., Greeley C. of C. Lodge: Rotary (bd. dirs.). Avocations: camping, phys. fitness. Oil and gas leasing, General corporate, Contracts commercial. Office: 1309 9th Ave Greeley CO 80631

ABBOTT, KENNETH WAYNE, legal educator; b. Albany, N.Y., July 25, 1944; s. Walter Miles and Ruth Bessie (Lasher) A.; m. Ann Wadsworth, June 8, 1968; children: Thomas A., Carolyn R.; m. Deborah deSchweitz, May 17, 1980. B.A., Cornell U., 1966; J.D. magna cum laude, Harvard U., 1969. Bar: Mass. 1969, N.Y. 1970. Vol., VISTA, 1969-70; assoc. Harris, Beach, Wilcox, Robin & Levey, Rochester, N.Y., 1970-77; research fellow Harvard U. Law Sch., 1977-78; assoc. prof. Northwestern U. Sch. Law, Chgo., 1978-82, prof., 1982—; vis. prof. Cornell U., 1983-84. Contbr. articles to profl. jours. and law revs. Mem. ABA, Am. Soc. Internat. Law, Am. Assn. for Comparative Study of Law. Private international, Public international. Office: Northwestern U Sch Law 357 Chicago Ave Chicago IL 60611 *

ABBOTT, WILLIAM ANTHONY, lawyer; b. Austin, Minn., May 25, 1951; s. Robert Elmer and Marion Iris (Edel) A.; m. Deborah Lynn Hunt, Apr. 23, 1982; 1 child, Whitney Hunt. B.B.A. with distinction, U. Wis., 1973, J.D. cum laude, 1975. Bar: Wis. 1976, U.S. Dist. Ct. (we. dist.) Wis. 1976, U.S. Tax Ct. 1981. Ptnr., Bell, Metzner & Gierhart, S.C., Madison, Wis., 1976—. Vice-pres. Briarpatch, Inc. for runaway youth, Madison, 1979—; ambassador Picada; sec. Energy Assistance, Inc., Madison, 1983; committeeman United Way Pres.'s Council, Madison, 1984. Mem. ABA, Wis. Bar Assn., Dane County Bar Assn., Middleton Jaycees (pres. 1978), Order of Coif, Phi Kappa Phi, Beta Gamma Sigma. Clubs: Bklyn. Flying (v.p. 1987—), Wis. Fun Flyers, Inc. (v.p. 1987—). Lodge: Optimists (bd. dirs. 1985-86). General corporate, Corporate taxation, Real property. Office: Bell Metzner & Gierhart SC 2472 Thatcher Ln McFarland WI 53558

ABBOTT, WILLIAM SAUNDERS, lawyer; b. Medford, Mass., June 2, 1938; s. Charles Theodoric and Evelyn (Saunders) A.; m. Susan Shaw, June 24, 1961; children: Cathryn, Stephen, David. AB, Harvard U., 1960, LLB, 1966. Bar: Mass. 1967, U.S. Dist. Ct. Mass., U.S. Ct. Appeals (D.C. cir.). White House fellow, 1966-67; reg. coordinator, U.S. Agrl. Programs, Asia, U.S. Dept. Agr., 1967-68; gen. counsel Cabot, Cabot & Forbes Co., Boston, 1968-77; prin. Simonds, Winslow, Willis & Abbott, Boston, 1977—; bd. dirs. Bay Tower Restaurant, Arlington Bd. Selectmen, 1970-73; pres., trustee Plymouth County Wildlands Trust. Served to lt. USN, 1963-66. Mem. Mass. Bar Assn., Boston Bar Assn., Phi Beta Kappa. Real property, General corporate. Office: 50 Congress St Boston MA 02109

ABBOTT, WILLIAM W., JR., lawyer; b. Delhi, La., Jan. 27, 1955; s. William W. Sr. and Margaret (Frame) A.; m. Risa Stevens Abbott, Feb. 4, 1977; children: Dawn Michelle, Kathrine, William W. III. BA, Hendrix Coll., 1977; JD, Tulane U., 1980. Bar: La. 1980, Miss. 1985, U.S. Dist. Ct. (ea. and we. dists.) La. 1980, U.S. Dist. Ct. (no. and so. dists.) Miss. 1985, U.S. Ct. Appeals (5th cir.) 1985. Atty. Fed. Land Bank, New Orleans, 1980-82, sr. atty., 1982-83, asst. v.p., asst. gen. counsel, 1983-84; v.p., dep. gen. counsel Fed. Land Bank, Jackson, Miss., 1984-86; ptnr. Brand & Abbott, Jackson, 1986—. Mem. ABA, La. Bar Assn., Miss. Bar Assn., Am. Agrl. Law Assn. (rural law and agribus. forum com.). Avocations: golf, reading. Bankruptcy, Federal civil litigation, State civil litigation. Home: 52 Wintergreen Rd Madison MS 39110 Office: Brand & Abbott Capital Towers Suite 111 Jackson MS 39205

ABDELLA, H. JAMES, lawyer; b. Gloversville, N.Y., June 21, 1934; s. Martin K. and Catherine (Skaff) A.; m. Susan Van Volkenburgh, Aug. 26, 1956; children: Cynthia, Stephen, Peter. BA, Coll. of William and Mary, 1956; JD, U. Mich., 1959. Bar: N.Y. 1960, U.S. Dist. Ct. (we. dist.) 1964, U.S. Supreme Ct. 1964. Assoc. Johnson, Peterson, Tener & Anderson, Jamestown, N.Y., 1959-63, ptnr., 1963-81; ptnr. Saperston, Day, Lustig, Gallick, Kirschner & Gaglione P.C., Jamestown, 1981-83, Abdella & Abdella, Jamestown, 1983—. Author: weekly non-legal discussions column Just Here 'n There, Mayville (N.Y.) Sentinel, 1974-80, 82—. Mem. Jamestown adv. bd. Buffalo Savs. Bank, 1971—; mgr. Babe Ruth League; numerous ch. positions; chmn. bd. dirs. Jamestown Youth Bur., 1974-80. Recipient outstanding newletter award N.Y. State Optimist Club, 1973-74. Mem. ABA, N.Y. State Bar Assn., Jamestown Bar Assn. (pres. 1978-79). Republican. Methodist. Club: Moon Brook Country (Jamestown). Lodge: Masons. General practice, Probate. Office: 901-903 Hotel Jamestown Bldg PO Box 3006 Jamestown NY 14701

ABDULAZIZ, SAM K., lawyer; b. Bagdad, Iraq, Apr. 10, 1939; came to U.S., 1946; s. Joseph S. Abdulaziz and Rachel J. Hawa; m. Joyce Joan, June 12; children: Michael Joseph, Deborah Ann. BBA, UCLA, 1962; JD, Loyola U., Los Angeles, 1971. Calif. 1972, U.S. Supreme Ct. 1981. Author: Contractors Guide to the Contractors Board Citation Procedure, 1974, Construction Law, 1985. Mem. Los Angeles County Bar Assn. (Lawyer of Yr. award Constl. Rights Found. 1977). Avocation: sports. Construction, Real property, Administrative and regulatory. Office: Abdulaziz & Grossbart 6454 Coldwater Canyon North Hollywood CA 91606

ABEDON, HERBERT JOSEPH, lawyer, investment counselor; b. Providence, Mar. 3, 1931; s. Bernard Bennett and Anna Beatrice (Seidman) A.; m. Paula Levin, July 11, 1954 (div.); children—Jon Howard, Robert Levin, Stephen Israel; m. 2d, Barbara Woods, June 3, 1979. A.B. cum laude, Harvard U., 1952; J.D., U. Pa., 1956. Bar: R.I. 1956, U.S. Dist. Ct. R.I. 1956, U.S. Ct. Appeals (1st cir.) 1956. Sole practice, Providence, 1956-78, 80—; ptnr. Zietz, Sonkin, Radin & Mittleman, Providence, 1978-79; investment banker, Mem. R.I. Gen. Assembly, 1961-63; registered rep. Mut. Benefit Fin. Service Co.; counsel to Cranston Redevel. Agy., 1963-75. Recipient Bur. Nat. Affairs award U. Pa. Law Sch., 1956. Mem. R.I. Bar Assn., ABA, Assn. Trial Lawyers Am. Jewish. Clubs: Harvard of R.I., U. Pa. of R.I., Masons. Probate, Real property, Securities. Home: 27 Fisher St East Providence RI 02914 Office: 100 Lafayette St Pawtucket RI 02860

ABEL, RICHARD L., legal educator, lawyer; b. 1941. B.A., Harvard U., 1962; LL.B. summa cum laude, Columbia U., 1965; Ph.D., U. London, 1974. Bar: N.Y. 1968, Conn. 1971. Asst. prof. Yale U., 1968-70, assoc. prof., 1970-74; prof. UCLA Law Sch., 1974—; atty. New Haven Legal Assistance Assn., Inc., 1971-72. Notes editor Columbia Law Rev.; editor-in-chief African Law Studies, Law and Soc. Rev. Legal education. Office: UCLA Law Sch 405 Hilgard Ave Los Angeles CA 90024 *

ABELITE, JAHNIS JOHN, lawyer; b. McMinnville, Tenn., Oct. 10, 1950; s. Augusts and Alexandrine Rita Olga (Tilga) A. BA, U. Wash., 1972; JD, U. Puget Sound, 1975. Bar: Wash. 1981, U.S. Dist. Ct. (we. dist.) Wash. 1983. Assoc. Dolack, Hansler et al, Tacoma, 1975-77; legal liaision State of Wash., Olympia, 1977-78; contract specialist State of Wash., Tacoma, 1978-80; contract adminstr. Data I/O Corp., Redmond, Wash., 1980—; sole practice Bothell, Wash., 1981—; counsel West Coast Latvian Edn. Ctr., Mountlake Terr., Wash., 1982—; bd. dirs. Latvian Credit Union, Seattle. Mem. ABA, Fed. Bar Assn., Seattle-King County Bar Assn. Lutheran. General corporate, Family and matrimonial, Contracts commercial. Office: PO Box 1062 Bothell WA 98041

ABELLE, PATSY CAPLES, lawyer; b. Waukegan, Ill., Aug. 20, 1935; d. Roy Lee Caples and Lee Self (Rosamond) Henderson. BS in Fin., DePaul U., 1964, JD, 1967; LLM, NYU, 1968. Bar: Ill. 1967, NY 1968, U.S. Dist. Ct. (no. dist.) Ill. 1967, U.S. Ct. Mil. Appeals 1968, U.S. Supreme Ct. 1968. Chief securities Fed. Res. Bank, N.Y.C., 1968-73; assoc. Willkie Farr & Gallagher, N.Y.C., 1973-78; sr. atty. Fed. Res. Bd, Washington, 1978-81; sr. assoc. Cravath, Swaine & Moore, N.Y.C., 1981—. Contbr. articles to law jours. Chmn. Fed. Women's Program Adv. Com., Washington, 1980. Mem. Blue Sky Lawyers Assn. (chmn. 1984-85). Securities. Office: Cravath Swaine & Moore 1 Chase Manhattan Plaza New York NY 10005

ABELMAN, ARTHUR F., lawyer; b. N.Y.C., June 12, 1933; s. Bert and Myra (Dickoff) A. A.B., Harvard U., 1954, J.D., 1957. Bar: N.Y. 1958, U.S. Dist. Ct. (so. dist.) N.Y. 1958, U.S. Ct. Appeals (2d cir.) 1958. Assoc. Casey Lane & Mittendorf, N.Y.C., 1957-59; counsel Am. Petroleum Inst., N.Y.C., 1959-61; corp. sec. Pocket Books, Inc., N.Y.C., 1961-65; assoc. Weil Gotshal Manges, N.Y.C., 1965-79; counsel Moses & Singer, N.Y.C., 1979—; pres. Millan House, Inc., N.Y.C., 1982—. Pres., Sculpture Ctr., Inc., N.Y.C., 1979-85; trustee Neighbors of the Seventh, Inc., James Beard Found., Inc. Mem. ABA, N.Y. Bar Assn., Assn. Bar City N.Y. Republican. Jewish. Club: Harvard. Libel, Trademark and copyright, Real property. Home: 116 E 68 St New York NY 10021 Office: Moses & Singer 1271 Ave of the Americas New York NY 10020

ABELS, JONATHAN BERLE, lawyer; b. Indpls., Feb. 22, 1944; s. Samuel and Frances (Falendar) A.; m. Linda Feiwell, May 6, 1973; children: Michelle, Benji, Matthew, Maribeth. Student, Wabash Coll., 1962-65; BA, Butler U., 1966; JD, Ind. U., 1969. Bar: Ind. 1970, U.S. Dist. Ct. 1970, U.S. Ct. Appeals 1970, U.S. Supreme Ct. 1980. Assoc. Dann, Pecar, Newman, Talesnick & Kleiman, Indpls., 1971-76, ptnr., 1976—. Author numerous legal articles. Bd. dirs. Jewish Welfare Fedn., Indpls., 1984; pres. Jewish Community Ctr., Indpls. 1986—. Recipient Martin L. Larner award Jewish Community Ctr., 1983, L.L. Goodman award Jewish Welfare Fedn., 1984. Mem. ABA, Ind. Bar Assn., Indpls. Bar Assn., Comml. Law League Am. Lodge: B'nai B'rith. Bankruptcy, Consumer commercial, General corporate. Home: 10245 Briar Creek Ln Carmel IN 46032 Office: Dann Pecar et al 2300 Am United Life Bldg Indianapolis IN 46204

ABELSON, MICHAEL ALLEN, lawyer; b. Wilkes-Barre, Pa.; s. Arthur Robert and Shirley (Fierman) A.; m. Lyndsay Carol Steffen, Aug. 10, 1980; children: Jeffrey S., Melissa S. BA, Pa. State U., 1971; JD cum laude, New Eng. Sch. Law, 1974. Bar: Mass. 1974, Pa. 1975, D.C. 1977, Md. 1977. Ptnr. Gelb, Abelson & Siegel, Washington, 1976-82; sole practice Washington, 1982—. Mem. Md. Bar Assn., D.C. Bar Assn., Assn. Trial Lawyers Am. (state del.), Trial Lawyers Met. Washington (bd. govs. 1979—). Jewish. Personal injury, Insurance, Federal civil litigation. Home: 9620 Reach Rd Potomac MD 20854 Office: 1000 16th St NW Suite 300 Washington DC 20036

ABERCROMBIE, THOMAS VERNON, municipal judge, tax consultant; b. Courtney, Tex., Mar. 26, 1919; s. Stephen Franklin and Jennie Emaline (Herring) A.; m. Rosie Lee Smith, Oct. 2, 1945; children—Thomas Vernon II, Catherine Elizabeth Abercrombie Griggs. B.S., Sam Houston State U., 1947, M.A., 1948; cert. Nat. Judicial Coll., 1981. Tchr. High Sch., Stafford, Tex., 1948-83; mcpl. judge City of Stafford, 1972—; prin. Abercrombie Tax Service, Stafford, 1950—. Author: (with others) Seed Sales and Service, 1965. Sec. city planning commn. City of Stafford, 1966-82. Served to s/sgt. USAF, 1941-45. Mem. Fort Bend County Tex. State Tchrs. Assn. (pres. 1972-73), Tex. Vocat. Agrl. Tchrs. Assn. Area III (pres.). Democrat. Baptist. Club: Oyster Creek (Missouri City Tex.). Lodge: Rotary, Masons (worshipful master 1964-65, high priest 1971-72). Local government, Personal income taxation. Home: PO Box 55 Stafford TX 77477 Office: City Stafford 2610 S Main Stafford TX 77477

ABERNATHY, HARRY HOYLE, JR., lawyer; b. Statesville, N.C., Mar. 28, 1925; s. Harry Hoyle and Annie Pearl (Frazier) A.; m. Martha Elizabeth Bell, Aug. 31, 1948; children—Harry H., Donna Cooper. A.A., Mitchell Jr. Coll., 1947; B.S., Appalachian State Tchrs. Coll., 1950; LL.B., U. S.C., 1958. Bar: S.C. 1958, U.S. Dist. Ct. S.C. 1958, U.S. Ct. Appeals (4th cir.) 1982. Sole practice, Great Falls, S.C., 1959—; city atty. Great Falls, 1968—; dir. Lancaster-Chester Public Defender Corp., 1978, Palmetto Legal Services, 1982. Chmn. Chester County Library Bd., 1962-76; pres. United Fund, 1973-74. Served with USAAF, 1943-46, USAF, 1950-51. Mem. S.C. Bar Assn., Chester County Bar Assn. (pres. 1982), Great Falls Bar Assn. (pres. 1960—), Phi Alpha Delta. Democrat. Methodist. Clubs: Masons (sec. Great Falls 1970—). Family and matrimonial, Real property, General practice. Home: 20 Argonne Ave Great Falls SC 29055 Office: 605 Dearborn St PO Box 488 Great Falls SC 29055

ABERSON, LESLIE DONALD, lawyer; b. St. Louis, May 30, 1936; s. Hillard and Adele (Wenneker) A.; m. Regene Jo Lowenstein, Oct. 16, 1960; children—Karen, Angie, Leslie. B.S., U. Ky., 1957, J.D., 1960. Bar: Ky. 1960, U.S. Dist. Ct. (we. dist.) Ky. 1964, U.S. Tax Ct. 1968, U.S. Supreme Ct. 1975. Assoc., Washer, Kaplan, Rothschild, Aberson & Miller, Louisville, 1963-65, ptnr., 1965—; dir. Bank of Louisville. Bd. dirs. Ky. Athletic Hall of Fame, 1965—, Jewish Hosp. Louisville, 1978—, Louisville Med. Research Found., 1975—, NCCJ; bd. dirs., past pres. B'rith Sholom Temple; bd. dirs., past v.p. Jewish Community Fedn. Louisville. Recipient Louis Cole Young Leadership award Louisville C. of C. Mem. Ky. Bar Assn., Louisville Bar Assn., Ky. Trial Lawyers Assn., Am. Trial Lawyers Assn., Louisville C. of C. (instl. rev. com.), U. Ky. Law Sch. Alumni Assn. (bd. dirs.). General corporate, Estate planning, Real property. Home: 2306 Merrick Rd Louisville KY 40207 Office: Washer Kaplan Rothschild Aberson & Miller 725 Marion E Taylor Bldg Louisville KY 40202

ABERY-WETSTONE, HOLLY ANN, lawyer; b. Hartford, Conn., July 8, 1954; d. Harry Hinton Jr. and Gertrude Marion (Wanic) A.; m. Mark L. Wetstone, Aug. 9, 1980; children: Benjamin Abery, Mallory Alyse. BA, St. Joseph Coll., West Hartford, 1976; JD cum laude, Western New Eng. Sch. of Law, 1980. Bar: Conn. 1980, U.S. Dist. Ct. Conn. 1985, U.S. Tax Ct. 1986. Trial atty. tax div., criminal sect. U.S. Dept. of Justice, Washington, 1980-84, FERC, Washington, 1984-85; ptnr. Clayman, Markowitz & Litman, Bloomfield, Conn., 1985—; lectr. Conn. Womens Ednl. and Legal Fund, Hartford, 1985, U. Hartford Tax Inst., West Hartford, Conn., 1985. Bd. dirs. Greater Hartford Montessori Sch. Mem. ABA, Conn. Bar Assn., Hartford Bar Assn., Hartford Assn. Women Attys. (nominating com., co-chmn. program com.). Democrat. Jewish. Family and matrimonial, Estate planning, Personal income taxation. Home: 55 Haynes Rd West Hartford CT 06117 Office: Clayman Markowitz & Litman 3 Regency Rd Bloomfield CT 06002

ABILHEIRA, RICHARD B., lawyer; b. Fall River, Mass., Oct. 6, 1949; s. Elias B. and Diolinda (Coelho) A.; m. Elvira Morra, Apr. 27, 1986. AB, Georgetown U., 1972; JD, Suffolk U., 1976. Bar: R.I. 1976, U.S. Dist. Ct. R.I. 1976, U.S. Supreme Ct. 1980. Sole practice Warren, R.I., 1976-86, Bristol, R.I., 1986—; asst. solicitor Town of Bristol, R.I., 1984—. Mem. Bristol Dem. Town Com., 1976—. Mem. ABA, R.I. Bar Assn. Democrat. Roman Catholic. Lodge: Lions (pres. Bristol chpt. 1981-82). General practice, Real property, Local government. Office: 970 Hope St Bristol RI 02809

ABINANTI, THOMAS J., ., lawyer; b. N.Y.C., Dec. 28, 1946. BA, Fordham Coll., 1968; JD, NYU, 1972. Bar: Conn. 1973, N.Y. 1975, U.S. Ct. Appeals (2d cir.), U.S. Dist. Ct. (so., ea. and no. dists.) Conn. Sole practice White Plains, N.Y., 1975—; prosecutor Village of Dobbs Ferry, N.Y., 1979; councilman Town of Greenburgh, N.Y., 1980-84; counsel N.Y. State Assembly, 1975, 77, 79, 84, Greenburgh Housing Authority, 1984—. Del. Nat. Dem. Conv., 1972; committeeman Westchester County Dem. Com., 1976—; vice chmn. Greenburgh Town Dem. Com., 1985—; pres. Greenburgh Town Dem. Club, 1985—. Mem. ABA, Westchester Bar Assn., White Plains Bar Assn., Columbian Lawyers Assn. Club: Soc. for Edn. Am. Sailors. State civil litigation, Real property, Labor. Office: 6 Chester Ave White Plains NY 10601

ABNEY, JOE L., lawyer; b. Wetumka, Okla., June 5, 1941; s. Virgil Lawrence and Wanda (Bachus) A.; m. Paula Katherine Fowler, Sept. 21, 1963; 1 child, Lisa Jo. B.A., E. Central U., 1963; J.D., S. Tex. Coll. Law, 1974. Bar: Tex. 1974. Prin., Lake Mt. Sch. Dist., Covelo, Calif., 1963; tchr. Davis Sch. Dist., Okla., 1964; claims supr. Liberty Mut. Ins., New Orleans, 1965-71, Home Ins. Co., Houston, 1971-74; mem. firm Smith, Abney & Woolf, Houston, 1974—. Advisor, Grangerland 4H Club, Conroe, 1981-83; pres. River Plantation Horse Owners Assn., 1980-81, Hughes County Young Dems., 1962-64; sec. E. Central U. Young Dems., Ada, Okla., 1963. Mem. So. Assn. Workmen's Compensation Adminstrs., Tex. Trial Lawyers Assn., Harris County Criminal Lawyers Assn. Baptist. Club: Montgomery County Genealogy, Soc. War of 1812. Lodge: Elks. Personal injury, Workers' compensation, Labor. Home: 150 Stonewall Jackson Dr Conroe TX 77302 Office: Smith Abney & Woolf 1331 Lamar Suite 1050 Houston TX 77010

ABRAHAM, ANDREW, lawyer; b. Phoenix, Jan. 14, 1958; s. Willard B. and Dale W. (Wiener) A.; m. Ann N. Boland, May 29, 1983. BA, Claremont McKenna, 1979; JD, Ariz. State U., 1982. Bar: Ariz. 1982, U.S. Dist. Ct. Ariz. 1982, U.S. Ct. Appeals (9th cir.) 1982. Law clk. Ariz. Supreme Ct., Phoenix, 1982-83; assoc. Burch and Cracchiolo, Phoenix, 1983—. Mng. editor Ariz. State U. Law Jour., 1981-82. Mem. Ariz. State U., Coll. Law Alumni Assn. (v.p. 1986—). State civil litigation, Condemnation, Zoning. Office: Burch & Cracchiolo 702 E Osborn PO Box 16882 Phoenix AZ 85011

ABRAHAM, DOUGLAS CLARK, lawyer; b. Detroit, Jan. 9, 1957; s. Philip Maurice and Genevieve Frances (Clark) A.; m. Katherine Gail Gaston, Mar. 31, 1984. BS, Eastern Mich. U., 1979; JD, U. Detroit, 1982. Bar: Mich. 1982. Sole practice Livonia, Mich., 1982—. Trustee Superior Twp. (Mich.) Bd., 1980-83; mem. Zoning Bd. Appeals, Superior Twp., 1980-83; precinct del. Washtenaw County (Mich.) Dems., 1980. Recipient Exceptional Service award City of Livonia, 1986, Dedicated Pub. Service award Superior Twp., 1983. Mem. Mich. Trial Lawyers Assn., Trial Lawyers Assn. Am., Superior Jaycees (pres. 1979, Disting. Service award 1982). Democrat. Lodge: Optimists. Civil rights, Personal injury, Real property. Office: 16832 Newburgh Rd Livonia MI 48154

ABRAHAM, JAMES ESBER, lawyer; b. Greensburg, Pa., Sept. 4, 1951; s. James Issa and Marian Joan (Kusinsky) A.; m. Mary Frances Dinneen Abraham, Feb. 29, 1980; children: Andrew Patrick, Amy Victoria. AB, Dickinson Coll., 1973; JD, Duquesne U., 1978. Bar: Pa. 1978, U.S. Tax Ct. 1981, U.S. Dist. Ct. (we. dist.) Pa. 1982, U.S. Supreme Ct. 1983. Compliance officer U.S. Dept. Labor/PWBA, Pitts., 1976-78; mgr. Touche Ross & Co., Pitts., 1978-83, 84-85; cons., counsel Buck Cons., Pitts., 1983-84; sr. assoc. Berkman Ruslander Pohl Lieber & Engel, Pitts., 1985—; adj. prof. Robert Morris Coll., Pitts., 1980—. Contbr. articles to profl. jours. Mem. Western Pa. Conservancy, Pitts., 1982, Trout Unltd., Washington, 1983. Dana Found. scholar, 1974. Mem. ABA (employee benefits com.), Allegheny County Bar Assn. (vice chmn. taxation sect.). Club: Rivers. Avocations: fly fishing, camping. Pension, profit-sharing, and employee benefits, Corporate taxation, Personal income taxation. Home: 4116 Millington Rd Pittsburgh PA 15217 Office: Berkman Ruslander Pohl Lieber & Engel One Oxford Ctr 40th Floor Pittsburgh PA 15219

ABRAHAM, NICHOLAS ALBERT, lawyer; b. Boston, Sept. 17, 1941; s. Nicholas and Ida (Ghiz) A.; m. Evie Stathopoulos, June 30, 1968; children: Annise, Nicholas. BS, Boston U., 1963, JD, 1966. Bar: Mass. 1966, U.S. Dist. Ct. Mass. 1968, U.S. Ct. Appeals (1st cir.) 1971. Sr. ptnr. Abraham-Hanna, P.C., Boston, 1968—; chief exec. officer Boston Investors Fund, 1972—. Author: Doing Business in Egypt, 1979, Doing Business in Saudi Arabia, 1980, Doing Business in Kuwait, 1982. Bd. of trustees Boston U. Coll. of Bus. Adminstrn., 1968; chmn. fund raising com. Boy Scouts Am., 1968; coach Weston Little League; founder of Weston Youth Hockey League, 1985. Served with U.S. Army, 1966-67; to lt. comdr. USN, 1967-74. Republican. Eastern Orthodox. State civil litigation, Real property, General corporate. Home: 21 Buckskin Dr Weston MA 02193 Office: Abraham Hanna PC 60 State St Boston MA 02109

ABRAHAMSON, A. CRAIG, lawyer; b. Washington, May 24, 1954; s. Joseph Labe and Helen Dorothy (Selis) A.; m. Mary Ellen Bernard, Dec. 29, 1979; children: Nicholas Eric, Amy Nicole. BA, U. Minn., 1976; JD, U. Tulsa, 1979. Bar: Minn. 1979, U.S. Dist. Ct. Minn. 1979, Okla. 1982, U.S. Dist. Ct. (no. dist.) Okla. 1983. Assoc. Law Office of Joseph L. Abrahamson, Mpls., 1979-82, Freese & March, Tulsa, 1982-83, Barlow & Cox, Tulsa, 1983-86; sole practice Tulsa, 1986—. Mem. ABA (litigation sect.), Okla. Bar Assn., Assn. Trial Lawyers Am., Tulsa County Bar Assn. Democrat. Jewish. Lodge: Masons. Avocations: fishing, camping, travel. Federal civil litigation, State civil litigation, Bankruptcy. Home: 2322 S 100th East Ave Tulsa OK 74129 Office: 707 S Houston Suite 308 Tulsa OK 74127

ABRAHAMSON, SHIRLEY SCHLANGER, justice Supreme Court Wisconsin; b. N.Y.C., Dec. 17, 1933; d. Leo and Ceil (Sauerteig) Schlanger; m. Seymour Abrahamson, Aug. 26, 1953; 1 son, Daniel Nathan. A.B., NYU, 1953; J.D., Ind. U., 1956; S.J.D., U. Wis., 1962. Bar: Wis. 1962. Asst. dir. Legis. Drafting Research Fund, Columbia U. Law Sch., 1957-60; since practiced in Madiso; mem. firm Lafollette, Sinykin, Anderson & Abrahamson, 1962-76; justice Supreme Ct. Wis., Madison, 1976—; prof. U. Wis. Sch. Law, 1966—, currently on leave; Mem. Wis. Bd. Bar Commrs.; mem. adv. bd. Nat. Inst. Justice, U.S. Dept. Justice, 1980-82; mem. Mayor's Adv. Com., Madison, 1968-70, Gov.'s Study Com. on Jud. Orgn., 1970-72; bd. visitors Ind. U. Sch. Law, 1972—, U. Miami Sch. Law, 1982—, Brigham Young U. Sch. Law, 1986—; bd. dirs. LWV, Madison, 1963-65; Union council Wis. Union, U. Wis., 1970-71. Editor: Constitutions of the United States (National and State) 2 vols, 1962. Bd. dirs. Wis. Civil Liberties Union, 1968-72, chmn. Capital Area chpt., 1969. Mem. ABA (council, sect. of legal edn. and admissions to the bar 1976-86, mem. commn. on undergrad. edn. in law and the humanities 1978-79), Wis. Bar Assn., Dane County Bar Assn., 7th Cir. Bar Assn., Nat. Assn. Women Judges, Am. Law Inst. (council), Order of Coif, Phi Beta Kappa. Jurisprudence. Home: 2012 Waunona Way Madison WI 53713 Office: Wis Supreme Ct PO Box 1688 Madison WI 53701

ABRAMOWITZ, ALTON LEE, lawyer; b. Bklyn., Jan. 19, 1948; s Julius and Jean (Isacson) A.; m. Susan Holly Greenhause, Jan. 19, 1980; m. Sherrie Rossberg, June 5, 1971 (div. Jan. 1979). B.A., American U., 1969; J.D., Rutgers U., 1972; LL.M., NYU, 1980. Bar: N.Y. 1973, U.S. Dist. Ct. (so. and ea. dists.) N.Y. 1974, U.S. Ct. Appeals (2d cir.) 1975, U.S. Tax Ct. 1975, U.S. Supreme Ct. 1976. Sr. staff atty. Legal Aid Soc. of Rockland Co., Inc., New City, N.Y., 1973-78; assoc. Erdheim, Shalleck & Frank, 1978-80, Fink, Weinberger, Fredman, Berman & Lowell, P.C., N.Y.C., 1980—. Mem. adv. com. Adult Homes, Rockland County, N.Y., 1976-78, legis. adv. com. Bd. Edn., White Plains, N.Y., 1982. Fellow Am. Acad. Matrimonial Lawyers; mem. Assn. Bar City of N.Y., N.Y. State Bar Assn. (exec. com. family law sect.), ABA. Democrat. Jewish. Family and matrimonial. Office: 551 Fifth Ave New York NY 10176

ABRAMOWITZ, ELKAN, lawyer; b. N.Y.C., Mar. 10, 1940; s. Harry and Claire L. (Liebreich) A.; m. Susan Isaacs, Dec. 7, 1943; children—Andrew, Elizabeth. A.B., Brown U., 1961; LL.B., NYU, 1964. Bar: N.Y. 1964. Law clk. U.S. Dist. Ct. (so. dist.) N.Y., 1964-66; asst. U.S. atty. for So. Dist. N.Y., 1966-70, chief criminal div., 1976-77; practice, N.Y.C., 1970-76, 77—; mem. Obermaier, Morvillo & Abramowitz, N.Y.C., 1979—; mem. faculty Nat. Inst. Trial Advocacy, 1977—. Mem. ABA, N.Y. State Bar Assn., Assn. Bar City of N.Y., Fed. Bar Council. Federal civil litigation, Criminal, State civil litigation. Home: 96 Middle Road Sands Point NY 11050 Office: 1120 Ave of Americas New York NY 10036

ABRAMOWITZ, ROBERT LESLIE, lawyer; b. Phila., May, 1950; s. Nathan P. and Lucille H. (Rader) A.; m. Susan Margaret Stewart, Dec. 1, 1974; children—David, Catherine. B.A., Yale U., 1971; J.D., Harvard U., 1974. Bar: Pa. 1974, N.J. 1975. Assoc. Ballard, Spahr, Andrews & Ingersoll, Phila., 1974-81, ptnr., 1981—; adj. prof. law Villanova U., 1986—. Trustee Moorestown (N.J.) Friends Sch., 1981—. Mem. ABA, Pa. Bar Assn., Phila. Bar Assn. (exec. com. probate sect. 1982-85, pension com. 1985—). Club: Yale (Phila.). Pension, profit-sharing, and employee benefits, Estate planning. Home: 623 Pembroke Rd Bryn Mawr PA 19010 Office: Ballard Spahr Andrews & Ingersoll 30 S 17th St 20th Floor Philadelphia PA 19103

ABRAMS, ALAN, corporate lawyer. Gen. counsel Witco Chem. Corp., N.Y.C. General corporate. Office: Witco Chem Corp 520 Madison Ave New York NY 10022 *

ABRAMS, BRENDA M., lawyer; b. N.Y.C., July 13, 1942; s. Nathan N. and Frances (Margulies) Greenberg; m. Ira Abrams, Mar. 1, 1962; 1 child, Jennifer. AB cum laude, U. Miami, 1964, JD cum laude, 1971. Bar: Fla. 1971, U.S. Ct. Appeals (5th cir.) 1971, U.S. Supreme Ct. 1976. Law clk. to chief judge U.S. Dist. Ct. Fla., Miami, 1971-72; sole practice Miami, 1972-74; ptnr. Abrams & Abrams P.A., Miami, 1974—; faculty U. Miami Law Sch., 1974—, Nova Law Sch., 1982-83. Author: 6 vols. Florida Family Law, 1986; contbr. articles to profl. jours. Fellow Am. Acad. Matrimonial Lawyers (mgr. 1983—, cert.); mem. ABA, Fla. Bar Assn. (chmn. family law sect. 1984-86, sec./treas. 1983-84, exec. council, Award Merit 1985), Dade County Bar Assn. (Pro Bono award 1985). Family and matrimonial, State civil litigation. Office: Abrams & Abrams PA 3341 Cornelia Dr Miami FL 33133

ABRAMS, BURT JAY, lawyer; b. Bklyn., Oct. 21, 1934; s. Samuel W. and Beatrice (Blick) A.; m. Fern Broida, Jan. 7, 1960; children: Janis Claire, Alison Sloan. A.B., Princeton U., 1955; J.D., Harvard U., 1958. Bar: N.Y. 1959, D.C. 1962, U.S. Supreme Ct. 1962, U.S. Tax Ct. 1963. Atty.-advisor Tax Ct. of U.S., Washington, 1958-60; atty. U.S. Dept. Justice, Washington, 1960-62; assoc. firm Milbank, Tweed, Hadley & McCloy, N.Y.C., 1962-68, ptnr., 1969—. Contbr. articles to profl. jours. Trustee Orange Valley Social Settlement, West Orange, N.J., 1972-82, pres., 1978-80; mem. Mayor's Task Force on Econ. Devel. Tax Policy, 1985—. Mem. ABA, N.Y. Bar Assn. (tax sect. exec. com. 1973-74), Bar Assn. City N.Y., Harvard Law Sch. Assn. N.Y.C., N.Y. C. of C. and Industry (chmn. com. on taxation 1983—, bd. dirs. 1986—), Princeton Alumni Assn. Essex County. Jewish. Clubs: Knoll Country, Wall St. Office: 1 Chase Manhattan Plaza New York NY 10005

ABRAMS, DOUGLAS BREEN, lawyer; b. Greenville, S.C., Mar. 18, 1954; s. Sol E. and Davitia F. (Fleishman) A.; m. Margaret M. Smith, May 15, 1976; children: Noah Breen, Elliott Sol. BA magna cum laude, Wake Forest U., 1976, JD, 1979. Bar: N.C. 1979, S.C. 1979, U.S. Dist. Ct. (ea. and mid. dists.) N.C. 1979, U.S. Ct. Appeals (4th cir.) 1979, U.S. Dist. Ct. (we. dist.) N.C. 1983. Assoc. Blanchard, Tucker, Twiggs & Abrams P.A., Raleigh, N.C., 1979-83, ptnr., 1983—; lectr. U. N.C., Chapel Hill, Wake Forest U., Winston-Salem, N.C., 1983—; mem. Ct. Info. System, Civil Adv. Com., Adminstrv. Office of Cts., 1986. Research editor Wake Forest U. Law Rev., 1978-79; co-author: Opening and Closing Statements, 1983; co-editor: Wake Forest U. Continuing Legal Education Civil Trial Manual, 1982; contbr. articles to profl. jours. Carswell scholar, 1973. Mem. ABA, N.C. Bar Assn. (products liability com.), N.C. Acad. Trial Lawyers (lectr., edn. com. 1982—, pub. service com. 1983—, victims rights com. 1985—), Phi Beta Kappa. Democrat. Jewish. Personal injury, Federal civil litigation, State civil litigation. Home: 5421 Huntingwood Dr Raleigh NC 27606 Office: Blanchard Tucker Twiggs & Abrams 134 Fayetteville St Mall Raleigh NC 27602

ABRAMS, ELLIOTT, government official; b. N.Y.C., Jan. 24, 1948; s. Joseph and Mildred (Kauder) A.; m. Rachel Decter, Mar. 9, 1980; children: Jacob, Sarah, Joseph. B.A., Harvard U., 1969, J.D., 1973; M.S. in Econs, London Sch. Econs., 1970. Bar: N.Y. 1974, U.S. Dist. Ct. (so. and ea. dists.) N.y. 1974, D.C. 1979. Atty. Breed, Abbott & Morgan, N.Y.C., 1974-75; asst. counsel U.S. Senate Permanent Subcom. on Investigations, Washington, 1975; spl. counsel Sen. Henry M. Jackson, 1975-76; spl. counsel Sen. Daniel P. Moynihan, 1977-78, chief of staff, 1978-79; atty. Verner, Liipfert, Bernhard & McPherson, Washington, 1979-80; asst. sec. for internat. orgn. affairs U.S. Dept. State, Washington, 1981, asst. sec. for human rights and humanitarian affairs, 1981-85, asst. sec. for InterAm. affairs, 1985—. Mem. Am. Jewish Com. Mem. Council Fgn. Relations. Administrative and regulatory, Private international, Public international. Office: US Dept State 2101 C St NW Washington DC 20520

ABRAMS, FRANKLIN STEPHEN, lawyer; b. N.Y.C., Sept. 17, 1942; s. Joseph Abrams and Mildred (Kauder) A.; m. Leslie Aura Goldstein, Mar. 6, 1947; children: Courtney, Jason. BA, Harvard U., 1963; LLB, Yale U., 1966; student, NYU, 1967-68. Bar: N.Y. 1967. Instr. law U.S. Mcht. Marine Acad., Kings Point, N.Y., 1966-69; ptnr. Abrams & Abrams P.C., N.Y.C., 1969—. Contbr. articles to profl. jours. Mem. Am. Immigration Lawyers Assn. Avocations: choral singing, running. Immigration, naturalization, and customs. Home: 2 Henhawk Rd Kings Point NY 11024 Office: Abrams & Abrams PC 1 Penn Plaza New York NY 10119

ABRAMS, JEFFREY ALAN, lawyer; b. Indpls., Mar. 28, 1956; s. Jerome Jeffrey and Barbara (Katz) A.; m. Pamela Flack, July 18, 1981 (div. Mar. 1986); 1 child, Grant Jeffrey. BS, Miami U., Oxford, Ohio, 1978; JD, Ind. U., 1981. Bar: Ind. 1981, U.S. Dist. Ct. (so. dist.) Ind. 1981. Assoc. Dann, Pecar, Newman, Talesnick & Kleiman, Indpls., 1981-86, ptnr., 1986—; lectr. landlord and tenant law, 1984-85. Pres., bd. mgrs. North Willow Park Co-Owners Assn., Indpls., 1982-85; bd. dirs. Bur. of Jewish Edn., Indpls., 1984—. Mem. ABA, Ind. Bar Assn., Indpls. Bar Assn. Republican. Club: Broadmoor (Indpls.) (bd. dirs. 1985—, sec. 1986—). Lodge: Optimists. Real property, Contracts commercial, Landlord-tenant. Home: 9041 Butternut Ct Indianapolis IN 46260 Office: Dann Pecar Newman et al Box 82008 Indianapolis IN 46282

ABRAMS, LEHN EDWARD, lawyer; b. Blue Island, Ill., Oct. 29, 1947; s. Everett Jr. and Edith (Lenderman) A.; m. Pamela K. Funck, Mar. 15, 1974. AB, Coll. William and Mary, 1970; JD, U. Fla., 1974. Bar: Fla. 1974, U.S. Dist. Ct. (mid. dist.) Fla. 1975, U.S. Ct. Appeals (5th cir.) 1977, U.S. Dist. Ct. (so. and no. dists.) Fla. 1981, U.S. Ct. Appeals (11th cir.) 1981, U.S. Tax Ct. 1983. Asst. pub. defender 9th jud. cir., Orange County, Orlando, Fla., 1974-80; ptnr. Arnold, Matheny & Eagan P.A., Orlando, 1980—. Mem. ABA, Assn. Trial Lawyers Am. Republican. Club: Orlando Lacrosse. Banking, Consumer commercial, Contracts commercial. Home: 319 Columbo Circle Orlando FL 32804 Office: Arnold Matheny & Eagan PA 853 N Orange Ave Orlando FL 32801

ABRAMS, NANCY, lawyer; b. Indiana, Pa., Dec. 14, 1954; d. Leonard Allen and Sally (Claster) A. AB cum laude, Harvard U., 1976; JD, U. Pitts., 1979. Bar: Pa. 1979, U.S. Dist. Ct. (mid. dist.) Pa. 1979, Fla. 1980. Assoc. Rosenberg & Ufberg, Scranton, Pa., 1979-84, Pechner, Dorfman, Wolffe, Rounick & Cabot, Phila., 1984—. Chmn. Red Cross Ctr. City Blood Council, Scranton, 1982-84. Mem. ABA (labor and employment law sect.), Pa. Bar Assn. (labor and employment law sect.), Fla. Bar Assn. (labor and employment law sect.), Phila. Bar Assn., Lackawanna County Bar Assn. (labor and employment law sect.). Avocation: theatre. Labor, Pension, profit-sharing, and employee benefits. Office: Pechner Dorfman et al 3 Benjamin Franklin Pkwy Philadelphia PA 19102

ABRAMS, NORMAN, legal educator; b. Chgo., July 7, 1933; s. Harry A. and Gertrude (Dick) A.; m. Toshka Alster, 1977; children: Marshall David, Julie, Hanna, Naomi. A.B., U. Chgo., 1952, J.D., 1955. Bar: Ill. 1956, U.S. Supreme Ct. 1967. Asso.-in-law Columbia U. Law Sch., 1955-57; research asso. Harvard Law Sch., 1957-59; sec. Harvard-Brandeis Coop. Research for Israel's Legal Devel., 1957-58, dir., 1959; mem. faculty Law Sch. UCLA, 1959—, prof. law, 1964—, co-dir. Ctr. for Internat. and Strategic Studies, 1982-83, chmn. steering com., 1985—; vis. prof. Hebrew U., 1969-70, Forchheimer vis. prof., Spring 1986; vis. prof. Bar Ilan U., 1970-71, spring 1978, U. So. Calif., summer 1972, spring 1973, Stanford U., fall 1977, U. Calif. at Berkeley, fall 1977, Loyola U., Los Angeles, summers 1974, 75, 76, 79; spl. asst. to U.S. atty. gen., also prof.-in-residence criminal div. Dept. Justice 1966-67; reporter for So. Calif. indigent accused persons study Am. Bar Found., 1963; cons. Gov. Calif. Commn. Los Angeles Riots, 1965; Pres.'s. Commn. Law Enforcement and Adminstrn. Justice, 1966-67, Nat. Commn. on Reform of Fed. Criminal Laws, 1967-69, Rand Corp., 1968-74, Center for Adminstrv. Justice, Am. Bar Assn., 1973-77, Nat. Adv. Commn. on Criminal Justice Standards, Organized Crime Task Force, 1976; spl. hearing officer, conscientious objector cases U.S. Dept. Justice, 1967-68. Author: (with others) Evidence--Cases and Materials, 1983, Federal Criminal Law and Its Enforcement, 1986. Chmn. Jewish Conciliation Bd., Los Angeles, 1975-81; bd. dirs. Bet Tzedek, 1975-85, Los Angeles Hillel Council, 1979-82; chmn. So. Calif. region Am. Profs. for Peace in Middle East, 1981-83; bd. dirs. met. region Jewish Fedn., 1982—, v.p. 1982-83; pres. Westwood Kehillah Congregation, 1985. Mem. Phi Beta Kappa. Criminal, Legal education. Office: 405 Hilgard Ave Los Angeles CA 90024

ABRAMS, RICHARD BRILL, lawyer; b. Mpls., Nov. 2, 1931; s. Joseph E. and Nettie (Brill) A.; m. Myrna Carole Noodleman, Dec. 5, 1965; children—Jennifer, Adam. B.B.A., U. Minn., 1958, B.S.L., 1958, J.D., 1958. Bar: Minn. 1958, U.S. Ct. Appeals (8th cir.) 1981, U.S. Dist. Ct. Minn. 1981, Wis. 1983. Sole practice Mpls., 1958-64; pres. Abrams & Spector, P.A., Mpls., 1964—; ad hoc instr. labor edn. U. Minn. Bd. dirs. Mpls. United Way; bd. dirs., v.p. Courage Ctr., 1977-83, 85-86; mem pain com. Nat. Acad. Sci., Nat. Inst. Medicine, 1986. Served with U.S. Army, 1955-57. Recipient Disting. and Devoted Service award Human Rights Com., Mpls. Central Labor Union Council, 1975; Meritorious Service award Minn. Rehab. Assn., 1978; Disting. Service award Courage Ctr., 1983. Mem. ABA, Minn. State Bar Assn., Wis. State Bar Assn., Assn. Trial Lawyers Am., Minn. Trial Lawyers Assn., Nat. Acad. Scis. (pain com.), Nat. Inst. Medicine. Personal injury, Workers' compensation. Office: Abrams & Spector PA 6800 France Ave S Suite 435 Minneapolis MN 55435

ABRAMS, ROBERT, state official; b. Bronx, N.Y., July 4, 1938; s. Benjamin and Dorothy A.; m. Diane B. Schulder, Sept. 15, 1974; children: Rachel Schulder, Becky Schulder. B.A., Columbia U., 1960; J.D., N.Y. U., 1963; LL.D. (hon.), Hofstra U., 1979; Lugum Doctoris (hon.), Yeshiva U., 1984. Mem. N.Y. State Assembly, 1965-69; pres. Borough of Bronx, 1970-78; atty. gen. State of N.Y., 1979—. Recipient Benjamin Cardozo award for legal excellence Jewish Lawyers Guild, Interfaith award Council of Chs. of N.Y.C., Brotherhood award B'nai B'rith, Man of Yr. award NAACP, Alumni Achievement award NYU Sch. Law, Enviromentalist of Yr., Environ. Planning Lobby N.Y., Disting. Pub. Service citation Bus. Council N.Y. State. Mem. N.Y. State Bar Assn. (Envitron. Achievement award), Assn. Bar City of N.Y., Bronx County Bar Assn., Nat. Assn. Attys. Gen. (gen. v.p., chmn. antitrust com., past chmn. environ. protection com.), Northeastern Regional Conf. Attys. Gen. (past chmn.), Nat. Assn. Attys. Gen. (gen. v.p.). Democrat. Law Enforcement Administration. Office: 120 Broadway New York NY 10271

ABRAMS, ROBERT ALLEN, lawyer; b. Newark, Aug. 25, 1937; s. Thomas and Dorothy (Belford) A.; m. Toby Alice Kaplan, Aug. 20, 1967; 1 child, Thomas Adam. Student, U. Miami, 1955-56; AB, Rutgers U., 1960, JD, 1963. Bar: N.J. 1963, U.S. Dist. Ct N.J. 1963, U.S. Supreme Ct. 1969, U.S. Ct. Appeals (3d cir.) 1972. Law clk. to presiding justice Monmouth County Ct., Freehold, N.J., 1963-64; assoc. Reusille, Cornwall, Mausner & Carotenuto, Red Bank, N.J., 1964-67; sole practice Newark, 1968-70; assoc. Skoloff & Wolfe, Newark, 1973-81; ptnr. Patterson & Abrams, Asbury Park, N.J., 1973-81; judge N.J. Ct. Mil. Rev., 1976—; ptnr. Abrams & Gatta, Ocean, N.J., 1981—; pres. LawWare Corp., Ocean, 1985—; lectr. various legal instns. Co-author: N.J Family Law, 1976, 3d ed.; inventor computer software Divorce Settlement Assistant, 1986. Atty. Wall (N.J.) Twp. Bd. Adjustment, 1973-81; v.p. Temple Beth Miriam, Elberon, N.J., 1983-84. Served to capt. JAGC, N.J. Army NG, 1968-74. Fellow Am. Acad. Matrimonial Lawyers; mem. ABA, N.J. Bar Assn., Monmouth County Bar Assn., Ocean County Bar Assn. Jewish. Avocations: golf, tennis. Family and matrimonial. Office: Abrams and Gatta PA 1127 Hwy 35 Ocean NJ 07712

ABRAMS, SAMUEL K., lawyer; b. Phila., May 31, 1913; s. Maurice and Mary (Hockstein) A.; m. Sylvia Lester, June 19, 1949; 1 son, Richard K. B.A., U. Okla., 1933, LL.B., 1936; postgrad., Wharton Sch., U. Pa. Bar: Okla. 1936, D.C. 1949. Asst. county atty. Logan County, Okla., 1937-41; atty. civil div. Dept. Justice 1947-49; asst. U.S. atty. D.C., 1949-50; acting asst. gen. counsel Econ. Stblzn. Agy., 1950; chief merger and clearance sect., antitrust div. Dept. Justice, 1951-52; partner firm Morison, Murphy, Abrams & Haddock (and predecessors), Washington, 1952-79, Baker & Hostetler, Washington, 1979—; adv. bd. antitrust and trade regulation report Bur. Nat. Affairs. Served to capt. AUS, 1942-46. Mem. Am. Bar Assn., D.C. Bar Assn., Okla. Bar Assn., Phi Beta Kappa, Order of Coif. Club: Internat. (Washington). Administrative and regulatory, Antitrust. Home: 5828 Lenox Rd Bethesda MD 20817 Office: Baker & Hostetler 1050 Connecticut Ave NW Washington DC 20036

ABRAMS, STUART, lawyer; b. N.Y.C., May 2, 1941; s. Hyman Sidney and Goldie (Abramowitz) A.; m. Eileen Sheingold, June 25, 1961 (div. 1977); children: Korri, Kevin; m. Peggy Lou Goodman Meyers, Jan. 10, 1982; 1 stepchild, Stefanie Meyers. BBA, CCNY, 1965; JD cum laude, New York Law Sch., 1968. Bar: N.Y. 1968, U.S. Dist. Ct. (ea. and so. dists.) N.Y. 1970, U.S. Ct. Appeals (2d cir.) 1970, U.S. Tax Ct. 1978, U.S. Supreme Ct. 1978. Ptnr. Schwartz, Rothman & Abrams P.C., N.Y.C., 1969-78; mng. assoc. Eisenberg, Honig & Meyer, N.Y.C., 1978-79; sole practice N.Y.C., 1979-84; counsel Finkelstein, Bruckman, Wohl & Rothman, N.Y.C., 1984-87; ptnr. Finkelstein, Bruckman, Wohl, Most & Rothman, N.Y.C., 1987—. Contbr. articles to profl. jours. Mem. N.Y. State Bar Assn. (mediation com., arbitration com., com. on continuing legal edn., family law sect.). State civil litigation, Family and matrimonial, General corporate. Office: Finkelstein Bruckman Wohl Most & Rothman 801 2d Ave New York NY 10017

ABRAMSON, HARVEY STANLEY, lawyer; b. Phila., Jan. 27, 1937; s. Leonard M. and Aurora (Segal); m. Irene E. Schaffel, Jan. 9, 1980; children: Mark J., Andrew J., Brett J. BA, U. Pa., 1958; JD, U. Miami, 1962. Pres. A. Abramson Law Office, P.A., Miami, Fla., 1962—, Broward, Brevard, Orange, Duval, Marion, Pasco and other counties, Fla., 1962—. Pres. Temple Menorah, Miami Beach, Fla., 1984—; bd. trustees Zool. Soc., Miami, 1985—. Served with USAFR, 1965-68, USCGR, 1965-68. Mem. Fla. Bar Assn., Dade County Bar Assn., Broward County Bar Assn., Assn. Trial Lawyers Am., N.Y. State Bar Assn. (sustaining), Acad. Fla. Trial Lawyers. Jewish. Lodge: Masons (worshipful master surfside chpt. 1970, 83). Avocations: stamps, art, autos. Personal injury, Workers' compensation. Office: A Abramson Law Office PA 3705 Biscayne Blvd Miami FL 33137

ABRAMSON, JOEL ELIOT, lawyer; b. N.Y.C., May 21, 1943; s. David Albert and Lillian (Salwen) A.; m. Blima Tuchmajer, Dec. 20, 1982; 1 child, Rachel. AB, Columbia U., 1964, MA in Econs., 1966; JD, NYU, 1969. Bar: N.Y. 1970, D.C. 1970, U.S. Supreme Ct. 1974. Atty. SEC, Washington, 1969-73; assoc. Phillips, Nizer, Benjamin, Krim & Ballon, N.Y.C., 1973-76; sole practice N.Y.C., 1976—; bd. dirs. Bronx (N.Y.) Legal Services Corp. Pres. Jewish Am. Polit. Affairs Com., N.Y.C., 1983-86. Mem. N.Y. County Lawyers Assn. (com. mem.). Real property, Securities, Family and matrimonial. Office: 25 W 43d St Suite 1011 New York NY 10036

ABRELL, JOSEPH KINDRED, marketing and media consultant, legal journalist, consultant; b. Freedom, Ind., July 24, 1934; s. Carl Calvin and Beatrice (Kindred) A; m. Judith Arlene Enlow, Aug. 9, 1959; children—Lisa, Bradford. A.B., Ind. U., 1960; M.A., Columbia U., 1966; J.D., U. Miami, 1976. Bar: Fla. 1976, U.S. Dist. Ct. (so. dist.) Fla. 1976, D.C. 1977, U.S. Ct. Appeals (5th cir.) 1977, U.S. Ct. Appeals (11th cir.) 1981. Reporter Terre Haute Star, Ind., 1959; corr. Newsweek mag., Chgo., N.Y.C., 1960-63; news dir., pub. affairs dir. Sta. WTVJ-TV, Miami, Fla., 1963-84; v.p. Miami Dolphins, 1984-86; pvt. practice mktg. and media cons., Miami, 1986—. Host, exec. producer Montage TV program, 1976-84, (12 Emmy awards). Chmn. Gov.'s Task Force on Cable TV, 1984—. Served as sgt. USAF, 1953-57. Ernie Pyle scholar, 1960; CBS fellow, 1965. Mem. Nat. Acad. TV Arts and Scis. (pres. 1982-84, nat. trustee 1983-85), Sigma Delta Chi (pres. 1972-73). Clubs: Miami, University. Communications, Libel. Home: 6245 SW 121st St Miami FL 33156 Office: 2649 S Bayshore Dr Suite 1906 Miami FL 33133 also Office: 2649 S Bayshore Dr #1906 Miami FL 33133

ABREU, LUIS ALBERTO, lawyer; b. Pinar Del Rio, Cuba, Apr. 20, 1956; came to U.S., 1961; s. Arnaldo Jesus and Justa (Villar) A.; m. Sallie Brown Shadrick, Aug. 23, 1980; 1 child, Sarah. BA, Davidson Coll., 1978; JD, U. Fla., 1981. Bar: Va. 1981, U.S. Bankruptcy Ct. 1981, U.S. Ct. Appeals (4th cir.) 1981. From assoc. to ptnr. Clement & Wheatley, Danville, Va., 1981—. Chmn. Local Human Rights Com., Danville, 1986—. Alex Hemby scholar Davidson Coll., 1974-78; recipient Bob Griese award Miami Touchdown Club, 1976. Mem. ABA, Va. Bar Assn., Danville Bar Assn., Hist. Soc., Danville Mus. Fine Arts. Republican. Roman Catholic. Lodge: Lions (pres. 1984-85). Avocations: racquetball, house restoration. Bankruptcy, Consumer commercial, Contracts commercial. Home: 169 Holbrook Ave Danville VA 24541 Office: Clement & Wheatley 400 Masonic Bldg Danville VA 24541

ABT, EVET SUE LOEWEN, lawyer; b. Borger, Tex., Sept. 13, 1952; s. Bruno Fritz and Tessibel Nadene (Collins) L.; m. Bruce Alan, June 12, 1973. BA in Cultural Studies, U. Tenn., 1974; JD, Santa Clara U., 1979. Bar: Calif. 1979, U.S. Dist. Ct. (no. dist.) Calif. 1979. Legal editor, assoc. Bancroft-Whitney, Inc., San Francisco, 1980; dep. atty. City of San Jose, Calif., 1980-85, sr. dep. city atty., 1985-86, chief dep. city atty., 1986—. Mem. ABA, Santa Clara Bar Assn. (pres. women lawyers com. 1986), Airport Ops. Council Internat. (legal com. 1981—). Democrat. Mennonite. Avocations: jogging, reading. Local government, Real property. Office: City Attys Office 151 W Mission St San Jose CA 95110

ABUT, CHARLES C., lawyer; b. Ankara, Turkey, Jan. 11, 1944; s. Vedat Abut and Eleanor (Klein) Von Landesberger); B.A., Columbia U., 1969; J.D., Cornell U., 1972. Bar: N.J. 1972, U.S. Supreme Ct. 1976, D.C. 1979, N.Y. 1980; cert. civil trial atty. Assoc. Hannoch & Weisman, Newark, 1972-74, Margolis & Bergstein, Verona, N.J., 1974-79; ptnr. Lowen & Abut, Ft. Lee, N.J., 1979—. Served with U.S. Army, 1964-67. Mem. ABA, Am. Acad. Matrimonial Lawyers, Assn. Trial Lawyers Am., N.J. Trial Lawyers Assn., Psi Upsilon. Lodge: Masons. State civil litigation, Federal civil litigation, Family and matrimonial. Home: 5 Horizon Rd Fort Lee NJ 07024 Office: Lowen & Abut One Executive Dr Fort Lee NJ 07024

ACERS, MAURICE WILSON, lawyer; b. Dallas, Aug. 27, 1907; B.A., So. Meth. U., 1929; LL.B., J.D., U. Tex., 1934; postgrad. Harvard U., 1929-30, 61, 76, Met. Police Coll., London, 1938. Bar: Tex. 1934. Successively spl. agt., personnel dir., insp. FBI, 1937-47; exec. sec. Govt. Allan Shivers of Tex., 1951-55; mem. Tex. Employment Commn., 1955-60; pres. Acers Investment Co., also chmn. bd.; pres., gen. counsel Ebby-Halliday Realtors, Dallas, 1961—; Tex. rep., vice chmn. Interstate Oil Compact Commn., 1950-55. Bd. dirs. S.W. Research Inst., San Antonio, 1947—, chmn. bd., 1971-75; pres. Tex. United Community Services, 1969-70, chmn. bd., 1971—; bd. dirs. Austin YMCA; pres. Greater Dallas Crime Commn., 1977-79; chmn. bd. 1979-80; mem. nat. adv. council USO; nat. assoc. Boys Clubs Am. Mem. ABA, Tex. Bar Assn., Dallas Bar Assn., Travis County Bar Assn., Jefferson County Bar Assn., Mid-Continent Oil and Gas Assn., Internat. Real Estate Fedn. (world pres. profl. and ednl. exchange com. 1977-80, chmn. congress com. 1982-83), Nat. Assn. Realtors, Tex. Assn. Realtors, Dallas C. of C., Tex. Assn. Bus., Dallas Hist. Soc., Dallas Council World Affairs. Named Hon. Houstonian; Ark Traveler; adm. Tex. Navy; hon. mayor Hollywood (Calif.); Knight of the Neches; ambassador at large San Antonio; spl. Tex. Ranger. Address: PO Box 12348 Dallas TX 75225 Office: 4455 Sigma Rd Dallas TX 75244-4597

ACKER, ALAN SCOTT, lawyer; b. Chgo., Mar. 14, 1953; s. Isreal and Loretta (Alter) A.; m. Lillian Grace Kacyn, Aug. 12, 1973; children: Steven, Kenneth, Jennifer, Daniel. BS, U. Ill., 1974; JD, IIT, 1977. Bar: Ill. 1977, Va. 1986. 2d v.p. AM. Nat. and Trust Co., Chgo., 1978-81; assoc. Reuben & Procter, Chgo., 1981-86, Hofheimer, Nusbaum, McPhaul & Brenner, Norfolk, Va., 1986—; adj. prof. law DePaul U., Chgo., 1984-85. Contbr. articles to profl. jours. Mem. ABA, Ill. Bar Assn., Chgo. Bar Assn. (David C. Hilliard award 1985), Va. Bar Assn., Norfolk-Portsmouth Bar Assn., Tidewater Estate Planning Council, Va. CPA Soc., Am. Inst. CPAs, Ill. CPAs Soc. Jewish. Estate taxation, Probate. Office: Hofheimer Nusbaum McPhaul & Brenner 1010 Plaza One Norfolk VA 23510

ACKER, WILLIAM MARSH, JR., judge; b. Birmingham, Ala., Oct. 25, 1927; s. William Marsh and Estelle (Lampkin) A.; m. Martha Walters, 1957; children—William Marsh III, Stacey Patricia. B.A., Birmingham So. Coll., 1949; LL.B., Yale U., 1952. Bar: Ala. Assoc. firm Graham, Bibb, Wingo & Foster, Birmingham, Ala., 1952-57; assoc. firm Smyer, White, Reid & Acker, 1957-72, Dominick, Fletcher, Yeilding, Acker, Wood & Lloyd, Birmingham, 1972-82; judge U.S. Dist. Ct. (no. dist.) Ala., 1982—. Mem. Ala. Republican Exec. Com.; del. to Repub. Nat. Convention, 1972, 76, 80. Judicial administration. Office: 354 Federal Courthouse Birmingham AL 35203 *

ACKERLY, BENJAMIN CLARKSON, lawyer; b. Lexington, Va., Aug. 25, 1942; s. John Paul Jr. and Marguerite Emmetta (Clarkson) A.; m. Lucile Wiltshire Moore; children: Benjamin, Cabell, Burns, Stewart. BA, U. Va., 1965, LLB, 1968. Bar: Va. 1968, U.S. Dist. Dist. Ct. (ea. dist.) Va. 1970, U.S. Ct. Appeals (4th cir.) 1976, U.S. Supreme Ct. 1976, U.S. Ct. Claims 1978. Assoc. Hunton & Wiilliams, Richmond, Va., 1970—. Pres., trustee, chmn. bd. dirs. Hist. Richmond Found., 1972—; bd. dirs. Richmond Goodwill Industries, 1971-76. Served to capt. U.S. Army. 1968-70. Mem. ABA, Va. BAr Assn., Richmond Bar Assn. (pres. bankruptcy sect. 1986—). Episcopalian. Clubs: Country Club of Va. (Richmond); Fishing Bay Yacht (Deltaville, Va.). Avocations: sailing, skiing, gardening. Bankruptcy, Consumer commercial, State civil litigation. Home: 6106 Three Chopt Rd Richmond VA 23226 Office: Hunton & Williams 707 E Main St PO Box 1535 Richmond VA 23212

ACKERMAN, ALAN THOMAS, lawyer, law educator; b. Detroit, Mich., Apr. 10, 1947; s. Irving and Feige (Goldberg) A.; m. Sharyl Lynne Taub, Dec. 15, 1984. BA, Mich. State U., 1968, M in Labor and Indsl. Relations, 1971; JD, U. Mich., 1972. Bar: Mich. 1972, Fla. 1972, D.C. 1975. Ptnr. Ackerman & Ackerman, Detroit, 1972—; adj. prof. U. Detroit Law Sch., 1983—; chmn. condemnation com. Mich. State Bar, 1980-81. Contbr. articles to profl. jours. Mem. ABA (real property sect. condemnation com. 1976—, chmn. 1987—), Mich. Bar Assn. (Rep. assembly 1984—), Detroit Bar Assn. (condemnation com. 1978-80). Condemnation. Office: Ackerman & Ackerman 3650 Penobscot Bldg Detroit MI 48226

ACKERMAN, BRUCE ARNOLD, lawyer, educator; b. N.Y.C., Aug. 19, 1943; s. Nathan and Jean (Rosenberg) A.; m. Susan Gould Rose, May 27, 1967; children: Sybil Rose, John Mill. BA summa cum laude, Harvard U., 1964; LLB with honors, Yale U., 1967. Bar: Pa. 1970. Law clk. U.S. Ct. Appeals, 1967-68; law clk. to assoc. justice John M. Harlan U.S. Supreme Ct., 1968-69; prof. law and public policy analysis U. Pa., 1969-74; prof. law Yale U., 1974-82; Beekman prof. law and philosophy Columbia U., 1982-87; Sterling prof. law and polit. sci. Yale U., New Haven, Conn., 1987—. Author: Private Property and the Constitution, 1977, Social Justice in the Liberal State, 1980 (Gavel award ABA), (with Hassler) Clean Coal/Dirty Air, 1981, Reconstructing American Law, 1984, (with others) The Uncertain Search for Environmental Quality, 1974 (Henderson prize Harvard Law Sch.). Guggenheim fellow, 1985, Nat. Acad. Arts and Scis. fellow, 1985. Fellow Am. Acad. Arts and Scis. Legal education. Office: Yale U Wall St New Haven CT 06501

ACKERMAN, HAROLD A., judge; b. 1928. Student, Seton Hall U., 1945-46, 48; LL.B., Rutgers U., 1951. Bar: N.J. 1951. Adminstrv. asst. to Commr. of Labor and Industry, State of N.J., 1955-56; judge of compensation State of N.J., 1956-62, supervising judge of compensation, 1962-65; judge Union County Dist. Ct., 1965-70, presiding judge, 1966-70; judge Union County Ct., 1970-73, Superior Ct. law div., 1973-75, Superior Ct. Chancery div., 1975-79, U.S. Dist. Ct., Dist. of N.J., 1980—; mem. Supreme Ct. Com. on Revision of Rules, 1967; chmn. Supreme Ct. Com. on County Dist. Cts., 1968; mem. faculty Nat. Jud. Coll., 1978. Office: US Dist Ct US Post Office and Courthouse 402 E State St PO Box 1688 Trenton NJ 08605 *

ACKERMAN, JOHN EDWARD, lawyer, educator; b. Sundance, Wyo., Sept. 11, 1939; s. John Evertt and Alice Elizabeth (Reynolds) A.; m. Deborah Ann Bartlett, Oct. 4, 1966; 1 dau., Leslie Donelle; m. 2d, Barbara Toby Baruch, May 26, 1979; 1 dau., Jessica Sundance. B.A., U. Wyo., 1961, J.D., 1967. Bar: Wyo. 1967, U.S. Dist. Ct. Wyo. 1967, U.S. Ct. Appeals (10th cir.) 1967, U.S. Supreme Ct. 1971, Tex. 1977, U.S. Dist. Ct. (so. dist.) Tex. 1977, U.S. Ct. Appeals (5th cir.) 1977. Assoc., Fagan & Fagan, Casper, Wyo., 1967-69; sole practice, Casper, 1969-74; dean Nat. Coll. for Criminal Def., Houston, 1974-82; sole practice, Houston, 1982—. Served with U.S. Army, 1961-64. Mem. ABA, (criminal justice council 1978-82), Nat. Assn. Criminal Def. Lawyers (pres. 1982-83), Tex. Criminal Def. Lawyers Assn. Democrat. Criminal, Administrative and regulatory, Federal civil litigation. Home: 5111 Briarbend Houston TX 77035 Office: 320 Main St Suite 100 Houston TX 77002

ACKERMAN, KENNETH EDWARD, lawyer, educator; b. Bronx, N.Y., May 25, 1946; s. Kenneth L. and Anna (McCarthy) A.; m. Kathryn H. Hartnett, July 10, 1972; children—Andrew, Carl, Sheila, Edward, Daniel, Kenneth. Student Talladega Coll., 1966; B.A., Fordham Coll., 1968; J.D. Cornell U., 1971. Bar: N.Y. 1972, U.S. Dist. Ct. (no. dist.) N.Y. 1975, U.S. Ct. Appeals (2d cir.) 1975, U.S. Supreme Ct. 1976. Clk. legal dept. Port Authority N.Y. and N.J., 1969; Clk. legal dept. IBM, 1970; ptnr. Mackenzie Smith, Lewis, Michell & Hughes, Syracuse, N.Y., 1971—; adj. prof. banking law and negotiable instruments Am. Inst. Banking program Onondaga Community Coll.; adj prof. Syracuse U. Coll., 1984—. Chmn. Central N.Y. chpt. March of Dimes, 1972-82; mem. A.A.-USSR Travel Group, 1987; bd. dirs. Central N.Y. Health Systems Agy., Inc., 1982-83. Mem. ABA, N.Y. State Bar Assn., Onondaga County Bar Assn. Banking, Bankruptcy, Contracts commercial. Office: 600 Onondaga Savs Bank Bldg Syracuse NY 13202

ACKERMAN, NEIL HARRIS, lawyer; b. Bklyn., Dec. 8, 1955; s. Jack and Estelle (Kuchlik) A. BA in Philosophy and Polit. Sci., SUNY, Binghamton, 1977; JD cum laude, Am. U., 1981. Bar: N.Y. 1982, U.S. Dist. Ct. (ea. and so. dists.) N.Y. 1982. Law clk. to judge U.S. Bankruptcy Ct. (ea. dist.) N.Y., Bklyn., 1982; assoc. Holland & Zinker, Smithtown, N.Y., 1982-84, Shaw, Goldman, Licitra, Levine & Weinberg P.C., Garden City, N.Y., 1984-86; sole practice Mineola, N.Y., 1986—; lectr. Suffolk Acad. Law, 1984, Nassau Acad. Law, 1985. Active Big Brother and Sisters of Nassau County, N.Y., 1985-87. Mem. ABA, N.Y. State Bar Assn., Nassau County Bar Assn., Suffolk County Bar Assn. (bankruptcy and insolvency law com., 1983-85), Phi Delta Phi. Democrat. Jewish. Avocations: running, reading, calisthenics. Bankruptcy, Consumer commercial, Contracts commercial. Home: 90 Westwood Dr #197 Westbury NY 11540 Office: 114 Old Country Rd Suite 152 Mineola NY 11501

ACKERMAN, ROBERT A(RTHUR), lawyer; b. Buffalo, Dec. 21, 1923; s. Thurston Fuller and Margaret (Myers) A.; divorced; children: Eric T., Konrad L. AB, Tufts U., 1946; JD, Columbia U., 1949. Bar: Mass. 1949, D.C. 1964, U.S. Ct. Appeals (D.C. cir.) 1966, U.S. Supreme Ct. 1971. With U.S. Govt., West Berlin, Fed. Republic of Germany, 1953-58, USN, Republic of China, 1959-61; trial atty. civil rights div. Dept. Justice, Washington, 1965-68, asst. U.S. atty. office of U.S.A., 1968-70, chief Students for Dem. Soc. task force internal security div., 1970-71; sole practice Washington, 1971—. Served to 1st lt. USMCR, 1945-46, PTO. Mem. ABA, Fed. Bar Assn., D.C. Bar Assn., Asst. U.S. Attys. Assn. Club: Torch (Washington) (sec. 1985-86, bd. dirs.). Avocation: rebuilding 1970 MG car. General practice, Private international, Personal injury.

ACKERSON, NELS J(OHN), lawyer, international consultant, arbitration counsel; b. Indpls., Apr. 12, 1944; s. Ralph D. and Mariel F. (Maze) A.; m. Sharon Carroll Ackerson, June 11, 1983; children by previous marriage: Betsy Virginia, Peter Nels; stepchildren: Stacia Carroll Loveall, Joshua Michael Loveall. BS with distinction, Purdue U., 1967; M Pub. Policy, Harvard U., 1971, JD cum laude, 1971. Bar: Ind. 1971, U.S. Dist. Ct. (so. dist.) Ind. 1971, U.S. Ct. Appeals (7th cir.) 1971. Advisor Harvard Adv. Mission to Republic of Columbia, 1970; assoc. Barnes, Hickam, Pantzer & Boyd, Indpls., 1971-76; chief counsel U.S. Senate Subcom. Constl. Amendments, Washington, 1976-77; chief counsel, exec. dir. U.S. Senate Subcom. on Constitution, Washington, 1977-79; ptnr. Campbell, Kyle & Proffitt, Noblesville, Ind., 1979-82; ptnr. Sidley & Austin, Washington, 1982—; mng. dir. Sidley & Austin & Naguib, Cairo, Egypt, 1982-84. Bd. editors Harvard Law Rev., 1968-1971. Mem. exec. bd. Am. Research Ctr., Egypt, 1982-84; U.S. mem., vice chmn. Binat. Fulbright Commn. U.S. and Egypt, 1982-84; Dem. nominee for U.S. Congress, 5th dist., Ind., 1980. Mem. ABA (litigation sect., bus. and banking sect., internat. law sect.), Am. Soc. Internat. Law, Internat. Law Soc., Am. C. of C. in Egypt (pres. 1984). Democrat. Presbyterian. General corporate, Private international, Civil litigation international. Office: Sidley & Austin 1722 Eye St NW Washington DC 20006 also: One First National Plaza Chicago IL 60603 also: 2049 Century Plaza E Los Angeles CA 90067 also: 520 Madison Ave New York NY 10022 also: Norfolk House, 31 St James's Sq, London SWIY 4JR, England also: UIC Bldg, 20th Floor, Suite 2008, 5 Shenton Way Singapore 0106 also: 12 Midan El Sheikh Youssef, Garden City, Cairo Egypt also: PO Box 8650, Riyadh Saudi Arabia also: PO Box 6750, Deira Dubai/UAE

ACKMAN, MILTON ROY, lawyer; b. N.Y.C., July 17, 1932; m. Carmela Suckow, July 14, 1959; children: David M., Daniel L. B.B.A., CCNY, 1953; LL.B, Columbia U., 1958. Bar: N.Y. 1958. Assoc. firm Fried, Frank, Harris, Shriver & Jacobson, N.Y., 1959-66; ptnr. Fried, Frank, Harris, Shriver & Jacobson, N.Y.C., 1967—; law sec. Judge William B. Herlands, U.S. Dist. Ct. (so.dist.), N.Y., 1958-59. Served with U.S. Army, 1953-55. Mem. Assn. Bar City N.Y. Federal civil litigation, State civil litigation, Securities. Home: 505 Laguardia Pl New York NY 10012 Office: Fried Frank Harris Shriver & Jacobson 1 New York Plaza New York NY 10004

ACKMAN, RICHARD LEROY, lawyer; b. Belvidere, Ill., Sept. 23, 1927; s. LeRoy William and Frances Ann (Redpath) A.; children: Kathleen, Jeffrey, Todd. JD, U. Ill., 1951. Bar: Ill. 1950, U.S. Supreme Ct. 1960, U.S. Dist. Ct. (ea. dist.) Ill. 1956. Pres. Ackman, Marek, Boyd & Simutis Ltd., Kankakee, Ill., 1970—. Served with U.S. Navy, 1945-47. Mem. Kankakee Bar Assn., Ill. Bar Assn., Chgo. Bar Assn., ABA, Am. Coll. Trial Lawyers. Episcopalian. Lodges: Elks, Moose, Masons, Shriners. Clubs: Kankakee Country, Retreat, The 100, Union League, Turtle Creek. Personal injury, Workers' compensation, General corporate. Office: Suite 400 1 Dearborn Sq Kankakee IL 60901

ACOBA, SIMEON RIVERA, JR., judge; b. Honolulu, Mar. 11, 1944; s. Simeon R. and Martina (Domingo) A. B.A., U. Hawaii, 1966; J.D., Northwestern U., 1969. Bar: Hawaii 1969, U.S. Dist. Ct. Hawaii, U.S. Ct. Appeals (9th cir.). Law clk. Hawaii Supreme Ct., Honolulu, 1969-70; housing officer U. Hawaii, Honolulu, 1970-71; dep. atty. gen., Honolulu, 1971-73; sole practice, Honolulu, 1973-80; judge 1st Cir. Ct., State of Hawaii, Honolulu, 1980—; atty. on spl. contract Div. OSHA, Dept. Labor, Honolulu, 1975-77, Pub. Utilities Div., State Hawaii, 1976-77, Campaign Spending Com., State Hawaii, 1976; staff atty. Hawaii State Legislature, 1975. Bd. dirs. Hawaii Mental Health Assn., 1975-77, Nuuanu YMCA, 1975-78; mem. Gov.'s Conf. on Yr. 2000, Honolulu, 1970, Citizens Com. on Adminstrn. of Justice, 1972, State Drug Abuse Commn., 1975-76. Recipient Liberty Bell award, 1964. Mem. ABA, Hawaii Bar Assn. (dir. young lawyers sect. 1973), Assn. Trial Lawyers Am. Criminal, Jurisprudence, Personal injury. Office: 1st Cir Ct 12th Div 777 Punchbowl St Honolulu HI 96813

ACOMB, JAMES RICHARD, II, lawyer; b. Athens, Ohio, Oct. 10, 1946; s. James Richard and Dorthy Ann (Schilling) A.; m. Lelia Maria Krstulovic, Mar. 23, 1974; 1 child, James Velimir. BS, U. Ky., 1969; JD, Capital U., 1973. Bar: Ohio 1973, N.Y. 1986. Atty., examiner Ohio Dept. Taxation, Columbus, 1973-74; asst. atty. gen. State of Ohio, Columbus, 1974—. Mem. ABA, N.Y. State Bar Assn. Democrat. Roman Catholic. Administrative and regulatory, Real property. Home: 1020 Timberbank Dr Westerville OH 43081 Office: Office Atty Gen 25 S Front St Columbus OH 43216

ACOSTA, RAYMOND LUIS, judge; b. N.Y.C., May 31, 1925; s. Ramon J. and Carmen J. (Acha-Jimenez) Acosta-Colon; m. Marie Hatcher, Nov. 2, 1957; children: Regina, Gregory, Ann Marie. Student, Princeton U., 1948; J.D., Rutgers U., 1951. Spl. agt. FBI, San Diego, Washington, Miami, Fla., 1954-58; asst. U.S. atty. San Juan, P.R., 1958-61; individual practice law 1961-67; trust officer Banco Credito y Ahorro Ponceno, San Juan, 1967-80; U.S. atty. Dist. P.R., Hato Rey, 1980-82; judge U.S. Dist. Ct. P.R., San Juan, 1982—; Alt. del. U.S.-P.R. Commn. on Status, 1962-63; mem. Gov.'s Spl. Com. to Study Structure and Orgn. Police Dept., P.R., 1969. Contbr. articles to profl. jours. Pres. United Fund, P.R., 1979. Served with USN, 1943-46. Recipient Meritorious Service certificate, 1976, Merit certificate Mayor San Juan, 1973. Mem. Fed. Bar Assn. (pres., P.R. 1967), P.R. Bankers Assn. (chmn. trust div. 1971, 75, 77), P.R. Bar Assn., Soc. Former Spl. Agts. FBI, Bergen County (N.J.) Bar Assn. Roman Catholic. Club: Rotary (San Juan). Office: PO Box 3671 Old San Juan Sta San Juan PR 00904

ADAIR, CHARLES ROBERT, JR., lawyer; b. Narrows, Va., Sept. 29, 1914; s. Charles Robert and Margaret (Davis) A.; m. Lillian Adele Duffee, Sept. 19, 1942. B.S., U. Ala., 1942, LL.B., 1948, J.D., 1969. Bar: Ala. bar 1948. Since practiced in Dadeville; solicitor Tallapoosa County, 1955-73; vice chmn. Ala. Securities Commn., 1969-71; commr., ; v.p., bd. dirs. Dadeville Industries, Inc.; bd. dirs. Bank of Dadeville, Ala.. Chmn. Dadeville One Drive, 1960; chmn. Horseshoe Bend Regional Library, 1960-65; mem., sec. planning commn. City of Dadeville, 1965-80; hon. life mem. Bethel Vol. Fire Dept. and Rescue Service; Jackson's Gap Vol. Fire Dept. and Rescue Service; trustee Ala. Law Inst., Ala. Bar Found. Served as officer USAAF, World War II. Mem. Ala. bar assn., Tallapoosa County bar assn., 5th Circuit bar assn. (pres.), Farrah Law Soc., V.F.W., Am. Legion, E. Ala. Peace Officers Assn. (hon. life), Scabbard and Blade, Omicron Delta Kappa, Delta Tau Delta, Phi Alpha Delta. Presbyn. Clubs: The Club, Relay House, Downtown, Still Waters, Quarterback (past capt.). Lodges: Masons, Kiwanis (dist. lt.-gov. 1980-81). Home: Duffee's Hill Dadeville AL 36853 Office: Old Bank of Dadeville Bldg Dadeville AL 36853

ADAIR, THOMAS SCARBOROUGH, lawyer; b. Gordo, Ala., Aug. 30, 1918; s. Thomas Scarborough and Bessie Ora (Pugh) A.; m. Mildred Margaret McLeskey, Aug. 22, 1940; children: Sheila Lynn, Thomas Steven. JD, U. Ala., 1942. Bar: Ala. 1942, U.S. Dist. Ct. (mid. dist.) Ala. 1947, Ga. 1950, U.S. Dist. Ct. (no. dist.) Ga. 1951, U.S. Ct. Appeals (5th cir.) 1951, U.S. Supreme Ct. 1958, D.C. 1981, U.S. Ct. Appeals (11th cir.) 1983. Ptnr. James, Elmore & Adair, Montgomery, Ala., 1946-50, Adair & Goldthwaite, Atlanta, 1950-83; pres. Adair, Scanlon & McHugh P.C., Atlanta and Washington, 1983—; gen. counsel Communications Workers of Am., Washington, 1980—; mem. adv. com. Fed. Mediation and Conciliation Service, Washington, 1973-82, lawyers adv. panel AFL-CIO, 1980—, exec. bd. lawyers coordinating com., 1984—. Chmn. exec. com. Fulton County Dems., Atlanta, 1966-72. Served to lt. (j.g.) USN, 1943-46, PTO. Mem. ABA, Ga. Bar Assn., D.C. Bar Assn. Club: Cherokee Town and Country (governing bd. 1967-71, v.p. 1970) (Atlanta). Labor. Home: 5095 Long Island Dr NW Atlanta GA 30327 Office: Adair Scanlon & McHugh PC 1430 W Peachtree St NW Atlanta GA 30309

ADAIR, WENDELL HINTON, JR., lawyer; b. Ft. Benning, Ga., Mar. 17, 1944; s. Wendell H. Sr. and Jacqueline (Moore) A.; m. Roberta Chapman, Sept. 3, 1966; children: Elizabeth Carroll, John Michael, Benjamin David. BA, Emory U., 1966, postgrad., 1966-67; JD, U. Chgo., 1969. Bar: Ill. 1969. Assoc. Ross, Hardies, O'Keefe, Babcock & Parsons, Chgo., 1969-72; ptnr. Mayer, Brown & Platt, Chgo., 1972—. Mem. Evanston Zoning Amendment Com., Ill, 1980-83. Mem. ABA (pub. utilities sect.), Ill. Bar Assn., Fed. Energy Bar Assn. (bd. dirs. 1985—), Fed. Energy Bar Assn. (v.p., bd. dirs. 1986—), AGA (bd. dirs. legal sect. 1986—), Am. Gas Assn.. Republican. Club: Econ. (Chgo.). Banking, Contracts commercial, FERC practice. Home: 1507 Colfax St Evanston IL 60201 Office: 190 S LaSalle St 37th Floor Chicago IL 60603

ADAIR, WILLIAM B. (BEN), lawyer, petroleum engineer; b. Lamesa, Tex., Sept. 12, 1927; s. Elvin Marshall and Ruth Harrell (Alldredge) A.; m. Barbara Reed, Sept. 9, 1950; children—William B., Marshall, Edward, Rebecca. Student Tex. A&M U., 1948; B.S. in Petroleum Engring., U. Tex., 1951; J.D., South Tex. Coll. Law, 1971. Bar: Tex. 1971; registered profl. engr., Tex. Various engring., cons. and sales positions with oil-related firms, 1952-72; ptnr. Brynes, Myers, Adair, Campbell & Sinex, and successor firm Adair & Myers, Houston, 1972—. Active Boy Scouts Am., Jr. Achievement; mem. Precinct Democratic Exec. Com., 1970-80. Served with AUS, 1946, to 2d lt., 1949. Mem. State Bar Tex., ABA, Houston Bar Assn., Houston Trial Lawyers Assn., Tex. Trial Lawyers Assn., Assn. Trial Lawyers Am., Tex. Aggie Bar Assn., South Tex. Coll. Law Alumni Assn. (past pres., chmn. bd. dirs.), Delta Theta Phi (vice dean). Clubs: Masons, Shriners. State civil litigation, Family and matrimonial, General practice. Home: 5242 Ariel Houston TX 77096 Office: 1980 Post Oak Blvd Suite 1095 Houston TX 77056

ADAMI, PAUL E., lawyer; b. Peoria, Ill., Oct. 7, 1950; s. Richard R. and Dorothy M. (Crawford) A.; m. Jane Flatley, Dec. 10, 1982; children: Mary Elizabeth, Megan Marie. BS, U. Ill., 1972, JD, 1975. Bar: Ill. 1975, U.S. Dist. Ct. (cen. dist.) Ill. 1976, U.S. Ct. Appeals (7th cir.) 1979. Law clk. to presiding justice U.S. Dist. Ct. (cen. dist.) Ill., Peoria, 1975-76; assoc. Mohan, Alewett & Prillaman, Springfield, Ill., 1976-81; ptnr. Mohan, Alewett & Prillaman, Springfield, 1981—. Ill. Bankers' Assn. scholar, 1971. Mem. ABA, Ill. State Bar Assn. General practice, Construction, Contracts commercial. Home: Rural Rt 1 Box 125 Tallula IL 62688 Office: Mohan Alewelt & Prillaman 325 INB Ctr Springfield IL 62701

ADAMS, ALFRED GRAY, lawyer, real estate developer; b. Winston-Salem, N.C., Feb. 28, 1946; s. Carlton Noble and Elizabeth (Walker) A.; m. Linda Hinson, Apr. 4, 1970; children—Alfred Gray Jr., Amanda Laing. B.A., Wake Forest U., 1968, J.D., 1973. Bar: N.C. 1973. Ptnr. Van Winkle, Buck, Wall, Starnes & Davis, P.A., Asheville, N.C., 1973—; sec., dir. Greystone Properties, Inc., Asheville, 1983—. Assoc. editor Wake Forest Law Rev., 1972. Chmn. Buncombe County Tax Adv. Com., Asheville, 1983. James Mason scholar Wake Forest U., 1972. Mem. N.C. Bar Assn. (real property sect. vice chmn. 1982-83, chmn. 1983-84, writer, lectr. real property and future interests bar rev. course 1981-83, mem. real property curriculum adv. com. 1984—, seminar planner and lectr. real property 1987), ABA. Democrat. Presbyterian. Club: Biltmore Forest Country (golf com. 1984—), Rhododendron Royal Brigade Guards (Asheville) (capt. Ensign Class). Real property, Banking. Home: 21 White Oak Rd Asheville NC 28803 Office: Starnes & Davis PA PO 7376 Van Winkle Buck Wall 11 North Market St Asheville NC 28802

ADAMS, CARY MEREDITH, lawyer; b. Memphis, Sept. 5, 1948; s. Thomas M. and Granville Lee (Meredith) A.; m. Carol Ann Nielsen, June 14, 1969; children: Allison Dale, Mary Healy. BA, U. Va., 1970; JD, U. Md., 1976. Bar: D.C. 1977, U.S. Ct. Appeals (9th and D.C. cirs.) 1978, U.S. Dist. Ct. (ea. and no. dists.) Calif. 1978, Calif. 1982, U.S. Supreme Ct. 1985. Law clk. to presiding justice U.S. Dist. Ct. Md., Balt., 1976-77; assoc. Arnold & Porter, Washington, 1977-81, Memel, Jacobs, Pierno, Gersh & Ellsworth, Sacramento, Calif., 1982-83; mng. ptnr. Memel, Jacobs, Pierno, Gersh & Ellsworth, Sacramento, 1984-87; ptnr., chmn. health law dept. Diepenbrock, Wulff, Plant & Hannegan, Sacramento, 1987—. Contbr. articles to profl. jours.; editor-in-chief U. Md. Law Rev., 1975-76. Chancellor St. Michael's Episc. Ch. and Day Sch., Carmichael, Calif., 1982—, sr. warden, 1985, chmn. rector search com., 1986—. Served with U.S. Army, 1971-73. Recipient Roger Howell award U. Md., 1876. Mem. ABA, Calif. Bar Assn., D.C. Bar Assn., Sacramento County Bar Assn., Calif. Soc. Healthcare Attys., Nat. Health Lawyers Assn., Order of Coif, Delta Sigma Phi. Democrat. Health, Administrative and regulatory, Antitrust. Office: Diepenbrock Wulff et al 300 Capitol Mall 17th Floor Sacramento CA 95814

ADAMS, DANIEL LEE, lawyer; b. Beaver, Ohio, Oct. 3, 1936; s. Paul D. and Margaret (Rhea) A.; m. Julianne Faller, Aug. 13, 1960; children: Cristin Adams Hyler, Meghan Kathleen. BA, Ohio State U., 1957, JD, 1960. Bar: Fla. 1962. Atty. Attys.' Title Services, Inc., Ft. Lauderdale, Fla., 1960-62, also bd. dirs.; ptnr. English, McCaughan and O'Bryan, Ft. Lauderdale, 1969—; trustee, dir. 17th Jud. Cir. of Attys.' Title Ins. Fund, Orlando, Fla.; mem. MRTA Commn., Tallahassee. Mem. ABA, Broward County Bar Assn., Fla. Bar Assn. (exec. council real property, probate and tax law sect., grievance com.), Broward County Com. of 100. Democrat. Roman Catholic. Club: Ft. Lauderdale Yacht. Avocations: bicycling, reading, wood working. Real property. Home: 600 Petunia Dr Plantation FL 33317 Office: English McCaughan & O'Bryan 100 NE Third Ave Fort Lauderdale FL 33301

ADAMS, DIRK STANDLEY, lawyer; b. Lynch, Nebr., May 19, 1951; s. Howard W. and Marilyn (Standley) A.; m. Anita Low, Feb. 14, 1984. BS, U. Tex., 1972; JD, Harvard U., 1976. Bar: N.Y. 1977, Calif. 1985. Ptnr. Sullivan, Johnson, Peters, Burns, Adams & Mullin, P.C., Rochester, N.Y., 1981-82; exec. v.p., treas., gen. counsel Suffolk County Fed. Savs & Loan Assn., Centereach, N.Y., 1982; ptnr. Phillips, Lytle, Hitchcock, Blaine & Huber, Rochester, 1982-83; sr. v.p., gen. counsel, corp. sec. Fed. Home Loan Bank of San Francisco, 1983—; acting counsel Fed. Asset Disposition Assn., San Francisco, 1985-86. Bd. dirs. Vol. Legal Services Project, Inc., Rochester, 1983. Mem. ABA (com. savs. and loan assns. sect. corp., banking and bus. 1983—), Calif. Bar Assn. (fin. instns. com. 1985). Banking, General corporate. Office: Fed Home Loan Bank San Francisco 600 California St San Francisco CA 94108

ADAMS, ELLIS PAUL, JR., lawyer; b. New Orleans, Nov. 13, 1947; s. Ellis Paul Sr. and Lucine Gladys (Barras) A.; m. Bettye Mizell, Aug. 13, 1966 (div. Sept. 1978); children: Timothy Joseph, Kristy Elizabeth; m. Diana Jones, Aug. 9, 1980. BA, La. State U., 1970, JD, 1974. Bar: La. 1974, U.S. Dist. Ct. (mid. dist.) La. 1978, U.S. Ct. Appeals (5th cir.) 1981, U.S. Supreme Ct. 1981. Staff atty. La. Dept. of Justice, Baton Rouge, 1974; staff atty. La. Dist. Atty.'s Assn., Baton Rouge, 1975-76, exec. dir., 1976—. Mem. ABA, Nat. Dist. Atty.'s Assn. (exec. com., bd. dirs. 1979—), Nat. Assn. Prosecutor Coordinators (past pres.), La. Child Support Enforcement Assn., La. Soc. of Assn. Execs., Gov.'s Task Force on Drug Enforcement. Club: Baton Rouge (La.) Ancient Athletic (pres. 1982-83). State civil litigation, Criminal, Legislative. Home: 3056 Zeeland Ave Baton Rouge LA 70808 Office: La Dist Attys Assn 1645 Nicholson Baton Rouge LA 70802

ADAMS, HAROLD FRANCIS, lawyer; b. Beaver, Ohio, July 8, 1900; s. Lewis W. and Arma F. (Halterman) A.; m. Ada Margaret Gregg, Dec. 4, 1929; children—John Marshall, Robert Gregg. A.B., Ohio State U., 1922, LL.B., 1926. Bar: Ohio 1926. Ptnr. Cowan & Adams, Columbus, Ohio, 1927—; mem. Ohio Bar Exam. Com., Columbus, 1937-42, chmn., 1942. Author: Workmen's Compensation, 1929; Trial and Appellate Practice in Ohio, 1934; Appellate Practice in Ohio, 1953. Trustee Columbus Pub. Library, 1958-74. Served with U.S. Army, World War I. Mem. ABA, Ohio State Bar Assn., Columbus Bar Assn., Lawyers Club Columbus Ohio, Am. Legion. Club: Downtown Sertoma (past pres.) Lodge: Masons (33 degree). Probate, Real property. Home: 3555 Chowning Ct Columbus OH 43220 Office: Cowan & Adams 3131 W Broad St Columbus OH 43204

ADAMS, HAROLD GENE, judge; b. Muskogee, Okla., July 1, 1926; s. William Clyde and Daisy (McAlister) A.; m. Carole Jean Harbuck, Feb. 10, 1962 (div.); 1 child, Patrick Andrew; Melissa Ann Graves, Dec. 22, 1986. B.S., Okla. State U., 1950; J.D., So. Meth. U., 1960, M.L.A., 1974. Bar: Tex. 1960, U.S. Dist. Ct. (no. dist.) Tex. 1962, U.S. Supreme Ct. 1968, U.S. Ct. Appeals (5th cir.) 1971, Okla. 1974. Regional mgr. Am. Arbitration Assn., 1957-60; asst. dist. atty., chief prosecutor Dallas County Criminal Ct., Dallas, 1961-62; Harold G. Adams, Inc., P.C., 1962-77; spl. asst. to Gov., dep. dir. Okla. Crime Commn., 1974; U.S. adminstrv. law judge, Santa Ana, Calif., 1977-79; U.S. adminstrv. law judge in charge Office of Hearings and Appeals, New Orleans, 1979-82; regional chief adminstrv. law judge Region VI, Office of Hearings and Appeals, Social Security Adminstrn., HHS, Dallas, 1982-85, hearing office, chief adminstrv. law judge, North Dallas, 1985—; instr. real estate law and oil and gas law Dallas County Community Coll.; instr. contracts and probate So. Meth. U. Dist. Served with USN, 1944-46; to lt. col. USAFR (ret.); with Tex. Air N.G., 1946-78. Decorated Air Force Res. medal World War II Victory medal, Combat Aircrew Wings, Am. Campaign medal; recipient Tex. Faithful Service medal. Mem. ABA, Dallas Bar Assn., Conf. Adminstrv. Law Judges, Fed. Adminstrv. Law Judges Conf. Methodist. Clubs: Tex. Game Fishing, Sonova Beach Rod and Reel, Sail Fish and Tarpon of Mex. Lodges: Masons, Shriners, Jesters. Grand champion Internat. Bill Fish Tournament, Alcapulco, Mex., 2 times. Administrative and regulatory, Pension, profit-sharing, and employee benefits, Real property. Office: 10830 N Central Expressway Suite 252 Dallas TX 75231

ADAMS, JAMES G., JR., lawyer; b. Hopkinsville, Ky., Nov. 4, 1954; s. J. Granville Sr. and Levina (Simmons) A.; children: James G. III, William H. II. AA, Hopkinsville Community Coll., 1974; BA, U. Ky., 1976; JD, No. Ky. U., 1979. Bar: Ky. 1979, U.S. Dist. Ct. (we. dist.) Ky. 1980. Assoc. Trimble, Soyars, Breathitt & Foster, Hopkinsville, Ky., 1979-80; ptnr. Trimble, Foster & Adams, Hopkinsville, 1980—; asst. atty. Commonwealth of Ky., Hopkinsville, 1982—; asst. atty. Christian County. Bd. chmn. Pennyroyal Area Mus., Hopkinsville, 1984—; pres. Buddies Inc., Hopkinsville, 1982-83. Named Boss of the Yr., Hopkinsville Legal Secs., 1983-84. Mem. ABA, Christian County Bar Assn. (pres. 1984-85), Assn. Trial Lawyers Am., Ky. Acad. Trial Atty.'s, Jaycees (pres. 1982-83, named Outstanding Local Pres. Ky. Jaycees, 1982-83). Democrat. Mem. Ch. Christ. Avocations: outdoor sports. General practice, Juvenile, Probate. Office: Trimble Foster & Adams 1103 S Main St PO Box 24 Hopkinsville KY 42240

ADAMS, JOHN EDMUND, lawyer; b. Pine Apple, Ala., Dec. 26, 1896; s. David Jr. and Lucy Dell (Lee) A.; m. Nan Coleman, May 27, 1925; 1 child, John Edmund Jr. AB, U. Ala., Tuscaloosa, 1917, MA, 1919, LLB, 1919. Bar: Ala. 1919, U.S. Supreme Ct. 1945. Jr. ptnr. Barnett & Adams, Florence, Ala., 1919-21, Pelham & Adams, Chatom, Ala., 1921-23, Bedsole & Adams, Grove Hill, Ala., 1923-25; pvt. practice Grove Hill, 1925-26; sr. ptnr. Adams & Gillmore, Grove Hill, 1926-52, Adams, Gillmore & Adams, Grove Hill, 1952-75, Adams, Adams & Kimbrough, Grove Hill, 1975-77, Adams & Adams, Grove Hill, 1977-81, Adams, Adams & Wilson, Grove Hill, 1981—; mem. State Bar Commn., 1941-51; sec., bd. dirs. First Bank of Grove Hill, 1965-84. Mem. State Dem. Exec. Com. 1923-41. Served as 2nd lt. F.A., U.S. Army, 1918. Mem. Ala. State Bar (pres. 1946), Clarke County Bar Assn. (pres. 1965—), Phi Beta Kappa, Sigma Chi. General corporate, General practice, Local government. Home and Office: PO Box 99 Grove Hill AL 36451

ADAMS, JOHN JILLSON, lawyer; b. Toledo, Nov. 12, 1934; s. Theodore Floyd and Esther (Jillson) A.; m. Barbara Barr, June 6, 1959; children: Leigh Ann Adams Miller, Leslie, Julie. BA, Denison U., 1956; LLB, U. Va., 1959. Bar: Va. 1959, D.C. 1967, U.S. Ct. Appeals (4th, 6th and D.C. cirs.), U.S. Supreme Ct. Assoc. Hunton & Williams, Richmond, Va., 1960-65; ptnr. Hunton & Williams, Washington, 1967—; assoc. dir. Am. United for Separation of Ch. and State, Washington, 1965-66; spl. asst. U.S. State Dept., Washington, 1966-67. Served with USAR, 1959-65. Mem. ABA, Va. Bar Assn., D.C. Bar Assn. Baptist. Administrative and regulatory, Federal civil litigation, Environment. Home: 8546 Georgetown Pike McLean VA 22102 Office: Hunton & Williams 2000 Penn Ave NW Washington DC 20036

ADAMS, JOHN JOSEPH, lawyer; b. Oct. 13, 1957; m. Joan Marie Sorbello, Jan. 9, 1982; 1 child, Richard Joseph. BA in English, History, U. Del., 1979; JD, Emory U., 1982. Bar: N.J. 1982, Pa. 1983, U.S. Dist. Ct. N.J. 1983, U.S. Dist. Ct. (ea. dist.) Pa. 1983. Law clk. Pa. Dept. HEW, Harrisburg, 1981-82; assoc. Offices of T.J. Kazlow, Villas, N.J., 1982-83, Hertzbach, Trichon & Silverstein, Phila., 1983-84, Offices of Paul N. Sandler, Phila. and Voorhees, Pa. and N.J., 1984—. TV appearance People Are Talking, 1986, AM San Francisco, 1986, The Phil Donahue Show, 1986. Regular speaker N.J. div. adoptees rights Youth and Family Services, Hammonton, 1984—; panelist, speaker Del. Valley Adoption Council Conf., Phila., 1985; legal advisor counseling and emergency accomodations for birth parents Connections Resource Ctr., also bd. dirs. Mem. ABA, Pa. Bar Assn. (telephone legal advisor Legal line 1984—), N.J. Bar Assn., Phila. Bar Assn., Atty. Adoption Network, Adoptees Liberty Movement, Concerned United Birth Parents, Swedesboro Rep. Assn. (chmn.), Phi Alpha Delta. Avocations: geneology, study of history, collect antique book and prints. Family and matrimonial, State civil litigation, Personal injury. Home: 605 Kings Hwy Swedesboro NJ 08085 Office: Offices of Paul N Sandler 1528 Walnut St Suite 1204 Philadelphia PA 19102

ADAMS, JOHN MARSHALL, lawyer; b. Columbus, Ohio, Dec. 6, 1930; s. H.F. and Ada Margaret (Gregg) A.; m. Janet Hawk, June 28, 1952; children: John Marshall, Susan Lynn, William Alfred. B.A., Ohio State U., 1952; J.D. summa cum laude, 1954. Bar: Ohio 1954. Mem. Cowan & Adams, Columbus, 1954-55; asst. city atty. City of Columbus, 1955-56; mem. Knepper, White, Richards & Miller, 1956-63; practiced in Columbus, 1963-74; partner Porter, Wright, Morris & Arthur, Columbus, 1975—; dir. Ohio Bar Liability Ins. Co.; Trustee Ohio Legal Center Inst., 1976-81, Ohio Lawpac, 1980—. Fellow Am. Coll. Trial Lawyers, Am. Bar Found., Ohio Bar Found. (trustee 1975-84); mem. ABA, Ohio Bar Assn. (exec. com. 1975-80, pres. 1978-79), Columbus Bar Assn. (gov. 1970-76 pres. 1974-75), Lawyers Club (pres. 1968-69), Order of Coif, Delta Upsilon, Phi Delta Phi. Republican. Clubs: Masons, Athletic, Scioto Country. Federal civil litigation, State civil litigation, Personal injury. Home: 1717 Arlingate Dr N Columbus OH 43220 Office: 41 S High St Columbus OH 43215

ADAMS, JOHN RICHARD, lawyer; b. Evanston, Ill., July 16, 1944; s. John R. and Norah Woodburn (Hardy) A.; m. Cynthia Marie Eggers, Aug. 3, 1974; children: Alison, Frank. BS, Calif. Inst. Technology, 1966; MEd, U. Ill., 1973; JD, Northwestern U., 1977. Bar: Ill. 1977, U.S. Dist. Ct. (no. dist.) Ill. 1977. Assoc. Spindell, Kemp & Kimmons, Chgo., 1977-80, Taylor, Miller, Sprowl, Hoffnagle & Merletti, Chgo., 1980—. Mem. ABA, Ill. Bar Assn., Chgo. Bar Assn. General corporate, Pension, profit-sharing, and employee benefits, Probate. Home: 258 Wood Ct Wilmette IL 60091

ADAMS, JOSEPH, lawyer, rail road company executive; b. N.Y.C., Sept. 11, 1945; s. Joseph J. and Wanda M. (Zak) Adams; m. Paula M. Eletto, Aug. 12, 1977; children: Elizabeth Jane, Emily Margaret, Douglas Joseph. BA cum laude, Brown U., 1967; JD, Stanford U., 1970. Atty. advisor Civil Aeronautics Bd., 1970-72; assoc. gen. counsel Inaugural Com., 1972-73; atty. office of counsel to Pres. The White House, Washington, 1973, asst. to gen. counsel, 1974-75; asst. to the under sec. U.S. Dept. Treasury, 1975-77; asst. gen. atty. Union Pacific R.R. Co., 1978-79, gen. atty., 1979-80; counsel Washington affairs Union Pacific Corp., 1981-83; assoc. gen. counsel govt. affairs Union Pacific R.R., 1983-84, asst. v.p. govt. affairs, 1984—. Legislative, General corporate. Home: 7940 Poppleton Ave Omaha NE 68124 Office: Union Pacific RR Co 1416 Dodge St Room 830 Omaha NE 68179

ADAMS, KENT MORRISON, lawyer; b. Houston, May 14, 1956; s. Duane Byron and Edith Marie (Giffen) A.; m. Joanne Catherine Brown, Dec. 30, 1981; 1 child, Mary Catherine. B.A. in Polit. Sci., George Washington U., 1978; J.D., La. State U., 1981. Bar: Tex. 1982, La. 1981, U.S. Ct. Appeals (5th cir.), U.S. Dist. Ct. (ea. and so. dists.) Tex. 1981, U.S. Dist. Ct. (we. dist.) La. 1983. Assoc. Brown and Adams, Beaumont, Tex., 1981-82, ptnr., 1985-86; ptnr. Adams and Assocs., Beaumont, 1986—; briefing atty. U.S. Dist. Ct., Beaumont, 1982-83; assoc. Benckenstein, Norvell, Bernsen and Nathan, Beaumont, 1983-85; instr. Lamar U., Beaumont, 1982-83. Del. Jefferson County Rep. Conv., 1984. Mem. ABA, Tex. Bar Assn., Maritime Law Assn. U.S., Am. Soc. Law and Medicine, Def. Research Inst., Tex. Assn. Def. Counsel, La. Bar Assn., Jefferson County Young Lawyers Assn. (bd. dirs. 1984-85, v.p. 1985-86, pres.-elect 1986-87, pres. 1987-88). Republican. Presbyterian. Lodge: Rotary. Insurance, Personal injury, Federal civil litigation. Home: 3675 Long Ave Beaumont TX 77706 Office: Adams and Assocs 2615 Calder Suite 220 Beaumont TX 77702

ADAMS, LEE STEPHEN, lawyer, banker; b. St. Louis, June 3, 1949; s. Albert L. and Margaret C. (Donoghue) A. A.B., Rutgers Coll., 1971; J.D., Georgetown U., 1974. Bar: D.C. 1975, Mo. 1975, Ohio 1982. Asst. dean Georgetown U. Law Ctr., Washington, 1974-76, adj. prof. law, 1973-76; sr. counsel to bd. govs. FRS, Washington, 1976-81; v.p., gen. counsel Fed. Res. Bank, Cleve., 1981-82, sr. v.p., gen. counsel, 1982-86; counsel Banc One Corp., Columbus, Ohio, 1986—; lectr. law Cath. U. Law Sch., Washington, 1977-81. Banking, Administrative and regulatory. Home: 2250 Adner Ct Upper Arlington OH 43220 Office: Banc One Corp 100 E Broad St Columbus OH 43271

ADAMS, LORI NELSON, lawyer; b. Ft. Meade, Md., Dec. 23, 1953; d. Jack G. and Arline L. (Shafer) Nelson; m. Jeffory E. Adams, Nov. 17, 1984. BA magna cum laude, U. Wash., 1976; JD, U. Puget Sound, 1979. Bar: Wash. 1979, U.S. Dist. Ct. (we. dist.) Wash. 1980. Law clk. to justice Wash. Supreme Ct., Olympia, 1979-80; ptnr. Reed, McClure, Moceri, Thonn & Moriarty, Seattle, 1981—. Mem. ABA, Wash. State Bar Assn., King County Bar Assn., Wash. Women Lawyers Assn., Phi Beta Kappa, Kappa Kappa Gamma. Club: Wash. Athletic (Seattle) (2d v.p.). Avocations: downhill skiing, cross country skiing, hiking, travel. Personal injury, State civil litigation, Insurance. Home: 2707 33d Ave S Seattle WA 98144 Office: Reed McClure Moceri Thonn & Moriarty 3600 Columbia Ctr Seattle WA 98104-7007

ADAMS, MARCIA HOWE, lawyer; b. Pasadena, Calif., Apr. 2, 1948; s. Paul Henry and Dorothy (Powell) H.; m. Jonathan Edwards Adams III, June 20, 1970; children: Natalie, Emily. BA, Wellesley Coll., 1970; postgrad., U. Calif., San Francisco, 1975-76; JD, Stanford U., 1978. Bar: Calif. 1978, U.S. Dist. Ct. (no. dist.) Calif. 1978. Paralegal Pepper, Hamilton & Scheetz, Phila., 1973-74, Petty, Andrews, Tufts & Jackson, San Francisco, 1974-75; assoc. Ware, Fletcher & Freidenrich, Palo Alto, Calif., 1978-80; atty. Hewlett-Packard Co., Palo Alto, 1980-84, sr. atty., 1984—. Elder 1st Presbyn. Ch. Palo Alto, 1981-83. Mem. ABA, Calif. Bar Assn., Palo Alto Bar Assn. Democrat. Club: West Bay Wellesley (v.p. Calif. 1980-81). Avocation: swimming. Computer, Contracts commercial, Antitrust. Office: Hewlett-Packard Co 3000 Hanover St 20BQ Palo Alto CA 94304

ADAMS, MARK HARRIS, lawyer; b. Portland, Oreg., Mar. 28, 1945; s. William Besley and Ruthe Eileen (Rolle) A.; m. Jane Ryder Staniford, June 18, 1966; children: Anne Hillman, Thomas William Mark, Susan Staniford. Student, U. Oreg., 1963; BA, Portland State U., 1967; JD, U. Calif., Berkeley, 1970. Bar: Wash. 1972, U.S. Dist. Ct. (we. dist.) Wash. 1972. Asst. atty. City of Tacoma, Washington, 1972-74; ct. commr. Wash. Ct. Appeals Div. 2, Tacoma, 1975—. Co-author: Washington Appellate Practice Handbook, 1980. Trustee Ctr. for Child Abuse Prevention, Tacoma, 1978-79. Mem. ABA (appellate handbook com.), Wash. State Bar Assn., Tacoma-Pierce County Bar Assn. (trustee young lawyers sect. 1975-77), Am. Heritage Assn. (bd. dirs. 1983—). Episcopalian. Judicial administration. Home: 4819 52d St Ct NW Gig Harbor WA 98335 Office: Ct Appeals Div 2 945 Market St Tacoma WA 98402

ADAMS, MICHAEL ROSS, lawyer; b. Detroit, June 24, 1957; s. Donald W. and Evelyn M. (Brown) A.; m. Debra K. Andrus, June 30, 1984. BA summa cum laude, Hillsdale Coll., 1979; JD, Vanderbilt U., 1982. Bar: Mich. 1982, U.S. Dist. Ct. (we. dist.) Mich. 1982. Assoc. Clary, Nantz & Wood, Grand Rapids, Mich., 1982—. Mem. ABA, Mich. Bar Assn., Grand Rapids Bar Assn., Nat. Pub. Employers Labor Relations Assn., Christian Legal Soc. Republican. Presbyterian. Labor. Office: Clary Nantz & Wood 500 Calder Plaza Grand Rapids MI 49503

ADAMS, OSCAR WILLIAM, JR., state justice; b. Birmingham, AL, Feb. 7, 1925; s. Oscar William and Ella Virginia (Eaton) A.; m. Ann-Marie Bradford, Jan. 1984; children: Oscar William, III, Gail Ingersoll Adams Harden, Frank T.; stepchildren: Kynath, Kevin. A.B., Talladega (AL.) Coll., 1944; LL.B., Howard U., 1947. Bar: Ala. bar. Practice in Birmingham, 1947-80; partner firm Adams & Adams, 1980; asso. justice Supreme Ct. Al., 1980—; past instr. Miles Coll. Sch. Law; bd. dirs. Lawyers Com. Civil Rights Under Law. Recipient Winner's award Talladega Coll.; award EEO Commn. Mem. Ala. Law Inst., Ala. Lawyers Assn. (award for outstanding public and profl. service), Nat. Bar Assn. (jud. council), Am. Trial Lawyers Assn., Omega Psi Phi, Phi Beta Boule. Democrat. Methodist. Clubs: Shriners, Elks. Jurisprudence. Office: Supreme Ct 445 Dexter Ave PO Box 218 Montgomery AL 36130

ADAMS, PHILIP JAMES, JR., lawyer; b. Bronx, N.Y., Feb. 22, 1947; s. Philip J. and Dorothy E. (Claire) A.; m. Linda K. Settles, Oct. 14, 1972; children—Katherine, Meredith, Jonathan and Daniel (twins), Kimberly. B.A., Seton Hall U., 1968; J.D., Suffolk U., 1971; LL.M., U. Mo.-Kansas City, 1972. Bar: Conn. 1971, Mo. 1984, U.S. Ct. Appeals (8th and 10th cirs.) 1974, U.S. Supreme Ct. 1975, U.S. Ct. Appeals (2d cir.) 1976, U.S. Dist. Ct. Conn. 1978, U.S. Dist. Ct. (we. dist.) Mo. 1984. Law clk. U.S. Dist. Ct. Kans., 1972-73; trial atty. Dept. Justice, Kansas City, Mo., 1973-76; assoc. RisCassi & Davis, Hartford, Conn., 1976-78; ptnr. Blume, Elbaum & Adams, Hartford, 1978-84; ptnr. Watson, Ess, Marshall & Enggas, Kansas City, Mo., 1984—. Mem. Conn. Bar Assn. (ho. of dels. 1980-84), ABA, Assn. Trial Lawyers Am., Mo. Bar Assn., Phi Alpha Delta (Felix Frankfurter chpt. Outstanding Mem. 1970). Club: Kansas City. Federal civil litigation, State civil litigation, Personal injury. Office: Watson Ess Marshall & Enggas 1010 Grand Ave Kansas City MO 64106

ADAMS, RALPH WYATT, SR., university chancellor, lawyer; b. Samson, Ala., June 4, 1915; s. Alfred E. and Eunice M. (Clements) A.; m. Dorothy Kelly, Sept. 5, 1942; children: Ralph Wyatt, Kelly Clements (Mrs. James B. Allen, Jr.), Samuel. A.B., Birmingham-So. Coll., 1937; LL.B., U. Ala., 1940, LL.D., 1965, J.D., 1969; postgrad., U. Colo., 1958, George Washington U., 1960, Princeton U., 1966, Harvard U., 1981, Jesus Coll., Oxford U., 1983. Bar: Ala. 1940, U.S. Supreme Ct. 1940. Atty., dep. supt. Ala. Dept. Ins., 1945-46; judge Tuscaloosa, Ala., 1946-47; founder Acad. Life Ins. Co., Denver, 1957; tchr. life ins. U. Colo.; dep. dean, acting dean Air Force Law Sch., Air U.; pres. Troy (Ala.) State U., 1964-85, chancellor, 1985—; chmn. Bankers Credit Life Ins. Co., Adams Life Ins. Co.; bd. dirs. South Trust Bank, First Ala. Bank of Troy. Former mem., chmn. State Personnel Bd. Ala., State Ins. Bd. Ala.; chmn. Ala. Oil and Gas Bd., Presdl. Clemency Bd.; commr. Edn. Commn. of States; past Ala. dir. Selective Service; past pres. Assn. Ala. Coll. and U. Pres.'s and Adminstrs., Gulf South Conf.; trustee, vice chmn. Lyman Ward Mil. Acad., Camp Hill, Ala.; mem. appeal bd. U.S. Dept. Edn. Served to capt. USAAF, 1941-45; maj. gen. Res.; maj. gen. also Ala. Air N.G. Recipient Silver Beaver award Boy Scouts Am.; Alumnus of Year award Birmingham-So. Coll., 1978; named to Ala. Acad. Honor, 1977, ICMS Newspaper Carrier Hall of Fame, 1979; Man of Yr. Troy, 1968, 75; Algernon Sydney Sullivan, 1982. Mem. English Speaking Union (former nat. bd. dirs.), Am. Legion (state comdr. 1977-78), Mortar Bd., Phi Alpha Delta, Kappa Delta Pi, Pi Delta Phi, Kappa Phi Kappa, Phi Kappa Phi, Lambda Chi Alpha, Omicron Delta Kappa, Pi Tau Chi. Methodist. Clubs: Alexandria Civitan (past pres.), Army-Navy Country (Alexandria, Va.); Montgomery (Ala.) Country, Troy Country; Metropolitan, Cosmos (Washington). Lodges: Masons, Rotary. Home: 110 McKinley Dr Troy AL 36081 Office: Troy State Univ Office of the Chancellor Troy AL 36082

ADAMS, RAY HARRIS, lawyer; b. Pascagoula, Miss., Oct. 17, 1945; s. Sykes Ray and Emily Jane (Hinman) A.; m. Linda Lee Barnes, Feb. 16, 1968; children: Jennifer Lee, Sara Catherine, James Michael. BS in Edn., Social Sci., S.W. Tex. U., 1968; JD, St. Mary's U., San Antonio, 1974. Bar: Tex. 1974, U.S. Dist. Ct. (we. dist.) Tex. 1976, U.S. Ct. Appeals (5th cir.) 1979, U.S. Supreme Ct. 1980. Sole practice San Antonio, 1974—. Mem. Tex. Bar Assn., San Antonio Bar Assn., Tex. Trial Lawyers Assn., San Antonio Trial Lawyers Assn. State civil litigation, Personal injury, Family and matrimonial. Home: 4350 Shallow Water San Antonio TX 78233 Office: 106 S St Mary's Suite 500 San Antonio TX 78205

ADAMS, RICHARD GLEN, lawyer; b. West Reading, Pa., Mar. 21, 1941; s. Daniel Snyder and Carrie B. (Vought) A.; m. Merrill Richards, June 13, 1964; children—Rebecca Elizabeth, Rachael Kate. A.B., cert. Woodrow Wilson Sch. Pub. and Internat. Affairs, Princeton U., 1963; LL.B., Yale U., 1967, M.A. in Econs., 1967. Bar: Conn. 1967, U.S. dist. ct. Conn. 1967, U.S. Ct. Apls. (2d cir.) 1967. Assoc. Jacobs, Jacobs, Grudberg & Clifford, New Haven, 1967-72; assoc. Ribicoff & Kotkin, Hartford, Conn., 1972-73, ptnr., 1973-78; mem. Adams & Tomc, Middletown, Conn., 1978-85; sole practice, Middletown, 1985—; sec., dir. Lyman Farm, Inc.; bar exam. reader and grader, 1982. Candidate Conn. Ho. of Reps., 1968; mem. Holiday Project, 1980—, Hunger Project, 1981—; mem. Lawyers Alliance Nuclear Arms Control, 1981—, profl. div. United Way, 1979; bd. dirs. Camp Hazen YMCA, 1984—. Mem. ABA, Conn. Bar Assn. (exec. coms. adminstrv. law and conservation and environ. quality sects.), Middlesex County Bar Assn., Cen. Conn. Bus. and Estates Planning Council, Conn. Sch. Attys. Council. Club: Middletown Exchange. Administrative and regulatory, State civil litigation, Real property. Home: 175 Powder Hill Rd Middlefield CT 06455 Office: 163 College St Middletown CT 06457

ADAMS, ROBERT MORFORD, JR., lawyer; b. Duluth, Minn., Feb. 13, 1916; s. Robert M. and Cherrill (McNeill) A.; m. Elizabeth Sweet, Mar. 23, 1940 (dec. Sept. 1980); children—Robert M., Clifford S., Richard M.; m. 2d, Joyce Halley, June 14, 1981. A.B., Stanford U., 1937, LL.B., 1940. Bar: Calif. 1941, U.S. Supreme Ct. 1958. Assoc. firm McCutchen, Olney, Mannon & Greene, San Francisco, 1941-47, Athearn, Chandler & Farmer, Hoffman & Angell, San Francisco, 1947-50; ptnr. firm Angell & Adams, San Francisco 1950-62, Angell, Adams and Holmes, San Francisco, 1962-70, Busterud, Draper & Adams, San Francisco, 1970-72, Draper, Adams & Huntington P.C., San Francisco, 1973-75, Draper, Adams & Zacher, P.C., San Francisco, 1975-76, Cotton, Seligman & Ray, San Francisco, 1976-79; sole practice, San Francisco, 1980—. Chancellor, Protestant Epis. Diocese Calif., 1973—; chmn. bd. dirs. St. Luke's Hosp., San Francisco, 1982—. Served with M.I., USNR, 1942-45. Mem. ABA, Bar Assn. San Francisco, Am. Judicature Soc., Engrs. Club San Francisco, Phi Beta Kappa, Theta Delta Chi, Phi Alpha Delta. Clubs: Bohemian, San Francisco Golf. Estate planning, Probate, Non-Profit organizations. Home: 529 W Poplar St San Mateo CA 94402 Office: 235 Montgomery St Suite 2500 San Francisco CA 94104

ADAMS, ROBERT WALKER, lawyer; b. Asheville, N.C., Oct. 28, 1950; s. Robert W. Phillips and Gloria B. E. (McAvoy) A.; m. Barbara Williams; children: Alexa McAvoy, Erica Walker. BA, U. Md., 1972; JD with honors, George Washington U., 1975. Bar: D.C. 1975, U.S. Dist. Ct. D.C. 1981, U.S. Ct. Appeals (4th cir.) 1982, U.S. Ct. Appeals (Fed. cir.) 1983, U.S. Ct. Appeals (D.C. cir.) 1984. Assoc. Cushman, Darby & Cushman, Washington, 1975-79, ptnr., 1979-86; ptnr. Nixon & Vanderhye, Arlington, Va., 1986—. Contbr. articles to profl. jours.; patentee. Mem. ABA, Bar Assn. of D.C. (chmn. patent law and litigation com. 1980-81), Am. Trial Lawyers Assn., Licensing Execs. Soc., Sigma Pi (v.p. 1971). Republican. Episcopalian. Patent, Trademark and copyright. Home: 322 11th St NE Washington DC 20002 Office: Nixon & Vanderhye 2000 N 15th St Arlington VA 22201

ADAMS, ROBERT WENDELL, lawyer; b. Shelbyville, Ind., June 29, 1942; s. Ralph and Rosalie (Stinson) A.; m. Donna Jean Adams, Oct. 23, 1971; 1 child, Benjamin Joseph. Student, London Sch. Econs., 1962-63; AB, Wabash Coll., 1964; JD, Northwestern U., 1967. Bar: Ind. 1968, U.S. Dist. Ct. Ind. 1968. Ptnr. Adams & Cramer, Shelbyville, 1968—. Pres. Shelby County Hist. Soc. 1976-78. Mem. ABA, Ind. Bar Assn., Shelby County Bar Assn. (pres. 1980-82), Ind. Bar Found., Am. Soc. Hort. Sci., Holly Soc. Am. (trustee), Magnolia Soc. (trustee 1984—, contbr. articles to jour.), Am. Rhododendron Soc. (pres. Ind. chpt. 1985—). Republican. Presbyterian. Avocations: plant physiology, horticulture. Estate planning, Probate, Estate taxation. Home: Rural Rt 2 PO Box 8 Shelbyville IN 46176 Office: Adams & Cramer 33 W Washington St PO Box 746 Shelbyville IN 46176

ADAMS, SAMUEL, lawyer; b. Colorado Springs, Colo., Dec. 12, 1955; s. Ralph Wyatt and Dorothy (Kelly) A.; m. Mary Virginia Martin, Aug. 16, 1986. Student, Oxford U., Eng., 1975, Harvard U., 1976; BA, U. Ala., 1979, JD, 1982. Bar: Ala. 1982. Law clk. to chief justice Ala. Supreme Ct., Montgomery, 1982; judge 12th Jud. Cir. Ct. Ala., Enterprise, 1984-87; assoc. Steiner, Crum & Baker, Montgomery, 1987—. Served to capt. JAGC, U.S. Army, 1976-82. Mem. ABA, Montgomery County Bar Assn., Assn. Cir. Judges, Am. Judicature Soc., Ala. Bar Assn., Coffee County Bar Assn., Nat. Jud. Coll. Alumni. Methodist. Avocations: tennis, golf, real estate, stocks. Home: 1849 Lockerbie St Montgomery AL 36106 Office: Steiner Crum & Baker PO Box 668 Montgomery AL 36101

ADAMS, STEPHEN THORNTON, lawyer; b. Jefferson City, Mo., Feb. 7, 1945; s. Joseph Thorton and Elsie Mae (Gollahon) A.; m. Judith Eileen Unruh, Dec. 20, 1969; children: Jennifer Rene, Jeffry Scott. BA in Indsl. Adminstrn., U. Kans., 1967, JD, 1970. Bar: Kans. 1970, U.S. Dist. Ct. Kans. 1970, Mo. 1971, U.S. Dist. Ct. (we. dist.) Mo. 1971. Assoc. Blackwell, Sanders, Matheny, Weary & Lombardi, Kansas City, Mo., 1970-76, ptnr., 1976-83; mng. ptnr. Blackwell, Sanders, Matheny, Weary & Lombardi, Overland Park, Kans., 1983—. Order of Coif Law Rev., 1968-70. Served to 1st lt. USAR, 1970. Mem. ABA, Mo. Bar Assn., Kans. Bar Assn., Lawyers Assn. Kansas City, Greater Kansas City Soc. Hosp. Attys. (pres. 1982-83). Republican. Real property, Health. Office: Blackwell Sanders Matheny Weary & Lombardi 9401 Indian Creek Pkwy Overland Park KS 66210

ADAMS, THOMAS LAWRENCE, lawyer; b. Jersey City, Apr. 14, 1948; s. Lawrence Ignatius and Dorothy Tekla (Halgas) A.; m. Elizabeth Anne Russell, June 14, 1969 (div. 1981); children—Thomas, Katherine; m. Deanna Louise Mollo, July 30, 1983; stepchildren—Kathy, Kerry. B.S., N.J. Inst. of Tech., 1969; J.D., Seton Hall U., 1975. Bar: N.J. 1975, N.Y. 1976, U.S. Dist. Ct. N.J. 1975, U.S. Patent Office 1975. Systems engr. Grumman Aerospace, Bethpage, N.Y., 1969-71; sr. engr. Weston Instruments, Newark, 1971-74; with patent staff RCA Corp., Princeton, N.J., 1974-75; corp. atty. Otis Elevator, N.Y.C., 1975-77; ptnr. Goebel & Adams, Morristown, N.J., 1978-80, Behr & Adams, Morristown & Edison, N.J., 1981—. Author, editor B & A Newsletter, 1984. Councilman Twp. Council, Livingston, N.J., 1985-89, dep. mayor, 1987; commr. Environ. Commn., Livingston, 1984-87; mem. Bd. Edn. Long Range Planning Com., Livingston, 1978; sec. Livingston Rep. Club, 1984. Recipient N.J. State Scholarship, 1965. Mem. N.J. Patent Law Assn., Morris County Bar Assn., West Essex C. of C. (rep.), Trial Attys. of N.J., Am. Arbitration Assn. (arbitrator), Seton Hall Law Rev., Tau Beta Pi, Eta Kappa Nu. Roman Catholic. Lodges: K.C. (Grand Knight 1980), Rotary. Patent, Trademark and copyright, State civil litigation.

ADAMS, WESLEY PRICE, JR., lawyer; b. N.Y.C., Oct. 4, 1935; s. Wesley Price and Dorothy (Campbell) A.; m. Marcia Shaw; children: Denise, Catherine, Wesley, Jennifer; m. Amelia Franklin; 1 child, Jennifer Leigh. AB, Dartmouth Coll.; LLB, U. Va. Bar: Ky. 1960, U.S. Dist. Ct. (we. dist.) Ky. 1968, U.S. Ct. Appeals (6th cir.) 1981, U.S. Dist. Ct. (ea. dist.) Ky. 1982. Ptnr. Ogden, Robertson & Marshall, Louisville, 1960-82, Goldberg & Simpson P.S.C., Louisville, 1982—. Federal civil litigation, State civil litigation, Insurance. Office: Goldberg & Simpson PSC 2800 1st Nat Tower Louisville KY 40202

ADAMS, WILLIAM GILLETTE, lawyer; b. Dallas, Oreg., July 26, 1939; s. Dwight B. and Ruth L. (Gillette) A.; m. Barbara A. Picoli, Jan. 24, 1970. B.A. in Econs., Stanford U., 1963; J.D., U. Utah, 1968. Bar: Calif. 1969; registered Conseie Juridique, France. Assoc. firm O'Melveny & Myers, Los Angeles, 1968-75; ptnr. O'Melveny & Myers, 1979—; resident ptnr. O'Melveny & Myers, Paris, 1979-84; ptnr. Erickson, Zerfas & Adams, Los Angeles, 1975-79; dir. Valentine Enterprises, Inc., 1983—. Editor-in-chief Utah Law Rev., 1967-68. Vol. U.S. Peace Corps, Morocco, 1963-65. Served with USCG, 1957-58. Mem. ABA, Los Angeles Bar Assn., Calif. Bar Assn., Los Amigo Del Pueblo (bd. dirs., gen. counsel 1974-76), Order of Coif, Phi Kappa Phi, Phi Delta Phi. Club: Cercle De l'Union Interalliee (Paris). Private international, General corporate, Contracts commercial. Office: O'Melveny & Myers 610 Newport Ctr Dr Newport Beach CA 92660

ADAMS, WILLIAM TENNANT, lawyer; b. Duluth, Minn., Oct. 21, 1941; s. John Tennant and Elizabeth (Collins) A.; m. Mary Gustafson, Nov. 15, 1980; children: Megan, Brandon, Amy. BA, Amherst Coll., 1967; JD, Georgetown U., 1970, LLM, 1971. Bar: N.Y. 1974, N.J. 1975. Atty. Gen. Instruments Corp., N.Y.C., 1973-75; counsel to Asia Warner-Lambert Co., Morris Plains, N.J., 1975—. Contbr. articles to profl. jours. Bd. of govs. Smoke Rise Club, Kinnelon, N.J., 1984—, bd. trustees, 1983-86; pres. bd. trustees, Community Church of Smoke Rise, 1985-86. Mem. ABA, N.J. Bar Assn., N.Y. State Bar Assn., Am. Soc. Internat. Law, Nat. Council on U.S.-China Trade. Avocation: sports. Private international. Office: Warner-Lambert Co 201 Tabor Rd Morris Plains NJ 07950

ADCOCK, LOUIE NORMAN, JR., lawyer; b. St. Petersburg, Fla., Dec. 8, 1930; s. Louie Norman Sr. and Lila (Anderson) A.; m. Mary Martha Shaw, Aug. 29, 1957; children: David Shaw, Margaret McClane, Joseph Wright. BA in Polit. Sci., Econs. and Sociology, U. Fla., 1952, JD, 1956. Bar: Fla., U.S. Dist. Ct. (so. and mid. dists.) Fla., U.S. Tax Ct., U.S. Ct. Mil. Appeals, U.S. Supreme Ct. From assoc. to ptnr. Fisher & Sauls P.A., St. Petersburg, 1956—; Pres. Fla. Lawyers Prepaid Legal Service Inc., Tallahassee, 1978-80. Contbr. articles to profl. jours. Pres. Pinellas County Vis. Nurse and Homemaker Service, St. Petersburg, 1962-64, Family Service Ctrs., St. Petersburg, 1968; v.p. region Family Service Assn. Am., N.Y.C., 1971-73; chmn. Com. of 100, St. Petersburg, 1974-76. Served with U.S. Army, 1952-54, Korea, lt. col. JAG, USAR, 1954-73. Fellow ABA; mem. Fla. Bar Assn. (bd. govs. 1980-84, cert. estate planning and probate), Fla. Bar Found. (bd. dirs. 1986—). Republican. Episcopalian. Clubs: St. Petersburg Yacht, Suncoasters (St. Petersburg). Avocations: camping, canoeing, jogging. Probate, Real property, General corporate. Office: Fisher & Sauls PA 100 2d Ave S Suite 701 Saint Petersburg FL 33701

ADDINGTON, DARREL BLAIR, lawyer; b. Kingsport, Tenn., June 7, 1945; s. Sutro K. and Gradalee (Blair) A.; m. Dorothy Coe, Nov. 23, 1963; children: Beth, Jenny, Emily, Betsy. BA, U. Tenn., 1966, JD, 1968. Bar: Tenn. 1969, Wash. 1973, U.S. Dist. Ct. (we. dist.) Wash. 1973, U.S. Ct. Claims 1984. Jud. clk. U.S. Dist. Ct. (we. dist.), Knoxville, Tenn., 1968-69; atty. U.S. Army JAGC, Ft. Lewis, Wash., 1969-73; dep. pros. atty. Pierce County, Tacoma, 1973-75; ptnr. Kane, Vandeberg, Hartinger & Walker, Tacoma, 1975—. Pres. Tacoma Community House, 1980-82, 86—, Pierce County Alliance, Tacoma, 1984; chmn. PAC panel United Way, Tacoma, 1983—. Served to capt. U.S. Army, 1969-73. Mem. ABA, Wash. State Bar Assn., Assn. Trial Lawyers Am., Wash. State Trial Lawyers Assn., Wash. Assn. Def. Counsel, Order of Coif, Phi Beta Kappa. Republican. Methodist. Avocations: hiking, camping, fishing, reading. Construction, State civil litigation, Local government. Home: 6523 47th St Ct W Tacoma WA 98466 Office: Kane Vandeberg Hartinger & Walker 2000 First Interstate Plaza Tacoma WA 98402-4391

ADDIS, LAUANE CLEO, corporate counsel; b. Delta, Colo., Jan. 13, 1956; s. Cleo Clinton and Kate Irene (Williams) A.; m. Jeanne Marie Suzuki, May 20, 1979; 1 child, Jennifer Anne. BA, Andrews U., 1978; JD, Baylor U., 1981; ML, U. Denver, 1982. Bar: Tex. 1981, Colo. 1981, U.S. Dist. Ct. Colo. 1981, U.S. Ct. Claims 1982, U.S. Ct. Appeals (10th cir.) 1982, Ill. 1984. Assoc. Waldbaum, Corn, Koff, Denver, 1981-84; corp. counsel, v.p. fin. Stevia Co., Inc., Arlington Heights, Ill., 1984-87; pres., corp. counsel Stevia Co., Inc., Arlington Heights, 1987—; corp. counsel, exec. v.p. Biosynergy, Inc., Arlington Heights, 1984—; bd. dirs. F.K. Suzuki Int., Inc., Arlington Heights. Mem. ABA, Ill. Bar Assn., Colo. Bar Assn., Tex. Bar Assn., Chgo. Bar Assn. General corporate, Securities, Probate. Office: Stevia Co Inc/Biosynergy Inc 746 W Algonquin Rd Arlington Heights IL 60005

ADDIS, RICHARD BARTON, lawyer; b. Columbus, Ohio, Apr. 9, 1929; s. Wilbur Jennings and Leila Olive (Grant) A.; m. Marguerite C. Christjohn, Feb. 9, 1957; children—Jacqueline Carol, Barton David. B.A., Ohio State U., 1954, J.D., 1955. Bar: Ohio 1956, U.S. Dist. Ct. (no. dist.) Ohio 1957, N.Mex. 1963, U.S. Dist. Ct. (N.Mex. 1963. Sole practice, Canton, Ohio, 1956-63, Albuquerque, 1963—. Served with USMC, 1946-48, 50-52. Mem. Ohio Bar Assn., N.Mex. Bar Assn., Am. Arbitration Assn. (arbitrator 1968—), Soc. Mining Engrs. General practice, Mining Law. Address: 1336 Wyoming Blvd NE Albuquerque NM 87112

ADDISON, LINDA LEUCHTER, lawyer; b. Allentown, Pa., Nov. 25, 1951; m. Max M. Addison, Sept. 10, 1977. BA with honors, U. Tex., 1969, JD, 1976. Ptnr. Fulbright & Jaworski, Houston. Mng. editor Tex. Law Rev. 1975-76; contbr. articles to profl. jours. Vol. Houston Ballet Found., 1980-81; vice-chmn. Mission Task Force of The Centennial Commn. of U. Tex., Austin, 1981-83; mem. bd. advisors Books for Texans, 1982-84; mem. pres.'s assocs. U. Tex., 1982—; mem. adv. council Tex. Union Found., U. Tex., 1984—. Named one of Outstanding Young Women Am., Outstanding Young Lawyer Houston, 1984-85. Mem. Tex. Bar Assn. (mem. bar convention com. 1980-81, mem. bar jour. com. 1981-82, mem. evidence inst. planning com. 1983-84), Houston Bar Assn. (mem. continuing legal edn. com. 1977—, chmn. continuing legal edn. insts. 1979-80, mem. jud. evaluations com. 1982-83), Tex. Young Lawyers Assn. (active in numerous coms.), Houston Young Lawyers Assn. (active in numerous coms.), Tex. Law Rev. Ex-Editors Assn., Friar Soc. (mem. steering com. Houston chpt. 1985—), Omicron Delta Kappa. Federal civil litigation, State civil litigation. Office: Fulbright & Jaworski 1301 McKinney Houston TX 77010

ADE, JAMES L., lawyer; b. Tampa, Fla., May 15, 1932; s. C. Theodore and Marguerite (Rood) A.; m. Mary Ann Vaughan, Sept. 11, 1954; children: Leanne, William Theodore, Elizabeth. BS in Bus. Adminstrn., U. Fla., 1954, JD, 1959. Bar: Fla. 1959, U.S. Dist. Ct. (so. and mid. dists.) Fla. 1959, U.S. Dist. Ct. (no. dist.) Fla. 1981, U.S. Tax Ct., U.S. Ct. Appeals (5th cir.) 1959, U.S. Ct. Appeals (11th cir.) 1981, U.S. Supreme Ct. 1970. Assoc. Buck, Drew & Glocker, Jacksonville, Fla., 1959-61; ptnr. Martin, Ade, Birchfield & Johnson, P.A. and predecessor firms, Jacksonville, 1961—. Pres. Gator Bowl Assn., Jacksonville, 1977, Greater Jacksonville Community Found., 1970-75; v.p. Jacksonville C. of C., 1971-72; mem. Jacksonville Area Com. of 100. Served to comdr. USNR, 1949—. Mem. ABA, Fla. Bar Assn., Jacksonville Bar Assn. (pres. 1968), U. Fla. Alumni Assn. (pres. 1962-65, Outstanding Alumnus award 1975), U. Fla. Alumni Club of Jacksonville (Outstanding Alumnus 1975). Democrat. Presbyterian. Lodge: Rotary (pres. local chpt. 1980-81). Avocation: sports. Corporate taxation, Probate, Public utilities. Home: 4831 Malpas Ln Jacksonville FL 32210 Office: Martin Ade Birchfield & Johnson 3000 Independent Sq Jacksonville FL 32202

ADELL, HIRSCH, lawyer; b. Novogrodek, Poland, Mar. 11, 1931; came to U.S., 1937; s. Nathan and Nachama (Wager) A.; m. Judith Audrey Fuss, Feb. 8, 1963; children—Jeremiah, Nikolas, Balthasar, Valentine. Student, City Coll. N.Y., 1949-52; B.A., UCLA, 1955; LL.B., U. Calif. at Los Angeles, 1963. Bar: Cal. bar 1963. Adminstrv. asst. to State Senator Richard Richards, 1956-60; partner law firm Warren & Adell, Los Angeles, 1963-75; mem. Reich, Adell & Crost (PLC), Los Angeles, 1975—; counsel AFTRA, Los Angeles. Served with AUS, 1953-55. Mem. ABA (labor and employment law sect.). Labor. Home: 545 S Norton Ave Los Angeles CA 90020 Office: Reich Adell & Crost 501 Shatto Pl Los Angeles CA 90020

ADELMAN, MICHAEL SCHWARTZ, lawyer; b. Cambridge, Mass., June 6, 1940; s. Benjamin Taft and Sally Frances (Schwartz) A.; m. Amy Kay, June 15, 1962; children: Robert, Jonathon. Student Boston U., 1958-59; BA with honors in English, U. Mich., 1962, JD cum laude. Bar: Mich. 1968, Miss. 1974. Assoc. Zwerdling, Miller, Klimist & Maurer, Detroit, 1968-69; ptnr. Philo, Maki, Ravitz, Glotta, Adelman, Cockrel & Robb, Detroit, 1969-70; ptnr. Glotta, Adelman & Dinges, Detroit, 1970-74; ptnr. Andalman, Adelman, & Steiner P.A., Hattiesburg, Miss., 1974—; sec., bd. dirs. SE Miss. Legal Services, Hattiesburg. Contbr. short stories: The Deputy, The Detention Center to New Renaissance. Treas., Hattiesburg Area Equal Rights Council. Recipient Ralph T. Abernathy award Jackson County (Miss.) SCLC, 1978. Mem. ABA, South Central Miss. Bar Assn. Criminal, Personal injury, Workers' compensation.

ADELMAN, ROBERT BARDWELL, lawyer; b. Tucson, Dec. 24, 1952; s. Stanley and Joan (Bardwell) A.; m. Merril Orenstein, June 6, 1982. BA, St. Lawrence U., 1975; JD, Cornell U., 1978. Bar: Conn. 1978, U.S. Dist. Ct. Conn. 1979, U.S. Dist. Ct. (so. dist.) N.Y. 1981, U.S. Ct. Appeals (2d cir.) 1981, U.S. Supreme Ct. 1982. Ptnr. Cohen and Wolf, Bridgeport, Conn., 1978—. Mem. Conn. Trial Lawyers Assn. (bd. dirs. 1984—, co-chmn. continuing legal edn. com. 1985—), Phi Beta Kappa. Personal injury, Federal civil litigation, State civil litigation. Home: 687 Mill Hill Rd Southport CT 06490 Office: Cohen and Wolf 1115 Broad St Bridgeport CT 06604

ADELMAN, STEVEN HERBERT, lawyer; b. Chgo., Dec. 21, 1945; s. Irving and Sylvia (Cohen) A.; m. Pamela Bernice Kozoll, June 30, 1968; children—David, Robert. B.S., U. Wis.-Madison, 1967; J.D., DePaul U., 1970. Bar: Ill. 1970, U.S. Dist. Ct. (no. dist.) Ill. 1970, U.S. Ct. Appeals (7th cir.) 1975. Ptnr. Keck, Mahin & Cate, Chgo., 1970—. Contbr. chpts. to books, articles to profl. jours. Bd. dirs. Bur. Jewish Employment Problems, Chgo., 1983—; employment relations com. Chgo. Assn. Commerce and Industry, 1982—. Mem. Chgo. Bar Assn. (chmn. liaison subcom. 1983—), ABA (Silver Key award 1969), Ill. State Bar Assn., Chgo. Council Lawyers, Decalogue Soc. Club: River (Chgo.). Labor. Office: Keck Mahin & Cate 8300 Sears Tower 233 S Wacker Dr Chicago IL 60606

ADELSON, BENEDICT JAMES, lawyer; b. Cleve., July 3, 1930; s. Joseph Stanley and Sara J. (Joffe) A.; m. Barbara Ford, Aug. 29, 1967 (div. Aug. 1977); children—Benjamin J., Melissa Lynn; m. Sybil Schar, Apr. 12, 1981. B.S. in Econs., U. Pa., 1952; J.D., Harvard U., 1955. Bar: Ohio 1955, Calif. 1970. Assoc., Schleshinger, Galvin, Kohn & Landefeld, Cleve., 1963-68, Gendel, Raskoff, Shapiro & Quittner, Los Angeles, 1970-77, Fierstein & Sturman, Los Angeles, 1977—. General corporate, Real property, Corporate taxation. Home: 146 Marguerita Santa Monica CA 90402 Office: Fierstein & Sturman 1875 Century Park E 15th Floor Los Angeles CA 90067

ADESS, MELVIN SYDNEY, lawyer; b. Chgo., May 9, 1944; s. Samuel and Evelyn E. (Bromberg) A.; m. Roberta L. Kaplan, Aug. 14, 1966; children: Jason, Stephanie, Matthew. BS with highest distinction, Northwestern U., 1966; JD cum laude, U. Chgo., 1969. Bar: Ill. 1969. Assoc. Kirkland & Ellis, Chgo., 1969-74; ptnr. &, &, 1974—; lectr. Northwestern U. Sch. Law, Chgo., DePaul U. Sch. Law, Chgo., DePaul U. Sch. Bus. Trustee Chgo. City Ballet. State Farm Exceptional Student fellow. Mem. ABA (com. fgn. activities of U.S. taxpayers), Ill. Bar Assn., Chgo. Bar Assn. (former vice chmn. corp. distributions, reorgns. and fgn. tax com.), Am. Law Inst. (cons. fed. income tax project on internat. aspects of U.S. income taxation), Phi Eta Sigma, Beta Gamma Sigma, Beta Alpha Psi, Order of Coif. Home: 211 Pine Point Dr Highland Park IL 60035 Office: Kirkland & Ellis 200 E Randolph Dr Chicago IL 60601

ADIN, RICHARD H(ENRY), lawyer, editor; b. Kingston, N.Y., May 19, 1948; s. Aaron and Lenore (Glasner) A.; m. Mary Grace Francioli, Nov. 10, 1972; children: Mariah Pompea, Justin Richard. BA, SUNY, Fredonia, 1970; JD, U. San Fernando Valley, 1977. Bar: Ind. 1977, U.S. Dist. Ct. (so. dist.) Ind. 1977, U.S. Ct. Appeals (7th cir.) 1979, U.S. Supreme Ct. 1980, U.S. Ct. Appeals (6th cir.) 1982. Assoc. Law Office of Jack Davis, Evansville, Ind., 1977-78; ptnr. Matthews, Shaw & Adin, Evansville, 1978-81, Fields & Adin, Evansville, 1981-82; assoc. Bates Law Office, Evansville, 1982-83; sole practice, Evansville, 1983-84; exec. editor, atty. Matthew Bender & Co., Inc., N.Y.C., 1984—; instr. in evidence, U. Evansville, 1979-80; bd. dirs. AmCor. Land Ltd., Plattekill, N.Y. Mem. U. San Fernando Valley Law Rev., 1976-77. Atty., bd. dirs. Deaf Social Services Agy., Evansville, 1978-80; bd. dirs. Evansville Legal Aid Soc., 1980-81, Plattekill Library Assn., Modena, N.Y., 1985, Plattekill Library, Modena, 1986—, AmCorland, Ltd., Plattekill, 1986—, Plattekill Library Chess Club, Modena, 1986—; litigation atty. Hoosiers for License Br. Reform, Evansville, 1981-83. Mem. ABA, Evansville Bar Assn., Gibson County Bar Assn., Ind. State Bar Assn. Republican. Club: Plattekill Library Chess (bd. dirs. 1986—). Legal writing, Criminal, Medical. Home: PO Box 588 Plattekill NY 12568-0588

ADINAMIS, GEORGE PETER, lawyer; b. Evergreen Park, Ill., Dec. 28, 1933; s. Peter George and Helen (Karavites) A.; m. Susan Campbell Coggeshall, Oct. 28, 1961; children—Ann H., Carol M., Susan L. B.S. in Bus. Adminstrn., Northwestern U., 1956; J.D., John Marshall Law Sch., 1959. Bar: Ill. 1963, U.S. Dist. Ct. (no. dist.) Ill. 1963, Ind. 1968, U.S. Dist. Ct. (so. dist.) Ind. 1968, U.S. Tax Ct. 1968, U.S. Supreme Ct. 1970. Spl. agt. IRS, Chgo., 1961-64, with chief counsel's office, Phila., 1964-66, trial atty. civil and civil fraud cases, Indpls., 1966-68; assoc. Kightlinger Young Gray and DeTrude, head tax dept., Indpls., 1968-71; sole practice bus. and corp. planning, estate planning, employee benefit plans, tax cases, Indpls., 1971—; lectr. in field. Served with U.S. Army, 1959-60. Mem. ABA, Ind. State Bar Assn., Ill. Bar Assn., Indpls. Bar Assn. Methodist. Clubs: Downtown Optimist, Masons, Shriners. Corporate taxation, Pension, profit-sharing, and employee benefits, Probate. Office: 320 N Meridian St Indianapolis IN 46204

ADKINS, EDWARD CLELAND, lawyer; b. Montgomery County, Iowa, Aug. 11, 1926; s. Esse Clarence and Elsie Mae (Cline) A.; m. Claudia Kangas, Sept. 17, 1955; children—Pamela, Philip, Paul. B.S., U.S. Naval Acad., 1949; J.D., U. Mich., 1957. Bar: Ohio 1957, U.S. Supreme Ct. 1961, Fla. 1963, Mich. 1965, U.S. Ct. Appeals (5th cir.) 1973 (8th cir.) 1974, (11th cir.) 1982. Assoc. Arter & Hadden, Cleve., 1957-64; trial counsel, Gen. Motors Corp., 1964-70; ptnr. litigation Carlton, Fields, Ward, Emmanuel, Smith & Cutler, Tampa, Fla., 1970—. Served to capt. USNR. Mem. ABA, Fla. Bar, Ohio Bar Assn., Mich. Bar Assn., Am. Judicature Soc. Republican. Lutheran. Clubs: Palma Ceia Golf and Country, Tower, Shrine. Antitrust, Federal civil litigation, State civil litigation. Address: 3938 Venetian Dr Tampa FL 33614

ADKINS, EDWARD JAMES, lawyer; b. Annapolis, Md., Oct. 18, 1947; s. Lee William and Lottie Elizabeth (Stevenson) A.; m. Cheryl Lynne Walcroft, Aug. 24, 1968; children: Helen Elizabeth, Susan Eileen. AB, U. N.C., 1969; JD, U. Md., 1972. Bar: Md. 1972, U.S. Mil. Ct. Appeals 1973, U.S. Dist. Ct. Md. 1974. Assoc. Smith, Somerville & Case, Balt., 1972-75; assoc. Venable, Baetjer & Howard, Balt., 1975-80, ptnr., 1980-81; ptnr. Miles & Stockbridge, Balt., 1982—; sr. cons. Yaffe & Offutt Assocs., Balt., 1981-82; adj. prof. Loyola Coll., Balt., 1980-83. Mem. Pension Oversight Commn., Anne Arundel County, Md., 1985; bd. dirs. United Way Cen. Md., Balt., 1980; bd. dirs., v.p. YMCA, Anne Arundel County, 1985. Served to capt. USAF, 1973. Named one of Outstanding Young Marylanders Jaycees, 1972. Mem. ABA, Md. Bar Assn., Balt. City Bar Assn., Order of Coif. Democrat. Presbyterian. Pension, profit-sharing, and employee benefits, Personal income taxation, Corporate taxation. Office: Miles & Stockbridge 10 Light St Baltimore MD 21202

ADKINS, MARILYN BIGGS, lawyer, consultant; b. East Greenwich, R.I., July 3, 1945; d. John Elmer and Merle Bonita (Irish) Biggs; m. John C. Adkins, Oct. 12. 1965 (div. Feb. 1978). BA, U. Denver, 1967, JD, 1982. Bar: Colo. 1982, U.S. Dist. Ct. Colo. 1982, U.S. Ct. Appeals (10th cir.) 1982. Owner Texaco Service Stas., Denver, 1971-78; legal asst., paralegal Law Offices of Hubert M. Safran, Denver, 1974-82; pvt. practice bookkeeping Denver, 1978-81; ptnr. Safran & Adkins, Denver, 1982—; leg. dir. Colo. Trial Lawyers Assn., Denver, 1982—; mem. Dist. Atty.'s Arbitration Panel, Denver, 1976; active Colo. Supreme Ct. Pub. Edn. Com., 1984—. Instr. Denver Inner City Parish, 1970-75; mem. Anti-Defamation League Civil Rights Commn., Denver, 1983—; del. Democratic County Convs., Denver, 1975-78, 86; advisor U.S. Senate Com., Washington, 1978; trustee Temple Sinai, Denver, 1986—. Mem. ABA, Colo. Bar Assn., Denver Bar Assn., Assn. Trial Lawyers Am., Colo. Trial Lawyers Assn. (bd. dirs. 1983—), Trial Lawyers for Pub. Justice, U. Denver Alumni Assn. Democrat. Jewish. Avocations: musician, gardening. Legislative, Personal injury, Family and matrimonial. Office: Safran & Adkins 1832 Clarkson St Denver CO 80218

ADLER, ALAN MICHAEL, lawyer; b. N.Y.C., Oct. 13, 1951; s. Horace N. and Renee (Streit) A.; m. Randee Elaine Hartz, July 12, 1973. BS in Bus. and Pub. Adminstrn., NYU, 1973; JD, Union U., Albany, N.Y., 1976. Bar: N.Y. 1977, U.S. Dist. Ct. (no. dist.) N.Y. 1977, U.S. Ct. Appeals (2d cir.) 1979, U.S. Supreme Ct. 1980, U.S. Dist. Ct. (so. dist.) N.Y. 1981, U.S. Dist. Ct. (ea. dist.) N.Y. 1983. Ptnr. Rosenblum & Leventhal, Albany, 1976-77; asst. atty. gen. State of N.Y., Albany, 1977-81; dep. counsel litigation N.Y. State Office of Mental Retardation, Albany, 1981—. Mem. ABA, N.Y. State Bar Assn. Avocations: cars, boats. Federal civil litigation, Civil rights, Administrative and regulatory. Home: 553 Clifton Park Center Rd Clifton Park NY 12065 Office: NY State Office Mental Retardation 44 Holland Ave Albany NY 12229

ADLER, A(RTHUR) MICHAEL, lawyer; b. Highland Park, Ill., Apr. 14, 1953; s. Arthur M. and Joan G. (Greenebaum) A. BA, Colo. Coll., 1975; JD, Lewis & Clark U., 1980. Bar: Oreg. 1980, U.S. Dist. Ct. Oreg. 1980, U.S. Ct. Appeals (9th cir.) 1981. Assoc. Des Connall P.C., Portland, Oreg., 1980-82; sole practice Portland, 1982-85; ptnr. Adler & Blount, Portland, 1986—. Mng. editor Lewis & Clark Law Rev., 1979-80. Bd. dirs. Friends of Columbia Gorge, Portland, 1984—. Mem. Oreg. Bar Assn. (treas. aviation sect. 1984-86), Multnomah Bar Assn. (bd. dirs. young lawyers sect. 1984), Assn. Trial Lawyers Am., Oreg. Trial Lawyers Assn. Avocations: aviation, skiing. Personal injury, State civil litigation, Environment. Office: Adler & Blount 1 Southwest Columbia 540 Benjamin Franklin Plaza Portland OR 97258

ADLER, EDWARD ANDREW KOEPPEL, lawyer; b. N.Y.C., Apr. 12, 1948; s. H. Henry and Geraldine (Koeppel) A.; m. Karen Stapf, Apr. 15, 1973; children: Heather, Trevor. BA, Trinity Coll., Hartford, Conn., 1969; JD, Columbia U., 1972. Bar: N.Y. 1973, U.S. Dist. Ct. (ea. and so. dists.) N.Y. 1973, U.S. Supreme Ct. 1977. Counsel Koeppel & Koeppel, N.Y.C., 1972—. Trustee Sands Point (N.Y.) Civic Assn., 1982—, also pres., 1986—, Buckley Country Day Sch., Roslyn, N.Y., 1984—, also treas., 1987—. Mem. ABA, N.Y. State Bar Assn., N.Y. County Lawyers Assn. Jewish. Club: Sands Point Bath and Racquet (v.p. 1978—). Avocations: sailing, skiing. Real property, Landlord-tenant. Home: 86 Barkers Point Rd Sands Point NY 11050

ADLER, ERWIN ELLERY, lawyer; b. Flint, Mich., July 22, 1941; s. Ben and Helen M. (Schwartz) A.; m. Stephanie Ruskin, June 8, 1967; children—Lauren, Michael, Jonathan. B.A., U. Mich., 1963, LL.M., 1967; J.D., Harvard U., 1966. Bar: Mich. 1966, Calif. 1967. Assoc. Pillsbury, Madison & Sutro, San Francisco, 1967-73; assoc. Lawler, Felix & Hall, Los Angeles, 1973-76, ptnr., 1977-82; ptnr. Rogers & Wells, Los Angeles, 1982-84, Richards, Watson & Gershon, Los Angeles, 1984—. Bd. dirs. Hollywood Civic Opera Assn., 1975-76, Children's Scholarships Inc., 1979-80. Mem. ABA (vice chmn. appellate advocacy com. 1982-86), Calif. Bar Assn., Phi Beta Kappa, Phi Kappa Phi. Jewish. Federal civil litigation, State civil litigation. Office: Richards Watson & Gershon 333 S Hope St 38th Floor Los Angeles CA 90071

ADLER, JACK PHILIP, lawyer; b. Long Branch, N.J., June 3, 1953; s. Samuel and Ruth (Berenbaum) A. BA, Rutgers U., 1975, JD, 1978. Bar: N.Y. 1979, U.S. Dist. Ct. (so. and ea. dists.) N.Y. 1979. Assoc. Mudge, Rose, Guthrie, Alexander & Ferdon, N.Y.C., 1978-82; assoc. counsel Western Union Corp., Upper Saddle River, N.J., 1983-85; assoc. gen. counsel Timeplex Inc., Woodcliff Lake, N.J., 1985—. Sec. N.J. Coll. Rep. Orgn., Trenton, 1973; chmn. N.J. Coll. Rep. Campaign, Trenton, 1973, Twp. Ocean Community Services Council, N.J., 1975; v.p. Ocean Twp. United Citizens Inc., 1974; bd. dirs. Greater Montvale Bus. Assn., N.J., 1985—. Mem. ABA (sect. of corp. banking and bus. law 1979—), N.Y. State Bar Assn., Assn. of Bar of City of N.Y., Bergen County Bar Assn. (assoc.), Phi Beta Kappa. General corporate, Computer. Office: Timeplex Inc 400 Chestnut Ridge Rd Woodcliff Lake NJ 07675

ADLER, KENNETH, lawyer; b. Queens, N.Y., Aug. 7, 1940; s. Alfred and Florence (Resnick) A.; m. Rita Klein, June 19, 1963; children—Howard, Andrew, Samantha. B.S., L.I. U., 1962; J.D., N.Y. U., 1968. Bar: N.Y. 1969, U.S Dist. Ct. (ea. and so. dists.) N.Y. 1973, U.S. Ct. Appeals (2d cir.) 1975, U.S. Ct. Mil. Appeals, 1980, U.S. Ct. Claims, 1980, U.S. Supreme Ct. 1980. Pub. accts. J.M. Levy & Co., CPAs, N.Y.C., 1961-63, Rashbar & Pokart CPAs, N.Y.C., 1963-64; v.p. Clobar Mfgf. Co., N.Y.C., 1964-69; sr. assoc. Morris H. Halpern, Esq., N.Y.C., 1969-72; founder, sr. ptnr. Kenneth Adler & Assocs., Melville, N.Y., 1972—; cons. to NEC Telephones, Inc. Mem., contbr. Coalition of Free Men. Recipient Am. Jurisprudence award, 1969, L.I. U. law award, 1962. Mem. Trial Lawyers Assn. Am., Nassau County Bar Assn., ABA, N.Y. State Bar Assn., Suffolk County Bar Assn., Matrimonial Bar Assn., N.Y. State Trial Lawyers Assn. Suffolk. Democrat. Jewish. Clubs: Match-Point Tennis (Huntington, N.Y.), K.P. Family and matrimonial, Federal civil litigation, State civil litigation.

ADLER, SIDNEY W., lawyer; b. Steubenville, Ohio, June 22, 1952. AB in Geography, Clark U., 1976; JD summa cum laude, Syracuse U., 1979. Bar: Mass. 1979, U.S. Dist. Ct. Mass. 1980. Ptnr. Morrison, Mahoney & Miller, Boston, 1979-85, Taylor, Anderson & Travers, Boston, 1985—. Professional liability litigation, Insurance, Personal injury. Office: Taylor Anderson & Travers 75 Federal St Boston MA 02110

ADLER, THEODORE ARTHUR, lawyer; b. Phila., Aug. 23, 1947; s. George and Gloria Doris (Cantor) A.; m. Shelley Lynn Chirsan, Aug. 21, 1971; children: Jessica Whitney, Bryan Jonathan. BA, Pa. State U., 1969; JD, Dickinson Sch. Law, 1972. Bar: Pa. 1972, U.S. Dist. Ct. (mid. dist.) Pa. 1974, U.S. Supreme Ct. 1977, U.S. Dist. Ct. D.C. 1980. Dep. atty. gen. Pa. Dept. Justice, Harrisburg, Pa., 1972-75; gen. counsel Drug & Alchohol Counsel, Harrisburg, Pa., 1975-76; chief counsel Pa. Dept. Gen. Services, Harrisburg, 1976-79; ptnr. Widoff, Reager, Selkowitz & Adler, P.C., Harrisburg, 1979—; cons. Pa. State Gov. Commn., Harrisburg, 1982-84, Pa. Legis. Budget & Fin. Com., 1984; commr. Harrisburg Tax and Rev. Study Commn., 1982-83. Contbr. articles to law revs. Fin. chmn. Dauphin Co. Dem. Com., Harrisburg, 1982-84. Mem. ABA (cons. model procurement code 1979-82, pub. contract sect., local govt.sect., forum com. on constrn.), Pa. Bar Assn. (vice chmn. pub. contract com. 1982-86, chmn. 1986—), Dauphin County Bar Assn. Avocations: golf, weight lifting. Construction, Government contracts and claims, Bankruptcy. Office: Widoff Reager Selkowitz & Adler PC 127 State St Harrisburg PA 17101

ADLERSTEIN, JO ANNE CHERNEV, lawyer; b. Bronx, N.Y., May 1, 1947; d. Bernard Arnold and Beatrice (Levin) Chernev; m. Lee Alan Adlerstein, Sept. 1, 1968; children: David Marshall, Laurie, Daniel Seth. BA in English and Am. Lit. magna cum laude, Brandeis U., 1969; MA, Columbia U., 1970, JD, 1976. Bar: N.Y. 1977, U.S. Dist. Ct. (so. and ea. dists.) N.Y. 1977, U.S. Ct. Claims 1977, U.S. Tax Ct. 1977, N.J. 1978, U.S. Dist. Ct. N.J. 1978. Assoc. Sullivan & Cromwell, N.Y.C., 1976-78; asst. U.S. atty., criminal tax coordinator Dist. of N.J., Newark, 1978-85; counsel Stern, Dubrow & Marcus, P.A., Maplewood, N.J., 1985-87, mem., 1987—. V.p. bd. govs. Solomon Schechter Day Sch., Cranford, N.J., 1985—, mem. bd. govs., 1980—. Harlan Fiske Stone scholar Columbia U., 1975; fellow Nat. Def. Edn. Act, 1970, Parkhurst Found., 1975; recipient Cert. of Appreciation U.S. Dept. Def., 1985, U.S. Customs Service, 1985. Mem. ABA (civil and criminal tax penalties com.), N.J. Bar Assn. (fed. practice and procedure com.), Brandeis U. Alumni Assn. (N.J. exec. bd. 1980—), Columbia Law Sch. Alumni Assn. (v.p. 1986—, sec. N.J. chpt. 1985—), Phi Beta Kappa. Criminal, Personal income taxation, Federal civil litigation. Home: 76 Glenview Rd South Orange NJ 07079 Office: Stern Dubrow & Marcus PA 111 Dunnell Rd Maplewood NJ 07040-2689

ADOMEIT, PETER LORING, law educator; b. Oak Park, Ill., Dec. 17, 1940; s. Bernard Loring and Frances (Coffin) A.; m. Katherine Freyburger, July 7, 1962 (div. 1979); children: Kristin, Hans, Paul. BA, Carleton Coll., 1962; JD, U. Minn., 1965. Bar: Calif. 1967, Conn. 1978. Law clk. to judge U.S. Ct. Appeals (9th cir.), San Francisco, 1965-66; assoc. Neyhart & Grodiv, San Francisco, 1967-72; prof. law U. Conn., W. Hartford, Conn., 1972-78, Western New Engl. Coll., Springfield, Mass., 1978—; mediator Conn. State Dept. Edn., 1972—; cons. U.S. Dist. Ct. Conn., 1978-79. Co-author: Connecticut Civil Procedure, 1978; contbr. articles to profl. jours. Mem. Am. Arbitration Assn. (arbitrator), Phi Beta Kappa. Labor, Judicial administration, Federal civil litigation. Office: Western New Engl Coll School Law Springfield MA 01119

ADRIAN, ROBERT MAC, lawyer; b. Salina, Kans., June 3, 1954; s. Paul Byron and Marian Elizabeth (Bair) A.; m. Janet Louise Vogelsberg, Feb. 7, 1986. BS cum laude, Kansas State U., 1976; JD with honors, Washburn U., 1979. Bar: Kans. 1979. Ptnr. King, Adrian, King & Brown, Salina, 1979—. Bd. dirs. Youthville, Salina, Big Bros./Big Sisters, Salina, 1986. Mem. ABA, Kans. Bar Assn., Saline County Bar Assn., Kans. Assn. Def. Counsel, Def. Research Inst., Phi Kappa Phi, Phi Delta Phi. Republican. Avocations: golfing, fishing, boating, hunting. State civil litigation, Insurance, Personal injury. Office: King Adrian King & Brown 116 W Iron Ave Salina KS 67401

ADUJA, PETER AQUINO, lawyer, business executive; b. Vigan, Philippines, Oct. 19, 1920; came to U.S., 1927, naturalized, 1944; s. Dionicio and Francisca (Aquino) A.; m. Melodie Cabalona, July 31, 1949; children—Jay, Rebecca. B.A., U. Hawaii, 1944; J.D., Boston U., 1951. Bar: Hawaii 1953, U.S. Supreme Ct. 1983. Individual practice law Hilo, Hawaii, 1953-60, Honolulu, from 1960; dep. atty. gen. State of Hawaii, 1957-60; judge Hawaii Dist. Ct., 1960-62; prin. broker AAP Realty, Inc., Honolulu, 1970—; pres. Aduja Corp., Las Vegas, Nev., 1972—, Travel-Air Internat., Honolulu, 1975—; mem. Hawaii Ho. of Reps., 1954-56, 67-74; del. Hawaii Constl. Conv., 1968; sec.-treas. Melodie Aduja, Inc., 1979—. Troop committeeman Aloha council Boy Scouts Am., 1959—; active ARC; chmn. Salvation Army Adult Rehab. Center, Honolulu, 1965—, Goodwill Industries, 1972. Served with U.S. Army, 1944-46. Mem. Bar Assn. Hawaii, Hawaii Bd. Realtors. Democrat. Methodist. Family and matrimonial, Immigration, naturalization, and customs, Juvenile. Home: 49 Niniko Pl Honolulu HI 96817 Office: AAP Realty Inc 1414 Dillingham Blvd Suite 102 Honolulu HI 96817

AFRICK, JOEL JAY, lawyer; b. Chgo., May 8, 1956; s. Richard I. and Diane (Lazow) A.; m. Caryn Katz. AB in Polit. Sci., U. Ill., 1978; JD, Harvard U., 1981. Bar: Ill. 1981, U.S. Dist. Ct. (no. dist.) Ill. 1981, U.S. Ct. Appeals (7th cir.) 1982; CPA, Ill. Law clk. to sr. judge U.S. Dist. Ct. (no. dist.) Ill., Chgo., 1981-82; assoc. Bell, Boyd & Lloyd, Chgo., 1982-84, Jenner & Block, Chgo., 1984—. Mem. ABA, Chgo. Bar Assn., Phi Beta Kappa. Federal civil litigation, State civil litigation, Criminal. Office: Jenner & Block 1 IBM Plaza Chicago IL 60611

AGATSTEIN, DAVID JOSEPH, judge; b. Anniston, Ala., Mar. 18, 1944; s. Samuel and Elayne Agatstein; m. Helene B. Hertzberg, June 12, 1966, divorced; children—Shari Leigh, Kevin Aron. B.A., Queens Coll., 1966; J.D., Coll. William and Mary, 1968; LL.M., NYU, 1971. Bar: Va. 1968, N.Y. 1969. Sole practice, N.Y.C., 1969-74; spl. counsel dept. law City of N.Y., 1974-75; adminstrv. law judge N.Y. State Dept. Labor, 1975—; chmn. Nat. Adminstrv. Law Judges Found., 1980-81. Mem. Nat. Assn. Adminstrv. Law Judges (pres. 1980-81, editor-in-chief jour. 1981—), N.Y. State Adminstrv. Law Judges Assn. (pres. 1978-80, 81-83). Administrative and regulatory, Labor. Office: 1 Main St Room 223 Brooklyn NY 11373

AGNICH, RICHARD JOHN, electronics company executive, lawyer; b. Eveleth, Minn., Aug. 24, 1943; s. Frederick J. and Ruth H. (Welton) A.; m. Victoria Webb Trescher, Apr. 19, 1969; children: Robert Frederick, Michael McCord, Jonathon Welton. A.B. in Econs., Stanford U., 1965; J.D., U. Tex., 1969. Bar: Tex. 1969. Legis. asst., legal counsel to John G. Tower U.S. Senate, 1969-70, adminstrv. asst. to John G. Tower, 1971-72; asst. counsel Tex. Instruments Inc., Dallas, 1973-78, asst. gen. counsel, 1978-82, v.p., sec., gen. counsel, 1982—. Mem. adv. council Sch. Social Scis., U. Tex.-Dallas, Dallas Assembly. Fellow Tex. State Bar; mem. ABA (com. corporate law depts.), Tex. Bar Assn. (corp. counsel sect.), Dallas Bar Assn., Am. Soc. Corp. Secs., Southwestern Legal Found. (adv. bd. Internat. and Comparative Law Ctr.), Machinery and Allied Products Inst. (law council). Republican. Presbyterian. General corporate, Patent. Home: 4934 Crooked Ln Dallas TX 75229 Office: Tex Instruments Inc PO Box 655474 MS 241 Dallas TX 75265

AGRANOFF, GERALD NEAL, lawyer; b. Detroit, Nov. 24, 1946; s. Carl and Frances (Solomon) A.; m. Ilene Beth Donin, May 15, 1980; children—Lindsay Sara, Dana Jill. B.S., Wayne State U., 1969, J.D., 1972; LL.M., NYU, 1973. Bar: N.Y. 1975, Mich. 1973, U.S. Tax Ct. 1974, U.S. Ct. Claims 1974. Atty.-advisor U.S. Tax Ct., Washington, 1973-75; assoc. law firm Baker & McKenzie, N.Y.C., 1975-79, Baer Marks & Upham, N.Y.C., 1979-80; counsel Pryor, Cashman et al, N.Y.C., 1980-82; gen. counsel Arbitrage Securities Co., Plaza Securities Co., N.Y.C., 1982—; gen. ptnr. ASCO Ptnrs., N.Y.C., 1984-87; gen. ptnr. Plaza Securities Co., N.Y.C., 1987—; trustee, Mgmt. Assistance Inc., Liquidating Trust ; dir. United Stockyards Corp., N.Y.C.; adj. instr. NYU Inst. on Fed. Taxation, 1980-81. Bd. dirs. Soho Repertory Theatre, N.Y.C., 1982. Corporate taxation, Personal income taxation, State and local taxation. Office: Arbitrage Securities Co 717 Fifth Ave New York NY 10022

AGUILA, ADOLFO ZACARIAS, lawyer; b. Las Martinas, Pinar del Rio, Cuba, Nov. 8, 1919; came to U.S., 1959; s. Jacinto and Herminia (Rojas) A.; m. Maria L. Higuera, Mar. 23, 1955; children: William, Luis, Alcida, Ramon, Aldo, Arnoldo. Cert. Diplomatic Consul, U. Havana, Cuba, 1951, Dr. Social Sci., 1952, JD, 1953; JD, U. Fla., 1975. Bar: Fla. 1978, U.S. Dist. Ct. (so. dist.) Fla. 1978, U.S. Ct. Appeals (11th cir.) 1984. Advisor Cuban Army, Camaguey, 1953-59; sole practice Camaguey, 1953-59, Miami, Fla., 1978—; acct. SBA, Miami, 1969-78; prof. adminstrv. and consular law Camaguey U., 1954-59. Author: Diplomatic and Administrative Law, 1954. Served to capt. Cuban Army, 1939-59. Mem. Fla. Bar Assn., Fed. Bar Assn., Cuban-Am. Bar Assn., U.S. C. of C., Fla. Accts. Assn. Republican. Roman Catholic. Avocations: swimming, boating. General practice, Criminal, State civil litigation. Home: 1225 Palermo Coral Gables FL 33134 Office: 6780 Coral Way Miami FL 33155

AGUILAR, HUMBERTO JUAN, lawyer; b. Havana, Cuba, Sept. 7, 1952; arrived in U.S., 1961; s. Hector and Fara (Gutierrez) A.; m. Christine DeSandolo, July 7, 1980. BA in History, U. Fla., 1975, JD, 1978. Bar: U.S. Ct. Appeals (5th cir.) 1980, U.S. Dist. Ct. (so., mid. and no. dists.) Ga. 1980, U.S. Ct. Appleasl (11th cir.) 1981, U.S. Ct. Internat. Trade 1981, U.S. Tax Ct. 1982, U.S. Ct. Claims 1982, U.S. Customs Ct. 1982, U.S. Ct. Appeals (4th cir.) 1984, U.S. Supreme 1984, U.S. Ct. Mil. Appeals 1984, U.S. Ct. Appeals (6th cir.) 1985, U.S. Ct. Appeals (8th cir.) 1985, U.S. Ct. Appeals (9th cir.) 1985, U.S. Ct. Appeals (10th cir.) 1985, U.S. Ct. Appeals (D.C. cir.) 1985. Law clk. to presiding justice Fla. Cir. Ct., Miami, 1978-79; ptnr. Fernandez Caubi, Fernandez & Aguilar, Miami, 1980-85, Fernandez Caubi, Fernandez, Aguilar, Berenguer & Cancio, Miami, 1985. Bd. dirs. Dialogo Familiares/Community Outreach VII, 1979-80, v.p., pres. 1980; bd. trustees Miami Mental Health Ctr. 1980-81, v.p. 1981, pres. alcohol adv. bd. 1980-82. Mem. ABA, Fla. Bar Assn., Nebr. Bar Assn., Cuban Am. Bar Assn., Nat. Assn. Criminal Def. Lawyers, Assn. Trial Lawyers Am., John Marshall Bar Assn. (pres., faculty-student com. minority affairs, faculty-student com. profl. responsibility, cert. appreciation, service award), U. Fla. Alumni Assn. (service award), Blue Key, Phi Delta Phi (service award), Sigma Delta Phi (service award), Sigma Alpha Epsilon (true gentleman award). Republican. Roman Catholic. Avocations: sailing, automobile racing, shooting, stamp collecting, music. Criminal, Probate, Private international. Office: Fernandez Caubi Fernandez Aguilar Cancio & Berenguer 1901 NW 17 Ave Miami FL 33125

AGUILAR, ROBERT P., U.S. district judge; b. Madera, Calif., Apr. 15, 1931. B.A., U. Calif., Berkeley, 1954; J.D., Hastings Coll. Law, San Francisco, 1958. Bar: Calif. 1960, U.S. Supreme Ct. 1966. Partner Aguilar & Edwards, San Jose, Calif., from 1960; judge U.S. Dist. Ct., No. Dist. Calif., San Francisco, 1980—; Mem. Regional Criminal Justice Planning Bd., from 1974; chmn. Santa Clara County (Calif.) Juvenile Justice Commn., 1975; mem. Santa Clara County Drug Abuse Task Force, 1974. Mem. Calif. Trial Lawyers Assn., Santa Clara County Criminal Trial Lawyers Assn., Am. Bar Assn., Calif. Bar Assn., Santa Clara County Bar Assn. (pres. 1972). Office: US Courthouse No Dist 280 S First St San Jose CA 95113 *

AGUIRRE, MICHAEL JULES, lawyer; b. San Diego, Sept. 12, 1949; s. Jules and Margaret Aguirre; m. Kathleen Jones, Jan. 16, 1982; children: Arthur Michael, Emilie Kathleen. BS, Ariz. State U.; JD, U. Calif., Berkeley. Bar: Calif. 1974, U.S. Dist. Ct. (so. dist.) Calif., U.S. Ct. Appeals (9th cir.). Asst. U.S. atty. State of Calif., San Diego; dep. legal counsel Calif. State Legislature, San Diego; asst. counsel U.S. Subcom. Investigation, Washington; assoc. Brobeck, Phleger & Harrison, Los Angeles, Silverberg, Rosco et al, Los Angeles; ptnr. Law Offices of Michael Jules Aguirre, San Diego, 1980—; adj. prof. history U. So. Calif., San Diego, chmn. conf. Kennedy, conf. organized crime. Contbg. editor Golden Hills Newspaper. Founding officer San Diego Crime Commn., 1982; mem. San Diego Speaker's Program on Ethical Practices, 1982; candidate U.S. Congress, 1982, 8th dist. San Diego City Council, 1986. Mem. Calif. Bar Assn., San Diego Bar Assn., LaRaza Lawyers Assn., San Diego County Urban League, World Affairs Counsel Assn., Bus. Practices Assn., Calif. Trial Lawyers Assn. Democrat. Roman Catholic. Club: City (San Diego). Federal civil litigation, State civil litigation, Securities. Office: Law Offices of Michael Jules Aguirre 1060 8th Ave Suite 300 San Diego CA 92101

AHEARN, CHARLES DENNIS, lawyer; b. Meriden, Conn., July 3, 1947; s. Charles Dennis and Helen Anne (Semolic) A.; m. Diane Kienast, Oct. 11, 1980; children: Brendan, Holly. BA in Physics, Yale U., 1969; JD cum laude, U. San Francisco, 1978. Bar: Calif. 1978, D.C. 1979. Assoc. Debevoise & Liberman, Washington, 1979-83; corp. counsel Transpace Carriers, Inc., Lanham, Md., 1983—. Served to capt. USAF, 1970-75. Nat. Merit scholar Yale U., 1965-69; State of Conn. scholar, 1965-69. Mem. ABA (chmn. new devels. in space law subcom. air and space law sect. 1983—), AAAS, AIAA, Space Studies Inst. (sr. assoc.), Nat. Space Club. Republican. Roman Catholic. Space commercialization, General corporate. Office: Transpace Carriers Inc 5900 Princess Garden Pkwy Lanham MD 20706

AHERN, GREGORY EMMETT, lawyer; b. Chgo., Mar. 27, 1944; s. John Thomas and Rita Agnes (McGarr) A.; m. Adrienne Deszcz, Nov. 5, 1966; children: Gregory Jr., Eric, Christopher, Mark, Adam. BS, DePaul U., 1966; JD, No. Ill. U., 1978. Bar: Ill. 1978, U.S. Dist. Ct. (no. dist.) Ill. 1978. Assoc. Kane, Doy & Harrington Ltd., Chgo., 1978. Served to sgt. U.S. Army, 1969-74. Mem. ABA, Ill. Bar Assn., Chgo. Bar Assn. Workers' compensation, Personal injury. Home: 636 Gannet Ln Bolingbrook IL 60439 Office: Kane Doy & Harrington Ltd 1 N LaSalle Chicago IL 60602

AHLENIUS, WILLIAM MATHESON, lawyer; b. Chgo., July 26, 1934; s. William Hilmer and Kathryn Marcella (Trenkle) A.; m. Jacqueline LaRue Painter, June 15, 1958; children—Lisa Jo, Kristen Sue. A.B., U. Ill., 1955, J.D., 1961; postgrad., Georgetown U., 1957-59; Bar:, Ill., 1961, Iowa, 1961. Bar: Ill. 1961, Iowa 1961. Assoc. Betty, Neuman, Heniger & McMahon/Davenport, Iowa, 1961-62; ptnr. Swain, Johnson & Gard, Peoria, Ill., 1962—; mem. faculty Ill. Inst. for Continuing Legal Edn., 1972—. Active Heart of Ill. United Fund.; mem. Peoria County Republican Central Com., 1966-70, 72-79, sec., 1974-79. Served with USN, 1955-59. Mem. ABA, Ill. Bar Assn., Iowa Bar Assn., Peoria County Bar Assn., Naval Res. Assn., Phi Delta Phi. Episcopalian. Club: Creve Coeur (Peoria). Real property, State civil litigation, Bankruptcy. Home: 1130 Multiflora Ln Peoria IL 61615 Office: Swain Johnson & Gard 411 Hamilton Blvd Suite 1900 Peoria IL 61602

AHLSTROM, BERT TAVELLI, JR., lawyer, educator; b. Sheridan, Wyo., Feb. 3, 1945; s. Bert Tavelli and Josephine Katherine (Legerski) A.; m. Susan Jeanne Fisher, Sept. 26, 1971; children: Kimberlee Jo, Whitney Marie. BA, U. Wyo., 1968, JD, 1971. Bar: Wyo. 1971, Colo. 1971. Asst. atty. gen. State of Wyo., 1972-74; asst. pros. atty. Laramie County,, Wyo., 1974-76; judge Mcpl. Ct., Wyo., 1976-77; city atty. City of Cheyenne,, Wyo., 1977-81; sole practice Cheyenne, 1976—; instr. Laramie County Community Coll., Law Enforcement Acad. State of Wyo. Assoc. editor Land and Water Law Rev. Watts Bros. scholar, 1971. Mem. ABA, Wyo. Bar Assn., Laramie County Bar Assn., Assn. Trial Lawyers Am., Wyo. Trial Lawyers Assn., Am. Judicature Soc., Cheyenne C. of C. Lodges: Kiwanis, Elks. General practice, State civil litigation, Personal injury. Office: 1807 Capitol Suite 204 PO Box 133 Cheyenne WY 82001

AHLSTROM, MICHAEL JOSEPH, lawyer; b. N.Y.C., June 1, 1953; s. Albert Warren and Bernadette Patricia (Flynn) A.; m. Mary Lou Donnelly, Apr. 19, 1980. BS, St. Francis Coll., 1975; JD, U. San Francisco, 1978. Bar: N.Y. 1980, U.S. Dist. Ct. (so. and ea. dists.) N.Y. 1980, Ga. 1982, U.S. Dist. Ct. (no. dist.) Ga. 1983, U.S. Ct. Appeals (11th cir.) 1984. Counsel Gear Design, Inc., N.Y.C., 1979-80; ptnr. Ahlstrom & Ahlstrom, N.Y.C., 1981-83; gen. counsel Network Rental, Inc., Atlanta, 1984-87; assoc. John Marshall and Assocs., P.C., Atlanta, 1987—. Named one of Outstanding Young Men Am. Mem. ABA, N.Y. State Bar Assn., Ga. Bar Assn., Atlanta Bar Assn., Am. Corp. Counsel Assn., Phi Delta Phi, Alpha Kappa Psi. Republican. Roman Catholic. Club: Ga. Croquet. Avocations: fishing, hunting, tennis, golf, croquet. General corporate, Contracts commercial, General practice. Home: 5340 Greenland Rd Atlanta GA 30342 Office: John Marshall and Assocs PC One Georgia Ctr 600 W Peachtree St NW Atlanta GA 30308

AHR, DEIRDRE O'MEARA, lawyer; b. N.Y.C., June 2, 1946; d. Thomas Francis and Mary Veronica (Meehan) O'Meara; m. Paul Robert Ahr, June 8, 1968 (div.); children—Thomas Brady, Andrew Travers. B.A. cum laude, Trinity Coll., 1968; M.Ed., Va. Commonwealth U., 1976; J.D., U. Mo., 1982. Bar: Mo. 1982, U.S. Dist. Ct. (we. dist.) Mo. 1982. Tchr. Prince George's County Schs., Md., 1968-70, St. Michael's Sch., Richmond, Va., 1976-78; staff lawyer Mo. Supreme Ct., Jefferson City, 1981-83; gen. counsel State of Mo. Detention Facilities Commn., Jefferson City, 1983; gen. counsel State of Mo. Jud. Fin. Commn., Jefferson City, 1983-85; clk. of the ct. Mo. Ct. Appeals Eastern Dist., St. Louis, 1985—. Recipient Acad. Excellance award in environ. law U. Mo. Sch. Law, 1981. Mem. ABA, Mo. Bar Assn., Boone County Bar Assn., Cole County Bar Assn., St. Louis County Bar Assn., Lawyers Assn. St. Louis, Met. St. Louis Bar Assn., Am. Judicature Soc., Phi Delta Phi. Roman Catholic. Office: Mo Ct Appeals 111 N 7th St Saint Louis MO 63101

AHRENS, FREDERICK, lawyer; b. Kansas City, Mo., Oct. 6, 1937; s. Fred Phillip and Adeline (Cutsford) A.; m. Carolyn Joan Thomas, Jan. 17, 1962 (div. 1977); children—Tracey Elizabeth, Sean Frederick; m. Kay Carter, Nov. 28, 1981. B.S., Xavier U., Cin., 1959, M.B.A., 1962; J.D., Marquette U., 1962. Bar: Wis. 1962, Mich. 1964, Tex. 1979, Calif. 1986. Dir. indsl. relations Paper Mate div. Gillette, Chgo., 1970-73, Gen. Instrument, Hicksville, N.J., 1973-74; v.p. indsl. relations Wylain Co., Dallas, 1974-80; v.p. human resources/legal Friedrich Air Conditioning, San Antonio, 1980-82; v.p. human resources/legal AMF/SOI, Irvine, Calif., 1982-84; exec. dir. Ball, Hunt, Hart, Brown & Baerwitz, Long Beach, Calif., 1984—; Mem. ABA, Wis. Bar Assn., Mich. Bar Assn., Tex. Bar Assn., Calif. Bar Assn., Am. Arbitration Assn. (arbitrator). Republican. Roman Catholic. Labor, Administrative and regulatory. Home: 1135 Canyon View Laguna Beach CA 92651 Office: Ball Hunt Hart Brown and Baerwitz 211 E Ocean Ave Long Beach CA 90802

AHRENSFELD, THOMAS FREDERICK, lawyer; b. Bklyn., June 30, 1923; s. Frederick Herman and Madeline Florence (Moffett) A.; m. Joan Ann McGowan, Mar. 17, 1944; 1 child, Thomas Frederick. A.B., Bklyn. Coll., 1948; LL.B., Columbia U., 1948. Bar: N.Y. 1948. Assoc., then partner Conboy, Hewitt, O'Brien & Boardman, N.Y.C., 1948-58; sec., assoc. gen. counsel Philip Morris Inc., N.Y.C., 1959-70; v.p., gen. counsel Philip Morris Inc., 1970-76, sr. v.p., gen. counsel, 1976—, also dir. Trustee Trinity-Pawling Sch. Corp., 1976—; mem. exec. com. Ctr. Pub. Resources; bd. visitors Columbia U. Sch. Law. Served to 1st lt. USAAF, 1942-45. Decorated D.F.C., Air medal with oak leaf clusters. Mem. Assn. Bar City N.Y., Am. Bar Assn. Presbyn. (elder). Club: New York (Athletic.). General corporate. Home: 85 Nannahagan Rd Pleasantville NY 10570 Office: 120 Park Ave New York NY 10017

AIBEL, HOWARD JAMES, diversified industry executive, lawyer; b. N.Y.C., Mar. 24, 1929; s. David and Anne (Fishman) A.; m. Katherine Walter Webster, June 6, 1952; children—David Webster, Daniel Walter, Jonathan Brown. A.B. magna cum laude, Harvard U., 1950, LL.B. cum laude, 1951. Bar: N.Y. 1952. Assoc. White & Case, N.Y.C., 1952-57; with Gen. Electric Co., 1957-64, litigation counsel, 1960-64; with ITT, 1964—, sr. v.p., gen. counsel; dir. ITT World Communications, Internat. Standard Electric Co., The Sheraton Corp.; trustee Fund for Modern Cts., Alliance of Resident Theatres N.Y. Mem. vis. com. Northwestern U. Law Sch., 1984—, also chmn. adv. com., 1986-87; mem. adv. com. Corp. Counsel Ctr., chmn. 1986—; bd. dirs. Alliance of Resident Theatres, N.Y.. Fellow Am. Bar Found.; mem. ABA (exec. council internat. law and practice sect.), Am. Arbitration Assn. (dir.). Club: Harvard (N.Y.C.). Home: 21 Berkely Rd Westport CT 06880 Office: ITT Corp 320 Park Ave New York NY 10022

AIDINOFF, M(ERTON) BERNARD, lawyer; b. Newport, R.I., Feb. 2, 1929; s. Simon and Esther (Miller) A.; m. Celia Spiro, May 30, 1956 (dec. June 28, 1984); children: Seth G., Gail M. B.A., U. Mich., 1950; LL.B., Harvard U., 1953. Bar: D.C. 1953, N.Y. 1954. Law clk. to Judge Learned

Hand, U.S. Ct. of Appeals, N.Y.C., 1955-56; with firm Sullivan & Cromwell, N.Y.C., 1956-63; partner Sullivan & Cromwell, 1963-; dir. Am. Internat. Group Inc., Gibbs & Cox, Inc., Goody Products, Inc.; adv. com. to IRS commr., 1979-80, 85-86. Editor-in-chief: The Tax Lawyer, 1974-77. Trustee Spence Sch., 1971-79; adv. com. Gibbs Bros. Fedn.; vis. com. Harvard U. Law Sch., 1976-82 Served as 1st lt. JAGC AUS, 1953-55. Mem. ABA (vice chmn. sect. taxation 1974-77, chmn.-elect 1981-82, chmn. 1982-83, chmn. commn. on taxpayer compliance 1983-87), N.Y. State Bar Assn., Assn. Bar City N.Y. (exec. com. 1974-78, chmn. exec. com. 1977-78, v.p. 1978-79, chmn. taxation com. 1979-81), Am. Law Inst. (cons. fed. income tax project 1974—), Council Fgn. Relations, Confrerie des Chevaliers du Tastevin, Commanderie de Bordeaux, East Hampton Hist. Soc. (trustee 1983—), Phi Beta Kappa. Clubs: Metropolitan (Washington), India House. Corporate taxation. Home: 1120 5th Ave New York NY 10128 Office: 125 Broad St New York NY 10004

AIKEN, J. DAVID, lawyer, agricultural economics educator; b. Sioux City, Iowa, May 21, 1950; s. John M. and Lois Jean (Larsen) A.; m. Kathleen Ann Sandall, July 29, 1981. B.A. cum laude, Hastings Coll., 1972; J.D. cum laude, George Washington U., 1975. Bar: Washington 1975, Nebr. 1976. Asst. prof. U. Nebr. 1975-79, assoc. prof., 1979—; legal cons. U.S. Fish and Wildlife Service, Ft. Collins, Colo., 1976-83, U.S. EPA, Washington, 1977-78, Nebr. Dept. Environmental Control, 1979-86 . Author: Nebraska Water Law Update, 1979-86. Contbr. articles to profl. jours. Mem. Nebr. State Bar Assn., Com. on Natural Resources (dir. 1981-85, chmn. 1983-85). Environment, Natural resources. Office: U Nebraska Dept Agricultural Econs Lincoln NE 68583

AIKEN, JEFFREY HOWARD, lawyer, accountant; b. Balt., July 14, 1958; s. Sidney Herbert and Janet Betty (Segall) A.; m. Diane Sheale Hutmacher, Jan. 6, 1985. B.A. magna cum laude, Towson State U., 1977; J.D. cum laude, U. Miami, Fla., 1980; LL.M., Georgetown U., 1982. Bar: Fla. 1980, D.C. 1981; C.P.A., Md., D.C. Mgr., mem. internat. tax team Arthur Andersen & Co., Washington, 1980—. Contbr. articles to profl. jours. Bd. govs. Anti Defamation League, Washington, 1984—. Mem. Internat. Fiscal Assn. (nat. reporter 1986), ABA (fgn. activities U.S. taxpayers com. and fgn. currency subcom. Taxation sect., vice-chmn. ann. reports com., editor Tax Lawyer 1984—), Am. Inst. C.P.A.s. Corporate taxation, Personal income taxation. Office: Arthur Andersen & Co 1666 K St NW Suite 400 Washington DC 20006

AIKEN, JEFFREY PAUL, lawyer; b. Milw., Dec. 19, 1946; s. Raymond J. and Patricia A. (Metter) A.; m. Suzanne Doering, Sept. 25, 1976; children: Michael D., Katherine M. BA, Marquette U., 1969, JD, 1972. Bar: Wis. 1972, U.S. Dist. Ct. (ea. and we. dists.) Wis. 1972, U.S. Ct. Appeals (7th cir.) 1977. Assoc. Frisch, Dudek & Slattery, Milw., 1972-83; gen. counsel Nat. Devel. and Investment, Inc., Brookfield, Wis., 1983—; organizer, bd. dirs. Community Nat. Bank, Mukwonago, Wis. Mem. ABA, Wis. Bar Assn. (reporter real estate forms com. 1981-83), Am. Coll. Mortgage Attys. (bd. of regents 1980-86), Am. Corp. Counsel Assn. Republican. Roman Catholic. Club: Tripoli Country (Milw.). Avocations: golf, skiing. General corporate, Real property, Securities. Office: Nat Realty Mgmt Inc 9800 W Bluemound Rd Wauwatosa WI 53226

AIN, SANFORD KING, lawyer; b. Glen Cove, N.Y., July 24, 1947; s. Herbert and Victoria (Ben Susan) A.; m. Miriam Luskin, July 12, 1980; children: David Lloyd, Daniel Jason. BA cum laude, U. Wis., 1969; JD, Georgetown U., 1972. Bar: Va. 1972, D.C. 1973, Md. 1982. Ptnr. Sherman, Meehan & Curtin, P.C., Washington, 1972—; mem. faculty continuing legal edn. program State Bar Va., D.C. Bar. Fellow Acad. Matrimonial Lawyers. Real property, Family and matrimonial. Office: Sherman Meehan & Curtin PC 1900 M St NW 601 Washington DC 20036

AINBINDER, MICHAEL COOPER, lawyer; b. Newark, Aug. 27, 1957; s. Seymour and Rose (Cooper) A. BA, Vanderbilt U., 1979; JD, U. Houston, 1981. Assoc. Walsh, Squires & Tompkins, Houston, 1982—. Mem. Tex. Trust Code Com., Austin, 1985—. Mem. Tex. Bar Assn. (real estate and banking sects.), Houston Bar Assn. (real estate and corp. counsel sects.), Houston Young Lawyers Assn. Clubs: Westwood Country, Texas (Houston). Avocations: tennis, golf, reading. Real property, General corporate, Banking. Office: Walsh Squires & Tompkins 5555 San Felipe Suite 900 Houston TX 77056

AISENBERG, IRWIN MORTON, lawyer; b. Worcester, Mass., Aug. 8, 1925; s. William and Esther (Lewis) A.; m. Lois P., Sept. 4, 1955 (div. Apr. 1986); children: Karen Sue Portner, Sondra Lee, David Craig, Steven Bennett. BS in Chem Engring., Carnegie Mellon U., 1946; JD, Georgetown U., 1977. Bar: D.C. 1958, N.J. 1965, Va. 1969, U.S. Supreme Ct. 1964. Patent examiner U.S. Patent and Trademark Office, Washington, 1954-57; assoc. atty. Wenderoth, Lind & Ponack, Washington, 1957-63; chief patent counsel Sandoz, Inc., Hanover, N.J., 1963-67; sole practice Washington, 1967-75; ptnr. Berman, Aisenberg & Platt, Washington, 1975—, mng. ptnr., 1980-85; lectr. Franklin Pierce Law Sch., Concord, N.H., 1980—. Mem. editorial adv. bd. IDEA, The Jour. of Law and Technology, 1981—; author: Attorney's Dictionary of Patent Claims, 1985; contbr. articles to profl. jours.; patentee in field. Served to cpl. U.S. Army, 1950-52. Mem. ABA, Asian-Pacific Lawyers Assn., Internat. Assn. Protection Indsl. Property, Am. Intellectual Property Law Assn., Appeal Bd. for Nat. Register of Health Service Providers in Psychology. Jewish. Club: Kenwood Golf and Country, Am. Contract Bridge League (life master). Patent, Trademark and copyright, Unfair Competition. Home: 6402 Kirby Rd Bethesda MD 20817 Office: Berman Aisenberg & Platt 1730 Rhode Island Ave NW Washington DC 20036

AISENSTOCK, BARRY ALAN, lawyer; b. Orange, N.J., Feb. 14, 1947; s. Mishel David and Judith (Follender) A.; m. Marquerite Yvette Policastro, Mar. 31, 1979. BS, Oklahoma City U., 1969; JD, Rutgers U., 1972. Bar: N.J. 1972, U.S. Dist. Ct. N.J. 1972, U.S. Ct. Appeals (3d cir.) 1975, U.S. Supreme Ct. 1976. Asst. counsel Newark Bd. Edn., 1972-74, acting gen. counsel, 1975-76; sole practice Bloomfield, N.J., 1976-77; assoc. counsel Oxfeld, Cohen & Blunda, Newark, 1978-85; assoc. Timins & Lesiak, ELizabeth, N.J., 1986—; lectr. Essex County Coll., Newark, 1981. Mem. ABA, N.J. Bar Assn., Essex County Bar Assn., N.J. Assn. Fed. Program Adminstrs. (gen. counsel 1978—), City Assn. Supervisors and Adminstrs.(gen. counsel 1978—). Jewish. Club: Israel Philathelist (Central, N.J.). Avocations: philately, photography. Labor, Education and civil service law, General practice. Home: 94 Baltusrol Rd Summit NJ 07901 Office: Timins & Lesniak 24-52 Rahway Ave Elizabeth NJ 07202

AITKEN, PHILIP MARTIN, lawyer; b. Lincoln, Nebr., Apr. 1, 1902; s. Martin Ingles and Clara (Lewis) A.; m. Josephine Adelia Lamaster, June 14, 1928; children: Philip Jr., Jean, James. AB, U. Nebr., 1923; LLB, Harvard U., 1926. Bar: Nebr. 1926, U.S. Ct. Appeals (5th and 8th cirs.) 1934, U.S. Supreme Ct. 1935. Ptnr. Woods, Aitken, Smith, Greer, Overcash & Spangler, Lincoln, 1926—; asst. U.S. atty. Dept. Justice, Lincoln, 1926-29; bd. dirs. Sahara Coal Co., Chgo. Mem. ABA, Nebr. Bar Assn., Lincoln Bar Assn. Republican. Congregationalist. Clubs: Lincoln Country (bd. dirs. 1958-59, treas. 1939-41), Lincoln U.; Chgo.; Thunderbird Country (Rancho Mirage, Calif.). Avocations: golf, fishing. General corporate, General practice, Probate. Home: 2733 Sheridan Blvd Lincoln NE 68402 Office: Woods Aitken Smith Greer et al 206 S 13th St 1500 American Charter Ctr Lincoln NE 68508

AJALAT, SOL PETER, lawyer; b. Chgo., July 12, 1932; s. Peter S. and Tesbina (Shahadie) Ajalat; m. Lily Mary Roum, Aug. 21, 1960; children: Stephen, Gregory, Denise, Lawrence. BS, UCLA, 1958, JD, 1962. Bar: Calif. 1963, U.S. Dist. Ct. (no., cen., ea. and so. dists.) Calif. 1963. Sole practice Los Angeles, 1965—. Pres. bd. dirs. St. Nicholas Orthodox Cath. Ch., Los Angeles, 1976-77; pres. Toluca Lake Elementary Adv. Council, Los Angeles, 1979, Los Angeles Unified Sch. Dist. Area I Adv. Council, 1980, Providence High Sch. Adv. Council, Los Angeles, 1985. Served with U.S. Army, 1955-57. Mem. Calif. Bar Assn., Los Angeles County Bar Assn. (chmn. mcpl. ct. com. 1985—), Calif. Trial Lawyers Assn., Los Angeles County Trial Lawyers Assn., Lawyers Club Los Angeles County (pres. 1985—), Calif. State Bar Ct. (referee 1984—), Wm. A. Neima Rep. Club (pres. 1978-79). Eastern Orthodox. Lodge: Masons, Shriners. Avocation: physical fitness. State civil litigation, General practice. Office: 3800 W Alameda Ave Suite 1150 Burbank CA 91505

AKAVICKAS, GARY ROBERT, lawyer; b. Wausau, Wis., May 7, 1956; s. Edward and Joanne M. (Curler) A. BA in Music Edn., BS in Polit. Sci. with high honors, U. Wis., Stevens Point, 1979; JD, U. Wis., Madison, 1982. Bar: Wis. 1982. Assoc. Terwilliger, Wakeen, Piehler, Conway & Klingberg S.C., Wausau, 1982-84; corp. counsel S.C. Johnson & Son Inc., Racine, Wis., 1984—. Mem. ABA, Wis. Bar Assn., Order of Coif. General corporate, Private international, Civil rights. Office: S C Johnson & Son Inc 1525 Howe St Racine WI 53403

AKERS, BROCK CORDT, lawyer; b. Milw., Oct. 30, 1956; s. John Norman (Akers) and Lucille Henrietta (Cordt) Galassini; m. Colleen Elizabeth Cullen, Nov. 24, 1984. BA, Tex. Christian U., 1978; JD, U. Tex., 1981. Bar: Tex. 1981, U.S. Dist. Ct. (so. and ea. dists.) Tex. 1981, U.S. Ct. Appeals (5th cir.) 1981. Assoc. Vinson & Elkins, Houston, 1981—. Mem. ABA, Houston Bar Assn., Assn. Trial Lawyers Am., Houston Young Lawyers Assn., Tex. Assn. Def. Counsel, Tex. R.R. Lawyers Trial Counsel, Def. Research Inst. Republican. Lutheran. Avocation: golf. Personal injury, Insurance, State civil litigation. Home: 3123 Southdown Dr Pearland TX 77584 Office: Vinson & Elkins 1001 Fannin 3106 1st City Tower Houston TX 77002

AKERS, CHARLES DAVID, lawyer; b. Atlanta, Jan. 6, 1948; s. James Ires and Lillian May (MacDonald) A. BA, Vanderbilt U., 1970, JD, 1973. Bar: Tenn. 1973. Legal analyst Tenn. Legis. Council Com., Nashville, 1974-76; staff atty. Tenn. Dept. Pub. Health, Nashville, 1976-80; gen. counsel Tenn. Human Rights Commn., Nashville, 1980—. Served to capt. USAR, 1970-85. Mem. ABA, Tenn. Bar Assn., Nashville Area C. of C., Music City IBM PC User Group (v.p. programs 1984—), Mensa. Avocations: computers, languages, reading, boating, tennis. Civil rights, Administrative and regulatory, Legislative. Office: Tenn Human Rights Commn Capitol Blvd Bldg 226 Capitol Blvd Suite 602 Nashville TN 37219-5095

AKIBA, LORRAINE HIROKO, lawyer; b. Honolulu, Dec. 28, 1956; d. Lawrence H. and Florence K. (Iwasa) Katsuyama. BS with honors, U. Calif., Berkeley, 1977; JD, U. Calif., San Francisco, 1981. Bar: Hawaii 1981, U.S. Dist. Ct. Hawaii 1981, U.S. Ct. Appeals (9th cir.) 1981, U.S. Supreme Ct. 1986. Ptnr. Cades, Schutte, Fleming & Wright, Honolulu, 1981—; mem. Hawaii State Jud. Conf., Honolulu, 1985—. Mem. Stivers Meml. Fund Distbn. Com., Honolulu, 1984—. Named one of Outstanding Young Women Am., 1985. Mem. ABA, Hawaii Bar Assn., Hawaii Women Lawyers Assn. (legis. com. 1985—, bd. dirs. 1985—, v.p., 1987—), Hawaii Women Lawyer's Found., Phi Beta Kappa. Club: Honolulu. State civil litigation, Federal civil litigation, Real property. Office: Cades Schutte Fleming & Wright 1000 Bishop St 12th floor Honolulu HI 96813

AKRE, STEVEN HEETLAND, lawyer; b. Jefferson City, Mo., Dec. 24, 1952; s. Donald E. and Arlis (Heetland) A.; m. Elizabeth I. Sugarbaker, Aug. 28, 1976; 1 child, Geneva Elaine. BSBA, U. Mo., 1975, JD, 1979; BA, U. Ala., 1976; LLM in Taxation, George Washington U., 1983. Bar: Mo. 1980, U.S. Dist. Ct. (we. dist.) Mo. 1980, U.S. Ct. Appeals (8th cir.) 1980, U.S. Ct. Claims 1982, U.S. Tax Ct. 1982, U.S. Ct. Appeals (Fed. cir.) 1983, U.S. Supreme Ct. 1984, U.S. Dist. Ct. (ea. dist.) Mo. 1985; Ordained deacon Presbyn. Ch., 1981. Law clk. to presiding justice Mo. Supreme Ct., Jefferson City, 1979-80; asst. atty. gen. Mo. Atty. Gen. Office, Jefferson City, 1980-82; spl. atty. Jefferson City, 1982; tax legis. aide U.S. Senate, Washington, 1982-84; assoc. Coburn, Croft & Putzell, St. Louis, 1985—; liaison Mo. Dept. Revenue Adv. Group, 1982—, IRS Dist. and Regional Commrs. Group, 1985—; bd. dirs. Culligan Water Conditioning Inc., Carter Swift Inc., Jefferson City. Contbr. articles to profl. jours. advisor Law Explorer Post, 1980; chmn. Explorer Scouts com. Great Rivers council Boy Scouts Am., 1980-82. Recipient Appreciation award Boy Scouts Am., 1981; named one of Outstanding Young Men Am., U.S. C. of C., 1984. Mem. ABA, Mo. Bar Assn. (editorial jour. 1984—, chmn. tax law com. 1985—, lectr. 1986—), St. Louis Bar Assn.. Republican. Avocations: sailing, flying. Corporate taxation, State and local taxation, General corporate. Home: 6810 Waterman Ave Saint Louis MO 63130 Office: Coburn Croft & Putzell 1 Mercantile Ctr Suite 2900 Saint Louis MO 63101

AKSEN, GERALD, lawyer, educator; b. N.Y.C., Feb. 16, 1930; s. David and Bess (Stein) A.; m. Phyllis Schwadron, June 3, 1957 (div.); 1 child, Lisa Susan. AB, CCNY, 1951; MA, Columbia U., 1952; LLB, NYU, 1958. Bar: N.Y. 1959, U.S. Dist. Ct. (so. and ea. dist.) N.Y. 1961, U.S. Supreme Ct. 1964. Assoc. Flood & Purvin, N.Y.C., 1958-61; assoc. gen. counsel Am. Arbitration Assn., N.Y.C., 1962-63, gen. counsel, 1964-80; ptnr. Reid & Priest, N.Y.C., 1981—; adj. prof. NYU, N.Y.C., 1968—; mem. First Dept. Jud. Screening Com., 1983—; bd. dirs. U.S. Council Internat. Bus., 1982—. Served to 1st lt. U.S. Army, 1952-55. Bd. dirs. Nat. Inst. Consumer Justice, 1971-72, World Arbitration Inst. 1984—. Fellow Am. Bar Found.; mem. ABA (chmn. sect. internat. law and practice 1982-83), N.Y. State Bar Assn., N.Y.C. Bar Assn., London Ct. Internat. Arbitration (v.p.), Am. Arbitration Assn. (bd. dirs. 1982—), Citizens Union (bd. dirs. 1983-86). International arbitration, Private international, Federal civil litigation. Office: Reid & Priest 40 W 57th St New York NY 10019

ALAIMO, ANTHONY A., judge; b. 1920. A.B., Ohio No. U.; J.D., Emory U. Bar: Ga. 1948. Now chief judge U.S. Dist. Ct. So. Dist. Ga., Brunswick. Office: US Courthouse US District Court PO Box 944 Brunswick GA 31521 *

ALALA, JOSEPH BASIL, JR., lawyer, accountant; b. Aleppo, Syria, Apr. 29, 1933; s. Joseph Basil and Waheda (Tall) A.; m. Nell Powers, Dec. 19, 1954; children: Sharon J., Tracy M., Joseph B. B.S. in Bus. Adminstrn., U. N.C., 1957, J.D. cum laude, 1959. Bar: N.C. 1959. Acct. Arthur Andersen & Co., Charlotte, N.C., 1959-62; pres. Garland & Alala, P.A., Gastonia, N.C., 1963—; dir. Branch Corp., Branch Banking & Trust Co.; lectr. various profl. assns. Contbr. articles to profl. jours. Bd. dirs. Garrison Community Found.; bd. dirs. Belmont Abbey Coll.; past mem. trustees, chmn. fin. com. St. Michael's Catholic Ch.; pres. Jaycees, 1964. Served with M.P. U.S. Army, 1954-55, Korea. Mem. Am. Judicature Soc., ABA, Am. Assn. Atty.-C.P.A.'s, N.C. Bar Assn., Gaston County Bar Assn., Am. Inst. C.P.A.'s, N.C. Assn. C.P.A.'s, Nat. Assn. Accts. Club: Gaston Country. Lodges: Knights of Malta; Rotary(Gastonia) (dir.). General corporate, Estate planning, Corporate taxation. Home: 1216 South St Gastonia NC 28052 Office: 192 South St Gastonia NC 28052

ALAN, SONDRA KIRSCHNER, lawyer; b. Pitts.; d. Andrew and Lora Frances (Hardy) Kirschner; divorced; 1 child, Gregory David. BA, SUNY, Buffalo, 1968; JD, Duquesne U., 1980. Bar: Pa. 1980, Va. 1983, U.S. Dist. Ct. (we. dist.) Va. 1982, U.S. Ct. Appeals (4th cir.) 1982. Art tchr. St. Gregory the Gt., Buffalo, 1966-68; mgr. visual arts lab Ind. U. Sch. of Optometry, Bloomington, 1969-71; law clk. to presiding justice Ct. Common Pleas, Waynesburg, Pa., 1979-80; assoc. Law Offices J.D. Bowie, Bristol, Va., 1980-83; sole practice Bristol, 1984—. Recipient 2d pl. award Pa. State Art Competition, 1976. Mem. ABA (family sect.), Pa. Bar Assn., Va. Bar Assn., Bristol Bar Assn. (pres. 1984-85). Lutheran. Avocations: pencil sketching, stained glass, home remodeling, gardening. Family and matrimonial, Probate, General practice. Home: 917 Arlington Ave Bristol VA 24201 Office: 510 Cumberland St Suite 306 Exec Plaza Bristol VA 24201

ALARCON, ARTHUR LAWRENCE, federal judge; b. Los Angeles, Aug. 14, 1925; s. Lorenzo Marques and Margaret (Sais) A.; m. Sandra D. Paterson, Sept. 1, 1979; children—Jan Marie, Gregory, Lance. B.A. in Polit. Sci, U. So. Calif., 1949, J.D., 1951. Bar: Calif. 1952. Dep. dist. atty. Los Angeles County, Los Angeles, 1952-61; exec. asst. to Gov. Pat Brown State of Calif., Sacramento, 1962-64, legal adv. to gov., 1961-62; judge Los Angeles Superior Ct., 1964-78; assoc. justice Calif. Ct. Appeals, Los Angeles, 1978-79; judge U.S. Ct. Appeals for 9th Circuit, Los Angeles, 1979—. Served with U.S. Army, 1943-46, ETO. Judicial administration. Office: US Ct Appeals 312 N Spring St Los Angeles CA 90012

ALARCON, TERRY QUENTIN, lawyer; b. New Orleans, July 6, 1948; s. Frederick Joseph and Ann Marie (Quentin) A.; m. Mollie Ann McCullough, June 2, 1972; children: Joseph McCullough, Joshua Holland. BS, Spring Hill Coll., 1970; MSW, U. Ala., 1974; JD, Loyola U., New Orleans, 1979. Bar: La. 1979. Asst. to criminal sheriff Orleans Parish, New Orleans, 1974-78, asst. dist. atty., 1978-83; asst. dist. atty. Jefferson Parish, Gretna, La., 1983-86; ptnr. Brandt, Alarcon & McDonald, Metairie, La., 1983—; trial adv. lectr. Tulane U. Sch. Law, New Orleans, 1981—; exec. counsel to mayor, New Orleans, 1986—. Mem. ABA, La. Bar Assn. Democrat. Roman Catholic. Criminal, Legislative, Local government. Home: 6225 St Bernard Ave New Orleans LA 70122 Office: City of New Orleans 1300 Perdido St New Orleans LA 70122

ALARID, ALBERT JOSEPH, judge; b. Albuquerque, Sept. 4, 1948; s. Albert Joseph and Evelyn Sylvia (Torres) A. B.A., U. N.Mex., 1970; J.D., Georgetown U., 1973. Bar: N.Mex. 1973, U.S. Dist. Ct. N.Mex. 1973, U.S. Supreme Ct. 1977. Civil rights atty. U.S. Dept. Justice, Washington, 1973-74; legis. counsel to U.S. Senator Joseph Montoya, Washington, 1974-77; asst. atty. gen. Office of N.Mex. Atty. Gen., Santa Fe, 1977-80; judge. Met. Ct., Albuquerque, 1980-81; 2d Jud. Dist., Albuquerque, 1981-83, N.Mex. Ct. Appeals, Santa Fe, 1984—; adj. prof. U. N.Mex. Sch. Pub. Adminstrn., Albuquerque, 1980-81. Mem. Gov.'s Com. on Disting. Service, Santa Fe, 1984; bd. dirs. N.Mex. Council on Crime and Delinquency, Albuquerque, 1983-84; mem. adv. bd. M.Mex. Law Related Edn. Project. Mem. N.Mex. Jud. Conf. (chmn. 1983-84), U. N.Mex.Alumni N.Mex. Alumni (bd. dirs. 1981-84), Delta Theta Phi. Democrat. Roman Catholic. Club: Kiwanis. Judicial administration. Office: N Mex Ct of Appeals PO Box 2008 Santa Fe NM 87501

ALATALO, RICHARD, lawyer; b. Detroit, Oct. 11, 1939; s. Richard A. and Allie A. (Porkka) A.; m. Evelyn S. Falatine, Aug. 13, 1971. B.B.A., Wayne State U., 1963, J.D., 1967. Bar: Mich. 1968, U.S. Dist. Ct. (ea. dist.) Mich. 1968, U.S. Ct. Appeals (6th cir.) 1983, U.S. Supreme Ct. 1984. Wayne County atty., Detroit, 1968-69; pros. atty. Ogemaw County, West Branch, Mich., 1969-71; asst. prosecutor Genesee County, Flint, Mich., 1971; sole practice, Redford Twp., Mich., 1971—. Civil rights, Federal civil litigation, General practice. Office: 24755 Five Mile Rd Redford Township MI 48239

ALBACH, HENRY JOHN, IV, lawyer; cons.; b. Dallas, Mar. 26, 1949; s. Henry John and Greta (Nobel) A.; m. Susan Albaugh, Oct. 2, 1971. B.A. magna cum laude, Tufts U.; LL.B., U. Tex., 1975. Bar: Tex., U.S. Dist. Ct. (no. dist.) Tex., U.S. Ct. Appeals (5th and 11th cirs.), U.S. Supreme Ct. Staff researcher Harvard U. Law Sch. Ctr. Criminal Justice, Cambridge, Mass., 1971-72; staff dir. Joint Com. on Prison Reform, Tex. Legislature, 1973-75; regional dir. Nat. Council Crime and Deliquency, 1975-77; exec. dir. Tex. Council Crime and Deliquency, 1977-78; spl. master U.S. Dist. Ct. (ea. dist.) Okla., U.S. Dist. Ct. (no. dist.) Tex; ptnr. Albach, Gutow & Blume, Dallas, 1978-85; sole practice, Dallas, 1985—; dir. Media Projects, Inc.; arbitrator Am. Arbitration Assn. Past pres. Tex. Coalition for Juvenile Justice; v.p. Tex. Civil Liberties Union, 1981-82; pres. E. Dallas Design Com., 1980-82. Recipient Sam Ziegler Found. award, 1974. Mem. ABA, Tex. Bar Assn., Dallas Bar Assn., Assn. Trial Lawyers Am., Tex. Assn. Trial Lawyers. Democrat. Unitarian. Author: Criminal Justice in Texas, 1975. State civil litigation, Personal injury, Family and matrimonial. Address: 3301 Elm St Dallas TX 75226

ALBANO, MICHAEL SANTO JOHN, lawyer; b. Bklyn., Jan. 13, 1944; s. Alexander Joseph and Josephine (Giannetto) A.; m. Grace Alma Hoelzel, Mar. 14, 1944; children—Christine Grace, Sarah Michelle. B.A., U. Mo.-Kansas City, 1965, J.D., 1968. Bar: Mo. 1968, U.S. Dist. Ct. (we. dist.) Mo. 1968. Successively assoc., ptnr. Paden, Welch, Martin, Albano & Graeff, Independence, Mo., 1968—. Contbr. numerous articles on family law to bar assns. publs. Tchrs. Assn. scholar, 1963-64; U. Mo.-Kansas City scholar, 1963-66. Mem. ABA (vice-chmn. family law sect., chmn.-elect 1983, chmn. 1984), Mo. Bar Assn., Kansas City Bar Assn., Internat. Acad. Matrimonial Lawyers (bd. of govs. Am. chpt. 1986—), Phi Delta Phi. Democrat. Lutheran. Family and matrimonial. Office: 311 W Kansas St Independence MO 64050

ALBANS, GABRIELLE VICTORIA, lawyer; b. Chapel Hill, N.C., Dec. 17, 1956; d. William Everett Albans and Jane Adele (Mabbott) Austrian; m. Michael Lane Hirschfeld, Sept. 29, 1985; 1 child, Edmund Ramsay. AB, Dartmouth Coll., 1977; JD, Harvard U., 1980. Bar: N.Y. 1981, U.S. Dist. Ct. (so. and ea. dists.) N.Y. 1981. Assoc. Donovan Leisure Newton & Irvine, N.Y.C., 1980-83, Seyfarth, Shaw, Fairweather & Geraldson, N.Y.C., 1983-84; corp. atty. Internat. Paper Co., N.Y.C., 1984—. Mem. ABA. Club: Harvard (N.Y.C.). Federal civil litigation, Legislative, General corporate. Office: Internat Paper Co 77 W 45th St New York NY 10036

ALBENDA, DAVID, lawyer; b. N.Y.C., June 27, 1936; s. Calef and Calo (Mizrachi) A. B.A., NYU, 1957; LL.B, Yale U., 1960. Bar: N.Y. Assoc. Proskauer, Rose, Goetz & Mendelsohn, N.Y.C., 1962-68; asst., assoc. gen. counsel N.Y. Life Ins. Co., N.Y.C., 1968-78, v.p., assoc. gen. counsel, 1980-83, sr. v.p., gen. counsel, 1983-85; v.p., gen. counsel Penn Cen. Corp., 1978-80; ptnr. Sonnenshein, Carlin, Nath & Rosenthal, 1985—. Contbr. articles to profl. jours. Trustee Jewish Bd. Family and Children's Services, N.Y.C.; vice chmn. Henry Ittleson Ctr. for Child Research, N.Y.C.; mem. governing bd. Plays for Living, N.Y.C. Fulbright scholar, 1960-62. Fellow Am. Bar Found; mem. Am. Law Inst., ABA (chmn. blanket authority com., bus. law sect.), Assn. of Bar of City of N.Y. (ad law com.), Am. Arbitration Assn., Am. Council of Life Ins., N.Y. State Bar Assn., Phi Beta Kappa Assocs. Clubs: Yale, University (N.Y.C.). Home: 405 E 54th St New York NY 10022 Office: Sonnenshein Carlin et al 900 3d Ave Suite 1600 New York NY 10022

ALBER, PHILLIP GEORGE, lawyer; b. Lansing, Mich., Dec. 10, 1948; s. Phillip Karl and Audrey Irene (Putnam) A.; m. Mary Margaret Konieczny, Oct. 10, 1979; children—Emily Nicole, Phillip George. B.A., U. Mich., 1971; J.D., Wayne State U., 1974. Bar: Mich. 1975, U.S. Dist. Ct. (ea. dist.) Mich. 1975, U.S. Ct. Appeals (6th cir.) 1978, U.S. Dist. Ct. (we. dist.) Mich. 1982. Assoc. Harvey, Kruse, Westen & Milan, Detroit, 1975-79, ptnr., 1979-84; ptnr. Mager, Monahan, Donaldson and Alber, Detroit, 1985—; lectr. Ill. Inst. Continuing Edn., Chgo., 1980. Mem. ABA, Detroit Bar Assn. (pub. adv. com. 1979—, cir. ct. com. 1978—), Mich. Bar Assn., (rep. assembly 1979-80), Internat. Assn. Def. Counsel (fidelity and surety com. 1984—), Assn. Def. Trial Counsel. Republican. Roman Catholic. Clubs: Athletic, Hundred, Goodfellows Old Newsboys (Detroit). Federal civil litigation, State civil litigation, Construction. Home: 411 Lakeland Rd Grosse Pointe MI 48230 Office: Mager Monahan Donaldson & Alber 2000 1st Nat Bldg Detroit MI 48226

ALBERGOTTI, SAMUEL FRETWELL, lawyer; b. Anderson, S.C.; s. William Greer and Lila (Fretwell) A.; m. Moyer Fairey, May 28, 1983.; children: William Greer III, Martha Fairey. BA, Washington & Lee U., 1975; JD, U. S.C., 1978. Bar: S.C. 1979, U.S. Dist. Ct. S.C. 1979, U.S. Ct. Appeals (4th cir.) 1979. Assoc. Law Offices of Gene R. Ellison, Columbia, S.C., 1978-81, Quinn, Brown, Staton & Boyle, Columbia, 1981-84; sole practice Anderson, S.C., 1984—. Bd. dirs. Piedmont chpt. Nat. Kidney Found., Anderson, S.C., 1984—. Mem. ABA. Methodist. Lodges: Rotary, Kiwanis. State civil litigation, Real property. Home: 902 Hiawatha Dr Anderson SC 29621 Office: PO Box 2786 Anderson SC 29622

ALBERS, FERN BETH, lawyer; b. Glencoe, Minn., Dec. 20, 1951; d. Anthony Raymond and Muriel June (Winter) A. BA summa cum laude, U. Minn., 1973, JD cum laude, 1976. Bar: Minn. 1976, U.S. Dist. Ct. Minn. 1977. Atty. Soo Line R.R., Mpls., 1976-82, atty., asst. sec., 1982-84, asst. gen. counsel, asst. sec., 1984-85, gen. counsel, corp. and asst. sec., 1985-86, gen. counsel, corp. and corp. sec., 1986—. Mem. ABA, Minn. Bar Assn., Hennepin County Bar Assn., Minn. Women Lawyers, Womens Transp. Seminar, Assn. Transp. Practitioners (pres. 9th dist. chpt. 1986—), Phi Beta Kappa. Roman Catholic. Club: Mpls. Athletic. General corporate, Securities, Contracts commercial. Home: 4560 S Cedar Lake Rd Apt #5 Saint Louis Park MN 55416 Office: Soo Line R R Co Box 530 Minneapolis MN 55440

ALBERS, RICK M., lawyer; b. Houston, Aug. 31, 1954; s. Melvin and Ruby (Graeter) A.; m. Susan Donovan, Aug. 15, 1981; 1 child, Joseph

D. BBA, U. Tex., 1975; MBA, JD, U. Houston, 1982. Bar: Tex. 1982, U.S. Dist. Ct. (so. dist.) Tex. 1982. Assoc. Kleberg, Dyer, Redford & Weil, Corpus Christi, Tex., 1982-84, Daugherty, Kuperman, Golden & Morehead, Austin, Tex., 1984—. Council mem. Trinity United Ch., Austin, 1986-88. Mem. ABA, Travis County Bar Assn., Austin Young Lawyers Assn. (bd. dirs. 1986-87), Nueces County Young Lawyers (bd. dirs. 1982-84). Avocation: sailing. Real property. Office: Daugherty Kuperman et al 221 W 6th St Suite 1500 Austin TX 78701

ALBERT, NEIL LAWRENCE, lawyer; b. Los Angeles, May 12, 1950; s. Herman Stewart and Sally Ann (Rapoport) A.; m. Linda S. Kling, May 27, 1979. BS, U. Oreg., 1972, MS, 1973; JD, Villanova U., 1976. Bar: Pa. 1976, U.S. Dist. Ct. (ea. dist.) Pa. 1976, U.S. Ct. Appeals (3d cir.) 1981. Law clk. to presiding judge Lancaster (Pa.) County Ct. Common Pleas, 1976-77; assoc. Geisenbecker, Zimmerman, Pfannebecker & Atlee, Lancaster, 1977-81; assoc. Zimmerman, Pfannebecker & Nuffort, Lancaster, 1982-83, ptnr., 1983—; mem. rules drafting com. Ct. Common Pleas, Lancater County, 1985—. Adult advisor Lancaster County Law Explorers Post, 1979-81; sec. Lancaster County Chpt. ACLU, 1981-83, pres., 1983—. Fellow Acad. Adv. Democrat. Personal injury, Criminal, Federal civil litigation. Office: Zimmerman Pfannebecker & Nuffort 22 S Duke St Lancaster PA 17602

ALBERT, WARD WIAN, lawyer; b. Glendale, Calif., Mar. 19, 1950; s. Ward Nevin and Frances (Gladwin) A.; 1 child, Wendy Amber. B.S., Western State U., San Diego, 1975, J.D., 1977. Bar: Calif. 1977, U.S. Tax. Ct. 1977, U.S. Dist. Ct. (so. dist.) Calif., 1977, U.S. Dist. Ct. (cen. dist.) 1980. Claims adjuster Allstate Ins. Co., San Diego, 1975-76; sole practice, Temecula, Calif., 1977—; dir., pres. Pub. Service Law Corp., Riverside, Calif., 1984—. Active Econ. Devel. Com., Temecula, 1982—. Served with USCG, 1970-74. Recipient Commendation State Bar Calif., 1977, 83. Mem. Temecula C. of C. (pres. 1985, 86,bd. dirs. 1982—), Calif. Young Lawyers (treas, bd. dirs. 1984—), ABA. Lodge: Kiwanis. Personal injury, State civil litigation, Criminal. Home: 27827 Tierra Vista Temecula CA 92390 Office: 27403 Ynez Rd Suite 203 Temecula CA 92390

ALBERTS, CELIA ANNE, lawyer; b. Denver, May 3, 1953; s. Robert Edward and Barbara Ellen (Wedge) A. BA in French, U. Colo., 1975, JD, 1979; LLM in Taxation, U. Denver, 1984. Bar: Colo. 1979, U.S. Dist. Ct. Colo. 1979, U.S. Ct. Appeals (10th cir.) 1979. Assoc. Dietze, Davis & Porter, Boulder, Colo., 1979-82; sole practice Boulder, 1983-84; assoc. George, Davies and Assocs., Denver, 1984-86; ptnr. Loser, Davies, Magoon & Fitzgerald, Denver, 1986—. Mem. ABA (tax div., real estate div., corp. div.), Colo. Bar Assn. (tax div.), Denver Bar Assn. (tax div.), Greater Denver Tax Counsel's Assn., Alliance of Profl. Women. Club: Toastmasters. Avocations: sports, crafts, reading, music. Real property, Corporate taxation, Estate planning. Home: 400 S Lafayette 807 Denver CO 80209 Office: Loser Davies Magoon & Fitzgerald 1512 Larimer St 600 Denver CO 80202

ALBERTS, HAROLD, lawyer; b. San Antonio, Tex., Apr. 3, 1920; s. Bernard H. and Rose (Cassel) A.; m. Rose M. Gaskin, Mar. 25, 1945; children—Linda Rae, Barry Lawrence. LL.B., U. Tex.-Austin, 1942. Bar: Tex. 1943, U.S. Sup. Ct. 1958, U.S. Ct. Mil. Apls. 1959. Tchr., U. Tex. 1942; legal officer Chase Field, 1944; sole practice, Corpus Christi, Tex. Pres. Jewish Welfare Fund, Corpus Christi, 1948; pres. Southwest Regional Anti-Defamation League, Tex. and Okla., 1953, chmn., 1969-72, chmn. Brotherhood Week, 1957; chmn. Nueces County (Tex.) Red Cross, 1959-61; mem. campaign exec. com., chmn. meetings United Community Services, 1961; v.p. Little Theatre, Corpus Christi, 1964; chmn. Corpus Christi NCCJ, 1967-69, nat. dir., 1974-76; bd. dirs. Tex. State Assn. Mental Health; pres. Combined Jewish Apl., Corpus Christi, 1974-76. Served to lt. USNR, 1942-46. Mem. ABA, Tex. Bar Assn., Nueces County Bar Assn. Clubs: Kiwanis (pres. 1962), B'nai B'rith (pres. 1955), Mason. General practice, State civil litigation, Probate. Home: 618 Dolphin Pl Corpus Christi TX 78411 Office: 903 First City Tower II Corpus Christi TX 78478

ALBERTY, STEVEN CHARLES, lawyer; b. Madison, Wis., Apr. 8, 1947; s. Robert Arnold and Lillian Jane (Wind) A.; m. Barbara Jeanne Thoele, Dec. 28, 1968; children—Jeffrey, Stephanie, Douglas, Emily. B.A. with distinction, U. Colo. 1969, J.D., 1972. Bar: Colo. 1973, Oreg. 1977. Law clk. to judge U.S. Ct. Appeals, Denver, 1972-73; assoc. Davis, Graham & Stubbs, Denver, 1973-77, Vonderheit, Hershner, Hunter, Miller, Moulton & Andrews, Eugene, Oreg., 1977-78; ptnr. Hershner, Hunter, Moulton , Andrews & Neill, Eugene, 1978—. Sect. editor: Advising Oregon Businesses, 1984; editor Jour. U. Colo. Law Review, 1971-72; contbr. articles to law review jour. Mem. City Joint Parks Com., Eugene; chmn. Lane County Law Library Com. Mem. Eugene/Springfield Tax Assn. (pres. 1981-82), Order of Coif, Phi Beta Kappa. Corporate taxation, Real property, Contracts commercial. Home: 2022 W 26th Pl Eugene OR 97405 Office: Hershner Hunter et al 180 E 11th Ave Eugene OR 97401

ALBRECHTA, MARK JEROME, lawyer; b. Bklyn., Apr. 21, 1956; s. L. Paul and Marjorie A. (Schenk) A.; m. Patricia R. Stackhouse, Aug. 30, 1980; 1 child, Steven M. Student, Villanova U., 1974-76; BA, Miami U., Oxford, Ohio, 1978; JD, U. Toledo, 1981. Bar: Fla. 1982, U.S. Dist. Ct. (mid. dist.) Fla. 1982. Asst. pub. defender Hillsboro County, Tampa, Fla., 1982-87; ptnr. Esposito & Albrechta, Tampa, 1987—. Contbr. articles to profl. jours. Adv. Law Explorer Post 243 Boy Scouts Am., Tampa, 1984—; bd. dirs. Country Place Civic Assn., Tampa, 1984-86. Mem. ABA, Fla. Bar Assn., Hillsbourough County Bar Assn. (com. chmn. 1986—), Assn. Trial Lawyers Am., Acad. Fla. Trial Lawyers, Soc. for Preservaton and Encouragment of Barbershop Singing in Am., Nat. Assn. Criminal Defense Lawyers. Republican. Lutheran. Avocations: singing, tennis, swimming, woodworking, bicycling. Criminal, General practice. Home: 4708 Fox Hunt Dr Tampa FL 33624 Office: Esposito & Albrechta 5035 N Lois Ave Tampa FL 33614

ALBRIGHT, CARL WAYNE, JR., lawyer; b. Birmingham, Ala., Apr. 27, 1944; s. Carl Wayne Sr. and Grace Charlotte (Teas) A.; m. Sally Rainer Lamar, Sept. 7, 1968; children: Sally, Carl W. III. BS in Aerospace Engring., U. Ala., 1967, JD, 1970. Bar: Ala. 1970, U.S. Dist. Ct. (no. dist.) Ala. 1973m U.S. Dist. Ct. (so. dist) Ala. 1978, U.S. Ct. Appeals (11th cir.) 1981. Ptnr. Rosen, Wright, Harwood, Albright & Cook P.A., Tuscaloosa, Ala., 1970-80; sr. v.p., gen. counsel 1st Nat. Bank Tuskaloosa, 1981-83, exec. v.p., 1984—, also bd. dirs.; v.p. 1st Tuscaloosa Corp., 1983—, bd. dirs.; judge Northport Mcpl. Ct., Ala., 1975-80; exec. v.p. AmSouth Bancorp., 1987—. V.p., treas. bd. dirs. Family Counseling Service; coordinator regional campaign Am. Heart Fund, Ala; mem. United Way, YMCA, Boy Scouts Am., DCH Found.; pres. Stillman Found., 1985—, Tuscaloosa Port Authority, 1985—; exec. com., bd. dirs. Industrial Devel. Authority; trustee Stillman Coll., 1984—; bd. dirs. Indian Rivers Community Mental Health Ctr. Mem. Tuscaloosa County Bar Assn. (pres. 1981-82), U. Ala. Law Sch. Alumni Assn. (pres. 1985), West Ala. C. of C. (chmn. 1986, vice chmn. 1985). Presbyterian. Clubs: NorthRiver Yacht, Indian Hills Country (Tuscaloosa). Avocations: golf, hunting. General corporate, Real property. Office: 1st Nat Bank Tuskaloosa 2330 University Blvd Tuscaloosa AL 35401

ALBRIGHT, CHARLES LLOYD, JR., lawyer; b. Pitts., Jan. 12, 1920; s. Charles and Mary (Jordan) A.; m. Virginia K. Kirby, July 20, 1963; children: John C. Kirby Jr., Kathleen Albright Wanke, Nancy L. Albright Souder, Anne K. Albright Glaid. AB, Pa. State U., 1941; JD, Harvard U., 1947. Bar: Pa. 1949, U.S. Dist. Ct. (we. dist.) 1949, U.S. Ct. Appeals (3d cir.) 1949, U.S. Supreme Ct. 1949. Assoc. Reed Smith Shaw & McClay, Pitts., 1947-53; atty. Mine Safety Appliances Co., Pitts., 1953—, sec. and gen. corp. counsel, 1973—. Served with USAF, 1942-46. Mem. ABA, Am. Soc. Corp. Secs., Pa. Bar Assn., Allegheny County Bar Assn., Am. Corp. Counsel Assn. Republican. Lodge: Masons. General corporate. Home: 65 Longue Vue Dr Pittsburgh PA 15228 Office: Mine Safety Appliances Co PO Box 426 Pittsburgh PA 15230

ALBRIGHT, WILLIAM JAMES, lawyer; b. San Antonio, Feb. 2, 1954; s. William Blaine and Barbro (Andren) A.; m. Kathryn Lee Barrett, Apr. 3, 1984. BA, U. Tex., 1976; JD, Harvard U., 1979. Bar: Tex. 1979, U.S. Dist. Ct. (no., so., ea., we. dists.) Tex. 1979, U.S. Ct. Appeals (5ht cir.) 1979. Assoc. Jenkens & Gilchrist, Dallas, 1979-80; v.p., assoc. gen. counsel Humble Exploration Co. Inc., Dallas, 1980-82; assoc. Johnson & Swanson, Dallas and Austin, 1983—, ptnr., 1986-87; ptnr. Figari & Davenport, Dallas, 1987—. Mem. Dallas Bar Assn. (council mem. oil and gas sect. 1982-83), Travis County Bar Assn., Austin Assn. Young lawyers. Federal civil litigation, State civil litigation, Oil and gas leasing. Office: Figari & Davenport 4800 InterFirst Plaza 901 Main St Dallas TX 75201

ALBURN, CARY RUDOLPH, III, lawyer; b. Cleve., Nov. 19, 1943; s. Cary Rudolph Jr. Alburn and Dorothy Jane (Sperry) Whiting; m. Nancy Ellen Herrold, Feb. 24, 1963 (div. Sept. 1981); children: Craig, Nathan; m. Nancy Faye Scoville, Jan. 2, 1983; 1 child, Charity. BA, U. Wyo., 1965, JD, 1967. Bar: Wyo. 1968, U.S. Dist. Ct. Wyo. 1968, U.S. Ct. Mil. Appeals 1968, U.S. Supreme Ct. 1971, U.S. Ct. Appeals (10th cir.) 1983. Sole practice Laramie, Wyo., 1973—; justice of the peace Albany County, Laramie, 1978; mcpl. judge City of Laramie, 1981-82. Mem. Albany County Red Cross, Laramie, 1978—; pres. Brees Field Airport Bd., Laramie, 1974-86, Albany Assn. for Mental Health, Laramie, 1975-85, Southeast Wyoming Mental Health Bd., Cheyenne, 1977-83. Served to capt. USAF, 1968-73. Mem. ABA, Wyo. Bar Assn., Albany County Bar Assn., Nat. Transp. Safety Bd. Bar Assn., Lawyer-Pilots Bar Assn. Republican. Lutheran. Lodge: Lions. Avocations: boating, home improvements, reading, electronics, piano playing. Family and matrimonial, General practice, Juvenile. Office: 410 Grand Ave Laramie WY 82070

ALCORN, HUGH MEADE, JR., lawyer, former chairman Republican National Committee; b. Suffield, Conn., Oct. 20, 1907; s. Hugh M. and Cora Terry (Wells) A.; m. Janet Hoffer, Oct. 21, 1933 (dec.); children: Thomas Glenn (dec.), Janet Eileen; m. Marcia Powell, Apr. 14, 1955. A.B., Dartmouth, 1930; LL.B., Yale, 1933; LL.D., U. Hartford, 1974. Bar: Conn. bar 1933. Ptnr. Alcorn, Bakewell & Smith (now Tyler, Cooper & Alcorn), Hartford, 1933—; asst. state's atty. Hartford County, 1935-42; state's atty. 1942-48; dir. United Bank & Trust Co., Hartford.; Mem. Conn. Ho. of Reps., 1937, 39, Rep. floor leader, 1939, speaker, 1941; chmn. Suffield Rep. Town Com., 1938-53; mem. Conn. Rep. State Central Com., 1948-57; del. Rep. Nat. Conv., 1940, 48, 52, 56, 60, alternate, 1944, vice chmn. arrangements com., 1956; mem. Rep. Nat. Com. from Conn., 1953-61, vice chmn., 1956-57, chmn., 1957-59, gen. counsel, 1960-61; Rep. floor leader constl. conv. 1965. Mem. Am. Coll. Trial Lawyers, ABA, Conn. Bar Assn. (pres. 1950-51), Hartford County Bar Assn., Sons Union Vets., Conn. Soc. S.A.R., Suffield Grange, Apollo Lodge, Phi Beta Kappa. Republican. Conglist. Club: Anglers (N.Y.C.). Lodges: Masons, Elks (N.Y.C.); Rotary (Hartford) (pres. 1949-50). General practice, State civil litigation, Condemnation. Home: 49 Russell Ave Suffield CT 06078 Office: 1 American Row Hartford CT 06103

ALCORN, WENDELL BERTRAM, JR., lawyer; b. Wharton, Tex., Dec. 19, 1939; s. Wendell Bertram Sr. and Gladys (Spell) A.; m. Sarah Katherine Joeris, June 15, 1963; children: Katherine Elizabeth, Nancy Ellen Wendell Bertram III. Student, Rice U., 1958-61; grad., U. St. Thomas, Houston, 1966; JD magna cum laude, U. Houston, 1969. Bar: Tex. 1969, N.Y. 1970, U.S. Dist. Ct. (so. and ea. dists.) N.Y. 1972, S.C. 1974, U.S. Dist. Ct. S.C. 1974, U.S. Ct. Appeals (4th cir.) 1974, U.S. Supreme Ct. 1974, Ga. 1975, U.S. Ct. Appeals (2d cir.) 1975. Assoc. Cadwalader, Wickersham & Taft, N.Y.C., 1969-73, 75-78, ptnr., 1978—; assoc. Hill, Towill, Norman, Barrett & Johnson, Augusta, Ga., 1973-75; adj. prof. Adelphi U., Hempstead, N.Y., 1975-78; spl. prof. Hofstra U., Hempstead, 1979—; gen. counsel Nat. Commn. for Rev. of Antitrust Laws & Procedures, Washington, 1978-79. Author: Asbestos Litigation, 1982; editor-in-chief U. Houston Law Rev., 1968-69 (highest merit award 1969); adv. bd. Hazardous Substances Jour., 1985—; contbr. articles to profl. jours. Recipient Academic Excellence award Houston Legal Found., 1985. Fellow Nat. Inst. Trail Advocacy, Def. Research Inst.; mem. ABA, Tex. Bar Assn., Ga. Bar Assn., S.C. Bar Assn., N.Y. State Bar Assn., N.Y. County Bar Assn., Fed. Bar Council (sustaining), N.Y. Acad. Scis. Democrat. Roman Catholic. Club: Darien Country (Conn.). Avocations: golf, tennis, sailing. Antitrust, Insurance, Personal injury. Home: 11 Old Oak Rd Darien CT 06820 Office: Cadwalader Wickersham & Taft 100 Maiden Ln New York NY 10038

ALDEN, RICHARD FREDRICK, lawyer, aerospace company executive; b. Cedar Falls, Iowa, Aug. 15, 1924; s. Raymond Fredrick and Gladys Marie (Severin) A.; m. Jeanne Latham (div.); children—Dana Latham, Amy Alden Glasgow, Anne Alden Clifford; m. Marjorie Ellen Lesnett, July 12, 1975. B.A., U. So. Calif., 1946, J.D., 1949. Bar: Calif. 1949. With Latham & Watkins, Los Angeles, 1949-85, sr. ptnr.; gen. counsel Hughes Aircraft Co., Los Angeles, 1974-85; vice. chmn., mem. exec. com., gen. counsel Hughes Aircraft Co., Los Angeles, 1985—; dir. Irvine Co. Mem. adv. bd. Calif. State Parks Found. Served as officer USN, World War II. Mem. ABA, Calif. State Bar, Los Angeles County Bar Assn. (trustee).

ALDEN, STEVEN MICHAEL, lawyer; b. Los Angeles, May 19, 1945; s. Herbert and Sylvia Zina (Hochman) A.; m. Evelyn Mae Subotky, Dec. 31, 1977; children: Carissa Louise, Bramley Marshall, Darym Alexander. AB, UCLA, 1967; JD, U. Calif.-Berkeley, 1970. Bar: Calif. 1971, N.Y. 1971. Assoc. Debevoise & Plimpton, N.Y.C., 1971-78, ptnr., 1979—; lectr., seminar panelist Practising Law Inst., N.Y.C., 1981—; panelist, lectr. N.Y. State Bar, Albany, 1984. Contbr. articles to profl. jours., 1982-83. Mem. ABA (real estate fin. com.), Assn. Bar City N.Y. (com. real property law), Am. Land Title Assn. (assoc. lender's counsel group), Am. Coll. Real Estate Lawyers, Order of Coif, Phi Beta Kappa. Republican. Club: Board Room (N.Y.C.). Real property. Office: Debevoise & Plimpton 875 Third Ave New York NY 10022

ALDERMAN, JOHN PERRY, lawyer; b. Mt. Airy, N.C., July 22, 1935; s. John and Elizabeth (Perry) A.; m. Marion Elizabeth Allen, Aug. 4, 1956; children: John Owen, Nancy Greene. B.A., Emory and Henry Coll., 1955; LL.B., U. Va., 1958. Bar: Va. 1958. Ptnr. Alderman & Alderman, Hillsville, Va., 1958-81; U.S. atty. Western Dist. Va., Roanoke, 1981—; Commonwealth atty. (Va. prosecutor) Hillsville, 1963-81. Author 1850 Census Annotated: Carroll County, Va., 1979, Carroll 1765-1815, The Settlements, 1985. Rector Radford U., Va., 1980-82, bd. visitors, 1974-82. Mem. Nat. Dist. Atty. Assn., Va. Commonwealth Atty. Assn., Order of Coif. Republican. Presbyterian. Lodge: Rotary (past pres.). Home: 3324 Penn Forest Blvd Roanoke VA 24018 Office: US Atty's Office Box 1709 Roanoke VA 24008

ALDERMAN, MARK LOUIS, lawyer; b. Washington, Nov. 26, 1952; s. Joseph and Cylvia (Friedland) A.; m. Sue Ellen Silverblatt, Aug. 5, 1978; children: Jesse Harlan, Holly Kate. AB, Brown U., 1975; JD, U. Pa., 1978. Bar: D.C. 1978, Mass. 1979, Pa. 1979. Law clk. to chief judge U.S. Dist. Ct. (ea. dist.) Pa., Phila., 1978-79; assoc. Choate, Hall & Stewart, Boston, 1979-80; from assoc. to ptnr. Wolf, Block, Schorr and Solis-Cohen, Boston, 1980—; bd. dirs. ABC Inc., Ardmore, Pa., 1985—. Chmn. Ams. with Gary Hart, Pa., 1982—. Mem. ABA, Pa. Bar Assn., Phila. Bar Assn. Avocation: music. Federal civil litigation, Real property, General corporate. Office: Wolf Block Schorr & Solis-Cohen Packard Bldg 12th Floor Philadelphia PA 19102

ALDERMAN, RICHARD MARK, legal educator, lawyer, television and radio commentator; b. Passaic, N.J., Feb. 18, 1947; s. Wilbur and Lois H. (Taub) A. B.A., Tulane U., 1968; J.D. cum laude, Syracuse U., 1971; LL.M., U. Va., 1973. Bar: N.Y. 1972, Tex. 1981. Staff atty. Legal Services, Syracuse, 1972-73; prof. law U. Houston, 1973—; vis. prof. Loyola Law Sch., Los Angeles, 1976-77, Boston Coll., 1980-81; People's Lawyer, Stas. KPRC-TV, KFMK-FM, Houston, 1980—; dir. council on Legal Edn. Opportunity Summer Inst., Houston, 1975. Author: A Transactional Guide to the Uniform Commercial Code, 1982; Creditors' Rights in Texas, 1978; Uniform Commercial Code Series, 1984; Know Your Rights! Answers to your most Common Legal Questions, 1985, Doing Business in Texas, 1987. Contbr. articles to profl. jours. Recipient M.D. Anderson Scholarship award U. Houston Law Ctr., 1977. Mem. ABA, State Bar Tex. (consumer law council 1984—, editor-in-chief Caveat Vendor 1984—; recipient Golden Gavel award 1985, Silver Gavel award 1986), Order of the Coif, Phi Delta Phi. Jewish. Consumer commercial, Contracts commercial. Home: 4402 Merwin St Houston TX 77027 Office: U Houston Law Ctr University Park 4800 Calhoun St Houston TX 77004

ALDISERT, RUGGERO JOHN, U.S. circuit judge; b. Carnegie, Pa., Nov. 10, 1919; s. John S. and Elizabeth (Magnacca) A.; m. Agatha Maria DeLacio, Oct. 4, 1952; children—Lisa Maria, Robert, Gregory. B.A., U. Pitts., 1941, J.D., 1947. Bar: Pa. bar 1947. Gen. practice law Pitts., 1947-61; judge Ct. Common Pleas., Allegheny County, 1961-68; judge U.S. Ct. Appeals (3d cir.), Pitts., 1968-84, chief judge, 1984-87, sr. judge, 1987—; adj. prof. law U. Pitts. Sch. Law, 1984-87 ; faculty Appellate Judges Seminar, N.Y.U., 1971-85 , asso. dir., 1979-85 ; lectr. internat. seminar legal medicine U. Rome, 1965, Law Soc. London, 1967, Internat. seminar comparative law, Rome, 1971; chmn. Fed. Appellate Judges Seminar; bd. dirs. Fed. Jud. Center, Washington, 1974-79; mem. Pa. Civil Procedural Rules Com., 1965-84 Jud. Conf. Com. on Adminstrn. Criminal Law, 1971-77; chmn. adv. com. on bankruptcy rules Jud. Conf. U.S., 1979-84; lectr. univs. in U.S. and abroad. Author: Il Ritorno al Paese, 1966-67, The Judicial Process, Readings, Materials and Cases, 1976. Allegheny dist. chmn. Multiple Sclerosis Soc., 1961-68; pres. Italian Sons and Daus. Am. Cultural Heritage Found., 1965-68; Trustee U. Pitts., 1968—; chmn. bd. visitors Pitts. Sch. Law, 1978—, Univ. Ctr. Internat. Studies, Grad. Sch. Pub. Internat. Affairs. Served to maj. USMCR, 1942-46. Recipient Outstanding Merit award Allegheny County Acad. Trial Lawyers, 1964. Fellow Internat. Acad. Law and Sci., Am. Coll. Legal Medicine; mem. Inst. Jud. Adminstrn., Am. Law Inst., Pitts. Legal Med. Inst., Italian Sons and Daus. of Am. (pres. 1954-68), Italian Sons and Daus. Am. Fraternal Assn. (nat. pres. 1960-68), Phi Beta Kappa, Phi Alpha Delta, Omicron Delta Kappa. Democrat. Roman Catholic. Home: 1000 Grandview Ave Pittsburgh PA 15211 Office: 831 Federal Bldg Liberty Ave Pittsburgh PA 15222

ALDRICH, ANN, federal judge; b. Providence, R.I., June 28, 1927; d. Allie C. and Ethel M. (Carrier) A.; m. Chester Aldrich, 1960 (dec.); children: Martin, William; children by previous marriage: James, Allen. B.A.; cum laude, Columbia U., 1948; LL.B. cum laude, N.Y. U., 1950, LL.M., 1964, S.J.D. Bar: D.C. bar, N.Y. bar 1952, Conn. bar 1966, Ohio bar 1973, Supreme Ct. bar 1956. Research asst. to mem. faculty N.Y. U. Sch. Law; asso. firm Samuel Nakasian, Washington, 1952-53; mem. gen. counsel's staff FCC, Washington, 1953-60; U.S. del. to Internat. Radio Conf., Geneva, 1959; practice law Darien, Conn.; asso. prof. law Cleve. State U., 1968-71, prof., 1971-80; also chmn. curriculum com.; U.S. Dist. Ct. (no. dist.) Ohio, 1980—;; bd. govs. Citizens' Communications Center, Inc., Washington; mem. litigation com.; guest lectr. Calif. Inst. Tech., Pasadena, summer 1971. Mem. Fed. Bar Assn., Nat. Assn. of Women Judges, Fed. Communications Bar Assn. Episcopalian. Jurisprudence. Office: U S Dist Ct 210 US Courthouse 201 Superior Ave NE Cleveland OH 44114 *

ALDRICH, LOVELL W(ELD), lawyer; b. Port Chester, N.Y., Dec. 21, 1942; s. Laurence Weld and Leota (Burton) A.; m. Sharon King, Aug. 20, 1966; children: Molly Colleen, Abigail Elizabeth. BBA in Fin., Tex. A&M U., 1965; JD, St. Mary's U., San Antonio, 1968. Bar: Tex. 1968, U.S. Dist. Ct. (so. dist.) Tex. 1971, U.S. Dist. Ct. (ea. dist.) Tex. 1980, U.S. Ct. Appeals (5th cir.) 1981. Assoc. Law Office of Fred Parks, Houston, 1970-72, Lloyd & Hoppess, Houston, 1972-75; sole practice Houston, 1975-78; ptnr. Aldrich & Buttrill, Houston, 1978-81, Aldrich, Buttrill & Kuhn, Houston, 1981—. Served to capt. U.S. Army, 1968-70, Vietnam. Mem. Assn. Trial Lawyers Am., Tex. Trial Lawyers Assn., Tex. Bar Assn. (cert. personal injury trial law). Episcopalian. Avocations: tennis, photography, reading. Personal injury, Federal civil litigation, State civil litigation. Home: 1007 Horseshoe Dr Sugar Land TX 77478 Office: Aldrich Buttrill & Kuhn 1919 Smith Suite 950 Concorde Tower Houston TX 77002

ALDRICH, RICHARD DENNIS, lawyer; b. Los Angeles, June 15, 1938; s. Floyd W. and Mary B. (Velez) A.; m. Joan Bernadette Sullivan, Oct. 31, 1979; children—Brooks, Brendan, Mark. B.S., Loyola U., Los Angeles, 1960; LL.B., UCLA, 1963. Bar: Calif. 1963. Assoc. Harney, Ford & Schlottman, Los Angeles, 1963-67; pres. and gen. counsel Casualty Ins. Co. of Calif., Los Angeles, 1967-68; gen. counsel LFC Fin. Corp., Los Angeles, 1969-70, Equitable Savs. and Loan Assn., Los Angeles, 1969-70; counsel Gt. Western Savs. and Loan Assn. Los Angeles, 1970-71; sole practice, Sherman Oaks, Calif., 1971—; spl. arbitrator apptd. by Los Angeles Superior Ct. to Superior Ct. Dependency Ct. Improvement Project; mem. Com. to Preserve the Jury System; mem. Los Angeles Superior Ct. Arbitration Panel. Fellow Am. Coll. Trial Lawyers; mem. Am. Bd. Trial Advs. (sec. 1976, v.p. 1985, pres. 1986, chmn. Calif. chpt. 1986, nat. bd. dirs. 1987), Calif. Trial Lawyers Assn. (cert. 1980, lectr. 1978, 79, 80, bd. govs. 1986-87), Los Angeles Trial Lawyers Assn. (lectr. 1979), Los Angeles County Bar Assn., Calif. Bar Assn., ABA, Founders (UCLA Sch. Law). Personal injury, State civil litigation, Insurance.

ALDRICH, THOMAS LAWRENCE, lawyer; b. Dubuque, Iowa, Feb. 10, 1948; s. Larry W. and Jeanne Blanche (Heitzman) A.; m. Janet Lee Proffer, Aug. 13, 1972; children: Jennifer Lee, Stephanie Christine. BA, Northwestern U., Evanston, Ill., 1970; JD, Northwestern U., 1973. Bar: Ill. 1973, U.S. Dist. Ct. (no. dist.) Ill. 1973, U.S. Ct. Appeals (7th cir.) 1974, U.S. Supreme Ct. 1980. Assoc. Chadwell, Kayser, Ruggles, McGee & Hastings Ltd., Chgo., 1973-81; staff counsel Household Merchandising, Inc., Des Plaines, Ill., 1981-83; asst. gen. counsel Household Mfg., Inc., Prospect Heights, Ill., 1983—. Articles editor Jour. Criminal Law and Criminology, 1972-73. Mem. choir Glenview (Ill.) Community Ch., 1976—, exec. bd., 1977—, chmn. music bd., 1977, 80, vice chmn. nominating com., 1986—. Mem. ABA, Chgo. Bar Assn., Machinery and Allied Products Inst. (hazardous materials mgmt. council 1983—) Psi Upsilon (trustee 1970-78). Mem. United Ch. Christ. Avocations: golf, cross-country skiing, reading, cooking, writing. General corporate, Federal civil litigation, Antitrust. Home: 707 Spruce St Glenview IL 60025 Office: Household Mfg Inc 2700 Sanders Rd Prospect Heights IL 60070

ALESEVICH, WALTER CHARLES, lawyer; b. Bridgeport, Conn., Oct. 8, 1954; s. Walter Simeon and Vera Charles (Kozulko) A. BA, Yale U., 1976, JD, 1980. Bar: N.Y. 1981, U.S. Dist. Ct. (so. and ea. dists.) N.Y. 1981, U.S. Ct. Appeals (4th cir.) 1981, U.S. Dist. Ct. Conn. 1985, Conn. 1986. Law clk. to presiding judge U.S. Ct. Appeals (2d cir.), New Haven, 1982; assoc. Lord, Day & Lord, N.Y.C., 1980-83, Milgrim, Thomajam, Jacobs & Lee, N.Y.C., 1983, Weingarten & Madden, N.Y.C., 1983-85, Carmody & Torrance, New Haven and Waterbury, Conn., 1985—. Mem. ABA. Republican. Russian Orthodox. Club: Yale (N.Y.C.) (mem. admissions com. 1981-85). Avocations: golf, tennis, squash. Federal civil litigation, State civil litigation, Insurance. Home: PO Box 190 Trumbull CT 06611 Office: Carmody & Torrance 59 Elm St New Haven CT 06509

ALESIA, JAMES H(ENRY), lawyer; b. Chgo., July 16, 1934; m. Kathryn P. Gibbons, July 8, 1961; children—Brian J., Daniel J. B.S. Loyola U., 1956; LL.B., IIT/Chgo.-Kent Coll. Law, 1960; grad. Nat. Jud. Coll., U. Nev.-Reno, 1976. Bar: Ill. 1960, Minn. 1970. Police officer City of Chgo., 1957-60; with Law Office Anthony Scariano, Chicago Heights, Ill., 1960-61; assoc. Pretzel, Stouffer, Nolan & Rooney, Chgo., 1961-63; asst. gen. counsel Chgo. & North Western Transp. Co., Chgo., 1963-70; assoc. Rerat Law Firm, Mpls., 1970-71; asst. U.S. atty. No. dist. Ill., Chgo., 1971-73, trial counsel Chessie System, Chgo., 1973; U.S. adminstrv. law judge, 1973-82; ptnr. Reuben & Proctor, Chgo., 1982-86, Isham, Lincoln & Beale, 1986—; faculty Nat. Jud. Coll., U. Nev.-Reno, 1979-80. Mem. ABA, Ill. Bar Assn. (assembly 1978-84), Fed. Bar Assn., Justinian Soc. Lawyers, Celtic Legal Soc. Republican. Roman Catholic. Contbr. articles to legal publs. Federal civil litigation, Criminal, State civil litigation. Home: 1025 S Lincoln Ave Park Ridge IL 60068 Office: Isham Lincoln & Beale 19 S LaSalle St Chicago IL 60603

ALEXANDER, BEVIN RAY, JR., lawyer; b. Evanston, Ill., Feb. 7, 1954; s. Bevin R. Sr. and Margaret (Bailey) A.; m. Pamela Craig, Aug. 6, 1977; children: Lauren Bradford, Bevin Craig. BA with distinction, U. Va., 1976; JD, Washington and Lee U., 1981. Bar: Va. 1982, U.S. Dist. Ct. (we. dist.) Va. 1982, U.S. Ct. Appeals (4th cir.) 1982. Law clk. to judge Va. Supreme Ct., Richmond, 1981-82; assoc. Edmunds & Williams, Lynchburg, Va., 1982—; bd. dirs. Va. Legal Services Corp., Richmond. Mem. Va. Bar Assn. (com. to commerate Va. statute religious freedom 1986), Va. Trial Lawyers Assn., Va. Assn. Def. Attys., 2d Regt. Va. Cavalry (lt. 1984—). Episcopalian. Avocations: hist. re-enactment, swimming, backpacking, antique firearms. State civil litigation, Insurance, Workers' compensation. Office: Edmund & Williams PO Box 958 Lynchburg VA 24505

ALEXANDER, CARLA J., lawyer; b. Superior, Nebr., Nov. 23, 1955; d. Leslie Dale Alexander and Betty J. (Haag) Ehlers. BA, U. Nebr., 1978, JD, 1981. Bar: Nebr. 1981, U.S. Dist. Ct. Nebr. 1981. Assoc. Downing & Alexander, Kearney, Nebr., 1981—. Mem. Nebr. Bar Assn., Buffalo County

Bar Assn., Big Bend Audobon Soc. General practice, Family and matrimonial, State civil litigation.

ALEXANDER, CHARLES JACKSON, II, lawyer; b. Winston-Salem, N.C., Nov. 20, 1946; s. Jack C. and Mary Ann (Smitherman) A.; m. Dawn L. Sattenfield; children—Kristen, Joseph. B.A., Wake Forest U., 1969, J.D., 1972. Bar: N.C. 1972, U.S. Dist. Ct. (mid. dist.) N.C. 1972. Sole practice, Winston-Salem, N.C., 1972-76; sr. ptnr. Alexander & Hinshaw, Winston-Salem, 1976-82, Alexander, Wright, Parrish, Hinshaw & Tash, Winston-Salem, 1982— Pres. Cystic Fibrosis Found., Winston-Salem, Am. Cancer Soc., Winston-Salem, 1984. Mem. ABA, Assn. Trial Lawyers Am., N.C. Acad. Trial Lawyers (patron), N.C. Bar Assn., Criminal Def. Lawyers (pres. 1982-83), N.C. Jaycees (legal counsel 1981-82; recipient Outstanding Pres. award 1977-78, Disting. Service award 1983), Greater Winston-Salem C. of C. (dir. 1978). Democrat. Presbyterian. Criminal, Family and matrimonial, Personal injury. Home: 7620 Penland Dr Clemmons NC 27012 Office: Alexander Wright Parrish Hinshaw & Tash 412 N Trade St Winston Salem NC 27101

ALEXANDER, CHRISTINE ANN, lawyer; b. Algoma, Wis., Apr. 16, 1956; d. Clarence Joseph and Anna Mae (Schmeling) A.; m. Peter R. Martin, July 23, 1983. BS, Boston Coll., 1979; JD, Harvard U., 1982. Bar: Wash. 1982, N.Y. 1985. Assoc. Karr, Tuttle, Koch et al, Seattle, 1982-84; asst. counsel SUNY, Albany, 1985—. Mem. ABA, N.Y. State Bar Assn., Wash. State Bar Assn., Capital Dist. Women's Bar Assn. (treas. 1986—). Labor, Legislative. Home: 11 Oak Tree Ln Schenectady NY 12309 Office: SUNY State U Plaza S329 Albany NY 12309

ALEXANDER, DAVE ALMON, lawyer; b. Decatur, Ala., Dec. 28, 1915; s. Truman Hudson and Helen Elizabeth (Almon) A.; m. Jane Bagley, Feb. 1, 1958; children—Suzanne Alexander Silva, Sarah A. Green, Dave A. Alexander Jr. B.A., Vanderbilt U., 1939, LL.B., 1942, J.D., 1969. Bar: Tenn. 1942. Sr. mem. firm Alexander, King & Williams, Franklin, Tenn., 1945—; dir., First Tenn. Bank. mem. Tenn. Gen. Assembly, 1945-47, floor leader, speaker pro tem, 1945-47. Mem. City Council, Franklin, 1951-52. Served as lt. comdr. USNR, 1942-45. Decorated Silver Star, Purple Heart. Mem. ABA (chmn. grievance com. 1951-52), Tenn. Bar Assn. (v.p. 1960-61, chmn. grievance com. 1960-61), Williamson County Bar Assn. (pres. 1960-61), Phi Delta Phi, Sigma Nu. Democrat. Methodist. Club: Lions (pres.). State civil litigation, General practice. Home: Isola Bella Farm 1112 Franklin Rd Brentwood TN 37027 Office: 203 3d Ave S Franklin TN 37064

ALEXANDER, DAVID CLEON, III, lawyer; b. New Orleans, July 13, 1941; s. David Cleon Alexander Jr. and Joyce (Bragg) Crane. BBA, U. Ga., 1963; MBA, Ga. State U., 1969; JD, U. Va., 1973; LLM in Taxation, NYU, 1976. Bar: N.Y. 1974, U.S. Tax Ct. 1974, Ariz. 1975. Assoc. White & Case, N.Y.C., 1973-75, Murphy & Posner, Phoenix, 1975-78; ptnr. Lewis & Roca, Phoenix, 1978—. Served to 1st lt. U.S. Army, 1962-64. Fellow Ariz. Bar Found; mem. ABA, Ariz. Bar Assn. (lectr., cert. specialist in taxation), Sports Car Club Am., Phi Kappa Phi, Beta Gamma Sigma. Republican. Episcopalian. Avocation: amateur road racing. Tax controversy work, Federal income taxation, Real property. Home: 8520 N 52d St Paradise Valley AZ 85253 Office: Lewis & Roca 100 W Washington Suite 2200 Phoenix AZ 85003

ALEXANDER, DONALD CRICHTON, lawyer; b. Pine Bluff, Ark., May 22, 1921; s. William Crichton and Ella Temple (Fox) A.; m. Margaret Louise Savage, Oct. 9, 1946; children: Robert C., James M. B.A. with honors, Yale U., 1942; LL.B. magna cum laude, Harvard U., 1948; LL.D., St. Thomas Inst., 1975. Bar: D.C. 1949, Ohio 1954, N.Y. 1978. Assoc. Covington & Burling, Washington, 1948-54, Taft, Stettinius & Hollister, Cin., 1954-56; ptnr. Taft, Stettinius & Hollister, 1956-66, Dinsmore, Shohl, Coates & Deupree, Cin., 1966-73; commr. IRS, 1973-77; mem. Commn. on Fed. Paperwork, 1975-77; ptnr. Olwine, Connelly, Chase, O'Donnell & Weyher, N.Y.C., Washington, 1977-79, Morgan, Lewis & Bockius, N.Y.C. and Washington, 1979-85, Cadwalader, Wickersham & Taft, Washington, 1985—; mem. adv. group to commr. IRS, 1969-70; cons. Treasury Dept., 1970-72; mem. adv. bd. NYU Tax Inst., 1969-73, 77—, Tax Mgmt., Inc., 1968-73, 77—; co-chmn. bd. advs. NYU/IRS Continuing Profl. Edn. Program, 1982-85. Author: The Arkansas Plantation, 1943; also articles on fed. taxation. Served to capt. AUS, 1942-45. Decorated Silver Star, Bronze Star. Mem. ABA (vice chmn. taxation sect. 1967-68), Am. Law Inst. (tax adv. group), U.S. C. of C. (taxation com. 1977—, bd. dirs. 1984—). Clubs: Chevy Chase (Md.); Metropolitan (Washington); Nantucket Yacht (Mass.); Mill Reef (Antigua, B.W.I.); Yale of N.Y. Corporate taxation, Personal income taxation, Pension, profit-sharing, and employee benefits. Home: 2801 New Mexico Ave NW Washington DC 20007 Office: 1333 New Hampshire Ave NW Washington DC 20036

ALEXANDER, ELLEN JO, lawyer; b. Detroit, 1943; d. Gabriel and Beatrice (Joshel) A. BA, U. Mich, 1964; MA, U. Ill., 1967; JD, DePaul U., 1974. Bar: Ill. 1975. City atty. City of Evanston, Ill., 1977-83; of counsel Shepp & Hellmann, Chgo., 1983-86; self-employed labor arbitrator Evanston, 1978—; pro-bono mediator Neighborhood Justice Ctr., Chgo.,1984—. Mem. City of Evanston Ethics Commn., 1980-83; bd. dirs. Family Counseling Services, Evanston, 1981-83. NEH Fellow, 1980. Mem. ABA, Am. Arbitration Assn. (mem. labor adv. panel Chgo. region 1983—), Soc. Profls. in Dispute Resolution (bd. dirs. Chgo. chpt. 1985—), Industrial Relations Research Assn. (bd. dirs. Chgo. chpt. 1982-85), Chgo. Bar Assn., Evanston Bar Assn. (pres. 1983-85). Arbitrator, mediator, General practice, Local government. Office: 1603 Orrington Suite 1047 Evanston IL 60201

ALEXANDER, FRITZ W., II, judge; b. Apopka, Fla., Apr. 24, 1926; m. Beverly Alexander; children: Karen, Kelly, Fritz Alexander III. Grad., Dartmouth Coll.; LLB, NYU; LLD, Pace U Sch Law, 1986, LL.D., 1986. Bar: N.Y. 1952, U.S. Supreme Ct., U.S. Ct. Appeals (2d cir.), U.S. Dist. Cts. (so. and ea. dists.) N.Y. Assoc. Demov, Morris, & Hammerling, 1952-54, Office of Thomas B. Dyett, 1954-58; founding ptnr. Dyett, Alexander & Dinkins, 1958-70; civil ct. judge 5th Mcpl. Ct. Dist., N.Y.C., 1970; acting justice N.Y. State Supreme Ct., 1972-75, justice, 1976, assoc. justice appellate div., 1982-85; assoc. judge N.Y. State Ct. Appeals, 1985—; adj. prof. law Cornell U., 1974-75; mem. N.Y. State Commn. on Jud. Conduct, 1979-85. Trustee NYU Law Ctr. Found.; bd. dirs. N.Y. Soc. for Prevention of Cruelty to Children. Recipient numerous awards and honors including Achievement award Fedn. Negro Civil Service Orgns., 1985, Golda Meir Meml. award Jewish Lawyers Guild, 1985, Outstanding Contbn. award Black and Latino Alumni Assn. of NYU Law Sch., 1985, Spl. Recognition award Met. Black Bar Assn., Inc., 1985, Arthur T. Vanderbilt gold medal award N.Y. Law Sch., 1985. Mem. ABA, Nat. Bar Assn. (exec. com. jud. council, William H. Hastie award 1985), N.Y. State Bar Assn., Bar City of N.Y. (past v.p.), Am. Law Inst., Dartmouth Coll. Black Alumni Assn. (past pres., founding mem., Spl. Recognition award 1985), Harlem Lawyers Assn. (past pres.), 100 Black Men, Inc., Am. Judicature Soc. (former adv. com. ctr. for jud. conduct orgns.), Order of Coif. Judicial administration. Office: Ct of Appeals Hall Eagle St Albany NY 12207

ALEXANDER, GEORGE JONATHON, legal educator, former dean; b. Berlin, Germany, Mar. 8, 1931; s. Walter and Sylvia (Grill) A.; m. Katharine Violet Sziklai, Sept. 6, 1958; children: Susan Katina, George Jonathon II. A.B. with maj. honors, U. Pa., 1953, J.D. cum laude, 1969; LL.M., Yale U., 1965, J.S.D., 1969. Bar: Ill. 1960, N.Y. 1961, Calif. 1974. Instr. law, Bigelow fellow U. Chgo., 1959-60; instr. internat. relations Naval Res. Officers Sch., Forrest Park, Ill., 1959-60; prof. law Syracuse U. Coll. Law, 1960-70, assoc. dean, 1968-69; vis. prof. law U. So. Calif., 1963; prof. law U. Santa Clara (Calif.) Law Sch., 1970—, dean, 1970-85; vis. scholar Stanford Law Sch., 1985-86; dir. Inst. Internat. and Comparative Law, 1986—; cons. in field. Author: Civil Rights, U.S.A., Public Schools, 1963, Honesty and Competition, 1967, Jury Instructing on Medical Issues, 1966, Cases and Materials on Space Law, 1971, The Aged and the Need for Surrogate Management, 1972, Commercial Torts, 1973, U.S. Antitrust Laws, 1980, also articles, chpts. in books, one film. Dir. Domestic and Internat. Bus. Problems Honors Clinic, Syracuse U., 1966-69, Regulations in Space Project, 1968-70; ednl. cons. Comptroller Gen., U.S., 1977—; Nat. Sr. Citizens Law Center, 1983—, pres., 1986—; co-founder Am. Assn. Abolition Involuntary Mental Hospitalization, 1970, dir., 1970-83. Served with USN, 1953-56. U.S. Navy scholar U. Pa., 1949-52; Law Boards scholar, 1956-59; Sterling fellow Yale, 1964-65; recipient Ralph E. Kharas Civil Liberties award, 1970, Owens award as Alumnus of Yr., 1984. Mem. Calif. Bar Assn. (first chmn. com. legal problems of aging), Assn. Am. Law Schs., Soc. Am. Law Tchrs. (dir., pres. 1979), AAUP (chpt. pres. 1962), N.Y. Civil Liberties Union (chpt. pres. 1965, dir., v.p. 1966-70), Am. Acad. Polit. and Social Sci., Order of Coif, Justinian Honor Soc., Phi Alpha Delta (chpt. faculty adviser 1967-70). Antitrust, Civil rights, Legal education. Home: 11600 Summit Wood Rd Los Altos Hills CA 94022 Office: Univ Santa Clara Santa Clara CA 95053

ALEXANDER, H. HEATH, lawyer; b. Charlotte, N.C., May 31, 1954; s. C. Heath and Billie Forester (Moore) A.; m. Elizabeth L. Brown, Feb. 7, 1981; 1 child, L. Heath. BS, U. N.C., 1976, JD, 1979. Bar: N.C. 1979, U.S. Dist. Ct. (wes. dist.) N.C. 1979, U.S. Ct. Appeals (4th cir.) 1981, U.S. Tax Ct. 1981. Assoc. Thigpen and Hines, P.A., Charlotte, 1979-84, Moore, Van Allen, Allen and Thigpen, Charlotte, 1984-86, Moore and Van Allen, Charlotte, 1986—. Herbert W. Jackson scholar U. N.C., 1972-76. Mem. ABA, N.C. Bar Assn., Mecklenburg County Young Lawyers Assn. (pres. 1986—), Order of Coif, Phi Beta Kappa. Republican. Episcopalian. Clubs: Toastmasters (Charlotte) (pres. 1983), Springdale Hall (Camden, S.C.). Corporate taxation, General corporate, Securities. Office: Moore and Van Allen 3000 NCNB Plaza Charlotte NC 28280

ALEXANDER, JAMES PATRICK, lawyer; b. Glendale, Calif., Oct. 14, 1944; s. Victor Elwin and Thelma Elizabeth (O'Donnell) A.; m. Jeanne Elizabeth Bannerman, June 10, 1967; children—Rene Leigh, Amy Lynne. A.B., Duke U., 1966, J.D., 1969. Bar: Ala. 1969. Assoc. law firm Bradley, Arant, Rose & White, Birmingham, Ala., 1969-75, ptnr., 1975—; adj. lectr. employment discrimination law U. Ala. Sch. of Law, 1981—; mem. adv. bd. div. paralegal studies Samford U. Trustee Ala. chpt. Nat. Multiple Sclerosis Soc. Mem. Birmingham Bar Assn., Ala. State Bar, ABA, Am. Arbitration Assn., Indsl. Relations Research Assn. (Ala. chpt.). Litigation, Labor, Antitrust.

ALEXANDER, JOHN DONALD, lawyer; b. Orange, N.J., Dec. 6, 1948; s. Thomas Walter and Grace (Hughes) A. BA, Boston Coll., 1971; JD, Rutgers U., 1975. Bar: N.J. 1975, Pa. 1979. Assoc. Okin, Pressler & Shapiro, Ft. Lee, N.J., 1975-78; gen. counsel Westwater, Gaston & Dunka, Pennington, N.J., 1978-80; sr. atty. Hoffmann LaRoche Inc., Nutley, N.J., 1980—. Mem. ABA, N.J. Bar Assn., Pa. Bar Assn. Environment, General corporate, Real property. Office: Hoffmann LaRoche Inc 340 Kingsland Ave Nutley NJ 07110

ALEXANDER, JOHN NICKOLAS, JR., lawyer; b. Phila., June 19, 1945; s. John Nickolas Sr. and Ruth A.; m. Sarah Harriet Bohr; children: Nicholas, Raechel, Meredith. BA in Fgn. Langs., Temple U., 1972; JD, Antioch Sch. Law, 1977. Bar: Pa. 1978, Fla. 1979. Staff atty. Jax (Fla.) Area Legal Aid, 1978-80, mng. atty., 1981-84; dir. recruitment and selection Howard U. Law Sch., Washington, 1980-81; sole practice Orange Park, Fla., 1984—. Buddhist. Family and matrimonial, Real property, Personal injury.

ALEXANDER, JOHN WILLIAM, lawyer; b. Murfreesboro, Tenn., Aug. 9, 1949; s. Jesse Milton and Cornelia (Reeves) A.; m. Susan Parks, Mar. 20, 1970; children: Lauren Anne, Shannon Leigh. BA, Mid. Tenn. State U., 1971; MA, Baylor U., 1974, JD, 1978. Bar: Tex. 1979, U.S. Tax Ct. 1980, U.S. Ct. Claims 1980, U.S. Dist. Ct. (ea. and we. dists.) Tex. 1981, U.S. Ct. Appeals (5th and 11th cirs.). Chmn. dept. English Blooming Grove (Tex.) High Sch., 1973-74; instr. McLennan Community Coll., Waco, Tex., 1974-76; asst. prof. Paul Quinn Coll., Waco, 1977-78; assoc. atty. Robert Bruce Law Office, Mineola, Tex., 1979; ptnr. Carlock & Alexander, Winnsboro, Tex., 1979-81; sole practice Winnsboro, 1981—; bd. advisors 1st Nat. Bank, Winnsboro, 1984—; atty. City of Winnsboro, 1981—; asst. atty. City of Mineola, 1979-81. Author (short story) Phoenix (1st Place Fiction award 1974, 77, 78). Bd. dirs. Wood County (Tex.) Child Welfare Bd., Quitman, 1982-84. McCartney-McSwain scholar, Baylor U. Sch. Law, 1977-78; named one of Outstanding Young Men Am., Nat. Jaycees, 1983. Mem. ABA, Tex. Criminal Def. Lawyers Assn., Northeast Tex. Bar Assn. (v.p. 1982-84, pres. 1986—), Wood County Bar Assn. (pres. 1982-83, v.p. 1986—), Assn. Trial Lawyrs Am., Tex. Bar Assn. (disciplinary com. grievance commn. 1985—), Winnsboro C. of C. (bd. dirs. 1982-84, pres. 1984-85), Autumn Trails Assn. Democrat. Methodist. Lodge: Rotary. (pres. elect 1982-83). State civil litigation, Criminal, Personal injury. Home: 701 N Main St Winnsboro TX 75494 Office: 318 N Main St PO Box 104 Winnsboro TX 75494

ALEXANDER, KATHARINE VIOLET, lawyer; b. N.Y.C., Nov. 19, 1934; d. George Clifford and Violet (Jambor) Sziklai; m. George Jonathon Alexander, Sept. 6, 1958; children: Susan Katina, George J. II. Student, Smith Coll., Geneva, 1954-55; BA, Goucher Coll., 1956; JD, U. Pa., 1959; student specialized courses, U. Santa Clara, 1974-76. Bar: Calif. 1974, U.S. Dist. Ct. (no. dist.) Calif., U.S. Ct. Appeals (9th cir.). Research dir., adminstr. Am. Bar Found., Chgo., 1959-60; lectr. law San Jose (Calif.) State U., 1972-74; sr. atty. Santa Clara County, San Jose, 1974—. Editor: Mentally Disabled and the Law, 1961; contbg. author: The Aged and the Need for Surrogate Management, 1969-70, Jury Instructions on Medical Issues, 1965-67. Community rep. Office Econ. Opportunity Com., Syracuse, N.Y., 1969-70. Mem. ABA (active various coms.), Calif. Bar Assn., Santa Clara County Bar Assn. (trustee 1981-82), Calif. Attys. for Criminal Justice, Calif. Pub. Def. Assn., Jr. League. Representative. Presbyterian. Avocations: stock market, gourmet, traveling. Criminal, Juvenile. Home: 11600 Summit Wood Rd Los Altos Hills CA 94022 Office: 70 W Hedding St County Govt Ctr West Wing San Jose CA 95110

ALEXANDER, KERRY DUANE, lawyer; b. Sault Ste. Marie, Mich., Apr. 21, 1935; s. Carl Alfred and Dorothy Jean (Franklin) A.; m. Marleen Grace Blau, Jan. 2, 1961; children: Kathleen, David, Kristen. BA, Augustana Coll., 1957; JD, Valparaiso U., 1960. Bar: Ohio 1960, Mich. 1960, U.S. Dist. Ct. (ea. and we.) dists. 1964, U.S. Supreme Ct. 1967. Law clk. to presiding justice Mich. Supreme Ct., Lansing, 1964; trial atty., ptnr. Mossner, Majoros & Alexander, P.C., Saginaw, Mich., 1964—. Mem. Valley Luth. High Sch. Bd. Edn., Saginaw, 1985—; bd. dirs. Am. Cancer Soc., Saginaw. Served to capt. JAGC, U.S. Army, 1961-64. Mem. ABA, Mich. Bar Assn., Assn. Trial Lawyers Am., Mich. Trial Lawyers Assn., Nat. Bd. Trial Advocacy (cert. civil trial specialist med. malpractice 1980). Democrat. Avocations: fishing, sailing, community service. Personal injury. Home: 5321 Overhill Dr Saginaw MI 48603 Office: Mossner Majoros & Alexander PC 4905 Berl Dr Box 5927 Saginaw MI 48608

ALEXANDER, LINDA DIANE (GRAHAM), lawyer, educator; b. Winchester, Va., May 10, 1953; d. Kenneth A. and Edna Frances (Whitlow) Graham; m. Patrick B. Alexander, May 8, 1975. B.A. in Govt., George Mason U., 1975, B.A. in Philosophy, 1975; J.D., U. Okla., 1978. Bar: Okla. 1978, U.S. Dist. Ct. (we. dist.) Okla. 1979, U.S. Ct. Appeals (10th cir.) 1980, U.S. Ct. Appeals (8th cir.) 1984, U.S. Ct. Claims 1980. Legal intern Foliart, Mills & Niemeyer, Oklahoma City, 1976-79, assoc., 1979-81; sole practice law, Oklahoma City, 1981-84; ptnr. firm Niemeyer, Edmonds, Noland, Alexander & Hargraves, Oklahoma City, 1983—; prof. Sch. Law, Oklahoma City U., 1981-83. Mem. Okla. Bar Assn., Oklahoma County Bar Assn., Assn. Trial Lawyers Am. Democrat. Mem. Ch. of Christ. Personal injury, Federal civil litigation, State civil litigation. Office: Niemeyer Noland & Alexander 300 N Walker St Oklahoma City OK 73102

ALEXANDER, MARY R., lawyer; b. Jersey City, Aug. 15, 1955; d. Robert A. and Marie (Gallagher) A.; m. Steven E. Parmelee, July 12, 1980. BA in Liberal Arts, U. Conn., 1977; JD, St. John's U., Jamaica, N.Y., 1982. Bar: N.Y. 1983, N.J. 1983. Assoc. Fried, Frank, Harris, Shriver & Jacobson, N.Y.C., 1982-86; assoc. tax counsel PepsiCo, Inc., Purchase, N.Y., 1986—. Corporate taxation, International taxation. Office: PepsiCo Inc 700 Anderson Hill Rd Purchase NY 10577

ALEXANDER, MELTON LEE, lawyer; b. Chester, Pa., Jan. 4, 1927; s. Richard Lincoln and Marie (Owens) A.; m. Beverly Ann Lankford, Apr. 18, 1969. B.A. in History, U. Ala., 1950, LL.B., 1954. Bar: Ala. 1954, U.S. Dist. Ct. for No. Dist. Ala 1954, U.S. Ct. Appeals (5th cir.) 1954, U.S. Supreme Ct. 1954, U.S. Dist. Ct. (we. dist.) Tenn. 1982, U.S. Dist. Ct. (mid. dist.) Ala. 1982, U.S. Ct. Appeals (6th and 11th cirs.) 1982. Spl. agt. FBI, Cleve., 1954-55, Washington, 1955-58; spl. agt., supr. FBI, Birmingham, Ala., 1958-66; criminal prosecutor, asst. U.S. atty. No. Dist. Ala., Birmingham, 1966—; 1st asst. U.S. atty. No. Dist. Ala., 1970-73, chief prosecutor, 1977-82, ret., 1982; mem. firm Collins and Alexander, 1982—; Nat. adv. bd. Am. Security Council. Mem. editorial bd.: Ala. Law Rev, 1951, 53-54. Served to sgt. paratroops World War II; capt. AUS, 1951-53, Korea. Decorated Bronze star, Combat Inf. Badge; recipient Atty. Gen.'s award, 1970, 82, U.S. Secret Service honor award, 1982. Mem. Farrah Order Jurisprudence, Nat. Criminal Def. Lawyers Assn., Ala. Criminal Def. Lawyers Assn., Assn. Trial Lawyers Am., Phi Beta Kappa. Criminal, Personal injury, Personal income taxation. Home: 2044 Cedarcrest Dr Birmingham AL 35214 Office: Suite 302 Park Place Tower Birmingham AL 35203

ALEXANDER, NEIL KENTON, JR., lawyer; b. Ft. Worth, Mar. 9, 1953; s. Neil Kenton and Alma (Widen) A.; m. Susan Perry, May 19, 1978; children: Matthew Kenton, Reid Smith. BA magna cum laude, Rice U., 1975; JD, Harvard U., 1978. Bar: Tex. 1978, U.S. Dist. Ct. (so. dist.) Tex. 1978, U.S. Ct. Appeals (5th cir.) 1981. Assoc. Baker & Botts, Houston, 1978-87, ptnr., 1987—; lectr. Rice U., Houston. Community assoc. Will Rice Coll. Rice U., 1979—. Mem. ABA (antitrust sect.), Houston Bar Assn., Houston Young Lawyers Assn. Episcopalian. Federal civil litigation, State civil litigation, Antitrust. Office: Baker & Botts 3000 One Shell Plaza Houston TX 77002-4995

ALEXANDER, RICHARD, lawyer; b. Cleve., Sept. 26, 1944; m. Nancy L. Biebel, Mar. 16, 1968; children—Marshall, Meredith. B.A., Ohio Wesleyan U., 1966; J.D. (Nat. Honor scholar), U. Chgo., 1969. Bar: Mich. 1969, U.S. Dist. Ct. (ea. and we. dists.) Mich. 1970, U.S. Dist. Ct. (so. dist.) Ind. 1970, Calif. 1971, U.S. Dist. Ct. (no. dist.) Calif. 1971, U.S. Ct. Appeals (9th cir.) 1971, U.S. Dist. Ct. (cen. dist.) Calif. 1972, U.S. Dist. Ct. (ea. dist.) Calif. 1973, U.S. Dist. Ct. D.C. 1980. Diplomate Nat. Bd. Trial Advocacy, 1980. Asst. prof. Grad. Sch. Bus., Mich. State U., 1969-71; assoc. Belli, Ashe, Ellison, Choulos & Lieff, San Francisco, 1971-72, Lieff, Alexander, Wilcox & Hill, San Francisco, 1972-74, Boccardo, Lull, Niland & Bell, San Francisco and San Jose, Calif., 1974-80; ptnr. Boccardo Law Firm, San Jose, 1980—; mem. Santa Clara County Criminal Justice Adv. Bd., 1978-82, chmn., 1978-80; mem. Santa Clara County Jail Over-crowding Task Force, 1978-81; mem. Santa Clara County Pub. Defender Charter Amendment Task Force, 1980; judge pro tem Santa Clara County Superior Ct., 1976-83, 85-86 arbitrator, 1976—; co-chmn. Superior Ct. Arbitration Adminstrn. Com., 1979—; spl. master State Bar Calif., 1980—, lectr. continuing edn., 1975, 78, 81, 82, 83, 84, 85, 86, bd. govs. 1985—, mem. com. profl. ethics, 1977-80; speaker legal seminars. Contbr. articles to profl. jours. Mem. Palo Alto (Calif.) Unified Sch. Dist. Task Force on Spl. Edn., 1975-79; vice chmn. sch. improvement program Palo Alto Unified Sch. Dist., 1977-78, mem. found. exploration com., 1984; mem. Santa Clara County Data Confidentiality Commn., 1976-78, chmn., 1977-78; mem. Santa Clara County Democratic Central Com., 1978-80; bd. dirs. Japanese Am. Environ. Conf., 1979-81. Recipient Santa Clara County Youth Commn. medal, 1980; commendation for disting. service Mayor San Jose, 1982; Roscoe Pound fellow; named one of Outstanding Young Men of Am. Mem. San Francisco Bar Assn., Santa Clara County Bar Assn. (pres. 1984), Calif. Attys. for Criminal Justice (founding; treas. 1972-74, gov. 1972-75), Calif. Trial Lawyers Assn. (recognized trial lawyer 1980-86), State Bar Calif., Assn. Trial Lawyers Am., Sierra Club, NAACP, Stanford Alumni Assn., Alexander Graham Bell Assn. for Deaf, Nat. Trust Hist. Preservation, San Jose Mus. San Jose Symphony. Clubs: U. Chgo. Alumni, San Jose Athletic. Jurisprudence, Personal injury, Federal civil litigation. Office: 111 W Saint John St Suite 1100 San Jose CA 95115

ALEXANDER, RICHARD ELMONT, lawyer; b. Yellow Springs, Ohio, Dec. 14, 1924; s. Joseph Arthur and Charlotte (Gunckel) A.; Student U. Dayton, 1942-43, Carnegie Inst. Tech., 1943-44, 46-47; J.D., U. Chgo., 1950. Bar: Ohio 1951, U.S. Ct. Customs and Patent Appeals 1955, Ill. 1956, U.S. Dist. Ct. (no. dist.) Ill. 1958, U.S. Patent Office 1958, U.S. Dist. Ct. (ea. dist.) Calif. 1968, U.S. Supreme Ct. 1971, U.S. Ct. Appeals (4th, 7th and 9th cirs.) 1975, U.S. Ct. Appeals (2d cir.) 1977, U.S. Ct. Appeals (1st cir.) 1980, U.S. Ct. Appeals (D.C. cir.) 1982. Patent atty. Gen. Motors Corp., Washington, 1953-55; assoc. Wilkinson, Huxley, Byron & Hume, Chgo., 1955-58; ptnr. Alexander & Slater, Chgo., 1958-59, Dawson, Tilton, Fallon, Lungmus & Alexander, Chgo., 1959-67, Alexander & Speckman, Chgo., 1967-74; prin. Richard E. Alexander, Chgo., 1975-81; ptnr. Alexander & Zalewa, Chgo., 1981-84, Alexander, Unikel, Bloom, Zalewa & Tenenbaum, Ltd., 1984—. Bd. dirs. St. Leonard's House, Chgo., 1979-87, v.p., 1980-82; chmn. Inst. Clin. Social Work, Chgo., 1981-84; trustee Episcopal Charities, Chgo., 1982—, v.p., 1984—. Served with U.S. Army, 1944-46. Decorated Purple Heart. Mem. ABA, Chgo. Bar Assn., U.S. Trademark Assn. (editorial bd. 1965-77), Chgo. Patent Law Assn. (chmn. trademark com. 1967-68), Sigma Alpha Epsilon. Episcopalian. Editor: Meditions of Andrew Morehouse, 1952. Trademark and copyright, Federal civil litigation, State civil litigation. Office: 55 W Monroe Chicago IL 60603

ALEXANDER, ROBERT LOUIS, lawyer; b. Jersey City, May 2, 1942; s. Michael A. and Margaret (Mayer) A.; m. Monica Mary Marazza, Nov. 24, 1965 (dec. 1973); children: Allison, Robert, Meredith; m. Ann R. Bartlett, Sept. 17, 1977; 1 stepchild, Kendall. BS in Econs., St. Peter's Coll., Jersey City, 1965; JD, N.Y. Law Sch., 1970. Bar: N.J. 1970, U.S. Dist. Ct. N.J. 1970, U.S. Tax Ct. 1971. Clerk Morgan Guaranty Trust, N.Y.C., 1960-67; mgmt. trainee CitiBank, N.Y.C., 1967-69; fin. planner Mfrs. Hanover, N.Y.C., 1969-70; assoc. Johnstone & O'Dwyer, Westfield, N.J., 1970-72; ptnr. Herrigel & Alexander, Clinton, N.J., 1972-82, Alexander & Bartlett, Clinton, 1982—; mediator Pub. Employment, N.J., 1982—; judge Flemington (N.J.) Mcpl. Ct., 1982-85. Mem., pres. Clinton Pub. Sch. Bd., 1976-82. Mem. N.J. Bar Assn., Hunterdon County Bar Assn. (pres. 1985-86), Assn. Trial Lawyers Am., Am. Arbitration Assn. (arbitrator 1982—). Republican. Lodge: Rotary. Banking, Contracts commercial, State civil litigation. Office: Alexander & Bartlett 46 Leigh St PO Box 5281 Clinton NJ 08809

ALEXANDER, WILLIAM HENRY, lawyer; b. Thomson, Ill., Nov. 16, 1902; s. Cyrus Hall and Mary Letitia (Livingston) A.; m. Jane Ashcraft, Dec. 22, 1934; children: Willa Jane, William Raymond, David Risdon, Sarah Susan and Peter Llewellyn (twins), Edwin Michael, James Livingston. B.S., Knox Coll., 1926; postgrad., U. Chgo. Law Sch., 1926-29. Bar: Ill. 1930. Law clk. to sr. judge U.S. Circuit Ct. Appeals, 1930-35; with firm Ashcraft & Ashcraft, Chgo., 1935-82; mem. Ashcraft & Ashcraft, 1936-82, Alexander & Alexander, 1982—. Trustee Village of Wilmette, Ill., 1941-45, pres., 1945-53; hon. mem. Wilmette Hist. Commn.; Bd. dirs., pres. Eleanor Assn.; trustee, pres. Chgo. Wesley Meml. Hosp.; trustee Northwestern U. Citizen fellow Inst. Medicine Chgo. Mem. ABA, Ill. Bar Assn., Chgo. Bar Assn. (pres. 1960-61), Chgo. Hist. Soc. (life), Chgo. Natural History Mus. (life), Scabbard and Blade, Phi Alpha Delta, Lambda Chi Alpha. Republican. Methodist. Clubs: Rotary, Wilmette Curling (Wilmette); Indian Hill (Winnetka); Law (Chgo.);. Home: 1025 Mohawk Rd Wilmette IL 60091

ALEY, CHARLES R., lawyer; b. Beaver Falls, Pa., Apr. 3, 1956; s. Charles L. and Lois E. (Teckemeyer) A.; m. Harriet M. Baker, June 21, 1986. BA in Econs., BSBA in Acctg. and Data Processing, BS in Info. Systems, Geneva Coll., 1978; JD, U. Pitts., 1981. Bar: Pa. 1981, U.S. Dist. Ct. (we. dist.) Pa. 1981, U.S. Tax Ct. 1981, U.S. Ct. Appeals (3d cir.) 1981, U.S. Ct. Appeals (fed. cir.) 1985, U.S. Supreme Ct. 1985. Tax atty. Arthur Young & Co., Pitts., 1981-82, Edward J. DeBartolo Corp., Youngstown, 1982-86, Alcan Aluminum Corp., Warren, Ohio, 1986—. Mem. ABA, Pa. Bar Assn., Allegheny County Bar Assn., Beaver County Bar Assn., Fed. Circuit Bar Assn., Assn. Trial Lawyers Am., Phi Alpha Delta. Mem. United Meth. Ch. Avocation: pipe organ restoration. Corporate taxation, Personal income taxation, State and local taxation. Home: 1212 6th Ave Beaver Falls PA 15010 Office: Alcan Aluminum Corp 280 N Park Ave Warren OH 44481

ALFORD, MARGARET SUZANNE, lawyer; b. New Orleans, Jan. 13, 1953; d. Charles Dalma and Margaret Ann (Waldrep) A.; m. Wayland Everett Loomis, Oct. 27, 1984. BA, La. State U., 1975; JD, Duke U., 1978. Bar: Tex. 1978, U.S. Dist. Ct. (no. dist. Tex. 1979, U.S. Ct. Claims 1979, U.S. Tax Ct. 1979. Ptnr. Thompson & Knight, Dallas, 1978—. Active Ctr. for Non-Profit Mgmt., Dallas. Mem. ABA, Tex. Bar Assn., Dallas Bar Assn., Dallas Internat. Law Soc., Dallas 500, Phi Alpha Delta, Phi Kappa Phi. Republican. Episcopalian. Club: Tower (Dallas). Avocations: run-

ning, reading, travel, antiques. Corporate taxation, Exempt organizations. Office: Thompson & Knight 3300 First City Center Dallas TX 75201

ALFRED, STEPHEN JAY, lawyer; b. N.Y.C., Aug. 15, 1934; s. George J. A. and Janet (Brenner) Miller; m. Nora Richman, June 24, 1956 (div. 1980); children: Deborah Susan, Lynda Beth, Bruce David, Julianne Richman; m. Lynne Belofsky Durchslag, Jan. 10, 1981. A.B., Princeton U., 1956; J.D., Harvard U., 1959. Bar: Ohio 1959, Fla. 1978. Assoc. Squire, Sanders & Dempsey, Cleve., 1959-69, ptnr., 1969—. Contbr. articles to profl. jours. Councilman City of Shaker Heights, Ohio, 1972-79, 81, mayor, 1984—; trustee Citizens League of Cleve., 1976-83; trustee Beech Brook Children's Home, Orange, Ohio, 1968-84, pres., 1971-72, treas., 1979-81; pres. Lomond Assn., Shaker Heights, 1965-67. Mem. ABA, Bar Assn. Greater Cleve., Cleve. Tax Inst. (gen. chmn. 1981), Harvard Law Sch. Assn. of Cleve. (pres. 1982). Democrat. Jewish. Corporate taxation. Home: 20856 S Woodland Rd Shaker Heights OH 44122 Office: Squire Sanders & Dempsey 1800 Huntington Bldg Cleveland OH 44115 also: City of Shaker Heights 3400 Lee Rd Shaker Heights OH 44120

ALIANO, RICHARD ANTHONY, lawyer; b. N.Y.C., Oct. 26, 1946; s. Albert Anthony and Ann (Barbera) A.; m. Elyse Janet Sonnenshein, Apr. 1, 1984. BA magna cum laude, Queens Coll., CUNY, 1968, MA, 1969; PhD, CUNY, 1973; JD, St. John's U., 1981. Bar: N.Y. 1982, U.S. Dist. Ct. (so. and ea. dists.) N.Y. 1982. Assoc. Fleck, Fleck and Fleck, Garden City, N.Y., 1981-86; mng. ptnr. L.I. office Weiner, Ostrager, Fieldman & Zucker, N.Y.C., 1986—; asst. prof. CUNY, 1973-78; cons. G.P. Putnam Sons, N.Y.C., 1977-80. Author: American Defense Policy, 1975, Crime of World Power, 1978. St. Thomas More fellow St. John's U. Law Sch., 1979. Mem. N.Y. Trial Lawyers Assn., N.Y. State Bar Assn., Phi Beta Kappa. Republican. Roman Catholic. State civil litigation, General practice, Personal injury. Home: 39 Sumter Ave East Williston NY 11596 Office: Weiner Ostrager Fieldman & Zucker 1 World Trade Ctr Suite 10251 New York NY 10048

ALICE, RONALD WILLIAM, lawyer; b. Highland Park, Mich., June 24, 1944; s. Don and Dorothy G. (Rufus) A.; m. Karen Joyce Nunamann, Aug. 27, 1976; children: Laura, Christopher. BS in Chem. Engring., U. Mich., 1970; JD magna cum laude, Wayne State U., 1974. Bar: N.Y. 1975. Assoc. Kenyon & Kenyon, N.Y.C., 1974-77; sr. counsel ITT Corp., N.Y.C., 1977-86; corp. licensing counsel Am. Home Products Corp., N.Y.C., 1986—. Served to 1st lt. U.S. Army, 1966-69. Federal civil litigation, Patent, Trademark and copyright. Home: 30 College Ave Upper Montclair NJ 07043 Office: Am Home Products Corp 685 Third Ave New York NY 10017

ALIDOR, GARY PAUL, SR., lawyer; b. Mobile, Ala., Nov. 5, 1943; s. Roy Francis and Mary Carolyn (Miller) A.; m. Janis Harding, July 16, 1966 (div. Feb. 1979); children: Gary Paul Jr., Michele Marie; m. Brenda Hankins, July 18, 1980 (div. July 1982); 1 child, Michael Benjamin Francis; m. Dayle Gladney, Sept. 8, 1983; 1 child, Samuel Grey. AB in Lib. Arts, Spring Hill Coll., 1965; JD, Ala. U., 1968. Bar: Ala. 1968, U.S. Supreme Ct. 1972. Assoc. Tyson, Marr & Friedlander, Mobile, 1968-72; sole practice Mobile, 1973—. Candidate State Ho. of Reps., Mobile, 1974, State Senate, Mobile, 1982. Mem. ABA, Ala. Bar Assn., Mobile Bar Assn., Assn. Trial Lawyers Am., Comml. Law League, U. Ala. Alumni Assn. (pres. Mobile chpt. 1981). Democrat. Roman Catholic. Lodge: Optimists (pres. Pleasant Valley chpt. 1985). Real property, General practice, Bankruptcy. Home: 2349 Huffman Dr E Mobile AL 36609 Office: 1110 Montlimar Dr Suite 965 Mobile AL 36616-0564

ALKE, JOHN, lawyer; b. Helena, Mont., Mar. 31, 1951; s. Leslie W. and Betty (Van Sice) A.; m. Mary Burnham, Sept. 16, 1972; children—Jonathan, Benjamin. B.A. in Econs., U. Mont., 1973, J.D., 1976. Bar: Mont. 1976, U.S. Dist. Ct. Mont. 1976. Ptnr. firm Hughes, Kellner, Sullivan & Alke, Helena, 1980—. Bd. editors U. Mont. Law Rev. 1974-76. Mem. ABA, State Bar Mont., Assn. Trial Lawyers Am. Public utilities, Administrative and regulatory, State civil litigation. Home: 201 S Hannaford St Helena MT 59601 Office: Hughes Kellner Sullivan & Alke 406 Fuller Ave Helena MT 59604

ALKIRE, RICHARD CHARLES, lawyer; b. Cleve., July 25, 1955; s. Walter Charles and Patricia Ann (Byrne) A.; m. Tina Marie Richmond, Sept. 3, 1983. AB, Coll. of Holy Cross, 1977; JD, Cleve. State U., 1980. Bar: Ohio 1980, U.S. Dist. Ct. (no. dist.) Ohio 1980, U.S. Ct. Appeals (6th cir.) 1981, U.S. Ct. Appeals (11th cir.) 1983, U.S. Ct. Appeals (4th cir.) 1985, U.S. Supreme Ct. 1985. Assoc. Nurenberg, Plevin, Heller & McCarthy L.P.A., Cleve., 1980—. Mem. ABA, Ohio Bar Assn., Greater Cleve. Bar Assn., Assn. Trial Lawyers Am., Ohio Assn. Trial Lawyers, Cleve. Acad. Trial Lawyers. Democrat. Roman Catholic. Personal injury, Federal civil litigation, State civil litigation. Home: 17513 Laverne Cleveland OH 44135 Office: Nurenberg Plevin Heller & McCarthy LPA 1365 Ontario 700 Engineers Bldg Cleveland OH 44114-1357

ALLAN, GERALDINE LYNNE, commissioner, referee; b. Pueblo, Colo., July 2, 1942; d. Roy Duncan and Geraldine (Shearer) A. B.S. in Journalism, Northwestern U., 1964; M.A., U. Denver, 1966, J.D. (scholar 1968-69), 1969. Bar: Colo. 1969, U.S. Dist. Ct. Colo. 1969. Sole practice, Denver, 1970-72; staff atty. Arapahoe County Legal Aid, Englewood, Colo., 1972-76; dep. city atty. Littleton, Colo., 1977-78; assoc. Miller & Leher, Littleton, 1978-81; sole practice, Littleton, 1982-83; assoc. judge Mcpl. Ct., Englewood, Colo., 1980, 82-84, referee, commr. Arapahoe County Dist. Ct., 1984—; instr. Colo. Law Enforcement Tng. Acad., 1978-81. Bd. dirs. Arapahoe Mental Health Ctr., Inc., 1978, Legal Aid Soc. Met. Denver, 1980-82, Arapahoe County Task Force on Youth and Drugs, 1981-82. Recipient Am. Jurisprudence award, 1969; scholar, Nat. Inst. Trial Advocacy, 1973. Mem. Colo. Bar Assn., Arapahoe County Bar Assn. Office: Arapahoe County Dist Ct 2069 W Littleton Blvd Littleton CO 80120

ALLAN, JOHN MALCOLM, JR., lawyer; b. Pitts., Aug. 7, 1955; s. John Malcolm and Marian (Lines) A. BA, Johns Hopkins U., 1977; postgrad., U. Md., 1977-78; JD, Case Western Res. U., 1981; LLM in Taxation, Georgetown U., 1986; postgrad., NYU, 1987—. Bar: Conn. 1982. Staff aide to Sen. Lowell P. Weicker, Jr. U.S. Senate, Washington, 1977-78; tax asst. Arthur Andersen & Co., Hartford, Conn., 1981-83, Washington, 1983-84; sr. tax specialist Peat, Marwick, Mitchell & Co., Washington, 1984-85; tax atty. Pechiney Corp., Greenwich, Conn., 1985—. Pres., treas. stewardship com. First Congl. Ch. Guilford (Conn.) 1986; pres. Johns Hopkins U. Alumni Assn. Mem. ABA (tax sect.), Conn. Bar Assn. (exec. com. tax sect. exec. com. liason with accts. com.), Am. Inst. CPA's (tax sect.), Conn. Soc. CPA's, D.C. Inst. CPA's, Greater Hartford Jaycees. Republican. Avocations: golf, tennis, lacrosse, swimming, politics. Corporate taxation, State and local taxation, International taxation. Home: 1465 E Putnam Ave Old Greenwich CT 06870 Office: Pechiney Corp 475 Steamboat Rd Greenwich CT 06836-1960

ALLAN, LIONEL MANNING, lawyer; b. Detroit, Aug. 3, 1943; s. Alfred C. and Sophie R. Allan; m. Marian Reid, Jan. 27, 1968; children—James, Margo. A.B. cum laude, U. Mich., 1965; J.D., Stanford U., 1968; student U. Paris. Bar: Calif. 1969, U.S. Tax Ct. 1970, U.S. Supreme Ct. 1972. Law clk. U.S. Dist. Ct. (no. dist.) Calif., 1969-70; assoc. Hopkins & Carley, San Jose, Calif., 1970-75, ptnr., 1975—; speaker and writer in field of corp. securities and pvt. internat. law; sec. adv. com. San Jose Fed. Ct., 1969—; bd. vis. Stanford Law Sch., 1985—; mem. com. comml. code State Bar Calif., 1974-77, corps. com., 1983—. Bd. dirs. San Jose Mus. Art, 1983—, v.p., 1984-86. Served to capt. JAGC, USAR, 1968-74. Mem. ABA (com. on small bus. 1980—, chmn. internat. bus. subcom. 1985—), Santa Clara County Bar Assn. (chmn. fed. ct. sect. 1971, 77), Internat. Bar Assn., Pi Sigma Alpha, Phi Sigma Iota, Phi Delta Phi. Co-author: How to Structure the Classic Venture Capital Deal, 1983, Equity Incentives for Start-up Companies, 1985.Incentives for Start-up Companies, 1985. General corporate, Private international, Securities. Office: 150 Almaden Blvd 15th Floor San Jose CA 95113

ALLAN, WALTER ROBERT, lawyer; b. Detroit, Aug. 1, 1937; s. Walter Francis and Henrietta (Fairchild) A. Bar: Calif. 1964, U.S. Ct. Appeals (9th cir.) 1964, U.S. Supreme Ct. 1972, U.S. Dist. Ct. (D.C. cir.) 1973, U.S. Dist. Ct. (5th cir.) 1977. From assoc. to ptnr. Pillsbury, Madison & Sutro, San Francisco, 1963—. State civil litigation, Federal civil litigation. Office: Pillsbury Madison & Sutro 225 Bush St San Francisco CA 94104

ALLARD, DAVID HENRY, judge; b. Snohomish, Wash., Jan. 10, 1929; s. Clayton Frederick and Ruth Elizabeth (Winston) A.; m. Elizabeth Ellen Burrill, Nov. 26, 1960; children: John M., Clayton Frederick II. A.B., Whitman Coll., 1951; LL.B., Duke U., 1956. Bar: Wash. 1957, U.S. Supreme Ct. 1965. Mem. staff ICC, Washington, 1958-67; adminstrv. law judge ICC, 1967-72, 73-80, Office Hearings and Appeals, Social Security Adminstrn., 1986—; chief adminstrv. law judge ICC, 1980-86; adminstrv. law judge HHS, Tucson, 1986—, FTC, 1972-73; law reporter Presdl. Task Force on Career Advancement, 1967; mem. comml. panel Am. Arbitration Assn. Served with AUS, 1951-53. Mem. ABA (Achievement award young lawyers sect. 1965), Fed. Bar Assn. (editor-in-chief jour. 1972, pres. 1974, chmn. edn. bd. 1976-82), Fed. Adminstrv. Law Judges Conf., Delta Tau Delta. Presbyterian. Administrative and regulatory. Home: 6273 E Via de la Yerba Tucson AZ 85715 Office: Room 3B Fed Bldg 301 W Congress St Tucson AZ 85701

ALLEMAN, RODGER NEAL, lawyer; b. Kansas City, Mo., July 27, 1930; s. Neal Dow and Mildred Maude (Hovey) A.; m. Lorraine Croft, April 26, 1956; children: Michael B., Linda Katherine. AA, Kansas City Jr. Coll., 1949; BA in Chemistry, U. Mo., 1951, JD, 1955; postdoctoral, George Washington U., 1955-56. Bar: Mo. 1955, U.S. Ct. Customs and Patent Appeals 1956, U.S. Patent Office 1957. Patent examiner U.S. Patent Office, Washington, 1955-57; assoc. Shlesinger, Arkwright, Garvey, Dinsmore & Dutton, Washington, 1957-58; patent counsel mgr. patents and licenses Lockheed Missiles and Space Co., Inc., Sunnyvale, Calif., 1958—. Bd. dirs. Calif. Inventors Council; v.p. exec. bd. Stanford Area Council Boy Scouts Am. Served with USNR, 1948-51, to cpl., AUS, 1951-53. Recipient Silver Beaver award Boy Scouts Am. Mem. ABA, Mo. Bar Assn., San Francisco Patent Law Assn., Aerospace Industries Assn., Am. Intellectual Property Law Assn., Lic. Execs. Soc., Peninsula Patent Law Assn. (bd. dirs. 1981), Phi Delta Phi, Beta Theta Pi. Republican. Methodist. Clubs: Nat. Beta. Lodge: Order of DeMolay. Patent, Trademark and copyright. Home: 1640 Elmhurst Dr Los Altos CA 94022 Office: PO Box 3504 Sunnyvale CA 94088-3504

ALLEN, ALBERT HERMAN, lawyer; b. Chgo., Nov. 9, 1907; s. Herman and Helen (Schroeder) A.; m. Marian Berk, Mar. 19, 1917; children: Judith Allen Springer, John Lawrence, Jeffery Earl. LLB, U. Chgo., 1930. Bar: Ill. 1930, Calif. 1934. Ptnr. Allen and Fasman, Beverly Hills, Calif., 1947—. Mem. ABA, Los Angeles County Bar Assn., Beverly Hills Bar Assn. Clubs: Hillcres Country (Los Angeles); Del Rey Yacht (Marine Del Rey). Real property, Probate, General practice. Office: Allen and Fasman 9595 Wilshire Blvd 9 Floor Beverly Hills CA 90210

ALLEN, CHARLES MENGEL, judge; b. Louisville, Nov. 22, 1916; s. Arthur Dwight and Jane (Mengel) A.; m. Betty Anne Cardwell, June 25, 1949; children: Charles Dwight, Angela M. B.A., Yale U., 1941; LL.B., U. Louisville, 1943. Bar: Ky. 1944. Practiced in Louisville, 1947-55; asst. U.S. atty. for Western Dist. Ky., 1955-59; mem. firm Booth & Walker, Louisville, 1959-61; circuit judge 4th Chancery div. Jefferson County, 1961-71; dist. judge U.S. Dist. Ct., Louisville, 1971—; then chief judge U.S. Dist. Ct., now sr. judge. Former pres. Ky. Ry. Mus.; past bd. dirs. Louisville Art Center; former mem. Ky. Humane Soc. Mem. ABA, Fed. Bar Assn., Ky. Bar Assn., Louisville Bar Assn., Nat. Ry. Hist. Soc. Office: Room 252 US Courthouse Louisville KY 40202

ALLEN, CLIVE VICTOR, communications company executive, lawyer; b. Montreal, Que., Can., June 11, 1935; s. John Arthur and Norah (Barnett) A.; m. Barbara Mary Kantor, Feb. 22, 1964; children—Drew, Blair. B.A., McGill U., 1956, B.C.L., 1959. Mem. firm Hackett, Mulvena,& Drummond & Fiske, 1960-63, Fiske, Emery, Allen & Lauzon, 1964-66; v.p., sec. Allied Chem. Can. Ltd., 1966-74; sr. v.p., gen. counsel No. Telecom Ltd., 1974—. Mem. editorial bd. Trade Law Topics Newsletter. Mem. Can. Bar Assn., Barreau du Quebec, Internat. Bar Assn. (chmn. corp. law depts. div.), Am. Soc. Corporate Secs., Assn. Can. Gen. Counsel, Can. Tax Found. Clubs: Montreal Badminton & Squash, St. James's (Montreal); Granite (Toronto). Home: 18A Deer Park, Crescent, Toronto, ON Canada M4V 2C2 Office: 33 City Centre Dr, Mississauga, ON Canada L5B 3A2

ALLEN, DAVID JAMES, lawyer; b. East Chicago, Ind., May 3, 1935; s. David F. and Emma (Soderstrom) A. B.S., Ind. U., 1957, M.A., 1959, J.D., 1965. Bar: Ind. 1965, U.S. Dist. Ct. (so. dist.) Ind. 1965, U.S. Ct. Appeals 1965, U.S. Tax Ct. 1965, U.S. Ct. Mil. Appeals 1966, U.S. Supreme Ct. 1968. Ptnr. Hagemier, Allen and Smith, Indpls., 1975—; adminstrv. asst. Gov. of Ind., 1961-65, 65-69; mem. Spl. Commn. on Ind. Exec. Reorgn., 1967-69; mem. Ind. Pub. Utility Commn., 1970-75; mem. Ind. Law Enforcement Acad. Bd. and Adv. Council, 1968-85; mem. Ind. State Police Bd., 1968—; mem. Ind. Commn. on Recodification and Revision of Ind. Adminstrv. Adjudication Act, 1985-86; nat. judge advocate Acacia Fraternity, 1980-86; chief counsel Ind. Ho. of Reps., 1975-76; spl. counsel Ind. Senate Majority, 1977-78; legis. counsel Ind. Ho. of Reps., Ind. Senate minority parties, 1979—; adj. prof. pub. law Ind. U., Bloomington. Mem. ABA, Ind. State Bar Assn. (mem. adminstrv. law com. 1968-77, chmn. adminstrv. lawa com., 1973-76, mem. law sch. liaison com. 1977-78, criminal justice law exec. com., 1966-72), Am. Soc. Pub. Adminstrn. Administrative and regulatory, Legislative, Public utilities. Office: 819 Circle Tower Bldg Indianapolis IN 46204

ALLEN, FREDERICK W., state supreme court justice. Bar: Vt. Justice Supreme Ct. Vt., Montpelier. Judicial administration. Office: Office of Supreme Ct 111 State St Montpelier VT 05602 •

ALLEN, H. WILLIAM, lawyer; b. Nevada, Mo., Apr. 7, 1944; s. Henry W. and Betty Jeane (Grover) A.; m. Kay Willis, Sept. 22, 1944; children—West, Farrell, Lindsay. B.A., Rhodes Coll., 1966; J.D., Washington U., St. Louis, 1969. Bar: Ark. 1969, Ill. 1969, Mo. 1969. Asst. U.S. atty. Chgo., 1969-70; spl. asst. to pres. ABA, 1970-71; assoc. Wright Lindsay & Jenninger, 1971-76, ptnr., 1976-80; sr. ptnr. Allen Cabe & Lester, Little Rock, 1980-86, H. William Allen, P.C., Little Rock, 1986—. Mem. ABA (ho. of dels., chmn. com. on ethics and profl. responsibility), Am. Bar. Found. (v.p., bd. dirs.), Am. Judicature Soc. (bd. dirs.). Administrative and regulatory, Federal civil litigation, State civil litigation. Office: 1200 Worthen Bank Bldg Little Rock AR 72201

ALLEN, HENRY SERMONES, JR., lawyer; b. Bronxville, N.Y., Aug. 26, 1947; s. Henry S. and Cecelia Marie (Chartrand) A.; A.B. magna cum laude, Washington U., St. Louis, 1969; M.P.A., Cornell U., 1973, J.D., 1974; m. Louann Beckman, June 25, 1976; children—David Beckman, Amy Louise, Jeffrey Roy. Bar: Ill. 1974. Adminstrv. resident Montefiore Hosp. and Med. Center, Bronx, N.Y., 1971; research trainee Nat. Center Health Services Research, HEW, 1974-75; adj. asst. prof. hosp. law Ithaca (N.Y.) Coll., 1974-75; lectr., adj. asst. prof. health services adminstrn. and law Sangamon State U., Springfield, Ill., 1975-82; adj. asst. prof. hosp. law Coll. of St. Francis, Joliet, Ill., 1980-81; assoc. firm Vedder, Price, Kaufman & Kammholz, Chgo., 1975-79; ind. practice law, health care cons., Chgo. and Springfield, 1979-81; ptnr. Allen & Reed, Chgo., 1981-86, McBride, Baker & Coles, 1986—; lectr. in field. Bd. dirs. Dr. Deepak K. Merchant Found. HUD fellow, 1969-71. Mem. Am. Soc. Hosp. Attys., Am. Acad. Hosp. Attys., Ill. Soc. Hosp. Attys., Nat. Health Lawyers Assn., Phi Beta Kappa, Omicron Delta Epsilon. Club: Cornell U. of Chgo. Health, Antitrust, Federal civil litigation. Home: 5223 Carpenter St Chicago IL 60515 Office: 3 First National Plaza 38th Floor Chicago IL 60602

ALLEN, HUNTER SMITH, JR., lawyer; b. Sheffield, Ala., Mar. 10, 1946; s. Hunter Smith and Mary Ellen (Guthrie) A.; m. Sandra Fraley Shuford, Apr. 26, 1980. B.S., U. S.C., 1967, J.D., 1970. Bar: Ga. 1970, S.C. 1971, U.S. Dist. Ct. (no. dist.) Ga. 1970, U.S. Ct. Appeals (5th cir.) 1970, U.S. Ct. Appeals (11th cir.) 1982. Assoc. Swift, Currie, McGhee & Hiers, Atlanta, 1970-72; mem. Thomas Marvin Smith Jr., P.C., 1972-79; ptnr. Allen & Ballard, 1979—. Served with N.G., 1967-71. Mem. ABA, Ga. Bar Assn., Atlanta Bar Assn., Def. Research Inst., Ga. Assn. Hosp. Attys., Ga. Def. Lawyers Assn., Am. Soc. Law and Medicine. Republican. Presbyterian. Clubs: Phoenix Soc., Ansley Golf, Lawyers. Health, Personal injury, Insurance. Office: Allen & Ballard 2 Midtown Plaza 1360 Peachtree St NE Suite 1700 Atlanta GA 30309

ALLEN, JAMES LEE, lawyer; b. Lakewood, Ohio, Apr. 21, 1952; s. Frank M. and Dorothy S. (Stone) A.; m. Sue Eveline Goble, July 25, 1981. B.A. with high distinction, U. Mich., 1974, J.D., 1977. Bar: Mich. 1977, U.S. Dist. Ct. (ea. dist.) Mich. 1978, U.S. Dt. Appeals (6th cir.) 1982, U.S. Tax Ct. 1981, U.S. Supreme Ct. 1984. Assoc. Hardig, Goetz, Heath, Merritt & Reebel, Birmingham, Mich., 1977-83, Plunkett, Cooney, Rutt, Watters, Stanczyk & Pedersen, P.C., Detroit, 1983—; instr. Walsh Coll., Troy, Mich., 1980. Vestryman Nativity Episcopal Ch., Birmingham, 1978-81; bd. dirs., treas. Common Ground, Birmingham, 1980; bd dirs. Birmingham Community House, 1983-86. Mem. U. Mich. Alumni Assn., Oakland County Bar Assn. (chmn. program com. (1979-82), Mich. Bar Assn. (mem. representation assembly 1978—), Phi Beta Kappa. Republican. Club: Detroit Yacht (mem. boating com. 1984). Banking, General corporate. Home: 3755 Ledge Ct Troy MI 48084 Office: Plunkett Cooney et al 900 Marquette Bldg Detroit MI 48226

ALLEN, JEFFREY MICHAEL, lawyer; b. Chgo., Dec. 13, 1948; s. Albert A. and Miriam (Feldman) A.; m. Anne Marie Guaraglia, Aug. 9, 1975; children: Jason M., Sara M. BA in Polit. Sci., U. Calif., Berkeley, 1970, JD, 1973. Bar: Calif. 1973, U.S. Dist. Ct. (no. and so. dists.) Calif. 1973, U.S. Ct. Appeals (9th cir.) 1973, U.S. Dist. Ct. (ea. dist.) Calif. 1974, U.S. Dist. Ct. (cen. dist.) Calif. 1977. Ptnr. Graves, Allen, Cornelius & Celestre and predecessor firms Graves & Allen and Graves & Mallory, Oakland, Calif., 1973—; lectr. St. Mary's Coll., Moraga, Calif., 1979—. Project editor U. Calif. Law Rev., 1971-73. Mem. ABA (vice chmn. com. and subcom. 1985-86, gen. practice sec.), Calif. Bar Assn., Alameda County Bar Assn., Assn. Trial Lawyers Am. Club: Commonwealth (San Francisco). Lodge: Rotary (chmn. com. Oakland club 1986—). Real property, State civil litigation, Bankruptcy. Office: Graves Allen & Cornelius 2101 Webster St Suite 1600 Oakland CA 94612

ALLEN, JEFFREY RODGERS, lawyer; b. West Point, N.Y., Aug. 15, 1953; s. James R. and Kathryn (Lewis) A.; m. Cynthia Lynn Colyer, Aug. 10, 1975; children: Emily Rodgers, Elizabeth Colyer. BA in History, U. Va., 1975; JD, U. Richmond, 1978. Bar: Va. 1978, U.S. Ct. Mil. Appeals 1981, U.S. Ct. Appeals (4th cir.) 1982, U.S. Supreme Ct. 1982. Trial atty. Michie, Hamlett, Donato & Lowry, Charlottesville, Va., 1982-86; chief counsel Va. Dept. Mil. Affairs, Richmond, 1986—; atty., advisor U.S. Army Mobile Air Surg. Transport Team, Savannah, Ga., 1980-82; mem. steering com. X-Car Litigation Group, 1983-85; lectr., organizer Law Everyone Should Know series Piedmont (Va.) Community Coll., Charlottesville, 1984-86; trial atty., of counsel Thorsen & Page, Richmond, 1986—. Pres. Regency Woods Condominium Assn., Richmond, 1976-78, Ashcroft Neighborhood Assn., Charlottesville, 1983-86. Served to capt. U.S. Army, 1978-82, to maj. JAGC, Va. Air N.G., 1982—. Mem. ABA (com. chair, 2d place project award), Assn. Trial Lawyers Am., Va. Bar Assn., Va. Trial Lawyers Assn. Democrat. Methodist. Avocations: jogging, mountain climbing, photography, fishing. Federal civil litigation, State civil litigation, Military. Home: 2255 Ridgeway Charlottesville VA 22901 Office: Dept Mil Affairs 501 E Franklin Richmond VA 23219

ALLEN, JOAN HOWARD, lawyer; b. Pensacola, Fla., Feb. 21, 1956; s. Jack Hal and Dixie Ann (Mason) H.; m. Douglas Philip Allen, Sept. 1, 1984. BA, U. Tex., 1977; JD, U. Houston, 1980. Bar: Tex. 1980, U.S. Ct. Appeals (5th cir.) 1985. Briefing atty. Gulf Oil Corp., Houston, 1980-81, leg. analyst, 1981-84; atty. Gulf States Utilities, Beaumont, Tex., 1984-85; legal counselor Tex. Edn. Agy., Austin, 1985-86, dir. hearing div., 1986—. Mem. ABA, Tex. Bar Assn., Travis County Bar Assn., Travis County Young Lawyers Assn., U. Tex. Alumni Assn. Avocations: travel, gardening. Administrative and regulatory, General corporate, Education law. Home: 3103 Sasparilla Cove Austin TX 78748 Office: Tex Edn Agy 1701 N Congress Ave Austin TX 78701

ALLEN, JOHN TREVETT, JR., lawyer; b. Ill., Apr. 9, 1939; s. John Trevett and Elinor Rose (Hatfield) A.; m. Marguerite DeHuszar, Jan 18, 1969; children—John Trevett, Samuel DeHuszar. AB in English summa cum laude and Spanish cum laude (double major), Williams Coll., 1961; LLB, Harvard U., 1964; postgrad., Central U. Ecuador, Quito, 1964-65. Bar: Ill. 1964, U.S. Supreme Ct., U.S. Ct. Appeals (7th cir.), U.S. Dist. Ct. (no. dist.) Ill., U.S. Dist. Ct. (ea. dist.) Ill. Assoc. Goodrich, Dalton, Little & Riquelme, Mexico City, 1962; assoc. Graham, James & Rolph, San Francisco, 1963; assoc. MacLeish, Spray, Price & Underwood, Chgo., 1963-71, ptnr., 1973-80; gen. atty. U.S. Gypsum Co., Chgo., 1971-73; ptnr. McBride, Baker & Coles, Chgo., 1980-86; assoc. Burditt, Bowles & Radzius, Ltd., Chgo., 1986—. Contbr. articles to profl. jours. Alderman City of Evanston, 1977-81; governing mem. Orchestral Assn. Chgo., 1980—; pres. Internat. Bus. Council MidAm., 1982-84, also mem. bd. dirs.; trustee Library Internat. Relations, 1983—, pres. 1986-87; vice chmn. Ill. Export Council, 1983—; counsel and dir. Ill. 4-H Found. Fulbright scholar, 1964-65. Mem. ABA, Ill. Bar Assn., Chgo. Bar Assn. (past chmn. internat. and fgn. law com., founder and past chmn. agri-bus. law com.), Vermilion County Bar Assn., Legal Club Chgo., Law Club Chgo., Phi Beta Kappa (exec. com. Chgo. area assn.). Republican. Presbyterian. Club: Union League (Chgo.). Private international, Antitrust, Administrative and regulatory. Office: Burditt Bowles & Radzins 333 W Wacker Dr Suite 1900 Chicago IL 60606

ALLEN, JOSEPH BERNARD, lawyer; b. Key West, Fla., Mar. 28, 1947; s. Joseph Bernard and Marjorie (holladay) A.; m. Rebecca Louise Caton, Nov. 27, 1976 (div. Oct. 1983); 1 child, Rebbecca Holladay. BS, U. Fla., 1965-69, JD with honors, 1973; MS in Chemistry, Ill. Inst. Tech., 1971. Bar: U.S. Patent Office 1973, Fla. 1974, U.S. Dist. Ct. (so. dist.) Fla. 1974, U.S. Ct. Appeals (5th and 11th cirs.) 1981. Assoc. Feldman & Eden, Key West, 1974-75, ptnr., 1975-80; sole practice Key West, 1980—; atty. City of Key West, 1975-86, Civil Service Bd., Key West, 1974-75. Atty. Monroe County Zoning Bd., Fla., 1974-75. Served with USAF, 1970-71. Democrat. Episcopalian. Banking, Local government, Real property. Home: 617 Canfield Ln Key West FL 33040 Office: 617 Whitehead St Key West FL 33040

ALLEN, KENNETH JAMES, lawyer; b. Gary, Ind., Sept. 12, 1956; s. Kenneth Edward and Joann (Christoff) A.; m. Nina Lajevardi, May 27, 1980. Student, Cambridge U., Eng., 1976; AB, Valparaiso U., 1979; JD, Ind. U., 1980. Bar: Ind. 1980, U.S. Dist. Ct. (no. and so. dists.) Ind. 1980, U.S. Ct. Appeals (7th cir.) 1980, U.S. Supreme Ct. 1980. Ptnr. Allen & Sarkisian, Merrillville, Ind., 1981—; pub. defender Lake County Ind., Crown Point, 1981—. Mem. ABA, Lake County Bar Assn., Ind. Bar Assn., E. Chgo. Bar Assn. (immigration and alien adminstrn. law com.). Republican. Personal injury, Immigration, naturalization, and customs, Workers' compensation. Home: 3906 Main East Chicago IN 46312 Office: Allen & Sarkisian 5825 Broadway Merrillville IN 46410

ALLEN, LAYMAN EDWARD, legal educator; b. Turtle Creek, Pa., June 9, 1927; s. Layman Grant and Viola Iris (Williams) A.; m. Christine R. Patmore, Mar. 29, 1950 (dec.); children: Layman G., Patricia R.; m. Emily C. Hall, Oct. 3, 1981; children: Phillip A., Kelly C. Student, Washington and Jefferson Coll., 1945-46; A.B., Princeton U., 1951; M.Pub. Admnstrn., Harvard U., 1952; LL.B., Yale U., 1956. Bar: Conn. 1956. Fellow Center for Advanced Study in Behavioral Scis., 1961-62; sr. fellow Yale Law Sch., 1956-57, lectr., 1957-58, instr., 1958-59, asst. prof., 1959-63, assoc. prof., 1963-66; assoc. prof. law U. Mich. Law Sch., Ann Arbor, 1966-71; prof. U. Mich. Law Sch., 1971—; research scientist Mental Health Research Inst., U. Mich., 1966—; cons. legal drafting Nat. Life Ins. Co., Mich. Blue Cross & Blue Shield (various law firms); quar. electronic data retrieval com. Am. Bar Assn.; ops. research analyst McKinsey & Co.; orgn. and methods analyst Office of Sec. Air Force.; Trustee Center for Study of Responsive Law. Editor-in-chief: Jurimetrics Jour; newspaper corr.; editor: Games & Simulations; Author: WFF 'n Proof: The Game of Modern Logic, 1961, latest rev. edit., 1973, (with Robin B.S. Brooks, Patricia A. James) Automatic Retrieval of Legal Literature: Why and How, 1962, WFF: The Beginner's Game of Modern Logic, 1962, latest rev. edit., 1973, Equations: The Game of Creative Mathematics, 1963, latest rev. edit., 1973, (with Mary E. Caldwell) Reflections of the Communications Sciences and Law: The Jurimetrics Conference, 1965, (with J. Ross and P. Kugel) Queries 'n Theories: The Game of Science and Language, 1970, altest rev. edit., 1973, (with F. Goodman, D. Hum-

phrey and J. Ross) On-Words: The Game of Word Structures, 1971, rev. edit., 1973; contbr. (with F. Goodman, D. Humphrey and J. Ross) articles to profl. jours.; inventee Diagnostic Instructional Gaming Math Program, 1985. Served with USNR, 1945-46. Mem. AAAS, Assn. Symbolic Logic, Nat. Council Tchrs. Math., Am. Bar Assn. (council sect. sci. and tech.), ACLU. Democrat. Unitarian. Legal education, Logic of legal writing. Home: 1407 Brooklyn Ave Ann Arbor MI 48104

ALLEN, LEON ARTHUR, JR., lawyer; b. Springfield, Mass., July 15, 1933; s. Leon Arthur Sr. and Elsie (Shoemaker) A.; m. Patricia Mellion, June 23, 1961; 1 child, Christopher L. BEE, Cornell U., 1955; LLB, NYU, 1964. Bar: N.Y. 1964, U.S. Dist. Ct. (so. and ea. dists.) N.Y. 1965. Tech. editor McGraw Hill Pub. Co., N.Y.C., 1958-62; constrn. engr. Gilbert Assocs., N.Y.C., 1962-64; assoc. LeBoeuf, Lamb, Leiby & MacRae, N.Y.C., 1964-70, ptnr., 1971—. Served with U.S. Army, 1956-58. Mem. ABA, Assn. of Bar of City of N.Y. (chmn. adminstrv. law com. 1972-74). Clubs: Racquet & Tennis (N.Y.C.); Tuxedo (Tuxedo Park, N.Y.). Administrative and regulatory, Public utilities. Home: 530 E 86th St New York NY 10028 Office: LeBoeuf Lamb Leiby & MacRae 520 Madison Ave New York NY 10022

ALLEN, MICHAEL DOUGLAS, lawyer; b. Sherman, Tex., Mar. 8, 1951; s. Elry Thurman and Mary Ann (Roberts) A.; m. Carol Nanette Lanham, Sept. 1, 1979; children: Lindsay Alyse, Caroline Michel. BA in Polit. Sci. and Bus. Adminstrn., Austin coll., 1973; JD, So. Meth. U., 1976. Bar: Tex. Congl. aid U.S. Congressman Ray Roberts, Washington, 1973; assoc. Richard Danner, Dallas, 1976-78; ptnr. Bain, Files, Allen & Caidwell, Tyler, Tex., 1978—; bd. dirs., officer East Tex. Estate Planning Council; mem. Tex. State Bar legal specialization, estate planning and probate law. Mem. planned giving council, Austin Coll., Sherman, Tex., 1985—, planned giving com. Grace Presbytery, Dallas, 1985—; bd. dirs. 1st Presbyn. Ch., Tyler, 1985—, chair Diaconate, 1986. Mem. Pi Gamma Mu. Democrat. Avocations: cattle, tennis, hunting, jogging. Estate planning, Probate, Real property. Office: Bain Files Allen & Caldwell 109 W Ferguson Tyler TX 75702

ALLEN, MICHAEL LEWIS, lawyer; b. N.Y.C., Dec. 14, 1937; s. Harry and Frances (Riesman) A.; m. Beverly Ackerman, June 26, 1960; children: Nancy, Richard, Jeffrey. AB, Columbia U., 1959; LLB, Harvard U., 1962; LLM in Internat. Law, NYU, 1969. Bar: N.J. 1962, N.Y. 1984, U.S. Dist. Ct. N.J. 1962, U.S. Tax Ct. 1981, U.S. Dist. Ct. (so. and ea. dists.) N.Y. 1984. Assoc. Clapp & Eisenberg, Newark, 1962-64, Hellring, Lindeman & Landau, Newark, 1964-68; ptnr. Kirsten, Simon, Friedman, Allen, Cherin & Linken (predecessor firm Simon & Allen), Newark, 1968—. Trustee Nat. Found. Ileitis and Colitis, N.Y.C., 1970—, Council for a Liveable World, Cambridge, Mass., 1978—. Mem. ABA, N.J. Bar Assn., Essex County Bar Assn., Am. Soc. Internat. Law, Union Internat. des Avocats. General corporate, Computer, Securities. Home: 139 Downey Dr Tenafly NJ 07670 Office: Kirsten Simon Friedman Allen Cherin & Linken One Gateway Ctr Newark NJ 07102

ALLEN, NADINE LOVELACE, judge; b. Columbus, Ohio, June 11, 1949; d. Eugene Lovelace and Norina F. (Vannucci) Lovelace Wolfe; m. George Allen, Mar. 22, 1975; 1 child, David George. Student Coll. Mt. St. Joseph, 1967-69; B.A., Ohio State U., 1972; J.D., Capital U., 1977. Bar: Ohio 1977, U.S. Dist. Ct. (so. dist.) Ohio 1983. Hearing officer Night Prosecutor Program, Columbus, 1975-76; law clk. Franklin County Pub. Defender's Office, Columbus, 1976-77; adminstrv. referee State Employee Compensation Bd., Columbus, 1977-78; atty. Legal Aid Soc., Cin., 1978-79, bd. dirs., 1983-85; atty. Hamilton County Pub. Defender's Office, Cin., 1979-85; judge, Hamilton County, Cin., 1985—; mem. Ohio Supreme Ct. Bd. Commrs. on Grievances and Discipline of Bar, Columbus, 1982—; adj. prof. U. Cin. Paralegal Program, 1980. Mem. Evendale Charter Rev. Com. (Ohio), 1984; bd. dirs. Children's Protective Soc., Cin., 1983—, Cin. chpt. NAACP, 1983—; mem. Big Bros./Big Sisters. Coll. Mt. St. Joseph French scholar at Universite de Laval, Que., Can., 1969; recipient Achievement award Ohio Senate, 1977. Mem. Nat. Bar Assn., Cin. Bar Assn. (Service award 1978), Black Lawyers Assn. Cin. (sec. 1979-83), Hamilton County Dem. Women, Burnet Area Bus. Assn., Coalition on Domestic Violence, Women Helping Women. Named 1st woman to Ohio Supreme Ct. Bd. Commrs. on Grievances. Criminal, Real property. Home: 10164 Kingsport Dr Cincinnati OH 45241 Office: 324 Reading Rd Cincinnati OH 45202

ALLEN, NEWTON PERKINS, lawyer; b. Memphis, Jan. 3, 1922; s. James Seddon and Sarah (Perkins) A.; m. Malinda Lobdell Nobles, Oct. 4, 1947 (dec. Nov. 1986); children: John Lobdell, Malinda Nobles, Newton Perkins, Cannon Fairfax. A.B., Princeton, 1943; LL.B., U. Va., 1948. Bar: Tenn. bar 1947. Assoc. Armstrong, Allen, Braden, Goodman, McBride & Prewitt (and predecessor firm), Memphis, 1948—; ptnr. Armstrong, Allen, Braden, Goodman, McBride & Prewitt (and predecessor firm), 1950—. Mem. Chickasaw council Boy Scouts Am., 1958-60, exec. bd. mem., 1961-69; Trustee LeBonheur Children's Hosp., Memphis, 1964-72, vice chmn. bd., 1965; mem. alumni council Princeton, 1954-64; pres. bd. trustees St. Mary's Episcopal Sch., 1966-67, v.p., 1972-73; chmn. Greater Memphis Council on Crime and Delinquency, 1976-80; co-chmn. Memphis conf. Faith at Work, 1975, bd. dirs., 1976-79; pres. Memphis Orchestral Soc., pres., 1979-81. Mem. Am. Coll. Probate Lawyers, Am., Tenn., Memphis, Shelby County bar assns., Tenn. Def. Lawyers Assn. Republican. Episcopalian sr. warden 1984,. Club: Memphis Lions (pres. 1956). General practice, Federal civil litigation, Probate. Home: 228 Windover Grove Memphis TN 38111 Office: One Commerce Sq Memphis TN 38103

ALLEN, NICHOLAS EUGENE, lawyer; b. Atlanta, July 24, 1907; s. Columbus Eugene and Maude Anne (Allen) A.; m. Adelaide Whitford, June 11, 1938; children: Sandra, Susanne. B.S., Princeton U., 1929; LL.B., Harvard U., 1932. Bar: N.J 1933, D.C 1940, Md. 1956. Pvt. practice N.J., 1933-35, D.C., 1953—, Md., 1957—; atty. Solicitor's Office, U.S. Dept. Labor, 1936-42, 1947; asst. gen. counsel Dept. of Air Force, 1948, asso. gen. counsel, 1949-51; steel industry div. adviser Office Gen. Counsel, NPA, 1951-52; spl. asst. to Sec. Commerce, dep. acting asst. sec. of commerce for internat. affairs, 1952-53; now of counsel Diuguid & Epstein; lectr. Am. U. and George Washington U. law schs., 1954-60. Served in Judge Adv. Gen.'s Dept. AUS, 1942-46; parachutist and staff judge advocate of 82d Airborne Div. in Ardennes, Rhineland and Central European campaigns; staff judge adv. U.S. Hdqtrs., Berlin Dist.; exec. officer ETO Judge Adv. Div.; brig. gen. USAF Res.; ret. dep. comdr. 1st (formerly 2d) Air Force Res. Region, 1960-67. Decorated Legion of Merit, Bronze Star Medal, commendation award U.S.; Belgian and Dutch fourrageres. Mem. Am., Fed. Md., D.C. bar assns., 82d Airborne Div. Assn., Judge Advocates Assn. (nat. pres. 1956-57), Phi Beta Kappa. Conglist. General practice, Probate, Copyright. Home: 5313 Blackstone Rd Westmoreland Hills Bethesda MD 20816 Office: 1000 Connecticut Ave NW Suite 1107 Washington DC 20036

ALLEN, RICHARD BLOSE, lawyer, editor; b. Aledo, Ill., May 10, 1919; s. James Albert and Claire (Smith) A.; m. Marion Treloar, Aug. 27, 1949; children: Penelope, Jennifer, Leslie Jean. B.S., U. Ill., 1941, J.D., 1947; LL.D., Seton Hall U., 1977. Bar: Ill. 1947. Staff editor ABA Jour., 1947-48, 63-66, exec. editor, 1966-70, editor, 1970-83, editor, pub., 1983-86; sole practice Aledo, 1949-57; gen. counsel Ill. State Bar Assn., 1957-63. Gen. editor Callaghan's Corp. Counsel Compliance Program Series, 1987&; editor (jour.) Sr. Lawyer, 1987—. Served from pvt. to maj. Q.M.C. AUS, 1941-46. Mem. Am. Bar Assn., Ill. Bar Assn. (mem. assembly 1972-74), Chgo. Bar Assn., Selden Soc., Scribes, Sigma Delta Chi, Kappa Tau Alpha, Phi Delta Phi, Alpha Tau Omega. Clubs: Michigan Shores (Wilmette); Law (Chgo.); Cosmos (Washington). Jurisprudence. Home: 702 Illinois Rd Wilmette IL 60091

ALLEN, RICHARD HOOPES, manufacturing executive, lawyer; b. Wilmington, Del., May 16, 1932; s. John William and Mildred Sample (Hoopes) A.; m. Mary Eller Allen, Sept. 8, 1962; 1 child, Christopher. AB, Bowdoin Coll., 1954; JD, U. Chgo., 1959. Bar: Del., Pa. Assoc. Morris, Nichols, Arsht & Tunnell, Wilmington, Del., 1959-63, Atlas Chem. Corp., Wilmington, 1963-66; asst. gen. counsel Rockwell Internat., Pitts., 1966-76; sec., gen. counsel Incom Internat. Inc., Pitts., 1976-85, pres., chief exec. officer, 1985—, also bd. dirs. Cons. Del. Human Relations Commn., Wilmington, 1964-66; bd. dirs. Del. Dept. Welfare, Dover, 1964-65; pres. bd. dirs. Fox Chapel Country Day Sch., Pitts., 1968-72. Served to 1st lt. U.S. Army, 1954-56. Mem. ABA, Allegheny County Bar Assn., Del. Bar Assn., Pa. Bar Assn., Order of Coif, Phi Beta Kappa. General corporate. Office: Incom Internat Inc 415 Holiday Dr Pittsburgh PA 15220

ALLEN, RICHARD LEE, JR., lawyer, consultant; b. Piqua, Ohio, Mar. 12, 1954; s. Richard Lee and Marcella Marie (Reaster) A.; m. Judith Ellen Simpkin, June 28, 1978; children—Richard Lee III, John Christopher. B.S. in Pharmacy, U. Cin., 1977; J.D., Capital Law Sch., 1980. Bar: Ohio 1980. Risk mgr. Med. Ctr. Hosp., Chillicothe, Ohio, 1978-79; Spl. counsel Ohio Hosp. Ins. Co., Columbus, 1980—; pharmacist Med. Ctr. Hosp., Chillicothe, 1977; adj. prof. Ohio State U., Columbus, 1982—. Mem. Assn. Trial Lawyers Am., Am. Soc. Law and Medicine, Ohio Bar Assn., Ohio Pharm. Assn., Columbus Bar Assn. Personal injury, Health, Insurance. Home: 678 Blackoak Ct Reynoldsburg OH 43068 Office: Ohio Hosp Ins Co 21 W Broad St Columbus OH 43216

ALLEN, RICHARD LEWIS, lawyer; b. Bryn Mawr, Pa., Dec. 4, 1954; s. Merton and Barbara (Goldstein) A.; m. Louise Jacowitz, Dec. 30, 1979; 1 child, Melissa. BA, Conn. Coll., 1976; JD, U. Miami, 1979. Bar: Tex. 1979, U.S. Dist. Ct. (no. dist.) Tex. 1979, Fla. 1980, U.S. Ct. Appeals (5th and 11th cirs.) 1980, U.S. Dist. Ct. (so. dist.) Fla. 1983, U.S. Tax Ct. 1983. Assoc. Shank, Irwin & Conant, Dallas, 1979-83, Rubin, Baum & Levin, Miami, Fla., 1983-84; ptnr. Solowsky & Allen PA, Miami, 1984—; adj. prof. law Cardozo Law Sch., N.Y.C., 1981-82. Editor U. Miami Law Rev., 1977-79. Regional chmn. Conn. Coll. Alumni Fundraising, East Coast Fla., 1985—. Mem. ABA, Fla. Bar Assn., Tex. Bar Assn., Dade County Bar Assn., Miami Children's Home Soc. (legal com.). Avocations: golf, swimming. Federal civil litigation, State civil litigation, Landlord-tenant. Office: Solowsky & Allen PA 9100 S Dadeland Blvd #1406 Miami FL 33156

ALLEN, RICHARD MARLOW, lawyer; b. Chgo., Sept. 26, 1940; s. Vern S. and Naomi C. Allen; children—Amanda, Brian. B.S., Purdue U., 1963; LL.B., Duke U., 1966. Bar: N.Y. 1967, U.S. Dist. Ct. (so. dist.) N.Y. 1968. Ptnr. Cravath, Swaine & Moore, N.Y.C., 1966—. Mem. Am. Coll. Investment Counsel. Bankruptcy, Contracts commercial, General corporate. Office: Cravath Swaine & Moore 1 Chase Manhattan Plaza New York NY 10005

ALLEN, ROBERT A., lawyer; b. Mobile, Ala., July 20, 1948; s. Francis H. and Elizabeth L. (Smith) A.; m. Sherry Y. Parsons, July 18, 1970; children: Austin Smith, Mary Elizabeth. BS, Auburn U., 1970; JD, U. Ala., 1975, LLM in Tax, 1982. Bar: Ala. 1975, U.S. Dist. Ct. (so. dist.) Ala. 1975, U.S. Ct. Appeals (11th cir.) 1978. Assoc. Nettles, Cox & Barker, Mobile, 1975-81; ptnr. Allen & Fernandez, Mobile, 1982—. Pres. Historic Mobile Preservation Soc., 1986—, Mobile Hist. Devel. Commn., 1982-86; advisor Ala. Hist. Commn., Montgomery, 1984—; mem. Nat. Trust for Historic Preservation, Washington, 1970—; bd. dirs. Mobile Hist. Devel. Found., 1982—, Mobile Arts Council, 1984—. Recipient Cert. of Merit Mobile Hist. Devel. Commn., 1985, Disting. Service award Alaska Hist. Commn., 1986. Mem. ABA, Ala. Bar Assn., Mobile Bar Assn., Nat. Assn. Bankruptcy Trustees. Episcopalian. Bankruptcy, Corporate taxation, General corporate. Home: 959 Charleston St Mobile AL 36604 Office: Allen & Fernandez PO Box 1945 Mobile AL 36633

ALLEN, ROBERT EUGENE BARTON, lawyer; b. Bloomington, Ind., Mar. 16, 1940; s. Robert Eugene Barton and Berth R. A.; m. Cecelia Ward Dooley, Sept. 23, 1960; children—Victoria, Elizabeth, Robert; m. Judith Elaine Hecht, May 27, 1979. B.S., Columbia U., 1962; LL.B., Harvard U., 1965. Bar: Ariz. 1965, U.S. Dist. Ct. Ariz. 1965, U.S. Tax Ct., 1965, U.S. Supreme Ct. 1970, U.S. Ct. Customs and Patent Appeals 1971, U.S. Dist. Ct. D.C. 1972, U.S. Ct. Appeals (9th cir.) 1974, U.S. Ct. Appeals (10th and D.C. cirs.) 1984, Ptnr., dir. Streich, Lang, Weeks and Cardon, Phoenix, 1965-83; ptnr., dir. Brown & Bain, Phoenix, Palo Alto (Calif.), 1983—. Nat. pres. Young Democrat Clubs Am., 1971-73; mem. exec. com. Dem. Nat. Com., 1972-73; mem. Ariz. Gov.'s Kitchen Cabinet working on wide range of state projects; bd. dirs. Phoenix Baptist Hosp. and Health Systems; bd. dirs. Phoenix and Valley of the Sun Conv. and Visitors Bur.; mem. Ariz. Aviation Futures Task Force; chmn. Ariz. Airport Devel. Criteria. Subcom.; mem. Apache Junction Airport Rev. Com., former mem Vestry and Sunday Sch. Tchr. Trinity Episcopal Cathedral; Am. rep. exec. bd. Atlantic Alliance of Young Polit. Leaders, 1973-77, 1977-80; trustee Am. Counsel of Young Polit. Leaders, 1971-76, 1981-85, mem. Am. delegations to Germany, 1971, 72, 76, 79, U.S.S.R., 1973, 76, France, 1974, 79, Belgium, 1974, 77, Can., 1974, Eng., 1975, 79, Norway, 1975, Denmark, 1976, Yugoslavia and Hungary, 1985; Am.observer European Parliamentary elections, Eng., France, Germany, Belgium, 1979. Mem. ABA, Ariz. Bar Assn., Maricopa County Bar Assn., N. Mex. State Bar, D.C. Bar Assn., Am. Judicature Soc., Fed. Bar Assn., Am. Arbitration Assn., Phi Beta Kappa. Democrat. Episcopalian (lay reader). Club: Harvard (Phoenix). Contbr. articles on comml. litigation to profl. jours. Antitrust. Office: 222 N Central Ave Phoenix AZ 85001

ALLEN, RONALD JAY, legal educator; b. Chgo., July 14, 1948; s. J. Mattison and Carolyn L. (Latchum) A.; m. Debra Jane Livingston, May 25, 1974 (div. 1982); children: Sarah, Adrienne; m. Julie O'Donnell, Sept. 2, 1984. BS, Marshall U., 1970; JD, U. Mich., 1973. Bar: Nebr. 1974, Iowa 1979, U.S. Ct. Appeals (8th cir.) 1980, U.S. Supreme Ct. 1981, Ill. 1986. Prof. law SUNY, Buffalo, 1974-79, U. Iowa, Iowa City, 1979-82, 83-84, Duke U., Durham, N.C., 1982-83, Northwestern U., Chgo., 1984—; pres. faculty senate U. Iowa, 1980-81. Author: Constitutional Criminal Procedure, 1985; contbr. articles to profl. jours. Mem. ABA (rules com. criminal justice sect.), Am. Law Inst. Federal civil litigation, Criminal, Jurisprudence. Home: 1812 N Hudson Chicago IL 60614 Office: Northwestern Sch Law 357 E Chicago Ave Chicago IL 60611

ALLEN, RONALD ROGER, JR., lawyer; b. Knoxville, Tenn., May 24, 1955; s. Ronald Roger and Flora Lee (Sheldon) A. BA, U. Tenn., 1977, MA, 1978; JD, Yale U., 1980. Bar: N.Y. 1982. Law clk. to presiding judge U.S. Dist. Ct. La., New Orleans, 1980-81; assoc. Hughes Hubbard & Reed, N.Y.C. and Paris, 1981-85, Curtis, Mallet-Prevost, Colt & Mosle, N.Y.C., 1985—. Mem. ABA, Union Internat. d' Avocats, Phi Beta Kappa, Phi Kappa Phi, Pi Delta Phi, Delta Phi Alpha. Private international, Federal civil litigation. Home: 331 W 16th St Apt 6 New York NY 10011 Office: Curtis Mallet-Prevost Colt & Mosle 101 Park Ave New York NY 10178

ALLEN, THOMAS D., lawyer; b. Detroit, June 25, 1926; s. Draper and Florence (Jones) A.; m. Joyce M. Johnson, July 18, 1953; children—Nancy A. Allen Bowser, Robert D., Rebecca D. B.S., Northwestern U., 1949; J.D., U. Mich., 1952. Bar: Ill. 1952, U.S. Supreme Ct. 1971. Assoc. Kirkland & Ellis, Chgo., 1952-60, ptnr., 1961-67; ptnr. Wildman, Harrold, Allen & Dixon, Chgo., 1967—. Chmn. Community Caucus, Hinsdale, Ill., 1960-61; mem. Hinsdale Bd. Edn., 1965-71, pres., 1970-71; pres. West Suburban Council, Boy Scouts Am., La Grange, Ill., 1980-82, mem. Internat. Com., 1980—, nat. boy scout com., 1975—, nat. exec. bd., 1986—, world program com., 1986—, chmn. World Jamboree com., 1980-83; moderator Union Ch., Hinsdale, 1983-84. Served with USN, 1944-46. Recipient Silver Beaver award Boy Scouts Am., 1964. Fellow Am. Coll. Trial Lawyers (state chmn. 1984-85); mem. ABA, Ill. Bar Assn., Chgo. Bar Assn., Law Club of Chgo., Legal Club of Chgo., Jaycees Internat. (senator, 1965). Mem. United Ch. of Christ. Clubs: Hinsdale Golf, Chgo. Athletic. Federal civil litigation, State civil litigation. Home: 940 Taft Rd Hinsdale IL 60521 Office: Wildman Harrold Allen & Dixon One IBM Plaza Chicago IL 60611

ALLEN, THOMAS ERNEST, lawyer; b. Salt Lake City, Sept. 30, 1939; s. Kenneth L. and Joyce Catherine (Thompson) A.; m. Elizabeth Harker Curtis, June 26, 1965; children: Kenneth, Susan, Gregory. AB, Dartmouth Coll., 1961; JD, U. Mich., 1967. Bar: Minn., 1967, U.S. Dist. Ct. Minn., 1968, U.S. Tax Ct., 1970, Mo., 1976, U.S. Dist. Ct. (ea. dist.) Mo., 1977. Assoc. Peterson, Peterson & Peterson, Albert Lea, Minn., 1967-69; ptnr. Peterson, Peterson & Allen, Albert Lea, Minn., 1969-76; assoc. Curtis, Casserly & Barnes, St. Louis, 1976-77; ptnr. Curtis & Crossen, St. Louis, 1977-84; of counsel Curtis, Bamburg & Crossen, St. Louis, 1984-87, Curtis, Bamburg, Oetting et al, St. Louis, 1987—; bd. dirs. Brooking Park Geriatrics, Inc., Sedalia, Mo., Geriatric Mgmt. Inc., Sedalia. Chmn. Freeborn County Rep. Com., Albert Lea, 1970-74. Served to 1st lt. U.S. Army, 1962-64. Mem. ABA, Mo. Bar Assn., Minn. Bar Assn., Bar Assn. Met. St. Louis, Phi Kappa Psi. Republican. Episcopalian. Club: Mo. Athletic (St. Louis). Lodge: Masons. Health, General corporate, General practice. Home: 423 Miriam Kirkwood MO 63122 Office: Curtis Bamburg & Oetting 325 N Kirkwood Rd Suite 203 Kirkwood MO 63122

ALLEN, W. RILEY, lawyer; b. Coral Gables, Fla., Oct. 24, 1953; s. William George and Winnie (Woodall) A. BA with honors, U. Cen. Fla., 1977; JD with honors, Fla. State U., 1981. Bar: Fla. 1982, U.S. Dist. Ct. (mid. dist.) Fla. 1982, U.S. Ct. Appeals (11th cir.) 1982. Assoc. Pitts, Eubank & Ross, P.A., Orlando, 1981-85; prin. W. Riley Allen & Assocs., Orlando, 1985—. Mem. ABA (tort and ins. practice com.), Fla. Bar Assn. (trial lawyers sect.), Assn. Trial Lawyers Am. (trial lawyers sect.), Acad. Fla. Trial Lawyers (trial lawyers sect.), Orange County Bar Assn. (law and edn., guardian ad litem coms. 1981—), Def. Research Inst., Am. Judicature Soc., Phi Delta Phi. Republican. Baptist. Avocations: softball, water and snow skiing, basketball, tennis, running. Federal civil litigation, State civil litigation, Personal injury. Office: W Riley Allen & Assocs 228 Annie St Orlando FL 32806

ALLEN, WILBUR COLEMAN, lawyer; b. Victoria, Va., Apr. 30, 1925; s. George Edward and Mary Lee (Bridgforth) A.; m. Frances Brockenbrough Gayle, Sept. 16, 1950; children—Frances Gayle Allen Fitzgerald, Wilbur Coleman, Robert Clayton, Edward Lefebvre, Courtney Bridgforth. B.A., U. Va., 1947, J.D., 1950. Bar: Va. 1949, D.C. 1954, U.S. Dist. Ct. (ea. and we. dists.) Va. 1951, U.S. Ct. Appeals 1950, U.S. Supreme Ct. 1954. Ptnr. Allen, Allen, Allen & Allen, Richmond, Va., 1950-69, pres., 1969—Served as lt. (j.g.) USN, 1942-45, PTO. Sunday Sch. supt. All Saints Episcopal Ch., Richmond, 1960-65, vestryman, 1964-68, 70-74, 80-83, sr. warden, 1967-68, chmn. stewardship com., 1980-81; bd. visitors Va. Commonwealth U., 1984-85, property com., 1984-85, audit com., 1984-85. Fellow Am. Coll. Trial Lawyers; mem. ABA, Assn. Trial Lawyers Am., Am. Judicature Soc., Va. State Bar, Va. Bar Assn., Va. State Bar Council, Va. Trial Lawyers Assn. (chmn. publicity com. 1968, chmn. spl. com. on ins. 1981), N.Y. State Trial Lawyers Assn., Richmond Bar Assn. (pres. 1979, outstanding contbn. award 1981). Clubs: Country of Va., Westwood (Richmond). Lodge: Rotary (pres. 1974-75, Rotarian of Yr. 1980). State civil litigation, Insurance, Personal injury. Home: 2 Gaymont Rd Richmond VA 23230 Office: Allen Allen Allen & Allen 1809 Staples Mill Rd Richmond VA 23230

ALLEN, WILBUR COLEMAN, JR., lawyer; b. Richmond, Va., Dec. 1, 1953; s. Wilbur Coleman and Frances (Gayle) A.; m. Anne Aras, June 6, 1980; children: Robert Sean, Kara Anne. BA, Yale U., 1976; JD, MBA, U. Va., 1980. Bar: Va. 1980, U.S. Dist. Ct. (ea. and we. dists.) Va. 1980, U.S. Ct. Appeals (4th cir.) 1980. Ptnr. Allen, Allen, Allen & Allen, Richmond, 1980—; bd. dirs. Profl. Images, Inc., Richmond. Mem. ABA, Assn. Trial Lawyers Am., Va. Bar Assn., Va. Trial Lawyers Assn. (exec. com. 1985—, bd. govs. 1985—, chmn. pub. affairs com. 1986), Richmond Bar Assn., Nat. bd. Trial Advocacy (cert. civil trial advocate). Democrat. Episcopalian. Avocations: sports, gardening, music, automobiles. State civil litigation, Libel, Personal injury. Office: Allen Allen Allen & Allen PC 1809 Staples Mill Rd Richmond VA 23230

ALLEN, WILLIAM HAYES, lawyer; b. Palo Alto, Calif., Oct. 19, 1926; s. Ben Shannon and Victoria Rose (French) A.; m. Joan Webster Emmett, July 16, 1950; children: Edwin Hayes, Neal French, William Kent. Student, Deep Springs Coll., 1942-44; B.A. with gt. distinction, Stanford U., 1948, LL.B., 1956. Bar: D.C. bar 1958. Corr. AP, Fresno, Calif., 1948-49; newsman AP, Sacramento, 1950-53; law clk. to Chief Justice Earl Warren U.S. Supreme Ct., Washington, 1956-57; assoc. Covington & Burling, Washington, 1957-64; partner Covington & Burling, 1964—; acting prof. law Stanford U. Law Sch., 1979; adj. prof. law Howard U. Sch. Law, 1981-83; lectr. George Mason U. Law Sch., 1983-86; chmn. jud. rev. com. Adminstrv. Conf. of U.S., 1972-82; sr. conf. fellow Adminstrv. Conf. of U.S., 1982—; mem. steering com. Nat. Prison Project, 1975—. Pres.: Stanford Law Rev., vol. 8, 1955-56; contbr. articles to legal jours. Mem. Fair Housing Bd., Arlington County, Va., 1974-79. Served with U.S. Army, 1945-47. Mem. Am. Law Inst., ABA (mem. council adminstrv. law sect. 1969-72, 79-81, chmn. 1982-83), Bar Assn. D.C., D.C. Bar (chmn. legal ethics com. 1976-78), Order of Coif. Democrat. Mem. United Ch. of Christ. Club: Fed. City. Administrative and regulatory, Federal civil litigation. Office: 1201 Pennsylvania Ave NW PO Box 7566 Washington DC 20044

ALLENDER, JOHN ROLAND, lawyer; b. Boone, Iowa, Oct. 22, 1950; s. John S. and C. Corinne (Hayes) A.; m. Ann P. Hippee, Nov. 24, 1972; children: Susan A., Andrew J. BS, Iowa State U., 1972; JD, U. San Diego, 1975; LLM in Taxation, NYU, 1976. Bar: Calif. 1976, Tex. 1977, U.S. Ct. Claims 1977, U.S. Tax Ct. 1977, U.S. Dist. Ct. (so. dist.) Tex. 1977. Assoc. Fulbright & Jaworski, Houston, 1976-83, ptnr., 1983—. State and local taxation, General corporate, Corporate taxation. Office: Fulbright & Jaworski 1301 McKinney Houston TX 77010

ALLEVA, PATTI ANN, lawyer, legal educator; b. N.Y.C., Apr. 10, 1955; d. Arthur Louis and Lee (Verrone) A. B.A., Hofstra U., 1976; J.D., 1979. Bar: N.Y. 1980, U.S. Dist. Ct. (so. dist.) N.Y. 1980, U.S. Dist. Ct. (ea. dist.) N.Y. 1980, U.S. Dist. Ct. (no. dist.) Calif. 1982. Law clk. U.S. Dist. Ct. N.J., 1980; assoc. Proskauer Rose Goetz & Mendelsohn, N.Y.C., 1981-87; asst. prof. U. N.D. Sch. Law, Grand Forks, 1987—. Articles editor Hofstra Law Rev., 1978-79. John Cranford Adams scholar, 1976; N.Y. State Regents scholar. Mem. Assn. Bar City N.Y. (sec. council jud. adminstrn. 1983-86, sex and law com. 1986-87), Am. Judicature Soc., Phi Beta Kappa, Phi Alpha Theta. Federal courts, Intellectual property, Securities. Office: U ND Sch Law Grand Forks ND 58202

ALLF, NANCY L., lawyer; b. Hackensack, N.J., Feb. 1, 1957; d. George William and Juanita (Ballard) A. BA, Transylvania U., 1979; JD, Chase Coll. of Law, 1982. Bar: Nev. 1983, U.S. Dist. Ct. Nev. 1983, U.S. Ct. Appeals (9th cir.) 1984. Assoc. John C. Whelton Chtd., Las Vegas, Nev., 1982-84, John Peter Lee Ltd., Las Vegas, 1984—; instr. Clark County Community Coll., Las Vegas, 1985—. Bd. dirs. Planned Parenthood So. Nev., Las Vegas, 1986—. Mem. Clark County Bar Assn., Nev. Bar Assn., Nev. Assn. Trial Lawyers, So. Nev. Assn. of Women Attys. (polit. action com.), ABA, Assn. Trial Lawyers Am., Am. Assn. of Univ. Women. Democrat. Club: A.W.W. Bankruptcy, Contracts commercial. Home: 670 Rolling Green Dr Las Vegas NV 89109-3773 Office: John Peter Lee Ltd 300 S Fourth St #1500 Las Vegas NV 89101

ALLGEYER, DAVID ALAN, lawyer; b. St. Paul, June 18, 1953; s. Louis Henry and Maybelle Teresa (Pearson) A.; m. Melinda Ann Look, Sept. 2, 1978; children: Matthew, Rebecca. BA in Anthropology, U. Minn., 1974, JD magna cum laude, 1980. Bar: Minn. 1980, U.S. Dist. Ct. Minn. 1981, U.S. Dist. Ct. (no. dist.) Calif. 1985, U.S. Ct. Appeals (8th and Fed. cirs.) 1985. Law clk. to presiding judge U.S. Dist. Ct. Minn., Mpls., 1980-82; assoc. Lindquist & Vennum, Mpls., 1982-86, ptnr., 1986—. Editor U. Minn. Law Rev., 1979-80. Mem. ABA, Fed. Bar Assn. (bd. dirs. Minn. chpt. 1986—), Minn. Bar Assn., Hennepin County Bar Assn. Lutheran. Federal civil litigation, State civil litigation. Office: Lindquist & Vennum 4200 IDS Ctr Minneapolis MN 55402

ALLISON, HOWARD MERVYN, lawyer; b. Akron, Ohio, June 27, 1943; s. Jack William and Sara (Goldstein) A.; m. Sandra Leslie, Aug. 26, 1965 (dec.); 1 son, Scott. B.A. in Edn., U. Akron, 1966, J.D., 1969. Bar: Ohio 1969, U.S. Dist. Ct. (no. dist.) Ohio 1970, U.S. Ct. Appeals (6th cir.) 1971. Claims adjustor CNA Ins. Co., 1965-71; assoc. Parker & Parker, 1969-71; ptnr. Allison & Miller, 1971-79; sole practice, Akron, 1979—. Chmn. ACLU, 1976, counsel Akron area, 1969—. Mem. Akron Bar Assn., Portage County Bar Assn., Stark County Bar Assn., Ohio Bar Assn., ABA. Criminal, General practice.

ALLISON, JAMES MCWILLIAMS, lawyer; b. Greenville, S.C., Oct. 5, 1948; s. Harold McWilliams and Elizabeth Cleveland (Williams) A.; m. Shirley Jeanne Schaeffer, June 20, 1970 (div. Sept. 1984); children: James McWilliams Jr., Patricia Schaeffer, William B. BA, Presbyn. Coll., Clinton, S.C., 1970; JD, U. S.C., 1976. Bar: S.C. 1976, U.S. Dist. Ct. S.C. 1977, U.S. Ct. Appeals (4th cir.) 1982. Assoc. Law Offices of Grover S. Parnell, Jr., Greenville, 1976-78; sole practice Greenville, 1978-79; ptnr. Yarborough, Mauldin & Allison, Greenville, 1979-81, Mauldin & Allison, Greenville,

1981—. Instr., speaker Leadership Greenville, 1984-85. Served to maj. USAR, 1971-73. Named one of Oustanding Young Men in Am., 1981. Mem. ABA, S.C. Bar Assn., Greenville County Bar Assn. (grievance com.), S.C. Trial Lawyers Assn. Republican. Roman Catholic. Clubs: Poinsett, Cotillion, Connestee Basin Yacht (Greenville); Chattooga River Raft. Avocation: white water rafting. State civil litigation, Family and matrimonial, Real property. Home: 213 Brookwood Dr Greenville SC 29601 Office: Mauldin & Allison 710 E McBee Ave Greenville SC 29601

ALLISON, JAMES STANLEY, lawyer; b. Greybull, Wyo., Aug. 29, 1947; s. Lester F. and Reva (Kincade) A.; m. Marva Gronberg, Oct. 16, 1982; 1 child: Derek James. AA, Northwest Community Coll., 1968; BA, U. Wyo., 1970, JD, 1974. Bar: Wyo. 1975, U.S. Dist. Ct. Wyo. 1975. Assoc. Ross D. Copenhaver, P.C., Powell, Wyo., 1975-76; sole practice Powell, 1976—; mcpl. judge City of Powell, Wyo., 1980—; alt. justice Peace for Park County, Wyo., 1980—; bd. dirs. Big Horn Enterprises, Inc., Thermopolis, Wyo. Bd. dirs. Park County Sch. Dist. 1, Powell, 1977-83, Northwest Bd. Coop. Services, Thermopolis, Wyo., 1977-82, Northwest Civic Orch., Powell, 1979-82; bd. of deacons Union Presbyn. Ch., Powell, 1977-80, bd. of elders, 1983-85; mem. Mayor's Com. on Disabled, Powell, 1985—; mem. planning council on devel. disabilities, State of Wyo., 1986—. Recipient Disting. Service award Powell Jaycees, 1979, Gov.'s Com. for the Employment of the Handicapped, Cheyenne, Wyo., 1982, Cert. Commendation Wyo. Sch. Bds. Assn., 1984; named one of Outstanding Young Men of Am., U.S. Jaycees, 1981, 82. Mem. Powell Jaycees (v.p. 1976-77), Wyo. Assn. Judges of Cts. Ltd. Jurisdiction (bench book com. 1985—), Powell Valley C. of C. (bd. dirs. 1985—, treas. 1986, pres. 1987—). Republican. Presbyterian. Lodges: Rotary (pres. 1980-81), Elks. General practice, Probate, Workers' compensation. Home: 928 Van Pl Powell WY 82435 Office: PO Box 926 126 N Bent St Powell WY 82435

ALLISON, JOHN ROBERT, law educator, author; b. Waco, Tex., Apr. 6, 1948; s. Lloyd Burton and Mary LaBertha (Fulps) A.; m. Margo Lu Armstrong, Dec. 22, 1971; children: Sarah Marie, Jill Elaine, Eric Forrest. Student Tex. A&M U., 1966-69; JD, Baylor U., 1972. Bar: Tex. 1972. Asst. prof. U. Tex., Austin, 1972-77, assoc. prof., 1977-81, prof. 1981-83, Mary John and Ralph Spence Centennial prof. in bus. adminstrn., 1983—. Staff editor Am. Bus. Law Jour., Austin, 1974-78, co-editor, 1978-79, articles editor, 1979-81, mng. editor, 1981-83, editor-in-chief 1983-85, adv. editor 1985—; author: Business Law: Text and Cases, 1978, 3d edit., 1985; Business Law: Alternate Edition, 1979, 3d edit., 1986; The Legal Environment of Business, 1984, 2d edit., 1987; Fundamentals of Business Law, 1984; contbr. articles to profl. jours. Mem. and contbr. Assn. for Retarded Citizens, 1974—, Am. Diabetes Assn., 1981—; parliamentarian and mem. supervisory com. Univ. Fed. Credit Union, Austin, 1975-84. Grantee Inst. Constructive Capitalism, 1978; named Outstanding Prof. Grad. Sch. Bus., U. Tex., 1984. Mem. Am. Bus. Law Assn. (exec. com. 1983-84). Democrat. Antitrust, Labor, Legal education. Home: 8616 Cameron Loop Austin TX 78745 Office: U Tex Grad Sch Bus Mgmt Sci & Info Systems Dept Austin TX 78712

ALLISON, JOHN ROBERT, lawyer; b. San Antonio, Feb. 9, 1945; s. Lyle (stepfather) and Beatrice (Kaliner) Forehand; m. Darlene Rush Allison, Oct. 4, 1975; 1 child, Katharine. B.S., Stanford U., 1966; J.D., U. Wash., 1969. Bar: Wash. 1969, D.C. 1973, U.S. Supreme Ct. 1973. Assoc., Garvey, Schubert, Adams & Barer, Seattle, 1969-73, ptnr., 1973-86, prin., Betts, Patterson & Mines, 1986—, mgr. Washington office, 1973-74, mng. ptnr., 1978; lectr. bus. law Seattle U., 1970, U. Wash., 1970-73; judge pro tem Seattle Mcpl. Ct., King County Superior Ct. Editorial bd. Hazardous Waste and Toxic Tort Law and Strategy Newsletter, 1985—. Mem. Seattle-King County Bar Assn. (chmn. jud. evaluation polling com. 1982-83), Wash. Bar Assn. (bd. bar examiners 1984—), D.C. Bar Assn., ABA (vice chmn. toxic and hazardous substances and environ. law com. 1986-87), Am. Judicature Soc. Republican. Episcopalian. Club: Washington Athletic (Seattle). State civil litigation, Federal civil litigation. Office: Financial Ctr 1215 Fourth Ave 8th Fl Seattle WA 98161-1090

ALLISON, RICHARD CLARK, lawyer; b. N.Y.C., July 10, 1924; s. Albert Fay and Anice (Clark) A.; m. Anne Elizabeth Johnston, Oct. 28, 1950; children: Anne Sidney, William Scott, Richard Clark. B.A., U. Va., 1944, LL.B., 1948. Bar: N.Y. 1948. Practiced in N.Y.C., 1948-52, 54-55, 55—; partner firm Reid & Priest, 1961—; with CIA, 1952-54. Trustee Buckley Country Day Sch. Served to ensign USNR, 1942-46. Mem. Am. Bar Assn. (chmn. com. Latin Am. Law 1964-68, vice chmn. internat. law sect. 1969-76, chmn. 1976-77, chmn. Nat. Inst. on Doing Bus. in Far East 1972, chmn internat. legal exchange program 1981-85), Internat. Bar Assn. (chmn. 1986 Conf., ethics com. 1986—), Société Internationale des Avocats, Inter-Am. Bar Assn., Am. Fgn. Law Assn. (dir.), Am. Arbitration Assn. (nat. panel), Southwestern Legal Found. (adv. bd.), Am. Soc. Internat. Law, Council on Fgn. Relations, Am. Bar Found., Assn. Bar City N.Y. (internat. law com.), Sec. State's Adv. Com. on Pvt. Internat. Law, Raven Soc., SAR, St. Andrew's Soc. N.Y., Phi Beta Kappa, Omicron Delta Kappa, Pi Kappa Alpha, Phi Delta Phi. Congregationalist. Clubs: Union League, Manhasset Bay Yacht. Private international, Federal civil litigation, General corporate. Home: 224 Circle Dr Plandome Manor NY 11030 Office: 40 W 57th St New York NY 10019

ALLISON, STEPHEN PHILIP, lawyer; b. Los Angeles, Jan. 4, 1947; s. Philip L. and Catherine (Lawder) A.; m. Margaret Ann Yochem, June 7, 1969; children—Brian Clayton, Todd Lawder. B.A., Tex. Christian U., 1969; J.D., U. Houston, 1972. Bar: Tex. 1972, U.S. Ct. Appeals (5th cir.) 1977, U.S. Supreme Ct. 1977, U.S. Dist. Ct. (we. dist.) Tex. 1981. Asst. dist. atty. Bexar County, San Antonio, 1973-77; assoc. Dobbins, Harris & Gonzalez, San Antonio, 1977-78, Sawtelle, Goode, Davidson & Troilo, San Antonio, 1978—; admissions com. Tex. Supreme Ct., 1978-82. Author: Texas Practice Guide, 1985. Pres., Tex. Christian U.-San Antonio Alumni Club, 1978-83. Mem. ABA, Def. Research Inst., State Bar of Tex. (peer com., court com. 1983—), Tex. Assn. Def. Counsel, San Antonio Bar Assn., N. San Antonio C. of C., Tex. Christian U. Alumni Assn. (bd. dirs. 1979-83). Republican. Episcopalian. Lodge: Olmos Kiwanis (San Antonio). Federal civil litigation, State civil litigation. Home: 201 Ridgemont San Antonio TX 78209 Office: #1000 Two SASA Center 613 NW Loop 410 San Antonio TX 78216

ALLISON, THOMAS D., JR., lawyer; b. Columbus, Ohio, Dec. 20, 1944; s. Thomas D. and Elizabeth (Tumbleson) A.; m. Sherry Holland. BA, Princeton U., 1966; JD, Yale U., 1969. Bar: Ill. 1969. Tchr. CUNY, 1969-71; ptnr. Cotton, Watt, Jones & King, Chgo., 1971—. Trustee Chgo. Police Pension Fund, 1985—; bd. dirs. Edgewater Community Council, Chgo., 1986—, 48th Ward Dems., Chgo. Mem. ABA, Chgo. Council of Lawyers, AFL-CIO. Federal civil litigation, Labor, Pension, profit-sharing, and employee benefits. Office: Cotton Watt Jones & King One IBM Plaza Chicago IL 60611

ALLORA, RALPH ANTHONY, insurance executive, lawyer; b. Newark, Aug. 6, 1946; s. Anthony Aloyisuis and Lucia (DiChiara) A.; m. Victoria Mary Rafanello, Oct. 28, 1966 (div. Jan. 1983); children: Ralph Jr., Lisa Marie, Michael Louis. BBA, Seton Hall U., 1976; JD, N.Y. Law Sch., 1980. Bar: N.Y. 1980, N.J. 1981, U.S. Dist. Ct. (N.J.) 1981. Account exec. Fisher-Stevens, Inc., Totowa, N.J., 1974-79, Direct Mktg. Agy., Stamford, Conn., 1979-80; atty. advt. underwriting Met. Life Ins. Co., N.Y.C., 1981; 2d v.p. Nat. Benefit Life Ins. Co., N.Y.C., 1982-85, v.p., 1986—; adj. prof. Coll. of Ins., N.Y.C., 1983-85. Roman Catholic. Avocations: tennis, skiing. Estate planning, State civil litigation, General practice. Office: Nat Benefit Life Ins Co 2 Park Ave New York NY 10016

ALLOTTA, JOSEPH JOHN, lawyer; b. Rochester, N.Y., May 1, 1947; s. Sam J. and Sarah L. (Cerrito) A.; m. Elizabeth Dingwall, July 17, 1971; children—John Joseph, Leslie Denise, Jeffrey James. B.A., Am. U., 1969; J.D., Case Western Reserve U., 1972. Bar: Ohio 1972. Law clk. to presiding justice U.S. Dist. Ct. (no. dist.) Ohio, 1972-74; assoc. Gallon, Kalniz & Iorio, 1974-79; sr. ptnr. Allotta & Farley, Toledo, 1979—; instr. U. Toledo, 1975-76. Dem. precinct committeeman Sylvania Twp., 1983—. Served with U.S. Army, 1969-75. Mem. Internat. Boilermakers (hon.), Ohio State Bar Assn. (labor law sect., bd. govs.), ABA (employment law sect.). Dem. Episcopalian. Club: Health. Lodge: Howard Johnson. Avocations: Logging; tennis; racquetball. Labor, Pension, profit-sharing, and employee benefits, Federal civil litigation. Home: 6127 Cross Trails Rd Sylvania Twp OH 43560 Office: Allotta & Farley 3450 W Central Ave Suite 366 Toledo OH 43606

ALLPORT, WILLIAM WILKENS, lawyer; b. Cleve., May 31, 1944; s. H. Burnham and Vernes Sophia (Wilkens) A.; m. Roberta Charlotte Warfield, Dec. 17, 1966; children—Christine Anne, Laura Warfield. A.B., Gettysburg Coll., 1966; J.D., Case Western Res. U., 1969. Bar: Ohio 1969, U.S. Ct. Appeals (6th cir.) 1971, U.S. Supreme Ct. 1973, U.S. Ct. Appeals (8th cir.) 1976, U.S. Ct. Appeals (7th cir.) 1978, U.S. Ct. Appeals (1st cir.) 1980, N.Y. 1981, U.S. Ct. Appeals (5th, 3d, 4th cirs.) 1981, U.S. Ct. Appeals (11th cir.) 1982, U.S. Ct. Appeals (2d cir.) 1983. Assoc. Baker & Hostetler, Cleve., 1969-75; chief labor counsel Leaseway Transp. Corp., Cleve., 1975-84, v.p. labor, 1984—. Ward chmn. Rep. Com.; explorer advisor Boy Scouts Am.; mem. Citizens League of Greater Cleve.; bd. govs. Case Western Res. Law Sch., 1983—, trustee Jr. Achievement of Greater Cleve. Mem. ABA, Ohio Bar Assn., N.Y. Bar Assn., Cleve. Bar Assn., Internat. Law Soc., Case Western Res. Law Sch. Alumni Assn. (pres. 1985—), Phi Delta Phi, Theta Chi, Pi Lambda Sigma. Club: Cleve. Athletic. Editor: Case Western Res. U. Law Rev., 1968-69. Labor. Home: 3337 Thomson Circle Rocky River OH 44116 Office: Leaseway Transp Corp 3700 Park East Dr Cleveland OH 44122

ALLRED, FORREST CARLSON, lawyer; b. Provo, Utah, Feb. 2, 1955; s. Forrest Rich and Emily Jesgwin (Carlson) A.; m. Catherine Elaine Redd, Aug. 26, 1978; four children. BS, Brigham Young U., 1979; JD, Am. U., 1982. Bar: S.D. 1982, U.S. Dist. Ct. S.D. 1982, U.S. Ct. Appeals (8th cir.) 1986. Sole practice Aberdeen, S.D., 1982—. Bd. edn. Sch. Dist. 6-1, Aberdeen, 1985—, v.p. 1986. Mem. ABA, S.D. Bar Assn., S.D. Trial Lawyers Assn., Brown County Bar Assn. Republican. Mormon. Lodge: Kiwanis (bd. dirs. Aberdeen club 1986—). Real property, Family and matrimonial, Personal injury. Office: Citizens Bldg Suite 500 Aberdeen SD 57401

ALLRED, STEVEN WESLEY, lawyer, consultant; b. Ogden, Utah, Sept. 4, 1947; s. Orland Wesley and Geneva (Pennington) A.; 1 son, Marshall Trent. B.S., U. Utah, 1969, J.D., 1971. Assoc. Roe, Fowler, Jerman, & Dart, 1971; practice, 1972—, now prin. Allred & Assocs., Salt Lake City; assoc. legis. gen. counsel Utah State Legislature, 1975-80; predisposition atty. Utah Supreme Ct., 1980-82; spl. counsel Intermountain Power Project; cons. White Pine Power Project; mem. various bar and bus-related adv. coms. Bd. dirs., chmn. bd. com. Salt Lake City Pub. Library. Environment, Legislative, Local government. Home: 1869 Yale Ave Salt Lake City UT 84108 Office: 185 S State Suite 400 Salt Lake City UT 84111

ALMON, RENEAU PEARSON, state justice; b. Moulton, Ala., July 8, 1937; s. Nathaniel Lee and Mary (Johnson) A.; m. Deborah Pearson, June 27, 1974; children by previous marriage: Jonathan, Jason, Nathaniel; 1 stepson-Tommy Preer. B.S., U. Ala., 1959; LL.B., Cumberland Sch. Law Samford U., 1964. Bar: Ala. bar 1964. Judge 36th Jud. Circuit Ala., 1965-69, Ala. Ct. Criminal Appeals, 1969-75; justice Ala. Supreme Ct., Montgomery, 1975—. Served with U.S. Army. Mem. Am., Ala. bar assns. Methodist. Office: Supreme Court 445 Dexter Ave PO Box 218 Montgomery AL 36130

ALMOND, DAVID R., corporate lawyer. BS, U. Va., 1962, LLB, 1967; student sr. exec. program, MIT, 1981. Assoc. Reid & Priest, N.Y.C., 1967-71; asst. gen. counsel Boise (Idaho) Cascade Corp., 1971-77; assoc. gen. counsel and asst. sec. Wilson Foods Corp., Oklahoma City, 1977-85, v.p. of gen. counsel and adminstrn., 1985—. Office: Wilson Foods Corp 4545 N Lincoln Blvd Oklahoma City OK 73105 *

ALONSO, ANDREA MARIA, lawyer; b. N.Y.C., Dec. 28, 1956; d. Manuel Daniel and Dolores (Sanchez) A. BA, St. John's U., 1978, JD, 1981. Bar: N.Y. 1982, U.S. Dist. Ct. (so. and ea. dists.) N.Y. 1982. Assoc. Morris & Duffy, N.Y.C., 1981—. Mem. Assn. of Bar of City of N.Y. (young lawyers com. 1983—, inter-Am. affairs com. 1984—), N.Y. County Lawyers Assn. Democrat. Roman Catholic. Federal civil litigation, State civil litigation, Personal injury. Office: Morris & Duffy 233 Broadway New York NY 10279

ALONSO, ANTONIO ENRIQUE, lawyer; b. Habana, Cuba, Aug. 31, 1924; came to U.S. 1959; s. Enrique and Inocencia (Avila) A.; m. Daisy Ojeda, July 20, 1949; children: Margarita, Antonio, Enrique, Jorge. Student, U. Fla., 1974-76; JD, U. Habana, Cuba, 1952; PhD, U. Habana, 1952. Bar: Fla. 1976. Pub. defendant High Ct. Las Villas, Cuba, 1946-49; atty. Provincial Gov., Cuba, 1950-52; under sec. Treasury, Cuba, 1952-54; mem. House of Reps. Congress of Cuba, 1954-58; sole practice Miami, 1976—. Author: (with others) History of the Communist Party of Cuba, 1970; Violation of Human Rights, 1962; contbr. articles to profl. jours. Mem. ABA, Fla. Bar Assn., Inter-Am. Bar Assn., Hispanic Nat. Bar Assn. Republican. Roman Catholic. Real property, General corporate, General practice. Home: 11125 SW 128th Ct Miami FL 33186 Office: 1699 Coral Way Suite 315 Miami FL 33145

ALPER, HARVEY MARTIN, lawyer; b. Bklyn., Nov. 19, 1946; s. Morris and Esther (Tanenbaum) A.; m. Judith Watkins, July 4, 1975; children: Susan Elizabeth, Benjamin Joseph. BSJM, U. Fla., 1968, JD, 1971. Bar: Fla. 1971, D.C. 1972, U.S. Dist. Ct. (mid. dist.) Fla. 1972, U.S. Ct. Appeals (5th and 11th cirs.) 1972, U.S. Supreme Ct. 1972. Asst. atty. City of Jacksonville, Fla., 1971-72; ptnr. Alper & Wack, Altamonte Springs, Fla., 1972-79, Massey, Alper & Walden, Altamonte Springs, 1979—; commr. domestice relations ct. Seminole County Cir. Ct., Fla., 1981—; adj. instr. Valencia Community Coll., Orlando, 1983—. Trustee Seminole County Law Library, Sanford, Fla., 1975—; bd. dirs. Seminole County Legal Aide Soc., Casselberry, Fla., 1975-84. Mem. ABA, Fla. Bar Assn., D.C. Bar Assn., Seminole County Bar Assn. (pres. 1981), Fla. Council Bar Assn. Pres.'s. Democrat. Avocations: stamp collecting, travel. General practice, Administrative and regulatory, General corporate. Home: 616 Hermits Trail Altamonte Springs FL 32701 Office: Massey Alper & Walden PA 112 W Citrus St Altamonte Springs FL 32701

ALPER, JOANNE FOGEL, lawyer; b. N.Y.C., Sept. 16, 1950; d. Ben R. and Florence D. (Schneider) Fogel; m. Paul Edward Alper, Aug. 4, 1973; children—Michael Ian, Brooke Lauren. B.A., Syracuse U., 1972; J.D., George Washington U., 1975. Bar: Va. 1975, U.S. Dist. Ct. (ea. dist.) Va. 1975, D.C. 1976, U.S. Dist. Ct. D.C. 1976, U.S. Ct. Appeals (4th and D.C. cirs.) 1978, U.S. Supreme Ct. 1980. Assoc. Leonard, Cohen & Gettings, Arlington, Va., 1975-79; ptnr. Cohen, Gettings, Alper & Dunham, Arlington, 1979—. Mem. Arlington County Fair Housing Bd., 1984—, mem. Commn. on Arlington's Future, 1986. Fellow Am. Acad. Matrimonial Lawyers; mem. Arlington Bar Assn. (pres. 1982-83), Va. State Bar (pres. conf. local bar assns. 1984-85 , chmn. family law sect. 1985-86), Va. Trial Lawyers Assn. (dist. gov. 1983-87, gov. at large 1987—), No. Va. Young Lawyers Assn. (pres. 1979, v.p. Arlington County 1978). Federal civil litigation, State civil litigation, Family and matrimonial. Home: 5601 Little Falls Rd Arlington VA 22207 Office: Cohen Gettings Alper & Dunham 1400 N Uhle St Arlington VA 22201

ALPERT, JONATHAN LOUIS, lawyer; b. Balt., Aug. 4, 1945; s. Leo M. and Louise (Altheimer) A.; m. Elizabeth Lapinta, June 12, 1979; children: Sara Louise, Rachel Leah. BA, Johns Hopkins U., 1966; JD, U. Md., 1969; LLM, Harvard U., 1970. Bar: Fla. 1969, Md. 1969, U.S. Supreme Ct. 1973, U.S. Ct. Appeals (11th cir.). Ptnr. Alpert & Alpert, Miami, Fla., 1970-77; judge indsl. claims State of Fla., St. Petersburg, 1977-79; assoc. prof. Stetson Law Sch., St. Petersburg, 1979-82; ptnr. Fowler & White, Tampa, Fla., 1982-86; sr. ptnr. Alpert, Josey et al, Tampa, 1986—; reporter Gov.'s Advisors on the Workers' Compensation Bill, 1979; lectr. numerous seminars, 1979-82; bd. dirs. Suncoast chpt. Am. Concrete Inst., Tampa. Pinellas Safety Council, Clearwater, Fla. Author: (with others) Florida Workmen's Compensation Law, 1978, 3d edit.; (with P. Murphy) Florida Law Damages, 1978, 2d edit., 1984, Automobile Reparations--The Law in Florida, 1980; Products Liability--The Law in Florida, 1979, Florida Real Estate, 1982, Florida Settlement and Release, 1982, Florida Motor Vehicle No Fault Law; contbr. numerous articles to profl. jours. Bd. dirs. Pinellas Safety Council, Clearwater, Fla., 1973—; chmn. coll. law admissions com. Stetson U., 1980-81; com. west Fla., Johns Hopkins U., Tampa, 1985-86. Mem. ABA, Am. Trial Lawyers Assn. (DRI Scribes), Am. Soc. Legal History, Fla. Bar Assn. (asst. sec. 1986—, co-chmn. adminstrv. law sect. 1981-82, others). Avocations: reading, video taping. Federal civil litigation, State civil litigation, Workers' compensation. Office: Alpert Josey et al Ashley Tower 100 S Ashley Dr Suite 2000 Tampa FL 33602

ALPERT, LEE KANON, lawyer. married; two sons. Student, Wayne State U., 1964-67; BS in Edn., U. So. Calif., 1971; JD, Loyola U., Los Angeles, 1972. Assoc. Newson and Wolfberg, Beverly Hills, Calif., Ruderman, Levin, Ballin, Plotkin & Graf, North Hollywood, Calif.; sole practic; prin. Mink, Alpert & Barr, Encino, Calif., 1976—; frequent lectr. on family law and litigation; past instr., lectr. bus law, Calif. State U., Northridge; mem. adv. bd. Bank of Granada Hills, 1985-86. Chairperson Citizen's Adv. Com. for Devel. of North Campus, Calif. State U., Northridge, 1984-87; bd. dirs. Calif. State U.-Northridge Athletic Assn., Valley Cable TV Inc., 1984-86, Valley Community Legal Found., 1986—; mem. Valley Coordinating Round Table, Valley Industry and Commerce Assn., Val-Pac, Town Hall Speakers Forum; past trustee Temple Ahavat Shalom, Northridge, Calif. Mem. ABA (family law div.), Am. Arbitration Assn. (panel of artitrators and mediators, named outstanding arbitrator of yr. 1984), Los Angeles County Bar Assn. (trustee 1984-85, sec. jud. evaluations com. 1983-86, spl. com. on pub. counsel 1984-85, past assoc., contbg. editor Family Law Quarterly, mem. family law sect.), San Fernando Valley Bar Assn. (pres. 1985-86, exec. com., family law exec. com., chmn. Stan Lintz community meml. award recipient selection com.). Avocations: sports, travel, residential decoration and renovation. Office: Mink Alpert & Barr 5435 Balboa Blvd Suite 211 Encino CA 91316-1560

ALPRIN, BRIAN DEAN, lawyer; b. Providence, Aug. 3, 1954; s. Jacob J. and Ruthe (Golburgh) A. BA, Yale U., 1976; JD with honors, George Washington U., 1979. Bar: R.I. 1979, U.S. Ct. Appeals (1st cir.) 1979, D.C. 1980, U.S. Dist. Ct. D.C. 1980, U.S. Ct. Appeals (D.C. cir.) 1981, U.S. Supreme Ct. 1985. Law clk. to justice R.I. Supreme Ct., Providence, 1979-80; atty. office of gen. counsel FDIC, Washington, 1980-82; from assoc. to ptnr. Metzger & Shadyac, Washington, 1982—; lectr. in field. Mem. ABA (corp., banking and bus. law sect.), R.I. Bar Assn. Banking, Antitrust, General corporate. Home: 1600 Prince St Alexandria VA 22314 Office: Metzger & Shadyac 1275 K St NW Washington DC 20005

ALSDORF, ROBERT HERMANN, lawyer; b. Ashland, Ohio, Mar. 5, 1946; s. Howard Alton and Henrietta (Bulleit) A.; m. Sarah Jane Schlick, Nov. 27, 1970; children—Matthew William, Paul August. B.A. magna cum laude, Carleton Coll., 1967; M.A. in U.S. History, Yale U., 1973, J.D., 1973. Bar: D.C. 1973, Wash. 1975, U.S. Dist. Ct. (we. dist.) Wash. 1975, U.S. Ct. Appeals (9th cir.) 1975, U.S. Dist. Ct. (ea. dist.) Wash. 1981, U.S. Supreme Ct. 1984. Trial atty. Dept. Justice, Washington, 1973-75; assoc. Culp, Dwyer, Guterson & Grader, Seattle, 1975-79; ptnr. Armstrong, Alsdorf, Bradbury & Maier P.C. and predecessor Armstrong & Alsdorf, Seattle, 1979-84, pres., 1984—; speaker continuing legal edn. seminars. Author continuing legal edn. materials. Bd. dirs. Stevens Neighborhood Housing Improvement Program, Seattle, 1979-82, pres., 1980-81. Mem. ABA (antitrust sect.), Wash. State Bar Assn. (franchise law revision subcom. corp. bus. and banking com. 1985—), Seattle-King County Bar Assn. (com. mem. young lawyers sect. 1978-80, continuing legal edn. 1984—), Phi Beta Kappa. Antitrust, Securities, Federal civil litigation. Home: 952 12th Ave E Seattle WA 98102 Office: Armstrong Alsdorf Bradbury & Maier 1300 Hoge Bldg Seattle WA 98104

ALSOBROOK, HENRY BERNIS, JR., lawyer; b. New Orleans, Nov. 9, 1930; s. Henry Bernis and Ethel (Smith) A.; m. Eugenie Loie Wilson, June 6, 1956; children—Eugenie Wilson, John Gleason, Emily Woodward. B.A., Tulane U., 1952, J.D., 1957. Bar: La. 1957. Since practiced in New Orleans; sr. partner firm Adams & Reese; past mem. faculty Tulane U. Law Sch.; bd. dirs. Def. Research Inst., 1978-81, chmn. med.-legal com., 1967-72; lectr. in field. Author articles in field; mem. editorial bds. legal jours. Chmn. dean's council Tulane U., 1983—; elder St. Charles Ave. Presbyn. Ch., New Orleans; first pres. Les Compagnons du Barreau de La Louisiane, 1985—; treas., bd. dirs. La. State Mus.; bd. dirs. New Orleans Philharm. Symphony Soc. Served with USNR, 1953. Fellow Am. Bar Found., Am. Coll. Trial Lawyers; mem. ABA (past chmn. standing com. commerce, ho. of dels. 1984—), La. Bar Assn. (pres. 1982-83), New Orleans Bar Assn., Internat. Assn. Def. Counsel (exec. com. 1982—, pres. 1986-87), Fedn. Ins. Counsel, New Orleans Assn. Def. Counsel, La. Assn. Def. Counsel (gov. 1965), La. Law Inst. (council 1963-64), Soc. Med. Assn. Counsel (charter), Soc. Hosp. Attys. (charter), AMA (hon.). Clubs: New Orleans Country, La, Avoca Duck, Lakeshore. Federal civil litigation, State civil litigation, Personal injury. Office: Adams & Reese 4500 One Shell Sq New Orleans LA 70139

ALSOP, DONALD DOUGLAS, federal judge; b. Duluth, Minn., Aug. 28, 1927; s. Robert Alvin and Mathilda (Aaseng) A.; m. Jean Lois Tweeten, Aug. 16, 1952; children—David, Marcia, Robert. B.S., U. Minn., 1950, LL.B., 1952. Bar: Minn. 1952. Practiced in New Ulm, 1952-75; mem. firm Gislason, Alsop, Dosland & Hunter, 1954-75; judge U.S. Dist. Ct. for dist. Minn., 1975—, now chief judge; Mem. Jud. Conf. Com. to Implement Criminal Justice Act, 1979—. Chmn. Brown County (Minn.) Republican Com., 1960-64, 2d Congl. Dist. Rep. Com., 1968-72, Brown County chpt. ARC, 1968-74. Served with AUS, 1945-46. Mem. ABA, Minn. Bar Assn., 8th Circuit Dist. Judges Assn. (pres. 1982-84, New Ulm C. of C. (pres. 1974-75), Order of Coif. Office: U S Dist Ct 760 Fed Bldg 316 N Robert St Saint Paul MN 55101

ALSTADT, LYNN JEFFERY, lawyer; b. Erie, Pa., Dec. 27, 1951; s. Willis Harry and Norma Margaret (Linn) A.; m. Nancy Ann Welz, Apr. 16, 1977. B.S., U. Pitts., 1973, B.A., 1973, J.D., 1976. Bar: Pa. 1976, U.S. Dist. Ct. (we. dist.) Pa. 1976, U.S. Patent and Trademark Office 1979, U.S. Ct. Appeals (3d cir.) 1980, U.S. Ct. Appeals (6th and Fed. cirs.) 1983, U.S. Supreme Ct. 1982, U.S. Ct. Internat. Trade 1983. Assoc. Blenko, Buell, Ziesenheim & Beck, Pitts., 1976-79; ptnr. Buell, Blenko, Ziesenheim & Beck, Pitts., 1979-84, Buell, Ziesenheim, Beck & Alstadt, Pitts., 1984—; dir. J.B. Res-Q, Inc., Moon Twp., Pa., 1984—, Internat. Congress on Tech., Pitts., 1983-84. Contbr. articles to legal jours. Treas. Moon Twp. Planning Agy., 1984. mem. Moon Twp. Vol. Fire Dept., 1981—. Recipient Samuel G. Wagner prize U. Pitts. Law Sch., 1976. Mem. ABA, Pa. Bar Assn., Allegheny County Bar Assn., Patent Law Assn. of Pitts. (pub. relations chmn. 1982-83), Phi Alpha Delta. Republican. Club: Rivers (Pitts.). Patent, Trademark and copyright, Trade regulation. Home: 102 Greenlea Dr Moon Township PA 15108 Office: Buell Ziesenheim Beck & Alstadt 322 Blvd of the Allies Pittsburgh PA 15222

ALTENHOFEN, CRAIG JOSEPH, lawyer; b. Seneca, Kans., Sept. 28, 1953; s. Joseph William and Elizabeth Virginia (Rettele) A.; m. Mary Bernice Floersch, July 2, 1977; children: Lisa Marie, Anthony Joseph, Jason Andrew. BA, Benedictine Coll., 1975; MA, U. Kans., 1979, JD, 1982. Bar: Kans. 1982, U.S. Dist. Ct. Kans. 1982, U.S. Ct. Appeals (10th cir.), 1982. Biologist Kans. Dept. Health and Environ., Topeka, 1977-80; ptnr. Harper, Hornbaker, Hepperly & Altenhofen, Junction City, Kans., 1982—. Mem. ABA, Kans. Bar Assn. Roman Catholic. Lodges: Kiwanis (pres. elect, Junction City 1985—), K.C. (deputy grand knight 1985—). Avocations: gardening, furniture restoring, hunting, fishing. General practice, Bankruptcy, Consumer commercial. Home: 201 South Bunker Hill Junction City KS 66441 Office: Harper Hornbaker et al 715 N Washington Junction City KS 66441

ALTER, ELEANOR BREITEL, lawyer; b. N.Y.C., Nov. 10, 1938; d. Charles David and Jeanne (Hollander) Breitel; children: Richard B. Zabel, David B. Zabel. B.A. with honors, U. Mich., 1960; postgrad., Harvard U., 1960-61; LL.B., Columbia U., 1964. Bar: N.Y. 1965. Atty., office of gen. counsel, ins. dept. State of N.Y., 1964-66; assoc. Miller & Carlson, N.Y.C., 1966-68, Marshall, Bratter, Greene, Allison & Tucker, N.Y.C., 1968-74; mem. firm Marshall, Bratter, Greene, Allison & Tucker, 1974-82, Rosenman & Colin, 1982—; adj. prof. law NYU Sch Law, 1983-87; lectr. in field. Editorial bd.: N.Y. Law Jour. Contbr. articles to profl. jours. Trustee Clients' Security Fund State of N.Y., 1983—, chmn., 1985—; bd. visitors U. Chgo. Law Sch., 1984-87. Mem. Am. Law Inst., Am. Bar Assn., N.Y. State Bar Assn., Assn. Bar City N.Y. (library com. 1978-80, com. on matrimonial law 1977-81, judiciary com. 1981-84), N.Y. County Lawyers Assn. (chmn.

com. on matrimonial law 1980-82), Am. Acad. Matrimonial Lawyers. Family and matrimonial. Office: Rosenman & Colin 575 Madison Ave New York NY 10022

ALTERMATT, PAUL BARRY, lawyer; b. New Haven, Apr. 18, 1930; s. Augustin M. Altermatt and Anna (Frances) McMahon; m. Ann Elizabeth Taylor, June 27, 1957; children: Paul A., Mark T., Thomas D., John F., Mary E. BA, Wesleyan U., Middlestown, Conn., 1951; LLB, Georgetown U., 1956. Bar: D.C. 1956, Ind. 1957, Conn. 1957. Assoc. Blacken & DeFur, Muncie, Ind., 1956-58; ptnr. Cramer & Anderson, New Milford, Conn., 1958—; ins. commr. State of Conn., Hartford, 1971-74; bd. dirs. Cologne Rev. of Am., Stamford, Conn. Pres., bd. dirs. Ellen Knowles Harcourt Found.; town atty. Sch. Bd., 1958—; bd. of govs. Tax Study Commn., 1973-74, Ins. Task Force, 1985-86. Served as capt. USMCR, 1951-56, Korea. Fellow Am. Bar Found.; mem. ABA (ho. of dels. 1985—), Conn. Bar Assn. (pres. 1986—, ho. of dels., 1983—, bd. govs.). Republican. Roman Catholic. Probate. Home: 9 S Main St New Milford CT 06776 Office: Cramer & Anderson 51 Main St New Milford CT 06776

ALTHAUSER, THOMAS CHARLES, lawyer; b. Centralia, Wash., Aug. 9, 1950; s. Stephen Rodney and Clara May (Riley) A.; m. Cheryl Lynn Hoelzer, July 28, 1973; children: Cassandra, Carolyn, Derek. BA, U. Puget Sound, 1972, JD, 1976. Bar: Wash. 1976, U.S. Dist. Ct. (we. dist.) Wash. 1976. Assoc. Olson & Pietig, Centralia, 1976-78; ptnr. Olson, Althauser & Dettmer, Centralia, 1978—; asst. atty. City of Centralia, 1976-84. Mem. Wash. State Bar Assn. (rules profl. conduct com.), Assn. Trial Lawyers Am., Wash. State Trial Lawyers Assn. Republican. Lodges: Rotary (pres. Centralia chpt. 1983-84), Elks. Avocation: sports. Personal injury, Real property, Family and matrimonial. Office: Olson Althauser & Dettmer PO Box 210 Centralia WA 98531

ALTIERI, PETER LOUIS, lawyer; b. Norwalk, Conn., Dec. 7, 1955; s. John L. and Eileen Mary (Rudden) A.; m. Sandra Shelton White, Sept. 3, 1983. AB, Georgetown U., 1977; JD, Fordham Sch. Law, 1980. Bar: N.Y. 1981, U.S. Dist. Ct. (so. dist., ea. dist.) N.Y. 1981, U.S. Dist. Ct. (no. dist. and we. dist.) N.Y. 1983, U.S. Dist. Ct. Conn. 1983, U.S. Sureme Ct. 1984, U.S. Ct. Appeals (2d. cir.) 1986. Law clk. to judge U.S. Dist. Ct., 1978; intern U.S. Attys. Office, N.Y.C., 1978; assoc. Law Firm Malcolm A. Hoffmann, N.Y.C., 1980—. Mem. ABA, N.Y.C. Bar Assn. (mem. com. Uniform State Laws, 1985—). Club: Patterson (Fairfield, Conn.). Antitrust, Federal civil litigation, General practice. Home: 155 W 68th St New York NY 10023 Office: Law Firm of Malcolm A Hoffmann 12 E 41st St New York NY 10017

ALTIMARI, FRANK X., judge; b. N.Y.C., Sept. 4, 1928; s. Antonio and Elvira (Stumpo) A.; m. Angela Scavuzzo, Sept. 23, 1951; children—Anthony, Nicholas, Vera, Michael. Student, St. Francis Coll., 1946-48, LL.D. (hon.), 1951; LL.B., Bklyn. Law Sch., 1951. Bar: N.Y. 1951, U.S. Dist. Ct. (so. and ea. dists.) N.Y. 1955, U.S. Supreme Ct. 1959, U.S. Ct. Appeals (2d cir.) 1962. Assoc. Austin & Dupont, 1951-56; ptnr. Hoffmann & Altimari, 1956-65; dist. ct. judge Nassau County, N.Y., 1966-70, acting county ct. judge, 1969-70, county ct. judge, 1970-73, adminstrv. judge, 1973, acting surrogate, 1975-77, supervising judge, 1981, adminstrv. judge, 1982; justice N.Y. State Supreme Ct., 1974-82; judge U.S. Dist. Ct. (ea. dist.) N.Y., 1982-85, U.S. Ct. Appeals (2d cir.), 1985—; faculty St. Francis Coll., 1954-64, 72-73; lectr. Hofstra Law Sch., St. John's Law Sch., Queens Coll.; also lectr., participant numerous panels, symposia. Former Westbury chmn. Am. Cancer Soc.; former dist. chmn. Cerebral Palsy Soc.; former regent, mem. speakers bur. St. Francis Coll.; former gen. counsel Westbury Bd. Edn., Lutheran High Sch. Assn., St. Francis Coll., St. Francis Monastery. Recipient Disting. Service award Alumni Assn. St. Francis Coll., 1967, 85, Pax et Bonum medal 1969, Norman F. Lent award Criminal Cts. Bar Assn., 1976, award Am. Acad. for Profl. Law Enforcement, 1981. Mem. ABA, N.Y. State Bar Assn., Nassau County Bar Assn., Jamaica Lawyers Club (past pres.). Roman Catholic. Judicial administration. Office: US Courthouse Uniondale Ave at Hempstead Turnpike Uniondale NY 11553

ALTMAN, JANE R., lawyer; b. Cambridge, Mass., Mar. 14, 1945; s. Nathan and Renee (Owlick) Rotman; m. Robert A. Altman, June 13, 1965; children: Jennifer Anne, John Scott. BA, Barnard Coll., 1966; MS, Bank Street Coll., 1967; JD, Rutgers U., 1978. Bar: N.J. 1978. Assoc. Carchman, Sochor & Carchman, Princeton, N.J., 1978-82; sole practice Skillman, N.J., 1982—; adj. prof. domestic relations law Mercer County Community Coll., West Windsor, N.J., 1986—. Advisor Womanspace, Trenton, N.J., 1979—; trustee Millhill Child and Family Devel. Ctr., 1979-83. Mem. ABA, N.J. Bar Assn. (exec. com., family law sect.), Mercer County Bar Assn. (trustee 1983—). Family and matrimonial. Office: 148 Tamarack Circle Skillman NJ 08558

ALTMAN, LOUIS, lawyer, author, educator; b. N.Y.C., Aug. 6, 1933; s. Benjamin and Jean (Zimmerman) A.; m. Sally J. Schlesinger, Dec. 26, 1955; m. Eleanor H. Silver, Oct. 30, 1966; children—Cynthia, Robert. A.B., Cornell U., 1955; LL.B., Harvard U., 1958. Bar: N.Y. 1959, Conn. 1970, Ill. 1973. Assoc. Amster & Levy, N.Y.C., 1958-60; patent atty. Sperry Rand, N.Y.C., 1960-63; chief patent csl. Gen. Time Corp., N.Y.C., 1963-67; ptnr. Altman & Reens, Stamford, Conn., 1967-72; chief patent csl. Baxter-Travenol Labs., Deerfield, Ill., 1972-76; assoc. prof. John Marshall Law Sch., 1976-79, adj. prof., 1979—; of counsel Gerlach, O'Brien & Kleinke, Chgo., 1981-83; ptnr. Laff, Whitesel, Conte & Saret, Chgo., 1983—. Author: Callmann on Unfair Competition, Trademarks & Monopolies, 4th edit., 1981; author Business Competition Law Adviser, 1983; Construction Law, 1986. Contbr. articles to legal jours. Patent, Trademark and copyright. Home: 3005 Manor Dr Northbrook IL 60062 Office: 401 N Michigan Ave Suite 2000 Chicago IL 60611

ALTMAN, MILTON HUBERT, lawyer; b. Mpls., July 18, 1917; s. Harry Edmund and Lee (Cohen) A.; m. Helen Horwitz, May 21, 1942; children—Neil, Robert, James. B.S., U. Minn., 1938, LL.B., 1947. Bar: Minn. bar 1947. Ptnr. firm Altman, Weiss & Bearmon, St. Paul, 1947-85; Mem. Minn. Gov.'s adv. com. on Constl. Revision, 1950, on Gift and Inheritance Tax Regulations, 1961-65; chmn. atty. gen.'s adv. com. on Consumer Protection, 1961-65; mem. U.S. Dist. Ct. Nominating Commn., 1979; spl. atty. Minn. Bd. Med. Examiners, 1963-75, U. Minn., 1963-75; dir. SPH Hotel Co.; Mem. nat. emergency com. Nat. Council on Crime and Delinquency, 1967-69; mem. Minn.-Wis. small bus. advisory council SBA, 1968-70; mem., v.p. Citizens' Council on Delinquency and Crime, 1968-76; bd. dirs. Correctional Service Minn., 1968-76; mem. Lawyers Com. for Civil Rights Under Law, 1965—; Chmn. Minn. Lawyers for Johnson and Humphrey, 1968. Author: Estate Planning, 1966. Bd. dirs. St. Paul Jewish Fund and Council, 1966-69, Minn. Soc. Crippled Children and Adults. Mem. Minn. Bar Assn. (chmn tax sect. 1960-62), Ramsey County Bar Assn. (exec. council 1968-71), Am. Arbitration Assn. (nat. panel arbitrators), Fgn. Policy Assn. (nat. council 1969), U. Minn. Law Sch. Alumni Assn. (dir. 1967-70), UN Assn. (nat. legacies com. 1967). Clubs: Minn. (dir. 1975-78), St. Paul Athletic. Contracts commercial, General corporate, Estate planning. Home: Galtier Plaza Apt 1702 172 E 6th St Saint Paul MN 55101 Office: 310 Cedar St Suite 200 Saint Paul MN 55101

ALTMAN, ROBERT HARRY, lawyer; b. Elmira, N.Y., Nov. 8, 1944; s. Harry and Madeline Maria (Limoncelli) A.; m. Susan C. Hecht, Aug. 18, 1968; children: Scott Robert, Jeremy Lawrence, Lee Rachel. B.A., U. Buffalo, 1966; J.D., U. Toledo, 1969. Bar: N.Y. 1970. Assoc. firm Silberfeld, Danziger & Bangser, N.Y.C., 1970-76; gen. counsel, sec. Fay's Drug Co., Inc., Liverpool, N.Y., 1976-80; partner firm Danziger, Bangser, Klipstein, Goldsmith & Greenwald, N.Y.C.; dir. Fay's Drug Co., Inc. Mem. Am. Bar Assn., N.Y. State Bar Assn. General corporate, Securities, Mergers and acquisitions. Office: 230 Park Ave New York NY 10017

ALTMAN, WILLIAM KEAN, lawyer; b. San Antonio, Feb. 18, 1944; s. Marion K. and Ruth (Nunely) A.; m. Doris E. Johnson, May 29, 1964; children: Brian, Brad, Blake. BBA, Tex. A&M U., 1965, MBA, 1967; JD, U. Tex., 1979. Bar: Tex., U.S. Dist. ct. (no. and ea. dists.) Tex., U.S. Ct. Appeals (5th and 11th cirs.), U.S. Supreme Ct. Prin., owner William K. Altman P.C., Wichita Falls, Tex., 1970—. Mem. ABA, Tex. Bar Assn., Assn. Trial Lawyers Am. (bd. of govs. 1980-83, active coms. and sects.), Tex. Trial Lawyers Assn. (assoc. bd. dirs. 1977-78, bd. dirs. 1978—, active various coms. and sect.). Democrat. Baptist. Personal injury, Insurance, Workers' compensation. Office: 500 Oil and Gas Bldg Wichita Falls TX 76301

ALUISE, TIMOTHY JOHN, lawyer; b. Hackensack, N.J., Apr. 9, 1956; s. Ralph Angelo and Regina Marie (DeMarco) A.; m. Amy S. Friend, Sept. 27, 1986. BA, Georgetown U., 1977; JD, U. Notre Dame, 1980. Bar: D.C. 1980, U.S. Ct. Appeals (D.C. cir.) 1981. Assoc. Brownstein, Zeidman & Schomer, Washington, 1980-85, Hale & Dorr, Washington, 1985—. Vol. Nat. Housing Law Project, Washington, 1985-86; atty. Community for Creative Non-Violence, Washington, 1986. Mem. ABA, D.C. Bar Assn. Democrat. Real property, Landlord-tenant, Legislative. Home: 3801 W St NW Washington DC 20007 Office: Hale & Dorr 1455 Pennsylvania Ave NW Washington DC 20004

ALUSHIN, MICHAEL STEPHEN, lawyer; b. Cleve., Aug. 13, 1947; s. Steve and Ann Marie (Matich) A.; m. Barbara Faye Ballantine, June 4, 1971 (div. Feb. 1976); m. Barbara Lynne Sirvetz, Apr. 2, 1983; 1 child, Gregory. BA, Oberlin Coll., 1969; JD, Harvard U., 1972. Bar: Pa. 1972, U.S. Ct. Appeals (9th cir.) 1974, U.S. Ct. Appeals (3d cir.) 1975, U.S. Dist. Ct. (no. dist.) Ohio 1978, U.S. Supreme Ct. 1980, D.C. 1983. Asst. atty. gen. Pa. Dept. Environ. Resources, Harrisburg, 1972-80; sr. environ. fellow EPA, Washington, 1980-81, dir. spl. programs, 1981-82, assoc. enforcement counsel for air, 1982—. Mem. ABA, Air Pollution Control Assn. Methodist. Avocations: music, hiking. Environment, Federal civil litigation. Home: 6605 44th Ave University Park MD 20782 Office: US EPA 401 M St SW Washington DC 20460

ALVARADO, RICARDO RAPHAEL, corporate executive, lawyer; b. Washington, Mar. 29, 1927; s. Alfonso and Beatrice (Raphael) A.; m. Rita Logue, Feb. 14, 1948; children—Donna, Bonita, Ricardo R. (dec.) Rita, Susan, Peter, Christina. B.S., U.S. Mcht. Marine Acad., 1948; J.D., Am. U., 1953; LL.M., Georgetown U., 1963; M.A., George Washington U., 1976. Bar: Va. 1953. Commd. 2d lt. U.S. Air Force, 1951, advanced through grades to col., 1969, dep. dir. Congl. liason Office Sec. Def., 1970-72; mgr. govt. relations Lockheed Corp., Washington, 1972-73, corp. dir. govt. affairs, 1973-82; v.p. The Signal Cos., Washington, 1982-85, Allied-Signal Inc., 1985—. Decorated Legion of Merit with cluster; recipient Outstanding Alumnus Profl. Achievement award U.S. Merchant Marine Acad., 1983. Mem. Air Force Assn. (life). Clubs: Aero; Army Navy (bd. dirs. 1975-76), Internat. (Washington); Army Navy Country (Arlington, Va.), City. Government contracts and claims, Legislative, General corporate. Home: 6108 Fort Hunt Rd Alexandria VA 22307 Office: 1001 Pennsylvania Ave NW Suite 700 Washington DC 20004

ALVAREZ, EDNA R. S., lawyer; b. Larchmont, N.Y., Mar. 16, 1939; d. Gustave and Edna (Rosenfeld) Simons; children: Anica, Amira. Student, Skidmore Coll., 1957-59; cert. in European studies, Inst. Am. U., France, 1960; AB, Calif. State U., San Francisco, 1961; JD, U. Wash., 1966. Bar: Conn. 1967, U.S. Dist. Ct. Conn. 1968, U.S. Tax Ct. 1971, U.S. Supreme Ct. 1971, Calif. 1973, U.S. Dist. Ct. Calif. 1974. Sr. assoc. Bergman, Horowitz, Reynolds & DeSarbo, New Haven, 1967-72; of counsel A. Reynolds Gordon, Bridgeport, Conn., 1973; sole practice Los Angeles, 1975—; instr. UCLA Extension, 1976—, UCLA Law Sch., 1979-81, U. So. Calif. Law Ctr., 1972, U. So. Calif. Bus. Sch., 1973-75, U. So. Calif. Sch. Continuing Edn., 1974; mem. Calif. Jud. Council Adv. Com. on Legal Forms, 1980-82, Los Angeles City Atty. Office Adv. Com., 1982; lectr. in field. Contbr. articles to profl. jours. Mem. adv. council-planned giving com. Am. Cancer Soc. San Fernando Valley unit, 1981-83; mem. adv. com. Arthritis Found. So. Calif., 1976-79; mem. adv. council Nat. Humanities Services Western Ctr. NEH, 1974-75; mem. legal com. Los Angeles Music Ctr. Found.; mem. cultural and fine arts adv. commn. Los Angeles Olympics Organizing Com., 1982; bd. dirs. Los Angeles Fed. Feminist Credit Union, 1976-77. Am. Coll. Probate Counsel fellow, 1984—; Wash. Sch. Law William Wallace Wilshire Meml. scholar, Mortar Bd. Grad. Alumnae scholar, 1964-65, H. Watson scholar, Carkeek scholar, 1965-66. Mem. ABA, ACLU (life), Nat. Assn. Women Lawyers, Nat. Assn. Latino Elected and Appointed Officials (founding mem.), Conn. Bar Assn., State Bar of Calif., Calif. Women Lawyers Assn. (incorporator, founder), C. of C. Los Angeles west, Nat. Audubon Soc. Democrat. Avocations: poetry, bird watching. Estate planning, Probate, Estate taxation. Office: 10850 Wilshire Blvd 4th floor Los Angeles CA 90024

ALVERSON, LUTHER, state superior court judge; b. Atlanta, Aug. 13, 1907; s. James Carroll and Minnie (Fleming) A.; m. Ruth Long, Mar. 21, 1942; children: Elizabeth Jacksonia, Patricia Ruth. Student, Emory U., 1929, Atlanta Law Sch., 1941. Bar: Ga. 1941. Assoc. Hooper, Hooper & Miller, Atlanta, 1940-43; ptnr. Woodruff, Alverson & O'Neil, Atlanta, 1943-48; mem. legis. office Ga. Ho. of Reps., Atlanta, 1947-52; criminal ct. judge Fulton County, Atlanta, 1952-56, superior ct. judge, 1956—. Chmn. Joint Info. Service Psychiatric and Mental Health, 1970-76. Served as 1st lt. U.S. Army, 1943-45. Named Outstanding Trial Judge, Am. Trial Lawyers Assn., 1974. Fellow Internat. Acad. Trial Judges (sec., treas. 1977, pres.1979); mem. Council Superior Ct. Judges (pres. 1968), ABA, Ga. Bar Assn., Atlanta BAr Assn., Nat. Assn. Mental Health (pres., chmn. bd. 1957-59, regular v.p.), Ga. Assn. for Mental Health (pres.). Democrat. Baptist. Club: Atlanta Lawyers. Lodge: Masons. Avocation: golf. Judicial administration. Home: 3635 Rembrandt Rd NW Atlanta GA 30327 Office: Fulton Superior County Ct 136 Pryor St SW Room 205 Atlanta GA 30303

AMABILE, JOHN LOUIS, lawyer; b. N.Y.C., Oct. 13, 1934; s. John A. and Rose (Singer) A.; m. Christine M. Leary, Nov. 23, 1963; children—Tracy Ann, John Christopher. B.S. cum laude, Coll. Holy Cross, 1956; LL.B., St. John's Sch. Law, 1959. Bar: N.Y. 1959, U.S. Dist. Ct. (so. and ea. dists.) N.Y. 1961, U.S. Supreme Ct. 1964, U.S. Ct. Claims 1964, U.S. Ct. Appeals (2d cir.) 1970, U.S. Tax Ct. 1984, U.S. Ct. Appeals (9th cir.) 1984. Assoc., Law Office of Allen Taylor, N.Y.C., 1959-62; assoc. Schwartz & Frohlich, N.Y.C., 1963-69, ptnr., 1970; ptnr. Summit, Rovins & Feldesman (and predecessor firms), N.Y.C., 1971—; co-chmn. ann. seminar Practising Law Inst. Regional commr. Am. Youth Soccer Orgn., Chappaqua, N.Y., 1975-84 ; mem. New Castle Recreation and Parks Commn., 1984—, chairperson, 1987—. Mem. ABA, N.Y. State Bar Assn., Assn. Bar City N.Y. (mem. com. on state legislation 1971-78, chmn. 1975-78, mem. com. of grievances 1979-80, mem. appellate div. disciplinary com. 1980-85, 87—), Fed. Bar Council. Democrat. Roman Catholic. Clubs: Mt. Kisco (N.Y.) Country. Articles editor St. John Law Rev. 1958-59. Federal civil litigation, State civil litigation. Home: 73 Westorchard Rd Chappaqua NY 10514 Office: 445 Park Ave New York NY 10022

AMADEO, NATIAL SALVATORE, lawyer; b. Jersey City, N.J., Oct. 2, 1955; s. Nataile Michael and Gussie (Calato) A.; m. Jane Marie Drafke, Aug. 16, 1980; children:—Nataile, Anthony, Amalia. A.B., U. Notre Dame, 1977; J.D., Duke U., 1980. Bar: N.J. 1980, Ill. 1981. Assoc. Arthur F. Lobbe, Jersey City, 1981-82; ptnr. Amadeo & Miller, Jersey City, 1982—. Officer bd. dirs. Hudson unit Assn. Retarded Citizens, Jersey City, 1983—; bd. dirs. N.J. Youth Correctional Facility, 1983—. Mem. Hudson C. of C. Republican. Roman Catholic. Lodge: Moose. State civil litigation, Family and matrimonial, Personal injury. Home: 28 E 47th St Bayonne NJ 07002 Office: Amadeo & Miller 1767 Kennedy Blvd Jersey City NJ 07305

AMAN, ALFRED CHARLES, JR., law educator; b. Rochester, N.Y., July 7, 1945; s. Alfred Charles, Sr. and Jeannette Mary (Czebatul) A.; m. Carol Jane Greenhouse, Sept. 23, 1976. A.B., U. Rochester, 1967; J.D., U. Chgo., 1970. Bar: D.C. 1971, Ga. 1972, N.Y. 1980. Law clk. U.S. Ct. Appeals, Atlanta, 1970-72; atty. Sutherland, Asbill & Brennan, Atlanta, 1972-75, Washington, 1975-77; assoc. prof. law Cornell U. Law Sch., Ithaca, N.Y., 1977-82, prof. law, 1982—; cons. U.S. Adminstrv. Conf., Washington, 1978-80, 86—; trustee U. Rochester, 1980—; vis. fellow Wolfson Coll., Cambridge U., 1983-84. Author: Energy and Natural Resources, 1983. Chmn. Ithaca Bd. Zoning Appeals, 1980-82. Mem. ABA, Am. Assn. Law Schs., D.C. Bar Assn., Ga. Bar Assn., N.Y. Bar Assn., Phi Beta Kappa. Democrat. Avocations: music; jazz drumming; piano; composition and arranging. Home: 404 Highland Rd Ithaca NY 14850 Office: Cornell U Law Sch Myron Taylor Hall Ithaca NY 14850 *

AMAN, GEORGE MATTHIAS, III, lawyer; b. Wayne, Pa., Mar. 2, 1930; s. George Matthias and Emily (Kalbach) A.; m. Ellen McMillan, June 20, 1959; children: James E., Catherine E., Peter T. A.B., Princeton U., 1952; LL.B., Harvard U., 1957. Bar: Pa. 1958. Assoc. Townsend Elliot & Munson, Phila., 1960-65; ptnr. Morgan Lewis & Bockius, Phila., 1965—. Commr. Radnor Twp., Pa., 1976-80, 86—, planning commr., 1981-86; pres. bd. trustees Wayne Presbyn. Ch., Pa., 1981-84. Served to 1st lt. U.S. Army, 1952-54. Mem. ABA, Pa. Mcpl. Authorities Assn., Phila. Regional Mcpl. Fin. Officers Assn. (dir. 1983—), Am. Law Inst. Republican. Clubs: Merion Cricket (Haverford, Pa.); Princeton (Phila.) (dir 1977-79, treas. 1985-86). General corporate, Local government, Municipal bonds. Home: 425 Darby Paoli Rd Wayne PA 19087 Office: Morgan Lewis & Bockius One Logan Sq Philadelphia PA 19103

AMARAL, MARY ELLEN, lawyer; b. Kenosha, Wis., Aug. 5, 1946; s. Nestor Johnson and Mary Louise (Parker) Thompson; m. Donald Earl Mielke, Apr. 27, 1968 (div. Jan. 1978); m. Charles Patrick Amaral, Aug. 31, 1980; children—Maura Patricia, Brian Patrick. B.A. in Journalism, U. Mich., 1968; postgrad. Temple U., 1968-69; M.S. in Mgmt., Pace U., 1979; J.D., U. Denver, 1973. Bar: Colo. 1974. With Mountain Bell, Denver, 1970-76; with regulatory matters AT&T, N.Y.C., 1976-79, regulatory matters dist. mgr., 1981-83, regional atty. govt. relations, Denver, 1983—; senate banking-internat. fin. minority staff mem. Conf. Bd. Congl. Asst., Washington, 1980. Mem. Gotham Bus and Profl. Women (legis. chmn. 1978-80, Outstanding Profl. Woman of Yr. 1982), ABA, Denver Bar Assn., Colo. Bar Assn., Colo. Women's Bar Assn., Alliance Profl. Women. Lodge: Zonta (N.Y. chpt. pres. 1983, Denver chpt. chmn. internat. and community relations com. 1984-86, 2d v.p. membership com. 1986-87). Legislative, Administrative and regulatory. Home: 1725 Fillmore Ct Louisville CO 80027 Office: AT&T 1331 17th St Suite 601 Denver CO 80202

AMBLER, THOMAS WILSON, lawyer; b. Allentown, Pa., Dec. 19, 1953; s. Franklin Marple and L. Dorethy (Guckes) A.; m. Martha Stewart Broadfoot, May 29, 1982. BA, SUNY, Potsdam, 1975; JD, U. Pitts., 1978. Bar: Pa. 1978, D.C. 1982, Ga. 1985, U.S. Dist. Ct. (no. dist.) Ga. 1986. Atty. real estate So. Ry. Co., Washington, 1978-82; atty. Norfolk So. Corp., Washington, 1981-84; solicitor Norfolk So. Corp., Atlanta, 1984-86, asst. gen. solicitor, 1986—. Mem. Arlington County Rep. Com., Va., 1979-84; 2d vice chmn. Young Reps., Arlington, 1983. Mem. ABA (conveyancing sect., probate and real estate sect.), Pa. Bar Assn., D.C. Bar Assn., Ga. Bar Assn. Presbyterian. Real property, Contracts commercial, Landlord-tenant. Office: Norfolk So Corp One Commercial Pl Norfolk VA 23510

AMBRISTER, JOHN CHARLES, lawyer; b. Norman, Okla., June 21, 1944; s. Charles Alexander and Rebecca Louise (Scott) A.; divorced; 1 child, Charles Scott; m. Peyron Ernette Miller, Sept. 3, 1977. B.A., Tulsa U., 1962-66; J.D., Washington U., St. Louis, 1969. Bar: Mo. 1969, Ill. 1978. Sole practice St. Louis, 1969-73; corp. atty. Sargent Welch, Skokie, Ill., 1973-74; corp. counsel, asst. sec. Bell and Howell, Chgo., 1974-80; gen. counsel, sec. Dayton Walther, Ohio, 1981; sr. exec. v.p., gen. counsel, sec. AM Internat., Chgo., 1981—. Mem. ABA, Ill. Bar Assn., Mo. Bar Assn., Am. Soc. Corp. Secs. Avocation: golf. General corporate. Home: 1170 Polo Dr Lake Forest IL 60045 Office: AM Internat Inc 333 W Wacker Dr Suite 900 Chicago IL 60606

AMBROSE, MYLES JOSEPH, lawyer; b. N.Y.C., July 21, 1926; s. Arthur P. and Anna (Campbell) A.; m. Elaine Miller, June 26, 1948 (dec. Sept. 1975); children: Myles Joseph, Kathleen Anne, Kevin Arthur, Elise Mary, Nora Jeanne Ambrose Baker, Christopher Miller; m. Joan Fitzpatrick, June 24, 1978. Grad., New Hampton Sch., N.H., 1944; B.B.A., Manhattan Coll., 1948, LL.D. (hon.), 1972; J.D., N.Y. Law Sch., 1952. Bar: N.Y. 1952, U.S. Supreme Ct. 1969, D.C. 1973, U.S. Ct. Appeals (fed. cir.) 1970, U.S. Ct. Internat. Trade 1970, D.C. Ct. Appeals 1973. Personnel mgr. Devenco, Inc., 1948-49, 51-54; adminstrv. asst. U.S. atty. So. dist., N.Y., 1954-57; instr. econs. and indsl. relations Manhattan Coll., 1955-57; asst. to sec. U.S. Treasury, 1957-60; exec. dir. Waterfront Commn. of N.Y. Harbor, 1960-63; pvt. practice law N.Y.C., 1963-69; chief counsel N.Y. State Joint Legislative Com. for Study Alcoholic Beverage Control Law, 1963-65; U.S. commr. customs Washington, 1969-72, spl. cons. to Pres., spl. asst. atty. gen., 1972-73; mem. firm Spear & Hill, 1973-75, Ambrose and Casselman, P.C., 1975-79; now mem. firm O'Connor & Hannan, Washington.; U.S. observer 13th session UN Commn. on Narcotics, Geneva, Switzerland, 1958; chmn. U.S. delegation 27th Gen. Assembly, Internat. Criminal Police Orgn., London, 1958, 28th Extraordinary Gen. Assembly, Paris, 1959; U.S. observer 29th Gen. Assembly, Washington, 1960; mem. U.S. delegation, Mexico City, 1969, Brussels, 1970, Ottawa, 1971, Frankfurt, 1972; chmn. U.S.-Mexico Conf. on Narcotics, Washington, 1960, mem. confs., Washington and; Mexico City, 1969, 70, 71, 72; chmn. U.S.-Canadian-Mexican Conf. on Customs Procedures, San Clemente, Calif., 1970; chmn. U.S. del. Customs Cooperation Council, Brussels, 1970; chmn., Vienna, 1971, U.S.-European Customs Conf. Narcotics, Paris and; Vienna, 1971; hon. consul Principality of Monaco, Washington, 1973—. Author: Primer on Customs Law. Bd. dirs. Daytop Village.; vice chmn. Reagan-Bush Inaugural Com. Recipient Presdl. Mgmt. Improvement certificate Pres. Nixon, 1970, Sec. Treasury Exceptional Service award, 1970; decorated knight comdr. Order Merit Italian Republic; recipient Distinguished Alumnus award N.Y. Law Sch., 1973, Alumni award for pub. service Manhattan Coll., 1972. Fellow Am. Bar Found.; mem. ABA (past chmn. standing com. on custom law), Assn. Bar City N.Y., Friendly Sons of St. Patrick, Alpha Sigma Beta, Phi Alpha Delta (hon.). Republican. Roman Catholic. Clubs: Metropolitan (N.Y.C.); University, Army-Navy (Washington). Criminal, Immigration, naturalization, and customs, Federal civil litigation. Home: 3101 Ballyeagna PO Box 801 Marshall VA 22115 Office: O'Connor & Hannan 1919 Pennsylvania Ave NW Suite 800 Washington DC 20006

AMDAHL, DOUGLAS KENNETH, justice Minnesota Supreme Court; b. Mabel, Minn., Jan. 23, 1919. B.B.A., U. Minn., 1945; J.D. summa cum laude, William Mitchell Coll. Law, 1951. Bar: Minn. 1951, Fed. Dist. Ct. 1952. Ptnr. Amdahl & Scott, Mpls., 1951-55; asst. county atty. Hennepin County, Minn., 1955-61; judge Mcpl. Ct., Mpls., 1961-62, Dist. Ct. 4th Dist., Minn., 1962-80; chief judge Dist. Ct. 4th Dist., 1973-75; assoc. justice Minn. Supreme Ct., 1980-81, chief justice, 1981—; asst. registrar, then registrar Mpls. Coll. Law, 1948-55; prof. law William Mitchell Coll. Law, 1951-65; moot ct. instr. U. Minn.; faculty mem. and advisor Nat. Coll. State Judiciary; mem. Nat. Bd. Trial Advocacy. Mem. ABA, Minn., Hennepin County bar assns., Internat. Acad. Trial Judges, State Dist. Ct. Judges Assn. (pres. 1976-77). Judicial administration. Home: 2322 W 53d St Minneapolis MN 55155 Office: Minn Supreme Ct 230 State Capitol Saint Paul MN 55155

AMDUR, ARTHUR R., lawyer; b. Houston, Jan. 19, 1946; s. Paul S. and Florence Amdur; m. Dora B.; children—Josh, Jonny, Shira. B.A., 1967; J.D., 1970; LL.M., 1974. Bar: Tex. 1970, D.C. 1974. Assoc. Black, Hebinck, Hargrove & Clark, Houston, 1970-72, Cramer, Haber & Becker, Washington, 1973-76; asst. U.S. atty, Houston, 1976-82; sole practice, Houston, 1982—; adj. prof. law South Tex. Coll. Law, Houston. Bd. dirs. YMCA Internat. Refugee Ctr., 1985—; spl. asst. to gen. counsel Republican Nat. Com., Washington, 1974. Named Adj. Law Prof. of Yr., South Tex. Coll. Law, 1983. Mem. Fed. Bar Assn. (pres. 1981), Am. Immigration Lawyers Assn. Jewish. Club: Georgetown U. Alumni (pres. 1984) (Houston). Immigration, naturalization, and customs, Private international, Federal civil litigation. Office: 1919 Smith St Suite 930 Houston TX 77002

AMDUR, MARTIN BENNETT, lawyer; b. N.Y.C., Aug. 19, 1942; s. Charles and Helen (Freedman) A.; m. Shirley Bell, May 25, 1975; children—Richard J., Stephen B. A.B., Cornell U., 1964; LL.B., Yale U., 1967; LL.M. in Taxation, NYU, 1968. Bar: N.Y. 1968, U.S. Tax Ct. 1970, U.S. Dist. Ct. (so. and ea. dists.) N.Y. 1971. With Weil, Gotshal & Manges, N.Y.C., 1968—, ptnr., 1975—. Mem. ABA, N.Y. State Bar Assn. (mem. exec. com.), Assn. Bar City N.Y., Internat. Fiscal Assn. Corporate taxation, Personal income taxation. Home: 28 Meadow Rd Scarsdale NY 10583 Office: Weil Gotshal & Manges 767 Fifth Ave New York NY 10153

AMDURSKY, ROBERT SIDNEY, lawyer, law educator; b. Syracuse, N.Y., July 7, 1937; s. Leonard H. and Sonya R. (Ross) Am.; m. Audrey S. Gertsman, May 27, 1964; children: Richard H., Eric J. B.A. with honors, Cornell U., 1959; J.D. cum laude, Harvard U., 1962. Bar: N.Y. 1962, U.S. Supreme Ct. 1974, D.C. 1975. Confidential law clk. N.Y. State Appellate Div., Rochester, 1962-63; ptnr. Amdursky & Amdursky, Oswego, N.Y.,

1963-70; dep. chmn., counsel State N.Y. Mortgage Agy., N.Y.C., 1970-72; ptnr. Sykes, Galloway & Dikeman, N.Y.C., 1972-76, Willkie Farr & Gallagher, N.Y.C., 1976—; adj. prof. law NYU Law Sch., N.Y.C., 1981—; mem. faculty U. Buffalo Law Sch., 1963-64, Syracuse U. Law Sch., N.Y., 1965-69; mem. N.Y. State Commn. on Urban Devel. Corp. and Other Financing Agys., 1975-76; mem. adv. panel N.Y. State Legis. Commn., 1979; mem. Gov.'s Commn. on Hazardous Waste Disposal, 1979-80; mem. adv. commn. on revision of state and local fin. laws N.Y. State Comptroller, 1987—; cons. Acad. for Ednl. Devel., 1971-72. Mem. editorial adv. bd. Housing Devel. Reporter, 1981-82; co-author: State and Local Government Debt Financing, 1985; contbr. articles to profl. jours. Counsel N.Y. State Joint Legis. Com. on Housing and Urban Devel., Albany, 1966-70; asst. counsel com. health, housing and social services N.Y. State Constl. Conv., Albany, 1967; assoc. counsel to majority leader N.Y. State Senate, Albany, 1970, spl. counsel, 1971-72, legal cons., 1977-79; mem. adv. commn. on rev. of state and local fin. laws to N.Y. State Comptroller, 1987—. Mem. ABA (chmn. subcom on mcpl. and govtl. obligations of com. on fed. regulation of securities 1981—), N.Y.C. Bar Assn., N.Y. State Bar Assn., Am. Law Inst., Practising Law Inst. (chmn. Annual Inst. Mcpl. Law 1980—). Clubs: University, Harvard (N.Y.C.). Municipal Bonds. Home: 6 Glen Dr Harrison NY 10528 Office: Willkie Farr & Gallagher 153 E 53d St New York NY 10022

AMELIO, LAURA LANE, lawyer; b. Akron, Ohio, Sept. 11, 1955; d. William George and Alice Joan (Beckett) Lane; m. Gary Alan Amelio, Nov. 13, 1982. BA, U. Pitts., 1977, JD, 1980. Bar: Pa. 1980, U.S. Dist. Ct. (we. dist.) Pa. 1980, U.S. Ct. Appeals (3rd cir.) 1980. Law clk. to presiding justice Commonwealth Ct. Pa., Pitts., 1980-82; assoc. Sullivan & Worcester, Pitts., 1982-84; atty. and asst. sec. Duquesne Light Co., Pitts., 1984—. Mem. Allegheny County Bar Assn. Democrat. Roman Catholic. General corporate, Securities, Public utilities. Office: Duquesne Light Co One Oxford Centre 30-3 Pittsburgh PA 15279

AMEND, JAMES MICHAEL, lawyer; b. Chgo., July 19, 1942; s. Nathan and Edith (Greenberg) A.; m. Sheila Rae Cohen, Apr. 4, 1971; children: Allison, Anthony. BSE, U. Mich., 1964, JD, 1967. Bar: Ill. 1968, U.S. Dist. Ct. (no. dist.) Ill. 1968, U.S. Ct. Appeals (7th cir.) 1969, U.S. Supreme Ct. 1970, U.S. Ct. Appeals (9th cir.) 1985. Ptnr. Kirkland & Ellis, Chgo., 1968—. Editor U. Mich. Law Rev., 1966; author: Intellectual Property Law, 1982. Chmn. Chgo. Lawyers Com. for Civil Rights Under Law, 1985—. Fulbright scholar, 1967. Mem. ABA, U.S. Trademark Assn. Jewish. Clubs: Saddle and Cycle, Mid-Am. (Chgo.). Avocations: tennis, running. Trademark and copyright, Federal civil litigation, Patent. Office: Kirkland & Ellis 200 E Randolph Dr Chicago IL 60601

AMENTO, CARL JOSEPH, lawyer; b. New Haven, Jan. 14, 1950; s. Carmine and Sophia Virginia (Golia) A.; m. Mary-Ellen Saracco, Jan. 26, 1980; children: Nicholas Carmine, Sarah Elaine. BA cum laude, Yale U., 1972; M in Arts and Teaching, Harvard U., 1973; JD cum laude, Boston Coll. Law Sch., 1977. Bar: Mass. 1977, Conn. 1978, D.C. 1981. Law clk. to presiding justice Mass. Superior Ct., Boston, 1977-78; assoc. Bulkeley, Richardson & Gelinas, Springfield, Mass., 1978-81, Tyler, Cooper & Alcorn, New Haven, 1981-84; ptnr. Amento, Kopetz & DiAngelo, New Haven, 1984—; asst. atty. Town of Hamden, Conn., 1984-85; instr. bus. law Quinnipiac Coll., Hamden, 1985. Pres. adv. council Hamden Regional Adult Day Care, 1986-87. Mem. ABA, Conn. Bar Assn., New Haven County Bar Assn., Hamden C. of C. (pres. 1986—). Democrat. Roman Catholic. Club: Unitas (Hamden) (sec. 1986—). General practice, Personal injury, State civil litigation. Home: 273 Highland Ave Hamden CT 06518 Office: Amento Kopetz & DiAngelo 41 Trumbull St New Haven CT 06510

AMERIKANER, STEVEN ALBERT, lawyer; b. N.Y.C., Sept. 28, 1947; s. Alfred and Gudula H. (Einstein) A.; m. Phyllis Gendel, May 29, 1977; children: David, Katherine. AB, Harvard U., 1969, JD, 1973. Bar: Calif. 1973. Asst. atty. City of Los Angeles, 1975-81; of counsel Cox, Castle & Nicholson, Los Angeles, 1981-82; city atty. City of Santa Barbara, Calif., 1982—. Mem. Calif. Bar Assn., Santa Barbara County Bar Assn. (bd. dirs.), League Calif. Cities Atty. Dept. Local government. Office: Office City Atty 735 Anacapa St Santa Barbara CA 93101

AMES, EDWARD ALMER, III, lawyer; b. Nassawadox, Va., Feb. 26, 1939; s. E. Almer Jr. and Elizabeth (Melson) A.; m. Elizabeth Henry Mumford, Sept. 9, 1967; children: Elizabeth Kenly, Katherine Henry, Edward A. IV. BA, Washington & Lee U., Lexington, Va., 1961; JD, Washington & Lee U., 1964. Bar: Va. 1964, U.S. Dist. Ct. (ea. dist.) Va. 1964. Assoc. E. Almer Ames. Jr., Onancock, Va., 1964; ptnr. Ames & Ames, Onancock, 1965—; bd. dirs. First Va. Bank of Tidewater, Norfolk. Trustee Northampton-Accomack Meml. Hosp., Nassawadox, 1975-87, pres.1983-85; chmn. Accomack County Welfare Bd., 1976-84. Served as 1st lt. JAGC USAR, 1964-70. Mem. ABA, Va. Bar Assn., Va. Trial Lawyers Assn., Accomack County Bar Assn. (pres. 1977-79), Phi Delta Phi. Presbyterian. Club: Eastern Shore Yacht & Country (Melfa, Va.). Lodge: Rotary. Real property, Probate, General practice. Home: Fairfield Onancock VA 23417 Office: PO Box 177 Onancock VA 23417

AMES, JAMES BARR, lawyer; b. Wayland, Mass., Apr. 20, 1911; s. Richard and Dorothy (Abbott) A.; m. Mary Ogden Adams, June 14, 1941 (dec. 1967); children: Elizabeth Bigelow (dec.), Richard, Charles Cabell; m. Suzannah Ayer Parker, Oct. 10, 1969. AB, Harvard U., 1932, JD magna cum laude, 1936. Bar: Mass. 1936. Assoc. Ropes & Gray, Boston, 1936-41, ptnr., 1947-83; of counsel Ropes & Gray, 1983—. Author: Boston: A City Upon a Hill, 1980; co-author: How to Live and Die with Massachusetts Probate, 1982. Pres. Hosp. Planning for Greater Boston Inc., 1965-71; pres. Mt. Auburn Hosp., Cambridge, 1953-59, Boston Athenaeum, 1961-81, Mass. Hist. Soc., 1975-78; trustee Boston Athenaeum; hon. trustee, past treas. Mus. Fine Arts; chmn. Animal Rescue League Boston, 1958-70, Greater Boston Charitable Trust, 1970-73; trustee Buckingham Sch., Cambridge, 1959-62; bd. dirs. Fiduciary Trust Co., Boston, 1954-87. Served to col. USAF, 1942-45. Decorated Legion of Merit, Bronze Star with oak leaf cluster. Fellow Am. Bar Found., Am. Coll. Probate Counsel (past state chmn.); mem. Am. Law Inst., ABA, Boston Bar Assn. (past chmn. probate com.), Cambridge Bar Assn. (past pres.), Phi Beta Kappa (past pres.). Unitarian. Clubs: Somerset, Tavern, Cohasset Yacht. Probate, Estate taxation, Estate planning. Home: 12 Browning Ln Lincoln MA 01773 Office: 225 Franklin St Boston MA 02110

AMES, JOHN WILLIAM, lawyer; b. Scranton, Pa., Feb. 2, 1946; s. John William and Eleanor Ames; m. Janet Spalding, Sept. 2, 1967; children: Christina, Caroline, John Paul, Jeffrey. BA in Internat. Affairs with honors, U. Louisville, 1967, JD magna cum laude, 1973. Bar: Ky. 1974, U.S. Dist. Ct. (we. and ea. dists.) Ky. Law clk. to presiding justice 1971-73; ptnr. Handmaker, Weber, Meyer & Rose, Goldberg & Simpson P.S.C., Louisville; lectr. in field. Past v.p. UN Assn. Louisville. Served to capt. USMC, 1967-71, Vietnam. Mem. ABA (executory contracts on chpt. 11 subcom. corp. banking and bus, law sect.), Ky. Bar Assn. (comml. banking com.), Louisville Bar Assn. (chmn. bankruptcy com.), Comml. Law League, Louisville Alumni Assn. (Outstanding Alumni award 1980, pres. 1983), Pi Sigma Alpha, Alpha Phi Omega, Phi Eta Sigma, Omicron Delta Kappa, Woodstock Soc., Phi Kappa Phi. Democrat. Roman Catholic. Bankruptcy. Home: 3715 Edmond Ln Louisville KY 40207 Office: Goldberg & Simpson 2800 1st Nat Tower Louisville KY 40202

AMES, MARC L., lawyer; b. Bklyn., Mar. 14, 1943; s. Arthur L. and Ray (Sardas) A.; m. Eileen, July 12, 1970; J.D., Bklyn. Law Sch., 1967; LL.M., NYU, 1968. Bar: N.Y. 1967, U.S. Dist. Ct. (ea. and so. dist.) N.Y. 1973, U.S. Ct. Appeals (2nd cir.) 1973, U.S. Supreme Ct. 1973, U.S. Ct. Appeals (3rd cir.) 1982; cert. arbitrator U.S. Dist. Ct. (ea. dist.) N.Y. Mem. faculty L.I. U., 1968-69, N.Y. C. Community Coll., 1969-70; practice, 1967—, now sole practice, N.Y.C.; cons. disability retirement and pensions; arbitrator Am. Arbitration Assn. Recipient cert. appreciation N.Y. State Trial Lawyers, commendation for disting. service as arbitrator. Mem. N.Y. State Trial Lawyers Assn., N.Y.C. Trial Lawyers Assn., N.Y. County Lawyers, N.Y. State Bar Assn., N.Y. Social Security Bar Assn., Electronic Technol. Soc. N.J. Inc. Contbr. articles to various publs.; patentee auto mirror. Disability matters, Personal injury, Labor. Office: 225 Broadway Suite 3005 New York NY 10007

AMES, STUART D., lawyer; b. Newark, Oct. 18, 1941; s. Martin and Helen (Fishler) A.; m. Frances J., July 7, 1963 (div. 1984); children—David, Jessica; m. Sandra Winters, 1984. B.S. in Acctg., Fairleigh Dickinson U., 1963; J.D., Rutgers U., 1966. Bar: N.J. 1966, N.Y. 1967, Fla. 1980. Assoc. Weil, Gotshal & Manges, N.Y.C., 1966-74, ptnr., 1974—; resident ptnr. Weil, Gotshal & Manges, Miami, Fla. Mem. ABA, Fla. Bar, Dade County Bar Assn., Greater Miami C. of C. (trustee), Miami City Ballet (bd. dirs.), U. Miami Citizens Bd. Club: Bankers (Miami). General corporate, Real property, Banking. Office: 701 Brickell Ave Suite 2100 Miami FL 33131

AMESTOY, JEFFREY LEE, lawyer, state official; b. Rutland, Vt., July 24, 1946; s. William Joseph and Diana (Wood) A.; m. Susan Claire Lonergan, May 24, 1980; 1 child, Katherine Leigh. B.A., Hobart Coll., 1968; J.D., U. Calif.-San Francisco, 1972; M.P.A., Harvard U., 1982. Bar: Vt. 1973, U.S. Dist. Ct. Vt. 1973. Assoc. Mahady & Klevana, Windsor, Vt., 1973-74; legal counsel Gov.'s Justice Commn., Montpelier, Vt., 1974-77; asst. atty. gen., chief of Medicaid fraud div. State of Vt., Montpelier, 1978-81, commr. labor and industry, 1982-84, atty. gen., 1985—; chmn. Vt. Passenger Tramway Bd., Montpelier, 1982-84, Vt. Electrician's Licensing Bd., Montpelier, 1982-84; mem. Vt. Criminal Rules Adv. Com., Montpelier, 1985—; mem. Vt. Bd. Forests and Parks, Montpelier, 1985—. Served with USAR, 1968-74. Mem. Nat. Assn. Attys. Gen., Vt. Bar Assn. Republican. Congregationalist. Criminal. Home: RD 2 Box 170 Waterbury VT 05676 Office: Office Atty Gen 109 State St Montpelier VT 05602 *

AMHOWITZ, HARRIS J., lawyer, educator; b. N.Y.C., Mar. 19, 1934. A.B., Brown U., 1955; LL.B., Harvard U., 1961. Bar: N.Y. 1961, U.S. Supreme Ct. 1967. Law clk. to judge U.S. dist. ct. N.Y., 1961-63; assoc. Hughes Hubbard & Reed, N.Y.C., 1963-69; gen. counsel Coopers & Lybrand, N.Y.C., 1970—; adj. prof. NYU Sch. Law, 1975-83; receiver, spl. master U.S. Dist. Ct., 1963—. Pres., bd. dirs. Prosher Group, Ltd., 1970—; trustee Citizens Budget Commn., Inc., 1983—. Mem. Assn. Bar City N.Y. (spl. com. lawyers' role in securities transactions 1975-77, com. profl. and jud. ethics 1983-86). General corporate, Legal education. Home: 955 Fifth Ave New York NY 10021 Office: 1251 Ave of Americas New York NY 10020

AMICK, STEVEN HAMMOND, lawyer; b. Ithaca, N.Y., May 13, 1947; s. Arthur Hammond and Marolyn Dee (Hollingshead) A.; m. Helen Louise Masten, Aug. 9, 1969. BA, Washington Coll., 1969; JD, Dickinson Sch. of Law, 1972. Bar: Del. 1972, U.S. Dist. Ct. Del. 1973. Assoc. Daley & Lewis, Wilmington, Del., 1972-74; atty. E.I. Dupont De Nemours and Co., Wilmington, 1974-85, counsel, 1986—. Pres. Com. of 39, Wilmington, 1978, Civic League for New Castle County, Wilmington, 1984-86; mem. Del. legis. Reps., Newark, 1986—. Mem. Del. Bar Assn. Presbyterian. Avocation: antique cars. Real property. Home: 449 W Chestnut Hill Rd Newark DE 19713 Office: EI DuPont de Nemours and Co Legal Dept 1007 Market St Wilmington DE 19898

AMIDON, ROBERT BRUCE, lawyer; b. Washington, Dec. 14, 1946; s. Robert Horace and Marjorie Louise (Owen) A; m. Valerie Laura Imbarrato, Dec. 21, 1985. BS, U.S. Naval Acad., 1968; MS, Cath. U. Am., 1972; JD, Georgetown U., 1976. Bar: Va. 1977, D.C. 1977, U.S. Ct. Appeals (4th and D.C. cirs.) 1977, U.S. Supreme Ct. 1980, Calif. 1982, U.S. Ct. Appeals (9th cir.) 1982, U.S. Ct. Appeals (Fed. cir.) 1987. Asst. U.S. atty. Dept. Justice, Roanoke, Va. and Washington, 1977-81; assoc. Belcher, Henzie, Biegenzahn, Chertok & Walker, P.C., Los Angeles, 1981-84, Rifkind, Sterling & Levin, Inc., Beverly Hills, Calif., 1984-85, Phillips, Nizer, Benjamin, Krim & Ballon, Los Angeles, 1985—; instr. Atty. Gen.'s Advocacy Inst., Dept. Justice, Washington, 1979; network atty. Commodities Futures Trading Commn., Washington, 1977-80. Contbr. articles to profl. jours. Chmn. Western Va. admissions com. Georgetown U., Washington, 1978-80. Served to lt. USN, 1968-76, to comdr. USNR, 1976—. Cath. U. Am. grad. fellow, 1968; recipient Outstanding Performance Rating and Spl. Achievement award U.S. Dept. Justice, 1979. Mem. ABA (vice chmn., chmn. legis. sub-com. 1979-80), Fed. Bar Assn. (nat. del. 1977-80), Lawyer-Pilots Assn., Internat. Bar Assn. (vice chmn. 1977-83), Am. Found. for Temple Bar (Eng.), Naval Res. Assn., U.S. Naval Inst. Republican. Lutheran. Federal civil litigation, State civil litigation, Criminal. Home: 10911 Bluffside Dr #23 Studio City CA 91604 Office: Phillips Nizer Benjamin et al 1880 Century Park E Suite 1150 Los Angeles CA 90067

AMMER, WILLIAM, common pleas judge; b. Circleville, Ohio, May 21, 1919; s. Moses S. and Mary (Schallas) A.; B.S. in Bus. Adminstrn., Ohio State U., 1941, J.D., 1946. Admitted to Ohio bar, 1947; atty., examiner Ohio Indsl. Commn. Columbus, 1947-51; asst. atty. gen. State of Ohio, Columbus, 1951-52; practiced in Circleville, 1953-57, pros. atty. Pickaway County, Circleville, 1953-57, common pleas judge, 1957—; asst. city solicitor Circleville, 1955-57. Past pres. Pickaway County ARC, Am. Cancer Soc. Served with inf., AUS, 1942-46. Mem. Am., Ohio (chmn. criminal law com. 1964-67), Pickaway County (pres. 1955-56) bar assns., Ohio Common Pleas Judges Assn. (pres. 1968). Methodist. Mason (K.T., Shriner), Kiwanian (Ohio dist. chmn., past lt. gov.). Criminal, Family and matrimonial, State civil litigation. Home: 141 Pleasant St Circleville OH 43113 Office: Courthouse PO Box 87 Circleville OH 43113

AMMERMAN, JAMES HARRY, II, lawyer; b. Corpus Christi, Tex., Jan. 30, 1951; s. James H. and Dolores Jean (Jones) A.; m. Linda Ann Ward, Nov. 17, 1980; children: Erik Blake, Marisa Lee. BA, U. Tex., 1976, JD, 1978. Bar: Tex. 1979, U.S. Dist. Ct. (ea. dist.) Tex. 1980, U.S. Ct. Appeals (11th cir.) 1983, U.S. Ct. Appeals (5th cir.) 1985. Ptnr. Ammerman & Ammerman, Marshall, Tex., 1979-81, Ammerman & Sanders, Marshall, 1981-82; sole practice Marshall, 1982—. Coach Marshall Youth Baseball Assn., Marshall, 1979—, bd. dirs. 1983—; Dem. precinct chmn., Harrison County, Tex., 1983-84; pres. Harrison County Council on Alcoholism, Marshall, 1986—; bd. dirs. Marshall-Harrison County Dist. Bd. of Health, 1985—. Served to sgt. Green Berets U.S. Army, 1971-73. Recipient Vol Service Cert. Appreciation Tex. Dept. Human REsources, 1982, Cert. Appreciation Tex. Assn. Alcoholism-Drug Abuse Counselors, 1984. Mem. Tex. Bar Assn. (dist. chmn. lawyers assistance com. 1985—). Northeast Tex. Bar Assn., Harrison County Bar Assn. (v.p. 1984-86, sec., treas. 1982-84, pres. 1986, local bar com. 1987—), Assn. Trial Lawyers Am., Tex. Trial Lawyers Assn. Democrat. Lutheran. Avocation: yard work. Personal injury, Workers' compensation, State civil litigation. Home: Rt 5 Box 707 Marshall TX 75670 Office: 209 W Rusk St Marshall TX 75670

AMODIO, JAMES ANTHONY, lawyer; b. South Bend, Ind., Jan. 20, 1952; s. Anthony V. and Theresa H. (Kaminski) A.; m. Bonnie A. Solowitch, May 13, 1978; children: Stephen C., Daniel J., Michael D. BA magna cum laude, Hofstra U., 1974; postgrad., U. Iowa, 1974-75; JD magna cum laude, U. Mich., 1978. Bar: Ohio 1978, U.S. Dist. Ct. (no. dist.) Ohio 1979, U.S. Ct. Appeals (6th cir.) 1981. Assoc. Jones, Day, Reavis & Pogue, Cleve., 1978-82, David N. Brown L.P.A., Cleve., 1982-85, Brown & Amodio, L.P.A., 1985—. Vol. United Way of Medina, Ohio, 1984. Mem. ABA, Medina County Bar Assn., Izaak Walton League Am., Order of Coif. Club: Toastmasters (Medina)(treas. 1986). Avocations: baseball card collecting, comic books, model building. General practice, Estate planning, General corporate. Home: 1016 Oakbrooke Dr Medina OH 44256 Office: Brown & Amodio LPA 109 W Liberty St Medina OH 44256

AMSCHLER, JAMES RALPH, lawyer, relocation company executive; b. Mpls., June 29, 1943; s. Ralph Frank Amschler and June Ann (Naslund) Petrovich; m. Judith Claire Ketterbaugh, Aug. 19, 1967; 1 child, Christy Hamilton. BS, U. Wis., 1965; LLB, Stanford U., 1968. Bar: Wis. 1968, U.S. Dist. Ct. (we. dist.) Wis. 1968, Utah 1969, U.S. Dist. Ct. Utah 1969, U.S. Supreme Ct. 1972, N.Y. 1975. Instr. law U. Wis., Madison, 1968-69; assoc. VanCott, Bagley, Cornwall & McCarthy, Salt Lake City, 1969-73; asst. gen. counsel Carrier Corp., Syracuse, N.Y., 1973-83; assoc. gen. counsel Federated Dept. Stores, Cin., 1983-85; v.p., gen. counsel Homequity Inc., Wilton, Conn., 1985—; adj. prof. law Syracuse U., 1981-82. Bd. dirs. Wilton (Conn.) United Way, 1985—. Mem. N.Y. State Bar Assn., Utah Bar Assn., Wis. State Bar Assn. Lutheran. Avocations: golf, tennis, sailing. Antitrust, Federal civil litigation, Real property. Home: 17 Cardinal Ln Westport CT 06880 Office: Homequity Inc 249 Danbury Rd Wilton CT 06897

AMSDEN, TED THOMAS, lawyer; b. Cleve., Dec. 11, 1950; s. Richard Thomas and Mary Agnes (Whitman) A.; m. Ruth Anna Rydstedt, May 1, 1982; children: Jennifer Rydstedt, Matthew Lars. BA, Wayne State U., 1972; JD, Harvard U., 1975. Bar: Mich. 1975, U.S. Dist. Ct. (ea. dist.) Mich. 1975, U.S. Ct. Appeals (6th cir.) 1975, U.S. Supreme Ct. 1979. From assoc. to ptnr. Dykema, Gossett, Spencer, Goodnow & Trigg, Detroit, 1975—. Served to lt. USNR, 1972-80. Mem. ABA, Mich. Bar Assn., Detroit Bar Assn., Macomb County Bar Assn., Assn. of Def. Counsel. Federal civil litigation, State civil litigation. Home: 19817 White Oaks Mount Clemens MI 48043 Office: Dykema Gossett Spencer Goodnow & Trigg 400 Renaissance Center Detroit MI 48243

AMSTERDAM, MARK LEMLE, lawyer; b. N.Y.C., June 10, 1944; s. Leonard M. and Erica (Lemle) A.; m. Valerie Szymanski, June 22, 1975; 1 dau., Lauren Jessica. A.B., Columbia Coll., 1966, J.D. cum laude, 1969. Bar: N.Y. 1969, U.S. Dist. Ct. (so. ea., no. dists.) N.Y. 1972, U.S. Dist. Ct. (no. dist.) Tex., U.S. Supreme Ct. 1973. Assoc. Fried, Frank, Harris, N.Y.C., 1969-70; staff atty. Ctr. for Constl. Rights, N.Y.C., 1970-75; sole practice law, N.Y.C., 1975-76, 81—; ptnr. Rubin Hanley & Amsterdam, 1976-79, Katz Amsterdam & Weinstein, N.Y.C., 1980; instr. N.Y. Law Sch., 1982-83. Contbr. articles to legal jours. Mem. N.Y. Criminal Bar Assn., Nat. Lawyers Guild. Club: Columbia. Criminal, Federal civil litigation, State civil litigation. Home: 400 West End Ave New York NY 10024 Office: 56 Thomas St New York NY 10013

ANAST, NICK JAMES, lawyer; b. Gary, Ind., Apr. 4, 1947; s. James Terry and Kiki (Pappas) A.; m. Linda K. Skirvin, Oct. 28, 1972; children: Jason, Nicole. AB, Ind. U., 1969, JD, 1972. Bar: Ind. 1972, U.S. Dist. Ct. (no. and so. dists.) Ind. 1972, U.S. Ct. Appeals (7th cir.) 1975, U.S. Supreme Ct. 1976. Ptnr. Pappas, Tokarski & Anast, Gary, 1972-74; ptnr. Tokarski & Anast, Gary, 1974-85, Schererville, Ind., 1985—; dep. pros. atty. Lake County Prosecutors Office, Crown Point, Ind., 1973-74; pub. defender Lake County Superior Ct., Gary, 1974-78; atty. Town of Schererville, 1982, Lowell, 1983, City of Lake Station, Ind., 1978. Pres. St. John (Ind.) Twp. Young Dems., 1980. Recipient Service to Youth award YMCA, 1980, Outstanding Service award Schererville Soccer Club, 1985. Fellow Ind. Bar Found.; mem. ABA, Ind. Bar Assn., Lake County Bar Assn. (bd. dirs.) 1983-85, Outstanding Service award 1985). Democrat. Greek Orthodox. Lodge: Lions (pres. Schererville chpt. 1985-86). Avocations: gardening, wood crafts, assisting children. Federal civil litigation, Contracts commercial, General corporate. Office: Tokarski & Anast 7803 W 75th Ave Suite 1 Schererville IN 46375

ANCEL, JERALD IRWIN, lawyer; b. Indpls., Jan. 29, 1944; s. Harry and Margaret (Schneider) A.; m. Gayle Elizabeth Vogel, Aug. 21, 1965; children—Jason, Jennifer, Marc. B.S. in Acctg., Ind. U.-Bloomington, 1965, J.D., 1968. Bar: Ind. 1968, U.S. Dist. Ct. (so. dist.) Ind. 1968, U.S. Dist. Ct. (no. dist.) Ind. 1980. Adjudicator, State of Ind., Indpls., 1965-68; assoc. Law Offices of Steven H. Ancel, Indpls., 1968-73; ptnr. Ancel & Ancel, Indpls., 1974-76; mng. ptnr. Ancel, Friedlander, Miroff & Ancel, Indpls., 1976-80; mng. ptnr. Ancel, Miroff & Frank, P.C., Indpls., 1981—; lectr. Ind. Continuing Legal Edn. Forum. Author: Save Our Farms, Farm Foreclosure Prevention and Reorganization, 1983; Survey of Bankruptcy Law from Creditor's View, 1983, 84; Farmer in Distress: Chapter 11 Plan and Disclosure Statement, 1986. Mem. Gov.'s Com. to Study Mental Health Laws, Indpls., 1974-76, com. chmn., 1978-80; bd. dirs., sec. Marion County Assn. Retarded Citizens, Indpls., 1978-80. Mem. ABA, Ind. Bar Assn., Indpls. Bar Assn., Comml. Law League Am., Assn. Trial Lawyers Am., Am. Bankruptcy Inst., Phi Delta Phi. Club: Broad Ripple Sertoma (pres. 1973-74). Bankruptcy, Federal civil litigation, Contracts commercial. Home: 11090 Queens Way Circle Carmel IN 46032 Office: Ancel Miroff & Frank 1000 Two Market Sq Ctr PO Box 44219 Indianapolis IN 46244

ANCEL, SORELLE JEAN LEWIS, lawyer; b. Chgo., Jan. 5, 1939; d. Harold and Anne (Levin) Lewis; m. Steven H. Ancel, Aug. 23, 1958; children: Robin Ilene, Kimberly Beth, Cori Lynne. Student, U. Ill., 1956-57, Butler U., 1957-58; BS with high distinction, Ind. U., 1959; JD magna cum laude, Ind. U., Indpls., 1979. Bar: Ind. 1979, U.S. Dist. Ct. (so. dist.) Ind. 1979. Sr. law clk. to presiding justice Ind. Ct. Appeals, Indpls., 1979-80; assoc. Ancel, Friedlander, Miroff & Ancel, Indpls., 1980-81; ptnr. Ancel, Dunlap & Traylor, Indpls., 1981—. Exec. editor Ind. Law Rev., 1979. Mem. ABA, Ind. Bar Assn., Indpls. Bar Assn. Banking, Bankruptcy, General corporate. Home: 440 Somerset Dr Indianapolis IN 46260 Office: Ancel Dunlap & Traylor PC 1770 Market Square Ctr Indianapolis IN 46204

ANCEL, STEVEN HARLAN, lawyer; b. Oak Park, Ill., Feb. 26, 1937; s. Harry and Margaret (Schneider) A.; m. Sorelle Jean Lewis, Aug. 23, 1958; children—Robin Ilene, Kimberly Beth, Cori Lynn. A.B., Ind. U., 1958, J.D., 1960. Bar: Ind. 1960, U.S. Ct. Apls. (7th cir.), U.S. Sup. Ct. 1982. Assoc., Craig & Pope, Indpls., 1960-62; sole practice, Indpls., 1962-64; sr. ptnr. Ancel & Kassenbrock, Indpls., 1964-68; sr. ptnr. Ancel & Ancel, Indpls., 1968-77; sr. ptnr. Ancel, Friedlander, Miroff & Ancel, Indpls., 1977-81; sr. ptnr. Ancel, Dunlap & Traylor, Indpls., 1981—; lectr. Ind. Continuing Legal Edn. Forum, 1976-80 , chmn. Ind. Continuing Legal Edn. Bankruptcy Seminars, 1981-86. Contbr. articles to legal jours. Mem. ABA, Ind. Bar Assn. (chmn. bankruptcy and creditors rights sect. 1984, chmn. bankruptcy and insolvency sect. 1985), Indpls. Bar Assn., Am. Judicature Soc., Phi Delta Phi. Contbr. articles to legal jours. Bankruptcy, Banking, Contracts commercial. Office: 1770 Market Sq Ctr Indianapolis IN 46204

ANDERS, MILTON HOWARD, lawyer; b. Shreveport, La., Apr. 28, 1930; s. Howard P. and Nora Lee (Whitman) A.; m. Patsy Ruth Hollis, Sept. 4, 1954; 1 child, Mary Alison. B.S., La. Tech. U., 1951; J.D., La. State U., 1957. Bar: La. 1957, Tex. 1971. Atty. Placid Oil Co., Shreveport, 1957-60, Barnwell Industries, Shreveport, 1960-65, Mobil Corp., Shreveport, 1965-69; ptnr. Vinson & Elkins, Houston, 1969—. Mem. La. Bar Assn., Tex. Bar Assn., La. Bank Counsel Assn., Tex. Assn. Bank Counsel. Baptist. Banking, Oil and gas leasing, Contracts commercial. Office: Vinson & Elkins 3300 1st City Tower 1001 Fannin St Houston TX 77002

ANDERSEN, CHARLES MATTHEW, lawyer; b. Dekalb, Ill., Mar. 21, 1949; s. Gilbert Kohrt and Mary Elizabeth (Cavanaugh) A.; m. Eleanor Ann Fassnacht. BS, Iowa State U., 1971; JD, Gonzaga U., 1976. Bar: Wash. 1976, U.S. Ct. Mil. Appeals 1977, U.S. Dist. Ct. Md. 1978, U.S. Dist. Ct. (ea. dist.) Wash. 1980, U.S. Ct. Claims 1980, U.S. Supreme Ct. 1982, Idaho 1986. Assoc. Winston & Cashatt, Spokane, 1980—. Del. caucus Wash. Dems., 1986—. Served to capt. U.S. Army, 1976-79. Mem. ABA, Wash. State Bar Assn., Spokane County Bar Assn., Fed. Bar Assn., Wash. Trial Lawyers Assn. Democrat. Avocations: sailing, biking, skiing. Federal civil litigation, State civil litigation, Contracts commercial. Home: West 224 16th Ave Spokane WA 99203 Office: Winston & Cashatt 1900 Seafirst Financial Ctr Spokane WA 99201

ANDERSEN, DANIEL JOHANNES, lawyer; b. Jamestown, N.Y., Nov. 3, 1909; s. Christian Johannes and Maria Bodil (Hansen) A.; m. Alice Klopstad, June 29, 1937; 1 dau., Dianne Andersen Tecklenbaerg. A.B., George Washington U., 1937, J.D., 1940; grad. JAG Sch., 1942, Army War Coll., 1965. Bar: D.C. 1939, U.S. Ct. Claims 1953, U.S. Tax Ct. 1953, U.S. Supreme Ct. 1947. Assoc. Baker, Beedy & Magee, 1940-42; ptnr. Magee, Bulow & Andersen, 1946-52; sole practice, Washington, 1952—; pres., treas. Dr. O.E. Howe Found., Washington. Served to col. USAFR, 1965. Mem. D.C. Bar Assn., Fed. Bar Assn., Air Force Judge Advocates Assn. (past pres.), Washington Bd. Trade, Christian Businessmen's Assn., Religious Heritage of Am., Nat. Lawyers Club, Sigma Chi. Republican. Lutheran. Club: Chevy Chase. Probate, Military, General practice. Home: 4441 Lowell St NW Washington DC 20016 Office: 430 Woodward Bldg Washington DC 20005

ANDERSEN, DAVID CHARLES, lawyer; b. Grand Rapids, Mich., Oct. 4, 1955; s. Daniel and Doris (Hoenninger) A.; m. Elestine Whittaker, July 10, 1982 (div. Dec. 1984); 1 child, Joseph. BS, Grand Valley State Coll., 1976; JD, Wayne State U., 1979; cert. paramedic, Davenport Coll., 1987. Bar: Mich. 1979, U.S. Dist. Ct. (we. dist.) Mich. 1979, U.S. Supreme Ct. 1987. Assoc. Dale R. Sprik, Grand Rapids, 1979-81; ptnr. Sprik & Andersen, Grand Rapids, 1981—; pres., chmn. Grand Rapids Pub. Broadcasting Sta. WEHB-FM, 1982-83. West Mich. Telecommunications Found., Grand

Rapids, 1984—. Personal injury, Health. Office: Sprik & Andersen PC 5 Lyon NW Grand Rapids MI 49503

ANDERSEN, JAMES A., justice; b. Auburn, Wash., Sept. 21, 1924; s. James A. and Margaret Cecilia (Norgaard) A.; m. Dolphina R. Novelli; children: James Blair, Tia Louise. BA, U. Wash., 1949, JD, 1951. Bar: Wash. 1952, U.S. Dist. Ct. (we. dist.) Wash. 1957, U.S. Ct. Appeals 1957. Dep. pros. atty. King County, Seattle, 1953-57; assoc. Lycette, Diamond & Sylvester, Seattle, 1957-61; ptnr. Clinton, Andersen, Fleck & Glein, Seattle, 1961-75; judge Wash. State Ct. of Appeals, Seattle, 1975-84; justice Wash. State Supreme Ct., Olympia, 1984—. Mem. Wash. State Ho. of Reps., 1958-67, Wash. State Senate, 1967-72. Served with U.S. Army, 1943-45, ETO. Decorated Purple Heart. Mem. ABA, Wash. State Bar Assn. Episcopalian. Judicial administration. Office: Wash State Supreme Ct Temple of Justice Olympia WA 98504-0511

ANDERSEN, MICHAEL PAGE, lawyer; b. Conway, S.C., Dec. 9, 1955; s. William Clarence and Mabel (Page) A.; m. Carla Tevis Mittwede, Apr. 27, 1985. BA summa cum laude, U. Ga., 1978, JD cum laude, 1981. Bar: Fla. 1981. Assoc. Kimbrell & Hamann, Miami, Fla., 1981-84; sr. assoc. investment counsel John Alden Life Ins. Co., Miami, 1984—. Vestry mem. St. Christophers By the Sea, Key Biscayne, Fla., 1985—. Mem. ABA. Republican. Episcopalian. Real property, Securities, Legal counsel for comprehensive investment department. Office: John Alden Life Ins Co 3655 NW 87th Ave Miami FL 33178

ANDERSEN, RICHARD ESTEN, lawyer; b. N.Y.C., Oct. 26, 1957; s. Arnold and Marianne (Singer) A. BA, Columbia U., 1978, JD, 1981. Bar: N.Y. 1982, U.S. Tax Ct. 1982. Assoc. Walter, Conston Alexander & Green, P.C., N.Y.C., 1981—; atty. Vol. Lawyers for Arts, N.Y.C., 1985—. John Jay scholar, Columbia U., N.Y.C., 1974. Mem. ABA, N.Y. State Bar Assn. Corporate taxation, Private international, General corporate. Office: Walter Conston Alexander & Green PC 90 Park Ave New York NY 10016

ANDERSON, ADELE KONKEL, lawyer; b. Winona, Minn., Jan. 25, 1949; d. Hubert John and Dorothy Margaret (Ries) Konkel; m. David S. Anderson, May 26, 1984. BA in English, St. Mary Coll., Leavenworth, Kans., 1971; JD, Washington U., St. Louis, 1981. Bar: Colo. 1981, U.S. Dist. Ct. Colo. 1981. Ptnr. Preston, Altman, et al, Pueblo, Colo., 1981—; instr. Nat. Bus. Coll., Pueblo, 1982, 84. Editor (newsletter): The Bar Tab, 1986, 87. Olin fellow, 1978-81. Mem. ABA, Pueblo County Bar Assn. (sec. 1983-84, bd. dirs. 1985—, young lawyer of yr. award 1985), Pueblo C. of C. Roman Catholic. Avocations: gardening, reading, music, theater. General practice. Office: Preston Altman et al 501 Thatcher Bldg Pueblo CO 81003

ANDERSON, ALISON GREY, legal educator; b. 1943. A.B., Radcliffe Coll., 1965; J.D., U. Calif.-Berkeley, 1968. Bar: Calif. 1969, D.C. 1969. Law clk. to judge U.S. Ct. Appeals (4th cir.), Balt., 1968-69; assoc. Covington & Burling, Washington, 1969-72; acting prof. UCLA Law Sch., 1972-77, prof., 1977—. Mem. Am. Law Inst., Order of Coif. Articles editor Calif. Law Rev. Legal education. Address: UCLA Law Sch 405 Hilgard Ave Los Angeles CA 90024 *

ANDERSON, ARNOLD STUART, lawyer, retail company executive; b. N.Y.C., June 4, 1934; s. David and Mary (Bilgoray) A.; m. Barbara Sapkowitz, Oct. 1, 1955; children: David Jay, Randi Lee. B.A., CCNY, 1956; J.D., Columbia U., 1959. Bar: N.Y. 1959, U.S. Supreme Ct. 1971. Gen. atty., office gen. counsel FAA, Washington, 1960-61; assoc. Fly, Shuebruck, Blume & Gaguine, N.Y.C., 1962-63; asst. counsel N.Y. Moreland Commn. on Alcoholic Beverage Control Law, N.Y.C., 1963-64; assoc. Winthrop, Stimson, Putnam & Roberts, N.Y.C., 1964-79; v.p., gen. counsel F.W. Woolworth Co., N.Y.C., 1979-80; sr. v.p., gen. counsel F.W. Woolworth Co., 1980-82, exec. v.p. adminstrn., gen. counsel, 1982—; asst. counsel investigation into jud. conduct Supreme Ct. Appellate Div. 2d Dept., 1970. Author: (with R.S. Taft) N.Y. Practice Series, Personal Taxation, Vol. I, 1975; contbr. (with R.S. Taft) articles to profl. jours. Mem. Am. Bar Assn., Fed. Bar Assn., N.Y. Bar Assn., N.Y.C. Bar Assn. General corporate. Office: F W Woolworth Co 233 Broadway Woolworth Bldg New York NY 10279

ANDERSON, AUSTIN GOTHARD, university adminstrator, lawyer; b. Calumet, Minn., June 30, 1931; s. Hugo Gothard and Turna Marie (Johnson) A.; m. Catherine Antoinette Spellacy, Jan. 2. 1954; children: Todd, Susan, Timothy, Linda, Mark. B.A., U. Minn., 1954, J.D., 1958. Bar: Minn. 1958, Ill. 1962, Mich. 1974. Mem. Spellacy, Spellacy, Lano & Anderson, Marble, Minn, 1958-62; dir. Ill. Inst. Continuing Legal Edn., Springfield, 1962-64; dir. dept. continuing legal edn. U. Minn., Mpls., 1964-70, assoc. dean gen. extension div., 1968-70; mem. Dorsey, Marquart, Windhorst, West & Halladay, Mpls., 1970-73; assoc. dir. Nat. Ctr. State Cts., St. Paul, 1973-74; dir. Inst. Continuing Legal Edn. U. Mich., Ann Arbor, 1973—; project dir. Select Com. on Judiciary State of Minn., 1974-76; adj. faculty U. Minn., 1974, Wayne State U., 1974-75, William Mitchell Coll. Law, 1973-74; mem. Am. Inst. Law Tng. within the Office, 1985—; cons. in field. Co-editor, contbg. author: Lawyer's Handbook, 1975; author: A Plan for Lawyer Development, 1986, Client Development: The Key to Successful Law Practice, 1986; cons. editor, contbg. author: Webster's Legal Secretaries Handbook, 1981; contbr. chpt. to book. Chmn. City of Bloomington Park and Recreation Adv. Commn., Minn., 1970-72; mem. adv. com. Ferris State Coll.; mem. Ann Arbor Citizens Recreation Adv. Com., 1983—, Ann Arbor Parks Adv. Com., 1983—. Served with U.S. Navy, 1950-51. Fellow Am. Bar Found., State Bar Mich. Found.; mem. Assn. Legal Adminstrs. (pres. 1969-70), ABA (chmn. sect. econ. of law practice 1981-82), Mich. Bar Assn., Ill. Bar Assn., Minn. Bar Assn., Washtenaw County Bar Assn., Am. Mgmt. Assn., Assn. Continuing Legal Edn. Adminstrs. Legal education, Law firm management. Home: 3617 Larchmont Dr Ann Arbor MI 48105 Office: U Mich 432 Hutchins Hall Ann Arbor MI 48109-1215

ANDERSON, BRUCE PAIGE, lawyer; b. Albany, Ga., Mar. 5, 1952; s. Paul Macon and Ruth Alice (O'neil) A.; m. Sandra Johnston, June 30, 1973; children: Christi Lauren, Sarah Alice. AB in Econs., Ga. So. Coll., 1973; JD, Loyola U., New Orleans, 1977. Bar: Ga. 1977, La. 1977, Fla. 1978. Asst. atty. gen. State of La., New Orleans, 1981; assoc. John A. Barley & Assocs., Tallahassee, 1981-83; sole practice Tallahassee, 1983-86; ptnr. Mowrey and Anderson, 1986—; guest lectr. Fla. A&M U. Sch. Architecture, Tallahassee, 1984-85. Mem. ABA, Fla. Bar Assn., La. Bar Assn., Ga. Bar Assn., Tallahassee Bar Assn. Roman Catholic. General practice, Construction, State civil litigation. Home: 3428 Castlebar Circle Tallahassee FL 32308 Office: 1017 Thomasville Rd Suite B Tallahassee FL 32303

ANDERSON, CAROL MCMILLAN, lawyer; b. Malone, Fla., Aug. 7, 1938; d. Fillmore Allen and Ernestine (Dickson) McMillan; m. Philip Sloan Anderson, Oct. 9, 1965; 1 child, Courtney Beth. BS, Fla. Atlantic U., 1969; JD, Cumberland Sch. Law, 1971. Bar: Fla. 1971. Asst. U.S. atty. Office of U.S. Atty., Miami, Fla., 1971-74; ptnr. Anderson & Anderson, Ft. Lauderdale, Fla. 1974—. Recipient Alumnae Achievement award Katharine Gibbs Sch., Boston, 1973. Mem. ABA, Assn. Trial Lawyers Am., Fed. Bar Assn., Fla. Assn. Trial Lawyers, Fla. Bar, Broward County Bar Assn., Broward County Women Lawyers (v.p. 1981), Royal Dames Cancer Research (trustee), Mus. Art, Gold Circle Nova U., Hospice Hundred (bd. dirs.). Presbyterian. Clubs: Thousand Plus, Coral Ridge Yacht. Personal injury. Home: 32 Isla Bahia Dr Fort Lauderdale FL 33316 Office: Anderson & Anderson PA 1313 S Andrews Ave Fort Lauderdale FL 33316

ANDERSON, CHARLES EDWARD, lawyer; b. Milw., Aug. 14, 1941; s. Edward Walter and Edna Alice A.; m. Sally J. Moriarty, Aug. 29, 1964; children: Erika, Seth. BBA, U. Wis., Madison, 1963, JD, 1966. Bar: Wis. 1966, U.S. Ct. Appeals (10th cir.) 1970, U.S. Ct. Appeals (9th cir.) 1972, N.Mex. 1974, U.S. Dist. Ct. N.Mex. 1974, U.S. Tax Ct. 1974, U.S. Supreme Ct. 1974. Tax atty., Arthur Anderson & Co., Milw., 1966-67; trial atty. appellate sect. tax div. U.S. Dept. Justice, Washington, 1970-74; ptnr. Schlenker, Parker, Wellborn & Anderson, Albuquerque, 1974-77; prin. Charles E. Anderson, P.A., 1977-83; shareholder, Eaves, Darling, Anderson & Porter, P.A., 1983—; adj. prof. law U. N.Mex., 1981-82. Served to 1st lt. USAF, 1967-70. Mem. ABA. Republican. Personal income taxation, State and local taxation, Estate taxation. Office: 6501 Americas Pkwy NE Suite 800 Albuquerque NM 87110

ANDERSON, CHRISTOPHER JAMES, lawyer; b. Chgo., Nov. 26, 1950; s. James M. and Margaret E. (Anderson) A.; m. Lyn R. Buckley, Jan. 3, 1976; 1 child, Vaughn Buckley. BA, Grinnell Coll., 1972; JD with highest distinction, U. Iowa, 1975. Bar: Mo. 1975. From assoc. to ptnr. Dietrich, Davis, Dicus, Schmitt & Gorman, Rowlands, Mo., 1975—. Mem. ABA, Mo. Bar Assn., Kans. City Bar Assn., Lawyers Assn. Kansas City, Estate Planning Council, Heart of Am. Tax Inst. (co-chmn. 1986—). Estate planning, General corporate, Personal income taxation. Office: Dietrich Davis Dicus et al 1100 Main St 1700 City Ctr Sq Kansas City MO 64105

ANDERSON, CRAIG W., lawyer; b. Idaho Falls, Idaho, Aug. 5, 1951; s. Wilford and Betty A.; m. Denise A. Dragoo, Nov. 25, 1977. B.S. magna cum laude, U. Utah, 1973, J.D., 1977. Bar: Utah 1977, U.S. Ct. Appeals (10th cir.), U.S. Supreme Ct. Research assoc. Environ. Law Inst., Washington, 1977; dep. county atty. Salt Lake County, 1978-81; ptnr. Suitter, Axland, Armstrong & Hanson, Salt Lake City, 1981-86, Van Wagoner & Stevens, Salt Lake City, 1986—. Contbr. articles to profl. jours. Editorial bd. Jour. Contemporary Law, 1976-77. Counsel, Children's Service Soc. Utah. U.S. Senate intern, 1974. Mem. Utah Bar Assn., Hinckley Inst. Politics Intern Alumni Assn., Salt Lake County Bar Assn., ABA. Federal civil litigation, State civil litigation, Local government. Home: 1826 Hubbard Ave Salt Lake City UT 84108 Office: Van Wagoner & Stevens 215 S State St Suite #500 Salt Lake City UT 84111

ANDERSON, CROMWELL ADAIR, lawyer; b. Palatka, Fla., Feb. 26, 1926; s. Cromwell Adair and Antoinette (Richardson) A.; m. Betty Ann Myers, July 27, 1957 (dec. Apr. 1981); children—Cromwell Adair, III, Bruce Myers, William Preston; m. Mary Alice Morgan, Aug. 22, 1984. B.A., U. Rochester, 1948; LL.B., U. Fla., 1950. Bar: Fla. 1950, U.S. Dist. Ct. (so. dist.) Fla. 1954, U.S. Ct. Appeals (5th cir.) 1956, U.S. Supreme Ct. 1973. Spl. agt. FBI, Washington, 1951-54; assoc. Smathers & Thompson, Miami, Fla., 1954-59, ptnr., 1959-82; ptnr. Patton & Kanner, Miami, 1982—; Served in USN, World War II. Mem. ABA (chmn. maritime ins. law com. 1974-75), Fla. Bar, Dade County Bar Assn. (dir. 1982—), Maritime Law Assn. (exec. com. 1979-82), Internat. Assn. Ins. Counsel, Fed. Bar Assn., Am. Judicature Soc. Clubs: Miami, Rod & Reel; Cat Cay (Bahamas); Met. S. Fla. Fishing Tournament Orgn. (pres. 1976-79). Contbr. articles to profl. jours. Admiralty, Banking, Federal civil litigation. Home: 1029 Hardee Rd Coral Gables FL 33146 Office: Patton & Kanner 150 SE 2d Ave Miami FL 33131

ANDERSON, DALE KENNETH, lawyer; b. Toledo, May 30, 1922; s. Ture B. G. and Astrid Annette (Pearson) A.; m. Barbara R. Phillips, Apr. 1, 1950; children: Sharon Anderson Sleight, Hollis Anderson Potere. Student, Miami U., Oxford, Ohio, 1940-41, 46; JD, U. Toledo, 1950. Bar: Ohio 1950, U.S. Dist. Ct. (no. dist.) Ohio 1951. Commd. 2d lt. USAF, 1942, advanced through grades to col., 1968, ret., 1968; ptnr. Anderson, Holder & Barkenquast, Toledo, 1968—. Recipient citation USAF Acad., 1966. Mem. Toledo Bar Assn., Assn. Trial Lawyers Am., Ret. Officers Assn., Res. Officers Assn. U.S., Mil. Order of U.S., Delta Theta Phi, Phi Kappa Tau, Silver Falcon Assn., Am. Legion. Republican. Lutheran. Club: Inverness (Toledo). Personal injury. Home: 2725 Pine Knoll Dr Toledo OH 43617 Office: Anderson Holder & Barkenquast 1020 Spitzer Bldg Toledo OH 43604-1395

ANDERSON, DAVID B., lawyer, steel company executive; b. Moorhead, Minn., Mar. 10, 1942; children—Kimberly, Erik, Jonathan, Caroline J. B.A., U. Minn., 1964, J.D., 1967; LL.M., DePaul U., 1983. Bar: Ill. Labor relations supr. Continental Can Co., N.Y.C., 1970-72; asst. gen. counsel Am. Hosp. Supply Co., Evanston, Ill., 1972-83; v.p. planning and gen. counsel Inland Steel Industries, Inc., Chgo., 1983—. Served as capt. U.S. Army, 1967-70. Home: 845 Moseley Rd Highland Park IL 60035 Office: Inland Steel Industries Inc 30 W Monroe St Chicago IL 60603

ANDERSON, DAVID BOWEN, lawyer; b. Seattle, Sept. 19, 1948; s. Gordon Browne and Elizabeth Josephine (Bowen) A.; m. Laura Ann Jorgensen, May 23, 1975; children: Elizabeth Christine, Christina Louise. BA with great distinction, Stanford U., 1970; JD, U. Mich., 1974; MBA, Western Wash. U., 1982. Bar: Wash. 1974, U.S. Dist. Ct. (we. dist.) Wash. 1974. Assoc. Bogle & Gates, Seattle, 1974-77; ptnr. Anderson & Connell, Bellingham, Wash., 1977—; instr. Pacific Northwest Admiralty Law Inst., Seattle, 1983, Nat. Fishery Law Symposium, Seattle, 1984. Mem. adv. com. Bellingham Sch. Bd., 1981-82, Bellingham Vocat. Tech. Inst., 1986. Mem. ABA, Wash. State Bar Assn., Whatcom County Bar Assn. (pres. 1986), Maritime Law Assn. U.S. (proctor), Phi Beta Kappa. Presbyterian. Clubs: Wash. Athletic (Seattle); Bellingham Yacht; Komo Kulshan Ski (bd. dirs. 1986—). Admiralty, Federal civil litigation, Personal injury. Home: 500 16th St Bellingham WA 98225 Office: Anderson & Connell 1501 Eldridge Ave Bellingham WA 98227-1063

ANDERSON, DAVID LAWRENCE, lawyer; b. Balt., Oct. 29, 1948; s. Robert L. and Ruth (Hahn) A.; m. Jeanne E. Albrecht. BS, Towson State U., 1970; JD, U. Md., 1973. Bar: Md. 1973, U.S. Dist. Ct. Md. 1976, U.S. Ct. Appeals (D.C. cir.) 1976, U.S. Dist. Ct. D.C. 1979. Asst. revisor Gov.'s Commn. to Revise Annapolis's Code, Md., 1973-74; counsel Gov.'s Task Force on Campaign Financing, Annapolis, 1974-75; atty. Fed. Election Commn., Washington, 1975-77, FEA, Washington, 1977; asst. chief counsel U.S. Dept. Energy, Washington, 1977-85, Environ. Enforcement Sect., Land and Natural Resources Div. U.S. Dept. Justice, Washington, 1986—; adj. prof. legal research and writing Am. U., 1985-87. Recipient Outstanding Performance award Dept. Energy, 1981, medal and award Dept. Energy, 1983. Mem. ABA (litigation sect.), D.C. Bar Assn. Democrat. Environment, Federal civil litigation. Office: US Dept Justice 10th & Pennsylvania Ave NW Washington DC 20580

ANDERSON, DORIS EHLINGER, lawyer; b. Houston, Dec. 1; d. Joseph Otto and Cornelia Louise (Pagel) Ehlinger; m. Wiley Newton Anderson, Jr., Aug. 26, 1946; children—Wiley Newton III, Joe E. Permanent high sch. tchr.'s cert. U. Houston, 1948; BA, Rice U., 1946; JD, U. Tex., 1950; MLS in Museology U. Okla. Bar: Tex. 1950, U.S. Supreme Ct. Assoc. Ehlinger & Anderson, Houston, 1950-52, ptnr., 1965—; assoc. Price, Guinn, Wheat & Veltmann, Houston, 1952-55, Wheat, Dyche & Thornton, Houston, 1955-65; life mem. Rice Assocs., Houston, 1984—; dir. Houston Bapt. Mus. Am. Architecture and Decorative Arts, 1980—, curator costume, 1980; hist. lectr. Editor, author Houston, City of Destiny, 1980. Contbr. articles to hist. publs. Partliamentarian Harris County Flood Control Task Force, Houston, 1975—; docent Bayou Bend Mus. Fine Arts, Houston. Recipient best interpretive exhibit award Tex. Hist. Commn., 1983, Outstanding Woman of Yr. award YWCA, Houston, 1983; named adm. Tex. Navy, 1980. Mem. ABA, Women Attys. Houston, UDC (pres. Jefferson Davis chpt.) Daus. Republic Tex. (parliamentarian gen.), Am. Mus. Soc. (bd. dirs. Houston 1981—), Harris County Heritage Soc. (librarian), Kappa Beta Pi. Episcopalian. Oil and gas leasing, Real property. Home: 5556 Cranbrook Houston TX 77056 Office: Ehlinger & Anderson 5556 Sturbridge Houston TX 77056

ANDERSON, E. KARL, lawyer; b. Huntington, W. Va., Mar. 30, 1931; s. Earle Karl and Helen Emerie (Johnson) A.; m. Mary Elizabeth Williams, Nov. 13, 1953; children—Sharon Elizabeth, Charles Wesley. B.B.A., So. Methodist U., 1953, LL.B., 1960. Bar: Tex. 1960, U.S. Dist. Ct. (no. dist.) Tex. 1963, U.S. Supreme Ct. 1971. Field supr. Travelers Ins. Co., Dallas, 1956-57; claim mgr. Allstate Ins. Co., Dallas, 1958-62; practiced in Dallas, 1963—; partner firm Lastelick, Anderson and Hilliard, 1968—. Served with USAF, 1954-56. Mem. Am. Bar Assn., Dallas Assn. Trial Lawyers (dir. 1964-65, 74-75), Tex. Trial Lawyers Assn., Assn. Trial Lawyers Am., Delta Theta Phi, Sigma Iota Epsilon, Sigma Alpha Epsilon. Presbyn. Club: Dallas Country. State civil litigation. Home: 3111 Drexel Dr Dallas TX 75205 Office: 1st Tex Bank Bldg PO Box 59105 Dallas TX 75229

ANDERSON, ELLIS B., lawyer; b. Michigan City, Ind., Aug. 30, 1926; s. A.B. and Esther (Nicholson) A.; m. Adrienne Scotchbrook, Aug. 6, 1955; children: Rebecca J., Katherine V. A.B. cum laude, Ind. U., 1949, J.D., 1952; grad., Advanced Mgmt. Program, Harvard U., 1970. Bar: Ind. bar 1952. Partner firm Butt, Bowers & Anderson, Evansville, Ind., 1952-60; with Baxter Labs. Inc., Morton Grove, Ill., 1961-65; sr. v.p., gen. counsel, dir., mem. exec. com. Hoffmann-La Roche Inc., Nutley, N.J., from 1965. Served with AUS, World War II. Mem. Phi Beta Kappa. Clubs: Nassau, Bay Head Yacht. General corporate. Home: 52 Elm Rd Princeton NJ 08540 Office: Hoffmann La Roche Inc 340 Kingsland St Nutley NJ 07110

ANDERSON, ERIC SEVERIN, lawyer; b. N.Y.C., Dec. 16, 1943; s. Edward Severin and Dorothy Elvira (Ekbloom) A. BA in History summa cum laude, St. Mary's San Antonio, 1968; JD cum laude, Harvard U., 1971. Bar: Tex. 1971. From assoc. to ptnr. Fulbright & Jaworski, Houston, 1971—. Served with USAF, 1961-65. Mem. ABA, State Bar Tex., Houston Bar Assn. Democrat. Clubs: Houston Ctr., Houston City. Avocations: classical music, theater, sports. General corporate, Securities, Municipal bonds. Home: 14 Greenway Plaza Apt 21-O Houston TX 77046 Office: Fulbright & Jaworski 1301 McKinney St Houston TX 77010

ANDERSON, EUGENE ROBERT, lawyer; b. Portland, Oreg., Oct. 24, 1927; s. Andrew E. and Ruth Beatrice (White) A.; m. Jenny Morgentham, Nov. 8, 1986: children—Matthew, Martin. B.S., UCLA, 1949; attended, Oreg. State Coll., 1945; J.D., Harvard U., 1952; LL.M., N.Y. U., 1960. Bar: N.Y. bar 1953, Mass., So. and Eastern dists. N.Y., Second Circuit, D.C. Circuit, U.S. Ct. Claims, U.S. Supreme Ct. bars 1953. Asso. firm Chadbourne, Parke, Whiteside & Wolff, N.Y.C., 1953-61; partner Chadbourne, Parke, Whiteside & Wolff, 1965-69; asst. U.S. atty. So. Dist. N.Y., Foley Square, 1961-65; chief civil div. So. Dist. N.Y., 1963-65; ptnr. firm Anderson Russell Kill & Olick (P.C.), N.Y.C., 1969—; asst. dist. atty. N.Y. County, 1977; dir. Keene Corp., N.Y.C., Am. Brands, Inc., N.Y.C., White Cap Inc., Lester, Pa.; Spl. hearing officer U.S. Dept. Justice, 1965-68; arbitrator Am. Arbitration Assn., 1965—, Small Claims Ct., 1970-76; mem. com. on trial practice and technique Second Circuit, 1967-73. Mem. St. George's Ch., vestryman, 1966-68. Served with AUS, 1946. Mem. Assn. Bar City N.Y., Fed., Am. bar assns., Police Athletic League (dir., gen. counsel). General practice. Home: 25 E 86th St New York NY 10028 Office: 666 3d Ave New York NY 10017

ANDERSON, FREDERICK RANDOLPH, JR., lawyer, legal educator; b. Rutherfordton, N.C., June 28, 1941; s. Frederick Randolph and Ophelia (Meeler) A.; m. Anne Clyde Hart, May 31, 1980. B.A. with highest honors (Morehead Scholar, Nat. Merit Scholar), U. N.C., 1963; B.A. In Jurisprudence (Marshall Scholar), Oxford (Eng.) U., 1965; J.D., Harvard U., 1968. Bar: D.C. 1969. Teaching fellow Harvard U., Cambridge, Mass.; editor-in-chief Environ. Law Reporter, Washington, 1970-73; exec. dir. Environ. Law Inst., Washington, 1973-78; pres. Environ. Law Inst., 1978-80, bd. dirs., 1980-86; prof. law U. Utah Coll. Law, Salt Lake City, 1980-85; dean Washington Coll. Law Am. U., 1985—; mem. panel on high-level radioactive waste disposal Nat. Acad. Scis., 1979-81, mem. congressional study of common law relief for hazardous waste injuries, 1980-82; bd. dirs. Environ. Law Inst., 1978—. Author: NEPA in the Courts, 1973, Environmental Improvement Through Economic Incentives, 1978, Environmental Protection: Law and Policy, 1984; contbg. author: Federal Environmental Law, 1974, Occupational and Environmental Health, 1982, The Southwest under Stress, 1981. Bd. dirs. Western Network, 1982—. Mem. ABA (standing com. on environ. law 1973-83, chmn. 1980-82, chmn. commn. on inter-am. affairs 1986—, chmn. 1986—), Am. Law Inst. Office: American Univ Washington Coll of Law 4400 Massachussetts Ave Washington DC 20016

ANDERSON, GEOFFREY ALLEN, lawyer; b. Chgo., Aug. 3, 1947; s. Roger Allen and Ruth (Teninga) A.; B.A. cum laude, Yale U., 1969; J.D., Columbia U., 1972. Bar: Ill. 1972. Assoc., Isham, Lincoln & Beale, Chgo., 1972-79, ptnr., 1980-81; ptnr. Reuben & Proctor, Chgo., 1981-85; dep. gen. counsel Tribune Co., Chgo., 1985—; gen. counsel Chgo. Cubs, 1986— . Mem. bd. deacons Fourth Presbyn Ch., Chgo. Recipient Citizenship award Am. Legion, 1965. Mem. Chgo. Bar Assn. (chmn. entertainment com. 1981-82, best performance award, 1977), Phi Delta Phi. Clubs: Yale (N.Y.C.); Attic (Chgo.). Securities, General corporate. Office: Tribune Co 435 N Michigan Ave Chicago IL 60611

ANDERSON, GEORGE ROSS, JR., fed. judge; b. Anderson, S.C., Jan. 29, 1929; s. George Ross and Eva Mae (Pooler) A.; m. Dorothy M. Downie, Dec. 2, 1951; 1 son, G. Ross. B.Comml. Sci., Southeastern U., 1949; postgrad., George Washington U., 1949-51; LL.B., U. S.C., 1954. Bar: S.C. bar 1954. Mem. identification div. FBI, Washington, 1945-47; clk. to U.S. Senator Olin D. Johnston, Washington, 1947-51, Columbia, S.C., 1953-54; individual practice law Anderson, S.C., 1954-79; U.S. dist. judge Dist. of S.C., Greenville, 1980—. Asst. editor: U. S.C. Law Rev, 1953-54. Bd. dirs. Salvation Army, 1968, YMCA, 1968-79, Anderson Youth Assn., 1978-80. Served with USAF, 1951-52. Fellow Internat. Acad. Trial Lawyers (dir. 1979-81), Internat. Soc. Barristers; mem. S.C. Bar Assn. (dir. 1977-80, past circuit v.p.), Am. Bar Assn., Assn. Trial Lawyers Am. (bd. govs. 1969-71), S.C. Trial Lawyers Assn. (v.p. 1970-71, pres. 1971-72), Ga. Trial Lawyers Assn., Am. Assn. Forensic Scientists. Democrat. Baptist. Jurisprudence. Office: US District Court PO Box 2147 Anderson SC 29622 *

ANDERSON, HENRY BRACKENRIDGE, lawyer; b. Wilkinsburg, Pa., May 30, 1918; s. Henry Brackenridge and Ida Adella (Stewart) A.; m. Audrey S. Anderson, June 25, 1952 (div. Mar. 1983); children: David L., Brooke S. Anderson Uminga, Bettina S. BA, Wesleyan U., Middletown, Conn., 1940, MA, 1948; LLB, U. Conn., 1948. Bar: Conn. 1948. Assoc. H.B. Bradbury, New Milford, Conn., 1949-51; ptnr. Ferriss & Anderson, New Milford, 1951-57, Anderson & Altermatt, New Milford, 1957-62, Cramer & Anderson, New Milford, 1962—; trial justice Town of Sherman, 1948-50, town counsel, 1948-76; corporator New Milford (Conn.) Svgs. Bank, 1961-86; bd. dirs. Conn. Atty.'s Title Guaranty Fund, Inc. Chmn. Bd. of Edn., Sherman, Conn., 1967-70; trustee New Milford Hosp., 1964—, U. of Conn. Law Sch. Found., Inc., 1974-81. Served to lt. comdr. USNR, 1941-46, PTO. Decorated Silver Star, Bronze Star. Mem. Conn. Bar Assn. (exec. com., real property sect., sec. examining com. 1975-77, chmn. examining com. 1977-80), Litchfield County Bar Assn. (pres. 1963-65, grievance com.), Nat. Conf. Bar Examiners (real property subcom.), Alpha Chi Rho. Probate, Estate planning, Real property. Home: Town Hill Rd Warren CT 06754 Office: Cramer & Anderson PO Box 330 New Milford CT 06776

ANDERSON, J. BLAINE, judge; b. Trenton, Utah, Jan. 19, 1922; s. Leslie Howard and Theo Ellen (Stocking) A.; m. Grace Little, Nov. 14, 1944; children—J. Eric, J. Blaine, Leslie Ann, Dirk Brian. Student, U. Idaho, 1940-41, U. Wash., 1945-46; LL.B., U. Idaho, 1949; J.D. (hon.), Lewis and Clark Coll., 1978. Bar: Idaho bar 1949. Practiced in Blackfoot, 1949-71; partner firm Furchner and Anderson (and predecessor law firms), 1955-71; U.S. dist. judge Dist. Idaho, Boise, 1971-76; U.S. circuit judge U.S. Ct. Appeals, 9th Circuit, 1976—. Chmn. Idaho Air Pollution Commn., 1959-60. Served with USCG, 1942-45. First Recipient Faculty award of Legal Merit, U. Idaho Coll. Law, 1974. Fellow Am. Coll. Trial Lawyers; mem. Am. Bar Assn. (mem. ho. of dels. 1959-60, 64-71, gov. 1971-74, mem. council gen. practice sect. 1962-66, 70-71, mem. adv. bd. editors Jour. 1969-71), Idaho State Bar (bd. commrs. 1958-61, pres. 1960-61, chmn. unauthorized practice of law com. 1955-58), S.E. Idaho Dist. Bar (pres. 1957-58), Am. Judicature Soc. (dir. 1961-66), Am. Coll. Probate Counsel. Jurisprudence. Office: US Court Bldg 550 Fort St Boise ID 83724

ANDERSON, J. TRENT, lawyer; b. Indpls., July 22, 1939; s. Robert C. and Charlotte M. (Pfeifer) A.; m. Judith J. Zimmerman, Sept. 8, 1962; children: Evan M., Molly K. BS, Purdue U., 1961; LLB, U. Va., 1964. Bar: Ill. 1965, Ind. 1965. Teaching asst. U. Cal. Law Sch., Berkeley, 1964-65; assoc. Mayer, Brown & Platt, Chgo., 1965-72, ptnr., 1972—; instr. Loyola U. Law Sch., Chgo., 1985. Mem. ABA, Ill. Assn. Hosp. Attys., Law Club. Clubs: Union League (Chgo.), Mich. Shores (Wilmette, Ill.). Banking, General corporate, Contracts commercial. Home: 2312 Lincolnwood Dr Evanston IL 60201 Office: Mayer Brown & Platt 190 S LaSalle St Chicago IL 60603

ANDERSON, JAMES HURD, lawyer; b. Mpls., June 1, 1950; m. Virginia Birskovich, June 3, 1972. BA in Polit. Sci., U. Notre Dame, 1972; JD, U. Puget Sound, 1975. Bar: Minn. 1975, U.S. Dist. Ct. Minn., U.S. Ct. Appeals (8th cir.),. Sr. atty. Minn. Power Co., Duluth, 1976-84; ptnr. Anderson & Anderson, Nisswa, Minn., 1985—. Pres. Gull Lake Sailing Sch., Nisswa, 1979-82; bd. dirs. St. Ann's Residence, Duluth, 1983-84. Mem. ABA, Minn. Bar Assn., Crow Wing County Bar Assn. Club: Gull Lake Yacht (Nisswa) (vice commodore, bd. dirs., 1978—). General corporate, Real property, Estate planning. Home: 1830 E Linden Blvd Nisswa MN 56468 Office: Anderson & Anderson PO Box 18 Nisswa MN 56468

ANDERSON, JOHN FOSTER, lawyer; b. Richmond, Va., Apr. 27, 1956; s. Hal and Emily (Peebles) A. BS MechE, U. Va., 1978, JD, 1981. Bar: Va. 1981, U.S. Dist. Ct. (ea. and we. dists.) Va. 1981, U.S. Ct. Appeals (4th cir.) 1982, D.C. 1985. Law clk. to presiding justice U.S. Dist Ct. (we. dist.) Va., Charlottesville, Va., 1981-82; assoc. McGuire, Woods Battle & Boothe (merger of McGuire Woods & Battle and Boothe, Prichard & Dudley), Alexandria, Va., 1982—. Bd. dirs. UVA Club No. Va., 1984-86. Mem. ABA, Va. Bar Assn., Alexandria Bar Assn. Federal civil litigation, State civil litigation, Contracts commercial. Office: McGuire Woods Battle & Boothe 1199 N Fairfax St Alexandria VA 22313

ANDERSON, JOHN FREDERICK, lawyer; b. Billings, Mont., Sept. 1, 1921; s. Walter O. and Katharine (McElligott) A.; m. Mary Maxwell Bond, Nov. 4, 1943 (div. Sept. 1971); children: John F. Jr., Katherine McElligott. Student, Harvard U., 1943; AB, Duke U., 1943; LLB, U. Va., 1948. Bar: Va. 1948, U.S. Ct. Appeals (4th cir.) 1948, U.S. Supreme Ct. 1948. Ptnr. Anderson, Larrick & Larrick, Winchester, Va., 1948—. Served to lt. USNR, 1943-46. General practice, Insurance, Federal civil litigation. Home: Rt 5 Box 534 Lake St Clair Winchester VA 22601 Office: 25 E Boscawen St PO Box 444 Winchester VA 22601

ANDERSON, JOHN MACKENZIE, lawyer; b. Newark, Ohio, Dec. 1, 1938; s. Samuel Albert Jr. and Margaret Lillian (MacKenzie) A.; m. Jane Venable Shelton, Aug. 17, 1963; children—Graham, Gregory, Jonathan. A.B. with high honors, Kenyon Coll., 1960; LL.B., Yale U., 1963. Bar: Ohio 1963. Assoc., Peck, Shaffer & Williams, Cin., 1963-70, ptnr., 1970—, also chmn. adminstrv. com.; lectr. Practising Law Inst., 1975-77. Chmn. Am. Scotch Highland Breeders Assn., 1985—; trustee Seven Hills Schs., 1976-81; del. Democratic Nat. Conv., 1976; trustee Ohio Nut Growers Assn., 1979—. Mem. Am. Bar Assn., Ky. Bar Assn., No. Ky. Bar Assn., Ohio State Bar Assn., Cin. Bar Assn., Assn. of Bar of City of N.Y. Democrat. Episcopalian. Clubs: Cincinnati, Bankers; Yale (N.Y.). Author: Next of Kin, 1980; The Kincade Chronicles, 1986; contbr. articles to profl. jours. Municipal bonds. Home: 2717 Johnstone Pl Cincinnati OH 45206 Office: 2200 1st Nat Bank Center Cincinnati OH 45202

ANDERSON, KEITH, lawyer, banker; b. Phoenix, June 21, 1917; s. Carl and Helen (Fairchild) A.; m. Grace R. VanDenburg, 1941 (div. 1957); m. Catherine Huber, 1960; children: Fletcher F., Warren, Nicholas H. A.B., Dartmouth Coll., 1939; LL.B., Harvard U., 1942. Bar: N.Y. 1942, Ariz. 1946, Colo. 1950. Ptnr. Baker & Hostetler. Mem. ABA, Denver Bar Assn., Colo. Bar Assn. Democrat. Clubs: University (Denver); Arapahoe Tennis. Office: Baker & Hostetler 303 E 17th Ave Denver CO 80203

ANDERSON, LAURENCE ALEXIS, lawyer; b. Willmar, Minn., July 20, 1940; s. Laurence Alexis and Ann Victoria (Carlson) A.; m. Elaine Mae Sather, Aug. 19, 1961; children—Jeanne Louise, Ross Laurence. B.A. in Polit. Sci. and Econs., Macalester Coll., 1962; J.D., U. Minn., 1965. Bar: Minn. 1965, U.S. Dist. Ct. Minn. Assoc., Olson, Kief & Kalar, Bemidji, Minn., 1965-67; spl. asst. atty. gen. State of Minn., St. Paul, 1967-69; ptnr., dir., Crawford & Anderson, West St. Paul, Minn., 1969-84; shareholder, dir. Bowman and London Ltd., 1984—; dir., officer Legal Assistance of Dakota County (Minn.). Active Greater St. Paul United Way. Mem. ABA, Minn. State Bar Assn., Dakota County Bar Assn., West St. Paul C. of C. Republican. Clubs: Southview Country, Optimists (West St. Paul). Real property, General corporate, Banking. Office: 1400 Conwed Tower 444 Cedar St Saint Paul MN 55101

ANDERSON, LAWRENCE OHACO, lawyer; b. Phoenix, Sept. 7, 1948; s. Jack M. and Viola (Ohaco) A. BS, U. San Francisco, 1971; JD, Ariz. State U., Tempe, 1974. Bar: Ariz. 1975. Prosecutor City of Phoenix, 1973-75; assoc. Jack M. Anderson, Phoenix, 1975-78; sole practice Phoenix, 1978—. Mem. ABA, Assn. Trial Lawyers Am., Ariz. Trial Lawyers Assn. (bd. dirs. 1985—). Republic. Roman Catholic. Avocations: fishing, hunting, sports. Personal injury, Insurance, State civil litigation. Home: 5001 E Rovey Paradise Valley AZ 85253 Office: 4500 N 32d St Suite 100 Phoenix AZ 85018

ANDERSON, LAWRENCE ROBERT, JR., lawyer; b. Minden, La., Oct. 30, 1945; s. Lawrence Robert and Elnora Dale (Fincher) A.; m. Constance Lorraine Fauver, Oct. 21, 1977; children—Lauren Constance, Frank Lawrence. B.S., La. State U., 1967, J.D., 1971. Bar: La. 1971, U.S. Dist. Ct. (ea. dist.) La. 1971, U.S. Dist. Ct. (mid. dist.) La. 1972, U.S. Dist. Ct. (we. dist.) La. 1975, U.S. Ct. Appeals (5th cir.) 1971, U.S. Supreme Ct. 1975. Assoc. Sanders, Miller, Downing & Kean, Baton Rouge, 1971; assoc. Talley, Anthony, Hughes & Knight, Bogalusa, La., 1971-74; ptnr. Newman, Duggins, Drolla, Gamble & Anderson, Baton Rouge, 1974-76, Anderson & Roberts, Baton Rouge, 1976-79, Anderson, Anderson, Hawsey, Rainach and Stakelum, Baton Rouge, 1979-83, Anderson & Rainach, 1983—. Served as 1st lt. U.S. Army, 1972. Mem. ABA, La. Bar Assn., Baton Rouge Bar Assn., Comml. Law League Am., La. Trial Lawyers Assn., Assn. Trial Lawyers Am. Democrat. Clubs: Lake Sherwood, Camelot (Baton Rouge). Contbr. articles to profl. jours. Bankruptcy, Contracts commercial, Federal civil litigation. Home: 11937 Lake Sherwood Ave N Baton Rouge LA 70816 Office: 3622 Government St Baton Rouge LA 70806

ANDERSON, LEE BERGER, lawyer; b. Holden, W.Va.; d. Arthur Frederick and Artie Frances (Covington) Berger; m. Donald Brown Anderson, Apr. 17, 1946; m. 2d, William Hooker Ryland Sr., Sept. 18, 1959. LL.B., Nat. U., Washington, 1939, LL.M., 1941; J.D. George Washington U., 1968. Law clk., sec. Office of Gen. Counsel Fed. Savs. & Loan Ins. Corp., Washington, 1933-42; atty. Office of Solicitor U.S. Dept. Labor, Washington, 1942-43; trial atty. U.S. Dept. Justice, 1943-48; ptnr. Anderson & Anderson, Caldwell, Idaho, 1948-53; trial atty. Office Alien Property U.S. Dept. Justice, 1953-60, app. atty. Internal Security div., 1960-72; sole practice, North Chevy Chase, Md., 1972—; lectr. in field; Chmn. legal sub.-com. D.C. Commn. on Status of Women, 1967-69. Recipient Cert. of award U.S. Dept. Justice, 1962, 69; Bar Assn. D.C. Chmn. of the Year award, 1981. Fellow Am. Bar Found.; mem. ABA, Fed. Bar Assn., Internat. Bar Assn. (council), Inter-Am. Bar Assn., Fed. Cir. Bar Assn., Md. Bar Assn., D.C. Bar, Bar Assn. D.C. (chmn. civil service law com.), U.S. Supreme Ct. Hist. Soc., Am. Judicature Soc., Am. Arbitration Assn., Nat. Assn. Women Lawyers (pres. 1976-77, exec. bd. 1972-80), Women's Bar Assn. D.C. (pres. 1969-70), Phi Delta Delta, Phi Alpha Delta. Editor: Women Lawyers Jour., 1972-73. Federal civil litigation, Constitutional. Address: 3809 Montrose Driveway North Chevy Chase MD 20815

ANDERSON, LLOYD VINCENT, JR., lawyer; b. Eau Claire, Wis., Apr. 5, 1943; s. Lloyd V. and Marion (Benner) A.; m. Mary Sue Wilson, June 19, 1965; children—Matthew, Kirsten, Sam. B.Mgmt.Engring., Rensselaer Poly. Inst., 1965; J.D., Georgetown U., 1969. Bar: Va. 1969, Alaska 1970, Minn. 1972, U.S. Ct. Appeals 1972, U.S. Dist. Ct. Minn. and Alaska 1972, Trust Ter. Pacific Islands 1972, D.C. 1969, U.S. Patent Office 1969. Law clk. Alaska Supreme Ct., Juneau, 1969-70; asst. U.S. atty. Dept. Justice, Agana, Guam, 1970-72; atty. Gray Plant Mooty & Anderson, Mpls., 1972-74; shareholder, dir. Birch Horton Bittner Pestinger & Anderson, Anchorage, 1974—; dir. Lightning Devel., Guam, Arrow Leasing, Anchorage. Mem. Anchorage Park Bd., 1976. Mem. ABA, Alaska Bar Assn., Am. Trial Lawyers Assn. Lutheran. Clubs: Wash. Athletic (Seattle); Capt. Cook Athletic (Anchorage). Personal injury, State civil litigation, Patent. Home: 370 Oceanview Dr Anchorage AK 99515 Office: Birch Horton Bittner Pestinger & Anderson 1127 W 7th Ave Anchorage AK 99501

ANDERSON, MARGRET ELIZABETH, lawyer; b. Port Chester, N.Y., Oct. 2, 1949; d. Samuel Glover and Evelyn (Oliver) A.; m. robert t. McDonald, May 16, 1980; children: Christina Anderson-McDonald, Meredith Anderson-McDonald. Student, Wellesley Coll., 1967-69; BA, Yale U., 1971; JD, U. Pa., 1974. Bar: Pa. 1974, U.S. Dist. Ct. (ea. dist.) Pa. 1975, U.S. Ct. Appeals (3rd cir.) 1976. Intern Pub. Defender, Phila., 1972-73, U.S. Civil Rights Commn., Washington, 1973; legal writing instr. U. Pa. Sch. Law, Phila., 1973-74; asst. atty. gen. Pa. Dept. of Justice, Phila., 1974-79; sr. atty. Merck & Co., Inc., West Point, Pa., 1979—. Mem. Zoning Hearing Bd., Abington, Pa., 1985—. Mem. Nat. Bar Assn., Pa. Bar Assn. Episcopalian. Environment, product liability, food and drug. Office: Merck & Co Inc Sumneytown Pike West Point PA 19486

ANDERSON, MARY VIRGINIA, lawyer; b. Chgo., Jan. 15, 1949; d. Roger Y. and L. Lee (Hubbell) A.; m. Terry Calvani (div.); children: Dominic, Howard; m. Jeffrey S. Harris, 1980; children: Sarah, Noah. BA, Elmira Coll., 1970; JD, Stanford U., 1975. Bar: Tenn. 1976. Tchr. Ithaca (N.Y.) City Schs., 1970-72; law clk. to presiding justice Tenn. Supreme Ct., Nashville, 1975-77; assoc. Dearborn & Ewing, Nashville, 1977-84; gen. counsel, v.p., sec. Health-Am., Nashville, 1984-86; ptnr. Gillmor, Anderson & Gillmor, Nashville, 1986—. Named one of Outstanding Young Women Am., 1984. Mem. ABA, Nashville Bar Assn., Lawyer's Assn. for Women, Nat. Health Lawyer's Assn., Am. Corp. Counsel Assn. Avocations: bluegrass and folk music, swimming, cross country skiing. General corporate, Health. Home: 223 Mockingbird Rd Nashville TN 37205 Office: Gillmor Anderson & Gillmor 3322 West End Ave Suite 414 Nashville TN 37203

ANDERSON, MICHAEL STEVEN, lawyer; b. Mpls., May 25, 1954; s. Wesley James and Lorraine Kathryn (Sword) A.; m. Gail Karin Miller, June 18, 1977; children: Mark, Steven. BA magna cum laude, Cornell U., 1976; JD, Washington U., St. Louis, 1980. Bar: Wis. 1980, U.S. Dist. Ct. (ea. and we. dists.) Wis. 1980, U.S. Ct. Appeals (7th cir.) 1986. Ptnr. Brynelson & Herrick, Madison, Wis., 1980—. Mem. exec. com. Dane County Reps., Madison, 1984. Mem. ABA, Order of Coif. Mem. Evangelical Free Ch. Avocation: family. State civil litigation, Federal civil litigation. Home: 6421 Portage Rd DeForest WI 53532 Office: Brynelson Herrick et al 122 W Washington Ave Madison WI 53701

ANDERSON, PETER JOSEPH, lawyer; b. Camden, N.J., Mar. 15, 1951; s. Lester Ryan and Rose Helen; 1 child, Elizabeth Rose. BA, Dickinson Sch. of Law, 1972, JD, 1975. Bar: Pa. 1975, Ga. 1978, U.S. Dist. Ct. (ea. dist.) Pa. 1978, U.S. Dist. Ct. (no. dist.) Ga. 1978, U.S. Ct. Appeals (11th cir.) 1978, U.S. Tax Ct. 1986. Dep. dist. atty. Dist. Attys. Office, Harrisburg, Pa., 1974-77; ptnr. Peterson, Young, Self & Asselin, Atlanta, 1977—. Mem. ABA (subcom. securities litigation 1978—), Ga. Bar Assn., Pa. Bar Assn., Atlanta Bar Assn., Assn. Trial Lawyers Am. Republican. Roman Catholic. Federal civil litigation, State civil litigation, Securities. Home: 900 Drewry St NE Atlanta GA 30306 Office: Peterson Young Self & Asselin 230 Peachtree St NW Suite 1100 Atlanta GA 30303

ANDERSON, R. LANIER, III, federal judge; b. Macon, Ga., Nov. 12, 1936; s. Robert L. and Helen A.; m. Nancy Briska, Aug. 18, 1962; children: Robert, William Hilliar, Browne McIntosh. A.B. magna cum laude, Yale U., 1958; LL.B., Harvard U., 1961. Judge U.S. Ct. Appeals (11th cir.), 1979—. Office: US Court Appeals PO Box 977 Macon GA 31202 *

ANDERSON, REESE C., lawyer; b. Nephi, Utah, Oct. 2, 1918; s. Andrew Peter and Mary Naomi (Reese) A.; m. Elizabeth Moore Devitt, Feb. 19, 1944 (dec. May 1983); 1 child, Christine Marie (dec.). Student, Utah State U., 1935-40; BS, U. Utah, 1947, JD, 1949. Bar: Utah 1949, U.S. Dist. Ct. Utah 1949, U.S. Ct. Mil. Appeals 1955, U.S. Supreme Ct. 1955. Ptnr. Anderson & Elkins, Salt Lake City, 1949-51, Jensen, Anderson & Jensen, Salt Lake City, 1951-53, Anderson, Taylor & Tanner, Salt Lake City, 1953-60, Anderson, Whitmer & McKee, Salt Lake City, 1960-72; sole practice Salt Lake City, 1972—; owner, mgr. sta. KWHO, Salt Lake City, 1956-79, sta. KWHO-FM, Salt Lake City, 1965-79. Author: State of the Business, 1961. Pres. Salt Lake City chpt. Nat. Cystic Fibrosis Found., 1959-61; mem. Salt Lake City Music Assn., 1966-69; bd. dirs. Utah Cystic Fibrosis Found., 1966-69. Served to maj. USAF, 1941-47, ETO, NATOUSA. Mem. Assn. Trial Lawyers Am., Salt Lake County Bar Assn., Am. Arbitration Assn. Club: Ft. Douglas Mil. (Salt Lake City). Administrative and regulatory, Probate, Personal income taxation. Office: 1241 E Brickyard Rd Suite 401 Salt Lake City UT 84106

ANDERSON, REUBEN V., state supreme court justice. Justice Miss. Supreme Ct., Jackson, 1985—. Office: Office of Supreme Court Miss Jackson MS 39205 *

ANDERSON, R(OBERT) BRUCE, lawyer; b. Effingham, Ill., Feb. 4, 1956; s. Robert Dee and Annalee (Schreiner) A.; m. Shannon Elizabeth Whitcomb, Mar. 19, 1983. BS in Polit. Sci., Ill. State U., 1977; JD, Stetson U., 1981. Bar: Ill. 1981, Fla. 1981. Assoc. Law Offices of James R. DePew, Bloomington, Ill., 1981-82; chief asst. county atty., utilities counsel Collier County, Naples, Fla., 1982—. Mem. editorial adv. com. Local Govt. Law Symposium, Stetson Law Rev., 1986—. State chmn. Ill. Teen-Age Rep. Fedn., Springfield, 1974; alt. del. Rep. Nat. conv., Kansas City, Mo., 1976, 80; mem. exec. com. Collier County Reps., Naples, Fla., 1986; treas. Collier County Rep. Exec. Com., 1987. Washington Crossing Found. scholar, 1974. Mem. Ill. Bar Assn., Fla. Bar Assn., Am. Coll. Trial Lawyers (Excellence in Advocacy medal 1981), Collier County Bar Assn., Nat. Inst. Mcpl. Law (chmn. com. on municipally-owned utilities 1984-86), Alpha Kappa Lamda (Holmes award 1978). Republican. Methodist. Local government, Public utilities, State civil litigation. Office: Office Collier County Atty 3301 Tamiami Trail E Naples FL 33962

ANDERSON, ROBERT LOUIS, lawyer; b. Aberdeen, S.D., Oct. 13, 1938; s. Louis Roland and Charlotte Maude (Valle) A.; m. Rosanne Jane Fritsche, Aug. 23, 1959; children—Erik Robert, Lars Robert. B.S., S.D. State U., 1960; J.D., U. Colo., 1966. Bar: Nebr. 1966, U.S. Dist. Ct. Nebr. 1966. Assoc. Mason, Knudsen, Berkheimer and Endacott, Lincoln, Nebr., 1966-70; ptnr. Knudsen, Berkheimer, Beam, Richardson and Endacott, 1970-82; sole practice, Lincoln, 1982—. Served to comdr. JAGC, USN, 1957-80, active duty, 1960-63. Mem. Lincoln Bar Assn., Nebr. Bar Assn. (past mem. and chmn. com. on ins.), ABA, Fedn. Ins. Counsel, Nebr. Assn. Trial Attys., Assn. Trial Lawyers Am. Republican. Insurance, Personal injury. Address: 3201 Pioneers Blvd Suite 216 Lincoln NE 68502

ANDERSON, SCOTT GALE, transp. corp. exec., lawyer; b. Steele, N.D., Apr. 27, 1937; s. Elmer L. and Velma E. (Woessner) A.; m. Rosemary Anderson, Dec. 7, 1963; children—Heather, Heidi. B.S., Jamestown Coll., 1959; J.D., U. N.D., 1966. Bar: N.D. 1966. Mem. N.D. Ho. of Reps., 1959-60; city atty. Fargo, N.D., 1967-70; pres. Scott Anderson Prodns., Reston, Va., 1970-77; with Burlington No. Inc., Washington, 1977—, v.p. legis. affairs, 1982—. Del., mem. platform com. Democratic Nat. Conv., 1960, conv. del., mem. rules com., 1968; Dem. candidate for Congress, 1962; bd. dirs. Nat. Soc. Food for Peace, 1961-63. Recipient numerous nat., internat. film awards including 6 Cine Golden Eagles. Mem. ABA, N.D. Bar Assn. Episcopalian. Clubs: Nat. Press (Washington); Elks (Fargo), Order of Coif. Author: (with Thomas Burgum) The Counselor and the Law, 1975. Writer, dir., producer 40 TV film documentaries. Legislative, General corporate, General practice. Home: 11431 Hook Rd Reston VA 22090 Office: Burlington No Inc 1050 Connecticut Ave NW Suite 200 Washington DC 20036

ANDERSON, STANTON DEAN, lawyer; b. Portland, Oreg., Oct. 18, 1940; s. Lloyd T. and Ruth M. (Brunes) A.; children: Stanton D. Jr., Mamie D.; m. Carol A. Serpa, June 14, 1985. BA, Westmont Coll., 1962; JD, Willamette U., 1969. Bar: D.C. 1969. Staff asst. to pres. White House, Washington, 1971-73; dep. asst. sec. State Dept., Washington, 1973-74; assoc. Surrey & Morse, Washington, 1975-76, ptnr., 1977-81; ptnr. Anderson, Hibey, Nauheim & Blair, Washington, 1981—; bd. dirs. Berkley Fed. Savings Bank, Norfolk, Va., Hay Systems Inc., Washington. Assoc. editor Willamette U. Law Rev. Mem. Ctr. for Internat. Pvt. Enterprise, D.C. Reps. Cen. Com., del., 1980. Mem. ABA, D.C. Bar Assn., Am. Soc. Interional Law, U.S. C. of C. (internat. trade subcom.). Clubs: University (Washington); Congl. Country (Bethesda, Md.).

ANDERSON, STEPHEN GUY, lawyer; b. Middletown, Ohio, Mar. 21, 1949; s. Jarold Guy and Nancy Ann (Metcalf) A.; m. Pamela Gail Steele, Dec. 22, 1975; children—Nathaniel, Benjamin. B.A., U. Cin., 1971; postgrad. Louisville Presbyn. Theol. Sem., 1971-72; J.D. cum laude, U. Louisville, 1975. Bar: Ky. 1975, U.S. Ct. Claims 1975, U.S. Ct. Appeals (Fed. cir.) 1982, U.S. Ct. Appeals (9th cir.) 1980, U.S. Ct. Appeals (8th cir.) 1984, U.S. Dist. Ct. D.C. 1984, U.S. Ct. Appeals (6th cir.) 1986, U.S. Supreme Ct. 1986. Trial atty. commercial litigation br. civil div. U.S. Dept. Justice, Washington, 1975-82, sr. trial counsel, 1982-83, asst. dir., 1983-84; assoc. Thompson & Mitchell, St. Louis, Washington, 1984-86; ptnr. Heiskell, Donelson, Bearman, Adams, Williams & Kirsch, Knoxville, Tenn., 1986—. Mem. ABA, Tenn. Bar Assn. (comml. litigation, banking, bankruptcy sect.). Home: 4196 Towanda Trail Knoxville TN 37919 Office: Heiskell Donelson Bearman Adams Williams & Kirsch Plaza Tower Suite 600 Knoxville TN 37929

ANDERSON, SUELLEN, lawyer; b. Los Angeles, Apr. 11, 1950; d. Robert Walter and Marian D. (Guild) Greiner; m. Dane Roger Anderson; children: Robert Joseph, Nicholas Drew. BA, Calif. State U., Los Angeles, 1974; JD, U. So. Calif., 1978. Bar: Calif. 1978, U.S. Dist. Ct. (cen. dist.) Calif. 1978. Corp. counsel, asst. sec. Tenneco West, Inc., Bakersfield, Calif., 1978-84; programs coordinator Greater Bakersfield Legal Assistance, 1985—; sec. Greater Bakersfield Legal Assistance, 1980-85. Assoc. dir. Alliance in Family Violence, Bakersfield, 1985—; bd. dirs. Tenneco Employees Fed. Credit Union, Bakersfield, 1981-83. Mem. Calif. Bar Assn. (pro bono devel. 1986), Kern County (Calif.) Bar Assn. (bd. dirs. 1985—), Kern County Women Lawyers Assn. (pres. 1982-83, bd. dirs. 1982—), Kern County Women Lawyers Scholarship Found. (v.p. 1986—). Democrat. General corporate, Voluntary legal services. Office: Greater Bakersfield Legal Assist 615 California Ave Bakersfield CA 93304

ANDERSON, TERENCE JAMES, law educator; b. Chgo., Feb. 26, 1940; s. James E. and Charlotte P. (Flatley) A.; children—Michael, Kathleen, Jamie, Andrew. B.A., Wabash Coll., 1961; J.D., U. Chgo., 1964. Bar: Ill. 1967, D.C. 1973, Fla. 1977. Local cts. commr., Zomba, Malawi, Africa., 1964-66; assoc. Goldberg, Weigle, Mallin & Gitles, Chgo., 1966-69, ptnr., 1970-73; atty. prof. Antioch Sch. of Law, Washington, 1973-78, acad. dean, 1975-76; vis. prof. U. Miami Sch. of Law, Coral Gables, Fla., 1976-78, prof., 1978—; spl. counsel to gen. counsel SEC, Washington, summers 1980-81; dir. Legal Services of Greater Miami, Inc., 1977-83. Bd. dirs. ACLU of South Fla., 1981-85; mem. dist. admissions com. U.S. Dist. Ct. (so. dist.) Fla. Mem. ABA, Am. Assn. Law Schs. Federal civil litigation, Legal education, Jurisprudence. Office: Univ Miami Sch Law PO Box 248087 Coral Gables FL 33124

ANDERSON, THOMAS ERNEST, lawyer; b. Detroit, May 1, 1945; s. Ernest Washington and Jeanne Elizabeth (Schoonover) A.; m. Janis M. Zembrzuski, Aug. 9., 1974. BA, Wayne State U., 1974; JD, U. Detroit, 1981. Bar: Mich. 1981, U.S. Dist. Ct. (ea. dist.) Mich. 1981, Fla. 1982, U.S. Patent and Trademark Office 1984. Assoc. Basile, Weintraub & Hanlon, Troy, Mich., 1980-82, James W. Goss P.C., Southfield, Mich., 1982-83, Gifford, Groh, Van Ophem et al, Birmingham, Mich., 1984—; assoc. prof. Walsh Coll., Troy, 1985—. Assoc. editor U. Detroit Law Rev. Mem. ABA, Alpha Sigma Nu. Roman Catholic. Avocation: sailing. Patent, Trademark and copyright, Entertainment. Home: 434 Whippers In Ct Bloomfield Hills MI 48013 Office: Gifford Groh Van Ophem et al 280 N Woodward Birmingham MI 48011

ANDERSON, THOMAS WILLMAN, lawyer; b. St. Paul, Feb. 27, 1950; s. Carl Willman and Ruth (Krogsrud) A.; m. Kathryn Jean Hagen, Feb. 14, 1981; children: Benjamin, Nicholas. Student, Case Western Res. U., 1968-69; B in Math. with distinction, U. Minn., 1972, JD cum laude, 1975. Bar: Minn. 1975, U.S. Dist. Ct. Minn. 1975, U.S. Dist. Ct. (no. dist.) Ill. 1984. Assoc. Oppenheimer, Wolff, Foster, Shepard & Donnelly, St. Paul, 1975-81; from legal counsel to gen. counsel Met. Airports Commn., Mpls., 1981—. Bd. dirs. Coordinated Health Care, St. Paul, 1985-86; counsel Met. Pub. Airport Found. Mem. ABA (local govt. sect., airport law com.), Minn. Bar Assn., Airports Operators Council Internat. (vice chmn. legal com. 1983-84, chmn. 1984-85). Avocations: fishing, skiing, running. Local government, Real property, Environment. Home: 4603 Drexel Edina MN 55424 Office: Met Airports Commn 6040-28th Ave S Minneapolis MN 55450

ANDERSON, TONI-RENEE, lawyer; b. Johnstown, Pa.; d. Stephen and Rita Mae (Bellavia) Hnatkovich; m. Mark Edward Anderson, Aug. 2, 1986. BS in Edn., Indiana U. of Pa., 1976, postgrad., 1976; JD, U. Pitts., 1979. Bar: Pa. 1980, U.S. Dist. Ct. (we. dist.) Pa. 1980, U.S. Supreme Ct. 1984. Sole practice Ebensburg, Pa., 1983—; master Orphans' Ct. Cambria County Ct. Common Pleas, Ebensburg, 1984—; mcpl. solicitor Cambria Twp., Ebensburg, 1984—. Jud. Legal asst. Ct. Common Pleas Cambria County, Ebensburg, 1981-86, asst. dist. atty., 1986—; speaker Jud. Retention Campaign, Cambria County, 1981, Jud. Superior Ct. Campaign, Cambria County, 1983, YWCA, Johnstown, Pa., 1981-83; coordinator legal div. Law Day/Red Mass, Cambria County, 1981—. Mem. ABA, Pa. Bar Assn. (Cambria County young lawyers' rep. 1986-87), Cambria County Bar Assn. (young lawyers' liason 1986-87), Cambria County Young Lawyers' Div. (sec., treas. 1981-83, v.p. 1983-84, pres. 1984-85), Am. Assn. Profl. Women (speaker 1982), Kappa Delta Phi. General practice, Probate, Legal research. Office: Courthouse Dist Attys Office Center St Ebensburg PA 15931

ANDERSON, WOLFGANG R., lawyer; b. Frankfurt, Fed. Republic Germany, June 2, 1941; came to U.S., 1953; s. Vincent O. and Irmgard C. (Happel) A.; m. Maria K. Butenko, Nov. 19, 1972; children: Theodore W., Benjamin J., Andrew C., Daniel A. BA in Prelaw, U. Wash., 1963, JD, 1966. Bar: Wash. 1966, U.S. Supreme Ct. 1971, U.S. Ct. Mil. Appeals. From assoc. to ptnr. Jonson & Jonson, Seattle, 1970-77; sr. ptnr. Anderson & Fields, Inc., P.S., Seattle, 1977—; judge pro tem superior and dist. cts., State of Wash., Seattle; speaker on divorce various tv programs, Seattle. Served to capt. JAGC, U.S. Army, 1966-70. Republican. Am. Orthodox. Club: Wash. Athletic Club. Lodge: Elks. Avocations: antique collecting, collecting art, stamps, family activities. Family and matrimonial. Office: Anderson & Fields 207 E Edgar St Seattle WA 98199

ANDERSSON, W. PAUL, lawyer; b. Bielefeld, Westphalia, Fed. Republic Germany, Apr. 28, 1946; s. Knud D. and Liselotte (Niemann) A.; m. Billie Venturatos, July 12, 1969; children: Dita, Elizabeth, Andrea. Student, La. State U., 1964-68; JD, Tulane U., 1971. Bar: La. 1972, U.S. Dist. Ct. (ea. dist.) La. 1973. From assoc. to ptnr. Hammett, Leake & Hammett, New Orleans, 1971—. Trustee Greek Orthodox Cathedral, New Orleans; mem. New Orleans Opera Chorus. Mem. ABA, La. Bar Assn., New Orleans Bar Assn. (chmn. civil rules com. 1985—), La. Assn. Def. Counsel (bd. dirs. 1985—), New Orleans Assn. Def. Counsel, Internat. Assn. Def. Counsel. Avocations: snow skiing, singing. Insurance, State civil litigation, Construction. Office: Hammett Leake & Hammett 1 Canal Pl Suite 2500 New Orleans LA 70130

ANDORKA, FRANK HENRY, lawyer; b. Lorain, Ohio, July 25, 1946; s. Frank Henry and Sue (Parham) A.; m. M. Jean Deliman, Aug. 10, 1968; children: Frank Henry Jr., Claire E. AB, Ohio U., 1968; postgrad., Ind. U., 1968-69; JD, Cornell U., 1975. Bar: Ohio 1975, U.S. Dist. Ct. (no. dist.) Ohio 1975. From assoc. to ptnr. Baker & Hostetler, Cleve., 1975—. Served to 1st lt. U.S. Army, 1969-72. Mem. ABA (chmn. internat. copyright laws and treaties com. 1984-86, chmn. govt. relations to copyright com. 1986—), Ohio Bar Assn., Greater Cleve. Bar Assn. Avocations: bowling, tennis. Trademark and copyright, Character merchandise licensing. Home: 31000 Clinton Dr Bay Village OH 44140 Office: Baker & Hostetler 3200 Nat City Ctr Cleveland OH 44114

ANDREOFF, CHRISTOPHER ANDON, lawyer; b. Detroit, July 15, 1947; s. Andon Anastas and Mildred Dimitry (Kolinoff) A.; m. Nancy Anne Krochmal, Jan. 12, 1980; 1 child, Alison Brianne. B.A., Wayne State U., 1969; postgrad. in law Washington U., St. Louis, 1969-70; J.D., U. Detroit, 1972. Bar: Mich. 1972, U.S. Dist. Ct. (ea. dist.) Mich. 1972, U.S. Ct. Appeals (6th cir.) 1974, Fla. 1978, U.S. Supreme Ct. 1980. Legal intern Wayne County Prosecutor's Office, Detroit, 1970-72; law clk. Wayne County Cir. Ct., Detroit, 1972-73; asst. U.S. atty. U.S. Dept. Justice, Detroit, 1973-80, asst. chief Criminal Div., U.S. Atty.'s Office, 1977-80, spl. atty. Organized Crime and Racketeering sect. U.S. Dept. Justice, 1980-84, dep. chief Detroit Organized Crime Strike Force, 1982-85, mem. narcotics adv. com. U.S. Dept. Justice, 1979-80; assoc. Evans & Luptak, Detroit, 1985—; lectr. U.S. Atty. Gen. Advocacy Inst., 1984. Recipient numerous spl. commendations FBI, U.S. Drug Enforcement Adminstrn., U.S. Dept. Justice, U.S. Atty. Gen. Mem. ABA, Fed. Bar Assn. (speaker criminal law sect. Detroit 1983—), Mich. Bar Assn., Fla. Bar Assn., Detroit Bar Assn. Greek Orthodox. Criminal, Federal civil litigation, State civil litigation. Home: 4661 Rivers Edge Dr Troy MI 48098 Office: Evans & Luptak 2500 Buhl Bldg Detroit MI 48226

ANDREOLI, PETER DONALD, lawyer; b. N.Y.C., July 31, 1919; s. Peter E. and Lucy C. (Scannapleco) A.; m. Catherine F. McCarthy, Aug. 25, 1945; children—Peter, Brian, Catherine, Christine, Francine. B.S., St. John's U., Bklyn., 1941; LL.B., Columbia U., 1947. Bar: N.Y. 1948, U.S. Dist. Ct. (ea. and so. dists.) N.Y. 1961, U.S. Supreme Ct. 1966, U.S. Ct. Appeals (2d cir.) 1975, U.S. Tax. Ct. 1977, U.S. Dist. Ct. (no. dist.) N.Y. 1978, Assoc. Kupfer, Silberfeld, Nathan & Danziger, N.Y.C., 1947-48; asst. dist. atty. New York County (N.Y.), 1948-76, dep. chief rackets bur., 1963-68, chief Criminal Ct. Trial Bur., 1969-70, chief Supreme Ct. Trial Bur., 1970-74, chief Frauds Bur., 1974-76; spl. state prosecutor Onondaga County (N.Y.), 1976-81; sole practice, Pelham, N.Y., 1981—; lectr. Practicing Law, Inst., Battelle Inst.; organized Crime Confs., 1966-68, Econ. Crim Conf., 1975-76, 1st Nat. Symposium in Law Enforcement, 1978. Served to col. USAAF, 1942-47; with USAFR, 1947-79. Decorated D.F.C. with oak leaf cluster, Air medal with 4 oak leaf clusters, Presl. citation (2). Mem. ABA, Assn. Bar City N.Y., New York County Lawyers, N.Y. State Trial Lawyers Assn., Columbia Law Alumni Assn., Xavier Alumnae Sodality, Phi Delta Phi. Club: K.C. Mem. editorial bd. St. John's Law Rev., 1941-42. General practice. Home and Office: 134 Harmon Ave Pelham NY 10803

ANDRESEN, MALCOLM, lawyer; b. Medford, Wis., July 26, 1917; s. Thomas Whelen and Ethel (Malkson) A.; m. Ann Kimball, Oct. 17, 1942 (deceased); children—Anthony M., Susan A. Bridges, Abbott K.; m. Barbara Brown, May 23, 1971; m. Nigi Sato, Dec. 12, 1979. B.A., U. Wis., 1940, LL.B., 1941. Bar: Wis. 1941, N.Y. 1946, U.S. Supreme Ct. 1958. Acct., J.D. Miller & Co., N.Y.C., 1946-47; jr. tax acct. Peat Marwick Mitchell & Co., N.Y.C., 1947-48; assoc. Davis Wagner Hallett & Russell, N.Y.C., 1948-52; tax counsel, then sr. tax counsel, then sr. govt. relations adviser Mobile Oil Corp., N.Y.C., 1952-70; dir. tax legal affairs Nat. Fgn. Trade Council, N.Y.C., 1970-73; of counsel Delson & Gordon, N.Y.C., 1973-77, Whitman & Ransom, N.Y.C., 1977-86; sole practice, 1986—. Trustee, treas. Cathedral Ch. of St. John the Divine, N.Y.C., 1977-84. Served to capt. USMCR, 1942-46. Decorated Bronze Star medal. Mem. Assn. Bar City N.Y., Internat. Fiscal Assn. (council U.S.A. br.), Tax Mgmt., Inc. (adv. bd.). Democrat. Episcopalian. Club: Univ. (N.Y.C.). Corporate taxation, State and local taxation. Home: Two Lincoln Sq Apt 24-D New York NY 10023 Office: 600 Third Ave New York NY 10016

ANDREW, JOHN HENRY, lawyer, retail corporation executive; b. Duluth, Minn., May 23, 1936; s. Frederick William and Florence Elizabeth (Phillips) A.; m. Floretta Claudette Townsend; children—Sean Townsend, Brett Townsend. B.A. cum laude with distinction, U. Minn., Duluth, 1958; J.D., Northwestern U., 1961. Bar: Ill. 1961, Calif. 1975, N.Y. 1980. Assoc., Pattishall, McAuliffe & Hofstetter, Chgo., 1961-71; sr. atty. J.C. Penney Co., Inc., N.Y.C., 1971-74, gen. atty., Western regional counsel, Los Angeles, 1974—. Chmn. pub. affairs com. Planned Parenthood Assn. of Chgo., 1970-71; mem. Calif. State Democratic Central Com., 1976-82. Mem. ABA, Ill. State Bar Assn. (chmn. internat. law sect. 1969-70), Calif. State Bar (com. on consumer fin. services 1982-84), Royal Instn. Cornwall, Am. Philatelic Soc., Calif. C. of C. (regulatory, consumer and legal affairs com. 1974—). Legislative, Consumer commercial, Administrative and regulatory. Home: 5930 S LaCienega Blvd Los Angeles CA 90056 Office: JC Penney Co Inc 350 S Figueroa St Suite 257 Los Angeles CA 90071

ANDREW, LEONARD DELESSIO, lawyer; b. N.Y.C., Nov. 16, 1941; s. Albert E. and Josephine (DeLessio) A.; m. Helen Fischer, June 25, 1966; children: Elizabeth Jane, Martha Carol. AB in History, Lafayette Coll., 1963; JD, St. John's U., 1969. Bar: N.Y. 1969, D.C. 1973, U.S. Supreme Ct. 1973, Calif. 1975. Staff atty. IBM Corp., Armonk, N.Y., 1969-72, various positions, 1976—; spl. asst. U.S. Solicitor of Labor, U.S. Dept. of Labor, Washington, 1972-73; regional counsel IBM Corp., Los Angeles, 1974-76; bd. dirs. Asbury Terr. Housing Corp., Tarrytown, N.Y. Trustee United Meth. Ch. of the Tarrytowns, 1976—. Served to 1st lt. U.S. Army, 1963-65. Antitrust, Computer, General corporate. Home: 11 Pokahoe Dr North Tarrytown NY 10591 Office: IBM Corp 44 S Broadway White Plains NY 10601

ANDREWS, BOLIVAR COLEMAN, JR., lawyer, executive; b. Dallas, Feb. 14, 1937; s. Bolivar Coleman and Nan (Dickinson) A.; m. Janet Guthrie, June 3, 1960; children—Bolivar Coleman III, Jeannette Dickinson, Mary Guthrie. B.A., U. Tex., 1960, J.D., 1961; A.M.P., Harvard U., 1982. Bar: Tex., U.S. Dist. Ct. (so. dist.) Tex., U.S. Ct. Appeals (5th cir.), U.S. Ct. Appeals (D.C. dir.). Enumerator Census Bur., Austin, 1960; librarian Atty. Gen.'s Office, Austin, 1960-61; atty. Tex. Eastern Corp., Houston, 1961-77; asst. gen. counsel Tex. Eastern Corp., 1977-81, v.p., asst. gen. counsel, 1981-84, v.p., gen. counsel, 1984—. Sr. warden of assoc. vestry Ch. of St. John the Divine, 1973; mem. Mus. Fine Arts, Zool. Soc., Cultural Arts Council of Houston. Fellow Houston Bar Found., Tex. Bar Found. (life); mem. ABA, Fed. Energy Bar Assn., Houston Bar Assn., Houston Jr. Bar Assn. (sec. 1966), State Jr. Bar Tex. (bd. dirs. 1968-72, chmn. bd. 1970-71), State Bar Tex. (corp. counsel sect. 1980-81), Southwestern Legal Found. (adv. bd. internat. oil and gas ednl. ctr. 1984), Exec. Assn. Houston, Phi Alpha Delta, Kappa Alpha Order (pres. 1959). Clubs: Houston Country, Forum, Houston Ctr., Houston, Houston Met. Racquet. Lodge: Kiwanis (chmn. program 1984-85). Avocations: tennis; golf. General corporate, FERC practice. Home: 5819 Shady River Houston TX 77057 Office: Tex Eastern Corp PO Box 2521 Houston TX 77001

ANDREWS, DALE CARTER, lawyer, b. St. Louis, Jan. 11, 1949; s. Wallace Carroll and Ruth Katherine (Moelling) A.; m. Patricia Marlene Black, Jan. 6, 1984; 1 child, Devon Andrews Black. B.A. in Sociology, George Washington U., 1971; J.D. cum laude, Am. U., Washington, 1976. Bar: D.C. 1976. Programmer/analyst McDonnell Douglas Corp., St. Louis, 1971-72, Washington, 1972-73; sr. research assoc. Am. U. Law Sch., 1974-76; clk. D.C. Ct. Apls., 1976-77; assoc. Galland, Kharasch, Calkins & Short, Washington, 1977-82; assoc. Short, Klein & Karas, P.C., Washington, 1982-84, ptnr, 1984—; adj. lectr. Am. U., 1980-84. Mem. ABA, Maritime Adminstrv. Bar Assn., Internat. Aviation Club, Sigma Phi Epsilon. Democrat. Club: Jefferson Islands (social chmn. 1978-83, bd. govs. 1980-84, bd. advs. 1984—) (Avenue, Md.). Maritime law, Aviation, Antitrust. Office: Short Klein & Karas PC 1101 30th St NW Washington DC 20007

ANDREWS, DAVID JOSEPH, lawyer; b. Providence, May 11, 1951; m. Susan G. Johnson, May 20, 1978; children: Christopher, Scott. BA, Brown U., 1972; JD, Boston U., 1977. Bar: Mass. 1977, U.S. Dist. Ct. Mass. 1980. Assoc. Harnish, MacDonald et al., Waltham, Mass., 1977-82; atty. Honeywell Inc., Waltham, 1982-84, counsel, 1984-86, sr. counsel, 1986—. J. Newton Esdaile scholar Boston U., 1974-77. Mem. Boston Bar Assn. (mem. computer law com. 1984-85), ABA (litigation sect.). Avocations: tennis, windsurfing. Federal civil litigation, State civil litigation, Computer. Office: Honeywell Inc 333 Wyman St Waltham MA 02154

ANDREWS, DEAN, lawyer; b. Andover, Ohio, July 18, 1931; s. C. Garry and Gladys Evelyn (Palmer) A.; m. Jeanne J., July 16, 1962; children—Laura Thompson, Frederick William. A.B., Ohio Wesleyan U., 1955, LL.B., Ohio State U., 1958. Bar: Fla. 1959. Assoc., Fleming, O'Bryan & Fleming, 1959; ptnr. Andrews & Lubbers, 1959-61, Andrews, Lubbers & Kilby, 1961-64, Andrews, Singer, Lubbers & Kilby, 1964-72, Andrews & Lubbers, Ft. Lauderdale, Fla., 1972—; chief mcpl. judge City of Ft. Lauderdale, 1963-64, gen. counsel, 1965-73; dir. Bank of Fla., Ocean Nat. Bank, 1966-73; founder, dir. Gt. Am. Bank of Broward County, 1973—. Bd. dirs. Ft. Lauderdale Symphony Soc., 1966-68, Broward League of Municipalities, 1967-68. Served with U.S. Army, 1950-53. Mem. ABA, Fla. Bar Assn., Broward County Bar Assn., Internat. Bar Assn., Am. Judicature Soc., Phi Delta Theta, Phi Delta Phi. Republican. Methodist. Clubs: Le Club, Coral Ridge Country (Ft. Lauderdale); Grandfather Golf and Country (Linville, N.C.). Author: You Can Beat City Hall, 1971. Banking, General corporate, Real property. Home: 3301 NE 16th St Fort Lauderdale FL 33304 Office: 2601 E Oakland Park Blvd Fort Lauderdale FL 33306

ANDREWS, GORDON CLARK, lawyer; b. Boston, Mar. 25, 1941; s. Loring Beal and Flora Spencer (Hinckley) A.; m. Deborah M. Devere, July 9, 1966; children: Christine Leigh, Cynthia Lyn, Carey Loring. B.A., Dartmouth Coll., 1963; J.D., N.Y. U., 1969. Bar: N.Y. State bar 1970, Conn. bar 1971. Assoc. firm Morgan Lewis & Bockius (and predecessor), N.Y.C., 1969-72; asst. sec., asst. gen. counsel Howmet Corp., Greenwich, Conn., 1973-75; sec., asst. gen. counsel Beker Industries Corp., Greenwich, 1976—; v.p. Beker Industries Corp., 1978-81; gen. counsel M&T Chems., Inc., Woodbridge, N.J., 1982-86, v.p. law dept., 1986—. Served to lt. USNR, 1963-69. Recipient Am. Law award, 1969. Mem. Am., N.Y. State, Conn. bar assns., Am. Soc. Corporate Secs., Westchester-Fairfield Corporate Counsel Assn. Republican. Club: Greenwich Country. Home: 46 Club Rd Riverside CT 06878 Office: M&T Chems Inc 1 Woodbridge Ctr Woodbridge NJ 07095

ANDREWS, H(OWARD) RAYMOND, JR., lawyer; b. Charleston, W.Va., Apr. 9, 1930; s. Howard Raymond and Juanita Mae (Armstrong) A.; m. Alice Ann Roush, Nov. 22, 1952; children: John Howard (dec.), Thomas Chester. AB, W.Va. U., 1952, JD, 1956. Bar: W.Va. 1956, Mich. 1979. Sole practice Ripley, W.Va., 1956-58; atty. United Fuel Gas Co., Charleston, 1958-73; sr. atty Columbia Gas Transmission Corp., Charleston, 1973-78; sr. corp. counsel Amway Corp., Ada, Mich., 1978—. Editor W.Va. Law Rev., 1955-56. Served to 1st lt. U.S. Army, 1952-54, Korea. Avocations: photography, computers, music, flying. General corporate. Home: 1505 Woodlawn SE East Grand Rapids MI 49506 Office: Amway Corp 7575 E Fulton Rd Ada MI 49355

ANDREWS, JOHN CHARLES, lawyer; b. Duncan, Okla., Oct. 24, 1926; s. John Charles and Eva L. (Loos) A.; m. Patricia Coffey, Nov. 22, 1952; children: John Charles, Patricia Kathleen, Michael Joseph, Margaret Ann, Daniel Coffey, Timothy Jerome. Student, Oklahoma City U., 1944; J.D., Okla. U., 1949. Bar: Okla. 1949. Asst. ins. commr. State of Okla., 1949-50; mem. firm Andrews Davis Legg Bixler Milsten & Murrah, Inc. (and predecessors), Oklahoma City, 1967—; bd. dirs. Founders Bank & Trust Co., Balliet's Inc., Cen. Cemetery Co. of Ill. Served with AUS, 1944-46. Mem. Am., Okla. bar assns., Phi Delta Phi. Roman Catholic. Club: Beacon. General corporate, Banking. Home: 1709 Wilshire Blvd Oklahoma City OK 73116 Office: 500 W Main St Oklahoma City OK 73102

ANDREWS, WILLIAM DOREY, lawyer, educator; b. N.Y.C., Feb. 25, 1931; s. Sidney Warren and Margaret (Dorey) A.; A.B., Amherst Coll., 1952, LL.D., 1977; LL.B., Harvard U., 1955; m. Shirley May Herrman, Dec. 26, 1953; children: Helen Estelle, Roy Herrman, John Frederick, Margaret Dorey, Susan Louise, Carol Mary. Bar: Mass. 1959. Practice in Boston, 1959-63; assoc. Ropes & Gray, 1959-63; lectr. Harvard Law Sch., Cambridge, Mass., 1961-63, asst. prof., 1963-65, prof., 1965—; assoc. reporter for accessions tax proposal Am. Law Inst. Fed. Estate and Gift Tax Project; gen. reporter for subchpt. C, Am. Law Inst. Fed. Income Tax Project, 1974—; cons. U.S. Treasury Dept., 1965-68. Mem. Zoning Bd. Appeals, Concord, 1966-73; bd. dirs., asso. gen. counsel Harvard Coop. Soc. Served to lt. USNR, 1955-58. Mem. Am. Law Inst., Am. Bar Assn., AAUP. Legal education. Office: Harvard Law Sch Cambridge MA 02138 *

ANDRIN, ALBERT ANTAL, lawyer; b. Chgo., Dec. 2, 1928; s. Antal and Helena (Lebda) A.; m. Sally Rose Cerkleski, Apr. 6, 1963; children—Lisa, Antal, Albert. B.A., Roosevelt U., 1952; LL.B., Chgo. Kent Coll. Law, 1956. Bar: Ill. 1956. Assoc. Axelrod, Goodman & Steiner, Chgo., 1956-61; ptnr. Levy, Andrin & Stillerman, Chgo., 1961-75, Burke, Kerwin, Towle & Andrin, Chgo., 1975-83. Served to sgt. USAF, 1946-49. Mem. ABA, Ill. Bar Assn., Chgo. Bar Assn., Motor Carrier Lawyers Assn., Mensa. Administrative and regulatory, General practice. Home: 9016 S Lemont Rd Downers Grove IL 60516 Office: 222 W Ontario St Suite 220 Chicago IL 60610

ANDRUS, KAY LEGRAND, law librarian; b. Idaho Falls, Idaho, Apr. 5, 1953; s. Thomas Edgar and Garda (Doman) A.; m. Cathy Ann Wells, Jan. 22, 1977; children: Kara, Callie. BA, Brigham Young U., 1977, JD, MLS, 1980. Asst. law librarian Oklahoma City (Okla.) U., 1980-81; sr. reference librarian So. Meth. U., Dallas, 1981-84; head of reader services So. Ill. U. Law Library, Carbondale, 1984—. Mem. Am. Assn. Law Libraries, Okla. Bar Assn. Avocations: gardening, camping, traveling, reading. Librarianship. Home: Rt 1 Box 66 Carterville IL 62918 Office: So Ill U Law Library Lesar Law Bldg Carbondale IL 62901

ANESTIS, ROBERT WILLIAM, transporation company executive; b. Pitts., Oct. 6, 1945; s. George and Virginia Margaret (Aspinall) A.; m. Janice Lee Allinder, June 22, 1968; children: Matthew Todd, Mark Christopher, Michael David. BA, Yale U., 1967; JD, MBA, Harvard U., 1971. Bar: Pa. 1971, U.S. Dist. Ct. (we. dist.) Pa. 1971. Assoc. Kirkpatrick & Lockhart, Pitts., 1971-77, ptnr., 1977-82; exec. v.p., chief fin. officer Guilford Transp. Industries Inc., Westport, Conn., 1982-84, pres., 1984—, also bd. dirs.; bd. dirs. Boston & Maine Corp., North Billerica, Mass., Maine Central R.R. Co., Portland, Del. & Hudson Railway Co., Albany, N.Y. Contbr. articles to profl. jours. Served to capt. USAF, 1972-74. Mem. ABA, Pa. Bar Assn., Allegheny County Bar Assn. Episcopalian. General corporate, Corporate taxation. Home: 23 White Oak Ln Weston CT 06883 Office: Guilford Transp Industries Inc 191 Post Rd W Westport CT 06880

ANGAROLA, ROBERT THOMAS, lawyer; b. N.Y.C., Nov. 4, 1945; s. Edward Gerard and Anne Louise (Sullivan) A.; m. Jane Lee, Sept. 14, 1985. AB with honors, Fordham U., 1967; postgrad., NYU, 1969-72; JD, U. Va., 1972. Bar: Va. 1972, D.C. 1979, U.S. Dist. Ct. D.C. 1979, U.S. Ct. Appeals (D.C. cir.) 1979. Atty. White Ho. Spl. Action office drug abuse prevention, Washington, 1972-73; legal adviser UN Internat. Narcotics Control Bd., Geneva, 1973-77; gen. counsel White Ho. Office of Drug Abuse Policy, Washington, 1977-81; mem. Hyman, Phelps & McNamara P.C., Washington, 1981—; bd. dirs. Internat. Televent, Inc., Washington. Washington rep. Dems. Abroad, 1981-83; bd. dirs. Am. Citizens Abroad, Geneva, 1981—. Mem. ABA, AMA (informal steering com. on prescription drug abuse), Nat. Council for Internat. Health, Assn. Former Fed. Narcotics Agts. (counsel 1984—). Democrat. Avocations: skiing, squash. Administrative and regulatory, Private international, Food and drug. Office: Hyman Phelps & McNamara PC 1120 G St NW Suite 1040 Washington DC 20005

ANGEL, ARTHUR RONALD, lawyer, consultant; b. Long Beach, Calif., May 10, 1948; s. Morris and Betty Estelle (Unger) A.; m. Karen L. Long, Mar. 13, 1982; 1 child, Jamie Kathryn. B.A., U. Calif.-Berkeley, 1969; J.D., Harvard U., 1972. Bar: Mass. 1972, D.C. 1975, Okla. 1979, U.S. Ct. Appeals (10th cir.) 1979, U.S. Dist. Ct. (we. dist.) Okla. 1980, U.S. Dist. Ct. (no. dist.) Okla. 1981, U.S. Supreme Ct. 1983. Atty. FTC, Washington, 1972-78; sole practice, Oklahoma City, 1978-87; ptnr., Angel, Ikard & Nash, Oklahoma City, 1987—; mem. adv. panel on cardiovascular devices, Washington, 1979-82; cons. FTC, 1978-79; mem. adv. bd. Health and Energy Learning Project, Washington, 1980—. Named Man of Yr., Am. Funeral Dirs., 1975; recipient Meritorious Service award FTC, Washington, 1978. Fellow Inst. Law and Social Scis.; mem. Assn. Trial Lawyers Am., Okla. Bar Assn., D.C. Bar Assn., Mass. Bar Assn. Democrat. Jewish. Federal civil litigation, Personal injury, General practice. Home: 4901 N Coltrane Rd Oklahoma City OK 73121 Office: Angel Ikard & Nash 101 N Robinson Suite 800 Oklahoma City OK 73102

ANGEL, DENNIS, lawyer; b. Bklyn., Feb. 14, 1947; s. Morris and Rosalyn (Sobiloff) A.; m. Linda Marlene Lobel, May 15, 1977; children: Stephanie Lee, Ilana Nicole, Michele Bari. B.A., St. Lawrence U., 1968; cert. pratique de langue francaise ler Degre U. Rouen (France), 1967, diplome d'etudes françaises (2e Degre), 1967; J.D., Washington and Lee U., 1972. Bar: N.Y. 1972, U.S. Dist. Ct. (so. dist.) N.Y. 1977. Assoc. Johnson & Tannenbaum, N.Y.C., 1972-77; sole practice, N.Y.C., 1977—. Contbr. articles to profl. jours. Served with USAR, 1969-75. Mem. ABA, N.Y. State Bar Assn., Bar Assn. City N.Y., Lawyers Alliance for Nuclear Arms Control, Phi Alpha Delta. Trademark and copyright, Entertainment. Home: 8 High Point Ln Scarsdale NY 10583 Office: Empire State Bldg 350 Fifth Ave New York NY 10118

ANGEL, STEVEN MICHAEL, lawyer; b. Frederick, Md., Sept. 19, 1950; s. Charles Robert and Laura Emily (Holland) A.; m. Joan Comproni, Dec. 7, 1972 (div. May 1975); m. Constance McCarthy, Apr. 24, 1981; children—Michael Sean, James Curtis. B.S., U. Md., 1972; J.D., Oklahoma City U., 1976; LL.M., George Washington U., 1979. Bar: Okla. 1976, Tex. 1981, U.S. Dist. Ct. Md. 1977, U.S. Dist. Ct. (no. dist.) Tex. 1979, U.S. Dist. Ct. (we. dist.) Okla. 1981, U.S. Dist. Ct. (we. dist.) Tex 1981, U.S. Ct. Claims 1981, U.S. Ct. Appeals (5th, 10th, and 11th cirs.) 1981, U.S. Ct. Appeals (D.C. cir.) 1983, U.S. Supreme Ct. 1984, D.C. 1986. Field atty. NLRB, Balt., 1976-79; supervising trial atty. Fed. Labor Relations Authority, Dallas, 1979-80; mem. Hughes & Nelson, Oklahoma City and San Antonio, 1980—. Articles editor Oklahoma City U. Law Rev., 1976, 77. Contbr. articles to profl. jours. Recipient cert. Spl. Confidence in Labor, Law Tex. Bd. Legal Specialization, 1982; various awards Oklahoma City U., 1975, 76; Spl. Achievement cert. Fed. Labor Relations Authority, 1980. Mem. ABA, Assn. Trial Lawyers Am., Okla. Bar Assn., Okla. Trial Lawyers Assn., State Bar Tex., Tex. Trial Lawyers Assn., Phi Delta Phi. Democrat. Baptist. Labor. Home: 4506 Karen Dr Edmond OK 73034 Office: Hughes & Nelson 5801 N Broadway Extension Suite 302 Oklahoma City OK 73118 Office: 6243 I H 10 Suite 290 San Antonio TX 78201

ANGELICO, DENNIS MICHAEL, lawyer; b. New Orleans, Dec. 19, 1950; s. John Blase and Gladys (Dehring) A.; B.A., Tulane U., 1974, J.D., 1974. Bar: La. 1974, U.S. Dist. Ct. (ea., mid. and we. dists.) La. 1974, U.S. Supreme Ct. 1983, U.S. Ct. Appeals (5th cir.) 1975. Assoc., then ptnr. Hess & Washofsky, New Orleans, 1974—. Bd. dirs. Dashiki Project Theatre, New Orleans, 1982-85. Mem. ABA, La. Bar Assn. (sec.-treas. labor law sect. 1983, vice chmn. labor law sect. 1984, chmn. labor law sect. 1985), De La Salle Alumni Assn. (rec. sec. 1982), Tulane Alumni Assn. (Fellows Club), Phi Alpha Delta. Democrat. Roman Catholic. Labor, Pension, profit-sharing, and employee benefits. Home: 58 Fontainebleau Dr New Orleans LA 70125 Office: Washofsky Angelico & Credo 421 Frenchman St New Orleans LA 70116

ANGELL, JAMES EDWARD, lawyer; b. Westfield, Mass., July 26, 1954; s. Carroll S. and Sophie T. Angell. B.A., U. Maine, 1975; J.D., Western New Eng. Coll., 1979. Bar: Mass. 1979, U.S. Dist. Ct. Mass. 1980. Sole practice, Westfield, 1979—. Mem. Westfield Planning Bd., 1985-86; city prosecutor City of Westfield 1986—; asst. city solicitor City of Westfield, 1986— . Mem. ABA, Mass. Bar Assn., Hampden County Bar Assn., Westfield Bar Assn. (treas. 1984—). Criminal, Real property, Personal injury. Home: 11 Cherry St Westfield MA 01085 Office: 43 Court St Westfield MA 01085

ANGELL, NICHOLAS BIDDLE, lawyer; b. N.Y.C., June 30, 1932; s. Montgomery Boynton and Ellen (Shipman) A.; m. Carley Paxton, June 15, 1957; children—Alexander, Michael, Samuel; m. Hanay Kang, May 20, 1972; children—Marisa, Jason. Grad., Princeton U., 1954; J.D., Harvard U., 1960. Assoc. Cahill Gordon Reindel & Ohl, N.Y.C., 1960-64; regional legal advisor, dep. dir. Pakistan mission AID, Washington, 1964-67; assoc. Chadbourne & Park and predecessor, N.Y.C., 1967-70, ptnr., 1970; resident ptnr. Chadbourne & Park and predecessor, Dubai, United Arab Emirates, 1979-86. Contbr. articles to profl. jours. Pres. bd. trustees Am. Sch., Karachi, Pakistan, 1966-67; mem. nat. adv. com. Am.-Arab Affairs Council, Washington, 1984—; Democratic candidate for U.S. Ho. of Reps., 1974; trustee Am. Crafts Council, N.Y.C., 1968-78, Day Sch., N.Y.C., 1970-76, Buckley Sch., N.Y.C., 1970-74. Served to 1st lt. U.S. Army, 1954-57. Mem. Bar Assn. City of N.Y., Internat. Bar Assn., ABA. Episcopalian. Avocations: travel; camping; canoeing; skiing; gardening. General corporate, Private international. Home: RD 3 Box 40 South Mountain Pass Peekskill NY 10566 Office: Chadbourne & Parke 30 Rockefeller Plaza New York NY 10112

ANGELLE, ROBERT, lawyer; b. New Orleans, Aug. 24, 1953; s. Robert Joseph and Shirely (Theisen) A. BBA, La. State U., BS, JD. Bar: La. 1979. Law clk. to presiding justice La. Dist. Ct. (24th dist.), Jefferson Parish; assoc. Henican, James & Cleveland, Metairie, La. Mem. ABA, La. Bar Assn. Democrat. Roman Catholic. State civil litigation, Federal civil litigation, Insurance. Home: 720 Athania Pkwy. Metairie LA 70001 Office: Henican James & Cleveland 111 Veterans Blvd Metairie LA 70005

ANGEL-SHAFFER, ARLENE BETH, lawyer; b. Bklyn., Jan. 24, 1951; d. Samuel and Ethel (Davis) A.; m. John Richard Shaffer, Feb. 14, 1981; 1 child, Daniel Brenden. BA in Philosophy, SUNY, Stony Brook, 1974; JD, Duquesne U., 1981. Bar: Ohio 1981, U.S. Dist. Ct. (so. dist.) Ohio 1982. Assoc. Green & Schiavoni, Steubenville, Ohio, 1981-83; ptnr. Shaffer & Shaffer, Steubenville, 1983—; speaker Gov.'s Task Force on Social Security Terminations, Athens, Ohio 1984. Mem. Jefferson County Task Force on Family Violence, 1986—, Youth Services Coordinating Council, Jefferson County, 1986—, Brook-Hancock Counties Task Force on Victims Abuse, 1987—; bd. dirs. ALIVE-Women's Shelter, Steubenville, 1982; bd. dirs., coordinator Jefferson County Victim's Assistance, Steubenville, 1985—. Mem. Ohio Bar Assn., Jefferson County Bar Assn. (treas. 1987), Assn. Trial Lawyers Am. Democrat. Social security disability, General practice, Administrative and regulatory. Home: Rd #1 Box 439D Steubenville OH 43952 Office: Shaffer & Shaffer 316 N 4th St Steubenville OH 43952

ANGEVINE, EARL FRANCIS, lawyer; b. Seattle, Sept. 28, 1940; s. Frank W. and Geraldine R. (Benshoof) A.; m. Jo Ann Angevine, Aug. 20, 1966; children—Sarah, Katy. Student Seattle U., 1958-62, U. San Francisco, 1962-63; LL.B., U. Wash., 1965. Bar: Wash. 1967, U.S. dist. ct. (we. dist.) Wash. 1971, U. S. Ct. Apls. (9th cir.) 1979, U.S. Sup. Ct. 1971. Sole practice, 1967-70; pros. atty. Skagit County, Wash., 1969-74; ptnr. Angevine, Johnson & Barth, Mt. Vernon, Wash., 1975-85; sole practice, Mt. Vernon, 1985—. Mem. Wash. State Trial Lawyers Assn. (bd. govs. 1974-75, 79-81, 82, v.p. 1982-85). Republican. Roman Catholic. State civil litigation, Personal injury, General practice. Home: 1490 Dunbar Ln Mount Vernon WA 98273 Office: 700 Main St Mount Vernon WA 98273

ANGLAND, JOSEPH, lawyer; b. N.Y.C., Sept. 1, 1949; s. Patrick and Josephine (Woods) A.; m. Ida Wolff, Aug. 4, 1984. BS, MIT, 1972; JD, Harvard U., 1975. Bar: N.Y. 1977, U.S. Dist. Ct. (so. and ea. dists.) N.Y. 1978, U.S. Ct. Appeals (2d cir.) 1982, U.S. Ct. Claims 1983, U.S. Tax Ct. 1985. Law clk. to presiding justice Calif. Supreme Ct., San Francisco, 1975-76; assoc. Dewey, Ballantine, Bushby, Palmer & Wood, N.Y.C., 1976-83, ptnr., 1984—. Mem. ABA, Assn. of Bar of City of N.Y. (com. on antitrust and trade regulation). Antitrust, Securities, Federal civil litigation. Home: 670 West End Ave New York NY 10025 Office: Dewey Ballantine Bushby Palmer & Wood 140 Broadway New York NY 10005

ANGLE, JOHN EDWIN, lawyer; b. Springfield, Ill., June 19, 1931; s. Paul McClelland and Vesta (Magee) A.; m. Shona Lederman, Aug. 15, 1959; children: Brad, Jennifer, Susan; m. Georgia Boss, Sept. 29, 1984. B.A., Brown U., 1953; J.D., Northwestern U., 1956. Bar: Ill. 1956. Assoc. Davis, Boyden, Jones & Baer, Chgo., 1957-59; ptnr. Kirkland & Ellis, Chgo., 1961—. Bd. dirs. Legal Aid Bur., Chgo., 1979—; mem. Caucus Nominating com. Village of Glencoe, Ill., 1979-80, mem. Bd. Zoning Appeals, 1981; mem. Spl. Commn. on Adminstrn. of Justice in Cook County, 1984—. Served with U.S. Army, 1957-58, 60. Mem. ABA, Ill. State Bar Assn. Club: Tavern (Chgo.). Home: 2130 Lincoln Park W Apt 17-S Chicago IL 60614 Office: Kirkland & Ellis 200 E Randolph Dr Chicago IL 60601

ANGLE, MARGARET SUSAN, lawyer; b. Lincoln, Nebr., Feb. 20, 1948; d. John Charles and Catherine (Sellers) A. BA with distinction in Polit. Sci., U. Wis., Madison, 1970, MA in Scandinavian Studies (scholarship, NDEA fellow), 1972, JD cum laude, 1976. Bar: Wis. 1977, Minn. 1978. Law clk., Madison, Mpls., Chgo., 1974-76; law clk. U.S. Dist. Ct., Mpls., 1977-78; mem. firm Faegre & Benson, Mpls., 1978-84; sr. atty. Nat. Car Rental System, Inc., Mpls., 1984—. Note and comment editor U. Wis. Law Rev.; contbr. articles to profl. publs. Mem. ABA, Minn. Bar Assn., Wis. Bar Assn., Hennepin County Bar Assn., Order of Coif, ACRA. General corporate, Contracts commercial, Private international. Home: 210 W Grant St No 221 Minneapolis MN 55403 Office: Nat Car Rental System Inc 7700 France Ave S Minneapolis MN 55435

ANGLIN, RICHARD LEE, JR., lawyer; b. Herrin, Ill., July 31, 1945; s. Richard Lee and Helen (Yanulavich) A. BSCE, Case Inst. Tech., 1967; M in Regional Planning, Cornell U., 1969; JD, Loyola U., Los Angeles, 1981. Bar: Calif. 1981, D.C. 1982, U.S. Supreme Ct. 1985. Sole practice Calif. General corporate, Computer, Environment. Office: 8601 Falmouth Ave #309 PO Box 5415 Playa Del Rey CA 90296

ANGST, GERALD L., lawyer; b. Chgo., Dec. 29, 1950; s. Gerald L. Sr. and Audrey M. (Hides) A.; m. Candace Simning, Jan. 29, 1983. BA magna cum

laude, Loyola U., Chgo., 1972, JD cum laude, 1975. Assoc. Sidley & Austin, Chgo., 1975-82, ptnr., 1982—. Mem. ABA (construction litigation com. litigation sect.), Ill. Bar Assn., Chgo. Bar Assn. (civil practice com.). Federal civil litigation, State civil litigation, Environment. Office: Sidley & Austin One First National Plaza Chicago IL 60603

ANGSTMAN, MYRON EUGENE, lawyer; b. Princeton, Minn., Nov. 5, 1947; s. Ezra and Edna (Balfanz) A.; m. Suzanne Lynn Gruhlke, July 21, 1973; children: Dolly, Sarah, Andy. BA, U. Minn., 1969, JD, 1974. Bar: Alaska 1974, U.S. Dist. Ct. Alaska 1979. Asst. state pub. defender State of Alaska, Bethel, 1974-77; sole practice Bethel, 1977—. Founder Kuskokwim 300 Sled Dog Race, Bethel, 1980; bd. dirs. Iditarod Race Com., 1982-84. Avocations: award winning dog sled racer, pvt. pilot. Criminal, Personal injury. Home and Office: Box 758 Bethel AK 99559

ANGULO, CHARLES BONIN, foreign service officer; b. N.Y.C., Aug. 6, 1943; s. Manuel R. and Carolyn C. (Bonin) A.; m. Penelope Snare, June 28, 1986. B.A., U. Va., 1966; cert., U. Madrid, 1966; J.D., Tulane U., 1969. Bar: Va. 1969. Assoc., Michael & Dent, Charlottesville, Va., 1969-73; assoc. editor The Michie Publishing Co., Charlottesville, 1973; fgn. service officer U.S. Dept. State, Washington, 1973-75, Am. Embassy, Brussels, 1976-78, Legal Advisor's Office, Dept. State, Washington, 1978-81, Am. Embassy, Santo Domingo, 1981-85; exec. dir. office of insp. gen. Dept. State, Washington, 1985-86, asst. chief protocol for U.S. Dept. State, Washington, 1986— . Mem. Council Fgn. Relations. Administrative and regulatory, Public international. Home: 200 N Picket St Apt 1107 Alexandria VA 22304

ANGULO, MANUEL RAFAEL, lawyer; b. N.Y.C., Sept. 5, 1917; s. Charles and Ysabel (Piedra) A.; m. Carolyn Louise Bonin, Nov. 6, 1937; children: Charles B., M. Ralph; m. Diana Hutchins Rockwell, June 12, 1970. BA, Yale U., 1939; LLB, Harvard U., 1942; postgrad., Columbia U., 1952. Bar: N.Y. 1947. Sole practice N.Y.C., 1942-48, 61—; assoc. Davis, Polk, Wardwell, Sunderland & Kiendl, 1942-48; attaché, econ. analyst Am. embassy, Santo Domingo, 1943-44; attaché embassy Lisbon, Portugal, 1944-46; with OSS, London, 1944; gen. solicitor Creole Petroleum Corp., Caracas, Venezuela, 1948-54; ptnr. Escritorio J.M. Travieso Paul, Caracas, 1954-61, Curtis, Mallet-Prevost, Colt & Mosle, N.Y.C., 1961—; lectr. Law Sch. U. Va., 1963-71. Contbr. profl. jours. Mem. council Boy Scouts Am., Venezuela, 1955-59; pres. N. Am. Assn. Venezuela, 1957-59. Mem. ABA, N.Y. State Bar Assn., N.Y.C. Bar Assn., Internat. Bar Assn., Inter Am. Bar Assn., N.Y. County Lawyers Assn., Am. Fgn. Law Assn., Pan Am. Soc. U.S., Sigma Xi. Clubs: Yale, Union League, Broad St. Met. (Washington); Farmington Country (Charlottesville, Va.); Merion Cricket (Haverford, Pa.); Gulph Mills Golf (King of Prussia, Pa.). Private international, Public international, Latin American law. Home: 301 Greenbank Rd Rosemont PA 19010 Office: 101 Park Ave New York NY 10178

ANICH, THOMAS MATTHEW, lawyer; b. Ashland, Wis., Aug. 31, 1918; s. Matt and Cecilia (Devcic) A.; m. Beverley Joan Boyle, Sept. 20, 1963; children: Nina Marie, Mary Katherine. Student, Northland Coll., 1936-38; PhB, U. Wis., Madison, 1942, LLB, 1942. Bar: Wis. 1942, U.S. Dist. Ct. (we. dist.) Wis. 1947, U.S. Ct. Appeals (7th) 1971, U.S. Supreme Ct. 1972. Mcpl. judge County of Ashland, 1950-61; ptnr. Anich & Peterson, Ashland. Chmn. Wis. Judicare, Inc., Wausau, Wis., 1973-75. Served with U.S. Army Signal 1942-46, PTO. Mem. Ashland-Wayfield Bar Assn., ABA, Assn. Trial Lawyers Assn. Democrat. Roman Catholic. Home: 1323 Vaughn Ave Ashland WI 54806 Office: Anich and Peterson 514 W 21nd St Ashland WI 54806-0388

ANIKEEFF, ANTHONY HOTCHKISS, lawyer; b. Washington, Dec. 30, 1952; s. Nicholas Michael and Nancy Brodie Wales (Hotchkiss) A. BA with distinction, U. Va., 1975; JD, Coll. William and Mary, 1980; LLM, U. London, Eng., 1981. Bar: Va. 1982, U.S. Ct. Appeals (4th cir.) 1982, D.C. 1983, U.S. Dist. Ct. D.C. 1986, U.S. Ct. Internat. Trade 1985. Law clk. U.S. Dist. Ct. (ea. dist.) Va., Richmond, Va., 1981-82; assoc. Kilpatrick and Cody, Washington, 1982—. Mem. ABA, S.R., Squadron A N.Y. Club: Army and Navy (Washington). Private international, Federal civil litigation, State civil litigation. Home: 928 Peacock Station Rd Mclean VA 22102 Office: Kilpatrick and Cody 2501 M St NW Suite 500 Washington DC 20037

ANNENBERG, TED MAX, lawyer; b. N.Y.C., Oct. 18, 1927; s. Ivan and Violet (Pacyna) A.; m. Janice Ornstein, June 3, 1949; 1 child, Matthew. BS, U.S. Naval Acad., 1949; JD, Columbia U., 1959. Bar: N.Y. 1960. Assoc. Aranow Brodsky et al, N.Y.C., 1959-60; atty. Sun Chem. Corp., N.Y.C., 1960-64, Am. Electric Power Co., N.Y.C., 1964-65; assoc. counsel Union Camp Corp., Inc., Wayne, N.J., 1965-76; labor counsel Nabisco Brands, Inc., East Hanover, N.J., 1976-83; v.p., dep. gen. counsel F.W. Woolworth Co., N.Y.C., 1983—. Served to lt. USN, 1949-56, PTO. Home: 531 E 20th St New York NY 10010 Office: FW Woolworth Co 233 Broadway New York NY 10279

ANSBACHER, LEWIS, lawyer; b. Jacksonville, Fla., Nov. 23, 1928; s. Morris and Lillian (Pinkus) A.; m. Sybil B. Ansbacher, Oct. 27, 1957; children—Richard I., Lawrence V., Barry B. B.S. in Bus. Adminstrn., U. Fla., 1948, J.D., 1951; LL.M., George Washington U., 1955. Bar: Fla. 1951. Assoc. Philip Selber, Jacksonville, 1955-62; ptnr. Selber & Ansbacher, 1963-73; sole practice, Jacksonville, 1973-80; ptnr. Ansbacher & Schneider, P.A., Jacksonville, 1981—. Vice pres. Jewish Family and Children's Service, Jacksonville, 1962-65, pres., 1965-68; v.p. Jacksonville Jewish Ctr., 1967-70; mem. planning bd. United Fund, 1965; mem. Duval County Legal Aid Assn., pres., 1964-65; mem. Gov.'s Ad Hoc Study Com. on Eminent Domain, 1984-85. Served to 1st lt. JAGC, U.S. Army, 1952-55. Named to Hall of Fame, U. Fla. Mem. Am. Arbitration Assn. Jewish. Author in field. General corporate, Probate, Real property. Home: 2008 Strand St Neptune Beach FL 32233 Office: 100 National Financial Bldg 4215 Southpoint Blvd Jacksonville FL 32216

ANSEL, WILLIAM HENRY, JR., lawyer; b. Springfield, W. Va., Jan. 23, 1914; s. William Henry and Alverda Catherine (Fields) A.; m. Helen Catherine Kauffman, Oct. 21, 1933; children: Connie Jean Keaton, Barbara Ann Carl, Vickie Jo Milleson. Grad. Potomac State Coll., Shepherd Coll.; LL.B., W. Va. U. Bar: W.Va. 1948. Mem. W.Va. Legislature, 1942-48; asst. atty. gen. State of W. Va., 1949; treas. State of W.Va., 1950-57; sole practice Romney, W. Va., 1957—; dir. Bank of Romney. Author: Frontier Forts Along the Potomac and Its Tributaries, 1984. Mem. ABA, C.&O. Canal Adv. Commn. General practice. Home: Box 107 Springfield WV 26763 Office: Box 46 Romney WV 26757

ANSELL, EDWARD ORIN, lawyer, university executive; b. Superior, Wis., Mar. 29, 1926; s. H. S. and Mollie (Rudnitzky) A.; m. Hanne B. Baer, Dec. 23, 1956; children: Deborah, William. B.S. in Elec. Engring, U. Wis., 1948; J.D., George Washington U., 1955. Bar: D.C. 1955, Calif. 1960. Electronic engr. FCC, Buffalo and Washington, 1948-55; patent atty. RCA, Princeton, N.J., 1955-57; gen. mgr. AeroChem. Research Labs., Princeton, 1957-58; patent atty. Aerojet-Gen. Corp., La Jolla, Calif., 1958-63; corp. patent counsel Aerojet-Gen. Corp., 1963-82, asst. sec., 1970-79, sec., 1979-82; dir. patents and licensing Calif. Inst. Tech., 1982—; adj. prof. U. La Verne (Calif.) Coll. Law, 1972-78; Spl. adv., task force chmn. U.S. Commn. Govt. Procurement, 1971. Contbr. articles profl. publns. Recipient Alumni Service award George Washington U., 1979. Mem. Am. Intellectual Property Law Assn., Assn. Corp. Patent Counsel, Nat. Assn. Coll. and Univ. Attys., Los Angeles Patent Law Assn., Licensing Execs. Soc., Soc. Univ. Patent Adminstrs., Patent, Trademark and Copyright Jour. (1971-76), State Bar Calif. (exec. com. intellectual property sect. 1983-86). Patent, Trademark and copyright. Home: 449 W Willamette Lane Claremont CA 91711 Office: 1201 E California Blvd Pasadena CA 91125

ANSLEY, SHEPARD BRYAN, lawyer; b. Atlanta, July 31, 1939; s. William Bonneau and Florence Jackson (Bryan) A.; m. Boyce Lineberger, May 9, 1970; children—Anna Rankin, Florence Bryan. B.A., U. Ga., 1961; LL.B., U. Va., 1964. Bar: Ga. 1967. Assoc. Carter & Ansley and predecessor firm Carter, Ansley, Smith & McLendon, Atlanta, 1967-73, ptnr., 1973-84, of counsel, 1984—; dir. DeKalb Fed. Savs. & Loan Assn.; chmn. bd. dirs. Sodamaster Co. Am. Bd. dirs. Jour. Pub. Law Emory U., 1961-62. Mem. vestry St. Luke's Episcopal Ch., Atlanta, 1971-74; treas., mem. exec. com., bd. dirs. Alliance Theatre Co., Atlanta, 1974-85; trustee Atlanta Music Festival Assn., Inc., 1975—; v.p. Atlanta Preservation Ctr., Inc. Served to capt. U.S. Army, 1965-67. Mem. ABA, Ga. Bar Assn., Atlanta Bar Assn., Atlanta Lawyers Club, Am. Coll. Mortgage Attys. Clubs: Piedmont Driving, World Trade (Atlanta). Real property, Probate.

ANSPACH, KENNETH GORDON, lawyer; b. Harvey, Ill., July 18, 1952; s. Kurt and Helen (Gordon) A. BA, U. Ill., 1974; JD, Washington U., St. Louis, 1977. Bar: Ill. 1977, U.S. Dist. Ct. (no. dist.) Ill. 1980, U.S. Ct. Appeals (7th cir.) 1981. Asst. atty. gen. State of Ill., Springfield and Chgo., 1977-82; assoc. Berman, Fagel et al, Chgo., 1982-85; sole practice Chgo., 1985—. Pres. Lincoln Park West Condominium, Chgo., 1986—; bd. dirs. Dawn Schuman Inst., Deerfield, 1984—. Mem. Chgo. Bar Assn. (environ. and comml. law coms.). Lodge: Anshe Emet Synagogue (group dir. 1982-84). Federal civil litigation, State civil litigation, Environment. Office: 20 N Clark St #3150 Chicago IL 60602

ANTHONY, ANDREW JOHN, lawyer; b. Newark, Jan. 26, 1950; s. Andrew and Mary (Norton) A.; m. Kathleen Turkenhopf, May 17, 1980. BA, Kean Coll., 1973; JD cum laude, U. Miami, 1976. Bar: Fla. 1977, U.S. Dist. Ct. (so. dist.) Fla. 1977. Assoc. Knight, Peters, Pickle, Hoeveler, Niemoeller & Flynn, Miami, Fla., 1977-79, Vernis & Bowling, Miami, 1979, Ligman, Martin, Shiley & McGee, Coral Gables, Fla., 1979-86; sole practice Coral Gables, 1986—. Mem. ABA, Fla. Bar Assn. Democrat. Roman Catholic. Avocations: numismatics, fishing, reading. State civil litigation, Insurance, Personal injury. Home: 5018 SW 149th Pl Miami FL 33185 Office: 301 Almeria Ave Suite #4 Coral Gables FL 33134

ANTHONY, DAVID VINCENT, lawyer; b. Erie, Pa., June 15, 1929; s. Frederick Peter and Marion Esther (Scharrer) A.; m. Rose Marie Mulvaney, Nov. 29, 1958; children—Joseph, Mary Catherine, Paul. B.A., Villanova U., 1951; J.D., Georgetown U., 1956, LL.M., 1960. Bar: D.C. 1956, U.S. Claims Ct. 1982, U.S. Ct. Appéals (D.C. cir.) 1956, U.S. Ct. Appeals 1982, U.S. Supreme Ct. 1963. Trial atty. civil div. U.S. Dept. Justice, Washington, 1956-63; ptnr. Sellers, Conner & Cuneo, Washington, 1963-74; ptnr. Pettit & Martin, Washington, 1974—; lectr. fed procurement, Fed. Pubs. Inc.; provider procurement courses NASA, Dept. of Navy; bd. advisors Bur. Nat. Affairs, Fed. Contracts Reports. Served to lt. USN, 1947-66. Mem. ABA, Fed. Bar Assn., Bar Assn. D.C., Assn. Trial Lawyers Am., Am. Judicature Soc., Nat. Security Industry Assn., Nat. Contract Mgmt. Assn. Republican. Roman Catholic. Clubs: Univ. (Washington), Belle Haven Country. Contbr. numerous articles on govt. contracts, claims, and litigation to profl. jours. Government contracts and claims, Contracts commercial, Public international. Office: Pettit & Martin 1800 Massachusetts Ave NW Washington DC 20036

ANTHONY, THOMAS DALE, lawyer; b. Cleve., July 23, 1952; m. Susan Shelly; children: Lara, Elizabeth. BS, Miami U., Oxford, Ohio, 1974; JD, Case Western Res. U., 1977. Bar: Ohio 1977. Tax specialist Ernst & Ernst, Cleve., 1977-79; ptnr. Walker, Chatfield & Doan, Cin., 1979—; speaker various orgns. Mem. Cin. Council on World Affairs, 1980-84; vol. fund-raising drive Sta. WVIZ, 1978-79, Sta. WCET, 1980-82; legal counsel Childrens Internat. Summer Villages, 1979—; account capt. United Appeal of Hamilton County, 1986—; v.p. State Library Bd., Ohio, 1984—. Mem. ABA (taxation sect., tax acctg. problems com., tax shelter subcom.), Ohio Bar Assn., Cin. Bar Assn. (tax inst. com.), Greater Cleve. Citizens League, Cleve. Bar Assn., Cin. C. of C., Miami U. Area Alumni Assn. (bd. dirs.), Nat. Health Lawyer's Assn., Sigma Phi Epsilon. Corporate taxation, Real property, Estate planning. Home: 1144 Halpin Ave Cincinnati OH 45208 Office: Walker Chatfield & Doan 1900 Carew Tower Cincinnati OH 45202

ANTON, DONALD C., lawyer; b. St. Louis, Mar. 26, 1931; s. Christian Joseph and Ann Louise (Thiel) A.; m. Aurora Ida Viglino, June 13, 1959; children: Donald Kris, Lynda Ann. BS, BA, Washington U., St. Louis, 1952, JD, 1955. Bar: Mo. 1955, U.S. Dist. Ct. (ea. dist.) Mo. 1955, U.S. Supreme Ct. 1961, U.S. Tax Ct. 1976. Atty. Corps of Engrs., St. Louis, 1957-58; assoc. Forgey & Sindel, St. Louis, 1958-59; officer probate and trust Mercantile Trust, St. Louis, 1959-60; assoc. Hall, Reaban, Siegel & Scheele, St. Louis, 1960-63; prin. Anton & Assocs., Clayton, Mo., 1968-87; sole practice Clayton, 1987—; counsel Mo. Senate, Jefferson City, 1969; spl. asst. atty. gen. Jefferson County, 1967, asst. pros. atty., 1968; gen. counsel staff Small Bus. Adminstrn., Washington, 1965-66. Dem. mayoral nominee St. Louis County, 1974; counsel Moline, Pattonville, Afton and Wellston Fire Dists., St. Louis, 1976-79; chmn. cen. com. St. Louis County, 1972-77, Mo. 3d Congl. Dist., 1982—; del. Dem. Nat. Conv., 1964, 72, 76, 80, 84; active Friends of St. Louis Art Mus., Mo. Hist. Soc., Friends of St. Louis Zoo, St. Louis Symphony, Shaws Garden, Confluence of St. Louis. Served to 1st lt. U.S. Army, 1955-57. Mem. ABA, Mo. Bar Assn., St. Louis Met. Bar Assn., St. Louis County Bar Assn., Lawyers' Assn. St. Louis, Mo. Assn. Trial Attys., Soc. Disting. Ams., Council World Affairs, DAV, Backstoppers, Wash. U. Law Alumni, Wash. U. Bus. Alumni. Roman Catholic. Clubs: Ambassadors (St. Louis). Avocations: jogging, swimming, tennis. General practice, Personal injury, Business. Office: 231 S Bemiston Suite 800 Clayton MO 63105

ANTON, RICHARD HENRY, lawyer; b. Ft. Worth, Aug. 30, 1946; s. Abe and Faye (Gernsbacher) A.; m. Merriessa Ratkin, June 23, 1968; children: Lane Elliot, Shirra Navit. BA with honors, U. Tex., 1968, JD, 1976; MS, Harvard U., 1973. Bar: Mo. 1976, U.S. Dist. Ct. (we. dist.) Mo. 1976, U.S. Ct. Appeals (10th cir.) 1978, U.S. Ct. Appeals (8th cir.) 1979, U.S. Supreme Ct. 1982, Tex. 1985, U.S. Dist. Ct. (we. dist.) Tex. 1985. Assoc. Koenigsdorf Kusnetzky, Kansas City, Mo., 1976-80; sole practice Kansas City, Mo., 1980-82; assoc. Law Offices of Gerald Rosen, Kansas City, Mo., 1982-84, Hancock Piedfort, Austin, Tex., 1985-87; ptnr. Hancock, Piedfort, Galton & McGill, Austin, 1987—. Served with USN, 1968-72. Mem. ABA, State Bar Assn. Tex., Assn. Trial Lawyers Am., Tex. Trial Lawyers Assn., Phi Beta Kappa. Democrat. Jewish. Avocations: golf, running. State civil litigation, Family and matrimonial, Bankruptcy. Home: 5005 Lodge View Ln Austin TX 78731-2633 Office: Hancock Piedfort Galton & McGill 9020 II Capital of Texas Hwy No STE 580 Austin TX 78759

ANTONIO, DOUGLAS JOHN, lawyer; b. N.Y.C., Sept. 14, 1955; s. John and Joan (Deitz) A.; m. Sarah Kathrine Nadelhoffer, Aug. 31, 1986. BS, BA, U. Md., 1977, JD, 1980, MBA, 1981; LLM in Taxation, Georgetown U., 1983. Bar: Md. 1980, D.C. 1981, Mo. 1983, U.S. Dist. Ct. (we. dist.) Mo. 1983, U.S. Tax Ct. 1983, U.S. Supreme Ct. 1983, U.S. Ct. Claims 1983, U.S. Ct. Appeals (8th cir.) 1984. Atty.-advisor U.S. Labor Dept., Washington, 1980-83; atty. Thompson & Mitchell, St. Louis, 1983-84; assoc. Blumenfeld, Sandweiss, Marx, Tureen, Ponfil & Kaskowitz, St. Louis, 1984-86; Sugar, Friedberg and Felsenthal Chgo., 1986—. Contbr. articles to profl. jours. Recipient Wabash Award Merit Wabash Coll., 1973. Mem. Beta Gamma Sigma. Democrat. Uniterian. Club: Mo. Athletic (St. Louis). Corporate taxation, Real property, Partnership taxation. Home: 555 W Madison St Tower #1 Apt 4010 Chicago IL 60606 Office: Sugar, Friedberg and Felsenthal 200 W Madison St Suite 3550 Chicago IL 60606

ANZALONE, FRANK ANTHONY, lawyer; b. St. Louis, Sept. 10, 1947; s. Anthony A. and Mary G. (Boscia) A.; divorced; 1 child, Anthony. BA, St. Louis U., 1968, JD cum laude, 1971; student, Georgetown U., 1971. Bar: Mo. 1971, U.S. Ct. Appeals (8th cir.) 1979. Pub. defender St. Louis County Pub. Defender, Clayton, Mo., 1971-79; ptnr. Anzalone & Fiser, Clayton, 1979—; instr. St. Louis U., 1974-75. Roman Catholic. Criminal. Office: Anzalone & Fiser 111 S Bemiston Clayton MO 63105

ANZELMO, DONALD JOSEPH, lawyer; b. New Orleans, Oct. 3, 1951; s. Salvador and Maribel (De Lucca) A.; m. Ana Delvalle, May 22, 1976; children: Michael, Margaret, Charles. BA, U. New Orleans, 1973; JD, Loyola U., New Orleans, 1976. Bar: La. 1976, U.S. Dist. Ct. (ea. dist.) La. 1976, U.S. Ct. Appeals (5th cir.) 1976, U.S. Dist. Ct. (we. dist.) La. 1978, U.S. Dist. Ct. (mid. dist.) La. 1980, U.S. Ct. Appeals (11th cir.) 1981. Law clk. to presiding justice U.S. Dist. Ct. (ea. dist.) La., New Orleans, 1976-78; assoc. McGlinchey, Stafford, Mintz, New Orleans, 1978-85, Bruscato, Loomis, Street & Anzelmo, Monroe, La., 1985—. Contbg. editor Loyola U. Law Rev., 1975-76. Mem. ABA, Assn. Trial Lawyers Am., Maritime Law Assn., Am. Judicature Soc., Loyola U. Law Alumni Assn. (pres. 1985-86). Democrat. Roman Catholic. Admiralty, Federal civil litigation, State civil litigation. Home: 2604 Birchwood Dr Monroe LA 71201 Office: Bruscato Loomis Street & Anzelmo 2011 Hudson Ln Monroe LA 71201

ANZUR, JOHN ANDREW, lawyer; b. Wilmington, Del., June 28, 1955; s. Edward Charles and Eleanor Theresa (Chaiko) A. BA, U. Santa Clara, 1977; MA, Oxford U., 1980; JD, Georgetown U., 1981. Bar: Calif. 1981. Assoc. Orrick, Herrington & Sutcliffe, San Francisco, 1981—. Rotary Found. scholar, 1978-79. Mem. ABA, San Francisco Bar Assn., Santa Clara County Bar Assn. (mem. exec. com. bus. law sect. 1986-87). Securities, General corporate, Pension, profit-sharing, and employee benefits. Office: Orrick Herrington & Sutcliffe 600 Montgomery St San Francisco CA 94111

APCEL, MELISSA ANNE, lawyer; b. Highland Park, Ill., Dec. 3, 1951; d. Edmund John and Leokadia (Kolasinski) A.; m. Kenneth R. Crooks (div. 1978). BA, Northwestern U., 1974, JD, 1977. Bar: Ill. 1977, U.S. Dist. Ct. (no. dist.) Ill. 1977, U.S. Dist. Ct. (cen. dist.) Ill. 1980, U.S. Ct. Appeals (7th cir.) 1982, U.S. Ct. Appeals (D.C. cir.) 1984. Assoc. Hedlund, Hunter & Lynch, Chgo., 1977-82; assoc. Latham & Watkins, Chgo., 1982-85, ptnr., 1985—. Editor Northwestern U. Law Rev., 1976-77. Recipient William Jennings Bryan award, Adlai E. Stevenson Jr. award, Lowden-Wigmore award, Lowden-Wigmore Writing prize, 1977. Mem. ABA, Chgo. Bar Assn. Club: Metropolitan (Chgo.). Federal civil litigation, State civil litigation. Office: Latham & Watkins 233 S Wacker Dr Suite 6900 Chicago IL 60606

APFEL, GARY, lawyer; b. N.Y.C., June 2, 1952; s. Willy and Jenny (Last) A.; m. Serena Jakobovits, June 16, 1980; children: Alyssa J., I. Michael, Alanna J. BA, NYU magna cum laude, 1973; JD, Columbia U., 1976. Bar: N.Y. 1977, U.S. Dist. Ct. (so. and ea. dists) N.Y. 1977. Assoc. Sullivan & Cromwell, N.Y.C., 1976-80; assoc. LeBoeuf, Lamb, Leiby & MacRae, N.Y.C., 1980-84, ptnr., 1985—. Kent scholar Columbia U., 1976. Mem. ABA, Phi Beta Kappa. Democrat. General corporate, Securities. Office: LeBoeuf Lamb Leiby & MacRae 725 S Figueroa St Los Angeles CA 90036

APJOHN, NELSON GEORGE, lawyer; b. N.Y.C., June 21, 1956; s. George N. and Catherine (Tonner) A.; m. Mary Joan Greene, June 3, 1978; children: Andrew, Eric, Allan. AB in Polit. Sci., Syracuse U., 1978; JD, Boston Coll., 1981. Bar: Mass. 1981, U.S. Dist. Ct. Mass. 1981, U.S. Ct. Appeals (1st cir.) 1984. Jr. ptnr. Nutter, McClennen & Fish, Boston, 1981—. Mem. ABA, Mass. Bar Assn., Boston Bar Assn., Phi Beta Kappa, Order of Coif. Federal civil litigation, State civil litigation, Products liabiltiy. Home: 24 Ticonderoga Ln Millis MA 02054 Office: Nutter McClennen & Fish 600 Atlantic Ave Boston MA 02210

APO, JAN KANANI, lawyer; b. Lahaina, Hawaii, Jan. 12, 1956; s. Albert Kalei (dec.) and Yukimi (Wakida) A.; m. Kelly S. Hogan, Aug. 14, 1982; 1 child, Taryn Keliaolele. BBA, Whittier Coll., 1978; JD, U. Honolulu, 1981. Bar: Hawaii 1981, U.S. Dist. Ct. Hawaii 1981. Dep. pub. defender Honolulu and Maui Pub. Defender's Office, 1981-85; ptnr. Tateishi & Apo, Wailuku, Hawaii, 1985—. Mem. ABA. Criminal, Personal injury, Juvenile. Home: PO Box 414 Lahaina HI 96761 Office: Tateishi and Apo 55 N Church St Wailuku HI 96793

APODACA, PATRICK VINCENT, lawyer; b. El Paso, Tex., Mar. 11, 1951; s. Richard Felix and Isabel (Ortega) A. B.S. in Fgn. Service, Georgetown U., 1972; J.D., Harvard U., 1975. Bar: D.C. 1975, N.Mex. 1984. Assoc. Silverstein & Mullens, Washington, 1975-76; spl. asst. Carter-Mondale Transition Group, Washington, 1976-77; assoc. counsel to pres., The White House, Washington, 1977-81; assoc. Finley, Kumble, Wagner, Washington, 1981-84, Keleher & McLeod, Albuquerque, 1984-86, ptnr., 1986—. Asst. coordinator get-out-the vote com. Dem. Nat. Com., Washington, 1976; voter registration coordinator N.Mex. Dem. Com., Albuquerque, 1984; mem. N.Mex. State Dem. Party Cen. Com., 1987—; mem. Pres.'s Adv. Com. on Arts, Washington, 1981; bd. dirs. Presbyn. Heart Inst., 1986—. Mem. D.C. Bar Assn. (chmn. internat. law com. young lawyers div. 1982-84), ABA, N.Mex. Bar Assn. Roman Catholic. General corporate, Administrative and regulatory, Securities. Office: Keleher & McLeod PO Drawer AA Albuquerque NM 87103

APPEL, ALFRED, lawyer; b. N.Y.C., May 8, 1906; s. Samuel and Sadie (Niedermann) A.; m. Beatrice C. Hoffman, Sept. 3, 1931; children—Alfred, Elizabeth (Mrs. Paul Schaffer), John S. A.B., Cornell U., 1926, J.D., 1928. Bar: N.Y. 1928. Practiced in N.Y.C., 1928—; asso. Proskauer Rose Goetz & Mendelsohn and (predecessor firms), 1928-40, partner, 1940—, now sr. partner; dir. McGregor Doniger, Inc., 1954-79, B. Manischewitz Co., 1954-70; Mem. Bd. Edn. Union Free Sch. Dist. 7, Great Neck, N.Y., 1954-60; mem. Cornell Law Sch. Adv. Council, 1967—, univ. council, 1979—; bd. dirs. Beatrice and Alfred Appel Found., Inc., Charles H. Oestreich Found.; former trustee Soc. of Hillside Hosp.; nat. chmn. Cornell Law Sch. Fund. Editor, bus. mgr.: Cornell Law Rev, 1927-28. Mem. Assn. Bar City N.Y., Internat. Bar Assn., N.Y. County Lawyers Assn., Am., N.Y. State bar assns., Order of Coif, Sigma Alpha Mu, Phi Kappa Phi. Clubs: Harmonie (N.Y.C.), Cornell (N.Y.C.). General corporate, Private international, Securities. Home: 200 E 57th St New York NY 10022 Office: Proskauer Rose Goetz & Mendelsohn 300 Park Ave New York NY 10022

APPEL, GARRY RICHARD, lawyer; b. Denver, Apr. 13, 1952; s. Robert S. and Virginia S. (Silver) A.; married, May 1, 1982; children: Jonathan, Henry. BA, U. Colo., 1974, JD, 1978. Bar: Colo. 1978, U.S. Dist. Ct. (Colo.) 1978, U.S. Ct. Appeals (10th cir.) 1979. Assoc. Rothgerber, Appel, Powers & Johnson, Denver, 1979-83, ptnr., 1983—; lectr. Nat Bus. Inst., Denver, 1983—, Wyo. Bar Assn., Casper, 1984, Colo. Credit Union League, Denver, 1985, various profl. ednl. seminars, 1983—. Contbr. articles to profl. jours. Mem. Denver Ctr. for Performing Arts, 1984, Denver Zool. Gardens, 1986. Mem. ABA, Colo. Bar Assn., Denver Bar Assn. Democrat. Jewish. Avocations: woodworking, hiking, skiing. Bankruptcy, Consumer commercial, Federal civil litigation. Home: 6424 E Eastman Ave Denver CO 80222 Office: Rothberger Appel Powers & Johnson 1200 17th Suite 2800 Denver CO 80202

APPEL, MARTIN SHERMAN, lawyer; b. Chgo., Mar. 15, 1933; s. Philip T. and Pearl (Goldman) A.; m. Audrey Blumenthal, Aug. 29, 1954; children—Lynne, Leslie, Leanne, Richard. B.S., Northwestern U., 1953, J.D., 1956. Bar: Ill. 1956, Calif. 1958. C.P.A., Godow & Lawrence, Chgo., 1953-56; assoc. Max Swerin, Chgo., 1956-58; tax mgr. Arthur Andersen & Co., Los Angeles, 1958-62; v.p. Ring Bros., Los Angeles, 1962; ptnr. Pacht, Ross, Warne, Bernhard & Sears, Inc., Los Angeles, 1962-82; ptnr. Rudin, Richman & Appel, Beverly Hills, Calif., 1982—; dir. Independence Bank, Los Angeles; lectr. acctg. Northwestern U., Roosevelt U., 1953-56; lectr. Practising Law Inst., U. So. Calif. Tax Inst.; mem. IRS Commr's Adv. Group. Bd. dirs. Jewish Fed. Council Greater Los Angeles, 1980—; mem. Pres.'s Commn. on Mental Retardation, 1986—; Jewish Community Found.; bd. govs. Cedars-Sinai Med. Ctr.; mem. U.S. Olympic Com. Mem. Los Angeles Bar Assn., Beverly Hills Bar Assn., Calif. Bar Assn., ABA. Republican. Club: Hillcrest Country. Corporate taxation, Personal income taxation, Real property. Home: 607 N Elm Dr Beverly Hills CA 90210 Office: Penthouse 9601 Wilshire Blvd Beverly Hills CA 90210

APPEL, T. ROBERTS, II, lawyer; b. Lancaster, Pa., Aug. 27, 1934; s. Robert R. and Alice (Edge) A.; m. Sandra F. Knack, Oct. 31, 1970. AB, U. Pa., 1957; LLB, Harvard U., 1960. Bar: Pa. 1981, U.S. Dist. Ct. (ea. dist.) Pa. 1970, U.S. Tax Ct. 1963. Mng. ptnr. Appel, Yost, Sorrentias and predecessor firms, Lancaster, 1960—. Pres. Lancaster (Pa.) City Council, 1966-67. General corporate, Real property, Probate. Home: 1425 Quarry Ln Lancaster PA 17603 Office: Appel Yost & Sorrentino 33 N Duke St Lancaster PA 17602

APPEL, THOMAS ALAN, lawyer, legal educator; b. Boston, June 28, 1950; s. Julius Mitchell and Pauline Ruth (Gould) A.; m. Theresa Anne Auerbach, July 16, 1978; children: Diane Marjorie, Lauren Elizabeth. BA in Econs., U. Pa., 1972; JD, Georgetown U., 1975. Bar: Va. 1975, U.S. Dist. Ct. Md. 1979, Md. 1979. Sr. research atty. Research Group, Inc., Charlottesville, Va., 1976-79; assoc. Wright & Parks, Balt., 1979-81; ptnr. Appel & Busick, Sykesville, Md., 1982-83; adj. prof. U. Balt. Sch. Law, 1982—; sole

practice, Sykesville, 1984—; referral atty. Ctr. for Auto Safety, Washington, 1981—, Md. Lawyer Referral Service, 1983—, Md. Vol. Lawyers, 1986—; pres. Imperial Gardens Improvement Assn., 1986-87. Contbr. articles to profl. jours. and newspapers. Editor Am. Criminal Law Rev., 1974-75. Mem. ABA, Md. Bar Assn., Md. Young Lawyers' Assn., Am. Trial Lawyers Assn., Carroll County Bar Assn. (Law Day lectr. 1984, pres. Imperial Garden's Improvement Assn. 1986-87). Jewish. Product liability, State civil litigation, Personal injury. Office: 1912 Liberty Rd Sykesville MD 21784

APPERSON, BERNARD JAMES, lawyer; b. Washington, June 28, 1956; s. Bernard James Jr. and Ann Wentworth (Anderson) A.; m. Deborah DeGrasse Abraham, July 7, 1984. BA in Polit. Sci., Am. U., 1978; JD, Samford U., 1981; LLM in Internat. Law, Georgetown U., 1985. Bar: Fla. 1981, Ga. 1981, D.C. 1983, U.S. Supreme Ct. 1985. Atty. office U.S. trustee so. dist. N.Y. Dept. Justice, N.Y.C., 1981; atty. EPA, Washington, 1981-83; atty. civil rights div. U.S. Dept. Justice, Washington, 1983-84, atty. office legis. affairs, 1986—; counsel to dir. Legal Services Corp., Washington, 1985-86. Assoc. editor Am. Jour. Trial Advocacy Cumberland Sch. Law, 1979-81. County chmn. Paula Hawkins for U.S Senate, Volusia County, Fla., 1974; nat. staff Citizens for Reagan, Fla., Kansas City, Mo., 1976; cons. Reagan for Pres., Detroit, 1980; dep. nat. dir. Reagan-Bush 1984, Washington, 1984. Lewis F. Powell Medal for Excellence in Advocacy Am. Coll Trial Lawyers, 1980. Mem. ABA, Fed. Bar Assn., Federalist Soc. for Law and Pub. Policy Studies, Order of Barristers, Delta Theta. Phi. Episcopalian. Lodge: St. Andrew's Soc. Public international, Legislative, Civil rights. Home: 11732 Amkin Dr Clifton VA 22024 Office: U S Dept Justice Office Legis Affairs 10th and Constitution Ave NW Washington DC 20530

APPERSON, JEFFREY ALLEN, lawyer; b. Zanesville, Ohio, July 1, 1954; s. Ronald L. and Rosemary (Carney) A.; m. Maureen C. Muddiman, Aug. 29, 1982; 1 child, Tara Michele. BA, High Point Coll., 1979; JD, Cumberland Sch. of Law, 1982. Bar: Ala. 1982. Atty. Adminstr. Office of U.S. Cts., Washington, 1982-85; clk. U.S. Bankruptcy Ct. (we. dist.) Ky., Louisville, 1985—. Chmn. Big Bros., Big Sisters, High Point, N.C., 1979. Served to sgt. USAF, 1972-76. Mem. ABA, Louisville Bar Assn., Bankruptcy Clk.'s Assn., Alpha Chi Omega (pres. 1979). Avocations: tennis, reading, hiking. Bankruptcy, Judicial administration, Legislative. Office: US Bankruptcy Ct 601 W Broadway Louisville KY 40202

APPLEGATE, KARL EDWIN, lawyer; b. Cicero, Ind., July 21, 1923; s. Karl Raymond and Gladys Mae (Worley) A.; m. Elizabeth Ann Dilts, June 10, 1944; children—Eric Edwin, Raymond Alan, Robert Dale, Beth Ann. B.S., Ind. U., 1946, J.D., 1948. Bar: Ind. 1949. U.S. commr. So. Dist. Ind., 1953-58; dep. prosecutor Monroe County, Ind., 1959; mcpl. judge, Bloomington, Ind., 1960-63; mem. Ind. Ho. of Reps., 1965-66; U.S. atty. So. Dist. Ind., 1967-70; sr. ptnr. Applegate Law Offices, Bloomington, 1970-86; legal cons. Ind. Masonic Home, Franklin. Trustee 1st United Methodist Ch., 1962-65. Served to sgt. AUS, 1941-44; ETO. Decorated Purple Heart. Named Outstanding Young Man of Bloomington, Jaycees, 1956, recipient Disting. Service award, 1956, Good Govt. award, 1961. Mem. Ind. Bar Assn., Monroe County Bar Assn., ABA, Tri-County Bar Assn., Alpha Kappa Psi. Democrat. Clubs: Kiwanis, Elks, Masons. State civil litigation, General practice, Personal injury. Home: 509 S Swain St Bloomington IN 47401 Office: Applegate Law Offices 321 E Kirkwood Bloomington IN 47401

APPLEGATE, WILLIAM RUSSELL, lawyer; b. Columbia, S.C., Oct. 18, 1946; s. William John and Vera (Lister) A.; m. Jerva Ann Watson, Dec. 20, 1969; children—Jennifer Corey, Amanda Ann. A.B., Wofford Coll., 1968; J.D., U.S.C., 1974, M.A. in Criminal Justice, 1978. Bar: S.C. 1974, U.S. Dist. Ct. S.C. 1974, U.S. Supreme Ct. 1979. Assoc. E. Pickens Rish, Esquire, Lexington, S.C., 1974-75; sole practice, West Columbia, S.C., 1975—; judge Town of Springdale, West Columbia, 1980—; atty. Town of Gaston, S.C., 1976—. Vice chmn. Episcopal Ch. Upper Diocese of S.C., Columbia, 1981—; sr. warden St. Mary's Ch., Columbia, 1979-81. Served to capt. U.S. Army, 1969-71. Mem. S.C. Bar Assn., ABA, Nat. Orgn. Social Security Claimant's Reps. Republican. Episcopalian. Consumer commercial, Family and matrimonial, Personal injury. Home: 123 Woodwinds W Dr Columbia SC 29210 Office: William R Applegate Esquire 1700 Sunset Blvd West Columbia SC 29169

APPLEMAN, JEFF THOME, lawyer; b. N.Y.C., Nov. 2, 1950; s. Nathan and Lillian (Thome) A.; m. Suzanne E. Engelberg, Oct. 25, 1981. BA, SUNY, Binghamton, 1972; JD, Golden Gate U., 1977. Bar: Calif. 1977, U.S. Dist. Ct. (no. dist.) Calif. 1977, U.S. Bd. Immigration Appeals 1977, U.S. Ct. Appeals (9th cir.) 1977. Assoc. Park & Litwin, San Francisco, 1978-79; sole practice San Francisco, 1979-80; ptnr. Berry & Appleman, San Francisco, 1980—. Mem. San Francisco Bar Assn., Am. Immigration Lawyers Assn. (exec. com., dist. liaison 1982-83, sec. 1983-84, chpt. chmn. 1984-85). Immigration, naturalization, and customs. Office: Berry & Appleman 463 Pacific Ave San Francisco CA 94133

APPLETON, RANDALL EUGENE, lawyer; b. Balt., Apr. 11, 1957; s. Robert Lee and Shirley (Winkler) A.; m. Debbie Olson, Aug. 16, 1980; 1 child, Randall Lee. BA in Govt., Hampden-Sydney Coll., 1979; JD, Wake Forest Coll., 1982. Bar: Va. 1982, U.S. Dist. Ct. (ea. dist.) Va. 1982, U.S. Ct. Appeals (4th cir.) 1982. Assoc. Moody, Strople & Lawrence, Portsmouth, Va., 1982—. Mem. ABA, Va. Bar Assn., Assn. Trial Lawyers Assn., Va. Trial Lawyers Assn. Democrat. Presbyterian. Lodge: Rotary. Personal injury, State civil litigation, Federal employer's liability act. Home: 4640 Winston Rd Portsmouth VA 23703 Office: Moody Strople & Lawrence Ltd PO Box 1138 Portsmouth VA 23705

APPLETON, R.O., JR., lawyer; b. San Francisco, Aug. 17, 1945; s. Robert Oser and Leslie Jeanne (Roth) A.; m. Susan Frelich, June 3, 1971; children: Jesse David, Seth Daniel. AB, Stanford U., 1967; JD, U. Calif., San Francisco, 1970; postgrad., NYU, 1971. Bar: Calif. 1971, U.S. Dist. Calif. (no. dist.) Calif. 1971, Mo. 1973, U.S. Dist. Ct. (ea. dist.) Mo. 1974, U.S. Ct. Appeals (8th cir.) 1975. Assoc. Dinkelspiel & Dinkelspiel, San Francisco, 1971-73; ptnr. Appleton, Newman & Kretmar, St. Louis, 1982-84, Appleton, Newman & Gerson, St. Louis, 1984—; adj. prof. pre-trial litigation Washington U. Sch. Law, St. Louis, 1985—. Arbitrator, vol. Better Bus. Bur. of St. Louis, 1980—; St. Louis Gymnastic Centre, 1984—. Mem. ABA, Calif. Bar Assn., Met. Bar Assn. of St. Louis. Democrat. Jewish. Club: Stanford (sec. 1986—). Avocations: jogging, swimming, cooking, model trains, reading. General corporate. Home: 8317 Cornell Ave Saint Louis MO 63105 Office: Appleton Newman & Gerson 225 S Meramec Ave Saint Louis MO 63105

APRIL, LEWIS BENJAMIN, lawyer; b. Bridgeton, N.J., Mar. 29, 1949; s. Max and Minnie (Weinstein) A.; m. Bunny Goldberg, Aug. 14, 1966; 1 child, Melissa. BS, W. Va. U., 1968; JB, Suffolk Law Sch., 1969. Bar: N.J., Mass., U.S. Dist. Ct.; cert. civil trial atty., N.J. Ptnr. Cooper, Perskie, April, Kieddmen, Wagskein & Weiss, Atlantic City, N.J., 1969—. Mem. ABA, N.J. Bar Assn., Mass. Bar Assn. Avocations: reading, running, sailing. Office: Cooper Perskie April et al 1125 Atlantic Ave Atlantic City NJ 08401

APRIL, RAND SCOTT, lawyer; b. Bklyn., Feb. 10, 1951; s. Arthur and Muriel (Marmorstein) A. BA, Northwestern U., 1972; JD, Columbia U., 1975. Bar: N.Y. 1976, U.S. Dist. Ct. (so. and ea. dists.) N.Y. 1976. Assoc. Marshall, Bratter, Greene, Allison & Tucker, N.Y.C., 1975-78, Gordon, Hurwitz, Butowsky, Baker, Weitzen & Shalov, N.Y.C., 1978-81; assoc. Skadden, Arps, Slate, Meagher & Flom, N.Y.C., 1981-83, ptnr., 1983—. Stone scholar Columbia U., 1974-75. Mem. Phi Beta Kappa. Avocation: skiing. Real property. Office: Skadden Arps Slate Meagher & Flom 919 3d Ave New York NY 10022

AQUILINO, THOMAS JOSEPH, JR., judge, law educator; b. Mt. Kisco, N.Y., Dec. 7, 1939; s. Thomas Joseph and Virginia Burr (Doughty) A.; m. Edith Luise Berndt, Oct. 27, 1965; children: Christopher T., Philip A., Alexander B. Student, Cornell U., 1957-59, U. Munich, 1960-61; BA, Drew U., 1962; postgrad., Free U., Berlin, 1965-66; JD, Rutgers U., 1969. Bar: N.Y. 1972, U.S. Dist. Ct. (so., ea. and no. dists.) N.Y. 1973, U.S. Ct. Appeals (2d cir.) 1973, U.S. Supreme Ct. 1976, U.S. Ct. Appeals (3d cir.) 1977, I.C.C. 1978, U.S. Ct. Claims 1979, U.S. Ct. Internat. Trade 1984. Law clk. to presiding justice U.S. Dist. Ct. (so. dist.) N.Y., N.Y.C., 1969-71; atty. Davis Polk & Wardwell, N.Y.C., 1971-85; judge U.S. Ct. Internat. Trade, N.Y.C., 1985—; adj. prof. law Benjamin N. Cardozo Sch. of Law, 1984—. Served with U.S. Army, 1962-65. Mem. N.Y. State Bar Assn., Fed. Bar Council. Roman Catholic. Avocations: sports, travel, linguistics, cinema. Office: US Ct Internat Trade One Fed Plaza New York NY 10007

ARABIA, PAUL, lawyer; b. Pittsburg, Kans., Mar. 28, 1938; s. John K. and Melva (Jones) A. B.A., Kans. State Coll.; J.D., Washburn U. Bar: Kans. 1966, U.S. Dist. Ct. Kans. 1966, U.S. Ct. Appeals (10th cir.) 1968. Ptnr., Fettis & Arabia, Wichita, 1968-74, Arabia & Wells, Wichita, 1974-78; sole practice, Wichita, 1978—. Talent for Peoples Lawyer Sta. KAKE TV. Mem. Kans. Bar Assn., Wichita Bar Assn. General practice, Contracts commercial. General practice. Office: 200 E First Suite 200 Wichita KS 67202

ARAGON, RUDOLPH FERMIN, lawyer; b. Albuquerque, N.Mex., Nov. 9, 1947; s. Fermin J. and Natalia (Jiron) A.; m. Lauren Jean Ridgeway, Aug. 20, 1971. BS, U.S. Air Force Acad., 1970; MA, Ind. U., 1971; JD, Yale U., 1979. Bar: Fla. 1979, U.S. Dist. Ct. (so. dist.) Fla. 1980, U.S. Ct. Appeals (5th cir.) 1980, U.S. Ct. Appeals (11th cir.) 1982, U.S. Ct. Appeals (9th cir.) 1986. Commd. 2d lt. USAF, 1970, advanced through grades to capt.; intelligence officer USAF, U.S., Panama, S.E. Asia, other locations; resigned USAF, 1976; assoc. Greenberg, Traurig, Askew et al, Miami, Fla., 1975-85, ptnr., 1985—. Assoc. editor: Florida Corporations Law and Practice (4 vols.), 1985. Mem. ABA, Fla. Bar Assn., Assn. Trial Lawyers Am. Democrat. Roman Catholic. Avocations: orchid growing, gardening, bird watching, exercise. Federal civil litigation, State civil litigation. Home: 7865 SW 161 St Miami FL 33157 Office: Greenberg Traurig Askew et al 1401 Brickell Ave Miami FL 33131

ARANA, KIMBERLY ANN, lawyer; b. Tucson, Nov. 11, 1957; d. Charles Wood and Ann (Hardesty) Howard; m. Hector G. Arana, Aug. 23, 1980. BA, Ariz. State U., 1979; JD, U. Ariz., 1982. Bar: Ariz. 1982, U.S. Dist. Ct. Ariz. 1982. Ptnr. Larson, Soto & Arana, Nogales, Ariz., 1982—. Mem. ABA, Santa Cruz County Bar Assn., Phi Beta Kappa. General practice. Office: Larson Soto & Arana 524 Grand L Nogales AZ 85621

ARANGO, ANA, lawyer; b. N.Y.C., Feb. 14, 1952; s. Anthony and Angela (Alcalde) Arango; m. Robert A. Chaffin, Sept. 1, 1984; 1 child, Angela V. BA in Econs., Stony Brook U., 1979; JD with high honors, Hofstra U., 1982. Bar: N.Y. 1982, Tex. 1985. Assoc. Speiser & Krause, N.Y.C., 1982-84, Houston, 1984—; sponsor Centro Latino, Houston, 1986—. Mem. ABA, Assn. Trial Lawyers Am., Tex. Trial Lawyers Assn., Women's Bar Assn., Lawyer Pilot Bar Assn., Hispanic Bar Assn., Aircraft Owners and Pilot Assn., League United Latin Am. Citizens, Phi Beta Kappa. Avocations: weight lifting, dance, swimming. Personal injury. Office: Speiser & Krause 3500 Travis Houston TX 77002

ARANGO, EMILIO, lawyer; b. Havana, Cuba, Mar. 4, 1927; came to U.S., 1960; s. Enrique Jose and Nyla Eulalia (Nuñez-Mesa) A.; m. Sylvia Fromm, Dec. 8, 1956 (div. June 1984); children: Sylvia Maria, Vivianne Victoria, Carolina Natalia. LLD, U. Havana, 1950. Assoc. Nuñez-Mesa & Machado, Havana, 1950-56; house counsel Standard Oil Ind., Havana, 1956-59, Standard Oil Calif., Havana, 1959-61; assoc. Reid & Priest, N.Y.C., 1961-69; gen. atty. Schlumberger, Caracas, Venezuela, 1969-78; asst. gen. counsel United Fruit Co., N.Y.C., 1978—. Coordinator ABA com. to help Cuban Lawyers, N.Y., 1962-64. Mem. Council of Ams. Republican. Roman Catholic. Contracts commercial, General corporate, Public international. Home: 322 W 57th St New York NY 10019 Office: United Fruit Co 1271 Ave of Americas New York NY 10020

ARANSON, MICHAEL J., lawyer, investment advisory and real estate services company executive; b. Pitts., Sept. 22, 1944; s. Milton H. and Pearl (Sacher) A.; m. Patti J. Greenberger, May 23, 1965; children—Richard P., Jill R. B.S. in Bus. Adminstrn., Duquesne U., 1966, J.D. Cum Laude, 1969. Bar: U.S. Dist. Ct. (we. dist.) Pa. 1969, sup. ct. Pa. 1969. Assoc., Berkman Ruslander Pohl Lieber & Engel, Pitts., 1969-72; jr., then gen. counsel Babb Investments, Inc., Pitts., 1972-75; sr. v.p., counsel Resource Investments, Inc., Pitts., 1975—; pres. GAF Realty, Inc., Pitts., 1975—; vis. prof. taxation Robert Morris Coll., 1982-83; mem. various real estate partnerships. Mem. Greater Pitts. Internat. Airport Adv. Com., 1982-84; bd. dirs., v.p. United Jewish Fedn. Greater Pitts., 1985-86, chmn. met. div., assoc. chmn. campaign, 1983-85; bd. dirs., chmn. Ambassador's Soc. Trustees State of Israel Bond Pa.; v.p., bd. dirs. Jewish Community Ctr., Pitts., 1981—, v.p., 1986—, chmn. new bldg. capital fund, 1985—; pres., v.p., bd. dirs. Zionist Orgn. Am., Pitts., 1982-84; trustee, 1982-86, chmn. capital devel. fund Tree of Life Congregation, 1982. Mem. ABA, Pa. Bar Assn., Allegheny County Bar Assn., Nat. Assn. Realtors, Pa. Assn. Realtors, Allegheny County Assn. Realtors. Republican. Clubs: Westmoreland Country (bd. dirs. 1979-86, Duqù esne, Concordia (bd. dirs. 1985-86), Masons, Shriners (Pitts.). Editor-in-chief Duquesne Law Rev., 1968-69. Real property. Home: 1072 Lyndhurst Dr Pittsburgh PA 15206 Office: 650 1 Allegheny Center Pittsburgh PA 15212

ARBER, HOWARD BRUCE, lawyer; b. N.Y.C., Sept. 7, 1949; s. Jack Charles and Rita (Cohen) A.; m. Linda Ellen Trapani, Oct. 2, 1983. B.S., NYU, 1972; J.D., Hofstra U., 1975. Bar: N.Y. 1976, U.S. Dist. Ct. (so. and ea. dists.) 1983. Engaged in real estate mgmt. Rose Assocs., N.Y.C., 1976-78; assoc. Entin & Rosenthal, N.Y.C., 1978-79, Jacobson & Goldberg, N.Y.C., 1979-81; sole practice, West Hempstead, N.Y., 1981-86, ptnr. Gerson & Arber, 1986—; gen. counsel Eastern Motor Racing Assn., N.Y.C., 1981—, L.I. Sports Car Assn., N.Y.C., 1981—; arbitrator Nassau County Dist. Cts., 1982—. Mem. Nassau County Bar Assn. (assigned counsel plan com.), Am. Arbitration Assn. (arbitrator 1986—). State civil litigation, Family and matrimonial, Real property. Office: 300 Hempstead Turnpike West Hempstead NY 11552

ARCARO, HAROLD CONRAD, JR., lawyer; b. Providence, Aug. 9, 1935; s. Harold Conrad and Ines (Cicerchia) A.; divorced; children—Harold Conrad III, Meredith, James E., John T., Elizabeth T.; m. Nancy M. Morris. A.B., Brown U., 1956; J.D., U. Va., 1959; LL.M. in Taxation, Boston U., 1963. Bar: R.I. 1959, U.S. Tax Ct. 1962, U.S. Dist. Ct. R.I. 1961, U.S. Ct. Appeals (1st cir.), U.S. Claims Ct. 1981, U.S. Supreme Ct. 1981. Assoc. Arcaro, Belilove & Kolodney, Providence, 1959-61; trial atty. Office of Regional Counsel, IRS, Boston, 1961-65; ptnr. Salter, McGowan, Arcaro & Swartz, 1965-81; propr. Law Offices of Harold C. Arcaro, Jr., Providence, 1981-85; ptnr. Arcaro & Reilly, 1985—; adj. prof. Bryant Coll. Grad. Tax Program, 1978—. Past pres. R.I. Civic Chorale, Arts R.I.; mem. corp. R.I. Hosp., Butler Hosp., Women's and Infants Hosp., Bradley Hosp, Blue Cross Assn. R.I.; mem. R.I. Senate, 1967-72; fed. bar examiner, U.S. Dist. Ct.; mem. R.I. Commn. on Criminal Justice, 1978-85. Mem. ABA (civil and criminal penalties com. sect. of taxation, white collar crime com. criminal justice sect, litigation sect.), R.I. Bar Assn. (IRS regional liaison mem. 1974-82, sect. taxation, fed. bench bar com.), Nat. Assn. Criminal Def. Lawyers. Democrat. Roman Catholic. Clubs: Aurora Civic Assn. (Providence); Dunes, Point Judith Country (Narragansett, R.I.). State and local taxation, Criminal, Federal civil litigation. Home: 687B Post Rd RR5 Matunuck RI 02879 Office: Arcaro & Reilly Suite 1040 Fleet National Bank Bldg Providence RI 02903

ARCENEAUX, GEORGE, JR., federal judge; b. New Orleans, May 17, 1928; s. George and Louise (Austin) A. B.A., La. State U., 1949; J.D., Am. U., 1957. Bar: La. 1959. Partner Duval, Arceneaux, Lewis and Funderburk, Houma, La., 1960-79; spl. counsel La. Mineral Bd., Baton Rouge, 1960-62; city atty. City of Houma, 1970-71; judge U.S. Dist. Ct. Eastern Dist. La., New Orleans, 1979—. Mem. Houma-Terrebonne Regional Planning Commn., 1963-65, chmn., 1963-71; mem. La. Ho. of Dels., 1973-74. Mem. Fed. Terrebonne Parish Bar Assn. (pres. 1964-65). Office: US Courthouse Chambers C-405 500 Camp St New Orleans LA 70130

ARCENEAUX, JAMES SHAW, lawyer; b. New Orleans, Oct. 30, 1936; s. James and Anita Ellen (Tate) A.; m. Alwyn Rose Toups, Nov. 27, 1965; children: Julie Marie, Michael John. BBA, Loyola U., New Orleans, 1960, JD, 1960. Bar: La. 1960, U.S. Dist. Ct. (ea. dist.) La. 1962, U.S. Ct. Appeals (5th cir.) 1962, U.S. Supreme Ct. 1977. Assoc. Bienvenu & Culver, New Orleans, 1961-64; landman Texaco, Inc., New Orleans, 1964-67; assoc. Mollere & Barbara, Metairie, La., 1967-73; ptnr. Mollere, Flanagan & Arceneaux, Metairie, 1973-82; sole practice Metairie, 1983—. Asst. parish atty. Jefferson Parish, Gretna, La., 1967—; bd. dirs. Legal Aid Bur., New Orleans, 1970—. Mem. ABA, La. Bar Assn., Jefferson Bar Assn. Democrat. Roman Catholic. Personal injury, Probate, Family and matrimonial. Home: 1700 Francis Ave Metairie LA 70003 Office: 2341 Metairie Rd Metairie LA 70001

ARCENEAUX, M. THOMAS, lawyer; b. Lake Charles, La., Oct. 8, 1951; s. Felix Felicien and Betty Gordon (Gunn) A.; m. Antoinette Langlois, Jan. 5, 1974; children: Anna Marie, Martin Thomas Jr. BS, La. State U., 1972, JD, 1976. Bar: La. 1976, U.S. Dist. Ct. (we. dist.) La. 1976, Tex. 1978, U.S. Ct. Appeals (5th cir.) 1980. Law clk. to presiding judge U.S. Dist. Ct., Shreveport, La., 1976-78; assoc. Vinson & Elkins, Houston, 1978-79; ptnr. Beard, Arceneaux & Sutherland, Shreveport, 1979-81; land mgr., gen. counsel Despot Exploration Inc., Shreveport, 1981-83; sole practice Shreveport, 1983—. Articles editor Law Rev., 1975-76. Chmn. utilities com. Shreveport City Council, 1983-87, chmn., 1985—; chmn. audit fin. com. Shreveport City Council, 1985—; vice chmn. Shrereport City Council, 1985-86; dir. Interfaith Com., Shreveport, 1983-85. Named Outstanding Young Man of Yr., Shreveport Jaycees, 1985. Republican. Roman Catholic. Avocations: aerobics, jogging, writing. Bankruptcy, Oil and gas leasing, Real property. Home: 828 E Kings Hwy Shreveport LA 71105 Office: PO Box 1657 Shreveport LA 71165

ARCHER, DENNIS WAYNE, judge; b. Detroit, Jan. 1, 1942; s. Ernest James and Frances (Carroll) A.; B.S., Western Mich. U., 1965; J.D., Detroit Coll. Law, 1970; m. Trudy Ann DunCombe, June 17, 1967; children—Dennis Wayne, Vincent DunCombe. Tchr. spl. edn. Detroit Bd. Edn., 1965-70; admitted to Mich. bar, 1970, assoc. Gragg & Gardner, 1970-71; ptnr. Hall, Stone, Allen & Archer, 1971-73; ptnr. Charfoos, Christensen & Archer, P.C., 1973-85; assoc. justice Mich. Supreme Ct. 1986—. Assoc. prof. Detroit Coll. Law, 1972-78; adj. prof. Wayne State U. Law Sch., Detroit, 1984-85. mem. Mich. Bd. Ethics, 1979-83; bd. dirs. Legal Aid and Defenders Assn. Detroit, 1980-82. Trustee Mich. Cancer Soc., 1980-84, bd. dirs., 1985—; co-chmn. Met. Detroit Community Coalition for Democratic Party, 1979-80; active numerous local Dem. campaigns, 1970-85; host local public service radio programs. Mem. ABA(ho. dels. 1979—, chmn. elect gen. practice sect. 1986-87, chair commn. on opportunities for minorities in the profession 1986-87, sect. legal edn. and admissions to the bar law sch. accreditation com. 1982-87, chmn. spl. com. prepaid legal services 1981-83), Nat. Bar Assn. (spl. asst. to pres. 1981-82, pres. 1983-84), Detroit Bar Assn., Am. Judicature Soc. (dir. 1977-81), State Bar Mich. (pres. 1984-85), Wolverine Bar Assn. (pres. 1979-80), Detroit Nat. Assn. (dir. 1973-75), Mich. Trial Lawyers Assn. (exec. bd. 1973-74), Am. Trial Lawyers Assn., Alpha Phi Alpha. Roman Catholic. Club: Economic, University. Contbr. articles to legal jours. General practice. Office: Mich Supreme Ct 1425 Lafayette Bldg Detroit MI 48226

ARCHER, GLENN LEROY, JR., judge, lawyer, government official; b. Densmore, Kans., Mar. 21, 1929; s. Glenn LeRoy and Ruth Agnes (Ford) A.; m. Vera Poe Wiseman, Dec. 29, 1956; children: Susan Elaine, Sharon Jane, Glenn LeRoy, Thomas Wiseman. B.A., Yale U., 1951; J.D. with honors, George Washington U., 1954. Bar: D.C. 1954. Ptnr. Hamel Park McCabe & Saunders, Washington, 1956-81; asst. atty. gen. U.S. Dept. Justice, Washington, 1981-85; judge U.S. Ct. Appeals (fed. cir.), Washington, 1985—. Served to 1st lt. USAF, 1954-56. Mem. ABA (sec. taxation sect. 1975-77), Fed. Bar Assn. D.C. Republican. Methodist. Judicial administration. Home: 6227 Lakeview Dr Falls Church VA 22041 Office: US Ct Appeals (fed cir) 717 Madison Washington DC 20439

ARDAM, DAVID MITCHELL, lawyer; b. Bronx, N.Y., Oct. 1, 1953; s. Seymour and Elaine (Kirshner) A.; m. Diane Cora Tonick, Aug. 15, 1976; children—Jacquelyn Wendy, Eric Barry. B.A., SUNY-Albany, 1975; J.D., John Marshall Law Sch., Chgo., 1979. Bar: N.Y. 1979, U.S. Dist. Ct. (ea. dist.) N.Y. 1980, U.S. Dist. Ct. (so. dist.) N.Y. 1982, U.S. Ct. Appeals (2d cir.) 1982, U.S. Ct. Claims 1986, U.S. Mil. Appeals 1986, U.S. Ct. Appeals (fed. cir.) 1986, U.S. Supreme Ct. 1986. Law clk. to justices, appellate div. N.Y. State Supreme Ct., Bklyn., 1979-81, sr. law clk., 1981; assoc. Flower & Plotka, Bay Shore, N.Y., 1981-84; sole practice, Hauppauge, N.Y., 1984-86; ptnr. Spada & Ardam P.C., 1986—. Mem. ABA, N.Y. State Bar Assn., Suffolk County Bar Assn. Democrat. Jewish. Lodge: Rotary. Personal injury, Family and matrimonial, Criminal. Office: Spada & Ardam PC 300 Wheeler Rd Hauppauge NY 11788

ARDEN, JOHN RÉAL, lawyer; b. Louisville, Aug. 17, 1944; s. Sylvan Sherwin and Marie Theresa (LaLiberté-Daigneau) A.; m. Margot deNise Elkin, Aug. 9, 1969; children: Michael John-Réal, Stephen Patrick, Catherine Elizabeth. AS in Engring., Flint Community Jr. Coll., 1964; BSEE, Mich. State U., 1967, postgrad., 1968-69; JD, U. Notre Dame, 1972. Bar: Mass. 1973, U.S. Dist. Ct. Mass. 1985. Assoc. Donald P. Conway, West Springfield, Mass., 1972-73; editorial asst. Ronald A. Anderson, Phila., 1973-74; tax atty. The Research Group Inc., Charlottesville, Va., 1974; corp. counsel Frank D. Wayne Assocs., Inc., Southampton, Mass., 1974-76; sole practice Southampton, Mass., 1974-77, Northampton, Mass., 1977—; adj. prof. Western New Eng. Law Sch., Springfield, 1977, Greenfield (Mass.) Community Coll., 1978. Mem. Town Fin. Com., Southhampton, 1978-80; coach, umpire Easthampton (Mass.) Little League, 1981—; candidate U.S. Ho. Reps., Mass., 1982; bd. dirs. Hampshire County Community Action, Northampton, 1978-80. Mem. ABA, Hampshire County Bar Assn., Eta Kappa Nu, Tau Beta Pi. Democrat. Roman Catholic. Avocations: politics, sports, travel, photography, stamps and coins. General practice, Real property, General corporate. Home: 23 Sterling Dr Easthampton MA 01027 Office: 181 Main St Suite 2 Northampton MA 01060

ARDERY, JOSEPH LORD TWEEDY, lawyer; b. Lexington, Ky., July 11, 1947; s. Philip Pendleton and Anne (Tweedy) A.; m. Anne Henneberry Lenihan, Sept. 16, 1978; children: Joseph Breckenridge, Rose Lenihan, James Lord. BA summa cum laude, Harvard U., 1972; JD, U. Louisville, 1976. Bar: Ky. 1976. Assoc. Brown, Todd & Heyburn, Louisville, 1976-81, ptnr., 1982—. Bd. dirs. Transit Authority of River City, Ky., 1977-81, exec. com., 1978-81; bd. overseers U. Louisville, 1979—, chmn. 1986—; mem. Leadership Louisville Found.; founding chmn. Third Century. Mem. ABA, Ky. Bar Assn., Louisville Bar Assn., Phi Beta Kappa. Democrat. Episcopalian. Clubs: Louisville Country, Pendennis, Jefferson (Louisville). General corporate, Corporate taxation, State and local taxation. Home: Mockingbird Valley Rd Louisville KY 40207 Office: Brown Todd & Heyburn 1600 Citizens Plaza Louisville KY 40202

ARDIFF, WILLIAM B., lawyer; b. Beverly, Mass., Feb. 20, 1937; s. Ralph E. Ardiff and Marjorie (Barrell) Ardiff Holmes; m. Susan Foy, Oct. 22, 1977. AB, Dartmouth Coll., 1959; JD, Cornell U., 1962; LLM, Boston U., 1963. Bar: Mass. 1962. Ptnr. Ardiff, Ardiff & Morse, Danvers, Mass., 1963-84; sole practice Danvers, 1984—; Incorporator Danvers Savs. Bank, 1964. Active Danvers Sch. Com., 1962-65; pres. Danvers Hist. Soc., 1968-71; bd. dirs. YMCA, Danvers, 1985; pres., bd. dirs. Ferncroft Tower Condominium Assn., 1981-86; trustee Gov. Drummer Acad., Byfield, Mass. 1972-86, Endicott Coll., Beverly, 1979-86,. Mem. North Shore C. of C. (bd. dirs. 1985), North Shore Dartmouth Club (pres. 1979-81). Lodge: Rotary (dist. gov. 1976-77). General corporate, Probate, Personal income taxation. Home: 606 Ferncroft Tower Middleton MA 01949 Office: 8 Cherry St Danvers MA 01923

ARDITO, LAURIE ANN, lawyer; b. Chgo., July 31, 1956; d. John and Catherine (Pieretti) A. BA, Rosary Coll., 1978; JD, No. Ill. U., 1981. Bar: Ill. 1981. Mgr. labor relations, counsel Dominick's Finer Foods, Inc., Northlake, Ill., 1982—. Mem. ABA, Ill. Bar Assn., DuPage County Bar Assn., Chgo. Bar Assn. Workers' compensation, Labor. Office: Dominicks Finer Foods Inc 333 Northwest Ave Northlake IL 60164

AREEDA, PHILLIP, lawyer, educator; b. Detroit, Jan. 28, 1930; s. Elias Herbert and Selma (Cope) A. A.B., Harvard U., 1951, LL.B., 1954; Harvard travelling fellow, 1954-55. Bar: Mich. 1954. Mem. White House staff, asst. spl. counsel to Pres. U.S. 1956-61; mem. faculty Harvard Law Sch., 1961, prof. law, 1963—, Langdell prof., 1981—; counsel to Pres. U.S., 1974-75; exec. dir. U.S. Cabinet Task Force on Oil Import Control, 1969.

Author: Antitrust Analysis, 1967, 3d edit., 1981, Antitrust Law, 3 vols., 1982, 85; co-author: Antitrust Law, 5 vols., 1978, 80. Served to 1st lt. USAF, 1955-57. Mem. Am. Law Inst., Am. Acad. Arts and Scis. Antitrust. Office: Langdell Hall Cambridge MA 02138

ARENCIBIA, RAUL A., lawyer; b. N.Y.C., Dec. 18, 1955; s. Raul and Elba (Petrovitch) A. BA cum laude, NYU, 1977; JD, Harvard U., 1980. Bar: Fla. 1980, U.S. Dist. Ct. (so. dist.) Fla. 1980, U.S. Ct. Appeals (5th and 11th cirs.) 1981, U.S. Dist. Ct. (mid. dist.) Fla. 1985. Assoc. Paul & Thomson, Miami, Fla., 1980-81, Mahoney, Hadlow, et al, Miami, 1981-82, Frates & Novey, Miami, 1983-84, Dady, Siegfried, et al, Coral Gables, Fla., 1984-85; sole practice Miami, 1985—. Recipient NYU Founders Day award, 1977, NYU scholar, 1973. Mem. ABA, Cuban Am. Bar Assn., Fla. Bar Assn., Dade County Bar Assn. Democrat. Roman Catholic. Avocations: chess, racquetball. Federal civil litigation, State civil litigation, Contracts commercial. Address: One Datran Ctr 9100 S Dadeland Blvd Suite 800 Miami FL 33156

ARENSBERG, CORNELIUS WRIGHT, lawyer; b. N.Y.C., June 19, 1951; s. Conrad Maynadier and Margaret (Walsh) A. BA, Columbia U., 1972; JD, Stetson U., 1977; M in Internat. Mgmt., Sch. of Internat. Mgmt., 1984. Bar: Fla. 1978, U.S. Ct. Mil. Appeals 1979. Asst. legal advisor NATO, Naples, Italy, 1981-83; mgmt. fellow Tokyo, 1984; pvt. practice cons. N.Y.C., 1985; ptnr. Hooper & Arensberg P.A., St. Petersburg, Fla., 1986—. Served to capt. U.S. Army (JAGC), 1979-83. Decorated D.S.M. Mem. ABA, Fla. Bar Assn., Internat. Bar Assn., Phi Delta Phi. Episcopalian. Avocations: languages, travel, art, horseback riding, hunting. Private international, Public international, Military. Home: 1876 1/2 Coffee Pot Blvd NE Saint Petersburg FL 33704 Office: Hooper & Arensberg PA Suite 1011 Plaza Bldg 111 2d Ave NE Saint Petersburg FL 33701

ARENSON, GREGORY K., lawyer; b. Chgo., Feb. 11, 1949; s. Donald L. and Marcia (Terman) A.; m. Karen H. Wattel, Sept. 4, 1970; 1 child, Morgan Elizabeth. BS in Econs., MIT, 1971; JD, U. Chgo., 1975. Bar: Ill. 1975, U.S. Dist. Ct. (no. dist.) Ill. 1975, N.Y. 1978, U.S. Dist. Ct. (so. and ea. dists.) N.Y. 1978, U.S. Supreme Ct. 1985. Assoc. Rudnick & Wolfe, Chgo., 1975-77; assoc. Schwartz, Klink & Schreiber P.C., N.Y.C., 1977-81, ptnr., 1982-87; ptnr. Proskauer, Rose, Goetz & Mendelsohn, N.Y.C., 1987—. Mem. N.Y. State Bar Assn. Federal civil litigation, Securities. Home: 125 W 76th St Apt 2A New York NY 10023 Office: Proskauer Rose Goetz & Mendelsoh 300 Park Ave New York NY 10022

ARENSTEIN, ROBERT DAVID, lawyer; b. N.Y.C., Jan. 16, 1947; s. Seymour and Sylvia Lillian (Rubenstein) A.; m. Judy Simonson, June 30, 1968; 1 dau., Amy Sue. B.S. in Acctg. cum laude, Ithaca Coll., 1968; J.D., St. John's U., Bklyn., 1972; LL.M. in Taxation, NYU, 1976. Bar: N.Y. 1973, D.C. 1976, N.J. 1979, Fla. 1979. Assoc. Hocheimer, Gartlir Gottlieb & Gross, N.Y.C., 1973-74; assoc. Shapiro Weiden & Mortman, P.C., N.Y.C., 1974-75; sole practice, N.Y.C., 1975-80; ptnr. Arenstein & Huston, P.C., N.Y.C., 1980-84; sole practice, 1984—. Fellow Am. Acad. Matrimonial Lawyers; mem. ABA (exec. council family sect., chmn. membership com., nominating com., chmn. policy and procedures handbook, chmn. research com.), N.Y. State Bar Assn. (chmn. long range planning com. family law sect.), Westchester County Bar Assn., N.J. Bar Assn., Fla. Bar, Assn. Bar City N.Y. Club: Masons. Family and matrimonial. Office: 295 Madison Ave New York NY 10017 also: 691 Cedar Ln Teaneck NJ 07666

ARESTY, JEFFREY MICHAEL, lawyer; b. Framingham, Mass., Dec. 31, 1951; s. Victor Joseph and Pola Aresty; m. Ellen Louise Gould, Aug. 15, 1976; children—Joshua, Abigail. B.A., Johns Hopkins U., 1973; J.D., Boston U., 1976, LL.M., 1978. Bar: Mass. 1977, D.C. 1982. Tax specialist Coopers & Lybrand, Boston, 1976-78; assoc. Meyers, Goldstein & Crossland, Brookline, Mass., 1978-79; ptnr. Crossland, Aresty & Levin, Boston, 1979-87, Aresty, Levin, Orenstein & Wernick, Boston, 1987—. Cons. editor Tax Shelter Investment Rev., 1981-85. Recipient Disting. Achievement award Boston Safe Deposit and Trust, 1976. Mem. ABA (membership chmn. 1981-84, council 1985—, vice chmn. computer div. 1985—, chmn. Mass. membership com. sect. econ. of law practice 1985—), Mass. Bar Assn. (bd. dels., exec. com. 1981-83, chmn. law practice sect. 1983-85), Mass. Bar Found. Contracts commercial, Private international, Real property. Home: 35 Three Ponds Rd Wayland MA 01788 Office: Aresty Levin Orenstein & Wernick Suite 105 World Trade Ctr Boston MA 02210

AREY, PATRICK KANE, lawyer; b. Mt. Holly, N.J., July 10, 1947; s. Richard Walton and Patricia (Kane) A.; m. Pamela Neill Henery, July 10, 1971; children: Lindsay, Anne, Molly, John Patrick. BA, Washington and Lee U., 1969, JD cum laude, 1976. Bar: Va. 1976, Md. 1983. Assoc. McGuire, Woods & Battle, Richmond, Va., 1976-82; ptnr. Miles & Stockbridge, Balt., 1982—. Served to capt. U.S. Army, 1969-73, Vietnam. Mem. ABA (com. chmn. urban, state and local govt. law sect.), Md. Bar Assn., Va. Bar Assn., Nat. Assn. Bond Lawyers (steering com.). Republican. Episcopalian. Municipal bonds, Securities, Contracts commercial. Office: Miles & Stockbridge 10 Light St Baltimore MD 21202

AREY, STEPHEN EDWARD, lawyer; b. Annapolis, Md., June 29, 1946; s. Richard Walton and Patricia (Kane) A.; m. Judy Lee Smith, Dec. 14, 1973; children: Jeremy Wayne, Jeffrey Alan, Amanda Dawn. BA, U. Va., 1968; JD, Washington & Lee U., 1975. Bar: Va. 1975. Law clk. to presiding justice Va. Supreme Ct., Pulaski, 1975-76; from assoc. to ptnr. Harman & Harman, Tazewell, Va., 1976-81; ptnr. Arey & Caldwell, Tazewell, 1981-82, Arey & Harman, P.C., Tazewell, 1985—; sole practice Tazewell, 1982-85; town atty. Town of Bluefield, Va., 1979—, Pocahontas, Va., 1981—. Lay reader, vestry mem. Stras Meml. Episcopal Ch., Tazewell; candidate Tazewell County Commonwealth's Atty., 1977. Served with U.S. Army, 1969-72; serves as lt. col. Va. Army N.G., 1972—. Decorated Meritorious Service medal. Mem. Va. Bar Assn., Tazewell Jaycees, U. Va. Alumni Assn., Va. Student Aid Found. Republican. Avocations: Civil War history, gardening. General practice, Local government, Administrative and regulatory. Home: 314 Fincastle Rd Tazewell VA 24651 Office: Arey & Harman PC 204 Main St PO Box 895 Tazewell VA 24651

ARGENTA, CRAIG JON, lawyer; b. Stafford, Conn., Apr. 3, 1952; s. Ronald William and Linda Catherine (Rui) A.; m. Nancy Oppenheim, Aug. 15, 1975 (div. Apr. 1983); 1 child, Ryan William. BA in Polit. Sci., Duquesne U., 1974, JD, 1977. Bar: Conn. 1978, U.S. Dist. Ct. Conn. 1980. Assoc. Law Offices of F. Joseph Paradiso, Stafford, 1977-79; sole practice Stafford, 1979—; trustee Johnson Meml. Hosp., Stafford, 1983. Bd. dirs. Stafford Pub. Health Nursing Assn., 1979-83, gov.'s appointee Farmland Preservation Com., State of Conn., 1979. Mem. Conn. Bar Assn., Tolland County Bar Assn. Roman Catholic. Real property, Family and matrimonial, Criminal. Home: 28 Woodland Dr Stafford Springs CT 06076 Office: 14 E Main St PO Box 64 Stafford Springs CT 06076

ARIS, JORAM JEHUDAH, lawyer; b. Haderah, Israel, Feb. 6, 1953; came to U.S., 1957; s. Joseph Koenigstein and Shoshanah (Lemberger) Aris; m. Gloria Bakash, Sept. 22, 1984; 1 child, Giselle Dina. Student, York U., Eng., 1972; BA magna cum laude, City Coll. of N.Y., 1972; JD, N.Y. Law Sch., 1978. Bar: N.J. 1978, N.Y. 1979. Asst. U.S. Dist. Ct. (so. dist.), N.Y.C., 1977; asst. atty. State of N.Y., N.Y.C., 1978; assoc. First & First, N.Y.C., 1978-79; atty. Empire Mut. Ins. Co., N.Y.C., 1979-80; law sec. U.S. Supreme Ct., N.Y.C., 1980-81; sole practice N.Y.C., 1981—; chmn. Collective, N.Y.C., 1971-72. Mem. Riverdale Dem. Club, Bronx, N.Y., 1975-86, N.Y.C. Community Bd. #8, Bronx, 1980-86, Pub. Safety Com., Bronx, 1980-84, Environ. Safety and Sanitation, Bronx, 1985-86, Housing Com., Bronx, 1980-82, law com. 1986—, ethics com. 1986—; pres. Windsor Tenants Assn., Bronx, 1980-86. Mem. ABA, N.Y. State Bar Assn., Am.-Sephardic Orgn., Phi Delta Phi. Democrat. Jewish. General practice, Personal injury, Family and matrimonial. Home and Office: 3671 Hudson Manor Terr Riverdale NY 10463

ARIZAGA, LAVORA SPRADLIN, lawyer; b. Garvin County, Okla., Apr. 29, 1927; d. Gervase Eugene and Donah Lavorah (Eddings) Spradlin; m. Francisco Depaula Arizaga, Aug. 10, 1946; children: Frisco D. III, Lavora Arizaga Ewan, Rebecca Arizaga Armour, Nicolas. BA, U. Okla., 1952; JD, U. Houston, 1979. Bar: Tex. 1979. Sole practice Houston, 1979—. Chmn. affirmative action adv. bd. City of Houston, 1984-86; bd. dirs. Wesley Community Ctr., Houston, 1983—, Gethsemane Sch. for Little Children, 1985—; pres. pta Sharpstown High Sch., Houston, 1975-76, United Meth. Women, 1984. Mem. ABA, Tex. Bar Assn., Houston Bar Assn., League of Women Voters (bd. dirs. 1980-83, v.p. 1983-85, pres. 1985—). Probate, General practice, Environment. Home and Office: 8911 Sandstone Houston TX 77036

ARKIN, HARRY LEE, lawyer, investment advisor; b. San Juan, P.R., Dec. 17, 1933; s. Benjamin and Rebecca (Schneiderman) A.; m. Sandra Loraine Fingold, June 30, 1962 (div. 1984); children: Pamela, Bradley; m. Jean Aaron Frankel, June 14, 1985. Student, U. Colo., 1951-54; BS, JD, U. Denver, 1956. Bar: Colo. 1957, U.S. Dist. Ct. Colo. 1957, U.S. Ct. Appeals (10th cir.) 1957, U.S. Ct. Mil. Appeals 1959, U.S. Supreme Ct. 1965. Ptnr. Linder & Arkin, Denver, 1959-63; sole practice Denver, 1963-71, 85—; sr. ptnr. Arkin, McGloin & Davenport, Denver, 1972-82; pres. Fin. Cons. Services Corp., Denver, 1983—. Served with USAF, 1957-59, with USAFR, 1955-85. Mem. ABA, Colo. Bar Assn., Internat. Bar Assn., Denver Bar Assn., Arapahoe County Bar Assn., Colo. Assn. Corp. Counsel (past pres.), Greater Denver Tax Counsels Assn., Denver Estate Planning Council, Licensing Execs. Soc., Am. Arbitration Assn. Republican. Jewish. Lodge: Shriners, Rotary. Avocations: skiing, racquetball, travel. General corporate, Probate, Private international. Office: 2 United Bank Ctr 1700 Broadway Suite 1500 Denver CO 80290

ARKIN, HENRY RUSSELL, lawyer; b. Chgo., Apr. 29, 1945; s. Sol E. and Beatrice J. (Wiener) A.; m. Barbara Ann Cronin, Feb. 29, 1980; 1 child, Sarah Elizabeth. BA, U. Wis., 1967, MA, 1971, MS, 1972; JD, DePaul U., 1977. Bar: Ill. 1977. Atty. Ill. Dept. Registration and Edn., Chgo., 1977-81, AMA, Chgo., 1981—. Mem. Am. Inst. Parliamentarians, Nat. Assn. Parliamentarians, Chgo. Bar Assn. Avocations: music. Health. Home: 5345 S Hyde Park Blvd #2E Chicago IL 60615 Office: AMA 535 N Dearborn St Chicago IL 60610

ARKIN, MICHAEL BARRY, lawyer, rancher; b. Washington, Jan. 11, 1941; s. William Howard and Zenda Lillian (Liebermann) A.; m. Gay Callan, July 3, 1982; children: Tracy Renee, Jeffrey Harris, Marcy Susan, Chatom Callan, Michael Edwin, Samuel Hopkins. A.A., George Washington U., 1961; B.A. in Psychology, U. Okla., 1962, J.D., 1965. Bar: Okla. 1965, U.S. Ct. Claims 1968, U.S. Supreme Ct. 1968, Calif. 1970, U.S. Tax Ct. 1970, U.S. Ct. Appeals (3d, 5th, 6th, 9th, 10th cirs.) 1970, U.S. Dist. Ct. (cen. dist.) Calif. 1970, U.S. Dist. Ct. (so. dist.) Calif. 1970, U.S. Dist. Ct. (ea. dist.) Calif. 1987. Trial atty. tax div. U.S. Dept. Justice, 1965-68, appellate atty., 1968-69; ptnr. Surr & Hellyer, San Bernardino, Calif., 1969-79; mng. ptnr. Wied, Granby Alford & Arkin, San Diego, 1979-82, Lorenz Alhadeff Fellmeth Arkin & Multer, San Diego, 1982, Finley, Kumble, Heine, Underberg, Manley & Casey, San Diego, 1983; sole practice Sacramento and San Andreas (Calif.), 1984-86; ptnr. McDonough Holland & Allen, Sacramento, 1986-87; sole practice San Andreas, Calif., 1987—. Bd. dirs. San Bernardino County Legal Aid Soc., 1971-73, sec., 1971-72, pres., 1973; mem. Calaveras County Adv. Com. on Alcohol and Drug Abuse, 1985—; treas. Calaveras County Legal Assistance Program, 1987—. Named to Hon. Order of Ky. Cols., 1967. Mem. ABA, Calif. Bar Assn. (com. on taxation), Sacramento County Bar Assn., San Diego County Bar Assn., San Bernardino County Bar Assn. (bd. dirs., sec.-treas. 1973-75, pilot drug abuse program 1970), Calaveras County Bar Assn., Am. Arbitration Assn. Republican. Jewish. Corporate taxation, Estate taxation, Personal income taxation. Office: PO Box 1210 7 N Main St Suite 206 San Andreas CA 95249 Office: 7 N Main St Suite 206 San Andreas CA 95249

ARKIN, ROBERT DAVID, lawyer; b. Washington, Feb. 15, 1954; s. William Howard and Zenda Lillian (Lieberman) A.; m. Rise Morgenstern, Dec. 29, 1974; 1 child, Chelsea Morgenstern-Arkin. BA, U. Pa., 1976, MA, 1976; JD, U. Va., 1979. Bar: Minn. 1980. Law clk. to chief justice Supreme Ct. Minn., St. Paul, 1979-80; assoc. Leonard, Street and Deinard, Mpls., 1980-84, ptnr., 1985-86; spl. asst. atty. gen. State of Minn., St. Paul, 1981; of counsel Trotter, Smith & Jacobs, Atlanta, 1986—; mem. Tech. Rev. Com. Seed Money Venture Capital Product Loan Program, Minn. Office of Software Tech. Devel., St. Paul, 1985-86; vice chmn. Minn. Software Tech. Commn. (gubernatorial appointee), St. Paul, 1985-86. Exec. editor: Va. Jour. Internat. Law, Charlottesville, 1978-79; contbr. articles to profl. jours. Participant Leadership Mpls. of Greater Mpls. C. of C., 1984-85; mem. steering com. Young Leadership Devel., Mpls. Fedn. for Jewish Service, 1982-85; bd. dirs., mem. exec. com. Community Housing and Service Corp., Mpls., 1981-85. Mem. ABA (computer law, corps., banking, bus. law and internat. sect.), Minn. Bar Assn. (chmn. internat. contracts com. 1985-86), Hennepin County Bar Assn., Computer Law Assn., Minn. Software Assn. (bd. dirs. 1986—), Minn. World Trade Assn., Pi Gamma Mu. Democrat. Jewish. Avocations: film, photography, running. Computer, General corporate, Securities. Home: 20 Battle Ridge Dr Atlanta GA 30342 Office: Trotter Smith & Jacobs 2400 Gas Light Tower 235 Peachtree St Atlanta GA 30303

ARLOW, ALLAN JOSEPH, lawyer; b. N.Y.C., Apr. 2, 1944; s. Jacob and Alice (Diamond) A.; m. Barbara Heather Graham, May 23, 1965; children—Joshua, Joanna. B.A., U. Mich., 1966; J.D., Georgetown U., 1969. Bar: U.S. Ct. Appeals (D.C. cir.) 1970, U.S. Dist. Ct. D.C. 1969, Ill. 1976. Assoc. Cohn & Marks, Washington, 1969-75; v.p., gen. counsel Nat. Soda Straw Co., Chgo., 1976; sr. atty. Centel Corp., Chgo., 1977, v.p. Washington office, 1978-81, v.p. staff Centel Video Services, Chgo., 1982; v.p., gen. counsel Ameritech Mobile Communications, Inc., Schaumburg, Ill., 1983—, also bd. dirs.; chmn., chief exec. officer Pan Canadian Communications Inc., Toronto, Ont., 1985—; bd. dirs. Joint Washington-Coordinating Com. Telephone Industry, Washington, 1978-81, chmn. legis. drafting com., 1979-81, Cantel Inc., Toronto; bd. dirs. Cellular Telecommunications Industry Assn., 1985—, legis. com., 1986—; Mem. citizens adv. bd Chgo. Pub. Radio Sta. WBEZ, 1982—, chmn. budget com. 1986—. Mem. Fed Communications Bar Assn., ABA, Chgo. Bar Assn., Ill. Bar Assn. Communications, Public utilities, Antitrust. Home: 400 Carriage Way Deerfield IL 60015 Office: Ameritech Mobile Communications Inv 1515 Woodfield Rd Suite 1400 Schaumburg IL 60173

ARLT, MARY ANN KOKOSZYNA, lawyer; b. Ludlow, Mass., Nov. 18, 1953; d. Peter Vincent and Stephanie Theresa (Nowak) Kokoszyna; m. Paul E. Arlt, Nov. 27, 1982. BA, Coll. New Rochelle, 1975; JD cum laude, Stetson U., 1982. Bar: Fla. 1982, U.S. Tax Ct. 1984, U.S. Dist. Ct. (mid. dist.) Fla. 1986m U.S. Ct. Appeals (11th cir.) 1986. News and feature asst. NBC News Radio, N.Y.C., 1975-77; news dir. WSUL Radio, Monticello, N.Y., 1977-79; atty. Gray, Harris & Robinson, P.A., Orlando, Fla., 1982—; mem. Employee Benefits Council Cen. Fla. Mem. ABA (tax sect.), Orange County Bar Assn. Pension, profit-sharing, and employee benefits, General corporate, Corporate taxation. Office: Gray Harris & Robinson PA 201 E Pine St Suite 1200 Orlando FL 32802

ARLT, PAUL EDWARD, lawyer; b. Elizabeth, N.J., July 11, 1956; s. Paul and Jessie Arlt; m. Mary Ann Kokoszyna, Nov. 27, 1982. BA in Polit. Sci., Muhlenberg Coll., 1978; JD, Stetson U., 1981. Bar: Fla. 1982. Chief trial atty. Pub. Defenders Office, Sanford, Fla., 1981—. Democrat. Baptist. Criminal. Home: 1000 Winderley Place # 121 Maitland FL 32751 Office: Office Pub Defender 301 N Park Ave Sanford FL 32771

ARMANI, FRANK HENRY, lawyer; b. Syracuse, N.Y., Sept. 12, 1927; s. Ezzelin M. and Edvige (Oliana) A.; m. Natalie Mary Mozo, July 1, 1950, children: Deborah M., Dorina A. AB, Syracuse U., 1950, JD, 1956. Bar: N.Y 1956, U.S. Dist. Ct. (no. dist.) N.Y. 1958, U.S. Ct. Appeals (2d cir.) 1962, U.S. Supreme Ct. 1964. Legal Aid counsel, Onondaga County, N.Y., 1956-57; sole practice, Syracuse, 1957-62; ptnr. Armani, Welch & Welch, Syracuse, 1962-68; asst. dist. atty., Onondaga County, 1961-70; sole practice, Syracuse, 1968—; lectr. on legal ethics, Albany Law Sch., Syracuse U., Detroit Law Sch., U. Va., U. La.; participant profl. confs. and symposia. Author: To Tell the Truth: Privileged Information, 1984; prodn. and tech. adv. (movie) Sworn to Silence, 1987. Membership chmn. Onondaga County Young Republicans, 1948-50, chmn. law day com., 1970; bd. dirs. Onondaga Council on Alcoholism, 1979—; del. 1980 Rep. Nat. Conv.; com. mem. VA Med. Ctr. Recipient Law Day award Catharagus County Bar Assn., 1985, Commendation State of La. Senate. Mem. N.Y. State Bar Assn. (chmn. 5th Jud. Dist., mem. alcohol and drug abuse com.), Onondaga County Bar Assn. (dir. 1979-81, chmn. alcohol and drug abuse com., 1977—), Assn. Trial Lawyers Am., Upstate Trial Lawyers Assn., N.Y. State Trial Lawyers Assn. Roman Catholic. Featured on WETA-TV documentary "Ethics on Trial." Personal injury, General practice, Criminal. Home: 121 Munro Dr Camillus NY 13031 Office: Armani Fitzpatrick Snyder & Armani 4300 W Genesee St Syracuse NY 13219

ARMOLD, JUDITH ANN, lawyer; b. Balt., Dec. 22, 1945; d. James Joseph and Mildred Louise (Swecker) A. BA, Western Md. Coll., 1967; JD, U. Md., 1971. Bar: Md. 1972, U.S. Dist. Ct. Md. 1972, U.S. Supreme Ct. 1980, U.S. Ct. Appeals (4th cir.) 1984. Tchr. French Balt. Pub. Schs., 1967-68; assoc. Venable, Baetjer and Howard, Balt., 1971-76; asst. atty. gen. Md. State Hwy. Adminstrn., Balt., 1976-77; asst. atty. gen., gen. counsel Md. Dept. State Planning, Balt., 1977—; trustee Md. Inst. for Continuing Profl. Edn. of Lawyers, Balt., 1979—, sec., 1986—; mem. inquiry com. Md. Atty. Grievance Commn., Annapolis, 1981-86, rev. bd., 1986—; mem. steering com. Md. Land Use Round Table, 1986—; trustee Bar Assn. Ins. Trust, Balt., 1985—, v.p., 1986—. Editor (notes and comments) Md. Law Rev., 1970-71. Mem. ABA, Am. Judicature Soc., Women's Bar Assn. of Md. (treas. 1974-78, sec. 1978-79), Md. Bar Assn. (state and local govt. law sect. council 1983—), Bar Assn. of Balt. City (exec. council 1979-80, young lawyers sect. council 1975-76, 78-80). Democrat. Presbyterian. Avocations: jogging, travel. Land use and planning, Local government, Administrative and regulatory. Home: 1428 John St Baltimore MD 21217 Office: Md Dept State Planning 301 W Preston St Baltimore MD 21201

ARMOUR, GEORGE PORTER, lawyer; b. Bryn Mawr, Pa., June 10, 1921; s. Charles Joseph and Florence (Eagle) A.; m. Isabel Blondet, Nov. 22, 1958; children—Luis O., Carlos O. B.A., Temple U., 1943, J.D., 1949. Bar: Pa. 1949, N.Y. 1969, Calif. 1975. Assoc. Bennett & Bricklin, Phila., 1949-59; atty. Atlantic Richfield Co., 1959-83, gen. atty., Phila., 1965-68, assoc. gen. counsel, Phila., N.Y.C., Los Angeles, 1968-78, dep. gen. counsel, Los Angeles, 1978-83; ptnr. Gregg & Armour, 1983—; chmn. Internat. and Comparative Law Ctr., Southwestern Legal Found., Dallas, 1980-82. Mem. Assocs. Calif. Inst. Tech., 1981—; mem. Soc. of Fellows Huntington Library and Art Gallery, San Marino, Calif., 1982—. Served with USAAF, 1943-46. Mem. ABA, Pa. Bar Assn., Phila. Bar Assn., N.Y. State Bar Assn., Calif. Bar Assn., Los Angeles County Bar Assn., Republican. Episcopalian. Clubs: California (Los Angeles); Calif. Inst. Tech. Athenaeum (Pasadena). Securities, Energy, oil and gas, Private international. Home: 1345 Circle Dr San Marino CA 91108 Office: 510 S Marengo Ave Pasadena CA 91101

ARMOUR, JAMES LOTT, lawyer; b. Jackson, Tenn., May 19, 1938; s. Quintin and Francis (Breeden) A.; m. Nancy Stokes Johnson, Mar. 17, 1962; 1 son, John Lawson. B.A., Vanderbilt U., 1961, LL.B., 1964; LL.M., So. Meth. U., 1967. Bar: Tenn. 1964, Tex. 1965, U.S. Supreme Ct. 1967, N.Y. 1969, Okla. 1972. Assoc. firm Turner & Rodgers, Dallas, 1965-66; internat. atty. Mobil Corp., N.Y.C., 1967-71, Phillips Petroleum Co., Bartlesville, Okla., 1972-73; asst. gen. counsel Conoco, Inc., Stamford, Conn., 1974-83; ptnr. firm Locke, Purnell Boren, Laney & Neely, Dallas, 1984—. Contbr. to So. Meth. U. Law Rev., 1965. Mem. Southwest Legal Found., 1985. Mem. Assn. Bar City N.Y., ABA, State Bar Tex., Dallas Bar Assn., Inst. Oil and Gas Law, Phi Delta Phi. Episcopalian. Clubs: City (Dallas); Field (New Canaan, Conn.). FERC practice, Oil and gas leasing, Private international. Home: 4541 Belfort Pl Dallas TX 75205 Office: Locke Purnell Boren Laney & Neely 3600 Republic Bank Tower Dallas TX 75201

ARMOUR, NORTON L., lawyer, newspaper executive; b. Grand Rapids, Mich., Nov. 12, 1929; s. Saul and Sarah (Rosenberg) A.; m. Monica Rosensweig, Aug. 28, 1957 (div. 1969); m. Marilyn Ruth Armour, Dec. 22, 1977; children—Greta, Jacob, Stephanie. LL.B., U. Mich., 1954, M.B.A., 1955; LL.M., Boston U., 1967. Atty. Office of Chief Counsel, IRS, Boston, 1957-61; assoc. Bundlie, Kelly & Torrison, St. Paul, 1961-64, Karlins, Grossman, Karlins & Siegel, Mpls., 1964-65; gen. counsel Mpls. Star & Tribune Co., 1965—; adj. prof. William Mitchell Coll. Law, St. Paul, 1963-80. Trustee William Mitchell Coll. Law, 1976—; bd. dirs. Minn. Civil Liberties Union, 1967-79, St. Paul Chamber Orch., 1975-80, Mpls. Soc. Fine Arts, 1982—, Urban Coalition, Mpls., 1984—. Mem. ABA, Minn. State Bar Assn. (chmn. joint bar press radio TV com. 1981-84). Home: 107 Arthur Ave SE Minneapolis MN 55414 Office: Mpls Star and Tribune Co 425 Portland Ave Minneapolis MN 55488

ARMS, BREWSTER LEE, business executive; b. Pasadena, Calif., Dec. 18, 1925; s. Louis Lee and Mae Warne (Marsh) A.; m. Shirley Smallwood, Mar. 17, 1962; children: Emily Diane, Stephen Brewster, Andrew Marsh. B.A., Stanford U., 1948, J.D., 1951. Bar: Calif. 1952. Atty., corp. sec. Bankline Oil Co., 1952-59; atty. The Signal Companies, Inc. (formerly Signal Oil and Gas Co.), Los Angeles, 1959-63; corp. sec. The Signal Companies, Inc. (formerly Signal Oil and Gas Co.), 1963-72, sr. v.p., gen. counsel, 1970—. Served with inf. AUS, 1944-45. Mem. Am., Calif., San Diego County bar assns., Am. Soc. Corp. Secs. (dir.). Club: Rotarian. Office: 11255 N Torrey Pines Rd La Jolla CA 92037 *

ARMSTRONG, DAVID LOVE, attorney general of Kentucky; b. Hope, Ark., Aug. 6, 1941; m. Carol Burress, 1963; 1 child, Bryce Shannon. B.S., Murray State U., 1966; J.D., U. Louisville, 1969; postgrad. Coll. Trial Advocacy, Harvard U., 1972; postgrad., U. Nev., 1973. Bar: Ky. 1969. Ptnr. firm Turner, McDonald & Armstrong Louisville, Ky., 1969-76; commonwealth atty. City of Louisville, 1976-83; atty. gen. State of Ky., 1983—; asst. prosecutor police ct., 1969-71; judge juvenile ct. Jefferson County, Ky., 1971-73; hearing officer Louisville-Jefferson County Bd. Health. Chmn. fund raising Brooklawn Home, Louisville. Fleur de Lis award City of Louisville, 1973, Recipient/Outstanding Achievement award Nat. Assn. County Ofcls., 1977. Mem. Ky. Commonwealth Attys. Assn. (pres.), Nat. Dist. Attys. Assn. (sec.), ABA. Criminal. Office: Office of Atty Gen 116 Capitol Bldg Frankfort KY 40601

ARMSTRONG, EDWIN ALAN, lawyer; b. Atlanta, June 20, 1950; s. Carl Edwin and Betty (Hawkins) A.; m. Marlene Bryant, Aug. 12, 1978. BA, Berry Coll., 1972; JD, Emory U., 1976. Bar: Ga. 1976, U.S. Dist. Ct. (no. dist.) Ga., 1977, U.S. Ct. Appeals (5th cir.) 1977, U.S. Ct. Appeals (11th cir.) 1981, U.S. Supreme Ct., 1982. Atty. Flynt Jud. Cir. Pub. Defenders Office, McDonough, Ga., 1976-77; assoc. Neely, Neely & Player, Atlanta, 1977; sole practice Atlanta, 1977-79, 81—; assoc. Stolz, Shulman & Loveless, Atlanta, 1979-81. Pres. Northcrest Pleasantdale Civic Assn., Chamblee and Doraville, Ga., 1984—. Mem. ABA, Assn. Trial Lawyers Am., Lawyer-Pilot's Bar Assn., Nat. Transp. Safety Bd. Bar Assn. (founding). Episcopalian. Avocation: flying. State civil litigation, General practice, Personal injury. Home: 3535 Hidden Acres Dr Doraville GA 30340

ARMSTRONG, EDWIN RICHARD, lawyer, publisher, editor; b. Chgo., Sept. 25, 1921; s. Robert S. and Ella (Bremer) A.; m. Catherine Claire Graeber, June 29, 1957; children—Catherine Jane, Diane Claire, Douglas Edwin, Gregory Charles. B.A., Knox Coll., 1942; J.D., Northwestern U., 1948. Bar: Ill. 1949, U.S. Dist. Ct. (no. dist.) Ill. 1949, U.S. Ct. Appeals (7th cir.) 1949, U.S. Supreme Ct. 1961. Ptnr. Reimers & Armstrong, 1949-55; assoc. Friedman & Friedman, 1957-62; ptnr. Friedman, Armstrong & Donnelly, 1962-78, Armstrong & Donnelly, Chgo., 1978—; lectr. Ill. Inst. Continuing Legal Edn., 1979—. Mem. Oak Park (Ill.) Elem. Sch. Bd. 1963-69, pres. 1964-67; mem. exec. bd. Thatcher Woods Area council Boy Scouts Am. 1978—, pres., 1983-84. Served to maj. USMCR 1942-46. Mem. Ill. Bar Assn., Chgo. Bar Assn., West Suburban Bar Assn. Club: Oak Park. Family and matrimonial, Probate, Estate planning. Home: 637 N Euclid St Oak Park IL 60302 Office: 77 W Washington St Suite 1717 Chicago IL 60602

ARMSTRONG, GRANT, lawyer; b. Raymond, Wash., Sept. 30, 1907; s. Oren G. and Clara (Knutson) A.; m. Elbertine Raymond Adams, Jan. 25, 1933 (dec. Jan. 1979). LL.B., U. Wash., 1929. Bar: Wash. 1930. Practiced in Chehalis, 1930—; mem. firm Armstrong, Vander Stoep & Remund (and predecessor firms), 1946—; Bd. regents U. Wash., 1950-57;. Served to lt. comdr. USNR, 1943-46. Fellow Am. Coll. Trial Lawyers, Am. Bar Found., Am. Coll. Probate Counsel; mem. Am. Bar Assn. (state del. 1965-74, gov. 1975-77), Wash. Bar Assn. (gov. 1958-61, pres. 1964-65), Sigma Nu, Phi Delta Phi, Order of Coif (hon.). Republican. Episcopalian. Clubs: Seattle Golf, Tacoma. Lodge: Rotary. General practice, Probate, Personal injury.

Home: 215 NE Glen Rd Chehalis WA 98532 Office: Armstrong Vander Stroep et al 345 NW Pacific Ave Chehalis WA 98532

ARMSTRONG, HENRY JERE, judge, lawyer; b. Dothan, Ala., Mar. 5, 1941; s. Henry Jordan and Lillian (Taylor) A.; m. Jeanne Bachmann, June 3, 1963; children—April Heather, Ashley Brooke. B.A., U. Ala.-Tuscaloosa, 1964; J.D., 1966; postgrad. JAG's Sch., Charlottesville, Va., 1972-73; grad. Armed Forces Staff Coll., 1978. Bar: Ala. 1966, U.S. Ct. Mil. Appeals 1967, U.S. Supreme Ct. 1972, D.C. 1974, Va. 1984. Commd. 2d lt. U.S. Army, 1964, advanced through grades to col., 1983; def. counsel/prosecutor, Ft. Ord, Calif., 1967-68; chief criminal law, chief civil law, mil. judge, Ft. Shafter, Hawaii, 1968-72; chief legis. br. criminal law div. Dept. Army, Washington, 1973-75; exec. asst. to JAG, Washington, 1975-77; staff judge adv. 2d Inf. Div., Korea, 1978-79; exec. officer U.S. Army Trial Def. Service, Falls Church, Va., 1979-82; exec. officer litigation div. Dept. Army, Washington, 1982-84, ret., 1984; counsel to chief Immigration Judge of U.S., 1984-86; judge, asst. chief immigration judge U.S. Dept. Justice, 1986—. Mem. profl. responsibility adv. com. dept. Army; guest lectr. on ethics and def. advocacy U.S. Army Europe Continuing Legal Edn. seminars. Elder Grace Presbyterian Ch., Springfield, Va. Decorated Army Commendation medal, Meritorious Service medal with 2 oak leaf clusters, Legion of Merit; named hon. Ky. Col., 1982. Mem. Ala. State Bar Assn., D.C. Bar Assn., Va. State Bar Assn., ABA, Assn. Trial Lawyers Am., Fed. Bar Assn., Judge Advs. Assn. (dir.), Kappa Sigma Alumni Assn., Phi Alpha Delta. Contbr. article to legal jour. General practice, Federal civil litigation, Immigration, naturalization, and customs. Home: 3391 Reedy Dr Annandale VA 22003

ARMSTRONG, JACK GILLILAND, lawyer; b. Pitts., Aug. 10, 1929; s. Hugh Collins and Mary Elizabeth (Gilliland) A.; m. Ellen Lee Gliem, June 10, 1951; children—Thomas G., Elizabeth Armstrong Pride. A.B., U. Mich., 1951, J.D., 1956. Bar: Pa. 1956, Mich. 1956, U.S. Supreme Ct. 1968, Fla. 1981. Assoc. Buchanan, Ingersoll, Rodewald, Kyle & Buerger, Pitts., 1956-65; ptnr. Buchanan Ingersoll P.C., 1965—; dir. Standard Steel Splty. Co., Beaver Falls, Pa.; lectr. profl. assns. Trustee Union Dale Cemetery, 1972—; elder Southminster Presbyterian Ch. Served to lt. U.S. Army, 1951-53. Mem. ABA (sects. taxation, real property, probate and trust law), Pa. Bar Assn. (real property, probate and trust law sect., mem. council 1981-84, treas. 1985, vice chmn. probate div. 1986—, tax law sect. 1986—), State Bar Mich. (probate and trust law sect., taxation sect.), Fla. Bar (real property, probate and trust law sect., tax sect.), Allegheny County Bar Assn. (taxation, probate and trust law), Estate Planning Council Pitts., Am. Coll. Probate Counsel, Am. Coll. Tax Counsel, U. Mich. Alumni Assn. (disting. alumni service award 1981), Am. Arbitration Assn. (nat. panel 1965—), Order of Coif, Phi Alpha Delta, Sigma Nu. Republican. Clubs: Duquesne, University, Chartiers Country, St. Clair Country, Masons, Shrines, Royal Order Jesters. Asst. editor Mich. Law Rev., 1955-56. Estate taxation, Probate, Personal income taxation. Home: 1500 Cochran Rd Apt 1010 Pittsburgh PA 15243 Office: 57th Floor 600 Grant St Pittsburgh PA 15219

ARMSTRONG, JAMES SINCLAIR, lawyer, banker; b. N.Y.C., Oct. 15, 1915; s. Sinclair Howard and Katharine Martin (LeBoutillier) A.; m. Charlotte Peirce Horwood Faircloth, Nov. 22, 1978. Grad., Milton (Mass.) Acad., 1934; A.B. cum laude, Harvard, 1938, J.D., 1941; postgrad., Northwestern U., 1942-44, 46-48. Bar: Ill. 1941, N.Y. 1959. Assoc. Isham, Lincoln & Beale, Chgo., 1941-45, 46-49; ptnr. Isham, Lincoln & Beale, 1950-53; commr. SEC, Washington, 1953-57; chmn. SEC, 1955-57; asst. sec. navy for fin. mgmt., also comptroller Dept. Navy, 1957-59; exec. v.p. U.S. Trust Co. of N.Y., 1959-80; ptnr. Whitman & Ransom, N.Y.C., 1980-84, of counsel, 1984—; exec. sec. Reed Found., 1986—. Sec. The Gunnery Sch., Washington, Conn.; pres. English-Speaking Union U.S.; chmn. internat. council English-Speaking Union Commonwealth; pres. Nat. Inst. Social Scis.; bd. dirs., past pres. St. Mark's Historic Landmark Fund, N.Y.C.; chmn., pres. Com. to Oppose Sale of St. Bartholomew's Ch. Served as lt. (j.g.) USNR, 1945-46. Decorated Order Orange-Nassau Netherlands. Mem. ABA, Am. Law Inst. (life), Practicing Law Inst., Assn. Bar City of N.Y. (nonprofit orgns. com.), Co. of Adventurers (Mass.) (sec.), Navy League U.S. (life), Hort. Soc. N.Y. (dir.), N.Y. Hist. Soc. (life), N.Y. Soc. Library (life), Pilgrims U.S., Am. Soc. Venerable Order St. John of Jerusalem, St. Andrews Soc. State N.Y. (life, vice chmn. standing com.), Huguenot Soc. Am. (life, historian), St. Nicholas Soc. City N.Y. (life, bd. dirs.), Soc. Colonial Wars of N.Y. (life). Clubs: Ch. of N.Y. (pres.), Century, Harvard, N.Y. Yacht, Thursday Evening, Union (N.Y.C.); Chevy Chase (Md.); Washington, Washington Garden (Conn.); Edgartown Yacht, Reading Room (Edgartown, Mass.); Metropolitan (Washington). Securities, Landmarks preservation, Banking. Home: 501 E 79th St Apt 3C New York NY 10021 Office: 30 Rockefeller Plaza Suite 4528 New York NY 10112-0119

ARMSTRONG, JOHN DOUGLAS, lawyer, educator; b. Dayton, Ohio, July 9, 1956; s. Stephen Daniel and Barbar J. (McCoy) A.; m. Patti Kay Berry, June 26, 1976; 1 child, Stephen Daniel. BS in Edn., George Washington U., 1978; JD, Oklahoma City U., 1981. Bar: Tex. 1982, U.S. Dist. Ct. (so. dist.) Tex. 1983. Intern U.S. Congress, Washington, 1974-75; mem. Law Offices of Knox W. Askins, LaPorte, Tex., 1981—; dir. devel. Bayshore Nat. Bank, LaPorte, 1984—. Mem. ABA, Houston Bar Assn., Bay Area Bar Assn. Republican. Lutheran. Lodge: Optimists (pres. La Porte 1985—). Local government, Family and matrimonial, Legislative. Office: Knox W Askins JD PC 702 W Fairmont PO Box 1218 LaPorte TX 77571

ARMSTRONG, JOHN KREMER, lawyer; b. Washington, Apr. 15, 1934; s. Stuart Morton and Marion Louise (Kreutzer) A.; m. A.M.E. (Mieke) van Haersma Buma, Apr. 1963; children: Marca Carine van Heloma, Jeb Stuart. B.A. with honors, Haverford Coll., 1956; postgrad. U. Delhi, 1956-57; LL.B., Yale U., 1960. Bar: N.Y. 1961. Assoc. Davies, Hardy and Schenck, N.Y.C., 1960-68; ptnr. Davies, Hardy, Ives and Lawther, N.Y.C., 1968-72, Armstrong and Ulrich, N.Y.C., 1973-81, Cole and Deitz, N.Y.C., 1981-85, Carter, Ledyard & Milburn, 1985—; dir., sec. Kinney Shoes Can. Ltd., 1973—. Bd. dirs. Chinese Lang. Study Inst., Inc.; trustee Bklyn. Bot. Garden, chmn. bd., 1982—; bd. regents L.I. Coll. Hosp., 1968-72, asst. sec., 1973—; Rotary Found. fellow 1956-57. Mem. ABA, N.Y. State Bar Assn., Assn. Bar City of N.Y., Phi Beta Kappa. Episcopalian. Republican. Clubs: Bronxville (N.Y.) Field, Church (N.Y.C.); Downtown Assn. General corporate, Private international, Trademark and copyright. Home: 14 Carlton Rd Bronxville NY 10708 Office: Carter Ledyard & Milburn 2 Wall St New York NY 10005

ARMSTRONG, ORVILLE A., lawyer; b. Austin, Tex., Jan. 21, 1929; s. Orville Alexander and Velma Lucille (Reed) A.; m. Mary Dean Macfarlane; children. B.B.A., U. Tex., Austin, 1953; LL.B., U. So. Calif., 1956. Bar: Calif., 1957, U.S. Ct. Appeals (9th cir.) 1958, U.S. Supreme Ct. 1980. Ptnr., Gray, Binkley & Pfaelzer, 1956-61, Pfaelzer, Robertson, Armstrong & Woodard, Los Angeles, 1961-66, Armstrong & Lloyd, Los Angeles, 1966-74, Macdonald, Halsted & Laybourne, Los Angeles, 1975—; lectr. Calif. Continuing Edn. of Bar. Served with USAF, 1946-49. Fellow Am. Coll. Trial Lawyers; mem. State Bar Calif. (gov. 1983-87, pres. 1986-87), ABA, Los Angeles County Bar Assn. (trustee 1971-72), Am. Judicature Soc., Chancery Club, Assn. Bus. Trial Lawyers, Am. Arbitration Assn. Democrat. Baptist. Clubs: Calif. Federal civil litigation, State civil litigation, Insurance. Home: 2385 Coniston Pl San Marino CA 91108 Office: 725 S Figueroa St 36th Fl Los Angeles CA 90017

ARMSTRONG, OWEN THOMAS, lawyer; b. Sheboygan, Wis., July 13, 1923; s. Dewey Thomas and Esther Marie (DeVille) A.; m. Jane Bowe Roessel, Sept. 3, 1949; children: Owen Thomas, Jr., William Dewey. BA, U. Wis., 1947, LLB, 1949; LLM, Harvard U., 1950. Bar: Wis. 1949, Mo. 1951, U.S. Dist. Ct. (ea. dist.) Mo. 1952, U.S. Ct. Appeals (8th cir.) 1953, U.S. Supreme Ct. 1958. Asst. prof. law Washington U., St. Louis, 1949, U. N.Mex., Albuquerque, 1950-51; assoc. Lowenhaupt & Chasnoff, St. Louis, 1951-58; ptnr. Lowenhaupt, Chasnoff, Armstrong & Mellitz, St. Louis, 1958—. Dem. twp. committeeman, Clayton, Mo., 1968-72. Served to 1st lt. (j.g.) JAGC, USNR, 1943-46, PTO. Mem. ABA, Mo. Bar Assn., St. Louis Bar Assn. Roman Catholic. General corporate, Pension, profit-sharing, and employee benefits, State and local taxation. Home: 1635 Dearborn Dr Warson MO 63122 Office: Lowenhaupt Chasnoff Armstrong & Mellitz 408 Olive St Saint Louis MO 63102

ARMSTRONG, RICHARD VOLKER, lawyer; b. Tulsa, Jan. 20, 1936; s. Max George and Mary Kathryn (Volker) A.; m. Ruth Eugene Johnston, Oct. 13, 1962 (div. July 1981); children: Sarah Kathryn, Rachel Johnston, Richard Volker II. BA, U. Okla., 1958; LLB, George Washington U., 1961. Bar: Okla. 1961, U.S. Dist. Ct. (no. dist.) Okla. 1962, U.S. Ct. Appeals (10th cir.) 1964. Assoc. Rucker, Taber, Shepherd and Palmer, Tulsa, 1961-65; ptnr. Palmer, Shepherd, Maner and Armstrong, Tulsa, 1965-70, Maner and Armstrong, Tulsa, 1970-72; spl. dist. judge 14th Dist. Ct. Okla., Tulsa, 1972, assoc. dist. judge, 1972-75, dist. judge, 1975-84; mem. W.C. Sellers Inc., Sapulpa, Okla., 1984—. Assoc. bd. dirs. Hillcrest Med. Ctr., Tulsa, 1973-76, Tulsa Arts & Humanities Council, Tulsa, 1973-75; vestryman Trinity Episcopal Ch., Tulsa, 1972-76. Served with USAR, 1961-67. Mem. Am. Trial Lawyers Assn., Am. Judicature Soc., Okla. Bar Assn., Okla. Trial Lawyers Assn., Tulsa County Bar Assn., Creek County Bar Assn., Kappa Alpha (pres. 1959-60), Delta Theta Phi. Democrat. Episcopalian. Avocations: fishing, swimming. Personal injury, State civil litigation, General practice. Home: 125 E 34th St Tulsa OK 74105 Office: WC Sellers Inc 708 S Main St Sapulpa OK 74066

ARMSTRONG, ROBERT ELMER, lawyer; b. Reno, Mar. 25, 1954; s. Raymond E. and Ruth J. (Baker) A.; m. Sallie Hill Bernard, Oct. 4, 1980. BS in Commerce, Santa Clara U., 1976; JD, Georgetown U., 1979; LLM in Taxation, NYU, 1980. Bar: Nev. 1979, U.S. Dist. Ct. Nev. 1980, U.S. Ct. Appeals (9th cir.) 1980, U.S. Supreme Ct. 1983, U.S. Ct. Appeals (D.C. cir.) 1987; CPA, Nev. Ptnr. McDonald, Carano, Wilson et al, Reno, 1980—; lectr. Golden Gate U., Reno, 1984—; bd. dirs. Desert Research Inst. Co-author: Nevada Practical Probate, 1986. Bd. dirs. Reno Philharm., 1980-86, U. Nev. Reno Found., 1986—. Mem. ABA, Nev. Bar Assn. (chmn. taxation sect. 1985-86), Am. Inst. CPA's, Nev. Soc. CPA's. Club: Wolf Pack Boosters (bd. dirs. 1985—). Estate planning, Corporate taxation, General corporate.

ARMSTRONG, ROBERT SITGREAVES, lawyer; b. Laurens, S.C., Aug. 12, 1956; s. Richard Manning Jr. and Catherine (Sitgreaves) Jefferies; m. Lauren MacDonald Porter, Aug. 2, 1986. BA, U. S.C., 1978, JD, 1982. Bar: S.C. 1982. Law clk. to presiding justice S.C. Cir. Ct., Walterboro, 1982-83; pub. defender Allendale, Hampton and Jasper County Pub. Defender Corp., Hampton, S.C., 1983-85; asst. solicitor 14th Cir. Solicitor's Office, Hampton, 1985—. Mem. ABA, Assn. Trial Lawyers Am., S.C. Bar Assn., Hampton County Bar Assn. Democrat. Episcopal. Criminal. Office: 14th Cir Solicitor's Office 307 1st St E Hampton SC 29924

ARMSTRONG, ROBERT WEAVER, judge; b. Burbank, Calif., Oct. 6, 1923. BA, Pepperdine U., 1947; JD, U. So. Calif., 1950. Bar: Calif. 1951, U.S. Supreme Ct. 1958. Ptnr. Armstrong & Wilbur and predecessor firm, Huntington Park, Calif., 1952-70, Armstrong, Wilbur, Knoll, Ratcliffe & Perkins and predecessor firm, Downey, Calif., 1970-85; judge County of Los Angeles Superior Ct., 1985—; lectr. seminars and symposia. Mem. Los Angeles County Bar Assn., Southeast Dist. Bar Assn., Nat. Assn. Def. Lawyers, Calif. Attys. for Criminal Justice, Am. Judicature Soc., Legion Lex. Office: Superior Ct 111 N Hill St Los Angeles CA 90012

ARMSTRONG, STEPHEN WALES, lawyer; b. Providence, Dec. 30, 1943; s. Gerald McIlroy and Alice Evelyn (Burnham) A.; m. Carol Joan Armstrong, Nov. 21, 1970; children: Jane Elizabeth, Susan Wales. AB, Brown U., 1965; JD, Georgetown U., 1972. Bar: Pa. 1972, U.S. Dist. Ct. (ea. dist.) Pa. 1973, U.S. Ct. Appeals (3d cir.) 1975, U.S. Ct. Appeals (5th cir.) 1978. Tchr. English U.S. Peace Corps, Washington and Thailand, 1966-69; asst. to solicitor NLRB, Washington, 1971-72; assoc. Morgan, Lewis & Bockius, Phila., 1972-80; assoc. Montgomery, McCraken, Walker & Rhoads, Phila., 1980-83, ptnr., 1983—. Bd. dirs. Wynnewood Civic Assn., 1974-80, sec. 1981-82, v.p., 1983-85, pres., 1986—; treas. PTA Friends Sch., Haverford, Conn., 1980-82; coach Merion Cricket Club, 1982-83. Mem. ABA (chmn. publs. com. 1983-84, monograph com. 1985), Pa. Bar Assn. (corp. law sect.), Phila. Bar Assn. (vice chmn. antitrust law com. corp., banking and bus. law sect. 1984-85, chmn. 1986—), Georgetown U. Law Alumni Bd., Brown U. Alumni Club, Brown U. Rowing Alumni Assn., Mayflower Soc. Avocations: squash, tennis. Antitrust, Federal civil litigation, Computer. Office: Montgomery McCracken Walker & Rhoads 3 Parkway 20th Floor Philadelphia PA 19102

ARMSTRONG, SUZANNE RAE, law professor; b. Laramie, Wyo., May 22, 1945; d. Charles Thomas and Evelyn (Pearson) A; m. Clayton E. Riley, June 26, 1968 (div. June 1976); m. Terry L. Hill, Jan. 1, 1985; 1 stepchild, Pamela Jean Hill. BA, U. Wyo., 1967; MA, U. S.C., 1971; JD, Mercer U., 1980. Bar: Ga. 1980, Fla. 1980, U.S. Dist. Ct. (so. dist.) Ga. 1980, U.S. Ct. Appeals (5th. and 11th. cirs.) 1980, U.S. Dist. Ct. (so. and mid. dists.) Fla. 1981, U.S. Supreme Ct. 1985. Law clk. to presiding justice U.S. Ct. Appeals (5th cir.) Fla., Miami, 1980-81; assoc. Carlton, Fields, Ward, Emmanuel, Smith & Cutler P.A., Tampa, 1981-83; assoc. prof. law Stetson U., St. Petersburg, Fla., 1983—; Contbr. articles to profl. jours. Mem. Am. Assn. Law Schs. (del. 1985-85), ABA, Scribes. Democrat. Presbyterian. Legal education, Federal civil litigation. Office: Stetson Coll of Law 1401 61th S Saint Petersburg FL 33712

ARMSTRONG, TIMOTHY JOSEPH, lawyer; b. Atlanta, June 17, 1945. B.A., Dartmouth Coll., 1967; J.D., U. Ga., 1970. Bar: Ga. 1970, Fla. 1971. Law clk. Hon. David W. Dyer, U.S. Ct. Appeals (5th cir.), Miami, 1970-71; assoc. Batchelor, Brodnax, Guthrie & Kindred, Miami, 1971-75; ptnr. Batchelor, Brodnax, Guthrie & Primm, Miami, 1975-83; ptnr. Armstrong & Mejer, 1983—. Mem. ABA, Fed. Bar Assn., Fla. Bar Assn., Ga. Bar Assn., Dade County Bar Assn., Maritime Law Assn U.S., Am. Judicature Soc., Internat. Assn. Def. Counsel. Contbr. articles to profl. jours. General practice. Office: Suite 1111 Douglas Centre 2600 Douglas Rd Coral Gables FL 33134

ARMSTRONG, WALTER PRESTON, JR., lawyer; b. Memphis, Oct. 4, 1916; s. Walter Preston and Irma Lewis (Waddell) A.; m. Alice Kavanaugh McKee, Nov. 3, 1949; children: Alice Kavanaugh, Walter Preston III. Grad., Choate Sch., Wallingford, Conn., 1934; A.B., Harvard U., 1938, J.D., 1941; D.C.L. (hon.), Southwestern at Memphis, 1961. Bar: Tenn. 1940. Practiced in Memphis, 1941—; assoc. firm Armstrong, Allen, Braden, Goodman, McBride & Prewitt (and predecessor firms), 1941-48, partner, 1948-86, of counsel, 1986—; Commr. for Promotion of Uniformity of Legislation in U.S. for Tenn., 1947-67. Author law rev. articles. Pres. bd. edn. Memphis City Schs., 1956-61; mem. Tenn. Higher Edn. Commn., 1967-84, chmn., 1974-75; mem. Tenn. Hist. Commn., 1969-80, hon. French consul, 1978-86 . Served from pvt. to maj. AUS, 1941-46. Fellow Am. Bar Found. (sec. 1960-62), Tenn. Bar Found. (chmn. 1983-84), Am. Coll. Trial Lawyers; mem. Am. Bar Assn. (ho. of dels. 1952-75), Tenn. Bar Assn. (pres. 1972-73), Memphis and Shelby County Bar Assn., Inter-Am. Bar Assn., Internat. Bar Assn., Fed. Bar Assn., Assn. Bar City N.Y., Am. Law Inst., Am. Judicature Soc., Nat. Conf. Commrs. on Uniform State Laws (pres. 1961-63), Harvard Law School Assn. (sec. 1957-58), Order of Coif, Scribes (pres. 1960-61), Phi Delta Phi, Omicron Delta Kappa. Federal civil litigation, State civil litigation, General corporate. Home: 1530 Carr Ave Memphis TN 38104 Office: 1900 One Commerce Sq Memphis TN 38103

ARNESEN, KENNETH GEORGE, banker, lawyer; b. Chgo., Nov. 24, 1928; s. George T. and Alva E. (Baier) A.; m. Lois Fisher, Sept. 28, 1957; children: Nancy Eileen, David Eric, Robert Kirk. B.S.C., State U. Iowa, 1951; LL.B., U. Ill., 1954. Bar: Ill. 1955. Atty., asso. gen. counsel, then sr. v.p., gen. counsel, cashier First Nat. Bank Chgo., 1956—, sr. v.p., gen. counsel, 1980—. Served with AUS, 1954-56. Clubs: Law (Chgo.), Legal (Chgo.). Office: 1st Chgo Corp 1 1st Nat Plaza Chicago IL 60670

ARNESON, JAMES H., lawyer; b. Winona, Minn., June 15, 1952; s. Herman Orlando and Vivian Agnes (Beardmore) A.; m. Ruth Helen Zimmerman, Sept. 2, 1979; children: Aaron Karl, Laura Rachel. BS, U. Wis., Eau Claire, 1974; JD, U. Mo., Kansas City, 1979. Bar: Mo. 1979, U.S. Dist. Ct. (we. dist.) Mo. 1979. Claims adjuster Crawford & Co., Columbia, Mo., 1974-76; assoc. Woolsey and Fisher, Springfield, Mo., 1979-82, Buck, Bohm & Stein, Kansas City, Mo., 1982-83, Shughart, Thompson & Kilroy, Kansas City, 1983—; adj. prof. law U. Mo., Kansas City, 1986—. Mem. youth com. Beth Shalom Synagogue, Kansas City, 1984—, memorialization com., 1985—, vice chmn. legal com. 1986—; mem. Sierra Club, 1981-85, legal chmn. Ozark chpt., 1981-83, chmn. Thomas Hart Benton Group, 1983-85; bd. dirs. Northwest Mo. Trauma Scholar, Kansas City, 1986—, Beth Shalom Synagogue, Kansas City, 1986—. Victor Wilson scholar, 1979. Mem. ABA, Mo. Bar Assn., Kansas City Bar Assn., Kansas City Lawyers Assn., Def. Research Inst., Phi Alpha Delta. Republican. Jewish. Insurance, Personal injury, Health. Home: 12823 High Dr Leawood KS 66209 Office: Shughart Thomson & Kilroy 120 W 12th St Kansas City MO 64105

ARNETT, FOSTER DEAVER, lawyer; b. Knoxville, Tenn., Nov. 28, 1920; s. Foster Greenwood and Edna (Deaver) A.; m. Jean Medlin, Mar. 3, 1951; children: Melissa Lee Arnett Campbell, Foster Deaver. BA, U. Tenn., 1946; LLB, U. Va., 1948. Bar: Va. 1948, Tenn. 1948, U.S. Dist. Ct. (ea. dist.) Tenn. 1949, U.S. Ct. Appeals (6th cir.) 1954, U.S. Supreme Ct. 1958. Practice law Knoxville, 1948—; partner Arnett, Draper & Hagood (and predecessors), 1954—; mem. Nat. Conf. Commrs. on Uniform State Laws, 1980-83; life mem. U.S. Ct. Appeals (6th cir.) Conf. Contbr. articles to profl. jours. Pres. Knox Children's Found., 1959-61, 75-76, East Tenn. Hearing and Speech Center, 1963-65, Knoxville Teen Ctr., 1969-71, Knoxville News-Sentinel Charities, 1985—; v.p. Ft. Loudon Assn., 1972-75; del. Republican Nat. Conv., 1964; nat. chmn. of appeals U. Va. Law Sch. Found., 1986—; active ARC, Am. Cancer Soc., United Fund. Served with AUS, 1942-46, PTO; to lt. col. USAR, ret. Decorated Silver Star, Bronze Star, Purple Heart. Fellow Am. Coll. Trial Lawyers (chmn. fed. rules of civil procedure com.), Internat. Acad. Trial Lawyers (bd. dirs., trustee Found.), Internat. Soc. Barristers, Am. Bar Found. (life), Tenn. Bar Found. (charter); mem. Southeastern Legal Found. (legal adv. bd.), ABA (unauthorized practice of law com., assn. communications com., aviation and space law com., state cert. of legal specialists com.), Tenn. Bar Assn. (pres. 1968-69), Knoxville Bar Assn. (pres. 1959-60), Internat. Assn. Def. Counsel (sec.-treas. 1981-84), S.E. Def. Counsel Assn. (v.p. 1966), Assn. Trial Lawyers Am., Am. Acad. Hosp. Attys. of Am. Hosp. Assn. (charter), Def. Research Inst., Fedn. Ins. and Corp. Counsel, Am. Bd. Trial Advs. (adv., pres. Tenn. chpt.), Def. Research Inst. (charter), Product Liability Adv. Council Inc. (sustaining), U. Tenn. Nat. Alumni Assn. (pres. 1961-62, chmn. nat. ann. giving program 1961-63), SAR, Scribes, Scabbard and Blade, Scarrabbean, Torchbearer, Phi Gamma Delta, Phi Delta Phi (hon.), Omicron Delta Kappa (hon.). Republican. Presbyterian. Clubs: Civitan (Knoxville); Farmington Country (Charlottesville, Va.); Cherokee Country, LeConte, U. Tenn. Faculty (hon.), Men's Cotillion (dir. 1960-61, 63-64, 66-68, trustee 1962—), Appalachian (pres. 1974-76). Lodge: Elks. Federal civil litigation, State civil litigation, Personal injury. Home: 4636 Alta Vista Way SW Knoxville TN 37919 Office: Arnett Draper & Hagood 2300 Plaza Tower Knoxville TN 37929-2300

ARNETT, RICHARD LYNN, lawyer; b. Dallas, Sept. 13, 1950; s. Richard Alden and Sarah Emma (Conner) A.; 1 child, John Alden. BS in Geophysics, Stanford U., 1972; JD, U. Tex., 1975. Bar: Tex. 1975, U.S. Ct. Appeals (5th cir.) 1977, U.S. Supreme Ct. 1979, U.S. Dist. Ct. (ea., no., so. and we. dists.) Tex. Research asst. dept. geophysics So. Methodist U., Dallas, 1969-72; law clk. to atty. gen. of Tex., Austin, 1974-75; asst. atty. gen. State of Tex., Austin, 1975-79; assoc. Roberts & Weldon, Austin, 1979-81; asst. atty. gen. State of Tex., Austin, 1981-82; dep. commr. for legal services Tex. Edn. Agy., Austin, 1982-84; ptnr. Brim, Tingley & Arnett, Austin, 1985-86, Brim & Arnett, Austin, 1986—. Mem. Tex. Bar Assn. (sch. law com.), 5th Circuit Bar Assn. Democrat. Methodist. Commercial litigation, Real property, Federal civil litigation. Home: 201 Westhaven Austin TX 78746 Office: Brim & Arnett 1012 Mopac Circle Austin TX 78746

ARNHOLD, THOMAS DEAN, lawyer; b. Hays, Kans., Dec. 1, 1954; s. Richard A. and Ann (Dechont) A.; m. Joleen Marie McNeive, Aug. 11, 1979; children: Colleen Marie, Kevin Thomas. BS in Polit. Sci., Ft. Hays State U., Kans., 1975; JD, Washburn U., 1978. Bar: Kans. 1979, U.S. Dist. Ct. Kans. 1979, U.S. Ct. Appeals (10th cir.) 1979. Assoc. McPherson Brown & Brown, Great Bend, Kans., 1978-79, Reno County Legal Aid Soc., Hutchinson, Kans., 1979-80; ptnr. Arnhold & McEwen, Hutchinson, 1980—. V.p. Hutchinson Human Rights Commn., 1982, Big Bros. for Boys, Hutchinson, 1982; sec. Downtown Devel. Bd., Hutchinson, 1986. Served to 1st lt. Kans. Army N.G., 1983—. Mem. ABA, Kans. Bar Assn., Reno County Bar Assn. Democrat. Roman Catholic. Lodge: KC (recorder Hutchinson 1986). Avocations: golf, cross-country skiing, basketball. Bankruptcy, Workers' compensation, Personal injury. Home: 81 Faircrest Hutchinson KS 67502 Office: Arnhold & McEwen PO Box 703 Hutchinson KS 67504-0703

ARNING, JOHN FREDRICK, lawyer; b. Lansing, Mich., 1925; s. Clarence W. and Leatha Mae (Stoner) A.; m. Mary Kiver, Apr. 6, 1947; children: Valerie P., John Frederick, William A. LL.B. magna cum laude, Harvard U., 1949. Bar: N.Y. 1949. Assoc. firm Sullivan & Cromwell, N.Y.C., 1949-57, ptnr., 1957—. Mem. ABA, Assn. Bar City N.Y., Union Internationale des Avocats. General practice. Home: 201 E 28th St New York NY 10016 Office: Sullivan & Cromwell 125 Broad St New York NY 10004

ARNO, JAMES, lawyer; b. Tyler, Tex., Aug. 3, 1940; m. Marguerite Johnston; children: James, Christina. BA, U. Tex., 1964, PhD, 1968; JD, George Washington, 1971. Bar: Ohio 1971, N.J. 1980, U.S. Patent Office 1971. Patent atty. Procter & Gamble, Cin., 1971-73; sr. patent counsel Merck & Co., Rahway, N.J., 1973-83; sr. dir. patents and lic. Alcon Labs., Ft. Worth, 1983—. NIH fellow, 1968. Mem. ABA, N.J. Bar Assn., AAAS, Dallas-Ft. Worth Patent Assn., Phi Beta Kappa. Patent, General corporate. Home: 2421 Stadium Dr Fort Worth TX 76109 Office: Alcon Labs Inc 6201 S Freeway Fort Worth TX 76134

ARNOLD, BRUCE GEORGE, lawyer; b. Milw., Sept. 22, 1956; s. Francis Martin and Rita Mary (Gildner) A.; m. Laurie Ann Doot, May 15, 1982. BBA summa cum laude, Georgetown U., 1978; JD cum laude, U. Mich., 1981. Bar: Wis. 1981, U.S. Dist. Ct. (ea. and we. dists.) Wis. 1981, U.S. Dist. Ct. (no. dist.) Calif. 1983, U.S. Ct. Appeals (7th cir.) 1981. Mem. Whyte & Hirschboeck, S.C., Milw., 1981—. Mem. ABA, Wis. Bar Assn., Milw. Bar Assn. (program chmn. 1985-86, chmn. 1986-87 bankruptcy sect.), Milw. Young Lawyers Assn., 7th Cir. Bar Assn. Roman Catholic. Avocations: obedience dog training, basketball, cooking, wine tasting. Federal civil litigation, State civil litigation, Bankruptcy. Home: 5000 W Beech Ct Brown Deer WI 53223 Office: Whyte & Hirschboeck SC 2100 Marine Plaza Milwaukee WI 53202-4894

ARNOLD, HARRY H., III, university adminstrator; b. Oklahoma City, Jan. 28, 1930; s. Harry H. and Lucille Lackey A.; m. Anne Morrison, Aug. 3, 1955; children—Harry H. IV, Mary Elizabeth, Daniel Steven, Tracy. B.A., U. Colo., 1952, LL.B., 1955. Bar: Colo. 1955. Staff asst. indsl. relations C F & I Steel, Pueblo, Colo., 1957-59, asst. supt., 1959-62, asst. sec., Denver, 1962-67, mgr. employee relations and communications, 1967-70, mgr. labor relations and personnel, 1970; dir. deferred giving U. Colo., Boulder, 1970-73, exec. sec. bd. regents, 1973—. Chmn., Boulder Housing Authority, 1981-82. Served to 1st lt. USMC, 1955-57. Recipient Alumni Recognition award U. Colo. Alumni Assn., 1965, Robert L. Stearns award, 1980. Republican. Presbyterian. Club: Rotary (Boulder, Colo.). Education and schools. Home: 4505 Ottawa Pl Boulder CO 80303 Office: Box B-3 Regent Hall U Colo Boulder CO 80309

ARNOLD, JEROME G., lawyer. U.S. atty. State of Minn., Mpls. Office: 234 US Courthouse 110 South 4th Street Minneapolis MN 55401 *

ARNOLD, JOHN FOX, lawyer; b. St. Louis, Sept. 17, 1937; s. John Anderson and Mildred Chapin (Fox) A.; m. Martha Ann Freeman, June 29, 1963; children—Lisa Chapin, Laura Wray, Lynne Farris, Lesli Freeman. A.B., U. Mo., 1959, LL.B., 1961. Bar: Mo. 1961, U.S. Dist. Ct. (ea. dist.) Mo. 1961, U.S. Ct. Appeals (8th cir.) 1961, U.S. Supreme Ct. 1971. Ptnr. Green, Hennings, Henry & Arnold, St. Louis, 1963-70; mem. Lashly, Baer & Hamel, P.C., St. Louis, 1970—. Mem. St. Louis County Charter Revision Com., Mo., 1968; chmn. St. Louis County Bd. Election Commrs., 1981-85. Recipient citation of merit U. Mo. Law Sch., Columbia, 1984. Mem. ABA (mem. house of dels. 1986—), Bar Assn. Met. St. Louis (pres. 1975-76), Mo. Bar (pres. 1984-85), Nat. Conf. Commrs. on Uniform State Laws (chmn. Securities Act 1978—). Am. Law Inst. Republican. Presbyterian. Securities, General corporate, Municipal bonds. Home: 210 Rosemont St Louis MO 63119 Office: Lashly Baer and Hamel 714 Locust St St Louis MO 63101

ARNOLD, KENNETH JAMES, lawyer, publishing company executive; b. Brighton, Colo., Sept. 10, 1927; s. Kenneth Wilburt and Frances Irene (Lloyd) A. Student, U. Paris, 1950-51, U. Rabat, Morocco, 1951-52; A.B., U. Calif., Berkeley, 1949; M.A., U. Calif., 1950; J.D., U. Calif., San Francisco, 1958. Bar: Calif. 1959. Sole practice San Francisco, 1959-60, 63—; sole practice Sacramento, 1960-62; owner Law Book Service Co., San Francisco, 1969—; research atty. Calif. Supreme Ct., Sacramento, 1960-62, Calif. Ct. Appeals 1st Appellate Dist., San Francisco, 1958-60; asst. sr. editor-in-chief Matthew Bender & Co., San Francisco, 1963-81, staff author, 1981-87, sr. staff author, 1987—; lectr. in field, 1972-81; cons. to Calif. State Jud. Council, 1970—, Calif. Ctr. Jud. Edn. and Research, 1974—, Calif. Coll. Trial Judges, 1975, McGeorge Coll. Law, U. Pacific, 1975-80; mem. Calif. Legal Forms Com., 1971-73. Author: California Courts and Judges Handbook, 1968, 4th revised edit., 1985; California Justice Court Manual, 1971 supplement; (with others) California Points and Authorities, 23 vols., 1964—, California Forms of Pleadings and Practice, 55 vols., 1966—, California Legal Forms, 25 vols., 1967-69; Commencing Civil Actions in California, 1975, and supplements; (with others) California Family Law Practice, 6 vols., 1977-78, California Civil Actions, 5 vols., 1982—; other manuals and handbooks; feature writer Barclays Law Monthly, 1979-82; editor Vector Mag., 1965-67. Bd. dirs. Soc. for Individual Rights, 1965-67, PRIDE Found., San Francisco, 1974-77. Served with AUS, 1952-55, Korea. Mem. State Bar Calif., Hastings Alumni Assn., San Francisco Gem and Mineral Soc. (bd. dirs.), Am. Legion, Soc. Individual Rights (bd. dirs. 1965-67). General practice. Home: 369 Harvard St San Francisco CA 94134 Office: 2101 Webster St Oakland CA 94612

ARNOLD, KENNETH ROBERT, lawyer; b. N.Y.C., June 7, 1938; s. Raymond Ellis and Anna Veronica (Maher) A.; m. Rosemarie Jenny, Nov. 14, 1964; children: Kenneth M., Gregory T., Elizabeth A. BS in Pharmacy, Fordham U., 1959, JD, 1962. Bar: N.Y. 1963, U.S. Dist. Ct. (so. dist.) N.Y. 1963, U.S. Dist. Ct. (ea. dist.) N.Y. 1967, U.S. Ct. Appeals (2d cir.) 1967. Atty. U.S. Bur. of Customs, N.Y.C., 1963-64; assoc. Kirlin, Campbell & Keating, N.Y.C., 1964-67; gen. atty. Nabisco Inc., N.Y.C., 1967-69; v.p., gen. counsel Wagner Electric Corp., Parsippany, N.J., 1969-86, Providence Mgmt. Group, Inc., Florham Park, N.J., 1986—. Mem. Paramus, N.J. Bd. of Edn., 1971-77, v.p., 1975-76, pres., 1976-77. Served with U.S. Army, 1962-68. Mem. ABA, N.Y. State Bar Assn. Avocations: scuba diving, hiking, fishing, boating, volleyball. General corporate, Environment, Real property. Office: Providence Mgmt Group Inc 248 Columbia Turnpike Florham Park NJ 07932

ARNOLD, MORRIS SHEPPARD, U.S. district judge; b. Texarkana, Tex., Oct. 8, 1941; student Yale U., 1959-61; BSEE, U. Ark., 1965, LLB, 1968; LLM, Harvard, 1969, SJD, 1971; MA (hon.) U. Pa., 1977, JD (hon.), 1986. Bar: Ark. 1968. Teaching fellow in law Harvard U., 1969-70; asst. prof. Ind. U. Law Sch., 1971-74, assoc. prof., 1974-76, prof., 1976-77, dean, fall 1985; prof. law & history, U. Pa., 1977-81, prof. law, 1984-85; Ben J. Altheimer disting. prof. law U. Ark., Little Rock, 1981-84; judge U.S. Dist. Ct. (we. dist.) Ark., Ft. Smith, Ark., 1985—; vis. fellow commoner Trintiy Coll, Cambridge, Mass., 1978; v.p., dir. office of pres. U. Pa., 1980-81; vis. prof. Stanford U. Law Sch., 1985. Editor: Old Tenures and Natura Brevium, 1974,Yearbook 2 Richard II, 1378-79, 1975, On the Laws and Customs of England, 1985, Unequal Laws Unto a Savage Race, 1985. Pres. Am. Soc. for Legal History, 1980-84; gen. Counsel Rep. Pary Ark., 1982, chmn., 1983; bd. dirs. Nature Conservancy of Ark., 1982—, Ark. Arts Ctr., 1981-84. Frank Knox fellow, Harvard U., London, 1970-71; fellow Mus. Sci. and Natural History, Little Rock, 1986; Harvey Levin Teaching award U. Pa. Law Sch., Phila., 1980, 85. Mem. Am. Law Inst. Clubs: Athenaeum (London); Union League (Phila.). Legal education. Office: US Courthouse PO Box 1606 Fort Smith AR 72902 *

ARNOLD, NANCY TARBUCK, lawyer; b. Pecos, Tex., Oct. 19, 1943; d. Laurence Edward and Helen Virginia (Clayton) Tarbuck; m. Donald Jay Hess, Mar. 25, 1984; 1 child, Ashley Ann Clayton. BA, Mills Coll., 1961; JD, U. Puget Sound, 1978. Bar: Wash. 1978, U.S. Dist. Ct. (we. dist.) Wash. 1978, U.S. Dist. Ct. (ea. dist.) Wash. 1981. Law clk. to chief judge U.S. Dist. Ct. (we. dist.) Wash., Seattle, 1978-80; assoc. Ryan, Swanson, Hendel & Cleveland, Seattle, 1980—. Mem. Jr. League, Seattle, 1972—; bd. visitors U. Puget Sound Sch. Law, Tacoma, Wash., 1979-85; bd. dirs. Achievement Rewards Coll. Scientists Found., Seattle, 1978—. Mem. ABA, Seattle-King County Bar Assn., Wash. Women Lawyers. Republican. Episcopalian. Avocations: skiing, horseback riding, sailing. General corporate, Estate planning, Real property. Home: 2134 40th Ave E Seattle WA 98112 Office: Ryan Swanson Hendel & Cleveland Bank Calif Ctr 32d Floor Seattle WA 98164

ARNOLD, RICHARD SHEPPARD, judge; b. Texarkana, Tex., Mar. 26, 1936; s. Richard Lewis and Janet (Sheppard) A.; children: Janet Sheppard, Lydia Palmer; m. Kay Kelley, Oct. 27, 1979. B.A. summa cum laude, Yale U., 1957; J.D. magna cum laude, Harvard U., 1960. Bar: D.C. 1961, Ark. 1960. Practiced in Washington 1961-64, Texarkana, 1964-74; law clk. to Justice Brennan, Supreme Ct. U.S., 1960-61; assoc. Covington & Burling, 1961-64; partner Arnold & Arnold, 1964-74; legis. sec. Gov. of Ark., 1973-74, staff coordinator, 1974; legis. asst. Senator Bumpers of Ark., Washington, 1975-78; judge U.S. Dist. Ct. Eastern and Western Dists. Ark., 1978-80, U.S. Ct. Appeals 8th Circuit, Little Rock, 1980—; part-time instr. U. Va. Law Sch., 1962-64; mem. Ark. Constl. Revision Study Commn., 1967-68. Case editor: Harvard Law Rev., 1959-60; contbr. articles to profl. jours. Gen. chmn. Texarkana United Way Crusade, 1969-70; pres. Texarkana Community Chest, 1970-71; mem. overseers com. Harvard Law Sch., 1973-79; mem. vis. com. U. Chgo. Law Sch., 1983-86; candidate for Congress 4th Dist. Ark., 1966, 72; del. Democratic Nat. Conv., 1968, Ark. Constl. Conv., 1969-70; chmn. rules com. Ark. Dem. Com., 1968-74, mem. exec. com., 1972-74; mem. Com. on Legis. Orgn., 1971-72; trustee U. Ark., 1973-74. Fellow Am. Bar Found.; mem. Am. Law Inst. (council), Cum Laude Soc., Phi Beta Kappa. Episcopalian. Jurisprudence. Home: 3901 Cedar Hill Rd No 5 Little Rock AR 72202 Office: US Court Appeals PO Box 429 Little Rock AR 72203

ARNOLD, STANLEY RICHARD, lawyer; b. Los Angeles, Apr. 20, 1932; s. Aaron Leon and Lucille May (Singer) A.; m. Jennie Ann Sabow, June 16, 1962; children: Abby Sue, James Andrew, Kathryn Rose, Julianna Marie. Student, UCLA, 1949-52; A.B., Stanford U., 1953, J.D., 1955; LL.M., McGill U., 1956. Bar: Calif. 1956. Practiced in Los Angeles, 1959—; trial atty. Dryden, Harrington, Horgan & Swartz, 1959-61; mem. firm Stapleton, Weinberg & Isen, 1961-63; partner firm Goldman, Goldman & Arnold, Los Angeles, 1967-75, Arnold & Fink, Encino, Calif., 1976-79; prin. Stanley R. Arnold P.C., Encino, 1979-83, Arnold & Singer, P.C., 1983-85, Stanley R. Arnold P.C., Los Angeles, 1986—; mem. bus. law arbitration panel Los Angeles Superior Ct. Mem. exec. com. Los Angeles County Com. to Re-Elect Pres., 1972—; Los Angeles chmn. Spl. Com. to Re-Elect Pres., 1972. Served to capt. USAF, 1956-59. Mem. Comml. Law League Am., State Bar Calif., Los Angeles County Bar Assn., Los Angeles bus. trial lawyers assns., Assn. Trial Lawyers Am., Internat. Bar Assn., Am. Arbitration Assn. (arbitrator), B'nai B'rith (past pres.). Office: 10960 Wilshire Blvd Suite 2134 Los Angeles CA 90024

ARNOLD, WILLIAM MCCAULEY, lawyer; b. Waco, Tex., May 3, 1947; s. Watson Caulfield and Mary Rebecca (Maxwell) A.; m. Karen Axtell, May 17, 1980; children: Margaret McCauley, William Axtell. BA, Duke U., 1969; JD, U. Tex., 1972. Bar: Tex. 1973, Va. 1975, D.C. 1977, Md. 1983, U.S. Dist. Ct. (ea. dist.) Va. 1975, U.S. Ct. Appeals (4th cir.) 1977, U.S. Ct. Claims 1977, U.S. Supreme Ct. 1978. Spl. atty. U.S. Dept. Justice, Newark, 1973-75; asst. county atty. County of Fairfax, Va., 1975-78; ptnr. Cowles, Rinaldi & Arnold, Ltd., Fairfax, 1978—; instr. No. Va. Community Coll., Alexandria. Pres. Clifton Betterment Assn., Va., 1979-81; chmn. Clifton Planning Comm., 1980-85; mem. Clifton Town Council, 1985—; bd. dirs. Clifton Gentlemen's Social Club, 1981-84. Mem. ABA, Va. State Bar Assn., Fairfax County Bar Assn., Va. Trial Lawyers Assn., Am. Arbitration Assn. (arbitrator), Associated Builders and Contractors (chmn. polit. action com.). State civil litigation, Construction, Local government. Office: Cowles Rinaldi & Arnold Ltd 10521 Judicial Dr Suite 204 Fairfax VA 22030

ARNOLD, WYNN EDMUND, utilities executive, lawyer; b. Ludlow, Mass., Sept. 27, 1947; s. William Edmund and Barbara Eileen (Smith) A.; m. Helen Janice Falkson, Aug. 27, 1978; children: Sara Lesley, Merrin Falkson. Student, Glasgow U., Scotland, 1968-69; BA, U. N.H., 1970; JD, Suffolk U., 1981. Bar: N.H. 1981, Mass. 1982, U.S. Dist. Ct. N.H. 1981. Vol. U.S. Peace Corps, Ecuador, 1970-73; specialist office for civil rights HEW, Boston, 1974-78; specialist equal opportunity Office fed. Contract and Compliance Programs, Boston, 1978-81; assoc. Tetler & Holmes, Hampton, N.H., 1981-83; exec. dir., sec. N.H. Pub. Utilities Commn., Concord, 1983—. Co-author, dir. (film) Despertad, 1972. Chmn. N.H. Episcopal Diosecan Stewardship Commn., Concord, 1986. Mem. Nat. Assn. Regulatory Utility Commrs. (exec. dirs. com.), N.H. Bar Assn. (long range planning com.). Episcopalian. Avocations: guitar, piano, folk music, water sports. Public utilities, General practice, Administrative and regulatory. Home: 3 Rocky Hill Rd Exeter NH 03833 Office: NH Pub Utilities Commn 8 Old Suncook Rd Bldg 1 Concord NH 03301

ARNOW, ARTHUR EMANUEL, lawyer; b. N.Y.C., Feb. 10, 1932; s. Harry and Beulah (Bobker) A.; m. Judith Ruth Cohen, June 3, 1956; children: Jessica Lynn, David Louis. BA, NYU, 1953, JD, 1956. Bar: N.Y. 1958, U.S. Dist. Ct. (so. and ea. dists.) N.Y. 1959, U.S. Ct. Mil. Appeals 1959, U.S. Supreme Ct. 1964, U.S. Ct. Appeals (2d cir.) 1975. Sole practice N.Y.C., 1962; ptnr. Michaels, Michaels, Wigdor & Arnow, N.Y.C., 1962-70, Miller & Arnow, Levittown, N.Y., 1970-86; sole practice 1986—; lectr. Hofstra U. Club. Contbr. articles to profl. jours. Served to capt. JAGC, USAF, 1956-62. Recipient Citations Town of Oyster Bay, 1983, Town of Hempstead, 1986, Humanitarian award State of Israel Bonds, 1986. Mem. ABA, N.Y. State Bar Assn., Nassau County Bar Assn. Republican. Jewish. Club: NYU (N.Y.C.). Avocations: lecturer, photography, tennis, swimming. State civil litigation, Military, Real property. Home: 29 Phipps Ln Plainview NY 11803 Office: 665 N Newbridge Rd Levittown NY 11756-1899

ARONIN, LOUIS, labor arbitrator; b. N.Y.C., Oct. 5, 1922; s. Isador and Dinah (Margolis) A.; m. Geraldine Alenik, Jan. 19, 1945 (div.); children—Marc Stephen, Ronni Lynn. B.A., Bklyn. Coll., 1945; LL.B., U. Balt., 1960. Bar: Md., 1960. Economist, N.Y. State Dept. Labor, 1946-49; examiner NLRB Region 5, Balt., 1949-68; exec. dir. N.J. Pub. Employee Relations Com., Trenton, 1968-70; dep. dir. Office Labor Mgmt. Relations, U.S. Civil Service Commn., Washington, 1970-79; labor arbitrator, Alexandria, Va., 1978—; adj. prof. Georgetown U. Law Center, 1975—, U. Md., 1974-78; chmn. Md. Task Force on Public Employee Relations, 1968. Served with AUS, 1944. Recipient Spl. citation U.S. Civil Service Commn., 1975. Mem. Am. Arbitration Assn., ABA (co chmn. com. fed. labor relations 1971-75), Fed. Bar Assn., Soc. Profls. in Dispute Resolution, Nat. Acad. Arbitrators, Soc. Fed. Labor Relations Profls., Indsl. Relations Research Assn. Jewish. Contbr. articles to profl. jours. Labor, Administrative and regulatory, Legal education. Home: 200 N Pickett St #812 Alexandria VA 22304

ARONOVITZ, SIDNEY M., judge; b. Key West, Fla., June 20, 1920; s. Charles and Ethel (Holtsberg) A.; m. Elinore Richman, Mar. 24, 1943; children—Elaine, Tod, Karen. B.A., U. Fla., 1942, J.D., 1943. Bar: Fla. Practice law Miami; judge U.S. Dist. Ct. (so. dist.) Fla., 1976—. Commr., City of Miami, 1962-66, vice-mayor, 1965. Mem. ABA, Am. Judicature Soc., Fla. Bar Assn., Dade County Bar Assn. Judicial administration. Office: PO Box 013069 Miami FL 33101 *

ARONSOHN, RICHARD FRANK, lawyer; b. Jersey City, Aug. 8, 1938; s. Isadore William and Elizabeth (Saltzman) A.; m. Deborah, Dec. 19, 1965; children—William John, Elizabeth Anne. A.B. Dartmouth Coll. 1960, J.D. Rutgers U. 1963. Bar: N.J. 1964; profl. cert.: civil trial lawyer, N.J. Law sec. Bergen County Ct., N.J., 1963-64; dep. atty. gen. State of N.J., 1964-66; spl. asst. prosecutor Bergen County, 1968-70; ptnr. Aronsohn & Springstead, and predecessors, Hackensack, N.J., 1970—; atty. Bergen Community Coll. 1967-69; chief legal counsel County of Bergen, Bergen Pines County Hosp.; lectr. Inst. for Continuing Legal Edn. 1968—. Mem. ABA, N.J. Bar Assn. (trustee 1979—), Bergen County Bar Assn. (trustee 1978—). Democrat. Jewish. Club: Indian Trail (Franklin Lakes, N.J.). Contbr. articles to legal jours. Administrative and regulatory, State civil litigation.

ARONSON, CRAIG DOUGLAS, lawyer; b. N.Y.C., June 10, 1956; s. Melvin Louis and Natalie (Brackman) A. BA summa cum laude, Dartmouth Coll., 1977; JD, U. Chgo., 1980. Bar: Calif. 1983. Legal analyst Battelle Research Inst., Seattle, 1980; assoc. Hagenbaugh & Murphy, Los Angeles, 1983—; cons., lectr. Dept. Energy Conf., Denver, 1981; organizer Energy Impacts Conf., U. B.C., Vancouver, Can., 1982. Vol. Singles for Charity, Los Angeles, 1980—. Mem. State Bar Calif., Dartmouth Alumni Assn. (recruiter 1980—), Phi Beta Kappa. Democrat. Jewish. State civil litigation, Insurance. Home: 403 N Crescent Beverly Hills CA 90210 Office: Hagenbaugh & Murphy 3701 Wilshire Los Angeles CA 90010

ARONSON, MARK BERNE, lawyer; b. Pitts., Aug. 24, 1941; s. Richard J. and Jean (DeRoy) A.; m. Ellen Jane Askin, July 20, 1970; children: Robert M., Andrew A., Michael D. BS in Econs., U. Pa., 1962; JD, U. Pitts., 1965. Bar: Pa. 1965, U.S. Dist. Ct. (we. dist.) Pa. 1965, U.S. Ct. Appeals (3d cir.) 1968, U.S. Ct. Claims 1978, U.S. Supreme Ct. 1966; lic. real estate broker, 1972. Sole practice, Pitts., 1965-66, 83—; sr. ptnr. Behrend & Aronson, Pitts., 1967-80, Behrend, Aronson & Morrow, 1980-83. Past pres. Community Day Sch., Pitts., Rodef Shalom Jr. Congregation; trustee Rodef Shalom Congregation, Pitts. Child Guidance Ctr. Found., 1987—. Mem. Am. Trial Lawyers Assn. (sustaining mem.; Pa. rep. to exchange commn.), Pa. Trial Lawyers Assn. (Pres.'s Club), Allegheny County Bar Assn., N.Y. State Trial Lawyers Assn., Pa. Bar Assn., Am. Arbitration Assn. (mem. Nat. Panel Arbitrators). Republican. Jewish. Clubs: Concordia, Rivers. Lodge: Masons (master). Personal injury, Real property, General practice. Office: 707 Law & Finance Bldg 429 4th Ave Pittsburgh PA 15219

ARONSON, MORTON HENRY, lawyer; b. Boston, May 17, 1935; s. Harry and Dorothy (Kraftchinsky) A.; m. Ellen Sandra Kaplan, Apr. 10, 1960; children—Stuart, Adam, Dorothy. A.B., Boston U., 1956, LL.B., 1959; LL.M., Harvard U., 1962. Bar: Mass. 1959, Ohio 1977, Tenn. 1981. Assoc. Widett & Kruger, Boston, 1960-61; asst. atty. gen. Mass., 1962-65; ptnr. Grabil & Ley, Boston, 1965-76; asst. counsel Federated Dept. Stores, Cin., 1976-78; assoc. gen. counsel Holiday Inns, Inc., Memphis, 1978—; chmn. Mass. Comm. Antenna Television Com., 1972-75. Pres. Temple Aliyah, Needham, Mass., 1966-68; mem. Needham Bd. Zoning Appeals, 1970-74, chmn., 1974-76; active No. Hills Synagogue, Cin., v.p., 1977; bd. dirs. Beth Shalom Synagogue, Memphis, 1980—. Mem. ABA, (franchise com.), Internat. Bar Assn. (franchise com.). Republican. Jewish. Club: Harvard (Boston) Contbr. articles to profl. jours. franchising, General corporate. Office: Holiday Inns Inc 3796 Lamar Ave Memphis TN 38118

ARONSTEIN, JAMES KARPELES, lawyer; b. Phila., Mar. 9, 1954; s. Martin Joseph and Sally (Rosenau) A.; m. Patricia Hauck, Jan. 12, 1985. AB summa cum laude, Dartmouth Coll., 1977; JD cum laude, Harvard U., 1981. Bar: Colo. 1981, U.S. Dist. Ct. Colo. 1981. Ptnr. Parcel & Mauro, Denver, 1981—. Mem. citizens adv. commn. S.E. Quadrant Transp. Study, City of Denver, 1986. Mme. ABA, Colo. Bar Assn., Denver Bar Assn., Rocky Mountain Mineral Law Found., Colo. Mining Assn. (environ. affairs com. 1984—), Assn. Comml. Fin. Attys. Mining and Public Lands, General corporate, Contracts commercial. Office: Parcel & Mauro 1801 California St Suite 3600 Denver CO 80202

ARONSTEIN, MARTIN JOSEPH, lawyer, educator; b. N.Y.C., Jan. 25, 1925; s. William and Mollie (Mintz) A.; m. Sally K. Rosenau, Sept. 18, 1948; children: Katherine Aronstein Porter, David M., James K. B.E., Yale U., 1944; M.B.A., Harvard U., 1948; LL.B., U. Pa., 1965. Bar: Pa. 1965. Bus. exec. Phila., 1948-65; assoc. firm Obermayer, Rebmann, Maxwell & Hippel, Phila., 1965-67; partner Obermayer, Rebmann, Maxwell & Hippel, 1968-69; assoc. prof. law U. Pa., 1969-72, prof., 1972-78; counsel firm Ballard, Spahr, Andrews & Ingersoll, Phila., 1978-80; partner Ballard, Spahr, Andrews & Ingersoll, 1980-81; prof. law U. Pa., 1981-86, prof. emeritus, 1986—; of counsel firm Morgan, Lewis & Bockius, Phila., 1986—. Contbr. articles to law revs.; mem.: Permanent Editorial Bd. Uniform Comml. Code, 1978—, Counsel, 1980—. Served with USN, 1943-46. Mem. Am. Law Inst., Am. Bar Assn. (reporter com. on stock certs. 1973-77, chmn. subcom. on investment securities 1982-84), Phila. Bar Assn., Order of Coif, Sigma Xi, Tau Beta Pi. Contracts commercial, Bankruptcy, Legal education. Home: 1820 Rittenhouse Sq Philadelphia PA 19103 Office: 2000 One Logan Sq Philadelphia PA 19103

AROUH, JEFFREY ALAN, lawyer; b. N.Y.C., May 2, 1945; s. Isaac E. and Jean J. (Halfon) A.; m. Karen Ann Wieder, Feb. 1, 1969; children: Russell Andrew, Ilonne A. BA, U. Mich., 1966; JD cum laude, NYU, 1969. Bar: N.Y. 1970. Assoc., Gilbert, Segall and Young, N.Y.C., 1969-74, ptnr., 1975—. Editor: NYU Law Rev., 1969; contbr. articles to legal publs. V.p. Westchester Jewish Ctr., Mamaroneck, N.Y. Mem. ABA, N.Y. State Bar Assn., Assn. Bar City N.Y., Order of Coif. Club: Hampshire Country. General corporate, Real property, General practice. Home: 3 Ridgeway Rd Larchmont NY 10538 Office: 430 Park Ave New York NY 10022

ARPS, LESLIE HANSEN, lawyer; b. Leipzig, Germany, July 14, 1907; s. George F. and Alice (Black) A.; m. Ruth Collicott, Oct. 26, 1959. A.B., Stanford, 1928; LL.B., Harvard, 1931. Bar: N.Y. bar 1932. Asso. Root, Clark, Buckner & Ballantine, N.Y.C., 1931-42, 46-48; mem. firm Skadden, Arps, Slate, Meagher & Flom, N.Y.C., 1948—; spl. asst. atty. gen. State of N.Y.; asst. chief counsel N.Y. State Crime Commn., 1951-52; asso. gen. counsel to N.Y. State Moreland Commn. to Investigate State Agys. in relation to Pari-Mutuel Harness Racing, 1953-54; cons. N.Y. State Moreland Commn. on Alcoholic Beverage Control law, 1963-64. Chmn. bd. trustees Gateway Sch. N.Y., 1965-67; trustee The Gunnery, Inc., 1978—. Served to lt. col. USAAF, 1942-45. Mem. Am. Bar Assn., N.Y. State Bar Assn., N.Y.C. Bar Assn. (chmn. exec. com. 1973-74), N.Y. County Lawyers Assn., Am. Bar Found., Am. Judicature Soc., Fed. Bar Council, Merc. Library Assn. (dir.), Am. Arbitration Assn. (dir.), Phi Beta Kappa. Clubs: Union League (N.Y.C.), Sky (N.Y.C.), Harvard (N.Y.C.). Antitrust, Federal civil litigation. Home: 530 Park Ave New York NY 10021 Office: 919 3d Ave New York NY 10022

ARRETT, OLIVER FORD, lawyer; b. Piney Fork, Ohio, Aug. 20, 1933; s. Ford Oliver and Margaret (Martin) A.; m. Kathryn Anne Allen, Jan. 2, 1960; children: Richard, Robert, Karen, Mary Anne, Elizabeth. BS, U. Detroit, 1958; JD, William Mitchell Coll. Law, 1965. Bar: Minn. 1965, U.S. Dist. Ct. Minn. 1965, Mich. 1969, U.S. Dist. Ct. (ea. dist.) Mich. 1972, U.S. Ct. Appeals (8th cir.) 1979, U.S. Ct. Appeals (Fed. cir.) 1982. Patent counsel Honeywell Inc., Mpls., 1965-69, Chrysler Corp., Detroit, 1969-77; ptnr. Schroeder, Siegfried, Vidas & Arrett, P.A., Mpls., 1977-85, Vidas & Arrett, P.A., Mpls., 1985—. Served with U.S. Army, 1958-60. Mem. Hennepin County Bar Assn., Am. Arbitration Assn., Minn. Intellectual Property Law Assn. Republican. Roman Catholic. Clubs: Minneapolis, Lafayette (Mpls.). Avocation: sailing. Patent, Trademark and copyright. Office: Vidas & Arrett PA 2925 Multifoods Tower Minneapolis MN 55402

ARRINGTON, JOHN LESLIE, JR., lawyer; b. Pawhuska, Okla., Oct. 15, 1931; s. John Leslie and Grace Louise (Moore) A.; m. Elizabeth Anne Waddington, 1956 (div.); children—Elizabeth Anne, John Leslie III, Winifred L., Katherine M.; m. 2d, Linda Vance, 1972. A.B., Princeton U., 1953; J.D., Harvard U., 1956, LL.M., 1957. Bar: Okla. 1956, U.S. Dist. Ct. (no. dist.) Okla. 1957, U.S. Dist. Ct. (we. dist.) Okla. 1958, U.S. Supreme Ct. 1960, U.S. Ct. Appeals (10th cir.) 1962, U.S. Dist. Ct. (ea. dist.) Okla. 1976. Assoc., Huffman, Arrington, Kihle, Gaberino & Dunn and predecessor firms, Tulsa, 1957-61, ptnr., 1961—; chmn. bd. Woodland Bank of Tulsa; prin. draftsman Okla. Supreme Ct. Rules Governing Disciplinary Proceedings, 1980-81. Bd. dirs. Tulsa County Legal Aid Soc., 1965-70, pres., 1967-70; bd. dirs. Tulsa Family and Children's Service, 1966-85, pres., 1974; bd. dirs. Tulsa Family Mental Health Ctr., 1982—. Mem. Tulsa County Bar Assn. (Young Lawyer award 1962, pres. 1970), Okla. Bar Assn. (mem. profl. responsibility commn. 1977-84, vice chmn. 1983-84), ABA, Fed. Energy Bar Assn., Motor Carrier Lawyers Assn., Am. Soc. Internat. Law. Republican. Episcopalian. Clubs: Tulsa, So. Hills Country (Tulsa); Princeton (N.Y.C.). General corporate, Public utilities, Administrative and regulatory. Home: 2136 E 26th Pl Tulsa OK 74114 Office: 1000 ONEOK Plaza Tulsa OK 74103

ARRINGTON, ROY DAVID, lawyer; b. Oak Hill, W.Va., Sept. 16, 1948; s. Roy Stanford and Mary Alice (Wolfe) A.; m. Theresa Carol Payne, June 20, 1975 (div. Nov. 1978). BS in Chemistry, W.Va. Inst. Tech., 1970; JD, W.Va. U., 1979. Bar: W.Va. 1979, U.S. Dist. Ct. (so. dist.) W.Va. 1979. Sole practice Marlinton, W.Va., 1979—; mcpl. judge Town of Marlinton, 1979—; fiduciary commr. Pocahontas County, W.Va., 1985—; bd. dirs. Marlinton R.R. Depot, Inc. Mental Hygiene Commr. Pocahontas County, 1984—; mem. Arts and Humanitites Council, Marlinton, 1980—; mem. Pioneer Days com., Marlinton, 1977—; active Girl Scouts U.S.A. and Boys Scouts Am. Mem. ABA, W.Va. Bar Assn. (family law com.). Democrat. Lodge: Lions. Avocations: photography, school lectr. Criminal, Family and matrimonial, Real property. Home and Office: PO Box 237 Marlinton WV 24954

ARROWOOD, LISA GAYLE, lawyer; b. Kansas City, Mo., Aug. 7, 1956; d. Paul Miller and Catherine Margaret (Alukas) A.; m. Philip D. O'Neill, June 25, 1983; children: Alexander Edwin O'Neill, Sean Matthew O'Neill. AB, Brown U., 1978; JD, Harvard U., 1982. Bar: Mass. 1982, U.S. Dist. Ct. Mass., U.S. Ct. Appeals (1st cir.). Assoc. Hale and Dorr, Boston, 1982—; instr. boston U. Sch. Law, 1984-85. Mem. ABA, Mass. Bar Assn., Boston Bar Assn., Am. Soc. Law and Medicine, Phi Beta Kappa. State civil litigation, Personal injury, Federal civil litigation.

ARTHUR, HARRY CORNELIUS, lawyer; b. Meridian, Tex., Apr. 1, 1941; s. George D. and Hattie (Lamb) A.; m. Donna Sue Vaughn, May 22, 1964 (dec. Oct. 1981); m. Kathryn Reynette Scott, July 1, 1982; children—Stephanie Arthur, Darrin Arthur. B.A., Tarleton State Coll., 1964; J.D., South Tex. Coll., 1970. Bar: Tex. 1970, U.S. Dist. Ct. (so. dist.) Tex. 1970, U.S. Ct. Appeals (5th cir.) 1975. Assoc., Brock & Williams, Houston, 1970-73; sole practice, Houston, 1973—; v.p., legal counsel Summit Life Ins. Co., 1975-80. Mem. Houston Bar Assn., Tex. Bar Assn., ABA, Tex. Trial Lawyers Assn. Republican. Mem. Society of Friends. Personal injury, Workers' compensation. Home: 704 Falling Leaf Friendswood TX 77546 Office: 1305 Prairie St Suite 300 Houston TX 77002

ARTHUR, JEANNE L., lawyer. BA, Stanford U., 1964; JD, U. Santa Clara, 1967. Bar: Calif. 1967, U.S. Dist. Ct. (no. dist.) Calif. 1967, U.S. Ct. Appeals (9th cir.) 1967. Assoc. Law Office of Morton P. MacLeod, Los Altos, Calif., 1968-70, Law Office of Skornia, Rosenblum & Gyemant, Palo Alto and San Francisco, Calif., 1970-72; sole practice Palo Alto, 1972-82; ptnr. Arthur, Pennix & Thompson, Palo Alto, 1983—; lectr. estate and fin. planning various colls. and Univs.; mem. faculty Foothill Coll. 1978-81; pres. Palo Alto Fin. Planning Forum, 1975-76; bd. dirs. Peninsula Estate Planning Council. Adv. com. Community Found. Santa Clara County, Calif., 1975—; mem. Allocations Rev. Com. United Way Santa Clara County, 1978-80. Mem. ABA (corp., banking and bus. law sect.), Calif. Bar Assn. (bus. law sect., conf. of dels. 1973—, com. on pub. affairs, chmn. 1982-83), Santa Clara Bar Assn. (treas. 1981, trustee 1973-75, 77-78, bench bar media police com. 1978, 83—), Palo Alto Area Bar Assn. (pres. 1977-78), Santa Clara County Fair Jud. Election Practices Com., Palo Alto C. of C. (bd. dirs. 1984—). General corporate, Probate. Office: Arthur Pennix & Thompson PO Box 60639 385 Sherman Ave Suite 5 Palo Alto CA 94306

ARTHUR, MICHAEL ELBERT, lawyer; b. Seattle, Oct. 9, 1952; s. Theodore E. and Gladys L. (Jones) A.; m. Claire C. Meeker, Dec. 23, 1974; children: Christine, Conor. BA, U. Calif., Santa Barbara, 1974; JD, Stanford U., 1977. Bar: Oreg. 1977, U.S. Dist. Ct. Oreg. 1977, U.S. Ct. Appeals (9th cir.) 1984. Assoc. Miller, Nash, Wiener, Hager & Carlsen, Portland, Oreg., 1977-84, ptnr., 1984—. Council, task forces St. Luke Luth. Ch., Portland, 1979-83. Mem. ABA, Oreg. Bar Assn., Multnomah Bar Assn., Order of Coif, Phi Beta Kappa. Club: Portland Golf. General corporate, Real property. Home: 13535 NW Lariat Ct Portland OR 97229 Office: Miller Nash Wiener Hager & Carlsen 111 SW 5th Ave Portland OR 97204

ARTIMEZ, JOHN EDWARD, JR., lawyer; b. Wheeling, W.Va., Aug. 20, 1956; s. John Edward and Wilma Mae (Wilson) A.; m. Linda Rae Richmond, Apr. 11, 1981; 1 child, Brittany Rae. BA magna cum laude, W.Va. U., 1978, JD, 1981. Bar: W.Va. 1981, U.S. Dist. Ct. (no. and so. dists.) W.Va. 1981. Assoc. Bachmann, Hess et al, Wheeling, 1981-85, ptnr.,

1986—. Mem. ABA, W.Va. Def. Trial Counsel, Def. Research Inst. Republican. Methodist. Club: Moundsville (W.Va.) Country Club. Lodge: Elks. Avocations: skiing, softball, basketball officiating. Federal civil litigation, State civil litigation, Personal injury. Home: 1200 4th St Moundsville WV 26041 Office: Bachmann Hess Bachmann & Garden PO Box 351 Wheeling WV 26003

ARTIS, GREGORY DWIGHT, lawyer, pharmaceutical consultant; b. Columbus, Ohio, July 8, 1952; s. Willie J. and Eloise I. (Smith) A.; m. Fredi Kay Johnson, Mar. 13, 1976; children—Kierstian D., Bethany S., Gregory Dwight Jr. B.S. in Pharmacy, Ohio State U., 1976; J.D., Emory U., 1982. Registered pharmacist, Ohio, Ga. Bar: Ga. 1982. Pharmacist, Thrift Drug Co., Atlanta, 1976-78, Eckerd Drugs, Atlanta, 1978-82; assoc. Smith, Cohen, Ringel, Kohler & Martin, Atlanta, 1982-84; atty. So. Bell, Atlanta, 1984—. Bd. dirs. Urban League, Columbus, 1974-75; mem. steering com. Progressive Alliance, Atlanta, 1985; commr. Housing Authority Fulton County, Ga., 1986—; mem. Ga. Asbestos Licensing Bd., 1986—. Recipient D. Robert Owen award Emory U., 1982, named coach Mugel Moot Court Tax Team, Moot Court Directorate, Coach of Yr., 1982, semi-finalist mem. Giles Sutherland Regional Moot Court Patent Team, 1982. Mem. ABA, Gate City Bar Assn. (exec. com. 1985-86, asst. sec. 1986—), State Bar Ga., Atlanta Bar Assn., Nat. Order Barristers. Avocation: travel. Federal civil litigation, Labor, Public utilities. Office: So Bell Telephone and Telegraph Co 675 W Peachtree St NE Atlanta GA 30375

ARTMAN, ERIC ALAN, lawyer; b. Jacksonville, Ill., Dec. 22, 1956; s. H. Dean and Cornelia Isabel (Green) A. BS in Math., Computer Sci., U. Ill., Urbana, 1978; JD, U. Ill., Champaign, 1981. Bar: Ill. 1981, U.S. Dist. Ct. (cen. dist.) Ill. 1983. Staff atty. Ill. Ho. of Reps., Springfield, 1981-83; assoc. Gramlich & Morse, Springfield, 1983-85, Saul J. Morse and Assoc., Springfield, 1985—; bd. dirs. State Bank of Auburn, Ill. Mem. Ill. Commerce Commn. Steering Com. on Ill. Universal Service Fund. Mem. ABA, Ill. Bar Assn., Sangamon County Bar Assn. Republican. Club: Island Bay Yacht. Lodge: Lions. Avocation: boating. Administrative and regulatory, State civil litigation, Legislative. Office: Saul J Morse and Assocs 828 S Second Suite 102 Springfield IL 62704

ARTURI, PETER A., II, lawyer; b. Greenwich, Conn., Dec. 10, 1953; s. Peter A. Sr. and Marillyn (Rathjen) A.; m. Denise Elizabeth Stevens, Sept. 12, 1981; 1 child, Peter Tobias. AB with honors, Hamilton Coll., 1975; JD with honors, U. Conn., 1979. Bar: Conn. 1979, U.S. Dist. Ct. Conn. 1980. Assoc. Albert, Pastore & Ward P.C., N.Y.C. and Greenwich, 1979-82; assoc. counsel Kero-Sun, Inc., Kent, Conn., 1982-83; ptnr. Cramer & Anderson, New Milford, Conn., 1986—. Mem. ABA, Conn. Bar Assn., New Milford Bar Assn. Democrat. Club: Washington (Conn.). Avocations: tennis, cross country skiing. Banking, General corporate, Trademark and copyright. Office: Cramer & Anderson 51 Main St New Milford CT 06776

ARTWICK, FREDERICK JOHN, lawyer; b. Chgo., June 4, 1944; s. Edward John and Evelyn Lorraine (Weymouth) A.; m. Judy Joan Kamps, Aug. 12, 1967; children: Elizabeth, Lindsay. AB, Harvard U., 1966; MA, U. Reading, Eng., 1967; JD, U. Chgo., 1970. Bar: Ill., Wis., U.S. Dist. Ct. (no. dist.) Ill, U.S. Ct. Appeals (7th cir.), U.S. Supreme Ct. Assoc. Leibman, Williams, Bennett, Baird & Minow, Chgo., 1971-72; assoc. Sidley & Austin, Chgo., 1972-75, ptnr., 1975—. Pres. Evanston United Way/Community Services, Ill., 1980-82, bd. dirs., 1978-84; mem. Evanston Mental Health Bd., 1982-85, Dist. 202 Bd. Edn., Evanston, 1984—. Mem. ABA, Wis. Bar Assn., Ill. Bar Assn., Chgo. Bar Assn., Chgo. Council Lawyers. Presbyterian. Club: Univ. (Chgo.). Federal civil litigation, State civil litigation. Office: Sidley & Austin One First National Plaza Chicago IL 60603

ARZT, LEE ROBERT, lawyer; b. Yonkers, N.Y., Sept. 23, 1948; s. Arthur A. and Marion (Bernstein) A.; m. Mary Wilson, Aug. 14, 1970; 1 child, Sarah Elizabeth. B.A., Hofstra U., 1970; J.D., Coll. William and Mary, 1973. Bar: Va. 1973, U.S. Dist. Ct. (ea. dist.) Va. 1973, U.S. Ct. Appeals (4th cir.) 1974, U.S. Supreme Ct. 1977. Assoc. Horwitz, Baer, Neblett, and successor firm, Richmond, Va., 1973-76; mng. ptnr. Arzt, Monahan, Sager, and predecessor firms, Richmond, 1977-80; sole practice, Richmond, 1981—; instr. J. Sargeant Reynolds Community Coll., Richmond, 1976-77. V.p. land trustee, chmn. various coms., bd. dirs. Congregation Or Ami, Richmond, 1974—; del. 3d Congl. Dist. and Va. Democratic Convs., Richmond, 1984; bd. dirs. Beth Sholom Home, Richmond, 1974-81. N.Y. State Regents scholar Hofstra U., 1966-70. Mem. ABA, Va. Bar Assn., Bar Assn. Richmond, Bar Assn. Henrico County. Democrat. Jewish. Contracts commercial, Real property, General practice. Office: 5001 W Broad St Richmond VA 23230

ASANTE, SAMUEL KWADWO BOATEN, lawyer, international official; b. Asokore, Ghana, May 11, 1933; s. Daniel Y. and Mary (Baafi) A.; m. Philomena Margaret Aidoo; children—Adlai, Joyce, Dominic, Philomena, Angela. J.S.D., Yale U., 1965; LL.M., U. London, 1958. Bar: Ghana 1960, Solicitor Sup. Ct. Eng. (hon.) 1960. Asst. state atty. Ghana, 1960-61; lectr. law U. Ghana, 1961-65, acting head dept. law, 1962; lectr. law U. Leeds, 1965-66; atty. legal dept. World Bank, Washington, 1966-69; adj. prof. law Howard U., 1967-69; solicitor gen. Ghana, 1969-77; chief adviser on legal matters UN Centre on Transnational Corp., N.Y.C., 1977-83, dir., 1983—; vis. prof. law and bus. Temple U., 1976; vis. fellow Clare Hall, mem. law faculty Cambridge U., 1978-79; lectr. in field. Fulbright fellow, 1963-65, Sterling fellow 1963-65. Bd. dirs. Internat. Development Law Inst. Fellow World Acad. Art and Sci., Ghana Acad. Art and Sci.; mem. Internat Law Assn., Am. Soc. Internat. Law, Soc. Pub. Tchrs. Law. Contbr. in field; mem. adv. bd. Jour. Fgn. Investment Law. Private international, Public international, Oil and gas leasing. Office: Room DC-1320 United Nations New York NY 10017

ASCHER, MARK LOUIS, legal educator; b. Junction City, Kans., Sept. 23, 1953; s. Martin Louis and Bertha May (Clark) A.; m. Kerry Elizabeth Muldowney, Feb. 6, 1982. BA, Marquette U., 1975; MA, Kans. State U., 1977; JD, Harvard U., 1978; LLM in Taxation, NYU, 1981. Bar: N.Y. 1979, Fla. 1980, Ariz. 1982. Assoc. White & Case, N.Y.C., 1978-82; assoc. prof. U. Ariz., Tucson, 1982-86, prof., 1986—; vis. prof. U. Tex., Austin, 1986. Contbr. articles to profl. jours. Served with USAF, 1971-73. Mem. So. Ariz. Estate Planning Council (bd. dirs. 1983—). Legal education, Estate planning, Personal income taxation. Office: U Ariz Coll Law Tucson AZ 85721

ASCHER, RICHARD ALAN, lawyer; b. Hartford, Conn., June 3, 1945; s. Richard Oscar and Bernice (Spiegel) A.; m. Barbara Haberman, May 22, 1967; children—Jonathan Colin, Andrew David. B.A., SUNY-Buffalo, 1967, J.D., 1970. Staff atty. Legal Aid Soc., Queens, N.Y., 1970-73; ptnr. Ascher & Goldstein, Queens, N.Y., 1973-83, Ascher & Novitt, Queens, 1983—; counsel Assemblyman L. Stavisky, Albany, N.Y., 1974-75, Assemblyman I. Lafayette, Albany, 1976—; counsel, bd. dirs. Jackson Heights Community Devel. Corp., Queens, 1980-82. Pres., Queens Ind. Democrats, 1976; mem. lawyers com. Hart presdl. campaign, 1984; chmn. Com. to Make Watergate Perfectly Clear, Queens, 1973-74. Mem. Queens County Bar Assn., Criminal Courts Bar Assn. Jewish. Club: JFK Democratic (Jackson Heights) (exec. bd. 1981-82). Criminal, Personal injury, Family and matrimonial. Office: Ascher & Novitt 125-10 Queens Blvd Kew Gardens NY 11415

ASCHKINASI, DAVID JAY, lawyer; b. N.Y.C.. BA, Brandeis U., 1972; JD, U. Colo., 1976. Bar: Colo. 1976, U.S. Dist Ct. Colo. 1976, U.S. Ct. Appeals (10th cir.) 1982. Sole practice Boulder, Colo., 1976-77; asst. atty. gen. State of Colo., Denver, 1977-83; sole practice Denver, 1983-84; div. counsel U.S. West Info. Systems, Denver, 1984—. Mem. ABA, Colo. Bar Assn., Denver Bar Assn., Am. Corp. Counsel Assn. General corporate, Contracts commercial. Office: US West Info Systems 6200 S Quebec St #210 Englewood CO 80111

ASCIONE, JOSEPH ANTHONY, lawyer; b. N.Y.C., Feb. 27, 1952; s. Alfred Michael and Joan (Petra) A.; m. Dorothy Eleanor Leptak, May 20, 1978; 1 child, Sarah Christine. BA, Manhattan Coll., 1973; JD, St. John's U., Jamaica, N.Y., 1976; LLM in Taxation, NYU, 1983. Bar: N.Y. 1977, U.S. Dist. Ct. (so. and ea. dists.) N.Y. 1977, N.J. 1978, U.S. Dist. Ct. N.J. 1978, D.C. 1980, U.S. Ct. Appeals (2d and 3d cirs.) 1981. Assoc. Cichanowicz & Callan, N.Y.C., 1976-79; ptnr. Fischer, Kagan, Ascione & Zaretsky, Clifton, N.J., 1979-87; prin. Sterns, Herbert, Weinroth & Petrino, P.C., Princeton, N.J., 1987—. Chmn. Juvenile Conf. Com., Chatham, N.J., 1984—; bd. dirs., exec. com. N.J. chpt. Am. Heart Assn., Fairfield, N.J., 1984-85. Mem. ABA, N.Y. State Bar Assn., Maritime Law Assn., Columbian Lawyers Assn., Chatham Jaycees (v.p., treas. 1982-84). Democrat. Roman Catholic. Corporate taxation, Estate taxation, State civil litigation. Office: Sterns Herbert Weinroth & Petrino PC 90 Nassau St Princeton NJ 08542

ASENCIO, DIEGO CARLOS, lawyer; b. San Antonio, May 23, 1956; s. Diego Cortés and Nancy (Rodriguez) A.; m. Norma Fehrmann, June 14, 1980; 1 child, Joshua. BA in Polit. Sci., Tex. A&I U., 1979; JD, U. Notre Dame, 1982. Bar: Fla. 1982, U.S. Dist. Ct. (so. dist.) Fla. 1986. Assoc. Law Offices of Jose Rodriguez, West Palm Beach, Fla., 1982-86, Slawson & Burman, North Palm Beach, Fla., 1987—. Dir. Notre Dame U. Migrant Program, South Bend, Ind. 1981-82; bd. dirs. Hispanic Human Resources, West Palm Beach, 1984-87, Hispanic Affairs Commn., West Palm Beach, 1985-87, various other commns.; officer Hispanic Dem. Club., West Palm Beach, 1985-86. Mem. ABA (family law sect.), Palm Beach County Bar Assn. (chmn. various coms.), Cuban Bar Assn., Hispanic Nat. Bar Assn., Assn. Trial Lawyers Am., Acad. Fla. Trial Lawyers. Roman Catholic. Personal injury, Wrongful death, Family and matrimonial. Home: 5679 Golden Eagle Circle Palm Beach Gardens FL 33418 Office: Slawson & Burman 712 US 1 Suite 300 North Palm Beach FL 33408

ASH, DAVID CHARLES, lawyer; b. Bklyn., Nov. 28, 1951; s. Jerome William and Bernice (Kibrick) A.; m. Karen Artz Ash, June 11, 1977; 1 child, Kimberly Barbara Ash. AB magna cum laude, Brandeis U., 1973; JD, Harvard U., 1976. Bar: N.Y. 1977, U.S. Dist. Ct. (so. dist.) N.Y. 1977. Assoc. Rosenman Colin Freund Lewis & Cohen, N.Y.C., 1976-79, Trubin Sillcocks Edelman & Knapp, N.Y.C., 1979-82, Corbin Silverman & Sanseverino, N.Y.C., 1982-85; v.p., gen. counsel Sam Ash Music Corp., Hempstead, N.Y., 1985—, Samson Techs. Corp. Mem. ABA, N.Y. State Bar Assn., Assn. Bar City of N.Y. Democrat. Jewish. Real property. Office: Sam Ash Music Corp 124 Fulton Ave Hempstead NY 11550

ASH, KAREN ARTZ, lawyer; b. Bklyn., Dec. 23, 1955; d. Bernard and Helen (Liff) Artz; m. David Charles Ash, June 11, 1977; 2 children. AB in Econs. with honors, Georgetown U., 1976; JD magna cum laude, N.Y. Law Sch., 1980. Bar: N.Y. 1981, U.S. Dist. Ct. (so. and ea. dists.) N.Y. 1981. Assoc. Kaye, Scholer, Fierman, Hays & Handler, N.Y.C., 1980-83, Amster, Rothstein & Ebenstein, N.Y.C., 1983—; lectr. in field. Author: Grey Goods and What Does It Mean to You, Trademark Licensing Do's and Don'ts, Rule 60(b)(4) F.R.C.P.; research editor N.Y. Law Rev., 1980 (cert. of merit 1980); contbr. articles to profl. jours. Fundraiser Assn. for Help Retarded Children, N.Y.C., 1978—. Mem. ABA (chairperson trademark com. 1982—), Women's Bar Assn., N.Y. State Bar Assn., U.S. Trademark Assn., NOW, N.Y. Humane Soc. Democrat. Trademark and copyright. Office: Amster Rothstein & Ebenstein 90 Park Ave New York NY 10016

ASHBY, KIMBERLY A., lawyer; b. Plainfield, N.J., Sept. 9, 1957; d. John L. and Patricia (Andrews) A. BA with high honors, U. Fla., 1978, JD, 1980. Bar: Fla. 1981. Research aide U.S. Ct. Appeals (2d cir.), Lakeland, Fla., 1981; assoc. Maguire, Voorhis & Wells, P.A., Orlando, Fla., 1981-86, ptnr., 1986—. Contbr. articles to profl. jours. Elder, trustee Park /Lake Presby. Ch., Orlando, 1984-86. Mem. Fla. Bar Assn. (appellate rules com., 1985, young lawyers jud. relations com., 1983-84), Fla. Def. Lawyers (Amicus brief writer 1984). Republican. Avocation: marathon running. State civil litigation, Federal civil litigation, Consumer commercial. Office: Maguire Voorhis & Wells 2 S Orange Orlando FL 32802

ASHCRAFT, JOHN MARION, III, lawyer; b. Charleston, W.Va., June 2, 1950; s. John Marion and Mary Helen (Skaggs) A.; m. Dorothy Emily Riley, Nov. 18, 1972; children: Emily Ellene, Julie Renee, Andrea Jean. BA, Mich. State U., 1972; JD, U. Colo., 1975. Bar: Pa. 1975, U.S. Dist. Ct. (ea. dist.) Pa. 1976, U.S. Ct. Appeals (3d cir.) 1982, U.S. Supreme Ct. 1986. Assoc. Dean L. Foote, Allentown, Pa., 1975-77; asst. county solicitor Lehigh County, Allentown, 1977-81; sole practice Allentown, 1981-86; assoc. Fitzpatrick & Assocs., Allentown, 1986—; bd. dirs., treas. Lehigh and Northampton Transp. Authority, Allentown. Bd. dirs., chmn. Lehigh and Northampton Transp. Authority. Republican. Avocations: walking, reading, ocean fishing, camping. Local government, General practice, Legal research. Home: 1363 Country Club Rd Wescoville PA 18106 Office: Fitzpatrick & Assocs 824 Walnut St PO Box 4485 Allentown PA 18105

ASHE, BERNARD FLEMMING, lawyer; b. Balt., Mar. 8, 1936; s. Victor Joseph and Frances Cecelia (Johnson) Flemming; m. Grace Nannette Pegram, Mar. 23, 1963; children—Walter Joseph, David Bernard. B.A., Howard U., 1956, J.D., 1961. Bar: Va. 1961, D.C. 1963, Mich. 1964, N.Y. 1971. Tchr., Balt. Pub. Schs., 1956-58; atty. NLRB, Washington, 1961-63; asst. gen. counsel Internat. Union United Auto Workers, Detroit, 1963-71; gen. counsel N.Y. State United Tchrs., Albany, 1971—; mem. adj. faculty Cornell Sch. Indsl. and Labor Relations, Albany div., 1981. Bd. dirs. Urban League Albany, 1979-85, 1st v.p., 1981-85; trustee N.Y. State Client Security Fund, 1981—. Mem. ABA (chmn. sect. labor and employment law sect. 1982-83, Ho. of Dels.), Am. Arbitration Assn. (dir. 1982—), Assn. Bar City N.Y., N.Y. State Bar Assn., Nat. Lawyers Club, Albany County Bar Assn. Contbr. articles on labor and constl. law to profl. jours. Labor, Administrative and regulatory. Office: 159 Wolf Rd Box 15-008 Albany NY 12212

ASHE, ROBERT LAWRENCE, JR., lawyer; b. Knoxville, Tenn., June 17, 1940; s. Robert Lawrence and Martha Victor (Henderson) A.; m. Kathleen Marie Blee, Dec. 22, 1972; children: Robert L. III, Sarah Cartter. AB magna cum laude, Princeton U., 1962; LLB cum laude, Harvard U., 1967. Bar: Ga. 1968, U.S. Dist. Ct. (no. dist.) Ga. 1968, U.S. Ct. Appeals (4th cir.) 1976, U.S. Supreme Ct. 1976, U.S. Dist. Ct. (mid. dist.) Ga. 1978, U.S. Ct. Appeals (D.C. cir.) 1978, U.S. Dist. Ct. (so. dist.) Ga. 1981, U.S. Ct. Appeals (5th and 11th cirs.) 1981, U.S. Dist. Ct. (so. dist.) Ind. 1983, U.S. Ct. Appeals (6th cir.) 1983, U.S. Dist. Ct. (ea. dist.) Ark. 1985, U.S. Ct. Appeals (2d, 3d, 9th and 10th cirs.) 1985, U.S. Dist. Ct. (ea. dist.) Mich. 1986. Assoc. Kilpatrick & Cody, Atlanta, 1967-72, ptnr., 1972-80; ptnr. Paul, Hastings, Janofsky & Walker, Atlanta, 1980—. Pres. Atlanta Urban League, 1977-80. Served to lt. USN, 1962-64. Mem. ABA (chmn. govt. liason employment law com. labor law sect.), Ga. Bar Assn., Gate City Bar Assn., Atlanta Lawyer's Club. Labor, Civil rights, Federal civil litigation. Office: Paul Hastings Janofsky & Walker 133 Peachtree St 42d Floor Ga Pacific Ctr Atlanta GA 30303

ASHER, LESTER, lawyer; b. Chgo., July 7, 1910; s. Jacob and Fannie (Robin) A.; m. Corinne S., Oct. 24, 1936; children—David Michael, Frances Leslie, Jonathan Daniel. B.A., U. Chgo., 1930. Bar: Ill. 1933. Assoc., Sonnenschein, Lautmann & Levinson, Chgo., 1933-37; rev. atty. regional atty. NLRB, Chgo., 1937-45, sec. 1945; gen. counsel Ill. Fedn. Labor, Chgo., 1955—; ptnr. Asher, Pavalon Gittler, Greenfield & Segall, Ltd., Chgo. and predecessors, 1951—, now sr. ptnr.; lectr. labor law U. Chgo., 1945—, U. Ill., 1950, Roosevelt U., Chgo., 1948, U. Wis., 1953; mem. Ill. Atty. Registration and Disciplinary Commn., 1973—, chmn., 1976-82. Mem. ABA, Ill. Bar Assn. (chmn. labor law sect.), Chgo. Bar Assn., Order of Coif, Phi Beta Kappa. Jewish. Labor.

ASHER, ROBERT MICHAEL, lawyer; b. Harvey, Ill., Aug. 27, 1956; s. Harry and Ardith (Weintraub) A.; m. Linda Ann Silverman, May 25, 1986. BSEE, MIT, 1978; JD, Harvard U., 1981. Bar: Ill. 1981, U.S. Dist. Ct. (no. dist.) Ill. 1981, Mass. 1983, U.S. Dist. Ct. Mass. 1983, U.S. Ct. Appeals (fed. and 1st cirs.) 1987. Assoc. Hume, Clement, Brinks, Willian & Olds, Chgo., 1981-83; assoc. Dike, Bronstein, Roberts, Cushman & Pfund, Boston, 1983-86, ptnr., 1987—. Mem. ABA, Am. Intellectual Property Law Assn., Boston Patent Law Assn., MENSA. Patent, Federal civil litigation, Trademark and copyright. Office: Dike Bronstein Roberts Cushman & Pfund 130 Water St Boston MA 02109

ASHFORD, CLINTON RUTLEDGE, lawyer; b. Honolulu, Mar. 23, 1925; s. Huron Kanoelani and Lillian Radcliffe (Cooke) A.; m. Joan Beverly Schumm, Aug. 24, 1951; children: Marguerite, Frank, Bruce, James. B.A., U. Calif.-Berkeley, 1945; J.D., U. Mich., 1950. Bar: Hawaii 1950, U.S. Supreme Ct. 1967. Ptnr. Lee & Ashford, Honolulu, 1951-53; dep. atty. gen. Hawaii, 1953-55; ptnr. Ashford & Wriston, Honolulu, 1955—. Pres., Child and Family Service Honolulu, 1971, bd. dirs., 1967-73; bd. dirs. Health and Community Services Council, 1973-75; bd. dirs. Aloha United Way, 1975-81, exec. com., 1977-79. Served with USN, 1943-46, USNR, 1950-64. Fellow Am. Bar Found., Am. Coll. Probate Counsel, Am. Coll. Real Estate Lawyers; mem. ABA (bd. govs. 1979-82, exec. com. 1981-82), Hawaii Bar Assn. (pres. 1972), Am. Law Inst., Am. Judicature Soc. (bd. dirs. 1981-86), Internat. Acad. Estate and Trust Law, Order of the Coif. State civil litigation, Probate, Real property. Home: 45-628 Halekou Pl Kaneohe HI 96744 Office: Ashford & Wriston 235 Queen St PO Box 131 Honolulu HI 96810 *

ASHFORD, THOMAS STEVEN, lawyer; b. Detroit, Sept. 14, 1951; s. James Thomas and Lucille Aspasia (Pappas) A.; children: James Thomas, Michael Garett. BA, Trinity Coll., Hartford, Conn., 1973; JD, Vanderbilt U., 1976; MBA, U. Chgo., 1977. Bar: Ill. 1976, U.S. Dist. Ct. (no. dist.) Ill. 1976, Ohio 1983; CPA, Ill. Assoc. Gardner, Carton & Douglas, Chgo., 1976-78, Coffield, Ungaretti, Harris & Slavin, Chgo., 1978-81; sr. atty. Am. Electric Power Service Corp., Columbus, Ohio, 1981—. Mem. ABA, Ohio Bar Assn., Columbus Bar Assn. Club: University (Chgo.). General corporate, Securities. Home: 5431 Aryshire Dr Dublin OH 43017 Office: Am Electric Power Service Corp 1 Riverside Plaza Columbus OH 43215

ASHIN, JEFFERY GORDON, lawyer; b. Phila., Dec. 31, 1955; s. Morris Meyer and Sheila Ashin; m. Mikki Z. Ashin, July 11, 1976; children: Brian Eric, Julie Heather. AB in Polit. Sci., Muhlenberg Coll., 1978; JD, Washington Coll. Law, 1981. Bar: Md. 1982, D.C. 1983, U.S. Dist. Ct. D.C. 1983, U.S. Dist. Ct. Md. 1984. Assoc. Howard Rensin P.A., Hyattsville, Md., 1978-83, Christian & Ashin P.A., Hyattsville, 1983-86; ptnr. Christian & Ashin P.A., College Park, Md., 1986—. Mem. ABA, Md. Bar Assn., D.C. Bar Assn., Prince George's County Bar Assn. Avocations: tennis, golf. Personal injury, Workers' compensation, Criminal. Office: Christian & Ashin PA 4511 Knox Rd College Park MD 20740

ASHLEMAN, IVAN RENO, II, health care executive, lawyer, mortgage banker; b. Kansas City, Mo., June 9, 1940; s. Ivan Reno and Ellen Lorraine (Fisher) A.; m. Susan Haase, July 25, 1986; children—Brian Eugene, Michael Scott. B.S., U. Nebr., 1963, J.D., 1963. Bar: Nev. 1963, U.S. Dist. Ct. Nebr. 1963, U.S. Dist. Ct. Nev. 1964, U.S. Tax Ct. 1975, U.S. Ct. Appeals (9th cir.) 1968, U.S. Supreme Ct. 1975. Sole practice, Las Vegas and Reno, Nev., 1966-69; ptnr. Davis, Cowell & Bowe, San Francisco and Las Vegas, 1969-80, Ashleman & Clontz, Las Vegas, 1982-83, Raggio, Ashleman, Wooster, Clontz & Lindell, Las Vegas and Reno, 1981; Clark County dep. dist. atty., Las Vegas, 1964-66; exec. v.p., dir. Equivest Mortgage Co., Inc., Reno, Las Vegas, 1981—; pres. Ins. Services, Inc., 1983—; bd. dirs., pres. Geriatric Health Resources, Inc., Consol. Hospitality Services, Inc.; sec.-treas., bd. dirs. Sierra Health Care Mgmt. Assocs., Inc.; exec. mem. Gov. Bryan's Fin. Com., 1980. Contbr. articles to profl. jours. Trustee Nev. Bd. Museums and History, Carson City; exec. bd. dirs., treas. Nathan Adelson Hospice, Las Vegas, 1981—; pres. Young Dems. of Las Vegas, 1970; bd. dirs. Sparks Family Hosp., 1980-83, Spring Valley Community Hosp. Mem. Assn. Trial Lawyers Assn. Am., Am. Judicature Soc., ABA, Nev. Bar Assn., Nebr. Bar Assn., Washoe County Bar Assn., Clark County Bar Assn., Nev. Homebuilders, So. Nev. Arbitration Assn., Indsl. Relations Reps. Assn., Reno C. of C. Episcopalian. Clubs: Las Vegas Country, Hualapai (Las Vegas); Virginia, Press (Reno). Administrative and regulatory, General corporate, Health. Home: 235 Country Club Reno NV 89509 Office: 350 S Center St Suites 542-544 Reno NV 89501

ASHLEY, DANIEL JOSEPH, lawyer; b. N.Y.C., Jan. 12, 1938; s. Daniel Elias Ashley and Lillian Marie (Ennis) Bell; m. Susan Andrée Finneran, Oct. 17, 1964; children: Daniel Christopher, Michael Lawrence, Elizabeth Noel. BS, Fordham U., 1959, JD, 1962. Bar: N.Y. 1962, U.S. Ct. Appeals (2d cir.) 1963, Calif. 1976, U.S. Dist. Ct. (cen. dist.) Calif. 1976, U.S. Ct. Appeals (9th cir.) 1976, U.S. Supreme Ct. 1986. Atty. IBM, N.Y.C., 1963-66; area counsel IBM Europe, S.A., Paris, 1966-69; western counsel IBM Corp., Los Angeles, 1969-74; counsel, gen. bus. group/internat. IBM Corp., White Plains, N.Y., 1974-83; counsel U.S. field ops. IBM Corp., White Plains, 1983-86; sr. group counsel Ams. IBM Corp., North Tarrytown, N.Y., 1986—; bd. dirs. Trimble-Mize Found., N.Y.C., 1980—. Commr. Zoning Bd. Appeals, Westport, Conn., 1985. Served to lt. JAGC, USNR, 1966-69. Mem. Westchester-Fairfield Corp. Counsel Assn. (bd. dirs. 1985—), Fordham U. Law Alumni Assn. (leadership com. 1986—), Fordham Coll. Alumni Assn., Gamma Eta Gamma, Omicron Chi Epsilon. Democrat. Roman Catholic. Club: Patterson (Fairfield, Conn.). Avocations: cinematic history, tennis, jogging. Antitrust, Computer, Private international. Home: 6 Tower Ridge Westport CT 06880 Office: IBM Corp Americas Group Town of Mount Pleasant Rt 9 North Tarrytown NY 10591

ASHLEY, JAMES WHEELER, lawyer; b. Chgo., Sept. 23, 1923; s. Frederick and Elizabeth (Wheeler) A.; m. Courtney Collidge, Dec. 27, 1947 (div. 1975); children: James W., Cooper S., Courtney, Christopher R., John M.; m. Joan Allbright, Sept. 25, 1975. Student, Fordham U., 1941-43; J.D., Northwestern U., 1948. Bar: Ill. 1948. Asst. sec. Continental Ill. Nat. Bank, Chgo., 1948-57; assoc. McDermott, Will & Emery, Chgo., 1957-59, ptnr., 1959—; dir. Madison-Kipp Corp., Chgo. Tube & Iron Co., Globe Corp. Contbr. articles to legal jours. Bd. dirs. Chgo. YMCA, 1964-85, chmn., 1974-75, mem. nat. bd. dirs., 1975—, chmn., 1985-87; bd. dirs. Bus. and Profl. People Pub. Interest, Chgo., 1973—, pres., 1982-86; trustee Village of Hinsdale, 1969-72. Served to capt. USAAF, 1943-45, ETO. Mem. ABA, Ill. Bar Assn., Chgo. Bar Assn., Chgo. Council Lawyers. Clubs: Monroe of Chgo. (pres., dir.), Met., Plaza. Estate planning, Probate. Home: 2400 Lake View Chicago IL 60614 Office: McDermott Will & Emery 111 W Monroe St Chicago IL 60603

ASHMALL, ROY ALFRED, lawyer; b. Yonkers, N.Y., Mar. 14, 1940; s. Roy Van Wart and Emma Matilda (Fox) A.; m. Marilyn Rosalie Nelson, Dec. 27, 1961 (div. Nov. 1969); children—Soren Peter, Kari Christine; m. Vicki Lyn Kowalski, Dec. 24, 1975. A.B., U. Mich., 1966, A.M.L.S., 1966; J.D., Wayne State U., 1978. Bar: Mich. 1969, U.S. Dist. Ct. (ea. dist.) Mich. 1982. Gen. mgr. Overseas Imported Cars Inc., Ann Arbor, Mich., 1971-79; sole practice, Ypsilanti, Mich., 1979—. Pres., U. Mich. Grad. Student Assembly, Ann Arbor, 1967. Mem. Mich. Bar Assn., Washtenaw County New Car Dealers' Assn. (exec. sec. 1980—), Beta Phi Mu, Tau Kappa Epsilon. General practice. Home: 5638 New Meadow Dr Ypsilanti MI 48197 Office: 27 N Washington Ypsilanti MI 48197

ASHMAN, ALLAN, lawyer; b. Boston, July 3, 1940; s. Joseph and Sylvia (Shatz) A.; m. Sandra Rachel Silverton, July 4, 1965; children: Laura Beth, Jonathan Ben. B.A. cum laude, Brown U., 1962; J.D., Columbia U., 1965. Bar: N.C. 1966, U.S. Supreme Ct. 1970. Asst. prof. public law and govt., asst. dir. Inst. Govt., U. N.C. at Chapel Hill, 1965-68; dir. research and spl. projects Nat. Legal Aid and Defender Assn., Chgo., 1968-71; dir. research Am. Judicature Soc., Chgo., 1971-77; asst. exec. dir. Am. Judicature Soc., 1977-80; exec. dir. Nat. Conf. Bar Examiners, Chgo., 1980-86; assoc. dean Ill. Inst. Tech., Chgo., 1986—; adj. prof. Ill. Inst. Tech. Author: The New Private Practice: A Study of Piper & Marbury's Neighborhood Law Office, 1972, (with James J. Alfini) The Key to Judicial Merit Selection: The Nominating Process, 1974, (with John P. Ryan) America's Trial Judges, 1980; Research editor: Columbia Jour. Law and Social Problems, 1964-65; Contbr. articles to law jours. Mem. Am. Law Inst. Legal education. Home: 748 Chilton Ln Wilmette IL 60091 Office: Ill Inst Tech Kent Coll Law 77 S Wacker Dr Chicago IL 60606

ASHMUS, KEITH ALLEN, lawyer; b. Cleve., Aug. 19, 1949; s. Richard A. and Rita (Petti) A.; m. Marie Sachiko Matsuoka, Dec. 15, 1973; children: Emmy Marie, Christopher Todd. BA in Polit. Sci., Mich. State U., 1971, MA in Econs., 1972; JD, Yale U., 1974. Bar: Ohio 1974, U.S. Dist. Ct. (no. dist.) Ohio 1975, U.S. Ct. Appeals (6th cir.) 1975, U.S. Supreme Ct. 1980. Assoc. Thompson, Hine & Flory, Cleve., 1974-82, ptnr., 1982—. Co-author: Public Sector Collective Bargaining: The Ohio System, 1984. Trustee community arts Baycrafters, Bay Village, Ohio, 1981-84, Hospice Council No. Ohio, 1982-84, Ctr. for Personal Health Skills, Cleve. 1985—; chmn. job placement for older persons Skills Available, Cleve., 1980—. Named one of

Outstanding Vols. award Nat. Hospice Orgn., 1982, Vol. of Yr. Vocat. Guidance and Rehab. Services, 1985, 86. Mem. ABA (litigation and labor sects.), Ohio Bar Assn. (labor sect., chmn. fed. law arbitration com. 1985-86), Cleve. Bar Assn. (trustee 1985—, chmn. labor law sect. 1983-84). Democrat. Avocation: fishing. Labor, Federal civil litigation, State civil litigation. Office: Thompson Hine & Flory 1100 Nat City Bank Bldg Cleveland OH 44114

ASHTON, MARK ALFRED, lawyer; b. Tulsa, July 18, 1944; s. Alfred Jackson and Margarette Carolyn (Green) A.; m. Linda Diane Stroud, May 15, 1971; children—Kathryn, Hillary, Courtney. B.B.A., U. Okla., 1966, J.D., 1969. Bar: Okla. 1969, U.S. Dist. Ct. (we. dist.) Okla. 1969, U.S. Ct. Appeals (10th cir.) 1970, D.C. Ct. Appeals 1970, U.S. Supreme Ct. 1973. Assoc. Rhoads, Ashton, Johnson & Schacher, Lawton, Okla., 1969-72; ptnr. Ashton and Ashton, Lawton, 1972-73; ptnr., pres. Ashton, Ashton, Wisener and Munkacsy, Inc., Lawton, 1975—; mem. com. appointed by Okla. Supreme Ct. to write civil instrn. manual for all trial judges, 1978—; lectr. continuing legal edn. of bar; mem. Okla. Supreme Ct. Com. on Media in the Courtroom, 1978; commr. Okla. Jud. Nominating Commn., 1983—; chmn., 1987. Mem. Comanche County Democratic Party; 4th congl. dist. Okla. del. Dem. Nat. Conv., 1984; mem. Centenary United Methodist. Ch., Lawton; chmn. City of Lawton Personnel Bd., 1975—; past chmn. Okla. chpt. Common Cause. Served to capt. Judge adv. Gen. USAF, 1969-72. Mem. Okla. Bar Assn. (lawyers ins. com. 1979, del. to ho. of dels. 1974—, chmn. pub. info. com. 1982, 83, assoc. editor jour. 1983—; named outstanding young lawyer 1974, award for outstanding performance 1976, Golden Gavel award 1982), SW Okla. Legal Inst. (pres. 1976), Okla. Trial Lawyers Assn. (pres. 1978, 87, bd. dirs. 1975-82, edn. chmn. 1976, pres. 1987—), ABA, Am. Trial Lawyers Assn., Okla. Bar Profl. Liability Co. (liability ins. com. 1979—, bd. dirs. 1979—, v.p. 1979-85, chmn. bd. 1985-87), Phi Delta Phi. Contbr. articles on law to prof. jours.; co-editor Okla. Bar Assn. Desk Manual, 1976. Personal injury, General practice, Federal civil litigation. Home: 907 Cheryl Circle Lawton OK 73505 Office: Ashton Ashton Wisener & Munkacsy Inc 711 C Ave Lawton OK 73501

ASHTON, ROBERT, lawyer; b. Memphis, Jan. 26, 1937; s. Robert Wilson and Ida Louise (Jones) A.; m. Jean Isabel Willoughby, Mar. 30, 1960; children—Katherine, Susanna, Emily, Isabel. B.A., U. Mich., 1960; LL.B., Vanderbilt U., 1964. Bar: N.Y. 1965. Assoc., Beekman & Bogue, N.Y.C., 1964-73, ptnr., 1973-81; ptnr. Gaston, Snow, Beekman & Bogue, N.Y.C., 1981—; v.p., dir. Conn. Railway & Lighting Co., 1976-80; exec. dir. The Bay Found., 1976—; dir. Josephine Bay Paul and C. Michael Paul Found., 1976-87. Treas., dir. St. Matthew's & St. Timothy's Neighborhood Ctr., N.Y.C., 1973—, The Fund for Artists Colonies, 1983—; trustee Marine Biol. Lab., Woods Hole, Mass., 1980—. Mem. ABA, N.Y. State Bar Assn., Assn. Bar City N.Y. Democrat. Clubs: Broad St. (N.Y.C.); Estate planning, Estate taxation. Home: 574 4th St Brooklyn NY 11215 Office: 14 Wall St New York NY 10005

ASHWORTH, BRENT FERRIN, lawyer; b. Albany, Calif., Jan. 8, 1949; s. Dell Shepherd and Bette Jean (Brailsford) A.; m. Charlene Mills, Dec. 16, 1970; children—Amy, John, Matthew, Samuel, Adam, David, Emily, Luke. B.A., Brigham Young U., 1972; J.D., U. Utah, 1975. Bar: Utah 1977. Asst. county atty. Carbon County, Price, Utah, 1975-76; assoc. atty. Frandsen & Keller, Price, 1976-77; v.p., gen. counsel Nature's Sunshine Products, Spanish Fork, Utah, 1977—; bd. mem., gen. counsel Carbon County Nursing Home, Price, 1976-77. Chmn. Utah County Cancer Crusade Com., 1981-83; city councilman Payson City, Utah, 1980-82, mem. planning commn., 1980-82, mayor pro tem, 1982. Mem. ABA, Assn. Trial Lawyers Am., Southeastern Utah Bar Assn. (sec. 1977), Utah State Bar, SAR, Phi Kappa Phi. Republican. Mormon. Lodge: Kiwanis. General corporate, Private international, Local government. Home: 1965 N 1400 E Provo UT 84604 Office: Nature's Sunshine Products 1655 N Main St Spanish Fork UT 84660

ASHWORTH, JOHN LAWRENCE, lawyer; b. Huntington, W.Va., Apr. 15, 1934; s. W.L.J. and Johnnie (Summers) A.; m. Rosemary L. Baxter, Aug. 10, 1957; children: Julie, Amy, Molly. B.A., Ohio Wesleyan U., 1956; J.D., U. Mich., 1959. Bar: Ky. 1962, Ohio 1960, U.S. Supreme Ct. 1976. Practice in Ashland, 1960-64, Marion, 1964—; staff atty. Ashland Oil & Refining Co., 1960-64. Comment editor: Pages Ohio Revised Code, 1978—. Chmn. Nat. Found. March of Dimes, 1970; chmn. profl. div. Marion County United Appeal, 1970, chmn. employee div., 1971; pres. United Way Marion County, 1972, drive chmn., 1973; mem. Marion City Bd. Edn., 1972-84, v.p., 1977-78, 82, pres., 1978-79, 83; Bd. dirs. Marion County United Community Services, 1970-72; bd. govs. Community Meml. Hosp., 1972-76; trustee Mary Elizabeth Smith Found., 1972-76. Recipient award of merit Ohio Legal Center Inst., 1964. Mem. Am. Bar Assn., Ohio Bar Assn. (past com. chmn.), Ky. Bar Assn., Marion County Bar Assn. (pres. 1973). Baptist. Club: Rotary (pres. Marion 1972-73). Federal civil litigation, State civil litigation, General corporate. Home: 725 King Ave Marion OH 43302 Office: Ashworth & McKinniss 255 Executive Dr Marion OH 43302

ASIJA, S(ATYA) PAL, patent lawyer, engineer; b. Leiah, India, Apr. 26, 1942; came to U.S., 1967, naturalized, 1972; s. Chander Bhanu and Radha Bai (Chugh) P.; m. Madeline Rich Magill, June 1, 1974 (dec. June 1982). Grad. IERE (Lond), Southampton, Eng., 1964; postgrad. diploma U. Wales, Cardiff, 1967; M.B.A., U. Dayton, 1970; J.D., No. Ky. State U., 1974. Bar: U.S. Patent Office 1974, U.S. Supreme Ct. 1978, Conn. 1983, U.S. Ct. Appeals (fed. cir.) 1984. Supr. electronics AEC Radiation Lab. U. Notre Dame, Ind., 1967-68; research & devel. systems engr. NCR, Dayton, Ohio, 1968-71; systems analyst Police Dept., Dayton, 1971-73; exec. dir. MINCIS, State of Minn., St. Paul, 1974-76; systems engr. Sperry Univac, Eagan, Minn., 1977-80; sr. mem. tech. staff ITT, Shelton, Conn., 1980—; advisor Computer Users Legal Reporter, Westport, Conn., 1984—, Yale Sci. Park Legal Clinic, New Haven, 1984—. Author: Software Patents, 1983. Editor newsletter Chasette, 1972. Inventor Swiftanswer, 1977 (3d pl. award 1977), Magicfold, 1976 (2d pl. award 1976). Candidate for Minn. Ho. of Reps., 1976; capt. CAP, 1979-80. Mem. Toastmasters Internat. (able toastmaster 1972, pres. 1972), Minn. Computer Soc. (pres. 1977), IEEE (sr.), Am. Arbitration Assn. (panelist 1972—), Internat. Bar Assn., ABA, Republican. Mormon. Patent, Trademark and copyright, Computer. Home: 7 Woonsocket Ave Shelton CT 06484

ASIMOW, MICHAEL R., lawyer, educator; b. Los Angeles, July 22, 1939; s. William E. and Frieda (Miller) A.; children: Daniel Bryan, Paul David. B.S., UCLA, 1961; LL.B., U. Calif., Berkeley, 1964. Bar: Calif. bar 1965. Asso. firm Irell & Manella, Los Angeles, 1964-66; acting prof. law UCLA, 1967-71, prof., 1971—; cons. Adminstrv. Conf. U.S. Sec., UCLA Faculty Assn.; bd. dirs. Tax Analysts and Advs., Washington. Author: Advice to the Public from Federal Administrative Agencies, 1973. Legal education. Office: Sch Law U Calif 405 Hilgard Ave Los Angeles CA 90024 *

ASKEW, JAMES ALBERT, lawyer; b. Oklahoma City, Oct. 10, 1949; s. James Albert and Verlia Mae (Harlin) A. B.A. in History, U. Calif.-Davis, 1971; J.D., U. Calif.-Berkeley, 1974. Bar: Calif. 1974, various fed. dist. cts. Prin., mng. prin. in litigation Neumiller & Beardslee, Stockton, Calif.; bd. arbitrators County of San Joaquin Superior Ct.; resolutions com. Calif. State Bar, 1980-81. Mem. San Joaquin County Bar Assn. (pres. 1979-80, bd. govs. 1977-79), ABA, State Bar Calif., Assn. Trial Lawyers Am., Calif. Trial Lawyers Assn., Def. Research Inst. Club: Yosemite (Stockton). Federal civil litigation, State civil litigation, Personal injury. Office: PO Drawer 20 Stockton CA 95201

ASMUNDSON, VIGFUS ANTHONY, lawyer; b. Sacramento, Aug. 28, 1936; s. Vigfus Samundur and Aline Mary (McGrath) A.; m. Ruthlane Uy, Oct. 6, 1973; children: Alinia, Irena, Vigdis, Sigrid. AA, U. Calif., Davis, 1956; BA with honors, U. Calif., Berkeley, 1958; LLB, Harvard U., 1961. Bar: Calif. 1962. Assoc., ptnr. Diepenbrock, Wulff, Plant & Hannegan, Sacramento, 1963-71; sole practice Sacramento, 1971-82, 84—; assoc. Downey, Brand, Seymour & Rohwer, Sacramento, 1984; prof. corp. law McGeorge Sch. Law, Sacramento, 1963-67. Mem. Davis City Council, 1968-72, mayor, 1970-72. Served with USAR, 1961-67. Mem. Calif. Bar Assn., Sacramento County Bar Assn., Yolo County Bar Assn., Phi Beta Kappa. Republican. Roman Catholic. General corporate, State civil litigation, Probate. Home: 545 Miller Dr Davis CA 95616 Office: 555 Capitol Mall Suite 1540 Sacramento CA 95814-4687

ASPEN, MARVIN EDWARD, U.S. dist. judge; b. Chgo., July 11, 1934; s. George Abraham and Helen (Adelson) A.; m. Susan Alona Tubbs, Dec. 18, 1966; children—Jennifer Marion, Jessica Maile, Andrew Joseph. B.S. in Law, Northwestern U., 1956, J.D., 1958. Bar: Ill. bar 1958. Individual practice Chgo., 1958-59; draftsman joint com. to draft new Ill. criminal code Chgo. Bar Assn.-Ill. Bar Assn., 1959-60; asst. state's atty. Cook County, Ill., 1960-63; asst. corp. counsel City of Chgo., 1963-71; individual practice 1971; judge Circuit Ct. Cook County, 1971-79; U.S. dist. judge No. Dist. Ill., Eastern div., Chgo., 1979—; mem. part-time faculty Northwestern U. Law Sch.; chmn. adv. bd. Inst. Criminal Justice, John Marshall Sch. Law; mem. Ill. Law Enforcement Commn., Gov. Ill. Adv. Commn. Criminal Justice, Cook County Bd. Corrections; chmn. coms. Commn. Ill. Supreme Ct. Appointments; mem. faculty Nat. Inst. Trial Advocacy, Nat. Jud. Coll.; past chmn. coms. Ill. Jud. Conf. Programs. Co-author: Criminal Law for the Layman-A Citizen's Guide, 2d edit, 1977, Criminal Evidence for the Police, 1972; Contbr. articles legal publns. Served with USAF, 1958-59. Mem. Am. Bar Assn., Am. Judicature Soc., Ill. Bar Assn. (past chmn. coms.), Chgo. Bar Assn. (bd. mgrs. 1978-79), Decalogue Soc. Lawyers (past chmn. coms.), John Howard Assn. (dir.). Jewish. Office: 219 S Dearborn St Chicago IL 60604

ASPERO, BENEDICT VINCENT, lawyer; b. Newton, N.J., Sept. 3, 1940; s. Umberto and Rose (Cerreta) A.; m. Sally Hennen, June 26, 1971; children—Benedict Vincent, Alexander Morgan. A.B., U. Notre Dame, 1962, J.D., 1966. Bar: N.J. 1970, U.S. Dist. Ct. N.J. 1970, N.Y. 1982, U.S. Supreme Ct. 1981, D.C. 1983. Assoc., then ptnr. Meyers, Lesser & Aspero, Sparta, N.J., 1971-76, Benedict V. Aspero, Sparta and Morristown, N.J., 1976-82; ptnr. Broderick, Newmark, Grather & Aspero, Morristown, N.J., 1982—. Trustee, pres. Harding Twp. Civic Assn., 1982-85; trustee Craig Sch. Mem. ABA, N.J. Bar Assn., Morris County Bar Assn., Sussex County Bar Assn. Republican. Roman Catholic. Clubs: Essex Hunt, Springbrook Country, Lake Mohawk Golf, Newton Tennis. Contracts commercial, General corporate, Probate. Address: Broderick Newmark Grather & Aspero 10 Park Pl Morristown NJ 07960

ASPINWALL, DAVID CHARLES, lawyer; b. Denver, Apr. 15, 1955; s. Darrell David and Gwendolyn Beth (Skeels) A.; m. Inez Bussey Merritt, Dec. 5, 1981; children: Courtney Merritt, Johnathan Westbrook. B.Arts and Sci., Denver U., 1977, J.D., 1980. Bar: Colo. 1980. Mem. Dunn, Crane & Burg, Denver, 1980-81, Michael S. Burg, P.C., Denver, 1981-83, Burg & Aspinwall, P.C., Denver, 1983—. Mem. ABA, Arapahoe County Bar Assn., Def. Research Inst., Colo. Bar Assn., Phi Beta Kappa. Democrat. Episcopalian. Insurance, Personal injury, Real property. Office: Burg & Aspinwall PC Regency Tower One 4643 S Ulster #900 Denver CO 80237

ASSAEL, MICHAEL, lawyer, accountant; b. N.Y.C., July 20, 1949; s. Albert and Helen (Hope) A.; m. Eiko Sato. B.A., George Washington U., 1971; M.B.A., Columbia U. Grad. Sch. Bus., 1973; J.D., St. John's Law Sch., 1977. Bar: N.Y. 1978, U.S. Dist. Ct. (so. and ea. dists.) N.Y. 1980, U.S. Supreme Ct. 1982; CPA, N.Y. Tax sr. Price Waterhouse & Co., N.Y.C. and Tokyo, 1977-78; pvt. practice law, N.Y.C., 1978—; pvt. practice acctg., N.Y.C., 1978—. Author: Money Smarts, 1982. Pres. bd. dirs. 200 Block East 74th Street Assn., 1982; bd. dirs. 200 E 74 Owners Corp., 1981—, treas., 1983-84, pres., 1984-85; mem. Yorkville Civic Council, tenant adv. com. Lenox Hill Neighborhood Assn., 1981-82. Recipient N.Y. Habitat/Citibank mgmt. achievement award, 1985. Mem. Am. Bar Assn., N.Y. State Bar Assn., N.Y. County Lawyers Assn., Am. Inst. CPA's, Am. Assn. Atty. CPA's, Inc. Nat. Assn. Accts., N.Y. State Soc. CPA's, Aircraft Owners and Pilots Assn. Clubs: N.Y. Road Runners, Columbia Bus. Sch. (N.Y.). Real property, Personal income taxation, Landlord-tenant.

ASSELIN, JOHN THOMAS, lawyer; b. Manshester, Conn., May 13, 1951; s. Oliver Joseph and MaryRose Mae (Dondero) A.; m. Jereslawa Senczikowska, Oct. 20, 1979; children: Jessica Lynn, Kristina Anne. BA, U. Conn., 1973, JD, 1976. Bar: Conn. 1976, U.S. Dist. Ct. Conn. 1976. Sole practice Willimantic, Conn., 1976—; lectr. Practicing Law Inst. N.Y., Profl. Edn. Systems Inc. Author: Connecticut Workers' Compensation Practice Manual, The Trial Handbook for Connecticut Lawyers; contbr. articles to profl. jours. Grantee Deerfield Found. Mem. ABA (lectr.), Conn. Bar Assn. (exec. com. civil justice sect.), Assn. Trial Lawyers Am., Conn. Trial Lawyers Assn. (bd. govs. 1981—), Phi Beta Kappa, Phi Kappa Phi, Pi Sigma Alpha. Roman Catholic. Avocation: skiing. Personal injury, Workers' compensation. Office: Asselin and Assocs PO Box 1 Willimantic CT 06226

ASTI, ALISON LOUISE, lawyer; b. Phila., July 25, 1954; d. Andrew Paul and Elsie Aileen (Sincavage) A.; m. Charles E. Bienemann Jr., Apr. 20, 1986. BA, Duke U., 1975, MA in Pub. Fin., 1976; JD, U. Md., 1979. Bar: Md. 1979. Assoc. Gordon, Feinblatt et al, Balt., 1979-86, ptnr., 1986—. Mem. ABA, Md. State Bar Assn. (bd. govs. 1986-87), Bar Assn. Balt. City, Womens Bar Assn. Md. (pres. Balt. chpt. 1986—), Balt. City Bar Found. (bd. dirs. 1984-87). Avocations: tennis, water sports, running, skiing, photography. General corporate, Securities, Contracts commercial. Office: Gordon Feinblatt et al 233 E Redwood St Baltimore MD 21202

ASTIGARRAGA, JOSE IGNACIO, lawyer; b. Habana, Cuba, July 20, 1953; came to U.S., 1960, naturalized 1974; s. Jose Agustin and Carolina (Vila) A.; m. Nancy Louise Upchurch, Aug. 11, 1979; 1 child, Carolina. AA with honors, Miami Dade Community Coll., 1973; BBA summa cum laude, U. Miami, 1975; JD magna cum laude, 1978. Bar: Fla. 1978, U.S. Dist. Ct. (so. dist.) Fla. 1978, U.S. Ct. Appeals (5th and 11th cir.) 1981. Chief bailiff Dade County Juvenile and Family Ct., Miami, Fla., 1972-74; law clk.-bailiff 11th Jud. Cir., Miami, 1974-77; with firm Steel, Hector & Davis, Miami, 1978—, ptnr., 1984—; adj. faculty U. Miami Sch. Law, Coral Gables, Fla., 1980-81; legal counsel Cuban Mus. Arts and Culture, 1985. Contbr. article to Dade County Young Lawyers Manual, 1980. Mem. biomedical tech. sci. panel High Tech. and Industry Council, 1984—, health care task force Beacon Council of Dade County, 1984—; adminstrv. hearing officer Dade County Sch. Bd., Miami, 1982—; bd. dirs. Miami Children's Hosp., 1985—, also chmn. quality assurance com., mem. fin. com.; bd. dirs. Miami Children's Hosp. Research Inst., Inc., 1986—, chmn. nominating com.; bd. dirs. Dade County Beacon Council Inc., 1985—. Named Harvey T. Reid scholar U. Miami Sch. Law, 1975-78, Leonard T. Abess scholar, U. Miami, 1974-75. Mem. ABA (com. on comml. fin. services, Uniform Comml. Code com., subcom. on comml. paper bank deposits and payment systems 1984), Fla. Bar Assn. (sec. civil procedure rules com. 1979-84), Dade County Bar Assn. (commr. jud. campaign practices commn. 1986—), Cuban-Am. Bar Assn., U. Miami Sch. Law Alumni Assn. (bd. dirs. 1981—), Greater Miami C. of C. (bd. govs. 1984—, group chmn. econ. devel. sect. 1986—, chmn. biotech task force 1984—, hispanic affairs com. 1984—). Banking, Federal civil litigation, State civil litigation. Office: Steel Hector & Davis 4000 Southeast Fin Ctr 200 S Biscayne Blvd Miami FL 33131

ASTRACHAN, JAMES BARRY, lawyer; b. New Haven, Dec. 25, 1948; s. Edwin Rolland Astrachan and Charlotte (Sherry) Astrachan Greene; m. Patricia Stiefel, May 27, 1973; children—Mark, Tracy. B.S., Bryant Coll., Providence, 1970; J.D., U. Balt., 1974; LL.M. in Tax, Georgetown U., 1978. Bar: Md. Lawyer, IRS, Washington, 1974-75; assoc. Burke, Gerber & Wilen, Balt., 1975-82; ptnr. Hall, Fronk & Astrachan P.A., Balt., 1982-85; ptnr. Astrachan & Landau, P.A., Balt., 1985—; adj. asst. prof. Loyola Coll., Balt., 1980-84; dir. MBR Internat., Inc. Irvine, Calif., TWI, Clinton, Md. Contbr. articles to profl. publs. Served with U.S. Army N.G., 1970-72. Mem. ABA, Md. Bar Assn. Republican. Jewish. Avocation: trout fishing. Corporate taxation, Entertainment, General corporate. Office: Astrachan & Landau PA 326 N Charles St Baltimore MD 20201

ASWAD, RICHARD NEJM, lawyer; b. Niagara Falls, N.Y., Apr. 23, 1936; s. Nejm M. and Najla A. (Anton) A.; m. Betsy Becker, Sept. 22, 1962; children—Richard N., Kristin D. B.A., SUNY-Binghamton, 1958; J.D., Cornell U., 1961. Bar: N.Y. 1962, U.S. Ct. Claims 1981, U.S. Dist. Ct. (no. and we. dists.) N.Y. 1982, U.S. Supreme Ct. Assoc. firm Twining & Fischer, Binghamton, N.Y., 1962; confidential law clk. to Justice Daniel J. McAvoy, N.Y. Supreme Ct., 1963-65; assoc. firm Rosefsky & D'Esti, Binghamton, 1965-68; solo practice, Binghamton, 1968-76; ptnr. firm Aswad & Ingraham, Binghamton, 1976—. Served with Army N.G., 1961-67. Mem. ABA, N.Y. Bar Assn., Broome County Bar Assn., Am. Judicature Soc. Presbyterian. General practice, Banking, State civil litigation. Office: Aswad and Ingraham 46 Front St Binghamton NY 13905

ATALLAH, ALBERT WADI, lawyer; b. Baghdad, Iraq, Apr. 9, 1956; came to U.S., 1959; s. Wadi David and Julia Zia (Kitchoo) A. BBA, U. Mich.; JD, U. Detroit. Bar: Mich. 1981, Calif. 1982, U.S. Dist. Ct. (ea. dist.) Mich. 1981, U.S. Dist. Ct. (so. dist.) Calif. 1983. Assoc. Law Offices of Paul Vincent P.C., Detroit, 1981-82; ptnr. Roehling & Atallah, Detroit, 1984-85; research atty. Macomb Cir. Ct., Mt. Clemens, Mich., 1985—. Mem. ABA, Mich. Bar Assn., Calif. Bar Assn., U.S. Golf Assn. Republican. Roman Catholic. Home: 8741 San Marco Sterling Heights MI 48078 Office: Macomb Cir Ct 40 N Gratiot Mount Clemens MI 48043

ATES, J. ROBERT, lawyer; b. New Orleans, Sept. 12, 1945; s. Loten Arthur Jr. and Eugenia Lea (Carpenter) A. BA, Tulane U., 1967; JD, Loyola U., New Orleans, 1972. Bar: La., U.S. Dist. Ct. (ea., mid. and we. dists.) La., U.S. Ct. Appeals (5th cir.), U.S. Supreme Ct. Prof., chmn. sci. dept. East Jefferson High Sch., Metairie, La., 1967-72; law clk. to presiding justice La. Ct. Appeals (4th cir.), New Orleans, 1972-73; assoc. Kierr, Gainsburgh, Benjsmin, Fallon & Lewis, New Orleans, 1974-78, ptnr., 1979—; lectr. in field; mem. faculty skills, continuing legal edn. programs. Mem. La. Bar Assn. (vice chmn. civil law sect. 1986—, sec., treas., 1985—), Orleans Bar Assn., Jefferson Bar Assn., Fed. Bar Assn., Assn. Trial Lawyers Am., La. Trial Lawyers Assn. (pres.'s adv. com.), Tex. Trial Lawyers Assn. Democrat. Baptist. Avocations: photography, snow skiing, water skiing, hunting, fishing. Personal injury, Admiralty, Federal civil litigation. Home: 1212 Aline St New Orleans LA 70115 Office: Kierr Gainsburgh Benjamin et al 1718 1st NBC Bldg New Orleans LA 70112

ATHERTON, BRUCE DWAIN, lawyer; b. Bethesda, Md., Aug. 24, 1954; s. B.T. and Winnie (Brown) A. BA, U. Louisville, 1976, JD, 1979. Bar: Ky. 1979, U.S. Dist. Ct. Ky. 1979. Law clk. to assoc. judge Ky. Ct. Appeals, Louisville, 1980; assoc. Morgan & Pottinger, Louisville, 1980-83; ptnr. Gallagher & Atherton, Louisville, 1983-85; assoc. Woodward, Hobson & Fulton, Louisville, 1985—; bd. dirs. Ky. Filter Co., Louisville; bd. dirs., sec. Ins. Field Co., Louisville. Mem. 3d Century of Louisville, 1984—; campaign mgr. Judge Robert Breetz, Louisville, 1980. Mem. Ky. Bar Assn. Democrat. Baptist. Contracts commercial, Federal civil litigation, Bankruptcy. Office: Woodward Hobson & Fulton 2500 1st Nat Tower Louisville KY 40202

ATKIN, JAMES BLAKESLEY, lawyer; b. Orange, N.J., Sept. 23, 1930; s. I.C. Raymond and Alice W. (Flanagan) A.; m. Margarita Leen, Jan. 29, 1957 (div. 1972); children: Deirdre Winifred, James Raymond, Blakesley; m. Eva Auchincloss, Aug. 1, 1972 (div. 1976). B.A., U. Va., 1953, LL.B., 1958. Bar: Calif. 1959, D.C. 1981. Assoc. Pillsbury, Madison & Sutro, San Francisco, 1958-66, ptnr., 1967-81; ptnr. Pillsbury, Madison & Sutro, Washington, 1981—; dep. dir. transition team Dept. Energy, Washington, 1980-81; project dir. com. on indsl. orgn. Am. Petroleum Inst., Washington, 1976-80. Trustee Women's Sports Found., San Francisco, 1978-86, Reed Union Sch. Dist., Belvedere-Tiburon, Calif., 1966-68; bd. dirs. Washington Performing Arts Soc., 1982—. Recipient Disting. Service medal Dept. Energy, 1981. Mem. Natural Gas Supply Assn. (chmn legal subcom. 1973-75, chmn. legal subcom. 1981-83). Republican. Episcopalian. Clubs: Bohemian (San Francisco); Union (N.Y.C.); Army and Navy (Washington). Home: PO Box 302 Sperryville VA 22740 Office: Pillsbury Madison & Sutro 1667 K St NW Washington DC 20006

ATKINS, PETER ALLAN, lawyer; b. N.Y.C., June 29, 1943. BA magna cum laude, CUNY, 1965; LLB cum laude, Harvard U., 1968. Bar: N.Y. 1969. Assoc. Skadden, Arps, Slate, Meagher & Flom, N.Y.C., 1968-74, ptnr., 1975—. Contbr. articles to profl. jours. Mem. ABA, N.Y. State Bar Assn., Assn. of Bar of City of N.Y. General corporate, Securities. Office: Skadden Arps Slate Meagher & Flom 919 3d Ave New York NY 10022

ATKINS, ROBERT ALAN, lawyer; b. N.Y.C., Apr. 30, 1944; s. David Atkins and Tabbie Crystal Sas; m. Carol Anne Pierson, Dec. 26, 1966 (div. Aug. 1975); children: Laura, Christopher; m. Mari Beth Loria, May 21, 1982; 1 child, Sascha. BS in Philosophy cum laude, CUNY, 1964; MA in Philosophy, U. Calif., Berkeley, 1967, PhD, 1973, JD, 1979. Bar: Calif. 1980, U.S. Dist. Ct. (no. dist.) Calif. 1980, U.S. Dist. Ct. (cen. dist.) Calif. 1985. From instr. to assoc. prof. philosophy Antioch Coll., Yellow Springs, Ohio, 1968-75; asst. Gordon Lapides, San Francisco, 1979-80; assoc. Erickson, Beasley & Hewitt, San Francisco, 1980—; prof. Union Grad. Sch., San Francisco, 1975—; lectr. U. Calif., Berkeley, 1983—, New Coll. Calif. Sch. Law, 1983—. Contbr. articles to profl. jours. Commr. Berkeley Citizens Budget Rev. Commn. 1985—; mem. adv. bd. U.S.-China Edn. Inst. 1981—; steering com. Bay Area Lawyers's Alliance for Nuclear Arms Control 1982-84, chmn. symposium com., internat. com.; trustee, sec. Ann Martin Ctr. 1982-84; commentator on pub. affairs for radio station WYSO, Yellow Springs, 1971-73, producer children's show 1974-75; mem. adminstrv. council Antioch Coll., 1973-75, chmn. humanities area, mem. Chancellor's Cabinet, 1974-75; mem. Union Grad. Sch. Council, 1979-84. Recipient Am. Jurisprudence award, 1979; Ford Found. grantee, 1969. Mem. Order of Golden Bear. Civil rights, Labor, Personal injury. Office: Erickson Beasley & Hewitt 12 Geary San Francisco CA 94108

ATKINS, RONALD RAYMOND, lawyer; b. Kingston, N.Y., Mar. 8, 1933; s. A. Raymond and Charlotte S. A.; m. Mary-Elizabeth Empringham, June 23, 1956; children—Peter Herrick, Timothy Barnard, Suzanne Elizabeth. B.S. in Econs., U. Pa., 1954; J.D., Columbia U., 1959. Bar: N.Y. 1959. Assoc. Pell, Butler, Curtis & LeViness, N.Y.C., 1959-61, ptnr., 1962-67; ptnr. Bisset, Atkins & Saunders, N.Y.C., 1967—, also Greenwich, Conn., 1982—; dir. Geyer-McAllister Publs., Inc., N.Y.C. Bd. overseers Old Sturbridge, Inc. (Mass.); vice chmn. Lower Hudson chpt. Nature Conservancy, chmn. Mianus River Gorge Conservation Com.. Served to 1st lt. U.S. Army, 1954-56. Mem. ABA, N.Y. State Bar Assn., Assn. Bar City N.Y. Republican. Episcopalian. Club: Univ. (N.Y.C.). Probate, Estate taxation, General corporate. Home: Hobby Hill Farm Mianus River Rd Bedford NY 10506 Office: 437 Madison Ave New York NY 10022 Office: 777 North St Greenwich CT 06830

ATKINS, SPENCER BERT, lawyer, real estate developer; b. Alamogordo, N.Mex., Aug. 20, 1951; s. Spencer Wyatt and Donnetta Jo (Reeves) A.; m. Eve M. Luteyn, Dec. 12, 1970; children: Mardelle, Erinna, Alissandra. BA in Univ. Studies, U. N.Mex., 1972, JD, 1977. Bar: N.Mex. 1981, U.S. Dist. Ct. N.Mex. 1981, U.S. Ct. Appeals (10th cir.) 1981. Asst. dist. atty. 12th jud. dist. State of N.Mex, Alamogordo, 1981-83, dist. pub. defender 12th jud. dist., 1983—; real estate developer Alamogordo, 1979—. Contbr. articles to profl. jours., 1977. Chmn. planning and zoning commn., Alamogordo, 1982-86; vice chmn. Young Dems. Otero County, Alamogordo, 1985, chmn. 1986-87. Mem. Nat. Criminal Def. Lawyers Assn., Delta Theta Phi, Sigma Phi Epsilon. Lodge: Masons. Avocations: music, electronics. Criminal. Home: PO Box 255 Alamogordo NM 88310 Office: State N.Mex Pub Defender Dept PO Box 1766 Alamogordo NM 88310

ATKINS, THOMAS JAY, lawyer, transportation equipment company executive; b. Detroit, Apr. 21, 1942; s. Robert Alfred and Dorothy Irene A.; m. Shirley Roberta Green, Dec. 21, 1968. BS in Engring., Wayne State U., 1965; MS in Engring., Rensselaer Poly. Inst., 1967; JD, San Joaquin Coll. Law, 1979; postgrad. Harvard Law Sch., 1979; MBA, UCLA, 1983. Bar: Calif. 1979. Cons. Ctr. for Advanced Studies, Gen. Electric Co., Santa Barbara, Calif., 1967-70; prin. Central Valley Distbrs., Visalia, Calif., 1970—, Thomas Jay Atkins, P.C., Visalia and Santa Barbara, 1979—, United Motor Supply, Inc., Fresno, Calif., 1986—; chmn. Calif. Merc. Inc., Tulare, 1980—. Recipient research commendation NASA, 1969. Mem. ABA, Am. Mgmt. Assn., Engring. Soc. Detroit. Republican. Clubs: Santa Barbara Yacht; Visalia Country; Regency (Los Angeles), Visalia Racquet. Contracts commercial, General corporate, Real property. Office: PO Box 3744 Visalia CA 93278 also: PO Box 524 Santa Barbara CA 93101

ATKINSON, JAMES PETER, lawyer; b. Jersey City, Sept. 25, 1947; s. James Anthony and Marjorie (Maher) A. BSCE, Worcester Poly. Inst., 1969; MCP, U. R.I., 1974; JD, New England Sch. Law, 1980. Bar: Mass.

1980, U.S. Dist. Ct. Mass. 1981, U.S. Ct. Appeals (1st cir.) 1981. Prin. transport planner Metro Area Planning Council, Boston, 1973-77; program devel. and constrn. contract analyst Mass. Bay Transp. Authority, Boston, 1979-81; asst. dir. legis. office of policy analysis N.J. Dept. Transp., Trenton, 1981-82; asst. to the sec. Exec. Office of Transp. and Constrn., Boston, 1983; asst. legal counsel Mass. Port Authority, Boston, 1983—; cons. White House Com. Rural Transp., Washington, 1978, U.S. Urban Mass Transp., Washington, 1978, Csaplar and Bok, Boston, 1981. Mem. Ward 4 Dem. Com., Cambridge, Mass., 1984—; coordinator transp. group Dukakis Com., Boston, 1982; asst. to policy dir. Kiley For Mayor Com., Boston, 1983. Served with U.S. Army, 1969-71. Mem. ABA, Mass. Bar Assn., Boston Bar Assn., Am. Inst. Cert. Planners, Am. Planning Assn. Roman Catholic. Avocations: tennis, swimming, running, amateur theatre. Real property, Environment, Administrative and regulatory. Office: Mass Port Authority Ten Park Plaza Boston MA 02116

ATKINSON, JEFF JOHN FREDERICK, lawyer, educator, writer; b. Mpls., Nov. 12, 1948; s. Frederick Melville Atkinson and Patricia (Bauman) Atkinson Farnes; m. Janis Pressendo, Dec. 22, 1982; children: Tara, Abigail, Grant. BS, Northwestern U., 1974; J.D. summa cum laude, DePaul U., 1977. Bar: Ill. 1977, U.S. Ct. Appeals (7th cir.) 1977, U.S. Dist. Ct. (no. dist.) Ill. 1978, U.S. Supreme Ct. 1982. Editor, reporter various Chgo. area newspapers and radio stas., 1967-71; assoc., Jenner & Block, Chgo., 1977-80; sole practice, Evanston and Chgo., 1980-83; instr. Loyola U. Law Sch., Chgo., 1982—. Author Modern Child Custody Practice, (2 vols.) 1986; contbr. articles on criminal, family, and constl. law to various publs. Mem. ABA (chmn. child custody com. 1983-84, 86—, mem. publs. devel. bd. 1984—, mem. task force on needs of children 1983-85, mem. research com. 1984—, chmn., 1987—, Merit award 1984, 86), Ill. Bar Assn., Chgo. Bar Assn., Chgo. Council Lawyers, Am. Trial Lawyers Assn., ACLU (bd. dirs. Ill. div. 1972-74), Northwestern U. Coll. Alumni Assn. (v.p. 1987—). Legal education, General practice, Family and matrimonial. Home: 903 S Ashland Ave Apt 107-B Chicago IL 60607

ATKINSON, JOHN BOND, lawyer, military reserve officer; b. Phila., July 27, 1950; s. John Bond and Eve (Adams) A.; m. Susan Goldschmidt, Aug. 11, 1979; children; John Bond, James Townsend. BA in History, U. Pa., 1972; JD, U. Miami, 1975. Bar: Pa. 1975, U.S. Dist. Ct. (ea. dist.) Pa.1975, U.S. Ct. Mil. Appeals 1976, Fla. 1979, U.S. Dist. Ct. (mid. and so. dists.) Fla. 1981, U.S. Ct. Appeals (5th and 11th cirs.) 1981. Assoc. Rawle & Henderson, Phila., 1975-76, Rumberger, Kirk, Caldwell, Cabaniss & Burke, Orlando, Fla., 1979-82, Rumberger, Wechsler & Kirk, Miami, 1984—. Served to maj. JAGC, USMCR, 1976-79, 82-84. Republican. Roman Catholic. Insurance, Personal injury, Military. Home: 1185 Campo Sano Coral Gables FL 33146 Office: Rumberger Wechsler & Kirk 2 S Biscayne Blvd Miami FL 33131

ATKINSON, SHERIDAN EARLE, lawyer, financial and management consultant; b. Oakland, Calif., Feb. 14, 1945; s. Arthur Sheridan and Esther Louise (Johnson) A.; m. Margie Ann Lehtin, Aug. 13, 1966. 1 son, Ian Sheridan. B.S., U. Calif.-Berkeley, 1966, M.B.A., 1971; J.D., U. San Francisco, 1969. Bar: Calif. 1970. Prin. Atkinson & Assocs., fin. and mgmt. cons., corp. and bus. valuations, San Francisco, 1968—; assoc. Charles O. Morgan, Jr., San Francisco, 1972-76; sole practice, San Francisco Bar Area, 1976—. Served with USAR, 1970-76. Mem. Calif. Bar Assn., ABA. Republican. State civil litigation, General corporate, General practice. Office: The Watergate 4 Commodore Dr #227 Emeryville CA 94608

ATKINSON, STEVEN DOUGLAS, lawyer; b. Rockford, Ill., Mar. 12, 1947; s. Donald Epperson and Edith (Wilson) A.; m. Cheri Violet Gill, Mar. 18, 1972; children: Matthew Scott, Melinda Trudi. BA, U. Fla., 1969, JD, 1972. Bar: Fla. 1972, Calif. 1974, U.S. Dist. Ct. (cen. dist.) Calif. 1976, U.S. Ct. Appeals (9th cir.) 1980, U.S. Supreme Ct. 1982. Field atty. Nat. Labor Relations Bd., Los Angeles, 1973-76; assoc. Tyre and Kamins, Century City, Calif., 1976-77; ptnr. Merrill and Atkinson, Newport Beach, Calif., 1977-79; sole practice Newport Beach, 1979-80; ptnr., pres. Atkinson, Andelson, Loya, Ruud and Romo, Cerritos, Calif., 1980—; pres. Elsinore Leasing, Inc., Cerritos, 1982—. Contbr. articles to L.A. Times, Bus. Week. Served to 1st. lt. U.S. Army, 1972-73. Mem. Associated Builders and Contractors (v.p. 1978—, Service awards 1978—), So. Calif. Contractors. Assn., Associated Gen. Contractors, U. Fla. Letterman's Assn. Republican. Methodist. Labor, Construction. Office: Atkinson Andelson Loya Ruud and Romo 13304 E Alondra Blvd Suite 200 Cerritos CA 90701

ATKINSON, WILLIAM EDWARD, lawyer; b. Cleve., Jan. 16, 1939; s. William Edward and Avis (Waterman) A.; m. Sandra Florence Rabe, Sept. 3, 1977; children—Kimberly Jeanne, William Edward. A.B., Dartmouth Coll., 1961; J.D., Harvard U., 1964. Bar: U.S. Dist. Ct. (no. dist.) Ohio 1966. Assoc. Baker & Hostetler, Cleve., 1966-73, ptnr., 1973—; bd. dirs. Capitol Am. Fin. Corp.; corp. sec. Independence BancCorp.; instr. European div. U. Md., 1964-66. Served as capt. U.S. Army, 1964-66. Mem. ABA, Ohio Bar Assn., Cleve. Bar Assn. General corporate, Securities. Office: Baker & Hostetler National City Center Suite 3200 Cleveland OH 44114

ATKINSON, WILLIAM WILDER, lawyer; b. Little Rock, May 18, 1910; s. William Wilder and Mary Byrne (Parrish) A.; m. Josephine Elizabeth Foster, Oct. 20, 1934; children—William Wilder, Richard Foster. B.A., U. N.Mex., 1936; J.D., U. Colo., 1948. Bar: N.Mex. 1948, U.S. Supreme Ct. 1975. Sole practice, Albuquerque, 1948-62; ptnr. Hernandez & Atkinson, Albuquerque, 1962-73; sr. ptnr. Atkinson & Kelsey, P.A., Albuquerque, 1973—. Mem. Albuquerque City Commn., 1955-63, vice chmn., 1962-63; chmn. City of Albuquerque Personnel Bd., 1964-65; mem. Albuquerque Human Rights Commn., 1974-80; del. N.Mex. Constl. Conv., 1969; mem. Gov.'s Task Force on Mcpl. Fin., 1976; mem. U. N.Mex. Governance Adv. Commn., 1970; mem. Albuquerque Community Council, 1963-78, pres., 1964-65; mem. Albuquerque-Bernalillo County Econ. Opportunity Bd., 1965-68, pres., 1967-68; trustee Bernalillo County Mental Health/Mental Retardation Ctr., 1968-73; bd. dirs. Goodwill Industries N.Mex., 1968-84, pres., 1973-76; mem. exec. com. Presbyn. Hosp. Found., 1977-80; bd. dirs. N.Mex. chpt. NCCJ, 1974-79, Sr. Citizens Legal Services, 1984—, Arthritis Found., 1987—. Recipient Brotherhood award NCCJ, 1972. Mem. ABA, N.Mex. Bar Assn., Albuquerque Bar Assn. (pres. 1970-71), Albuquerque Lawyers Club (pres. 1954), U. N.Mex. Alumni Assn. (dir. 1960-66), Order of Coif, Phi Kappa Phi, Phi Delta Phi. Democrat. Congregationalist. Clubs: Optimists, Knife and Fork (Albuquerque). Real property, Probate, General practice. Home: 1637 Kit Carson Ave SW Albuquerque NM 87104 Office: 1300 First Interstate Bank Bldg PO Box 1126 Albuquerque NM 87103

ATLAS, ALLAN JAY, lawyer; b. Bklyn., Jan. 29, 1952; s. Irving Isaac and Julia (Salem) A. B.A., Queens Coll., Flushing, N.Y., 1976; J.D., U. Miami, Coral Gables, Fla., 1979. Bar: Fla. 1979, U.S. Dist. Ct. (so. and no. dists.) Fla. 1979, U.S. Claims Ct. 1979, U.S. Tax Ct. 1979, U.S. Ct. Mil. Appeals 1979, U.S. Ct. Appeals (D.C. and 2d cirs.) 1979, N.Y. 1980, U.S. Dist. Ct. (mid. dist.) Fla. 1980, U.S. Ct. Internat. Trade 1980, U.S. Ct. Appeals (11th cir) 1982, U.S. Ct. Appeals (fed. cir.) 1982. Legal research aide to presiding justice Fla. Supreme Ct., Tallahassee, 1979-80; asst. gen. counsel dept. banking and fin. Office of Comptroller, State of Fla., Tallahassee and Miami, 1980-82; assoc. Schwartz & Nash, P.A., Miami, 1982-84; prin. Allan Jay Atlas, P.A., Miami, 1984—; assoc. Buchbinder & Elegant, P.A., Miami, 1986—. Mem. regional bd. of dirs. Anti-Defamation League, B'nai B'rith, Fla., 1983—; v.p. bench and bar unit B'nai B'rith, 1986—. Named hon. asst. atty. gen. Ark., Atty. Gen. Ark., 1983. Recipient Stojan A. Bayitch Internat. Law Service award U. Miami Sch. Law, Internat. Law Soc., 1979. Mem. ABA, Assn. Trial Lawyers Am., Comml. Law League Am., Acad. Fla. Trial Lawyers, Dade County Bar Assn., Dade County Trial Lawyers Assn., U. Miami Law Alumni Assn. (bd. dirs. 1982—, bd. dirs. 1982-87, treas. 1987—Dade County chpt.), Phi Alpha Delta (dist. justice 1980-84, justice S. Dade County Alumni chpt. 1982-86, dep. internat. justice 1984—, outstanding mem. 1979, outstanding alumnus 1980, 85, justice emeritus, treas. 1986—). Republican. Jewish. Lodge: Masons. Commercial litigation, Banking, Family and matrimonial. Home: 8415 SW 107 Ave #16W Miami FL 33173

ATLAS, MORRIS, lawyer; b. Houston, Dec. 25, 1926; s. Sam and Bluma (Cohen) A.; m. Rita Jeanne Wilner, Aug. 31, 1947; children: Scott Jerome, Debra Lynne Emans, Lauren Teri, Lisa Gayle. BBA, U. Tex., 1948, LLB, 1950. Bar: Tex. 1950. Practiced law McAllen, Tex., since 1950, sole practice, 1953; sr. ptnr., mng. ptnr. Atlas and Hall, McAllen. Mem. U. Tex. Centennial Commn.; trustee U. Tex. Law Sch. Found., 1978—; mem. Gulf Coast Adv. Council on Water Resources, New Century Fund; chmn. fund drive McAllen Internat. Mus.; chmn. Hidalgo County Dem. Exec. Com., 1968-80; del. to 1968 and 1972 Dem. Nat. Convs. Fellow Am. Coll. Trial Lawyers, Tex. Bar Found. (life, dist. 15-B grievance com. 1960-71, chmn. 1963-65, mem. fed. ct. systems study com. 1972-75, chmn. 1974-75, liaison with fed. judiciary, compensation and tenure of state judges 1973-75, co. for new state law ctr.); mem. ABA, Tex. Bar Assn., Assn. Def. Counsel (bd. dirs. 1967), Assn. Ins. Attys., Hidalgo County Bar Assn. (pres. 1960), McAllen C. of C. (bd. dirs. 1955), Rio Grande Valley C. of C. (bd. dirs. 1956), Phi Delta Phi. Jewish. Federal civil litigation, State civil litigation, Contracts commercial. Home: 1600 Iris McAllen TX 78501 Office: Atlas and Hall 818 Pecan McAllen TX 78501

ATLAS, SCOTT JEROME, lawyer; b. Austin, Jan. 15, 1950; s. Morris and Rita Jean (Willner) A.; m. Nancy Ellen Friedman, Mar. 26, 1983; children: Ryan, David. BA, Yale U., 1971; JD, U. Tex., 1975. Bar: Tex. 1975, U.S. Dist. Ct. (so. dist.) Tex. 1976, U.S. Ct. Appeals (5th cir.) 1976, U.S. Supreme Ct. 1979, U.S. Ct. Appeals (11th cir.) 1981. Law clk. to judge U.S. Ct. Appeals (5th cir.), Austin, 1975-76; assoc. Vinson & Elkins, Houston, 1976-82, ptnr., 1982—. Pres., founder Houston Shakeseare Festival, 1980-82; v.p., founder Tex. Lyceum Assn. Inc., 1983-85; exec. com. Alley Theater, Houston, 1983—; bd. dirs. Cultural Arts Council Houston, 1982-85. Named Outstanding Young Houstonian, Houston Jaycees, 1984-85. Fellow Houston Bar Found. (founder); mem. ABA (chmn. appellate practice com. litigation sect. 1985—, antitrust com. 1976—, Pro Bono Publico award 1986), Tex. Bar Assn. (jud. selection com. 1985—, legal aid to indigent com. 1986—), Houston Bar Assn. (litigation and continuing legal edn. coms. 1986—), Tex. Law Rev. Assn. (past pres., bd. dirs. 1977—), Houston Young Lawyers Assn. (Outstanding Young Lawyer in Houston 1983-84). Democrat. Jewish. Club: Yale (Houston) (bd. dirs. 1982—). Avocation: tennis. Federal civil litigation, Antitrust, State civil litigation. Home: 2420 Brentwood Houston TX 77019 Office: Vinson & Elkins 3300 1st City Tower 1001 Fannin Houston TX 77002-6760

ATTERBURY, LEE RICHARD, lawyer; b. Newark, Aug. 25, 1948; s. Harold Blackburn and Annabel Rose (Lee) A.; m. Michana Mosler Buchman, June 5, 1971; 1 child, Alex Blackburn. BA cum laude, Lawrence U., 1970; JD, U. Wis., 1974. Bar: Wis. 1974, U.S. Dist. Ct. (we. dist.) Wis. 1974. Assoc. Callahan & Arnold Law Office, Columbus, Wis., 1974-80; ptnr. Johnson, Swingen, Atterbury, Riley & Luebke S.C., Madison, Wis., 1980—. Note and comment editor U. Wis. Law Rev., 1974. Mem. Dane County Bar Assn., Assn. Trial Lawyers Am., ACLU, The Planetary Soc., Union of Concerned Scientists. Federal civil litigation, State civil litigation, Personal injury. Office: Johnson Swingen Atterbury et al 411 W Main St Madison WI 53703

ATTERMEIER, FREDRIC JOSEPH, lawyer; b. Milw., Mar. 27, 1946; s. Fredric J. and Olga B. (Uldrian) A. BA, Rice U., 1968; MS, U. Houston, 1976; JD, South Tex. Coll. Law, 1975; LLM in Taxation, DePaul U., 1987. Bar: Tex. 1975, U.S. Tax Ct. 1975, U.S. Ct. Appeals (5th, 7th, 10th and 11th cirs.) 1975, U.S. Ct. Claims 1976, U.S. Ct. Internat. Trade 1976, U.S. Supreme Ct. 1979, Ill. 1984; CPA, Ill., Tex., Wyo. Sole practice Houston, 1975-78; tax supr. Alexander Grant and Co., Houston, 1978-79; tax atty. Texaco Inc., Houston, 1979—. Contbr. articles to profl. jours. lectr. continuing edn. programs bar and acctg. groups, Nationwide, 1978—; cooperating atty. Houston Vol. Lawyers Program, 1986. Mem. ABA, State Bar Tex. (tax sect. continuing edn. com. 1983—), Ill. State Bar Assn., Chgo. Bar Assn., Houston Bar Assn. Avocation: raising parrots. State and local taxation, Corporate taxation, Personal income taxation. Home: PO Box 52910 Houston TX 77052 Office: Texaco Inc PO Box 1404 Houston TX 77251

ATTRIDGE, DANIEL F., lawyer; b. Washington, Oct. 4, 1954; s. Patrick J. and Teresa (Glynn) A.; m. Anne Asbill, Aug. 23, 1980; 1 child, James Winchester. BA magna cum laude, U. Pa., 1976; JD cum laude, Georgetown U., 1979. Bar: D.C. 1980, U.S. Dist. Ct. D.C. 1980, U.S. Ct. Appeals (D.C. cir.) 1980, U.S. Supreme Ct. 1983, U.S. Dist. Ct. Md. 1985, U.S. Ct. Appeals (fed. cir.) 1985. Law clk. U.S. Dist. Ct. D.C., Washington, 1979-80; assoc. Kirkland & Ellis, Washington, 1980-85, ptnr., 1985—; mem. Jud. Conf. D.C. Cir., 1982, 86, 87. Exec. editor Georgetown U. Law Jour., 1978-79. Mem. ABA, D.C. Bar Assn., St. Anselm's Alumni Assn. (bd. dirs. 1985—). Roman Catholic. Federal civil litigation, State civil litigation. Home: 6701 Honesty Dr Bethesda MD 20817 Office: Kirkland & Ellis 655 15th St NW Washington DC 20005

ATWOOD, CHARLES STARR, lawyer, consultant; b. Bellefonte, Pa., Jan. 9, 1941; s. Sanford S. and Nora Elizabeth (Long) A.; m. Lois Jean Myers, April 23, 1966 (div. Jan. 1983); m. Rebecca Anne Stanfill, Feb. 19, 1983; children: Jay B., Craig S. BS in Hotel Adminstrn., Cornell U., 1969; JD, Case Western Res. U., 1972. Bar: Wash. 1974. Asst. sec. Westin Hotels, Inc., Seattle, 1973-76; mgr. Papa's Pasta, Inc., Everett, Wash., 1976-77, Alderbrook Inn, Union, Wash., 1977; various positions Holiday Inns, Inc., Memphis, 1978-82; of counsel Gunnar and Assoc., P.C., Portland, Oreg., 1982-84; cons. in field Lake Oswego, Oreg., 1985-87; project officer Internat. Fin. Corp. div. World Bank, Washington, 1987—. Served with USN, 1961-66. Mem. ABA, Wash. Bar Assn., Am. Hotel and Motel Assn. (affiliate), Cornell Soc. Hotelmen. Lodge: Rotary. Avocations: golf, tennis, skiing. Securities, Hotels and motels. Home: 19603 River Run Dr Lake Oswego OR 97034 Office: Internat Fin Corp div World Bank 1818 H St NW Washington DC 20433

ATWOOD, HOLLYE STOLZ, lawyer; b. St. Louis, Dec. 25, 1945; d. Robert George and Elise (Sauselle) Stolz; m. Frederick Howard Atwood III, Aug. 12, 1978; children: Katherine Stolz, Jonathan Robert. BA, Washington U., St. Louis, 1968; JD, Washington U., 1973. Bar: Mo. 1973. Jr. ptnr. Bryan, Cave, McPheeters & McRoberts, St. Louis, 1973-82, ptnr., 1983—. Bd. dirs. St. Louis council Girl Scouts U.S., 1976-86; trustee John Burroughs Sch., St. Louis, 1983-86. Mem. ABA, Met. St. Louis Bar Assn., Washington U. Law Sch. Alumni Assn. (pres. 1983-84). Club: Noonday (St. Louis) (bd. govs. 1983-86). Labor, Federal civil litigation, Administrative and regulatory. Office: Bryan Cave McPheeters & McRoberts 500 N Broadway Saint Louis MO 63102

ATWOOD, JAMES R., lawyer; b. White Plains, N.Y., Feb. 21, 1944; s. Bernard D. and Joyce Rose A.; m. Wendy Fisler, Aug. 22, 1981; children—Christopher Charles, Carl Fisler. B.A., Yale U., 1966; J.D., Stanford U., 1969. Bar: Calif. 1969, D.C. 1970. Law clk. to judge U.S. Ct. Appeals, Los Angeles, 1969-70; law clk. to Chief Justice Warren Burger U.S. Supreme Ct., 1970-71; mem. firm Covington & Burling, Washington, 1971-78; partner Covington & Burling, 1977-78, 81—; dep. asst. sec. for transp. affairs Dept. State, Washington, 1978-79, dep. legal adviser, 1979-80; acting prof. Stanford Law Sch., 1980. Author: (with Kingman Brewster) Antitrust and American Business Abroad, 2d edit, 1981. Mem. ABA, D.C. Bar Assn., Am. Soc. Internat. Law, Internat. C. of C. (vice chmn. air transp. com.), Washington Inst. Fgn. Affairs, U.S. Council for Internat. Bus. (chmn. air transp. com.). Club: Met. (Washington). Antitrust, Private international, Public international. Home: 8020 Greentree Rd Bethesda MD 20817 Office: 1201 Pennsylvania Ave NW PO Box 7566 Washington DC 20044

ATWOOD, RAYMOND PERCIVAL, JR., lawyer; b. Ossining, N.Y., June 25, 1952; s. Raymond Percival and Berniece Lucille (Beach) A.; m. Theresa Carol Goeken, Aug. 13, 1977; children—Shannon, Heather, Sarah, Raymond III, Jennifer. B.S. cum laude, U. Nebr., 1972, J.D., 1974; cert. Trial Advocacy, Hastings Coll. Law, U. Calif.-San Francisco, 1978. Bar: Nebr. 1975, Mo. 1978, U.S. Dist. Ct. Nebr. 1975, U.S. Ct. Appeals (8th cir.) 1979, U.S. Bankruptcy Ct. 1975. Agy. legal counsel Nebr. Workmen's Compensation Ct., Lincoln, 1975-77; staff counsel Hartford Ins. Co., Kansas City, Mo., 1977-78; ptnr. McCord, Janssen & Atwood, Lincoln, 1978-80, Healey, Wieland, Kluender, Atwood & Jacobs, Lincoln, 1980—; educator Lincoln Sch. Commerce, Nebr., 1978-81; dir. legal studies Lincoln Sch. Commerce, Nebr., 1979-81; educator U. Nebr. Coll. Law, Lincoln, 1982—; legal seminar lectr., 1976-86. Contbr. articles to profl. jours. Organizer United Way, Lincoln, 1975-77; campaign chmn. Larson for Legislature, Lincoln, 1984. Mem. ABA (com. workmen's compensation), Nebr. Order Barristers, Nebr. Trial Lawyers Assn., Am. Trial Lawyers Assn. (sustaining), Nebr. State Bar (com. workman's compensation), Delta Theta Phi. Methodist. Club: Lincoln U. State civil litigation, Insurance, General practice. Office: 1141 H St PO Box 83104 Lincoln NE 68501

ATWOOD, RONALD WAYNE, lawyer; b. Eugene, Oreg., Nov. 25, 1950; s. Wayne Riley and Phoebe Hall (Smith) A.; m. Rebecca Ada Youngstrom, Sept. 9, 1978; 1 child, Kira Juda Phoebe. BA, Lewis & Clark Coll., 1973; JD, U. Oreg., 1978. Bar: Oreg. 1978, U.S. Dist. Ct. Oreg. 1978, U.S. Ct. Appeals (9th cir.) 1980. Assoc. Gearin, Landis & Aebi, Portland, Oreg., 1978-79; ptnr. Rankin, Vav Rosky, Doherty, MacColl and Mersereau, Portland, Oreg., 1979—. Contbr. (book) Workers Compensation, 1980. Mem. ABA, Oreg. State Bar, Am. Soc. Law and Medicine, Assn. Workers Compensation Def. Attys. (mem. exec. com.), Mult County Bar Assn., Internat. Brotherhood of Knights of Vine, Oreg. Wine Tasters Guild (cellarmaster, v.p.). Democrat. Presbyterian. Club: City (chair bus. and labor standing com.) (Portland). Avocations: wine tasting, sculling, reading, video. Civil rights, Labor, Workers' compensation.

AUCHTER, JOHN RICHARD, lawyer; b. Springfield, Mass., May 1, 1922; s. Frank and Alfaretta (Thurston) A.; m. Norma Jean Ledger Wood; children: Susan Adrienne (dec.), Richard Hagen, Ellen Laura, John Lovejoy, Sarah Jean. BA, Amherst Coll., 1947; JD, Northeastern U., 1950. Bar: U.S. Supreme Ct. 1964, U.S. Dist. Ct. Mass. 1965. Agt. and title atty. Commonwealth Land Title Ins. Co., First Am. Title Ins. Co.; title atty. Lawyers Title Ins. Co.; ptnr. Auchter, Bozenhard, Socha & Ely and predecessor firms, Springfield and Palmer, Mass., 1959-85; counsel Bozenhard, Socha, Ely & Kolber, West Springfield, Mass., 1985—; sole practice Palmer, 1985—; instr. real estate law Western New Eng. Coll., Springfield, Mass., 1966-69; land ct. examiner, 1956—; justice of peace, 1974—. Contbr. articles to profl. jours. Bd. dirs. Goodwill Industries of Springfield/Hartford Area, Inc., 1952-75, 77—, pres. 1961-67, 73, chmn bd. 1974-75, counsel 1966—; bd. dirs. Alcoholism Services of Greater Springfield, 1973-75, hon. dir. 1975—; bd. dirs. Palmer Ambulance Service, 1984—. Served to cpl. CAC, AUS, 1943-46. Mem. ABA, Mass. Bar Assn., Hampden County Bar Assn., Am. Judicature Soc., Mass. Conveyancers Assn., Estate Planning Council Hampden County, Quaboag Valley C. of C., Inc. (bd. dirs. 1978—, pres. 1978-81, chmn. legis. com. 1981—), Home Builders Assn. Greater Springfield (bd. dirs. 1956-58, counsel). Club: Exchange (Springfield)(pres. 1959-60, bd. dirs. New Eng. dist. 1982-85). Real property, Estate planning, Probate. Home: 32 Country Club Dr Monson MA 01057 Office: 32 Thorndike St Palmer MA 01069

AUCOIN, BARNEY R., lawyer; b. Pasadena, Tex., Oct. 15, 1951; s. Edward and Hazel (Bellon) A. BA in Sociology, McNeese State U., 1974; JD, La. State U., 1982. Bar: La. 1982, U.S. Dist. Ct. (we. dist.) La. 1984, U.S. Dist. Ct. (mid. dist.) La. 1986, U.S. Ct. Appeals (5th cir.) 1986. Law clk. to presiding justice 16th Jud. Dist. Ct., New Iberia, La., 1982-83; assoc. Corne and Aucoin, Lafayette, La., 1983-85, David S. Cook, Profl. Law Corp., Lafayette, 1985—. Recipient cert. of distinction La. Am. Legion, 1986. Mem. La. Bar Assn., La. Trial Lawyers Assn., Lafayette Bar Assn. Democrat. Roman Catholic. Insurance, Personal injury, State civil litigation. Office: David S Cook PLC PO Box 5107 Lafayette LA 70502

AUDETT, THEOPHILUS BERNARD, lawyer; b. Giltedge, Mont., Feb. 12, 1905; s. Joseph Abraham and Katherine Amanda (Johnson) A.; m. Beverly Corinne Lowery, Sept. 21, 1939 (dec.); m. Barbara M. Terini, Nov. 6, 1976 (div. Mar. 1978); 1 dau., Katherine Ann Audett MacCluer. J.D., U. Wash., 1926. Bar: Wash. 1926, Calif. 1964. With U.S. Customs Service, 1930-63, asst. dep. commr., hdqrs., Washington, 1951-63; of counsel Stein, Shostak, Shostak & O'Hara, Los Angeles, 1965—; customs expert with U.S. del. GATT, Geneva, 1956, 61; U.S. rep. on panel of experts on antidumping and countervailing duties GATT, Geneva, 1959, 60; chmn. Interdepartmental Com. for Study Antidumping Legis., Washington, 1962. Served to capt. U.S. Army, 1942-45. Recipient Exceptional Service award Dept. Treasury, 1963. Mem. ABA, Calif. State Bar, Am. Judicature Soc., Assn. Customs Bar. Republican. Club: Los Angeles Athletic. Immigration, naturalization, and customs. Home: 348 S Orange Grove Blvd Pasadena CA 91105 Office: 3580 Wilshire Blvd Los Angeles CA 90010

AUDLIN, DAVID JOHN, JR., lawyer; b. Alexandria Bay, N.Y., July 2, 1957; s. David John Sr. and Eleanor (Vock) A. AB magna cum laude, Eisenhower Coll., 1978; JD, U. So. Calif., 1981. Bar: Calif. 1981, U.S. Dist. Ct. (cen. dist.) Calif. 1981, U.S. Ct. Appeals (9th cir.) 1981, Fla. 1984. Assoc. Memel, Jacobs, Pierno & Gersh, Los Angeles, 1981-84; asst. pub. defender 16th jud. cir. State of Fla., Key West, 1984—. Mem. ABA. Democrat. Episcopalian. Criminal, Civil rights, Jurisprudence. Office: Pub Defenders Office 424 Fleming St Key West FL 33040

AUERBACH, ERNEST SIGMUND, lawyer, ins. co. exec.; b. Berlin, Dec. 22, 1936; s. Frank L. and Gertrude (Rindzkopf) A.; m. Norma Carol Lipscomb, Aug. 21, 1981; 1 son, Hans Kevin. A.B., George Washington U., 1958, J.D., 1961. Bar: D.C. 1962, Pa. 1978, U.S. Dist. Ct. D.C. 1962, U.S. Ct. Appeals (D.C. cir.) 1962, U.S. Supreme Ct. 1971. Atty., So. Ry. Co., Washington, 1961-62; commd. 1st lt. U.S. Army, 1962, advanced through grades to maj., 1968; asst. staff judge adv. 1st Logistical Command, Saigon, Vietnam, 1966-67; internat. affairs div. Hdqrs. U.S. Army Europe, Heidelberg, Ger., 1967-70, chief, 1969-70; resigned, 1970; div. counsel Xerox Corp., Stamford, Conn., 1970-75; mng. atty. NL Industries, Inc,. N.Y.C., 1975-77; asst. gen. counsel INA Corp., Phila., 1977-78, staff v.p. and assoc. gen. counsel, 1978-79, sr. v.p. INA Service Co., 1979-82, sr. v.p. CIGNA Worldwide Corp. div. CIGNA Corp., 1982-84, pres. internat. life and group ops., 1984—; mng. dir. Crusader Life Ins. PLC, Reigate, Eng., 1984-86, chmn. 1986—. Mem. computer systems tech. adv. com. Dept. Commerce, 1974-76. Served to col. USAR, 1970-85 . Decorated Legion of Merit with oak leaf cluster, Bronze Star. Contbr. articles to news and def. jours. Mem. ABA, Westchester-Fairfield Corp. Counsel Assn. Clubs: University, Nat. Arts (N.Y.C.). Private international, General corporate, Public international. Office: CIGNA Worldwide Inc 1600 Arch St JFK 14 Philadelphia PA 19103

AUERBACH, JOSEPH, business educator, lawyer; b. Franklin, N.H., Dec. 3, 1916; s. Jacob and Besse Mae (Reamer) A.; m. Judith Evans, Nov. 10, 1941; children: Jonathan L., Hope B. Pym. A.B., Harvard U., 1938, LL.B., 1941. Bar: N.H. 1941, Mass. 1952, U.S. Ct. Appeals (1st, 2d, 3d, 5th, 7th and D.C. cirs.), U.S. Supreme Ct. 1948. Class of 1957 prof. Harvard Bus. Sch., Boston, 1983—; atty. SEC, Washington and Phila., 1941-43, prin. atty., 1946-49; fgn. service staff officer U.S. Dept. State, Dusseldorf, W. Ger., 1950-52; ptnr. Sullivan & Worcester, Boston, 1952-82, counsel, 1982—; lectr. Boston U. Law Sch., 1975-76; lectr. Harvard Bus. Sch., Boston, 1980-82, prof., 1982-83. Author: (with S.L. Hayes, III) Investment Banking and Diligence, 1986, also papers and articles in field. Mem. editorial bd., Harvard Bus. Rev. Bd. dirs. Friends of Boston U. Libraries; vice-chmn., bd. dirs., mem. exec. com. Eastern br. Shakespere Globe Ctr. (N.A.), N.Y.C., 1983—; trustee Mass. Eye and Ear Infirmary, Boston, 1981—, chmn. devel. com., 1985—; trustee Old Colony Charitable Found., 1976—; mem. adv. bd. Am. Repertory Theatre, Cambridge, Mass., 1985—, also chmn. endowment com. Served with AUS, 1943-46. Decorated Army Commendation medal. Mem. ABA, Mass. Bar Assn., Boston Bar Assn., Assn. Transp. Practitioners, Harvard Mus. Assn. Clubs: Federal, Harvard of N.Y.C., Sky, Grolier, Shop. Administrative and regulatory, General corporate, Federal civil litigation. Home: 23 Lime St Boston MA 02108 Office: Harvard Bus Sch Soldiers Field Boston MA 02163 also Office: 1 Post Office Sq Boston MA 02109

AUERBACH, MARSHALL JAY, lawyer; b. Chgo., Sept. 5, 1932; s. Samuel M. and Sadie (Miller) A.; m. Carole Landsberg, July 3, 1960; children—Keith Alan, Michael Ward. Student, U. Ill.; J.D., John Marshall Law Sch., 1955. Bar: Ill. 1955. Sole practice Evanston, Ill., 1955-72; ptnr. in charge matrimonial law sect. Jenner & Block, Chgo., 1972-80; mem. firm Marshall J. Auerbach & Assocs., Ltd., Chgo., 1980—; mem. faculty Ill. Inst. Continuing Legal Edn. Author Illinois Marriage and Dissolution of Marriage Act, enacted into law, 1977; (with Albert E. Jenner, Jr.) Historical and Practice Notes to Illinois Marriage and Dissolution of Marriage Act, 1980—; contbr. chpts. to Family Law, Vol. 2. Fellow Am. Acad. Matrimonial Lawyers; mem. Ill. State Bar Assn. (chmn. family law sect. 1971-72), ABA (vice-chmn. family law sect. com. for liaison with tax sect. 1974-76). Family

and matrimonial. Home: 2314 Orrington Ave Evanston IL 60201 Office: 180 N LaSalle St Chicago IL 60601

AUERBACH, SHERYL LYNN, lawyer; b. Phila., July 20, 1952; d. Nathan and Rhoda (Silverstein) A.; m. Jerome R. Richter, Nov. 5, 1977; children: Lauren, Jonathan. BA magna cum laude, Wesleyan U., 1973; JD cum laude, U. Pa., 1976. Bar: Pa. 1976, U.S. Dist. Ct. (ea. dist.) Pa. 1976, U.S. Ct. Appeals (3d cir.) 1977. Assoc., mem. exec. com. Dilworth, Paxson, Kalish & Kauffman, Phila., 1977-82, ptnr., 1982—. Mem. ABA, Pa. Bar Assn. (del. 1977—), Phila. Bar Assn. (past chmn. state civil procedures commn.), Phi Beta Kappa. State civil litigation, Construction, Banking. Office: Dilworth Paxsonet al 2600 Fidelity Bldg Philadelphia PA 19109

AUGELLO, WILLIAM JOSEPH, lawyer; b. Bklyn., Apr. 5, 1926; s. William J. and Catherine (Ehalt) A.; m. Elizabeth Deasy, July 1, 1950; children: Thomas, Charles, Patricia, William, Peggy Ann, James. LL.B., Fordham U., 1950; B.A., Dartmouth Coll., 1946. Bar: N.Y. 1951. Individual practice law N.Y.C., 1953-71; mem. firm Augello, Deegan & Pezold, Huntington, N.Y., 1971-78; sr. mem. firm Augello, Pezold & Hirschmann, Huntington, 1978—; treas., dir. Transp. Arbitration Bd., Inc., 1978-81; chmn. accreditation com. Certified Claims Profl. Accreditation Council, Inc., Washington, 1981-85; exec. dir., gen. counsel Shippers Nat. Freight Claim Council, Inc., Huntington, 1974—. Author: Freight Claims in Plain English, 1979, 82; author, lectr.: Course I - The Beginning of Freight Claims - The Bill of Lading Contract, 1979, Course II - Documenting Claims, 1980, Course III - Liability Rules and Shipping/Receiving Practices Affecting Loss, Damage and Delay, 1981, Course IV - Changes in Carrier Liability: Court Decisions, Statutes and Regulations, 1983, Transportation Insurance in Plain English, 1985. Served with USN, 1944-46. Named Nat. Transp. Man of Yr. Delta Nu Alpha, 1980-81. Mem. Maritime Lawyers Assn., Transp. Lawyers Assn., Suffolk County Bar Assn., Assn. Transp. Practitioners, Delta Nu Alpha. Republican. Roman Catholic. Club: Indian Hills Country. Transportation, Administrative and regulatory. Office: Augello Pezold & Hirschmann 120 Main St Huntington NY 11743

AUGUST, ANN, lawyer; b. Cleve., Mar. 17, 1934; d. Charles Joseph and Esther Dorothy (Goffene) A.; m. Thomas James Higgins, May 23, 1981. BA, U. Dayton, 1955; JD, U. Cin., 1958. Bar: Ohio 1958, Calif. 1966, U.S. Ct. Appeals (9th cir.) 1966, U.S. Supreme Ct. 1973. Sole practice Sydney, Ohio, 1958-64; asst. atty. City of Sunnyvale, Calif., 1964-65; assoc. Paul N. McCloskey Jr., McCloskey, Wilson, Mosher & Martin, Palo Alto, Calif., 1965-66; sole practice Palo Alto, 1966-80; ptnr. August & Landay, San Diego, 1980—. Judge Dudley V. Sutphen scholar 1955. Mem. ABA (family law sect.), Calif. Bar Assn. (family law sect.), San Diego County Bar Assn. (arbitration com., client relations and profl. ethics com.), Calif. Trial Lawyers Assn., San Diego Trial Lawyers Assn., St. Thomas More Soc. San Diego, Phi Alpha Delta. Republican. Roman Catholic. Personal injury, Family and matrimonial, Probate. Office: August & Landay Suite 1720 Cen Savings Tower 225 Broadway San Diego CA 92101-5009

AUKLAND, DUNCAN DAYTON, lawyer; b. Delaware, Ohio, July 6, 1954; s. Merrill Forest and Elva Sampson (Dayton) A.; m. Diane Sue Clevenger, Aug. 7, 1982. BA, Va. Polytech. Inst., 1978; JD, Capitol U., 1982. Bar: Ohio 1982, U.S. Dist. Ct. (so. dist.) Ohio 1982. Legal intern Ohio EPA, Columbus, 1982, staff atty., 1982-83, legal cons., 1983; sole practice Columbus, 1983— atty. Clean Up & Recycling Backers of Clintonville, Columbus, 1983—; deacon Overbrook Presbyn. Ch., Columbus, 1986—. Served with JAGC, USAR, 1984—. Mem. ABA, Ohio Bar Assn., Columbus Bar Assn., Assn. Trial Lawyers Am. (winner environ. law essay contest 1980), Va. Polytech. Alumni Assn. Cen. Ohio (pres. 1984—), Ohio Gamma Alumni Corp. (trustee 1983—). Republican. Avocations: golf, home repairs. Administrative and regulatory, General practice, Environment. Home: 353 E Weber Rd Columbus OH 43202 Office: 6500 Busch Blvd Suite 110 Columbus OH 43229-1738

AULD, BRUCE, lawyer; b. Denver, Dec. 30, 1954; s. David and Virginia (Waters) A.; m. Lexa Anne Bond, Aug. 9, 1980. BA, U. Del., 1977; JD, So. Meth. U., 1980. Bar: Tex. 1980. Assoc. Pace, Chandler & Rickey, Dallas, 1980-81; ptnr. Auld & Mansfield, Ft. Worth, 1981-85, Auld, Koenig, Stephenson & Mansfield, Bedford, Tex., 1985—. City councilman Richland Hills, Tex., 1983-86. Mem. ABA, Tex. bar Assn., Northeast Tarrant County Bar Assn., Northeast Tarrent County C. of C. (bd. dirs.). Republican. Methodist. Club: Arlington (Tex.) Amateur Radio (edn. dir. 1985—). Lodge: Rotary (bd. dirs.). Avocations: amateur radio, sailing. Federal civil litigation, State civil litigation, Contracts commercial. Office: Auld Koenig Stephenson & Manfield 1909 Centrel Dr Suite 300 Bedford TX 76021

AULENBACH, W(ILLIAM) CRAIG, lawyer; b. Louisville, June 17, 1951; s. William Francis and Margaret Jean (Cummins) A.; m. Nancy Elizabeth Tovell, Jan. 10, 1979; 1 child, Warren Craig. AS, U. Louisville, 1970, U. Ky., Lexington, 1972; JD, U. Louisville, 1977. Bar: Ky. 1978, Ind. 1978, U.S. Dist. Ct. (we. dist.) Ky. 1978, U.S. Dist. Ct. (so. dist.) Ind. 1978, U.S. Dist. Ct. (ea. dist.) Ky. 1980. Staff counsel Credithrift Fin. Mgmt., Evansville, Ind., 1978-80; assoc. Pallo, White & Prizant, Louisville, 1980-81, Mapother & Mapother, Louisville, 1981-83, Shapero and Assocs., Louisville, 1983—; legal counsel Am. Radio Relay League, Newington, Conn., 1985—. Mem. ABA, Ky. Bar Assn., Ind. Bar Assn., Louisville Bar Assn., Phi Beta Kappa. Democrat. Avocations: amateur radio, electronics. Bankruptcy, Consumer commercial, Communications. Home: 12814 Ledges Dr Louisville KY 40243 Office: Shapero and Assocs 539 W Market St Louisville KY 40202

AULT, CHARLES ROLLIN, lawyer; b. Cleve., Aug. 2, 1923; s. Charles Maurice and LoRena Minnie (Wiswell) A.; m. Janice Mary McLeod, Apr. 9, 1949; children: Charles R., Marcia A., Jonathan M. Student, Brown U., 1941-43; A.B. in Polit. Sci., Case Western Res. U., 1948, J.D., 1951. Bar: Ohio 1951. Assoc. Falsgraf, Reidy, Shoup & Ault, Cleve., 1951-58, ptnr., 1959-71; ptnr. Baker & Hostetler, Cleve., 1971—; dir., officer various privately held corps.; mem. bd. trustees Dyke Coll., 1979—; vis. com. Case Western Res. U., Cleve., 1976-78. Contbr. articles to profl. jours. Pres. Citizens League of Cleve., 1972; v.p., life trustee YMCA, Cleve., 1971—; pres., dir. Eastern Cleve. Rotary, 1968; v.p., trustee Forest Hill Ch. Housing Corp., Cleve., 1971-73. Served to capt. U.S. Army, 1941-45, 51-53. Recipient Soc. Benchers Case Western Res. U., 1981; John Hay fellow, 1941-42. Fellow ABA; mem. Ohio Bar Assn., Bar Assn. Greater Cleve. Republican. Presbyterian. Clubs: Cleve. Playhouse, Cheshire Cheese, Walden Country. Home: 624-7 Fairington Oval Aurora OH 44202 Office: 3200 National City Ctr Cleveland OH 44114

AURELL, JOHN KARL, lawyer; b. Tulsa, Sept. 26, 1935; s. George E. and Maxine (Reagor) A.; m. Janet Brevard Collins, Oct. 1, 1960; 1 child, Jane B. BA, Washington and Lee U., 1956; LLB, Yale U., 1964. Bar: Fla. 1964, D.C 1971, U.S. Dist. Ct. (no., cen. and so. dists.) Fla., U.S. Ct. Appeals (5th and 11th cirs.), U.S. Supreme Ct. Gen. counsel to Gov. State of Fla., Tallahassee, 1979-80; ptnr. Aurell, Fons, Radey & Hinkle, Tallahassee, 1985—. Mem. exec. com., v.p. Yale Law Sch. Assn., 1975-80. Served to 1st lt. U.S. Army, 1956-57. Fellow Am. Bar Found., Internat. Soc. Barristers, Am. Coll. Trial Lawyers; mem. ABA, Fla. Bar (bd. govs. young lawyers sect., 1966-71), Am. Law Inst. Democrat. Episcopalian. Clubs: Biscayne Bay Yacht (Miami, Fla.); Governor's (Tallahassee), Golden Eagle Golf (Talahassee), Yale (N.Y.C.). Federal civil litigation, State civil litigation, Administrative and regulatory. Home: 920 Live Oak Plantation Rd Tallahassee FL 32312 Offcie: Aurell Fons Radey & Hinkle PO Drawer 11307 Tallahassee FL 32302

AURNOU, JOEL MARTIN, lawyer; b. Bronx, N.Y., May 3, 1933; s. Herman Ely and Rae (Soloff) A.; m. Rosemary Arunou; children: Heather, Marshall, Scott. BA, CCNY, 1954; LLB cum laude, NYU, 1959. Bar: N.Y. 1959, U.S. Dist. Ct. (so. dist.) N.Y. 1960, U.S. Dist. Ct. Conn. 1965, U.S. Dist. Ct. (we. dist.) N.Y. 1967, U.S. Ct. Appeals (2d and 3d cirs.) 1968, U.S. Dist. Ct. (no. dist.) Ohio 1971, U.S. Ct. Appeals (5th and 10th cirs.) 1973m U.S. Dist. Ct. (ea. dist.) N.Y. 1976. Law clk. to presiding justice U.S. Dist. Ct. (so. dist.) N.Y., N.Y.C., 1959-60; assoc. Smith, Ranscht & Croake, White Plains, N.Y., 1960-64; ptnr. Greenspan & Aurnou, White Plains, 1964-77; sole practice White Plains, 1977—; judge Westchester County, White Plains, N.Y., 1977. Commr. Human Rights Commn., White Plains, 1972-79. Served with U.S. Army, 1954-56. Mem. Order of Coif. Democrat. Jewish. General practice, Criminal. Office: 50 Main St White Plains NY 10601

AUSER, WALLACE VAN CORTLANDT, III, lawyer; b. Fulton, N.Y., Apr. 16, 1950; s. Wallace Van Cortlandt and Elizabeth Frances (Morin) A.; m. Sharon Lee Trask, May 2, 1981; 1 child, Trevor Trask. BA, Cornell U., 1972; JD, Coll. William and Mary, 1975. Bar: N.Y. 1976, U.S. Dist. Ct. (no. dist.) N.Y. 1976, U.S. Supreme Ct. 1980, U.S. Ct. Appeals (2d cir.) 1981. Assoc. Auser Law Office, Fulton, 1976-80; ptnr. Auser, Sumner & Auser, Fulton, 1980-83, Sumner & Auser, Fulton, 1983—; adv. bd. mem. Ticor Title Guarantee Co., Syracuse, N.Y., 1986—. Mem. N.Y. State Bar Assn., Oswego County Bar Assn., Young Polish Men's Amatuer Edn. Soc. Inc. Repubican. Baptist. Avocation: sports. Real property, Probate, General practice. Home: RR9 Box 79 Fulton NY 13069 Office: Sumner & Auser 226 Oneida St PO Box 549 Fulton CA 13069

AUSNEHMER, JOHN EDWARD, lawyer; b. Youngstown, Ohio, June 26, 1954; s. John Louis and Patricia Jean (Liguore) A.; m. Margaret Mary Kane, Oct. 17, 1981; 1 child, Jill Ellen. BS, Ohio State U., 1976; JD, U. Dayton, 1980. Bar: Ohio 1980, U.S. Dist. Ct. (no. dist.) Ohio 1981, U.S. Supreme Ct. 1984, U.S. Ct. Appeals (6th cir.) 1984. Law clk. Ohio Atty. Gen., Columbus, 1978, Green, Schiavoni, Murphy, Haines & Sgambati Co., L.P.A., 1978; assoc. Dickson Law Office, Petersburg, Ohio, 1979-85 ; sole practice, Youngstown, Ohio, 1984—; asst. prosecuting atty. Mahoning County, Ohio, 1986—. Mem. Am. Trial Lawyers Assn., Ohio Acad. Trial Lawyers, ABA, Ohio State Bar Assn., Nat. Assn. Criminal Def. Lawyers, Mahoning County Bar Assn., Columbiana County Bar Assn., Phi Alpha Delta. Democrat. Roman Catholic. Club: Mahoning Valley Soccer (rep. 1982-84). State civil litigation, Criminal, Personal injury. Home: 310 Ewing Rd Youngstown OH 44512 Office: 14 Boardman-Poland Rd Youngstown OH 44512-4601

AUSTGEN, DAVID MICHAEL, lawyer; b. Gary, Ind., Sept. 4, 1955; s. Ronald E. and Doris M. (Lawson) A. BA, U. Notre Dame, 1977; JD, John Marshall Law Sch., 1981. Bar: Ind. 1981, U.S. Dist. Ct. (so. and no. dists.) Ind. 1981. Assoc. Hand, Muenich & Wilk, Hammond, Ind., 1981-82, John M. O'Drobinak, P.C., Crown Point, Ind., 1983—. Bd. dirs. Cedar Lake (Ind.) Boys Club, 1982—, Boys Club of Northwest Ind., Gary, 1983—. Mem. ABA, Ind. Bar Assn., Lake County Bar Assn., South Lake County Bar Assn., Jaycees. Avocations: running, officiating high sch. athletics. Local government, General practice, Banking. Office: John M O'Drobinak PC 5191 W Lincoln Hwy Crown Point IN 46307

AUSTIN, DANIEL WILLIAM, lawyer; b. Springfield, Ill., Feb. 24, 1949; s. Daniel D. and Ruth A. (Ahrenkiel) A.; m. Lois Ann Austin, June 12, 1971; 1 child, Elizabeth Ann. BA, Millikin U., 1971; JD, Washington U., 1974. Bar: Ill. 1974, U.S. Dist. Ct. (cen. dist.) Ill. 1979, U.S. Ct. Appeals (7th cir.) 1980, U.S. Supreme Ct. 1980, U.S. Tax Ct. 1986. Assoc. Miley & Meyer, Taylorville, Ill., 1974-78; ptnr. Miley, Meyer & Austin, Taylorville, 1978-81; v.p. Miley, Meyer, Austin, Spears & Romano P.C., Taylorville, 1981—. Pres. United Fund, Taylorville, 1980, Christian County YMCA, Taylorville, 1983-85. Named one of Outstanding Young Men Am., 1985. Mem. ABA, Ill. Bar Assn., Christian County Bar Assn., Ill. Appellate Lawyers Assn., Order of Barristers. Democrat. Presbyterian. Club: Taylorville Country (pres. 1985). Lodge: Sertoma (Taylorville pres. 1976). Avocations: golf, photography. State civil litigation, Probate, Real property. Home: 14 Westhaven Ct Taylorville IL 62568 Office: Miley Meyer Austin Spears Romano PC 210 S Washington Taylorville IL 62568

AUSTIN, JOHN DELONG, lawyer, genealogist, judge; b. Cambridge, N.Y., May 31, 1935; s. John DeLong and Mabel Cowles (Bascom) A.; m. Marcia Kay Behan, Aug. 15, 1969; children—John DeLong, Susan Behan. A.B., Dartmouth Coll., 1957; postgrad. U. Minn., 1959; J.D., Albany Law Sch., 1969. Bar: N.Y. 1970. Editorial dir. Glens Falls (N.Y.) Times, 1960-66; sole practice, Glens Falls, 1970-79; law asst. Warren County Judge and Surrogate, 1975-79; law asst. N.Y. State Supreme Ct., 1980-84; judge Warren County Family Ct. (N.Y.), 1984—; instr. Adirondack Community Coll., Glens Falls. Councilman, Town of Queensbury (N.Y.), 1969-71, supr., 1972-74; budget officer Warren County, N.Y., 1974. Served with U.S. Army, 1958-60. Recipient Adminstrv. Law prize Albany Law Sch., 1969. Mem. N.Y. State Bar Assn., Warren County Bar Assn. Republican. Clubs: Mohican Grange, Elks. Editor, New Eng. Hist. and Geneal. Register, 1970-73; contbr. hist. and geneal. articles to various periodicals. Legal history. Office: Warren County Municipal Center Lake George NY 12845

AUSTIN, MARGARET SCHILT, lawyer; b. Buffalo, June 5, 1950; d. Earl Alfred and Mary Margaret (Belk) Schilt; children: Emily Jean, Nathan Earl. BA, U. Mich., 1972, JD, 1979; MA, Northwestern U., 1973. Bar: Mich. 1979. Ptnr. Dobson, Hammond, Griffin, Roach, Ziegelman & Sotiroff, P.C. (and predecessor firm Dobson, Griffin, Austin & Berman, P.C.), Ann Arbor, Mich., 1979—; bd. dirs. Ann Arbor Student Bldg. Industry Program, Inc. Mem. ABA, Mich. Bar Assn. General corporate, Family and matrimonial, Local government. Home: 930 Duncan Ann Arbor MI 48103 Office: Dobson Griffin Austin & Berman PC 500 City Center Bldg Ann Arbor MI 48104

AUSTIN, PAGE INSLEY, lawyer; b. Balt., May 1, 1942; d. John Webb and Sallie Byrd (Massey) Insley; m. William H. Austin, June 10, 1967. BA in Philosophy, Valparaiso U., 1962; MA in Philosophy, Washington U., St. Louis, 1963; postgrad., Yale U., 1963-66; JD, U. Tex., 1977. Bar: Tex. 1977, U.S. Dist. Ct. (so. dist.) Tex. 1978, U.S. Ct. Appeals (10th cir.) 1980, U.S. Ct. Appeals (5th cir.) 1981, U.S. Supreme Ct. 1986. Instr. Yale U., New Haven, 1966-67, U. Houston, 1967-73; assoc. Vinson & Elkins, Houston, 1977-84, ptnr., 1984—. Mem. ABA, Tex. Bar Assn., Houston Bar Assn., Order of Coif, Chancellors. Federal civil litigation, State civil litigation, Antitrust. Home: 7510 Prestwick Houston TX 77025 Office: Vinson & Elkins 1001 Fannin 3300 First City Tower Houston TX 77002

AUSTIN, RICHARD DAVID, lawyer; b. Springfield, Ill., Sept. 13, 1953; s. Daniel D. and Ruth A. (Ahrenkiel) A.; m. Sheryl L. Kroeger, Dec. 20, 1974. BA, Vanderbilt U.; JD, Tulane U. Bar: Tenn., U.S. Dist. Ct. (ea. and mid. dists.) Tenn., U.S. Ct. Appeals (5th, 6th, 11th and D.C. cirs.), U.S. Supreme Ct. Atty. TVA, Knoxville, 1978-83; sr. atty. Combustion Engring. Inc., Windsor, Conn., 1984—. Mem. Order of Coif, Phi Delta Phi. Contracts commercial, Financing, General corporate. Home: 5 Whitman Dr Granby CT 06035 Office: Combustion Engring Inc 1000 Prospect Hill Rd Windsor CT 06095

AUSTIN, ROBERT EUGENE, JR., lawyer; b. Jacksonville, Fla., Oct. 10, 1937; s. Robert Eugene and Leta Fitch A.; div. Feb. 86; children: Robert Eugene, George Harry Talley. B.A., Davidson Coll., 1959; J.D., U. Fla., 1964. Bar: Fla. 1965, D.C. 1983, U.S. Supreme Ct. 1970; cert. in civil trial law Nat. Bd. Trial Advocacy, Fla. Bar. Legal asst. Fla. Ho. Reps., 1965; assoc. firm Jones & Sims, Pensacola, Fla., 1965-66; ptnr. firm Warren, Warren & Austin, Leesburg, Fla., 1966-68, McLin, Burnsed, Austin & Cyrus, Leesburg, 1968-77, Austin & Burleigh, Leesburg, 1977-81; sole practice Leesburg, 1981-83, Leesburg and Orlando, Fla., 1984-86; ptnr. firm Austin & Lockett P.A., 1983-84; ptnr. Austin, Lawrence & Landis, Leesburg and Orlando, 1986—; asst. state atty., 1972; mem. Jud. Nominating Commn. and Grievance Com. 5th Dist. Fla.; gov. Fla. Bar, 1983—. Chmn. Lake Dist. Boy Scouts Am.; asst. dean Leesburg Deanery, Diocese of Central Fla.; trustee Fla. House, Washington, U. Fla. Law Center, 1983—. Served to capt. U.S. Army, 1959-62. Mem. Acad. Fla. Trial Lawyers, Am. Arbitration Assn., ABA, Am. Judicature Soc., Am. Law Inst., Assn. Trial Lawyers Am., Nat. Inst. Trial Advocacy, Def. Research Inst., Fed. Bar Assn., Lake County Bar Assn., Roscoe Pound Am. Trial Found., Kappa Alpha, Phi Delta Phi. Democrat. Episcopalian. Clubs: Timuquana Country (Jacksonville, Fla.); University (Orlando, Fla.). Trial practice. Home: 6300 N Silver Lake Dr Leesburg FL 32788 Office: Austin Lawrence & Landis 1321 W Citizens Blvd Leesburg FL 32748

AUSTIN, THOMAS NELSON, banker, lawyer; b. Athens, Ga., Oct. 7, 1945; s. William D. and Gladys B. (McDaniel) A.; m. Mary Ellen Holbrook, June 9, 1968; children—Ellen Sherman, Lydia Erwin. B.A. in Journalism cum laude, U. Ga., 1966, M.A. in Polit. Sci., 1968, J.D., 1975. Bar: Ga. 1975, U.S. Dist. Ct. (mid. dist.) Ga. 1975, U.S. Ct. Appeals (5th and 11th cirs.). Asst. city atty. Columbus, Ga., 1976-82; asst. v.p., asset mgmt. officer, head asset mgmt. services Columbus Bank & Trust, 1982-86, Columbus Coll. Found., Inc., 1986—. Served with USAF, 1969-72. Mem. State Bar Ga., ABA, Columbus Lawyers Club. Presbyterian. Clubs: Country of Columbus, Rotary, Breakfast. Author: Perceptions of Reapportionment in the Georgia General Assembly, 1968. Banking, Estate planning, Personal income taxation. Address: 1615 18th Ave Columbus GA 31901

AUSUBEL, MARVIN VICTOR, lawyer; b. N.Y.C., June 30, 1927; s. Adolph and Frances (Einwohner) A.; m. Marion L. Levine, Aug. 13, 1955; children: Eric, Warren, Lauren. BA, NYU, 1948; JD, Harvard U., 1951. Bar: N.Y. 1951, U.S. Dist. Ct. (ea. and so. dists.) N.Y. 1956, U.S. Dist. Ct. (no. and we. dists.) N.Y. 1980. Ptnr. Berman & Frost, N.Y.C., 1953-74, Trubin, Sillcocks, Edelman & Knapp, N.Y.C., 1975-84, Fried, Frank, Harris, Shriver & Jacobson, N.Y.C., 1984—. Contbr. articles to profl. jours. Chmn., mem. Planning Bd. Village of Lake Success, N.Y., 1968-87. Fellow Am. Coll. Trial Lawyers; mem. ABA, N.Y. State Bar Assn., Nassau County Bar Assn., Assn. of Bar of City of N.Y. (state legis. com. 1968-70, state cts. and superior jurisdiction com. 1971-74, fed. cts. com. 1974-77, judiciary com. 1982—, profl. and jud. ethics 1986—), N.Y. County Young Lawyers Assn. (aeronautical law com. 1971-78), Fed. Bar Council, Am. Judicature Soc., Am. Law Inst., Scribes, Phi Beta Kappa. Federal civil litigation, State civil litigation, Insurance. Home: 8 Grenfell Dr Great Neck NY 11020 Office: Fried Frank Harris Shriver & Jacobson 1 New York Plaza New York NY 10004

AUTEN, DAVID CHARLES, lawyer; b. Phila., Apr. 4, 1938; s. Charles Raymond and Emily Lillian (Dickel) A.; m. Suzanne Crozier Plowman, Feb. 1, 1969; children: Anne Crozier, Meredith Smedley. B.A., U. Pa., 1960, J.D., 1963. Bar: Pa. 1963. Mng. ptnr. firm Reed Smith Shaw & McClay (and predecessor), Phila., 1963—. Author articles in field. Vice pres. Northeast Community Mental Health Center, 1971-72; vice chmn. alumni ann. giving U. Pa., 1975-77, 81-82, chmn. alumni ann. giving, 1982-84, trustee, 1977-80, 83—; pres. Gen. Alumni Soc., 1977-80; chmn. Benjamin Franklin Assos., 1975-77, 81-82; trustee Springside Sch., 1985—; pres. Soc. of Coll., 1975-77; v.p. Assn. Republicans for Educated Action, 1971-79; bd. mgrs. Presbyn.-U. Pa. Med. Center, 1980—, vice chmn., 1983-85; bd. mgrs. Phila. City Inst., 1981—, Kearsley Home, 1974—; bd. mgrs. St. Peter's Sch., 1975—, pres., 1978-79. Mem. ABA, Pa. Bar Assn. (vice chmn. real property sect. 1985—), Phila. Bar Assn. (vice chmn. young lawyers sect. 1971-72), Juristic Soc. (pres.), Interfrat. Alumni Council U. Pa. (pres. 1970-74), Phi Beta Kappa, Theta Xi (pres. 1974-76, chmn. found. 1977-86). Episcopalian (vestryman). Clubs: Rittenhouse (pres.), Union League (bd. dirs.), Fourth St., Philadelphia, Philadelphia Cricket. Home: 120 Delancey St Philadelphia PA 19106 Office: Reed Smith Shaw & McClay 1600 Ave of the Arts Bldg Broad and Chestnut Sts Philadelphia PA 19107

AUTHER, JERI LYNN KISHIYAMA, lawyer; b. Phoenix, Mar. 30, 1955; d. Charles Y. and Barbara Geraldine (Howard) K.; m. David Charles Auther, Mar. 26, 1983; 1 child, Claire. BS in Polit. Sci., Ariz. State U., 1977, JD, 1980. Bar: Ariz. 1981, U.S. Dist. Ct. Ariz. 1981, U.S. Ct. Appeals (9th cir.) 1981. Atty. Ariz. Atty. Gen.'s Office, Phoenix, 1981-85; assoc. Tower, Byrne & Beaugureau, Phoenix, 1985-86; sole practice Phoenix, 1986—. Mem. Jr. League Phoenix, 1986, Ariz. State U. Student Relations Com., Tempe, 1983-85. Mem. ABA (govt. litigation sect.), Ariz. Bar Assn. (writer Ariz. Legal Skills 1985-86, vol. disciplinary counsel 1986), Maricopa County Bar Assn. (med.-legal com. 1984-85), Assn. Trial Lawyers Am., Def. Research Inst., Phoenix Assn. Def. Counsel, Exec. Bus. and Profl. Women, Ariz. State U. Alumni Assn. (bd. dirs. 1986), Delta Gamma (panhellenic rep. 1984-85, advisor 1985—). Democrat. Roman Catholic. Avocations: snowskiing, sailing, jogging, needlepoint. Personal injury, State civil litigation, Federal civil litigation.

AUTIN, DIANA MARIE THERESE KATHERINE, lawyer, educator; b. Golden Meadow, La., Sept. 16, 1954; d. Alphonse Adam and Lorraine (Leydecker) A.; m. W. Keith Hefner, Sept. 15, 1979; 1 child, Peter Richard Lefas Autin-Hefner. BA, U. Mich., 1974, JD, 1977. Bar: Mich. 1977, U.S. Dist. Ct. (ea. dist.) Mich. 1978, N.Y. 1982. Atty. Transp. Employees Union, Ann Arbor, Mich., 1977-79; atty., asst. dir. Downtown Welfare Adv. Ctr., N.Y.C., 1979-81; exec. dir. Fund Open Info. Accountability, Inc., N.Y.C., 1981-84; dep. gen. counsel N.Y.C. Bur. Labor Services, 1984—; adj. prof. Indsl. Labor Relations Sch. Cornell U.; apptd. mem. Mich. Ad Hoc Com. Juvenile Justice, Ann Arbor, 1978. Author: Young People and Law, 1979; also articles. Named Woman to Watch in the 1980's, Mademoiselle Mag., 1982. Mem. N.Y. Women's Bar Assn., Assn. Trial Lawyers Am., N.Y. Trial Lawyers Assn., Nat. Lawyers Guild (cons. 1984). Civil rights, Labor, Juvenile. Home: 650 Warren St Brooklyn NY 11217 Office: NYC Bur of Labor Services 66 Leonard St 4th Floor New York NY 10013

AVANT, GRADY, JR., lawyer; b. New Orleans, Mar. 1, 1932; s. Grady and Sarah (Rutherford) A.; m. Katherine Willis Yancey, Feb. 23, 1963; children: Grady M., Mary Willis Yancey. B.A. magna cum laude, Princeton U., 1954; J.D., Harvard U., 1960. Bar: N.Y. 1961, Ala. 1962, Mich. 1972. Assoc. Bradley, Arant, Rose & White, Birmingham, Ala., 1961-63; assoc., ptnr. Long, Preston, Kinnaird & Avant, Detroit, 1972—. Contbr. articles to legal jours. Served to lt. USMC, 1954-57. Mem. Am. Law Inst., ABA (antitrust sect., corp., fin. and bus. law sect., fed. regulation of securities com.), State Bar of Mich. (council sect. antitrust law 1978-85, chmn. sect. 1983-84), Detroit Com. on Fgn. Relations (exec. com. 1979—, chmn. 1986—). Episcopalian. Clubs: Grosse Pointe, Detroit Athletic; Mountain Brook (Ala.); Knickerbocker (N.Y.C.); Metropolitan (Washington); Princeton of Mich. (pres. 1976-77). Securities, Antitrust. Home: 406 Lincoln Rd Grosse Pointe MI 48230 Office: Long Preston Kinnaird & Avant 4300 Penobscot Bldg Detroit MI 48226

AVERY, BRUCE EDWARD, military officer, lawyer; b. Boonville, N.Y., Aug. 16, 1949; s. Edward Cecil and Marian Alma (Pierce) A.; m. Margaret Calvert, June 21, 1969; children: Sarah, Prudence. BA in Sociology, Polit. Sci., Hobart Coll., 1971; JD, U. Louisville, 1976. Bar: Ky. 1976, U.S. Ct. Mil. Appeals 1977, U.S. Army Ct. Mil. Rev. 1984, U.S. Supreme Ct. 1984. Researcher U.S. Army Research Inst., Ft. Knox, Ky., 1972-76, atty., 1976-77; atty. U.S. Army, Camp Zama, Japan, 1977-80, U.S. Army Recruiting, Ft. Meade, Md., 1980-83, U.S. Army Claims Service, Ft. Meade, Md., 1984-87, U.S. Armed Forces Claims Service, Seoul, Korea, 1987—. Mem. Ft. Knox Bd. Edn., Ky., 1975-76. Served to maj. U.S. Army, 1971—. Mem. ABA, Fed. Bar Assn., Assn. Trial Lawyers Am., Assn. of U.S. Army. Personal injury, Military, Public international.

AVERY, DARRELL ROBERT, lawyer; b. San Antonio, Aug. 22, 1957; s. Durward Robert Jr. and Frances (Miles) A.; m. Donna Marie Robinson, June 21, 1985. BS, La. Tech. U., 1979; JD, La. State U., 1982. Bar: :a. 1982, U.S. Ct. Appeals (5th cir.) 1983, U.S. Dist. Ct. (we. dist.) La. 1984. Assoc. Culpepper, Teat & Caldwell, Jonesboro, La., 1982-83; ptnr. Culpepper, Teat, Caldwell & Avery, Jonesboro, 1983—. Named one of Outstanding Young Men in Am., 1986. Mem. ABA, Assn. Trial Lawyer Am., La. Trial Lawyers Assn., Bar Assn. U.S. Ct. Appeals (5th cir.), Jackson Parish Bar Assn. (treas. 1983—). Democrat. Baptist. Lodge: Kiwanis (v.p. Jonesboro 1985-86, pres. 1986—). General practice. Home: PO Box 306 Jonesboro LA 71251 Office: Culpepper Teat Caldwell & Avery 525 E Court Jonesboro LA 71251

AVERY, JAMES THOMAS, III, management consultant, lawyer; b. Richmond, Va., July 21, 1945; s. James Thomas Jr. and Hester Vail (Kraemer) A.; m. Nancy Carolyn Hoag, June 22, 1968; children: James Thomas IV, Carolyn Sears, John Dolph II. AB magna cum laude, Princeton U., 1967; MBA, JD, Harvard U., 1975. Bar: Mass. 1975, U.S. Dist. Ct. Mass. 1975, U.S. Ct. Appeals (1st cir.) 1975. Assoc. Choate, Hall & Stewart, Boston, 1975-79; dir. Cambridge (Mass.) Research Inst., 1979-85; pres. The Avery Co., Boston, 1985—; bd. dirs. Boston Pub. Co. Treas. All Saints Ch., Brookline, Mass., 1976-78; vestry Ch. of the Redeemer, Chestnut Hill, Mass., 1985—. Served to capt. U.S. Army, 1967-71, Vietnam. Decorated Bronze Star, Air medal. Mem. ABA, Phi Beta Kappa. Republican. Episcopalian. Clubs: Somerset, Harvard, The Second (trustee, sec. 1980-85) (Boston). Avocations: tennis, golf, skiing. Antitrust, General corporate, Securities.

AVERY, MICHAEL AARON, lawyer; b. Chgo., Dec. 5, 1944; s. B. Leonard and June Ethel (Monroe) A.; m. Margaret A. O'Reilly; children: Katherine Jeanne, David Monroe. BA, Yale U., 1966, LLB, 1970. Bar: Conn. 1970, U.S. Dist. Ct. Conn. 1970, U.S. Ct. Appeals (2d cir.) 1972, Mass. 1977, U.S. Dist. Ct. Mass. 1977, U.S. Supreme Ct. 1978, U.S. Ct. Appeals (1st cir.) 1979, U.S. Ct. Appeals (4th and 9th cirs.) 1984. Staff atty. ACLU, Conn., 1970-71; ptnr. Roraback, Williams & Avery, New Haven, 1971-74, Williams, Avery & Wynn, New Haven, 1974-77; sole practice Boston, 1977-84; ptnr. Avery & Friedman, Boston, 1984—; mem. adj. faculty Northeastern U., 1977—. Author: Police Misconduct Law and Litigation, 1978. Bd. dirs. Civil Liberties Mass. Mem. Nat. Lawyers Guild. Civil rights, Criminal, Personal injury. Office: Avery & Friedman 6 Beacon St Boston MA 02110-0008

AVERY, PATRICIA I., lawyer; b. N.Y.C., Nov. 3, 1951; s. Anthony J. and Dorothy F. (Irish) A. BA, NYU, 1973, JD, 1976. Bar: N.Y. 1977, U.S. Dist. Ct. (so. and ea. dists.) N.Y. 1977, U.S. Ct. Appeals (2d cir.) 1978, U.S. Dist. Ct. (no. dist.) Tex. 1979, U.S. Ct. Appeals (9th cir.) 1979, U.S. Supreme Ct. 1980. Assoc. with firm N.Y.C., 1976-82; assoc. Wolf Popper Ross Wolf & Jones, N.Y.C., 1982-86, ptnr., 1986—. Mem. ABA, N.Y. County Lawyers Assn. Avocations: zoology, travel. Federal civil litigation, Securities, State civil litigation. Office: Wolf Popper Ross Wolf & Jones 845 3d Ave New York NY 10022

AVNER, JUDITH I., lawyer; b. N.Y.C., Mar. 19, 1952. BA in Polit. Sci. cum laude, SUNY, Albany, 1972; JD, Antioch Sch. Law, 1975. Bar: D.C. 1976, U.S. Dist. Ct. D.C. 1976, U.S. Ct. Appeals (D.C. cir.) 1976, U.S. Ct. Mil. Appeals 1977, U.S. Supreme Ct. 1980, N.Y. 1984. Assoc. Drew & Garfinkle, Washington, 1976-78; asst. to Congresswoman Elizabeth Holtzman N.Y.C., 1978-79; atty. NOW Legal Def. and Edn. Fund, N.Y.C., 1979-84; asst. dir. NOW Legal Def. and Edn. Fund, Albany, N.Y., 1984-85; dir. div. for women State of N.Y., Albany, 1985—; lectr. various law schs. and colls., 1976—. Contbr. numerous articles to profl. jours. Mem. adv. com. Inst. on Women and Work Cornell U., adv. com. Nat. Ctr. Women and Family Law, adv. bd. Inst. on Women and Work, adv. bd. Paralegal Studies Program Marymount Manhattan Coll., N.Y.C. Commn. on Status of Women, Manhattan Women's Polit. Caucus. Named one of Outstanding Young Women of Am., 1979, 80. Mem. ABA (family law sect., individual rights and responsibilities sect.), N.Y. Women's Bar Assn. (rec. sec. 1985-86, matrimonial law com.), N.Y. State Bar Assn., D.C. Bar Assn., Assn. of Bar of City of N.Y. (sex and law com.), Women's Legal Def. Fund, NOW, Sierra Club, SUNY Alumni Assn. (chairperson council 1981-85, vice chairperson ann. fund 1982-85, bd. dirs. 1981-85). Family and matrimonial. Office: State of NY Div for Women Exec Chamber Albany NY 12224

AXELRAD, DAVID M., lawyer; b. Salt Lake City, Mar. 5, 1950; s. Robert Gabriel and Ruth Grace (Axelrath) A.; m. Liza Felice Bercovici, Aug. 10, 1980; children: Joseph David, Gabriella Elizabeth. BA, Stanford U., 1972; JD, U. Calif., San Francisco, 1977. Bar: Calif. 1977, U.S. Ct. Appeals (9th cir.) 1978, U.S. Dist. Ct. Calif. (cen. dist.) 1982, U.S. Supreme Ct. 1983. Staff atty. U.S. Ct. Appeals, San Francisco, 1977-78; staff atty. FTC, Washington, 1978-81, asst. to dir. bur. of consumer protection, 1981; assoc. McKenna, Connor & Cuneo, Los Angeles, 1981-82, Horvitz & Levy, Los Angeles, 1982-85; ptnr. Horvitz, Levy & Amerian, Los Angeles, 1986—. Mem. ABA, Los Angeles County Bar Assn. Federal civil litigation, State civil litigation. Office: Horvitz Levy & Amerian 16000 Ventura Blvd # 401 Encino CA 91436

AXELROD, CHARLES PAUL, lawyer; b. N.Y.C., Oct. 23, 1941; s. Abraham and Lillian Rose (Neidetch) A.; m. Gail Y. Buksbaum, June 24, 1965; children: Seth Jordan, Tracy Brooke. BS, NYU, 1963; JD, Bklyn. Law Sch., 1966. Bar: N.Y. 1966, U.S. Ct. Appeals (2d cir.) 1967, U.S. Dist. Ct. (so. dist.) N.Y. 1970, U.S. Supreme Ct. 1974, U.S. Dist. Ct. (ea. dist.) N.Y. 1975, U.S. Ct. Appeals D.C. 1979. Assoc. Kane, Kessler & Proujansky, N.Y.C., 1970-72, Law Offices of Richard Frank P.C., N.Y.C., 1972-79; ptnr. Goldstein & Axelrod, N.Y.C., 1980—; chmn. legis. sub-com. study of securities laws N.Y. State Assembly, 1972; bd. dirs. Temco Home Health Care Products Inc.; adj. prof. law Pace U., Pleasantville, N.Y., 1976-77. Vol. atty. City of N.Y. Com. on Human Rights, 1972. Mem. ABA, N.Y. State Trial Lawyers Assn., N.Y. County Lawyers Assn., N.Y. State Bar Assn. Democrat. Jewish. Lodge: B'Nai Brith. Securities, General corporate, Contracts commercial. Office: Goldstein & Axelrod 369 Lexington Ave New York NY 10017

AXELROD, JONATHAN GANS, lawyer; b. N.Y.C., Oct. 23, 1946; s. Arthur and Rosalind (Gans) A.; m. Carol Jean Zachary, Jan. 16, 1983; children: Zachary Arthur, Tristan Gans. A.B. Dartmouth Coll. 1968; J.D. Columbia U. 1971; LL.M. in Labor Law George Washington U. 1975. Bar: N.Y. 1971, D.C. 1975. Trial atty. App. ct. br. NLRB 1971-74; asst. gen. csl. Ea. Conf. Teamsters 1974-80; ptnr. Beins, Axelrod & Osborne, P.C., Washington 1980—. Mem. ABA, Fed. Bar Assn. Contbr. articles to legal publs. Labor, Federal civil litigation. Office: 1200 15th St NW Suite 505 Washington DC 20005

AXELSON, JEFFREY MARK, lawyer; b. N.Y.C., Oct. 20, 1951; s. Hyman Morris and Rose (Shanes) A.; m. Justine Elizabeth Wilcox, May 22, 1982. AB, Colgate U., 1972; JD, Am. U., 1975. Bar: Md. 1975, D.C. 1977, U.S. Dist. Ct. D.C. 1977, U.S. Dist. Ct. Md. 1977, U.S. Ct. Appeals (D.C. cir.) 1977, U.S. Supreme Ct. 1980, Fla. 1981, U.S. Ct. Appeals (4th cir.) 1982. Assoc. Schwarzbach & Wortman, Washington, 1976-78; ptnr. Axelson & Williamowsky, Rockville, Md., 1978-80, Van Grack, Axelson & Williamowsky, Rockville, 1980—. Mem. Homeowner Assn. task force Montgomery County Council, Rockville, 1983-85; bd. dirs. Washington Met. chpt. Community Assns. Inst., 1976-84. Mem. Md. Bar Assn., Montgomery County Bar Assn. (chmn. comml. law and banking sect.), Atty. Grievance Commn. of Md. General corporate, Contracts commercial, Condominium homeowner association. Home: 10310 Snowpine Way Potomac MD 20854 Office: Van Grack Axelson & Williamowsky 110 N Washington St Suite 404 Rockville MD 20850

AXINN, STEPHEN MACK, lawyer; b. N.Y.C., Oct. 21, 1938; s. Mack N. and Lili H. (Tannenbaum) A.; m. Stephanie Chertok, May 12, 1963; children: Audrey, David, Jill. BS, Syracuse U., 1959; LLB, Columbia U., 1962. Bar: N.Y. 1962, U.S. Supreme Ct. 1962. Assoc. Cahill & Gordon, N.Y.C., 1963-64, Malcolm A. Hoffman, N.Y.C., 1964-66; assoc. Skadden, Arps, Slate, Meagher & Flom, N.Y.C., 1966-69, ptnr., 1970—; adj. prof. NYU Law Sch., 1981-83. Author: Acquisitions Under H-S-R, 1980; contbr. articles to profl. jours. Chmn. lawyers div. United Jewish Appeal, N.Y.C., 1985—. Served to capt. U.S. Army, 1965-68. Mem. ABA (council antitrust sect. 1983-85), N.Y. State Bar Assn. (chmn. antitrust sect. 1982-83). Antitrust, Securities, Federal civil litigation. Office: Skadden Arps Slate Meagher & Flom 919 3rd Ave New York NY 10022

AXLEY, FREDERICK WILLIAM, lawyer; b. Chgo., June 23, 1941; s. Frederick R. and Elena (Hoffman-Pinther) A.; m. Cinda Jane Russell, Apr. 29, 1969; children: Sarah Elizabeth, Elizabeth Jane. BA, Holy Cross Coll., 1963; MA, U. Wis., 1966; JD, U. Chgo., 1969. Bar: Ill. 1969, U.S. Dist. Ct. (no. dist.) Ill. 1969, U.S. Ct. Appeals (7th cir.) 1970. Assoc. McDermott, Will & Emery, Chgo., 1969-74, jr. ptnr., 1974-80, sr. ptnr., 1980—. Trustee Wilmette Elem. Sch. Dist. #39, Ill., 1976-81, Ill. chpt. Nature Conservnacy, 1983—; bd. dirs. Bus. and Profl. People for the Pub. Interest, Chgo., 1984—. Served to lt. USN, 1963-65. Democrat. Roman Catholic. Club: Union League (Chgo.). General corporate, Securities. Home: 112 Lawndale Ave Wilmette IL 60091 Office: McDermott Will & Emery 111 W Monroe St Chicago IL 60603

AYCOCK, FELIX ALFRED, lawyer; b. San Antonio, June 14, 1933; s. Felix Alfred Sr. and Ellen Antoinette (Dimeline) A.; m. Nancy Becker, Mar. 17, 1957 (div.); children: Lindy Lou, Daniel Alan, Susan Lynn; m. Linnea Marie Nunn. AA, Fresno City Coll., 1957; BS with highest honors, Calif. State U., 1959; JD, San Francisco Law Sch., 1963. Bar: Calif. 1964, Iowa 1973. Sole practice Fresno, Calif. and Oxford, Iowa, 1964-73, 1977-78; farmer South Amana, Iowa, 1973-77; ptnr. Hanna, Brophy, MacLean, McAleer & Jensen, Oakland and Fresno, Calif., 1978—; dep. U.S. Marshal U.S. Dept. Justice, San Francisco, 1961-62. Contbr. articles on discrimination and workers' compensation to Los Angeles Daily Journal. Served with USN, 1950-54. Recipient Letters of Commendation from Pres. John Kennedy and Atty. Gen. Robert Kennedy, 1962. Mem. ABA, Iowa Bar Assn., Calif. Bar Assn., Fresno Bar Assn., Phi Kappa Phi. Avocations: sailing, fishing. Workers' compensation, Labor, Insurance. Office: Hanna Brophy MacLean McAleer & Jensen PO Box 1312 Fresno CA 93715

AYCOCK, WILLIAM ROBERT, lawyer; b. Trenton, Mich., July 6, 1950; s. Benjamin F. and Esther L. (Limon) A.; m. Doris Aston, June 17, 1972 (div. May 1982); 1 child, Kristen G. B.B.A. cum laude, Eastern Mich. U., 1971; J.D. cum laude, Ohio State U., 1974. Bar: Mich. 1975, U.S. Dist. Ct. (ea. dist.) Mich. 1975, U.S. Supreme Ct. 1980. Assoc., D'Avanzo & Danko, Southgate, Mich., 1974-77; ptnr. D'Avanzo, Danko & Aycock, 1978-82; prin. William R. Aycock & Assocs., P.C., Lincoln Park, Mich., 1982—; dir. Actron Security Alarm Systems, Inc. adj. prof. law U. Detroit Sch. Law. Mem. ABA, State Bar Mich., Downriver Bar Assn., Stoic Hon. Soc. Republican. Roman Catholic. Clubs: Grosse Ile Golf and Country (house com. 1981-82); Detroit Athletic. General corporate. Home: 22037 W River Rd Grosse Ile MI 48138 Office: William R Aycock & Assocs PC 2868 Fort St Lincoln Park MI 48146

AYLSWORTH, ROBERT REED, lawyer; b. Evansville, Ind., Oct. 24, 1953; s. Robert Earl and Loraine L. (Simmons) A.; m. Carolyn Sue Cundiff, Mar. 6, 1976; children—Beth Anne, Benjamin Reed. B.S., Ind. State U.-Evansville, 1976; J.D. magna cum laude, Ind. U.-Indpls., 1979. Bar: Ind. 1979, U.S. Dist. Ct. (so. dist.) Ind. 1979. Assoc. Phillips and Long, Boonville, Ind., 1979-82; dep. pros. atty. Warrick County-2d Jud. Cir. Ind., Boonville, 1980—; sole practice, Boonville, 1982—. Mem., v.p. Bd. Health of Warrick County, Boonville, 1980—; bd. dirs. Boonville Jr. Football League, 1982-83. Mem. ABA, Ind. State Bar Assn., Warrick County Bar Assn. (pres. 1983). Democrat. General practice. Home: 824 S 4th St Boonville IN 47601 Office: PO Box 461 316 S 2nd St Boonville IN 47601

AYLWARD, PAUL LEON, lawyer, banker, rancher; b. Stonington, Ill., Mar. 1, 1908; s. Dennis E. and Via (Holben) A.; m. Karma Golden, Oct. 30, 1929; children—Paul, Patricia Thompason, Peter. B.S., U. Ill., 1928; LL.B., Chgo. Kent Coll. Law, 1930. Bar: Ill. 1930, Kans. 1931, U.S. Dist Ct. Kans. 1931, U.S. Ct. Appeals (10th cir.) 1941. Sole practice, Elsworth, Kans., 1931-40; county atty. Ellsworth, 1933-39; atty. city of Ellsworth, 1938-63, 66-72; spl. atty. U.S. Dept. Justice, 1940-53; ptnr. Aylward, Svaty & Sherman, Ellsworth, 1940—; dir. First Nat. Bank Holcomb (Kans.). Trustee, past pres. Ellsworth County Vet. Meml. Hosp., 1946—; bd. dirs. Ellsworth Devel. Assn.; past chmn. Kans. Park Resources Authority; chmn. Kans. Joint Council on Recreation, 1967-74; active Rural Area Devel. Nat. Adv. Com., 1963-63; trustee, past pres. Smoky Hills Art Found., 1968-74; mem. exec. com. Coronado council Boy Scouts Am., 1970—, pres., 1977-78; county chmn. Democratic party, 1946-74, chmn. 1st Dist., 1964-68, 70-74; del. Dem. Nat. Conv., 1960, 68, 72, 76; chmn. Kansans for Carlin for Gov., 1977; mem. Kans. for Carter Com., 1976, Kans. Vets. Commn., 1986—. Served to lt. USN, 1943-45. Mem. ABA, Kans. Bar Assn., Kans. Assn. Def. Counsel (dir. 1967-72), Am. Legion (comdr. Kans. 1953; nat. legis. com. 1954-57; others). Roman Catholic. Condemnation, Estate planning, Contracts commercial. Home: 306 Forest Dr Ellsworth KS 67439 Office: Aylward Svaty & Sherman Box 83 Ellsworth KS 67439

AYLWARD, TIMOTHY MICHAEL, lawyer; b. Kansas City, Mo., Feb. 5, 1954; s. James Patrick and Betty (Bourk) A.; m. Jane Elizabeth Parks, Jan. 29, 1977; children: Sarah, Michael. BA in Journalism, U. Mo., 1975; JD, Washburn U., 1982. Bar: Mo. 1982, U.S. Dist. Ct. (we. dist.) Mo. 1982. Assoc. Blackwell, Sanders, Matheny, Weary & Lombardi, Kansas City, 1982—. Mem. ABA, Mo. Bar Assn., Kansas City Met. Bar Assn. Democrat. Roman Catholic. Personal injury, Federal civil litigation, State civil litigation. Home: 444 W 68th St Kansas City MO 64113 Office: Blackwell Sanders Matheny et al 2480 Pershing Rd Kansas City MO 64108

AYNES, JAMES PAUL, JR., lawyer; b. Long Beach, Calif., Feb. 6, 1945; s. James Paul Sr. and Malva Joon (Gay) A.; m. Patricia Ann Cassidy, Dec. 18, 1977; children: Alia Vera, Mira June. AA in Polit. Sci., Orange Coast Coll., 1970; BA in Polit. Sci., Calif. State U., Long Beach, 1973; JD, Western State U., 1977. Bar: Calif. 1978, U.S. Dist. Ct. (cen. dist.) Calif. 1978, U.S. Dist. Ct. (so. dist.) Calif. 1983, U.S. Supreme Ct. 1984. From law clk. to sr. dep. atty. City of Orange, Calif., 1977-83; atty. Orange County Dept. Edn., Costa Mesa, Calif., 1983—; legal officer CAP Squadron #88, Orange, 1980-83; staff judge adv. 3d aviation group Calif. Mil. Res., Van Nuys, Calif., 1982—; judge pro tem Orange County Mcpl. Ct., Santa Ana, Calif., 1982-83. Mem. Rep. Cen. Com. Orange County, 1983, appointed mem., Costa Mesa, Calif., 1984; bd. dirs. polit. action com. Mesa Action, Costa Mesa, 1984. Served with U.S. Army, 1966-69, Vietnam. Decorated Bronze Star, Air medal. Mem. ABA, Calif. Bar Assn., Christian Legal Soc., VFW, Am. Legion, Delta Theta Phi. Presbyterian. Lodge: Mason. Avocations: sailing, sports cars. Local government, Government contracts and claims, Legal education. Home: 2811 Loreto Ave Costa Mesa CA 92626 Office: Orange County Dept Edn 200 Kalmus Dr Costa Mesa CA 92628

AYOOB, RICHARD JOSEPH, lawyer; b. Los Angeles, Apr. 16, 1953. BS, U. So. Calif., 1975; JD, U. Calif., San Francisco, 1978. Bar: Calif. 1978, U.S. Dist. Ct. (no, so., and cen. dists.) Calif. Assoc. Law Offices of James A. Kaddo, Los Angeles, 1978-80; sole practice Los Angeles, 1980-82; assoc. Ajalat & Polley, Los Angeles, 1982-85, ptnr., 1985—; adj. prof. Golden Gate U., Los Angeles, 1985—. Mem. ABA (taxation sect.), State Bar Calif. (taxation sect.), Los Angeles County Bar Assn. (vice-chmn. state and local tax com. 1984-86). Republican. Mem. Antiochian Orthodox Christian Ch. Clubs: Lakeside Golf (Toluca Lake, Calif.); Los Angeles Athletic. State and local taxation, State civil litigation. Office: Ajalat & Polley 643 S Olive St Suite 200 Los Angeles CA 91104

AYRES, JEFFREY PEABODY, lawyer; b. Waltham, Mass., Sept. 23, 1952; s. John Cecil and Dora Hoxie A.; m. Janet Diehl, May 31, 1980; children: Brendan Peabody, Caroline Bradfield, Gordon Pettit. BA, Harvard U., 1974; JD, George Washington U., 1977. Bar: D.C. 1977, Md. 1978, U.S. Ct. Appeals (3d, 4th and D.C. cirs.), U.S. Dist. Ct. Md., U.S. Dist. Ct. D.C., U.S. Supreme Ct. 1985. Assoc. Arent, Fox, Kintner, Plotkin & Kahn, Washington, 1977-78; assoc. Venable, Baetjer & Howard, Balt., 1978-85, ptnr., 1986—. Contbr. articles to profl. jours. Treas. Harvard Club of Md., 1985—. Mem. ABA, Md. Bar Assn., Balt. Bar Assn. Republican. Episcopalian. Avocations: running, kayaking. Labor, Federal civil litigation, State civil litigation. Home: 7120 Sheffield Rd Baltimore MD 21212 Office: Venable Baetjer & Howard 2 Hopkins Plaza Baltimore MD 21201

AYRES, STEVEN EDWARD, lawyer, naval reserve officer; b. Decatur, Ill., Sept. 12, 1945; s. Robert Lynn and Amy Elizabeth (Almfelt) A.; m. Elizabeth Jean McCullough, Aug. 26, 1967; children: Amy Elizabeth, Rebecca Ruth. AB, Dartmouth Coll., 1967; MA, Syracuse U., 1969; postgrad., U. Minn., 1973-74; JD, Cornell U., 1978. Bar: Conn. 1978. Assoc. Durey & Pierson, Stamford, Conn., 1978-80, Winthrop, Stimson, Putnam & Roberts, Stamford, 1980-86; ptnr. Mead, Bromley & Bishop, Stamford, 1987—; instr. U. Conn. Law Sch., Stamford, 1983-86; adj. prof. U. Bridgeport Law Sch., Conn., 1986. Comdr. USNR, 1978—. Served as lt. USN, 1969-75, Vietnam. Mem. Conn. Bar Assn. (probate and estate sect., instr. 1983-86), Phi Beta Kappa. Republican. Congregationalist. Avocations: hiking, bicycling, stamp collecting. Probate, Estate taxation, Real property. Home: 105 Tower Ave Stamford CT 06907 Office: Mead Bromley & Bishop 41 Bank St Stamford CT 06901

AYSCUE, EDWIN OSBORNE, JR., lawyer; b. Monroe, N.C., May 21, 1933; s. Edwin Osborne and Grace Elizabeth (Fields) A.; m. Emily Mizell Urquhart, Aug. 17, 1957; children: Grace Thompson, E. Osborne, Emily Urquhart, Margaret Mizell. Grad. cum laude, Phillips Acad., Andover, Mass., 1951; AB in Polit. Sci., U. N.C., Chapel Hill, 1954, LLB with honors, 1960. Bar: N.C. 1960, U.S. Supreme Ct. 1979. Assoc., Helms, Mulliss, McMillan & Johnston, Charlotte, N.C., 1960-65, ptnr., 1965-68; ptnr. Helms, Mulliss & Johnston, Charlotte, 1968-85; ptnr. Smith Helms Mulliss & Moore, Charlotte, 1986—. Editor-in-chief N.C. Law Rev., 1959-60. Contbr. articles to profl. jours. Alumni rep. Phillips Acad., 1964—; bd. dirs. Legal Services of So. Piedmont, 1983-85, Legal Services of N.C., 1984-85. Served as lt. USNR, 1955-57. Fellow Am. Coll. Trial Lawyers, Am. Bar Found.; mem. Order of the Coif, Am. Judicature Soc. (bd. dirs. 1985—), Order Golden Fleece, ABA, Nat. Conf. Bar Presidents, So. Conf. Bar Presidents, Fourth Cir. Judicial Conf., N.C. Bar Assn. (Pres. 1984-85), Mecklenburg County Bar Assn. (pres. 1980-81), Phi Beta Kappa. Democrat. Episcopalian. Clubs: Charlotte Country, Charlotte Athletic. Federal civil litigation, State civil litigation, Libel. Office: 227 N Tryon St PO Box 31247 Charlotte NC 28231

BAADE, HANS WOLFGANG, legal educator, law expert; b. Berlin, Dec. 16, 1929; s. Fritz and Edith (Wolff) B.; m. Anne Adams Johnston; children—Friedrich James, Hans Alastair. A.B., Syracuse U., 1949; J.D., Kiel U. (Germany), 1951; LL.B., LL.M., Duke U., 1955, diploma Hague Acad. Internat. Law, 1956. Assoc. Inst. Internat. Law, Kiel, 1955-60; assoc. prof. law Duke U., 1960-64, prof. law, 1964-70; prof. law U. Toronto, 1970-71; Hugh Lamar Stone prof. civil law U. Tex., Austin, 1971—; arbitrator internat. comml. matters; dir. Am. Assn. Comparative Study Law. Mem. Am. Arbitration Assn. (nat. panel arbitrators); assoc. mem. Internat. Acad. Comparative Law Am. Acad. Fgn. Law (dir.). Editor: Law and Comparative Problems, 1961-66; bd. editors Am. Jour. Comparative Law, 1960—; editorial sec. German Yr. Book Internat. Law, 1956-60; contbr. numerous articles to profl. jours. Legal history, Private international, Public international. Home: 6002 Mountain Climb Dr Austin TX 78731 Office: U Tex Sch Law Austin TX 78705

BABB, FRANK EDWARD, lawyer; b. Maryville, Mo., Dec. 22, 1932; s. Dale Victor and Esther (Hull) B.; m. Patricia McClaren, June 6, 1953; children: Frank Edward Jr., George. B.S., Northwest Mo. State U., Maryville, 1954; LL.B., Harvard U., 1959. Bar: Ill. 1959, D.C. 1980, Fla. 1980, Va. 1980. Ptnr. McDermott, Will & Emery, Chgo., 1959—. Served with CIC U.S. Army, 1954-56, C.Z. Mem. ABA, Chgo. Bar Assn., D.C. Bar Assn., Fla. Bar Assn., Va. Bar Assn. Clubs: Chicago, University. General corporate, Securities. Office: McDermott Will & Emery 111 W Monroe St Chicago IL 60603

BABB, GUY LEE, lawyer; b. Dalton, Ga., Aug. 6, 1951; s. Samuel Edward and Elsie (Carney) B.; m. Pauline A. Hollinworth, Aug. 2, 1979. B in Indsl. Engring., Ga. Inst. Tech., 1973; JD, South Tex. Coll., 1981. Bar: Tex. 1981, U.S. Dist. Ct. (so. dist.) Tex. 1982, Vt. 1986. Counsel Clyde W. Woddy Atty. At Law, Houston, 1982-84; sole practice Houston, 1985; assoc. Law Offices of Jonathan B. Lash, Houston, 1985—. Mem. State Bar Tex., Vt. Bar Assn., Alpha Pi Mu. Club: Toastmasters, Dhahran Saudi Arabia (founder, 1st pres. 1978-79). Avocations: birdwatching, hiking. Real property, Personal injury. Home: Rt 4 Box 4352 Shelburne VT 05482 Office: Law Offices Jonathan B Lash 217 Union St Burlington VT 05402

BABBITT, DAVID BERKELEY, judge; b. Phoenix, Ariz., Dec. 23, 1927; s. David Joseph Babbitt and Mabel Elizabeth (Fuqua) Smith; m. Jil D. Mason, Jun 10, 1970 (div. 1987); children: Heather, David, Susan, Scott, Michael. BS, U. Ariz., 1949, JD, 1972. Bar: Ariz. 1972, U.S. Dist. Ct. Ariz. 1973. Sole practice Parker, Ariz., 1972-75, Lake Havasu City, Ariz., 1975-77, 79-85; atty. Mohave County, Kingman, Ariz., 1977-79; justice of the peace Kingman, 1985—; magistrate City of Lake Havasu City, Ariz., 1985—; active jud. coordinating comnn. Ariz. Supreme Ct., 1978-81. State rep. Ariz. Ho. of Reps., Phoenix, 1955-56. Served to lt. USCGR, 1950-52. Mem. Ariz. Bar Assn. (adminstrv. com. 1982-85, chmn. 1985), Mohave County Bar Assn. (pres. 1981-82), VFW, Am. Legion. Republican. Lodges: Rotary, Elks. Judicial administration. Office: Justice of the Peace 2060 N Acoma Blvd Lake Havasu City AZ 86403

BABBITT, EDWARD JOSEPH, lawyer; b. Cin., May 7, 1952; s. Edward Gerard and Mary Grace (Groneman) B.; m. Maureen Bohlen, Nov. 27, 1982. BBA, U. Cin., 1975; JD, Southwestern U., 1978. Bar: Calif. 1980, D.C. 1985. Legis. asst. U.S. Ho. of Reps., Washington, 1979-81; subcom. counsel Ho. Pub. Works Com., Washington, 1981-83, asst. counsel, 1983-84; congl. relations officer U.S. Dept. Transp., Washington, 1984-86, dir. office of congl. affairs, 1986—. Mem. ABA, D.C. Bar Assn. Roman Catholic. Legislative, Administrative and regulatory. Home: 9324 Glenbrook Rd Fairfax VA 22031 Office: US Dept Transp 400 7th St SW Washington DC 20590

BABCOCK, BARBARA ALLEN, lawyer, educator; b. Washington, July 6, 1938; d. Henry Allen and Doris Lenore (Moses) B.; m. Thomas C. Grey, Aug. 19, 1979. A.B., U. Pa., 1960; LL.B., Yale U., 1963. Bar: Md. 1963, D.C. 1964. Law clk. U.S. Ct. Appeals D.C., 1963; assoc. Edward Bennett Williams, 1964-66; staff atty. Legal Aid Agy., Washington, 1966-68; dir. Pub. Defender Service of D.C. 1968-72; assoc. prof. Stanford U., 1972-77, prof., 1977—; asst. atty. gen. U.S. Dept. Justice, 1977-79. Ernest W. McFarland Prof. Law, 1986—. Democrat. Author: (with others) Sex Discrimination and The Law, 1975; (with Carrington) Civil Procedure, 1977; contbr. articles to profl. jours. Federal civil litigation, Criminal. Home: 835 Mayfield Ave Stanford CA 94305 Office: Stanford Law Sch Stanford CA 94305

BABCOCK, BRUCE EDWARD, legal educator, lawyer; b. Loma Linda, Calif., Dec. 30, 1954; s. Harold Edward and Betty Lou (Sanders) B.: m. Susan Crofts, Nov. 17, 1979; children: Sarah, Mark, Alan, Timothy. BS, Brigham Young U., 1977, JD, 1980; LLM in Taxation, NYU, 1981. Bar: Utah 1980, Ohio 1981, U.S. Tax Ct. 1983, U.S. Ct. Claims 1986. Assoc. Smith & Schnaake, Dayton, Ohio, 1981-84; assoc. Jones, Waldo, Holbrook & McDonough, Salt Lake City, 1984-86, ptnr., 1986—. Editor Brigham Young U. Law Rev., 1979-80. Mem. ABA. Republican. Mormon. Pension, profit-sharing, and employee benefits, Corporate taxation, Personal income taxation. Home: 2242 E Wilmott Dr Salt Lake City UT 84109 Office: Jones Waldo Holbrook & McDonough 1500 First Interstate Plaza Salt Lake City UT 84111

BABCOCK, CHARLES WITTEN, lawyer; b. Kansas City, Mo., Dec. 6, 1941; s. Charles W. and Esther L. (Marcy) B.; m. Sharon K. Chamberlain, June 26, 1976; children: David, William, Susan, Stephen. BA with honors, U. Mo., 1963; JD, Harvard U., 1966. Bar: Mo. 1966, Mich. 1971. Judge advocate USMC, various locations, 1966-69; assoc. Blackwell, Sanders, Kansas City, 1969-71; staff atty. Gen. Motors Corp., Detroit, 1971-78, atty.-in-charge, 1978-83, asst. gen. counsel, 1983—. Contbr. articles to profl. jours. Vestryperson Christ Episcopal Ch., Grosse Pointe, Mich., 1983-86; mem. Detroit Symphony Orch. Chorale. Served as capt. JAGC USMC, 1966-69, Vietnam. Republican. Episcopalian. Club: Recess (Detroit). Avocation: amateur radio. Personal injury, General corporate, Product liability litigation. Home: 917 Grand Marais Grosse Pointe MI 48230 Office: Gen Motors Corp PO Box 33143 Detroit MI 48232

BABCOCK, GARY D., lawyer, state official. Pub. defender State of Oreg., Salem. Office: Pub Defenders Office 1655 State St Salem OR 97310 *

BABCOCK, KEITH MOSS, lawyer; b. Camden, N.J., Aug. 5, 1951; s. William Strong Jr. and Dinah Leslie (Moss) B.; m. Jacquelyn Sue Dickman, Aug. 16, 1975; children: Michael Arthur, Max William. AB, Princeton U., 1973; JD, George Washington U., 1976. Bar: S.C. 1977, U.S. Dist. Ct. S.C. 1977, U.S. Ct. Appeals (4th cir.) 1977, U.S. Supreme Ct. 1980. Staff atty. S.C. Atty. Gen.'s Office, Columbia, 1977-78, state atty., 1978-79, asst. atty. gen., 1979-81; ptnr. Barnes & Austin, Columbia, 1981-82, Austin & Lewis, Columbia, 1982-84, Lewis, Babcock, Pleicones & Hawkins, Columbia, 1984—. Bd. dirs. Columbia Jewish Community Pre-Sch., 1984, chmn. 1985-86; bd. dirs. Columbia Jewish Community Ctr., 1986—. Mem. ABA, S.C. Bar Assn. (chmn. profl. standard subcom. 1983—), Richland County Bar Assn., Princeton Alumni Assn. of S.C. (v.p. 1980—), George Washington U. Law Sch. Alumni Assn. (bd. dirs. 1983—). Democrat. Episcopalian. Club: Summit, Spring Valley Country (Columbia). Federal civil litigation, State civil litigation, Condemnation. Home: 233 W Springs Rd Columbia SC 29223 Office: Lewis Babcock Pleicones & Hawkins 1513 Hampton St Columbia SC 29211

BABER, WILBUR H., JR., lawyer; b. Shelby, N.C., Dec. 18, 1926; s. Wilbur H. and Martha Corinne (Allen) B.; B.A., Emory U., 1949; postgrad. U. N.C., 1949-50, U. Houston, 1951-52; J.D., Loyola U., New Orleans, 1965. Bar: La. 1965, Tex. 1966. Sole practice, Hallettsville, Tex., 1966—. Served with U.S. Army. Mem. ABA, La. Bar Assn., Tex. Bar Assn., La. Engring. Soc., Tex. Surveyors Assn. Methodist. Lodge: Rotary. Probate, Oil

and gas leasing, State civil litigation. Office: PO Box 294 Hallettsville TX 77964

BABINEAU, ANNE SERZAN, lawyer; b. Jersey City, Dec. 16, 1951; d. Joseph Edward and Mary (Golding) Serzan; m. Paul A. Babineau, Apr. 7, 1973; children: John Regis, Matthew Paul. BA, Coll. New Rochelle, 1973; JD, Seton Hall U., 1977. Bar: N.J. 1977, N.Y. 1983, U.S. Ct. Appeals (3d cir.) 1984. Staff atty. rate counsel div. N.J. Dept. Pub. Adv., Newark, 1977-78; assoc. Wilentz, Goldman & Spitzer, P.C., Woodbridge, N.J., 1979-85, ptnr., 1985—. Mem. ABA, N.J. State Bar Assn., Fed. Bar N.J., Middlesex County Bar Assn. Roman Catholic. Avocations: antiques, museums, gardening. Administrative and regulatory, Public utilities, Real property. Office: Wilentz Goldman & Spitzer 900 Rt 9 Woodbridge NJ 07095

BABIRAK, MILTON EDWARD, JR., lawyer; b. Blue Island, Ill., Sept. 27, 1946; s. Milton and Mildred B.; m. Helen Badonna Savitzky, B.S., U. Ill., 1968; J.D., John Marshall Law Sch., 1973; LL.M., Georgetown U., 1979. Bar: Ill. 1973, D.C. 1979, Va. 1987. Assoc. firm Billig Sher & Jones, Washington, 1979-80; ptnr. Babirak & Fisher, Washington, 1980—. Mem. ABA (taxation sect.), Fed. Bar Assn., D.C. Bar Assn. (com. on emerging bus.). General corporate, Corporate taxation. Home: 2059 Huntington Ave 1509 Alexandria VA 22303 Office: Babirak & Fisher 2111 Wilson Blvd Suite 550 Arlington VA 22201

BABLER, WAYNE E., retired telephone company executive; b. Orangeville, Ill., Dec. 8, 1915; s. Oscar E. and Mary (Bender) B.; m. Mary Blome, Dec. 27, 1940; children: Wayne Elroy Jr., Marilyn Anne Evans, Sally Jane Sperry. B.A., Ind. Central Coll., 1936; J.D., U. Mich., 1938; LL.D., Ind. Central U., 1966. Bar: Mich. bar 1938, N.Y. bar 1949, Mo. bar 1955, Wis. bar 1963, also U.S. Supreme Ct. bar 1963. Asso. firm Bishop & Bishop, Detroit, 1938-42; partner Bishop & Bishop, 1945-48; atty. AT&T, 1948-55; gen. solicitor Southwestern Bell Telephone Co., St. Louis, 1955-63; v.p., gen. counsel, sec. Southwestern Bell Telephone Co., 1965-80, ret., 1980; v.p., gen. counsel Wis. Telephone Co., Milw., 1963-65. Bd. dirs., chmn. St. Louis Soc. Crippled Children; bd. dirs. St. Louis Symphony Soc. Mem. ABA (chmn. pub. utility sect. 1978-79), Fed. Communications Bar Assn., Wis. Bar Assn., St. Louis Bar Assns., Mo. Bar. Assn. Clubs: Delray Dunes Country, Delray Beach. Antitrust, Federal civil litigation, State civil litigation. Home: 11943 Date Palm Dr Boynton Beach FL 33436

BABLITCH, WILLIAM, state supreme court justice; b. Stevens Point, Wis., Mar. 1, 1941. B.S., U. Wis., Madison, 1963, J.D., 1968. Bar: Wis. 1968. Practice law Stevens Point, Wis.; mem. Wis. Senate, 1972-85, senate majority leader, 1976-82; justice Wis. Supreme Ct., Madison, 1985—; dist. atty. Portage County, Wis., 1969-72. Mem. Nat. Conf. State Legislators (exec. com. 1979). Democrat. Office: Office of Supreme Ct Wis Madison WI 53702 *

BACALL, ELLIOT STEPHEN, lawyer, accountant; b. Oak Park, Ill., Oct. 26, 1945; s. Harold L. and Renarda (Gable) B.; 1 dau., Renee Dawn. B.S. in Acctg., U. Ill., 1967; J.D., Ill. Inst. Tech., 1970. Bar: Ill. 1971, U.S. Ct. Appeals (7th cir.) 1972, U.S. Tax Ct. 1972, U.S. Supreme Ct. 1980. Gen. counsel Florsheim Shoe Co., Chgo., 1971-72; asst. states atty. Lake County, Ill., 1972-75; sole practice, Deerfield, Ill., 1975—; chmn., chief exec. officer Shylock Investment Co., Chgo., 1972—. Editor: U.S. Tax Reports, 1970. Bd. dirs. Jewish United Fund, Chgo., 1981-82; asst. treas. Lake County Forest Preserve, 1980-82, commr., 1978-82; commr. Lake County Bd., 1978-82. Served with USAR, 1969-75. Mem. Ill. Bar Assn. Republican. Jewish. Lodges: Lions, Moose. Criminal, General practice, General corporate. Home and Office: 934 Waukegan Rd Deerfield IL 60015

BACCINI, LAURANCE ELLIS, lawyer; b. Darby, Pa., Nov. 16, 1945; s. Alfred Ellis and Elizabeth Tarbet (Butler) B. B.S., Drexel U., 1968; J.D., Villanova U., 1971. Bar: Pa. 1971, U.S. Dist. Ct. (ea. dist.) Pa. 1973, U.S. Ct. Appeals (3d cir.) 1979. Law clk. to chief judge U.S. Dist. Ct. (ea. dist.) Pa., 1971-73; assoc. Schnader, Harrison, Segal & Lewis, Phila., 1973-78, ptnr., 1979—; speaker, faculty mem. on labor law Practising Law Inst., N.Y.C.; trustee Phila. Bar Found., 1986—. Author: NLRA Supervisor's Handbook; assoc. editor Villanova Law Rev. Mem. Phila. Bar Assn. (bd. govs. 1978—, chmn. 1982, vice chancellor 1986, commn. on jud. selection, retention and evaluation 1978-79, vice chancellor 1986—), Pa. Bar Assn. (ho. of dels. 1983—), ABA (former chair, and dir. young lawyers div. 1981-82, mem. exec. council Sect. Labor and Employment Law 1981-82, exec. council 1980-81, chancellor-elect 1987, chancellor, 1978, chair long-range planning com., young lawyers div.'s Fed. practice com., fed. jucicial standards com., judicial conf. for 3d cir.). Labor. Office: 1600 Market St Suite 3600 Philadelphia PA 19103

BACCUS, TONYA LYNN, judge; b. Granite City, Ill., Apr. 13, 1956; d. Markus Vernell and Shirley (Pohl) Baccus; m. Giles D. Rainwater, Oct. 29, 1983; 1 child, Sabrina. BS, Fla. State U., 1976; JD, U. Fla., 1976. Bar: Fla., 1979. Asst. atty. State of Fla., Titusville, 1979-80; sole practice Indian Harbor Beach, Fla., 1981-86; county judge Brevard County, Melbourne, 1987—; adj. faculty mgmt. and humanities, Fla. Inst. Tech., Melbourne. Pres., bd. dirs. Mental Health Assn., Brevard County, Fla., 1985; campaign treas. Judicial Election, Brevard County, 1983; mem. devel. council Holmes Regional Med. Ctr., Melbourne, 1984-85. Mem. ABA, Fla. Bar Assn. (bd. govs. young lawyers sect., 1982-84), Brevard County Bar Assn. Republican. Lutheran. Real property, General corporate, Family and matrimonial. Office: Brevard County Courthouse 50 S Neiman Ave Melbourne FL 32901

BACH, STEVE CRAWFORD, lawyer; b. Jackson, Ky., Jan. 31, 1921; s. Bruce Grannis and Evelyn (Crawford) B.; m. Rosemary Husted, Sept. 6, 1947; children—John Crittenden, Greta Christine. A.B., Ind. U., 1943, J.D., 1948; postgrad. Eastern studies, U. Mich., 1944, Nat. Trial Judges Coll., 1966; U. Minn. Juvenile Inst., 1967. Bar: Ky. 1948, Ind. 1948. Atty. Bach & Bach, Jackson, Ky., 1948-51; investigator U.S. CSC, Indpls., 1951-54; sole practice Mt. Vernon, Ind., 1954-65; judge 11th Jud. Circuit, Mt. Vernon, 1965-82; pres. Internat. Inst. for Youth, Inc., Mt. Vernon, 1985—; spl. overseas rep. Nat. Council Juvenile and Family Ct. Judges, bd. trustees, 1978-82; moderator Ind. Conf. Crime and Delinquency, Indpls., 1968; tchr. seminar on juvenile delinquency, Ind. Trial Judges Assn., 1969, del. Internat. Youth Magistrates Conf., Geneva, 1970, Oxford, Eng., 1974, Can., 1977; faculty adviser Criminal Law Inst., Nat. Trial Judges Coll., 1973; treas. Ind. Council Juvenile Ct. Judges, 1975, v.p., 1976, pres., 1978-79, mem. juvenile study com., 1976; bd. dirs. Jud. Conf., Ind. Jud. Ctr.; faculty adviser Nat. Jud. Coll., 1978; mem. faculty Seminar for Inst. for New Judges, State of Ind., 1979. Pres. Greater Mt. Vernon Assn., 1958-59; bd. dirs. Regional Mental Health Planning Commn., Criminal Justice Planning Commn. 8th Region Ind., Evansville, Ind.; mem. Juvenile Justice div. Ind. Jud. Study Commn.; mem. Ind. Gov.'s Juvenile Justice Delinquency Prevention Adv. Bd., 1976-78, community adv. council Ind. U. Sch. Medicine, 1986—. Served with intelligence Signal Corps, AUS, 1943-46. Mem. Nat. Council Juvenile Ct. Judges, Am. Legion, Ind. Soc. Chgo., Ind. Bar Assn. (del.), Ind. Judges Assn. (bd. mgrs. 1966-71), Sigma Delta Kappa, Delta Tau Delta. Democrat. Methodist. Lodges: Masons, Shriners, Kiwanis, Elks. Oil and gas leasing, State civil litigation, Probate. Home: 512 Walnut St Mount Vernon IN 47620 Office: 203 E 4th St Mount Vernon IN 47620

BACH, THOMAS HANDFORD, lawyer; b. Vineland, N.J., Dec. 25, 1928; s. Albert Ludwig and Edith May (Handford) B. A.B., Rutgers U., 1950; LL.B., Harvard U., 1956. Bar: N.Y. State bar 1957. Asso. firm Hawkins, Delafield & Wood, N.Y.C., 1956-61, Reed, Hoyt, Washburn & McCarthy, N.Y.C., 1961-62; partner Bach & Condren, N.Y.C., 1963-71, Bach & McAuliffe, N.Y.C., 1971-79, Stroock & Stroock & Lavan, N.Y.C., 1979—; co-counsel N.Y. State Senate Housing and Urban Devel. Com., 1971; fiscal cons. N.Y.C. Fin. Adminstrn., 1967-70; asst. counsel State Fin. Com., N.Y. State Constl. Conv. of, 1967. Contbr. articles to profl. jours. Mem. N.Y. State Commn. to Study Constl. Tax Limitations, 1974-75. Served with U.S. Army, 1951-53. Mem. Am. Bar Assn., N.Y. State Bar Assn., Assn. of Bar of City of N.Y., N.J. Bar Assn., N.Y. Mcpl. Analysts Group (chmn. 1973-74), Mcpl. Forum of N.Y., Mcpl. Fin. Officers Assn. of U.S. and Can., Mcpl. Fin. Officers Assn. N.J. Episcopalian. Municipal bonds. Home: 4 E 89th St New York NY 10128 Office: Stroock & Stroock & Lavan 7 Hanover Sq New York NY 10004

BACHMAN, KENNETH LEROY, JR., lawyer; b. Washington, Aug. 24, 1943; s. Kenneth Leroy and Audrey Teresa (Torrence) B.; m. Sharon Abel, June 18, 1966; children—Laura Ann, Eric Kenneth. A.B. summa cum laude, Ohio U., 1965; J.D. cum laude, Harvard U., 1968. Bar: D.C. 1968, U.S. Ct. Appeals (D.C. cir.) 1971, U.S. Supreme Ct. 1981. Law clk. to judge U.S. Dist. Ct. So. Dist. N.Y., 1968-70; assoc. Cleary, Gottlieb, Steen & Hamilton, Washington, 1970-76, ptnr., 1976—. Mem. ABA. Contbg. editor Oil and Gas Price Regulation Analyst, 1978—; contbr. articles to profl. jours. FERC practice, Banking, Administrative and regulatory. Home: 5412 Duvall Dr Bethesda MD 20816 Office: Cleary Gottlieb Steen & Hamilton 1752 N St NW Washington DC 20036

BACHRACH, EVE ELIZABETH, lawyer; b. Oakland, Calif., July 3, 1951; d. Howard Lloyd and Shirley Faye (Lichterman) B. AB cum laude, Boston U., 1972; JD with honors, George Washington U., 1976. Bar: D.C. 1976, U.S. Dist. Ct. D.C. 1976, U.S. Ct. Appeals (D.C. cir.) 1976. Assoc. Stein, Mitchell & Mezines, Washington, 1976-79; assoc. gen. counsel Cosmetic, Toiletry, and Fragrance Assn., Washington, 1979-85, The Proprietary Assn., Washington, 1985—; guest lectr. Am. U., Washington, 1986—, George Washington Nat. Law Ctr., Washington, 1986—. Author, Editor: Small Business Resource Manual, 1984. Vol. lawyer Legal Counsel for the Elderly, Washington, 1978—. Mem. ABA (food and drug com., antitrust sect., patent, copyright, trademark com.), D.C. Bar Assn., Women's Bar Assn. D.C., Fed. Bar Assn. (chmn. food and drug com. 1986—), Food and Drug Law Inst. (chmn. writing awards com. 1982—). Avocations: classical pianist, sailing. Antitrust, Health, Legislative. Home: 2400 Virginia Ave NW C423 Washington DC 20037

BACHSTEIN, HARRY SAMUEL, lawyer, educator; b. Oakland, Calif., Aug. 6, 1943; s. Elizabeth (Rodenhouse) B.; m. Kathy Ann Hill; children—Harry S. III, David Jason, Shane Thomas, Jacob William, Gretchen Leah. BS in Bus. Adminstrn., No. Ariz. U., 1966; JD with honors, U. Ariz., 1969. Bar: Ariz. 1969, U.S. Supreme Ct. 1973, U.S. Ct. Customs and Patent Appeals, U.S. Dist. Ct. Ariz., U.S. Ct. Appeals (9th cir.), U.S. Bankruptcy Ct. Spl. investigator ethics com. Pinal County Bar Assn., 1971; juvenile ct. referee Ariz. Superior Ct., 1972-76; mem. Superior Ct. Med. Liability Rev. Panel, 1981; lawyer arbitrator Better Bus. Tucson. Mem. Devel. Authority for Tucson's Expansion, 1970-76; mem. U.S. Presdl. Task Force, 1981—; faculty Pima Coll., 1982-83. Mem. State Bar of Ariz. (sec., exec. council young lawyers' sect. 1972-73), ABA (Ariz. rep. com. on div. law and procedures 1976), Pima County Bar Assn. (grievance com. 1978—, spl. investigator for ethics com. 1971), Profl. Assn. of Diving Instrs. (cert. divemaster), Delta Chi (sec., pledgemaster 1961-65). Clubs: Optimist Internat. (state gov. Ariz. 1976, lt. gov. 1972-73, pres. 1971-72, Outstanding Gov. and Disting. Gov. 1976), Mason. Editor: Ariz. Law Rev., 1967-69. Avocations: hunting, deep sea diving (cert. openwater scuba diver). Family and matrimonial, Consumer commercial, State civil litigation. Office: PO Box 43188 Tucson AZ 85733-3188

BACIGAL, RONALD JOSEPH, law educator; b. Pitts., Jan. 13, 1943. BA, Concord Coll., 1964; LLB summa cum laude, Washington and Lee U., 1967; postgrad. in Internat. Law, The Hague, The Netherlands, 1967-68. Bar: D.C. 1967, Va. 1985. Law clk. to presiding judge U.S. Dist. Ct. (we. dist.) Va., 1967, 68; prof. law U. Richmond (Va.), 1971—; vis. prof. law Duke U. Sch. Law, Durham, N.C., 1976; lectr. Cir. Judges Confs., Dist. Judges Confs., Magistrates Confs., seminars. Author: The Virginia Magistrates' Manual, 1974, rev. edit. 1978, Goals for Virginia's Criminal Justice System: Report of the Governor's Task Force, 1977, Cases and Materials on Criminal Procedure, 1979, (with Moenssens and Singer) supplement 1984, Virginia Criminal Procedure, 1983, supplement 1985, Virginia Criminal Procedure Forms, 1984, supplement 1985; (with others) Virginia Magistrates' Orientation Manual, 1976; also articles. Exec. dir. Va. Task Force on Criminal Justice Standards and Goals, 1975-76; reporter Joint Bar Com. Study of ABA Standards for Criminal Justice, 1975-76, Com. on Jury Use and Mgmt. Jud. Council Va., 1983-84; mem. Drafting Com. Va. Rules Evidence Va. Supreme Ct., 1984-85. Served to lt. JAGC, USN, 1968-71. Fulbright scholar, 1967-68. Home: 6000 York Rd Richmond VA 23226 Office: Univ Richmond TC Williams Sch Law Richmond VA 23173

BACKSTEIN, ROBERT JOSEPH, lawyer, municipal government official; b. Phoenix, Apr. 25, 1932; s. Milton Joseph and Martha Susana (Huber) B.; m. Mary Lee Coy, Sept. 5, 1956; children—Sharon Backstein Woodhouse, Robin Backstein Smith, Robert Samuel, Julie Johnson, Jennifer, Mark Aaron. B.S., U. Ariz., 1954, J.D., 1959. Bar: Ariz. 1959, Wash. 1970. City atty. Phoenix, 1966-70. assoc. Short, Cressman & Cable, Seattle, 1970-73; chief civil dep. Pierce County Prosecutor, Tacoma, Wash., 1973-75; hearing examiner City of Tacoma, 1975-78; sole practice, Tacoma, 1978-83; hearing examiner Pierce County, Thurston County, Cities of Olympia and Lacy (Wash.), 1978-83; city atty. City of Tacoma, 1983—; cons. mcpl. and govtl. law. Served to 1st lt. JAG, U.S. Army, 1954-56, 59. Mem. Am. Arbitration Assn., ABA, Tacoma-Pierce County Bar Assn., Pi Alpha Delta. Republican. Mem. Ch. Jesus Christ of Latter-day Saints. Club: Elks (Tacoma). Real property, Administrative and regulatory, General practice. Home: 1400 Weathervane Dr Tacoma WA 98466 Office: 747 Market St Tacoma WA 98402-3767

BACKUS, BRADLEY, lawyer; b. Bklyn., Sept. 12, 1950; s. Thomas and Bernice (Smith) B.; m. Stephanie Delores George, Dec. 13, 1975; 1 child, Crystal Olivia. B.A., Lincoln U., 1972; J.D., George Washington U., 1975. Bar: N.Y. 1976, U.S. Supreme Ct. 1979, U.S. Tax Ct. 1981. Advanced underwriting cons. Met. Life Ins. Co., N.Y.C., 1977-81, dir. bus. and estate analysis, 1981—; corp. sec. Bedford-Stuyvesant Legal Services Corp., Bklyn., 1983—. Mem. ABA, Met. Black Bar Assn. (v.p. 1984-86, pres. 1986—), Bedford-Stuyvesant Lawyers Assn. (pres. 1980-81), N.Y. Soc. Ethical Culture (parliamentarian 1982—), Crown Heights Jaycees (of counsel 1976). Democrat. Estate planning, Estate taxation, Pension, profit-sharing, and employee benefits. Home: 667 Park Pl Brooklyn NY 11216 Office: Met Life Ins Co 1 Madison Ave New York NY 10010

BACON, BRETT KERMIT, lawyer; b. Perry, Iowa, Aug. 8, 1947; s. Royden S. and Aldeen A. (Zuker) B.; m. Peggy Darlene Smith, July 30, 1972; children: Jeffrey Brett, Scott Michael. BA, U. Dubuque, 1969; JD, Northwestern U., 1972. Bar: Ohio 1972, U.S. Ct. Appeals (6th cir.) 1972, U.S. Supreme Ct. 1980. Assoc., Thompson, Hine & Flory, Cleve., 1972-80, ptnr., 1980—; speaker in field. Author: Computer Law, 1982, 1984. Vice-pres. profl. sect. United Way, Cleve., 1982-86; pres. Shaker Heights Youth Ctr., Inc., Ohio, 1984-86. Mem. Bar Assn. Greater Cleve. Federal civil litigation, State civil litigation, Personal injury. Home: 2924 Manchester Rd Shaker Heights OH 44122 Office: Thompson Hine & Flory 1100 Nat City Bank Bldg Cleveland OH 44114

BACON, DOUGLAS ARMS, lawyer; b. Northampton, Mass., Dec. 1, 1949; s. Theodore Spaulding and Sarah Shields (Hogate) B.; m. Stephanie Kerr Sewall, July 1, 1972; children: Nicholas, Anna. BA, Amherst Coll., 1971; JD, Syracuse U., 1975. Bar: Mass. 1975, U.S. Dist. Ct. Mass. 1975, U.S. Ct. Appeals (1st cir.) 1975. Assoc. Choate, Hall & Stewart, Boston, 1975-80; sr. counsel Bank of Boston, 1981—. Trustee The Park Sch., Brookline, Mass., 1985—. Mem. Order of Coif, Justinian Soc. Republican. Episcopalian. Clubs: The Country (Brookline, Mass.); Hillsboro (Pompano Beach, Fla.). Real property, General corporate, Banking. Home: 541 Hammond St Chesnut Hill MA 02167 Office: 1st Nat Bank Of Boston 100 Federal St Boston MA 02110

BACON, JAMES THOMAS, lawyer; b. Tokyo, June 4, 1957; came to U.S., 1960; s. Norman James and Angie M (Mooshian) B. BBA cum laude, Olivet Nazarene U., 1979; JD, Am. U., 1982. Bar: Va. 1982, U.S. Dist. Ct. (ea. dist.) Va. 1982, U.S. Tax Ct. 1982, U.S. Ct. Appeals (4th cir.) 1982, U.S. Supreme Ct. 1985. Assoc. Hall, Surovell, Jackson & Colten, P.C., Fairfax, Va., 1982. Del. com. Fairfax County Reps., 1986—. Mem. ABA (corp. sect., bus. and banking law sect., litigation sect. 1982—), Nat. Rep Lawyers Assn., Va. Bar Assn. (tax manual com.), Fairfax County Bar Assn., Phi Beta Kappa. Republican. Lodge: Rotary (bd. dirs. Springfield, Va. 1984—). Avocation: youth baseball. Contracts commercial, Federal civil litigation, State civil litigation. Home: 4314 Dehaven Dr Chantilly VA 22021 Office: Hall, Surovell et al 4010 University Dr Fairfax VA 22030

BACOT, JOHN PAISLEY, JR., lawyer; b. Conway, S.C., July 14, 1947; s. John P. and Lucia (Cross) B.; m. Jancie Patterson, May 14, 1983. BS, U.S. Mil. Acad., 1969; JD, U. S.C., 1978. Bar: S.C. 1979, U.S. Ct. Appeals (4th cir.) 1982. Commn. 2d lt. U.S. Army, 1969; advanced through grades to capt. U.S. Army, Europe, Vietnam; resigned U.S. Army, 1975; assoc. Willcox, Hardee, McLeod, Buyck & Baker, Surfside Beach, S.C., 1979-85, Parsons & Patrick, Surfside Beach, 1985-86; sole practice Surfside Beach, 1986—. Mem. ABA, Am. Trial Lawyers Assn., S.C. Trial Lawyers Assn., Surfside Merchants Assn. (bd. dirs. 1983). Presbyterian. Lodge: Sertoma (sec. local club 1980-81). Avocations: hunting. athletics. State civil litigation, Real property, Personal injury. Office: PO Box 15439 Surfside SC 29587

BADEL, JULIE, lawyer; b. Chgo., Sept. 14, 1946; d. Charles and Saima (Hyrkas) B. Student, Knox Coll., 1963-65; BA, Columbia Coll., Chgo., 1967; JD, DePaul U., 1977. Bar: Ill. 1977, U.S. Dist. Ct. (no. dist.) Ill. 1977, U.S. Ct. Appeals (7th and D.C. cirs.) 1981, U.S. Supreme Ct. 1985. Hearings referee State of Ill., Chgo., 1974-78; assoc. Cohn, Lambert, Ryan, Schneider & Harman, Chgo., 1978-80; assoc. McDermott, Will & Emery, Chgo., 1980-84, ptnr., 1985—; legal counsel, adv. bd. Health Evaluation Referral Service, Chgo., 1980—. Author: Hospital Restructuring: Employment Law Pitfalls, 1985; editor DePaul U. Law Rev., 1976-77. Mem. ABA, Chgo. Bar Assn., Ill. State C. of C., Columbia Coll. Alumni Assn. (1st v.p., bd. dirs. 1981-86), Pi Gamma Mu. Club: Monroe (Chgo.). Labor, Civil rights, Federal civil litigation. Office: McDermott Will & Emery 111 W Monroe St Chicago IL 60603

BADEN, EARL W., JR., lawyer; b. Bradenton, Fla., Jan. 31, 1939; s. Earl W. Sr. and Daisy (Brown) B.; m. Ina Holley, April 23, 1964; children: Holley M., Heather N. BS, Fla. State U., 1965; JD, Stetson U., 1968. Bar: Fla. 1969, U.S. Dist. Ct. (mid. dist.) Fla. 1969, U.S. Supreme Ct. 1982. Assoc. Pratt Atty., Palmetto, Fla., 1969-70; sole practice Bradenton, Fla., 1970—. Mem. Boys Clubs Manatee County, Bradenton, Fla. Mem. 4-H. Republican. Methodist. Lodge: Kiwanis. Avocations: hunting, fishing, welding. Home: 1210 99th St NW Bradenton FL 33529 Office: 1101 6th Ave W Bradenton FL 33506

BADER, ALBERT XAVIER, JR., lawyer; b. Bklyn., Oct. 19, 1932; s. Albert Xavier and Elizabeth Dolores (Campion) B.; m. Patricia Anne Keeler, June 27, 1959; children: Albert X. III, Christopher F., Thomas J., Paul L. B.S. magna cum laude, Georgetown U., 1953; LL.B., Columbia U., 1956. Bar: N.Y. 1956, U.S. Supreme Ct. 1965. Assoc. Simpson Thacher & Bartlett, N.Y.C., 1956-69, ptnr., 1969—. Bd. dirs. St. Christopher-Jennie Clarkson Child Care Services, Dobbs Ferry, N.Y., 1980—, Tolentine-Zeiser Community Life Ctr., Bronx, N.Y. Served with U.S. Army, 1956-58. Mem. ABA, N.Y. State Bar Assn., Assn. of Bar of City of N.Y., Fed. Bar Council. Clubs: Larchmont Shore, Down Town Assn. Federal civil litigation, Labor, FERC practice. Home: 30 Masterton Rd Bronxville NY 10708 Office: Simpson Thacher & Bartlett 1 Battery Park Plaza New York NY 10004

BADER, GREGORY VINCENT, lawyer; b. Puyallup, Wash., Feb. 6, 1948; s. Frederick A. and Patricia W. (Burns) B. BA, Mont. State U., 1970; MA, Washington State U., 1972; JD, Harvard U., 1978. Bar: Tex. 1979, Idaho 1980, U.S. Dist. Ct. (so. dist.) Tex. 1981, U.S. Dist. Ct. (ea. dist.) Tex. 1982, U.S. Ct. Appeals (5th cir.) 1982. Assoc. Foreman & Dyess, Houston, 1978-79; counsel Boise (Idaho) Cascade Corp., 1979-81; atty. Texaco Inc., Houston, 1981-84, Conoco Inc., Houston, 1984-85; atty. Am. Gen. Corp., Houston, 1985-86, sr. atty., 1986—. Del. Idaho State Dem. Conv., Pocatello, 1980. NSF fellow, 1970-73. Mem. ABA, U.S. Def. Com., MENSA, Sierra Club, U.S. English. Roman Catholic. Club: Am. Athletic (Houston). Avocations: travel, stamp collecting, polit. affairs. Labor, Pension, profit-sharing, and employee benefits, Environment. Office: Am Gen Corp Law Dept 2929 Allen Pkwy Houston TX 77019

BADER, HOWARD DAVID, lawyer; b. N.Y.C., Jan. 14, 1949; s. Edward and Georgette (Dick) B.; m. Linda Anderson, Sept. 10, 1977; 1 child, Robert Benjamen. B.A., Adelphi U., 1970; J.D., Ohio State U., 1973. Bar: N.Y. 1975, U.S. Dist. Ct. (so. and ea. dists.) N.Y. 1975, U.S. Ct. Appeals (2d cir.) 1975. U.S. Supreme Ct. 1980. Atty. Shank & Bader, Hempstead, N.Y., 1975-79; sole practice, N.Y.C., 1980; sr. ptnr. Mannarino, Bader & Bloom, P.C., N.Y.C., 1980—. Chmn. lawyers sect. Assn. to Help Retarded Children, N.Y.C., 1983—. Recipient award of appreciation St. Albans VA, 1984. Mem. ABA (chmn. litigation subcom. 2d cir.), N.Y. State Bar Assn., N.Y. State Trial Lawyers (com. on litigation), N.Y.C. Bar Assn., Nassau County Bar Assn., Comml. Law League of Am. Federal civil litigation, State civil litigation, Bankruptcy. Office: Mannarino Bader & Bloom PC 275 Madison Ave New York NY 10016

BADER, IZAAK WALTON, lawyer; b. N.Y.C., June 20, 1922; s. Maximillian Bader and Ida (Sussman) B.; m. Betty Sands Bader, Mar. 26, 1972. A.B. in Chemistry, NYU, 1942, J.D., 1968. Bar: N.Y., D.C., U.S. Supreme Ct. Atty., FTC, Washington, 1948-50; asst. counsel N.Y. State Rent Com., N.Y.C., 1950-54; patent counsel Swingline Inc., 1954-72; sr. ptnr. Bader & Bader, White Plains, N.Y., 1972—; counsel Heart Disease Found., 1970-76; gen. counsel Ind. Protection League, N.Y.C., 1972—. Mem. ABA, N.Y. State Bar Assn., Westchester County Bar Assn. Democrat. Patent, Securities, State civil litigation. Home: 19 Beech Tree Rd Brookfield Center CT 06805 Office: 65 Court St White Plains NY 10601

BADER, JOHN MERWIN, lawyer; b. Wilmington, Del., June 29, 1919; s. Merwin Oldrin and Escelyn (Connell) B.; m. Constance Wulffaert, Dec. 27, 1944 (div. Oct. 1965); children: Andrew M., Mary Drakely, Eileen Williams, Matthew J.; m. Anne S. Shane, Jan. 10, 1973. BA, Villanova U., 1941; LLB, U. Pa., 1948. Bar: Del. 1948, U.S. Supreme Ct. 1956. Sole practice Wilmington, 1948-56, 59-70; assoc. Bader & Biggs, Wilmington, 1959-66; ptnr. Balick & Bader, Wilmington, 1956-59, Bader, Dorsey & Kreshtool, Wilmington, 1970-81, Bader & Williams, Wilmington, 1985—. Counsel Rep. State Com., Wilmington, 1975-85. Served to 1st lt. U.S. Army, 1941-45. Mem. Del. Bar Assn. (v.p. 1969-71), Assn. Trial Lawyers Am. (bd. govs. 1969-73, 75-80), Del. Trial Lawyers Assn. (pres. 1977-80). Club: Univ., Whist (Wilmington). Lodge: Elks, Kiwanis. State civil litigation, Personal injury, General practice. Home: 402 Rockwood Rd Wilmington DE 19802 Office: Bader & Williams 800 Washington St Wilmington DE 19801

BADER, MICHAEL HALEY, lawyer; b. Tacoma, Aug. 28, 1929; s. Francis William and Gertrude Mary (Haley) B.; m. Joan Marie Berry, Aug. 21, 1954; children: Michael Haley, Brian Raymond, Mary Jennifer, Margaret Patricia, Joan Kerry. LL.B., George Washington U., 1952; M.Liberal Studies, Georgetown U., 1980. Bar: D.C. 1954. Since practiced in Washington; partner firm Haley, Bader & Potts, 1959—; pres. Sta. WTID, Suffolk, Va., 1980—, Sta. WGLL, Mercersburg, Pa., 1983—; mng. ptnr. Sta. WGTO, Cypress Gardens, Fla., 1986—; bd. dirs. MCI Communications Corp., Washington. Bd. advs. Georgetown Visitation Prep. Sch., Washington; co-chmn. bd. dirs. Georgetown Symphony Orch., Washington, 1986—. Served to capt. AUS, 1952-54. Mem. Fed. Communications Bar Assn. (exec. com. 1971-74), D.C. Bar Assn. Republican. Roman Catholic. Administrative and regulatory, Federal civil litigation, Public utilities. Home: 5211 Wehawken Rd Bethesda MD 20816 Office: Haley Bader & Potts 2000 M St NW Washington DC 20036

BADER-YORK, JUDITH, lawyer; b. N.Y.C., May 24, 1939; m. Louis B. York, Dec. 17, 1967; 1 dau., Elizabeth York. B.A. with honors, Queens Coll., 1961; J.D., NYU, 1964. Bar: N.Y. 1964, U.S. Ct. Appeals (2d cir.) 1966, U.S. Dist. Ct. (so. dist.) N.Y. 1967, U.S. Dist. Ct. (ea. dist.) N.Y. 1967, U.S. Supreme Ct. 1968. Sr. trial atty. civil div. Legal Aid Soc., N.Y.C., 1964-67; trial counsel Com. Grievances of Assn. of the Bar, N.Y.C., 1967-69; gen. counsel N.Y.C. Dept. Probation, Family and Criminal Cts., 1969-72; sole practice, N.Y.C., 1972-74, 79—; dir. N.Y. State Div. Criminal Justice Services, N.Y.C., 1974-79; adj. asst. prof. Grad. Sch., Lehman Coll., CUNY, 1970-74; adminstrv. law judge N.Y.C. Environ. Control Bd., 1980-82; hearing examiner Family Ct. N.Y. County, 1979-81. Vice pres., trustee Fair Harbor Community Assn., Fire Island, N.Y.; mem. N.Y. County Democratic Com., 1975—. Mem. Assn. Bar City of N.Y., N.Y. Women's Bar Assn., ABA (family law sect.). Editor of profl. jours. State civil litigation, Family and matrimonial, General practice. Office: 21st Floor 415 Madison Ave New York NY 10017

BADGER, DAVID RUSSELL, lawyer; b. South Weymouth, Mass., May 30, 1947; s. Russell Weston Badger and Marie (McGowan) Barnes; m. Tommi West, Aug. 21, 1971; children: Chris, Erin. AB in Polit. Sci., U. N.C., 1969, JD, 1972. Bar: N.C. 1972, U.S. Dist. Ct. (we. dist.) N.C. 1972, U.S. Ct. Appeals (4th cir.) 1972, U.S. Dist. Ct. (mid. dist.) N.C. 1978, U.S. Dist. Ct. (ea.dist.) N.C. 1980, U.S. Supreme Ct. 1983. Ptnr. Whitfield, McNeely, Norwood & Badger, Charlotte, N.C.; pres. Badger, Blackford, McNeely & Tepper P.A., Charlotte, Badger & Johnson P.A., Charlotte, 1986—. Author: North Carolina Post-Judgment Collection Law, 1985, North Carolina Collection Law for Creditors, 1987. Mem. N.C. Bar Assn. (chmn. bankruptcy sect. 1984-85), Assn. Trial Lawyers Am., N.C. Acad. Trial Lawyers, Nat. Bd. Trial Advocacy (diplomate), Am. Bankruptcy Inst. Democrat. Presbyterian. Clubs: Hornet's Nest, Sertoma (Charlotte). Avocations: sailing, tennis, scuba diving. Bankruptcy, Criminal. Home: 525 N Poplar St Charlotte NC 28202 Office: Badger & Johnson PA 701 E Trade St Suite 7 Charlotte NC 28202

BADGER, JEFFREY EWEN, lawyer; b. Greenville, S.C.; s. Russell Weston and Alice Kathryn (Smith) B.; m. Kathryn John Badger, Nov. 21, 1981. BA, Boston Coll., 1977; JD, Washington & Lee U., 1980. Bar: Md. 1980, Va. 1980, U.S. Dist. Ct. Md. 1982. Assoc. Webb, Burnett & Duvall, Salisbury, Md., 1980-82; asst. state's atty. Wicomico County, Md., 1983; assoc. Long, Hughes, Bahen & Dashiell, Salisbury, 1983—; 2d v.p., bd. dirs. Lower Shore Sheltered Workshop, Inc., Salisbury, 1984—. Bd. dirs., legal counsel Johnson's Lake Neighborhood Assn., Inc., 1985—. Mem. ABA, Va. Bar Assn., Md. Bar Assn., Wiccmico County Bar Assn. Avocations: sports, photography. State civil litigation, Criminal, Personal injury. Home: 713 Lakeside Dr Salisbury MD 21801 Office: Long Hughes Bahen & Dashiell 124 E Main St Salisbury MD 21801

BADGER, RAYMOND LOUIS, JR., lawyer; b. Boston, Oct. 11, 1951; s. Raymond Louis Sr. and Dorothy C. (Clemens) B.; m. Sharon E. Miller; children: Sabrina K., Jessica M. BA in English, U. Notre Dame, 1973; JD, U. of Pacific, 1977. Bar: Calif. 1978, Nev. 1979, U.S. Dist. Ct. Nev. 1979. Drafter bills Nev. Legis., Carson City, 1979; gen. counsel Nev. Indsl. Ins. System, Carson City, 1979-83; sole practice Carson City, 1983—; ptnr. Badger & Baker, Carson City, 1985—. Mem. Nev. Trial Lawyers Assn. (bd. dirs. 1985—). Democrat. Workers' compensation, Personal injury, Insurance. Home: 1110 Cabrolet Dr Carson City NV 89701 Office: Badger & Baker 312 W 3d St Carson City NV 89701

BADGEROW, JOHN NICHOLAS, lawyer; b. Macon, Mo., Apr. 7, 1951; s. Harry Leroy Badgerow and Barbara Raines (Buell) Novaria; m. Teresa Ann Zvolanek, Aug. 7, 1976; 1 child, Anthony Thornton. BA in Bus. and English with honors, Principia Coll., 1972; JD, U. Mo., Kansas City, 1975. Bar: Kans. 1976, U.S. Dist Ct. Kans. 1976, U.S. Ct. Appeals (10th cir.) 1977, U.S. Ct. Appeals (4th cir.) 1979, U.S. Ct. Appeals (fed. cir.) 1985, U.S. Supreme Ct. 1982, Mo. 1986. Ptnr. McAnany, VanCleave & Phillips, P.A., Kans. City, Kans., 1975-85, Spencer, Fane, Britt & Browne, Kans. City, Mo. and Overland Park, Kans., 1986—. Mem. ABA, Kans. Bar Assn. (employment seminar 1985, bd. of editors 1982—), Kansas City Met. Bar Assn., Lawyers' Assn. of Kansas City, Kans. Assn. Def. Counsel (age discrimination seminar). Republican. Christian Scientist. Club: Mission Valley Hunt (Stilwell, Kans.). Avocations: horseback riding, carpentry, reading. Federal civil litigation, Civil rights, State civil litigation. Office: Spencer Fane Britt & Browne 9401 Indian Creek Pkwy Overland Park KS 66225

BAECHTOLD, ROBERT LOUIS, lawyer; b. Jersey City, Dec. 18, 1937; s. Fred Jacob and Catherine (Lenning) B.; m. Henrietta Thelma Hornbaker, Jan. 24, 1959; children—Kathi Ann, Christina Lee, Theresa Lynn. B.S., Rutgers U., 1958, J.D. summa cum laude, Seton Hall U., 1966. Bar: N.Y. 1967, N.J. 1971, U.S. Dist. Ct. (so. and ea. dists.) N.Y. 1967, U.S. Ct. Appeals (fed. cir.) 1971, U.S. Ct. Appeals (2d cir.) 1967. Research chemist Am. Cyanamid Co., Bound Brook, N.J., 1958-62; patent agt. M & T Chems., Inc., Rahway, N.J., 1962-65; assoc. Ward, Haselton, Orme, McElhannon, Brooks & Fitzpatrick, N.Y.C., 1965-68, ptnr., 1969-71; ptnr. Fitzpatrick, Cella, Harper & Scinto, N.Y.C., 1971—; lectr. Am. Patent Law Assn., 1979, Practising Law Inst., 1981, others. Mem. Cranford (N.J.) Bd. Edn., 1970-73. Nat. Starch Products scholar, Leopold Schepp Found. grantee, 1954-58. Mem. ABA, Am. Patent Law Assn. (com. chmn. 1981), Fed. Cir. Bar Assn., N.J. Patent Law Assn. (pres. 1978-80), N.Y. Patent Law Assn., N.Y. Bar Assn., N.J. Bar Assn. Contbg. author course handbook Practising Law Inst., 1981; patentee chemistry field. Patent, Federal civil litigation, Trademark and copyright. Office: Fitzpatrick Cella Harper & Scinto 277 Park Ave New York NY 10172

BAER, BENJAMIN FRANKLIN, federal official, criminologist; b. Peoria, Ill., Jan. 2, 1918; s. Henry and Emma (Siebenthal) B.; m. Dorothea Frances Heisman, Mar. 20, 1942; children: Marc Bradley, Meredith Jan, Bartley Benjamin F. B.A., San Diego State U., 1941; M.S.W., U. So. Calif., 1947, postgrad., 1964. Camp dir. Probation Dept., Los Angeles, 1942-47; staff Calif. Dept. Corrections, Sacramento, 1947-54; assoc. warden San Quentin, 1954-60; dir. Dept. Corrections State of Iowa, Des Moines, 1960-64, Correctional Decision Info. Project, Sacramento, 1965-67; dep. commr., chmn. youth commn. Minn. Dept. Corrections, St. Paul, 1967-72; staff U.S. Parole Commn., 1972; commr. U.S. Parole Commn., Washington, 1981—; chmn. U.S. Parole Commn., 1982—; bd. mem. Nat. Inst. Corrections, 1982—; bd. dirs. Adv. Correctional Council, Washington, 1982—; commr., ex officio U.S. Sentencing Commn., 1984—; mem. Pres. Kennedy's Juvenile Delinquence Commn., 1961-63. Author (with Harlan Hill) California Correctional Information System: Preliminary Information System Design, 1967. Mem. Am. Correctional Assn. Home: 10925 Wickshire Way Rockville MD 20852 Office: U S Parole Commn 5550 Friendship Blvd Chevy Chase MD 20815

BAER, DAVID, JR., lawyer; b. Belleville, Ill., Sept. 24, 1905; s. David and Sunshine (Lieber) B.; LL.B., Washington U., 1928; m. Mary Lynne Cockrell Sweet, Apr. 18, 1938 (dec.); m. 2d, Jane Caulfield, Sept. 11, 1982. Ptnr. Lashly, Baer & Hamel, P.C., St. Louis; dir. Lindell Trust Co.; former pres., dir. Mo.-Lincoln Trust Co.; former dir. Scullin Steel Co., St. Louis. Former mem. St. Louis Boy Scout Endowment Fund Com. Served as sgt. AUS, 1943-45. Mem. Estate Planning Council St. Louis (past pres., dir.), Am., Mo., St. Louis (past chmn. group ins. com.) bar assns., Washington U. Law Alumni Assn., Jr. (life), Ill. Jr. (past pres.), U.S. Jr. Cs. of C. (senator). Clubs: Mo. Athletic, University. Lodges: Masons, De Molay (sr., Legion of Honor, past master councilor). Banking, Probate, Estate planning. Home: 625 S Skinker Blvd Saint Louis MO 63105 Office: 714 Locust St Saint Louis MO 63101

BAER, JOHN RICHARD FREDERICK, lawyer; b. Melrose Park, Ill., Jan. 9, 1941; s. John Richard and Zena Edith (Ostreyko) B.; m. Linda Gail Chapman, Aug. 31, 1963; children—Brett Scott, Deborah Jill. B.A., U. Ill.-Champaign, 1963, J.D., 1966. Bar: Ill. 1966, U.S. Dist. Ct. (no. dist.) Ill. 1967, U.S. Ct. Appeals (7th cir.) 1969, U.S. Ct. Appeals (D.C. cir.) 1975, U.S. Ct. Appeals (9th cir.) 1979, U.S. Supreme Ct. 1975. Assoc. Keck, Mahin & Cate, Chgo., 1966-73, ptnr., 1974—; instr. Advanced Mgmt. Inst., Lake Forest Coll., 1975-76; speaker various legal seminars, 1975, 76, 77, 80, 81; mem. adv. com. legal asst. program. Nat. Coll. Edn., 1980-83, chmn., 1982-83. Mem. Plan Commn., Village of Deerfield (Ill.), 1976-79, chmn., 1978-79, mem. Home Rule Study Commn., 1974-75, mem. home rule implementation com., 1975-76. Mem. Ill. State Bar Assn. (competition dir. region 8 Nat. Moot Ct. Competition 1974, co-chmn. nat. moot competition 1976, profl. ethics com. 1977-84, chmn. 1982-83, spl. com. on individual lawyre advt. 1981-83, profl. responsibility com. 1983-84), ABA, Fed. Bar Assn., Am. Judicature Soc., Nat. Lawyer's Club. Clubs: River (Chgo.). Editorial bd. U. Ill. Law Forum, 1964-65, asst. editor, 1965-66; contbg. editor: Commercial Liability Risk Management and Insurance, 1978. Administrative and regulatory, Contracts commercial, General practice. Office: 8300 Sears Tower 233 S Wacker Dr Chicago IL 60606

BAER, LUKE, lawyer; b. Portage La Prarie, Man., Can., Aug. 7, 1950; came to U.S., 1951; s. Allan and Edna (Brubacher) B.; m. Leslie Ann Swazee, Sept. 11, 1982; 1 child, Jessica Ann. Student, U. Wis., Whitewater, 1971-73; BA in German, History, U. Wis., 1974; student, Rheinische Fredrich Wilhems U., Bonn, Fed. Republic of Germany, 1973-74; JD, William Mitchell Coll. Law, 1978. Bar: Minn., Nev., U.S. Dist. Ct. Nev., U.S. Ct. Appeals (9th cir.). Law clk. to chief judge U.S. Dist. Ct., St. Paul, 1979-81; assoc. Dorsey & Whitney, Mpls., 1981-86; v.p., gen. counsel Porsche Cars N.Am., Inc., Reno, 1986—. Recipient West Pub. Book award, 1976, 1977, Am. Jurisprudence Book award, 1977, , Hornhood award, 1977; CJS scholar, 1977, Space Ctr. Acad. scholar, 1977, 3M Acad. scholar, 1978. Mem. ABA, Minn. Bar Assn., Nev. Bar Assn., Hennepin County Bar Assn., Nat. Order Barristers (Excellence in Appellate Adv. award). Republican. Avocations: pvt. pilot, reading and speaking German, skiing. General corporate. Office: Porsche Cars N Am Inc 200 S Virginia St Reno NV 89501

BAER, PETER EDWARD, lawyer; b. North Bend, Oreg., July 19, 1937; s. Samuel Edward and Charlotte Jane (Quist) B.; m. Carol Jane Schimschok, July 15, 1977 (div. July 1983); children: Samuel Peter, Andrea Charlotte. BS, Oreg. State U., 1959, postgrad., 1961-62; B in Fgn. Trade, Am. Grad. Sch. Internat. Mgmt., Glendale, Ariz., 1966; JD, Lewis & Clark U., 1974. Bar: Oreg. 1974, U.S. Dist. Ct. Oreg. 1974, U.S. Ct. Appeals (9th cir.) 1974, U.S. Ct. Internat. Trade 1981. Geologist Litton Industry Western Geophys., Calif., 1962-64; planner City of Phoenix, 1964-65; cargo booker Matson Navigation, Portland, Oreg., 1966; wholesale staff Chevron Corp., Portland, 1967-74; sole practice Portland, 1974—; adj. prof. Western Oreg. State Coll., Monmouth, 1979—. Legal advisor Percent for Arts lobby, Portland, 1974-76, Mt. Hood Pops Orch., Gresham, Oreg., 1983—; bd. dirs., pres. Vol. Bur. United Way, Portland, 1968-76. Served with USNR, 1954-62. Recipient Cert. of Appreciation Stop Oreg. Littering and Vandalism, 1971, Western Oreg. State Coll. Art Dept., 1979. Mem. ABA, Oreg. Bar Assn. (lectr. continuing legal edn. on art authentication 1975), Greater Gresham Bar Assn. (pres. 1985, com. on computerization 1986), Multnomah Bar Assn., AIME (chmn. Oreg. sect. 1986), Assn. Engring. Geologists, Portland Jaycees (bd. dirs. 1967-71, Silver Key award 1970), Geol. Soc. Oreg. Country (legal advisor to bd. dirs.), Ducks Unltd. (bd. dirs. 1983—), Chi Phi. Republican. Episcopalian. Avocations: fly fishing, bird hunting. Contracts commercial, Mining, General practice. Home: 1026 US Hwy 26 Gresham OR 97030 Office: 838 NE 10th St Gresham OR 97030

BAFFES, THOMAS GUS, heart surgeon, lawyer; b. New Orleans, Apr. 3, 1923; s. Gus and Tina (Bores) B.; m. Mary Lou Amann, Feb. 23, 1958; children: Kathleen, Christine, Paul, Andrew. B.S., Tulane U., 1943, M.D., 1945; J.D., DePaul U., 1975, LL.M. in Taxation, 1978. Bar: Ill. 1975, La. 1975. Rotating intern Charity Hosp., New Orleans, 1945-46, residency tng. gen. surgery, 1948-51, residency tng. thoracic surgery, 1951-52; residency pediatric pathology Children's Meml. Hosp., Chgo., 1952, residency pediatric surgery, 1953, fellow cardiovascular research, 1954-56, now mem. staff; mem. staff Swedish Covenant Hosp., 1960-84; prof. surgery Rush Med. Coll.; chmn. dept. surgery Mt. Sinai Med. Ctr.; staff Augustana Hosp., Luth. Gen. Hosp., Ill. Cen. Hosp., Mt. Sinai Hosp., all Chgo.; mem. law firm Pierce, Daley & Penn, Chgo., 1975-85, Daley, Baffes, O'Sullivan and Mussar, 1985. Author med. and legal articles. Served as capt. M.C., AUS, 1946-48; psychiatry and surgery VA hosps. Recipient Beta Mu award biology; Alpha Chi Sigma award chemistry; Isadore Dyer scholastic award Tulane U., 1945; chosen one of Ten Outstanding Young Men, 1957. Mem. AMA, ACS, Am. Acad. Pediatrics, Am. Coll. Chest Physicians, Chgo. Surg. Soc., Am. Soc. Artificial Organs, Am. Assn. Thoracic Surgery, Soc. Thoracic Surgeons, Western Surg. Soc., Chgo. Med. Soc., Protective Med. Assn. Ill. (pres. 1975—), Am. Coll. Law and Medicine, Phi Beta Kappa, Alpha Omega Alpha. Mem. Hellenic Orthodox Ch. Admiralty, Health, Personal income taxation. Home: 1701 Woodland Ave Park Ridge IL 60068 Office: 4055 Main St Skokie IL 60076 Office: 180 N LaSalle St Chicago IL 60601

BAGAN, GRANT ALAN, lawyer; b. Chgo., Dec. 27, 1953; s. Seymour Jack and Joyce (Klass) B. m. Laurie Beth Weiss, Aug. 19, 1978; children: Stacy, Michelle, Ashley. BS cum laude, Tulane U., 1976; JD magna cum laude, U. Ill., 1979. Bar: Ill. 1979. Assoc. McDermott, Will & Emery, Chgo., 1979-85, ptnr., 1985—. General corporate, Securities.

BAGBY, WILLIAM RARDIN, lawyer; b. Grayson, Ky., Feb. 19, 1910; s. John Albert and Nano A. (Rardin) B.; m. Mary Carpenter, Sept. 3, 1939; 1 son, John Robert; m. Elizabeth Hinkel, Nov. 22, 1975. A.B., Cornell U., 1933; J.D., U. Mich., 1936. Bar: Ky. 1937, Ohio 1952, U.S. Tax Ct. 1948, U.S. Supreme Ct. 1950, U.S. Ct. Appeals (6th cir.) 1952. Sole practice, Grayson, Ky., 1937-43; city atty., judge City of Grayson, 1939-43; counsel Treasury Dept., Chgo., Cleve. and Cin., 1946-54; sole practice Lexington, Ky., 1954—; prof. U. Ky., 1956-57; gen. counsel Headley-Whitney Mus., 1974-84. Mem. Bd. of Adjustment, Lexington-Urban County City Govt., 1965—, chmn. 1981—; trustee Bagby Music Found., N.Y.C., 1963-74; trustee, gen. counsel McDowell Cancer Found., 1979—. Served to lt. USN, 1943-46. Mem. ABA, Am. Judicature Soc., Ky. Bar Assn., Lexington Bar Assn. Democrat. Episcopalian. Clubs: Rotary, Spindletop, Keeneland, Lexington, Iroquois Hunt. Estate taxation, Personal income taxation, State and local taxation. Home: 228 Market St Lexington KY 40508 Office: 1107 1st Nat Bank Bldg Lexington KY 40507

BAGGE, DOUGLAS MALCOLM, lawyer; b. Ridgewood, N.J., Oct. 15, 1953. AB, Syracuse U., 1975; JD, Georgetown U., 1978. Bar: D.C. 1978, Fla. 1982. Assoc. Reid & Priest, Washington, 1979-81; asst. counsel Fla. Power Corp., St. Petersburg, 1981-82; corp. counsel, asst. sec. Fla. Progress Corp., St. Petersburg, 1983—. General corporate, Contracts commercial, High technology and venture capital. Office: Fla Progress Corp Box 33042 Saint Petersburg FL 33733

BAGGE, MICHAEL CHARLES, lawyer; b. Westfield, Mass., June 30, 1950; s. Roy Rudolph and Margaret Mary (Coyle) B. BA, Tufts U., 1973; JD, Tulane U., 1976. Bar: Mo. 1976, U.S. Dist. Ct. (ea. dist.) Mo. 1977, N.Y. 1979, U.S. Dist. Ct. (no. dist.) N.Y. 1979, U.S. Ct. Appeals (2d cir.) 1982. Atty. Bootheel Area Legal Assistance Program, Caruthersville, Mo., 1976-77, staff. atty., 1977-78; staff. atty. Legal Aid Soc. Oneida County, Utica, N.Y., 1978-80, sr. atty., 1980—. Mem. Nat. Lawyers Guild. Socialist. Roman Catholic. Administrative and regulatory, Federal civil litigation, Pension, profit-sharing, and employee benefits. Home: 1314 Rutger St Utica NY 13501 Office: Legal Aid Soc Oneida County 185 Genesee St Utica NY 13501

BAGGETT, STEPHEN DALLAS, lawyer; b. Atlanta, Sept. 23, 1950; s. Julius Herbert and Evelyn Ruth (Heacox) B.; m. Sara Elizabeth Strom, June 16, 1974; children: Stephen Dallas Jr., Martha Elizabeth, Sara Evelyn. BA, Furman U., 1972; JD, U. S.C., 1976. Bar: S.C. 1976, U.S. Dist. Ct. S.C. 1976, U.S. Ct. Appeals (4th cir.) 1976. Assoc. Whaley, McCutchen, Blanton & Rhodes, Columbia, S.C., 1976-80, Burns, McDonald, Bradford, Patrick & Dean, Greenwood, S.C., 1980—; ptnr. Burns, McDonald, Bradford, Erwin & Patrick, Greenwood, S.C., 1983—; atty. Greenwood County, 1980—. Notes editor S.C. Law Rev., 1975-76. Deacon First Bapt. Ch., Greenwood, 1982-86; bd. dirs. Hospice of Greenwood, 1982—, chmn., 1986—; bd. dirs. Lander Coll. Found., Greenwood, 1986—; mem. adv. bd. Salvation Army, Greenwood, 1983-86. Mem. ABA, S.C. Bar Assn., S.C. Def. Trial Attys. Assn., Greenwood County Bar Assn. Baptist. Lodge: Rotary (bd. dirs. Greenwood 1986—). State civil litigation, Insurance, Workers' compensation. Office: Burns McDonald et al 201 Park Plaza Greenwood SC 29648

BAGGETT, W. MIKE, lawyer; b. Waco, Tex., Nov. 8, 1946; s. Bill R. and Jenna (Robertson) B.; m. Jo Kilpatrick, May 28, 1968; children: Carl, Cary. BBA, Tex. A&M U., 1968; JD cum laude, Baylor U., 1973. Bar: Tex. 1973. Briefing atty. Tex. Supreme Ct., Austin, 1973-74; ptnr. Winstead, McGuire, Schrest & Minick, Dallas, 1974—; bd. dirs. MBank Abilene (Tex.), N.A., Allied Bank of Dallas. Author: Texas, Foreclosure: Law & Practice. Bd. dirs. former students Tex. A&M Assn., Coll. Sta., 1982-86, pres., 1987—. Served to 1st lt. U.S. Army, 1968-71, Vietnam. Decorated Bronze Star. Fellow Tex. Bar Found.; mem. Tex. Bar Assn. (adminstrn. of justice com., bd. certified civil trial com.). Republican. Lutheran. Clubs: City, Lancers, Royal Oaks (Dallas). Federal civil litigation, State civil litigation, Banking. Home: 10116 Estate Ln Dallas TX 75238 Office: MBank 1700 MBank Dallas Bldg Dallas TX 75201

BAGGETT BOOZER, LINDA DIANNE, lawyer; b. Pascagoula, Miss., Jan. 22, 1956; d. Grady Milton and Ruby Constance (Hunter) Baggett; m. John Singleton Boozer, June 14, 1986. Student, Universidad de Filosofia y Letras, Valencia, Spain, 1976; BA in Spanish and Secondary Edn. with highest honors, U. So. Miss., 1978; JD cum laude, U. Miss., 1981. Bar: Miss. 1981, U.S. Dist. Ct. (no. and so. dists.) Miss. 1981, U.S. Ct. Appeals (5th cir.) 1982. Assoc. Megehee, Brown, Williams & Mestayer, Pascagoula, 1981-84; atty. Ingalls Shipbuilding div. Litton Systems Inc., Pascagoula and Beverly Hills, Calif., 1984—. Mem. Miss. div. Am. Cancer Soc., pres. Jackson County Unit, 1983-85; appointed to com. on care offered to Pascagoula elderly by Pascagoula City Council, 1983; participant 1987 Leadership Miss. Program Miss. Econ. Council. Named one of Outstanding Young Women Am., 1983, 84, Outstanding Young Careerist Pascagoula Bus. and Profl. Women's Club, 1985. Mem. ABA, Miss. Bar Assn., Jackson County Bar Assn. (treas. 1984-85, sec. 1985-86), Jackson County Young Lawyers Assn. (treas. 1982-83), Phi Kappa Phi, Phi Delta Phi, Omicron Delta Kappa (sec./treas.), Phi Delta Rho, Pi Tau Chi (pres.), Cwens/Lambda Sigma (pres.), Alpha Lambda Delta, Kappa Delta Pi, Chi Omega (corresponding sec., scholarship award). Baptist. Avocation: bicycling. Environment, General corporate. Home: 2212 Sandalwood Pl Gautier MS 39553 Office: Litton Systems Inc Ingalls Shipbldg Div PO Box 149 Pascagoula MS 39567

BAGLEY, CONSTANCE ELIZABETH, lawyer; b. Tucson, Dec. 18, 1952; d. Robert Porter Smith and Joanne Snow-Smith. AB in Polit. Sci. with distinction, with honors, Stanford U., 1974; JD magna cum laude, Harvard U., 1977. Bar: Calif. 1978, N.Y. 1978. Tchg. fellow Harvard U., 1975-77; assoc. Webster & Sheffield, N.Y.C., 1977-78, Heller, Ehrman, White & McAuliffe, San Francisco, 1978-79; assoc. McCutchen, Doyle, Brown & Enersen, San Francisco, 1979-84, ptnr., 1984—; mem. Bur. Nat. Affairs Corp. Practice Series Adv. Bd., 1984—; lectr. bus. bd. dirs. exec. program Stanford (Calif.) U. Grad. Sch. of Bus., 1985—; lectr., mem. planning com. Calif. Continuing Edn. of the Bar, Los Angeles, San Francisco, 1983, 85—. Author: Mergers, Acquisitions and Tender Offers, 1983, (with others) Proxy Contests, 1983, supplement, 1987; contbg. editor Calif. Bus. Law Reporter, 1983—; also articles. Vestry mem. Trinity Episcopal Ch., San Francisco, 1984-85; vol. Moffit Hosp. U. Calif., San Francisco, 1983-84. Teaching fellow Harvard U., 1975-77. Mem. ABA, San Francisco Bar Assn., Phi Beta Kappa. Republican. Clubs: Golden Gateway Tennis and Swim, Commonwealth (San Francisco), Peninsula Stanford. General corporate, Securities. Office: McCutchen Doyle Brown & Enersen 3 Embarcadero Ctr San Francisco CA 94111

BAGLEY, WILLIAM THOMPSON, lawyer; b. San Francisco, June 29, 1928; s. Nino J. and Rita V. (Thompson) Baglietto; m. Diane Lenore Oldham, June 20, 1965; children—Lynn Lorene, William Thompson, Walter William, Shana Angela, Tracy Elizabeth. A.B., U. Calif.-Berkeley, 1949, J.D., 1952. Bar: Calif. 1953, U.S. Supreme Ct. 1967. Atty., Pacific, Gas & Electric Co., 1952-56; assoc. Gardiner, Riede & Elliott, San Rafael, Calif., 1956-60; ptnr. Bagley & Bianchi, San Rafael, 1960-74; mem. Calif. Legis., 1960-74; chmn. Commodity Futures Trading Commn., Washington, 1975-78; ptnr. Nossaman, Guthner, Knox and Elliott, San Francisco, 1980—; ; mem. Calif. Pub. Utilities Commn., Calif. Transp. Commn., 1983-86. Bd. dirs. Nat. Futures Assn., Calif. Council Environ. and Econ. Balance, Edmund G. Brown Inst. Govtl. Affairs, Los Angeles; chmn. bd. Calif. Republican League, 1980-82. Recipient Freedom of Info. award Sigma Delta Chi, 1970; Golden Bear award Calif. Park Commn., 1973; named Most Effective Assemblyman, Capitol Press Corps, 1969, Legislator of Yr., Calif. Trial Lawyers Assn., 1970. Mem. ABA, Calif. State Bar Assn., San Francisco Bar, Marin County Bar Assn., Phi Beta Kappa. Presbyterian. Clubs: World Trade, Elks (life). Bd. editors Calif. Law Rev., 1951-52. Administrative and regulatory, Legislative, Government contracts and claims. Office: 100 The Embarcadero San Francisco CA 94105

BAHLS, STEVEN CARL, lawyer, legal educator; b. Des Moines, Sept. 4, 1954; s. Carl Robert and Dorothy Rose (Jensen) B.; m. Jane Emily Easter, June 18, 1977; children: Daniel David, Timothy Carl. BBA, U. Iowa, 1976; JD, Northwestern U., Chgo., 1979. Bar: Wis. 1979; CPA, Iowa. Assoc. Frisch, Dudek & Slattery, Milw., 1979-84, dir., 1985; asst. prof. U. Mont. Sch. of Law, Missoula, 1985—; bd. dirs. Musebeck Shoe Co., Oconomowoc, Wis. Coordinating exec. editor Northwestern U. Law Rev., 1979. Mem. ABA, Wis. Bar Assn., Order of Coif. Republican. Presbyterian. Avocations: photography, skiing, hiking. General corporate, Legal education, Securities. Home: 3300 Pattee Canyon Rd Missoula MT 59803 Office: U Mont Sch of Law Missoula MT 59812

BAHNER, THOMAS MAXFIELD, lawyer; b. Little Rock, Nov. 26, 1933; s. Carl Tabb and Catharine (Garrott) B.; m. Sara Minta McIntyre, Sept. 28, 1957; children: Maxfield Tabb, Minta Susan, Margaret Catharine. B.S., Carson-Newman Coll., 1954; B.D., So. Baptist Theol. Sem., 1957; J.D., U. Va., 1960. Bar: Va. 1960, Tenn. 1960. Assoc. Kefauver, Duggan and McDonald, Chattanooga, 1960-62; ptnr. Duggan, McDonald and Bahner, Chattanooga, 1962-64, Chambliss, Bahner, Crutchfield, Gaston and Irvine, Chattanooga, 1964—; mem. adv. commn. civil rules Tenn. Supreme Ct., chmn., 1982—; mem. bd. profl. responsibility, 1982-85 , chmn. fin. com., 1984-85. Bd. dirs. United Cerebral Palsy Greater Chattanooga, 1963-70, pres., 1966-67; mem. allocations steering com. United Fund Greater Chattanooga, 1970, vice-chmn. com., 1972-73; founding bd. dirs. Chattanooga Council on Alcoholism, 1964-65; bd. dirs. Team Evaluation Ctr., Inc., Chattanooga, 1965-70, Chattanooga Symphony, 1978-81, Orange Grove Ctr., Chattanooga, 1962—, pres. 1973-75, chmn. bldg. com., various other coms.; mem. Hamilton County Sch. Bd., 1969-73; trustee Carson-Newman Coll., Jefferson City, Tenn., 1975—, chmn. bd., 1983—, pres. search com., 1982; chmn. pulpit com., deacon Signal Mountain Baptist Ch., also Sunday sch. supt. Recipient Disting. Alumni award, Carson-Newman Coll., 1984. Fellow Am. Bar Found., Tenn. Bar Found. (founding); mem. Am. Coll. Trial Lawyers, Am. Bd. Trial Advocates, Chattanooga Bar Assn. (pres. 1969-70), Tenn. Bar Assn. (lectr. 1965, bd. govs. 1975-82, pres. 1980-81, long range planning com.), Conf. So. Bar Pres. (chmn. 1980-81), ABA (Tenn. del.), Va. State Bar, Tenn. Def. Lawyers Assn., Am. Judicature Soc., Estate Planning Council (bd. dirs. 1971-72), Chattanooga Trial Lawyers Assn. Clubs: Mountain City, Walden, Signal Mountain Golf and Country. Federal civil litigation, State civil litigation, General corporate. Home: 718 Parsons Ln Signal Mountain TN 37377 Office: 1000 Tallan Bldg Two Union Sq Chattanooga TN 37402

BAIER, DAVID DONALD, lawyer; b. Milw., Mar. 17, 1954; s. Donald Gordon and Anna Lee (Scott) B.; m. Barbara Ann Schmitt, Jan. 8, 1977; children: Justin, Andrea. BS, Marquette U., 1976; JD, John Marshall Law Sch., 1980. Bar: Ill. 1980, U.S. Dist. Ct. (no. dist.) 1980, Wis. 1985, U.S. Ct. Appeals (7th cir.) 1985. Sr. tax atty. IRS, Chgo., 1980-85; asst. tax counsel Gen. Dynamics Corp., St. Louis, 1985—. Mem. ABA, Ill. Bar Assn., Wis. Bar Assn., Chgo. Bar Assn., Phi Delta Phi. Republican. Lutheran. Avocation: amateur athletics. Corporate taxation, Personal income taxation, Trademark and copyright. Office: Gen Dynamics Corp Pierre Laclede Ctr Saint Louis MO 63105

BAIGENT, JULIA MARIE, lawyer; b. Toronto, Ont., Can., Jan. 17, 1958; d. Lyle Roger and Mary Frances (Daniel) B.; m. William F. Moison, Aug. 10, 1980 (div. Jan. 1983). BS magna cum laude, U. Calif., Berkeley, 1979; JD cum laude, U. Calif., San Francisco, 1982. Bar: Calif. 1982. Assoc. Ware & Freidenrich, Palo Alto, Calif., 1982-86; sr. legal counsel De Monet Industries, San Mateo, Calif., 1986—. Mem. ABA, Calif. Bar Assn., Palo Alto Bar Assn. Real property, Contracts commercial, Construction. Office: De Monet Industries 1450 Fashion Island Blvd San Mateo CA 94404

BAILEY, ANN LESLIE, lawyer; b. Louisville, Mar. 3, 1958; d. John Lee and Mildred Ann (Wheeler) B. Student, Morehead State U., 1975-77; BA, U. Louisville, 1979, JD, 1982. Bar: Ky. 1982. Staff atty. Jefferson Dist. Pub. Defender, Louisville, 1982-86; assoc. Goldberg & Simpson P.S.C., Louisville, 1986—. Mem. ABA, Ky. Bar Assn., Louisville Bar Assn. Democrat. Mem. Christian Ch. Avocation: piano. State civil litigation, Family and matrimonial, General practice. Home: 1291 Willow Ave Apt 4 Louisville KY 40204 Office: Goldberg & Simpson PSC 2800 1st Nat Tower Louisville KY 40202

BAILEY, BRANT ALLAN, lawyer; b. Kansas City, Kans., May 7, 1948; m. Analyn Ruth Bailey; children: Benjamin, Tirzah. BA, U. Ga., 1970; JD, Sanford U., 1978; LLM, Washington U., 1984. Asst. counsel gen. counsel's office City of Jacksonville, Fla., 1978-80; law clk. to presiding justice 2d Dist. Ct. Appeals, Lakeland, Fla., 1980-81; asst. state atty. Fla. 10th Jud. Cir., Lakeland, 1981-82; sole practice Lakeland, 1982-83; research atty. IRS Appeals, St. Louis, 1984; tax atty. Battaglia, Ross et al, St. Petersburg, Fla.,

1985—. Mem. ABA, Fla. Bar Assn., St. Petersburg Bar Assn., U.S. Profl. Tennis Assn. Republican. Corporate taxation, Probate, General corporate. Office: Battaglia Ross et al 980 Tyrone Blvd Saint Petersburg FL 33710

BAILEY, CRAIG BERNARD, lawyer; b. Camden, N.J., Aug. 20, 1952; s. Bernard Thomas and Nora Frances (DiDomenico) B. BA and BS, Bucknell U., 1975; JD, George Washington U., 1978. Bar: U.S. Patent Office 1977, D.C. 1978, Calif. 1984, U.S. Ct. Claims, U.S. Ct. Internat. Trade, U.S. Tax Ct., U.S. Ct. Mil. Appeals, U.S. Ct. Appeals (1st, 4th, 5th, 7th, 8th, 9th, 10th, D.C. and fed. cirs.), U.S. Supreme Ct. Law clk. to chief judge U.S. Ct. Customs and Patent Appeals, Washington, 1978-80; assoc. Brenner & Wray, Arlington, Va., 1980-83; patent atty. Hughes Aircraft Co., El Segundo, Calif., 1983-86; assoc. Fulwider, Patton, Rieber, Lee & Utecht, Los Angeles, 1986—. Mem. ABA, Los Angeles Patent Law Assn., Tau Beta Pi. Patent, Trademark and copyright, Government contracts and claims. Office: Fulwider Patton Rieber et al 3435 Wilshire Blvd Suite 2400 Los Angeles CA 90010

BAILEY, DANIEL ALLEN, lawyer; b. Pitts., Aug. 31, 1953; s. Richard A. and Virginia R. Bailey; m. Janice Abraham, Oct. 10, 1981. BBA, Bowling Green State U., 1975; JD, Ohio State U., 1978. Bar: Ohio 1978, U.S. Dist. Ct. (so. dist.) 1978, U.S. Tax. Ct. 1979. Ptnr. Arter & Hadden, Columbus, Ohio, 1978—. Contbg. author: Handbook for Corporate Directors, 1985. Bd. dirs. Columbus Met. Community Action Orgn., 1979-80, Franklin County Head Start, Columbus, 1979-80, Faith Luth. Ch., Whitehall, Ohio, 1985—. Mem. ABA, Ohio Bar Assn., Columbus Bar Assn., Phi Kappa Phi, Beta Gamma Sigma, Omicron Delta Kappa. General corporate, Securities, Director and officer liability. Office: Arter & Hadden 10 W Broad St Columbus OH 43215

BAILEY, FRANCIS LEE, lawyer; b. Waltham, Mass., June 10, 1933; m. Florence Gott (div. 1961); m. Froma Victoria (div. 1972); 1 child, Scott Frederic; m. Lynda Hart, Aug. 26, 1972 (div. 1980); m. Patricia Shiers, June 10, 1985. Student, Harvard U.; LL.B., Boston U. Bar: Mass. 1960. Ptnr. Bailey & Broder, Boston, N.Y.C., Bailey & Fishman, Boston, Bailey, Gerstein, Rashkind & Dresnick, Miami; dir. Murray Chris Craft. Author: (with Harvey Aronson) The Defense Never Rests, 1972, Cleared for the Approach, 1977, (with John Greenya) For the Defense, 1976; novel Secrets, 1979; How to Protect Yourself Against Cops In California and Other Strange Places, 1982, To Be a Trial Lawyer, 1983. Mem. Am. Bar Assn. Address: 823 N Olive Ave West Palm Beach FL 33401 *

BAILEY, FRANK HENRY, lawyer, farmer; b. Memphis, Mar. 7, 1946; s. Robert Henry and Leone (Mooney) B.; m. Cynthia Coffman, Apr. 1, 1978 (div. Apr. 1983); 1 child, Frank Coffman. BBA, U. Ark., 1969, JD, 1972. Bar: Ark. 1974, U.S. Dist. Ct. (ea. and we. dists.) Ark. 1977. Sole practice Mt. Home, Ark., 1974-75; sr. ptnr. Bailey & Paden P.A., Mt. Home, 1975—. Bd. dirs. No. Ark. Concert Assn., Harrison, 1978-82, No. Ark. Counsel for Arts, Mt. Home, 1985—. Served to sgt. U.S. Army, 1969-71, Vietnam. Mem. ABA, Ark. Bar Assn., Baxter-Marion County Bar Assn., Assn. Trial Lawyers Am., 4-H (recipient State Achievement award 1964, Cora Dillard Leadership award 1965). Presbyterian. Lodges: Masons, Rotary. Avocations: fly fishing, cross country skiing. Banking, Personal injury, Family and matrimonial. Home: Rt 9 PO Box 362 Mountain Home AR 72653 Office: Bailey & Paden PA 310 1st Nat Bank Bldg Mountain Home AR 72653

BAILEY, FRANK JOSEPH, JR., lawyer, educator; b. Kingston, N.Y., May 20, 1955; s. Frank Joseph Sr. and Marilyn (Reynolds) B.; m. Susan L. Cahill, Aug. 4, 1984. BS in Fgn. Service, Georgetown U., 1977; JD cum laude, Suffolk U., 1980. Bar: Mass. 1980, N.Y. 1981, U.S. Dist. Ct. Mass. 1981, U.S. Ct. Appeals (1st cir.) 1981. Law clk. to presiding justice Mass. Supreme Jud. Ct., Boston, 1980-81; assoc. Sullivan & Worcester, Boston, 1981-85, Powers & Hall, Boston, 1985—; lectr. Boston U. Sch. Law, 1981—; bd. dirs. Fed. Dorchester Neighborhood Houses Inc., Boston. Mem. ABA, Mass. Bar Assn., Boston Bar Assn. Roman Catholic. Avocation: golf. Federal civil litigation, State civil litigation, Bankruptcy. Home: 23 Union St Natick MA 01760 Office: Powers & Hall PC 100 Franklin St Boston MA 02110

BAILEY, HENRY JOHN, III, lawyer, educator; b. Pitts., Apr. 4, 1916; s. Henry J. and Lenore Powell Bailey Cahoon; m. Marjorie Jane Ebner, May 30, 1949; children: George W., Christopher G., Barbara W., Timothy P. Student, U.S. Naval Acad., 1934-36; B.A., Pa. State U., 1939; J.D., Yale U., 1947. Bar: N.Y. 1948, Mass. 1963, Oreg. 1974. Ins. investigator Liberty Mut. Ins. Co., N.Y.C., 1941-42; atty. Fed. Res. Bank of N.Y., N.Y.C., 1947-55; asst. v.p. Empire Trust Co., N.Y.C., 1955-56; atty., legal dept. Am. Bankers Assn., N.Y.C., 1956-62; editor Banking Law Jour., Boston, 1962-65; asso. prof. law Willamette U., Salem, Oreg., 1965-69; prof. Willamette U., 1969-81, prof. emeritus, 1981—, adj. prof., 1981—; counsel firm Churchill, Leonard, Brown & Donaldson, Salem, 1981-85; vis. prof. U. Akron Sch. Law, 1983-84, Fla. State U. Coll. Law, 1984-85, Rutgers Sch. Law, Camden, N.J., 1985—; cons., lectr. to bar and banking groups; lectr. Banking Sch. of South, Baton Rouge, 1972, 73, 75. Author: The Law of Bank Checks, 1960, 5th edit., 1979; periodic supplements Modern Uniform Commercial Code Forms, 1963; (with Clarke and Young) Bank Deposits and Collections, 1972, UCC Deskbook: A Short Course in Commercial Paper, 1973, (with Robert D. Hursh) The American Law of Products Liability, 3d edit, 1984, (with William D. Hawkland) The Sum and Substance of Commercial Paper, 1976, 80, Secured Transactions in a Nutshell, 1976, 2d edit., 1981, Oregon Uniform Commercial Code, 3 vols., 1983, 84, 86; Contbr. articles on sales, products liability, comml. paper and secured transactions to legal jours. Served to 1st lt. USAAF, 1942-45; lt. col. Res.; ret. Mem. Am. Bar Assn. (chmn. subcom. on comml. paper 1965-66, 79-81), Am. Law Inst. (mem. editorial bd. The Practical Lawyers 1981—), Oreg. State Bar, Lambda Chi Alpha. Republican. Roman Catholic. Banking, Bankruptcy, Contracts commercial. Office: 530 Center St NE PO Box 804 Salem OR 97308 Office: Fla State U Coll Law Tallahassee FL 32306

BAILEY, JAMES FREDERICK, JR., lawyer; b. Phila., Apr. 11, 1950; s. James Frederick Sr. and Dawn (Lundsted) B.; children—Lauren Elizabeth, Vanessa Ann, Robin M. B.A. in Polit. Sci., Wake Forest U., 1972; J.D., 1975. Bar: Del. 1975, U.S. Dist. Ct. Del. 1976. Dep. atty. gen. State of Del., Wilmington, 1975-77, dir. Div. Bus. Adminstrn. and Gen. Services, 1977-79; assoc. firm Berg Heckler & Cattie, Wilmington, 1979-83; ptnr. firm Elzufon & Bailey, P.A., Wilmington, 1983-87, James Bailey & Assocs., 1987—; lectr. honors program U. Del. Contbr. articles to profl. jours. Bd. dirs. Leukemia Soc. Del., 1981-83; mem. usher com Christ Ch. Christiana Hundred, Wilmington, 1982—. Mem. Del. Bar (family law com. 1977—, ins. law com. 1980—, corps. com. 1980-83), Del. Bar Assn., Fed. Bar Assn. (dist. Del.), ABA, Del. Claims Adjusters, Phi Delta Phi, Sigma Phi Epsilon. Republican. Episcopalian. General corporate, State civil litigation. Home: PO Box 2034 Wilmington DE 19899 Office: James Bailey & Assocs PA 818 Marine Midland Plaza 824 Market St Mall Wilmington DE 19899

BAILEY, NANCY HAWKINS, lawyer; b. Albemarle, N.C., Sept. 2, 1952; d. Leo Franklin and Willie Geneva (Witherspoon) Hawkins; m. Dalcho Fields Bailey, July 27, 1974; children: John Rhodes, Katherine Crowder, Susan Covington. BA, Wake Forest U., 1974; JD, U. S.C., 1977. Bar: S.C. 1977, N.C. 1978, U.S. Dist. Ct. S.C. 1978. Assoc. Alan R. Garris, Dillon, S.C., 1977-79, A. Glenn Greene Jr., Latta, S.C., 1979; ptnr. Greene, Lockemy & Bailey, Dillon, 1979—; treatment adv. team S.C. Dept. Social Services, Dillon, 1983—. Mem. ABA, S.C. Bar Assn., N.C. Bar Assn., Am. Trial Lawyers Assn., S.C. Trial Lawyers Assn. Democrat. Episcopalian. Family and matrimonial, Personal injury, Insurance. Office: 112 N MacArthur Ave PO Box 1658 Dillon SC 29536

BAILEY, PATRICIA SEASOR, lawyer; b. Indpls., Mar. 22, 1956; d. Darrell Eugene and H. Fay (Hayes) Seasor; m. Mark Allen Bailey, Nov. 21, 1981. BA and BS in Social Work, Anderson Coll., 1978; JD, Ind. U., 1981. Bar: Ind. 1981, U.S. Dist. Ct. (no. dist.) Ind. 1981. Lectr. law Ind. U., Indpls., 1981-82; assoc. Stark, Doninger, Mernitz & Smith, Indpls., 1982—. Editor Ind. U. Law Rev., 1980-81. Vol. spl. campaigns Marion County Heart Assn., Indpls., 1983—; chmn. bd. ch. growth Ch. at the Crossing, Indpls., 1982—, chmn. stewardship campaign, 1984; mem. Indpls. Civil War Round Table, 1984—. Mem. ABA, Ind. Bar Assn., Indpls. Bar Assn. (legal ethics com., probate and corps. sects.), Phi Alpha Delta. Republican. Mem. Ch. of God. Club: Indpls. Econ. Avocations: running, writing. Probate, General corporate, Securities. Home: 9151 Fireside Ct Indianapolis IN 46250 Office: Stark Doninger Mernitz & Smith Suite 700 50 S Meridian St Indianapolis IN 46204

BAILEY, PATRICK JOSEPH, lawyer; b. San Francisco, Dec. 13, 1954; s. James Curtis and Opal Irene (Van Houtan) B.; m. Cheryl Teruko Kobata, Aug. 21, 1976; 1 child, Doriana Michiko. BA, U. Calif., Berkeley, 1976; JD, U. Calif., San Francisco, 1979. Bar: Calif. 1979, U.S. Ct. Appeals (9th cir.) 1979, U.S. Ct. Mil. Appeals 1980. Commd. capt. U.S. Army, 1980; asst. staff judge adv. U.S. Army, Ft. Davis, Republic of Panama, 1980-83; sr. def. counsel trial def. service U.S. Army, Ft. Bliss, Tex., 1983-86; assoc. Thornton, Taylor & Downs, San Francisco, 1986—. Mem. Nat. Assn. Criminal Def. Lawyers. Republican. Roman Catholic. Lodge: Elks. Insurance. Home: 3526 Rivera St San Francisco CA 04116

BAILEY, ROBERT SHORT, lawyer; b. Bklyn., Oct. 17, 1931; s. Cecil Graham and Mildred (Short) B.; m. Doris Furlow, Aug. 29, 1953; children—Elizabeth Jane Goldentyer, Robert F., Barbara A. A.B., Wesleyan U., Middletown, Conn., 1953; J.D., U. Chgo., 1956. Bar: Ill. 1965, U.S. dist. ct. D.C. 1956, U.S. Supreme Ct. 1960. With U.S. Dept. Justice, 1956-61; asst. U.S. atty. No. Dist. Ill., 1961-65; ptnr. LeFevour & Bailey, Oak Park, Ill., 1965-68; sole practice, Chgo., 1968—; mem. faculty Nat. Coll. Criminal Def. Lawyers, 1975-78; panel atty. Fed. Defender Program, 1965—. Mem. Nat. Assn. Criminal Def. Lawyers (legis. chmn. 1976-78). Criminal. Home: 17 Timber Trail Streamwood IL 60103 Office: 53 W Jackson Blvd Suite 1220 Chicago IL 60604

BAILEY, ROBERT THEODORE RUSS, lawyer, legal educator; b. Fairbanks, Alaska, July 22, 1952; s. James Edmund and Elizabeth (Russ) B. BA, Auburn U., 1974; JD, Samford U., 1977. Bar: Ala. 1977, U.S. Dist. Ct. (mid. dist.) Ala. 1980, U.S. Ct. Appeals (11th cir.) 1982. Asst. dist. atty. Montgomery County, Ala., 1977-79; assoc. Ballard & Ballard, Montgomery, Ala., 1979-82; sole practice Montgomery, 1982—; ct. referee Juvenile Ct. Montgomery County, 1979—; adj. prof. Auburn U., Montgomery, 1980, 81, 85, 86. Mem. ABA, Ala. Trial Lawyers Assn. Avocations: reading, tennis. Real property, Bankruptcy, Consumer commercial. Home: 1610 Salisbury Place Montgomery AL 36117 Office: 623 S McDonough Montgomery AL 36102

BAILEY, RONALD E., lawyer; b. Portland, Oreg., Aug. 12, 1937; s. Thomas H. and Helen J. (Johnson) B.; m. Joanne L. Bailey, Jan. 2, 1960; children: Griffin T., Brad E. BS, U. Oreg., 1959; JD, Willamette U., 1963. Bar: Oreg. 1963, U.S. Dist. Ct. Oreg. 1963. Assoc. Bullivant, Houser, Bailey, Hanna, Pendergrass, Hoffman, O'Connell & Goyak, Portland, 1963-68, ptnr., 1969—; bd. dirs. Litigations Services Inc., Waltham, Mass. Editor Willamette Law Rev., 1959. Pres. Metro. Business Assn., 1986—. Served to 1st lt. U.S. Army, 1960. Fellow Oreg. Law Found.; mem. ABA, Oreg. Bar Assn. (bd. govs. 1981-84, v.p. 1983-84), Multnomah Bar Assn., Oreg. Assn. Def. (bd. dirs. 1985—). Republican. Roman Catholic. Clubs: Multnomah Athletic, Columbia Edgewater Golf and Country, Univ. (Portland). Insurance, Federal civil litigation, State civil litigation. Home: 11 SW Ridge Dr Portland OR 97219 Office: Bullivant Houser Bailey Hanna et al 1211 SW Fifth Ave 1400 Pacwest Ctr. Portland OR 97204-3797

BAILEY, TIMOTHY GORDON, lawyer; b. St. Paul, Nov. 1, 1950; s. Gordon Edward and Virginia Lois (Parlin) B.; m. Linda L. Holstein, May 28, 1986. BS, U. Minn., 1979, JD cum laude, 1982. Bar: Minn. 1982, U.S. Dist. Ct. Minn. 1983, U.S. Ct. Appeals (8th cir.) 1983. Assoc. Robins, Zelle, Larson & Kaplan, St. Paul, 1982—. Atty. Ramsey County Vol. Atty. Panel, St. Paul, 1983—; mem. Minn. Civil Liberties Union, 1986—. Mem. ABA, Assn. Trial Lawyers Am., Minn. Trial Lawyers Assn., Minn. Bar Assn., Ramsey County Bar Assn., Hennepin County Bar Assn. Democrat. Personal injury. Home: 210 W Grant St Apt 402 Minneapolis MN 55403 Office: Robins Zelle Larson & Kaplan 1500 Amhoist Tower 345 St Peter St Saint Paul MN 55102

BAILEY, WILLIAM SCHERER, lawyer, educator; b. St. Charles, Ill., July 28, 1948; s. Robert Wilbank and Josephine Grant (Scherer) B.; m. Sylvia Lillian Sherry, July 15, 1977; children: Robert, Mimy Ann. BS, U. Oreg., 1970; JD, Northwestern U., 1974. Bar: Ill. 1974, U.S. Dist. Ct. (no. dist.) Ill. 1976, Wash. 1977, U.S. Dist. Ct. (we. dist.) Wash. 1977. Legal counsel govt. com. Ill. Mental Health Code, 1974-76; asst. pub. defender State of Wash., Seattle, 1976-80, asst. atty. gen., 1980-82; ptnr. Levinson, Friedman, Vhugen, Duggan, Bland & Horowitz, Seattle, 1982-87, Schroeter, Goldmark & Bender, Seattle, 1987—; adj. prof. civil trial advocacy U. Puget Sound Sch. Law, Tacoma, 1981-85; judge pro tem Seattle Mcpl. Ct., 1983—. Contbr. articles to profl. jours. Mem. jud. evaluation com. Mcpl. League, Seattle, 1980-82, Mayor's Jud. Merit Selection Com., Seattle, 1981-82; legal counsel Wash. Dems., Seattle, 1985—. Mem. ABA, Wash. State Bar Assn. (editor jour. 1985), Seattle-King County Bar Assn., Wash. State Trial Lawyers Assn., Assn. Trial Lawyers Am. Democrat. Avocations: jogging, writing, tennis, music. State civil litigation, Personal injury, Legal education. Home: 805 W Blaine St Seattle WA 98119 Office: Schroeter Goldmark & Bender Central Bldg Suite 540 810 Third Ave Seattle WA 98104

BAILLY, DAVID RYAN, lawyer; b. Fargo, N.D., Sept. 22, 1950; s. Charles Edward and Helen Louise (Aasen) B.; m. Janet Lynn Wenner, Feb. 24, 1979; 1 child, Nicole Lyon. BBA, BA, U. N.D., 1972, JD, 1976. Bar: N.D. 1976, U.S. Dist. Ct. N.D. 1976, Minn. 1984, U.S. Dist. Ct. Minn. 1984, U.S. Ct. Appeals (8th cir.) 1984. Assoc. Tenneson, Serkland, Lundberg, Erickson & Marcil, Ltd., Fargo, N.D., 1976-84; ptnr. Crockett & Anderson, Fargo, 1984—; instr. bus. and acctg. Moorhead (Minn.) State U., 1977-80. Sr. editor N.D. Law Rev., 1976. Active various arts orgns.; clk. Fargo Park Dist. 1979—; chmn. emeritus Red River Dance and Performing Co., 1985—; bd. dirs. Ronald McDonald House, 1983-85, Dakota chpt. Arthritus Found., 1980-84, YMCA Found., 1978—; mem. adv. bd. Ctr. for Parents and Children 1985—; pres. Senn's Beach Propert Owners Assn. 1981—, active Broadmoor Condominium Owners Assn.; pres. United Way of Cass-Clay, Fargo, 1986—, trustee 1985—; choir mem. Gethsemane Episc. Cathedral, 1976—, chancellor 1979—, trustee 1983-86; 46th dist. Rep. precinct committeeman, 1980—. Mem. ABA (taxation, bus. law and econs. sects.), Minn. Bar Assn., N.D. Bar Assn. (taxation, corps. and bus., banking, trust and real estate sects., chmn. ethics com. east 1980—, sec.-treas. 1983-84, sec.-treas. young lawyers sect. 1980-82, pres. 1982—), Cass County Bar Assn. (sec.-treas. 1977-78), Fargo Law Library Assn. (pres. 1981-84), Advt. Fedn. Fargo-Moorhead (bd. dirs.), N.D. Jaycees (state legal dir. 1979-84, Outstanding Young North Dakotan 1984, Roughrider award 1985), Fargo Jaycees (pres. 1982-83; (life); Pioneer award) U.S. Jaycees (Senator award 1985, Ambassador award 1986), Fargo C. of C., Phi Delta Phi, Beta Alpha Psi, Alpha Tau Omega. Clubs: Fargo Country, Pelican Lake Yacht . Lodge: Elks (exalted ruler 1985—). Avocations: snow and water skiing, golf, sailing. General corporate, Estate planning, Pension, profit-sharing, and employee benefits. Home: PO Box 2581 Fargo ND 58108 Office: Crockett & Anderson Fed Bldg 112 Roberts St Suite 300 Fargo ND 58102

BAINBRIDGE, JOHN SEAMAN, law school administrator; b. N.Y.C., Nov. 1, 1915; s. William Seaman and June Ellen (Wheeler) B.; m. Katharine Barker Garrett, Feb. 3, 1943 (div. July 24, 1968); 1 son, John Seaman; m. 2d, Elizabeth Kung-Ji Liu, May 13, 1978. B.S., Harvard U., 1938; LL.B., J.D., Columbia U., 1941. Bar: N.Y. 1941, Md. 1946, U.S. Dist. Ct. Md. 1946, U.S. Supreme Ct. 1946, U.S. Dist. Ct. (so. dist.) N.Y. 1948. Gen. practice law, Md. and N.Y., 1945-56; asst. dean Columbia U. Law Sch., 1956-65, assoc. dir. Internat. Fellows Program, 1960-62, asst. to pres. Columbia U., 1965-66; dir. Project on Staffing of African Instns. of Legal Edn. and Research, 1962-72; assoc. dir. Ctr. for Adminstrn. of Justice, Wayne State U., Detroit, 1972-74; dir. planning Sch. Law, Pace U., Westchester County, N.Y., 1974-76; assoc. dean, dean, prof. law No. Ill. U. Coll. Law, Glen Ellyn, 1976-81; vis. prof., assoc. dean Del. Law Sch., Wilmington, 1981-82; dean, prof. law Touro Coll. Sch. Law, Huntington, N.Y., 1982-85; cons. Edward John Noble Found., 1959-61, Inst. Internat. Edn., 1962-67; mem. adv. com. Peace Corps Lawyers Project, 1963; founder, dir. African Law Assn. in Am., Inc., 1965-72. Served to lt. comdr. USNR, 1940-46. Mem. ABA, Sons of Revolution, S.R. Presbyterian. Club: Harvard (N.Y.C.). Author: The Study and Teaching of Law in Africa, 1972. Legal education. Home: 17 Ringfield Chadds Ford PA 19317

BAINS, DAVID PAUL, lawyer; b. Shreveport, La., Oct. 9, 1950; s. John Calvin and Alice (Mixon) B.; m. A. Sue Book, Aug. 27, 1971; children: J. Ashley, D. Andrew, E. Abigail. BA, La. Coll., 1972; JD, Mercer U., 1975; LLM, Tulane U., 1982. Bar: La. 1975, Ga. 1975, U.S. Dist. Ct. (ea. dist.) La. 1975, U.S. Dist. Ct. (so dist.) Ala. 1976, U.S. Ct. Appeals (5th cir.) 1976, U.S. Ct. Appeals (11th cir.) 1982, Fla. 1984, S.C. 1984, Miss. 1985, U.S. Dist. Ct. (we. dist.) La. 1985, Ala. 1986, Ill. 1987. Assoc. Law Offices of David Vosbein, New Orleans, 1975-80; ptnr. Hilleren, Bains & Smith, New Orleans, 1980—. Mem. future studies com. Chamber New Orleans & River Region, 1983-85, C. of C. E. St. Mary Parish, 1986, The Chamber, New Orleans, 1986; bd. dirs. New Orleans Traffic & Transp. Bur., 1986—. Mem. ABA, Assn. Trial Lawyers Am., Fed. Bar Assn., La. Trial Lawyers Assn., Miss. Trial Lawyers Assn., Norwegian C. of C. Admiralty, Federal civil litigation, Personal injury. Home: 5209 Elmwood Pkwy Metairie LA 70003 Office: Hilleren Bains & Smith 1432 Magazine St New Orleans LA 70130

BAINS, LEE EDMUNDSON, lawyer, state official; b. Birmingham, Ala., June 18, 1912; s. Herman Lipsey and Myrtle (Edmundson) B.; m. Ruel Eneida Burton, Jan. 1, 1938; children: Sandra Anita (Mrs. Henry Barnard Hardegree), Myrtle Lee, Lee Edmundson. Student, Birmingham So. Coll., 1930-31; B.S., U. Ala., 1934, J.D., 1936. Bar: Ala. 1936, U.S. Supreme Ct 1936; diplomate: Nat. Coll. Advocacy. Practiced in Bessemer, 1936—, city atty., 1950-58; instr. Birmingham Sch. Law, 1937-41; faculty Nat. War Coll., 1960; atty. for Ala. Power Co., South Central Bell Telephone Co., Phillips Petroleum Co., AmSouth Bank; apptd. by gov. as spl. asst. atty. gen. State of Ala., 1980—. Contbr. article to profl. jour.; Author: Basic Legal Skills, 1976. Pres. Bessemer Bd. Edn., 1955-58, Bessemer YMCA, 1961; Mem. Nat. Naval Res. Policy Bd., 1952-53; advisor Bd. Family Ct., Jefferson County, 1966—; chmn. finance com. Nat. Vets. Day for Birmingham, 1973; Alternate del. Democratic Nat. Conv., 1941; tchr. Men's Bible class First United Meth. Ch., 1966—. Served to rear adm. USNR, 1941-46, ETO, PTO; rear adm. Res. Fellow Am. Coll. Trial Lawyers; mem. Am., Ala. assns. trial lawyers, ABA (vice chmn. environ. law sect. 1979—), Ala. Bar Assn. (chmn. unauthorized practice com. 1977-79), Bessemer Bar Assn. (pres. 1983-84), Birmingham Bar Assn., Res. Officers Assn., Naval Res. Assn., Soc. Colonial Wars (state gov. 1972-73, corr. sec. 1976—), SAR (pres. Ala.), Phi Gamma Delta, Beta Gamma Sigma. Clubs: Kiwanian; Birmingham Ski (Birmingham), Downtown (Birmingham), The Club (Birmingham). Winner numerous swimming, jogging, skiing and figure skating awards, Presdl. sports award. State civil litigation, Federal civil litigation, Family and matrimonial. Home: 621 Melody Ln Bessemer AL 35020 Office: 1813 3d Ave Bessemer AL 35020

BAIR, BRUCE B., lawyer; b. St. Paul, May 26, 1928; s. Bruce B. and Emma N. (Stone) B.; m. Jane Lawler, July 19, 1952; children—Mary Jane, Thomas, Susan, Barbara, Patricia, James, Joan, Bruce, Jeffrey. B.S., U. N.D., 1950, J.D. 1952. Bar: N.D. 1952, U.S. Dist. Ct. N.D. 1955, U.S. Ct. Appeals (8th cir.) 1971, U.S. Supreme Ct. 1974. Assoc. Lord and Ulmer, Mandan, N.D., 1955-57; ptnr. Bair, Brown & Kautzmann and predecessors, Mandan, 1957—; spl. asst. atty. gen. State of N.D., 1967—; chmn. bd. Bank of Tioga, 1984—, also dir. Rep. precinct committeeman, 1956-70, chmn. Morton County Rep. Com., 1958-62, mem. N.D. Rep. State Cen. Com., 1962-67; pres. sch. bd. St. Joseph's Cath. Ch., 1967-68; mem. bd. Mandan Pub. Sch. Dist. #1, 1971-77; mem. exec. com. Internat. Assn. Milk Control Agys., 1970—; mem. bd. regents U. Mary, Bismarck, N.D., 1984—. Served to 1st lt. JAG Corps USAF, 1952-55. Fellow Am. Coll. Probate Counsel; mem. ABA, N.D. Bar Assn., Morton County Bar Assn., Am. Legion, Assn. Trial Lawyers Am. Roman Catholic. Lodges: Rotary, Elks. State civil litigation, Condemnation, Probate. Home: 901 3d St NW Mandan ND 58554 Office: 210 1st St NW Mandan ND 58554

BAIRD, BRUCE ALLEN, lawyer; b. Cin., Mar. 26, 1948; s. William Wendell and Audrey (Geignetter) B.; m. Erica Borden, July 27, 1975; 1 child, Jessica. BA, Cornell U., 1970; JD, NYU, 1975. Spl. asst. to dep. atty. gen. U.S. Dept. Justice, Washington, 1975-76; law clk. to presiding judge U.S. Ct. Appeals (2d cir.), Brattleboro, Vt. and N.Y.C., 1976-77; assoc. Davis, Polk & Wardwell, N.Y.C., 1977-80; asst. U.S. atty. U.S. Attys. Office (so. dist.) N.Y., N.Y.C., 1980-86, dep. chief criminal div., 1986-87, chief narcotics unit, 1987—. Editor in chief NYU Law Rev., 1974-75. Mem. ABA, N.Y. State Bar Assn. (profl. jud. ethics com. 1982—), Assn. Bar of City of N.Y. (profl. jud. ethics com. 1979-82, 86—), Fed. Bar Council. Republican. Presbyterian. Criminal, Federal civil litigation, Jurisprudence. Home: 12 Dante St Larchmont NY 10538 Office: US Attys Office 1 St Andrews Plaza New York NY 10007

BAIRD, CHARLES BRUCE, lawyer, consultant; b. DeLand, Fla., Apr. 18, 1935; s. James Turner and Ethelyn Isabelle (Williams) B.; m. Barbara Ann Fabian, June 6, 1959 (div. Dec. 1979); children—C. Bruce, Jr., Robert Arthur, Bryan James; m. Byung-Ran Cho, May 23, 1982; children—Merah-Iris, Haerah Violet. B.S. in M.E., U. Miami, 1958; postgrad UCLA, 1962-64; M.B.A., Calif. State U., 1966; J.D., Am. U., 1971. Bar: Va. 1971, U.S. Dist. Ct. (ea. dist.) Va. 1971, D.C. 1973, U.S. Dist. Ct. D.C. 1973, U.S. Ct. Appeals (4th cir.) 1974, U.S. Supreme Ct. 1975. Research engr. Naval Ordnance Lab., Corona, Calif., 1961-67; aerospace engr. Naval Air Systems Command, Washington, 1967-69; cons. engr. Bird Engring. Research Assts., Vienna, Va., 1969-71; prof. Def. Systems Mgmt. Coll., Ft. Belvoir, Va., 1982; spl. asst. for policy compliance USIA Voice of Am., Washington, 1983-84; cons. Booz, Allen & Hamilton, Inc., Bethesda, 1975-82, IBM, Bethesda, Md., 1984; Logistics Mgmt. Inst., Bethesda, 1986—. Contbr. articles to profl. jours. Inventor computer-based communications systems for the gravely handicapped. Bd. govs. Sch. Engring. U. Miami, 1957; trustee Galilee United Meth. Ch., Arlington, Va., 1983-87. Mem. Assn. Trial Lawyers Am., Soc. Gen. Systems Research, Sigma Alpha Epsilon. Republican. Federal civil litigation, Personal injury, Computer. Home and Office: 2728 Sherwood Hall Ln Alexandria VA 22306

BAIRD, DOUGLAS GORDON, law educator; b. Phila., July 10, 1953; s. Henry Welles and Eleanora (Gordon) B. B.A., Yale U., 1975; J.D., Stanford U., 1979. Law clk. U.S. Ct. Appeals (9th cir.), 1979, 80; asst. prof. law U. Chgo., 1980-83, prof. law, assoc. dean, 1984—. Author: (with others) Security Interests in Personal Property, 1984, Bankruptcy, 1985. Mem. Order of Coif. Bankruptcy, Contracts commercial. Office: U Chgo Law Sch 1111 E 60th St Chicago IL 60637

BAIRD, EDWARD ROUZIE, JR., lawyer; b. Norfolk, Va., Aug. 29, 1936; s. Edward Rouzie and Eleanor Gray (Perry) B.; m. Nell McGlaughon, Oct. 8, 1967 (dec. Oct. 1973); 1 child, Eleanor Gray; m. Abby St. John Starke, Feb. 5, 1977; children—Abby St. John, Edward Rouzie V. B.A., U. Va., 1960, LL.B., 1967. Bar: Va. 1967. Assoc. Baird, Creshaw & Ware, Norfolk, 1967-68; asst. dist. counsel U.S. Army C.E., Norfolk, 1968-73; asst. U.S. atty. U.S. Atty.'s Office, Norfolk, 1973-77; sole practice, Norfolk, 1977-82; ptnr. Willcox & Baird, Norfolk, 1982—. Served to lt. (j.g.) USN, 1960-63. Mem. ABA, Va. Bar Assn., Norfolk-Portsmouth Bar Assn., Assn. Trial Lawyers Am., Soc. of Cincinnati. Club: Virginia (Norfolk). Environment, Federal civil litigation, General corporate. Home: 1711 Cloncurry Rd Norfolk VA 23507 Office: Willcox & Baird 210 Monticello Arcade Norfolk VA 23510

BAIRD, JAMES KENNETH, telephone holding company executive; b. Tanta, Egypt, Jan. 10, 1917; came to U.S., 1926; s. James Wallace and Maude Rebecca (Edgerton) B.; m. Marian Elisabeth Irish, Sept. 7, 1940 (dec.); children—J. Stacey, Bruce Wallace, Darcy Jean; m. Sally Ann Maenza, Feb. 2, 1957; children—Joan Marie, Robert K. B.A., Monmouth Coll., 1937; M.B.A., Northwestern U., 1938; J.D., 1941. Bar: Ill. 1941, Wis. 1968, Fla. 1975, U.S. Supreme Ct. 1949. Assoc., atty. U.S. Govt. Dept. of Labor, Washington, 1941-42; asst. to judge U.S. Tax Ct., 1942-43; law practice with K. Raymond Clark, Chgo., 1946-51, Baird & Lundquist, Zion, Ill., 1958-67; gen. mgr., gen. counsel Turtle Wax Auto Polish Co., Chgo., 1953-57; sr. v.p., gen. counsel Universal Telephone, Inc., Milw., 1967—, also dir. Mem. Zion Sch. Bd., 1964. Mem. ABA, Ill. Bar Assn., Wis. Bar Assn., Milw. Bar Assn., Chgo. Bar Assn., Fla. Bar Assn., Am. Corp. Counsel Assn., Am. Legion. Republican. Presbyterian. Clubs: St. Andrew's Soc., Telephone Pioneer Assn. (Milw.), Am.-Scottish Found. Lodge: Masons, Shriners, Lions. General corporate, Personal income taxation, Securities.

BAIRD, RUSSELL MILLER, lawyer; b. Chgo., Aug. 4, 1916; s. Frederick Rogers and Ruth Estelle (Miller) B.; m. Martha Steere, Mar. 28, 1942; children—Lindsay, Scott, Frederick. A.B., U. Chgo., 1938; LL.B., Harvard U., 1941. Bar: Ill. 1941, U.S. Dist. Ct. (no. dist.) Ill. 1948, U.S. Supreme Ct. 1982. Ptnr., mem. exec. com. Sidley & Austin, and predecessors, Chgo., 1941—. Served to lt. USNR, 1942-45. Mem. ABA, Ill. Bar Assn., Chgo. Bar Assn., Bar 7th Fed. Cir. Presbyterian. Clubs: Racquet, Univ. (Chgo.); Crystal Downs Country (Mich.); River Forest (Ill.) Tennis; Oak Park (Ill.) Country. Author: Chgo. Bar Christmas Spirits Gridiron Show, 1956-66. Administrative and regulatory, General corporate, Trademark and copyright. Office: Sidley & Austin One First Nat Plaza Suite 4500 Chicago IL 60603

BAIRD, THOMAS BRYAN, JR., lawyer; b. Newport News, Va., June 21, 1931; s. Thomas Bryan and Mary Florence (Rieker) B.; m. Mildred Katherine Clark, June 23, 1956; children—Sarah, Thomas Bryan, William, Laura. B.A., U. Va., 1952; LL.B., U. Tenn., 1960. Bar: Tenn. 1964, Va. 1969, U.S. Dist. Ct. (we. dist.) 1970. With State Farm Ins., Knoxville, Tenn., 1960-68; asst. commonwealth atty., Wytheville, Va., 1969-71; commonwealth atty. Wythe County, 1972—; prin. Thomas B. Baird, Jr. Trustee, Simmerman Home for the Aged, 1972-83. Served with U.S. Army, 1953-55. Mem. ABA, Nat. Dist. Attys. Assn., Va. Bar Assn., Assn. Am. Trial Lawyers, Am. Judicature Soc., Va. Trial Lawyers Assn., Phi Alpha Delta. Democrat. Presbyterian. Criminal, Insurance, Real property. Home: 875 N 18th St Wytheville VA 24382

BAISLEY, JAMES MAHONEY, manufacturing company executive; b. Dec. 21, 1932; s. Charles Thomas and Katherine (Mahoney) B.; m. Barbara Brosnan, Sept. 7, 1960; children—Mary Elizabeth, Katherine, Barbara, Paul, Genevieve, Charles, James. B.S., Fordham U., 1954, LL.B., 1961. Bar: N.Y. 1961, Ill. 1969. Assoc. Naylon, Aronson, Huber & Magill, N.Y.C., 1961-66; asst. counsel GTE Corp, 1966-69; v.p., gen. counsel GTE Automatic Electric Inc., Northlake, Ill., 1969-81; gen. counsel, v.p. W. W. Grainger Inc., Skokie, Ill., 1981—; dir. EAC, Inc. Served with USMC, 1954-57. Decorated Nat. Def. medal. Mem. ABA, Chgo. Bar Assn. Republican. Roman Catholic. Club: North Shore Country. Home: 530 Longwood Ave Glencoe IL 60022 Office: W W Grainger Inc 5500 W Howard St Skokie IL 60077

BAISLEY, JOAN ANN, lawyer; b. New Haven, Aug. 14, 1956; d. Robert W. and Jean S. Baisley. BA, Pa. State U., 1977; JD, Columbia U., 1981. Bar: N.Y. 1982. Assoc. Willkie Farr & Gallagher, N.Y.C., 1981-83, Baer Marks & Upham, N.Y.C., 1983-85, Winston & Strawn, Chgo., 1985. Mem. ABA, N.Y. State Bar Assn. Private international. Home: 400 E Randolph St 1026 Chicago IL 60601 Office: Winston & Strawn 1 First National Plaza Suite 5000 Chicago IL 60603

BAKALY, CHARLES GEORGE, JR., lawyer; b. Long Beach, Calif., Nov. 15, 1927; s. Charles G. and Doris (Carpenter) B.; m. Patricia Murphey, Oct. 25, 1952; children: Charles G., John W., Thomas B. A.B., Stanford U., 1949; J.D., U. S.C., 1952. Assoc. firm O'Melveny & Myers, Los Angeles, 1956-63, ptnr., 1963—; mem. equal opportunity law com. Def. Research Inst. Author: (with Joel M. Grossman) Modern Law of Employment Contracts: Formation, Operation and Remedies for Breach, 1983; contbr. chpts to books. Bd. advisors Calif. Rep. League; bd. dirs. Children's Hosp. of Los Angeles; mem. exec. com. Calif. Rep. Com.; trustee, mem. exec. com. Scripps Coll., 1986-87; bd. fellows Claremont U. Ctr., 1986-87. Served to capt. JAG U.S. Army, 1952-56. Fellow ABA (chmn. sect. labor and employment law 1982); mem. Am. Coll. Trial Lawyers, Los Angeles County Bar Assn. (trustee, chmn. labor law sect. 1976-77), Mchts. and Mfrs. Assn. (exec. com.), NAM (labor adv. task force), Am. Arbitration Assn., U.S. C. of C. (Labor reations com.), Internat. Soc. Labor Law and Social Legis., Chancery Club, Law Soc. Club: Valley Hunt (Pasadena, Calif.). Labor, Federal civil litigation, State civil litigation. Office: O'Melveny & Myers 400 S Hope St Los Angeles CA 90071

BAKEMAN, WILLARD PATRICK, III, lawyer; b. Syracuse, N.Y., Dec. 9, 1953; s. Willard Patrick and Mary Elisabeth (Hallinan) B.; m. Irma Alvarez, Aug. 28, 1983; children: Israel, Homer, Willard Patrick IV, Evaleen. BA, Eisenhower Coll., 1975; JD, U. San Diego, 1978. Bar: Calif. 1978. Dep. dist. atty. Stanislaus County, Modesto, Calif., 1978-79; assoc. Carroll & Berk, Ventura, Calif., 1979-80; atty. So. Calif. Law Ctr., Compton, Calif., 1981-83; sole practice Vista, Calif., 1983—. Mem. Calif. Trial Lawyers Assn., Assn. Trial Lawyers Am., Los Angeles Trial Lawyers Assn., S.D. Trial Lawyers Assn. Democrat. Avocations: running, travel. Personal injury, Insurance. Office: 400 S Melrose Dr Suite 105 Vista CA 92083

BAKER, ANITA DIANE, lawyer; b. Atlanta, Sept. 4, 1955; d. Byron Garnett and Anita (Swanson) B. BA summa cum laude, Oglethorpe U., 1977; JD with distinction, Emory U., 1980. Bar: Ga. 1980. Assoc. Hansell & Post, Atlanta, 1980—. Mem. ABA, Atlanta Bar Assn., Ga. Bar Assn., Atlanta Hist. Soc., Order of Coif, Phi Alpha Delta, Phi Alpha Theta, Alpha Chi, Omicron Delta Kappa. Real property, Administrative and regulatory, General corporate. Office: Hansell & Post 56 Perimeter Ctr E Suite 500 Atlanta GA 30346

BAKER, BARTON, lawyer, lecturer; b. Webster, N.Y., Jan. 9, 1901; s. Charles John and Emma (Martin) B.; m. Bernice Maude Dennis, June 6, 1925; 1 dau., Betty Baker Trost. LL.B., Cornell U., 1922; D.C.L. cum laude, Chgo. Law Sch., 1926, Ph.D., 1928. Bar: N.Y. 1923, U.S. Sup. Ct. 1926. Asst. law librarian Cornell U., 1921-22; asst. Rochester (N.Y.) Legal Aid Soc., 1921; atty. MacFarlane & Harris, 1922-26; atty. Baker & Carver, Baker & Weldgen; now gen. counsel Auditing Bur. Rochester; columnist Damascus News, 1982. Bd. dirs. Internat. Bell Orch., 1952—; formerly council chief N.Y. and N.J. Boy Scouts Am. Lone Scout Div.; founder Barton Baker Youth Edn. Center, Monroe County Fair Park, 1973; trustee Minett Fund; past pres. Rochester Internat. Friendship Council, Inc.; mem. adv. bd. Salvation Army. Recipient Monroe County Citizens Civic Com. Achievement citation, 1977; achievement award Internat. Assn. Fairs and Expns., Reagan Republican Task Force Citation, 1985; Order of Lincoln. Methodist. Clubs: Shrine Lunch (past pres.), Masons (past master), Cornell (past pres.). Contbr. articles to profl. jours.; former assoc. editor Cornell Law Rev., Reveille, Universal Scout, Universal Tribune. Consumer commercial, Real property, Probate. Home: 100 Brookwood Rd Rochester NY 14610 Office: 1030 Times Square Bldg Rochester NY 14614

BAKER, BENJAMIN JOSEPH, lawyer; b. N.Y.C., Jan. 5, 1954; s. Harry and Stella Baker; m. Carmelyn D. Civiletto, Aug. 7, 1975; 1 child, Matthew. BS, Pa. State U., 1973; MS, Ohio State U., 1974; MBA, JD, U. Ill., 1979. Bar: Ill. 1979. Ptnr. McDermott, Will & Emery, Chgo., 1979—. General corporate, Securities, Municipal bonds. Home: 2341 Hampton Ln Northbrook IL 60062 Office: McDermott Will & Emery 111 W Monroe St Chicago IL 60603

BAKER, BENNETT JOEL, lawyer; b. Chgo., Jan. 20, 1954; s. Ira and Gertrude (Schor) B.; m. Tammy J. Bark, June 6, 1982. BA, U. Colo., 1975; JD, John Marshall Sch. Law, 1978. Bar: Ill. 1978, U.S. Dist. Ct. (no. dist.) Ill. 1978. Assoc. Gordon, Schaeffer, Gordon, Chgo., 1978-79, Law Office Richard I. Bass & Assocs., Chgo., 1979-80, Law Office Harvey L. Walner & Assocs., Chgo., 1980-86, Goldberg, Fohrman & Weisman, Chgo., 1986—; lectr. Voir Dire, 1987. Mem. ABA, Ill. Bar Assn., Chgo. Bar Assn. (cert. appreciation 1985,chmn. trial techniques com. young lawyers div. 1986—, vice chmn. trial techniques com. 1986, lectr. tort com. seminar 1985, lectr. trial techniques seminar 1986, lectr. "voir dire" 1986), Ill. Trial Lawyers Assn. Democrat. State civil litigation, Personal injury. Home: 872 Swallow Ct Deerfield IL 60015 Office: Goldberg Fohrman & Weisman 221 N LaSalle Chicago IL 60601

BAKER, BERNARD ROBERT, state district court judge; b. Chgo., Apr. 5, 1937; s. Bernard F. and Pearl L. (Beesley) B.; m. Caroline Spanier, Mar. 22, 1958; children—Susan Caroline, Deborah Ann, Pamela Ruth. B.S.B.A., Northwestern U., 1958; J.D., Ind. U., 1964. Bar: Colo. 1968, Ind. 1964, U.S. Supreme Ct. 1969, U.S. Ct. Mil. Appeals 1965, U.S. Dist. Ct. Colo. 1968, Ind. 1964; ins. counselor Equitable Life Ins., N.Y.C., 1958-60; acct. Chevrolet div. Gen. Motors Corp., Indpls., 1960-61; claims investigator, supr. Allstate Ins. Co., Indpls., 1961-64; assoc. firm Agee & Fann, Colorado Springs, Colo., 1968; dep., chief dep. dist. atty. Office Dist. Atty., State of Colo., 1968-75; dist. ct. judge 4th Jud. Dist., State of Colo., Colorado Springs, 1976—; guest prof. Nat. Jud. Coll., Reno, Nev., 1982. Pres., Citizens Lobby for Sensible Growth, 1974; bd. dirs. Salvation Army, 1973-78, Mental Retardation Found., 1972-76. Served to capt. JAG Corps, U.S. Army, 1965-67. Decorated Army Commendation medal; recipient Presdl. citation Colo. Health Dept., 1975. Mem. ABA, Colo. Bar Assn., El Paso County Bar Assn., Am. Judicature Soc. Democrat. Methodist. Club: Moose. Contbg. editor, bd. editors Colo. Environ. Law Handbook, 1971-72. State civil litigation, Criminal, Jurisprudence. Address: El Paso County Courthouse 20 E Vermijo St Colorado Springs CO 80903

BAKER, BRUCE J., lawyer; b. Balt., Apr. 2, 1954; s. John J. and Kathryn (Fusetti) B.; m. Pamela Ross Fennell, Nov. 17, 1984. BA, U. Pa., 1976; JD, Harvard U., 1979. Bar: N.Y. 1980, U.S. Dist. Ct. (so. and ea. dists.) N.Y. 1980, U.S. Dist. Ct. (we. dist.) N.Y. 1986. Assoc. Milbank, Tweed, Hadley & McCloy, N.Y.C., 1979-83; sr. atty. office of gen. counsel U.S. Synthetic Fuels Corp., Washington, 1983-85; assoc. Nixon, Hargrave, Devans & Doyle, Rochester, N.Y., 1985—. Dist. committeeman Monroe County Reps., Rochester, 1986—. Mem. ABA, N.Y. State Bar Assn., Assn. of Bar of City of N.Y., Monroe County Bar Assn., Rep. Nat. Lawyers Assn. Roman Catholic. Banking, General corporate, Securities. Home: 20 Castlebar Rd Rochester NY 14610 Office: Nixon Hargrave Devans & Doyle PO Box 1051 Rochester NY 14603

BAKER, BRUCE JAY, lawyer; b. Chgo., June 18, 1954; s. Kenneth and Beverly (Gould) B.; m. Lynn Sylvia Preece, July 18, 1976. Student, U. Leeds, Eng., 1974-75; BS, U. Ill., 1976; JD, Washington U., 1979. Bar: Ill. 1979, U.S. Dist. Ct. (no. dist.) Ill. 1984. Asst. atty. gen., antitrust div. State of Ill., Chgo., 1979-83; assoc. Mass, Miller & Josephson Ltd., Chgo., 1983-86; assoc. counsel Discover Card Services Inc., Lincolnshire, Ill., 1986—. Contbr. bi-weekly column to Ill. Bank News; contbr. articles to profl. jours. Registered lobbyist Ill. Legislature, Springfield, 1985—. Ill. State scholar, 1972. Mem. ABA (antitrust com.), Chgo. Bar Assn. (fin. insts. com.), Ill. Bankers Assn. (legis. counsel 1985-86), Ill. Bar Assn. Banking, Legislative, Administrative and regulatory. Office: Discover Card Services Inc 333 Knightsbridge Pkwy Lincolnshire IL 60069

BAKER, C. EDWIN, law educator; b. 1947. BA, Stanford U., 1969; JD, Yale U., 1972. Asst. prof. U. Toledo, 1972-75; asst. prof. U. Oreg., Eugene, 1975-79, assoc. prof., 1979-81, prof., 1981-82; prof. U. Pa., Phila., 1982—. Fellow Harvard U., Cambridge, Mass., 1974-75. Office: U Penn Law Sch 3400 Chestnut St Philadelphia PA 19104 *

BAKER, CAMERON, lawyer; b. Chgo., Dec. 24, 1937; s. David Cameron and Marion (Fitzpatrick) B.; m. Katharine Julia Solari, Sept. 2, 1961; children: Cameron III, Ann, John. Student, U. Notre Dame, 1954-57; AB, Stanford U., 1958; LLB, U. Calif., Berkeley, 1961. Bar: Calif. 1962, U.S. Dist. Ct. (so. dist.) Calif. 1962, U.S. Dist. Ct. (no. dist.) Calif. 1963, U.S. Ct. Appeals (9th) 1963. Assoc. Adams, Duque & Hazeltine, Los Angeles, 1961-62; mng. ptnr. Pettit & Martin, San Francisco,, 1972-81, 84—; mem. exec. com Pettit & Martin, San Francisco, 1971-82, 84—; del. Union Internat. des Avocats, 1983—; mayor City of Belvedere, Calif., 1978-79. Mem. City Council, Belvedere, 1976-80, fin. com. San Francisco Lawyers Com. for Urban Affairs, 1986—, bd. dirs., 1975-83; bd. dirs. San Francisco Legal Aid Soc., 1971-72, Boalt Hall Alumni Assn., 1982-84. Mem. ABA (partnership and unincorporated bus. orgns. com., internat. bus. law com., law and acctg. com., small bus. com., law firms com.), Calif. Bar Assn. (partnership and unincorporated bus. entities com., corp. com.), Bar Assn. of San Francisco (bd. dirs. 1966, 72-73, client relations com., chmn. pub. relations com., chmn. governing com. continuing edn. 1975). Clubs: Bohemian (san Francisco), Belvedere Tennis (Calif.), Tiburon Peninsula. Home: 38 Alcatraz Ave Belvedere CA 94920 Office: Pettit & Martin 101 California 35th Floor San Francisco CA 94111

BAKER, DARRYL ELLIS, lawyer; b. Corinth, Miss., Mar. 2, 1952; s. Billy Clay and Geraldine (Ellis) B.; m. Lorie Ann Hollingsworth, Dec. 30, 1978; children: Emily, Elizabeth. BS in Pub. Adminstrn., U. Ark., 1974, JD, 1978. Bar: Ark. 1978, U.S. Dist. Ct. (ea. dist.) Ark. 1978, U.S. Ct. Appeals (8th cir.) 1984. Assoc. Napper, Hardin & Wood P.A., North Little Rock, 1978-80, Gary Eubanks & Assocs., Little Rock, 1980—. Named One of Outstanding Young Men in Am., U.S. Jaycees. Mem. ABA, Ark. Bar Assn., Ark. Trial Lawyers Assn. (bd. govs. 1981-86), Assn Trial Lawyers Am., Pulaski County Bar Assn., North Pulaski County Bar Assn. (sec. 1979-80). Democrat. Federal civil litigation, State civil litigation. Home: 1201 Adell Little Rock AR 72212 Office: Gary Eubanks & Assocs 708 W 2d St Little Rock AR 72201

BAKER, DAVID HARRIS, lawyer; b. Rome, N.Y., Aug. 27, 1955; s. Abraham Harris and Ruth Elizabeth (Flanagan) B. BA in History and French, Hamilton Coll., 1976; JD, George Washington U., 1979. Bar: D.C. 1979, N.Y. 1985. Assoc. Pope Ballard & Loos, Washington, 1978-81; ptnr. Holland & Knight, Washington, 1982—; instr. U.S. Dept. Def., Falls Church, Va., 1983—. Mem. ABA (vice chmn. rate-making com. 1985-86), D.C. Bar Assn. (chmn. adminstrn. law sect. 1986-87, editor jour. 1986), Assn. Transp. Practioners (chmn. 1984-85). Republican. Roman Catholic. Club: Capitol Hill (Washington). Administrative and regulatory, Private international. Home: 4601 N Park Ave Chevy Chase MD 20815 Office: Holland & Knight 888 17th St NW Wahington DC 20006

BAKER, DAVID REMEMBER, lawyer; b. Durham, N.C., Jan. 17, 1932; s. Roger Denio and Eleanor Elizabeth (Ussher) B.; m. Myra Augusta Mullins, Nov. 2, 1955. Ph.B., U. Chgo., 1949; B.A., Birmingham-So. Coll., 1951; J.D., Harvard Law Sch., 1954. Bar: Ala. 1954, N.Y. 1963, U.S. Supreme Ct. 1972. Assoc. Cabaniss & Johnston, Birmingham, Ala., 1957-62; assoc. Chadbourne, Parke, Whiteside & Wolff (now Chadbourne & Parke), N.Y.C., 1962-66, ptnr., 1967-86; ptnr. Jones, Day, Reavis & Pogue, N.Y.C., 1986—; gen. counsel Econ. Club of N.Y., N.Y.C., 1977—; pres. Remember Baker Corp.; bd. dirs., sec. Philon, Inc. Contbr. articles to profl. jours. Pres. N.Y. Legis. Service, N.Y.C., 1975—; sec., counsel Jr. Achievement of N.Y., 1974—; bd. dirs., v.p. World of Musicians, Ltd., N.Y.C., 1981—; trustee Birmingham-So. Coll., 1985—. Served with U.S. Army, 1954-57. Mem. Am. Law Inst., ABA, Assn. of Bar of City of N.Y. (chmn. com. on state legislation 1968-70), Internat. Bar Assn. (vice chmn. bus. orgn. com. 1986—), N.Y. State Bar Assn. (exec. com. banking, corp. and bus. law sect. 1986—). Democrat. Unitarian. Clubs: Harvard, Metropolitan, The Club at Citicorp Ctr. Avocation: bridge (life master Am. Contract Bridge League). General corporate, Private international, Administrative and regulatory. Home: 599 Lexington Ave 32d Floor New York NY 10022 Office: Jones Day Reavis & Pogue 599 Lexington Ave New York NY 10022

BAKER, DAVID S., lawyer; b. Jacksonville, Fla., Feb. 25, 1937; s. Benjamin E. and Esther (Fendrich) B.; m. Betsy Cohen, Nov. 18, 1961; children—Stuart I., Curtis A., Trudy L. B.S. in Econs., U. Pa., 1958; LL.B., Harvard U., 1961. Assoc. Cleary, Gottlieb, Steen & Hamilton, N.Y.C., 1962-65; assoc. Powell, Goldstein, Frazer & Murphy, Atlanta, 1965-68, ptnr., 1968—; dir. Harvard Legal Aid Bur., Cambridge, Mass., 1959-61; lectr. on corp. and environ. law. Contbr. articles to profl. jours. Mem. exec. com. Theatrical Outfit, Atlanta, 1982-85; trustee Am. Jewish Com., Atlanta, 1982-85, Rich Found., 1983—. Mem. ABA (council gen. practice sect. 1979-82, chmn. gen. practice sect. 1986-87), Ga. Bar Assn. Democrat. Jewish. Clubs: Standard (bd. dirs. 1977-81, 85), Ashford (bd. dirs. 1985—), Commerce (Atlanta). General corporate, Environment, Banking. Home: 4501 Harris Trail NW Atlanta GA 30327 Office: Powell Goldstein Frazer & Murphy 400 Perimeter Ctr Terrace Suite 1050 Atlanta GA 30346

BAKER, DONALD, lawyer; b. Chgo., May 28, 1929; s. Russell and Elizabeth (Wallace) B.; m. Gisela S. Carli, Oct. 6, 1960; children: Caryna, Andrew, Russell. Student, Deep Springs Coll., Calif., 1947-49; J.D.S., U. Chgo., 1954. Bar: Ill. 1955, N.Y. 1964. Ptnr. Baker & McKenzie, Chgo., 1955—; bd. dir. Trimedyne, Inc., Pharmatec, Inc., Great Pacific Holdings, Inc. Bd. dirs. exec. com. Mid-Am. Com., Chgo., 1980—; bd. dirs. Internat. Bus. Council Mid-Am., 1982-84. Mem. ABA, Ill. Bar Assn., Chgo. Bar Assn. Club: Michigan Shores (Wilmette, Ill.). Private international, Corporate taxation. Home: 544 Earlston Rd Kenilworth IL 60043 Office: Baker & McKenzie 2800 Prudential Plaza Chicago IL 60601

BAKER, ELIZABETH STATUTA, lawyer; b. Worcester, Mass., July 8, 1948; d. Joseph James and Mildred Marie (Reynolds) S.; m. Edward Keefer Baker III, Apr. 14, 1973; children: Emily Katherine, Sarah Elizabeth. BA, Goucher Coll., 1970; JD, U. Md., 1973. Bar: Md. 1973, U.S. Dist. Ct. Md. 1974, D.C. 1977, U.S. Supreme Ct. 1978, Fla. 1978, U.S. Dist. Ct. (so. dist.) Fla. 1979, U.S. Ct. Appeals (5th cir.) 1980, U.S. Ct. Appeals (5th and 11th cirs.) 1981. Staff atty., mng. atty., chief atty. Legal Aid Bur. Balt., 1973-78; unit mgr., dep. dir., acting dir. Legal Services of Greater Miami (Fla.), Inc., 1978-81; sole practice Miami, 1981—; adj. prof. law U. Miami Law Sch., 1979-81; mem. King Com. on Standards for Admission to Practice in Fed. Ct., Miami, 1981. Mem. Fla. Bar Assn., Md. State Bar Assn., D.C. Bar Assn., Dade County Bar Assn., Fla. Assn. Women Lawyers, NOW, Supreme Ct. Hist. Soc. (founding mem.). Avocations: crosswords, mystery books, cross stitching. Family and matrimonial, State civil litigation. Home: 615 Gondoliere Ave Coral Gables FL 33143 Office: 6701 Sunset Dr Suite 101D South Miami FL 33143

BAKER, FRANK ADAMS, III, lawyer; b. Balt., July 6, 1950; s. Frank Adams Jr. and Mary Isabel (Randall) B.; m. Peggy Ruth Dreher, June 21, 1980; children: Adams Dreher, Yvonne Elizabeth. BA, U. Pa., 1972; JD, Villanova U., 1977. Bar: Pa. 1977, U.S. Dist. Ct. (ea. dist.) Pa. 1977, U.S. Ct. Appeals (3d cir.) 1978. Law clk. to presiding justice Northampton County Ct., Easton, Pa., 1977-78; assoc. Butz, Hudders & Tallman, Allentown, Pa., 1978-85; ptnr. Margolis, Smith & Baker, Bethlehem, Pa., 1985—. Trustee Pastoral Inst. Lehigh Valley, Bethlehem, 1982—, Moravian Acad., Bethlehem, 1980—, fundraising chmn. 1982-82. Mem. Assn. Trial Lawyers Am., Pa. Trial Lawyers Assn., Def. Research Inst., Pa. Def. Inst. Republican. Federal civil litigation, State civil litigation, Insurance. Office: Margolis Smith & Baker 2158 Ave C PO Box 2728 Bethlehem PA 18001

BAKER, FREDERICK MILTON, JR., lawyer; b. Flint, Mich., Nov. 2, 1949; s. Frederick Milton Baker and Mary Jean (Hallitt) Rarig; m. Irene Taylor; children: Jessica, Jordan. BA, U. Mich., 1971; JD, Washington U., St. Louis, 1975. Bar: Mich. 1975, U.S. Dist. Ct. (we. dist.) Mich. 1980, U.S. Dist. Ct. (ea. dist.) Mich. 1981, U.S. Ct. Appeals (6th cir.) 1983, U.S. Supreme Ct. 1986. Instr. law Wayne State U., Detroit, 1975-76; research atty. Mich. Ct. Appeals, Lansing, 1976-77, law clk. to chief judge, 1977; asst. prof. T.M. Cooley Law Sch., Lansing, Mich., 1978-80; ptnr. Honigman, Miller, Schwartz & Cohn, Lansing, Mich., 1986—. Author: Michigan Bar Appeal Manual, 1982; editor Mich. Bar Jour., 1984-86; contbr. articles to profl. jours. Founder, pres. Sixty Plus Law Ctr., Lansing, 1978—; mem. community adv. bd. Lansing Jr. League, 1983—. Mem. ABA (Outstanding Single Project award 1980), Mich. Bar Assn. (vice chmn. jour. adv. bd. 1984—, mem. young lawyers sect. council 1980-84, grievance com. 1982-84, John W. Cummiskey award 1984), Ingham County Bar Assn. Unitarian. Club: Big Oak (Baldwin, Mich.). Avocations: photography, fishing, running, frisbee, squash. Federal civil litigation, State civil litigation, Insurance. Home: 640 Oakwood Dr East Lansing MI 48823 Office: Honigman Miller Schwartz & Cohn Mich National Tower Suite 636 Lansing MI 48933

BAKER, GAIL DYER, lawyer; b. West Point, N.Y., Mar. 16, 1954; s. Hillier Locke Jr. and Miriam Jane (Dyer) B. BA magna cum laude, U. Minn., 1978; JD, Suffolk U., 1981. Bar: Minn. 1981, U.S. Dist. Ct. Minn. 1981. Assoc. R.C. Ploetz & Assocs., Mpls., 1981-82; exec. dir., staff atty. Legal Assistance of Olmsted County, Rochester, Minn., 1982-85; assoc. Steward, Perry, Mahler & Bird, P.A., Rochester, 1985—. Class agt. Suffolk U. Law Sch. Mem. ABA (young lawyers div.), Minn. Bar Assn. (family law sect., young lawyers sect.), Olmsted County Bar Assn. (treas., chairperson law day 1983-84), U. Minn. Alumni Assn., Phi Delta Phi, Phi Beta Kappa. Republican. Presbyterian. Family and matrimonial, General practice. Home: 1412 Berkman Ct SE Rochester MN 55904 Office: Steward Perry Mahler & Bird PA 300 3d Ave SE Rochester MN 55904

BAKER, HAROLD ALBERT, fed. judge; b. Mt. Kisco, N.Y., Oct. 4, 1929; s. John Shirley and Ruth (Sarmiento) B.; m. Dorothy Ida Armstrong, June 24, 1951; children: Emily, Nancy, Peter. A.B., U. Ill., 1951, J.D., 1956. Bar: Ill. bar 1956. Practiced in Champaign, Ill., 1956-78; partner firm Hatch & Baker, 1960-78; judge U.S. Dist. Ct. for Central Dist. Ill., Danville, 1978—; adj. mem. faculty Coll. Law, U. Ill., 1972-78; sr. counsel Presdl. Commn. on CIA Activities within U.S., 1975. Pres. Champaign Bd. Edn., 1967-76, pres., 1967-76. Served to lt. j.g. USN, 1951-53. Mem. Am. Bar Assn., Ill. Bar Assn. Democrat. Episcopalian. Jurisprudence. Office: U S Dist Ct PO Box 125 Danville IL 61832 *

BAKER, HELEN, lawyer; b. Cleve., May 6, 1922; d. Harry and Belle (Speiser) Manheim; m. Marvin Baker, Nov. 10, 1944 (div. 1973); children—Jon, Scott, Lauren. B.S. cum laude, Northwestern U., 1943; J.D. summa cum laude, Cleve. State U., 1977. Bar: Ohio 1979, U.S. Dist. Ct. (no. dist.) Ohio 1979. Staff children's rights project ACLU of Ohio Found., Inc., Cleve., 1977-78; staff counsel ACLU of Greater Cleve. Found., 1979-80, dir. children's rights advocacy project, 1980-81; cons., adv. ACLU, others, 1982—. Contbr. to books, articles to profl. jours. Active politics, civil rights, anti-war movement, nuclear freeze movement, others. Recipient Wall St. Jour. award, 1978; Civil Libertarian award ACLU of Ohio, 1981; Civil Libertarian of Yr. award ACLU of Greater Cleve. Mem. Ohio Bar Assn., ABA, Assn. Trial Lawyers Am., Nat. Lawyers Guild. Civil rights, Juvenile, Rights of Handicapped; Family Rights. Home: 440 Addison Ave Elmhurst IL 60126

BAKER, HORACE ROSS, JR., lawyer; b. Akron, Ohio, Mar. 8, 1924; s. Horace Ross and Helen (Baldwin) B.; m. Phyllis Laurence Green, Dec. 18, 1948; children: Robert Clarkson, Warren Ross, David Ware, Emily Laurence. AB, Harvard U., 1947, LLB, 1951. Bar: Mass. 1951. Lawyer John Hancock Mut. Life Ins. Co., Boston, 1951-55, asst. counsel, 1955-57, assoc. counsel, 1957-60, counsel, 1960-65, gen. solicitor, 1965-67, v.p. and gen. solicitor, 1967-72, sr. v.p. and gen. solicitor, 1972-79, sr. v.p. and sec., 1979-83, exec. v.p. and gen. counsel, 1983—, also bd. dirs.; bd. dirs. John Hancock subs., Inc., Boston, John Hancock Property & Casualty Holding Co., John Hancock Property and Casualty Ins. Co., John Hancock Indemnity Co., John Hancock Variable Life Ins. Co., Hanseco Ins. Co., Unigard Security Ins. Co., Bellevue, Washington. Chmn. Hingham (Mass.) Bd. Appeals, 1967-75; clerk Hingham Planning Bd., 1961-62; mem. Hingham Planning Bd., 1960-67. Served as tech. sgt. U.S. Army, 1943-46, ETO, PTO. Mem. ABA, Mass. Bar Assn., Boston Bar Assn., Assn. Life Ins. Counsel (chmn. ins. section 1977-79), Am. Corp. Counsel Assn., New Eng. Legal Found. Clubs: Algonquin (Boston), Harvard (pres. Hingham chpt. 1970-71). Avocations: fishing, boating, photography. General corporate, Insurance, Administrative and regulatory. Home: 367 Main St Hingham MA 02043 Office: John Hancock Mut Life Ins Co PO Box 111 Boston MA 02117

BAKER, JAMES EDWARD SPROUL, lawyer; b. Evanston, Ill., May 23, 1912; s. John Clark and Hester (Sproul) B.; m. Eleanor Lee Dodgson, Oct. 2, 1937 (dec. Sept. 1972); children: John Lee, Edward Graham. A.B., Northwestern U., 1933, J.D., 1936. Bar: Ill. 1936, U.S. Supreme Ct. 1957. Practice in Chgo., 1936—; assoc. Sidley & Austin, and predecessors, 1936-48, ptnr., 1948-81; of counsel Sidley & Austin, 1981—; lectr. Northwestern U. Law Sch., 1951-52; Nat. chmn. Stanford U. Parents Com., 1970-75; mem. vis. com. Stanford Law Sch., 1976-79, 82-84, Northwestern U. Law Sch., 1980—, DePaul U. Law Sch., 1982—. Served to comdr. USNR, 1941-46. Fellow Am. Coll. Trial Lawyers (regent 1974-81, sec. 1977-79, pres. 1979-80); mem. ABA, Bar Assn. 7th Fed. Circuit, Ill. State Bar Assn., Chgo. Bar Assn., Soc. Trial Lawyers Ill., Northwestern U. Law Alumni Assn. (past pres.), Order of Coif, Phi Lambda Upsilon, Sigma Nu. Republican. Methodist. Clubs: John Evans (Northwestern U.) (chmn. 1982-85); University (Chgo.); John Henry Wigmore (past pres.); Midday (Chgo.), Legal (Chgo.), Law (Chgo.) (pres. 1983-85); Westmoreland Country (Wilmette, Ill.). Federal civil litigation, Antitrust, State civil litigation. Home: 1300 N Lake Shore Dr Chicago IL 60610 Office: 1 First Nat Plaza Chicago IL 60603

BAKER, JAMES EDYRN, lawyer; b. Wenatchee, Wash., Dec. 13, 1951; s. John Robert and Barbara Jean (Shawcross) B.; m. Linda F. Nichols, Apr. 1, 1972; children: John Nicholas, Joseph Orry-Leroy, Paul Smithmoore. BA, Eastern Wash. U., 1975; JD, Gonzaga U., 1979. Bar: Wash. 1979, U.S. Dist.

Ct. (ea. dist.) Wash. 1979, U.S. Dist. Ct. (we. dist.) Wash. 1980, U.S. Ct. Appeals (9th cir.) 1980, U.S. Ct. Claims 1984, U.S. Tax Ct. 1985, U.S. Ct. Mil. Appeals 1985. Law clk. to U.S. Magistrate Spokane, Wash., 1979-80; assoc. Lyon, Beaulaurier, Weigand, Suko & Gustafson, Yakima, Wash., 1980-83; ptnr. Lyon, Beaulaurier, Weigand, Suko & Gustafson, Yakima, 1984-85; sole practice Port Townsend, Wash., 1985-86; assoc. Miracle, Pruzan and Morrow, Seattle, 1986—. Mem. ABA (law and media com. young lawyers div. 1985—, exec. com. human rights 1985—), Wash. State Bar Assn. (bd. trustees youg lawyers sect. 1981-84, continuing legal edn. com. 1985—), Assn. Trial Lawyers Am. Democrat. Lutheran. Avocations: reading, writing, photography, music, fishing. Personal injury, Insurance. Home: 3211 43d Ave W Seattle WA 98199 Office: Smith Tower 23d Floor Seattle WA 98104

BAKER, JAMES JAY, lawyer, trade association adminstrator; b. Washington, Aug. 12, 1953; s. John Edward and Barbara (Freney) B. BA, U. N.Mex., 1975; JD, Cath. U., 1978. Bar: D.C. 1978, Mo. 1978. Prosecutor Ray County, Mo., 1979-81; dep. dir. govtl. affairs Nat. Rifle Assn., Washington, 1981-86, dir. govtl. affairs, 1986—. Mem. ABA. Republican. Roman Catholic. Avocation: photo journalism. Legislative, Criminal. Office: Nat Rifle Assn 1600 Rhode Island Ave NW Washington DC 20036

BAKER, JOSIAH CARR EGGLESTON, lawyer; b. Nashville, Apr. 2, 1929; s. Robert Howell and Julia (Plummer) E.; m. Elizabeth Harper Ruble, Sept. 14, 1957; children—Wade Eggleston, Edward Harper, Julia Plummer. B.E., Vanderbilt U., 1951, J.D., 1953. Bar: Tenn. 1955. Dep. clk. and master 7th Chancery Div. Tenn., 1957-58; prin. Baker & Kinsman, P.C.1958—; spl. counsel to atty. gen. Tenn., 1963-65; spl. counsel Chattanooga-Hamilton County Air Pollution Control Bd., 1970—; spl. counsel City of Chattanooga. Bd. dirs. Chattanooga Symphony, 1965; chmn. Carter St. Corp., 1981. Served to lt. (j.g.) USNR, 1953-57; to lt. comdr. USNR, 1957-64. Mem. Chattanooga Bar Assn. (bd. govs. 1965-72, pres. 1970-71), Tenn. Bar Assn., ABA, Def. Research Inst., Fed. Ins. and Corp. Counsel, Tenn. Def. Lawyers Assn., Baylor Sch. Alumni (bd. dirs., sec. treas., 1960), Vanderbilt Law Sch. Alumni (bd. dirs. 1981-83). Methodist (1st Centenary bd. mem. and tchr.). Clubs: Chattanooga Golf and Country, Mountain City (Chattanooga), Mason (33 deg. Scottish Rite). Insurance, Personal injury, Environment. Office: 1st Tennessee Bldg Suite 724 Chattanooga TN 37402

BAKER, KEITH BRIAN, lawyer, consultant; b. Chgo., Mar. 10, 1956; m. Maurine Joy. BS in Acctg. with honors, U. Ill., Champaign, 1978, JD, 1982. Bar: Ill. 1982, U.S. Dist. Ct. (no. dist.) Ill. 1982; CPA, Ill. Tax mgr. Arthur Andersen and Co., Chgo., 1982—. Information rep. United Way, Chgo., 1982-83. Mem. ABA, Ill. Bar Assn., Chgo. Bar Assn., Am. Inst. CPA's, Ill. CPA Soc. Corporate taxation, Personal income taxation, Estate taxation. Home: 2020 Lincoln Park W Chicago IL 60614 Office: Arthur Andersen and Co 33 W Monroe St Chicago IL 60603

BAKER, KEITH LEON, lawyer; b. Columbus, Ind., Jan. 22, 1950; s. Richard Leon and Sarah Elizabeth (Wisehart) B. A.B., Princeton U., 1972; J.D., Syracuse U., 1975; LL.M. with highest honors, George Washington U., 1978. Bar: N.Y. 1976, D.C. 1976, U.S. Ct. Appeals (D.C. cir.) 1983, U.S. Ct. Internat. Trade 1983. Asst. bank examiner U.S. Treasury Dept., N.Y.C., 1974; law clk. U.S. Dept. of Justice, Syracuse, N.Y., 1974-75; atty.-adviser GAO, Washington, 1975-78; atty.-adviser U.S. EPA, Washington, 1978-80; assoc. Brownstein, Zeidman & Schomer, Washington, 1980-82; ptnr. Trammell, Chase & Lambert, Washington, 1982-84, Barnett & Alagia, Washington, 1984—; dir. Small Bus. Financing Inst., Washington, 1983—. Author: Small Business Financing, 1983; contbr. articles to profl. jours. Mem. ABA, Fed. Bar Assn., Nat. Contract Mgmt. Assn. Methodist. Government contracts and claims, Private international, General corporate. Home: 2811 S 12th St Arlington VA 22204 Office: Barnett & Alagia 1000 Thomas Jefferson St NW Washington DC 20007

BAKER, LLOYD HARVEY, lawyer; b. Bklyn., Sept. 17, 1927; s. George William and Marion (Souville) B.; m. Barbara I. Gustafson, Sept. 4, 1955; children—Laurie, Jeffrey. Student Colgate U., 1945-48; LL.B., NYU, 1951. Bar: N.Y. 1951, U.S. Dist. Ct. (so. and ea. dists.) N.Y. 1953, U.S. Ct. Apls. (2d cir.) 1970. Assoc. Milligan, Reilly, Lake & Schneider, Babylon, N.Y., 1952-53; staff Fgn. Claims Commn., Washington, 1954; spl. atty. windfall investigations FHA, Washington, 1955; asst. U.S. atty. for Eastern Dist. N.Y., 1955-59; sole practice, Bayshore and Islip, N.Y., 1959-67; atty. Suffolk County (N.Y.) Legal Aid Soc., 1967-69; dep. chief civil div. U.S. Atty.'s Office for Eastern Dist. N.Y., 1969-74; asst. counsel met. region Penn Central R.R. and Conrail, N.Y.C., 1975-81; ptnr. Bleakley, Platt, Remsen, Millham and Curran, N.Y.C., 1982—. Mem. Suffolk County Republican Com., 1963-71. Mem. Suffolk County Bar Assn. (chmn. fed. ct. com.). Episcopalian. Club: Bay Shore (N.Y.) Yacht. Federal civil litigation, State civil litigation. Home: 5 Mulberry Rd Islip NY 11751 Office: 80 Pine St New York NY 10005

BAKER, MARK BRUCE, lawyer, educator; b. Bridgeport, Conn., Dec. 27, 1946; s. Phillip and Lillian (Islovitz) Bader; m. Sandra Fay Wolf, June 9, 1968 (div. 1982); 1 dau., Rachel Barrett Bader; m. 2d Nora Kay Mandell, Dec. 30, 1984; 1 dau., Lisa Anne Baker. B.B.A., U. Miami, Coral Gables, Fla., 1968; J.D., So. Meth. U., 1974. Bar: Tex. 1974. Assoc. firm Herndon, Girand and Dooley, Dallas, 1974-76; ptnr. firm Pailet and Bader, Dallas, 1976-80; prof. internat. law U. Tex., Austin, 1980—; of counsel firm Bard and Groves, Houston, 1981-83. Contbr. articles to legal publs. Bd. dirs. Jewish Community Council Austin, 1983—. Recipient Outstanding Asst. Prof. award U. Tex., 1982, Outstanding Class Lectr. award, 1984; Tex. Excellence Teaching award U. Tex. Alumni Assn., 1983. Mem. ABA, Union Internationale des Avocats, Am. Friends of Wilton Park (sec.-treas. 1982-84), Tex. Bar Assn. (internat. law sect.), Austin Fgn. Trade Council. Private international, General corporate, Contracts commercial. Home: 1112 Quaker Ridge Dr Austin TX 78746 Office: CBA 5 202 Univ Texas Austin TX 78712

BAKER, MAX ALLEN, lawyer; b. Atlantic City, June 18, 1946; s. Samuel and Thelma (Rich) B.; m. Elyse Bank, Sept. 18, 1970 (div. Mar. 1984); 1 child, Jessica. BA, NYU, 1968; JD, Boston U., 1974. Bar: N.J. 1974, U.S. Dist. Ct. N.J. 1974. Jud. clerk to presiding justice chancery div. Atlantic County Superior Ct., N.J., 1974-75; assoc. Feinberg & Ginsberg, Atlantic City, 1975-76, Sherman Kendis, Atlantic City, 1976-81; ptnr. Kendis & Baker, P.A., Atlantic City, 1981-85; sole practice Pleasantville, N.J., 1986—; chmn. dist. 1 fee arbitration com. Supreme Ct. N.J., Pleasantville, 1982—. Bd. dirs. Hebrew Acad. Atlantic County, Atlantic City, 1979-83, Seashore Gardens, Atlantic City, 1984-85. Served with U.S. Army, 1969-71, Vietnam. Mem. ABA, N.J. Bar Assn., Atlantic County Bar Assn. Family and matrimonial, General practice, Personal injury. Home: 127 London Ct Pleasantville NJ 08232 Office: 1009 S Shore Rd PO Box 905 Pleasantville NJ 08232

BAKER, PAUL VIVIAN, judge, editor; b. Southgate, Middlesex, Eng., Mar. 27, 1923; s. Vivian Cyril and Maud Lydia (Jiggins) B.; m. Stella Paterson Eadie, Jan. 2, 1957; children: Ian David, Alison Joyce. BA, Univ. Coll., Oxford, 1948, BCL, 1949, MA, 1954. Bar: Eng. 1950, Queen's Counsel 1972. Sole practice Eng., 1950-83, cir. judge, 1983—. Asst. editor Law Quarterly Review, 1960-70, editor, 1971—, co-editor Snell's Principles of Equity, 1954, latest edition, 1982. Served to flight lt. Royal Air Force, 1941-46. Mem. Honourable Soc. Lincoln's Inn (life tenure bencher). Clubs: Athenaeum, Authors (London). Avocations: gardening, music. Landlord-tenant, Real property, Probate. Home: 27 Peaks Hill, Purley CR2 3JG, England Office: Law Quarterly Review, 9 Old Sq Lincolns Inn, London WC2A 3SR, England

BAKER, RICHARD SOUTHWORTH, lawyer; b. Lansing, Mich., Dec. 18, 1929; s. Paul Julius and Florence (Schmid) B.; m. Marina Joy Vidoli, July 24, 1965; children: Garrick Richard, Lydia Joy. Student, DePauw U., 1947-49; A.B. cum laude, Harvard, 1951; J.D., U. Mich., 1954. Bar: Ohio 1957, U.S. Dist. Ct. (no. dist.) Ohio 1958, U.S. Tax Ct. 1960, U.S. Supreme Ct. 1971, U.S. Ct. Appeals (6th cir.) 1972. Since practiced in Toledo; mem. firm Fuller & Henry, and predecessors, 1956—; Chmn. nat. com. region IV Mich. Law Sch. Fund, 1967-69, mem.-at-large, 1970-85. Bd. dirs. Asso. Harvard Alumni, 1970-73. Served with AUS, 1954-56. Fellow Am. Coll. Trial Lawyers; mem. Am., Ohio, Toledo bar assns., Phi Delta Theta, Phi Delta Phi. Clubs: Toledo (Toledo), Harvard (Toledo) (pres. 1968-77), Inverness (Toledo). Federal civil litigation, State civil litigation, Workers' compensation. Home: 2819 Falmouth Rd Toledo OH 43615 Office: 1200 Edison Plaza Toledo OH 43604

BAKER, ROBERT KENNETH, lawyer; b. Anderson, Ind., Mar. 20, 1940; s. James Leslie and Bernadine (Bright) B.; m. Sally Jean Kauffman, Dec. 13, 1971 (div.); children: Alexis Bright, Sarah Elizabeth. AB in Econs., Stanford U., 1962, LLB, 1965. Bar: Calif. 1966, N.Y., 1971, U.S. Dist. Ct. (cen. dist.) Calif. 1966, U.S. Dist. Ct. (so. dist.) N.Y. 1972, U.S. Dist. Ct. (ea. dist.) N.Y., 1974, U.S. Dist. Ct. (so. dist.) Calif. 1979, U.S. Dist. Ct. (ea. dist.) Calif. 1983, U.S. Ct. Appeals (2d cir.) 1972, U.S. Ct. Appeals (5th cir.) 1976, U.S. Ct. Appeals (9th cir.) 1976, U.S. Supreme Ct. 1976. Instr. Columbia Law Sch., N.Y.C., 1965-66; staff mem. Antitrust div. U.S. Dept. Justice, Washington, 1966-67, spl. asst. to Dep. Atty. Gen., 1967-68; dep. gen. counsel, co-dir. Media Task Force, Nat. Commn. on Causes Prevention of Violence, Washington, 1968-69; assoc. Cravath, Swaine & Moore, N.Y.C., 1970-76; ptnr. Agnew, Miller & Carlson, Los Angeles, 1976-79; ptnr. Baker & Wilson, Los Angeles, 1980-82; ptnr. Alef, Baker, Grunfeld & Wilson, Beverly Hills, Calif., 1982-86. Mem. Calif. State Bar Assn., Los Angeles County Bar Assn., ABA. Club: Regency (Los Angeles). Federal civil litigation, Antitrust, General corporate. Home: 234 S Figueroa St Los Angeles CA 90012 Office: 190 N Canon Dr 4th Floor Beverly Hills CA 90210

BAKER, RONALD LEE, folklore educator; b. Indpls., June 30, 1937; s. Delbert Everett and Ellen (Harrison) B.; m. Catherine Anne Neal, Oct. 21, 1960; children: Susannah Jill, Jonathan Kemp. B.S., Ind. State U., Terre Haute, 1960; M.A., Ind. State U., 1961; postgrad., U. Ill., 1963-65; Ph.D., Ind U., 1969. Instr. English U. Ill., Urbana, 1963-65; teaching assoc. Ind. U., Ft. Wayne, 1965-66; prof. English Ind State U., Terre Haute, 1966—; chmn. dept. Ind State U., 1980—; vis. lectr. U. Ill., 1972-73; vis. assoc. prof. Ind. U., Bloomington, 1975; vis. prof. Ind. U., 1978, 84. Author: Folklore in the Writings of Rowland E. Robinson, 1973, Hoosier Folk Legends, 1982; Jokelore, 1986; (with others) Indiana Place Names, 1975. Mem. Am. Folklore Soc., MLA, Am. Name Soc. (v.p. 1981-82), Hoosier Folklore Soc. (pres. 1970-79). Estate planning, Bankruptcy, Family and matrimonial. Home: RD 51 Box 434 Terre Haute IN 47805 Office: Indiana State University Terre Haute IN 47809

BAKER, RONALD LEE, lawyer; b. North Vernon, Ind., Jan. 14, 1927; s. Albert Louis and Mary (Wilkerson) B. m. Clara Marie Johnson, Nov. 1, 1969. BS, Ind. U., 1951, JD, 1959. Bar: Ind. 1959, U.S. Dist. Ct. (so. dist.) Ind. 1966. From mgmt. trainee asst. to mgr. J.C. Penny Co., Jeffersonville, Ind., 1951-56; trust adminstrn. officer Merchants Nat. Bank, Indpls., 1959-66; sr. commr. Marion County (Ind.) Probate Ct., 1967-68; chief counsel Mass Transp. Authority, Indpls., 1969; dep. corp. counsel City of Indpls., 1970-77; sole practice Indpls., 1977—. Chmn. precinct Indpls. Reps., 1966-69, chmn. ward, 1967-76. Served with U.S. Army, 1945-47. Mem. ABA, Ind. Bar Assn., Indpls. Bar Assn., Indpls. Estate Planning Council, Assn. Trial Lawyers Am., Ind. Trial Lawyers Assn., Am. Judicature Soc. Mem. Christian Ch. (Disciples of Christ). Lodges: Kiwanis, Masons. Avocations: bowling, skiing. Estate planning, Contracts commercial, Family and matrimonial. Home: 819 W Banta Rd Indianapolis IN 46217 Office: 11 S Meridian St #919 Indianapolis IN 46204

BAKER, SCOTT RUSSELL, lawyer; b. Cleve., Apr. 9, 1952; s. Hugh Russell Baker and Elsie Georgienne (Gergel) Macko; m. Joni Adelle Davis, May 25, 1974; children: Emily Sara, Jefferson Bentley, Evan Russell. BA, U. Tex., 1975; JD, So. Meth. U., 1980. Bar: Tex. 1980, U.S. Dist. Ct. (no. dist.) Tex. 1981. Tennis pro T Bar M Aerobics Ctr., Dallas, 1976-80; counsel Fidelity Union, Dallas, 1981-86; sole practice Dallas, 1986—. Precinct chmn. campaign of Kent Hance for Gov., Dallas, 1985-86; atty. Ctr. for Non Profit Mgmt., Dallas, 1982-83; bd. dirs. Hockaday Sch. Parents Assn., Dallas, 1986. Recipient Outstanding Service award Ctr. for Non Profit Mgmt., 1983. Fellow Life Mgmt. Inst.; mem. ABA (com. investment services), Tex. Bar Assn., Coll. State Bar of Tex., Dallas Bar Assn. Republican. Mem. Northwest Bible Ch. Club: Dallas Legal Edn. Ctr. Avocations: triathlons, tennis, home remodelling, Bible study. Securities, General corporate, Insurance. Office: 10000 North Central Expressway Suite 1002 Lock Box 10 Dallas TX 75231

BAKER, SIDNEY, lawyer; b. Pitts., Oct. 25, 1926; a. Charles and Bess (Schwartz) B.; m. Judith R. Baker, Feb. 21, 1946; children: Karen, Steven, Larry, Wendy. JD, U. Notre Dame, 1951. Bar: Pa. 1952, U.S. Ct. Appeals (3d cir.) 1976, U.S. Supreme Ct. 1980. Sole practice Pitts., 1952—. Served with USN, 1944-46. Mem. Pa. Bar Assn., Allegheny County Bar Assn. (chmn. various coms.), Assn. Trial Lawyers Am. (pres. Pitts. chpt. 1985-86), Pa. Trial Lawyers Assn. (bd. govs. 1974-80), Acad. Trial Lawyers Allegheny County. State civil litigation, Federal civil litigation, General corporate. Office: 700 Manor Bldg Pittsburgh PA 15219

BAKER, SUSAN ELAINE NEHER, lawyer, legal educator; b. Gooding, Idaho, Feb. 23, 1952; d. Royal Glen and Juanita Irene (Byerly) Neher; m. Delwyn Richard Baker, Jan. 31, 1981; 1 child, Jonathan Richard. BS, Coll. of Idaho, 1974; JD, U. Idaho, 1978. Bar: Idaho 1979, U.S. Dist. Ct. Idaho 1979. Legal analyst Idaho Dept. Health and Welfare, Boise, Idaho, 1979; law clk. Idaho State Ct., Boise, 1979-81; tax preparer Arthur Young, Athens, Ga., 1982; prof. City Coll. of Chgo., Athens, Greece, 1981-84, U. Md., Athens, 1981-84. Author: Child Support Enforcement Manual in Idaho, 1979. Vol. Spokane County Prosecutors Office, 1985-86. Mem. ABA, Idaho Bar Assn., Assn. Trial Lawyers Am. Episcopalian. Estate taxation. Home: 701 San Jose Way Boise ID 83712

BAKER, THOMAS EDWARD, lawyer, accountant; b. Washington, July 24, 1923; s. John Thad and Angelina E. (Rappa) B.; m. Mildred M. Younglove, Dec. 26, 1944; children—Jean Ann Baker Holland, Cindy Baker Goralewicz, Linda Hogan. B.S. U. Okla., 1950, J.D., 1950. Bar: Okla. 1950; C.P.A., Okla. Sole practice, Oklahoma City, 1950; IRS agt., spl. agt., 1951-53; ptnr. Shutler Baker Simpson & Logsdon, Kingfisher, Okla., 1953-79, Baker Logsdon & Schulte, Kingfisher, 1979—. Trustee U. Okla. Found., Inc., 1987—. Served with AUS, 1943-46. Mem. ABA, Am. Inst. C.P.A.s, Am. Legion (past service officer). Democrat. Mem. Christian Ch. (Disciples of Christ). Clubs: Hennessey Country, Elks. General practice, Probate, Oil and gas law. Home: 903 Park Ln Kingfisher OK 73750 Office: Baker Logsdon & Schulte 302 Main St Kingfisher OK 73750

BAKER, THOMAS EUGENE, law educator; b. Youngstown, Ohio, Feb. 25, 1953; s. John M. and Helen Marie B.; m. Jane Marie Schussler, June 15, 1974; 1 child, Thomas Athanasius. BS cum laude, Fla. State U., 1974; JD with high honors, U. Fla., 1977. Bars: Fla. 1979, U.S. Dist. Ct. (no. dist.) Tex. 1979, U.S. Supreme Ct. 1982, U.S. Ct. Appeals (5th cir.) 1979, U.S. Ct. Appeals (11th cir.) 1981. Law clk. to presiding justice U.S. Ct. Appeals (5th cir.) Ga., Atlanta, 1977-79; faculty Tex. Tech. U., Lubbock, 1979—; jud. fellow U.S. Supreme Ct., Washington, 1985—; mem. adv. bd. Am. Criminal Law Rev., Washington, 1981-85. Contbr. articles to profl. jours. Recipient Faculty Research award Tex. Tech. U., 1983; Justice Tom C. Clark fellow Jud. Fellows Commn., Washington, 1986. Mem. ABA (various sects. and coms.), Am. Law Inst. (elected). Byzantine Catholic. Club: Sachems (Lubbock). Avocations: photography, racquet sports. Legal education, Civil rights, Federal civil litigation. Home: 3414 91st St Lubbock TX 79423 Office: Tex Tech U Sch Law Lubbock TX 79409

BAKER, VERLYN CHILDS, lawyer; b. Atlanta, July 20, 1929; s. Mert Lee and Ethel Pauline (Childs) B.; m. Joyce Valeria Sikes, Jan. 26, 1950; children: Garrett Verlyn, Scott Steven. LLB, Atlanta Law Sch., 1953; BA, Ga. State U., 1972. Bar: Ga. 1956, U.S. Dist. Ct. (no. dist.) Ga. 1965, U.S. Ct. Appeals (5th cir.) 1978, U.S. Ct. Appeals (11th cir.) 1981, U.S. Supreme Ct. 1983. Claims mgr. Hartford Accident & Indemnity Co., Montgomery and Columbia, Ala. and S.C., 1955-63; real estate negotiator F.W. Woolworth Co., Atlanta, 1963-65; sole practice Decatur, Ga., 1965—. Mem. Ga. State Bar Assn. (gen practice and trial sect., 4th. dist. council mem. 1982—), Ga. Trial Lawyers Assn. (v.p. 1982-86), Decatur-DeKalb Bar Assn. Republican. Baptist. Lodges: Masons, Civitan (local pres. 1971). Avocations: reading, music. State civil litigation, Personal injury, Workers' compensation. Office: 509 Medlock Rd Decatur GA 30030-1513

BAKER, WILLIAM DUNLAP, lawyer; b. St. Louis, June 17, 1932; s. Harold Griffith and Bernice (Kraft) B.; m. Kay Stokes, May 23, 1955; children: Mark William, Kathryn X., Beth Kristie, Frederick Martin. A.B., Colgate U., 1954; J.D., U. Calif. at Berkeley, 1960. Bar: Calif. 1961, Ariz. 1961, U.S. Supreme Ct. 1969. Practice in Coolidge, 1961, Florence, 1961-63, Phoenix, 1963—; law clk. Stokes & Moring, 1960; spl. investigator Office Pinal County Atty., 1960-61, dep. county atty., 1961-63; partner McBryde, Vincent, Brumage & Baker, 1961-63; assoc. atty. Rawlins, Ellis, Burrus & Kiewit, 1963-65, partner, 1965-81; pres., atty. Ellis & Baker, P.C., 1981-84, Ellis, Baker, Lynch, Clark & Porter P.C., 1984-86, Ellis, Baker, Clark & Porter, P.C., 1986—; referee Juvenile Ct. Maricopa County Superior Ct., 1966-85. Mem. Gov.'s Adv. Council, Phoenix, 1969-71, Ariz. Environ. Planning Commn., 1974-75; bd. dirs. Agri-Bus. Council, 1978—, sec., 1978-82; Spl. legal counsel Ariz. Com. Republican Party, 1964; legal counsel Ariz. Com. Rep. Party, 1965-69, mem. exec. com., 1972-78; vice-chmn. Maricopa County Rep. Com., 1968-69, chmn., 1969-71; bd. dirs. San Pablo Home for Youth, 1964-72, pres., 1971; bd. dirs. Maricopa County chpt. Nat. Found. March of Dimes, 1966-71, campaign chmn., 1970; trustee St. Luke's Hosp., 1976-85, sec., 1978-82, chmn., 1982-85; bd. dirs. Luke's Men, 1971-80, pres., 1976-77; bd. dirs. Combined Health Resources, 1982-85; bd. dirs. St. Luke's Health Systems, 1985—, chmn., 1985—; bd. dirs., v.p. Ariz. Anglican Cursillo Movement, 1982-86; regional v.p. Colgate Alumni Corp., 1977-82; vice chancellor Episcopal Diocese of Ariz., 1970—; sr. warden Christ Ch. of Ascension, 1983-86. Served to 1st lt. USAF, 1954-57. Mem. Am., Ariz., Calif., Maricopa County bar assns., Ariz. Acad., Sigma Chi, Phi Delta Phi. Clubs: Ariz., Phoenix Country. Real property, Local government, Contracts commercial. Home: 5309 N 34th St Phoenix AZ 85018 Office: 4444 N 32d St Suite 200 Phoenix AZ 85018

BAKER, WILLIAM PARR, lawyer; b. Balt., Sept. 5, 1946; s. George William and Jane (Parr) B.; m. Christine Corbett, Oct. 23, 1982; children: William Corbett, Brendan Parr. B.A., St. Francis Coll., Loretto, Pa., 1968; J.D., U. Md., 1971. Bar: Md. 1971, U.S. Dist. Ct. Md. 1972, U.S. Tax Ct. 1978, U.S. Sup. Ct. 1980, U.S. Ct. Apls. (4th cir.) 1982. Law clk. Md. Ct. Apls., 1971-72; ptnr. Baker and Baker, P.A. and predecessors, Balt., 1972—. Vice pres. bd. dirs. Santa Claus Anonymous, 1973-76; bd. dirs. Balt. Assn. Retarded Citizens, 1981—. Mem. ABA, Md. Bar Assn., Bar Assn. Balt. City. Roman Catholic. Clubs: Balt. Country. Contracts commercial, General practice, Federal civil litigation. Office: 10 Charles Plaza Suite 200 Baltimore MD 21201

BAKES, ROBERT ELDON, justice Idaho Supreme Ct.; b. Boise, Jan. 11, 1932; s. Warren H. and Oral Bakes; m. Lurlene M. Fisher; children—Juliann, Colleen, Diane, Rachel. Bar: Ida. 1956, U.S. Ct. Appeals (9th cir.) 1963. Instr., U. Ill., 1956-57; legal counsel Idaho State Tax Commn., Boise, 1959-61; asst. U.S. atty., Boise, 1961-66; sr. ptnr. Bakes, Ward & Bates, Boise, 1969-71; justice Idaho Supreme Ct., 1971—, chief justice, 1981-82. Jurisprudence. Office: Supreme Ct Bldg 451 W State St Boise ID 83702

BAKKEN, GORDON MORRIS, legal educator; b. Madison, Wis., Jan. 10, 1943; s. Elwood S. and Evelyn A. H. (Anderson) B.; m. Erika Reinhardt, Mar. 24, 1943; children—Angela E., Jeffrey E. B.S., U. Wis., 1966, M.S., 1967, Ph.D., 1970, J.D., 1973. Asst., then assoc. prof. history Calif. State U.-Fullerton, 1969-74, dir. faculty affairs, 1974-86, prof. history, 1974—; cons. Calif. Sch. Employees Assn., 1976-78; cons. Calif. Bar Commn. Hist. Law., 1985—; mem. mgmt. task force on acad. grievance procedures Calif. State Univ. and Colls. Systems, 1975. Placentia Jusa referee coordinator, 1983. Russell Sage resident fellow law, 1971-72; Am. Council Learned Socs. grantee-in-aid, 1979-80; Am. Bar Found. fellow in legal history, 1979-80, 84-85. Mem. Orgn. Am. Historians, Am. Soc. Legal History, Law and Soc. Assn., Western History Assn. Democrat. Lutheran. Contbr. aritcles to profl. jours. Legal history, Labor. Office: Calif State U 800 N State College Blvd Fullerton CA 92634

BAKKER, THOMAS GORDON, lawyer; b. San Gabriel, Calif., Aug. 18, 1947; s. Gordon and Eva Marie (Hoekstra) B.; m. Charlotte Anne Kamstra, Aug. 1, 1969; children: Sarah, Jonathan. AB in History, Calvin Coll., Grand Rapids, Mich., 1969; JD, U. Mich., 1973. Bar: Ariz. 1973, U.S. Dist. Ct. Ariz. 1973, U.S. Ct. Appeals (9th cir.) 1973. Staff reporter Ariz. Criminal Code Revision Com., Phoenix, 1973-75; asst. atty. gen. State of Ariz., Phoenix, 1975-77; staff atty. div. 1 Ariz. Ct. Appeals, Phoenix, 1977-79; assoc. Burch, Cracchiolo et al, Phoenix, 1979-80; from assoc. to ptnr. Weyl, Guyer, MacBan & Olson, Phoenix, 1980—; v. chmn. tort and ins. practice sect. Appellate Advocacy Commn., 1982-83; judge pro tempore div. 1 Ariz. Ct. Appeals, 1985. Served with U.S. Army, 1969-71. Fellow Ariz. Bar Found. (founding fellow); mem. ABA, Ariz. Bar Assn., Maricopa County Bar Assn., Am. Judicature Soc., Def. Research Inst. Democrat. Mem. Christian Reformed Ch. Club: Mansion (Phoenix). Avocations: reading, golf, aerobics. State civil litigation, Federal civil litigation, Personal injury. Office: Weyl Guyer MacBan & Olson 7243 N 16th St Phoenix AZ 85020

BALA, GARY GANESH, lawyer; b. Madras, India, Feb. 10, 1958; came to U.S. 1960; s. T.N. and Susila Bala. BA summa cum laude, Temple U., 1979; JD, Villanova U., 1982. Bar: Pa. 1982, U.S. Dist. Ct. (ea. dist.) Pa. 1982, U.S. Ct. Appeals (3d cir.) 1982, N.J. 1986, U.S. Dist. Ct. N.J. 1986, U.S. SUpreme Ct. 1986. Law clk. to presiding judge Phila. Common Pleas Ct., 1982-84; assoc. Harvey, Pennington, Herting & Renneisen Ltd., Phila., 1985-86, Thompson & Pennell, Phila., 1986—. Editor Phila. County Reporter, 1983—. Pres.'s scholar, 1979. Mem. ABA, Pa. Bar Assn., Phila. Bar Assn. Democrat. Avocations: sports, reading, travel. Federal civil litigation, State civil litigation, Insurance. Office: Thompson & Pennell 410 Public Ledger Bldg 6th and Chestnut Sts Philadelphia PA 19106

BALABANIAN, DAVID MARK, lawyer; b. Wenatchee, Wash., July 29, 1938; s. Mark Sarkis and Ibraxie (Elmas) B.; m. Christine Madath, June 27, 1962; children: Lisa Marie, Mark Sarkis. A.B., Harvard Coll., 1960; B.Phil. (Rhodes scholar), Oxford U., 1962; LL.B., Harvard U., 1965. Bar: Calif. 1966. Partner firm McCutchen, Doyle, Brown & Enersen, San Francisco, 1973—; chmn. Conf. of Dels., Calif. State Bar, 1981-82. Mem. Bar Assn. San Francisco (dir. 1974-76, pres. 1986), San Francisco Barristers Club (pres. 1972), Practising Law Inst. (trustee 1983—). Home: 641 Spruce St Berkeley CA 94707 Office: 3 Embarcadero Center San Francisco CA 94111

BALABER-STRAUSS, BARBARA, lawyer; b. N.Y.C., July 30, 1938; d. Philip Balaber and Clara (Rund) Balaber; children—Nancy C., Elizabeth A. A.B. cum laude, Hunter Coll., 1960; J.D. Brooklyn Law Sch., 1978. Bar: N.Y. 1979, U.S. Dist. Ct. (so. and ea. dists.) N.Y. 1979. Law clk. to presiding justices U.S. Bankruptcy Ct., 1977-78; law asst., assoc. Law Office of R. Dryer, N.Y.C., 1978-79; sole practice, N.Y.C., 1979—; apptd. bankruptcy trustee U.S. Trustee Panel, U.S. Dist. Ct. (so. dist.) N.Y., N.Y.C., 1979—. Mem. Bankruptcy Lawyers Bar Assn., Comml. Law League, Bar Assn. City N.Y., N.Y. County Lawyers Assn. (com. on bankruptcy), Phi Beta Kappa. Bankruptcy, General corporate, Contracts commercial. Home: 20 Irene Ct Demarest NJ 07627 Office: 2 Park Ave Suite 2204 New York NY 10016

BALAGNA, STEVEN DAVID, lawyer; b. Detroit, Feb. 19, 1955; s. Marvin Anthony and Edith (Bernise) B.; m. Susan Marie Fresard, Aug. 2, 1986. AB, U. Mich., 1977; JD, U. Oreg., 1980. Bar: Oreg. 1980, U.S. Dist. Ct. Oreg. 1980, Mich. 1981, U.S. Dist. Ct. (ea. dist.) Mich. 1981, U.S. Ct. Appeals (6th cir.) 1982, U.S. Ct. Appeals (9th cir.) 1983. Paralegal specialist land and natural resource div. U.S. Dept. of Justice, Washington, 1979; sole practice Bend, Oreg., 1980-81; assoc. Cooke & Hickox P.C., Bloomfield Hills, Mich., 1982; ptnr. Balagna & Dinnerman P.C., Eugene, Oreg., 1983-84; atty. Waste Mgmt., Inc., Southfield, Mich., 1984—. Author: Fisheries Management, 1981. Mem. ABA (solid and hazardous waste com.), Am. Soc. Civil Engrs. Avocations: snow and water skiing, soccer, racquetball, music, golf. Environment, FERC practice, General corporate. Office: Waste Mgmt. Inc. 22166 W Nine Mile Rd Southfield MI 48034

BALD, LEROY, lawyer; b. Balt., Nov. 8, 1918; s. George Henry and Bertha (Taylor) B.; m. Sarah Harriet Showell, June 14, 1947; children—Gary, Barbara, Jeffrey. B.A., Colgate U., 1942; J.D., U. Md., 1949. Bar: Md. 1949, U.S. Dist. Ct. Md. 1949, U.S. Ct. Appeals 1949, U.S. Ct. Mil. Appeals 1951. Assoc. Levy, Burns & Gordon, Balt., 1949-52; ptnr. Childs & Bald, Annapolis, Md., 1952-65, Bald, Smith & Lucke, Annapolis, 1965-75; sr. ptnr.

Bald & Hale, Annapolis, 1975—; dir. First Am. Bank of Md. Bd. govs. YMCA, Annapolis. Served to col. USMC. Decorated Bronze Star. Mem. Md. Bar Assn., ABA, Anne Arundel County Bar Assn. (pres. 1965-66), Mil. Order of World Wars (comdr. Annapolis chpt. 1961-62), So. Md. Soc., Beta Theta Pi (pres. 1941). Democrat. Episcopalian (vestry St. Martin's Ch.). Club: Rotary (pres. Annapolis 1976-77). General practice, Probate, Real property. Home: Rugby Hall Arnold MD 21012 Office: 192 Duke of Gloucester St Annapolis MD 21401

BALDINO, JOHN JOSEPH, lawyer; b. Lodi, N.J., June 4, 1942; s. Joseph J. and Wilda E. (Sharp) B.; m. Gloria J. DeSimone, June 11, 1966; children: Joseph, Melissa Beth, John J. B.A., U. Pa., 1963; J.D., Seton Hall U., 1966. Bar: N.J. 1966, U.S. dist. ct. N.J. 1966. Law sec. Superior Ct. Judge Morris Malech, 1966-67; ptnr. Cuccio, Clinger & Baldino, Hackensack, N.J., 1971-75; ptnr. Baldino & DeMaria, Hackensack, 1976—; lectr. N.Y. Law Sch., 1974—. Named Young Lawyer of Yr., Bergen County N.J., 1972. Mem. ABA, N.J. Bar Assn., Bergen County Bar Assn., Am. Trial Lawyers Assn., Am. Judicature Soc. Roman Catholic. General corporate, Real property, Personal injury. Office: 118 Hudson St Hackensack NJ 07601

BALDOCK, BOBBY RAY, federal judge; b. Rocky, Okla., Jan. 24, 1936; s. W. Jay and S. Golden (Farrell) B.; m. Mary Jane (Spunky) Holt, June 2, 1956; children—Robert Jennings, Christopher Guy. Grad., N.Mex. Mil. Inst., 1956; J.D., U. Ariz., 1960. Bar: Ariz. 1960, N.Mex. 1961, U.S. Dist. Ct. N.Mex., 1965. Ptnr. Sanders, Bruin & Baldock, Roswell, N.Mex., 1960-83; adj. prof. Eastern N.Mex. U., 1962-81; judge U.S. Dist. Ct. N.Mex., Albuquerque, 1983-86, U.S. Ct. Appeals (10th cir.), 1986—. Mem. ABA, N.Mex. Bar Assn., Chaves County Bar Assn., Ariz. Bar Assn., Phi Alpha Delta. Office: Fed Bldg & US Courthouse Rm 167 PO Box 2388 Roswell NM 88202

BALDWIN, CAROLYN WHITMORE, lawyer; b. Newton, Mass., July 9, 1932; d. Henry Jr. and Grace M. (Chase) W.; m. Peter Arthur Baldwin, Sept. 3, 1955; children: Sarah M., Robert H., Judith H. Student, U. Coll. of Southwest, Exeter, Eng., 1952-53; BA cum laude, Middlebury Coll., 1954; MA in Library Sci., U. Chgo., 1971; JD, Franklin Pierce Coll., Concord, N.H., 1977. Bar: N.H., 1977, U.S. Dist. Ct. N.H. 1977. Exhibits dir. U. Chgo. Library, 1970-73; manuscripts librarian N.H. Hist. Soc., Concord, 1973-74; library cataloger Franklin Pierce Law Ctr., Concord, 1973-77, dir. environ. law clinic, 1978-82; assoc. Murphy and McLaughlin, Laconia, N.H., 1977-78; sole practice Concord, 1983-86; ptnr. Baldwin & Dunn, Concord, 1986—; of counsel, McGregor, Shea & Doliner, PC, Boston, 1982—. Supervising editor: Historic Districts in New Hampshire, a Handbook for Establishing and Administering Historic Districts, 1980; contbr. articles to profl. and other jours. Mem. Lakes Region Planning Commn., Meredith, N.H., 1977—, chmn. 1982-83, 86—; chmn. N.H. Natural Resources Forum, Concord, 1983-86, Water Resources Action Project, 1985, Gilmanton (N.H.) Conservation Commn., 1974-80; mem. N.H. Commn. for Humanities, Concord, 1977-80, Gilmanton Planning Bd., 1982—, chmn., 1986—; bd. dirs. Granite State Pub. Radio, 1980-83, N.H. Pub. Radio Sta. WEVO, Concord, 1981-84; exec. dir. Environ. Law Council N.H., 1978-82; vice-chmn. N.H. Hist. Preservation Task Force, 1983-84. Recipient Pres.'s medal N.H. Planner's Assn., 1985. Mem. N.H. Bar Assn. (mcpl., govt. law sect.), N.H. Assn. Regional Planning Commns. (chmn. legis. com. 1984-86), Am. Planner's Assn. (assoc.), Franklin Pierce Law Ctr. Alumni Assn. (pres. 1979-80). Democrat. Mem. Unitarian Universalist Ch. Avocations: skiing, family, gardening. Environment, Real property, Planning and zoning. Home: Box 101 RFD 2 Gilmanton Pittsfield NH 03263 Office: 41 S Main St Concord NH 03301

BALDWIN, FRANK BRUCE, III, lawyer; b. Phila., Oct. 18, 1939; s. Frank Bruce and Eleanor Elizabeth (Dutton) B.; m. Joan L. Crowell, June 23, 1962; children—Elisa Rose, Bruce Andrew, Christopher Dutton. A.B. cum laude, Harvard U., 1961; LL.B. magna cum laude, U. Pa., 1964; LL.M., U. London, 1965. Bar: Pa. 1966, Calif. 1967, U.S. Ct. Appeals (3d cir.) 1982. Vis. asst. prof. law U. Pa., 1965-66; acting assoc. prof. law U. Calif.-Davis, 1966-69; assoc. Morgan, Lewis & Bockius, Phila., 1969-72, 73-74; v.p., gen. counsel A.V.C. Corp., Phila., 1972-73; asst. gen. counsel IU Internat. Corp., Phila., 1974-82; ptnr. Saul, Ewing, Remick & Saul, Phila., 1982-83, Ehmann & Baldwin, 1983-85, Obermayer, Rebmann, Maxwell & Hippel, 1985—; legal counsel Trustees of Presbytery of Phila. Sec., mem. bd. govs. Southeastern Pa. chpt. Am. Heart Assn. Gowen fellow, 1964-65. Mem. ABA, Pa. Bar Assn., Phila. Bar Assn., State Bar Calif., Order of Coif. Republican. Presbyterian. Club: Union League of Phila. Reporter Del. Criminal Code, Proposed Ofcl. Draft, 1967. General corporate, Contracts commercial, Private international. Office: Packard Bldg 14th Floor Philadelphia PA 19102

BALDWIN, GORDON BREWSTER, educator, lawyer; b. Binghamton, N.Y., Sept. 0, 1929; s. Schuyler Forbes and Doris Ambeline (Hawkins) B.; m. Helen Louise Hochgraf, Feb., 1958; children—Schuyler, Mary Page. LL.B., Cornell U., 1953; B.A., Haverford Coll., 1950. Bar: N.Y. 1953, Wis. 1965. Practiced in Rochester and Rome, N.Y., 1953-57; prof. law U. Wis.-Madison, 1957—, assoc. dean law, 1968-70; dir. officer edn. U. Wis., 1972—; of counsel Murphy & Desmond, S.C., Madison, Wis., 1986—; chmn. internat. law U.S. Naval War Coll., 1963-64; Fulbright prof., Cairo, 1966-67, Tehran, Iran, 1970-71; lectr. State Dept., Cyprus, 1967, 1969, 1971; counselor internat. law U.S. Dept. State, Washington, 1975-76, cons., 1976-77; vis. prof. Chuo U., Tokyo, 1984, Gressen U., Fed. Republic Germany, 1987; cons. U.S. Naval War Coll., 1961-65; chmn. screening com. on law Fulbright Program, 1974; mem. constl. law com. Multi-State Bar Exam.; chmn. State Public Def. Bd., 1980-83. Served to capt. AUS, 1953-57. Ford Found. fellow, 1962-63. Fellow Am. Bar Found.; mem. Wis. Bar Assn. (vice chmn. sect. on individual rights 1973-75), Fulbright Alumni Assn. (dir. 1979-82), AAUP (nat. council 1975-78, pres. Wis. conf. 1986-87), Order of Coif, Phi Beta Kappa. Club: Madison Lit. (pres. 1985-86), University. Lodge: Rotary (pres. Madison 1980). Legal education, Public international, Admiralty. Office: Law Sch Univ Wis Madison WI 53706

BALDWIN, JANICE MURPHY, lawyer; b. Bridgeport, Conn., July 16, 1926; d. William Henry and Josephine Gertrude (McKenna) Murphy; m. Robert Edward Baldwin, July 31, 1954; children: Jean Margaret, Robert William, Richard Edward, Nancy Josephine. AB, U. Conn., 1948; MA, Mt. Holyoke Coll., 1950; postgrad. U. Manchester, Eng., 1950-51; MA, Fletcher Sch., Tufts U., 1952; JD, U. Wis., 1971. Bar: Wis. 1971, U.S. Dist. Ct. (we. dist.) Wis. 1971. Staff atty. Legis. Council, State of Wis., Madison, 1971-74, 75-78, sr. staff atty., 1979—; atty. adviser HUD, Washington, 1974-75, 78-79. Mem. Dane County Bar Assn. (legis. com. 1980-81), Wis. Bar Assn. (pres. govt. lawyers div. 1985—, bd. govs.), Wis. Women's Network, AAUW, NOW, LWV, Legal Assn. for Women, Wis. Women's Polit. Caucus, U. Wis. Univ. League, Older Women's League. Health, Marital property, State and local taxation. Home: 125 Nautilus Dr Madison WI 53705 Office: Legis Council Room 147N State Capitol Madison WI 53702

BALDWIN, MICHAEL WENDEL, lawyer; b. N.Y.C., Mar. 13, 1954; s. Theodore Gregory and Ellen (Wendel) B.; m. Jodene Louise Frey, June 18, 1983. BBA, U. Nebr., 1976; JD, Creighton U., 1979. Bar: Nebr. 1980. Sole practice Kearney, Nebr., 1980—. Bd. dirs. Kearney (Nebr.) Area Community Ctr., 1984—. Republican. Episcopalian. Avocations: golf, racquetball, skiing. General practice. Office: 1419 Central Ave PO Box 922 Kearney NE 68848

BALDWIN, ROBERT FREDERICK, JR., lawyer; b. Syracuse, N.Y., Sept. 25, 1939; s. Robert F. and M. Elizabeth (Thompson) B.; m. Margaret Melissa Richards, Aug. 20, 1962; m. Jeanella M. Mastrobattisto, Apr. 26, 1980; children—Robert F., Melissa Brooke. Student Hamilton Coll., 1957-59; B.S. in Bus. Adminstrn., Syracuse U., 1962, LL.B., 1964. Bar: N.Y. 1964, U.S. Ct. Mil. Appeals 1965, U.S. Tax Ct. 1968, U.S. Supreme Ct. 1968, U.S. Dist. Ct. (no. dist.) N.Y. 1980, U.S. Ct. Claims 1980, Fla. 1982. Assoc., Hancock, Estabrook, Ryan, Shove & Hust, Syracuse, 1968-73, ptnr., 1974-84; ptnr. Green & Seifter, Syracuse, 1984—; village atty. Village of Fayetteville, N.Y., 1974—; adj. prof. Syracuse U. Coll. Law, 1977. Trustee Village of Fayetteville, N.Y., 1972-74, Fayetteville Library Assn., 1976-79, Fayetteville Cemetery Assn., 1974-80; bd. dirs. UN Assn. Central N.Y., 1971-74, Planned Parenthood Ctr. of Syracuse, Inc., 1978-84, Assn. Retarded Citizens, 1976-79, 86—; bd. govs. Citizens Found., 1973-76, 86—, Sta. WCNY-TV, 1987—; mem. steering com. Syracuse U. Tax Inst., 1980—; mem. deferred gifts com. Central N.Y. Chpt. ARC. Served with JAGC, USNR, 1965-68, to comdr., 1965—. Fellow Am. Coll. Probate Counsel; mem. ABA (sect. taxation, real property, probate and trust law sect., vice chmn. death tax problems of estates and trusts com. 1981-82, chmn. 1982—), N.Y. State Bar Assn. (trusts and estates sect. com. on adminstrn. expense chmn. 1976-77, vice chmn. com. on life ins. 1980-84, mem. exec. com. sect. taxation 1982—, chmn. com. sales, property and miscellaneous taxes 1983-84, Co-chmn. com. estate and gift taxes 1984—), Onondaga County Bar Assn. (chmn. com. on continuing legal edn. 1975, chmn. bank liaison com. 1979, chmn. surrogate's ct. com. 1981, bd. dirs. 1976-79), Estate Planning Council Central N.Y. (pres. 1973-74), Nat. Assn. Estate Planning Councils (bd. dirs. 1974-80, pres. 1982-83). Contbg. author articles in profl. publs. Estate planning, Estate taxation, Corporate taxation. Office: 900 Lincoln Ctr Syracuse NY 13202

BALES, JOHN FOSTER, III, lawyer; b. Springfield, Mass., July 17, 1940; s. John Foster II and Jean (Torrence) B.; m. Jane Lee Black, Sept. 11, 1965; children: Patricia, Elizabeth, Susan. BS in Enring., Princeton U., 1962; LLB, U. Va., 1965; LLM, Georgetown U., 1972. Bar: U.S. Supreme Ct. 1972. Staff atty. U.S. SEC, Washington, 1970-72; assoc. Morgan, Lewis & Bockius, Phila., 1972-76, ptnr., 1976—; bd. dirs. Independent Publs., Inc., Phila. Served to lt. USN, 1965-69. Mem. ABA, Va. Bar Assn., Pa. Bar Assn., Phila. Bar Assn., Colo. Bar Assn. Republican. General corporate, Securities, Health. Office: Morgan Lewis & Bockius 2000 One Logan Square Philadelphia PA 19103

BALESTER, VIVIAN SHELTON, law librarian, lawyer, legal research consultant; b. Pine Bluff, Ark., Dec. 10, 1931; d. Marvin W. and Mary Lena (Burke) Shelton; m. James Beverly Stanberfer, Aug. 1, 1951 (dec. 1952); 1 son, Walter Eric; m. 2d, Raymond James Balester, Oct. 19, 1956; children—Carla Maria, Mark Shelton. B.A. cum laude, Vanderbilt U., 1955; M.S.L.S., Case Western Res. U., 1972, J.D., 1975. Bar: Ohio 1975, U.S. Dist. Ct. (no. dist.) Ohio 1975. Ind. bibliographic and legal research cons., Cleve., Nashville, 1959—; head law librarian Squire, Sanders & Dempsey, Cleve., 1975-86; Ohio del. White House Conf. Libraries/Information Services, 1979; speaker Law Librarians Nat. Conf., 1978, 80, 82; mem. adv. com. on profl. ethics Case Western Res. U., 1982-85. Lay reader St. Alban's Episcopal Ch., 1978—, mem. vestry, 1977-79, 84-86, warden, 1979, 84; mem. council Diocese of Ohio, 1980-82, chmn. racial justice com., 1980-86, chmn. nominating com., 1982, del. Nat. Confs. on Faith Pub. Policy, Racism, 1982; dep. gen. Conv. of Episcopal Ch. in U.S., 1985; mem. Women's Polit. Caucus, 1978—; founder and co-chmn. Greater Cleve. Ann. Martin Luther King Celebration, 1980—; mem. County Commrs. adv. com. on handicapped, 1980-84; chmn. adolescent health coalition Fedn. Community Planning, 1979-81, mem. health concerns commn., 1981—, vice chair, 1986—; regional chmn. alumni edn. Vanderbilt U., 1982-83; mem. community adv. com. Cleve. Orch., 1983—; bd. dirs. Hospice Council No. Ohio, 1979-81, vol. atty., 1982-85; bd. dirs. Interch. Council Greater Cleve., 1978-84, 86—; mem. Ohio Com. Nat. Security, 1983; bd. dirs. WomenSpace, 1979-83. Recipient Outstanding Community Service award Fedn. Community Planning, 1980, Woman of Profl. Excellence award YWCA, 1983; Cleve. Mayor's award for volunteerism, 1984; Nat. Endowment for Humanities fellow, 1980. Mem. ABA, Cleve. Bar Assn. (Merit Service award 1979) Am. Assn. Law Libraries, Am. Soc. Info. Sci. (chmn. law sect. 1978). Democrat. Librarianship, Jurisprudence. Home and Office: 2460 Edgehill Rd Cleveland Heights OH 44106

BALESTRACCI, PAUL NOEL, lawyer; b. San Francisco, May 24, 1953; s. Leo and Margaret Jane (Creek) B.; m. Leslie Spoon, Oct. 20, 1984. AB, U. Calif., Davis, 1975; JD, U. Pacific, 1978. Bar: Calif. 1978, U.S. Dist Ct. (ea. dist.) Calif. 1978. Dep. dist. atty. San Joaquin County, Calif., 1979-84; assoc. Neumiller & Beardslee, Stockton, 1984—. Mem. ABA. Democrat. Roman Catholic. Avocations: running, spectator sports. State civil litigation, Insurance, Federal civil litigation. Office: Neumiller & Beardslee PO Drawer 20 Stockton CA 95201

BALICK, BERNARD, judge; b. Wilmington, Del., May 14, 1940; s. Simon and Jennie (Rubenstein) B.; m. Helen Shaffer, June 29, 1967. AB cum laude, Columbia U., N.Y.C., 1962; JD, Dickinson Sch. of Law, 1966; LLM, U. Va., 1986. Bar: Del. 1966. Assoc. Aerenson and Balick, Wilmington, Del., 1966-69; part-time staff atty. Legal Aid Soc., Wilmington, 1968-69; chief asst. pub. defender Office of Pub. Defender, Wilmington, 1969-71; ptnr. Aerenson, Balick and Balick, Wilmington, 1971-73; city solicitor City of Wilmington, 1973; assoc. judge Del. Superior Ct., Wilmington, 1973—. Mem. ABA, Del. State Bar Assn., Am. Judicature Soc., Am. Inns of Ct. (Richard S. Rodney chpt.). Democrat. Jewish. Avocations: classical music, travel, collecting used books. Office: Superior Ct of Del Ct House Wilmington DE 19801

BALICK, STEVEN JEFFREY, lawyer; b. Wilmington, Del., Aug. 18, 1956; s. Norman and Joan (Liebert) B. BA, U. Del., 1978; JD, Boston U., 1981. Bar: Del. 1982, U.S. Dist. Ct. Del. 1982, U.S. Ct. Appeals (3d cir.) 1983. Law clk. Del. Superior Ct., Wilmington, 1981-82; dep. atty. gen. State of Del., Wilmington, 1982-86; assoc. Ashby, Mckelvie & Geddes, Wilmington, 1986—. Mem. ABA, Del. Bar Assn., Del. Trial Lawyers Assn. Democrat. Jewish. Avocations: tennis, skiing. Federal civil litigation, State civil litigation, General corporate. Home: 7 Rockford Rd Apt B-17 Wilmington DE 19806 Office: Ashby McKelvie & Geddes One Rodney Sq PO Box 1150 Wilmington DE 19899

BALIKOV, HENRY R., lawyer; b. Bayshore, N.Y., May 23, 1946; s. Harold and Esther (Chernow) B.; m. Mary L. McMahon, 1976; children—Benjamin, Molly. B.A., Grinnell Coll., 1967; J.D., U. Chgo., 1971. Bar: Ill. 1971, U.S. Supreme Ct. 1976. Adminstrv. asst. to chmn. Ill. Pollution Control Bd., 1972-73; enforcement atty. U.S. EPA, 1973-75, chief legal br., 1975-77; environ. counsel J.M. Huber Corp., 1977-79, govt. relations counsel, Edison, N.J., 1979—; of counsel Synthetic Amorphous Silica and Silicates Industry Assn., 1985—. Mem. Nat. Cooling Lake Policy Com., 1974-75; Nat. Noise Enforcement Adv. Com., 1975-76; Nat. Water Enforcement Policy Group, 1976-77; chmn. Environ. Com. Nat. Limestone Inst., 1983; bd. dirs. Hazardous Waste Treatment Council, 1985-87; counsel Synthetic Amorphous Silica and Silicates Industry Assn., 1986—. Recipient EPA Bronze medal, 1975; named an outstanding Young Man in Am., Nat. Jaycees, 1976; U.S. Congl. fellow, 1977. Mem. ABA, Ill. State Bar Assn., N.J. Assn. Corp. Counsel, AAAS, N.Y. Acad. Sci. Environment, Health, Legislative. Home: 304 Evergreen Dr Moorestown NJ 08057 Office: J M Huber Corp 333 Thornall St Edison NJ 08818

BALKA, SIGMUND RONELL, lawyer; b. Phila., Aug. 1, 1935; s. I. Edwin and Jane (Chernicoff) B.; m. Elinor Bernstein, May 29, 1966. A.B., Williams Coll., 1956; J.D., Harvard U., 1959. Bar: Pa. 1961, D.C. 1961, N.Y. 1970, U.S. Supreme Ct. 1966, other fed. cts. Sr. atty. Lilco, Mineola, N.Y., 1969-70; v.p., gen. counsel Brown Boveri Corp., North Brunswick, N.J., 1970-75; asst. gen. counsel Power Authority State N.Y., N.Y.C., 1975-80; gen. counsel Krasdale Foods, Inc., N.Y.C. 1980—. bd. dirs. Am. Corp. Counsel Assn., Met. N.Y. chpt. pres. Graphic Arts Council N.Y., 1980—; co-chmn. Hunts Point Environ. Protection Council, N.Y.C., 1980—; mem. N.Y.C. Community Bd. 6-Queens and chmn. law com., 1980—; chmn. Soc. for a better Bronx, 1985—; bd. dirs. Bronx Council on Arts, 1981—, Greater N.Y. Met. Food Council, 1986—. Mem. Assn. Bar City N.Y., ABA (co-chmn. corp. law dept. pro bono project 1986—), Fed. Bar Assn. General corporate. Office: Krasdale Foods Inc 400 Food Center Dr New York NY 10474

BALKANY, CARON LEE, lawyer; b. Miami, Fla., Apr. 4, 1950; d. John W. and Marilyn R. Balkany; m. Harvey M. Goldstein, Sept. 26, 1976. A.A., U. Fla., 1970; B.A., George Washington U., 1972; J.D., U. Miami-Fla., 1977. Bar: D.C. 1979, Fla. 1977, Colo. 1980. Ptnr. Goldstein Profl. Assn., Miami, Fla., 1977—; mem. Dade County Pub. Defender's Office; cons. Dade County, 1973. Contbr. articles to profl. jours. atty. Dade County Rape Treatment Ctr., Safe Space for Battered Women. Chairperson White House Conf. on Youth, 1970; mem. Rape Treatment Center Task Force; youth dir. women's bur. U.S. Dept. Labor, 1971. Mem. ABA, Acad. Fla. Trial Lawyers, Assn. Trial Lawyers Am., Assn. Women Lawyers, Fla. Assn. Women Lawyers, Am. Judicature Soc. State civil litigation, Personal injury. Home: 850 San Pedro Coral Gables FL 33156 Office: 1540 NW 15th St Rd Miami FL 33125

BALKIN, JEFFREY GILBERT, lawyer; b. Chgo., Mar. 29, 1943; s. David R. and Sari S. (Sol) B.; m. Sylvia Hazan, Dec. 21, 1973; children—Stephanie, Jeremy. B.A., Wayne State-Monteith Coll., 1965; J.D. with honors, Wayne State U., 1968. Bar: Mich. 1968, D.C. 1972, Calif. 1975, U.S. Sup. Ct. 1982; cert. tax specialist, Calif.; C.P.A., Calif. Atty. office internat. ops. IRS, Washington, 1970-73; dir. internat. tax ops. Touche Ross & Co., Los Angeles, 1974-77; sole practice, Los Angeles, 1977-81; ptnr. Bronson, Bronson & McKinnon, Los Angeles, 1981-85; sole practice, Los Angeles, 1985—; U.S. Trade rep., 1982-86; mem. tax mgmt. editorial adv. bd. Fgn. Income Portfolio series Bur. Nat. Affairs, 1977—; instr. Sch. Public Adminstrn. U. So. Calif., 1978-85; mem. Industry Sector Adv. Com. on services for Trade Policy Matters, Dept. Commerce and U.S. Trade Rep., 1982—. Mem. ABA, Calif. Bar Assn., D.C. Bar Assn., Mich. Bar Assn., Internat. Fiscal Assn. Republican. Jewish. Club: Braemar Country (Tarzana, Calif.). Contbr. articles to profl. jours. Private international, Corporate taxation, State and local taxation. Home: 19534 Greenbriar Dr Tarzana CA 91356 Office: One Wilshire Bldg Suite 2650 Los Angeles CA 90017

BALL, CRAIG DOUGLAS, lawyer, educator; b. Bronxville, N.Y., Sept. 1, 1957; s. Herbert Morton and Joan (Cameron) B. BA, Rice U., 1979; JD, U. Tex., 1982. Bar: Tex. 1982, U.S. Dist. Ct. (so. dist.) Tex. 1982, U.S. Ct. Appeals (5th cir.) 1983, U.S. Dist. Ct. (no. dist.) Tex. 1985. Assoc. Abraham, Watkins et al, Houston, 1982—; adj. prof. So. Tex. Coll. Law, Houston, 1984—. Counsel standing com. on student affairs Rice U., Houston, 1985-86. Mem. ABA, Tex. Bar Assn. (jury charge com., continuing legal edn. com.), Houston Bar Assn., Assn. Trial Lawyers Am., Tex. Trial Lawyers Assn. (membership com. 1986—), Houston Trial Lawyers Assn., Rice U. Alumni Assn. (chmn. student-alumni liason 1984-86). Club: Texas (Houston). Personal injury, Legal education, Federal civil litigation. Home: 6719 Cindy Ln Houston TX 77008 Office: Abraham Watkins et al 800 Commerce St Houston TX 77002

BALL, JORDAN MITCHELL, lawyer; b. Alliance, Nebr., Mar. 23, 1947; s. Emil Leopold and Evelyn Ernestine (Robbins) B.; m. Patricia Susan Hedrick, Aug. 7, 1976; children: Jason Mitchell, Melanie Marie. BA in Music Edn., Colo. State Coll., 1969; MA in Music Edn., U. No. Colo., 1970; JD, U. Nebr., 1975. Bar: Nebr. 1976, U.S. Dist. Ct. Nebr. 1976. Tchr. Sidney (Nebr.) Pub. Sch. System, 1969-73; adminstrv. asst. to supt./pres. Des Moines Area Community Coll., 1976-79; county atty. County of Cheyenne, Sidney, 1979-85; city prosecutor City of Sidney, 1979-85; sole practice Sidney, 1985—. Pres. High Plains Arts Council, Sidney, 1985-86; bd. dirs. First United Meth. Ch. Choir, Sidney, 1979—; pres. Ft. Sidney Cols. Men's Chorus, 1983-85. Mem. ABA, Comml. Law League Am., Nebr. Bar Assn., Cheyenne County Lawyers Assn. Republican. Methodist. Lodge: Kiwanis Internat. Avocations: music, golf, travel. Consumer commercial, Real property, Family and matrimonial. Home: 535 Keller Dr Sidney NE 69162 Office: 1025 10th Ave Sidney NE 69162

BALL, OWEN KEITH, JR., lawyer; b. Louisville, Feb. 19, 1950; s. Owen Keith and Martha Katherine (Guntherberg) B.; m. Shirley Marie Galinski, Sept. 16, 1972. BSCE, U. Kans., 1972, JD, 1980. Bar: Mo. 1980, U.S. Dist. Ct. (we. dist.) Mo. 1980. Ptnr. Smith, Gill, Fisher & Butts Inc., Kansas City, Mo., 1980—. Mem. staff Hyatt Regency Hotel com. to investigate safety of the Hyatt Regency Hotel, Kansas City C. of C., 1981. Served to lt. USN, 1972-77. Mem. ABA, Kansas City Met. Bar Assn., Mo. Bar Assn. Avocation: classical music. Securities, General corporate, Contracts commercial. Office: Smith Gill Fisher & Butts Inc 1400 Commerce Trust Bldg Kansas City MO 64106

BALL, WILLIAM KENNETH, lawyer; b. DeQueen, Ark., Jan. 15, 1927; s. William P. and Lucille (Jeter) B.; m. Ella Hubbard Scaife, Dec. 28, 1950; children—Lucy Jane, William Ramsay, Charles Scaife. J.D., U. Ark., 1953. Bar: Ark. bar 1953. Law clk. to assoc. justice Ark. Supreme Ct., 1953-54; practice in Monticello, 1954—; partner firm Ball & Bird, 1958—; city atty. Monticello, 1961—. Served with AUS, 1945-47, 50-52. Fellow Am. Coll. Probate Counsel, Ark. Bar Found.; mem. ABA, Ark. Bar Assn., S.E. Ark. Bar Assn. (pres. 1957-58), Kappa Sigma, Delta Theta Phi. Presbyterian. Lodge: Rotary (pres. 1962-63). General practice, Probate, Contracts commercial. Home: 104 Westwood Ln Monticello AR 71655 Office: Ball and Bird 106 W Oakland Ave Monticello AR 71655

BALLANFANT, RICHARD BURTON, lawyer; b. Houston, Aug. 15, 1947; s. Richard Edward and Selma Autrey (Lewis) B.; m. Kathleen Gamber, June 9, 1974; children: Andrea Lavon, Benjamin Burton. BA, U. Tex., 1969, JD, 1972. Bar: Tex. 1972, U.S. Ct. Appeals (5th cir.) 1976, U.S. Ct. Appeals (11th cir.) 1981, U.S. Dist. Ct. (so. dist.) Tex. 1974. Atty. FCC, Washington, 1973-74; asst. U.S. atty. Dept. Justice, Houston, 1974-78; sr. asst. city atty. City of Houston, 1978-80; atty. Shell Oil Co., Houston, 1980—. Mem. Citizens Adv. Bd. Met. Transit Authority, Houston, 1979-83; del. Rep. State Conv., 1978, 80, 82; chmn. Personnel Bd., West University Pl., Tex., 1975-85. Served to capt. USAR, 1972-82. Named Outstanding Asst. U.S. Atty., Dept. Justice, Houston, 1976, 77. Mem. Fed. Bar Assn. (pres. 1979-80), ABA, Houston C. of C. (govt. relations com.). Episcopalian. Federal civil litigation, State civil litigation, Environment. Home: 3123 Amherst St Houston TX 77005 Office: Shell Oil Co PO Box 2463 Houston TX 77001

BALLANTINE, THOMAS AUSTIN, JR., judge; b. Louisville, Sept. 22, 1926; s. Thomas Austin and Anna Marie (Pfeiffer) B.; m. Nancy A. Armstrong, June 10, 1953; children: Thomas A., Nancy Adair, Brigid A., Joseph A. Student, Northwestern U., 1944-46; B.A., U. Ky., 1948; J.D., U. Louisville, 1954. Bar: Ky. bar 1954. Asso. firm McElwain, Dinning, Clarke & Winstead, Louisville, 1954-64; dep. commr. Jefferson Circuit Ct., 1958-62; commr. Jefferson Fiscal Ct., 1962-64; judge Jefferson Circuit Ct., 1964-77, U.S. Dist. Ct., Western Dist. Ky., 1977—; instr. U. Louisville Law Sch., 1969-75. Bd. dirs. Louisville Urban League, 1958-64, chmn., 1963-64; bd. dirs. NCCJ, 1960-65, Health and Welfare Council, 1969, Louisville Theatrical Assn., 1970, Father Maloney's Boys Haven, 1983—. Mem. Louisville Bar Assn., Ky. State Bar. Democrat. Roman Catholic. Club: Pendennis. Jurisprudence. Home: 48 Hill Rd Louisville KY 40204 Office: US District Court U S Courthouse Room 247 Louisville KY 40202 *

BALLANTYNE, RICHARD L(EE), lawyer; b. Evanston, Ill., Dec. 10, 1939; s. Frank and Grace (Bowles) B.; children: Richard L(ee) Jr., Brant. BS in Engring., U. Conn., 1965, MBA, 1967; JD with honors, George Washington U., 1969. Bar: Mass. 1970, U.S. Dist. Ct. Mass. 1976, U.S. Patent Office 1982. Dir. corp. devel. Itek Corp., Lexington, Mass., 1969-73, assoc. counsel, 1975; corp. counsel, sec. Goodhope Industries, Springfield, Mass., 1975-77; gen. counsel, asst. treas., sec. Compugraphic Corp., Wilmington, Del., 1977-82; v.p., gen. counsel, sec. Prime Computer Inc., Natick, Mass., 1982—; pres. Rt. 128 Corp. Lawyers Inc., 1984—. Served with U.S. Army, 1958-61. Mem. Licensing Execs. Soc., Am. Soc. Corp. Secs. Republican. Avocations: jogging, golf. General corporate, Computer, Patent. Office: Prime Computer Inc Prime Park Way Natick MA 01760

BALLARD, MARY BETH, lawyer; b. Cleve., Dec. 21, 1954; d. John Edward and Mary Stewart (Eaton) Frey; m. John Farlow Ballard, July 1, 1977 (div. May 1982). AB in Spanish, BA in Polit. Sci., Cleve. State U., 1974; JD, Case Western Res. U., 1978. Bar: Ohio 1978, U.S. Dist. Ct. (no. dist.) Ohio 1979. Assoc. DuLaurence & DuLaurence, Cleve., 1978-80, Benesch, Friedlander, Coplan & Aronoff, Cleve., 1980-84, Ziegler, Metzger & Miller, Cleve., 1984—; instr. Cleve. Area Bd. Realtors, 1985-86. Trustee N.E. Ohio Apartment Assn., Cleve., 1978—, pres., 1985-86; trustee Ohio Apartment Condominium Assn., 1982—, sec., 1985-86. Mem. ABA, Ohio State Bar Assn., Cleve. Bar Assn. (speakers bur. 1985-86), Greater Cleve. Round Table. Roman Catholic. Avocations: golf, boating, music, theater. Contracts commercial, Landlord-tenant, Real property. Home: 22670 Detroit Rd Rocky River OH 44116 Office: Ziegler Metzger & Miller 1900 Huntington Bldg Cleveland OH 44115

BALLARD, WADE EDWARD, lawyer; b. Tallassee, Ala., Feb. 20, 1957; s. Kay B. and Alice Nelson (Lawless) B.; m. Karen Cecile Studstill, Oct. 10, 1984. BA, Wofford Coll., 1979; JD, Duke U., 1982. Bar: N.C. 1982, S.C. 1983, U.S. Dist Ct S.C. 1984, U.S. Ct. Appeals (5th cir.) 1985, U.S. Dist. Ct. (ea. dist.) N.C. 1986, U.S. Ct. Appeals (4th cir.) 1986. U.S. Assoc. Haynsworth, Baldwin, Miles, Johnson, Greaves & Edwards, Greenville, S.C.,

1982—. Editor (book) Florida Employment Law Manual, 1987. Mem. ABA, N.C. Bar Assn., S.C. Bar Assn., Greenville Young Lawyers Club (social chmn. 1984, v.p. 1985, pres. 1986—), Phi Beta Kappa. Avocations: racquet sports, reading, hunting, fishing. Civil rights, Labor. Home: 27 Rowley St Greenville SC 29601 Office: Haynsworth Baldwin Miles Johnson Greaves & Edwards PO Box 10888 Greenville SC 29603

BALLEN, ROBERT GERALD, lawyer; b. Bridgeport, Conn., Dec. 20, 1956; s. Myron Ronald and Joan Ruth (Miller) B.; m. Debra Ruth Tarnapol, Jan. 5, 1986. AB, Princeton U., 1978; JD, Harvard U., 1981. Bar: D.C. 1981, U.S. Dist. Ct. D.C. 1982, U.S. Ct. Appeals (D.C. cir.) 1982. Atty. Fed. Res. Bd., Washington, 1981-85; assoc. Morrison & Foerster, Washington, 1985—. Contbr. articles to profl. jours. Mem. Fed. Bar Assn., Am. Bankers Assn., Audubon Soc. Club: Princeton Tower (N.J.) (sec. 1980-81). Banking, Consumer commercial, Securities. Office: Morrison & Foerster 2000 Pennsylvania Ave NW Washington DC 20006

BALLENTINE, KATHRYN E., lawyer; b. Wright Patterson AFB, Ohio, Apr. 4, 1949; d. Robert H. Ballentine and Evelyn Rae (Smith) B.; m. Mark Healy Naftalin, Feb. 3, 1970 (div. Apr. 1983); 1 child, David Jerome. LLB, New Coll. Calif., San Francisco, 1978. Bar: Calif. 1978. Assoc. Law Offices of Sandra Sennett, San Rafael, Calif., 1978-80; sole practice San Rafael, 1980-84; assoc. Krause, Baskin, Shell & Grant, Larkspur, Calif., 1984-85; ptnr. Krause, Baskin, Grant & Ballentine, Larkspur, 1985—; bd. dirs. Bay Area Legal Found., San Francisco, 1983-84. Assoc. editor: (reference manual) Human Rights Casefinder, 1978; (jour.) The Practitioner, 1983. Pres. bd. trustees Marin County Law Library, San Rafael, 1980-86; sec. National Women's Polit. Caucus, Marin County, Calif., 1974-75; instr. Domestic Violence Clinic, San Francisco, 1986, various unions on Occupational Safety and Health Act; organizer Com. to Retain Justice Cruz Reynoso, Marin County, Calif., 1986. Mem. ABA (child custody com. 1983-85), San Francisco Bar Assn. (adoptions com. 1985—), Marin County Bar Assn. (com. to revise local family ct. rules 1987—, chair family law sect. 1986—), No. Calif. Thoroughbred Assn. Democrat. Roman Catholic. Avocations: horseracing, writing, film, running. Equine Law. Office: Wood Island 60 E Sir Francis Drake Blvd #207 Larkspur CA 94939

BALLER, JAMES, lawyer; b. West Berlin, Fed. Republic Germany, Jan. 19, 1947; s. Samuel and Irene (Lusczanowska) B.; m. Marlene Gilda Berlin, May 21, 1972; 1 child, Erica Berlin Baller. AB, Dartmouth Coll., 1969; JD, Cornell U., 1972. Bar: D.C. 1973, U.S. Dist. Ct. D.C. 1973, U.S. Supreme Ct. 1978. assoc. Covington & Burling, Washington, 1972-79; ptnr. Baller & Downey, Washington, 1979-81; sole practice Washington, 1981-83; ptnr. Baller & Hammett, Washington, 1983-84; pres. Baller, Hammett, Williams & Grammer, P.C., Washington, 1984—; cons. in field. Contbr. articles to profl. jours. Past legal counsel, past bd. dirs., past chmn. bd. dirs. Spl. Approaches to Juvenile Assistance, Washington, 1975-81, Sun Found., 1986—. Mem. ABA. Avocations: hockey, swimming, tennis, reading. FERC practice, General corporate, Environment. Home: 1517 Corcoran St NW Washington DC 20009 Office: Baller Hammett Williams & Gramner PC 1726 M St NW Washington DC 20036

BALLEW, WILLIAM VIRGIL, JR., lawyer, rancher; b. Abilene, Tex., July 9, 1918; s. William Virgil and Ada Alice (Cunningham) B.; m. Iris Lytle, May 15, 1953; children—Alice Ballew McAlpine, William Virgil III, Helen B., Emily B. B.A., Rice U., 1940; LL.B., Yale U., 1947. Bar: Tex. 1947, U.S. Ct. Appeals (5th cir.) 1954, U.S. Dist. Ct. (so. dist.) Tex. 1950. Assoc. Baker & Botts, Houston, 1947—; dir. Spaw-Glass, Inc., Houston, Clarewood House, Inc., Houston. Contbr. articles on edn. and fgn. policy to newspapers. Co-chmn. Houston and Harris County campaign Johnson for Pres., 1964; chmn. Houston-Harris County Econ. Opportunity Com., 1966-67, Citizens Tex. Constl. Revision Com., 1969-70. Served to lt. cmdr. USNR, 1941-45, PTO. Decorated Bronze Star. Mem. Houston-Harris County Bar Assn., Tex. State Bar Assn., Houston Jr. Bar Assn. (v.p. 1950-51), Houston Philos. Soc. (pres., bd. dirs. 1970), Houston Com. on Fgn. Relations, Assn. Rice U. Alumni (pres. 1970). Democrat. Unitarian. Clubs: Allegro, Inns of Court. Public utilities, Condemnation, Construction. Home: 4131 Meadowlake Dr Houston TX 77057 Office: Baker & Botts 3000 One Shell Plaza Houston TX 77002

BALLIET, SUSAN JACKSON, lawyer; b. San Francisco, Dec. 10, 1943; d. Dean Brooks and Betty June (Lindsay) Jackson; m. John Howard Balliet; children: Sarah Jackson, Andrew Max. BA in English, Stanford U., 1966; JD, U. San Francisco, 1975. Bar: Calif. 1976, U.S. Dist. Ct. (ea. dist.) Calif. 1976, U.S. Dist. Ct. (no. dist.) Calif. 1978, U.S. Ct. Appeals (9th cir.) 1982. Atty. Calif. Rural Legal Assistance, Marysville, 1975-77; atty. Legal Aid Soc. San Mateo County, Redwood City, Calif., 1977-81, directing atty., 1981-84, dir. litigation, 1987—; exec. dir. East Palo Alto (Calif.) Community Law Project, 1984-87. Co-author: Domestic Violence Practical Manual, 1982. Co-founder La Casa de las Madres Women's Shelter, San Francisco, 1975, Casa de Esperanza Women's Shelter, Yuba City, Calif., 1976, Yuba Sutter Legal Ctr., Marysville, 1977, San Mateo Women's Shelter, 1978. Mem. San Mateo County Bar Assn. Democrat. Presbyterian. Avocation: swimming. General practice, Pension, profit-sharing, and employee benefits, Family and matrimonial. Office: Legal Aid Soc San Mateo County 298 Fuller St Redwood City CA 94063

BALLOT, ALISSA E., lawyer; b. N.Y.C., Nov. 25, 1955; s. I. Martin and Barbara E. (Bendet) B. BA, Williams Coll., 1977; JD, Harvard U., 1980. Bar: N.Y. 1981, U.S. Dist. Ct. (so. and ea. dists.) N.Y. 1981. Assoc. Kramer, Levin et al, N.Y.C., 1980-83; counsel Lincoln Savs. Bank, N.Y.C., 1983-85; assoc. gen. counsel Am. Savs. Bank, N.Y.C., 1985-86, dep. gen. counsel, 1987—. Mem. ABA, Assn. Bar of City of N.Y. Democrat. Jewish. Banking, General corporate. Home: 140 E 56th St 11-L New York NY 10022 Office: Am Savs Bank FSB 380 Madison Ave New York NY 10016

BALLOU, JOHN WALDO, lawyer; b. Bangor, Maine, Sept. 29, 1925; s. William R. and Gladys M. (Lowell) B. B.A., U. Maine, 1949; LL.B., Yale U., 1952. Bar: Maine 1952, U.S. Dist. Ct. Maine 1953, U.S. Ct. Appeals (1st cir.) 1954, U.S. Ct. Claims 1977, U.S. Tax Ct. 1977. Assoc. James E. Mitchell, Bangor, Maine, 1952-54; ptnr. Mitchell & Ballou, Bangor, 1954-74, Mitchell, Ballou & Keith, Bangor, 1974-80; ptnr. Mitchell & Stearns, P.A., Bangor, 1980—, now pres., sr. ptnr.; chmn. bd. overseers State Bar Maine, 1984-86, chmn. grievance commn. bd. overseers, 1978-84. Mayor of Bangor, 1970; mem. Bangor City Council, 1967-76; trustee Bangor Water Dist., 1960-67; mem. Gov.'s Adv. Council on Mental Health, 1978—. Served with U.S. Army, 1943-46. Named Exemplary Citizen, Bangor-Brewer Indsl. Mgmt. Club, 1979; recipient Greater Bangor C. of C. Pub. Service award, 1979. Mem. Penobscot County Bar Assn., Maine Bar Assn. (chmn. grievance com. 1968-79), ABA, Nat. Assn. R.R. Trial Counsel. Republican. Unitarian. Clubs: Tarratine (Bangor); Penobscot Valley Country (Orono, Maine). State civil litigation, Federal civil litigation, Personal injury. Home: 52 Montgomery St Bangor ME 04401 Office: 1 Merchants Plaza PO Box 702 Bangor ME 04401

BALLOW, JOHN EDWARD, lawyer; b. Buffalo, June 24, 1959. BA in History with honors and Polit. Sci., Canisius Coll., 1981; JD, Capital U., 1983; vis. student, SUNY, Buffalo, 1983-84. Bar: N.Y. 1985, U.S. Dist. Ct. (we. dist.) N.Y. 1986. Law clk. Erie County Attys. Office, Buffalo, 1981-84; atty., spl. agt. FBI, U.S. Justice Dept., Mont. and Idaho, 1984-86; assoc. Thielman & Thielman, Buffalo, 1986, Paul William Beltz P.C., Buffalo, 1986—; faculty law and jurisprudence SUNY, Buffalo, 1983-84; cert. fitness instr. FBI SWAT, Mont. and Idaho, 1984—. Mem. ABA, N.Y. State Bar Assn., Assn. Trial Lawyers Am., N.Y. State Trial Lawyers Assn., Western N.Y. Trial Attys. Assn. (trial technique award 1984), FBI Agts. Assn., Soc. Former Spl. Agents FBI, Phi Alpha Theta. Avocation: triathlons. Personal injury, Criminal, State civil litigation. Home: 4800 Crittenden Rd Akron NY 14001 Office: Paul William Beltz PC 36 Church St Buffalo NY 14202

BALLSUN, KATHRYN ANN, lawyer; b. Calif., May 8, 1946; d. Zan and Doris (Pratt) B.; m. Paul L. Stanton, June 1, 1981; 1 child, Brian Paul. BA, U. So. Calif., 1969, MA, 1971; JD, Loyola U., Los Angeles, 1976. Bar: Calif. 1976, U.S. Dist. Ct. (cen. dist.) Calif. 1977. Sole practice Los Angeles; ptnr. Stanton & Ballsun, Los Angeles; vis. prof. UCLA Law Sch., Loyola U. Law Sch., Los Angeles; adj. prof. U. So. Calif. Law Sch.; lectr. various schs. Editor: How to Live and Die with California Probate; contbr. articles to profl. jours. Mem. graphic arts council Los Angeles County Mus. Art; co-chmn. for Class of 1976 Greater Loyola Law Sch. Devel. Program, 1983; advisor Am. Cancer Soc. Program; radio vol. sta. KUSC; bd. dirs. Planned Protective Services Inc.; bd. dirs. Los Angeles Philharm. Orch., com. profl. women, treas. 1985-86. Mem. ABA (real property, probate and trust law, taxation sects.), State Bar Calif. (estate planning, trust and probate, bus. law, taxation sects., law revision study team 1983-85), Los Angeles County Bar Assn. (trust and probate, taxation sects.), Beverly Hills Bar Assn. (treas. 1985-86, bd. govs. 1982-84, 84-86, probate and trust com., del. State Bar Conv. 1981-85), Calif. Women Lawyers, Los Angeles Women Lawyers, Women in Business, West Los Angeles C. of C., ACLU (Los Angeles chpt.), Kappa Alpha Theta. Probate. Office: Stanton and Ballsun AVCO Ctr 6th Floor 10850 Wilshire Blvd Los Angeles CA 90024

BALLUFF, JOHN JOSEPH, lawyer; b. Tooele, Utah, Oct. 25, 1910; s. Joseph Peter and Anne Marie (Johnston) B.; m. Minette Lillian LeClerg, Oct. 3, 1933 (dec. June 1976); children—John Edward, Douglas Paul, Robert Charles; m. 2d, Billie Jo Brown, Feb. 9, 1979. Student St. Mary's Coll., Moraga, Calif., 1928-29; J.D., Chgo. Kent Coll. Law, 1933. Bar: Ill. 1933, U.S. Dist. Ct. (no. dist.) Ill. 1934, U.S. Dist. Ct. (so. dist.) Calif. 1948, Calif 1948, U.S. Supreme Ct. Assoc. Chapman & Culter, Chgo., 1936-41, 45-48; Ill. counsel Douglas Aircraft Co., Chgo., System labor counsel, Santa Monica, Calif., 1941-45; gen. atty. Atcheson, Topeka & Santa Fe Ry. Co., Los Angeles, 1948-62, gen. atty., Calif., chief counsel for Santa Fe, in Calif., 1962-76; sole practice, part-time, San Diego, 1976—; mem. Calif. Law Revision Commn., 1971-77; chmn. Product Liability Sect. of Legis. Adv. Com. on Tort Reform, 1978-79. Bd. dirs. Multiple Sclerosis Soc. Calif., corp. mem. Calif. Blue Shield, 1979—. Mem. Calif. State Bar. Club: Rancho Bernardo Golf. Republican. General corporate, Real property. Home and Office: 12458 Caleta Way San Diego CA 92128

BALMER, JAMES W., lawyer; b. Pipestone, Minn., Sept. 26, 1948. BA, U. Minn., 1970, JD, 1973. Bar: Minn. 1973, U.S. Dist. Ct. Minn. 1974, U.S. Dist. Ct. Wis. 1984, U.S. Dist. Ct. (we. dist.) Wis. 1985, U.S. Ct. Appeals (8th cir.) 1985, U.S. Ct. Appeals (7th cir.) 1986. Assoc. Donovan, McCarthy, Crassweller, Larson, Barnes & Magie, Duluth, Minn., 1973-75; ptnr. Falsani, Balmer, Berglund & Merritt, Duluth, 1975—. Chmn. Seventh Legis. Dist. Conv., 1982. Mem. Minn. State Bar Assn., Minn. Trial Lawyers Assn. (bd. of govs. 1986—), Minn. Acad. Cert. Trial Lawyers, Eleventh Dist. Bar Assn., Duluth Trial Lawyers Assn. (sec. 1986), Assn. Trial Lawyers Am., Nat. Bd. Trial Adv. (cert. specialist 1986—), Duluth Jaycees (pres. 1977-78). Republican. Roman Catholic. Clubs: Duluth Power Squadron, Duluth Keel. Avocations: sailing, jogging, reading. Federal civil litigation, State civil litigation, Insurance. Office: 414 Providence Bldg Suite 414 Duluth MN 55802

BALOUGH, RICHARD CHARLES, lawyer; b. South Bend, Ind., Apr. 25, 1947; s. Rudolph Frances and Mary Magedaline (Riba) B.; m. Margaret Mae Craig, June 28, 1969. BA, Ind. U., 1969; JD, John Marshall Law Sch., 1976. Bar: Ill. 1976, U.S. Dist. Ct. (no. dist.) Ill. 1976, Fla. 1977, Tex. 1978, U.S. Dist. Ct. (we. dist.) Tex. 1978. Asst. states atty. Will County, Joliet, Ill., 1976-77; asst. atty. City of Austin, Tex., 1977-83; mng. ptnr. Heron, Burchette, Ruckeert & Rothwell, Austin, 1983—. Administrative and regulatory, Public utilities, Local government. Home: 2402 Kathy Cove Austin TX 78704 Office: Heron Burchette Ruckert & Rothwell 221 W 6th St Suite 1400 Austin TX 78701

BAM, FOSTER, lawyer; b. Bridgeport, Conn., Jan. 11, 1927; s. Frederick and Alma (Foster) B.; children: Sylvia Carol, Sheila Catherine, Eric Foster. Grad., Loomis Sch., 1944; A.B., LL.B., Yale, 1950. Bar: N.Y. 1954, Conn. Mem. faculty acctg. Yale, 1952-53; with firm Spence & Hotchkiss, N.Y.C., 1954-55; asst. U.S. dist. atty. So. Dist. N.Y., 1955-58; partner firm Feldman, Kramer, Bam Nessen, N.Y.C., 1958-67; now partner Cummings & Lockwood.; Bd. dirs. Interstate Bakeries Corp., Cities Service Co., Evergreen Fund, Evergreen Total Return Fund, Chartwell Group Ltd. Trustee Phoenix Sci. Ctr., Am. Mus. Fly Fishing. Recipient Johny Foyle Meml. award, 1969. Mem. ABA, Conn. Bar Assn., Greenwich Bar Assn., Oceanic Soc. (chmn. bd. trustees), N.Y. County Lawyers Assn., N.Y. State Dist. Attys. Assn., Exptl. Aircraft Assn., Phi Beta Kappa. Home: 51 Londonderry Dr Greenwich CT 06830 Office: Cummings & Lockwood 2 Greenwich Plaza Greenwich CT 06830

BAMBACE, ROBERT SHELLY, lawyer; b. Spokane, Wash., Sept. 23, 1930; s. Felix Shelly and Constance Marion (Vandervert) B.; m. Madelyn Constance Saxer, May 11, 1957; children—Michelle Suzanne, Mark Shelly, Robert Sean, Peter Joseph, Constance Diane. B.S., Georgetown U., 1953; LL.B. St. Mary's U., San Antonio, 1961. Bar: Tex. 1961, U.S. Dist. Ct. (so. dist.) Tex. 1967, U.S. Ct. Appeals (5th cir.) 1967, U.S. Ct. Appeals (11th cir.) 1981, U.S. Supreme Ct. 1983; cert. labor law specialist, Tex. Trial atty. NLRB, Region 23, Houston, 1961-63; assoc. Fulbright & Jaworski Houston, 1963-71, ptnr., 1971—, chmn. labor sect., 1974—; panelist profl. seminars speaker on devels. in labor law for law students, mgmt. groups. Fellow Tex. Bar Found.; mem. Houston Bar Assn., Houston Mgmt. Lawyers Forum, State Bar Tex., Tex. State Bar (labor law com. 1970-71), ABA, S.W. Found. Research and Edn. Republican. Roman Catholic. Clubs: Argyle (San Antonio); Houstonian, Tex. Tech. U. Dad's. Contbr. numerous articles to mgmt. publs. Labor. Office: Fulbright & Jaworski 1301 McKinney St Houston TX 77010

BAMBERG, JONATHAN BAKER, lawyer, real estate developer; b. Harlington, Tex., Apr. 18, 1954; s. John Baker and Jeanette Catherine (Simmang) B. AA, Fla. Tech. U., 1974; BA in History, U. Fla., 1976; BE, U. Cen. Fla., 1977; JD, St. Mary's U., San Antonio, 1980. Bar: Tex. 1980, Fla. 1981. Corp. counsel Sand Dollar Devel., Inc., Orlando, Fla., 1980-83, v.p., 1981-83; v.p. Crescent Sand Dollars, Inc., Orlando, 1983-84, corp. counsel, 1983—, pres., 1984—; sec., bd. dirs. Sand Dollar II, Inc., St. Augustine, Fla., 1986—; bd. dirs. Sand Dollar IV, Inc., St. Augustine. Mem. ABA, Orange County Bar Assn. Democrat. Lutheran. Avocations: tennis, golf, numismatics. Real property. Home: 420 Madeira Ave Orlando FL 32817

BAMBERGER, MICHAEL ALBERT, lawyer; b. Berlin, Feb. 29, 1936; s. Fritz and Kate (Schwabe) B.; m. Phylis Skloot, Dec. 19, 1965; children—Kenneth A., Richard A. A.B. magna cum laude, Harvard U., 1957, LL.B. magna cum laude, 1960. Bar: N.Y. 1960, D.C. 1982. Assoc. Proskauer Rose Goetz & Mendelsohn, N.Y.C., 1960-69; assoc. Finley, Kumble, Wagner, Heine, Underberg, Manley, Myerson & Casey, N.Y.C., 1970, ptnr., 1971—; mem. faculty various legal seminars and insts. Co-editor: State Limited Partnership Laws (4 vols.), 1986; contbr. articles to profl. jours. Trustee, v.p. Central Synagogue; overseer Hebrew Union Coll.-Jewish Inst. Religion, N.Y.C.; pres. Brewery Hill Block Assn.; bd. dirs. Leo Baeck Inst. Mem. First Amendment Lawyers Assn., ABA (com. on ltd. partnerships 1980—), N.Y. State Bar Assn. (com. on fed. legislation 1970-73), Assn. Bar City N.Y. (com. on fed. legislation 1979-82, com. on civil rights 1982-86, chmn. 1983-86), N.Y. County Lawyers Assn. (securities com. 1980-82). Jewish. General corporate, Libel, Publishing.

BAMBERTH, HUGO ARNOLD, lawyer; b. Albion, Ill., July 31, 1948; s. Peter and Alice (Wolsky) B.; m. Diane Kay Young, Feb. 27, 1971; children: Kristen, Wendy. BA, Carthage Coll., 1970; JD, Valparaiso U., 1974. Bar: Ind. 1974, U.S. Dist. Ct. (no. dist.) Ind., U.S. Tax Ct. 1977. Assoc. Law Office of John J. Davie, La Porte, Ind., 1974-82; sole practice La Porte, 1982—; with Firm of Hugo A. Bamberth and Assocs., La Porte, 1983—. Mem. facility study com. La Porte Sch. Bd., 1986-87; bd. dirs. Youth Service Bur., past pres., La Porte; Christian edn. com. Bethany Luth. Ch., La Porte, 1986-87, leader 4H Club, La Porte. Named one of Outstanding Young Men Am, 1986. Mem. ABA, La Porte County Bar Assn., La Porte City Bar Assn. (past sec., pres. elect 1987), La Porte C. of C. (mktg. com.). Avocations: golf, swimming, antique cars. Personal injury, Family and matrimonial, General practice. Office: 809 Jefferson St La Porte IN 46350

BAMBRICK, JOSEPH THOMAS, JR., lawyer, corporation executive; b. Chgo., Oct. 9, 1941; s. Joseph Thomas and Frances Mae (Whittaker) B. B.S., Manhattan Coll., 1963; J.D., Villanova U., 1966. Bar: N.Y. 1967, U.S. Supreme Ct., 1979, Pa. 1985. Mgmt. assoc. Fuller Brush Co., East Hartford, Conn., 1973-74; v.p. ops. Am. Delivery Systems, Inc., Detroit, 1974-75; pres. N.P. Express, Inc., Douglassville, Pa., 1975—, Thrifty Home Decoration Center, Inc., Douglassville, 1976—, N.P. Express of Fla., Inc., Sebastian, 1979—, Bambrick Enterprises, Inc., Douglasville, 1982—, Thrifty Express, Inc., Atlanta, 1980—; prin. Joseph T. Bambrick & Assocs., Douglassville, 1975—. Served to capt. AUS, 1966-69. Decorated Bronze Star with 2 oak leaf clusters. Mem. ABA, So. Shipper and Motor Carrier Conf., Middle West Shipper and Motor Carrier Conf. Democrat. Roman Catholic. Administrative and regulatory, Contracts commercial, Corporate taxation. Office: NP Express Inc 529 Reading Ave West Reading PA 19611

BAMBUROWSKI, THOMAS JOSEPH, lawyer; b. Batavia, N.Y., Mar. 28, 1944; s. John and Jean Ann (Cudney) B.; m. Jean Marie Swartzlander, Aug. 8, 1970; children—Brent Thomas, David Scott. B.S., Bowling Green State U., 1965, M.B.A., 1969; J.D., U. Toledo, 1975. Bar: Ohio 1975, U.S. Dist. Ct. (no. dist.) Ohio 1977. Trust adminstr. Toledo Trust Co., 1975-77; asst. prosecutor Wood County, Ohio, 1978-80; sole practice, Bowling Green, Ohio, 1977—; domestic relations referee Wood County Ct. of Common Pleas, 1984—. Bd. dirs. Am. Lung Assn. of Northwestern Ohio, 1983—. Served to capt. U.S. Army, 1965-67. Mem. Wood County Bar Assn. (pres. 1984), Weston C. of C., Am. Legion. Republican. Roman Catholic. Lodge: Kiwanis (pres. Bowling Green chpt. 1986-87). Probate, Family and matrimonial, General practice. Home: 733 Brittany St Bowling Green Oh 43402 Office: Thomas J Bamburowski 920 N Main St Bowling Green OH 43402

BAMBURY, JOSEPH ANTHONY, JR., lawyer, insurance executive; b. N.Y.C., June 14, 1932; s. Joseph Anthony and Rose Mary (McGinness) B.; m. Mary Elizabeth Forde, Dec. 29, 1956. AB, Holy Cross Coll., 1953; JD, Columbia U., 1956. Bar: N.Y. 1956, U.S. Dist. Ct. (ea. and so. dists.) N.Y. 1961, U.S. Ct. Appeals (2d cir.) 1961. Corp. sec., asst. gen. counsel Royal Ins., N.Y.C., 1970-78, v.p., gen. counsel, 1978-81, gen. counsel, 1982—; bd. dirs. Am. and Fgn. Ins. Co., Globe Indemnity Co., Royal Indemnity Co., Safeguard Ins. Co., Newark Ins. Co., Royal Ins. Co. Am., Royal Life Ins. Co. Am., B.E.I. Services Inc., Royal Surplus Lines Ins. Co., Comml. Mktg. Systems Inc., Shield Intermediaries Inc., Royal Excess and Spl. Risks Inc., Royal Excess an Spl. Risks of Ill. Inc., Royal Excess and Spl. Risks of Ga. Inc., U.S. Transp. Underwriters Inc., Royal Ins. Service Corp., Royal Excess and Spl. Risks Ins. Services Inc., Protected Settlements Inc. Co-author: The Business Insurance Handbook, 1981, Handling Property and Casualty Claims, 1985. Mem. Dem. County Com., N.Y.C., 1961-73; pres. Horatio Seymour Dem. Club, N.Y.C., 1965-75, Community Planning Bd. 2, N.Y.C., 1966-70. Served to capt. USMC, 1956-60. Mem. ABA, N.Y. State Bar Assn., N.Y. County Lawyers Assn. (bd. dirs. 1979—). Democrat. Roman Catholic. Club: Merchants (N.Y.C.). Insurance, General corporate, Antitrust. Office: Royal Ins 9300 Arrowpoint Blvd Charlotte NC 28210

BAMFORD, DAVID ELLERY, lawyer; b. New Salem, Pa., Sept. 5, 1921; s. George Kyle and Hazel (Reid) B.; m. Theodora Mary Kenny, Jan. 7, 1949; children: Mary Ann, David Reid, James Douglas. LLB with honors, George Washington U., 1949. Bar: D.C. 1949, Ill. 1960. Assoc. Law Offices C.S. Rhyne, Washington, 1949-51; counsel Gen. Electric Co., N.Y.C., 1951-66; v.p., gen. counsel Gen. Electric Credit Corp., Stamford, Conn., 1966-76; corp. counsel Gen. Electric Co., Fairfield, Conn., 1976—. Served to sgt. U.S. Army, 1942-46, CBI. Mem. Ill. State Bar Assn., D.C. Bar Assn., Order of Coif. Presbyterian. Club: Patterson (Fairfield). Antitrust, General corporate, Securities. Home: 1 Wedgewood Rd Westport CT 06880 Office: Gen Electric Co 3135 Easton Turnpike Fairfield CT 06431

BANALES, J(OSE) MANUEL, judge; b. El Paso, Tex., Sept. 17, 1950; s. Margarito and Consuelo (Villalobos) B.; m. Margaret Sandra Moreno, Dec. 28, 1974; children—Josemanuel Edmundo, Margarita Consuelo, Alejandro Xicotencatl, Juanmarcos Patrocinio. B.A., U. Tex.-El Paso, 1972; J.D., U. Houston, 1974. Bar: Tex. 1975 (bd. cert. specialist criminal law), U.S. Dist. Ct. (so. dist.) Tex. 1976, U.S. Ct. Appeals (5th cir.) 1976, U.S. Supreme Ct. 1983. Assoc. Ramsey, Muniz, Corpus Christi, Tex., 1975, Huerta, Pena & Beckman, Corpus Christi, 1976-78; sole practice with Daniel V. Alfaro, Corpus Christi, 1979; ptnr. Banales & Cavada, Corpus Christi, 1980; sole practice, Corpus Christi, 1981-87, judge 105th Dist. Ct., Nueces, Kleberg and Kenedy Counties, 1987—. Mem. Jr. League of United Latin Am. Citizens, El Paso, 1966-72, nat. pres., 1968-70. Recipient Presdl. citation State Bar Tex., 1981, Appreciation award, 1979. Mem. Mexican Am. Bar Assn. Tex. (founder, treas. 1984—), Chicano Bar Assn. of So. Tex. (founder, pres. 1979-80), Nueces County Bar Assn. (bd. dirs. 1978-80), State Bar Tex. (chmn. sect. on concerns of spanish-speaking community Tex. 1980-81). Democrat. Roman Catholic. Criminal, Personal injury, General practice. Home: 3134 Seven Tree St Corpus Christi TX 78410 Office: 105th Dist Ct Nueces County Courthouse 901 Leopard 8th Floor Corpus Christi TX 78401

BANCROFT, ALEXANDER CLERIHEW, lawyer; b. N.Y.C., Feb. 6, 1938; s. Harding F. and Jane (Northrop) B.; m. Margaret A. Armstrong, Mar. 14, 1964; 1 dau., Elizabeth. A.B., Harvard U., 1960, LL.B., 1963. Mem. Shearman & Sterling, N.Y.C., 1964—, ptnr., 1973—. Home: 15 E 91st St New York NY 10128 Office: 53 Wall St New York NY 10005

BANCROFT, DAVID PHILLIPS, lawyer; b. Hartford, Conn., Sept. 14, 1937; s. P.S. and Mildred Ann (Provost) B.; m. Cheryl Marjorie Hagenberger, July 27, 1963; children: Jennifer, James, Jessica. Trial atty. criminal div. U.S. Dept. Justice, Washington, 1963-66; asst. U.S. atty. criminal div. State of Calif., San Francisco, 1966-69; asst. U.S. atty., chief spl. projects State of Calif.fice, San Francisco, 1971-78; assoc. dir. Nat. Commn. Reform of Fed. Criminal Laws, Washington, 1960-71; ptnr. Sideman & Bancroft, San Francisco, 1978—. Contbr. articles to profl. jours. Mem. Calif. Bar Assn. (advisor litigation sect., exec. com. 1982—), San Francisco Bar Assn. (bd. dirs. 1984—), Fed. Bar Assn. (v.p. San Francisco chpt. 1986—). Republican. Avocations: mountain hiking, cross country skiing, travelling, art history. Criminal, Federal civil litigation, Government contracts and claims. Office: Sideman & Bancroft 3 Embarcadero Ctr San Francisco CA 94111

BANDUCCI, THOMAS ANTHONY, lawyer; b. San Mateo, Calif., Oct. 15, 1954; s. Candido A. and Marjorie Von (Baird) B.; m. Lori Gibson, June 19, 1977; 1 child, Andrea Lorain. AB, Stanford U., 1976; JD, U. Calif., San Francisco, 1979. Bar: Idaho 1979, U.S. Dist. Ct. Idaho 1979, U.S. Ct. Appeals (9th cir.) 1979. Ptnr. Eberle, Berlin, Kading, Turnbow & Gillespie, Chartered, Boise, Idaho, 1979—. Mem. ABA (chmn. young lawyers div. 1981-82), Def. Research Inst., Idaho Bar Assn. (evidence com. 1980-85), Idaho Def. Counsel, Boise Bar Assn. (pres. 1986—). Federal civil litigation, Construction, Insurance. Office: Eberle Berlin et al 300 N 6th St Boise ID 83702

BANDY, JACK D., lawyer; b. Galesburg, Ill., June 19, 1932; s. Homer O. and Gladys L. (Van Winkle) B.; m. Betty McMillan, Feb. 18, 1956; children—Jean A. Bandy Dodie, D. Michael, Jeffery K. B.A., Knox Coll., 1954; LL.B., U. San Fernando Valley, 1967. Bar: Calif. 1972. Safety engr. Indsl. Indemnity Co., Los Angeles, 1960-65, sr. safety engr., 1965-69, resident safety engr., 1969-72; trial atty. Employers Ins. of Wausau, Los Angeles, 1972-79; mng. atty. Wausau Ins. Cos., Los Angeles, 1979—. Youth leader YMCA, Mission Hills, Calif., 1965-72; active PTA, Little League. Served with U.S. Army, 1954-56. Mem. Def. Research Inst., Calif. State Bar, Assn. So. Calif. Def. Counsel, Am. Soc. Safety Engrs. (cert. safety profl.). Contbr. articles to profl. jours. Personal injury, Workers' compensation, Insurance. Office: 74 N Pasadena Ave Pasadena CA 91103

BANDY, THOMAS ROCHELLE, III, lawyer; b. Johnson City, Tenn., May 17, 1940; s. Thomas Rochelle Jr. and Betty Harmon (Preas) B.; m. Judy Carol Snapp, Sept. 6, 1965. BA, Va. Mil. Inst., 1962; JD, U. Tenn., 1965. Bar: Tenn., U.S. Dist. Ct. Tenn. Sole practice Kingsport, Tenn. Served to capt. Med. Service Corps, 1965-67, Vietnam. Mem. Tenn. Bar Assn., Tenn. Trial Lawyers Assn. (bd. govs. 1985—). Democrat. Baptist. Lodge: Masons (local jr. warden 1986—). Bankruptcy, Personal injury, Criminal. Office: PO Box 1127 Kingsport TN 37662

BANGEL, HERBERT K., lawyer; b. Norfolk, Va., May 29, 1928; m. Carolyn Kroskin; children: Nancy Jo, Brad J. BS in Commerce, U. Va.,

1947, JD, 1950. Bar: Va. 1949, U.S. Dist. Ct. (ea. dist.) Va., U.S. Ct. Appeals (4th cir.), U.S. Tax Ct., U.S. Bd. Immigration Appeals, D.C., U.S. Supreme Ct. Ptnr. Bangel, Bangel & Bangel, Portsmouth, Va., 1950; bd. dirs. Portsmouth Enterprises, Inc., Portsmouth Local Devel. Co., Inc., TVX Broadcast Group, Inc., Dominion Bank Greater Hampton Roads, Tidewater Profl. Sports Inc.; commr. chancery Portsmouth Cir. Ct., 1973—; substitute judge Portsmouth Gen. Dist. Ct., 1979-84; mem. U.S. Ct. Appeals (4th cir.) Jud. Conf. Commr. Eastern Va. Med. Authority, 1983—, vice chmn., 1987—; pres., chmn. Portsmouth Area United Fund, 1971-73; bd. dirs. Portsmouth Indsl. Found., 1968—, bd. dirs. Urban League Tidewater (Va.), 1978-79, Tidewater chpt. Am. Heart Assn., 1983-84, Portsmouth Community Trust Distbn. Com., 1977—, chmn., 1985-86; bd. dirs. Maryview Hosp., 1969; trustee Portsmouth-Chesapeake Area Found., 1968-72, United Community Funds and Councils Va., 1970-71, others; chmn. Portsmouth Redevel. and Housing Authority, 1977-83. Named First Citizen of Portsmouth City of Portsmouth, 1974. Mem. ABA, Va. Bar Assn., Portsmouth Bar Assn. (pres. 1964), Norfolk Bar Assn., Tidewater Trial Lawyers Assn. (bd. dirs. 1968-73), Va. Trial Lawyers Assn. (bd. govs. 1970), Assn. Trial Lawyers Am. Democrat. Jewish. Clubs: Suburban Country (pres. 1961-62), Oceans (bd. dirs. 1973-76), Town Point (bd. govs. 1983—), Downtown Athletic (Portsmouth). Lodges: Elks, Moose, B'nai B'rith. Personal injury. Home: 4201 Faigle Rd Portsmouth VA 23703 Office: Bangel Bangel & Bangel PO Box 760 Portsmouth VA 23705-0760

BANGEL, STANLEY JEROME, lawyer; b. Norfolk, Va., July 16, 1925; s. Abraham Arthur and Florence (Block) B.; m. Frances Dorf, Dec. 22, 1946; children: Keith Harrison, Karen Bangel Burnell. J.D., U. Va., 1947. Bar: Va. 1947. Ptnr. Bangel & Bangel, Portsmouth, Va., 1947-49, Bangel, Bangel & Bangel, Portsmouth, 1949—. Mem. pres.'s adv. council Va. Wesleyan Coll. Served to ensign USN, 1945-46. Fellow Internat. Acad. Trial Lawyers; mem. ABA, Va. Bar Assn., Portsmouth Bar Assn. (pres. 1967), Norfolk-Portsmouth Bar Assn., Assn. Trial Lawyers Am. (v.p. 1953-57, bd. govs. 1957-59), Va. Trial Lawyers Assn. (pres. 1967-68, bd. govs.), Tidewater Trial Lawyers Assn. (bd. govs. 1958-70), Jud. Conf. U.S., Am. Judicature Soc., Law Sci. Acad. Am. Jewish. Club: Harbor (Norfolk). Lodge: Elks. Personal injury, Criminal. Home: 204 Park Rd Portsmouth VA 23707 Office: Bangel Bangel & Bangel 505 Court St PO Box 760 Portsmouth VA 23705

BANK, MALVIN E., lawyer; b. Phila., May 22, 1930; s. Herman and Fannie (Miller) B.; m. Lea Betty Plessett, Sept. 2, 1951; children—Herman, Jonathan, Douglas, Steven. B.A., Pa. State U., 1952; LL.B., Yale U., 1957. U.S. Dist. Ct. (no. dist.) Ohio, 1957, U.S. Ct. Appeals (6th cir.), 1959. Ptnr. Thompson, Hine & Flory, Cleve., 1957—; dir. Revco D.S., Inc., Twinsburg, Ohio, Oglebay Norton Co., Cleve., Am. Consumer Products, Inc., Cleve. Contbr. articles to profl. jours. Served to 1st lt. U.S. Army, 1952-54. Decorated Bronze Star. Mem. Phi Beta Kappa, Phi Kappa Phi. Club: Union (Cleve.). Estate taxation, Personal income taxation, Estate planning. Office: Thompson Hine & Flory 1100 National City Bank Bldg Cleveland OH 44114

BANKER, BARBARA L., lawyer; b. Manitowoc, Wis., Jan. 26, 1951; s. Robert Joseph and Marilyn Delores (Lange) B.; m. Robert Paul Redemann, June 15, 74 (div. Jan. 1983). Student, Miami U., Oxford, Ohio, 1969-71; BA, U. Wis., 1973; MA, U. Tulsa, 1978, JD, 1982. Bar: Okla., U.S. Dist. Ct. (no. dist.) Okla. Tchr. D.C. Everest Middle Sch., Schofield, Wis., 1973-75; legal sec. Spradling, Stagner, Alpern & Friot, Tulsa, 1975-76; dept. mgr. Tulsa Job Corps Ctr., 1976-79; assoc. Conner & Winters, Tulsa, 1982—; adj. prof. U. Tulsa, 1986—; judge-oral advocacy U. Tulsa, 1983—; guest lectr. Oral Roberts U., Tulsa, 1985,86. Editor: Tulsa Law Jour., 1981-82. Account chmn. Tulsa Area United Way campaign, 1985; active Tulsa Ballet Theatre Guild, 1985—, Vol. Council of Tulsa Philharmonic, 1985—. Mem. ABA, Okla. Bar Assn., Okla. Assn. Women Lawyers (treas. 1985-86), Tulsa Bar Assn., Tulsa Women Lawyers Assn. (spl. project com. 1983-85, treas. 1985-87), Tulsa Banking Lawyers (program com. 1985—). Republican. Unitarian. Avocations: reading, camping, music, theatre, bicycling. Banking, Bankruptcy, Contracts commercial. Office: Conner & Winters 2400 First Nat Tower Tulsa OK 74103

BANKER, STEPHEN M., lawyer; b. Flushing, N.Y., Apr. 20, 1952; s. Abraham and Dorothy (Fuhr) B.; m. Amy Beth Cohen, June 29, 1975; children: Meredith Elaine, Allison Jane. BA, Cornell U., 1974; JD, U. Pa., 1977. Bar: N.Y. 1978, U.S. Dist. Ct. (so. and ea. dists.) N.Y. 1978. Assoc. Skadden, Arps, Slate, Meagher & Flom, N.Y.C., 1977-85, ptnr., 1985—. Contbr. articles to profl. jours. Mem. ABA, N.Y. State Bar Assn. General corporate, Securities. Home: 50 E 89th St New York NY 10128 Office: Skadden Arps Slate Meagher & Flom 919 3d Ave New York NY 10022-9931

BANKERT, JOSEPH EDWARD, lawyer; b. Planfield, N.J., Jan. 12, 1949; s. Frederick Ball and Mary Jane (Rodgers) B.; m. Barbara Jane Moriarty, May 17, 1974; children: Amanda Jane, Honora Mary. BSBA, Georgetown U., 1971; JD, U. Pitts., 1974. Bar: Va. 1974, D.C. 1975, U.S. Supreme Ct. 1977. Assoc. Christmas & Schulze, Washington, 1974-78, Mackey & Klein, Washington, 1978-79, Taylor & Clemante, Alexandria, Va., 1979-81; ptnr. Brock & Bankert, Alexandria, 1981-85; sole practice Fairfax, Va., 1985—. Bd. dirs. Barker Found., Washington, 1985—, Pinecrest Sch., Fairfax, 1985—. Mem. Va. Bar Assn., D.C. Bar Assn., Assn. Trial Lawyers Am., Va. Trial Lawyers Assn., Am. Arbitration Assn. Roman Catholic. Avocations: boating, basketball. State civil litigation, Real property, Contracts commercial. Home: 5845 Colfax Ave Alexandria VA 22311 Office: 3025 Hamaker Ct Fairfax VA 22031

BANKS, CECIL JAMES, lawyer; b. Des Moines, Sept. 27, 1947; s. Otis and Mary Louise (Watkins) B.; m. Margot Elaine Harper; children: Kimberly, Imani, Jamaal. Student, Sophia U., Tokyo, 1965-66; BA, Duquesne U., 1970; M in Pub. Adminstrn., U. Pitts., 1974; JD, Rutgers U., 1976. Bar: N.J. 1976, U.S. Dist. Ct. N.J. 1976. Assoc. McCarter & English, Newark, 1976-78; gen. counsel Newark Bd. Edn., 1978-82; sole practice Newark, 1982-84; ptnr. Sills, Beck, Cummis, Zuckerman, Radin et al, Newark, 1984—; atty. City of Orange, N.J., 1984—; asst. treas. The Leaguers Inc., Newark, 1986; bd. dirs. Essex Legal Services, Newark. Bd. dirs. United Community Corp., Newark, 1976-78, Community Coop. Found., Bridgeport, Conn., 1986—. Recipient Community Service award Bethel Bapt. Ch., Community Service award United Community Corp., 1977, Disting. Service award Orange Mcpl. Council. Mem. ABA, Nat. Bar Assn. (regional dir.), Essex Bar Assn. (co-founder young lawyers div.), Assn. Trial Lawyers Am., Omega Psi Phi. Federal civil litigation, Municipal bonds, Real property. Home: 238 Elmwynd Dr Orange NJ 07052 Office: Sills Beck Cummis Zuckerman Radin et al 33 Washington St Newark NJ 07102

BANKS, ERIC KENDALL, lawyer; b. St. Louis, Aug. 21, 1955; s. Willie James Banks Jr. and Grace (Kendall) Palmer; m. Diana Yvonne Parran, Apr. 8, 1984. BSBA, U. Mo., St. Louis, 1977; JD, U. Mo., Columbia, 1980. Bar: Mo. 1980, U.S. Dist. Ct. (we. dist.) Mo. 1980, U.S. Dist. Ct. (ea. dist.) Mo. 1984, U.S. Ct. Appeals (8th cir.) 1984. Asst. gen. counsel Mo. Pub. Service Commn., Jefferson City, 1980-84; asst. atty. Office Cir. Atty., St. Louis, 1984-87; assoc. Law Office of William A. Brasher, St. Louis, 1987—; sec., bd. dirs. Black Leadership Tng. Program, St. Louis, 1975-77. Mem. Laclede West Pine Neighborhood Assn., St. Louis, Vols. in Corrections, Jefferson City, Mo. St. Louis Met. Leadership Program fellow, 1975-77. Mem. ABA, Mo. Bar Assn. (adminstrv. law com., com. counsel), Mound City Bar Assn., Bar Assn. Met. St. Louis, Mo. Assn. Pros. Attys., NAACP (sustaining, life). Democrat. Lutheran. Club: Toastmasters Internat. (adminstrv. v.p. 1983, William Tellman award 1982). Lodge: Rosicrucians. Avocations: karate, reading, photography, public speaking, community work. Administrative and regulatory, Criminal, General corporate. Home: 4236 W Pine #102 Saint Louis MO 63108 Office: Office of William A Brashee 1 Centerre Plaza Suite 1660 Saint Louis MO 63101

BANKS, FRED LEE, JR., judge; b. Jackson, Miss., Sept. 1, 1942; s. Fred L. and Violet (Mabry) B.; m. Taunya Lovell, June 5, 1967 (div. 1975); children: Rachel R., Jonathan L.; m. Pamela Gipson, Jan. 28, 1978. BA, Howard U., 1965, JD cum laude, 1968. Bar: Miss. 1968, U.S. Dist. Ct. (no. and so. dists.) Miss. 1968, U.S. Ct. Appeals (5th cir.) 1968, D.C. 1969. Ptnr. Banks & Nichols, Jackson, 1968, Banks, Owens & Byrd and predecessor firms Anderson, Banks, Nichols & Stewart; Anderson, Banks, Nichols & Leventhal; Anderson & Banks, Jackson, 1968-85; judge Miss. Cir. Ct., Hinds County and Yazoo County, 1985—; mem. Miss. Bd. Bar Admissions, 1978-79; pres. and bd. dirs. State Mut. Fed. Savs. and Loan, Jackson, 1976—. Bd. dirs. NAACP, 1981—; active Nat. Adv. Com. for the Edn. of Disadvantaged Children, 1978-80; del. Dem. Nat. Conv., 1976, 1980; co-mgr. Miss. Carter-Mondale presidl. campaign, 1976; legislator Miss. Ho. of Reps., Jackson, 1976-85. Mem. ABA, Magnolia Bar Assn., Nat. Bar Assn., Hinds County Bar Assn. Roman Catholic. Avocation: tennis. Home: 976 Metairie Rd Jackson MS 39209 Office: Box 327 Jackson MS 39205

BANKS, ROBERT SHERWOOD, lawyer; b. Newark, Mar. 28, 1934; s. Howard Douglas and Amelia Violet (Del Bagno) B.; m. Judith Lee Henry; children—Teri, William; children by previous marriage—Robert, Paul, Stephen, Roger, Gregory, Catherine. A.B., Cornell U., 1956, LL.B., 1958. Bar: N.J. bar 1959, N.Y. State bar 1968. Practice law Newark, 1958-61; atty. E.I. duPont, Wilmington, Del., 1961-67; with Xerox Corp., Stamford, Conn., 1967—; v.p., gen. counsel Xerox Corp., 1976—; exec. com. Center for Public Resources, N.Y.C., chmn., 1984-87; mem. com. on pretrial phase of civil cases Jud. Council U.S. Ct. Appeals (2d cir.), fed. jud. com. on gifts, 2d cir. standing com on improvement of civil litigation. Mem. adv. council Cornell Law Sch.; bd. dirs. U. Conn. Research and Devel. Corp. Mem. Am. Bar Assn., Am. Arbitration Assn., Practicing Law Inst., Cornell Law Assn., Am. Corporate Counsel Assn. (chmn. 1982-83), Conn. Bar Assn., Machinery and Allied Products Inst. (law council), Westchester Fairfield Corp. Counsel Assn., Tau Kappa Epsilon. Clubs: Aspetuck Valley Country, Jonathan's Landing. General corporate. Home: 29 Laurel Rd New Canaan CT 06840 Office: Xerox Corp Stamford CT 06904

BANKS, ROLAND FITZGERALD, JR., lawyer; b. Portland, Oreg., May 2, 1932; s. Roland F. and Doris D. Pixley (Dezendorf) B.; m. Janet M. Sinclair, June 14, 1955; children—Kathryn Kelly, Jeffrey, Sarah. Student, Stanford, U., 1950-53; B.A., U. Oreg., 1955, LL.B., 1958. Bar: Oreg. 1958, U.S. Dist. Ct. Oreg. 1958, U.S. Supreme Ct. 1972. Assoc., Schwabe, Williamson, Wyatt, Moore & Roberts, Assocs., Portland, 1958-68, ptnr., 1968—, sr. ptnr., 1978—. Bd. dirs. Fruit and Flower Child Care Ctr., 1977—, pres., 1979-80; bd. dirs. Ascension Chapel. Served to 1st lt. U.S. Army, 1955-57. Mem. ABA (chmn. products, gen. liability, and consumer's law com. 1982-83), Oreg. State Bar Assn. (bd. of govs. 1978-81), Multnomah County Bar Assn., Def. Research Inst., Oreg. Assn. of Def. Counsel (pres. 1977), Am. Bd. Trial Advs. Republican. Episcopalian. Clubs: Univ. (pres. 1977), Multnomah Athletic, Waverley Country. Contbr. articles to law jours. State civil litigation, Federal civil litigation, Personal injury. Office: 1600 Pacwest Ctr 1211 SW 5th Ave Portland OR 97204

BANKS, THEODORE LEE, lawyer; b. Chgo., Nov. 5, 1951; s. Morris M. and Ruth Lilly (Gray) B.; m. Cheryl Deborah Steinhardt, Aug. 20, 1972; children: Miriam, Rebecca, Sarah. BA, Beloit Coll., 1972; JD, U. Denver, 1975. Bar: Colo. 1976, Ill. 1976, U.S. Dist. Ct. (no. dist.) Ill. 1976, U.S. Supreme Ct. 1981, U.S. Ct. Appeals (6th cir.) 1985. Atty. Kraft, Inc., Glenview, Ill., 1976-80, gen. atty., 1980-81; corp. counsel Dart & Kraft, Inc., Northbrook, Ill., 1981-86, sr. counsel litigation and trade regulation, 1986—. Author: International Antitrust Law, 1981, Distribution Law for the Practitioner, 1987. Mem. ABA (young lawyer liaison to antitrust sect. council 1985—, chmn. fgn. antitrust subcom. 1981-84, chmn. young lawyer antitrust com. 1982-84). Club: Windy City BMW (Chgo.) (gen. counsel 1979-86). Antitrust, General corporate, Private international. Office: Kraft Inc Kraft Ct 4W Glenview IL 60025

BANKSTON, ARCHIE MOORE, JR., lawyer, utility executive; b. Memphis, Oct. 12, 1937; s. Archie M. and Elsie Bernice (Shaw) B.; m. Emma Ann Dejan, Apr. 16, 1966; children—Louis, Alice. B.A., Fisk U., 1959; LL.B., Washington U., St. Louis, 1962, M.B.A., 1964. Bar: Mo. 1963, N.Y. 1966. Asst. div. counsel Gen. Foods Corp., White Plains, N.Y., 1964-67, product mgr. Maxwell House div., 1967-69; asst. sec. and corp. counsel PepsiCo, Inc., Purchase, N.Y., 1969-72; div. counsel Xerox Corp., Stamford, Conn., 1973; sec. and asst. gen. counsel Consol. Edison Co. of N.Y. Inc., N.Y.C., 1974—. Bd. dirs. Mental Health Assn. Westchester County; trustee Beth Israel Med. Ctr.; former bd. dirs. Urban League of Westchester; mem. 100 Black Men, Inc., N.Y.C.; bd. of trustees Coll. of New Rochelle, N.Y. Recipient Black Achievers in Industry award Harlem br. YMCA, 1971, Merit award Black Exec. Exchange Program Nat. Urban League, 1974. Mem. Am. Soc. Corp. Secs. (N.Y. regional group adv. com., securities industry com., former dir., chmn. budget com., edn. com., N.Y. regional group adv. com.), Stockholder Relations Soc. N.Y. (past pres. and dir.), Am. Mgmt. Assn. (former trustee), ABA, Phi Delta Phi, Sigma Pi Phi, Alpha Phi Alpha. Club: Westchester Clubmen. Administrative and regulatory, General corporate, Public utilities. Office: Consol Edison Co NY Inc 4 Irving Pl New York NY 10003

BANKSTON, WILLIAM MARCUS, lawyer; b. San Angelo, Tex., Feb. 16, 1946; s. Wyatt Lester and Mary Alice (Powell) B.; m. Janna Coe Herridge, Aug. 15, 1965 (div.); children—Darla Kae, Kendra Lynne; m. Judith Ann Railsback, Nov. 20, 1981. B.A., Tex. Tech U., 1968, B.S., 1968; J.D., U. Tex., 1971. Bar: Alaska 1971, Tex. 1971, U.S. Tax Ct. 1983, U.S. Ct. Claims 1984, U.S. Supreme Ct. 1986. Assoc. Croft & Bailey, Anchorage, 1971-73; ptnr. Croft, Bailey, Guetschow & Bankston, 1973-74; instr. Anchorage Community Coll., 1972-74; ptnr. Greene & Bankston, Anchorage, 1974—. Mem. ABA, Alaska Bar Assn., State Bar Tex. Methodist. State civil litigation, Construction, Securities. Home: PO Box 102713 Anchorage AK 99510 Office: Bankston McCollum & Fossey PC 550 W 7th Suite 1800 Anchorage AK 99501

BANNON, BRIAN ANTHONY, lawyer; b. Bklyn., Sept. 27, 1951; s. John Joseph and Vivian (Jesse) B.; m. Hedy Ilene Seligman, July 23, 1978; children: Tristan Alexander, Colin John. BA, Bklyn. Coll., 1973; JD, George Washington U., 1981. Bar: D.C. 1981. Spl. asst. to comdr. small bus. affairs Def. Contract Adminstrn. Services, N.Y.C., 1974-77; asst. chief contracts U.S. Arms Control and Disarmament Agy., Washington, 1977-82; assoc. Epstein, Becker, Borsody & Green, Washington, 1982—. Author: Loss of Efficiency, 1985, Government Contract Cost, 1986, Calculating Loss of Efficiency Claims, 1986. Mem. ABA, D.C. Bar Assn. Computer, Government contracts and claims, Public international. Office: Epstein Becker Borsody & Green 1140 19th St NW Washington DC 20036

BANOS, JOSE LUIS, banker, lawyer, sugar planter; b. New Orleans, Aug. 25, 1918; s. Jose Rodrigo and Julia Sussmann (del Olmo) B.; m. Catherine Dunbar, Mar. 29, 1927; children—Catherine, Julia, Margot, J. Luis, George. B.B.A., Tulane U., 1939, LL.B., 1946. Bar: La. 1946, U.S. Supreme Ct. 1970. With Whitney Nat. Bank of New Orleans, 1946—, v.p., 1960-83; of counsel Jones Walker Waechter Poitevent Carrere & Denegre, 1984—; past lectr. Sch. Banking of South, Baton Rouge, Midwest Sch. Banking, Madison, Wis., Emory U., Atlanta, Online Resource Exchange, Inc. Past pres. pres.'s council St. Mary's Dominican Coll., New Orleans; exec. com., past pres. Internat. House; bd. dirs. Internat. Trademart, World Trade Assns.; bd. dirs. New Orleans Symphony; vice chmn. devel. com. Tulane U. Served to lt. comdr. USNR 1941-46; PTO, ETO. Decorated knight comdr. Isabel La Catolica (Spain); knight Grand Cross, Bacula de la Paz (Vatican), knight grand cross Mil. and Hospitaller Order of St. Lazarus of Jerusalem (Malta); knight Sovereign order of St. John of Jerusalem knight comdr. Equestrian Order of the Holy Sepulchre (Rome). Mem. ABA, La. Bar Assn., La. Bankers Assn., New Orleans C. of C. (past sec.-treas. exec. com.), Phi Delta Theta. Roman Catholic. Clubs: Boston, Southern Yacht, Pickwick, New Orleans Country, Bayou Country, Plimsoll, Lake Shore. Home: 9 Richmond Pl New Orleans LA 70115 Office: Place St Charles 201 St Charles Ave New Orleans LA 70170

BANSE, ROBERT LEE, lawyer; b. Phila., Mar. 11, 1927; s. Robert John and Esther Elizabeth (Warren) B.; m. Anne Windels, Dec. 17, 1955; children—Robert L., Amy L., John W. B.S., U. Pa., 1949; LL.B. cum laude, Washington and Lee U., 1953. Bar: N.Y. bar, Pa. bar. Mem. firm Townsend & Lewis, 1953-55; with Merck & Co., Inc., Rahway, N.J., 1955—; counsel Merck & Co., Inc. (Merck Sharp & Dohme div.), 1960-73, sr. counsel, 1973-75, gen. counsel, 1975—, v.p., 1977-86, sr. vp., 1986—. Mem. ABA,, Assn. Bar City N.Y., Pharm. Mfrs. Assn. (chmn. law sect. 1977-78), N.J. Gen. Counsel's Group, Assn. Gen. Counsel. Clubs: Phila. Cricket, Eagles Mere Country, Springdale Golf. Antitrust, General corporate, Administrative and regulatory. Office: Merck & Co Inc PO Box 2000 Rahway NJ 07065-0900

BANTIVOGLIO, THOMAS NICHOLAS, lawyer; b. Camden, N.J., Sept. 30, 1925; s. Thomas J. and Marie E. (Hoer) B.; m. Patricia M. Parker, Apr. 10, 1950; children: Christine A. Bantivoglio Czech, Joy A., Judith A. Dwornik, Barbara J. AB, Princeton U., 1946; JD, Harvard U., 1948. Bar: N.J. 1949. Assoc. Archer, Greiner, Hunter and Read, Camden, 1949-53, ptnr., 1954-77; pres. Archer, Greiner and Read, Haddonfield, N.J., 1978-84; also chmn. bd. dirs. Archer & Greiner; bd. dirs., sec. Camden Iron and Metal Co., Bantivoglio Investment Co. Republican. Roman Catholic. General corporate, Probate, Corporate taxation. Home: 142 Heritage Rd Haddonfield NJ 08033 Office: Archer and Greiner One Centennial Sq Haddonfield NJ 08033

BANTON, STEPHEN CHANDLER, lawyer; b. St. Louis; s. William Conwell and Ruth (Chandler) B. AB, Bowdoin Coll., 1969; JD, Washington U., St. Louis, 1973, MBA, 1974. Bar: Mo. 1973, U.S. Dist. Ct. (ea. and we. dists.) Mo. 1973. Asst. pros. atty. St. Louis County, 1973-75; sole practice Clayton, Mo., 1975-83; ptnr. Quinn, Ground & Banton, Manchester, Mo., 1983—. Exploring chmn. St. Louis council Midland Dist. Scouts, 1975-77; pres. Am. Youth Hostels Ozarks area, 1976-80; bd. trustees St. Louis Art Mus., 1985—. Served with USMC. Recipient Leadership award Lafayette Community Assn., 1983, Service award The Meramec Palisades Community Assn., 1985, Service award Profl. Remodeling Assn., 1985, Service award St. Louis Symphony Orch., 1985. Mem. ABA, Mo. Bar Assn., St. Louis County Bar Assn., Bar Assn. Met. St. Louis, Assn. Trial Lawyers Am., St. Louis County League of C. of C. (pres. 1978), West Port C. of C. (bd. dirs. 1978-81, Service award 1983). Republican. Club: Toastmasters (Clayton) (adminstrv. v.p.). Lodge: Lions (pres. 1977). General practice, Workers' compensation, Legislative. Home: 929 Saint Paul Rd Ellisville MO 63021 Office: Quinn Ground & Banton 14611 E Manchester Manchester MO 63011

BAPPE, DANIEL EUGENE, lawyer; b. Ames, Iowa, July 10, 1950; s. Virgil E. and Margaret E. (Davidson) B.; m. Karen Evenson, May 29, 1976; 1 child, Adam Daniel. BS, U.S. Mil. Acad., 1972; MBA, U. Iowa, 1979, JD, 1981. Bar: Iowa 1981. Commd. 2d lt. U.S. Army, 1972, advanced through ranks to capt., 1976, resigned, 1977; sole practice Nevada, Iowa, 1977—; corp. atty. El Paso (Tex.) Natural Gas Co.; atty. City of Maxwell, Iowa, 1985-86. Mem. ABA, Fed. Bar Assn., Iowa Bar Assn., Story County Bar Assn., Assn. Trial Lawyers Am., Fm. Jurisprudence Soc. Lodge: Kiwanis. Avocations: tennis, softball, basketball, fishing, running. Probate, Real property, General practice. Home: 1222 2d St Nevada IA 50201 Office: PO Box 127 Nevada IA 50201

BARACK, PETER JOSEPH, lawyer, educator; b. Cleve., Nov. 3, 1943; s. Louis Barry and Florence (Schenberg) B.; m. Elise Hoffman, June 6, 1971; children—Sarah, Jonathan, David. A.B. summa cum laude, Princeton U., 1965; B.Phil. Oxford U. (Eng.), 1967; J.D. magna cum laude, Harvard U., 1970. Bar: Ill. 1970, U.S. Ct. Appeals (7th cir.) 1976, U.S. Supreme Ct. 1978. Asst. prof. bus. adminstrn. Harvard U. Grad. Sch. Bus. Adminstrn., Cambridge, Mass., 1970-72; asst. prof. law Northwestern U. Sch. Law, Chgo., 1972-74, dir. J.D.-M.M. joint degree program, 1972-80, assoc. prof., 1974-79, adj. prof. corp. law, 1979—; ptnr. Levy and Erens, Chgo., 1979-84, Barack, Ferrazzano, Kirschbaum & Perlman, Chgo., 1984—; of counsel Mayer, Brown & Platt, Chgo., 1977-79; lectr. in field; pres. Chgo. Mgmt. Group, Inc., 1972—. Pres. Highland Park (Ill.) Library, 1982-84. Recipient Lt. John A. Larkin, Jr. Meml. prize, 1965; Marshall scholar, 1965; Nuffield scholar, 1966. Mem. Chgo. Bar Assn., Chgo. Council Lawyers, Ill. State Bar Assn., ABA, Assn. Marshall Scholars. Contbr. articles to legal jours. General corporate, Securities, Private international. Home: 1379 Sheridan Rd Highland Park IL 60035 Office: 333 W Wacker Dr Suite 1120 Chicago IL 60606

BARAD, EDWARD NELSON, lawyer; b. St. Louis, Feb. 12, 1947; s. Melvin S. and Susan R. (Funk) B.; m. Marlin Anne Pulaski, Apr. 12, 1970; children: Meredith Jewel, Jonathan Aaron, Caroline Beth. BA, U. Colo., 1969, JD, 1973. Bar: Colo. 1973. Assoc. Hindry & Meyer, Denver, 1973-76; ptnr., chmn. real estate dept. Roath & Brega P.C., Denver, 1976-86, also bd. dirs.; ptnr. Brownstein, Farber & Madden, Denver, 1986—. Bd. dirs. Jewish Family and Children's Service, Denver, 1984—. Mem. ABA (corp. banking and bus. law sect., real property, probate and trust law sect.), Colo. Bar Assn. (corp. banking and bus. law sect., real property, probate and trust law sect., ethics com. 1980-83, chmn. rules com. 1983), Denver Bar Assn. (corp. banking and bus. law sect., real property, probate and trust law sect., exec. council real estate sect. 1983-86, co-chmn. real estate sect. 1986, opinion letter standard com.), Internat. Council Shopping Ctrs. Jewish. Clubs: Green Gables Country, Met. (Denver). Real property. Home: 13 Sedgwick Dr Englewood CO 80110 Office: Roath & Brega PC 1873 S Bellaire Suite 1700 Denver CO 80222 Mailing Address: PO Box 5560 TA Denver CO 80217

BARAN, JAN WITOLD, lawyer; b. Ingolstadt, Germany, May 14, 1948; came to U.S., 1951; s. Jerzy Leopold and Leonce Sidonie (Vanden Bussche) B.; m. Kathryn Kavanagh, June 16, 1979; children—Brendan Jerzy, Maria Leonce, Elise Jett. B.A., Ohio Wesleyan U., 1970; J.D., Vanderbilt U., 1973. Bar: Tenn. 1973, D.C. 1976, U.S. Dist. Ct. D.C. 1980, U.S. Ct. Appeals D.C. 1980, U.S. Supreme Ct. 1980. Legal counsel Nat. Republican Congressional Com., Washington, 1975-77; exec. asst. Fed. Election Commn., Washington, 1977-79; assoc. Baker & Hostetler, Washington, 1979-81, ptnr., 1981-85; ptnr. Wiley, Rein & Fielding, Washington, 1985—; lectr. Practicing Law Inst., Washington, 1978—. Author: (booklet) The Election Law Primer for Corporations, 1984. Chmn. nat. adv. bd. Jour. of Law and Politics, 1983—. Patrick Wilson scholar, 1970-73. Mem. ABA (chmn. com. election law 1981—), D.C. Bar Assn., Fed. Bar Assn. (chmn. polit. campaign and election law com. 1981-83). Roman Catholic. Administrative and regulatory, Federal civil litigation, Legislative. Home: 1608 Walleston Ct Alexandria VA 22302 Office: Wiley Rein & Fielding 1776 K St NW Washington DC 20006

BARANDES, ROBERT, lawyer; b. Bklyn., May 15, 1947; s. Max and Helen (Berger) B.; m. Joan Noveck, May 28, 1970 (div. Jan. 1981); m. Kathleen Lindsey, Aug. 22, 1982 (div. Jan. 1986). Student, U. Coll., London, 1967-68; BA magna cum laude, Union Coll., Schenectady, N.Y., 1969; JD, Harvard U., 1972. Bar: N.Y. 1973, U.S. Dist. Ct. (so. and ea. dists.) N.Y. 1976. From assoc. to ptnr. Barandes, Rabbino & Arnold, N.Y.C., 1972-81; ptnr. Roper & Barandes, N.Y.C., 1981—. Lyricist musical Etched in Stone, 1984; writer, lyricist musical Star Crossed Lovers, 1984. Mem. ABA, Copyright Soc. U.S., Phi Beta Kappa. Jewish. Avocations: writing, skiing, golf, tennis. Entertainment, Securities, General corporate. Office: Roper & Barandes 130 W 42d St Suite 2600 New York NY 10036

BARANOWKSI, EDWIN MICHAEL, lawyer; b. Utica, N.Y., Jan. 26, 1947; s. Edwin Joseph and Mary Jane (Ostrouch) B.; m. Shelley Osmun, Dec. 27, 1969. B.A., Hamilton Coll., 1968; J.D., U. Va., 1971. Bar: N.Y. 1972, Ohio 1982. Assoc. Kenyon & Kenyon, N.Y.C., 1971-81; counsel Porter Wright Morris & Arthur, Columbus, Ohio, 1981-83, ptnr., 1983—; v.p. Plaskolite, Inc., Columbus, 1981-82. Mem. Republican Nat. Com., 1975—. Mem. ABA, Ohio Bar Assn., N.Y. State Bar Assn., Columbus Bar Assn., Assn. Bar City of N.Y., Columbus Patent Assn. (past pres.), Chi Psi. Clubs: Hamilton, St. Michael's Lancers, Rocky Fork Hunt and Country Club, Capital. Federal civil litigation, Patent, Trademark and copyright. Home: 75 Marrus Dr Gahanna OH 43230 Office: 41 S High St Columbus OH 43215

BARASH, ANTHONY HARLAN, lawyer; b. Galesburg, Ill., Mar. 18, 1943; s. Burrel B. and Rosalyne J. (Silver) B.; m. Jean E. Anderson, May 17, 1965; children—Elizabeth, Christopher, Katherine, Andrew. A.B. cum laude, Harvard Coll., 1965; J.D., U. Chgo., 1968. Bar: Calif. 1969. Assoc., Irell & Manella, Los Angeles, 1968-71; assoc. Cox, Castle & Nicholson, Los Angeles, 1971-74, ptnr., 1975-80; ptnr. Barash & Hill, Los Angeles, 1980-84; ptnr. Wildman, Harrold, Allen, Dixon, Barash & Hill, Los Angeles, 1984—; dir. Bank of Beverly Hills, Deauville Restaurants, Inc.; trustee Pitzer Coll., 1981—; nat. adv. bd. Ctr. Nat. Policy, 1981—. Mem. State Bar Calif., ABA, Los Angeles County Bar Assn., Beverly Hills Bar Assn. (bd. dirs. found. 1979—, bd. govs. 1979-81), Pub. Counsel (dir. 1980—). Clubs: Regency (Los Angeles); Harvard of So. Calif. Real property, Administrative and regulatory, General corporate. Home: 825 Amalfi Dr Pacific Palisades CA

90272 Office: Wildman Harrold et al 2029 Century Park E Suite 2050 Los Angeles CA 90067

BARBABELATA, ROBERT D., lawyer; b. San Francisco, Jan. 9, 1925; s. Dominic Barbagelata and Jane Z. Frugoli; m. Doris V. Chatfield, June 8, 1956; children: Patricia, Robert, Michael. Student, U. San Francisco, 1942-43, 46-47, Gonzaga U., 1943-44, Notre Dame U., 1944; BS, U. San Francisco, 1947, JD, 1950. Bar: Calif., U.S. Ct. Appeals (9th cir.), U.S. Supreme Ct. Ptnr. Barbabelata & Howard, San Francisco, 1950—. Served with USN, 1943-46. Fellow Am. Coll. Trial Lawyers, Internat. Soc. Barristers; mem. Am. Bd. Trial Advs. (pres. no. Calif. chpt. 1970, nat. pres. 1981-82, chmn. nat. membership com. 1978, Trial Lawyer of Yr., Calif. chpt. 1986), Assn. Trial Lawyers Am., Calif. Trial Lawyers Assn. (v.p. 1969, 70, 71), Lawyers Club of San Francisco (bd. dirs. 1958-62), San Francisco Trial Lawyers Assn. (pres. 1959), World Assn. Lawyers of World Peace Through Law Ctr., San Francisco Superior Ct. (jud. arbitration policy com.). State civil litigation, Federal civil litigation, Personal injury. Home: 819 Holly Rd Belmont CA 94002 Office: Barbagelata & Howard 109 Geary St 4th Floor San Francisco CA 94108-5699

BARBANEL, JACK A., lawyer, business executive; b. Jan. 19, 1950; s. Edward and Gilda (Tokarewa) B. B.A., U. Md.; J.D., Del. Law Sch.; LL.M. in Corps., NYU. Bar: N.J., Fla., D.C. Trial atty. SEC, 1975-79; assoc. gen. counsel Smith Barney, Harris Upham Inc., N.Y.C., 1979-80, counsel, dir. commodity ops., 1980-81; v.p., gen. counsel Commodities Corp., Princeton, N.J., 1981-83, sr. v.p., dir. futures trading div., 1983-84, 84—; lectr. on econs., securities and commodities law; cons. to fund mgrs. and corps. Mem. Congl. Adv. Bd. Mem. ABA (com. on commodities regulations), Fla. Bar Assn., D.C. Bar Assn., N.J. Bar Assn., Fed. Bar Assn., Am. Arbitration Assn., Nat. Futures Assn. (bus. conduct com.), Internat. Platform Assn., Phi Delta Theta. Editor: Commodities Law Letter. General corporate, Private international, Securities. Home: 29 Sayre Dr Princeton NJ 08540 Office: Gruntal & Co Inc 14 Wall St New York NY 10005

BARBAROWICZ, ROBERT PAUL, lawyer, finance company executive; b. Ellwood City, Pa., Dec. 10, 1946; s. Joseph Stanley Barbarowicz and Victoria Barbara (Ferrese) Scialdone. B.A., Pa. State U., 1968; J.D., Dickinson Sch. Law, 1971. Bar: Pa. 1971, Calif. 1980. Assoc. Eckert, Seamans, Cherin & Mellott, Pitts., 1971-77; corp. counsel Whittaker Corp., Los Angeles, 1978-81; v.p., corp. counsel H.F. Ahmanson & Co., Los Angeles, 1981-85; v.p., asst. gen. counsel Ahmanson Ins. Cos., Los Angeles, 1985-86, sr. v.p., asst. gen. counsel, 1986-87, 1st v.p., asst. gen. counsel, 1987—. Assoc. editor Dickinson Law Rev., 1970-71. Served to capt. USAF, 1968-72. Mem. ABA, Los Angeles Bar Assn., Calif. State Bar Assn. General corporate, Real property, Insurance. Home: 1025 N Kings Rd #203 Los Angeles CA 90069 Office: H F Ahmanson & Co 3731 Wilshire Blvd Los Angeles CA 90010

BARBEE, JOE E., lawyer; b. Pharr, Tex., Feb. 27, 1934; s. Archie Allen and Concha (Leal) B.; m. Yolanda Margaret Atonna, Feb. 17, 1962; children—Cindy, Adam, Walter. B.S.E.E., U. Ariz., 1961; J.D., Western New Eng. Coll., 1973. Bar: Mass. 1973, U.S. Patent Office 1973, U.S. Ct. Appeals (fed. cir.) 1982. Engr. Gen. Electric Co., Pittsfield, Mass., 1961-73, patent atty., Fort Wayne, Ind., 1973-75; patent atty. Magnavox, Fort Wayne, 1975-76, Motorola, Inc., Phoenix, 1976—. Served to sgt. U.S. Army, 1953-56. Mem. ABA, Am. Patent Law Assn. Republican. Patent, Trademark and copyright. Home: 7611 N Mockingbird Ln Paradise Valley AZ 85253 Office: Motorola Inc 4250 E Camelback Rd Phoenix AZ 85018

BARBEOSCH, WILLIAM PETER, lawyer; b. N.Y.C., Nov. 25, 1954; s. Peter Joseph and Marie Delores (Slesiona) B.; m. Marta B. Varela, Sept. 6, 1986. AB magna cum laude, Brown U., 1976; JD, Columbia U., 1979. Bar: N.Y. 1980, U.S. Tax Ct. 1985. Assoc. Casey, Lane and Mittendorf, N.Y.C., 1979-82, Casey, Haythe and Krugman, N.Y.C., 1982-84, Haythe and Curley, N.Y.C., 1984-86, Milbank, Tweed, Hadley and McCloy, N.Y.C., 1986—. Mem. ABA, N.Y. State Bar Assn., Assn. of the Bar of City of N.Y., Phi Kappa Psi (sec. 1974-75). Republican. Roman Catholic. Club: Brown (N.Y.C.). Avocations: tennis, bridge. Probate, Estate taxation, Real property. Home: 878 West End Ave Apt 15C New York NY 10025 Office: Milbank Tweed Hadley and McCloy 1 Chase Manhattan Plaza New York NY 10025

BARBER, FRANK DAVID, lawyer; b. Hot Springs, Ark., Apr. 2, 1929; s. Frank David and Mary Margaret (Venus) B.; m. Sarah Frances McMullan, Dec. 23, 1953 (div. 1967); children—Amanda, Frank David, Melanie, Anabel, John Paul; m. Mary Jane Burch, Dec. 28, 1974; children—Mary Jane Burch, William Cameron. Student U. Miss., 1947-48, postgrad., 1954-55; B.A., U. So. Miss., 1954; J.D., George Washington U., 1957. Bar: Miss. 1958, D.C. 1958, U.S. Dist. Ct. D.C. (D.C. Circuit), 1958, U.S. Supreme Ct. 1978, U.S. Ct. Appeals (5th, 11th cirs.) 1981. Atty. Gen. Legis. Investigating Com., Jackson, Miss., 1958-59; mem. Miss. State Senate, Jackson, 1960-64; exec. asst. to gov. of Miss., Jackson, 1964-68; atty. Miss. Agr. and Indsl. Bd., Jackson, 1968-72; legis. asst. U.S. Sen. James O. Eastland, Washington, 1972-78; sole practice, Jackson, 1978—. Author: The Pursuit of Excellence: Summary of Administration of Governor Paul B. Johnson, 1968. Del. Dem. Nat. Conv., Los Angeles, 1960. Served with U.S. Army, 1948-49, 50-52. Recipient Project Cairo award Am. Assn. States and Local History, 1967. Mem. ABA, Miss. State Bar Assn., Fed. Bar Assn., Miss. Hist. Soc., Hinds County Bar Assn., Omicron Delta Kappa, Phi Alpha Delta, Sigma Nu, Pi Kappa Delta, Alpha Gamma Rho. Roman Catholic. Clubs: University, Capital City Petroleum (Jackson); Nat. Capital Democratic (Washington). Lodges: Masons, Royal Arch., Scottish Rite, York Rite. General practice, Administrative and regulatory, Legislative. Home: 4061 Roxbury Rd Jackson MS 39211 Office: 316 Heritage Bldg Congress at Capitol St Jackson MS 39201

BARBER, JANICE ANN, lawyer; b. Buffalo, May 30, 1947; d. Warren Richard and Betty A. (Stabler) B. BA with high distinction, U. Ky., 1969; JD cum laude, SUNY, Buffalo, 1977. Bar: N.Y. 1978, U.S. Dist. Ct. (we. dist.) N.Y. 1978. Reporter The Times-Union, Rochester, N.Y., 1969-74; assoc. Smith, Murphy & Schoepperle, Buffalo, 1977-84, ptnr., 1985—. Mem. N.Y. State Bar Assn., Erie County Bar Assn., Phi Beta Kappa, Alpha Lambda Delta. Democrat. Episcopalian. Personal injury, Insurance, State civil litigation. Home: 139 Woodward Ave Buffalo NY 14214 Office: Smith Murphy & Schoepperle 786 Ellicott Sq Buffalo NY 14203

BARBER, MONTY CLYDE, lawyer, cosmetice executive; b. Rockdale, Tex., Jan. 12, 1931; s. Clyde and Estelle (Montague) B.; m. Kay Wallace, June 29, 1963; children: Kelty Lynn, Brandon Chase. BBA, U. Tex., 1953, JD, 1955. Bar: Tex. 1957, U.S. Dist. Ct. (no. dist.) Tex. 1965. Ptnr. Biggers, Baker, Lloyd & Carver, Dallas, 1957-67; v.p., gen. counsel Liquid Paper Co., Dallas, 1967-68; exec. v.p., gen. counsel Mary Kay Cosmetics, Inc., Dallas, 1968—, also bd. dirs., sec.; mgr., trustee Mary Kay Found., Dallas, 1968—; vice chmn. Direct Selling Edn. Found., Washington, 1985-86. Served to sgt. U.S. Army, 1955-57. Mem. ABA, Tex. Bar Assn., Dallas Bar Assn., Am. Soc. Corp. Secs. Republican. General corporate, Public international, Pension, profit-sharing, and employee benefits. Office: Mary Kay Cosmetics Inc 8787 Stemmons Dallas TX 75247

BARBER, PERRY OSCAR, JR., lawyer; b. Ft. Worth, Aug. 23, 1938; s. Perry Oscar and Laura Lee (Spires) B.; m. Mary Diane Petrella, Oct. 4, 1975; children: Perry Oscar III, Caroline Killough; 1 dau. by previous marriage, Shelley Anne. B.B.A., U. Tex., 1960, J.D., 1963. Bar: Tex. 1963. Law clk. U.S. Ct. Appeals for 5th Circuit, Houston, 1963-64; staff asst. to Pres. of U.S., Washington, 1964-66; assoc. Baker & Botts, Houston and Washington, 1966-71; ptnr. Baker & Botts, 1972-77, 84—; gen. counsel, dir., mem. exec. com. Pennzoil Co., Houston, 1977-84. Mem. adv. bd. Internat. and Comparative Law Center, Southwestern Legal Found.; trustee Houston Legal Found., 1970-71; bd. dirs. Soc. Performing Arts, 1980-84; adv. dir. New Century Fund, U. Tex. Law Sch., 1974-75; mem. Harris County Democratic Exec. Com., 1972-73. Mem. ABA, Bar Assn., Am. Judicature Soc., Fed. Bar Assn., State Bar Tex., Tex. Bar Found., Houston Bar Found., Houston Bar Assn.; Council on Fgn. Relations, U. Tex. Law Sch. Assn. (dir. 1977-79). Methodist. Clubs: Ramada (Houston); Georgetown (Washington). Office: Baker & Botts 1701 Pennsylvania Ave NW Washington TX 20006

BARBER, ROBERT CUSHMAN, lawyer; b. Columbus, Ga., Aug. 30, 1950; s. Robert Kennard and Kathleen (Cushman) B.; m. Bonnie A. Neilan, Apr. 30, 1983; children: Nicholas, Benjamin. AB, Harvard U., 1972, M in City Planning, 1977; JD, Boston U., 1977. Bar: Mass. 1978, N.Y. 1978, U.S. Dist. Ct. Mass. 1981, U.S. Dist. Ct. (ea. and so. dist.) N.Y. 1981. Asst. dist. atty. N.Y. County, N.Y.C., 1977-81; assoc. Looney & Grossman, Boston, 1981-84, ptnr., 1985—; trial advisor Harvard Law Sch., 1985—. Mem. adv. com. Cambridge (Mass.) rezoning study, 1985-86; campaign chmn. com. for Francis Duehay for City Council, Cambridge, 1983-86. Mem. ABA, Mass. Bar Assn., Mass. Conveyancers Assn., Boston Bar Assn., Middlesex Bar Assn. Federal civil litigation, Computer, Real property. Office: Looney & Grossman 50 Congress St Boston MA 02109

BARBER, STEPHAN ALLEN, lawyer; b. San Jose, Calif., July 1, 1950; s. E. Allen and Carole E. (Andersen) B.; m. Lauren S. Haflinger, Oct. 8, 1983; one child. BA in Econs., U. Calif., 1972; JD, U. Pacific, 1976. Bar: Calif 1976, U.S. Dist. Ct. (no. dist.) Calif. 1976. Assoc. Popelka, Allard, et al, San Jose, 1976-80, ptnr., 1981-84; assoc. Ropers, Majeski, et al, San Jose, 1984-87; ptnr. Ropers, Majeski et al, San Jose, 1987—; judge pro temp Santa Clara County Superior Ct., 1984—. Mem. Santa Clara County Bar Assn., Assn. Def. Counsel, Nat. Assn. R.R. Trial Counsel. Republican. State civil litigation, Insurance, Personal injury. Office: Ropers Majeski Kohn Bentley Wagner & Kane 80 N First St Suite 300 San Jose CA 95113

BARBIN, RYTHER LYNN, lawyer; b. Port Arthur, Tex., July 15, 1943; s. L.B. and Edna Mae (Ryther) B.; m. Claire Kreger, June 19, 1970 (div.). BBA, Tex. Tech U., 1966; JD, Baylor U., 1968. Bar: Tex. 1968, Hawaii, 1976, U.S. Dist. Ct. Hawaii, 1976; lic. realtor, Hawaii. Law clk. U.S. Dept. Justice, Washington, 1967; officer trust dept. Bank of Am., San Francisco, 1968-71; officer Investors Bank & Trust Co., Boston, 1972-74; sole practice, Wailuku, Hawaii, 1974-82, 84—; ptnr. Barbin & Ball, Wailuku, 1982-84. Bd. dirs. Maui United Way, 1980-84, v.p., 1987-88; mem. sch. bd. Maui Dist. Sch., 1980-84; state del., dist. council Hawaii Dems., Wailuku, 1978-84; field rep. for U.S. senator Daniel K. Inouye; campaign mgr. Dem. Presdl. Campaigns Maui County, 1983; vice-chmn. Maui County Dem. Party, 1986—; bd. dirs. Maui Humane Soc., Maui Kokua Service. Recipient cert. of appreciation Gov. State of Hawaii, 1981. Mem. ABA, Hawaii Bar Assn. (bd. dirs.), Maui Bar Assn. (pres. 1984-86), Upcountry Jaycees Makawao (officer 1979-83). Episcopalian. Lodge: Rotary (pres. Wailuku club 1986-87). Bankruptcy, Family and matrimonial, Contracts commercial. Home: 57 Lino Pl Pukalani HI 96788 Office: 61 N Church St Wailuku HI 96793

BARBOUR, WILLIAMS H., JR., judge; b. 1941. B.A., Princeton U., 1963; J.D., U. Miss., 1966; postgrad., NYU, 1966. Bar.: Miss. Ptrn. firm Henry, Barbour & DeCell, Yazoo City, Miss., 1966-83; youth counselor Yazoo City, 1971-82; judge U.S. Dist. Ct. (so. dist.) Miss., 1983—. Office: US Dist Ct PO Box 2247 Jackson MS 39225 *

BARCELLA, ERNEST LAWRENCE, JR., lawyer; b. Washington, May 23, 1945; s. Ernest Lawrence and Louise Marion (Berniere) B.; m. Mary Elizabeth Lashley, June 1, 1970; 1 child, Laura Louise. AB, Dartmouth U., 1967; JD, Vanderbilt U., 1970. Bar: D.C. 1971, U.S. Dist. Ct. D.C. 1971, U.S. Ct. Appeals (D.C. cir.) 1971, U.S. Supreme Ct. 1976. Asst. U.S. atty. Washington, 1970-86; ptnr. Finley, Kumble, Wagner et al, Washington, 1986—. Recipient John Marshall award, U.S. Dept. Justice, 1983. Mem. ABA (white collar crime com. criminal justice sect.), Assn. Trial Lawyers Am., Fed. Bar Assn. (youger lawyer award, 1979). Roman Catholic. Criminal. Office: Finley Kumble Wagner et al 1140 Connecticut Ave NW Washington DC 20008

BARCELO, JOHN JAMES, III, law educator; b. New Orleans, Sept. 23, 1940; s. John James Jr. and Elfrieda Margaret (Bisso) B.; m. Lucy L. Wood, July 14, 1974; children—Lisa, Amy, Steven. B.A., Tulane U., 1962, J.D., 1966; S.J.D., Harvard U., 1977. Bar: La. 1967, D.C. 1974, U.S. Supreme Ct. 1974, N.Y. 1975. Fulbright scholar U. Bonn, Fed. Republic Germany, 1966-67; research assoc. Harvard U. Law Sch., Cambridge, Mass., 1968-69; prof. law Cornell U. Law Sch., Ithaca, N.Y., 1969—, A. Robert Noll. prof. of law, 1984—, dir internat. legal studies, 1972—; cons. Import Trade Adminstrn., Dept. Commerce. Author: (with others) Law: Its Nature, Functions and Limits, 3rd edit., 1986; contbr. articles to profl. jours. Mem. Am. Assn. for Comparative Study of Law (bd. dirs.), Am. Soc. Internat. Law, Maritime Law Assn. U.S. Private international, Public international, Admiralty. Office: Cornell Law Sch Ithaca NY 14853-4901

BARCLAY, H(UGH) DOUGLAS, lawyer, former state senator; b. N.Y.C., July 5, 1932; s. Hugh and Dorothy (Moody) B.; B.A., Yale U., 1955; J.D., Syracuse U., 1961; D.Sc., Clarkson U., Tech., 1981; LL.D., St. Lawrence U., 1985; m. Sara Seiter, Aug. 15, 1959; children—Kathryn D., David H., Dorothy G., Susan M., William A. Bar: N.Y. 1962; ptnr. firm Hiscock & Barclay, Syracuse, N.Y.; sec., gen. counsel Key Corps and subs., Albany, N.Y., 1971—; mem. N.Y. State Senate, 1965-84, chmn. Judiciary com., chmn. Select Task Force on Ct. Reogn.; dir., chmn. bd. Astradyne Computer Industries Inc., Syracuse Supply Co. Bd. dirs. Crouse Irving Meml. Found.; trustee, vice chmn. Syracuse U., Clarkson U.; overseer N.A. Rockefeller Inst. Govt. Served to lt. arty. U.S. Army, 1955-57; Korea. Mem. ABA, N.Y. State Bar Assn., N.Y. County Bar Assn. Office: Fin Plaza PO Box 4878 Syracuse NY 13221

BARD, STEPHEN ALLAN, lawyer; b. Mpls., Apr. 1, 1941; s. Joseph Leonard and Helen A. (Goldblatt) B.; children: Lisa Joy, Benjamin Adam, Joel Alexander. BA magna cum laude, U. Minn., 1962, LLB, 1965. Bar: Minn. 1965, U.S. Dist. Ct. Minn. 1965, U.S. Tax Ct. 1972, U.S. Ct. Appeals (8th cir.) 1982. Atty. GSA, Washington, 1966-68; ptnr. Nathanson, Bard & Levy, Mpls., 1969-80, Bard & BardLtd., Mpls., 1980—; arbitrator Minn. Pub. Employment Relations Bd., St. Paul, 1979—, Hennepin County Dist. Ct., Mpls., 1985—. Served with U.S. Army, 1966-72. Mem. ABA, Minn. Bar Assn., Hennepin County Bar Assn., Assn. Trial Lawyers Am., Minn. Trial Lawyers Assn., Phi Beta Kappa. Jewish. Avocations: skiing, golf, music, writing. State civil litigation, Family and matrimonial, Entertainment. Office: Bard & Bard Ltd 431 S 7th St Centre Village Suite 2415 Minneapolis MN 55415

BARDACK, PAUL ROITMAN, lawyer; b. N.Y.C., Nov. 13, 1953; s. Lawrence Stanley and Charlotte (Sebold) B.; m. Esther Roitman, May 27, 1979; 1 child, David. BA, Yale U., 1975; JD, Am. U., 1978. Bar: D.C. 1980. Gen. counsel to U.S. congressman Robert Garcia, Washington, 1978-81; assoc. atty. Barrett Smith Schapiro Simon & Armstrong, N.Y.C., 1981-83; mgr. econ. devel. dept. City of Cleve., 1983-84; chief exec. officer Econ. Devel. Resources, Inc., Washington, 1984-86; sr. policy advisor Gov. Thomas Kean, Trenton, N.J., 1986—; campaign adviser to various Rep. presdl. and congl. candidates, 1981—. Contbr. numerous articles on local econ. devel. to profl. jours. Mem. ABA (urban, state and local govt. law sect.), D.C. Bar Assn., Greater Phila. C. of C. (enterprise zones com.). Republican. Jewish. Local government, Venture capital, Economic development. Home: 111 The Gatehouse Andalusia PA 19020 Office: State House Trenton NJ 08625

BARDEN, KENNETH EUGENE, lawyer, educator; b. Espanola, N.Mex., Nov. 21, 1955; s. Lloyd C. and Beverly A. (Coverdale) B.; m. Janice Reece, 1986. B.A. cum laude, Ind. Central U., 1977; J.D., Ind. U., 1977; cert. Harvard U. Law Sch., 1983. Bar: Ind. 1981, U.S. Dist. Ct. (so. dist.) Ind. 1981, U.S. Tax Ct. 1983, U.S. Ct. Mil. Appeals 1983, U.S. Ct. Appeals (7th cir.) 1983, U.S. Ct. Internat. Trade 1983. Law clk. Marion County Prosecutor's Office, Ind., 1976-78, Krieg Devault Alexander & Capehart, Indpls., 1978-79; bailiff Marion County Mcpl. Ct. 7, 1979-81, commr.-judge pro tem, 1981; pub. defender criminal div. 1, Marion County Superior Ct., 1981; asst. to U.S. magistrate, U.S. Dist. Ct. (so. dist.) Ind. Indpls., 1982-84; city atty. City of Richmond, Ind., 1984—; corp. counsel Richmond Power and Light Co., 1984—; adj. prof. law Ind. Central U., Indpls., 1983. Nat. v.p. Coll. Democrats of Am., 1979-82; ward chmn. Marion County Dem. Party, 1977-81; precinct committeeman Wayne County Dem. Party, 1985—, treas. 2d dist. 1986— ; del. to NATO European Youth Leadership Conf., 1980; co-founder Hubert H. Humphrey Tng. Inst. for Campaign Politics, 1980; treas. Perry Twp. Dem. Club, 1980-83; alt. del. Dem. Nat. Conv., 1980; del. White House Forum on Domestic and Econ. Policy, 1975; del. Youth Conf. on Nat. Security and the Atlantic Alliance, Mt. Vernon Coll., Washington, 1976; mem. U.S. Youth Council under Pres. Carter, 1980; mem. Ind. Gov.'s Community Corrections Com., 1973-75; mem. adv. council Friends of the Battered, 1985—; mem. personnel policies forum Bur. Nat. Affairs, 1985—. Recipient Youth In Govt. award, Optimist Club, 1972. Mem. ABA (com. on industry regulation, Young lawyers div. labor law com., lawyers and arts com., chmn. town hall com. 1987—), Fed. Bar Assn., Ind. State Bar Assn., Indpls. Bar Assn., Wayne County Bar Assn., Ind. Council on World Affairs, Phi Alpha Delta, Epsilon Sigma Alpha, Alpha Phi Omega. Methodist. Clubs: Athenaeum (Indpls.): World Trade of Ind., Kiwanis. Local government, Family and matrimonial, Private international. Home: 426 S 23d St Richmond IN 47374 Office: 50 N 5th St Richmond IN 47374

BARDENWERPER, WILLIAM BURR, lawyer; b. Milw., Jan. 12, 1952; s. H. William and Dorothy W. B.; m. Gail Smith, Apr. 11, 1959. B.A., U. Va., 1974; J.D., U. Louisville, 1977. Bar: Ky. 1978, Wis. 1985, U.S. Dist. Ct. (western dist.) Ky. 1978. Assoc. Marlin M. Volz, Louisville, 1977-78; counsel, dir. intergovtl. affairs Jefferson County, Louisville, 1978-84; mem. Rice, Porter & Seiller, Attys., 1984—; chmn. operating co. Louisville Gardens. Vice chmn. bd. Wesley Community House. Cons. to ABA, 1980-85. Recipient Disting. Service award U. Louisville Sch. Law, 1977. Mem. ABA, Wis. Bar Assn., Ky Bar Assn., Louisville Bar Assn. (award of merit 1980). Republican. Episcopalian. Editor-in-chief Louisville Lawyer mag. General corporate, Entertainment, Local government. Home: 122 Southampton St Louisville KY 40223 Office: Rice Porter & Seiller 2200 Meidinger Tower Louisville KY 40202

BARDIN, DAVID J., lawyer; b. N.Y.C., June 2, 1933; s. Shlomo and Ruth (Jonas) B.; m. Livia Goldeen, Mar. 12, 1961; children—Jacob, Matthew, Joseph, Sarah. A.B., Columbia U., 1954, J.D., 1956. Bar: N.Y. 1956, D.C. 1966, Israel 1970. Atty., dep. gen. counsel FPC, Washington, 1958-69; asst. to atty. gen. Jerusalem, 1970-72; counsel Environ. Protection Service, Jerusalem, 1973; commr. N.J. Dept. Environ. Protection, Trenton, 1974-77; dep. adminstr. FEA, Washington, 1977; adminstr. Econ. Regulatory Adminstrn., Dept. Energy, Washington, 1977-80; counsel, ptnr. Arent, Fox, Kintner, Plotkin & Kahn, Washington, 1980—; lectr. law Bar-Ilan U., Tel Aviv U., U. Va. Extension. Co-author: AGA Select Gas Use Handbook; Natural Gas for Environmental Control, 1985. Served with U.S. Army, 1956-58. Mem. ABA, Fed. Bar Assn., Fed. Energy Bar Assn., Internat. Bar Assn., Am. Gas Assn.,. Democrat. Jewish. Club: Columbia U. (N.Y.C.). FERC practice, Environment, Energy. Office: 1050 Connecticut Ave NW Washington DC 20036-5339

BARDWELL, STANFORD O., JR., federal agency administrator; b. Baton Rouge, La., July 2, 1940; s. Stanford and Loyola Ann (Munson) B.; m. Leslie Kay Groves, Mar. 16, 1968; children: Brian, Patrick, Erin. B.S., La. State U., 1962, J.D., 1965. Bar: La. 1965, U.S. Supreme Ct. 1971. Instr. La. State U., Baton Rouge, 1970-72; asst. atty. gen. La. Dept. of Justice, Baton Rouge, 1970-74; sole practice Baton Rouge, 1969-81, U.S. atty., 1981-86; dep. gen. counsel U.S. Dept. Energy, Washington, 1986—. Bd dirs. Cancer Soc. Greater Baton Rouge, 1973-82; counselor, assoc. dir. La. Boys State and Girls State, 1957-79; mem. Govs. Commn. on Criminal Justice, 1981-82; chmn. East Baton Rouge Parish Polit. Action Council, 1975-77; east Baton Rouge Parish chmn. Ford/Dole Campaign, 1976; La. chmn. ballot security Reagan/Bush Campaign, 1980; mem. La. Del. Selection Procedure Com. for 1980 Rep. Nat. Conv.; chmn. rules com. Rep. State Central Com., 1980-81. chmn. Charter Rev. Com. La. Rep. Political Action Council, 1980-81. Served to capt. USAF, 1965-69. Mem. Baton Rouge Bar Assn., La. Bar Assn., Com. on Bar Admissions (asst. examiner 1976-82), Baton Rouge C. of C. (govtl. affairs com.). Roman Catholic. Avocations: swimming; reading. Civil litigation, Bankruptcy, Real property. Home: 514 Council Ct Vienna VA 22180 Office: US Dept Energy 1000 Independence Ave SW Washington DC 20585 *

BARE, JOSEPH EDWARD, lawyer; b. Jackson, Miss., Dec. 27, 1923; s. Joseph Edward and Marguerite (Thompson) B.; m. Meta Rose Bramer, Dec. 25, 1947; children: Marguerite, David, James, John, Robert. B.A., U. Rochester, 1947; J.D., Harvard U., 1950. Bar: Calif. 1953. Atty. U.S. High Commn. Germany, Frankfurt, 1950-51, Bad Godesberg, 1951-53; assoc. firm Pillsbury, Madison & Sutro, San Francisco, 1953-63, ptnr., 1963-67, 70—; v.p. Chevron Oil Europe, Inc., N.Y.C., 1967-70. Served with AC U.S. Army, 1942-46. Mem. ABA, State Bar Calif., Bar Assn. San Francisco, Phi Beta Kappa. Clubs: Mill Valley Tennis; Stock Exchange (San Francisco). Office: Pillsbury Madison & Sutro 225 Bush St San Francisco CA 94104

BARHAM, CHARLES DEWEY, JR., electric utility executive, lawyer; b. Goldsboro, N.C., July 7, 1930; s. Charles Dewey and Helen Wilkinson (Douglass) Barham Hughes; m. Margaret Wright Crow, June 17, 1960; children: Margaret Douglass, Charles Dewey III. B.S., Wake Forest U., 1952, J.D., 1954. Bar: N.C. 1954. Asst. atty. gen. N.C. Dept. Justice, Raleigh, 1958-66; assoc. gen. counsel Carolina Power & Light Co., Raleigh, N.C., 1966-73; ptnr. Douglass & Barham, Raleigh, 1974-80; v.p., sr. counsel Carolina Power & Light Co., Raleigh, 1981-82, sr. v.p., gen. counsel, 1982—; chmn. bd., pres. Nuclear Mut., Ltd., Hamilton, Bermuda, 1981-86 , dir.; gen. counsel World Nuclear Fuel Market, Atlanta, 1974-80, Meredith Coll., Raleigh, 1977-80. Pres. Raleigh YMCA, 1982—. Served to capt. USNR, 1955-77. Mem. ABA, N.C. Bar Assn., Fed. Energy Bar Assn. Democrat. Baptist. Clubs: Raleigh Civitan (dir. 1974-77), Glen Forest (pres. 1977). General corporate. Office: Carolina Power & Light Co PO Box 1551 Raleigh NC 27602

BARILLA, FRANK (ROCKY), lawyer, consultant, educator; b. Los Angeles, Jan. 26, 1948; s. Bruno Frank and Lucera (Campos) B. Student Glendale Coll., 1966-68; B.A., U. So. Calif., 1970, J.D., 1975; M.B.A., Stanford U., 1972. Bar: Calif. 1975, Oreg. 1976, U.S. Dist. Ct. (no. dist.) Calif. 1976, U.S. Dist. Ct. Oreg. 1976, U.S. Ct. Appeals (9th cir.) 1977. Adj. asst. prof. immigration law Sch. Law, U. Oreg., Eugene, 1976—; adj. asst. prof. Willamette U., Salem, Oreg., 1979, 83, 86—; instr. bus. law Linfield Coll., McMinnville, Oreg., 1983; adminstr. labor and edn. com. Oreg. Legislature, Salem, 1979, 81, 83, legal counsel joint judiciary com., 1984-86, legislator, state rep. Oreg. Legis. Assembly, 1986—; cons. Interface Cons., Portland, Oreg., 1981-84; hearings officer Oreg. Employment Div., Salem, 1982-83; adj. instr. Lewis and Clark Law Sch., Portland, Oreg., 1977, 80; cons. in field; vice chmn. Housing and Urban Devel. Com., mem. various other coms. Oreg. State Legislature; bd. dirs. La Alianza Legal de Oregon, 1983—. Author tng. manual Enabling Legislation for Multicultural Education, 1981. Mem. Salem Pub. Schs. Affirmative Action, 1976-78; chmn. Salem Chpt. Hispanic Polit. Action Com., 1983-84; bd. dirs. Oreg. Soccer Assn., Salem, 1978, United Way, Portland, 1980. Recipient Civil Liberties award Oreg. chpt. ACLU, 1984. Calif. State fellow/scholar, 1968-72; fellow Merrill Trust, 1970-72, Council Grad. Mgmt. Edn., 1970-72, Kellogg Found., 1981-82. Mem. Oreg. State Bar (com. on affirmative action 1978-80, com. on fgn. and internat. law 1980-83, com. on legal aid 1983—), Calif. State Bar, Marion County Bar Assn. Legal education, Immigration, naturalization, and customs, Civil rights. Home: 1113 Waller SE Salem OR 97302 Office: State Capitol Room 1-1471 Salem OR 97310

BARIS, JAY G., lawyer; b. N.Y.C., Jan. 29, 1954; s. Philip and Shelley (Glaser) B.; m. Carole Gould, Oct. 12, 1980; 1 child, Sam Gould. BA, SUNY, Stony Brook, 1975; JD, Hofstra U., 1978. Bar: N.Y. 1979, U.S. Dist. Ct. (so. and ea. dists.) N.Y. 1979, U.S. Dist. Ct. N.J. 1979, N.J. 1984, U.S. Ct. Appeals (2d cir.) 1984, U.S. Supreme Ct. 1984. Assoc. West Pub. Co., Mineola, N.Y., 1978-80, Buckley, Kremer, Mineola, 1980-82; atty. 1st Investors Corp., N.Y.C., 1982—; sec., counsel 1st Fin. Savs., Woodbridge, N.J., 1985—. Contbr. articles to profl. jours. Mem. ABA, N.Y. State Bar Assn., N.J. Bar Assn., Phi Beta Kappa. Securities, Banking, General corporate.

BARISH, GEORGE, lawyer, developer, record producer, lecturer, writer; b. Outwood, Ky., Aug. 11, 1938; s. Samuel Shep and Ruth B.; m. Edith Garfinkle, Aug. 19, 1962; m. 2d Sheila Marchant, Sept. 12, 1975; children—Marilyn Jean, Robert William. B.B.A., U. Miami, 1960, J.D., 1963. Bar: Fla. 1963. Assoc. John V. Christie, Miami, 1963-65; sole practice, Miami, 1965—; pres. Planetary Prodns. Inc., Miami. Exec. producer sound recording Planetary Person. Recipient Disting. Service award S.W. Miami Jaycees, 1966, Senator, Jaycees Internat. Mem. Fla. Bar, Dade County Bar

Assn., U. Miami Band Alumni (pres. 1964-65), Greater Miami Community Concert Band (dir. 1980-81). Real property, Workers' compensation. Address: 9020 SW 140th St Miami FL 33176

BARIST, JEFFREY, lawyer; b. Jersey City, Dec. 29, 1941; s. Irving and Lillian (Finkelstein) B.; m. Joan Travers, Feb. 19, 1967; children: Jessica, Alexis. AB, Rutgers U., 1963; JD, Harvard U., 1966. Bar: N.Y. 1967, U.S. Ct. Appeals (2d cir.) 1968, U.S. Dist. Ct. (so. dist.) N.Y. 1969, U.S. Supreme Ct. 1975. Ptnr. White & Case, N.Y.C., 1974—. Fellow Am. Coll. Trial Lawyers. Federal civil litigation, Private international. Office: White & Case 1155 Ave of Americas New York NY 10036

BARKAI, JOHN LEE, legal educator; b. Detroit, July 11, 1945; s. John and Livia (Fanchini) B. BBA, U. Mich., 1968, MBA, 1969, JD, 1971. Bar: Mich. 1972, Calif. 1973, Hawaii 1978. Trial atty. State of Mich. Defenders Office, Detroit, 1972-73; assoc. prof. Wayne State U., Detroit, 1973-78; prof. U. Hawaii, Honolulu, 1978—; cons. judiciary Federated States of Micronesia, 1983-85. Pres., bd. dirs. Legal Aid Soc. of Hawaii, 1984-85. Legal education, State civil litigation, Criminal. Home: 4433 Sierra Dr Honolulu HI 96816 Office: U Hawaii Law Sch 2515 Dole Honolulu HI 96822

BARKAN, LEONARD, lawyer; b. Phila., June 2, 1926; s. Isreal Barkan and Esther (Lieberman) Gurowitz; m. Estelle Katz, Aug. 15, 1955; children: June, Lorna, Justine, Irene. BS, Temple U., 1949; JD, U. Pa., 1953. Sole practice Phila., 1953-66; v.p. Strick Corp., Fairless Hills, Pa., 1965—; legal asst. Pa. Ct. Common Pleas, Phila., 1953-66; prof. U. Pa., Phila., 1955-59. Thomsa Skelton Harrison Found. grantee. Jewish. General corporate. Home: Spencer Rd and Glenwood Dr Washington Crossing PA 18977 Office: Strick Corp 225 Lincoln Hwy Fairless Hills PA 19030

BARKER, CHARLES THOMAS, lawyer; b. Pitts., Aug. 13, 1946; s. Harry Heintz and Dorothy Marie (Johns) B.; m. Nancy L. Loeckel, June 17, 1966 (div. 1970); m. Hannelore M. Ickert, Sept. 28, 1974; children: Lisa Ann, Lindsay Marie. Student, Wittenburg U., 1965; BA in Polit. Sci., Ohio State U., 1972; postgrad., Ohio No. U., 1977-78; JD cum laude, U. Miami, 1979. Bar: Fla. 1979, U.S. Dist. Ct. (so. dist.) Fla. 1980, U.S. Tax Ct. 1980, U.S. Ct. Appeals (5th cir.) 1980, U.S. Ct. Appeals (11th cir.) 1981. Account exec. Mansfield (Ohio) News Jour., 1973-76; assoc. Lavalle & Wochna, Boca Raton, Fla., 1979-80, Buchanan & Ingersol P.C., Boca Raton, 1980-84; ptnr. Hodgson, Russ, Andrews, Woods & Goodyear, Boca Raton, 1984—; bd. dirs. WXEL-TV and Radio, Palm Beach, Fla. Mem. Boca Raton Zoning Bd. Adjustment, 1986—. Mem. ABA, Fla. Bar Assn. Palm Beach Bar Assn., South Palm Beach Bar Assn. (bd. dirs. 1982—, editor newsletter, 1983—), Assn. Immigration Lawyers Am., Am. Arbitration Assn. (arbitrator), Boca Raton Bd. Realtors (bd. dirs. realtor accord com. 1981-83, cert. recognition 1981-83), Attys. Title Ins. Fund, Am. Fedn. Musicians, Soc. Wig and Robe, Boca Raton C. of C. (participant Leadership Boca Raton 1985). Presbyterian. Avocations: music, reading, swimming. Real property, Securities, Immigration, naturalization, and customs. Home: 135 NE Olive Way Boca Raton FL 33432 Office: Hodgson Russ Andrews Woods & Goodyear 2000 Glades Rd Suite 400 Boca Raton FL 33431

BARKER, J(OHN) EMERY, lawyer, judge pro tempore; b. Phoenix, Jan. 28, 1936; s. John Wiley and Eddyth (Gallogly) B.; m. Jacqueline Jean Creecy, June 3, 1956; children—Mark, Craig, Susan, Brett. B.A., U. Ariz., 1957, J.D., 1960. Bar: Ariz. 1960, U.S. dist. ct. Ariz. 1960, U.S. Tax Ct. 1974, U.S. Ct. Appeals (9th cir.) 1968, U.S. Supreme Ct. 1971. Assoc. Merchant, Parkman, Miller & Pitt, 1960-63; sole practice, 1963-65; ptnr. Odgers & Barker, 1965-70; sole practice, Tucson, 1970—; ptnr. Mesch, Clark & Rothschild, P.C.; spl. superior ct. commr., 1977-80; judge pro tem superior ct. appeals, 1981-86; pres. Pima County Legal Aid Soc., 1969-71; mem. Ariz. Legal Service Adv. Comm., 1976, Ariz. Commn. Jud. Qualifications, 1983-86. Pres. Met. YMCA of Tucson, 1978-80. Mem. Pima County Bar (pres. 1975-76), State Bar Ariz., ABA, Assn. Trial Lawyers Am., Ariz. Trial Lawyers, Phi Gamma Delta. Republican. Lutheran. Club: Rotary (Tucson). State civil litigation, Real property, Construction. Home: 6241 N Camino Santa Valera Tucson AZ 85718 Office: 259 N Meyer Tucson AZ 85701

BARKER, JOSEPH RANSOM, lawyer; b. Hardeeville, S.C., Oct. 5, 1946; s. Joseph Ransom and Allie Belle B.; m. Barbara Lassiter, Dec. 22, 1968; 1 dau., Lauren Leigh. B.A., U. S.C., 1968, J.D., 1973. Bar: S.C. 1973, U.S. Dist. Ct. S.C. 1973, U.S. Ct. Appeals (4th cir.) 1983. Sr. asst. atty. gen. S.C. Atty. Gen.'s Office, Columbia, 1974-79; asst. legal counsel U.S. Senate Com. on Judiciary, Washington, 1980; assoc. Bethea, Jordan & Griffin, P.A., Hilton Head Island, S.C., 1981-83, ptnr., 1983—. Mem. Beaufort County Bar Assn., S.C. State Bar, ABA, S.C. Trial Lawyers Assn., Assn. Trial Lawyers Am. State civil litigation, Personal injury, Criminal. Home: 23 Brown Thrasher Hilton Head Island SC 29928 Office: Bethea Jordan & Griffin PA 23-B Shelter Cove Ln PO Box 5666 Hilton Head Island SC 29928

BARKETT, ROSEMARY, justice; b. Ciudad Victoria, Tamps, Mex., Aug. 29, 1939; came to U.S., 1958; BS summa cum laude, Spring Hill Coll., 1967; JD, U. Fla., 1970. Bar: Fla., U.S. Dist. Ct. (so. dist.) Fla., U.S. Ct. Appeals (5th cir.), U.S. Supreme Ct. Sole practice 1971-79; judge 15th Jud. Cir. Ct., Palm Beach County, Fla., 1979-84, 4th Dist. Ct. Appeal, West Palm Beach, Fla., 1984-85; justice Supreme Ct. Fla., Tallahassee, 1985—; mem. faculty U. Nev., Reno, Fla. Jud. Coll.; former mem. sentencing guidelines commn. State of Fla., Statewide Prosecution Function Commn., Consumer Affairs Hearing Bd., Palm Beach County. Mem. editorial bd. The Florida Judges Manual. Former mem. Mental Health Bd. No. 9, Inc., Palm Beach County, Palm Beach County Adult Corrections Research and Evaluation Steering Com. Recipient Woman of Achievement award Palm Beach County Commn. on Status of Women, 1985. Fellow Acad. Matrimonial Lawyers; mem. Fla. Bar Assn. (family law sect., com. on civil procedure, com. on appellate rules, lectr. on matrimonial media and criminal law continuing legal edn.), Palm Beach County Bar Assn. (com. on needs of children, Hispanic Affairs com.), Assn. Trial Lawyers Am. (Jud. Achievement award 1986), Am. Acad. Matrimonial Lawyers (award 1984), Fla. Assn. Women Lawyers (Palm Beach chpt.), Nat. Assn. Women Judges, Palm Beach Marine Inst. (former chairperson, bd. trustees). Named to Fla. Women's Hall of Fame, 1986. Office: Supreme Ct Fla Supreme Ct Bldg Tallahassee FL 32301

BARKLEY, BRIAN EVAN, lawyer, political consultant; b. Teaneck, N.J., Jan. 30, 1945; s. Henry E. and Alice M. (Schultz) B.; m. Pamela A. Martin, May 5, 1979; 1 child, Leigh Elizabeth, Mar. 3, 1986. B.A., U. Md., 1967; J.D. with honors, George Washington U., 1970. Bar: Md. 1970, D.C. 1976, U.S. Dist. Ct. Md. 1973. Assoc., Everngam & Goldstein, Silver Spring, Md., 1970-72; sole practice, Silver Spring, 1972-80, Rockville, Md., 1980—; spl. asst. Rep. Michael Barnes, Washington, 1981-84; ptnr. Barkley and Kennedy, Chartered 1987—. Vice chmn. Nat. Capital chpt. Nat. Multiple Sclerosis Com., Washington, 1980-84; chmn. Montgomery County Multiple Sclerosis Com., Rockville, Md., 1980; campaign mgr. Barnes for Congress, Rockville, 1980, campaign chmn., 1982-84. Mem. Montgomery County Bar Assn. Democrat. Methodist. Club: Bethesda Country (Md.). Lodge: Masons. Bankruptcy, Family and matrimonial, State civil litigation. Home: 1202 Azalea Dr Rockville MD 20850 Office: 51 Monroe St Suite 1407 Rockville MD 20850

BARKLEY, THIERRY VINCENT, lawyer; b. Paris, Mar. 21, 1955; s. Jacques and Michéline Marié (Rossi) B.; came to U.S., 1967, naturalized, 1974; m. Mary Ellen Gamble, June 18, 1983; children: Richard A., Robert V. B.A. in Polit. Sci., UCLA, 1976; J.D., Calif. Western Sch. Law, San Diego, 1979. Bar: Nev. 1980, U.S. Dist. Ct. Nev. 1982, U.S. Supreme Ct. 1986. Intern, Calif. Ct. Appeals 4th Circuit, San Diego, 1978-79; law clk. Nev. Dist. Ct., 7th Jud. Dist., Ely, 1979-81; assoc. firm C.E. Horton, Ely, 1982-83; asst. city atty. Ely, 1982-83; assoc. firm Barker, Gillock & Perry, Reno, 1983—. Assoc. editor Internat. Law Jour., 1979. Mem. Internat. Moot Ct. Team, 1978; recipient Dean's award Calif. Western Sch. Law, 1979. Mem. ABA, Nev. Bar Assn., Washoe Bar Assn., U.S. Jaycees (past pres. White Pine, Nev.). Republican. Roman Catholic. Lodge: Elks (past treas. Ely club). Federal civil litigation, State civil litigation, Insurance. Office: Barker Gillock Perry Koning & Spann 620 Humboldt St Reno NV 89509

BARKMAN, JON ALBERT, lawyer; b. Somerset, Pa., Oct. 8, 1947; s. Blair Albert and Billie (Dietz) B.; m. Annette E. Shaulis, Dec. 1, 1983. B.A., Washington and Jefferson U., 1969; J.D., Duquesne U., 1975. Bar: Pa. 1975, U.S. Dist. Ct. (we. dist.) Pa. 1975, U.S. Supreme Ct. 1984. Mem. claims dept. Liberty Mut. Ins. Co., Pitts., 1969-71; dist. justice Commonwealth of Pa., Somerset, 1973—; sole practice, Somerset, 1975—. Advisor Com. Against Sexual Assault, Somerset, Pa., 1984. Mem. ABA, Assn. Trial Lawyers Am., Pa. Bar Assn., Pa. Trial Lawyers Assn., Somerset County Bar Assn., Allegheny County Bar Assn. Republican. Methodist. Lodges: Elks, Moose, Rotary. General practice, Personal injury, State civil litigation. Home: RD #8 Somerset PA 15501 Office: 118 N Center Ave Suite 2 Somerset PA 15501

BARKOFSKE, FRANCIS LEE, lawyer, coal company executive; b. Kansas City, Mo., Feb. 4, 1939; s. Francis and Mildred (Wagner) B.; m. Mary Anne Potts, Apr. 4, 1964; children—Peter, John, Paul, Anne. A.B., Rockhurst Coll., 1960; LL.B., St. Louis U., 1963. Bar: Mo. bar 1963, D.C. bar 1973. Asso., then partner firm Keefe, Schlafly, Griesedieck & Ferrell, St. Louis, 1963-72; atty. Mo. Pacific Corp., St. Louis, 1972-79; corp. sec. Mo. Pacific Corp., 1975-79; asst. gen. counsel Mo. Pacific R.R. Co., St. Louis, 1979-80; sr. v.p. legal and pub. affairs Peabody Coal Co., St. Louis, 1980-82; sr. v.p. legal and pub. affairs, sec. Peabody Holding Co., St. Louis, 1983—. Mem. Am., Fed. Energy bar assns., Mo. Bar, Bar. Assn. Met. St. Louis, Am. Soc. Corp. Secs. Roman Catholic. Clubs: Racquet, Noonday. General corporate, Administrative and regulatory, General practice. Office: Peabody Holding Co Inc 301 N Memorial Dr Saint Louis MO 63166

BAR-LEVAV, DORON MORDECAI, lawyer; b. Detroit, May 28, 1954; s. Reuven Bar-Levav and Sylvia (Savin) Iwrey; m. Sandra Gonzalez, June 13, 1982. Bar: N.Y. 1980. Assoc. Brown & Wood, N.Y.C., 1979-87, Donavan, Leisure, Newton & Irvine, N.Y.C., 1987—. Mem. ABA, N.Y. State Bar Assn., Nation Assn. of Bond Lawyers. Avocations: playing and composing music, bridge, wine, racquetball. Municipal bonds, Securities. Home: 154 DeKalb Ave Brooklyn NY 11217 Office: Donavan Leisure Newton & Irvine 1 World Trade Center 30 Rockefeller Ctr New York NY 10019

BARLEY, JOHN ALVIN, lawyer; b. Jacksonville, Fla., Oct. 16, 1940; s. Lewis Alvin Barley and Catherine Alberta (Curran) McKendree; m. Mary Freida Szarowicz, Nov. 30, 1974; children: Jared Scott, Jessica Lauren. BS, Fla. State U., 1963; JD, U. Fla., 1968. Bar: Fla. 1969, U.S. Dist. Ct. (mid. and no. dists.) Fla. 1973, U.S. Ct. Appeals (5th and 11th cirs.) 1973, U.S. Supreme Ct. 1973. Law clk. to presiding justice U.S. Dist. Ct. (so. dist.), Miami, Fla., 1968-69; exec. asst. to Hon. Ray C. Osborne Lt. Gov. Fla., Tallahassee, 1969-70; asst. dir. div. of labor U.S. Dept. of Commerce, Tallahassee, 1971; assoc. Maquire, Voorhis & Wells, Orlando, Fla., 1972-73; asst. atty. gen. Dept. of Legal Affairs, Tallahassee, 1974-75; gen. counsel Dept. of Gen. Services, Tallahassee, 1976-78; sole practice Tallahassee, 1978—. Mem. ABA (litigation sect., pub. contract sect., corp., banking and bus. law sect.), Fla. Bar Assn. (trial lawyers sect., adminstrv. law sect., bd. of govs. young lawyers 1974, rules of civil procedure com. 1974—), Tallahassee Bar Assn., Am. Judicature Soc., Tallahassee C. of C., Phi Delta Phi. Roman Catholic. Avocations: camping, hunting, fishing, swimming, running. Construction, State civil litigation, Contracts commercial. Home: 4927 Heathe Dr Tallahassee FL 32308 Office: 400 N Meridian St PO Box 1016632301 Tallahassee FL 32302

BARLINE, JOHN, lawyer; b. Tacoma, Dec. 29, 1946; s. John Dean Barline and Jane (Greiwe) Moosey; m. Sally Harris, Oct. 21, 1984. B.A., Netherland Sch. Internat. Bus., Breukelen, 1968; B.A., U. Puget Sound, 1969; J.D., Willamette U., 1972; LL.M. in Taxation, NYU, 1973. Bar: Wash. 1972, U.S. Dist. Ct. (we. dist.) Wash. 1974. Ptnr., Dolack, Hansler, et al, Tacoma, 1973-85, ptnr. Williams, Kastner & Gibbs, Tacoma, 1985—. Bd. dirs., treas. Bldg. a Scholastic Heritage, Tacoma, 1980-85; bd. dirs., chmn. Bellarmine Prep. Sch., 1981—; bd. dirs. Tacoma Community Coll. Found. Named among Leaders of Tomorrow, Time Mag., 1983. Mem. Wash. State Bar (com. mem.), Pierce County Bar Assn., ABA, U. Puget Sound Alumni Assn. (bd. dir. 1984). Republican. Roman Catholic. Clubs: Tacoma, Tacoma Yacht (bd. dirs. 1978-80), Tacoma Country and Golf. Lodge: Elks. Probate, Corporate taxation, General practice. Office: Williams Kastner & Gibbs 1000 Financial Ctr 1145 Broadway Tacoma WA 98402

BARLOW, DONALD EUGENE, lawyer; b. Odessa, Tex., June 12, 1947; s. A.K. Barlow and Virginia Ruth (Thomas) B.; divorced; children: Lesley Clair, Benjamin Paul. BA, U. Tex., 1969, JD, 1972; MBA, So. Meth. U., 1973. Bar: Tex. 1972. Comml. mgr. Southwestern Bell Telephone Co., Odessa, 1973-75, Austin, Tex., 1975-78; gen. counsel Perry Gas Cos., Inc., Odessa, 1978-80, pres., 1980-82; v.p., gen. counsel Capitan Enterprises, Inc., Odessa, 1983—. Bd. dirs. First United Meth. Ch., Odessa. Named Outstanding Dir. Odessa Jaycees 1975, Outstanding Officer Odessa Jaycees 1975, Outstanding Rookie Odessa Jaycees, 1975. Mem. ABA, Tex. Bar Assn., Ector County Bar Assn., C. of C. (bd. dirs. Odessa). Lodge: Rotary (Odessa chpt. dir. 1985—). General corporate, Contracts commercial, Oil and gas leasing. Home: 2719 Pagewood Odessa TX 79762 Office: Capitan Engerprises Inc PO Box 6967 Odessa TX 79762

BARLOW, W. P., JR., lawyer; b. Washington, July 29, 1945; s. W.P. and Elaine Virginia (Zweifel) B.; m. Kathryn L. Prescott, June 13, 1977; children: Ashley Prescott, Matthew Wallace. BA, U. Wis., 1967; JD, Marquette U., 1970. Bar: Wis. 1970, Tex. 1981, U.S. Ct. Appeals (5th, 7th, 11th cirs.) 1971, U.S. Dist. Ct. (ea. and we. dists.) Wis. 1970, U.S. Dist. Ct. (no. and so. dists.) Tex. 1981. Assoc., Ames, Riordan, Crivello & Sullivan, Milw., 1970-74; sr. ptnr. Barlow, Russo & Felker, Milw., 1974-78, Dallas, 1978-83; sr. ptnr. Barlow & Lippe, Dallas, 1983-84; pres. W.P. Barlow Jr., P.C., Dallas, 1984—; chmn. bd. dirs. 1st Savs. & Loan, Burkburnett, Tex. Mem. Fellowship of Christian Athletes, Friends Pub. Library, Dallas, 1983—; bd. dirs. Tex. Spl. Olympics, Austin, 1984—. Served to lt. comdr. USN, 1971-74. Recipient Most Disting. Vol. award Tex. Spl. Olympics, 1986. Fellow Sequoyah, Am. Indian Sci. and Engring. Soc.; mem. ABA, Fed. Bar Assn., Assn. Trial Lawyers Am., Tex. Trial Lawyers Assn., Tex. Bar Assn., Dallas Bar Assn., Dallas Trial Lawyers Assn., Houston Bar Assn., Houston Trial Lawyers Assn., Nat. Interfraternity Conf. (bd. dirs. 1985—), Sigma Tau Gamma (dir. 1972-84, pres. 1978-80, Ellsworth C. Dent award 1967), Sigma Tau Gamma Found. (dir., pres. 1984—, Wilson C. Morris award 1982, Marvin M. Millsap award 1983), Delta Theta Phi, Alpha Epsilon Rho. Clubs: Lincoln City, Energy. Legislative, Administrative and regulatory, Banking. Home: 9502 Bill Browne Ln Dallas TX 75243 Office: 8080 N Central Expressway 13th Floor Lock Box 13 Dallas TX 75206

BARNARD, GEORGE SMITH, lawyer, former IRS official; b. Opelika, Ala.; s. George Smith and Caroline Elizabeth (Dowdell) B.; m. Muriel Elaine Outlaw, July 26, 1945; children—Elizabeth Elaine, Charles Dowling, Beverly Laura Barnard Parker, Andrew Carey. B.A., U. Ala., 1948, LL.B., 1950. Bar: Fla. 1978, Ala. 1950, U.S. Tax Ct. 1950, U.S. dist. ct. Ala. 1950, Fla. 1978, U.S. Supreme Ct. 1965, U.S. Ct. Claims 1979 U.S. Ct. Appeals (Fed. cir.) 1984, U.S. Ct. Appeals (11th cir.) 1985. Sole practice, Opelika, 1950-51; with IRS, 1951-78; attache, revenue service rep., Sao Paulo Brazil, 1965-71, Mexico City, 1971-77; ptnr. Barnard, P.A., Miami, Fla., 1978—; lectr. taxation U. Ala., 1958-60. Pres. Rocky Ridge Vol. Fire Dept., 1956-58, Rocky Ridge Civic Club, 1959, Ala. chpt. Nat. Assn. Internal Revenue Employees, 1962; commr. Rocky Ridge Civic Water Works, 1960-62. Served in USAAF, 1942-46. Recipient Albert Gallatin award U.S. Treasury Dept., 1978; named Hon. Citizen of Tex., 1979, Hon. Admiral in Tex. Navy, 1979. Mem. Kappa Sigma. Republican. Personal income taxation, Estate taxation, Private international. Home: 2761 SE 9th St Pompano Isles Pompano Beach FL 33062 Office: Barnard PA 9769 S Dixie Hwy Miami FL 33156

BARNARD, HOLLINGER FARMER, lawyer; b. Troy, Ala., Mar. 17, 1943; d. Curren Adams and Margaret Downer (Pace) Farmer; m. William Dean Barnard, Dec. 21, 1964; children: William Harrison II, Margaret Pace, Joshua Bates. BA, Birmingham So. Coll., 1965; MEd, U. Va., 1967; JD, U. Ala., 1982. Bar: Ala. 1982, U.S. Dist. Ct. (no. dist.) Ala. 1983. Law clk. to chief judge U.S. Dist. Ct. (no. dist.) Ala., Birmingham, 1982-83; assoc. Johnston, Barton, Proctor, Swedlaw & Naff, Birmingham, 1983—; lectr. various student and media groups, Birmingham, 1983—. Editor: Outside the Magic Circle—The Autobiography of Virginia Foster Durr, 1985; contbr. Ala. Law Rev., 1981. Founding mem. The Progressive Alliance, Inc., Birmingham, 1985—. Mem. ABA, Ala. Bar Assn., Birmingham Bar Assn., Order of Coif, Phi Beta Kappa. Democrat. Methodist. Avocations: tennis, house repairs, gardening, reading. Libel, Federal civil litigation, State civil litigation. Home: 4324 Overlook Rd Birmingham AL 35222 Office: Johnston Barton et al 1100 Park Place Tower Birmingham AL 35203

BARNARD, ROBERT C., lawyer; b. 1913; s. Robert C. and Elsie (Francis) B.; m. Helen Hurd, Dec. 25, 1939; children—Robert Christopher, Mary Anne. B.A., Reed Coll., 1935; postgrad. Columbia U. Law Sch. 1935-36; B.A., Oxford (Eng.) U., 1938, B.C.L. (Rhodes scholar), 1939, M.A., 1951. Bar: Wash., 1940, D.C., 1947, U.S. Sup. Ct., 1943. Chief app. sect. antitrust div., chief legal adv. Office of Asst. Solicitor Gen., Dept. Justice, Washington, 1939-47; assoc. Cleary, Gottlieb, Steen & Hamilton, Washington, 1947-49, in charge Paris office, 1949-52, Washington, after 1952, sr. ptnr., 1961-84, counsel, 1984—. Mem. ABA, Fed. Bar Assn., D.C. Bar Assn., Wash. Bar Assn., Washington Inst. Fgn. Affairs. Clubs: Capitol Hill, Internat. Contbr. articles to profl. jours. Administrative and regulatory, Antitrust, Environment. Home: 5409 Dorset Ave Chevy Chase MD 20815 Office: 1752 N St NW Washington DC 20036

BARNES, DENNIS NORMAN, lawyer; b. Kingston, Pa., Feb. 10, 1940; s. Leslie Orland and Mary Whitney (Brown) B.; m. Ingrid Daubitz, Oct. 5, 1961; children: Richard, Kendra. AB, Dartmouth Coll., 1962; JD, Georgetown U., 1965. Bar: D.C. 1966, U.S. Ct. Appeals (D.C. cir.) 1966. Assoc. Morgan, Lewis & Bockius, Washington, 1970-75, ptnr., 1975—. Bd. dirs. Bucknell U. Parents Assn., Lewisburg, Pa., 1985. Served to capt. JAGC, U.S. Army, 1966-70. Mem. ABA, D.C. Bar Assn., Maritime Adminstrv. Bar Assn., Assn. Transportation Practitioners. Administrative and regulatory. Office: Morgan Lewis & Bockius 1800 M St SW Washington DC 20036

BARNES, DONALD KING, lawyer; b. N.Y., June 22, 1908; s. Edwin Allen and Maude (King) B.; m. Ruth Chadwick, June 1936 (dec. 1983); m. 2d, Libretta L. Reece, Jan. 1984. A.B., Harvard U., 1927; M.B.A., NYU, 1931; LL.B., Fordham U., 1938; S.J.D., St. Johns, 1940. Bar: N.Y. 1939, Mich. 1947, U.S. Dist. Ct. (so. dist.) N.Y. 1946, U.S. Dist. Ct. (ea. dist.) Mich. 1947, U.S. Ct. Appeals (6th and 8th cirs.) 1948, U.S. Customs Ct. 1948, U.S. Ct. Customs and Patent Appeals 1949, U.S. Tax Ct. 1940, U.S. Supreme Ct. 1950. Assoc. Bankers Trust Co., N.Y.C., 1927-42; assoc. Gen. Motors Corp., N.Y.C. and Detroit, 1946-73; sole practice pro bono, Pompano Beach, Fla., 1973—. Served as maj. U.S. Army, 1942-46. Mem. Detroit Bar Assn., Mich. Bar Assn., ABA, U.S. Power Squadrons. Republican. Clubs: Palm Yacht and Beach (Pompano Beach); Harvard (Eastern Mich., N.Y.C. and Broward County, Fla.); Coral Ridge Yacht (Ft. Lauderdale); Delray Beach (Fla.). Civil rights, General corporate, State and local taxation. Home: 26 Palm Club Pompano Beach FL 33062

BARNES, DONALD MICHAEL, lawyer; b. Hazleton, Pa., June 15, 1943; s. Donald A. and Margaret (Resuta) B.; m. Mary Catherine Gibbons, June 3, 1967; children: Donald M., Stephanie A., Susan E. BS in Indsl. Engring., Pa. State U., 1965; JD cum laude, George Washington U., 1970. Bar: D.C. 1970, U.S. Dist. Ct. D.C. 1970, U.S. Ct. Appeals (D.C. cir.) 1970, U.S. Supreme Ct. 1975, U.S. Ct. Appeals (5th cir.) 1975, U.S. Ct. Appeals (4th cir.) 1980, U.S. Ct. Appeals (8th cir.) 1981. Assoc. Arent, Fox, Kintner, Plotkin & Kahn, Washington, 1970-78; ptnr. Arent, Fox, Kintner, Plotkin & Kahn, 1978—. Notes editor George Washington Law Rev., 1969-70. Mem. ABA (crminial justice, antitrust, litigation and adminstrv. law sects.), Fed. Bar Assn., D.C. Bar Assn., Order of Coif, Phi Delta Phi. Antitrust, Federal civil litigation, Administrative and regulatory. Office: Arent Fox Kintner Plotkin & Kahn 1050 Connecticut Ave NW Washington DC 20036

BARNES, HERSCHIEL SEVIER, lawyer; b. Cookeville, Tenn., Dec. 19, 1919; s. Herschiel Sevier and Susan Gertrude (Tinnon) B.; m. Vivian Hicks, Dec. 22, 1950; children: Amy Barnes Walters, Joel, Thomas. Student, Tenn. Tech. U., 1936-39; BS, George Peabody Coll., 1940; JD, Vanderbilt U., 1948. Bar: Tenn. 1947, U.S. Dist. Ct. (mid. dist.) Tenn. 1948. Ptnr. Crawford & Barnes, Cookeville, 1949-71, Crawford, Barnes & Acuff, Cookeville, 1971-79, Barnes, Acuff & O'Mara, Cookeville, 1979-82, Barnes & Acuff, Cookeville, 1982—; atty. City of Cookeville, 1948-52; referee in bankruptcy U.S. Dist. Ct., 1954-54-58; bd. dirs. Citizens Bank, Cookeville. Editor in chief Vanderbilt U. Law Rev., 1947. Bd. dirs. Cookeville Gen. Hosp., 1962-72, chmn. 1968-72. Served with U.S. Army, 1941-45, ETO. Mem. ABA, Tenn. Bar Assn., Putnam County Bar Assn. (past pres.), Tenn. Bar Found., Order of Coif, VFW. Democrat. Methodist. Lodge: Lions (pres. Cookeville 1952—). Probate, Real property, General corporate. Home: 957 Sunset Dr Cookeville TN 38501 Office: Barnes & Acuff 101 S Jefferson Ave Cookeville TN 38501

BARNES, JAMES GARLAND, JR., lawyer; b. Ga., Mar. 3, 1940; s. James Garland Sr. and Carolyn L. (Stewart) B.; m. Lucy Curtis Ferguson, Nov. 1976; children—Susan Whitney, David Lawrence, Matthew Martin. B.A., Yale U., 1961; LL.B., U. Mich., 1966. Bar: Ill. 1967. With firm Baker & McKenzie, Chgo., 1966—, ptnr., 1973—. Mem. adv. com. Ill. Sec. of State's Corp. Acts, 1981. Mem. ABA, Ill. Bar Assn. (chmn. corp. and security law sect. 1977-78), Chgo. Bar Assn. (chmn. corp. law com. 1982-83, chmn. profl. responsibility com. 1983-84), Legal Club Chgo. Contracts commercial, General corporate, Private international. Office: Baker & McKenzie Suite 2800 Prudential Plaza Chicago IL 60601

BARNES, JOHN BREASTED, lawyer; b. Peoria, Ill., Sept. 17, 1926; s. George Zebulon and Mary (Fitzgerald) B.; divorced; children, John N., Rachel. AB, Harvard U., 1949, LLB, 1952. Bar: Calif. 1981. Sr. mng. counsel Wells Fargo Bank, San Francisco, 1954-82; sole practice San Francisco, 1983—; sec., gen. counsel, bd. dirs., Vestek Systems, Inc., San Francisco, 1983, Capital Fund Advisors, San Francisco, 1983—. Sec., treas., bd. dirs. Marin Poetry Ctr., San Rafael, Calif., 1981—. Mem. ABA, Calif. Bar Assn., San Francisco Bar Assn., San Francisco Photography Ctr. Avocation: art history. Computer, Securities, Probate. Office: 480 Vallejo St Rm 5 San Francisco CA 94133

BARNES, KAREN KAY, lawyer; b. Independence, Iowa, June 22, 1950; s. Walter William and Vashti (Greenlee) Sessler; m. James Alan Barnes, Feb. 12, 1972; children: Timothy Matthew, Christopher Michael. B.A., Valparaiso U., 1971; J.D., DePaul U., 1978, LL.M. in Taxation, 1980. Bar: Ill. 1978, U.S. Dist. Ct. (no. dist.) Ill. 1978. Ptnr. McDermott, Will & Emery, Chgo., 1978—. instr. John Marshall Grad. Sch. Law, Chgo., 1986-87. Contbr. case note to DePaul Law Rev., 1976, note and comment editor DePaul Law Rev., 1976-77, editor Taxation For Lawyers, 1986-87. Mem. ABA, Ill. State Bar Assn., Chgo. Bar Assn., Midwest Pension Conf., Women in Employee Benefits (pres. Chgo. chpt. 1986-87). Mem. Christian Ch. Club: Chgo. Soc. Pension, profit-sharing, and employee benefits. Home: 705 Crescent Ct Glen Ellyn IL 60137 Office: McDermott Will & Emery 111 W Monroe Chicago IL 60603

BARNES, LOUIE BURTON, III, lawyer; b. Jackson, Ms., Sept. 5, 1948; s. Louie Burton Jr. and Julia (Herring) B.; m. Melanie Barrentine, Aug. 18, 1973; children: Carlyle, Sidney, Christopher. BA, Ms. State U., 1970, MA, 1974; JD, Cornell U., 1976. Bar: D.C. 1976, Ala. 1980. Staff atty. Comptroller of Currency, Washington, 1976-78; regional counsel Comptroller of Currency, Cleve., 1978-79; assoc. Lange, Simpson, Robinson & Somerville, Birmingham, Ala., 1979-82, ptnr., 1982-85; gen. counsel, corp. sec. 1st Ala. Bancshares Inc., Birmingham, 1985—; bd. dirs. 1st Ala. Investments Inc., 1st Ala Ins. Agy., 1st Ala. Life Ins. Co. Counsel Jefferson County Reps., Birmingham, 1984—, exec. com., 1984—. Served to 1st lt. U.S. Army, 1971-73. Mem. ABA, Ala. Bar Assn., Birmingham Com. Fgn. Relations. Episcopalian. Banking. Home: 2881 Balmoral Rd Birmingham AL 35223 Office: 1st Ala Bancshares Inc 417 N 20th St Box 10247 Birmingham AL 35203

BARNES, MARK JAMES, lawyer; b. Oak Park, Ill., Jan. 10, 1957; s. James W. and Lorraine (Brady) B. BS in Polit. Sci. summa cum laude, Ariz. State U., 1978; JD, UCLA, 1981. Staff atty. Senator Ted Stevens U.S. Senate, Washington, 1981-83, chief counsel Senator Ted Stevens, 1983-84; assoc. Davis, Wright & Jones, Anchorage, 1984-86; dep. gen. counsel U.S. Office of Personnel Mgmt., Washington, 1986—. Alaska ambassador organizing com.

Anchorage Olympics, 1986. Mem. ABA, Alaska Bar Assn., Ariz. Bar Assn., D.C. Bar Assn., Phi Beta Kappa. Republican. Roman Catholic. Avocations: travel, movies, stamps. Administrative and regulatory, Federal civil litigation, Legislative. Office: Office Personnel Mgmt Office Gen Counsel 1900 E St NW #7F08 Washington DC 20415

BARNES, ROBERT NORTON, lawyer; b. Magnolia, Ark., Jan. 14, 1949; s. Bill Newland and Mary Lou (Wagner) B.; m. Susan Eileen Ensch, Oct. 16, 1976; children—Megan Desiree, Allison Nichole. B.A. in English, U. Okla., 1970, J.D., 1974. Bar: Okla. 1974, U.S. Dist. Ct. (we. dist.) Okla. 1983, (no. dist.) Okla. 1976, U.S. Ct. Appeals (10th cir.) 1984. Sole practice, Tulsa, 1974-75; ptnr. Gibbon, Gladd, Clark, Barnes & Taylor, Tulsa, 1976-78; sr. dist. counsel Tex. Oil & Gas Corp., Oklahoma City and Dallas, 1978-80; v.p. Tex. Internat. Petroleum Corp., Oklahoma City, 1980-81; pres. Carson Petroleum Corp., Oklahoma City, 1981-82; co-founder, atty. Stack & Barnes PC, Oklahoma City, 1982—. Mem. Okla. Bar Assn., ABA, Oklahoma County Bar Assn., Okla. Mineral Lawyers Soc. Democrat. Episcopalian. Oil and gas leasing, Federal civil litigation, State civil litigation. Office: Stack & Barnes 701 NW 63d St Suite 500 Oklahoma City OK 73116

BARNES, RUDOLPH COUNTS, lawyer; b. Prosperity, S.C., Jan. 9, 1917; s. Willie Claudius and Marie Nichols (Counts) B.; m. Ella Caroline Carson, Aug. 15, 1941; children: Rudolph C. Jr., Susan Marie. BA, U. S.C., 1937, LLB, 1940. Bar: S.C. 1940, U.S. Ct. Appeals (4th cir.) 1948. Atty. U.S. Dept. Justice, Columbia, S.C., 1941-42; sr. ptnr. Barnes, Alford, Stork & Johnson, Columbia, 1945—; founder, chmn. bd. dirs. Bank of Commerce, Prosperity, 1950-73. Editor S.C. Nat. Tech. Publ. Inc., 1970-73. Pres. Greater Columbia C. of C., 1971, United Way of The Midlands, Columbia, 1977; chmn. bd. dirs. Epworth Children's Home, Columbia, 1976, Greenwood (S.C.) Meth. Home, 1986—. Served as lt. USN, 1942-45, PTO. Named Trustee of Yr. Nat. Assn. Health and Welfare Ministries of United Meth. Ch., 1979. Mem. ABA (S.C. editor Bank Tax Study and Bank Tax Bulletin 1982—), S.C. Bar Assn., Richland County Bar Assn. Banking, General corporate, Real property. Home: 1829 Senate 10 C Columbia SC 29201 Office: Barnes Alford Stork & Johnson 1613 Main St Columbia SC 29202

BARNES, THOMAS ARTHUR, JR., lawyer; b. Los Angeles, Jan. 4, 1949; s. Thomas Arthur and Katherine Marian (Gillman) B.; m. Mary Therese Grant, Aug. 10, 1974; 1 child, Grant Thomas. B.A., U. Colo., 1971; J.D., Ohio Northern U., 1974. Bar: Colo. 1975, U.S. Dist. Ct. Colo. 1975, U.S. Ct. Appeals (10th cir.) 1981, U.S. Supreme Ct. 1980. Atty., VISTA, Denver, 1976-77; dep. dist. atty. Dist. Atty.'s Office, Colorado Springs, Colo., 1977-81; sole practice, Colorado Springs, 1981-87, assoc. Law Firm of Lloyd C. Kordick, 1987—; instr. criminal justice Pikes Peak Community Coll., 1978. Mem. Gov.'s Juvenile Justice Council, Denver, 1976-80; organizer Shape-Up Prison Visitation Program, Canon City, Colo., 1980-81; advisor Minority Council for Arts, 1983-85. Recipient Commendation award Colo. Gov., 1980. Mem. Colo. Bar Assn., El Paso County Bar Assn., Assn. Trial Lawyers Am., Colo. Trial Lawyers Assn. Democrat. Club: U.S. Fencing. Workers' compensation, Personal injury, Civil rights. Office: Law Firm of Lloyd C Kordick 805 S Cascade St Colorado Springs CO 80903

BARNES, THOMAS G., legal educator; b. 1930. A.B., Harvard U., 1952; D.Phil., Oxford U., 1955. Asst. prof. to assoc. prof. Lycoming Coll., Williamsport, Pa., 1956-60; lectr. to prof. history U. Calif., Berkeley, 1960—, humanities research prof., 1971-72, prof. history and law, 1974—, co-chmn. Canadian Studies program, 1982—; project dir. legal history project Am. Bar Found., 1965-86; editor Pub. Record Office, London; mem. com. on ct. records 9th Cir. Ct.; fellow Huntington Library, 1960. Am. Council Learned Socs. fellow, 1962-63; John Simon Guggenheim Found. fellow, 1970-71. Fellow Royal Hist. Soc.; mem. Selden Soc. (councillor, state corr.), Am. Soc. Legal History, Am. Hist. Assn. Author: Somerset 1625-1640; A County's Government During the Personal Rule, 1961; List and Index to Star Chamber Procs., James I, 3 vols., 1975; Lawes and Libertyes of Massachusetts, 1975; Hastings College of Law: The First Century, 1978; chmn. editorial adv. bd. Gryphon Legal Classics Library; Legal education. Address: Univ Calif Law Sch 355 Boalt Hall Berkeley CA 94720

BARNES, TIMOTHY LEE, lawyer; b. Orange, N.J., Sept. 20, 1951; s. William Oliver and Marilyn Louise (Isenberg) B.; m. Virginia Lee Peterson, July 15, 1978; children: Christopher, Andrew. BA, Wake Forest U., 1973; JD, U. Richmond, 1978. Bar: N.J. 1978, U.S. Dist. Ct. N.J. 1978, N.Y. 1985. Ptnr. Barnes & Barnes, Newark, 1978—. Mem. ABA, N.J. Bar Assn., Essex County Bar Assn., Am. Trial Lawyers Assn., Am. Bd. Trial Advs. (assoc.), N.J. Bd. Civil Trial Attys. (cert.), Trial Attys. N.J. (trustee), Wake Forest U. Alumni Assn. (council 1982-85), Phi Delta Phi. Republican. Presbyterian. Personal injury, Health, State civil litigation. Home: 200 Sagamore Dr New Providence NJ 07974 Office: Barnes & Barnes 1180 Raymond Blvd Newark NJ 07102

BARNES, WALLACE RAY, lawyer; b. Easton, Pa., Nov. 7, 1928; s. Charles Hicks and Erma (Saylor) B.; m. Helen Honey Bartley, July 2, 1958; children: Charles Calvin, Elizabeth McKee, Douglas Wittmer. A.B., Duke U., 1950; LL.B., Harvard U., 1957. Bar: Pa. 1958, Ohio 1973. Atty. Allegheny Ludlum Steel, Pitts., 1957-62; atty. Columbia Gas, Md., N.Y., Pa., Pitts., 1962-73; sec., gen. counsel Columbia Gas, Ky., Md., N.Y., Ohio, Pa., Va., W.Va., Columbus, Ohio, 1973-78; sr. counsel Columbia Gas, 1978-81, asso. gen. counsel, 1981—; corp. dir. Columbia Gas Ohio, 1973-78, N.Y., 1973-78. Bd. dirs. Pitts. Better Bus. Bur., 1972-74. Served with USN, 1951-54. Mem. Fed. Bar Assn. (pres. chpt. 1961), ABA, Franklin County Bar Assn., Allegheny County Bar Assn., Phi Beta Kappa. Clubs: Fox Chapel Racquet (Pitts.); Racquet (Columbus). Home: 2438 Sandover Rd Columbus OH 43220 Office: 200 Civic Center Dr Columbus OH 43216-0117

BARNETT, BARRY HOWARD, lawyer; b. Columbus, Ohio, Apr. 19, 1954; s. Harold Sanford and Delores Mae (Stein) B.; m. Melissa Diane Perry, July 14, 1979. BS in Bus. and Mgmt., U. Md., 1975; JD, Loyola U., Chgo., 1979. Bar: Ill. 1979, U.S. Dist. Ct. (no. dist.) Ill. 1979, Fla. 1983, U.S. Ct. Appeals (7th cir.) 1983, U.S. Dist. Ct. Md. 1984, U.S. Dist. Ct. (mid. dist.) Fla. 1984, N.Mex. 1985. Staff atty. U.S. SEC, Chgo., 1979-83; assoc. Messer, Rhodes & Vickers, P.A., Tallahassee, 1983-84, Johnson & Lanphere, P.C., Albuquerque, 1984-86; ptnr. Barnett, Leverick & Musselman P.C., Albuquerque, 1986—. Served with U.S. Army, 1972-75. Mem. ABA, Fla. Bar Assn., N.Mex. Bar Assn., Internat. Assn. Fin. Planners (bd. dirs., regulatory coordinator N.Mex. chpt. 1985—). Avocations: photography. Securities, General corporate, Contracts commercial. Office: Barnett Leverick & Musselman PC 4600-A Montgomery Blvd NE Suite 101 Albuquerque NM 87109

BARNETT, BERNARD HARRY, lawyer; b. Helena, Ark., July 13, 1916; s. Harry and Rebecca (Grossman) B.; BA U. Mich., 1934-36; J.D., Vanderbilt U., 1940; m. Marian Spiesberger, Apr. 9, 1949; 1 son, Charles Dawson. Bar: Ky. 1940, D.C. Practiced in Louisville, 1940-42; assoc. firm Woodward, Dawson, Hobson & Fulton, 1946-48; partner firm Bulitt, Dawson & Tarrant, 1948-52, firm Greenbaum, Barnett, Wood & Doll, 1952-70, firm Barnett & McConnell, 1972, firm Barnett, Greenebaum, Martin & McConnell, 1972-74, firm Barnett, Alagia, Greenebaum, Miller & Senn, 1974-75; sr. ptnr. Barnett & Alagia, 1975—; bd. dirs. Fuqua Industries, Inc., Hasbro, Inc., Advanced World Techs. Inc., U.S. Container Corp.; mem. adv. group Joint Com. on Internal Revenue Taxation, U.S. Congress, 1953-55, Com. on Ways and Means, U.S. Ho. of Reps., 1956-58. Chmn., Louisville Fund, 1952-53; mem. Louisville and Jefferson County Republican Exec. Com., 1954-60; chmn. Ky. Rep. Fin. Com., 1955-60; nat. exec. com., nat. campaign cabinet United Jewish Appeal, 1959-71, nat. chmn., 1967-71, campaign chmn., Louisville, 1968-69; trustee Spalding Coll., Louisville, 1975-82, Benjamin N. Cardozo Sch. Law, 1979-84, Ford's Theatre, 1981—; bd. dirs. Norton Gallery and Sch. Art, 1980—. Served as lt. USNR, 1942-45. Mem. ABA, D.C. Bar, Louisville Bar Assn., Ky. Bar Assn., Fellows of Am. Bar Found. Public international, Corporate taxation. Office: Barnett & Alagia 250 S County Rd Palm Beach FL 33480 Office: 1000 Thomas Jefferson St NW Suite 600 Washington DC 20007

BARNETT, CHARLES DAWSON, lawyer; b. Louisville, Jan. 27, 1951; s. Bernard Harry and Marian (Spiesberger) B.; m. Maureen Liel Stewart, Nov. 17, 1980; children: Rachel Barnett Langfeld, Jacob Bernard. B.S. in Commerce, U. Louisville, 1973; J.D., U. Fla., 1976. Bar: Fla. 1977, Ky. 1977, D.C. 1977, U.S. Dist. Ct. (so. dist.) Fla. 1981. Assoc. Barnett & Alagia, Louisville, 1977-81, ptnr., Palm Beach, Fla., 1981—; Ind.-Fla. Realty Trust, Indpls. Bd. dirs. Ralph E. Mills Found., Frankfort, Ky., 1980—. Active Louisville-Jefferson County Republican Exec. Com., 1978-80. Served with USCG, 1969-74. Jewish. General corporate, Private international, Corporate taxation. Home: 231 Seaspray Ave Palm Beach FL 33480 Office: Barnett & Alagia 250 S County Rd Suite 201 Palm Beach FL 33480

BARNETT, CHARLES E., lawyer. Vice pres., gen. counsel Combustion Engrng., Stamford, Conn. General corporate. Office: Combustion Engrng Inc PO Box 9308 Stamford CT 06904 *

BARNETT, EDWARD WILLIAM, lawyer; b. New Orleans, Jan. 2, 1933; s. Phillip Nelson and Katherine (Wilkinson) B.; m. Margaret Mauk, Apr. 3, 1933; children: Margaret Ann Stern Edward William. B.A., Rice U., 1955; LL.B., U. Tex.-Austin, 1958. Bar: Tex. 1958. Mng. ptnr. Baker & Botts, Houston, 1958—; dir. Tex. Commerce Bank. Fellow Am. Coll. Trial Lawyers; mem. ABA (chmn. sect. antitrust law 1981-82), State Bar Tex., Houston Bar Assn. Clubs: Coronado, Houston Philos (Houston); Headliners (Austin). Office: Baker & Botts 3000 One Shell Plaza Houston TX 77002

BARNETT, GEORGE DAVID, lawyer; b. Baytown, Tex., July 21, 1948; s. Charles Sidney and Irma Virginia (Burnett) B.; m. Nancy Carol Graham, Aug. 19, 1978. AA, Lee Jr. Coll., 1973; BA, U. Houston, 1975, JD, 1978. Bar: Tex. 1978, U.S. Ct. Appeals (5th and 11th cirs.) 1980. Assoc. atty. Fed. Land Bank of Tex., Houston, 1979-81; asst. regional counsel Title Ins. Co. of Minn., Houston, 1981-82; gen. counsel Houston Title Co., Houston, 1982-85; assoc. Pruitt & Cowden, Houston, 1985-86; gen. counsel Vanguard Title Co., Houston, 1986; v.p. region B Am. Surveying Co. Houston, Inc., 1987—. Served to sgt. USAF, 1967-71. Mem. ABA, Tex. Bar Assn. (legal forms com.), Nat. Rifle Assn. Methodist. Club: N.Am. Hunting. Avocations: hunting, fishing, golf. Real property, Insurance. Office: Am Surveying Co Houston Inc 2200 W Loop S #600 Houston TX 77056

BARNETT, HOLLIS H., lawyer; b. Seattle, May 27, 1939; s. Hollis Hall and Elizabeth Catherine (Devitt) B.; m. Patricia Joan Anderson, May 18, 1968; children: Hollis E., Aaron P., Beritt Ann. BA in Bus., Seattle U., 1962; JD, Gonzaga U., 1969. Bar: Wash. 1969. Law clk. to atty. gen. State of Wash., Spokane, 1967-68; dep. prosecuting atty. Pierce County, Tacoma, 1969-71; assoc. Campbell, Manning & Price, Puyallup, Wash., 1971; ptnr. Campbell, Dille & Barnett, Puyallup, 1971-75; ptnr. Campbell, Dille, Barnett, McCarthy & Adams, Puyallup, 1975-79, mng. ptnr., 1979—; judge City of Puyallup, 1976-80; atty. City of Orting, Wash., 1971-83, 87—, City of Eatonville, Wash., 1971-83, 87—. Chmn. Puyallup Valley United Way campaign, 1976, Puyallup Sch. Dist. Levy campaign, 1986; bd. dirs. Puyallup Valley YMCA, 1977-80. Served with U.S. Army, 1962-64. Mem. ABA, Wash. State Bar Assn., Assn. Trial Lawyers Am., Wash. State Trial Lawyers Assn. Roman Catholic. Lodges: Rotary (Puyallup pres. 1978-79), Elks. Avocations: skiing, snowmobiling, fishing, hiking, boating. Personal injury, Probate, Real property. Home: 13521 118th St E Puyallup WA 98374 Office: Campbell Dille Barnett McCarthy & Adams 317 Meridian S Puyallup WA 98371

BARNETT, JAMES MONROE, lawyer; b. Hulah, Okla., Dec. 24, 1933; s. Irvin M. and Ida Ruth (Loy) B.; m. Vicki L. Smith, Dec. 30, 1985. B.B.A., Washburn U., 1955, J.D., 1959. Bar: Kans. 1959. Mem. firm Ross & Wells, Kansas City, Kans., 1959-63, Ross, Wells & Barnett, Kansas City, Kans., 1963-73; pres. Barnett & Ross, Chartered, Kansas City, Kans., 1973—. Bd. govs. Washburn Law Sch., 1974—, pres., 1982-83. Served with U.S. Army, 1956-58. Mem. ABA, Am. Judicature Soc., Kans. Bar Assn., Johnson County Bar Assn., Wyandotte County Bar Assn., Kansas Bar Assn., Kans. Trial Lawyers Assn., Assn. Trial Lawyers Am. Republican. Methodist. Personal injury, Medical malpractice. Home: 10330 Manor Rd Leawood KS 66206 Office: 705 N 8th St Kansas City KS 66101 also: 9800 Metcalf St Gen Sq Bldg Overland Park KS 66206

BARNETT, RICHARD ALLEN, lawyer; b. Akron, Ohio, Dec. 26, 1949; s. James Joseph and Beverly Muriel (Gergel) B.; m. Jacalyn Sherriton, July 1, 1978. BS in Econs., U. Pa., 1971; JD, Harvard U., 1975. Law clk. to presiding justice U.S. Dist Ct. Calif., San Diego, 1975-76; assoc. Krupnick & Campbell, Ft. Lauderdale, Fla., 1978-81; sole practice Hollywood, Fla., 1981—. Author: Tort Trend Newsletter, 1984—. mem. steering com. Bob Parks for Broward Sch. Bd., Ft. Lauderdale, Fla., 1985-86; Hollywood Hills Dem. Club, 1984—; bd. dirs. Liberia Econ. and Social Devel. Inc., Hollywood, Fla., 1979—, Jewish Fedn. South Broward (chmn. community relations com. 1984—, bd. dirs.). Served with U.S. Army, 1970-72. Mem. Assn. Trial Lawyers Am., Calif. Bar assn., Fla. Bar Assn., Acad. Fla. Trial Lawyers (Amicus Curiae Com. 1985-86), Broward County Trial Lawyers, Fed. Bar Assn. (pres. Broward County chpt. 1986-87). Avocations: golf, tennis, reading, travel. Personal injury, State civil litigation, Libel. Home: 3111 N Ocean Dr #1401 Hollywood FL 33019 Office: 4651 Sheridan St Suite 325 Hollywood FL 33021

BARNETT, STEPHEN R., legal educator; b. 1935. A.B., Harvard U., 1957, LL.B., 1962; postgrad. St. Anthony's Coll., Oxford U., 1958-59. Bar: N.Y. 1963, D.C. 1966, Calif. 1977. Law clk. to judge U.S. Cir. Ct. Appeals, 1962-63; law clk. to Justice Brennan, U.S. Supreme Ct., 1963-64; sole practice, N.Y.C. and Washington, 1965-67; spl. asst. to asst. sec. def. for internat. affairs U.S. Dept. Def., 1967; dep. solicitor gen. U.S. Dept. Justice, 1977-79; mem. task force on justice, publicity, and the 1st amendment 20th Century Fund, 1975-76; prof. law U. Calif.-Berkeley, 1979—, chmn. com. on acad. freedom, 1976-77. Bd. dirs. Sta. KQED, 1976-77. Mem. Am. Law Inst. Legal education. Address: Univ Calif Law Sch 225 Boalt Hall Berkeley CA 94720 *

BARNETT, WAYNE G., legal educator; b. 1928. A.B., Harvard U., 1950, LL.B., 1953. Bar: D.C. 1953. Law clk. to Justice Harlan, U.S. Supreme Ct., 1955-56; assoc. Covington & Burling, Washington, 1956-58; asst. to solicitor gen. Dept. U.S. Dept. Justice, 1958-65, 1st asst. Office Legal Counsel, 1965-66; prof. Stanford U., 1966—. Articles editor Harvard Law Rev. Legal education. Address: Stanford U Law Sch Stanford CA 94305 *

BARNETT, WILLIAM A., lawyer; b. Chgo., Oct. 13, 1916; s. Leo James and Anita (Olsen) B.; LL.B., Loyola U., Chgo., 1941; m. Evelyn Yates, June 23, 1945; children—William, Mary Leone (Mrs. John J. Fahey), Therese, Kathleen (Mrs. William D. Norwood). Admitted to Ill. bar, 1941; with U.S. IRS, 1948-54, atty. chief counsel's office, Chgo., 1948-52, dist. counsel penal div., Detroit, 1952-54; chief tax atty. U.S. Atty's Office, Chgo., 1955-60; practitioner before the 6th Circuit Court of Appeals, since 1954, 7th Circuit Ct. Appeals, since 1955, U.S. Supreme Ct., since 1959. Fellow Internat. Acad. Trial Lawyers; mem. Am., Fed., Ill. and 7th Circuit bar assns., Am. Judicature Soc., Nat. Assn. Criminal Def. Lawyers, Ill. Trial Lawyers Assn. Criminal, Federal civil litigation. Home: 1448 Norwood St Chicago IL 60660 Office: 135 S LaSalle St Chicago IL 60603

BARNETTE, CURTIS HANDLEY, lawyer, steel company executive; b. St. Albans, W.Va., Jan. 9, 1935; s. Curtis Franklin and Garnett Drucella (Robinson) B.; m. Loris Joan Harner, Dec. 28, 1957; children: Curtis Kevin, James David. A.B. with High Honors, W.Va. U., 1956; postgrad. (Fulbright scholar), U. Manchester, 1956-57; J.D., Yale U., 1962; grad. advanced mgmt. program, Harvard U., 1974-75. Bar: Conn. 1962, Pa. 1968. Mem. Wiggin & Dana, New Haven, Conn., 1962-67; atty. Bethlehem Steel Corp., Pa., 1967-70; gen. atty. Bethlehem Steel Corp., 1970-72, asst. sec., 1972-76, asst. gen. counsel, 1972-77, asst. to v.p., 1974-76, sec., 1976—, asst. v.p., 1976-77, v.p., gen. counsel, 1977-85, sr. v.p., 1985—, also bd. dirs.; lectr. U. Md., 1958-59; law tutor Yale U., 1962-67; dir. Sta. WLVT-TV. bd. dirs., vice chmn. Yale Law Sch. Fund; mem. adv. bd. Minsi Trails council Boy Scouts Am.; bd. dirs. Pa. Bus. Roundtable, 1986—; bd. govs. Bethlehem Area Found. Served with U.S. Army Intelligence, 1956-57, USAR, 1958-67. Mem. ABA, Fed. Bar Assn., Pa. Bar Assn., Conn. Bar Assn., Northampton County Bar Assn., Am. Iron and Steel Inst., Assn. Gen. Counsel (v.p. 1986—), Am. Soc. Corp. Secs. (chmn. 1986), Am. Law Inst., Stockholder Relations Soc. N.Y., Pa. C. of C. (dir. 1985—), Pa. Bus. Roundtable (dir. 1986—), Phi Beta Kappa, Beta Theta Pi, Phi Alpha Theta, Phi Delta Phi. Clubs: New Haven, Lawn, Saucon Valley, Bethlehem, Blooming Grove Hunting and Fishing; Yale (N.Y.C.); University (Washington). Home: 1112 Prospect Ave Bethlehem PA 18018 Office: Bethlehem Steel Corp Martin Tower Room 2018 Bethlehem PA 18016

BARNETTE, DAVID ALLEN, lawyer; b. Wilmington, Del., Jan. 10, 1952; s. Gordon Lee and Mary Alice (Echols) B.; m. Cynthia Wegley, May 23, 1983; 1 child, Elizabeth Alice. BA, Concord Coll., 1973; MA, Marshall U., 1975; JD, U. Dayton, 1979. Bar: W.Va. 1979, Ohio, U.S. Ct. Appeals (4th cir.) 1979, U.S. Ct. Appeals (3d cir.) 1981, U.S. Ct. Appeals (6th and 8th cirs.) 1982, U.S. Supreme Ct. 1984. Ptnr. Jackson & Kelly, Charleston, W.Va., 1979—. Administrative and regulatory, Antitrust, General corporate. Office: PO Box 553 Charleston WV 25322

BARNEY, JOHN CHARLES, lawyer; b. N.Y.C., Nov. 18, 1939; s. Harold Lamont and Sara Eleanor (Johnston) B.; m. Joyce Marie Ebbinge; children—John C., Karen E., William L. B.A., Wesleyan U., 1961; LL.B., Columbia U., 1964. Bar: N.Y. 1964, U.S. Dist. Ct. (so. and ea. dists.) N.Y. 1966, U.S. Dist. Ct. (no. and we. dists.) N.Y. 1977, U.S. Ct. Appeals (2d cir.) 1973, U.S. Supreme Ct. 1979. Assoc. Donovan, Leisure, Newton and Irvine, N.Y.C., 1964-66; staff atty. N.Y. State Law Revision Commn., Ithaca, 1966-68; ptnr. Barney, Grossman, Roth & Dubow, Ithaca, 1968—; asst. dist. atty. Tompkins County, N.Y., 1968-70; mem. N.Y. State Com. on Profl. Standards, 3d Jud. Dept., 1984—. Chmn. Bd. Zoning Appeals, Lansing, N.Y., 1975—; v.p. Bd. Edn., Lansing, 1981—; bd. dirs. Challenge Industries (sheltered workshop), Ithaca, 1970-80. Mem. Tompkins County Bar Assn. (pres. 1983-84), N.Y. State Bar Assn. Republican. Unitarian. General practice, Contracts commercial, Real property. Home: 12 Stormy View Rd Ithaca NY 14850 Office: Barney Grossman Roth & Dubow 315 N Tioga St Ithaca NY 14850

BARNEY, PATRICK EARL, lawyer; b. Sheridan, Wyo., Nov. 3, 1954; s. J. Reid and Ruth Frances (Olson) B.; m. Victoria Sumerlin, Nov. 20, 1982; 1 child, Daniel Jay. BS magna cum laude, U. Utah, 1976; JD, Stanford U., 1980. Bar: Colo. 1980, U.S. Dist. Ct. Colo. 1980. Assoc. Welborn, Dufford, Brown & Tooley, Denver, 1980-84, Sharp & Black, Steamboat Springs, Colo., 1984-86; ptnr. Sharp & Casson, Steamboat Springs, 1986—. Named one of Outstanding Young Men of Am., 1985. Mem. ABA, Colo. Bar Assn., Denver Bar Assn. (chmn. election com. 1984), Routt County Bar Assn., N.W. Colo. Bar Assn., Phi Beta Kappa. Republican. Episcopalian. Lodge: Optimists Internat. Avocations: downhill skiing, stamp collecting, fishing. Contracts commercial, General corporate, Real property. Office: Sharp & Casson PC PO Box 774608 Steamboat Springs CO 80477

BARNHART, FORREST GREGORY, lawyer; b. Alpine, Tex., Sept. 11, 1951; d. F. Neil and Jody (Ogg) B. A.B., Vassar Coll., 1973; J.D., Cornell U., 1976. Bar: Fla. 1976, U.S. Dist. Ct. (so. dist.) Fla. 1977, U.S. Cts. Appeals (5th and 11th cirs.) 1977; Cert. civil trial lawyer. Assoc. Levy, Plisco, Perry, Shapiro, Kneen & Kincade, West Palm Beach, Fla., 1976-78; assoc. Montgomery Searcy & Denney, P.A., West Palm Beach, 1978-81, ptnr., 1981—; lectr. in field; moderator TV show Call the Lawyer, 1983—; dir. WXEL-TV and FM, Pub. Radio and TV, West Palm Beach. Speaker and com. mem. Floridians Against Constl. Tampering, 1984. Mem. Jud. Nominating Commn., 1986—. Fellow Fla. Bar, ABA (jud. nominating commn. 1986—), Fed. Bar Assn. (treas. 1983-84, sec., v.p. 1984-85, pres. 1986-87), Palm Beach County Bar Assn. (vice chmn. fed. ct. practice com. 1981-82, media law com. 1981-82, bench bar com. 1980-81; chmn. pub. relations com. 1983-84, TV com. 1984—), Palm Beach Trial Lawyers Assn. (founding dir.), Assn. Trial Lawyers Am., Acad. Fla. Trial Lawyers (bd. dirs. 1986—, chmn., key man legis. com. 1986—, mem. coll. of diplomates, steering counsel continuing edn. com., Eagle Benefactor). Clubs: Cornell, Governor's, Collette. Federal civil litigation, State civil litigation, Personal injury. Home: 236 MiraFlores Dr Palm Beach FL 33480 Office: Montgomery Searcy & Denney 2139 Palm Beach Lakes Blvd West Palm Beach FL 33402

BARNHART, KATHERINE LOUISE, lawyer; b. Detroit, Mar. 18, 1940; d. Joseph D. and Mae (MacNeill) B.; m. Feliciano Colista, Oct. 31, 1968; children: Gian A. Colista, Celia Diana Colista, Joseph Aaron Colista. BA, U. Mich., 1962; postgrad. in urban planning, Wayne State U., 1969-70, JD, 1976. Bar: Mich. 1976, U.S. Dist. Ct. (ea. dist.) Mich. 1976. Sr. social planner City of Detroit, 1964-67; sole practice Detroit, 1977—. Mem. ABA, Mich. Bar Assn., Detroit Bar Assn., Womens Econ. Club, Women Lawyers Assn. (treas. 1978-80), Detroit NOW (sec. 1983). Democrat. Family and matrimonial. Office: 975 E Jefferson Detroit MI 48207

BARNHILL, CHARLES J., JR., lawyer; b. Indpls., May 22, 1943; s. Charles J. and Phyllis (Landis) B.; m. Elizabeth Louise Hayek, Aug. 14, 1971; children—Eric Charles, Colin Landis. B.S. in Econs., U. Pa., 1965; J.D., U. Mich., 1968. Bar: Ill. 1968, U.S. Dist. Ct. (no. dist.) Ill. 1968, U.S. Ct. Appeals (7th cir.) 1969, U.S. Supreme Ct. 1972. Assoc. Kirkland & Ellis, Chgo., 1968; Reginald Heber Smith fellow Chgo. Legal Aid, 1968-69; assoc. Katz & Friedman, Chgo., 1969-72; ptnr. Davis, Miner, Barnhill, & Galland, P.C., Chgo., 1972—. Assoc. editor Mich. Law Rev., 1968. Bd. dirs. Legal Assistance Found., Chgo., 1972-74, Old Town Triangle Assn., Chgo., 1972-75. Mem. ABA (chmn. employment litigation of litigation sect. 1975-78), Chgo. Council Lawyers (bd. dirs. 1974-76), Barristers Soc., Order of Coif. Antitrust, Civil rights. Office: Davis Barnhill & Galland PC 14 W Erie St Chicago IL 60610

BARNHILL, ROBERT EDWIN, III, lawyer; b. Lubbock, Tex., Dec. 29, 1956; s. Robert Edwin Jr. and Karen Sue (Green) B.; m. Jana Susan Barnett, Aug. 9, 1980. BBA, Tex. Tech U., 1976, MBA, JD, 1980. Bar: Tex. 1980, U.S. Dist. (no. dist.) Tex. 1980. Staff acct. Peat, Marwick & Mitchell, Dallas, 1980-82; assoc. Blackledge Law Offices, Lubbock, 1982-83, Walters and Assocs., Lubbock, 1983-85; sole practice Lubbock, 1985—; sec., treas. Innovative Money Adv. Inc., 1985—; instr. Lubbock Christian Coll., 1982-83, So. Plains Coll., Lubbock, 1982-83, Tex. Tech U., Lubbock, 1986—. Bd. dirs. So. Plains chpt. ARC, Lubbock, 1984—, Big Bros./ Big Sisters, Lubbock, 1984—. Mem. ABA (tax sect.), Tex. Bar Assn. (tax sect.), Tex. Soc. CPA's, Order of Coif, Phi Kappa Phi. Republican. Mem. Christian Ch. Club: Toastmasters (dist. gov. 1986-87). Personal income taxation, Corporate taxation, Probate. Home: 2506 61st Lubbock TX 79413 Office: PO Box 2583 Lubbock TX 79408-2583

BARNHORST, HOWARD JOSEPH, II, lawyer; b. Indpls., Oct. 19, 1948; s. Howard and Helen Nora (Killilea) B.; m. Margery Wright, Aug. 15, 1970; children: Kiley Ann, Amy Vanessa, Zachary Andrew, Nicholas Scott. BA, Ind. U., 1970; JD cum laude, U. San Diego, 1975. Bar: Calif. 1975, U.S. Dist. Ct. (so. dist.) Calif. 1975, U.S. Dist. Ct. Nebr. 1978, U.S. Dist. Ct. (no. dist.) Calif. 1979, U.S. Tax Ct. 1981, U.S. Ct. Claims 1982, U.S. Ct. Appeals (9th cir.) 1983, U.S. Dist. Ct. (ea. dist.) Calif. 1984, U.S. Dist. Ct. (cen. dist.) 1985. Claims adjuster Aetna Life & Casualty Ins. Co.N.Am., 1972-74, Ind. Nat. Bank, Indpls., 1974-76; assoc. Seltzer, Caplan, San Diego, 1976-77; ptnr. Dorazio, Barnhorst & Bonar, San Diego, 1977—; lectr. in field, San Diego; adj. prof. sch. law U. San Diego. Contbr. articles to profl. jours. Mem. ABA (litigation discovery com.), Calif. Bar Assn. (law office acct. relations com., lectr.), San Diego Trial Lawyers Assn. Club: La Jolla Country (San Diego). Avocations: golf, tennis, skiing. Federal civil litigation, State civil litigation, Real property. Home: 1155 Savoy St San Diego CA 92107 Office: Dorazio Barnhorst & Bonar 438 Camino Del Rio S Suite B223 San Diego CA 92108

BARNTHOUSE, WILLIAM JOSEPH, lawyer; b. Jefferson City, Mo., Nov. 25, 1948; s. William Robison and Genevieve L. (Nacke) B.; children: Joseph, Jonathon, Jamie. AB, Rockhurst Coll., 1970; JD, U. Mo., 1973, LLM in Trial and Criminal Law, 1976. Bar: Mo. 1973, U.S. Dist. Ct. (we. dist.) Mo. 1973, U.S. Ct. Appeals (8th cir.) 1973, Colo. 1976, U.S. Dist Ct. (ea. dist.) Mo. 1976, U.S. Dist. Ct. Colo. 1976, U.S. Ct. Appeals (10th cir.) 1976, U.S. Supreme Ct. 1977. Trial clk. to presiding justice Mo. 16th Jud. Cir., Kansas City, 1972-73; pros. atty. Jackson County, Kansas City, 1973; research atty. Mo. Ct. Appeals, Kansas City, 1974; counsel Gulf Oil Co., Denver, 1975-77; sole practice Denver, 1978, 84—; regional counsel Conoco Oil Corp./Consol Coal Co., Denver, 1979-84; gen. counsel ChemTech Corp., Denver, 1984—; teaching fellow law U. Mo., Kansas City, 1974. Author: Product Liability Law, 1976, Energy Litigation, 1985, Colorado Dissolution,

1986. Served to maj. NG, 1970-86. Nat. Inst. Trial Adv. scholar, 1974. Mem. ABA (vice chmn. natural resources sect. 1980—), Colo. Bar Assn., Denver Bar Assn., Mo. Bar Assn., Colo. Trial Lawyers Assn. Roman Catholic. Federal civil litigation, State civil litigation, Oil and gas leasing. Office: PO Box 3322 Littleton CO 80161

BARNUM, CAROL LEE, lawyer; b. Columbus, Ohio, June 8, 1951; d. Frank Lon Jr. and Dorothy Helen (Gross) B. B.A. cum laude, Ohio State U., 1973, post-grad., 1973-74, J.D., 1977. Bar: Ohio 1977. Staff atty. Buckeye Internat. Inc., Columbus, Ohio, 1977-80; Worthington Industries, Inc., Columbus, 1980-83, Carpenter Tech. Corp., Reading, Pa., 1984. Mem. Columbus Bar Assn., Ohio State Bar Assn., ABA, Phi Beta Kappa. Home: 1608 Sandy Side Dr Worthington OH 43085 Office: 100 E Wilson Bridge Rd Suite 204 Worthington OH 43085

BARNUM, JOHN WALLACE, lawyer; b. N.Y.C., Aug. 25, 1928; s. Walter and Frances (Long) B.; m. Nancy Russell Grinnell, Sept. 13, 1958; children: Alexander Stone, Sarah Kip, Cameron Long. B.A., Yale U., 1949, LL.B., 1957. Analyst 1st Banking Corp., Tangier, Morocco, 1950; rep. Bache & Co., London and Paris, 1951-52; assoc. Cravath, Swaine & Moore, N.Y.C., 1957-62, ptnr., 1963-71; gen. counsel U.S. Dept. Transp., Washington, 1971-73, undersec., 1973-74, dep. sec., 1974-77; resident fellow Am. Enterprise Inst. for Pub. Policy Research, Washington, 1977-78, vis. fellow, 1978—; ptnr. White & Case, Washington, 1978—; lectr. Practising Law Inst.; U.S. del. Inter-Am. Comml. Arbitration Commn., 1969-71; adv. mem. Council on Wage and Price Stability, 1974-77; mem. Council Adminstrv. Conf. U.S., 1973-77; bd. dirs. Palmer Nat. Bancorp and Bank, Washington, 1982—. Bd. editors Regulation: AEI Jour. on Govt. and Society, 1977-86. Chmn. bd. Internat. Play Group, 1962-77; bd. dirs., exec. com. N.Y.C. Center Music and Drama, 1969-75; trustee Washington Drama Soc. (Arena Stage), 1983—. Served as lt. AUS, 1952-54. Mem. Am Arbitration Assn. (bd. dirs., exec. com. 1968—), N.Y. State (exec. com., chmn. antitrust law sect. 1969-70), ABA, D.C. Bar Assn., Am. Bar Found., Assn. Bar City N.Y., Nat. Def. Transp. Assn. (chmn. mil. airlift com. 1983—). Clubs: Metropolitan, Fed. City, Nat. Aviation (Washington); Waquoit Bay Yacht, Chevy Chase; Amateur Ski, Yale, India House, N.Y. Yacht, Madison Sq. Garden (N.Y.C.). Home: 5175 Tilden St NW Washington DC 20016 Office: White & Case 1747 Pennsylvania Ave NW Washington DC 20006

BARON, FREDERICK DAVID, lawyer; b. New Haven, Dec. 2, 1947; s. Charles Bates and Betty (Leventhal) B.; m. Kathryn Green Lazarus, Apr. 4, 1982; children—Andrew K. Lazarus, Peter D. Lazarus, Charles B. B.A., Amherst Coll., 1969; J.D., Stanford U., 1974. Bar: Calif. 1974, D.C. 1975, U.S. Supreme Ct. 1978, U.S. Dist. Ct. D.C. 1979, U.S. Ct. Appeals (D.C. cir.) 1979, U.S. Dist. Ct. (no. dist.) Calif. 1982, U.S. Ct. Appeals (9th cir.) 1982. Counsel select com. on intelligence U.S. Senate, Washington, 1975-76; spl. asst. to U.S. atty. gen., Washington, 1977-79; asst. U.S. atty. for D.C., 1980-82; ptnr. Clark, Baron & Korda, San Jose, Calif., 1982-83, Cooley, Godward, Castro, Huddleson & Tatum, San Francisco, 1983—; mem. presdl. transition team, 1976-77; mem. research com. Bay Area Internat. Forum; lectr. U.S. Info. Service, 1979-80; pres. bd. trustees Keys Sch., Palo Alto, Calif., 1983—; bd. dirs. Retail Resources Inc. Co-author, editor U.S. Senate Select Com. on Intelligence Reports, 1975-76; also articles. Issues dir. election com. U.S. Senator Alan Cranston, 1974, Gov. Edmund G. Brown Jr., 1976. Mem. ABA, Calif. Bar Assn., San Francisco Bar Assn., D.C. Bar Assn., Palo Alto Bar Assn., Santa Clara County Bar Assn., D.C. Bar (chmn. criminal justice legis. com. 1981). Club: University. Federal civil litigation, State civil litigation. Office: Cooley Godward Castro Huddleson & Tatum 5 Palo Alto Sq Suite 400 Palo Alto CA 94306

BARON, RICHARD MARK, lawyer; b. N.Y.C., Feb. 1, 1954; s. Seymour and Florence (Chill) B. BA, Dickinson Coll., 1976; JD, Cath. U., 1979. Bar: N.J. 1980, D.C. 1980, U.S. Dist. Ct. N.J. 1980, Fla. 1981, U.S. Ct. Appeals (D.C. cir.) 1981, N.Y., 1984. Atty. Burns & Roe, Engrs. and Constructors, Oradell, N.J.; assoc. Berman, Paley, Goldstein & Berman, N.Y.C., 1983-85, Peckar & Abramson, Hackensack, N.J., 1985—. Mem. ABA (forum com. on construction), N.J. Bar Assn. Construction, Contracts commercial, Government contracts and claims. Office: Peckar & Abramson 223 Moore St Hackensack NJ 07601

BARON, ROGER FREDERICK, lawyer; b. Brigham City, Utah, July 22, 1952; s. Rex Clark and LeOra (Petersen) B.; m. Christine Bowen, June 26, 1975; children: Teresa, LeAnn, Bryan, Janette. BS, Weber State Coll., 1976; JD, Brigham Young U., 1979. Bar: Utah 1979, U.S. Dist. Ct. Utah, 1979. Assoc. Jack H. Molgard, Brigham City, 1979-80; ptnr. Bunderson & Baron, Brigham City, 1980—; dep. atty. Box Elder County, Utah, 1980—. Dist. chmn. Reps., Brigham City, 1986; vice-chmn. Bear River Mental Health Assn., Logan, Utah, 1984—. Mem. ABA, Assn. Trial Lawyers Am., Box Elder County Bar Assn. (pres. 1985—, sec. 1983-85), Brigham City C. of C. (bd. dirs. 1986—). Mormon. Avocations: gardening, motorcycling. Contracts commercial, Probate, Criminal. Home: 552 N 5th W Brigham City UT 84302 Office: Bunderson & Baron 45 N 1st E Brigham City UT 84302

BARR, CHARLES JOSEPH GORE, lawyer; b. Saginaw, Mich., Sept. 17, 1940; s. Joseph Gore and Maja T. (Strand) B.; m. Carolyn Conn, Aug. 26, 1961; children: Maja Irene, Shannon Conn, Meaghan Won. BA, U. Mich., 1962, LLB, 1965. Bar: Mich. 1965, U.S. Dist. Ct. (ea. dist.) Mich. 1965, U.S. Ct. Appeals (6th cir.) 1968. Assoc. Clark Klein Winter, Detroit, 1965-67, Goodman, Eden, Millender & Bedrosian, Detroit, 1967-73; ptnr. Moore, Barr & Kerwin, Detroit, 1974-78, Barr & Walker, Detroit, 1978-83, Barr & Arsenault, Detroit, 1984—. Mem. ABA, State Bar of Mich. (chmn. negligence sect. 1985-86), Assn. Trial Lawyers Am. (gov. 1982-85), Mich. Trial Lawyers Assn. (sec. 1986-87), Nat. Lawyers Guild (pres. Detroit chpt. 1983-84, exec. bd.). Personal injury. Home: 19430 Cumberland Way Detroit MI 48203 Office: 2715 Cadillac Tower Detroit MI 48226

BARR, HARRY E., lawyer; b. Lexington, Ky., June 10, 1941; s. Charles Haseldon and Martha (Lowe) B.; m. Virginia Glynn, May 18, 1974. BS in Indsl. Engring., U. Ala., 1964, JD, 1974. Bar: Ala. 1974, Fla. 1974, U.S. Dist. Ct. (no. dist.) Fla. 1974, U.S. Ct. Appeals (5th and 11th cirs.). Engr. Brown & Root, New Orleans, 1964-65; law clk. to presiding justice U.S. Dist. Ct. (no. dist.) Fla., Tallahassee, 1974-75; assoc. Law Office Charles R. Timmel, Ft. Walton Beach, Fla., 1975-79; ptnr. Chesser, Wingard, Barr & Townsend, Ft. Walton Beach, 1979—. Bd. dirs. Camp Walton Sch. House, Fort Walton Beach, 1985-86, Krewe of Bowlegs, Ft. Walton Beach, 1980-86. Served to capt. USAF, 1965-71, Vietnam. Mem. Ala. Bar Assn., Fla. Bar Assn., Okaloosa/Walton Bar Assn. (pres. 1978), Assn. Trial Lawyers Am., Acad. Fla. Trial Lawyers. Avocation: sailing. Personal injury, Insurance. Office: Chesser Wingard Barr & Townsend 838 N Eglin Pkwy Suite 601 Fort Walton Beach FL 32548

BARR, JAMES HOUSTON, JR., lawyer; b. Louisville, Nov. 2, 1941; s. James Houston Jr. and Elizabeth Hamilton (Pope) B.; m. Sara Jane Todd, Apr. 16, 1970; 1 child, Lynn Jamison. Student U. Va., 1960-63, U. Tenn., 1963-64; B.S.L., J.D., U. Louisville, 1966. Bar: Ky. 1966, U.S. Ct. Appeals (6th cir.) 1969, U.S. Supreme Ct. 1971, U.S. Ct. Mil. Appeals 1978. Law clk., Ky. Ct. Appeals, Frankfort, 1966-67; asst. atty. gen. Ky., Frankfort, 1967-71, 1979-82; asst. U.S. atty. U.S. Dept. Justice, Louisville, 1971-79, 1983—; 1st asst. U.S. Atty., 1978-79; asst. dist. counsel U.S. Army C.E., Louisville, 1982-83. Served to lt. comdr. USNR, 1967-81, to lt. col. USAR, 1981—. Mem. Fed. Bar Assn. (pres. Louisville chpt. 1975-76, Younger Fed. Lawyer award 1975), Ky. Bar Assn., Louisville Bar Assn., Soc. Colonial Wars, SAR, Soc. Ky. Pioneers, Delta Upsilon. Republican. Episcopalian. Clubs: Pendennis, Louisville Boat, Filson (Louisville). Federal civil litigation, Criminal, Military. Home: 218 Choctaw Rd Louisville KY 40207 Office: US Atty 211 US Courthouse Louisville KY 40202

BARR, JAMES VICTOR, III, lawyer; b. Nashville, July 9, 1947; s. James Victor Jr. and Mary (Maddy) B.; m. Wanda Carole Midgett, Feb. 18, 1978 (div. 1980); 1 child, Mary Elizabeth; m. Sarah Susan Baker, July 14, 1984. Student Southwestern U., Memphis, 1965-66; B.A., Vanderbilt U., 1969; J.D. Nashville Sch. of Law YMCA Night Sch., 1974. Bar: Tenn. 1974, U.S. Dist. Ct. (mid. dist.) Tenn. 1977, U.S. Ct. Appeals (6th cir.) 1976. Assoc. Steltemeier & Westbrook, Nashville, 1984-86; ptnr. James V. Barr III and Assocs., Nashville, 1986—. Bd. dirs. Green Hills YMCA, Nashville, 1976-83, fin. chmn., 1979-81, sustaining campaign chmn., 1978, 79, 81, chmn. bd. dirs., 1981-82; bd. dirs. Met. Nashville YMCA, 1984, chmn. internat. com., 1984—, Pres. award 1986; bd. dirs. Martha O'Bryan Presbyn. Community Ch., Nashville, 1981-84, 1986—. Recipient Service to Youth award, 1979, Vol. of Yr. award, 1980-81, Outstanding Mem. award, 1981, Pres.'s award, 1986 (all Nashville YMCA). Mem. Tenn. Trial Lawyers Assn. (bd. govs., treas. 1980-82, exec. com. 1979-82, 85-86, chmn. pub. relations com. 1985-86, Presdl. award 1986), Nashville Bar Assn., Assn. Trial Lawyers Am., Tenn. Assn. Criminal Def. Lawyers, Nat. Assn. Criminal Def. Lawyers, Melvin M. Belli Soc. (trustee), Christian Legal Soc. State civil litigation, Federal civil litigation, Criminal. Home: 1809 Hillmont Ave TH A2 Nashville TN 37215 Office: 2120 Crestmoor Rd Suite 306 Nashville TN 37215

BARR, JOHN H., lawyer; b. June 22, 1955; s. Burt and Marge (Oare) B.; m. Celia Van Voorhees, July 20, 1980. BBA, St. Mary's U., San Antonio, 1978, JD, 1980. Bar: Tex., U.S. Dist. Ct. (no. and we. dists.) Tex., U.S. Ct. Appeals (5th cir.), U.S. Supreme Ct. Assoc. Westbrook & Goldston, San Antonio, Tex., 1980-81; ptnr. Burt, Barr & Assocs., Dallas, 1981—. chmn. juvenile justice com. Greater Dallas Crime Commn., 1984—; bd. dirs. selection com. Austin (Tex.) Dems. Mem. Tex. Bar Assn. (speaker practice skills course 1986), Dallas Bar Assn. (bd. dirs. family law sect. 1981—, author, chmn. civil ct. rules 1986, chmn. rules com. 1986). Democrat. Methodist. Family and matrimonial, State civil litigation, Probate. Office: Burt Barr & Assocs 306 S Record St Dallas TX 75202

BARR, JOHN MONTE, lawyer; b. Mt. Clemens, Mich., Jan. 1, 1935; s. Merle James and Wilhelmina Marie (Monte) B.; student Mexico City Coll., 1955; B.A., Mich. State U., 1956; J.D., U. Mich., 1959; m. Marlene Joy Bielenberg, Dec. 17, 1954; children—John Monte, Karl Alexander, Elizabeth Marie. Admitted to Mich. bar, 1959, since practiced in Ypsilanti; mem. firm Ellis B. Freatman, Jr., 1959-61; partner, chief trial atty. Freatman, Barr, Anhut & Moir and predecessor firm, 1961-63; pres. Barr, Anhut, Sacks, P.C., 1963—; city atty. City of Ypsilanti, 1981. Lectr. bus. law Eastern Mich. U., 1968-70. Pres., Ypsilanti Family Service, 1967; mem. Ypsilanti Public Housing Com., 1980-84; sr. adviser Explorer law post Portage Trail council Boy Scouts Am., 1969-71, commr. Potawatomi dist., 1973-74, commr. Washtenong dist., 1974-75, dist. committeeman, 1984; bd. dirs. Mich. Mcpl. League Legal Def. Fund. Served with AUS, 1959-60. Mem. State Bar Mich. (grievance bd. 1969—, state rep. assembly 1977-82), Am., Ypsilanti, Washtenaw County (pres. 1975-76) bar assns., Am., Mich. trial lawyers assns., Mich. Mcpl. Attys. Assn. (bd. dirs.), U.S. (instr. piloting, seamanship, sail), Ann Arbor (comdr. 1972-73) power squadrons. Lutheran. Club: Washtenaw Country. Contbr. articles to boating mags. Local government, General practice. Home: 1200 Whittier Rd Ypsilanti MI 48197 Office: 105 Pearl St Ypsilanti MI 48197

BARR, JOHN ROBERT, lawyer; b. Gary, Ind., Apr. 10, 1936; s. John Andrew and Louise (Stentz) B.; children: Mary Louise, John Mills, Jennifer Susan. A.B., Grinnell Coll., 1957; LL.B. cum laude, Harvard U., 1960. Bar: Ill. 1960. Assoc. Sidley & Austin, Chgo., 1960-69, ptnr., 1970—; mem. Ill. Ho. of Reps., 1981-83, Commn. on Presdl. Scholars, Washington, 1975-77. Chmn. Ill. Bd. Regents, 1971-77; mem. Ill. Bd. Higher Edn., 1971-77; chmn. Ill. State Scholarship Commn., 1985—; chmn. Republican Central Com. of Cook County, Chgo., 1978-85; mem. Rep. state central committee 9th Congl. Dist. Ill., 1986—. Mem. ABA, Ill. Bar Assn. (chmn. state tax sect. council 1986—), Chgo. Bar Assn. (chmn. com. on state and mcpl. taxation 1974-75), Law Club, Legal Club Chgo., Selden Soc., Nat. Assn. State Bar Tax Sects. (exec. com. 1986—), Internat. Assn. Assessing Officers, Inst. Property Taxation, Phi Beta Kappa. Episcopalian. Clubs: Chgo, Monroe. State and local taxation, Legislative, Administrative and regulatory. Home: 1501 Oak Ave Evanston IL 60201 Office: Sidley & Austin 1 First National Plaza Chicago IL 60603

BARR, MICHAEL BLANTON, lawyer; b. Freeport, N.Y., July 24, 1948; s. Harry Kyle and Rosemary (Blanton) B.; m. Nancy Nickeson, Aug. 11, 1979; children: Nicholas Upton, Jessica Nickeson. B.S., Georgetown U., 1970; J.D., George Washington U., 1973. Bar: D.C. 1973. U.S. Dist. Ct. D.C. 1973, U.S. Ct. Appeals (D.C. cir.) 1974, U.S. Ct. Appeals (3d cir.) 1979, U.S. Ct. Appeals, (4th cir.) 1976, U.S. Ct. Appeals (6th cir.) 1981, U.S. Supreme Ct. 1980. Assoc. LeBoeuf, Lamb, Lieby & McRae, Washington, 1973-76, Hunton & Williams, Washington, 1976-80; ptnr. Hunton & Williams, Washington, 1980—, also mem. exec. com., 1985—. Contbr. articles to profl. jours. Bd. dirs. Episcopal Ctr. for Children, Washington, 1980—. Mem. ABA ,Internat. Bar Assn., Fed. Communication Bar Assn., D.C. Bar Assn. Democrat. Club: City Tavern (Washington). Administrative and regulatory, Communications, Private international. Home: 7203 Exfair Rd Bethesda MD 20814 Office: Hunton & Williams 2000 Pennsylvania Ave NW PO Box 19230 Washington DC 20036

BARR, ROBERT LAURENCE, JR., lawyer; b. Iowa City, Nov. 5, 1948; s. Robert Laurence and Beatrice Emily (Radenhausen) B.; m. Gail Vogel, Oct. 9, 1976; children: Adrian Robert, Derek Ryan. B.A. in Internat. Relations, U. So. Calif., 1970; M.A. in Internat. Affairs (grad. fellow), George Washington U., 1972; J.D., Georgetown U., 1977. Bar: Ga. 1977, Fla. 1979. Analyst, atty., chief legis. staff CIA, Washington, 1970-78; asso. Law Offices of Edwin Marger, Atlanta, 1979-81; sole practice, Marietta, Ga., 1981—; gen. counsel Cobb County Republican Com., 1981-83, 1st vice-chmn., 1983—U.S. attorney for Northern Georgia, 1986—. Mem. ABA, Ga. Bar Assn., Fla. Bar Assn., Cobb County Bar Assn., Atlanta Bar Assn., Assn. Trial Lawyers Am., Ga. Assn. Criminal Def. Lawyers, Cobb County C. of C., Assn. Former Intelligence Officers, Phi Alpha Delta, Delta Phi Epsilon. Episcopalian. Clubs: Kiwanis, Metro Marietta. Mem. editorial staff Am. Criminal Law Rev., 1974-77. Criminal, State civil litigation, Private international. Home: 4320 Revere Circle Marietta GA 30062 Office: 248 Washington Ave Marietta GA 30060 *

BARR, THOMAS DELBERT, lawyer; b. Kansas City, Mo., Jan. 23, 1931; s. Harold D. and Emma M. (Sanders) B.; m. Cornelia Harrington, Sept. 26, 1953; children: Daniel C., Phoebe Anne Hotz, Robert A., Sara E. B.A., U. Mo., Kansas City, 1953; LL.B., Yale U., 1958. Bar: N.Y. State 1959, U.S. Supreme Ct. 1964. Assoc. firm Cravath, Swaine, & Moore, N.Y.C., 1958-65; partner firm Cravath, Swaine, & Moore, 1965—; bd. dirs. Salzburg Seminar. Dep. dir. Nat. Commn. on Causes and Prevention of Violence, 1968-70; mem. exec. com. Lawyers' Com. for Civil Rights Under Law, nat. co-chmn., 1977-79. Served to lt. USMC, 1953-55. Mem. Am., N.Y. State bar assns., Assn. Bar of City of N.Y., Am. Coll. Trial Lawyers, Internat. Acad. Trial Lawyers, Am. Bar Found., Council Fgn. Relations. Home: 18 Meadowcroft Ln Greenwich CT 06830 Office: One Chase Manhattan Plaza New York NY 10005

BARRANGER, GARIC KENNETH, lawyer; b. New Orleans, La., Dec. 7, 1934; s. Dalton and Miriam (Garic) B.; m. Mildred Slater, Aug. 26, 1961 (div. Dec. 1985); 1 child, Heather Dalton. BA in Philosophy, Yale U., 1956; JD, Tulane U., 1959. Bar: La., U.S. Dist. Ct. (mid. and ea. dists.) La. Ptnr. Barranger, Barranger, Jones & Fussell, Covington, La., 1962-80; sole practice Covington, 1980—; bd. dirs. New Orlean Jazz and Heritage Found., Sta. WWNO Radio, WWOZ Radio. Founding mem., gen. counsel Hospice of St. Tammany; bd. dirs., pres., chmn. fund raising com. Playmakers, Inc.; gen. counsel, bd. dirs. performer Puppet Playhouse, Inc.; bd. dirs. Southeastern La. Legal Services Corp.; chmn. solicitation dr. Am. Cancer Soc., 1976-77. Mem. ABA, La. Bar Assn. (Ho. of Dels. 1971-73), Covington Bar Assn., St. Tammany Bar Assn. (chmn. ethics and grievances com. 1959-67-76, courthouse location and design com.), Assn. Trial Lawyers Am., La. Trial Lawyers Assn., Am. Judicature Soc., Law Sci. Acad. of Am., Internat. Barristers Soc., Supreme Ct. Hist. Soc., Am. Theatre Assn., La. Mental Health Assn. (chmn. ad hoc com. 1973, v.p. pub. affairs), Yale U. Alumni Assn. (bd. dirs. 1967-77, pres. 1972-76). Roman Catholic. Clubs: Covington Ct., Smithsonian. Family and matrimonial, Personal injury. Home: 1414 S Jahncke Ave Covington LA 70433 Office: 325 E Lockwood St Covington LA 70433

BARRECA, CHRISTOPHER ANTHONY, lawyer; b. Pittsfield, Mass., Sept. 15, 1928; s. Christopher Joseph and Jennie (Cannici) B.; m. Alice Hazlehurst, Sept. 5, 1953; children—Christopher, Alice, Jennifer. A.A., Boston U., 1950, J.D., 1953; LL.M., Northwestern U., 1968. Bar: Mass 1954, Ky. 1969, U.S. Dist. ct. (we. dist.) Ky. 1970, U.S. Ct. Apls. (6th cir.) 1970. With Gen. Electric Co., Fairfield, Conn., 1953—, labor arbitration and litigation csl., 1971-80, labor and employment law csl., 1980—; mem. arbitration services adv. com. Fed Mediation and Conciliation Service, 1973—; adj. prof. U. Louisville, 1970-71, U. Bridgeport (Conn.) Sch. of Law, 1986—. Chmn., Weston (Conn.) Bd. Edn., 1977-82; trustee exec. com., chmn. com. legal affairs Boston U., 1977—. Served with AUS, 1946-47. Mem. ABA (co-chmn. labor and employment law sect. com. labor arbitration advocacy, elected to governing council of labor and employment law sect. 1986—), Boston U. Sch. Law Alumni Assn. (Silver Shingle award 1982). Club: Aspetuck Valley Country (Weston). Co-author, editor: Labor Arbitrator Development, 1983. Contbr. articles to profl. jours. Labor, Administrative and regulatory, General corporate. Home: 6 Aspetuck Hill Ln Weston CT 06883 Office: 3135 Easton Tpk Fairfield CT 06431

BARRETT, BRUCE ALAN, lawyer; b. Pitts., Aug. 9, 1950; s. Hugh Horner and Ethel (McCrea) B.; m. Gayle Gray, Sept. 24, 1974; children: Eric, Sarah, Brian. BA, U. Pa., 1972; JD, Cleve. State U., 1975. Bar: Pa. 1975, U.S. Dist. Ct. (we. dist.) Pa. 1978. Ptnr. Magee & Barrett, Meadville, Pa., 1975-79; sole practice Meadville, 1979-85; ptnr. Barrett & Dratler, Meadville, 1985—; 1st asst. pub. defender Crawford County, Meadville, 1978—. Chmn. parade com. Meadville Meml. Day Celebration, 1980-82. Named one of Outstanding Young Men Am., 1986. Mem. Pa. Bar Assn., Crawford County Bar Assn., Meadville Jaycees (pres. 1979-80). Republican. Presbyterian. State civil litigation, General practice, Criminal. Office: Barrett & Dratler 965 S Main St Meadville PA 16335

BARRETT, CYNTHIA LOUISE, lawyer; b. Portland, Oreg., Jan. 18, 1949; d. Eugene Francis and Frances Barbara (Tobin) B. BA in Polit. Sci., U. Pa., 1970; JD, Lewis and Clark Coll., 1976. Bar: Oreg. 1976, U.S. Dist. Ct. Oreg. 1976, U.S. Ct. Appeals (9th cir.) 1978. Assoc. Haley & Haley, Portland, 1976-77; sole practice Portland, 1977-83, 86—; ptnr. Fellows, McCarthy, Friedman, Odman & Barrett, Portland, 1984-86. Mem. Tax Supervising and Conservation Commn., Portland, 1978-85, chmn. 1982; mem. Multnomah County Bd. Equalization, Portland, 1982. Mem. ABA, Oreg. Bar Assn., Multnomah Bar Assn. Democrat. Roman Catholic. Avocations: fishing, mil. history, writing. Real property, Probate, State civil litigation. Home: 6710 N Michigan Portland OR 97217 Office: 711 Mead Bldg 421 SW Fifth Ave Portland OR 97204

BARRETT, DAVID CARROLL, lawyer; b. Delaware, Ohio, Jan. 17, 1956; s. David Carroll and Friedel Laura (Reintjens) B.; m. Theresa Clare Creighton, Apr. 2, 1982. BS in Agr. with honors, Ohio State U., 1978; JD cum laude, U. Toledo, 1981. Bar: Ohio 1981, U.S. Dist. Ct. (no. dist.) Ohio 1982, U.S. Tax Ct. 1983, U.S. Ct. Appeals (6th cir.) 1984. From assco. to ptnr. Wasserman, Wasserman, Bryan & Landry, Toledo, 1981-85; ptnr. Arnold & Barrett, Toledo, 1985—; bd. dirs. farm div. Mid Am. Nat. Bank and Trust Co., Bowling Green, Ohio. Contbr. articles to profl. jours. Chmn. agri. bus. com. Mid Am. Council Econ. Devel., Bowling Green, 1982—, bd. of trustees, 1986—. Recipient Young Profl. Achievement award Ohio State U. Coll. Agr. Alumni Assn., 1985. Mem. ABA (agr. bus. fin. subcom. sect. corp., banking and bus. law), Ohio Bar Assn. (sec. agrl. law com. 1987—), Toledo Bar Assn. (taxation, bankruptcy and lawyers life underwriters com.), Am. Agrl. Law Assn., Alpha Zeta Alumni Assn. (bd. trustees 1987—). Republican. Roman Catholic. Club: Exchange (West Toledo) (pres. 1987—). Agricultural, Estate planning, Bankruptcy. Home: 4419 Westway St Toledo OH 43612 Office: Arnold & Barrett 425 Jefferson Ave Suite 804 Toledo OH 43604

BARRETT, DAVID EUGENE, lawyer; b. Hiawassee, Ga., June 25, 1955; s. Homer and Laura Arispah (Wilson) B.; m. Nell Mills, June 17, 1978; children: Laura Elizabeth, Thomas Jeffrey. BA summa cum laude, U. Ga., 1977, JD cum laude, 1980. Assoc. Erwin, Epting, et al, Athens, Ga., 1980-84, Blasingame, Burch, et al, Athens, 1984; sole practice Hiawassee, 1984—; counsel Towns County Humane Soc., Hiawassee, 1985—; bd. dirs. Mountain Bank of Ga., Towns County Hosp. Authority. counselor Alzheimer Support, Hiawassee, 1985; fin. supr. N. Ga. for Sen. Mattingly, 1986. Mem. ABA, Ga. Bar Assn., Mountain Bar Assn., Western Bar Assn. (sec. 1983-84), Trial Lawyers Assn., Towns County C. of C. (bd. dirs. 1985—), Demosthenian Lit. Soc. (bd. dirs., sec. bd. trustees 1978—), Athens Jaycees (v.p. 1983-84). Republican. Baptist. State civil litigation, Real property, Family and matrimonial. Home: Sequoia Point Hiawassee GA 30546 Office: The Mall-Main St Hiawassee GA 30546-0261

BARRETT, DENNIS CHRISTOPHER, lawyer; b. N.Y.C., June 14, 1942; s. Norman Joseph and Maryalce (Smith) B.; m. Kathryn Watt; children: Megan, Kelly, Brendan, Christopher. BA, U. Calif., Santa Barbara, 1964; JD, U. Calif., San Francisco, 1967. Bar: Calif. 1968, U.S. Dist. Ct. Calif. 1968, U.S. Tax Ct. 1969. Staff atty. Legal Aid Soc., Santa Cruz, Calif., 1968-70; pub. defender Santa Clara, Calif., 1970-72; sole practice San Jose, Calif., 1972—. Mem. Calif. Attys. for Criminal Justice, Calif. Trial Lawyers Assn. Criminal, Federal civil litigation, State civil litigation. Office: 510 N 3rd St San Jose CA 95112

BARRETT, JAMES E., judge; b. Lusk, Wyo., Apr. 8, 1922; s. Frank A. and Alice C. (Donoghue) B.; m. Carmel Ann Martinez, Oct. 8, 1949; children—Ann Catherine Barrett Sandahl, Richard James, John Donoghue. Student, U. Wyo., 1940-42, LL.B., 1949; student, St. Catherine's Coll., Oxford, Eng., 1945, Cath. U. Am., 1946. Bar: Wyo. 1949. Mem. firm Barrett and Barrett, Lusk, 1949-67; atty. gen. State of Wyo., 1967-71; judge U.S. Circuit Ct. Appeals, 10th Circuit, 1971—; county and pros. atty. Niobrara County, Wyo., 1951-62; atty. Town of Lusk, 1952-64, Niobrara Sch. Dist., 1950-64. Active Boy Scouts Am.; sec.-treas. Niobrara County Republican Central Com.; bd. dirs. St. Joseph's Children's Home, Torrington, Wyo., 1971-85; trustee ch. Served as cpl. AUS, 1942-45, ETO. Recipient Distinguished Alumni award U. Wyo., 1973. Mem. VFW, Am. Legion. Office: US Ct of Appeals PO Box 1288 Cheyenne WY 82001

BARRETT, JAMES P., lawyer; b. N.Y.C., Sept. 22, 1936; s. Timothy J. and Margaret (Nevins) B.; m. Rosemary Rush, June 7, 1958; children: Brian, Susan, Deirdre, Robert, Raymond. BBA, St. John's U., N.Y.C., 1958, LLB, 1961. Bar: N.Y., U.S. Dist. Ct. (so. and ea. dists.). Atty. Royal Ins. Co., N.Y.C., 1962-67; assoc. Kroll, Edelman & Lawzone, N.Y.C., 1967-68; assoc. Simpson, Thachen & Bartlett, N.Y.C., 1968-80, ptnr., 1980—. Acting judge Village of Munsey Park, Nassau County, N.Y., 1983—. Mem. N.Y. State Bar Assn. Avocation: golfing. Personal injury, Insurance. Home: 208 Nassau Ave Manhasset NY 11030

BARRETT, JANE H., lawyer; b. Dayton, Ohio, Dec. 13, 1947; d. Walter J. and Jane H. Barrett. B.A., Calif. State U.-Long Beach, 1969; J.D., U. So. Calif., 1972. Bar: Calif. 1972, U.S. Dist. Ct. (cen. dist.) Calif. 1972, U.S. Ct. Appeals (9th cir.) 1982, U.S. Supreme Ct. Assoc. Lawler, Felix & Hall, Los Angeles, 1972-79, mng. ptnr., 1979-85, ptnr., 1985—; lectr. bus. law Calif. State U., 1973-75. Fellow Am. Bar Found.; mem. ABA (gov. 1980-84, chmn. young lawyers div. 1980-81, chair com. on delivery of legal services 1985—, sec. Am. Bar Endowment), Legion Lex. Democrat. General practice, Federal civil litigation, State civil litigation. Office: 700 S Flower St 30th Floor Los Angeles CA 90017

BARRETT, KAREN MOORE, lawyer; b. Pitts., Jan. 16, 1950; d. James Newton and Grace Naomi (Gigax) Moore; m. Jay Elliott Barrett, June 24, 1972; children: Catherine Grace, Elizabeth Alice. AB, Bryn Mawr Coll., 1972; JD, Harvard U., 1977. Bar: Pa. 1977, U.S. Dist. Ct. (we. dist.) Pa. 1977. Assoc. Buchanan Ingersoll Profl. Corp., Pitts., 1977-84, ptnr., 1984—. Bd. dirs. Planned Parenthood of Pitts. Inc., 1983—; v.p. Bryn Mawr Club of Western Pa., Pitts., 1984-87, pres., 1987—. Mem. ABA, Pa. Bar Assn., Allegheny County Bar Assn. Democrat. Presbyterian. Club: Harvard-Yale-Princeton of Western Pa.(Pitts.) (bd. dirs. 1986—). Securities, Banking, General corporate. Office: Buchanan Ingersoll Profl Corp 600 Grant St 57th Floor Pittsburgh PA 15219

BARRETT, ROBERT MATTHEW, lawyer; b. Bronx, N.Y., Mar. 18, 1948; s. Harry and Rosalind B. AB summa cum laude, Georgetown U., 1976, MS in Fgn. Service, JD, 1980. Bar: Calif. 1981. Assoc. Latham & Watkins, Los Angeles, 1980-82, Morgan, Lewis & Bockius, Los Angeles, 1982-84, Skadden, Arps, Slate, Meagher & Flom, Los Angeles, 1984—. Mem. ABA,

Los Angeles Bar Assn. (bd. advisors vols. in parole com. 1981—). Mass product liability litigation, State civil litigation, Private international. Home: 13816 Bora Bora Way #137A Marina del Rey CA 90292 Office: Skadden Arps Slate Meagher Flom 300 S Grand #3400 Los Angeles CA 90071-3144

BARRETT, ROGER WATSON, lawyer; b. Chgo., June 26, 1915; s. Oliver R. and Pauline S. B.; m. Nancy N. Braun, June 20, 1940; children—Victoria Barrett Bell, Holly, Oliver. A.B., Princeton U., 1937; J.D., Northwestern U., 1940. Bar: Ill. bar 1940. Mem. firm Poppenhusen, Johnson, Thompson & Raymond, Chgo., 1940-43; 45-50; charge documentary evidence Nuremberg Trial, 1944-45; regional counsel Econ. Stablzn. Agy., Chgo., 1951-52; partner firm Mayer, Brown & Platt, Chgo., 1952—; dir. John M. Smyth Co. Vice pres. Mus. Contemporary Art, Chgo., 1972—. Served with AUS, 1943-45. Mem. Am. Bar Assn., Am. Coll. Trial Lawyers, Ill. Bar Assn., Chgo. Bar Assn. Clubs: Indian Hill (Winnetka); Commonwealth (Chgo.), Caxton (Chgo.), Confrerie des Chevaliers du Tastevin (Chgo.). Antitrust, Federal civil litigation. Home: 84 Indian Hill Rd Winnetka IL 60093 Office: 231 S LaSalle St Chicago IL 60604

BARRICK, DONALD MICHAEL, surgeon, lawyer; b. Washington, Nov. 21, 1931; s. George Peter and Matilda Marie (Dora) B.; m. Donna Michelle Kinzer, Feb. 14, 1985; children: Donald Michael Jr., Robert George, James Ross. AA, George Washington U., 1954, AB, 1958; MD, U. Md., 1962, JD, 1977. Bar: Md. 1977, U.S. Dist. Ct. Md. 1978, D.C. 1980. Intern in internal medicine U. Md. Hosp., Balt., 1962-63, resident in surgery, 1964-67; practice medicine specializing in surgery Balt., 1967—; assoc. Seiland & Jednorski, Balt., 1978—; bd. dirs. Balt. City Profl. Standards Rev. Orgn.; chief of med. staff Md. Gen. Hosp., Baron, 1982—. Served with USAF, 1951-53. Mem. ABA, AMA, ACS, Am. Coll. Legal Medicine, Aircraft Owners and Pilots Assn. Republican. Eastern Orthodox. Lodge: Masons. Office: 25 W Chesapeake St Towson MD 21204

BARRICKMAN, UHEL OVERTON, lawyer; b. Bedford, Ky., Sept. 4, 1920; s. Roy F. and Sadie Lee (Overton) B.; m. Ann Clinton Gandy, Feb. 17, 1 943; children: John, Nancy, Don, Bruce. AB, U. Ky., 1941, JD, 1947. Bar: Ky. 1942, U.S. Dist. Ct. (we. dist.) Ky. 1948, U.S. Ct. Appeals (6th cir.) 1955. Sr. ptnr. Richardson, Barrickman, Dickinson & Ropp, Glasgow, Ky., 1957—. Served to maj. U.S. Army, 1942-46. Fellow Am. Coll. Trial Lawyers; mem. ABA, Ky. Bar Assn. (civil rules com.), Barren County Bar Assn., Fed. Bar Assn., Council Sch. Bd. Attys., Internat. Soc. Barristers, Jud. Ethics Com. Ky., Civil Rules Com. Ky., Glasgow C. of C. Presbyterian. Lodge: Rotary (pres., past dist. gov. 1971-72; Paul Harris fellow Glasgow 1978). Federal civil litigation, State civil litigation, Insurance. Home: 412 Garmon Ave Glasgow KY 42141

BARRIE, JOHN PAUL, lawyer, educator; b. Burbank, Calif., Oct. 7, 1947; s. John and Virginia (Feagans) B.; m. Deanna Phippen, June 21, 1969; children: Sean, Tyler. AB in Pol. Sci., UCLA, 1969; JD, U. Calif., San Francisco, 1972; LLM in Tax, NYU, 1973. Bar: Calif. 1972, D.C. 1975, Mo. 1977. Atty. advisor to judge U.S. Tax Ct., Washington, 1973-75; atty. office of gen. counsel Renegotiation Bd., Washington, 1975-77; assoc. Lewis & Rice, St. Louis, 1977-82, ptnr., 1982-86; ptnr. Gallop, Johnson & Neuman, St. Louis, 1986—; adj. prof. Washington U. Sch. Law, St. Louis, 1979—. Contbr. various tax articles to jours. Mem. ABA (tax sect. task force, com. on affiliated and related corps., chmn. subcom. on interco. allocations), Mo. Bar Assn. (tax sect., past chmn. tax com., Pres.'s award 1983), Calif. Bar Assn. (tax sect.), D.C. Bar Assn., Bar Assn. Met. St. Louis (tax sect.), Nat. Assn. State Bar Tax Sects. (chmn. 1983-84), St. Louis Regional Commerce and Growth Assn. (spending and taxes com.). Episcopalian. Clubs: Noonday, Whittemore House (St. Louis). Corporate taxation, Personal income taxation, State and local taxation. Home: 6379 Waterman Saint Louis MO 63130 Office: Gallop Johnson & Neuman 101 S Hanley 1600 Intern Tower Saint Louis MO 63105

BARRON, CAROLINE JOAN, lawyer, editor; b. Orinda, Calif., Jan. 4, 1958; d. John Francis and Carolyn Patricia (Dunn) B.; m. Christopher Mead, Aug. 27, 1983. BA, Stanford U., 1978, JD, 1981. Bar: Calif. 1982, Ariz. 1983. Assoc. Brobeck, Phleger & Harrison, San Francisco, 1981-83, Beus, Gilbert, Wake & Morrill, Phoenix, 1983—; editor, ptnr. Mead Ventures, Inc., Phoenix, 1983—; bd. dirs. 1st Cen. Bank, Phoenix. Editor: (newsletter) Japan High Tech Rev., 1983—, Korean High Tech Rev., 1986—, Korean Automotive Rev., 1986—, Taiwan High Tech Rev., 1986—, Southeast Asia Tech Rev., 1986—, Japanese Auto Manufacturingin North America, 1986—. Vol. Phoenix Art Mus. Contemporary Forum, 1985—, Taliesin West/Frank Lloyd Wright Found., Phoenix, 1986—, Ariz. north br. Am. Soc. Interior Designers, Phoenix, 1985—, also speaker, arbitrator. Mem. ABA, Calif. Bar Assn., Ariz. Bar Assn., Maricopa County Bar Assn., Assn. Trial Lawyers Am. Avocations: horseback riding, squash, windsurfing, polo. State civil litigation, Federal civil litigation, General practice. Office: Beus Gilbert Wake & Morrill 3300 N Central Suite 1000 Phoenix AZ 85012

BARRON, FRANCIS PATRICK, lawyer; b. Boston, Apr. 17, 1951; s. Francis P. and Audrey (Lutz) B.; m. Eve Brandis Sundelson, Sept. 13, 1981; 1 child, Elisha Brandis. AB, Harvard U., 1973, JD, 1978. Bar: N.Y. 1979, U.S. Dist. Ct. (so. dist) N.Y. 1979, U.S. Dist. Ct. (ea. dists.) N.Y. 1981, U.S. Ct. Internat. Trade 1982, U.S. Ct. Appeals (2d cir.) 1981, U.S. Ct. Appeals (6th cir.) 1983, U.S. Supreme Ct. 1983. Asst. dir. film Sta. WCVB-TV, Boston, 1973-75; assoc. Cravath, Swaine & Moore, N.Y.C., 1978-85, ptnr., 1985—. Mem. Harvard Vol. Defenders, Cambridge, 1977-78. Athletic scholar Nat. Football Found. Hall of Fame, 1969. Mem. ABA, N.Y. State Bar Assn., N.Y. County Bar Assn., Assn. of Bar of City of N.Y. Federal civil litigation, Antitrust, Libel. Office: Cravath Swaine & Moore 1 Chase Manhattan Plaza New York NY 10005

BARRON, HOWARD ROBERT, lawyer; b. Chgo., Feb. 17, 1930; s. Irwin P. and Ada (Astrahan) B.; m. Marjorie Shapira, Aug. 12, 1953; children: Ellen J., Laurie A. Ph.B., U. Chgo., 1948; B.A., Stanford U., 1950; LL.B., Yale U., 1953. Bar: Ill. 1953. Assoc. Jenner & Block, Chgo., 1957-63, ptnr., 1964—. Contbr. articles in field to profl. jours. Mem., then pres. Lake County Sch. Dist. 107 Bd. Edn., Highland Park, 1964-1971; pres. Lake County Sch. Bd. Assn., 1970-71; mem. Lake County High Sch. Dist. 113 Bd. Edn., Highland Park, 1973-77, Highland Park Zoning Bd. Appeals, 1984—. Served to lt. j.g. USNR, 1953-57. Mem. ABA (chmn. subcom. labor matters, com. corp. counsel litigation sect.), Ill. State Bar Assn. (chmn. antitrust sect. 1968-69), Fed. Bar Assn., Chgo. Bar Assn., Yale Law Sch. Assn. (v.p. 1978-81), Yale Law Sch. Assn. Ill. (pres. 1962). Democrat. Clubs: Standard, Cliff Dwellers (Chgo.). Labor, Federal civil litigation, State civil litigation. Home: 433 Ravine Dr Highland Park IL 60035 Office: Jenner & Block 1 IBM Plaza Chicago IL 60611

BARRON, JEROME AURE, university dean, law educator, lawyer; b. Tewksbury, Mass., Sept. 25, 1933; s. Henry and Sadie (Shafmaster) B.; m. Myra Hymovich, June 18, 1961; children—Jonathan Nathaniel, David Jeremiah, Jennifer Leah. A.B. magna cum laude, Tufts Coll., 1955; LL.B., Yale U., 1958; LL.M., George Washington U., 1960. Bar: Mass. 1959, D.C. 1960. Law clk. to chief judge U.S. Ct. Claims, Washington, 1960-61; assoc. firm Cross, Murphy & Smith, Washington, 1961-62; asst. prof. law U. N.D., 1962-64; vis. assoc. prof. U. N.Mex., 1964-65; assoc. prof. George Washington U., from 1965, prof., 1973—, dean, 1979—, Lyle T. Alverson prof. law, 1987—; dean Syracuse U. Coll. Law, 1972-73. Author books including: (with C. Thomas Dienes) Handbook of Free Speech and Free Press, 1979, (with Donald Gillmor) Mass Communication Law, Cases and Comment, 4th edit., 1984, Public Rights and the Private Press, 1981; contbr. articles, chpts. to profl. publs.; mem. adv. bd. Media Law Reporter. Served with U.S. Army, 1959-60. Mem. ABA, D.C. Bar, Phi Beta Kappa. Democrat. Jewish. Clubs: Cosmos, Nat. Lawyers. Legal education, Communications. Office: George Washington U 2000 H St NW Washington DC 20052

BARRON, MYRA HYMOVICH, lawyer; b. Stamford, Conn., July 5, 1938; d. Leo and Lillian Estelle (Berman) Hymovich; m. Jerome Aure Barron, June 18, 1961; children—Jonathan Nathaniel, David Jeremiah, Jennifer Leah. A.B. cum laude, Smith Coll., 1959; student L'Institut des Hautes Etudes, Geneva, 1957-58; M.A., Johns Hopkins U., 1961; J.D., Georgetown U., 1970. Bar: Va. 1970, D.C. 1972, N.Y. 1973. Instr. econs. U. N.D., Grand Forks, 1962-64; econ. research asst. U. N.Mex., Albuquerque, 1964-65; legal aid staff atty., Fairfax County, Va., 1971-72; assoc. Melvin & Melvin, Syracuse, N.Y., 1973; asst. county atty., Fairfax County, 1974-81; counsel Fairfax County Redevel. and Housing Authority, Fairfax, Va., 1981—. Recipient Samuel Bowles award Smith Coll., 1959. Mem. LWV (local chmn. nat. events 1962-64). Mem. Georgetown Law Jour., 1967-68. Local government, Real property, General corporate. Home: 3231 Ellicott St NW Washington DC 20008 Office: One University Plaza Fairfax VA 22030

BARROWS, RONALD THOMAS, lawyer; b. Detroit, Jan. 19, 1954; s. Harland Wayne and Jeanette Edith (Authier) B. BA in English and Polit. Sci. magna cum laude, Oakland U., 1976; JD, Wayne State U., 1979. Bar: Mich. 1979, U.S. Dist. Ct. (ea. dist.) Mich. 1979, U.S. Ct. Appeals (6th cir.) 1983, U.S. Tax Ct. 1986. Assoc. Abbott, Nicholson, Quilter, Esshaki & Youngblood, P.C., Detroit, 1979-80; counsel Lindon Land Co., Inc., Harper Woods, Mich., 1980-82; sole practice St. Clair Shores, Mich., 1981—; cons./counselor to corporate and pvt. real estate investors. Mem. ABA (real property probate and trust law sect. 1979—, corp. banking and bus. sect. 1979—, econs. of law sect. 1985—), Mich. Bar Assn. (title standards com. 1985—, real property sect. 1980—, riparian rights com. 1985—, corp. banking and bus. sect. 1979—, econs. of law sect. 1985—, chmn. water law com. 1985—), Macomb County Bar Assn., Am. Trial Lawyers Assn., Nat. Assn. Realtors, Mich. Assn. Realtors (sr. instr. 1980—), Nat. Order Barristers. Republican. Presbyterian. Avocations: sailing, billiards, theater. Real property, Investments. Office: 21631 E Nine Mile Rd Saint Clair Shores MI 48080

BARRY, CHARLES BYRON, lawyer; b. St. Paul, Feb. 12, 1952; s. Stanley James and Claire Louise (Sather) B.; m. Paula Marie Peick, June 22, 1974; children: David, Andrew, Colleen. AA in Human Services, Inver Hills Community Coll., 1973, AA, 1974; B in Applied Studies, U. Minn., 1975; JD, Hamline U., 1979. Bar: Minn. 1979, U.S. Dist. Ct. Minn. 1979. Procurement legal counsel Honeywell Corp., Hopkins, Minn., 1980-81, asst. contracts counsel, 1981-82, contracts counsel, 1982-86; staff atty. GNB Inc., Mendota Hts., Minn., 1986—. Team mgr. Highland Area Hockey Assn., St. Paul, 1984—; bd. dirs. Total Life Clinics, St. Paul, 1982—, v.p. 1984-85. Mem. ABA (pub. contract law and internat. law and practice sects.), Minn. Bar Assn. (internat. bus. law sect., computer law sect. 1984—), Am. Corp. Counsel Assn. Roman Catholic. Avocations: biking, sports, reading, vol. work. Contracts commercial, General corporate, Private international. Home: 1422 Wellesley Ave Saint Paul MN 55105 Office: GNB Inc PO Box 64100 Saint Paul MN 55164-0100

BARRY, DESMOND THOMAS, JR., lawyer; b. N.Y.C., Mar. 26, 1945; s. Desmond Thomas and Kathryn (O'Connor) B.; m. Patricia Mellicker, Aug. 28, 1971; children—Kathryn, Desmond Todd. A.B., Princeton U., 1967; J.D., Fordham U., 1973. Bar: N.Y. 1974, U.S. Dist. Ct. (so. and ea. dist.) N.Y. 1974, U.S. Ct. Appeals (2d cir.) 1974, U.S. Ct. Appeals (9th cir.) 1980, U.S. Ct. Appeals (5th cir.) 1983, U.S. Ct. Appeals (3d cir.) 1984, U.S. Supreme Ct. 1985. Assoc. firm Condon & Forsyth, N.Y.C., 1973-79, ptnr., 1979—. Trustee Canterbury Sch., New Milford, Conn., 1970-80. Served to capt. USMC, 1967-70, Vietnam. Decorated Navy Commendation medal with combat V; Combat Action medal, 1969, Vietnamese Cross of Gallantry, 1969. Mem. Assn. Bar City N.Y., ABA, N.Y. State Bar Assn., Internat. Assn. Ins. Counsel. Republican. Roman Catholic. Club: Winged Foot Golf (Mamaroneck, N.Y.). Federal civil litigation, State civil litigation, Insurance. Home: 5 Point O'Woods St Darien CT 06820 Office: Condon & Forsyth 1251 Ave of Americas New York NY 10020

BARRY, EDWARD LOUIS, lawyer; b. Greenville, Mich., Mar. 20, 1951; s. Edward H. and Gertrude (Hamper) B.; m. Mary Lynn Berger, Mar. 16, 1974; children—Jane, Laura, Anne Marie. B.A. with high honors, Mich. State U., 1975; postgrad. U. So. Calif., 1977, Oxford U., 1975; J.D., Ariz. State U., 1979. Bar: Ariz. 1979, U.S. Dist. Ct. Ariz. 1979. Sole practice law, Phoenix, 1979—. Recipient Am. Jurisprudence award, 1977. Mem. Assn. Trial Lawyers Am., Ariz. Trial Lawyers Assn., Fed. Bar Assn. Personal injury, State civil litigation, Federal civil litigation. Office: 3300 N Central Ave 14th fl Phoenix AZ 85012

BARRY, FRANCIS JULIAN, JR., lawyer; b. New Orleans, Oct. 7, 1949; s. Francis Julian and Bertha Anna (Lion) B.; m. Janice Leigh Gonzales, May 8, 1976; children: Francis III, Maria. BA, Tulane U., 1970, JD, 1973. Bar: La. 1973, U.S. Dist. Ct. (ea. dist.) La. 1973, U.S. Ct. Appeals (5th cir.) 1973, U.S. Dist. Ct. (we. dist.) La. 1978, U.S. Ct. Appeals (11th cir.) 1982. Assoc. Deutsch, Kerrigan & Stiles, New Orleans, 1973-78, ptnr., 1978—; Editor Admiralty Law Inst. Symposium Tulane U., 1973. Adv. editor The Maritime Lawyer, New Orleans, 1975—. Served to capt. USAR. Mem. ABA, La. Bar Assn., New Orleans Bar Assn., Fed. Bar Assn., Maritme Law Assn. U.S. (proctor, carriage of goods com. 1982-87, transp. hazardous substances com. 1987—), Assn. Henri Capitant, Southeastern Admiralty Law Inst. Democrat. Roman Catholic. Clubs: Army & Navy (Washington); City, Petroleum, Plimsoll, Internat. House, Mariners, Paul Morphy Chess (New Orleans). Admiralty. Home: 4301 Dumaine St New Orleans LA 70119 Office: Deutsch Kerrigan & Stiles 755 Magazine St New Orleans LA 70130

BARRY, JOHN KEVIN, lawyer; b. Akron, Ohio, Mar. 23, 1925; s. John Henry and Mary Ellen (O'Hara) B.; m. Ann L. Trainer, June 14, 1952 (div. 1958); children: Mona A., Barry de Sayve; m. Barbara Ann Lacek, Dec. 15, 1973; children: J. Kevin, Nicholas A., Liza M. A.B., Princeton U., 1947; J.D., Northwestern U., 1951. Bar: Ohio 1951, Pa. 1963. Assoc. Brouse, McDowell Inc., Akron, 1951-54; trial atty. IRS, Washington, 1954-57; atty., mem. legal adv. staff U.S. Treasury Dept., Washington, 1957-60, mem. office of tax legis. counsel, 1960-62; assoc. Reed Smith Shaw & McClay, Pitts., 1962-66, ptnr., 1966-86, inactive ptnr., 1987—. Bd. dirs. Pitts. Symphony Soc., 1981—; trustee Sewickley (Pa.) Acad., 1982—. Served with USN, 1943-46. Mem. ABA, Fed. Bar Assn., Pa. Bar Assn., Am. Coll. Tax Counsel, Am. Arbitration Assn., Northwestern U. Sch. Law Alumni Assn. (regional v.p. 1979-87). Republican. Roman Catholic. Clubs: Allegheny Country (Sewickley Heights, Pa.); Duquesne, Harvard-Yale-Princeton (Pitts.); Columbia Country (Chevy Chase, Md.); Portage Country (Akron); Princeton (N.Y.C.). Home: Scaife Rd Sewickley PA 15143 Office: Reed Smith Shaw & McClay Mellon Sq 435 6th Ave Pittsburgh PA 15219

BARRY, MARYANNE TRUMP, judge; b. 1937. BA, Mt. Holyoke Coll., 1958; MA, Columbia U., 1962; JD, Hofstra U., 1974. Asst. U.S. Atty., 1974-75, dep. chief appeals div., 1976-77, chief appeals div., 1977-82, exec. asst. U.S. Atty., 1981-82, 1st asst., 1981-83, judge U.S. Dist Ct., N.J., 1983—. Judicial administration. Office: US Courthouse Bldg PO Box 419 Newark NJ 07102

BARRY, MICHAEL FRANCIS, lawyer; b. New Orleans, Nov. 30, 1943; s. Francis Julian and Bertha Anna (Lion) B. BA, Loyola U., New Orleans, 1965, JD, 1968. Bar: La. 1968, U.S. Dist. Ct. (ea. dist.) La. 1968, U.S. Ct. Appeals (5th cir.) 1970, U.S. Supreme Ct. 1973. Sole practice New Orleans, 1968—. Democrat. Roman Catholic. Criminal, Federal civil litigation, State civil litigation. Office: 1005 Maison Blanche Bldg New Orleans LA 70112

BARRY, RICHARD WILLIAM, lawyer; b. Quincy, Mass., May 2, 1934; s. Richard J. and Mary J. (Prendergast) B.; m. Maryellen Martell, Dec. 27, 1958; children—Richard G., Jill M. Student, Coll. Holy Cross, 1956; A.B., Boston Coll., 1959. Bar: Mass. 1959, U.S. Dist. Ct. Mass. Dist. 1959, U.S. Supreme Ct. 1959. City councillor City of Quincy 1960-66, city solicitor, 1978-79; 1st asst. dist. atty. Norfolk County, Quincy, 1967-69; ptnr. Barry, Masterson & Harrington and Barry, Masterson, Sullivan & Largey, Quincy, 1979—. Mem. Mass. Trial Lawyers Assn., Mass. Bar Assn. Democrat. Roman Catholic. Office: Barry Masterson Sullivan & Largey 339 Hancock St Quincy MA 02171

BARSAMIAN, J(OHN) ALBERT, lawyer, lecturer educator, criminologist, arbitrator; b. Troy, N.Y., May 1, 1934; s. John and Virginia (Tachdjian) B.; m. Alice Missirlian, Apr. 21, 1963; children—Bonnie, Tamara. B.S. in Psychology, Union Coll., 1956; LL.B., Albany Law Sch., 1959; J.D., Union U., 1968. Bar: N.Y. 1961, U.S. Dist. Ct. (no. dist.) N.Y. 1961, U.S. Supreme Ct. 1967; fire tng. cert. N.Y. State Exec. Dept. Sole practice, Troy, 1961—; founder, chmn. dept. police sci. Hudson Valley Community Coll., 1961-69; dir. criminal sci. Russell Sage Coll., 1970—, assoc. prof. criminal sci., 1977-82, prof., 1982-87, Emeritus prof., 1987—; faculty Nelson A. Rockefeller Coll. Pub. Affairs and Policy, 1986—, Cornell U. Sch. Labor Relations, 1986; spl. counsel Office of Police Chief, Cohoes, N.Y. 1986— ; counsel North Greenbush Police Assn., 1985—, Office of Police Chief, Syracuse, N.Y., 1986—, Fire Dept. Union, Albany, N.Y., 1986; police and media cons.; public sector and negligence arbitrator; gen. counsel Internat. Narcotic Enforcement Officers Assn., 1982-83, Troy Uniformed Firefighters Assn. 1977—; spl. investigator Rensselaer County Dist. Atty., 1959-61. Mem. Union Coll. Alumni Council, 1981-86; mem. parish council St. Peter Armenian Ch., Watervliet, N.Y. 1979-83, chmn., 1981-83, vice chmn., 1984; evaluator N.Y. State Edn. Dept. Office of Non-Collegiate Programs, 1985—; hon. dep. sheriff St. Mary Parish (La.). Decorated chevalier, knight comdr. Sovereign Order Cyprus; recipient Police Sci. Students' award Hudson Valley Community Coll., 1968; award for meritorious service to law enforcement Law Enforcement Officers Soc. N.Y., 1969, Archbishop's cert. merit Armenian Ch. Am., 1973; Union Coll. Tarzian scholar, 1952-56, Porter scholar, 1954-56; Albany Law Sch. Saxton scholar, 1956-59; Lawyers Coop. Pub. Co. prize in criminal law, 1957. Mem. ABA (com. on police selection and tng. 1967-69), Rensselaer County Bar Assn., Acad. Criminal Justice Scis., N.Y. State Bar Assn. (chmn. com. on police criminal justice sect. 1970-72, trial lawyers sect com. continuing legal edn. 1977—), Assn. Trial Lawyers Am., N.Y. State Trial Lawyers Assn., Am. Correctional Assn., Am. Arbitration Assn., N.Y. State Chiefs of Police Assn., Internat. Assn. Chiefs of Police, Northeastern Chiefs of Police Conf., Am. Assn. Fed. Investigators, Internat. Assn. Identification, N.Y. State Tng. Dirs. Assn., Union Coll. Alumni Assn. (Silver medal 1956), Les Amis d'Escoffier Soc., Internat. Narcotic Enforcement Officers Assn., Northeastern Assn. Criminal Justice Educators, Masonic Vet. Assn. Troy (life), N.Y. Vet. Police Assn. (life, hon. counsel), Phi Delta Theta, Psi Chi, Alpha Phi Sigma. Clubs: Mason (32 degree), Rose Croix (most wise master Delta chpt. 1986), Royal Order Jesters, Shriners, Albany Country. Contbr. articles to legal jours. Criminal, Legal education, Labor. Home: 5 Sage Hill Ln Albany NY 12204 Office: 21 2d St Troy NY 12180

BARSON, STEPHEN PAUL, lawyer; b. Phila., July 4, 1947; s. Samuel and Florence (Sollot) B.; m. Evalyn Lois Stein, Sept. 16, 1969; children: Nicole Renae, Andrew Chad. BA, Adelphi U., 1969; JD, Villanova U., 1972. Bar: Pa. 1972, U.S. Dist. Ct. (ea. dist.) Pa. 1972. Ptnr. Robinson, Greenberg & Lipman, Phila., 1972-81; sole practice Phila., 1981—. Served to sgt. USAR, 1968-74. Mem. ABA, Pa. Bar Assn., Pa. Trial Lawyers Assn. Avocations: coaching little leaguers, weight lifting, music, art. Personal injury. Home: 621 Heather Ln Bryn Mawr PA 19010 Office: 1712 Locust St Philadelphia PA 19103

BART, RANDALL KERR, lawyer; b. Lakeland, Fla., Aug. 17, 1952; s. Roger and Elaine (Bickford) B.; m. Barbara Susan Davne, May 19, 1974; children: Daniel Bennett, Matthew Stewart. BA, U. Rochester, 1974, MBA, 1975; JD, U. Ga., 1978. Bar: Ga. 1978, Fla. 1979, U.S. Dist. Ct. (so. dist.) Ga. 1979, U.S. Tax Ct. 1979, U.S. Ct. Appeals (11th cir.) 1981. Assoc. Bouhan, Williams & Levy, Savannah, Ga., 1978-84, ptnr., 1984—. Mng. editor U. Ga. Law Rev., 1977-78; editorial bd. The Jour. of State Taxation, 1980—. Mem. ABA, Fla. Bar Assn., Ga. Bar Assn., Savannah Bar Assn. General corporate, State and local taxation, Estate planning. Home: 2912 Atlantic Ave Savannah GA 31405 Office: Bouhan Williams & Levy 447 Bull St Savannah GA 31401

BARTFELD, ARNOLD L., corporate lawyer. BA, CUNY, 1970; JD, Bklyn. Law Sch., 1974. Atty. regional counsel IRS, 1974-75; sr. v.p., gen. counsel Fidelity Bank & Fidelcor Inc., 1975-84; exec. v.p., gen. counsel, corp. sec. European Am. Bank, Uniondale, N.Y., 1984—. Office: European Am Bank EAB PLaza Uniondale NY 11555 *

BARTH, ROGER VINCENT, lawyer; 1983-85, b. Buffalo, Nov. 10, 1938; s. Philip Charles and Mary Katherine (Eustace) B.; m. Mary Carol Manion, July 2, 1960; children—Mary Katherine, Roger Vincent, Krista, Marci; m. 2d, Christina E. Brown, June 20, 1979. B.A., Princeton U., 1960; LL.B. cum laude, SUNY-Buffalo, 1963. Bar: N.Y. 1963, D.C. 1970, Md. 1976, U.S. Supreme Ct. 1970. Ptnr., Hodgson, Russ, Andrews, Woods & Goodyear, Buffalo, 1963-69; asst. to commr. IRS, Washington, 1969-72, dept. chief counsel, 1972-74; ptnr. Bird & Tansill, Washington, 1975-79, Jackson, Campbell & Parkinson, Washington, 1979-83, Barrett & Hanna, Washington, 1983-85, Curtis, Mallet-Prevost, Colt & Mosle, Washington, 1985—; counsel N.Y. State Senate Social Services Com., 1966-67, N.Y. Joint Legis. Com. to Revise Social Services Law, 1967-68; mem. Adminstrv. Conf. U.S., 1982—. Dir. credentials Presdl. Inaugural Com., 1981, 85; tax counsel csl. Republican Nat. Com., 1979—; dep. gen. counsel for Reagan-Bush '84. Mem. ABA, Fed. Bar Assn. (vice chmn. gen. counsels com. 1981—, mem. nat. council 1983—), N.Y. State Bar Assn. (exec. com. tax sect. 1971-74). Roman Catholic. Clubs: Princeton (N.Y.C.); Capitol Hill (Washington); Kenwood (Bethesda, Md.). Corporate taxation, Personal income taxation, Administrative and regulatory. Office: Curtis Mallet-Prevost Colt & Mosle 1735 I St NW Washington DC 20006

BARTHELD, RICHARD HENRY, lawyer; b. Seattle, Jan. 10, 1955; s. James Harold and Patricia Eileen (Nord) B.; m. Jacqulyn Kay Martin, Aug. 16, 1975; children: Christopher, Jeremy. AA, Yakima Valley Community Coll., 1975; BA, U. Wash., 1977; JD, Gonzaga U., 1980. Bar: Wash. 1980. Ptnr. Dauber & Bartheld, Yakima, Wash., 1982—. Mem. Assn. Trial Lawyers Am., Wash. Trial Lawyers Assn. Republican. Lodge: Eagles. Family and matrimonial, Personal injury. Home: 507 Bittner Yakima WA 98901 Office: Dauber & Bartheld 413 N 2d St Yakima WA 98901

BARTHOLDT, WILLIAM EDWARD, JR., lawyer; b. Frankfurt, Fed. Republic Germany, Dec. 24, 1951; s. William E. and Marion (Bruner) B.; m. Laura Ann Kelemanik, Dec. 29, 1976. BA, Westminster Coll., 1974; JD magna cum laude, Washburn U., 1982. Bar: Tex. 1982. Assoc. Winstead & McGuire, Dallas, 1982-83, Eldridge, Goggins & Weiss, Dallas, 1983-84, Carrington, Coleman, Sloman & Blumenthal, Dallas, 1984—. Editor-in-chief Washburn Law Jour., 1981-82. Served to capt. U.S. Army, 1974-79. Mem. ABA, Tex. Bar Assn., Dallas Bar Assn., Phi Kappa Phi, Phi Alpha Delta. Club: 500, Inc. (Dallas). General corporate, Securities. Home: 3945 Frontier Dallas TX 75214 Office: Carrington Coleman Sloman & Blumenthal 200 Crescent Ct Suite 1500 Dallas TX 75201

BARTHOLET, ELIZABETH, law educator; b. N.Y.C., Sept. 9, 1940; d. Paul and Elizabeth (Ives) B.; divorced; children: Derek DuBois, Christopher. BA in English, Radcliffe Coll., 1962; LLB, Harvard U., 1965. Bar: Mass., D.C., N.Y., U.S. Dist. Ct. (so. and ea. dists.) N.Y., U.S. Ct. Appeals (2d cir.), U.S. Supreme Ct. Law clk. to judge U.S. Ct. Appeals, Washington, 1965-66; spl. asst. to exec. dir. Pres. Commn. on Law Enforcement, Washington, 1966-67; staff atty. Legal Aid Agcy., Washington, 1967; staff atty. legal defense fund NAACP, N.Y.C., 1968-72; counsel VERA Inst. of Justice, N.Y.C., 1972-73; pres., dir. Legal Action Ctr., N.Y.C., 1973-77; assoc. prof. law Harvard U., Cambridge, Mass., 1977-83, prof. law, 1983—; bd. dirs. Legal Action Ctr., N.Y.C. Contbr. articles to profl. jours. Mem. equality com. ACLU, 1970-72, N.Y. com of U.S. Commn. on Civil Rights, 1970-76, N.Y. State Task Force on Law Enforcement, 1975-76, overseers com. to visit Harvard Law Sch., 1971, bd. overseers Harvard U., 1973-77, Civil Rights Rev. Authority U.S. Dept. Edn., 1979-81; bd. dirs. Advs. for Pub. Interest., Washington, 1985—. Mem. Mass. Bar Assn., D.C. Bar Assn., N.Y. State Bar Assn., Assn. of Bar of City of N.Y. (exec. com. 1973-77), Boston Bar Assn., Am. Arbitration Assn. (labor panel 1980—), Soc. Am. Law Tchrs. (bd. govs. 1977—). Democrat. Club: Harvard (N.Y.C.). Civil rights, Employment discrimination. Office: Harvard U Law Sch 1545 Massachusetts Ave Cambridge MA 02138

BARTHOLOMEW, JAMES IRA, lawyer; b. Raton, N.Mex., Oct. 11, 1938; s. Charles and Helen Mildred (Paulsen) B.; B.A., U. N.Mex., 1961; J.D., Oklahoma City U., 1967. Bar: N.Mex. 1967. Assoc. Sheehan & Duhigg, Albuquerque, 1967-68; sole practice, Albuquerque, 1968—. Mem. Am. Trial Lawyers, ABA, Am. Judicature Soc., N.Mex. Trial Lawyers, Phi Delta Phi. Democrat. Episcopalian. Club: Albuquerque Lawyers. Bankruptcy, Consumer commercial, Personal injury. Office: 708 Marquette NW Albuquerque NM 87102

BARTIMUS, JAMES RUSSELL, lawyer; educator; b. Trenton, Mo., Oct. 21, 1949; s. James Leeper and Dixie Lee (Swearinger) B.; m. Mary Dana

Quick, Sept. 8, 1979; children—Adam James, Philip David. B.A., U. Mo.-Columbia, 1971; J.D., U. Mo.-Kansas City, 1977, postgrad. Med. Sch., 1978-80. Bar: Mo. 1977, U.S. Dist. Ct. (we. dist.) Mo. 1977. Sole practice, limited to med. negligence plaintiffs, Kansas City, Mo., 1977—; adj. prof. U. Kansas City Sch. Law, 1983, 84, 85; adj. grad. faculty, non-nurse mem. U. Mo. Sch. Nursing, 1986; lectr. U. Mo. Kansas City Sch. Nursing, 1983, 85, U. Mo. Kansas City Law Sch., 1986, Kansas City Coll. Med. Assts., 1977-80, 82, Truman Med. Ctr. Health Scis. Library, 1986, numerous other law and health related groups; mem. profl. liability rev. bd. State of Mo., 1978, Jackson County Med.-Legal Com., 1980-81. Contbg. author sects. in books; contbr. articles to profl. jours.; mem. U. Mo.-Kansas City Law Rev., 1976-77. Trustee U. Mo. Kansas City Law Found., 1986. 87; mem. Lyric Opera Guild, Kansas City, Mo., Friends of Zoo, Friends of Art, Children's Place, Kansas City, Mo. Served to lt. USNR, 1971-74, Vietnam, Japan. Fellow Am. Bd. Profl. Liability Attys.; mem. Am. Coll. Legal Medicine, Am. Soc. Law and Medicine, Am. Bd. Trial Advocates, Pitts. Inst. Legal Medicine, Mo. Assn. Trial Attys. (gov. 1980-86, exec. com. 1985-87, med. malpractice legis. com. 1987), Lawyer's Pilots Bar Assn., Assn. Trial Lawyers Am. (com. of 25, 1986,87), ABA, Mo. Bar Assn. (tort law com. 1985-87), Kansas City Met. Bar Assn. (lectr. med. malpractice program 1980-84, disability law com. 1978-80, mcpl. cts. compensation com., 1979, others), Am. Bd. Trial Advocates, Phi Delta Phi. Clubs: Kansas City, Blue Hills Country (Mo.). Office: James Bartimus PC 29th Floor City Center Square 1100 Main St Kansas City MO 64105

BARTLE, ROBERT FRANKLIN, lawyer, legal educator; b. St. Paul, Nebr., June 22, 1950; s. Edward Franklin and Alice May (Christensen) B.; m. Mary E. Tait, Apr. 30, 1977 (div. Jan. 1979); m. Barbara J. Maline, May 25, 1985; stepchildrn: Megan L., Allen Andrew III. BA in English, Pub. Address, Wesleyan U., Lincoln, Nebr., 1972; JD, U. Nebr., 1976. Bar: Nebr. 1976, U.S. Dist. Ct. Nebr. 1976, U.S. Ct. Appeals (8th cir.) 1978, U.S. Supreme Ct. 1980. Asst. atty. gen. antitrust div. Dept. of Justice, Lincoln, 1976-81; ptnr. Nelson & Harding, Lincoln, 1981—; adj. prof. law U. Nebr., Lincoln, 1982-86. Chmn. program ethics com. Region V Mental Retardation Services, Inc., Lincoln, 1981-86; bd. dirs. Brownville (Nebr.) Village Theatre, Inc., 1977-86; deacon First Plymouth Ch., Lincoln, 1986—. Mem. ABA (antitrust sect.), Nebr. Bar Assn., Lincoln Bar Assn. Democrat. Congregationalist. Avocations: softball, tennis, basketball, theatre. Federal civil litigation, Antitrust, State civil litigation. Home: 2401 Van Dorn St Lincoln NE 68502 Office: Nelson & Harding 1200 N St Lincoln NE 68501

BARTLETT, ALEX, lawyer; b. Warrensburg, Mo., Aug. 7, 1937; s. George Vest and May (Woolery) B.; m. Sue Gloyd, June 5, 1961 (div. June 1978); children: Ashley R., Nathan G.; m. Eleanor M. Veltrop, Oct. 27, 1978. BA, Cen. Mo. State U., 1959; LLB, U. Mo., 1961. Bar: Mo. 1962, U.S. Ct. Mil. Appeals 1963, U.S. Supreme Ct. 1965, U.S. Dist. Ct. (we. dist.) Mo. 1966, U.S. Ct. Appeals (8th cir.) 1968. From assoc. to ptnr. Hendren & Andrae, Jefferson City, Mo., 1965-79; mem. Bartlett, Venters, Pletz & Toppins, P.C., Jefferson City, 1980—; lectr. law U. Mo., Columbia, 1965-66. Contbr. editor Mo. Law Rev., 1960-61. Served to capt. JAGC, U.S. Army, 1962-65. Mem. ABA, Fed. Bar Assn., Mo. Bar Assn. (chmn. young lawyers sect. 1972-73, ct. modernization com. 1972-74, jud. reform com. 1974-76, chmn. cts. and jud. com. 1978-79, chmn. legis. com. 1981-84, Pres.'s award 1976, Smithson award 1976), Cole County Bar Assn., Am. Coll. Trial Lawyers, Order of Coif. Democrat. Federal civil litigation, State civil litigation, Administrative and regulatory. Office: Bartlett Venters Pletz & Toppins 325 Jefferson ST PO Box 1586 Jefferson City MO 65102

BARTLETT, CHARLES JOHN, lawyer; b. Oak Park, Ill., Feb. 18, 1954; s. Thomas Harold and Ida Therese (Ensweiler) B. AA, Manatee Jr. Coll., 1974; BS, Fla. State U., 1976; JD, U. Fla., 1978. Bar: Fla. 1979, U.S. Dist. Ct. (mid. dist.) Fla. 1979, U.S. Ct. Appeals (5th and 1th cirs.) 1983. From assoc. to sr. ptnr. Icard, Merrill, Cullis, Timm & Furen P.A., Sarasota, Fla., 1979—; assoc. prof. Manatee Jr. Coll., Bradenton, Fla., 1981-83. Mem. Fla. Bar Assn. (bd. gov. young lawyers sect., chmn. conv. 1983-84, chmn. publ. 1984-85, chmn. scholarship com. 1985-86), Sarasota County Bar Assn. (bd. dirs. young lawyers sect. 1981-83, sec. 1983-84, bd. dirs. 1982-86, pres. 1985-86), Sarasota C. of C. (trustee 1984—). Republican. Roman Catholic. Lodge: Kiwanis. Avocations: golf, water sports. State civil litigation, Federal civil litigation, Contracts commercial. Home: 5147 Oxford Dr Sarasota FL 34242 Office: Icard Merrill Cullis Timm & Furen 200 S Washington Blvd Sarasota FL 33577

BARTLETT, CODY BLAKE, lawyer, law educator; b. Syracuse, N.Y., Apr. 21, 1939; s. Stanley Jay and Izora Elizabeth (Blake) B.; m. Claudine Germaine Bouthillette, Dec. 27, 1968; 1 child, Cody Blake. A.A.S., Auburn Community Coll., 1960; B.A. with high honors, Mich. State U., 1963; J.D., Harvard U., 1966. Bar: Mich. 1967, N.Y. 1967, U.S. Dist. Ct. (no. dist.) N.Y. 1967, U.S. Dist. Ct. (ea. dist.) Mich. 1967, U.S. Supreme Ct. 1984, U.S. Dist. Ct. (we. dist.) N.Y. 1985. Law clk. Onondaga County Dist. Atty.'s Office, Syracuse, N.Y., 1965; assoc. atty. Touche, Ross, Bailey & Smart, Detroit, 1966; law clk. Onondaga County Family Ct., Syracuse, 1967; assoc. atty. Melvin & Melvin, Syracuse, 1967; budget and accounts officer Appellate Div., 4th Dept., Rochester, N.Y., 1967-69, dep. dir. adminstrn., 1969-72, dir. adminstrn., 1972-80; chief atty. State Commn. on Jud. Conduct, 1980-84; ptnr. Newman, Kehoe, Wunder, Bartlett & Gosdeck, Lyons, N.Y., 1984—; spl. adminstr. N.Y. State Dangerous Drug Program, Western N.Y., 1973-75; adj. prof. polit. sci. dept. and Grad. Sch. Pub. Adminstrn., SUNY-Brockport, 1983-87; adj. prof. Syracuse U. Coll. Law, 1980-84, Coll. Criminal Justice, Rochester Inst. Tech., 1979-80; grad. asst. polit. sci. dept. Mich. State U., 1962-63. Mem. adv. com. Regional Criminal Justice Edn. and Tng. Ctr., Monroe Community Coll., Rochester, N.Y., 1974-80; div. leader YMCA, Midtown Rochester Membership drive, 1976; mem. East Bloomfield Planning Bd., 1984-87, chmn., 1985-87; trustee Village of East Bloomfield, 1985-87; mem. Zoning Bd. of Appeals, Village of Sodus Point, 1986—. Recipient Disting. Alumni award Assn. Bds. Trustees of SUNY, 1980. Mem. N.Y. State Bar Assn. (spl. com. on jud. conduct 1984—), Wayne County Bar Assn., Onondaga County Bar Assn. (chmn. Syracuse City Ct. com. 1968-72), Phi Kappa Phi, Pi Sigma Alpha. Club: Sodus Bay Heights Country. Lodge: Lyons. General practice, State civil litigation, Administrative and regulatory. Home: 7094 Overlook Dr Sodus Point NY 14555 Office: Newman Kehoe Wunder Bartlett & Gosdeck 12 William St PO Box 404 Lyons NY 14489

BARTLETT, D. BROOK, federal judge; b. 1937. B.A., Princeton U., 1959; LL.B., Stanford U., 1962. Assoc. Stinson, Mag, Thomson, McEvers & Fizzell, 1962-67, ptnr., 1967-69; asst. atty. gen. Mo., 1969-73, 1st asst. atty. gen., 1973-77; assoc. Blackwell, Sanders, Matheny, Weary & Lombardi, 1977-78, ptnr., 1978-81; judge U.S. Dist. Ct. (we. dist.) Mo., Kansas City, 1981—. Judicial administration. Office: U S Dist Ct US Courthouse 811 Grand Ave Room 654 Kansas City MO 64106 *

BARTLETT, JAMES WILSON, III, lawyer; b. Pasadena, Calif., Mar. 21, 1946; s. James Wilson Jr. and Helen (Archbold) B.; m. Jane Edmunds Graves; children: Matthew Archbold, Polly Graves. BA, Washington & Lee U., 1968; JD, Vanderbilt U., 1975. Bar: Md. 1975, U.S. Dist. Ct. Md. 1975, U.S. Ct. Appeals (4th cir.) 1976, U.S. Claims Ct. 1984. Assoc. Semmes, Bowen & Semmes, Balt., 1975-85; sole practice Balt., 1985-86; ptnr. Kroll & Tract, Balt., 1986—; permanent mem. jud. conf. 4th Cir. Contbr. articles to profl. jours. Chmn. law firm campaign United Fund, Balt., 1979; bd. dirs. Roland Park Civic League, 1987—. Served to 1st lt. U.S. Army, 1969-71. Mem. ABA (vice chmn. admiralty and maritime litigation com. litigation sect. 1985—), Md. Bar Assn., Balt. City Bar Assn., Fed. Bar Assn., Maritime Law Assn. U.S. (proctor), Md. Assn. Def. Trial Counsel, St. Andrews Soc. Republican. Presbyterian. Clubs: 12-30, Propeller U.S. (gov. 1984-87, v.p. 1987—) (Balt.). Admiralty, Federal civil litigation, Insurance. Home: 307 Edgevale Rd Baltimore MD 21210 Office: Kroll & Tract 201 N Charles St Suite 900 Baltimore MD 21201

BARTLETT, MICHAEL JOHN, lawyer; b. Paterson, N.J., June 8, 1943; s. Ernest John and Alice Edith (Schrell) B.; m. Carol Ann Bishop, June 10, 1967; children: Tara Christine, Jessica Simons, Darren Michael. BA cum laude, Amherst Coll., 1965; JD, U. Va., 1969. Bar: Va. 1969, D.C. 1971, U.S. Sup. Ct. 1976. Atty., Office Gen. Counsel, NLRB, Washington, 1969-71; atty. law offices Joseph C. Wells, Washington, 1971-74, atty. Vedder, Price, Kaufman, Kammholz & Day, Washington, 1974-76, ptnr., 1976-80; ptnr. (Michael J. Bartlett, P.C.), Ogletree, Deakins, Nash, Smoak & Stewart, Washington, 1980-86; staff v.p. employee relations Eastern Airlines, Inc., 1986—. Mem. exec. bd. Arlington (Va.) YMCA, 1982-86, treas., 1984-86. Andrew D. Lawrie scholar, Amherst Coll., 1964-65; Am. Jurisprudence award in labor law Lawyer Coop. Pub. Co., 1969. Mem. Va. State Bar, D.C. Bar, Fed. Bar Assn., ABA (sect. on labor law). Contbr. articles to profl. jours. Labor. Home: 5860 SW 116th St Miami FL 33156 Office: Eastern Airlines Inc (MIALV) Miami Internat Airport Miami FL 33148

BARTLETT, RICHARD JAMES, lawyer, former university dean; b. Glens Falls, N.Y., Feb. 15, 1926; s. George Willard and Kathryn M. (McCarthy) B.; m. Claire E. Kennedy, Aug. 18, 1951; children: Michael, Amy. B.S., Georgetown U., 1945; LL.B., Harvard U., 1949; LL.D. (hon.), Union Coll., 1974; Sc.D. (hon.), Albany Med. Coll., 1986. Bar: N.Y. State 1949. Practice law Glens Falls, 1949-73; mem. firm Clark Bartlett & Caffry, 1962-73; justice N.Y. State Supreme Ct., 1973-79; chief adminstr. of courts N.Y. State, 1974-79; dean Albany Law Sch., Union U., Albany, 1979-86; ptnr. Bartlett, Pontiff, Stewart, Rhodes & Judge P.C., Glens Falls, N.Y., 1986—; Mem. N.Y. State Assembly, 1959-66, N.Y. Bd. Law Examiners, 1987—; chmn. N.Y. Commn. on Revision of Penal Law, 1961-70; del. N.Y. Constl. Conv., 1967. Served to capt. USAF, 1951-53. Fellow Am. Bar Found.; mem. Am. Law Inst., Am. Bar Assn., N.Y. State Bar Assn., Assn. Bar City of N.Y., Warren County Bar. Republican. Roman Catholic. Clubs: Lake George; Ft. Orange (Albany); Harvard (N.Y.C.). Home: Bolton Landing NY 12814 Office: Bartlett Pontiff Stewart Rhodes & Judge PC Box 380 Glens Falls NY 12801

BARTLETT, RICK E., lawyer; b. Connersville, Ind., Mar. 27, 1956; s. Richard L. and Doris (Perkins) B.; m. Sandra Lynn Heeke, June 25, 1978. BS, Ind. U., 1978, JD, 1981. Bar: Ind. 1981, U.S. Dist. (so. dist.) Ind. 1981. Assoc. Roemer & Mintz, South Bend, Ind., 1981-82, Fox & Smith, Jeffersonville, Ind., 1983—. Vol. United Way, Clark County, Ind., 1984-86; mem. Leadership Clark County, 1984-85; mem. Clark-Floyd Estate Planning Council, 1984—, sec., treas., 1986-87. Mem. ABA, Ind. Bar Assn., Clark County Bar Assn. Evang. Free Ch. Avocations: tennis, golf, softball. Probate, General corporate, General practice. Home: 3215 Julian Dr New Albany IN 47150 Office: Fox & Smith 209 E Chestnut PO Box 98 Jeffersonville IN 47131-0098

BARTLETT, STEPHEN SHEPPARD, judge; b. San Diego, Apr. 23, 1952; s. Stephen Olmstead and Dana (Sheppard) B.; m. Elizabeth Adele Anthony, Jan. 12, 1980; 1 child, Stephen Wyman. BS, Cen. Mo. State U., 1974; JD, U. S.C., 1977. Bar: S.C. 1977, U.S. Dist. Ct. S.C. 1979, U.S. Ct. Appeals (4th cir.) 1979. Asst. atty. City of Greenville, S.C., 1977; asst. solicitor City of Greenville, 1978-80; judge Greenville Mcpl. Ct., 1980—. Bd. dirs. Family Services of Greenville, 1985—. Mem. ABA (faculty Nat. Jud. Coll., 1986—), S.C. Bar Assn. (continuing legal edn. com.). Criminal, Judicial administration. Home: 111 Teal Ln Mauldin SC 29662 Office: Greenville Mcpl Ct 22 W Broad St Greenville SC 19601

BARTLEY, ALBERT LEA, JR., lawyer, oil company executive; b. Ladonia, Tex., July 19, 1927; s. Albert Lea and Gladys (Oakley) B.; m. Virginia Ann Burnett, Feb. 14, 1959; children—Thomas G., Christopher A., Pamela A. B.A., N. Tex. State U., 1947; J.D., U. Tex., 1950. Bar: Tex. 1950, U.S. dist. ct. (ea. dist.) Tex. 1951, U.S. dist. ct. (so. dist.) Tex. 1962, U.S. dist. ct. (no. dist.) Tex. 1975, U.S. Ct. Appeals (5th cir.) 1982. Dist. and county atty. Fannin County, Tex., 1951-54; asst. v.p. Citizens Bank, Greenville, Tex., 1955; contract adminstr. Gen. Dynamics, Ft. Worth, 1956-60; with Continental Emsco Co. (now LTV Energy Products Co.), Dallas, 1960—, gen. counsel, 1977-80, v.p. and group counsel, 1980—; dir. Farmers and Merchants State Bank, Ladonia. Honored guest Democratic Nat. Conv., Chgo., 1952. Mem. ABA, Tex. Bar Assn., Dallas Bar Assn. Republican. Episcopalian. Clubs: Chapparal (Dallas); Masons (Ladonia). General corporate. Home: 2220 Eastwood St Richardson TX 75080 Office: 2441 Forest Ln PO Box 469016 Garland TX 75040

BARTOLINI, JAMES DANIEL, lawyer; b. New Haven, Apr. 13, 1946; s. Dante J. and Mariella (Cestaro) B.; m. Roni Goldstein, Dec. 22, 1975; 1 child, Jessica Marie. B.A., Trinity Coll., Hartford, Conn., 1968; M.A., Hartford Sem., 1970, M.Div., 1972; J.D., U. Conn., 1975. Bar: Conn. 1975, U.S. Ct. Appeals (2d cir.) 1975. Assoc. RisCassi and Davis, Hartford, Conn., 1975—. Recipient Book award Harvard U., 1964. Mem. Nat. Bd. Trial Advocates (cert. Civil trial Specialist), Conn. Bar Assn. (bd. dirs. civil law sect. 1984—), Conn. Trial Lawyers Assn. (dir. 1982—), Hartford County Med. Soc. (co-chmn. legal com. 1982—). Roman Catholic. Personal injury. Home: 56 Strickland Glastonbury CT 06033 Office: PO Box 6550 Hartford CT 06106

BARTOLONE, FRANK SALVATORE, lawyer; b. Cornwall, N.Y., May 6, 1952; s. Joseph and Antonetta (Di Salvo) B.; m. Priscilla Ann Dunson, July 2, 1983. BA in Latin, Catholic U. Am., 1974; JD, Nova U., 1977. Bar: Fla. 1977, U.S. Dist. Ct. (so. dist.) Fla. 1979. Assoc. Tylander, de Claire, Van Kleeck, Boca Ratoan, Fla., 1977-79; asst. atty. City of Boca Raton, 1979-83, atty., 1984—; assoc. MarchBanks and Eisen, Boca Raton, 1983-84; lectr. in field. Chmn. City Boca Raton United Way Campaign, 1985. Mem. Fla. Bar Assn., Palm Beach County Bar Assn. (chmn. lawyer referral com. 1984-86), South Palm Beach County Bar Assn., Palm Beach County Planning Congress. Republican. Roman Catholic. Club: Loggehead. Lodges: Rotary. Local government, Administrative and regulatory, Growth mamgement, land use planning and zoning. Office: City Boca Raton 201 W Palmetto Park Rd Boca Raton FL 33432

BARTON, ANTHONY BLACKSHAW, lawyer; b. Los Angeles, Apr. 29, 1947; s. Richard Thomas Barton and Patricia Pearl (Caddell) Barton Macomb; m. Janet McNicol, Dec. 27, 1969; children: Christopher Paul, Scott Donald. AB cum laude, Harvard U., 1969; JD, Georgetown U., 1972. Bar: D.C. 1973, U.S. Dist. Ct. D.C. 1973, U.S. Ct. Appeals (D.C. cir.) 1973, U.S. Supreme Ct. 1973, N.Y. 1977, U.S. Dist. Ct. (so. and ea. dists.) N.Y. 1977. Spl. asst. to asst. gen. counsel, multi-family housing Dept. Housing and Urban Devel., Washington, 1973-74, spl. asst. to assoc. gen. counsel for housing, 1975-76; assoc. Hall, McNicol, Hamilton & Clark, N.Y.C., 1976-78, ptnr., 1978—, mem. exec. com., 1984—. Gov. Groton Sch., Mass., 1982—; trustee Hoosac Sch., Hoosac Falls, N.Y., 1978-79; mem. planning bd. Village of Oyster Bay Cove, N.Y., 1985—; bd. dirs. John Sloan Found., N.Y.C., 1979—. Mem. ABA, D.C. Bar Assn., N.Y. State Bar Assn., Nassau County Bar Assn. Republican. Episcopalian. Club: Harvard (N.Y.C.) (gov. 1982-85). Securities, Municipal bonds, Real property. Office: Hall McNicol Hamilton & Clark 220 E 42d St New York NY 10017

BARTON, BABETTE B., lawyer, educator; b. Los Angeles, Apr. 30, 1930; d. Milton Vernon and Ruth (Schreiber) Barancik; m. John K. McNulty, Mar. 23, 1978; children: Jeffrey B. Barton, David R. Barton, Baird R. Barton. B.S., U. Calif., Berkeley, 1951, LL.B., 1954. Bar: Calif., U.S. Dist. Ct., U.S. Ct. Appeals 1955. Law clk. to Chief Justice Phil S. Gibson, Calif. Supreme Ct., San Francisco, 1954-55; lectr., acting prof. Sch. of Law, U. Calif., Berkeley, 1961-72; prof. law Sch. of Law, U. Calif., 1972—; cons. Calif. Inter Agy. Task Force on Electronic Funds Transfers, 1978-79, Dept. Treasury, 1963; mem. adv. com. Calif. Bd. Legal Specialization, 1980-83. Contbr. chpts. to books in field. Mem. adv. com. Alameda County Dir. Welfare, 1970-73; bd. dirs. Family Service Berkeley, 1967-74, Univ. Students' Coop. Assn., 1966-74. Fellow Am. Law Inst., Am. Bar Found.; mem. Am. Bar Assn. (mem. council Real Property, Probate and Trust sect. 1977-79), Calif. State Bar (chmn. taxation sec. 1976-77), Western Regional Bar Assn. (chmn. 1978-79), Am. Coll. Tax Counsel, San Francisco Tax Club, San Francisco Estate Planning Council. Democrat. Corporate taxation, Estate planning, Personal income taxation. Home: 620 Spruce Berkeley CA 94707 Office: Univ Calif Berkeley Sch of Law Berkeley CA 94720

BARTON, HUGH MITCHELL, III, lawyer; b. Bartlesville, Okla., Aug. 16, 1952; s. Hugh Mitchell Jr. and Margaret Ann (Nance) B.; m. Joyce Anne Mayfield, May 13, 1981. BBA, So. Meth. U., 1974; JD, U. Tulsa, 1977. Bar: Tex. 1979, U.S. Dist. Ct. (no. dist.) Tex. 1984, U.S. Dist. Ct. (we. dist.) Tex. 1985. Assoc. Law Office of Calvin A. Barker, Dallas, 1979-80; sole practice Dallas, 1980-81; asst. dist. atty. 258th jud. dist. State of Tex., Groveton, 1982-84; asst. atty. gen. medicaid fraud control unit State of Tex., Austin, 1984—. Vol. United Action for Elderly Inc., Austin, 1985—. Mem. ABA, Tex. Dist. and County Attys. Assn., Polk County Bar Assn., Tex. Young Lawyers Assn., Austin Young Lawyers Assn. Democrat. Avocations: theater, backpacking. Criminal, Health. Office: Tex Atty Gen 1101 Camino LaCosta Suite 257 Austin TX 78752

BARTON, JAMES CARY, lawyer; b. Raymondville, Tex., Sept. 1, 1940; s. Dewey Albert and Dorothy Marie (Keene) B.; m. Isabel Pattee Critz, Sept. 12, 1964 (div. June 1975); children: Hamilton Keene, John Franklin, James Albert; m. Carolyn Ann Cox, Dec. 20, 1975; stepchildren: Holly Ann Adams, Laura Lee Adams, Jennifer Lynn Adams. BA, Baylor U., 1962; LLB, Harvard U., 1965. Bar: Tex. 1965, U.S. Dist. Ct. (so. dist.) Tex. 1972, U.S. Tax Ct. 1977. Trial atty. FPC, Washington, 1965-67; atty.-advisor U.S. Tax Ct., Washington, 1967-68; from assoc. to ptnr. Kleberg, Mobley, Lockett & Weil, Corpus Christi, Tex., 1969-75, Brown, Maroney, Rose, Baker & Barber, Austin, Tex., 1975-82; from ptnr. to of counsel Johnson & Swanson, Austin and Dallas, 1982—; speaker in field. Served to sgt. USAF, 1968-69. Mem. ABA, State Bar Tex. (council real estate probate and trust law sect. 1982-85), Am. Coll. Real Estate Lawyers. Democrat. Episcopalian. Clubs: Capital, Univ., Westwood Country (Austin). Real property, General corporate. Office: Johnson & Swanson 1400 100 Congress Bldg Austin TX 78701

BARTON, JOHN HAYS, legal educator; b. Chgo., Oct. 27, 1936; s. Jay and Agnes (Heisler) B.; m. Julianne Marie Gunnis, June 13, 1959; children: John II, Robert, Anne, Thomas, David. B.S., Marquette U., 1958; J.D., Stanford U., 1968. Bar: D.C. 1969. Engr., Sylvania Electronic Def. Labs., Mountain View, Calif., 1961-68; assoc. Wilmer, Cutler and Pickering, Washington, 1968-69; prof. Stanford (Calif.) U. Law Sch., 1969—; vis. prof. U. Mich. Law Sch., fall 1981. Served to lt. (j.g.) USN, 1958-61. Rockefeller Found. fellow, 1976-77. Mem. ABA, AAAS, Am. Soc. Internat. Law, Am. Soc. Agrl. Cons. Author: Politics of Peace, 1981, co-author International Trade and Investment, 1986, Law in Radically Different Cultures, 1983 (Am. Soc. Internat. Law award 1984); co-editor: International Arms Control, 1976, Law and High Technology, 1983. Private international, Public international. Home: 1340 Harwalt Dr Los Altos CA 94022 Office: Stanford U Law Sch Stanford CA 94305

BARTON, JUDITH MARIE, lawyer; b. Grosse Pointe, Mich., Feb. 19, 1953; d. Joseph J. and Shirley (Fisher) B.; m. A. Scott MacGuidwin, Sept. 19, 1980; children: Stephen Fisher, Richard Joseph. BA, U. Mich., 1975; JD, Thomas M. Cooley Sch. Law, 1979. Bar: Mich. 1981, U.S. Dist. Ct. (we. dist.) Mich. 1982. Mgr. bus. and circulation Football News/Basketball Weekly, Grosse Pointe, 1975-77; legis. asst. Mich. Ho. of Reps., Lansing, 1977-80, legal specialist, 1980-81; staff dir. Mich. State Senate, Lansing, 1981-83; sole practice Lansing, 1983—. Bd. dirs. Common Cause, Lansing, 1983—, state chairperson, Mich.; bd. dirs. Landlords of Mid-Mich., Lansing, 1985—. Mem. ABA, Mich. Bar Assn., Ingham County Bar Assn., Women's Law Assn., Pub. Action Com., Capitol Area Women's Network (bd. dirs. 1983-84), Pi Beta Phi. Republican. Roman Catholic. Club: Civitan Internat. Real property, Legislative, Family and matrimonial. Home: 4317 Manitou Dr Okemos MI 48864

BARTON, RICHARD LEE, lawyer; b. Norfolk, Va., Mar. 30, 1941; s. Elvin L. and Pauline B. (Carroll) B.; m. Donna Elizabeth Pyle, Aug. 25, 1963 (div. 1974); children—Richard Lee, Robert Thomas; m. Donna Lee Lounsberry, Aug. 5, 1978. B.A., Willamette U., 1962, J.D. cum laude, 1965. Bar: Oreg. 1965, U.S. Dist. Ct. Oreg. 1966, U.S. Ct. Mil. Appeals 1968, U.S. Ct. Appeals (9th cir.) 1969, U.S. Supreme Ct. 1975. Dep. dist. atty. Dist. Atty's Office, Portland, Oreg., 1965-70, chief dep. dist. atty., 1970-72; sr. ptnr. Barton & Loennig, Portland, 1973—; instr. advanced trial practice, criminal procedure Northwestern Coll. Law, Lewis and Clark U., Portland, 1974-77. Assoc. editor, contbg. author Willamette U. Law Jour., 1965; editor, contbg. author: CLE Criminal Law, 1969—. Served to capt. JAGC, USAR, 1966-74. Sr. scholar dept. econs. Willamette U., Salem, Oreg., 1962. Mem. Oreg. Trial Lawyers Assn. (parliamentarian 1981-82, treas. 1982-83, v.p. 1983-84, pres. 1984-85), Order of Purple. Republican. Personal injury, Criminal, State civil litigation. Home: 5335 SW 150th Ct Beaverton OR 97007 Office: Barton & Loennig 1600 Orbanco Bldg 1001 SW 5th Portland OR 97204

BARTON, WILLIAM ARNOLD, lawyer, educator; b. Morton, Wash., Mar. 15, 1948; s. Marvin Buryl and Jo Ellen (Wilson) B.; m. Almine De Villiers, Dec. 4, 1974; children: Monique, Almine, Brent. BS, Pacific U., 1969; JD, Willamette U., 1972. Bar: Oreg. 1972. Sole practice Newport, Oreg., 1973—; adj. prof. Willamette U. Coll. Law, Salem, Oreg., 1983—; trial judge pro tem all state cts. Author: Recovering for Psychological Injuries, 1985. Brooks scholar, 1971. Mem. Oreg. State Bar Assn. (v.p. 1986—), Western Trial Lawyers Assn. (pres. 1985), Oreg. Trial Lawyers Assn. (pres. 1983), Lincoln County Bar Assn. (pres. 1987). Personal injury, Federal civil litigation, State civil litigation. Home: 2114 NE Crestview Newport OR 97365 Office: 214 SE Coast Hwy Newport OR 97365

BARTON, WILLIAM HARVEY, lawyer; b. Pascagoula, Miss., Aug. 13, 1955; s. William Harvey Barton and Juanita (Tutt) Hesford; m. Renee Smith, Jan. 19, 1985. BS, U. So. Miss., 1976; JD, U. Miss., 1980; Cert. of Completion(hon.), London Sch. Econs., 1976. Bar: Miss. 1980, U.S. Dist. Ct. Miss. 1980, U.S. Ct. Appeals (5th and 11th cirs.) 1981. Counselor Jackson County Youth Ct., Pascagoula, 1977; assoc. Cumbest, Cumbest & Hunter P.A., Pascagoula, 1980-86; sole practice Pascagoula, 1986—. Recipient Group Study Exchange award Rotary Internat., Brazil, 1984; named Outstanding Young Man of Pascagoula, Jaycees, 1986. Mem. Miss. Bar Assn., Jackson County Bar Assn. (treas. 1984, sec. 1985), Assn. Trial Lawyers Am., Miss. Trial Lawyers Assn., U. So. Miss. Alumni Assn. (pres. Jackson County chpt. 1986—). Baptist. Lodge: Kiwanis (local pres. 1985-86). Federal civil litigation, State civil litigation, Personal injury. Home: 2012 Old Oaks Dr Gaviter MS 39553 Office: 3203 Pascagoula St Suite 103 Ritz Pascagoula MS 39567

BARTOS, JOHN BURY, lawyer; b. Los Angeles, May 23, 1944; s. John Bury and Pauline Elizabeth (Rose) B.; m. Harriet Kai-ma Sun, Nov. 23, 1974; 1 child, William Harry. BA in Polit. Sci., UCLA, 1966, JD, 1973. Bar: Calif. 1973, U.S. Dist. Ct. (cen. dist.) Calif. 1974, U.S. Ct. Appeals (9th cir.) 1975, U.S. Supreme Ct. 1977. Atty. U.S. Immigration and Naturalization Service, Los Angeles, 1973-75, 76-82; assoc. Otto F. Swanson, Inc., Marina del Rey, Calif., 1975-76; asst. regional counsel U.S. Immigration and Naturalization Service, San Pedro, Calif., 1982-84; dist. counsel U.S. Immigration and Naturalization Service, Phoenix, 1984—. Served to 1st lt. U.S. Army, 1966-69, Vietnam, USAR, 1975—. Mem. ABA, Fed. Bar Assn., Res. Officers Assn., Am. Legion. Democrat. Presbyterian. Immigration, naturalization, and customs, Government contracts and claims, Federal civil litigation. Office: US Immigration Naturalization Service 230 N 1st Ave Phoenix AZ 85025-0090

BARTOSIC, FLORIAN, lawyer, university dean; b. Danville, Pa., Sept. 15, 1926; s. Florian W. and Elsie (Woodring) B.; m. Eileen M. Payne, 1953 (div. 1969); children: Florian, Ellen, Thomas, Stephen. B.A., Pontifical Coll., 1948; B.C.L., Coll. William and Mary, 1956; LL.M., Yale U., 1957. Bar: Va. 1956, U.S. Supreme Ct. 1959. Asst. instr. Yale U., 1956-57; assoc. prof. law Coll. William and Mary, 1957, Villanova U., 1957-59; atty. NLRB, Washington, 1956, 57, 59; counsel Internat. Brotherhood of Teamsters, Washington, 1959-71; prof. law Wayne State U., 1971-80; dean, prof. law U. Calif. at Davis, 1980—; adj. prof. George Washington U., 1966-71, Cath. U. Am., 1960-71; mem. panel arbitrators Fed. Mediation and Conciliation Service, Nat. Mediation Bd., 1972—; hearing officer Mich. Employment Relations Commn., 1972-80, Mich. Civil Rights Commn., 1974-80; bd. dirs. Mich. Legal Services Corp., 1973-80, Inst. Labor and Indsl. Relations, U. Mich., Wayne State U., 1976-80; mem. Steering com. Inst. on Global Conflict and Cooperation, 1982-83; mem. adv. bd. Assn. for Union Democracy Inc., 1980—, adv. coms. Calif. Jud. Council, 1984-85, 87—; visiting scholar Harvard Law Sch., 1987, Stanford Law Sch., 1987. Co-author: Labor Relations Law in the Private Sector, 1977, 2d edit., 1986; contbr. articles to law jours. Mem. ABA (sec. labor relations law sect. 1974-75), Am. Law Inst. (acad. mem. labor law adv. com. on continuing profl. edn.), Soc. Profls. in Dispute Resolution (regional v.p. 1979-80), Indsl. Relations Research Assn., Internat. Soc. Labor Law and Social Legis., Internat. Indsl. Relations Assn., Am. Arbitration Assn. (panel), Fed. Bar Assn., Nat. Bar Assn, Nat Lawyers Guild, ACLU (dir. Detroit chpt. 1976-77), Order of Coif, Scribes. Legal

education, Labor, Workers' compensation. Home: 235 Ipanema Pl Davis CA 95616 Office: U Calif Law Sch Davis CA 95616

BARTUNEK, JOSEPH WENCESLAUS, lawyer; b. Cleve., Feb. 16, 1924; s. Otto Joseph and Anna Barbara (Hlavin) B.; m. Pauline Frances Evans, Jan. 15, 1945; children—Kenneth J., Rod, Deborah Hees, Donna Kissner. B.S., Case Western Reserve U., 1948; L.L.B., Cleveland-Marshall Coll., 1955. Sole practice, Cleve., 1955-64; probate judge Ohio courts, Cleve., 1964-70; of counsel Ginsberg, Guren & Merritt, Cleve., 1970-75; ptnr. Bartunek, Garofoli & Hill, Cleve., 1975-86, U.S. Magistrate U.S. Dist. Ct. (no. dist.) Ohio, Cleve., 1986—; trustee Cleve. State U., 1964-77, chmn. 1975-76. State senator Ohio Gov., Columbus, 1949-58, 59-64; county chmn. Democratic Party, Cleve., 1971-72. Served with U.S. Army, 1943-46. Cleve. State U. Law Library named in his honor. Recipient Alumni Disting. Service award Cleve. State U., 1973, Outstanding Alumnus award Cleveland-Marshall Alumni Assn. Mem. ABA, Am. Judicature Soc., Ohio Bar Assn. Assn. Trial Lawyers Am., Bar Assn. Greater Cleve. Democrat. Roman Catholic. Clubs: Hermit, Athletic (Cleve.)

BARVICK, WILLIAM MICHAEL, lawyer; b. Kansas City, Mo., Jan. 20, 1938; s. Michael Patrick and Ann Loretta (Pietrzyk) B.; m. Mary Bridget Foley, July 22, 1967; children: Bridget Anne, Sheila Kathleen, Michael John, William Vincent. BA, St. Mary's Coll., 1958; JD, Northwestern U., 1961; postdoctoral., Columbia U., 1970-71. Bar: Mo. 1961, U.S. Dist. Ct. (we. dist.) Mo. 1963, U.S. Supreme Ct. 1966. With firm Kansas City, 1962-66; regional dir. Legal Services, Kansas City, 1966-71; assoc. prof. law U. S.C., Columbia, 1971-74; pub. counsel State of Mo., Jefferson City, Mo., 1974-81; sole practice Jefferson City, 1981—; spl. asst. Pub. Defender, Jefferson City, 1981-84; hearing officer Dept. Natural Resources, Jefferson City, 1986. Pres. Mo. Lawyers Credit Union, Jefferson City, 1982. Served with U.S. Army, 1961-67. Mem. ABA, Mo. Bar Assn. (profl. specialization com., ins. programs com.), Polish Inst. Arts and Scis. Am., Am. Arbitration Assn. (arbitrator), Nat. Legal Aid and Defender Assn. (cons. 1970-74). Roman Catholic. Lodge: KC. Avocations: racquetball, bicycling, coaching boys sports, reading. Administrative and regulatory, Public utilities, General practice. Home: 309 Binder Dr Jefferson City MO 65101

BARZ, PATRICIA, lawyer; b. Mattoon, Ill., Oct. 18, 1953; d. William E. Barz and Rosemary A. (Easton) Scott.; m. Herbert P. Wiedemann, Feb. 12, 1983. BA, Yale U., 1974; JD, U. Va., 1978. Bar: Va. 1979, Conn. 1982, Ohio 1985. Assoc. Hunton & Williams, Richmond, Va., 1978-81, Davis, Graham & Stubbs, Denver, 1981-82; counsel legal dept. Aetna Life and Casualty Co., Hartford, Conn., 1982-84; assoc. Jones, Day, Reavis & Pogue, Cleve., 1984—. Trustee St. Anthony Trust Assn., New Haven, 1983-86; class agt. Yale Alumni Fund, New Haven, 1985—. Mem. Ohio Bar Assn., Cleve. Bar Assn., Conn. Bar Assn., Va. Bar Assn., Yale Alumni Assn. Cleve. (v.p.). Methodist. Avocations: figure skating, raquetball, theater, reading, travel. Real property, Landlord-tenant, Contracts commercial. Home: 3008 Claremont Rd Shaker Heights OH 44122 Office: Jones Day Reavis & Pogue 1700 Huntington Bldg Cleveland OH 44115

BARZA, HAROLD A., lawyer; b. Montreal, Que., Can., July 28, 1952; came to U.S., 1969; s. Solomon A. and Evelyn (Elkin) B. BA, Boston U., 1973; JD, Columbia U., 1976. Bar: N.Y. 1977, Calif. 1978, U.S. Dist. Ct. (cen. dist.) Calif. 1978. Law clk. to judge U.S. Dist. Ct. (so. dist.) N.Y., 1976-77; assoc. Munger, Tolles & Rickershauser, Los Angeles, 1978-81; ptnr. Gelles, Singer & Johnson, Los Angeles, 1982-83, Gelles, Lawrence & Barza, Los Angeles, 1983-87, Loeb & Loeb, 1987—; adj. prof. mass communications law Southwestern U. Sch. Law, Los Angeles, 1979-82; judge pro tem., Los Angeles Mcpl. Ct., 1985—. Mem. bd. editors Columbia Law Rev., 1975-76. Mem. steering com. Jewish Nat. Fund, Los Angeles, 1983. James Kent scholar, 1974-76, Harlan Fiske Stone scholar, 1973-74. Mem. Los Angeles County Bar Assn. (trial lawyers and litigation sects., mem. antitrust com. on antitrust litigation), ABA. Antitrust, Federal civil litigation, State civil litigation. Office: Loeb & Loeb 624 S Grand Ave #1600 Los Angeles CA 90017

BASHAM, MARSHALL DENVER, judge, educator; b. Ponca City, Okla., Nov. 16, 1943; s. Orville and Mary Frances (Stubblefield) B.; m. Judith Ann Alexander, June 6, 1964; children: Tim, Chris, Erin. BA, Cen. State U., 1965; MA, U. Okla., 1968, JD, 1980. Bar: Okla. 1980, U.S. Dist. Ct. (we. dist.) Okla. 1980. Assoc. Henry, West & Sill, Shawnee, Okla., 1980-81, Ingram & Lewis, Shawnee, 1981-82; ptnr. Lewis & Basham, Shawnee, 1982-84; assoc. dist. judge 23d Jud. Dist. Pottawatomie County, Shawnee, 1984—. Pres. Shawnee Camp Fire, Inc., 1984—. Mem. ABA, Pottawatomie County Bar Assn. (pres. 1986—), Am. Judicature Soc. Democrat. Baptist. Lodge: Lions. Avocation: hunting. Judicial administration, Family and matrimonial, State civil litigation. Office: 325 N Broadway S #307 Shawnee OK 74801

BASHAW, STEVEN BRADLEY, lawyer; b. Chgo., Mar. 2, 1951; s. Raymond P. and Neila M. (Booth) B.; m. Laura L. Liptrot, Mar. 18, 1972; children—Jennifer, Kimberly, Andrew, Daniel. B.A. in History, U. Ill. 1973; J.D., Chgo. Kent Coll. Law, 1976. Bar: Ill. 1976, U.S. Dist. Ct. (no. dist.) Ill. 1976. Atty. Shapiro & Kreisman, Northbrook, Ill., 1974-77, Denis B. Pierce, Atty., Chgo., 1977-78; ptnr. Pierce & Bashaw, Chgo., 1978-83, Bashaw & Assocs., Hinsdale, Ill., 1983—; teaching asst. Chgo. Kent Coll. Law, 1975-77; lectr. U.S. League of Savs., Chgo., 1979—; lectr., panelist Mortgage Bankers Assn. Am., Washington, 1980—; panelist Ill. Mortgage Bankers Assn., Chgo., 1982—, Ill. Continuing Legal Edn., Ill. Inst. Tech., Chgo., 1985-86; instr. Inst. Fin. Edn. Coorespondence. Study Dept., 1986—. Sect. chmn. Hinsdale Village Caucus, 1983-85. Mem. ABA, Ill. Bar Assn. Republican. Roman Catholic. Real property, State civil litigation, Contracts commercial. Office: 211 W Chicago Ave Suite 210 Hinsdale IL 60521

BASHLINE, JAMES DUANE, lawyer; b. Butler, Pa., Aug. 16, 1942; s. Bernard and Dorothy Mae (Regal) B.; m. RoEllen Bashline, Apr. 1972 (div. July 1974); m. Helen Sampson, Mar. 21, 1980. BA, Cameron U., 1975; JD, Baylor U., 1980. Bar: Tex. 1980, U.S. Dist. Ct. (so. and ea. dists.) Tex. 1980, U.S. Dist. Ct. (no. dist.) Okla. 1980, U.S. Ct. Appeals (5th cir.) 1980. Enlisted USAF, 1961; legal tech. USAF, Turkey and U.K., 1961-64; resigned USAF, 1964; enlisted U.S. Army, 1966, advanced through grades to maj., 1982; aviator U.S. Army, Fed. Republic of Germany and Vietnam, 1966-77; resigned active duty U.S. Army, 1977; assoc. Mcleod, Alexander, Powell & Apffel, Galveston, Tex., 1980—, firm officer, 1986. Serves as maj. USAR, 1982—. Mem. ABA (law office econs. sect.), Tex. Assn. Def. Counsel. Avocations: running, weight lifting, racquetball. State civil litigation, Personal injury, Insurance. Office: McLeod Alexander Powel & Apffel 802 Rosenberg Galveston TX 77550

BASHWINER, STEVEN LACELLE, lawyer; b. Cin., Aug. 3, 1941; s. Carl Thomas and Ruth Marie (Burlis) B.; m. Arden J. Lang, Apr. 24, 1966 (div. 1978); children: Heather, David; m. Donna Lee Gerber, Sept. 13, 1981; children: Margaret, Matthew. AB, Holy Cross Coll., 1963; JD, U. Chgo., 1966. Bar: Ill. 1966, U.S. Dist. Ct. Ill. 1967, U.S. Ct. Appeals (7th cir.) 1968, U.S. Supreme Ct. 1970. Assoc. Kirkland & Ellis, Chgo., 1966-72, ptnr., 1972-76; ptnr. Friedman & Koven, Chgo., 1976-86, Katten, Muchin, & Zavis, Chgo., 1986—. Served to sgt. USAFR, 1966-72. Mem. ABA, Fed. Bar Assn., Ill. State Bar Assn., Chgo. Bar Assn., Legal Club Chgo. Clubs: Tavern, University (Chgo.). Securities, Federal civil litigation, State civil litigation. Home: 834 Green Bay Rd Highland Park IL 60035 Office: Katten Muchin et al 525 W Monroe Chicago IL 60606

BASILE, PAUL LOUIS, JR., lawyer; b. Oakland, Calif., Dec. 27, 1945; s. Paul Louis and Roma Florence (Paris) B.; m. Linda Lou Paige, June 20, 1970; m. 2d Diane Chierichetti, Sept. 2, 1977. B.A., Occidental Coll., 1968; postgrad. U. Wash., 1969; J.D., UCLA, 1971. Bar: Calif. sup. ct. 1972, U.S. Dist. Ct. (cen. dist.) Calif. 1972, U.S. Sup. Ct. 1978, U.S. Tax Ct. 1977, U.S. Ct. Clms. 1978, U.S. Customs Ct. 1979, U.S. Ct. Customs and Patent Appeals 1979, U.S. Ct. Internat. Trade 1981. Assoc., Parker, Milliken, Kohlmeier, Clark & O'Hara, Los Angeles, 1971-72; corporate counsel TFI Cos., Inc., Irvine, Calif., 1972-73; sole practice, Los Angeles, 1973-80; ptnr., Basile & Siener, Los Angeles, 1980—; ptnr. Clark & Trevithick, Los Angeles, 1986—; sec. J.W. Brown, Inc., Los Angeles, Calif.; sec. Souriau, Inc., Valencia, Calif.; v.p., sec. Pvt. Fin. Assocs., Los Angeles. Trustee, sec. Nat. Repertory Theatre Found., 1975—, mem. exec. com. 1976—; active Los Angeles Olympic Organizing Com.; dir. March Dimes Birth Defects Found., Los Angeles County, 1982—; dir. Canadian Soc. Los Angeles, 1980-83, sec., 1982-83; dist. fin. chmn. Los Angeles Area council Boy Scouts Am., 1982-83. Mem. ABA, State Bar Calif., Los Angeles County Bar Assn., Canada Calif. C. of C. (dir. 1980—, 2d v.p. 1983-84, 1st v.p. 1984-85, pres. 1985-87), French-Am. C. of C. (councilor 1979-84, v.p. 1980, 82-84), Los Angeles Area C. of C. (dir. 1980-81), Grand Peoples Co. (bd. dirs., 1985—, chmn. bd. 1986—). Democrat. Baptist. General corporate, Corporate taxation, Private international. Home: 3937 Beverly Glen Blvd Sherman Oaks CA 91403 Office: Clark & Trevithick 800 Wilshire Blvd 13th Floor Los Angeles CA 90017

BASINGER, RICHARD LEE, lawyer; b. Canton, Ohio, Nov. 24, 1941; s. Eldon R. and Alice M. (Bartholomew) B.; m. Rita Evelyn Gover, May 14, 1965; children—David A., Darron M. B.A. in Edn., Ariz. State U., 1963; postgrad. Macalester Coll., 1968-69; J.D., U. Ariz., 1973. Bar: Ariz. 1973, U.S. Dist. Ct. Ariz. 1973, U.S. Tax Ct. 1977, U.S. Ct. Appeals (6th cir.) 1975, U.S. Ct. Appeals (9th cir.) 1976, U.S. Supreme Ct. 1977. Assoc. law offices, Phoenix, 1973-74; sole practice, Scottsdale, Ariz. 1974-75; mem., pres. Basinger & Assocs., P.C., Scottsdale, 1975—. Contbr. articles to profl. jours. Bd. dirs. Masters Trail Ventures, Scottsdale, 1984-85, Here's Life, Ariz., Scottsdale, 1976—; precinct committeeman Republican Party, Phoenix, 1983—. NSF grantee, 1968-69. Mem. ABA, Ariz. Bar Assn., Maricopa County Bar Assn., Ariz. State Horseman's Assn. (bd. dirs. 1984-86, 1st up 1986), Scottsdale Bar Assn. Baptist. Clubs: Western Saddle (Phoenix) (bd. dirs. 1983-86, pres. 1985-86); Scottsdale Saddle, Saguaro Saddle. Real property, General corporate, Probate. Office: Basinger & Assocs PC 4120 N 70th St Suite 211 Scottsdale AZ 85251

BASINSKI, ANTHONY JOSEPH, lawyer; b. Pitts., Apr. 11, 1947; s. Anthony F. and Emily C. (Klocko) B.; m. Elisabeth Fawcett, Oct. 4, 1980; children: Ann Elisabeth, Robert Anthony. BA, U. Pitts., 1969, JD, 1974. Bar: Pa. 1974, U.S. Dist. Ct. (we. dist.) Pa. 1974, U.S. Ct. Appeals (3d cir.) 1981. Law clk. to presiding justice Pa. Supreme Ct., Pitts., 1974-76; ptnr. Reed, Smith, Shaw and McClay, Pitts., 1976—. Served with U.S. Army, 1969-71, Vietnam. Mem. Allegheny County Bar Assn., Am. Arbitration Assn. (arbitrator 1983—). Democratic. Roman Catholic. Federal civil litigation, State civil litigation, Securities. Home: 438 Marlin Dr Pittsburgh PA 15228 Office: Reed Smith Shaw & McClay 435 6th Ave Pittsburgh PA 15219

BASKETTE, WILLIAM L., JR., lawyer; b. Balt., July 11, 1955; s. William L. Sr. and Josephine K. (Marino) B.; m. Maria Cristina Matthews, Aug. 14, 1982. BA cum laude, Tex. Luth. Coll., 1977; JD, St. Mary's U., San Antonio, 1982. Bar: Tex. 1982, U.S. Dist. Ct. (ea. dist.) Tex. 1983. Briefing atty. U.S. Ct. Appeals (12th cir.), Tyler, Tex., 1982-83; asst. atty. Kerr County, Kerrville, Tex., 1983—; assoc. Jons & Parker, P.C., Kerrville, 1983—. Mem. Trial Lawyers Assn. Tex., Am. Judicature Soc., Nat. Dist. Attys. Assn., Tex. Dist. and County Attys. Assn., Tex. Prosecutor Council, Alpha Phi Omega (life), Phi Alpha Theta, Alpha Chi. Republican. Lutheran. Lodge: Rotary. State civil litigation, Criminal, Juvenile. Home: PO Box 364 Kerrville TX 78028 Office: Kerr County Courthouse Kerrville TX 78028

BASKIN, DAVID GREEN, lawyer; b. Detroit, July 30, 1949; s. Harry and Dorothy (Green) B.; m. Cynthia Baskin, Aug. 19, 1974; children: Caleb, Alexander. BA, U. Mich., 1970; JD, Wayne State U., 1974. Asst. dist. atty.'s office Santa Cruz County, Calif., 1974; sole practice Santa Cruz, 1979—; ptnr. Baskin, Hultzen & Grant, Santa Cruz. Mem. Calif. Bar Assn., Santa Cruz County Bar Assn., Assn. Trial Lawyers Am. State civil litigation, Federal civil litigation, Personal injury. Office: Baskin Hultzen & Grant 730 Mission St #1 Santa Cruz CA 95060

BASON, GEORGE FRANCIS, JR., judge; b. Chapel Hill, N.C., June 30, 1931; s. George Francis and Mary Isabel (Reuther) B.; m. Sheilah Margaret Weavis, Oct. 12, 1961; children—Neil William, Iain George. A.B. cum laude, Davidson Coll., 1953; J.D. cum laude, Harvard U., 1956. Bar: NC 1956, D.C. 1958, U.S. Supreme Ct. 1961. Assoc. Royall, Koegel and Harris, Washington and N.Y.C., 1958-61, Martin, Whitfield and Thaler, Washington, 1962-66; asst. prof. law Am. U., 1966-69, assoc. prof., 1969-72; sole practice, Washington, 1972-78; pres. George F. Bason Jr. P.C., Washington, 1978-84; judge U.S. Bankruptcy Ct. for D.C., 1984—; chmn. bankruptcy and reorgn. com. D.C. Bar, 1974-75; standing trustee for D.C. Wage Earner Plans Under Chapter XIII Bankruptcy Act, 1972-75. Recipient Am. Bar Found. Constl. Law Essay Contest 1st prize, 1973. Mem. ABA, D.C. Bar Assn. Contbr. articles to profl. jours. Pension, profit-sharing, and employee benefits. Office: US Courthouse Room 2106 Constitution Ave and 3d St Washington DC 20001

BASS, FRED, lawyer; b. Saddle Brook, N.J., July 19, 1957. BS, Cornell U., 1978; JD, Columbia U., 1981. Bar: N.Y. 1982, N.J. 1982, U.S. Dist. Ct. (so. dist.) N.Y. 1982. Assoc. Dewey, Ballantine, Bushby, Palmer & Wood, N.Y.C., 1981—. Mem. ABA. Avocations: squash, tennis. Securities, General corporate, Contracts commercial. Office: Dewey Ballantine et al 140 Broadway New York NY 10005

BASS, LEWIS, lawyer; b. Bklyn., Oct. 22, 1947; s. Alexander and Doris (Aranowitz) B.; m. Sharon Diane Abdallah; 1 child, Michael. BSME, CCNY, 1969; MS in Indsl. Engring., U. So. Calif., 1971; JD, U. Santa Clara, 1976. Bar: Calif. 1976, U.S. Dist. Ct. (no. dist.) Calif. 1976. Mech. engr. Rockwell Internat., Los Angeles, 1969-70; project engr. Aerospace Corp., Los Angeles, 1970-71; safety engr. Lockheed, Sunnyvale, Calif., 1971-77; assoc. Caputo, Liccardo, Rossi, Sturges & McNeil, San Jose, Calif., 1977-78; corp. counsel Rose Mfg. Co., Englewood, Calif., 1978-79; sole practice Mountain View, Calif., 1979—; pres. Kairos Co. Safety Engring., Mountain View, 1979—; adj. asst. prof. safety sci. U. So. Calif., Los Angeles, 1979—. Author: Products Liability Design and Manufacturing Defects, 1986; contbr. articles to profl. jours. Named Outstanding Teaching award U. So. Calif., 1984. Mem. ABA, Am. Soc. Quality Control, Am. Soc. Safety Engrs., System Safety Soc. Personal injury, General corporate, Insurance. Office: 1001 N Rengstroff Ave Suite 100 Mountain View CA 94043-1715

BASS, SHIRLEY ANN, lawyer; b. Brockton, Mass., Mar. 1, 1938; d. Ernest Francis and Clarissa May (Atwood) Marcotte; m. Jerry J. Bass, Dec. 26, 1959; children: Thomas, Robert, John. Cert. Katharine Gibbs Sch., 1958; student San Diego State U., 1963-64; BA, Portland State U., 1975; JD, Lewis and Clark Law Sch., 1979. Bar: Oreg. 1980. Assoc., Cyr, Moe & Benner, P.C., 1980-85; lectr. Portland Community Coll. (Oreg.), 1983—. Bd. dirs. Oreg. Fair Plan, 1982-86, The Samaritan Counseling Ctr., Inc., 1986—; vol. lawyer Sr. Law Project, 1985—; mem. planned giving com. Loaves and Fishes, Inc., 1985—. Recipient Estate Planning award Am. Jurisprudence, 1979. Mem. Oreg. Bar (editorial bd., legis. com. estate planning sect.), ABA, Multnomah Bar Assn., Washington County Bar Assn., Estate Planning Council Portland, Inst. for Managerial and Profl. Women, P.E.O., Phi Alpha Delta. Republican. Episcopalian. Club: Portland City, Altrusa (Portland). Probate, Estate taxation, Personal income taxation. Office: Cyr Moe & Benner PC 1230 SW 1st Ave Suite 300 Portland OR 97204

BASSETT, CRAIG JAY, lawyer; b. Walnut Creek, Calif., Jan. 6, 1955; s. Richard Andre and Sandra Diane (Foley) B.; m. Lynda Lyman, Apr. 14, 1978; children: Amber, Richard, Elise, Cameron. BS in Econs., Brigham Young U., 1979, JD, 1982. Bar: Calif. 1982. Assoc. William H. Brown, Morgan Hill, Calif., 1983-85; ptnr. Sullivan & Bassett, Morgan Hill, 1985—. Republican. Mormon. Avocation: guitar. State civil litigation, Probate, Real property. Home: 2470 Gitana Ct Morgan Hill CA 95037 Office: Sullivan & Bassett 25 W First St Morgan Hill CA 95037-4501

BASSETT, JEFFREY MICHAEL, lawyer; b. Baton Rouge, Oct. 8, 1953; s. Aubrey Jefferson and Lauranell (Fleming) B.; m. Cecette Smith, July 17, 1982; children: Laura Elizabeth, Taylor Jefferson. JD, La. State U. Bar: U.S. Dist. Ct. (ea. and mid. dists.) La., U.S. Ct. Appeals (5th and 11th cirs.), U.S. Supreme Ct. Asst. dist. atty. Dist. Atty's Office, New Orleans, 1978-81; ptnr. Morrow & Morrow, Opelousas, La., 1981—. Page, La. Ho. of Reps., Baton Rouge, 1970-71. Mem. ABA, Assn. Trial Lawyers Am., La. State Bar Assn., La. Trial Lawyers Assn., St. Landry Parish Bar Assn. (v.p. 1986-87). Democrat. Roman Catholic. Lodge: Elks. Avocations: hunting, fishing, tennis. Admiralty, Personal injury, Criminal. Office: Morrow & Morrow 324 W Landry St Opelousas LA 70570

BASSETT, JOEL ERIC, lawyer; b. Adrian, Mich., Feb. 15, 1944; s. Carroll William and Creita (Eayrs) B.; m. Cynthia Rae Slager, Aug. 31, 1968; children—Eric William, Nicole Rae, Jodi Lynn, Ethan Christopher, Victoria Renee. B.A., Northwestern U., 1966, J.D., 1969; LL.M. in Taxation, Georgetown U., 1973. Bar: D.C. 1969. Intern Office of Regional Counsel IRS, San Francisco, 1968; atty. interpretive div. Office Chief Counsel IRS, Washington, 1969-74; asst. chief internat. tax br. Legis. and Regulations div. IRS, 1974-75, chief corp. tax br. Refund Litigation div., 1975; assoc. firm Arent, Fox, Kintner, Plotkin & Kahn, Washington, 1975-80; ptnr. Arent, Fox, Kintner, Plotkin & Kahn, 1980—; adj. prof. law Georgetown U., 1977-78. Mem. editorial bd. Jour. Criminal Law, Criminology and Police Sci., 1968-69; contbr. articles to profl. publs. Mem. council City of Chevy Chase View, Md., 1979-81; sr. warden Christ Episcopal Ch., Chevy Chase View, 1980-81. Mem. ABA, Washington Tax Group. Democrat. Corporate taxation, Personal income taxation, Estate taxation. Office: Arent Fox Kintner Plotkin & Kahn 1050 Connecticut Ave NW Washington DC 20036

BASSETT, JOHN WALDEN, JR., lawyer; b. Roswell, N.Mex., Mar. 21, 1938; s. John Walden and Evelyn (Thompson) B.; m. Patricia Lubben, May 22, 1965; children—John Walden III, Loren Patricia. A.B. in Econs., Stanford U., 1960; LL.B. with honors, U. Tex., 1964. Bar: Tex. 1964, N.Mex. 1964. Assoc. Atwood & Malone, Roswell, 1964-66; White House fellow, spl. asst. to U.S. atty. gen., Washington, 1966-67; ptnr. Atwood, Malone, Mann & Turner and predecessors, P.A., Roswell, 1967—; dir., chmn. Sunwest Bank of Roswell, N.A., dir. A.H. Belo Corp., Dallas; chmn. N.Mex. State Bd. of Edn., 1987—. Pres., chmn. bd. United Way of Chaves County, N.Mex., 1973; bd. dirs. St. Mary's Hosp., Roswell, 1976-86. Served to 1st lt. U.S. Army, 1961-68. Mem. ABA, Tex. Bar Assn., N.Mex. Bar Assn., Chaves County Bar Assn., Order of Coif. Republican. Episcopalian. Club: Rotary (pres. 1976) (Roswell). General practice. Home: 602 Rosemary Ln Roswell NM 88201 Office: PO Drawer 700 Roswell NM 88201

BASSETT, WILLIAM RANDALL, lawyer; b. Montgomery, Ala., May 23, 1937; s. Julian Morris and Neva Carmichael (Johnson) B.; m. Dorothy Sue Gideon, June 13, 1959; children: Dianne, Randy, Susanne. BSCE, Auburn U., 1959; JD, Emory U., 1967. Bar: Ga. 1968, U.S. Dist. Ct. (no. dist.) Ga. 1968, U.S. Ct. Appeals (5th and 11th cirs.) 1968, U.S. Supreme Ct. 1968. Assoc. Wiggins & Smith, Atlanta, 1968-73; ptnr. Bassett, Gerry, Friend & Koenig, Atlanta, 1973—. Mem. ABA, Ga. Bar Assn., Atlanta Bar Assn., Lawyers Club of Atlanta. Presbyterian. Lodge: Kiwanis (pres. 1972-73). Real property, Securities. Home: 1157 Hampton Hall Dr Atlanta GA 30319 Office: Bassett Gerry Friend & Koenig 57 Executive Park S Atlanta GA 30329

BASSFORD, CHARLES ADDISON, retired lawyer; b. St. Paul, Oct. 29, 1914; s. Charles Asher and Helen Faye (Lamoreaux) B.; m. Ruby Hendrickson Bassford, Dec. 4, 1918; children—Charles Addison, Faye Louise. B.A., U. Minn. 1935, LL.B. magna cum laude, St. Paul Coll. 1939, JD magna cum laude, William Mitchell Coll. Law. Bar: Minn. 1939, U.S. dist. ct. Minn. 1939, U.S. Ct. Apls. (8th cir.) 1951. Assoc. Richards, Janes, Montgomery & Cobb, Mpls. 1950-60; ptnr. Richards, Montgomery, Cobb & Bassford, Mpls. 1960-79; ptnr. Bassford, Heckt, Lockhart & Mullin, Mpls. 1979—; lectr. in field. Served to capt. War Dept., 1942-45. Mem. ABA, Minn. Bar Assn., Hennepin County Bar Assn., Am. Judicature Soc., Am. Coll. Trial Lawyers, Internat. Soc. Barristers, Am. Bd. Trial Advocates, Internat. Assn. Ins. Counsel, Minn. Def. Attys., Minn. Hosp. Attys. Republican. Presbyterian. Clubs: Mpls. Athletic, Luck Wis. Country; Palmbrook Country (Sun City, Ariz.). Personal injury, Federal civil litigation, Insurance. Home: 18229 103d Ave N Sun City AZ 85373 Home: Route 2 PO Box 239 Balsam Lake WI 54810 Office: 3550 Multifoods Tower 33 S 6th St Minneapolis MN 55402

BASSICK, EDGAR WEBB, III, judge; b. Bridgeport, Conn., Sept. 26, 1927; s. Edgar Webb and Christine (Newman) B.; m. Dorothy Taylor, May 23, 1968; children—Edgar Webb Gayle T., Rae Bassick Bogusky; stepchildren—Leslie J. Bosse, Paul A. Johnson, Jay J. Purcell, Stephen G. Johnson. B.A., Yale U., 1950; J.D., Harvard U., 1955. Bar: Conn. 1955, U.S. dist. ct. Conn., 1956, U.S. Ct. Appeals (2d cir.) 1957, U.S. Supreme Ct. 1959. Assoc. Pullman, Comley, Bradley & Reeves, Bridgeport, Conn., 1955-60, ptnr., 1960-86; judge superior ct. State of Conn., 1986—; atty. state trial referee, 1984-85; spl. master Family Ct., 1983-85. Pres. Barnum Festival Soc., 1972, dir., 1964-78, hon. dir., 1966—, ringmaster Barnum Festival, 1966; bd. dirs. Mt. Grove Cemetary Assn., 1982—. Served to 1st lt., inf. AUS, 1946-48, 50-52. Fellow Am. Acad. Matrimonial Lawyers (bd. mgrs. Conn. 1976-79); mem. ABA, Conn. Bar Assn. (ho. of dels. 1983-86), Bridgeport Bar Assn. (chmn. family law sect. 1978-80, 83, bd. govs. 1980-85), Am. Arbitration Assn., Am. Judicature Soc. Clubs: Algonquin (pres. 1980-81, trustee 1983-87), Exchange (pres. 1967-68), Masons. Home: 510 Barlow Rd Fairfield CT 06430 Office: 855 Main St Bridgeport CT 06604

BASSITT, JANET LOUISE, lawyer; b. Macomb, Ill., Oct. 8, 1941; d. James Russell Hoover and Louise Loretta (Lawrence) Hoover Reed; children: Teri Beth Bassitt Robertshaw, William Jefferson, Margaret Louise. BA in Psychology with honors, U. Ill., Chgo., 1976; JD, John Marshall Law Sch., 1980. Bar: Ill. 1981, U.S. Dist. Ct. (no. dist.) Ill. 1982, U.S. Ct. Appeals (7th cir.) 1982, U.S. Supreme Ct. 1985. Sole practice Roselle, Ill., 1982—; instr. Harper Coll., Palatine, Ill., 1983—; legis. asst. to Ill. rep. K. Wojcik, Schaumburg, Ill., 1985—. Author: Attorney Conduct, 1985; contbr. articles to profl. jours. Vol. lawyer Constl. Rights Found., Chgo., 1982—; chmn. March of Dimes, Wenatchee, Wash., 1972-72; leader Wenatchee Troop Boy Scouts Am., 1971-72. Mem. ABA, Ill. Bar Assn., Chgo. Bar Assn., Woodfield Bar Assn. (chmn. pub. relations 1985—), Internat. Assn. Fin. Planners. Entertainment, General corporate, Criminal. Home: 7155 Orchard Ln Hanover Park IL 60103 Office: 672 E Irving Park Rd #103 Roselle IL 60172

BASSLER, HARRY WARREN, lawyer; b. Nashville, Mar. 7, 1948; s. Fred Gilbert and Mary Frances (Gotto) B.; m. Emma Wardlyn Mills, Dec. 4, 1976; 1 child, Jonathan Warren. BA, Emory U., 1970, JD, 1973. Bar: Ga. 1974. Assoc. Horton & Crim, Atlanta, 1973-77, Hopkins & Gresham, Atlanta, 1977-80; ptnr. Scroggins, Brizendine & Bassler, Atlanta, 1980-86, Crim & Bassler, Atlanta, 1986—. Vice chmn. Marietta (Ga.) Clean City Commn., 1984-85. Served to capt. U.S. Army, 1972-80. Mem. ABA, Ga. Bar Assn., Atlanta Bar Assn., Lawyers Club of Atlanta. Republican. Presbyterian. Insurance, Personal injury, Family and matrimonial. Home: 647 Hickory Dr Marietta GA 30064 Office: Crim & Bassler 6201 Powers Ferry Rd Suite 320 Atlanta GA 30339

BASSMAN, ROBERT STUART, lawyer; b. N.Y.C., Dec. 12, 1947; s. Benjamin and Eva (Pinck) B.; m. Sofia Yank, Sept. 12, 1971; 1 child, B. Zachary. BA, U. Pitts., 1969; JD, George Washington U., 1972. Bar: D.C. 1973, U.S. Dist. Ct. D.C. 1973, U.S. Ct. Appeals (D.C. cir.) 1973, U.S. Ct. Appeals (4th cir.) 1974, U.S. Supreme Ct. 1977. Counsel environ. Nat. Forest Products Assn., Washington, 1972-75; counsel Nat. Oil Jobbers Council, Washington, 1975-79; mng. ptnr. Bassman, Mitchell & Alfano, Washington, 1979—. Mem. ABA, D.C. Bar Assn., Gulf Oil Wholesale Marketers Assn. (counsel 1979—), Nat. Assn. Union Oil Co. Jobbers (counsel 1981—). Administrative and regulatory, Antitrust, Environment. Home: 1819 Q St NW Washington DC 20009 Office: Bassman Mitchell & Alfano 1707 H St NW Suite 1000 Washington DC 20006

BASSO, RONALD MATTHEW, administrative law judge, property tax consultant; b. Passaic, N.J., June 12, 1948; s. Orpheo and Victoria Mary (Russin) B.; m. Sara Jane Angeli, Apr. 14, 1973; children—Gabriel, Nora Mae. B.B.A., U. Notre Dame, 1970, J.D., 1973. Bar: Mich. 1975, U.S. Dist. Ct. (we. dist.) Mich. 1977. Tax cons. Mich. Senate, Lansing, 1975-78; adminstrv. law judge Mich. Tax Tribunal, Lansing, 1978-82; chief adminstrv. law judge Mich. Dept. Licensing and Regulation, Lansing, 1982—; property tax cons. Basso & Basso, Okemos, Mich., 1983—; adj. prof. Cooley Law Sch., Lansing, 1978-80. Contbr. articles to profl. jours. Candidate for dist. judge of Mich., 1980; mediator Neighborhood Justice Ctr., Lansing, 1983—; mem. Civilian Rev. Bd. Mem. ABA, State Bar Mich., Adminstrv. Law

Judges Assn., So. Poverty Law Ctr. Roman Catholic. Clubs: Notre Dame, Mich. State U. Administrative and regulatory, Judicial administration, State and local taxation. Home: 1381 Sebewaing St Okemos MI 48864 Office: Mich Dept Licensing and Regulation PO Box 30018 Lansing MI 48909

BASTEDO, WAYNE WEBSTER, lawyer; b. Oceanside, N.Y., July 13, 1948; s. Walter Jr. and Barbara Catherine (Manning) B.; m. Bina Shantilal Mistry, Dec. 29, 1978. AB in Polit. Sci. cum laude, Princeton U., 1970; postgrad., NYU, 1977-78; JD, Hofstra U., 1978. Bar: N.Y. 1980. Mgr. adminstrv. Law Jour. Seminars Press, N.Y.C., 1978-79; editor decisions and legal digests N.Y. Law Jour., N.Y.C., 1979-81; sole practice N.Y.C., 1981-82; atty. Western Union Corp., Upper Saddle River, N.J., 1983—; cons. litigation Exxon Corp., N.Y.C., 1982, Western Union Corp., Upper Saddle River, 1983. Author: A Comparative Study of Soviet and American World Order Models, 1978, Who Has the Edge on Justice? Computer Services Alter Fair Play, 1979; edit. editor Princeton U. Law Rev., 1969-70; assoc. editor Hofstra U. Law Rev. 1976-77; editor (directory series) Outside Counsel: Inside Director, 1976-81; contbr. articles to profl. jours. Mem. policy com. Roosevelt Island (N.Y.) Residents Assn., 1981-82. Served to lt. USN, 1970-75, Vietnam. N.Y. State Regents scholar, 1966-70, USN Officer Tng. scholar, 1967-70. Mem. ABA, N.Y. County Lawyers Assn. Democrat. Methodist. Avocations: internat. law and politics, cinema, writing. General corporate, Contracts commercial, General practice. Home: 370 Park St Apt 203 Hackensack NJ 07601 Office: Western Union Corp One Lake St Upper Saddle River NJ 07458

BASTEK, JOHN ANTHONY, coast guard officer, lawyer; b. Ridgewood, N.J., Sept. 30, 1946; s. Stanley A. and Eileen M. (Doran) B.; m. Susan Henry, Mar. 13, 1971; children—Neal J., Ian A. B.S., U.S. Coast Guard Acad., 1968; J.D., U. Miami, 1974. Bar: Fla. 1974, U.S. Ct. Mil. Appeals, 1974, N.J. 1977. Commd. ensign U.S. Coast Guard, 1968, advanced through grades to comdr., 1984; asst. legal officer 9th Coast Guard Dist., Cleve., 1974-76; base legal officer Coast Guard Tng. Ctr., Cape May, N.J., 1976-78; exec. officer U.S. Coast Guard Cutter Duane, Portland, Maine, 1978-80; dist. legal officer 14th Coast Guard Dist., Honolulu, 1980-83; 1st comdg. officer U.S. Coast Guard Cutter Northland, Portsmouth, Va., 1984-86, chief gen. law enforcement br., Washington, 1986—; mil. judge, 1981-83 . Decorated Coast Guard Commendation medal, Coast Guard Achievement medal. Mem. ABA, Fed. Bar Assn. Roman Catholic. Military, Public international, Admiralty. Home: 6723 Passageway Pl Burke VA 22015 Office: US Coast Guard Commandant G-OLE-3 Washington DC 20593

BASTIAANSE, GERARD C., lawyer; b. Holyoke, Mass., Oct. 21, 1935; s. Gerard C. and Margaret (Lally) B.; m. Paula E. Paliska, June 1, 1963; children: Elizabeth, Gerard. BSBA, Boston U., 1960; JD, U. Va., 1964. Bar: Mass. 1964, Calif. 1970. Assoc. Nutter, McClennen & Fish, Boston, 1964-65; counsel Campbell Soup Co., Camden, N.J., 1965-67; gen. counsel A&W Internat. (United Fruit Co.), Santa Monica, Calif., 1968-70; ptnr. Kindel & Anderson, Los Angeles, 1970—. Mem. ABA, Calif. Bar Assn., Mass. Bar Assn., Japan Am. Soc., Asia Soc., World Trade Ctr. Assn., Lincoln Club. Clubs: California (Los Angeles); Big Canyon Country (Newport Beach, Calif.). General corporate, Private international. Home: 2 San Sebastian Newport Beach CA 92660 Office: Kindel & Anderson 1301 Dove St Suite 1050 Newport Beach CA 92660

BATA, RUDOLPH ANDREW, JR., lawyer; b. Akron, Ohio, Jan. 9, 1947; s. Rudolph Andrew and Margaret Eleanor (Ellis) B.; m. Genevieve Ruth Brannam, Aug. 25, 1968 (div. May 1985); 1 child, Seth Andrew; m. Linda Lee Waldo, May 7, 1985. BS, So. Coll., Collegedale, Tenn., 1969; JD, Emory U., 1972. Bar: D.C. 1973, N.C. 1978. Assoc. ICC, Washington, 1972-73; in house counsel B.F. Saul Real Estate Investment Trust, Chevy Chase, Md., 1973-74; staff atty. Martha, Cafferky, Powers & Jordan, Washington, 1974-75; asst. corp. counsel Hardee's Food Systems, Inc., Rocky Mount, N.C., 1975-78; ptnr. Bata & Blomeley, Murphy, 1978—. Bd. dirs. Cherokee County United Fund, Murphy, N.C., 1981-83. Mem. ABA, N.C. Bar Assn., D.C. Bar Assn., 30th Jud. Dist. Bar Assn., So. Soc. of Adventist Attys. (pres. 1984-85), Cherokee County C. of C. (bd. dirs. 1980-82). Avocations: golf, tennis, hiking. Real property, Banking, Probate. Office: Bata & Blomeley 302 Valley River Ave Murphy NC 28906

BATCHELDER, ALICE M., federal judge; b. 1944; m. William G. Batchelder III; children: William G. IV, Elisabeth. BA, Ohio Wesleyan U., 1964; JD, Akron U., 1971. Tchr. Plain Local Sch. Dist., Franklin City, Ohio, 1965-66, Jones Jr. High Sch., 1966-67, Buckeye High Sch., Medina County, 1967-68; ptnr. Williams & Batchelder, Medina, Ohio, 1971-83; judge U.S. Bankruptcy Ct., Ohio, 1983-85, U.S. Dist. Ct. (no. dist.) Ohio, Cleve., 1985—. Mem. ABA. Office: US District Court 256 US Courthouse 201 Superior Ave NE Cleveland OH 44114 *

BATCHELDER, WILLIAM F., state supreme court justice; b. 1926. A.B., U. N.H.; LL.B., Boston U. Bar: N.H. 1952. Former judge N.H. Superior Ct.; assoc. justice N.H. Supreme Ct., Concord, 1982—. Former pres., trustee Sci. Ctr. N.H. Fellow Am. Bar Found.; mem. Am. Judicature Soc. (bd. dirs.). Judicial administration. Office: NH Supreme Ct Noble Dr Concord NH 03301 *

BATCHELOR, JAMES KENT, lawyer; b. Long Beach, Calif., Oct. 4, 1934; s. Jack Morrell and Edith Marie (Ottinger) B.; m. Jeanette Lou Dyer, Mar. 27, 1959; children—John, Suzanne; m. 2d, Susan Mary Leonard, Dec. 4, 1976. A.A., Sacramento City Coll., 1954; B.A., Long Beach State Coll., 1956; J.D., Hastings Coll. Law, U. Calif., 1959. Bar: Calif. 1960, U.S. Dist. Ct. (cen. dist.) Calif. 1960, U.S. Supreme Ct. 1968. Dept. dist. atty., Orange County, Calif., 1960-62; assoc. Miller, Nisson, Kogler & Wenke, Santa Ana, Calif., 1962-64; ptnr. Batchelor, Cohen & Oster, Santa Ana, 1964-67, Kurilich, Ballard, Batchelor, Fullerton, Calif., 1967-72; pres. James K. Batchelor, Inc., Santa Ana, 1972—; tchr. paralegal sect. Santa Ana City Coll.; judge pro-tem Superior Ct., 1974—. Fellow Acad. Am. Matrimonial Lawyers; mem. ABA, Calif. Trial Lawyers Assn., Calif. State Bar (placque chmn. family law sect. 1975-76, advisor 1976-78), Orange County Barristers (founder, pres., placque 1963), Calif. State Barristers (placque 1965, v.p.), Orange County Bar Assn. (plaque sec. 1977). Republican. Methodist. Family and matrimonial. Office: 1200 N Main Suite 916 Santa Ana CA 92701

BATCHELOR, JAMES WILEY, lawyer; b. Washington, Nov. 5, 1946; s. Kerney Davis and Dorothy Elaine (Berry) B.; m. Theresa Marie Wasierski, Sept. 22, 1979; children: Geoffrey Robert, Rebecca Anne. BA, Oakland U.; JD, U. Va. Bar: Va. 1975, Mich. 1975, U.S. Dist. Ct. (ea. and we. dists.) Mich. 1975, U.S. Ct. Appeals (6th cir.) 1975. Assoc. Russell & Ward, Grand Rapids, Mich., 1975-80; ptnr. Russell & Batchelor, Grand Rapids, 1980—; instr. Inst. Continuing Legal Edn., 1979-80; tchr. Am. Paralegal Inst., Detroit, 1984-85. Contbr. articles to profl. jours. Del. County and state Rep. Conventions, Mich., 1976, 80, 84; mem. State Rep. Conv., 1986—. Served to staff sgt. USAF, 1969-72, Vietnam. Mem. ABA (real property law sect., creditors rights com.), Mich. Bar Assn. (real property law sect., mechanics lien and bankruptcy com.), Victorian Mil. Soc., Am. Bus. Club, West Mich. Bus Club (pres., sec., treas. 1978-85). Congregationalist. Avocations: victorian military history, collecting rare books on military history. Real property, Bankruptcy, Contracts commercial. Home: 3173 Wildridge NE Grand Rapids MI 49505 Office: Russell & Batchelor 200 Monroe NW Suite 555 Grand Rapids MI 49503

BATE, CHARLES THOMAS, lawyer; b. Muncie, Ind., Nov. 14, 1932; s. Thomas Elwood and Vina Florence (Jackson) B.; m. Barbara Kay Dailey, June 17, 1955; children—Charles Thomas, Gregory Andrew, Jeffrey Scott. A.B., Butler U., 1955, postgrad., 1955-56; student, Christian Theol. Sem., Indpls., 1956-57; J.D., Ind. U., 1962. Bar: Ind. 1962. Staff adjuster State Automobile Ins. Assn., Indpl., 1953-57; claim supr. State Automobile Ins. Assn., 1958-59, office mgr., 1960-61, casualty claim mgr., 1961-62, atty., 1962-63; mem. firm Smith & Yarling, Indpls., 1963-67; sr. ptnr. Bate, Harrold & Meltzer, Shelbyville, Ind., 1967—; city atty. City of Shelbyville, 1981-86; dir., v.p., gen. counsel Discovery Life Ins. Co., Indpls., 1966-70. Bd. dirs. Nat. Pensions Bd. of Ch. of God, 1970-74; bd. dirs. Glendale Ch. of God Inc. 1958-80, lay speaker, 1962—, sec. nat. by-laws com. 1968-72); trustee emeritus Warner Pacific Coll., Portland, Oreg., 1984—; trustee Anderson Coll., Ind., 1982—. Recipient Merit award Ind. Jud. Council, 1962, Outstanding Student award Ind. U. Law Week, 1962. Fellow Ind. Bar Found.; mem. ABA, Ind. Bar Assn. (ho. of dels. 1978-80), Indpls. Bar Assn., Shelby County Bar Assn. (pres. 1979), Am. Judicature Soc., Am. Arbitration Assn. (panel arbitrators), Assn. Trial Lawyers Am., Ind. Trial Lawyers Assn. (dir. 1979—), Tex. Trial Lawyers Assn., Pa. Trial Lawyers Assn., Am. Bd. Trial Advocates. Republican. Lodge: Elks. State civil litigation, Personal injury, General practice. Home: Box 26 Shelbyville IN 46176 Office: 505 S Harrison Shelbyville IN 46176

BATE, DAVID SOULE, lawyer; b. Montclair, N.J., Mar. 15, 1918; s. Oscar Mortimer and Gladys (Soule) B., m. Janet Mallon, May 29, 1942; children: Suzanne Bate Morris, David S. Jr., Nancy Bate Bayne, Catherine D. AB, Hamilton U., 1939; LLB, Harvard U., 1946. Bar: N.J. 1947, U.S. Supreme Ct. 1963. Assoc. Stryker Tams & Horner, Newark, N.J., 1946-48; ptnr. Booth Bate & Grieco, Montclair, N.J., 1948—; atty. Township of Essex Fells, N.J. 1966—; bd. dirs. Glen Ridge (N.J.) Svs. & Loan Assn. Trustee The Florence and John Schumann Found., Montclair, 1967—, the Internat. Found., Butler, N.J., 1984—. Served to lt. comdr. USN, 1940-45. Mem. ABA, N.J. Bar Assn., Essex County Bar Assn., Am. Coll. of Probate Counsel. Republican. Episcopalian. Probate, Local government, General practice. Home: 368 Roseland Ave Essex Falls NJ 07021 Office: Booth Bate & Grieco 31 Park St Montclair NJ 07042

BATEMAN, DAVID ALFRED, lawyer; b. Pitts., Jan. 28, 1946; s. Alfred V. and Ruth G. (Howe) B.; m. Trudy A. Heath, Mar. 13, 1948; children—Devin C., Mark C. A.B. in Geology, U. Calif.-Riverside, 1966; J.D., U. San Diego, 1969; LL.M., Georgetown U., 1978. Bar: Calif. 1970, U.S. Dist. Ct. (so. dist.) Calif. 1970, U.S. Ct. Mil. Appeals 1972, Wash. 1973, U.S. Dist. Ct. (we. dist.) Wash. 1973, U.S. Supreme Ct. 1974, D.C. 1976, U.S. Dist. Ct. D.C. 1977, U.S. Ct. Claims 1979, U.S. Ct. Appeals (9th cir.) 1981. Assoc. Daubney, Banche, Patterson and Nares, Oceanside, Calif., 1969-72; asst. atty. gen. State of Wash., Olympia, 1977-81; ptnr. Bateman & Woodring, Olympia, 1981-85, Woodring, Bateman & Westbrook, 1985—; instr. Am. Inst. Banking, San Diego, 1972, U. Puget Sound, Olympia campus, spring, 1979. Served to capt. JAGC, USAF, 1972-77; maj. JAGC, USAFR, 1977—. Mem. ABA (internat. law and environ. law sect.), Am. Soc. Internat. Law (environ. law sect.), Wash. State Bar Assn. Roman Catholic. Club: Rotary (past chmn. internat. services com.). Real property, Private international, Personal injury.

BATEMAN, HAL MARION, educator, lawyer; b. Dallas, Dec. 22, 1931; s. Harold Ayars and Anita Albertine (Taylor) B.; m. Martha Joan Hansen, June 10, 1959; children—John Robert, James Daniel, Michael Benjamin. B.A., Rice U., 1954; J.D. cum laude, So. Methodist U., 1956. Bar: Tex. 1954, Mo. 1970. Assoc. Kilgore and Kilgore, Dallas, 1956-59, Carrington, Johnson and Stephens, Dallas, 1960-65; asst. prof. U. Mo. Sch. Law, 1965-68, assoc. prof. 1968-70, prof. 1970-72; prof. Tex. Tech U. Sch. Law, Lubbock, 1972—; mem. Tex. State Securities Bd., 1981—. Author: (with Elliott) West's Texas Forms, Vol. 8A, Partnerships and Unincorporated Business Associations. Contbr. articles to profl. jours. Active South Plains council Boy Scouts Am., 1978—; asst. dist. commr. 1980-83, chpt. advisor Order of Arrow, 1980-86. Mem. ABA (corp., banking, bus. law sect.), Tex. State Bar Assn. (past chmn., vice chmn. corp. banking and bus. law sect.), Dallas Bar Assn., Lubbock County Bar Assn. Presbyterian. Bankruptcy, Securities, General corporate. Office: Tex Tech U Sch Law Lubbock TX 79409

BATEMAN, THOMAS ROBERT, lawyer; b. Winchester, Mass., Dec. 9, 1944; s. Richard Holt and Phyllis (Brown) B.; m. Katherine Elizabeth Elliott, Sept. 9, 1972; children: Kyra Elizabeth, Richard Holt, Robert Elliott. BA, Harvard U., 1967; JD, NYU, 1971. Bar: N.Y. 1972, U.S. Dist. Ct. (so. dist.) N.Y. 1973, U.S. Ct. Appeals (2d cir.) 1974, Mass. 1978, U.S. Dist. Ct. Mass. 1978, U.S. Ct. Appeals (1st cir.) 1978. Assoc. Winthrop, Stimson, Putnam & Roberts, N.Y.C., 1971-77; assoc. Skadden, Arps, Slate, Meagher & Flom, Boston, 1977-79, ptnr., 1980—. Class agent Phillips Exeter Acad., N.H., 1969—; class steering com. Harvard U., Cambridge, Mass. 1985—. Mem. ABA, N.Y. State Bar Assn., Assn. of Bar of City of N.Y. Episcopalian. Club: Harvard (Boston). General corporate, Securities, Public international. Home: 33 Bullard Rd Weston MA 02193

BATES, ALBERT KEALIINUI, lawyer; b. Honolulu, Jan. 1, 1947; s. Albert Willard and Dorothy Ann (Roost) B.; m. Cynthia Adele Winkler, June 1973; children: Gretchen Brook, Will. BA, Syracuse U., 1969; JD, NY Law Sch., 1972. Bar: Tenn. 1981, U.S. Ct. Appeals (D.C. cir.) 1981, U.S. Ct. Appeals (6th cir.) 1983, U.S. Ct. Appeals (11th cir.) 1985, U.S. Supreme Ct. 1986. Emergency med. technician Farm Ambulance Service, Summertown, Tenn., 1974-75; corp. counsel The Found., Summertown, 1972—, also bd. dirs.; sole practice Summertown, 1972—; pres. Albert Bates Profl. Corp., Summertown, 1984—; adv. panel Tenn. Criminal Justice Standards and Goals, 1975; research assoc. Ethos Research Group, Summertown, 1979; bd. dirs., sec., counsel Plenty USA, Summertown, 1980—; bd. dirs. The Natural Rights Ctr., Summertown, 1980—. Author: Honicker Vs. Hendrie, 1978, Shutdown: Nuclear Power on Trial, 1979, Your Rights to Victims Compensation, 1984; co-author: The Grass Case, 1974; producer: (film) Helen Caldicott: Creators of Life, 1978. Pres. Global Village Inst. for Apprpriate Tech., 1985—; bd. dirs. Tenn. Environ. Council, 1982—; trustee Farm Sch., Summertown, 1983—. Grantee U.S. Dept. Energy, 1981, 82, 83. Mem. Phi Gamma of Delta Kappa Epsilon (pres. 1968-69). Avocations: horseback riding, motorcycling, canoeing. Environment, Civil rights, Nuclear power. Home: 10 The Farm Summertown TN 38483 Office: The Natural Rights Ctr PO Box 90 Summertown TN 38483-0090

BATES, HAROLD MARTIN, lawyer; b. Wise County, Va., Mar. 11, 1928; s. William Jennings and Reba (Williams) B.; m. Audrey Rose Doll, Nov. 1, 1952 (div. Mar. 1978); children—Linda, Carl. m. Judith Lee Farmer, June 23, 1978. B.A. in Econs., Coll. William and Mary, 1952; LL.B., Washington and Lee U., 1961. Bar: Va. 1961, Ky. 1961. Spl. agt. FBI, Newark and N.Y.C., 1952-56; tech. sales rep. Hercules Powder Co., Wilmington, Del., 1956-58; practice law, Louisville, 1961-62; sec.-treas., dir., house counsel Life Ins. Co. of Ky., Louisville, 1962-66; practice law, Roanoke, Va., 1966—; sec., dir. James River Limestone Co., Buchanan, Va., 1970—; sec. Eastern Ins. Co., Roanoke, 1984—. Pres., Skil, Inc., orgn. for rehab. Vietnam vets., Salem, Va., 1972-75. Served to cpl. U.S. Army, 1946-47, PTO. Mem. Va. Bar Assn., Roanoke Bar Assn., William and Mary Alumni Assn. (bd. dirs. 1972-76), Soc. Former Spl. Agts. of FBI (chmn. Blue Ridge chpt. 1971-72). Republican. Presbyterian. General corporate, Corporate taxation, Estate planning. Home: 2165 Laurel Woods Dr Salem VA 24153 Office: Dominion Bank Bldg Suite 1213 Roanoke VA 24011

BATES, JOHN BURNHAM, lawyer; b. Oakland, Calif., Mar. 2, 1918; s. Charles David and lucretia Margaret (Burnham) B.; m. Nancy Witter; children: John Burnham, Catharine Bates Kreitler, Charles W. A.B., Stanford U., 1940; J.D., U. Calif.-Berkeley, 1947. Bar: Calif. 1947, U.S. Supreme Ct. 1953. Assoc. firm Pillsbury, Madison & Sutro, San Francisco, 1947-53, ptnr., 1953—, sr. ptnr., 1977—, chmn. mgmt. com., 1979-83; mem. Am. team Anglo-Am. Legal Exchange, 1973; lectr. continuing edn. of bar, 1953-56. Mem. Piedmont City Council (Calif.), 1959-62; bd. dirs. Bay Area Council, 1979—; trustee Pacific Legal Found., 1985—; co-chmn. United San Francisco Republican Fin. Com., 1967-70. Served to lt. USNR, 1942-45. Fellow ABA; mem. Bar Assn. San Francisco (chmn. jud. com. 1962, chmn. trial practice com. 1963-64), Am. Coll. Trial Lawyers (chmn. Gumpert award com. 1973-78, regent 1969-73). Clubs: Commonwealth of Calif. (gov. 1973—, pres. 1977), Pacific Union (pres. 1969-70), Claremont Country (dir., v.p. 1954-58), Cypress Point (dir. 1975-83), Bohemian, San Francisco Golf. Home: 20 Bellevue Ave Piedmont CA 94611 Office: Pillsbury Madison & Sutro 225 Bush St San Francisco CA 94104

BATES, LAWRENCE FULCHER, lawyer; b. Evanston, Ill., June 1, 1954; s. Edwin Ricker and Elizabeth (Moseley) B.; m. Geri Lynn Wickelhaus, May 8, 1982; 1 child, Graham Edward. BA, Denison U., 1976; JD, Emory U., 1980. Bar: Ga. 1981. Atty. Fed. Deposit Ins. Co., Washington, 1981-84, counsel, 1984—. Chmn. Denison U. Area Recruiting Team, Washington, 1984—. Mem. ABA, Fed. Bar Assn., Ga. Bar Assn., Omicron Delta Kappa (v.p. Denison 1975-76), Alpha Kappa Delta. Republican. Congregationalist. Banking, Administrative and regulatory, Federal civil litigation. Office: Fed Deposit Ins Co 550 17th St NW Washington DC 20429

BATES, R. EDWARD, lawyer, author; b. Princeton, Ill., July 28, 1943; s. Schuyler C. and Betty Jane (Werner) B.; m. E. Ann Smith, Dec. 30, 1964 (div. 1984); children—Kristin, Kevin. B.A. in Fin., So. Ill. U., 1965; J.D., Wayne State U., 1971. Bar: Mich. 1971, Ill. 1973, U.S. Dist. Ct. (no. dist.) Ill. Fin. analyst Ford Motor Co., Dearborn, Mich., 1965-71, lawyer, 1971-73; counsel Lane Banking Group, Chgo., 1973-78; dir. law Tiger Leasing Corp., Chgo., 1978-80; sole practice, Naperville, Ill., 1980—. Author: Social Security Disability and SSI Claims-Your Need for Representation, 1981; Facts Regarding United States Immigration-Investors, Businesses, Workers, 1982; Facts Regarding Your Social Security Disability and SSI Hearing, 1982; Obtaining Immigration Benefits through Marriage, 1983; Illinois Workers' Compensation Act and Illinois Occupational Disease Act, 1983; Understanding Medical Malpractice and Understanding Hospital Malpractice, 1984: also articles in profl. jours. Bd. dirs. Nat. Head Injury Found., 1982—. Mem. Am. Immigration Lawyers Assn. (assoc.), Assn. Trial Lawyers Am., Ill. Bar Assn., Nat. Orgn. Social Security Reps. (state rep. 1982-83), DuPage County Bar Assn., U.S. Polo Assn. Roman Catholic. Clubs: Green Valley Polo (v.p. 1978-80). Immigration, naturalization, and customs, Pension, profit-sharing, and employee benefits, Bankruptcy. Home: 25 W 314 Hobson Rd Naperville IL 60540 Office: 190 E 5th Ave Naperville IL 60540

BATES, RICHARD WARDEN, lawyer; b. Petoskey, Mich., Apr. 24, 1929; s. Harold Storey and Mary (Warden) B.; m. Joan Margaret Mace, Sept. 19, 1953 (dec.); 1 child, Harold Scott. BA, Stetson U., 1950; LLB, 1953. Bar: Fla. 1953, U.S. Dist. Ct. (so. dist.) Fla. 1958, U.S. Dist. Ct. (mid. dist.) Ga. 1954, U.S. Ct. Mil. Appeals 1955, U.S. Ct. Appeals (5th cir.) 1960, U.S. Ct. Appeals (11th cir.) 1984; diplomate Nat. Bd. Trial Advocacy; cert. civil trial lawyer, Fla. Assoc. Gurney, McDonald & Handley, Orlando, 1956-61; ptnr., McCarty & Bates, Orlando, 1961-63; sole practice, Orlando, 1963-72, 75-84; ptnr. Maguire Voorhis & Wells, Orlando, 1972-75, Bates & Bates P.A., Orlando, 1984-87, Mateer, Harbert & Bates, P.A., 1987— (merged with Mateer & Harbert, P.A. Trustee Orlando Regional Med. Ctr., 1977—; bd. mgrs. YMCA, 1979-83. Served to maj. AUS, 1953-56. Fellow Fla. Acad. Trial Lawyers; mem. Fla. Bar Assn. (bd. cert. trial lawyer), ABA. Democrat. Methodist. Personal injury, Insurance, State civil litigation. Home: 2354 Lake Shore Dr Orlando FL 32803 Office: Mateer Harbert & Bates PA 255 S Orange Ave Orlando FL 32801

BATES, WILLIAM HUBERT (BERT), lawyer; b. Lexington, Mo., Apr. 14, 1926; s. George Hubert and Ernestine Norma (Comer) B.; m. Joy Lorue Godbehere, Aug. 10, 1927; children—William Brand, Joy Ann. B.A., U. Mo., 1949; J.D., U. Mich., 1952. Bar: Mo. 1952. mng. ptnr. Lathrop, Koontz & Norquist, Kansas City, Mo., 1960—, ; gen. counsel Midwest Gas Users Assn; asst. gen. counsel Kansas City Terminal Ry. Co.; past sec.-counsel Bd. Police Commrs. of Kansas City; counsel greater Kansas City C. of C.; past counsel Cen. Meth. Coll.; dir. Centerre Bank of Kansas City. Pres. bd. of curators U. Mo.; mem. Kansas City Civic Council. Served with AUS, 1944-46. Mem. ABA, Am. Judicature Soc., Mo. Bar Integrated (bd. of govs.), Kansas City Bar Assn., Lawyers Assn. Kansas City, Mo. State C. of C. (exec. com.), Kansas City C. of C. (exec., bd. dirs.). Democrat. Methodist. Clubs: Mercury, Vanguard, River, Mission Hills Country, Masons. General corporate, FERC practice, Legislative. Office: 2345 Grand Ave Suite 2600 Kansas City MO 64108

BATEY, DOUGLAS LEO, lawyer; b. Portland, Oreg., Oct. 23, 1947; s. Frank and Dorothy Frances (Hoffman) B.; m. Patricia Johnson, May 27, 1967 (div. 1982); 1 child, Jonathan Samuel; m. Marian Virginia Gaynor, Sept. 24, 1983; 1 child, Thomas Gaynor. BS summa cum laude, U. Wash., 1972, JD with honors, 1980. Bar: Wash. 1980, U.S. Dist. Ct. (we. dist.) Wash. 1980. Prin. Jones, Grey & Bayley P.S., Seattle, 1980—. Served to sgt. USMC, 1965-69. Mem. Wash. State Bar Assn., Seattle-King County Bar Assn., Phi Beta Kappa. Computer, General corporate, Securities. Office: Jones Grey & Bayley PS 777 108th Ave NE Bellevue WA 98004

BATLA, RAYMOND JOHN, JR., lawyer; b. Cameron, Tex., Sept. 1, 1947; s. Raymond John and Della Alvina (Jezek) B.; m. Susan Marie Clark, Oct. 1, 1983; children: Sara, Charles, Michael. BS with highest honors, U. Tex., 1970, JD, with honors, 1973. Bar: Tex. 1973, D.C. 1973, U.S. Dist. Ct. D.C. 1974, U.S. Dist. Ct. (so. dist.) Tex. 1982, U.S. Ct. Appeals (D.C. cir.) 1974, U.S. Ct. Appeals (5th cir.) 1982, U.S. Ct. Appeals (10th cir.) 1978, U.S. Supreme Ct. 1977. Structural engr. Tex. Hwy. Dept., Austin, 1970; assoc. Hogan & Hartson, Washington, 1973-82, gen. ptnr., 1983—; dean's adv. bd. com. U. Tex. Law Sch., Austin, 1983—. Author: Petroleum Regulation Handbook, 1980; contbr. articles to profl. jours. Chmn. bd. deacons Meml. Bapt. Ch., Arlington, 1978-80; pres., bd. dirs. Randolph Sq. Condominium Assn., Arlington, 1986—. Mem. ABA (vice chmn. energy com. 1981), Fed. Energy Bar Assn., Fed. Bar. Assn., D.C. Bar Assn., State Bar Tex., Nat. Lawyers Club. U. Tex. Law Sch. Assn. (bd. dirs.), Assn. Energy Engrs., Order of Coif, Phi Delta Phi, Chi Epsilon, Tau Beta Pi. Episcopalian. Club: City of Wash. (founder), Nat. Lawyers. FERC practice, Oil and gas leasing, Administrative and regulatory. Home: 1025 N Stafford St Arlington VA 22201 Office: Hogan & Hartson 555 13th St NW Washington DC 20004

BATOFF, STEVEN IRVING, lawyer; b. Phila., June 5, 1951; s. Milton Arthur and Ingeborg Virginia (Baumgarten) B.; m. Marlene Paul, June 21, 1981 (dec. Feb. 1982); m. Carol Renee Gross, June 19, 1983; children: Justin Alexander, Jeremy Alden. Student, Villanova U., 1969-71; BA, U. Conn., 1973; JD, Hofstra U., 1977. Bar: N.Y. 1978, Md. 1979, D.C. 1979, U.S. Dist. Ct. Md. 1979, U. Ct. Appeals (4th cir.) 1979. Atty. IRS, Washington, 1977-78; assoc. Venable, Baetjer and Howard, Balt., 1978-80, Whiteford, Taylor and Preston, Balt., 1980—; atty Office Spl. Counsel, Balt., 1985-86; asst. prof. Loyola Coll., Balt., U. Balt. Contbr. articles to profl. jour. and mags. Mem. ABA, Md. Bar Assn., Bar Assn. Balt. City. Democrat. Jewish. Lodge: Rotary. Pension, profit-sharing, and employee benefits, Banking, Personal income taxation. Home: 3304 Redspire Ln Baltimore MD 21208 Office: Whiteford Taylor and Preston Seven Saint Paul St Baltimore MD 21202

BATOR, PAUL MICHAEL, lawyer, educator; b. Budapest, Hungary, July 2, 1929; came to U.S., 1939, naturalized, 1945; s. Victor and Franciska Elisabeth (Sichermann) B.; m. Alice Garrett Hoag, June 2, 1956; children—Thomas Ewing, Michael G., Julia F. Grad., Groton Sch., 1947; A.B., Princeton, 1951; M.A. in History, Harvard, 1953, LL.B., 1956. Bar: N.Y. bar 1958. Law clk. to Supreme Ct. Justice Harlan, 1956-57; assoc. firm Debevoise, Plimpton & McLean, N.Y.C., 1957-59; asst. prof. law Harvard Law Sch., 1959-62, prof., 1962-85, assoc. dean, 1971-75, Bromley prof., 1981-85; dep. solicitor gen., counselor Solicitor Gen. of U.S., 1983-84; John P. Wilson prof. of law U. Chgo., 1985—; of counsel Mayer, Brown & Platt, Chgo., 1985—; vis. prof. law U. Calif., Berkeley, 1966, Stanford U., 1971-72, U. Chgo., 1978-79. Co-editor: Hart and Wechsler's Federal Courts and the Federal System, 2d edit, 1973; author: The International Trade in Art, 1983. Mem. Am. Law Inst. Legal education, Federal civil litigation, State civil litigation. Home: 4950 Chicago Beach Dr Chicago IL 60615 Office: U Chgo Law Sch 1111 E 60th St Chicago IL 60637

BATSON, DAVID WARREN, lawyer; b. Wichita Falls, Tex., Jan. 4, 1956; s. Warren M. Batson and Jacqueline (Latham) Rhone; m. Anglea Deanne Yow, May 19, 1983. BBA, Midwestern State U., 1976; JD, U. Tex., 1979. Bar: Tex. 1980, U.S. Dist. Ct. (no. dist.) Tex. 1981, U.S. Tax Ct. 1981, U.S. Ct. Appeals (5th cir.) 1983, U.S. Ct. Appeals (D.C. cir.) 1983, U.S. Ct. Claims 1984, U.S. Supreme Ct. 1984. Atty. Arthur Andersen & Co., Ft. Worth, 1980-81; tax atty. The Western Co. of N.Am., Ft. Worth, 1981-85; sr. tax atty. Alcon Labs., Inc., Ft. Worth, 1985; gen. counsel Data Tailor, Inc., Ft. Worth, 1985—; lectr. U. of Tex., Arlington, 1984-85; of counsel Means & Means, Corsicana, Tex., 1985-86. Contbr. articles to profl. jours. Speaker A Wish With Wings, Arlington, Tex., 1984-85. Mem. Tex. Bar Assn., Christian Legal Soc., Phi Delta Phi. Avocations: racquetball, weight lifting, self improvement, guitar. Contracts commercial, Oil and gas leasing, Corporate taxation. Office: 810 Houston St Suite 610 Fort Worth TX 76102

BATT, NICK, lawyer; b. Defiance, Ohio, May 6, 1952; s. Dan and Zenith (Dreher) B. BS, Purdue U., 1972; JD, U. Toledo, 1976. Bar: Ohio 1976. Asst. prosecutor Lucas County, Toledo, 1976-80, civil div. chief, 1980-83; village attorney, Village of Holland, Ohio, 1980—; law dir. City of Oregon, Ohio, 1984—. Mem. Maumee Valley Girl Scout Council, Toledo, 1977-80;

bd. mem. Bd. Community Relations, Toledo, 1975-76; mem. Lucas County Democratic Exec. Com., 1981-83. Named One of Toledo's Outstanding Young Men, Toledo Jaycees, 1979. ABA, Ohio Bar Assn., Mem. Toledo Bar Assn., Ohio Council of Sch. Bd. Attorneys, Ohio Mcpl. Attorneys Assn. Democrat. Roman Catholic. Club: Toledo. Lodge: K.C. Local government, Government contracts and claims, Municipal bonds. Office: 325 10th St Toledo OH 43624

BATTAGLIA, PHILIP MAHER, lawyer; b. Pasadena, Calif., Jan. 18, 1935; s. Philip N. and Helen Margaret (Maher) B.; m. Lorraine Marie Moore, Dec. 29, 1962; children—Karen, Steven, Kristen, Scott. B.S.L., U. So. Calif., 1956, LL.B., 1958. Bar: Calif. 1959, U.S. Dist. Ct. (cen. dist.) Calif. 1959, U.S. Supreme Ct. 1967. Assoc., then sr. ptnr. Flint & MacKay, Los Angeles, 1960—; adminstrv. asst. to Gov. Ronald Reagan, 1966-67; dir. First Colony Life Ins. Co. (Va.), Alco Battery, Newport Beach, Calif., others. Served to 1st lt. USAF. Mem. Los Angeles County Bar Assn., U. So. Calif. Law Alumni Assn. (pres.), Trojan Barristers (pres.), Calif. Jr. Chamber (named Outstanding Young Man of Yr. 1967-68), Los Angeles Jr. Chamber, Phi Alpha Delta. Republican. Roman Catholic. Clubs: Chancery, Lincoln (Los Angeles); Elks (Santa Inez, Calif.). General corporate, Libel, Real property. Office: Donovan Leisure Newton & Irvine 333 S Grand Los Angeles CA 90071

BATTAGLIA, TIMOTHY JOSEPH, lawyer; b. Belleville, Ill., Mar. 14, 1947; s. Olis Alfred and Ann Agnes (Frey) B.; m. Dorothy Traphagen, Dec. 5, 1970; children—Nicole Ann, Bradley Joseph. B.A., Cornell U., 1969, J.D., 1972. Bar: 1972. Assoc. Emens, Hurd, Kegler & Ritter, Columbus, Ohio, 1972-76, ptnr., 1976—; lectr. on energy law. Mem. Energy Task Force, Ohio, 1978, Natural Gas Task Force Ohio, 1986—. Mem. Columbus Bar Assn. (profl. ethics and grievance com. 1977-81, energy com. 1979—, chmn. energy com. 1986—), Ohio State Bar Assn. (vice chmn. natural resources law com. 1982-85, chmn. 1985—), ABA (natural resources and pub. utility law sects. 1986—) Eastern Mineral Law Found. (trustee 1981—, chmn. ann. inst. program com. 1982-83, chmn. spl. insts. com. 1984-85, exec. com. 1985—, chmn. memberhip com. 1986—, v.p. 1987—), Ohio Oil and Gas Assn.(chmn. natural gas and crude oil com. 1984-85, co-chmn. legal com. 1986—, trustee 1987—, exec. com. 1987—), Independent Petroleum Assn. Am. (affiliate), Ohio Gas Assn. Republican. Roman Catholic. Clubs: Athletic of Columbus (Ohio); Muirfield Village Golf (Dublin, Ohio), Swiss (Columbus, Ohio). Co-mng. editor Cornell Law Forum, 1971. FERC practice, Oil and gas leasing, Public utilities. Office: Capitol Square 65 E State St Columbus OH 43215

BATTERSBY, GREGORY JOHN, lawyer; b. Bklyn., Mar. 22, 1947; s. Frank X. and Margot R. (Satriana) B.; m. Susan Ann Strockis, July 11, 1970; children—Damian Paul, Adam Jonathan. B.A., Seton Hall U., 1968; J.D., Fordham U., 1972. Bar: N.Y. 1973, U.S. Ct. Appeals (2d cir.) 1973, U.S. Ct. Appeals (D.C. cir.) 1978, U.S. Supreme Ct. 1978, U.S. Ct. Appeals (Fed. cir.) 1982, Conn. 1984, U.S. Ct. Appeals (11th cir.) 1985. Chemist Grumman Aerospace Corp., Bethpage, N.Y., 1968-71; assoc. Fitzpatrick, Cella, Harper & Scinto, N.Y.C., 1972-74; patent atty. Amerace Corp., N.Y.C., 1974-75; assoc. patent counsel Gulf & Western Industries, N.Y.C., 1975-82; ptnr. firm Kontler, Grimes & Battersby, Stamford, Conn., 1982-84, Grimes & Battersby, Stamford, 1984—. Co-author: The Law of Merchandising and Character Licensing, 1985; Licensing Law Handbook, 1985. Editor, Fordham U. Urban Law Jour., 1971-72, The Merchandising Reporter, 1982—; legal editor Toy and Hobby World, 1985—, Bobbin, 1985-86, N.Y. Patent, Trademark Copyright Law Assn. Bull., 1986—. Gen. counsel H. Arnold chpt. Air Force Assn., L.I., N.Y., 1978-80, Cold Spring Hills Civic Assn., Huntington, N.Y., 1980-83. Mem. ABA, Conn. Bar Assn., N.Y. Patent, Trademark and Copyright Law Assn., Am. Intellectual Property Law Assn., Conn. Patent Law Assn. Republican. Roman Catholic. Patent, Trademark and copyright, Government contracts and claims. Home: 25 Poplar Plain Rd Westport CT 06880 Office: Grimes & Battersby 184 Atlantic St Stamford CT 06901

BATTEY, RICHARD HOWARD, federal judge; b. 1929; m. Shirley Ann Battey; children: David, Russell, Dianne. BA, U. S.D., 1950, JD, 1953. Atty. City of Redfield, S.D., 1956-63; state's atty. Spinti County, S.D., 1959-65, 81-85; judge U.S. Dist. Ct. S.D., Rapid City, 1985—; ptnr. Gallagher & Battey, Redfield, 1956-85. Served with AUS, 1953-55. Office: U S Dist Ct 318 Fed Bldg 515 9th St Rapid City SD 57701 *

BATTIN, JAMES FRANKLIN, judge, former congressman; b. Wichita, Kans., Feb. 13, 1925; m. Barbara Choate; children: Loyce Battin Peterson, Patricia Battin Pfeiffer, James Franklin. J.D., George Washington U., 1951. Bar: D.C. and Mont. bars. Practice in Washington, 1951-52; now in Billings; past dep. county atty.; past sec.-counsel City-County Planning Bd.; past asst. city atty. Billings; then city atty.; mem. Mont. Ho. of Reps., 1958-59; mem. 87th-91st congresses 2d Dist., Mont.; resigned when apptd. U.S. dist. judge Mont. Dist., 1969; chief judge 1978—. Served with USNR, World War II. Mem. Am. Legion, DeMolay Legion of Honor. Presbyterian. Club: Mason (Shriner). Office: US Dist Ct Mont 5428 Federal Bldg 316 N 26th St PO Box 1476 Billings MT 59103

BATTISTI, FRANK JOSEPH, federal judge; b. Youngstown, Ohio, Oct. 4, 1922; s. Eugene and Jennie (Dalesandro) B. B.A., Ohio U., 1947; LL.B., Harvard U., 1950. Bar: Ohio 1950. Asst. atty. gen. Ohio, 1950; atty. adviser C.E. U.S. Army, 1951-52; 1st asst. dir. law Youngstown, 1954-59; judge Common Pleas Ct., Mahoning County, Ohio, 1959-61; judge U.S. Dist. Ct. (no. dist.) Ohio, Cleve., 1961-69, chief judge, 1969—. Served with C.E., U.S. Army, 1943-45; ETO. Mem. ABA, Mahoning County Bar Assn., Cleve. Bar Assn., Am. Judicature Soc. Roman Catholic. Judicial administration. Office: US District Court 302 US Courthouse Cleveland OH 44114 *

BATTLE, LEONARD CARROLL, lawyer; b. Toronto, Ont., Can., Oct. 25, 1929; s. Leonard Conlon and Beatrice Hester B.; m. Marjory Estelle Holland, Dec. 28, 1953; children—David, Tracy, Thomas, Patricia, John, Mary. A.B., U. Mich., 1950; J.D., Ind. U., 1958. Bar: Mich. 1961, Ind. 1961, U.S. Ct. Mil. Appeals 1964, U.S. Supreme Ct. 1964. Claims adjuster State Farm Ins. Co., 1959-61; asst. pros. atty. Midland County (Mich.), 1961-67; sole practice, Midland, Mich., 1967—. Served to lt. col. JAG USAFR, 1950-84, USAFRR, 1984—. Mem. Midland County Bar Assn. (pres.), Mich. State Bar Assn. (mil. law com.), Judge Advs. Assn., Am. Trial Lawyers Assn. Clubs: Kiwassee Kiwanis, Elks (Midland). Personal injury, State civil litigation, Military. Home: 408 Harper Ln Midland MI 48640 Office: 200 E Main St Midland MI 48640

BATZER, JAMES MARTIN, circuit judge; b. Manistee, Mich., Dec. 14, 1943; s. William Rheinold and Rose Ethell (Dontz) B.; m. Nancy L. Housman, Feb. 20, 1965; children: Margaret, Martha, Christine. Student, Albion Coll., 1961-63; BA, U. Mich., 1968; MS, Mich. State U., 1976; JD cum laude, Wayne State U., 1978. Bar: Mich. 1978, U.S. Dist. Ct. (ea. dist.) Mich. 1979, U.S. Ct. Appeals (6th cir.) 1979, U.S. Dist. Ct. (we. dist.) Mich. 1983. Law clk. to presiding justice U.S. Dist. Ct. (ea. dist.) Mich., Detroit, 1978-79; asst. atty. gen. State of Mich., Lansing, 1979-84; judge 19th jud. cir. State of Mich., Manistee and Benzie Counties, 1985—. Teaching fellow legal research and writing Detroit Coll. Law, 1979-81. Teaching fellow legal research and writing Detroit Coll. Law, 1979-81. State civil litigation, Criminal, Judicial administration. Office: Cir Ct 415 3d St PO Box 484 Manistee MI 49660

BAUCH, THOMAS JAY, lawyer, apparel company executive; b. Indpls., May 24, 1943; s. Thomas and Violet (Smith) B.; m. Ellen L. Burstein, Oct. 31, 1982; children: Chelsea, Elizabeth. B.S., U. Wis., 1964, J.D., 1966. Bar: Ill. 1966, Calif. 1978. Assoc. Lord, Bissell & Brook, Chgo., 1966-72; lawyer, asst. sec. Marcor-Montgomery Ward, Chgo., 1973-75; spl. asst. to solicitor Dept. Labor, Washington, 1975-77; dep. gen. counsel Levi Strauss & Co., San Francisco, 1977-81, sr. v.p., gen. counsel, 1981—; mem. U. Wis. Law Review, Madison, 1964-66. Bd. dirs. The Urban Sch., San Francisco, 1986. Mem. Am. Assn. Corp. Counsel (dir. 1982—), Order of Coif. Democrat. Clubs: Univ. (San Francisco); Racquet (Chgo.). General corporate. Office: Levi Strauss & Co Levi's Plaza Box 7215 San Francisco CA 94120

BAUCOM, SIDNEY GEORGE, utility executive, lawyer; b. Salt Lake City, Oct. 21, 1930; s. Sidney and Nora (Palfreyman) B.; m. Mary B., Mar. 5, 1954; children—Sidney, George, John. B.S., J.D., U. Utah, 1953. Bar: Utah. Sole practice Salt Lake City, 1953-55; asst. city atty. Salt Lake City Corp., 1955-56; asst. atty. Utah Power and Light Co., Salt Lake City, 1956-60, asst. atty., asst. sec., 1960-62, gen. counsel, asst. sec., 1962-68, v.p., gen. counsel, asst. sec., 1974-79, sr. v.p., 1974-79, exec. v.p., gen. counsel, 1979—; dir. Utah Power and Light Co., Salt Lake City. Past chmn. Utah Coordinating Council Devel., Utah Taxpayers Assn.; past mem. Mayor's Council Capitol Improvements, Utah Hoover Commn., Airport Bond Commn. Mem. Phi Delta Phi. Mormon. Club: Alta. Lodge: Lions. General corporate. Home: 2248 Logan Ave Salt Lake City UT 84108 Office: Utah Power and Light Co 1407 W North Temple St Salt Lake City UT 84116

BAUDIER, ADELAIDE, lawyer; b. New Orleans, Feb. 24, 1912; d. Louis Maurice and Adelaide (Thompson) B.; m. James A. Madigan, Nov. 6, 1943 (dec. 1973); 1 child, Nina. J.D., Loyola U., New Orleans, 1935. Sole practice, New Orleans, 1935-72, Metairie, La., 1972—. Vice-chmn. Bd. Aging. Mem. La. State Bar Assn., Jefferson Bar Assn., Women's Bar Assn., Assn. Trial Lawyers Am., Naim Conf. (pres. Metairie chpt.), Phi Alpha Delta. Roman Catholic. Club: St Ann's Over 50 (past pres.). State civil litigation, General practice, Probate. Office: 3917 Clearview Pkwy Metairie LA 70006

BAUDLER, DAVID EVAN, lawyer; b. Austin, Minn., Nov. 13, 1941; s. William J. and Katherine (Simpson) B.; m. Anne Morgan, Dec. 28, 1967; children: Mark, Jay, Matthew. BA, U. Minn., 1963, JD, 1966. Bar: Calif. 1966. Assoc. Morrison & Foerster, San Francisco, 1966-72, ptnr., 1972—. Mem. ABA (banking law com., bus. banking and corp. law sect.). Avocations: golf, skiing, travel. Banking, General corporate, Securities. Office: Morrison & Foerster 345 California St San Francisco CA 94104

BAUDLER, WILLIAM JOHN, lawyer; b. Austin, Minn., Dec. 13, 1914; s. Otto and Katherine (Kenevan) B.; m. Katherine Elizabeth Simpson, May 13, 1939; children—Bryan, David, John, William, Scott. B.S.L., U. Minn., 1936, LL.B., 1938. Bar: Minn. 1938, U.S. Dist. Ct. Minn. 1940. Ptnr. Baudler, Baudler & Maus, and predecessor, Austin, 1939-71, sr. ptnr. 1971—; mem. adv. com. on drafting rules of civil procedure Minn. Supreme Ct. 1966-70, mem. adv. com. on drafting Minn. rules of evidence, 1975-79. Sec. Mower County Pub. Health Assn. 1946-60; chmn. citizens adv. com. Austin Pub. Schs. 1956. Fellow Am. Coll. Trial Lawyers; mem. ABA, Minn. Bar Assn., Mower County Bar Assn. Mem. Democrat-Farmer-Labor Party. Clubs: Austin Country, Kiwanis, Elks (Austin); Mpls. Athletic. State civil litigation, Probate.

BAUER, EDWARD GREB, JR., lawyer, utilities executive; b. Jeannette, Pa., Aug. 10, 1928; s. Edward Greb and Virginia (Euwer) B.; m. Carolyn Large Isbell, May 8, 1954; children: Charlotte Large, Barbara Greb, Edward Greb III. B.A., Princeton U., 1951; LL.B., Harvard U., 1957. Bar: Pa. 1958. Atty. Ballard, Spahr, Andrews & Ingersoll, Phila., 1957-62; exec. asst. to Mayor James H.J. Tate, Phila., 1962-63; city solicitor Phila., 1963-70; v.p., gen. counsel Phila. Electric Co., 1970—; dir. Susquehanna Power Co., Susquehanna Electric Co., Adwin Realty Co., Adwin Equipment Co., Continental Bank, Eastern Pa. Devel. Co.; Bd. dirs. Phila. Crime Commn. Served with USAF, 1951-54. Mem. ABA, Pa., Phila. bar assns. Clubs: Union League (Phila.); Boca Raton Hotel and Club. Public utilities, General corporate, General practice. Home: 1913 River Park House 3600 Conshohocken Ave Philadelphia PA 19131 Office: Phila Electric Co 2301 Market St Philadelphia PA 19101 *

BAUER, GEORGE A., III, lawyer; b. Queens, N.Y., Nov. 2, 1954; s. George A. Jr. and Mariella (Hoffman) B.; m. Marcy F. Greenberg, Aug. 6, 1978; children: Garrett J., Melissa I., Maren A.A. BBA magna cum laude, CUNY, 1976; JD, NYU, 1979. Bar: N.Y. 1980, U.S. Dist. Ct. (so. and ea. dists.) N.Y. 1980. Assoc. Milberg, Weiss, Bershad, Specthrie & Lerach, N.Y.C., 1979—. Mem. ABA, N.Y. State Bar Assn., N.Y. County Lawyers Assn. Federal civil litigation, Securities, State civil litigation. Office: Milberg Weiss Bershad et al One Pennsylvania Plaza New York NY 10119-0165

BAUER, HENRY LELAND, lawyer; b. Portland, Oreg., June 7, 1928; s. Henry and Emma L. (Peterson) B.; m. Doris Jane Philbrick, May 21; children—Henry Stephen, Thomas Leland. B.S. in Bus., Oreg. State U., 1950; J.D., U. Oreg., 1953. Bar: Oreg. 1953, U.S. Dist. Ct. Oreg., 1956; U.S. Ct. Appeals (9th cir.), 1960. Mem. Bauer & Bauer, Portland, Oreg., 1955-70, Bauer, Murphy, Bayless & Fundingsland, and successor firms, Portland, 1970-75; now sr. mem. Bauer, Hermann, Fountain & Rhoades P.C., Portland. Mem. adv. council Oreg. State U. Coll. Bus.; bd. dirs., vice chmn. St. Vincent Hosp. and Med. Ctr.; mem., vice chmn. council of trustees St. Vincent Med. Found.; bd. dirs., sec. Nat. Interfrat. Conf.; pres. Columbia Pacific council Boy Scouts Am.; past pres. Portland Civic Theatre; bd. visitors U. Oreg. Sch. Law, 1979-83. Served to 1st lt. USAF, 1953-55. Mem. ABA, Oreg. Bar Assn., Multnomah County Bar Assn., Am. Judicature Soc., Oreg. State U. Alumni Assn. (bd. dirs.), Delta Theta Phi, Kappa Sigma (past nat. pres.). Republican. Presbyterian. Clubs: Multnomah Athletic, Arlington, Masons, Rotary. Banking, Probate, Real property. Office: Commonwealth Bldg Suite 1100 Portland OR 97204

BAUER, JEFFRY MARK, lawyer, consultant; b. Pontiac, Mich., Mar. 21, 1955; s. Russell Edward and Adelaide Bernice (Cooke) B. AB cum laude, Boston Coll., 1977; JD, U. Detroit, 1980. Bar: Mich. 1981, U.S. Dist. Ct. (ea. dist.) Mich. 1981, U.S. Ct. Mil. Appeals 1981, U.S. Ct. Claims 1982, U.S. Dist. Ct. (we. dist.) Tenn. 1982, U.S. Ct. Appeals (D.C. cir.) 1982, U.S. Dist. Ct. (we. dist.) Mich. 1983, U.S. Ct. Appeals (6th cir.) 1984, U.S. Supreme Ct. 1984, U.S. Ct. Appeals (7th cir.) 1985. Assoc. Baumgardner & Oravec, Southfield, Mich., 1983-84; sole practice Detroit, 1984-86; assoc. Berry, Moorman, King, Cooke & Hudson, Detroit, 1986—. Mem. Disaster commn. ARC, Detroit, 1984—. Served to lt. JAGC, USNR, 1980-83. Mem. ABA, Fed. Bar Assn., Fed. Communications Bar Assn., Oakland County Bar Assn., Assn. Trial Lawyers Am., Detroit Bar Assn., Am. Arbitration Assn. (arbitrator), Nat. Assn. Securities Dealers Inc. (arbitrator), Am. Judicature Soc., Judge Advs. Assn., U.S. Naval Inst., Constrn. Assn. Mich., Nat. Assn. Bus. and Edn. Radio. Republican. Episcopalian. Clubs: University, Bayview Yacht (Detroit), Boston Yacht (Marblehead, Mass). Securities, Real property, Contracts commercial. Home: 860 Trombley Rd Grosse Pointe Park MI 48230

BAUER, JOSEPH LOUIS, lawyer; b. Danville, Ill., Jan. 4, 1950; s. Joseph Louis and Jean (Fahey) B. BS, St. Louis U., 1972, JD, 1975. Bar: Mo. 1975, Ill. 1984, U.S. Dist. Ct. (we. dist.) Mo. 1975, U.S. Dist. Ct. (ea. dist) Mo. 1976, U.S. Dist. Ct. (so. dist.) Ill. 1984, U.S. Ct. Appeals (8th cir.) 1977, U.S. Supreme Ct. 1980. Staff atty. Legal Aid Soc., St. Louis, 1975-77; asst. atty. gen. State of Mo., St. Louis, 1977, asst. cir. atty., 1977-83; assoc. Carr, Korein, Schlichter, Kunin & Montroy, East St. Louis, Ill., 1983—; guest lectr. St. Louis U. Law Sch., 1981. Roman Catholic. Personal injury, Admiralty, Criminal. Home: 6917 Waterman Ave University City MO 63130 Office: Carr Korein et al 412 Missouri Ave East Saint Louis IL 62201 Office: 916 Olive St Saint Louis MO 63103

BAUER, LAWRENCE MICHAEL, lawyer; b. Rockford, Ill., Oct. 18, 1950; s. George Frank and Eufalia Rose (Viola) B.; m. Sharlene Kay Johnson, Dec. 18, 1982; 1 child, Laurel Renee. AA, Rock Valley Coll., 1970; BA, Carthage Coll., 1972; JD, Valparaiso U., 1975. Bar: Ill. 1976, U.S. Dist. Ct. (no. dist.) Ill. 1976. Staff atty. Legal Aid Winnebago County, Rockford, 1976-77; sole practice Rockford, 1977-85; asst. state's atty. Winnebago County, Rockford, 1985—. Contbr. articles to profl. mag. Mem. Rockford Clergy Youth Task Force, 1976—; bd. dirs. Girl Scouts Am., Rock Valley, 1985, Rock River Valley Epilepsy Assn., 1985—. Served with USMC, 1972-74. Mem. ABA, Ill. Bar Assn., Winnebago County Bar Assn., Jaycees (named one of Outstanding Young Men of Am., 1984, 85). Lutheran. Criminal, Juvenile. Home: 11506 Tanawingo Trail Roscoe IL 61073 Office: Winnebago County State's Atty 400 W State Suite 619 Rockford IL 61101

BAUER, MARK EUGENE, lawyer; b. Great Falls, Mont., Apr. 20, 1952; s. Raymond Eugene and Denise Joan (Zunchich) B.; m. Anne Patricia Perron, Nov. 14, 1982; 1 son, Matthew Paul Perron. AB in Geol. Sci., Harvard U., 1974; JD, U. Mont., 1977. Bar: Mont. 1977, U.S. Dist. Ct. Mont. 1977. Immigration insp. Immigration and Naturalization Service, Roosville, Mont., 1975; law clk. to presiding justice 8th Jud. Dist. Ct., 1977-78; sole practice Great Falls, 1978—. State civil litigation, Construction, Family and matrimonial. Home: PO Box 1423 Great Falls MT 59403 Office: 304 Strain Bldg Great Falls MT 59401

BAUER, WILLIAM JOSEPH, chief judge; b. Chgo., Sept. 15, 1926; s. William Francis and Lucille (Gleason) B.; m. Mary Nicol, Jan. 28, 1950; children—Patricia, Linda. A.B., Elmhurst Coll., 1949; J.D., DePaul U., 1952. Bar: Ill. bar 1951. Partner firm Erlenborn, Bauer & Hotte, Elmhurst, Ill., 1953-64; asst. state's atty. Du Page County, Ill., 1952-56; 1st asst. state's atty. 1956-58, state's atty., 1959-64; judge 18th Jud. Cir. Ct., 1964-70; U.S. dist. atty. No. Ill. Chgo., 1970-71; judge U.S. Dist. Ct., Chgo., 1971-75; judge U.S. Ct. Appeals, 7th Circuit, 1975-86, chief judge, 1986—; instr. bus. law Elmhurst Coll., 1952-59; adj. prof. law DePaul U., 1978—. Pres. Elmhurst Young Republicans, 1958-59; trustee Elmhurst Meml. Hosp., Elmhurst Coll., 1979—, De Paul U., 1984—; mem. bd. govs. Mercy Hosp. Served with AUS, 1945-47. Mem. ABA, Ill. Bar Assn., Du Page County Bar Assn. (pres.), Ill. State's Attys. Assn. (dir.). Roman Catholic. Club: Union League (Chgo.). Criminal. Home: 213 Grace St Elmhurst IL 60126 Office: U S Ct of Appeals 219 S Dearborn St Chicago IL 60604

BAUGHER, PETER V., lawyer; b. Chgo., Oct. 2, 1948; s. William and Marilyn (Sill) B.; m. Robin Stickney, Nov. 25, 1978; children: Julia Allison, Britton William Herbert. AB, Princeton U., 1970; JD, Yale U., 1973. Bar: Ill. 1974, U.S. Dist. Ct. (no. dist.) Ill. 1974, U.S. Ct. Appeals (7th cir.) 1974. Law clk. to presiding judge U.S. Ct. Appeals (7th cir.), Chgo., 1973-74; from assoc. to ptnr. Schiff Hardin & Waite, Chgo., 1974-85; ptnr. Adams, Fox, Adelstein & Rosen, Chgo., 1985—; trustee Sta. WTTW Channel 11, Chgo., 1976-81, Kendall Coll., Evanston, Ill., 1980—. Mem. adv. com. Rep. Nat. Commn., Washington, 1976-81; alt. del. Rep. Nat. Convention, Detroit, 1980. Mem. ABA, Chgo. Council on Fgn. Relations, Am. Council on Germany, Ripon Soc. (chmn. 1975-76). Republican. Club: University (Chgo.). Federal civil litigation, State civil litigation, Private international. Home: 1310 Sheridan Rd Wilmette IL 60091 Office: Adams Fox Adelstein & Rosen 208 S LaSalle St Chicago IL 60604

BAUGHN, ALFRED FAIRHURST, lawyer; b. Florence, Ariz., May 1, 1912; s. Otis James and Mary Holman (Fairhurst) B.; m. Barbara Hobbs, June 17, 1935; children—Brent F., Barbara Hendershot. A.B., U. So. Calif., 1935, J.D., 1938. Bar: Calif. 1938, Ariz. 1959, U.S. Dist. Ct. (so. dist.) Calif. 1939, U.S. Ct. Appeals (9th cir.) 1945, U.S. Dist. Ct. Ariz. 1948, U.S. Supreme Ct. 1967. With Title Guarantee & Trust, Los Angeles, 1937-41; corp. counsel Pacific Western Oil Co., 1942-43; practice, Los Angeles and Hollywood, Calif., 1943-56; Ariz. chief corp. counsel Garrett Corp., 1956-77, ret., 1977; sole practice, Ariz. and Calif., 1959—; Ariz. Assn. Industries spl. counsel utility rate hearings Ariz. Corp. Commn., 1977-80; investment counselor. Bd. dirs. EPI-HAB, Inc., 1974—. Adopted by Hopi Indian Chief Seletstewa and Squaw (2d Mesa), 1967; Pres. U. So. Calif. scholar, 1931-35. Mem. Calif. Bar Assn., Ariz. Bar Assn., Maricopa County Bar Assn., Los Angeles Philanthropic Found., Skull and Scales, Phi Alpha Delta (chpt. pres. 1938), Kappa Sigma (pres. Los Angeles alumni 1945, pres. Phoenix Alumni 1960), Phi Alpha Delta (pres. 1938—). Republican. Mem. Christian Ch. Clubs: Hollywood Exchange (pres. 1947); Kiwanis (Phoenix pres. club 1965); Kachina Klub (organizer, charter v.p. 1974), Hon. Order Ky. Cols. (pres. chpt. 1980—), Phoenix Teocali of Order Quetzalcoatl (pres. 1984), Ariz. Bola Tie Soc., Masons (Master 1953), Shriners (pote 1971), Jesters (bd. dirs. 1969), Internat. Gorillas (chief 1971—). Probate, Real property. Address: 5530 E Valley Vista Rd Phoenix AZ 85018

BAUM, JOSEPH A., lawyer; b. N.Y.C., July 24, 1928; s. Adolph and Pauline (Roth) B.; m. Sherry Meyerson; Dec. 5, 1959; children: Debra, Jane, Jonathan. BBA, Adelphi U., 1951; BBL, Bklyn. Law Sch., 1956. Bar: N.Y. 1957, U.S. Dist. Ct. (ea. and so. dists.) N.Y. 1959, U.S. Supreme Ct. 1962. Counsel Allstate Ins. Co., N.Y.C., 1956-59, U.S. Fidelity & Guaranty Ins. Co., N.Y.C., 1959; sole practice Flushing, N.Y., 1959-63; ptnr. Pliskin, Rubano & Baum, Flushing, 1963—; cons. counsel Volvo Am., Rockleigh, N.J., Reichold Chem., White Plains, N.Y., Allied Stores, N.Y.C., Hartford Ins. Co., N.Y.C.; mem. appellate div. grievance com., Bklyn., mem. grievance com. Queens County, Jamaica, N.Y. Mem. ABA, Assn. Trial Lawyers Am., N.Y. State Trial Lawyers Assn., Queens County Bar Assn. (bd. mgrs.). Jewish. Avocation: salt water fishing. State civil litigation, Real property, Personal injury. Office: Pliskin Rubano & Baum 137-11 Northern Blvd Flushing NY 11354

BAUM, JOSEPH THOMAS, lawyer; b. Amsterdam, N.Y., May 25, 1944; s. Joseph W. and Margaret M. (Wilt) B.; children—Jason, Daniel. B.A., Siena Coll., 1966; J.D., Albany Law Sch., 1972. Bar: N.Y. 1973, U.S. Dist. Ct. (no. dist.) N.Y. 1973. Instr. Alfred U., N.Y., 1973-74; assigned counsel Allegeny County, Belmont, N.Y., 1973-74; law sec. Family Ct., Allegeny County, 1974; asst. atty. gen. N.Y. State, Albany, 1974-79; clin. dir. Albany Law Sch., 1981—. Town atty. Town of Sand Lake, N.Y., 1980-82, 84; bd. dirs. YMCA, Albany, 1984—. Mem. ABA, N.Y. State Bar Assn. (gen. practice sect.), Rensselaer County Bar Assn., Am. Assn. Law Schs. (clin. sect., externship subcom.). Clubs: Adirondack Mountain (Albany); U.S. Snowshoe Assn. (Corinth, N.Y.). State civil litigation, Legal education. Office: Albany Law Sch 80 New Scotland Ave Albany NY 12208

BAUM, PETER ALAN, lawyer; b. Jamaica, N.Y., Sept. 22, 1947; s. Morris and Elsa (Sturtz) B.; m. Barbara Hartman, Nov. 29, 1969; children: Benjamin, Lisa, Alexander. BA, Colgate U., 1969; JD, Syracuse U., 1972. Bar: N.Y. 1973, U.S. Dist. Ct. (no. dist.) N.Y. 1974. House counsel William Porter Real Estate Co., Syracuse, N.Y., 1972-73; sole practice Syracuse, 1973-82; ptnr. DiStefano and Baum, Syracuse, 1983-85, Baum and Woodard, Syracuse, 1985—; lectr. Onandaga Community Coll., Syracuse, 1976-79. Chmn. bd. dirs. Syracuse Area Landmark Theater, 1982-83; bd. dirs. Syracuse Opera Co., 1979-85. Mem. N.Y. State Bar Assn., Madison County Bar Assn., Onondaga County Bar Assn. (continuing edn. chmn. 1977-78), Onondaga Title Assn. Real property, Landlord-tenant. Office: Baum and Woodard 224 Harrison St Syracuse NY 13202

BAUM, STANLEY M., lawyer; b. Bronx, N.Y., Mar. 6, 1944; s. Abraham S. and Mae (Weiner) B.; m. Louise Rae Iteld, Aug. 30, 1970; children: Rachel Jennifer, Lauren Amy. BS in Commerce, Rider Coll., 1966; JD summa cum laude, John Marshall Law Sch., 1969. Bar: Ga. 1970, U.S. Dist. Ct. (no. dist.) Ga. 1970, U.S. Ct. Appeals (5th cir.) 1970, U.S. Supreme Ct. 1973, U.S. Ct. Appeals (11th cir.) 1981, U.S. Tax Ct. 1983. Law clk. to U.S. atty. No. Dist. Ga., 1969; legal aide Ga. Gen. Assembly, 1970-71; asst. U.S. atty. No. Dist. Ga., 1971-74; ptnr. Bates & Baum, 1974-76, Bates, Baum & Landey, 1976—. Mem. Southeast regional bd. Anti-Defamation League; pres. Congregation Shearith Israel, 1976-78; chmn. Rep. Party of DeKalb County, 1983-85, 4th Dist. Rep. Party, 1985—. Mem. ABA (criminal justice sect. grand jury com.), Ga. Bar Assn., Atlanta Bar Assn. (chmn. criminal law sect. 1985-86, bd. dirs. 1986—), Fed. Bar Assn. (pres. Atlanta chpt. 1976-77, nat. council 1974-77), Decatur-Dekalb Bar Assn. (sec. 1985-86, treas. 1986-87), Am. Judicature Soc., Nat. Dist. Attys. Assn. Clubs: Nat. Lawyers, Atlanta Lawyers. Lodges: Masons, B'nai B'rith. Office: Suite 3500 101 Marietta Tower Atlanta GA 30303

BAUMAN, ARNOLD, lawyer; b. N.Y.C., July 25, 1914; s. William and Betty (Kraft) B.; m. Bernice Rechtman, Aug. 7, 1938; children—Jane Dorothy (Mrs. James W. Phillips), William Kraft. B.B.A. cum laude, St. Johns U., 1934; J.D., N.Y. U., 1937. Bar: N.Y. bar 1938. Asst. dist. atty. N.Y. County, 1938-41, 45-47; pvt. practice law N.Y.C., 1947-53; chief counsel U.S. Senate Com. Investigating Crime and Law Enforcement in D.C., 1951-52; chief criminal div. U.S. Atty.'s Office, So. dist. N.Y., 1953-55; chief counsel Joint Legis. Com. on Govt. Ops., N.Y. State Legislature, 1955-58; mem. firm Christy, Bauman & Christy, 1965-68, Bauman & Marcheso, N.Y.C., 1968-72; judge U.S. Dist. Ct., So. dist. N.Y., 1972-74; partner Shearman & Sterling, N.Y.C., 1974—; trustee Practising Law Inst. Served from ens. to lt. comdr. USNR, 1941-45. Fellow Inst. Jud. Adminstrn., Am. Coll. Trial Lawyers; mem. Am., N.Y. State bar assns., Assn. Bar City N.Y. (chmn. com. on judiciary 1974-77), Fed. Bar Council (pres. 1966-68, chmn. bd. trustees 1968-70). Clubs: Univ. (N.Y.C.), Down Town Assn. (N.Y.C.), Broad Street (N.Y.C.). Federal civil litigation. Home: 20 Chester Dr Rye NY 10580 Office: Shearman & Sterling 53 Wall St New York NY 10005

BAUMAN, JOHN ANDREW, legal educator; b. 1921. B.S.L., U. Minn., 1942, LL.B., 1947; J.S.D., Columbia U., 1958. Bar: Wis. 1947, Minn. 1948. Spl. fellow Columbia U., 1950-51; assoc. prof. U. N. Mex., 1947-54; assoc. prof. Ind. U., 1954-59, prof., 1959-60; prof. UCLA, 1960—; exec. dir. Assn. Am. Law Schs., Washington, 1980-83, Mem. Order of Coif (sec.-treas.). Author: (with York) Cases and Materials on Remedies, 1967, 4th edit., 1985. Legal education. Address: UCLA Law Sch 405 Hilgard Ave Los Angeles CA 90024

BAUMAN, SUSAN JOAN MAYER, lawyer; b. N.Y.C., Mar. 2, 1945; d. Curt H. J. and Carola (Rosenau) Mayer; m. Ellis A. Bauman, Dec. 29, 1968. BS, U. Wis., 1965, JD, MS, 1981; MS, U. Chgo., 1966. Bar: Wis. 1981, U.S. Dist. Ct. (we. dist.) Wis. 1981, U.S. Ct. Appeals (7th cir.) 1983, U.S. Dist. Ct. (ea. dist.) Wis. 1985. Tchr. Madison (Wis.) Pub. Sch., 1970-78; research asst. U. Wis. Law Sch., Madison, 1981; ptnr. Thomas, Parsons, Schaefer & Bauman, Madison, 1981-84; sole practice Madison, 1984-85; ptnr. Bauman & Massing, Madison, 1985—. Alderman Madison Common Council, 1985—; commr. Madison Equal Opportunities Com., 1985—, Madison Econ. Devel. Com., 1986—. Mem. ABA, Wis. Bar Assn., Dane County Bar Assn., Indsl. Relations Research Assn., Wis. Indsl. Relations Alumni Assn. (pres. 1985-86). Democrat. Avocations: knitting, reading, backpacking, cross-country skiing. Pension, profit-sharing, and employee benefits, Labor, General practice. Home: 4809 Hillview Terr Madison WI 53711 Office: Bauman & Massing 116 King St Madison WI 53703

BAUMANN, CHRISTOPHER JOHN, lawyer; b. Lead, S.D., May 23, 1955; married. BS, U. S.D., 1977; postgrad. anthropology, U. Oreg., 1978; JD, U. S.D., 1981. Bar: S.D. 1981, U.S. Dist. Ct. S.D. 1983. Staff atty. Pennington County Pub. Defender's Office, Rapid City, S.D., 1981-82, asst. dir., 1982-83; ptnr. Baumann & Claggett, Spearfish, S.D., 1983-85; sole practice Spearfish, 1985—. Mem. ABA, S.D. Trial Lawyers Assn. Lodge: Optimists. Criminal, Family and matrimonial, Personal injury. Office: 504 Main St PO Box 555 Spearfish SD 57783

BAUMANN, LARRY R(OGER), lawyer; b. Chadron, Nebr., Feb. 19, 1946; s. Robert R. and Mary Nadine (Simpson) B.; children—Brenda Sue, Andrea Lynn; m. Susan Jo Luebbe, July 16, 1981; 1 child, Abigail Lynn. B.A., Chadron State Coll., 1968; J.D., U. Nebr., 1974. Bar: Nebr. 1974, U.S. Dist. Ct. Nebr. 1974, U.S. Tax Ct. 1983. Ptnr. Fillman & Baumann, York, Nebr., 1974-80; ptnr. Kelley, Scritsmier, Moore & Byrne, North Platte, Nebr., 1981—. Pres. York Jaycees, 1976. Served with U.S. Army, 1968-71, Vietnam. Mem. Nebr. Bar Assn., Assn. Trial Lawyers Am., Lincoln County Bar Assn., Western Nebr. Bar Assn. Democrat. Methodist. Federal civil litigation, State civil litigation, Construction. Office: Kelley Scritsmier Moore & Byrne 221 W 2nd North Platte NE 69103

BAUMGARDNER, JOHN ELLWOOD, JR., lawyer; b. Balt., Jan. 6, 1951; s. John Ellwood and Nancy G. (Brandenburg) B.; m. Astrid Rehl, Sept. 9, 1974; children: Jeffrey Mark, Julia Alexis. Bar: N.Y. 1976. Assoc. Sullivan & Cromwell, N.Y.C., 1975-83, ptnr., 1983—. Mem. ABA, N.Y. State Bar Assn., Assn. of Bar of City of N.Y. Club: Princeton (N.Y.C.). General corporate. Office: Sullivan & Cromwell 125 Broad St New York NY 10004

BAUMGART, RICHARD ALAN, lawyer; b. Cleve., Dec. 30, 1953; s. Herman Charles and Ethel Rae (Sicherman) B.; m. Debra Andrea Winston, Aug. 25, 1979; children: Melissa Gayle, Jared Scott. BA, U. Rochester, 1975; JD, Ohio State U., 1978. Bar: Ohio 1978, U.S. Dist. Ct. (no. dist.) Ohio 1978. Assoc. Dettelbach & Sicherman Co. L.P.A., Cleve., 1978—. Mem. Ohio Bar Assn., Cleve. Bar Assn. (bankruptcy and comml. law com., bar applicants' com.). Democrat. Jewish. Avocations: basketball, photography, running. Bankruptcy, Contracts commercial. Home: 2434 Cedarwood Rd Pepper Pike OH 44124 Office: Dettelbach & Sicherman Co LPA 1801 E 9th St 1300 Ohio Savs Plaza Cleveland OH 44114-3169

BAUMGARTEN, RONALD NEAL, lawyer; b. Chgo., May 13, 1942; s. Albert and Beatrice (Loseff) B.; m. Aloha Herman, Aug. 27, 1966; children: Brett, Reed, Jaclyn, Blake. BA, U. Ill., 1964, JD, 1966. Bar: Calif. 1970, U.S. Dist. Ct. (cen. dist.) Calif. 1970, U.S. Ct. Appeals (9th cir.) 1973, U.S. Supreme Ct. 1975. Gen. counsel, chief ops. officer Elgin Jewelry Distbrs. Inc., Los Angeles, 1967-72, also bd. dirs.; assoc. Grobe, Rinestein, Freid & Katz P.L.C., Beverly Hills, Calif., 1972-75; ptnr. Jacobs & Baumgarten P.L.C., Beverly Hills, 1975-80, Baumgarten & Greene P.L.C., Santa Monica, Calif., 1980—; chmn. bd. dirs., chief exec. officer J.D. Alexander & Assocs. Inc., Santa Monica, 1980—; asst. prof. law U. San Fernando Valley, Calif., 1974. Mem. Los Angeles World Affairs Council, 1974—, Los Angeles Olympic Citizens Adv. Commn., 1982-84, Town Hall, 1983—; v.p., gen. counsel, bd. dirs. Varity Club So. Calif., 1974—, Variety Boy's and Girl's Club, Los Angeles, bd. dirs., 1981—; founder 1st Bus. Bank, Los Angeles, 1981. Mem. ABA, Calif. Bar Assn., Los Angeles County Bar Assn., Beverly Hills Bar Assn., Santa Monica Bar Assn., Phi Delta Phi. Contracts commercial, General corporate, Real property. Office: Baumgarten & Greene 2951 28th St #3000 Santa Monica CA 90405

BAUMGARTEN, SIDNEY, lawyer; b. N.Y.C., July 30, 1933; s. Abraham and Doris (Kanarick) B.; m. Sylvia Rosen, June 26, 1955; children: Douglas, Fredrick, Roger, Julia. AB, Brown U., 1954; JD, NYU, 1960. Bar: N.Y. 1961, U.S. Dist. Ct. (ea. and so. dists.) N.Y. 1961, U.S. Ct. Claims 1961, U.S. Ct. Appeals (2d cir.) 1961. Asst. mgmt., field underwriter Home Life Ins. Co., 1957-61; sole practice 1961-67; asst. dist. atty. Queens County, N.Y., 1967-68; law sec. to presiding justice State of N.Y., Queens, 1968-73; asst. to Mayor City of N.Y., 1974-77; gen. counsel Phoenix House Found., 1978-80; sr. ptnr. Baumgarten, Swiedler & Waxman, N.Y.C., 1980—; lectr. various seminars, assns. and ednl. instns; adj. prof. law N.Y. Inst. Tech. Co-chmn. area interviews alumni schs. program Brown U.; committeeman county Boy Scouts Am.; bd. dirs. N.Y.'s Finest Found.; bd. dirs., chmn. N.Y. Therapeutic Communities, Inc.; trustee Lawrence Country Day Sch. (pres. 1985—). Served with U.S. Army, 1954-56, with Res. 1956-73. Mem. Queens County Bar Assn., Nat. Council Crime and Delinquency, Nat. Dist. Attys. Assn., N.Y. Law Sch. Alumni Assn., East Side C. of C. (pres. 1983—), VFW, Nat. Rifle Assn. (life). Club: Brown U. (N.Y.C.). General practice, Criminal, Local government. Office: Baumgarten Swiedler & Waxman 291 Broadway New York NY 10007

BAUMGARTNER, WILLIAM HANS, JR., lawyer; b. Chgo., July 24, 1955; s. William H. and Charlotte Burnette (Lange) B.; m. Andrea Jean Coath, Oct. 6, 1984. B.A., U. Chgo., 1976; J.D. magna cum laude, Harvard U., 1979. Bar: Ill. 1979, U.S. Dist. Ct. (no. dist.) Ill. 1979. Assoc. Sidley & Austin, Chgo., 1979-86, ptnr., 1986—. Mem. ABA, Chgo. Bar Assn., Phi Beta Kappa. Antitrust. Office: Sidley & Austin One 1st Nat Plaza Chicago IL 60603

BAUMOHL, HARRY ALAN, lawyer; b. Balt., Sept. 2, 1957; s. Norman Howard and Beverly Sylvia (Waxman) B. BS, Rider Coll., 1979; JD, U. Balt., 1981. Sole practice Towson, Md., 1981—. Mem. ABA, Md. Bar Assn. Family and matrimonial, State civil litigation, General practice.

BAUR, DONALD CHRISTIAN, lawyer; b. Meriden, Conn., Oct. 31, 1954; s. David I. and Agnes T. (Kokoska) B.; m. Phebe C. Jensch, May 11, 1985. BA in History, Trinity Coll., 1976; JD, U. Pa., 1979. Bar: Pa. 1979, D.C. 1985. Legal advisor office of solicitor U.S. Dept. Interior, Washington, 1979-84; gen. counsel U.S. Marine Mammal Commn., Washington, 1984—. Mem. D.C. Bar Assn. (environ. energy and natural resources div.), Soc. Marine Mammalogy, Phi Beta Kappa, Pi Gamma Mu. Environment, Administrative and regulatory, Public international. Office: US Marine Mammal Commn 1625 I St NW Washington DC 20006

BAVERMAN, ALAN JEROLD, lawyer; b. Balt., May 19, 1956; s. Edward James and Carolyn Lee (Kermisch) B.; m. Elida Blaine Steele, Aug. 7, 1982; children: Ariel Jenna, Jessica Raquel. BA in History, U. Md., 1978; JD, Emory U., 1981. Bar: Ga. 1981, U.S. Dist. Ct. Ga. 1981, U.S. Ct. Appeals (11th cir.) 1981, U.S. Ct. Claims 1984. Law clk. to presiding judge U.S. Dist. Ct. Ga., Rome, 1981-83; ptnr. Kadish & Kadish, Atlanta, 1983-86; assoc. Chilivis & Grindler, Atlanta, 1986—. Mem. Fed. Bar Assn., Nat. Assn. Criminal Def. Lawyers, Ga. Assn. Criminal Def. Lawyers, Ga. Trial Lawyers Assn., Atlanta Bar Assn. Democrat. Jewish. Avocations: swimming, baseball, boating. Criminal, Federal civil litigation, State civil litigation. Office: Chilivis & Grindler 2964 Peachtree Rd Suite 500 Atlanta GA 30305

BAVERMAN, ELIDA BLAINE, lawyer; b. Bklyn., May 13, 1957; s. David Douglas and Anne (Nagel) Steele; m. Alan Jerold Baverman, Aug. 7, 1982; 1 child, Ariel Jenna. BA, SUNY, Binghamton, 1979; postgrad., Brunel U., 1978; JD, Emory U., 1981. Bar: Ga. 1982, N.J. 1982, U.S. Dist. Ct. (no. dist.) Ga. 1983. Asst. dist. atty. Conasauga Judicial Cir., Dalton, Ga., 1982-83; assoc. Law Office Clifford J. Steele, Atlanta, Ga., 1982—. Mem. Assn. Trial Lawyers Am., Atlanta Bar Assn., Ga. Trial Lawyers Assn. Personal injury, State civil litigation, Workers' compensation. Office: Law Office of Clifford J. Steele 5505 Roswell Rd Atlanta GA 30342

BAVERO, RONALD JOSEPH, lawyer, legal educator; b. N.Y.C., Jan. 11, 1950; s. Joseph Carmine and Nancy (Martino) B.; m. Carolyn Angela Grippi, Aug. 20, 1972; children—Christen, Theresa, James, Joanna. B.A., Fordham U., 1971; J.D., St. John's U., N.Y.C., 1974. Bar: N.Y. 1975, U.S. Ct. Appeals (2d cir.) 1975, U.S. Dist. Ct. (ea. and so. dists.) N.Y. 1975. Law asst. appellate div. N.Y. State Supreme Ct., 1974-76; asst. dist. atty. Westchester County Dist. Atty.'s Office, White Plains, N.Y., 1976-82; prin. law sec. N.Y. State Family Ct., White Plains, 1982-85; assoc. Fink, Weinberger, Fredman, Berman & Lowell, P.C., 1985—; acting village justice Village of Gunsford, 1987—; asst. prof. law Pace U., Pleasantville, N.Y., 1982—. Editor Symposium on Law of Condominiums, 1974; assoc. editor St. John's Law Rev., 1974. Mem. N.Y. State Bar Assn., Westchester County Bar Assn., Columbian Lawyers Assn. Republican. Roman Catholic. Family and matrimonial, Legal education, Criminal. Home: 11 Prospect St Elmsford NY 10523 Office: Fink Weinberger Fredman Berman & Lowell 81 Main St White Plains NY 10601 also: 555 5th Ave New York NY 10017

BAXENDALE, JAMES CHARLES LEWIS, lawyer; b. Batley, Yorkshire, Eng., Dec. 1, 1945; came to Can., 1953; came to U.S., 1961; s. Stanley and Dora Maria (Day) B. BA in Econs., Rutgers U., 1967, JD, 1970, MBA, 1975; postgrad. law, Oxford U., Eng., 1971-72. Bar: N.J. 1971, U.S. Dist. Ct. N.J. 1971, Oreg. 1981, U.S. Ct. Appeals (9th cir.) 1982, U.S. Supreme Ct. 1983. Sr. law clk. to presiding judge U.S. Dist. Ct. N.J., 1973; dep. pub. adv. State of N.J., 1974-77; ptnr. Strauss, Wills & Baxendale, Princeton, N.J., 1977-78; sr. trial atty. U.S. Dept. Transp., Washington, 1978-80; mem. Stoll, Stoll & Baxendale, Portland, Oreg., 1980-81; assoc. gen. counsel Portland Gen. Elec. Co., 1981—. Mem. joint conf. com. United Hosps. of Newark, 1972-75; bd. dirs. West Coast Chamber Orch., Portland, 1982—; pres. bd. trustees Pacific Ballet Theatre, Portland, 1983—. Served to 1st lt. USAR, 1967-71. Mem. ABA, Oreg. Bar Assn., N.J. Bar Assn. (gen. council 1973). Republican. Episcopalian. Administrative and regulatory, General corporate, FERC practice. Home: 77 Touchstone Lake Oswego OR 97035 Office: Portland Gen Elec Co 121 SW Salmon St Portland OR 97204

BAXTER, HARRY STEVENS, lawyer; b. Ashburn, Ga., Aug. 25, 1915; s. James Hubert and Anna (Stevens) B.; m. Edith Ann Teasley, Apr. 4, 1943; children: Anna Katherine Stevens Worley (dec.), Nancy Julia Baxter Sibley. A.B. summa cum laude, U. Ga., 1936, LL.B. summa cum laude, 1939; postgrad., Yale U., 1939-40. Bar: Ga. 1941. Instr. U. Ga. Law Sch., Athens, 1941; assoc. Smith Kilpatrick Cody Rogers & McClatchey, Atlanta, 1942-51; ptnr. Kilpatrick & Cody, Atlanta, 1951-86, of counsel, 1986—; mem. State Bd. Bar Examiners Ga., 1960-66; chmn. State Bd. Bar Examiners, 1961-66; mem. Ga. Jud Qualifications Commn., 1979-86, chmn., 1984-85. Pres. Atlanta Community Chest, 1963; mem. bd. visitors U. Ga. Law Sch., 1965-68, chmn., 1965-66, chmn. alumni adv. com. on reorgn., 1963-64; chmn. chancellor's alumni adv. com. on selection of pres. U. Ga., 1966-67; gen. co-chmn. Joint Ga. Tech.-Ga. Devel. Fund, 1967; trustee U. Ga. Found., chmn., 1973-76; former William E. Honey Found., St. Joseph's Hosp., Atlanta, 1976-84. Served with AUS, 1942-45. Recipient Disting. Alumnus award U. Ga. Law Sch., 1967. Fellow Am. Bar Found.; mem. Am. Law Inst., ABA, Ga. Bar Assn., Atlanta Bar Assn., Atlanta C. of C. (dir. 1959-62), Atlanta Legal Aid Soc. (pres. 1956-57), Phi Beta Kappa, Phi Beta Kappa Assocs., Phi Kappa Phi, Omicron Delta Kappa, Phi Delta Phi. Clubs: Capital City (pres. 1965-67), Lawyers (pres. 1958-59), Piedmont Driving, Commerce, University Yacht. General corporate, Government contracts and claims, Public utilities. Home: 3197 Chatham Rd NW Atlanta GA 30305 Office: Equitable Bldg 100 Peachtree St NW Atlanta GA 30043

BAXTER, RANDOLPH, lawyer; b. Columbia, Tenn., Aug. 15, 1946; s. Lenon Pillow and Willie Alexine (Hood) B.; m. Yvonne Marie Williams, Nov. 26, 1980; children—Mark, Melissa, Scott; m. Rebecca Terrell, Oct. 10, 1968; (div. Apr. 1976); 1 dau., Kimberly Lynn. B.S., Tuskegee Inst., 1967; J.D., U. Akron, 1974. Bar: Ohio 1976, U.S. Dist. Ct. (no. dist.) Ohio 1978, U.S. Ct. Appeals (6th cir.) 1978, U.S. Supreme Ct. 1980. Salary analyst B.F. Goodrich Co., Akron, 1971-73; courts planner Criminal Justice Commn., Akron, 1973-76; dep. dir., pub. service dept. City Akron, 1976-78; asst. U.S. atty. U.S. Dept. Justice, Cleve., 1978-86, chief appellate litigation, 1982-86; judge U.S. Bankruptcy Court (no. dist.) Ohio, 1985—; instr. real estate law Kent State U., 1974-78; v.p., dir. Alpha Phi Alpha Homes, Inc., Akron, 1971—. Bd. dirs. Western Res. Legal Services, Inc., Akron, 1982—, Boy Scouts Am., Akron 1982—; mem. Ohio Republican Council, 1981—. Served to capt. AUS, 1968- 71, Vietnam. Named Man of Yr., Akron Jaycees, 1977; recipient Disting. Service award City Akron, 1978, Spl. Achievement award U.S. Dept. Justice, 1981, 82, Disting. Vets. award Fed. Exec. Bd. Cleve., 1982. Mem. Akron Barristers Club (pres. 1978-79), ABA, Fed. Bar Assn., Assn. Trial Lawyers Am., Nat. Bar Assn., Akron Bar Assn., Alpha Phi Alpha. Clubs: Cascade, Blue Coats. Federal civil litigation, Personal injury, Administrative and regulatory. Home: 243 S Miller Rd Akron OH 44313 Office: US Attys Office 1404 E 9th St Suite 500 Cleveland OH 44114

BAXTER, RICHARD BRIAN, lawyer; b. Detroit, Feb. 22, 1927; s. Charles Lewis and Madelyn (Kilburtus) B.; m. Margaret Elizabeth, May 28, 1949; children—Judith Ann, Janet Carole, Richard Brian, Jr. A.B., U. Mich., 1951, J.D., 1954. Bar: Mich. 1954. ptnr. Dykema, Gossett, Spencer, Goodnow & Trigg and predecessor, Grand Rapids, 1965—, sr. ptnr., 1979—; mem. faculty, participant continuing legal edn., Advocacy Inst. Served with USAAC, 1944-46. Recipient Exceptional Performance citation Def. Research Inst., 1981. Mem. Fellow Mich. Bar Found., Am. Bar Found.; mem. Grand Rapids Bar Assn. (pres. 1977), Mich. Def. Trial Counsel (pres. 1981), Am. Coll. Trial Lawyers, Internat. Acad. Trial Lawyers (dir. 1985—), Internat. Soc. Barristers, Fedn. Ins. Counsel Internat. Assn. Ins. Counsel Am. Judicature Soc. Club: Cascade Hills Country (Grand Rapids). Author: Michigan Continuing Legal Education Defenses in Legal Malpractice, 1974; Defenses in Wrongful Death Cases, 1975; contbr. chpts. and articles to legal publs. Federal civil litigation, State civil litigation. Home: 1318 Woodcliff Dr SE East Grand Rapids MI 49506 Office: Dykema Gossett Spencer et al 200 Oldtown Riverfront Bldg 348 Louis Campau Promenade NW Grand Rapids MI 49503

BAXTER, WILLIAM FRANCIS, lawyer; b. N.Y.C., July 13, 1929; s. William F. and Ruth C. B.; children—William Francis, Marcia, Stuart Carlton; m. Carol Cairns Treanor, Mar. 27, 1987. A.B., Stanford U., 1951, J.D., 1956. Bar: Calif. 1956, U.S. Supreme Ct. 1960, D.C. 1983. Asst. prof. law Stanford U., 1956-58, prof., 1960—; asst. atty. gen. of U.S. for antitrust Washington, 1981-83; assoc. firm. Covington & Burling, Washington, 1958-60; vis. prof. Yale U. Law Sch., 1964-65; fellow Center for Advanced Study in Behavioral Scis., 1972-73; cons. in field; fellow Brookings Inst., 1968-72; mem. Pres.'s Task Force on Communications Policy, 1968, Pres.'s Task Force on Antitrust Policy, 1968; of counsel Shearman & Sterling, 1984—. Author: People or Penguins, An Optimum Level of Pollution, 1974, (with others) Retail Banking in Electronic Age: The Law and Economics of Electronic Funds Transfer, 1977. Served with USN, 1951-54. Mem. Am. Econ. Assn. Antitrust. Office: Stanford U Law Sch Stanford CA 94305

BAY, WILLIAM ROBERT, lawyer; b. St. Louis, Nov. 5, 1953; s. Robert Dewey and Peggy Alene (Hampton) B.; m. Angela Sue Toole, May 27, 1978; children: Julia Elizabeth, Peter William. BA in Polit. Sci., U. Mo., 1975; JD, U. Mich., 1978. Bar: Mo. 1978, U.S. Dist. Ct. (ea. dist.) Mo. 1978, Ill. 1981, U.S. Ct. Appeals (8th cir.) 1981. Assoc. Armstrong, Teasdale, Kramer & Vaughan, St. Louis, 1978-80; assoc. Thompson & Mitchell, St. Louis, 1980-86, ptnr., 1987—. V.p. Southwest Bapt. Ch., St. Louis, 1985-86, pres. 1986-87. Mem. ABA (exec. com. admiralty law commn. young law div. 1986-87, affiliate outreach project pamphlet editor, 1986-87), Ill. Bar Assn., Mo. Bar Assn., Bar Assn. Metro St. Louis (sec. 1982-83, exec. com. 1984-87, chmn. young lawyers sect. 1986-87, award of merit 1985-86). Club: Mo. Athletic (St. Louis). Admiralty, Federal civil litigation, State civil litigation. Home: 6526 Delor Ave Saint Louis MO 63109 Office: Thompson & Mitchell One Mercantile Ctr Suite 3400 Saint Louis MO 63101

BAYARD, ALTON ERNEST, III, lawyer; b. New Orleans, La., Mar. 25, 1952; s. Alton Ernest Jr. and Elvy Alys (Backer) B.; m. Mary Watkins, Jan. 8, 1983; 1 child, Andrew Ernest. BS, La. State U., 1975, JD, 1976; LLM in Taxation, So. Meth. U., 1980. Bar: La. 1977, U.S. Dist. Ct. (mid. dist.) La. 1977. Ptnr. Calongne & Bayard, Baton Rouge, La., 1977-80, Jones, Walker, Waechter, Poitevent, Carrere & Deneare, Baton Rouge, 1981—. Served to tech. sgt. La. Air N.G., 1970-76. Mem. ABA, La. Bar Assn., Baton Rouge Bar Assn. Avocation: sailing. Probate, Estate taxation, Pension, profit-sharing, and employee benefits. Office: Jones Walker Waechter Poitevent et al One American Pl Suite 1614 Baton Rouge LA 70825

BAYBAYAN, RONALD ALAN, lawyer; b. Paia, Hawaii, July 4, 1946; s. Celedonio Ludrano and Carlina (Domingo) B.; m. Dianne Lea, June 14, 1969 (div. June 1985); children: Alycia Kay, Amber Lea; m. Sharyn Dee Huckins, Dec. 31, 1985. BA, Coe Coll., 1968; JD, Drake U., 1974. Bar: Iowa 1977, U.S. Dist. Ct. (so. dist.) Iowa 1977, U.S. Tax Ct. 1978, U.S. Dist. Ct. (no. dist.) Iowa 1980, U.S. Ct. Appeals (8th cir.) 1985, U.S. Supreme Ct. 1985, U.S. Dist. Ct. Hawaii 1986. Asst. law librarian Drake U., Des Moines, 1974-77; assoc. Law Office Mike Wilson, Des Moines, 1977-78; sole practice Des Moines, 1978—. Served with USAF, 1969-73. Mem. ABA, Iowa Bar Assn., Polk County Bar Assn., Am.-Filipino Assn. Iowa (bd. dirs. 1986), Bass Anglers Sportsman Soc. (Iowa chpt. pres. 1979-82). Republican. Mem. Wakonda Christian Ch. Club: Mid-Iowa Bassmasters (past pres., past v.p., past sec.) (Des Moines). State civil litigation, Family and matrimonial, General practice. Home: 1520 Birch Norwalk IA 50211 Office: 5609 Douglas Des Moines IA 50310

BAYER, ELMER VALENTINE, lawyer; b. St. Louis, Sept. 6, 1912; s. Valentine Anthony and Rose Alma (Helfrich) B.; m. Mary Marcella Charleville, May 10, 1941; children—Marcia Ann, Georgia Lea, Carole Lynne, Pamela Jean, Thomas Elmer, James Andrew, Valerie Rose, Joyce Marie, Joseph Victor, Michael Gerard. B.A., Glennon Coll., St. Louis, 1935; LL.B., City Coll. Law and Fin., St. Louis, 1940, LL.M., 1941. Bar: Mo. 1940, U.S. Dist. Ct. (ea. dist.) Mo. 1941, U.S. Supreme Ct. 1976. Ill. claims atty. New Amsterdam Casualty Co., St. Louis, 1941-47; operated liability claims office for various ins. cos., St. Louis, 1947-75; sole practice, St. Louis, 1975—. Mem. Republican Nat. Com. Mem. ABA, Mo. Bar, Lawyers Assn., Met. St. Louis Bar Assn., Mo. Assn. Trial Attys. Roman Catholic. Club: Jefferson Twp. Republican. Family and matrimonial, General practice, Workers' compensation. Office: 3920 Lindell Blvd Saint Louis MO 63108

BAYER, RICHARD STEWART, lawyer; b. Laurel, Md., July 7, 1951; s. James Theodore and Patricia Ruth (Stewart) B.; m. Roberta Ann Cruise, July 9, 1977; children—Andrew Stewart, Henry Eliot. A.B., Middlebury Coll., 1973; J.D., Colo. U., 1976. Bar: Colo. 1976, U.S. Dist. Ct. Colo. 1976, U.S. Ct. Appeals (10th cir.) 1976. Assoc. Brownstein Hyatt, Farber & Madden, Denver, 1976-81, ptnr., 1981-86; with firm Kutak, Rock & Campbell, Denver, 1987—. Author: Colorado Appellate Advocacy, 1984. Contbr. articles to legal jours. Mem. ABA (chmn. 10th cir. comml., banking, fin. transactions subcom., litigation sect. 1984—), Denver Bar Assn., Denver Law Club (sec. 1982-83). Democrat. Federal civil litigation, State civil litigation. Home: 4917 Montview Blvd Denver CO 80207 Office: Kutak Rock & Campbell 2400 Arco Tower 707 17th St Denver CO 80202

BAYKO, EMIL THOMAS, lawyer; b. Pitts., Mar. 5, 1947; s. Emil and Ruth (Alberti) B.; m. Ruth Ann Loucks, Nov. 5, 1967; children: Anthony M., Keith C., Paul S. BA in Polit. Sci., Kent State U., 1970; JD cum laude, U. Ill., Champaign, 1973. Bar: Ill. 1973, U.S. Dist. Ct. (no. dist.) Ill. 1973, U.S. Ct. Appeals (7th cir.) 1974, D.C. 1975, N.Y. 1975, U.S. Ct. Appeals (2d cir.) 1975, U.S. Ct. Claims 1976, U.S. Dist. Ct. (so. dist.) N.Y. 1976, U.S. Ct. Appeals (D.C. cir.) 1976, U.S. Supreme Ct. 1976, U.S. Dist. Ct. (ea dist.) Pa. 1978, U.S. Ct. Appeals (3d cir.) 1978, Tex. 1980, U.S. Dist. Ct. (so. dist.) Tex. 1981, U.S. Ct. Appeals (5th cir.) 1981. Assoc. Chapman & Cutler, Chgo., 1973-74, White & Case, N.Y.C., 1975-80; ptnr. Liddell, Sapp & Zivley, Houston, 1981, Holtzman & Urquhart, Houston, 1982—. Co-author: Essays on American Law, 1971, Home Rule, 1972. Harno fellow U. Ill., 1971-73. Mem. ABA, Assn. of Bar of City of N.Y., Houston Bar Assn., Chgo. Bar Assn., Tex. Bar Assn., D.C. Bar Assn., Order of Coif. Democrat. Presbyterian. Clubs: Tex., Houston. Federal civil litigation, State civil litigation, Environment. Office: Holtzman & Urquhart 900 Two Houston Ctr Houston TX 77010

BAYLEY, THOMAS WAY, JR., lawyer; b. Mpls., Feb. 27, 1915; s. Thomas Way and Agnes Gertrude (O'Brien) B.; m. Suzanne Ludey, Feb. 7, 1942; children—Patty Ruth Bayley Dhondt, Charlotte Ann, Thomas W. B.A., UCLA, 1936; LL.B., U. Calif.-Berkeley, 1939. Bar: Calif. 1940, W.Va. 1946, U.S. Dist. Ct. (no dist.) W.Va., U.S. Dist. Ct. (no. dist.) Ohio. Assoc. W. Blair Gibbens, Santa Monica, Calif., 1939-42, Ambler, McCluer & Davis, Parkersburg, W.Va., 1946-52; ptnr. Burk and Bayley, Parkersburg, 1952—, sr. ptnr., 1970—; city atty. Williamstown, 1946-71; asst. pros. atty. Wood County (W.Va.), 1952-54. Co-founder Parkersburg Community Found., 1963. Served with U.S. Army, 1942-46. Mem. ABA, Calif. Bar Assn., W.Va. Bar Assn., Wood County Bar Assn. Republican. Roman Catholic. General practice, General corporate, Estate planning. Office: Burk and Bayley Box 287 Parkersburg WV 26101

BAYLISS, MALCOLM B., corporate lawyer; b. 1928. AB, Harvard U., 1949, JD, 1955. Assoc. Burns, Blake and Rich, 1955-59; ptnr. Reid & Priest, 1959-70; with Amax Inc., Greenwich, Conn., 1970-73, dir. legal dept., 1973-74, v.p. legal dept., 1974-77, v.p. gen. counsel, 1977-81, sr. v.p. gen. counsel, 1981-82, exec. v.p., gen counsel, 1982—. Office: Amax Inc Amax Ctr PO Box 1700 Greenwich CT 06836 *

BAYLY, JOHN HENRY, lawyer; b. Washington, Jan. 26, 1944; s. John Henry and Salome Carole (Winters) B.; m. Barbara Jean Downey, Feb. 16, 1974 (dec. Jan. 1977); 1 child, Anne Louise; m. Katherine Bridget Kenny, Dec. 1, 1979; children: Johanna, Georgia. AB, Fordham U., 1966; JD, Harvard U., 1969. Bar: U.S. Dist. Ct. D.C. 1969, U.S. Ct. Appeals (D.C. cir.) 1969, D.C. 1971, U.S. Supreme Ct. 1974. Atty., advisor FCC, Washington, 1969-71; asst. atty. Office of U.S. Atty., Washington, 1971-75, 78-85; dep. minority counsel Senate Select Com. on Intelligence, Washington, 1975-76; acting asst. gen. counsel Corp. for Pub. Broadcasting, Washington, 1976-78; gen. counsel Legal Services Corp., Washington, 1985-87, pres., 1987—. Mem. D.C. Bar Assn., Phi Beta Kappa. Republican. Roman Catholic. Clubs: City Tavern, Georgetown (Washington). Administrative and regulatory, Federal civil litigation, General corporate. Home: 3512 Runnymede Pl NW Washington DC 20015 Office: Legal Services Corp 400 Virginia Ave SW Washington DC 20024-2751

BAYNARD, ERNEST CORNISH, III, lawyer; b. Washington, Aug. 8, 1944; s. Ernest Cornish Jr. and Ann Rives (Evans) B.; m. Karen Dawalt, Apr. 4, 1970 (div. Mar. 1973); 1 child, Ernest C. IV; m. Wendy Elizabeth Fee, Sept. 6, 1975; children: Jackson P.F., Elizabeth R., William T. Mac. BA, Trinity Coll., 1966; JD, Georgetown U., 1971. Bar: D.C. 1971, U.S. Dist. Ct. D.C. 1971, U.S. Ct. Appeals (7th cir.) 1972, U.S. Ct. Appeals (5th cir.) 1975, U.S. Ct. Appeals (fed. cir.) 1982, U.S. Supreme Ct. 1986. Assoc. Connole & O'Connell, Washington, 1972-80, ptnr., 1980-83; assoc. soliciter U.S. Dept. Interior, Washington, 1983-84; dep. gen. counsel FERC, Washington, 1984-86; of counsel Newman & Holtzinger, Washington, 1986—; mem. adv. com. U.S. Ct. Appeals (fed. cir.) 1982-83. Author: Public Land Law and Procedure, 1986; editor in chief Natural Resources and Environ., 1984-86. Served with USN, 1966-68. Mem. ABA (council mem. natural resources sect. 1983-86, vice chmn. 1986). Republican. Episcopalian. Club: Mill Reef (Antigua, West Indies). Avocations: hunting, fishing. FERC practice, Administrative and regulatory, Environment. Home: 613 N Overlook Dr Alexandria VA 22305 Office: Newman & Holtzinger 1615 L St NW Washington DC 20036

BAYS, ALBERT BERNARD, lawyer; b. Pomona, Calif., Oct. 13, 1944; B.A., U. So. Calif., 1966; J.D., Stanford U., 1969. Bar: Calif. 1969, Hawaii 1970, U.S. Dist. Ct. Hawaii 1970, U.S. Supreme Ct. 1976. Assoc., ptnr. Padgett, Greeley, Honolulu, 1970-75; ptnr. Carlsmith, Wichman, Case, Mukai & Ichiki, Honolulu, 1975—; active in devel. of residential leasehold law in Hawaii. Editor Stanford U. Law Rev. Served to capt. USMC, 1969-78. Mem. Hawaii Bar Assn. Clubs: Honolulu, Outrigger. State civil litigation, Real property, General corporate. Office: Bays Deaver Hiatt Kawachika & Lezak 9th Floor Hawaii Bldg Honolulu HI 96813

BAZERMAN, STEVEN HOWARD, lawyer; b. N.Y.C., Dec. 12, 1940; s. Solomon and Miriam (Kirschenberg) B.; m. Christina Ann Gray, Aug. 28, 1981. BS in Math., BS in Sci. and Engring., U. Mich., 1962; JD, Georgetown U., 1966. Bar: D.C. 1967, N.Y. 1968. Assoc. Arthur, Dry & Kalish, N.Y.C., 1967-80, Offner & Kuhn, N.Y.C., 1980-83; ptnr., head litigation dept. Kuhn, Muller & Bazerman, N.Y.C., 1983-87; ptnr. Moore, Berson, Lifflander & Mewhinney, N.Y.C., 1987—. Vol. counsel community law offices Legal Aid Soc., N.Y.C., 1974-82, treas., 1979-82. Mem. Assn. of Bar of City of N.Y., Am. Intellectual Property Law Assn., N.Y. Patent, Trademark & Copyright Law Assn. Jewish. Avocations: horses, classic automobiles. Patent, Trademark and copyright, Federal civil litigation. Home: 2 W 67th St New York City NY 10023 Office: Moore Berson Lifflander & Mewhinney 595 Madison Ave New York NY 10022

BAZYLER, MICHAEL J., legal educator; b. Tashkent, Uzbekistan, USSR, Nov. 28, 1952; came to U.S., 1964; s. Ben and Jenny (Gasner) B.; m. Anna Dosik, Dec. 20, 1980. BA, UCLA, 1974; JD, U. So. Calif., 1978. Bar: Calif. 1979, U.S. Dist. Ct. (cen. dist.) Calif., U.S. Ct. Appeals (9th cir.). Law clk. to presiding justice U.S. Ct. Appeals (9th cir.), San Francisco, 1978-79; assoc. Morrison & Foerster, Los Angeles, 1979-81; law prof. Loyola U., Los Angeles, 1981-82, Whittier Coll., Los Angeles, 1982—. Contbr. articles to profl. jours. Vol. atty. ACLU, Los Angeles, 1985—; internat. law cons. legal support network Amnesty Internat., N.Y.C., 1984—, chmn. legal edn. com., 1983. Mem. AAAS, Am. Soc. Internat. Law, Phi Beta Kappa, Pi Gamma Mu. Private international, Public international. Office: Whittier Coll Sch Law 5353 W 3d St Los Angeles CA 90020

BEACH, BARBARA PURSE, lawyer; b. Washington, D.C., June 12, 1947; d. Clifford John and Lillian (Natarus) B. BA, U. Ky., 1968; MSW, U. Md., 1972; JD, Am. U., 1980. Bar: D.C. 1980, Va. 1980. Law clk. to presiding justice benefit rev. bd. U.S. Dept. Labor, Washington, 1980; asst. city atty. City of Alexandria, Va., 1981-85; atty. Ross, Marsh & Foster, Alexandria, 1985—. Mem. Dem. Com., Arlington, Va., 1985-86. Mem. ABA, Va. Trial Lawyers Assn., Alexandria Bar Assn. (pres. elect 1986-87, pres. 1987—). State civil litigation, General corporate, Local government. Office: Ross Marsh & Foster 324 N Fairfax St Alexandria VA 22314

BEACH, CHARLES ADDISON, lawyer; b. Albany, N.Y., Apr. 21, 1945; s. Charles A.W. and Eleanor (Johnston) B.; m. Jane L. Shlionsky, June 8, 1968; children: James E. and Jonathan M. BA, Hamilton Coll., 1967; JD, Cornell U., 1973. Bar: N.Y. 1974, U.S. Dist. Ct. (no., ea., we. and so. dists.) N.Y. 1974, U.S. Ct. Appeals (2d and 10th cirs.) 1975, U.S. Supreme Ct. 1982. Assoc. Shearman & Sterling, N.Y.C., 1973-81; counsel Exxon Corp., N.Y.C., 1981—. Vol. Peace Corps., Libya and Tunisia, 1968-71. Mem. ABA, N.Y. State Bar Assn., Assn. Bar City N.Y., Am. Arbitration Assn. (arbitrator 1985—). Presbyterian. Private international, Federal civil litigation, State civil litigation. Home: 19 Cornell Way Upper Montclair NJ 07043 Office: Exxon Corp 1251 Ave of Americas New York NY 10020-1198

BEACH, CHESTER PAUL, JR., lawyer; b. Memphis, Oct. 4, 1954; s. Chester Paul Sr. and Gertrude (Lloyd) B.; m. Carol Elizabeth Swanson, July 14, 1979 (div. Sept. 1982). Student, Va. Mil. Inst., 1972-73; BA magna cum laude, Vanderbilt U., 1976; JD, U. Chgo., 1980. Bar: Ill. 1980, U.S. Dist. Ct. (no. dist.) Ill. 1980, U.S. Ct. Mil. Appeals 1985, U.S. Ct. Appeals (fed. cir.) 1986. Commd. 2d lt. U.S. Army, 1976, advanced through grades to capt., 1981; legal assistance officer U.S. Army, Mannheim, Fed. Republic Germany, 1981-82, prosecutor, 1982-83, chief prosecutor, 1983-84; spl. asst. to chief litigation div. U.S. Army, Washington, 1984-85, litigation atty., 1985-87; atty.-advisor office of gen. counsel U.S. Dept. of Def., 1987—; visiting instr. Ill. Inst. Tech.-Kent Coll. Law, Chgo., 1980-81. Fellow Danforth Found., 1976. Mem. ABA (chmn. young lawyers div. com. 1985—), Am. Soc. for Legal History, Judge Advs. Assn., Omicron Delta Kappa. Republican. Episcopalian. Club: Army Navy Country (Arlington, Va.). Lodge: Masons. Avocations: hist. research and writing, hiking, golf, travel. Federal civil litigation, Military, Legal history. Home: 7909 Carrousel Ct Annandale VA 22003-1414 Office: OAGC (P&HP) 3E999 Pentagon Washington DC 20301

BEACH, JOHN ARTHUR, lawyer; b. Syracuse, N.Y., Apr. 30, 1932; s. Arthur Myron and Norma Irene (Vergason) B.; m. Victoria Regina Gorcoff, 1954 (div. 1985); children: Carolyn, Ann, Ellen, George; m. Joyce Ann Gruka, 1985. AB summa cum laude, Syracuse U., 1954; JD, U. Mich., 1957. Bar: N.Y. 1958, U.S. Dist. Ct. (no. dist.) N.Y. 1965, Fla. 1983. Assoc. Bond, Schoeneck & King, various cities in N.Y. and Fla., 1957-65, ptnr., 1965—; interim dean Syracuse U. Coll. Law, 1973-74. Sr. editor U. Mich. Law Rev., 1957; contbr. articles to profl. jours. Mem. ABA, N.Y. State Bar Assn., Albany County Bar Assn., Onondaga County Bar Assn., Fla. Bar Assn., Nat. Assn. Coll. and Univ. Attys. (pres. 1985-86), Phi Alpha Delta, Phi Beta Kappa, Phi Kappa Phi. General corporate, Health. Home: 420 Sand Creek Rd #132 Albany NY 12205 Office: Bond Schoeneck & King 111 Washington Ave Albany NY 12210

BEACHLER, EDWIN HARRY, III, lawyer; b. Pitts., Nov. 21, 1940; s. Edwin H. and Mercedes S. B. B.A., Georgetown U., 1962; J.D., U. Pitts., 1965. Bar: Pa. 1965, U.S. Dist. Ct. (we. dist.) Pa. 1965, U.S. Ct. Appeals (3d cir.) 1966. Assoc., McArdle, McLaughlin, Palettea & McVay, Pitts., 1966-72; ptnr. Caroselli, Spagmolli & Beachler, Pitts., 1972—. Mem. ABA, Allegheny County Bar Assn., Allegheny County Acad. Trial Lawyers, Pa. Trial Lawyers Assn. (gov. 1982-83), Assn. Trial Lawyers Am. Federal civil litigation, State civil litigation, Personal injury. Home: 5660 Darlington Rd Pittsburgh PA 15217

BEACHLEY, CHARLES EDWARD, III, lawyer; b. N.Y.C., Apr. 14, 1951; s. Charles Edward Jr. and Joan Elizabeth (Nichols) B.; m. Harriet Jane Bowen, Feb. 10, 1979; children: William C. Martin Jr., Kay Cathrynne Martin, Charles E. Beachley IV. AA, Paris (Tex.) Jr. Coll., 1971; BA, Trinity U., 1973, MFA, 1976; JD, So. Meth. U., 1982. Bar: Tex. 1982, U.S. Dist. Ct. (no. dist.) Tex 1983, U.S. Ct. Appeals (5th cir.) 1984, U.S. Dist. Ct. (ea. dist.) 1986. Asst. city atty. City of Garland, Tex., 1982; assoc. Joann Peters Law Offices, Dallas, 1983-85; staff atty. Hyatt Legal Services, Irving, Tex., 1985; mng. atty. Hyatt Legal Services, Dallas, 1985-86; sole practice Carrollton, Tex., 1986—; lectr. Lewisville (Tex.) Library Law Lectures, 1985—. Author: (plays) Preserve, Protect and Defend, 1975, A Marvelous War, 1976, Close to Home, 1976, The Cause of this Effect, 1977. Mem. Tex. Bar. Assn., Dallas Bar Assn. (pro bono service award 1984, 85), Denton Bar Assn., Am. Judicature Soc., Phi Alpha Delta. Democrat. Roman Catholic. Avocation: writing. General practice, Family and matrimonial, State civil litigation. Office: 3740 N Josey Suite 210B Carrollton TX 75007

BEACHY, ROBERT M., lawyer; b. Kansas City, Mo., Aug. 27, 1946; s. Robert S. Jr. and Betty S. (Smith) B.; m. Mary Don, June 8, 1974; children: Laura, Jane, Robert. BS, Colo. U., 1968; JD, U. Mo., Kansas City, 1972, LLM, 1975. Bar: Mo. 1973, U.S. Dist. Ct. Mo. 1973, U.S. Ct. Appeals (8th cir.) 1973, U.S Ct. Appeals (10th cir.) 1980. Ptnr. Van Osdol, Magruder, Erickson & Redmond, Kansas City, 1973—; dir. Legal Aid of Western Mo., Kansas City, 1976-81. Dir. Estate Planning Council, Kansas City, 1985—; dir. Rehab. Inst., 1979, Red Cross, 1984-85; mem. Econ. Devel. Com., Leawood, Kans., 1985-86. Served to sgt. U.S. Army, 1969-71, Thailand. Mem. Nat. Health Lawyers Assn., Mercury Club (dir., v.p. 1984—), Vis. Nurse Assn. (dir., pres. 1974-80), Phi Kappa Phi, Sigma Chi. Presbyterian. Avocations: hunting, fishing, wine, golf. General corporate, Health, Estate planning. Home: 9215 Ensley Ln Leawood KS 66206 Office: Van Osdal Magruder Erickson & Redmond 515 Commerce Trust Bldg Kansas City MO 64106

BEACROFT, PERCIVAL THOMAS, lawyer; b. Freeport, Tex., Apr. 21, 1935; s. Percival Thomas and Pollye (Maddox) B. B.A., So. Meth. U., 1957, J.D., 1960; cert. internat. law, Univ. Coll., London, 1961. Bar: Tex. 1960. With internat. dept. Chase Manhattan Bank, N.Y.C., 1963-65; mem. legal staff Ashley Famous Agy., N.Y.C., 1965-67; sole practice, N.Y.C., 1967-71, Freeport, 1971—, Woodville, Miss., 1971—; trustee Stringfellow Trusts, Freeport, 1971-85. Mem. exec. com. So. Meth. U., 1985-86; trustee Tex. Hist. Found., Austin, 1981-85. Recipient Jefferson Davis medal DAC, 1974, mem. Jefferson Davis Assn. (trustee 1978-84). Republican. Episcopalian. Private international, Real property. Home: Rosemont Plantation Woodville MS 39669 Office: REL Stringfellow Interests 225 Park Ave Freeport TX 77541

BEAIRD, JAMES RALPH, legal educator, dean; b. 1925. B.S., U. Ala., 1949, LL.B., 1951; LL.M., George Washington U., 1953. Bar: Ala. 1951, D.C. 1973. Atty. U.S. Dept. Labor, 1951-56, asst. solicitor, 1956-69; assoc. gen. counsel NLRB, 1959-60; assoc. solicitor U.S. Dept. Labor, 1960-65; vis. prof. U. Ga., 1965-66, prof. law, 1967—, dean, 1977—; mem. Sec. Labor's Adv. Council on Welfare and Pension Plans, 1968—. Mem. adv. com. for Ga. SBA, 1969—. Mem. Farrah Order Jurisprudence. Legal education. Office: Univ of Ga Sch of Law Athens GA 30602

BEAKLEY, ROBERT PAUL, lawyer; b. Millville, N.J., Sept. 29, 1946; s. John A. Jr. and Eleanor Jayne (Schanck) B.; m. Susan McClure Besinger, April 8, 1972; children: Timothy Andrew, Tara Anne. BA, W.Va. Wesleyan U., Buckhannon, 1969; JD, Washington & Lee U., 1972. Bar: N.J. 1972, U.S. Ct. Appeals (3d cir.) 1980. Assoc. Albert M. Ash, Ocean City, N.J., 1972-73; mgmt. trainee Coastal State Bank, Ocean City, 1973-74; staff atty. Cape-Atlantic Legal Services, Atlantic City, N.J., 1974-79; ptnr. Middlesworth, Beakley & Barry, Atlantic City, 1979-82; sole practice Atlantic City, 1982-84, Wallen & Beakley, Atlantic City, 1984—. Bd. dirs. Jr. Achievement, Cape Atlantic County, 1978; jr. warden Holy Trinity Episc. Ch., Ocean City, 1981-82; trustee Am. Diabetes Assn., Atlantic County, 1985. Served to 1st lt. U.S. Army, 1970-78. Mem. Atlantic County Bar Assn., Assn. Trial Lawyers Am., N.J. Trial Lawyers Assn. Republican. General practice, Civil rights. Home: 244 W Seaspray Rd Ocean City NJ 08226 Office: Wallen & Beakley 1125 Atlantic Ave Suite 421 Atlantic City NJ 08401

BEAL, BRUCE CURTIS, lawyer; b. Boston, Dec. 25, 1950; s. Harold Bruce and Shirley Eunice (Armstrong) B.; m. Jennifer Jean Morris, May 28, 1973; children: Nathaniel Bruce, Alissa Carol. BA, Ill. Coll., 1973; JD, Western New Eng. Sch. of Law, 1976. Bar: Ill. 1976, U.S. Dist. Ct. (cen. dist.) Ill. 1980, Wis. 1986. Assoc. Claudon, Lloyd & Barnhart, Canton, Ill., 1976-80; jr. ptnr. Claudon, Lloyd, Barnhart & Beal, Ltd., Canton, 1980-84, sr. ptnr., 1984—. Trustee Wesley United Meth. Ch., Canton, 1982—; bd. dirs. Canton Friendship Festival Assn., Canton, 1978-84, Attention Home of Fulton County, Canton, 1980. Mem. ABA, Ill. Bar Assn. (council labor law sect.), Fulton County Bar Assn. (sec. 1976). Lodge: Kiwanis (pres. 1982-83). Labor, Estate taxation, Family and matrimonial. Home: 236 Van Dyke Dr Canton IL 61520 Office: Claudon Lloyd Barnhart & Beal Ltd 121 W Elm St Canton IL 61520

BEAL, JOHN ARTHUR, lawyer, educator, dentist, pharmacist; b. Methuen, Mass., Feb. 2, 1937; s. John C. and Gertrude E. (Mahoney) B.; m. Dolores M. Nolet, Oct. 23, 1960; children: Johnna Ann, Ryan Thomas. BS, Mass. Coll. of Pharmacy, 1960, MS, 1962; DMD, U. Pa., 1966; JD, Suffolk U., 1977; MPH, Harvard U., 1980; cert., Boston U., 1983. Bar: Mass. 1977, U.S. Dist. Ct. Mass. 1978, U.S. Ct. Appeals 1978; licensed pharmacist, Mass.; licensed dentist Mass. Pharmacist Mass., 1960-62; dentist Methuen, Mass., 1966—; sole practice Lawrence, Mass., 1977—; asst. clin. prof. biomed. law and ethics Boston U. and Forsyth Dental Sch., Mass., 1980—; prof. law. Commonwelath Sch. Law, Lowell, Mass., 1986—. Assoc. editor: Jour. Dental Law; contbr. articles on biomedical law to profl. jours. Served to pvt. 1st class USMC, 1954-56. Mem. ABA, ADA, New Eng. Pub. Health Assn. (officer 1980—, mem. com.). Health, Personal injury, Inter-professional relationship dilemmas. Home: 11 Donald Circle Andover MA 01810 Office: 45 Jackson St Methuen MA 01844

BEALE, J. BURKHARDT, lawyer, educator; b. Suffolk, Va., May 12, 1955; s. J. Vaughan and Marydele Jane (Stulting) B. Student, U. Va., 1977; BA, Gonzaga U., 1978; JD, Washington and Lee U., 1980. Bar: Va. 1980, U.S. Dist Ct. (ea. dist.) Va. 1981, U.S. Ct. Appeals (4th cir.) 1981. Assoc. Willis F. Hutchens, Richmond, Va., 1980-81; assoc. Boone & Warren, Richmond, 1982-83, ptnr., 1983-86; ptnr. Boone, Beale, Cosby & Hyder, Richmond, 1986—; adj. prof. J. Sargeant Reynolds Community Coll., Richmond, 1983—. Mem. Richmond Jaycees (legal counsel 1980-81, bd. dirs. 1981-82). Criminal, Personal injury. Office: Boone Beale Cosby & Hyder 11 S 12th St Suite 500 Richmond VA 23219

BEALL, INGRID LILLEHEI, lawyer; b. Cedar Falls, Iowa, June 18, 1926; d. Ingebrigt Larsen and Olive (Allison) Lillehei; m. George Brooke Beall, Dec. 21, 1951 (div. 1971). A.B., U. Chgo., 1945, M.A., 1948, J.D., 1956. Bar: Ill. 1956. Assoc. firm McDermott, Will & Emery, Chgo., 1956-58, Baker & McKenzie, Chgo., 1958-61; ptnr. Baker & McKenzie, Chgo., Brussels and Paris, 1961—. Mem. ABA, Ill. Bar Assn., Chgo. Bar Assn., Internat. Fiscal Assn. Home: 175 Delaware St Chicago IL 60611 Office: Baker & McKenzie 2800 Prudential Plaza Chicago IL 60601

BEALL, KENNETH SUTTER, JR., lawyer; b. Evanston, Ill., Aug. 9, 1938; s. Kenneth Sutter and Helen Cantlon (Koenig) B.; m. Blair Hamilton Bissett, May 25, 1975; children—Kevina Anne, Hunter Bissett, Baret Bissett. B.A., Washington and Lee U., 1961, LL.B., 1963. Bar: Fla. 1964. With Gunster, Yoakley, Criser & Stewart, P.A., Palm Beach, Fla., 1964—, ptnr., 1970—. Bd. dirs. Palm Beach Habilitation Center, The Whitehall Found.; chmn. Palm Beach County Environ. Control Hearing Bd., 1970—. Served with USMCR, 1963-68. Mem. Fla. Bar (recipient Pres. Pro Bono Service award 1982), Palm Beach County Bar Assn., ABA, Fed. Bar Assn. (pres. Palm Beach County chpt. 1981). Democrat. Roman Catholic. Clubs: Bath and Tennis, Everglades, Saulfish (Palm Beach). Contracts commercial, General corporate, Probate. Office: 777 S Flagler Dr Suite 500 West Palm Beach FL 33901-6194

BEAM, C. ARLEN, judge; b. Stapleton, Nebr., Jan. 14, 1930; s. Clarence Wilson and Cecile Mary (Harvey) B.; m. Betty Lou Fletcher, July 22, 1951; children—Randal, James, Thomas, Bradley, Gregory. B.S., U. Nebr., 1951, J.D., 1965. Feature writer Nebr. Farmer Mag., Lincoln, 1951; with sales dept. Steckley Seed Co., Mount Sterling, Ill., 1954-58, advt. mgr., 1958-63; ptnr. Knudsen, Berkheimer, Beam, et al, Lincoln, 1965-82; judge U.S. Dist. Ct. Nebr., Omaha, 1982-86, chief judge, 1986—; mem. com. on lawyer discipline Nebr. Supreme Ct., 1974-82; mem. Conf. Commrs. on Uniform State Laws, 1979—, chmn. Nebr. sect., 1980-82. Contbr. articles to profl. jours. Chmn., Nebr. Young Republicans, 1960-62; mem. Nebr. Rep. Central Com., 1970-78. Served to capt. U.S. Army, 1951-53, Korea. Regents scholar U. Nebr., Lincoln, 1947, Roscoe Pound scholar U. Nebr., Lincoln, 1964. Mem. ABA, Nebr. State Bar Assn. Lodges: Kiwanis, Masons. Judicial administration. Office: US Dist Ct PO Box 1297 DTS Omaha NE 68101

BEAM, ROBERT CHARLES, lawyer; b. Phila., Dec. 21, 1946; s. Thomas Joseph and Jeannette Hortense (Templin) B.; m. Maureen McCauley, Aug. 21, 1976.; children—Davis McCauley B., Morgan McCauley B. BS in Commerce and Engring. Scis., Drexel U., 1970; JD, Temple U., 1977. Bar: U.S. Patent Office 1976, Pa. 1977, U.S. Dist. Ct. (ea. dist.) Pa. 1977, N.Y. 1978, D.C. 1979, U.S. Ct. Customs and Patent Appeals 1980, U.S. Ct. Appeals (3d and fed. cirs.) 1982, N.J. 1983, U.S. Dist. Ct. N.J. 1983, Can. Patent Office 1985. Law clk. U.S. Dist. Ct., Phila., 1976-77; assoc. Firzpatrick, Cella, Harper & Scinto, N.Y.C., 1977-79; patent atty. Hercules Inc., Wilmington, Del., 1979-81, CPC Internat. Inc., Englewood Cliffs, N.J., 1981-83; patent counsel Congoleum Corp., Kearny, N.J., 1983-85, counsel and asst. gen. counsel, 1983-85; atty. Paul & Paul, Phila., 1985-86; sr. atty. Armstrong World Industries, Lancaster, Pa.. Mem. ABA, Phila. Bar Assn., D.C. Bar Assn., Phila. PatentLaw Assn., Am. Intellectual Property Law Assn. Patent, Trademark and copyright, Contracts commercial. Home: 78 HighGate Lane Blue Bell PA 19422 Office: Armstrong World Industries PO Box 3001 Lancaster PA 17604

BEAMAN, ANDREW VARNUM, lawyer; b. Jackson, Mich., Sept. 25, 1958; s. James Comstock and Catherine Kimball (Varnum) B. B.A., Simon's Rock Coll., 1978; J.D., U. Mich., 1981. Bar: Hawaii 1981, U.S. Dist. Ct. Hawaii 1981, U.S. Ct. Appeals (9th cir.) 1985. Summer assoc. Shea, Gould, Climenko & Casey, N.Y.C., 1979; law clk. Antitrust div., U.S. Justice Dept., Washington, 1980; atty., Chun, Kerr & Dodd, Honolulu, 1981—. Big Bro. Big Bros./Big Sisters of Honolulu, 1982—. Mem. ABA, Assn. Trial Lawyers Am., Hawaii Bar Assn. Federal civil litigation, State civil litigation. Office: Chun Kerr & Dodd 700 Bishop St Amfac Bldg Honolulu HI 96813

BEAMAN, GLEN EDWARD, lawyer; b. Ft. Worth, Sept. 20, 1958; s. Kenneth E. and Clara E. (Butts) B.; m. Darlene S. Beaman, Aug. 17, 1979. BBA, Baylor U., 1979, JD, 1981. Bar: Tex. 1981, U.S. Dist. Ct. (so. dist.) Tex. 1981. Sole practice Houston, 1981—. Rep. candidate U.S. Congress, Houston, 1984; panelist anti-dryg campaign Chem. People, Houston, 1984. Mem. ABA, Tex. Bar Assn. (vice chmn. lawyer referral com. 1984, chmn. 1985—), Houston Bar Assn., Harris County Bar Assn., Assn. Trial Lawyers Am., Tex. Trial Lawyers Assn. Republican. Mem. Ch. Christ. Personal injury. Home: 926 Saddlerock Houston TX 77088 Office: 14511 Falling Creek Dr Suite 406 Houston TX 77014

BEAN, BRUCE WINFIELD, lawyer; b. Albany, N.Y., Dec. 19, 1941; s. William Joseph and Ruth Elizabeth (Lafferty) B.; m. Barbara Hunting; children: Austin Bryant, Ashley Elizabeth. AB, Brown U., 1964; JD, Columbia U., 1972. Bar: N.Y. 1973, Calif. 1981. Law clk. to judge U.S. Ct. Appeals (2d cir.), 1972-73; assoc. Simpson Thacher & Bartlett, N.Y.C., 1973-76, Patterson, Belknap, Webb & Tyler, N.Y.C., 1976-80; counsel fin. and planning Atlantic Richfield, Los Angeles, 1980-85; v.p., gen. counsel The Home Group Inc., N.Y.C., 1985—; bd. dirs. 5th Generation Computer Corp., N.Y.C., Cole, Haan, Yarmouth, Maine. Served to col. USAFR, 1964-86, Vietnam. Mem. N.Y. State Bar Assn. (chmn. spl. com. on mil. and veterans affairs). General corporate, Banking, Securities. Office: The Home Group Inc. 59 Maiden Ln 28th Floor New York NY 10038-4548

BEANE, FRANK LLEWELLYN, lawyer; b. Canton, Ohio, Feb. 17, 1943; s. Frank Clarence and Lillian Ruth (Powell) B.; m. Patricia Jean Johnson, Sept. 16, 1967; children—Frank Clarence II, Adam Tyler. B.A., Central State U., Wilberforce, Ohio, 1965; J.D., U. Toledo, 1972. Bar: Ohio 1973, U.S. Dist. Ct. (no. dist.) Ohio 1973, U.S. Ct. Appeals (6th cir.) 1973. Asst. prosecutor Canton Police, 1973-74; pub. defender U.S. Dist. Ct. (no. dist.) Ohio, Cleve., 1974-81; assoc. Matecheck, Ferrero, and Stefanko, Massillon, Ohio, 1981—. Bd. dirs. Urban League, Massillon, 1981—, Boy's Club, Massillon, 1984—. Republican. Criminal. Home: 1134 3d St SE Massillon OH 44646 Office: Matecheck Ferrero and Stefanko 46 Federal Ave NW Massillon OH 44646

BEANE, JERRY LYNN, lawyer; b. Winnsboro, Tex., Mar. 3, 1944; s. Von Rhea and Charlene (Hawkins) B.; children from previous marriage—Lucynda, Todd. B.A., Baylor U., 1965, J.D., 1967. Bar: Tex. 1967, U.S. Dist. Ct. (no. dist.) Tex. 1968, U.S. Dist. Ct. (ea. dist.) Tex. 1972, U.S. Dist. Ct. (so. dist.) Ga. 1971, U.S. Ct. Appeals (5th cir.) 1970, U.S. Ct. Appeals (11th cir.) 1982, U.S. Ct. Appeals (10th cir.) 1979, U.S. Supreme Ct. 1972. Assoc. Strasburger & Price, Dallas, 1967-73, ptnr., 1974—. Mem. Dallas Commn. on Children and Youth, 1977-78, Dallas County Health Com., 1978. Mem. Dallas Assn. Young Lawyers (pres. 1973, chmn. continuing legal edn. com. 1979, chmn. bar activities com. 1980), ABA, Baylor Ex-Editors Assn., Baylor Law Sch. Alumni Assn., Tex. Bar Assn. Baptist. Clubs: City, DAC Country. Contbr. articles to profl. jours. Editor in chief Baylor Law Rev. 1967. Federal civil litigation, Antitrust, State civil litigation. Address: 4300 InterFirst Plaza 901 Main St Dallas TX 75202

BEAR, DINAH, lawyer; b. Lynnwood, Calif., Oct. 22, 1951; d. Henry Louis and Betty Jean (Isenhart) B. BJ, U. Mo., 1974; JD, McGeorge Sch. Law, 1977. Bar: Calif. 1978, D.C. 1981, U.S. Supreme Ct. 1982. Dep. gen. counsel Council on Environ. Quality, Washington, 1981-83, gen. counsel, 1983—. Staff asst. Dems. for Ronald Reagan, Arlington, Va., 1980. Recipient Am. Jurisprudence award Bancroft Whitney Co., 1975. Mem. ABA, D.C. Bar Assn. (environ. energy and natural resource sect. 1986—). Republican. Jewish. Avocation: gardening. Environment. Office: Council on Environ Quality 722 Jackson Pl NW Washington DC 20503

BEAR, HENRY LOUIS, lawyer; b. Kansas City, Kans.; s. Max and May (Kagon) B.; m. Betty Jean Isenhart, Jan. 4, 1951; 1 dau., Dinah. J.D., U. Mo., 1939. Bar: Mo. 1939, Calif. 1949, U.S. Dist. Ct. (so. dist.) Calif. 1949, U.S. Supreme Ct. 1959. Assoc., O'Hern & O'Hern, Kansas City, Mo., 1939-42; ptnr. Bear, Kotob, Ruby & Gross, and predecessors, Downey, Calif., 1949—; sec., dir. Pyrotronics Corp.; dir. Bank of Irvine. Chmn. Midland dist. council Boy Scouts Am., 1954; active Community Chest, Lynwood, Calif. Served to lt. USAF, 1942-46. Named Lynwood Man of Yr. 1952. Fellow Am. Coll. Probate Counsel; mem. Mo. Bar Assn., Calif. Bar Assn., Los Angeles County Bar Assn., Calif. Trial Lawyers Assn. Clubs: Rotary (Downey); Exec. Dinner (Pres. Lynwood, Calif.); Elks. Author: California Law of Corporations, Partnerships and Associations, 1970. Banking, General corporate, Probate. Office: PO Box 747 Downey CA 90241

BEARAK, COREY B(ECKER), lawyer; b. Forest Hills, N.Y., Oct. 7, 1955; s. Stephen Irwin Bearak and Phyllis (Stone) Stark; m. Rachelle Pamela Confino, Mar. 24, 1985; 1 child: Jonathan Marc. BA in Polit. Sci., Hofstra U., 1977, JD, 1981. Bar: N.Y. 1982. Asst. to sec. of state N.Y. State, Albany and N.Y.C., 1978; sole practice Queens, N.Y., 1982—. Mem. Community Planning Bd. #13, Queens and N.Y.C., 1980—, N.Y. State Dems., 1986—; alt. del. Dem. Nat. Convention, San Francisco, 1984, Queens Jewish Community Council, 1978—, Northeast Queens Jewish Community Council; v.p. Greater N.Y. Raoul Wallenberg Com., N.Y.C., 1985—, trustee, 1983-84; assoc. v.p. Temple Sholom, Floral Park, 1986—; trustee Lost Community Civic Assn., Floral Park and Hyde Park; 1st v.p. Queens County Line Dem. Assn., Glen Oaks, N.Y., 1980-82, pres. 1982-84, exec. sec. 1985—; counsel, chief of staff to N.Y.C. councilman Sheldon S. Leffler, 1982—. Recipient Cert. of Merit Boy Scouts Am., 1983; named one of Outstanding Young Men Am., 1985. Mem. ABA (state and local govt. law sect.), N.Y. State Bar Assn., Queens Bar Assn. (assoc. editor jour. 1983—, real property com.), N.Y. County Lawyers Assn. (legis. com., real property com.), Brandeis Assn. Avocations: family, friends, softball, music, football. Legislative, Administrative and regulatory, Environment. Home: 82-35 251st St Bellerose NY 11426 Office: Councilman Sheldon S Leffler 205-07 Hillside Ave Hollis NY 11423

BEARD, CHARLES RICHARD, lawyer; b. St. Louis, July 30, 1929; s. John William and Nellie Marie (Trullinger) B.; m. Phyllis James Church, Dec. 29, 1956; children: Carolyn Emily, Charles Richard, Elizabeth Church. BA, Washington U., St. Louis, 1950, JD, 1955. Bar: Mo. 1955, U.S. Ct. Mil. Appeals 1963, U.S. Supreme Ct. 1963. With various law firms St. Louis, 1955-68; counsel, asst. sec. The May Dept. Stores Co., St. Louis, 1968—. Chmn. parks and recreation commn. City of Clayton, Mo., 1970-71; liaison officer to admissions office U.S. Mil. Acad., West Point, N.Y., 1976-80. Served as col. USAR, 1975-80. Mem. Bar Assn. Met. St. Louis (chmn. probate com. 1965, admissions com. 1969, pub. contracts com. 1978), Am. Retail Fedn. (credit com.), Merchants Research Council (bd. dirs. 1969—), Nat. Retail Merchants Assn. (lawyers com., legis. steering com. credit mgmt. div.), Ill. Retail Merchants Assn., Mo. Retail Merchants Assn., Mo. C. of C. (taxation and fiscal affairs council), Phi Delta Phi, Kappa Sigma. Republican. Presbyterian. Club: Toastmasters (award 1973). Lodges: Masons, Shriners. General corporate, Consumer commercial, Federal civil litigation. Home: 440 Edgewood Dr Clayton MO 63105 Office: The May Dept Stores Co 611 Olive St Saint Louis MO 63101

BEARD, DAVID BENJAMIN, lawyer; b. Cleve., Nov. 4, 1954; s. John Samuel and Clare (Sloniker) B.; m. Katherine Lewis, Dec. 31, 1977; children: Meghan Lewis, Michael Benjamin, Peter Nicholas. BA with high honors, U. Cin., 1977; JD, Case Western Res. U., 1982. Bar: Ohio 1982, U.S. Dist. Ct. (no. dist.) Ohio 1982. Assoc. Calfee, Halter & Griswold, Cleve., 1982-87; assoc. prof. law U. Idaho, 1987—. Pres. Coventry Youth Ctr., Cleveland Heights, Ohio, 1985-87, bd. trustees, 1983-87. Recipient Soc. Benchers award, Guardian Title award Guardian Title Ins. Co., 1982. Mem. ABA, Ohio Bar Assn., Cleve. Bar Assn., Order of Coif, Phi Beta Kappa. Republican. Lutheran. Contracts commercial, Bankruptcy. Office: U Idaho Coll of Law Moscow ID 83843

BEARD, GLENDA RAINWATER, lawyer; b. Lebanon, Ky., July 23, 1947; d. Ernest and Agnes M. (Perkins) Rainwater; m. Kenneth P. Beard, Feb. 14, 1971; 1 child, Allison E. BS, U. Ky., 1968; JD, U. Louisville, 1974. Bar: Ky. 1974, U.S. Dist. Ct. (ea. dist.) Ky. 1975, U.S. Ct. Appeals (6th cir.) 1975, N.C. 1982, Tex. 1982, U.S. Dist. Ct. (no. dist.) Tex. 1983, U.S. Dist. Ct. (so. dist.) Tex. 1984. Assoc. Tarrant, Combs & Bullitt, Louisville, 1974-76; exec. officer Ky. Atty. Gen.'s Office, Frankfort, 1976-80; atty. Southeast region Gen. Telephone Co., Durham, N.C., 1980-82; atty. Southwest region Gen. Telephone Co., San Angelo, Tex., 1982-84; assoc. gen. counsel Southwest region Gen. Telephone Co., Irving, Tex., 1984—. Public utilities, Administrative and regulatory. Home: 500 Shalamar Pl Irving TX 75061 Office: Gen Telephone Co Southwest 290 E Carpenter Freeway Irving TX 75015-2013

BEARD, JANE ANN VARNER, lawyer; b. Wichita, Kans., Oct. 11, 1952; d. Sterling Verl and Paula Jean (Kennedy) Varner; m. Russell Creighton Beard, Jan. 25, 1986. BS in Edn., Abilene Christian U., 1974; JD, U. Tex., 1977. Bar: Tex. 1977, U.S. Dist. Ct. (no. dist.) Tex. 1977, U.S. Ct. Appeals (5th and 11th cirs.) 1981. Assoc. Rhodes, Doscher, Chalk & Heatherly, Abilene, Tex., 1977-78, Wagstaff, Harrell, Alvis, Erwin, Stubbeman & Baker, Abilene, 1978-79; ptnr. Ghandon, Erwin, Baker, Choate & Elmore, Abilene, 1979-80, McMahon, Smart, Surovik, Suttle, Buhrmann & Cobb, Abilene, 1980—. Pres. Taylor County Red Cross, Abilene, 1981-83; trustee Community Found., Abilene, 1985—, Hendrick Med. Ctr. Found., Abilene, 1985—, West Tex. Rehabilitation, Abilene, 1985—. Named Outstanding Young Woman of Tex., Tex. Jaycees, 1983. Mem. Tex. Bar Assn., Abilene Bar Assn. (sec., treas. 1980-81), Tex. Young Lawyers Assn. (bd. dirs. 1983-85, Outstanding Young Lawyer Tex. 1986, Outstanding Dir. 1985), Abilene Young Lawyers Assn. (pres. 1984-85, Outstanding Young Lawyer 1986), Nat. Health Lawyers, Am. Acad. Hosp. Attys., Tex. Council Sch. Bd. Attys., Am. Judicature Soc. Republican. Mem. Ch. of Christ. Avocations: travel, raquetball. Health, General corporate, Probate. Office: McMahon & Law Firm PO Box 3679 Abilene TX 79604

BEARD, RONALD STRATTON, lawyer; b. Flushing, N.Y., Feb. 13, 1939; s. Charles Henry and Ethel Mary (Stratton) B.; m. Karen Asselta, June 24, 1961; children: D. Karen, Jonathan D., Dana K. BA, Denison U., 1961; LLB, Yale U., 1964. Bar: Calif. 1975, U.S. Ct. Appeals (9th cir.) 1980, U.S. Dist. Ct. (cen. dist.) Calif. 1964. Ptnr. Gibson, Dunn & Crutcher, Los Angeles, 1964—; chmn. Interac Corp., Woodland Hills, Calif., 1985—. Trustee Denison U., Granville, Ohio, 1975—. Mem. ABA, Calif. Bar Assn., Los Angeles Bar Assn., Beverly Hills Bar Assn. (chmn. internat. law com. 1976). Avocations: sports, travel. General corporate, Private international, Securities. Home: 14904 Corona del Mar Pacific Palisades CA 90272 Office: Gibson Dunn & Crutcher 333 S Grand Ave Los Angeles CA 90071

BEARG, MARTIN LEE, lawyer; b. N.Y., Mar. 15, 1952; s. Arnold and Esther M. Bearg; m. Deborah Rae Rothfeld, June 6, 1976; children: Avia Hannah, Isaac Yochanan Noam. BA in Polit. Sci., Am. U., 1973; M in Pub. Adminstrn., Syracuse U., 1974, JD, 1977; LLM in Taxation, Villanova U., 1985. Bar: N.J. 1977, U.S. Dist. Ct. N.J. 1977, Fla. 1978, U.S. Tax Ct., U.S. Supreme Ct. 1980, U.S. Ct. Claims 1981, N.Y. 1982. Law clk. to presiding judge Superior Ct. N.J., 1977-78; asst. counsel Hudson County, Jersey City, 1978-80; sole practice Summit, N.J., 1980-84, 86—; counsel tax dept. Leonard G. Birnbaum & Co., Summit, 1980-84; sr. assoc. Herbert M. Gannet, Newark, 1984-85, Bendit, Weinstock & Sharbaugh P.A., West Orange, N.J., 1985-86; sole practice Livingston, N.J., 1986—; adj. lectr. St. Peter's Coll., Jersey City; lectr. Inst. Paralegal Studies, Linden, N.J.; writer Matthew Bender & Co. Contbr. articles to profl. jours.; bd. editors Jour. of Taxation. Asst. treas. Juvenille Diabetes Found., No. Jersey; mem. steering com. New Leadership Campaign, Israel Bonds; bd. dirs. Bethel Menorah Golden Rule Found., Congregation Oheb Shalom, South Orange, N.J. Mem. ABA, N.J. Bar Assn., Fla. Bar Assn., Essex County Bar Assn., Pi Sigma Alpha. Lodge: Masons. Corporate taxation, Estate taxation, Personal income taxation. Office: 154 S Livingston Ave Suite 207 Livingston NJ 07039

BEASLEY, FREDERICK ALEXANDER, lawyer; b. Salley, S.C., July 23, 1943; s. Percy Eugene and Amelia (Schroder) B.; m. Susan Mobley McGarity, Aug. 10, 1974; children—Sarah Elizabeth, Amelia Schroder. A.B., Duke U., 1965; J.D., U. S.C., 1970. Bar: S.C. 1970, Ga. 1971, U.S. Dist. Ct. (no. dist.) Ga. 1972, U.S. Ct. Appeals (5th cir.) 1974, U.S. Dist. Ct. S.C. 1981, U.S. Ct. Appeals (4th cir.) 1981, U.S. Ct. Appeals (11th cir.) 1982. Atty., trust examiner Fed. Res. Bank, Atlanta, 1970-72; assoc. Jones & Somers, Atlanta, 1972-74; ptnr. Somers & Altenbach, Atlanta, 1974-75; trust officer So. Bank & Trust Co., Columbia and Orangeburg, S.C., 1975-81; sole practice, Aiken, S.C., 1981-85; master in equity Aiken County, 1981-85; ptnr. Williams, Johnson, Buchanan & Beasley, Aiken, 1986—. Bd. dirs. Childrens Bur. S.C., Columbia, 1977-81, vice chmn., 1978; bd. dirs. Child Devel. Ctr., Aiken, 1981-84, Tri Devel. Ctr., Aiken, 1984-86. Served to lt. USN, 1965-67. Mem. S.C. Bar Assn. (chmn. 1987—, sec. corps., banking and securities law sect.), Aiken County Bar Assn. (pres. 1987—), Am. Bus. Club Aiken, Phi Delta Phi, Sigma Chi. Episcopalian. Club: Fermata (Aiken). Lodge: Kiwanis. General practice, Real property, Estate planning. Home: 118 Surrey Circle Aiken SC 29801 Office: 526 Richland Ave W PO Box 463 Aiken SC 29801

BEASLEY, JAMES EDWIN, lawyer; b. Buffalo, July 2, 1926; s. James Edwin and Margaret Ann (Patterson) B.; m. Helen Mary, Jan. 1, 1958 (div.); children—Pamela Jane, Kimberly Ann, James Edwin. B.S., Temple U., 1953, J.D., 1956. Bar: Pa. 1956. Law clk. to judge U.S. Dist. Ct. Ea. Dist. Pa., Phila., 1954-56; mem. Beasley, Hewson, Casey, Colleran, Erbstein & Thistle, 1966—; instr. law Temple U., 1979-81; mem. Philadelphia County Bd. Law Examiners; permanent del. 3d Cir. Jud. Conf.; chmn. com. standard jury instrns. Pa. Supreme Ct. Author: Products Liability and Unreasonably Dangerous Doctrine; contbr. articles to legal jours. Served with USN, 1943-45, USAR, 1951-57; ETO, PTO. Mem. Am. Judicature Soc., ABA, Pa. Bar Assn., Phila. Bar Assn., Fed. Bar Assn., Am. Law Inst., Phila. Trial Lawyers Assn. (pres. 1970-71), Pa. Trial Lawyers Assn. (pres. 1969-70), Aircraft Owners and Pilots Assn., Inner Circle of Advocates, Am. Trial Lawyers Assn., Phila. Trial Lawyers Assn. (Justice Michael Musmanno award), Am. Bd. Profl. Liability Attys., Temple U. Gen. Alumni Assn. (cert. of honor), Pa. Soc. Republican. Episcopalian. Clubs: Masons, Union League. Personal injury, Libel. Office: 21 S 12th St Philadelphia PA 19107

BEASLEY, NORMA LEA, lawyer, title insurance and real estate executive; b. Springdale, Ark., Sept. 6, 1931; d. Alpha F. and Minnie Lee (Parham) B. LLB, U. Ark., 1953, BS in law, 1960; postgrad. So. Meth. U., 1958-60. Bar: Ark. 1953, Tex. 1958. With legal dept. Mid-Continent Petroleum Corp., Tulsa, 1953; with claims dept. Res. Life Ins. Co., Dallas, 1955-56; chief exec. legal dept. Tex. Title Co., 1956-61; sole practice, Dallas, 1958—; gen. counsel, exec. v.p. Fidelity Title Co., Dallas, 1961-68; ptnr. B&W Investments, Dallas, 1962—; chief exec. officer, chmn. bd. Trinity Abstract & Title Co., Waxahachie, Tex., 1966—; owner, mgr. Hillcrest office Hexter-Fair Title Co., Dallas, 1968-79; chmn. bd., chief exec. officer Safeco Land Title of Dallas, 1979—, Safeco Land Title of Kaufman, Safeco Land Title of Rockwall, N. Tex. Title of Hunt, Safeco Land Title of Collin, Safeco Land Title of Denton, Safeco Land Title of Tarrant County; vice chmn. bd. Tex. Am. Bank-Prestonwood; mem. adv. bd. Tex. Nat. Bank, Dallas; dir. Coming Attractions, Inc., Jami, M.D. Labs. and Verarex Med. Corp.; co-ptnr. B P W Investments; chmn. bd., chief exec. officer Flame/Pruf, Inc. Campaign helper Multiple Sclerosis Soc., Dallas, 1967; lectr. to various colls. and organizations; charter mem. Charter " 100" Club of Dallas; Marie Mivelaz Scholarship fund founder at So. Meth. U.; bd. dirs. Dallas Chpt. Juvenile Diabetes Found. Internat.; founder Norma Lea Beasley endowed scholarship U. Ark. Mem. Comml. Real Estate Women (charter), Ark. Bar Assn., Nat. Women's Econ. Alliance (bd. govs.), Tex. Bar Assn., Dallas County Jr. Bar Assn., Bus. and Profl. Women's Club, Kappa Beta Phi (Eta Sigma Phi chpt.). Republican. Baptist. Clubs: Altrusa (treas. 1964-65), Bent Tree Country (Dallas). Contbg. author: Organizational Behavior, Understanding and Managing Pople at Work, America's New Women Entrepreneurs. Real property, Banking, General corporate. Office: Safeco Land Title of Dallas 8080 N Central Expressway Suite 120 Dallas TX 75206

BEASLEY, OSCAR HOMER, lawyer; b. Denver, Sept. 30, 1925. BA, U. Omaha, 1949; JD, U. Iowa, 1950. Bar: Iowa 1949, N. Mex., 1952, Calif. 1964, Hawaii 1982. Assoc. Joseph L. Smith, Albuquerque, 1955-59; ptnr. Ertz & Beasley, Albuquerque, 1959-62, Beasley & Colberg, Albuquerque, 1962-64; atty. 1st Am. Title Ins. Co., Santa Ana, Calif., 1964-70, sr. v.p., sr. title counsel, 1970—; mem. N.Mex. Ho. of Reps., 1958-62; dir. Title Guaranty of Wyo.; instr. Western State U. Coll. Law, Fullerton, Calif., 1970—, also mem. adv. bd. Mem. ABA, Calif. Bar Assn., Orange County Bar Assn., Los Angeles County Bar Assn., N. Mex. Bar Assn., Iowa Bar Assn., Am. Coll. Real Estate Lawyers, Assn. Trial Lawyers Am., Am. Land Title Assn. (chmn. title ins. forms com.). Real property. Home: 13432 Eton Place Santa Ana CA 92705 Office: First Am Title Ins Co 114 E Fifth St Santa Ana CA 92701

BEASLEY, REBECCA OCTAVIA, lawyer; b. Wilmington, Del., Dec. 10, 1954; d. John Knox and Octavia (Moses) B.; m. Michael Curtis Malone, Apr. 28, 1984. BA, Duke U., 1976; JD, Boston U., 1979. Bar: Tex. 1979, U.S. Dist. Ct. (no. dist.) Tex. 1979. Assoc. Denton & Davis, Dallas, 1979-83, Spradley, Rushing & Davis, Dallas, 1983-84; div. counsel Nat. Gypsum Co., Dallas, 1984—. Mem. Tex. Bar Assn., Dallas County Bar Assn. General corporate. Office: Nat Gypsum Co 4500 Lincoln Plaza Dallas TX 75201

BEASLEY, THOMAS TARRY, II, lawyer, consultant; b. Memphis, Aug. 26, 1939; s. Houston Dixon and Urcile (Powell) B.; m. Janet Welch, June 28, 1964; children: Janet Lee, Thomas Tarry III. BS, U. Tenn., 1961; LLB, So. Law U., 1964; BL, Memphis State U., 1966. Asst. mgr. br. Union Planters Nat. Bank, Memphis, 1961-67; trust officer 1st Nat Bank, Memphis, 1967-69; dir. franchise sales Holiday Inns, Inc., Memphis, 1969-76; assoc. Neely, Green, Fargarson et al, Memphis, 1976-84; v.p., gen. counsel J.H. Shoemaker & Co., Memphis, 1984-86; sole practice Memphis, 1984—. Pres. Balmoral Civic Assn., Memphis, 1968-74; bd. dirs. YMCA, Memphis, 1967; chmn. bd. dirs. Steinberg Handicap Ministries, Memphis, 1979—; trustee Evangelical Christian Sch., Memphis, 1978—. Mem. Tenn. Bar Assn., Memphis Shelby County Bar Assn., SCV (commr. 1964-72). Avocations: real estate devel., skiing, camping, travel, photography. General practice, General corporate, Probate. Home: 5978 McQueen Cove Memphis TN 38119

BEATIE, RUSSEL HARRISON, JR., lawyer; b. Lawrence, Kans., Jan. 20, 1938; s. Russel Harrison and Mary Louise (Zimmerman) B.; children—Benjamin Wilson Parkhill, Amy Wilder. B.A. cum laude, Princeton U., 1959, LL.B. cum laude Columbia U., 1964. Bar: N.Y., U.S. Dist. Ct. (so. and ea. dists.) N.Y., U.S. Ct. Appeals (2d cir.), U.S. Supreme Ct. Assoc., Dewey, Ballantine, Bushby, Palmer & Wood, N.Y.C., 1964-66, 68-72; assoc. Rogers & Wells, 1966-68; mem. Dewey Ballantine, 1972-83; sole practice, 1983—. Served to 1st lt., arty. U.S. Army, 1959-61. Mem. Assn. Bar City N.Y. Republican. Christian Scientist. Clubs: Union, University, Verbank Hunting and Fishing. Author: Road to Manassas—The Growth of Union Command in the Eastern Theatre from the Fall of Fort Sumter to the First Battle of Bull Run, 1961. Federal civil litigation, State civil litigation. Office: 10 E 53d St Suite 3200 New York NY 10005

BEATON, NEAL N., lawyer; b. N.Y.C., Feb. 11, 1953; s. Daniel and Shirley Ruth (Sobelman) B.; m. Ann Renee Rosovsky, June 6, 1976; children: Eric Barry, Gregory David. AB magna cum laude, Harvard U., 1975, JD cum laude, 1978. Bar: N.Y. 1979, U.S. Dist. Ct. (so. and ea. dists.) N.Y. 1979. Assoc. Gilbert Segall & Young, N.Y.C., 1978-84, ptnr., 1985—. Mem. ABA, Internat. Bar Assn., Assn. Bar City N.Y. General corporate, Private international, Trademark and copyright. Home: 250 E 87th St Apt 14 F New York NY 10128 Office: Gilbert Segall & Young 430 Park Ave New York NY 10022

BEATTIE, CHARLES ROBERT, III, lawyer; b. Red Wing, Minn., Aug. 25, 1948; s. Charles Robert Jr. and Dorothy Catherine (Shepherd) B.; m. Camilla Lawther Foot, Aug. 26, 1972; children: Virginia, Anne, Charles. BA with honors, U. Mich., 1970; JD, Yale U., 1973. Bar: Minn. 1973, U.S. Dist. Ct. Minn. 1973, U.S. Ct. Appeals (8th cir.) 1975. Assoc. Doherty, Rumble & Butler, St. Paul, 1973-78; ptnr. Doherty, Rumble & Butler, St. Paul and Mpls., 1978—; lectr. on partnerships and banking, 1983-85. Contbr. articles on ltd. partnerships to profl. jours., 1983-85. Mem. Citizens League, St. Paul and Mpls., 1979—; officer Leadership St. Paul, 1981—; bd. dirs. Civic Symphony Assn., 1976-80, St. John the Evangelist Episc. Ch., St. Paul, officer, 1981—. Mem. ABA, Minn. Bar Assn. (corp. banking and bus. law sects.). Club: Athletic (St. Paul). Avocations: sailing, skiing, tennis. Contracts commercial, Banking, Securities. Office: Doherty Rumble & Butler PA 3750 IDS Tower Minneapolis MN 55402

BEATTIE, DONALD GILBERT, lawyer; b. Des Moines, Nov. 30, 1947; s. Max and Rowena Jean (Gilbert) B.; m. Kristi Louise Nellans, June 6, 1975; children: Brett Joseph, Ryan Troy, Adam Ross. BA, Simpson Coll., 1970; JD, Drake U., 1977. Bar: Iowa 1977, U.S. Dist. Ct. (no. and so. dist.) Iowa 1977. Ptnr. Skinner, Beattie & Wilson P.C., Altoona, Iowa, 1975—. City atty. Runnells, Iowa, 1977—. Mem. Am. Trial Lawyers Assn., Assn. of Trial Lawyers of Iowa, Iowa Bar Assn., Polk County Bar Assn., Drake Law Rev. Alumni Assn. (bd. dirs.), Am. Legion, Order of Coif. Democrat. Lodge: Masons (master 1980). Personal injury, State civil litigation, Federal civil litigation.

BEATTIE, RICHARD IRWIN, lawyer; b. N.Y.C., Mar. 24, 1939; s. Richard I. Beattie and Ruth (Fisher) McCarthy; m. Diana Lewis, Dec. 21, 1963; children: Lisa C., Nina M. BA, Dartmouth Coll., 1961; LLB, U. Pa., 1968. Bar: N.Y. 1969, U.S. Dist. Ct. (so. and ea. dists.) N.Y. 1972, U.S. Ct. Appeals (2d cir.) 1975, U.S. Ct. Appeals (D.C. cir.) 1977, U.S. Supreme Ct. 1978, U.S. Ct. Appeals (5th cir.) 1979. Assoc. Simpson, Thacher & Bartlett, N.Y.C., 1968-75, ptnr., 1975-77, 80—; dep. gen. counsel U.S. Dept. Health, Edn. and Welfare, Washington, 1977-78, exec. asst. to sec., 1978-79, gen. counsel, 1979; spl. counsel to sec., dir. transition U.S. Dept. Edn., Washington, 1980; chmn. Commn. Reorganization of Human Resources Adminstrn., N.Y.C., 1984-85, Commn. on Spl. Edn., N.Y.C., 1984-85; mem. Council Fgn. Relations, N.Y.C. Bd. dirs. Human Resources Ctr., Albertson, N.Y., 1982—, WNET/Channel 13, N.Y.C., 1983—, Natural Resources Def. Counsel, N.Y.C., 1984-86, Bd. Edn., N.Y.C. Served to capt. USMC, 1961-65. Avocations: skiing, mountain climbing, ballet. General corporate, Environment, Health. Office: Simpson Thacher & Bartlett One Battery Park Plaza New York NY 10004

BEATTIE, STEVEN MACK, lawyer; b. Boulder, Colo., Aug. 23, 1946. BA, Tufts U., 1968; JD, Colo. U., 1973. Bar: Colo. 1973, U.S. Dist. Ct. Colo. 1973, Ariz. 1974, U.S. Dist. Ct. Ariz. 1974. Atty. legal staff Tucson Gas and Electric, 1973-79; assoc. Waterfall, Economidis, Caldwell & Hanshaw, Tucson, 1979-82; ptnr. Larson & Beattie, Glenwood Springs, Colo., 1982—; counsel Colo. Mountain Coll., Glenwood Springs, 1982—; atty. Town of Silt, Colo., 1982—. Served with U.S. Army, 1969-71, Vietnam. Mem. ABA, Ariz. Bar Assn., Colo. Bar Assn., Colo. Trial Lawyers Assn. Methodist. Avocations: golf, river running, mountain activities. Contracts commercial, State civil litigation, Educational law. Home: 90 Tanager Dr Glenwood Springs CO 81601 Office: Larson & Beattie 201 Centennial St Suite 203 Glenwood Springs CO 81601

BEATTY, SAMUEL ALSTON, state justice; b. Tuscaloosa, Ala., Apr. 23, 1923; s. Eugene C. and Rosabelle (Horton) B.; m. Maude Applegate, Jan. 19, 1949; children: Rosa Beatty Lord, Eugene A. B.S. in Commerce and Bus. Adminstrn, U. Ala., 1948, J.D., 1953; LL.M., Columbia U., 1959, J.S.D., 1964. Bar: Ala. bar 1953. Pvt. practice Tuscaloosa, 1953-56; mem. faculty U. Ala. Law Sch., 1955-70, prof. law, 1963-70, asst. dean, 1959-63; vis. prof. law U. Cin. Law Sch., 1966-67; assoc. dir. Ala. Defender Project, 1967-70; dean, prof. law Mercer U. Law Sch., 1970-72, adj. prof., 1972-74; v.p., trust officer First Nat. Bank & Trust Co., Macon, Ga., 1972-74; asst. atty. gen., chief civil div. State of Ala., 1974; partner firm Henley & Beatty, Tuscaloosa, Northport, Ala., 1975-76; asso. justice Ala. Supreme Ct., 1976—; adj. prof. U. Ala. Grad. Sch., since 1975; speaker, lectr. in field. Contbr. legal jours. Served to maj. USAAF, 1942-45, PTO. Decorated Air medal with 9 oak leaf clusters. Mem. Am., Ala., Tuscaloosa County bar assns., Nat. Orgn. Legal Problems Edn., Farrah Order Jurisprudence, Order of Coif, Phi Alpha Delta. Democrat. Methodist. Jurisprudence. Address: Supreme Court 445 Dexter Ave PO Box 218 Montgomery AL 36130 *

BEATTY, WILLIAM GLENN, lawyer; b. Moline, Ill., July 13, 1953; s. Glenn Willard and Mary Frances (Karlson) B.; m. Carla Ann Busse, Feb. 25, 1978; children—Andrew Glenn, Mark William. B.A. cum laude, Augustana Coll., Rock Island, Ill., 1975; postgrad. Creighton U., 1975-76; J.D. with honors, Chgo.-Kent Coll. Law, 1978. Bar: Ill. 1978, U.S. Dist. Ct. (no. dist.) Ill. 1979, U.S. Ct. Appeals (7th cir.) 1979, U.S. Ct. Claims 1979. Assoc. Johnson, Cusack & Bell, Ltd., Chgo., 1978-84, ptnr., 1985—; asst. instr. Chgo.-Kent Coll. Law, 1978; lectr. in field. Mem ABA, Ill. Bar Assn., Chgo. Bar Assn., Ill. Def. Counsel, Trial Lawyers Club Chgo., Def. Research Inst. Republican. Roman Catholic. Personal injury, State civil litigation, Insurance. Office: Johnson Cusack & Bell Ltd 211 W Wacker Dr Chicago IL 60606

BEATTY, WILLIAM LOUIS, federal judge; b. Mendota, Ill., Sept. 4, 1925; s. Raphael H. and Teresa A. (Collins) B.; m. Dorothy Jeanne Starnes, June 12, 1948; children: William S., Steven M., Thomas D., Mary C. Student, Washington U., St. Louis, 1945-47; LL.B., St. Louis U., 1950. Bar: Ill. 1950. Gen. practice law Granite City, 1950-68; circuit judge 3d Jud. Circuit Ill., 1968-79; U.S. dist. judge So. Dist. Ill., 1979—. Served with AUS, 1943-45. Mem. Am. Bar Assn., Ill. Bar Assn., Madison County Bar Assn., Tri-City Bar Assn. Roman Catholic. Jurisprudence. Office: U S Dist Ct 501 Belle St Alton IL 62002

BEAUCHAMP, GARY FAY, lawyer; b. Waco, Tex., Oct. 21, 1951; s. Fay Harry and Mary Elva (Gaunt) B. BBA, So. Meth. U., 1975; JD, South Tex. Coll. Law, 1980. Bar: Tex. 1980, U.S.Dist. Ct (so. dist.) Tex. 1980, U.S. Supreme Ct. 1983. Sole practice The Woodlands, Tex., 1980—. Avocation: scuba diving. Personal injury, Criminal, General practice. Office: 1776 Woodstoad Ct #111 Woodlands TX 77380

BEAUCHAMP, JAMES HARRY, lawyer; b. Stillwater, Okla., Sept. 19, 1942; s. Raymond O. and Helen Ruth (Pennington) B.; m. Frances Reams, Sept. 1, 1943; children—Gregory, Colleen, John. B.S., Okla. State U., 1965; J.D., Tulane U., 1968. Bar: Ohio 1968, U.S. Supreme Ct. 1976, Okla. 1978, U.S. Dist. Ct. (we. dist.) Okla. 1971, U.S. Dist. Ct. (so. dist.) Ohio, U.S. Ct. Appeals (6th cir.) 1974, U.S. Ct. Appeals (10th cir.) 1978, U.S. Dist. Ct. (no. dist.) Okla. 1980, U.S. Dist. Ct. (ea. dist.) Okla., 1984, U.S. Tax Ct. Assoc., Bieser, Greer & Landis, Dayton, Ohio, 1971-77, Miller, Dollarhide & Beauchamp, 1978-79; spl. counsel Profl. Investors Corp., 1980-81; sole practice, Tulsa, 1981—. Served to capt. U.S. Army, 1969-70. Recipient Am. Jurisprudence award, 1977. Mem. Okla. Bar Assn., Tulsa Bar Assn., ABA. Author: What if Karen Quinlan Had Lived in Oklahoma? Office: Suite 900 4500 S Garnett Tulsa OK 74145

BEAUTYMAN, MICHAEL JOHN, lawyer; b. Klagenfurt, Austria, Sept. 30, 1946; came to U.S., 1951; s. William and Daphne (Hawkes) B.; m. Megan Sanford, Sept. 8, 1985. BA in English, Trinity Coll., Hartford, Conn., 1969; JD, U. Va., 1975. Bar: Mass. 1975, U.S. Dist. Ct. Mass. 1976, U.S. Ct. Appeals (1st cir.) 1976, Pa. 1985. Assoc. Ropes & Gray, Boston, 1975-81; chmn. health law group Drinker, Biddle & Reath, Phila., 1985—; bd. dirs. Limelight Prodns., Stockbridge, Mass., Sports Dynamic Labs., Cambridge, Mass., Computer Aided Communications, Waltham, Mass. Contbr. articles to profl. jours. Bd. dirs. Christ Ch. Hosp., Kearsley Nursing Home, Phila. Eastern Coll. Athletic Conf. scholar, Trinity Coll. Mem. ABA, Am. Acad. Hosp. Attys., Nat. Health Lawyers Assn., Mass. Bar Assn. (health law com.), Boston Bar Assn. (health law com.), Phila. Bar Assn. (health law com.), Pa. Soc. Hosp. Attys., Order of Coif. Avocations: tennis, squash, skiing. Health. Office: Drinker Biddle & Reath 1100 Phila Nat Bank Bldg Broad & Chestnuts Sts Philadelphia PA 19107

BEAUZAY, VICTOR H(ILTON), lawyer; b. Waverly, N.Y., Mar. 28, 1924; s. Eugene Louis and Edith (Peet) B.; m. JoEllen, Apr. 17, 1946; children—Victor H. II, Victoria Ellen Beauzay Bova. Student Syracuse U., 1947; A.B. in Polit. Sci., Stanford U., 1948, J.D., 1951. Bar: Calif. 1952, U.S. Sup. Ct. 1957. Sr. ptnr. Beauzay, Ezgar, Bledsoe, Levin & O'Laughlin, San Jose, Calif. and Salinas, Calif., 1952—; lectr. in workers' compensation law; chmn. Workers' Compensation Adv. Commn., Calif. State Bar Specialization Program; exec. com. State BarCalif., conf. of dels. 1984—. Served with U.S. Army, 1943-46. Recipient Golden Banana award P & L Seminar Soc., 1979, Gene Marias Lifetime Achievement award. Mem. Santa Clara County Bar Assn. (pres. 1981), Calif. Applicants' Attys. Assn. (pres. 1968-69, chmn. legis. com. 1968-71). Clubs: Century (pres.), Masons (San Jose). Workers' compensation. Office: 300 W Hedding St San Jose CA 95110

BEBCHICK, LEONARD NORMAN, lawyer; b. New Bedford, Mass., Dec. 11, 1932; s. Samuel and Frances (Hait) B.; m. Gabriela Meyerhoff, Aug. 31, 1968; children—Ilana, Brian. A.B., Cornell U., 1955; LL.B., Yale U., 1958. Bar: Mass. 1958, D.C. 1960. Atty. CAB, Washington, 1959-60; assoc. Ginsburg & Leventhal, Washington, 1960-64; ptnr. Bebchick, Sher & Kushnick, Washington, 1964-74, Martin, Whitfield, Smith & Bebchick, Washington, 1974-82; pres. Leonard N. Bebchick P.C., Washington, 1982—; joint co. sec. Brit. Caledonian Airways, Eng., 1963—; dir. British Caledonian Group, Eng., 1978—; spl. counsel D.C. Pub. Service Commn., Washington, 1965-66, V.I. Pub. Utilities Commn., 1967-70. Served to capt. U.S. Army, 1959-60. Mem. ABA (chmn. adv. com. on aero. law 1982-83), Fed. Bar Assn., Internat. Bar Assn., Bar Assn. City N.Y. Democrat. Jewish. Clubs: City Tavern, Nat. Lawyers (Washington); Directors (London). Administrative and regulatory, General corporate, Private international. Home: 6321 Lenox Rd Bethesda MD 20817 Office: 1220 19th St NW Washington DC 20036

BEBOUT, BRADLEY CAREY, lawyer; b. Convoy, Ohio, Oct. 8, 1950; s. Eugene Harold and Carol C. (Carey) B.; m. Carol Anne Hall, Aug. 2, 1975; 1 child, Stephen Eugene. B.A., Bowling Green State U., 1972; J.D., Ohio No. U., 1979. Bars: Ohio 1980, U.S. Dist. Ct. (no. dist.) Ohio 1980. Vol. Peace Corps, Washington, 1972; market auditor Market Facts, Fort Wayne, Ind., 1972-73; claims rep. Crawford & Co., Cleve., 1973-77; ptnr. Hall & Bebout, Marion, Ohio, 1980—; ct. referee Juvenile Ct. for Marion County. Sec. bd. dirs. Marion Goodwill Industries, 1983-87; treas., v.p. bd. dirs. Handicap Awareness Assn., Marion; pres., bd. dirs. Marionaires, Marion Area Counseling Ctr.; pres. A Spl. Wish Found. Recipient Disting. Citizen of Marion County award, 1985. Mem. Marion County Bar Assn., Ohio State Bar Assn., ABA, Marion C. of C. (bd. dirs. 1985-87), Willis Soc., Phi Kappa Phi. Lodge: Kiwanis (bd. dirs. 1982-84). General practice, Family and matrimonial, Personal injury. Home: 515 Virginia Ave Marion OH 43302 Office: Hall and Bebout Law Offices 125 S Main St Marion OH 43302

BECCI, MICHAEL NELSON, lawyer. BME, U. Notre Dame, 1972; JD with honors, Villanova U., 1976, LLM in Taxation, 1984. Bar: Pa. 1976, U.S. Dist. Ct. (ea. dist.) Pa. 1976. Assoc. Lentz Riley, Paoli, Pa., 1976-77, Malcolm & Riley, West Chester, Pa., 1977-79; div. counsel Litton Industries, Inc., Wayne, Pa., 1979-86; corp. counsel SPS Techs., Inc., Newton, Pa., 1986—. Editor Villanova U. Law Rev., 1976. Mem. ABA, Am. Corp. Counsel Assn., Pa. Bar Assn. General corporate, Contracts commercial. Office: SPS Techs. Inc. Newtown PA 18940

BECHER, PAUL EUGENE, lawyer; b. Mishawaka, Ind., Apr. 1, 1947; s. Richard Paul and Agatha Margaret (Anthony) B.; m. Heidemarie Pesendorfer, Oct. 25, 1969; 1 child, Teresa Annette. AB, Ind. U., 1969; JD, U. Notre Dame, 1978. Bar: Ind. 1978, U.S. Dist. Ct. (no. and so. dists.) Ind. 1978. Assoc. Barnes & Thornburg, Elkhart, Ind., 1978-84, ptnr., 1984—. Bd. dirs. Elkhart Concert Club, 1980—. Mem. ABA, Ind. Bar Assn., Elkhart City Bar Assn., Elkhart County Bar Assn. Personal injury, Federal civil litigation, State civil litigation. Office: Barnes & Thornburg 301 S Main St Elkhart IN 46516

BECHTLE, LOUIS CHARLES, U.S. district judge; b. Phila., Dec. 14, 1927; s. Charles R. and Gladys (Kirchner) B.; m. Margaret Beck, Sept. 5, 1978; children: Barbara, Nancy, Amy; stepchildren: Joanne, Tara, Samuel. B.S., Temple U., 1951, LL.B., 1954. Bar: Pa. 1954. Asst. U.S. atty. U.S. Dept. Justice, Phila., 1957-59, U.S. atty., 1969-72; pvt. practice law Jacoby & Maxmin, Phila., 1959-62; pvt. practice Wisler, Pearlstine, Talone, Gerber, Norristown, Pa., 1962-69; U.S. dist. judge U.S. Dist. Ct., Phila., 1972—; mem. adj. faculty Temple U. Law Sch., Phila., 1974—, Villanova Law Sch., 1985. Served with U.S. Army, 1946-47. Mem. Montgomery County Bar Assn., Fed. Bar Assn. Republican. Presbyterian. Judicial administration. Office: US Dist Ct Eastern Dist Pa 601 Market St Philadelphia PA 19106

BECHTOLD, PAULA MILLER, lawyer; b. San Luis Obispo, Calif., Oct. 18, 1946; d. Leland Franklin and Barbara May (Stallcup) Miller; m. Robert Dean Laird, Oct. 23, 1976; children: Deven McKenzie, Brenna Catherine. BS in History, Lewis and Clark Coll., 1967; postgrad., Portland State U., 1968-69; JD, Northwestern Sch. of Law, 1975. Bar: Oreg. 1975, U.S. Dist. Ct. Oreg. 1975. Law clk. to presiding justice Oreg. Supreme Ct., Salem, 1975-76; ptnr. Bechtold & Laird, Coos Bay, Oreg., 1976—; city atty. City of Coos Bay, 1978—; bd. dirs., officer Southwestern Oreg. Pub. Defender, North Bend; bd. dirs. Oreg. Legal Services Corp., Portland. Pres. Herb Shepard Rehabilitation Ctr. Inc, Coos Bay, 1983-84; bd. dirs. Goodwill Industries of Lane County, Eugene, Oreg., 1978-81, United Way of Southwestern Oreg., Coos Bay, 1980—. Mem. Oreg. Bar Assn. (pres. legal aid com. 1979-80, joint press and broadcasting com. 1982-85, unlawful practice law com. 1985—), Oreg. Law Found. (bd. dirs. 1986—), Oregon City Attys. Assn. (pres. elect 1986—). Democrat. Unitarian. Lodge: Zonta Internat. (pres. Coos Bay 1984—). Local government, General practice, Probate. Home: 1755 N 8th Coos Bay OR 97420 Office: Bechtold & Laird PC PO Box 3295 Coos Bay OR 97420

BECK, ANDREW JAMES, lawyer; b. Washington, Feb. 19, 1948; s. Leonard Norman and Frances (Greif) B.; m. Gretchen Ann Schroeder, Feb. 14, 1971; children: Carter, Lowell, Justin. BA, Carleton Coll., 1969; JD, Stanford U., 1972; MBA, Long Island U., 1975. Bar; Va. 1972, N.Y. 1973. Assoc. Casey, Lane & Mittendorf, N.Y.C., 1972-80, ptnr., 1980-82; managing ptnr. Haythe & Curley, N.Y.C., 1982—. Trustee Bklyn. Heights Synagogue, 1980-81. Mem. ABA, Va. State Bar Assn., New York State Bar Assn., Assn. of Bar of City of N.Y. Avocations: squash, bridge. General corporate, Securities. Home: 71 Willow St Apt 1 Brooklyn NY 11201 Office: Haythe & Curley 437 Madison Ave New York NY 10022

BECK, EDWARD WILLIAM, lawyer; b. Atchison, Kans., Aug. 19, 1944; s. Russell Niles and Lucille Mae (Leighton) B.; m. Marshia Ablon, June 24, 1966; children: Michael Adam, David Gordon, Stephen Jared. B.A. cum laude, Yale Coll., 1967; J.D. cum laude, Harvard U., 1972. Bar: Calif. 1972. Assoc. firm Pillsbury, Madison & Sutro, San Francisco, 1972-77; gen. counsel Pacific Lumber Co., San Francisco, 1977-86; sec. Pacific Lumber Co., 1978-86, v.p., 1980-86, dir., 1985-86; v.p., gen. counsel, sec. Shaklee Corp., San Francisco, 1986-87, sr. v.p., gen. counsel, sec., 1987—. Mem. ABA, Calif. Bar Assn., Bay Area Gen. Counsels Group, Am. Soc. Corp. Secs., San Francisco Bar Assn., San Francisco Leadership Group, San Francisco C. of C. Office: Shaklee Corp 444 Market St San Francisco CA 94111

BECK, JAMES HAYES, lawyer; b. Canton, Ohio, Aug. 29, 1935; s. Harry W. and Helen E. Beck; m. Monika Feld, June 12, 1965; children—Barbara E., James R. A.B., Wittenberg U., 1956; LL.B., U. Va., 1959, J.D., 1970. Bar: Ohio 1959, U.S. Dist. Ct. (no. dist.) Ohio 1960, U.S. Supreme Ct. 1971. Sole practice, Cleve., 1959-63; jr. ptnr. Leanza, Longano, Farina & Mendelson, Cleve., 1963-66; assoc. Nadler & Nadler, Youngstown, Ohio, 1966-73, Beck & Tyrrell, Canfield, Ohio, 1973-83; sr. ptnr. Beck & Vaughn, Canfield, 1984—; instr. real estate law Youngstown State U., 1972. Precinct committeeman, ward leader, Bay Village, Ohio, 1962-66, Canfield, Ohio, 1976-78; v.p. Canfield Civic Assn., 1972-74; mem. stewardship and fin. coms. Lord of Life Lutheran Ch.; comdr., Youngstown Power Squadron, 1985-86. Mem. Am. Arbitration Assn. (panel of arbitrators and regional adv. council 1969—), ABA (sect. on econs. of law practice 1978—), ACLU (legal com. Youngstown chpt. 1966—), Assn. Trial Lawyers Am., Commercial Law League Am., Ohio State Bar Assn. (unauthorized practice of law com. 1978-85, profl. econs. com. 1980-84), Mahoning County Bar Assn. (chmn. profl. econs. com. 1979-82, chmn. unauthorized practice of law com. 1976-79, grievance com. 1984, ins. com. 1986), Beta Theta Pi, Phi Alpha Theta, Pi Sigma Alpha, Tau Kappa Alpha. Clubs: Ashtabula Yacht; Point Yacht. Lodge: Lions. Avocations: tennis; bridge; boating. Bankruptcy, General corporate, Contracts commercial. Home: 265 Saw Mill Run Rd Canfield OH 44406 Office: Beck & Vaughn Olde Courthouse Bldg Canfield OH 44406

BECK, JAN SCOTT, lawyer; b. Newark, May 5, 1955; s. Robert William and Dorothy (Warhaftig) B.; m. Marla Terri Klein, Sept. 27, 1981; children: Jamie Kyle, Bryan Michael. BA in Acctg., Rider Coll., 1977; JD, Villanova U., 1980, LLM in Taxation, 1983. Bar: N.J. 1980, U.S. Dist. Ct. N.J. 1980, N.Y. 1981, U.S. Tax Ct. 1981, D.C. 1985, U.S. Supreme Ct. 1986. Sole practice Westfield, N.J., 1980-86; atty. Inspiration Resources Corp., N.Y.C., 1986—; atty. Laventhol & Horwath, Phila., 1979-80, Touche Ross & Co., N.Y.C., 1980-86; dir. taxation Inspiration Resources Corp., N.Y.C. Author: The Strike: Student Involvement, 1975. Mem. ABA, N.Y. State Bar Assn., N.J. Bar Assn., N.Y. County Lawyers Assn., Am. Inst. CPAs, N.J. Soc. CPAs, Tax Exec. Inst., Am. Mining Congress, Omicron Delta Epsilon, Delta Epsilon Kappa. Avocations: camping, backpacking, mountain climbing, writing, skiing. Corporate taxation, Mergers, acquisitions and divestitures. Home: 437 E Dudley Ave Westfield NJ 07090 Office: Inspiration Resources Corp 250 Park Ave New York NY 10177

BECK, JOSEPH JAMES, lawyer; b. Johnson City, N.Y., Feb. 27, 1946; s. Joseph Lee and Anne Eileen (O'Malley) B.; m. Linda Ann Flores, Apr. 13, 1973 (div. 1980); children: Joseph Lee, Renee Lee, Sean Patrick; m. Debbie Lee Koch, June 6, 1985. BA, Clemson U., 1968; JD, U. S.C., 1972; postgrad., U. Richmond, 1986—. Bar: S.C. 1972, N.Y. 1975. From asst. counsel reins. to counsel reins. Lawyers Title Ins. Corp., Richmond, Va., 1980-85, asst. v.p. reins., 1985-86, v.p. reins., customer liaison, 1986—. Advisor, recruiter, solicitor Jr. Achievement Richmond, 1979-84. Mem. S.C. Bar Assn., N.Y. Bar Assn., Am. Land Title Assn. (chmn. reins. and coins. com. 1986-87). Republican. Roman Catholic. Avocations: golf, pool, stamps, books. Real property, Insurance, General corporate. Home: 8701 Wadsworth Ct Richmond VA 23236 Office: Lawyers Title Ins Corp 6630 W Broad St Richmond VA 23230

BECK, PAUL AUGUSTINE, lawyer; b. Pitts., Aug. 16, 1936; s. August W. and Agnes (Heyl) B.; children: Jennifer, Bradford, Michael. BS, Carnegie-Mellon U., 1957; LLB, Duquesne U., 1962. Bar: Pa. 1962, U.S. Ct. Appeals (4th cir.) 1963, U.S. Supreme Ct. 1966, U.S. Ct. Appeals (2d and 3d cirs.) 1971, U.S. Ct. Appeals (7th cir.) 1974, U.S. Ct. Appeals (Fed. cir.) 1982. Ptnr. Buell, Ziesenheim, Beck & Alstadt, Pitts., 1962—. Chmn. alumni forum com. Carnegie-Mellon U., Pitts., 1966-67. Served to capt. U.S. Army, 1957-59. Mem. ABA, Nat. Council Patent Law Assn., Pitts. Patent Law Assn. (bd. dirs.), Allegheny County Bar Assn. (gov. 1977-79, chmn. intellectual property law sect. 1979-84). Club: Duquesne (Pitts.). Patent, Trademark and copyright. Office: Buell Ziesenheim Beck & Alstadt 322 Blvd of the Allies Pittsburgh PA 15222

BECK, ROBERT DAVID, lawyer; b. Pitts., July 22, 1941; s. Erwin and Frances Lenore (Urbanek) B.; m. Carole N. Beck, Oct. 1, 1971 (div. 1979); m. Gloria S. White, Jan. 22, 1982. Student, Princeton U., 1959-61; BS, Allegheny Coll., 1964; LLB, U. Pitts., 1967. Bar: Pa. 1967, U.S. Dist. Ct. (we. dist.) Pa. 1968, U.S. Supreme Ct. 1971. Assoc. Patrono, Ceisler & Edwards, Washington, Pa., 1967-74; sole practice Washington, 1975-77; ptnr. Beck and DeHaven, Washington, 1977—; Mem. bd. viewers Washington County, 1975-76, asst. dist. atty., 1977-79. Pres. Greater Washington Area YMCA, 1978-79; mem. budget com. Greater Washington County United Way, 1974-80. Mem. ABA, Pa. Bar Assn. (ho. of dels. 1978-82, 86—), Pa. Trial Lawyers Assn., Washington County Bar Assn. (pres. 1984), Greater Washington Area Jaycees (pres. 1975). Democrat. Jewish. Avocations: golf, oenology. State civil litigation, Family and matrimonial, Personal injury. Office: Beck and DeHaven 30 S Main St Suite 103 Washington PA 15301

BECK, ROBERT EDWARD, lawyer; b. Collingdale, Pa., Mar. 20, 1910; s. Herman C. and Laura A. (Speck) B.; m. Marion Gibson, Aug. 20, 1938. A.B., Rutgers U., 1931, LL.B., 1934. Bar: N.J. 1935, U.S. Supreme Ct. 1957. Gen. counsel Llewellyn-Edison Savs. and Loan Assn., West Orange, N.J., 1978—; ptnr. Grosso and Beck, Orange, N.J., 1946-77; sole practice, Orange, 1978-84; mem. Livingston Twp. Commn., 1947-50. Served to col. USAAF, 1941-46; col. U.S. Army ret. Decorated Bronze Star medal, Croix de Guerre. Mem. N.J. State Bar Assn., Essex County Bar Assn. Republican. Probate, Real property, Banking.

BECK, THOMAS HENRY, lawyer; b. Carrington, N.D., Dec. 26, 1953; s. Keith Duane Beck and Florence Ruth (Watson) Johnson; m. diane Marie Brault, June 16, 1984. BS, N.D. State U., 1975; JD, Harvard U., 1979. Bar: N.Y. 1980, U.S. Dist. Ct. (so. and ea. dists.) N.Y. 1980. Assoc. Fish & Neave, N.Y.C., 1979—. Mem. fundraising com. Stanley M. Issacs Neighborhood Ctr. Inc., N.Y.C., 1985—. Mem. ABA, N.Y. Patent Trademark and Copyright Assn. Lutheran. Patent. Office: Fish & Neave 875 3d Ave 29th floor New York NY 10022

BECK, WILLIAM HAROLD, JR., lawyer; b. Clarksdale, Miss., Aug. 18, 1928; s. William Harold and Mary (McGaha) B.; m. Nancy Cassity House, Jan. 30, 1954; children—Mary, Nancy, Katherine. B.A., Vanderbilt U., 1950; J.D., U. Miss., 1954. Bar: Miss. 1954, La. 1960. Atty., Clarksdale, Miss., 1954-57; asst. prof. Tulane U., 1957-59; ptnr. Foley Judell Beck Bewley Martin & Hicks, New Orleans, 1959—. Served to capt., AUS, 1951-53. Mem. ABA, La. Bar Assn., Miss. Bar Assn., SAR, Sons Colonial Wars, S.R. Local government. Office: 535 Gravier St New Orleans LA 70130

BECKER, BRANDON, lawyer; b. Berwyn, Ill., Mar. 19, 1954. BA summa cum laude, U. Minn., 1974; JD magna cum laude, U. San Diego, 1977; LLM, Columbia U., 1979. Bar: Calif. 1978, D.C. 1978. Legal asst. SEC, Washington, 1981-82, assoc. dir. div. market regulation, 1986—. Mem. ABA (fed. regulation of securities com.). Avocation: chess. Administrative and regulatory, General corporate, Securities. Office: SEC 450 5th St NW Washington DC 20549

BECKER, EDWARD ROY, judge; b. Phila., May 4, 1933; s. Herman A. and Jeannette (Levit) B.; m. Flora Lyman, Aug. 11, 1957; children: James Daniel (dec. 1969), Jonathan Robert, Susan Rose, Charles Lyman. B.A., U. Pa., 1954; LL.B., Yale U., 1957. Bar: Pa. 1957. Ptnr. Becker, Becker & Fryman, Phila., 1957-70; U.S. Dist. Judge 1970-82; U.S. Circuit Judge 3d Cir., 1982—; counsel Rep. City Com., Phila., 1965-70; mem. task force on implementation of new jud. article Joint State Govt. Commn., 1969; lectr. law U. Pa. Law Sch., 1978-83; mem. edn. adv. com. concerning Comprehensive Crime Control Act, Fed. Jud. Ctr. Bd. editors: Manual for Complex Litigation. Trustee Magna Carta Found., Phila. Mem. ABA (jud. rep. antitrust sect. 1983-86), Phila. Bar Assn., Am. Judicature Soc., Am. Law Inst. (adv. com. restatement conflict of laws 2d; ALI-ABA continuing edn. adv. com. on trial practice), Jud. Conf. U.S. (com. on adminstrn. probation system), Phi Beta Kappa. Jewish. Jurisprudence. Home: 936 Herbert St Philadelphia PA 19124 Office: 19613 US Courthouse Philadelphia PA 19106

BECKER, FRANK GREGORY, lawyer; b. Detroit, Nov. 20, 1950; s. Frank L. and Estelle M. (Roznak) B.; 1 child, Mark G. BA, Wayne State U., 1972, JD cum laude, 1975. Bar: Mich. 1975. Ptnr. Becker & Van Cleef, PC, Southfield, Mich., 1975—. Mem. Mich. Bar Assn. Civil rights, Personal injury.

BECKER, FRED REINHARDT, JR., lawyer, military officer; b. Louisville, June 14, 1949; s. Fred Reinhardt and Olivia Louise (Nicklies) B.; m. Barbara Lee Sheinhouse, Sept. 20, 1973; children: Kimberly Lee, Lori Michelle, Melissa Olivia. BS, U.S. Naval Acad., 1971; JD, Coll. William and Mary, 1979. Bar: Va. 1979, U.S. Ct. Appeals (4th cir.) 1979. Commd. ensign USN, 1971, advanced through grades to comdr., 1987; aide-de-camp Jr. Armed Forces Staff Coll., Norfolk, Va., 1974-76; from pros. atty. to head pros. atty. Naval Legal Service Office, Norfolk, 1979-81; exec. officer Naval Legal Service Office, Guam, 1981-83; head procurement and plans div. Office of JAG, Alexandria, Va., 1983-85; atty. office of legis. affairs USN, Washington, 1985-87, mil. advisor to assoc. dir. Nat. Security and Internat. Affairs, Office of Mgmt. and Budget, Exec. Office of Pres., 1987—; adj. instr. bus. mgmt. dept. U. Md., College Park, 1982—. Mem. ABA (award of profl. merit 1979), Va. Bar Assn., Assn. Trial Lawyers Am., Judge Advs. Assn., Order of Coif, Phi Alpha Delta. Democrat. Mem. Disciples of Christ Ch. Military, Legislative, Legal education. Home: 7606 Maritime Ln Springfield VA 22153 Office: USN Nat Security & Internat Affairs Office of Mgmt and Budget Exec Office of Pres Washington DC 20503

BECKER, JOHN ERNEST, JR., lawyer; b. Mt. Holly, N.J., Dec. 4, 1945; s. John Ernest and Eleanor Mae (Johnson) B. B.A., Rutgers U., 1968, J.D., 1971. Bar: N.J. 1971, U.S. Dist. Ct. N.J. 1971, U.S. Tax Ct. 1973, U.S. Supreme Ct. 1980, N.Y. 1984. Sr. trial atty. Manhattan Dist. Counsel, IRS, N.Y.C., 1971—. Republican. Lutheran. Club: American Three Quarter Midget Racing Assn. (dir. 1981—). Federal civil litigation, Estate taxation, Personal income taxation. Home: 519 8th St Riverside NJ 08075 Office: Manhattan Dist Counsel 26 Federal Plaza 12th Floor New York NY 10278

BECKER, JOHN FRANCIS, lawyer; b. Pitts., Nov. 17, 1943; s. Edward DeFalco and Catherine M. (Dolan) B.; m. Genevieve M. McNally, Feb. 1967; children: Genevieve L., Elizabeth A., John E., Margaret C. AB, U. Notre Dame, 1965; JD, St. John's U., N.Y.C., 1968. Bar: N.Y. 1969, Pa. 1971, U.S. Dist. Ct. (we. dist.) Pa. 1972, U.S. Ct. Appeals (3d cir.) 1978. House counsel Allstate Ins. Co., N.Y.C., 1969-70; asst. dist. atty. Kings County Dist. Atty.'s Office, Bklyn., 1970-73; from assoc. to ptnr. Sikou & Love P.A., Pitts., 1973—. Mem. zoning hearing bd. Borough of Greentree, 1981—; v.p. parish council St. Margaret's Ch., Pitts., 1978, pres. Holy Name Soc., 1982. Mem. ABA, Allegheny County Bar Assn. (profl. ethics com. 1985—, medical-legal com. 1986, ad hoc com. on ct. adminstrn. 1986, vice chmn. continuing legal edn. com. 1986), Assn. Trial Lawyers Am., Pa. Trial Lawyers (pres. western Pa. chpt. 1985, 86, v.p., treas., sec., bd. dirs. 1977-85, state bd. dirs. 1982-86), Acad. Trial Lawyers Allegheny County (bd. dirs. 1986). Republican. Roman Catholic. Clubs: Montour Heights Country (Coraopolis, Pa.); Notre Dame (Pitts.). Avocation: golf. Workers' compensation, State civil litigation, Federal civil litigation. Home: 12 E Manilla Ave Pittsburgh PA 15220 Office: Sikov & Love PA 1400 Lawyers Bldg Pittsburgh PA 15219

BECKER, KARL MARTIN, holding company executive; b. Glenridge, N.J., May 30, 1943; s. Alfred Martin and Helen K. (Gramse) B.; m. Barbara A. Benton, Feb. 19, 1966; children—Glenn M., Mark W. A.B., Yale U., 1965; J.D., U. Chgo., 1968. Bar: Ill. Assoc. Vedder Price Kaufman Kammholz, Chgo., 1968-75, ptnr., 1975-78; asst. gen. counsel Esmark, Inc., Chgo., 1978-83, assoc. gen. counsel, 1983-84; v.p., gen. counsel, sec. Swift Ind. Corp., Chgo., 1985-86, sr. v.p., gen. counsel, sec., 1986; sr. v.p., gen. counsel Beatrice Cos., Inc. and BCI Holdings Corp., Chgo., 1986—. Mem. Chgo. Bar Assn., ABA. Club: Monroe. Avocations: skiing; sailing. Home: 924 Forest Ave Wilmette IL 60091 Office: Beatrice Cos Inc 2 N LaSalle St Chicago IL 60602

BECKER, RALPH ELIHU, lawyer, diplomat; b. N.Y.C., Jan. 29, 1907; s. Max Joseph and Rose (Becker) B.; m. Ann Marie Watters; children: William Watters, Donald Lee, Pamela Rose, Ralph Elihu. LL.B., St. John's U., 1928; L.L.D., St. Johns U., 1983; LL.D. (hon.), South Eastern U., Washington. Bar: N.Y. 1929, U.S. Supreme Ct. 1940, D.C. 1949. Practice in Washington, 1948-76; spl. counsel to Landfield, Becker & Green, 1978—; gen. counsel, founding trustee John F. Kennedy Center for Performing Arts, 1958-76, hon. trustee, 1980—; U.S. ambassador to Honduras, 1976-77; cons. NASA; Disting. lectr. Strom Thurmond Inst., Clemson U., S.C.; assoc. mem. council NASA Task Force for the Comml. Use of Space. Author numerous booklets, articles on constl. law, ins., space law, atomic energy. Chmn. and former bd. dirs., gen. counsel Met. Washington Bd. of Trade, 1964-71; bd. dirs., gen. counsel, sec. Albert Schweitzer Found., 1955; pres. bd. dirs. Voice Found., 1976—, Friends of LBJ Library; adv. com. L.B. Johnson Meml. Grove on the Park; founding dir., former gen. counsel Wolf Trap Found., 1964-76; mem. adv. com. Sec. Interior Wolf Trap Farm Park for Performing Arts; dir. emeritus Nat. Bank Washington; rep. of Pres. L.B. Johnson with rank spl. ambassador Independence Ceremonies, Swaziland, 1968; mem. Arctic Expdn. for polar bears Washington Zoo, 1962, Antarctic-South Pole Operation Deepfreeze, 1963; nat. chmn. Young Republicans, 1946-49; mem. Rep. Nat. Exec. Com., 1948-51, Pres.'s Inaugural Com., 1953, 57, 69, 73, 80, 83, Vice Pres. Rockefeller Inaugural Medal Com., Rep. Senatorial Inner Circle, fin. com. Rep. Eagle, Presdl. Task Force; charter mem. Nat. Rep. Congl. Com.; donor collection polit. Americana to Smithsonian Instn., Dartmouth Coll., St. Albans Sch., L.B.J. Library, U. Tex., Austin., Strom Thurmond Inst., Clemson U. (S.C.); founder, dir. Inter-Am. Music Festival. Served to capt. AUS, 1942-45, ETO. Decorated Bronze Star medal U.S.; chevalier Legion of Honor; Croix de Guerre with palm France; Belgian Fourragere; Order Morazon 1st class Honduras; chevalier and officer So. Cross of Brazil; Knight's Cross Order of Dannebrog, Denmark; Gt. Cross for Meritorious Services to Austrian Republic; Royal Order de Vasa Sweden; Netherlands Resistance Meml. Cross; Order Rising Sun Japan; recipient Smithsonian Instn. Benefactor medal, 1975; Antarctic Service medal; honored with award by OAS, 1968. Fellow Corcoran Gallery Art, Aspen Inst. Humanistic Studies; mem. ABA (mem. major coms., del. Internat. Bar Assn. com. meeting Monte Carlo 1954, Oslo, 1956, chmn. Vienna post conv. Am. Bar Assn. meeting London 1957), D.C. Bar Assn., N.Y. State Bar Assn., Internat. Bar Assn., Fed. Bar Assn. (nat. council), Am. Law Inst. (life mem.), 30th Inf. Div. Assn. (pres. 1958), U.S. Capitol Hist. Soc. (founding dir.), N.Y. State Soc. (pres. 1963-64), Columbia Hist. Soc., Arctic Polar Inst. (hon.), Smithsonian Assn. (nat. mem.), Supreme Ct. Hist. Soc. (founding dir., mem. exec. com., chmn. ann. meetings 1978, 79, 80), Am. Fedn. Musicians (hon.), James Smithson Soc. of Smithsonian Assocs. (life), Friends of the Folger Library, Ctr. For Study of Presidency, Nat. Wildflower Research Ctr., Dacor-Bacon House Found., Am. Chamber Orch. Soc. (hon.), Choral Arts Soc. (hon.), Council Am. Ambassadors, Am. Fgn. Service Officers Assn., Am. Fgn. Service Assn., Diplomatic and Consular Officers Ret. Clubs: International, Capitol Hill; Bald Peak Colony (N.H.). Lodge: Masons. Public international, Private international, Insurance. Home: 4000 Massachusetts Ave NW Washington DC 20016 Office: 1818 N St NW Suite 300 Washington DC 20036

BECKER, WILLIAM HENRY, judge; b. Brookhaven, Miss., Aug. 26, 1909; s. William Henry and Verna (Lilly) B.; m. Geneva Moreton, June 9, 1932; children—Frances Becker Mills, Patricia Becker Hawkins, Nancy Becker Hewes, Geneva Becker Jacks, William Henry III. Student, La. State U., 1927-28; LL.B., U. Mo., 1932. Bar: Miss. 1930, Mo. 1932, U.S. Supreme Ct. 1937. Assoc. firm Clark & Becker, Columbia, Mo., 1932-36; mem. firm Clark & Becker, 1936-44, 46-61; judge U.S. Dist. Ct. Western Dist. Mo., 1961—, chief judge, 1965-77, sr. judge, 1977—; judge U.S. Temp. Emergency Ct. Appeals, 1977—; spl. master Supreme Ct. of U.S., 1979-83; counsel to Gov. Lloyd Stark; counsel to Gov. Lloyd Stark in Kansas City Criminal Investigation, 1938-39; spl. asst. to dir. econ. stblzn. Office of War Mobilization and Reconversion, Washington, 1945-46; spl. commr. Mo. Supreme Ct., 1954-58; spl. counsel Mo. Ins. Dept., 1936-44; chmn. Mo. Supreme Ct. Com. to Draft Rules of Civil Procedure for Mo., 1952-59, mem. coordinating com. for multiple litigation, 1962-68, vice chmn., 1967-68; chmn. subcom. drafting Jury Selection and Service Act, 1968; mem. jud. panel on multidist. litigation Jud. Conf. U.S., 1968-77, mem. com. on operation of jury system, 1966-68; faculty Fed. Jud. Center seminars and workshops for U.S. Dist. judges, 1968—; chmn. subcom. drafting Jury Selection and Service Act of 1968. Bd. editors Manual for Complex Litigation, 1968—; chmn., 1977-81. Served with USN, 1944-45, PTO; with Res. 1944-52. Decorated Phillipines Liberation Ribbon with Bronze Star. Fellow Am. Bar Found., Am. Coll. Trial Lawyers, Am. Coll. Probate Counsel; mem. ABA, Am. Judicature Soc., Fed. Bar Assn. (award 1977), Mo. Bar Assn., Kansas City Bar Assn. (spl. award 1977), Lawyers Assn. Kansas City (award 1977, Charles Evans Whittaker award 1979). Office: US Courthouse 811 Grand Ave Kansas City MO 64106

BECKER-LEWKE, LAURA VIRGINIA, lawyer; b. Bklyn., Jan. 12, 1955; d. Gordon Lyon and Virginia Frances (Hochette) Becker; m. Reynold Hans Lewke. BA, Wellesley Coll., 1977; LLB, McGill U., Montreal, Quebec, Can., 1980. Assoc. Burlingham, Underwood & Lord, N.Y.C., 1980-83; counsel Navios Mgmt. Inc., Greenwich, Conn., 1983—. Mem. ABA, Maritime Law Assn., Westchester and Fairfield County Corp. Counsel Assn. General corporate, Contracts commercial, Admiralty. Home: 105 Sturbridge Ln Trumbull CT 06611

BECKERMAN, RAY, lawyer; b. Bronx, N.Y., Mar. 12, 1948. AB, Herbert H. Lehman Coll., 1968; JD cum laude, St. John's U., 1978. Bar: N.Y. 1979, U.S. Dist. Ct. (ea. and so. dist.) N.Y. 1979, U.S. Ct. Appeals (2d cir.) 1984. Assoc. Phillips, Nizer, Benjamin, Krim & Ballon, N.Y.C., 1978-80; assoc. litigation Lowey, Dannenberg & Knapp, N.Y.C., 1980-81; assoc. Squadron, Ellenoff, Plesent & Lehrer, N.Y.C., 1981-83; sole practice N.Y.C., 1983—; mem. panel of arbitrators Civil Ct. City of N.Y., 1984—. Mem. regional civil rights com. Anti-Defamation League, B'nai B'rith, N.Y.C., 1980-86; gen. counsel History of N.Y.C. Project, Bronx, 1983—; spl. copyright counsel Bronx County Hist. Soc., 1983—. Recipient Am. Jurisprudence award 1976, 77, Cornelius W. Wickersham Jr. award Fed. Bar Council, 1978. Mem. N.Y. State Bar Assn., Assn. of Bar of City of N.Y., Am. Arbitration Assn. (panel of comml. arbitrators), Lehman Coll. Alumni Assn. (gen. counsel). State civil litigation, Federal civil litigation, Consumer commercial. Office: 156 Fifth Ave New York NY 10010

BECKETT, ALICE TALBIRD, lawyer; b. Beaufort, S.C., Sept. 11, 1908; d. George W. and Elinor Louise (Mansfield) B. Student assoc. Lionel K. Legge, justice Supreme Ct. S.C., 1940-46. Bar: S.C. 1946. Sole practice, Walterboro, S.C., 1946—; sec., treas. Colleton County Bar, Walterboro, S.C., 1947-76; govt. appeal agt. Selective Service, Walterboro, 1949-69. Pres., treas. Colleton County Hist. Soc., 1942-85, sec. 1985—; mem. S.C. Hist. Soc.; active local ARC programs; alderman Walterboro, 1952-58; county chmn. Crusade for Freedom. Mem. S.C. Bar Assn., Colleton County Bar Assn. Republican. Roman Catholic. Real property, Probate, Estate planning. Office: 122 Hampton St PO Box 531 Walterboro SC 29488

BECKETT, AMY LOUISE, lawyer; b. Ypsilanti, Mich., Mar. 14, 1957; d. Robert Dudley and Muriel Margaret (Friedhoff) B. AB, Mt. Holyoke Coll., 1979; JD, NYU, 1982. Bar: Mo. 1982, Ill. 1983, U.S. Dist. Ct. (we. dist.) Mo. 1982, U.S. Dist. Ct. (no. dist.) Ill. 1984, U.S. Ct. Appeals (D.C.) 1986. Law clk. to presiding justices Mo. Supreme Ct., Jefferson City, 1982-83; assoc. Schiff, Hardin & Waite, Chgo., 1983-85; asst. corp. counsel dept. of law City of Chgo., 1985—. Bd. dirs. Network 44, Chgo., 1985—; mem. Cook County Dem. Women, Chgo., 1986—. Mem. Mo. Bar Assn., Chgo. Bar Assn., Chgo. Council Lawyers, Phi Beta Kappa. Club: Mt. Holyoke (Chgo.). Avocations: classical piano, lit., women's studies, polit. economy. Government contracts and claims, Local government, State civil litigation. Office: City of Chgo Dept of Law Affirmative Litigation Div 180 N LaSalle Rm 704 Chicago IL 60601

BECKETT, THEODORE CHARLES, lawyer; b. Boonville, Mo., May 6, 1929; s. Theodore Cooper and Gladys (Watson) B.; m. Daysie Margaret Cornwall, 1950; children: Elizabeth Gayle, Theodore Cornwall, Margaret Lynn, William Harrison, Anne Marie. B.S., U. Mo., Columbia, 1950, J.D., 1957. Bar: Mo. 1957. Since practiced in Kansas City; mem. firm Beckett & Steinkamp; instr. polit. sci. U. Mo., Columbia, 1956-57; asst. atty. gen. State of Mo., 1961-64. Former mem. bd. dirs. Kansas City Civic Ballet; mem. City Plan Commn., Kansas City, 1976-80. Served to 1st lt. U.S. Army, 1950-53. Mem. Am., Mo., Kansas City bar assns., Lawyers Assn. Kansas City, Newcomen Soc. N.Am., SAR, Order of Coif, Sigma Nu, Phi Alpha Delta. Presbyterian. Clubs: Kansas City (Kansas City, Mo.), Blue Hills Country (Kansas City, Mo.). Federal civil litigation, State civil litigation. Office: Beckett & Steinkamp 600 Commerce Trust Bldg PO Box 13425 Kansas City MO 64199

BECKEY, SYLVIA LOUISE, lawyer; b. Los Angeles, Feb. 8, 1946; d. Andrew Gabriel and Rita Jane (Mayer) B. B.A. with spl. honors, U. Texas-Austin, 1968, postgrad., 1968-69; J.D., Duke U., 1971; M.A. candidate Johns Hopkins Sch. Advanced Internat. Studies, 1973-74; LL.M., NYU, 1981. Bar: D.C. 1972, N.Y. 1975, U.S. Dist. Ct. (so. and ea. dist.) N.Y. 1975, U.S. Supreme Ct. 1975, U.S. Ct. Appeals (2d cir.) 1980. Legis. atty. Am. law div. Congl. Research Service, Library of Congress, Washington, 1971-74; assoc. Cole & Deitz, N.Y.C., 1975-76, Milberg, Weiss, Bershad & Specthrie, N.Y.C., 1976-78; law. clk. to judge U.S. Dist. Ct. (so. dist.) N.Y., 1979-80; asst. chief div. comml. litigation Office of Corp. Counsel of City of N.Y., 1980-86; spl. master Supreme Ct. State of N.Y.-N.Y. County, 1984-86; spl. counsel-enforcement U.S. Securities and Exchange Commn., N.Y.C., 1986—; guest speaker U. Witerwatersrand Sch. Law, Johannesburg, S. Africa, 1973; guest researcher Ct. Library, Nairobi, Kenya, 1973; pro bono Internat. League Human Rights, N.Y.C., 1974-75, 8th ann. Conf. for World Peace through Law, Abidjan, Ivory Coast, W. Africa, 1973. Co-author Handbook for Drafting Jury Instructions, U.S. Dept. Justice Civil Rights Div., 1970; assoc. editor The Constitution of the United States of America-Analysis and Interpretation, 1972; author legis. reports on Equal Credit Opportunity Act;

referee Am. Bus. Law Jour., 1980-81. Bd. dirs. Chalon Cooperative Bldg., Washington, 1972-73; chmn. fine arts com., mem. bd. dirs. St. Bartholomew's Community Club, St. Bartholomew's Episcopal Ch., N.Y.C., 1982-83. Grantee EEO, 1966, Hinds Webbs Fund, 1967. Mem. Women's Bar Assn. City of N.Y., NYU Law Alumni Assn., Duke U. Law Alumni Assn., Fed. Bar Council, Am. Fgn. Law Assn., Consular Law Soc., Dramatists Guild. Protestant Lawyers Guild, English Speaking Union, Met. Mus. Art, Chelsea Block Assn. and Hist. Soc. Democrat. Federal civil litigation, State civil litigation, Construction. Home: 235 W 22d St Apt 4T New York NY 10011 Office: US SEC NY Regional Office 26 Federal Plaza New York NY 10278

BECKHAM, WALTER HULL, lawyer; b. Albany, Ga., Apr. 18, 1920; m. Ethel Koger, Mar. 13, 1943; children: Barbara, Walter III, James K. AB, Emory U., 1941; LLB cum laude, Harvard U., 1948. Bar: Fla. 1949, U.S. Supreme Ct. 1956, D.C. 1978. Assoc. prof. law U. Miami, Fla., 1948-49; ptnr. Nichols, Gaither, Beckham et al, 1950-67; of counsel Podhurst, Orseck, Parks, Josefsberg, Eaton, Meadow & Olin P.A., Miami, 1967—; prof. law U. Miami, 1967-82, prof. emeritus, 1982—. Editor Harvard U. Law Rev. Pres. Greater Miami YMCA, 1963-68, Crippled Children's Soc. Dade County, 1968-69; mem. Dade County Mental Health Bd., 1971-73; chmn., bd. of trustees YMCA Blue Ridge Assembly, 1977-79. Served with USNR, 1941-46; capt. USNR, ret. Recipient The Perry Nichols award, Acad. Fla. Trial Lawyers, 1984. Mem. ABA (spl. com. on tort liability system 1979-84, spl. commn. on assn. grievance 1983-84, chmn. tort and ins. practice sect. 1974-75, Ho. of Dels. 1979-82, sec.-elect 1986-87, sec. 1987—), Am. Bar Found., Am. Coll. Trial Lawyers, Am. Law Inst., Assn. Trial Lawyers Am. (chmn. aviation sect. 1966-68), Fla. Bar Assn. (past mem. bd. of govs. jr. bar sect.), Dade County Bar Assn. (pres. jr. bar sect. 1952-53, bd. dirs., exec. com. 1953-54), Internat. Acad. Trial Lawyers (pres. 1973), Internat. Acad. Law and Sci., Law Sci. Inst., Maritime Law Assn. U.S., Nat. Inst. Trial Adv. (trustee 1976, chmn. 1983—), Inner Circle of Advs., Med. Inst. for Attys. (bd. dirs. 1968-83), Nat. Bd. Trial Adv. (founding mem.), Phi Beta Kappa, Omicron Delta Kappa, Phi Alpha Delta, Chi Phi. Lodge: Kiwanis. Home: 3612 SW 57th Ave Miami FL 33155 Office: Podhurst Orseck Parks et al 25 W Flagler St 1201 City National Bank Bldg Suite 800 Miami FL 33130

BECKLER, RICHARD WILLIAM, lawyer; b. Bklyn., Mar. 30, 1940; s. William Francis and Mary (Lohrmann) B.; children—Katherine, Lindsey. B.A., Williams Coll., 1961; J.D., Fordham U., 1968. Bar: N.Y. 1968, Conn. 1972, D.C. 1978. Asst. dist. atty. N.Y. County Dist. Atty.'s Office, 1968-72; with fraud sect., criminal div. Dept. Justice, Washington, 1973-78, chief, 1978-79, dep. chief, 1976-78; ptnr. Fulbright & Jaworski, Washington, 1979—. Served to lt. comdr. USNR, Recipient Spl. Achievement award Dept. Justice, 1975, Meritorious award, 1979, Spl. Commendation for Outstanding Service, 1978, Outstanding Service and Leadership, 1973-79. Mem. ABA. Federal civil litigation, Criminal, Labor. Office: Fulbright & Jaworski 1150 Connecticut Ave NW Washington DC 20036

BECKMAN, ALLEN JOEL, lawyer; b. Phila., Aug. 21, 1943; s. David Jacob and Miriam (Shanefield) B.; m. Cynthia Zelinski, June 7, 1981. BA in English, Temple U., 1965; JD, Villanova U., 1968. Bar: Pa. Assoc. Freedman, Borowsky & Lorry, Phila., 1968-70, Richter, Syken, Ross, Binder & O'Neill, Phila., 1970-73; ptnr. Shuster & Beckman, Phila., 1973-84, Allen J. Beckman & Assocs., Phila., 1984—. bd. dirs., officer Phila. Civic Museums Corp., Phila Hist. Commn., spl. steering com. Phila. City Planning Commn., Friends of Museums; active Green for Mayor, Senate, Congress, Phila., 1971, 72, 74, 76, 79, Gray for Congress, Phila., 1978, 80, 82, 84, 86, Rendell for Dist. Atty., Gov., Phila., 1982, 86. Mem. ABA, Pa. Bar Assn., Phila. Bar Assn., Assn. Trial Lawyers Am., Pa. Trial Lawyers Assn. (bd. govs.), Phila. Trial Lawyers Assn. (bd. govs.), Nat. Health Lawyers Assn., Nat. Inst. Trial Advocacy. Democrat. Jewish. Lodge: B'nai B'rith. Avocation: golf. Personal injury, Health, General practice. Home: 1811 N Parktowne Pl Philadelphia PA 19130 Office: Allen J Beckman & Assocs 1339 Chestnut St Philadelphia PA 19107

BECKMAN, DONALD, lawyer; b. Phila., Feb. 1, 1932; s. Meyer Robert and Ada Edith (Horwitz) B.; m. Aileen Kohn, July 14, 1952; children: Howard, Richard (dec.), Bradley. B.A., U. Pa., 1953; LL.B. magna cum laude, 1959. Bar: Pa. 1959, Mass. 1985. Assoc. Dechert Price & Rhoads, Phila., 1959-65, ptnr., 1965-84; partner Csaplar & Bok, Phila. and Boston, 1984—; dir. Teleflex Inc., Limerick, Pa., Altman Bros., Inc., Glenside, Pa. Mem. allocation com. United Way, Phila., 1978, 79, 82—; pres. Bala Cynwyd Library Assn., Pa., 1974, Main Line Reform Temple, Wynnewood, Pa., 1974-76, trustee; scout leader Valley Forge council Boy Scouts Am., 1960-71. Served to lt. USN, 1953-56. Mem. ABA, Phila. Bar Assn., Am. Arbitration Assn., U. Pa. Law Alumni Assn. (trustee 1987—), Order of Coif. Democrat. Jewish. Clubs: Phila. Racquet; London RAC. General corporate, Securities, Banking. Home: One Independence Pl Apt 1601 6th St and Locust Walk Philadelphia PA 19106 Office: Csaplar & Bok 1600 Market St Suite 3315 Philadelphia PA 19103

BECKMAN, DOUGLAS GARY, lawyer; b. Portland, Oreg., Sept. 24, 1944; s. Reinhold Emanuel and Lorraine Audrey (Rittenhouse) B.; m. Evelyn Maria Beckman, Dec. 27, 1970 (div. June 1980); 1 child, Karen Elizabeth; m. Karen Steinbock, Jan. 2, 1982; children: Rachel Lauren, Heather Rebecca. BA, Yale U., 1966; JD, U. Calif., Berkeley, 1972. Bar: Oreg. 1972, U.S. Dist. Ct. Oreg. 1972, U.S. Ct. Appeals (9th cir.) 1972, U.S. Supreme Ct. 1975. Assoc. Black, Kendall, Tremaine, Boothe & Higgins, Portland, 1972-85; ptnr. Ragen, Tremaine et al, Portland, 1985—. Served with U.S. Army, 1967-70, Vietnam. Mem. ABA (teaching trial advocacy com.), Oreg. Bar Assn. (chmn. continuing legal edn. publs. 1982-83, author publ. 1980, program planning plaque 1981), Multnomah County Bar Assn. (chmn. continuing legal edn. com. 1986—), Profl. Liability Fund Def. Panel, Multnomah County Panel Arbitrators, Yale Alumni Assn. Oreg. (pres. 1976). Democrat. Jewish. Avocation: running. State civil litigation, Federal civil litigation, Insurance. Home: 5417 SW Seymour St Portland OR 97221 Office: Ragen Tremaine et al 2300 1st Interstate Tower Portland OR 97201

BECKMAN, JILL MARIE, lawyer; b. Pitts., Mar. 29, 1956; d. Charles E. and Jean R. (Reid) B. BS, Pa. State U., 1978; JD, Pepperdine U., 1981. Bar: Pa. 1981, U.S. Dist. Ct. (mid. dist.) Pa. 1981. Assoc. McNees, Wallace & Nurick, Harrisburg, Pa., 1981-83; gen. atty. eastern group United Telephone, Carlisle, Pa., 1983—; instr. Franklin & Marshall Coll., Lancaster, Pa., 1983—, Pa. State U., Hershey, 1986—. Served with USNR, 1985—. Mem. ABA, Pa. Bar Assn., Masters Swim Team. Club: Harrisburg (Pa.) Bike. Avocations: biking, skiing, swimming. General corporate, Public utilities. Office: United Telephone 1170 Harrisburg Pike Carlisle PA 17013

BECKNER, DONALD LEE, lawyer; b. New Orleans, Dec. 18, 1939; s. Marion L. and Rose Ann (Lee) B.; m. Paulette White, Apr. 22, 1978; children: Donald Glynn, Kristin Dawn, Brittany Lee. B.S. in Econs., La. State U., 1959, J.D., 1965; grad., Nat. Coll. Dist. Attys., 1972, Nat. Jud. Coll., U. Nev., 1979. Bar: La., Calif., D.C., U.S. Dist. Ct. (so. dist.) Miss., U.S. Supreme Ct., U.S. Tax Ct. 1982. Vice pres., gen. mgr. Shells, Inc., 1957-65; partner firm Foil, Gill & Beckner, 1965-69; asst. dist. atty. E. Baton Rouge (La.) Parish, 1969-72; individual practice law 1972-74, Baton Rouge, 1981—; partner firm Gill, Lindsay, Seago & Beckner, Baton Rouge, 1974-77; U.S. atty. Middle Dist. La., 1977-81; guest speaker various civic orgns. Served with U.S. Army, 1957. Named Man of Year, Asso. Builders & Contractors La., 1981; Baton Rougeon of Yr., 1982. Mem. La. Bar Assn. (Ho. Dels.), Bar Assn. Fifth Fed. Circuit (bd. govs., lawyers adv. com. Fifth Circuit Ct. Appeals). Democrat. Clubs: City, Country of La. Lodge: Rotary (Baton Rouge). Federal civil litigation, General corporate, Criminal. Office: 9300 Bluebonnet Blvd Baton Rouge LA 70810

BECKSTEAD, JOHN A., lawyer; b. Murray, Utah, July 23, 1950; s. Farol W. and Ruth I. (Elieson) B.; m. Deborah Heiner, June 28, 1972; children: Alexander, Spencer, Taylor, Christopher. BA, U. Utah, 1972, JD, 1975. Bar: Ariz. 1975, U.S. Dist. Ct. Ariz. 1976, Utah 1977, U.S. Dist. Ct. Utah 1977, U.S. Ct. Appeals (10th cir.) 1977. Dep. county atty. Maricopa County (Ariz.) Atty.'s Office, 1975-76, spl. dep. county atty., 1976-80; assoc. Callister, Greene & Nebeker, Salt Lake City, 1977-80; ptnr. Callister, Duncan & Nebeker, Salt Lake City, 1981—. Mem. ABA (sub. com. creditor's rights, inventory and accounts receivable financing factor, comml. fin. services com.), Utah State Bar Assn. (sec. banking and fin. sect. 1983-84, vice chmn. 1984-85, chmn. 1985-86), Salt Lake County Bar Assn. Contracts commercial. Office: Callister Duncan & Nebeker 800 Kennecott Bldg Salt Lake City UT 84133

BECKSTROM, CHARLES G., lawyer; b. Jamestown, N.Y., July 14, 1940; s. Charles Wilbert and Dorothy Helen (Carlson) B.; m. Marie Jane Trebilcock, Nov. 28, 1964; children—Kimberly Leigh, Erika Lynn, Kristyn Marie, Stephanie Rae. B.A., Mich. State U., 1962; M.B.A., Wayne State U., 1966; J.D., SUNY-Buffalo, 1969. Bar: Mich. 1969, N.Y. 1971. Ptnr. Johnson, Peterson, Tener & Anderson, Jamestown, 1970—; fin. analyst Fisher Body div. Gen. Motors Corp., Warren, Mich., 1963-66; lawyer Ernst & Ernst, Detroit, 1969-70; town atty. Town of Ellery, N.Y., 1972-83. Trustee, chmn. 1st Covenant Ch. Jamestown, 1976-82; chmn., bd. pensions Evangelical Covenant Ch. Nat. Pension Plan, Chgo., 1979-84; mem. exec. bd. Evangelical Covenant Ch., 1986—. Served with U.S. Army, 1963-64. Mem. Jamestown Bar Assn., N.Y. Assn. Sch. Attys., Jamestown Estate Planning Council (pres., v.p., sec.), Internat. Found. Employee Benefit Plans. Republican. Clubs: Norden; Chautauqua Lake Yacht. Labor, Pension, profit-sharing, and employee benefits, General corporate. Home: 125 Westminster Dr WE Jamestown NY 14701 Office: 4th Floor Key Bank Bldg Jamestown NY 14701

BECKSTROM, JOHN H., lawyer, educator; b. 1932. B.A., U. Iowa, 1954, J.D., 1959; LL.M., Harvard U., 1966; M.A. U. London, 1971-72. Bar: Iowa 1959, N.Y. 1960, Ill. 1961. Assoc. Dewey, Ballantine, N.Y.C., 1959-64; teaching fellow Harvard U., 1964-66; assoc. prof. Northwestern U., Chgo., 1966-73, prof., 1973—; Fulbright postdoctoral research fellow U. London, 1971-72. Mem. Order of Coif. Article and note editor U. Iowa Law Rev. Legal education. Office: Northwestern U Law Sch 357 E Chicago Ave Chicago IL 60611 *

BECKWITH, KAREN LU, lawyer; b. Kingston, Pa., June 28, 1956; d. Chung-tai and Chi-hui (Ching) Lu; m. Jeffrey John Beckwith, Aug. 20, 1983. BA in Polit. Sci., Carleton Coll.; JD, U. Wis. Bar: Wis., Mich., U.S. Dist. Ct. (we. dist.) Wis. Atty. Dow Chem. Co., Midland, Mich., 1981-83, Merrell Dow Pharms. Inc., Cin., 1983—. Mem. Big Sisters Am. Environment, Federal civil litigation, State civil litigation. Office: Merrell Dow Pharms Inc 2110 E Galbraith Cincinnati OH 45215

BECKWITH, LEWIS DANIEL, lawyer; b. Indpls., Jan. 30, 1948; s. William Frederick and Helen Lorena (Smith) B.; m. Marcia Ellen Ride, June 27, 1970; children: Laura, Gregory. BA, Wabash Coll., 1970; JD, Vanderbilt U., 1973. Bar: Ind. 1973, U.S. Dist. Ct. (so. dist.) Ind. 1973. Assoc. Baker & Daniels, Indpls., 1973-80, ptnr., 1981—; bd. dirs. Electric Steel Castings Co., Indpls. Articles editor Vanderbilt Law Rev., 1972-73. Mem. ABA, Ind. Bar Assn., Indlps. Bar Assn., Ind. C. of C. (chmn. subcom. right-to-know laws 1985—, com occupations safety and haelth law1982—), Order of Coif, Eta Sigma Phi. Republican. Lutheran. Club: Indpls. Athletic. Avocation: sports. Environment, Labor, Administrative and regulatory. Office: Baker & Daniels 810 Fletcher Trust Bldg Indianapolis IN 46204

BECNEL, PHILIP ALFRED, III, lawyer; b. Schenectady, N.Y., Nov. 27, 1942; s. Philip Alfred Becnel Jr. and Dorothy Madeline Knobloch; m. Joan Baker, Feb. 22, 1981; 1 child from previous marriage, Philip A. IV. BS, U.S. Naval Acad., 1964; JD, U. San Francisco, 1972. Bar: Calif. 1972, La. 1976; registered profl. engr., La., Calif. Commd. ensign USN, 1964, advanced through grades to lt., resigned, 1969; engr., then engring. supr. Bechtel Corp., San Francisco, 1969-72, counsel, 1972-84; atty. Adams & Reese, New Orleans, 1984—. Mem. ABA (mem. corp., banking, bus. law sects., forum com. on construction indsutry), Calif. Bar Assn., La. Bar Assn. (corp., bus. law sects.). General corporate, Construction. Office: Adams & Reese One Shell Square Suite 4500 New Orleans LA 70139

BEDDOW, JOHN WARREN, lawyer; b. Washington, Apr. 8, 1952; s. Thomas John and Virginia Coleburn (Fenton) B.; m. Mary Christine Jackson, July 28, 1974; children: Blair Kristen, Christopher John. BS, U. N.C., 1974, JD, 1977. Bar: N.C. 1977, U.S. Dist. Ct. (we. dist.) N.C. 1977, U.S. Tax Ct. 1979. Assoc. Lindsey, Schrimsher, Erwin, Bernhardt & Hewitt, Charlotte, 1977-79; ptnr. Lindsey, Schrimsher, Erwin, Bernhardt, Hewitt & Beddow, Charlotte, 1979-80, Erwin & Beddow, Charlotte, 1980-85, Erwin, Beddow & Reese, Charlotte, 1985-86, Weinstein & Sturges, Charlotte, 1986—. Mem. ABA, N.C. Bar Assn. (council mem. tax sect. 1981—), Phi Beta Kappa, Phi Eta Sigma. Democrat. Episcopalian. Club: Carmel Country (Charlotte). Lodge: Civitan. Avocations: hunting, fishing, golf. Probate, Personal income taxation, Real property. Home: 2208 Colony Rd Charlotte NC 28209 Office: Weinstein & Sturges 810 Baxter St Charlotte NC 28202

BEDFORD, DANIEL ROSS, lawyer; b. Berwyn, Ill., Aug. 19, 1945; s. Fred Doyle and Nelda Elizabeth (Dittrich) B.; m. Susan Rives, Mar. 25, 1967; children: Ian, Kate. BS, Stanford U., 1967, JD, 1971, MBA, 1971. Bar: Calif. 1972. Assoc. Thelen & Marrin, San Francisco, 1971-78, ptnr., 1979-86; ptnr. Orrick, Herrington & Sutcliffe, San Francisco, 1986—. Mem. ABA, Calif. Bar Assn., San Francisco Bar Assn., Am. Coll. of Investment Counsel. Democrat. Episcopalian. Contracts commercial, General corporate. Home: 1661 Ascension Dr San Mateo CA 94402 Office: 600 Montgomery St San Francisco CA 94111

BEDINGER, FRANK CLEVELAND, JR., lawyer; b. Boydton, Va., May 12, 1916; s. Frank Cleveland and Lena (Reekes) B.; m. Martha Ingram Smith, Oct. 6, 1951; children: Martha, William, Frank, Lucy. BA, Hampden-Sydney Coll., 1937; LLB, Washington and Lee U., 1941. Bar: Va. 1940. Spl. agt. FBI, 1941-44; ptnr. Bedinger, Bedinger & Lipscomb, Boydton, 1946—; mem. disciplinary bd. Va. State Bar, 1976-81. Served to cpl. USMC, 1944-46, PTO. Mem. ABA, Va. Bar Assn., Mecklenburg County Bar Assn. Episcopalian. General practice, Criminal, Real property. Home and Office: PO Drawer 310 Boydton VA 23917

BEEBY, KENNETH JACK, lawyer, food company executive; b. Peoria, Ill., May 21, 1936; s. Harold J. and L. and Elizabeth (Otten) B.; m. Shelley Jean Seip, June 14, 1959; children—Kathryn Jean, Sara Jane, Christine Vivian. B.A., Beloit (Wis.) Coll., 1958; J.D., Northwestern U., 1961. Bar: Ind. 1961, Ill. 1961, Mo. 1962, Mass. 1974. Staff atty. Seven-Up Co., St. Louis, 1961-73; house counsel, then chief legal officer Ocean Spray Cranberries, Inc., Hanson, Mass., 1973-77; v.p., gen. counsel Ocean Spray Cranberries, Inc., Plymouth, Mass., 1977—, sec., 1982—. Mem. ABA, Mass. Bar Assn., Am. Corp. Counsel Assn. Antitrust, General corporate, Trademark and copyright. Office: Ocean Spray Cranberries Inc Water St Plymouth MA 02360

BEECH, JOHNNY GALE, lawyer; b. Chickasha, Okla., Sept. 18, 1954; s. Lovell Gale and Lucille L. (Phillips) B.; m. Judy Carol Schroeder, Dec. 31, 1977. BS, Southwestern Okla. State U., 1977; JD, U. Ark., Little Rock, 1980; LLM in Energy-Environment, Tulane U., 1985. Bar: Okla. 1980, U.S. Dist. Ct. (we. dist.) Okla. 1982, U.S. Dist. Ct. (no. dist.) Tex. 1983, U.S. Dist. Ct. (no. dist.) Okla. 1986. Assoc. Meacham, Meacham and Meacham, Clinton, Okla., 1980-84, Ford & Brown, Enid, Okla., 1985-86, Wright & Sawyer, Enid, 1986—; mcpl. judge town of Arapaho, Okla., 1982-84. bd. dirs. Jr. Achievement Garfield County, Enid, 1986—. Mem. ABA (real property, probate and trusts sect.), Assn. Trial Lawyers Am., Okla. Bar Assn., Garfield County Bar Assn., Am. Bus. Club, Southwestern Okla. State U. Alumni Assn. (pres. 1983—), Southwestern Sch. Bus. Alumni Assn. (v.p. 1980—), Jaycees, Phi Alpha Delta (sec. 1979). Democrat. Methodist. Club: Am. Bus., Enid. Avocations: hunting, fishing, weight lifting. Banking, State civil litigation, Oil and gas leasing. Home: 702 N Cook Cordell OK 73632 Office: Wright & Sawyer 1010 W Maple Enid OK 73702

BEEKMAN, WILLIAM BEDLOE, lawyer; b. N.Y.C., July 8, 1949; s. Robert Struthers and Mary (Marckwald) B.; m. Helen Hinckley, June 7, 1980; children: Izaak, Hugo. BA magna cum laude, Harvard U., 1971; JD, Yale U., 1980. Bar: N.Y. 1981. Assoc. Debevoise & Plimpton, N.Y.C., 1980-86; bd. dirs. Lafayette Studios Corp., N.Y.C. Mem. ABA, Assn. of Bar of City of N.Y. (copyright com.). Democrat. Episcopalian. General corporate, Securities, Trademark and copyright. Home: 284 Lafayette St Apt 4B New York NY 10012 Office: Debevoise & Plimpton 875 3d Ave New York NY 10022

BEELER, THOMAS JOSEPH, lawyer, manufacturing company executive; b. Marion, Ind., June 5, 1933; s. Thomas James and Margaret B. (Milford) B.; children: Kristin, Mark, Laura. B.S. in Bus. Adminstrn. cum laude, Notre Dame U., 1956, J.D., 1957. Bar: Ind. 1957. Sole practice Anderson, 1958-61; asst. sec., counsel The Weatherhead Co., Cleve., 1961-68; asst. gen. counsel, corp. sec. A-T-O Inc., Willoughby, Ohio, 1968-74; corp. atty., sec. Outboard Marine Corp., Waukegan, Ill., 1974-76; v.p., gen. counsel, sec. Outboard Marine Corp., 1976—. Served to 1st lt. AUS, 1957-58. Mem. Am., Ind. bar assns., Am. Soc. Corp. Secs. Home: 701 E Prospect Ave Lake Bluff IL 60044 Office: 100 Sea-Horse Dr Waukegan IL 60085

BEEM, JACK DARREL, lawyer; b. Chgo., Nov. 17, 1931. A.B., U. Chgo., 1952, J.D., 1955. Bar: Ill. 1955. Assoc. firm Wilson & McIlvaine, Chgo., 1958-63; ptnr. firm Baker & McKenzie, Chgo., 1963—. Mem. ABA, Ill. Bar Assn., Chgo. Bar Assn. Home: 175 E Delaware Pl Apt 8104 Chicago IL 60611 Office: Baker & McKenzie Suite 2800 Prudential Plaza Chicago IL 60601

BEEMER, JOHN BARRY, lawyer; b. Scranton, Pa., Sept. 4, 1941; s. Ellis and Rose Mary (Costello) B.; m. Diane Montgomery Fletcher, July 18, 1964; children—David, Bruce. B.S., U. Scranton, 1963; LL.B., George Washington U., 1966. Bar: Pa. 1966; cert. civil trial advocate Nat. Bd. Trial Advocacy. Law clk. trial div. U.S. Ct. Claims, 1966-67; clk. to judge U.S. Dist. Ct. Middle Dist. Pa., 1967-68; assoc. Warren, Hill, Henkelman & McMenamin, Scranton, 1968-72; pres. Beemer, Rinaldi, Fendrick & Mellody, P.C., Scranton, 1972-83; ptnr. Beemer & Beemer, 1984—. Chmn. com. constn. and by-laws revision Lackawanna (county, Pa.) United Fund, 1971. Mem. ABA, Pa. Bar Assn., Lackawanna Bar Assn., Assn. Trial Lawyers Am., Pa. Trial Lawyers Assn. Criminal, Federal civil litigation, State civil litigation. Home: 320 Tulip Circle Clarks Summit PA 18411 Office: 334 N Spy Rd Clarks Summit PA 18411

BEENS, RICHARD ALBERT, lawyer; b. Tracy, Minn., Sept. 7, 1941; s. Albert Charles and Dolores (Burnham) B.; m. Lynn Margaret Baker, Aug. 20, 1966 (dec. June 1973); 1 child, Jennifer Lois; m. Laura Lee Marie Geraghty, Aug. 9, 1974. BA, Coll. St. Thomas, St. Paul, 1965; JD, U. Minn., 1968. Bar: Minn. 1968, U.S. Ct. Appeals (8th cir.) 1968. From assoc. to ptnr. Babcock & Locher, Anoka, Minn., 1968-77; ptnr. Steffen, Munstentieger, Beens & Peterson, Anoka, 1977—; instr. U. Minn. Law Sch., Mpls., 1972-73; asst. pub. defender State of Minn., Anoka, 1977-83, State Bd. PUb. Defenders 1986—. Vol. Peace Corps, West Pakistan, 1962-64; commr. Met. Waste Control Com., St. Paul, 1974-83; mem. Aviation Adv. Task Force, St. Paul, 1984-85; chmn. adv. com. Met. Council Solid Waste, St. Paul, 1986—. Mem. Assn. Trial Lawyers Am., Minn. Trial Lawyers Assn., Minn. Bar Assn., Anoka County Bar Assn. (chmn. ethics com. 1982—, chmn. judicial evaluation com. 1987—), Am. Arbitration Assn. (arbitrator 1970—). Avocations: reading, hunting, fishing. Federal civil litigation, State civil litigation, Criminal. Office: Steffen Munstentieger Beens & Peterson 403 Jackson St Anoka MN 55303

BEER, BETTY LOUISE, lawyer; b. Waco, Tex., July 17, 1943; d. William Lester and Ruth (Parks) B.; m. Sherwood James Franklin, June 16, 1979; 1 son, Jacob Harrison. B.A., Oberlin Coll., 1965; J.D., St. Louis U., 1974. Bar: Ill. 1974. Assoc. Kavanagh Scully Sudow White & Frederick, Peoria, Ill., 1974-78; owner Allen and Beer, Aledo, Ill., 1978—; asst. states atty. Mercer County, Aledo, 1979-84. Editor St. Louis U. Law Jour., 1974. Bd. dirs. Mo. Pub. Interest Research Group, 1973-74, Peoria Civic Opera, 1975-78, Prairie State Legal Services, Inc., 1975-77; bd. dirs., pres. Peoria City Beautiful, 1975-78; active Tri County Women Strength, Peoria, 1975-76; founding mem. Mercer County Coalition Against Domestic Violence, 1984-85, Greasepaint Guild Theater, Aledo, 1980-83. Mem. ABA, Ill. State Bar Assn. (estate planning council 1982, lawyer referral com 1975-82, ins. com., 1987, pres. 1981), Mercer County Bar Assn. (pres. 1985—). Republican. Baptist. Lodge: PEO. General practice, Probate, Estate planning. Home: 207 SE 6th St Aledo IL 61231

BEER, LAWRENCE WARD, government and law educator; b. Portland, Oreg., May 11, 1932; s. Norman Henry and Lucile Mary (Hodges) B.; m. Keiko Juliana Harada, Oct. 21, 1961; children—David, Christopher, Kimberley, Lawrence. A.B., Gonzaga U., 1956, M.A., 1957; postgrad. Fordham U., summer 1957; grad. 2 yr. program Japanese Lang. Sch., Tokyo, 1960; Ph.D., U. Wash., 1966. Tng. dir. Calif. Credit Union League, Oakland, 1961-62; instr. English and philosophy Sophia U., Tokyo, 1957, 60-61; mem. faculty U. Colo., Boulder, 1966-82, prof. polit. sci., 1974-82; Fred Morgan Kirby prof. civil rights Lafayette Coll., Easton, Pa., 1982—, head dept. govt. and law, 1982-85; vis. research scholar Faculty of Law, U. Tokyo, 1969-70, 73, 78-79, 82, 84; Fulbright prof. law Hokkaido U., Sapporo, Japan, 1986-87; mem. Am. adv. com. Japan Found., Washington, 1982-84. Author: (with Hiroshi Itoh) The Constitutional Case Law of Japan, 1978; Freedom of Expression in Japan, 1984; author (with others), editor (with Colin Chilton): Credit Union Family Financial Counseling, 1962; author (with others), editor: Constitutionalism in Asia, 1979, Japanese edit., 1981. Mem. editorial adv. com. Law in Japan, 1978—; mem. internat. adv. com. Pacific Basin Law Jour., 1985—. Contbr. articles to profl. jours. and books. Mem. Assn. for Asian Studies (chmn. com. on Asian law 1973-78, 82-85, mem. exec. com. Mid-Atlantic region 1984-85), Am. Polit. Sci. Assn., World Assn. Law Profs. (co-chmn. 1985—). Democrat. Roman Catholic. Legal education, Japanese, Civil rights. Home: 929 Powder Mill Rd Bethlehem PA 18017 Office: Dept Govt and Law Lafayette Coll Easton PA 18042

BEER, PETER HILL, judge; b. New Orleans, Apr. 12, 1928; s. Mose Haas and Henret (Lowenburg) B.; children: Kimberly Beer Bailes, Kenneth, Dana Beer Long-Innes; m. Marjorie Barry, July 14, 1985. B.B.A., Tulane U., 1949, LL.B., 1952; LL.M., U. Va., 1986. Bar: La. 1952. Successively assoc., partner, sr. partner Montgomery, Barnett, Brown & Read, New Orleans, 1955-74; judge La. Ct. Appeal, 1974-79; U.S. dist. judge Eastern Dist. La., 1979—; vice chmn. La. Appellate Judges Conf.; apptd. by chief justice of U.S. to state-fed. com. Jud. Conf. of U.S., 1985; cir. rep. bd. of govs. (5th cir.) Fed. Judges Assn. Bd. mgrs. Touro Infirmary, New Orleans, 1969-74; exec. com. Bur. Govtl. Research, 1965-69; chmn. profl. div. United Fund New Orleans, 1966-69; mem. New Orleans City Council, 1969-74, v.p., 1972-74. Served to capt. USAF, 1952-55. Decorated AF Commendation medal, Bronze Star. Mem. ABA (ho. of dels.), Am. Judicature Soc., Fed. Bar Assn., La. State Bar Assn., Fed. Judges Assn. of U.S. (bd. dirs. 1985). Jewish. Clubs: Nat. Lawyers, So. Yacht, Audubon Golf. Home: 5855 Bellaire Dr New Orleans LA 70124 Office: US Courthouse 500 Camp St New Orleans LA 70130

BEERBOWER, CYNTHIA GIBSON, lawyer; b. Dayton, Ohio, June 25, 1949; d. Charles Augustus and Sara (Rittenhouse) Gibson; m. John Edwin Beerbower, Aug. 28, 1971; 1 son, John Eliot. B.A., Mt. Holyoke Coll., 1971; J.D., Boston U., 1974; LL.B., Cambridge U., Eng., 1976. Bar: N.Y. 1975. Assoc., Cadwalader, Wickersham & Taft, N.Y.C., 1975-76; assoc. Simpson, Thacher & Bartlett, N.Y.C., 1977-81, ptnr., 1981—. Mem. Assn. Bar City N.Y., N.Y. State Bar Assn., ABA. Corporate taxation. Home: 720 Park Ave New York NY 10021 Office: Simpson Thacher & Bartlett 1 Battery Park Plaza New York NY 10004

BEERMAN, BERNARD MARVIN, lawyer; b. N.Y.C., Apr. 23, 1936; s. Michael and Ester Flora (Goodman) B.; m. Frances Ann Ferrall; children: Rachel, Michael, David, Jenifer. BA, Princeton U., 1958; LLB, George Washington U., 1962. Bar: D.C. 1983, Md. 1983. Ptnr. Morison, Murphy, Abrams & Haddock, Washington, 1968-71, mng. ptnr., 1971-79; ptnr. Baker & Hostetler, Washington, 1979-82, Stein, Miller, Brodsky & Beerman, Washington, 1982-85, Stein, Stills & Brodsky, Washington, 1986—; cons. Strategic Resources, Inc., Stamford, Conn., 1985—; counsel The Nat. Burglar & Fire Alarm Assn., Washington, 1986—, Cen. Sta. Elec. Assn., 1986—; pres. Alarm Industry Telecommunications Cons., Washington, 1986—. Spl. counsel D.C. Rep. Com., Washington, 1965-66; mem. pvt. security adv. panel Law Enforcement Assistance Adminstrn., Washington, 1975-77; bd. dirs. Choral Arts of Washington, 1966—. Mem. ABA, Am. Judicature Soc., Princeton Terr. (bd. dirs. 1985—). Clubs: International (Washington), Princeton Terr. (bd. dirs. 1985—), Nassau of Princeton.

Avocations: landscaping, photography. Antitrust, Administrative and regulatory. Home: 13206 Chestnut Oak Dr Darnestown MD 20878-2553 Office: Nat Burglar & Fire Alarm Assn 1120 19th St NW Washington DC 20036

BEERS, DONALD OSBORNE, lawyer; b. Sodus, N.Y., May 28, 1949; s. John Taylor and Edna Viola (DuMond) B.; m. Deborah Constance Merkamp, Mar. 16, 1974; children: Laura DuMond, Emily Katherine, Michael Osborne. AB, Dartmouth Coll., 1971; JD, Columbia U., 1974. Bar: N.Y. 1975, U.S. Ct. Appeals (10th cir.) 1978, U.S. Ct. Appeals (D.C. cir.) 1979, U.S. Ct. Appeals (5th cir.) 1980, D.C. 1986, U.S. Dist. Ct. D.C. 1986, U.S. Supreme Ct. 1986. Law clk. to judge U.S. Dist. Ct. (so. dist.) N.Y., N.Y.C., 1974-75; atty. office chief counsel FDA, Rockville, Md., 1975-85; of counsel McCutchen, Doyle, Brown & Enersen, Washington, 1985—; lectr. U. Pa. Law Sch., Phila., 1982-84. Contbr. articles to profl. jours. Mem. ABA. Democrat. Methodist. Administrative and regulatory, Food and drug, Federal civil litigation. Office: Willard Office Bldg 1455 Pennsylvania Ave NW Suite 650 Washington DC 20004

BEERY, FRED JEROME, lawyer; b. Cin., July 5, 1955; s. Forrest Frederick and Jeanne Maxine (Johnson) B.; m. Michele Sue Manifold, Aug. 20, 1977; 1 child, Jo Beth Ellen. BCE, Ohio State U., 1978; postgrad., Franklin U., 1979; JD, Capital U., 1982. Bar: Ohio 1982, U.S. Dist. Ct. (so. dist.) Ohio 1983. Engr. planning Ohio Dept. Transp., Columbus, 1978-80; ptnr. Beery & Beery, Hillsboro, Ohio, 1982—; law dir. City of Hillsboro, 1984—; solicitor Village of Mowrystown, Ohio, 1985—. Sch. atty. Bd. of Edn., Hillsboro, 1984—; chmn. fin. United Meth. Ch., Hillsboro, 1986—; v.p., pres. bd. dirs. Rural Legal Aid, Springfield, Ohio, 1983—. Mem. ABA, Ohio Bar Assn., Assn. Trial Lawyers Am., Ohio Assn. Sch. Bd. Attys., Profl. Land Surveyors of Ohio. Club: Aircraft Owners and Pilots Assn. Lodge: Rotary. Personal injury, Probate, Real property. Office: Beery & Beery 125 N High St Hillsboro OH 45133

BEESLEY, BRUCE THOMAS, lawyer; b. Salem, Oreg., Feb. 15, 1952; s. Richard C. and Ruth Irene (Goodrich) B.; m. Mary Ann Morgan. BA, U. Nev., 1975; JD, U. Pacific, 1978. Bar: Calif. 1978, Nev. 1979, U.S. Dist. Ct. (no. dist.) Nev. 1979, U.S. Dist. Ct. (no. and ea. dists.) Calif. 1984, U.S. Ct. Appeals (9th cir.) 1984, U.S. Dist. Ct. (cen. dist.) Calif. 1985, U.S. Supreme Ct. 1985. Law clk. to presiding justice U.S. Dist. Ct., Reno, 1978-79; pub. defender Washoe County, Reno, 1979-80; assoc. Woodburn, Wedge, Blaky & Jeppson, Reno, 1980-82; assoc. Robison, Lyle, Belaustegui & Robb, Reno, 1982-84, ptnr., 1984—. Trustee Washoe County Law Library, Reno, 1983—; mem. No. Nev. Disciplinary Bd., Reno, 1984—. Mem. ABA, Washoe County Bar Assn. (bd. dirs. 1983—). Republican. Bankruptcy, Contracts commercial. Office: Robison Lyle Belaustegui & Robb 71 Washington St Reno NV 89503

BEEZER, ROBERT RENAUT, judge; b. Seattle, July 21, 1928; s. Arnold Roswell and Josephine (May) B.; m. Hazlehurst Plant Smith, June 15, 1957; children—Robert Arnold, John Leighton, Mary Allison. Student, U. Wash., 1946-48, 51; B.A., U. Va., 1951, LL.B, 1956. Bar: Wash. 1956, U.S. Supreme Ct. 1968. Ptnr. Schweppe, Krug, Tausend & Beezer, P.S., Seattle, 1956-84; judge U.S. Ct. Appeals (9th cir.), Seattle, 1984—; alt. mem. Wash. Jud. Qualifications Commn., Olympia, 1981-84. Served to 1st lt. USMCR, 1951-53. Fellow Am. Coll. Probate Counsel, Am. Bar Found.; mem. ABA, Seattle-King County Bar Assn. (pres. 1975-76), Wash. Bar Assn. (bd. govs. 1980-83). Clubs: Rainier, Tennis (Seattle). Office: US Ct Appeals 9th Cir 1010 5th Ave Suite 802 Seattle WA 98104

BEEZLEY, THEODORE, lawyer; b. Cooks Sta., Mo., June 2, 1914; s. John and Amanda (Springer) B.; m. Virginia Elizabeth Roberts, July 5, 1941; children: Robert Theodore, John Bruce. JD, U. Mo., 1938. Bar: Mo. 1938, U.S. Dist. Ct. (so. dist.) Mo. 1940, U.S. Ct. Appeals (8th cir.) 1940. City atty. City of Springfield, Mo., 1941-45, atty., 1945-48; ptnr. Beezley & Beezley, Springfield, 1948—. Mem. ABA, Mo. Bar Assn., Greene County Bar Assn. (pres. 1968), Fed. Bar Assn., Assn. Trial Lawyers Am. (sustaining). Democrat. Personal injury, Product liabilty, Workers' compensation. Home: 1522 S Virginia Springfield MO 65807 Office: Beezley & Beezley 226 Woodruff Bldg Springfield MO 65806

BEGAM, ROBERT GEORGE, lawyer; b. N.Y.C., Apr. 5, 1928; s. George and Hilda M. (Hirt) B.; m. Helen C. Clark, July 24, 1949; children—Richard, Lorinda, Michael. B.A., Yale U., 1949, LL.B., 1952. Bar: N.Y. bar 1952, Ariz. bar 1956. Assoc. firm Cravath, Swaine & Moore, N.Y.C., 1952-54; spl. counsel State of Ariz., Colorado River Litigation in U.S. Supreme Ct., 1956-58; ptnr. Langerman, Begam, Lewis & Marks, Phoenix, 1958—. Pres. Ariz. Repertory Theater, 1960-66; treas. Ariz. Democratic Party, 1964-70, chief counsel, 1970-76; bd. dirs. Phoenix Theater Center, 1955-60; chmn. Attys. Congl. Campaign Trust, 1979—; trustee Atla Roscoe Pound Found. Served as 1st lt. USAF, 1954-56. Fellow Internat. Soc. Barristers; mem. Assn. Trial Lawyers Am. (pres. 1976-77), Western Trial Lawyers Assn. (pres. 1970), Am. Bd. Trial Advocates. Clubs: Yale (N.Y.C.); Ariz. Biltmore Country (Phoenix); Desert Highlands Country (Scottsdale, Ariz.); Palmetto Dunes Country (Hilton Head, S.C.). Personal injury, Federal civil litigation, State civil litigation. Home: 77 E Missouri #12 Phoenix AZ 85012 Office: Langerman Begam Lewis & Marks 1400 Ariz Title Bldg Phoenix AZ 85003

BEGER, JOHN DAVID, lawyer; b. St. Charles, Mo., Oct. 12, 1954; s. Carl Harold and Elizabeth Mae (Heye) B.; m. Cynthia Ann Morris, June 7, 1981. BSBA, U. Mo., 1976, JD, 1978. Bar: U.S. Dist. Ct. (we. dist.) Mo. 1979, U.S. Dist. Ct. (ea. dist.) Mo. 1981. Asst. pros. atty. Phelps County, Rolla, Mo., 1979-82; gen. ptnr. Beger & White, Rolla, 1981-82, Price & Beger, Salem, Mo., 1982-86; sole practice Rolla, Mo., 1986—; city atty. City of Doolittle, Mo., 1980-81; mcpl. judge City of Bourbon, Mo., 1980-85; chmn. Rolla Police Personal Bd., 1983—; cons. Salem Police Personal Bd., 1985. Mem. ABA., Mo. Bar Assn. (criminal law com.), Assn. Trial Lawyers Am., Mo. Assn. Trial Attys. Republican. Club: Bennett Springs (Mo.) Barristers. Criminal, State civil litigation, Insurance.

BEGGS, HARRY MARK, lawyer; b. Los Angeles, Nov. 15, 1941; s. John Edgar and Agnes (Kentro) B.; m. Sandra Lynne Mikal, May 25, 1963; children—Brendan, Sean, Corey, Michael. Student, Ariz. State U., 1959-61, Phoenix Coll., 1961; LL.B., U. Ariz., 1964. Bar: Ariz. 1964, U.S. Dist. Ct. Ariz. 1964, U.S. Ct. Appeals (9th cir.) 1973. Assoc. Carson Messinger, Elliott, Laughlin & Ragan, Phoenix, 1964-69, ptnr., 1969—; mem. Civil Practice and Procedure Com., State Bar of Ariz., 1969-80, Fin. Insts. Counsels Com., 1980-83; founding fellow Ariz. Bar Found. Recipient award for highest grade on state bar exam. Atty. Gen. Ariz., 1964; Fegtly Moot Ct. award, 1963, 64; Abner S. Lipscomb scholar U. Ariz. Law Sch., 1963. Mem. State Bar of Ariz., Maricopa County Bar Assn., ABA. (litigation, antitrust sects.), Ariz. Acad. Clubs: Plaza, LaMancha Racquet. Mem. editorial bd. Ariz. Law Rev. 1963-64; contbr. articles to profl. jours. General practice, Federal civil litigation, Banking. Address: PO Box 33907 Phoenix AZ 85067

BEGHE, RENATO, lawyer; b. Chgo., Mar. 12, 1933; s. Bruno and Emmavve (Frymire) B.; m. Bina House, July 10, 1954; children: Eliza Ashley, Francesca Forbes, Adam House, Jason Deneen. B.A., U. Chgo., 1951, J.D., 1954. Bar: N.Y. bar 1955. Mng. editor U. Chgo. Law Review, 1953-54; since practiced in N.Y.C.; assoc. Carter, Ledyard & Milburn, 1954-65, ptnr., 1965-83; ptnr. Morgan, Lewis & Bockius, 1983—; lectr. N.Y. U. Fed. Tax Inst., 1967, 78, U. Chgo. Fed. Tax Conf., 1974, 80, 86, also other profl. confs. Contbr. articles to profl. jours. Mem. ABA, Am. Law Inst., Internat. Bar Assn., Internat. Fiscal Assn., N.Y. State Bar Assn. (chmn. tax sect. 1977-78), Am. Coll. Tax Counsel, Assn. Bar City N.Y. (chmn. art law com. 1980-83), Phi Beta Kappa, Order of Coif, Phi Gamma Delta. Clubs: Lakeside Golf (N.Y.); America-Italy Society Inc. (dir 1980—). Home: 300 West End Ave New York NY 10023

BEGLEY, LOUIS, lawyer; b. Stryj, Poland, Oct. 6, 1933; came to U.S., 1948, naturalized, 1953; s. Edward David Begley and Frances Hauser; m. Sally Higginson, Feb. 11, 1956 (div. May 1970); children—Peter Higginson, Amey B. Larmore, Adam C.; m. Anne Muhlstein Dujarric dela Riviere, Mar. 30, 1974. AB summa cum laude, Harvard U., 1954, LLB magna cum laude, 1959. Bar: N.Y. 1961. Assoc. Debevoise & Plimpton, N.Y.C., 1959-67, ptnr., 1968—; sr. vis. lectr. Wharton Sch., U. Pa., Phila., spring, 1985, 86. Bd. dirs., mem. steering com. French Am. Found., N.Y.C., 1975-82; mem. adv. com. Inst. French Studies, N.Y.C., 1981—. Served with U.S. Army, 1954-56. Mem. Assn. Bar of City of N.Y. (various coms. 1960—), Union Internationale des Avocats, Council on Fgn. Relations. Democrat. Club: Century Assn. (N.Y.C.). General corporate, Private international. Home: 925 Park Ave New York NY 10028 Office: Debevoise & Plimpton 875 3d Ave New York NY 10022

BEGOS, WALTER ANTHONY, lawyer, consultant; b. N.Y.C., Aug. 8, 1930; s. Walter and Catherine (Canney) B.; m. Katheleen O'Kelly, Oct. 29, 1959; children—Dennis G., Patrick W., Brian J., Michael V. B.S., Fordham Coll., 1955, J.D., 1959. Bar: N.Y. 1960, U.S. Dist. Ct. (ea. and so. dists.) N.Y. 1968, U.S. Supreme Ct. 1975. Asst. mgr. claims Allstate Ins. Co., Bronx, N.Y., 1955-61; assoc. A.L. D'Sernia, N.Y.C., 1961-63; trial atty. Liberty Mut. Ins. Co., N.Y.C., 1963-68, Bower, O'Connor & Gardiner, N.Y.C., 1969; ptnr., trial atty. Anthony J. DeVito, White Plains, N.Y., 1970-74; ptnr. Schiavetti Begos & Nicholson, N.y.C., 1974—. Mem. Soc. Med. Jurisprudence, Def. Research Inst., ABA, N.Y. State Bar Assn., Bronx County Bar Assn., Westchester County Bar Assn. Roman Catholic. Personal injury, Health, State civil litigation. Home: 521 Scarsdale Rd Crestwood NY 10707 Office: Schiavetti Begos & Nicholson 1633 Broadway New York NY 10019

BEGOUN, MICHAEL JAY, lawyer; b. Chgo., Nov. 11, 1956; s. Sherwin Terry and Ina Jean (Lefstin) B.; m. Jacqueline Mary Randazza, Sept. 21, 1986. BS in Advt., U. Ill., 1978; JD, Loyola U., New Orleans, 1981. Bar: La. 1981, U.S. Dist. Ct. (ea. dist.) La. 1982, U.S. Ct. Appeals (5th cir.) 1984. Asst. dist. atty. Orleans Parish, New Orleans, 1981-84; assoc. Herman, Herman, Katz & Cotlar, New Orleans, 1984—. Mem. ABA, La. Bar Assn., Assn. Trial Lawyers Am., La. Trial Lawyers Assn., Sigma Alpha Mu. Democrat. Jewish. Personal injury, Consumer commercial, Bankruptcy. Home: 1425 Wisteria Dr Metairie LA 70005 Office: Herman Herman Katz & Cotlar 820 OKeefe Ave New Orleans LA 70113

BEHA, JAMES ALEXIUS, II, lawyer; b. N.Y.C., July 3, 1949; s. James J. and Macy Ann (Reilly) B.; m. Nancy Ryan, June 10, 1972; children: Mary Alice, James J., Christopher R. BA, Princeton U., 1971; MA, Harvard U., 1974, JD, 1975, PhD, 1986. Bar: N.Y. 1976, U.S. Dist. Ct. (so. and ea. dists.) N.Y. 1976, U.S. Tax Ct. 1981. Assoc. Cravath, Swaine & Moore, N.Y.C., 1976-78; of counsel Gasser & Hayes, N.Y.C., 1978—; ptnr. Hertzog, Calamari & Gleason, N.Y.C., 1980—; cons. criminal justice coordinating council City of N.Y., 1978-80; bd. dirs. Draw Investment Co., Montreal, Can., Huntsham Investment Co., Montreal. Trustee Loyola Sch., N.Y.C., 1983—, Children of Bellevue, Inc., N.Y.C., 1986—. Mem. ABA, N.Y. State Bar Assn., New York County Lawyers Assn. Roman Catholic. Federal civil litigation, State civil litigation, Probate. Office: Hertzog Calamari & Gleason 100 Park Ave New York NY 10017

BEHA, RALPH WERNER, lawyer; b. Racine, Wis., Oct. 10, 1950; m. Judith Hope Spirer, Aug. 8, 1976; children: Jonathan Michael, Janine Elizabeth. AB, Princeton U., 1972; JD, Georgetown U., 1975, LLM, 1977. Bar: Va. 1975, D.C. 1977, N.Y. 1978. Assoc. Alexander & Green, N.Y.C, 1977-82; counsel Control Data Corp., Mpls., 1982-85, asst. gen. counsel, 1985—; adj. faculty in internat. mgmt. Coll. St. Thomas, St. Paul, 1986—. Schulte Zur Hausen fellow Georgetown U. Law Ctr., 1975-77. Avocations: windsurfing, personal computing. Private international, Computer, General corporate. Home: 6609 Pawnee Rd Edina MN 55435 Office: Control Data Corp 8100 34th Ave S Minneapolis MN 55420

BEHRENDT, JOHN THOMAS, lawyer; b. Syracuse, Kans., Oct. 26, 1945; s. Thomas Franklin and Anna Iola (Carrithers) B. m. Martha Jean Montgomery, Dec. 28, 1967 (div.); children—Todd Thomas, Gretchen Jean; m. Theresa Ann Elmore, Oct. 27, 1985. B.A., Sterling Coll.; J.D. cum laude, U. Minn. Bar: Calif. 1971, Tex. 1973. Assoc., then ptnr. Gibson, Dunn & Crutcher, Los Angeles, 1970-71, 1974—. Served to capt. JAGC, U.S. Army, 1971-74. Mem. ABA, Los Angeles County Bar Assn. Republican. Presbyterian. Clubs: Jonathan (Los Angeles); Union League (N.Y.). Federal civil litigation, General corporate, Private international. Office: Gibson Dunn & Crutcher 2029 Century Park East Los Angeles CA 90067 also: 200 Park Ave New York NY 10001

BEHRLE, SANDRA GALE, lawyer; b. Bayonne, N.J., May 16, 1933; d. Joseph Gale and Ceil (Berger) Goldfarb; m. Frederick Joseph Behrle, Nov. 12, 1955 (div. Jan. 1980); children: Scott Jeffrey, Keith Douglas. AB, Douglass Coll., 1954; postgrad., NYU, 1955-56; JD, Fordham U., 1971. Bar: N.Y. 1974, U.S. Dist. Ct. (so. and ea. dists.) N.Y. 1974, U.S. Ct. Appeals (2d cir.) 1974. Assoc. Barrett, Smith, Shapiro, Simon & Armstrong, N.Y.C., 1971-77; ptnr. Austrian, Lance & Stewart, N.Y.C., 1977-86; founding ptnr. Cooper, Brown & Behrle, P.C., N.Y.C., 1986—. Mem. ABA, Assn. of Bar of City of N.Y., Assn. Trial Lawyers Am., Am. Arbitration Assn. (arbitrator). Federal civil litigation, State civil litigation. Home: 301 E 87th St New York NY 10128 Office: Cooper Brown & Behrle 30 Rockefeller Plaza New York NY 10112

BEIDLER, JOHN NATHAN, lawyer; b. Biloxi, Miss., Aug. 5, 1945; s. Henry Landis and Pauline Henrietta (Yerger) B.; m. Marsha Susan Wolf, Aug. 18, 1974. BSE, Princeton U., 1967; JD, Rutgers U., 1973. Bar: N.J. 1973, U.S. Dist. Ct. N.J. 1973, U.S. Ct. Appeals (3d cir.) 1978. Assoc. Smith, Stratton, Wise & Heher, Princeton, 1973-78, ptnr., 1978-81; gen. atty. Johnson & Johnson, New Brunswick, N.J., 1981—. Served with U.S. Army, 1967-70, Vietnam. Decorated Bronze Star. Mem. ABA, N.J. Bar Assn., Def. Research Inst. Federal civil litigation, Health, Personal injury. Home: 155 Montadale Dr Princeton NJ 08540 Office: Johnson & Johnson One Johnson & Johnson Plaza New Brunswick NJ 08933

BEIDLER, MARSHA WOLF, lawyer; b. Bridgeton, N.J., Feb. 29, 1948; d. Benjamin and Esther (Lourie) Wolf; m. John Nathan Beidler, Aug. 18, 1974. BA, Dickinson Coll., Carlisle, Pa., 1969; JD, Rutgers U., Camden, N.J., 1972; LLM in Taxation, NYU, 1979. Bar: Pa. 1972, Fla. 1973, N.J. 1975. Estate and gift tax atty. IRS, Phila., 1972-74, Trenton, N.J., 1974-76; atty. McCarthy & Hicks, Princeton, N.J., 1976-81; ptnr. Pinto & Beidler, Princeton, 1981-83; prin. Smith, Lambert, Hicks & Miller, Princeton, 1983—; Sec. Mercer County Estate Planning Council, 1977-86; prof. paralegal studies Rider Coll., Trenton, 1982; lectr. estate planning various corps. and univs. Bd. dirs. Birth Alternatives, Princeton, 1980; bd. dirs. Mercer Council on Alcoholism, Trenton, 1985-86. Mem. ABA (taxation sect.), Fla. Bar Assn., N.J. Bar Assn. (taxation sect.). Lodge: Soroptimists. Estate planning, Probate, Corporate taxation. Office: Smith Lambert Hicks & Miller PO Box 627 Princeton NJ 08542

BEIGHLE, DOUGLAS PAUL, aerospace company executive; b. Deer Lodge, Mont., June 18, 1932; s. Douglas Paul Beighle and Clarice Janice (Driver) Kiefer; m. Gwendolen Anne Dickson, Oct. 30, 1954; children: Cheryl, Randall, Katherine, Douglas J. B.S. in Bus. Adminstrn., U. Mont., 1954; J.D., U. Mont, 1958; LL.M., Harvard U., 1960. Bar: Mont. 1958, Wash. 1959, U.S. Supreme Ct. 1970. Assoc. Perkins, Coie, Stone, Olsen & Wilson, Seattle, 1960-67, ptnr., 1967-80; v.p. contracts Boeing Co., Seattle, 1980-81, v.p. contracts, gen. counsel, sec., 1981-86; sr. v.p., sec. Boeing Co., 1986—; chief legal counsel Puget Sound Power & Light Co., Bellevue, Wash., 1970-80, dir., 1981—; dir. Peabody Holding Co., St. Louis. Nat. dir. Jr. Achievement, Conn., 1981—; trustee Mcpl. League Seattle, 1983—, U. Mont. Found., Missoula, 1983—. Served to 1st lt. USAF, 1954-56. Harvard U. Law Sch. fellow, 1959. Mem. ABA, Mont. Bar Assn., Wash. State Bar Assn. (chmn. advt. law sect. 1959-60), Seattle-King County Bar Assn., Nat. Assn. Mfrs. (state dir. 1986—). Republican. Presbyterian. Clubs: Rainier; Yacht (Seattle). Office: Boeing Company 7755 E Marginal Way S Seattle WA 98124

BEIRNE, MARTIN DOUGLAS, lawyer; b. N.Y.C., Oct. 24, 1944; s. Martin Douglas and Catherine Anne (Rooney) B.; m. Kathleen Harrington; children—Martin, Shannon, Kelley. B.S., Spring Hill Coll., 1966; J.D., St. Mary's Sch. Law, 1969. Bar: Tex. 1969, U.S. Dist. Ct. (ea. dist.) Tex. 1972 U.S. Dist. Ct. (so. dist.) Tex. 1971, U.S. Ct. Appeals (5th cir.) 1974, U.S. Dist. Ct. (ea. dist.) Calif., U.S. Dist. Ct. (ea. dist.) N.Y., U.S. Supreme Ct. 1975. Ptnr. Fulbright & Jaworski, Houston, 1971-85; sr. ptnr. Beirne, Maynard & Parsons, Houston, 1985—. Served to capt. Signal Corps, U.S. Army, 1969-71. Fellow Tex. Bar Found.; mem. ABA, Tex. Bar Assn., Houston Bar Assn. Roman Catholic. Clubs: Coronado, Houston Athletic, Meml. Drive Country. Federal civil litigation, State civil litigation, General corporate. Office: 1300 Post Oak Blvd 24th Floor Allied Bank Tower Houston TX 77056

BEISSER, LOUIE FREDERICK, judge; b. Ft. Dodge, Iowa, July 7, 1924; s. Conrad Christian Gotlieb and Anna Marie (Oleson) B.; m. Corinne Ann Andrews, June 4, 1949; children—Mary Lou, Ann Marie, William Conrad. Grad. Ft. Dodge Jr. Coll., 1948; postgrad., U. S.D., 1948-49, J.D., 1952. Bar: S.D. 1952, Iowa, 1952. Assoc. Rider & Bastian, Ft. Dodge, 1952-54; mem. Rider, Bastian & Beisser, Ft. Dodge, 1954-64; ptnr. Bastian, Beisser & Carlson, Ft. Dodge, 1964-72, McCarville, Bennett, Beisser & Wilke, Ft. Dodge, 1972-81; judge Dist. Ct. State of Iowa, Ft. Dodge, 1981—; asst. county atty. Webster County, Ft. Dodge, 1955-59; county atty., 1971-75; justice of peace Wahkonsa Twp., Ft. Dodge, 1961-71. Author manual Trial Procedures for OMVUI cases, 1973. Treas. North Central Alcoholism Found., Ft. Dodge, 1969-75; pres. Ft. Dodge Catholic Charities, 1967; bd. dirs. Ft. Dodge Residential Facility, 1979-81, 2nd Jud. Dist. Dept. Correction, Ft. Dodge, 1979-81, 84-86. Served to 1st lt. USAF, 1943-46. Recipient Outstanding Community Service award Ft. Dodge United Fund, 1966, Outstanding Contribution to Law Enforcement award Iowa Law Enforcement Acad., 1971, Outstanding Service to Iowa award Cen. Community Coll., 1983. Mem. Webster County Bar Assn. (pres. 1973-74), 2b Bar Assn. (v.p. 1980-81), Iowa Bar Assn., Iowa Judges Assn., Am. Jud. Soc., Am. Legion (commdr. 1966-68), Delta Theta Phi (dean 1951-52). Republican. Roman Catholic. Lodge: Sertoma (Americanism chmn. 1968-71). State civil litigation, Family and matrimonial, Personal injury. Home: 1928 N 22nd St Fort Dodge IA 50501 Office: PO Box 1857 Fort Dodge IA 50501

BEISTLINE, RALPH ROBERT, lawyer; b. Fairbanks, Alaska, Dec. 6, 1948; s. Earl Hoover and Dorothy Ann (Hering) B.; m. Peggy Ann Griffin, Aug. 29, 1972; children: Carrie, Daniel, Tamara, Rebecca, David. BA, U. Alaska, 1972; JD, U. Puget Sound, 1974. Bar: Alaska 1975. From assoc. to ptnr. Hughes, Thorsness, Gantz, Powell & Brundin, Fairbanks, 1974—; mem. Alaska Pro Bono Panel, Fairbanks, 1985—. Mem. Alaskaland Commn., Faibanks, 1980—; leader Boy Scout Am., Fairbanks, 1986—. Mem. ABA, Alaska Bar Assn. (bd. govs. 1985—, pres. 1986—), Tanana Valley Bar Assn. (sec. 1976, treas. 1977, v.p. 1978, pres. 1979). Republican. State civil litigation, Personal injury, Workers' compensation. Office: Hughes Thorsness Gantz et al 590 University Ave Suite 200 Fairbanks AK 99701 Home: 1071 Bruhn Rd PO Box 60796 Fairbanks AK 99701

BEISWANGER, GARY LEE, lawyer; b. Billings, Mont., May 31, 1938; s. Howard H. and Mollie (Pope) B.; m. Judith J. Buckland, Sept. 14, 1963. B.A. in Philosophy, History and Polit. Sci., U. Mont., 1960, LL.B., 1963. Bar: Mont. 1963, U.S. Dist. Ct. Mont. 1963. Ptnr. Harwood, Galles, Gunderson & Beiswanger, Billings, 1965-73, Ryan & Beiswanger, Billings, 1973-75, Beiswanger & Wilson, Billings, 1976-77, Beiswanger & Jarussi, Billings, 1978-80; sole practice, Billings, 1980—; dep. county atty. for environ. law Yellowstone County (Mont.). Served to capt. U.S. Army, 1963-65. Decorated Army Commendation medal; named Outstanding Young Man of Mont., U.S. Jaycees, 1972. Mem. State Bar Mont., Yellowstone County Bar Assn., Mont. Trial Lawyers Assn., ABA, Assn. Trial Lawyers Am. Republican. Mem. Faith Evangelical Ch. Club: Kiwanis (dist. lt. gov. 1977-78) (Billings). General corporate, State civil litigation, Real property. Office: Rocky Village Ctr I 1500 Poly Dr Billings MT 59102

BEISWENGER, ALLAN DAVID, lawyer; b. Fisher, Minn., Oct. 4, 1948; s. Walter Edwin and Harriet Anna (Christianson) B.; m. Susan Jane ADams, Jan. 6, 1978; children: Elizabeth Anna, David Walter. B in Aero. Enging., U. Minn., 1970, JD cum laude, 1976. Bar: Minn. 1976, Alaska 1977, Trust Territory Pacific Islands 1979, U.S. Dist. Ct. No. Mairannas 1979, U.S. Dist. Ct. Alaska 1981. Legal intern Alaska Pub. Defender, Bethel, 1976-77, supervising atty., 1977-79; supervising atty. Alaska Pub. Defender, Kenai, 1980-82; chief pub. dender Federated State of Micronesia, Kolonia, Ponape, 1979-80; ptnr. Robinson & Beiswenger, Soldotna, Alaska, 1982—; prof. Kenai Peninsula Community Coll., Soldotna, 1982—. Pres. bd. dirs. Peninsula Home Health Care, Soldotna, 1984—. Mem. Kenai Peninsula Bar Assn. (pres. 1984). Democrat. Lutheran. Avocations: flying, canoing, gardening, fishing. Criminal, Real property, State civil litigation. Home: Box 636 Soldotna AK 99669 Office: Robinson & Beiswenger 35401 Kenai Spur Soldotna AK 99669

BEKMAN, PAUL D., lawyer; b. Washington, Mar. 31, 1946; s. Israel J. and Clara O. (Ostrinsky) B.; m. Arlene J. Nagel, June 8, 1969. BA, U. Md., 1968, JD, 1971. Bar: Md. 1972, U.S. Dist. Ct. Md. 1972, U.S. Ct. Appeals (4th cir.) 1972. From assoc. to ptnr. Kaplan, Heyman, Greenberg, Engelman & Belgrad P.A., Balt., 1971-85; ptnr. Israelson, Salsbury, Clements & Bekman, Balt., 1985—. Mem. adv. com. U.S. Dist. Ct. Md., 1981—, adv. com. U.S. Dist. Ct., 1985, trial cts. Jud. Nominating Commn. for 8th Jud. Cir., 1983—; chmn. lawyer assistance com. U.S. Dist. Ct. Md., 1984—; pres. Har Sinai Congregation Brotherhood, Balt., 1986—. Mem. Md. Bar Assn. (chmn. correctional reform sect. 1981-82, bd. of govs. 1983-85, chmn. negligence ins. and workmen's compensation sect., Dist. Service award 1982-83), Fed. Bar Assn. (bd. of govs. 1978—, Dist. Service award 1985), Balt. City Bar Assn. (chmn. young lawyers sect. 1981-82), Md. Trial Lawyers Assn. (pres. 1986—), Loophole Law Club, Sgt.'s Inn Club. Democrat. Jewish. Personal injury, Admiralty, Workers' compensation. Home: 1302 Hickory Spring Circle Catonsville MD 21228 Office: Israelson Salsbury Clements & Bekman 2 E Fayette St Suite 600 Baltimore MD 21202

BEKRITSKY, BRUCE ROBERT, lawyer; b. Utica, N.Y., Nov. 9, 1946; s. Morris and Dorothy (Horowitz) B.; m. Helene Marcia Andrews, June 23, 1968; children: Brett Jonathan, Amy Beth, Seth Benjamin. BA, Yeshiva U., 1968; JD, Bklyn. Law Sch., 1973. Bar: N.Y. 1974, U.S. Dist. Ct. (ea. and so. dists.) N.Y. 1975, U.S. Ct. Appeals (2d cir.) 1975, U.S. Supreme Ct. 1978. Atty. Legal Services Bklyn., 1974-81; assoc. Law Offices of Richard Hartman, Little Neck, N.Y., 1981-86; sole practice Far Rockaway, N.Y., 1986—. Mem. ABA, N.Y. State Bar Assn., Queens County Bar Assn., Nassau County Bar Assn. Democrat. Jewish. Civil litigation, General practice, Personal injury. Home and Office: 730 Mador Ct Far Rockaway NY 11691

BELCHER, DENNIS IRL, lawyer; b. Wheeling, W.Va., Aug. 24, 1951; s. Finley Duncan Belcher and Ellen Jane (Huffman) Good; m. Vickie Marie Early, Aug. 2, 1975; children: Sarah Anne, Matthew Irl, Benjamin Scott. BA, Coll. William and Mary, 1973; JD, T.C. Williams Law Sch., 1976. Bar: Va. 1976, U.S. Tax Ct. 1978. Assoc. McGuire, Woods, Battle & Boothe, Richmond, Va., 1976-83; ptnr. McGuire, Woods & Battle, Richmond, Va., 1983—; adj. prof. taxation Va. Commonwealth U., Richmond, 1985—. Co-author: Business Tax Planning Forms for Businesses and Individuals, 1985. Chmn. Richmond chpt. Am. Heart Assn., 1984-85. Fellow Am. Coll. Probate Counsel; mem. ABA (real property and probate sect., taxation sect., chmn. marital deduction com., vice chmn. lifetime transfers com.), Va. Bar Assn. (wills and trusts and taxations sects.). Presbyterian. Clubs: Bull & Bear, Willow Oaks (Richmond). Avocations: golf, farming. Estate taxation, Probate, General corporate. Office: McGuire Woods Battle & Boothe 1 James Ctr Richmond VA 23219

BELCHER, JOHN ARTHUR, lawyer; b. Pasadena, Calif., Mar. 3, 1956; s. Arthur Henshaw and Silva (Campbell) B. Student, U. Edinburgh, 1977; AB in Econs., U. Calif., Berkeley, 1978, JD, 1981. Bar: Calif. 1981, U.S. Ct. Appeals (9th cir.) 1981, U.S. Dist. Ct. (no. dist.) Calif. 1981, U.S. Dist. Ct. (cen. dist.) Calif. 1983. Dep. dist. atty., felony trial team Contra Costa County, Martinez, Calif., 1981-83; assoc. Morgan, Lewis & Bockius, Los Angeles, 1983-85, Richards, Watson, Dreyfuss & Gershon, Los Angeles, 1985—. Mem. ABA, Los Angeles County Bar Assn. Republican. Baptist. Federal civil litigation, State civil litigation, Insurance. Office: Richards Watson et al 333 S Hope St Los Angeles CA 90071

BELDEN, H. REGINALD, lawyer; b. Arnold, Pa., Dec. 23, 1907; s. Arhtur Ernest and Otilla Christiana (Sode) B.; m. Irene, Jan 15, 1938; children: H. Reginald Jr., Marcia I. Belden Lappas. BS in Econs., Thiel Coll., 1929; JD, U. Pa., 1932. Bar: Pa. 1933, U.S. Dist. Ct. (we. dist.) Pa. 1943, U.S. Ct.

Appeals (3d cir.) 1954, U.S. Supreme Ct. 1960. Author: (with others) Lawyers Professional Liability, 1981. Recipient Disting. Alumnus award Thiel Coll., 1973. Fellow Am. Bar Found. (life), Pa. Bar Found. (life), Am. Coll. Trial Lawyers (state chmn. 1975-76); mem. ABA (mem. Ho. of Dels. 1971-72), Pa. Bar Assn. (pres. 1971-72, mem. Ho. of Dels.), Westmoreland Bar Assn. (pres. 1961), Westmoreland Acad. Trial Lawyers (founder, pres. 1969-70), Internat. Assn. Ins. Counsel (state chmn. 1972—), Nat. Conf. Bar Pres., Jud. Conf. for Third Cir. U.S. (life), Def. Research Inst., Pa. Def. Inst. Republican. Lutheran. Club: Greensburg (Pa.) Country, Pinehurst (N.C.) Country, Belleview Biltmore Country (Belleair, Fla.). Avocations: golf, legal research. State civil litigation, Insurance, Workers' compensation. Office: Stewart Belden & Belden 117 N Main St Greensburg PA 15601

BELDOCK, MYRON, lawyer; b. N.Y.C., Mar. 27, 1929; s. George J. and Irene (Goldstein) B.; m. Elizabeth G. Pease, June 28, 1953 (div. 1969) children—David, Jennifer, Hannah, Benjamin; m. Karen L. Dippold, June 19, 1986. B.A., Hamilton Coll., 1950; LL.B., Harvard U., 1958. Bar: N.Y. 1958, U.S. Dist. Ct. (ea. and so dists.) N.Y. 1960, U.S. Ct. Appeals (2d cir.) 1960, U.S. Supreme Ct. 1973, U.S. Dist. Ct. (no. dist.) N.Y. 1983, U.S. Ct. Appeals (3d cir.) 1985. Asst. U.S. atty. U.S. Atty.'s Office, Eastern Dist., N.Y., 1958-60; assoc. Geist, Netter & Marx, N.Y.C., 1960-62; sole practice, N.Y.C., 1962-64; ptnr. Beldock, Levine & Hoffman, N.Y.C., 1964—. Bd. dirs., v.p. Brother-hood-In-Action, N.Y.C., 1972—; bd. dirs. Brookdale Revolving Fund, N.Y.C. 1973-76. Served with U.S. Army, 1951-54. Mem. Assn. Bar City N.Y., (spl. com. penology 1974-80), Kings County Criminal Bar Assn., New York County Criminal Bar Assn., Nat. Assn. Criminal Def. Lawyers. Criminal, Federal civil litigation, State civil litigation.

BELEW, DAVID OWEN, JR., federal judge; b. Ft. Worth, Mar. 27, 1920; s. David Owen and Mazie Desporд (Erskine) B.; m. Marjorie Dale Mitchell; children: Marjorie Dale Belew Peterson, Susan Elizabeth Belew Arnoult, David Mitchell. B.A., U. Tex., 1946, LL.B., 1948. Bar: Tex. 1948. Practice with father Ft. Worth, 1948-49; asst. U.S. atty. No. Dist. Tex., 1949-52; partner firm Cantey, Hanger, Gooch, Munn & Collins, Ft. Worth, 1952-79; U.S. dist. judge No. Dist. Tex., 1979—. Served with AUS, 1942-45. Decorated Silver Star, Purple Heart (3). Mem. Am. Bar Assn., Fed. Bar Assn., State Bar Tex., Ft. Worth-Tarrant County Bar Assn. (pres. 1970). Jurisprudence. Office: US Dist Ct 201 US Courthouse Fort Worth TX 76102 *

BELFER, ANDREW BENJAMIN, lawyer, real estate developer; b. Forest Hills, N.Y., Nov. 11, 1953; s. Norman Charles and Elinor (Renfield) B.; m. Karen Bernstein, Aug. 11, 1985. BA, Cornell U., 1975; JD, Boston U., 1979. Bar: N.Y. 1980, N.J. 1980, Fla. 1980. Exec. v.p., gen. counsel Belfer Realty and Devel. Co., Great Neck, N.Y., 1979—; Bd. dirs., gen. counsel United Feather and Down, Inc., Bklyn., 1979—. Mem. ABA. Jewish. Club: Fresh Meadow Country (Great Neck, N.Y.). Avocations: tennis, skiing. Real property. Office: Belfer Realty & Devel Co 40 Cutter Mill Rd Great Neck NY 11021

BELFIGLIO, JEFF, lawyer; b. St. Louis, Nov. 17, 1957; s. Nick J. and Gertrude (Bounk) B.; m. Lee Evan Evans, June 12, 1982; 1 child, Evan Jeffrey. BA, St. Louis U., 1979; JD, Stanford U., 1982. Bar: Wash. 1982, U.S. Dist. Ct. (we. dist.) Wash. 1982. Assoc. Davis, Wright & Jones, Seattle, 1982—. Co-author: Siting Hazardous Waste Facilities, 1981; assoc. mng. editor Stanford U. Law Rev., 1981-82. Trustee Seattle Philharm. Orch., 1985—. Mem. ABA, Wash. State Bar Assn., Order of Coif. Episcopalian. Avocation: viola player with Seattle Philharm. Orch. Pension, profit-sharing, and employee benefits, Contracts commercial, Environment. Home: 12629 NE 2d St Bellevue WA 98005 Office: Davis Wright & Jones 110 110th Ave NE Suite 700 Bellevue WA 98004

BELFORD, LLOYD EARL, lawyers; b. Fall River, Mass., May 7, 1930; s. Frederick and Sarah (Strolsky) B.; m. Aileen Hirschman, Aug. 14, 1955; 1 child, Kyle Alexandra. BS, Boston U., 1950, JD, 1953. Bar: Mass. 1953, U.S. Dist. Ct. Mass. 1954, US.. Supreme Ct. 1967. Ptnr. Belford & Belford, Fall River, 1957—; bd. dirs. registered voters City of Fall River, 1964-68; pub. adminstr. Bristol County, Fall River, 1971-75; first asst. corp. counsel, 1971-77. Served to capt. USAF, 1954-57. Mem. ABA (corp., banking and bus. law sect., criminal law div.), Mass. Bar Assn. (unauthorized practice law com., bankruptcy com.), Fall River Bar Assn. (exec. bd. 1963-65, treas. 1965-67, sec. 1967-69, v.p. 1969-71, pres. 1971-72), Bristol County Bar Assn. (exec. bd. 1971-72), Comml. Law League of Am. Bankruptcy, Consumer commercial, General practice. Home: 1135 Highland Ave Fall River MA 02720 Office: Belford & Belford 279 N Main St Fall River MA 02720

BELIN, DAVID WILLIAM, lawyer; b. Washington, June 20, 1928; s. Louis I. and Esther (Klass) B.; m. Constance Newman, Sept. 14, 1952 (dec. June 1980); children—Jonathan L., James M., Joy E., Thomas R., Laura R. B.A., U. Mich., 1951, M.B.A., 1953, J.D., 1954. Bar: Iowa 1954. Sole practice Des Moines; ptnr. Herrick & Langdon, 1955-62, Herrick, Langdon, Sandblom & Belin, 1962-66; sr. ptnr. Herrick, Langdon, Belin, Harris, Langdon & Helmick, 1966-78, Belin, Harris, Helmick, Tesdell, Lamson & McCormick, Des Moines, 1978—; dir. Kemper Mut. Funds.; counsel President's Commn. on Assassination of President Kennedy (Warren Commn.), 1964; exec. dir. Commn. on CIA Activities within the U.S. (Rockefeller Commn.), 1975; mem. Pres.'s Com. on Arts and Humanities, 1984—. Author: November 22, 1963: You Are the Jury, 1973. Bd. dirs. Des Moines Civic Music Assn., 1959-61, Des Moines Community Drama Assn., 1961-64, Des Moines Symphony, 1968-70, U. Mich. Alumni Assn., 1963-66. Served with AUS, 1946-47. Recipient Henry M. Bates Meml. award U. Mich. Law Sch., Brotherhood award NCCJ, 1978; hon. orator U. Mich., 1950. Mem. Soc. Barristers, Order of Coif, Phi Beta Kappa, Phi Kappa Phi, Delta Sigma Rho, Beta Alpha Psi. Club: Michigamua. Federal civil litigation, General corporate, State civil litigation. Home: 1705 Plaza Circle Des Moines IA 50322 Office: 2000 Financial Ctr Des Moines IA 50309

BELKIN, JEFFREY A., lawyer, arbitrator; b. Cleve., May 10, 1940; s. Louis Sindell and Anne (Adler) B.; m. Jane Phillips, June 22, 1963; children: Aaron C., Joanna. AB, Brown U., 1961; JD, U. Mich., 1964. Atty. NLRB, Detroit, 1964-66; ptnr. Belkin & Belkin Co., LPA, Cleve., 1967-75, Kelley, McCann & Livingstone, Cleve., 1975-79, Millisor, Belkin & Nobil, Akron, Columbus and Cleve., 1979—; arbitrator Cleve., 1975—, lectr. Cleve. State U. Law Sch., 1977. Mem. bd. trustees Bur. Jewish Edn., Cleve., 1976-79, Fairmount Temple, Cleve. 1985—. Mem. ABA, Ohio State Bar Assn. (bd. govs., mem. labor law sect., sec.), Am. Arbitration Assn. Democrat. Club: Commerce (Cleve.). Labor. Home: 19901 Shelburne Rd Shaker Heights OH 44118 Office: Millisor Belkin & Nobil 620 National City E 6th Bldg Cleveland OH 44114

BELKNAP, JERRY P., lawyer; b. Napoleon, Ohio, Aug. 22, 1917; s. Nathaniel J. and Mary E. (Ragan) B.; m. Maryellen Pilliod, Nov. 29, 1945; children—Nathaniel J., Raymond V., Caroline M. Belknap Russell, Mary Elizabeth Belknap Brann, Sarah A. Belknap Boonstra. A.B., U. Mich., 1939, J.D., 1941. Bar: Ohio 1941, Ind. 1942, U.S. Ct. Appeals (7th cir.) 1942, U.S. Supreme Ct. Ptnr. Barnes, Hickam, Pantzer & Boyd, and successor firm Barnes & Thornburg, Indpls., 1941—; chmn. Ind. Supreme Ct. com. on rules and practice. Mem. Indpls. Sch. Bd., 1968-72; treas. Episcopal Diocese of Indpls., 1964-71. Served with USAAF, 1942-45. Decorated Bronze Star, Air medal. Mem. Ind. State Bar Assn., ABA, Indpls. Bar Assn., Bar Assn. 7th Fed. Cir. Republican. Contbr. articles to legal jours. Public utilities, Federal civil litigation, State civil litigation. Home: 7039 Warwick Rd Indianapolis IN 46220 Office: 11 S Meridian St Merchants Bank Suite 1313 Indianapolis IN 46204

BELL, ALLEN ANDREW, JR., lawyer; b. Paris, Ill., June 23, 1951; s. Allen Andrew and Mary Elizabeth (Charley) B.; m. Carol Anne Larson, June 15, 1974; children—Sara Elizabeth, Emily Anne, David Allen. B.A., DePauw U., 1973; J.D. cum laude, Ind. U.-Indpls., 1980. Bar: Ill. 1980, Ind. 1980, U.S. Dist. Ct. (so. dist.) Ind. 1980, U.S. Dist. Ct. (cen. dist.) Ill. 1980. Underwriter Am. States Ins. Co., Indpls., 1973-80; assoc. Dillavou Overaker Asher & Smith, Paris, Ill., 1980-85; ptnr. Ruff, Garst & Bell, Paris, 1985-87; asst. state's atty. Edgar and Clark Counties, 1987—; pub. defender Edgar County, Ill., 1982-84, Clark County, Ill., 1982-84. Mem. ABA, Ill. State Bar Assn., Ind. State Bar Assn., Edgar County Bar Assn. (pres. 1982-83). Republican. Lodges: Kiwanis (treas. local club 1981-83), Masons (master local lodge 1986). General practice, Consumer commercial, Criminal. Home: 802 Shaw Ave Paris IL 61944

BELL, CHARLES D., lawyer; b. McKeesport, Pa., Jan. 23, 1923; s. Charles R. and Bertha Beatrice (Davis) B.; m. Mary Porter Wilkin, Mar. 17, 1945 (dec. 1971); children—Betty Bell Williams, Peggy Jean Hrach, Charles William, Julie Bell Caldwell; m. 2d Marjorie Wicks, Mar. 26, 1977. B.S. in Chemistry, Bethany Coll., 1944; J.D., U. Mich., 1949. Bar: W.Va., 1951. Assoc. Schroeder, Merriam, Hofgren & Brady, Chgo., 1950-51; ptnr. Bell, McMullen and Cross, Wellsburg, W.Va., 1951—; asst. pros. atty. Brooke County, W.Va., 1960-68, 72-76, 81—; dir., sec. Banner Fibreboard Co., Wellsburg; v.p., dir. Wellsburg Nat. Bank. Mem. bd. dirs. W.Va. Rehab. Found.; bd. dirs. N. Cent. Region Boy Scouts Am., also mem. nat. bd., coms.; mem. W.Va. Ind. Coll. Found.; chmn. bd. trustees Bethany Coll. Served with AUS, 1944-46. Mem. Brooke County Bar Assn., W.Va. State Bar Assn., ABA. Republican. Clubs: Masons, Elks. General corporate, General practice, Insurance. Home: 1222 Pleasant Ave Wellsburg WV 26070 Office: Bell McMullen & Cross 67 7th St Wellsburg WV 26070

BELL, DENNIS ARTHUR, lawyer; b. Chgo., July 5, 1934; s. Samuel Arthur and Frances (Gordon) B.; m. Judith Gail Young, Nov. 6, 1977. B.S. in Accountancy, U. Ill., 1955; J.D., DePaul U., 1961. Bar: Ill. 1961, U.S. Supreme Ct., 1964. C.P.A., Ill., 1956. C.P.A. Peat, Marwick Mitchell, Chgo., 1957-62; staff acct., atty. SEC, Washington, 1957-62; capital devel. officer U.S. AID, Ankara, Turkey, 1966-68; pvt. cons., Chgo., 1968-70; group controller Nat. Student Mktg. Corp., Chgo., 1970-72; dir. corp. fin. dept. and house counsel Rothschild Securities Corp., Chgo., 1973-74; corp. sec., assoc. gen. counsel Midwest Stock Exchange, 1974-79; pres. Dennis A. Bell & Assocs. Ltd., Chgo., 1979—; dir., sec., treas. Joy Internat. Corp., 1977—, Lyric Internat. Corp., Chgo. and Hong Kong, 1983—. Bd. dirs. Mental Health Assn., Chgo. Clarence Darrow Community Ctr. Served with USAR, 1957-62. Mem. ABA, Fed. Bar Assn., Ill. Bar Assn., Ill. C.P.A. Soc., Am. Soc. Corp. Secs. Democrat. Jewish. Club: Attic (Chgo.); International (Chgo.). General corporate, Commodities, Securities. Home: 1325 N State Pkwy 10F Chicago IL 60610 Office: 140 S Dearborn St Suite 800 Chicago IL 60603

BELL, DERRICK ALBERT, legal educator, author, lecturer; b. Pitts., Nov. 6, 1930; s. Derrick Albert and Ada Elizabeth (Childress) B.; m. Jewel Allison Hairston, June 26, 1960; children—Derrick Albert III, Douglass Dubois, Carter Robeson. A.B., Duquesne U., 1952; LL.B., U. Pitts., 1957; hon. degree in law, Toogaloo Coll., 1983, Northeastern U., 1985. Bar: D.C. 1957, Pa. 1959, N.Y. State 1966, Calif. 1969. Atty. civil rights div. Dept. Justice, Washington, 1957-59; 1st asst. counsel NAACP Legal Defense Edn. Fund, N.Y.C., 1960-66; dep. dir. Office Civil Rights, HEW, Washington, 1966-68; exec. dir. Western Ctr. on Law and Poverty 1968-69; lectr. law Harvard U., 1969-71, prof. law, 1971-80, 86—; dean U. Oreg. Law Sch., 1981-85. Author: Race, Racism and American Law, 1973, 2d edit., 1980, Shades of Brown: New Perspectives on School Desegregation, 1980. Served to 1st lt. USAF, 1952-54. Ford Found. grantee, 1972, 75; Nat. Endowment Humanities grantee, 1980-81. Civil rights, Legal education. Home: 9 Walden Mews Cambridge MA 02140 Office: Harvard Law Sch Cambridge MA 02138

BELL, DOUGLAS MCCALL, lawyer; b. Somerset, Pa., June 23, 1955; s. David McCall and Kathryn Jeanette (Countryman) B.; m. Kathleen Joan Smith. BA, Dickinson Coll., 1978; JD, Dickinson Sch. Law, 1981. Assoc. Bruacher, Keim & Saylor, Somerset, 1981-82, Keim & Bowman, Somerset, 1982-83; assoc. counsel Somerset County Pub. Defender, 1982; assoc. Keim, Bowman & Bell, Somerset, 1983-84, ptnr., 1984-86; ptnr. Bowman & Bell, Somerset, 1986; sole practice Berlin, Pa., 1986—; exec. officer Somerset County (Pa.) Homebuilders and Suppliers Assn. Rep. committeeman, Somerset County, 1978-80; sec. Berlin Fife and Drum Corps, 1982—; exec. com. Somerset County Single County Authority Drug and Alcohol Commn., 1984-86; pro-bono counsel Berlin (Pa.) Area Ambulance Assn., Inc., 1984—, Berlin Vol. Fire Dept., 1984. Named one of Outstanding Young Men of Am., 1985. Mem. Pa. Bar Assn., Somerset County Bar Assn. (exec. com. 1986—), Sigma Alpha Epsilon. Lutheran. Lodge: Lions (3d v.p. Berlin club 1986—). Avocations: skiing, sailing, hunting, fishing, martial music. Home: PO Box 51 Berlin PA 15530 Office: 500 Main St Berlin PA 15530

BELL, FRANK OURAY, JR., lawyer, state public defender; b. San Francisco, Aug. 13, 1940; s. Frank Ouray, Sr. and Clara Belle (McClure) B.; m. Sherrie A. Levie, Mar. 29, 1981; children—Aimee, David; children from previous marriage—Carin, Laurie. A.B., San Francisco State U., 1963; J.D., Hastings Coll. Law, 1966. Bar: Calif. 1966. Dep. atty. gen. Calif. State's Atty.'s Office, Sacramento, 1966-68; ptnr. Goorjian & Bell, San Francisco, 1968-70; chief asst. Pub. Defender's Office, San Francisco, 1970-82; pub. defender Pub. Defender's Office, 1984—; sole practice San Francisco, 1982-84. Mem. ABA (criminal justice sect.), San Francisco Bar Assn., Nat. Assn. Criminal Def. Lawyers, Calif. Attys. for Criminal Justice, Calif. Pub. Defenders Assn. Club: Lawyers. Criminal, Federal civil litigation, State civil litigation. Office: Office of State Pub Defender 1390 Market St Suite 425 San Francisco CA 94102

BELL, HANEY HARDY, III, tobacco company executive; b. Staunton, Va., Aug. 20, 1944; s. Haney Hardy Jr. and Maud (Deekens) B.; m. Alice Tester, Feb. 17, 1968; 1 son, Landon D. Grad., Gilman Sch., Balt., 1962; B.A., U. Va., 1966; JD cum laude, U. Wis., 1973. Bar: Va. 1974. Group ins. rep. Prudential Ins. Co. Am., Milw., 1969-70; asso. firm Woods, Rogers, Muse, Walker & Thornton, Roanoke, Va., 1973-78; asso. counsel R.J. Reynolds Industries, Inc., Winston-Salem, N.C., 1978-79; sec., gen. counsel RJR Foods, Inc., 1979-80; sr. internat. counsel R.J. Reynolds Tobacco Internat., Inc., 1980—. Served to lt. AUS, 1967-69. Mem. Am. Bar Assn., Va. State Bar, Order of Coif. Clubs: Twin City; Bermuda Run Country (Winston-Salem). Contracts commercial, Private international.

BELL, HARRY FULLERTON, JR., lawyer; b. Charleston, W.Va., Nov. 17, 1954; s. Harry Fullerton and Kathryn Laura (Lewis) B.; m. Pamela Cynthia Deem., Aug. 23, 1980. BS in Econs., W.Va. U., 1977, JD, 1980. Bar: W.Va. 1980, U.S. Dist. Ct. (so. dist.) W.Va. 1980, U.S. Dist. Ct. (no. dist.) W.Va. 1986, U.S. Ct. Appeals (4th cir.) 1986. Asst. pros. atty. Kanawka County, Charleston, 1980-82; assoc. Kay, Casto & Chaney, Charleston, 1982-85, ptnr., 1986—; instr. Marshall U., Huntington, W.Va., 1984—. Contbr. articles to profl. jours. Pres. fireman's civil service commn. City of Charleston, 1985-86; mem. adminstrv. bd. Christ Meth. Ch., Charleston, 1985—, bd. trustees, 1986—; bd. dirs. Charleston Civic Ctr., 1987—. Mem. W.Va. Bar Assn. (vice chmn. com. on lawyers profl. liability ins. 1984-85, chmn. 1985-87, young lawyers bd. 1985, cert. merit 1985, young lawyers sect. 1985), Kanawka County Bar Assn. (chmn. courthouse renovation com. 1984-85), Def. Trial Counsel of W.Va., Def. Research Inst., W.Va. U. Alumni Assn. (treas. 1985, v.p. Kanawha County chpt. 1986, pres. 1986—), W.Va. U. Blue & Gold Barristers Club (founder), Beta Gamma Sigma, Omicron Mu Epsilon. Republican. Club: Berry Hills Country (Charleston). Avocations: sports car racing, flying, golf, tennis, skiing. Federal civil litigation, State civil litigation, Insurance. Home: 410 Abbey Dr Charleston WV 25314 Office: Kay Casto & Chaney 1600 Charleston Nat Plaza Charleston WV 25301

BELL, HENRY NEWTON, III, lawyer, rancher; b. Temple, Tex., Mar. 5, 1941; s. Henry Newton and Mildred (Smith) B.; m. Pamela Roberts, July 25, 1964; children—Regina Eleanor, Henry Newton IV. B.B.A., U. Tex., 1965; J.D., Baylor U., 1968. Bar: Tex. 1970, U.S. Ct. Mil. Appeals. Sole practice, Austin, Tex., 1970—; sr. trial counsel Tips Grant Steel Co., Austin, 1977—; owner Bell Ranches, Bastrop and Burleson Counties, Tex., 1970—; owner, gen. capital ptnr. Henry Newton Bell III, Austin, 1970—; oil and gas operator, Bastrop and Burleson Counties, Tex., 1979—; judge Internat. Moot Ct. Competition, U. Tex. Sch. Law, 1980. Served with U.S. Army, 1968-70; served to lt. col. JAGC, U.S. Army, 1982—. Decorated Bronze Star; recipient cert. of honor Tex. Dept. Agr., 1974. Mem. Internat. Bar Assn., Fed. Bar Assn., ABA, Am. Judicature Soc., Assn. Trial Lawyers Am., SAR (sec. 1979), Tex. Bar Assn., Tex. Trial Lawyers Assn., Sons Republic Tex., Phi Delta Phi. Democrat. Episcopalian. Consumer commercial, Family and matrimonial, State civil litigation. Home: PO Box H Bastrop TX 78602 Office: 300 E Huntland St Suite 214 Austin TX 78752

BELL, JAMES FREDERICK, lawyer; b. New Orleans, Aug. 5, 1922; s. George Bryan and Sarah Barr (Perry) B.; m. Jill Cooper Arden, Apr. 14, 1951; children: Bradley Cushing, Sarah Perry, Ashley Arden. A.B. cum laude, Princeton U., 1943; LL.B., Harvard U., 1948. Bar: D.C. 1949. Assoc. firm Pogue & Neal (name changed to Jones, Day, Reavis & Pogue 1967), Washington, 1948-53; partner Pogue & Neal (name changed to Jones, Day, Reavis & Pogue 1967), 1953—; gen. counsel Conf. State Bank Suprs., 1951—. Chmn. com. on canons and other bus. Episcopal Diocese of Washington, 1960-78; pres. Episc. Center for Children, Washington, 1966-67. Served to lt. USNR, 1943-46. Mem. Am., Fed., D.C. bar assns. Club: Metropolitan (Washington). Banking, FERC practice. Home: 2103 R St NW Washington DC 20008 Office: 655 15th St NW Washington DC 20005

BELL, JOHN WRIGHT, lawyer; b. Pontiac, Mich., June 19, 1925; s. Robert William and Bernice Verdella (Hoskins) B.; m. Catherine Eloise Duffy, Jan. 16, 1946; children—Leslie Bell Maslowski, Dawson, Zachary, Hilary, Nicholas; m. 2d, Suzanne Elizabeth Conat, Aug. 28, 1970; Kimberly, Elizabeth. B.A., U. Rochester, 1946; J.D., U. Mich., Ann Arbor, 1949. Bar: Mich. 1949, U.S. Dist. Ct. (ea. dist.) Mich. 1949, U.S. Ct. Appeals (6th cir.) 1973, U.S. Supreme Ct. 1964. Twp. atty. Waterford, Independence and Springfield Twps., Mich., 1951-57; sole practice, Pontiac, 1949-56; ptnr. Bell & Hertler, P.C., Pontiac, also sec.-treas. Pres. Oakland County Young Republicans, 1952-54, Oakland County Animal Welfare Soc., 1950-52. Served to ensign, USN, 1943-46. Mem. Oakland County Bar Assn., Mich. Bar Assn., Def. Research Inst., Mich. Def. Trial Counsel. Personal injury, Insurance. Office: Bell & Hertler PC Suite 1001 Pontiac State Bank Bldg Pontiac MI 48058

BELL, JONATHAN ROBERT, lawyer; b. Bklyn., Oct. 2, 1947; s. Saul A. and Hope R. (Rosenblat) B.; children—Gabriel J., Nicholas R. B.A., Yale U., 1969; J.D., Harvard U., 1973. Bar: Mass. 1974, U.S. Tax Ct. 1977, N.Y. 1978, U.S. Dist. Ct. (so. dist.) N.Y. 1980. Assoc. Nutter, McClennen & Fish, Boston, 1973-77; assoc. Debevoise & Plimpton, N.Y.C., 1977-84, ptnr., 1984—. Mem. planned giving com. United Way, N.Y.C., 1983—, bd. dirs., 1984—. Mem. N.Y. State Bar Assn. (vice-chmn. trusts and estates law sect.). Probate, Tax exempt organizations, Banking. Home: 35 Bethure St New York NY 10014 Office: Debevoise & Plimpton 875 3d Ave New York NY 10022

BELL, KEITH WHITMAN, lawyer; b. Washington, Sept. 13, 1946; s. William Eugene and Betty Brooks (Hays) B.; m. Rebecca Lee Howe, Aug. 9, 1973; children—Rebecca Brooks, Sarah Elizabeth, Scott Alexander. B.A., Duke U., 1968; J.D., U. Md., 1973. Bar: Md. 1973, Alaska 1974, U.S. Dist. Ct. Alaska 1974, U.S. Ct. Appeals (9th cir.) 1974, U.S. Supreme Ct. 1979, Wash. 1978, D.C. 1979. Asst. mcpl. atty. Municipality of Anchorage, 1974-77; ptnr. Burton, Crane & Bell, Seattle, 1978-82; sole practice Seattle, 1983-84, Anchorage, 1984—; lectr. immigration law Wash. State Bar, Hawaii State Bar, U. Wash. Law Sch., 1981—; pro bono atty. for Cuban refugees Seattle-King County Bar Assn., 1981. Mem. Anchorage Sister Cities Commn., 1986—, Alaska World Affairs Council, 1984—, bd. dirs., 1986. Mem. Am. Immigration Lawyers Assn. (state chmn. 1980-81, 82-83). Congregationalist. Immigration, naturalization, and customs. Office: 12350 Industry Way Suite 203 Anchorage AK 99515

BELL, MARY-KATHERINE, lawyer; b. Los Angeles, July 7, 1910; d. Weldon Branch and Vina (Cowan) Morris; m. Robert Collins Bell, Mar. 22, 1941; children—Robert Collins III, Marianne Bell Reifenheiser. B.A., Stanford U., 1934; J.D., George Washington U., 1943. Bar: D.C. 1943, N.Y. 1952, Conn. 1960. Atty., Cummings & Lockwood, Stamford, Conn., 1944-45, Shearman & Sterling, N.Y.C., 1948-77, Ivey, Barnum & O'Mara, Greenwich, Conn., 1978-83; asst. sec. to Assn. Bar City of N.Y., 1946-47; atty. to Conf. on Personal Fin. Law, N.Y.C., 1947-48; sole practice, New Canaan, Conn., 1983-84; mem. Tax Adv. Com. of Am. Law Inst. Co-editor: U.S. Bankruptcy Guide, 1948. Mem. Democratic Town Com., Conn. Bar Assn., Delta Gamma. Clubs: Cosmopolitan (N.Y.C.), Tokeneke (Darien). Estate planning, Probate, Estate taxation. Home: 528 Main St New Canaan CT 06840 Office: 16 Forest St New Canaan CT 06840

BELL, MILDRED BAILEY, law educator; b. Sanford, Fla., June 28, 1928; d. William F. and Frances E. (Williford) Bailey; m. J. Thomas Bell, Jr., Sept. 18, 1948 (div.); children—Tom, Elizabeth, Ansley. A.B., U. Ga., 1950, J.D. cum laude, 1969; LL.M. in Taxation, N.Y. U., 1977. Bar: Ga. 1969. Law clk. U.S. Dist. Ct. No. Dist. Ga., 1969-70; prof. law Mercer U., Macon, Ga., 1970—; mem. Ga. Com. Constl. Revision, 1978-79. Mem. ABA, Ga. Bar Assn., Phi Beta Kappa, Phi Kappa Phi. Republican. Episcopalian. Bd. editors Ga. State Bar Jour., 1974-76; contbr. articles to profl. jours., chpts. in books. Corporate taxation, Estate taxation, Personal income taxation. Home: 516 High Point North Rd Macon GA 31210 Office: Mercer U Law School Macon GA 31207

BELL, NAPOLEON ARTHUR, lawyer; b. Dublin, Ga., June 17, 1927; s. Arthur Lee and Ethel Lee (Coleman) B.; m. Dorothy J. Lyman, May 5, 1956; children: Kayethel Bell Mason, Napoleon A. II. BA, Mt. Union Coll., 1951; LLB, Case Western Res. U., 1954. Bar: Ohio. Atty. examiner Indsl. Commn. Ohio, 1955-58; ptnr. Bell, White & Ross, Columbus, Ohio, 1958—; spl. counsel Ohio Atty. Gen., 1972-74; pres., chmn. Beneficial Acceptance Corp., chmn. bd. dirs. Tax Appeals, 1971-74; lectr. Seminar on Workers' Compensation, Ohio Legal Ctr.; bd. dirs. Columbia Gas Ohio. Mem. exec. com. Franklin County Dems., 1965, Columbus Traffic and Transp. Commn., 1965, Columbus Urban Renewal Commn., 1968; committeeman 5th Ward; chmn. Concerned Citizens for Columbus Com., 1969-78, Capital Dist. Boy Scouts Am., 1974-78, Ohio United Negro Coll. Fund, 1972, 76, 79; bd. dirs. Cen. Ohio Boy Scouts Am., Columbus Tech. Inst. Devel. Found., Inc., 1982-85, United Way, 1982-85, Columbus Urban League, treas. 1965-66, pres. 1969-72; bd. trustees Mt. Union Coll., Columbus Tech. Inst., 1984-85. Served with U.S. Army, 1946-47. Recipient Merit award Ohio Legal Ctr., Mahoning County Youth Club, 1964, United Negro Coll. Fund; recipient Mt. Union Coll. Alumni Chmn. award, 1974, Alumni award, 1976; Gov.'s Community Service award, 1974, Silver Anniversary award Nat. Collegiate Athletic Assn., 1976; named to Youngstown Coach's Hall of Fame, 1986. Mem. Columbus Bar Assn., NAACP (life applicant), Columbus Area C. of C. (bd. dirs. 1970-73, sch. issues com.), Blue Key, Kappa Alpha Psi (Man of Yr. 1964, polemarch 1963-64, 78-79). Avocation: golf. Workers' compensation, Personal injury, General practice. Home: 1975 Sunbury Rd Columbus OH 43219 Office: Bell White & Ross 180 E Broad St Suite 1716 Columbus OH 43215-3735

BELL, OLIN NILE, lawyer; b. Jefferson City, Mo., Jan. 31, 1939; s. Olin N. and Alice E. (Penn) B.; m. Joanne Mackey, Aug. 27, 1960; 1 child, Ashley. AB in History with distinction, U. Mo., 1960; LLB, Harvard U., 1963. Bar: N.Y. 1964, D.C. 1979. Assoc. Dewey, Ballantine, Bushby, Palmer & Wood, N.Y.C., 1964-71, ptnr., 1971-79; ptnr. Dewey, Ballantine, Bushby, Palmer & Wood, Washington, 1979—. Mem. Dem. Nat. Fin. Council, Washington, 1983—. Mem. ABA, N.Y. State Bar Assn., D.C. Bar Assn., Assn. Bar City of N.Y., Phi Beta Kappa. Democrat. Episcopalian. Clubs: Congl. Country (Bethesda, Md.); University, Down Town (N.Y.C.); Internat. (D.C.); Montclair Golf (N.J.); Tournament Players-Avenel (Potomic, Md.). General corporate, Securities. Office: Dewey Ballantine et al 1775 Pennsylvania Ave NW Washington DC 20006 Office: Dewey Ballantine et al 140 Broadway New York NY 10005

BELL, PAUL ANTHONY, II, lawyer; b. Latrobe, Pa., Mar. 12, 1954; s. Paul Anthony and Marcia Chloe (Martin) B.; m. Arlene Rotella, Aug. 19, 1978; children: Montgomery Vincent, Elyse Maureen, Alexa Marie. AB cum laude, Princeton U., 1975; JD, U. Pitts., 1978. Bar: Pa. 1978, U.S. Dist. Ct. (we. dist.) Pa. 1978. Assoc. Scales and Shaw, Greensburg, Pa., 1978, Laurel Legal Services, Indiana, Pa., 1978-81; sole practice Blairsville, Pa., 1981—; asst. public defender Indiana County, 1984-86, asst. dist. atty., 1986—; bd. dirs. Laurel Legal Services. Pres. Saints Simon and Jude Council, Blairsville, 1982-85; dir. rights com. Torrance (Pa.) State Hosp., 1984—. Mem. ABA, Pa. Bar Assn., Indiana County Bar Assn. Republican. Roman Catholic. Avocations: golf, bridge, reading, basketball. Real property, Personal injury, Probate. Office: 135 E Market St Blairsville PA 15717

BELL, PAUL BUCKNER, lawyer; b. Charlotte, N.C., July 29, 1922; s. George Fisher and Carrie (Savage) B.; m. Betty Sue Trulock, May 3, 1952;

children—Paul B., Morris Trulock, Betty Fisher, Douglas Savage. B.S., Wake Forest U., 1947, J.D. cum laude, 1948. Bar: N.C. 1948. Pres. Bell, Seltzer, Park & Gibson, Charlotte, 1948—; dir. Southland Investors Inc., Idlewild Farms, Inc.; pres., dir. Charpat Investment Corp.; lectr. Practising Law Inst., 1974, N.C. Bar, 1985; adj. prof. patent law Wake Forest U. Sch. Law, 1974—. Trustee, Mecklenburg Presbytery, Alexander Children's Ctr., Presbyn. Home of Charlotte, Mountain Retreat Assn.; pres. Presbyn. Found. Served to 1st lt. USAAF, 1943-46. Mem. ABA, N.C. Bar Assn., Mecklenburg Bar Assn., Am. Intellectual Property Law Assn., Licensing Execs. Soc., Federation Internationale Des Conseils Propriete Industrielle (pres. U.S.A.), Sigma Phi Epsilon, Phi Alpha Delta. Presbyterian. Charlotte City (past pres.), Charlotte Country, Charlotte Textile (past pres.), Grandfather Golf and Country; Union League (N.Y.C.). Federal civil litigation, Patent, Trademark and copyright. Home: 4001 Foxcroft Rd Charlotte NC 28211 Office: 1211 E Morehead St PO Box 34009 Charlotte NC 28234

BELL, RICHARD, state supreme court justice; b. Iva, S.C., July 5, 1920; s. Frank Montgomery and Margaret (Blaine) B.; m. Naomi Whittemore, 1954; children: Richard, Carol Anne, Naomi Jean and Margaret Jane (twins). B.S., Presbyterian Coll. S.C.; LL.B., Emory U. Bar: Ga. 1950. Rep., Ga. Gen. Assembly from DeKalb County, 1950-54; solicitor City Ct. of Decatur, 1954-56; solicitor gen. Stone Mountain Jud. Circuit, 1956-76; exec. dir. State Bar Ga., 1976-80; judge Superior Ct. Stone Mountain Jud. Circuit, 1980-82; assoc. justice Ga. Supreme Ct., Atlanta, 1982—; past mem. Jud. Council Ga.; past adminstrv. judge 4th dist. Served to capt. U.S. Army, World War II, PTO, lt. col. Res. ret. Mem. State Bar Ga. (bd. govs. 1963-71, treas. 1971-76), Ga. Dist. Attys. Assn. (pres.), Nat. Dist. Attys. Assn. (bd. dirs.), Decatur-DeKalb Bar Assn. Clubs: Old Warhorse Lawyers, Atlanta Lawyers, Masons, Decatur Lions. Judicial administration. Office: George Supreme Ct State Jud Bldg Atlanta GA 30334 *

BELL, ROBERT BROOKS, lawyer; b. Norman, Okla., Aug. 31, 1953; m. Lisa M. Griffin, Aug. 24, 1978. BA, Dartmouth Coll., 1975; MA, Cambridge U., 1977; JD, Stanford U., 1980. Bar: U.S. Dist. Ct. D.C. 1981, U.S. Ct. Appeals (D.C. cir.) 1981, U.S. Dist. Ct. Md. 1985. Law clk. to judge U.S. Dist. Ct. D.C., 1980-81; law clk. to justice Byron White U.S. Supreme Ct., Washington, 1981-82; atty. Sullivan & Cromwell, Washington, 1982—. Contbr. articles to profl. jours. Deacon Georgetown Presbyn. Ch., 1983—, trustee Nat. Capital Chpt. Trout Unltd., Washington, 1984—. Mem. ABA (litigation, antitrust sects.), Order of the Coif, Phi Beta Kappa. Democrat. Environment, Federal civil litigation. Office: Sullivan & Cromwell 1775 Pennsylvania Ave NW Washington DC 20006

BELL, ROBERT CECIL, lawyer; b. San Francisco, June 1, 1951; s. Robert Elmer and Lillian Marie (Petrik) B. BJ, U. Nev., 1973; JD, U. Pacific, 1980. Bar: Nev. 1980, U.S. Dist. Ct. Nev. 1980, U.S. Bankruptcy Ct. 1981, U.S. Ct. Appeals (9th cir.) 1982. Investigator, legal asst. Washoe County Dist. Atty.'s Office, Reno, 1975-77; law clk. to presiding justice Washoe County Dist. Ct., Reno, 1980-81; sole practice Reno, 1981—; judge pro tem Reno Mcpl. Ct., 1985—; bd. dirs. Washoe Legal Services, Reno, Sparks Mcpl. Ct., 1986—. Bd. dirs. March of Dimes, Reno, 1985—. Mem. ABA, Washoe County Bar Assn., Assn. Trial Lawyers Am., Nev. Trial Lawyers Assn., Reno Rodeo Assn., Reno Air Races, Union Pacific U. Law Alumni Assn. (bd. dirs. 1986—). Democrat. Lutheran. Avocations: photography, flying, skiing, golf. General practice, State civil litigation, Criminal. Home: 4635 Aster Dr Reno NV 89502 Office: 121 California Ave Reno NV 89509

BELL, ROBERT COLLINS, lawyer; b. St. Joseph, Mo., Sept. 19, 1912; s. Robert Cook and Mamie Burke (Collins) B.; m. Mary-Katherine Morris, Mar. 22, 1941; children—Robert III, Marianne. Student Carleton Coll., 1929-32; A.B., U. Minn., 1933; J.D., Harvard U., 1936. Bar: Minn. 1936, Conn. 1942, D.C. 1949, N.Y. 1953. Assoc. Fowler, Youngquist, Furber, Taney and Johnson, Mpls., 1936-37; atty. U.S. Wage and Hour Div.-Minn., N.D., S.D., Mont., 1939-40; chief tax amortization sect. War Prodn. Bd., 1940-42; assoc. Cummings and Lockwood, Stamford, Conn., 1942-52; ptnr. Smith Mathews, Bell and Solomon, N.Y.C., 1952-62; practice, New Canaan, Conn., 1962—; pros. atty., New Canaan, 1948-50. Mem. War Dept. Bd. Contract Appeals, Office of Under Sec. of War, 1944-45. Mem. ABA, Conn. Bar Assn., Internat. Bar Assn. Democrat. Congregationalist. Clubs: Harvard (N.Y.C.); Tokeneke (Darien, Conn.); Masons. Obtained judgments totalling over 25 million dollars on behalf of the Pottawatomi, Miami and Chippewa Indian Tribes in U.S. Ct. Claims and U.S. Indian Claims Commn. General corporate, Private international, Indian. Home: 528 Main St New Canaan CT 06840 Office: 528 Main St New Canaan CT 06840

BELL, ROBERT MORRALL, lawyer; b. Graniteville, S.C., Feb. 15, 1936; s. Jonathan F. and Ruby Lee (Carpenter) B.; m. Cecelia Richardson Coker, June 11, 1965 (dec.). A.B., U. S.C., 1958, LL.B., 1965. Bar: S.C. 1965, U.S. Dist. Ct. S.C. 1965, U.S. Ct. Appeals (4th cir.) 1970. With Watkins, Vandiver, Kirven & Long, Anderson, S.C., 1965-67; sr. law clk. to chief judge U.S. Dist. Ct. S.C., Greenville, 1967-69; mem. firm Abram, Bowen & Townes, Greenville, 1969-71, Bell & Surasky, Langley, S.C., 1971—, sr. ptnr., 1976—; county atty. Aiken County (S.C.), 1982—. Mem. S.C. Hwy. Commn., 1982—; state exec. committeeman S.C. Democratic Com., 1980—; mem. S.C. Bd. Chiropractic Examiners, 1978-80; mem. Service Council of Aiken County, 1976-82, Aiken County Planning Commn., 1976-80; bd. dirs. Aiken County Crippled Children's Soc., 1976-82. Served with USAR, 1959-60. Mem. Aiken County Bar Assn., S.C. Bar Assn., ABA, S.C. Trial Lawyers Assn., Am. Trial Lawyers Assn., Kappa Sigma Kappa, Tau Kappa Alpha, Phi Delta Phi. Democrat. Methodist. Club: Masons, Shriners. Personal injury, Workers' compensation, Local government. Home: PO Drawer 1 Langley SC 29834

BELL, RONALD LEE, lawyer, consultant; b. Chgo., Dec. 30, 1955; s. Harold and Elinor D. Bell; m. Doreen S. Hirsch; children: Heather A., Ashley. BA in History and Polit. Sci., Lake Forest (Ill.) Coll., 1976; JD, John Marshall Law Sch., Chgo., 1980. Bar: Ill. 1980, U.S. Dist. Ct. (no. dist.) Ill. 1980, U.S. Ct. Appeals (7th cir.) 1981, U.S. Tax Ct. 1984, U.S. Supreme Ct. 1984. Asst. atty. gen. State of Ill., Chgo., 1980-84; assoc. Franzin & Colombik, Deerfield, Ill., 1984-85; mem. Colombik & Bell, Palatine, Ill., 1985-87, Ronald L. Bell & Assocs., P.C., Palatine, 1987—; cons. in field. Research editor John Marshall Law Sch. Review, 1980. Bd. dirs. Maine Twp. (Ill.) Rep. Orgn., 1982. Mem. ABA, Ill. Bar Assn., 7th Cir. Bar Assn., Lake County Bar Assn., Northwest Suburban Bar Assn., Chgo. Bar Assn., Assn. Trial Lawyers Am., Ill. Trial Lawyers Assn. Jewish. Club: Meadows (Rolling Meadows, Ill.). Avocations: Appellate work, writing, tennis. Federal civil litigation, State civil litigation, Criminal. Office: Ronald L Bell & Assocs PC 1530 E Dundee Rd Suite 150 Palatine IL 60067

BELL, SAMUEL H., federal judge; b. Rochester, N.Y., Dec. 31, 1925; s. Samuel H. and Marie C. (Williams) B.; m. Joyce Elaine Shaw, 1948 (dec.): children—Henry W., Steven D.; m. Jennie Lee McCall, 1983. B.A., Coll. Wooster, 1947; J.D., U. Akron, 1952. Practice law Cuyahoga Falls, Ohio, 1956-68; asst. pros. atty. Summit County, Ohio, 1956-58; judge Cuyahoga Falls Mcpl. Ct., Ohio, 1968-73, Ct. of Common Pleas, Akron, Ohio, 1973-77, Ohio Ct. Appeals, 9th Jud. Dist., Akron, 1977-82, U.S. Dist. Ct. (no. dist.) Ohio, Akron, 1982—; mem. adv. bd. U. Akron Sch. Law, trustee Dean's Club. Recipient Disting. Alumni award U. Akron, 1983, St. Thomas More award, 1987. Mem. ABA, Fed. Bar Assn., Akron Bar Assn., Ohio Bar Assn., Akron U. Sch. Law Alumni Assn. (disting. alumni award 1983), Phi Alpha Delta. Republican. Presbyterian. Club: Akron City. Lodge: Masons. Judicial administration. Office: US Courthouse 2 S Main St Akron OH 44308

BELL, THOMAS LEE, lawyer; b. Holton, Kans., Sept. 24, 1955; s. Ray Thomas and Lulu LaVerne (Kling) B.; m. Valerie Ann Schirmer, Mar. 11, 1978; 1 child Catherine Anne. BS magna cum laude, Kans. State U., 1978; JD cum laude, Washburn U., 1978-81. Bar: Kans. 1981, U.S. Dist. Ct. Kans. 1981. Research atty. Kans. Supreme Ct., Topeka, 1981-83; assoc. Goodell, Stratton, Edmands & Palmer, Topeka, 1981-83; v.p. Kans. Hosp. Assn., Topeka, 1986—; Mem. Lou Douglas Lectr. Series, Manhattan, Kans., 1984—. Vol. Kans. Children's Service League, Topeka, 1983-85; bd. dirs. Topeka Housing Info. Ctr., 1985; pres., bd. dirs. Community Youth Homes, Inc., 1986. Mem. ABA, Nat. Health Lawyers Assn., Am. Acad. Hosp. Attys., Kans. Bar Assn., Topeka Bar Assn. (pres. young lawyers 1984-86). Democrat. Methodist. Avocations: sports, reading, fishing. Health, Legislative. Office: Kans Hosp Assn 1263 Topeka Blvd Topeka KS 66601

BELL, THOMAS REUBEN, lawyer; b. Birmingham, Ala., Feb. 15, 1918; s. Thomas Reuben and Ola Ann (Reeves) B.; m. Helen Louise Norris, July 6, 1940 (div. June 1966); children: Thomas Reuben III; m. Anne Jenkins, Dec. 27, 1977. BA, U. Ala., 1938, LLB, 1940; ML, Harvard U., 1948, JD, 1969. Bar: Ala. 1940, U.S. Supreme Ct. 1951. Ptnr. Brown & Bell, Birmingham, 1940-42; staff atty. Avondale Mills, Sylacauga, Ala., 1946-52; sole practice Sylacauga, 1952-85; ptnr. Bell & Landers, Sylacauga, 1986—. Served to 1st lt. USAF, 1942-45, PTO. Mem. ABA, Ala. Bar Assn., Talladega Bar Assn. (pres. 1955), Bd. of Bar Commrs. (ho. of dels. 1979-82). Democrat. Episcopalian. Clubs: Mountain Brook (Birmingham), Coosa Valley (Sylacauga). General corporate, Banking, Probate. Home: 7 Forest Dr Sylacauga AL 35150 Office: Bell & Landers 223 N Norton Ave Sylacauga AL 35150

BELL, WAYNE STEVEN, lawyer; b. Los Angeles, June 24, 1954; s. Joseph and Jane Barbara (Barsook) B. BA magna cum laude, UCLA, 1976; JD, Loyola U., Los Angeles, 1979. Bar: Calif. 1980, U.S. Dist. Ct. (cen. dist.) 1981, U.S. Tax Ct. 1981, U.S. Ct. Appeals (9th cir.) 1981, U.S. Dist. Ct. (so. and no. dists.) Calif. 1983, U.S. Supreme Ct. 1984, D.C. 1986. Assoc. Levinson, Rowen, Miller, Jacobs & Kabrins, Los Angeles, 1980-82; sr. assoc. Montgomery, Gascou, Gemmill & Thornton, Los Angeles, 1982-84; of counsel Greenspan, Glasser & Medina, Santa Monica, Calif., 1984-86; assoc. gen. counsel Am. Diversified Cos., Costa Mesa, Calif., 1985—; counsel, project developer Thomas Safran & Assocs., Los Angeles, 1984-85. Chief note and comment editor Loyola U. Law Rev., 1978-79. Vol. atty. Westside Legal Services, Santa Monica, 1982-87; mem. Calif. adv. council Legal Services Corp., 1982—, Nat. Soc. for Children and Adults with Autism, Los Angeles and Washington, Calif. Dems. for New Leadership, Los Angeles; contbg. mem. Dem. Nat. Com., So. Poverty Law Ctr.; assoc. Immaculate Heart Coll. Ctr., Los Angeles; bd. dirs. Am. Theatre Arts, Hollywood, Calif., 1983-84, Programs for the Developmentally Handicapped Inc., Los Angeles, 1985—; chmn. bd. appeals handicapped accommodations City of Manhattan Beach, 1986—. Mem. ABA, Calif. Bar Assn. (standing com. legal problems of aging 1983-86, chmn. legis. subcom. 1984-86, legal services sect.), Los Angeles County Bar Assn. (olympics ombudsman 1984, barristers sect.), Legal Assistance Assn. Calif. (bd. dirs., exec. com., legis. strategy com. 1984-86), UCLA Alumni Assn., Loyola Law Sch. (assoc. adv.), Phi Beta Kappa, Pi Gamma Mu, Pi Sigma Alpha, Phi Alpha Delta, Sierra Club. Democrat. Lodge: Lions. Avocations: cycling, hiking, rowing, sailing. General corporate, Real property, State civil litigation. Home: 3008 Palm Ave Manhattan Beach CA 90266 Office: Am Diversified Cos 3200 Park Center Dr Costa Mesa CA 92626

BELL, WILLIAM HALL, lawyer; b. Greeneville, Tenn., July 16, 1951; s. Charles B. and Peggy (Hall) B.; m. Ellen Bell, July 3, 1981; children: Burnley, Bethany. BA in Psychology, BA in Polit. Sci. with honors, U. Tenn., 1975, JD, 1978; LLM, Cambridge (Eng.) U., 1979; cert. d'Assiduite, Hague (The Netherlands) Acad. Internat. Law, 1984. Bar: Tenn 1978, U.S. Dist. Ct. Tenn. 1980. Ptnr. Bell & Mills, Greeneville, 1979—; adv. com. Macro Engring. Group, MIT Sch. Engring.; co-counsel on Macro-Engring. Law, Internat. Law Collaborative, Cambridge, Mass.; legal advisor to solicitor-at-law in Cambridge U., Eng., 1978-79; law lectr. Cambridge Inst. Arts and Techs., 1978-79. Mem. Tenn. Trial Lawyers Assn. (bd. dirs.), Greeneville Bar Assn. (pres.). Private international, Public international, General corporate. Office: 128 S Main St Greenville TN 37743

BELL, WILLIAM HENRY, lawyer; b. Yenangyaung, Burma, Dec. 15, 1926; came to U.S., 1932; s. William R. and Beulah Joyce (Girsham) B.; m. Rita Ely, 1950; children: Sharon, Martin, David, Leta. BA, Duke U., 1947; BBA, Texas A&I U., 1950; JD, Tulsa U., 1954; DHL (hon.), Okla. Christian Coll., 1973. Bar: Okla. 1954, U.S. Dist. Ct. (no. dist.) 1954, U.S. Ct. Appeals (10th cir.) 1954, U.S. Supreme Ct. 1968. Assoc. John Rogers, Tulsa, 1954-64; ptnr. Rogers and Bell, Tulsa, 1964—; Bd. dirs. Bank Okla., Tulsa, Red River Oil Co. Trustee Hillcrest Med. Ctr., Okla., 1964—, Okla Med. Research Found., 1964—, Tulsa U., 1966—, various colls. and univs.; past pres., chmn. Tulsa Area United Way; past pres. Tulsa Edn. Found., Tulsa Med. Edn. Found., others. Served with USNR, 1944-46. Recipient Disting. Service award U.S. Jr. C. of C., 1961, Medallion Boys Clubs Am., 1962; named Man of Yr. Downtown Tulsa Unlimited, 1973, named to Okla. Hall of Fame, 1974. Fellow Am. Bar Found., Am. Coll. Probate Counsel, Southwestern Legal Found. , Okla. Bar Found. (past pres.); mem. ABA (resource devel. council), Fed. Energy Bar Assn., Okla. Bar Assn. (past pres.), Tulsa County Bar Assn. (past pres., outstanding jr. mem. 1960, outstanding sr. mem. 1972). Republican. Episcopalian. Clubs: So. Hills, Summit, Tulsa. Probate, Oil and gas leasing, Tax exempt organizations. Home: 4612 S Birmingham Ave Tulsa OK 74105

BELL, WILLIAM WOODWARD, lawyer; b. Brownwood, Tex., May 15, 1938; s. Charles Smith and Janie Mae (Woodward) B.; m. Mary Elizabeth Beniteau, May 31, 1969; children—Susan Elizabeth, Carol Ann. B.B.A., Baylor U., 1960, J.D., 1965. Bar: U.S. Dist. Ct. (we. dist.) Tex. 1967, U.S. Supreme Ct. 1971. Ptnr. Sleeper, Boynton, Bueleson, Williams & Johnson, Waco, Tex., 1965-68, Holloway, Slagle & Bell, Brownwood, 1968-71; ptnr. Johnson, Slagle & Bell, Brownwood, 1971-74; sole practice, Brownwood, 1974-80; atty. City of Brownwood, 1980—; ptnr. Bell and Ellis, Brownwood, 1980—; v.p. Bell Mortgage and Investment Co., Brownwood, 1962—. Served to capt. USMC, 1960-63. Fellow Tex. Bar Found.; mem. Tex. Bar Assn. (chmn. dist. 15B grievance com. 1986—), Brown County Bar Assn., Am. Judicature Soc., Assn. Trial Lawyers Am., Phi Alpha Delta. Baptist. Club: Rotary. General practice, State civil litigation, Local government. Home: PO Box 1564 Brownwood TX 76804 Office: Bell and Ellis 115 S Broadway PO Box 1726 Brownwood TX 76804

BELLAH, C. RICHARD, lawyer; b. San Antonio, Jan. 11, 1955; s. Max and Charlotte (Arant) B. BS in Gen. Bus. Adminstrn., Ariz. State U., 1977; JD, U. Ariz., 1980. Bar: U.S. Dist. Ct. Ariz. 1980, U.S. Ct. Appeals (9th cir.) 1981, U.S. Tax Ct. 1985, U.S. Supreme Ct. 1985. Law clk. to presiding justice Ariz. Supreme Ct., Phoenix, 1980-81; assoc. Crotts & Laird, Phoenix, 1981-82; ptnr. Charles, Smith & Bellah, Glendale, Ariz., 1982-86; sole practice Glendale, 1986—; councilman City of Glendale, 1984—; justice of peace pro tem Maricopa County Justice Ct., Glendale, 1985—. Committeeman precinct Maricopa County Reps. Recipient Outstanding Service award Am. Legion, 1979, Cert. of Appreciation Ariz. State Legis., 1979, Maricopa Services Commn., 1985, Phoenix of Realtors, 1985, Soroptimist Internat., 1985, City of Glendale, 1985, Glendale Sr. Ctr., 1986. Mem. ABA (Silver Key award 1979), Ariz. Bar Assn., Assn. Trial Lawyers Am., Ariz. Trial Lawyers Assn., Phi Alpha Delta (chpt. justice, vice justice alumni assn.). Baptist. Lodge: Rotary (chmn. installation banquet). Avocation: jogging. Family and matrimonial, General practice, Juvenile. Home: 4554 W Maryland Glendale AZ 85301 Office: 5724 W Palmaire Ave Glendale AZ 85301

BELLAH, KENNETH DAVID, lawyer; b. Joliet, Ill., Aug. 17, 1955; s. Virgil and Joyce (Allen) B.; m. Lori Ann Piazza, Nov. 26, 1983. B.A., Augustana Coll., 1977; J.D., Chgo. Kent Coll. Law, Ill. Inst. Tech., 1980. Bar: Ill. 1980, U.S. Dist. Ct. (no. dist.) Ill. 1980, U.S. Ct. Appeals (7th cir.) 1980. Assoc. Matthias & Matthias, Chgo., 1980-83; ptnr. Matthias & Bellah, Chgo., 1983—. Republican. Methodist. State civil litigation, Federal civil litigation, Insurance. Office: Matthias & Bellah 230 W Monroe St Suite 2220 Chicago IL 60606

BELLAK, RICHARD CHARLES, lawyer; b. Phila., Feb. 7, 1945; s. Carl and Ona (Rappaport) B. BA, U. Pa., 1966, PhD, 1976; MFA, Princeton U., 1968; JD, Fla. State U., 1981. Bar: Fla. 1981, U.S. Dist. Ct. (no. dist.) Fla. 1984, U.S. Dist. Ct. (mid. dist.) Fla. 1985. Faculty mem. Franconia (N.H.) Coll., 1970-77; asst. atty. gen. State of Fla., Tallahassee, 1981—. Mem. ABA, Fla. Bar Assn. Avocations: musician, composer, pianist. Antitrust, Trademark and copyright, Entertainment. Office: The Capitol Dept Legal Affairs Tallahassee FL 32301

BELLAMY, FREDERICK ROBERT, lawyer; b. Newark, Jan. 28, 1954; s. Roy Canfield and Rita Grace (Schmidt) B.; m. Mary Kathryn Crook, Nov. 26, 1983; 1 child, Franklin Roy. BA, U. Va., 1976; JD magna cum laude, Cornell U., 1979. Bar: D.C. 1979, U.S. Ct. Appeals (4th cir.) 1980. Law clk. to presiding justice U.S. Ct. Appeals (4th cir.), Abingdon, Va., 1979-80; assoc. Sutherland, Asbill & Brennan, Washington, 1980-86, ptnr., 1986—. Mem. ABA, Fed. Bar Assn. Securities, Insurance, Investment companies. Home: 112 Saint Andrews Dr NE Vienna VA 22180 Office: Sutherland Asbill & Brennan 1666 K St NW Washington DC 20006

BELLAMY, WILLIAM MURRAY, JR., tax lawyer; b. Bklyn., July 14, 1931; s. William Murray Sr., and Florence Jane (Eibel) B.; m. Jan Peifer; children—Susan I., Laura E., William III. A.B., Cornell U., 1953, M.B.A., 1958, LL.B., 1959; LL.M. in Taxation, NYU, 1965. Bar: N.Y. 1960, U.S. Tax Ct. 1964. Tax assoc. Willkie Farr & Gallagher, N.Y.C., 1959-66; tax atty. Union Carbide Corp., N.Y.C., 1966-74, assoc. tax counsel, 1974-78, chief tax counsel, Danbury, Conn., 1978—; mem. Chem. Mfrs. Assn.-Tax Policy Com., Washington, 1978—, chmn. Tax Policy Com., 1984-86. Mem. Cornell U. Council, Ithaca, N.Y., 1974—. Served to 1st lt., U.S. Army, 1953-55. Mem. ABA, N.Y. State Bar Assn., Phi Kappa Phi, Phi Delta Phi, Sigma Phi Epsilon. Republican. Episcopalian. Club: Seven Bridges Field (Chappaqua) (treas. 1972-73, pres. 1973-74); Mt. Kisco Country. Corporate taxation. Home: 34 Cross Ridge Rd Chappaqua NY 10514 Office: Union Carbide Corp Old Ridgebury Rd Danbury CT 06817

BELLER, BARRY, lawyer, trust company executive; b. N.Y.C., Feb. 14, 1945; s. Charles S. and Shirley (Green) B. BA, Mich. State U., 1966; JD, Bklyn. Law Sch., 1969; LLM in Internat. Legal Studies, NYU, 1980. Bar: N.Y. 1970, U.S. Dist. Ct. (so. dist.) N.Y. 1974, U.S. Ct. Appeals (2d cir.) 1974, U.S. Supreme Ct. 1976. V.ps. assoc. gen. counsel Mfrs. Hanover Trust Co., N.Y.C., 1971—. Mem. ABA (sect. internat. law, chmn. com. on internat. fin. transactions), Nat. Fgn. Trade Council (internat. investment com.). Private international, Banking, Contracts commercial. Home: 435 E 65th St New York NY 10021 Office: 270 Park Ave New York NY 10017

BELLER, CHARLES ROSCOE, III, lawyer; b. Radford, Va., Nov. 13, 1947; s. Charles Roscoe Jr. and Dorothy (Boswell) B.; m. Paula Tabarini, Aug. 5, 1978; children: Jennifer Neale, Joanna Garst. BA, Va. Tech. U., 1970; JD, U. Richmond, 1978. Bar: Va. 1978, U.S. Ct. Appeals (4th cir.) 1978. Tax appraiser Chesterfield (Va.) County, 1970-71; aid, tchr. St. Albans Hosp., Radford, 1971-72; com. clk. Gen Assembly of Va., Richmond, 1972; legal asst. Richard W. Davis, Atty., Radford, 1972, 74; systems analyst U.S. Ho. of Reps., Washington, 1972-73; sole practice Christianburg, Va., 1982—; instr. Va. Tech. U., Blacksburg, 1979-82. Mem. Va. Bar Assn., Va. Trial Lawyers Assn., Assn. Trial Lawyers Am., Am. Arbitration Assn., Christianburg C. of C. (small. bus. com. 1985). Avocation: golf. Federal civil litigation, State civil litigation, Personal injury. Office: 114 N Franklin St Christianburg VA 24073

BELLER, GARY A., financial services company executive; b. N.Y.C., Oct. 16, 1938; s. Charles W. and Jeanne A. B.; m. Carole P. Wrubel, Nov. 22, 1967; 1 child, Jessie Melissa. B.A., Cornell U., 1960; LL.B., NYU, 1963, LL.M., 1971; postgrad. in Advanced Mgmt., Harvard Bus. Sch., 1967-68. Bar: N.Y. 1963. Various postiions gen. counsel's office Am. Express Co., N.Y.C., 1968-82, exec. v.p. and gen. counsel, 1983—. Editorial bd. Ctr. Pub. Resources (Alternatives), N.Y.C. Bd. dirs. Lenox Hill Neighborhood Assn.; mem. Citizens' Crime Commn. of N.Y. Mem. ABA, Bar Assn. City N.Y., N.Y. County Bar Assn. (com. corp. law depts.), Am. Corp. Counsel Assn. (dir.). Clubs: Harvard Bus. Sch. (N.Y.C.), Downtown Athletic (N.Y.C.). General corporate. Office: American Express Co Am Express Tower World Fin Ctr New York NY 10004 *

BELLEVILLE, PHILIP FREDERICK, lawyer; b. Flint, Mich., Apr. 24, 1934; s. Frederick Charles and Sarah (Adelaine) B.; m. Geraldean Bickford, Sept. 2, 1953; children—Stacy L., Philip Frederick II, Jeffrey A. B.A. in Econs. with high distinction and honors, U. Mich., 1956, J.D., 1960. Bar: Calif. 1961. Assoc. Latham & Watkins, Los Angeles, 1960-68; ptnr. Latham & Watkins, Los Angeles and Newport Beach, Calif., 1968-73; ptnr., chmn. litigation dept. Latham & Watkins, Los Angeles and Newport Beach, 1973-80; sr. ptnr. Latham & Watkins, Los Angeles, Newport Beach, San Diego, Washington,, 1980—, Chgo., 1983—, N.Y.C., 1985—. Asst. editor Mich. Law Rev., U. Mich. Law Sch., Ann Arbor, 1959-60. Mem. So. Calif. steering com. NAACP Legal Def. Fund, Inc., Los Angeles, 1979—; mem. community adv. bd. San Pedro Peninsula Hosp., Calif., 1980—. James B. Angell scholar U. Mich., 1955-56. Mem. ABA (antitrust law and criminal justice sects.), Calif. State Bar Assn. (antitrust and trade regulation and bus. law sects.), Los Angeles County Bar Assn. (bus. trial lawyers sect.), Assn. Trial Lawyers Am., Assn. Bus. Trial Lawyers, Order of Coif, Phi Beta Kappa, Phi Kappa Phi, Alpha Kappa Psi. Republican. Clubs: University (Los Angeles); Jack Kramer Tennis (Rolling Hills Estates, Calif.); Portuguese Bend (Calif.); Caballeros (Rollings Hills), Rolling Hills (Calif.). Avocations: antique and classic autos; human behavior study; tennis; art; antiques. Federal civil litigation, State civil litigation, Antitrust. Office: Latham & Watkins 555 S Flower St Los Angeles CA 90071

BELLI, MELVIN MOURON, lawyer, lecturer, writer; b. Sonora, Calif., July 29, 1907; s. Caesar Arthur and Leonie (Mouron) B.; m. Betty Ballantine, 1933; children: Richard R., Melvin Mouron, Jean, Susan; m. 2d Joy Maybelle Turney, May 3, 1956; 1 son, Caesar Melvin; m. 3d Lia G.T. Triff, June 3, 1972; 1 dau., Melia. A.B., U. Calif. - Berkeley, 1929; LL.B., Boalt Hall, 1933; J.D. (hon.), New Eng. Sch. Law. Bar: Calif. 1933. Sr. partner Belli Law Offices, San Francisco, 1933—; condr. Belli Seminars in Law, 1953—; pres. Belli Found. Lectrs., 1960—; provost Belli Soc.; Mem. Calif. Bldg. Standards Commn.; Bd. dirs. Disability & Casualty Inter-Ins. Exchange, N.W. Affairs Council; mem. exec. bd. Western State U. Coll. Law. Author: Modern Trials and Modern Damages, 6 vols, 1954, abridged edit., 1962, 2d edit., 1981, Ready for the Plaintiff, 1956, Trial and Tort Trends, 14 vols, 1954-62, The Adequate Award, 1953, Demonstrative Evidence and The Adequate Award, 1955, Malpractice, 1955, Modern Trials (student edition), (with Danny Jones) Life and Law in Japan, (with Maurice Carroll) Dallas Justice, 1964, The Law Revolt, 2 vols, 1968, Melvin Belli My Life on Trial, 1976, The Belli Files: Reflections on the Wayward Law, 1983, (with Allen Wilkinson) Everybody's Guide to the Law, 1986; contbr.: numerous articles, also syndicated column So That's The Law; Asso. editor: Am. Trial Lawyers Assn. Law Jour, 1950—; adv. editor: Negligence and Compensation Service, 1955—; legal adv. bd.: Traumatic Medicine and Surgery for the Atty., 1958—; mem. bd. editors: Trial Diplomacy Jour; mem. editorial bd.: The Common Law Lawyer; bd. dirs.: Am. Jour. Forensic Psychiatry. Named dean emeritus Coll. Law, Riverside U.; decorated grand ofcl. St. Brigidian Order. Fellow Internat. Acad. Trial Lawyers (dir., past dean); mem. Authors Guild, Am. Acad. Forensic Scis., Tuolumne County Hist. Soc., Inter-Am. Bar Assn., ABA, Calif. Bar Assn., San Francisco Bar Assn., Fed. Bar Assn., Internat. Bar Assn. (patron), Internat. Legal Aid Assn., San Diego, Hollywood, Beverly Hills bars, Am. Trial Lawyers Assn. (past pres., chmn. torts sect. 1959), Barristers Club San Francisco (past dir.), La Asociacion Nacional de Abogados Mexico (hon.), Societe Driot (pres.), Phi Delta Phi, Delta Tau Delta. Clubs: Mason (San Francisco) (Shriner), Olympic (San Francisco), The Commonwealth (San Francisco), Lawyers (San Francisco). General practice. Office: Belli Bldg 722 Montgomery St San Francisco CA 94111 also: The Belli Bldg 9952 Santa Monica Bldg Suite 9000 Beverly Hills CA 90212 also: 317 Ash St San Diego CA 92101 also: The Belli Bldg 405 Forest Ave Pacific Grove CA 93950 also: The Belli Bldg 215 N San Joaquin Stockton CA 95202

BELLINGER, EDGAR THOMSON, lawyer; b. N.Y.C., Sept. 23, 1929; s. John and Margaret Steiner (Thomson) B.; m. Adrian Dunn, Nov. 27, 1957; children—Edgar Jr., Robert, Margaret. B.A., Haverford Coll., 1951; J.D., George Washington U., 1955. Bar: D.C. 1955, Md. 1955. Law clk. to chief judge U.S. Dist. Ct. D.C., 1955-57; asst. U.S. atty. for Washington, 1957-59; ptnr. Pope Ballard and Loos, Washington, 1959-81, Zuckert, Scoutt, Rasenberger and Johnson, Washington, 1981—; chmn. unauthorized practice com. D.C. Ct. Appeals, 1972-78; mem. D.C. jud. conf., 1972—; bd. dirs. D.C. chpt. ARC; bd. mgrs. Chevy Chase Village, 1983-86. Mem. ABA, D.C. Bar Assn. (org. com. 1972), Montgomery County Bar Assn., Md. Bar Assn., Am. Judicature Soc. Clubs: Metropolitan, Chevy Chase (Md.) (bd. govs. 1972-77, pres. 1976-77). Barristers. State civil litigation, Insurance, Probate. Office: 888 17th St NW Washington DC 20006

BELLO-MONACO, DEBORAH ANN, lawyer; b. Jersey City, Sept. 20, 1956; d. Richard Anthony and Anna (Barberio) B.; m. Carl Anthony Monaco, July 17, 1977; 1 child, Carl. BS in Mgmt. summa cum laude, St.

Peter's Coll., 1976; JD cum laude, Seton Hall U., 1979. Bar: N.J. 1979, U.S. Dist. Ct. N.J. 1979, U.S. Ct. Appeals (3d cir.) 1979. Assoc. gen. counsel, asst. sec. Prudential Reins. Co., Newark, 1979—. Mem. Fedn. Ins. Counsel. Roman Catholic. General corporate, Insurance, Reinsurance. Office: Prudential Reins Co 100 Mulberry St Newark NJ 07102

BELLO-TRULAND, ROSEMARIE, lawyer; b. Bklyn., June 3, 1947; d. John W. and Marie (Perry) Bello; children: Jacqueline Joy, Jon Jason. BA in Spanish, Marymount Manhattan Coll., 1969; JD, Fordham U., 1976; postdoctoral, Seton Hall U., 1982—. Bar: N.J. 1976, N.Y. 1977. Sole practice Little Falls, N.J., 1976—; trustee Passaic County Legal Aid Soc., Paterson, N.J. Mem. ABA, N.J. Bar Assn., Passaic County Bar Assn. (trustee). Family and matrimonial.

BELLOTTI, FRANCIS XAVIER, state official, lawyer; b. Dorchester, Mass., May 3, 1923; s. Peter Vincent and Mary J. (Petrocelli) B.; m. Margarita E. Wang, Feb. 22, 1949; children: Francis X., Kathleen A., Mary E., Nina M., Peter V., Therese A., Margarita E., Joseph R., Thomas, Patricia A., Michael G., Sheila A. A.B., Tufts U., 1947; LL.B. (Univ. fellow), Boston Coll., 1952; J.D. (hon.), New Eng. Sch. Law, 1977, Tufts U., 1979. Bar: Mass. 1952, U.S. Supreme Ct. 1965, U.S. Dist. Ct. 1975. Practiced law Quincy, Mass., 1952-74; lt. gov. Commonwealth of Mass., 1963-64, atty. gen., 1975—; chmn. Criminal History Systems Bd., Comm. on Criminal Justice, Organized Crime Control Council, Com. on Privacy and Consumer Rights; mem. Mass. Council on Juvenile Behavior, Consumers' Council, Criminal Justice Tng. Council, Select Com. on Jud. Needs (Cox Com.), Motor Vehicle Ins. Merit Rating Bd. Served to lt. (j.g.) USN, 1942-46. Recipient Silver medal VFW, 1978, comdr. in chief gold medal and citation VFW, 1979. Fellow Internat. Acad. Trial Lawyers, Am. Coll. Trial Lawyers; mem. Nat. Assn. Attys. Gen. (Louis C. Wyman award 1981, pres. 1984-85), Harvard Inst. Politics, Nat. Coll. Criminal Def. Lawyers, Profl. Journalists, New Eng. Law Inst., Am. Judicature Soc., Justinian Law Soc. Roman Catholic. Criminal, Legislative. Home: 120 Hillside Ave Quincy MA 02170 Office: Dept of Atty Gen 1 Ashburton Pl Boston MA 02108

BELLOW, GARY, lawyer, educator; b. 1935. B.A., Yale U., 1957; LL.B., Harvard U., 1960; LL.M., Northwestern U., 1961. Bar: N.Y. 1962, D.C. 1962, Calif. 1966, Mass. 1974. Dep. dir. Legal Aid Agy., Washington, Washington, 1962-65; adminstrv. dir. United Planning Orgn., Washington, 1965, dep. exec. dir., 1965-66; dep. dir. Calif. Rural Legal Assistance, Los Angeles, 1966-68; assoc. prof. U. So. Calif., 1966-68; vis. prof. Harvard U., Cambridge, Mass., 1971-72, prof. law, 1972—. Bd. dirs. Vera Inst., Mass. Advocacy Ctr.; mem. Nat. Adv. Com. on Law and Poverty, OEO. Mem. ABA (mem. com. on legal aid and indigent defendants). Author: (with Beatrice Moulton) The Lawyering Process, 1978; (with J. Kettleson) The Mirror of Public Interest Ethics, 1978, (with Beatrice Moulton) Preparing and Presenting the Case, 1980, Professional Responsibility, 1981, Clinical Studies in Law, in Looking at Law School, 1984. Legal education. Office: Harvard U Sch of Law Cambridge MA 02138

BELLOWS, LAUREL GORDON, lawyer; b. Chgo., Apr. 9, 1948; d. Michael M. Gordon and Lois (Loren) Gross; m. Joel J. Bellows, June 9, 1978. BA, U. Pa., 1969; JD, Loyola U., Chgo., 1974. Bar: Ill. 1974, Fla. 1975, U.S. Dist. Ct. (no. dist.) Ill. 1975, U.S. Dist. Ct. (no. dist.) Ga. 1980, Calif. 1981, U.S. Dist. Ct. (cen. dist.) Calif. 1980. Ptnr. Bellows and Bellows, Chgo., 1975—. Editor Loyola U. Law Rev., 1973-74. Past pres. women's bd. Traveller's Aid Soc., Chgo.; bd. dirs. SCORE Music Conservatory. Mem. ABA, Ill. Bar Assn., Chgo. Bar Assn. (chmn. membership com. 1982-83, vice chmn. young lawyer's sect. 1982-83, bd. mgrs. 1983-85, chmn. sustaining mem. program 1984, chmn. pub. relations com. 1985, chmn. long range planning 1986—, vice chmn. assn. meetings 1986—, sec. 1987-88), Chgo. Pops Orch. Assn. Club: The Arts. Federal civil litigation, State civil litigation, Securities. Office: Bellows and Bellows 79 W Monroe Suite 800 Chicago IL 60603

BELMORE, F. MARTIN, lawyer; b. N.Y.C., Mar. 17, 1944; s. Frederick M. and Charlotte Lee (Munn) B.; m. Suzanne Corkedale, July 24, 1981. A.B., Princeton U., 1966; postgrad., Oxford U., 1966-67; J.D., Harvard U., 1970; LL.M. in Taxation, NYU, 1975. Bar: N.Y. 1971, Ill. 1976. Assoc. Dewey, Ballatine, Bushby, Palmer & Wood, N.Y.C., 1970-75; assoc. Mayer, Brown & Platt, Chgo., 1975-77, ptnr., 1978—. Mem. ABA, Assn. Bar City N.Y., N.Y. State Bar Assn., Internat. Fiscal Assn. Clubs: Law, Racquet (Chgo.); Princeton (N.Y.C.). Corporate taxation, Private international. Office: Mayer Brown & Platt 190 S LaSalle St Chicago IL 60603

BELNAP, MICHAEL GARY, lawyer; b. Ogden, Utah, June 19, 1953; s. Gary DeVar Belnap and Lois B. (Standing) Howell; m. Diane Francom, June 23, 1983; 1 child, Brandon Michael. BA, U. Utah, 1977; JD, Brigham Young U., 1981. Bar: Utah 1982, U.S. Dist. Ct. Utah 1982. Sole practice Ogden, 1982—. Mem. ABA, Utah Bar Assn. (employment law sect.). LDS. Avocations: outdoor sports, music, farming, gardening. Probate, Real property, Personal injury. Office: 2610 Washington Blvd Ogden UT 84401

BELNICK, MARK ALAN, lawyer; b. Elizabeth, N.J., Oct. 30, 1946; s. Ben B. and Rhoda Helen (Dubrowsky) B.; m. Randy Lee Birer, Mar. 23, 1974; children: Kelly Ann, Cory Frances, Jason Todd. BA cum laude, Cornell U., 1968; JD, Columbia U., 1971. Bar: N.Y. 1972, U.S. Tax Ct. 1972, U.S. Ct. Appeals (2d cir.) 1972, U.S. Dist. Ct. (so. dist.) N.Y. 1973, U.S. Supreme Ct. 1975, U.S. Dist. Ct. (ea. dist.) N.Y. 1978, U.S. Ct. Appeals (9th cir.) 1980, D.C. Bar 1981. Assoc. Marshall, Bratter, Greene et al, N.Y.C., 1971-72; assoc. Paul. Weiss, Rifkind, Wharton & Garrison, N.Y.C., 1972-79, ptnr., 1979—; adj. prof. law Banjamin N. Cardozo Sch. Law, N.Y.C. 1982—; mem. panel mediators and fact finders N.Y. State Pub. Employment Relations Bd., Albany, 1972—; exec. asst. to chief counsel, dep. counsel U.S. Senate select com. on secret mil. assistance to Iran and the Nicaraguan oppositon, 1987. Co-chmn. Westchester Com. for Am. Israel Pub. Affairs Com., Westchester County, N.Y., 1985—, Harrison/Purchase Div. United Jewish Appeal Fedn., Yonkers, N.Y., 1985—; mem. United Jewish Appeal, N.Y.C., 1985—, nat. young leadership cabinet, 1985-86; pres. Jewish Community Ctr. Harrison, N.Y., 1986—; bd. dirs. Children's Blood Found., N.Y.C., 1980—, United Jewish Appeal of Greater N.Y. Harlan Fiske Stone scholar, 1971. Mem. ABA, N.Y. State Bar Assn., Assn. of Bar of City of N.Y. Club: Univ. (N.Y.C.). Federal civil litigation, State civil litigation, Securities. Office: Paul Weiss Rifkind Wharton & Garrison 1285 Avenue of the Americas New York NY 10019

BELSHEIM, HAROLD GULBRAND, II, lawyer; b. Ft. Dodge, Iowa, July 4, 1948; s. Harold G. and Loretta Christine (Lehman) B. AA, St. Paul Jr. Coll., 1969; BA, Concordia Coll., 1971; MBA, Washington U., 1974, JD, 1977. Bar: Ill. 1978, Mo. 1978, U.S. Dist. Ct. (so. dist.) Ill., U.S. Dist. Ct. (ea. dist.) Mo., U.S. Ct. Appeals (7th and 8th cirs.). Staff atty. Mo. Ct. Appeals, St. Louis, 1977-79; assoc. Bernard & Davidson, Granite City, Ill., 1979; sole practice Fairview Heights, Ill., 1980-86; ptnr. Pessin, Baird, Belsheim & Wells, Belleville, Ill., 1986—. Chmn. Children's Wing Fund Raising Drive, O'Fallon Pub. Library, Ill., 1982; alderman O'Fallon City Council, 1980-82; bd. dirs. O'Fallon Pub. Library, 1982—. Mem. Ill. Bar Assn. (chmn. statewide membership and bar activities 1982-85), Mo. Bar Assn., St. Louis Met. Bar Assn. (bd. editors bar jour. 1979-80), Fairview Heights C. of C. Lodges: Optimists, Rotary. General practice, Real property. Office: Pessin Baird Belsheim & Wells 105 N Illinois Belleville IL 62222

BELSKY, MARTIN HENRY, dean, law educator, lawyer; b. Phila., May 29, 1944; s. Abraham and Fannie (Turnoff) B.; m. Kathleen Waits, Mar. 9, 1985; 1 child, Allen Frederick. B.A. cum laude, Temple U., 1965; J.D. cum laude, Columbia U., 1968; cert. of study Hague (Netherlands) Acad. Internat. Law, 1968; diploma in criminology Cambridge (Eng.) U., 1969. Bar: Pa. 1969, Fla. 1983, U.S. dist. ct. (ea. dist.) Pa. 1969, U.S. Ct. Appeals (3d cir.) 1970, U.S. Supreme Ct. 1973, N.Y. 1987. Chief asst. dist. atty. Phila. Dist. Atty.'s Office, 1969-74; assoc. Blank, Rome, Klaus & Comisky, Phila., 1975; chief counsel U.S. Ho. of Reps., Washington, 1975-78; asst. adminstr. NOAA, Washington, 1979-82; dir. Ctr. for Govtl. Responsibility, assoc. prof. law U. Fla. Holand Law Ctr., 1982-86; dean Albany Law Sch., 1986—; bd. advs. Ctr. Oceans Law and Policy; mem. corrections task force Pa. Gov.'s Justice Commn., 1971-75; adv. task force on cts. Nat. Adv. Commn. on Criminal Justice Standars and Goals, 1972-74; mem. com. on proposed standard jury instrns. Pa. Supreme Ct., 1974-81; lectr. in law Temple U., 1971-75; mem. faculty Pa. Coll. Judiciary, 1975-77; adj. prof. law Georgetown U., 1977-81. Chmn. Phila. council Anti-Defamation League, 1975, mem. D.C. bd., 1977-78, now mem. nat. leadership Council. Stone scholar and Internat. fellow Columbia U. Law Sch. Mem. Phila. Bar Assn. (chmn. young lawyers sect. 1974-75), Pa. Bar Assn. (exec. com. young lawyers sect. 1973-75), ABA (del. young lawyers sect. exec. bd. 1973-75), Fla. Bar Assn., Fed. Bar Assn., Am. Judicature Soc., Nat. Dist. Attys. Assn., Am. Soc. Internat. Law, Am. Arbitration Assn., Temple U. Liberal Arts Alumni Assn. (v.p. 1971-75), Sword Soc. Jewish. Club: B'nai B'rith (v.p. lodge 1973-75). Author: (with Steven H. Goldblatt) Analysis and Commentary to the Pennsylvania Crimes Codes, 1973; Handbook for Trial Judges, 1976; contbr. articles to legal publs.; editor-in-chief Jour. Transnat. Law, Columbia Law Sch., 1968, now bd. dirs. Legal education, Public Interest Research. Office: Albany Law Sch of Union Univ Office of the President 80 New Scotland Ave Albany NY 12208

BELSON, JAMES ANTHONY, judge; b. Milw., Sept. 23, 1931; s. Walter W. and Margaret (Taugher) B.; m. Rosemary P. Greenslade, Jan. 11, 1958; children—Anthony James, Marie Taylor, Elizabeth Ann, Stephen Griffin. A.B. cum laude, Georgetown U., 1953, J.D., 1956, LL.M., 1962. Bar: D.C. 1956, Md. 1962. Law clk. U.S. Ct. Appeals (D.C. cir.), 1956-57; Passoc. Hogan & Hartson, Washington, 1960-67, ptnr., 1967-68; trial judge D.C. Superior Ct., 1968-78, presiding judge Civil Div., 1978-81, assoc. judge D.C. Ct. Appeals, 1981—; faculty mem. Nat. Judicial Coll., 1973-80 ; bd. dirs. Council for Ct. Excellence, 1982—; bencher Am. Inn of Ct. VI, 1983—. Bd. editors Georgetown Law. Jour., 1955-56. Served with JAGC, U.S. Army, 1957-60. Mem. Am. Judicature Soc. (dir. 1980-85), ABA (jud. adminstrn. sect., ins. sect., negligence and compensation law sect., criminal law sect.), World Peace Through Law Ctr., Am. Bar Found., John Carroll Soc. (bd. govs. 1978-85). Home: 2220 46th St NW Washington DC 20007 Office: 500 Indiana Ave NW Washington DC 20001

BELTON, JOHN THOMAS, lawyer; b. Yonkers, N.Y., Feb. 24, 1947; s. Harry James and Anne Marie (Kupko) B.; m. Linda Susanne Cheugh, Jan. 6, 1973; 1 child, Joseph Timothy. B.A., Ohio State U., 1972; postgrad. in bus. adminstrn. 1972-73; J.D., Ohio No. U., 1976. Bar: Ohio 1977. Sole practice, Columbus, Ohio, 1976-83; ptnr. Belton, Wherry, Dougherty, Golowin & Cheugh and predecessor firm Belton, Goldwin & Cheugh, Columbus, 1983—; arbitrator Franklin County Ct. Common Pleas, 1983—; dir. Weeks-Finneran Inc. Republican precinct chmn., 1983; v.p. Far Northwest Coalition, 1984; mem. ch. council St. Peter's Parish, 1984—; pres. Dublin youth Athletics, 1985—. Served with USAF, 1968-71. Mem. Dublin Jr. C. of C., ABA, Columbus Bar Assn. (com. chmn. 1976—), U.S. Dist. Ct. Fed. Bar, Ohio Bar Assn., Assn. Trial Lawyers Am., Order of Barristers, Omicron Delta Kappa, Phi Alpha Delta (justice 1975). Clubs: The Pres., Ohio State Alumni, Republican Glee. Republican. Roman Catholic. Lodge: K.C. Avocations: reading; chess; golf; racquetball; recreational activities. State civil litigation, Criminal, Personal injury. Home: 2510 Slateshire Dr Dublin OH 43017 Office: Belton Wherry Dougherty et al 2066 W Henderson Rd Columbus OH 43220

BELTON, ROBERT, law educator; b. 1935. BA, U. Conn., 1961; JD, Boston U., 1965. Asst. counsel legal def. fund NAACP, N.Y.C., 1966-70; ptnr. Chambers, Stein, Ferguson & Lanning, Charlotte, N.C., 1970-75; lectr., dir. fair employment clinic Vanderbilt U., Nashville, 1975-77, assoc. prof., 1977-82, prof., 1982—; vis. prof. Harvard U., Cambridge, Mass., 1986-87. Office: Vanderbilt U Sch of Law Nashville TN 37240 *

BELTRE, LUIS OSCAR, lawyer; b. Azua, Dominican Republic, Apr. 30, 1954; came to U.S., 1966; s. Rafael Euribiades and Maria Remedios (Ramirez) B.; m. Olga Maria Martinez, Oct. 5, 1975; children: Yadira Eurisa, Luis Oscar Jr. BS, Pace U., 1977; JD, Case Western Res. U., 1981. Bar: N.Y. 1982, N.J. 1982, Fla. 1982, U.S. Dist. Ct. (so. and ea. dists.) N.Y. 1982, U.S. Dist. Ct. N.J. 1982, U.S. Supreme Ct. 1986. Assoc. Kaplan, Russin, Vecchi & Kirkwood, N.Y.C., 1981-82, Kaplan, Russin, Vecchi & Heredia-Bonetti, Santo Domingo, Dominican Republic, 1982; sole practice N.Y.C., 1982—; bd. dirs. Banco Dominico Hispano, Dominican Republic. Cons. Desfile Festival Dominicano, N.Y.C., 1984—, Assn. Prensa Turistica, N.Y.C., 1984—; bd. dirs. Fed. Com. Ind. Dominicano, N.Y.C., 1983—. Republican. Roman Catholic. Avocations: trumpet, swimming, tennis. Contracts commercial, Criminal, Immigration, naturalization, and customs. Home: 198 Nimitz Rd Paramus NJ 07650 Office: 605 W 181st St New York NY 10033

BELTZ, PAUL WILLIAM, lawyer; b. Nov. 23, 1925; s. Edward Joseph and Margaret Elizabeth (Ryan) B.; m. Catherine Adell Mitchell, Oct. 2, 1954; children: Anne, Margaret, Catherine, John, Mary, Sara. BBA, St. Bonaventure U., 1950; JD, Cornell U., 1953. Assoc. McDonough, Boasberg, McDonough & Beltz, Buffalo, 1953-72; sole practice Buffalo, 1972—; lectr. N.Y. State Bar Assn., SUNY Buffalo Law Sch. Mem. Am. Trial Lawyers Assn., Am. Bd. Profl. Liability Attys., Erie County Bar Assn. (lectr.), N.Y. State Trial Lawyers Assn. (bd. dirs.), Western N.Y. Trial Lawyers Assn., Pa. State Trial Lawyers Assn. Clubs: Wanakah Country, Buffalo Exec. Lodge: KC. Personal injury, Admiralty, Product liability. Home: 262 Stonehedge Dr Orchard Park NY 14127 Office: 36 Church St Buffalo NY 14202-3905

BELVILLE, BARBARA ANN, lawyer; b. Urbana, Ohio, Mar. 11, 1957; d. Evan Dale and Evelyn Marjorie (Vaught) B. BA, Ohio Wesleyan U., Delaware, Ohio, 1977; JD, Ohio State U., 1980. Bar: Ohio 1980, U.S. Dist. Ct. (so. dist.) Ohio 1980. Assoc. Emens, Hurd, Kegler & Ritter Co., LPA, Columbus, Ohio, 1980-86; atty. Am. Electric Power Service Corp., Columbus, 1986—. Mem. adv. bd. Wesleyan U. Ctr. Econs. and Bus., Ohio, 1985—. Mem. ABA, Ohio Bar Assn., Columbus Bar Assn. Democrat. Club: Capital (Columbus). Avocations: squash, photography. Contracts commercial, Pension, profit-sharing, and employee benefits, Personal injury. Home: 901 Birchmont Rd Columbus OH 43220 Office: Am Electric Power Service Corp 1 Riverside Plaza Columbus OH 43215

BELZ, HERMAN JULIUS, history educator; b. Camden, N.J., Sept. 13, 1937; s. Irvin Carl and Ella (Engler) B.; m. Mary Martin, Aug. 5, 1961 (div.); children—Kristin, Aaron; m. Valerie O'Brian, Aug. 25, 1985. A.B., Princeton U., 1959; M.A., U. Washington, 1963, Ph.D., 1966. Asst. prof. to prof. history, U. Md., College Park, 1966—; vis. assoc. prof. U. Colo., summer 1969. Active Com. for the Free World. Served to lt. j.g. USNR, 1959-61. John Simon Guggenheim Meml. fellow, 1980-81; Project '87 fellow for research in constl. history, 1980-81; Am. Bar Found. fellow in legal history, 1973-74. Mem. Am. Hist. Assn. (Albert J. Beveridge award 1966), Orgn. Am. Historians, Am. Soc. for Legal History, So. Hist. Assn. Republican. Lutheran. Club: Nassau (Princeton). Author: Reconstructing the Union, 1969, Emancipation and Equal Rights: Politics and Constitutionalism in the Civil War Era, 1978, A New Birth of Freedom: The Republican Party and Freedmen's Rights 1881-1866, 1976; Affirmative Action from Kennedy to Reagan: Redefining American Equality, 1984; co-author: The American Constitution, 6th edit., 1983. Legal history. Office: Dept History Univ Maryland College Park MD 20742

BEMILLER, F. LOYAL, lawyer; b. Mansfield, Ohio, Nov. 1, 1933; s. Clarence C. and Esther (crall) B.; m. Judith E. Baer, Aug. 16, 1958; children: Kimberly, Susan, James, Jennifer. AB, Ohio U., 1955; JD, U. Mich., 1958. Bar: Ohio 1958, U.S. Dist. Ct. (no. dist.) Ohio 1963, U.S. Tax Ct. 1980. Ptnr. to sr. ptnr. Brown, Bemiller, Murray & McIntyre, Mansfield, 1961—; cre; lectr. Ohio State U., Mansfield, 1984; mem. adv. bd. First Buckeye Bank, Masfield, 1975—; bd. dirs. Mansfield Brass & Aluminum, D&S Creative Advt., Remcor, Inc., Mansfield Paint Co. Trustee The Pryor Found., Ann Arbor, 1978—, The Richland County Found., Mansfield, 1980—, Mansfield-Richland Edn. Found., 1979—; mem. exec. com., trustee Mansfield Gen. Hosp., 1980—, Richland County Reps., 1986—; v.p., trustee Mansfield-Richland County Pub. Library, 1978—; nat. chmn. YMCA Drug Abuse Task Force, 1969-71. Served to capt. USAF, 1958-61. Recipient Service to Youth award Mansfield YMCA, 1969, Outstanding Service award Rehab. Services N. Cen. Ohio, 1977. Mem. ABA, Ohio Bar Assn., Richland County Bar Assn., U. Mich. Pres.'s Club. Republican. Congregationalist. Club: WestBrook Country. Lodge: Sertoma. Avocations: tennis, golf. General corporate, Probate, General practice. Home: 800 S Home Rd Mansfield OH 44906 Office: Brown Bemiller Murray & McIntyre 70 Park Ave W Mansfield OH 44902

BEMIS, LAWRENCE PERRY, lawyer; b. Chgo., June 15, 1949; m. Cheryl L. Jelinek, Mar. 19, 1971; children: Lauren, Justin. Bar: Ill. 1974, Fla. 1986. Law clk. to presiding justice U.S. Dist. Ct., Chgo., 1974-76; ptnr. Kirkland & Ellis, Chgo., 1976-86, Steel, Hector & Davis, Miami, 1986—. Mem. ABA. Club: Univ. (Chgo.). Bankruptcy, State civil litigation, Federal civil litigation. Office: Steel Hector & Davis 4000 SE Fin Ctr Miami FL 33131-2398

BENAK, JAMES DONALD, lawyer; b. Omaha, Jan. 22, 1954; s. James R. and Norma Lea (Roberts) B.; m. Mari Lu Petersen, Sept. 15, 1979. BA, U. Nebr., 1977; JD, Creighton U., 1980. Bar: Nebr. 1980, U.S. Dist. Ct. Nebr. 1980. Assoc. Kennedy, Holland, DeLacy & Svoboda, Omaha, 1980-84; asst. gen. atty. Union Pacific R.R. Co., Omaha, 1984-87, gen. atty., 1987—. Fin. dir. Hugh O'Brian Youth Found., Omaha, 1983-84; co-incorporator Nebr. Leadership Seminar Inc., Omaha, 1984; bd. dirs. Combined Health Agencies Drive/Nebr., Omaha, 1985—. Mem. ABA, Nebr. Bar Assn., Omaha Bar Assn. (chmn. law day 1986—). Republican. Roman Catholic. General corporate, Federal civil litigation, Bankruptcy. Home: 15353 Page St Omaha NE 68154 Office: Union Pacific RR Co 1416 Dodge St Room 830 Omaha NE 68179

BENCKENSTEIN, JOHN HENRY, lawyer; b. Detroit, Nov. 28, 1903; s. Leonard Fredrick and Genevieve (Peterson) B.; m. Agnes Merle Halpin, June 27, 1936; children: Mary Agnes Benckenstein Cain, Jacqueline Louise. JD, U. Va., 1928. Bar: Tex. 1928, U.S. Dist. Ct. (ea. dist.) Tex. 1928, U.S. Ct. Appeals (5th cir.) 1931, U.S. Dist. Ct. (we. dist.) La. 1948, U.S. Supreme Ct. 1952, U.S. Dist. Ct. (so. dist.) Tex. 1957, U.S. Dist. Ct. (ea. dist.) La. 1957, U.S. Dist. Ct. (we. dist.) Tex. 1980, U.S. Ct. Appeals (11th cir.) 1981. Ptnr. Benckenstein & Norvell, Beaumont, Tex., 1966-80; of counsel Benckenstein, Norvell, Bernsen & Nathan, Beaumont, 1981—; tchr. Interstate Commerce Practice & Procedure Lamar State Coll., Beaumont; bd. dirs. Gulf Coast Machine & Supply Co., Beaumont. Recipient Selective Service medal U.S. Congress. Fellow Tex. Bar Found.; mem. ABA (sr. lawyers sect.), Tex. Bar Assn., Jefferson County Bar Assn., Assn. Trial Lawyers Am., Fedn. Ins. Counsel, Tex. Assn. Def. Counsel, Thomas Jefferson Soc. Alumni U. Va., Phi Delta Phi. Republican. Episcopalian. Clubs: Beaumont (pres. 1980-81), Beaumont Country; Tower. Avocation: golf. Federal civil litigation, State civil litigation, Labor. Home: 2625 Gladys Beaumont TX 77702 Office: Benckenstein Norvell Bernsen & Nathan 2615 Calder Beaumont TX 77702

BENDELL, JAMES MICHAEL, lawyer; b. Camden, N.J., Feb. 2, 1951; s. Sidney Leo and Laura V. (Marini) B.; m. Marianne Bendell. AB, William and Mary U., 1973; JD, Rutgers U., 1976. Bar: Alaska 1976, U.S. Dist. Ct. Alaska 1976, U.S. Ct. Appeals (9th cir.) 1976. Assoc. Robinson, McCaskey, Reynolds & Frankel, Anchorage, 1976-78; ptnr. Erwin, Smith, Garnett & Bendell, Anchorage, 1979-83, Bendell, Bendell & Holmes, Anchorage, 1983-85; prin. James Bendell & Assocs., Anchorage, 1985—; city prosecutor, Anchorage, 1978-79. Bd. dirs. Gov.'s Mental Health Adv. Com., Alaska, 1981-83. Mem. ABA, Anchorage Bar Assn., Alaska Bar Assn. (law examiners com., editor Alaska Bar Rag), Internat. Assn. Chiefs of Police. Republican. Roman Catholic. Personal injury, Workers' compensation. Office: James Bendall & Assocs 2525 Blueberry Suite 106 Anchorage AK 99503

BENDER, ALAN RONALD, lawyer; b. N.Y.C., Nov. 29, 1954; s. Herman and Joan (Leicher) B.; m. Joyce S. Fain, June 2, 1985. AB, Washington U., St. Louis, 1975; JD, Duke U., 1979. Bar: N.Y. 1980, U.S. Dist. Ct. (so. dist.) N.Y. 1983, U.S. Tax Ct. 1980, Va. 1985. Assoc. Otterbourg, Steindler, et.al., N.Y.C., 1979-81, Seward & Kissel, N.Y.C., 1981-83; v.p., chief legal counsel Nat. Realty Services, Inc., Washington, 1983-86, The Patrician Group, N.Y.C., 1986—. Mem. N.Y. State Bar Assn., ABA, Va. State Bar Assn. Avocations: tennis, golf. Real property, Securities, General corporate. Home: 112 W 18th St 4C New York NY 10011 Office: The Patrician Group 919 Third Ave New York NY 10022

BENDER, CHARLES WILLIAM, lawyer; b. Cape Girardeau, Mo., Oct. 2, 1935; s. Walter William and Fern Evelyn (Stroud) B.; m. Carolyn Percy Gavagan, June 20, 1961 (div. 1983); children: Theodore Marten, Christopher Percy; m. Betty Lou Port, May 5, 1983; stepchildren: Courtney Elizabeth, Cameron Ann. AB magna cum laude, Harvard U., 1960, LLB magna cum laude, 1963. Bar: Calif. 1965, U.S. Dist. Ct. (cen. dist.) Calif. 1965, U.S. Ct. Appeals (9th cir.) 1969, U.S. Supreme Ct. 1979, D.C. 1984. Assoc. O'Melveny & Myers, Los Angeles, 1965-71, ptnr., 1972-84, mng. ptnr., 1984—. Editor Harvard U. Law Rev., 1961-62, articles editor, 1962-63. Advisor campaign Alan Cranston for Senator, Calif., 1968, 74, 80; mgr. campaign Jess Unruh for Gov., Calif., 1970; trustee Los Angeles Legal Aid Found., 1971, Lawyers' Com. for Civil Rights Under Law, Washington, 1985—. Served with U.S. Army, 1956-57. Sheldon Traveling fellow Harvard U., 1963-64. Mem. ABA, Calif. Bar Assn., Los Angeles Bar Assn. Democrat. Administrative and regulatory, Federal civil litigation, State civil litigation. Home: 2831 The Strand Hermosa Beach CA 90254 Office: O'Melveny & Myers 400 S Hope St Los Angeles CA 90071

BENDER, DIANE LOUISE WOLF, lawyer; b. Evansville, Ind, Oct. 21, 1955; d. Thomas Joseph and Margaret Gertrude (Horn) Wolf; m. John Frederick Bender, June 15, 1985. BBA with highest honors, U. Notre Dame, 1977, JD cum laude, 1980. Bar: Ind. 1980. Ptnr. Kahn, Dees, Donovan & Kahn, Evansville, Ind., 1980—. Bd. dirs. Vis. Nurses Assn. of Southwestern Ind., Inc., 1983—, United Way of Southwestern Ind., Inc., 1984—, Health Skills, Inc., Evansville, 1984—, Cath. Press of Evansville, Inc., 1985—. Mem. ABA, Ind. Bar Assn., Evansville Bar Assn., Am. Inst. CPA's, Ill. CPA Soc. Home: PO Box 9164 Evansville IN 47710 Office: Kahn Dees Donovan & Kahn PO Box 3646 Evansville IN 47735-3646

BENDER, JOEL CHARLES, lawyer; b. Bklyn., Dec. 12, 1939; s. Harry and Edna (Bogolowitz) B.; div. July 1984; children: Andrew, Gary. BA, Cornell U., 1961; JD, NYU, 1964. Bar: N.Y. 1964, U.S. Supreme Ct. 1970, Fla. 1980. Ptnr. Bender, Bodnar & Frucco, White Plains, N.Y. Councilman Greenburgh, N.Y. 1976—; dep. supv., police commr. Greenburgh, 1979—. Fellow Am. Acad. Matrimonial Law; mem. N.Y. State Bar Assn., Westchester County Bar Assn. Family and matrimonial, State civil litigation, General corporate. Home: 4 Mohican Ln Irvington NY 10533 Office: Bender Bodnar & Frucco 11 Martine Ave White Plains NY 10606

BENDER, JOHN TIMOTHY, lawyer; b. Akron, Ohio, July 26, 1949; s. John William and June Lee (Heffelfinger) B.; m. Michele Anne Postak, Jan. 7, 1969; 1 child, John Michael. BS in Acctg., U. Akron, 1973, JD, 1978. Bar: Ohio 1978, U.S. Tax Ct. 1979, U.S. Dist. Ct. (no. dist.) Ohio 1980, U.S. Ct. Appeals (6th cir.) 1982. Agt. IRS, Cleve., 1973-79; assoc. Kadish & Krantz, Cleve., 1979-82, ptnr., 1982-84; ptnr. Kadish and Bender, Cleve., 1984—. Mem. ABA, Ohio Bar Assn., Greater Cleve. Bar Assn., Fed. Bar Assn., Tax Club of Cleve., Beta Alpha Psi. Republican. Club: Cleve. Athletic. Personal income taxation, General corporate. Home: 2196 Edgerton Rd University Heights OH 44118 Office: Kadish and Bender 2112 E Ohio Bldg Cleveland OH 44114

BENDER, KENNETH N., lawyer; b. Far Rockaway, N.Y., Sept. 14, 1945; s. Moe and Mildred (Goodman) B.; m. Linda Gabbe; children—Jonathan, Andrew. B.A., Pa. State U., 1967; J.D., NYU, 1971. Bar: N.Y. 1971, U.S. Dist. Ct. (so. dist.) N.Y. 1972, (ea. dist.) N.Y. 1972, Ariz. 1978. Assoc. Law Offices of Ira J. Greenhill, N.Y.C., 1971-75; counsel office gen. counsel, Honeywell Inc., N.Y.C., 1975-77, sr. counsel, Phoenix, 1978—; founder, chmn. adv. bd. Ariz. Law and Tech. Inst. Ariz. State U. Coll. Law, Tempe, 1982-84, lectr. computer law, negotiation studies for sr. execs. Mem. N.Y. State Bar Assn., State Bar Ariz., Maricopa County Bar Assn. (founder, pres. corp. counsel sect. 1981-82, bd. dirs. 1982-83), ABA (sci. and tech. sect.), Alpha Epsilon Pi, Pi Sigma Alpha. Democrat. Jewish. General corporate, Contracts commercial, Computer. Office: Honeywell Inc PO Box 8000 Phoenix AZ 85066

BENDER, PAUL EDWARD, lawyer; b. Decatur, Ill., June 5, 1951; s. Kenneth Donald and Martha Rosalie (Heinzelmann) B.; m. Anne Marie Scartabello, Dec. 31, 1976 (div. 1978). B.A., Millikin U., 1973; J.D. cum laude, Hamline U., 1976. Assoc. Halloran & Alfuby, Mpls., 1976-77; sole

practice Bender Law Office, Arthur, Ill., 1977-79; sr. title atty. Chgo. Title Ins. Co., Peoria, Ill., 1979-82, Champaign, Ill., 1984—; ptnr. Cordis & Bender, Princeville, Ill., 1982-84. Pres. Peoria Evening Optimist Club, 1981-82, lt. gov. zone 6 Ill. Optimists, 1982-83. Mem. Peoria Bar Assn. (chmn. real estate com. 1983-84, mem. continuing legal edn. 1981-83), Champaign County Bar Assn., Ill. Bar Assn., ABA. Republican. Methodist. Lodges: Masons, Shriners. Real property, Legal history, Bankruptcy. Home: 2711 Clayton Blvd Champaign IL 61821

BENDER, RICHARD JOHN, asst. U.S. attorney; b. Washington, Mar. 9, 1953; s. Henry John and Georgia Mae (Jolly) B.; m. Janice May Knoblett, Dec. 20, 1981; 1 child, Eric John. BA, U. Md., 1975; JD, Georgetown U., 1978. Bar: Md. 1978, U.S. Dist. Ct. Md. 1979, U.S. Ct. Appeals (4th cir.) 1979, Hawaii 1981, U.S. Dist. Ct. Hawaii 1981, U.S. Ct. Appeals (9th cir.) 1982, U.S. Tax Ct. 1983, U.S. Ct. Claims 1983. Law clk. to judge U.S. Dist. Ct. Md., Balt., 1978-80; assoc. Cades Schutte Fleming & Wright, Honolulu, 1980-86; asst. U.S. atty. U.S. Dist. Ct. (ea. dist.) Calif., Sacramento, 1986—. Mem. Am. Waterski Assn. (cert. tournament driver and judge). Avocations: tournament water skiing, basketball, softball, swimming. Office: US Atty's Office 650 Capitol Mall Rm 3305 Sacramento CA 95814

BENDES, BARRY JAY, lawyer; b. N.Y.C., Sept. 8, 1950; s. Arnold R. and Shirley (Shnitman) B.; m. Tamara Shulman, Jan. 14, 1984. B.A. cum laude, Queens Coll., 1971; J.D. cum laude, NYU, 1974, cert. in real property law, 1980. Bar: N.Y. 1975, U.S. Dist. Ct. (so. dist.) N.Y. 1975, U.S. Dist. Ct. (ea. dist.) N.Y. 1975, U.S. Ct. Appeals (2d cir.) 1975, U.S. Supreme Ct. 1978, U.S. Ct. Internat. Trade 1985. Assoc. firm Leon, Weill & Mahony, N.Y.C., 1974-78; ptnr. firm Certilman Haft Lebow Balin Buckley & Kremer and predecessor firms, N.Y.C., 1978—. Research editor NYU Rev. Law and Social Change, 1972-73. Mem. ABA (com. on computer contracting, sect. sci. and tech. 1983—), Am. Arbitration Assn. (nat. panel arbitrators), Assn. Bar City N.Y. (computer law com. 1986—), N.Y. State Bar Assn. Contracts commercial, Securities, Real property. Home: 340 E 64th St New York NY 10021 Office: Certilman Haft Lebow Balin et al 805 3d Ave New York NY 10022

BENEDETTO, WILLIAM RALPH, lawyer; b. Livermore Falls, Maine, May 11, 1928; s. Fiorindo DiBenedetto and Erminia Gonella; m. Barbara Audrey Sherlock, Sept. 4, 1948; children: Cheryl, Liana Sharon, Valerie Choinire, William R. Jr. BS in Polit. Sci., Portland State U., 1977; JD, U. Oreg., 1980. Bar: Oreg. 1981. Sole practice Beaverton, Oreg., 1981—. Mem. Washington County (Oreg.) Civil Service Commn., 1980-84, chmn. 1985—. Served with USCG, 1946-70. Mem. ABA, Oreg. Bar Assn., Multnomah County Bar Assn., Washington County Bar Assn., Assn. Trial Lawyers Am., Ret. Officers Assn. Roman Catholic. Lodge: Elks. Avocations: golf, jogging, chess, skiing. General practice. Home: 11920 SW Faircrest Portland OR 97225 Office: 12655 SW Center St Suite 305 Beaverton OR 97005

BENEDICT, JAMES NELSON, lawyer; b. Norwich, N.Y., Oct. 6, 1949; s. Nelson H. and Helen (Wilson) B.; m. Janet E. Fagal, May 8, 1982. B.A. magna cum laude, St. Lawrence U., 1971; J.D., Albany Law Sch. of Union U., 1974. Bar: N.Y. 1975, U.S. Dist. Ct. (no., ea. and so. dists.) N.Y. 1975, U.S. Ct. Appeals (2d cir.) 1975, U.S. Ct. Appeals (8th cir.) 1977, U.S. Ct. Appeals (10th cir.) 1978, U.S. Ct. Appeals (11th cir.) 1982, U.S. Supreme Ct. 1978. Assoc. Rogers & Wells, N.Y.C., 1974-82, ptnr., 1982—. Mem. bd. contbg. editors and advisors The Corp. Law Rev., 1976—. Contbr. articles to profl. jours. Bd. dirs. Reece Sch., N.Y.C., 1984—, Stanley Isaacs Neighborhood Ctr., N.Y.C., 1984—; trustee St. Lawrence U., Canton, N.Y., 1985—. Mem. ABA (chmn. securities litigation subcom. on 1940 Act matters 1984—), Fed. Bar Council, N.Y. State Bar Assn., Assn. Bar City N.Y. (mem. fed. legislation com., fed. cts. com.) Am. Soc. Writers on Legal Subjects, Phi Beta Kappa. Clubs: Princeton (N.Y.C.); New Haven Country (Hamden, Conn.). Federal civil litigation, State civil litigation, Securities. Home: 435 E 79th St Apt 5-C New York NY 10021 Office: Rogers & Wells Pan Am Bldg 200 Park Ave New York NY 10166

BENEDICT, PETER BEHRENDS, lawyer; b. Pittsfield, Mass., Feb. 28, 1951; s. Bruce Merrill and Eleanor Jean (Hamel) B.; m. Jan Elizabeth Roina, May 20, 1972; children—Seth Behrends, Sarah Krapf. B.A. in English, Central Conn. State Coll., New Britain, 1973; J.D. cum laude, New Eng. Sch. Law, Boston, 1976. Bar: Conn. 1976, U.S. Dist. Ct. Conn. 1978, Mass. 1977, U.S. Supreme Ct. 1980. Atty., R. Richard Roina, Norwalk, Conn., 1976-78, Roina & Benedict, Norwalk, 1978, Roina, Benedict & Fiore, Norwalk, 1979, Rapaport & Manheim, Stamford, Conn., 1979-83, Rapaport, Manheim & Benedict, Stamford, 1983—. Bd. dirs. Norwalk YMCA, 1979-82, Literacy Vols. of Stamford, 1981—. Mem. ABA, Conn. Bar Assn., Stamford Bar Assn., Assn. Trial Lawyers Am., Conn. Trial Lawyers Assn. Independent. Congregational. Clubs: Bridgeport Rifle, Greenwich Boat and Yacht. State civil litigation, General practice, Personal injury. Home: 33 Sachem Ln Greenwich CT 06830 Office: Rapaport & Benedict PC 750 Summer St Stamford CT 06901

BENEDICT, RONALD LOUIS, lawyer; b. Cin., Feb. 22, 1942; s. Harold Lloyd and Thelma (Bryant) B.; m. Carol Joyce Worthington, Sept. 9, 1961 (div. Sept. 1980); children—Karen Elizabeth Benedict Sterwerf, Jennifer Lynn; m. Deborah Ann Taggart, Aug. 14, 1982. B.A. in Polit. Sci., U. Cin., 1964; J.D., Salmon P. Chase Coll., 1968. Bar: Ohio 1968, U.S. Supreme Ct. 1985. Methods analyst Western-So. Life Ins. Co., Cin., 1964-69; atty. Ohio Nat. Life Ins. Co., Cin., 1969-71, sr. atty., 1971-73, asst. gen. counsel, 1973-80, assoc. counsel, 1980—; sec., dir. Ohio Nat. Fund, Inc., Cin., 1973—; sec. Ohio Nat. Investment Mgmt. Co., Cin., 1971—, sec., bd. dirs. Ohio Nat. Equity Sales Co., Cin., 1971—, also bd. dirs. Author, lectr.: (treatise and course) Trial and Execution of Jesus, 1978; Pseudochristian Cults, 1977. Pres. Young Democrats, U. Cin., 1964; arbitrator Ct. Common Pleas, Hamilton County, Ohio, 1973—; mem. and counsel Tri-State Billy Graham Crusade Com., Cin., 1977. Recipient cert. Adult Christian Edn. Found., 1977; Life Office Mgmt. Inst. fellow, 1971. Mem. ABA, Ohio State Bar Assn. (corp. counsel com.), Cin. Bar Assn. (securities law com., speakers' bur.), Assn. Life Ins. Counsel (securities law com.), Investment Co. Inst. (SEC rules com.), Alpha Tau Omega. Democrat. Presbyterian. Avocations: theology; Bible teaching; church leadership; outdoor activities. Securities, General corporate, Insurance. Home: 7029 Gaines Rd Cincinnati OH 45247 Office: Ohio Nat Life Ins Co 237 William Howard Taft Rd Cincinnati OH 45219

BENEDICT, THANE, III, lawyer; b. Ionia, Mich., Mar. 28, 1940; s. Thane and Margaret Elizabeth (Bergstrom) B.; m. Kathryn Louise MacMullen, June 23, 1962; children—Tracy Louise, Thane IV, Heidi Brooke. Student, Sorbonne, 1959-60; B.A., Yale U., 1961, LL.B., 1964; LL.M. in Taxation, NYU, 1979. Bar: N.Y. 1965. Assoc. Olwine, Connelly, Chase, O'Donnell & Weyher, N.Y.C., 1964-73; asst. gen. counsel Sperry & Hutchinson Co., N.Y.C., 1973-81; sec. The S&H Found., Inc., N.Y.C., 1981—. ptnr. Contino Ross & Benedict, N.Y.C., 1982-86; ptnr. Benedict & Aiello, P.C., N.Y.C., 1986—. Trustee, McBurney Sch., N.Y.C., 1982-85; dir. Norwalk Youth Symphony, Conn., 1981—, chmn., 1984-86; vice chmn., 1982-84, 86—; cellist Wilton Chamber Orch., Conn., 1981—. Mem. N.Y. State Bar Assn., Phi Beta Kappa. Corporate taxation, Securities. Home: 27 Sachem Rd Weston CT 06883 Office: Benedict & Aiello PC 320 Park Ave 27th Floor New York NY 10022

BENEKE, WILLIAM SCOTT, lawyer; b. Ft. Dodge, Iowa; s. Leland Franklin and Shirley Jean (Siefken) B.; m. Sallee Jean Skinner, Dec. 23, 1975; children: Margaret Rose, Alice Catherine. BA, Cornell Coll., 1975; JD, U. Okla., 1978. Bar: Iowa 1979, Ill. 1982. Assoc. Mealy, Metcalf & Conlon, Muscatine, Iowa, 1979-81; exec. dir. Legal Aid Soc. of Story County, Nevada, Iowa, 1981-82; ptnr. Skinner & Beneke, Princeton, Ill., 1982—; adv. bd. mem. Prairie State Legal Services, Ottawa, Ill., 1985—. Bd. dirs. Mid-Iowa Community Action Bd., Marshalltown, Iowa, 1981-82. Mem. ABA, Ill. State Bar Assn., Bur. County Bar Assn. Probate, Real property, Family and matrimonial. Home: 1105 S Main Princeton IL 61356 Office: Skinner & Beneke 717 S Main Princeton IL 61356

BENGOECHEA, SHANE ORIN, lawyer, educator; b. Jerome, Idaho, Jan. 21, 1956; s. Richard Victor and Marcia Lenore (Beddall) B.; m. DiAnn Beverly Harritt, June 20, 1981; children: Amaya Lenore, Micaela Cassidy. BA in Econs., Boise State U.; JD, Gonzaga U., 1982. Bar: Idaho 1982, U.S. Dist. Ct. Idaho 1982. Pub. defender Ada County, Boise, Idaho, 1982-83; asst. atty. City of Boise, 1983-84; dep. atty. gen. revenue and tax State of Idaho, Boise, 1984-85; atty. City of Twin Falls, Idaho, 1985—; prof. law Coll. So. Idaho, Twin Falls, 1986—. Asst. sergeant at arms, Idaho Legislature, Boise, 1978-79; precinct committeeman Reps., Boise, 1982, worker various campaigns, Boise and Twin Falls, 1976, 78, 80, 82, 84, 86. Recipient citation U.S. Dept. Interior, 1977. Mem. ABA (various coms.), Assn. Trial Lawyer Am., Idaho Pros. Attys. Assn., Assn. Idaho Cities, Nat. Inst. Mcpl. Lawyers (various coms.), Phi Alpha Delta (vice justice 1980-81), Alpha Kappa Psi. Republican. Roman Catholic. Avocations: running, snow skiing, weighlifting, biking, classic cars. Criminal, General practice, Local government. Home: 1049 Twin Parks Dr Twin Falls ID 83301

BENGTSON, KARL WAYNE, lawyer; b. Thibodeaux, La., Aug. 23, 1955; s. Robert W. and Bonnie Jean R. (Dunbar) B. BA, La. State U., 1977, JD, 1980. Bar: La. 1980, U.S. Dist. Ct. (ea. dist.) La. 1980, U.S. Dist. Ct. (mid. and we. dists.) 1981, U.S. Ct. Appeals (5th cir.) 1981, U.S. Ct. Appeals (11th cir.) 1982, U.S. Supreme Ct. 1985. Tankerman Canal Barge Co., New Orleans, 1976-78; assoc. George & George, Baton Rouge, 1978-80; ptnr. Shelton & Legendre, Lafayette, La., 1981—. Served with USCG, 1973-76. Mem. ABA, La. Bar Assn., LaFayette Bar Assn., Assn. Trial Lawyers Am., La. Trial Lawyers Assn., LaFayette Trial Lawyers Assn., Practicing Law Inst., Am. Soc. Law and Medicine. Democrat. Methodist. Avocations: sailing, fishing. Admiralty, Personal injury, Federal civil litigation. Home: 732 Mudd Ave LaFayette LA 70501 Office: Shelton & Legendre 2448 Johnston St Lafayette LA 70503

BENJAMIN, EDWARD A., lawyer; b. N.Y.C., May 30, 1938; s. Martin and Ruth B. (Rich) B.; m. Roberta Rose, Jan. 16, 1960 (div.); children—Robert, Michael, Ted; m. Toni Wheelis, May 18, 1980. B.A., U. Pa., 1958; LL.B., Harvard U., 1961. Assoc. Ropes & Gray, Boston, 1961-65, assoc., 1967-69; ptnr. Ropes & Gray, Boston and Washington, 1969—; atty., adviser AID, Washington, 1965-67; dir. IPC Limited Partnership, Bristol, N.H. Mem. ABA. Clubs: University (Washington); Downtown (Boston). General corporate, Private international, Securities. Office: Ropes & Gray 1001 22d St NW Suite 700 Washington DC 20037

BENJAMIN, EDWARD BERNARD, JR., lawyer; b. New Orleans, Feb. 11, 1923; s. Edward Bernard and Blanche (Sternberger) B.; m. Adelaide Wisdom, May 11, 1957; children: Edward Wisdom, Mary Dabney, Ann Leith, Stuart Minor. B.S., Yale U., 1944; J.D., Tulane U., 1952. Bar: La. 1952. Since practiced in New Orleans; ptnr. firm Jones, Walker, Waechter, Poitevent, Carrere & Denegre; pres. Am. Coll. Probate Counsel, 1986-87, Internat. Acad. Estate & Trust Law, 1976-78; chmn. bd. Starmount Co., Greensboro, N.C., 1968—. Editor-in-chief: Tulane Law Rev, 1951-52. Vice chmn. bd. trustees Southwestern Legal Found., 1980—; trustee Hollins Coll., 1966—; chancellor Episcopal Diocese of La., 1984—, Trinity Ch., New Orleans, 1974—; mem. adv. bd. CCH Estate & Fin. Planning Service. Served to 1st lt. U.S. Army, 1943-46. Mem. Am. Coll. Tax Counsel, Am. Law Inst., La. Law Inst., ABA (sec. taxation sect. 1967-68, council 1976-79, council real property, probate and trust law sect. 1978-81), La. Bar Assn. (chmn. taxation sect. 1959-60). Clubs: New Orleans Country, Greensboro Country, So. Yacht, New Orleans Lawn Tennis. Probate, Corporate taxation, Estate taxation. Home: 1837 Palmer Ave New Orleans LA 70118 Office: 201 St Charles Ave 51st Floor New Orleans LA 70170

BENJAMIN, JAMES GILBERT, lawyer; b. Washington, Aug. 7, 1949; s. Gilbert Giddings and Ruth (Swanson) B.; m. Isabella Leml, Oct. 27, 1979; 1 child, Troy Matthew. BA, U. So. Calif., 1971; JD, Loyola U., Los Angeles, 1976. Bar: Calif. 1976, U.S. Ct. Appeals (9th cir.) 1976, Colo. 1977, U.S. Ct. Appeals (10th cir.) 1977. Mgr. Security Pacific Bank, Los Angeles, 1971-75, atty., 1975-76; ptnr. Towey & Zak, Denver, 1976-81; dir. Roath & Brega, P.C., Denver, 1981—. Author: Commercial Law II, 1976; lectr. Fin. Comml. Real Estate, 1986. Mem. ABA, Denver Bar Assn. (bd. dirs. young lawyers sect. 1979-82, sec. young lawyers sect. 1981), Adams County Bar Assn., Colo. Bar Assn., Calif. Bar Assn. Lutheran. Banking, Real property. Office: Roath & Brega PC PO Box 5560 TA Denver CO 80217

BENJAMIN, JEFFREY, chemical manufacturing corporation executive, lawyer; b. Bklyn., Dec. 28, 1945; s. Haskell and Lillian (Sikofski) B.; m. Betty Gae Meckler, Mar. 21, 1971; children—Lily Meckler, Ross Meckler. B.A., Cornell U., 1967; J.D. cum laude, NYU, 1971. Bar: N.Y. 1971, U.S. Dist. Cts. (so. and ea. dists.) N.Y. 1972. Assoc., Kronish, Lieb, Shainswit, Weiner & Hellman, N.Y.C., 1971-74; atty. CIBA-GEIGY Corp., Ardsley, N.Y., 1974—, counsel for regulatory affairs, 1976—, div. counsel, 1978—, asst. gen. counsel, 1985—; dir. legal dept. and assoc. gen. counsel, 1986—. Served with USAR, 1969-74. Mem. ABA, Order of Coif. Antitrust, General corporate, Labor. Home: 13 Park Ave New City NY 10956 Office: CIBA-GEIGY Corp 444 Saw Mill River Rd Ardsley NY 10502

BENKERT, ARTHUR C., lawyer. m. Delphine S. Heston, Oct. 18, 1937; children: Carolyn Benkert Bishop, Ruth Ann Benkert Bailey, Roberta Benkert Bernet. BA in Commerce, U. Wis., 1934, LLB, 1936. Bar: Wis. 1936. Atty. City of Monroe, Wis., 1939-59; ptnr. Benkert, Spielman, Asmus & Deininger, Monroe, 1959-85, of counsel, 1986—. Mem. St. John's Ch. of Christ, Monroe. Mem. ABA, Wis. Bar Assn., Green County Bar Assn. (past pres.), Iron Cross, Sigma Phi Epsilon, Alpha Kappa Psi, Phi Kappa Phi. Home and Office: 1403 17th Ave Monroe WI 53566

BENN, SARA KITCHEN, lawyer, educator; b. Holden, Mass., Jan. 25, 1949; d. Charles Grant and Helen (Mansfield) Kitchen; m. Joel Dennis Benn, Feb. 14, 1976; children—Julia Ruth, Leon Matthew. A.B., Trinity Coll., 1971; J.D., Villanova U., 1975. Bar: Pa. 1975. Asst. pub. defender Pub. Defender's Office, Bucks County, Pa., 1975-77; mem. adj. faculty Gwynedd-Mercy Coll., Gwynedd Valley, Pa., 1977-85; asst. prof., chair sociology dept. Chestnut Hill Coll., Phila., 1985—; instr. Beaver Coll., Glenside, Pa., 1979; instr. in criminal law Temple U., Ambler, Pa., 1984-85; resource person Juvenile Justice Ctr. Pa., Phila., 1975-77; cons. Youth Services Agy., Doylestown, Pa., 1979; sec. bd. dirs. Alpha Pregnancy Services, Phila., 1983—. Editor: Bucks County on Youth Diversion, 1979. Mem. Nat. Right to Life Com., Washington, 1981—. Mary D. Walsh scholar Trinity Coll., 1967-71; Thomas J. Watson fellow, 1971-72. Mem. ABA (criminal justice div. and family law sect.), Pennsylvanians for Human Life. Roman Catholic. Legal education, Juvenile, Criminal. Home: 10 Oak Rd Philadelphia PA 19118

BENNETT, ANDY DWANE, lawyer; b. Charlotte, Tenn., July 12, 1957; s. Freeman Dwane and Doris May (Patey) B.; m. Sidney Suzanne Forester, June 20, 1981; 1 child, Adam Forester. BA, Vanderbilt U., JD. Bar: Tenn. 1982, U.S. Dist. Ct. (mid. dist.) Tenn. 1983. Asst. atty. gen. State of Tennessee, Nashville, 1982-86; dep. state atty. gen. State of Tenn., Nashville, 1986—. Mem. ABA. Democrat. Methodist. Tennessee constitutional law, Legislative, Government contracts and claims. Office: Tenn Atty Gen's Office 450 James Robertson Parkway Nashville TN 37219

BENNETT, BRUCE SCOTT, lawyer; b. Bkln., Oct. 3, 1958; s. Allan E. and Marlene B. (Leisner) B.; m. Wendy Swartz, June 20, 1982 (div. June 1986); 1 child, Joel Alex. ScB magna cum laude, Brown U., 1979; JD cum laude, Harvard U., 1982. Bar: Calif. 1982, U.S. Dist. Ct. (cen., no., so. and ea. dists.) Calif., U.S. Ct. Appeals (9th cir.). Assoc. Stutman, Treister & Glatt, Los Angeles, 1982-87, atty., 1987—. Mem. ABA (corps., banks and bus. law sect., bus. bankruptcy com.), Calif. Bar Assn. (comml. law sect.), Los Angeles Bar Assn. (comml. law and bankruptcy sect.), Fin. Lawyers Conf. Jewish. Bankruptcy, Insolvency and out of court financial workouts. Office: Stutman Treister & Glatt PC 3699 Wilshire Blvd #900 Los Angeles CA 90010-2739

BENNETT, CLARENCE J., lawyer; b. Springfield, Mass., Oct. 6, 1946; s. Nathaniel N. and Bess E. (Schneiderman) B.; m. Leslie G. Kimball, Aug. 31, 1969; children—Jonathan D., Alissa P. B.A., McGill U., 1972, LL.B., 1975. Bar: Mass. 1975, U.S. Dist. Ct. Mass. 1975. Assoc. Kimball, Bennett & Brooslin, Springfield, Mass., 1975—. Served with U.S. Army, 1967-69, Vietnam. Decorated Purple Heart, Bronze Star. Mem. DAV, Mil. Order Purple Heart, Jewish War Vets., Mass. Bar Assn., Hampden County Bar Assn. Republican. Jewish. Personal injury, Workers' compensation, Criminal. Home: 96 White Oaks Dr Longmeadow MA 01106 Office: Kimball Bennett & Brooslin 101 State St Suite 708 Springfield MA 01103

BENNETT, DAVID H., lawyer; b. Portage, Wis., Sept. 18, 1928; s. Ross and Helen (Hinkley) B.; m. LaVonne Bennett, Feb. 3, 1955; children: Mark H., Todd W., John D. BBA, U. Wis., 1952, LLB, 1956. Bar: Wis. 1956, U.S. Ct. Appeals (7th cir.), U.S. Supreme Ct. Ptnr. Bennett & Bennett, Portage, 1956—; dist. atty. Columbia County, Wis., 1959-67; regent Wis. State Univs., 1965-71. Served to 2d lt. AUS. Mem. ABA, Wis. Bar Assn. Republican. Presbyterian. Lodge: Masons. General practice, Personal injury, Estate planning. Home: 215 W Franklin St Portage WI 53901 Office: Bennett and Bennett 139 W Cook St PO Box 30 Portage WI 53901

BENNETT, DONN, lawyer; b. Rapid City, S.D., July 19, 1922; s. Wynn Millard and Anne Jane (Sparks) B.; m. Anita Jane Crockett; children—David, Michael, Kim, Robert, Kirstin, Megan. Student U. N.Mex., 1943; B.A., U. Colo., 1946, J.D., 1949. Bar: S.D. 1949, U.S. Dist. Ct. (so. dist.) S.D. 1950, U.S. Ct. Apls. (8th cir.) 1960, U.S. Tax Ct. 1959, U.S. Ct. Mil. Apls. 1953. Sole practice, Buffalo, S.D., 1949-50, 53-71; state's atty. Harding County (S.D.), 1955-59, 60-72; ptnr. Bennett & Main and predecessor Belle Fourche, S.D., 1972—; instr. justice U.S. Naval Sch. Naval Justice, 1949-53; lectr. Inst. Energy Devel., 1982. Served to lt. USNR, 1943-46, 50-53. Mem. S.D. Bar Assn. (commr. 1960-63), ABA, Rocky Mountain Mineral Law Found. (trustee 1964—, pres. 1979-80). Republican. Clubs: Lions (Belle Fourche), Masons (Buffalo, S.D.); Elks (Deadwood, S.D.). Oil and gas leasing, Probate, Personal income taxation. Home: 1212 Walworth Belle Fourche SD 57717 Office: 618 State St Belle Fourche SD 57717

BENNETT, HAROLD KIMSEY, lawyer; b. Mooresville, N.C., Aug. 14, 1914; s. Oscar Kimsey and Ethel Genevieve (Robinson) B.; m. Elsie Dunn Allport, Apr. 27, 1942; children—Randolph A., Stephen D. A.B., U. N.C., 1935, LL.B., 1937. Bar: N.C., 1936. Ptnr., Bennett & Bennett, 1937-41; sole practice, Asheville, N.C., 1946-49; judge Superior Cts., of N.C., 1949-52; ptnr. Ward & Bennett, Asheville, 1952-65; sole practice, Asheville, 1965-69; ptnr. Bennett, Kelly & Long, Asheville, 1969-74; sr. ptnr. Bennett, Kelly & Cagle, Asheville, 1974-84; of counsel Patla, Straus, Robinson & Moore, P.A., 1984—; county atty., atty. Bd. Tax Supervision, Buncombe County, 1946-49; chmn. disciplinary hearing commn. N.C. State Bar, 1975-80; vice chmn. N.C. Jud. Standard Commn., 1973-75. Served to lt. USN, 1942-45. Fellow Am. Bar Found. Am. Coll. Trial Lawyers; mem. ABA, N.C. Bar Assn. (pres. 1972-73), N.C. State Bar. Buncombe County Bar Assn. (pres. 1967-68). Democrat. Episcopalian. Club: Biltmore Forest Country (Biltmore, N.C.). Federal civil litigation, State civil litigation, Personal injury. Home: 47 Windsor Rd Asheville NC 28804 Office: Patla Straus Robinson & Moore PA 29 N Market St Asheville NC 28801

BENNETT, HORACE MICHAEL, lawyer, educator, consultant; b. Nashville, May 12, 1949; s. Horace E. and Violet (Reasoner) B.; m. Janice Elinor MacFarlane, July 8, 1972; children: Jason Alexander, Lindsay Allyson. BA, Vanderbilt U., 1971, JD, 1974. Bar: Tenn. 1974, U.S. Dist. Ct. (mid. dist.) Tenn. 1974, U.S. Ct. Appeals (6th cir.) 1977. Ptnr. Schulman, LeRoy & Bennett, Nashville, 1974—, Cox, Simpson & Bennett, Memphis, 1985—; ptnr. Health Law Inst., Little Rock, 1977—; instr. Critical Care Edn. Ctr., Nashville, 1976—, Southeast Paralegal Inst., Nashville, 1985—. Contbg. editor: Practices, 1984; legal editor (column) Critical Care Nurse, 1980-85. Bd. dirs. Tenn. Baptist Conv., Nashville, 1983—. Recipient Cert. of Appreciation, Am. Soc. Law and Medicine, 1980, Cert. of Appreciation So. Bap. Conv. Fgn. Mission Bd., 1981. Mem. ABA (forum com. health law), Tenn. Bar Assn., Nashville Bar Assn. (medicolegal affairs com.), Order of Coif. Republican. Avocation: stamp collecting. Health, Legal education, Personal injury. Home: 808 Steeplechase Dr Brentwood TN 37027 Office: Schulman LeRoy & Bennett 501 Union St Nashville TN 37219

BENNETT, JAMES DAVISON, lawyer; b. Mineola, N.Y., Dec. 2, 1938. B.A., Cornell U., 1960, J.D., 1963. Bar: N.Y. 1963. Ptnr. Bennett Scholly Pape Rice & Schure, Rockville Centre, N.Y., 1968—. Councilman, Town of Hempstead, 1968-78, supr., 1978—; mem. Nassau County Bd. Suprs., 1978—; apptd. to N.Y. State Conservation and Wildlife Fund. Recipient citation Practising Law Inst., 1972, 73, others. Mem. ABA, N.Y. State Bar Assn., Nassau County Bar Assn. Estate planning, Probate, Estate taxation. Home: 34 Hilton Ave City NY 11530 Office: 255 Merrick Rd Rockville Centre NY 11570

BENNETT, JAMES MARTIN, lawyer; b. Hackensack, N.J., Apr. 11, 1948; s. Elmer James and Mary Ann (Martin) B.; m. Christine Lora Gerber, Nov. 25, 1971; children: Stephan, Karin, John David. BA, Lafayette Coll., 1970; JD, New York Law Sch., 1973. Bar: N.J. 1973, U.S. Ct. Mil. Appeals 1974. Mem. Gerling-Konzern Allgemeine, Cologne, Fed. Republic Germany, 1977-80; v.p. Gerling-Konzern Am. Service Corp., N.Y.C., 1980-86, Colonia Ins. Co., N.Y.C., 1986—. Chmn., trustee Deutsche Sprachschule of Cen. N.J., Inc., South Plainfield, 1981—; assoc. Rep. City Com., Summit, N.J., 1983—; chmn. Substandard Housing and Property Maintainence Bd., Summit, 1984—. Served to capt. JAGC, U.S. Army, 1974-77. Mem. ABA. Lodge: Optimists (pres. Summit-New Providence club 1985-86). Avocation: sailing. Insurance, Private international. Home: 38 Fairview Ave Summit NJ 07901 Office: Associated Ins Mgmt Corp 116 John St New York NY 10038

BENNETT, JAMES PATRICK, lawyer; b. San Francisco, Sept. 26, 1950; s. William Morgan and Jane Evangeline (Grey) B.; m. Paula Marie Hagan, June 7, 1986. Grad., U. Calif., Berkeley, 1972; JD, U. Calif., San Francisco, 1975. Ptnr. Morrison & Foerster, San Francisco, 1975—. Mem. Order of Coif, Thurston Soc. Democrat. Roman Catholic. Federal civil litigation, State civil litigation. Office: Morrison & Foerster 345 California St San Francisco CA 94104

BENNETT, KEVIN DANE, lawyer; b. Mpls., Apr. 11, 1954; s. Dane Jason and Marlene (Thuringer) B.; m. Rayne Rochell Stott, Aug. 6, 1976 (div. Dec. 1982); children: Melanie Raine, Kandis Kristine, Heather Michelle; m. Kathryn Elaine Hall, Feb. 16, 1985. BA, Brigham Young U., 1977; JD, U. Tex., 1980. Bar: Tex. 1980, U.S. Dist. Ct. (so. dist.) Tex. 1981, U.S. Ct. Appeals (5th cir.) 1982. Assoc. Covington & Reese P.C., Houston, 1977-85; ptnr. Reese, Meyer & Cribbs P.C., Houston, 1985—. Editor Urban Law Rev., 1978; exec. editor Am. Jour. Criminal Law, 1979. Edwin S. Hinkley scholar Brigham Young U., 1976. Mem. ABA (real property div., com. on significant lit.), Tex. Bar Assn., Houston Bar Assn., Brigham Young U. Mgmt. Soc. of Houston (sec. 1986-87, pres. 1987—). Republican. Mormon. Avocations: running, travel, basketball. Real property, Contracts commercial, Landlord-tenant. Home: 2010 Feather Ridge Dr Missouri City TX 77489 Office: Reese Meyer & Cribbs PC 1700 W Loop S Suite 1100 Houston TX 77027

BENNETT, LAWRENCE ARTHUR, lawyer; b. Windsor, Ont., Can., Oct. 18, 1941; s. Edwin Joseph and Rosmary Agnes (Lawrence) B.; m. Rosemary Therese Eglin, June 24, 1967; m. 2d, Althea Lynette Miller, May 16, 1981; 1 dau., Erin Colleen. B.S., U. San Francisco, 1964, M.B.A., 1969; J.D., U. of Pacific, 1976. Bar: Calif. 1976, U.S. dist. ct. (no., cen. and so. dists.) Calif., U.S. Ct. Appeals (9th cir.). With Crosby, Heafey, Roach & May, Oakland, Calif., 1976-78; with Maloney, Chase, Fisher & Hurst, San Francisco, 1978-81; ptnr. Morton, Bennett & Lacy, San Francisco, 1982—. Mem. ABA, San Francisco Bar Assn., Assn. Def. Counsel, Def. Research Inst. Assoc. editor Pacific Law Jour., 1975-76. State civil litigation, Federal civil litigation, Insurance. Office: Morton Bennett & Lacy One Embarcadero Ctr Suite 950 San Francisco CA 94111

BENNETT, MARIANNE, health coverage company executive, lawyer; b. Bklyn., Oct. 9, 1948; d. Thomas Maurice and Mary Jo (Freese) D.; m. Charles N. Rapson, Sept. 25, 1971; children—Sean Maurice Bennett Rapson, Liam Terrence Bennett Rapson. B.A., Coll. of New Rochelle, 1970; J.D., Bklyn. Law Sch., 1975. Bar: N.Mex., 1976. Dir. Pre-Paid Legal Services, Albuquerque, 1975-76; research asst. prof. Inst. Pub. Law, Albuquerque, 1976-77; dir. Comserv. Ctr. for Legal Rep., Los Lunas, N.Mex., 1977-80, Legal Services-Albuquerque Bar Assn., 1980-81; v.p., gen. counsel N.Mex. Blue Cross and Blue Shield, Albuquerque, 1981—. Contbr. chpt. to book, articles to publs. Pres. bd. dirs. S.W. Maternity Ctr., Albuquerque, 1977-80; bd. dirs. Assn. for Children with Learning Disabilities, 1982-83; mem. Bernalillo

County Foster Parents, 1977-78, Am. Assn. on Mental Deficiency, N.Mex. Assn. for Retarded Citizens. Mem. ABA, N.Mex. Bar Assn., Albuquerque Bar Assn. Democrat. Roman Catholic. Office: NMEx Blue Cross and Blue Shield 12800 Indian School NE Albuquerque NM 87110

BENNETT, MARION TINSLEY, U.S. court appeals judge; b. Buffalo, Mo., June 6, 1914; s. Philip Allen and Bertha (Tinsley) B.; m. June Young, Apr. 27, 1941; children: Ann Bennett Guptill, William Philip. A.B., Southwest Mo. State U., 1935; J.D., Washington U., 1938. Bar: Mo. 1938, D.C. 1956, U.S. Supreme Ct. 1956, other fed. cts. 1956. Sole practice 1938-43, Congl. adminstrv. asst. to father, 1941-43; commr. U.S. Ct. Claims, 1949-64, chief commr. trial div., 1964-72; judge Appellate div. Ct. Claims, 1972-82, U.S. Ct. Appeals Fed. Circuit, 1982-86; sr. U.S. Circuit Ct. judge 1986—. Author: American Immigration Policies, A History, 1963, U.S. Court of Claims, A History, 1976. Mem. Greene County Republican Central Com., 1938-42; mem. 78th-80th Congresses from 6th Mo. Dist. Col. USAF Res.; ret. Decorated Legion of Merit; recipient Outstanding Alumnus award S.W. Mo. State U., 1964. Mem. Fed. Bar Assn. (nat. council 1958-76), ABA, D.C. Bar Assn., Res. Officers Assn., Delta Theta Phi. Republican. Methodist (ofcl. bd.). Clubs: Exchange, Nat. Lawyers. Federal civil litigation, Jurisprudence, Government contracts and claims. Home: 3715 Cardiff Rd Chevy Chase MD 20815 Office: US Court Appeals Nat Courts Bldg Washington DC 20439

BENNETT, MARSHALL ALTON JR., lawyer; b. Toledo, May 19, 1955; s. Marshall Alton and Irma Bennett; m. Pamela Sue Regan, July 1, 1978; children: Natalie Elizabeth, Nicole Elaine. Student, Wittenberg U., 1973-74; BA magna cum laude, U. Toledo, 1977; JD with honors, Ohio State U., 1980. Bar: Ohio 1980, U.S. Dist. Ct. (no. dist.) Ohio 1981, U.S. Ct. Appeals (6th cir.) 1983. Assoc. Marshall and Melhorn, Toledo, 1980-86, ptnr., 1987—; Sec., bd. dirs. Bennett Funeral Home, Toledo. Bd. dirs. Toledo Legal Aid Soc., 1984—. Mem. ABA, Ohio State Bar Assn. (bd. govs. litigation sect.), Toledo Bar Assn. (pro bono bd. dirs., grievance investigator). Republican. Avocation: golf. Federal civil litigation, State civil litigation, Insurance. Home: 3845 Farmbrook Dr Sylvania OH 43560 Office: Marshall and Melhorn 4 SeaGate 8th Floor Toledo OH 43604

BENNETT, MAXINE TAYLOR, lawyer; b. Owensboro, Ky., Apr. 6, 1938; d. John Clevis and Alice Elizabeth (Siebe) Taylor; m. Wilford Thomas Bennett, Jan 19. 1957 (div. Dec. 1976); children: Cynthia Bennett Liosi, Jonathan Taylor Bennett; m. Edwin R. Druker, May 13, 1978. BA, Ky. Wesleyan Coll., 1959; MA, Western Ky. U., 1967; JD, Ind. U., 1977. Bar: Ind. 1977, U.S. Dist. Ct. (so. dist.) Ind. 1977, U.S. Ct. Appeals (7th cir.) 1984, U.S. Supreme Ct. 1986. Clk. Indpls. Corp. Counsel, 1975-77; atty. Commodities Dealers Licensing Bur. State of Ind., Indpls., 1977-78; sole practice Indpls., 1977-84; assoc. Buck, Berry, Landau & Breunig, Indpls., 1984—. Mem. People of Vision (Soc. to Prevent Blindness), Indpls., 1986—, Indpls. Symphony Guild, 1986—, Family Support Ctr. Aux., Indpls., 1985—, Block Lecture Soc.; mem. steering com. Indpls. Hebrew Congregation, 1982—; bd. dirs. Women's Haven, Indpls., 1981-82; trustee E.A. Block Charitable Trust, Indpls., 1982—. Mem. ABA, Assn. Trial Lawyers Am., Ind. State Bar Assn., Ind. Trial Lawyers Assn. Indpls. Bar Assn. Republican. Club: Skyline (Indpls.). Avocations: world travel, reading, creative needlework, gourmet cooking. Family and matrimonial, Personal injury, Probate. Office: Buck Berry Landau & Breunig 302 N Alabama Indianapolis IN 46204

BENNETT, RICHARD EDWARD, lawyer; b. Boston, Nov. 19, 1954. AB, Boston Coll., 1975, JD, 1978. Bar: Mass. 1978, U.S. Dist. Ct. Mass. 1979, U.S. Ct. Appeals (1st cir.) 1979. Assoc. Willcox, Pirozzolo & McCarthy, Boston, 1979—. Federal civil litigation, State civil litigation, Antitrust. Office: Willcox Pirozzolo & McCarthy PC 50 Federal St Boston MA 02140

BENNETT, ROBERT, lawyer; b. Yonkers, N.Y., Mar. 5, 1952; s. Neil Francis and Claire Marie (Hunter) B.; m. Mary Marjorie Adams, June 28, 1974 (div. Aug. 1984); 1 child, Matthew Adams; m. Rebecca Ann Jerred, Nov. 23, 1984; 1 child, Kathryn Hunter. AB in English, U. Notre Dame, 1973; JD, U. Minn., 1976. Bar: Minn. 1976, U.S. Dist. Ct. Minn. 1976, U.S. Ct. Appeals (8th cir.) 1982. Assoc. Delaney & Thompson & O'Rourke, Mpls., 1976-79; ptnr. Delaney & Solum, Mpls., 1980-84, Bennett, Ingvaldson & McInerny P.A., Mpls., 1984—; panel Fed. Pub. Defenders, 1980—, Hennepin Countuy Pub. Defenders, 1980—. Mem. ABA, Minn. Bar Assn., Hennepin County Bar Assn. (criminal law com.), Assn. Trial Lawyers Am., Minn. Trial Lawyers Assn. Clubs: Edina (Minn.) Country. Federal civil litigation, State civil litigation, Personal injury. Home: 7113 Shannon Dr Edina MN 55435 Office: Bennett Ingvaldson & McInerny PA 7900 Xerxes Ave S Suite 820 Minneapolis MN 55431

BENNETT, ROBERT WILLIAM, lawyer; b. Chgo., Mar. 30, 1941; s. Lewis and Henrietta (Schneider) B.; m. Harriet Trop, Aug. 19, 1979. B.A., Harvard U., 1962, LL.B., 1965. Bar: Ill. bar 1966. Legal asst. FCC commr. Nicholas Johnson, 1966-67; atty. Chgo. Legal Aid Bur., 1967-68; asso. firm Mayer, Brown & Platt, Chgo., 1968-69; faculty Northwestern U. Sch. Law, Chgo., 1969—; prof. law Northwestern U. Sch. Law, 1974—, dean, 1985—. Author: (with LaFrance, Schroeder and Boyd) Hornbook on Law of the Poor, 1973. Knox Meml. fellow London Sch. Econs., 1965-66. Fellow Am. Bar Fedn. (bd. dirs., treas.); mem. Chgo. Council Lawyers (pres. 1971-72), Am. Law Inst., ABA. Constitutional, Contracts commercial, Legal education. Home: 501 W Armitage Ave Chicago IL 60614 Office: Sch Law Northwestern U 357 E Chicago Ave Chicago IL 60611

BENNETT, ROGER WILLIAM, lawyer; b. Lafayette, Ind., Nov. 12, 1948; s. William Kenneth and Mary Evelyn (Waye) B.; m. Jane Anne Rheinwald, May 27, 1972; 1 child, Jason Wade. Student, Wheaton Coll., 1967-68, John Brown U., 1968-70; BS, Bradley U., 1972; JD, Ind. U., 1982. Bar: Ind. 1982, U.S. Dist. Ct. (no. and so. dists.) Ind. 1982, U.S. Ct. Appeals (7th cir.) 1984. Resident mgr. Service Master Industries, Downers Grove, Ill., 1973-76; owner, operator Service Master by Bennett, Prescott, Ariz., 1976-79; assoc. Bennett, Boehing, Poynter & Clary, Lafayette, 1981—. Articles editor Ind. Law Jour., 1981. Bd. dirs. New Directions Inc., Lafayette, 1984-86, Lafayette Christian Sch., 1986—, Tippecanoe County Right to Life, Lafayette, 1985—; gen. counsel Ind. Right to Life, Indpls., 1983—; chmn. adv. bd. Matrix Lifeline, Lafayette, 1985—. Mem. ABA, Ind. State Bar Assn., Christian Legal Soc., Assn. Trial Lawyers of Am. Republican. Mem. Christian Reformed Ch. Civil rights, Federal civil litigation, State civil litigation. Home: 2710 Elizabeth St Lafayette IN 47904-2747 Office: PO Box 469 133 N 4th St Lafayette IN 47902

BENNETT, SCOTT LAWRENCE, lawyer; b. N.Y.C., July 8, 1949; s. Allen J. and Rhoda (Maltz) B. A.B. with high distinction, U. Mich., 1971; J.D., Cornell U., 1974. Bar: N.Y. 1975, U.S. Dist. Ct. (so. dist.) N.Y. 1976, U.S. Ct. Appeals (2d cir.) 1976, U.S. Supreme Ct. 1977. Assoc. Donovan, Leisure, Newton & Irvine, N.Y.C., 1974-79; assoc. gen. counsel McGraw-Hill, Inc., N.Y.C., 1979—. Mem. Assn. Am. Pubs. (lawyers com.), Assn. of Bar of City of N.Y. (corp. law com.), ABA, N.Y. State Bar Assn., Phi Beta Kappa. General corporate, Real property, Securities. Home: 101 W 12th St Apt 10J New York NY 10011 Office: McGraw Hill Inc 1221 Ave of Americas New York NY 10020

BENNETT, THOMPSON, lawyer; b. Kalamazoo, Mich., July 9, 1912; s. Lorenzo Thompson and Helen Mary (Timerman) B.; m. Ann Garrett, Aug. 19, 1948; children—Kathryn Bennett Solley, Charles Garrett, Thomas Timerman, Elizabeth Ann. B.A., George Washington U., 1938, J.D. with honors, 1936, LL.M., 1939. Bar: D.C. 1935, Mich. 1940, U.S. Dist Ct. (we. dist.) Mich. 1946, U.S. Ct. Appeals (6th cir.) 1950, U.S. Supreme Ct. 1940. Chief atty. U.S. Mktg. Laws Survey, Washington, 1939-41; asst. solicitor Dept. Interior, Washington, 1941-42; spl. agt. FBI, 1942-46; assoc. Howard Howard & Bennett, Kalamazoo, 1947-52; ptnr. Bennett LaParl & Milligan, Kalamazoo; assoc. judge Mcpl. Ct., Kalamazoo, 1954-57. Chmn. Kalamazoo ARC, 1964-68, chmn. Delano Psychiat. Clinic; chmn. Borgess Mental Health Ctr., Kalamazoo, 1976—; city commr. City of Kalamazoo, 1961-63; mem. Kalamazoo County Bd. Suprs., 1961-62; vice chmn. Kalamazoo chpt. Mich. Children's Aid; mem. curriculum council Kalamazoo Pub. Schs.; pres. Western Mich. U. Campus Sch. PTA; trustee, bd. dirs. Sr. Citizens Fund, 1969-78; trustee, chmn. Kalamazoo Symphony Soc.; trustee Dorothy U. Dalton Found., 1978—. Mem. Kalamazoo County Bar Assn. (pres. 1966-67), ABA, State Bar Mich. (chmn. negligence sect. 1966-67), Am. Judicature Soc., Am. Trial Lawyers Assn., Kalamazoo C. of C. (pres. 1966-67), Phi Delta Phi. Republican. Roman Catholic. Contbr. numerous articles to profl. jours. Personal injury, Probate, Estate planning. Office: 415 W Michigan Ave Kalamazoo MI 49007

BENNINGHOFF, CHARLES FRANKLYN, III, lawyer, accountant; b. San Bernadino, Calif., May 28, 1944; s. Charles Franklyn Jr. and Ella Corella (Hinshaw) B.; m. Nancy Lee Summerhays, July 3, 1971; children—Charles Franklyn IV, Nancy Whitmel. A.A., Chaffey Coll., 1969; B.S., U. So. Calif., 1971, M.Acctg., 1974, J.D., 1974. Bar: Calif. 1975. C.P.A., Calif. Tax acct. Touche Ross & Co., Los Angeles, 1974-76; sole practice, So. Calif., 1976—; venture capitalist; chmn. bd. Video Comdr., Inc., Santa Ana, Calif., 1981-83 , Casino Bancorp., Las Vegas, Nev., 1983-85, also chmn. bd., chief exec. officer So. Equites Corp, Newport Beach, 1982—; chmn. bd., chief exec. officer Am. Fgn. Exchange & Telegraph Co., Inc., Los Angeles, 1984—; Carben Munitions Co., 1983—, also vice chmn.; gen. ptnr. Cadar-Benninghoff Gen. Ptnr., 1982—; founder, vice chmn. Money Transmitters Assn. Contbr. articles to profl. jours. Bd. dirs. Homeowners Assn., 1982-83, Dollars for Scholars, Huntington Beach, Calif., 1980—; fund raiser Patrick J. Nolan for Assembly, Glendale, 1978; fin. com. Nina N. Pierce for Congress, Ontario, Calif., 1984; adv. com. Dr. Arthur B. Laffer for U.S. Senate, 1985; bd. dirs. South Coast Community Clinic, San Juan Capistrano. Served to E-5 USN, 1965-68, Vietnam. Randolph Hearst Found. scholar, 1964; recipient Mar of Yr. award Mira Casta Coll., 1969; Law Rev. invitee U. San Diego, 1972. Mem. Calif. Soc. C.P.A.'s (ethics com.), Huntington Beach C. of C. (bd. dirs. 1980), Beta Alpha Psi. Republican. Mem. Christian Ch. Securities, Corporate taxation, Venture capital. Office: 350 S Figueroa St 120 World Trade Ctr Los Angeles CA 90071

BENNINGTON, ALFRED JOSEPH, JR., lawyer; b. Glen Ridge, N.J., Nov. 30, 1952; s. Alfred J. Sr. and Ann Katherine (Walsh) B.; m. Patricia M. Cofer, Sept. 21, 1985. BA, Marietta Coll., 1974; JD, Ohio No. U., 1977. Bar: N.J. 1977. Asst. prosecutor, sr. trial atty. Essex County Prosecutor's Office, N.J., 1978-79; assoc. Blatt, Blatt, Mairone & Biel, Atlantic City, 1978-82; sole practice Northfield, N.J., 1983—; mcpl. prosecutor Cities of Ventnor, Linwood & Somers Point, N.J.; asst. solicitor prosecutor, Egg Harbor Twp. Contbr. articles to profl. jours. Candidate 2d congl. dist. N.J., U.S. Ho. of Reps., 1986. Mem. ABA (criminal justice div.), Assn. Trial Lawyers Am., N.J. Bar Assn., Atlantic County Bar Assn., Jaycees. Roman Catholic. Office: 200 Jackson Ave Northfield NJ 08225

BENNION, DAVID JACOBSEN, lawyer; b. Glendale, Calif., Jan. 29, 1940; s. Donald Clark and Margaret (Jacobsen) B.; m. Constance Wilson, Jan. 27, 1966; children—Marian, Margaret, Elizabeth, David, Sarah, Heidi. B.A., Stanford U., 1964, J.D., 1966. Bar: Calif. 1966. Ptnr. Boccardo Law Firm, San Jose, Calif., 1966-79; mission pres. Ch. of Jesus Christ of Latter-day Saints, Geneva, Switzerland, 1979-82; ptnr. Packard, Packard & Bennion, Palo Alto, Calif., 1982—; instr. continuing edn. of bar, personal injury trial. Mem. ABA, Calif. State Bar, Assn. Trial Lawyers Am., Am. Bd. Trial Advs. Republican. Personal injury, Products liability, Civil litigation. Home: 441 Maple Palo Alto CA 94301 Office: 260 Sheridan Ave Suite 208 Palo Alto CA 94306

BENSER, FRANK LEROY, lawyer; b. Balt., June 2, 1945; s. Frank and Ilene (Long) B.; m. Sharon Anne Willoughby, Dec. 17, 1966; children: Kathryn Elizabeth, Stephanie Lynne. BA, U. Va., 1967; JD, Coll. of William and Mary, 1975. Bar: Va. 1975. Assoc. Julien J. Mason, Bowling Green, Va., 1975-79; ptnr. Mason & Benser, Bowling Green, 1980—; atty. Town of Bowling Green, Va., 1975—, County of Caroline, Bowling Green, 1979-86. Chmn. Caroline County Rep. Com., Bowling Green, 1977—; chmn. Germanna Community Coll. Bd., Locust Grove, Va., 1986-87; pres. Caroline Hist. Soc., Bowling Green, 1981-82. Served to capt. U.S. Army, 1968-72, Vietnam. Decorated Bronze Star. Lodges: Lions (pres. Bowling Green 1983-85), Ruritan (pres. Bowling Green 1980). Real property, Local government, Criminal. Home: 215 Milford St Bowling Green VA 22427 Office: Mason & Benser PO Box 118 Bowling Green VA 22427

BENSINGER, CARL JOSEPH, lawyer; b. Baden, Germany, May 19, 1935; s. Fred and Judith (Schloessinger) B. Student Northwestern U., 1952-54; B.A., U. Louisville, 1956, J.D., 1958. Bar: Ky. 1958, U.S. Supreme Ct. 1972, U.S. Dist. Ct. (we. dist.) Ky. 1977, U.S. Tax Ct. 1977, U.S. Ct. Appeals (6th cir.) 1986. Law clk. Ky. Ct. Appeals, 1958-59; assoc. Morris, Garlove, Waterman & Johnson, Louisville, 1959-69; ptnr. Carl J. Bensinger & Assocs., Louisville, 1969—; sec.-counsel Ky. Real Estate Commn., 1973-75; probate commr., 1970-77; instr. real estate law Jefferson Community Coll., Louisville, 1975. Bd. dirs. Bridgehaven, 1969-77, Jewish Community Fedn., 1975-79; pres. Am. Jewish Com., 1974-75, mem. nat. exec. com., 1970—; mem. exec. com. Jefferson County Dem. Party, 1968-76, 80—; pres. East End Dem. Club, 1977, 78; bd. dirs. NCCJ, 1974-80; regional bd. dirs. Anti-Defamation League, 1969—, chmn. chpt., 1983; commr. Jefferson County Human Relations Com., 1978-80; commr. Jefferson County Crime Commn., 1982-83; mem. Jefferson County Community Improvement Dist. Commn., 1986, Govs. Adv. Council for Vol. Services, 1986. Served with U.S. Army, 1958-59. Mem. ABA, Louisville Bar Assn. (grievance, probate, civil practice, continuing legal edn. and litigation coms.), Ky. Bar Assn., Phi Alpha Delta, Phi Kappa Phi, Phi Eta Sigma. Clubs: B'nai B'rith (Warden), Masons. Real property, Probate, State civil litigation. Home: 2621 Byron Ave Louisville KY 40205 Office: Ky Home Life Bldg Suite 1517 Louisville KY 40202

BENSON, GREGG CARL, lawyer; b. Norwich, Conn., Feb. 2, 1953; s. Lester William Benson and Mona Marie (Magner) Blitz; m. Deborah Fay Horwitz, May 30, 1976; children: Sarah N., Joshua K. BA, U. Conn., 1974, MS, 1975, JD, 1981. Bar: Conn. 1981, U.S. Dist. Ct. Conn. 1981, U.S. Patent Office 1983. Scientist Pfizer Inc., Groton, Conn., 1975-81; assoc. Horwitz & Benson P.C., Norwich, 1981-84; patent counsel Am. Cyanamid Co., Stamford, Conn., 1984-87; patent atty. Pfizer Inc., Groton, 1987—. Bd. dirs. Am. Cancer Soc., Norwich, 1983. Mem. ABA, Conn. Bar Assn., Assn. Trial Lawyers Am., N.Y. Patent, Trademark and Copyright Law Assn., Am. Intellectual Property Law Assn. Lodge: Masons. Avocations: racquetball, golf, woodworking. Patent. Home: 20 Riverbend Rd Trumbull CT 06611 Office: Pfizer Inc Eastern Point Rd Groton CT 06304

BENSON, JAMES ROBERT, lawyer; b. Bloomington, Ill., June 16, 1947; s. John M. and Martha F. (Schroeder) B.; m. Mary E. Gushwa, June 21, 1973. AS, Vincennes U., 1967; BS, U. Ill., 1969, JD, 1974. Bar: Ill. 1974. Asst. states atty. State of Ill., Watseka, 1974-76; states atty. Ford County, Paxton, Ill., 1976—. Mem. ABA, Ill. Bar Assn., Ill. States Atty. Assn. Republican. Methodist. Avocations: bee-keeping, pilot. Criminal, Local government. Home: 607 S Washington Paxton IL 60957 Office: Ford County States Atty Office State St Courthouse Paxton IL 60957

BENSON, JOHN SCOTT, lawyer; b. Atlanta, Sept. 17, 1947; s. Lawrence Walker and Betty Lamar (Chick) B.; m. Louise Kathryn Sweet, July 22, 1984; children: Nathaniel Michael, Elisabeth Sweet. BA magna cum laude, Vanderbilt U., 1969; JD, U. Va., 1974. Bar: Fla. 1974. Assoc. Martin, Ade, Birchfield & Johnson, Jacksonville, Fla., 1974-78, ptnr., 1978—. Bd. dirs. Cerebral Palsy of Jacksonville, 1980-86, pres., 1986; mem. Fedn. Council YMCA Indian Guides, 1985-86; bd. dirs. Children's Services of Jacksonville, 1986. Served to 1st lt. U.S. Army, 1969-71, Vietnam. Decorated Air medal; named one of Outstanding Young Men in Am., 1979. Mem. ABA, Fla. Bar Assn., Jacksonville Bar Assn., Phi Beta Kappa, Phi Kappa Sigma. Republican. Club: Fla. Yacht (Jacksonville). Avocations: sunday school teaching, camping, canoeing. Real property, General corporate, Environment. Office: Martin Ade Birchfield & Johnson 3000 Independent Sq Jacksonville FL 32202

BENSON, LARRY JOHN, lawyer; b. New Orleans, Aug. 21, 1945; s. Thomas Milton and Carmalita Maria (Pintado) B.; m. Nuala Carolyn Morris, Oct. 5, 1974; 1 son, Larry John. B.S., La. State U.-Baton Rouge, 1969; J.D., St. Mary's U., San Antonio, 1972. Bar: Tex 1972. Sole practice, San Antonio, 1973-81, 82—; ptnr. Benson & Yedor, San Antonio, 1981-82; dir. Groos Bank, N.A., San Antonio, San Pedro Bank, San Antonio, Hill Country Motors, Kerrville, Tex., Comml. Nat. Bank, San Antonio, Benson Motor Cos., Ltd. Mem. adv. council St. Mary's U., San Antonio, 1984; mem. legacy council Incarnate Word Coll., San Antonio, 1981-84. Mem. ABA, Tex. Bar Assn., Tex. Trial Lawyers Assn., San Antonio Bar Assn., Phi Alpha Delta. Republican. Roman Catholic. General corporate, Real property, Banking. Office: 1100A Gill Plaza 9601 McAllister Freeway San Antonio TX 78216

BENSON, LAWRENCE KERN, JR., lawyer, real estate exec.; b. New Orleans, May 16, 1938; s. Lawrence Kern and Adele (Foster) B.; m. Alta Sarah Bechtel, June 10, 1961; children—Robert Foster, Andrew Thompson, Marion Alta. Student Washington & Lee U., 1956-58; B.A., Tulane U., 1960, J.D., 1962. Bar: La. 1962, U.S. Dist. Ct. (ea. and mid. dists.) La. 1962, U.S. Ct. Mil. Appeals 1963, U.S. Ct. Appeals (5th cir.) 1969, U.S. Supreme Ct. 1971, U.S. Dist. Ct. (we. dist.) La. 1977. Assoc. Milling, Benson, Woodward, Hillyer, Pierson & Miller, New Orleans, 1962-66, ptnr., 1966-85, asst. dist. atty. U.S. Dist. Ct. (ea. dist.) La., 1986—; adj. lectr. Tulane U. Law Sch., 1980. Served with USAR, 1963-64. Mem. ABA, La. Bar Assn. (ho. of dels. 1978-81), New Orleans Bar Assn. (exec. com. 1979-81), Order of Coif. Republican. Methodist. Clubs: City, Boston (New Orleans). General practice, State civil litigation, Federal criminal prosecution. Office: US Dist Atty's Office Hale Boggs Fed Bldg New Orleans LA 70130

BENSON, STUART WELLS, III, lawyer; b. Sewickley, Pa., Jan. 6, 1951; s. Stuart Wells and Rosalie (Sassin) B.; m. Ruthanne Ackerman, July 15, 1978; children—Kate Eileen, Laura Elizabeth, Sarah Wells. B.A., Northwestern U., 1972; J.D., U. Pitts., 1975. Bar: Pa. 1975, U.S. Dist. Ct. (we. dist.) Pa. 1975, U.S. Supreme Ct. 1982. Assoc. Brandt McManus Brandt & Malone, Pitts., 1975-80; ptnr. Dickie, McCamey & Chilcote, P.C., Pitts., 1980—. Contbr. articles to legal jours. Bd. dirs. North Hills YMCA, Pitts., 1981-84. Mem. Am. Arbitration Assn. (Appreciation award 1980, arbitrator), Pa. Def. Inst., Pa. Claims Assn., Pitts. Claims Assn., Allegheny County Bar Assn., Pa. Bar Assn., ABA, Internat. Assn. Indsl. Accident Bds. and Commns. Republican. Episcopalian. Clubs: Oakmont Country (Pa.); Wildwood Golf (Allison Park, Pa.). Lodge: Rotary (pres. 1985, bd. dirs. 1979—) (North Boroughs). Workers' compensation, Insurance, Personal injury. Home: 4256 Laurel Ridge Dr Allison Park PA 15101 Office: Dickie McCamey & Chilcote PC 2 PPG Pl Suite 400 Pittsburgh PA 15222

BENT, DANIEL A., lawyer; b. New Orleans, May 24, 1947; s. Edward and Alberta (Fabacher) B.; m. Maribeth Reader, Mar. 9, 1974; children: Laurance Elizabeth, Johnathan Binnings. B.S. in Mech. Engring., La. State U., 1970; J.D., Georgetown U., 1974. Bar: La., D.C., Hawaii, U.S. Supreme Ct., U.S. Ct. Appeals (9th cir.), U.S. Ct. Appeals (5th cir.), U.S. Dist. Ct. (ea. dist.) La., U.S. Dist. Ct. Hawaii, U.S. Patent Office. Patent examiner U.S. Patent Office, Washington, 1970-72; patent adviser Naval Ship Research and Devel. Ctr., Bethesda, Md., 1972-74; asst. U.S. atty. Eastern Dist. La., New Orleans, 1974-77; chief criminal div. Eastern Dist. La., 1977, 1st asst. U.S. atty., 1977-78; spl. atty. organized crime and racketeering sect. U.S. Dept. Justice, Honolulu Field Office, 1978-82; U.S. atty. Dist. of Hawaii, 1982—; lectr. Sch. Law U. Hawaii, Fed. Agy. Tng. Sessions; lectr. and instr. Atty. Gen's Advocacy Inst., Washington, 1977—; instr. Hasting Ctr. for Trial and Appellate Advocacy, Civil Advocacy Programs; mem. com. on local rules U.S. Dist. Ct., Hawaii; mem. com. on course design and revision Atty. Gen's. Advocacy Inst.; organizer, presenter trial advocacy tng. programs County Prosecutors State of Hawaii; co-instr. Patent Trial Advocacy Inst., 1980; mem. com. on penal code reform, Honolulu, 1983. Rowan Oil Co. scholar, 1969; NSF summer research grantee. Mem. ABA, Assn. Trial Lawyers Am., D.C. Bar Assn., La. Bar Assn., Hawaii Bar Assn., Fed. Bar Assn., Tau Beta Pi, Pi Tau Sigma. Republican. Club: Rotary. Office: US Dept Justice 300 Ala Moana Blvd Box 50183 Honolulu HI 96850 *

BENT, STEPHEN ANDREW, lawyer; b. Chelsea, Mass., Sept. 12, 1951; s. Charles Linley and Maude (Andrews) B.; m. Barbara Miller Schwartz, June 2, 1974; children: Max, Robert. BS, Earlham Coll., 1973; MS, U. Conn., 1976; JD with high honors, George Washington U., 1981. Bar: D.C. 1981, U.S. Ct. Appeals (Fed. cir.) 1982. Tech. asst. U.S. Ct. Appeals (Fed. cir.), Washington, 1981-83; ptnr. Schwartz, Jeffery, Schwaab, Mack, Blumenthal & Evans P.C., Alexandria, Va., 1983—; lectr. Patent Resources Inst., Washington, 1985—. Co-author: Protecting Biotechnology Property Rights Worldwide, 1986, Biotechnology Patent Practice, 1985; contbr. articles to profl. jours. Mem. ABA, Am. Intellectual Property Law Assn., Md. Patent Law Assn., AAAS. Phi Beta Kappa. Avocation: writing. Patent, Trademark and copyright, Personal injury. Home: 3008 Gumwood Dr Hyattsville MD 20783 Office: Shcwartz Jeffery Schwaab et al PC 1800 Diagonal Rd Alexandria VA 22314

BENTLEY, ANTHONY MILES, lawyer; b. N.Y.C., July 16, 1945; s. Herbert A. and Dorothy Dene (Hyman) B. AB, U. Pa., 1967; JD, Fordham U., 1971. Bar: N.Y. 1971, U.S. Ct. Appeals (2d cir.) 1971, Pa. 1973, U.S. Dist. Ct. (so. and ea. dists.) N.Y. 1973, U.S. Tax Ct. 1976, U.S. Supreme Ct. 1976. Assoc. Hughes Hubbard & Reed, N.Y.C., 1970, Cahill Gordan & Reindel, N.Y.C., 1971-75, Goldstein Shames Hyde, N.Y.C., 1975-76; sole practice N.Y.C., 1977—; spl. master N.Y. County Supreme Ct. Editor Fordham Law Rev., 1970-71, founding editor Fordham Urban Law Jour., 1971. Mem. ABA, Assn. of Bar of City of N.Y., Assn. Trial Lawyers Am., Pa. Bar Assn., Phila. Bar Assn., Mensa. Jewish. Landlord-tenant, Federal civil litigation, Bankruptcy.

BENTLEY, ANTOINETTE COZELL, insurance executive, lawyer; b. N.Y.C., Oct. 7, 1937; d. Joseph Richard Cozell and Rose (Lafata Cozell) Vila; children: Robert S., Anne W. B.A. with distinction, U. Mich., 1960; LL.B., U. Va., 1961. Bar: N.Y. 1962, N.J. 1971. Asso. Sage Gray, Todd & Sims, N.Y.C., 1961-65; of counsel Farrell, Curtis, Carlin & Davidson, Morristown, N.J., 1971-73; asst. sec. Crum and Forster, N.J., 1973; sec. Crum and Forster, 1973—, v.p., counsel, 1975-87, sr. v.p., assoc. gen. counsel, 1987—. Mem. policy com. N.J. Future, 1986; trustee Crum and Forster Found., 1979—; vice pres. Mendham Borough (N.J.) Bd. Edn., 1976-79; trustee N.J. Conservation Found., 1981—, pres., 1986—; trustee Morris Mus., 1982, St. Peter's Coll. Mem. ABA, N.J. Bar Assn., Am. Soc. Corp. Secs. (v.p. and program chmn. regional group, mem. adv. com.), Women's Econ. Roundtable, LWV, Order of Coif, Chi Omega. Home: Fowler Rd Far Hills NJ 07921 Office: 305 Madison Ave Morristown NJ 07960

BENTLEY, FRED DOUGLAS, SR., lawyer; b. Marietta, Ga., Oct. 15, 1926; s. Oscar Andrew and Ima Irene (Prather) B.; m. Sara Tom Moss, Dec. 26, 1953; children: Fred Douglas, Robert Randall. BA, Presbyn. Coll., 1949; JD, Emory U., 1948. Bar: Ga. 1948. Sr. mem. Bentley & Dew, Marietta; ptnr. Bentley, Awtrey & Bartlett, Marietta, Edwards, Bentley, Awtrey & Parker, Marietta, Bentley & Schindelar, Marietta, Bentley & Bentley, Marietta. Mem. Ga. Ho. of Reps., 1951-57, Ga. Senate, 1958; past pres. Cobb County (Ga.) C. of C. Served with USN. Named Citizen of Yr., C. of C., 1951, Leader of Tomorrow, Time mag., 1953, Vol. Citizen of Yr., Atlanta Jour./Constn., 1981. Mem. Nat. Trial Lawyers Assn., Assn. Trial Lawyers Am., Ga. Trial Lawyers Assn., ABA, Ga. Bar Assn., Am. Jurisprudence Soc. Democrat. Methodist. Clubs: Rotary (Marietta); Georgian (Atlanta). Jurisprudence, General practice. Home: 1441 Beaumont Dr Kennesaw GA 30144 Office: 260 Washington Ave Marietta GA 30060

BENTLEY, JOHN MARTIN, lawyer; b. San Francisco, June 29, 1929; s. Mark and Daisie Elizabeth (Martin) B.; m. Ruth Catherine Marshel, Nov. 17, 1951; children—John M., Juliana, James, Joseph, Joshua, Mark. J.D., U. San Francisco, 1955. Bar: Calif. 1955, U.S. Dist. Ct. (no. dist.) Calif. 1955, U.S. Ct. Appeals (9th cir.) 1955, U.S. Dist. Ct. (ea. dist.) Calif. 1967. Diplomate Am. Bd. Profl. Liability Attys. Assoc., James J. Duryea, San Francisco, 1956-59; assoc. Duryea, Bentley & Hartman, San Francisco, 1959-64; assoc. Ropers, Majeski & Phelps, Redwood City, Calif., 1964-67; ptnr., dir. Ropers Majeski Kohn Bentley Wagner & Kane, Redwood City, 1967—. Fellow Am. Coll. Trial Lawyers, Internat. Acad. Trial Lawyers; mem. Am. Bd. Trial Advocates, Internat. Assn. Ins. Counsel, Fedn. Ins. Counsel, Assn. Def. Counsel No. Calif. Club: Olympic (San Francisco). Federal civil litigation, State civil litigation, Personal injury. Home: 15 Bear Gulch Dr Portola Valley CA 94025 Office: Ropers Majeski Kohn Bentley Wagner & Kane 1125 Marshall St Redwood City CA 94063

BENTLEY, PETER, lawyer; b. Jersey City, Sept. 1, 1915; s. Peter and Emma (Patterson) B.; m. Signe Von Krusenstierna, Apr. 15, 1944 (dec. Mar. 1984); 1 child, Frederique Bentley Boire; m. Jane Morfoot Chapman, Apr. 19, 1986. B.A., Princeton U., 1938; LL.B., Yale U., 1941. Bar: Conn.,

N.Y., U.S. Dist. Ct. Conn., U.S. Dist. Ct. N.Y., U.S. Ct. Appeals (2d cir.). Assoc. Simpson, Thacher & Bartlett, N.Y.C., 1941-52, Maguire, Cole, Bentley & Babson (and predecessors), Stamford, Conn., 1952-54; ptnr. Bentley, Mosher & Babson, P.C. and predecessors, Stamford, 1954—. Rep. Greenwich (Conn.) Town Meeting, 1966-68; bd. dirs. Am. Red Cross, Greenwich, 1985—, Greenwich Emergency Med. Service, 1986—; bd. dirs., pres. The Carl J. Herzog Found. Inc., 1978—; bd. dirs., sec. Feris Found. Am. Inc., 1983—. Mem. Stamford Bar Assn. (pres. 1971-72), Conn. Bar Assn., ABA. Republican. Mem. Soc. of Friends. General practice, General corporate, Probate. Home: 130 Shore Rd Old Greenwich CT 06870 Office: Bentley Mosher & Babson PC 970 Summer St Stamford CT 06905

BENTLEY, PETER JOHN HILTON, lawyer; b. Bournemouth, Eng., Nov. 8, 1934; came to U.S., 1965; s. James Hilton and Marjorie (Wimpress) B.; m. Barbara Brokaw Lamb (div. Aug. 1970); m. Kaye Bensinger, Sept. 11, 1979; children: Marion Elisabeth, Paul Richard, Rebecca Catherine. BA, Cambridge U., Eng., 1957, MA, 1965. Bar: Solicitor of the Supreme Ct. of Eng. and Wales 1965, Ill. Assoc. Linklaters & Paines, London, 1960-65, Sullivan & Cromwell, N.Y.C., 1960-61; assoc. Baker & McKenzie, Chgo., 1965-67, ptnr., 1967—; hon. lectr. law Northwestern U., Evanston, Ill., 1969-70. Bd. dirs. Legal Assistance Found. Chgo., 1975-83. Served as midshipman Royal Navy, 1953-54. Mem. Law Soc. of Eng. and Wales, Ill. Bar Assn., Chgo. Bar Assn., Am. Arbitration Assn. (nat. panel). Private international, English and British commonwealth. Home: 90 Meadow Hill Rd Barrington Hills IL 60010 Office: Baker & McKenzie Prudential Plaza Suite 2800 Chicago IL 60601

BENTON, ANDREW KEITH, university administrator, lawyer; b. Hawthrone, Nev., Feb. 4, 1952; s. Darwin Keith and Nelda Lou (Cochran) B.; m. Deborah Sue Strickland, June 22, 1974; children: Hailey Michelle, Christopher Andrew. BS in Am. Studies, Okla. Christian Coll., 1974; JD, Oklahoma City U., 1979. Bar: Okla. 1979, U.S. Dist. Ct. (we. dist.) Okla. 1982. Sole practice Edmond, Okla., 1979-81, 83-84; ptnr. Benton & Thomason, Edmond, 1981-83; asst. v.p. Pepperdine U., Malibu, Calif., 1984, v.p., 1984—. Chmn. precinct, state conv. del. Okla. Reps., 1980. Mem. ABA, Okla. Bar Assn. (contbr. articles to ednl. community), Malibu C. of C., Santa Monica C. of C. Republican. Mem. Ch. of Christ. Real property, Legal education, Environment. Home: 24450 Tiner Ct Malibu CA 90265 Office: Pepperdine U 24255 Pacific Coast Hwy Malibu CA 90265

BENTON, DONALD STEWART, publishing company executive; b. Marlboro, N.Y., Jan. 2, 1924; s. Fred Stanton and Agnes (Townsend) B.; B.A., Columbia U., 1947, J.D., 1949; LL.M., N.Y.U., 1953; student U. Leeds (Eng.), 1945. Admitted to N.Y. State bar, 1953; practiced in N.Y.C., 1953-56; atty. N.Y. State Banking Dept., 1954-55; v.p. Found. Press, Inc., Bklyn., 1957-60; exec. asst. to exec. v.p. N.Y. Stock Exchange, 1960-61; dir. reference book dept. and spl. projects editor Appleton Century Crofts, N.Y.C., 1962-71; sr. editor Matthew Bender & Co., Inc., N.Y.C., 1974-77; sr. legal editor Warren, Gorham & Lamont, Inc., N.Y.C., 1977—. Author: Federal Banking Laws, 2d edit., 1987. Real Estate Tax Digest, 1984, Criminal Law Digest, 3d edit., 1983. Mem. Cresskill (N.J.) Zoning Bd. Adjustment, 1969-71, 82-83; 86—. Mem. Cresskill Planning Bd., 1971-74; councilman City of Cresskill, 1972-74. Served with AUS, 1943-46, 50-52. Decorated Bronze Star. Mem. Phi Delta Phi. Mem. Reformed Ch. in Am. Banking, Consumer commercial, Real property. Home: 117 Heatherhill Rd Cresskill NJ 07626 Office: Warren Gorham & Lamont Inc 1 Penn Plaza New York NY 10119

BENTON, JOHN BUNYAN, lawyer; b. Sabinal, Tex., Dec. 2, 1932; s. Francis Marian and Willie Mae (Cooner) B.; m. Rosa Marie Guajardo, Nov. 22, 1974; children—Jeffrey Franc, Amy Denise, Marie Denise, Anna Marie. B.B.A., U. Tex., 1958, LL.B., 1959, LL.M. (Humble award 1960), 1963. Bar: Tex. bar 1959, N.Y. State bar 1963. Atty. FTC, Washington, 1960-65; exec. vice chmn. gen. counsel Jewelers Com., N.Y.C., 1965-69; sr. counsel NBC, N.Y.C., 1969-73; asst. gen. counsel Montgomery Ward & Co., Inc., Chgo., 1973-76; v.p., gen. counsel, sec., dir. Gimbel Bros., Inc., N.Y.C., 1976-78; v.p., gen. counsel Howell Corp. and Howell Petroleum Corp., Houston, 1978-83; individual bus. practice Houston, 1983-86; ptnr. Manitzas & Benton, San Antonio, 1986—. Author articles in field. Democrat candidate for N.Y. State Assembly, 1968. Served with USMC, 1953-56, Korea. Mem. Am. Bar Assn., Tex. Bar Assn., Assn. Bar City N.Y., Houston Bar Assn., Phi Alpha Delta. Unitarian. Clubs: Houston, Nat. Lawyers. Labor, Pension, profit-sharing, and employee benefits, State civil litigation. Home: 3322 Le Blanc San Antonio TX 78247 Office: 900 Isom Rd Suite 208 San Antonio TX 78216

BERARD, DOUGLAS CLAY, lawyer; b. Lynn, Mass., Aug. 30, 1945; s. Anthony Dwight and Lucille (Clay) B.; m. Linda Margaret Allison, June 28, 1968. BA in History and Polit. Sci., The Citadel, 1968; JD, Southwestern U., Los Angeles, 1978. Bar: Calif. 1979, U.S. Dist. Ct. (cen. dist.) Calif. 1980, U.S. Ct. Appeals (9th cir.) 1980. Assoc. Revere, Citron and Wallace, Los Angeles, 1979-81, Law Office of Barry Zalma, Los Angeles, 1981-85; ptnr. Zalma and Berard, Culver City, Calif., 1985—. Served to capt. USAF, 1968-73, Vietnam. Mem. ABA, Calif. Bar Assn., Los Angeles County Bar Assn. Democrat. Office: Zalma and Berard 6319 W Slauson Ave Culver City CA 90230

BERARDINELLI, DAVID JOSEPH, lawyer; b. Santa Fe, Dec. 3, 1948; s. Joseph Anthony and Patricia (Boyd) B.; m. Deborah Lee Ortiz, June 9, 1979. BS, U. Santa Clara, 1971, JD cum laude, 1974. Bar: N.Mex. 1974, U.S. Dist. Ct. N.Mex. 1974, U.S. Supreme Ct. 1980. Assoc. Standley, Witt & Quinn, Santa Fe, 1974-75; asst. dist. atty. 1st Jud. Dist., Santa Fe, 1975-80; sole practice Santa Fe, 1980-85; ptnr. Berardinelli & Martinez, Santa Fe, 1985—. Commr. County Devel. Rev. Commn., Santa Fe, 1985-86. Mem. ABA, N.Mex. Bar Assn., Assn. Trial Lawyers Am., N.Mex. Trial Lawyers Assn. Democrat. Roman Catholic. Lodge: Rotary. Avocations: poetry composition, Mozart. Federal civil litigation, Personal injury, State civil litigation. Office: Berardinelli & Martinez 1462 St Francis Santa Fe NM 87504-1725

BERCHELMANN, DAVID ADOLPH, JR., judge; b. San Antonio, July 14, 1947; s. David A. and Nancy (Dole) B.; m. Dona Becker, June 12, 1971; children—Ashley, Shelby, David III, B.A., St. Mary's U., 1970, J.D., 1973. Bar: Tex. 1973, U.S. Dist. Ct. (we. dist.) Tex. 1976, U.S. Ct. Appeals (5th cir.) 1976, U.S. Supreme Ct. 1977. Asst. criminal dist. atty. Bexar County, Tex., San Antonio, 1973-80; assoc. firm Cobb, Thurmond, Bain & Clark, San Antonio, 1980-81; judge 290th Dist. Ct., San Antonio, 1981—. Mem. San Antonio United Way Vol. Ctr., 1984; bd. dirs. San Antonio YMCA, 1984. Named Outstanding Young Man of Am., U.S. Jaycees, 1982; recipient Community Service Restitution Week award, San Antonio, 1983. Mem. State Bar Tex., San Antonio Bar Assn. (vice chmn.), San Antonio Young Lawyers, Catholic Lawyers Guild (pres. 1983), Young Republicans Club, Tex. Dist. and County Attys. Criminal, Family and matrimonial, General practice. Office: 290th Dist Ct Bexar County Courthouse Main Plaza San Antonio TX 78228

BEREN, DANIEL EDWARD, lawyer; b. Phila., Nov. 3, 1929; s. Arthur and Frances (Shapiro) B.; m. Joan M. Cranmer, July 7, 1956; children: Day, Sandra, Jane. BA, Baldwin-Wallace Coll., 1952; JD, Temple U., 1956. Bar: Pa. 1955, U.S. Dist. Ct. (ea. dist.) Pa. 1963. Sole practice Phila., 1958-64; assoc. Waters, Fleer, Cooper & Gallagher, Jenkintown, Pa., 1971-76; ptnr. Beren, Deane & Clancey, Abington, Pa., 1964-70, Dilworth, Paxson, Kalish & Kauffman, Phila., 1976-86, Baskin Flaherty Elliott Mannion & Beren, Harrisburg, Pa., 1986—. Rep. Pa. Gen. Assembly, Harrisburg, 1967-76; chmn. Montgomery County Rep. Com., Norristown, 1971-78. Served to cpl. U.S. Army, 1955-57. Mem. Pa. Bar Assn., Montgomery Bar Assn., Dauphin County Bar Assn., Assn. Trial Lawyers Am., Am. Judicature Soc. Republican. Jewish. Legislative, Administrative and regulatory. Office: Baskin Flaherty Elliott Mannion & Beren 128 Walnut St Harrisburg PA 17101

BEREND, ROBERT WILLIAM, lawyer; b. Miami Beach, Fla., Dec. 31, 1931; s. George Harry and Miriam (Wagner) B. A.B., N.Y. U., 1952; LL.B., Yale U., 1955. Bar: N.Y. State 1955. Asst. gen. atty. to trustee Hudson & Manhattan R.R., N.Y.C., 1958-61; assoc. firm Delson & Gordon, N.Y.C., 1961-65; ptnr. Delson & Gordon, 1965-76; dir. Mgmt. Assistance Inc., N.Y.C., 1971-84; sec. Mgmt. Assistance Inc., 1970-86, sr. v.p., gen. counsel, 1976-86, trustee, counsel liquidating trust, 1986—; trustee, counsel Mgmt. Assistance, Inc., Liquidating Trust, 1986—. Served with U.S. Army, 1956-58. Mem. Am., N.Y. State bar assns., Assn. Bar City N.Y., Phi Beta Kappa. Clubs: Jewish. (N.Y.C.), Yale (N.Y.C.). General corporate. Home: 132 E 35th St New York NY 10016 Office: 900 3d Ave New York NY 10022

BERENDT, ROBERT T., lawyer; b. Chgo., Mar. 8, 1939. BA, Monmouth Coll., 1961; JD with distinction, U. Iowa, 1965. Bar: Iowa 1965, Ill. 1968, U.S. Dist. Ct. (no. dist.) Ill. 1968, U.S. Ct. Appeals (7th cir.) 1968, Mo. 1979, U.S. Dist. Ct. (ea. dist.) Mo. 1979. Assoc. Schiff, Hardin & Waite, Chgo., 1968-73, ptnr., 1973-78; litigation counsel Monsanto Co., St. Louis, 1978-83, asst. gen. counsel, 1983-85, assoc. gen. counsel, 1986—. Served to lt. USN, 1965-68. Mem. ABA, Ill. Bar Assn., Iowa Bar Assn., Mo. Bar Assn., St. Louis Met. Bar Assn. Federal civil litigation, State civil litigation, Personal injury. Office: Monsanto Corp 800 N Lindbergh Blvd Saint Louis MO 63167

BERENS, MARK HARRY, lawyer; b. St. Paul, Aug. 4, 1928; s. Harry C. and Gertrude M. (Scherkenbach) B.; m. Barbara Jean Steichen, Nov. 20, 1954; children: Paul J., Joseph F. (dec.), John M., Stephen M., Thomas M., Michael M., Lisa M., James M., Daniel. B.S.C. in Acctg. magna cum laude, U. Notre Dame, 1950, J.D. magna cum laude, 1951; postgrad., U. Chgo., 1951-53. Bar: Ill. 1951, D.C. 1955, U.S. Supreme Ct. 1971; C.P.A., Ill. James Nelson Raymond grad. research fellow U. Chgo. Law Sch., 1951-53; assoc. Mayer, Brown & Platt, and predecessors, Chgo., 1956-61; ptnr. Mayer, Brown & Platt, and predecessors, 1961—; chmn. bd. Attys.' Liability Assurance Soc. Ltd., Hamilton, Bermuda, 1979—, bd. dirs. Lancer Fin. Group Inc., Accts.' Liability Assurance Co.; nat. chmn. Nat. Assn. Law Rev. Editors, 1950-51; mem. nat. adv. com. Office Fgn. Direct Investment, U.S. Dept. Commerce, 1969-71. Contbr. articles to law publs.; editor-in-chief: Notre Dame Law Rev, 1950-51. Served as 1st lt. Judge Adv. Gen. Corps, U.S. Army, 1953-56. Mem. Am. Law Inst., ABA; mem. Internat. Bar Assn.; Mem. D.C. Bar Assn., Chgo. Bar Assn., Am. Assn. Atty.-C.P.A.'s, Japan-Am. Soc. Republican. Roman Catholic. Clubs: Union League, Law, Legal, Metropolitan (Chgo.). Private international, Corporate taxation, General corporate. Home: 1660 North Ln Northbrook IL 60062 Office: Mayer Brown & Platt 190 S LaSalle St Chicago IL 60603

BERENSON, WILLIAM KEITH, lawyer; b. Nashville, Nov. 23, 1954. BA with honors, U. Tex., 1976; JD, So. Meth. U., 1979. Bar: Tex. 1979, U.S. Dist. Ct. (no. dist.) Tex., U.S. Ct. Appeals (5th and 11th cirs.), U.S. Supreme Ct. Sole practice Ft. Worth, 1979—. Chmn. explorers dist. Longhorn Council Boy Scouts Am., Ft. Worth, 1986—. Mem. ABA, Tex. Bar Assn., Tarrant County Bar Assn., Assn. Trial Lawyers Am., Tarrant County Young Lawyers Assn. General practice, Family and matrimonial, Bankruptcy. Home: 3232 Wabash Ave Fort Worth TX 76109 Office: 900 River Plaza Tower Fort WOrth TX 76107

BERENZWEIG, JACK CHARLES, lawyer; b. Bklyn., Sept. 29, 1942; s. Sidney A. and Anne R. (Dubowe) B.; m. Susan J. Berenzweig, Aug. 8, 1968; children—Mindy, Andrew. B.E.E., Cornell U., 1964; J.D., Am. U., 1968. Bar: Va. 1968, Ill. 1969. Examiner U.S. Pat. Off., Washington, 1964-66; pat. adviser U.S. Naval Air Systems Command, Washington, 1966-68; ptnr. William Brinks Hofer Gilson & Lione Ltd. and predecessor firm, Chgo., 1968—. Editorial staff Am. U. Law Rev., 1966-68; contbr. articles to profl. jours. Mem. Chgo. Bar Assn., Ill. State Bar Assn., ABA, Bar Assn. 7th Fed. Cir., Va. State Bar, U.S. Trademark Assn. (bd. dirs. 1983-85), Delta Theta Phi. Club: Meadow (Rolling Meadows, Ill.). Patent, Trademark and copyright, Federal civil litigation. Home: 4119 Terramere Ave Arlington Heights IL 60004 Office: One IBM Plaza Suite 4100 Chicago IL 60611

BERESFORD, ROBERT, retired judge, arbitrator; b. Buenos Aires, Nov. 20, 1912; (parents Am. citizens); s. Robert and Janet Coats (Barrett) B.; m. Janet Coggeshall, Mar. 7, 1943. BA, 1934; LLB, Yale U., 1937. Bar: N.Y. 1938, Calif. 1946, U.S. Dist. Ct. (so. dist.) N.Y. 1941, U.S. Dist. Ct. (no. dist.) Calif. 1946. Assoc. Donovan, Leisure, Newton & Lumbard, N.Y.C., 1937-41; sole practice San Jose, Calif., 1946-63; judge Calif. Mcpl. Ct., San Jose, 1963-79; ret. judge, arbitrator 1979—; chmn. statutory Calif. Small Claims Ct. Exptl. Project, 1977-79; chmn. adv. council Friends Outside, 1976-81; jud. founder Neighborhood Small Claims Ct., San Jose, 1976, advisor, 1977—; arbitrator Am. Arbitration Assn., 1963, 79—, Calif. Statutory Ct. Annexed Arbitration Program, 1979—; mem. faculty Nat. Jud. Coll., 1972, 1971-76; mem. adv. council Nat. Ctr. for State Cts., 1971-76, assoc., 1985—. Served with USNR, 1940-45; commdr. JAGC, USNR (ret.), 1972—. Mem. ABA (dispute resolution com. liaison 1976-80, advisor 1980-86, council jud. adminstrn. div. 1970-71, 74-76), Am. Judicature Soc., U.S. Dist. Ct. Calif. Hist. Soc. (bd. dirs. 1979—), Nat. Conf. Spl. Ct. Judges (co-founder 1969, chmn. 1970-71, chmn. small claims ct. com. 1976-80, chmn. Flaschner award bd. 1981-85, co-chmn. 1986—, Chief Justice Flaschner award 1979), Calif. Judges Assn., Santa Clara County Bar Assn. (Justice Salsman award 1976). Clubs: Met. University, Commonwealth. Home: 2004 Adele Pl San Jose CA 95125

BEREZNOFF, GREGORY MICHAEL, lawyer; b. Grand Rapids, Mich., Aug. 10, 1951; s. Walter and Marjorie Ann (Nash) B. BA with high honors, Mich. State U., 1974; JD, U. Detroit, 1978. Bar: Mich. 1978, U.S. Dist. Ct. (ea. dist.) Mich. 1978. Assoc. Schureman, Frakes, Glass & Wulfmeier, Detroit, 1978-85, ptnr., 1986—. Mem. Wayne County Bar Assn., Oakland County Bar Assn. Avocations: tennis, fly casting. State civil litigation, Personal injury, Employment Litigation-Wrongful Discharge. Home: 3892 Old Creek Troy MI 48084 Office: Schureman Frakes Glass & Wulfmeier 400 Renaissance Ctr Suite 1800 Detroit MI 48243

BERG, ALAN, lawyer, government official; b. Scranton, Pa., June 5, 1947; s. Donald and Lucile (DeLugo) B.; m. Rita A. Samin, June 15, 1975; children—Thomas M., Matthew P., Andrew J. B.A., Hartwick Coll., Oneonta, N.Y., 1969; J.D., St. John's U., 1972; LL.M. in Labor Law, NYU, 1975. Bar: N.Y. 1973, U.S. Dist. Ct. (dists. N.Y.) 1973, U.S. Ct. Appeals 1973, U.S. Supreme Ct. 1976. Atty., N.Y. State Labor Relations Bd., 1972-79, adminstrv. law judge, 1979-80, chief judge, 1980-84, gen. counsel, 1984—; judge N.Y. Law Sch. Wagner Moot Ct., 1981—; advisor NYU Law Sch. student adv. program, 1983—. Trustee, Freeport Meml. Library (N.Y.), 1976-81; coach Freeport High Sch. summer basketball team, 1973—(9 league championships), N.Y. all-star team 30th and 31st ann. N.Y.-Phila. basketball festival, 1985, 86; arbitrator Better Bus. Bur. Mem. N.Y. State Bar Assn., Indsl. Relations Research Assn., St. John's Law Sch. Alumni Assn. Labor, Administrative and regulatory, State civil litigation. Home: 861 Lorenz Ave Baldwin NY 11510 Office: NY State Labor Relations Bd 400 Broome St New York NY 10013

BERG, DAVID HOWARD, lawyer; b. Springfield, Ohio, Mar. 4, 1942; s. Nathan Stewart Berg and Mildred (Besser) Berg-Filion; m. Dayle Black, Sept. 15, 1965 (div. Sept. 1977); children: Geoffrey Alan, Gabriel Adam. Student, Tulane U., 1963; BA, U. Houston, 1964, Jd, 1967. Bar: Tex., U.S. Dist. Ct. Tex., U.S. Ct. Appeals (2d, 4th, 5th and 11th) cirs., U.S. Supreme Ct. Law clk. NLRB, Washington, 1967-68; ptnr. Berg & Androphy and predecessor firm David Berg & Assocs., Houston, 1968—. Contbr. essays to mags. Issues staff Jimmy Carter Campaign, Atlanta, 1976; adv. Jimmy Carter Transition Govt., Washington, 1976, Kathy Whitmire Campaign, 1980, 85. Fellow Houston Bar Found.; mem. Tex. Bar Assn. (vice chmn. grievance com. 1984-85, chmn. 1985-86), Assn. Trial Lawyers Am., Nat. Assn. Criminal Def. Lawyers. Democrat. Jewish. Avocations: writing, running. Criminal, Federal civil litigation, Civil rights. Home: 2211 Inwood Houston TX 77019 Office: Berg & Androphy 3702 Travis Houston TX 77002

BERG, GALE DIANE, lawyer; b. Bklyn., June 24, 1951; d. Sidney and Evelyn (Schulman) B.; m. Joel Hochdorf, Feb. 8, 1981. B.A., Am. U., 1972; J.D., Vt. Law Sch., 1976. Bar: N.Y. 1977, D.C. 1978, U.S. Dist. Ct. (so. and ea. dists.) N.Y. 1978, U.S. Ct. Appeals (2d cir.) 1978. Asst. atty. gen. N.Y. State Dept. Law, N.Y.C., 1977-80; assoc. Fischbein Olivieri, Rozenholc & Badillo, N.Y.C., 1980; sole practice, N.Y.C., 1981-84; asst. counsel N.Y. State Racing and Wagering Bd., N.Y.C., 1984—; asst. adj. prof. bus. contract law Baruch Coll., 1982, asst. adj. prof. domestic relations, 1983; arbitrator N.Y.C. Civil Ct., 1983-84. Vol. Friends of Mario Cuomo, N.Y.C., 1984. Mem. ABA (chmn. subcom. on atty.'s fees of com. sole practitioners and small firms 1981-84, N.Y. State Bar Assn., N.Y. State Women's Bar Assn. (chmn. membership 1981-82). Administrative and regulatory, General practice, Judicial administration. Office: NY State Racing and Wagering Bd 400 Broome St New York NY 10013

BERG, JULIUS HARRY, lawyer; b. St. Louis, June 19, 1925; s. Ben and Sophie (Sokolik) B.; m. Marjorie R. Rosenbloom, Dec. 26, 1948; children—Andrew, Janice. B.S., St. Louis U., 1947; LL.B., Harvard U., 1950. Bar: Mo., 1950. Sole practice, St. Louis, 1950-74; pres. Julius H. Berg P.C., St. Louis, 1973—. Served with U.S. Army, 1943-46. Mem. Am. Bar Assn., Mo. Bar Assn., St. Louis Bar Assn. Jewish. Clubs: Meadowbrook Country, Masons, Elks (St. Louis). Real property, Probate, General corporate. Home: 83 Stoneyside Ln Olivette MO 63132 Office: 7777 Bonhomme St Suite 2222 Saint Louis MO 63105

BERG, NANCY ZALUSKY, lawyer; b. Mpls., June 1, 1951; d. Thomas John and Josephine (Lucas) Zalusky; m. Thomas Sherman Berg, Nov. 6, 1976; 1 child, Zachary Zalusky. BA, Antioch Coll., 1976; JD, Wm. Mitchell Coll. of Law, 1980. Bar: Minn. 1980, U.S. Dist. Ct. Minn. 1980, U.S. Ct. Appeals (8th cir.) 1980. Asst. city atty. Mpls., 1980-81, sole practice, 1981—; v.p., bd. dirs. Response to Abuse of Children. Mem. Minn. State Bar Assn. (chmn. child abuse, 1983), Henn. County Bar Assn. (chmn. juvenile law 1985). Avocation: competitive dressage style horseback riding. State civil litigation, Family and matrimonial, Juvenile. Office: Suite 620 Nat City Bank 510 Marquette Minneapolis MN 55402

BERG, THOMAS SIDNEY, lawyer; b. Washington, Mar. 19, 1952; s. Richard M. and Doris (Alexander) B.; 1 child, Amanda. BA, Rice U., 1974; JD, U. Houston, 1977. Bar: Tex. 1978, U.S. Dist. Ct. (so. dist.) Tex. 1978, U.S. Ct. Appeals (5th cir.) 1978, U.S. Ct. Appeals (11th cir.) 1981, U.S. Supreme Ct. 1982. Ptnr. Smith, Berg & Assocs., Houston, 1978-82; asst. atty. Fed. Pub. Defender, Houston, 1982-85, 1st asst. atty., 1985—. Del. Tex. Dem. Conv., Dallas, 1982; bd. dirs. Chinquapin, Houston, 1985—. Served to 1st lt. USAR, 1986—. Mem. ABA, Houston Bar Assn., Nat. Assn. Criminal Def. Lawyers, XV Inns of Ct. Criminal, Military. Office: Fed Pub Defender PO Box 61508 Houston TX 77208

BERGAMO, CHARLES, lawyer; b. Lakewood, N.J., Nov. 16, 1955; s. Thomas John and Antoinette (Tedesco) B. BA, Montclair State Coll., 1976; MA, Fordham U., 1979, JD, 1980. Bar: N.J. 1980, U.S. Dist. Ct. N.J. 1980, U.S. Tax Ct. 1982. Assoc. Breslin & Breslin, Hackensack, N.J., 1980-85; ptnr. Bergamo & Buonocore, Hackensack, 1985—. Sec. Dist. IIA Fee Arbitration com., Hackensack, 1985—; mem. Bergan County Legal-Medical com., Hackensack, 1984—. Mem. ABA, N.J. Bar Assn., Bergan County Bar Assn., Assn. Trial Lawyers Am., Trial Attys. N.J., Montclair State Coll. Law Alumni Assn. (co-chmn. 1986—), Fordham Law Sch. No. N.J. Alumni Assn. (bd. dirs. 1984—). Roman Catholic. Avocations: fishing, golf. State civil litigation, Real property, Contracts commercial. Home: 403 Anderson Ave Apt 2B Fairview NJ 07601 Office: Bergamo & Buonocore 61 Hudson St Hackensack NJ 07601

BERGEN, G. S. PETER, lawyer; b. Mineola, N.Y., Apr. 17, 1936; s. Hugh G. and Helen (Sawin) B.; m. Katherine Guthrie, July 28, 1964; children: Jennifer Guthrie, Anne Sawin, Lydia Kunkle. Geol. engr., Colo. Sch. Mines, 1958; J.D., Columbia U., 1962. Bar: N.Y. 1963, U.S. Dist. Ct. (ea. dist.) N.Y. 1964, U.S. Dist. Ct. (so. dist.) N.Y. 1964, U.S. Ct Appeals (2d cir.) 1966, D.C. 1968, U.S. Ct. Appeals (5th cir.) 1979, U.S. Ct. Appeals (D.C. cir.) 1973, U.S. Supreme Ct. 1968. Ptnr. LeBoeuf, Leiby & MacRae, N.Y.C.; bd. dirs. EA Engring. Sci. and Tech. Inc. Served as 2d lt. C.E. U.S. Army, 1958-59. Mem. ABA, N.Y. Bar Assn., Assn. Bar City N.Y., Fed. Energy Bar Assn. Club: Manhasset Bay Yacht, University. Environment, FERC practice, Nuclear power. Office: LeBoeuf Lamb Leiby & MacRae 520 Madison Ave New York NY 10022

BERGEN, KENNETH WILLIAM, lawyer; b. Harlingen, N.J., Sept. 13, 1911; s. Edward Burgess and Adelia (Mertz) B.; m. Emily Fetter; children—Bruce, Carol Franklin, Nancy, Roger. A.B., Rutgers U., 1934; LL.B., Harvard U., 1937; D.H.L. (hon.), Colby Coll., 1983. Bar: N.Y. 1938, Mass. 1943. Assoc., White & Case, N.Y.C., 1937-42; atty. Tax Ct. U.S., 1942-43; ptnr. Bingham, Dana & Gould, Boston, 1954—; pres. Mass. Continuing Legal Edn.-New Eng. Law Inst., Inc., 1974-77, trustee, 1969-78; co-chmn. Conf. Reps. of Am. Bar Assn. and trust div. Am. Bankers Assn., 1974-78; mem. adv. com. U.S. Ho. of Reps. Ways and Means Com. on Adminstrn. Fed. Tax Laws, 1956, income taxation estates and trusts, 1958; bd. dirs., co-founder Fed. Tax Inst. New Eng., 1948—; mem. adv. com. Tax Lawyer, 1975—; mem. planning com., co-founder Colby Coll. Estate Planning and Tax Inst., 1953—; mem. Mass. Bd. Registration C.P.A.s, 1956-60; dir., lectr. grad. tax program Northeastern U. Sch. Law, 1946-52; adv. com., lectr. Boston U. Law Sch. Grad. Tax Program; mem. adv. group Commr. of IRS. Moderator, Town of Lincoln (Mass.), 1966-78; mem. Lincoln-Sudbury Regional High Sch. Com., 1956-62; mem. Lincoln Rep. Town Com., 1950—, chmn., 1954-62. Mem. Am. Law Inst., Am. Bar Found., ABA (past sec., mem. council tax sect., tax sect.), Am. Coll. Probate Counsel (past regent), Am. Judicature Soc., Mass. Bar Assn., Boston Bar Assn. (mem. council, chmn. sect. profl. responsibility, chmn. com. on legislation), Mass. Soc. CPA's (hon.). Corporate taxation, Estate taxation. Office: 35th Floor 100 Federal St Boston MA 02110

BERGEN, THOMAS JOSEPH, lawyer, nursing home executive, association executive; b. Prairie du Chien, Wis., Feb. 7, 1913; s. Thomas Joseph and Emma Marilla (Grelle) B.; m. Jean Loraine Bowler, May 29, 1941 (dec. Aug. 1972); children—Kathleen Bergen McElwee, Eileen Bergen Bednarz, Patricia Bergen Buss, Thomas Joseph, Patrick Joseph, John Joseph. Student, U. Wis., 1930-32; J.D., Marquette U., 1937, postgrad., 1937-38. Bar: Wis. 1937, U.S. Supreme Ct. 1972. Practice law Milw., 1937—; exec. sec. Wis. Assn. Nursing Homes, 1957-71; legal counsel, exec. dir. Am. Coll. Nursing Home Adminstrs., Milw., 1967-68; sec., dir. Bayside Nursing Home, Milw., 1967—; pres., dir. N.W. Med. Ctrs., Inc., Milw., 1968—, Northland Med. Ctrs., Inc., Milw., 1968—; treas., exec. dir. Nat. Geriatrics Soc., Milw., 1971—; pres. Sen. Joseph R. McCarthy Found., Inc., 1983, pres. bd. dirs., 1979—; mem. program planning com. Nat. Conf. on Aging, del. to conf., 1974; panel speaker Nat. Justice Found. Conv., 1974. Editor: Silver Threads, Wis. Assn. Nursing Homes publ., 1963-71, News Letter, Am. Coll. Nursing Home Adminstrs., 1967-68; Views and News, Nat. Geriatrics Soc., 1971—; mem. editorial bd. Educational Gerontology, 1973-85; contbr. articles to nursing home publs. Bd. dirs., treas. Nat. Geriatrics Ednl. Soc., 1971—; bd. dirs., pres. Wis. Justice Found., 1971—. Served with AUS, 1943, 44. Recipient Merit award Wis. Assn. Nursing Homes, 1962, Outstanding Leadership award Nat. Geriatrics Soc., 1976. Mem. ABA, Wis. Bar Assn., Milw. Bar Assn. (pres., exec. dir.), Real Estate Profls. Assn. (pres. 1974—), Am. Med. Writers Assn., Delta Theta Phi, Delta Sigma Rho. Roman Catholic. Federal civil litigation, State civil litigation, Probate. Home: 10324 W Vienna Ave Wauwatosa WI 53222 Office: 212 W Wisconsin Ave Milwaukee WI 53203

BERGER, C. JAYE, lawyer; b. N.Y.C.. BA summa cum laude, SUNY, Buffalo, 1974; JD, Syracuse U., 1977; postdoctoral, Cornell U., 1977. Bar: Mich. 1978, Mass. 1982, N.Y. 1983. Ptnr. Lewis, White & Clay, Detroit, 1978-83; sr. assoc. Barry, LePatner & Assocs., N.Y.C., 1983-85; sole practice N.Y.C., 1985—. Contbr. articles on architecture to mags. Mem. forum com. on constrn. law, 1984—. Rackman fellow U. Mich., 1974-75. Mem. AIA, Inst. Bus. Designers, Assn. Women in Real Estate, N.Y.C. Bar Assn. (real estate com.), Art Deco Soc., Phi Beta Kappa. Construction, Computer, Real property. Office: 110 E 59th St 29th Floor New York NY 10022

BERGER, C. WILLIAM, lawyer; b. Pitts., Feb. 29, 1932; s. Morris M. and Dorothy June (Barkin) B.; m. Margaret R. Hornick, Aug. 20, 1957 (div. Nov. 1983); children: Jonathan Harvey, Jennifer Alix; m. Doreen Ann Yurik, Sept. 22, 1984. BA magna cum laude, Yale U., 1954, JD, 1957. Bar: Pa. 1957, U.S. Dist. Ct. (we. dist.) Pa. 1957, U.S. Ct. Appeals (3d cir.) 1972, U.S. Supreme Ct. 1974, Fla. 1981. Ptnr. Berger, Kapetan, Malakoff & Meyers, P.C. and predecessors, Pitts., 1957-82; sole practice Boca Raton, Fla., 1982—; mem. probationary officers selection bd. Dept. State, Washington, 1969-70; bd. dirs. Bay Fin. Savs. & Loan, Tampa, Fla. Chmn. 14th ward Reps., Pitts., 1969-70; gen. counsel Boca Raton Airport Authority, 1982—; candidate Pa. Legislature, Pitts., 1968. Mem. Fla. Bar, Allegheny

County Bar Assn., Lawyer Pilots Bar Assn., Assn. Trial Lawyers Am., Am. Acad. Forensic Sci., Phi Beta Kappa. Lodge: Masons (master 1967). Avocations: piloting own aircraft, skiing, cooking. Personal injury, Federal civil litigation, Aviation. Home: 8653 Twin Lake Dr Boca Raton FL 33434 Office: 412 Interstate Plaza Bldg 1499 W Palmetto Park Rd Boca Raton FL 33432

BERGER, CAROLYN, lawyer, judge; b. N.Y.C., Dec. 20, 1948; d. Melvin and Elaine Joyce (Ritter) B.; m. Fred S. Silverman, Feb. 15, 1981; children: Danielle Alexis, Michael Louis. B.A., U. Rochester, 1969; M.Ed., Boston U., 1971, J.D., 1976. Bar: Del. 1976, U.S. Dist. Ct. Del. 1976, U.S. Ct. Appeals (3d cir.) 1981, U.S. Supreme Ct. 1981. Dep. atty. gen. Del. Dept. Justice, Wilmington, 1976-79; assoc. firm Prickett, Ward, Burt & Sanders, Wilmington, 1979, Skadden, Arps, Slate, Meagher & Flom, Wilmington, 1979-84; vice-chancellor Ct. of Chancery, Wilmington, 1984—. Mem. Bd. Bar Examiners (assoc.), Del. Bar Assn., ABA. Office: Ct Chancery Pub Bldg Wilmington DE 19801

BERGER, CHARLES LEE, lawyer; b. Evansville, Ind. Oct. 14, 1947; s. Sydney L. and Sadelle (Kaplan) B.; m. Leslie Lilly, Apr. 20, 1973; children—Sarah, Rebecca, Leah. B.A., U. Evansville, 1969; J.D. cum laude, Ind. U., 1972. Bar: Ind. 1972, U.S. Dist. Ct. (so. dist.) Ind. 1972, U.S. Ct. Appeals (7th cir.) 1972, U.S. Ct. Appeals D.C. 1975, U.S. Supreme Ct. 1977, U.S. Dist. Ct. (we. dist.) Ky. 1981, U.S. Ct. Appeals (6th cir.) 1984. Ptnr., Berger & Berger, Evansville, 1972—. Bd. dirs. Leadership Evansville, 1977. Fellow Ind. Bar Found.; mem. Ind. Bar Assn. (chmn. trial lawyers sect. 1982-83), Am. Bd. Trial Advocates, Ind. Trial Lawyers Assn. (bd. dirs. 1973-77, 77-84, v.p. 1984—). Jewish. Personal injury, Federal civil litigation, State civil litigation. Home: 723 SE Riverside Evansville IN 47713 Office: Berger & Berger 313 Main St Evansville IN 47708

BERGER, CURTIS JAY, legal educator; b. Rochester, N.Y., Apr. 16, 1926; s. Samuel and Ruth (Taksen) B.; m. Constance Lindau, June 29, 1953 (div.); children: Ellen, John, Cathy, Wendy; married, Vivian O. Adler; June 17, 1973. A.B. with high honors, U. Rochester, 1948; J.D., Yale U., 1951. Bar: N.Y. 1951. Practice in Rochester, 1951-58; instr. law Yale U. Law Sch., 1958-60, vis. lectr., 1966; asso. prof. U. So. Calif. Law Sch., 1960-62; mem. faculty Columbia U. Law Sch., 1962—, prof. law, 1964—; now Lawrence A. Wien prof. real estate law, chmn. div. urban planning Sch. Architecture Columbia U., 1969-70; spl. cons. Nassau (N.Y.) County, 1964-66; lectr. U. Miss., 1967, Leiden U., Netherlands, 1968, NYU, 1969, Amsterdam U., Netherlands, 1971, 79, 85, Cornell U., 1978; vis. prof. public and internat. affairs Princeton U., 1975-82. Author: Land Ownership and Use, 1968, 2d edit., 1975, 3d edit., 1982, Law and Poverty, 1969, (with Axelrod and Johnstone) Land Transfer and Finance, 1971, 2d edit., 1978, 3d edit., 1986; bd. editors: Jour. Real Estate Taxation, Jour. Partnership Taxation; Contbr. profl. jours. Exec. dir. N.J. Commn. to Study Meadowland Devel., 1964-67; chmn. Englewood Redevel. Agy., 1968-69; Democratic candidate for N.Y. State Senate, 1956; Bd. dirs. Citizens Housing and Planning Council; chmn. Adv. Services for Better Housing, 1978-82, D.C. 37 Mcpl. Employees Legal Services Adv. Bd., 1977-82, The Bridge, 1981-86; mem. N.Y. Citizens Adv. Com. on Housing; exec. dir. West Side Task Force, 1986. Served with USNR, 1944-46. Mem. ABA, N.Y. State Bar Assn., Am. Coll. Real Estate Lawyers, Am. Law Inst., Order of Coif, Phi Beta Kappa, Phi Alpha Delta, Zeta Beta Tau. Club: Columbia Men's Faculty. Legal education, Real property, Estate taxation. Home: 20 W 64th St New York NY 10023 Office: Columbia U Law Sch New York NY 10027

BERGER, DAVID, lawyer; b. Archbald, Pa., Sept. 6, 1912; s. Jonas and Anna (Raker) B.; children—Jonathan, Daniel. A.B. cum laude, U. Pa., 1932, LL.B. cum laude, 1936. Bar: Pa. 1938, D.C., N.Y. Asst. to prof. U. Pa. Law Sch., Phila., 1936-38, spl. asst. to dean; law clk. Pa. Supreme Ct., Phila., 1939-40; spl. asst. to dir. enemy alien identification program U.S. Dept. Justice, Washington, 1941-42; law clk. U.S. Ct. Appeals, 1946; pvt. practice Phila., Washington and N.Y.C.; city solicitor Phila., 1956-63; former counsel Sch. Dist. Phila.; former chmn. adv. com. Pa. Superior Ct.; mem. adv. com. fed. rules evidence U.S. Supreme Ct.; lectr. on legal subjects including antitrust, securities, mass torts and class actions; founder, chmn. Berger & Montague, P.C. Author numerous articles on law. Nat. commr. Anti-Defamation League, B'nai B'rith; chmn. Anti-trust Inst.; mem. adv. bd. anti-trust and trade regulation report Bur. Nat. Affairs, Inc. Served to comdr. USNR, 1942-45. Decorated Silver Star, Presdl. Unit Citation. Fellow Am. Coll. Trial Lawyers, Internat. Acad. Trial Lawyers, Internat. Soc. Barristers; mem. ABA, Phila. Bar Assn. (pres., bd. govs., chancellor), Phila. Bar Found. (past pres.), Order of Coif. Antitrust, Securities, Class actions, commercial litigation, mass torts, toxic torts litigation. Home: One Breakers Row Palm Beach FL 33480 Office: Berger & Montague PC 1622 Locust St Philadelphia PA 19103

BERGER, HAROLD, engineer, lawyer; b. Archbald, Pa., June 10, 1925; s. Jonas and Anna (Raker) B.; m. Renee Margareten, Aug. 26, 1951; children: Jill Ellen, Jonathan David. B.S. in Elec. Engring, U. Pa., 1948, J.D., 1951. Bar: Pa. 1951. Since practiced in Phila.; judge Ct. of Common Pleas, Phila. County, 1971-72; Chmn., moderator Internat. Aerospace Meetings Princeton U., N.J., 1965-66; chmn. Western Hemisphere Internat. Law Conf., San Jose, Costa Rica, 1967; chmn. internat. Confs. on Aerospace and Internat. Law, Coll. William and Mary; permanent mem. Jud. Conf. 3d Circuit Ct. of Appeals; mem. County Bd. Law Examiners, Phila. County, 1961-71; chmn. World Conf. Internat. Law and Aerospace, Caracas, Venezuela, Internat. Conf. on Environ. and Internat. Law, U. Pa., 1974, Internat. Confs. on Global Interdependence, Princeton U., 1975, 79; mem. Pa. State Conf. Trial Judges, 1972-80, Nat. Conf. State Trial Judges, 1972—; chmn. Pa. Com. for Independent Judiciary, 1973—. Mem. editorial advisory bd.: Jour. of Space Law, U. Miss. Sch. of Law, 1973—; Contbr. articles to profl. jours. Mem. We the People 200 Com. for Constn. Bicentennial. Served with Signal Corps AUS, 1946-48. Recipient Alumnus of Year award Thomas McKean Law Club, U. Pa. Law Sch., 1965, Gen. Electric Co. Space award, 1966, Nat. Disting. Achievement award Tau Epsilon Rho, 1972, Spl. Pa. Jud. Conf. award, 1981. Mem. Inter-Am. Bar Assn. (past chmn. aerospace law com.), Fed. Bar Assn. (chmn. class action and complex litigation com. Phila. chpt. 1986—, past nat. chmn. com. on aerospace law, pres. Phila. chpt. 1983-84, nat. exec. council, nat. chmn. fed. and state jud. com., Presdl. award 1970, Nat. Distinguished Service award 1978), ABA (Spl. Presdl. Program medal 1975, past chmn. aerospace law com., mem. state and fed. ct. com., nat. conf. of state trial judges), Phila. Bar Assn. (chmn. jud. liaison com. 1975, past chmn. internat. law com. 1977), Assn. U.S. Mems. Internat. Inst. Space Law Internat. Astronautical Fedn. (dir.), Internat. Acad. Astronautics Paris (past v.p.). Office: 1622 Locust St Philadelphia PA 19103

BERGER, HARVEY CHARLES, lawyer; b. N.Y.C., Mar. 28, 1953; s. Richard and Lore (Polak) B.; m. Janice F. Mulligan, July 26, 1986. BA, SUNY, Stony Brook, 1974; MS, MIT, 1976; JD, U. San Diego, 1981. Bar: Calif. 1982, U.S. Dist. Ct. (so. dist.) Calif. 1982, U.S. Ct. Appeals (9th cir.) 1984. Rep. labor relations Stop & Shop Inc., Boston, 1976-78; mgr. personnel Zayre Corp., St. Paul, 1978-79; mgr. labor relations Fed Mart Stores, San Diego, 1979-80; cons. labor relations Mark D. Roberts & Assocs., San Diego, 1980-82; assoc. McInnis, Fitzgerald, Rees, Sharkey & McIntyre, San Diego, 1982-84, Haasis, Pope & Correll, San Diego, 1984—; organizer, mem. program com. MIT Enterprise Forum, San Diego, 1985—. Mem. San Diego County Bar Assn. (chmn. labor law subcom. legis. com., del. conv. 1984-85, 87), San Diego Trial Lawyers Assn., San Diego Def. Lawyers Assn. Libertarian. State civil litigation, Insurance, Personal injury. Office: Haasis Pope & Correll 101 W Broadway Suite 1130 San Diego CA 92101

BERGER, HOWARD CHARLES, lawyer; b. Bartlesville, Okla., Aug. 26, 1953; s. Donald Edwin Sr. and Alice Lynn (Street) B.; m. Diane Harris, Aug. 18, 1976; children: William Harris, Mark Nicholas, Jacob Grey. BA, Trinity U., 1974; JD, Washington U., St. Louis, 1977; postgrad., U. Tex., San Antonio, 1982—. Bar: Tex. 1977. Atty. Wilson County Child Welfare Bd., Floresville, Tex., 1980-85, vice chmn., 1982-84; sole practice Floresville, 1979—; atty. Wilson County, Floresville, 1985—; bd. dirs. Murray Guaranty Title Co., Floresville. County coordinator Hightower re-election campaign, Wilson County, 1980-84. Mem. ABA (natural resource sect., gen. practice sect.), Tex. Bar Assn. (family law sect., real estate and probate sect., oil and gas sect.), San Antonio Bar Assn., ACLU. Democrat. Avocations: history, jogging, politics. Oil and gas leasing, Real property, Local government. Home: Rt 2 Box 141-D Floresville TX 78114 Office: PO Box 299 Floresville TX 78114

BERGER, JOEL, lawyer; b. Bklyn., Apr. 16, 1944; s. M. Marvin and Lillian Berger; m. Barbara R. Pollack, Nov. 13, 1983. A.B., Columbia U., 1965; J.D., U. Chgo., 1968. Bar: N.Y. 1968, U.S. Dist. Ct. (so. and ea. dists.) N.Y. 1970, U.S. Ct. Appeals (2d cir.) 1970, U.S. Dist. Ct. (no. and we. dists.) N.Y. 1971, U.S. Supreme Ct. 1972, U.S. Ct. Appeals (5th cir.) 1977, U.S. Ct. Appeals (11th cir.) 1981, U.S. Ct. Appeals (6th cir.) 1982, U.S. Ct. Appeals (D.C. cir.) 1983, U.S. Ct. Appeals (8th cir.) 1985. Assoc. appellate counsel Legal Aid Soc., N.Y.C., 1968-71, dir. prisoners' rights project, 1971-77; atty. NAACP Legal Def. Fund, N.Y.C., 1977—; mem. exec. com. Citizens' Inquiry on Parole, N.Y.C., 1974-76, N.Y. State Council on Criminal Justice, N.Y.C., 1973-77; guest speaker. Mem. commn. on local candidates Citizens Union, N.Y.C. Recipient Karl Menninger award Fortune Soc., 1986. Mem. Assn. Bar City of N.Y. (legal assistance com.), Nat. Council on Crime and Delinquency, Correctional Assn. N.Y. Democrat. Jewish. Avocations: jogging; hiking; bicycle riding. Civil rights, Criminal.

BERGER, LAWRENCE DOUGLAS, lawyer; b. Phila., Oct. 2, 1947; s. Milton and Nellie Leah (Kean) B.; m. Caroline Eggerding, Jan. 14, 1984; 1 child, Jonathan Philip. BA, U. Pa., 1969; JD, Yale U., 1972. Bar: Pa. 1972, U.S. Dist. Ct. (ea. dist.) Pa. 1975, U.S. Ct. Appeals (3d cir.) 1976, U.S. Supreme Ct. 1978. Assoc. Dilworth, Paxson, Kalish & Kauffman, Phila., 1972-78, ptnr., 1978—. Mem. ABA (litigation sect., antitrust sect.), Pa. Bar Assn., Phila. Bar Assn. Club: Racquet. Federal civil litigation, State civil litigation.

BERGER, LAWRENCE HOWARD, lawyer; b. Phila., May 19, 1947; s. Howard Merrill Berger and Doris Eleanor Cummins; m. Julie Mitchell Collins, Aug. 8, 1970; children: Colby Shaw, Ryan Lawrence, Lindsey Wade. BS, Mich. State U., 1969; JD, U. Va., 1972. Bar: Pa. 1972, U.S. Dist. Ct. (ea. dist.) Pa. 1973. Assoc. Morgan, Lewis & Bockius, Phila., 1972-79, ptnr., 1979—; mem. adv. bd. Extended Care Inc., Bryn Mawr, Pa., 1985—; bd. dirs. INROADS/Phila. Bd. dirs. Agnes Irwin Sch., Rosemont, Pa., 1985—. Mem. ABA (sec. com. on nonprofit corps. 1980—), Pa. Bar Assn. (chmn. com. on uniform comml. code 1978-80), Phila. Bar Assn., Banking Law Inst. (lectr. 1985), Pa. Bankers Assn. (lectr. 1980), Blue Key, Omicron Delta Kappa. Clubs: Martins Dam (Wayne, Pa.), U. Va. (v.p. Phila. club 1985—). Banking, Consumer commercial, General corporate. Home: 360 Pond View Rd Devon PA 19333 Office: Morgan Lewis & Bockius 2000 One Logan Sq Philadelphia PA 19103

BERGER, MELVIN GERALD, lawyer; b. Bklyn., June 13, 1943; s. Louis and Lillian (Shapiro) B.; m. Ellen Terry Chelmow, Jan. 24, 1965; children—Michael R., Andrew R., Lee M. B.S., CCNY, 1965; M.S., NYU, 1967; J.D., George Washington U., 1971, LL.M., 1975. Bar: Md. 1972, U.S. Ct. Claims 1973, U.S. Ct. Customs and Patent Appeals 1972, D.C. 1986. Patent examiner U.S. Patent Office, Washington, 1967-69; patent advisor Dept. of Navy, Naval Ordnance Lab., White Oak, Silver Spring, Md., 1969-72, patent atty., 1972-73; law clk. U.S. Ct. Claims, Washington, 1973-74; trial atty. Antitrust div. Dept. of Justice, Washington, 1974-79; trial atty. Office of Gen. Counsel, Fed. Energy Regulatory Commn., Washington, 1979-84; atty. Brand & Leckie, 1984—. Cub Scout leader, 1977-79, 81-82; com. mem. Boy Scouts Am., 1979-86. Recipient Superior Performance award Dept. of Navy, 1973; Spl. Achievement award Dept. of Justice, 1976; Superior Job Performance award Fed. Energy Regulatory Commn., 1980, 82. Mem. ABA, Phi Beta Kappa, Order of Coif. Club: B'nai B'rith. Antitrust, FERC practice, Administrative and regulatory. Home: 6147 New Leaf Ct Columbia MD 21045 Office: 1730 K St NW Washington DC 20006

BERGER, ROBERT BERTRAM, lawyer; b. N.Y.C., Sept. 1, 1924; s. Edward William and Sophie (Berkowitz) B.; m. Phyllis Ann Korona, June 14, 1947; children—Barry Robert, Mark Alan, Karen Elizabeth, James Michael; m. 2d, Arlene Kidder Wills, Dec. 27, 1980; 1 step-dau., Kimberly Kidder Wills. B.S., Georgetown U., 1948; J.D., U. Conn., 1952. Bar: Conn. 1952, U.S. Dist. Ct. Conn. 1953, U.S. Tax Ct. 1967, U.S. Ct. Appeals (2d cir.) 1968. Sole practice, 1952-56; ptnr. Berger & Alaimo, Enfield, Conn., 1956-82, Berger, Alaimo & Santy, 1982—; bd. dirs., mem. exec. com. First Nat. Bank of Conn., Conn. Attys. Title Ins. Co., Rocky Hill, Conn.; sec., bd. dirs., exec. com. First Regional Bancorp, Inc. Chmn., Enfield Dem. Town Com., 1979-87, Conn. Psychiat. Security Review Bd., 1985—; pres. United Way of N. Cen. Conn., 1981-84; trustee St. Bernard's Roman Cath. Ch., 1977—, Johnson Meml. Hosp., Stafford, Conn.; corporator Bay State Med. Ctr., Springfield, Mass.; bd. dirs. United Way of Capitol Area, 1981-85. Served with USMCR, 1942-45. Decorated Purple Heart. Recipient Disting. Service award Enfield Jr. C. of C., 1955, Clayton Frost award U.S. Jr. C. of C., 1959-60. Mem. ABA, Conn. Bar Assn., Hartford County Bar Assn., Enfield Lawyers Assn. (pres. 1973-74), Am. Judicature Soc. Club: Enfield Rotary (pres. 1970-71, Paul Harris fellow 1984). Contbr. monthly polit. column Enfield Press, 1980-84. Probate, Real property, General corporate. Office: 709 Enfield St PO Box 98 Enfield CT 06082-0098

BERGER, SANFORD JASON, lawyer, securities dealer, real estate broker; b. Cleve., June 29, 1926; s. Sam and Ida (Solomon) B.; m. Bertine Mae Benjamin, Aug. 6, 1950 (div. Dec. 1977); children—Bradley Alan, Bonnie Jean. B.A., Case Western Res. U., 1950, J.D., 1952. Bar: Ohio 1952, U.S. Supreme Ct. 1979. Field examiner Ohio Dept. Taxation, Cleve., 1952; sole practice, Cleve., 1952—; real estate cons., Cleve., 1960—; investment cons., Cleve., 1970—. Contbr. author: Family Evaluation in Child Custody Litigation, 1982, Child Custody Litigation, 86. Copyright 10 songs, 1977. Candidate police judge, East Cleve., 1955, Bd. Edn., Beachwood, Ohio, 1963, mayor, Beachwood, 1967, judge ct. common pleas, Cuyahoga County, Ohio, 1984, 1986. Successful lawyer in U.S. Supreme Ct. Case of Cleveland Bd. of Edn. vs. Loudermill, 1985. Served with USMC, 1944-45; PTO. Recipient cert. Appreciation Phi Alpha Delta, 1969. Mem. Ohio State Bar Assn. (family law com.). Republican. Jewish. Lodge: B'nai B'rith (editor 1968-70). Avocations: poet; lyricist; legal writer; drag racer; scuba diving. Family and matrimonial, Civil rights, Constitutional. Home: 6809 Mayfield Rd Apt 972 Mayfield Heights OH 44124 Office: Berger and Fertel 1836 Euclid Ave #305 Cleveland OH 44115

BERGER, STEVEN R., lawyer; b. Miami, Fla., Aug. 23, 1945; s. Jerome J. and Jeanne B. B.; m. Francine Blake, Aug. 20, 1966; children—Amy, Charlie. B.S., U. Ala., 1967, J.D., 1969. Bar: Fla. 1969, U.S. Dist. Ct. (no. dist.) Fla. 1969, U.S. Dist. Ct. (so. dist.) Fla. 1971, U.S. Ct. Appeals (5th cir.) 1971, U.S. Supreme Ct. 1972, U.S. Ct. Claims 1977, U.S. Ct. Appeals (11th cir.) 1981. Assoc., W. Dexter Douglass, Tallahassee, Fla., 1969-71; assoc. William R. Dawes, Miami, 1971; ptnr. Carey, Dwyer, Cole Selwood & Bernard, Miami, 1971-81; sole practice, Miami, 1981—; mem. faculty Nat. Appellate Advocacy Inst., Washington, 1980. Chmn. City Miramar Planning Bd., 1975-76. Mem. ABA (vice chmn. app. practice com. litigation sect. 1981-83, chmn. 5th cir. subcom. appellate practice com. 1978-81), Tallahassee Bar Assn., Kendall-South Miami Dist. Bar Assn., Am. Judicature Soc., Dade County Def. Bar Assn., Fla. Def. Lawyers Assn., Def. Research Inst., Am. Arbitration Assn. (vice chmn. 4th dist. Ct. Appeals bench and bar adv. com. 1986—). Mem. editorial bd. Trial Adv. Quar.; contbr. articles to legal jours. State civil litigation, Insurance, Personal injury. Address: 8525 SW 92d St Miami FL 33156

BERGER, SYDNEY L., lawyer; b. N.Y.C., May 29, 1917; s. Abraham I. and Ruth (Levine) B.; m. Jean Danenberg, May 16, 1985; children: Charles Lee, Jeri Beth. B.S., Coll. City N.Y., 1936; J.D., Columbia U., 1940. Bar: N.Y. 1941, Ind. 1947, U.S. Supreme Ct. 1952. Atty. REA, 1941-43; individual practice law Evansville, Ind., 1946-72; ptnr. firm Berger & Berger, 1972—; adj. instr. law and polit. sci. Ind. State U., Evansville, 1971—; adj. lectr. legal medicine Ind. U. Med. Sch., Evansville, 1973—; adj. prof. law Ind. Law Sch., Indpls., 1974—. Mem. Mayor's Commn. on Human Relations; mem. Gov.'s advisory com. for Evansville State Psychiat. Treatment Center for Children, 1961-68; pres. Legal Aid Soc., Evansville, 1965. Served with AUS, 1943-45. Recipient James Bethel Gresham freedom award, 1971; Human Rights award City of Evansville, 1978. Mem. Am. Judicature Soc., ABA, Ind. Bar Assn. (Presdl. citation 1975, chmn. Ho. of Dels. 1980-81), Evansville Bar Assn. (pres. 1966), Am. Trial Lawyers Assn. (editor law jour. 1959-69, bd. govs. 1968-70), Ind. Trial Lawyers Assn. (pres. 1971-72), Am. Polit. Sci. Assn., Am. Arbitrators Assn. (nat. panel), Wilderness Soc., U. Evansville Acad. Arts and Scis. Personal injury, Federal civil litigation, State civil litigation. Home: 430 S Kelsey St Evansville IN 47714 Office: 313 Main St Evansville IN 47708

BERGERBEST, NATHAN STEVEN, lawyer; b. Bklyn., Oct. 4, 1957; s. Harry and Jeanette (Krinsky) B. BA, City Coll. of N.Y., 1979; JD, U. So. Calif., 1981. Bar: Calif. 1981, D.C. 1984. Atty. Exxon Co. USA, Thousand Oaks, Calif., 1981-84; assoc. Cotten, Day & Doyle, Washington, 1984—; pres. Suburban Radio News Service, Washington, 1985—. Contbg. reporter Intermountain Network, Salt Lake City, Utah, 1985—. Mem. transition adv. com. to Calif. Gov. George Deukmejian, Sacramento, 1983; mem. exec. com. Calif. Reps., Sacramento, 1982-84; pres. Calif. Rep. League, Los Angeles, 1982-84; bd. dirs. N.Y. Pub. Interest Research Group, N.Y.C., 1977-78. Mem. ABA, Radio-TV News Dirs. Assn. Republican. Jewish. General practice, Environment, Legislative. Office: Cotten Day & Doyle 1899 L St NW Washington DC 20036

BERGERSON, J. STEVEN, corporate lawyer; b. 1942. BA, U. Minn., 1965, JD, 1968. Asst. counsel Econs. Lab., 1969-73; gen. counsel Waste Mgmt. Inc., Oak Brook, Ill., 1973-84, v.p. gen counsel, 1984—. Office: Waste Mgmt Inc 3003 Butterfield Rd Oak Brook IL 60521 *

BERGHEL, VICTORIA SMOUSE, lawyer; b. Oakland, Md., Nov. 20, 1952; d. Edward Fraley Smouse and Martha Jean (Engelbach) Royer; m. Robert John Berghel Jr., Feb. 1, 1981; children: Brett Fraley, CLaire Louise. AA, Montgomery Coll., 1972; BA, U. Md., 1974, JD, 1977. Bar: Md. 1978. Assoc. Weinberg & Green, Balt., 1977-84, ptnr., 1985—; instr. legal writing U. Md. Sch. Law, Balt., 1977-78, real estate drafting and negotiation, 1986—. Bd. dirs. Wyman Park Community Assn., Balt., 1982-85, Travelers Aid Soc., Balt., 1983—. Mem. ABA (chmn. subcom. 1986—), Md. Bar Assn., Balt. City Bar Assn., Comml. Real Estate Women, Phi Beta Kappa. Episcopalian. Real property. Office: Weinberg & Green 100 S Charles St Baltimore MD 21201

BERGHOFF, PAUL HENRY, lawyer; b. Chgo., Aug. 25, 1956; s. John Colerick Sr. and Doris Margaret (Anderson) B.; m. Kathryn Elaine Thompson, May 30, 1981. B.A. cum laude in Chemistry, Lawrence U., 1978; J.D. cum laude, U. Mich., 1981. Bars: Ill. 1981, U.S. Dist. Ct. (no. dist.) Ill. 1981, U.S. Ct. Appeals (fed. cir.) 1983, U.S. Supreme Ct. 1986. Assoc. Allegretti, Newitt, Witcoff & McAndrews, Ltd., Chgo., 1981-85, ptnr. 1985—. Mem. ABA, Ill. Bar Assn., Chgo. Bar Assn., Patent Law Assn. Chgo. Mem. United Ch. of Christ. Federal civil litigation, Patent, Trademark and copyright. Office: Allegretti Newitt Witcoff & McAndrews 125 S Wacker Dr Chicago IL 60606

BERGHOLZ, WARREN ERNEST, JR., lawyer; b. Ft. Lewis, Wash., June 8, 1945; s. Warren Ernest Sr. and Doris Vera (Ripoli) B.; m. Natalie Sumter Tisdale, June 27, 1970; children: Rebecca, Peter. BA, U. Pitts., 1967; JD, U. Wyo., 1976. Bar: Wyo. 1976. Atty., advisor U.S. Dept. of Energy, Washington, 1976-83; chief counsel Savannah River ops. office Dept. of Energy, Aiken, S.C., 1983—. Served to lt. USNR, 1967-73, Vietnam. Mem. ABA, Fed. Bar Assn. Democrat. Avocations: golf, computers. Environment, Government contracts and claims, Nuclear power. Home: 724 Winged Foot Dr Aiken SC 29801 Office: Savannah River Ops Office PO Box A Aiken SC 29802

BERGMAN, ARLIE WALTER, lawyer; b. Escondido, Calif., Mar. 20, 1937; s. Orlando Arlie and Annie Esther Bergman; m. Coral Rhodes, Jan. 2, 1959; children: Carol Anne, Abigail Esther Kunz, Mary Rachel. BS in Acctg., San Diego State U., 1960; JD, Calif. Western Sch. Law, 1964. Bar: Calif. 1965, U.S. Dist. Ct. (so. dist.) Calif. 1965, U.S. Tax Ct. 1965. Assoc. Cox, Pendleton & Swan, Hemet, Calif., 1965; ptnr. Bergman & Lisi and predecessor firm Bergman & Roick, Escondido, 1966-86; sole practice Aguanga, Calif., 1986—. Estate taxation, Probate, Estate planning.

BERGMAN, BRUCE JEFFREY, lawyer; b. N.Y.C., May 15, 1944; s. Lawrence A. and Myrna (Coe) B.; m. Linda A. Cantor, May 30, 1971; children: Jennifer Dana, Jason Cole. BS, Cornell U., 1966; JD, Fordham U., 1969. Bar: N.Y. 1970, U.S. Dist. Ct. (so. dist.) N.Y. 1971, U.S. Supreme Ct. 1973, U.S. Dist. Ct. (ea. dist.) N.Y. 1973, U.S. Ct. Appeals (2d cir.) 1973. Assoc. law firm Jarvis, Pilz, Buckley & Treacy, N.Y.C., 1970-76; ptnr. law firm Pedowitz & Bergman, Garden City, N.Y., 1976-80; dep. county atty. Nassau County, Mineola, N.Y., 1980-84; counsel Jonas Libert & Weinstein, Garden City, 1981-84; ptnr. Roach & Bergman, 1984—; adj. assoc. prof. NYU Real Estate Inst., N.Y.C., 1981—. Author: New York Mortgage Foreclosures, 1983; contbr. numerous articles to legal jours.; contbg. editor: Mortgages and Mortgage Foreclosure in New York, 1982. Councilman, City of Long Beach, N.Y., 1980—. Mem. ABA, N.Y. State Bar Assn., Nassau County Bar Assn. (dir., chmn. real property law com.). Republican. Club: Cornell of L.I. (past pres.). Real property, Legal education, Construction. Home: 457 E Pine St Long Beach NY 11561 Office: Roach & Bergman 600 Old Country Rd Garden City NY 11530

BERGMAN, CAROL AMY, lawyer; b. Newark, Mar. 14, 1954; s. Jacob and Judith (Horowitz) B. BA, Hampshire Coll., 1976; JD, Golden Gate U., 1979. Bar: Mass. 1981, U.S. Dist. Ct. Mass. 1982. Dir. Help for Abused Women and Children, Salem, Mass., 1980-81; D.C. coordinator nat. moratorium on prison constrn. Unitarian Universalist Service Com., Washington, 1981-84, dir. nat. moratorium on prison constrn., 1984-86, dir. U.S. programs, 1986—. Editor Jericho Jour., 1981—. Steering com. Nat. Coalition for Jail Reform, Washington, 1981—; participant Congl. Black Caucus-Criminal Justice Braintrust, Washington, 1983—; bd. dirs. Offender Aid and Restoration Nat., Alexandria, Va., 1985—. Rockefeller Found. grantee, 1974. Mem. Nat. Lawyers Guild D.C. (pres. 1983-85, exec. bd. 1981—), Am. Correctional Assn., Nat. Orgn. Women, ACLU. Avocations: bicycling, gardening. Civil rights, Criminal, Legislative. Office: Unitarian Universalist Service Com 309 Pennsylvania Ave SE Washington DC 20003

BERGMAN, GREGORY MARK, lawyer; b. Los Angeles, Sept. 12, 1947; s. Lloyd A. Bergman and Norma Koskoff; m. Leah Schneider Bergman; children: Brian, Alex. BA, UCLA, 1970; JD, S.W. U., Los Angeles, 1975. Bar: Calif. 1975, U.S. Dist. Ct. (cen. dist.) Calif. 1975, U.S. Ct. Appeals (9th cir.) 1975, U.S. Ct. Claims 1977, U.S. Supreme Ct. 1985. Assoc. Fadem, Berger & Norton, Santa Monica, Calif., 1975, Irmas, Simke & Chodos, Los Angeles, 1983; ptnr. Bergman & Wedner, Los Angeles, 1983—. Contbr. articles to profl. jours. Mem. ABA, Assn. Trial Lawyers Am., Assn. Real Estate Attys., Los Angeles County Bar Assn., Chancellor's Assn. Avocation: Tai Kwon Do. Federal civil litigation, State civil litigation. Office: Bergman & Wedner Inc 10880 Wilshire Blvd Suite 1011 Los Angeles CA 90024

BERGMANN, LARRY EDWARD, lawyer; b. Bklyn., Mar. 20, 1949; m. Zaida D. Atanacio, Jan. 21, 1978; children: Heather Brooke, Lauren Whitney. BS, MIT, 1971; JD, Boston Coll., 1975. Bar: Mass. 1975, D.C. 1978. Atty. enforcement SEC, N.Y.C., 1975-78, br. chief enforcement, 1978-84; asst. dir., market regulation SEC, Washington, 1984—. Bd. dirs. Leewood Homeowners Assn., Inc., Springfield, Va., 1980—. Mem. ABA, Order of Coif. Securities. Home: 7058 Leebrad St Springfield VA 22151 Office: SEC 450 Fifth St NW Washington DC 20549

BERGNER, WILLIAM JOSEPH, lawyer; b. Sidney, Nebr., Aug. 17, 1948; s. Lyle Francis and Marilyn Lucille (Wood) B.; m. M. Denise, Sept. 23, 1982; children: Nicole Leah Harris, William Joseph Jr. BS in Distributive Edn., U. N.D., 1970; JD, U. Okla., 1981. Bar: Okla. 1981, U.S. Dist. Ct. (we. dist.) Okla. 1981, U.S. Ct. Appeals (10th cir.) 1982, U.S. Dist. Ct. (no. dist.) Okla. 1983, U.S. Dist. Ct. (ea. dist.) 1985, U.S. Supreme Ct. 1986. Mgr. trainee Northwestern Bell, Grand Forks, N.D., 1971-73; mgr. Northwestern Bell Co., Williston, N.D., 1973-74; assoc. Stewart & Elder, Oklahoma City, 1981—. Pres. Distributive Edn. Clubs Am., Williston, 1970-71. Served to sgt. USAF, 1974-78. Mem. ABA, Okla. Bar Assn., Okla. Assn., Def. Counsel, Okla. County Bar Assn. Democrat. Federal civil litigation, State civil litigation, Insurance. Office: Stewart & Elder 1329 Classen Dr PO Box 2056 Oklahoma City OK 73101

BERGONIA, RAYMOND DAVID, investment banker; b. Spring Valley, Ill., May 21, 1951; s. Raymond A. and Elva M. (Bernadini) B. B.B.A., U.

Notre Dame, 1973; J.D., Harvard U., 1976. Bar: Ill. 1976, U.S. Dist. Ct. (no. dist.) Ill. 1976, U.S. Tax Ct. 1977; C.P.A., Ill. Assoc. Winston & Strawn, Chgo., 1976-79; legal counsel, v.p. adminstrn. Heizer Corp., Chgo., 1979-86; v.p. corp. fin. Chgo. Corp., 1986—. Treas. Wrigthwood Dayton Condominium Assn., 1982-86. Recipient Elijah Watts Sells award Am. Inst. C.P.A.s, 1973. Mem. ABA, Chgo. Bar Assn. General corporate, Securities, Corporate taxation. Home: 842 W Wrightwood Apt 3 Chicago Il 60614 Office: Chgo Corp 208 S LaSalle St Chicago IL 60604

BERGSTEIN, DANIEL GERARD, lawyer; b. Nice, France, May 1, 1943; came to U.S., 1952; s. Max and Suzanne (Fenigstein) B.; m. Barbara J. Rabiner, June 20, 1965; children: Jordan, Elizabeth C. BA, CUNY, 1965; JD, Bklyn. Law Sch., 1968. Bar: N.Y. 1968, Fla. 1974. From assoc. to ptnr. Greenbaum, Wolff & Ernst, N.Y.C., 1982; ptnr. Reavis & McGrath, N.Y.C., 1982-85, Finley, Kumble, Wagner, Heine, Underberg, Manley, Myerson & Casey, N.Y.C., 1985—; bd. dirs. Robeson Industries Corp., Mineola, N.Y. Bd. dirs. The Vitas Gerulaitis Youth Found., Great Neck, N.Y. Mem. ABA, French-Am. C. of C. in U.S. Venture capital, General corporate, Securities. Office: Finley Kumble Wagner Heine et al 425 Park Ave New York NY 10022

BERGSTROM, ROBERT WILLIAM, lawyer; b. Chgo., Nov. 8, 1918; s. C. William and Ellen (Anderson) B.; m. Betty Howard; children: Mark Robert, Philip Alan, Bryan Scott, Cheryl Lee, Jeffrey Alan. M.B.A., U. Chgo., 1947; LL.B., Ill. Inst. Tech.-Chgo. Kent Coll. Law, 1940, J.D., 1970. Bar: Ill. 1940, U.S. Supreme Ct. 1950. Ptnr. Bergstrom, Davis & Teeple (and predecessors), 1951—; founder Ill. Statewide Com. on Cts. and Justice, 1971—; bd. dirs. Ill. Com. for Constl. Conv., 1969, Ill. Constl. Research Group, 1970; spl. counsel Ill. Joint Legislative Com. to Investigate Met. San. Dist. of Cook County, 1967, Ill. Senate Mcpl. Corp. Com., 1970. Co-author: The Law of Competition in Illinois, 1962, Antitrust Developments, 1955-68, Antitrust Advisor, 1985; author Marxism, Senator Sherman, and Our Economic System, 1968, and numerous articles on antitrust, constl. law, and econs.; Editor: Chgo. Bar Record, 1971-72. Served to lt. USNR, 1941-46. Named Chicagoan of Yr. in Law and Judiciary Chgo. Jaycees, 1969; recipient medal Ill. Constl. Conv., 1970, Disting. Pub. Service award Union League Club, 1981. Mem. ABA, Ill. Bar Assn., Chgo. Bar Assn. (sec. 1969-71). Club: Union League (pres. 1971-72). As chmn. Com. for Legis. Reform, drafted constl. amendment enacted 1980, reducing Ill. Ho. of Reps. by 1/3 and abolishing cumulative voting. Antitrust, Federal civil litigation, State civil litigation. Office: Bergstrom Davis & Teeple 39 S LaSalle St Suite 800 Chicago IL 60603

BERINGER, WILLIAM ERNST, electrical equipment manufacturing company executive, lawyer; b. Madison, Wis., Oct. 24, 1928; s. William and Martha M. (Wupper) B.; m. Marilyn J. Walter, Aug. 4, 1984; children: Amy, Julia, Barry, Thomas, Maureen. BA summa cum laude, Lawrence Coll., 1950; JD with distinction, U. Mich., 1953. Bar: Mich. 1953, Wis. 1953, Ill. 1955, Ga. 1978. Assoc. firm Vedder, Price, Kaufman & Kammholz, Chgo., 1953-56; atty. law dept. Swift & Co., Chgo., 1956-71; dir. gen. law dept. Allis-Chalmers Corp., Milw., 1971-77; v.p., gen. counsel, sec. Siemens Energy & Automation, Inc. and Utility Power Corp., Atlanta, 1978—; bd. dirs. corp. banking and bus. law sect. Wis. Bar, 1976-78; mem. antitrust and corp. policy com. U.S. C. of C., 1974-80. Editorial bd. Mich. Law Rev, 1952-53. Bd. dirs. Hinsdale (Ill.) Community Concert Assn., 1969-71, Dupage County (Ill.) Girl Scouts U.S., 1969-71, Clarendon Hills (Ill.) Community Chest, 1968-70; vice chmn. Clarendon Hills Human Relations Commn., 1968-70; mem. Chgo. study team Nat. Commn. on Causes and Prevention Violence, 1968. Mem. ABA, Ga. Bar Assn., Atlanta Bar Assn., Am. Corp. Counsel Assn. (bd. dirs. Ga. chpt.), Order of Coif. Republican. Congregationalist. Club: Cherokee Town and Country. Antitrust, Contracts commercial, General corporate. Home: 9010 River Run Atlanta GA 30350 Office: 223 Perimeter Center Pkwy Atlanta GA 30346

BERK, JOHN STEVEN, lawyer; b. Ft. Lauderdale, Fla., July 26, 1950; s. Theodore and Tookie (Heyboer) B.; m. Natalie Barone, Aug. 1, 1970; 1 son, Justin. B.A., U. Miami, 1972, J.D., 1974. Bar: Fla. 1975, U.S. Dist. Ct. (so. dist.) Fla. 1975, U.S. Ct. Appeals (5th cir.) 1975, U.S. Dist. Ct. (we. dist.) Tex. 1979, U.S. Dist. Ct. (ea. dist.) Mich. 1981, U.S. Tax Ct. 1981, U.S. Ct. Appeals (9th cir.) 1981, U.S. Supreme Ct. 1982. Asst. atty. U.S. Dist. Ct. (so. dist.) Fla., Miami, 1974-77; sole practice, Ft. Lauderdale, 1977—. Mem. ABA, Assn. Trial Lawyers Am., Broward County Trial Lawyers Assn., Fed. Bar Assn. (pres. Broward County chpt. 1977-78), Fla. Bar Assn., Acad. Fla. Trial Lawyers, Fla. Criminal Def. Lawyers Assn. (past bd. dirs.), Nat. Assn. Criminal Def. Lawyers, Internat. Platform Assn. Club: African Safari Fla., Delta Theta Phi. Criminal. Office: 633 S Federal Hwy Ft Lauderdale FL 33301

BERKELHAMMER, ROBERT BRUCE, lawyer; b. Providence, Oct. 27, 1949; s. Cyril Lester and Anne Louise (Rossman) B.; m. Miriam June Finkelstein, Mar. 9, 1975; children: Jessi, Max, Abby. BA, U. Rochester, 1971; JD, Boston U., 1974. Bar: R.I. 1975, U.S. Dist. Ct. R.I. 1977. Atty. NLRB, Pitts., 1974-77; ptnr. Licht & Semonoff, Providence, 1977—. V.p. Jewish Family Service, Inc.; Providence, 1985—. Mem. ABA, R.I. Bar Assn. Jewish. Real property, Contracts commercial, General corporate. Home: 131 Laurel Ave Providence RI 02906 Office: Licht & Semonoff 1 Park Row Providence RI 02903

BERKIN, JEFFREY JACK, lawyer, educator; b. Washington, Jan. 1, 1957; s. Gerald Landon and Harriet (Lichter) B.; m. Stephanie Leigh Buchanan, Oct. 9, 1982. AB, Coll. William and Mary, 1978; JD, Am. U., 1981. Bar: Va. 1981, U.S. Dist. Ct. (ea. dist.) Va., 1981, U.S. Ct. Appeals (4th cir.) 1981, U.S. Bankruptcy Ct. 1981. Trial atty. Compton, Bergere & Lubeley, Woodbridge, Va., 1981-83; supervisory spl. agt. FBI, Los Angeles, 1983—; legal advisor, instr. FBI, Los Angeles, 1986—. Named hon. officer Compagnie Republicaine de Securite, France, 1985. Mem. FBI Agent's Assn. Administrative and regulatory, Federal civil litigation, Government contracts and claims. Office: FBI Hdqrs 10th and Pennsylvania Aves NW Washington DC 20535

BERKLAND, ROGER ALAN, lawyer; b. Cylinder, Iowa, Nov. 1, 1938; s. Amos and Pearl (Knudson) B.; m. Linda L. Freeman, June 25, 1961; children: Terry, Pamela, Jackie, Roger Grant. BBA, U. Iowa, 1960, JD, 1968. Bar: Iowa, 1968. Assoc. Carl L. Spies Law Office, Emmetsburg, Iowa, 1968-70; ptnr. Berkland & Brown, Emmetsburg, 1970—; atty. County of Palo Alto, Emmetsburgh, 1969-76. Chmn. Palo Alto County Reps., Emmetsburg, 1970-74. Served to sgt. USNG, 1962-67. Mem. ABA, Iowa Bar Assn., Palo Alto County Bar Assn., Assn. Trial Lawyers Iowa, Ducks Unltd. Republican. Lutheran. Clubs: Iowa Lakes. Avocations: fishing, hunting. General practice, Probate, Personal income taxation. Home: Rural Rt Emmetsburg IA 50536 Office: Berkland & Brown 2112 Main St PO Box 246 Emmetsburg IA 50536

BERKLEY, PETER LEE, lawyer; b. Newark, Mar. 10, 1939; s. Irving S. and Goldie (Karp) B.; m. Nancy Margolis, Aug. 2, 1964; children—James, Alison, John. B.A., Williams Coll., 1960; J.D., Harvard U., 1963. Bar: N.J. 1963, U.S. Dist. Ct. (N.J.) 1963. Assoc. Riker, Danzig, Scherer & Brown, Newark, 1963-68; ptnr. Riker, Danzig, Scherer, Hyland & Perretti, Newark, 1969—, sr. ptnr. Morristown, N.J., 1980—, mng. ptnr., 1984—; dir. Newark Watershed Conservation & Devel. Corp., Newark, 1973-85. Trustee Livingston Symphony Orch (N.J.), 1975—, Morristown & Morris Twp. Library Found., 1983—. Mem. ABA, N.J. State Bar Assn., Essex County Bar Assn., Harvard Law Sch. Assn. N.J. (pres. 1980-81), Williams Coll. Alumni Assn. Cen. N.J. (pres. 1986—), Am. Coll. Real Estate Lawyers, Phi Beta Kappa. Club: Mountain Ridge Country (West Caldwell, N.J.). Real property, Landlord-tenant, Contracts commercial. Home: 16 Fordham Rd Livingston NJ 07039 Office: Riker Danzig Scherer Hyland & Perretti 1 Speedwell Ave Headquarters Plaza Morristown NJ 07960

BERKOW, MICHAEL, legal advisor; b. San Antonio, Tex., Apr. 13, 1955; s. Robert and Esther (Leavitt) B. BA, Kalamazoo Coll., 1978; JD, Syracuse U., 1981. Officer Rochester (N.Y.) Police Dept., 1976-82, legal advisor, 1983-86, sgt., 1986—; law clk. to presiding justice U.S. Dist. Ct. N.Y., Rochester, 1982-83. Mem. Monroe County Human Rights Com. Task Force on Police, Rochester, 1975—, Bristol Mountain Ski Patrol, Nat. Ski Patrol; bd. dirs. Community Partners for Youth, Rochester, 1985—. Mem. ABA, N.Y. State Bar Assn. (criminal justice-police com.), Monroe County Bar Assn. (continuing legal edn. com., bd. dirs. VISION 1985—), Internat. Assn. Chiefs of Police (legal officers sect.). Criminal, Civil rights. Office: Rochester Police Dept 150 S Plymouth Ave Rochester NY 14614

BERKSON, JACOB BENJAMIN, lawyer, writer, conservationist; b. Washington County, Md., Dec. 6, 1925; s. Meyer and Ida Evelyn (Berman) B.; m. Ann Goldstein, June 25, 1955 (div.); children—Daniel Jeremy, Susan Kay, Meyer James; B.A., U. Va., 1947, LL.B., 1949, J.D., 1970; grad. Fed. Exec. Inst., Charlottesville, Va., 1972. Bar: Md. 1949, Va. 1949, U.S. Supreme Ct. 1965, Calif. 1975. Sole practice, Hagerstown, Md., 1949-52, 54-65; ptnr. McCauley, Cooey, Berkson & Wright, Hagerstown, 1964-70; dep. gen. counsel GSA, Washington, 1970-76; sole practice, Hagerstown, Md., 1976—; instr. Law Hagerstown Bus. Coll.; trial magistrate, Hagerstown and Washington County, Md., 1951-52; mem. Legis. Council Md., 1955-58; del. Md. Legislature, 1955-58; trial magistrate, Hagerstown, Md., 1958-59. Author: Shingahi Saburo and Short Stories, 1978; contbr. address to Congrl. Record. Organizer, dir. County Youth Conservation Corps; active Big Bros.; developer Doub's Woods County Park, Devil's Backbone County Park; assisted in establishment of C&O Canal Nat. Hist. Park, 1954-70; camp sponsor YMCA; adv. Model Youth Legislature; pres. PTA; active Boy Scouts Am.; chmn. Washington County Pk. Commn., 1961-66. Recipient commendation for service to U.S. Naval Acad. and pub. interest Chief of Naval Personnel, 1956. Served to lt. USNR, 1944-46, 52-54. Mem. ABA, Calif. Bar, Va. Bar, Md. Assn. County Civil Attys. (pres., award for services as pres. 1966), Bar Assn. Washington County (pres.). Republican. Jewish. Clubs: Hagerstown, Am. Legion. Lodges: Lions, Moose. State civil litigation, General practice, Personal injury. Home and Office: 1419 Potomac Ave Hagerstown MD 21740

BERLEY, DAVID RICHARD, lawyer; b. Bklyn., Apr. 9, 1942; s. Alexander and Ruth (Ginsburg) B.; m. Sharon Lee Freeman, Aug. 10, 1964 (div. 1975); children—Steven N., Barbara Robin. B.S., Boston U., 1963; J.D., Boston Coll., 1966. Bar: Mass. 1966, Fla. 1977. Corp. and pvt. practice, 1966-77; gen. counsel Econocar Internat. Inc., Miami, Fla., 1976-77; v.p., gen. counsel Emergency Med. Services Assn., Inc., Miami, 1977-79; sole practice, Miami, 1979-85; ptnr. Berley & Littman, P.A., 1985— . Bd. dirs. Community Habilitation Ctr.; active Greater Miami Heart Assn., Jewish Fedn. Greater Miami. Mem. ABA, Mass. Bar Assn., Am. Trial Lawyers Assn., Fla. Bar Assn., Boston Coll. Law Sch. Alumni Assn. Commercial, Banking, Real property. Office: 202 Brickell Exec Tower 1428 Brickell Ave Miami FL 33131

BERLIN, ALAN DANIEL, lawyer, oil company executive; b. Bklyn., Oct. 20, 1939; s. Joseph Jacob and Rose (Smith) B.; m. Renee Wellinger, Dec. 22, 1962; children—Nicole Suzanne, Allison Leigh. B.B.A., CCNY, 1960; LL.B., NYU, 1963, LL.M., 1968. Bar: N.Y. 1963. Assoc. Aranow, Brodsky, Bohlinger, Einhorn & Dann, N.Y.C., 1965-68; asst. counsel Gen. Electric Co., N.Y.C., 1968-70; tax counsel Norton Simon Inc., N.Y.C., 1970-77; pres. Belco Petroleum Corp., N.Y.C., 1977—; asst. prof. Pace U. Grad. Sch. Bus., 1977-85. Author monographs on fed. income tax. Bd. dirs. Mental Health Assn., Westchester; vice chmn. Briarcliff Manor (N.Y.) Peoples Caucus. Served with U.S. Army, 1963-65. Mem. Am. Bar Assn., N.Y. State Bar Assn., Assn. Bar City N.Y., Inter-Am. Bar Assn. Lodge: Masons. General corporate, Corporate taxation, Private international. Office: 1 Dag Hammarskjold Plaza New York NY 10017

BERLIN, MARK A., lawyer; b. Bklyn., Nov. 1, 1944; s. Roy and Bess (Wolfe) B.; m. Renee D., June 7, 1970; children—Robert, Brian, Steven. B.S. in Econs., N.Y.U., 1966; LL.M., 1973; J.D., Bklyn. Law Sch., 1969. Bar: N.Y. 1970, Fla. 1979. With Touche Ross & Co., 1969-73; asso. Seidman & Seidman, N.Y.C., 1973-75; ptnr. Schulman & Berlin P.C., N.Y.C., 1975—, mng. atty. Mem. ABA, N.Y. State Bar Assn., Fla. Bar Assn., Am. Inst. C.P.A.s, N.Y. State Soc. C.P.A.s, Faculty Fedn. for Acctg. Estate taxation, Personal income taxation, Probate. Home: 21180-13 Mainsail Circle North Miami Beach FL 33180

BERLINER, L. JED, lawyer; b. Bklyn., Oct. 14, 1950; s. Emanuel R. and Ruth Leah (Tabacoff) B.; m. Karen F. Blair, Dec. 29, 1984. AB, Cornell U., 1972; JD, U. Kans., 1977. Bar: Mich. 1978, U.S. Dist. Ct. (we. dist.) Mich. 1978, U.S. Dist. Ct. (ea. dist.) Mich. 1979, Mass. 1982, U.S. Dist. Ct. Mass. 1982, U.S. Ct. Appeals (1st cir.) 1985, U.S. Dist. Ct. Conn. 1986. Atty. Upper Penisula Legal Services Inc., Sault Ste. Marie, Mich., 1977-80, Thompson, Zirnhett, Bowron & Senger, Traverse City, Mich., 1980-81; assoc. Silverman & Kudisch, Boston, 1982-84, Kamberg, Berman & Gold, Springfield, Mass., 1985—. Mem. Mass. Bar Assn. (rules ct. com.). Federal civil litigation, State civil litigation, Bankruptcy. Home: 291 Bennett Rd Hampden MA 01036-9653 Office: Kamberg Berman & Gold 31 Elm St Springfield MA 01103

BERLY, JOEL ANDERSON, III, lawyer; b. Clinton, N.C., Aug. 13, 1956; s. Joel Anderson Jr. and Betty Carl (Ussery) B. BS in Zoology, Clemson U., 1978; JD, Wake Forest U., 1981. Bar: S.C. 1982, U.S. Dist. Ct. S.C. 1982, U.S. Ct. Appeals (4th cir.) 1982, N.C. 1986. Staff asst.judiciary com. U.S. Senate, Washington, 1980; assoc. Hyman, Morgan, Brown et al, Florence, S.C., 1981-84; trial atty. environ. occupational disease litigation group, torts br. civil div. U.S. Dept. Justice, Washington, 1984-86; assoc. Blatt & Fales, Charleston, S.C., 1986—. Named one of Outstanding Young Men in Am., 1978. Mem. ABA, S.C. Bar Assn., Assn. Trial Lawyers Am., Blue Key. Republican. Methodist. Avocations: golf, travel, biking, history. Federal civil litigation, Personal injury. Home: 1164 Shadow Lake Circle Mount Pleasant SC 29464 Office: Blatt & Fales 174 E Bay St PO Box 1137 Charleston SC 29402

BERMAN, BENNETT I., lawyer; b. Chgo., Oct. 29, 1918; s. Reuben and Lillian (Diamond) B.; m. Nancy Baer, Nov. 16, 1944; 1 dau., Cynthia Ann Berman Watson. B.S., U. Ill., 1940; LL.B., Harvard U., 1943. Bar: Ill. bar 1947. Gen. counsel Investors Realty & Mgmt. Co., Chgo., 1963-66; chief counsel, v.p. Nat. Tea Co., Rosemont, Ill., 1966—. Contbr. articles to profl. publs. Served to lt. USNR, 1942-46. Mem. Ill. Bar Assn., Chgo. Bar Assn. (chmn. landlord and tenant subcom., lectr. continuing legal edn., Certificate of Appreciation). Clubs: Harvard of Chgo. (Chgo.) (dir.), Harvard of N.Y. Home: 860 N Lake Shore Dr Chicago IL 60611 Office: 9701 W Higgins Rd Rosemont IL 60018

BERMAN, DAVID, lawyer, poet; b. N.Y.C., Sept. 11, 1934; s. Joseph and Sophie (Hersh) B. B.A. with honors, U. Fla., 1955; postgrad. Johns Hopkins U., 1955-56; J.D., Harvard U., 1963. Bar: Mass. 1963. Law clk. to justice Mass. Supreme Ct., 1963-64; asst. atty. gen. Commonwealth of Mass., 1964-67; assoc. Zamparelli & White, 1967, ptnr., 1968-74; sole practice, 1974-82; ptnr. Berman and Moren, Medford, Mass., 1982—. Author: Future Inperfect, 1982. Trustee Cantata Singers, 1981—. Mem. ABA, Mass. Bar Assn., Middlesex Bar Assn. Republican. Unitarian. Clubs: Harvard (Boston and N.Y.C.); Masons. State civil litigation, Federal civil litigation, Criminal. Home: 33 Birch Hill Rd Belmont MA 02178 Office: 100 George P Hassett Dr Medford MA 02155

BERMAN, DAVID IRA, lawyer; b. Chgo., June 25, 1939; s. Irving and Lillian (Root) B.; m. Sharlene Joyce Zemen, Dec. 26, 1964; children: Lisa Ann, Daniel Max. BA, U. Ill., 1960; JD, Harvard U., 1963. Bar: Ill. 1963, Calif. 1964, U.S. Supreme Ct. 1980. Sole practice San Diego, 1963—. Pres. San Diego Gas Lamp Quarter Assn., 1977-78. Served to 1st lt. U.S. Army, 1963-65. Club: Harvard of San Diego (sec. 1984—). Criminal, Personal injury. Home: 6268 Lance Pl San Diego CA 92120 Office: 401 W A St Suite 1300 San Diego CA 92101

BERMAN, HOWARD JONATHAN, lawyer; b. N.Y.C., June 13, 1943; s. Samuel and Vivian (Kerner) B.; m. Stephanie Jaffe, Aug. 1, 1974; children: Zachary, Ezra. AB, Princeton U., 1965; JD, U. Calif., 1971. Bar: Calif. 1972. Staff atty. Prison Law Project, Oakland, Calif., 1971-72; ptnr. Berman & Glenn, San Francisco, 1972—; arbitrator Marin County Superior Ct., San Rafael, Calif., 1981—, San Francisco Superior Ct., 1981—; judge pro tem San Francisco Mcpl. Ct., 1982—. Served with Peace Corps, 1965-67, India. Mem. San Francisco Bar Assn. (bd. dirs. 1976-77), Barristers Club (pres. San Francisco 1977). Real property, Family and matrimonial, Contracts commercial. Office: 3d and Market Suite 1100 San Francisco CA 94103

BERMAN, JOHN ARTHUR, lawyer; b. Hartford, Conn., Feb. 29, 1932; s. Jacob and Anna (Woike) B.; m. Beverly Fuller; children: Jay, Virginia Emily. AB, Wheaton Coll., 1954; LLB, U. Conn., 1957. Bar: Conn. 1960, U.S. Dist. Ct. Conn. 1960, U.S. Ct. Appeals (2nd cir.) 1962, U.S. Supreme Ct. 1967. Ptnr. Berman & Berman, Hartford, 1957-70, Berman & Bourns, Hartford, 1970-85, Berman, Bourns & Currie, West Hartford, Conn., 1985—; corp. counsel Town of West Hartford, 1980-82. State rep. Conn. Gen. Assembly, Hartford, 1976-81. Republican. Presbyterian. Family and matrimonial, Probate, General practice. Home: 37 Glenwood Rd West Hartford CT 06107 Office: Berman Bourns & Currie 970 Farmington Ave West Hartford CT 06107

BERMAN, MARK NILES, lawyer; b. Pitts., Jan. 13, 1952; s. George and Evelyn (Robin) B.; m. Beth Ann Stamell, Aug. 12, 1973; children: Lia Michelle, Daniel Scott. BA, Northwestern U., 1973; JD, Boston Coll., 1976. Bar: Mass. 1977, U.S. Dist. Ct. Mass. 1977, U.S. Ct. Appeals (1st cir.) 1985, U.S. Supreme Ct., 1985. From assoc. to ptnr. Widett, Slater & Goldman, P.C., Boston, 1976—, also bd. dirs. Mem. ABA, Mass. Bar Assn., Boston Bar Assn., Comml. Law League Am. Bankruptcy, Contracts commercial. Home: 98 Falmouth Rd West Newton MA 02165 Office: Widett Slater & Goldman PC 60 State St Boston MA 02109

BERMAN, MICHAEL DAVID, lawyer; b. Washington, Feb. 4, 1948; s. Hyman and Ann (Cohn) B. BA, U. Wis., 1970; MA, U. Md., College Park, 1977; JD with honors, U. Md., Balt., 1980. Law clk. to presiding justice U.S. Dist. Ct. Md., Balt., 1980-81; assoc. Kaplan, Heyman, Greenberg, Engelman & Belgrad, P.A., Balt., 1981—. Served to capt. U.S. Army, 1971-75. Mem. ABA, Md. Bar Assn., Am. Assn. Trial Lawyers, Md. Assn. Trial Lawyers. Jewish. Federal civil litigation, State civil litigation, Civil rights. Home: 628 S Hanover St Baltimore MD 21230 Office: Kaplan Heyman Greenberg et al 20 S Charles St Baltimore MD 21201

BERMAN, MICHAEL DEXTER, lawyer; b. Boston, May 26, 1952; s. Max A. and Anita Ruth (Berman) B.; m. Melinda Meadow, June 7, 1981; children: Emily, Peter. BA, Harvard U., 1974; JD, U. Pa., 1977. Bar: Mass. 1977, Calif. 1981. Assoc. Gaston, Snow & Ely Bartlett, Boston and Palo Alto, Calif., 1977-85; exec. v.p., gen. counsel Continental Wingate Capital Corp., Boston, 1985—, also bd. dirs.; bd. .dirs., gen. counsel Continental Wingate Co. (parent co. Wingate Capital Corp.). Mem. ABA, Boston Bar Assn. Real property, Securities, Corporate taxation. Office: Continental Wingate Capital Corp 75 Central St Boston MA 02109

BERMAN, MICHAEL HOWARD, lawyer; b. Bklyn., Mar. 28, 1945; s. George and Sylvia (Wiener) B.; m. Susan Lynn Klass, Mar. 14, 1982; children: Debbie, Steven. BS in Polit. Sci., Loyola U., Chgo., 1966; JD, John Marshall Law Sch., 1969. Bar: Ill. 1969, U.S. Dist. Ct. (no. dist.) Ill. 1969, U.S. Supreme Ct. 1976. From assoc. to ptnr. Brody & Gore, Chgo., 1972-79; ptnr. Berman & Trachtman, P.C., Chgo., 1979—. Served to capt. U.S. Army, 1969-71, Vietnam. Mem. ABA, Ill. Bar Assn., Chgo. Bar Assn., Assn. Trial Lawyers Am., Ill. Trial Lawyers Assn. Personal injury. Office: Berman & Trachtman PC 100 N LaSalle Chicago IL 60602

BERMAN, PAMELA JILL, lawyer; b. Los Angeles, Apr. 2, 1947; d. William MacArthur Robertson and Virginia Lee (Mathews) Winford; m. Ronald Berman, Jan 10, 1982 (div. Apr. 1986). BA, UCLA, 1969; MSW, U. Hawaii, 1973, JD, 1977. Bar: Hawaii 1977, U.S. Dist. Ct. Hawaii 1977, U.S. Supreme Ct. 1985. Dep. Office of Pub. Defender, Honolulu, 1977-79; ptnr. Wilson & Berman, Honolulu, 1979-82; sole practice Honolulu, 1982—. bd. dirs. ACLU, Honolulu, 1977-85, Salvation Army, Honolulu, 1979-82, Protection and Advocacy, Honolulu, 1983-84; pres. bd. dirs. Parents' Anonymous, Honolulu, 1985—. Named Pacesetter of the Pacific, Honolulu Star Bull., 1985. Mem. ABA, Assn. Trial Lawyers Am., Hawaii Bar Assn., Honolulu C. of C. Democrat. Club: Honolulu. Avocations: hiking, snorkeling, weightlifting, opera, crossword puzzles. Personal injury, Family and matrimonial, Criminal. Home: 1028 Iopono Loop Kailua HI 96734 Office: 1001 Bishop Suite 2010 Honolulu HI 96813

BERMAN, RICHARD BRUCE, lawyer; b. Freeport, N.Y., Sept. 26, 1951; s. Nathan and Helen Dorothy (Raiden) B.; m. Laurie Michael, Nov. 2, 1985. BA in Speech Communication, Am. U., 1973; JD, U. Miami, 1976. Bar: Fla. 1976, U.S. Dist. Ct. (so. dist.) Fla. 1976, D.C. 1978. Atty. Travelers Ins. Co., Ft. Lauderdale, Fla., 1977-84; assoc. Frank & Flaster P.A., Sunrise, Fla., 1984—. Mem. panel health care Dem. Legis. Task Force, Ft. Lauderdale, 1985—. Mem. ABA, Fla. Bar Assn., Assn. Trial Lawyers Am., Am. Abitration Assn., Broward County Trial Lawyers Assn. Lodge: B'nai B'rith. Avocations: writing and performing music, theatre. Personal injury, Workers' compensation, Insurance. Office: Frank & Flaster PA 7770 W Oakland Park Blvd Sunrise FL 33321

BERMAN, RONALD CHARLES, accountant; b. Chgo., July 7, 1949; s. Joseph and Helen (Neiderman) BBS with highest honors, U. Ill., 1971, JD with honors, 1974. Bar: Ill. 1974, Wis. 1976; CPA, Wis. Tax staff Grant Thornton, Chgo., 1974-76, tax supr., Madison, Wis., 1976-78, tax mgr., 1978-81; ptnr. tax dept. Grant Thornton, Madison, 1981—. Mem. editorial adv. bd. Physician's Tax Advisor Newsletter, 1986—; Scoutmaster Boy Scouts Am., Middleton, Wis., 1978—; fin. chmn. Mohawk Dist. Four Lakes council Boy Scouts Am., Madison, 1981-85, endowment fund chmn., 1984—, exec. bd., 1982—; bd. dirs. Scouts on Stamps Soc. Internat., 1986—, Madison Pension Council, 1986—. Recipient Bronze Tablet, U. Ill., 1971, Silver Beaver Boy Scouts Am., 1981. Mem. ABA (employee benefits com. taxation sect), Am. Inst. CPA's (Sells award Hon. mention 1971), Wis. Soc. CPA's, State Bar of Wis., Ill. Bar Assn., Order of Coif, Alpha Phi Omega, Phi Kappa Phi, Phi Alpha Delta. Lodge: Optimist. Avocations: photography, philately, camping. Corporate taxation, Pension, profit-sharing, and employee benefits, Personal income taxation. Home: 3906 Rolling Hill Dr Middleton WI 53562 Office: Grant Thornton 2 E Gilman PO Box 8100 Madison WI 53708

BERMAN, STANFORD WARNER, lawyer; b. Washington, June 22, 1928; s. Hyman and Ida (Koblen) B.; m. Marilyn Ruth Miller, May 27, 1956; children: Scott, Marcy, Brian. BS in Mech. Engring., U. Md., 1950; JD, George Washington U., 1953. Bar: D.C. 1954, U.S. Supreme Ct. 1954. Commd. USAR, 1950, advanced through grades to lt., resigned, 1963; ptnr. McMorrow, Berman & Davidson, Washington, 1956-63, Berman, Davidson & Berman, Washington, 1963-72, Berman, Bishoff & Platt, Washington, 1972-75; sr. ptnr. Berman, Aisenberg & Platt, Washington, 1975—; prof., lectr. patent law for engrs. U. Md., 1977—. Adv. bd. dirs. Tech. Advancement Program, U. Md.; bd. dirs. Hebrew Home Greater Washington, Rockville, Md., Washington Jewish Community Found. Served lt. USAR. Mem. ABA, D.C. Bar Assn., Am. Intellectual Property Law Assn., Internat. Intellectual Assn., U.S. Trademark Assn., Alumni Internat. U. Md. (v.p.), Engring. Alumni chpt. U. Md. (pres. 1979-80). Club: Woodmont Country (Rockville). Avocations: tennis, golf, racketball, squash. Unfair competition, Patent, Trademark and copyright. Home: 7429 Arrowood Rd Bethesda MD 20817 Office: Berman Aisenberg & Platt 1730 Rhode Island Ave NW Washington DC 20036

BERMAN, STEVE WILLIAM, lawyer; b. Chgo., Nov. 13, 1954; s. Mert E. and Lois Ann (Eliot) B.; m. Janet S. Friend, June 18, 1979. BS, U. Mich., 1976; JD, U. Chgo., 1980. Bar: Ill. 1980, U.S. Dist. Ct. Ill. 1980, U.S. Ct. Appeals (7th cir.) 1980, Wash. 1982, U.S. Dist. Ct. 1982, U.S. Ct. Appeals (3d and 9th cirs.), U.S. Supreme Ct. 1986. Assoc. Jenner & Block, Chgo., 1980-82, Shidler & Gates, Seattle, 1982-85; resident atty. Bernstein, Litowitz, Berger & Grossman, Seattle, 1986—; adj. prof. law U. Puget Sound, Tacoma, 1983—. Mem. com. Juvenile Conf., Seattle, 1984. Mem. ABA (trial practice com., discovery com.). Jewish. Club: Lake Washington Rowing (Seattle). Avocations: running, rowing, hiking, skiing. Federal civil litigation, Securities, Criminal. Office: Bernstein Litowitz Berger & Grossman First Interstate 44th Floor Seattle WA 98107

BERMAN, STEVEN PAUL, lawyer; b. Bklyn., June 8, 1942; s. Harold and Sylvia (Reiner) B.; m. Carolyn Pearl Flacks, Feb. 23, 1969; children: Mark

Robert, Lisa Michelle. BS in Chemistry, CCNY, 1963; JD, Bklyn. Law Sch., 1966; postgrad., NYU, 1969-70. Bar: Ohio 1967, N.Y. 1969, U.S. Dist. Ct. (ea. and so. dists.) N.Y. 1969, U.S. Ct. Appeals (2d cir.) 1969, N.J. 1977, U.S. Ct. Appeals (fed. cir.) 1982. Patent atty. Procter and Gamble, Cin., 1966-68, Nabisco, Inc., N.Y.C., 1968-69; assoc. Fitzpatrick, Cella, Harper and Scinto, N.Y.C., 1970-74, Johnson and Johnson, New Brunswick, N.J., 1974—; bd. dirs. Devro, Inc., Somerville, N.J., asst. sec., 1980—; asst. sec. Pitman and Moore, Inc., Washington Crossing, N.J., 1980—, Johnson and Johnson Baby Products Co., 1981—. Mem., v.p. then pres. sch. bd. Bridgewater (N.J.)-Raritan Regional Sch. Dist., 1980-84. Mem. ABA, Am. Intellectual Property Law Assn., N.Y. Patent, Trademark and Copyright Law Assn., Am. Arbitration Assn. (panel of arbitrators N.Y. and N.J. 1976—). Jewish. Avocations: sports, reading, philately. Patent, licensing, General corporate. Home: 705 Red Lion Way Bridgewater NJ 08807 Office: Johnson and Johnson 1 Johnson and Johnson Plaza New Brunswick NJ 08933

BERMANN, GEORGE ALAN, law educator, lawyer; b. Fall River, Mass., Dec. 2, 1945; s. Sigmund Dressler and Mae (Gordon) B.; m. Sandra Lekas, Dec. 28, 1969; children: Sloan, Suzanne, Grant. B.A., Yale U., 1967, J.D., 1971; LL.M., Columbia U., 1975. Bar: N.Y. 1972, U.S. Dist. Ct. (So. Dist.) N.Y. 1980, U.S. Dist. Ct (ea. dist.) N.Y. 1980. Assoc. Davis Polk & Wardwell, N.Y.C., 1970-73; asst. prof. law Columbia U., N.Y.C., 1975-79, assoc. prof., 1979-81, prof., 1981—; vis. prof. law U. Paris and U. Rouen, France, 1981-82; lectr. Internat. Faculty for Teaching Comparative Law, Strasbourg, France, 1975; exec. dir. Columbia Summer Program, Netherlands, 1979-82; cons. Nat. Ctr. Adminstrv. Justice, Washington, 1979-82, Adminstrv. Conf. of U.S., 1983—; internat. comml. arbitrator Am. Arbitration Assn., N.Y.C., 1982—; sec. Am. Acad. Fgn. Law, Stanford, Calif., 1983—. Contbr. chpt. to book, articles to profl. jours.; editor: Am. Jour. Comparative Law, 1976—. Cons., Operation Crossroads Africa, 1983—. Marshall scholar Sussex, Eng., 1967-68; Jervey fellow Parker Sch. Fgn. and Comparative Law, N.Y.C., 1973-75. Mem. Am. Fgn. Law Assn. (bd. dirs. 1983—), Deutsch-Amerikanische Juristen Vereingung, ABA, German Am. Law Assn. (bd. dirs. 1979—), Phi Beta Kappa. Legal education, Private international, Administrative and regulatory. Home: 115 Prospect Ave Princeton NJ 08540 Office: Columbia U Sch Law 435 W 116th St New York NY 10027

BERMANT, GEORGE WILSON, lawyer; b. Los Angeles, July 2, 1926; s. Ira G. and Josephine (Wilson) B.; m. Laurel Ardyce Knight, Aug. 19, 1950; 1 child, James G.; m. Neely Wagner, Oct. 22, 1970; m. Ann Taylor Corley, Dec. 19, 1985. B.A. magna cum laude, U. So. Calif., 1950; LL.B. cum laude, Yale U., 1953. Bar: Calif. 1954, Colo. 1981. Assoc. Gibson, Dunn & Crutcher, Los Angeles, 1953-61, ptnr., 1962-81; ptnr. Gibson, Dunn & Crutcher, Denver, 1981—. Bd. dirs., vice chmn. Hist. Denver, Inc., 1983—. Served with USNR, 1944-46. Mem. ABA, Los Angeles Bar Assn., Colo. Bar Assn., Denver Bar Assn., Fin. Lawyers Conf. Los Angeles. Republican. General corporate, Contracts commercial, Securities. Home: 1512 Larimer St Apt 33 Denver CO 80202 Office: Gibson Dunn & Crutcher 1801 California St Suite 4200 Denver CO 80202

BERN, MARC JAY, lawyer; b. Milw., June 19, 1950; s. James Ellis and Harriet (Kramer) B.; m. Janis Mechanic, June 29, 1974 (div. Mar. 1983); children—Lindsay, Jesse, Noah; m. Roberta Roth, May 20, 1984; 1 child, Erica. B.A., with distinction, U. Wis., 1972; J.D., Ill. Inst. Tech., 1975. Bar: Wis. 1975, U.S. Dist. Ct. (ea. and we. dists.) Wis. N.Y. 1983, U.S. Dist. Ct. (so. and ea. dists.) N.Y. Assoc. Habush, Gillick, Habush & Murphy, Milw., 1975-79; ptnr. Gillick, Murphy, Gillick, Bern & Wicht, Milw., 1979-82; assoc. Lipsig, Sullivan, Liapakis, N.Y.C., 1983-84; sr. trial assoc. Julien & Schlesinger, P.C., N.Y.C., 1984-86, Trolman & Glaser, P.C., 1986—; lectr. Milw. Area Tech. Coll., 1979-80, Continuing Edn. State Bar Wis., 1978—, Melvin Belli Seminar, Am. Trial Lawyers Assn., 1982—, Hahneman Med. Coll., 1980, Practicing Law Inst., 1984—, Wis. Acad. Trial Lawyers, Madison, 1981—, NYU Sch. Continuing Edn., 1985—, Inst. Continuing Profl. Edn., 1981-82. Mem. ABA, Am. Trial Lawyers Assn., State Bar Wis., Wis. Acad. Trial Lawyers, State Bar N.Y., Am. Judicature Soc., Am. Soc. Law and Medicine, N.Y. State Trial Lawyers Assn., Milw. Bar Assn., Milw. Young Lawyers, Delta Theta Phi. Personal injury, State civil litigation. Home: 130 Barrow St Apt 101 New York NY 10014 Office: Trolman & Glaser PC 9 E 40th St 13th Fl New York NY 10016

BERNABO, RAYMOND ANDREW, lawyer; b. N.Y.C., Jan. 1, 1930; s. Ernest L. and Ethel (Volpi) B. AB, Harvard U., 1951; LLB, Columbia U., 1955. Bar: N.Y. 1955. Assoc. Winthrop, Stimson & Roberts, N.Y.C., 1955-58; gen. counsel, sec. M&T Chems. Inc., N.Y.C., 1958-77; v.p., gen. counsel packaging, corp. dep. gen. counsel Primerica Corp, Greenwich, Conn., 1977-86, v.p., dep. gen. counsel, 1986—. Fulbright scholar U. Rome, 1951-52. Mem. ABA, N.Y. State Bar Assn., Assn. of Bar of City of N.Y. Office: Primerica Corp American Ln Greenwich CT 06830

BERNARD, BRUCE WILLIAM, lawyer; b. Erie, Pa., Feb. 3, 1951; s. Barney and Barbara Jean (Wurst) B.; m. Valerie Jean Noziglia, June 2, 1978 (div.); children: Elizabeth Anne, Brandon Wallace; m. Catherine Ann Blore, May 4, 1984. B.A., Case Western Res. U., Cleve., 1972, J.D., 1975. Bar: Pa. 1975, U.S. Dist. Ct. (we. dist.) Pa. 1975, U.S. Supreme Ct. 1980. Assoc. Silin, Eckert & Burke, Erie, 1975-77; ptnr. Ely & Bernard, Erie, 1978-85, Bernard & Stuczynski, Erie, 1985—; instr. Am. Inst. Banking, Erie, 1981—. Bd. dirs., Erie Civic Music Assn., 1976-83, Florence Crittendon Services, Erie, 1978-84, Meth. Towers, Erie, 1979—. Named Vol. of yr., Erie chpt. ARC, 1982. Mem. ABA, Pa. Bar Assn., Erie County Bar Assn., Assn. Trial Lawyers Am., Pa. Trial Lawyers Assn., Comml. Law League Am., Phi Delta Phi. Republican. Methodist. Club: Kiwanis (bd. dirs. 1978-81, Disting. Service award 1976, 79). Personal injury, Contracts commercial, Workers' compensation. Home: 1211 St Mary Dr Erie PA 16509 Office: Bernard & Stuczynski 234 W 6th St Erie PA 16507-1319

BERNARD, DONALD RAY, lawyer, author; b. San Antonio, June 5, 1932; s. Horatio J. and Amber (McDonald) B.; children—Doren, Kevin; m. Elizabeth Priscilla Gilpin, 1986. Student U. Mich., 1950-52; B.A., U. Tex., 1954, J.D., 1958, LL.M., 1964. Bar: Tex. 1958, U.S. Ct. Mil. Appeals, U.S. Supreme Ct. Briefing atty. Supreme Ct. Tex., Austin, 1958-59; asst. atty. gen. State of Tex., Austin, 1959-60; ptnr. Bernard & Bernard, Houston, 1960-80; sole practice, Houston, 1980—; mem. faculty S.W. Sch. Real Estate, 1968-77; past dir. Micro-Gage, Inc., Maencor, Inc. Bd. dirs. Nat. Kidney Found., Houston, 1960-63; chmn. Bd. Adjustment, Hedwig Village, Houston, 1972-76. Served to comdr. U.S. Navy, 1950. Mem. Lawyers Soc. Houston (pres. 1973-74), Houston Bd. Realtors, ABA, Inter-Am. Bar Assn., Tex. Bar Assn., Houston Bar Assn., Lawyer-Pilot Bar Assn., Sons of the Republic of Tex., Alpha Tau Omega, Phi Delta Phi. Methodist. Clubs: St. James's (London); Masons, Shriners. Lic. comml. pilot. Author: Origin of the Special Verdict As Now Practiced in Texas, 1964; co-author: (novel) Bullion, 1982. Private international, General corporate, Bankruptcy. Office: 1212 Main St Suite 851 Houston TX 77002

BERNARD, HUGH Y(ANCEY), JR., law librarian, educator; b. Athens, Ga., July 17, 1919; s. Hugh Yancey and Marguerite Louise (Vonderau) B. A.B., U. Ga., 1941; B.S. in L.S., Columbia U., 1947; J.D. with honors, George Washington U., 1961. Bar: D.C. 1961, U.S. Ct. Appeals (D.C. cir.) 1962, U.S. Supreme Ct. 1969. Librarian, Library of Congress, 1947-60; law librarian George Washington U., Washington, 1960-81, asst. and assoc. prof. law, 1962-70, prof., 1970-81, prof. emeritus, 1981—; cons. law sch. history, 1981-83; cons. AID, Kabul, Afghanistan, 1974. Served with USAF, 1942-46. Recipient profl. achievement award George Washington Law Assn., 1981. Mem. Am. Assn. Law Libraries, Law Librarians Soc. Washington, Univ. Profs. for Acad. Order, Phi Beta Kappa, Phi Alpha Delta, Kappa Delta Pi. Republican. Baptist. Clubs: Nat. Lawyers (Washington), Masons, K.T., Shriners. Author: The Law of Death and Disposal of the Dead, 1966, 2d ed. 1979; Public Officials, Elected and Appointed, 1968; contbr. to Your Complete Guide to Estate Planning, 1971. Librarianship, Legal history, Legal education. Home: 3563 S Leisure World Blvd Apt 1A Silver Spring MD 20906

BERNARD, LAWRENCE JAY, lawyer; b. Melbourne, Fla., Feb. 15, 1952; s. Edward Ephraim and Rena Joyce (Harris) B.; m. Carla Bea Moskovitz, Aug. 17, 1975; children: Joshua Aaron, Geri Dana. BA, U. Fla., 1974; JD, Mercer U., 1977. Bar: Fla. 1978, U.S. Dist. Ct. (no. and mid. dists.) Fla. 1978. Assoc. Harold B. Halmowitz P.A., Jacksonville, Fla., 1977-80; ptnr. Morris & Bernard, Jacksonville, 1980—. Mem. Jacksonville Bar Assn., Jacksonville Bd. of Realtors, Am. Congress of Real Estate. Democrat. Jewish. Avocations: water skiing, racquetball, fishing. General corporate, Probate, Real property. Office: Morris & Bernard 2064 Park St Jacksonville FL 32204

BERNARD, LINDA DIANE, legal services executive; b. Detroit, Nov. 1, 1949; d. John Robert and Dorthea Cleo (Graves) B. BA, Wayne State U., 1970, JD, 1973; LLM, U. Pa., 1975. Bar: Mich. 1973, Pa. 1974, U.S. Supreme Ct. 1979, Mass. 1981. Staff atty. Ford Motor Co., Detroit, 1974-76; supr. asst. corp. counsel City of Detroit, 1976-81; gen. counsel Mass. Port Authority, Boston, 1981; ptnr. L.D. Bernard & Assocs., Boston, 1982-84; exec. dir. Wayne County Neighborhood Legal Services, Detroit, 1984—. bd. dirs. Black Family Devel., Inc. 1985—, Parents Anonymous Mich., 1986—; mem. host com. Rep. Nat. Com., Detroit, 1980; bd. regents Eastern Mich. 1976-80. Recipient Resolution of Tribute, Mich. Ho. Reps., 1976, named one of Outstanding Young Women Am., 1979. Mem. ABA, Nat. Bar Assn. (life mem.), Detroit Bar Assn., Wolverine Bar Assn., Am. Arbitration Assn. (law panel com.), Urban League, NAACP, Mass. Black Women Lawyer Assn. Roman Catholic. Club: Detroit Econ. Home: 17355 Warrington Detroit MI 48221-2766

BERNARD, MICHAEL MARK, city planning consultant, lawyer; b. N.Y.C., Sept. 5, 1926; s. H.L. and Henryetta (Siegel) B.; m. Laura Jane Pincus, Aug. 28, 1958; 1 dau., Daphne Michelle. A.B., U. Chgo., 1949; J.D., Northwestern U., 1953; M.City Planning, Harvard U., 1959. Bar: Ill. 1952, U.S. Dist. Ct. (no. dist.) Ill. 1953, N.Y. 1955, U.S. Ct. Appeals (1st cir.) 1956. Gen. practice law Chgo. and N.Y.C., 1953-55; research Harvard Law Sch., 1955-56; city planning cons., atty.-adviser Puerto Rico, 1956-58; research assoc. Model Laws Project Am. Bar Found., 1959-60; city planner, legal adviser Chgo. Dept. City Planning, 1960-64; cons. planning and land regulation 1964—, lectr. in field, 1959—; Mem. exec. faculty Boston Archtl. Center, 1967—; vis. prof. urban and regional planning U. Iowa, 1969-70; mem. faculty Am. Law Inst., 1978—; adv. to Gov.'s Exec. Office on reorgn. Commonwealth Mass., 1968-72; cons. A.I.A. Research Corp., 1974; cons. Mass. Atty. Gen., 1981—; Mem. com. urban devel. and housing World Peace Through Law Center, 1965—; mem. com. transp. law transp. research bd. NRC-Nat. Acad. Scis., 1966—; cons. White House Policy Adv. Com. to D.C., 1966; del. World Congress Housing and Planning, Paris, France, 1962, Tokyo, Japan, 1966; fellow Ctr. Advanced Visual Studies, M.I.T. Author: Constitutions, Taxation and Land Policy, 2 vols., 1979-80, Airspace in Urban Development, 1963; co-editor: Policy Studies Jour.; editor, pub.: Reflections on Space; revision project mgr.: Constitutional Uniformity & Equality in State Taxation, 1984; spl. editor: Urban Law Ann. of Washington U. Sch. Law.; columnist: Jour. Real Estate Devel. Contbr. articles to profl. jours. Patron Hull House Assn., Chgo., 1965; v.p., trustee Cambridge Community Art Center, 1971-73. Served with USN, 1944-46. Recipient cert. of Commendation for teaching Boston Archtl. Ctr., 1984. Fellow Lincoln Inst. Land Policy; mem. ABA (land use, planning and zoning com., chmn. T.D.R. subcom. 1984—), Internat. Fedn. Housing and Planning, Am. Soc. Pub. Administrn., Policy Studies Orgn., Am. Planning Assn. (chmn. legislative com. Met. Chgo. sect. 1963-65, state reporter planning and law div. 1980—), Am. Underground Space Assn., Internat. Centre for Land Policy Studies (London), Urban Affairs Assn. (jour. rev. editor), Am. Crafts Council, Mass. Assn. Craftsmen (v.p. 1975-78), Boston Visual Artists Union (sec.-gen. 1971-72, hon. mem. 1984—), New Eng. Poetry Club (life, fin. chmn.), NRC-Nat. Acad. Scis. (grantee 1964-66). Unitarian (mem. standing com.). Real property, Local government. Home: 25 Stanton Ave Newton MA 02166 Office: MIT Br PO Box 49 Cambridge MA 02139-0901

BERNARD, PAMELA JENKS, lawyer; b. Montgomery, Ala., Nov. 27, 1955; d. Harford Perry and Mable (Sawyer) Jenks; m. Geoffrey Pedrick Bernard, Sept. 19, 1981. BA, U. Fla., 1976, JD, 1981. Bar: Fla. 1982, U.S. Dist. Ct. (mid. dist.) Fla. 1983, U.S. Ct. Appeals (11th cir.) 1983. Asst. atty. U. Fla., Gainesville, 1982-83, assoc. gen. counsel, 1983—; pvt. investment trustee, Gainesville, 1976-83. Mem. Nat. Assn. Coll. and Univ. Attys. Legal education, Administrative and regulatory, State civil litigation.

BERNARD, RICHARD PHILLIP, lawyer; b. Chgo., May 29, 1950; s. Martin Joseph Jr. and Ruth (Hadka) B.; m. Karen Elizabeth Oas, June 12, 1971; children: Rachel, Benjamin. BA, Mich. State U., 1972; JD, NYU, 1976; MBA, Princeton U., 1976. Bar: N.Y. 1977. Assoc. Milbank, Tweed, Hadley & McCloy, N.Y.C., 1976-84, ptnr., 1985—. Participating atty. Legal Aid Soc. Community Law Offices, N.Y.C., 1977—. Mem. ABA (banking and bus. sects., com. on fed. regulation of securities), N.Y. State Bar Assn. (banking, corp. and bus., young lawyers sects., Pres. Pro Bono Service award 1986). Democrat. Avocations: carpentry, children. General corporate, Private international, Securities. Home: 52 Gordonhurst Ave Upper Montclair NJ 07043 Office: Milbank Tweed Hadley & McCloy 1 Chase Manhattan Plaza New York NY 10005

BERNARD, ROBERT LOUIS, lawyer; b. Fall River, Mass., Mar. 20, 1936; s. John J. and Margaret (Bernard) De Costa; m. Diolinda B. Abilheira, Oct. 20, 1967. AB, Providence Coll., 1957; JD, Boston U., 1964. Bar: R.I. 1965, Mass. 1965, Tex. 1983, U.S. Dist. Ct. R.I., U.S. Dist. Ct. Mass., U.S. Supreme Ct. Spl. asst. atty. gen. Dept. Atty. Gen., R.I., 1966-71, asst. atty. gen., 1971-1975; atty. corp. litigation Shell Oil Co., Houston, 1975-86; sr. litigation counsel Browning & Ferris Industries, Houston, 1987—. Federal civil litigation, State civil litigation. Home: 12342 Wrenthorpe Dr Houston TX 77031 Office: Browning & Ferris Industries PO Box 3151 Houston TX 77253

BERNARDI, DONALD DELPHO, lawyer; b. Spring Valley, Ill., May 8, 1951; s. Donald James and Celia Rose (Gualandri) B. BA, Knox Coll., 1973; JD, Western New Eng. Coll., 1978. Bar: Ill. 1978, U.S. Dist. Ct. (cen. dist.) Ill. 1980, U.S. Supreme Ct. 1985. Asst. solicitor City of Springfield, Mass., 1977-78; asst. state's atty. Livingston County, Pontiac, Ill., 1978-82; state's atty. Livingston County, Pontiac, 1982—; mem. Ill State's Atty. Assn. liaison com. with Atty. Gen., Springfield, Ill., 1982-84. Pres. Young Reps. Livingston County, Pontiac, 1980-81; chmn. div. project 85 Boys and Girls Club, Pontiac, 1985. Mem. ABA, Ill. Bar Assn. (vice chmn. correctional facilities com. 1980-85), Assn. Trial Lawyers Am., Nat. Dist. Attys. Assn. Lodge: Elks. Avocations: antique automobiles, fishing. Criminal, Juvenile, Local government. Home: 804 C Deerfield Rd Pontiac IL 61764 Office: Livingston County State's Atty Livingston County Cthouse Pontiac IL 61764

BERNDT, KAREN ANN, lawyer; b. Houston, Jan. 12, 1947; d. Walter Frey and Bernice Helen (Kocurek) B. B.Journalism in Advt., U. Tex., 1968, J.D., 1970. Bar: Tex. 1971, D.C. 1971, U.S. Ct. Appeals (2nd, 3rd, 5th, 10th, 11th, D.C. cir.) 1972; U.S. Ct. Claims 1971, U.S. Mil. Ct. Appeals 1972, U.S. Ct. Customs and Patent Appeals 1972, U.S. Supreme Ct. 1973. Trial atty. U.S. Dept. Justice, Washington, 1971-74; atty. corp. and securities Childs, Fortenback, Beck & Guyton, Houston, 1974-76; ptrn. Woodward, Berndt & Teeter, Houston, 1976-78; sr. atty. Texaco Inc., Houston, 1978-87, asst. to pres., 1987— ; chmn. joint adv. com. of Natural Gas Producers, 1982-83; v.p. bd. govs. The Texaco Round Table, 1983-84. Assoc. editor U. Tex. Law Review, 1969-70. Active mem. State Bar Grievance Com., Harris County, Tex., 1977-81. Mem. ABA (vice chmn. natural gas com. 1985—), Houston Bar Assn., Fed. Energy Bar Assn. Administrative and regulatory, FERC practice, Federal civil litigation. Office: Texaco Inc PO Box 52332 Houston TX 77052

BERNDT, RICHARD OLAF, lawyer; b. Balt., Dec. 27, 1942; s. Olaf Fritz and Matilda Louise (Amrhein) B.; m. Rita Jean Sloan, Aug. 22, 1964; 1 child, Richard John. BS, Villanova U., 1964; JD, U. Md., 1967; M in Liberal Arts, Johns Hopkins U., 1970. Assoc. Gallahger, Evelius & Jones, Balt., 1967-74, mng. ptnr., 1974—; bd. dirs., trustees Mercantile-Safe Deposit and Trust Co., Balt., Mercantile Bankshares Corp., Balt., Mercantile Mortgage Co., Balt., Mercy Hosp., Inc., Balt., Jenkins Meml., Inc., Balt., Enterprise Social Investment Corp., Balt., Struever Bros., Eccles & Rouse, Inc., Balt. Campaign mgr. 3d Cong. Dist. Md. for Paul Sarbanes, 1970; campaign chmn. Citizens for Harborplace, 1978; for congresswoman 3d Cong. Dist. Md. Barbara Mikulski, 1980, 82, 84, campaign chmn., 1986; bd. dirs., trustees Good Samatarian Hosp. Endowment Fund, Inc., Cardinal Shehan Ctr. for the Aging, Inc., Archdiocesan Bd. of Fin. Adminstrn., Goucher Coll., Ctr. Stage, Associated Cath. Charities, Inc., Good Samatarian Hosp., Inc., Stella Maris Hospice Operating Corp., Inc., St. Ambrose Housing Aid Ctr., Inc., Legal Aid Bur. Recipient Outstanding Community Service award Greater Balt. Com., 1978, Mayor's Bus. Recognition award City of Balt., 1980, Outstanding Pub. Service award, Associated Cath. Charities, 1983. Mem. ABA, Md. Bar Assn., Balt. City Bar Assn. Club: Center (Balt.). General corporate, Health, Real property. Home: 3523 N Calvert St Baltimore MD 21218 Office: Gallagher Evelius & Jones 218 N Charles St Suite 400 Park Charles Baltimore MD 21201

BERNER, FREDERIC GEORGE, JR., lawyer; b. Washington, May 7, 1943; s. Frederic George and Florence Grace (Carlton) B.; m. Lorraine Ann (Ouellette) Sept. 28, 1968; children—Frederic George, III, Christina Lorraine, Jennifer Jane. B.A., Middlebury Coll., 1965, M.B.A., Am. U., 1970, J.D., George Washington U., 1973. Bar: D.C. 1973, U.S. Dist. Ct. (D.C. dist.) 1973, U.S. Ct. Appeals (D.C. cir.) 1974, U.S. Ct. Appeals (4th cir.) 1977, U.S. Ct. Appeals (11th cir.) 1984, U.S. Supreme Ct. 1980. Econ. intelligence officer CIA, Washington, 1965-67, 70; assoc. Sidley & Austin, Washington, 1973-80, ptnr., 1980—. Contbr. articles to legal publs. Gen. counsel, bd. dirs. Washington chpt., Nat. Hemophilia Found., 1976-80. Served to 1st lt. U.S. Army, 1967-70. Mem. Fed. Energy Bar Assn. (com. chmn. 1983—), D.C. Bar, ABA, Order of Coif. Republican. Presbyterian. FERC practice, Antitrust, Administrative and regulatory. Home: 7804 Fairfax Rd Bethesda MD 20814 Office: Sidley & Austin 1722 Eye St NW Washington DC 20006

BERNER, ROBERT LEE, JR., lawyer; b. Chgo., Dec. 9, 1931; s. Robert Lee and Mary Louise (Kenney) B.; m. Sheila Marie Reynolds, Jan. 12,. 1957; children: Mary, Louise, Robert, Sheila, John. A.B., U. Notre Dame, 1953; LL.B., Harvard U., 1956. Bar: Ill. 1956. With Petit, Olin, Overmyer & Fazio, Chgo., 1956-63; ptnr. Baker & McKenzie, Chgo., 1963—; mem. vis. com. Northwestern U. Law Sch., 1981-85. Mem. adv. bd. Catholic Charities, Chgo., 1971—; mem. vis. com. U. Chgo. Div. Sch., 1972—; mem. legal aid com. United Charities, Chgo., 1971—, bd. dirs., 1982—, chmn., 1983-85; bd. dirs. Link Unltd., Chgo., 1975—; mem. adv. bd. Loyola U., 1972—. Mem. ABA, Chgo. Bar Assn., Ill. State Bar Assn., Legal Club Chgo. (pres. 1974-75), Law Club Chgo. General corporate, Private international, Federal civil litigation. Home: 932 Euclid Ave Winnetka IL 60093 Office: Baker & McKenzie 2800 Prudential Plaza Chicago IL 60601

BERNER, THOMAS FRANKLYN, lawyer; b. Freeport, N.Y., July 20, 1954; s. Howard Everett and Elizabeth Ann (Phelan) B.; m. Ariel Holdsworth, May 8, 1982. BA, U. Wis., 1976; JD, Columbia U., 1979. Bar: N.Y. 1980, U.S. Dist. Ct. (so. dist.) N.Y. 1981. Assoc. Dewey, Ballantine, Bushby, Palmer & Wood, N.Y.C., 1979—. Pres. Seventh Ch. Christ, Scientist, N.Y.C., 1984-85, bd. trustees, 1985—. Harlan Fiske Stone scholar, 1979. Mem. ABA, Nat. Arts Club, Phi Beta Kappa. Republican. Banking, General corporate, Real property. Home: 255 W 108th St #11B New York NY 10025 Office: Dewey Ballantine Bushby Palmer & Wood 101 Park Ave New York NY 10178

BERNEY, LONN E., lawyer; b. Apr. 13, 1948. Sr. Ptnr. Berney & Chase, N.Y.C., 1977—; host weekly radio pub. affairs show Sta. WOR; nat. lectr. to hosps., schs. and orgns.; past or present faculty Hunter Coll., New Sch. Social Research, Met. Hosp., Downstate Hosp., NYU Med. Ctr., N.Y. Law Sch.; legal adviser to patient and consumer orgns. including Health-Rite, Ms. Found., Ctr. for Med. Consumers; legal adviser WNET, NBC, ABC, CBS TV; mem. criminal justice panels fed. and State cts. N.Y. State. chmn. bd. Med. Legal Research Team Corp. Contbr. articles to profl. jours.; pub. Litigation Letter; author poetry. Chmn. Commn. Consumer Rights; founder, chmn. bd. Miracle Found.; founder Legal Outreach Team; bd. dirs. Rush Dance Co. Recipient media award N.Y. Heart Assn. Mem. N.Y. Acad. Scis., Am. Med. Soc., AMA, Soc. Law and Medicine, Com. on Med. Jurisprudence. Federal civil litigation, State civil litigation, Criminal. Office: Berney & Chase 220 Fifth Ave 16th Fl New York NY 10001

BERNFELD, JEFFREY ALAN, lawyer; b. Bklyn., May 9, 1957; s. Hyman and Doris (Tash) B.; m. Mary-Kathleen O'Connell, Aug. 7, 1983; 1 child, Jeremy David. BA, Brandeis U., 1978; JD, NYU, 1981. Bar: Mass. 1981, U.S. Dist. Ct. Mass. 1982, U.S. Ct. Appeals (1st cir.) 1982. Assoc. Goldstein & Manello, Boston, 1981-86, ptnr., 1987—. Bd. dirs. Arts in Progress, Boston, 1984—. Mem. ABA, Mass. Bar Assn., Boston Bar Assn. Avocations: sports, music, films. General corporate, Securities, Entertainment. Home: 60 Browne St Brookline MA 02146 Office: Goldstein & Manello 265 Franklin St Boston MA 02110

BERNHARD, ALEXANDER ALFRED, lawyer; b. New Orleans, Sept. 20, 1936; s. John Helanus and Dora (Solosko) B.; m. Martha Ruggles, Nov. 21, 1959 (div.); m. Joyce Harrington, Dec. 30, 1976 (div.); children—John, Jason, Frederic; m. Myra Mayman, Nov. 1986. B.S., MIT, 1957; LL.B., Harvard U., 1964. Bar: Calif. 1964, Oreg. 1965, Mass. 1966. Law clk. to judge U.S. Ct. Appeals (9th cir.), 1964-65; assoc. Johnson, Johnson & Harrang, Eugene, Oreg., 1965-66, Bingham, Dana & Gould, Boston, 1966-71, Hale and Dorr, Boston, 1971-73, jr. ptnr., 1973-75, sr. ptnr., 1975—. Trustee Mass. Eye and Ear Infirmary. Served to lt. USNR, 1957-61. Mem. ABA, Boston Bar Assn. Democrat. Clubs: Union Boat, Manchester Yacht, Longwood Cricket. General corporate, Private international, Corporate taxation. Office: Hale and Dorr 60 State St Boston MA 02109

BERNHARD, BERL, lawyer; b. N.Y.C., Sept. 7, 1929; s. Morris and Celia B.; children—Peter Berl, Robin Churchill, Andrew Morris. B.A. in Govt. magna cum laude (Rufus Choate scholar), Dartmouth Coll., 1951, A.M., 1974; J.D., Yale U., 1954; LL.D., Central Ohio State Coll., 1963. Bars: D.C., 1954, U.S. Supreme Ct., 1957. Assoc. Davis, Polk, Wardwell, Sunderland & Kiendl, N.Y.C., summer 1953; law clk. to U.S. dist. judge 1954-56; assoc Turney & Turney, 1956-59; staff dir. U.S. Commn. on Civil Rights, 1961-63; ptnr. Verner, Liipfert, Bernhard, McPherson and Hand and predecessor firms, 1959, 63—, Hughes, Hubbard & Reed, Washington, 1972-75; gen. counsel, dir. Evening Star Newspaper Co., Washington, 1974-78, WJLA, Inc., Washington, 1976-80, Allbritton Communications Co., 1976-80; staff dir. U.S. Commn. on Civil Rights, 1961-63, cons. under sec. polit. affairs Sec. State, 1963-65; adj. prof. law Georgetown U. Law Ctr., 1963-65; spl. counsel, dir. White Ho. Conf. "To Fulfill These Rights," 1966; counsel Lawyers Com. for Civil Rights Under Law; mem. audit, trust, human resources com. Nat. Bank of Washington. Contbr. articles to profl. jours. Gen. counsel Democratic Senatorial Campaign Com., 1965-71; spl. counsel Dem. Nat. Com., 1965-71; staff dir. Senator Edmund S. Muskie, 1971, nat. campaign mgr., 1972; mem. D.C. Bd. Higher Edn., chmn. fin. com.; trustee Dartmouth Coll., 1974-84, Joe Davies Found., 1968—; sr. advisor to Sec. of State, 1980-81; chmn., chief exec. officer Washington Federals, U.S. Football League; bd. dirs. Harriman Polit. Action Com., 1980—, Nat. Bank Washington, 1983—, bd. visitors Nelson A. Rockefeller Ctr. for Social Scis., 1983—; bd. overseers The Amos Tuck Sch. Bus. Adminstrn. Dartmouth Coll. 1985—. Recipient Arthur S. Flemming award D.C. Jr. C. of C., 1960, Ten Outstanding Young Men award U.S. Jr. C. of C., 1962. Mem. Am. Bar Assn., Bar Assn. D.C., Assn. Interstate Practitioners, Nat. Panel Arbitrators, Am. Arbitration Assn., Casque and Gauntlet, Phi Beta Kappa, Sigma Nu, Phi Delta Phi. Clubs: Metropolitan (Washington); Yale (N.Y.C.). Administrative and regulatory, Banking, Legislative. Home: PO Box 4905 Annapolis MD 21403 Office: Verner Liipfert Bernhard McPherson and Hand 1660 L St NW #1000 Washington DC 20036

BERNHARD, HERBERT ASHLEY, lawyer; b. Jersey City, Sept. 24, 1927; s. Richard C. and Amalie (Lobl) B.; m. Nancy Ellen Hirschaut, Aug. 8, 1954; children: Linda, Alison, Jordan, Melissa. Student, Mexico City Coll., 1948; BEE, N.J. Inst. Tech., 1949; MA in Math., Columbia U., 1950; JD cum laude, U. Mich., 1957. Bar: Calif. 1958, U.S. Dist. Ct. (cen. dist.) Calif. 1958, U.S. Dist. Ct. (no., ea. and so. dists.) Calif., U.S. Dist. Ct. (ea. dist.) Wis., U.S. Dist. Ct. (ea. and we. dists.) Ark., U.S. Dist. Ct. Nebr., U.S. Ct. Claims, U.S. Ct. Internat. Trade, U.S. Tax Ct., U.S. Ct. Appeals (2d, 3d, 4th, 5th, 7th, 8th, 9th, 10th, 11th and D.C. cirs.), U.S. Supreme Ct. 1965. Research engr. Curtis-Wright Co., Caldwell, N.J., 1950-52, Boeing Aircraft Co., Cape Canaveral, Fla., 1952-55; assoc. O'Melveny & Myers, Los Angeles, 1957-62; ptnr. Greenberg, Bernhard, et al, Los Angeles, 1962-85,

Jeffer, Mangels & Butler, Los Angeles, 1985—; instr. math. U. Fla., Cape Canaveral, 1952-55, elec. engring. U. Mich., Ann Arbor, 1955-57. Contbr. articles to profl. jours. Chmn. adv. com. Skirball Mus.; bd. overseers Hebrew Union Coll.; bd. govs. Am. Jewish Congress, 1986—. Served with USAF, 1946-47. Mem. Jewish Publ. Soc. (trustee 1986—). Club: Mulholland Tennis (Los Angeles). Federal civil litigation, State civil litigation, Antitrust. Home: 1105 Tower Rd Beverly Hills CA 90210 Office: Jeffer Mangels & Butler 1900 Ave of Stars 4th Floor Los Angeles CA 90067

BERNHARDSON, IVY SCHUTZ, lawyer; b. Fargo, N.D., Aug. 22, 1951; d. James Newell and Phyllis Harriet (Iverson) Schutz; m. Mark Elvin Bernhardson, Sept. 1, 1973; children: Andrew Schutz, Jenna Clare. BA, Gustavus Adolphus Coll., 1973; JD, U. Minn., 1978. Bar: Minn. 1978, U.S. Dist. Ct. Minn. 1978. Staff atty. Gen. Mills, Inc., Mpls., 1978-83, assoc. counsel, 1983-85, sr. assoc. counsel, 1985—; asst. sec. to bd. dirs. Gen. Mills, Inc., Mpls., 1982—. Mem. ABA, Minn. Bar Assn., Hennepin County Bar Assn., Am. Soc. Corp. Secs., Gustavus Adolphus Alumni Assn. (Class Agt. of Yr. 1978, bd. dirs. 1978-84). Lutheran. General corporate, Securities, Pension, profit-sharing, and employee benefits. Office: Gen Mills Inc PO Box 1113 Minneapolis MN 55440

BERNHEIM, PEGGY, judge; b. Newark, Feb. 2, 1929; d. Charles E. and Eva (Kempner) B. A.B., U. Miami, Coral Gables, Fla., 1950; LL.B., NYU, 1965. Bar: N.Y. 1965, U.S. Dist. Ct. (so. dist.) N.Y. 1968, U.S. Ct. Appeals (2d cir.) 1968. Mdse. exec. A. Bohrer, Inc., 1956-66; staff atty. Civil Legal Aid, 1966-70; law sec. to Civil Ct. Judge, 1970-73, to Supreme Ct. Justice, 1973-78; civil ct. judge, Bronx County, N.Y., 1978—; acting justice, 1st Dept., N.Y. Supreme Ct., N.Y.C., 1980—. State Democratic committeewoman 82d Dist. N.Y., 1970-74. Mem. ABA, Nat. Assn. Women Judges, N.Y. State Bar Assn., Bronx County Bar Assn. (dir.), N.Y. State Trial Lawyers Assn., NYU Law Alumni, Nat. Council Jewish Women, Delta Phi Epsilon (nat. exec. council). Democrat. Jewish. State civil litigation, Jurisprudence, Criminal.

BERNHEIM, SADYE KERN, lawyer; b. Monroe, La., Aug. 10, 1955; d. Sadrian Kern and Arvenia (May) B.; m. Gerald Wayne Merritt, Nov. 7, 1981; children—Sadrian Kern, Cale Alexander. B.A., Northeast La. U., Monroe, 1976; J.D., Loyola U., New Orleans, 1979. Bar: La. 1980, U.S. Dist. Ct. (we. dist.) La. 1980. Assoc. Law Offices James A. Norris, West Monroe, La., 1979-80; atty., Law Offices Sadye Kern Bernheim, Monroe, 1980—; cooperating atty. N. La. Legal Assistance Corp., Monroe, 1983—, Gen. Motors-UAW, Detroit, 1983-85, Pro Bono Elderly Project. Mem. Northeast La. U. Student Correctional Assn. (v.p., organizer), ABA, La. State Trial Lawyers Assn., La. State Bar Assn., Fourth Jud. Dist. Bar Assn. (mem. com. on profl. responsibility 1985-86), Am. Trial Lawyers Assn., Alpha Phi Sigma, Phi Alpha Delta (pres., sec. O'Niell chpt.), Blue Key. Republican. Jewish. Family and matrimonial, Bankruptcy, General practice. Home: 1420 Park Ave Monroe LA 71201 Office: 1401 Hudson Ln Suite 139 La Bank Bldg Monroe LA 71201

BERNING, LARRY D., lawyer; b. Kendallville, Ind., Oct. 21, 1940; s. Melvin and Dolores (Sorge) B.; m. Zola Sue Makrauer, Feb. 21, 1969 (div. Aug. 1984); children—Emily Lyn, Scott Michael. A.B., Ind. U., 1963, J.D., 1968. Bar: Ill. 1968, Ind. 1968. Assoc. Sidley & Austin, Chgo., 1968-74, ptnr., 1974—. Trustee, v.p. Old People's Home of Chgo.; trustee The Georgian, William H. Miner Found., Medic Alert Records Trust (Chgo.). Served with U.S. Army, 1963-65. Mem. ABA, Ill. Bar Assn., Chgo. Bar Assn., Ind. Bar Assn., Am. Coll. Probate Counsel, Chgo. Estate Planning Council. Clubs: Mid-Day, Law, Legal. (Chgo.). Probate, Estate planning, Personal income taxation. Office: Sidley & Austin 1 First Nat Plaza Chicago IL 60603

BERNS, BONNIE AVA, lawyer; b. N.Y.C., July 31, 1951; d. Murray and Muriel (Kirshner) B.; m. Gary Leland Cadle, Dec. 2, 1976 (div. Feb. 1983); 1 child, Harris M.; m. Timothy James Conner, June 24, 1983; 1 child, Monica D. BA, NYU, 1973; JD, Antioch Sch. of Law, 1977. Bar: Fla. 1978, U.S. Dist. Ct. (mid. dist.) Fla. 1982. Sole practice Naples, Italy, 1978-80; atty. Cen. Fla. Legal Services, Daytona Beach, 1982-85; sole practice Palm Coast, Fla., 1985—. Named one of Outstanding Young Women in Am., 1983. Mem. ABA, Fla. Bar Assn. (vice chmn. com. on the elderly 1985—), Volusia County Bar Assn., NOW (pres. 1981—, del. convention 1984, rep. polit. action com. Fla. 1984), Fla. Assn. for Women Lawyers (Gift of Appreciation Outstanding Community Service 1983), Flagler County Bar Assn. (chair com. on elderly 1985-86), Phi Beta Kappa. Democrat. Jewish. Civil rights, State civil litigation, Family and matrimonial. Office: PO Box 2530 Palm Coast FL 32037-2530

BERNSTEIN, BERNARD, lawyer, corporate executive; b. Bklyn., Feb. 9, 1929; s. Irving and Esther (Schriro) B.; m. Carmel Roth, June 24, 1973. AB, Syracuse U., 1950; JD, Harvard U., 1953. Bar: N.Y. With Philipp Bros., Inc. subs. Philbro-Salomon Inc. (formerly Minerals and Chems. Philipp, Englehard Minerals & Chems. Corp., Phibro Corp.), N.Y.C., 1965—; now gen. counsel, bd. dirs., sec. Philipp Bros., Inc. subs. Philbro-Salomon Inc. (formerly Minerals and Chems. Philipp, Englehard Minerals & Chems. Corp., Phibro Salomon, Inc.), N.Y.C. Served with AUS, 1953-55. Mem. ABA, Am. Arbitration Assn. (bd. dirs., mem. exec. com.). dir. Speculum Musicae. Home: 25 E 86th St New York NY 10028 Office: Philipp Bros Inc 1221 Ave of Americas New York NY 10020 *

BERNSTEIN, BERNARD EMANUEL, lawyer; b. Newark, Feb. 3, 1931; s. Joseph Solomon and Bertha (Eichler) B.; m. Barbara Winick, June 21, 1956; children: Barri Eichler, Mark Winick. BS in Econs., U. Pa., 1952; JD, U. Tenn., 1958. Bar: Tenn. 1959, U.S. Dist. Ct. (ea. dist.) Tenn. 1959, U.S. Ct. Appeals (6th cir.) 1961, U.S. Supreme Ct. 1966. Sr. ptnr. Bernstein, Susano & Stair, Knoxville, Tenn., 1959—. Del. constl. convention State of Tenn., Nashville, 1977. Served to 1st lt. USAF, 1952-54. Fellow Am. Coll. Trial Lawyers, Tenn. Bar Found.; mem. ABA, Tenn. Bar Assn., Knoxville Bar Assn. (pres. 1968—). Democrat. Jewish. Club: LeConte. Avocation: wildflower gardening. State civil litigation, Federal civil litigation, General corporate. Home: 8014 Corteland Dr Knoxville TN 37909 Office: Bernstein Susano & Stair 1st Tennessee Bank Bldg 6th Floor Knoxville TN 37902

BERNSTEIN, CARYL SALOMON, lawyer; b. N.Y.C., Dec. 22, 1933; d. Gustav and Rosalind (Aron) Salomon; m. William D. Terry, June 12, 1955 (div. 1967); children: Ellen Deborah, Mark David; m. Robert L. Cole, Jr., Oct. 25, 1970 (div. 1975); m. George K. Bernstein, June 17, 1979. B.A. with honors, Cornell U., 1955; J.D., Georgetown U., 1967. Bar: D.C. 1968, U.S. Dist. Ct. D.C. 1968, U.S. Ct. Appeals (D.C. cir.) 1968, U.S. Supreme Ct. 1971. Atty. Covington & Burling, Washington, 1967-73; staff atty. Overseas Pvt. Investment Corp., Washington, 1973-74, asst. gen. counsel, 1974-77, v.p. for ins., 1977-81; sr. v.p., gen. counsel, sec. Fed. Nat. Mortgage Assn., Washington, 1981-82, exec. v.p., gen. counsel, sec., 1982—; dir. Nat. Housing Conf., 1983—. Contbr. articles to profl. jours., chpt. to book; mem. bd. editors Georgetown Law Jour., 1966; mem. editorial adv. bd. Housing and Devel. Reporter, 1986—. Mem. bd. regents Georgetown U., 1986—; bd. dirs. Council for Ct. Excellence, Washington, 1986—. N.Y. Regents scholar, 1951-55. Mem. ABA, Fed. Bar Assn., D.C. Bar Assn., Am. Soc. Internat. Law, Phi Beta Kappa, Phi Kappa Phi. General corporate, Real property. Office: Fed Nat Mortgage Assn 3900 Wisconsin Ave NW Washington DC 20016

BERNSTEIN, CHARLES BERNARD, lawyer; b. Chgo., June 24, 1941; s. Norman and Adele (Shore) B.; A.B., U. Chgo., 1962; J.D., DePaul U., 1965; m. Roberta Luba Lesner, Aug. 7, 1968; children—Edward Charles, Louis Charles, Henry Jacob. Admitted to Ill. bar, 1965, U.S. Supreme Ct. bar, 1972; asso. firm Axelrod, Goodman & Steiner, Chgo., 1966-67, Max & Herman Chill, Chgo., 1967-74, Bellows & Assos., Chgo., 1974-81, Marvin Sacks Ltd., Chgo., 1981; individual practice law, 1981—; basketball press dir. U. Chgo., 1967-74. Vice pres. Congregation Rodfei Zedek, 1979, bd. dirs., 1978—. Recipient Am. Jurisprudence award, 1963; citation meritorious service Dist. Grand Lodge 6 B'nai B'rith, 1969; My Brothers Keeper award Am. Jewish Congress, 1977. Mem. Chgo., Ill. State bar assns., Chgo. Jewish Hist. Soc. (treas. 1977-79, v.p. 1979-82, dir. 1977—), Chgo. Pops Orch. Assn. (treas., exec. com. 1975-81), Am. Jewish Hist. Soc., Art Inst. of Chgo., Chgo. Hist. Soc., Jewish Geneal. Soc. (dir. 1977—), Nu Beta Epsilon. Club: B'nai B'rith. Contbr. articles to profl. jours. and mags. Landlord-tenant, Probate, General practice. Home: 5400 S Hyde Park Blvd Apt 10-C Chicago IL 60615 Office: 120 W Madison St Chicago IL 60602

BERNSTEIN, EDWARD ALLAN, lawyer; b. Bklyn., Feb. 6, 1948; s. Sol and Evelyn (Weinstein) B.; m. Roberta Ellen Cohen, Mar. 28, 1970; children: Scott Peter, Jarrod Neal. BA, L.I. U., 1969; JD, Bklyn. Law School, 1972. Bar: N.Y. 1973, U.S. Dist. Ct. (ea. and so. dists.) N.Y. 1973, U.S. Ct. Appeals (2d cir.) 1979. Assoc. Stanley Finder, Queens, N.Y., 1972-73, Glassman & Elias, N.Y.C., 1973-83; ptnr. Glassman, Elias & Bernstein, N.Y.C., 1983—; instr. Nassau County Community Coll., Garden City, N.Y., 1983—. v.p. Merrick (N.Y.) Community Council, 1982—; exec. bd. Merrick Police Boys Club Soccer, 1983-86. Served to sgt. USAR, 1969-75. Recipient Appreciation citation Nassau County Police Boys Club Soccer, 1984. Mem. Am. Assn. Immigration Lawyers, N.Y. State Bar Assn., N.Y. County Bar Assn. Immigration, naturalization, and customs, Real property, Contracts commercial. Office: Glassman Elias & Bernstein 49 W 24th St New York NY 10010

BERNSTEIN, EDWIN S., judge; b. Long Beach, N.Y., Aug. 15, 1930; s. Harry and Lena (Strizver) B.; m. Mira Frost, Dec. 25, 1974; children—Debora, Andrea, David. B.A., U. Pa., 1952; LL.B., Columbia U., 1955. Bar: N.Y. 1955, U.S. Ct. Appeals (2d cir.) 1962, U.S. Dist. Ct. (ea. and so. dists.) N.Y. 1962, U.S. Tax Ct. 1962, U.S. Supreme Ct. 1964, Md. 1981, D.C. 1982. Mem. bd. contract appeals Dept. Army, Heidelberg, Fed. Republic Germany, 1968-72; regional counsel U.S. Navy, Quincy, Mass., 1972-73; adminstrv. law judge U.S. Dept. Labor, Washington, 1973-79, Fed. Mine Safety and Health Rev. Commn., Washington, 1979-81, U.S. Postal Service, Washington, 1981—; liaison rep. Administrv. Conf. of U.S., Washington, 1983-84; guest lectr. SUNY-Albany, 1978, U. Md., 1982, George Washington U., 1984. Author: U.S. Army Procurement Handbook, 1971; Establishing Federal Administrative Law Judges as an Independent Corps, 1984, also articles. Bd. dirs. Washington Hebrew Congregation, 1985—. Recipient Meritorious Civilian Service award Dept. Army, 1972. Mem. ABA, Fed. Bar Assn., D.C. Bar Assn., Fed. Adminstr. Law Judges Conf. (pres. 1983-84), Papermill Assn. (pres. 1980-81). Lodge: Masons. Avocations: golf; bridge; sailing; wines; opera. Administrative and regulatory, Federal civil litigation, Real property. Home: 7032 Buxton Terr Bethesda MD 20817 Office: US Postal Service 475 L'Enfant Plaza West SW Washington DC 20260

BERNSTEIN, H. BRUCE, lawyer; b. Omaha, Dec. 9, 1943; s. David and Muriel (Krasne) B.; m. Janice Ostroff, Aug. 27, 1967; children: Daniel J., Jill M. AB, Cornell U., 1965; JD, Harvard U., 1968. Bar: Ill. 1968. Ptnr. Sidley & Austin, Chgo., 1974—; lectr. Practicing Law Inst. 1978-79. Mem. ABA, Ill. Bar Assn., Chgo. Bar Assn., Nat. Bankruptcy Conf. Clubs: Monroe (Chgo.); Northmoor Country (Highland Park, Ill.). Avocations: golf, tennis. Office: Sidley & Austin One First National Plaza Chicago IL 60603 Home: 1740 W Summit Ct Deerfield IL 60015

BERNSTEIN, HOWARD MARK, lawyer; b. Washington, May 3, 1952; s. Howard and Mary Delia (Sliney) B.; m. Alice Ruth Huneycutt, Nov. 28, 1981; 1 child, Ashley Laughton. Bar: Fla. 1976, U.S. Dist. Ct. (so. dist.) Fla. 1976, U.S. Ct. Appeals (5th cir.) 1981, U.S. Ct. Appeals (11th cir.) 1981, U.S. Dist. Ct. (mid. dist.) Fla. 1982, U.S. Ct. Claims 1982, U.S. Supreme Ct. 1982, U.S. Ct. Appeals (fed. cir.) 1982. Assoc. Bradford, Williams, McKay, Kimbrell, Hamman & Jennings, P.A., Miami, Fla., 1976-78, Lane, Mitchell & Harris, P.A., Miami, 1978-81, Jacobs, Robbins, Gaynor, Hampp, Burns, Cole & Shasteen, P.A., St. Petersburg, Fla., 1981-83, Schultz & Walsh, P.A., Brandenton, Fla., 1983-85; asst. county atty. Pinellas County, Clearwater, Fla., 1985—. Mem. ABA, Clearwater Bar Assn., Barristers Soc. (lord high chancellor 1975-76). Democrat. Roman Catholic. State civil litigation, Insurance, Local government. Home: 526 21st Ave NE St Petersburg FL 33704 Office: Office of County Atty 315 Court St Clearwater FL 33516

BERNSTEIN, JACOB, lawyer; b. Glen Cove, N.Y., Dec. 23, 1932; s. David and Ida (Miller) B.; m. Eva Belle Smolokoff, June 28, 1959; children—Diane Susan, Neal Robert. A.B., U. Rochester, 1954; J.D., U. Mich., 1957. Bar: N.Y. 1957. Mem. Ralph J. Marino, 1959-64, Marino & Bernstein, 1964-73; mem. Marino, Bernstein & La Marca, P.C., Oyster Bay, N.Y., 1973—; lectr. in field. Founding mem., trustee Community Found., 1962—; trustee Oyster Bay Jewish Ctr., 1962—, pres. 1965-67; sec., bd. dirs. Oyster Bay Youth and Family Counseling Agy., 1975—; pres. Oyster Bay E. Norwich Youth Council , 1976-78; actor Sagamore Players, 1972—; mem., chief legal officer Sagamore Yacht Club, 1973—; div. chmn. United Jewish Appeal, 1965-74. Served with U.S. Army, 1958-59. Recipient United Jewish Appeal award of honor, 1972, Man of Yr. award Oyster Bay Jewish Ctr., 1986. Mem. N.Y. Bar Assn., U.S. Dist. Ct. Bar Assn., ABA, Nassau County Bar Assn., Nassau Lawyers Assn., North Shore Lawyers Assn. Republican. Lodge: Rotary (dist. parliamentarian 1986-87). Land Use and planning, Real property, Probate. Address: P O Box 180 Oyster Bay NY 11771

BERNSTEIN, JEREMY MARSHALL, lawyer; b. Denver, Dec. 29, 1952; s. Harry S. and Belle R. (Sperling) B.; m. Elyse A. Elliott, Aug. 23, 1985. BA with honors, Stanford U., 1975; JD, Boston U., 1979. Bar: Colo. 1979, U.S. Dist. Ct. D.C. 1979, U.S. Ct. Appeals (10th cir.) 1986. Law clk. to presiding justice Colo. Ct. Appeals, Denver, 1979-80; assoc. Grant, McHendrie, Haines & Crouse, Denver, 1980-82; jr. assoc. Cogswell & Wehrle, Denver, 1982-84; assoc. and head of litigation Garfield & Hecht, P.C., Aspen, Colo., 1984-87; ptnr. Wright, Schumacher & Bernstein, Aspen, 1987—. Mem. Colo. Trial Lawyers' Assn., Am. Trial Lawyers' Assn., ABA, Colo. Bar Assn., Pitkin County Bar Assn. (sec. 1985-86), Phi Beta Kappa. Avocations: skiing, fly fishing. Federal civil litigation, State civil litigation, Family and matrimonial. Office: Wright Schumacher & Bernstein 201 N Mill St Suite 106 Aspen CO 81611

BERNSTEIN, JOHN THOMAS, lawyer; b. Cleve., June 11, 1929; s. Maurice Bernstein and Dorothy (Fleishman) Kahn; m. Nancy Ross, Oct. 8, 1961; children: John T., Douglas J. BA, U. Cin., 1951; JD, Harvard U., 1954. Bar: Ohio 1954; CPCU. Asst. v.p. Prog. Casualty Ins. Co., Cleve., 1968-72; asst. gen. counsel State Farm Mut. Automobile Ins. Co., Bloomington, Ill., 1972—; mem. Joint Industry Com. on Automobile Theft and Fraud, 1981—; chmn. Ins. Industry Com. on Model Uninsured Motorist Law, 1985—. Chmn. Heart of Ill. region ARC Blood Services, Peoria, 1984-86. Served with U.S. Army, 1954-56. Recipient Pres.'s award Fla. Ins. Council, 1980-81; named Outstanding Vol. ARC, 1982. Mem. Ohio Bar Assn., Soc. CPCU's. Jewish. Insurance, Legislative, Administrative and regulatory. Home: 2625 Hall Ct Bloomington IL 61701 Office: State Farm Ins Cos 1 State Farm Plaza Bloomington IL 61701

BERNSTEIN, KENNETH ALAN, lawyer; b. Bklyn., Oct. 11, 1956; s. Jay M. and Marjorie J. (Rosenthal) B.; m. Joy S. Smilon, Aug. 10, 1980; 1 child, Lisa. BA, SUNY, Binghamton, 1978; JD, Am. U., 1981. Bar: N.Y. 1982, U.S. Dist. Ct. (so. and ea. dists.) N.Y. 1982. Asst. dist. atty. N.Y. County Dist. Atty's. Office, N.Y.C., 1981-86; assoc. Law Office of Robert I. Elan, Lake Success, N.Y., 1986—. Mem. ABA, N.Y. Bar Assn., Nassau County Bar Assn. Criminal, State civil litigation, Personal injury. Home: 309 Syosset-Woodbury Rd Woodbury NY 11797 Office: Law Offices of Robert I Elan 5 Dakota Dr Lake Success NY 11042

BERNSTEIN, LEWIS, lawyer; b. Bklyn., May 18, 1916; s. Muttle and Lillian (Friedman) B.; m. Elaine Gordon, Feb. 13, 1949. B.S., St. John's U., 1935, LL.B., 1938. Bar: N.Y. 1938, Maine 1948, U.S. Dist. Ct. Maine 1948, U.S. Supreme Ct. 1958, U.S. Dist. Ct. D.C. 1977, U.S. Dist. Ct. (ea. and so. dists.) N.Y. 1978, U.S. Ct. Appeals (3d cir.) 1982. Sole practice, Bklyn., 1938-41; ptnr. Roberts & Bernstein, Ft. Fairfield, Maine, 1947-53; trial atty. Antitrust div. U.S. Dept. Justice, Washington, 1953-58, chief spl. litigation sect., 1958-77, spl. asst. to atty. gen., 1978—; pres. Lewis Bernstein, P.C., 1978—. Served with AUS, 1941-46. Decorated Bronze Star. Mem. ABA, Fed. Bar Assn. Antitrust. Office: 1667 K St NW 8th Floor Washington DC 20006

BERNSTEIN, MARC ALAN, lawyer; b. Omaha, Dec. 9, 1955; s. Sandor L. and Florene E. (Cohen) B. AB, Duke U., 1977; JD, Georgetown U., 1980. Bar: D.C. 1980, U.S. Dist. Ct. (D.C. dist.) 1981, U.S. Ct. Appeals (D.C. Cir.) 1985, U.S. Ct. Appeals (11th cir.) 1986. Atty./advisor U.S. Dept. Energy Office Hearings and Appeals, Washington, 1980-82, dep. asst. dir., 1982-84; atty. Short, Klein and Kasas, Washington, 1984—. Mem. ABA, D.C. Bar Assn. (adminstrv. law div.). Administrative and regulatory, Transportation. Home: 1820 T St NW #3 Washington DC 20009 Office: Short Klein and Kasas 1101 30th St NW Suite 303 Washington DC 20007

BERNSTEIN, MICHAEL ALAN, lawyer; b. Detroit, Oct. 31, 1956; s. Frederick Bernard and Sandra Diane (Meier) B. BS in Psychology with honors, Mich. State U., 1978; JD, Nova U., 1981. Bar: Fla. 1981, U.S. Dist. Ct. (so. dist.) Fla. 1981, U.S. Ct. Appeals (5th and 11th cirs.) 1981, Mich. 1986. Assoc. Pyszka & Kessler P.A., Ft. Lauderdale, Fla., 1982-83; prin. Law Offices of Michael A. Bernstein P.A., Ft. Lauderdale, 1983—. Mem. ABA, Fla. Bar Assn., Broward Bar Assn., Assn. Trial Lawyers Am., Fla. Trial Lawyers Assn., Mich. Bar Assn., Mich. State U. Alumni Assn., Phi Delta Phi. Jewish. Club: Gold Coast Masters Swimming (Ft. Lauderdale). Avocations: athletics, triathelete, tennis, body fitness, health. State civil litigation, Personal injury, Federal civil litigation. Office: Law Offices Michael Bernstein PA 2734 E Oakland Park Blvd Suite 200 Fort Lauderdale FL 33306

BERNSTEIN, PAUL MURRAY, lawyer; b. N.Y.C., Dec. 24, 1929; s. Emanuel Klein and Anne Krasner-Glauber; m. Mae P. Bernstein, June 10, 1950; children: Jane Shapiro, Richard S. BA, Columbia U., 1951, LLB, 1953. Assoc. Chadbourne Parke W&W, N.Y.C., 1953-63; gen. mgr. Saks Fifth Ave, N.Y.C., 1964-68; ptnr. Kreindler & Kreindler, N.Y.C., 1969-83; sr. ptnr. Bernstein Litowitz Berger & Grossmann, N.Y.C., 1983—. Contbr. articles to N.Y. Law Jour., 1972—. Trustee Fed. Bar Council. Mem. ABA, Assn. of Bar of City of N.Y., Practicing Law Inst., ABA. Litigation, Securities. Home: 2526 Williams Ct Bellmore NY 11710 Office: Berstein Litowitz Berger & Grossmann 875 3d Ave New York NY 10022

BERNSTEIN, RICHARD FORBES, lawyer; b. Providence, Mar. 23, 1946; m. Beth A. Mandelbaum, June 29, 1980. BA, Williams Coll., 1967; MA, U. Chgo., 1971, PhD, 1976; JD, Harvard U., 1979. Bar: Ill. 1979, U.S. Dist. Ct. (no. dist.) Ill. 1979, U.S. Ct. Appeals (D.C. cir.) 1980, N.Y. 1983, U.S. Dist. Ct. (so. and ea. dists.) N.Y. 1983, U.S. Ct. Appeals (2d cir.) 1984. Assoc. Jenner & Block, Chgo., 1979-82, Guggenheimer & Untermyer, N.Y.C., 1982-85, Rosenman & Colin, N.Y.C., 1985—. Author: Legal Utilitarianism, 89 Ethics, 1979. Mem. ABA (com. on constrn. law and litigation), Bklyn. Bar Assn. (ethics com.), N.Y. County Lawyers Assn. (ethics and civil rights coms.). Contracts commercial, Construction, Federal civil litigation. Office: Rosenman & Colin 575 Madison Ave New York NY 10022

BERNSTEIN, ROBERT BRUCE, lawyer; b. N.Y.C., Oct. 5, 1955; s. Alfred and Sara June (Zoota) B. BA in History cum laude, Cornell U., 1977; JD, U. Va., 1981. Bar: N.Y. 1982, U.S. Ct. Appeals (9th cir.) 1982, U.S. Dist. Ct. (so. and ea. dists.) N.Y. 1983, U.S. Ct. Appeals (2d cir.) 1986. Legis. asst. to senator Harrison A. Williams, Washington, 1977-78; assoc. Kaye, Scholer, Fierman, Hays & Handler, N.Y.C., 1981—; v.p., treas., bd. dirs. 301 E. 22d St. Tenants Corp., N.Y.C., 1985—. Mem. ABA, Assn. of Bar of City of N.Y., Am. Judicature Soc. Democrat. Jewish. Avocations: skiing, windsurfing. Antitrust, Federal civil litigation, FERC practice. Home: 301 E 22d St Apt 4D New York NY 10010 Office: Kaye Scholer Fierman Hays & Handler 425 Park Ave New York NY 10022

BERNSTEIN, ROBERT GARY, lawyer, legal educator; b. San Antonio, Mar. 26, 1945; s. Benjamin and Sylvia (Flayer) B.; m. Zelda Steinberg, Aug. 31, 1968; children: Laura, Neil, Michael. BA, NYU, 1966; JD, Columbia U., 1970, MIA, 1970, MBA, 1971. Bar: N.Y. 1971, U.S. Dist. Ct. (so. and ea. dists.) N.Y. 1973, U.S. Ct. Appeals (2d cir.) 1973, Conn. 1979. Assoc. Gilbert, Segall & Young, N.Y.C., 1971-74; corp. atty., asst. sec. Chem. Constrn. Corp., N.Y.C., 1974-76; assoc. Layton & Sherman, N.Y.C., 1976-77; counsel Pitney Bowes Inc., Stamford, Conn., 1977-80, sr. counsel, 1980-84, asst. gen. counsel, 1984-86, assoc. gen. counsel, asst. sec., 1986—; adj. prof. bus. law U. Bridgeport, 1981-83. V.p. Congregation Beth El, Fairfield, Conn. Mem. ABA, N.Y. State Bar Assn., Westchester-Fairfield Corp. Counsel Assn. Jewish. Securities, General corporate, Real property. Office: Walter H Wheeler Jr Dr Stamford CT 06926

BERNSTEIN, ROBERT STEVEN, lawyer; b. Pitts., June 18, 1954; s. Joseph Jacob and Marlene Judith (Karsh) B.; m. Ellie Kay Broz, June 29, 1974; children: Katherine Arielle, Alex Steven. BA in Philosophy, U. Pitts., 1976; JD, Duquesne U., 1981. Bar: Pa. 1981, U.S. Dist. Ct. (we. dist.) Pa. 1981, Fla. 1983, U.S. Ct. Appeals (3d cir.) 1985, U.S. Supreme Ct. 1985. Ptnr. Apple & Bernstein P.C., Pitts., 1981-83, Bernstein & Bernstein P.C., Pitts., 1983—. Trustee Nat. Multiple Sclerosis Soc., Pitts., 1984—. Mem. Comml. Law League Am. (chmn. young members sect. 1986—, chmn. various coms.), Allegheny County Bar Assn. (council bankruptcy and comml. law sect. 1984—). Democrat. Jewish. Lodge: Masons (master 1981-84). Bankruptcy, Contracts commercial. Office: Bernstein and Bernstein PC 1133 Penn Ave Pittsburgh PA 15222

BERNSTEIN, SCOT D(AVID), lawyer; b. Los Angeles, Nov. 4, 1955. BA in Econs., UCLA, 1977; JD, U. Calif., Berkeley, 1980. Bar: Calif. 1980, U.S. Dist. Ct. (ea. dist.) Calif. 1980. Assoc. Van Camp & Johnson, Sacramento, 1980-82, Bolling, Walter & Gawthrop, Sacramento, 1982-84; sole practice Sacramento, 1984—. Mem. ABA, Calif. Bar Assn., Sacramento County Bar Assn., Capital City Trial Lawyers Assn., Sacramento Valley Venture Capital Forum. Securities, General corporate. Office: 1010 Hurley Way Suite 300 Sacramento CA 95825

BERNSTEIN, SIDNEY, lawyer; b. Bronx, N.Y., May 3, 1938; s. Meyer and Ethel (Sloop) B.; m. Joyce Elaine Blum, July 7, 1963; children: Michael Louis, Sheryl Lyn; m. 2d Andra Jane Schutz, June 6, 1982. B.A., Columbia U., 1960; J.D., Cornell U., 1964. Bar: N.Y. 1966, U.S. Dist. Ct. (we. dist.) N.Y. 1966, U.S. Dist. Ct. (so. dist.) N.Y. 1978, U.S. Ct. Appeals (D.C. cir.) 1980, U.S. Supreme Ct. 1971. Jr. editor Lawyer's Coop. Pub. Co., Rochester, N.Y., 1964-65, asst. mng. editor, 1966-71, editor Case and Comment Mag., 1966-71; sr. mng. editor Matthew Bender & Co., N.Y.C., 1971-75, asst. to pres., 1976-83; chief exec. officer, pres. Kluwer Law Book Pubs., Inc., N.Y.C., 1984—; faculty Nat. Coll. Advocacy, 1977—; adj. faculty Sch. Continuing Edn., NYU, 1980-81. Mem. editorial bd. Trial Mag.; mem. editorial adv. bd. Am. Criminal Law Rev., 1972-74; exec. editor: Nat. Law Rev. Reporter, 1981-83; editor-in-chief: Belli Soc. Internat. Law Jour.; editor: Criminal Defense Techniques, 6 vols., 1977-83; Columnist Supreme Ct. Rev., Trial Mag. contbr. articles to profl. jours. Mem. Roscoe Pound. Found.; pres. Bell Soc. Mem. ABA, Am. Law Inst., Am. Soc. Writers on Legal Subjects (past pres.), Assn. Trial Lawyers Am., N.Y. Trial Lawyers Assn., Nat. Assn. Criminal Def. Lawyers, Am. Judicature Soc., Trial Lawyers for Pub. Justice. Republican. Jewish. Clubs: Netherlands, Columbia. Lodge: Masons. Home: W Shore Towers Apt 6B 101 Gedney St Nyack NY 10960 Office: 36 W 44th St New York NY 10036

BERNSTEIN, STEPHEN MICHAEL, lawyer, real estate developer; b. Bklyn., Feb. 10, 1941; s. Murray P. and Harriet L. (Rosenberg) B.; m. Lois Blitzer Kleinerman, July 15, 1984; 1 stepchild, Matthew. B.A., Bklyn. Coll., 1962; LL.B., Columbia U., 1965. Bar: N.Y. 1965. Atty. HUD, N.Y.C., 1966-69; asst. counsel N.Y. State Urban Devel. Corp., N.Y.C., 1969-72, assoc. dir. housing devel., 1972-75; practice law, N.Y.C., 1975—; real estate developer, N.Y.C., 1975—; vis. prof. real estate fin. Pratt Inst., 1985. Bd. dirs. Am. Cancer Soc., N.Y.C., 1980—; bd. dirs. Florence Court Corp., Bklyn., 1982—, pres., 1982—. Mem. Nat. Housing Conf., Citizens Housing and Planning Council, N.Y. State Bar Assn. Club: City N.Y. Avocations: baseball, history. Real property, Local government, Construction. Home: 187 Hicks St Brooklyn Heights NY 11201 Office: 10 E 40th St New York NY 10016

BERNSTEIN, STUART, lawyer; b. Chgo., Nov. 23, 1919; m. Doris Golding. A.B., U. Chgo., 1942, J.D., 1947. Bar: Ill. 1947. Assoc. Mayer, Brown & Platt, Chgo., 1947-58, ptnr., 1958—; mem. United Air Lines Pilots System Bd., 1958-72. Pres. Dist. 113 Bd. Edn., Lake County, Ill., 1970-72; mem. Plan Commn. and Zoning Bd. Appeals, Highland Park, Ill., 1966-72. Served to 1st lt. USAAF, 1942-46. Decorated Air medal (5). Mem. ABA, Ill. Bar Assn., Chgo. Bar Assn., Chgo. Council Lawyers, Order of Coif, Phi Beta

Kappa. Clubs: Law, Standard (Chgo.). Editor-in-chief U. Chgo. Law Rev., 1947. Labor, Civil rights, Federal civil litigation. Office: Mayer Brown & Platt 190 S LaSalle St Chicago IL 60603

BERNSTEIN, ZAYLE ABRAHAM, lawyer, accountant; b. Morristown, N.J., Apr. 8, 1940; s. Charles and Gloria Bernstein; m. Cynthia Sue Pitterman, Jan. 25, 1964 (div.); children—Robert, Steven, Janet. B.B.A., U. Miami 1962, J.D. cum laude, 1971. Bar: Fla. 1971, U.S. Tax Ct., U.S. Ct. Appeals (5th, 9th and 11th cirs.), U.S. Supreme Ct. C.P.A., Fla. with IRS, 1962-69; sole practice, also cert. pub. acct., Hollywood, Fla., 1969-71; ptnr. DiGiulian, Spellacy & Bernstein, Ft. Lauderdale, Fla., 1971-79; sr. ptnr. Bernstein, Bernstein & Stein P.A., and predecessors, Ft. Lauderdale, 1979—; lectr., speaker tax seminars. Served with N.G. Recipient several Am. jurisprudence awards 1970; Govt. Relations award Fla. Inst. C.P.A.'s 1979. Mem. Lawyers Title Guaranty Fund, U. Miami Tax Law Soc., Am. Inst. C.P.A.'s, Broward County Bar Assn., Fla. Inst. C.P.A.s. Clubs: Inverrary (Lauderhill, Fla.); Tower (Ft. Lauderdale); Emerald Hills Country (Hollywood, Fla.); Ocean Reef (Key Largo, Fla.). Corporate taxation, Personal income taxation, Real property. Office: Bernstein Bernstein & Stein 1164 E Oakland Park Blvd 3d Floor Fort Lauderdale FL 33334

BERNTHAL, DAVID GARY, judge; b. Danville, Ill., Apr. 18, 1950; s. Albert F. and Mary Lou (Ackelmire) B.; m. Vicki Lynn Taylor, May 1, 1976. B, U. Ill., 1972, JD, 1976. Bar: U.S. Dist. Ct. (cen. dist.) Ill. Assoc. Brittingham, Sadler & Meeker, Danville, 1976-78; ptnr. Brittingham, Sadler, Meeker & Bernthal, Danville, 1979-80, Meeker & Bernthal, Danville, 1980-84, Snyder Meeker & Bernthal, Danville, Ill., 1984-86; assoc. judge 5th Jud. Cir. Ct., Danville, 1986—. Bd. dirs. Vermilion County chpt. ARC, 1982—, Lakeview Meml. Found., 1984—, Danville Area Community Coll. Found., 1985—; mem. Danville Zoning Com., 1982-86. Mem. ABA, Ill. State Bar Assn., Vermilion County Bar Assn., Assn. Trial Lawyers Am., Jaycees (Dist. Service award 1984). Republican. Lutheran. Club: Danville Country. Lodge: Rotary (pres. and bd. dirs. Danville club 1980-84). Avocations: golf, traveling. Home: 1418 Golf Terr Danville IL 61832 Office: Cir Ct 7 N Vermilion Danville IL 61832

BERRES, TERRENCE ROBERT, lawyer; b. Milw., Apr. 21, 1950; s. Robert Kenneth and Shirley June (Barker) B.; m. Karen Christine Engels, June 6, 1970; children: Paul Sean, Timothy Robert. BA, Marquette U., 1972; JD, U. Wis., 1976. Bar: Wis. 1976, U.S. Ct. Appeals (7th cir.) 1977, U.S. Dist. Ct. (ea. dist.) Wis. 1979. Assoc. Seher & Seher, Milw., 1976-77, Kasdorf, Dall, Lewis & Swietlik, S.C., Milw., 1977-83, Lloyd, Phenicie & Lynch S.C., Burlington, Wis., 1983-84; sr. trial atty. Am. Family Ins. Group, Brookfield, Wis., 1984—. Mem. ABA, Wis. Bar Assn., Civil Trial Counsel Wis. Roman Catholic. Personal injury, State civil litigation, Insurance. Home: 4070 S Packard Ave Saint Francis WI 53207 Office: Am Family Ins Group 440 S Exec Dr Brookfield WI 53005

BERREY, ROBERT WILSON, III, lawyer, judge; b. Kansas City, Mo., Dec. 6, 1929; s. Robert Wilson and Elizabeth (Hudson) B.; A.B., William Jewell Coll., 1950; M.A., U. S.D., 1952; LL.B., Kansas City U., 1955; LL.M., U. Mo. at Kansas City, 1972; grad. Trial Judges Coll., U. Nev., 1972; m. Katharine Rollins Wilcoxson, Sept. 5, 1950; children—Robert Wilson IV, Mary Jane, John Lind. Admitted to Mo. bar, 1955, Kans. bar, 1955, since practiced in Kansas City; asso. mem. firm Shugert and Thomson, 1955-56, Clark, Krings & Bredehoft, 1957-61, Terry and Welton, 1961-62; judge 4th Dist. Magistrate Ct., Jackson County, Mo., 1962-79; asso. cir. judge 16th Jud. Cir. Ct., Jackson County, Mo., 1979-81, cir. judge, 1981-83, mem. mgmt.-exec. com., 1979-83; judge Mo. Ct. Appeals-Western Dist., Kansas City, 1983—; mem. Supreme Ct. Com. to Draft Rules and Procedures for Mo.'s Small Claims Ct., 1976-86. Vol. legal cons. Psychiat. Receiving Center. Del. Atlantic Council Young Polit. Leaders, Oxford, Eng., 1965; Kansas City rep. to President's National Conference on Crime Control; del.-at-large White House Conf. Aging, 1972; former pack chmn. Cub Scouts Am.; counselor, com. mem. Boy Scouts Am., sponsor Eagle Scouts; vice chmn. water fowl com. Mo. Conservation Fedn., 1968-69, chmn. water fowl com., 1971-73; v.p. Cook PTA, 1967-68; mem. cts. and judiciary com. Mo. bar, 1969-73; mem. Midwest region adv. com. Nat. Park Service, 1973-78, chmn., 1973-78; mem. Mo. State Judicial Planning Commn., 1977; bd. dirs., founder Kansas City Open Space Found., 1976. Regional dir. Young Rep. Nat. Fedn., 1957-59, gen. counsel, 1959-61, nat. vice-chmn.; chmn. Mo. Young Rep. Fedn., 1960, nat. committeeman, 1959-60, 61-64; Mo. alternate at large Republican Nat. Conv., 1960, asst. gen. counsel, 1964, del. state and dist. convs., 1960, 64, 68. Bd. dirs. Naturalization Council, Kansas City, pres., 1973—; trustee Kansas City Mus., 1972-73, Hyman Brand Hebrew Acad., 1983—; hon. life dir. Rockhurst Coll. Mem. Mo. Bar (Disting. Service award 1973, agr. law com., com. council 1980-81), Kansas City Bar Assn., Urban League (exec. com., dir.), S.A.R., Kansas City Mus. Natural Sci. Soc. (charter), Tex. Longhorn Breeders Assn. (life), Am. Royal (bd. of govs. 1986), Mo. Longhorn Breeders Assn. (life), Alpha Phi Omega, Delta Theta Phi, Pi Gamma Mu, Tau Kappa Epsilon. Mem. Christian Ch. Mason, mem. DeMolay Legion Honor. Clubs: Kansas City; Waldo Optimist (v.p. 1967-68); Capitol Hill (Washington); Ducks Unltd. (state com. 1981—, nat. trustee 1986—), The Explorers. Family and matrimonial, State civil litigation, Legal history. Home: Rural Rt 2 Box 1078 Excelsior Springs MO 64024 Home (summer): Route 2 Battle Lake MN 56515 Office: Mo Ct Appeals Bldg 1300 Oak St Kansas City MO 64106

BERRY, ALONZO FRANKLIN, JR, lawyer; b. Nashville, June 29, 1944; s. Alonzo Franklin and Ruby Madison (Gum) B.; m. Mary Ann Kessler, Aug. 24, 1974; 1 dau., Jennie Ann. BBA, U. Miami, 1966, LLM, 1972; JD, U. Ky., 1969. Bar: Ky. 1969, D.C. 1973, Fla. 1973, U.S. Dist Ct. (mid. dist.) Fla. 1973, U.S. Ct. Claims 1973, U.S. Tax Ct. 1973, U.S. Supreme Ct. 1973, U.S. Ct. Appeals (11th cir.) 1981, Ga. 1985. Tax law specialist IRS, Washington, 1972-73; assoc. Giles, Hedrick & Robinson, Orlando, Fla., 1973-76; ptnr. Graham, Market & Scott, Orlando, 1976-77; sole practice, Orlando, 1977-81; ptnr. Smith, Mackinnon, Mathews & Berry, Orlando, 1981-82; gen. counsel Days Inns of Am., Inc., Atlanta, 1982-85; sole practice atty., cons., Atlanta, 1985—. Chmn. adult rehab. ctr. adv. com. Orlando Salvation Army, 1980-81. Served to capt. AUS, 1969-71. Decorated Bronze Star with oak leaf cluster. Mem. ABA. Democrat. Presbyterian. Corporate taxation, General corporate, Real property. Home and Office: 345 Quiet Water Ln Atlanta GA 30350

BERRY, BUFORD PRESTON, lawyer; b. Wichita Falls, Tex., Nov. 20, 1935; s. Buford P. and Fayette Jane (Herron) B.; m. Jane Carolyn Cato, Nov. 29, 1958; children—Laura Lynn, Buford Preston III. B.B.A., U. Tex., 1958, LL.B., 1963. Bar: Tex. 1963, U.S. Tax Ct. 1963, U.S. Dist. Ct. (no. dist.) Tex. 1965, U.S. Dist. Ct. (we. dist.) Tex. 1968, U.S. Ct. Appeals (5th cir.) 1969, U.S. Ct. Claims 1974, U.S. Ct. Appeals (3d cir.) 1977, U.S. Ct. Appeals (10th cir.) 1981. Assoc. Thompson & Knight, Dallas, 1963-69, ptnr., 1969-74, sr. ptnr., 1974—; lectr. in field. Active Goodwill Industries of Dallas, 1979—. Served to lt. USNR, 1958-60. Fellow Am. Coll. Tax Counsel; mem. ABA (chmn. natural resource com. tax sect. 1983-85), Tex. Bar Assn., Southwestern Legal Found. (chmn. tax sect. 1984-85). Clubs: Dallas, Brook Hollow Golf. Methodist. Corporate taxation, Personal income taxation. Office: Thompson & Knight 3300 1st City Ctr Dallas TX 75201

BERRY, CHARLES GORDON, lawyer; b. N.Y.C., Nov. 14, 1950; s. Rynn and Nancy (Ward) B.; m. Kathryn McGraw, April 23, 1983; children: Samuel Ward, Nicholas McGraw. BA, Yale U., 1972; MA, Cambridge U., 1974; JD, Columbia U., 1977. Bar: N.Y. 1978, U.S. Dist. Ct. (so. and ea. dists.) N.Y. 1978, D.C. 1979. Assoc. Milbank, Tweed, Hadley & McCloy, N.Y.C., 1977-86, ptnr., 1986—. Active Vol. Lawyers for Arts; founder, bd. dirs. Ollantay Ctr. for Arts, Queens, N.Y. Mem. ABA, N.Y. State Bar Assn., Assn. of Bar of City of N.Y. (transp. com. 1983—). Club: The River (N.Y.C.). Federal civil litigation, State civil litigation, Probate. Office: Milbank Tweed Hadley & McCloy One Chase Manhattan Plaza New York NY 10005

BERRY, CHARLES RICHARD, lawyer; b. Louisville, Apr. 19, 1948; s. Charles Russell and Lillie Juanita (Crady) B.; m. Joan Phyllis Rosenberg, Aug. 29, 1970; children: Kevin Charles, Ryan Andrew. BA, Northwestern U., 1970, JD, 1973. Bar: Ariz. 1973, U.S. Dist. Ct. Ariz. 1973, U.S. Ct. Appeals (9th cir.) 1983. Assoc. Snell & Wilmer, Phoenix, 1973-77; ptnr. Tilker, Burke & Berry, Scottsdale, Ariz., 1978-80, Norton, Berry, French & Perkins, P.C. and predecessor firm Norton, Burke, Berry & French, P.C., Phoenix, 1980-86; dir. Fennemore, Craig, von Ammon, Udall & Powers P.C., Phoenix, 1986—; bd. dirs. Cir. Research Labs Inc., Tempe, Ariz. Mem. Unitarian Ch. Lodge: Rotary. Securities, General corporate, Real property. Home: 6148 E Mountain View Rd Scottsdale AZ 85253 Office: Fennemore Craig 2 N Central Ave Suite 2200 Phoenix AZ 85004

BERRY, DEAN CLEMENT, lawyer; b. Sigourney, Iowa, Sept. 10, 1955; s. Dean Clement and Margaret Clare (Murphy) B. BS with distinction, U.S. Mil. Acad., 1977; JD, U. Calif., Berkeley, 1982; LLM with highest honor, George Washington U., 1986. Bar: Calif. 1982, U.S. Ct. Mil. Appeals 1984. Commd. 2d lt. U.S. Army, 1977, advanced through grades to capt., 1981; field artillery officer U.S. Army, Ft. Ord, Calif., 1977-79; trial def. counsel JAGC U.S. Army, Tongduchon, Republic of Korea, 1983; appellate atty. JAGC U.S. Army, Falls Church, Va., 1984-85, commr. ct. rev., 1985-86; chief, adminstrv. and civil law field artillery ctr. U.S. Army, Ft. Sill, Okla., 1986—. Bd. dirs. Indsl. Relations Law Jour., Berkeley, 1981-82. Mem. ABA, Assn. Trial Lawyers Am. Roman Catholic. Avocation: outdoor sports. Labor, Criminal. Home: 704 SW Gaylord Lawton OK 73505 Office: Office Staff Judge Adv Fort Sill OK 73503

BERRY, DOUGLAS CLAYTON, lawyer; b. Ft. Wayne, Ind., Jan. 30, 1952; s. D.C. and Mona L. (O'Shaughnessey) B.; m. Mary Helen Berry, Aug. 28, 1981; 1 child, Nicholas Wade. BS, Bowling Green State U., 1974; JD, U. Toledo, 1978. Law clk. to presiding justice U.S. Dist. Ct. (no. dist.) Ohio, Toledo, 1978-80, U.S. Ct. Appeals (6th cir.), Cin., 1980-81; assoc. Graham & Dunn, Seattle, 1981—. Republican. Federal civil litigation, State civil litigation, Antitrust. Home: 132 236th SW Bothell WA 98021 Office: Graham & Dunn 3400 Ruinier Bank Tower Seattle WA 98101

BERRY, GERALD THOMAS, lawyer; b. Miami, Fla., May 15, 1954; s. Grady Thomas and Pauline Octavia (Ellison) B.; m. Catherine Laich, Sept. 12, 1980; children: Taylor, Casey. BA, U. Fla., 1976; JD, Fla. State U., 1979. Bar: Fla. 1979, U.S. Dist. Ct. (mid. dist.) Fla. 1981, U.S. Dist. Ct. (so. dist.) Fla. 1984. Asst. states atty. State of Fla., Bartow, 1979-81, Naples, 1981-83; ptnr.. McDonnell & Berry, Naples, 1983—. Fellow Am. Trial Lawyers Assn., Acad. Fla. Trial Lawyers, Fla. Bar Assn.; mem. Collier County Bar Assn. (law library chmn. 1982-84, treas. 1983-84, bd. dirs. 1984-85, sec. 1985—). Avocations: softball, tennis, golf. Criminal, Personal injury, State civil litigation. Office: McDonnell & Berry 720 Goodlette Rd Naples FL 33940

BERRY, JAMES W. BILL, lawyer; b. Oklahoma City, Feb. 6, 1922; s. James Wilson and Elsie (Tratchel) B.; m. Lelah Maytubby, Feb. 14, 1946; children—Rebecca, James, Lauren, Jenifer. Student Cumberland U., 1946-47, U. Okla., 1947. Bar: Okla. 1949, U.S. Dist. Ct. (we. dist.) Okla. 1950, U.S. Ct. Appeals (10th cir.) 1951, U.S. Dist. Ct. (ea. dist.) Okla. 1952, U.S. Dist. Ct. (no. dist.) Okla. 1953, U.S. Supreme Ct. 1986. Practice, Oklahoma City, 1949-57, 60—; dist. atty. Oklahoma County, 1957-60; lectr. criminal law Oklahoma City U. and U. Okla. Coll. Law, 1968, 69, 71, 80, 81. Served to 1st lt. USAAF, 1941-45. Decorated D.F.C., Air medal with 3 oak leaf clusters, Purple Heart. Fellow Am. Coll. Trial Lawyers, Am. Judicature Soc., Am. Bd. Criminal Lawyers, Nat. Coll. Def. Lawyers; mem. ABA (criminal justice sect.) Okla. Bar Assn. (lectr. Seminars on Civil Appellate Procedure 1978, mem. coms.), Oklahoma County Bar Assn. (bd. dirs. 1978-71, bench and bar screening com. 1980-81), Okla. Trial Lawyers Assn., Assn Trial Lawyers Am., Am. Bd. Trial Advs. Democrat. Criminal, Personal injury, General practice. Office: 2500 First City Pl Oklahoma City OK 73102

BERRY, JAMES WILSON, lawyer; b. Oklahoma City, Apr. 15, 1950; s. James William and Lelah (Maytubby) B.; m. Nancy Paige Marshall, May 15, 1982; 1 child, Marshall Reid. BA, Rollins Coll., 1972; JD, Oklahoma City U., 1975. Bar: Okla. 1975, U.S. Dist. Ct. (we. and ea. dists.) Okla. 1985, U.S. Ct. Appeals (10th cir.) 1975. Legal intern Berry & Berry Atty.'s, Oklahoma City, 1974-75, ptnr., 1974-79; ptnr. James W. Bill Berry & Assocs., Oklahoma City, 1979—; arbitrator U.S. Dist. Ct. (we. dist.) Okla., 1985—. Bd. dirs. Okla. Go Hunter Jumper Charity Show, Oklahoma City, 1985—. Fellow Okla. Bar Found., mem. Am. Bd. Trial Advocacy (assoc.), Nat. Assn. Criminal Def. Lawyers, Okla. Bar Assns., Okla. Trial Lawyers Assn. Democrat. Methodist. Avocations: horseback riding, hunter-jumping competitions, flying, fly fishing. Criminal, Personal injury, Federal civil litigation. Office: James W Bill Berry and Assocs 2500 1st City Pl Oklahoma City OK 73102

BERRY, JAN VANCE, lawyer; b. Ames, Iowa, Mar. 14, 1951; s. Burl V. and Helen I. (Messer) B. B.A., Drake U., 1973, J.D., 1977. Bar: Iowa 1978, U.S. Dist. Ct. (so. dist.) Iowa 1978, U.S. Ct. Appeals (8th cir.) 1978, U.S. Dist. Ct. (no. dist.) Iowa 1986. Asst. Polk County Atty., Polk County Attys. Office, Des Moines, 1978-81; ptnr. Handley, Berry & Eisenhauer, Ankeny, Iowa, 1981-85, Handley & Berry, Ankeny, 1985—. Mem. Assn. Trial Lawyers Iowa, Iowa Bar Assn. Club: Ankeny Golf and Country. State civil litigation, Workers' compensation, Pension, profit-sharing, and employee benefits. Office: Handley & Berry 110 SE Grant St Suite 205 Ankeny IA 50021

BERRY, JOHN FREDRICK, lawyer; b. Memphis, June 15, 1955; s. Fred S. and Joan Luella (Noyes) B.; m. Peggy Anne Berry Parker, May 31, 1980; children: Parker, Anne. BBA, U. Tex., 1977, JD, 1980. Bar: Tex. 1980, U.S. Dist. Ct. (ea. dist.) Tex. 1981, U.S. Tax Ct. 1983. Lectr. U. Tex., Tyler, 1982-83; ptnr. Pye, Dobbs, Johnson & Berry, Tyler, 1980—. Contbr. articles to profl. jours. Mem. Tex. Assn. Bank Counsel, ABA, Smith County Bar Assn., Smith County Tex. Execs. (pres. 1986), Phi Alpha Delta. Episcopalian. Lodge: Lions (pres. Tyler Eve. club). Banking, Bankruptcy, Real property. Office: Pye Dobbs Johnson & Berry 100 Independence Pl Suite 400 Tyler TX 75703

BERRY, LESTA JEAN, lawyer, holding company executive; b. Iowa City, Iowa, June 7, 1940; d. Lester Jacob and Mary Viola (Droll) Gafeller; m. William Joseph Berry, Mar. 21, 1964. B.B.A., U. Iowa, 1964; J.D., DePaul U., 1978. C.P.A., Ill.; bar: Ill. 1978. Tax acct., sr. income tax acct. United Airlines, Inc., Chgo., 1964-73, mgr. income taxes, 1977-80, dir. taxes, 1980-85, v.p. taxes, 1986—; sr. tax acct. Sears Roebuck & Co., Chgo., 1973-77. Mem. ABA, Ill. Bar Assn., Chgo. Bar Assn., Tax Execs. Inst. Office: Allegis Corp PO Box 66919 Chicago IL 60666

BERRY, MARY FRANCES, history and law educator; b. Nashville, Feb. 17, 1938; d. George Ford and Frances Southall (Wiggins) B. B.A., Howard U., 1961, M.A., 1962; Ph.D., U. Mich., 1966, J.D., 1970; hon. degree, Cen. Mich. U., 1977, Howard U., 1977, U. Akron, 1977, Benedict Coll., 1979, U. Md., 1979, Grambling State U., 1979, Bethune-Cookman Coll., 1980, Clark Coll., 1980, Del. State Coll., 1980, Oberlin Coll., 1983, Langston U., 1983, Marian Coll., 1984, Haverford Coll., 1984, Colby Coll., 1986, CUNY, 1986, DePaul U., 1987. Bar: D.C. 1972. Asst. prof. history Central Mich. U., Mt. Pleasant, 1966-68; asst. prof. Eastern Mich. U., Ypsilanti, 1968-69; assoc. prof. Eastern Mich. U., 1969-70, U. Md., College Park, 1969-76; acting dir. Afro-Am. studies, 1970-72, dir., 1972-74, acting chmn. div. behavioral and social scis., 1973-74, provost div. behavioral and social scis., 1973-76; prof. history, prof. law U Colo. at Boulder, 1976-80, chancellor, 1976-77; prof. history and law Howard U., Washington, 1980—; asst. sec. for edn. HEW, Washington, 1977-80; mem. U.S. Commn. on Civil Rights, 1980—; adj. assoc. prof. U. Mich., 1970-71; mem. com. visitors U. Mich. Law Sch., 1976-80; mem. nat. adv. panel on minority concerns Coll. Bd., 1980-84; mem. adv. bd. Feminist Press, 1980—; mem. research adv. com. Joint Ctr. for Polit. Studies, 1981—; mem. editorial adv. com. Marcus Garvey Papers, 1981—; mem. adv. bd. Inst. for Higher Edn. Law and Governance, U. Houston, 1983—; Geraldine R. Segal prof. of am. social thought U. Pa., 1987—. Author: Black Resistance/White Law, 1971, Military Necessity and Civil Rights Policy, 1977, Stability, Security and Continuity, Mr. Justice Burton and Decision-Making in the Supreme Court, 1945-58, 1978, (with John Blassingame) Long Memory: The Black Experience in America, 1982; Why ERA Failed, 1986; asso. editor Jour. Negro History, 1974-78; contbr. articles, revs. to profl. jours. Bd. dirs. ARC, Washington, 1980—; trustee Tuskegee U., 1980—; mem. adv. bd. Project '87, 1978—; mem. council UN U., 1986—. Recipient Athena (disting. alumni) award U. Mich., 1977, Roy Wilkins Civil Rights award NAACP, 1983, Image award, 1983, Allard Lowenstein award, 1984, President's award Congl. Black Caucus Found., 1985, Woman of Yr. award Nat. Capital Area YWCA, 1985, Hubert H. Humphrey Civil Rights award Leadership Conf. on Civil Rights, 1986, Rosa Parks award SCLC, Black Achievement award Ebony Mag., Woman of Yr. award Ms. Mag., 1986. Mem. Nat. Acad. Public Adminstrn., Orgn. Am. Historians (exec. bd. 1974-77), Assn. Study of Afro-Am. Life and History (exec. bd. 1973-76), Am. Hist. Assn. (v.p. for profession 1980-83), Am. Soc. Legal History, ABA, Nat., D.C. bar assns., Coalition 100 Black Women (hon.), Delta Sigma Theta (hon.). Civil rights, Legal education, State civil litigation. Office: Commn on Civil Rights Office of the Chairman 1121 Vermont Ave NW Washington DC 20425

BERRY, RICHARD MORGAN, lawyer; b. Newport, R.I., Jan. 29, 1945; s. George Morgan and Eleanor (Prior) B.; m. Jane Elizabeth D'Esti, Jan. 22, 1972; 1 child, David Alric. BA, Pa. State U., 1967; MS in Mgmt. Scis., SUNY, Binghamton, 1973; JD, Bklyn. Law Sch., 1973. Bar: N.Y. 1974, Ill. 1982. Staff atty. med. soc. State of N.Y., Lake Success, 1973-77; mgr. profl. relations med. soc. County of N.Y., N.Y.C., 1977-78; sr. research atty. The Research Group, Inc., Charlottesville, Va., 1978-81; state legis. counsel ADA, Chgo., 1981-85, asst. gen. counsel, 1984-85, assoc. gen. counsel, 1985—; lectr. various nat. health orgns., 1982—. Columnist legis. and litigation JADA, 1981—. Mem. ABA. Roman Catholic. Avocations: golf, travel, writing, soccer referee. Health, Legislative, General corporate. Home: 1430 Brandon Rd Glenview IL 60025 Office: ADA 211 E Chgo Ave Chicago IL 60611

BERRY, ROBERTA MARIE, lawyer; b. Bellefonte, Pa., Jan. 5, 1955; d. Robert Charles and Beth Marie (King) Eck; m. William Warren Berry, Aug. 26, 1977. BA, Swarthmore (Pa.) Coll., 1976; JD cum laude, U. Wis., 1982. Bar: Wis. 1982, U.S. Dist. Ct. (we. and ea. dists.) Wis. 1982. Ptnr. Berry & Berry, Madison, Wis., 1982-83; legis. atty. Wis. Legislature, Madison, 1983-86; assoc. Whyte & Hirschboeck, S.C., Madison, 1986—. Mem. ABA, Wis. Bar Assn., Order of Coif. Health, General corporate, Insurance. Home: 7317 Sawmill Rd Madison WI 53717 Office: Whyte & Hirschboeck SC 44 E Mifflin St Suite 301 Madison WI 53703

BERRY, RYNN, lawyer; b. Los Angeles, Mar. 24, 1915; s. Ray Chamberlain and Ann (Rynn) B.; m. Anne Moorehead (div. 1946); 1 child, Rynn; m. Nancy Ward, Nov. 21, 1947; children: Eliot Ward, Charles Gordon, Peter Chamberlain. BA, Yale U., 1937, LLB, 1941. Bar: N.Y. 1942, D.C. 1948, U.S. Dist. Ct. (so. dist.) N.Y. 1949, U.S. Dist. Ct. Md. 1950, U.S. Dist. Ct. (ea. dist.) N.Y. 1952, U.S. Dist. Ct. (no. dist.) Ohio 1957, U.S. Dist. Ct. N.J. 1957, U.S. Ct. Appeals (4th cir.) 1959, U.S. Dist. Ct. (we. dist.) 1960, U.S. Dist. Ct. (no. dist.) Ind. 1960, U.S. Ct. Appeals (2d and 6th cirs.) 1960, U.S. Dist. Ct. Del. 1963, U.S. Dist. Ct. R.I. 1966, U.S. Dist. Ct. (we. dist) Okla. 1971, U.S. Dist. Ct. Conn. 1973, U.S. Dist. Ct. (no. dist.) Ill. 1973, U.S. Dist. Ct. (ea. dist.) N.C. 1974, U.S. Dist. Ct. (cen. dist.) Calif. 1975, U.S. Ct. Appeals (7th and 9th cirs.) 1977, U.S. Supreme Ct. 1977, U.S. Dist. Ct. (ea. dist.) Va. 1980, U.S. Ct. Appeals (8th cir.) 1980, U.S. Ct. Appeals (Fed. cir.) 1985. Assoc. Fish, Richardson & Neave, N.Y.C., 1941-42, 1946-55; ptnr. Fish & Neave, N.Y.C., 1955-85. Served to capt. U.S. Army, 1942-46, PTO. Republican. Congregationalist. Patent, Trademark and copyright. Office: Fish & Neave 875 3d Ave New York NY 10022-6250

BERRY, SAMUEL HARPER, JR., lawyer; b. Oakland, Calif., Nov. 23, 1956; s. Samuel Harper and Dorothy (Konkin) B. AB, Harvard U., 1978, JD, 1981. Bar: Calif. 1982, N.Y. 1982, U.S. Dist. Ct. (ea. dist.) Calif. 1985, U.S. Dist. Ct. (no. dist.) Calif. 1986, U.S. Tax Ct. 1986. Assoc. Shearman & Sterling, N.Y.C., 1981-83, Morgan, Lewis & Bockius, N.Y.C., 1983-84, Lempres & Wulfsberg P.C., Oakland, 1985-86, Lewis, D'Amato, Brisbois and Bisgaard, Los Angeles, 1987—. Mem. ABA, Phi Beta Kappa. State civil litigation, Federal civil litigation, Corporate taxation. Office: Lewis D'Amato Brisbois & Bisgaard 261 S Figueroa St Suite 300 Los Angeles CA 90012

BERRY, STEVEN CRAIG, lawyer; b. Elmhurst, Ill., Oct. 29, 1950; s. Roy Edwin and Myra (Kleis) B.; m. Nancy June Burke, Jan. 28, 1972; children: Christopher Shea, Hilary Ann, Meredith Hope, Brooke Morgan. BA, Hope Coll., 1972; JD, U. Detroit, 1976. Bar: Mich. 1976, U.S. Dist. Ct. (ea. dist.) Mich. 1976. Assoc. Keller, Thoma, Toppin & Schwarz P.C., Detroit, 1976-77; ptnr. Franklin, Bigler, Berry & Johnston P.C., Troy, Mich., 1977—. Commr., Mayor pro tem City of Pleasant Ridge, Mich. C.L. Burton scholar U. Detroit, 1976. Mem. Mich. Bar Assn., Assn. Trial Lawyers Am., Def. Research Inst. Club: Birmingham (Mich.) Country. Federal civil litigation, State civil litigation, Personal injury. Home: 1592 Buckingham Birmingham MI 48008 Office: Franklin Bigler Berry & Johnston PC 900 Tower Dr 14th Floor Troy MI 48098

BERRY, THOMAS EUGENE, lawyer; b. San Antonio, July 26, 1923; s. Kearie Lee and Alice Celeste (Fleming) B.; m. Joan Jester, June 30, 1951; children: James Buchanan, Janet, Alice. BBA, Southwestern U., Georgetown, Tex., 1944, U. Tex., 1949; LLB, U. Tex., 1951. Bar: Tex. 1951, U.S. Dist. Ct. (so. dist.) Tex. 1951, U.S. Ct. Appeals (5th cir.) 1953, U.S. Supreme Ct. 1960. Ptnr. Baker & Botts, Houston, 1963—. Trustee Goodrich Art Found., Houston, 1963—, M.B. Flake Home For Old Ladies, Houston, 1965—, Turner Charitable Found., Houston, 1975—, Isla Carroll Turner Friendship Trust, Houston, 1975—, Hope Ctr. For Youth, 1976—. Served with USMC, 1942-48, lt. col. Tex. NG, 1938-65. Fellow Am. Coll. Probate Counsel; mem. N.G. Assn. Tex. (minuteman award 1967), Phi Delta Phi, Delta Kappa Epsilon. Democrat. Episcopalian. Clubs: Coronado (Houston), Yale (N.Y.C.). Avocations: hunting, running, collecting stamps. Estate planning, Probate, Estate taxation. Home: 6151 Del Monte Houston TX 77057 Office: Baker & Botts 3000 One Shell Plaza 910 Louisiana Houston TX 77002-4995

BERRY, WILLIAM WELLS, lawyer; b. Nashville, Sept. 10, 1917; s. Allen Douglas and Agnes Wilkie (Vance) B.; m. Mary John Atwell, May 31, 1941 (dec.); children: William W., Edith Allen Berry Kain; m. Virginia N. Buntin, Jan. 4, 1986. B.A., Vanderbilt U., 1938, LL.B., 1940. Bar: Tenn. 1940. Practice Nashville, 1940-42, 46—; ptnr. Bass, Berry & Sims, 1965—; dir. Ingram Industries, Inc., Franklin Industries, Inc. Mem. Tenn. Inheritance Tax Study Com., 1977, 82; mem. adv. com. dental div. Tenn. Dept. Pub. Health, 1953-57; pres. Bill Wilkerson Hearing and Speech Ctr., 1959-67; bd. dirs. Noel Meml. Found., 1954-68; trustee Tenn. Fed. Tax Inst., 1973-79, pres., 1976-77; trustee Monroe Harding Home, 1971—, Washington Found., 1978—, Nashville Found., 1965-82. Served to capt. AUS, 1942-46. Decorated Air medal with oak leaf cluster. Fellow Am. Coll. Probate Counsel (Tenn. state chmn. 1975-81 bd. regents 1979-85), Internat. Acad. Trial Lawyers, Am. Bar Found., Tenn. Bar Found.; mem. ABA, Tenn. Bar Assn., Nashville Bar Assn. (dir. 1969-72, v.p. 1971-72), Am. Judicature Soc., Nashville C. of C., Nashville Srs. Golf Assn. (pres. 1978-80), Nat. Soc. SAR. Democrat. Presbyterian (deacon, elder). Clubs: Belle Meade Country (Nashville), Cumberland (Nashville), Capitol City (Nashville); Highlands Country (N.C.). General corporate, Probate, Corporate taxation. Home: 5110 Boxcroft Pl Nashville TN 37205 Also Home: 130 Pipers Ct Highlands NC 28941 Office: Bass Berry & Sims 2700 First American Ctr Nashville TN 37238

BERRYHILL, W. WADE, law educator. BS in Bus. Adminstrn. and Acctg., Ark. State U., 1967; JD, U. Ark., 1972; LLM, Columbia U., 1976. Adj. prof. estate planning North Ark. Community Coll., 1974-75; ptnr. Moore, Logan & Berryhill, 1972-76, of counsel, 1976; prof. law T.C. Williams Sch. Law, U. Richmond (Va.), 1976—; lectr. environmental law Richmond area middle and high schs., 1979-85; rep. Va. Fisheries and the Environment conf., 1979, Land Use Planning conf. U. N.C., Nat. Oceanic and Atmospheric Adminstrn. conf., 1980. Articles editor Ark. Law Rev., 1972. Mem. Va. Bar Assn. (bd. govs. real property sect., chmn. com. on wetlands legislation). Office: Univ Richmond TC Williams Sch Law Richmond VA 23173

BERSOFF, DONALD NEIL, lawyer, psychologist; b. N.Y.C., Mar. 1, 1939; s. Irving and Mina (Cohen) B.; children: David, Judith. B.S., N.Y. U., 1958; M.A., NYU, 1960, Ph.D., 1965; student, U. Va. Law Sch., 1973-74; J.D., Yale U., 1976. Bar: Md., D.C. Asst. prof. Ohio State U.; asso. prof. U. Ga., U. Md. Sch. Law; ptnr. Ennis, Friedman & Bersoff, Washington; coordinator joint J.D. and Ph.D. program in law and psychology U. Md. Sch. Law and

Johns Hopkins U. Dept. Psychology., 1976-86. Author: Learning to Teach: A Decision-Making System, 1976. Served with USAF, 1965-68. N.Y. State Regents coll. teaching fellow. Mem. Am. Psychology-Law Soc. (pres. 1980-81), Am. Psychol. Assn., ABA (com. mentally disabled), Nat. Health Lawyers Assn. Federal civil litigation, Health, Antitrust. Home: 1502 Vermont Ave NW Washington DC 20005 Office: 1200 17th St NW Washington DC 20036

BERSON, NORMAN SCOTT, lawyer; b. N.Y.C., Nov. 19, 1926; s. Joseph A. and Theresa (Levinsky) B.; m. Lenora Ersner, Aug. 26, 1955; children: Peter, Erica. BA, Temple U., 1950; LLB, U. Pa., 1953. Bar: Pa. 1953. Assoc. Folz, Bard, Kamsler, Goodis & Greenfield, Phila., 1953-60; ptnr. Friedman, Berson & O'Donnell, Phila., 1960-80, Hunt & Fineman, Phila., 1981—; mem. Pa. Ho. Reps., Harrisburg, 1966-82, chmn. judiciary com., 1976-80. Served with U.S. Army, 1944-46, PTO. Mem. Pa. Bar Assn., Phila. Bar Assn. Democrat. Jewish. Real property. Office: Hunt & Fineman 1608 Walnut St Philadelphia PA 19103

BERTAIN, G(EORGE) JOSEPH, JR., lawyer; b. Scotia, Calif., Mar. 9, 1929; s. George J. and Ellen Veronica (Canty) B.; m. Bernardine Joy Galli, May 11, 1957; 1 son, Joseph F. A.B., St. Mary's Coll. of Calif., 1951; J.D., Cath. U. Am., 1955. Bar: Calif. Assoc. Joseph L. Alioto, San Francisco, 1955-57, 59-65; asst. U.S. Atty. No. Dist. Calif., 1957-59; pvt. practice of law San Francisco, 1966—. Editor-in-chief, Law Rev. Cath. U. Am. (vol. 5), 1954-55. Chmn. San Francisco Lawyers Com. for Elections of Gov./Pres. Ronald Reagan, 1966, 70, 80, 84; spl. confidential adviser to Gov. Reagan for jud. selection, San Francisco, 1967-74; chmn. San Francisco Lawyers for Better Govt., 1978-87; confidential adv. on jud. selection to Senator Hayakawa, 1981-82, Gov. Deukmejian, 1983—; bd. regents St. Mary's Coll. of Calif., 1980—; mem. civilian adv. com. U.S. 6th Army, Presidio, San Francisco. Recipient De La Salle medal St. Mary's Coll. of Calif., 1951, Signum Fidei award St. Mary's Coll. of Calif., 1976. Mem. ABA, Calif. Bar Assn., Fed. Bar Assn. (del. 9th Circuit Jud. Conf. 1967-76), Am. Judicature Soc., St. Thomas More Soc. San Francisco, Calif. Acad. Scis., Mus. Soc., Assn. Former U.S. Attys. and Asst. U.S. Attys. of No. Calif. (past pres.), Supreme Ct. Hist. Soc., Western Assn. Republican. Roman Catholic. Clubs: Commonwealth, Commercial, Olympic, 1st Friday Group. Lodges: K.C., Order of Knights of Malta. Antitrust, Federal civil litigation. Office: 1250 Alcoa Bldg Suite 1600 One Maritime Plaza San Francisco CA 94111

BERTELSMAN, WILLIAM ODIS, judge; b. Cin., Jan. 31, 1936; s. Odis William and Dorothy (Gegan) B.; m. Margaret Ann Martin, June 13, 1959; children: Kathy, Terri, Nancy. B.A., Xavier U., 1958; J.D., U. Cin., 1961. Bar: Ky. bar 1961. Law clk. firm Taft, Stettinius & Hollister, Cin., 1960-61; mem. firm Bertelsman & Bertelsman, Newport, Ky., 1962-79; judge U.S. Dist. Ct. Eastern Dist. Ky., Covington, 1979—; instr. Coll. Law U. Cin., 1965-72; city atty., prosecutor Highland Heights, Ky., 1962-69. Contbr. articles to profl. jours. Served to capt. AUS, 1963-64. Mem. No. Ky. C. of C. (pres. 1974, dir. 1969-77), Ky. Bar Assn. (bd. govs. 1978-79), Am. Bar Assn., Campbell County Bar Assn. Republican. Roman Catholic. Club: Optimist. Jurisprudence. Home: 78 W Vernon Ln Fort Thomas KY 41075 Office: US Distrcit Ct 7th & Scott Sts PO Box 1012 Covington KY 41012 *

BERTHOLD, ROBERT VERNON, JR., lawyer; b. Charleston, W.Va., June 23, 1951; s. Robert V. and Betty Jeanne (Harkins) B.; m. Jacqueline G. Baisden, Aug. 9, 1976; children—Robert V., III, Matthew Chandler. B.S. cum laude, W.Va. U., 1973; J.D., 1976. Bar: W.Va. 1976, U.S. Dist. Cts. (no. and so. dists.) W.Va. 1976, U.S. Ct. Appeals (4th cir.) 1977. Assoc. Hoyer & Sergent, Charleston, W.Va., 1976-79; ptnr. Hoyer, Hoyer & Berthold, Charleston, 1979—; arbitrator Am. Arbitration Assn., 1978—. Mem. ABA, W.Va. Bar Assn., W.Va. Trial Lawyers Assn., (bd. dirs. 1984—), Assn. Trial Lawyers Am., Kanawha County Bar Assn. Democrat. Presbyterian. Personal injury, Federal civil litigation, State civil litigation. Home: 1605 Wilshire Pl Charleston WV 25301 Office: Hoyer Hoyer and Berthold 22 Capitol St Charleston WV 25301

BERTHOLF, TERRY DONALD, lawyer; b. Kingman, Kans., Dec. 15, 1947; s. Donald Earl and Phyllis Irene (Dennet) B.; m. Linda M. Beebe, June 11, 1977; children: Matthew, Todd. BA, Kans. U., 1970, JD, 1973. Bar: Kans. 1973, U.S. Dist. Ct. Kans. 1973, U.S. Ct. Appeals (10th cir.) 1985. Sole practice Hutchinson, Kans., 1974—; cons. Kans. Farmers Service Assn., Hutchinson, 1974—; sec. Agri-Bus. Benefit Group, Hutchinson, 1984—. Mem. Nat. Council Farmer Coops., Nat. Soc. Accts. for Coops. (past v.p., sec., pres. 1987 midwest chpt.). General corporate, Contracts commercial, Consumer commercial. Office: 100 E 1st PO Box 2560 Hutchinson KS 67504-2560

BERTRAND, LOUIS ROBERTSON, lawyer; b. Wilmington Del., July 16, 1942; m. Sharon Ann Clark, June 1966; children—Robertson, Elisa, Laura. B.A. in History, SUNY-Buffalo, 1965; J.D., U. Toledo, 1968. Bar: Ohio 1968, Mich. 1969, U.S. Dist. Ct. (no. dist.) Ohio 1970; diplomate Nat. Bd. Trial Advocacy. Investigator, Toledo Police Dept., 1967-68; probation officer Portage County Juvenile Ct., Ravenna, Ohio, 1968-69; asst. pros. atty. Portage County, 1969-72; instr. Dept. Mgmt. Kent State U., Ohio, 1969-70; ptnr. Bertrand & Zavinski, Ravenna, 1971—. Councilman, Hiram, Ohio, 1973—, mem. fin. com., chmn. safety com., pres. Village Council, 1976-78; bd. dirs. Portage County Hospice Council. Mem. Assn. Trial Lawyers Am., Ohio Acad. Trial Lawyers, Akron Bar Assn., Portage County Bar Assn. (chmn. grievance com. 1975), Summit-Portage Football Offcials Assn. (assoc.) Clubs: Ohio State Athletic Assn. (lic. official baseball, 1983, football, 1980). Personal injury, State civil litigation, Bankruptcy. Office: Bertrand & Zavinski PO Box 268 409 S Prospect Ravenna OH 44266

BERTSCH, GENE CLAIR, lawyer; b. Pitts., Feb. 4, 1950; s. George R. and Gladys J. (Ressler) B.; m. Mary L. Wilhite, Aug. 12, 1972; children: Lara, Lisa, David. BA in Internat. Studies, Am. U., 1972; JD magna cum laude, U. Pitts., 1975. Bar: Pa. 1975, U.S. Dist. Ct. (we. dist.) Pa. 1979, U.S. Supreme Ct. 1982. Law clk. to presiding justice Ct. Common Pleas, Pitts., 1975-77; head legal sect. Bur. Air Pollution Control, Pitts., 1977-81; sr. atty. Duquesne Light Co., Pitts., 1981—. Officer YMCA, Pitts., 1983—. Recipient Law and Medicine prize Teplitz Found., 1975. Mem. Allegheny County Bar Assn. (annual prize 1975), Environ. Lawyers Group. Lutheran. Avocation: music, skiing, outdoor activities. General corporate, Labor, Environment. Home: 124 Elmore Rd Pittsburgh PA 15221 Office: Duquesne Light Co One Oxford Centre Pittsburgh PA 15279

BERTSCHE, COPELAND GRAY, lawyer; b. N.Y.C., Aug. 8, 1941; s. William I. and Louise Copeland (Gray) B.; m. Andree Gowen Wright; children: Alane Wright, Brijit Meehan, Victoria Gray, Jessica Harper. BA, Colgate U., 1963; JD, Seton Hall U., 1971; MBA, NYU, 1976. Bar: N.J. 1971, U.S. Dist. Ct. N.J. 1971, U.S. Supreme Ct. 1977, U.S. Ct. Appeals (3d cir.) 1979, N.Y. 1980. Mgr. Lawyers & Merchants Transl. Bur., N.Y.C., 1966-71; assoc. Law Offices of John B.M. Frohling, Newark, 1971-74, Connell, Foley & Geiser, Newark, 1974-76; atty. N.J. Bell Telephone Co., Newark, 1976-81; gen. atty. AT&T, N.Y.C., 1981—; v.p., gen. counsel AT&T Resource Mgmt. Corp., Berkeley Heights, N.J., 1986—; assoc. prof. Seton Hall U., Newark, 1976-77. V.p. Montclair (N.J.) Bd. Edn., 1979-82. Served to 1st lt. U.S. Army, 1963-66. Mem. ABA, N.Y. State Bar Assn., N.J. Bar Assn., Essex County Bar Assn. Roman Catholic. Club: Montclair Golf. General corporate, Real property, Contracts commercial. Home: 147 S Mountain Ave Montclair NJ 07042 Office: AT&T Resource Mgmt Corp 1 Oak Way Berkeley Heights NJ 07922-2727

BERWICK, PHILIP CREGAR, law librarian; b. Phila., July 25, 1951; s. Leonard and Mary (Cregar) B.; m. Carol Ann Fichtelman, Aug. 18, 1978; 1 child, Meredith Shaffer. BA, U. Pa., 1973; JD, U. Toledo, 1978; AMLS, U. Mich., 1979. Bar: Ohio 1978. Evening circulation supr. U. Toledo Law Library, 1977-79; assoc. law librarian U. Toledo Coll. Law, 1979-81; head law library reading room Law Library of Congress, Washington, 1981-84; asst. librarian for pub. services Georgetown U. Law Library, Washington, 1984—; head research and writing program. U. Toledo, 1979-81, tchr. criminal law, 1980. Mem. Am. Assn. Law Libraries, Am. Soc. Legal History, Law Librarians Soc. of D.C. Librarianship, Legal education. Home: 324 South Carolina Ave SE Washington DC 20003

BERZOW, HAROLD STEVEN, lawyer; b. Bklyn., Oct. 22, 1946; s. Julius and Lillian (Hershkowitz) Brzozowsky; m. Lynore Kushner, Aug. 22, 1970; children—Alan, Jason, Rachel. B.A., Bklyn. Coll., 1968; J.D., Bklyn. Law Sch., 1971. Bar: N.Y. 1972, U.S. Dist. Ct. (so. and ea. dists.) N.Y. 1973, U.S. Ct. Appeals (2d cir.) 1975, U.S. Supreme Ct. 1978. Assoc. Finkel, Nadler & Goldstein, N.Y.C., 1971-77; ptnr. Finkel, Goldstein & Berzow, N.Y.C., 1977—. Mem. ABA, N.Y. County Bar Assn., N.Y. State Bar Assn., Bankruptcy Bar Assn., Nassau County Bar Assn. Jewish. Bankruptcy, Contracts commercial, General corporate. Home: 15 Acorn Ln Plainview NY 11803 Office: Finkel Goldstein & Berzow 67 Wall St New York NY 10005

BESCHLE, DONALD L., legal educator; b. Danbury, Conn., Oct. 15, 1951; s. Donald J. and Marian (Tomaino) B. BA, Fordham U., 1973; JD, NYU, 1976; LLM, Temple U., 1983. Bar: N.Y. 1977, U.S. Dist. Ct. (so. and ea. dists.) N.Y. 1977. Assoc. Philips, Nizer, Benjamin, Krim & Ballon, N.Y.C., 1976-79; teaching fellow Temple U. Sch. Law, Phila., 1979-81; asst. prof. The John Marshall Law Sch., Chgo., 1981-86, assoc. prof., 1986—. Contbr. articles to law revs. Mem. ABA, Order of the Coif. Democrat. Roman Catholic. Antitrust, Civil rights, Legal education. Home: 850 N State St #4D Chicago IL 60610 Office: The John Marshall Law Sch 315 S Plymouth Ct Chicago IL 60604

BESHAR, CHRISTINE, lawyer; b. Paetzig, Germany, Nov. 6, 1929; came to U.S., 1952, naturalized, 1957; d. Hans and Ruth (vonKleist-Retzow) von Wedemeyer; m. Robert P. Beshar, Dec. 20, 1953; children: Cornelia, Jacqueline, Frederica, Peter. Student, U. Hamburg, 1950-51, U. Tuebingen, 1951-52; B.A., Smith Coll., 1953. Bar: N.Y. 1960, U.S. Supreme Ct. 1971. Asso. firm Casey, Lane & Mittendorf, N.Y.C., 1960-63; assoc. firm Cravath, Swaine & Moore, N.Y.C., 1964-70; partner Cravath, Swaine & Moore, 1971—. Bd. dirs. Catalyst for Women Inc., 1977—; trustee Colgate U., 1978-84. Inst. Internat. Edn. fellow, 1952-53; recipient Disting. Alumnae medal Smith Coll., 1974. Fellow Am. Coll. Probate Counsel, Am. Bar Found.; mem. Assn. Bar City N.Y. (exec. com. 1973-75, v.p. 1985-86), N.Y. State Bar Assn. (ho. of dels. 1971-80, v.p. 1979-80), N.Y. State Bar Found. (bd. dirs. 1977—), UN Assn. (bd. dirs. 1975—), Fgn. Policy Assn. (bd. dirs. 1978-87). Presbyterian. Clubs: Wall St., Downtown Assn., Cosmopolitan, Gipsy Trail. Home: 120 East End Ave New York NY 10028 : Stone House Box 533 Somers NY 10589 Office: Cravath Swaine & Moore 1 Chase Manhattan Plaza New York NY 10005

BESHAR, ROBERT PETER, lawyer; b. N.Y.C., Mar. 3, 1928; m. Christine von Wedemeyer, Dec. 20, 1953; children: Cornelia, Jacqueline, Frederica, Peter. A.B. (Scholar of the House, honors with exceptional distinction), Yale U., 1950, LL.B., 1953. Bar: N.Y. 1954. Asst. gen. counsel Waterfront Commn. N.Y. Harbor, 1954-55; law sec. Hon. Charles D. Breitel, Appellate div. 1st dept. N.Y. Supreme Ct., N.Y.C., 1956-58; spl. hearing officer Justice Dept., 1967-68; dep. asst. sec. Commerce; dir. Bur. Internat. Commerce; nat. export expansion coordinator Commerce Dept., Washington, 1971-72; pvt. practice N.Y.C., 1972—; Dir. Nat. Semiconductor Corp., Nat. Investor Data Services, Inc.; dir. Deep Ocean Tech., Inc.; mem. bus. adv. panel Nat. Commn. for Rev. of Antitrust Laws, 1978-79; mem. Mcpl. Securities Rulemaking Bd., 1982-85. Author: Current Legal Aspects of Doing Business With Sino-Soviet Nations, 1973; Editor: Manhattan Auto Study, 1973; contbg. editor: Boardroom Reports, 1974—. Trustee United Bd. Christian Higher Edn. in Asia, 1981—. Mem. ABA (chmn. corporate and antitrust law com. 1982-85), Internat., N.Y. State bar assns., Assn. Bar City N.Y., Westchester and No. Westchester Bar Assn., N.Y. County Lawyers Assn. (dir.), Phi Beta Kappa. Presbyterian. Clubs: Down Town (N.Y.C.); Gipsy Trail (Carmel, N.Y.); Elizabethan (New Haven). Federal civil litigation, General corporate, General practice. Home: 120 East End Ave New York NY 10028 Office: 100 Maiden Lane Ste 1608 New York NY 10038 Office: PO Box 533 Somers NY 10589

BESOZZI, PAUL CHARLES, lawyer; b. N.Y.C., Aug. 22, 1947; s. Alfio Joseph and Lucy Agnes (Ducibella) B.; m. Caroline Lisa Hesterberg, Oct. 7, 1978; 1 child, Christina Claire. B.S. cum laude in Fgn. Service, Georgetown U., 1969, J.D., 1972; M.B.A. in Bus./Govt. Relations, George Washington U., 1977. Bar: Va. 1972, D.C. 1973, U.S. Ct. Mil. Appeals 1972, U.S. Supreme Ct. 1977, U.S. Ct. Appeals (4th cir.) 1978. Assoc. Arnold & Porter, Washington, 1977-80; gen. counsel, minority counsel U.S. Senate Com. on Armed Services, Washington, 1980-83; ptnr. Hennessey, Stambler & Siebert, P.C., Washington, 1984-86, Besozzi & Gavin, 1987—. Contbr. articles and revs. to legal jours. Editor Georgetown Law Jour., 1971-72. Alumni interviewer Georgetown U. Alumni Assn., Washington, 1981—. Served as capt. JAGC, U.S. Army, 1972-76. Mem. ABA, Am. Soc. Internat. Law, Arms Control Assn., Phi Beta Kappa, Phi Alpha Theta, Pi Sigma Alpha. Administrative and regulatory, Legislative, Private international. Office: Besozzi & Gavin 1901 L St Suite 200 Washington DC 20036

BESSER, AMY HELENE, lawyer; b. Reading, Pa., July 11, 1956; d. Wallace and Trina Mae (Daniels) Rudolph; m. Marcus Peter Besser, Dec. 15, 1985. BS in Econs., U. Pa., 1978; JD, Rutgers U., 1981. Bar: Pa. 1981, N.J. 1981, U.S. Dist. Ct. N.J. 1981, U.S. Dist. Ct. (ea. dist.) Pa. 1986. Assoc. Sauer, Boyle, Dwyer & Canellis, Westfield, N.J., 1982-83, Korn, Kline & Kutner, Phila., 1983-86; house counsel Am. Equity Devel. and Mgmt. Cos., North Wales, Pa., 1986—. Democrat. Jewish. Avocations: reading, sports. Real property, General corporate. Home: 7413 Overhill Rd Melrose Park PA 19126 Office: Am Equity Devel and Mgmt Cos English Village Profl Ctr Suite 104 North Wales PA 19454

BESSER, HOWARD RUSSELL, lawyer; b. Cleve., Sept. 12, 1941; s. Morris Milton and Florence Helen (Sandler) B.; m. Barbara Kaye, Sept. 3, 1972; 1 child, Matthew Emerson Doublas. B.A., Ohio State U., 1963, J.D., 1966. Bar: Ohio 1966, U.S. Dist. Ct. (no. dist.) Ohio 1967, U.S. Ct. Appeals (6th cir.) 1975, U.S. Supreme Ct. 1977. Assoc. Griff, Weiner & Orkin, Cleve., 1966-68; asst. dir. law, counsel to mayor City of Cleve., 1968-71; U.S. dist. counsel EEOC, 1971-76; trial atty. Ohio Bell Telephone Co., 1976—; lectr. law Cleve. State U., 1971-85, adj. prof., 1985—. Contbr. articles to profl. jours. State pres. ACLU, 1973-75, 83—, v.p., 1982-83, 70-73, bd. dirs., 1968-77, 80—; mem. adv. council Mus. Arts Assn., 1983—; vice-chmn. New Democratic Coalition Cuyahoga County, 1969-71; trustee No. Ohio Unit Am. Jewish Congress, 1983—. Recipient Outstanding Civil Libertarian of Yr. award ACLU, 1975. Mem. ABA, Ohio Bar Assn. (chmn. civil rights com. 1980—), Cuyahoga County Bar Assn. (trustee 1983—), Cleve. Bar Assn., Sphinx, Tau Epsilon Rho. Labor, Civil rights, Legal education. Home: 3554 Stoer Rd Shaker Heights OH 44122 Office: Ohio Bell Telephone Co 45 Erieview Plaza Room 1448 Cleveland OH 44114

BESSON, PAUL SMITH, lawyer; b. N.Y.C., May 11, 1953; s. Frederick A. and Patricia (Smith) B. BS, Cornell U., 1975, MBA, 1976; JD, Northwestern U., 1980. Bar: Ill. 1980, N.Y. 1981. Mktg. planning analyst Cummins Engine Co., Columbus, Ind., 1976-77; labor relations counsel Jewel Cos., Chgo., 1980-83, mgr. personnel, labor relations, 1983-84; mgr. labor relations NBC Inc., Chgo., 1984—; arbitrator AAA Panel Comml., Chgo., 1985—; hearing officer State Univ. Ill. Civil Service commn., Chgo., 1983—. Contbr. articles to Black Enterprise mag. Mem. ABA, Ill. Bar Assn., N.Y. State Bar Assn., Chgo. Bar Assn., Cook County Bar Assn., Chgo. Black Cornell Alumni Assn. (pres. 1984-86). Roman Catholic. Avocations: photography, travel. Labor, Entertainment, General practice. Home: 4900 Marine Dr Chicago IL 60640 Office: NBC Merchandise Mart Chicago IL 60654

BEST, FRANKLIN L., JR., lawyer; b. Lock Haven, Pa., Dec. 14, 1945; s. Franklin L. and Hazel M. (Yearick) B.; m. Kimberly R., May 1, 1982. B.A., Yale U., 1967; J.D., U. Pa., 1970. Bar: Pa. 1970. Assoc. MacCoy, Evans & Lewis, Phila., 1970-74; asst. counsel Penn Mutual Life Ins. Co., Phila., 1974-77, asst. gen. counsel, 1978-84, assoc. gen. counsel, 1985—; counsel, asst. sec. Penn Ins. and Annuity Co., Phila., 1983—; lectr. Pa. Bar Inst. Bd. dirs. Center City South Neighborhood Assn., 1979-80; pres. Center City South Neighborhood Assn., 1978-79; mem. Com. of Seventy, 1978-84; sec. Washington Sq. Assn., 1977—; mem. 30th Ward Republican Exec. Com., 1972-84. Mem. Phila. Bar Assn., ABA, Internat. Claim Assn. (exec. com. 1980-81, 85—). Presbyterian. Club: Yale of Phila. Contbr. articles to profl. jours. Insurance, Federal civil litigation, Probate. Office: Penn Mutual Life Ins Co Independence Sq Philadelphia PA 19172

BEST, GEORGE BULLOCK, JR., lawyer; b. Tacoma, July 25, 1949; s. George Bullock and Louise Lavina (Mournout) B.; m. Shirley Marie Brooke, June 11, 1973; children: Wendy M., Anthony G., Nicholas M. BA with honors, U. Mont., 1971, JD, 1974. Bar: Mont., U.S. Ct. Appeals (9th cir.), U.S. Tax Ct. Assoc. Murphy Robinson Heckathorn & Phillips, Kalispell, Mont., 1974-76, ptnr., 1976-81; sole practice Kalispell, Mont., 1981—; prof. U. Mont., Missoula, 1974; speaker Law Day Flathead Community High Sch., Kalispell, 1976-78; advisor and cons. Mont. Med. Malpractice Panel, Helena, 1985. Bd. dirs. Flathead Valley Pee Wee League, Kalispell, 1974-80; committeeman Bigfork Bambino Baseball League, Mont., 1986. Mem. Mont. Bar Assn., Assn. Trial Lawyers Am., Buffalo Hill Golf Assn. (committeeman 1986), Phi Delta Phi (chmn. spl. coms.). Roman Catholic. Avocations: fishing, hunting, golf. Federal civil litigation, State civil litigation, Criminal. Office: George B Best PO Box 278 Kalispell MT 59903

BETH, KENNETH NORMAN, lawyer; b. Elgin, Ill., Jan. 13, 1943; s. Norman William and Ethel Carolyn (Albrecht) B.; m. Mary Ellen Read, May 1, 1971; children—Phillip K., Matthew C., Michael A. B.A., Valparaiso (Ind.) U., 1965, J.D., 1968; M.B.A., U. Ill., Urbana, 1979. Bar: Ill. 1968, U.S. Ct. Mil. Apls. 1970, U.S. Sup. Ct. 1972. Ct. commr. U.S. Ct. Mil. Apls., Washington, 1973-75; assoc. Tepper & Gwinn, P.C., Urbana, 1979—; city atty., Urbana, 1975—; instr. U. Md., 1974-75. Served to lt. comdr. JAGC, USNR, 1969-73. Mem. ABA, Ill. Bar Assn., Champaign County Bar Assn., Nat. Inst. Mcpl. Law Officers, Ill. Mcpl. League. Lutheran. Local government, Real property, State civil litigation. Home: 1205 S Orchard St Urbana IL 61801 Office: 209 W Elm St Urbana IL 61801

BETHEA, WILLIAM LAMAR, JR., lawyer; b. Dillon, S.C., June 2, 1940; s. William Lamar and Lillie (Hotchkiss) B.; m. Margaret McInnis, June 23, 1962 (div. Mar. 1977); children—William Lamar, Margaret Amanda; m. Paula Mikell Harper, Aug. 12, 1977. A.B., Newberry Coll., 1962; J.D. magna cum laude, U. S.C., 1969. Bar: S.C. 1969, U.S. Dist. Ct. S.C. 1969, U.S. Ct. Appeals (4th cir.) 1974, U.S. Supreme Ct. 1981. Assoc., Harvey Battey & Bethea, P.A., and predecessors, 1969-71, ptnr., 1971-81; prin. Bethea Jordan & Griffin, P.A., Hilton Head Island, S.C., 1981—, sr. ptnr., 1981—; dir. Citizens & So. Trust Co., Citizens & So. Nat. Bank S.C., Citizens and So. Trust Co. Chmn. bd. trustee Hilton Head Hosp.; trustee, chmn. acad. affairs and faculty liaison com. U. S.C.,; trustee U. S.C. Bus. Partnership Found. Served with USMCR, 1958-63, USMC, 1963-66. Mem. ABA, Beaufort County Bar Assn. (past pres), Hilton Head Island Bar Assn. (past pres.), Am. Land Devel. Assn., Communities Assn. Inst., Order Wig and Robe, Phi Beta Kappa, Phi Alpha Delta (Outstanding Scholastic Achievement award 1969). Episcopalian. Clubs: Gamecock, U. S.C. Alumni, Masons. Banking, Contracts commercial, Real property. Home: 3 Gray Fox Ln Hilton Head Island SC 29928

BETOW, JOEL THOMAS, lawyer; b. Lake Charles, La., Apr. 8, 1955; s. Lowell H. and Wanda Fay (Lunsford) B. BA in Journalism, U. Okla., 1977; JD, St. Mary's U., San Antonio, 1980. Bar: Tex. 1980. Petroleum landman Houston, 1981-82, sole practice, 1982—. Del. Cleveland County Dem. Conv., Okla., 1976, Senate Dist. Conv. for Gary Hart, 1984, Senate Dist. Conv., Houston, 1986, Dem. State Conv. Austin, 1986, Tex. State Dem. Conv., 1986; mem. Harris County Dems., Houston, 1985—, also Southwest Dems.; staff mem. John Pouland for R.R. Commn., Harris County, 1986. Served with Tex. NG, 1980-86. Fellow John F. Kennedy Library (hon.); mem. ABA, Houston Bar Assn., Delta Theta Phi, Delta Upsilon Alumni Assn. Methodist. Club: Braeburn Terr. Civic (Houston) (treas. 1986—). Avocations: tennis, jogging, horseback riding. Oil and gas leasing, Real property, Probate. Home: 5906 Carew Houston TX 77074

BETTMANN, FRANK ADAM, JR., lawyer; b. Junction City, Kans., July 25, 1955; s. Frank Adam Sr. and Josefine Anna (Enders) B.; m. Rebecca Jean Lind, Aug. 14, 1976; 1 child, Frank Adam III. BA, U. S.D., 1977, MPA, 1978; JD, U. Idaho, 1981. Bar: S.D. 1981, U.S. Dist. Ct. S.D. 1981, U.S. Ct. Appeals (8th cir.) 1982. Dep. states atty. Pennington County States Attys.'s Office, Rapid City, S.D., 1981-83; ptnr. Bettmann & Feehan P.C., Rapid City, 1983—. Co-author: Operationalization of Indicators for Public Policyand Quality of Life Analysis, 1978. Coach Rapid City (S.D.) Youth Soccer League, 1982-85. Mem. ABA, S.D. Bar Assn., Pennington County Bar Assn., Assn. Trial Lawyers Am., Black Hills Criminal Def. Bar Assn. (bd. dirs. 1986—), Phi Alpha Delta. Republican. Roman Catholic. Lodge: Elks. Avocations: hunting, fishing, skiing, baseball, soccer. General practice, Personal injury, Real property. Office: Bettmann & Feehan PC 636 St Anne PO Box 5506 Rapid City SD 57709

BETTS, JAMES ROBERT, lawyer; b. Des Moines, Apr. 23, 1955; s. Robert Clinton and Rita Kathleen (Fowler) B.; m. Mary Christine Van Deelen, June 20, 1981; 1 child, Sarah Elizabeth. BA, U. Wis., Milw., 1978; JD with honors, U. Wis., Madison, 1981. Bar: Fla. 1981, Wis. 1981, U.S. Dist. Ct. (mid. dist.) Fla. 1982, U.S. Ct. Appeals (11th cir.) 1982. Ptnr. Fowler, White, Gillen, Boggs, Villareal and Banker P.A., Tampa, Fla., 1981—. Bd. dirs. Northside Community Mental Health Ctr., Tampa, 1984-87. Mem. ABA, Fla. Bar Assn., Hillsborough County Bar Assn. Democrat. Roman Catholic. Avocations: basketball, golf, baseball. State civil litigation, Federal civil litigation, Commercial collections. Home: 710 South Blvd Tampa FL 33606 Office: Fowler et al 501 E Kennedy Blvd Tampa FL 33602

BETTS, KIRK HOWARD, lawyer; b. Jersey City, Mar. 5, 1951; s. Fred Semour and Mary Elizabeth (Morrell) B.; m. Christine Marlene Sheridan, Mar. 19, 1976; 1 child, Abigail Sheridan. BA, George Washington U., 1973; JD, Am. U., 1979. Bar: D.C. 1980, U.S. Dist. Ct. (D.C. dist.) 1980, U.S. Ct. Appeals (D.C., 5th and 11th cirs.) 1980, U.S. Supreme Ct. 1984, Md. 1986. Assoc. Northcut Ely, Washington, 1979-82; mng. ptnr. Ely, Ritts, Pietrowski & Brickfield, Washington, 1982-84, Ely, Ritts, Brickfield & Betts, Washington, 1984-86; counsel Dickinson, Wright, Moon, Van Dusen & Freeman, Washington, 1986—; asst. counsel U.S. Senat subcom. on intergovtl. relations, Washington, 1974-76; legis. aide to Hon. William V. Roth, Washington, 1973-74. Chmn. bd. mgrs. for Hallowood, St. Luke Luth. Ch., Silver Spring, Md., 1985—, ch. council, 1987—. Mem. ABA (sects. on natural resource law, pub. utility law, econs. of law practice, Best Article in Series award 1980), D.C. Bar Assn., Md. Bar Assn., Fed. Energy Bar Assn. (alumni relations com.). Republican. Lutheran. Club: Podickory Yacht (Annapolis, Md.) (vice commodore 1975-76). Avocations: sailing, woodworking, collecting lit. about Chesapeake Bay. FERC practice, Public utilities. Home: 1415 Crestridge Dr Silver Spring MD 20910 Office: Dickinson Wright Moon et al 1901 L St NW Washington DC 20036

BETTWY, SAMUEL WILLIAM, lawyer; b. Phoenix, Oct. 8, 1954; s. Andrew Leo and Janice Kathryn (Kennerly) B.; m. Susan Raines Benninghoff, May 26, 1984; 1 child, Christopher Bix. BA in Econs., Pomona Coll., 1976; JD, Calif. Western Sch. of Law, 1980; LLM in Internat. Law, Georgetown U., 1985. Bar: Calif. 1980, U.S. Dist. Ct. (so. dist.) Calif. 1980, Ariz. 1981, U.S. Dist. Ct. Ariz. 1981, D.C. 1984, U.S. Dist. Ct. (no. dist.) Calif. 1987. Gen. counsel North Am. Coin and Currency, Ltd., Phoenix, 1981-82; legal counsel Medevac, San Diego, 1982-83; editor The Law Mag., Bethesda, Md., 1984-85; atty. Dept. Justice, Washington, 1986—; asst. editor Internat. Legal Materials, Washington, 1985—; adj. prof. Antioch Sch. of Law, Washington, 1986. Contbr. articles to profl. jours. Serves as lt. USAR. Mem. ABA, Phi Alpha Delta Legal. Roman Catholic. Public international, Legal education, Immigration, naturalization, and customs. Home: 778 30th Ave San Francisco CA 94121 Office: Immigration Naturalization Service 630 Sansome St San Francisco CA 94111

BEU, WILLIAM RAYMOND, lawyer; b. Chgo., Oct. 3, 1940; s. Morice E. and Kathleen M. (Welch) B.; m. Lorna M. Koenig, Apr. 15, 1967; children: Gregory T., Jonathan R. BA, Valparaiso U., 1963, JD, 1966. Bar: Ill. 1966, Ind. 1966., U.S. Dist. Ct. (no. dist.) Ill. 1975, U.S. Ct. Appeals (7th cir.) 1985, U.S. Ct. Appeals (11th cir.) 1985, Wis. 1986. Asst. city atty. City of Gary, Ind., 1966-67; atty. Roth & Yonover, Gary, 1967-68; asst. state's atty. Winnebago County, Rockford, Ill., 1968-71, pub. defender, 1971-73; sole practice Rockford, 1973—. Bd. dirs. Rockford sickle Cell Assn., 1985—, Rockford Mus. Assn., 1982-84, Rockford Luth. High Sch., 1984-86. Mem. Ill. Bar Assn., Wis. Bar Assn., Winnebago County Bar Assn., Nat. Orgn. Social Security Claimants Reps. Republican. Avocations: metal dectecting, golf, fishing. Criminal, Social security disability, Bankruptcy. Home: 5219

Marion Ave Rockford IL 61108 Office: 631 N Longwood Rockford IL 61107

BEUCHERT, EDWARD WILLIAM, lawyer; b. N.Y.C., Feb. 13, 1937; s. August Vincent and Anna (Jaufmann) B.; m. Elizabeth Sadowsky, Aug. 5, 1961; children—Edward William, Jon, Philip, Suzanne, Alexandra. B.A. cum laude, Fordham U., 1958; J.D. cum laude, Harvard U., 1961. Bar: N.Y. 1962. Assoc., ptnr. Seward & Kissel, N.Y.C., 1963—. Bd. dirs. Cotswold Assn., Inc., 1977-85, v.p., 1979-80, pres., 1980-82; bd. dirs. Greenville Community Council, Inc., 1984—, sec., 1984-86 . Served to 1st lt. U.S. Army, 1961-63. Mem. Internat. Bar Assn., ABA, N.Y. State Bar Assn., Assn. Bar City N.Y. Republican. Roman Catholic. Club: Downtown Assn. (N.Y.C.). Contbr. articles to profl. jours. Real property, General corporate. Home: 53 Inverness Rd Scarsdale NY 10583 Office: Wall St Plaza New York NY 10005

BEUTEL, RICHARD ARMSTRONG, lawyer; b. Mt. Pleasant, Mich., Jan. 6, 1954; s. Richard Armstrong and Martha (Solomons) B.; m. Donna Marie Beutel, June 10, 1985. BA, Pomona Coll., 1976; JD, Georgetown U., 1981. Bar: D.C. 1980, Calif. 1983. Law clk., assoc. Howry & Simon, Washington, 1980-82; assoc. Hopkins, Mitchell & Carly, Palo Alto and San Jose, Calif., 1982-84, Dow, Lohnes & Albertson, Washington, 1984-85; motions staff atty. U.S. Ct. Appeals, Washington, 1985-86; of counsel Abrams, Westermeier & Goldberg, Washington, 1986—. Contbr. articles to profl. jours. Mem. IEEE (task force for protection of proprietary tech.), Computer Law Assn., Software Pubs. Assn., D.C. Computer Law Forum, Boston Computer Soc. (law spl. interest group), Washington Apple Users Group (law spl. interest group). Federal civil litigation, Computer. Home: 2622 Redcoat Dr C-2 Alexandria VA 22303

BEUTTENMULLER, RUDOLF WILLIAM, lawyer; b. St. Louis, Dec. 20, 1953; s. Paul A. and Doris R. (Henle) B.; m. Ragina Lee Winters, July 14, 1984. AB cum laude, Princeton U., 1976; JD with distinction, Duke U., 1980. Bar: Tex. 1980, U.S. Dist. Ct. (no. dist.) Tex. 1980. Assoc. Jenkens & Gilchrist, Dallas, 1980-83; ptnr. Gregory, Self & Beuttenmuller, Dallas, 1983—; Bd. dirs. Pkwy. Capital Investments, Inc. Articles editor Duke Law Jour., Durham, 1979-80. Mem. Dean's adv. council Duke Law Sch., Durham, N.C., 1983—; mem. Rep. Nat. Com., Washington, 1984, 500 Inc., Dallas, 1985. Mem. ABA, Dallas Bar Assn., Duke Law Alumni Assn., Princeton Alumni Assn. Club: Internat. Athletic (Dallas). Banking, General corporate, Real property. Home: 4118 Briargrove Dallas TX 75252 Office: Gregory Self & Beuttenmuller 14180 Dallas Pkwy Suite 900 Dallas TX 75240

BEVAN, KENT MORGAN, lawyer; b. Kansas City, Mo., Mar. 17, 1950; s. Phillip H. and Jean (Sivers) B.; m. Peggy Layne Antry, Aug. 12, 1972; children: Jean, Layne. BA, U. Mo., Kansas City, 1972, JD, 1974. Bar: Mo. 1975, U.S. Dist. Ct. (we. dist.) Mo. 1975. Assoc. Knipmeyer, McCann, Fish & Smith, Kansas City, 1975-83, ptnr., 1984—. Victor Wilson scholar U. Mo. Kansas City, 1968. Mem. ABA, Mo. Bar Assn., Kansas City Bar Assn., Lawyers Assn. Kansas City. Insurance, State civil litigation, Federal civil litigation. Home: 5221 Ward Pkwy Kansas City MO 64112 Office: Knipmeyer McCann Fish & Smith 1800 Power and Light Bldg Kansas City MO 64105

BEVER, ROBERT LYNN, lawyer; b. Richmond, Ind., Apr. 30, 1953; s. Lucien C. and M. Elizabeth (Hawley) B.; m. Alice L. Reath, Oct. 20, 1979 (div. Mar. 1985). BA with distinction, DePauw U., 1975; JD magna cum laude, Ind. U., Indpls., 1978. Bar: Ind. 1978, U.S. Dist. Ct. (no. and so. dists.) Ind. 1978. Assoc. Harlan, Schussler, Keller & Boston, Richmond, Ind., 1978-81; ptnr. Harlan, Schussler, Keller, Boston & Bever, Richmond, 1982—. Chmn. Wayne County Rep. Party, 1986; bd. dirs., sec. Leadership Wayne County, 1978-85; bd. dirs. Wayne County Hist. Soc., 1983—, Jr. Achievement Eastern Ind., 1984—; trustee DePauw U., 1975-78, Cen. United Meth. Ch., Richmond, 1984—. Named one of Outstanding Young Men of Am., U.S. Jaycees, 1983. Mem. ABA, Ind. State Bar Assn. (legal edn. com. 1980—), Ind. Trial Lawyers Assn. Lodge: Rotary. Avocations: tennis, piano, politics, reading. Banking, Contracts commercial, Insurance. Home: 2105 Oak Park Dr Richmond IN 47374 Office: Harlan Schussler et al 400 First Nat Bank Bldg Richmond IN 47374

BEX, RICHARD ELMER, lawyer, insurance company executive; b. Portland, Oreg., July 27, 1921; s. Harry Louis and Lora Imogene (Frisbie) B.; m. Rena Joan Calzavara, Apr. 3, 1943; 1 child, Lora Catherine Bex Lempert. Student, Kalamazoo Coll., 1944; AA, Am. U., 1946; JD, John Marshall Law Sch., 1953. Bar: Ill. 1953. Officer nat. service DAV, Inc., Chgo., 1946-50; rep. vets. employment State of Ill., Chgo., 1950-53; asst. gen. counsel Continental Assurance Co., Chgo., 1953-75; asst. v.p., asst. gen. counsel Fireman's Fund Ins., San Rafael, Calif., 1976-85; v.p., asst. gen. counsel AMEX Life Assurance Co., San Rafael, 1985-86. Served to sgt. U.S. Army, 1941-45. Mem. ABA (vice chmn. life ins. com. TIPS sect. 1972-74, sr. counsel sect., vice chmn. corp. law com.), Ill. Bar Assn., Assn. Life Ins. Counsel, Am. Council Life Ins. (legal sect.). Avocations: sports, reading. Insurance, Pension, profit-sharing, and employee benefits, General corporate. Home: 51 Shannon Ct Novato CA 94947 Office: AMEX Life Assurance Co 1650 Los Gamos Dr San Rafael CA 94903

BEYDA, DANIEL, lawyer; b. N.Y.C., Aug. 3, 1953; s. Gabriel David Beyda and Paula (Douek) Aboutboul; m. Joan Coughlin, Sept. 16, 1984. BA magna cum laude, Ithaca Coll., 1975; JD, U. Miami, 1979. Bar: N.Y. 1980, Fla. 1980. Assoc. Mazur & Carp, N.Y.C., 1980-81; atty. N.Y. Stock Exchange, Inc., N.Y.C., 1981-82, spl. counsel, 1982-83, arbitration counsel, 1983-84, sr. arbitration counsel, 1984—. Chmn. Beekman East Tenants Assn., N.Y.C., 1983-85. Mem. ABA, Fla. Bar Assn. Club: Hampshire Country (Mamaroneck, N.Y.). Avocations: skiing, tennis, golf. Securities. Office: NY Stock Exchange Inc 11 Wall St New York NY 10005

BEZET, GARY ANTHONY, lawyer; b. White Castle, La., Sept. 25, 1952; s. Randolph Anthony and Beulah Ann (Bijeaux) B.; m. Cassandra Kay Major, Aug. 16, 1975; children: Gary Andrew, Alan Major. BA in Econs., La. State U., 1976, JD, 1979. Bar: La. 1979, U.S. Ct. Appeals (5th cir.), 1979, U.S. Dist. Ct. (middle dist.) La., 1980, U.S. Dist. Ct. (ea. dist.) La., 1979, U.S. Dist. Ct. (we. dist.) La., 1982. Assoc. Jones, Walker, New Orleans, 1979-80; assoc. Sanders, Downing, Baton Rouge, 1980-82, ptnr., 1982-83; ptnr. Kean, Miller, Hawthorne, D'Armond, McCowan & Jarman, Baton Rouge, 1983—. Mem. ABA, La. Bar Assn., Baton Rouge Bar Assn. Republican. Avocations: running, piano. Bankruptcy, Federal civil litigation, State civil litigation. Home: 2350 Olive St Baton Rouge LA 70806 Office: Kean Miller Hawthorne et al 22d Floor One American Pl Baton Rouge LA 70825

BEZIKOS, LYNNE A., lawyer; b. N.Y.C., June 12, 1956; d. Richard Peter and Carole Emma (Williams) B. BA, St. Lawrence U., 1978; JD, Suffolk U., 1981. Bar: N.Y. 1982, U.S. Dist. Ct. (so., ea., no. and we. dists.) N.Y. 1982. Atty. Superior Electronics Inc., New Rochelle, N.Y., 1982-84; from atty. to counsel North Am. Philips Corp., N.Y.C., 1984—. Mem. ABA, N.Y. State Bar Assn. General corporate, Antitrust. Office: North Am Philips Corp 100 E 42d St New York NY 10017

BIAETT, DODDRIDGE HEWITT, III, corporate lawyer; b. Aurora, Ill., Nov. 20, 1942; s. Doddridge Hewitt and Ruthanne (Migley) B.; m. Jean Iden, Apr. 13, 1969; children—Elizabeth Iden, Doddridge Hewitt, Maryanne Migley. B.S., Hampden-Sydney Coll., 1965; LL.B., U. Va., 1968. Bar: Va. 1968. Atty., Govt. Employees Ins. Co., Washington, 1970-73, sr. counsel, 1973-76; atty., Crum & Forster Corp., Morristown, N.J., 1976-79, v.p., counsel, 1979—. Chmn. Fin. Com. Mendham United Meth. Ch., 1982—, chmn. 1986—. Served to comdr. USNR, 1968—; Vietnam. Mem. ABA, N.J. Assn. Corp. Counsel. Republican. General corporate, Pension, profit-sharing, and employee benefits, Insurance. Address: 36 Dean Rd Mendham NJ 07945

BIALKIN, KENNETH J., lawyer; b. N.Y.C., Sept. 9, 1929; s. Samuel and Lillian (Kastner) B.; m. Ann Eskind, Aug. 19, 1956; children: Lisa Beth, Johanna. A.B., U. Mich.-Ann Arbor, 1950; cert. of attendance, London Sch. Econ., 1952; J.D., Harvard U., 1953. Bar: N.Y. 1953, U.S. Dist. Ct. (ea. dist.) N.Y. 1955, U.S. Supreme Ct. 1964, U.S. Dist. Ct. (so. dist.) N.Y. 1972, U.S. Ct. Appeals (2d cir.) 1976. Assoc. Willkie Farr & Gallagher, N.Y.C., 1953-60, ptnr., 1960—; adj. prof. law NYU., 1969—; lectr., commentator legal and fin. symposia; dir. E.M. Warburg, Pincus & Co., Inc., Gulf Resources & Chem. Corp., Shearson-Lehman Bros. Express Inc., The Mcpl. Assistance Corp. City of N.Y. Editor: The Business Lawyer, 1980; contbr. articles on corp., fin. investment law to profl. jours. Chmn. Conf. of Pres. of Maj. Am. Jewish Orgns., 1984—; nat. chmn. Anti-Defamation League of B'nai B'rith, 1982-84; vice chmn., dir. Jerusalem Found., Inc., 1975; mem. distbn. com. Fedn. Jewish Philanthropies of N.Y., 1979-82; bd. govs. Tel-Aviv U., 1979; trustee Am. Friends of the Hebrew U., 1980; bd. dirs. United Jewish Appeal Greater N.Y., 1979; mem. report coordinating group SEC, 1974-77. Mem. ABA (chmn. fed. regulation of securities com. 1974-79, chmn. com. to study fgn. investment in U.S. 1978-80, chmn. sect. of corp. banking and bus. law 1981), N.Y. County Lawyers Assn. (pres. 1986—), Am. Bar Retirement Assn. (dir. 1981—). Club: Harvard. General corporate, Administrative and regulatory, Banking. Home: 211 Central Park W New York NY 10024 Office: Willkie Farr & Gallagher One Citicorp Ctr 153 E 53d St New York NY 10022

BIARS, MARK MARTIN, lawyer; b. Balt., Jan. 3, 1951; s. Kopel S. and Myrtle R. (Goldberg) B.; Rosanne Thomas, Aug. 22, 1976; children: Rachel Christine, Julia Wynne. BA, Case Western Res. U., 1973, JD, 1977. Bar: Ohio 1977, U.S. Dist. Ct. (no. dist.) Ohio 1977. Atty. Nat. City Bank, Cleve., 1977-82, v.p., atty., 1982-86, v.p., sr. atty., 1986—. Mem. Ohio Bar Assn., Cleve. Bar Assn. Banking, Consumer commercial, General corporate. Home: 3320 Bradford Rd Cleveland Heights OH 44118 Office: Nat City Bank 1900 E 9th St Cleveland OH 44114

BICE, SCOTT HAAS, lawyer, educator; b. Los Angeles, Mar. 19, 1943; s. Fred Haas and Virginia M. (Scott) B.; m. Barbara Franks, Dec. 21, 1968. B.S., U. So. Calif., 1965, J.D., 1968. Bar: Calif. bar 1971. Law clk. to Chief Justice Earl Warren, 1968-69; successively asst. prof., assoc. prof., prof. law., Carl Mason Franklin prof. U. So. Calif., Los Angeles, 1969—; assoc. dean U. So. Calif., 1971-74, dean, 1980—; vis. prof. polit. sci. Calif. Inst. Tech., 1977; vis. prof. U. Va., 1978-79. Contbr. articles to law jours. Affiliated scholar Am. Bar Found., 1972-74. Fellow Am. Bar Found.; mem. Am. Law Inst., Calif. Bar, Los Angeles County Bar Assn., Am. Judicature Soc. Club: Chancery. Home: 787 S San Rafael Ave Pasadena CA 91105 Office: U So Calif Law Center University Park Los Angeles CA 90089-0071

BICKEL, DWIGHT FRANKLIN, lawyer, escrow company exec.; b. Trilla, Ill., Feb. 1, 1931; s. Melvin and Ethel M. (Hackley) B.; m. Cynthia Ann, Aug. 2, 1969; children—Dwight A., Deborah A., Justin D. B.S., U. Ill., 1955, J.D., 1957. Bar: Ill. 1957, Idaho 1958, Hawaii 1981. Asst. atty. gen. Idaho, Boise, 1958-61; exec. v.p. Idaho Investment Corp., Twin Falls, 1963-64; v.p., sec. Mich. Chem. Corp., Chgo., 1965-67; pres. Inc., Inc., Seattle and Santa Ana, Calif., 1969-71; sole practice, Boise, 1971—; lectr. Boise Community Schs., continuing legal edn. Served with USAF, 1950-54. Mem. Idaho Bar Assn., Ill. State Bar Assn., Hawaii State Bar Assn. Club: Mason (Charleston, Ill.). Editor and contbg. author: Idaho Real Estate Practice, 1977, 80. Real property, Estate planning, Personal income taxation. Home: 3087 N Mountain Rd Boise ID 83702 Office: PO Box 7943 Boise ID 83707 Office: 101 Aupuni Suite 202 Hilo HI 96720

BIDDLE, ERIC HARBESON, JR., lawyer; b. Bryn Mawr, Pa., Feb. 10, 1928; s. Eric Harbeson and Katharine Clover (Rogers) B.; A.B. cum laude (scholar), Harvard U., 1950; J.D., George Washington U., 1977; m. Mary Churchill, 1948 (div.); 1 son, Michael C. Soviet Area intelligence officer CIA, Washington and overseas, 1951-60; contract negotiator Smith Kline & French Labs., Phila., 1960-61; editor and estimator Bechtel Corp., San Francisco, 1961-64; insp. govt. programs OEO and ACTION, Washington, 1969-80; admitted to Va. bar, 1979, D.C. bar, 1980; individual practice law, Arlington, Va., 1980—; cons. fed. grants and program audits; apptd. commr. Commn. for the Study of Internat. Migration and Cooperative Econ. Devel., 1987. Served as officer USNR, 1951-71. Mem. Va. Bar Assn., D.C. Bar Assn., Am. Bar Assn., Fed. Bar Assn., Assn. Trial Lawyers Am., Inter-Am. Bar Assn., Am. Immigration Lawyers Assn. Anglican. Club: Harvard (D.C.). Immigration, naturalization, and customs, Private international, Public international. Office: 2251 N Vermont St Arlington VA 22207

BIDEAU, EDWIN HALE, III, lawyer; b. Chanute, Kans., Oct. 1, 1950; s. Edwin H. and Beverly Maxine (Semon) B.; m. Margaret E. Fritton, June 30, 1973; children: Scott E., Sarah M., Jenny E. AA, Neosho Community Coll., 1970; BBA, Washburn U., 1972, JD, 1975. Bar: Kans. 1975, U.S. Dist. Ct. Kans. 1975, U.S. Dist. Ct. Okla. 1984. Law clk., atty. Kans. Ins. Commn., Topeka, 1973-75; asst. county atty. Neosho County Atty.'s Office, Chanute, Kans., 1975-76, county atty., 1976-85; sole practice, Chanute, 1975-83, sr. ptnr., Bideau Law Offices, 1983—; adj. instr. Washburn U., Topeka, 1974-75, Neosho Community Coll., Chanute, 1975-83; pres. Profl. Software Assocs., Inc., Chanute; state rep. Kans. Legis. 5th Dist., 1985—. Mem. adv. com. bus. dept. Neosho Community Coll., Chanute, 1984—; Rep. precinct committeeman Neosho County, 1984; mem. adv. com. Social and Rehab. Services, 1980; bd. dirs. Chanute Pub. Library, 1980; mem. Neosho County Law Library Com., 1978-83; mem. Kans. Legislature from 5th dist., 1985—; chmn. House Jud. and Legis. Appointment com., 1987—; deacon First Presbyn. Ch., Chanute. Named Outstanding Young Man, Chanute Jaycees, 1978, 83. Mem. ABA, Assn. Trial Lawyers Am., Nat. Dist. Atty.'s Assn., Kans. Dist. Atty.'s Assn., Kans. Bar Assn., Southeast Kans. Bar Assn., Neosho County Bar Assn. (pres. 1978-79), Kans. Trial Lawyers Assn., Neosho Valley Hist. Soc. (pres. 1980), Neosho River Muzzle Loaders, Sigma Phi Epsilon (bd. dirs. Kans. Delta chpt. 1972-78). Lodge: Elks. Criminal, Insurance, Workers' compensation. Home: 14 S Rutter St Chanute KS 66720 Office: 18 N Forest Chanute KS 66720

BIDWELL, JAMES TRUMAN, JR., lawyer; b. N.Y.C., Jan. 2, 1934; s. James Truman and Mary (Kane) B.; m. 2d Gail S. Bidwell, Mar. 6, 1965 (div.); children: Hillary Day, Kimberly Wade, Courtney E. B.A., Yale U., 1956; LL.B., Harvard U., 1959. Bar: N.Y. 1959. Atty. U.S. Air Force, Austin, Tex., 1959-62; assoc. firm Donovan, Leisure, Newton & Irvine, N.Y.C., 1962-68, ptnr., 1968-84; ptnr. White & Case, N.Y.C., 1984—. Pres. Youth Consultation Service, 1973-78. Mem. ABA, Fed. Bar Assn., N.Y. State Bar Assn., N.Y. County Lawyers Assn. Club: Ch. N.Y.C. (pres. 1983—). General corporate, Private international. Home: 301 E 69th St New York NY 10021 Office: White & Case 1155 Ave of the Americas New York NY 10036

BIEDERMAN, DONALD ELLIS, lawyer; b. N.Y.C., Aug. 23, 1934; s. William and Sophye (Groll) B.; m. Marna M. Leerburger, Dec. 22, 1962; children: Charles Jefferson, Melissa Anne. AB, Cornell U., 1955; JD, Harvard U., 1958; LLM in Taxation, NYU, 1970. Bar: N.Y. 1959, Calif. 1977, U.S. Dist. Ct. (so. dist.) N.Y. 1967. Assoc. Hale, Russell & Stentzel, N.Y.C., 1962-66; asst. corp. counsel City of N.Y., 1966-68; assoc. Delson & Gordon, N.Y.C., 1968-69; ptnr. Roe, Carman, Clerke, Berkman & Berkman, Jamaica, N.Y., 1969-72; gen. atty. CBS Records, N.Y.C., 1972-76; v.p. legal affairs and adminstrn. ABC Records, Los Angeles, 1977-79; ptnr. Mitchell, Silberberg & Knupp, Los Angeles, 1979-83; v.p. legal and bus. affairs Warner Bros. Music, Los Angeles, 1983—; adj. prof. law Southwestern U., 1982—, Pepperdine U., 1985—. Editor: Legal and Business Problems of the Music Industry, 1980. Bd. dirs. Calif. Chamber Symphony Soc., Los Angeles, 1981—, AMC Med. Ctr., Los Angeles, 1986. Served to 1st lt. U.S. Army, 1959. Recipient Hon. Gold Record, Recording Industry Assn. Am., 1974, Trendsetter award Billboard Mag., 1976. Mem. N.Y. State Bar, State Bar Calif. Democrat. Jewish. Club: Riviera Country (Pacific Palisades, Calif). Avocations: golf, skiing, travel, reading. Entertainment, Legal education. Home: 2406 Pesquera Dr Los Angeles CA 90049 Office: Warner Bros Music 9000 Sunset Blvd Los Angeles CA 90069

BIEGEN, ARNOLD IRWIN, lawyer; b. N.Y.C., Apr. 9, 1933; s. Sol and Eva (Trupine) B.; m. Anne R. Friedenberg, Feb. 19, 1967; children—Richard S., Peter, Mathew, Elissa. B.A., Bklyn. Coll., 1954; J.D., N.Y.U., 1959. Bar: N.Y. 1959, U.S. Supreme Ct. 1964. Assoc., Booth, Lipton & Lipton, N.Y.C., 1959-63, ptnr., 1964-87, Chapin, Flattau & Klimpl, 1987—; faculty Grad. Sch. John Jay Coll. Mem. casino gambling study panel, N.Y., 1979; trustee John Jay Coll. Criminal Justice, 1982; mem. Commn. on Jud. Nomination, 1983—; bd. dirs. N.Y. Urban League, 1984—; mem. adv. bd. PBS Channel 13, N.Y.C., 1983—. Served as cpl. U.S. Army, 1954-56. Mem. Assn. Bar City of N.Y. (commr. council on jud. adminstrn.), N.Y. State Bar Assn., N.Y.U. Sch. Law Alumni Assn. (dir. 1977-82). Democrat. Hebrew. General corporate, Securities. Office: 405 Park Ave New York NY 10022

BIEHL, KATHY ANNE, lawyer; b. Pitts., Jan. 27, 1956; d. Edward Robert and Julianne (Addis) B. BA with highest honors, So. Meth. U., 1976; JD with honors, U. Tex., 1979. Bar: Tex. 1979, U.S. Dist. Ct. (so. dist.) Tex. 1986, U.S. Ct. Appeals (5th cir.) 1986. Assoc. Schlanger, Cook, Cohn, Mills & Grossberg, Houston, 1979-82; sole practice Houston, 1982—; lectr. Rice U., Houston, 1982. Contbr. articles to profl. jours. Mem., vol. Tex. Accts. and Lawyers for Arts, Houston, 1981—, Orange Show Found., Houston, 1985—; performing mem. Houston Folklore Soc., 1985—. Mem. ABA, Tex. Bar Assn., Houston Bar Assn., Sierra Club, Wilderness Soc., Friends of Goethe (founding bd. dirs., pres. 1983—), Phi Beta Kappa. Democrat. Mem. Unitarian Ch. General practice, Probate, General corporate. Office: 909 Kipling Houston TX 77006

BIEHL, MICHAEL M., lawyer; b. Milw., Feb. 24, 1951; s. Michael Melvin Biehl and Frieda Margaret (Krieg) Davis. AB, Harvard U., 1973, JD, 1976; DD (hon.), Ch. of Modern Apostles, 1984. Bar: Wis. 1976, U.S. Dist. Ct. (ea. dist.) Wis. 1976. Assoc. Foley & Lardner, Milw., 1976-84, ptnr., 1984—. Mem. Mt. Sinai Med. Ctr. Clin. Investigations Com., Hastings Ctr. Mem. ABA, Nat. Health Lawyers Assn., Am. Soc. Law and Medicine. Mem. Unitarian Ch. Health, Real property. Home: 3467 N Hackett Ave Milwaukee WI 53211 Office: Foley & Lardner 777 E Wisconsin Ave Milwaukee WI 53202

BIEL, MARK, lawyer; b. N.Y.C., May 3, 1944; s. Jack and Renee (Rappaport) B.; children: Justin M., Jordan K. BA in History, Bates Coll., 1966; JD, Rutgers U., 1972. Bar: N.J. 1972, U.S. Dist. Ct. N.J. 1972, U.S. Tax Ct. 1975, U.S. Supreme Ct. 1976, U.S. Ct. Appeals (3d cir.) 1983. Assoc. Blatt, Mairone, Biel, Zlotnick, Feinberg & Griffith, Atlantic City, 1972-74; ptnr. Mairone, Biel, Zlotnick, Feinberg & Griffith and preceding law firm Blatt, Mairone, Biel, Zlotnick, Feinberg & Griffith, Atlantic City, 1974—; solicitor City of Somers Point, N.J., 1974-80, City of Ventnor, N.J., 1974-80, indsl. commn. Hamilton Twp., N.J., 1978—, Hamilton Twp. Indsl. Commn. Mem. spl. gifts com. Am. Cancer Soc., Atlantic County, 1978-82, scholarship com. Stockton State Coll., Gallowy, N.J., 1983—; fund raiser profls. com. United Way, Atlantic County, N.J. Served to sgt. U.S. Army, 1969-70, Vietnam. Decorated Bronze Star. Mem. N.J. Bar Assn. (trustee 1984—, fund raising com. bar ctr. meeting 1985—, exec. com. family law sect. 1986—, travel and arrangements com. 1986—), Atlantic County Bar Assn. (sec., treas., v.p., pres., trustee 1978-82), Somers Point Jaycees (bd. dirs. 1972-76). Jewish. Avocations: tennis, travel, running, gardening. Family and matrimonial, State civil litigation, Local government. Home: 2520 Cedarbridge Rd Northfield NJ 08225 Office: Mairone Biel Zlotnick Feinberg & Griffith 3201 Atlantic Ave Atlantic City NJ 08401

BIELORY, ABRAHAM M., lawyer, financial service executive; b. Modena, Italy, Sept. 20, 1946; came to U.S., 1948; s. Motel and Basia (Spielberg) B.; m. Beverly B. Berkowitz, Jan. 26, 1969; children—Jennifer Rebecca, Debra Elizabeth, David Ethan. B.S., N.J. Inst. Tech., 1968; J.D., U. Denver, 1973. Bar: N.J. 1974, U.S. Dist. Ct. N.J. 1974, U.S. Supreme Ct. 1979. Field engr. Control Data Corp., Mpls., 1968-69; assoc. Paschow & Feurey, Toms River, N.J., 1973-77; ptnr. Paschow & Feurey, 1978, VanSicle & Bielory, Toms River, 1978—; owner ABEV Fin. Service, Toms River, 1976—. Vice pres. Lakewood Hebrew Day Sch., N.J., 1975-82, pres., 1982-86 ; trustee Hillel High Sch., Deal, N.J., 1983-84; v.p. Congregation Sons of Israel, Lakewood, 1984-86, pres. 1986—. Served to sgt. USAF, 1969-73. Fellow ABA; mem. Assn. Trial Lawyers Am., N.J. State Bar Assn., Trial Atty. N.J., Ocean County Bd. Realtors, Ocean County Bar Assn. (chmn. ins. com. 1975), Hudson County Bar Assn. (sr. citizen com. 1984), Internat. Lawyers Assn. Jewish War Vets. Republican. State civil litigation, Personal injury, Real property. Home: 1422 14th St Lakewood NJ 08701

BIELUCH, WILLIAM CHARLES, judge; b. Hartford, Conn., Nov. 12, 1918; s. Joseph and Catherine (Galazka) B.; m. Nellie Sidor, July 4, 1942 (dec. Dec. 1982); children—William Charles, Virginia M., Philip J.; m. 2d Pauline O'Connor, Nov. 25, 1983. A.B. magna cum laude, Brown U., 1939; J.D., Yale U., 1942. Bar: Conn. 1942. Assoc. Covington, Burling, Rublee, Acheson & Shorb, Washington, 1942-43; ptnr. Bieluch, Barry & Ramenda and predecessors, Hartford, 1946-68; judge Cir. Ct. Conn., 1968-73, Ct. Common Pleas Conn., 1973-76; judge Superior Ct. Conn., 1976-85, Appellate Session, 1979-83, Appellate Ct. Conn., 1985—. Trustee S. S. Cyril and Methodius Roman Catholic Ch., Hartford; corporator St. Francis Hosp. and Med. Ctr., Hartford. Served to lt. (j.g.) USCG, World War II. Decorated Knight St. Gregory (Pope Paul VI); recipient Merit award Polish Legion Am. Vets., 1952; Man of Yr. award United Polish Socs., 1968; Archdiocesan medal of appreciation Archbishop John F. Whealon, 1970. Mem. Conn. Bar Assn. (chmn. Jr. Bar Sect. 1948-49), Hartford County Bar Assn. Republican. Club: K.C. Jurisprudence. Office: 95 Washington St Hartford CT 06106

BIENENSTOCK, MARTIN J., lawyer; b. N.Y.C., Nov. 14, 1952; s. Arthur H. and Elaine (Schulman) B. BS in Econs., U. Pa., 1974; JD, U. Mich., 1977. Bar: N.Y. 1978, U.S. Dist. Ct. (so. dist.) N.Y. 1978, U.S. Ct. Appeals 1986. Assoc. Weil, Gotshal & Manges, N.Y.C., 1977-85, ptnr., 1985—. Mem. ABA. Jewish. Bankruptcy. Office: Weil Gotshal & Manges 767 Fifth Ave New York NY 10153

BIENSTOCK, JOSHUA ELLIOTT, lawyer; b. N.Y.C., Apr. 16, 1955; s. Herbert and June May (Klein) B. BA, CUNY, 1977; JD, Hofstra U., 1980; LLM, N.Y. Law Sch., 1986. Bar: N.Y. 1981, U.S. Dist. Ct. (so. and ea. dists.) N.Y. 1981, U.S. Ct. Appeals (2d cir.) 1985, U.S. Supreme Ct. 1986. Assoc. Quinn & Lilly P.C., N.Y.C., 1981—. Recipient Am. Jurisprudence award in Labor Law, 1980, Hofstra Law Sch. Citation of Excellence in Labor Law, 1980. Mem. ABA, N.Y. State Bar Assn. Avocation: aeronautics. Federal civil litigation, State civil litigation, Labor. Office: Quinn & Lilly PC 300 Garden City Plaza Garden City NY 11364

BIERBOWER, MARK BUTLER, lawyer; b. Washington, May 26, 1951; s. James Jospeh and Ellen Katherine (Butler) B.; m. Eleanor Dodds Deane, June 12, 1982; children: Laura Haskell, James Joseph II. BA, Northwestern U., 1976; JD, Georgetown U., 1979. Bar: D.C. 1980, U.S. Dist. Ct. D.C. 1981, Va. 1983, U.S. Dist. Ct. (ea. dist.) Va. 1983, U.S. Ct. Appeals (D.C. cir.) 1983, U.S. Ct. Appeals (4th cir.) 1984, Md. 1986. Assoc. Bierbower & Rockefeller, Washington, 1979-82; ptnr. Bierbower & Bierbower, Washington, 1982—. Founding mem. Capitol Forum Legis. Discussion Group, Washington, 1981—; founder Empaths Washington chpt. Multiple Sclerosis Soc., 1984; gen. counsel Nebr. Soc. of Washington, Inc., 1983-86. Recipient Merit citation Nat. Multiple Sclerosis Soc., 1983. Mem. ABA (com. on entertainment and sports industries, litigation sect., gen. practice sect., standing com. law and nat. security), D.C. Bar Assn. (chmn. young lawyers sect., cert. appreciation 1981-84), Sigma Alpha Epsilon. Republican. Roman Catholic. Club: Metropolitan (Washington). Avocations: golf, tennis, squash, jogging. General practice, Federal civil litigation, State civil litigation. Home: 8101 Merrick Rd Bethesda MD 20817 Office: Bierbower & Bierbower 1875 Eye St NW Washington DC 20006

BIERCE, JAMES MALCOLM, judge; b. Columbus, Ohio, July 5, 1931; s. Bruce Wallace and Glyde Vivian (Brown) B.; m. Frances M., June 19, 1953; children—James M., Teresa A.; m. 2d, Fern C., July 22, 1967. LL.B., U. Akron, 1963. Bar: Ohio 1965, Mich. 1971. Asst. dir. law City of Cuyahoga Falls (Ohio), 1966-68; sr. ptnr. Bierce & Kortze and predecessor firms, Akron, 1968-77; judge Cuyahoga Falls Mcpl. Ct., 1977—; instr. Ohio Jud. Coll., 1979—; faculty adviser Nat. Jud. Coll., 1983—. Bd. dirs. Am. Diabetes Assn., 1982-83; pres. Cuyahoga Valley Community Mental Health Center, 1982-83, Cuyahoga Falls Fraternal Order of Police Assn., 1977. Mem. Phi Alpha Delta Internat. (dist. justice 1969-76, tribune 1976-78, internat. exec. bd. dirs. 1978-82). Republican. Club: Lions (Cuyahoga Falls). Jurisprudence. Home: 1724 Chestnut Blvd Cuyahoga Falls OH 44223 Office: 2310 2d St Cuyahoga Falls OH 44222

BIERCE, WILLIAM BLAIKIE, lawyer; b. Englewood, N.J., Dec. 15, 1949; s. Thurber Hoffman and Joy Bierce; m. Martha Kenerson, Aug. 24,

1985. BA, Yale U., 1971; Licence en Droit, U. Grenoble, France, 1972; JD, NYU, 1975. Bar: N.J. 1975, N.Y. 1976, U.S. Ct. Internat. Trade 1980, U.S. Ct. Appeals (D.C. and 9th cirs.) 1984. Assoc. Coudert Bros., N.Y.C., 1975-78, Pisar and Huhs, N.Y.C., 1978-80; assoc. Windels, Marx, Davies and Ives, N.Y.C., 1980-85, ptnr., 1985—; adj. asst. prof. Pace U. Grad. Sch. Bus., N.Y.C., 1981—; bd. advisors Silex jour. Computer Law, Paris, 1985—. Editor articles NYU jour. Internat. Law Politics, 1974-75; contbr. articles to profl. jours. Trustee Dwight-Englewood Sch., 1982-84. Grad. fellowship Rotary Found., 1971-72. Mem. ABA, Licensing Execs. Soc. Computer, Private international, General corporate. Office: Windels Marx Davies & Ives 51 W 51st St New York NY 10019

BIERIG, JACK R., lawyer; b. Chgo., Apr. 10, 1947; s. Henry J. and Helga (Rothschild) B.; m. Barbara A. Winokur; children: Bobby, Sarah. BA, Brandeis U., 1968; JD, Harvard U., 1972. Bar: Ill., U.S. Dist. Ct. (no. dist.) Ill., U.S. Ct. Appeals (1st, 2d, 7th, 10th, 11th and D.C. cirs.), U.S. Supreme Ct. Ptnr. Sidley & Austin, Chgo., 1972—. Contbr. articles to profl. jours. Pres. Neighborhood Justice Chgo., 1983—. Mem. Chgo. Bar Assn. (bd. govs). Jewish. Club: Standard (Chgo.). Health, Antitrust, Administrative and regulatory. Office: Sidley & Austin One First National Plaza Chicago IL 60603

BIERMAN, NORMAN, lawyer; b. St. Louis, July 1, 1907. BA, Washington U., St. Louis, 1929; LLB, Washington U., 1929, JD, 1929. Bar: Mo. 1929. Assoc. Anderson, Gilbert, Wolfort, Allen & Bierman, St. Louis, 1929-36, ptnr., 1936—. Contbr. articles to legal jours. Mem. Mo. Council Nat. Civil Service League, 1940—; chmn. bd. Mo. Fedn. for Merit System, 1938-43; pres. Jewish Med. Soc. Service Bur., 1947-51, Mo. Assn. for Social Welfare, St. Louis, 1948; v.p. Jewish Child Welfare Assn., 1950, Jewish Orthodox Old Folks Home, 1954-55; vice chmn. St. Louis Child Welfare Adv. Com., 1952-55, Health and Welfare Council Met. St. Louis, 1952-55; bd. govs. Community Chest of Greater St. Louis, 1950-52; sec., gen. counsel Jewish Hosp., St. Louis, 1977—; mem. life bd. dirs. 1951—; Vocat. Counselling Service, 1957— ; chmn. Univ. City (Mo.) Plan Commn., 1971-77, Univ. City Civil Service Commn., 1965-71. Served as maj. USAF, 1942-46. Mem. ABA, Mo. Bar Assn., St. Louis Bar Assn., Am. Judicature Soc., Judge Advs. Assn. Am. Soc. Internat. Law, Pi Lambda Phi. Health, Hospital and physician's malpractice defense, General corporate. Office: 705 Olive St Saint Louis MO 63101

BIESTEK, JOHN PAUL, lawyer; b. Chgo., May 28, 1935; s. John P. and Selma (Glick) B.; m. Elizabeth Mary Frer, Dec. 31, 1956; children—Scott, Becky. B.S., Loyola U., Chgo., 1957, J.D., 1964. Bar: Ill. 1964, U.S. dist ct. (no. dist.) Ill. 1964. Sr. ptnr. Biestek & Facchini, Chgo., 1965-74; founding ptnr. Biestek & Assocs., Arlington Heights, Ill., 1974—. Atty. Wheeling Twp. Republican. Orgn., 1978, fin. chmn., 1982-84; founder, chmn. Arlington Heights Econ. Devel. Commn., 1983-84. Mem. NW Suburban Bar Assn. (pres. 1977-78), Arlington Heights C. of C. (pres. 1982-84, dir. and atty., 1972-86, award Extraordinary Commitment and Leadership 1984), Bridgeview C. of C. (pres. 1969). Roman Catholic. Clubs: Rolling Green Country (sec. 1978-81, atty. 1980-84). Lodge: Rotary (sec. Arlington Heights chpt. 1987—). Family and matrimonial, Real property, Personal injury. Home: 805 S Salem Ave Arlington Heights IL 60005 Office: John P Biestek & Assocs Ltd 115 N Arlington Heights Rd Arlington Heights IL 60004

BIESTERFELD, CRAIG STEWART, lawyer; b. Chicago Heights, Ill., Nov. 6, 1953; s. Howard Martin and Ula J. (Ginn) B.; m. Isabel von Phul Hall, June 6, 1981; children: Christopher, Lindsay. BA, Westminster Coll., 1975; JD, U. Mo., 1978. Bar: Mo. 1978. Ptnr. Peper, Martin, Jensen, Maichel & Hetlage, St. Louis, 1978—. Mem. ABA, Mo. Bar Assn., Bar Assn. of Met. St. Louis. Lutheran. Real property, Construction, Local government. Office: Peper Martin Jensen Maichel & Hetlage 720 Olive St 24th Floor Saint Louis MO 63101

BIGELOW, ROBERT P., lawyer, journalist; b. N.Y.C., Jan. 17, 1927; s. Robert R.L. and Doris W.S. (Bissell) B.; m. Katharine M. MacKenty, Apr. 14, 1951; children—Katharine R., Robert S., Sanford W., Edward G. AB cum laude, Harvard U., 1950, JD, 1953. Bar: Mass. 1953, N.Y. 1980. Law clk. Supreme Ct. Mass., 1953-54; assoc. Bingham Dana & Gould, Boston, 1954-56; atty., asst. counsel John Hancock Mut. Life Ins. Co., Boston, 1956-66; pvt. practice, Woburn, Mass., 1966-86 ; of counsel Hennessy Kilburn Killgoar & Ronan, Boston, 1973-84; ptnr. Bigelow & Saltzberg, Woburn, 1980-86; counsel Warner & Stackpole, Boston, 1986—; adj. prof. Dartmouth Coll., 1982-84, Suffolk Law Sch., 1986-87; acting dir. New Eng. Law Inst., 1974-75. Served with U.S. Army, 1945-46, 51-67. Fellow AAAS, Brit. Computer Soc.; mem. ABA (editor Computers and the Law 1966, 69, 81, Jurimetrics Jour. 1971-74, Bull. Law, Sci. and Tech. 1977-80; chmn. com. law relating to computers 1979-80), Mass. Bar Assn. (chmn. econs. com. 1969-73, mem. com. profl. ethics 1973-79, mem. council of law practice 1981-84 chmn. bus. law sect. 1984-85), Computer Law Assn. (pres. 1977-79, dir. 1973-84), FCC Bar Assn., Can. Bar Assn. (assoc.), ACM (nat. lectr. 1969-70, chmn. computers and soc. group 1969-71), Data Processing Mgmt. Assn., Computer Soc. IEEE (sr.), Australian Computer Soc., Can. Info. Processing Soc., N.Z. Computer Soc., Soc. Computers and Law (U.K.), Soc. Computers and Law (New South Wales), Authors Guild. Author: (with Susan Nycum) Your Computer and the Law, 1975, Contracting for Computer Hardware, Software and Services, 1985, Computer Contracts, 1987; editor Law Office Economics and Management, 1969-78; Computer Law Service, 1973-81; Computer Law and Tax Report, 1974-84, Computer Law Newsletter, 1979—; contbr. articles to profl. jours. Computer, Private international, copyright. Office: 28 State St Boston MA 02109

BIGGERS, NEAL BROOKS, JR., U.S. district judge; b. Corinth, Miss., July 1, 1935; s. Neal Brooks and Sara (Cunningham) B.; m. Jo Ann, 1970; 1 child, Sherron. B.A., Millsaps Coll., 1956; J.D. cum laude, U. Miss., 1963. Sole practice law, Corinth, 1963-68; pros. atty. Alcorn County, 1964; dist. atty. 1st Jud. Dist. Miss., 1968-75; cir. judge, 1975-84; U.S. dist. judge No. Miss., Oxford, 1984—. Contbr. articles to profl. jours. Judicial administration. Office: US Dist Ct PO Box 1238 Oxford MS 38655-1238 *

BIGGINS, FRANKLIN N., lawyer; b. Lebanon, Pa., Oct. 20, 1946; s. N. Stocking and Clarice M. (Franklin) B.; m. J. Veronica Williams, July 1970; children: Dawn E., Kenzie M. AA, Daytona Beach Jr. Coll., 1967; BA, U. South Fla., 1969; JD, Cath. U., Washington, 1974. Bar: Ga. 1974, U.S. Dist. Ct. (no. dist.) Ga. 1974, U.S. Ct. Appeals (5th cir.) 1977, U.S. Ct. Appeals (11th cir.). Asst. atty. gen. State of Ga., Atlanta, 1974-77; sole practice Atlanta, 1977-78, 80-83, 86—; ptnr. Webb, Young, Daniel & Murphy, Atlanta, 1978-80, Arrington, Biggins & Horne P.C., Atlanta, 1983-86; spl. asst. atty. gen. State of Ga., Atlanta, 1978-84; assoc. atty. Fulton County, Atlanta, 1978—. Bd. dirs. Council for Children, Atlanta, 1983, Travelers Aid Met. Atlanta, 1978—. Recipient Disting. Alumni award U. South Fla., 1976. Episcopalian. Avocation: golf. Federal civil litigation, State civil litigation, Criminal. Home: 569 Cherokee Ave Atlanta GA 30312 Office: 1400 Bank S Bldg 55 Marietta St NW Atlanta GA 30303

BIGGS, THOMAS SANFORD, JR., lawyer; b. Georgetown, Fla., Oct. 18, 1932; s. Thomas Sanford and Clara Belle (Summersill) B. LL.B., U. Fla., 1959. Bar: Fla. 1959, U.S. Dist. Ct. (so. dist.) Fla. 1960, U.S. Dist. Ct. (mid. dist.) Fla. 1963, U.S. Dist. Ct. (no. dist.) Fla. 1969, U.S. Ct. Appeals (5th cir.) 1960, U.S. Ct. Appeals (11th cir.) 1982. Assoc., Milam, Ramsay & Martin, Jacksonville, Fla., 1959-63, ptnr., 1963-66; gen. counsel U.S. Senate Spl. Com. on Aging, Washington, 1966-67; sole practice, Jacksonville, Fla., 1967-69; gen. counsel U. Fla.-Gainesville, 1969-82; sole practice, Naples, Fla., 1982—. Mem. Fla. Bd. Bar Examiners, 1982-83. Served with AUS, 1954-57. Mem. ABA, The Fla. Bar, Assn. Trial Lawyers Am., Fla. Blue Key. Litigation. Federal civil litigation, State civil litigation, Personal injury. Office: 849 7th Ave S Suite 202 Naples FL 33940

BIGLER, GLADE S., government agency lawyer; b. Brigham City, Utah, Apr. 21, 1928; s. Horace J. and Marie (Schow) B.; m. Lois A., Sept. 4, 1951; children—Cathy, Nadine, Elaine, Thad, Pat. B.S. in zoology, U. Utah 1950, J.D. 1956. Bar: Utah 1956, U.S. Dist. Ct. Utah 1956, U.S. Ct. Appeals (10th cir.) 1956, U.S. Supreme Ct. 1970. Ins. adjuster Travelers Ins. Co. 1956-58; gen. atty. VA, Salt Lake City 1958-60, loan guaranty atty. 1960-68, dist. counsel 1974—, adminstrv. law judge 1971-74; lectr. in field; pres. Nat. Fedn. Fed. Employees Local 990, 1961-62. Served with USN, 1950-53, USNR 1953-81. Fellow Am. Coll. Legal Medicine; mem. Fed. Bar Assn. (pres. 1964-65), Res. Officers Assn. (pres. Salt Lake chpt. 1978-79). Mormon. Personal injury, Real property, Government contracts and claims. Home: 3003 Kenwood St Salt Lake City UT 84106 Office: 125 S State St Salt Lake City UT 84138

BIGLER, ROSS LOWELL, judge; b. Helena, Mont., Feb. 21, 1923; s. Roy Lapp and Irene Elizabeth (Shook) B.; m. Bridgetta Theresa Boyle, May 7, 1947; 1 son, Randal Lawrence. Student U. Mont., 1940-42, 48; J.D., San Francisco Law Sch., 1953. Bar: Calif., U.S. Dist. Ct. (ea. dist.) Calif. Sole practice, San Francisco, 1954-56; ptnr. Charles Lederer, Alturas, Calif., 1956-60; ptnr. Messner, Hurley and Bigler, Yreka, Calif., 1960-62, Hurley and Bigler, Yreka, 1962-64; sole practice, Yreka, 1964-77; judge Shasta Valley Jud. Dist., Siskiyou County, Calif., 1977—; U.S. magistrate U.S. Dist. Ct., 1971-78; juvenile referee Siskiyou County Superior Ct., 1972—; instr. real estate law Coll. of Siskiyous, 1962-78. Chmn. adv. com. Calif. Legal Services, 1976-79; chmn. Siskiyou County Rep. Central Com., 1961-65; mem. Calif. State central com. Republican Party, 1962-65; chmn. Siskiyou County Air Pollution Hearing Bd., 1972—; chmn. Siskiyou County Assessment Appeals Bd., 1973—. Mem. Calif. Judges Assn., Judges, Marshalls and Constables (bd. dirs. 1985-87). Methodist. Clubs: Lions, Masons, Elks. State civil litigation, Criminal, Jurisprudence. Address: 326 Herzog Blvd Yreka CA 96097

BIGMAN, ANTON W., lawyer; b. Braddock, Pa., Apr. 6, 1929. AB cum laude, U. Pitts., 1951; LLB, Harvard U., 1954. Bar: Pa. 1955, U.S. Supreme Ct. 1965. Sole practice Pitts., 1955—; solicitor Braddock Sch. Dist., 1956-71, 57-69, No. Braddock Sch. Bldg. Authority, 1960-69, Gen. Braddock Area Sch. Dist., 1971-72, 1980-81. Mem. ABA, Pa. Bar Assn., Allegheny County Bar Assn., Assn. Trial Lawyers Am. Personal injury, Family and matrimonial, State civil litigation. Home: 15-H Chatham Tower Apts Pittsburgh PA 15219 Office: 210 Fort Pitt Commons Pittsburgh PA 15219

BILBY, RICHARD MANSFIELD, federal judge; b. Tucson, May 29, 1931; s. Ralph Willard and Marguerite (Mansfield) B.; m. Ann Louise Borchert, July 6, 1957; children: Claire Louise, Ellen Markley. B.S., U. Ariz., 1955; J.D., U. Mich., 1958. Bar: Ariz. bar 1959. Since practiced in Tucson; law clk. to Chief Judge Chambers, 9th Circuit Ct. Appeals, San Francisco, 1958-59; mem. firm Bilby, Thompson, Shoenhair & Warnock, 1959-79, partner, 1967-79; judge U.S. Dist. Ct., Dist. Ariz., Tucson, 1979—; chief judge U.S. Dist. Ct., Dist. Ariz., 1985—; conscientious objector hearing officer Dept. Justice, 1959-62; chmn. (Pima County Med.-Legal panel), 1968-70; Mem. Tucson Charter Revision Com., 1965-70. Chmn. United Fund Profl. Div., 1968; chmn. Spl. Gift Div., 1970, St. Joseph Hosp. Devel. Fund Drive, 1970; Republican state chmn. Vols. for Eisenhower, 1956; Rep. county chmn., Pima County, Ariz., 1972-74; Past pres. Tucson Conquistadores; bd. dirs. St. Josephs Hosp., 1969-77, chmn., 1972-75. Served with AUS, 1952-54. Fellow Am. Coll. Trial Lawyers; mem. Ariz. Acad., Town Hall (dir. 1976-79). Jurisprudence. Home: 4717 Brisa Del Sur Tucson AZ 85718 Office: US Courthouse 55 E Broadway Tucson AZ 85701 *

BILDERSEE, ROBERT ALAN, lawyer; b. Albany, N.Y., Jan. 22, 1942; s. Max U. and Hannah (Marks) B.; m. Ellen Bernstein, June 9, 1963; 1 child, Jennifer M. A.B., Columbia Coll., 1962, M.A., 1964; LL.B., Yale U., 1967. Assoc. Wolf Block Schorr & Solis-Cohen, Phila., 1967-72; sole practice, Phila., 1972-73; assoc., then ptnr. Fox Rothschild, O'Brien & Frankel, Phila., 1973-80; ptnr. Morgan Lewis & Bockius, Phila., 1980—; lectr. Temple U. Sch. Law, Phila., 1978—; asst. in instrn. Yale U. Law Sch., New Haven, 1966; lectr., Phila., 1968—. Author: Pension Regulation Manual; contbg. author: Employee Benefits Handbook, 1982—; editor: Beyond the Fringes; contbr. articles to profl. jours. Woodrow Wilson fellow, 1962. Mem. ABA, Pa. Bar Assn., Phila. Bar Assn. Avocation: wildlife photography. Pension, profit-sharing, and employee benefits, Corporate taxation. Office: Morgan Lewis & Bockius 2000 One Logan Sq Philadelphia PA 19103

BILLAUER, BARBARA PFEFFER, lawyer; b. Aug. 9, 1951; d. Harry George and Evelyn (Newman) Pfeffer; B.S. with honors, Cornell U., 1972; J.D., Hofstra U., 1975; M.A., N.Y. U., 1982. Admitted to N.Y. bar, 1976, Fed. Dist. Ct. N.Y., 1977, U.S. Ct. Appeals for 2d circuit, 1978, U.S. Supreme Ct. 1984; assoc. firm Bower & Gardner, N.Y.C., 1974-78; sr. trial atty. Joseph W. Conklin, N.Y.C., 1978-80; assoc. dept. head firm. Curtis, Mallet-Prevost, Colt & Mosle, N.Y.C., 1980-82; partner firm Anderson, Russell, Kill & Olick, N.Y.C., 1982-86, Stroock & Stroock & Lavan, N.Y.C., 1986—; adj. assoc. prof. N.Y.U. Grad. Sch., 1982—; lectr. Rutger's U. Med. Sch.; adminstrv. law judge N.Y.C. Dept. Transp., 1981-85; mem. jud. screening com. Coordinated Bar Assn., 1982-84; mem. Spl. Panel on Citywide Ct. Adminstrn. Mem. Met. Women's Bar Assn. (v.p. 1981-82, pres. 1983-84, chmn. bd. 1985—), ABA, Nat. Conf. Womens Bar Assn. (bd. dirs.), N.Y. State Bar Assn., Nat. Assn. Bar Presidents, Am. Soc. Law and Medicine, Network Bar Leaders State of N.Y. and City of N.Y., Assn. of Bar of City of N.Y. (products liability com. 1983-86, sex and the law com. 1986—), Am. Soc. Microbiology, Am. Arbitration Assn., Brit. Occupational Hygiene Soc., N.Y. Acad. Scis., AAUW, AAAS, Weizmann League of Weizmann Inst. Sci. (exec. com.). Personal injury, Environment, Health. Office: Stroock & Stroock & Lavan 7 Hanover Sq New York NY 10004

BILLICK, BROOKE JAY, lawyer; b. Des Moines, Nov. 18, 1953; s. Lyle Larkin and Florence Lenore (Carlson) B.; m. Susan Diane Bickert, Aug. 11, 1984. BS in Fin., Iowa State U., 1976; JD, U. Iowa, 1979. Bar: Wis. 1979, U.S. Dist. Ct. (we. and ea. dists.) Wis. 1979. From assoc. to ptnr. Gibbs, Roper, Loots & Williams, Milw., 1979—. Pres., bd. dirs. Vol. Ctr. of Greater Milw., Inc., 1981-87; bd. dirs. Instl. Rev. Bd. U. Wis., Milw., 1983-86. Mem. ABA (fed. regulation securities com.), Wis. Bar Assn. Republican. Presbyterian. Avocations: photography, cycling. Securities, General corporate. Office: Gibbs Roper Loots & Williams 735 N Water St Milwaukee WI 53202

BILLINGS, BRUCE ARTHUR, lawyer; b. Whittier, Calif., Dec. 24, 1952; s. David Devore and Eileen Margaret (Cox) B.; m. Joyce Elaine Barros, Nov. 12, 1983; children: Jodi Marie, Hilary Eileen. BA, Colo. State U., 1974; JD, U. Nebr., 1977. Bar: Colo. 1977, U.S. Dist. Ct. Colo. 1977, U.S. Ct. Appeals (10th cir.) 1985. Dep. dist. atty. Dist. Atty.'s Office, Montrose, Colo., 1978-81; sole practice Trinidad, Colo., 1981—; instr. Trinidad (Colo.) State Jr. Coll., 1983, Colo. Law Enforcement Tng. Acad., Trinidad, 1983-84; judge Nucla Mcpl. Ct., Colo., 1980; dep. dist. atty. Dist. Atty.'s Office, Trinidad, 1981-82; atty. child support enforcement Las Animas County, Trinidad, 1981—, City of Trinidad, 1983—. Pres., v.p., bd. dirs. Trinidad for Youth, 1981-84; bd. dirs. Fishers Peak Alcoholic Treatment Ctr., Trinidad, 1982-83; regional v.p. Colo. Family Support Council, 1979. Mem. Colo. Bar Assn., So. Colo. Bar Assn., Nat. Inst. Mcpl. Law Officers. Democrat. Avocations: hiking, reading. Local government, Family and matrimonial, General practice. Home: 216 W First St Trinidad CO 81082 Office: McCormick Bldg Room 4 Trinidad CO 81082

BILLINGS, FRANKLIN SWIFT, JR., judge; b. Woodstock, Vt., June 5, 1922; s. Franklin S. and Gertrude (Curtis) B.; m. Pauline Gillingham, Oct. 13, 1951; children: Franklin, III, Jireh Swift, Elizabeth, Ann. S.B., Harvard U., 1943; postgrad., Yale U. law Sch., 1945; J.D., U. Va., 1947. Bar: Vt. 1948. With dept. electronics Gen. Electric Co., Schenectady, N.Y., 1943-45; bldg. dept. Vt. Marble Co., Proctor, 1945-46; individual practice law Woodstock, 1948-52; mem. firm Billings & Sherburne, Woodstock, 1952-66; asst. sec. Vt. Senate, 1949-55, sec., 1957-59; sec. civil and mil. affairs State of Vt., 1959-61; exec. clk. to gov. 1955-57; judge Hartford Mcpl. Ct., 1955-63; mem. Vt. Ho. of Reps., 1961-66, chmn. jud. com., 1961, speaker of ho., 1963-66; judge Vt. Superior Ct., 1966-75; assoc. justice Vt. Supreme Ct., Montpelier, 1975-83, chief justice, 1983-84; judge U.S. Dist. Ct. Vt., 1984—. Bd. dirs. Norman Williams Library, Woodstock, 1950—, active, Town of Woodstock, 1948-72. Served as warrant officer 1st class attached Brit. Army, 1944-45. Decorated Purple Heart U.S.; Brit. Empire medal. Mem. Vt. Bar Assn., Delta Theta Phi. Club: Rotary (past pres.). Office: PO Box 218 Rutland VT 05701

BILLINGS, WILLIAM HOWARD, chief justice; b. Kennett, Mo., Aug. 21, 1921; s. James. v. and Leora (Sapp) B. Student naval aviator program, U. Iowa, 1942-43; LL.B., U. Mo., 1952. Bar: Mo., U.S. Dist. Ct. (ea. dist.) Mo., U.S. Supreme Ct. Ptnr. McHaney, Billings & Welman, Kennett, 1952-66; judge 35th jud. cir., Kennett, 1966-73, so. dist. Mo. Ct. Appeals, Springfield, 1973-82, Mo. Supreme Ct., Jefferson City, 1982—; lectr. Mo. State Hwy. Patrol, 1971-72. Pres., v.p. bd. curators U. Mo., Columbia, 1965-74. Served to capt. USMCR, 1942-45. Mem. ABA, Mo. Bar. Assn., Dunklin County (Mo.) Bar Assn., Am. Legion, VFW, Amvets, Order of Coif, Phi Delta Phi, Pi Kappa Alpha. Methodist. Lodge: Masons. Judicial administration. Home: 1500 Rosewood Jefferson City MO 65101 Office: Supreme Ct Mo Supreme Ct Bldg Jefferson City MO 65101 *

BILLINGSLEY, CURTIS ASHLEY, lawyer; b. Wadsworth, Ohio, Oct. 5, 1950; s. Jack Fenton Billingsley and Dora Frances (Swisher) Adam. BA, U. South Fla., 1972; postgrad., St. Catherines Coll., Oxford, Eng., 1973; JD, Fla. State U., 1974. Bar: Fla. 1975. Atty. Fla. Senate, Tallahassee, 1973-76; hearing officer Pub. Employees Relations Commn., Tallahassee, 1977-80; atty. Dept. of Health and Rehabilitative Services, Tallahassee, 1980-82, Dept. of Ins., Tallahassee, 1982-84; atty. office of gov. Hosp. Cost Containment Bd., Tallahassee, 1984—. Author: Soft Regulation: A Concept for the 80's?, 1986. Democrat. Presbyterian. Avocations: athletics, art, photography. Administrative and regulatory, State civil litigation, Health. Home: 218 Teal Ln Tallahassee FL 32308 Office: Hosp Cost Containment Bd 325 John Knox Rd #101L Tallahassee FL 32303

BILLINGSLEY, ROBERT THAINE, lawyer; b. Wichita, Kans., Jan. 9, 1954; s. Thaine Edward and Anita (Moore) B.; m. Anna Barron, Dec. 31, 1983. AB, Coll. of William and Mary, 1976; JD, U. Richmond, 1980. Bar: Va. 1980. Law clk. to presiding justice U.S. Dist. Ct., Roanoke, Va., 1980-81; assoc. McGuire, Woods & Battle, Richmond, Va., 1981-87, Hirschler, Fleischer, Weinberg, Cox & Allen, Richmond, Va., 1987—; mem. com. on legal edn. and admission to bar, bd. govs. Young Lawyers Conf. Va. State Bar, 1985—. Bd. editors: The Virginia Lawyer, 1984—; mem. adv. bd. U. Richmond Law Rev., 1986—. Bd. dirs. Bethlehem Ctr., Richmond, 1985—; mem. adminstrv. bd. Trinity United Meth. Ch., Richmond, 1986—. Mem. ABA (state membership chmn. young lawyers div. 1985—), Virginia Bar Assn. (com. on alternative dispute resolution), Richmond Bar Assn., Richmond Jaycees (bd. dirs. 1984-86). Club: Va. Reel (Richmond). Avocations: running, golf, basketball, theatre, movies. Federal civil litigation, State civil litigation. Home: 4633 Leonard Pkwy Richmond VA 23226 Office: Hirschler Fleischer Weinberg Cox & Allen Main St Centre 629 E Main St Richmond VA 23202

BILLINGTON, BARRY E., lawyer; b. Bruceton, Tenn., June 24, 1940; s. Charles Raymond and Edith Virginia (Bowles) B.; m. Bonnie Leslie Johnson, Oct. 16, 1971; children—Erin Alexis, Barry E. A.B. in Econs, Davidson Coll., 1964; J.D., Emory U., 1968. Bar: Calif. 1969, Ga. 1971, U.S. Dist. Ct. (cen. dist.) Calif. 1969, U.S. Dist. Ct. (no. dist.) Ga. 1971. Assoc. Surr & Hellyer, San Bernardino, Calif., 1968-70; with Mfrs. Life Ins. Co., Atlanta, 1970-71; assoc. Carter, Ansley, Smith & McClendon, Atlanta, 1971-72; of counsel Raiford & Hills, Decatur, Ga., 1972-75; ptnr. Raiford, Hills, Billington & McKeithen, Atlanta, 1975-77; mem. Rich, Bass, Kidd, Witcher & Billington, Decatur, 1977-82; ptnr. Billington & Beasley, Decatur, 1982-83, Billington & Turner, Atlanta, 1983-85, Barry E. Billington & Assocs., Atlanta, 1985—. Republican candidate for Ga. Ho. of Reps., 52d Dist., 1978, U.S. Congress, 4th Dist. Ga., 1980; editor Ga. Rep. Party Newsletter, 1968, Fulton County Young Rep. Club Newsletter, 1971-72; publicity dir. San Bernardino County Rep. Party, 1969-70, San Bernardino County for Ronald Reagan Com., 1970; alt. del. Rep. Central Com. of Calif., 1969-70; fin. dir. Ga. Fedn. Young Rep. Clubs, 1971-72; pres. Fulton County Young Rep. Club, 1972; chmn. 4th Dist. Conservative Caucus, 1977-79. Served with U.S. Army, M.P. Corps, 1958-60. Mem. Atlanta Bar Assn. (speaker's com. 1974-77, litigation, family law, criminal law sects.), Decatur-DeKalb Bar Assn. (chmn. speaker's com. 1977-78), ABA (litigation sect. 1969—), Ga. Trial Lawyers Assn., Assn. Trial Lawyers Am. Mormon. Clubs: Conservative League, Masons. Personal injury, Federal civil litigation, State civil litigation. Home: 922 Dunbar Dr Dunwoody GA 30338 Office: Barry E Billington & Assocs 5901 C Peachtree Dunwoody Rd Suite 77 Atlanta GA 30328

BINDER, DAVID A., lawyer, educator; b. 1934. B.A., UCLA, 1956; LL.B., Stanford U., 1959. Bar: Calif. 1960. Ptnr. Brown & Brown, Los Angeles, 1965-69; litigation dir. Western Ctr. on Law and Poverty, 1969-70; faculty UCLA, 1970—, prof. law, 1970—. Author: (with Price) Legal Interviewing and Counseling: A Client-Centered Approach, 1977. Legal education. Office: UCLA Law Sch 405 Hilgrad Ave Los Angeles CA 90024 *

BINDER, DAVID FRANKLIN, lawyer, author; b. Beaver Falls, Pa., Aug. 1, 1935; s. Walter Carl and Jessie Maivis (Bliss) B.; m. Deana Jacqueline Pines, Dec. 25, 1971; children—April, Bret. B.A., Geneva Coll., 1956; J.D., Harvard U., 1959. Bar: Pa. 1960, U.S. Ct. Appeals (3d cir.) 1963, U.S. Supreme Ct. 1967. Law clk. to chief justice Pa. Supreme Ct., 1959-61; counsel Fidelity Mut. Life Ins. Co., Phila., 1964-66; ptnr. Bennett, Bricklin & Saltzburg, Phila., 1967-68; mem. Richter, Syken, Ross, and Binder, Phila., 1969-72, Raynes, McCarty, Binder, Ross and Mundy, Phila., 1972—; mem. faculty Pa. Coll. Judiciary; lectr., course planner Pa. Bar Inst. Recipient Disting. Alumnus award Geneva Coll., 1981. Mem. ABA, Pa. Bar Assn., Phila. Bar Assn., Assn. Trial Lawyers Am., Pa. Trial Lawyers Assn. (lectr.), Phila. Trial Lawyers Assn., Harvard Law Sch. Assn. Clubs: Peale, Union League. Author: Hearsay Handbook, 1975, ann. supplements, 2d edit., 1983. Federal civil litigation, State civil litigation, Personal injury. Office: 1845 Walnut St Suite 2000 Philadelphia PA 19103

BINDLEY, RICHARD STEPHEN, lawyer; b. Marion, Ohio, Feb. 22, 1951; s. Robert Edward and Irenaea (Norris) B.; m. Sheryl Anne Sullivan, Mar. 22, 1975; children: Lauren Elizabeth, Shaun Robert. BS in Edn., Ohio State U., 1974; JD, Capital U., 1978. Bar: Ohio 1978, U.S. Dist. Ct. (so. dist.) Ohio 1980. Ptnr. Morrison, Myer & Bindley, Heath, Ohio, 1978—; law dir. City of Heath, Ohio, 1982—; solicitor Village of Hanover, Ohio, 1980—. Crusade chmn. Am. Cancer Soc., Licking County, Ohio, 1982, bd. dirs. 1982—, pres. 1983-84; trustee Harbor Hills Civic Assn., Hebron, Ohio, 1984—. Mem. ABA, Ohio State Bar Assn., Licking County Bar Assn. Republican. Roman Catholic. Lodge: Lions (bd. dirs. Newark club 1986). Local government, General practice, Probate. Home: 48 Hillcrest Dr Hebron OH 43025 Office: Morrison Myer & Bindley 987 Professional Pkwy Unit B Heath OH 43056

BINGHAM, LISA BLOMGREN, lawyer, educator; b. Lansing, Mich., Jan. 4, 1955; d. Arthur Charles and Lola (Bonacio) Blomgren; m. Geoffrey Parker Bingham, Aug. 7, 1977. BA magna cum laude, Smith Coll., 1976; JD with high honors, U. Conn., 1979. Bar: Conn. 1979, U.S. Dist. Ct. Conn. 1980. Ptnr. Shipman & Goodwin, Hartford, 1979—; bd. dirs. Arioso Prodns., Inc.; adj. prof. Western New Eng. Coll. Law, Springfield, Mass., 1985—. Fulbright Scholar, 1983. Mem. ABA, Conn. Bar Assn., Hartford County Bar Assn., U. Conn. Law Sch. Alumni Assn. (bd. dirs., v.p. 1981—), Hartford Women's Network, Conn. Sch. Atty.'s Council. Club: Hartford Smith Coll. Labor, Local government, Edn. law (school bds.). Home: 29 Griswold Dr West Hartford CT 06119 Office: Shipman & Goodwin 799 Main St Hartford CT 06103

BINGHAM, LOYD EDWARD, JR., lawyer; b. San Antonio, Oct. 8, 1942; s. Loyd Edward and Marie Louise (Olfers) B.; m. Susan Harper, Nov. 29, 1981; 1 son, Edward Allen. A.A., San Antonio Coll., 1962; B.B.A., St. Mary's U., 1965, J.D., 1967. Bar: Tex. 1967, U.S. Dist. Ct. (we. dist.) Tex. 1972, U.S. Dist. Cts. (so. and no. dists.) Tex. 1978, U.S. Ct. Appeals (5th cir.) 1972. Assoc. House, Mercer, House & Brock, San Antonio, 1967-75; ptnr. House, Mercer, House, Brock & Wilson, San Antonio, 1975-77, Brock, Bingham & Person, San Antonio, 1977-83, Brock & Kelfer, 1983—. Bd. dirs. Bexar County Legal Aid Assn., 1970-75. Mem. State Bar Tex., San Antonio Bar Assn., Tex. Assn. Def. Counsel. Democrat. Baptist. Federal civil litigation, State civil litigation, Insurance. Office: Brock & Kelfer 1700 One Riverwalk Pl San Antonio TX 78205

BINGMAN, TERRENCE L., lawyer; b. Miami, Fla., Feb. 29, 1948; s. Samuel Bernard Bingman and Jeanne Eloise (Yerty) Beattie; m. Lynne Aylward, May 20, 1978. BS, U.S. Naval Acad., 1969; JD, U. San Diego, 1975. Commd. ensign USN, 1969, advanced through grades, res., 1980, combat infantry ctr. officer, 1969-72; JAGC USN, San Diego, 1975-80; ptnr. Roger & Wells, San Diego, 1980—; lectr. continuing edn. of bar, San Diego,

1984—. Federal civil litigation, State civil litigation, Insurance. Office: Rogers & Wells 101 W Broadway #2000 San Diego CA 92101 Home: 710 Loring St San Diego CA 92109

BINNING, J. BOYD, lawyer; b. N.Y.C., July 7, 1944; s. James Edward and Lillian (Doughty) B.; m. Penelope Elizabeth Lancione, July 22, 1977; children—Alicia, Peter. A.A., Wesley Coll., 1964; B.S. cum laude, Urbana Coll., Ohio, 1970; M.A. in Polit. Sci., Eastern Ky. U., 1971; J.D., Ohio No. U., 1974. Bar: Ohio 1976, U.S. Dist. Ct. (so. dist.) Ohio 1977, U.S. Ct. Appeals (6th cir.) 1977, U.S. Dist. Ct. (no. dist.) Ohio 1979, U.S. Supreme Ct. 1979. Dep. sheriff Miami County, Troy, Ohio, 1971-74; investigator, legal intern Miami County prosecutor's office, Troy, 1973-75; spl. counsel for the Ohio Senate Jud. Com.; instr., advisor Iowa State Law Enforcement Acad., Des Moines, 1976; sole practice law, Columbus, 1976—; spl. counsel jud. com. Ohio Senate; judge moot ct. Capital Law Sch., Columbus. Author: Civil Rights and the Federal Courts, 1971. Grad. scholar Eastern Ky. U., 1970-71 Mem. Ohio State Bar Assn., Columbus Bar Assn., Nat. Assn. Criminal Def. Lawyers. Republican. Criminal, Civil rights, State civil litigation. Office: 592 S 3d St Columbus OH 43215

BIOFF, ALLAN LEWIS, lawyer; b. Chgo., June 5, 1930; s. Allen and Mary (Shemitis) B.; m. Sarah Susanne (div.); children—Linda, John. B.S., Northwestern U., 1952; J.D., U. Mich., 1958. Bar: Mo. 1958, U.S. Dist. Ct. (we. dist.) Mo. 1958, U.S. Dist. Ct. Kans., 1958, U.S. Ct. Appeals (8th cir.) 1960, U.S. Ct. Appeals (10th cir.) 1960, U.S. Ct. Appeals (7th cir.) 1965, U.S. Ct. Appeals (5th cir.) 1979, U.S. Supreme Ct. 1977. Assoc., Watson, Ess, Marshall & Enggas, Kansas City, Mo., 1958-65, ptnr., 1965—. Served to lt. (s.g.) USNR, 1952-55. Mem. ABA (chmn. labor and employment law sect. 1986—), Mo. Bar Assn., Kansas City Bar Assn., Lawyers Assn. Kansas City, Mo. C. of C., ABA (council labor and employment law sect. 1979—). Clubs: University, Saddle and Sirloin. Editor: The Developing Labor Law, 2d edit., 1983; contbr. articles to profl. jours. Labor. Office: 1006 Grand St 15th Floor Kansas City MO 64106

BIOLCHINI, ROBERT FREDRICK, lawyer; b. Detroit, Sept. 22, 1939; s. Alfred and Erma (Barbetti) B.; m. Francis L., June 5, 1965; children—Robert F., Douglas C., Frances E., Tobin M., Thomas A, Christine M. B.A., U. Notre Dame, 1962; LL.B., George Washington U., 1965. Bar: Okla., Mich. 1965. Assoc. Doerner, Stuart, Saunders, Daniel & Anderson, Tulsa, 1968-71, ptnr., 1971—; dir. Pennwell Pub. Co., Lawrence Electronics Inc., Bank of the Lakes, Bank Jackson Hole, Valley Nat. Bank, Centrifugal Casting Machine Co., Inc., also chmn. bd.; temp. appeals judge Okla. Supreme Ct., 1981—; bd. chmn. Lloyds London . Bd. dirs. Thomas Gilcrease Mus. Assn., past pres. and chmn. bd., 1977-80, dir. emeritus, 1980—; bd. dirs., sec., legal cls. Tulsa Ballet Theatre, Inc., 1976-84; bd. trustees and pres. Monte Cassino Sch., 1970-78; bd. dirs. legal com. Tulsa Area United Way, 1986—; chmn. Christ the King Parish Council, 1974-75; mem. adv. council U. Notre Dame Law Sch., 1982—; legal counsel, bd. dirs. United Way, 1986—. Served to capt. U.S. Army, 1965-67. Mem., ABA, Okla. Bar Assn., Mich. Bar Assn. Roman Catholic. Clubs: Tulsa, Southern Hills Country (Tulsa). General corporate, Federal civil litigation, Securities. Home: 1744 E 29th St Tulsa OK 74114 Office: 1000 Atlas Life Bldg Tulsa OK 74103

BIONDO, VINCENT F., JR., lawyer. BA in History, Polit. Sci., Econs., San Diego State U., 1964; JD, Stanford U., 1967. Bar: Calif. 1967, U.S. Dist. Ct. (so. dist.) Calif., U.S. Ct. Appeals (9th cir.), U.S. Supreme Ct. Dep. city atty. criminal div. City of San Diego, 1967-68, 70-71; asst. atty. City of Escondido, Calif., 1971-72; city atty. City of Carlsbad, Calif., 1972—; lectr. League of Calif. Cities, 1981-82; arbitrator San Diego County Superior Ct., 1982—; judge pro tem North San Diego County, 1983—; pres. City Attys. Dept. League Calif. Cities, 1983-84. Contbr. articles to profl. jours. Served to lt. JAGC, USNR. Mem. ABA (local govt. sect.), Calif. Bar Assn. (exec. com. pub. law sect. 1985-87), Nat. League Mcpl. Law Officers, San Diego County Bar Assn., San Diego-Imperial County City Attys. Assn. (pres. 1977-78). Office: City Attys Office 1200 Elm Ave Carlsbad CA 92008

BIRCH, TERRELL COLHOUN, lawyer; b. Washington, Mar. 23, 1935. B.S.E.E., George Washington U., 1959, J.D., 1963. Bar: D.C. 1964, Md. 1972, Va. 1980. Ptnr. Birch & Birch, Washington, 1964-76; ptnr. Birch, Stewart, Kolasch & Birch, Falls Church, Va., 1976—; arbitrator Am. Arbitration Assn., Fed. Insecticide, Fungicide and Rodenticide Act, disputes Fed. Mediation and Conciliation Service. Federal civil litigation, Patent, Trademark and copyright. Office: 301 N Washington St Falls Church VA 22046

BIRCHER, EDGAR ALLEN, manufacturing company executive; b. Sprinfield, Ohio, Apr. 28, 1934; s. John Clark and Ethel Ann (Speakman) B.; m. Lavinia Brock, Sept. 30, 1978; children: Douglas, Stephen, Todd, Karen. B.A., Ohio Wesleyan U., 1956; J.D., Ohio State U., 1961. Bar: Tex. 1973, Ohio 1962. Assoc. Fuller, Seney, Henry & Hodge, Toledo, 1962-64; with Cooper Industries, Inc., Houston, 1964—; v.p. Cooper Industries, Inc., Houston, 1977—; gen. counsel Cooper Industries, Inc., Houston, 1977—. Served with USAF, 1956-59. Mem. ABA, Ohio Bar Assn., Tex. Bar Assn., Am. Corp. Counsel Assn. (bd. dirs.), Knights of Momus, Phi Delta Theta, Phi Delta Phi. Clubs: Houston, Bob Smith Yacht. Contracts commercial, Antitrust. Home: 1501 Harborview Circle Galveston TX 77550 Office: 4000 First City Tower PO Box 4446 Houston TX 77210

BIRCHFIELD, J. KERMIT, JR., forest products company executive, lawyer; b. Roanoke, Va., Jan. 8, 1940; s. John Kermit and Christine (Luke) B.; m. Glenys Garnell, Nov. 14, 1964; 1 child, Guthrie Kathryn. B.S. in Econs., Roanoke Coll., 1968; J.D., U. Va., 1971. Bar: N.Y., 1972, U.S. Dist Ct. (so. dist.) N.Y., 1972, U.S. Ct. Appeals (2d cir.), 1972. Assoc. Shearman & Sterling, N.Y.C., 1971-81; ptnr. Holtzmann, Wise & Shepard, N.Y.C., 1981-83; sr. v.p. legal and govtl. affairs, gen. counsel Ga. Pacific Corp., Atlanta, 1983—; bd. dirs. WSHCB Properties, Inc. Author: How to Borrow on the Eurodollar Market, 1981. Bd. dirs., exec. com. Atlanta Ballet, 1984—, chmn., 1987—, vice chmn., 1986-87; bd. dirs. Atlanta Music Festival Assn., 1984—; Friends of Piedmont Hosp., 1985—; bd. dirs., exec. com. Assn. Am. Indian Affairs, 1983-86; bd. dirs. The High Mus. of Art, 1986—; bd. visitors Emory U., 1985—. Served to capt. USAF, 1959-67, Vietnam. Mem. ABA, Am. Arbitration Assn. (bd. dirs.), Atlanta Bar Assn., N.Y.C. Bar Assn., N.Y. Bar Assn., Am. Law Inst. Clubs: Racquet and Tennis, India House, Piedmont Driving, Capital City; Carlton (London); Farmington Country; Roanoke (Va.) Country; Annisquam Yacht. General corporate, Securities. Office: Ga Pacific Corp 133 Peachtree St NE Atlanta GA 30303

BIRD, AGNES THORNTON, lawyer; b. Wichita Falls, Tex., Sept. 15, 1921; d. Ernest Grady and Ann McNulty (Renfro) Thornton; m. Frank Babington Bird, Mar. 10, 1946; 1 dau., Patricia Ann. B.S., Tex. Womans U., 1943; M.A., U. Tenn., 1959, Ph.D., 1967, J.D., 1974. Bar: Tenn. bar 1975. Draftsman Humble Oil Co., Wichita Falls, Tex., 1943-45; clk. Aluminum Co. Am., Alcoa, Tenn., 1947-49; tchr. public schs. Blount County, Tenn., 1950-52; instr. polit. sci. U. Tenn., 1961-64; asst. prof. polit. sci. Maryville (Tenn.) Coll., 1969-72; partner firm Bird, Navratil & Bird, Maryville, 1975—; Mem. Tenn. Human Rights Commn., 1965-68; mem. Tenn. adv. com. U.S. Civil Rights Commn., 1963-72, vice chmn., 1968; chmn. Tenn. Commn. on Status of Women, 1977-79; pres. Tenn. Fedn. Dem. Women, 1964-65; parliamentarian Nat. Fedn. Dem. Women, 1974-83; mem. Nat. Assn. Dem. State Chairs, 1976-84; vice chmn. Tenn. Dem. Party, 1976-84; Dem. nat. committeewoman for, Tenn., 1976-84; bd. dirs. Nat. Assn. Commns. on Women, 1977-78; mem. adv. council Maryville Coll., 1979—. Recipient Disting. Alumna award Tex. Women's U., 1980; Citizens Research Found. of Princeton; N.J., grantee, 1965. Mem. Am. Bar Assn., Tenn. Bar Assn., Blount County Bar Assn. (treas. 1978-79), Am. Trial Lawyers Assn., Tenn. Trial Lawyers Assn., Am. Polit. Sci. Assn., AAUW (pres. Maryville br. 1967-69, chmn. assn. topic com. 1970-72, pres. Tenn. div. 1985-87), ACLU, NOW, LWV, DAR, Common Cause. Unitarian. Club: Chilhowee (pres. 1965-66). Contracts commercial, Probate, General corporate. Home: Cold Springs Rd Walland TN 37801 Office: Bird Navratil Bird & Kull Box 647 100 N Court St Maryville TN 37803-0647

BIRD, FRANCIS MARION, lawyer; b. Comer, Ga., Sept. 4, 1902; s. Henry Madison and Minnie Lee (McConnell) B.; m. Mary Adair Howell, Jan. 30, 1935; children—Francis Marion, Mary Adair Bird Kennedy, Elizabeth Howell Bird Hewitt, George Arthur. A.B., U. Ga., 1922, LL.B., 1924; LL.M., George Washington U., 1925; LL.D., Emory U., 1980, U. St. Andrews, 1982. Bar: Ga. bar 1924, D.C. bar 1925. Since practiced in Atlanta; with U.S. Senator Hoke Smith, 1925; individual practice 1930-45; mem. firm Bird & Howell, 1945-59, Jones Bird & Howell, 1959-82, Alston & Bird, 1982—; served as part-time U.S. referee in bankruptcy, 1945-54; spl. asst. to U.S. atty. gen. as hearings officer Nat. Selective Service Act.; Mem. commn. for preparation plan of govt. City of Atlanta and county area; mem. permanent rules com. Ga. Supreme Ct.; mem. Met. Atlanta Commn. Crime and Juvenile Delinquency, chmn., 1969-70; formerly Ga. co-chmn. Tech.-Ga. Devel. Fund.; Trustee Young Harris Coll., U. Ga. Found., Atlanta Lawyers Found., Interdenominational Theol. Center; trustee, past mem. exec. com. Emory U., Atlanta.; Chmn. Ga. Bd. Bar Examiners, 1954-61. Mem. permanent editorial bd.: Uniform Comml. Code, 1962-77, Fed. Jud. Conf., 5th Circuit, Fed. Jud. Conf., 11th Circuit, 1960-81, 1981—. Recipient Distinguished Service citation U. Ga. Law Sch.; Distinguished Service award Atlanta Bar Assn., 1977; Pres.'s award Assn. Pvt. Colls. and Univs., 1979. Fellow Am. Bar Found; mem. Am. Judicature Soc. (past dir.), Am. Law Inst. (council 1949-82, emeritus, past chmn. com. membership), ABA, Ga. (past pres.), Atlanta), Am., Ga. (past pres.) bar assns.), Assn. Bar City N.Y., Atlanta C. of C. (past pres., Atlanta Civic Service award 1957), U. Ga. Alumni Assn. (past pres., certificate of merit 1952), George Washington U. Alumni Assn. (achievement award 1965), Phi Kappa Phi, Sigma Chi, Phi Delta Phi. Methodist. Clubs: Peachtree Golf, Atlanta Athletic (past pres.), Kiwanis, Piedmont Driving, Capital City, Lawyers (past pres.), Augusta (Ga.) Nat. Golf (gov.). General practice. Home: 89 Brighton Rd NE Atlanta GA 30309 Office: 1200 The Citizens and So Nat Bank Bldg Atlanta GA 30335

BIRD, FRANK BABINGTON, lawyer; b. Athens, Tenn., Mar. 12, 1917; s. James T. and Emily (Merrill) B.; m. Agnes Thornton, Mar. 10, 1946; 1 child, Patricia Anne. JD, U. Tenn., 1941. Bar: Tenn. 1941, U. Dist. Ct. (ea. dist.) Tenn. 1946, U.S. Supreme Ct. 1968, U.S. Ct. Appeals (6th cir.) 1968. Atty. Tenn. Valley Authority, Knoxville, 1942, Office of Price Adminstrn., Washington, 1942-46; ptnr. Bird, Navratil, Bird & Kull, Maryville, Tenn., 1946—. pres. Blount County C. of C., 1956-57. Served to sgt. USAF, 1943-46. Mem. ABA, Tenn. Bar Assn., Blount County Bar Assn. (pres. 1951-72), World Assn. Lawyers. Democrat. Unitarian. Contracts commercial, Estate planning, Bond issues. Home: Cold Springs Rd Walland TN 37886 Office: Bird Navratil Bird & Kull PO Box 647 100 N Court St Maryville TN 37803

BIRD, ROSE ELIZABETH, former chief justice California Supreme Court; b. Tucson, Nov. 2, 1936. B.A. magna cum laude, L.I. U., 1958; J.D., U. Calif., Berkeley, 1965. Bar: Calif. 1966. Clk. to chief justice Nev. Supreme Ct., 1965-66; successively dep. public defender, sr. trial dep., chief appellate div. Santa Clara County (Calif.) Pub. Defenders Office, 1966-74; tchr. Stanford U. Law Sch., 1972-74; sec. Calif. Agr. and Services Agy., also mem. governor's cabinet, 1975-77; chief justice Calif. Supreme Ct., 1977-86; chairperson Calif. Jud. Council, Commn. Jud. Appointments; pres. bd. dirs. Hastings Coll. Law, U. Calif.; bd. councilors U. So. Calif. Law Center, 1975-77; Past mem. Western regional selection panel President's Commn. White House Fellowships; bd. assos. San Fernando Valley Youth Found. Named Most Outstanding Sr. L.I. U., 1958; Ford Found. fellow, 1960. Democrat. Address: PO Box 51376 Palo Alto CA 94306 *

BIRD, TERRY CORNELIUS, lawyer; b. Knoxville, Tenn., Aug. 20, 1946; s. Roy Selman and Helen Virginia (Kerby) B. Bar: Tenn. 1975, Ga. 1977. Instr. math. Castle Heights Mil. Acad., Lebanon, Tenn., 1968-72; assoc. David Bolin, Atty., Smyrna, Tenn., 1975-76; dist. counsel U.S. Dept. Immigration and Naturalization Services, Atlanta, 1976—. Mem. Fed. Bar Assn., Ga. Trial Lawyers Assn. Immigration, naturalization, and customs, Federal civil litigation, Public international. Office: US Immigration Naturalization Service 1408 Richard Russell Bldg Atlanta GA 30303

BIRENBAUM, DAVID ELIAS, lawyer; b. Waterbury, Conn., Nov. 30, 1937. AB cum laude, Brown U., 1959; JD, Harvard U., 1962. Bar: Conn. 1962, D.C. 1963. Law clk. to presiding justice U.S. Dist. Ct. Conn., Hartford, 1962-63; asst. gen. counsel Nat. Adv. Commn. on Civil Disorders, 1967-68; resident ptnr. Fried, Frank, Harris, Shriver & Jacobsen, London, 1970-73; ptnr. Fried, Frank, Harris, Shriver & Jacobsen, Washington, 1973—; lectr. internat. trade law U. Pa.; chmn. subcom. Extraterritorial Provisions of Restatement of Fgn. Law, 1984; mem. program com. Ctr. for Nat. Policy. Contbr. articles to profl. jours. Coordinator domestic policy issues Humphrey for Pres., 1968; issues dir., gen. counsel Shriver for Pres. com., 1975-76; mem. Montgomery County, Md. Dem. Cen. Com., 1975-76; gen. counsel, bd. dirs. Handgun Control Inc.; pres. Handgun Info. Ctr. Mem. ABA (co-chmn. ad hoc task force extraterritorial application of U.S. law internat. law sect. 1984), U.S. C. of C. (internat. service industry com.), Phi Beta Kappa. Home: 2804 34th Pl NW Washington DC 20007 Office: Fried Frank Harris et al 1001 Pennsylvania Ave NW Suite 800 Washington DC 20004-2505

BIRIBAUER, RICHARD FRANK, lawyer; b. Cranford, N.J., May 30, 1950; s. Frank Anton and Mary M. (Valle) B.; m. Linda Carey, Aug. 26, 1972; 1 child, James Richard. A.B., Rutgers U., 1972; J.D., Washington and Lee U., 1975. Bar: Va. 1975, D.C. 1976. Assoc. Law Offices of Fulton Brylawski, Washington, 1975-77; trademark counsel Johnson & Johnson, New Brunswick, N.J., 1977-83, internat. trademark counsel, 1984—. Contbr. articles to Washington and Lee U. Law Rev. Mem. ABA, D.C. Bar Assn., Va. State Bar Assn., U.S. Trademark Assn., Pharm. Trade Marks Group. Trademark and copyright, Private international. Office: Johnson & Johnson One Johnson & Johnson Plaza New Brunswick NJ 08933

BIRIBIN, RENATO RAYMOND, lawyer; b. Jersey City, July 29, 1940; s. Theodore A. and Anna L. (DeStefano) B.; m. Elaine M. Serido, Mar. 26, 1966; children: Renee, Renato R. Jr., Elaine M., Theodore John, Marianna G. BS, Rutgers U., 1967; JD, Seton Hall U., 1974. Bar: N.J. 1974, U.S. Dist. Ct. (no. dist.) N.J. 1974. Sole practice Plainfield, N.J., 1974—; tchr. Taylor Bus. Inst., Plainfield, N.J., 1975, 76. Atty. planning bd. Borough of South Plainfield, 1981-82. Served with U.S. Army, 1963-65, ETO. Mem. ABA, N.J. Bar Assn., Union County Bar Assn., Assn. Trial Lawyers Am., UNICO (pres. Plainfield chpt. 1971-73, nat. pres. 1980-81), Phi Alpha Delta. Republican. Roman Catholic. Avocations: travel, reading, service club membership. State civil litigation, Criminal, Probate. Office: 404 E Front St Plainfield NJ 07060

BIRKENBUEL, MARCIA LEE, lawyer; b. Billings, Mont., Dec. 8, 1953; d. Ralph G. and Gertrude E. (Evarts) Grooms; m. Brian H. Birkinbuel, June 9, 1979; 1 child, William L. BA in History, Mont. State U., 1976; JD, U. Mont., 1979. Bar: Mont. 1979, U.S. Dist. Ct. Mont. 1979, U.S. Ct. Appeals (9th cir.) 1984. Atty. Cascade County Office of Pub. Defenders, Great Falls, Mont., 1979-81; sole practice Great Falls, 1981—. Criminal, Family and matrimonial, Juvenile. Office: 410 Central Ave Strain Bldg Suite 606 Great Falls MT 59401

BIRMINGHAM, RICHARD FRANCIS, lawyer; b. S.I., N.Y., July 9, 1949; s. Francis J. and Margaret M. (Pannetta) B.; m. Sharon R. Harkins, Aug. 15, 1969; children: Richard F. Jr., Lauren M., Marissa Beth. BA in English Lit., Fordham Coll., 1971; JD, Fordham U., 1977. Bar: N.Y. 1978, U.S. Ct. Internat. Trade 1978, U.S. Dist. Ct. (ea. and so. dists.) N.Y. 1978, Fla. 1979, Pa. 1980, U.S. Supreme Ct. 1986. Assoc. Freeman, Meade, Wasserman, N.Y.C., 1977-78, Sandler & Travis, N.Y.C., 1978-80; ptnr. Cawse & Birmingham, S.I., 1980—; spl. counsel Minority Leader, N.Y.C. Council, 1986—; arbitrator N.Y. City Civil Ct., 1984—. Candidate N.Y. State Assembly, 1982; counsel Childrens Harbor Pre-Sch., S.I., 1983—; lector coordinator Our Lady Good Counsel Parish, S.I., 1983—; adv. bd. Bayley Seton Hosp., S.I., 1984—; law chmn. Richmond County Conservatives, 1985—, mem. exec. com. 1984—; bd. dirs. March of Dimes, S.I., 1985—. Mem. ABA, N.Y. State Bar Assn., Richmond County Bar Assn., N.Y. County Lawyers Assn., Am. Arbitrators Assn. (arbitrator 1984—). Conservative. Roman Catholic. Avocations: camping, sports. Family and matrimonial, Personal injury, Probate. Office: Cawse & Birmingham 3974 Amboy Rd Staten Island NY 10308

BIRMINGHAM, RICHARD JOSEPH, lawyer; b. Seattle, Feb. 26, 1953; s. Joseph E. and Anita (Loomis) B. BA cum laude, Wash. State U., 1975; JD, U. Puget Sound, 1978; LLM in Taxation, Boston U., 1980. Bar: Wash. 1978, Oreg. 1981, U.S. Dist. Ct. (we. dist.) Wash. 1978, U.S. Tax Ct. 1981. Assoc. Burt & Hagen, Portland, Oreg., 1980-82; ptnr. Davis, Wright & Jones, Seattle, 1982—; mem. King County Bar Employee Benefit Com., Seattle, 1986. Contbg. editor: Compensation and Benefits Mgmt., 1985—; contbr. articles to profl. jours. Mem. ABA (employee benefits and exec. compensation com. 1982—), Wash. State Bar Assn. (speaker 1984-86, tax sect. 1982—), Oreg. State Bar Assn. (tax sect. 1982—), Western Pension Conf. (speaker 1986), Seattle Pension Round table. Democrat. Avocations: jogging, bicycling, photography. Pension, profit-sharing, and employee benefits, Personal income taxation. Home: 505 Belmont Ave E #204 Seattle WA 98102 Office: Davis Wright & Jones 1501 Fourth Ave 2600 Century Sq Seattle WA 98101

BIRMINGHAM, WILLIAM JOSEPH, lawyer; b. Lynbrook, N.Y., Aug. 7, 1923; s. Daniel Joseph and Mary Elizabeth (Tighe) B.; m. Helen Elizabeth Roche, July 23, 1955; children—Deirdre, Patrick, Maureen, Kathleen, Brian. M.E., Stevens Inst. Tech., 1944; M.B.A., Harvard U., 1948; J.D., DePaul U., 1953. Bar: Ill. 1953, U.S. Patent and Trademark Office, 1953, U.S. Dist. Ct. (no. dist.) Ill. 1960, U.S. Supreme Ct. 1961, U.S. Ct. Appeals (7th cir.) 1962, U.S. Ct. Appeals (3d cir.) 1968, U.S. Ct. Appeals (D.C. cir.) 1973, U.S. Ct. Mil. Appeals 1973, U.S. Ct. Appeals (fed. cir.) 1982, U.S. Ct. Claims 1986. Chem. engr. Standard Oil Co. (Ind.), Chgo., 1948-53, patent atty., 1953-59; assoc. Neuman, Williams, Anderson & Olson, Chgo., 1959-60, ptnr., 1961—. Served to capt. USNR, 1942-75. Mem. ABA, Ill. Bar Assn., Chgo. Bar Assn., Bar Assn. Seventh Fed. Cir., Fed. Cir. Bar Assn. Am. Intellectual Property Law Assn., Patent Law Assn. Chgo. (bd. mgrs. 1976-77), Internat. Patent and Trademark Assn., Licensing Execs. Soc. Club: Mid-Day (Chgo.). Registered profl. engr., Ill., Ind. Patent, Trademark and copyright, Federal civil litigation. Home: 233 Pine St Deerfield IL 60015 Office: Neuman Williams Anderson & Olson 77 W Washington St Chicago IL 60602

BIRNBAUM, EDWARD L., lawyer; b. Bklyn., Aug. 2, 1939; s. Isaac and Rita (Kuris) B.; m. Madeleine, Apr. 10, 1965; children—Amanda, Jordan. B.A., Queens Coll., CUNY, 1961; LL.B., N.Y.U., 1964. Bar: N.Y. 1964, U.S. Dist. Cts. (so. and ea. dists.) N.Y. 1967, U.S. Ct. Appeals (2d cir.) 1970, U.S. Supreme Ct. 1971, U.S. Dist. Ct. (we. dist.) 1983. Assoc. Korkus & Korkus, N.Y.C., 1964-66, I. Richman, Esq., N.Y.C., 1966-67; ptnr. Herzfeld & Rubin, P.C., N.Y.C., 1967—; lectr. in field; faculty NYY Sch. Continuing Edn., Law and Taxation, fall 1987; arbitrator small claims night ct. Contbr. articles on law to profl. jours. Coach Little League Baseball and Little League Basketball; candidate trustee Village of Saddle Rock, town counsel, N. Hempstead, N.Y.; pres., v.p. Village of Saddle Rock Civic Assn.; mem. Liberal Party County com., del. to jud. conv. Mem. ABA, N.Y. State Bar Assn. (chmn. com. on Supreme Ct., ho. of dels.), N.Y. County Bar Assn., Queens County Bar Assn., Nassau County Bar Assn., Am. Arbitration Assn. (arbitrator), Am. Trial Lawyers Assn., N.Y. State Trial Lawyers Assn., N.Y. Bar Found. Federal civil litigation, State civil litigation, Personal injury. Home: 70 Shelley Ln Great Neck NY 11023 Office: Herzfeld & Rubin PC 40 Wall St New York NY 10005

BIRNBAUM, RICHARD MICHAEL, lawyer; b. N.Y.C., Aug. 6, 1941; s. Philip and Rosalind (Horowitz) B.; children—David L., Jason M. Student Ithaca Coll., 1959-60, Syracuse U., 1960-63, N.Y.U., summer 1961; B.A., C.W. Post Coll., 1964; postgrad. Bernard Baruch Grad. Sch. Bus. Adminstrn., N.Y.C., 1964-65; J.D., U. Fla., 1968. Bar: Fla. 1968, U.S. Dist. Ct. (so. dist.) Fla. 1968, U.S. Ct. Appeals (4th cir.) 1969, U.S. Ct. appeals (5th cir.) 1972, U.S. Ct. Appeals (11th cir.) 1981, U.S. Ct. Appeals (D.C. cir.) 1982, U.S. Supreme Ct. 1973. Clk., assoc. Maloney & Frazier, Ft. Lauderdale, Fla., 1968-70; assoc. Johnson & Heller, Ft. Lauderdale, 1970-75; sole practice, Ft. Lauderdale, 1975-80; prin. Richard M. Birnbaum, P.A., 1980-85; ptnr. Birnbaum & Beilly P.A., Ft. Lauderdale, 1986—; adj. prof. Coll. Law, Nova U., 1977. Panel mem., lectr. Fla. Forum. Fellow Am. Acad. Matrimonial Lawyers; mem. ABA, Fla. Bar (family law sect.), Broward County Bar Assn. (family law com., past chmn.), Acad. Fla. Trial Lawyers (chmn. family law sect. 1984), Assn. Trial Lawyers, Bankruptcy Bar Assn. So. Dist. Fla., Broward County Women Lawyers Assn., Am. Arbitration Assn., Phi Alpha Delta. Contbr. articles to legal jours. State civil litigation, General corporate, Family and matrimonial. Office: 2810 E Oakland Park Blvd Suite 250 Fort Lauderdale FL 33306

BIRNBAUM, ROY BENNETT, lawyer; b. Newark, Oct. 22, 1953; s. Harold and Elaine (Fein) B.; m. Jungae Park, Sept. 29, 1984. BA, Brandeis U., 1974; JD, Harvard U., 1977. Bar: D.C. 1977, U.S. Dist. Ct. D.C. 1978, U.S. Ct. Appeals (D.C. cir.) 1979. Assoc. Kaler, Worsley, Daniel & Hollman, Washington, 1977-81; fgn. legal cons. Kim & Chang, Seoul, Republic of Korea, 1981-84; internat. atty. The Upjohn Co., Kalamazoo, Mich., 1985—. Mem. ABA, Phi Beta Kappa. Jewish. Private international. Home: 4011 E Hillandale Kalamazoo MI 49008 Office: Upjohn Internat Inc 7000 Portage Rd Kalamazoo MI 49001

BIRNBAUM, SHEILA L., lawyer, educator; b. 1940. B.A., Hunter Coll., 1960, M.A., 1962; LL.B. NYU, 1965. Bar: N.Y. 1965. Legal asst. Superior Ct., N.Y.C., 1965; assoc. Berman & Frost, N.Y.C., 1965-70, ptnr., 1970-72; prof. Fordham U., N.Y.C., 1972-78; prof. NYU, N.Y.C., 1978-86; ptnr. Skadden, Arps, Meagher, Slate & Flom, 1984—; assoc. dean NYU, 1982-84. N.Y.C Bar Assn. (mem. exec. com. 1978—, jud. com. 1977), ABA (chmn. product gen. liability, consumer land coms.), Assn. of Bar of City of N.Y. (exec. com. 1978—, 2d century com. 1984-86), Phi Beta Kappa, Phi Alpha Theta, Alpha Chi Alpha. Author: (with Rheingold) Products Liability, Law, Practice Science, 1974. Legal education. Office: Skadden Arps Slate Meagher et al 919 3d Ave New York NY 10022

BIRNE, KENNETH ANDREW, lawyer; b. Englewood, N.J., Apr. 2, 1956; s. Alvin Aaron and Rita May (Gorsky) B.; m. Pamela Beth Ross; 1 child, Jennafer Sara. BA in Polit. Sci., Ohio State U., 1978; JD, Case Western Res. U., 1981. Bar: Ohio 1981, U.S. Dist. Ct. (no. dist.) Ohio 1981. Sole practice Cleve., 1981-85; with Peltz & Birne, Cleve., 1985—; instr. Am. Inst. Paralegal Studies, Cleve., 1982—, personnel dir. Cleve. area 1984—; cons. in field. Mem. ABA, Ohio Bar Assn., Cleve. Bar Assn. (chmn. practice and procedure clinic 1984—, vol. Call for Action 1986, meritorious service award 1986), Cuyahoga County Bar Assn., Phi Eta Sigma, Zeta Beta Tau, Phi Delta Phi. Lodge: Masons. Personal injury, Workers' compensation, State civil litigation. Office: Peltz & Birne 843 Terminal Tower Cleveland OH 44113

BIRNEY, WILLIAM JOSEPH, JR., lawyer; b. Torrington, Conn., Mar. 29, 1931; s. William Joseph and Lina (Valli) B.; m. Barbara Allen, Aug. 12, 1967; children: William III, Mark. BA, St. Bonaventure U., 1952; LLB, Southwestern U., 1960. Bar: Calif. 1961. Dep. atty. City of Los Angeles, 1961-62; dep. counsel Los Angeles County, 1962-68; gen. counsel Vons Grocery Co., El Monte, Calif., 1968—; asst. sec. The Vons Cos. Inc., El Monte, 1986—. Served with U.S. Army, 1954-56. Mem. ABA, Calif. Bar Assn., Los Angeles County Bar Assn. General corporate, Real property. Office: Vons Grocery Co 10150 Lower Azusa Rd El Monte CA 91731

BIRNKRANT, HENRY JOSEPH, lawyer; b. Phila., Jan. 24, 1955; s. Harry Philip and Myra Arlene (Hendler) B.; m. Lynn Rachel Goldin, Oct. 23, 1983. BA magna cum laude, U. Rochester, 1976; JD, Columbia U., 1979; LLM, NYU, 1983. Bar: D.C. 1979, U.S. Dist. Ct. D.C. 1980; U.S. Ct. Appeals (D.C. cir.) 1980, U.S. Tax Ct. 1984. Assoc. Bergson, Borkland, Margolis & Adler, Washington, 1979-82, Covington & Burling, Washington, 1983—. Editor: Columbia Jour. Law and Social Problems, 1979. Mem. ABA (tax section). Estate taxation, Corporate taxation, Personal income taxation. Home: 7723 Old Chester Rd Bethesda MD 20817 Office: Covington & Burling 1201 Pennsylvania Ave NW Washington DC 20004

BIRRELL, GEORGE ANDREW, oil company executive; b. Warren, Ohio, Apr. 25, 1921; s. George Henry and Mary Ann (Rook) B.; m. Lelia Torrey Pannill, Aug. 7, 1948; children: Lelia Carter, Amanda Griswold, Ellen Torrey, Laura Tudor, George William. BA, Yale U., 1942, LLB, 1947. Bar: N.Y. 1948. Assoc. Donovan, Leisure, Newton and Irvine, N.Y.C., 1947-55, ptnr., 1956-58; with Mobil Oil Corp., 1959-86, gen. counsel, 1970-86, sec., 1972-75, v.p., 1975-86; v.p., gen. counsel Mobil Corp., 1976-86; counsel Dorsey and Whitney, N.Y.C., 1986—; Mem. Rye (N.Y.) Planning Comm., 1957-60, Rye Bd. Zoning Appeals, 1962-67, city council, 1968-72, acting mayor, 1970-72. Served to 1st lt. USAAF, 1943-45. Fellow Am. Bar

Found.; mem. ABA, Am. Law Inst., Assn. Bar City N.Y., Assn. Gen. Counsel (pres. 1982-84). Republican. Clubs: Apawamis, Blind Brook, Am. Yacht (Rye). Lodge: Masons. General corporate, Antitrust. Home: Pecksland Rd Greenwich CT 06831 Office: 350 Park Ave New York NY 10022

BISBEE, DAVID GEORGE, lawyer; b. Council Bluffs, Iowa, June 7, 1947; s. George Kimball and Margaret Ruth (McMurry) B.; m. Rita Ann Bentley, May 21, 1981; children: Michael, Christopher, Tyler. Student Iowa State U., 1965-67; BA, Augusta Coll., 1973; JD, U. Ga., 1975. Bar: Ga. 1975, U.S. Dist. Ct. (no. dist.) Ga. 1976, U.S. Ct. Appeals (5th cir.) 1978, U.S. Ct. Appeals (11th cir.) 1981. Assoc. Troutman, Sanders, et al, Atlanta, 1975-81; ptnr. Bisbee, Parker & Rickertsen, Atlanta, 1981—. Served to capt. U.S. Army, 1968-72. Mem. ABA (bus. bankruptcy com.), Am. Bankruptcy Inst. (subcom. on. internat. insolvencies), Atlanta Bankruptcy Bar Assn. (bd. dirs. 1980—), Order of Coif. Republican. Methodist. Bankruptcy, General corporate. Home: 926 Plymouth Rd Atlanta GA 30306 Office: Bisbee Parker & Rickertsen 400 Candler Bldg Atlanta GA 30303

BISCAY, MARCEL PIERRE, lawyer; b. San Francisco, Mar. 18, 1913; s. Frank and Genevieve (Mariande) B.; m. Frances Rhodes Watson, Mar. 14, 1942. BA, Stanford U., 1945; JD, U. Santa Clara, 1948. Bar: Calif. 1948, U.S. Dist. Ct. (no. dist.) Calif. 1948, U.S. Ct. Appeals (9th cir.) 1948. Sole practice Burlingame, Calif., 1948-57; judge mcpl. ct. San Mateo County, Calif., 1957-73; ptnr. Galligan & Biscay, Millbrae, Calif., 1973—; atty. City of San Bruno, Calif., 1956-57; corp. counsel SDI, San Mateo, 1980—; bd. dirs. Chrissa Imports, Brisbane, Calif., Spaten West Inc., Brisbane. Bd. dirs. San Francisco Basque Cultural Ctr., 1979-80. Served with U.S. Army, 1942-43. Recipient Legion of Honor award DeMolay Internat., 1983. Mem. San Mateo County Bar Assn. (v.p. 1956-57). Republican. Presbyterian. Clubs: Green Hills Country (Millbrae) (bd. dirs., sec. 1955-57), Cercle de L'Union (San Francisco). Lodges: Lions (pres. Burlingame 1948—), Masons (sec. 1976-77), Shriners. Probate, Personal injury, General corporate. Office: Galligan & Biscay 1795 El Camino Real Millbrae CA 94030

BISCHOFF, RALPH FREDERIC, lawyer; b. Boston, May 16, 1906; s. Rudolph Paul and Louise (Burkhardt) B.; m. Elizabeth Fay Fauver, Sept. 11, 1937; children: David F., Elizabeth Ann Bischoff Sunderland, John F. BS, Wesleyan U., Middletown, Conn., 1927; LLB, Harvard U., 1930, MA, 1931, PhD, 1937. Bar: Mass. 1930, N.H. 1974. Asst. prof. law Wesleyan U., Middletown, 1934-46; assoc. prof. law NYU, N.Y.C., 1946-49, prof., 1949-65, Denison prof. law, 1965-74, prof. emeritus, 1975—; prof. Vt. Law Sch., South Royalton, 1975-86, prof. emeritus, 1986—. Legal education. Office: Vt Law Sch South Royalton VT 05068

BISETTI, RICHARD L., lawyer; b. Santa Monica, Calif., Jan. 11, 1948. BA, U. So. Calif., 1970; JD, U. West Los Angeles, 1975. Bar: Calif. 1975, U.S. Dist. Ct. (cen. and so. dists.) Calif. 1976, U.S. Ct. Appeals (9th cir.) 1976. Assoc. Magana, Cathcart, McCarthy & Pierry, Los Angeles, 1975—. Mem. Calif. Bar Assn., Assn. Trial Lawyers Am. Personal injury. Office: Magana Cathcart McCarthy & Pierry 1801 Ave of Stars #810 Los Angeles CA 90067

BISGARD, EILEEN BERNICE REID, lawyer; b. Portland, Oreg., July 30, 1944; d. Elbert Hann and Bernice Elizabeth (Smythe) Reid; m. Stanley Howard Hargrove, Aug. 11, 1963 (div. 1973); children—Michael Dean, Kimberly Diane; m. William Harlow Bisgard, Nov. 27, 1974; children—Jeffery Beecher, Corrine Elizabeth. B.S. with highest distinction, Colo. State U., 1966; J.D., U. Denver, 1977. Bar: Colo. 1977. Sole practice, Longmont, Colo., 1977-81; pres. Eileen B. Bisgard, P.C., Longmont, 1982—. Bd. dirs. Parents United, Boulder, Colo., 1983—; founding pres., bd. dirs. Longmont Coalition Women in Crisis, 1979-82; bd. mgrs. St. Vrain Valley YMCA, Longmont, 1981—; mem. youth ctr. adv. bd. City of Longmont, 1983—; exec. dir. The Family Extension, Inc., Longmont, 1986—. Mem. ABA, Colo. Bar Assn., Boulder County Bar Assn. (chmn. juvenile law com. 1984-85), Nat. Assn. Council Children. Club: Soroptimists. Family and matrimonial, Juvenile. Office: 515 Kimbark Suite 201 Longmont CO 80501

BISHAR, JOHN JOSEPH, JR., lawyer; b. N.Y.C., Jan. 22, 1950; s. John Joseph Sr. and Mildred (Marron) B.; m. Noreen Ellen Leddy, Aug. 5, 1972; children: Kimberly, Kelly, Lauren. BA, Georgetown U., 1971; JD, Fordham U., 1974. Bar: N.Y. 1975, U.S. Dist. Ct. (ea. dist.) N.Y. 1975. Assoc. Cullen & Dykman, Garden City, N.Y., 1974-80; sr. v.p., gen. counsel North Am. Bancorp., Garden City, 1980-87; ptnr. Cullen & Dykman, Garden City, 1987—. Bd. dirs. YMCA of Long Island, Huntington, N.Y., 1981—; bd. of trustees Family Life Ctr., Garden City, 1985—; gov. Cath. Sch. of St. Mary, Garden City, 1985—. Named Man of Yr. YMCA of Long Island, 1986. Mem. ABA, N.Y. State Bar Assn., Nassau County Bar Assn., N.Y. State Bankers Assn. (lawyers adv. com.), Assn. Bank Holding Cos. (lawyers com.). Republican. Roman Catholic. Clubs: Cherry Valley (Garden City), Atlantic Beach (N.Y.). Avocations: sports, golf, basketball, tennis, coaching kids. Banking, General corporate. Home: 53 Chestnut St Garden City NY 11530 Office: North Am Bancorp Inc 1010 Franklin Ave Garden City NY 11530

BISHIN, WILLIAM ROBERT, lawyer, legal consultant, educator; b. N.Y.C., Sept. 1, 1939; s. Arthur Abraham and Jean (Dashevsky) B.; m. Sharlee Field, Jan. 23, 1967 (div.); children—Benjamin, Susannah; m. 2d, Adeline Safyan, Apr. 6, 1976. A.B. cum laude, Columbia U., 1960; LL.B. magna cum laude, Harvard U., 1963. Bar: Wash. 1978, N.Y. 1964, Calif. 1965, U.S. Dist. Ct. (cen. dist.) Calif. 1965, U.S. Dist. Ct. (we. dist.) Wash. 1978. Am. history editor Columbia Ency., 1960; assoc. Paul, Weiss, Rifkind, Wharton & Garrison, N.Y.C., 1960; asst. prof. law U. So. Calif. Law Ctr., Los Angeles, 1963-65, assoc. prof., 1965-67, prof., 1967-80; sole practice, Seattle, 1980-86; prin. Bishin, Vane & Skone, Seattle, 1986—; syndicated columnist Los Angeles Times, 1968-70; juvenile ct. referee Superior Ct. County of Los Angeles, 1971-75; ptnr. Edwards & Bishin, Los Angeles, 1973-76; litigator Pacht, Ross, Warne, Bernhard & Sears, Inc., Los Angeles, 1977-78; prof. law U. Puget Sound Law Sch., 1978-80; instr. Bd. dirs. Met. Democratic Club Seattle; chmn. legal com. People Opposed to One-Newspaper Town. Am. Council Learned Socs. fellow, 1968; Columbia U. scholar, 1968; recipient Dart award U. So. Calif., 1969. Mem. ABA, Fed. Bar Assn. (pres. 1984-85), Western Wash. (sec., chmn. continuing legal edn. com.), Seattle King County Bar Assn., Wash. State Bar Assn. (chmn. subcom. continuing legal edn. goals), N.Y. State Bar Assn. Contbr. to The Weekly, 1981-82; author: (with C. Stone) Law, Language and Ethics, 1972; contbg. author Mass Media and the Supreme Court, 2d edit., 1976; contbr. articles to legal jours. Antitrust, Federal civil litigation, State civil litigation. Home: 1404 E Lynn Seattle WA 98112 Office: 520 Pike St Suite 1501 6th and Pike Tower Seattle WA 98101

BISHINS, LARRY V., lawyer; b. Bklyn., May 6, 1945; s. Arthur and Sylvia (Brauer) B.; m. Jan Farber, Dec. 27, 1975; 1 child, Spencer. BS, Syracuse U., 1967; JD, Suffolk U., 1970; LLM in Tax, Boston U., 1971. Bar: Mass. 1970, U.S. Dist. Ct. Mass. 1971, U.S. Ct. Claims 1972, U.S. Tax Ct. 1972, U.S. Ct. Appeals (1st cir.) 1972, Fla. 1974, U.S. Dist. Ct. (so. dist.) Fla. 1974, U.S. Ct. Appeals (5th cir.) 1974, U.S. Supreme Ct. 1974, U.S. Ct. Appeals (11th cir.) 1981. Sole practice Ft. Lauderdale, Fla., 1972—. Personal income taxation, Corporate taxation, Estate taxation.

BISHOP, ALFRED CHILTON, JR., lawyer; b. Alexandria, Va., Oct. 3, 1942; s. Alfred Chilton and Margaret (Marshall) B.; divorced; 1 son, Alfred Chilton III; m. 2d Catherine Ann Keppel, May 17, 1980. B.A. with distinction, U. Va., 1965, LL.B., 1969; LL.M. in Taxation, Georgetown U., 1974. Bar: N.Y. 1970, U.S. Ct. Appeals (2d cir.), 1970, U.S. Tax Ct. 1971, U.S. Ct. Claims 1971, D.C. 1977. Assoc. Shearman and Sterling, N.Y.C., 1969-70; assoc. trial atty., Office of Chief Counsel IRS, Washington, 1970-74, sr. trial atty., 1974-80, sr. technician reviewer, 1980-81, br. chief, 1981—. Recipient Am. Jurisprudence award 1968, 1968. Mem. ABA (tax sec.), D.C. Bar Assn., Sr. Exec. Service Candidate Network (v.p. 1980-81, pres. 1981-82, dir. 1983), Sr. Exec. Assn., Phi Delta Phi. Episcopalian. Corporate taxation, Personal income taxation, Administrative and regulatory. Home: 7523 Thistledown Trail Fairfax Station VA 22039

BISHOP, BRYAN EDWARDS, lawyer; b. Providence, Nov. 29, 1945; s. Charles Frederick Jr. and Emma Kirtley (Edwards) B.; m. Martha Jo Maben, June 12, 1970; children: Jennifer, Adam. BSME, U. Tex., Arlington, 1968; JD, Harvard U., 1972. Bar: Tex. 1972, U.S. Ct. Appeals (5th cir.) 1972. Ptnr. Rain, Harrell, Emery, Young & Doke, Dallas, 1972—. Mem. ABA, Tex. Bar Assn. Club: Chaparral (Dallas). General corporate, Securities, Banking. Home: 7031 Roundrock Rd Dallas TX 75248 Office: Rain Harrell Emery Young & Doke 4200 Republic Bank Tower Dallas TX 75201

BISHOP, LAWRENCE RAY, lawyer; b. Douglas, Wyo., May 10, 1934; s. Cecil Lawrence and Mabel Ruby (Spracklen) B.; m. Sharleen Jo Bishop; m. Nancy Delight Nixon, June 2, 1979; 1 child, Somer Lauren. Student, U. Wyo., 1952-53; BS, U. Utah, 1956; postgrad., Duke U. Sch. Psychology, 1956-57; JD, U. Mich., 1963. Bar: Mich. 1963, U.S. Supreme Ct. 1969. Asst. pros. atty. Washtenaw County, 1964-66; ptnr. Thompson & Bishop, 1966-69, Thompson, Bishop, Tryand & Thompson and predecessor firm Thompson, Bishop & Tyrand, 1969-73, Forsythe, Campbell, Vandenberg, Clevenger & Bishop, P.C., 1973-78, Bishop & Shelton, P.C., Ann Arbor, Mich., 1978—; ptnr. Mich. Law Clinic, 1978-80, Washington St. Assocs., Tech. Ctr., DTR Assocs.; sec. bd. dirs. Cen. Title Service Inc.; pres., chmn. bd. dirs. Legal Edn. Services. Asst. editor U. Mich. Law Rev.; contbr. articles to profl. jours. Past mem. Mich. Mental Health Adv. Bd., chmn. subcom. recipient rights, chmn. select panel on abuse; hon. mem. Ann Arbor Police Officers Assn.; past chmn. Ann Arbor Cancer Crusade, Ann Arbor Mich. Week; past treas. Ann Arbor Rep. City Com., Washtenaw County Rep. Com.; past campaign mgr. numerous polit. candidates; past bd. dirs. Ann Arbor Am. Cancer Soc. Served to lt. USN, 1957-60. Mem. ABA (chmn. publs. div., chmn. products media bd., liaison with Assn. Trial Lawyers Am., governing council econs. sect., lectr.), Mich. Bar Assn. (chmn. econs. law practice sect., counsel to hearing panel of grievnace bd.), Washtenaw County Bar Assn. (past pres., chmn. mediation and cir. ct. coms.), Assn. Trial Lawyers Am., Mich. Trial Lawyers Assn., Washtenaw Trial Lawyers Assn., Inst. for Study Profl. Risk (founding, bd. dirs., exec. dir.), MENSA, Scabbard and Blade, Tau Epsilon Rho, Sigma Chi. Personal injury, Federal civil litigation, State civil litigation. Home: 2172 Spruceway Ln Ann Arbor MI 48103 Office: Bishop & Shelton PC 709 W Huron Ann Arbor MI 48103

BISHOP, REGINALD B., lawyer, consultant; b. Indpls., Apr. 29, 1951; s. Annual B. and Lovie (Ussery) B.; m. Diane Elaine Bishop, June 25, 1970 (div. May 1980); children: Reginald L., Dionne L. BS in Communications, Boston U., 1972; JD, Ind. U., 1977. Bar: Ind. 1977, U.S. Dist. Ct. (so. dist.) Ind. 1977. Columnist Indpls. News, 1972-83; ptnr. Bishop & Schwebel, Indlps., 1977—; cons. polit. campaign developers, Indpls., 1983—. Gen. counsel Indpls. Black Rep. Counsel, 1985—; regional treas. Nat. Black Rep. Counsel, Washington, 1985—. Recipient Casper award Community Service Counsel Met. Indpls., 1978, Profl. Achievement award Ctr. for Leadership, 1981. Republican. Club: Indpls. Athletic. Lodges: Kiwanis, Masons (32 degree), Trinity (John P. Powers award 1985). State civil litigation, General practice, Consumer commercial. Home: 5226 Staughton Dr Indianapolis IN 46226 Office: Bishop & Schwebel 4720 Kingsway Dr #425 Indianapolis IN 46205

BISHOP, ROBERT WHITSITT, lawyer; b. Atlanta, Jan. 7, 1949; s. James Clarence and Dorothy Davis (Whitsitt) B.; m. Cynthia Graham, Aug. 23, 1970; children: Jessica Levesque, Joshua Davis, Amanda Joyce. Student, Duke U., 1966-68; BA with high distinction, U. Ky., Lexington, 1973; postgrad. George Washington U., 1973-74; JD, U. Ky., 1976. Bar: Ohio 1976, Ky. 1981. Mem. Squire, Sanders & Dempsey, Cleve., 1976-80, Barnet & Alagia, Louisville, 1980-84; ptnr. Greenebaum, Young, Treitz & Maggiolo, Louisville, 1984-87, founding mem. Friedman, Evans & Bishop, Louisville, 1987—; founder, dir., officer Indoor Soccer of Louisville Inc., (The Louisville Thunder), 1984-85; bd. dirs., officer Louisville Thunder, Inc., 1985—, Cen. Indoor Soccer League, 1984. Author: The Interdict. Bd. dirs., mem. personnel and fin. coms. Louisville Central Community Ctrs. Inc., 1985. Mem. ABA, Ky. Bar Assn., Ohio Bar Assn., Louisville Bar Assn. (chmn. fed. practice sect. 1987—), Cleve. Bar Assn., Order of Coif, Phi Beta Kappa, Sigma Alpha Epsilon. Avocations: mountain and rock climbing, soccer, creative writing. Federal civil litigation, State civil litigation. Home: 13108 Settlers Point Trail Prospect KY 40059 Office: Friedman Evans & Bishop The Republic Bldg Suite 1000 Louisville KY 40202

BISHOP, WAYNE STATON, lawyer; b. Tarboro, N.C., Oct. 30, 1937; s. Lionel Lyston and Lelia Ruth (Staton) B.; children: John, Jeffrey, Scott. A.B., U. N.C., 1959, J.D., 1964. Bar: D.C. 1964, U.S. Supreme Ct. 1968. Appellate litigation atty. NLRB, Washington, 1964-68; sole practice Washington, 1968—; ptnr. Bishop, Cook, Purcell & Reynolds, Washington, 1980—, firm chmn., 1982—; mem. adv. com. U.S. Trade Rep., 1984—. Coauthor: Authorization Cards and the National Labor Relations Board, 1969. Transition ofcl. Office of Pres.-Elect Reagan, 1980; nat. dir. Dems. for Reagan/Bush, 1980; mem. adv. council Am. Productivity Ctr. Mem. ABA, Fed. Bar Assn., D.C. Bar Assn. Private international, Administrative and regulatory, Labor. Home: 3338 Reservoir Rd Washington DC 20007 Office: 1200 17th St Washington DC 20036

BISSELL, JEAN GALLOWAY, circuit judge; b. Due West, S.C., June 9, 1936; d. Robert Stone and Clara Elizabeth (Agnew) G.; m. Gregg Claude Bissell, June 11, 1969. Student, Erskine Coll., 1952-54; B.S. magna cum laude, U. S.C., 1956, LL.B., 1958; LL.D., Converse Coll., 1976. Bar: S.C. 1958. With Haynsworth, Perry, Bryant, Marion and Johnston, Greenville, S.C., 1958-71; ptnr. McKay, Sherrill, Walker & Townsend, Columbia, S.C., 1971-76; sr. v.p., gen. counsel S.C. Nat. Bank, Columbia, 1976-80, exec. v.p., gen. counsel, 1980-81, vice chmn., chief adminstrv. officer, gen. counsel, 1981-84; sr. v.p., gen. counsel S.C. Nat. Corp., Columbia, 1976-80, exec. v.p., gen. counsel, 1980-81, vice chmn., chief adminstrv. officer, gen. counsel, 1981-84, dir., 1982-84; circuit judge U.S. Ct. Appeals Fed. Circuit, Washington, 1984—; lectr. Sch. Law U.S.C., 1971-78, 80-84. Mem. adv. council S.C. State Library, 1971-76, Erskine Coll., 1971-74, Columbia Coll., 1974-78, Furman U., 1972-84; mem. pres.'s nat. adv. council U. S.C., 1981-84; mem. bd. Columbia Philharm. Orch., 1975-78, Greater Columbia Community Relations Council, 1976-79; regent Leadership S.C., 1979-81; mem. merit selection panel S.C. Pub. Service Commn., 1980-84; chmn. Richland County Pub. Library, 1975-78; mem. S.C. Library Bd., 1982-84; mem. bd. S.C. Council Econ. Edn., 1984. Recipient Disting. Service award S.C. Library Assn., 1973, 1st ann. Friend of Libraries award, 1976, Algernon Sydney Sullivan award. Mem. ABA, S.C. Bar Assn. Clubs: City Tavern (Washington). Office: US Court of Appeals 717 Madison Pl NW Washington DC 20439

BISSELL, JOHN W., federal judge; b. Exeter, N.H., June 7, 1940; s. H. Hamilton and Sarah W. B.; m. Caroline M.; July 15, 1967; children—Megan L., Katharine W. A.B., Princeton U., 1962; LL.B., U. Va., 1965. Law clk. U.S. Dist. Ct., N.J., 1965-66; assoc. Pitney, Hardin & Kipp, Morristown, N.J., 1966-69, ptnr., 1972-78; asst. U.S. atty. N.J., 1969-71; judge Essex County, N.J., 1978-81, N.J. Superior Ct., 1981-82, U.S. Dist. Ct. N.J., Trenton and Newark, 1983—. Office: US PO and Courthouse Fed Sq Newark NJ 07102

BISSEX, WALTER EARL, lawyer; b. Uvalde, Tex., Feb. 16, 1950. AB, Princeton U., 1972; JD, U. Houston, 1975. Bar: Tex. 1975. Staff atty. Browning Ferris Industries, Houston, 1975-79; gen. counsel Lifemark Corp., Houston, 1979-84; ptnr. Clark, Thomas, Winters & Newton, Austin, Tex., 1984—; gen. counsel Travis County Health Facilities Devel. Corp., Houston, 1985—, Travis County Housing Fin. Corp., Houston, 1985—; bd. dirs. Curaflex Health Services, Houston. Mem. Am. Acad. Hosp. Attys., Nat. Health Lawyers Assn., Tex. Health Care Assn., Assn. Internat. des Etudiantsen Scis. Econs. and Commerce (adv. dir. 1986—). Securities, Health, General corporate. Office: Clark Thomas Winters & Newton PO Box 1148 Austin TX 78767

BISTLINE, STEPHEN, justice; b. Pocatello, Idaho, Mar. 12, 1921; s. Ray D. and Martha (Faber) B.; m. Sharon Mooney; children: Patrick, Paul, Arthur, Claire, Susan, Shelley, Diana, Leslie. LL.B., U. Idaho, 1949. Bar: Idaho bar 1949. Individual practice law Sandpoint, Idaho, 1950-76; justice Idaho Supreme Ct., Boise, 1976—. Served with USN, 1941-45. Office: Supreme Ct Bldg State Capitol Boise ID 83720 *

BITSKY, JASON ISIDORE, lawyer; b. Bklyn., Nov. 28, 1950; s. Louis and Gladys (Mintz) B. B.S., MIT, 1972; M.A., Princeton U., 1977; J.D., U. Chgo., 1980. Bar: N.Y. 1981, U.S. Dist. Ct. (so. and ea. dists.) N.Y. 1981. With Shea & Gould, N.Y.C., 1980-82, Golenbock and Barell, N.Y.C., 1982-84, Cooperman, Levitt & Winikoff, N.Y.C., 1984-85, Bell, Kalnick, Beckman, Klee & Green, N.Y.C., 1985—. Legis. intern Mass. Ho. of Reps., Boston, 1972; law clk. to U.S. Bankruptcy Ct. (so. dist.) N.Y., 1978. NSF fellow, 1967, 72-75. Mem. ABA, N.Y.C. Bar Assn., Sigma Xi. Republican. Jewish. General corporate, Securities, Contracts commercial. Office: Bell Kalnick Beckman Klee & Green 300 Park Ave New York NY 10022

BITTEL, PATRICIA THOMAS, labor arbitrator, educator; b. Montgomery, Ala., May 23, 1951; d. James Edwin and Doris Patricia (Sewell) Thomas; m. Timothy Marion Bittel, Oct. 9, 1982; 1 child, Timothy James. BA, Emory U., 1973; JD, U. Va., 1976. Bar: Ala. 1976, Ohio 1983, Fla. 1985. With legal devel. program Gen. Electric, Louisville, 1976-78, labor atty., 1978-79; labor atty. Gen. Electric, Cleve., 1979-82, labor counsel, 1982-84; labor educator Cleveland State U., 1985—; labor arbitrator Cleve., 1986—. Active Jr. League, Cleve.; layreader St. Peter's Epis. Ch., Lakewood, Ohio, 1985—. Mem. ABA (arbitration and law of collective bargaining agreements com., labor sect.), Cleve. Bar Assn. (labor sect.), Am. Arbitration Assn., Soc. Profls. in Dispute Resolution, Indsl. Relations Research Assn., Pub. Sector Labor Relations Assn. Sierra Club. Clubs: Playhouse, Edgewater Yacht (Cleve.). Office: PO Box 40218 Cleveland OH 44140-0218

BITTING, WILLIAM MCCLURE, lawyer; b. Santa Monica, Calif., Apr. 17, 1939; s. Richard Edward and Joan Emma (Jenner) B.; m. Kathleen Joan Pell, July 15, 1940; children—William F., Michelle C., John P. LL.B., UCLA, 1961, J.D., 1965. Bar: U.S. Supreme Ct. 1979, U.S. Ct. Appeals (9th cir.) 1977, U.S. Tax Ct. 1979, U.S. Dist. Ct. (cen. and so. dists.) 1966, Calif. 1966. Ptnr., Hill, Farrer & Burrill, Los Angeles, 1973—; trial counsel Fed. Home Loan Bank Bd., Los Angeles, 1970-72. Fellow Am. Coll. of Trial Lawyers. State civil litigation, Condemnation. Office: 445 S Figueroa St 34th Floor Los Angeles CA 90017

BITTMAN, MITCHELL DAVID, patent lawyer; b. Bronx, N.Y., Jan. 13, 1953; s. Lawrence and Delores (Gura) B.; m. Marcia Ann Glicksman, Aug. 4, 1975; children: Scott, Eric, Craig. BS, SUNY, Stony Brook, 1974; JD, NYU, 1978. Bar: U.S. Patent Office 1975, N.Y. 1979, U.S. Dist. Ct. (so. dist.) N.Y. 1979, U.S. Ct. Customs and Patent Appeals 1979, U.S. Ct. Appeals (2d cir.) 1979. Sr. patent atty. Gen. Foods Corp., White Plains, N.Y., 1974-81; patent atty. Exxon Chem. Corp., Florham Park, N.J., 1981-85; patent counsel Sun Chem. Corp., Carlstadt, N.J., 1985—. Mem. ABA, N.Y. State Bar Assn., N.Y. Patent Law Assn. Patent, General corporate, Trademark and copyright. Home: 27 London Terr New City NY 10956 Office: Sun Chem Corp 631 Central Ave Carlstadt NJ 07072

BITZEGAIO, HAROLD JAMES, lawyer; b. Coalmont, Ind., Jan. 29, 1921; s. Nicholas Gilbert and Dora Belle (Burns) B.; m. Betty Jean Law, Apr. 15, 1950; children: Judith L. Bitzegaio Wallin, Gail Ann, Susan R. Bitzegaio Denyer, James R., Jane E. Bitzegaio Siders. BS, Ind. State U., 1948; JD, Ind. U., 1953; grad., Ind. Jud. Coll., 1980. Bar: Ind. 1953, U.S. Dist. Ct. (so. dist.) Ind. 1953, U.S. Ct. Appeals (7th cir.) 1956. Sole practice Terre Haute, Ind., 1953-58, 81—; judge Vigo Superior Ct., Terre Haute, 1959-80. Editor, contbr.: Indiana Pattern Jury Instructions, 1966. Mem. Ind. Adv. Com. Civil Rights, Indpls., 1961-70, Mayor's Com. Civil Rights, Terre Haute, 1967-68; bd. dirs. Wabash Valley Council Boy Scouts Am., Terre Haute, 1960-80. Served to lt. comdr. USN, 1941-46, PTO. Decorated D.F.C. with gold star, Air medal with two gold stars, Purple Heart. Mem. ABA, Ind. Bar Assn., Terre Haute Bar Assn., Ind. Judges Assn. (bd. mgrs. 1961-80, pres. 1977-78), Ind. U. Law Alumni Assn. (pres. 1973-74, recipient disting. service award 1974), VFW (life), Nat. Rifle Assn. (life), Ducks Unltd. (nat. trustee, emeritus). Democrat. Club: Terre Haute Country (bd. dirs. 1974-76). General practice. Home: Rural Rt 24 Box 523 Terre Haute IN 47802 Office: 1 Courthouse Sq PO Box 1910 Terre Haute IN 47808

BIVENS, DONALD WAYNE, lawyer; b. Ann Arbor, Mich., Feb. 5, 1952; s. Melvin Donley and Frances Lee (Speer) B.; m. Sandra Elise Gale, Mar 6, 1983; children: Jody, Lisa. BA magna cum laude, Yale U., 1974; JD, U. Tex., 1977. Bar: Ariz. 1977, U.S. Dist. Ct. Ariz. 1977, U.S. Ct. Appeals (9th cir.) 1977, U.S. Supreme Ct. 1982, U.S. Dist. Ct. (Fed. cir.) 1984. Ptnr. Meyer, Hendricks, Victor, Osborn & Maledon, Phoenix, 1977—; judge pro tem Maricopa County Superior Ct., Ariz., 1987—; bd. dirs. Ctr. for Law in Pub. Interest, Phoenix, 1983-85. Note & Comment editor Tex. Law Rev., Austin, 1976-77. Pres. Ariz. Young Dems., 1980-82, Scottsdale Men's League, 1980-82; v.p., bd. dirs. Phoenix Symphony Assn., 1980-86; bd. dirs. Scottsdale Arts Ctr. Assn., 1981-84. Recipient Consul award U. Tex. Sch. Law, 1977, Three Outstanding Young Men award Phoenix Jaycees, 1981. Mem. State Bar Ariz., Ariz. Trial Lawyers Assn., Maricopa County Bar Assn. (bd. dirs. 1985—, chmn. Trial Adv. Inst. 1986-87). Democrat. Avocations: music, theater. Federal civil litigation, Computer, Securities. Home: 7118 N 3d Ave Phoenix AZ 85021 Office: Meyer Hendricks et al 2700 N 3d St Suite 4000 Phoenix AZ 85004

BIXBY, FRANK LYMAN, lawyer; b. New Richmond, Wis., May 25, 1928; s. Frank H. and Esther (Otteson) B.; m. Katharine Spence, July 7, 1951; children—Paul, Thomas, Edward, Janet. A.B., Harvard U., 1950; LL.B., U. Wis., 1953. Bar: Ill. 1953, Wis. 1953, Fla. 1974. Since practiced in Chgo.; partner firm Sidley & Austin, 1963—. Editor-in-chief: Wis. Law Rev, 1952-53; editorial bd.: Chgo. Reporter, 1973—. Trustee MacMurray Coll., Jacksonville, Ill., 1973-85; bd. dirs. Chgo. Urban League, 1962—, v.p., 1972-86, gen. counsel, 1972—, chmn. 1986—; bd. dirs. Community Renewal Soc., 1973-86; chmn. trustees Unitarian Ch., Evanston, Ill., 1962-63; bd. dirs. Spencer Found., 1967—, chmn., 1975—; mem. dist. 202 bd. edn. Evanston Twp. High Sch., 1975-81, pres., 1977-79. Recipient Man of Year award Chgo. Urban League, 1974. Mem. Am., Ill., Chgo., Wis., Fla. bar assns., Chgo. Council Lawyers, Chgo. Council Fgn. Relations, Order of Coif, Phi Beta Kappa. Clubs: Harvard (Chgo.) (pres. 1962-63), Mid-Day (Chgo.). Probate. Home: 1100 Ridge Rd Evanston IL 60202 Office: Sidley & Austin 1 First National Plaza Chicago IL 60603

BIXBY, JOSEPH NATHAN, lawyer; b. Geneva, Nebr., Apr. 6, 1950; s. Joseph and Glenna Melba (Pilkey) B.; m. Debra Sue Dondlinger, Aug. 6, 1971; children: Joseph Jonathan, Angela Marie, Deanna Kay, Monica Sue, Paul Nathan. BS, Wesleyan U., Lincoln, Nebr., 1972; JD, U. Nebr., 1975. Bar: Nebr. 1975, U.S. Dist. Ct. Nebr. 1975. Assoc. Gewacke Law Office, Geneva, Nebr., 1975-76; ptnr. Gewacke & Bixby, Geneva, 1976—; asst. atty. City of Geneva, Nebr., 1976-78, atty., 1978—. Mem. ABA, Nebr. Bar Assn., 7th Jud. Bar Assn., Geneva C. of C. (pres. 1980). Republican. Roman Catholic. Club: Hidden Hill (pres., bd. dirs. 1978-80). Lodge: Lions (pres., bd. dirs. 1980—); K.C. (pres., bd. dirs. 1980—, grand knight 1980-81). Avocations: plate collecting, clock making, radio controlled models. Local government, Personal income taxation, General practice. Home: 319 N 9th Geneva NE 68361 Office: Gewacke & Bixby Geneva State Bank Bldg Geneva NE 68361

BIXENSTINE, KIM FENTON, lawyer; b. Providence, Feb. 26, 1958; d. Barry Jay Fenton and Gail Louise (Traverse) Weinstein; m. Barton Aaron Bixenstine, June 25, 1983; 1 child, Paul Jay. BA, Middlebury Coll., 1979; JD, U. Chgo., 1982. Bar: Ohio 1982, U.S. Dist. Ct. (no. and so. dists.) Ohio 1983, U.S. Ct. Appeals (6th cir.) 1983. Law clk. to presiding judge U.S. Dist. Ct. (so. dist.) Ohio, Cin., 1982-83; assoc. Jones, Day, Reavis & Pogue, Cleve., 1983—. Mem. ABA, Ohio Bar Assn., Cleve. Bar Assn. Avocation: jogging. Federal civil litigation, State civil litigation. Office: Jones Day Reavis & Pogue 1700 Huntington Bldg Cleveland OH 44115

BIZAR, IRVING, lawyer; b. N.Y.C., June 30, 1932; s. Samuel Bizar and Julia Weinberg; m. Eileen Joy Schwartz, June 30, 1985; children from previous marriage: Steven E., Carolyn S. BA in Acctg., CUNY, 1953; JD cum laude, Bklyn. Law Sch., 1956. Bar: N.Y. 1957, U.S. Ct. Appeals (2d cir.) 1958, U.S. Ct. Appeals (5th cir.) 1974, U.S. Supreme Ct. 1977, U.S. Ct. Appeals (3d and 9th cirs.) 1983. Assoc. Pomerantz, Levy & Haudek, N.Y.C., 1957-62, Cravath, Swaine & Moore, N.Y.C., 1962-63, Demov & Morris, N.Y.C., 1963-68; ptnr. Demov, Morris, Levin & Shein, N.Y.C., 1968-77, Pincus, Ohrenstein, Bizar & D'Alessandro, N.Y.C., 1978-83, Bizar, D'Alessandro, Shustak & Martin, N.Y.C., 1983—. Dem. dist. leader 84th Assembly Dist., N.Y.C., 1966-68. Mem. Assn. of Bar of City of N.Y., N.Y.

State Bar Assn. Federal civil litigation, State civil litigation, Securities. Office: Bizar D'Alessandro Shustak & Martin 485 Madison Ave New York NY 10022

BIZZELL, KINCHEN CAREY, lawyer; b. Goldsboro, N.C., July 1, 1954; s. J. Eustace and Harriet Simpson (Powers) B.; m. Eileen Marie Dacey, Jan. 1, 1984. B.A. magna cum laude, N.C. State U., 1972; J.D., Duke U., 1975. Bar: N.C. 1975, N.Y. 1977. Ptnr. Bizzell Bros., Goldsboro, N.C., 1975-76; atty. Home Ins., N.Y.C., 1976-78; assoc. Mendes & Mount, N.Y.C., 1978-84, jr. ptnr., 1985—; mem. N.Y. Futures Exchange, N.Y.C., 1983-84. Mem. exec. com. Met. Republican Club, N.Y.C., 1978-81, county com. N.Y. Young Rep. orgn., N.Y.C., 1982-84; chmn. bd. assessment rev. Town of Woodbury, 1986—. Mem. ABA, N.C. State Bar, N.Y. State Bar Assn. Republican. Club: English Speaking Union (N.Y.C.). Insurance. Office: Mendes & Mount 3 Park Ave New York NY 10016

BJORK, ROBERT DAVID, JR., lawyer; b. Evanston, Ill., Sept. 29, 1946; s. Robert David and Lenore Evelyn (Loderhose) B.; m. Linda Louise Reese, Mar. 27, 1971; children: Heidi Lynne, Gretchen Anne. BBA, U. Wis., 1968; JD, Tulane U., 1974. Bar: La. 1974, U.S. Dist. Ct. (ea. dist.) La. 1974, U.S. Ct. Appeals (5th cir.) 1974, U.S. Dist. Ct. (mid. dist.) 1975, U.S. Supreme Ct. 1977, U.S. Dist. Ct. (we. dist.) 1978, U.S. Ct. Appeals (11th cir.) 1981, Calif. 1983, U.S. Dist. Ct. (no. dist.) Calif. 1983, U.S. Dist. Ct. (ea. dist.) Calif. 1984. Ptnr. Adams & Rees, New Orleans, 1974-83; assoc. Crosby, Heafey, Roach & May, Oakland, Calif., 1983-85; ptnr. Bjork, Fleer & Lawrence, Oakland, 1985—; instr. paralegal studies Tulane U., New Orleans, 1979-82. Mem. Tulane U. Law Rev., 1973-74; editor Med. Malpractice newsletter, 1983—. Bd. dirs. Piedmont (Calif.) Council of Camp Fire, 1984—; treas. Couhig Congl. Com., New Orleans, 1980-82. Served to lt., USNR, 1968-71. Mem. ABA, Calif. Bar Assn., La. Bar Assn. (chmn. young lawyers sect. 1982-83), Am. Soc. Law and Medicine. State civil litigation, Federal civil litigation, Personal injury. Home: 1909 Oakland Ave Piedmont CA 94611 Office: Bjork Fleer & Lawrence 192 Tenth St Oakland CA 94607

BLACHLY, JACK LEE, oil company executive, lawyer; b. Dallas, Mar. 8, 1942; s. Emery Lee and Thelma Jo (Budd) B.; m. Lucy Largent Rain, Jan. 15, 1972; 1 son, Michael Talbot. B.B.A., So. Meth. U., 1965, J.D., 1968. Bar: Tex. 1968, U.S. Ct. Appeals (5th cir.) 1969, U.S. Supreme Ct. 1975, U.S. Tax Ct. 1977. Trust officer InterFirst Bank Dallas, N.A., 1968-70; ptnr. firm Reese & Blachly, Dallas, 1970-71; assoc. firm Rain Harrell Emery Young & Doke, Dallas, 1971-76; staff atty. Sabine Corp., Dallas, 1976-77, mgr. legal dept., 1977-80, v.p., gen. counsel, 1980—. Mem. ABA, Tex. Bar Assn., Dallas Bar Assn., Am. Soc. Corp. Secs. Baptist. Clubs: Chaparral, Dallas Gun, Northwood, Dallas Petroleum (Dallas). General corporate, Oil and gas leasing, Securities. Office: 1000 LTV Ctr 2001 Ross Ave Dallas TX 75201

BLACHOR, ISAAC, lawyer; b. N.Y.C., Nov. 2, 1939; s. Irving Blachor and Jean Resnikoff; m. Evelyn Blatt, Aug. 23, 1984; children: Adam, Adena, Deborah. BA, Bklyn. Coll., 1961; JD, St. John's U., N.Y.C., 1964. Bar: N.Y. 1964, U.S. Dist. Ct. (ea. and so. dists.) N.Y. 1966, U.S. Supreme Ct. 1970, U.S. Ct. Appeals (2d cir.) 1971, U.S. Dist. Ct. (no. dist.) N.Y. 1984. Assoc. Lindenbaum & Young, N.Y.C., 1964-66; sole practice N.Y.C., 1967—. Editor: Collected Opinions on Profl. Ethics, 1980; contbr. articles to profl. jours. Chmn. bd. dirs. Heritage Endowment Fund, Uniondale, N.Y., 1984—; nat. exec. bd. Jewish Nat. Fund Am., 1986; v.p. Hebrew Acad. of Nassau County, West Hempstead, N.Y., 1973—; sustaining mem. Rep. Nat. Com., N.Y. State Nat. Com. Recipient Markowitz award Hebrew Acad. of Nassau County, 1982, Award for Service, Nassau Acad. of Law, 1984-86. Mem. ABA, N.Y. State Bar Assn., Bar Assn. Nassau County (Merit award 1982), Jewish Lawyers Assn. Bankruptcy, Real property, Contracts commercial. Home: 381 Roosevelt Blvd West Hempstead NY 11552 Office: 350 Old Country Rd Garden City NY 11530

BLACK, ALEXANDER, lawyer; b. Pitts., Nov. 19, 1914; s. Alexander and Ruth (Hay) B.; m. Jane Mevay McIntosh, Apr. 23, 1955; children: F. Kristin Hoeveler, Kenneth M., Elizabeth H. Black Watson. AB, Princeton U., 1936; LLB, Harvard U., 1939. Bar: Pa. 1940, U.S. Supreme Ct. 1955, U.S. Ct. Appeals (3d cir.) 1957, U.S. Ct. Claims 1959, U.S. Ct. Appeals (Fed. cir.) 1982. Law clk. Buchanan, Ingersoll P.C. and predecessors, Pitts., summers 1936-39, assoc., 1939-51, ptnr., 1951-85, shareholder, 1980-85, of counsel, 1985—. Served to lt. USNR, 1942-46, PTO. Mem. ABA, Pa. Bar Assn., Allegheny County Bar Assn., Am. Law Inst., Am. Coll. Trial Lawyers, Am. Coll. Real Estate Lawyers, Am. Bar Found., Am. Judicature Soc. Republican. Presbyterian. Clubs: Harvard/Yale/Princeton, Duquesne (Pitts.); Princeton (N.Y.C.); Edgeworth (Sewickley, Pa.). Federal civil litigation, State civil litigation, Real property. Home: 1309 Beaver Rd Sewickley PA 15143 Office: Buchanan Ingersoll PC 600 Grant St 57th Floor Pittsburgh PA 15219

BLACK, AUGUST BERNARD, lawyer; b. Morris, Ill., Aug. 1, 1915; s. Frank and Kate (Ryan) B.; m. Marie Weber, Oct. 19, 1944; children: George, Don, Frank, Jean, Ed, Linda, Jim, Mike, Richard. AB, U. Ill., 1938, JD, 1940. Bar: Ill. 1940, Wis. 1984. States atty. Grundy county, Ill., 1948-64; ptnr. Black & Black, Morris, Ill., 1964—. Served with MI Corps, 1941-45. Mem. VFW, Am. Legion. Clubs: Union League (Chgo.); Morris Country. Lodges: Elks, Eagles, KC. General practice. Home: 320 George Apt E24 Morris IL 60450 Office: PO Box 148 Morris IL 60450

BLACK, BARBARA ARONSTEIN, legal history educator; b. Bklyn., May 6, 1933; d. Robert and Minnie (Polenberg) A.; m. Charles L. Black, Jr., Apr. 11, 1954; children—Gavin B., David A., Robin E. B.A., Bklyn. Coll., 1953; LL.B., Columbia U., 1955; M.Phil., Yale U., 1970, Ph.D., 1975; LL.D. (hon.), Marymount Manhattan Coll., 1986. Assoc. in law Columbia U. Law Sch., N.Y.C., 1955-56; lectr. history Yale U., New Haven, 1974-76, asst. prof. history, 1976-79, assoc. prof. law, 1979-84; George Welwood Murray prof. legal history Columbia U. Law Sch., N.Y.C., 1984—, dean faculty of law, 1986—. Editor: Columbia Law Rev., 1953-55. Mem. editorial bd. Law and History Rev. Recipient Fed. Bar Assn. prize Columbia Law Sch., 1955. Mem. Am. Soc. Legal History (pres. 1986—), Law and Soc. Assn. (bd. trustees 1984—), Selden Soc. Club: Com. of 13 (New Haven). Office: Columbia U Law Sch 435 W 116th St New York NY 10027

BLACK, CHARLES LUND, JR., legal educator; b. Austin, Tex., Sept. 22, 1915; s. Charles Lunn and Alzada Helena (Bowman) B.; m. Barbara Ann Aronstein, Apr. 11, 1954; children: Gavin Bingley, David Alan, Robin Elizabeth. B.A., U. Tex., 1935, M.A., 1938; LL.B., Yale, 1943; LL.D., Boston U., 1975. Bar: N.Y. 1946, U.S. Supreme Ct. 1960. Practiced N.Y.C., 1946-47; asst. prof. law Columbia U., 1947-49, asso. prof., 1949-52, prof., 1952-56; Henry R. Luce prof. jurisprudence Yale U., 1956-75, Sterling prof. law, 1975—; mem. cast Yale Repertory Theater, 1976, 78; vis. prof. law U. Tex., 1955; mem. faculty Salzburg Seminar in Am. Studies, 1956; Edward Douglass White lectr. La. State U., 1968; mem. faculty Orientation Program in Am. Law, 1969; Holmes Devise lectr. U. Washington, 1970; Morris Ames Soper lectr. U. Md., 1972; Baum lectr. U. Ill., 1975; Tucker lectr. Washington and Lee U., 1975; Pope John XXIII lectr. Cath. U. Sch. Law, 1976; Dreyfus lectr. Tulane U., 1977; Alumni Disting. lectr. U. Tenn. Coll. Law, 1978; Holmes lectr. Harvard Law Sch., 1979; Phi Beta Kappa vis. scholar, 1980-81, Tex. lectr. on the Humanities, 1983; Coen lectr. U. Colo., 1984; counsel Supreme Ct. briefs in school segregation, civil rights cases; legal cons. N.A.A.C.P. Legal Def. and Edn. Fund.; Mem. adv. com. on admiralty rules Jud. Conf. U.S., 1960-70. Author: (with Grant Gilmore) The Law of Admiralty, 1957, 2d edit., 1975, The People and the Court, 1960, The Occasions of Justice, 1963, Perspectives in Constitutional Law, 1963, rev. edit., 1970; poetry Telescopes and Islands, 1963; Structure and Relationship in Constitutional Law, 1969, Impeachment: A Handbook, 1974, Capital Punishment: The Inevitability of Caprice and Mistake, 1974, 2d edit., 1981; (with Bob Eckhardt) Tides of Power, 1976; poetry Owls Bay In Babylon, 1980; Decision According to Law, 1981; poetry The Waking Passenger, 1983; also articles and poems in mags. and jours. Named Disting. Alumnus U. Tex., 1975; Conn. Law Rev. award, 1980; Soc. Am. Law Tchrs. award, 1983; Fellow Jonathan Edwards Coll., Yale U.; Bye-fellow Queens' Coll., Cambridge U., 1966-67. Mem. Maritime Law Assn. U.S., Am. Acad. Arts and Scis., Conn. Acad. Arts and Scis., Order of Coif, Phi Delta Phi, Kappa Sigma. Club: Elizabethan (gov. bd. 1971-72). Admiralty. Office: Yale U Law Sch New Haven CT 06520 *

BLACK, CLAIRE ALEXANDER, lawyer; b. Fayette, Ala., May 11, 1953; d. Gorman Jackson and Margaret (Alexander) B. BA in Spl. Studies magna cum laude, U. Ala., 1974, JD, 1978. Bar: Ala. 1979, U.S. Dist. Ct. Ala. 1979, U.S. Ct. Appeals 1979, U.S. Supreme Ct. 1985. Assoc. Lee, Barrett & Mullins, Tuscaloosa, Ala., 1978-80; ptnr. Prince & Black, Tuscaloosa, 1980-82, Crownover & Black, Tuscaloosa, 1982-87, Dishuck, Rodenberry & Black, P.C., Tuscaloosa, 1987—. Mem. Jr. League of Tuscaloosa, 1980—, Christ Episc. Ch., Soc. for the Fine Arts, 1979—; advisor Boy Scout Am., 1979-80. Named one of Outstanding Young Women in Am., 1979, 80. Mem. ABA (family law sect., trial practice com.), Ala. Bar Assn. (young lawyers sect. chmn. continuing legal edn. com. 1980-83, treas. 1983-84, sec. 1984-85, pres.-elect 1985-86, pres. 1986-87), Tuscaloosa County Bar Assn. (chmn. continuing legal edn. com. 1980-81, sec., treas. 1981-84), Assn. Trial Lawyers Am., Tuscaloosa Trial Lawyers Assn. (pres. 1984-85), U. Ala. Alumni Assn. Tuscaloosa County (sec., treas. 1979-80, v.p. 1980-81, pres. 1981-82), Farrah Law Soc., Phi Beta Kappa, Alpha Gamma Delta. Avocations: music, ballet, horseback riding. Family and matrimonial, General practice, Personal injury. Home: 2125 Glendale Gardens Tuscaloosa AL 35401 Office: Dishuck Rodenberry & Black PC 810 27th Ave PO Box Drawer 7 Tuscaloosa AL 35402

BLACK, DONALD BRUCE, lawyer, arbitrator, ice cream manufacturer; b. Los Angeles, June 25, 1932; s. Freeman Carleton and Elizabeth (Bergstrom) B.; children: Jeanine, Debra, Lawrence Bently. A.B., UCLA, 1954; J.D., U. So. Calif., 1960. Bar: Calif. 1960. Mem. firm Shield and Smith, 1960-72, Williams and Black, Los Angeles, 1972-75; individual practice law Donald B. Black, Inc., Los Angeles and Laguna Beach, Calif., 1976—; arbitrator Superior Ct.; regional adviser Am. Arbitration Assn. Pres. Parent-Tchr. Council, 1968-70; sec. Betts Found., 1970—, Panel judge pro tem Los Angeles Mcpl. Ct.; bd. dirs. Friendship Housing, Inst. for Victims, Inner Resources. Served with USAF, 1955-56. Mem. Am. Bd. Trial Advocates (nat. pres. 1975-76), Assn. So. Calif. Def. Counsel (pres. 1972-73, joint legis. commns. on structure of judiciary 1974-77, tort reform 1977-79), ABA (com. chmn.), Laguna Beach C. of C. (bd. dirs. 1986, pres.), Phi Delta Phi, Delta Tau Delta. Republican. Presbyterian. Clubs: Jonathan, Calcutta Saddle and Cycle (founding gov. 1971—); Balboa Bay (Newport Beach, Calif.). Insurance, Banking, Securities. Office: Village Business Center 301 Forest Ave Laguna Beach CA 92651

BLACK, FREDERICK EVAN, lawyer; b. N.Y.C., Oct. 1, 1944; s. Harry Newhouse and Gertrude (Marston) B.; m. Christine Barron MacKinnon, Aug. 26, 1967; children—Alexis MacKinnon, Caroline Frances Dorothy. B.A. in History, U. N.C., Chapel Hill, 1967; J.D., Syracuse U., 1973. Bar: Pa. 1973, U.S. Dist. Ct. (ea. dist.) Pa. 1973, U.S. Supreme Ct. 1978, N.J., 1986. Atty., Nationwide Ins. Co., Phila., 1973-75, Margolis, Edelstein & Scherlis, Phila., 1975-77; ptnr. Post & Schell, Phila., 1977 —. Bd. dirs. Friends of Holy Cross Monastery, Inc., 1986—. Served to lt. USNR, 1967-82. Mem. Pa. Bar Assn., Pa. Def. Inst., Phila. Bar Assn., Def. Research Inst. Health, Insurance, Personal injury. Office: Post & Schell PC 1800 J F Kennedy Blvd Philadelphia PA 19103

BLACK, HOWARD, lawyer; b. Bklyn., June 29, 1947; s. Bernard and Frieda (Wapner) B.; m. Roberta A. Linder, June 22, 1969; children: Frann, Jason, Stacy. BA in Econs., Hofstra U., 1968; JD, Bklyn. Law Sch., 1971. Bar: N.Y. 1972, U.S. Tax Ct. 1972. Advanced under cons. Mutual of N.Y., N.Y.C., 1971-72, Met. Life Ins. Co., N.Y.C., 1972-76; tax cons. Multiple Funding, N.Y.C., 1976-78; sole practice Mineola, N.Y., 1978—; adj. assoc. prof. cert. fin. planning program Adelphi U., Garden City, N.Y., 1978—. Served to capt. U.S. Army, 1971-83. Mem. ABA, Registry of Fin. Planning Practitioners, Internat. Assn. Fin. Planners (v.p. membership 1978—). Democrat. Jewish. Estate planning, Pension, profit-sharing, and employee benefits, Real property. Home: 85-15 Somerset St Jamaica NY 11432 Office: 100 E Old Country Rd Mineola NY 11501

BLACK, JAMES ISAAC, III, lawyer; b. Lakeland, Fla., Oct. 26, 1951; s. James Isaac Jr. and Juanita (Feemster) B.; m. Vikki Harrison, June 15, 1973; children: Jennifer Leigh, Katharine Ann, Stephanie Marie. BA, U. Fla., 1973; JD, Harvard U., 1976. Bar: Fla. 1976, N.Y. 1977, U.S. Tax Ct. 1984. Assoc. Sullivan & Cromwell, N.Y.C., 1976-84, ptnr., 1984—. Mem. N.Y. State Bar Assn. (persons under disability com. trusts and estates law sect. 1984—) Assn. of Bar of City of N.Y. (sec. 1980-81, trusts estates and surrogates ct. com. 1980-83). Real property, Estate planning, Probate. Home: 23 Chesterfield Rd Scarsdale NY 10583 Office: Sullivan & Cromwell 250 Park Ave New York NY 10177

BLACK, JOHN VICTOR, lawyer; b. Pratt, Kans., Jan. 8, 1937; s. Cyril Victor and Margaret Joan (Koppers) B.; m. Janet Sue McKinney, Jan. 14, 1961; children: Thomas V., John P., Robert D., Rebecca S. BS in Psychology and Sociology, U. Kans., 1959; JD, Washburn U., 1963. Bar: Kans. 1963, U.S. Dist. Ct. Kans. 1963, U.S. Ct. Mil. Appeals 1964, U.S. Supreme Ct. 1968. Sr. ptnr. Black Law Office P.A., Pratt, 1968—; gen. counsel W.K. Black Inc., Pratt, 1978—; atty. Pratt County, Kans., 1969-77, counselor, 1980-84. Served to capt. JAGC, U.S. Army, 1963-68. Mem. VFW (service officer 1968—). Democrat. Roman Catholic. Lodges: Rotary, Elks. State civil litigation, Probate, Oil and gas leasing. Home: Rt 2 Pratt KS 67124 Office: Black Law Office PA 306 S Oak Pratt KS 67124

BLACK, LEON DAVID, JR., lawyer; b. Saluda, S.C., Nov. 11, 1926; s. Leon David and Ruth W. (Wheeler) B.; m. Margaret Louise Flynn, Dec. 1, 1956; children—Rebecca Black Freeman, David, Julia. B.A., Miami U., Oxford, Ohio, 1948; LL.B., Yale U., 1952. Bar: Fla. 1952, U.S. Dist. Ct. (so. dist.) Fla. 1954, U.S. Ct. Appeals (5th cir.) 1966, U.S. Supreme Ct. 1972. Mem. Brigham, Black, Niles & Wright, 1952-58, Kelly, Black, Black, Byrne & Beasley, P.A. and predecessor firms, Miami, Fla., 1958—. Chmn. bd. Heart Assn. of Greater Miami, 1976-78; bd. dirs. Am. Heart Assn. of Greater Miami, 1979—. Served to lt. USNR, 1944-46. Fellow Am. Coll. Trial Lawyers; mem. ABA (chmn. com. on condemnation, zoning and property use litigation, litigation sect. council 1985—), Internat. Soc. Barristers, Fla. Bar, Dade County Bar Assn. Congregationalist. Clubs: Biscayne Bay Yacht, Royal Palm Tennis, Riviera Country, Miami, Ocean Reef. Contbr. chpts., articles to profl. publs. in field. Condemnation, State civil litigation. Office: Kelly Black Black Byrne & Beasley PA 1400 Alfred I duPont Bldg Miami FL 33131

BLACK, LOUIS ENGLEMAN, lawyer; b. Washington, Aug. 5, 1943; s. Fischer Sheffey and Elizabeth (Zemp) B.; m. Cecelia Whidden, Sept. 5, 1966; 1 child, Kerrison Todd. BA, NYU, 1968, JD, 1971, LLM in Taxation, 1978. Bar: N.Y. 1972. Assoc. Carter, Ledyard & Milburn, N.Y.C., 1972-79; ptnr. Van Ginkel & Benjamin, N.Y.C., 1979-83; of counsel Zimet, Haines, Moss & Friedman, N.Y.C., 1983-84; of counsel DeForest & Duer, N.Y.C., 1984-86, ptnr., 1986—; vice chmn. bd. dirs. MacMillan Ring-Free Oil Co., Inc., 1987—. Editor: NYU Jour. Internat. Law and Politics, 1970-71; author: Partnership Buy/Sell Agreements, 1977. Mem. ABA, N.Y. State Bar Assn. General corporate, Corporate taxation, Personal income taxation. Home: 41 Commerce St New York NY 10014 Office: DeForest & Duer 90 Broad St New York NY 10004

BLACK, NORMAN WILLIAM, judge; b. Houston, Dec. 6, 1931; s. Dave and Minnie (Nathan) B.; m. Berne Rose Efron, Feb. 21, 1959; children: Elizabeth Ann, Diane Rebecca. B.B.A., U. Tex., Austin, 1953, J.D. (Frank Bobbitt scholar 1954), 1955. Bar: Tex. 1955. Law clk. to Houston judge 1956; asst. U.S. atty. Houston, 1956-58, pvt. practice, 1958-76; U.S. magistrate 1976-79; U.S. dist. judge So. Dist. Tex., Houston, 1979—; adj. prof. South Tex. Coll. Law. Served with AUS, 1955-56. Mem. Fed. Bar Assn., State Bar Tex., Houston Bar Assn., Houston Philos. Soc. Judicial administration. Office: U S Courthouse 515 Rusk Ave Suite 9114 Houston TX 77002

BLACK, ROBERT ALLEN, lawyer; b. Ocala, Fla., Aug. 15, 1954; s. Allen Harrison and Rose Marie (Dupree) B. BA, U. Tex., El Paso, 1977; JD summa cum laude, Tex. Tech U., 1980. Bar: Tex. 1980, U.S. Ct. Appeals (5th and 11th cirs.) 1980, U.S. Supreme Ct. 1985. Ptnr. Mehaffy, Weber, Keith & Gonsoulin, Beaumont, Tex., 1980—; adj. prof. law Lamar U., Beaumont, Tex., 1981-84. Case note editor Tex. Tech Law Rev., 1979-80. Pres. Humane Soc. Southeast Tex., Beaumont, 1983-87; bd. dirs. YMCA, Beaumont, 1985-87; host TV show Pets on Parade, Beaumont, 1986—. Named one of Outstanding Young Men of Am., Jaycees, 1982. Mem. ABA, Tex. Young Lawyers Assn (treas. 1983-84), Tex. Assn. Def. Counsel, Jefferson County Young Lawyers Assn. (bd. dirs. 1982-83, treas. 1983-84). Democrat. Episcopalian. Avocations: bridge, tennis, history. Federal civil litigation, Libel, Personal injury. Home: 601 22d St Beaumont TX 77706 Office: Mehaffy Weber Keith & Gonsoulin 2615 Calder Beaumont TX 77702

BLACK, ROBERT L., JR., state judge; b. Cin., Dec. 11, 1917; s. Robert L. and Anna M. (Smith) B.; m. Helen Charfield, July 27, 1946; children—William C., Stephen L., Luther F. A.B., Yale U., 1939; LL.B., Harvard U., 1942. Bar: Ohio 1946, U.S. Ct. Appeals (6th cir.) 1947, U.S. Supreme Ct. 1955. Sole practice, Cin., 1946-53; ptnr. Graydon, Head & Ritchey, Cin., 1953-72; judge Ct. Common Pleas, Cin., 1973-77, Ct. Appeals, Cin., 1977—; chmn. jury instrns. com. Ohio Jud. Conf. 1973-86 (chmn. 1986—), Councilman Village Indian Hill (Ohio), 1953-65, mayor, 1959-65; chmn. Cin. Human Relations Commn., 1967-70. Served to capt. U.S. Army, 1942-45. Decorated Bronze Star. Mem. Cin. Bar Assn., Ohio Bar Assn., ABA, Am. Judicature Soc., Nat. Legal Aid and Defender Assn., Ohio Cts. of Appeals Judges Assn. Republican. Episcopalian. Clubs: Queen City, Camargo, Commonwealth (Cin.). Contbr. articles on law to profl. jours. Jurisprudence. Home: 5900 Drake Rd Cincinnati OH 45243 Office: 300 Hamilton Country Courthouse Cincinnati OH 45202

BLACK, SUSAN HARRELL, judge; b. Valdosta, Ga., Oct. 20, 1943; d. William H. and Ruth Elizabeth (Phillips) Harrell; m. Louis Eckert Black, Dec. 28, 1966. B.A., Fla. State U., 1964; J.D., U. Fla., 1967. Bar: Fla. 1967. Asst. state atty. 4th Jud. Circuit Fla.; asst. gen. counsel City of Jacksonville, Fla.; judge County Ct. of Duval County, Fla.; judge 4th Jud. Circuit Ct. of Fla.; U.S. dist. judge Middle Dist. Fla., Jacksonville, 1979—; faculty Fed. Jud. Ctr. Mem. adv. bd., former trustee Jacksonville Hosp. Ednl. Program; mem. Jacksonville Council Citizen Involvement; trustee Law Sch. U. Fla. Mem. Am. Bar Assn., Fla. Bar Assn., Jacksonville Bar Assn., Conf. Circuit Judges (former chmn. edn. com., dean New Judges Coll.). Episcopalian. Jurisprudence. Office: PO Box 53135 Jacksonville FL 32201

BLACK, WALTER EVAN, JR., judge; b. Balt., July 7, 1926; s. Walter Evan and Margaret Luttrell (Rice) B.; m. Catharine Schall Foster, June 30, 1951; children: Walter Evan III, Charles Foster, James Rider. A.B. magna cum laude, Harvard U., 1947, LL.B., 1949. Bar: Md. 1949. Assoc. Hinkley & Singley, Balt., 1949-53; ptnr. Hinkley & Singley, 1957-67; asst. U.S. atty. Dist. Md., Balt., 1953-55; U.S. atty. Dist. Md., 1956-57; ptnr. Clapp, Somerville, Black & Honemann, Balt., 1968-82; U.S. dist. judge Dist. Md., Balt., 1982—; Sec.-treas. Parkwood Cemetery Co., Balt., 1967-82; also dir.; sec. So. Mech. Inc., Balt., 1971-82; also dir.; pres. Charles T. Brandt Inc., Balt., 1972-82; also dir. Chmn. Bd. Municipal and Zoning Appeals, Balt., 1963-67; mem. Jail Bd., Balt., 1971-73, Atty. Grievance Commn., 1978-82, Rev. Bd., 1975-78, chmn., 1975-76; mem. Gov.'s Commn. to Revise Annotated Code, 1975-82. Alt. Md. del. Republican Nat. Conv., 1960; chmn. Rep. City Com., Balt., 1962-66; Md. del. Rep. Nat. Conv., 1964; Bd. dirs. Balt. Urban League, 1963-69, 76-82; bd. dirs. Union Meml. Hosp., Hosp. for Consumptives of Md. Mem. Bar Assn. Balt. City, ABA, Md. Bar Assn., Rule Day Club, Lawyers' Round Table. Baptist. Clubs: Speaker's, Harvard-Radcliffe of Md. Office: US Dist Ct 101 W Lombard St Baltimore MD 21201

BLACK, WARREN JOHN, lawyer; b. N.Y.C., July 14,1929; s. Charles Warren and Gladys Belle (Lord) B.; m. Dorothy Windle, Oct. 29, 1955; children —Neal S., Warren L. B.A., NYU, 1949; LL.B., St. John's U., 1952. Bar: N.Y. 1954, U.S. Supreme Ct. 1970. Sole practice, N.Y.C., 1954—; also lectr. Fellow Am. Acad. Matrimonial Lawyers (bd. mgrs.); mem. N.Y. State Bar Assn., Internat. Soc. Family Law, N.Y. Criminal and Civil Cts. Bar Assn., Internat. Platform Assn. Men of Achievment. Presbyterian. Family and matrimonial, State civil litigation, General practice. Office: 4930 Broadway New York NY 10034

BLACK, WILLIAM EARL, lawyer; b. Port Arthur, Tex., Mar. 15, 1951; s. Earl Milton and Lola (Fuller) B.; m. Martha Talbot Rain, Aug. 11, 1972; children: Katherine Gano, Robert William. BA, U. Tex., 1973; JD, St. Mary's U., San Antonio, 1976. Legal examiner R.R. Commn. of Tex., Austin, 1977-80; ptnr. Lynch, Chappell, Allday & Alsup, Austin, 1980—. Mem. ABA, Tex. Bar Assn., Travis County Bar Assn. (treas. oil, gas and mineral sect. 1987). Presbyterian. Clubs: Austin Country, Metropolitan, Austin. Avocations: music, exercise. Oil and gas leasing, Administrative and regulatory, Entertainment. Home: 1404 Ridgecrest Dr Austin TX 78746 Office: Lynch Chappell et al 900 Littlefield Bldg Austin TX 78701

BLACKBURN, JOHN D(AVID), legal educator, lawyer; b. Connersville, Ind., Dec. 19, 1949; s. James Edwin and Julia Jane (Hubbard) B.; m. Rebecca Sue Mehling, June 2, 1973; children—Jennifer Anne, Melissa Christine. B.S., Ind. State U., 1971; J.D., U. Cin., 1974. Bar: Ohio 1974. Instr. bus. adminstrn. U. Cin., 1974-75; asst. prof. bus. Ohio State U., Columbus, 1975-80, assoc. prof., 1981—; vis. asst. prof. U. Pa., Phila., 1980-81, Ind. U., Bloomington, summer 1980. Author (with Elliot I. Klayman and Martin H. Malin): Legal Environment of Business, 2d edit. 1985 ; (with Julius Getman) Labor Relations: Law, Practice, and Policy, 1983; editor (with others): Modern Business Law, 1984, Law and Business, 1987; (with Jack Steiber) Protecting Unorganized Employees Against Unjust Discharge, 1984; staff editor: Jour. Legal Studies Edn., 1985—, Am. Bus. Law Jour., 1986—. Mem. Am. Bus. Law Assn. (best article award 1980). Legal education, Labor. Home: 1766 Dorsetshire Rd Columbus OH 43229 Office: Ohio State Univ 1775 College Rd Columbus OH 43210

BLACKBURN, JOHN GILMER, lawyer; b. Opelika, Ala., Oct. 21, 1927; s. John A. and Vera (Isley) B.; m. Phyllis Blackburn, May 12, 1951; children: Gay Blackburn Maloney, Beth Allison, Lisa Blackburn Ayerst. BS in Acctg., Auburn U., 1950; JD, U. Ala., 1954; LLM in Taxation, NYU, 1956. Bar: Ala. 1954. Sole practice Decatur, Ala., 1955-79; ptnr. Blackburn & Maloney, Decatur, 1979—; lectr. various tax seminars. Mayor, City of Decatur, 1962-68; mem. exec. com. Ala. Dems.; vice chmn. Auburn U. Found.; vice chmn. Ala. Rev. Com. on Higher Edn. Served with U.S. Army, 1946-47, to 1st lt., 1951-52, ETO. Mem. ABA (com. on life ins., cos. sect. taxation), Ala. Bar Assn. (chmn. tax sect.). Methodist. Lodge: Kiwanis. Estate planning, Corporate taxation, Estate taxation. Office: PO Box 1469 Decatur AL 35602

BLACKBURN, MILFORD GENE, lawyer; b. Grand Juction, Iowa, July 27, 1922; s. George Samuel and Geneva Isabel (Terrill) B.; m. Edna S. Blackburn, Mar. 17, 1947; children: Paul Scott, Justin Evan. BA, Drake U., 1953, JD, 1955. Ptnr. Guthrie & Blackburn, Webster City, Ia., 1955-65; prof. law Drake U., Des Moines, 1965-75; ptnr. Murray & Blackburn, Ft. Dodge, Iowa, 1975-81; sr. ptnr. Blackburn, Stockdale & Brownlee, Ft. Dodge, 1981-85, Law Offices of M. Gene Blackburn, Ft. Dodge, 1985—; atty. Hamilton County, Iowa, 1958-59, Webster City, 1961-65. Contbr. articles to profl. jours. Trustee Polk County Legal Aid Soc., Des Moines, 1967-70. Served with USNR, 1942-46. Named Alumnus of Yr., Drake U., 1984, one of Outstanding Educators of Am., 1975. Fellow Am. Coll. Trial Lawyers, Iowa Acad. Trial Lawyers (pres. 1985-86); mem. Iowa State Bar Assn. (bd. govs.), Iowa Def. Counsel Assn., Assn. Trial Lawyers Iowa, Assn. Trial Lawyers Am., Order of Coif, Phi Beta Kappa. Republican. Lutheran. Lodge: Elks. Avocation: photography. Federal civil litigation, State civil litigation, Insurance. Office: 142 N 9th Fort Dodge IA 50501

BLACKBURN, THOMAS IRVEN, lawyer; b. Columbus, Ohio, May 4, 1949; s. Ervin C. and Dorothy E. (Wonn) B.; m. Sharon C. Mahoney, July 7, 1973; children: Ashley Anne, Christopher Ryan. BS, Ohio State U., 1972, JD, 1979. Bar: Ohio 1979, U.S. Dist. Ct. (so. dist.) Ohio 1980, U.S. Tax Ct. 1986. Computer software developer IBM, Atlantic City, 1972-76; assoc. Williams & Deeg, Columbus, 1979-81, Denmead, Gerrity & Tsitouris, Columbus, 1981-86; ptnr. Denmead, Blackburn & Willard, Columbus, 1986—; trustee Newsreel Club Inc., Columbus, 1986—. Pres. Strawberry Farms Civic Assn., Columbus, 1986—, v.p., 1984-86; mem. steering com. Westerville (Ohio) Sch. Levy Com., 1984; mem. steering com. Westerville Sch. Bond Issue, 1986. Mem. ABA, Ohio Bar Assn., Columbus Bar Assn. (admissions com. 1985—, mcpl. ct. com. 1982-85, common pleas ct. com. 1982-85), Columbus Claims Assn., Ohio Assn. Civil Trial Attys., Def. Research Inst. Avocations: golf, running. State civil litigation, Insurance,

General corporate. Home: 3927 Chickory Ave Gahanna OH 43230 Office: Denmead Blackburn & Willard 37 W Broad St Suite 1150 Columbus OH 43215

BLACKMAN, GORDON N., JR., lawyer; b. Tampa, Fla., Dec. 18, 1957; s. Gordon N. and Mary E. (Pingree) B.; m. Linda L. Smith, May 29, 1982; 1 child, Rachel R. BA in English, Centenary Coll., 1980; JD, La. State U., 1983. Bar: La. 1983, U.S. Dist. Ct. (we. dist.) La. 1985. Law clk. to presiding judge 1st Jud. Dist. Ct., Shreveport, La., 1983-84, U.S. Ct. Appeals (2d cir.), Shreveport, 1984-85; assoc. M. Thomas Arceneaux P.L.C., Shreveport, 1985—; bd. dirs. Centenary Coll. Alumni Bd., Shreveport, Crimestoppers, Shreveport. Mem. Leadership Council of Shreveport, 1986—; vol. Project Justice, Shreveport, 1986—. Mem. ABA, Shreveport Trial Lawyers Assn., Assn. Trial Lawyers Am., La. Trial Lawyers Assn., Omicron Delta Kappa. Republican. Presbyterian. Avocations: computers. General practice, Federal civil litigation, State civil litigation. Office: M Thomas Arceneaux PLC PO Box 1657 Shreveport LA 71165-1657

BLACKMAN, JOHN CALHOUN, IV, lawyer; b. Monroe, La., Dec. 13, 1944; s. John Calhoun III and Marie (Collens) Bernstein; m. Paula Perry, Aug. 19, 1966 (div. Mar. 1986); children: Carrie Marie, Caroline Frances, Mary Winston; m. Judy Swayze, Apr. 19, 1986. BA, La. State U., 1966, JD, 1969. Bar: La. 1969, U.S. Ct. Appeals (5th cir.) 1969, U.S. Tax Ct. 1972, U.S. Supreme Ct. 1976. Ptnr. Hudson, Potts & Bernstein, Monroe, 1969-79, Blackman, Arnold & Pettway, Monroe, 1979—; bd. dirs. Premier Bancorp, Inc., Baton Rouge; bd. dirs., mem. exec. trust and discount coms. Ouachita Nat. Bank in Monroe, La.; mem. adv. council Ctr. of Civil Law Studies Paul M. Hebert Law Ctr., La. State U., 1984—. Fellow Am. Coll. Probate Counsel; mem. La. Bar Assn. (cert. tax specialist, chmn. taxation sect. 1976-77, chmn. liaison com. with dist. dir. IRS 1981-82, liaison com. with regional commrs. office), ABA (estate and gift tax com., taxation sect.), Estate Planning Council of Northeast La. (pres. 1975-76). Democrat. Episcopalian. Clubs: Lotus (pres. 1979-80), Bayoe Desiard Country Tower. Corporate taxation, Estate taxation, Personal income taxation. Office: Blackman Arnold & Pettway 1603 Lamy Ln Monroe LA 71201

BLACKMAN, KENNETH ROBERT, lawyer; b. Providence, May 19, 1941; s. Edward and Beatrice (Wolf) B.; m. Meryl June Rosenthal, June 7, 1964; children: Michael, Susan, Kevin. A.B., Brown U., 1962; LL.B., Columbia U., 1965, M.B.A., 1965. Bar: N.Y. 1966. Law clk. to U.S. Dist. Judge 1965-66; ptnr. Fried, Frank, Harris, Shriver & Jacobson, N.Y.C., 1966—. Mem. ABA, N.Y. Bar Assn., Assn. Bar City of N.Y., Phi Beta Kappa, Beta Gamma Sigma. General corporate, Securities, Bankruptcy. Office: Fried Frank Harris Shriver & Jacobson 1 New York Plaza New York NY 10004

BLACKMAR, CHARLES BLAKEY, state justice; b. Kansas City, Mo., Apr. 19, 1922; s. Charles Maxwell and Eleanor (Blakey) B.; m. Ellen Day Bonnifield, July 18, 1943 (dec. 1983); children—Charles A., Thomas J., Lucy E. Blackmar Alpaugh, Elizabeth S., George B.; m. Jeanne Stephens Lee, Oct. 5, 1984. A.B. summa cum laude, Princeton U., 1942; J.D., U. Mich., 1948. Bar: Mo. bar 1948. Practiced in Kansas City; mem. firm Swanson, Midgley, Jones, Blackmar & Eager, and predecessors, 1952-66; professorial lectr. U. Mo. at Kansas City, 1949-58; prof. law St. Louis U., 1966-82, prof. emeritus; judge Supreme Ct. Mo., 1982—; spl. asst. atty. gen. Mo. 1969-77, labor arbitrator.; Chmn. Fair Pub. Accommodations Commn. Kansas City, Mo., 1964-66; mem. Commn. Human Relations Kansas City, 1965-66. Author: (with Volz and others) Missouri Practice, 1953, West's Federal practice Manual, 1957, 71, (with Devitt) Federal Jury Practice and Instructions, 1970, 3d edit., 1977; contbr. (with Devitt) numerous articles on probate law to profl. publs. Mem. Jackson County Republican Com., 1952-58; mem. Mo. Rep. Com., 1956-58. Served to 1st lt., inf. AUS, 1943-46. Decorated Silver Star, Purple Heart. Mem. Am. Law Inst., Nat. Acad. Arbitrators, Mo. Bar (spl. lectr. insts.), Disciples Peace Fellowship, Scribes (pres. 1986-87), Order of Coif, Phi Beta Kappa. Mem. Disciples of Christ Ch. Home: 612 Hobbs Rd Jefferson City MO 65101 Office: Supreme Ct Bldg Jefferson City MO 65102

BLACKMUN, HARRY ANDREW, associate justice U.S. Supreme Court; b. Nashville, Ill., Nov. 12, 1908; s. Corwin Manning and Theo H. (Reuter) B.; m. Dorothy E. Clark, June 21, 1941; children: Nancy Clark, Sally Ann, Susan Manning. B.A. summa cum laude in Math, Harvard U., 1929, LL.B., 1932; numerous hon. degrees. Bar: Minn. 1932. Law clk. to presiding justice John B. Sanborn; judge 8th circuit U.S. Ct. of Appeals, St. Paul, 1932-33; assoc. Dorsey, Colman, Barker, Scott & Barber, Mpls., 1934-38, jr. ptnr., 1939-42, gen. ptnr., 1943-50; instr. St. Paul Coll. Law, 1935-41, U. Minn. Law Sch., 1945-47; resident counsel Mayo Clinic, Mayo Assn., Rochester, 1950-59; mem. sect. adminstrn. Mayo Clinic, 1950-59; judge 8th Circuit U.S. Ct. of Appeals, 1959-70; assoc. justice U.S. Supreme Ct., 1970—; chmn. faculty Salzburg Seminar in Am. Studies, July 1977; Mem. bd. members Mayo Assn. Rochester, 1953-60; mem. adv. com. on jud. activities Jud. Conf., 1969-79; co-moderator seminar on justice and soc., Aspen (Colo.) Inst., 1979-87, seminar on constl. justice and soc., Aspen Inst. Italia, Rome, 1986; vis. instr. Constl. Law, La. State U. Law Sch., Summer Session at Aix-en-Provence, France, 1986; participant seminar on the role of cts. in soc. Hebrew Univ., 1986. Contbr. articles to legal, med. jours. Bd. dirs., mem. exec. com. Rochester Meth. Hosp., 1954-70; trustee Hamline Univ., St. Paul, 1964-70, William Mitchell Coll. Law, St. Paul, 1959-74; jud. mem. Nat. Hist. Publs. and Records Commn., 1975-82, 86—; participant Franco-Am. Colloquium on Human Rights, Paris, 1979. Mem. ABA, Minn. Bar Assn., Olmsted County Bar Assn., 32 Jud. Dist. Bar Assn., Phi Beta Kappa. Jurisprudence. Office: Supreme Ct US Washington DC 20543

BLACKSHEAR, A.T., JR., lawyer; b. Dallas, July 5, 1942; s. A.T. and Janie Louise (Florey) B.; m. Stuart Davis Blackshear. B.B.A. cum laude, Baylor U., 1964, J.D. cum laude, 1968. Bar: Tex. 1968, U.S. Ct. Appeals (5th cir.) 1970, U.S. Tax Ct. 1970; C.P.A., Tex. Acct. Arthur Andersen & Co., Dallas, 1964-66; ptnr. Fulbright & Jaworski, Houston, 1969—. Mem. ABA, State Bar Tex., Houston Bar Assn. Baptist. Clubs: Houston Ctr., Coronado. Corporate taxation, Personal income taxation. Office: Fulbright & Jaworski 1301 McKinney 51st Floor Houston TX 77010

BLACKSTOCK, JERRY BYRON, lawyer; b. Monticello, Ga., Mar. 9, 1945; s. J.B. and Eugenia (Jones) B.; m. Margaret Owen, June 10, 1967; children: Towner Anson, Michael Owen, Kendrick. BA, Davidson Coll., 1966; JD, U. Ga., 1969. Bar: Ga. 1969, U.S. Ct. Appeals (5th cir.) 1969, U.S. Supreme Ct. 1978, U.S. Ct. Appeals (11th cir.) 1981, U.S. Ct. Appeals (fed. cir.) 1984. Ptnr. Powell, Goldstein, Frazer & Murphy, Atlanta, 1969—; adj. prof. law Emory U., Atlanta, 1975-81. Served to 2d lt. USAR, 1966-68. Mem. Ga. Bar Assn. (editor in chief jour. 1984-85, bd. of govs. 1982—), Atlanta Bar Assn. (editor-in-chief Atlanta Lawyer, 1972-73), Am. Law Inst., Atlanta Lawyers Club, Ga. Def. Lawyers Assn., Am. Bd. Trial Advs. (adv.). Methodist. Clubs: Commerce, Cherokee Town and Country Club (Atlanta). Avocation: running. Federal civil litigation, State civil litigation, Personal injury. Home: 3364 Chatham Rd NW Atlanta GA 30305 Office: Powell Goldstein Frazer & Murphy 900 Circle 75 Pkwy Suite 800 Atlanta GA 30339

BLACKSTONE, SANDRA LEE, lawyer, educator, former govt. ofcl.; b. Washington; d. Fred J. and Madeline S. Blackstone; B.A., U. Vt., 1969; J.D., U. Denver, 1977; Ph.D., Colo. Sch. Mines, 1979. Systems analyst Martin Marietta Aerospace, Denver, 1969-74; cons. legal, econ. and regulatory matters W.R. Grace & Co., Colo. Energy Research Inst., Colo. Sch. Mines, Dawson, Nagel, Sherman & Howard, Denver, 1976-79; mgr. bus. devel. for synthetic fuels Rocky Mountain Energy subs. Union Pacific Corp., Denver, 1979-81; dep. dir. energy and mineral resources Bur. Land Mgmt., Dept. Interior, Washington, 1981-83; prof. Denver Coll. Law, 1983—; mem. Colo. Adv. Council on Energy and Energy-Related Mineral Research, 1980-82; mem. Bd. on Mineral and Energy Resources, Nat. Acad. Scis., 1983—. Republican precinct committeewoman, 1970-74; del. Denver County Rep. Conv., 1971, 74, Colo. State Rep. Conv., 1972. Colo. Energy Research Inst. fellow, 1974-76; Mobil Oil Co. natural resources fellow, 1975-76; Kennecott Corp. fellow, 1976-77. Mem. Am. Bar Assn., Colo. Bar Assn., Denver Bar Assn. Republican. Contbr. articles to profl. jours. Administrative and regulatory, Legal education, Oil and gas leasing. Office: U Denver Coll Law 1900 Olive St Denver CO 80220

BLACKWELL, HENRY BARLOW, II, lawyer; b. Salem, Ill., Feb. 15, 1928; s. Carl G. and Goldie Blanche (Hill) B.; m. Nancy Neckers, June 21, 1952; children: Nancy Anne, James Stokely, Thomas Barlow. B.S., U. Ill., 1952; J.D., Ind. U., 1956. Bar: Ind. 1956, U.S. Supreme Ct. 1961. Asst. auditor Mchts. Nat. Bank, Indpls., 1952-53; indsl. engr., personnel rep., atty. Eli Lilly & Co., 1953-62; atty., asst. sec. Eli Lilly Internat. Corp., 1962-70, sec., asst. gen. counsel, 1970-77, sec., gen. counsel, 1977—. Dir. Indpls. Indians, Inc., baseball team, 1967—, chmn. bd., 1971-75; Mem. exec. council Brebeuf Prep. Sch., Indpls., 1972—; bd. dirs. Happy Hollow Children's Camp, 1964—, pres., 1968-71; bd. govs. ARC; bd. dirs., mem. exec. com. Indpls. chpt. ARC, 1975—, chmn. bd. dirs., 1979—, mem. Midwest Adv. Council; bd. dirs. Hoosier Salon Patrons Assn., 1980. Served with USNR, 1946-48. Mem. Am., Ind., Indpls. bar assns., Indpls. Legal Aid Soc., English Speaking Union, Ind. State Mus. Soc., Indpls. Zool. Soc., Indpls. Children's Mus., Ind. State Symphony Soc., U. Ill. Alumni Assn. (pres. 1977, dir), Ind. Hist. Soc., U.S. Trotting Assn., Ind. Trotting and Pacing Horse Assn., Phi Delta Phi, Phi Sigma Kappa. Clubs: Meridian Hills Country, Econ. Indpls, Lawyers. Private international, General corporate. Home: 3835 West 116th St Zionsville IN 46077 Office: Lilly Corporate Ctr Indianapolis IN 46285

BLACKWELL, MENEFEE DAVIS, lawyer; b. Lexington, Mo., Feb. 17, 1916; s. Horace F. and Berrien (Menefee) B.; m. Mary Louise Harris, Apr. 25, 1942; 1 son, Stephen M. (dec.). A.B., U. Mo., 1936; J.D., U. Mich., 1939. Bar: Mo. bar 1939. Since practiced in Kansas City; ptnr. firm Blackwell, Sanders, Matheny, Weary & Lombardi; dir. Kansas City Title div. Chgo. Title Ins. Co., Inter-State Holdings Inc., Interstate Prodn. Co., Continental Potash Co., Percy Kent Bag Co. Bd. dirs. Greater Community Kansas City Found., Chas. R. Cook and Minnie K. Cook Found., Starlight Theatre Assn.; trustee William Rockhill Nelson Trust, Nelson Gallery Found., Louetta M. Cowden Found., Jacob L. and Ella C. Loose Found., Midwest Research Inst.; bd. govs. Am. Royal Assn. Served from 2d lt. to maj., 14th Armored Div. AUS, 1942-46. Decorated Silver Star, Bronze Star with cluster, Purple Heart. Mem. Am., Mo., Kansas City bar assns., Order of Coif, Phi Beta Kappa, Phi Delta Theta, Phi Delta Phi. Episcopalian. Clubs: Kansas City Country (Kansas City), Kansas City (Kansas City), River (Kansas City). General corporate, Probate, Banking. Home: 1215 W 57th Terr Kansas City MO 64113 Office: Five Crown Center 2480 Pershing Rd Kansas City MO 64108

BLACKWELL, WILLIAM LEGGETT, lawyer; b. Bushnell, Fla., Mar. 18, 1936; s. Newton Floyd and Fay (Hamilton) B.; m. Doris Elizabeth Zieman, July 1, 1961; children—Teresa, Stanley, Patrick. B.S., U. Fla., 1960; J.D., S. Tex. Coll. Law, 1976. Bar: Tex. 1976, Fla. 1977, U.S. Dist. Ct. (so. dist.) Tex. 1976, U.S. Dist. Ct. (so. and mid. dists.) Fla. 1977, U.S. Ct. Appeals (5th and 11th cirs.) 1981. Ptnr., Turner and Blackwell, Port Lavaca, Tex., 1976-77, Boardman and Blackwell, Immokalee, Fla., 1977-78; atty. Collier Cos., Naples, Fla., 1978-80; sole practice, Naples, 1980-82; ptnr. Blackwell and Beal, P.A., Naples, 1982—. Patentee hydraulic insert. Contbr. articles to legal jours. Mem. ABA, Collier County Bar Assn. (pres.-elect), Assn. Trial Lawyers Am., Acad. Fla. Trial Lawyers. Republican. Roman Catholic. Criminal, Oil and gas leasing, Federal civil litigation. Office: Blackwell and Beal PA 3301 Davis Blvd Suite 301 Naples FL 33942

BLAINE, DOROTHEA CONSTANCE RAGETTÉ, lawyer, b. N.Y.C., Sept. 23, 1930; d. Robert Raymond and Dorothea Ottilie Ragetté; B.A., Barnard Coll., 1952; M.A., Calif. State U., 1968; Ed.D., UCLA, 1978; J.D., Western State U., 1981; postgrad. in taxation Golden Gate U. Bar: U.S. Dist. Ct. (ea., so. and cen. dists.) Calif., 1986—. Mem. tech. staff Planning Research Corp., Los Angeles, 1964-67; asso. scientist Holy Cross Hosp., Mission Hills, Calif., 1967-70; career devel. officer and affirmative action officer County of Orange, Santa Ana, Calif., 1970-74, sr. adminstrv. analyst, budget and program coordination, 1974-78; spl. projects asst. CAO/Spl. Programs Office, 1978-80, sr. adminstrv. analyst, 1980-83; admitted to Calif. bar, 1982; sole practice, 1982—; instr. Am. Coll. Law, Brea, Calif., 1987. Bd. dirs. Deerfield Community Assn., 1975-78, Orange YMCA, 1975-77. Mem. Assn. Trial Lawyers Am., Calif. Trial Lawyers Assn., Orange County Trial Lawyers Assn., Calif. Women Lawyers, Nat. Women's Polit. Caucus, ABA, Calif. Bar Assn., Orange County Bar Assn., Orange County Women Lawyers Assn. ACLU, Delta Theta Phi, Phi Delta Kappa. Office: 2121 S Coast Hwy Suite 200 Corona Del Mar CA 92625

BLAIR, ALLEN STUART, lawyer; b. Houston, Apr. 29, 1945; s. Arnold Gans and Isabel (Hecht) B.; m. 2d Mary Loeb Block, Sept. 5, 1979; children—Brian John, Peter Martin, Kevin Arnold. B.S., U. Wis.-Madison, 1967; J.D., Vanderbilt U., 1970. Bar: Tenn. 1970, U.S. Dist. Ct. (we. dist.) Tenn. 1970, U.S. Ct. Appeals (6th cir.) 1974, U.S. Supreme Ct. 1982. Law clk. to chief judge U.S. Dist. Ct. (we. dist.) Tenn., 1970-71; assoc. Hanover, Walsh, Barnes & Jalenak, Memphis, 1971-74; ptnr. Hanover, Walsh, Jalenak & Blair, 1974—; lectr. in law Memphis State U., 1973-76. Mem. Leadership Memphis, Class of 1981. Served to sgt. USAR, 1968-74. Mem. Memphis Bar Assn., Shelby County Bar Assn., Tenn. Bar Assn. (chmn. labor law sect. 1981-82), Internat. Found. Employee Benefit Plans, ABA. Democrat. Jewish. Labor. Office: 219 Adams Ave Memphis TN 38103

BLAIR, ANDREW LANE, JR., lawyer, educator; b. Charleston, W.Va., Oct. 10, 1946; s. Andrew Lane and Catherine (Shaffer) B.; m. Catherine Lynn Kessler, June 21, 1969; children—Christopher Lane, Robert Brook. B.A., Washington & Lee U., 1968; J.D., U. Denver, 1972. Bar: Colo. 1972, U.S. Dist. Ct. Colo. 1972, U.S. Ct. Appeals (10th cir.) 1972. Assoc., Dawson, Nagel, Sherman & Howard, Denver, 1972-78; ptnr. Sherman & Howard, Denver, 1978-84; ptnr. Sherman, Howard, Baker & Wendelken, Colorado Springs, 1984—; lectr. U. Denver Law Sch., 1980-83, U. Colo., Colorado Springs, 1984. Author: Uniform Commercial Code sects. for Colorado Methods of Practice, 1982. Contbr. articles to profl. jours. Mem. ABA (small bus. subcom.), Colo. Bar Assn. Democrat. Methodist. Securities, General corporate, Contracts commercial. Home: 9 Broadmoor Ave Colorado Springs CO 80906 Office: Sherman Howard Baker & Wendelken 102 S Tejon Colorado Springs CO 80903

BLAIR, ANDREW LANE, lawyer; b. Buckhannon, W.Va., Dec. 5, 1915; s. Herbert McClaskey and Madge Breckenridge (Chidester) B.; m. Catherine Hester Shaffer, May 23, 1942; children: Catherine B. Ferguson, Andrew L. Jr., Barbara B. Henson. Student, W.Va. U., 1932-34, LLB, 1939; AB, Duke U., 1936. Bar: W.Va. 1939, U.S. Dist. Ct. (no. and so. dists.) W.Va. 1939, U.S. Ct. Appeals (4th cir.) 1955, U.S. Supreme Ct. 1974. Sole practice Weston, W.Va., 1939-42; assoc. Jackson, Kelly, Holt & O'Farrell, Charleston, W.Va., 1946-50, ptnr., 1950—; chmn. bd. dirs. Weston Nat. Bank; bd. dirs. Heritage Bancorp, Glenville, W.Va. Chancellor W.Va. Annual Conf. United Meth. Ch., Charleston, 1968—; trustee W.Va. Wesleyan Coll., Buckhannon, 1963—; chmn. bd. adminstrs. Christ Ch. United Meth., Charleston, 1969-76; bd. dirs., sec. United Meth. Charities W.Va., Charleston, 1973—. Served to lt. comdr. USNR, 1942-46. Fellow Am. Bar Found.; mem. ABA, W.Va. Bar Assn., Kanawha County Bar Assn. (pres. 1964-65), Am. Judicature Soc. (bd. dirs. 1981-85), Am. Counsel Assn., Charleston Area C. of C. (bd. dirs., sec. 1967-72), Order of Coif. Democrat. Clubs: Exchange, Edgewood Country (Charleston). Lodges: Masons, Shriners. Avocations: golf, fishing, boating. Banking, General corporate, Church law. Home: 1400 Connell Rd Charleston WV 25314 Office: Jackson Kelly Holt & O'Farrell 1600 Laidley Tower PO Box 553 Charleston WV 25322

BLAIR, CLIFFORD JENNINGS, II, lawyer; b. Oklahoma City, Sept. 27, 1953; s. Clifford Jennings and LaRue (McAnally) B.; m. Alma Echols, Dec. 21, 1979; children: William Michael Tisdal, Kelly Dian Tisdal. BA in English, Okla. State U., 1975; JD, U. Okla., 1979; student, Am. Banker's Assn. Nat. Trust Sch., 1981. Legal intern Okla. Supreme Ct., Oklahoma City, 1979-80; trust officer First Interstate Bank of Del City, Okla., 1980-83; v.p., trust officer First Interstate Bank of Norman, Okla., 1983-84; legal coordinator, spl. trust account adminstr. First Interstate Bank of Oklahoma City, Oklahoma City, 1984—; adj. prof. Oklahoma City Community Coll., 1984-86; legal cons. Oliver & Assocs., Oklahoma City, 1984—; exec. dir. Oklahoma City Monday Tax Luncheon, 1984-86; pub. speaker in field. Co-producer: (television series) Being of Sound Mind, 1982; author: A Covenant with Life, 1987, also short stories; contbr. articles to profl. jours. Mem. Humane Soc. U.S., Vols. for Animal Welfare, Oklahoma City, Juvenile Services Inc., Norman, Union Baptist Layman's Corp., Norman, Oklahoma City Estate Planning Council. Mem. ABA, Okla. Bar Assn., Okla. County Bar Assn., Cleveland County Bar Assn., Christian Legal Soc. Republican. Avocations: ch. work, profl. fiction writing, humane work, tae kwon do. Probate, Estate taxation, Pension, profit-sharing, and employee benefits. Home: 12 Valley View Norman OK 73069 Office: 1st Nat Bank and Trust Co PO Box 25189 Oklahoma City OK 73125

BLAIR, GRAHAM KERIN, lawyer; b. Shirley, Mass., Aug. 20, 1951; s. Joseph William and Ruth Marilyn (Shore) B.; 1 child, Elizabeth. B.A., So. Meth. U., 1973; J.D., U. Tex.-Austin, 1976. Bar: Tex. 1976, U.S. Ct. Appeals (5th cir.) 1977, U.S. Dist. Ct. (so. dist.) Tex. 1977. Assoc. Bracewell & Patterson, Houston, 1976-79; ptnr., co-chmn. litigation sect. Chamberlain, Hrdlicka, White, Johnson & Williams, Houston, 1979-82; sr. ptnr., chmn. litigation sect. Boyar, Norton & Blair, Houston, 1982—. Served to lt. (j.g.) USNR, 1973-76. Dir. advocacy, bd. advocates U. Tex. Sch. Law, Austin, 1976. Mem. ABA, Houston Bar Assn., Houston Young Lawyers Assn., State Bar Tex., Am. Arbitration Assn., Alpha Tau Omega. Democrat. Methodist. Federal civil litigation, State civil litigation, Construction. Office: Boyar Norton & Blair 4th Floor Five Post Oak Park Houston TX 77027

BLAIR, JAMES F., lawyer; b. Lima, Ohio, Mar. 3, 1947; s. James C. and E. Helen (Lippincott) B.; m. Lena Mae Hefner, May 17, 1974; children: Justin, Elizabeth, Thom. BA in Polit. Sci., Ohio No. U., 1969, JD, 1974. Bar: Ohio 1974, U.S. Dist. Ct. (no. dist.) Ohio 1982. Ptnr. Everett & Blair, Lima, 1974-82, Blair & Cornwell, Lima, 1982—. Served to sgt. U.S. Army, 1969-71. Mem. ABA, Ohio Bar Assn., Allen County Bar Assn., Assn. Trial Lawyers Am., Ohio Acad. Trial Lawyers. Republican. Roman Catholic. Lodge: Elks. General practice, Probate, Personal injury. Office: Blair & Cornwell 2100 Lost Creek Blvd Lima OH 45804

BLAIR, JOHN HOUSTON, lawyer; b. Amory, Miss., Aug. 20, 1954; s. James Houston and Billie Grace (Johnson) B.; m. Constance Louise Cox, July 17, 1982; 1 child, Jeannie Letitia. BBA, U. Miss., 1976, JD, 1979. Bar: Miss. 1979, U.S. Dist. Ct. (no. dist.) Miss. 1979, U.S. Dist. Ct. (so. dist.) Miss. 1980, Tex. 1985. Assoc. Wilbourne & Rogers, Meridian, Miss., 1979-80, Peterson, Harper & Bellan, Jackson, Miss., 1980-82; staff atty. Tex. Oil and Gas Corp., Dallas, 1982-83; sr. atty. Natural Resource Mgmt. Corp., Dallas, 1983—. Mem. ABA, Tex. Bar Assn., Miss. Bar Assn., Dallas Bar Assn., Phi Delta Phi. Methodist. Oil and gas law. Office: Natural Resource Mgmt Corp 2121 San Jacinto Dallas TX 75201

BLAIR, RICHARD EUGENE, lawyer; b. Loudon, Tenn., Mar. 7, 1923; s. John Thomas and Minnie Laura (Jones) B.; m. Marjorie Ann Bechtel, Apr. 17, 1954; children—Catherine Elizabeth, Marilynne L. B.A., U. Wash., 1948; J.D., Georgetown U., 1956; LL.M., So. Meth. U., 1962. Bar: Va. 1956, U.S. Supreme Ct. 1962, U.S. Dist. Ct. (ea. dist.) Va. 1972, U.S. Ct. Appeals (4th cir.) 1981. Commd. ensign, U.S. Navy, 1944, advanced through grades to capt., 1967, ret., 1972; sole practice, Fairfax, Va., 1972-79, McLean, Va., 1979-82; of counsel Light & Harrison, P.C., McLean, 1982—; dir. McLean Savs. & Loan Assn., 1977—, gen. counsel, 1975-82; dir. McLean Fin. Corp., 1982—; chmn. bd. dirs. Unifed Land Title Co., 1986—; adj. prof. oil and gas law Georgetown U., 1962-75; vis. prof. Duke U. Law Sch., 1964-68. Recipient Navy Lawyer award Navy League U.S., 1961. Mem. Va. Bar Assn., Fairfax County Bar Assn., Va. Trial Lawyers Assn., Georgetown U. Law Sch. Alumni Assn. Republican. Presbyterian. Contbr. articles to profl. jours. Banking, Probate. Address: 6849 Old Dominion Dr Suite 410 PO Box 6625 McLean VA 22106

BLAIR, ROBERT ALLEN, lawyer, savings and loan executive; b. Suffolk, Va., June 25, 1946; s. Thomas Francis Jr. and Ossie (Southern) B.; m. Linda Britt, Dec. 27, 1970; children—Robert Allen II, Thomas Edward. B.A. in Math., Coll. William and Mary, 1968; J.D., U. Va., 1973. Bar: Mass. 1974, U.S. Dist. Ct. Mass. 1974, U.S. Ct. Appeals (D.C. cir.) 1976, U.S. Dist. Ct. D.C. 1980. Assoc. Goodwin, Procter & Hoar, Boston, 1973-74; assoc. Surrey & Morse, Washington, 1974-78, ptnr., 1979-81; mng. ptnr. Anderson, Hibey, Nauheim & Blair, Washington, 1981—; vice-chmn. Enterprise Fed. Savs. & Loan Assn., Clearwater, Fla., 1984—, chmn. 1987—; dir. Palmer Tech. Services, Inc., Washington; pres., dir. Performance Evaluation Assocs., Inc., Va. Editorial bd. Law Rev. U. Va., 1971. Chmn. Inst. on Terrorism and Subnat. Conflict, Washington, 1982—; active Dupont Circle Citizens Assn., Washington, 1982—, 1700 S St. Assn., Washington, 1982-87; co-counsel Citizens for Democratic Alternatives in 1980, Washington, 1979-81; mem. adv. panel on fgn. policy, def. and arms control Dem. Nat. Com., Washington, 1982-85; mem. drafting team for fgn. policy, def. and arms control issue workshop Dem. Nat. Conf., Phila., 1982; mem. exec. com. Senate Dem. Roundtable, Washington, 1983—; mem. Senate Dem. Leadership Circle, Washington, 1983—; vice chmn. Potomac Group, Washington, 1983-84, chmn., 1984-85; mem. adv. council Dem. Platform Com., Washington, 1984; spl. counsel 1984 Dem. Nat. Conv., San Francisco, 1984; spl. counsel to nat. fin. chmn. Dem. Nat. Com., Washington, 1984-85, mem. fin. bd. dirs., 1982-85 ; mem. Nat. Dem. Club; vice chmn. Washington Fgn. Affairs Soc., 1984—; mem. Gov.'s Econ. Adv. Council, Va., 1986—; bd. dirs. Operation Up and Coming, Washington, 1984-86, Project Accessibility, Washington, 1984-86, Youth Leadership Inst., Washington, 1984-86. Named to Outstanding Young Men Am., U.S. Jaycees, 1976. Mem. Am. Soc. Internat. Law, ABA. Roman Catholic. Club: University (Washington). General corporate, Private international, Administrative and regulatory. Home: 1748 S St NW Washington DC 20009 Office: Anderson Hibey Nauheim & Blair 1708 New Hampshire Ave NW Washington DC 20009

BLAIR, WILLIAM HENRY, lawyer; b. Ft. Worth, Oct. 15, 1948; s. Aubrey Ray and Lennijo Ruth (Goldsberry) B.; m. Susan Norman, May 20, 1979. BBA, North Tex. State U., 1971; JD, Baylor U., 1976; LLM in Taxation, So. Meth. U., 1981. Bar: Tex. 1976. Asst. sec., br. mgr. Western Svgs. and Loan Assn., Ft. Worth, 1972-74; ptnr. Maples & Blair, Ft. Worth, 1976-80, McLean, Sanders, Price, Head & Ellis, Ft. Worth, 1981—. Editor Baylor U. Law Rev., 1975-76. Mem. adv. bd. Salvation Army, Ft. Worth, 1983-86, Downtown Ft. Worth, Inc., 1986—. Mem. Tex. Bar Assn. (partnership com., real estate taxation sect.). Club: Woodhaven (Ft. Worth). Avocations: tennis, music, photography. Corporate taxation, Personal income taxation, State and local taxation. Home: 3705 Holland St Fort Worth TX 76118 Office: McLean Sanders Price Head & Ellis 100 Main Pl Fort Worth TX 76102

BLAIS, JAN DAVID, lawyer; b. Providence, May 2, 1938; s. J.A.N. and Myrthle (Jache) B.; m. Barbara Marie Keane, Dec. 28, 1968; children: Ann Elizabeth, Andrew Nicholas. BS, Coll. Holy Cross, 1959; MPA, Harvard U., 1962, LLB, 1963; postgrad., U. Calif., Berkeley, 1963-64. Bar: Mass. 1964, D.C. 1972, Wash. 1986. Atty. Mass. Crime Commn., Boston, 1964; assoc. Goodwin, Proctor & Hoar, Boston, 1965; adminstrv. dean U. Calif., Berkeley, 1966-70; cons. Western Edn. Cons., Richmond, Calif., 1970-71; atty. FAA, Washington, 1971-73; adminstrv. proceedings counsel, atty., dir. properties United Airlines, Inc., Chgo. and San Francisco, 1973-80; aviation cons. Peat, Marwick, Mitchell & Co., San Mateo, Calif., 1980-82, Palo Alto, Calif., 1982-84; v.p. legal, gen. counsel, asst. sec. Alaska Airlines, Inc., Alaska Air Group, Seattle, 1984—. General corporate, Contracts commercial, Administrative and regulatory. Office: Alaska Airlines Inc PO Box 68900 Seattle WA 98168

BLAKE, FRANCIS STANTON, lawyer; b. Boston, July 30, 1949; s. George Baty and Rosemary (Shaw) B.; m. Anne McChristian, Jan. 1, 1977; children: Francis S., Margaret D. BA, Harvard U., 1971; JD, Columbia U., 1976. Bar: D.C. 1978. Law clk. to presiding justice Washington, 1976-77, 1977-78; assoc. Leva, Hawes, Symington, Washington, 1978-81; dep. counsel Vice Pres. George Bush, Washington, 1981-83; ptnr. Swidler & Berlin, Washington, 1983-85; gen. counsel U.S. EPA, Washington, 1985—. Republican. Episcopalian. Environment. Home: 5309 Locust Ave Bethesda MD 20814

BLAKE, HARLAN MORSE, law educator; b. Huron, S.D., Oct. 21, 1923; s. Ambrose Barnum and Martha (Fardig) B.; B.A., U. Chgo. 1946, M.A., 1947, J.D., 1954; student Yale, 1947-48; m. Barbara Barke, July 17, 1957. Asst. dean, lectr. econs. Univ. Coll., U. Chgo., 1948-52, acting dean, 1950-51; admitted to N.Y. bar, 1955; with firm Cravath, Swaine & Moore, N.Y.C., 1954-57; prof. law U. Minn., 1957-59; mem. faculty Columbia Law Sch., 1960—, prof. law, 1963-84, Arthur Levitt prof., 1984—. Mem. joint

com. econs. and law Am. Econ. Assn.-Assn. Am. Law Schs., 1965—; mem. trade regulation council Assn. Am. Law Schs., 1964—; cons. Inter-Am. Law Center, 1968—, FTC, 1970—, Center for Law and Econ. Studies, 1976—. Bd. dirs. Am. Dance Found., 1974—. Served to lt. (j.g.) USNR, 1943-46. Mem. Assn. Bar City N.Y. (dir. European common market research project 1964-68), Soc. Am. Law Tchrs., Phi Beta Kappa, Sigma Chi, Order of Coif. Club: Taurino (founder, dir.) (N.Y.C.). Author: Cases and Materials on Antitrust Law, 1967, 3d edit., 1982. Contbr. articles to mags., jours. including Fortune, Harper's. Editor: Business Regulation in the Common Market Nations, 3 vols., 1969. Antitrust, Constitutional law, Public international. Home: 125 Riverside Dr New York NY 10024 Office: Columbia U Law Sch 435 W 116 St NY NY 10027

BLAKE, JONATHAN DEWEY, lawyer; b. Long Branch, N.J., June 14, 1938; s. Edgar Bond and Haven (Johnstone) B.; m. Prudence Anne Rowsell, Dec. 22, 1964 (div. June 1977); children: Juliet Haven, Deborah Anne, Susanna Rowsell; m. Elizabeth L. Shriver, Dec. 9, 1977; children: Jonathan Shriver-Blake, Molly Shriver-Blake. BA, Yale U., 1960, LLB, 1964; BA, MA, Oxford U., Eng., 1962. Bar: D.C. 1965, U.S. Supreme Ct. 1969, U.S. Dist. Ct. D.C., U.S. Ct. Appeals (1st and D.C. cirs.). From assoc. to ptnr. Covington & Burling, Washington, 1964—; tchr. Howard U., U. Va., 1965-70; bd. dirs. Telocator Found., Washington. Pres. Great Falls Citizens Assn., Va., 1967-68; exec. com., bd. dirs. Deerfield Acad, Mass., 1980-85. Mem. Fed. Communications Bar Assn. (pres. 1984-85). Administrative and regulatory, Communications. Home: 4926 Hillbrook Ln Washington DC 20016 Office: Covington & Burling 1201 Pennsylvania Ave NW PO Box 7566 Washington DC 20044

BLAKE, STANFORD, lawyer; b. Detroit, Sept. 13, 1948; s. Morris and Betty (Yaffe) B.; m. Ellen Perkins, Mar. 5, 1978; children—Cary, Brandon, Stephanie. B.S., U. Fla. 1970; J.D., U. Miami, 1973. Bar: Fla. 1973, U.S. Dist. Ct. (so. dist.) Fla. 1973, U.S. Supreme Ct. 1980, U.S. Ct. Appeals (5th and 11th cirs.) 1981. Asst. pub. defender Dade County, Miami, Fla., 1973-78; ptnr. Todd, Rosinek & Blake, Miami, 1978-84, Rosinek & Blake, Miami, 1984-86; sole practice, Miami, 1986—. Chmn. Jr. Maccabiah Games S. Fla., Miami, 1984—. Co-chmn. Dade County Outstanding Citizen award, 1986. Mem. ABA, Fla. State Bar Assn. (grievance com.), Fed. Bar Assn., Nat. Assn. Criminal Def. Lawyers, Fla. Criminal Def. Attys. Assn. (pres. 1982-83), so. Miami Kendall Bar Assn. (pres. 1984-85). Lodge: B'nai B'rith (pres. 1980-81). Democrat. Jewish. Criminal. Home: 7810 SW 164th St Miami FL 33157 Office: 9200 S Dadeland Blvd Suite 617 Miami FL 33156

BLAKESLEE, JULIA FAY, lawyer; b. Maryville, Mo., June 30, 1949; d. Barton Jr. and Mary Esther (Wolff) B. BS, U. Kansas, 1971; JD, U. Mo., 1977. Bar: Mo. 1977, U.S. Dist. Ct. (we. dist.) Mo. 1977, U.S. Ct. Appeals (8th cir.) 1980. Assoc. Spencer, Fane, Britt & Browne, Kansas City, Mo., 1977-80; assoc. Rich, Granoff, Levy & Gee, Kansas City, 1980-82, ptnr., 1982—; teaching asst. U. Mo., Kansas City, 1981. Co-author: Kansas City Court Handbook, 1983. Mem. Kansas City Tomorrow, 1984—; active in fund raising Rose Brooks Ctr. for Battered Women, Kansas City, 1982—. Named one of 40 Most Influential Women in Kansas City, Kansas City Mag., 1984. Mem. ABA, Mo. Bar Assn. (various coms.), Kansas City Met. Bar Assn. (bd. dirs. 1984, pres. young lawyers sect. 1984, sec. young lawyers sect. 1983, law day chmn. 1981, co-chmn. continuing legal edn. com. 1982, disting. service award 1984, 82), Lawyers Assn. Kansas City (nominating com. 1986), Phi Beta Kappa. Roman Catholic. Lodge: Zonta Internat. (v.p. Kansas City 1984, membership chmn. 1983). Avocation: travel. Federal civil litigation, State civil litigation, Contracts commercial. Office: Rich Granoff Levy & Gee 1100 Main St 2300 City Ctr Sq Kansas City MO 64105

BLAKESLEE, WESLEY DANIEL, attorney, consultant; b. Wilkes-Barre, Pa., May 28, 1947; s. Daniel Leo and Anne (Gabura) B.; m. Georgia Carroll Croft, July 28, 1973; children—Jaime Kiersten, Christopher Justin, Shaun Michael. B.S., Pa. State U., 1969; J.D. (hon.), U. Md.-Balt., 1976. Bar: Md. 1976, U.S. Dist. Ct. Md. 1977, U.S. Tax Ct. 1984. Systems analyst NASA, Greenbelt, Md., 1969-76; assoc. Semmes, Bowen & Semmes, Balt., 1976-78; assoc. Dulany & Davis, Westminster, Md., 1978-83, ptnr., 1983; sole practice, Westminster, 1984—; lectr., dir. computer devel. U. Md. Law Sch., Balt., 1984—. Contrbg. author, editor; Maryland District Court Practice, 1981, revised 1983. Author: Understanding Computers, 1984. Contrbg. author: Computers, 1984. Rep. Carroll County, Md. State Employment and Tng. Council, 1980-82; bd. dirs. Carroll County chpt. Am. Heart Assn., Westminster 1981—; bd. govs. Md. Law Sch. Fund, Balt., 1982—. Mem. ABA, Fed. Bar Assn. (treas. Balt. chpt. 1984—), Md. Bar Assn. (young lawyers sect. council 1982-84, Outstanding Service award 1984, litigation sect. council 1982—), Carroll County Bar Assn. (treas. 1984), Assn. Trial Lawyers Am., Def. Research Inst., Order of Coif, Delta Theta Phi. Democrat. Roman Catholic. Club: Carroll County Democratic. Personal injury, Contracts commercial. Home: 1702 Bachman Valley Dr Westminster MD 21157 Office: 117 E Main St 1st Floor Westminster MD 21157

BLAKEY, MILTON KEITH, district attorney; b. Rupert, Idaho, Apr. 26, 1945; s. Howard Whyte and Lou Ella (Glenn) B.; m. Suzanne Kate Wells, Aug. 20, 1970 (div. Mar. 1976); 1 child, Elisa Lou; m. Patricia Joan Maher Mangone, Sept. 5, 1981; stepchildren—John P., Robert P. B.A., U. Colo., 1967, J.D., 1970. Bar: Colo. 1970, U.S. Ct. Appeals (10th cir.) 1979, U.S. Supreme Ct. 1979. Dep. city atty. City of Colo. Springs, 1970-71, chief pros. atty., 1971-72; dep. dist. atty. 4th Jud. Dist. Colo., 1973-76, chief dep. dist. atty., 1976-79, asst. dist. atty., 1979-81; dist. atty. 9th Jud. Dist. Colo., Glenwood Springs, 1981—. Republican. Lodge: Elks. Criminal, State civil litigation, Federal civil litigation. Home: PO Box 177 Glenwood Springs CO 81602 Office: Dist Atty Court House PO Box 961 Glenwood Springs CO 81602

BLAKLEY, BENJAMIN SPENCER, III, lawyer; b. DuBois, Pa., Sept. 1, 1952; s. Benjamin Spencer Jr. and Mary Jane (Campney) B.; 1 child, Benjamin Spencer IV. BA, Grove City Coll., 1974; JD, Duquesne U., 1977. Bar: Pa. 1977. Ptnr. Blakley & Jones, DuBois, 1977—; pub. defender Clearfield (Pa.) County, 1977-84; instr. Pa. State U., DuBois, 1979—. Bd. dirs. Salvation Army Pa. Corp., DuBois, 1978—, DuBois Area Youth Aid Panel, 1984—, Citizens for Effective Govt., DuBois, 1985—; trustee DuBois Vol. Fire Dept., 1986—. Mem. ABA, Pa. Bar Assn., Clearfield County Bar Assn., Nat. Assn. Criminal Def. Lawyers. Democrat. Methodist. Family and matrimonial, Criminal, General practice. Office: Blakley & Jones 406 Deposit Bank Bldg DuBois PA 15801

BLAN, KENNITH WILLIAM, JR., lawyer; b. Detroit, Dec. 15, 1946; s. Kennith William and Sarah Shirley (Shane) B.; m. Rebbeca Jo McCraken, Mar. 6, 1981; 1 son, Noah Winton. B.S., U. Ill., 1968, J.D., 1971. Bar: Ill. 1972, U.S. Supreme Ct. 1978. With Office State's Atty., Vermilion County, Ill., 1971-72; atty. Chgo. Title & Trust Co., 1972; asso. firm Graham, Meyer, Young, Welsch & Maton, Chgo., Springfield and Danville, Ill., 1972-74; individual practice law, Danville, 1975—; spl. asst. atty. gen. Ill., 1974-76; atty. City of Georgetown, Ill., 1985— . Chmn. Vermilion County Young Republican Club, 1975-77; founding sponsor Civil Justice Found.; capt. CAP. Mem. ABA, Ill. Bar Assn., Vermilion County Bar Assn., Lawyer-Pilots Bar Assn., Assn. Trial Lawyers Am., Ill. Trial Lawyers Assn., Ind. Trial Lawyers Assn., Am. Soc. Law and Medicine. Republican. Mem. Ch. of Christ. Club: Danville Country. Lodge: Elks. Personal injury, Federal civil litigation, State civil litigation. Office: Towne Ctr Suite 206 2 E Main St Danville IL 61832

BLAN, OLLIE LIONEL, JR., lawyer; b. Ft. Smith, Ark., May 22, 1931; s. Ollie Lionel and Eva Ocie (Cross) B.; m. Allen Conner Gillon, Aug. 19, 1960; children: Bradford Lionel, Elizabeth Ann, Cynthia Gillon. A.A., Ft. Smith Jr. Coll., 1951; LL.B., U. Ark., 1954. Bar: Ark. 1954, Ala. 1959. Research analyst Ark. Legis. Council, 1954-55; law clk. to Judge U.S. Dist. Ct. Ala., 1959-60; assoc. Spain, Gillon, Tate, Grooms & Blan and predecessor firms, Birmingham, Ala., 1960—, ptnr., 1965—; tchr. Am. Inst. Banking, 1965-68. Contbr. articles to legal jours. Treas. Jefferson County Hist. Commn., 1972-81, vice chmn., 1981-87, chmn., 1987—; mem. Jefferson County Rep. Exec. Com., 1973-76. Served with USMCR, 1955-58. Mem. ABA, Ark. Bar Assn., Ala. Bar Assn. (com. admissions and legal edn. 1971-74, com. jud. office 1972-76, com. ins. programs), Birmingham Bar Assn. (exec. com. 1987—), Ala. Def. Lawyers Assn. (v.p. 1983-84), Am. Life Ins. Assn., Internat. Assn. Ins. Counsel, Def. Research Inst. Baptist. Clubs: Birmingham Tip Off (charter); Relay House. Insurance, Personal injury, State civil litigation. Home: 2100 22d Ave S Birmingham AL 35223 Office: Spain Gillon Tate Grooms & Blan 2117 2d Ave N Birmingham AL 35203

BLANC, ROGER DAVID, lawyer; b. N.Y.C., Dec. 26, 1945; s. Robert Smith and Ara Jeanne (Ponchelet) B.; m. June Chunchin Ku, Sept. 17, 1972; children: David Jung-Wei, Gregory Jung-Lee, Cynthia Jung-Lin. BA, Yale U., 1967; JD, Columbia U., 1970. Bar: N.Y. 1971. Assoc. Chadbourne & Parke, N.Y.C., 1970-74; asst. chief counsel market regulation div. SEC, Washington, 1974-76, chief counsel market regulation div., 1976-80, assoc. dir. market regulation div., 1980-81; assoc. Willkie, Farr & Gallagher, N.Y.C., 1981-82, ptnr., 1982—; lectr. various profl. orgns. Contbr. articles to profl. jours. Mem. Bd. Edn., Chappaqua, N.Y., 1985—. Mem. ABA, Assn. of Bar of City of N.Y. Clubs: University (N.Y.C.); Whippoorwill (Armonk, N.Y.). General corporate, Securities, Administrative and regulatory. Office: Willkie Farr & Gallagher 1 Citicorp Ct 153 E 53d St New York NY 10022

BLANCATO, LYDIA COX, lawyer; b. Washington, July 27, 1954; d. Earl French and Gloria Parthenia (Swanson) Cox; m. Robert John Blancato, Sept. 23, 1982. AB, Vassar Coll., 1976; JD, U. Pa., 1979. Bar: Pa. 1979, D.C. 1981, Del. 1985. Jr. atty. E.I. duPont deNemours, Wilmington, Del., 1979-80; assoc. Kaye, Scholer, Fierman, Hays & Handler, Washington, 1980-82; acct. exec. AT&T Informations Systems, Wilmington, 1982-83; assoc. legal counsel Bank of Del., Wilmington, 1984—; asst. sec. Christina Life Ins. Co., Wilmington, 1986—. Bd. dirs. Kingswood Community Ctr., Wilmington, 1985—. Mem. ABA, Nat. Bar Assn., Am. Corp. Counsel Assn., Delaware Valley Am. Corp. Counsel Assn., Brandywine Profl. Assn. Banking, Consumer commercial, Contracts commercial. Office: Bank of Del 300 Delaware Ave Wilmington DE 19899

BLANCHARD, KIMBERLY STAGGERS, lawyer; b. Ann Arbor, Mich., May 17, 1954; d. Theodore R. and Bette Lee (Clark) Staggers; m. John Sears Blanchard, May 31, 1980; 1 child, Charles Stuart. BA, Dartmouth Coll., 1976; MS, U. Wis., 1978; JD, NYU, 1981. Bar: N.Y. 1982. Assoc. Paul, Weiss, Rifkind, Wharton & Garrison, N.Y.C., 1981-83, Haythe & Curley, N.Y.C., 1983—; adj. prof. NYU Sch. Continuing Edn., 1982—. Recruitment officer Dartmouth Coll., Hanover, N.H., 1985—. Mem. ABA, Assn. Bar of City of N.Y. Democrat. Baptist. Club: Pelham Country (Pelham Manor, N.Y.). Avocation: golf. Corporate taxation, Personal income taxation, Private international. Home: 535 Stellar Ave Pelham Manor NY 10803 Office: Haythe & Curley 437 Madison Ave New York NY 10022

BLANCHETTE, JAMES GRADY, JR., lawyer; b. Dallas, Apr. 29, 1922; s. James Grady and Thelma (Keys) B.; m. Bess Neblett, May 29, 1944; children—Linda Blanchette Ponti, Kay Blanchette Hill, Martha Blanchette Caschette. B.B.A., U. Tex., 1943, LL.B., 1947; M.B.A., Harvard U., 1948. Bar: Tex. 1947. Ptnr. Blanchette & James, Dallas. Chmn. exec. com. Chancellor's Council U. Tex. System, 1983; pres. Dad's Assn. U. Tex., 1972-73. Served to lt., USNR, 1943-45. Fellow Tex. Bar Found., Am. Coll. of Probate Counsel; mem. ABA, Dallas Bar Assn. Tex. Bar Assn. Presbyterian. Clubs: The Dallas (pres., 1978-79), Northwood (pres., 1971), Dallas Petroleum. General corporate, Probate, Estate taxation. Address: 8330 Meadow Rd Dallas TX 75231

BLANCO, FRANKLIN AUGUSTO, lawyer; b. La Maya, Cuba, Aug. 5, 1948; came to U.S., 1962; s. J. Amador Blanco and Maria C. (Alonso) Seisdedos. BA, Hunter Coll., 1978; JD, Bklyn. Law Sch., 1981. Bar: N.Y. 1982, N.J. 1982. Assoc. Barst & Mukamal, N.Y.C., 1981-83, Mailman & Ruthizer, N.Y.C., 1983, Tibby Blum, N.Y.C., 1984-86, Sandra G. Levitt, P.C., N.Y.C., 1986—. Mem. Am. Immigration Lawyers Assn., Phi Beta Kappa. Immigration, naturalization, and customs. Home: 3519 New York Ave Union City NJ 07087-4713

BLAND, JAMES THEODORE JR., lawyer; b. Memphis, June 16, 1950; s. James Theodore and Martha Frances (Downen) B.; m. Pattie L. Martin, Apr. 12, 1974. BBA magna cum laude, Memphis State U., 1972, JD, 1974. Bar: Tenn. 1975, U.S. Dist. Ct. (we. dist.) Tenn. 1976, U.S. Tax Ct. 1976, U.S. Supreme Ct. 1983. Estate tax atty. IRS, Memphis, 1974-76; assoc. Armstrong, Allen, Braden, Goodman, McBride & Prewitt, Memphis, 1976-81, ptnr., 1981—; instr. taxation, bus. law State Tech. Inst., Memphis, 1975-83; adv. bd. dirs. Thomas W. Briggs Found., Memphis. Mem. ABA (legis. initiatives com. taxation sect., specialization in estate planning real property, probate and trust section, achievement award 1983, 1985), Fed. Bar Assn. (pres. elect 1986—, 1st v.p. 1985-86, nat. council 1979—, bd. dirs. young lawyers div. 1979-84, pres. Memphis mid-south chpt. 1979-80), Am. Assn. Attys.-CPA's, Tenn. Bar Assn. (chmn. tax sect. 1984-85, bd. govs. 1984-85), Tenn. Young Lawyers Conf. (bd. dirs. 1978—, pres. 1984-85), Tenn. Soc. CPAs (scholar 1971-72), Memphis and Shelby County Bar Found. (chmn. 1982-86). Republican. Methodist. Probate, Corporate taxation, Estate taxation. Office: Armstrong Allen et al 1900 One Commerce Sq Memphis TN 38103

BLANDING, SANDRA ANN, lawyer; b. Providence, June 16, 1951; d. Joseph Viti and Gloria Carmen (Montella) Comiskey; 1 child, James Pearson. BS, Tufts U., 1973; JD, George Washington U., 1978. Bar: R.I. 1978, U.S. Dist. Ct. R.I. 1978, U.S. Ct. Appeals (1st cir.) 1979, U.S. Supreme Ct. 1983. Assoc. Revens & DeLuca, Warwick, R.I., 1978-84, ptnr., 1984—; legal counsel R.I. chpt. Children's Code Commn., 1980—; bd. dirs. R.I. Legal Services Corp. Bd. dirs. ACLU, Providence, 1981—. Mem. Fed. Bar Assn. (asst. sec. 1982-83, sec. 1983-85, pres. 1987), R.I. Bar Assn. (ho. dels. 1981—), R.I. Women's Bar Assn., Assn. Trial Lawyers Am., Nat. Assn. Women Lawyers, R.I. Women Lawyers Assn. (sec. 1979-80, pres. 1980-81), R.I. Women's Network, Nat. Orgn. Social Security Claimant's Reps., Indls. Research and Relations Assn., Phi Beta Kappa, Psi Chi. Avocations: gardening, boating. Civil rights, State civil litigation, Personal injury. Home: 199 S Pierce St East Greenwich RI 02818 Office: Revens & DeLuca Ltd 946 Centerville Rd Warwick RI 02886

BLANGIARDO, FRANK J., judge; b. N.Y.C., May 5, 1923; s. John and Teresa (Spano) B.; m. Amelia Blangiardo, Sept. 10, 1950; children; Theresa, Bernice, Joan, John, Frank, Louis. Student, The Citadel, 1941-43; JD, Bklyn. Law Sch., 1949. Bar: N.Y. 1950, U.S. Dist. Ct. (so. and ea. dists.) N.Y. 1957. Sole practice N.Y.C., 1950-56; asst. dist. atty. N.Y. County, N.Y.C., 1956-58, mcpl. ct. justice, 1959-62, civil ct. judge, 1962—; acting justice Supreme Ct. N.Y. County, N.Y.C., 1972—. Served to sgt. U.S. Army, 1943-46, ETO. Criminal, State civil litigation. Office: NYC Civil Ct 111 Centre St New York NY 10013

BLANK, A(NDREW) RUSSELL, lawyer; b. Bklyn., June 13, 1945; s. Lawrence and Joan B.; children—Adam, Marisa. Student U. N.C., 1963-64; B.A., U. Fla., 1966, postgrad. Law Sch., 1966-68; J.D., U. Miami, 1970. Bar: Ga. 1971, Fla. 1970; cert. civil trial advocate Nat. Bd. Trial Advocacy. Law asst. Dist. Ct. Judge, Atlanta, 1970-72; sole practice, 1972—. Contbr. articles to profl. jours. Mem. pub. adv. com. Atlanta Regional Commn., 1972-74. Recipient Merit award Ga. Bar Assn., 1981. Mem. Atlanta Bar Assn., Ga. Bar Assn., Ga. Trial Laywers Assn. (officer), Fed. Assn. Atlanta, Lawyers Club Atlanta, ABA, Am. Trial Lawyers Assn., Fla. Bar Assn., Am. Bd. Trial Advocates (advocate, v.p., pres. Ga. chpt.). Federal civil litigation, State civil litigation, Personal injury. Office: 1020 Equitable Bldg Atlanta GA 30303

BLANK, GARY L., lawyer; b. Chgo., July 24, 1944; s. Morton and Jeanne Blank; m. Sandra Karen Farber, Dec. 22, 1968; children: Melissa, Marcey, Mindy. BS, Ohio State U., 1966; JD, John Marshall Law Sch., 1970. Bar: Ill., D.C., U.S. Dist. Ct. (no. dist.) Ohio, U.S. Ct. Appeals (7th cir.), U.S. Tax Ct., U.S. Supreme Ct.; CPA, Ill. Tax cons., acct. Alexander Grant & Co., Chgo., 1968-72; sole practice Chgo., 1972—; bd. dirs. Coalstar Enterprises, Chgo. and Carlise, Ind. Served to capt. U.S. Army, 1966-75. Fellow North Suburban Bar Assn.; mem. ABA, Assn. Trial Lawyers Am., Ill. Bar Assn., Chgo. Bar Assn., Phi Alpha Epsilon, Alpha Epsilon Pi. Jewish. General corporate, Real property, Personal injury. Office: 33 N LaSalle St Chicago IL 60602

BLANK, IRVING MICHAEL, lawyer; b. Richmond, Va., Dec. 29, 1943; s. Lewis and Evelyn (Rosenstein) B.; m. Rhona Mandel, June 26, 1966; children—Lisa Rae, Jonathan Todd. B.S. in Pub. Adminstrn., Va. Tech., 1965; J.D., U. Richmond, 1967. Bar: Va. 1967, U.S. Supreme Ct. 1972, D.C. 1978, U.S. Ct. Appeals (4th cir.) 1983. Assoc. Paul & Smith and predecessors, Richmond, 1967-71; ptnr. Paul, Smith & Blank, Richmond, 1972-83, Smith, Blank, Isaacs & Hinton, 1983-85, Smith, Moncure, Blank, Isaccs & Hinton, 1985—. Chmn. community relations com. Richmond Jewish Fedn.; mem. community relations com. Richmond Jewish Community Ctr.; mem. exec. com., bd. dirs. Richmond Multiple Sclerosis Soc.; bd. dirs. Jewish Family Services, Richmond Jewish Community Fedn.; mem. internat. affairs commn. and equal opportunity commn. Anti-Defamation League, 1981—; mem. Tom Bliley adv. com. Richmond Tennis Patrons, 1982; mem. exec. com. Nat. Jewish Community Relations Adv. Com., 1980-84 ; mem. Nat. Jewish Community Relations Adv. Council, Nat. Council Am.-Israel Pub. Affairs. Served to capt. JAGC, U.S. Army. Mem. Assn. Trial Lawyers Am., Va. Trial Lawyers Assn., ABA (com. privacy, com. specialization, criminal justice sect. 1974-76, environ. matters in criminal law com., criminal justice sect. 1974-76), Va. Bar Assn., Richmond Bar Assn. (exec. com. 1982-85 , com. adminstrn. of justice 1981-83), Am. Arbitration Assn. (panel arbiters), Am. Judicature Soc., Richmond Criminal Law Assn. (sec. 1973), Va. Assn. Def. Attys. State civil litigation, Criminal, Insurance. Home: 405 Branway Dr Richmond VA 23229 Office: 1804 Staples Mill Rd Richmond VA 23226

BLANK, MARK, JR., lawyer; b. Phila., June 25, 1946; s. Mark and Grace (Rabinowitz) B.; m. Jill Seltzer, Aug. 10, 1984. BA, Tulane U., 1968; MA, Temple U., 1972; JD, Del. Law Sch., 1975; LLM, NYU, 1982. Bar: Pa. 1976, U.S. Dist. Ct. (ea. dist.) Pa. 1976, U.S. Ct. Appeals (3d cir.) 1976, N.Y. 1982, U.S. Supreme Ct. 1984. Prof. law, Cheyney U., Pa., 1971—; atty. Goldberg & Evans, West Chester, Pa., 1977-78; sole practice, Paoli, 1978—. Asst. editor Chester County Law Reporter, 1980-86, editor, 1986—. Hearing officer Chester County Housing Authority, 1980—; spl. master divorce Chester County, 1986—; bd. dirs. Friend Advocacy Network, West Chester, 1979—. Mem. ABA, Am. Judicature Soc., Am. Arbitration Assn. (panel of arbitrators), Assn. Trial Lawyers Am., Chester County Bar Assn. (chmn. law reporter com. 1982), Pa. Bar Assn., Pa. Trial Lawyers Assn., Comml. Law League Am. Republican. General practice, Consumer commercial. Office: 19 E Lancaster Ave Paoli PA 19301

BLANK, NELSON DOUGLAS, lawyer; b. Wilmington, Del., June 15, 1955; s. Raymond A. and Betty Gay (Gerber) B.; m. Deborah Ann Lukowski, Nov. 17, 1979; 1 child, Andrew Paul. BS in Physics, BS in Math., MIT, 1977; JD cum laude, U. Pa., 1980. Bar: Fla. 1980, U.S. Dist. Ct. (mid. dist.) Fla. 1980, U.S. Ct. Appeals (11th cir.) 1981, U.S. Dist. Ct. (no. dist.) Fla. 1985, U.S. Dist. Ct. (so. dist.) Fla. 1986. Assoc. Trenam, Simmons, Kemker, Scharf, Barkin, Frye & O'Neill, P.A., Tampa, Fla., 1980-85, ptnr., 1985—. Mem. civil rules com. Hillsborough County, Tampa, 1982-83, Tampa Preservation Inc., 1985-86. Mem. Hillsborough County Bar Assn., MIT Alumni Assn. (v.p. 1985-86). Federal civil litigation, State civil litigation, Trademark and copyright. Home: 134 Bosphorous Tampa FL 33606 Office: Trenam Simmons Kemker et al 111 E Madison St Tampa FL 33602

BLANK, RALPH JOHN, JR., lawyer; b. Lake City, Fla., Apr. 2, 1922; s. Ralph John Sr. and Stella Pauline (Kleinbeck) B.; m. Merry H. Lake, May 17, 1952; children: Pamela Hellin, Liisa Pauline, Michelle Susan. BS in Bus. Adminstrn., U. Fla., 1942, LLB cum laude, 1948. Bar: Fla. 1948, U.S. Dist. Ct. (so. dist.) Fla. 1948, U.S. Supreme Ct. 1951. Assoc. Morehead, Pallot, Smith, Green & Phillips, Miami, Fla., 1948-49; counsel home office Am. Fire & Casualty Co., Orlando, Fla., 1950-51; sole practice West Palm Beach, Fla., 1952-72; sr. ptnr. Blank % Benn, West Palm Beach, 1972—. mem. Fla. Ho. of Reps., Tallahassee, 1956-60, Civil Service Bd., West Palm Beach, 1965-74; senator Fla. State Senate, Tallahassee, 1960-64; trustee, bd. dirs. Fla. Atlantic U. Endowment Corp., Boca Raton, 1960-80. Served to lt. col. U.S. Army, 1942-45, 51-52, ETO. Decorated Air medal with 5 oak leaf clusters. Mem. ABA, Fla. Bar Assn., Assn. Trial Lawyers Am., Palm Beach County Bar Assn., Phi Kappa Phi, Phi Delta Phi. Democrat. Presbyterian. Real property, Probate, State civil litigation. Home: 122 Forest Hill Blvd West Palm Beach FL 33405 Office: Blank & Benn 1016 Clearwater Pl West Palm Beach FL 33401

BLANKE, RICHARD B., lawyer; b. St. Louis, Oct. 28, 1954; s. Robert H. and Phyllis I. (Kessler) Schaffler. BA, U. Pa., 1977; JD, U. Mo., 1980. Bar: U.S. Dist. Ct. (ea. and we. dists.) Mo. 1980, Mo. 1980. Ptnr. Blanke & Assocs., St. Louis County, Mo., 1980—. Mem. Assn. Trial Lawyers Am., ABA, Mo. Bar Assn., Mo. Assn. Trial Attys., St. Louis Met. Bar Assn. General practice, Personal injury, Family and matrimonial. Office: Blanke & Assocs 8420 Delmar Suite 405 Saint Louis MO 63124 Office: 8420 Delmar Blvd, Suite 405, University City 63114

BLANKENHEIMER, SUSAN LESLIE, government lawyer; b. Washington, Aug. 25, 1952; d. Bernard and Rosalind (Drescher) B.; m. Joseph J. Geraci, Jan. 9, 1982. Student Johannesburg, South Africa, 1968-70, London Polytech. 1973; B.A. with honors, Syracuse U., 1974; J.D., Vanderbilt U., 1977. Bar: Pa. 1979, U.S. Ct. Appeals (D.C. cir.) 1980, U.S. Ct. Appeals (fed. cir.) 1982, D.C. 1984, N.Y. 1984, U.S. Supreme Ct. 1984. Law clk. presdl. clemency bd., White House, Washington, summer 1975, FCC, Washington, summer 1976, Office Opinions and Rev., FCC, Washington, 1977-78; atty. Civil Aeronautics Bd., CAB, Washington, 1979-84, law dept., Comptroller of the Currency, Washington, 1985—. Assoc. editor Vanderbilt Jour. Transnat. Law, 1975-76, contbr. article to law jour. Recipient Spl. Achievement award CAB, 1980. Mem. Fed. Bar Assn., D.C. Bar Assn., Eta Pi Upsilon, Pi Sigma Alpha, Alpha Chi Omega. Club: Internat. Aviation (Washington). Banking, Antitrust, Administrative and regulatory. Home: 5413 DuVall Dr Bethesda MD 20816 Office: Comptroller of the Currency Law Dept 490 L'Enfant Plaza E SW Washington DC 20219

BLANKENSHIP, JERI BURNETTE, judge; b. Atlanta, Sept. 28, 1944; d. Henry Paul and Norma Helen (Brittingham) Burnette; m. Clyde Alan Blankenship, Feb. 27, 1980. B.A., U. Ala., 1966, J.D., 1976; postgrad. Cultural Inst., Madrid, 1966. Tchr. pub. and pvt. schs., Wichita, Kans. and Sumter, S.C., 1967-72; ptnr. Stephens, Millirons, Harrison & Walker, P.C., Huntsville, Ala., 1977-81; dist. judge Ala. Unified Jud. System, 23d Jud. Circuit, Huntsville, 1981—; mem. faculty Ala. Jud. Coll., Tuscaloosa, 1981—. Mem. adv. bd. J.C. Calhoun State Coll., Decatur, Ala., 1979-82; bd. dirs. Big Bros./Big Sisters Madison County, Am. Heart Assn., Huntsville, 1983, Girls Club, Huntsville, 1983, Girl Scouts of North Ala., Inc.; trustee Humana Hosp. Ala.; mem. women's div. Huntsville Democratic Com. Mem. ABA, Huntsville-Madison County Bar Assn., Am. Bus. Women's Assn., Bus. and Profl. Women's Club (sec. Huntsville 1983-84), Phi Beta Kappa. Presbyterian. Judicial administration. Office: Madison County Courthouse Huntsville AL 35801

BLANKER, ALAN HARLOW, lawyer; b. Montague, Mass., Sept. 15, 1951; s. William Charles and Ann (Harlow) B.; B.A., Colby Coll., 1973; J.D., Georgetown U., 1976. Bar: Mass. 1977, U.S. Dist. Ct. Mass. 1977. Ptnr. Levy, Winer, Hodos, Berson, Blanker and Bishop, Greenfield, Mass., 1977—; clk. Esleeck Mfg. Co., Inc., Montague, 1980—, also dir.; clk., bd. dirs. Valley Tire Co., Ltd., Greenfield; incorporator Heritage Bank for Savs., Greenfield, 1980-86, Greenfield Savs. Bank, 1986—; Editor Georgetown Law Jour., 1975-76. Mem. Greenfield Fin. Com., 1980-84; chmn. Greenfield Sch. Bldg. Com., 1977-81; mem. Greenfield Republican Town Com., 1976-85; incorporator Franklin Med. Ctr., 1979—; bd. dirs., clk. Greenfield Indsl. Devel. Area Corp.; Mem. Franklin County C. of C. (chmn. tech. services com. 1982—), Phi Beta Kappa, Pi Sigma Alpha. Congregationalist. Lodge: Kiwanis. General corporate, Real property, Contracts commercial. Home: 4 Adams Ct South Deerfield MA 01373 Office: Levy Winer et al PO Box 1538 Greenfield MA 01302

BLANKINGSHIP, A. HUGO, JR., lawyer; b. Norfolk, Va., Aug. 9, 1930; s. Alex Hugo and Antoinette (Woodward) B.; m. Sally Redding, Sept. 1, 1956; children: Page, Hugo III. BA, U. Va., 1952, LLB, 1957. Bar: Va. 1957, U.S. Dist. Ct. (ea. dist.) Va., U.S. Ct. Appeals (4th cir.), U.S. Supreme Ct. Ptnr. Blankingship & Keith, Fairfax, Va., 1957—; atty. City of Fairfax, 1964-68; mem. Va. Bd. Bar Examiners. Chancellor Episcopal Diocese Va., 1977—; sr. warden Truro Episcopal Ch. 1973-74; trustee Va. Theol. Sem.,

Alexandria. Served to lt. USNR, 1952-54. Fellow Am. Bar Found., Va. Law Found.; mem. Va. Bar Assn. (pres. 1977-78), Fairfax County Bar Assn. (pres. 1974). Condemnation, General practice, Real property. Home: 10400 Towlston Rd Fairfax VA 22030 Office: Blankingship & Keith 4020 University Dr PO Box 280 Fairfax VA 22030

BLANTON, MARY RUTHERFORD, lawyer, educator; b. Alexandria, Va., July 4, 1950; d. Arthur J. and Margaret (Cockrell) Rutherford; m. Theodore A. Blanton, May 27, 1972; children: William F., John A., Thomas Pennington, Mary Elizabeth. BA, Wake Forest U., 1972; postgrad., St. John's Grad. Inst., Santa Fe, 1973; JD, Georgetown U., 1981. Bar: Va. 1982, N.C. 1985. Tchr., chmn. English dept. Martin Spalding High Sch., Severn, Md., 1972-75; Legis. aide Ho. of Reps., Washington, 1976-77; sole practice Springfield, Va., 1982-83; assoc. Ketner & Rankin, Salisbury, N.C., 1984-86; ptnr. Crowell, Porter, Blanton & Blanton, Salisbury, 1986—; instr. continuing edn. program Catawba Coll., Salisbury, 1985. Carswell scholar, 1969-71. Mem. ABA, N.C. State Bar Assn., Va. State Bar Assn., Rowan County Bar Aux. (pres. 1985—), Phi Beta Kappa. Episcopalian. Avocations: aerobics, music, teaching. General practice. Home: 320 W Thomas St Salisbury NC 28144 Office: Crowell Porter Blanton & Blanton 516 W Innes St Salisbury NC 28144

BLASER, STEPHEN JEFFERY, lawyer; b. Rigby, Idaho; s. Clair E. and Rosemary (Polson) B.; m. Rena Hooper, Mar. 12, 1981; children: Justin, Shawn, Ryan, Jennifer, Andrew, Danielle. Assoc. in Sci., Ricks Coll., 1969; BS, U. Idaho, 1972, JD, 1976. Bar: Idaho 1976, U.S. Dist Ct. Idaho 1976. Sole practice Blackfoot, Idaho, 1976-79; ptnr. Blaser & Sorenson, Blackfoot, 1979—. Chmn., bd. dirs. United Way, Blackfoot, 1979-82. Named one of Outstanding Young Men in Am. U.S. Jaycees, 1983, 84, 85. Mem. ABA, Am. Trial Lawyers Assn., Idaho Trial Lawyers Assn., Idaho State Bar Assn., Exchange Club (sec., treas. 1979-82). Republican. Mormon. Avocations: cattle ranching. Bankruptcy, General practice, Estate planning. Home: 300 E 325 N Blackfoot ID 83221 Office: Blaser & Sorensen PO Box 1047 Blackfoot ID 83221

BLASIER, PETER COLE, lawyer; b. Munich, Fed. Republic Germany, Sept. 27, 1953; (parents Am. citizens); s. Stewart Cole and Martha (Hiett) B.; m. Ann Lewis Scully, June 12, 1982; 1 child, Emily Hiett. BA cum laude, Harvard U., 1975; JD, Fordham U., 1980. Bar: Pa. 1980, U.S. Dist. Ct. (we. dist.) Pa. 1980. Mgmt. trainee Morgan Guaranty Trust Co. N.Y., N.Y.C., 1975-77; atty. comml./corp. litigation Thorp, Reed & Armstrong, Pitts., 1980-85; sr. counsel corp. fin./transactions Westinghouse Credit Corp. subs. Westinghouse Electric Corp., Pitts., 1985—; sec. Westinghouse Securities Corp., Pitts., 1985—, bd. dirs. Mem. World Affairs Council Pitts., 1983—. Clubs: Pitts. Golf, Rolling Rock (Ligonier, Pa.). Avocations: racket sports, polit. and social hist. General corporate, Contracts commercial, Securities. Home: 5446 Kipling Rd Pittsburgh PA 15217 Office: Westinghouse Credit Corp One Oxford Centre 301 Grand St Pittsburgh PA 15219

BLASKE, E. ROBERT, lawyer; b. Battle Creek, Mich., June 4, 1945; s. Edmund Robert and Wilma Jayne (Hill) B.; m. Vicki Lyn Rayner, Aug. 11, 1968. BA with distinction, U. Mich., 1966, JD cum laude, 1969. Bar: Mich. 1969, U.S. Dist. Ct. (we. dist.) Mich. 1970, U.S. Ct. Appeals (6th cir.) 1983. Ptnr. Blaske & Blaske, Battle Creek, 1969—; mem. Mich. Bd. Law Examiners, 1976—, drafting com. for rules to implement Mich. mental health code, 1978-79, multi-state bar exam. com. Nat. Conf. Bar Examiners, 1983-85, multi-state profl. responsibility exam. com., 1985—; instr. trial advocacy program steering com. U.S. Dist. Ct. (we. dist.) Mich., 1982—; lectr. Inst. Continuing Legal Edn., 1983—. Mem. U. Mich. Law Rev., 1968-69. Bd. dirs. Calhoun County Legal Aid Soc., Battle Creek, 1976, Mich. Audubon Soc., Kalamazoo, 1981, Blaske-Hill Found., Battle Creek, 1983—; bd. govs. Lawyers Club U. Mich. Law Sch., 1985—. Mem. ABA, State Bar Mich., Calhoun County Bar Assn. (pres. 1977-78), Assn. Trial Lawyers Am., Mich. Trial Lawyers Assn., Order of Coif. Roman Catholic. Personal injury, State civil litigation. Home: 25001 Battle Creek Hwy Bellevue MI 49021 Office: Blaske & Blaske 1509 Comerica Bldg Battle Creek MI 49017

BLASKE, THOMAS HUGH, lawyer; b. July 25, 1951; m. Mary Stef-fek. BA with high honors, U. Mich., 1973, JD magna cum laude, 1976. Bar: Mich. 1976, U.S. Dist. Ct. (ea. dist.) Mich. 1977, U.S. Dist. Ct. (we. dist.) Mich. 1977, U.S. Ct. Appeals (6th cir.) 1982. Ptnr. Blaske & Blaske, Battle Creek, Mich., 1976-77; assoc. O'Brien, Moran & Dimond, Ann Arbor, Mich., 1977-79; ptnr. Bishop & Shelton, Ann Arbor, 1979—; grader, proctor Mich. Bd. Law Examiners; lectr. in field. Contbr. articles to profl. jours.; contbr. poems to New Yorker mag. Counsel Wolverine Council Boy Scouts Am., v.p. for fin., mem. exec. bd., exec. com., endowment com.; sec. Washtenaw Community Coll. Found., mem. exec. bd., exec. com.; mem. Hist. Soc. Mich., Ann Arbor Wine and Food Soc.; bd. trustees Blaske-Hill Scholarship Found. Recipient Silver Beaver award Boy Scouts Am. Mem. ABA (various sects.), Mich. Bar Assn. (select com. on civil procedure, chmn. select com. on medicolegal affairs, profl. devel. task force, various sects.), Washtenaw County Bar Assn. (treas., exec. bd. dirs., judiciary com.), Pine River Bar Assn., Assn. Trial Lawyers Am., Mich. Trial Lawyers Assn. (new legis. evaluation com., med. malpractice adv. com.), Washtenaw Trial Lawyers Assn. (editor newsletter), Am. Soc. Law and Medicine, Inst. for Study of Profl. Risk (bd. dirs.), Nat. Trust for Hist. Preservation, Original Mich. Fiddlers Assn., Mich. Audubon Soc., U. Mich. Band Alumni Assn., Baker St. Irregulars, Trout Unltd., Phi Eta Sigma. Avocations: fishing, legal and constitutional history, wine making, athletics, poetry. Federal civil litigation, Personal injury, Government contracts and claims. Home: 820 3d St Ann Arbor MI 48103 Office: Bishop & Shelton 709 W Huron Ann Arbor MI 48103

BLASZAK, MICHAEL WILLIAM, lawyer; b. Chgo., Jan. 19, 1953. BA, Northwestern U., 1973; postgrad. in law, U. So. Calif., 1973-74; JD, U. Chgo., 1976. Bar: Ill. 1976, U.S. Dist. Ct. (no. dist.) Ill. 1976, U.S. Dist. Ct. (ea. dist.) Wis. 1980, U.S. Ct. Appeals (10th cir.) 1981. Atty. The Atchison Topeka & Santa Fe Ry. Co., Chgo., 1976-78; atty. Santa Fe Industries, Chgo., 1978-79, asst. gen. atty., 1980-83, gen. atty., 1984-85; gen. atty. Santa Fe So. Pacific Corp., Chgo., 1985—; bd. dirs. Joliet Union Depot Co., Ill. Contbr. articles on R.R. and R.R. history to profl. jours. Mem. ABA, Assn. of Transp. Practitioners. Contracts commercial, Administrative and regulatory, Bankruptcy. Office: Santa Fe So Pacific Corp 224 S Michigan Ave Chicago IL 60604

BLATCHFORD, JOSEPH HOFFER, lawyer, consultant; b. Milw., June 7, 1934; s. George and Zoe (Hoffer) B.; m. Winifred Marich, Dec. 27, 1967; children—Andrea Nicole, Nicholas George, Antonia Nason. B.A. in Polit. Sci., UCLA, 1956; J.D., U. Calif.-Berkeley, 1961; L.H.D. (hon.), Seton Hall U., 1969, Kenyon Coll., 1970; H.H.D. (hon.), Chapman Coll., 1969, Westminster Coll., 1972; LL.D. (hon.), Fairfield U., 1972. Bar: D.C. 1977, U.S. Ct. Internat. Trade 1981. Legis. asst. com. edn. and labor U.S. Congress, Washington, 1957-58; founder, exec. dir. Acció n en Venezuela, Caracas, 1961-64; founder Aç ã o Communitaria do Brasil, Rio de Janeiro, Brazil, 1966-67; Acció n Internat., N.Y.C., 1964-69; dir. U.S. Peace Corps, Washington, 1969-72; founding dir. Action, Washington, 1971-72; internat. mgmt. cons., Los Angeles, 1973-75; dep. under sec. Dept. Commerce, Washington, 1976-77; ptnr. Blatchford, Epstein & Brady, Washington, 1980-83, O'Connor & Hannan, Washington, 1983—; prof. polit. sci. Whittier (Calif.) Coll., 1973; producer, commentator Sta. KNBC-TV (NBC), Los Angeles, 1973-74; gen. counsel East-West Trade Council, 1977-80; pres. Ventana Assocs., Inc., Washington, 1980—, Com. for the Caribbean, 1978-79, also trustee; trustee Caribbean/Central Am. Action, 1983—; chmn. regional commn. White House Fellows, 1975-77; spl. cons. on social policy Bank Am., 1973-75, Pres. cabinet com. opportunities for Spanish Speaking, 1974; cons. Latin Am. policy Inst. Strategic and Internat. Studies, Georgetown U., 1969; dir. Applied Solar Energy Corp., 1979—, Inter-Am. Devel. Inst., 1978—; mem. Ctr. Study Hemispheric Priorities, Am. Enterprise Inst., 1979—, Commn. of Califs., 1978-80, internat. adv. bd. U.S.-Mex. Studies Ctr., U. Calif.-San Diego, 1980—, Pres. Cabinet Com. on the Aging, 1971-72, spl. envoy to Peru for Earthquake Relief, 1970; lectr. Inter-Am. Def. Coll., 1978; mem. adv. bd. Nat. Victims of Crime, 1983—. Organizer sports and music goodwill tour Latin Am., People to People Found. and Inst. Internat. Edn., 1959; mem. adv. council Latin Am. Inst. Heritage Found., 1986—; Rep. candidate for Congress, 1969, 76; mem. Rep. State Cen.Com., Calif., 1973-76, steering com. Bush for Pres., 1979-80, adv. council Rep. Nat. Com., mem. com. nat. security and internat. affairs, 1978—. Served to 2d lt. U.S. Army, 1956-57. Clubs: Regency Racquet (McLean, Va.), Federal City (Washington). Immigration, naturalization, and customs, Private international, Public international. Office: O'Connor & Hannan 1919 Pennsylvania Ave NW Suite 800 Washington DC 20006

BLATT, SOLOMON, JR., judge; b. Sumter, S.C., Aug. 20, 1921; s. Solomon and Ethel (Green) B.; m. Carolyn Gaden, Sept. 12, 1942; children—Gregory, Sheryl Blatt Hooper, Brian. A.B., U. S.C., 1941, LL.B., 1946. Bar: S.C. Ptnr. Blatt & Fales, Barnwell, S.C., 1946-71; judge U.S. Dist. Ct. S.C., Charleston, 1971-86, chief judge, 1986—. Judicial administration. Office: PO Box 835 Charleston SC 29402

BLATTNER, JEFFREY HIRSH, lawyer; b. Pitts., Nov. 13, 1954; s. Walter M. and Edith (Hamburger) B.; m. Deborah Kaple, Aug. 11, 1985. BA summa cum laude, U. Pa., 1975; JD magna cum laude, Harvard U., 1980. Bar: D.C. 1981, U.S. Dist. Ct. D.C. 1982, U.S. Ct. Appeals (D.C. cir.) 1982. Law clk. to judge U.S. Dist. Ct. Mass., Boston, 1980-81; assoc. Wald, Harkrader & Ross, Washington, 1982; legis. fellow Sen. Gary Hart, Washington, 1982; law clk. to assoc. justice Potter U.S. Supreme Ct., Washington, 1982-83; assoc. Rogovin, Huge & Lenzner, Washington, 1983-87; counsel subcom. on immigration and refugee affairs U.S. Senate, Washington, 1987—. Mem. ABA, Phi Beta Kappa. Jewish. Office: US Senate Subcom Immigration Senate Office Bldg Room 518 Washington DC 20510

BLAUSTEIN, FRANCES JAN, lawyer; b. Detroit, Nov. 15, 1949; d. Eugene Paul and Mary (Sylvester) Malinowski; m. John L. Blaustein, Apr. 14, 1979; children: Peter L., Michael J. BA, U. Mich., 1970; JD, U. Calif., Berkeley, 1977. Bar: Calif. 1977. From assoc. to ptnr. Heller, Ehrman, White & McAuliffe, San Francisco, 1977-86; ptnr. Gordon & Rees, San Francisco, 1987—. Mem. ABA, Internat. Bar Assn., Internat. Fiscal Assn., Boalt Hall Alumni Assn. (bd. dirs. 1980—, pres.). Personal income taxation, Corporate taxation, Private international. Office: Gordon & Rees 601 Montgomery St San Francisco CA 94104

BLAZEK, DORIS DEFIBAUGH, lawyer; b. Easton, Md., Nov. 17, 1943; d. George W. and Nola M. (Buterbaugh) Defibaugh; m. Edwin L. Blazek, Aug. 11, 1967; children—Christine T., Judson M. B.A., Goucher Coll., 1965; J.D., Georgetown U., 1968. Bar: D.C. 1969, Virgin Islands 1969, U.S. Ct. Appeals (3d cir.) 1969, U.S. Ct. Appeals (D.C. cir.) 1971, Md. 1979. Gen. practice with Warren H. Young, U.S. Virgin Islands, 1968-70; assoc. Covington & Burling, Washington, 1970-76, ptnr., 1976—. Mem. Am. Coll. Probate Counsel. Estate planning, Probate, Estate taxation. Office: Covington & Burling 1201 Pennsylvania Ave NW PO Box 7566 Washington DC 20044

BLAZEK, GEORGE THOMAS, lawyer; b. Omaha, Nebr., Mar. 31, 1951; s. George Rudolph and Mary Irene (Shramek) B.; m. Donna Jean Cavanaugh, Dec. 27, 1975; children: Mary Frances, Bridget Anne. BSBA, Creighton U., 1973; MHA, St. Louis U., 1975; JD, Creighton U., 1978. Bar: Nebr. 1978, U.S. Dist. Ct. Nebr. 1978. Assoc. Ellick, Spire & Jones, Omaha, 1978-84; ptnr. Ellick & Jones, Omaha, 1985—; bd. dirs. Health Ventures, Omaha, HPCM, Omaha. Mem. ABA, Nebr. Bar Assn., Omaha Bar Assn. Republican. Roman Catholic. Avocations: fishing, camping, outdoor activities. Estate planning, Probate, General corporate. Home: 674 N 58th St Omaha NE 68132-2002 Office: Ellick & Jones 8805 Indian Hills Dr Suite 280 Omaha NE 68114-4070

BLAZIER, JOHN CHARLES, lawyer; b. El Paso, Tex., June 5, 1944; s. John Charles and Bertha (DeLeeuw) B.; m. Fleur Annette Christensen, Apr. 7, 1972; children—John Christensen, Bernard Michael. B.S., U. Tex.-El Paso, 1966; J.D., U. Tex.-Austin, 1969; LL.M. in Taxation, NYU, 1973. Bar: Tex. 1969, U.S. Dist. Ct. (no. dist.) Tex. 1973, U.S. Dist. Ct. (we. dist.) Tex. 1976, U.S. Dist. Ct. (so. dist.) Tex. 1978. Gift estate tax atty. IRS, Austin, 1972; assoc. Nieman & Nieman, 1974-77; sole practice, Austin, 1977—. Editor-in-chief Tex. Law Forum, U. Tex., 1969. Served with JAGC, U.S. Army. Decorated Bronze Star (2), Army Commendation medal, Meritorious Service medal. Mem. ABA, State Bar Tex., Travis County Bar Assn. Real property, Probate, General corporate. Office: 1600 MBank Tower Suite 1600 Austin TX 78701

BLAZZARD, NORSE NOVAR, lawyer; b. St. Johns, Ariz., July 8, 1937; s. Howard N. and Viola (Greer) B.; m. Mary Elizabeth Jecker, June 15, 1958; children—Howard Norse, Mary Catherine; m. 2d, Judith A. Hasenauer, July 2, 1977. A.B., Stanford U., 1959; J.D., U. Calif. Hastings 1962; C.L.U. Bar: Calif. 1963, U.S. Dist. Ct. (no. dist.) Calif. 1966, Conn. 1974, U.S. Dist. Ct. Conn. 1975, U.S. Supreme Ct. 1975, U.S. Ct. Appeals (2d cir.) 1978, U.S. Ct. Appeals (D.C. cir.) 1977. Counsel, Calif. Western Life Ins. Co., Sacramento, 1966-70; sr. v.p., gen. counsel NARe Life Service Co., Palo Alto, Calif., 1970-74; mng. ptnr. Blazzard, Grodd & Hasenauer, Westport, Conn., 1974—. Bd. govs. Norwalk Symphony, 1979. Served to capt. JAGC, U.S. Army, 1692-66. Decorated Army Commendation medal. Mem. ABA, Calif. Bar Assn., Fed. Bar Assn., Conn. Bar Assn., D.C. Bar Assn., Am. Soc. C.L.U.s (pres. Fairfield County chpt. 1977-79). Republican. Mormon. Insurance, Corporate taxation, Securities. Office: Blazzard Grodd & Hasenauer PC PO Box 5108 Westport CT 06881

BLECK, MICHAEL JOHN, lawyer; b. Michigan City, Ind., Apr. 8, 1950; s. Eugene and Joan (Mathias) B.; m. Sally Bulleit, Aug. 19, 1972; children—Andrew, Erica. A.B. with distinction, DePauw U., 1972; J.D. cum laude, Ind. U., 1975. Bar: Ind. 1975, Minn. 1977, U.S. Dist. Ct. Ind. 1975, U.S. Dist. Ct. Minn. 1977, U.S. Ct. Appeals (8th cir.) 1978. Law clk. to judge U.S. Ct. Appeals (8th cir.), Des Moines, 1975-76; assoc. Oppenheimer, Wolff & Donnelly, Mpls., 1977-82, ptnr. 1983—. Articles editor Ind. Law Rev., 1974-75. Trustee Mayflower Community Congregational Ch. Mem. Minn. State Bar Assn. (ct. rules com. 1981—), Hennepin County Bar Assn. (ct. rules com. 1981—), Ind. State Bar Assn., Ramsey County Bar Assn., ABA (civil litigation sect.). Democrat. Federal civil litigation, Securities, Labor. Home: 4650 W 44th St Edina MN 55424 Office: Oppenheimer Wolff & Donnelly 4800 IDS Ctr Minneapolis MN 55402

BLEICH, DAVID LLOYD, lawyer; b. Bklyn., Dec. 14, 1943; s. Martin and Dorothy (Reman) B.; m. Karen Christine Manson, Jan. 21, 1978; children: Brian Andrew, Katherine Anne. BS in Econs., Rensselaer Polytech. Inst., 1964; LLB, NYU, 1967. Bar: N.Y. 1968, U.S. Dist. Ct. (so. and ea. dists.) N.Y. 1969. From assoc. to ptnr. Shearman & Sterling, N.Y.C., 1967—. Served to capt. U.S. Army, 1967-69, Vietnam. Mem. ABA (bus. bankruptcy com.), N.Y. State Bar Assn. (lectr. 1982—, chmn. bankruptcy com. 1985—), Assn. of Bar of City of N.Y., Practising Law Inst. (lectr. 1982-84). Bankruptcy, Banking, Contracts commercial. Home: 17 Hampton Rd Scarsdale NY 10583 Office: Shearman & Sterling 153 E 53d St New York NY 10022

BLEIWEISS, SHELL J., lawyer; b. Chgo., Mar. 7, 1950; s. Ben and Berte (Melin) B.; m. Patricia Lynn Heck, Dec. 19, 1970 (div. 1976); m. Jo Ellen Rosencrans, May 21, 1985; 1 child, Michael Lawrence. BA, So. Ill. U., 1971, MS, 1974; JD, Northwestern U., 1982. Bar: Ill. 1982, U.S. Dist. Ct. (no. dist.) Ill. 1982. Wildlife ecologist Jack McCormick & Assoc., Devon, Pa., 1973-76; project mgr. Betz Converse Murdoch, Plymouth Meeting, Pa., 1976-78; cons. McGraw Hill Publ., N.Y.C., 1978-79; assoc. Sidley & Austin, Chgo., 1981-85, Coffield, Ungaretti, Harris & Slavin, Chgo., 1985—. Environ. advisor Roland Burris for Atty. Gen. Campaign, Ill., 1986. NSF fellow, 1970. Mem. ABA, Chgo. Bar Assn. Environment, Health, Administrative and regulatory. Office: Coffield Ungaretti Harris & Slavin 3500 Three 1st National Plaza Chicago IL 60602

BLENKO, DON BALMAN, lawyer; b. Pitts., May 25, 1929; s. Walter John and Ardis Leah (Jones) B.; m. Katherine Crawford MacDonald, July 16, 1952; children: David B., Thomas M., Katherine A., Don B. Jr., James C. BA, Amherst Coll., 1950; JD, U. Pa., 1953. Bar: Pa. 1954, U.S. Dist. Ct. (ea. dist.) Pa. 1954, U.S. Ct. Appeals (3d cir.) 1954, U.S. Supreme Ct. 1958. Assoc. Morgan, Lewis & Bockius, Phila., 1954-62; assoc. counsel Ford Motor Co., Phila., 1962-75; sr. counsel Atlantic Richfield Co., Phila., 1975—. Mem. ABA, Pa. Bar Assn., Phila. Bar Assn., Phi Beta Kappa. Republican. Presbyterian. Antitrust, Administrative and regulatory, General corporate. Home: 512 Rose Ln Haverford PA 19041 Office: Atlantic Richfield Co 1500 Market St Philadelphia PA 19101

BLENKO, WALTER J(OHN), JR., lawyer; b. Pitts., June 15, 1926; s. Walter J. and Ardis Leah (Jones) B.; m. Joy Kinneman, Apr. 9, 1949; children—John W., Andrew W. B.S., Carnegie-Mellon U., 1950; J.D., U. Pitts., 1953. Bar: Pa. 1954. Practice Law, Pitts., 1954—; ptnr. Eckert, Seamans, Cherin & Mellott. Served with U.S. Army, 1944-46. Decorated Bronze Star. Fellow Am. Coll. Trial Lawyers; mem. ABA, Pa. Bar Assn., Allegheny County Bar Assn., Am. Patent Law Assn., Patent Law Assn. Pitts. (pres. 1977-78), Assn. Bar City of N.Y. Clubs: Duquesne, University. Patent, Trademark and copyright, Federal civil litigation. Home: 4073 Middle Rd Allison Park PA 15101 Office: 600 Grant St 42d Floor Pittsburgh PA 15219

BLEVINS, JEFFREY ALEXANDER, lawyer; b. Forest Hills, N.Y., June 18, 1955; s. William E. and Mary J. Blevins; m. Pamela A. Manos, Nov. 26, 1983. BA, Denison U., 1977; JD, DePaul U., 1981. Bar: Ill. 1981, U.S. Dist. Ct. (no. dist.) Ill. 1981, U.S. Dist. Ct. (we. dist.) Wis. 1984, U.S. Ct. Appeals (7th cir.) 1984. Personnel specialist Comerica Bank, Detroit, 1979-80; assoc. Bell, Boyd & Lloyd, Chgo., 1981—. Editor in chief DePaul Law Rev., 1980. Mem. ABA (litigation and labor sects.), Chgo. Bar Assn., Omnicron Delta Epsilon. Republican. Congregationalist. Labor, Federal civil litigation, State civil litigation.

BLEWETT, ROBERT NOALL, lawyer; b. Stockton, Calif., July 12, 1915; s. Stephen Noall and Bess Errol (Simard) B.; m. Virginia Weston, Mar. 30, 1940; children—Richard Weston, Carolyn Blewett Lawrence. LL.B., Stanford U., 1936, J.D., 1939. Bar: Calif. bar 1939. Dep. dist. atty. San Joaquin County, 1942-46; practice law Stockton, 1946—; mem. firm, pres. Blewett, Garretson & Hachman, Stockton, 1971—. Chmn. San Joaquin County chpt. ARC, 1947-49; v.p. Goodwill Industries, 1967-68; vice chmn. Stockton Sister City Commn., 1969-70; adv. bd. bus. adminstrn. dept. U. Pacific; trustee San Joaquin Pioneer and Haggin Galleries. Fellow Am. Coll. Probate Counsel, Am. Bar Found.; mem. State Bar Calif. (mem. exec. com. of conf. of dels. 1969-72, vice chmn. 1971-72), Am. Bar Assn., Am. Judicature Soc., Am. Law Inst., Stockton C. of C., Delta Theta Phi, Theta Xi. Republican. Clubs: Rotary, Yosemite, San Francisco Comml, Masons, Shriners. Estate planning, Probate, General corporate. Home: 3016 Dwight Way Stockton CA 95203 Office: 141 E Acacia St Stockton CA 95202

BLEY, JOSEPH RUSSELL, JR., lawyer; b. St. Louis, Mar. 23, 1939; s. J. Russell Sr. and Esther H. (Ashdown) B.; m. Nina Valmonte, Aug. 9, 1969; children: J. Russell III, Maya Christina. BA, St. Louis U., 1961; JD, U. Notre Dame, 1964. Bar: Mo. 1964, U.S. Dist. Ct. (ea. dist.) Mo. 1966. Law clk. to presiding justice U.S. Ct. Appeals (7th cir.), Chgo., 1964-65; atty. Monsanto Co., St. Louis, 1965-75, asst. corp. counsel, 1975-77, assoc. corp. counsel, 1977-86, asst. sec., 1978—, asst. gen. counsel corp., 1986—. Survey editor U. Notre Dame Law Rev., 1963-64; contbr. articles to profl. jours. Chmn. St. Louis U. Alumni Council, 1976-80. Mem. ABA, Mo. Bar Assn., Bar Assn. Met. St. Louis, Am. Soc. Corp. Secs. (pres. St. Louis Regional Group 1984-85, nat. bd. dirs 1986—). Roman Catholic. Avocation: tennis. General corporate, Securities. Home: 14 Williamsburg Rd Saint Louis MO 63141 Office: Monsanto Co 800 N Lindbergh Blvd Saint Louis MO 63167

BLINDER, ALBERT ALLAN, judge; b. N.Y.C., Nov. 27, 1925; s. William and Sarah (Gold) B.; m. Meredith Zaretzki, Nov. 16, 1961 (dec.); 1 son, Adam Z.; m. Joan Goodman, Jan. 20, 1985. A.B., N.Y. U., 1944, postgrad., 1944-45; J.D., Harvard U., 1948. Bar: N.Y. 1949, U.S. dist. ct. (so. dist.) N.Y. 1953, U.S. Ct. Apls. (2d cir.) 1953; U.S. Sup. Ct. 1967. Asst. U.S. atty. so. dist. N.Y., 1950-53; asst. dist. atty. County of Bronx, N.Y., 1954-60; ptnr. Saxe, Bacon & O'Shea, N.Y.C., 1960-64; ptnr. Blinder, Steinhaus & Hochhauser, N.Y.C., 1965-73; judge N.Y. State Ct. Clms., N.Y.C., 1973—; asst. counsel N.Y.C. Bd. High Edn., 1953-54; research counsel N.Y. Commn. on the Law of Estates, 1965; assoc. counsel N.Y. Commn. Revision of Penal Law, 1966-70; asst. counsel N.Y. Commn. on Eminent Domain, 1970-73.; research asst. N.Y. Commn. State Ct. System, 1971-73. Mem. ABA, Internat. Bar Assn., N.Y. State Bar Assn., Assn. Bar City N.Y., N.Y. County Lawyers Assn., Am. Arbitration Assn. (mem. nat. panel arbitrators 1965-73). Assoc. editor: Am. Criminal Law Quarterly, 1968-70; mem. adv. bd. Am. Criminal Law Quarterly, 1969-70. State civil litigation, Government contracts and claims, Real property. Office: Chambers Two World Trade Center Suite 8403 New York NY 10047

BLINKOFF, JAMES BLADEN, lawyer; b. Buffalo, Aug. 4, 1941; s. Maurice and Goldene P. (Jacobstein) B.; m. Jeanne E. Eckardt, May 21, 1966; children: Rachel, Andrew. A.B., Princeton U., 1963; LL.B., U. Pa., 1966. Bar: D.C. 1967. Law clk. to assoc. justice Pa. Supreme Ct., 1966-67; assoc. Fried, Frank, Harris, Shriver & Jacobson, Washington, 1967-75, ptnr., 1975-87; ptnr. Content, Tatusko, Patterson, Siegel & Blinkoff, Washington, 1987—. Vice chmn. Montgomery County Human Relations Commn., also chmn. employment panel. Mem. ABA, D.C. Bar Assn., Bar Assn. D.C., Internat. Council Shopping Ctrs. Real property. Home: 10601 Shady Circle Silver Spring MD 20903 Office: Fried Frank Harris Shriver & Jacobson 1001 Pennsylvania Ave NW Washington DC 20004

BLISH, JOHN HARWOOD, lawyer; b. Racine, Wis., May 9, 1937; s. Wesley Wainwright and Lois Margaret (Jensen) B.; m. Edith Josephine Smith, Aug. 5, 1961; children—Geoffrey Harwood, Catherine Elizabeth. A.B., Brown U., 1959; J.D., U. Mich., 1965. Bar: R.I. 1965, U.S. Dist. Ct. R.I. 1967, U.S. Ct. Appeals (1st cir.) 1973, U.S. Ct. Appeals (Fed. cir.) 1985. Assoc. Edwards & Angell, Providence, 1965-73, ptnr., 1973-86, Blish & Cavanagh, Providence, 1986—. Bd. overseers Moses Brown Sch., Providence, 1978-81; bd. dirs., past pres. Sophia Little Home, Cranston, R.I.; trustee Providence Country Day Sch., East Providence, R.I. Served to lt. j.g. USN, 1959-62. Fellow Am. Coll. Trial Lawyers; mem. R.I. Bar Assn., ABA, Am. Judicature Soc., Assoc. Alumni Brown U. (past bd. dirs., sec.), Order of Coif, Phi Delta Phi. Clubs: Univ., Brown of R.I. (trustee, past pres.) (Providence); Agawam Hunt (East Providence); Acoaxet (Westport, Mass.). Federal civil litigation, State civil litigation. Home: 66 Catlin Ave Rumford RI 02916 Office: Blish & Cavanagh 30 Exchange Terr Providence RI 02903

BLISS, DONALD TIFFANY, JR., lawyer; b. Norwalk, Conn., Nov. 24, 1941; s. Donald Tiffany and Marina (Popova) B.; m. Nancy Arnold, Sept. 14, 1974; children—Evan Hale, Bion Northam. J.D., Harvard U., 1966. Bar: D.C. 1971, N.Y. 1969, U.S. Supreme Ct. 1975, U.S. Dist. Ct. D.C. 1975, U.S. Ct. Appeals (D.C. cir.) 1971, U.S. Ct. Appeals (5th cir.) 1979, U.S. Ct. Appeals (11th cir.) 1981, U.S. Ct. Appeals (3rd cir.) 1981, U.S. Ct. Appeals (9th cir.) 1984. Peace Corps atty. Micronesia, 1966-67; legis. counsel Congress of Micronesia, 1968; cons. judiciary Am. Samoa, 1968; assoc. firm LeBoeuf, Lamb, Leiby & McCrae, N.Y.C., 1969; asst. to sec. HEW, 1969-72; spl. asst. to adminstr. EPA, 1972-73; exec. sec. AID, 1973-74; dep. gen. counsel U.S. Dept. Transp., 1975-77, acting gen. counsel, 1976-77; ptnr. firm O'Melveny & Myers, Washington, 1977—; Maritime Adv. Com., 1984-85; pres. Harvard Law Sch. Assn. D.C., 1985-86; dep. chmn. Transp. Sect. FBA; mem. interior task force Grace Commn.; mem. governing bd., exec. com. Rippon Soc. Recipient spl. citation HEW, 1972, 73; Pres.'s Cert. Exec. Mgmt., 1973; Superior Achievement award Dept. Transp., 1976. Mem. ABA, Fed. Bar Assn., D.C. Bar Assn. Club: Capitol Hill. Author: Making Transportation Policy, 1976; No Fault Insurance Legislation, 1977; Regulatory Retorm, 1978. Administrative and regulatory, Federal civil litigation. Home: 5809 Bradley Blvd Bethesda MD 20814

BLISS, JAMES IRELAND, lawyer; b. Milw., June 10, 1944; s. Rodger Lewis Bliss and Marian Duane (Ireland) Littrell; m. Rose Marie Ranney, Aug. 21, 1965; children: Rodger Lee, William Ireland. BS, U. Ill., 1965, JD, 1967. Bar: Ill. 1967, Mo. 1970, U.S. Dist. Ct. (no. dist.) Ill. 1967, U.S. Ct. Appeals (7th cir.) 1968. Assoc. Keck, Mahin & Cate, Chgo., 1967-69, Monsanto Co., St. Louis, 1969-71; pres. Bliss Group Co., Bloomington, Ill., 1971—; bd. dirs. Nat. Fire and Casualty Co., Bloomington, 1980—; pres. Govtl. Ins. Mgrs., Inc., Bloomington, 1977—. Contbr. articles to profl. jours. Mem. ABA, Ill. State Bar Assn., Mo. Bar Assn., Ind. State Bar Assn., Inter-Am. Bar Assn. Office: Bliss Group Cos 2801 E Empire Bloomington IL 61702

BLITZ, STEPHEN MICHAEL, lawyer; b. N.Y.C., July 29, 1941; s. Leo and Dorothy B.; m. Ellen Sue Mintzer, Sept. 23, 1962; children: Catherine Denise, Thomas Joseph. B.A., Columbia U., 1962, B.S. in Elec. Engring., 1963; LL.B., Stanford U., 1966. Bar: Calif. 1967, U.S. Dist. Ct. (cen. dist.) Calif. 1967. Law clk. to judge U.S. Dist. Ct. Central Dist. Calif., 1966-67; ptnr. Gibson, Dunn & Crutcher, Los Angeles, 1967—; adj. prof. law U. West Los Angeles Sch. Law, 1978-80. Mem. ABA, Los Angeles County Bar Assn. (exec. com. real property section 1986—) , Order of Coif. Real property, General corporate. Office: Gibson Dunn & Crutcher 2029 Century Park E Suite 4100 Los Angeles CA 90067

BLIXT, ROY ELOF, retired judge; b. Etna, Nebr., Apr. 12, 1915; s. Elof E. and Alice D. (Oman) B. AB, U. Nebr., 1940, JD, 1941. Bar: Nebr. 1940, U.S. Dist. Ct. Nebr. 1946, U.S. Supreme Ct. 1962. County atty. Blaine County, Brewster, Nebr., 1941-50; dep. county atty Custer County, Nebr., 1965-74; judge County Ct., Ord, Nebr., 1976-87. Mem. Nebr. Rep. State Com., 1957; city treas., Arnold, Nebr., 1951-73. Served with U.S. Army, 1943-46. Mem. ABA. Presbyterian. Club: Rotary. Lodges: Moose, Masons, Shriners, K.T., Elks. Home: 1514 1/2 L St Ord NE 68822

BLOCH, ALAN NEIL, federal judge; b. Pitts., Apr. 12, 1932; s. Gustave James and Molly Dorothy B.; m. Elaine Claire Amdur, Aug. 24, 1957; children: Rebecca Lee, Carolyn Jean, Evan Amdur. B.S. in Econs, U. Pa., 1953; J.D., U. Pitts., 1958. Bar: Pa. 1959. Indsl. engr. U.S. Steel Corp., 1953; pvt. practice, then individual practice Pitts., 1959-79; U.S. judge Western Dist. Pa., Pitts., 1979—. Contbr. articles to legal publs. Vice chmn. Stadium Authority Pitts., 1970—; bd. dirs. St. John's Gen. Hosp., Pitts., 1975—. Served with AUS, 1953-55. Mem. Am. Bar Assn., Pa. Bar Assn., Allegheny County Bar Assn., Acad. Trial Lawyers Allegheny County. Jewish. Club: Allegheny. Office: US District Court 1014 US Post Office and Courthouse Pittsburgh PA 15219 *

BLOCH, MARC JOEL, lawyer; b. Cleve., Feb. 14, 1943; s. David R. and Sylvia C. (Levof) B.; m. Barbara Ann Bandler; children—Stephen, Robin. B.A., Miami U., 1965; J.D., Cleve. State Law Sch., 1969. Bar: Ohio 1969. Field atty NLRB, Cleve., 1969-72; assoc. Robert P. Duvin & Assocs., Cleve., 1973-79; prin. Duvin, Flinker & Cahn, Cleve., 1979—. Pres. Pub. Sector Labor Relations Assn. Cleve. Mem. Greater Cleve. Bar Assn., ABA, Fed. Bar Assn., Phi Alpha Delta. Club: Beechmont Country. Contbr. numerous articles in field to profl. publs. Labor. Office: 1400 TransOhio Bank Bldg Cleveland OH 44115

BLOCH, SUSAN LOW, law educator; b. N.Y.C., Sept. 15, 1944; d. Ernest and Ruth (Frankel) Low; m. Richard I. Bloch, July 10, 1966; children—Rebecca, Michael. B.A. in Math., Smith Coll., 1966; M.A. in Math., U. Mich., 1968, M.A. in Computer Sci., Ph.C., 1972, J.D., 1975. Bar: D.C. 1975. Law clk. to chief judge U.S. Ct. Appeals, Washington, 1975-76; law clk. to assoc. justice Marshall, U.S. Supreme Ct., Washington, 1976-77; assoc. Wilmer, Cutler & Pickering, Washington, 1978-82; assoc. prof. Georgetown U. Law Ctr., Washington, 1983—; contbr. Mich. Law Rev., Wis. Law Rev., Supreme Ct. Preview, 1984, Voice of Am., 1983. Active, Common Cause, ACLU, Women's Legal Def. Fund. Mem. ABA, D.C. Bar (Bicentennial of Constn.), Bar Assn., Soc. Am. Law Tchrs., Inst. Pub. Representation (bd. dirs.), Order of Coif, Phi Beta Kappa, Sigma Xi. Legal education, Legal history. Home: 4335 Cathedral Ave NW Washington DC 20016 Office: Georgetown U Law Ctr 600 New Jersey Ave NW Washington DC 20001

BLOCK, DENNIS JEFFERY, lawyer; b. Bronx, N.Y., Sept. 1, 1942; s. Martin and Betty (Berger) B.; m. Hedy Elizabeth Troupin, Nov. 27, 1967; children: Robert, Tracy, Meredith. B.A., U. Buffalo, 1964; LL.B., Bklyn. Law Sch., 1967. Bar: N.Y. 1968, U.S. Dist. Ct. (ea. dist.) N.Y., U.S. Dist. Ct. (so. dist.) N.Y., U.S. Ct. Appeals (2d, 3d and 8th cirs.). Br. chief SEC, N.Y.C., 1967-72; assoc. Weil, Gotshal & Manges, N.Y.C., 1972-74, ptnr., 1974—. Co-editor: The Corporate Counselor's Desk Book, 1982, 2d edit, 1985, The Business Judgment Rule: Fiduciary Duties of Corporate Directors and Officers, Law & Business, Inc., 1987; contbr. articles to profl. jours. Mem. ABA, Am. Law Inst. Home: 22 Maple Dr Port Washington NY 11050 Office: Weil Gotshal & Manges 767 Fifth Ave New York NY 10153

BLOCK, FREDERIC, lawyer; b. Bklyn., June 6, 1934; s. Norman Louis and Florence (Ferman) B.; m. Estelle Lenora Kaufman, Dec. 18, 1960; children: Neil M., Nancy L. AB, Ind. U., 1956; LLB, Cornell U., 1959. Bar: N.Y. 1959, U.S. Supreme Ct. 1967, U.S. Ct. Appeals (2d cir.) 1971, U.S. Dist. Ct. (ea. and so. dists.) N.Y. 1975. Law clk. appellate div. N.Y. State Supreme Ct., Albany, 1960-61; ptnr. Block & Hamburger, Smithtown, N.Y.; lectr. Cornell U. Law Sch., Ithaca, N.Y., 1984—. Composer mus. show Professionally Speaking, 1986. Counsel edn. com. N.Y. State Constl. Conv., 1967; mem. Suffolk County Charter Rev. Commn., N.Y., 1968-70. Named Man of Yr., Cystic Fibrosis Found., 1984. Fellow Am. Bar Found., N.Y. Bar Found.; mem. N.Y. State Bar Assn. (spl. counsel 1981, v.p. 1983-86), Suffolk County Bar Assn. (pres. 1979-80, Pres.'s award 1985), N.Y. State Assn. Sch. Attys. (pres. 1982), N.Y. State Conf. Bar Leaders (chmn. 1980-82). Avocation: musical composition. Home: 15 Stern Dr Port Jefferson NY 11777 Office: Block & Hamburger 202 E Main St Smithtown NY 11787

BLOCK, LESTER H., lawyer; b. Buffalo, Sept. 14, 1906; s. Barnett and Deborah Block; children: Bruce, Brian. Student, NYU, 1923-24; BA, U. Va., 1927; LLB, U. Ga., 1928; postdoctoral, Yale U., 1931. Bar: Ga. 1928, N.Y. 1931, U.S. Dist. Ct. (we. dist.) N.Y. 1931. Ptnr. Block & Colucci, Buffalo, 1931—; Pres. Rosa Coplan Home, 1966-68. Mem. bd. of trustees Columbus Hosp., 1973-78, Temple Beth Zion; bd. dirs. Lakes Area Regional Med. Program, Inc.; v.p. United Jewish Fedn., Buffalo, 1973. Mem. ABA, Am. Arbitration Assn. (panel of arbitrators), Alpha Epsilon Pi. Club: Montepiore (pres. 1973—). General practice, Bankruptcy, Consumer commercial. Home: 78 Hallam Rd Buffalo NY 14216 Office: Block & Colucci 518 Statler Towers Buffalo NY 14202

BLOCK, MARTIN, lawyer; b. N.Y.C., July 14, 1937; s. Leonard and Rose (Tenzer) B.; m. Linda Zuckerman, Dec. 25, 1965 (div. 1979); children—Sarin, Bryson. Student Bklyn. Coll., 1959-61, NYU, 1962-63; LL.B., Bklyn. Law Sch., 1965. Bar: N.Y. 1965, U.S. Dist. Ct. (so. and ea. dists.) N.Y. 1966, U.S. Ct. Appeals (2d cir. 1979). Assoc. Seymour L. Colin, N.Y.C., 1965-70; assoc. then ptnr. Queller, Fisher, Block & Wisotsky, N.Y.C., 1970-85; ptnr. Sanders, Sanders, Block & Byrne, P.C. 1985—; guest lectr. Lawline-Cable TV, N.Y.C., 1984. Served as staff sgt. USNG, 1959-64. Mem. Nassau County Bar Assn., Met. Women's Bar Assn., N.Y. State Trial Lawyers Assn. (lectr. 1984), N.Y. County Lawyers Assn., Assn. Trial Lawyers Am., Am. Arbitration Assn. Democrat. Jewish. Personal injury. Home: 375 South End Ave Apt 10P New York NY 10280 Office: Sanders Sanders Block & Byrne PC 332 Willis Ave Mineola NY 11501

BLOCK, NELSON RICHARD, lawyer; b. San Antonio, Tex., Mar. 24, 1951; s. Norman and Ethel (Poliakoff) B.; m. Linda Freedman, Aug. 22, 1976; children: Adam S., Brian I., Jordan A. BA, Johns Hopkins U., 1973; JD, U. Tex., 1976. Bar: Tex. 1976. Law clk. to judge 14th Ct. Appeals, Houston, 1976-77; assoc. Sheinfeld, Maley & Kay, Houston, 1977-82, ptnr., 1982—; speaker various insts. Mem. exec. bd. Sam Houston area council Boy Scouts Am., Houston, 1984—. Mem. ABA, Tex. Bar Assn. (chmn. uniform comml. code com. 1982-84), Houston Bar Assn., Tex. Bar Found., Selden Soc. (state correspondent 1978—). Avocations: camping, hiking, reading, history, sketching. Banking, Contracts commercial. Office: Sheinfeld Maley & Kay 1st City Tower Suite 3700 Houston TX 77002

BLOCK, STEVEN ROBERT, lawyer; b. Miami Beach, Fla., Dec. 6, 1955; s. Mason J. Block and Joan Sandra (Bromberg) Gitlin; m. Sharla Rae Wright, Oct. 16, 1983. BA in Polit. Sci., Ind. U., 1977; JD, Emory U., 1980. Bar: Tex. 1980. Assoc. Johnson & Swanson, Dallas, 1980-85; assoc. Akin, Gump, Strauss, Hauer & Feld, Dallas, 1985-87, ptnr., 1987—; tchr. So. Meth. U. Southwestern Graduate Sch. Banking, Dallas, 1985. Research editor Emory U. Law Rev., 1979. Wendell Wilkie fellow Ind. U., 1977. Mem. ABA (bank holding cos. and related nonbank matter subcom. corp. banking and bus. law sect.), Tex. Bar Assn. (speaker 1983), Dallas Bar Assn., N.J. Bankers' Assn. (speaker 1983), Okla. Bankers' Assn. (speaker 1984), Phi Beta Kappa. Republican. Jewish. Avocations: chess, golf, sports, reading. Banking, General corporate, Securities. Office: Akin Gump Strauss Hauer & Feld 4100 1st City Ctr Dallas TX 75201-4618

BLOEDE, VICTOR CARL, lawyer, university executive; b. Woodwardville, Md., July 17, 1917; s. Carl Schon and Eleanor (Eck) B.; m. Ellen Louise Miller, May 9, 1947; children—Karl Abbott, Pamela Elena. A.B., Dartmouth Coll., 1940; J.D. cum laude, U. Balt., 1950; LL.M. in Pub. Law, Georgetown U., 1967. Bar: Md. 1950, Fed. Hawaii 1958, U.S. Supreme Ct. 1971. Sole practice Balt., 1950-64; mem. Goldman & Bloede, Balt., 1959-64; Md. counsel Seven-Up Bottling Co., Balt., 1958-64; dep. atty. gen. Pacific Trust Ter., Honolulu, 1952-53; asst. solicitor for ters. Office of Solicitor, U.S. Dept. Interior, Washington, 1953-54; atty. U.S. Justice, Honolulu, 1955-58; asst. gen. counsel Dept. Navy, Washington, 1960-61, 63-64; spl. legal cons. Md. Legislature, Legis. Council, 1963-64, 66-67; assoc. prof. U. Hawaii, 1961-63, dir. property mgmt., 1964-67; house counsel, dir. contracts and grants U. Hawaii System, 1967-82; house counsel U. Hawaii Research Corp., 1970-82; legal counsel Law of Sea Inst., 1978-82; legal cons. Research Corp. and research div., U. Hawaii, 1982—; spl. counsel to Holifield Congl. Commn. on Govt. Procurement, 1970-73. Author: Hawaii Legislative Manual, 1962, Maori Affairs, New Zealand, 1964, Oceanographic Research Vessel Operations, and Liabilities, 1972, Hawaiian Archipelago, Legal Effects of a 200 Mile Territorial Sea, 1973, Copyright-Guidelines to the 1976 Act, 1977, Forms Manual, Inventions: Policy, Law and Procedure, 1982; writer, contbr. Coll. Law Digest and other publs. on legislation and pub. law. Mem. Gov.'s Task Force Hawaii and The Sea, 1969, Citizens Housing Com. Balt., 1952-64; bd. govs. Balt. Community YMCA, 1954-64; bd. dirs. U. Hawaii Press, 1964-66, Coll. Housing Found., 1968-80; internat. rev. commn. Canada-France Hawaii Telescope Corp., 1973-82, chmn., 1973, 82; co-founder, incorporator First Unitarian Ch. Honolulu. Served to lt. comdr. USNR, 1942-45, PTO. Grantee ocean law studies NSF and Dept. Energy, 1970-80. Mem. ABA, Balt. Bar Assn., Fed. Bar Assn., Am. Soc. Internat. Law, Nat. Assn. Univ. Attys. (chmn. patents and copyrights sect. 1974-76). Government contracts and claims, Legal education, Geothermal. Home: 635 Onaha St Honolulu HI 96816

BLOEDEL, PHILIP JOHN, lawyer; b. San Antonio, May 4, 1931; s. Henry John and Clara (Knudson) B.; m. Marilyn Ann Carlson, Mar. 28, 1959; children—Holly, Eric, Cynthia, Carrie, Matthew, Thor. B.B.A., U. Minn., 1953; J.D. with honors, William Mitchell Coll., 1960. Bar: Minn. 1960, U.S. Ct. Appeals (8th cir.) 1964. Corp. counsel No. States Power Co., Mpls., 1960-62; asst. county atty. Hennepin County, Minn., 1962-65; ptnr. Bloedel, Sundberg, Slade, Mpls., 1965-70, Bloedel, Nelson, Slade, Volstad & Hawkinson, Mpls., 1970-83; ptnr. Bloedel, Slade & Hawkinson, 1983—; dir. corps. Regional commr. Region IV, U.S. Volleyball Assn., 1972-73; co-chmn. AAU Volleyball Nat. Championships, St. Paul, 1972. Served with U.S. Army, 1954-56. Mem. Hennepin County Bar Assn., Minn. Bar Assn., ABA. Clubs: Internat. Brotherhood of Magicians. General corporate, Criminal. Address: Suite 390 301 4th Ave S Minneapolis MN 55415

BLOM, DANIEL CHARLES, lawyer, investor; b. Portland, Oreg., Dec. 13, 1919; s. Charles D. and Anna (Reiner) B.; m. Ellen Lavon Stewart, June 28, 1952; children: Daniel Stewart, Nicole Jan. B.A. magna cum laude, U. Wash., 1941, postgrad., 1941-42; J.D., Harvard U., 1948; postgrad., U. Paris, 1954-55. Bar: Wash. bar 1949. Teaching fellow speech U. Wash., 1941-42; law clk. to justice Supreme Ct. Wash., 1948-49; since practiced in Seattle; asso. Graves, Kizer & Graves, 1949-51; gen. counsel Northwestern Life Ins. Co., 1952-54; partner Case & Blom, 1952-54; assoc., ptnr. Ryan, Swanson & Cleveland, 1956—; exec. v.p., gen. counsel Family Life Ins. Co., 1977-85, spl. counsel, dir., 1985—; vice chmn. Wash. Bd. Bar Examiners, 1970-72, chmn., 1972-75; mem. industry adv. com. Nat. Assn. Ins. Commrs., 1966-68; pres. Wash. Ins. Council, also Ins. Fund Found., 1971-73, gen. counsel, 1975-78; bd. dirs. Family Life Ins. Co. (sec. 1985—). Editor: Wash. State Bar Jour, 1951-52; assoc. editor: The Brief, 1975-76; Author: Life Insurance Law of the State of Washington, 1980. Chmn. jury selection Wash. Gov.'s Writer's Day Awards, 1976; bd. dirs. Crisis Clinic; trustee Bush Sch., 1971-79, v.p., 1976-77; trustee, v.p. Frye Mus., Seattle, 1976-82, World Affairs Council Seattle, 1972—, Friends of Freeway Park, 1976—; trustee Friends of Seattle Pub. Library, 1982—. Served to 2d lt. AUS, 1942-45, PTO. Decorated Bronze Star. Mem. ABA (vice chmn. com. on life ins. law, sect. ins., negligence and compensation law 1971-76, chmn. 1976-78, sect. program chmn. 1978-79, mem. council 1979-83, pub. relations com. 1981-83 com. on profl. independence of the lawyer 1984-85, com. on scope and correlation 1985-86, del. ABA to Union Internat. Des Avocats 1986—, policy coordinator Tips sect. 1986—), Wash. Bar Assn. (award of merit 1975, chmn. legal edn. liason com. 1977-78), Seattle Bar Assn., WAsh. Ins. Council (pres. 1971-73, trustee 1971-85), Am. Judicature Soc., Assn. Life Ins. Counsel, Harvard Law Sch. Assn., Am. Council Life Ins. (legis. com. 1982-85), Am. Arbitration Assn., Harvard Assn. Seattle and Western Wash. (trustee 1976-77), Phi Beta Kappa, Tau Kappa Alpha. Club: Rainier (Seattle), Harvard of Seattle, Western Washington. Insurance, General corporate. Home: 2424 Magnolia Blvd W Seattle WA 98199 Office: 3201 Bank of Calif Ctr Seattle WA 98164

BLOMELEY, JAMES LEE, JR., lawyer; b. Atlanta, Nov. 14, 1956; s. James Lee Sr. and Mary Louise (Roberts) B.; m. Susan Patricia Beall; 1 child, Allyson Faith. BS in Community Devel., Ga. State U., 1978; JD, Wake Forest U., 1981. Bar: N.C. 1981, U.S. Dist. Ct. (we. dist.) N.C. 1982. Assoc. Rudolph A. Bata, Jr., Andrews, N.C., 1981-82; ptnr. Bata & Blomeley, Andrews, 1982—. Mem. Cherokee County Bd. Elections, Murphy, N.C., 1985—; bd. dirs. Valleytown Cultural Arts and Hist. Soc., Andrews, 1986—. Mem. N.C. Bar Assn. (environ. law com.), N.C. Trial Lawyers Assn., Andrews C. of C. (pres. 1985). Democrat. Presbyterian. Criminal, State civil litigation, Local government. Home: Main Street Andrews NC 28901 Office: 302 Valley River Ave Murphy NC 28906

BLOMQUIST, ROBERT FRANK, lawyer, educator; b. Elizabeth, N.J., Oct. 9, 1951; s. Robert Andrew and Patricia Anne (Weidknecht) B.; m. Maura Crawford, June 23, 1973; children: Andrew Robert, Courtney Patricia. B.S. in Econs., U. Pa., 1973; J.D., Cornell U., 1977. Bar: N.J. 1977, U.S. Dist. Ct. N.J. 1977, U.S. Ct. Appeals (3d cir.) 1979, U.S. Supreme Ct. 1981, Ind. 1986. Assoc. Law Offices of William Wells, Mt. Holly, N.J., 1977-78; v.p., dir. firm Davis, Reberkenny & Abramowitz, Cherry Hill, N.J., 1978-86; assoc. prof. sch. law Valparaiso (Ind.) U. Editor: New Jersey Appellate Practice, 1984 (Disting. service award 1984). Bd. dirs. United Way of Burlington County, Mt. Holly, 1978-86, Medford Bd. Edn. (N.J.), 1983-86; mem. citizen adv. com. Evesham Sludge Mgmt. Study (N.J.), 1983-86; mem. Burlington County Republican Com., 1983-86. Mem. N.J. Bar Assn. (Young Lawyer of Yr. award 1985). Lutheran. Environment, Bankruptcy, Torts. dffice: Valparaiso Univ Sch Law Valparaiso IN 46383

BLOODWORTH, A(LBERT) W(ILLIAM) FRANKLIN, lawyer; b. Atlanta, Sept. 23, 1935; s. James Morgan Bartow and Elizabeth Westfield (Dimmock) B.; m. Elizabeth Howell, Nov. 24, 1967; 1 child, Elizabeth Howell. A.B. in History and French, Davidson Coll., 1957; J.D. magna cum laude with 1st honors, U. Ga., 1963. Bar: Ga. 1962, U.S. Supreme Ct. 1971. Asst. dir. alumni and pub. relations Davidson Coll., N.C., 1959-60; assoc. Hansell & Post, Atlanta, 1963-68, ptnr., 1969-84; ptnr. Bloodworth & Nix, Atlanta, 1984—; counsel organized crime com. Met. Atlanta Commn. on Crime, 1965-67; asst. sec., counsel Met. Found. Atlanta, 1968-76. Bd. dirs. Atlanta Presbytery, 1974-78; trustee Synod of Southeast, Presbyn. Ch. in U.S.A., Augusta, Ga., 1982—; trustee Big Canoe Chapel, Ga., 1983-86, chmn. bd. trustees, 1985-86. Served to 1st lt. Intelligence Corps, USAR, 1957-59. Recipient Jessie Dan MacDougal Scholarship award U. Ga. Found., 1963, Outstanding Student Leadership award Student Bar Assn., U. Ga., 1963. Fellow Am. Coll. Probate Counsel; mem. ABA, State Bar Ga., Atlanta Bar Assn., Atlanta Estate Planning Council, N. Atlanta Estate Planning Council, Phi Beta Kappa, Phi Kappa Phi, Omicron Delta Kappa, Alpha Tau Omega (pres. chpt. 1957), Phi Delta Phi (grad. of yr. 1963, pres. chpt. 1963). Republican. Presbyterian (elder). Clubs: Capital City, Lawyers (Atlanta); Sphinx, Gridiron (Athens, Ga.). Probate, Estate planning, Estate taxation. Home: 3784 Club Dr NE Atlanta GA 30319 Office: Bloodworth & Nix 3414 Peachtree Rd Suite 706 Monarch Plaza Atlanta GA 30326

BLOOM, ARNOLD SANFORD, lawyer; b. Syracuse, N.Y., Sept. 3, 1942; s. Benjamin and Sarah (Kushner) B.; m. Cirelle Dvorin, July 20, 1967; children: Brooke, Jessica, Evan. B.S., Syracuse U., 1964, M.B.A., 1967, J.D., 1967; LL.M., NYU, 1968. Bar: N.Y. 1967, U.S. Dist. Ct. (so. dist.) N.Y. 1972, U.S. Supreme Ct. 1986. Assoc. Marshall, Bratter, Greene, Allison & Tucker, N.Y.C., 1968-74; sr. atty. Kane-Miller Corp., Tarrytown, N.Y., 1974-78, gen. counsel, 1978—, v.p., 1980—. Mem. ABA, N.Y. State Bar Assn., Am. Meat Inst. (legal Com.), Westchester-Fairfield Corp. Counsel Assn., Order of Coif, Justinian Soc., Beta Alpha Psi, Alpha Kappa Psi. General corporate, General practice, Securities. Home: 8 Suzanne Ln Chappaqua NY 10514 Office: Kane-Miller Corp 555 White Plains Rd Tarrytown NY 10591

BLOOM, CHRISTOPHER ARTHUR, lawyer; b. Chgo., May 25, 1951; s. Charles G. and Lyra Anne (Eells) B.; m. Jo Anne Gazarek, Apr. 21, 1979; children: Anna Victoria, Mary Olivia. B.A. cum laude, Kenyon Coll., 1973; J.D., Ind. U., 1975. Bar: Ind. 1975, Pa. 1976, Ill. 1976, U.S. Dist. Ct. (so. dist.) Ind., 1975, U.S. Dist. Ct. (no. dist.) Ill. 1976, U.S. Dist. Ct. (no. dist.) Ind. 1980, U.S. Ct. Appeals (7th cir.) 1975, U.S. Ct. Appeals (2d cir.) 1976, U.S. Supreme Ct. 1979. Assoc. Green & Brandwein, Chgo., 1976-78; assoc. Fox & Grove, Chartered, Chgo., 1978-82, ptnr., 1982-84; ptnr. Alexander, Unikel, Bloom, Zalewa & Tenenbaum, Ltd., Chgo., 1984-86, ptnr. Meck, Mahin & Cate, 1986—; instr. Loyola U., Chgo., 1976-79; gen. counsel Orch. of Ill., Chgo., 1976—, Grant Park Concerts Soc., Chgo., 1977—. Mem. ABA, Ill. Bar Assn., Chgo. Bar Assn. (fed. tax commn.). General corporate, Computer, Corporate taxation. Home: 5490 S Shore Dr Chicago IL 60615

BLOOM, JEFFREY BRIAN, lawyer; b. Oceanside, N.Y., Dec. 14, 1953; s. Lowell and Estelle Helen (Reich) B. BS, Lehigh U., 1976; JD, Hofstra U., 1979. Bar: N.Y. 1980, U.S. Dist. Ct. (so. and ea. dists.) N.Y. 1980. Ptnr. Gair, Gair & Conason, N.Y.C., 1979—. Mem. Nassau Dem. County Com., Mineola, N.Y., 1974-85; del. Dem. Nat. Com. Conv., N.Y.C., 1980, Memphis, 1978; alt. del. N.Y. State Dem. Jud. Dist. Conv., Nassau County, N.Y., 1976-84; bd. dirs. Five Towns Dem. Club, Hewlett, N.Y., 1974-85. Mem. ABA, N.Y. State Bar Assn., Nassau County Bar Assn., Assn. Trial Lawyers Am., N.Y. State Trial Lawyers Assn., Sigma Alpha Mu (pres. 1975-76, undergraduate nat. frat. bd. govs. 1976). Jewish. Avocations: golf, tennis, football, basketball. State civil litigation, Federal civil litigation, Personal injury. Home: 340 E 64th St New York NY 10021 Office: Gair Gair & Conason 80 Pine St New York NY 10005

BLOOM, ROBERT AVRUM, lawyer; b. N.Y.C., Jan. 24, 1930; s. Samuel and Rose (Ladenheim) B; m. Joan Pivar, Apr. 19, 1959; children: Jonathan, Matthew. BA summa cum laude, Princeton U., 1951; LLB, Harvard U., 1957; PhD, N.Y.U., 1974. Bar: N.Y. 1957, U.S. Dist. Ct. (ea. dist.) N.Y. 1958. Assoc. Senator Edward J. Speno, Mineola, N.Y., 1957-59; sole practice Great Neck, N.Y., 1959-62; ptnr. Martin Bloom & Van De Walle, Great Neck, 1962-75, Hollenberg Levin Marlow & Bloom, Mineola, N.Y., 1975-79, Bloom & Amrod, Garden City, 1979-85; pres. Bloom & Esterces, P.C., Garden City, 1985-87; with Blodnick Pomeranz Schultz & Abromowitz, P.C., N.Y.C., 1987—. Pres. Pederson-Krag Mental Health Clinic, Huntington, N.Y., 1978-80; sec., treas. Found. for the Establishment of an Internat. Criminal Ct., Boston, 1972-79. Served as lt. USN, 1954-57. Mem. Internat. Space Law Inst., Nassau County Bar Assn., N.Y. State Trial Lawyers Assn. Democrat. Jewish. Personal injury, Family and matrimonial, Probate. Home: 40 E 83rd St Apt 10W New York NY 10028 Office: Blodnick Pomeranz et al 477 Madison Ave New York NY 10022 Office: 3111 New Hyde Park Rd Lake Success NY 11042

BLOOM, ROBERT THOMAS, lawyer; b. Bklyn., May 28, 1945; s. Daniel and Ruth Sarah (Kleinberg) B.; m. Roberta, Aug. 24, 1968; 1 son, Gregory Scott. B.A., Hofstra U., 1967; J.D., George Washington U., 1970; postgrad. Adelphi U., 1972-73. Bar: N.Y. 1972, U.S. Supreme Ct. 1979. Legal editor Bur. Nat. Affairs, Inc., Washington, 1970-71; dep. county atty. dep. bur. chief Tax Certiorari Bur., Nassau County Attys.' Office, Mineola, N.Y., 1971—; guest lectr. N.Y.U. Sch. Continuing Edn.; lectr. Nassau Acad. Law. Committeeman Nassau County Republican Committeemen's council, 1972-80, 1982—; mem. selection com. Homestead Housing Improvement Program, Urban Renewal Agy., Hempstead, N.Y., 1979-81; mem. Hempstead Rep. Club, 1972-80, Plainview Rep. Club, 1980—. Mem. Nassau County Bar Assn., N.Y. State Bar Assn., ABA, ASCAP, Am. Soc. Writers Legal Subjects (SCRIBES). Co-author theme song Internat. Games for Disabled, 1984. Contbr. articles on law to profl. jours. and treatises. Real property, Estate taxation. Home: 58 Sylvia Ln Plainview NY 11803 Office: Nassau County Attys Office West St Mineola NY 11501

BLOOM, STEPHEN, lawyer; b. San Francisco, June 10, 1948; s. Allan I. and Wilma Ann (Morgan) B.; m. Rebecca Joan Nelson, June 19, 1976; children: Benjamin Jacob, Molly Marie, John Robert. Student, Dartmouth Coll., 1966-68; BA in Eng., Stanford U., 1970; JD, Willamette Coll. of Law, 1977. Bar: Oreg., U.S. Dist. Ct. Oreg. Assoc. Joyce & Harding, Corvallis, Oreg., 1977-78; dep. dist. atty. Umahua County Dist. Atty.'s Office, Pendleton, Oreg., 1978-79; assoc. Morrison & Reynolds, Hermiston, Oreg., 1979-81; ptnr. Kottkamp & O'Rourke, Pendleton, 1981—. Served to lt. J.G. USNR, 1970-72. Lodges: Rotary, Elks. General practice. Office: Kottkamp & O'Rourke 331 SE 2d Pendleton OR 97801

BLOOMGARDEN, PAUL M., lawyer; b. Albany, N.Y., Apr. 8, 1943; s. Leo and Selma Bloomgarden; m. Joan R. Braderman, Mar. 14, 1974; children: Jessica, Jami. BA, U. Miami, 1965; JD, Bklyn. Law Sch., 1970. Bar: N.Y. 1970, Fla. 1972, U.S. Dist. Ct. (so. dist.) Fla. 1972. Atty. Legal Aid, N.Y.C., 1970-71; assoc. Bloom & Sachs, Miami, Fla., 1071-73; atty. Am. Title Ins. Co., Miami, Fla., 1973-75; sole practice Ft. Lauderdale, 1975-77; ptnr. Fiore & Blommgarden, Ft. Lauderdale, 1977-84, Fiore, Bloomgarden & Forman, Ft. Lauderdale, 1984—. Mem. Fla. Bar Assn., N.Y. State Bar Assn., Broward County Bar Assn., Attys.' Title Ins. Fund. Democrat. Jewish. General corporate, Probate, Real property. Office: Fiore Bloomgarden & Foreman 800 E Broward Blvd Suite 408 Fort Lauderdale FL 33301

BLOOMINGDALE, ARTHUR LEE, JR., insurance company executive; b. Omaha, Sept. 20, 1930; s. Arthur Lee and Johanna Cecilia (Coady) B.; m. Teresa Burrowes, July 2, 1955; children: Arthur Lee III, John Joseph, Michael Gerard, James Burrowes, Mary Teresa, Daniel Coady, Margaret Mary, Ann Cecilia, Timothy Cooney, Patrick Templeton. BS in Commerce cum laude, Creighton U., 1954, JD cum laude, 1954; LLM, U. Mich., 1955. CLU; bar: Nebr., 1954, U.S. Supreme Ct., 1961. Asst. prof. Creighton U., Omaha, 1955-59, assoc. prof., 1959-62, prof., 1962-71; dir. Mut. Protective Ins. Co., Omaha, 1961, exec. v.p., sec., 1969, pres., chief operating officer, treas., 1983—; chief operating officer, sr. v.p., sec. Medico Life Ins. Co., Omaha, 1983—, also bd. dirs.; counsel Omaha Charter Revision Com., 1973. Mem. Nebr. State Bar Assn., Omaha Bar Assn., Am. Trial Lawyers Assn., Internat. Assn. Ins. Counsels, Am. Arbitration Assn. General practice, Insurance, General corporate. Office: Mutual Protective Ins Co 1515 S 75th St Omaha NE 68124

BLOOMQUIST, DENNIS HOWARD, lawyer; b. Mpls. Sept. 18, 1942; s. Howard Richard and Ingrid Marit (Brostrom) B.; m. Shirley Anne Ruemele, Aug. 22, 1964; children—Michael Dennis, Eric William. B.A., Albion Coll., Mich., 1964; M.B.A., Mich. State U., 1965; J.D. cum laude, Wayne State U., 1968; LL.M., NYU, 1975. Bar: Mich. 1968, U.S. Dist. Ct. (ea. dist.) Mich. 1968, N.Y. 1971. Assoc. Parsons, Tennent, Hammond, Hardig & Ziegelman, Detroit, 1968-70, Alexander and Green, N.Y.C., 1970-73; tax counsel Mobil Oil and Mobil Corp., N.Y.C., 1973-81, gen. counsel Mobil Land Devel. Corp., N.Y.C., 1981—, real estate and land devel., Mobil Corp., 1984—; lectr. continuing legal edn. Mem. ABA, Bar Assn. Mich., N.Y. State Bar Assn. (sect. taxation, corps.) Congregationalist. Corporate taxation, Real property, General corporate. Home: 32 Edgewood Rd Scarsdale NY 10583 Office: 150 E 42d St New York NY 10017

BLOUNT, MICHAEL EUGENE, lawyer; b. Camden, N.J., July 9, 1949; s. Floyd Eugene and Dorothy Alice (Geyer) Durham; m. Janice Lynn Brown, Aug. 22, 1969; children—Kirsten Marie, Gretchen Elizabeth. B.A., U. Tex., 1971; J.D., U. Houston, 1974. Bar: Tex. 1974, Ill. 1980, D.C. 1981, U.S. Ct. Appeals (D.C. cir.) 1978, U.S. Ct. Mil. Appeals 1975, U.S. Supreme Ct. 1977. Atty. advisor Office of Gen. Counsel SEC, Washington, 1977-78, legal asst. to chmn., 1978-79; assoc. Gardner, Carton & Douglas, Chgo., 1980-84; ptnr. Arnstein, Gluck, Lehr, Barron & Milligan, Chgo., 1984-86, Seyfarth, Shaw, Fairweather & Geraldson, Chgo., 1987—. Served as lt. JAGC, USN, 1974-77. Mem. ABA (fed. regulation of securities com.), Chgo. Bar Assn.,

Order of Barons, Phi Alpha Delta (chpt. treas. 1973.) Club: Univ. of Chgo. Securities, General corporate. Home: 1432 S Highland Ave Arlington Heights IL 60005 Office: Seyfarth Shaw Fairweather & Geraldson 55 E Monroe Chicago IL 60603

BLUE, DONALD SHERWOOD, lawyer; b. Danville, Pa., Jan. 17, 1956; s. Samuel Bruce and Ellen Grace (Salsbury) B.; m. Catherine Anne Mahoney, Oct. 4, 1980; children: Mairead, Pierce. BA in Govt., Shippensburg State Coll., 1977; JD, U. Pitts., 1980. Bar: Pa. 1980, U.S. Dist. Ct. (we. dist.) Pa. 1980. Assoc. Kirkpatrick & Lockhart, Pitts., 1980-82, Papper, Hamilton & Scheetz, Harrisburg, Pa., 1982-85; gen. atty. Koppers Co. Inc., Pitts., 1985-86; assoc. Reed, Smith, Shaws & McClay, Pitts., 1986—. Mem. Order of Coif. Republican. Episcopalian. Clubs: Pitts. Athletic Assn., Fox Chapel Yacht. General corporate, Municipal bonds, Securities. Office: Reed Smith Shaw & McClay 435 6th Ave Pittsburgh PA 15219

BLUEMLE, ROBERT LOUIS, lawyer; b. Anderson, Ind., Nov. 6, 1933; s. Orville Wesley and Marguerite (Fadely) B.; children: Tiffany Windsor, Elizabeth Hayden; m. Carol Gillard Bidstrup, Aug. 6, 1979. B.S. with distinction, Ind. U., 1955, M.B.A., 1956; J.D., U. Mich., 1959. Bar: Ariz. 1959, U.S. Supreme Ct 1964. Practiced in Phoenix, 1961—; partner in charge Ariz. office Furth Fahrner Bluemle & Mason, Scottsdale; atty., fin. analyst SEC, Washington, 1959-61; contbg. film critic Phoenix Mag., 1977-80; pres. Chalk Hill Winery, Sonoma, Calif., 1983—. Past bd. dirs. Scottsdale (Ariz.) Arts Center Assn.; bd. dirs. Valley Shakespeare Theater, 1979, Ariz. State U. Found., 1987—; past bd. dirs., past pres. Greater Phoenix Summer Festival-Images: USA; bd. dirs. Am. Light Opera Co., Washington, 1960, Jr. Achievement, Phoenix, 1970-73, SW Ensemble Theater, 1975, Valley Forward Assn., Phoenix, 1972-76, Friends Mexican Art, 1973, Western Opera Theater, San Francisco, 1975-78; pres. Shakespeare on the Desert, Phoenix, 1968; chmn. Scottsdale Com. on Cable TV, 1979-81; mem. nat. cabinet Ariz. State U., 1986—; bd. dirs. Ariz. State U. Found., 1987; mem. Council of 100 Sch. Bus. Ariz. State U., 1987—. Served with USAF, 1959. Recipient Disting. Achievement award Coll. Fine Arts Ariz. State U., 1987. Mem. Phoenix Soc. Financial Analysts, Assn. for Corp. Growth, Ariz. Innovation Network, The Enterprise Network, English Speaking Union, Newcomen Soc., Fed., Am. bar assns., State Bar Ariz. (chmn., sec. law com. 1969-85), Bar Assn. San Francisco, Scottsdale Bar Assn. (dir. 1986—). Clubs: Plaza (Phoenix), Ariz. (Phoenix), Phoenix (Phoenix), Univ. (Phoenix) (pres. 1967-68). Antitrust, General corporate, Securities. Office: Furth Fahrner Bluemle & Mason 7373 N Scottsdale Rd Suite B252 Scottsdale AZ 85253

BLUESTEIN, EDWIN A., JR., lawyer; b. Hearne, Tex., Oct. 16, 1930; s. Edwin A. and Frances Grace (Ely) B.; m. Marsha Kay Meredith, Dec. 21, 1957; children: Boyd, Leslie. B.B.A., U. Tex., 1952, J.D., 1958. Bar: Tex. 1957, U.S. Ct. Appeals (5th cir.) 1960, U.S. Dist. Ct. (so. dist.)Tex. 1959, U.S. Dist. Ct. (ea. dist.)Tex. 1965, U.S. Supreme Ct. 1967, U.S. Ct. Appeals (11th cir.) 1982. Law clk. U.S. Dist. Ct., Houston, 1958-59; assoc. Fulbright & Jaworski, Houston, 1959-65, participating atty., 1965-71, ptnr., 1971—; head admiralty dept. Fulbright & Jaworski, 1985—; mem. permanent adv. bd. Tulane Admiralty Law Inst., New Orleans, 1983—; mem. planning com. Houston Marine Ins. Seminar, 1970-76; lectr. profl. seminars. Contbr.: articles to profl. jours. Mem. Tex. Coastal Mgmt. Adv. Com., Austin, 1975-78. Served with U.S. Army, 1952-54. Recipient Yachtsman of Yr. award Houston Yacht Club, 1978. Mem. Tex. Bar Found., Maritime Law Assn. U.S. (mem. exec. com 1980-83), Houston Mariners Club (pres. 1970), Southeastern Admiralty Law Inst. (dir. 1983-85), Houston C. of C. (chmn. ports and waterways com. 1978-79), Propeller Club U.S. Methodist. Club: Houston Yacht (commodore 1979-80). Home: 203 Bay Colony Circle La Porte TX 77571 Office: Fulbright & Jaworski 1301 McKinney St Houston TX 77010

BLUESTEIN, LOUIS ALLEN, lawyer; b. Chgo., June 20, 1944; s. Richard N. and Eleanor G.; m. Tessa M. Bensew, Apr. 20, 1986. Student, U. So. Calif., 1961-62; BA, U. Calif., Berkeley, 1966; student, Brandeis U., Jerusalem, 1964; JD, U. Colo., 1969. Bar: Colo. 1969, U.S. Dist. Ct. Colo. 1969, U.S. Ct. Appeals (10th cir.) 1969. Asst. to exec. v.p., lectr. SUNY, Stony Brook, 1969-71; dep. state pub. defender State of Colo., Denver, 1972-74; ptnr. Bluestein, Simon & Schulman, Denver, 1975—; resource lectr. Nat. Inst. Corrections, Boulder, Colo., 1976-80; lectr. Denver Sheriff Dept., 1976-84; chmn., bd. dirs. Community Police Partnership, Denver, 1983-85. Editor: U. Colo. Law Rev., 1968-69. Vol. counsel Colo. Pub. Interest Research Group, Colo. Common Cause, Denver, 1977, ACLU Colo., Denver, 1976-85, officer, bd. dirs., 1980-85; chmn. Coalition for Effective Law Enforcement, Denver, 1978. Recipient Radetsky award ACLU Colo., Denver, 1986. Mem. Colo. Bar Assn. (chmn. Bill of Rights Com. 1980-82), Denver Bar Assn. (chmn. Community Concerns Com. 1978), Nat. Assn. Realtors, Colo. Assn. Realtors, Denver Assn. Realtors. Clubs: Hillel Council (pres. 1981-83), Mayfair Neighbors (Denver) (pres. 1979). Avocations: competitive volleyball (player and coach), recreational softball, tennis, racquetball. General practice, General corporate, Real property. Office: Bluestein Simon & Schulman 1653 Vine St Denver CO 80206

BLUESTONE, ANDREW LAVOOTT, lawyer; b. N.Y.C., Feb. 16, 1951; s. Henry Robert and Joan (Lavoott) B. BA, Alfred U., 1973; MA, SUNY, Oswego, 1975; JD, Syracuse U., 1978. Bar: N.Y. 1979, U.S. Dist. Ct. (so. and ea. dists.) N.Y. 1979. Sr. trial asst. dist. atty. Kings County Dist. Atty., Bklyn., 1978-84; sr. assoc. Davis & Hoffman, N.Y.C., 1984-86, Donald Ayers, N.Y.C., 1986—. Mem. ABA, Assn. Trial Lawyers Am. Home: 150 Remsen St Brooklyn NY 11201 Office: Donald Ayers 15 Maiden Ln New York NY 10038

BLUM, IRVING RONALD, lawyer; b. Phila., Mar. 3, 1935; s. William and Dorothy B.; m. Rochelle S. Klempner, June 17, 1956; children—Loren, Karen, Jill, Jason. B.A., Wayne State U., 1956; J.D., Detroit Coll. Law, 1959. Bar: Mich. 1959, U.S. Dist. Ct. (ea. dist.) Mich. 1959. Ptnr., Akerman, Kaplan & Blum, Detroit, 1959-62, Blum, Brady & Rosenberg, Detroit, 1962—. Fellow Assn. Trial Lawyers Am. Republican. Jewish. Federal civil litigation, State civil litigation, Personal injury. Home: 4681 Cove Rd West Bloomfield MI 48033

BLUM, JEFFREY STUART, lawyer; b. Pitts., June 26, 1947; s. Max and Eleanor (Frommer) B.; m. Eva Tansky, May 6, 1973; 1 child, Hannah Elizabeth. BA, U. Pitts., 1969, JD, 1973; LLM, George Washington U., 1978. Bar: Pa. 1973. Atty. U.S. Dept. Justice, Washington, 1973-77; assoc. Thorp, Reed & Armstrong, Pitts., 1977-81, ptnr., 1982-86; ptnr. Berkman Ruslander Pohl Lieber & Engel, Pitts., 1986—. Bd. dirs. Am. Jewish Com., Pitts., 1982, United Jewish Fedn. Young Bus. and Profls. Div., Pitts., 1984, B'nai Brith Hillel Found., Pitts., 1984, Pitts. Children's Festival, 1986. Served as capt. USAFR, 1973-83. Mem. ABA, Pa. Bar Assn., Allegheny County Bar Assn. (tax sect.), Pitts. Tax Club. Republican. Club: Concordia; Rivers (Pitts.); Westmoreland Country. State and local taxation, Corporate taxation, Personal income taxation. Office: Berkman Ruslander Pohl Lieber & Engel One Oxford Centre 40th Floor Pittsburgh PA 15219-6498

BLUM, MAURICE HENRY, lawyer; b. Buenos Aires, Argentina, Dec. 10, 1948; came to U.S., 1963, naturalized, 1974; s. Isaac and Rose (Glik) B.; m. Maxine Alice Cohen, Feb. 15, 1976; children—Marcel, Jesse. B.A., CUNY, 1975; J.D., N.Y. Law Sch., 1979. Bar: N.Y. 1980, U.S. Dist. Ct. (ea. and so. dists.) N.Y. 1981, U.S. Ct. Appeals (2d cir.) 1984, U.S. Supreme Ct. 1984. Fellow, counsel's asst. N.Y.C. Planning Commn., 1977-78; assoc. Reich & Reich, N.Y.C., 1980-81; sole practice, N.Y.C., 1981—; state advisor U.S. Congl. Adv. Bd., Washington, 1984. N.Y.C. mayoral fellow, 1977-78; appd. hon. lt. col. aide-de-camp Ala. State Militia. Mem. ABA, N.Y. State Bar Assn. (com. mem. real property sect., domestic relations sect., internat. tax sect., banking com. 1980-81), Assn. Trial Lawyers Am., Assn. of Bar of City of N.Y., New York County Bar Assn., Internat. Platform Assn. Real property, Private international, General practice. Office: 24 W 40th St 10th Floor New York NY 10018

BLUM, MELANIE RAE, lawyer; b. N.Y.C., Aug. 6, 1949; d. Theodore and Gertrude (Brawer) Sands; m. Michael Phillip Blum (div. Oct. 1986); 1 child, Megan Alyse; m. Mark E. Roseman, Apr. 12, 1987. BA, Calif. State, Northridge, 1971; MBA, Calif. State U., Long Beach, 1978; JD, Loyola U., Los Angeles, 1981. Bar: Calif. 1981. Acct. Shain & Cohen, Los Angeles, Calif., 1969-71, INA, Los Angeles, 1971-72, Louis Kelso, San Francisco, 1972-75, O Asian, Inglewood, Calif., 1975-78; assoc. Law Offices of Richard Dickson, Newport Beach, Calif., 1982-83; sole practice Newport Beach, 1983—. Mem. ABA, Calif. Bar Assn., Orange County Bar Assn., Assn. Trial Lawyers Am., Calif. Trial Lawyers Assn., Phi Kappa Phi, Beta Gamma Sigma. General practice, Insurance, Personal injury. Office: 4041 MacArthur Blvd Suite 250 Newport Beach CA 92660

BLUM, PAUL J., lawyer; b. N.Y.C., Sept. 14, 1952; s. Nathan and Ruth (Bregman) B.; m. Judith M. Goldstein, July 2, 1978; 1 child, Deborah Suzanne. BA, SUNY, Stony Brook, 1973; JD cum laude, N.Y. Law Sch., 1981. Bar: N.Y. 1981, Ariz. 1985. Assoc. Turk, Marsh, Kelly & Hoare, N.Y.C., 1981-84; gen. counsel JRS Devel. Inc., Phoenix, 1985—. Mem. ABA, Ariz. Bar Assn., Maricopa County Bar Assn. Real property, Landlord-tenant. Office: Anchor Ctr Three 2231 E Camelback Rd Phoenix AZ 85016

BLUM, WALTER J., lawyer, educator; b. Chgo., Aug. 17, 1918; m. Natalie Richter; children: Wendy (Mrs. David R. Coggins, Jr.), Catherine (Mrs. James Dennis Scott). A.B., U. Chgo., 1939, J.D., 1941. Bar: Ill., D.C. Atty. OPA, 1941-43; faculty U. Chgo. Law Sch., 1946—, prof., 1953—, mem. planning com. tax conf., 1947—; legal counsel Bull. Atomic Scientists, 1949—; Mem. steering com. IRS project Adminstrv. Conf. of U.S., 1974-76. Author: (with Harry Kalven, Jr.) The Uneasy Case for Progressive Taxation, 1953, Public Law Perspectives on a Private Law Problem, Auto Compensation Plans, 1964, (with Stanley A. Kaplan) Corporate Readjustments and Reorganizations, 1976; also articles. Trustee Coll. Retirement Equity Fund, 1970-82. Mem. ABA (mem. council tax Sect. 1972-75), Chgo. Bar Assn. (past bd. mgrs.), Am. Law Inst. (cons. fed. income tax project 1974-82), Am. Acad. Arts and Scis., Chgo. Fed. Tax Forum, Order of Coif, Phi Beta Kappa. Club: Law (Chgo.). Legal education. Home: 5724 S Kimbark Ave Chicago IL 60637

BLUMBERG, EDWARD ROBERT, lawyer; b. Phila., Feb. 15, 1951. B.A. in Psychology, U. Ga., 1972; J.D., Coll. William and Mary, 1975. Bar: Fla., 1975, U.S. Dist. Ct. Fla., 1975, U.S. Ct. Appeals, 1975, U.S. Supreme Ct., 1979; cert. civil trial adv. Nat. Bd. Trial Advocacy. Assoc., Knight, Peters, Hoeveler, Pickle, Niemoeller & Flynn, Miami, Fla., 1976-78; assoc. Goldfarb, Deutsch & Blumberg, Miami, 1976-78; ptnr. Deutsch & Blumberg, P.A., Miami, 1978—; adj. prof. U. Miami Sch. Paralegal Studies. Mem. Dade County Bar Assn., Assn. Trial Lawyers Am., Acad. Fla. Trial Lawyers. Personal injury, State civil litigation, Federal civil litigation. Office: 100 N Biscayne Blvd 28th Floor Miami FL 33132

BLUMBERG, GERALD, lawyer; b. N.Y.C., July 25, 1911; s. Saul and Amelia (Abramowitz) B.; m. Rhoda Shapiro, Jan. 6, 1945; children: Lawrence, Rena, Alice, Leda. A.B. cum laude, Cornell U., 1931; J.D. cum laude, Harvard, 1934. Bar: Mass. 1934, N.Y. 1934. Practiced in N.Y.C., 1934—; mem. firm Gerald & Lawrence Blumberg; instr. econs. Cornell U., 1931; mem. Harvard Legal Aid Bur., 1934; mem. nat. estate affairs com. Cornell U., 1974—. Bd. dirs., v.p., exec. com. Am. Com. Weizmann Inst. Sci., internat. bd. govs. Weizmann Inst. Sci., 1982—. Mem. Am., N.Y. State, Westchester, Yorktown bar assns., Phi Beta Kappa, Phi Kappa Phi. General corporate, Probate, Real property. Home: Baptist Church Rd Yorktown Heights NY 10598 Office: Gerald & Lawrence Blumberg 1 Rockefeller Plaza New York NY 10020

BLUMBERG, GRACE GANZ, educator, lawyer; b. N.Y.C., Feb. 16, 1940; d. Samuel and Beatrice (Finkelstein) Ganz; m. Donald R. Blumberg, Sept. 9, 1959; 1 dau., Rachel. B.A. cum laude, U. Colo., 1960; J.D. summa cum laude, SUNY, 1971; LL.M., Harvard U., 1974. Bar: N.Y. State bar 1971. Confidential law clk. Appellate Div., Supreme Ct., 4th Dept., Rochester, N.Y., 1971-72; teaching fellow Harvard Law Sch., Cambridge, Mass., 1972-74; prof. law SUNY, Buffalo, 1974-81, UCLA, 1981—; cooperating atty. ACLU. Editorial bd.: Am. Jour. Comparative Law, 1977; contbr. articles to profl. jours. Baldy Summer Research fellow in law and social policy, 1977-78; SUNY research Found. summer faculty fellow, 1975. Mem. Am. Soc. Comparative Law, Am. Assn. Law Schs., NOW, ACLU. Address: UCLA Law Sch 405 Hilgard Ave Los Angeles CA 90024

BLUMBERG, JOHN PHILIP, lawyer; b. Mpls., Dec. 6, 1949; s. Myron and Shirley (Hartmann) B.; children: Heather Rachel, Adam Joseph. BA cum laude, Calif. State U., Long Beach, 1972; JD, Western State U., Fullerton, Calif., 1976. Bar: Calif. 1976, U.S. Dist. Ct. (cen. dist.) Calif. 1978, U.S. Ct. Appeals (9th cir.). Atty. Long Beach, Calif., 1976—; judge pro tempore Long Beach Mcpl. Ct., 1979-82; arbitrator Los Angeles County Supr. Ct., civil litigation settlement officer; del. Calif. State Bar Conf., 1985-87; pres. Legal Aid Found. Long Beach, 1986, also bd. dirs.; lectr. various profl. and edn. groups. Assoc. editor Western State U. Law Review, 1975-76; contbr. articles to profl. jours. Mem. Calif. Trial Lawyers Assn., Assn. Trial Lawyers of Am., Long Beach Bar Assn. (arbitrator atty.-client disputes, mem. legis., legal aid, law in a free soc., youth and the law coms.), Nat. Bd. Trial Advocacy (bd. cert. civil trial specialist), Los Angeles County Bar Assn., Los Angeles Trial Lawyers Assn., Am. Arbitration Assn., Screen Actors Guild. Avocations: music, theater, acting. State civil litigation, Personal injury, Insurance. Office: Blumberg Law Offices 444 W Ocean Blvd Suite 1600 Long Beach CA 90802

BLUMBERG, LEONARD RICHARD, lawyer; b. Bayonne, N.J., July 12, 1915; s. Jacob and Fannie (Joseph) B.; m. Adele Rosenberg, June 16, 1940; children—Joyce Kozloff, Bruce A., Allen. B.Philosophy, Dickinson Coll., 1936, J.D., 1938. Bar: N.J. 1939, U.S. Dist. Ct. N.J. 1939, U.S. Supreme Ct. 1983. Sr. ptnr. Blumberg & Rosenberg, Manville, N.J., 1939—; chmn. bd. Manville Nat. Bank; dir. 1st Nat. Bank of Central Jersey. Chmn. allocations com. United Way; past pres. Bridgewater (N.J.) Bd. Edn. Fellow ABA, Am. Bar Found.; mem. N.J. State Bar (mem. council 1959—), Somerset County Bar Assn. pres. 1963), World Peace Through Law. Club: Elks. Probate, Banking, Real property. Office: 203 S Main St Manville NJ 08835

BLUMBERG, PHILLIP IRVIN, legal educator; b. Balt., Sept. 6, 1919; s. Hyman and Bessie (Simons) B.; m. Janet Helen Mitchell, Nov. 17, 1945 (dec. 1976); children: William A.M., Peter M., Elizabeth B., Bruce M.; m. Ellen Ash Peters, Sept. 16, 1979. A.B. magna cum laude, Harvard U., 1939, J.D. magna cum laude, 1942. Bar: N.Y. 1942, Mass. 1970. Assoc. Willkie, Owen, Otis, Farr & Gallagher, N.Y.C., 1942-43, Szold, Brandwen, Meyers and Blumberg, N.Y.C., 1946-66; pres., chief exec. officer United Ventures Inc., 1962-67; pres., chief exec. officer, trustee Federated Devel. Co., N.Y.C., 1966-68, chmn. fin. com., 1968-73; prof. law Boston U., 1966-74; dean U. Conn. Sch. Law, Hartford, 1974-84, prof. law, 1984—; dir. Verde Exploration Ltd. Author: Corporate Responsibility in a Changing Society, 1972, The Megacorporation in American Society, 1975, The Law of Corporate Groups: Procedure, 1983, The Law of Corporate Groups: Bankruptcy, 1985, The Law of Corporate Groups: Substantive Common Law, 1987; bd. editors Harvard Law Rev., 1940-42, treas., 1941-42; contbr. articles to profl. jours. Mem. White House Conf. Indsl. World Ahead, 1972; chmn. Com. to Rev. Conn. Law of Bus. Corps., 1975-77, Fed. Bankruptcy Judge Merit Screening Com. Conn., 1979-81; mem. Conn. Gov.'s Commn. to Rev. Jud. Nominations, 1975-84, Essex County (N.J.) Democratic Com., 1956-57; pres., trustee Edward A. Filene Goodwill Found. Served with USAAF, 1943-46, ETO. Decorated Bronze Star. Mem. ABA, Conn. Bar Assn., Conn. Bar Found. (trustee), Am. Law Inst., Phi Beta Kappa, Delta Upsilon. Clubs: Harvard (Boston); University (Hartford). General corporate, Legal education. Home: 71 Sycamore Rd West Hartford CT 06117 Office: U Conn Sch Law 65 Elizabeth St Hartford CT 06105

BLUME, KAROLYN VREELAND, lawyer; b. N.Y.C., Aug. 16, 1952; d. Donald Walker and Margaretta (Waller) Vreeland; m. Peter Frederick Blume, Oct. 4, 1980; 1 dau., Susanna Vreeland. B.A., Skidmore Coll., 1974; J.D., Villanova U., 1977. Bar: Pa. 1977. Sole practice law, Allentown, Pa., 1977-83; ptnr. Blume and Schwartz, Allentown, 1983—. Bd. dirs. United Way Lehigh County, Allentown, 1983—, pres. Women's Div., 1983-86, pres. women's div., 1983-86; mem. Allentown Zoning Hearing Bd., 1978-84; dir., sec. Old Allentown Preservation Assn., 1980-82, pres., 1987—. Mem. ABA, Pa. Bar Assn., Lehigh County Bar Assn. (dir. 1980—, treas. 1987, service award 1982). Democrat. Presbyterian. General practice, Family and matrimonial, Real property. Address: 420 N 8th St Allentown PA 18102

BLUME, LAWRENCE DAYTON, lawyer; b. Kansas City, Mo., July 7, 1948; s. Dayton G. and Meredith L. (Bruns) B.; m. Marilyn L. Moore, Sept. 6, 1975. B.A., U. Ariz., 1970; J.D., U. Mo., 1974. Bar: Mo. 1974, U.S. Dist. Ct. (we. dist.) Mo. 1974, U.S. Supreme Ct. 1978, U.S. Tax Ct. 1980, U.S. Ct. Internat. Trade 1981, U.S. Ct. Customs and Patent Appeals 1982. Ptnr., Swanson, Midgley, Gangwere, Clarke & Kitchin, Kansas City, 1973-80; prin. Miller & Blume, P.C., Kansas City, 1980—; instr. Kansas City Sch. Dist., 1974-76; lectr. Nat. Assn. Fgn. Trade Zones, Washington, 1981—, gen. counsel, 1982—; lectr. U.S. Small Bus. Adminstrn., Kansas City, 1983—, Am. Assn. Exporters and Importers, N.Y.C., 1984—, various colls., univs. and trade groups, 1980—; chmn. Ad Hoc Com. on Internat. Trade, Kansas City, 1983—; prin. instr. Seminar on Internat. Bus. Transactions and Litigation Techniques, Monte Carlo, 1984; dir. Internat. Trade Club, Kansas City. Mem. Friends of Art, Kansas City, 1978—, United Cerebral Palsy Assn., Kansas City, 1981-83; bd. dirs. Kansas City Philharmonic Orch. 1981-83, Am. Royal Assn., Kansas City, 1984—; sponsor Cystic Fibrosis Assn., Kansas City, 1980-81; pres. Lakas, Kansas City, 1981-82. Recipient Regional Advocacy award Coll. Trial Lawyers, 1974. Mem. ABA (adv. bd. disability law project 1981-82), Kansas City Bar Assn. (chmn. law sch. com. 1975-80, co-chmn. speakers bur. 1980-83), Inter-Am. Bar Assn. (sr.), Am. Immigration Lawyers Assn., Internat. Trade Bar Assn., Am. Assn. Exporters and Importers, Lawyers Assn. Kansas City, Order of Barristers. Democrat. Private international, Immigration, naturalization, and customs. Office: Miller & Blume PC 911 Main St Suite 2320 City MO 64105

BLUME, PAUL CHIAPPE, lawyer; b. Omaha, Oct. 11, 1929; s. Herman Alexander and Marie (Simoni) B.; m. Mary Lou Higgins, June 28, 1958; children—Nancy, Julia, Paul II, William. B.S. in Commerce, Loyola U., Chgo., also J.D. Bar: Ill. 1957. Legal sect. mgr. Aldens Inc., 1957-58; assoc. Lord, Bissell & Brook, 1958-63, 83—. v.p., gen. counsel Nat. Assn. Ind. Insurers, Des Plaines, Ill., 1963-83. Served to capt. U.S. Army, 1951-53. Mem. ABA, Ill. State Bar Assn., Chgo. Bar Assn., Internat. Assn. Ins. Counsel, Fedn. Ins. Counsel, Ill. Def. Counsel. Club: Turnberry Country (Crystal Lake, Ill.). Insurance, Administrative and regulatory, Legislative. Office: 115 S La Salle St Chicago IL 60603

BLUMENFELD, ELI, lawyer; b. N.Y.C., May 17, 1933; s. William E. and Bessie (Rappaport) B.; m. Nancy Sue Greenberg, Dec. 2, 1973; children—Beth C., Robert K., Jennifer P., Whitney S., Kevin Jonathan. J.D., UCLA, 1963. Bar: Calif., 1964. Dist. counsel IRS, Portland, Oreg. and Los Angeles, 1964-69; mem. firm Mitchell, Silberberg & Knupp, Los Angeles, 1969; acct., bus. mgr. Charles Goldring, Esq., Los Angeles, 1962-64; sole practice, Los Angeles, 1969—. Served with USN, 1951-55. Mem. Calif. Bar Assn., Los Angeles Bar Assn., Beverly Hills Bar Assn., ABA, others. Clubs: Hillcrest Country, Lake Arrowhead Country, Vista Del Mar Pres.'s (chmn. fund raising activities 1979—, v.p. 1981-84, chmn. bd. 1985—). Estate planning, Corporate taxation, Estate taxation. Office: 1900 Ave of the Stars 2440 Los Angeles CA 90067

BLUMENTHAL, CAROL, lawyer; b. Oakland, Calif., Feb. 19, 1951; m. Lloyd T. Shanley III, Jan. 25, 1982. AB, Bryn Mawr Coll., 1973; postgrad., Yale U., 1973-74; JD, Georgetown U., 1980. Bar: D.C. 1981, U.S. Dist. Ct. D.C. 1981, U.S. Ct. Appeals 1981, U.S. Ct. Internat. Trade 1982, U.S. Supreme Ct. 1984, W.Va. 1987, U.S. Supreme Ct. Appeals W.Va. 1987, U.S. Dist. Ct. (so. dist.) W.Va. 1987. Assoc. Preston, Thorgrimson, Ellis & Holman, Washington, 1980-82; ptnr. Blumenthal & Shanley, Washington, 1982-86; judge moot ct. competitions George Washington U., 1984-85. Contbr. articles to profl. jours. Mem. ABA, Fed. Bar Assn. Trademark and copyright, Landlord-tenant, Probate. Office: Blumenthal & Shanley 1322 18th St NW #300 Washington DC 20036

BLUMENTHAL, RICHARD ALLEN, lawyer; b. Phila., Aug. 7, 1948; s. Herbert and Florence (Gross) B.; m. Ceil Shapiro, Mar. 15, 1975; children: Amy, Rebecca. AB, Temple U., 1970, JD, 1974. Bar: Pa. 1974. Assoc. Wexler, Weisman, Maurer & Forman, Phila., 1974-76; corp. counsel, sec. Aydin Corp., Ft. Washington, Pa., 1976-79; corp. counsel, asst. sec. Commodore, West Chester, Pa., 1979-83; asst. gen. counsel, sec. Coleco, West Hartford, Conn., 1983-85; assoc. v.p., gen. counsel, sec. Systems and Computer Tech. Corp., Malvern, Pa., 1985—. Mem. ABA, Phila. Bar Assn. Republican. Jewish. Avocation: skiing, tennis, spectator sports. Home: 432 Roundhill Saint Davids PA 19087

BLUMKIN, LINDA RUTH, lawyer; b. N.Y.C., Aug. 25, 1944; d. Louis and Edith (Fortus) Blumkin. A.B. cum laude, Barnard Coll., 1964; LL.B. cum laude, Harvard U., 1967, LL.M., 1973. Bar: N.Y. 1968, U.S. dist. ct. (so. dist.) N.Y. 1969, U.S. Ct. Apls. (2nd cir.) 1969, U.S. Supreme Ct. 1982. Assoc. Fried, Frank, Harris, Shriver & Jacobson, N.Y.C., 1967-71, ptnr., 1979—; lectr. Boston U., 1971, asst. prof. mgmt., 1972-73; assoc. Breed, Abbott & Morgan, N.Y.C., 1973-77; asst. dir. Bur. Competition FTC, 1977-79. Mem. ABA, Internat. Bar Assn., N.Y.C. Bar Assn., Fed. Bar Council. Antitrust, Federal civil litigation. Office: Fried Frank Harris Shriver & Jacobson One New York Plaza 26th Floor New York NY 10004

BLUMOFF, THEODORE YALE, legal educator; b. St. Louis, Jan. 27, 1947; s. Jack George and Esther (Klaman) B.; m. Jane Correll McNamee, Sept. 28, 1974; children: Katherine, Meredith. BS, St. Louis U., 1969, AM, 1971, PhD, 1976; JD, Washington U., St. Louis, 1982. Instr. St. Louis U., 1972-73; asst. prof. history St. Louis Community Coll., 1974-79; assoc. Gallop, Johnson & Neuman, St. Louis, 1982-85; asst. prof. Mercer U. Law Sch., Macon, Ga., 1985—. Co-author: Modern Discovery- Stately and Tactics, 1986. Henry Semple Ames fellow, 1981-82. Mem. Mo. Bar Assn. Legal history, Legal education, Contracts commercial. Home: 1071 Underwood Dr Macon GA 31210 Office: Mercer U Sch of Law 1025 Georgia Ave Macon GA 31207

BLUMROSEN, ALFRED WILLIAM, lawyer, educator; b. Detroit, Dec. 14, 1928; s. Sol and Frances (Netzorg) B.; m. Ruth L. Gerber, July 3, 1952; children: Steven Marshall, Alexander Bernet. B.A., U. Mich., 1950, J.D., 1953. Bar: Mich. 1953, N.J. 1961, N.Y. 1981. Sole practice Detroit, 1953-55; mem. faculty Rutgers Law Sch., Newark, 1955—, prof., 1961—, acting dean, 1974-75, Herbert J. Hannoch scholar, 1984, Thomas A. Cowan prof., 1986—; dir. fed.-state relations, chief of conciliations U.S. EEO Commn., 1965-67; adv. U.S. Dept. Justice, Dept. Labor, Dept. HUD, 1968-72; cons. to chmn. EEOC, 1977-79; of counsel firm Kaye, Scholer, Fierman, Hays & Handler, N.Y.C., 1979-82. Author: Black Employment and The Law, 1971; contbr. articles to profl. jours. Mem. U.S. Nat. Com., Internat. Soc. for Labor Law and Social Security, Indsl. Relations Research Assn., ABA (Ross essay prize 1983), Order of Coif. Labor, Administrative and regulatory, Legislative. Office: Rutgers Law Sch 15 Washington St Newark NJ 07102

BLUMROSEN, RUTH GERBER, lawyer, educator, arbitrator; b. N.Y.C., Mar. 7, 1927; d. Lipman Samuel and Dorothy (Finklebrand) Gerber; m. Alfred William Blumrosen, July 3, 1952; children—Steven Marshall, Alexander B. B.A. in Econs., U. Mich., 1947, J.D., 1953. Bar: Mich. 1953, U.S. Supreme Ct. 1967, U.S. Ct. Appeals (3d cir.). Sole practice, Detroit, 1953-55; cons. civil rights litigation, 1958-65; acting chief advice and analyses, acting dir. compliance EEOC, Washington, 1965; asst. dean Howard U., Washington, 1965-67; consul to chmn. EEOC, 1979-80; expert EEO HHS, Washington, 1980-81; assoc. prof. Grad. Sch. Mgmt., Rutgers U., Newark, 1972—. Adviser, N.J. Commn. on Sex Discrimination in the Statutes, 1983—. Mem. ABA, Fed. Bar Assn., Indsl. Relations Research Assn., Nat. Com. Pay Equity. Author: (with A. Blumrosen) Layoff or Worksharing: The Civil Rights Act of 1964 in the Recession of 1975; The Duty to Plan for Fair Employment Revisited: Worksharing in Hard Times, 1975; Wage Discrimination, Job Segregation and Title VII of Civil Rights Act of 1964, 1979; Wage Discrimination and Job Segregation: The Survival of a Theory, 1980; An Analysis of Wage Discrimination in N.J. State Service, 1983; Worksharing, STC and Affirmative Action in Shorttime Compensation: A Formula for Work-sharing, Remedies for Wage Discrimination., 1987. Labor, Administrative and regulatory. Home: 54 Riverside Dr New York NY 10024 Office: Grad Sch Mgmt 180 University Ave Newark NJ 07021

BLUMSTEIN, EDWARD, lawyer; b. Phila., Aug. 24, 1933; s. Isaac and Mollye (Rodofsky) B.; m. Susan Perloff, Aug. 13, 1983; 1 child, Daniel Blumstein. BS in Econs., U. Pa., 1955; JD, Temple U., 1958. Bar: U.S. Dist. Ct. (ea. dist.) Pa. 1959, U.S. Ct. Appeals (3rd cir.) 1959. Sole practice

Phila., 1959-85; ptnr. Blumstein, Block, Vanore & Pease, Phila., 1985—. Gen. counsel Beth Jacob Schs. of Phila., 1986. Served to sgt. U.S. Army, 1958-64. Mem. ABA (family law sect. task force on div. mediation), Pa. Bar Assn., Phila. Bar Assn. (bd. govs. 1984-85, past chmn. family law sect. 1984), Assn. Trial Lawyers Am., Pa. Trial Lawyers Assn., Phila. Trial Lawyers Assn., Acad. Family Mediators and Family Mediation Assn. Del. Valley. Republican. Jewish. Club: Margate City Yacht Club (N.J.). Lodge: B'nai B'rith. Avocations: skiing, sailing, reading, photography. Family and matrimonial, Personal injury. Office: Blumstein Block et al 1500 Chestnut St Suite 700 Philadelphia PA 19102

BLUMSTEIN, JAMES FRANKLIN, legal educator, lawyer, consultant; b. Bklyn., Apr. 24, 1945; s. David and Rita (Sondheim) B.; m. Andree Kahn, June 25, 1971. B.A. in Econs., Yale U., 1966, M.A. in Econs., LL.B., 1970. Bar: Tenn. 1970, U.S. Ct. Appeals (6th cir.) 1970, U.S. Dist. Ct. (mid. dist.) Tenn. 1971, U.S. Supreme Ct. 1974, N.Y. 1985. Instr. econs. New Haven Coll., 1967-68; pre-law adviser Office of Yale Coll. Dean, New Haven, 1968-69; sr. pre-law adviser Office of Yale Coll. Dean, 1969-70; asst. in instrn. Law Sch., Yale U., 1969-70; asst. prof. law Vanderbilt U., Nashville, 1970-73; assoc. prof. Vanderbilt U., 1973-76, prof., 1976—, spl. advisor to chancellor for acad. affairs, 1984-85; assoc. dir. Vanderbilt Urban and Regional Devel. Ctr., 1970-72, dir. ctr., 1972-74; sr. research assoc. Vanderbilt Inst. for Pub. Policy Studies, 1976-85, sr. fellow, 1985—; Commonwealth Fund fellow, vis. assoc. prof. law and policy scis. Duke U. Law Sch. and Inst. of Policy Scis. and Pub. Affairs, 1974-75; vis. prof. health law Dartmouth U. Med. Sch., 1976, scholar-in-residence intermittently, 1976-78; cons. law, health policy, land use, state taxation, torts; lectr. in field. Editor: (with Eddie J. Martin) The Urban Scene in the Seventies, 1974, (with Benjamin Walter) Growing Metropolis: Aspects of Development in Nashville, 1975, (with Lester Salamon) Growth Policy in the Eighties (Law and Contemporary Problems Symposium), 1979, (with Frank A. Sloan and James M. Perrin) Uncompensated Hospital Care: Rights and Responsibilities, 1986; mem. bd. editors Yale Law Jour., 1968-70; mem. editorial bd. Jour. Health Politics, Policy and Law, 1981—; mem. pub.'s adv. bd. Nashville Banner, 1982—; contbr. numerous articles to profl. jours., op-ed articles to newspapers. Instr econs. Health Econs. Force, Middle Tenn. Health Systems Agy., 1979; mem. adv. bd. LWV, 1979-80; mem. Nashville Mayor's Commn. on Crime, 1981; cons. Leadership Nashville, 1977—, Tenn. Motor Vehicle Commn., 1986-87; panelist Am. Arbitration Assn., 1977—; chmn. Tenn. adv. com. U.S. Commn. on Civil Rights, 1985—; sec. Martin Luther King Jr. Holiday Com., State of Tenn., 1985-87; bd. dirs. Jewish Fedn. Nashville and Middle Tenn., 1981—, chmn. community relations com., 1980-82; chmn. Yale Alumni Schs. Com. Middle Tenn., 1983—. Named one of Outstanding Young Men in Am., U.S. Jaycees, 1971; recipient award Univ. Research Council, 1971-72, 73-74, 79-80, Paul J. Hartman award as outstanding prof. Vanderbilt U., 1982; Bates jr. fellow, 1968-69; grantee Ford Found./Rockefeller Found. Population Program, 1970-73; health policy grantee HCA Found., 1986—. Mem. ABA (sec. sect. legal edn. and admissions to bar 1982-83 , chmn. subcom. on state and local taxation com. on corp. law and taxation sect. on corp., banking and bus. law 1983—, mem. accreditation com. sect. legal edn. and admissions to bar 1983—, mem. com. on state and local taxation sect. on taxation 1983—), Assn. Am. Law Schs. (chmn. law and medicine sect. 1987—, 2d vice chmn. sect. local govt. law 1976-78, mem. sect. council 1980-86), Tenn. Bar Assn., N.Y. State Bar Assn., Hastings Ctr., Assn. for Pub. Policy Analysis and Mgmt., Assn. Yale Alumni (del.), Yale Law Sch. Alumni Assn. (exec. com. 1985—). Club: University (Nashville). Health, Civil rights, Legal education. Home: 2113 Hampton Ave Nashville TN 37215 Office: Vanderbilt Univ Law Sch Nashville TN 37240

BLUNT, RONALD L., lawyer; b. Springfield, Mo., Sept. 23, 1953; s. Leroy and Neva (Letterman) B.; m. Theresa Ann Ferrugia, June 24, 1972 (div. Apr. 1985); 1 child, Benjamin Walter. BA, Westminster Coll., 1975; JD cum laude, U. Mo., 1981. Bar: Mo. 1981, U.S. Ct. Appeals 1982, U.S. Supreme Ct. 1985. Law clk. Criminal Div. Mo. Atty. Gen.'s Office, Jefferson City, 1979; law clk. to presiding judge U.S. Ct. Appeals (D.C. cir.), Washington, 1981-82; law clk. to justice William H. Rehnquist U.S. Supreme Ct., Washington, 1982-83; counselor, spl. asst. to Atty. Gen. U.S. Dept. Justice, Washington, 1983-85; ptnr. Gaar & Bell, Kansas City, Mo., 1985—. Editor-in-chief U. Mo. Law Rev., 1980-81; contbr. articles to profl. jours. Campaign mgr. Roy Blunt Rep. condidate for Mo. Lt. Gov., 1980, Leroy Blunt Rep. candidate for Mo. Ho. Reps., 1978. Earl F. Nelson Meml. scholar U. Mo., 1980-81, Kenneth Teasdale Meml. scholar U. Mo., 1979-80. Mem. ABA (urban state and local govt. sect.), Mo. Bar Assn., Nat. Assn. Bond Lawyers, Order of Coif. Municipal bonds, Local government, Securities. Home: 318 Hunnington Kansas City MO 64113 Office: Gaar & Bell 1100 Main St Suite 1600 Kansas City MO 64105

BLYTHE, JAMES DAVID, II, lawyer; b. Indpls., Oct. 20, 1940; s. James David and Marjorie M. (Horne) B.; m. Sara S. Frantz, Nov. 21, 1974; 1 dau., Amanda Renee. B.S., Butler U., 1962; J.D., Ind. U., 1966; diploma Ct. Practice Inst., 1974. Bar: Ind. 1966, U.S. Dist. Ct. (so. dist.) Ind. 1966. U.S. Congressional staff asst., 1965-69, also majority atty. Ind. Ho. of Reps., 1967, 69; dep. prosecutor Marion County Prosecutor's Office, 1966, 68; travel agt. Skyline Travel, Inc., 1972-86; sole practice, Indpls., 1966—; with firm Butler, Brown & Blythe, 1984—; mem. com. on character and fitness Ind. Supreme Ct., 1974—; host TV show Ask a Lawyer, 1977-79. Bd. dirs. Marion County chpt. Am. Cancer Soc., 1971-76, pres., 1975-76, cert. of merit, 1971, 74, 75, Outstanding Service award Indpls. br. 1972, 73, Man of Yr., 1974; Ind. chmn. West Indies Ambassador Exchange, Jaycees, 1972-73, Richard E. Rowland award, 1971-72, Stanley K. Lacy Meml. award, 1974, Disting. Service award, 1974; bd. dirs. Central Ind. council Boy Scouts Am., 1969-72, exec. com., 1969-71, bd. dirs. Crossroads of Am. council, 1972-87, exec. com., 1976-84, pres., 1979-81, Silver Beaver award, 1981; mem. lawyers fund raising com. Indpls. Mus. Art, 1973-74; co-membership chmn. Friends of Channel 20, 1975; bd. dirs. Salvation Army, 1977—, vice chmn., 1986, chmn., 1987; assoc. mem., entertainment chmn. 500 Hundred Festival, 1977-78. Recipient commendation Gov. State of Ind., 1973; Jim Blythe Day named in his honor, Mayor of Indpls., 1976; named Sagamore of the Wabash, 1981. Mem. Indpls. Bar Assn. (bd. mgrs. 1978-81, chmn. grievance com. 1980-87), Kappa Sigma, Phi Delta Phi. Republican. Presbyterian. Lodge: Kiwanis (v.p. Indpls. 1986-87, pres. 1987—). General corporate, Family and matrimonial, Probate. Home: 11028 Lakeshore Dr E Carmel IN 46032 Office: 155 E Market St Suite 301 Indianapolis IN 46204

BOAL, ELLIS, lawyer; b. Evanston, Ill., Sept. 27, 1944; s. Stewart and Susan (Ballard) B.; m. Marilyn Hendrick Morehead, Aug. 11, 1979. A.B., Bowdoin Coll., 1966; J.D., Wayne State U., 1972. Bar: Mich. 1973, U.S. Dist. Ct. (ea. dist.) Mich. 1973, U.S. Ct. Appeals (D.C. and 6th cirs.) 1978, U.S. Ct. Appeals (1st cir.) 1981. Sole practice, Detroit, 1974—. Author: Teamster Rank and File Legal Rights Handbook, rev. edit., 1984. Mem. Nat. Lawyers Guild, Belle Isle Runners, Finland Station, Phi Beta Kappa. Labor, Civil rights. Office: 925 Ford Bldg 615 Griswold St Detroit MI 48226

BOAND, CHARLES WILBUR, lawyer; b. Bates County, Mo., Aug. 19, 1908; s. Albert and Edith Nadine (Pipes) B.; m. Phoebe Bard, Aug. 2, 1980; children: Bard, Barbara. AA, Jr. Coll. Kansas City; JD summa cum laude, U. Mo., Kansas City; MBA, LLB cum laude, U. Chgo. Bar: Mo. 1931, D.C. 1936, Ill. 1937, U.S. Supreme Ct. 1935, U.S. Ct. Appeals (1st, 2d, 5th, 7th, 9th, 10th, 11th and D.C. Cirs.), trial bar of U.S. Dist. Ct. (no. dist.) Ill. Assoc. Moore & Fitch, St. Louis, 1933; atty. Gen. Counsel's Office, U.S. Treasury Dept., 1933-36; assoc. Wilson & McIlvaine, 1937-42, ptnr., 1945—, chmn. exec. com., 1974-86, sr. ptnr., 1982—; mem. Nat. Conf. Lawyers and CPA's, 1976-82. Mem. grad. sch. bus. council U. Chgo., 1961-68, citizens bd., vis. com. to libraries, 1985—; trustee Muskingum Coll., 1965-79; stated clk. Presbyn. Ch. Barrington, 1962-65. Served as officer USNR, 1942-45, lt. comdr. Res. (ret.). Mem. ABA, Ill. Bar Assn. (chmn. exec. com. corp. securities law sect. 1954-56), Chgo. Bar Assn. (chmn. com. corp. law 1963-64), Fed. Bar Assn., 7th Circuit Bar Assn., U. Chgo. Alumni Assn. (pres. 1975-80, alumni cabinet 1964-70, 72-80, v.p. 1973-74, 1st Alumni Disting. Service award 1981), U. Chgo. Law Sch. Alumni Assn. (pres. 1968-70, bd. dirs. 1950-72), Order of Coif, Beta Gamma Sigma, Sigma Chi, Phi Alpha Delta. Clubs: Chgo., Mid-Am., Met., Law, Legal (Chgo.); Barrington Hills (Ill.) Country (bd. dirs. 1947-55); Los Caballeros Golf (Ariz.). Federal civil litigation. Home: 250 W County Line Rd PO Box 567 Barrington Hills IL 60011 Office: 135 S LaSalle St Chicago IL 60603

BOARDMAN, HAROLD FREDERICK, JR., lawyer; b. Darby, Pa., Nov. 23, 1939; s. Harold Frederick and Juanita (Sorzano) B.; m. Martha Eltie; 1 dau., Kimberly. B.S., Trinity Coll., Hartford, Conn., 1961; J.D. with honors, George Washington U., 1964. Bar: D.C. 1964, U.S. Dist. Ct. D.C. 1964, U.S. Ct. Appeals (D.C. cir.) 1965, U.S. Ct. Mil. Appeals 1964, Hawaii 1971, N.J. 1974, U.S. Supreme Ct. 1974. Gen. atty. Fed. Home Loan Bank Bd., Washington, 1964-65; atty. Hoffmann-LaRoche, Inc., Nutley, N.J., 1965-66; with Hoffmann-LaRoche, Inc., Nutley, 1973—, sec., 1979—, assoc. gen. counsel, 1981—, asst. v.p., 1983—. Served to capt. JAGC, USAF, 1966-73. Mem. ABA, N.J. Bar Assn. Republican. Episcopalian. General corporate. Home: 19 Holly Ln Essex Fells NJ 07021

BOARDMAN, MARK SEYMOUR, lawyer; b. Birmingham, Ala., Mar. 16, 1958; s. Frank Seymour and Flora (Sarinopoulos) B.; m. Cathryn Dunkin, Feb. 26, 1983. BA cum laude, U. Ala., 1979, JD, 1982. Bar: Ala. 1982, U.S. Dist. Ct. (no. dist.) Ala. 1982, U.S. Ct. Appeals (11th cir.) 1983. Assoc. Spain, Gillon, Riley, Tate & Etheredge, Birmingham, 1982-84; ptnr. Porterfield, Scholl, Bainbridge, Mims & Harper, Birmingham, 1984—. Mem. Hellenic Cultural Soc., Birmingham, 1986—. Mem. ABA, Birmingham Bar Assn., Am. Jud. Soc., Ala. Def. Lawyers Assn., Ala. Claims Assn., Order of Barristers, Phi Beta Kappa, Delta Sigma Rho-Tau Kappa Alpha, Pi Sigma Alpha. Greek Orthodox. Avocations: studying fgn. langs. Insurance, State civil litigation, Federal civil litigation. Home: 1915 Wellington Rd Homewood Birmingham AL 35209 Office: Porterfield Scholl et al 2 Office Park Circle Birmingham AL 35253

BOARDMAN, MICHAEL NEIL, lawyer, educator; b. N.Y.C., Jan. 7, 1942; s. Martin Vincent and Hannah (Greisman) B.; m. Constance Hallie Kramer, Aug. 28, 1966; children—Adam Lawrence, Amy Suzanne. A.B., Syracuse U., 1964; J.D., Seton Hall U., 1967. Bar: N.J. 1968, U.S. Dist. Ct. N.J. 1968, U.S. Supreme Ct. 1971. Assoc., Liebowitz, Krafte & Liebowitz, Englewood, N.J., 1968-69; ptnr. Boardman & Epstein, Saddle Brook, N.J., 1969-75; sole practice, Saddle Brook and Ridgewood, N.J., 1975—; designated counsel State of N.J. Office of Pub. Defender, 1970-77; mem. skills tng. course faculty Inst. Continuing Legal Edn., Newark, 1976—; mem. Bergen County dist. fee arbitration com. Supreme Ct. N.J., 1986—; lectr. Inst. Continuing Legal Edn., Newark, 1979—. Democratic committeeman County of Bergen, N.J., 1974-76; mem. Citizens Com. to Study Declining Enrollment, Glen Rock, N.J., 1975-77; panelist Matrimonial Early Settlement Program, Bergen County, 1978—; mem. Glen Rock Jewish Ctr.; mem. profl. adv. bd. Nat. Hypoglycemia Assn., Inc., 1985—. Mem. ABA, N.J. State Bar Assn., Bergen County Bar Assn., Am. Judicature Soc., NOW. Club: Adoptive Parents Orgn. Bergen County. General practice, Family and matrimonial, Real property. Home: 48 Glen Blvd Glen Rock NJ 07452 Office: 4 Franklin Ave Box 782 Ridgewood NJ 07451

BOATWRIGHT, DAVID CROFT, lawyer; b. Albuquerque, Aug. 8, 1956; s. Donald C. and JoAnne (Croft) B.; m. Camille Guerin, June 19, 1982; 1 child, Catherine JoAnne. BS in Acctg. with honors, No. Ariz. U., 1978; JD, Pepperdine U., 1981. Bar: Calif. 1981, U.S. Dist. Ct. Calif. 1981, U.S. Ct. Claims 1982, U.S. Tax Ct. 1982. Acct. Nathan & Mattice, Ariz., 1976-78; assoc. Gray, Cary, Ames & Frye, San Diego, 1981-83; assoc. Aylward, Kintz, Stiska, Wassenaar & Shannahan, San Diego, 1983-85, ptnr., 1985—. Contbr. articles to profl. jours. Bd. dirs. planned giving com U. San Diego, 1983—. Mem. ABA (taxation sect.), San Diego Bar Assn., La Jolla Bar Assn. Republican. Episcopalian. Avocation: water sports. Corporate taxation, Personal income taxation, State and local taxation. Office: Aylward Kintz Stiska Wassenaar & Shannahan 225 Broadway Suite 2100 San Diego CA 92101

BOBAK, DONALD JOHN, patent lawyer; b. Cleve., Aug. 1, 1943; s. Joseph John and Mary Ann (Gogol) B.; m. Vivian Sue O'Brien, June 1, 1968. Student John Carroll U., 1961-63; B.S., U. Akron, 1968, J.D., 1973. Bar: Ohio, 1973, U.S. Dist. Ct. (no. dist.) Ohio 1974, U.S. Ct. Appeals (6th cir.) 1975, U.S. Supreme Ct. 1976, Ct. Customs and Patent Appeals 1979, U.S. Ct. Appeals (fed. cir.) 1983. Law clk. Hamilton, Renner & Kenner, Akron, Ohio, 1970-73, assoc., 1973-75, ptnr., 1975-83; sr. ptnr. Renner, Kenner, Greive & Bobak, Akron, 1984-85; sec., treas. Renner, Kenner, Greive & Bobak, L.P.A., 1985-86, Renner, Kenner, Greive, Bobak & Taylor L.P.A., 1986—. Mem. ABA, Ohio Bar Assn. (bd. govs. patent trademark and copyright sect.), Am. Chem. Soc., Akron Rubber Group, Am. Intellectual Property Law Assn., Cleve. Patent Law Assn. Republican. Patent, Trademark and copyright. Home: 6522 Amblewood St NW Canton OH 44718 Office: 1610 First Nat Tower Akron OH 44308

BOBBITT, PHILLIP LAMAR, lawyer; b. Jacksonville, Fla., July 11, 1948; s. Lamar Vivian Bobbitt and Wynette (Phillips) Dodson; m. Mildred Gail Coffee, May 26, 1973; children: Jacqueline Wynette. Ila Britt. AA in Pre Law, Brewton Parker Coll.; JD, Ogleothorpe U. Classified courier FBI U.S. Dept. Justice, Washington, 1967-68; mgr. legal dept. Credit Bur., Inc., Atlanta, 1974-78; mng. atty. Hyat, Hyat & Landau, Atlanta, 1978-79; ptnr. Baggerly, Bobbitt & Bray, Marietta, Ga., 1979-81; ptnr., owner Bobbitt & Assocs., Marietta, 1981—; owner, bd. dirs. Credit Interaction Agy., Marietta, 1985—. Served with CIA, U.S. Army, 1968-71, Vietnam. Decorated Vietnam Campaign Bar with four bronze stars, 1970, Vietnam Campaign Bar with oak leaf cluster, 1970. Mem. ABA, Ga. Bar Assn., The Comml. Bar Assn., The Comml. Law League, Lawyer Pilots Bar Assn. Avocations: falconry, canoeing, hunting, fishing. Consumer commercial, State civil litigation, Real property. Home: 3770 Shallow Ct Marietta GA 30067 Office: Bobbitt & Assocs 1297 Johnson Ferry Rd Marietta GA 30067

BOBLICK, SHELBY SUSAN, lawyer; b. Detroit, July 13, 1952; d. Frederick Dudley Holcombe and Mary Elizabeth (Green) Robeson; m. William Edward Boblick Jr., Dec. 27, 1975; children: Sara, Matthew, Kristen. AB with high honors, Smith Coll., 1974; MA, U. Ill., 1976; JD with honors, DePaul U., 1981. Bar: Ill. 1981, U.S. Dist. Ct. (no. dist.) Ill. 1981. Tchr. English Proviso E. High Sch., Maywood, Ill., 1976-78; assoc. McDermott, Will & Emery, Chgo., 1981-86, ptnr., 1987—. Mem. ABA, Women's Bar Assn., Ill. Bar Assn., Chgo. Bar Assn., Smith Coll. Alumni Assn. of Chgo. (bd. dirs.). Roman Catholic. Contracts commercial, Landlord-tenant, Real property. Office: McDermott Will & Emery 111 W Monroe St Chicago IL 60603

BOBROFF, HAROLD, lawyer; b. Bronx, N.Y., Apr. 29, 1920; s. Max and Mary (Platofsky) B.; m. Marion Hemendinger, Nov. 25, 1945; children: Caren Spital, Fredric Jon. B.B.A., City U. N.Y., 1947; J.D., N.Y. Law Sch., N.Y.C., 1951. Bar: N.Y. State 1952. Ptnr. Bobroff & Olonoff (C.P.A.s), 1949-51, 52-61; auditor U.S. Army Audit Agy., N.Y.C., 1951—; ptnr. Bobroff, Olonoff & Scharf (Attys.), N.Y.C., 1962—; chief dep. county atty. Nassau County, N.Y., 1962-63; chief counsel joint legis. com. on ins. N.Y. State Legislature, 1965-67; chief counsel com. on intergovt. relations N.Y. State Constl. Conv., 1967. Fin. sec. Nassau County Dem. Com., 1973; former chmn. bd. Trustees Nassau Community Coll.; former pres., trustee Temple Sinai of L.I.; former v.p. N.Y. Fedn. Reform Synagogues. Served with AUS, 1942-45. Decorated Bronze Star medal with oak leaf cluster, Presdl. Unit citation with oak leaf cluster; Belgium Fouraggere; Honored by United Jewish Appeal Fedn. Mem. B'nai B'rith. Lodge: Masons. Probate, General corporate, Contracts commercial. Home: 795 Hampton Rd Woodmere NY 11598 Office: Bobroff Olonoff & Scharf 122 E 42d St New York NY 10017

BOBROW, ALVAN LEE, lawyer; b. Bklyn., Oct. 16, 1949; s. Aaron and Kitty (Maltzman) B.; m. Elisa Susan Orlick, Aug. 20, 1972. BBA, City Coll. N.Y., 1969; JD, Bklyn. Law Sch., 1972; LLM in Taxation, U. Miami, 1973. Bar: N.Y. 1974, U.S. Tax Ct. 1974, U.S. Ct. Appeals (2d cir.) 1974, U.S. Supreme Ct. 1980. Tax counsel CBS Inc., N.Y.C., 1973—. Served wtih USCGR, 1968-74. Mem. ABA (taxation sect.), N.Y. State Bar Assn. (tax sect.). Jewish. Avocations: target shooting, stamp collecting, sports. Corporate taxation, State and local taxation, International taxation. Office: CBS Inc 51 W 52d St New York NY 10019

BOCK, JEFFREY WILLIAM, lawyer; b. Mpls., Mar. 26, 1950; s. Frederick Garland Bock and Vera (Lewer) Randall; m. Elaine Drinkwater, Dec. 5, 1976 (div. 1981); m. A. Thayer Cheatham, Oct. 17, 1986. BA, Dartmouth Coll., 1972; JD, U. Chgo., 1975. Bar: Oreg. 1975. Assoc. Tonkon, Torp & Galen, Portland, Oreg., 1975-78, McEwen, Hanna & Gisuld, Portland, 1978-81; corp. counsel Thermo Electron, Waltham, Mass., 1981-83; assoc. Perkins, Coie, Stone, Olsen & Williams, Portland, 1983—. Club: University. Contracts commercial, Securities, Real property. Office: Perkins Coie Stone Olsen & Williams 111 SW 5th Ave Portland OR 97204

BOCKELMAN, JOHN RICHARD, lawyer; b. Chgo., Aug. 8, 1925; s. Carl August and Mary (Ritchie) B. Student, U. Wis., 1943-44, Northwestern U., 1944-45, Harvard U., 1945, U. Hawaii, 1946; B.S. in Bus. Adminstrn, Northwestern U., 1946; M.A. in Econs, U. Chgo., 1949, J.D., 1951. Bar: Ill. 1951. Atty.-advisor Chgo. ops. office AEC, 1951-52; asso. firm Schradzke, Gould & Ratner, Chgo., 1952-57, Brown, Dashow & Langeluttig, Chgo., 1957-59, Antonow & Weissbourd, Chgo., 1959-61; partner firm Burton, Isaacs, Bockelman & Miller, Chgo., 1961-69; individual practice law Chgo., 1970—; prof. bus. law Ill. Inst. Tech., Chgo., 1950-82; lectr. econs. DePaul U., Chgo., 1952-53; dir., v.p., sec. Secretaries, Inc., Beale Travel Service, Inc; dir., sec. Arlington Engring. Co.; dir., v.p. Universal Distbrs., Inc. Pres. 1212 Lake Shore Dr. Condo Assn. Served with USNR, 1943-46. Mem. Am. Bar Assn., Ill. Bar Assn., Chgo. Bar Assn., Cath. Lawyers Guild Chgo., Phi Delta Theta. Clubs: Lake Point Tower (Chgo.), Barclay Ltd. (Chgo.), Whitehall (Chgo.), Internat. (Chgo.); Anvil (East Dundee, Ill.). General corporate, Probate, Real property. Home: 1212 Lake Shore Dr Chicago IL 60610 Office: Suite 808 104 South Michigan Ave Chicago IL 60603

BOCKSTEIN, HERBERT, lawyer; b. N.Y.C., Jan. 27, 1943; s. Stanley Joseph and Sylvia (Tannenbaum) B.; m. Bonnie Sue Ritt, Sept. 2, 1967; children: Andrew, Michelle. BA, NYU, 1963, JD cum laude, 1971, MBA, 1966. Bar: N.Y. 1972, Mo. 1979. Assoc. Stroock & Stroock & Lavan, N.Y.C., 1971-78, Stolar, Heitzmann & Eder, St. Louis, 1978-80; ptnr. Finley, Kumble, Wagner, Heine, Underberg, Manley & Casey, N.Y.C., 1980—. Mem. ABA, N.Y. State Bar Assn., Mo. Bar Assn., Order of Coif. Avocations: tennis, golf. Estate planning, Probate. Home: 14 Cat Rocks Dr Bedford NY 10506 Office: Finley Kumble Wagner et al 425 Park Ave New York NY 10022

BODANSKY, ROBERT LEE, lawyer; b. N.Y.C.. BA cum laude, Syracuse U., 1974; JD with honors, George Washington U., 1977; cert. postgrad. studies, Ctr. Internat. Legal Studies, Salzburg, Austria, 1978. Bar: Md. 1978, D.C. 1978, U.S. Dist. Ct. Md. 1978, U.S. Ct. Appeals (D.C. cir.) 1980, U.S. Dist. Ct. D.C. 1980, U.S. Ct. Appeals (4th cir.) 1981, U.S. Supreme Ct. 1982. First assoc., then ptnr. Feldman, Krieger, Goldman & Tish, Washington, 1978-83; ptnr. Feldman, Bodansky & Feldman, Washington, 1984—; advisor McGeorge Sch. Law, Sacramento, Calif., 1985—. Author: Special Problems of Subcontractors and Suppliers, 1987. Legal advisor Parkwood Resident's Assn., Kensington, Md., 1984; tchr. Adas Israel Congregation, Washington, 1975—. Mem. ABA (chmn. subcom. internat. and foreign bus. law young lawyers div. 1978-80), Md. State Bar Assn., D.C. Bar Assn. General corporate, Private international, Real property. Office: Feldman Bodansky & Feldman 2019 Que St NW Washington DC 20009

BODDEN, THOMAS ANDREW, lawyer; b. Lafayette, Ind., Dec. 18, 1945; s. William A. and Dorothy (Schlacks) B.; m. Irene S. Hiye; children: Wendee, Todd, Christopher. AB, Cornell U., 1968; JD, U. Miami, 1974. Bar: Hawaii 1975. Assoc. Torkildson, Katz et al, Honolulu, 1975-78, ptnr., 1978-81; pres. Bodden Law Corp., Kihei and Wailuku, Hawaii, 1981—. Author: Taxation of Real Estate in Hawaii, 1979, Taxation of Real Estate in U.S., 1982, Selling DPP Programs, 1983. Pres. Kihei Community Assn., 1984—. Served to lt. USN, 1969-72. Mem. ABA (tax, real property, probate and trust sects.), Hawaii Bar Assn., Nat. Assn. Realtors/RESSI (pres. 1986—). Lodge: Rotary. Estate planning, Probate, Real property. Home: 2694 Ohina St Kihei HI 96753 Office: Bodden Law Corp 1993 S Kihei Rd Kihei HI 96753 Office: Bodden Law Corp 270 Hookahi St Wailuku HI 96791

BODENSTEIN, IRA, lawyer; b. Atlantic City, Nov. 9, 1954; s. William and Beverly (Grossman) B. Student, Tel Aviv U., 1974-75; BA in Govt., Franklin & Marshall Coll., 1977; JD in Econs., U. Miami, 1980. Bar: Ill. 1980, U.S. Dist Ct. (no. dist.) Ill. 1980, U.S. Ct. Appeals (7th cir.) 1982, Fla. 1983. Assoc. James S. Gordon Ltd., Chgo., 1980-85, mem., 1985—. Mem. Lawyers for Mayor Byrne, Chgo. 1983. Named one of Outstanding Young Men Am., 1986. Mem. ABA (antitrust com., rep. young lawyers div. dist. 15 1986-87), Chgo. Bar Assn. (bd. dirs. young lawyers sect. 1985-87, chmn.-elect 1987—, antitrust com., chmn. athletics com. 1984-85, Cert. of Appreciation 1984), Trial Lawyers Assn. Democratic. Jewish. Antitrust, Securities, Federal civil litigation. Home: 2820 N Racine Chicago IL 60657 Office: James S Gordon Ltd 404 S Dearborn Suite 104 Chicago IL 60603

BODINE, LAURENCE, lawyer; b. Kissimmee, Fla., Nov. 4, 1950; s. Cornelius and Tatiana (Krupenin) B.; m. Christine Marie Lizanich, June 30, 1979; 1 child, Theodore Laurence. Student, Universitat Munchen, Munich, Germany, 1970-71; BA, Amherst Coll., 1972; JD, Seton Hall U., 1981. Bar: Wis. 1981, U.S. Dist. Ct. (we. dist.) Wis. 1981. Reporter The Star-Ledger, Newark, 1973-76, N.Y. Daily News, N.Y.C., 1976-78; reporter, asst. editor Nat. Law Jour., N.Y.C., 1978-81; assoc. Stafford, Rieser, Rosen & Hansen, Madison, Wis., 1982; assoc. editor ABA Jour., Chgo., 1982-85, editor, pub., 1986—. Chmn. ABA campaign United Way, Chgo., 1985. Recipient Media award N.J. Bar Assn., 1977, Enterprise award N.J. Press Assn., 1977, 78, Extended Deadline award Sigma Delta Chi, 1977. Mem. ABA, Wis. Bar Assn., Am. Soc. Bus. Press Editor, Mag. Pub. Assn. Office: ABA Jour 750 N Lake Shore Dr Chicago IL 60611

BODKER, STUART ELIOT, lawyer; b. Kansas City, Mo., Sept. 11, 1953; s. Stanley Paul and Dorothy (Gorelick) B.; m. Hortensia Marcos, Nov. 16, 1985. BA cum laude, Tulane U., 1975; JD, Columbia U., 1978. Bar: Mo. 1978. Assoc. Shughart, Thomson & Kilroy, Kansas City, 1978-82, ptnr., 1982—; counsel numerous shopping ctr. devels. Chmn. assn. bd. Jewish Geriatric Convalescent Ctr., Kansas City, 1979-82; bd. govs. Kansas City Citizens Assn., 1986; bd. dirs. Shalom Geriatric Ctr., Kansas City, 1982—. Real property, Banking, Commodities. Office: Shughart Thomson & Kilroy 120 W 12th St Suite 1800 Kansas City MO 64105

BODKIN, HENRY GRATTAN, JR., lawyer; b. Los Angeles, Dec. 8, 1921; s. Henry Grattan and Ruth May (Wallis) B.; m. Mary Louise Davis, June 28, 1943; children: Maureen L. Dixon, Sheila L. McCarthy, Timothy Grattan. B.S. cum laude, Loyola U., Los Angeles, 1943, J.D., 1948. Bar: Calif. 1948. Practiced Los Angeles, 1948-51, 53—; mem. firm Bodkin, McCarthy, Sargent & Smith (and predecessor), Los Angeles, 1948-51, 53—. Mem. Los Angeles Bd. Water and Power Commrs., 1972-74, pres., 1973-74; Regent Marymount Coll., 1962-67; trustee Loyola-Marymount U., 1967—, vice chmn., 1985—. Served with USNR, 1943-45, 51-53. Fellow Am. Coll. Trial Lawyers; Mem. Calif. State Bar (mem. exec. com. conf. of dels. 1968-70, vice chmn. 1969-70), Phi Delta Phi. Republican. Roman Catholic. Clubs: Calif, Riviera Tennis, Tuna, Chancery. Federal civil litigation, State civil litigation, Insurance. Home: 956 Linda Flora Dr Los Angeles CA 90049 Office: Bodkin McCarthy Sargent & Smith 707 Wilshire Blvd 51st Floor Los Angeles CA 90017

BODKIN, ROBERT THOMAS, lawyer; b. Anderson, Ind., Jan. 26, 1945; s. Robert G. and Marggie Jean (Whelchel) B.; m. Penny Ann Nichols, June 17, 1967; children: Beth Ann, Bryan Thomas. BS, Ind. U.-Bloomington, 1967; JD, Ind. U.-Indpls., 1973. Bar: Ind. 1973, U.S. Dist. Ct. (so. dist.) Ind. 1973, U.S. Dist. Ct. (no. dist.) Ind. 1975, U.S. Ct. Appeals (7th cir.) 1974, U.S. Supreme Ct. 1977. Law clk. U.S. Dist. Ct., Indpls., 1973-75; assoc. Bamberger Foreman Oswald & Hahn, Evansville, Ind., 1975-80, ptnr., 1980—; town atty., Newburgh, Inc., 1984. Bd. dirs. Evansville Dance Theatre, 1983, Evansville Philharm. Orch., 1983-85; trustee Evansville Day Sch., 1983-86. Served with U.S. Army, 1968-70. Named Vol. of Yr., Hist. Newburgh, Inc., 1983. Fellow Ind. Bar Found., 1983. Mem. Def. Research Inst., ABA, Ind. Bar Assn., Ind. Def. Lawyers Assn., Evansville Bar Assn., Bar Assn. of 7th Fed. Cir., Ind. Mcpl. Lawyers Assn. (bd. dirs. 1986—). Democrat. Federal civil litigation, State civil litigation, Personal injury. Home: 2011 Old Plank Rd Newburgh IN 47630 Office: Bamberger Foreman Oswald & Hahn 708 Hulman Bldg Evansville IN 47708

BODLE, JOHN FREDERICK, lawyer; b. Mishawaka, Ind., Dec. 14, 1924; s. Alexander Thurston and Caroline (Grimes) B.; m. Mary Alice Kayser, Jan. 13, 1951; children—David J., Thomas J., Michael J., Kathleen A., Stephen

K. B.S. in Commerce magna cum laude, U. Notre Dame, 1949, J.D. magna cum laude, 1950. Bar: Ind., 1950, U.S. Dist. Ct. (no. and so. dists.) Ind. 1950, U.S. Ct. Appeals (7th cir.) 1961, U.S. Supreme Ct. 1962. Assoc. Stuart & Branigin and predecessor firm Stuart, Branigin, Ricks & Schilling, Lafayette, Ind., 1950-53, ptnr., 1953—; dir. Gen Telephone Co. of Ind., 1964-69; counsel to trustees Purdue U., 1977—. Past dir., mem. Greater Lafayette C. of C.; mem. West Lafayette Bd. Zoning Appeals, 1968-83. Served with USAAF, 1943-45. Mem. ABA (utility, anti-trust sects.), Ind. State Bar Assn., Tippecanoe County Bar Assn. (past pres.), Nat. Assn. Coll. and Univ. Attys., Notre Dame U. Alumni Assn. Republican. Roman Catholic. Clubs: Lafayette Country, Elks. Federal civil litigation, State civil litigation, General corporate. Home: 132 Wheeler Ln West Lafayette IN 47906 Office: PO Box 1010 Stuart & Branigin 8th Floor The Life Bldg Lafayette IN 47901

BODNAR, PETER O., lawyer; b. Queens, N.Y., Mar. 19, 1945; s. John and Edith (Schultz) B.; children—Lauren, James. B.A., NYU, 1966; J.D., Fordham U., 1970. Bar: N.Y. 1971. Confidential law sec. Hon. Evans V. Brewster, Family and County Ct., Westchester County, N.Y., 1970-73; sole practice, White Plains, N.Y., 1973-77; mem. Bodnar & Greene, P.C., 1977-80, Bender & Bodnar, 1980-85, Bender, Bodnar & Frucco, 1985—. Mem. ABA, N.Y. Bar Assn., Westchester County Bar Assn. Family and matrimonial. Office: Bender Bodnar & Frucco 11 Martine Ave White Plains NY 10606

BODNEY, DAVID JEREMY, lawyer; b. Kansas City, Mo., July 15, 1954; s. Daniel F. and Retha (Silby) B. BA cum laude, Yale U., 1976; MA in Fgn. Affairs, U. Va., 1979, JD, 1979. Bar: Ariz. 1979, U.S. Dist Ct. Ariz. 1980, U.S. Ct. Appeals (9th cir.) 1980, U.S. Supreme Ct. 1983. Legis. asst., speechwriter U.S. Senator John V. Tunney, Washington, 1975-76; sr. editor Va. Jour. of Internat. Law, 1978-79; assoc. Brown and Bain PA, Phoenix, 1979-85, ptnr., 1985—; vis. prof. Ariz. State U., Tempe, 1985. Co-author: Libel Defense Resource Center: 50-State Survey, 1982-86. Bd. dirs. Ariz. chpt. ACLU, Phoenix, 1984-85, Ariz. Ctr. for Law in the Pub. Interest, Phoenix, 1983—; chmn. Yale Alumni Schs. Com., Phoenix, 1984—; vice chmn. City of Phoenix Solicitation Bd., 1986—. Mem. ABA (forum com. on communication law 1984—, concerned correspondents network com. 1979—), Ariz. Bar Assn. Democrat. Clubs: Yale (bd. dirs. Phoenix club 1979—), Ariz. Acad. Libel, Federal civil litigation, Media law. Office: Brown and Bain 222 N Central Ave Phoenix AZ 85004

BOE, MYRON TIMOTHY, lawyer; b. New Orleans, Oct. 30, 1948; s. Myron Roger and Elaine (Tracy) B. BA, U. Ark., 1970, JD, 1973; LLM in Labor, So. Methodist U., 1976. Bar: Ark. 1974, Tenn. 1977, U.S. Ct. Appeals (4th, 5th, 6th, 7th, 8th, 9th, 10th, 11th cirs.) 1978, U.S. Supreme Ct. 1978. City atty. City of Pine Bluff, Ark., 1974-75; sec.-treas. Ark. City Atty. Assn., 1975; labor atty. Weintraub-Dehart, Memphis, 1976-78; sr. ptnr. Rose Law Firm, Little Rock, 1980—. Author: Handling the Title VII Case Practical Tips for the Employer, 1980; contbr. book supplement: Employment Discrimination Law, 2d edit., 1983. Served to 2d lt. USAR, 1972-73. Recipient Florentino-Ramirez Internat. Law award, 1975. Mem. ABA (labor sect. 1974—, employment law com. 1974—), Ark. Bar Assn. (sec., chmn. labor sect. 1978-81, ho. of dels. 1979-82, Golden Gavel award 1983), Def. Research Inst. (employment law com. 1974—), Assn. Trial Lawyers Am., Ark. Trial Lawyers Assn., Ark. Assn. of Def. Counsel, Ark. Bd. of Legal Specialization (sec. 1982-85, chmn. 1985—). Labor, Employment discrimination, Civil rights. Office: Rose Law Firm 120 E Fourth Little Rock AR 72201

BOECKER, SYLVIA JEAN, lawyer; b. Aurora, Ill., Nov. 24, 1939; d. Theodore Ferdinand and Verna (Vaux) B. BA, U. Denver, 1961; MA, Oberlin Coll., 1965; JD, DePaul U., 1977. Bar: Ill. 1978, U.S. Dist. Ct. (no. dist.) Ill. 1978. Sole practice Chgo., 1978—. Mem. ABA, Chgo. Bar Assn. (chmn. immigration com. 1981-82), Latin Am. Bar Assn., Am. Immigration Lawyers Assn. (pres. Chgo. chpt. 1985-86). Immigration, naturalization, and customs. Office: 405 N Wabash 1006 Chicago IL 60611

BOEHM, STEVEN BRUCE, lawyer; b. N.Y.C., May 22, 1954; s. Henry and Irene (Jonas) B. BA, Rutgers U., New Brunswick, N.J., 1975; JD, Rutgers U., Newark, 1978. Bar: N.J., 1978, D.C., 1982, U.S. Dist. Ct. N.J., U.S. Dist. Ct., D.C. Atty. SEC, Washington, 1978-81, atty. office gen. counsel, 1982, counsel to commr. Barbara S. Thomas, 1982-83; assoc. Sutherland, Asbill & Brennan, Washington, 1983—. Philip J. Levin scholar Rutgers U., 1975-78. Mem. ABA (corp., banking and bus. law com.), D.C. Bar Assn., Phi Beta Kappa, Pi Sigma Alpha. Securities, General corporate, Insurance. Office: Sutherland Asbill & Brennan 1666 K St NW Washington DC 20006

BOEHNEN, DANIEL A., lawyer; b. Mitchell, S.D., Aug. 5, 1950; s. Lloyd and Mary Elizabeth (Buche) B.; m. Joan Bensing, May 22, 1976; 1 child, Christopher. BS in Chem. Engring. cum laude, Notre Dame U., 1973; JD, Cornell U., 1976. Bar: Ill., U.S. Dist. Ct. (no. dist.) Ill., U.S. Ct. Appeals (7th and fed. cirs.). Atty. Allegretti, Newitt, Witcoff & McAndrews Ltd., Chgo., 1976—, assoc., 1982—; mem. adv. com. Shearson-Am. Venture Ptnrs., Boston, 1984. Voting mem. Northbrook Caucus, Ill., 1980—; bd. dirs. Mitchell (S.D.) Prehist. Indian Village Soc., 1983—. Mem. ABA, Chgo. Bar Assn., Chgo. Patent Law Assn. Avocations: skiing, photography, woodworking. Patent, Trademark and copyright, Federal civil litigation. Home: 1244 Blue Hill Terrace Northbrook IL 60062 Office: Allegretti Newitt et al 125 S Wacker Dr Chicago IL 60606

BOEHNER, LEONARD BRUCE, lawyer; b. Malvern, Iowa, Apr. 19, 1930; s. Bruce and Flora (Kruse) B. A.B., Harvard U., 1952, J.D., 1955. Bar: N.Y. 1956, U.S. Dist. Ct. (so. dist.) N.Y. 1963, U.S. Ct. Appeals (2d cir.) 1963, U.S. Supreme Ct. 1964. Assoc. Dewey, Ballantine, Bushby, Palmer & Wood, N.Y.C., 1959-66; ptnr. Clare & Whitehead, N.Y.C., 1966-73, Morris & McVeigh, N.Y.C. 1973—. Served to lt. USN, 1955-59. Mem. Assn. Bar City N.Y. Club: Union (N.Y.C.). General corporate, Securities, Estate planning. Office: 767 3d Ave New York NY 10017

BOELTER, ALLEN BOYD, lawyer; b. Saginaw, Mich., Oct. 17, 1956; s. Allen Helmuth and Margaret (Nelson) B. BA, U. Mich., 1978; JD, U. So. Calif. Bar: Calif. 1982, U.S. Dist. Ct. (cen. and so. dists.) Calif. 1982. Pres. Am. Entertainment Ventures, Corp., Hollywood, Calif., 1982-84; assoc. Law Offices of Arthur Leeds, Century City, Calif., 1984—. Mem. ABA, Calif. Bar Assn., Los Angeles County Bar Assn., Century City Bar Assn., Sierra. Club: Polar/Equator (Mich.). Avocations: trekking, rafting, sports, music, film. Entertainment, General corporate, General practice. Office: Law Offices of Arthur Leeds 10100 Santa Monica Blvd #2500 Los Angeles CA 90067

BOENSCH, ARTHUR CRANWELL, lawyer; b. Charleston, S.C., Nov. 9, 1933; s. Frank Neville and Mary Alice (Cranwell) B.; m. Katherine Hume Lucas, June 16, 1956; children—Arthur Cranwell, Katherine Pierce, Alice, Frances, Benjamin; m. 2d, Annelle Yvonne Beach, July 27, 1979. B.S. in Gen. Engring., U.S. Naval Acad., 1956; J.D., U. S.C., 1970. Bar: S.C. 1970, U.S. Dist. Ct. (so. dist.) Ga. 1970, U.S. Dist. Ct. S.C. 1971. Ptnr., Ackerman & Boensch, 1970-73, Bogoslow & Boensch, 1973-75; sole practice, Walterboro, S.C., 1975—; city recorder, mcpl. ct. judge, Walterboro, 1973-78. Vice chmn. Colleton County Alcohol and Drug Abuse Commn., 1981—; dist. chmn., exec. bd. Coastal Carolina council Boy Scouts Am., 1975—; vestry St. Jude's Episcopal Ch. Served to lt. comdr. USN, 1956-67. Recipient Silver Beaver award and dist. award of merit Boy Scouts Am., 1982. Mem. S.C. Bar Assn., Phi Alpha Delta. Republican. Club: Rotary. General practice. Address: 108 Hamton St Walterboro SC 29488

BOER, ELLEN S(TRAUSS), lawyer; b. N.Y.C., Oct. 15, 1941; d. Michael E. and Cecilia (Rosen) Strauss; m. F. Peter Boer, Aug. 9, 1963; children: Alexandra, Andrew. BA, Mt. Holyoke Coll., 1963; JD, South Tex. Coll. Law, 1977. Bar: Tex., Conn., U.S. Dist. Ct. Of counsel Simmons & Zwernemann, Houston, 1977-78; asst. town atty. Town of Greenwich (Conn.), 1980-83; sole practice law specializing in spl. edn. law, Washington, 1983-86, Greenwich, 1986—. Planning commr. Midland, Mich., 1972-73. Mem. Law Rev., South Tex. Coll. Law, 1977. Mem. ABA, Tex. Bar Assn., Conn. Bar Assn., Greenwich Bar Assn., Nat. Sch. Bd. Assn. (council sch. attys.), Order of Lytae. Home: 325 Taconic Rd Greenwich CT 06830

BOES, LAWRENCE WILLIAM, lawyer; b. Bklyn., Aug. 3, 1935; s. Lawrence and Elizabeth (Schaefer) B.; m. Joan Mary Elward, July 21, 1941; children—Lawrence, Siobhan, Thomas. A.B., Columbia Coll., 1961; J.D., Columbia U., 1964. Bar: N.Y. 1965, U.S. Dist. Ct. (ea. dist.) N.Y. 1968, U.S. Dist. Ct. (so. dist.) N.Y. 1968, U.S. Ct. Appeals (2d cir.) 1971, U.S. Ct. Appeals (8th cir.) 1974, U.S. Supreme Ct. 1974, U.S. Ct. Appeals (9th cir.) 1982. Law clk., 1964-65; assoc. firm Reavis & McGrath, N.Y.C., 1965-70, ptnr., 1970—; sec. Computer Lessors Assn., 1974-80. Mem. Village of Westbury Code Rev. Commn., N.Y., 1983—. Served with U.S. Army, 1958-60. Pulitzer Scholar, N.Y.C. Bd. Edn., 1954; nat. scholar Sch. Law Columbia U., 1962. Mem. ABA, N.Y. State Bar Assn., Bar Assn. Nassau County. Democrat. Roman Catholic. Revs. editor Columbia Law Rev., 1963-64. Antitrust, Federal civil litigation, State civil litigation. Office: Reavis & McGrath 345 Park Ave New York NY 10154

BOESE, JAMES STEPHEN, lawyer; b. Keokuk, Iowa, Aug. 10, 1940; s. Robert Otto and Janet Evelyn (Thulin) B.; m. Cynthia Ann McFarlin, Sept. 14, 1984. B.S.B.A., Kans. State Coll., 1963; J.D., U. Tulsa, 1970. Bar: Okla. Spl. agt. Nebr. Western Ins. Co., 1962-67; intern to atty. Rogers, Bell & Robinson, Tulsa, 1968-75; ptnr., then mng. ptnr. Robinson, Boese, Orbison & Lewis, Tulsa, 1975—; sec. BancOklahoma Corp., Tulsa; adv. dir. Bank of Okla., Southwest Tulsa, Tulsa. Trustee Tulsa Airport Authority, Tulsa Airport Improvements Trust. Served with USAFR, 1963-69. Mem. Okla. Bar Assn., ABA, Tulsa County Bar Assn., Com. of 500 C. of C. (govtl. affairs div. planning group 1987). Republican. Club: Golf of Okla. (Tulsa). Avocations: sailing; jogging; skiing. Office: Robinson Boese Orbison & Lewis One Williams Ctr Suite 1500 PO Box 1046 Tulsa OK 74101

BOESEN, JOHN MICHAEL, lawyer; b. Stamford, Conn., Oct. 21, 1946; s. John James and Ann Josephine (Obzud) B. BA, St. Michael's Coll., Winooski, Vt., 1968; JD, U. Conn., 1972. Bar: Conn. 1972, U.S. Ct. Appeals (2d cir.) 1975. Staff atty. Conn. Legal Services, Norwalk, 1972-73; mng. atty. Conn. Legal Services, Stamford, 1973—. Co-chmn. Community Housing Coalition, Stamford, 1986—. Mem. Stamford Darien Bar Assn. (exec. com.). Democrat. Landlord-tenant, State civil litigation. Office: Conn Legal Services 20 Summer St Stamford CT 06901

BOGAARD, WILLIAM JOSEPH, lawyer; b. Sioux City, Iowa, Jan. 18, 1938; s. Joseph and Irene Mary (Hensing) B.; B.S., Loyola Marymount U., Los Angeles, 1959; J.D. with honors, U. Mich., 1965; m. Claire Marie Whalen, Jan. 28, 1961; children—Michele, Jeannine, Joseph, Matthew. Bar: Calif. 1966. Ptnr. firm Hufstedler, Miller, Carlson & Beardsley, Los Angeles, 1971-82; exec. v.p., gen. counsel First Interstate Bancorp., Los Angeles, 1982—. Mem. Pasadena (Calif.) City Council, 1978-86; mayor City of Pasadena, 1984-86. Served to capt. USAF, 1959-62. Mem. Am. Bar Assn., Los Angeles County Bar Assn., Pasadena C. of C. Address: First Interstate Bancorp 707 Wilshire Blvd PO Box 54068 Los Angeles CA 90017

BOGAN, NEIL EARNEST, lawyer; b. Des Moines, Oct. 21, 1945; s. William Eldirage and Cynthia Marie (Faulkner) B.; m. Carolyn Sue Martin, Aug. 9, 1968; children: Tiffany Lynn, Tyler Douglas, Tadd Justin Pace. BA, U. Okla., 1967; JD, U. Tulsa, 1970. Bar: Okla. 1970, U.S. Dist. Ct. (no. dist.) Okla. 1970, U.S. Ct. Appeals (10th cir.) 1975, U.S. Supreme Ct. 1980. Legal intern Jones, Givens, Brett, Gotcher & Doyle, Tulsa, 1970, assoc., 1970-75; v.p. Jones, Givens, Gotcher, Bogan & Hiborne, Tulsa, 1975—, mng. atty., 1987—; bd. dirs. Tulsa Nat. Bank; lectr. in field. Captain Indian Nations council Boy Scouts Am., 1987; patron N.E. Okla. chpt. Am. Heart Assn., 1987; com. mem. annual fund drive Philbrook Art Ctr., 1985, 86; office coordinator annual fund drive United Way, 1986. Fellow Okla. Bar Found.; mem. ABA, Am. Judicature Soc., Okla. Bar Assn. (v.p. 1984, gov. 1984—), Tulsa County Bar Assn. (bd. dirs 1985—, pres. elect 1986—, Pres. award 1984, Disting. Service award 1986), Tulsa Bus. Builders Assn. (pres. 1985). Republican. Methodist. Avocations: water sports, hunting, fishing, antique collecting. General corporate, Real property, Contracts commercial. Office: Jones Givens Gotcher Bogan & Hilborne 3800 1st National Tower Tulsa OK 74103

BOGDANSKI, JOHN ANDREW, III, lawyer, law educator, columnist; b. Newark, Jan. 15, 1954; s. John Andrew Jr. and Anne Teresa (Hoare) B.; m. Georgene Deraeve, Mar. 21, 1981. AB, St. Peter's Coll., 1975; postgrad., Yale U., 1977; JD, Stanford U., 1978. Bar: Calif. 1978, Oreg. 1980, U.S. Tax Ct. 1984. Law clk. to judge U.S. Ct. Appeals (9th cir.), Portland, Oreg., 1978-79; from assoc. to ptnr. Stoel Rives et al, Portland, 1980-82, 83-86; from vis. asst. prof. to assoc. prof. Lewis & Clark Law Sch., Portland, 1982-83, 86—; lectr. numerous continuing legal and tax edn. programs, Oreg., 1984—. Columnist Jour. of Corp. Taxation, 1982—; contbr. articles to profl. jours. Bd. dirs. People Against Nuclear Dumping at Hanford Inc., 1986—. Mem. ABA (taxation sect.), Oreg. Bar Assn. (taxation sect.). Personal income taxation, Corporate taxation, General corporate. Office: Lewis & Clark Law Sch 10015 SW Terwilliger Portland OR 97219

BOGERT, GEORGE TAYLOR, lawyer; b. Ithaca, N.Y., Sept. 20, 1920; s. George Gleason and Lolita Eleanor (Metzger) B.; m. Adelyn Mayo Russell, July 22, 1950; children: Nicholas Snowden, Amy Gleason, Carroll Russell. A.B., Cornell U., 1941; LL.B., Harvard U., 1948. Bar: Ill. 1949. Assoc. Hopkins, Sutter, Halls, DeWolfe & Owen, Ill., 1948-51; gen. counsel, asst. to pres. Guardian Electric Mfg. Co., Chgo., 1951-54; mem. Crowell & Leibman, and predecessors, Chgo., 1954-60, ptnr., 1960-66; ptnr. Mayer, Brown & Platt, Chgo., 1966—. Co-author, editor: Trust and Trustees, 1959-66, author, 2d rev. edit., 1974-84. Mem. ABA, Ill. Bar Assn., Chgo. Bar Assn., Am. Law Inst., Chgo. Estate Planning Council, Am. Coll. Probate Counsel, Internat. Acad. Estate and Trust Law. Estate planning, Probate. Home: 2440 N Lakeview Ave Chicago IL 60614 Office: Mayer Brown & Platt 190 S LaSalle St Chicago IL 60603

BOGGS, JAMES CALEB, lawyer; b. Cheswold, Del., May 15, 1909; s. Edgar Jefferson and Lettie (Vaughn) B.; m. Elizabeth Muir, Dec. 26, 1931; children—James Caleb, Marilu. B.A., U. Del., 1931; LL.B., Georgetown U., 1937; LL.D. (hon.), Del. State Coll., 1959; LL.D. (hon.), Bethany Coll., 1967, U. Del., 1981. Bar: Del. 1938, U.S. Supreme Ct. 1946. Sole practice, Dover, Del., 1938-40; ptnr. Logan & Duffy, later Logan, Duffy & Boggs, 1940-41, Logan & Duffy, Wilmington, 1946; part-time assoc. judge Family Ct., New Castle County, Del., 1946; of counsel Bayard, Handelman & Murdoch, P.A., Wilmington, Del., 1973—; dir. Rollins Environ. Services, Inc., R.L.C. Corp., Beneficial Nat. Bank. U.S. Senator from Del., 1961-73; gov. State of Del., 1953-61; chmn. Nat. Govs. Conf., 1959; pres. Council of State Govts., 1960; U.S. Rep. from Del., 1947-53; mem. Joint Com. on Orgn. of Congress, 1965-66; mem. White House Conf. on Internat. Coop., 1965; mem. U.S. Nat. Commn. for UNESCO, 1964-66; bd. visitors U.S. Mil. Acad., 1965, U.S. Naval Acad., 1966, 72, U.S. Air Force Acad., 1970; bd. dirs. Del. Safety Council, Blood Bank of Del., Goldey Beacom Bus. Coll., Greater Wilmington Devel. Council, Del. chpt. Arthritis Found.; trustee Wilmington Med. Center; hon. trustee Boy Scouts Am.; mem. Salvation Army Regional Adv. bd. and former mem. nat. adv. council; trustee Freedoms Found., Inc. Served with Del. N.G., 1926-31, U.S. Army, 1941-46. Decorated Legion of Merit, Croix de Guerre with Palm, Bronze Star with oak leaf cluster. Recipient Marvel Cup award Del. C. of C., 1979; SAR gold Medal award, 1962; State of Del. Gold Medal award for pub. service, 1973; Jaycees Awards of Senator, 1953, Ambassador, 1974, others. Mem. Del. Bar Assn., Am. Judicature Soc., ABA. Republican. Methodist. Clubs: Nat. Republican, Univ., Whist, Nat. Lawyers, Masons (33 deg.). Administrative and regulatory, Environment, Legislative. Home: 1203 Grinnell Rd Green Acres Wilmington DE 19803 Office: 1300 Del Trust Bldg PO Box 25130 Wilmington DE 19899

BOGGS, RALPH STUART, lawyer; b. Toledo, June 6, 1917; s. Nolan and Sarah (MacPhie) B.; m. Mary Frances Sharp Wiggins, Sept. 7, 1940; children: Sally Ann Boggs Bashore, William S., Robert A. A.B., Denison U., 1939; LL.B., U. Mich., 1942. Bar: Ohio 1942, U.S. Supreme Ct. 1960. Spl. agt. FBI, 1942-45; practiced in Toledo 1946—; partner Boggs, Boggs & Boggs (P.A.), 1946-74, now pres., treas., dir.; sec., dir. Master Chem. Corp., Cousino Metal Products Inc. Mem. Maumee Bd. Edn., 1953-69; mem. Maumee Recreation Com., 1954-69; v.p. Toledo adv. com. Salvation Army, 1970-81, pres., 1981-83; pres. Maumee Men's Republican Club, 1947-48; former chmn. bd. trustees Presbytery of Maumee, Inc. Mem. X-FBI Agts. Soc., Ohio Acad. Trial Lawyers, Am., Ohio, Lucas County, Toledo bar assns., Am. Judicature Soc., Assn. Trial Lawyers Am. Presbyterian (elder). Clubs: Masons (Toledo) (33 deg.); Shriners; Heather Downs Country (Toledo) (past pres., dir.). State civil litigation, Federal civil litigation, Probate. Home: 5920 Swan Creek Dr Toledo OH 43614 Office: 413 Michigan St Toledo OH 43624

BOGUE, JEFFREY A., lawyer; b. Mpls., Nov. 13, 1943; s. Robert A. and Shirley (Brown) B.; divorced; children: Zachary, Katie. BA, Wesleyan U., Nebr., 1965; JD, Cath. U., 1973. Bar: Nebr. 1973, Colo. 1977, U.S. Supreme Ct. 1977, U.S. Dist. Ct. Colo., U.S. Dist. Ct. Nebr., U.S. Ct. Appeals (8th and 10th cirs.). Counsel judiciary com. U.S. Senate, Washington, 1973; asst. atty. U.S. Dept. Justice, Lincoln, Nebr., 1973-74; ptnr. O'Connor, Miller & Bogue, Denver, 1977-83, Leventhal & Bogue, Denver, 1983—. Served to 1st lt. USMC. 1969-72, Vietnam. Named one of Outstanding Young Men Am., U.S. Jaycees, 1976. Mem. Colo. Bar Assn., Nebr. Bar Assn., Colo. Trial Lawyers Assn., Nebr. Trial Lawyers Assn., Denver C. of C. Republican. Avocations: golf, sports, reading. Personal injury. Office: Leventhal & Bogue PC 950 S Cherry #711 Denver CO 80222

BOGUE, RUSSELL S., lawyer; b. Tampa, Fla., Sept. 11, 1954; s. Russell S. and elaine (Seibert) B.; m. Virginia Ballenger, Sept. 9, 1978; children: Sarah Virginia, Mary Reid. BA in Acctg., Duke U., 1976; JD, U. Fla., 1979. Bar: Fla., U.S. Dist. Ct. (mid. and so. dists.) Fla., U.S. Ct. Appeals (11th cir.). Assoc. to ptnr. Carlton, Fields, Ward, Emmanuel, Smith Cutler & Kent, Tampa, Fla., 1979-86; ptnr. Smith, Helms, Mulliss & Moore, Tampa, Fla., 1986—. Contbr. articles to profl. jours. Mem. ABA, Hillsborough County Bar Assn. (bd. dirs. 1981-85). Democrat. Presbyterian. Banking, Bankruptcy, Consumer commercial. Home: 2625 Jetton Ave Tampa FL 33629 Office: Smith Helms Mulliss & Moore Box 1842 Tampa FL 33629

BOGUS, CARL THOMAS, lawyer; b. Fall River, Mass., May 14, 1948; s. Isidore E. and Carolyn (Dashoff) B.; m. Dale Shepard, Sept. 5, 1970 (div. 1987); children—Elizabeth Carol, Ian Troy. A.B., Syracuse U., 1970, J.D., 1972. Bar: Pa. 1973, U.S. Dist. Ct. (ea. dist.) Pa. 1973, U.S. Ct. Appeals (3d cir.) 1976, U.S. Supreme Ct. 1977. Assoc. Steinberg, Greenstein, Gorelick & Price, Phila., 1973-79, ptnr., 1979-83; assoc. Mesirov, Gelman, Jaffe, Cramer & Jamieson, Phila., 1983-84, ptnr., 1985—; mem. bd. Visitors Coll. Law, Syracuse U., N.Y., 1976—. Bd. govs. Phila. chpt. Lawyers Alliance for Nuclear Arms Control, 1984—. Mem. ABA, Pa. Bar Assn., Phila. Bar Assn., Syracuse Law Coll. Assn. (exec. sec. 1979-83, 2d v.p. 1983-85). Democrat. Jewish. Federal civil litigation, State civil litigation, Antitrust. Home: 1420 Locust St Apt #16-I Philadelphia PA 19102 Office: Mesirov Gelman Jaffe Cramer & Jamieson Fidelity Bldg 15th Floor Philadelphia PA 19109

BOGUTZ, JEROME E., lawyer; b. Bridgeton, N.J., June 7, 1935; s. Charles and Gertrude (Lahn) B.; m. Helene Carole Ross, Nov. 20, 1960; children—Marc Lahn, Tami Lynne. B.S. in Finance, Pa. State U., 1957; J.D., Villanova U., 1962. Assoc. Dash & Levy, Phila., 1962-63; assoc. Abrahams & Loewenstein, Phila., 1963-64; dep. dir., chief of litigation Community Legal Services, Phila., 1964-68; sole practice law Phila., 1968-71; ptnr. Bogutz & Mazer, Phila., 1971-81, Fox Rothschild O'Brien & Frankel, Phila., 1981—; adj. clin. prof. law Villanova U., Pa., 1969-72, lectr.; pres., dir. Internat. Mobile Machines, Phila., 1980-81; dir., sec. Westpark Hosp., Phila., 1982—; bd. consultors Villanova Law Sch., 1983—. Commr. ABA Commn. on Advt., 1985—, vice chmn., 1987—; Am. Friends Hebrew U. Served with USAR, 1955-60; with Res. Fellow Am. Bar Found. (life), Pa. Bar Found. (pres. 1986—, dir. 1983—); mem. Phila. C. of C. (dir. 1980-83), ABA (ho. of dels. credtials and admission com., chair ABA/JAD bench bar com., co-chair mid yr. meeting com. 1987—, mem. admissions and credentials com.), Am. Judicature Soc., Pa. Bar Assn. (pres. 1985-86), Pa. Bar Found. (pres. 1986—), Phila. Bar Assn. (pres. 1980), Phila. Bar Found. (pres. 1981), Nat. Met. Bar Leaders (founder, pres. 1979-82), Nat. Conf. Bar. Republican. Jewish. Avocations: golf; sailing. General corporate, Oil and gas leasing, General practice. Home: 509 Hamilton Rd Merion PA 19066 Office: Fox Rothschild O'Brien and Frankel 2000 Market St 10th Floor Philadelphia PA 19103

BOHAN, THOMAS LYNCH, lawyer, physicist; b. Terre Haute, Ind., Feb. 12, 1938; s. Richard Timothy and Anna Elizabeth (Lynch) B.; m. Linda Ann Sian, Nov. 26, 1960 (div. Dec. 1981); children: Richard Michael, Cecilia Anne, John Charles. BS in Physics, U. Chgo., 1960; MS in Physics, U. Ill., 1964, PhD in Physics, 1968; JD, Franklin Pierce Law Ctr., 1980. Bar: Maine 1980, Mass. 1980, U.S. Dist. Ct. Maine 1980, U.S. Patent Office 1980. Research assoc. U. Ill., Urbana, 1968-69; prof. physics Bowdoin Coll., Brunswick, Maine, 1969-76; assoc. Sunenblick, Fontaine and Reben, Portland, Maine, 1980-82; ptnr. Med. and Tech. Cons., Portland, 1982—. Contbr. articles to profl. jours. Chmn. Community Devel. Com., Brunswick, 1976-78. Research grantee Am. Heart Assn., 1970-76, The Research Corp., 1972-74, NSF/NATO, 1967; fellow Tex. Instruments, 1965; Fulbright scholar 1972-73. Mem. AAAS, Am. Chem. Soc., Am. Phys. Soc., Assn. Trial Lawyers Am., Cumberland County Bar Assn., Maine State Bar Assn., Maine Trial Lawyers Assn. Sigma Xi. State civil litigation, Federal civil litigation, Patent. Home: Centennial Ave Peaks Island ME 04108 Office: Med & Tech Cons 371 Fore St Portland ME 04101

BOHANNON, PAUL, lawyer; b. Cushing, Okla., May 20, 1950; s. Marvin J. and Marscia (Hughes) B.; m. Cynthia J. James, June 1, 1974; 1 child, Brenton. B.A., Okla. State U., 1972; J.D., So. Meth. U., 1975. Bar: Tex. 1975, N.Mex. 1976, U.S. Ct. Appeals (5th and 10th cirs.) 1975, U.S. Dist. Ct. N.Mex. 1976, U.S. Dist. Ct. (we. and no. dists.) Tex. 1983. Ptnr. Hinkle, Cox, Eaton, Coffield & Hensley, Roswell, N.Mex., 1975-83, Midland, Tex., 1983—. Bd. dirs. council # 212 Girl Scouts U.S., Roswell, 1982-83. Mem. ABA (mem. water quality com. environ. law sect. 1980), Am. Mgmt. Assn., Am. Arbitration Assn. (panel arbitrators), Roswell Jaycees, Order of Coif. Democrat. Episcopalian. Lodges: Mason, Order of DeMolay (legion of honor, bd. govs. 1981-83). Environment, Federal civil litigation, State civil litigation. Home: 2203 Princeton Midland TX 79701 Office: Hinkle Cox Eaton Coffield & Hensley PO Box 5105 Midland TX 79704

BOHANON, RICHARD L., federal bankruptcy judge; b. Oklahoma City, Feb. 9, 1935; s. Luther L. and Marie F. (Swatek) B.; m. Margaret Herrmann, Aug. 12, 1959; children—Christopher, David, Philip. A.B., Dartmouth Coll., 1957; LL.B., Okla. U., 1960; LL.M., N.Y.U., 1962. Bar: Okla. 1960, U.S. Ct. Appeals (10th cir.) 1961, U.S. Supreme Ct. 1976. Ptnr., Bohanon & Barth, Oklahoma City, 1964-79, Andrews, Davis, Legg, Bixler, Milsten & Murrah, Oklahoma City, 1979-82; chief judge U.S. Bankruptcy Ct., Western Dist. Okla., Oklahoma City, 1982—. Mem. Nat. Conf. Bankruptcy Judges (bd. of govs.). Club: Oklahoma City Golf and Country. Bankruptcy. Office: US Bankruptcy Ct US Courthouse Oklahoma City OK 73102

BOHARIC, ROBERT VINCENT, judge; b. Chgo., July 7, 1945; s. John Charles and Marie A. (Leben) B.; m. Kathleen JoAnn Kane, June 19, 1971; children: Marie Grace, Margaret Clare, Thomas Joseph. AB, John Carroll U., 1967; JD, U. Ill., 1973. Bar: Ill. 1973, U.S. Dist. Ct. (no. dist.) Ill. 1973. Asst. states atty. Cook County States Atty.'s Office, Chgo., 1973-81; ptnr. Boharic & Theobald, Chgo., 1981-83; assoc. Clausen, Miller, Gorman, Caffrey & Witous P.C., Chgo., 1983-84; judge Cir. Ct. Cook. County, Chgo., 1984—. Served with USMC, 1967-69. Mem. ABA, Ill. Bar Assn., Chgo. Bar Assn., Am. Judicature Soc. Republican. Roman Catholic. Lodge: Lions. Avocations: softball, weightlifting. Criminal, Jurisprudence. Office: 2600 S California Room 303 Chicago IL 60608

BOHLEN, CHRISTOPHER WAYNE, lawyer; b. Decatur, Ill., July 24, 1949; s. Martin Orlando and Mamie Virginia (Andrews) B.; m. Rosemary Pistorius, June 4, 1972; children: Harper Pistorius, Andrew Pistorius, Elizabeth Pistorius. BA, U. Ill., 1970; JD, Northwestern U., 1973. Bar: Ohio 1973, U.S. Dist. Ct. Ohio 1974, Ill. 1977, U.S. Dist. Ct. (cen. dist.) Ill. 1977, U.S. Supreme Ct., 1977, U.S. Dist. Ct. (no. dist.) Ill. 1986, U.S. Ct. Appeals (7th cir.) 1986. Atty. Legal Aid/Pub. Defender's Office, Cleve., 1973-77; assoc. Blanke & Blanke, Kankakee, Ill., 1977-78; ptnr. Blanke, Norden, Barmann & Bohlen P.C., Kankakee, 1978—. Mem. exec. bd. Kankakee YMCA, 1984, Kankakee Valley Park Dist., 1983—, pres. 1986—; Rep. precinct committeeman, Kankakee, 1985—. Recipient Claude E.

Clarke award 1976. Mem. Ill. State Bar Assn. (young lawyers div.), Ill. State Trial Lawyers Assn., Riverview Hist. Dist. (sec.). Mem. United Ch. Christ. Federal civil litigation, Personal injury, State civil litigation. Home: 949 S Chicago Ave Kankakee IL 60901 Office: Blanke Norden Barmann & Bohlen 189 E Court St PO Box 1787 Kankakee IL 60901

BOHLMANN, DANIEL ROBERT, financial planner, lawyer; b. Portland, Oreg., Apr. 28, 1948; s. Walter Richard and Nora Laticia (DeCandido) B.; m. Sylvia Maria Martha Bachand, June 20, 1981. A.A. with honors, Multnomah Jr. Coll., 1969; B.S. in Bus. Adminstrn. and Polit. Sci., Lewis & Clark Coll., 1970; J.D., Northwestern Sch. Law, 1974. Bar: Oreg. 1976, U.S. Dist. Ct. (9th cir.) Oreg., U.S. Ct. Appeals, U.S. Supreme Ct. Supr., Bohlmann & Bohlmann Investment Trust, 1970—; sole practice, Oreg., 1976—; chief exec. Atlas Internat. Investments, Ltd., 1981—; officer, co-owner, investor Investors Gen. Computer Software, Inc., 1981—; investor, founder Rangefinder Petroleu, Ltd., Black Giant Mining & Petroleum; founder, owner Sun West Energy, Inc.; owner Gem-Con, Inc., 1979-81, Hopps Body and Paint Shop, Inc., 1976-80; owner Racquet Club Cove Hotel/Apts. of Palm Springs; bd. dirs. Shakey's Pizza, Palm Springs. Internat. fin. advisor U.S. Presdl. Task Force, 1981-84; mem. subcom. Oreg. Bd. Edn., 1973-75; bd. dirs. Willamette Democratic Soc., 1979-81; precinct committeeman, Oreg., 1976, 78, 80; mem. U.S. Senatorial Bus. Adv. Bd., 1981-83; active Oreg. Arts Found.; mem. Los Angeles Bicentennial Coordinating Com., 1975-76. Served with USAR, 1967. Mem. Assn. M.B.A. Execs., Assn. Trial Lawyers Am., Oreg. Trial Lawyers Assn., Am. Judicature Soc., Am. Soc. Agrl. Engrs., Oreg.-U.S. and Palm Springs C. of C., Internat. Assn. Fin. Planners, U.S. Hist. Soc., Smithsonian Assocs., Am. Mgmt. Assn., Nat. Fedn. Ind. Businessmen, Nat. Life Underwriters Assn., Oreg. Environ. Council, U.S. Antique and Collectors Automobile Assn., Am. Legion, Calif. Apt. Owners Assn., U.S. Restaurant Owners Assn., Phi Alpha Delta, Phi Theta Kappa. Republican. Lutheran. Clubs: Palm Springs Rotary, Elks (nat. found. outstanding benefactor 1980); Columbia River Yacht, Desert Mus., Living Desert Reserve, Oreg. Auto Body Craftsmen Assn. Contbr. articles to fin. jours. Estate planning, Insurance, Real property. Address: Vista Las Palmas 1022 Friar Ct Palm Springs CA 92262

BOHM, JOEL LAWRENCE, lawyer, securities industry executive; b. N.Y.C., Dec. 27, 1942; s. Ernest Jonas and Laura (Ullman) B.; m. Karen Rea Brandt, July 3, 1966; children—Michelle Elizabeth, Lori Allison. B.A. in Polit. Sci., Bklyn. Coll., 1965; J.D., Bklyn. Law Sch., 1970. Bar: N.Y. 1971, U.S. Ct. Appeals (2d cir.) 1972, U.S. Dist. Ct. (so. and ea. dists.) N.Y. 1975, U.S. Supreme Ct. 1976. Staff atty. Mohawk Data Scis. Corp., N.Y.C., 1971-72; asst. gen. counsel Gen. Cable Corp., N.Y.C., 1972-73; v.p., sec., gen. counsel Securities Industry Automation Corp., N.Y.C., 1973—; referee, arbitrator small claims N.Y.C. Civil Ct., 1984—. Trustee Temple Shaari Emeth, Englishtown, N.J., 1981. Served with USN, 1961. Mem. ABA, Am. Judges Assn., Assn. Arbitrators, N.Y. State Bar Assn., N.Y. County Lawyers Assn., Assn. Bar City N.Y. General corporate, Computer, Contracts commercial. Office: Securities Industry Automation Corp 55 Water St 22d Floor New York NY 10041

BOHN, ROBERT HERBERT, lawyer; b. Austin, Tex., Sept. 2, 1935; s. Herbert and Alice (Heinen) B.; m. Gay P. Maloy, June 4, 1957; children—Rebecca Shoemaker, Katherine, Robert H., Jr. B.B.A., U. Tex., 1957, LL.B., 1963. Bar: Tex. 1963, Calif. 1965. Ptnr. Boccardo Law Firm, San Jose, Calif., 1965—; speaker Calif. Continuing Edn. of Bar; judge pro tem Superior Ct. of Calif., San Jose, 1975-86. Sustaining mem. Republican Nat. Com., Washington, Nat. Rep. Senatorial Com., Washington, Rep. Presdl. Task Force, Washington. Mem. Calif. Trial Lawyers Assn., Assn. Trial Lawyers Am., Santa Clara County Bar Assn., Calif. State Bar Assn., Internat. Platform Assn., Phi Gamma Delta. Personal injury, State civil litigation. Home: 14124 Pike Rd Saratoga CA 95070 Office: Boccardo Law Firm 111 W St John San Jose CA 95115

BOHNER, ROBERT JOSEPH, lawyer; b. Bklyn., Nov. 11, 1934. B.A., St. John's U., 1956, J.D., 1958. Bar: N.Y. 1959, U.S. Supreme Ct. Ptnr. Bohner & Bohner, P.C., Rego Park, N.Y., 1960—; mem. malpractice panel N.Y. State Supreme Ct.; Contbr. articles on dram shop litigation and civil lawsuits to profl. jours.; lectr. trial practice. Pres. sch. bd. Sacred Heart Sch., Merrick, N.Y., 1975-79; candidate Right to Life party for gov. State of N.Y., 1982. Mem. Queens County Bar Assn., N.Y. State Bar Assn. (chair trial lawyers sect., exec. com. ins. negligence and compensation law sect., chmn. continuing legal edn. com. trial lawyers sect.), Nassau County Bar Assn., ABA, Assn. Trial Lawyers Am., N.Y. Trial Lawyers Assn. (bd. govs.), Am. Arbitration Assn. (arbitrator), Blackstone Lawyers Club (pres.). Office: 62-55 Woodhaven Blvd Rego Park NY 11374

BOHREN, MICHAEL OSCAR, lawyer; b. Appleton, Wis., Feb. 27, 1947; s. Oscar Robert and Martha (Anderson) B.; m. Mary Joset Morse, Nov. 26, 1977; children: Juliana Rose, Katherine Elizabeth. AB, Ripon Coll., 1969; JD, Marquette U., 1975. Bar: U.S. Dist. Ct. (ea. and we. dists.) Wis. 1975, U.S. Ct. Appeals (5th and 7th cirs.) 1976, Wis. 1978. Atty. U.S. Dept. Agr., Washington, 1975; gen. counsel Aries Ltd., Milw., 1975-78; atty. Marola & Bohren, Milw., 1978—. Bd. dirs. Kettle Moraine Sch. Dist. (pres. 1986), Wales, Wis., 1982—; v.p. Greenfield Sch. Dist., Wis., 1977-81. Mem. ABA, Wis. Bar Assn., Assn. Trial Lawyers Am., Wis. Trial Lawyers Assn. Republican. Lodge: Masons. Avocations: geology, politics, reading. Family and matrimonial, Personal injury, General practice. Home: W315 S496 Christopher Way Delafield WI 53018 Office: Marola & Bohren 10401 W Lincoln Ave Milwaukee WI 53227

BOHRER, NANCY KING, lawyer; b. Evanston, Ill., May 24, 1950; d. Charles Edward King and Annamabel Tyner; m. Douglas R. Bohrer, Sept. 5, 1972; children: Charlotte, Victoria. Student, De Pauw U., 1968-70; BS in Communications, U. Ill., 1972; JD, John Marshall Law Sch., 1979. Bar: Ill. 1979, U.S. Dist. Ct. (no. dist.) Ill. 1979. Sole practice Wilmette, Ill., 1979—. Precinct capt. New Trier Rep. Orgn., Kenilworth, Ill., 1978—; mem. exec. com. various Rep. campaigns, Ill, 1982—. Mem. ABA, Ill. Bar Assn., Chgo. Bar Assn., Wilmette Jr. Aux., Woman's Club of Wilmette (various coms.). Republican. Congregationalist. General practice.

BOHRER, ROBERT A., legal educator; b. Chgo., Apr. 28, 1949; s. Ira Morris and Charlotte (Davis) B.; m. Karen Sue Birstein, Feb. 6, 1977. BA, Haverford Coll., 1971; JD, U. Ill., 1974; LLM, Harvard U., 1979. Bar: Ill. 1974, U.S. Dist. Ct. (no. dist.) Ill. 1974. Assoc. Bell, Boyd & Lloyd, Chgo., 1974-78; asst. prof. Hofstra U. Law Sch., Hempstead, N.Y., 1979-82; from assoc. prof. to prof. Calif. Western Sch. Law, San Diego, 1982—; chmn. San Diego Biotech Conf., 1985, 86. Contbr. articles to profl. jours. Mem. ABA (real property sects. on environ. law and role of lawyer), Pi Alpha Delta. Democrat. Jewish. Avocations: swimming, history. Legislative, Real property. Home: 6288 Calle Vera Cruz La Jolla CA 92037 Office: Calif Western Sch Law 350 Cedar St San Diego CA 92037

BOIES, WILBER H., lawyer; b. Bloomington, Ill., Mar. 15, 1944; s. Wilbur H. and Martha Jane (Hutchison) B.; m. Victoria Joan Steinitz, Sept. 17, 1966; children: Andrew Charles, Carolyn Ursula. A.B., Brown U., 1965; J.D., U. Chgo., 1968. Bar: Ill. 1968, U.S. Dist. Ct. (no. dist.) Ill. 1968, U.S. Dist. Ct. (ea. dist.) Wis. 1973, U.S. Ct. Appeals (7th cir.) 1974, U.S. Ct. Appeals (5th cir.) 1975, U.S. Ct. Appeals (3d cir.) 1977, U.S. Supreme Ct. 1978. Assoc. Altheimer & Gray, Chgo., 1968-71; ptnr. McDermott, Will & Emery, Chgo., 1971—. Contbr. articles to profl. jours. Served with USAR, 1968-74. Mem. Legal Club Chgo., Law Club Chgo., Bar Assn. 7th Fed. Cir., ABA, Chgo. Bar Assn., Chgo. Council Lawyers. Clubs: Chgo. Athletic, Monroe. Federal civil litigation, State civil litigation, Bankruptcy. Office: McDermott Will & Emery 111 W Monroe St Chicago IL 60603

BOIGON, HOWARD LAWRENCE, lawyer; b. Detroit, Dec. 4, 1946; s. Irving I. and Frances (Glazer) B.; m. Carol Ann Spickler, Dec. 30, 1969; children: Jared, Hannah. BA cum laude, U. Mich., 1968, JD magna cum laude, 1971. Bar: Mich. 1971, U.S. Dist. Ct. (ea. dist.) Mich. 1971, Colo. 1974, U.S. Ct. Appeals (6th and 10th cirs.) 1974, U.S. Supreme Ct. 1974. Law clk. to judge U.S. Ct. Appeals (6th cir.), Detroit, 1971-73; assoc. Davis, Graham & Stubbs, Denver, 1973-78, ptnr., 1978—; bd. dirs. Provenance Petroleum, Inc., Denver, HBB Inc., Denver, Kerikorp, Inc., Denver; lectr. and chair Rocky Mountain Mineral Found. Spl. Insts., 1979, 1983, 1987; lectr. Denver Assn. Petroleum Landmen Workshops, 1985-87. Administrv. editor U. Mich. Law Rev., 1970-71; contbr. articles to profl. jours. Committeeman precinct Denver Dems., 1984—. Mem. ABA, Colo. Bar Assn. (chmn. mineral law sect.), Denver Assn. Petroleum Landmen (lectr.), Rocky Mountain Mineral Law Found. (spl. insts. com., ann. program com.), SW Legal Found. (lectr. 37th and 38th ann. Inst. 1986, 87, ann. program com.), Order of Coif. Democrat. Jewish. Avocations: running, triathlons, reading. Energy, Oil and gas leasing. Home: 2001 Ivy Denver CO 80207 Office: Davis Graham & Stubbs 370 17th St #4700 Denver CO 80202

BOKAT, STEPHEN A., lawyer; b. Washington, July 30, 1946; s. George and Golda (Shurack) B.; m. Karen Gilbert, June 17, 1972; children: Christina, Rebecca. BA, Adams State Coll., 1968; JD, George Washington U., 1972. Bar: D.C. 1973, U.S. Dist. Ct. D.C. 1974, U.S. Ct. Appeals (D.C., 7th and 9th cirs.) 1976, U.S. Supreme Ct. 1976, U.S. Ct. Appeals (8th cir.) 1977, U.S. Ct. Appeals (4th cir.) 1979, U.S. Ct. Appeals (5th cir.) 1980, U.S. Ct. Appeals (3d cir.) 1985. Atty., advisor NLRB, Washington, 1972-74, Occupational Safety and Health Rev. Commn., Washington, 1974-76; appellate atty. solicitors office U.S. Dept. of Labor, Washington, 1976-77; sr. labor counsel Nat. Chamber Lit Ctr., Washington, 1977-82; v.p., gen. counsel U.S. C. of C., Washington, 1983—. V.p. Nat. Chamber Lit. Ctr., Washington, 1985—. Served with U.S. Army, 1969-70. Mem. ABA (co-chmn. occupational safety and health com. 1983-86), Am. Corp. Counsel Assn. (bd. dirs. 1983—, treas. 1987—). Avocations: photography, sailing. Labor, Federal civil litigation, General corporate. Office: US C of C 1615 H St NW Washington DC 20062

BOLAN, THOMAS ANTHONY, lawyer; b. Lynn, Mass., May 30, 1924; s. Thomas J. and Margaret (Cremin) B.; m. Marie T. Gerst, Nov. 25, 1950; children: Sean, Douglas, Mary, Jacqueline, William. B.A. summa cum laude, St. John's U., 1952, LL.B. summa cum laude, 1950, LL.D. (hon.), 1985. Bar: N.Y. 1951. Assoc. firm Burroughs & Brown, N.Y.C., 1951-53; asst. U.S. atty. Dept. Justice, N.Y.C., 1953-57; assoc. Roy M. Cohn, N.Y.C., 1957-59; mem. firm Saxe, Bacon & Bolan, N.Y.C., 1960-71; counsel Saxe, Bacon & Bolan, 1972—; lectr. law St. John's U., 1957-61; pres., chmn. bd. 5th Ave. Coach Lines, N.Y.C., 1967-68, Championship Sports, Inc., N.Y.C., 1961—; treas., exec. dir. Feature Sports, Inc., 1959-61; chmn. bd. Merc. Nat. Bank, Chgo., 1967-68, Gateway Nat. Bank, Chgo., 1966-67; sec. Balt. Paint and Chem. Corp., N.Y.C., 1966-68, TelePro Industries Inc., N.Y.C., 1966-68; sec., dir. B.S.F. Co., N.Y.C., 1966-68, Defiance Industries, N.Y.C., 1966-68; v.p. Am. Steel and Pump Corp., N.Y.C., 1966-68, WRNJ Assocs., Atlantic City, 1961-68, Harrisburg Broadcasting Co., Palmyra, Pa., 1966-68; sec., treas., dir. Berwick Broadcasting Corp., Reading, Pa., 1967-68; dir. Overseas Pvt. Investment Corp., 1982-86. Bd. editors: Nat. Law Jour., 1983—; Contbr. articles to legal jours. Co-chmn. N.Y. Reagan Fin. Com., 1980, N.Y. Reagan-Bush Campaign Com., 1984; founder law chmn., mem. exec. com. Conservative Party, N.Y. State, 1962—; chmn. E. Side Conservative Club, N.Y.C., 1973—; v.p. Crusade for Am., Rockville Center, N.Y., 1957-62; bd. regents St. Francis Coll., Bklyn., 1968—; treas. Ednl. Reviewer, 1960—; pres. Cambria Heights (N.Y.) Parish Council, 1968-70; pres., dir. Pro Ecclesia Found., 1972-73; trustee Cambria Heights Boys Club Assn., 1968-72, St. John's U., 1987—, deans bd. of visitors, 1987—; v.p., dir. Heiser Found., 1955-73; mem. Com. to Restore Internal Security, 1979—; bd. govs. Council for Nat. Policy, 1983—; mem. Am. Council on Germany, 1983—, U.S. Commn. for UNESCO, 1983-85; bd. visitors Eureka Coll., 1983—; nat. adv. council Actors Youth Fund, 1982—; mem. U.S. Senator Alfonse D'Amato's Jud. Screening Com., 1980—; bd. dirs. Global Econ. Action Inst., 1986—. Served with USAF, 1943-45. Decorated Air medal with 5 oak leaf clusters; recipient Medal of Honor The 52 Assn., 1981; Bella V. Dodd Meml. award N.Y. County Conservative Party, 1981; Ann. award Bronx County Conservative Party, 1984; Disting. Service award Nat. Cath. War Vets, 1985. Mem. Fed. Bar Council, Am., N.Y. State, N.Y. County bar assns., Am. Judicature Soc., Cath. Lawyers Guild, Nat. Assn. Coll. and Univ. Attys., Cath. War Vets. (Queens County judge advocate 1965—, nat. judge advocate 1984—, Service award Queens County chpt. 1968, 77, elected to Order St. Sebastian, nat. assn. 1981), Am. African Affairs Assn. (sec., dir. 1975—), Internat. Assn. Jurists, Ret. Officers Assn. (Knickerbocker chpt.). Club: Knights of Malta. General practice, Probate, Private international. Office: 39 E 68th St New York NY 10021

BOLAND, CHRISTOPHER THOMAS, II, lawyer; b. Scranton, Pa., June 10, 1915; s. Patrick J. and Sarah (Jennings) B.; m. Nora Cusick, Jan. 23, 1943; m. Cornelia Bingham Maury, Mar. 1, 1980. B.S.S. cum laude, Georgetown U., 1937; LL.B., Harvard, 1940. Staff dir. Spl. Senate Com. on Atomic Energy, 1945-47; staff dir., counsel Joint Senate-House Com. on Atomic Energy, 1947; practice law Washington, 1947—; now sr. partner firm Gallagher, Boland, Meiburger & Brosnan; utility specialist Dept. Energy. Served to lt. col., intelligence USAAF, 1941-45. Mem. Fed. Energy Bar Assn. (pres. 1970), ABA, D.C. Bar Assn. Clubs: Congressional Country (pres. 1974), Harvard (Washington); Burning Tree (Bethesda, Md.). FERC practice. Home: 5309 Cardinal Ct Spring Hill Bethesda MD 20816 Office: 821 15th St NW Washington DC 20005

BOLAND, JOHN DANIEL, lawyer; b. Carbondale, Pa., June 8, 1948; s. Floran J. and Stella (Andrews) B.; m. Susan Preston, May 12, 1973; children: Daniel, Vanessa, Sarony. BA magna cum laude, U. Conn., 1971, MA, 1975; JD, Georgetown U., 1977. Bar: Conn. 1977, Mass. 1978, U.S. Dist. Ct. Mass. 1978. Assoc. Gross, Hyde & Williams, Putnam, Conn., 1977-83, ptnr., 1982-83; ptnr. Cummings, McNally, Boland & St. Onge, Putnam, 1983—; counsel Town of Chaplin, Conn., 1979—, Town of Ashford, Conn., 1986—, Town of Bklyn., Conn., 1986—. Columnist (newspaper) Windham County Observer Patriot, 1986—. Mem. Pomfret (Conn.) Bd. Edn., 1979—; pres. United Social and Mental Health Services, Inc., Danielson, Conn., 1981-84; chmn. Pomfret Dem. Com., 1986. Mem. Conn. Bar Assn. (internat. law and world peace sect., mem. exec. com.), Windham County Bar Assn. State civil litigation, General practice, Local government. Home: RFD 2 Carter Rd Pomfret Center CT 06259 Office: Cummings McNally Boland & St Onge 211 Kennedy Dr PO Box 550 Putnam CT 06260

BOLCH, SUSAN BASS, lawyer; b. Phila., Mar. 8, 1953; d. Herbert Jerome and Lillian (Margolis) B.; m. Carl Edward Bolch, Aug. 2, 1981; children: Natalie Jane, Melanie Caroline, Jordan Bass. BA in history magna cum laude, Columbia U., 1974; JD, Georgetown U., 1977. Bar: Pa. 1977, U.S. Dist. Ct. (ea. dist.) Pa. 1977, D.C. 1979, U.S. Ct. Appeals (D.C. cir.) 1979, Ga. 1982, U.S. Dist. Ct. (no. dist.) Ga. 1982, U.S. Ct. Appeals (11th cir.) 1982, U.S. Supreme Ct. 1982. Assoc. Collier Shannon Rill & Scott, Washington, 1977-81, Kinj & Spalding, Atlanta, 1981-82; gen. counsel, sec. Racetrac Petroleum, Inc., Atlanta, 1982—, also bd. dirs. Mem. D.C. Bar Assn., Pa. Bar Assn., Ga. Bar Assn., Atlanta Bar Assn. Avocations: family, interior design, travel. General corporate, Administrative and regulatory, Environment.

BOLD, FREDERICK, JR., lawyer; b. Los Angeles, May 24, 1913; s. Frederick Charles and Ruby Jane (Morrison) B.; m. Carol Randall, Jan. 17, 1939 (div. 1960); children: Frederick III, Jane E.; m. Helene Myers, June 17, 1961. AB, Stanford U., 1935; JD, Harvard U., 1938. Bar: Calif. 1938, U.S. Supreme Ct. 1941. Assoc. Pillsbury, Madison & Sutro, San Francisco, 1938-46; ptnr. Carlson, Collins & Bold, Richmond, Calif., 1946-70; sr. ptnr. Bold & Polisner, Walnut Creek, Calif., 1970—. Mem. faculty U. Calif. Hastings Coll. Law, San Francisco, 1946-49. Contbr. articles to profl. jours. Bd. dirs. Brookside Community Hosp., San Pablo, Calif. Served to col. U.S. Army, 1941-46, ETO. Mem. ABA, Contra Costa Bar Assn. (pres. 1958-59). Clubs: St. Francis Yacht (San Francisco), Los Altos Hunt (Woodside, Calif.) (pres. 1975-76). Avocation: sailing. Water rights, Environment, Probate. Home: 1201 California St San Francisco CA 94109

BOLDEN, MELVIN WILBERFORCE, JR., lawyer; b. N.Y.C., Sept. 11, 1941; s. Melvin Wilberforce and Eloise (Thomas) B.; children—Danielle Lillian, Melvin Wilberforce, III. B.A., Morgan State Coll., Balt., 1964; J.D., Howard U., 1970. Bar: D.C. 1971, U.S. Dist. Ct. D.C. 1976, U.S. Ct. Appeals (D.C. cir.) 1976, U.S. Supreme Ct. 1987. Asst. gen. counsel NAACP, N.Y.C., 1970-72; atty. Commn. Human Rights City of N.Y., 1973-76; mng. atty. Neighborhood Legal Services, Washington, 1977-79; asst. chief Office of Corp. Counsel, Washington, 1980-82, chief, 1982—; mem. mental health rules com. D.C. Superior Ct., jud. conf. of D.C., 1982-87. Co-author The Search for Military Justice. Mem. ABA, Washington Bar Assn., D.C. Bar Assn., NAACP, Alpha Phi Alpha, Sigma Delta Tau. Democrat. Mem. African Methodist Episcopal Ch. State civil litigation, Federal civil litigation, Personal injury. Office: Office of Corp Counsel DC 500 Indiana Ave NW Room 4450 Washington DC 20601

BOLES, DAVID LAVELLE, corporate lawyer; b. Tulia, Tex., May 22, 1937; s. Jerry Hoytt and Irma Ruth (Walker) B.; m. Kerstin Gunilla Stenrudh, May 25, 1959 (div. 1984); children—David LaVelle Jr., Kerstin Regina Boles Davenport, William Gail-Holger. Student North Tex. U., 1955-57; B.S., Trinity U., 1959; J.D., U. Tex., 1963. Bar: Tex. 1963. Asst. atty. gen. Tex., Austin, 1963-67; sole practice, Denton, Tex., 1967-69; house counsel, corp. officer Sam P. Wallace Co., Inc., Dallas, 1969-73, adminstrv. mgr. contracts, labor, indsl. relations, ins., 1973-85, house counsel, corp. officer MMR/Wallace Group, Inc., 1985—. Deacon Presbyterian Ch., Austin, Denton, 1963-74. Mem. Tex. Bar Assn., Denton County Bar Assn., Trinity Alumni Assn. (pres. 1965), Denton C. of C. Construction, Labor, Administrative and regulatory. Home: 3831 Furneaux Carrollton TX 75007 Office: MMR/Wallace Group Inc 2535 Walnut Hill Ln Dallas TX 75229

BOLES, EDGAR HOWARD, II, lawyer; b. Cleve., Mar. 2, 1947; s. Laurence Huey and Blossom (Miller) B.; m. Elizabeth Young, Dec. 27, 1974; children—Gwendolyn H., Edgar H. III, Mary H., Elizabeth A. B.A., Ohio Wesleyan U., 1969; J.D., Case Western Res. U., 1973. Bar: Ohio 1973. Law clk. Ct. of Appeals of Ohio, Cleve., 1973-75; asst. county prosecutor Cuyahoga County, Cleve., 1975-76; mem. firm Calfee, Halter & Griswold, 1976-84; ptnr. Thomas & Boles, Chagrin Falls, 1985—. Mem. bd. govs. Case Western Res. U. Sch. Law, Cleve., 1981—. Mem. ABA, Ohio Bar Assn., Greater Cleve. Bar Assn. Republican. Episcopalian. Club: Hermit. Federal civil litigation, State civil litigation. Home: 2221 Delaware Dr Cleveland Heights OH 44106 Office: Thomas & Boles 36 S Franklin St Chagrin Falls OH 44022

BOLGER, JOEL HAROLD, lawyer; b. Carroll, Iowa, Feb. 16, 1955; s. Glenn Harold and Ada Ruth (Thomas) B.; m. Cheryl Rita Poore, July 31, 1983; children: Stephanie, Michelle. BS in Econs., U. Iowa, 1976, JD, 1978. Bar: Iowa 1978, Alaska 1979, U.S. Dist. Ct. Alaska, U.S. Ct. Appeals (9th cir.). Staff atty. Alaska Legal Services Corp., Dillingham, 1978-80; supervising atty. Alaska Legal Services Corp., Kodiak, 1980-81; asst. pub. defender Town of Barrow, Alaska, 1981-82; ptnr. Jamin & Bolger, Kodiak, 1982-85, Jamin, Ebell, Bolger & Gentry, Kodiak, 1985—. Avocations: trumpet, softball. Criminal, Local government, Real property. Office: Jamin Ebell Bolger & Gentry 326 Center St Suite 202 Kodiak AK 99615

BOLGER, T(HOMAS) MICHAEL, lawyer; b. Minocqua, Wis., Dec. 23, 1939; s. Patrick Edward and Mary Frances (McConville) B.; A.B., Marquette U., 1961; M.A., St. Louis U., 1966, Ph.L., 1966; J.D., Northwestern U., 1971; m. Virginia Kay Empey, Aug. 24, 1968; children—John, Jennifer. Admitted to Wis. bar, 1971; mem. firm Quarles & Brady, Milw., 1971—, partner, 1978—; instr. philosophy Marquette U., Milw., 1967-68. Vice chmn. United Performing Arts Fund drive, 1976-77; bd. dirs. Kearney Negro Welfare Found., 1974—, Milw. Repertory Theatre, 1977—, Milw. Ballet Found., Inc., 1981—, Permanent Diaconate Program of Milw. Archdiocese, 1977—; pres. Artreach, Inc., 1979—, Milw. Repertory Theater, 1980—; pres. bd. trustees Highland Community Sch., 1976—; trustee, sec.). U. Wis.-Milw. Found., 1976—; pres. bd. dirs. Hickory Hollow, 1978—. Mem. Am. Bar Assn., Milw. Bar Assn., Wis. Bar Assn., Fed. Bar Assn., Marquette U Alumni Assn. (pres. 1982-84), Alpha Sigma Nu, Phi Sigma Tau. Clubs: Univ., The Town. Contbr. articles in field to profl. jours.; editor Northwestern Jour. of Criminal Law, 1970-71. Antitrust, Health, General practice. Home: 137 E White Oak Way Mequon WI 53092 Office: 780 N Water St Milwaukee WI 53202

BOLICK, CLINT DANIEL, lawyer; b. Elizabeth, N.J., Dec. 26, 1957; s. Donald Lee and Emily Martha (Cotter) B.; m. Joanne Beth Felder, Jan. 3, 1981; 1 child, Evan Drew. BA, Drew U., 1979; JD, U. Calif., Davis, 1982. Bar: Calif. 1982, U.S. Supreme Ct. 1986, U.S. Ct. Appeals (2d, 6th, 7th, 9th and 10th cirs.). Atty. Moutain States Legal Found., Denver, 1982-85; spl. asst. to commr. EEOC, Washington, 1985-86; atty. civil rights div., appellate sect. U.S. Dept. Justice, Washington, 1986-87, asst. to atty. gen., 1987—. Contbr. articles to profl. jours. Counsel Colo. Homeschooling Network, 1983-85; campaign activist Pres. Reagan, N.J., Colo., 1976, 84. Barry Goldwater scholar, 1978, Am. Leaders scholar, 1983; Richard Weaver Fellow, 1979. Mem. ABA, Calif. Bar Assn., Federalist Soc. Republican. Civil rights, Labor, Jurisprudence. Home: 3801 Ridge Rd Annandale VA 22003 Office: Dept Justice 9th and Pennsylvania NW Room 5545 Washington DC 20530

BOLLES, DONALD SCOTT, lawyer; b. Buffalo, Dec. 17, 1936; s. Theodore H. amd Marie (Heth) B.; m. Jean Waytulonis Oct. 24, 1963 (dec. May 1983); children: Scott, Matthew. BA, Alfred U., 1960; JD cum laude, U. San Diego, 1970. Bar: Calif. 1971, U.S. Dist. Ct. (so. and no. dists.) Calif. 1971. Ptnr. Hutton, Foley, Anderson & Bolles Inc., King City, Calif., 1971—. Editor lead articles San Diego Law Rev., 1969-70. Trustee Mee Meml. Hosp., King City, 1974-78, chmn., 1978-80; chmn. King City Recreation Commn., 1974-77; candidate mcpl. ct. judge primary and gen. election, Monterey County, Calif., 1986—. Served to capt. U.S. Army, 1961-67, Vietnam. Mem. Monterey County Bar Assn. (exec. com. 1985-86). Republican. Club: Toastmasters (King City) (pres. 1972-74). Lodge: Lions (pres. 1975-76, sec. 1984-86 King City club). Avocations: tennis, raquetball, golf, pool, bridge. General practice, State civil litigation, Consumer commercial. Home: 111 River Dr King City CA 93930 Office: Hutton Foley Anderson & Bolles Inc 510 Broadway King City CA 93930

BOLLIGER, RALPH WENDELL, lawyer; b. Portland, Oreg., Sept. 22, 1931; s. William G. and Frieda U. (Zurbuchen) B.; m. Sally Lichty, Sept. 6, 1952; children: Judy Bolliger Anderson, Laurie Bolliger Boyer, Rondi. BA, Willamette U., 1953, JD, 1955. Bar: Oreg. 1955, U.S. Dist. Ct. Oreg. 1959, U.S. Ct. Appeals (9th cir.) 1971, U.S. Supreme Ct. 1972. Assoc. Peterson, Pozzi & Lent, Portland, Oreg., 1959, Reiter, Day & Anderson, Portland, 1960-63; ptnr. Bolliger, Hampton & Tarlow, Portland, 1963—. Chmn. bd. dirs. Wash. County Edn. Service Dist., Hillsboro, Oreg., 1966-78; trustee Collins Found., Portland, 1980—, Marylhurst Coll., Portland, 1985—. Served to capt. USNR, 1955-85. Mem. ABA, Oreg. Bar Assn. (chmn. com. on probate practice and procedure), Wash. County Bar Assn. Republican. Methodist. Clubs: Columbia Edgewater Country (Portland). Real property, Estate planning. Home: 11190 SW Foothill Dr Portland OR 97225 Office: Bolliger, Hampton & Tarlow 1600 SW Cedar Hills Blvd Suite 102 Portland OR 97225

BOLLINGER, BARRY GILBERT, lawyer; b. Peoria, Ill., Mar. 7, 1943; s. Harold Wilson and Eleanor Lynette (Brunig) B.; m. Modesta Lea Lovejoy, Aug. 13, 1966; 1 child, Jennifer Lea. BS, U. Wis., 1965, JD, 1973. Bar: Wis. 1973, Ill. 1973, U.S. Dist. Ct. (no. dist.) Ill. 1973, U.S. Dist. Ct. (we. dist.) Wis. 1973. Assoc. Wildman, Harrold, Allen & Dixon, Chgo., 1973-79, ptnr., 1980-85; ptnr. Brinton & Bollinger, Chgo., 1986—; bd. dirs. Mgmt. and Care Services, Inc., Norwegian-Am. Hosp.; instr. Loyola Law Sch., Chgo., 1985. Mem. ABA, Ill. Bar Assn., Fed. Trial Bar, Chgo. Trial Lawyers Club. Personal injury, Insurance, State civil litigation. Office: Brinton & Bollinger 303 E Wacker Dr Suite 739 Chicago IL 60601

BOLLINGER, LEE C., legal educator; b. 1946. B.S., U. Oreg., 1968; J.D., Columbia U., 1971. Law clk. U.S. Ct. Appeals (2d cir.), 1971-72; law clk, Chief Justice Warren Burger, U.S. Supreme Ct., 1972-73; asst. prof. law U. Mich., 1973-76, assoc. prof., 1976-78, prof., 1978—; research assoc. Clare Hall, Cambridge U., 1983. Author: (with Jackson) Contract Law in Modern Society, 1980; The Tolerant Soc., 1986. Mem. Rockefeller Humanities Fellowship. Office: U Mich Law Sch 304 Hutchins Hall 621 S State St Ann Arbor MI 48109

BOLT, J. DENNIS, lawyer; b. Anderson, S.C., Dec. 13, 1947; s. Joseph Roy and Frances Lucy (Holley) B.; m. Lynn Wright, July 3, 1971; 1 child, Mary Elizabeth. BA, Clemson U., 1970; JD, U. S.C., 1973. Bar: S.C. Asst. v.p. C & S Nat. Bank, Columbia, S.C., 1973-75; pros. atty., solicitor U.S. Ct. Appeals (5th cir.), Columbia, 1975-79; ptnr. Bolt & Smith, Columbia, 1979—; asst. atty. Richland County, S.C., 1979-83. Mem. Sentencing Alternatives Adv. Com., S.C., 1985—; exec. committeeman Richland County

Dems., Columbia, 1974-76, chmn. 1976-77. Mem. ABA, Richland County Bar Assn., S.C. Trial Lawyers Assn. (chmn. criminal law commn. 1984-85). Democrat. Club: German (Columbia, S.C.) (pres. 1984—). Avocation: photography. Criminal, State civil litigation, Personal injury. Home: 1731 Crestwood Dr Columbia SC 29205 Office: Bolt & Smith PO Box 1699 Columbia SC 29202

BOLTON, JOHN ROBERT, lawyer, federal agency administrator; b. Balt., Nov. 20, 1948; s. Edward Jackson and Virginia (Godfrey) B.; m. Gretchen Brainerd, Jan. 1987; 1 child, Jennifer Sarah. BA, Yale U., 1970, JD summa cum laude, 1974. Bar: D.C. 1975, U.S. Dist. Ct. D.C. 1975, U.S. Ct. Appeals (D.C. cir.) 1975, U.S. Ct. Appeals (4th cir.) 1977, U.S. Ct. Appeals (3d cir.) 1978, U.S. Supreme Ct. 1978, U.S. Ct. Appeals (5th and 11th cirs.) 1981, U.S. Ct. Appeals (10th cir.) 1983. Assoc. Covington & Burling, Washington, 1974-81, ptnr., 1983-84; legal cons. The White House, Washington, 1981; gen. counsel Agy. for Internat. Devel., Washington, 1981-82, asst. adminstr., 1982-83; exec. dir. com. on resolutions Rep. Nat. Com., Washington, 1983-84; ptnr. Covington and Burling, Washington, 1984-86; asst. atty. gen. legis. affairs U.S. Dept. Justice, 1986—. Contbr. articles to profl. jours. Mem. Phi Beta Kappa, Pi Sigma Alpha. Home: 9107 Fernwood Rd Bethesda MD 20817 Office: Dept of Justice Legis Affairs 10th Constitution Ave NW Washington DC 20530

BOLTON, ROBERT SAUL, lawyer; b. Detroit, Dec. 25, 1936; s. Irving and Ruth (Wolf) B.; m. Ruth Ellen Schmiedl, Sept. 29, 1967; children: Anya, Karine, Gabrielle, Tami. BA, U. Mich., 1958, JD, 1961. Bar: Mich. 1962, Calif. 1962. Research asst. Mich. Constl. Conv., Lansing, 1961-62; assoc. Butzel, Keiden, Simon, Myers & Graham, Detroit, 1965-73; ptnr. Butzel, Keiden, Simon, Myers & Graham, Detroit and Bloomfield Hills, Mich., 1973—. Contbr. articles to profl. jours. Served to capt. JAGC, USAF, 1962-65. Mem. Mich. Bar Assn. (treas. real property sect. 1981-84), Calif. Bar Assn., Oakland County Bar Assn., Detroit Bar Assn., Am. Coll. Real Estate Lawyers Comml. Law League. Bankruptcy, Contracts commercial, Real property. Home: 4689 Patrick West Bloomfield MI 48033 Office: Butzel Keiden Simon Myers & Graham 505 N Woodward #1100 Bloomfield Hills MI 48013

BOLTON, WARREN ROBERT, lawyer; b. Plymouth, Mass., Aug. 12, 1923; s. Charles L.E. and Mary Jane (Mattie) B.; m. Doris Ann Besso, Aug. 31, 1946; children—David Warren, Carol Ann, Janice Rebecca, Nancy Marie. B.A., Suffolk U., 1948, J.D., 1951. Bar: Mass. 1951, U.S. Dist. Ct. Mass. 1955, U.S. Ct. Appeals (1st cir.) 1957, U.S. Supreme Ct. 1960, N.H. 1976. Sr. ptnr. Bolton & Trebat, P.C., Waltham, Mass., 1954—, Chatham, Mass., 1977—; legis. counsel Mass. Assn. Land Surveyers and Civil Engrs., Boston, 1959-72, legis. agt. atty., 1959-72, atty. Boston Survey Cons., 1955—; def. counsel on infamous Brinks case, 1955; trustee Coastal and Suburban Trust, Waltham, Chatham, 1960—; corporator Waltham Sav. Bank, 1984—. Served as sgt. USAAF, 1943-46, ETO. Decorated Air medal with 4 oak clusters. Mem. ABA, Mass. Bar Assn., N.H. Bar Assn., Assn. Trial Lawyers Am., Assn. Mass. Trial Lawyers, Boston Bar Assn. Republican. Roman Catholic. Lodge: Kiwanis (gov. New Eng. dist. 1970-71). State civil litigation, Personal injury, Real property. Home: 560 Orleans Rd North Chatham MA 02650 Office: 132 Vernon St Waltham MA 02154

BOLTZ, GERALD EDMUND, lawyer; b. Dennison, Ohio, June 1, 1931; s. Harold E. and Margaret Eve (Hecky) B.; m. Janet Ruth Scott, Sept. 19, 1959; children—Gretchen, Eric, Jill. B.A., Ohio No. U., 1953, J.D., 1955. Bar: Ohio 1955, U.S. Supreme Ct. 1964, Calif. 1978, U.S. Dist. Ct. (cen. dist.) Calif. 1978. Asst. atty. gen. State of Ohio, 1958; trial atty. SEC, 1959-60, legal asst. to commr., 1960-61, sr. trial and spl. counsel, Denver, 1961-66, regional adminstr., Ft. Worth, 1967-71, regional adminstr., Los Angeles, 1972-78; ptnr. Fine, Perzik & Friedman, Los Angeles, 1979-83; ptnr. Rogers & Wells, Los Angeles, 1983—. Served with U.S. Army, 1955-57. Recipient SEC Disting. Service award, 1971. Mem. ABA, Fed. Bar Assn., Los Angeles Bar Assn., Ohio Bar Assn., Calif. Bar Assn. Republican. Presbyterian. Club: Calif. Yacht (Marina Del Rey, Calif.). General corporate. Office: Rogers & Wells 201 N Figueroa St Floor 15 Los Angeles CA 90012-2638

BOLTZ, RUSS EDWARD, lawyer; b. Detroit, Sept. 30, 1947; s. Edward Davilla and Frances Barbara (Russ) B.; m. Amy Gere, Mar. 22, 1969; children: Edward C., Rebecca Anne. BA, Kalamazoo Coll., 1969; cert., U. London, 1971; JD, U. Notre Dame, 1972. Bar: Mich. 1972, U.S. Supreme Ct. 1977, D.C. 1978. Assoc. Riley & Roumell, Detroit, 1972-73; ptnr. Beer & Boltz, Bloomfield Hills, Mich., 1973-81, Boltz & Roth, Bloomfield Hills, 1978-81; sr. counsel Mich. Nat. Corp., Clawson, Mich., 1981-85; ptnr. Pepper, Hamilton & Scheetz, Detroit, 1985—. Mem. State Bd. Med., Lansing, 1985—. Mem. D.C. Bar Assn., Mich. Bar Assn., Mich. Bankers Assn. Methodist. Club: Detroit Athletic. Banking, Federal civil litigation, Consumer commercial. Home: 487 E Gunn Rd Rochester MI 48063 Office: Pepper Hamilton & Scheetz 100 Renaissance Ctr 36th Floor Detroit MI 48243

BOLY, JEFFREY ELWYN, lawyer; b. Portland, Oreg., Mar. 16, 1942; s. Elwyn and Frances Rolland (Hulse) B.; m. Mary Ione Van Beckum, Sept. 4, 1965; children—Jeffrey Elwyn, Justin; m. 2d, Diane Edna Davis, Jan. 8, 1976; children—Teresa, Craig. A.B., Georgetown U., 1964; J.D., U. Calif.-San Francisco, 1967. Bar: U.S. Dist. Ct. (no. dist.) Calif. 1967, Calif. 1967, U.S. Ct. Appeals (9th cir.) 1967, U.S. Tax Ct. 1968, Oreg. 1971, U.S. Dist. Ct. Oreg. 1971, U.S. Supreme Ct. 1971. Trial atty. office of chief counsel to commr. IRS, San Francisco, 1967-71; ptnr. Wood Tatum Mosser Brooke & Landis, Portland, Oreg., 1971—; chmn. estate planning sect. Oreg. State Bar. Trustee Portland Civic Theatre, 1975-81, pres. bd. trustees, 1979-80; bd. dirs. Oreg. Advs. for Arts, 1980—, pres. bd. dirs., 1981-82; chmn. bd. dirs. Ballet Oreg. Mem. ABA, Calif. Bar Assn., Multnomah County Bar Assn., Oreg. Bar Assn. Democrat. Roman Catholic. Club: Georgetown U. Alumni Assn. (pres. Portland chpt. 1977). Estate planning, Corporate taxation, Personal income taxation. Office: 1001 SW 5th Ave Suite 1300 Portland OR 97204

BOMBERGER, RUSSELL BRANSON, lawyer, educator; b. Lebanon, Pa., May 1, 1934; s. John Mark and Viola (Aurentz) B.; divorced; children—Ann Elizabeth, Jane Carmel. B.S., Temple U., 1955; M.A., U. Iowa, 1956, U. Iowa, 1961; Ph.D., U. Iowa, 1962; M.S., U. So. Calif., 1960; LL.B., J.D., LaSalle U. Bar: Calif. also various fed. cts., U.S. Supreme Ct. Mem. editorial staff Phila. Inquirer, 1952-54; lectr. U. Iowa, 1955-57, U. So. Calif., 1957-58; asst. prof. U.S. Naval Postgrad. Sch., Monterey, Calif., 1958-62; assoc. prof. U.S. Naval Postgrad. Sch., 1963-75, prof., 1975—; practice law 1970—; free lance writer, 1952—, communications cons., 1963—; safety cons. internat. program U. So. Calif. Inst. Safety and Systems Mgmt., 1983—; cons. Internat. Ctr. for Aviation Safety, Lisbon, 1984—. Author: broadcast series The World of Ideas; motion picture Strokes and Stamps; abstracter-editor: Internat. Transactional Analysis Assn. Served to capt. USNR., 1966—. Am. Psychol. Found. fellow Columbia U., 1954-55; CBS fellow U. So. Calif., 1957-58. Mem. ABA. Aviation, Federal civil litigation, Legal education. Office: PO Box 8741 Monterey CA 93943

BOMBINO, ISABEL PIÑERA, lawyer; b. Havana, Cuba, Jan. 6, 1954; came to U.S., Jan. 1971; d. Osvaldo V. Piñera and Lidia (Ayala) Molina; m. Hector L. Bombino, June 9, 1972 (div. Apr. 1980). AA with honors, Hillsborough Community Coll., 1974; BA with honors, U. S. Fla., 1977; postgrad., Nova Law Ctr., 1977-78; JD with honors, Fla. State U., 1980. Recipient Am. Jurisprudence award in Criminal Law, 1977, Fed. Jurisdiction, 1978, Adminstrv. Law, 1978. Mem. ABA, Cuban-Am. Bar Assn., Fla. Trial Lawyers Assn., Phi Alpha Delta. Republican. Roman Catholic. Criminal, Personal injury, Family and matrimonial. Home: 1412 Ortega Ave Coral Gables FL 33134 Office: 1702 SW 15th St Miami FL 33145

BOMMER, TIMOTHY J., magistrate; b. Columbus, Ohio, Dec. 9, 1940; s. Thomas F. and Susan L. (Proper) B.; m. Sandra K. Bartlett, May 16, 1964; children: Breton J., Kevin A., Melissa K. BA, U. Wyo., 1963, JD, 1970. Bar: Wyo. 1970, Colo. 1970. Dep. county and pros. atty. Teton County Prosecutor's Office, Jackson, Wyo., 1970-74; ptnr. Ranck & Bommer, Jackson, 1970-77; magistrate U.S. Dist. Ct., Jackson, 1976—; sole practice Jackson, 1977—; regional dir. Govs.'s Planning Com. on Criminal Adminstrn., Wyo., 1973-74. Served to capt. USAF, 1963-67. Mem. ABA, Assn. Trial Lawyers Am., Wyo. Trial Lawyers Assn. (bd. dirs. 1976-79), Wyo. State Bar Ethics Com., Wyo. State Bar Fee Arbitration Com. (chmn. 1980-84), Wyo. Jud. Nominating Commn. Republican. Episcopalian. Avocations: boating, hunting, fishing, skiing. Federal civil litigation, State civil litigation, Personal injury. Home: 575 W Aspen Dr PO Box 1728 Jackson WY 83001 Office: 172 Center St PO Box 1728 Jackson WY 83001

BONACCI, EDWARD HOWARD, JR., lawyer; b. Bklyn., May 17, 1955; s. Edward Howard and Nancy Anna (Oliva) B. BA in English, Villanova U., 1977, JD, 1980. Bar: N.Y. 1981, U.S. Dist. Ct. (ea. and so. dists.) N.Y. 1984. Assoc. Iannuzzi, Russo & Iannuzzi, N.Y.C., 1981-82; staff atty. Empire Mut. Ins. Group, N.Y.C., 1982—. Mem. ABA, N.Y. County Lawyers Assn. Republican. Roman Catholic. Avocations: traveling, theater, nature, writing prose and poetry, legal courses. State civil litigation, Insurance, Personal injury. Home: 1322 44th St Apt A15 Brooklyn NY 11219 Office: Raymond J MacDonnell 122 Fifth Ave New York NY 10011

BONAPARTE, RONALD H., lawyer; b. Los Angeles, Apr. 7, 1935; s. Haig K. and Gladys (Torosian) B.; m. H. Aileen Ingram, Dec. 2, 1977. BA, Pomona Coll.; JD, Stanford U.; postgrad., UCLA. Bar: Calif. 1960, U.S. Supreme Ct. 1965. Sole practice Los Angeles, 1960-81; sr. ptnr. Bonaparte & O'Kane, Los Angeles, 1981-86; sole practice Los Angeles, 1987—; lectr. law Practising Law Inst., N.Y.C., 1968—, UCLA, 1971-77, U. So. Calif., Los Angeles, 1974—, Southwestern U. Sch. Law, Los Angeles, 1983-84. Contbr. articles to profl. jours. Served with USAF. Mem. ABA (internat. law sect., chmn. immigration com. 1976-84), Calif. Bar Assn. (chmn. organizing com. to recognize immigration law as a specialized practice 1983-86), Am. Immigration Lawyers Assn. (chmn. 1968-69, 86-87). Republican. Clubs: Town Hall of Calif., Riviera Country (Los Angeles); Balboa Bay (Newport Beach, Calif.). Avocations: golf, boating, skiing. Immigration, naturalization, and customs. Home: 350 N Gunston Los Angeles CA 90049

BONAVENTURA, MARK GABRIEL, lawyer; b. Columbus, Ohio, Dec. 6, 1952; s. Angelo Paul and Virginia Eunice (McGowan) B.; m. Kathleen Ann Cahill, Aug. 25, 1979; 1 child, Bridget Ann. BS in Adminstrv. Sci., Ohio State U., 1974; JD cum laude, Capital U., 1979. Bar: Ohio 1979, U.S. Dist. Ct. (so. dist.) Ohio 1980, U.S. Dist. Ct. (no. dist.) Ohio 1982. Asst. atty. gen. State of Ohio, Columbus, 1979—. Mem. Columbus Symphony Chorus, 1979—. Mem. ABA, Ohio Bar Assn., Columbus Bar Assn., Order of Curia. Roman Catholic. Avocations: vocal performance, scuba diving, woodworking. Administrative and regulatory, State civil litigation, Bankruptcy. Office: Div of Reclamation Fountain Sq Bldg B3 Columbus OH 43224

BOND, GEORGE CLINE, lawyer, oil company executive; b. Abingdon, Ill., May 30, 1920; s. George Clair and Bertha Rose (Cline) B.; m. Winifred Commack, Dec. 27, 1942; children—Kathryn Bond Holden, Walter Cochran, Margaret, Bruce. A.B., Swarthmore Coll., 1942; J.D., Stanford U., 1949. Bar: Calif. 1949, D.C. 1954. Assoc. counsel Union Title Ins. & Trust Co., San Diego, 1949-51; asst. sec., atty. Consol. Vultee Aircraft Corp., San Diego, 1951-53; sec., gen. counsel Pacific Airmotive Corp., Burbank, Calif., 1953-55; asst. to chmn. bd. Union Oil Co. of Calif., Los Angeles, 1960-62, v.p., gen. counsel, 1973—. Del. Republican Nat. Conv., 1952. Served to lt. comdr. USNR, 1942-45. Mem. ABA, Chancery Club Los Angeles, Am. Corp. Counsel Assn. (dir.), S.W. Legal Found. (chmn. Internat. Oil and Gas Edn. Ctr. 1979-81), Am. Petroleum Inst. (chmn. com. on law 1979-80). Clubs: Calif. (Los Angeles); Annandale Golf (Pasadena, Calif.). General corporate, Oil and gas leasing, Private international. Office: 725 S Figueroa St Los Angeles CA 90017

BOND, KENNETH WALTER, lawyer; b. Eugene, Oreg., Apr. 18, 1947; s. Daniel Bernard and Mildred Iris Bond; m. Gloria Lynn Veeder, Jan. 20, 1979; children: Kenneth Sandler, Elizabeth Veeder, Allison Martin. BA, Johns Hopkins U., 1969; JD, U. Calif. Hastings Coll. of Law, 1972; LLM, NYU, 1976. Bar: N.Y., Fla., U.S. Dist. Ct. (so. dist.) Fla., U.S. Ct. Appeals (2d cir.), U.S. Tax Ct. Assoc. LeBoeuf, Lamb, Leiby & Macrae, N.Y.C., 1975-79, Roger & Wells, N.Y.C., 1980-84; ptnr. Sullivan, Donovan, Hanrahan & Silliere, N.Y.C., 1984—. Contbr. articles to Fordham Urban Law Jour., 1976, N.Y. Law Jour., 1983. Served to capt. U.S. Army, 1972-76. Mem. N.Y. State Bar Assn., Fla. Bar Assn., Assn. of the Bar of the City of N.Y. Presbyterian. Clubs: University (N.Y.C.); Tuxedo (N.Y.). Avocation: gardening. Municipal bonds, State and local taxation, Real property. Office: Sullivan Donovan Hanrahan & Silliere 780 Third Ave New York NY 10017

BOND, MARC DOUGLAS, lawyer; b. Spokane, Wash., July 3, 1954; s. Richard Milton and Patricia (Hendrikson) B.; m. Cathy Sue Kasner, July 16, 1977. BA in Polit. Sci., Willamette U., 1975, JD cum laude, 1978. Bar: Wash. 1978, Alaska 1979, U.S. Dist. Ct. Alaska 1979, U.S. Ct. Appeals (9th cir.) 1984. Law clk. to presiding judge Alaska Ct. System, Anchorage, 1978-79; assoc. Delaney, Wiles, Hayes, Reitman & Brubaker Inc., Anchorage, 1979-83, ptnr., 1983—. Legal advisor Alaska div. Nat. Ski Patrol System Inc., Denver, 1982—; dir. Sourdough Ski Patrol, Girdwood, Alaska, 1983-86; bd. dirs. ARC, Anchorage, 1983-86. Mem. ABA, Wash. State Bar Assn., Alaska Bar Assn. Republican. Mem. Evangelical Christian Ch. Avocations: skiing, hiking, camping. Contracts commercial, Natural resources, Landlord-tenant. Office: Delaney Wiles Hayes et al 1007 W 3d Ave #400 Anchorage AK 99501

BOND, RICHARD EWING, lawyer; b. Elkhart, Ind., Sept. 2, 1953; s. James Ewing Jr. and Rosemary (Kryder) B.; m. Elizabeth Keyser Elliott, Aug. 2, 1975; 1 child, Elliott Ewing. AB, Ind. U., 1976; JD, Willamette U., 1979. Bar: Oreg. 1979, Ind. 1981, U.S. Dist. Ct. (no. dist.) Ind. 1981. Assoc. Schlegel, Milbank, Wheeler, Jarman & Hilgemann, Salem, Oreg., 1979-81, Spahn, Atwater, Arko & Yoder, Elkhart, Ind., 1981-84; v.p., asst. gen. counsel Holiday Rambler Corp., Wakarusa, Ind., 1984-86, v.p., gen. counsel, corp. sec., 1987—. Articles editor Willamette U. Law Rev., 1978-79. Pres. bd. dirs. Elkhart Youth Services Bur. Inc., 1985—. Mem. ABA, Ind. State Bar Assn., Elkhart City Bar Assn. Republican. State civil litigation, General corporate. Home: 2207 E Jackson Blvd Elkhart IN 46516 Office: Holiday Rambler Corp 65528 State Rd 19 Wakarusa IN 46573

BOND, THOMAS RICHARD, lawyer; b. Abington, Pa., Apr. 24, 1945; s. Richard Charles Bond and Elizabeth M. (Mellott) Yerkes; m. Suzanne Elizabeth Seif, Apr. 15, 1967; children: Christopher Thomas, Paul J., Jean Marie, Michael. BA, U. Pa., 1967; JD, Temple U., 1973. Bar: Pa. 1973. Asst. dist. atty. Bucks County, Doylestown, Pa., 1973-74; house counsel Employers Ins. of Wausau, Phila., 1974-76; ptnr. LaBrum & Doak, Phila., 1976-86, Manta & Welge, Phila., 1986—; lectr. numerous assns. and orgns. Contbr. articles to profl. jours. Adult advisor Chalfont (Pa.) Youth Orgn., 1985—. Mem. ABA, Pa. Bar Assn. (compensation sect., editor-in-chief newsletter 1982—), Phila. Bar Assn., Phila. Workers Compensation Claim Assn., Pa. Def. Inst. (bd. govs.1983—), Phil.-Lower Bucks County Claim Assn. Republican. Roman Catholic. Lodge: KC. Avocations: reading, tennis, nautilis. Workers' compensation. Home: 119 Brittany Drive Chalfont PA 18914 Office: Manta & Welge 3 Penn Center Plaza Suite 1818 Philadelphia PA 19102

BONDOC, ROMMEL, lawyer; b. Pomona, Calif., June 23, 1938; s. Nicholas Rommel and Gladys Sue (Buckner) B.; m. Ariel Guiberson, Aug. 20, 1960 (div. 1963); m. alberta Linnea Young, Dec. 13, 1967; children—Daphne, Patience, Margaret, Nicholas. A.B., Stanford U., 1959, J.D., 1963. Bar: Calif. 1964, U.S. Ct. Appeals (9th cir.) 1965, U.S. Supreme Ct. 1969. Assoc. Melvin Belli, San Francisco, 1964-66, Vincent Hallinan, San Francisco, 1966-69; sole practice, San Francisco, 1969—. Mem. San Francisco Bar Assn. (judiciary com. 1982-85), No. Calif. Criminal Trial Lawyers Assn. (bd. dirs. 1972—, pres. 1978-79), Calif. Attys. for Criminal Justice (bd. dirs. 1975-80). Democrat. Methodist. Criminal. Home: 509 Canyon Rd Novato CA 94947 Office: 899 Ellis St San Francisco CA 94109

BONE, MAURICE EDGAR, lawyer; b. East St. Louis, Ill., Mar. 1, 1924; s. Edgar W. and Margaret T. (Jett) B.; m. Phyllis J. Frick, June 7, 1955; children: Stephen, Gregory, Larry, David. BS, St. Louis U., 1947, JD, 1951. BAr: Mo. 1951, Ill. 1953, U.S. Dist. Ct. (ea. dist.) Ill. 1953. Sole practice East St. Louis, 1953-56; ptnr. Kassly, Carr & Bone, East St. Louis, 1956-60, Kassly, Weihl, Carr & Bone, East St. Louis, 1960-67, Kassly, Bone, Becker, Dix, Tillery & Reagan, Belleville, Ill., 1967—; bd. dirs. trustee Magna Trust Co., Ill. State Trust Co., Belleville, Bank of Belleville. Contbr. articles to profl. jours. Served to maj., USAF, 1943-45, ETO, 51-53. Mem. Ill. Bar Assn. (bd. govs. 1984—), Ill. Bar Found. (pres. 1984). State civil litigation, Landlord-tenant, Personal injury. Home and Office: 5111 W Main St Belleville IL 62223

BONEBRAKE, CAROL BUCHELE, lawyer; b. Arkansas City, Kans., Dec. 28, 1949; d. Julian Milton and Vergie May (Bryant) Buchele; m. Charles Richard Bonebrake, May 23, 1971; children: Michael, Ashley, Natalie, Matthew. BA, Kans. State U., 1971; JD cum laude, DePaul U., 1975. Bar: Minn. 1975, Kans. 1980, U.S. Dist. Ct. Kans. 1980, U.S. Ct. Appeals (10th cir.) 1981, U.S. Supreme Ct. 1983. Assoc. Dorsey, Windhorst, Hannaford, Whitney & Halladay, Rochester, Kans., 1975-79; atty. Kans. Dept. Revenue, Topeka, 1979-83; dir. of taxation State of Kans., Topeka, 1983—. Mem. Topeka Jr. League, 1985—; bd. dirs. Topeka YMCA, 1986—. Mem. Kans. Bar Assn., Minn. Bar Assn., Topeka Bar Assn., Olmsted County Bar Assn., Kans. Trial Lawyers Assn., Alpha Chi Omega. Democrat. Methodist. State and local taxation. Office: Kans Dept Revenue State Office Bldg Topeka KS 66611

BONEE, JOHN LEON, III, lawyer; b. Hartford, Conn., Dec. 16, 1947; s. John Leon, Jr. and M. Elaine (Sheridan) B. B.A., Trinity Coll., Hartford, 1970; J.D., Suffolk U., 1974; postgrad. Hague Acad. Internat. Law, The Netherlands, 1975. Bar: Conn. 1974, U.S. Dist. Ct. Conn. 1974; U.S. Ct. Appeals (2d cir.) 1975, U.S. Supreme Ct. 1979. Assoc. Kenyon, Bonee & Greenspan, Hartford, 1974-78, ptnr., 1979—; corp. counsel Town of West Hartford, Conn., 1983. Contbr. articles to profl. jours. Mem. West Hartford Bd. of Edn., 1981-83, Community Planning Adv. Com., West Hartford, 1984, exec. com., bd. dirs. World Affairs Ctr., Hartford, 1980-87; mem. West Hartford Town Council, 1985—. Mem. ABA (gen. practice and Internat. Law sects.), Conn. Bar Assn. (editor-at-large jour. 1978-84), Greater Hartford C. of C. (internat. trade com. 1984), Hartford County Bar Assn. (bar/media com. 1984), Loomis-Chaffee Nat. Alumni Assn. (v.p. Loomis affairs 1978-82), Trinity Coll. Alumni Assn. (class pres. and sec. 1986—). Federal civil litigation, Probate, State civil litigation. Office: Kenyon Bonee & Greenspan 1 State St Hartford CT 06103

BONESIO, WOODROW MICHAEL, lawyer; b. Hereford, Tex., Dec. 27, 1943; s. Harold Andre and Elizabeth (Ireland) B.; m. Michaele Ann Dougherty; children: Elizabeth Eaton, Jo Kristin, William Michael. B.A., Austin Coll., 1966; J.D., U. Houston, 1971. Bar: Tex. 1971, U.S. Dist. Ct. (we. and no. dists.) Tex. 1973, U.S. Ct. Appeals (5th cir.) 1973, U.S. Ct. Appeals (11th cir.) 1981. Law clk. to U.S. dist. Judge Western Dist. Tex., San Antonio, 1971-73; ptnr. Akin, Gump, Strauss, Hauer & Feld, Dallas, 1973—; speaker profl. confs. Democratic precinct chmn. Dallas County; mem. Dallas County Dem. Exec. Com., 1982—; elder Northminster Presbyterian Ch., 1981-85; bd. dirs. Grace Presbytery Devel. Bd., 1986—. Mem. ABA, Fed. Bar Assn., Am. Judicature Soc., Dallas Bar Assn., Phi Alpha Delta, Order of Barons, Austin Coll. Alumni Assn. (bd. dirs. 1983—); U. Houston Law Alumni Assn. (chpt. pres. 1982). Federal civil litigation, Antitrust, State civil litigation. Office: Akin Gump Strauss Hauer & Feld 1700 Pacific Ave Suite 4100 Dallas TX 75201

BONESTEEL, MICHAEL JOHN, lawyer; b. Los Angeles, Dec. 22, 1939; s. Henry Theodore Samuel Becker and Kathleen Mansfield (Nolan) B.; children—Damon Becker, Kirsten Kathleen; m. Susan Elizabeth Schaff, June 1, 1980. A.B. in History, Stanford U., 1961; J.D., U. So. Calif., 1966. Bar: Calif. 1967, U.S. Dist. Ct. (cen. and so. dists.) Calif. 1967, U.S. Dist. Ct. (no. dist.) Calif. 1969, U.S. Dist. Ct. (ea. dist.) Calif. 1983. Assoc., Haight, Dickson, Brown & Bonesteel and predecessors, Los Angeles and Santa Monica, Calif., 1967-71, ptnr. 1972—. Sustaining mem. Republican Nat. Com. Fellow Internat. Acad. Trial Lawyers; mem. State Bar Calif., Fedn. Ins. Counsel, Def. Research Inst., Assn. of So. Calif. Def. Counsel. Episcopalian. Club: Bel Air Bay (Santa Monica). Federal civil litigation, State civil litigation, Insurance. Office: Haight Dickson Brown & Bonesteel 201 Santa Monica Blvd Santa Monica CA 90406

BONESTEEL, RICHARD DAVID, lawyer; mortgage banker; b. Seattle, May 26, 1931; s. Wendell and Jeanne (Eppley) B.; m. Charlotte Marie Hunt, Aug. 16, 1958 (div.); children—Richard David Jr., Linda Jayne, Wendy Ann. B.A. in Bus. Adminstrn., U. Wash., 1953, J.D., 1956; cert. Sch. Mortgage Banking, Northwestern U., 1966. Bar: Wash. 1956, U.S. Dist. Ct. (no. dist.) Wash. 1956, U.S. Ct. Appeals (9th cir.) 1956. Assoc., Evans, McLaren, Lane, Powell & Beeks, Seattle, 1956-61; with Seafirst Mortgage Corp., Seattle, 1961—, now v.p., sr. counsel, sec.-treas., sec. bd. Pres. Wash. State Badminton Assn., 1961-62. Served with USAF, 1951-52. Fellow Am. Coll. Mortgage Attys.; mem. Wash. Mortgage Bankers Assn. (pres. 1973-74), Seattle Mortgage Bankers Assn. (pres. 1979-80), Am. Land Title Assn. (founder, chmn. lender counsel group 1976—), Am. Coll. Real Estate Lawyers (charter 1979—), Mortgage Bankers Assn. Am. (legal issues com. 1987—), ABA, Wash. State Bar Assn. (chmn., lectr. and panelist real estate law seminars), Seattle-King County Bar Assn., Phi Delta Phi, Alpha Delta Phi. Republican. Episcopalian. Club: Wash. Athletic (Seattle). Revisions editor Wash. Law Rev., 1955-56; mem. seminar panel N.Y. Law Jour., 1980; contbr. chpts. to books, articles on real property to legal jours. Real property, Banking, Contracts commercial. Home: 3044 37th Ave W Seattle WA 98199 Office: Seafirst Real Estate Group PO Box C 34103 Seattle WA 98124-1103 Address: PO Box C-34103 Seattle WA 98124-1103

BONGIORNO, ANDREW WILLIAM, lawyer; b. N.Y.C., Sept. 7, 1945; s. Joseph and Rose (DeRicco) B.; m. Donna Lee Striffler, Aug. 24, 1968; children: Jessica Lee, Andrea Lorin. BA, Queens Coll., 1966; JD, Fordham U., 1969. Bar: N.Y. 1970, U.S. Supreme Ct. 1974. Assoc. Wormser, Koch, Kiely etc., N.Y.C., 1968-71; atty. AT&T Western Electric, N.Y.C., 1971-85; sr. atty. AT&T Info. Systems, Parsippany, N.J., 1985—. Served with U.S. Army, 1969-75. Mem. ABA, N.Y. State Bar Assn. Republican. Contracts commercial, Antitrust, Immigration, naturalization, and customs. Office: AT&T Info Systems 5 Wood Hollow Rd Parsippany NJ 07054

BONHAM, TERRENCE JAMES, lawyer, hearing officer; b. Richmond, Calif., June 8, 1938; s. Harry L. and Helen G. (Gately) B.; m. Joyce E. Trout, July 28, 1968; 1 dau., Teresa J. B.A. in Econs., St. Mary's Coll., 1960; J.D., U. Calif., Hastings Coll. Law, San Francisco, 1963. Bar: Calif. 1964, U.S. Dist. Ct. (no. dist.) Calif. 1964, U.S. Ct. Mil. Appeals 1964, U.S. Ct. Appeals (9th cir.) 1964, U.S. Supreme Ct. 1983. Assoc. Halde, Battin, Barrymore & Stevens, Santa Barbara, Calif., 1968-73; ptnr. Barrymore, Stevens & Bonham, Santa Barbara, 1973-74; mem. Riley, Holzhauer, Denver & McClain, Santa Barbara, 1974-80; ptnr. Lawler & Ellis, Ventura, Calif., 1980-85, ptnr. Lawler, Bonham & Walsh, 1985—; judge protem Santa Barbara-Goleta Mcpl. Ct., Ventura County Superior Ct.; hearing officer County of Santa Barbara Civil Service Com., Santa Barbara Bd. Retirement; lectr. Bridging the Gap, Ventura County; lectr. to assns. Mem. Civil Arbitration Panel Ventura County, 1979—; mem. Republican Presdl. Task Force, Nat. Rep. Senatorial Com. Served to capt. U.S. Army, 1964-68. Decorated Bronze Star. Mem. Assn. So. Calif. Def. Counsel, Am. Bd. Trial Advs. (pres. 1984-85), Ventura County Bar Assn. (formerly exec. com., co-chmn. atty./client com.), ABA, Am. Soc. Law and Medicine. Roman Catholic. Clubs: KC (past faithful navigator) (Santa Barbara); Elks (Ventura). State civil litigation, Insurance, Personal injury. Home: 2851 Seahorse Ave Ventura CA 93001 Office: PO Box 1269 Ventura CA 93002

BONHAM-YEAMAN, DORIA, business law educator; b. Los Angeles, June 10, 1932; d. Carl Herschel and Edna Mae (Jones) Bonham Emanuel; widowed; children—Carl Q., Doria Valerie-Constance. B.A., U. Tenn., 1953, J.D., 1957, M.A., 1958; Ed.S. in Computer Edn., Barry U., 1984. Instr. bus. law Palm Beach Jr. Coll., Lake Worth, Fla., 1960-69; instr. legal environment Fla. Atlantic U., Boca Raton, 1969-73; lectr. bus. law Fla. Internat. U., North Miami, 1973-83, assoc. prof. bus. law, 1983—. Editor: Anglo-Am. Law Conf., 1980; Developing Global Corporate Strategies, 1981; editorial bd. Attys. Computer Report, 1984-85, Jour. Legal Studies Edn., 1985—. Contbr. articles to profl. jours. Bd. dirs. Palm Beach County Assn. for Deaf Children, 1960-63; mem. Fla. Commn. on Status of Women, Tallahassee, 1969-70; mem. Broward County Democratic Exec. Com., 1982—; pres. Dem. Women's Club Broward County, 1981; mem. Marine Council of Greater Miami, 1978—, Service award, 1979. Recipient Faculty Devel. award Fla. Internat. U., Miami, 1980; grantee Notre Dame Law Sch., London, summer 1980. Mem. Am. Bus. Law Assn., No. Dade C. of C., Am. Acctg. Assn.,

Inst. Mgmt. Sci. (pres. alumnae chpt.), AAUW (pres. Palm Beach County 1965-66), Alpha Chi Omega (chpt. pres. 1968-71), Tau Kappa Alpha. Episcopalian. Legal education, Computer. Office: Fla Internat Univ North Miami FL 33181

BONILLA, TONY, league executive, lawyer; b. Calvert, Tex., Mar. 2, 1936. Grad., Del Mar. Coll., 1955; B.A. in Edn., Baylor U., 1958; LL.B., U. Houston, 1960. Bar: Tex. 1960, U.S. Dist. Ct. (so. dist.) Tex. 1960. Mem. firm Bonilla, Read, Bonilla & Berlanga, Inc., and predecessors, Corpus Christi, Tex., 1960—; mem. Tex. Legislature, 1964-66, Tex. Constn. Revision Commn., 1973; pres. League of United Latin Am. Citizens, Washington; bd. dirs. League of United Latin Am. Citizens, Washington, 1972-75; chmn. Nat. Hispanic Leadership Conf., Tex. Bilingual Task Force, Task Force on Pub. Edn.; rep. USIA tour S.Am. to discuss drug issues, 1986. Appeared, Today Show, McNeil-Lehr Report, Phil Donohue Nightline, CBS News; lectr. on Hispanic issues colls. and univs. Mem. coordinating bd. Tex. Coll. and Univ. System, 1973-79. Recipient Cecil Burney Humanitarian award Nueces County Bar Assn., 1986. Mem. ABA, Tex. Trial Lawyers Assn., Corpus Christi C. of C. (dir. 1973-78). General practice. Home: 327 Baycliff Corpus Christi TX 78412 Office: Nat Hispanic Leadership Conf 2590 Morgan Corpus Christi TX 78405

BONNER, EUGENE ALOYSIUS, lawyer; b. Bryn Mawr, Pa., Oct. 2, 1951; s. Francis John and Marion Kirk (Henderson) B.; m. Isabel Jean Finkbiner, Aug. 18, 1979; children: Michael Eugene, Charles Rodman, John Francis. BS, U. Dayton, 1974, JD, 1977. Bar: Pa. 1977, U.S. Dist. Ct. (ea. dist.) Pa. 1977, U.S. Supreme Ct. 1982. Law clk. to presiding justice Pa. Ct. Common Pleas, Media, 1977-78, pub. defender, 1978-83, juvenile ct. master, 1984-85; sole practice Media, 1985—. Advisor, Law Explorers Post, 1980-86. Mem. Rep. com., Upper Providence, Pa., 1986. Mem. Pa. Bar Assn., Del. County Bar Assn. (pres. young lawyers' sect.), Pa. Trial Lawyers Assn. Lodge: K.C. State civil litigation, Criminal, Personal injury. Office: 111 N Olive St Media PA 19063

BONNER, LEONARD JOHN, lawyer; b. Wilmington, Del., May 23, 1938; s. Edward Daniel and Josephine Ann B.; children—Sean Leonard, Joseph Edward. B.A., LaSalle Coll., 1960; J.D., U. Md., 1965. Bar: D.C. 1968, Md. 1973, U.S. Supreme Ct. 1971. Claims atty. Nationwide Mut. Ins. Co., Annapolis, Md., 1964-68; assoc. Macleay, Lynch, Bernhard & Gregg, Washington, 1969-70; asst. gen. counsel D.C. Transit System, Inc., Washington, 1970-72; assoc. Giordano, Alexander, Haas, Mahoney & Bush, Oxon Hill, Md., 1972-76; gen. counsel Prince George's Del., Md. Ho. of Dels., 1976-78. Mem. ABA, Md. Bar Assn., Prince George's County Bar Assn., Assn. Trial Lawyers Am. Democrat. Roman Catholic. Club: KC. State civil litigation, Criminal, Insurance. Office: 5811 Baltimore Ave Riverdale MD 20737

BONNER, MARY CATHERINE, lawyer; b. Youngstown, Ohio, Dec. 11, 1945; d. Edgar J. and Helen Louise (Wick) Mahar; m. Glen L. Bonner, Dec. 16, 1967. BA, U. Fla., 1966; JD cum laude, U. Miami, 1979. Bar: Fla. 1979, U.S. Dist. Ct. (so. dist.) Fla. 1979, U.S. Ct. Appeals (5th cir.) 1980, U.S. Dist. Ct. (mid. dist.) Fla. 1981, U.S. Ct. Appeals (11th cir.) 1981, U.S. Ct. Appeals (7th cir.) 1986. Asst. fed. pub. defender Office Pub. Defender, Miami, Fla., 1979-80; sole practice Ft. Lauderdale, Fla., 1980—. Mem. Nat. Assn. Criminal Def. Lawyers. Democrat. Roman Catholic. Criminal. Home: 1315 S Ocean Dr Fort Lauderdale FL 33316 Office: 207 SW 12th Ct Fort Lauderdale FL 33315

BONNER, ROBERT CLEVE, lawyer; b. Wichita, Kans., Jan. 29, 1942; s. Benjamin Joseph and Caroline (Kirkwood) B.; m. Kimiko Tanaka, Oct. 11, 1969; 1 child, Justine M. B.A., Md. U., 1963; J.D., Georgetown U., 1966. Bar: D.C. 1966, Calif. 1967, U.S. Dist. Ct. (no., so. and cen. dists.) Calif., U.S. Ct. Appeals (4th, 9th and 10th cirs.), U.S. Supreme Ct. Law clk. to judge U.S. Dist. Ct., Los Angeles, 1966-67; asst. U.S. atty. U.S. Dist. Ct. (cen. dist.) Calif., Los Angeles, 1971-75, U.S. atty., 1984—; ptnr. Kadison, Pfaelzer, et al, Los Angeles, 1975-84. Served to lt. comdr. USN, 1967-70. Fellow Am. Coll. Trial Lawyers, Fed. Bar Assn. (pres. Los Angeles chpt. 1982-83). Republican. Roman Catholic. Clubs: University, Chancery. Office: U S Atty's Office 312 N Spring St 1200 US Courthouse Los Angeles CA 90012

BONNER, WALTER JOSEPH, lawyer; b. N.Y.C., Nov. 18, 1925; s. Walter John and Marie Elizabeth (Guerin) B.; m. Barbara E. Degnan, Dec. 27, 1951; children: Kevin P., Keith M., Barbara A., Susan E. A.B. cum laude, Cath. U. Am., 1951; J.D., Georgetown U., 1955. Bar: U.S. Supreme Ct., D.C., Va. Law clk. to judge U.S. Ct. Appeals D.C. Circuit, 1954-55; judge U.S. Dist. Ct., Washington, 1955-56; asst. U.S. dist. atty. for D.C., 1956-60; ptnr. firm Bonner & O'Connell, Washington.; Adj. prof. Georgetown U. Law Center, 1957-58, 67-83; appt. to D.C. Jud. Conf. 1987. Trustee Lawrence E. Dean Meml. Scholarship Fund, Georgetown U. Med. Center. Served with USNR, 1943-46; ret. capt. JAGC. Fellow Am. Coll. Trial Lawyers; mem. ABA, Fed. Bar Assn., Bar Assn. of D.C., Va. State Bar, Va. Trial Lawyers Assn., Res. Officers Assn., Naval Res. Lawyers Assn., Naval Res. Assn., Phi Delta Phi. Roman Catholic. Clubs: Officers and Faculty (U.S. Naval Acad.). Criminal, Federal civil litigation. Home: 9628 Parkwood Dr Bethesda MD 20814 Office: 900 17th St Washington DC 20006

BONNER, WILLIAM JOEL, JR., lawyer; b. Camden, Ala., Aug. 30, 1956; s. William Joel and Sarah (Patterson) B.; m. Dawne Roche, Aug. 12, 1978; 1 child, William Joel III. BS in Acctg., U. Ala., 1977, JD, 1981. Bar: Ala. 1982. Sole practice Camden, 1982—. Asst. scoutmaster Boy Scouts Am., Camden, 1982-83. Named Eagle Scout with multiple palms, one of Outstanding Young Men Am., 1985. Mem. Am. Trial Lawyers Assn., Ala. Bar Assn., Ducks Unltd. Avocations: hunting, fishing, restoration of real estate. Consumer commercial, Criminal, General practice. Office: PO Box 88 Camden AL 36726

BONNES, CHARLES ANDREW, industrial and medical products company executive, lawyer; b. Bklyn., Jan. 23, 1941; s. Charles Andrew and Beverly (Bade) B.; m. Cynthia Crane Rich, Aug. 7, 1965; children—Jocelyn Winthrop, Andrew Rich. B.A., Dartmouth Coll., 1962; LL.B., Yale U., 1965. Bar: N.Y. 1965. Assoc. Olwine, Chase, O'Donnel & Weyher, N.Y.C., 1965-76; corp. sec. Airco, Inc., Montvale, N.J., 1977-84; v.p. gen. counsel The BOC Group, Inc., Montvale, 1984—. Mem. ABA. Home: 154 Carlisle Terr Ridgewood NJ 07450 Office: The BOC Group Inc 85 Chestnut Ridge Rd Montvale NJ 07645

BONNEY, GEORGE WILLIAM, judge; b. Midwest, Wyo., Aug. 22, 1923; s. George William and Bertha Anne (Ormsby) B.; m. Kerminette Schweers, Aug. 27, 1949; children—Susan Mary, George William III, Michael Kermit. A.B., U. Wis., 1950, LL.B., 1952. Bar: Calif. bar 1952. Since practiced in San Jose; partner firm Rankin, Oneal, Luckhardt, Center, Ingram, Bonney, Marlais & Lund, 1967-72; judge Santa Clara Municipal Ct., 1972-80, presiding judge, 1979-80; judge Santa Clara County Superior Ct., 1980—. Dist. chmn. Santa Clara County chpt. Boy Scouts Am., 1967—, mem. exec. bd., 1967—; commr. Parks and Recreation Commn., City of Saratoga, 1970—. Served as pilot USAAF, 1942-46. Mem. Conf. Calif. Judges, Wis. Alumni Assn., Santa Clara County Trial Lawyers Assn. (pres. 1971), Santa Clara County Conf. Municipal Judges (pres. 1977), Sigma Phi Epsilon. Club: San Jose Rotary. Personal injury, State civil litigation, Criminal. Home: 12740 Carniel Ave Saratoga CA 95070 Office: 191 North First St San Jose CA 95113

BONO, ANTHONY SALVATORE EMANUEL, lawyer, legal educator; b. Sciacca, Sicily, Italy, Oct. 12, 1913; came to U.S., 1914, naturalized, 1936; s. Pellegrino and Domenica (Marciante) B.; m. Lola Mae Riddle, Jan. 27, 1946; children: Anthony S.E., Marc W. LLB, St. John's U., Bklyn., 1936. Bar: N.Y. 1941, U.S. Dist. Ct. (so. and ea. dists.) N.Y. 1952, U.S. Ct. Appeals (2d cir.) 1942, U.S. Supreme Ct. 1958, U.S. Ct. Mil. Appeals 1961, cert. trial and def. counsel JAG of Navy. Sole practice, N.Y.C. and Irvington, N.Y., 1941—; clearance counsel Title Guarantee Co. and Title Ins. Co., White Plains, N.Y., 1970-79; village prosecutor Irvington, 1960-61; acting police justice Police Ct., Irvington, 1962-63; assoc. prof. bus. law Pace U., N.Y.C., 1968-87, prof., 1987—. Served with USMCR, 1931-39, 42-73, active duty, 1942-46, 49-53, col. Res. ret. Mem. Marine Corps Fathers Assn. (hon. life mem., award 1963), USMCR Officers Assn., Ret. Officers Assn. Democrat. Criminal, Family and matrimonial, Probate.

BONO, GASPARE JOSEPH, lawyer; b. Phila., Dec. 9, 1950; s. Joseph and Eva (Aidone) B.; m. Kathryn Leigh Fichenberg, Aug. 3, 1974; children: Michael, Melissa. BS in Econs., U. Pa., 1972; JD, Georgetown U., 1976. Bar: N.Y. 1977, U.S. Dist Ct. (we. dist.) N.Y. 1977, D.C. 1978, U.S. Dist. Ct. D.C. 1979, U.S. Ct. Appeals (D.C. cir.) 1979, U.S. Supreme Ct. 1980, U.S. Ct. Appeals (4th cir.) 1986. Assoc. Howrey & Simon, Washington, 1978-83, ptnr., 1984—. Mem. ABA, Fed. Bar Assn., D.C. Bar Assn. Democrat. Roman Catholic. Club: International (Washington). Avocations: tennis, golf, sailing. Antitrust, Federal civil litigation, State civil litigation. Home: 7704 River Falls Dr Potomac MD 20854 Office: Howrey & Simon 1730 Pennsylvania Ave NW Washington DC 20006

BONOMI, JOHN GURNEE, lawyer; b. N.Y.C., Aug. 13, 1923; s. Felix A. and Bessie (Gurnee) B.; m. Patricia Updegraff, Aug. 22, 1953; children: Kathryn, John. B.A., Columbia U., 1947; J.D., Cornell U., 1950; LL.M., N.Y.U., 1957. Bar: N.Y. bar 1952. Asst. dist. atty. N.Y. County, 1953-60; spl. counsel subcom. antitrust and monopoly Kefauver Com. U.S. Senate, 1960-61; spl. asst. atty. gen. N.Y. State, 1961-62; chief counsel com. grievances Assn. Bar City N.Y., 1963-76; vis. scholar Harvard U. Law Sch., 1976-77; counsel firm Anderson, Russell, Kill & Olick, N.Y.C., 1977-80; practice law N.Y.C., 1980—; mem. com. grievances and admissions U.S. Circuit Ct. Appeals for Second Circuit, 1983—. Columnist: N.Y. Law Jour; contbr. articles to legal jours. Trustee Village of Tarrytown, N.Y., 1965-67, 68-72; councilman, dep. supr. Town of Greenburgh, 1974. Served with USAAF, 1943-45. Mem. ABA (spl. com. on evaluation disciplinary enforcement Clark Com. 1967-70, cons. spl. com. on evaluation ethical standards), N.Y. State Bar Assn. (vice-chmn. com. grievances 1970-71), Am. Law Inst. (spl. com. peer rev. 1978-80), Assn. Bar City N.Y., Inst. Jud. Adminstrn., Nat. Orgn. Bar Counsel (pres. 1970-71, chmn. spl. com. on Watergate discipline 1974-76). Democrat. Club: Harvard (N.Y.C.). Atty. and Jud. disciplinary law, Med. disciplinary law. Home: 131 Deertrack Ln Irvington NY 10533 Office: 41 E 42d St New York NY 10017

BONSAL, DUDLEY BALDWIN, judge; b. Bedford, N.Y., Oct. 6, 1906; s. Stephen and Henrietta Fairfax (Morris) B.; m. Lois Abbott Worrall, May 16, 1931 (dec. Aug. 1981); children: Lois (Mrs. Frederic B. Osler, Jr.), Stephen.; m. Lucia Turner Faithfull, Mar. 5, 1983. A.B., Dartmouth Coll., 1927; LL.B., Harvard, 1930. Bar: N.Y. bar 1932. Asso. firm Curtis, Mallet-Prevost, Colt & Mosle, N.Y.C., 1930-38; mem. firm Curtis, Mallet-Prevost, Colt & Mosle, 1938-42, 45-61; U.S. dist. judge So. dist. N.Y., 1961—; judge Temporary Emergency Ct. Appeals of U.S., 1977—; chief counsel Office Inter-Am. Affairs, Washington, 1942-45; mem. U.S. del. Inter-Am. Conf. on Problems of War and Peace, Mexico City, 1945; legal adviser Fgn. Bondholders Protective Council, Conf. on German Debts, London, 1951, 52; mem. Internat. Commn. of Jurists, Geneva, Switzerland, 1953-73; chmn. spl. com. on fed. loyalty-security program Assn. Bar City N.Y., 1955-57; mem. com. on criminal justice act Jud. Conf. of U.S., 1964-79, chmn., 1974-79. Trustee Inst. Internat. Edn., 1948-64, Sterling and Francine Clark Art Inst., Williamstown, Mass., 1960-73, William Nelson Cromwell Found., Practising Law Inst., 1969-85. Fellow Am. Bar Found. (dir. 1967-75); mem. Am., N.Y. bar assns., Assn. Bar City N.Y. (pres. 1958-60), N.Y.C. Council on Fgn. Relations. Club: Century Assn. (N.Y.C.). Home: St Mary's Church Rd Bedford NY 10506 Office: US Ct House Foley Sq New York NY 10007

BONSKY, JACK ALAN, chemical exec., lawyer; b. Canton, Ohio, Mar. 12, 1938; s. Jack H. and Pearl E. Bonsky; A.B., Ohio U., 1960; J.D., Ohio State U., 1964; m. Carol Ann Portmann, Sept. 2, 1960; children—Jack Raymond, Cynthia Lynn. Bar: Ohio 1964, U.S. Dist. Ct. (so. dist.) Ohio 1969. With Metcalf, Thomas & Bonsky, Marietta, Ohio, 1964-69, Addison, Fisher & Bonsky, Marietta, 1969-70; asst. counsel GenCorp., Inc. (formerly Gen. Tire & Rubber Co.), Akron, Ohio, 1970-75, assoc. gen. counsel, 1975-86, asst. sec., 1977-86, v.p. and sec., 1986; v.p.. sec., gen. counsel DiversiTech Gen., Inc., 1986—; solicitor City of Marietta, Ohio, 1966-67; legal advisor City of Marietta Bd. of Edn., 1966-67; police prosecutor, Belpre, Ohio, 1969-70; comml. law instr. Am. Inst. Banking, 1969; dir. Frontier Holdings, Inc., Denver, Frontier Airlines, Denver, 1985 (merged with People Express Airlines, 1985). Mem. Marietta Income Tax Bd. of Rev., 1966-67; mem. Traffic Commn., 1966-69, chmn., 1967; mem. Civil Service Commn., 1969; trustee Urban League, 1978-81, pres., 1980-81; trustee Akron Community Service Ctr., 1978-81, United Way of Summit County, 1982—; bd. dirs. Washington County Soc. for Crippled Children, 1964-70; bd. dirs. S.E. Ohio unit Arthritis Found., 1967-70, chmn., 1968-70; mem. Washington County Health Planning Com., 1968-70; mem. ho. of dels. Ohio Easter Seal Soc., 1968-70. Recipient Akron Community Service Ctr. and Urban League Leadership award, 1981. Mem. Ohio Bar Assn. General corporate. Home: 4234 Idlebrook Dr Akron OH 44313 Office: GenCorp Inc 1 General St Akron OH 44329

BONVENTRE, VINCENT MARTIN, lawyer, legal educator; b. Bklyn., Nov. 11, 1948; s. Martin Victor and Raffaela (Sabella) B.; m. Karen Bonner, Feb. 4, 1978; children: Martin Peter, Richard Joseph. BS, Union Coll., 1970; JD, Bklyn. Law Sch., 1976; MA in Pub. Adminstrn., U. Va., 1981, postgrad., 1987. Bar: N.Y. 1977, U.S. Ct. Mil. Appeals 1977, U.S. Supreme Ct. 1980. Asst. prof. govt. U. Va., Charlottesville, 1982-83; law clk. to judge N.Y. State Ct. of Appeals, Albany, 1983-86; jud. fellow U.S. Supreme Ct., Washington, 1986—; instr. Cochise Coll., Sierra Vista, Ariz., 1978-80, U. Va., Charlottesville, 1980-82. Served to capt. U.S. Army Intelligence, 1970-73, (JAGC) 77-80. U. Va. fellow, 1981-82. Mem. ABA, N.Y. State Bar Assn., Am. Judicature Soc., Mensa. Democrat. Roman Catholic. Avocations: classical music, great books, running. Jurisprudence, Civil rights, Criminal. Home: 42-30 Douglaston Pkwy Douglaston NY 11363 Office: US Supreme Ct Jud Fellows Program Washington DC 12207

BONVILLIAN, WILLIAM BOONE, lawyer; b. Honolulu, Mar. 7, 1947; s. William Doughty and Florence Elizabeth (Boone) B.; m. Janis Ann Sposato, Apr. 12, 1980; 1 child, Raphael William Boone. AB, Columbia U., 1969; MA in Religion, Yale U., 1972; JD, Columbia U., 1974. Bar: Conn. 1975, D.C. 1976, U.S. Supreme Ct. 1983. Assoc. Steptoe & Johnson, Washington, 1975-77; dep. asst. sec., dir. congl. affairs U.S. Dept. Transp., Washington, 1977-81; ptnr. Brown, Roady, Bonvillian & Gold, Washington, 1981-85, Jenner & Block, Washington, 1985—; Editor Columbia Law Rev. 1973-74; contbr. articles to law jours. Recipient Outstanding Performance award U.S. Sec. Transp., Washington, 1979, 80. Mem. ABA, Conn. Bar Assn., D.C. Bar Assn. Democrat. Presbyterian. Administrative and regulatory, Legislative, Real property. Home: 1325 19th Rd S Arlington VA 22202 Office: Jenner & Block 21 Dupont Circle NW Washington DC 20036

BONYHADI, ERNEST, lawyer; b. Salzburg, Austria, Jan. 9, 1924; came to U.S., 1939, naturalized, 1943; s. Fred and Elsa (Steindler) B.; m. Ilo Lehman, Sept. 5, 1948; children—Lyn Bonyhadi-Schleicher, Mark Lehmann. B.A., Reed Coll., 1948; J.D., Columbia U., 1951. Bar: Oreg. 1952, U.S. Dist. Ct. Oreg. 1953, U.S. Ct. Appeals (9th cir.) 1957, U.S. Supreme Ct. 1961. Assoc. Rosenberg, Swire & Coan, Portland, Oreg., 1952-56; sole practice, Portland, 1956-60; ptnr. Bonyhadi & Hall, Portland, 1956-67; ptnr. Rives, Bonyhadi & Smith, Portland, 1968-79; ptnr. Stoel, Rives, Boley, Fraser Jones & Grey (merger Rives, Bonyhadi & Smith and Davies, Biggs, Strayer, Stoel & Boley), Portland, 1979—; faculty law U. Cambridge, 1986; vis. scholar Max Planck Inst., Munich, 1986; participant programs on antitrust, libel and other bus. litigation. Trustee Reed Coll., 1971—; bd. dirs. Good Samaritan (Hosp.) Found., Portland, 1972—. Served with Mil. Intelligence, U.S. Army, 1943-46. Mem. ABA, Oreg. Bar Assn., Multnomah County Bar Assn., Am. Soc. Internat. Law, Columbia Law Sch. Alumni Assn. (v.p.). Democrat. Jewish. Clubs: Multnomah Athletic, Arlington (Portland); Marines Meml. (San Francisco); B'nai B'rith. Antitrust, Federal civil litigation, Libel. Office: 900 SW 5th Ave Portland OR 97204

BOOCHEVER, ROBERT, federal judge; b. N.Y.C., Oct. 2, 1917; s. Louis C. and Miriam (Cohen) B.; m. Lois Colleen Maddox, Apr. 22, 1943; children: Barbara K., Linda Lou, Ann Paula, Miriam Deon. A.B., Cornell U., 1939, LL.B., 1941; HHD (hon.), U. Alaska, 1981. Bar: N.Y. 1944, Alaska 1947. Asst. U.S. atty. Juneau, 1946-47; partner firm Faulkner, Banfield, Boochever & Doogan, Juneau, 1947-72; asso. justice Alaska Supreme Ct., 1972-75, 78-80, chief justice, 1975-78; judge U.S. Ct. Appeals for 9th Circuit, 1980—; chmn. Alaska Jud. Council, 1975-78; mem. appellate judges seminar N.Y.U. Sch. Law, 1975; mem. Conf. Chief Justices, 1975-79, vice chmn., 1978-79; mem. adv. bd. Nat. Bank of Alaska, 1968-72. Chmn. Juneau chpt. ARC, 1949-51, Juneau Planning Commn., 1956-61; mem. Alaska Devel. Bd., 1949-52, Alaska Jud. Qualification Commn., 1972-75; mem. adv. bd. Juneau-Douglas Community Coll. Served to capt. inf. AUS, 1941-45. Named Juneau Man of Year, 1974. Fellow Am. Coll. Trial Attys.; mem. ABA, Alaska Bar Assn. (pres. 1961-62), Juneau Bar Assn. (pres. 1971-72), Am. Judicature Soc. (dir. 1970-74), Am. Law Inst., Juneau C. of C. (pres. 1952, 55), Alaskans United (chmn. 1962). Clubs: Marine Meml, Wash. Athletic, Juneau Racket, Altadena Town and Country. Home: 336 Orange Grove Blvd Pasadena CA 91105 Office: US Ct Appeals 9th Cir 125 S Grand Ave Pasadena CA 91109-1510

BOOCOCK, STEPHEN WILLIAM, lawyer; b. Wilkinsburg, Pa., Sept. 25, 1948; s. William Samuel and Zelda Elizabeth (Heginbotham) B.; m. Carol Ann Bennett, July 11, 1970; children: Eric Alan, Allison Anne, Megan Leigh. BS in Acctg., Pa. State U., 1970; JD, U. Pitts., 1973. Bar: Pa. 1974, U.S. Dist. Ct. (we. dist.) Pa. 1973. Supervising tax specialist Coopers & Lybrand, Pitts., 1973-76; tax counsel Incom Internat., Inc., Pitts., 1977-81; asst. treas., dir. tax Allegheny Ludlum Corp., Pitts., 1981—. Mem. adv. bd. Ann. Pitts. Tax Conf., 1985. Served to capt. U.S. Army, USAR, 1970-79. Mem. ABA (tax sect.), Pa. Bar Assn. (tax sect.), Allegheny County Bar Assn. (tax sect.), Am. Inst. CPA's (tax div.), Pa. Inst. CPA's, Tax Exec. Inst., Inc. (treas. Pitts. chpt. 1985-86, v.p., sec. 1986—). Republican. Methodist. Avocations: golf, hunting, fishing, camping. Corporate taxation, Pension, profit-sharing, and employee benefits, State and local taxation. Home: 2625 Woodmont Ln Wexford PA 15090 Office: Allegheny Ludlum Corp 1000 Six PPG Place Pittsburgh PA 15222-5479

BOODELL, THOMAS JOSEPH, JR., lawyer; b. Chgo., Sept. 29, 1935; s. Thomas J. and Mary Elizabeth (Houze) B.; m. Beata Bergman Boodell, Aug. 4, 1962; children—Beata, Mary, Peter, David. A.B., Princeton U., 1957; J.D., Harvard U., 1964. Bar: Ill. 1964. Assoc. Boodell, Sears et al. Chgo., 1964-68; fellow Adlai Stevenson Inst. Internat. Affairs, Chgo., 1968-71; ptnr. Boodell, Sears, Giambalvo & Crowley, Chgo., 1971-84; ptnr. Keck, Mahin & Cate, Chgo., 1984—. Publisher, contbr. articles New City Mag., 1967-71. Pres. bd. dirs. Chgo. Children's Choir, 1979—; bd. dirs. Wendy Will Case Cancer Fund, 1983—, Law in Am. Soc. Found., Chgo., 1972—; trustee Chi Psi Ednl. Trust, Chgo., 1978-84. Served to lt. (j.g.) USN, 1957-60. Recipient Disting. Service award Chi Psi 1984, Disting. Service award Princeton Club Chgo., 1979. Fellow Am. Bar Found.; mem ABA, Chgo. Bar Assn., Ill. Bar Assn., Law Club City Chgo., Legal Club Chgo., Democrat. Clubs: University, Metropolitan. General corporate, Federal civil litigation, Private international. Home: 1229 E 56th St Chicago IL 60637 Office: Keck Mahin & Cate 8300 Sears Tower Chicago IL 60606

BOOHER, LAWRENCE J., JR., lawyer; b. Tucson, Nov. 6, 1942; s. Lawrence J. Booher; m. Karen C. Booher; 3 children. BA, U. Calif., Berkeley, 1964; JD, UCLA, 1967. Bar: Calif. Atty. Calif. Dept. Transp., Los Angeles, 1970-74, Los Angeles County Counsel, 1974-80, Texaco Inc., Los Angeles, 1980—. Co-author: Landslide and Subsidence Liability Supplement, 1981. Coach, referee Am. Youth Soccer Orgn., Palos Verdes. Club: Palos Verdes Breakfast. Avocations: sports, music. Federal civil litigation, State civil litigation, Contracts commercial. Office: Texaco Inc 10 Universal City Plaza Universal City CA 91603

BOOK, RONALD LEE, lawyer; b. Pleasanton, Calif., Dec. 3, 1952; s. Harold Book and Delores Betty (Koret) Rosen; m. Patricia Ann Duda, Mar. 31, 1984; children: Lauren, Samantha. Student, U. Fla., 1971-73; BA in Polit. Sci., Fla. Internat. U., 1974; JD, Tulane U., 1977. Bar: Fla. 1978, U.S. Dist. Ct. (so. and mid. dists.) Fla. 1978 , U.S. Ct. Appeals (11th cir.) 1978. Mem. gov.'s transition team State of Fla., 1978-79, officer cabinet and legis. affairs, 1979, acting dir. cabinet and legis. affairs, 1979, dir. legis. affairs, 1979-80; ptnr. Sparber, Shevin, Shapo, Heilbronner & Book P.A., Miami, 1981-86, spl. counsel, 1987—; sole practice 1987—. Exec. dirs. 5 for Fla.'s Future, Tallahassee; mem. presdl. search adv. com. Fla. Internat. U., 1986; bd. dirs., Carey Tech. Inst., Miami, 1984—, Truman Savings and Loan Assn., Miami, 1984—, Young Dems., Dade County, 1970—; bd. dirs., trustee Milton Littman Found., Miami; Fla. delegation whip Dem. Nat. Conv., 1980. Mem. Fla. Bar Assn. (familty law and govtl. law sects., Dade County Bar Assn., Maritime Law Assn., Am. Judicature Soc., Tulane Almni Assn., Fla. Internat. U. Alumni Assn. (bd. dirs. 1982-83), Tulane Alumni Assn., Delta Theta Phi, Internat. Platform Assn. Jewish. Avocations: polit. memorabilia collector, skiing, swimming. Local government, Banking, Health. Home: 2251 NE 201st St North Miami Beach FL 33180 Office: Sparber Shevin Shapo et al 1 SE 3d Ave 30th Floor AmeriFirst Bldg Miami FL 33131 Office: 20801 Biscanine Blvd. North Miami Beach FL 33180

BOOKBINDER, RONALD ERIC, lawyer; b. Phila., July 23, 1949; s. Clarence and Esther (Hoffman) B.; m. Sylvia Haber, Apr. 8, 1978; children: Julie P., Linda S. BA in Polit. Sci., Colgate U., 1971; JD, George Washington U., 1974. Bar: N.J. 1974, U.S. Dist. Ct. N.J. From assoc. to ptnr. Bookbinder & Colaguori, Burlington, N.J., 1974-81; sole practice Burlington, 1981-82; ptnr. Bookbinder & Guest, Burlington, 1982-83, Bookbinder, Guest & Domzalski, Burlington, 1983—. Exec. com. Burlington County Red Cross 1975—; chmn. Burlington County Heart Assn., Mt. Holly, N.J., 1976-79; mem. Dem. Nat. Platform Com., Washington , 1984—; chmn. Burlington County Dem. Com., Mt. Holly, 1981-86. Mem. ABA, N.J. Bar Assn., Burlington County Bar Assn. (Robert W. Criscuolo award, Outstanding Young Lawyer 1979). Democrat. Jewish. Local government, Real property, General practice. Home: 1319 Tanner Ave Burlington NJ 08016 Office: Bookbinder Guest & Domzalski 235 High St Burlington NJ 08016

BOOKER, JAMES FOSTER, lawyer; b. Richmond, Va., Aug. 4, 1947; s. George William and Jackie (Crute) B.; m. Nelda L. Joplin, Aug. 20, 1977; children: Dawn Lanelle, George William. BA, Old Dominion U., 1973; JD, Coll. William and Mary, 1977. Bar: Va. 1977, U.S. Dist. Ct. Va. 1978. Ptnr. Ashe, Booker, Hallock, Norfolk, Va., 1977-85; sole practice Norfolk, 1985—. Mem. ABA, Va. Bar Assn., Va. Rugby Union (pres. 1985—). Club: Norfolk Blues Rugby (pres. 1983, 86). Personal injury, Federal civil litigation, State civil litigation. Home: 759 W 51st St Norfolk VA 23508

BOOKER, LEWIS THOMAS, lawyer; b. Richmond, Va., Sept. 22, 1929; s. Russell Eubank and Leslie Quarles (Sessoms) B.; m. Nancy Electa Brogden, Sept. 29, 1956; children: Lewis Thomas, Virginia Frances, Claiborne Brogden, John Quarles. B.A., U. Richmond, 1950, LL.D., 1977; J.D., Harvard U., 1953. Bar: Va. 1953, U.S. Ct. Mil. Appeals 1954, U.S. Supreme Ct. 1958, D.C. 1980, N.Y. 1985. Assoc. Hunton & Williams, Richmond, Va., 1956-63; ptnr. Hunton & Williams, 1963—; lectr. in law Seinan Gakuin U., Fukuoks, Japan, 1985; dir. Daily Press Inc., 1986. Commr., chmn. Richmond Redevel. and Housing Authority, 1961-70; vice chmn. Richmond Sch. Bd., 1970-78; trustee U. Richmond, 1972—, rector, 1973-77, 81-85, vice rector, 1985-87, chmn. exec. commn., 1977-81; brig. gen., mil. aide to gov. Va., 1983—. Served with U.S. Army, 1953-56; to col. USAR, 1975-83. . Fellow Am. Coll. Trial Lawyers, Am. Bar Found.; mem. ABA, Fed. Bar Assn., Va. Bar Assn., Richmond Bar Assn. Democrat. Baptist. Clubs: Westwood Racquet, Bull & Bear, Harvard of N.Y. Federal civil litigation, State civil litigation. Office: Hunton and Williams 707 E Main St PO Box 1535 Richmond VA 23212

BOOKER, R. MICHAEL, lawyer; b. McKenzie, Ala., Mar. 8, 1948; s. Manning Milfred and Joye (Coleman) B.; m. Renee Williams, May 26, 1972; children—R. Michael Jr., Mary Ruth. B.S., Auburn U., 1969; J.D. cum laude, Samford U., 1974; LL.M. in Taxation, U. Ala., 1979. Bar: Ala. 1974, U.S. Dist. Ct. (no., so. and mid. dists.) Ala., U.S. Ct. Appeals (5th, 10th and 11th cirs.). Law clk. to judge U.S. Dist. Ct. (no. dist.) Ala., Birmingham, 1974-75; assoc. firm Johnston & Shores, Birmingham, 1975-79; ptnr. firm Shores & Booker, Birmingham, 1979—, Fairhope, Ala. 1983—. Mem. Cumberland Law Rev. Deacon 1st Baptist Ch., Birmingham, 1983—. Served to capt. U.S. Army, 1969-71, Vietnam. Decorated Bronze Star, Combat Infantryman's badge. Mem. ABA, Nat. Orgn. Social Security Claimants Reps. (Ala. chmn. 1981—), Omicron Delta Kappa, Delta Theta Phi. Administrative and regulatory, Workers' compensation, Estate taxation. Home: 2502 Elizabeth Dr Helena AL 35080 Office: Shores & Booker 2157 14th Ave S Birmingham AL 35205

BOOKMAN, MARK, lawyer; b. Englewood, N.J., Oct. 19, 1952; s. Herbert and S. Florence (Kreps) B.; m. Marsha W. Bookman, Aug. 26, 1973; children: Andrea, Matthew, Stephanie. AB, Boston U., 1974; JD, Duke U., 1977. Ptnr. Reed, Smith, Shaw & McClay, Pitts., 1977—. Bd. dirs. Am. Wind Symphony Orch., Pitts., 1985—. Mem. ABA (chmn. real property probate and trust sect., various coms.), Pa. Bar Assn., Fla. Bar Assn., PLI (lectr.), ACBA (lectr.), Order of Coif. Clubs: Harvard-Yale-Princeton, Rivers (Pitts). Estate planning, Probate, Estate taxation. Home: 80 Standish Blvd Pittsburgh PA 15228 Office: Reed Smith Shaw & McClay PO Box 2009 Pittsburgh PA 15230

BOOKSH, ROBERT WILLIAM, JR., lawyer; b. San Marcos, Tex., May 30, 1951; s. Robert W. Sr. and Shirley Ann (Newport) B.; m. Jan Meyer, Dec. 26, 1973 (div. Dec. 1982); m. Nancy J. Allman, Jan. 3. 1983; children: Scott Tyler, Christopher Newport, Holly Elizabeth, Elizabeth Ann. BA, U. Southwestern La., 1973; JD, La. State U., 1976. Bar: La. 1976, New Orleans 1976. Law clk. to chief justice La. Supreme Ct., New Orleans, 1976-77; ptnr. Liskow & Lewis, New Orleans, 1977—. Assoc. editor La. State U. Law Rev., 1975-76. Mem. Maritime Law Assn. U.S. (assoc.), La. Assn. Def. Counsel, Order of Coif, Phi Kappa Phi. Republican. Clubs: Chateau Golf and Country (Kenner, La.); Racquetball One (New Orleans). Avocations: golf, tennis, canoeing. Admiralty, Federal civil litigation, Personal injury. Home: 67 Verde St Kenner LA 70065 Office: Liskow & Lewis 1 Shell Sq 50th Floor New Orleans LA 70139

BOONE, DAVID EASON, lawyer; b. Raleigh, N.C., July 5, 1948; s. Devan Duke and Virgil (Eason) B.; m. Beverly Ann Deem, Feb. 3, 1968; children: Rebecca Ann, Jacob Elisha, Courtney Keriann. BA, U. Va., 1970; JD, U. Richmond, 1975. Bar: Va. 1976, U.S. Dist. Ct. (ea. dist.) Va. 1976, U.S. Ct. Appeals (4th cir.) 1976, U.S. Supreme Ct. 1982. Law clk. to presiding justice U.S. Dist. Ct., Richmond, Va., 1976-78; assoc. Francis, Hubard & Tice, Richmond, 1978-80; ptnr. Boone, Beale, Cosby & Hyder, Richmond, 1980—; adj. instr. J. Sargeant Reynolds Community Coll., Richmond, 1977—. Served to lt. USN, 1970-73, Vietnam. Recipient NAACP Freedom Fund award, Richmond, 1983. Mem. ABA, Richmond Criminal Bar Assn., Nat. Assn. Criminal Def. Lawyers, Va. Coll. Criminal Def. Attys., Lawyers Pilots Bar Assn. Republican. Baptist. Club: Hermitage Country (Goochland, Va.). Avocations: flying, travel, horse breeding. Criminal. Office: Boone Beale Cosby & Hyder 11 S 12th St Suite 500 Richmond VA 23219

BOONE, HAROLD THOMAS, lawyer; b. Oak Hill, W. Va., Dec. 14, 1921; s. Thomas thumb and Cora Anna (McGlamery) B.; m. Ferne Miller, July 31, 1948; 1 dau., Cheryl Ann. B.S., W. Va., 1943; J.D., U. Va., 1948. With Md. Casualty Co., Balt., 1948—, v.p., gen. counsel, corp. sec., 1979—, dir., 1979—; dir. N.C. Guaranty Fund, Calif. Def. Counsel; arbitrator Def. Research Inst., Inc., v.p. ins., 1986-87. Served to 2d lt. USAAF, 1943-46. Mem. Internat. Assn. Ins. Counsel (v.p. 1979-81), Am. Arbitration Assn. (arbitrator). Republican. Club: Hunt Valley Golf. General corporate, Federal civil litigation, State civil litigation. Home: 551 Piccadilly Rd Towson MD 21204 Office: Md Casualty Co 3910 Keswick Rd Baltimore MD 21211

BOONE, TAYLOR SCOTT, lawyer; b. Houston, Dec. 27, 1948; s. B. H. and Joyce T. Boone; m. Alison Wenger; children: Catherine L. Student, Washington & Lee U., 1967-68; BBA, U. Tex., 1971; JD, St. Mary's Sch. of Law, San Antonio, 1980. Bar: Tex. 1980; CPA, Tex.; cert. in estate planning and probate law Tex. Bd. Legal Specialization. Chief econ. devel. and transp. sect. Tex. Gov.'s Budget and Planning Office, Austin, 1971-75; pvt. pracitce acctg. San Antonio, 1976-77; assoc. Oppenheimer, Rosenberg, Kelleher & Wheatley, Inc., San Antonio, 1980—. Contbr. articles to profl. jours. Mem. adv. council Coll. of Bus., 1985—; chmn. various allocation com. United Way of San Antonio, 1981—; trustee Laurel Heights United Meth. Ch., 1984—, Southwest Tex. Meth. Hosp., 1985—; bd. dirs., treas. Hospice San Antonio, 1985—; bd. dirs. Boysville, Inc., San Antonio, 1984—, Am. Diabetes Assn., 1984-86; bd. dirs., chmn. devel. com. Am. Diabetes Assn. (Alamo area chpt.), 1983—. Named one of Outstanding Young Men of Am., 1985. Fellow Tex. Bar Found., San Antonio Bar Found.; mem. ABA (estate planning and drafting com., inter vivos transfers and property ownership subcom.), Tex. Bar Assn. (newsletter on taxation com., real estate, probate and trust law com.), San Antonio Bar Assn., Am. Inst. CPA's, Tex. Soc. CPA's (relations with bar com.), San Antonio Soc. CPA's, San Antonio Estate Planning Council, Barristers, Phi Delta Phi. Probate, Estate taxation, Personal income taxation. Office: Oppenheimer Rosenberg Kelleher & Wheatley Inc 711 Navarro 6th Floor San Antonio TX 78205

BOONE, TIMOTHY J., lawyer; b. Bellefontaine, Ohio, Mar. 5, 1947; s. Raymond Lee and Ella M. (Taylor) B. BS in Acctg. cum laude, Ohio State U., 1973; JD cum laude, Capitol U., 1976. Bar: Ohio 1976, U.S. Dist. Ct. (so. dist.) Ohio 1977, U.S. Supreme Ct. 1980, U.S. Dist. Ct. S.C. 1981, U.S. Dist. Ct. (no. dist.) Ohio 1983, U.S. Dist. Ct. N.J. 1983, U.S. Dist. Ct. N.D. 1983, U.S. Dist. Ct. Ala. 1983, U.S. Dist. Ct. (ea. and we. dists.) Wis. 1984, U.S. Dist. Ct. (we. dist.) Mo. 1984, U.S. Dist. Ct. Nebr. 1984, U.S. Ct. Appeals (5th, 6th, 7th and 8th cirs.) 1984. Assoc. Rownd, Dimond & Shea, Columbus, Ohio, 1976-77; sole practice Columbus, 1977-86; ptnr. Sellman & Boone, Columbus, 1986—. Bd. advisors Cert. Legal Assts. Program, Capitol U. Law Sch., Columbus, 1986—. Served to tech. sgt. USAF, 1967-71. Mem. ABA, Ohio Bar Assn., Columbus Bar Assn., Assn. Trial Lawyers Am., Ohio Acad. Trial Lawyers, Am. Agrl. Law Assn., Order of Curia, Order of Barristers, Beta Gamma Sigma, Beta Alpha Psi. Republican. Methodist. Avocations: cycling, tennis, rock climbing, snow skiing, flying. Federal civil litigation, Personal injury, State civil litigation. Home: 387 Olentangy Forest Dr Columbus OH 43214-1419 Office: Sellman & Boone Capitol Sq Suite 1600 65 E State St Columbus OH 43215-4213

BOONE, WILLIAM DANIEL, lawyer; b. Atlanta, Aug. 25, 1947; s. William E. Boone and Catherine (Hupman) Jackman. BA, Williams Coll., 1969; JD, Cornell U., 1972. Bar: N.Y. 1973, U.S. Dist. Ct. (no., so., and ea. dists.) N.Y. 1973, U.S. Ct. Appeals (2d cir.) 1973. Assoc. Shearman & Sterling, N.Y.C., 1972-77; sr. corp. atty. Union Pacific Corp., N.Y.C., 1978-79, asst. gen. counsel, 1979-84, counsel pub. affairs, 1984—. Exec. dir. Alliance Clean Energy, Roslyn, Va., 1984—. Mem. ABA, N.Y. State Bar Assn. Methodist. Club: Sandbar (Quogue, N.Y.). General corporate, Legislative, Public affairs. Office: Union Pacific Corp 345 Park Ave New York NY 10154

BOORSTEIN, BEVERLY WEINGER, lawyer; b. Chgo., Apr. 25, 1941; d. Morris Aaron and Bess (Meisel) Weinger; m. Sidney L. Boorstein, July 3, 1962; children—Robin Anne, Michelle Loren. B.A., Brandeis U., 1961; J.D., Boston U., 1964. Bar: Mass. 1964, U.S. Dist. Ct. Mass. 1967. Assoc. Siskind & Siskind, Boston, 1965-70; sole practice, Boston, 1971-79; ptnr. Boorstein & Del Vecchio, P.C., Boston, 1980—. Bd. overseers Commonwealth of Mass.; mem. Jud. Condust Commn., Mental Health Legal Advisors Com. Mem. ABA, Mass. Bar Assn., Middlesex County Bar Assn., Mass. Assn. Women Lawyers (dir.), Boston Bar Assn. Contbr. articles to legal publs. General corporate, Real property, General practice.

BOOS, ARTHUR CHARLES, lawyer; b. N.Y.C., Oct. 6, 1954; s. Roy Peter and Rose Carlein (Schneider) B.; m. Rose Angeli, Apr. 27, 1985. BS in Chemistry magna cum laude, Valparaiso U., 1975, JD magna cum laude, 1978. Bar: Tex. 1979, U.S. Patent Office 1980, U.S. Dist. Ct. (so. dist.) Tex. 1981, U.S. Dist. Ct. (we. dist.) Tex. 1984. Patent atty. Shell Oil Co., Houston, 1978-81; atty. Merichem Co., Houston, 1981-87, also bd. dirs. and sec. polit. action com., 1982-84; assoc. Johnson, Bromberg & Leeds, Houston, 1987—. Vol. March of Dimes, Houston, 1979; assoc. mem. Crimestoppers, Inc. Dow Chem. Patent Law scholar, 1975-77. Mem. ABA, Houston Bar Assn., Houston Young Lawyers Assn., Houston Intellectual Property Lawyers Assn., Lic. Exec. Soc., Assn. for Community TV, Am. Chem. Soc. (cert. by profl. tng. com. 1975). Republican. Lutheran. General corporate, Contracts commercial, Patent. Home: 2350 Bering Dr 124 Houston TX 77057 Office: Johnson Bromberg & Leeds 2600 Lincoln Plaza Dallas TX 75201

BOOTH, EDGAR CHARLES, lawyer; b. Gainsville, Fla., July 13, 1934; s. Clyde V. and Bertha H. Booth; m. Anne Cawthon, Sept. 6, 1958; children: Rainey, John. BBA, U. Fla., 1956, JD, 1962. Bar: Fla. 1962. Sole practice Tallahassee, 1962—; judge small claims ct. Tallahassee, 1963-64; city judge Tallahassee, 1964-70. Served to capt. USAF, 1957-60. Mem. Fla. Bar Assn. (continuing legal edn. com. 1975—), Tallahasse Bar Assn. (sec., treas. 1970-71), Fla. Def. Lawyers Assn., Def. Research Inst., Fla. Mcpl. Judges Assn. (pres. 1969-70). Democrat. Episcopalian. Avocations: sailing, tennis, hiking, camping. State civil litigation, Federal civil litigation, Administrative and regulatory. Home: 900 High Rd Tallahassee FL 32302 Office: PO Drawer 840 Tallahassee FL 32302

BOOTH, EDGAR HIRSCH, lawyer; b. Bklyn., June 8, 1926; s. Benjamin H. and Lee (Benzman) B.; m. Joan E. Blumberg, Oct. 7, 1956; children—Charles, Janet. Student, U. Va., 1944, 46-47; B.A., Stanford, 1949; LL.B., Harvard, 1953. Bar: N.Y. State bar 1954. Since practiced in N.Y.C.; assoc. firm Booth, Lipton & Lipton, 1954-65, mem. firm, 1965-84; mem. firm Booth, Marcus & Pierce,, 1984—; Mem. nat. panel lawyers Am. Arbitration Assn. Mem. Glen Rock Bd. Edn., 1971-77, pres., 1973-74; bd. dirs. S.M. Louis Fund, Inc., N.Y.C. Served with AUS, 1944-46. Mem. Am., N.Y. State bar assns., Assn. Bar City N.Y., N.Y. County Lawyers Assn., Fed. Bar Council, Bankruptcy Lawyers Bar Assn. Bankruptcy, Contracts commercial, Federal civil litigation. Home: 25 Belmont Rd Glen Rock NJ 07452 Office: 79 Fifth Ave New York NY 10003

BOOTH, MITCHELL B., lawyer; b. N.Y.C., June 26, 1927; s. Samuel and Rose (Waxman) B.; m. Barbara C. Ribman, July 13, 1952; 1 son, Brian S. A.B., Clark U., 1949; J.D., N.Y. U., 1952. Bar: N.Y. 1952. Since practiced in N.Y.C.; asso. I. Moldauer, 1952-54; with firm Sol A. Rosenblatt, 1954-67; individual practice 1967—; minority counsel joint legis. com. unsatisfied judgments N.Y., 1958-59, joint legis. com. preservation restoration hist. sites N.Y., 1960-64; med. malpractice mediator First Jud. Dept. Supreme Ct. State N.Y., 1980—; bd. dirs. Burgos Art Galleries Ltd., Dorolyat Corp. Asst. to chmn. Dem. law com., N.Y. County, 1961-65; rep. admissions N.Y., N.J., Conn. Clark U., 1968-71. Served to lt. USNR, 1945-46, 51, 52. Named judge adv. and life companion Mil. Order Fgn. Wars of U.S. Mem. ABA, N.Y. State Bar Assn., Assn. of Bar of City of N.Y. (mem. com. profl. discipline). Family and matrimonial, Probate, Estate taxation. Home: 75 East End Ave New York NY 10028 Office: 1290 Ave of Americas New York NY 10019

BOOTH, ROBERT ALVIN, editor, lawyer; b. Cin., July 24, 1949; s. Robert Leslie Jr. and Etta Jo (Myers); m. Catherine Roth, 1973 (div. 1974). BA with honors, U. Cin., 1971; JD, Salmon P. Chase Coll. Law, 1975. Bar: Ohio 1975, U.S. Dist. Ct. (so. dist.) Ohio 1975. Reference librarian Chase Coll. of Law, Highland Heights, Ky., 1971-72; ptnr. Dunn & Booth, Cin., 1975-80; sole practice Cin., 1980—; asst. mng. editor Anderson Pub. Co., Cin., 1972—; Arbitrator, Cin. Bd. Arbitrators, 1975—. Author, editor numerous publs. on Ohio, Ind., Ky. and fed. law. Asst. dir. Cin. Experience, U. Cin., 1973-75. Mem. ABA, Order of Curia, Greater Cin. Sports Assn. (pres. 1985, 87), Pi Alpha Theta. Republican. United Methodist. Avocations: English riding, tennis. Legal Publishing, Probate, General corporate. Home: 526 E Mitchell Ave Cincinnati OH 45217 Office: Anderson Pub Co 646 Main St Cincinnati OH 45201

BOOZ, NINA ROBIN, lawyer; b. Sellersville, Pa., June 25, 1956; s. Robert Ernest and Nancy Jeanne (Hill) B. BA, Ursihus Coll., 1978; JD, Villanova U., 1982. Bar: Pa. 1982. Trust account mgr. 1st Pa. Bank N.A., Phila., 1982-84; law clk. to presiding justice Bucks County Ct. of Common Pleas, Doylestown, Pa., 1984-85; assoc. Scott & Lyons, Warrington, Pa., 1985—. Mem. Pa. Bar Assn., Bucks County Bar Assn., Bucks County Estate Planning Council. Probate, Insurance. Office: Scott & Lyons 850 Easton Rd Warrington PA 18976

BOPP, THOMAS ROE, lawyer; b. Tampa, Fla., Jan. 17, 1957; s. Edward Lee and Evelyn (Wiggonton) B. BA, U. Fla.; JD, Samford U. Bar: U.S. Dist. Ct. (mid. dist.) Fla., U.S. Ct. Appeals (11th cir.). Aast. atty. Hillsborough County, Tampa, 1981-83; assoc. Fowler & White, Tampa, 1983—. Bd. dirs. Boys Clubs Tampa, 1981—. Mem. ABA (pres., chmn. com. young lawyers sect., family law sect.), Assn. Trial Lawyers Am. Democrat. Roman Catholic. State civil litigation, Personal injury, Insurance. Office: Fowler & White 501 E Kennedy PO Box 1438 Tampa FL 33606

BOR, DANIEL, lawyer; b. Prague, Czechoslovakia, Mar. 6, 1956; came to U.S., 1966; s. Imrich and Eva (Albrechtova) B. BA, Wesleyan U., Middletown, Conn., 1978; JD, U. Calif., San Francisco, 1981. Bar: Wash. 1981, U.S. Dist. Ct. (we. dist.) Wash. 1981, U.S. Ct. Appeals (Fed. cir.) 1981. Assoc. Dodel, Skone & Leonardson, Seattle, 1981-85, Hight & Green, Seattle, 1985-86; sole practice Seattle, 1986—; assoc. mem. Associated Gen. Contractors (Wash. chpt.) Seattle, 1981—. Extern senator Henry M. Jackson, Washington, 1979. Mem. ABA, Wash. State Bar Assn. Clubs: Washington Athletic, College (Seattle). Insurance, Construction, State civil litigation. Home: 1525 Grand Ave Seattle WA 98122 Office: 2101 Fourth Ave Suite 2400 Fourth and Blanchard Bldg Seattle WA 98121

BORCHERS, MARION JACK, lawyer; b. Lavaca County, Tex., July 11, 1933; s. William and Mary (Schaeg) B.; m. Robbie Walters, Sept. 3, 1960; children: Mary Ann, Brenda Ruth, William Robert, T Charles. BBA, U. Tex., Austin, 1956, JD, 1962. Bar: Tex. 1962, U.S. Dist. ct. (we. dist.) Tex. 1973, U.S. Supreme Ct. 1973. Assoc. Wm. H. Borchers, New Braunfels, Tex., 1962-64; ptnr. Borchers & Borchers, New Braunfels, 1964-69; sole practice New Braunfels, 1969-74; mem. Marion J. Borchers P.C., New Braunfels, 1975; ptnr., pres. Borchers & Taylor, New Braunfels, 1977-83; pres. Marion J. Borchers, PC, New Braunfels, 1983—; chmn. elect Sch. Law Sect., State Bar of Tex., 1982-83. Mem. governing bd., officer Gonzales Warm Springs REhab. Hosp., Inc., Ottine, Tex., 1970-80, pres., 1973-75. Served with U.S. Army, 1956-58. Mem. Am. Judicature Soc., Tex. Bar Assn. (pres. 1973-74), Tex. Jaycees (state legal counsel 1967-68, dir. 1966-67, state v.p. 1968-69). Republican. Methodist. Clubs: Elk, Lions, Masons. Consumer commercial, Real property, State civil litigation. Office: 493 S Seguin Ave New Braunfels TX 78130

BORDEN, MARK STANLEY, lawyer; b. Santa Monica, Calif., July 29, 1952; s. Harold and Ruth (Weiss) B.; m. Patricia Ann Borden, Feb. 16, 1986; 1 child, George Chaplin. BA, U. Calif., Davis, 1974; JD, Western State U., San Diego, 1977. Bar: Calif. 1978, U.S. Dist. Ct. (so. dist.) Calif. 1978, U.S. Dist. Ct. (ea. dist.) Calif. 1986. Atty. Los Angeles County Pub. Defenders, 1979-84; sole practice Long Beach, Calif., 1984-85, 86—; assoc. Law Offices of William MacCabe, Torrance, Calif., 1985-86. Bd. dirs. One in Long Beach, 1986—. Criminal. Office: 5855 Naples Plaza Suite 101 Long Beach CA 90803

BORDEN, RANDOLPH TYSON, lawyer; b. Balt., Jan. 13, 1948; s. Eldon Louis and Rhea Natalie (Tyson) B.; m. Dede Mariruth Smith, July 25, 1970 (div. July 1984); m. Gwen Ellen Kleinbauer, Sept. 1, 1984. B.A., Baylor U., 1970; J.D., U. Ark., 1973; LL.M., U. Mich., 1974. Assoc. Ballard, Spahr, Andrews & Ingersoll, Phila., 1973-76; sole practice, Hawley, 1976—. Committeeman Democratic party, Milford, Pa., 1982—. Mem. ABA, Pa. Bar Assn., Phila. Bar Assn., Pa. Trial Lawyers Assn. (mem. criminal lawyer com. 1982—), Pike County Bar Assn. (v.p. 1984-85, pres. 1985-87), Pocono Mountain C. of C., Wallenpaupack C. of C., Phi Alpha Delta. Methodist. Criminal, Personal injury, General corporate. Home: RD 3 Box 1064 Honesdale PA 18431 Office: Star Route 2 Box 24 Hawley PA 18428

BORDERS, SIDNEY RICHARD, lawyer; b. Pontiac, Mich., Dec. 7, 1945; s. Carl Edison and Elsie Dewey (Baugh) B.; m. Lynne Rae Stoner, Aug. 21, 1971. Student, U. Mich., 1964-66; AS, Port Huron Jr. Coll., 1967; BS, Eastern Mich. U., 1969; JD, Wayne State U., 1972. Bar: Mich. 1972, U.S. Dist. Ct. (ea. dist.) Mich. 1973. Assoc. Frank R. Langton, Warren, Mich., 1972-75; ptnr. Borders, Boyer & Schwarb, P.C., Utica, Mich., 1976-79, Borders, Givens and Justin, P.C., Utica, 1979-81, Borders, Beadle and Eizelman, P.C., Utica, 1981-83; sole practice Utica, 1983—. Mem. Zoning Bd. Appeals, Charter Twp. of Shelby, Utica, 1986—, commr. Police and Fire CSC, 1986—. Mem. ABA, Am. Trial Lawyers Assn., Mich. Trial Lawyers Assn. Republican. Lodge: Frat. Order of Police. (assoc.). Real property, General corporate, Personal injury. Home: 53714 Sherwood Ln Utica MI 48087 Office: 48635 Van Dyke Ave Utica MI 48087

BORELL, KAREN LORRAINE, lawyer; b. Salina, Kans., June 11, 1950; d. Charles Milton and Geneva B. (Nelson) B.; m. Jonathan D. Spicher, Nov. 14, 1969 (div. June 1976). BA, U. Kans., 1974, JD, 1977. Bar: Kans. 1977, U.S. Dist. Ct. Kans. 1977, Calif., 1987. Atty. Kans. Dept. Revenue, Topeka, 1977-78, Solbach Law Offices, Lawrence, Kans., 1979-81; supervising atty., teaching fellow Douglas County Legal Aid Soc., Lawrence, 1981-82; mng. atty. Hyatt Legal Services, Lenexa, Kans., 1982-85; regional ptnr. Hyatt Legal Services, San Francisco, 1985—. Mem. ABA, San Mateo County Bar Assn., Bar Assn. San Francisco, Queen's Bench, Calif. Bar Assn., Santa Clara County Bar Assn. General practice, Family and matrimonial, Bankruptcy. Office: Hyatt Legal Services 32 W 25th Ave 102 San Mateo CA 94403

BORELLI, B. MICHAEL, lawyer; b. Vineland, N.J.. BA, Bucknell U., 1978; JD, Widener U., 1981. Bar: N.J. 1981, U.S. Dist. Ct. N.J. 1981. Sole practice Pitman, N.J., 1981—. Mem. ABA, N.J. State Bar Assn., Gloucester County Bar Assn., N.J. Sch. Bds. Assn. General practice, Personal injury, Family and matrimonial. Office: 121 W Jersey Ave Pitman NJ 08071

BORENSTEIN, MILTON CONRAD, corporation executive, lawyer; b. Boston, Oct. 21, 1914; s. Isadore Sidney and Eva Beatrice B.; m. Anne Shapiro, June 20, 1937; children: Roberta, Jeffrey. A.B. cum laude, Boston Coll., 1935; J.D., Harvard U., 1938. Bar: Mass. 1938, U.S. Dist. Ct. 1939, U.S. Ct. Appeals 1944, U.S. Supreme Ct. 1944. Gen. practice law Boston, 1938—; officer, dir. Sweetheart Paper Products Co., Inc., Chelsea, Mass., 1944-61, pres., 1961-83, chmn. bd., 1984; with Sweetheart Plastics, Inc., Wilmington, Mass., 1958—, v.p., 1958-84, also dir.; v.p. Md. Cup Corp., Owings Mills, 1960-77, exec. v.p., treas., 1977-84, also dir.; Bd. dirs. Am. Assos. Hebrew U., 1968—, Ben Gurion U., 1975—. Trustee Boston Coll., 1979—, chmn. estate planning council, 1981-83; trustee Combined Jewish Philanthropies, Boston, 1969—, N.E. Sinai Hosp., Stoughton, Mass., 1974—, Ben-Gurion U., 1975-85, 87—; bd. overseers Jewish Theol. Sem. Am., 1971—; mem. pres.'s council Sarah Lawrence Coll., 1970-79; pres. Congregation Kehillath Israel, Brookline, Mass., 1977-79, hon. pres., 1979—; mem. pres.'s council Brandeis U., 1979—, fellow, 1981—; v.p. Assoc. Synagogues of Mass., 1980-81; bd. dirs. nat. governing council Am. Jewish Congress, 1984—. Recipient Community Service award Jewish Theol. Sem. Am., 1970. Mem. ABA, Boston Bar Assn. (bicentennial com. 1986-87), Mass. Bar Assn., Single Service Inst., Chelsea C. of C. (dir.). Clubs: Harvard (Boston and N.Y.C.), Harvard Faculty, 100, Masons, Shriners. General corporate, Estate planning. Home: 273 Eliot Chestnut Hill MA 02167 Office: 1 Devonshire Pl Suite 2912 Boston MA 02109

BORESI, RICHARD L(EO), lawyer; b. Des Moines, Oct. 19, 1951; s. Leo Joseph and Margery Evelyn (Miles) B.; m. Janet Carlson, May 18, 1975; 1 child, Kristen Carlson. BA, U. Iowa, 1973; JD, Drake U., 1979. Bar: Iowa 1980, U.S. Dist. Ct. Iowa 1980. Assoc. Flagg, hockett, Benhart & Golden, Des Moines, 1980-82, King & Smith, Cedar Rapids, Iowa, 1982-84; ptnr. King, Smith & Boresi, Cedar Rapids, 1984—. Bd. dirs. Big Brothers/Big Sisters, Cedar Rapids, 1982-84, Found. II, Inc., 1982—, Linn County Advocate, 1986—. Mem. ABA, Iowa Bar Assn., Linn County Bar Assn., Cedar Rapids Jaycees. Democrat. Roman Catholic. Avocations: sports, music, chess. Family and matrimonial, Consumer commercial, Real property. Office: King Smith & Boresi 121 3d St SW Cedar Rapids IA 52404

BORG, JOSEPH PHILIP, lawyer; b. N.Y.C., Nov. 20, 1952; s. Philip Joseph and Dorothy Ann (Chircop) B.; widowed; 1 child, Chelly. BS in Polit. Sci., CCNY, 1974; JD, Hofstra U., 1977. Bar: N.Y., Ala., Fla., U.S. Dist. Ct. (no. dist.) Ala., U.S. Dist. Ct. (mid. dist.) Ala., U.S. Ct. Appeals (5th cir.), U.S. Ct. Appeals (11th cir.), U.S. Supreme Ct. Asst. corp. counsel Hagan Industries, Inc., Montgomery, Ala., 1977-79; corp. counsel, legal officer First Ala. Bank of Montgomery, 1979-85; sr. assoc. Capouano, Wampold, Prestwood & Sansone, P.A., Montgomery, 1985—; prof. law uniform comml. code Faulkner U.; lectr. Jones Bar Review Course, Ala. Continuing Ed. Program. Bd. dirs. Consumer Credit Counseling Serv. of Ala., Inc., 1981-85, pres. , 1982-84; bd. dirs. Ala. Youth Found., 1982-85, programs chmn., 1983-84. Mem. ABA, N.Y. State Bar Assn., Ala. State Bar Assn., Fla. State Bar Assn., Am. Trial Lawyers Assn., N.Y. Trial Lawyers Assn., Montgomery County Bar Assn., Montgomery County Trial Lawyers Assn., Montgomery County Young Lawyers Assn. (sec. 1984, v.p. 1985), N.Y. Acad. Sci. Banking, Consumer commercial, Contracts commercial. Home: 2656 Woodley Rd Montgomery AL 36111 Office: Capouano Wampold Prestwood & Sansone PA 359 Adams Ave Montgomery AL 36104

BORGER, JOHN EMORY, lawyer; b. Warren, Pa., Apr. 26, 1952; s. Lee James and Patricia Marie (Ulam) B.; m. Melissa May Hurley, May 30, 1981. BA, Dickinson Coll., 1974; JD, Fordham U., 1982. Bar: Conn. 1982, N.Y. 1983. Assoc. Walter, Couston, N.Y.C., 1982-83, Law Offices of J. Russell Clune, Harrison, N.Y., 1983—. MEm. ABA, N.Y. Bar Assn., West Chester County Bar Assn., Conn. Bar Assn. Avocations: coin collecting, sports. Contracts commercial, General corporate, Real property. Home: 1007 King St Greenwich CT 06831-3207 Office: J. Russell Clune PC 480 Mamaroneck Ave Harrison NY 10528

BORGES, DAVID JOSEPH, lawyer; b. Tulare, Calif., May 10, 1955; s. Joseph R. Jr. and Rosemary (Rogers) B.; m. Kirstine E. Keel, June 18, 1977; children: David J. Jr., Derek J., Dylan J. BA in History magna cum laude, Calif. State U., Northridge, 1977; JD magna cum laude, U. So. Calif., 1980. Bar: Calif. 1980, U.S. Dist. Ct. (ea. dist.) Calif. 1980, U.S. Supreme Ct. 1986. Assoc. Stringham, Rogers & Graves, Tulare, 1980-83; ptnr. Stringham, Rogers & Borges, Tulare, 1983-86; sole practice Visalia, Calif., 1985—. Mem. Rep. Nat. Com. (life), Washington, 1980—. Mem. ABA, Calif. Bar Assn. (del. 1983—), Tulare County Bar Assn. (bd. dirs. 1982—), Small Bars of Calif. (bd. dirs. 1987—), Assn. Trial Lawyers Am., Calif. Trial Lawyers Assn., Tulare County Trial Lawyers Assn. (v.p. 1984—), Rep. Nat. Lawyers Assn. (life). Avocation: karate. Family and matrimonial, State civil litigation, Probate. Home: 3710 W Mineral King Visalia CA 93291 Office: 3710 W Mineral King Ave Visalia CA 93291

BORGESE, JOHN A., lawyer; b. Bklyn., Oct. 4, 1951; s. Salvatore A. and Mary A. (Sciarrillo) B.; m. Miriam D. Dutkiewicz, Aug. 4, 1974; children: Michelle, Rebecca. BA, CUNY, 1973; JD, New Eng. Sch. Law, Boston, 1978. Bar: N.Y. 1979; U.S. Dist. Ct. (ea. and so.) N.Y. 1979. Asst. dist. atty. Kings County, N.Y.C., 1978-81; asst. gen. counsel E.F. Hutton & Co. Inc., N.Y.C., 1981, asst. v.p., asst. gen. counsel, 1982, v.p., asst. gen. counsel, 1983, first v.p., assoc. gen. counsel, 1984—; arbitrator N.Y. Stock Exchange, N.Y.C., 1983—, Nat. Assn. Securities Dealers, N.Y.C., 1983—, Nat. Futures Assn., N.Y.C., 1985—. Mem. ABA, Securities Industry Assn., Futures Industry Assn., N.Y. State Bar Assn. Securities, Commodities, Administrative and regulatory. Home: 188 Dahlia St Staten Island NY 10312 Office: E F Hutton & Co Inc One Battery Park Plaza New York NY 10004

BORGESON, EARL CHARLES, law librarian, law educator; b. Boyd, Minn., Dec. 2, 1922; s. Hjalmar Nicarner and Dohris (Donaldson) B.; m. Barbara Ann Jones, Sept. 21, 1944; children—Barbara Gale, Geoffrey Charles, Steven Earl. B.S. in Law, U. Minn., 1947, LL.B., 1949; B.A. in Law Librarianship, U. Wash., 1950. Librarian Harvard U. Law Sch. Library, 1952-70; assoc. dir. Stanford U. Libraries, 1970-75; law librarian Los Angeles County (Calif.) Law Library, 1975-78; prof. and law librarian So. Meth. U., Dallas, 1978—; lectr. UCLA Grad. Sch. Library Sci., 1975-78; adj. prof. Tex. Women's U., 1979-80; cons. in field. Served with USNR, 1943-46. Mem. Am. Assn. Law Libraries. Legal education, Librarianship. Home: 2801 Binkley #102 Dallas TX 75205 Office: Underwood Law Library So Meth U Dallas TX 75275

BORGHOFF, JOHN JOSEPH, lawyer, tax manager; b. Omaha, Nov. 9, 1955; s. Joseph John and Katherine Ann (Wolf) B.; m. Rosemary Ann Lanspa, June 20, 1980; 1 child, Joseph John. BA, Creighton U., 1978, JD, 1981; LLM, U. Mo., Kansas City, 1985. Bar: Nebr. 1981, U.S. Dist. Ct. Nebr. 1981. Sole practice Omaha, 1982-84; tax adminstr. 1st Nat. Bank Omaha, 1986—. Mem. ABA (tax. sect.), Nebr. State Bar Assn. Democrat. Roman Catholic. Avocations: golf, fishing, reading, gardening. Estate planning, Probate, Estate taxation. Office: 1st Nat Bank Omaha 16th and Dodge Omaha NE 68102

BORGOGNONI, GREGORY PAUL, lawyer; b. Coral Gables, Fla., Apr. 21, 1952; s. Mario and Jessica (Stoner) B.; m. Georgia Prokos, Jan. 12, 1986;

1 child, Christopher Paul. BBA, Fla. Internat. U., 1974; JD, U. Fla., 1978. Bar: Fla. 1978, U.S. Dist. Ct. (no., so. and mid. dists.) Fla. 1979, U.S. Ct. Appeals (5th cir.) 1979, U.S. Ct. Appeals (11th cir.) 1981, U.S. Supreme Ct. 1985. Law clk. to presiding justice Fla. Supreme Ct., Tallahassee, 1978-79; assoc. Shutts & Bowen, Miami, Fla., 1979-83; ptnr. Finley, Kumble, Wagner, Heine, Underberg, Manley, Myerson & Case, Miami, 1983—. Trustee Italians Found., Miami, 1984—. Mem. ABA (chmn. various coms.), Fla. Bar Assn. (bd. govs. young lawyers sect. 1983—, chmn. appellate ct. rules com. 1984—, chmn. jud. adminstrn. selection and tenure com. 1987—), Dade County Bar Assn. (service award 1982-85, pro bono service award 1983), Leadership Miami/C. of C. (task force 1984-85). Federal civil litigation, State civil litigation, Banking. Home: 6950 SW 107th St Miami FL 33155 Office: Finley Kumble Wagner Heine Underberg Manley Myerson & Casey 777 Brickell Ave Suite 1000 Miami FL 33131

BORISH, ARNOLD PETER, lawyer; b. Phila., Sept. 3, 1948; s. Bernard Marten and Annette (Peck) B.; m. Linda Carrie, Nov. 30, 1974; children: Carrie Ellen, Catherine Louise. BA, U. Pa., 1970; JD cum laude, U. Mich., 1974. Bar: Pa. 1975, U.S. Dist. Ct. 1975, U.S. Ct. APpeals (3d cir.) 1980, U.S. Supreme Ct. 1986. Law clk. to chief judge U.S. Dist. Ct. (ea. dist.), Phila., 1974-75; mem. Hangley, Connolly, Epstein, Chicco, Foxman & Ewing, Phila., 1975—. Mem. United Way Family Service Rev. Com., Phila., 1985—. Mem. ABA, Pa. Bar Assn. (jud. retention subcom. 1985—), Phila. Bar Assn. (civil jud. com. 1983—). Federal civil litigation, State civil litigation. Home: 604 Vassar Rd Strafford PA 19087 Office: Hangley Connolly Epstein et al 1429 Walnut St Philadelphia PA 19102

BORK, ROBERT HERON, judge, educator; b. Pitts., Mar. 1, 1927; s. Harry Philip and Elizabeth (Kunkle) B.; m. Claire Davidson, June 15, 1952 (dec. 1980); children: Robert Heron, Charles E., Ellen E.; m. Mary Ellen Pohl, Oct. 30, 1982. B.A., U. Chgo., 1948, J.D., 1953; LL.D. (hon.), Creighton U., 1975, Notre Dame Law Sch., 1982; L.H.D., Wilkes-Barre Coll., 1976; J.D. (hon.), Bklyn. Law Sch., 1984. Bar: Ill. 1953, D.C. 1977. Asso. and ptnr. firm Kirkland, Ellis, Hodson, Chaffetz & Masters, Chgo., 1955-62; asso. prof. Yale Law Sch., 1962-65, prof. law, 1965-75, on leave, 1973-75, Chancellor Kent prof. law, 1977-79; Alexander M. Bickel prof. public law 1979-81; ptnr. Kirkland & Ellis, Washington, 1981-82; judge U.S. Ct. Appeals (D.C. cir.), 1982—; solicitor gen. U.S. Dept. Justice, Washington, 1973-77; acting atty. gen. U.S., 1973-74; resident scholar Am. Enterprise Inst., Washington, 1977, adj. scholar, 1977-82; Mem. Presdl. Task Force on Antitrust, 1968; cons. Cabinet Com. on Edn., 1972. Author: The Antitrust Paradox: A Policy at War with Itself, 1978. Trustee Woodrow Wilson Internat. Center for Scholars., 1973-78. Served with USMCR, 1945-46, 50-52; 945-46, 50-52. Recipient Francis Boyer award Am. Enterprise Inst., 1984. Fellow Am. Acad. Arts and Scis. Home: United States Courthouse Washington DC 20001

BORNMANN, CARL M(ALCOLM), lawyer; b. Somerville, N.J., Aug. 13, 1936; s. John Carl Bornmann and Dorothy Louise (Balliet) Capparelli; m. Billie Wollen, Aug. 24, 1985; children: Carl, Gregory, Melissa. BS, Ohio U., 1958; JD with distinction, Ind. U., 1961. Bar: Ind. 1961, N.Y. 1962, U.S. Dist. Ct. (so. and ea. dists.) N.Y. 1962, U.S. Ct. Appeals (2d cir.) 1962, U.S. Supreme Ct. 1965. Assoc. Cahill, Gordon, Reindel & Ohl, N.Y.C., 1961-69; ptnr. Cahill, Gordon & Reindel, N.Y.C., 1970—; bd. dirs. Donald B. Cook & Assocs., New Brunswick, N.J. Co-founder LaTrappe Creek Hist. and Ecological Soc., Rochester, N.Y., 1971. Mem. ABA (corp. banking and bus. law sect.), N.Y. State Bar Assn., Order of Coif. Clubs: N.Y. Athletic, Whitehall (N.Y.C.). Securities, Banking, General corporate. Home: 125 Chestnut Ridge Rd Saddle River NJ 07458 Office: Cahill Gordon & Reindel 80 Pine St New York NY 10005

BORNS, CLARENCE, lawyer, consultant; b. Chgo., July 24, 1931; s. I.J. and Sylvia (Mackoff) B.; m. Barbara L. Critchfield, Aug. 14, 1955; children: Michael, Laura. AB, U. Mich., 1953; LLB, Ind. U., 1956. Bar: Ind. 1956, U.S. Dist. Ct. (no. dist.) Ind. 1959, U.S. Supreme Ct. 1969. Ptnr. Call, Call & Borns, Gary, Ind., 1959-71, Borns, Quinn, Kopko & Lindquist, Merrillville, Ind., 1971-75; pres. Borns, Quinn & Lindquist P.C., Merrillville, 1975-83; chmn. bd. dirs. Borns & Quinn P.C., Merrillville, 1983—; sec., treas. Cambridge Cons., Inc., 1980—. Pres. Gary (Ind.) Indsl. Found., 1969-70; mem. Econ. Devel. Commn. of Gary, 1973-75. Mem. Am. Soc. Hosp. Attys., Assn. Trial Lawyers Am. (sustaining), Ind. Trial Lawyers Assn. (bd. dirs. 1982-85), Nat. Bd. Trial Advocacy (diplomate), Greater Gary C. of C. (pres. 1969-70). Lodge: Rotary. Personal injury, Insurance, State civil litigation. Office: Borns & Quinn PC 1000 E 80th Pl Merrillville IN 46410

BOROD, DONALD LEE, lawyer; b. Cleve., June 22, 1947; s. Jules Arthur and Hortense Edith (Cowan) B.; m. Jane Duclos Hudson, Nov. 11, 1978; children: James Hudson, Catherine Duclos. B.A., U. Mich., 1969; J.D., Columbia U., 1972. Bar: N.Y. 1973, Conn. 1984. Assoc. firm Dewey, Ballantine, Bushby, Palmer & Wood, N.Y.C., 1972-81; assoc. gen. counsel Kollmorgen Corp., Hartford, Conn., 1981-83, gen. counsel, 1983-86, v.p., gen. counsel, 1986—. Harlan Fiske Stone scholar Columbia U., 1971. Mem. ABA, Conn. Bar Assn., Am. Corp. Counsel Assn., Assn. Bar City N.Y. Club: Hartford Golf. Federal civil litigation, General corporate, Private international. Office: Kollmorgen Corp 10 Mill Pond Ln Simsbury CT 06070

BOROWITZ, ALBERT IRA, lawyer, author; b. Chgo., June 27, 1930; s. David and Anne (Wolkenstein) B.; m. Helen Blanche Osterman, July 29, 1950; children: Peter Leonard, Joan, Andrew Seth. B.A. in Classics (Detur award 1948) summa cum laude, Harvard U., 1951, M.A. in Chinese Regional Studies, 1953, J.D. (Sears prize) magna cum laude, 1956. Bar: Ohio 1957. Asso. firm Hahn, Loeser, Freedheim, Dean & Wellman, Cleve., 1956-62; partner Hahn, Loeser, Freedheim, Dean & Wellman, 1962-83, Jones, Day, Reavis & Pogue, Cleve., 1983—. Author: Fiction in Communist China, 1955, Innocence and Arsenic: Studies in Crime and Literature, 1977, The Woman Who Murdered Black Satin: The Bermondsey Horror, 1981, A Gallery of Sinister Perspectives: Ten Crimes and a Scandal, 1982; The Jack the Ripper Walking Tour Murder, 1986, The Thurtell-Hunt Murder Case: Dark Mirror to Regency England, 1987; contbr. articles to profl. jours. Recipient Cleve. arts prize for lit., 1981. Mem. Am. Law Inst., Am. Bar Assn., Ohio State Bar Assn., Bar Assn. Greater Cleve. Clubs: Union (Cleve.), Rowfant (Cleve.), Ct. of Nisi Prius (Cleve.); Harvard N.Y.C. Antitrust, General corporate. Office: 1700 Huntington Bldg Cleveland OH 44115

BOROWITZ, PETER, lawyer; b. Boston, May 2, 1953; s. Albert Ira and Helen (Osterman) B.; m. Talanat Lapid, Aug. 7, 1982; 1 child, Dana Arielle. AB, Harvard U., 1974, JD, 1978. Bar: N.Y. 1979, U.S. Dist. Ct. (so. and ea. dists.) N.Y. 1979. Assoc. Debevoise and Plimpton, N.Y.C., 1978-86, ptnr., 1986—. Contbr. articles to profl. jours. Mem. ABA (com. bus. bankruptcy), Phi Beta Kappa. Bankruptcy. Home: 24 Ilinka Ln Irvington NY 10533 Office: Debevoise and Plimpton 875 3d Ave New York NY 10022

BOROWSKY, PHILIP, lawyer; b. Phila., Oct. 9, 1946; s. Joshua and Gertrude (Nicholson) B.; m. Judith Lee Goldwasser, Sept. 5, 1970; children—Miriam Isadora, Manuel, Nora Jo. B.A., UCLA, 1967; J.D., U. San Francisco, 1973. Bar: Calif. Assoc. Cartwright, Saroyan, Slobodin & Fowler, San Francisco, 1973-78; ptnr. Cartwright, Sucherman, Slobodin & Fowler, Inc., San Francisco, 1978-87; ptnr. Cartwright, Slobodia, Bokelman, Borowsky, Wartnick, Moore & Harris, 1987—; mem. faculty Practicing Law Inst., N.Y.C., 1983-84; mem. adj. faculty Hastings Coll. Law, San Francisco, 1982-83; arbitrator Superior Ct., San Francisco, 1982—, Am. Arbitration Assn., 1982—. Co-author: Unjust Dismissal and At-Will Employment, 1985; mem. bd. editorial cons. Bad Faith Law Update, 1986. Served with U.S. Army, 1968-70; Vietnam. Mem. Calif. Trial Lawyers Assn. Democrat. Jewish. Federal civil litigation, State civil litigation, General practice. Office: 101 California St 26th Floor San Francisco CA 94111

BORTECK, ROBERT D., lawyer; b. Boston, May 14, 1947; s. Jack and Beatrice (Drucker) B.; m. Lynn R. Stier, June 6, 1971; children: Andrew Evan, Jill Allison. Student, Colby Coll., 1965-67; BA, NYU, 1969, JD, 1972. Bar: N.J. 1972, U.S. Dist. Ct. N.J. 1972, U.S. Tax Ct. 1977, U.S. Supreme Ct. 1978, N.Y. 1982. Assoc. Pitney, Hardin & Kipp, Morristown, N.J., 1972-77; assoc. Shanley & Fisher, Morristown, 1977-79, ptnr., 1980-83; ptnr. Gern, Dunetz, Davison, Borteck & Weinstein, Roseland, N.J., 1983—. Fellow Am. Coll. Probate Counsel; mem. ABA (real property, probate and trust law sect.), N.J. Bar Assn. (real property, probate and trust law sect., chmn. estate planning com. 1986—, taxation sect., co-chmn. death tax com. 1982—, N.J. practice and procedure com. co-chmn. 1979-81, sub-com. to consider existing court rules and surrogate's practice with regard to settlement of accounts), Northwestern N.J. Estate Planning Council, (bd. dirs. 1978-80, pres. 1980), N.J. Soc. Hosp. Attys. (ad hoc com. on Quinlan case). Jewish. Club: Orange Lawn Tennis (South Orange, N.J.). Probate, Estate taxation, General corporate. Office: Gern Dunetz Davison et al 103 Eisenhower Pkwy Roseland NJ 07068

BORTMAN, DAVID, lawyer; b. Detroit, Mich., Sept. 17, 1938; s. Erwin Arne and Miriam Elaine (Shapiro) B. BA, U. Mich., 1962, JD, 1965. Bar: Mich. 1965, Ill. 1971. Asst. prosecuter Wayne County, Detroit, 1965-71; staff atty. Fed. Defender, Chgo., 1971-73; trial atty. SEC, Chgo., 1974-77; sole practice Chgo., 1977-79; ptnr. Bortman, Meyer & Barasa, Chgo., 1980—; mem. Fed. Ct. Jury Instructions Con., Chgo., 1984-85. Chmn. telethon com. Muscular Dystrophy Assn., Chgo., 1984; pres. Met. Chgo. Air Force Community Council, 1986. Mem. ABA, Ill. Bar Assn., Chgo. Bar Assn. (chmn. lawyer referral service 1985), Fed. Bar Assn., Chgo. Council Lawyers, Assn. Trial Lawyers Am., Bar Assn. 7th Cir., Ill. Trial Lawyers Assn., Chgo. Council Fgn. Relations. Republican. Jewish. Clubs: U. Mich., Executives Union League (Chgo.). Lodges: Masons, Shriners. Securities, Federal civil litigation, Criminal. Home: 1340 N Astor #1903 Chicago IL 60603 Office: Bortman Meyer & Barasa 140 S Dearborn #810 Chicago IL 60603

BOS, JOHN EARL, lawyer; b. Lansing, Mich., July 7, 1938; s. Hilbert J. and Katherine Elizabeth (Ellwood) B.; m. Jewel Theresa Clabuesch, June 24, 1961; children: Julie, Jonathan, Jeffrey. BA, Mich. State U., 1960; JD, U. Mich., 1964. Bar: Mich. 1964, U.S. Supreme Ct. 1968, U.S. Dist. Ct. (we. and ea. dists.) Mich., U.S. Ct. Appeals (6th cir.), U.S. Tax Ct. Assoc. Foster, Lindemer, Campbell & McGurrin, Lansing, 1964-66; ptnr. O'Brien, Skehan & Bos, Lansing, 1966-71, Dood & Bos, Lansing, 1972-78, Bos & Hanes P.C., Lansing, 1979—; adj. prof. Cooley Law Sch., Lansing, 1978-80. Mem. Ingham County (Mich.) Bd. Commrs., 1974-78; bd. dirs. YMCA, Lansing, 1972—, Lansing Art Gallery, 1985—. Fellow Am. Coll. Probate Council; mem. Mich. Bar Assn. (probate and estate planning council, treas.), Greater Lansing Estate Planning Council (pres. 1978-79) . Lodge: Lions. Family and matrimonial, Probate, Real property. Home: 1240 Whittier East Lansing MI 48823 Office: Bos & Hanes PC 6920 S Cedar Suite 8 Lansing MI 48910

BOSE, THOMAS LEWNAU, lawyer; b. Indpls., Jan. 2, 1944; s. Carl Christian and Dorothy (Lewnau) B.; m. Barbara Ellen Kark, Oct. 4, 1969; children: Susan Ellen, Julie Ellen. BA, Butler U., 1966; JD, Ind. U., 1969. Bar: Ind. 1969, U.S. Dist. Ct. (so. dist.) Ind. 1969, U.S. Ct. Appeals (7th cir.) 1970, Ill. 1983. Chief dep. securities commr. Ind. Sec. of State, Indpls., 1969-71; asst. U.S. atty. U.S. Dept. Justice, Indpls., 1971-78; atty. Eli Lilly and Co., Indpls., 1978-81; dir. product litigation G.D. Searle & Co., Skokie, Ill., 1981-83, asst. gen. counsel, 1983—. Mem. ABA, Ill. Bar Assn., Ind. Bar Assn., Phi Alpha Delta. Republican. Lutheran. Federal civil litigation, General corporate, Insurance. Home: 319 E Winchester Rd Libertyville IL 60048 Office: GD Searle & Co PO Box 1045 Skokie IL 60076

BOSETTI, GUY C., corporate lawyer. AB, Holy Cross Coll., 1949; JD, Fordham U., 1952. Assoc. Stryker, Tams & Dill, N.Y.C., 1952, Newark, 1955-61; with Mut. Benefit Life Ins. Co., Newark, 1961-77, v.p., gen. counsel, 1977-85, sr. v.p., gen. counsel, 1985—. Office: Mut Benefit Life Ins Co 520 Broad St Newark NJ 07101 *

BOSICK, JOSEPH JOHN, JR., lawyer; b. Phila., May 13, 1947; s. Joseph John and Kathleen Christina (O'Dwyer) B.; m. Mary Ellen Chajkowski, Apr. 6, 1974; children: Michael, Brian, Jennifer. BA in Econs., St. Joseph's U., Phila., 1969; JD, U. Pitts., 1973. Bar: Pa. 1973, U.S. Supreme Ct. 1978, U.S. Dist. Ct. (we. dist.) Pa. 1973, U.S. Ct. Appeals (3d cir.) 1973. Law clk. to presiding justice civil div. Allegheny County Ct. Common Pleas, Pitts., 1973-74; assoc. Meyer, Darragh, Buckler, Bebenek & Eck, Pitts., 1975-80, ptnr., 1980-87; ptnr. Pietragallo, Bosick & Gordon, Pitts., 1987—. Mem. ABA, Pa. Bar Assn., Allegheny County Bar Assn., Assn. Trial Lawyers Am., Delta Sigma Pi. Democrat. Roman Catholic. Club: Pitts. Athletic. State civil litigation, Federal civil litigation, Insurance. Office: Pietragallo Bosick & Gordon 1 Oxford Centre 13th Floor Pittsburgh PA 15219

BOSKEY, JAMES BERNARD, law professor; b. Alexandria, La., Mar. 27, 1942; s. Loeser M. and Grace (Gottlieb) B.; m. Adele Ludin, June 28, 1970; 1 child, Elizabeth Rona. AB, Princeton U., 1964; JD, U. Mich., 1967; LLM, London Sch. Econs., 1972. Bar: N.J. 1967, Ind. 1967, Ohio 1968, N.Y. 1982. Lectr. Indpls. Law Sch. Ind. U., 1967-68; asst. prof. Cleve. State U. Law Sch., 1968-70; from asst. prof. to prof. Seton Hall Law Sch., Newark, 1971—. Author: (with others) Teaching About Aging, 1982; editor: Child Abuse Manual, 1980; co-editor (series of books) N.J. Transactions Guide, 1984-86. Chmn., bd. trustees N.J. Div. of Youth and Family Services, 1984—; bd. dirs. Assn. Children N.J., Newark, 1975—; mem. govs. com. on Children's Service Planning, 1983—, Child Care Adv. Council, 1985—. Mem. ABA, N.J. State Bar Assn., Am. Arbitration Assn. Family and matrimonial, Legal education, Workers' compensation. Home: 4 Winding Way North Caldwell NJ 07006 Office: Seton Hall Law Sch 1111 Raymond Blvd Newark NJ 07102

BOSLAUGH, LESLIE, judge; b. Hastings, Nebr., Sept. 4, 1917; s. Paul E. and Ann (Herzog) B.; m. Elizabeth F. Meyer, Aug. 10, 1943; children: Marguerite Ann, Sarah Elizabeth, Paul Robert. B.B.A., U. Nebr., 1939, LL.B., 1941. Bar: Nebr. bar 1941. Mem. staff Nebr. Statute Revision Commn., 1941-43; pvt. practice law Hastings, 1946-47; asst. atty. gen. Nebr., 1947-48; mem. firm Stiner & Boslaugh, Hastings, 1949-60; judge Nebr. Supreme Ct., Lincoln, 1961—. Served to lt. AUS, 1943-46. Mem. Nebr. Bar Assn., Am. Judicature Soc., Inst. Jud. Adminstrn., Appellate Judges Conf., Order of Coif. Jurisprudence. Office: Supreme Court Box 4638 Lincoln NE 68509 *

BOSS, STEVEN SPRAGUE, lawyer, energy company executive; b. San Mateo, Calif., Apr. 16, 1946; s. Stanley Sprague and Barbara H. (Schade) S.; m. Dorothy Daignault, Oct. 6, 1973; children—Brittany Allison, Sloan Sprague. B.S. in Aerospace Engring., U. Tex.-Austin, 1968; J.D., U. So. Calif., 1974. Bar: Calif. 1974, U.S. Dist. Ct. (cen. dist.) Calif. 1974. Atty. Pacific Lighting Corp., Los Angeles, 1974-77, Tex. Oil & Gas Corp., Dallas, 1977-80; gen. counsel Lear Petroleum Corp., Dallas, 1980-84; pres. Sunshine Energy Co., Dallas, 1984—, also dir.; of counsel firm Cameron & Guy, Los Angeles, 1984—. Chmn. Los Angeles United Way, 1976. Mem. Nat. Transp. and Exchange Conf. (steering com. chmn. 1984-85), Natural Gas Soc. North Tex. (pres. 1984), ABA, Natural Gas Men of Houston, Natural Gas Men of Okla., Omicron Delta Kappa, Tau Beta Pi, Sigma Gamma Tau. Republican. FERC practice, General corporate, Energy, oil and gas contracts. Home: 5922 Bent Trail Dallas TX 75248 Office: Sunshine Energy Co 8150 N Central Expressway Suite 645 Dallas TX 75206

BOSSE, RICHARD EDWARD, lawyer; b. Dayton, Ohio, Jan. 20, 1947; s. Earl William and Helen Nina (Armstrong) B.; m. Susan Kelly, Aug. 25, 1973; 1 child, Kirsten Blair. BA, U. Cin., 1969; JD, Case Western Res. U., 1972. Bar: Fla. 1972, U.S. Dist. Ct. (so. dist.) Fla. 1975, U.S. Ct. Appeals (11th cir.) 1983, U.S. Supreme Ct. 1984. Assoc. Eubanks & Ricky, Boca Raton, Fla., 1972-73, Kurzinger & Honchell, Boca Raton, 1976-77, Honchell, Rappaport & Bosse, Boca Raton, 1977-79, Rappaport & Bosse, Boca Raton, 1979-82; sole practice Boca Raton, 1973-76, 82—. Pres. Ctr. Family Services, West Palm Beach, Fla. 1979-80, Big Bros./Big Sisters, West Palm Beach, 1979-80, Travelers Aid, West Palm Beach, 1979-80; Vestryman, St. Paul's Episcopal Ch., Delray Beach, Fla., 1985—. Mem. South Palm Beach County Bar Assn. (sec. 1979-80, pres. 1980-81), Palm Beach County Bar Assn. (bd. dirs. 1980-83). Federal civil litigation, State civil litigation, Personal injury. Home: 3125 Lakeview Dr Delray Beach FL 33444 Office: 5301 N Federal Hwy Suite 200 Boca Raton FL 33431

BOSSELMAN, FRED PAUL, lawyer; b. Oak Park, Ill., June 14, 1934; s. Fred and Beulah (Chamberlain) B.; m. Kay Wilson, 1956; children: Judith, Carol, Mark. B.A., U. Colo., 1956; J.D., Harvard U., 1959. Bar: Ill. 1959, Fla. 1985. Assoc. firm Ross & Hardies, Chgo., 1959-67; partner Ross, Hardies, O'Keefe, Babcock & Parsons, 1967-83, Burke, Bosselman & Weaver,, Chgo., 1983—; asso. reporter Am. Law Inst., 1969-75; dir. Met. Planning Council Chgo., 1971—; commr. Housing Authority Cook County (Ill.), 1973—. Author: (with David Callies) The Quiet Revolution in Land Use Control, 1971, (with David Callies and John Banta) The Taking Issue, 1973, (with Richard Babcock) Exclusionary Zoning, 1974, In the Wake of the Tourist, 1978. Mem. ABA (chmn. environ. law com. sect. real property, probate and trust law 1974-77), Am. Soc. Planning Ofcls. (dir. 1977-78), Am. Planning Assn. (sec. 1978-79, pres. 1982-83), Urban Land Inst. (dir. Fed. Policy Council 1982—), Nat. Audubon Soc. (dir. 1985—). Environment. Home: 2715 Woodbine Ave Evanston IL 60201 Office: Burke Bosselman & Weaver 55 W Monroe St Chicago IL 60603

BOSSES, STEVAN J., lawyer; b. Bronx, N.Y., July 29, 1937; s. Fred and Frieda (Picard) B.; m. Abbye Z. Bosses, May 24, 1964; children—Donna Lynne, David Keith, Gary Philip. B.M.E., Cornell U., 1960; LL.B., Columbia U., 1963. Bar: N.Y. 1963, U.S. Dist. Ct. (so. dist.) N.Y. 1964, U.S. Dist. Ct. (ea. dist.) N.Y. 1964, U.S. Dist. Ct. (we. dist.) Wis. 1981, U.S. Patent Office 1964, U.S. Ct. Appeals (2d cir.) 1970, U.S. Ct. Appeals (3rd cir.) 1979, U.S. Ct. Appeals (D.C. cir.) 1982. Assoc., Watson Leavenworth Kelton & Taggart, N.Y.C., 1963-71, ptnr., 1972-81; ptnr. Fitzpatrick, Cella, Harper & Scinto, N.Y.C., 1981—. Mem. ABA, N.Y. State Bar Assn., Westchester County Bar Assn., Am. Intellectual Property Law Assn., Fed. Bar Council, N.Y. Patent, Trademark and Copyright Law Assn., ASME. Patent, Trademark and copyright, Federal civil litigation. Home: 19 Springdale Rd Scarsdale NY 10583 Office: 277 Park Ave New York NY 10172

BOSSHARD, JOHN, lawyer, banker; b. LaCrosse, Wis., Sept. 28, 1920; s. John Bosshard and Effie Kremmer; m. Rylla Jane Hattan, June 15, 1944; children: John III, Sabina, William Hattan, Kurt Robert. PhB, U. Wis., 1942; MBA, Harvard U., 1947, LLB, 1947. Bar: Wis. 1947, U.S. Dist. Ct. (we. dist.) Wis. 1947. Ptnr. Bosshard and Assocs., La Crosse, 1947—; pres. Spartek Inc., Sparta, Wis., 1983—, Kickapoo Oil Co., Hillsboro, Wis., 1978—, La Crosse Devel. Corp., 1978-80; v.p. Intercity Bank, Schoenfield, Wis., 1985—, Community Nat. Bank, Oregon, Wis., 1978—; exec. v.p. LaFarge State Bank, 1969—; pres., bd. dirs. 1st Nat. Bank, Bangor, Wis., 1972—, Farmers State Bank, Hillsboro, 1970—; chmn. bd. dirs. Bank of Mauston, Wis., 1972—, Grand Marsh (Wis.) State Bank, 1977—, Bank of Alma, Wis., 1986—; judge Small Claims Ct., La Crosse, 1954-60; dist. atty. La Crosse County, 1950-54. Sec. La Crosse County Reps., 1952-56. Named Man of Yr. LaCrosse Area, 1986. Mem. La Crosse County Bar Assn. (pres.). Lodge: Kiwanis. Banking, State civil litigation, Probate. Office: Bosshard and Assocs PO Box 966 La Crosse WI 54601

BOSSIER, LARRY SHERMAN, lawyer; b. Baton Rouge, May 18, 1952; s. J.J.E. and Joan (Sherman) B.; m. Brenda Kay Jones, Apr. 13, 1985. BA, Nicholls State U., 1974; student, La. State U., 1979; JD, So. U., Baton Rouge, 1980. Bar: La. 1981, U.S. Dist. Ct. (mid. and ea. dists.) La. 1983. Archarist Sec. State of La., Baton Rouge, 1978-80; law clk. to presiding justice div. C 18th Jud. Dist. Ct., Plaquemine, La., 1980-81; sole practice Grosse Tete, La., 1981—; atty. Village of Grosse Tete, 1981—; bd. dirs. Cap. Area Legal Service, Baton Rouge, 1984—. Asst. chief Grosse Tete Vol. Fire Dept., 1976-86; bd. dirs. Iberville Parish (La.) Planning Commn., 1982-86, Iberville Mental Health Bd., 1982-86. Mem. La. Bar Assn., La. Trial Lawyers Assn., 18th Jud. Dist. Bar Assn. Democrat. Baptist. Lodges: Lions (legal counsel), Masons. Avocation: model ship building. General practice, Personal injury. Office: PO Box 56 Grosse Tete LA 70740

BOST, DEBORAH JACOBS, lawyer; b. Greensboro, N.C., May 11, 1950; d. Cyril and Eugenie (Goodman) Jacobs; m. John C. Bost, June 18, 1972. BA in Econs. and Acctg., N.C. State U., 1972; JD, Wake Forest U., 1979. Bar: N.C. 1979; CPA, N.C. Research asst. N.C. State U., Raleigh, 1968-72; comptroller Maverick Mobile Homes, Greensboro, 1972-73; field agt. IRS, Winston-Salem, N.C., 1973-76; pvt. practice cons., acctg. Greensboro, Winston-Salem, 1976-79; assoc. Tuggle, Duggins, Meschan & Elrod, Greensboro, 1979-86, ptnr., 1986—; speaker in field. Contbr. articles to profl. jours. Fellow Am. Inst. CPA's; mem. ABA, N.C. Bar Assn. (treas. young lawyers div.), N.C. Assn. CPA's (speaker symposium 1985). Democrat. Jewish. Corporate taxation, Personal income taxation, General corporate. Home: 3935 Starmount Dr Greensboro NC 27410 Office: Tuggle Duggins Meschan & Elrod PA PO Drawer X Greensboro NC 27402

BOST, THOMAS GLEN, lawyer; b. Oklahoma City, July 13, 1942; s. Burl John and Lorene Belle (Croka) B.; m. Sheila K. Pettigrew, Aug. 27, 1966; children: Amy Elizabeth, Stephen Luke, Emily Anne, Paul Alexander. BS in Acctg. summa cum laude, Abilene Christian U., 1964; JD, Vanderbilt U., 1967. Bar: Tenn. 1967, Calif. 1969. Instr. David Lipscomb Coll., Nashville, 1967; asst. prof. law Vanderbilt U., Nashville, 1967-68; ptnr. Latham & Watkins, Los Angeles, 1968—; lectr. on taxation subjects. Chmn. bd. regents, law sch. bd. visitors Pepperdine U., Malibu, Calif., 1980—. Mem. ABA (standards of tax practice com., sec. taxation), Calif. Bar Assn., Los Angeles County Bar Assn. (chmn. taxation sect. 1981-82). Republican. Mem. Ch. of Christ. Club: Calif. (Los Angeles). Personal income taxation, Corporate taxation, State and local taxation. Office: Latham & Watkins 555 S Flower St Los Angeles CA 90071

BOSTIC, HARRIS CLEMON, lawyer; b. Atlanta, Sept. 21, 1938; s. Clemon and Lizzie Mae (Daniel) B.; m. Joyce Elaine Pauline, Sept. 9, 1960; children—Kenneth G., Harris Clemon, II, Joi LaTrice, Anthony T. B.A., Morehouse Coll., 1960; M.A., Atlanta U., 1962; J.D., Howard U., 1966; LL.M., George Washington U., 1967. Bar: Ga. 1970, U.S. Ct. Appeals (5th cir.) 1971, U.S. Ct. Appeals (11th cir.) 1977, U.S. Supreme Ct. 1977. Atty. Neighborhood Legal Ctr., Washington, 1966; atty., researcher Garland & Garland, Atlanta, 1966-70; counsel EEOC, Atlanta, 1970-71; ptnr. Johnson & Bostic, Atlanta, 1971-74; prin., counselor at law Harris C. Bostic & Assocs. P.C., Atlanta, 1974—; dir., gen. counsel Southeastern Tng. Corp., Atlanta, 1977—; gen. counsel U.S. Vet. Clubs, Atlanta, 1983—, Fulton County Devel. Authority, Atlanta, 1983—. Pres. Omega chpt. Y Men Internat., Atlanta, 1972; bd. dirs. Butler St. YMCA, 1978; v.p. Democratic Clubs of Ga., 1973. Recipient Disting. Alumnus award Morehouse Coll., Atlanta, 1975, Chief Justice award, Sigma Delta Tau, 1972, Man of Yr. award Y's Men Internat., 1976. Fellow Nat. Bar Assn.; mem. Atlanta Bar Assn., Gate City Bar Assn. (v.p. 1979-80), Ga. Trial Lawyers Assn., Ga. Conf. Black Lawyers (v.p., 1978-79, Lawyer of Yr. 1980), NAACP (bd. dirs. Atlanta chpt. 1976), Morehouse Coll. Alumni Assn. (gen. counsel 1975—). Democrat. Methodist. Clubs: Loch Lomond (pres. 1980-81), Bay Country (treas. 1978-80). Lodge: Masons (32 deg.). Personal injury, Criminal, Family and matrimonial. Home: 1765 Loch Lomond Trail SW Atlanta GA 30331 Office: The Bostic Bldg 980 M L King Jr Dr SW Atlanta GA 30314

BOSTICK, CHARLES DENT, law educator; b. Gainesville, Ga., Dec. 28, 1931; s. Jared Sullivan and Charlotte Catherine (Dent) B.; m. Susan Oliver, Sept. 8, 1956; children: Susan, Alan. Student, Emory-at-Oxford U., 1948-49; B.A., Mercer U., 1952, J.D., 1958. Bar: Ga. 1957, Tenn. 1974, U.S. Dist. Ct. (no. dist.) Ga. 1958, U.S. Ct. Appeals (5th cir.) 1959. Individual practice law Gainesville, Ga., 1958-66; asst. prof. law U. Fla., Gainesville, 1966-68, assoc. prof., 1968; assoc. prof. Vanderbilt U., Nashville, 1968-71, prof., 1971—, assoc. dean, dir. admissions, 1975-79, acting dean, 1979-80, dean, 1980-85; vis. prof. law U. Leeds, Eng., 1985-86. Served to lt. USNR, 1952-55. Mem. Tenn. Bar. Assn. Episcopalian. Probate, Real property. Office: Vanderbilt U Law Sch Nashville TN 37240

BOSTICK, GEORGE HALE, lawyer; b. Birmingham, Ala., Dec. 9, 1944; s. Raymond Ellis and Marion Elizabeth (George) B.; m. Rebecca Ann Vernon, Dec. 28, 1968; children—Matthew Ellis, Katherine Martin. B.A. in Econs., Emory U., 1967; J.D., U. Va., 1973. Bar: Va. 1973, D.C. 1974, U.S. Tax Ct. 1977, U.S. Ct. Claims 1978, U.S. Supreme Ct. 1979. Law clk. to presiding judge U.S. Ct. Appeals (5th cir.), Montgomery, Ala., 1973-74; assoc. Sutherland, Asbill & Brennan, Washington, 1974-79, ptnr., 1979—; adj. prof. law Georgetown U. Law Sch., Washington, 1978-80; speaker in field. Mem., notes editor U. Va. Law Rev., 1971-73; contbr. articles to profl. jours. Mem. Barkley Forum Found., Atlanta, 1968—; alumni rep. Emory U. Admissions Office, Washington, 1978—; treas. MacArthur Elem. Sch. PTA, Alexandria, Va., 1982-84 . Stipe scholar, 1963-64, Lockheed Leadership scholar, 1963-67. Mem. ABA (vice chmn. corp. sect. employee benefits com., corp. section rep. to joint com. on employee benefits, chair of tax sect. subcom. on unfunded

deferred compensation). Democrat. Presbyterian. Pension, profit-sharing, and employee benefits, Corporate taxation. Home: 920 Vicar Ln Alexandria VA 22302 Office: Sutherland Asbill & Brennan 1666 K St NW Washington DC 20006

BOSTON, ROBERT EARL, lawyer; b. Lawrenceburg, Tenn., Aug. 27, 1957; s. William E. and Thelma Sue (Benson) B.; m. Dixie A. La Grone, Dec. 20, 1980. BA, Vanderbilt U., 1979; JD, U. Tenn., 1981. Bar: Tenn. 1982, U.S. Dist. Ct. (mid. dist.) Tenn. 1982, U.S. Ct. Appeals (6th cir.) 1985, U.S. Dist. Ct. (11th cir.) 1986, U.S. Supreme Ct. 1987. Ptnr. Waller, Lansden, Dortch & Davis, Nashville, 1982—. Vol. Tenn. Soc. to Prevent Blindness, Nashville, 1984—. Mem. ABA, Assn. Trial Lawyers Am., Tenn. Bar Assn., Tenn. Trial Lawyers Assn., Nashville Bar Assn., Nat. Rifle Assn., Order of Coif. Republican. Methodist. Club: Ducks Unltd., Nashville City. Avocations: sports, reading, travel. Labor, Federal civil litigation, State civil litigation. Office: Waller Landsden Dortch & Davis 2100 One Commercial Pl Nashville TN 37239

BOSTWICK, RICHARD RAYMOND, lawyer; b. Billings, Mont., Mar. 17, 1918; s. Leslie H. and Maude (Worthington) B.; m. Margaret Florence Brooks, Jan. 17, 1944; children: Michael, Patricia, Ed, Dick. Student, U. Colo., 1937-38; A.B., U. Wyo., 1943, J.D., 1947. Bar: Wyo. 1947. Claim atty. Hawkeye Casualty Co., Casper, Wyo., 1948-49; partner Murane & Bostwick, Casper, 1949—; Lectr. U. Wyo. Coll. Law; mem. 10th Cir. Jud. Adv. Com. Contbr. articles profl. jours. Past trustee Casper YMCA; dep. dir. Civil Def., 1954-58; chmn. local SSS, 1952-70; mem. curriculum coordinating com. Natrona Co. Sch. Dist. 2, High Sch. Dist. Served to capt. AUS, 1943-46. Decorated Bronze Star medal; recipient Silver Merit awards Am. Legion. Mem. ABA, Wyo. Bar Assn. (pres. 1964-65), Natrona County Bar Assn. (pres. 1956), Am. Judicature Soc. (exec. com. 1973-75, sec. 1975-77 Herbert Harley award), Internat. Assn. Def. Counsel, Fedn. Ins. and Corp. Counsel, Nat. Conf. Bar Pres. (exec. council 1970-72), Internat. Soc. of Barristers (dir. 1971-76, pres. 1975), Am. Legion (dir. 1951-58, post comdr. 1953-54), Wyo. Alumni Assn. (trustee 1955-57), Casper C. of C. (chmn. legis. com. 1955-57, dir. 1959-62, v.p.). Presbyn. Club: Mason (Shriner, KT). Personal injury, Federal civil litigation, State civil litigation. Home: 1137 Granada Ave Casper WY 82601 Office: Wyoming Bldg 350 West A St Suite 100 Casper WY 82601

BOSWELL, GEORGE HARVEY, lawyer; b. Medina, Tenn., July 8, 1947; s. George Finley and Edna Luola (Kirk) B.; m. Jenny Lynn Butler, Aug. 11, 1967; 1 child, Julie Annice. BS, U. Tenn., 1969; JD, Memphis State U., 1978. Bar: Tenn. 1979, U.S. Dist. Ct. (no. dist.) Tenn. 1979. Assoc. Law Office of Dwight Hawks, Humboldt, Tenn., 1979-80; sole practice Milan, Tenn., 1980-83; ptnr. Kizer, Bonds & Boswell, Milan, 1983-85, Kizer, Bonds, Boswell & Crocker, Milan, 1985—; asst. atty. City of Milan, 1985—; bd. dirs., sec. Tenn. Plastics Corp., Milan, 1986—; bd. dirs. Milan Raceway Inc., 1985—. Mem. Capital Club Reps., Nashville, 1983—; bd. dirs. Gibson County Reps., Humboldt, 1985-86. Named Young Man of Yr. Jaycees, 1982. Mem. ABA, Tenn. Bar Assn., Gibson County Bar Assn. (pres. 1983-84), Tenn. Trial Lawyers Assn., Milan C. of C. (bd. dirs. 1982-85). Republican. Methodist. Lodge: Lions (pres. 1982-83). Avocations: fishing, golf, flowers. Bankruptcy, Contracts commercial, Personal injury. Home: Rt 2 Box 446 Milan TN 38358 Office: Kizer Bonds Boswell & Crocker PO Box 320 Milan TN 38358

BOSWELL, JOHN HOWARD, lawyer; b. Houston, Mar. 22, 1932; s. Henry Oliver and Opal Everest (Wineburg) B.; m. Sharon Lee Ueckert, Dec. 19, 1959; children—John Brooke, Mark Richard. B.B.A., U. Houston, 1955; J.D., U. Houston, 1963. Bar: Tex. 1962, U.S. Supreme Ct. 1970, U.S. Ct. Appeals (5th cir.) 1970. Ptnr. Boswell and Hallmark, Houston; lectr. State Bar Tex. Continuing Legal Edn. Program, 1978-84, Pepperdine U. Coll. Law, 1981[3 ; faculty Tex. Coll. of Trial Advocacy, 1980-86. Served to lt. USNR, 1955-58. Mem. Am. Bd. Trial Advocates, Internat. Assn. Ins. Counsel, Tex. Assn. Def. Counsel, Def. Research Inst. Personal injury, Federal civil litigation, State civil litigation. Home: 405 Chapelwood Ct Houston TX 77024 Office: 2100 InterFirst Plaza 1100 Louisiana St Houston TX 77002

BOSWELL, WILLIAM DOUGLAS, lawyer; b. Harrisburg, Pa., June 7, 1918; s. Ralph Everett and Edna Stansberry (Heller) B.; m. Doris M. Lutz, June 9, 1945; children—William D. Jr., Jeffrey R., Nancy Jeanne, Joanne Elizabeth. PhB, Dickinson Coll., 1940, LLB, 1943. Bar: Pa. 1943, U.S. Dist. Ct. (mid. dist.) Pa. 1946, U.S. Dist. Ct. (ea. dist.) Pa. 1965, U.S. Ct. Appeals (3d cir.) 1966, U.S. Ct. Appeals (4th cir.) 1981, U.S. Supreme Ct. 1962. Ptnr. Compton, Handler, Berman & Boswell, Harrisburg, Pa., 1946-71, Berman, Boswell & Titner, Harrisburg, 1971-86, Berman, Boswell, Tintner & Piccola, 1986—; lectr. Pa. Bar Inst., Am. Soc. C.L.U.s, Pa. Banker's Assn.; bd. dirs. Iceland Seafood Corp., Byers Lumber Co., Inc. Pres. Tri-County United Way, 1963-64, Tri-County Welfare Council, 1960-61, Josiah W. and Bessie H. Kline Found.; v.p. Dauphin County unit Am. Cancer Soc., 1970-72; pres. Children's Home of Harrisburg, Inc., 1965-68, 75—, Estate Planning Council Central Pa., 1970. Served as master sgt. AUS, 1942-46. Fellow Am. Coll. Probate Counsel, mem. ABA, Pa. Bar Assn., Dauphin County Bar Assn. (pres. 1962-63), Am. Judicature Soc. Republican. Methodist. Clubs: Executive of Central Pa. (pres. 1978); Masons, K.T., Shriners, Tuesday, Country (pres. 1974-76) (Harrisburg). General practice, Probate, General corporate. Office: Berman Boswell Tintner & Piccola PO Box 3787 Harrisburg PA 17105

BOSWELL, WILLIAM PARET, lawyer; b. Washington, Oct. 24, 1946; s. Yates Paret and Mary Frances (Hyland) B.; m. Barbara Stelle Schroeder, Sept. 6, 1969; children: Susan Anne, Sarah Mary, Christina Catherine. BA cum laude, Cath. U., 1968; JD, U. Va., 1971. Bar: Va. 1971, D.C. 1972, U.S. Ct. Mil. Appeals 1972, U.S. Supreme Ct. 1975, Pa. 1978. Atty. Peoples Natural Gas Co., Pitts., 1978-82, asst. sec., gen. atty., 1982-85, sec., gen. counsel, 1985—, also bd. dirs.; bd. dirs. Met. Pitts. Pub. Broadcasting Inc. V.p. Borough council Osborne, Pa., 1984—. Served to capt. JAGC, USAF, 1971-78. Mem. ABA, Pa. Bar Assn., D.C. Bar Assn., Va. Bar Assn., Am. Gas Assn., Pa. Gas Assn. (vice chmn. 1985—), Am. Corp. Counsel Assn., Am. Soc. Corp. Secs. Republican. Roman Catholic. Clubs: Rivers, City (Pitts.). Avocations: reading, sailing, walking. General corporate, Public utilities, Oil and gas leasing. Home: 405 Hare Ln Sewickley PA 15143 Office: Peoples Natural Gas Co Two Gateway Ctr Pittsburgh PA 15222

BOTHAM, LISA ANNE, lawyer; b. Mankato, Minn., Aug. 20, 1957; d. Kaye John and Ruth G. Botham; m. David G. Westling, Apr. 16, 1983. BE, S.W. State U., Marshall, Minn., 1978; JD, U. Wyo., 1981. Bar: Wyo. 1981, U.S. Dist. Ct. Wyo. 1981, U.S. Ct. Appeals (10th cir.) 1986, U.S. Supreme Ct. 1986. Asst. pub. defender State of Wyo., Casper, 1981-82; sole practice Green River, Wyo., 1983—; prosecutor City of Green River, 1982—. Firefighter Green River Vol. Fire Dept., 1985—. Mem. ABA, Wyo. Bar Assn., Assn. Trial Lawyers Am. Lutheran. Criminal, Federal civil litigation, Civil rights. Office: Green River City Hall 50 E 2d N Green River WY 82935

BOTTGER, WILLIAM CARL, JR., lawyer; b. Roanoke, Va., Oct. 18, 1941; s. William Carl and Anne Harrison (Sneed) B.; m. Shirley Jean Tietjen, Feb. 10, 1968; children: W. Carl III, Christina K., Frederick B., Erica M. BA, Dartmouth Coll., 1966; JD, U. Va., 1971. Bar: Calif. 1972, U.S. Dist. Ct. (cen. dist.) Calif. 1972, U.S. Ct. Appeals (9th cir.) 1976, U.S. Supreme Ct. 1982. Assoc. Latham & Watkins, Los Angeles, 1971-79, ptnr., 1979—. Served to 1st lt., U.S. Army, 1962-64. Republican. Episcopalian. Avocations: karate, rock climbing. Labor, Federal civil litigation, State civil litigation. Office: Latham & Watkins 555 S Flower St Los Angeles CA 90071

BOTTI, ALDO E., lawyer; b. Bklyn., Dec. 27, 1936; s. Ettore and Filomena (DeLucio) B.; m. Sheila Higgins, Aug. 5, 1967; children: Michael, Joseph, Mark, Sarah, Elizabeth, John. BA, Rockhurst Coll., 1962; JD, St. Louis U., 1965. Bar: Ill. 1966, U.S. Dist. Ct. (no. and so. dists.) Ill. 1967, U.S. Supreme Ct. 1973, U.S. Ct. Appeals (7th cir.) 1979. Assoc. Frank Glazer & William O'Brien, Chgo., 1966-69; asst. states atty. DuPage County, Wheaton, Ill., 1969-71, pub. defender, 1971-72; sr. ptnr. Botti, Marinaccio & DeSalvo Ltd., Oak Brook, Ill., 1972—; atty. Village of Villa Park, 1985—. Mem. picnic plus com. Hinsdale (Ill.) Community House, 1985; bd. dirs. Opera Theatre Ill., 1981-84; chmn. bd. dirs. Hinsdale Community Services, 1972-73. Served with U.S. Army, 1955-58. Mem. ABA, Ill. Bar Assn., Chgo. Bar Assn., DuPage County Bar Assn. (chmn. speakers bur. 1975-78, chmn. pub. relations 1973-75), Am. Judicature Soc., Assn. Trial Lawyers Am., Internat. Platform Assn. Republican. Roman Catholic. Club: Butterfield Country (Oak Brook). Avocations: oil painting, reading. State civil litigation, Criminal, Federal civil litigation. Office: Botti Marinaccio & DeSalvo Ltd 720 Enterprise Dr Oak Brook IL 60521

BOTTITTA, JOSEPH ANTHONY, lawyer; b. Newark, Mar. 9, 1949; s. Anthony S. and Elizabeth (Bellisano) B.; m. Lynda Joan Kloss, Apr. 14, 1979; children—Michelle Emma, Gregory Joseph. B.S. in Bus. Adminstrn., Seton Hall U., 1971, J.D., 1974. Bar: N.J. 1974, U.S. Dist. Ct. N.J. 1974, U.S. Supreme Ct. 1981. Ptnr. Rusignola & Pugliese, Newark, 1974-78; sr. ptnr. Joseph A. Bottitta, West Orange, N.J., 1979—; chmn. Supreme Ct. Fee Arbitration Com. Dist. V-B., 1984-85. Mem. ABA, Assn. Trial Lawyers Am., N.J. State Bar Assn., Essex County Bar Assn. (sec. 1983-84, treas. 1984-85, pres. elect 1985-86, pres. 1986—). Republican. Roman Catholic. Criminal, Personal injury, Real property. Office: 91 Main St West Orange NJ 07052

BOUCEK, GEORGE WASHINGTON, lawyer; b. Berwyn, Ill., Jan. 11, 1912; s. Frank and Hattie (Horacek) B.; m. Blanche Korecek, Dec. 2, 1942; 1 child, Melinda Kathy. Paralegal cert., Morton Jr. Coll., 1930; LLB, LLD, Chgo. Kent Coll. Law, 1930-33; LHD (hon.), Carroll Coll., 1978. Bar: Ill. 1934, U.S. Dist. Ct. (no. dist.) Ill. 1936. Law clk. to Robert F. Bradburn, Chgo., 1930-33; assoc. Bradburn & Dammann, 1934-37; ptnr. Bradburn, Dammann & Boucek, 1938-59, Bradburn & Boucek, 1960-67; sole practice, Berwyn, Ill., 1967—. Nat. dir. CSA Frat. Life, Berwyn, Ill., 1942-46, 77—; treas. Berwyn Pub. Health Dist., 1958-77; active Boy Scouts Am., 1924—; twp. assessor Berwyn Twp., 1958-77; cemetery care adv. bd. Comptroller of Ill., 1972—. Served as 1st lt. U.S. Army, 1944-46, ETO. Recipient Commendation Ribbon for war crimes duty, London, 1945. Mem. Am. Legion (nat. fin. commn. 1978—, vice chmn. 1983-86, chmn. 1986—), Ill. dept. judge advocate 1979—), Ill. Bar Assn., West Suburban Bar Assn., Bohemian Lawyers Assn., Chgo. Law Inst., Judge Advocates Assn., Twp. Ofcls. Ill. (assoc.), 40 and 8, VFW, Am. Czechoslovak Legion, Sokol Tabor Gymnastic Assn., Bohemian Nat. Cemetery Assn. (gen. counsel 1935—), Unity of Czech Ladies and Men (gen. counsel 1963-77), Czechoslovak Soc. Am. (pres. T.A. Edison chpt. 1942-44, trustee 1944—). Democrat. Lodge: Elks. Probate, Real property, General practice. Home: 1938 Maple Ave Berwyn IL 60402 Office: 6915 W Cermak Rd Berwyn IL 60402

BOUCHER, JOSEPH WILLIAM, lawyer, accountant, business owner, teacher, writer; b. Menominee, Mich., Oct. 28, 1951; s. Joseph W. and Patricia (Coon) B.; m. Susan M. DeGroot, June 4, 1977; children: Elizabeth, Bridget. BA, St. Norbert Coll., 1973; JD, U. Wis., 1977, MBA in Fin., 1978. Bar: Wis. 1978, U.S. Dist. Ct. (we. dist.) Wis. 1978; CPA, Wis. Adminstrv. aide to Senator Wis. Senate, Madison, 1977; ptnr. Murphy, Stolper et al., Madison, 1978-84, Stolper et al., Madison, 1985—; lectr. bus. U. Wis., Madison, 1980—. Bd. dirs. United Way, Dane County, Wis., 1986—. Named one of Outstanding Young Men Am., 1978, Wis. Lawyer Adv. Yr., SBA, 1983. Mem. ABA, Wis. Bar Assn., Dane County Bar Assn., Am. Inst. CPA's, Wis. Inst. CPA's, U. Wis. Bus. Alumni Assn. (bd. dirs. 1980-87). Roman Catholic. Avocations: sports, reading. Contracts commercial, General corporate, Corporate taxation. Home: 5925 S Hill Dr Madison WI 53705 Office: 7617 Mineral Point Rd Madison WI 53717

BOUDIN, MICHAEL, lawyer; b. N.Y.C., Nov. 29, 1939; s. Leonard B. and Jean (Roisman) B.; m. Martha A. Field, Sept. 14, 1984. B.A., Harvard Coll., 1961, LL.B., 1964. Bar: N.Y. 1964, D.C. 1967. Clk. U.S. Ct. Appeals, 2 d cir., 1964-65, U.S. Sup. Ct., 1965-66; assoc. firm Covington & Burling, Washington, 1966—, ptnr., 1972—; vis. prof. Harvard Law Sch., 1982-83, lectr., 1983-84, 85-87; lectr. U. Pa. Law Sch., 1984-85. Contbr. revs. to law jours. Mem. ABA, Am. Law Inst. Administrative and regulatory, Antitrust, Federal civil litigation. Office: Covington & Burling 1201 Pennsylvania Ave NW PO Box 7566 Washington DC 20044

BOUDREAUX, ANDREE ANITA, lawyer; b. New Orleans, Dec. 14, 1956; d. Allen I. and Doris C. (McGinity) B. BBA, Loyola U., New Orleans, 1977, JD, 1980. Bar: La. 1980, U.S. Dist. Ct. (ea. dist.) La. 1981, U.S. Dist. Ct. (mid. and we. dists.) La. 1983. Sole practice New Orleans, 1980-83; atty. Dist. Counsel VA, New Orleans, 1983-85, Gen. Counsel VA, Washington, 1985—. Mem. ABA, La. State Bar Assn., La. Trial Lawyers Assn., Am. Soc. of Women Accts. (program chmn. 1984-85). Democrat. Roman Catholic. Administrative and regulatory, Labor, Health. Home: 6611 E Wakefield Dr Alexandria VA 22307 Office: Vets Adminstrn 810 Vermont Ave NW Washington DC 20420

BOULANGER, CAROL SEABROOK, lawyer; b. N.Y.C., Sept. 14, 1942; d. John M. and Anne (Schlaudecker) Seabrook; m. Jacques P. Boulanger, June 1, 1974; children: Rodolphe, Adriana. BA, Swarthmore Coll., 1964; LLB, U. Pa., 1969. Bar: N.Y. 1970, U.S. Tax Ct. 1970. Assoc. Baker & McKenzie, N.Y.C., 1969-71; assoc. Wender, Murase & White, N.Y.C., 1971-75, ptnr., 1975-82; ptnr. Boulanger, Finley & Hicks, N.Y.C., 1982-84, Drinker, Biddle & Reath, N.Y.C., 1984—. Founding mem. ARCS Found. Inc., N.Y.C., sec. 1973-75, v.p. 1975-80; bd. dirs. Swarthmore Coll., 1977-81. Mem. ABA (tax sect., internat. law sect.), Assn. Bar City of N.Y. (internat. law com. 1980-84, fgn. and comparative law com., 1984-85, chmn. 1985—). Private international, Corporate taxation, Estate taxation. Office: Drinker Biddle & Reath 405 Park Ave New York NY 10022

BOULGER, WILLIAM CHARLES, lawyer; b. Columbus, Ohio, Apr. 2, 1924; s. James Ignatius and Rebecca (Laughlin) B.; m. Ruth J. Schachtele, Dec. 29, 1954; children—Brigid Carolyn, Ruth Mary. A.B., Harvard Coll., 1948; LL.B., Law Sch. Cin., 1951. Bar: Ohio, 1951, U.S. Dist. Ct. (so. dist.) Ohio 1952, U.S. Supreme Ct. 1957. Ptnr. with Thomas A. Boulger, Chillicothe, Ohio, 1951-73; sole propr. Law Offices of William C. Boulger, Chillicothe, 1974—. Pres. Ross County Welfare Assn., Chillicothe, 1954-60; mem. Chillicothe. ARC, 1958-84, chmn., 1959-63, 1985—; mem. Democratic Exec. Com., Chillicothe, 1950s. Served as pfc. U.S. Army, 1943-45, ETO. Mem. Ross County Bar Assn. (pres. 1971), Ohio Bar Assn., ABA. Roman Catholic. Clubs: Sunset, Symposiarchs (pres.). Avocations: tennis, golf. Personal injury, Probate, General practice. Home: 31 Club Dr Chillicothe OH 45601 Office: 10-14 Foulke Block Chillicothe OH 45601

BOUMA, ROBERT EDWIN, diversified company executive, lawyer; b. Ft. Dodge, Iowa, July 19, 1938; s. Jack and Gladys (Cooper) B.; m. Susan Lawson, Nov. 26, 1963; children: James, Whitley. B.A., Coe Coll., 1960; J.D., U. Iowa, 1962. Bar: Iowa 1962, N.Y. 1964, Ill. 1985. Asso. Cravath, Swaine & Moore, N.Y.C., 1962-70; gen. counsel Xerox Data Systems Co., Los Angeles, 1970-73; sr. group counsel Xerox Corp., Rochester, N.Y., 1973-76; asso. gen. counsel Monsanto Co., St. Louis, 1976-78; sr. v.p., gen. counsel Household Internat., Prospect Heights, Ill., 1978-84; ptnr. McDermott Will & Emery, Chgo., 1984—. Trustee Coe Coll. Served with USN, 1962-63. Mem. ABA, Internat. Bar Assn., Chgo. Bar Assn., Am. Judicature Soc., Legal Club Chgo. Clubs: Riviera Tennis (Pacific Palisades, Calif.); Mid-Day (Chgo.); Winter (Lake Forest, Ill.), Onwentsia (Lake Forest, Ill.). General corporate, Antitrust, Federal civil litigation. Home: 901 Church Rd Lake Forest IL 60045 Office: McDermott Will & Emery 111 W Monroe St Chicago IL 60603

BOUSCAREN, TIMOTHY LINCOLN, lawyer; b. N.Y.C., Apr. 10, 1943; s. Henri V. and Katherine (McNulty) B. A.B., Holy Cross Coll., 1965; J.D., U. Cin., 1968. Bar: Ohio 1969, U.S. Dist. Ct. (so. dist.) Ohio 1969, U.S. Ct. Appeals (6th cir.) 1970, U.S. Ct. Appeals (5th cir.) 1981, U.S. Ct. Appeals (7th cir.) 1984. Asst. city solicitor City of Cin., 1971-78; ptnr. Walker, Chatfield & Doan, Cin., 1978—. Mem. advance team Republican Nat. Com., Washington, 1976-80. Mem. ABA, Ohio Bar Assn., Ohio Acad. Trial Lawyers, Assn. Trial Lawyers Am. Federal civil litigation, State civil litigation, Securities. Home: 2484 Observatory Ave Cincinnati OH 45208 Office: Walker Chatfield & Doan 1900 Carew Tower Cincinnati OH 45202

BOUSQUET, THOMAS GOURRIER, lawyer; b. Houston, Oct. 18, 1934; s. John A. and Ophelia Ann (Tucker) B.; m. Katherine Lynn Cummings, Aug. 22, 1959 (div. 1970); children: Thomas Gourrier, Robert Brant, Katherine Lynn; m. Duke Ellen Taylor, Nov. 27, 1970 (div. 1973); m. Rebecca Boatwright, May 1, 1986. B.A., U. Tex., 1956, J.D., 1958. Bar: Tex. 1958, U.S. Supreme Ct. 1971, U.S. Ct. Appeals (5th cir.); Cert. family law specialist, civil trial specialist Tex. Bd. Legal Specialization. Practiced in Houston, 1958—; ptnr. Wandel & Bousquet, 1958-70, firm Bousquet & Assocs., Inc., 1970—. Author: Become an Effective Player at Casino Craps, 1973. Mem. Houston Family Law Forum, Houston Martini Fund & Trust, 1984—, chmn., 1986-87. Served to maj. USAF, 1958-64; maj. Res. Fellow Tex. Bar Found. (life); Mem. Houston Bar Assn. (sec. 1960, v.p. 1961), Lawyers Soc. Houston (pres. 1973), Gulf Coast Family Law Specialist Assn. (sec. 1975-78, v.p. 1978-79), Tex. Assn. Cert. Civil Trial Lawyers (pres. 1979-81), Tex. Assn. Cert. Family Lawyers (pres. 1978-79), Am. Acad. Matrimonial Lawyers, Order Stars and Bars, Magna Charta Barons, SAR (chancellor 1966), Plantagenet Soc., SCV, Order Descs. Colonial Govs., Phi Alpha Delta. Clubs: Cadre (pres. 1975-76, 82), Space City Ski, Caribbee Dance. State civil litigation, Family and matrimonial, Real property. Home: 4642 Richmond Ave Houston TX 77027 Office: 2500 West Loop S Suite 480 Houston TX 77027

BOVAIRD, BRENDAN PETER, lawyer; b. N.Y.C., Mar. 9, 1948; s. John Francis and Margaret Mary (Endrizzi) B.; m. Carolyn Warren Boyle, Dec. 18, 1971; children—Anne Warren, Sarah Grant. B.A., Fordham U., 1970; J.D., U. Va., 1973. Bar: N.Y. 1974, U.S. Dist. Ct. (so. and ea. dists.) N.Y. 1974, U.S. Ct. Appeals (2d cir.) 1974, D.C. 1980, Pa. 1983. Atty., Dewey, Ballantine, Bushby, Palmer & Wood, N.Y.C., 1973-82; asst. gen. counsel Campbell Soup Co., Camden, N.J., 1982—. Mem. Grocery Mfrs. Am. (legal com. 1983—), ABA (com. on corp. counsel, litigation sect., antitrust law sect.), Assn. Bar City N.Y., Phi Delta Phi. Antitrust, Labor, General corporate. Office: Campbell Soup Co Campbell Pl Camden NJ 08103-1799

BOVARNICK, PAUL SIMON, lawyer; b. N.Y.C., Sept. 15, 1952; s. Murray Elliott and Esther (Waters) B.; m. Nan Garner Waller, Aug. 31, 1980; 1 child, Polly Ames. BA, Claremont Men's Coll., 1974; JD, U. Oreg., 1979. Bar: Oreg. 1979, Mont. 1980, U.S. Dist. Ct. Mont. 1980, U.S. Ct. Appeals (9th cir.) 1981, U.S. Dist. Ct. Oreg. 1983. Staff atty. Mont. Legal Services, Billings, 1979-80, mng. atty., 1980-82; mng. atty. Oreg. Legal Services, Hillsboro, 1982-83; assoc. Bricker, Zakovics, Portland, Oreg., 1983-85; sole practice Portland, 1985—; mem. com. on legal aid State Bar Oreg. Chmn., bd. dirs. Forest Park Children's Ctr., Portland, 1986—; treas. Yellowstone Valley Dem. Club, Billings, 1982; bd. dirs. Oregonians for Individual Rights, Portland, 1984, ACLU, Billings, 1981-82. Mem. ABA, Oreg. Bar Assn., Mont. Bar Assn., Multnomah County Bar Assn., Assn. Trial Lawyers Am., Oreg. Trial Lawyers Assn., Assn. Immigration Lawyers Am. Club: City (Portland). Avocations: fly fishing, skiing, softball. Personal injury, Workers' compensation, Immigration, naturalization, and customs. Home: 7460 SW Canyon Ln Portland OR 97225 Office: 400 SW 6th Ave Suite 907 Portland OR 97204

BOVÉ, EDWARD JOSEPH, lawyer; b. Bklyn., Mar. 21, 1954; s. Edward Richard and Joan (Severini) B.; m. Donna Ann Sciortino, July 16, 1978. BA, St. John's U., 1976; JD, Potomac Sch. Law, 1980. Bar: Ga. 1980, Md. 1982, U.S. Dist Ct. Md. 1982, U.S. Dist. Ct. (no. dist.) Ga. 1980, U.S. Tax Ct. 1982, U.S. Ct. Appeals (4th and 11th cirs.) 1982. Sole practice Washington, 1980-82; assoc. Law Offices of David L. Wortman, College Park, Md., 1983; staff atty. Banner Life Ins., Rockville, Md., 1983—. Mem. ABA, Ga. Bar Assn., Md. Bar Assn. Republican. Roman Catholic. Club: Lido Civic, (Washington). General corporate, State and local taxation, Pension, profit-sharing, and employee benefits. Office: Banner Life Ins Co 1701 Research Blvd Rockville MD 20850

BOWDRE, JOHN BIRCH, JR., lawyer; b. Macon, Ga., Apr. 28, 1954; s. John Birch and Becky (Watson) B.; m. Karon Owen, Apr. 7, 1979; 1 child, John Neville Birch III. BA, Furman U., 1976; JD cum laude, Samford U., 1979; LLM in Taxation, U. Ala., 1985. Bar: Ga. 1979, Ala. 1979, U.S. Dist. Ct. (no. dist.) Ala. 1979, U.S. Tax Ct. 1981, U.S. Ct. Appeals (11th cir.) 1981. Assoc. Spain, Gillon, Tate, Grooms & Blan, Birmingham, Ala., 1979-84; ptnr. Spain, Gillon, Tate, Grooms & Blan, Birmingham, 1985—. Bd. deacons, chmn. legal com. Southside Bapt. Ch., Birmingham, 1986. Mem. ABA (taxation sect.), Ala. Bar Assn. (taxation sect.), Ga. Bar Assn., Birmingham Bar Assn., Order of Barristers. Republican. Club: Birmingham Sailing. Avocations: sailing, tennis, backpacking. Estate planning, Contracts commercial, General corporate. Home: 2613 Acton Dr Birmingham AL 35243 Office: Spain Gillon Tate Grooms & Blan 2117 2d Ave N Zinszer Bldg Birmingham AL 35203

BOWEN, BROOKS JEFFERSON, lawyer; b. Wilmington, Del., Aug. 5, 1949; s. Hardy Jefferson and Pauline (Street) B.; m. Nancy Barbara Rogers, Oct. 18, 1975; children: Brooks Jr., Christopher Pendleton. BA cum laude, Yale U., 1971; JD, U. Va., 1974. Bar: D.C. 1975. Legal cons. BDM Corp., Vienna, Va., 1975-76; sr. counsel ocean minerals and energy, Nat. Oceanic and Atmospheric Adminstrn. U.S. Dept. of Commerce, Washington, 1976-83; minority counsel merchant marine and fisheries com. U.S. Ho. of Reps., Washington, 1983-86; spl. asst. to adminstr. and dep. adminstr. EPA, Washington, 1986—; U.S. del. United Nations Conf. on Law of the Sea, 1981-82, Internat. Maritime Orgn., 1983-85. Mem. ABA, D.C. Bar Assn., Am. Soc. Internat. Law. Club: City Tavern (Washington). Avocations: tennis, squash, jogging. Environment, Public international, Legislative. Home: 8308 Bells Mill Rd Potomac MD 20854 Office: US EPA A-100 401 M St SW Washington DC 20460

BOWEN, DEBRA LYNN, lawyer; b. Rockford, Ill., Oct. 27, 1955; d. Robert Calvin and Marcia Ann (Crittenden) Bowen. B.A., Mich. State U., 1976; Rotary Internat. fellow Internat. Christian U., Tokyo, 1975; J.D., U. Va., 1979. Bar: Ill. 1979, Calif. 1983. Assoc., Winston & Strawn, Chgo., 1979-82, Washington, 1985-86, Hughes Hubbard & Reed, Los Angeles, 1982-84; sole practice, Los Angeles, 1984—; pres., Debco Enterprises, Inc., Methesda, Md., 1986—; gen. counsel, mem. exec. com. State Employee's Retirement System Ill., Springfield, 1980-82; pres. Bowen & Assocs., Marina del Rey, Calif., 1984-85 ; adj. prof. Watterson Coll. Sch. Paralegal Studies, 1985. Exec. editor Va. Jour. Internat. Law, 1977-78; contbr. articles to profl. jours. Mem. mental health law com. Chgo. Council Lawyers, 1980-82. Wigmore scholar Northwestern U. Sch. Law, Chgo., 1976. Mem. ABA, Los Angeles County Bar Assn., Calif. Bar Assn., Phi Kappa Phi. Unitarian. Corporate taxation, Personal income taxation, General corporate. Office: 4807 Bethesda Ave Suite 329 Bethesda MD 20814 Other: 279 S Beverly Dr Suite 453 Beverly Hills CA 90212

BOWEN, DUDLEY HOLLINGSWORTH, JR., U.S. district judge; b. Augusta, Ga., June 25, 1941; s. Dudley Hollingsworth and Edna (Maury) B.; m. Madeline Martin, Aug. 14, 1963; children: Laura Madeline, Anna Maury. A.B in Fgn. Lang., U. Ga., 1964, LL.B., 1965. Bar: Ga. 1965. Gen. practice law Augusta, 1968-72; bankruptcy judge So. Dist. Ga., 1972-75; partner firm Dye, Miller, Bowen & Tucker, Augusta, 1975-79; U.S. dist. judge So. Dist. Ga., 1979—; tchr. seminars; panelist Atlanta Bar Assn., S.C. Bar and Inst. Continuing Legal Edn., 1976-78; bd. dirs. Southeastern Bankruptcy Law Inst., 1976—. Served to 1st lt. inf., U.S. Army, 1966-68. Decorated Commendation medal. Mem. Am. Bar Assn., State Bar Ga. (chmn. bankruptcy law sect. 1977), Fed. Judges Assn. (bd. dirs. 1985—). Presbyterian. Jurisprudence. Address: PO Box 2106 Augusta GA 30903

BOWEN, EDDIE HOWARD, lawyer; b. Monroe, La., Feb. 21, 1949; s. Howard Johnny and Flora Eunice (Bradshaw) B.; m. Sharon Elizabeth Blackledge, Sept. 25, 1981; children: Jonas Edwards, Caleb Bradshaw. BS, Miss. State U., 1977; JD, U. Miss., 1980. Bar: Miss. 1980, U.S. Dist. Ct. (no. and so. dists.) Miss. 1980. Ptnr. Varnado & Bowen, Jackson, Miss., 1980-81; sole practice Raleigh, Miss., 1982—. Co-author: Our World's Most Beloved Poems, 1985 (Golden Poet award 1985). Pres. Lit. Arts Soc., Canton. Miss., 1966-67, Indsl. Arts Soc., Canton, 1967. Served to 1st lt. U.S. Army, 1970-72, Vietnam. Pres.'s scholar Miss. State U., 1977. Mem. ABA, Miss. Bar Assn., Assn. Trial Lawyers Am., Miss. Trial Lawyers Assn., Am. Legion (commr. post #22 1984-85). Republican. Methodist. Lodge: Masons. Avocations: writing songs, writing poetry, guitar, tennis, canoeing. Home and Office: PO Box 115 Raleigh MS 39153

BOWEN, GERALD L., lawyer; b. Phila., July 3, 1936. Grad., La Salle Coll., 1957; JD, Villanova U., 1960. Asst. dist. atty. City of Phila., 1961-66; ptnr. Esgan & Bowen, Willow Grove, Pa., 1966-78; sole practice Southampton, Pa., 1978—. Mem. ABA, Phila. Bar Assn., Montgomery County Bar Assn., Bucks County Bar Assn., Am. Trial Lawyers Assn., Pa. Trial Lawyers Assn., Phila. Trial Lawyers Assn. Roman Catholic. Avocations: golf, fishing, snorkeling, travel. Personal injury, Probate, Real property. Home: 8325 Roberts Rd Elkins Park PA 19117 Office: 1160 Street Rd Southampton PA 18966

BOWEN, JOHN WESLEY EDWARD, IV, lawyer; b. Columbus, Ohio, July 11, 1954; s. John Wesley Edward III and Jeanne (Lehar) B. BBA, So. Meth. U., 1976; JD, Columbia U., 1979. Bar: N.Y. 1980, U.S. Ct. Claims 1982, U.S. Supreme Ct. 1983, U.S. Dist. Ct. (so. and ea. dists.) N.Y. 1985, U.S. Ct. Appeals (fed. cir.) 1986. Trial atty. antitrust div. U.S. Dept. Justice, Washington, 1979-85; of counsel Howard & Rhone, N.Y.C., 1985—. Contbr. articles to profl. jours. Mem. Martin Luther King Jr. Dem. Club, N.Y.C., 1985—; bd. dirs., sec., legal counsel Manhattan Jr. Assn. Commerce and Industry, N.Y.C., 1985—. Named one of Outstanding Young Men in Am., U.S. Jaycees, 1981-84. Mem. ABA, Fed. Bar Assn., Nat. Bar Assn., N.Y. County Lawyers Assn., Blue Key, Alpha Phi Alpha, French Inst./Alliance Francaise, Columbia U. Club. Methodist. Federal civil litigation, State civil litigation, General corporate. Home: 2186 Fifth Ave New York NY 10037 Office: Howard & Rhone 10 Columbus Circle Suite 1503 New York NY 10019

BOWEN, STEPHEN STEWART, attorney; b. Peoria, Ill., Aug. 23, 1946; s. Gerald Raymond and Frances Arlene (Stewart) B.; m. Ellen Claire Newcomer, Sept. 23, 1972; children—David, Claire. B.A. cum laude, Wabash Coll., 1968; J.D. cum laude, U. Chgo., 1972. Bar: Ill. 1972, U.S. Dist. Ct. (no. dist.) Ill. 1972, U.S. Tax Ct. 1977. Assoc. Kirkland & Ellis, Chgo., 1972-78, ptnr., 1978-84; ptnr. Latham & Watkins, Chgo., 1985—; adj. prof. DePaul U. Masters in Taxation Program, Chgo., 1976-80. Lectr. Practicing Law Inst., N.Y.C., Chgo., Los Angeles, 1978-84. Mem. vis. com. U. Chgo. Div. Sch., 1984; bd. dirs. Samaritan Ctr., Evanston, Ill., 1984—; elder Northminster Presbyterian Ch., Evanston, 1985—; mem. planning com. U. Chgo. Tax Conf., 1985—. Mem. ABA, Ill. State Bar Assn., Order of Coif, Phi Beta Kappa. Presbyterian. Club: Mich. Shores (Wilmette, Ill.); Metropolitan (Chgo.). Corporate taxation, Personal income taxation, General corporate. Office: Latham & Watkins 6900 Sears Tower Chicago IL 60606

BOWEN, THOMAS ALLAN, tax executive; b. Janesville, Wis., May 13, 1951; s. Francis Allan and Elaine Doris (Anderson) B. BBA, U. Wis., Whitewater, 1973; MS in Taxation, DePaul U., 1976; JD, U. Wis., 1979. Bar: Wis. 1979, U.S. Dist. Ct. (we. dist.) Wis. 1979, U.S. Tax Ct. 1979. Revenue agent IRS, Chgo., 1974-77; pres. Tax Report Clearinghouse, Inc., Madison, Wis., 1977-80; pres., tax atty. Bowen Ltd., Madison, 1979-81; tax mgr. Arthur Young & Co., Oklahoma City, 1981-84; asst. tax mgr. AMP Inc., Harrisburg, Pa., 1984—. Editor IRS Practice and Procedures, 1977-80. Mem. Wis. Bar Assn., Am. Inst. CPA's (taxation sect.), Delta Mu Delta. Republican. Presbyterian. Avocations: church, music, bus. and econ. investment interests. Corporate taxation. Home: RD #3 Hummelstown PA 17036 Office: AMP Inc 470 Friendship Rd Harrisburg PA 17111

BOWEN, WILLARD GENE, lawyer; b. Union City, Ind., Oct. 31, 1921; s. Henry Willard and Mary Frances (Hill) B.; m. Jane Hartman, June 28, 1944; children—Steven H., Cynthia M. Bowen Dorell, Sarah F. Bowen Stevens, Susanne J. B.S. in Bus. Administrn., Ohio State U., 1947; J.D., U. Mich., 1949. Bar: Ind. 1949, U.S. Dist. Ct. (so. dist.) Ind. 1949. Ptnr., Bowen & Duning, 1949-55, Bowen & O'Maley, 1955-67, Bowen, Cecere & O'Maley, 1967-75, pres. Bowen, Cecere and O'Maley, P.C., 1975-84, Bowen, Cecere & Horn, P.C., 1984—; mem. Ind. Ho. Reps., 1955-57. Served to capt. USAF, 1942-46. Fellow Ind. Bar Found.; mem. ABA, Ind. Bar Assn. (past mem. bd. mgrs.), Wayne County Bar Assn. (past pres.), Republican. Lutheran. Club: Forest Hills Country (bd. dirs., past pres.), Rotary. Real property, Probate, General corporate. Home: 2026 Minneman Rd Richmond IN 47374 Office: Bowen Cecere and Horn PC 101 South 10th St Richmond IN 47374

BOWER, GLEN L., lawyer; b. Highland, Ill., Jan. 16, 1949; s. Ray Landis and Evelyn Ferne (Ragland) B. BA, So. Ill. U., 1971; JD with honors, Ill. Inst. Tech., 1974. Bar: Ill. 1974, U.S. Ct. Mil. Appeals 1975, U.S. Ct. Appeals (7th cir.) 1976, U.S. Dist. Ct. (so. dist.) Ill. 1977, U.S. Supreme Ct. 1978, U.S. Tax Ct. 1984, U.S. Ct. Claims 1986. Sole practice Effingham, Ill., 1974-83; prosecutor Effingham County, Ill., 1976-79; mem. Ill. House of Reps., Springfield, 1979-83; asst. dir., gen. counsel Ill. Dept. Revenue, Springfield, Ill., 1983—; mem. U.S. Dept. Justice Nat. Adv. Com., Washington, 1976-80, U.S. Econ. Adv. Bd., Washington, 1982-85, Ill. Gen. Assembly State Adv. Com. on Cir. Ct. Fin., Springfield, 1984, Revenue Bd. Appeals, Chgo., 1985—, chmn., 1986—; mem. com. of 50 on Ill. Constn., 1987—. Alt. del. Rep. Nat. Conv., Miami Beach., Fla., 1972; vice chmn. Effingham County Rep. Cen. Com., Illinois, 1976—. Served as maj. USAFR, 1974—. Recipient Outstanding Legislator award Ill. Conservative Union, 1980, Cert. of Appreciation, Ill. Fedn. for Right to Life, 1980, 82, Outstanding Freshman Legislator award Ill. Edn. Assn., 1980, Legis. of Yr., Ill. Assn. Rehab. Facilities, 1981, 82, cert. of Appreciation Ill. chpt. Prevention of Child Abuse, 1981, Recognition and Appreciation award Ill. Sheriff's Assn., 1981, Presdl. Citation, Ill. Environ. Health Assn., 1981, Cert. of Appreciation for extraordinary service Ill. Pharmacist Assn., 1981, Outstanding Legislator award Ill. Pub. Health Assn., 1982, Dist. Service award Ill. Assn. Homes for the Aging, 1984, Dist. Service award Ill. Petroleum Marketers Assn., 1984. Mem. ABA (adminstrv. practice com. of taxation sect.), Ill. State Bar Assn. (state taxation sect. council, labor law sect. council), Effingham County Bar Assn. (sec. 1976-77, pres. 1983-84), Chgo. Bar Assn., Nat. Assn. Tax Adminstrs. (vice chmn. attys. sect. 1985-86, chmn. 1986—), Effingham County Old Settlers Assn. (pres., bd. dirs. 1983-86), Ill. State Hist. Soc. (v.p. 1979-81, bd. dirs. exec. com. 1983-86), Effingham Regional Hist. Soc., SBA Adv. council (bd. dirs. 1973-77), Effingham County Mental Health Assn. (bd. dirs. 1975-77), Effingham County Operation Drug Alert Council (bd. dirs. 1975-77), Effingham County C. of C. (chmn. legis. com. 1976-78), Ill. Mental Health Assn. (pub. affairs com. 1977-78), U.S. Capitol Hist. Soc. (charter), So. Ill. Univ. Alumni Assn. (life), Am. Legion, Ill. Farm Bur. Methodist. Lodges: Shriners, Kiwanis (pres. 1977-78), Elks, SAR, Fraternal Order Police. Corporate taxation, Personal income taxation, State and local taxation. Home: PO Box 1106 Effingham IL 62401 Office: Ill Dept Revenue 101 W Jefferson 6 SW Springfield IL 62794

BOWER, MARK RICHARD, lawyer. BA, SUNY, Binghamton, 1969; JD, NYU, 1972. Bar: N.Y. 1973, U.S. Dist. Ct. (so. dist.) 1974, U.S. Dist. Ct. (ea. dist.) N.Y. 1975, U.S. Supreme Ct. 1978. Corp. counsel City of N.Y., 1972-79; sr. assoc. Fuchsberg & Fuchsberg, N.Y.C., 1975-78; assoc. Morris & Duffy, N.Y.C., 1978-79; ptnr. Queller, Fisher, Bower & Wisotsky, N.Y.C., 1979—. Author: Crystallization of Beliefs in the Conscientious Objector; contbr. articles to legal jours. Mem. Queens County Bar Assn. (mem. speakers panel 1976-78), N.Y. State Trial Lawyers Assn. (mem. med. malpractice com. 1981-83). Office: Queller Fisher Bower & Wisotsky 110 Wall St New York NY 10005

BOWER, PAUL GEORGE, lawyer; b. Chgo., Apr. 21, 1933; s. Chester L. and Retha (Dausmann) B.; m. Elreen L. Thurlow, June 23, 1962; children: Stephanie, Julienne, Aimee. B.A., Rice U., 1955; postgrad., Calif. Inst. Tech., 1959-60; LL.B., Stanford U., 1963. Bar: Calif. 1964, U.S. Sureme Ct. 1969. Assoc. Gibson, Dunn & Grutcher, Los Angeles, 1963-67, ptnr., 1970—. Asst. dir. Nat. Adv. Com. Civil Disorder, 1967-68; spl. asst. to dep. atty. gen. U.S. Dept. Justice, 1968-69, consumer counsel, 1969; bd. dirs. Legal Aid Found.; trustee Sierra Club Legal Def. Fund, 1982—. Served with U.S. Army, 1956-59. Mem. ABA, Calif. Bar Assn., Los Angeles County Bar Assn., Beverly Hills Bar Assn., Order of Coif. Democrat. Antitrust, Federal civil litigation, Entertainment. Office: Gibson Dunn & Crutcher 2029 Century Park E Los Angeles CA 90067

BOWER, WARD ALAN, mgmt. consulting co. exec.; b. Carlisle, Pa., Feb. 10, 1947; s. Dale Luther and Margaret Louise (Chapman) B.; B.A. in Econs., Bucknell U., 1969; J.D., Dickinson Sch. Law, 1975; m. Judith DiSerafino, June 26, 1976; children—Miles Robert, Chase Batchelor. Admitted to Pa. bar, 1975; group pension adminstr. Prudential Ins. Co., Newark, 1969-70; methods analyst Liberty Mut. Ins. Co., Boston, 1972; prin., v.p. Altman & Weil, Inc., Ardmore, Pa., 1975—, also dir. Served with U.S. Army, 1970-71. Mem. Am. Arbitration Assn., Internat. Bar Assn., ABA, Pa. Bar Assn., Inst. Mgmt. Cons. Author: (with Frank Arentowicz, Jr.) Law Office Automation and Technology, 1980. General corporate, Law office management and marketing. Office: Altman & Weil Inc 600 Haverford Rd PO Box 472 Haverford PA 19041

BOWERMAN, DONALD BRADLEY, lawyer; b. Portland, Oreg., Aug. 15, 1934; s. Milton Willard and Anna Louise (Keehn) B.; m. Elizabeth Dawn Kneestad, Mar. 18, 1956; children: Donald Marcus, Steven David, Bradley James. JD, Lewis & Clark Coll., 1959. Bar: Oreg. 1959, U.S. Ct. Appeals (9th cir.) 1960, U.S. Supreme Ct. 1971. Dist. atty. Clackamas County, Oregon City, Oreg., 1960-63; ptnr. Rask, Hefferin & Bowerman, Portland, 1963-67, Misko, Njust & Bowerman, 1967-72, Hibbard, Caldwell, Bowerman, Schultz & Hergert, Oregon City, 1972—; chmn. Profl. Liability Fund, 1979-85. Chmn. West Linn (Oreg.) Sch. Dist. Bd. Edn., 1967-76; bd. dirs. West Linn YMCA, 1962-64. Fellow Am. Bar Found., Oreg. Bar Found., Oreg. Bar Assn. (bd. govs. 1977-79, v.p. 1979), Oreg. Assn. Def. Counsel. Republican. Baptist. Club: University (Portland). Insurance, Medical legal malpractice, Aviation business litigation. Home: 1285 Marylhurst Dr West Linn OR 97068 Office: 1001 Molalla Ave Suite 200 Oregon City OR 97045

BOWERS, MICHAEL JOSEPH, state attorney general; b. Jackson County, Ga., Oct. 7, 1941; s. Carl Ernest and Janie Ruth (Bolton) B.; m. Bette Rose Corley, June 8, 1963; children: Carl Wayne, Bruce Edward, Michelle Lisa. B.S., U.S. Mil. Acad., 1963; M.S., Stanford U., 1965; M.B.A., U. Utah-Wiesbaden, Germany, 1970; J.D., U. Ga., 1974. Bar: Ga. 1974. Sr. asst. atty. gen. State of Ga., Atlanta, 1975-81, atty. gen., 1981—. Served to capt. USAF, 1963-70. Mem. Lawyers Club. Democrat. Methodist. Lodge: Kiwanis. Home: 817 Allgood Rd Stone Mountain GA 30083 Office: State Judicial Bldg Atlanta GA 30334

BOWLES, JERRY JAY, lawyer; b. Arkansas City, Kans., July 3, 1957; s. Jarrell F. and Doris G. (Reeves) B.; m. Anita Ragan, Aug. 12, 1977. BA, U. Ky., 1979; JD, U. Louisville, 1982. Bar: Ky. 1982. Trial def. atty. Jefferson County Pub. Defender's Office, Louisville, 1982-84; prosecutor Jefferson County Atty.'s Office, Louisville, 1984—; civil atty. Miller, Conliffe & Sandmann, Louisville, 1984-86, Black, Carle, Maze & Wilmes, Louisville, 1986—. Lectr. Caring Connection, Louisville, 1984-85; group leader Jefferson County Dems. 47th Legis. Dist., 1985-86. Named one of Outstanding Young Men Am., 1984. Mem. ABA, Ky. Bar Assn., Louisville Bar Assn. Avocations: swimming, boating, water skiing. Criminal, Family and matrimonial, Personal injury. Home: 112 Chadwick Rd Louisville KY 40223 Office: Black Carle Maze & Wilmes 310 W Liberty St Suite 510 Louisville KY 40202

BOWLING, DAVID JOSEPH, lawyer; b. Louisville, Sept. 13, 1949; s. William Jospeh and Helen (Kost) B.; m. Joan Margaret Kreimborg, Sept. 21, 1974; children: Monika, Emilie. AB, Bellarmine Coll., 1971; MBA, U. Ky., 1972; JD, U. Louisville, 1981. Bar: Ky. 1981, U.S. Tax Ct. 1981. Mgr. tax Am. Comml. Barge Line Co., Jeffersonville, Ind., 1973-81; dir. taxes Tex. Gas Transmission, Owensboro, Ky., 1981-86; dir. research and planning CSX Corp., Richmond, Va., 1986—. Patterson fellow U. Ky., 1971. Mem. ABA, Ky. Bar Assn. Republican. Roman Catholic. Corporate taxation, State and local taxation. Home: 14103 Spring Gate Terr Midlothian VA 23113 Office: CSX Corp 901 E Cary St Richmond VA 23219

BOWMAN, CAROL ANN, lawyer; b. Marion, Ind., Jan. 20, 1952; d. James Russell and Carol Joan (Horner) B. BA with honors, Georgetown Coll., 1974; JD, Valparaiso U., 1977; postdoctoral, John Marshall Law Sch., 1980-81. Bar: Ind. 1977, U.S. Dist. Ct. (so. dist.) Ind. 1977, U.S. Dist. Ct. (no. dist.) Ind. 1978, U.S. Ct. Appeals (7th cir.) 1979. Dep. atty. gen. State of Ind., Indpls., 1977-79; asst. gen. counsel Whiteco Industries, Inc., Merrillville, Ind., 1979—; mem. adv. com. Atty. Gen. Ind., 1980—. Mem. ABA, Ind. Bar Assn., Women's Lawyers Assn. of Lake and Porter Counties (pres. 1982), Lake County Bar Assn., South Lake County Bar Assn., Valparaiso U. Law Sch. Alumni Assn. (bd. dirs 1980-85). Avocations: reading, golf, tennis, sailing, theater. Real property, Contracts commercial, General corporate. Home: 8140 Cedar Point Dr Apt D89 Crown Point IN 46307 Office: Whiteco Industries Inc 1000 E 80th Pl Suite 700 N Merrillville IN 46410

BOWMAN, C(HARLES) ALAN, lawyer; b. Oneonta, Ala., Feb. 12, 1953; s. Charles Floyd and Maxie Mae (Morris) B.; m. Tamara A. Westphal, Aug. 4, 1979; 1 child, Sarah Ann. BS, Ariz. State U., 1976, JD, 1979. Bar: Ariz. 1979, U.S. Dist. Ct. Ariz. 1980, U.S. Ct. Appeals (9th cir.) 1980, Colo. 1986. Assoc. Richards & Smith P.C., Yuma, Ariz., 1979-81, Law Offices of Brian E. Smith Ltd., Yuma, 1981-87; ptnr. Bowman and Smith, Yuma, 1987—. Contbg. author: Bridge the Gap, 1985. Mem., bd. dirs. Red Cross, Yuma, 1980. Mem. Ariz. Bar Assn. (vol. bar counsel 1984—), Yuma County Bar Assn. (sec. 1983, pres. 1984), Assn. Trial Lawyers Am., Ariz. Trial Lawyers Assn. Democrat. Avocations: water and snow skiing, softball, over-the-line, weight lifting. Personal injury, State civil litigation, Insurance. Home: 1417 Ridgeview Dr Yuma AZ 85364 Office: Bowman and Smith 290 S 1st Ave Yuma AZ 85364

BOWMAN, MICHAEL ALLEN, lawyer; b. Jacksonville, N.C., Nov. 3, 1952; s. Hugh G. and Mary L. (Whitmore) B.; m. Deborah Stewart, Aug. 15, 1975; children: Rebecca, Elizabeth. BA, Coe Coll., 1975; JD, Washington & Lee U., 1978. Bar: Iowa 1978. Assoc. Erdahl Law Office, Monticello, Iowa, 1978-80; ptnr. Shimanek & Bowman, Monticello, 1981—. Mem. ABA, Iowa Bar Assn. Estate taxation, Consumer commercial, Criminal. Office: Shimanek & Bowman PO Box 351 Monticello IA 52310

BOWMAN, MICHAEL FLOYD, lawyer; b. Lafayette, Ind., Jan. 31, 1953; s. Harry Ellsworth and Sara Jane (Snyder) B.; m. Deborah Lou Gardner, Dec. 20, 1975; children: Joshua Stewart, Sarah Elizabeth. BA, Purdue U., 1975, MA, 1977; JD, U. Puget Sound, 1980. Bar: Wash. 1980, U.S. Dist. Ct. (we. dist.) Wash. 1980, U.S. Ct. Claims 1982, U.S. Ct. Appeals (9th cir.) 1982. Assoc. Noble & Johnson, Tacoma, 1980-81; asst. counsel Naval Supply Ctr. Puget Sound, Bremerton, Wash., 1981-82; counsel Naval Weapons Support Ctr., Crane, Ind., 1982-85, Spl. Asst. Naval Inspector Gen. for Contract Law, Washington, 1985—; instr. Ft. Steilaloom Community Coll., Tacoma, 1977-81, Navy Office Gen. Counsel, Washington, 1981—, Naval Inspector Gen. Sch., Washington, 1985—, Naval Investigative Service Contract Fraud Sch., Athens, Ga., 1985—. Leader Boy Scouts Am., Tacoma, Wash., Ft. Wayne, Ind., 1971-78. Mem. Wash. State Bar Assn., U.S. Naval Inst., Phi Delta Phi, Alpha Phi Omega, Phi Alpha Theta. Episcopalian. Government contracts and claims, Administrative and regulatory, Military. Home: 5832 Valley View Dr Alexandria VA 22310 Office: Counsel Naval Inspector Gen Bldg 200 Washington Navy Yard DC 20374-2001

BOWMAN, PASCO MIDDLETON, II, judge; b. Timberville, Va., Dec. 20, 1933; s. Pasco Middleton and Katherine (Lohr) B.; m. Ruth Elaine Bowman, July 12, 1958; children: Ann Katherine, Helen Middleton, Benjamin Garber. B.A., Bridgewater Coll., 1955; J.D., NYU, 1958; LLM, U. Va., 1986. Bar: N.Y. 1958, Ga. 1965, Mo. 1980. Assoc. firm Cravath, Swaine & Moore, N.Y.C., 1958-61, 62-64; asst. prof. law U. Ga., 1964-65, assoc. prof., 1965-69, prof., 1969-70; prof. Wake Forest U., 1970-78, dean, 1970-78; vis. prof. U. Va., 1978-79; prof., dean U. Mo., Kansas City, 1979-83; judge U.S. Ct. Appeals (8th cir.), Kansas City, MO., 1983—. Mng. editor: NYU Law Rev, 1957-58; Reporter, chief draftsman: Georgia Corporation Code, 1965-68. Served to col. USAR, 1959-84. Fulbright scholar London Sch. Econs. and Polit. Sci., 1961-62, Root-Tilden scholar, 1958. Mem. N.Y. Bar, Ga. Bar, Mo. Bar. General corporate, Antitrust, Contracts commercial. Home: 11109 Blue River Rd Kansas City MO 64131 Office: US Courthouse Rm 819 811 Grand Ave Kansas City MO 64106

BOWMAN, PHILLIP BOYNTON, lawyer; b. Ames, Iowa, Feb. 28, 1936; s. Alfred Boynton and Susan Jean (Foxworthy) B.; m. Elizabeth Wales Porter, June 20, 1959; children—Susan Foxworthy, William Porter, Peter Wales. B.S. in Engring., Princeton U., 1958; J.D., U. Mich., 1961. Bar: Ill. 1961, U.S. Dist. Ct. (no. dist.) Ill. 1962, U.S. Ct. Appeals (7th cir.) 1965. Assoc. then ptnr. Gorham, Adams, White & DeYoung, Chgo., 1961-75; ptnr. Gorham, Metge, Bowman & Hourigan, Chgo., 1976—. Pres., commr. Northbrook Park Dist., Ill., 1968-76; pres., bd. dirs., referee, coach, Northbrook Hockey League, 1962-86. Mem. ABA, Ill. Bar Assn., Chgo. Bar Assn., Chgo. Soc. Assn. Execs. (edn. com. 1984—). Republican. Episcopalian. Clubs: Skokie Country (Glencoe, Ill.) (golf com. 1984); Chgo. Curling (Northbrook) (bd. dirs., sec. 1980-87), Tavern (Chgo.), Law, Legal. Antitrust, General corporate, General practice. Home: 2330 Crabtree Ln Northbrook IL 60062 Office: 300 W Washington Chicago IL 60606

BOWMER, JIM DEWITT, lawyer; b. Temple, Tex., May 4, 1919; s. DeWitt and Linnie B. (Morgan) B.; m. Daurice Spoonts, Mar. 26, 1961; children: Bonnie Nell Neal, Mary Helen Bowmer Schreiner, IV. B.A. cum laude, Baylor U., Waco, Tex., 1940, LL.B. cum laude, 1942. Bar: Tex. 1942. County atty. Bell County, Tex., 1946-47; lectr. Baylor U. Law Sch., 1949-50, 56-57; pres. firm Bowmer, Courtney, Burleson, Normand & Moore, Temple, 1964—. Contbr. articles to legal jours. Bd. dirs. Nat. Park Found., 1968-69. Served with AUS, 1942-46. Mem. Am. Law Inst., Am. Judicature Soc., Tex. Assn. Def. Counsel, State Bar Tex. (chmn. bd. 1970-71, pres. 1972-73), Bell-Lampasas-Mills Counties Bar Assn. (past pres.), Temple C. of C. (past pres.), Baylor U. Law Alumni Assn. (past pres.), Phi Alpha Delta. Democrat. Baptist. Clubs: Masons, K.P. (past grand chancellor Tex.), Kiwanis. General practice, Probate, Federal civil litigation. Home: Bowmer's Ranch Route 2 Killeen TX 76541 Office: First Nat Bank Bldg Temple TX 76501

BOWNES, HUGH HENRY, judge; b. N.Y.C., Mar. 10, 1920; s. Hugh Gray and Margaret (Henry) B.; m. Irja C. Martikainen, Dec. 30, 1944; children—Barbara Ann, David and Ernest (twins). B.A., Columbia U., 1941, LL.B., 1948. Bar: N.H. bar 1948. Since practiced in Laconia; partner firm Nighswander, Lord & Bownes, 1951-66; asso. justice N.H. Superior Ct., 1966-68; U.S. dist. ct. judge Concord, N.H., 1968-77; circuit judge 1st Circuit Ct. Appeals, 1977—. Mem. Laconia City Council, 1953-57; chmn. Laconia Democratic Com., 1954-57; mayor, Laconia, 1963-65; mem. Dem. Nat. Com. from N.H., 1963-66; Chmn. Laconia chpt. A.R.C., 1951-52; pres. bd. Laconia Hosp. Assn., 1963-64. Served to maj. USMCR, 1941-46. Decorated Silver Star. Mem. ABA, N.H. Bar Assn., Belknap County Bar Assn. (pres. 1965—), Laconia C. of C. (past pres.). Club: Lion (past pres. Laconia). Jurisprudence. Home: 4 Poor Richard's Dr Concord NH 03301 Office: Federal Courthouse Concord NH 03301

BOXER, HAROLD S., lawyer; b. Port Chester, N.Y., Oct. 7, 1951; s. Murray and Doris (Skluth) B.; m. Alice Elizabeth Hintz, Apr. 1, 1978; 1 dau., Sarah Elizabeth. B.A. in History, Harpur Coll., SUNY-Binghamton, 1973; J.D., SUNY-Buffalo, 1976. Bar: N.Y. 1977, U.S. Dist. Ct. (so. dist.) N.Y. 1984. Title officer Precise Abstract Co. Inc., Scarsdale, N.Y., 1977-82; ptnr. McMahon and Boxer, Mamaroneck, N.Y., 1983-84, McMahon, Boxer and Brannigan, Harrison, N.Y., 1984-85; asst. counsel Commonwealth Land Title Ins. Co., N.Y.C., 1985—. Mem. N.Y. State Bar Assn., Westchester County Bar Assn. General practice, Real property, Probate. Office: Commonwealth Land Title Ins Co 655 3d Ave New York NY 10017

BOXER, JEFFREY VICTOR, lawyer; b. Port Chester, N.Y., Sept. 26, 1943; s. Samuel and Elizabeth Ann (Whitman) B.; m. Joyce Elaine Schleicher, Jan. 30, 1950; children—Andrew, Jonathan, Jason, Sarah. B.S., Fordham Coll., 1965; J.D., N.Y. Law Sch., 1968. Bar: N.Y. 1968, U.S. Dist. Ct. (so. dist.) N.Y. 1970, U.S. Dist. Ct. (ea. dist.) N.Y. 1971, U.S. Ct. Appeals (2d cir.) 1971, Mass. 1980, U.S. Dist. Ct. Mass. 1980, U.S. Ct. Appeals (1st cir.) 1980, U.S. Supreme Ct. 1980, U.S. Dist. Ct. (we. dist.) N.Y. 1983. Ptnr., Lilly Sullivan & Purcell, P.C., N.Y.C., 1970-79; v.p., gen. counsel First Commodity Corp., Boston, 1979-82; Jeffrey V. Boxer & Assocs., Boston and N.Y.C., 1983—. Mem. ABA (subcom. on commodity regulation), Maritime Law Assn., Mass. Bar Assn. (subcom. on banking and security regulation). Jewish. Securities. Office: 129 South St Boston MA 02111 Office: 485 Fifth Ave New York NY 10001

BOYCE, EDWARD WAYNE, JR., lawyer; b. Tuckerman, Ark., June 20, 1926; s. Edward Wayne and Sylla Jo (Harvey) B.; m. Phyllis Elayne Williams, Oct. 29, 1951; children: Elayne Boyce Zellmer, Edward Wayne III. Student, The Citadel, Charleston, S.C., 1943-44; A.B., U. Ark., 1950, LL.B. (later J.D.), 1951. Bar: Ark. 1951, U.S. Supreme Ct. 1960. Assoc. Pickens & Pickens, Newport, Ark., 1951-53; sole practice Tuckerman, Ark., 1954-59; pros. atty. 3d Jud. Circuit of Ark., 1956-60; ptnr. Pickens, Boyce, McLarty & Watson, Newport, 1959-84; sr. ptnr. Boyce & Boyce, 1984—; del. Nat. Conf. on Continuing Legal Edn., 1968; dir. Ark. Law Rev., 1980—. Dep. Episcopal Gen. Conv., 1979, 82; pres. standing com. Diocese of Ark., 1983-84; trustee Epis. Sem. of S.W., Bapt. Med. System Found. Served with U.S. Army, 1944-47. Decorated Bronze Star, Combat Medic badge. Mem. ABA, Am. Law Inst., Ark. Bar Assn. (pres. 1978-79), Ark. Bar Found. (dir. 1970-73). Democrat. Club: Newport Country (pres. 1963-64). General practice. Office: Boyce & Boyce 515 2d St Newport AR 72112

BOYCE, KATHARINE RANDOLPH, lawyer; b. Princeton, N.J., Feb. 17, 1949; d. Wallace Campbell Boyce and Margaret Randolph (Merrick) Barrett; m. Joe Robert Reeder, Jan. 1, 1983; children: Rachael Anne, Aubrilyn, Julia Randolph. BA, Wheaton Coll., 1971; JD, Cath. U., 1979. Bar: D.C. 1980, U.S. Dist. Ct. D.C. 1980. Legis. aide Rep. James G. O'Hara, Washington, 1971-73; press sec., legis. asst. Rep. Brock Adams, Washington, 1973-77; assoc. Patton, Boggs & Blow, Washington, 1979-86, ptnr., 1987—. Mem. Ballston Partnership, Arlington, Va., 1985—, Arlington Dem. Com., 1986, Women's Congl. Council, Washington, 1985—. Mem. ABA, D.C. Bar Assn., Fed. Bar Assn., Women's Bar Assn. D.C., Am. League Lobbyists. Episcopalian. Avocations: running, ballet, art. Legislative, Federal election law, Government contracts and claims. Home: 2301 Fort Scott Dr Arlington VA 22202 Office: Patton Boggs & Blow 2550 M St NW Washington DC 20037

BOYD, CRAIG STEPHEN, lawyer; b. Coatesville, Pa., Jan. 3, 1948; s. Clarence Clifford and Ellen (Hunsicker) B.; m. Pamela Kline, Aug. 30, 1969; children—David C., Jeffrey R., Steven D. B.S., Shippensburg U., Pa., 1970, M.S., Bowling Green State U., Ohio, 1971; J.D., U. Notre Dame, 1974; L.L.M. in Taxation, Villanova U., 1987. Bar: Pa. 1974, U.S. Dist. Ct. (ea. dist.) Pa. 1974. Assoc., E. Kenneth Nyce, Boyertown, Pa., 1974-77; sole practice law, Boyertown, Pa., 1977-83; mng. ptnr. Boyd & Karver, Boyertown, Pa., 1983—; lectr. law Ursinus Coll., Collegeville, Pa., 1974-76, Pa. State U., 1978-80; solicitor Hereford (Pa.) Twp. Zoning Bd., 1978—. Author: Domestic Relations Guide, 1984; research asst. book Lawyers, Law Students and People, 1974. Bd. dirs. Boyertown Area Community Trust, 1984—, Helping Hands, Inc., 1984-84; pres. Boyertown Area YMCA, 1978-83. Spencer Found. grantee, 1973-74; YMCA Service award, 1983, Red Triangle award, 1982, Exec. award, 1980. Mem. Pa. Bar Assn., Berks County Bar Assn., ABA. Democrat. Home: PO Box 114 Boyertown PA 19512 Office: 7 E Philadelphia Ave Boyertown PA 19512

BOYD, DAVID PARKER, lawyer; b. Pitts., Oct. 25, 1957; s. Richard Moody and Dale (Crowe) B.; m. Judith Seeber, May 6, 1984. AB, Duke U., 1979; JD, Yale U., 1982. Bar: Ill. 1982. Assoc. Kirkland & Ellis, Chgo., 1982—. Mem. ABA, Phi Beta Kappa, Phi Kappa Psi. Republican. Presbyterian. Club: University (Chgo). Antitrust, Federal civil litigation, Securities. Home: 415 Aldine #15A Chicago IL 60657 Office: Kirkland & Ellis 200 E Randolph Chicago IL 60601

BOYD, F. KEATS, JR., lawyer; b. N.Y.C., Feb. 18, 1936; s. F. Keats Sr. and Sally B.; m. Ina Creagh, Aug. 20, 1960; children: F. Keats III, Bonnie J., J. Christopher. BS cum laude, Holy Cross Coll., 1957; JD, Stanford U., 1962. Bar: Mass. 1964, U.S. Dist. Ct. Mass. 1966, U.S. Ct. Appeals (1st cir.) 1980, U.S. Supreme Ct. 1980. With legal dept. Liberty Mut. Ins. Co., Boston, 1962-64; v.p. B.A. Corbin & Son Co., Marlboro, Mass., 1964-73; prin. Newton, Mass., 1974-86, Weston, Mass., 1986—. Mem. ABA, Mass. Bar Assn., Am. Arbitration Assn. (arbitrator). General practice, Consumer commercial, Probate. Office: Riverside Office Park 13 Riverside Rd Suite 201 Weston MA 02193

BOYD, JOSEPH ARTHUR, JR., former state justice, lawyer; b. Hoschton, Ga., Nov. 16, 1916; s. Joseph Arthur and Esther Estelle (Puckett) B.; m. Ann Stripling, June 6, 1938; children: Joanne Louise Boyd Goldman, Betty Jean Boyd Jala, Joseph Robert, James Daniel, Jane Nan. Student, Piedmont

Coll., Demorest, Ga., 1936-38, LL.D., 1963; student, Mercer U., Macon, Ga., 1938-39; J.D., U. Miami, Coral Gables, Fla., 1948; LL.D., Western State U. Coll. Law, San Diego, 1981. Bar: Fla. 1948, D.C. 1973, N.Y. 1982, U.S. Supreme Ct. 1959. Practice law Hialeah, 1948-68, city atty., 1951-58; mem. Dade County Commn., Miami, Fla., 1958-68; chmn. Dade County Commn., 1963; vice mayor Dade County, 1967; justice Fla. Supreme Ct., Tallahassee, 1969-87, chief justice, 1984-86; assoc. Boyd & Thompson, P.A., Tallahassee, 1987—; mem. Hialeah Zoning Bd., 1946-48; juror Freedoms Found., Valley Forge, Pa., 1971, 73. Bd. dirs. Bapt. Hosp., Miami, 1962-66, Miami Council Chs., 1960-64. Served with USMCR, 1943-46, PTO. Recipient Nat. Top Hat award Bus. and Profl. Women in U.S. for advancing status of employed women, 1967. Mem. ABA, Fla. Bar Assn., Hialeah-Miami Springs Bar Assn. (pres. 1955), Tallahassee Bar Assn., Hialeah-Miami Springs C. of C. (pres. 1956), Am. Legion (comdr. Fla. 1953-54), VFW, Wig and Robe, Iron Arrow, Phi Alpha Delta, Alpha Kappa Psi. Democrat. Baptist (deacon). Lodges: Mason; Shrine (33 degree); Lion; Moose; Elk. Probate, Federal civil litigation. Office: Boyd & Thompson 2441 Monticello Dr Tallahassee FL 32303

BOYD, JOSEPH ROBERT, lawyer; b. Springfield, Mo., July 17, 1937; s. John Hamilton and Helen Tower (Reed) B.; m. Catherine Ann Nacario, Aug. 4, 1962; children: Joseph R. Jr., Erin H. BA, Tulane U., 1961; JD, Loyola U., New Orleans, 1967. Bar: La., U.S. Dist. Ct. (ea. dist.) La., U.S. Ct. Appeals. Sole practice New Orleans, 1967-71; gen. counsel, v.p. Internat. Auto Sales/Serivce, New Orleans, 1971-75; gen. counsel Southern Scrap Material Co., Ltd., New Orleans, 1975—. Bd. dirs. Friends Alliance for Mentally Ill, New Orleans, 1980—, pres. 1984-85, La. Alliance for Mentally Ill, New Orleans, 1984-85, Alliance for Mentally Ill Services, New Orleans, v.p. 1984-85. Republican. Roman Catholic. General corporate, Insurance, Labor. Home: 9886 Wheaton Circle New Orleans LA 70127 Office: Southern Scrap Material Co Ltd 4801 Florida Ave New Orleans LA 70186

BOYD, MARY OLERT, lawyer, educator, journalist; b. Holland, Mich., Aug. 28, 1930; d. Frederick H. and Sarah (Klooster) Olert; m. Joseph M. Boyd, Jr., Dec. 29, 1953; children—Andrew Martin, David Alexander, Martha Lucile. B.A., Hope Coll., 1952; postgrad. Johns Hopkins Med. Sch., 1952-53, Am. U., 1953-54, Sch. Law Vanderbilt U., 1955-56; J.D., Memphis State U., 1977. Bar: Tenn. 1977, U.S. Dist. Ct. (we. dist.) Tenn. 1977, U.S. Ct. Appeals (6th cir.), 1982. Tchr. schs. Nashville, Dyer County, and Dyersburg, Tenn., 1954-61; legal asst. Joseph M. Boyd, Jr., Dyersburg, 1965-74; ptnr. firm Boyd and Boyd, 1977—; asst. dist. atty. Dyer County (Tenn.), 1980—; head Child Support Div. for 29th Jud. Cir., Dyer and Lake County (Tenn.); instr. bus. law and other paralegal courses, Dyersburg State Community Coll., 1977—; free-lance writer, Dyersburg, 1961—. Chmn. Dyer County Democratic Party, 1979-83; mem. exec. com. Tenn. Dems., 1986—. Recipient Labor prize Memphis State Law Sch., 1977. Mem. ABA (family law sect.), Tenn. Bar Assn. (chmn. family law sect. 1985—), Dyer County Bar Assn. (pres. 1982-83), Tenn. Jaycettes (pres. 1961-62). Methodist. Club: Dyersburg Woman's (pres. 1964-65). Contbr. photos and articles to Memphis Press-Scimitar and other newspapers; contbr. articles to profl. jours. and popular mags. Family and matrimonial, General corporate, Criminal. Home: 607 Troy Ave Dyersburg TN 38024 Office: Dyer County Court House Dyersburg TN 38025

BOYD, ROLAND, lawyer; b. Lavon, Tex., Sept. 10, 1908; s. William F. and Fannie Belle (Stimson) B.; m. Nannette Gay, Sept. 6, 1935; children: Bill, Betty Boyd Skelton. BA, U. Tex., 1931; LLB, Southern Meth. U., 1933. Bar: Tex. 1940, U.S. Dist. Ct. (no. dist.) Tex. 1940, U.S. Supreme Ct. 1950, U.S. Ct. Appeals (5th cir.) 1986. Ptnr. Boyd, Veigel & Hance, McKinney, Tex., 1933—; criminal dist. atty. Collin County, 1939-42. Mem. Pres.'s Emergency Bd.; del. econ. and social counsel UN, Geneva, 1967. Democrat. Condemnation, Personal injury, Legal education. Home: 616 Finch St McKinney TX 75069 Office: Boyd Veigel & Hance 218 E Louisiana St McKinney TX 75069

BOYD, STANLEY JEFFREY, JR., lawyer; b. Florence, S.C., July 22, 1950; s. Stanley Jeffrey Sr. and Cloy Dell (Little) B.; m. Terri Lynn Langley, Sept. 28, 1985. BS, U. S.C., 1972, JD, 1977. Bar: S.C. 1977, U.S. Dist. Ct. S.C. 1978. Assoc. Marshall & Flom, Myrtle Beach, S.C., 1977-78; mortgage originator August, Kohn & Co., Inc., Columbia, S.C., 1979-81; ptnr. Young, Boyd & Caughman, Sumter, S.C., 1981-83; chief staff atty. S.C. Ct. Adminstrn., Columbia, 1983-86; claims mgr. Am. Mutual Liability Ins. Co., Columbia, 1987—; recording sec. S.C. Appellate Def. Commn., Columbia, 1983-86, Jud. Council of S.C., 1983-86. Mem. Govs. Hwy. Traffic Safety Com., 1984, Trenholm Road United Meth. Ch. Mem. S.C. Bar Assn. (speaker continuing legal edn. 1984), Nat. Assn. State Jud. Educators. Club: U. S.C. Sport Parachute (Columbia) (chartered). Insurance, Education for summary court judges, Personal injury. Home: 3829 Linbrook Dr Columbia SC 29204 Office: Am Mutual Liability Ins Co 111 Executive Ctr Dr Columbia SC 29210

BOYD, WILLIAM CLARK, lawyer; b. Edom, Tex., Jan. 8, 1940; s. Fred W. and Annice H. Boyd; m. Linda Capps, June 15, 1963; children—William Clark, Stanford Scott. B.S. in Math., Tex. Tech U., 1962; postgrad. U. N.Mex., 1962-63; J.D., U. Houston, 1968. Bar: U.S. Dist. Ct. (so. dist.) Tex. 1968, U.S. Dist. Ct. (we. dist.) Tex. 1973. Data analyst T.S.I., White Sands, N.Mex., 1962-64; aerospace technologist NASA, Houston, 1964-68; assoc. Woodard Hall & Primm, Houston, 1969-72; ptnr. Patterson Boyd Lowery & Aderholt, Houston, 1972—. Trustee Tex. Tech. U. Mem. Houston Bar Assn. (dir. 1974-75, liaison 1981-82), State Bar Tex. (dir. 1979-82), ABA, Phi Delta Theta. Presbyterian. Club: Kiwanis (Houston). General practice, Consumer commercial, Real property. Office: 2101 Louisiana Houston TX 77002

BOYD, WILLIAM SPROTT, lawyer; b. San Francisco, Feb. 12, 1943; s. R. Mitchell S. and Mary (Mitchell) B.; m. Marion Sagar, Aug. 25, 1973; children: Mitchell Sagar, Sterling McMicking. AB, Stanford U., 1964, JD, 1971. Bar: Calif. 1972, U.S. Dist. Ct. (no. dist.) 1972, U.S. Ct. Appeals (9th cir.) 1972, U.S. Dist. Ct. (cen. dist.) Calif. 1974, U.S. Dist. Ct. (ea. dist.) Calif. 1976. Assoc. Brobeck, Phleger & Harrison, San Francisco, 1971-77, ptnr., 1977—. Mem. Lawyers Com for Urban Affairs, San Francisco, 1979—; bd. dirs. San Francisco Legal Aid Soc., 1980-85. Served to lt. USNR, 1975-78, Vietnam. Mem. ABA, Calif. Bar Assn., San Francisco Bar Assn. Antitrust, Federal civil litigation, State civil litigation. Home: 101 Eye St San Rafael CA 94901 Office: Brobeck Phleger & Harrison One Market Plaza Spear St Tower San Francisco CA 94105

BOYER, DAVID RANDALL, lawyer, educator; b. Montreal, Que., Can., Feb. 20, 1956; s. William H. and Helen (Dokus) B.; m. Victoria Gabriel, Aug. 16, 1986. BA magna cum laude, U. Minn., 1977; JD cum laude, Hamline U., 1981. Bar: Minn. 1981, U.S. Dist. Ct. Minn. 1982, U.S. Ct. Appeals (8th cir.) 1982. Assoc. Schlesinger & Assocs., St. Paul, 1981-83, Leonard, Street & Deinard, Mpls., 1983-85, Popham, Haik Law Firm, Mpls., 1985—; adj. prof. Hamline U. Sch. Law, St. Paul, 1985—; Minn. software ind. trade rep. to Peoples Republic of China, 1985—. Mng. editor Hamline Law Rev., 1980-81; contbr. articles to law jours. State del. Dem. Farmer Labor Party Conv., Duluth, Minn., 1982. Mem. ABA, Minn. Bar Assn. (chmn. computer law sect. 1983-85), Hennepin County Bar Assn., Computer Law Assn., Minn. Software Assn. (pres. 1986—). Computer, Private international, Trademark and copyright. Office: Popham Haik Law Firm 3300 Piper Jaffray Tower Minneapolis MN 55402

BOYER, ELROY GEORGE, lawyer; b. Balt., May 5, 1920; s. J. LeRoy and Cora Ellen (Hodges) B.; m. Laura Hogans, Mar. 15, 1952; children: Elroy G. Jr., V. Brooke, Rebecca Boyer Lawson, H. Stacey. AB, Washington Coll., 1942; LLB, U. Md., 1945. Bar: U.S. Supreme Ct. 1961. Sole practice Chestertown, Md., 1945—; atty. Town of Rock Hall, Md., 1954—, Town of Betterton, Md., 1962—; del. Md. Gen. Assembly, Annapolis, Md., 1958-70, senate, 1970-78; bd. dirs. Millington (Md.) Bank; adv. bd. Farmers Nat. Bank, Annapolis, 1978—. Chmn. gen. provisions com. Constl. Convention of Md., Annapolis, 1967-68; mem. Bd. of Visitors and Gov. Washington Coll., Chestertown, Md., 1978-84, Md. Hist. Trust, Chestertown; Patron Eastern Star. Named Legislator of Yr. Md. Mcpl. League, 1976. Mem. ABA, Md. Bar Assn. (bd. of gov. 1979), Kent County Bar Assn. (v.p. 1962), Md. Bar Assn. Fellows, Kent County C. of C. (pres. 1983, Outstanding Man of Yr. 1985). Democrat. Methodist. Lodges: Lions (pres. 1959), Masons (worshipful master 1959). Avocations: golf, reading. General practice, Probate, Real property. Home and Office: 107 Court St PO Box 480 Chestertown MD 21620

BOYER, WILLIAM GILBERT, lawyer; b. May 2, 1941; m. Lisa DeBoard; children: William G., Kelly Lynn, Jay Christian. Student, Western Mich. U., 1958-59, U. Mich., 1959-61; JD, Detroit Coll. Law, 1965. Bar: Mich. 1967, U.S. Dist. Ct. (we. dist.) Mich. 1967, U.S. Ct. Appeals (6th cir.) 1971, U.S. Supreme Ct. 1983. Assoc. Sugar, Schwartz, Silver, Schwartz & Tyler, Detroit, 1966-70; ptnr. Hopping and Boyer P.C., Detroit, 1970-78; pres. Boyer and Churilla, P.C., Detroit, 1978—; lectr. continuing legal edn. programs on jury selection, mediation and no-fault ins.; mem. Wayne County Mediation Tribunal, 1982—. Mem. ABA (com. litigation 1970—), Mich. Bar Assn. (rep. assembly 1980-83, task force com. attys. for indigent clients), Macomb County Bar Assn. (bd. dirs. 1980-82, sec. 1982-83, treas. 1983-84, pres. 1985—, author monthly article Bar Briefs, mediator selection com. 1980—), Detroit Bar Assn. (com. legal services for indigent), Am. Trial Lawyers Assn., Mich. Trial Lawyers Assn. (bd. dirs. 1984—), Macomb County Trial Lawyers Assn. (bd. dirs. 1985-86, pres. 1984-85), Met. Trial Lawyers Assn. (bd. dirs. 1980—), Detroit Coll. Law Alumni Assn., Detroit Coll. Law 2d Century Club, Sigma Phi Epsilon Alumni Assn. Clubs: Great Oak and Country (bd. dirs. 1980-82), Detroit Athletic. Home: 1202 Oakwood Ct Rochester MI 48063 Office: Boyer and Churilla PC 43805 Van Dyke Ave Sterling Heights MI 48078

BOYKO, CHRISTOPHER ALLAN, lawyer, assistant prosecutor; b. Cleve., Oct. 10, 1954; s. Andrew and Eva Dorothy (Zepko) B.; m. Roberta Ann Gentile, May 29, 1981; 1 child, Philip. B in Polit. Sci. cum laude, Mt. Union Coll., 1976; JD, Cleve. Marshall Coll. Law, 1979. Bar: Ohio 1979, U.S. Dist. Ct. (no. dist.) Ohio 1979, Fla. 1985, U.S. Tax Ct. 1986. Ptnr. Boyko & Boyko, Parma, Ohio, 1979—; asst. prosecutor City of Parma, 1981—; v.p., gen. counsel BKL Industries, Cleve., 1983—, also bd. dirs.; guardian ad litem Juvenile Ct., 1979—; legal advisor spl. weapons and tactics div. City of Parma Police Dept., 1984—. Bi-monthly columnist Parma Police Newsletter, 1985—. Active Citizens League of Greater Cleve., 1985—; cen. committeeman Democratic Party, Parma, 1984—; mem. Parma Drug Task Force, 1987—. Mem. ABA, Fla. Bar Assn., Ohio Bar Assn., Cleve. Bar Assn., Parma Bar Assn. (trustee, treas. 1985—), Ukrainian Bar Assn., Cuyahoga County Police Chief Assn. (assoc.), Narcotics Law Officers Assn., Cleve. Am. Middle Eastern Orgn., Mt. Union Coll. Alumni Assn., Cleve. Marshall Law Sch. Alumni Assn. Byzantine Catholic. Lodge: Rotary (bd. dirs. Parma 1986—), Sons of Am. Legion. Avocations: martial arts, running, weightlifting, hand guns. General practice, Probate. Home: 7451 Meadow Ln Parma OH 44134 Office: Boyko & Boyko Attys 6741 Ridge Rd Parma OH 44129

BOYLAN, MICHAEL LEE, lawyer, educator; b. Jeffersonville, Ind., May 28, 1950; s. Veron Lee and Mary Ann (Evans) B.; m. Mary Ann Quick, June 3, 1972; children: Rebecca, Jonathan, Christopher, Patrick, Jennifer. BS in Commerce with honors, U. Louisville, 1972, MBA with high honors, 1973, JD, 1978. Bar: Ky. 1978, U.S. Dist. Ct. (we. dist.) Ky. 1982, U.S. Ct. Appeals (6th cir.) 1983, U.S. Supreme Ct. 1983, U.S. Dist. Ct. (ea. dist.) 1985. Mktg. adminstr. Brown-Forman Distillers Corp., Louisville, 1973-77, labor relations mgr., 1977-82; sole practice Louisville, 1982—; instr. Ind. U., New Albany, 1983—; atty. City of Coldstream, Ky., 1983—, Coldstream Homeowners Assn., 1981-83. Dem. candidate magistrate, Jefferson County., Ky., 1985. Mem. Ky. Bar Assn., Louisville Bar Assn., Assn. Trial Lawyers Am., Ky. Acad. Trial Lawyers, Ky. Acad. Mcpl. Attys. Roman Catholic. Club: Viking Canoe (Louisville) (treas. 1979). Avocations: whitewater canoeing, camping, hiking, photography. Civil rights, Labor, Federal civil litigation. Home: 11819 Olde Spring Rd Louisville KY 40223 Office: 807 W Market St Louisville KY 40202

BOYLAN, WILLIAM ALVIN, lawyer; b. Marshalltown, Iowa, Sept. 18, 1924; s. Glen D. and Dorothy I. (Gibson) B.; m. Nancy Dickson, Aug. 5, 1950; children: Ross, Laura. Student, U. Iowa, 1943-44; B.A., Drake U., 1947; LL.B., Harvard U., 1950. Bar: Ill. 1950, N.Y. bar 1952. Practiced in N.Y.C., 1952—; mem. firm Boylan & Evans, and predecessor firms, 1963-86; spl. counsel Sage Gray Todd & Sims, N.Y.C., 1986-87; mem. firm Gould & Wilkie, N.Y.C., 1987—; bd. dirs. Tribune Oil Corp. Contbr. articles to profl. jours. Served with USAAF, 1943-46. Mem. ABA, N.Y. State Bar Assn., Assn. Bar City N.Y., Fed. Bar Council, Phi Beta Kappa, Sigma Alpha Epsilon. Episcopalian. Club: Harvard. General practice, General corporate. Home: 108 E 82d St New York NY 10028 Office: Gould & Wilkie One Wall St 34th Floor New York NY 10005

BOYLAND, HERBERT LAYTON, lawyer; b. Dallas, Jan. 2, 1927; s. Herbert Layton and Bessie Deborah (Jones) B.; m. Peggy Jane Porter, Mar. 5, 1949; children: Rex, Laurie Boyland Collins, Kurt, Sharon. LLB, Baylor U., 1950. Bar: Tex. 1950, U.S. Dist. Ct. (ea. dist.) Tex. 1953, U.S. Ct. Appeals (5th cir.) 1958. Sole practice, Longview, Tex., 1951; asst. dist. atty. Gregg County, Tex., 1952-53; assoc. Kenley, Sharp and Ritter; ptnr., 1956—. Dem. chmn., Gregg County, 1976-80. Served with U.S. Army, 1945-47. Fellow Tex. Bar Found. (peer com. 1983—, vice-chmn. tort and compensation com. 1969-70); mem. ABA, Tex. Bar Assn. (bd. dirs. 1968-70, 76-78, 84—), Tex. Assn. Def. Counsel, Phi Delta Phi. Mem. Ch. of Christ. Lodges: Masons (32 degree), Shriners. Federal civil litigation, State civil litigation, Insurance. Office: Kenley & Boyland 2020 Bill Owens Pkwy PO Box 312 Longview TX 75606

BOYLE, EDWARD MICHAEL, lawyer; b. Kansas City, Mo., Feb. 27, 1939; s. Edward G. and Monica I. (Murphy) B.; children—Katherine, Edward, James, John, Andrew. A.B. magna cum laude, U. Notre Dame, 1960; J.D., U. Kans., 1965. Bar: Kans. 1965, Mo. 1965, U.S. Dist. Ct. (we. dist.) Mo. 1965, U.S. Ct. Appeals (8th cir.) 1965, U.S. Ct. Appeals (10th cir.) 1966. Assoc. Payne & Jones, Overland Park, Kans., 1965—; spl. asst. atty. gen. Kans. antitrust program, 1971-74. Served to lt. USN, 1960-62. Mem. Johnson County Bar Assn. (sec. 1967), Kans. Bar Assn. (sec. discipline com. 1978-80), Mo. Bar Assn., ABA, Kans. Assn. Def. Counsel. Democrat. Roman Catholic. Club: Milburn Country. Editor-in-chief: Kans. Law Rev., 1965. Personal injury, Federal civil litigation, State civil litigation. Home: PO Box 26625 Overland Park KS 66225

BOYLE, ELIZABETH MARY HUNT, lawyer; b. Oak Park, Ill., Apr. 12, 1956; d. Lawrence Halley and Mary Hamilton (Johnson) Hunt; m. Francis Anthony Boyle Jr., May 27, 1982. BA, Wellesley Coll., 1978; JD, U. Ill., 1982. Bar: Ill. 1982, U.S. Dist. Ct. (cen. dist.) Ill. 1983, U.S. Ct. Appeals (7th cir). 1985. Assoc. Craig & Craig, Mattoon, Ill., 1982-86. Mem. ABA, Ill. Bar Assn., Coles-Cumberland Bar Assn. (sec.-treas. 1983-84), Bar Assn. for 7th Fed. Cir. Avocations: swimming, tennis, windsurfing, skiing. Federal civil litigation, State civil litigation, Personal injury.

BOYLE, FRANCIS ANTHONY, law educator; b. Chgo., Mar. 25, 1950. AB in Polit. Sci., U. Chgo., 1971; JD magna cum laude, Harvard U., 1976, AM, 1978, PhD, 1983. Bar: Mass. 1977. Tax atty. Bingman, Dana & Gould, Boston, 1977-78; asst. prof. U. Ill., Champaign, 1978-81, assoc. prof., 1981-84, prof., 1984—; mem. exec. com. Program in Arms Control, Disarmament and Internat. Security, U. Ill., 1979—; assoc. African Studies Program, U. Ill., 1981—; assoc. Ctr. for Latin Am. Studies, U. Ill., 1984—; judge provisional dist. World Ct., 1984—. Author: World Politics and International Law, 1985 (outstanding acad. book Choice mag. 1985-86), Defending Civil Resistance Under International Law, 1987; contbr. legal articles and book revs. to profl. jours. Mem. bur. polit.-mil. affairs (scholar-diplomat program) U.S. Dept. State, 1981;bd. dirs. coordinating council Lawyers Com. on Nuclear Policy, 1981—; adv. com. on human rights in Lebanon Am. Friends Service Com., 1982—; cons. Amnesty Internat., 1983—; chmn., panel of jurists IPO Brussels Conf. on Reagan Adminstrns. Fgn. Policy, 1984; mem. steering com. Concerned Acads. for Peace and Justice in the Middle East, 1984—; mem. adv. bd. Am. Bibliog. Ctr. Polit. Sci., 1985—. Fellow Harvard U. Mem. Am. Soc. Internat. Law (ad hoc guidelines and mem. coms. 1978-80, Lieber group on Laws of War 1979—), ABA (human rights com., young lawyer's div.), Internat. Third World Legal Studies Assn. (bd. dirs.), Internat. Law Assn. (internat. terrorism com. am. br.). Public international. Office: Coll of Law 504 E Pennsylvania Ave Champaign IL 61820

BOYLE, FRANCIS J., chief judge; b. 1927. Grad., Providence Coll.; LL.B., Boston Coll. Bar: bar 1952. Judge U.S. Dist. Ct. for R.I., Providence, 1977—, now chief justice. Mem. Am. Bar Assn. Office: US District Ct US Courthouset Providence RI 02903 *

BOYLE, GERARD JOSEPH, lawyer; b. Cambridge, Mass., June 26, 1949; s. James John and Eleanor Marie (Mahler) B.; m. Barbara Ann Cahill, Oct. 20, 1979; children: Bridgid, Brianna. BS, Boston Coll., 1971; M in Pub. Adminstrn., JD, Suffolk U., 1979; diploma, USMC Command and Staff Coll., 1984. Bar: N.H. 1979, Maine 1979, U.S. Dist. Ct. N.H. 1979, U.S. Ct. Mil. Appeals 1979, U.S. Supreme Ct. 1983. Commd. 2d lt. USMC, 1972, advanced through grades to major, 1981; judge adv. USMC, Quantico (Va.) and Okinawa (Japan), 1972-85; resigned USMC, 1985; legal and cost analyst Office of Sec. of Def., Washington, 1984-85; sole practice Plymouth, N.H., 1985—; major USMCR, 1985—. Mem. Grafton County (N.H.) Rep. com., 1985—; eucharistic minister St. Matthew's Cath. Ch., Plymouth, N.H., 1985—. Mem. ABA, Am. Trial Lawyers Assn., N.H. Trial Lawyers Assn., Maine Trial Lawyers Assn., Maine Bar Assn., N.H. Bar Assn., Am. Legion, Nat. Assn. Criminal Def. Lawyers, White Mountain Gateway C. of C. Republican. Roman Catholic. Criminal, General practice, Real property. Home: 48 Highland St Plymouth NH 03264 Office: 50 Highland St Suite A Plymouth NH 03264

BOYLE, JOHN EDWARD, lawyer; b. Denver, Feb. 4, 1948; s. Herbert M. and Anne E. (Rockwell) B.; m. Christy Ann Stambaugh, Apr. 20, 1974; children: John Alexander, Mary Elizabeth. BA, U. Colo., 1970, JD, 1973. Bar: Colo. 1973, U.S. Dist. Ct. Colo. 1973, U.S. Ct. Appeals (10th cir.) 1973, U.S. Tax Ct. 1974, U.S. Supreme Ct. 1986. Sole practice Denver, 1973—; lectr. estate planning Iliff Sch. Theology, Denver, 1985—; monitor Legal Services Corp., Denver, 1985—. Chmn. bd. trustees St. Andrew United Meth. Ch., Denver, 1982—; trustee Rocky Mountain Conf. United Meth. Ch., Denver, 1985—; Rep. committeeman, Englewood, Colo., 1977—. Mem. ABA, Colo. Bar Assn., Denver Bar Assn., Am. Judicature Soc., Denver Law Club. Avocations: skiing, tennis, jogging, reading, classical music. Probate, Real property, Family and matrimonial. Office: 4704 Harlan #500 Denver CO 80212

BOYLE, MATTHEW ANTHONY, lawyer; b. Flushing, N.Y., June 23, 1944; s. Gerald Michael and Adele Catherine (Cassidy) B.; m. Kathleen Lorretta Briggles, Aug. 2, 1975; children: Tracie Diane, Matthew Franklin. BA, U. Notre Dame, 1966; JD, Fordham U., 1977. Bar: N.Y. 1978. Commd. 2d lt. USAF, 1966, advanced through grades to maj., 1971; assoc. Haight, Gardner, Poor & Havens, N.Y.C., 1977-79; pilot N.Y. Air N.G., Newburgh, N.Y, 1976—; gen. counsel, sec. Falon Jet Corp., Tetrboro, N.J., 1979—. Democratic committeeman Bergen County, Ramsey, N.J., 1985—. Mem. N.Y. Bar Assn., Assn. of the Bar of the City of N.Y. Roman Catholic. Avocations: flying. Contracts commercial, General corporate, Aviation. Home: 57 Snyder Ave Ramsey NJ 07446 Office: Falcon Jet Corp Teterboro Airport Teterboro NJ 07608

BOYLE, PATRICIA JEAN, judge. Student, U. Mich., 1955-57; B.A., Wayne State U., 1963, J.D., 1963. Bar: Mich. Practice law with Kenneth Davies, Detroit, 1963; law clk. to U.S. Dist. judge, 1963-64; asst. U.S. atty., Detroit, 1964-68; asst. pros. atty. Wayne County; dir. research, tng. and appeals Wayne County, Detroit, 1969-74; Recorders Ct. judge City of Detroit, 1976-78; U.S. dist. judge Eastern Dist. Mich., Detroit, 1978-83; justice Mich. Supreme Ct., Detroit, 1983—. Active Women's Rape Crisis Task Force, Vols. of Am. Named Feminist of Year Detroit chpt. NOW, 1978; recipient Outstanding Achievement award Pros. Attys. Assn. Mich., 1978; Spirit of Detroit award Detroit City Council, 1978. Mem. Women Lawyers Assn. Mich., Fed. Bar Assn., Mich. Bar Assn., Detroit Bar Assn., Wayne State U. Law Alumni Assn. (Disting. Alumni award 1979). Federal civil litigation, Criminal. Office: Mich Supreme Ct 1425 Lafayette Bldg Detroit MI 48226

BOYLE, PATRICK OTTO, lawyer; b. St. Louis, Nov. 15, 1935; s. Otto William and Wilma Louise (Bowers) B.; m. Jane Adeline Roberts, Nov. 22, 1966; children—Laura Jane, Daniel Patrick. B.S.B.A., Washington U., 1957, J.D., 1960. Bar: Mo. 1960, Ill., 1970. Assoc. firm Lucas & Murphy, St. Louis, 1963-67; assoc. csl. Interco Inc., St. Louis, 1967-69; csl. Energy Systems div. Olin Corp., East Alton, Ill., 1969-74; assoc. Winchester Group Csl., 1974-77; asst. sec., 1970-77; partner Boyle & Stillwell, East Alton, 1977-80; sole practice, St. Louis and E. Alton, 1980—. Bd. dirs. Ferguson-Florissant Sch. Bd., 1981—. Served to comdr. USCGR, 1960—. Mem. Mo. Bar Assn., Ill. Bar Assn., Madison County Bar Assn., Metro. Bar St. Louis, Beta Gamma Sigma. Mem. United Ch. Christ. Club: Mo. Athletic. General practice, Admiralty, Environment. Office: 210 Smith Ave East Alton IL 62024 Home: 3715 Greengrass Dr Florissant MO 63033

BOYLE, TERRENCE W., U.S. district judge; b. 1945. B.A., Brown U., 1967; J.D., Am. U., 1970. Minority counsel housing subcom., banking and currence com. U.S. Ho. of Reps., 1970-73; legis. asst. U.S. senator J. Helms, 1973; ptnr. law firm LeRoy, Wells, Shaw, Hornthal & Riley, Elizabeth City, N.C., 1974-84; U.S. dist. judge, Fayetteville, N.C., 1984—; lectr. Wake Forest Law Sch. Mem. 1st Jud. Dist. Bar Assn. (sec.-treas. 1982-83, v.p. 1983-84). Judicial administration. Office: US Dist Ct PO Box 1148 Fayetteville NC 28302 *

BOYLES, KEVAN KENNETH, lawyer; b. Providence, Dec. 1, 1954; s. Kenneth George and Mildred (Eddleston) B.; m. Rosemary Cooney, Nov. 28, 1981; 1 child, Carling Cooney. BA, U. R.I., 1976; JD, Stetson U., 1979. Bar: R.I. 1979, Fla. 1979, U.S. Dist. Ct. (so. dist.) Fla. 1980. Assoc. Nason, Gildaw, Yeager & Gerson P.A., West Palm Beach, Fla., 1980-84; founding ptnr. Boyles & McCarthy, West Palm Beach, 1984—. Pres. Young Reps. of the Palm Beaches, 1985-86; treas. Palm Beach chpt. Juvenile Diabetes Found., 1985—. Mem. Fla. Bar Assn., R.I. Bar Assn., Assn. Trial Lawyers Am., Fla. Trial Lawyers Assn. Republican. State civil litigation, Family and matrimonial, Personal injury. Home: 1716 17th Way West Palm Beach FL 33407 Office: Boyles & McCarthy 5725 Corp Way Suite 103 West Palm Beach FL 33407

BOYNTON, FREDERICK GEORGE, lawyer; b. Yokohama, Japan, May 9, 1948; s. Fred Wenderoth and Buelah Eleanor (Nygaard) B.; m. Nancy Jeanne McLendon, Aug. 3, 1985. BA, The Citadel, 1970; JD, Tulane U., 1973. Bar: SC 1973, Ga. 1976, U.S. Dist. Ct. Ga. 1976, U.S. Ct. Appeals (5th and 11th cirs.). Assoc. Smith, Gambrell & Russell, and predecessors, Atlanta, 1976-82, ptnr., 1982—. Author: Criminal Defense Techniques, 1976. Mem. exec. com. Southside Progress Assn., Atlanta, 1983-84. Served to capt. JAGC, U.S. Army, 1973-76. Articles editor Tulane Sch. Law Rev. Mem. Fed. Bar Assn. (pres. Atlanta chpt. 1981-82, dep. chmn. adminstrv. law sect. 1986-87, bd. dirs. younger lawyers div. 1981-84, v.p. 11th Cir. 1985-87), ABA, State Bar Ga. (chmn. adminstrv. law sect. 1987—), Lawyers Club of Atlanta, Am. Judicature Soc., Order of Coif. Republican. Presbyterian. Club: Commerce (Atlanta). Administrative and regulatory, Federal civil litigation, State civil litigation. Home: 4860 Northway Dr NE Atlanta GA 30342 Office: Smith Gambrell & Russell 2400 First Atlanta Tower Atlanta GA 30383

BOYNTON, GARY JOHN, lawyer; b. Atlanta, Sept. 29, 1954; s. John H. Jr. and Martha (Murray) B.; m. Amy Goff, Aug. 18, 1979; 1 child, Michael. AA, U. Cen. Fla., 1973; BA, Emory U., 1975; JD, Stetson U., 1978. Bar: Fla. 1978, Ga. 1978, U.S. Dist. Ct. (mid. dist.) Fla., U.S. Ct. Appeals (11th and 15th cirs.), U.S. Supreme Ct. Assoc. Meyers, Mooney & Adler, Orlando, Fla., 1979-81; sole practice Orlando, 1981-85, Winter Park, Fla., 1985—. Mem. Orange County Bar Assn., Sigma Alpha Epsilon (pres. 1983). Personal injury, Workers' compensation, Family and matrimonial. Home: 1711 Gay Dr Orlando FL 32803 Office: 1150 Louisiana Ave #3 Winter Park FL 32789

BOZARTH, ROBERT STEPHEN, lawyer; b. Glendale, Calif., May 21, 1945; s. Marion Farrell and Elna Josephine (Haynes) B.; m. Marsha Ketcham, June 8, 1968; children—Howard Austin, Robert Belden. B.S., U. Va., 1967, J.D., 1975. Bar: Va. 1975. Law clk. Supreme Ct. Va., Richmond, 1975-76; assoc. McDonald & Crump, P.C., Richmond, 1976-81; assoc. counsel law div. Lawyers Title Ins. Corp., Richmond, 1982—. Vol. referee,

coach Three Chopt Youth Soccer League, Richmond, 1981-83. Served to lt. USN, 1969-73. Mem. Va. Bar Assn., Richmond Bar Assn. Republican. Episcopalian. Club: Ridgetop Recreation Assn. Real property, Insurance, Land titles. Home: 1103 E Durwood Crescent Richmond VA 23229 Office: Lawyers Title Ins Corp 6630 W Broad St PO Box 27567 Richmond VA 23261

BOZE, URIELE L., lawyer; b. Houston, Nov. 1, 1949; s. Uriele Lebanon and Iva (Stewart) B.; m. Joyce Menard, Aug. 4, 1979; children: Darrin Lawrence, Andrea Simone. BS, U. Houston, 1973; JD summa cum laude, MBA summa cum laude, Tex. So. U., 1978. Bar: Tex. 1978, U.S. Ct. Appeals (5th and 11th cirs.) 1981, U.S. Dist. Ct. (so. and no. dists.) Tex. Law clk. to presiding justice City of Houston, 1974-75, U.S. Dept. of Justice, Dallas, 1976; atty. Gulf Oil Corp., Houston, 1978-85, Chevron USA Inc., Houston, 1985-86; v.p., bankruptcy counsel Allied Bancshares, Inc., Houston, 1987—; moot ct. judge U. Houston, Tex. So. Law Schs., 1980—, business law instr. Tex. So. U., 1981—; state bar grader State Bar Tex., Austin, 1983—. Lectr., panelist Nat. Urban League (black exec. exchange program), N.Y.C., 1981—; panelist energy braintrust Congl. Black Caucus, Washington, 1984—. Named one of Outstanding Young Men in Am., U.S. Jaycees, 1979. Mem. ABA (vice chmn. energy, gen. practice div. 1985—), Nat. Bar Assn. (vice chmn. energy and environ. sect. 1984-86, exec. com.), Assn. of Blacks in Energy, Houston Bar Assn., Houston Lawyers Assn. (bd. dirs. 1985-86), Omega Psi Phi. Democrat. Baptist. Bankruptcy, Contracts commercial, Oil and gas leasing. Office: Allied Bancshares Inc 808 Travis Suite 1349A Houston TX 77002

BOZORTH, SQUIRE NEWLAND, lawyer; b. Portland, Oreg., Oct. 25, 1935; s. Squire Smith and Ethel Elizabeth (Newland) B.; B.S., U. Oreg., 1958; LL.B., N.Y. U., 1961; m. Louise Crosby Mathews, Aug. 9, 1967; children—Squire Mathews, Caroline Rutgers. Admitted to N.Y. bar, 1961; assoc. firm Milbank, Tweed, Hadley & McCloy, N.Y.C., 1961-70, partner, 1970—; assoc. counsel Rockefeller U., 1973-83. Bd. dirs., mem. exec. com., v.p. Fedn. Protestant Welfare Agencies. Mem. Am., N.Y. State bar assns., Assn. of Bar of City of N.Y., Phi Beta Kappa. Democrat. Episcopalian. Clubs: Century Assn., Down Town Assn. (N.Y.C.). Education, Probate, Estate taxation. Home: 38 Olmsted Rd Scarsdale NY 10583 Office: Milbank Tweed Hadley & McCloy 1 Chase Manhattan Plaza New York NY 10005

BOZZO, PAUL PETER, lawyer; b. Queens, N.Y., July 31, 1953; s. Aldo Paul and Ida (Morelli) B.; m. Louise Ann Brunetti, June 26, 1976; children: Amy Elizabeth, Brian. BA, St. John's U., Jamaica, N.Y., 1975, JD, 1979. Bar: N.Y. 1980. Assoc. Law Offices of Joseph M. Mattone, Queens, 1979-81; assoc. counsel The Lefrak Orgn., Inc., Queens, 1981—. Mem. ABA, N.Y. State Bar Assn., Queens County Bar Assn. Real property, General corporate. Home: 1 Blacksmith Rd Levittown NY 11756 Office: The Lefrak Orgn Inc 97-77 Queens Blvd Rego Park NY 11374

BRAAFLADT, ARNIE ROLF, lawyer; b. Moorhead, Minn., Oct. 17, 1951; s. Halvor John Braafladt and Arlene Olga (Johnson) Lumley; m. Nancy Jeanne Holmes, Aug. 1, 1976; children: Nicole Yvonne Holmes Braafladt, Sarah Arlene Holmes Braafladt. AB in Polit. Sci. and Journalism magna cum laude, Humboldt State U., 1974; MA in Urban Studies, Occidental Coll., 1976; JD, Willamette U., 1978. Bar: Oreg. 1978, Calif. 1980, Wash. 1981, U.S. Dist. Ct. (no. dist.) Calif. 1984, U.S. Ct. Appeals (9th cir.) 1984. Law clk. to presiding justice Wash. Supreme Ct., Olympia, 1979-80; dep. legis. counsel Oreg. Legislature, Salem, 1980-82; ptnr. Shields & Braafladt, Eureka, Calif., 1982—; lectr. media law Humboldt State U., Arcata, Calif., 1983; legal counsel The Lumberjack student newspaper, 1984—. Assoc. editor Willamette Law Jour., 1977-78; contbr. articles to profl. jours. Chmn., vice chmn. Humboldt County Dem. Cen. Com., Calif., 1974; active various polit. campaigns, 1972-78; bd. dirs. Redwood Community Action Agy., 1985-86. Fellow Coro Found., 1974-75. Mem. Calif. Bar Assn., Oreg. Bar Assn., Wash. State Bar Assn., Assn. Trial Lawyers Am., Calif. Trial Lawyers Assn., Humboldt State U. Alumni Assn. (bd. dirs. 1985-86, v.p. 1986—), Green and Gold Key Soc. Lutheran. General practice, Personal injury, Civil rights. Home: 238 Ponderosa Ct Eureka CA 95501 Office: Shields & Braafladt 1125 3d St Eureka CA 95501

BRAATZ, DAVID EDWARD, lawyer; b. Berwyn, Ill., Oct. 22, 1956; s. Edward M. and Virginia H. Braatz; m. Rhonda Diane Jackson, Aug. 22, 1986. AA, Coll. of Dupage, 1976; BA, Valparaiso U., 1978, JD, 1981. Bar: Ill. 1981, Ind. 1981. Dep. pros. atty felony div. Lake County Prosecutors Office, Crown Point, Ind., 1981-85; atty. Sims & Braatz, Cedar Lake, Ind., 1985—; pub. defender Lake County Div 2, Crown Point, 1986; legal advisor Lake County Arson Task Force, Crown Point, 1985. Mem. Fed. Bar Assn., Lake County Bar Assn., Assn. Trial Lawyers Am., Delta Theta Phi (bd. dirs. 1986). Lutheran. Avocations: fishing, waterskiing. State civil litigation, Criminal, General practice. Home: 9984 Olcott Ave Saint John IN 46307 Office: Sims & Braatz 11108 W 133rd Ave Cedar Lake IN 46303

BRACETE, JUAN MANUEL, judge; b. Mayaguez, P.R., Sept. 10, 1951; s. Manuel and Norma (Mari) B.; m. Sonia Rivera, Apr. 5, 1974. BS in Bus. Adminstrn. summa cum laude, Georgetown U., 1971; JD magna cum laude, U. P.R., Rio Piedras, 1976. Bar: P.R. 1976, D.C. 1976, U.S. Tax Ct. 1978, Fla. 1986. Mgmt. trainee First Fed. Savs., San Juan, P.R., 1972; pro mgr. CitiBank, N.A., San Juan, 1972-74; law clk. U.S. Dept. Justice, Washington, 1975; atty., advisor Bd. of Immigration Appeals, Washington, 1976-78; assoc. Goldman & Antonetti, San Juan, 1979-84; immigration judge U.S. Dept. Justice, Miami, 1985—; treas. Am. Immigration Lawyer's Assn. Puerto Rico chpt., Washington, 1982-84, chairperson, 1984. Contbr. articles to profl. jours. Sec., supr. Dept. Justice Fed. Credit Union, Washington, 1976-78; sec. real estate commn.; Alliance Francaise, San Juan, 1980-84; treas. Magdalena 1305 Owners Assn., San Juan, 1983-84; alt. bd. dirs. Harbour Club Villas, Miami, 1986. Recipient Sustained Achievement award U.S. Dept. Justice, Washington, 1977, Spl. award Fed. Credit Union, Washington, 1979. Mem. Fed. Bar Assn., Am. Immigration Judges Assn. (sec. 1985), P.R. Bar Assn., Canon Law Soc. Am. Republican. Roman Catholic. Avocation: philately. Judicial administration, Immigration, naturalization, and customs, Administrative and regulatory. Office: Office of the Immigration Judge 7880 Biscayne Blvd 8th Fl Miami FL 33138

BRACEY, WILLIE EARL, lawyer, university program director; b. Jackson, Miss., Dec. 21, 1950; s. Dudley and Alvaretta (King) B. AA, Wright Jr. Coll., 1971; BS, Mt. Senario Coll., 1974; MS, Eastern Ill. U., 1976; JD, So. Ill. U., 1979. Bar: Ill. 1979. Dir. student legal services Western Ill. U., Macomb, 1979-86, adj. prof., 1981-84, asst. v.p. student affairs, spl. services, 1986—; asst. pub. defender McDonough County, Macomb, 1983-84. Mem. Ill. Com. on Concern of Blacks in Higher Edn., 1984—, Chgo. Com. on Fgn. Realtions, 1986—, McDonough/Fulton County Youth Service Bd., Macomb, 1985-86. Mem. ABA, Ill. Bar Assn., McDonough County Bar Assn., Assn. Trial Lawyers Am., Nat. Legal Aid and Defender Assn., Ill. Student Atty. Assn., (v.p. 1984—), Nat. Assn. Student Personnel Adminstrs., NAACP. Avocations: chess, cooking. State civil litigation, Criminal, Family and matrimonial. Home: 1006 Derry Ln Macomb IL 61455 Office: Western Ill U Student Legal Services Sherman Circle Macomb IL 61455

BRACHTENBACH, ROBERT F., state justice; b. Sidney, Nebr., Jan. 28, 1931; s. Henry W. and Elizabeth A. (Morfeld) B.; m. Marilyn; children: Rick, Jeff, Randal, Curtis, David. B.S., U. Wash., 1953, LL.B., 1954. Bar: Wash. bar 1954. Instr. U. Calif. Sch. Law, Berkeley, 1954-55; practiced in Selah, Wash., 1955-72; justice Wash. Supreme Ct., 1972-81, chief justice, 1981—. Contbr. articles to law revs. Mem. Selah Sch. Bd., 1960-72; mem. Wash. State Ho. of Reps., 1963-67; trustee Eastern Wash. State Coll. Office: Wash Supreme Ct Temple of Justice Olympia WA 98504 *

BRACKEN, NANETTE BEATTIE, lawyer; b. Poughkeepsie, N.Y., Mar. 12, 1950; d. John Lindley and Margaret Jane (Brickner) Beattie; m. Paul Bracken, May 25, 1974; children: Kathleen John, James Beattie, Margaret Logue. BA, Vassar Coll., 1972; JD, U. Balt., 1975. Bar: N.Y. 1976, Conn. 1978, U.S. Dist. Ct. Conn. 1980. Chief clk. estate tax dept. Surrogate's Ct. Westchester County, N.Y. Dept. Taxation and Fin., White Plains, N.Y., 1976-78; assoc. Grehan & Fricke, Ridgefield, Conn., 1978—. Active Birthright, Danbury, Conn., 1978-80, Housatonic Mental Health Commn., Conn., 1980-83, Ridgefield Youth Commn., 1978-81. Mem. N.Y. State Bar Assn., Conn. Bar Assn., Assn. Trial Lawyers Am. Republican. Roman Catholic. Avocations: traveling, gardening, cooking. General practice, Family and matrimonial, Real property. Home: 14 Mulberry St Ridgefield CT 06877 Office: Crehan & Fricke 181 Main St Ridgefield CT 06877

BRACKETT, RONALD E., lawyer; b. Rockford, Ill., May 10, 1942; s. F. Earl Brackett and Anne (Christenberry) Townsend; m. Susan Carol Tucker, June 11, 1966 (div. June 1972); m. Susan Catherine Stichnoth, May 31, 1975; 1 child, Charles William. BA, Trinity Coll., 1964; JD, U. Mich., 1967. Bar: N.Y. 1968. Assoc. Rogers & Wells, N.Y.C., 1968-74, ptnr., 1974—; bd. dirs. King Kullen Grocery Co. Inc., Westbury, N.Y. Mem. ABA, N.Y. State Bar Assn., Phi Beta Kappa. Republican. Presbyterian. Contracts commercial, General corporate, Securities. Office: Rogers & Wells 200 Park Ave New York NY 10166

BRADBURY, JOHN HOWARD, lawyer; b. Orofino, Idaho, Aug. 7, 1936; s. John Howard and Helen Vivian (Molloy) B. BA, U. Idaho, 1958; LLB, U. Mich., 1961. Bar: Wash. 1964, Idaho 1964, U.S. Dist. Ct. (we. dist.) Wash. 1964, U.S. Ct. Appeals (9th cir.) 1965, U.S. Supreme Ct. 1970, Alaska 1973, U.S. Dist. Ct. Alaska 1973. From assoc. to ptnr. Howard, LeGros, Buchanan & Paul, Seattle, 1964-73; ptnr. Bradbury, Bliss & Riordan, Anchorage, 1973—. Assoc. editor Am. Maritime Cases, Balt., 1973—. Served with U.S. Army, 1961-64. Recipient Carnegie Heroism Found. award, 1961. Mem. Maritime Law Assn. U.S. Roman Catholic. Club: Wash. Athletic. Admiralty, Contracts commercial, Securities. Home: 221 E 7th Ave Anchorage AK 99501 Office: Bradbury Bliss & Riordan 431 7th Ave Anchorgae AK 99501

BRADBURY, TIMOTHY DEWET, lawyer; b. Seattle, June 2, 1944; s. George Wolcott and Louise Margaret (Link) B. B with honors, Wash. State U., 1966; M, Roosevelt U., 1970; JD, U. Chgo., 1972. Bar: Wash. 1972, U.S. Dist. Ct. (we. dist.) Wash. 1972, U.S. Ct. Appeals (9th cir.) 1973, U.S. Tax Ct. 1975. Assoc. Reed, McClure, Moceri & Thonn, Seattle, 1973-78; sole practice Seattle, 1978-87; ptnr. Armstrong, Alsdorf, Bradbury & Maier P.C., Seattle, 1987—. Civilian mem. Seattle Police Disiplinary Rev. Bd., 1978-82; chmn. Wash. State U. Honors Program Endowment Fund, Pullman, 1983-85; bd. dirs. Pike Pl. Market Hist. Commn., Seattle, 1986—. NEH Fellow, 1981. Mem. Wash. State Bar Assn., Seattle-King County Bar Assn. (trustee 1980-83, chmn., treas., trustee young lawyers sect. 1979-83), Wash. Vol. Lawyers for the Arts, Muscular Distrophy Assn. (nat. bd. dirs. 1982—). Democrat. Club: Wash. Athletic (Seattle). State civil litigation, Contracts commercial, Probate. Home: 2723 Boylston Ave E Seattle WA 98102 Office: 705 2d Ave 710 Belmont Pl E Seattle WA 98104

BRADDOCK, DONALD LAYTON, lawyer, accountant; b. Jacksonville, Fla., Dec. 14, 1941; s. John Reddon and Harriet (Burgess) B.; children—Stella Helene, Leslie Ann, Donald Layton. B.S. in Bus. Adminstrn., U. Fla., 1963, J.D., 1967. Bar: Fla. 1968, U.S. Dist. Ct. (mid. and no. dists.) Fla. 1968, U.S. Tax Ct. 1970, U.S. Ct. Appeals (5th cir.) 1968, U.S. Ct. Appeals (4th and 11th cirs.) 1983, U.S. Supreme Ct., 1976; C.P.A., Fla. Staff acct. Coopers and Lybrand, C.P.A.s, 1964-65, Keith C. Austin, C.P.A., 1965-67; assoc. Kent, Durden & Kent, attys. at law, 1967-71; sole practice, 1971-73; ptnr. Howell, Kirby, Montgomery, D'Aiuto & Dean, attys. at law, 1974-76; pres. Howell, Liles, Braddock & Milton, attys. at law, Jacksonville, Fla., 1976—. Bd. dirs. Jacksonville Vocat. Edn. Authority, 1971-75; mem. Jacksonville Bicentennial Commn., 1976; bd. govs. Fla. Bar Found., 1984-86, sec.-treas., 1986—. Served with Air N.G., 1963-69. Mem. Fla. Bar Assn. (bd. govs. young lawyers sect. 1972-77), Fla. Inst. C.P.A.s, Jacksonville C. of C. (com. of 100), Jacksonville Bar Assn. (pres. 1983-84, bd. govs. 1978-84), U. Fla. Alumni Assn. (pres. 1975, bd. dirs. 1968-75), Fla. Blue Key, Phi Delta Phi, Alpha Tau Omega. Clubs: Seminole, Friars, University. Democrat. Baptist. Estate taxation, Civil litigation, General corporate. Office: Howell Liles Braddock & Milton 901 Blackstone Bldg PO Box 420 Jacksonville FL 32201

BRADEN, DANA DANIELLE, Braden, Dana Danielle, lawyer; b. Detroit, June 8, 1951; d. William A. and Majorie L. (Badertscher) B. BA, Mich. State U., 1973; JD, Detroit Coll. Law, 1977; postgrad. U. Miami, 1979-81. Bar: Mich. 1977, Fla. 1978. Asst. bank mgr. Community Nat. Bank, Pontiac, Mich., 1973-76; asst. trust officer Genesee Bank, Flint, Mich., 1976-78; trust officer Sun Banks of Fla., Orlando, 1978-79; assoc. Storms Krasny et al, Melbourne, Fla., 1979, Lake Worth, Fla., 1986—; sole practice, West Palm Beach, 1981-85.Contbr. articles on estate planning and planned giving to profl. jours. Rep. precinct del., 1972; 2d vice chmn. Oakland County Reps., Mich., 1972; bd. dirs. Big Bros./Big Sisters Brevard County, Fla., 1978. Joseph S. Burak scholar, 1977. Mem. ABA, Mich. Bar Assn., Fla. Bar Assn., Martin County Estate Planning Council (co-founder), Planned Giving Council Palm Beach County (co-founder, pres. 1982—), Nat. Assn. Planned Giving Council (co-founder). Congregationalist. Corporate taxation, Estate taxation, Probate. Home: 4000 Shelley Rd S West Palm Beach FL 33407 Office: Raymond & Dillon PC 2290 10th Ave N Penthouse Suite 600 Lake Worth FL 33461-3208

BRADEN, EFREM MARK, lawyer; b. Youngstown, Ohio, June 1, 1951; s. Frank and Margaret (Archer) B.; m. Mckayla Dockum, Aug. 28, 1976; children: Amanda, Marshall. BA, Washington & Lee U., 1973, JD, 1976. Bar: Ohio 1976, U.S. Supreme Ct. 1983. Asst. election counsel Sec. of State, Columbus, Ohio, 1978; elections counsel Sec. of State, Columbus, 1978-79; dep. chief counsel Rep. Nat. Comm., Washington, 1979-81, chief counsel, 1981—. Mem. bi-partisan assessment team Ctr. for Democracy, Boston, 1985, internat. observed delegation U.S. Congress, 1986—. Served as capt. USAR. Mem. ABA, Am. Polit. Sci. Assn., Nat. Rep. Lawyers Assn. Episcopalian. Avocations: golf, skiing. Election law. Home: 3413 Weyssington Way Alexandria VA 22309 Office: Rep Nat Com 310 First St SE Washington DC 20003

BRADEN, EVERETTE ARNOLD, judge circuit court Cook County; b. Chgo., Nov. 3, 1932; s. Zedrick Thomas and Bernice (Beckwith) B.; m. Mary Jeanette Hemphill, Sept. 26, 1964; 1 dau., Marilynne. B.S., Northwestern U., 1954; J.D., John Marshall Law Sch., Chgo., 1961. Bar: Ill. 1969, U.S. Dist. Ct. (no. dist.) Ill. 1969. Trial atty. Cook County Pub. Defender's Office, Chgo., 1969-76, supervising trial atty., 1976-77; assoc. judge Circuit Ct. Cook County, Chgo., 1977—; property and ins. cons. Cook County Dep. Pub. Aid, Chgo., 1961-69. Pres., South Shore Valley Community Orgn.; v.p. Southeast Community Orgn.; bd. dirs. Legal Assistance Found. Chgo., 1977. Mem. Cook County Bar Assn. (pres. 1975-76), Ill. State Bar Assn. (chmn. gen. practice sect. 1979-80), Ill. Bar Found., Ill. Judges Assn. (treas. 1980-81), Ill. Judicial Council (sec. 1982-84, chmn. 1985-86), Phi Alpha Delta, Kappa Alpha Psi. Clubs: Chicago Assembly, Internat. Lions (past v.p.). Judicial administration, Family and matrimonial, Criminal. Office: Circuit Ct Cook County Richard J Daley Center Chicago IL 60602

BRADFORD, BARBARA R., lawyer, business specialist; b. Cleve., June 13, 1948; s. William C. and Martha (Horn) B.; m. Warren N. Davis, Oct. 9, 1976. BA, Pitzer Coll., 1970; JD, Georgetown U., 1975, MBA, 1985. Bar: N.Y. 1976, D.C. 1976. Atty. advisor Agy. Internat. Devel. Dept. State, Washington, 1978-83, asst. dir. trade and devel. program, 1986—; pres. Georgetown Export Trading Co., Washington, 1984—. Bd. dirs. Jr. League, Washington, 1977-78; com. chairperson Fed. Bar Assn., 1981-82. Office: US Dept State Room 301 SA-16 Washington DC 20523

BRADFORD, CHARLES STEVEN, lawyer, educator; b. Waxahachie, Tex., Mar. 14, 1956; s. Charles Randel Bradford and Bettie Jean (Adams) Johnston; m. Meg Clark, Sept. 16, 1977; children: Jason Clark, Allison Marie, John David. BS magna cum laude, Utah State U., 1978; JD magna cum laude, M Pub. Policy, Harvard U., 1982. Bar: Tex. 1982, U.S. Dist. Ct. (no. dist.) Tex. 1982, U.S. Ct. Appeals (5th cir.) 1983. Assoc. Jenkens & Gilchrist, Dallas, 1982-86; asst. prof. U. Nebr., Lincoln, 1987—; vis. asst. prof. So. Meth. U. Law Sch., Dallas, 1986-87. Mem. Duncanville (Tex.) Transp. Task Force, 1983, Southwest Dallas County Dems.; del. Tex. Dem. Conv., Austin, 1986. Mem. Dallas Bar Assn. (speakers com. 1986), Tex. Young Lawyers Assn. (legis. com. 1983-84, moot ct. com. and consumer affairs com. 1985-86). Avocations: religious studies, basketball, photography. Federal civil litigation, State civil litigation, General corporate. Home: 426 Blueridge Dr Duncanville TX 75137 Office: U Nebr Lincoln Coll of Law Lincoln NE 68583-0902

BRADIE, PETER RICHARD, lawyer, engineer; b. Bklyn., Feb. 19, 1937; s. Alexander Robert and Blanche Sylvia (Silverman) B.; m. Anna Barbara Corcoran, Jan. 22, 1960; children: Suzanne J., Barbara L., Michael S. BSME, Fairleigh Dickinson U., 1960; JD, South Tex. Coll. Law, 1978. Bar: Tex. 1978, U.S. Dist. Ct. (so. dist.) Tex. 1981; registered profl. engr. Ala., Tex. Performance engr. Pratt & Whitney Aircraft, West Palm Beach, Fla., 1961-63; sr. engr. Hayes Internat. Corp., Huntsville, Ala., 1963-64, Lockheed Missiles and Space, Huntsville, 1964-68; fluids engr. Double A Products Co., Manchester, Mich., 1968-69; cons. Spectrum Controls, Montvale, N.J., 1969-72; sr. project mgr. Materials Research Corp., Orangeburg, N.Y., 1972-74; sr. contracts adminstr. Brown & Root Inc., Houston, 1974-85; sole practice Houston, 1985—; counsel Inverness Forest C.A., Houston, 1978-80; sr. counsel Raymond-Brown & Raymond-Molem, J.V., Houston, 1982-84. Contbr. articles on fluidic controls to mags.; patentee. Dem. committeeman Bergen County, Haworth, N.J., 1959; del. Harris County Reps., Houston, 1984; officer, bd. dirs. Inverness Forest Civic Assn., Houston, 1975-78. Served to 2d lt. USMCR, 1958-61. Mem. ABA, Tex. Bar Assn., Houston Bar Assn., Houston Northwest Bar Assn. (treas. 1986), Assn. Trial Lawyers Am., Houston Trial Lawyers Assn., Comml. Law League Am. Republican. Jewish. Lodges: Rotary (Montvale bd. dirs. 1973-74). Avocations: classical music, history, computers. Consumer commercial, Contracts commercial, General practice. Home: 22007 Kenchester Houston TX 77073 Office: 400 FM 1960 W #154 Houston TX 77090

BRADIGAN, BRIAN JAY, lawyer; b. Dunkirk, N.Y., Mar. 3, 1951; s. Neal Andrew and Patricia Ann (Drake) B. m. Pamela Louise Schiffer, July 24, 1982; 1 child, Laura Anne. BA, Grove City Coll., 1973; JD, Capital U., 1981. Bar: Ohio 1981, U.S. Dist. Ct. (so. dist.) Ohio 1982, U.S. Ct. Appeals (6th cir.) 1983, U.S. Supreme Ct. 1986. Tchr. Akron (N.Y.) Central Sch., 19778; assoc. Hamilton, Kramer, Myers & Cheek, Columbus, Ohio, 1981-85, ptnr., 1985—. Mem. ABA, Ohio Bar Assn., Columbus Bar Assn. (common pleas ct. com. 1985—), Ohio Acad. Civil Trial Attys., Def. Research Inst. (ins. law com. 1985—). Republican. Club: Athletic (Columbus). Avocations: golf, travel, history. Insurance, State civil litigation, Federal civil litigation. Home: 1136 Kingslea Rd Columbus OH 43209 Office: Hamilton Kramer Myers & Cheek 17 S High St Suite 920 Columbus OH 43215

BRADING, STANLEY GATEWOOD, JR., lawyer; b. Sumter, S.C., Apr. 5, 1954; s. Stanley Gatewood Sr. and Gene (Boyle) B.; m. Nancy Clark, July 4, 1981; children: Mary Blair, Stanley Clark. AB, Duke U., 1974; JD, Washington & Lee U., 1979; LLM, Emory U., 1984. Bar: Ga. 1979. Assoc. McClain, Mellen, Bowling & Hickman, Atlanta, 1979-81; assoc. O'Callaghan, Saunders & Stumm, Atlanta, 1981-84, ptnr., 1984—; legal counsel Atlanta Jaycees, 1981-84. Mem. Ga. Bar Assn. (bd. dirs. younger lawyers sect. 1984-86), Atlanta Council Younger Lawyers (bd. dirs. 1984-86), Atlanta Duke Alumni Assn. (pres. 1984—), Washington & Lee Atlanta Alumni Club (bd. dirs. 1984—). Securities, Corporate taxation, Real property. Home: 2171 Brookview Dr NW Atlanta GA 30318 Office: O'Callaghan Saunders & Stumm 6201 Powers Ferry Rd Suite 330 Atlanta GA 30339

BRADLEY, CHARLES HARVEY, JR., lawyer; b. Indpls., July 17, 1923; s. Charles Harvey and Carolyn (Coffin) B.; m. Mary Jo Albright, Aug. 26, 1944; children: Sally A., Jane C. A.B., Yale U., 1945, LL.B., 1949. Bar: Ind. 1949. Ptnr., Thomson, O'Neal & Smith, Indpls., 1950-60; mgr. legal dept. Eli Lilly and Co., Indpls., 1960-63, asst. sec., dir. legal div., 1963, sec., gen. counsel, 1964-84, v.p., gen. counsel, 1984—, also dir.; bd. dirs. Indpls. Water Co. Mem. com. on character and fitness Ind. Supreme Ct. Served to 2d lt. USMC, 1943-45, to capt., 1952-53. Decorated Air medal with 8 oakleaf clusters, D.F.C. with 3 oakleaf clusters. Fellow Ind. Bar Found.; mem. ABA (com. on corp. law depts.), Ind. Bar Assn., Indpls. Bar Assn., Assn. Gen. Counsel (exec. com.), Indpls. Lawyers Club, Indpls. Legal Aid Soc., Yale Law Sch. Assn., Indpls. C. of C. (bd. dirs.). Clubs: Yale of Ind., Indpls. Athletic, Meridian Hills Country, University (Indpls). Home: 1310 S State Rd 421 Zionsville IN 46077 Office: Eli Lilly and Co Lilly Corporate Ctr Indianapolis IN 46285

BRADLEY, GEORGE HAVIS, lawyer; b. Warren, Ark., May 31, 1937; s. James Harvey Hawley and Dixie (Stringer) B. AB, Mercer U., 1959; JD, U. Tenn., 1971. Atty. estate tax IRS, Wilmington, Del., 1972-75; tax law specialist legis. and regulations div. office of chief counsel IRS, Washington, 1975—; fed. register liaison officer IRS, Washington, 1977—. Pres. Literacy Council No. Va., Alexandria, 1980-81, v.p., 1982; sec. Alexandria Community Mental Health Ctr., 1978; literacy tutor Refugee Edn. and Employment Program, Arlington, Va., 1985—. Served to lt. USN, 1962-66. Recipient Outstanding Service award, Literacy Council No. Va., 1980-83, Vol. Learning Program, 1978-81, Alexandria Community Mental Health Ctr., 1978-80, Refugee Unaccompanied Minors Program, 1986. Mem. ABA, Tenn. Bar Assn., Phi Alpha Delta. Episcopalian. Avocations: tennis, squash, literacy tutoring, refugee assistance. Personal income taxation. Home: 3800 N Fairfax Dr #401 Arlington VA 22203 Office: IRS Legis and Regulations Div Office of Chief Counsel 1111 Constitution Ave NW Washington DC 20224

BRADLEY, LEE CARRINGTON, JR., lawyer; b. Charlottesville, Va., Sept. 27, 1897; s. Lee C. and Eleanor (Lyons) B.; m. Mary Allen Northington, Jan. 9, 1924; children—Lee Carrington, Merrill Northington, Mary Earle (Mrs. Murray). Litt.B., Princeton, 1918; LL.B., Harvard, 1921. Bar: Ala. bar 1921. Since practiced in Birmingham; partner firm Bradley, Arant, Rose & White (and predecessors), 1922—. Mem. Phi Beta Kappa. Episcopalian. Club: Rotarian. Home: 2844 Carlisle Rd Birmingham AL 35213 Office: Park Pl Tower Birmingham AL 35203

BRADLEY, PAUL ANTHONY, lawyer; b. Wilmington, Del., Aug. 17, 1955; s. Charles H. and Mary L. (Brunhammer) B.; m. Karen Anne Murphy, Jan. 24, 1981; 1 child, Kathryn Anne. Bar: Ill. 1981, U.S. Dist. Ct. (no. dist.) Ill. 1981, Del. 1983, U.S. Dist. Ct. Del. 1983. Law clk. to presiding justice Illinois Supreme Ct., Ottawa, 1981-82; assoc. Howard M. Berg & Assocs., Wilmington, 1982-85, Biggs & Battaglia, Wilmington, 1985—. Mem. ABA (chmn. subcom. on bad faith claims 1985—, vice chmn. comml. torts com. 1986), Del. Bar Assn., Am. Judicature Soc. State civil litigation, Personal injury, Contracts commercial. Office: Biggs & Battaglia 1206 Mellon Bank Ctr Wilmington DE 19801

BRADNER, JAMES HOLLAND, JR., lawyer; b. Cleve., Nov. 28, 1941; s. James Holland and Georgena Knight (Gray) B.; m. Elizabeth Jean Elliot, Mar. 12, 1968; children: Alexandra Elizabeth, James Elliot, Carolyn Holland. BA, Bowdoin Coll., 1963; JD, Ohio State U., 1966; MBA, U. Chgo., 1977. Bar: Ohio 1967, U.S. Dist. Ct. (no. dist.) Ohio 1969, U.S. Ct. Mil. Appeals 1973, U.S. Supreme Ct. 1975, Ill. 1979, D.C. 1979, U.S. Dist. Ct. (no. dist.) Ill. 1981. Assoc. Stephen J. Knerly, Cleve., 1969-72; counsel Bar Assn. Greater Cleve., 1972-74; asst. dir. Ctr. Profl. Discipline ABA, Chgo., 1974-78; sr. atty. Econ. Crime Project Nat. Dist. Attys. Assn., Chgo., 1979-80; practice law, Highland Park, Ill., 1980; ptnr. Bradner & Studzinski, Chgo., 1981; practice law, Chgo., 1982, Lake Forest, Ill., 1982-84; counsel Alliance of Am. Insurers, Schaumburg, Ill., 1984-86, asst. gen. counsel 1986—; pres. Heller-Aller Co., Napoleon, Ohio, 1981-85, chief exec. officer, 1985—; lectr. law Ill. Inst. Tech./Chgo. Kent Coll. Law, Chgo., 1979-83; mem. bd. control com. for Inter-Dist. Cooperation Ins. Coop., Highland Park, 1985—; mem. Task Force on Alternate Dispute Resolution of Spl. Commn. Adminstrn. of Justice, Cook County, Ill., 1985—. Rep. committeeman Deerfield Twp. Precinct 63, Lake County, Ill., 1978—; commr., East Skokie Drainage Dist., Lake County, 1981—; deacon First Presbyn. Ch., Lake Forest, 1983; community organizer Woodlands Assn., Highland Park, 1975-77. Served to capt. U.S. Army, 1967-69. Mem. ABA, D.C. Bar Assn., Bar Assn. Greater Cleve., Theta Delta Chi. Republican. Presbyterian. Club: Union League (Chgo.). Contbr. articles to profl. jours. State civil litigation, Federal civil litigation, General corporate. Home: 695 Euclid Ave Highland Park IL 60035 Office: 1501 Woodfield Rd Suite 400 W Schaumburg IL 60173-4980

BRADSHAW, ALICE LINDA, lawyer; b. Salem, Ind., June 11, 1957; d. James Russell and Ella Watson (Browne) B. BA, Georgetown Coll., 1979; JD, U. Ky., 1982. Bar: Ky. 1982, U.S. Tax Ct. 1983, U.S. Dist. Ct. (ea. dist.) Ky. 1984, U.S. Supreme Ct. 1986. Counsel Hist. Themson Subdiv.,

Winchester, 1982-86; Blue Grass Turst, Lexington, 1984-86. Mem. ABA, Ky. Bar Assn., Am. Trial Lawyers Assn., LWV, Hon. Order Ky. Cols., Rockhounds of Cen. Ky. (v.p. 1987). Republican. Presbyterian. Club: Blue Grass Gem & Mineral (Lexington) (sec. 1984). Avocations: lapidary, stained glass. Bankruptcy, Family and matrimonial, Criminal. Office: 31 N Main St Winchester KY 40391

BRADSHAW, LESLIE ARNOLD, lawyer; b. Louisville, Dec. 3, 1938; s. Tuncill Walker Bradshaw and Ruth (Arnold) Bradshaw Haefling; m. Susan Conrad Edgerton, Apr. 27, 1962 (div. June 1975); children—S. Elizabeth E. Bradshaw DiPasquale, Mary M., Eric E.; m. Sharon Kelly Sayers, July 16, 1975. A.B., Ind. U., 1959, J.D., 1962. Bar: Ind. 1962, N.Y. 1968, U.S. Dist. Ct. (so. dist.) Ind. 1962, U.S. Dist. Ct. (we. dist.) N.Y. 1968, U.S. Ct. Appeals (3d cir.) 1976, U.S. Ct. Appeals (2d cir.) 1979, U.S. Ct. Mil. Appeals 1969, U.S. Supreme Ct. 1969. Law clk. Ind. Ct. Appeals, Indpls., 1962; editor, research writer Lawyers Co-op. Pub. Co., Rochester, N.Y., 1965-69; appellate atty. Monroe County Pub. Defenders Office, Rochester, 1969-75; assoc. Presutti & Leonardo, Rochester, 1975-76; ptnr. Bradshaw & Sayers, Rochester, 1979-82; sole practice, Rochester, 1976-79, 82—. Contbr. articles to profl. jours. Bd. dirs. Jail Ministry, Rochester; legal cons. Prison Action Group, Rochester. Served to capt. USAF, 1962-65. Mem. N.Y. State Bar Assn., N.Y. State Defenders Assn., Phi Delta Phi. Democrat. Unitarian. Criminal, Family and matrimonial. Home: 65 Sunset Dr Rochester NY 14618 Office: 100 Exec Office Bldg 36 W Main St Rochester NY 14614

BRADSHAW, PENNI PEARSON, lawyer; b. Bradenton, Fla., Oct. 14, 1954; d. Walter Loyall and Lois Elna (Grumstrup) P.; m. Michael Ray Bradshaw, May 3, 1986. AB, Randolph-Macon Woman's Coll., 1977; JD, U. N.C., 1980. Bar: N.C. 1980, U.S. Dist. Ct. (mid. dist.) N.C. 1980, U.S. Ct. Appeals (4th cir.) 1981, U.S. Supreme Ct. 1985. Assoc. Petree, Stockton & Robinson, Winston-Salem, N.C., 1980-86, ptnr., 1987—; adj. instr. U. N.C. Law Sch., Chapel Hill, 1980-85, Wake Forest U. Law Sch., Winston-Salem, 1986—. Research editor N.C. Law Rev., 1979-80. Vice chmn. Habitat for Humanity Forsyth County, Inc., Winston-Salem, 1985-86; vice chmn. Food Bank Northwest N.C., Winston-Salem, 1985, bd. dirs., 1981—; bd. dirs. Crimestoppers, Winston-Salem, 1984—, northwest N.C. Chpt. ARC, Winston-Salem, 1985—; sec. Salvation Army Girl's Club Council, Winston-Salem, 1982—. Mem. ABA, N.C. Bar Assn. (litigation sect., labor and employment sect.), Forsyth County Bar Assn., Forsyth County Young Lawyers Assn. (sec. 1984-85). Democrat. Baptist. Avocations: tennis, whitewater rafting, backpacking. Labor, Federal civil litigation, State civil litigation. Home: 2631 Forest Dr Winston-Salem NC 27104 Office: Petree Stockton & Robinson 1001 W 4th St Winston-Salem NC 27101

BRADSHAW, THOMAS MICHAEL, lawyer; b. St. Louis, Dec. 12, 1942; s. William J. and Sheila (Hannon) B.; m. Marilyn J. Gulotta; children: Patrick J., Jodie A., Sean W., W. Michael. BA, Rockhurst Coll., 1964; JD, U. Mo., 1969. Bar: Mo. 1969, U.S. Dist. Ct. (we. dist.) Mo. 1969, U.S. Ct. Appeals (8th cir.) 1973, U.S. Supreme Ct. 1979, U.S. Tax Ct. 1982, U.S. Ct. Appeals (10th cir.) 1982. Fed. pub. defender, Kansas City, Mo., 1973-79; ptnr. Hoskins, King, McGannon, & Hahn, Kansas City, 1980—; instr. Ct. adminstrn. and criminal process, Rockhurst Coll., 1977-79. Mem. Kansas City Bar Assn., ABA (litigation sect.), Mo. Bar Assn., Lawyers Assn. Kansas City, Assn. Trial Lawyers Am., Nat. Bd. Trial Advocacy (cert. criminal trial advocate), Def. Research Inst. Democrat. Roman Catholic. Clubs: Kansas City Athletic, Hibernians. Contbr. articles to profl. jours. Business litigation, Criminal, Personal injury. Office: Hoskins King et al Commerce Trust Bldg Suite 1100 Kansas City MO 64106

BRADSHAW, WILLIAM ELBERT, lawyer; b. Kingsport, Tenn., Oct. 7, 1947; s. Hugh Lowell and Margaret Louise (Wolfe) B.; m. Grace Currie, Jan. 27, 1973; children—Sara Elizabeth, Rachel Margaret. B.A., U. Va., 1970, J.D., 1973. Bar: Va. 1973, Pa. 1979. Sole practice, 1973-75; with Westmoreland Coal Co., 1975—, counsel eastern ops., Big Stone Gap, Va., 1975-78, dir. legal and govtl. affairs, 1978-79, gen. counsel, Phila., 1979—, sec., 1982—. Mem. ABA, Va. Bar Assn., Pa. Bar Assn., Am. Soc. Corporate Secs. Republican. Presbyterian. Club: Racquet (Phila.). Administrative and regulatory, General corporate, Environment. Office: Westmoreland Coal Co 2500 Fidelity Bldg Philadelphia PA 19109

BRADY, EDMUND MATTHEW, JR., lawyer; b. Detroit, Apr. 24, 1941; s. Edmund Matthew and Thelma (McDonald) B.; m. Marie Pierre Wayne, May 14, 1966; children—Edmund Matthew III, Meghan, Timothy. B.S.S., John Carroll U., 1963; J.D., U. Detroit, 1966; postgrad. Wayne State U., 1966-69. Bar: Mich. 1966, U.S. Dist. Ct. (ea. dist.) Mich. 1966, U.S. Ct. Appeals (6th cir.) 1973, U.S. Supreme Ct. 1974. Ptnr. Vandeveer, Garzia, Tonkin, Kerr, Heaphy, Moore, Sills & Poling, P.C., Detroit, 1973—. Village clk. Grosse Pointe Shores, Mich., 1975-80, trustee, 1980—; trustee St. Clair Ambulatory Care Corp., Detroit, 1984—; trustee Grosse Pointe Acad., Mich., 1977-83, adv. trustee, 1983—; pres., dir. Grosse Pointe Hockey Assn., 1969-70; bd. dirs., chmn. major gifts div. First Fund, St. John Hosp. Guild; bd. dirs., pres. Friends of Bon Secours Hosp. Recipient award of distinction U. Detroit Law Alumni, 1981. Mem. Am. Arbitration Assn., ABA, Internat. Assn. Ins. Counsel, Am. Judicature Soc., Am. Soc. Law and Medicine, Assn. Def. Trial Counsel (dir. 1975-80, pres. 1980-81), Mich. Defense Trial Counsel (dir. 1980-81), Def. Research Inst. (Exceptional Performance citation, Detroit, 1981), Catholic Lawyers Soc., Soc. Irish-Am. Lawyers (founding dir. 1979-81), Mich. Soc. Hosp. Attys., Mediation Tribunal Assn. (mem. panel Wayne County), Detroit Bar Assn. (dir. 1986—), State Bar Mich., Delta Theta Phi. Republican. Roman Catholic. Clubs: Country of Detroit (Grosse Pointe); Detroit Athletic. State civil litigation, Federal civil litigation, Personal injury. Office: 333 W Fort St Suite 1600 Detroit MI 48226

BRADY, GEORGE CHARLES, III, lawyer; b. Darby, Pa., Mar. 13, 1947; s. George Charles Jr. and Lillian (Foster) B.; m. Joan Ann Kilkenny, Apr. 27, 1973; children—Jeffrey, Stephanie, Brent. A.B., Holy Cross Coll., 1969; J.D., Villanova U., 1972. Bar: Pa. 1972, U.S. Dist. Ct. (ea. dist.) Pa. 1972. Assoc. McDonnell & McDonnell, Drexel Hill, Pa., 1972-74; asst. dist. atty. Montgomery County, Pa., 1974-76; ptnr. Cox & Brady, Conshohocken, Pa., 1976-81; sole practice, Conshohocken, 1981-83; ptnr. Baughman & Brady, Conshohocken, 1983-85, Pizonka & Brady, Norristown, Pa., 1985—; dir. Personnel Data Systems, Conshohocken. Mem. Villanova Law Sch. Alumni Assn. (pres. 1980). Republican. Roman Catholic. Club: Whitemarsh Valley Country. General corporate, State civil litigation, General practice. Home: 372 Jamestown Circle Eagleville PA 19403 Office: Pizonka & Brady 18 W Airy St Norristown PA 19401

BRADY, LAWRENCE JOSEPH, lawyer; b. Mt. Kisco, N.Y., Nov. 24, 1954; s. Lawrence Peter and Mary Frances (Sellmeyer) B.; m. Debbie Reva Kagan, May 26, 1980; 1 child, Benjamin Kagan. BA in Polit. Sci., U. Ark., Fayetteville, 1977; JD, Washington U., St. Louis, 1980. Bar: Ark. 1980, U.S. Dist. Ct. Ark. 1981. Law clk. to presiding justice Ark. Supreme Ct., Little Rock, 1980-81; from assoc. to ptnr. Hoover, Jacobs & Storey, Little Rock, 1981—. Mem. ABA, Ark. Bar Assn., Pulaski County Bar Assn., Phi Beta Kappa. Roman Catholic. General practice, Banking, Real property. Office: Hoover Jacobs & Storey 945 Savers Bldg Little Rock AR 72201

BRADY, MATTHEW JOSEPH, lawyer; b. Springfield, Mass., May 19, 1952; s. Bernard D. and Alice M. (McKenna) B.; m. Susan O. Storey, Sept. 8, 1984. BA, U. Mass., 1974; JD, U. Conn., 1981. Bar: Conn. 1981, U.S. Dist. Ct. Conn. 1981, Mass. 1982. Assoc. Caruso and Brady, Farmington, Conn., 1981-82, The Marcus Law Firm and Marcus and Burns, New Haven, 1982—. Mem. ABA (forum com. on construction industry), Conn. Bar Assn. (exec. com. Young Lawyers sect. 1984—), New Haven County Bar Assn., Mass. Bar Assn., Assn. Trial Lawyers Am., Conn. Trial Lawyers Assn. Democrat. Roman Catholic. Club: Duck Island Yacht (Westbrook, Conn.). Avocations: sailing, backpacking, writing. Construction, Federal civil litigation, State civil litigation. Home: Rural Rt 2 #334 Durham CT 06042 Office: The Marcus Law Firm 111 Whitney Ave New Haven CT 06510

BRADY, ROBERT LINDSAY, publisher; b. Titusville, Pa., July 3, 1946. BA, U. Notre Dame, 1971; JD, U. Conn., 1978. Bar: Conn. 1980. Mng. editor Official Assoc. Polit. Almanac, Essex, Conn., 1971-74; v.p. editorial Inst. for Mgmt., Old Saybrook, Conn., 1974-78; pres., pubs. Bus. and Legal Reports, Madison, Conn., 1978—. Labor. Office: Bus and Legal Reports 64 Wall St Madison CT 06443

BRADY, ROBERT MICHAEL, lawyer; b. Pawtucket, R.I., Apr. 2, 1949; s. Frank J. and Doris I. (DonCarlos) B. BA, Providence Coll., 1971; JD, New England Sch. Law, 1978. Bar: Mass. 1978, R.I. 1978, U.S. Dist. Ct. R.I. 1978. Law clk. R.I. Supreme/Superior Cts., 1978-79; assoc. Alan T. Dworkin, Ltd., Warwick, R.I., 1980-82; ptnr. Dworkin & Brady, Warwick, 1982—. Mem. Assn. Trial Lawyers Am., R.I. Bar Assn., Mass. Bar Assn. Roman Catholic. Personal injury, Real property, Probate. Home: 8 Beach Tree Rd Rumford RI 02916 Office: Dworkin & Brady 164 Airport Rd Warwick RI 02920

BRADY, RUPERT JOSEPH, lawyer; b. Washington, Jan. 24, 1932; s. John Bernard and Mary Catherine (Rupert) B.; m. Maureen Mary MacIntosh, Apr. 20, 1954; children: Rupert Joseph Jr., Laureen, Kevin, Warren, Jeanine, Jacqueline, Brian, Barton. BEE, Cath. U. Am., 1953; JD, Georgetown U., 1959. Bar: Md. 1961, D.C. 1962, U.S. Patent Office 1961, D.C. 1962, U.S. Supreme Ct. 1969, U.S. Ct. Appeals (fed. cir.) 1961. Elec. engr. Sperry Gyroscope Co., L.I., 1953-56; patent specifications writer John B. Brady, patent atty., 1956-59; patent agt. B.P. Fishburne, Jr., Washington, 1959-61; pvt. practice patent agt., Washington, 1961; practice, Washington, 1961—; sr. ptnr. Brady, O'Boyle & Gates, Washington, 1963—. Mem. ABA, Am. Patent Law Assn., Md. Patent Law Assn., Am. Intellectual Property Law Assn. Republican. Roman Catholic. Club: Senator's Alumni. Patentee crane, booms, moldboard support assembly. Patent, Trademark and copyright. Home: 7201 Pyle Rd Bethesda MD 20817 Office: 920 Chevy Chase Bldg 5530 Wisconsin Ave Chevy Chase MD 20815

BRADY, WILLIAM JOHN, JR., lawyer; b. Rockville Center, N.Y., Aug. 9, 1946; s. William John Sr. and Marie Elizabeth (Downing) B.; m. Helen Kourlis, Dec. 30, 1973; children: Stephanie, Aristea. BA, St. John's U., N.Y.C., 1968; MA, U. Denver, 1974, JD, 1977. Bar: Colo. 1978, U.S. Dist. Ct. Colo. 1978, U.S. Ct. Appeals (10th cir.) 1978. Mng. ptnr. Berkowitz, Berkowitz & Brady, Denver, 1977—; asst. atty. Lakewood (Colo.) City Atty.'s Office, 1978-79, 79—; asst. city atty. Littleton, Colo., 1979—. Dir., writer: The Cornerston, 1975. Mem. Assn. Trial Lawyers Am., Colo. Trial Lawyers Assn. Personal injury, Local government, State civil litigation. Office: Berkowitz Berkowitz & Brady 1775 Sherman Suite 1700 Denver CO 80203

BRAGAR, RAYMOND AARON, lawyer; b. Long Branch, N.J., Apr. 12, 1946; s. Paul and Arline N. (Goldberg) B.; m. Sandy Ellen Schenkman, Aug. 12, 1972; children: Courtney Hope, Adam Ross. BA in Philosophy, Rutgers U., 1968; JD, Harvard U., 1972. Bar: N.Y. 1973, U.S. Dist. Ct. (so. and ea. dists.) N.Y. 1974, U.S. Ct. Appeals (2d cir.) 1974. Law clk. U.S. Dist Ct. (so. dist.) N.Y., N.Y.C., 1972-73; assoc. Rosenman, Colin, Freund et al, N.Y.C., 1973, Hammond & Schreiber, N.Y.C., 1973-75, Otterbourg, Steindler, Houston et al, N.Y.C., 1976-79; ptnr. Bragar, Spiegel, Garfunkel, Rubin & Driggin, N.Y.C., 1979-82; sole practice N.Y.C., 1982-84; ptnr. Bragar & Wexler, N.Y.C., 1984—. Co-author: Sanctions Rule 11 and Other Powers, 1986. Mem. ABA (fed. procedure com.), N.Y. State Bar Assn. (civil practice law and rules com.). Democrat. Jewish. Federal civil litigation, State civil litigation, Real property. Office: Bragar & Wexler 900 3d Ave New York NY 10022

BRAGG, ELLIS MEREDITH, JR., lawyer; b. Washington, Jan. 30, 1947; s. Ellis Meredith Sr. and Lucille (Tingstrum) B.; m. Judith Owens, Aug. 18, 1968; children: Michael Andrew, Jennifer Meredith. BA, King Coll., 1969; JD, Wake Forest U., 1973. Bar: N.C. 1973, U.S. Dist. Ct. (we. and mid. dists.) N.C. 1974, U.S. Ct. Appeals (4th cir.) 1980. Assoc. Bailey, Brackett & Brackett, P.A., Charlotte, N.C., 1973-76; ptnr. Howard & Bragg, Charlotte, 1976-77, McConnell, Howard, Johnson, Pruitt, Jenkins & Bragg, Charlotte, 1977-79; sole practice Charlotte, 1979—. Dist. chmn. Mecklenburg County Dems., Charlotte, 1978; coach youth soccer program YMCA, Charlotte, 1982-83; mem. Headstart Policy Council, Charlotte, 1985—. Mem. ABA, N.C. Bar Assn., N.C. Acad. Trial Lawyers, Am. Judicature Soc. Presbyterian. Avocations: reading, jogging, gardening. General practice, State civil litigation, Family and matrimonial. Home: 6407 Honegger Dr Charlotte NC 28211 Office: 210 Barclays Am Ctr 500 E Morehead St Charlotte NC 28202

BRAGG, MICHAEL ELLIS, lawyer; b. Holdrege, Nebr., Oct. 6, 1947; s. Lionel C. and Frances E. (Klinginsmith) B.; m. Nancy Jo Aabel, Jan. 19, 1980; children: Brian Michael, Kyle Christopher. B.A., U. Nebr., 1971, J.D., 1975. Bar: Alaska 1976, U.S. Dist. Ct. Alaska 1976, Nebr. 1976, U.S. Dist. Ct. Nebr. 1976. Assoc. White & Jones Anchorage, 1976-77; field rep. State Farm Ins., Anchorage, 1977-79, atty. corp. law dept., Bloomington, Ill., 1979-81, sr. atty., 1981-84, asst. counsel, 1984-86, counsel, 1986—. Contbr. articles to profl. jours. Bd. dirs. Friends of Arts, Bloomington, 1984-85. lectr., contbr. legal seminars; Served with USNG, 1970-76. Mem. ABA (vice chmn. property ins. com., corp. counsel and antitrust coms., arrangement chmn. torts and ins. practices sect. 1987), Am. Corp. Counsel Assn., Internat. Platform Assn. Republican. Mem. Unitarian Ch. Club: Crestwicke Country. Insurance, Administrative and regulatory, Legislative. Office: State Farm Ins Cos 1 State Farm Plaza Suite E-6 Bloomington IL 61710

BRAID, FREDERICK DONALD, lawyer; b. N.Y.C., Aug. 10, 1946; s. Donald Michael and Margaret Anna (Fluty) B.; m. Eleanor Mae Friedman, Oct. 23, 1980; children: Andrew Harris, Roy Leal. BS in Econs., St. John's U., Jamaica, N.Y., 1968; JD, St. John's U., Bklyn., 1971; LLM, NYU, 1979. Bar: N.Y. 1972, U.S. Dist. Ct. (so. and ea. dists.) N.Y. 1973, U.S. Ct. Appeals (2d cir.) 1973, U.S. Supreme Ct. 1975. Assoc. Rains & Pogrebin, Mineola and N.Y.C., N.Y., 1971-77, ptnr., 1978—; bd. dirs. Rains & Pogrebin, P.C., Mineola and N.Y.C., N.Y. Contbr. articles to profl. jours. Served to capt. USAR, 1972-80. St. Thomas More scholar, St. John's U. Sch. Law, 1968-71. Mem. ABA, N.Y. Bar Assn., Assn. Trial Lawyers Am., Nassau County Bar Assn., Omicron Delta Epsilon, Delta Mu Delta. Labor, Federal civil litigation, State civil litigation. Home: 17 E 96th St New York NY 10128 Office: Rains & Pogrebin PC 210 Old Country Rd Mineola NY 11501

BRAINARD, H OGDEN, lawyer; b. Vincennes, Ind., Mar. 6, 1905; s. Claude O. and Myrtle Elizabeth (Newman) B.; m. Bertie Elizabeth Tate, Feb. 6, 1937. JD, U. Ill., 1933; LLD (hon.), Eastern Ill. U., 1973. Bar: Ill. 1933, U.S. Dist. Ct. (ea. dist.) Ill. 1938, U.S. Supreme Ct. 1954. Ptnr. Brainard, Bower & Kramer, Charleston, Ill., 1935—; fed. conciliation commr. U.S. Dist. Ct. (ea. dist.) Ill., Danville, 1939-41; city atty., Charleston, 1941-44; twp. atty., Charleston, 1941-58. Precinct committeeman Ill. Reps., Charleston, 1959-82; pres. Eastern Ill. U. Found., Charleston, 1981-82, bd. dirs., 1955-73, 1980—. Named Alumnus of Month U. Ill. Law Sch., 1970. Fellow Am. Bar Found., Ill. Bar Found.; mem. ABA (vice chmn. ct. modernization com. 1972-75, standing com. on profl. career devel., ho. dels. 1969-79), Ill. Bar Assn. (pres. 1970-71, v.p. 1969-70, bd. govs. 1963-67, chmn. inst. legal edn. 1962-69, chmn. fed. judiciary appointments com. 1971-75, various others), Coles County Bar Assn. (pres. 1952-53), Am. Judicature Soc., Eastern Ill. U. Alumni Assn. (pres. 1957-58), Phi Alpha Delta. Lodges: Rotary (pres. Charleston), Masons (worshipful master Charleston 1938). Avocations: golf, reading. General practice, State civil litigation, Probate. Home: 1202 Monroe Ave Charleston IL 61920 Office: Brainard Bower & Kramer 600 Jackson Ave Charleston IL 61920

BRAINARD, JAMES C., lawyer; b. Manhattan, Kans., June 8, 1954; s. Jack D. and Dortha R. (Stucky) B.; m. Elizabeth Hackl, Oct. 19, 1985; 1 child, John Walter. BA, Butler U., 1976; postgrad., U. San Diego, Oxford, Eng., 1981; JD, Ohio No. U., 1982. Bar: Ind. 1982, U.S. Dist. Ct. (no. and so. dists.) Ind. 1982, U.S. Ct. Appeals (7th cir.) 1982. Sole practice Indpls., 1982—; adj. faculty U. Indpls., 1984—. Mem. ABA, Ind. Bar Assn., Indpls. Bar Assn. General corporate, Real property, Consumer commercial. Office: 1 N Capitol Suite 444 Indianapolis IN 46204

BRAINIS, LEON IRVING, lawyer; b. Shreveport, La., Feb. 25, 1937; s. Z. and Betty Brainis; m. Jacqlyn Moore, Jan. 16, 1981; children: Jan, Melissa, Benjamin. BS in Geology, La. State U., 1959; JD, Loyola U., New Orleans, 1965. Bar: La. 1965, U.S. Dist. Ct. (ea. dist.) La. 1965, U.S. Ct. Appeals (5th cir.) 1968, U.S. Supreme Ct. 1972. Ptnr. Le Brun, Karno, Lockhart and Brainis, New Orleans, 1965-72; mem. Karno, Lockhart and Brainis, 1972-75; ptnr. Lea, Lilley and Brainis, 1975-77; sole practice New Orleans, 1977—; juvenile judge ad hoc, 1975, first Parish Ct. judge ad hoc, 1976. Mem. Jefferson Parish (La.) Sch. Bd., 1970-74, 77-80. Served to capt. U.S. Army, 1959-67. Recipient Martin Luther King Jr. Atty. award, 1983. Mem. ABA, Assn. Trial Lawyers Am., La. Trial Lawyers Assn. (bd. govs. 1969, Recognition award 1980). Republican. Presbyterian. Lodges: Rotary, Shriners. Personal injury, Criminal, Family and matrimonial. Office: 716 Williams Blvd PO Box 111 Kenner LA 70063

BRAKE, ROBERT M., lawyer; b. Detroit, Sept. 30, 1926; m. Eileen Murphy, Nov. 15, 1952; children: Daniel, Katrina, Christopher, Eileen Roberta. Student, Wayne State U., 1944-47, U. Chgo., 1947-48; JD, U. Mich., 1950. Bar: Fla. 1951, Mich. 1951, U.S. Dist. Ct. (ea. dist.) Mich. 1951, U.S. Dist. Ct. (so. dist.) Fla. 1952, U.S. Ct. Appeals (5th cir.) 1952, U.S. Supreme Ct. 1958, U.S. Ct. Appeals (11th cir.) 1981. Assoc. Turner, Hendrick & Fascell, 1952-55; ptnr. Turner, Hendrick, Fascell & Brake, 1956-59; sole practice Coral Gables, Fla., 1960—; assoc. mcpl. judge City of Coral Gables, 1958; atty. Dade County League of Mcpls., 1964, City of Sweetwater, Fla., 1966; spl. asst. atty. City of Miami Springs, Fla., 1972; hearings examiner Met. Dade County Personnel System, 1976—. Mem. Fla. Ho. of Reps., 1966-67; commr. Dade County, 1962-64, City of Coral Gables, 1971-79; founding pres. Dade County Council on Adoptable Children, 1970-74; mem. adv. council U.S. Cath. Bishops, 1974-76, vice chairperson, 1976; bd. dirs. Fla. Right to Life, Inc., 1975—. Served with U.S. Army, 1945-46; USAR; USAF JAGR, 1951-83. Recipient Good Govt. award Coral Gables Jaycees, 1976, Joshua award Concerned Christian Mothers, 1979. Mem. ABA, Fla. Bar Assn. (grievance com., panel mem. 1976-79), Dade County Bar Assn. (pub. interest law bank com., Haitian Refugees com., Disting. Service award for pro bono legal services 1984, Disting. Service award from Haitain Refugee Program 1984), Coral Gables Bar Assn. (pres. 1959), Am. Arbitration Assn. (panel mem.), ACLU (cooperating atty. 1965-71), NAACP (cooperating atty. legal def. fund. 1965), Coral Gables C. of C. (bd. dirs. 1968-69, v.p. 1970-71), Res. Officers Assn., Greater Miami United C. of C. (founding pres. 1968), Serra of Miami (pres. 1977-78, dist. 30 gov. 1982-83). Clubs: 200 (Miami), Toastmasters (founding pres. 1960). Lodges: K.C., Kiwanis (Outstanding Community Services award Coral Gables chpt. 1977), K.M. Home: 1300 Coral Way Coral Gables FL 33134 Office: 1830 Ponce de Leon Blvd Coral Gables FL 33134

BRAKEBUSCH, MARGARET GUILL, lawyer; b. McKenzie, Tenn., Feb. 29, 1948; d. Maurice A. and Freda Ruth (Rodgers) G.; m. Eric C. Theiner, July 16, 1977 (div. Nov. 1985); m. Dirk K. Brakebusch, Jan. 16, 1986. BA in Psychology, Bethel Coll., 1969; M in Social Work, U. Tenn., 1971; JD, Memphis State U., 1980. Bar: Tenn. 1981, U.S. Dist. Ct. Tenn. Social worker family planning div. Memphis and Shelby County Health Dept., 1971-72; psychiatric social worker Porter Leath Children's Ctr., Memphis, 1972-73; clin. social worker and foster home specialist Child Service and Family Counseling Ctr., Atlanta, 1973-75; community social worker VA Med. Ctr., Memphis, 1975-77, coordinator hosp. based home care program, 1977-79; atty. NLRB, Memphis, 1979—. Served as 1st lt. USAR, 1976-78. Mem. Assn. Trial Lawyers Am. Labor. Home: 18 S Idlewild Memphis TN 38104 Office: NLRB 1407 Union Ave Memphis TN 38104

BRAMES, ARNOLD HENRY, lawyer; b. St. Marks, Ind., Apr. 12, 1943; s. Herman A. and Leona B.; m. Carol Carter, Aug. 17, 1965; children: Mary Elizabeth, Hillary Ann. BS, Ind. State U.-Terre Haute, 1965; JD, Ind. U.-Indpls., 1970. Bar: Ind. 1970, U.S. Dist. Ct. (so. dist.) Ind. 1970, U.S. Ct. Appeals (7th cir.) 1972, U.S. Supreme Ct. 1980. Ptnr. Brames, McCormick, Bopp, Haynes & Abel and predecessor Terre Haute, Ind., 1971—; judge Vigo County Juvenile Ct., 1977-79; welfare atty., Vigo County, Ind., 1980-82; dep. atty. gen. Ind., 1970-71. Mem. bd. dirs. Lifeline Inc., 1978-80; mem. parish council Cath. Ch., 1975-81, past pres.; del., Rep. State Conv., 1976, 78, 80, 82. Mem. ABA, Ind. State Bar Assn., Vigo County Bar Assn., Sierra Club. Republican. Clubs: Strawberry Hill Cannoneers, Pachyderm. Lodge: Elks. Banking, Real property, Probate. Home: 133 McKinley Blvd Terre Haute IN 47803 Office: Brames McCormick Bopp Haynes & Abel 191 Harding Ave PO Box 410 Terre Haute IN 47808

BRAMLEY, JEFFREY LEE, lawyer; b. Medina, Ohio, Apr. 5, 1956; s. Clarence Donald and Marlene May (Muntz) B.; m. Suzanne Louise Kelly, Nov. 17, 1984; Aaron Christopher. BS in Bus., Econs., Miami U., Oxford, Ohio, 1978; JD, Akron U., 1981. Bar: Ohio 1981, U.S. Dist. Ct. (no. dist.) Ohio. Law clk. to presiding judge Ct. of Common Pleas, State of Ohio, Medina, 1979-81; assoc. Law Offices of David N. Brown, Medina, 1981; sole practice Medina, 1981—; tchr. Medina County Joint Vocational Sch., 1982; law librarian Medina County Law Library, 1983—. Pres. Highland Meadows Condominium Assn., Medina, 1983-84; vol. United Way Medina, 1981—. Mem. ABA, Ohio Bar Assn., Medina County Bar Assn. (treas. 1985—), Jaycees of Medina. Republican. Lutheran. Avocations: racquetball, tennis, skiing, sailing, swimming. General practice. Home: 4015 Marks Rd #3-D Medina OH 44256 Office: 209 S Broadway Medina OH 44256

BRAMLEY, WILLIAM ALEXANDER, III, lawyer; b. Bronxville, N.Y., Aug. 14, 1947; s. William Alexander Bramley II and Lois (Monroe) Sutherland; m. Cheryl Akins, July 29, 1978; children: Kendra Elizabeth, Gavin William. BS, U.S. Naval Acad., 1969; JD, U. San Diego, 1976. Bar: Calif. 1976, U.S. Dist. Ct. (so. dist.) Calif. 1976. Commd. ensign USN, 1969, advanced through grades to lt., 1972, resigned, 1974; ptnr. Sullivan, Delafield, McDonald & Middendorf, San Diego, 1977—; chmn. bd. dirs. Los Ninos Inc., San Ysidro, Calif., 1986—, past bd. dirs. Mem. adv. bd. Vols. in Parole, San Diego, 1985—, fund raising com. Christian Childrens Fund Inc., Los Angeles, 1981—. Recipient Atty. Match award Vols. in Parole, 1981. Mem. ABA, San Diego County Bar Assn. Episcopalian. Avocations: sports, travel. Contracts commercial, Bankruptcy, Real property. Office: Sullivan Delafield McDonald & Middendorf Security Pacific Plaza 1200 3d Ave Suite 1405 San Diego CA 92101

BRAMMELL, WILLIAM HARTMAN, lawyer; b. Shelbyville, Ky., Dec. 11, 1955; s. Billy Duard and Helen Combs (Hartman) B.; m. Eleanor Agnes Pesek, Apr. 3, 1982; children: William Hartman Jr., Katherine Elizabeth. BA, Transylvania U., 1977; JD, U. Louisville, 1980. Bar: Ky. 1980. Ptnr. Brammell, Croley, Moore & Yates, New Castle, Ky., 1980—; city atty. Eminence and Pleasureville, Ky., 1982—; pub. defender Henry and Trimble Counties, Ky., 1983; asst. atty. commr. 12th Jud. Dist., LaGrange, Ky., 1984; trial commr. 12th Jud. Dist., Henry County, 1985—. Sec. Protect Our Children, Inc., Henry County, 1981-82; bd. dirs. Eminence Christian Ch., 1986; pres. Henry County Heart Assn., 1985-86, Henry County Hist. Soc., 1987—. Mem. ABA, Ky. Bar Assn., Carroll County Bar Assn. Avocations: civil war history, fishing, travel. Consumer commercial, Real property, General practice. Home: 118 Tolle Ct Eminence KY 40019 Office: PO Box 629 Main Cross St New Castle KY 40050

BRAMNIK, ROBERT PAUL, lawyer; b. N.Y.C., Nov. 17, 1949; s. Abe and Ruth (Richman) B.; m. Sheryl Ann Kalus, Aug. 12, 1973; children: Michael Lawrence, Andrew Martin. BA, CCNY, 1970; JD, Bklyn. Law Sch., 1973. Bar: N.Y. 1974, U.S. Ct. Appeals (2d cir.) 1974, U.S. Dist. Ct. (so. and ea. dists.) N.Y. 1974, U.S. Supreme Ct. 1977, Ill. 1980, U.S. Dist. Ct. (no. dist.) Ill. 1980, U.S. Dist. Ct. (cen. dist.) Ill. 1982. Sr. trial atty. NYSE, Inc., N.Y.C., 1973-75; asst. gen. counsel E.F. Hutton & Co., Inc., N.Y.C., 1975-77, Nat. Securities Clearing Corp., N.Y.C., 1977-79; with Arvey, Hodes, Costello and Burman, Chgo., 1979-86, ptnr., 1982-86; ptnr. Wood, Lucksinger & Epstein, Chgo., 1987—; lectr. Securities Industry Assn. Compliance and Legal div., N.Y.C., 1980—. Vice-chmn. Ill. Adv. Com. on Commodity Regulation, Chgo., 1985—. Fellow Ill. Bar Found.; mem. ABA (coms. on futures regulation and fed. regulation of securities, subcom. on broker-dealer matters), Chgo. Bar Assn. (futures regulation), Assn. of Bar of City of N.Y., Nat. Assn. of Sec. Dealers (arbitrator 1981—), Nat. Futures Assn. (arbitrator 1981-86). Jewish. Masons. Securities, Federal civil litigation, Futures regulation-financial services. Office: Wood Lucksinger & Epstein 333 W Wacker Dr Chicago IL 60606

BRAMWELL, HENRY, judge; b. Bklyn., Sept. 3, 1919; s. Henry Hall and Florence Elva (MacDonald) B.; m. Ishbel W. Brown, Jan. 29, 1966. LL.B.,

Bklyn. Law Sch., 1948, LL.D. (hon.), 1979. Bar: N.Y. bar 1948. Asst. U.S. atty. Bklyn., 1953-61; asso. counsel N.Y. State Rent Commn., 1961-63; judge Civil Ct., N.Y.C., Bklyn., 1966, 69—; asst. adminstrv. judge Kings County, Bklyn., 1974—; judge U.S. Dist. Ct., Bklyn., 1975—; Mem. Community Mayors N.Y. State; trustee Bklyn. Law Sch., 1978—. Served with AUS, 1941-45. Mem. Am., N.Y. State, Bklyn. (trustee 1968-74), Nat. (life) bar assns., Am. Judicature Assn. Federal civil litigation, Criminal, General practice. Home: 101 Clark St Brooklyn NY 11201 Office: US Courthouse 225 Cadman Plaza East Brooklyn NY 11201

BRANAGAN, JAMES JOSEPH, lawyer, electronics and distribution company executive; b. Johnstown, Pa., Mar. 5, 1943; s. James Francis and Caroline Bertha (Schreier) B.; m. Barbara Jeanne Miller, June 19, 1965; children: Sean Patrick, Erin MacKay, David Michael. B.A. in English Lit. with honors magna cum laude (Woodrow Wilson fellow), Kenyon Coll., Gambier, Ohio, 1965; LL.B. cum laude, Columbia U., 1968. Bar: Ohio 1968. Asso. firm Jones, Day, Reavis & Pogue, Cleve., 1968-72; with Leaseway Transp. Corp., Cleve., 1972-81; gen. counsel Leaseway Transp. Corp., 1975-80, sec., 1979-81, v.p. corp. affairs, 1980-81; also officer, dir. Leaseway Transp. Corp. (subsidiaries); v.p. Premier Indsl. Corp., Cleve., 1981-82; sr. counsel TRW Inc., 1982—. Mem. ABA, Ohio Bar Assn., Cleve. Bar Assn., Phi Beta Kappa. General corporate, Real property, Securities. Office: 1900 Richmond Rd Cleveland OH 44124

BRANAN, CAROLYN BENNER, accountant, lawyer; b. Wiesbaden, Fed. Republic Germany, Mar. 7, 1953; came to U.S., 1958; d. Huebert Harrison and Kathryn Wilfreda (Diggs) Benner; m. Robert Edwin Branan, Oct. 3, 1981. B.A. in Philosophy, U. S.C., 1973, J.D., 1976. Bar: S.C. 1977, U.S. Dist. Ct. S.C. 1977, U.S. Ct. Appeals (4th cir.) 1977; C.P.A., N.C. Sole practice law, Columbia, S.C., 1977-79; mgr. Deloitte Haskins & Sells, Charlotte, N.C., 1979—; cons. Gov.'s Bus. Council Task Force on Infrastructure Financing, 1983. Contbr. articles to profl. jours. Mem. exec. com., former treas., v.p., chmn. budget com. Charlotte Opera Assn., 1981—; v.p. Opera Carolina 1986—; exec. com., chmn. 1st and 2d ann. funding campaigns N.C. Opera, 1982—; exec. com. mayor's study com. Performing Arts Ctr., Charlotte, 1983—; former mem. adv. council, bd. dirs., chmn. performing arts Springfest, Charlotte, 1982—; fin. chmn. Opening of New Charlotte Transit Mall, 1984-85; bus. adv. council Queens Coll., Charlotte, 1984—. Mem. ABA (chmn. important devels., gen. acctg. matters, regulated pub. utilities tax sect. 1984—), N.C. Bar Assn., S.C. Bar Assn., Charlotte Estate Planning Council, Nat. Assn. Accts. (bd. dirs., dir. profl. devel., dir. community affairs 1979-84), N.C. Assn. C.P.A.s, Founders Soc. of Charlotte Opera Assn. (life). Episcopalian. Club: Charlotte City. Corporate taxation, Estate taxation, Personal income taxation. Home: 530-A N Poplar St Charlotte NC 28202 Office: Deloitte Haskins & Sells 2100 So Nat Ctr Charlotte NC 28202

BRANCA, JOHN GREGORY, lawyer, consultant; b. Bronxville, N.Y., Dec. 11, 1950; s. John Ralph and Barbara (Werle) B. AB in Polit. Sci. cum laude, Occidental Coll., 1972; JD, UCLA, 1975. Bar: Calif. 1975. Assoc. Kindel & Anderson, Los Angeles, 1975-76, Hardee, Barovick, Konecky & Braun, Beverly Hills, Calif., 1977-81; ptnr. Ziffren, Brittenham & Branca, Los Angeles, 1981—; bd. dirs. Brother Records, Los Angeles, MJJ Prodns., Los Angeles. Editor-in-Chief UCLA Law Rev., 1974-75; contbr. articles to profl. jours. Cons. United Negro Coll. Fund; bd. dirs. Michael Jackson Burn Ctr., UCLA Law Com. Recipient Bancroft-Whitney award; named Entertainment Lawyer of Yr. Am. Lawyer Mag. Mem. ABA (patent trademark and copyright law sect.), Calif. Bar Assn., Beverly Hills Bar Assn. (entertainment law sect.), Phi Alpha Delta, Sigma Tau Sigma. Avocations: art, antiques, music, real estate. Entertainment. Office: Ziffren Brittenham & Branca 2049 Century Park E #2350 Los Angeles CA 90067

BRANCH, JAMES ALEXANDER, JR., lawyer, educator; b. Houston, Sept. 26, 1942; s. James A. and Juanita (Wilson) B. B.A., U. N.Mex., 1966, J.D., 1971; LL.M., U. Ga., 1979. Bar: N.Mex., 1976, Trust Terr. Pacific Islands 1978, U.S. Ct. Appeals (10th cir.) 1978, North Mariana Islands 1979, U.S. Dist. Ct. North Mariana Islands 1979, Colo. 1982, U.S. Dist. Ct. Colo. 1982, Marshall Islands 1985, Federated States of Micronesia 1985. Latin Am. teaching fellow, Brazil, 1972; ptnr. Branch & Branch, 1973-76; atty. Micronesian Legal Service Corp., 1976; pub. defender Trust Ter. Pacific Islands, 1977-78; instr. law U. Ga., 1979; asst. prof. law U. Denver, 1979-82, assoc. prof., 1982-83; sole practice, Denver, 1979; mem. faculty U. Denver Coll. Law; 1983-84; vis. prof. law U. N.Mex., summer 1983, 84; assoc. Am. Bd. Trial Advs.; lectr. continuing legal edn. Bd. dirs. Legal Aid Soc. Met. Denver, Colo.-Minas-Gerais Ptnrs. Articles editor: N.Mex. Law Rev. and Natural Resources Jour., 1970-71; contbr. articles to profl. jours. Served with USAF, 1968-69, Vietnam. Decorated Air Force Commendation medal; Fulbright-Hays travel grantee, 1972. Mem. ABA, Colo. Bar Assn. (inter-profl. com. 1982-83), Denver Bar Assn. (com. on availability of legal services 1980-81, com. on jud. appointments and benefits 1980-81, inter-profl. com. 1982-83), Albuquerque Bar Assn., Nat. Inst. Trial Advocacy (cert., instr. 1981-85, of counsel to br. law firms), Assn. Trial Lawyers Am. (sustaining), Phi Alpha Delta. Legal education, Federal civil litigation, State civil litigation. Home: 1717 Avenida Las Canpanas NW Albuquerque NM 87107 Office: 2501 Yale St SE Suite 301 Albuquerque NM 87106 Office: U Denver Coll Law 1900 Olive St Denver CO 80220

BRANCH, JOHN ELLISON, lawyer; b. Atlanta, Sept. 17, 1915; s. William Harllee and Bernice (Simpson) B.; m. Jean McKay, Nov. 19, 1938; children—Jean Elizabeth, Barbara Ann, Patricia Elaine, John Ellison. B.S., Davidson Coll., 1937; J.D., Emory U., 1940. Bar: Ga. 1939. Assoc., Gambrell and White, Atlanta, 1940-49; ptnr. Wilson, Branch and Barwick, Atlanta, 1949-70; sr. ptnr. Branch and Swann, Atlanta, 1970-81; of counsel Ogletree, Deakins, Nash, Smoak and Stewart, Atlanta, 1981—; guest lectr. Ga. State U. Atlanta, 1960-70; employer mem. U.S. del. ILD, Geneva, 1960-62. Bd. dirs. Ga. Hospitality and Travel Assn.; past trustee Atlanta council Boy Scouts Am.; mem. governing bd. Bus. Council Ga. Served to maj. U.S. Army, 1942-45. Mem. ABA, State Bar Ga., Atlanta Bar Assn., Lawyers Club Atlanta, U.S. C. of C. (past mem. employee relations com.), Council State Chambers Commerce (chmn. employee relations com.), Ga. C. of C. (mem. governing bd.), Atlanta C. of C. (past bd. dirs., chmn. govt. affairs dept.), Phi Beta Kappa, Omicron Delta Kappa. Presbyterian. Clubs: Capital City, Commerce, Cherokee, Athletic (Atlanta); University Yacht (Lake Lanier, Ga.); Amelia Plantation (Amelia Island, Fla.). Author: (with J.P. Swann) The Wage and Hour Law Handbook, 1980. Labor, Administrative and regulatory. Home: 3648 Peachtree Rd NE 1G Atlanta GA 30319 Office: 1st Atlanta Tower 2 Suite 3920 Atlanta GA 30383

BRANCH, MARGARET MOSES, lawyer; b. Salzburg, Austria, Feb. 28, 1953; d. Thomas Lyons and Willie (Singleton) Moses; m. Turner Williamson Branch, Oct. 4, 1984. B of Univ. Studies, U. N.Mex., 1976, JD, 1979. Bar: N.Mex. 1978. Assoc. Glascock, McKim & Head, Gallup, N.Mex., 1978-80; gen. counsel Carbon Coal Co., Albuquerque, 1980-83; assoc. Branch Law Firm, Albuquerque, 1984—. Mem. citizen's adv. bd. N.Mex. Fed. Savs. & Loan, Albuquerque, 1985; bd. dirs. YMCA, Albuquerque, 1983. Mem. ABA (v.p. young lawyers div. N.Mex. chpt. 1982-83), Albuquerque Bar Assn., Assn. Trial Lawyers Am. (cert. advanced trial advocacy 1985), N.Mex. Trial Lawyers Assn. Democrat. Episcopalian. Clubs: Albuquerque Country, Women's Investment (Albuquerque). Avocations: golf, tennis, art collecting. Personal injury, Workers' compensation, Real property. Home: 8635 Rio Grande NW Albuquerque NM 87107 Office: 2025 Rio Grande Blvd NW Albuquerque NM 87104

BRANCH, THOMAS BROUGHTON, III, lawyer; b. Atlanta, June 5, 1936; s. Thomas Broughton Jr. and Alfred Iverson (Dews) B.; m. Trudi Schroetter, Dec. 27, 1963; children: Maria Barbara, Thomas B. IV. BA cum laude, Washington and Lee U., 1958, JD, 1960. Bar: Ga. 1960, U.S. Dist. Ct. (no. dist.) Ga. 1960, U.S. Ct. Appeals (5th cir.) 1960, U.S. Dist. Ct. (mid. dist.) Ga. 1980, U.S. Ct. Appeals (11th cir.) 1980, U.S. Dist. Ct. (so. dist.) N.Y. 1984, U.S. Ct. Appeals (2d cir.) 1984. Assoc. Kilpatrick & Gody, Atlanta, 1960-63; ptnr. Greene, Buckley et al, Atlanta, 1963-79, Wildman, Harrold, Allen, Dixon & Branch, Atlanta, 1979—; asst. prof. Woodrow Wilson Law Sch., Atlanta, 1964-68; trustee Washington and Lee U., Lexington, Va., 1979—; trustee, chmn. Atlanta Lawyers Found., Atlanta, 1980-81, Atlantis Aurora, Inc., 1970-74. Mem. Citizens Adv. Council on Urban Devel., Atlanta, 1977; trustee The Children's Sch., Inc., Atlanta, 1980-85; elder, clk. First Presbyn. Ch., Atlanta, 1967-79, 81-85. Served to capt. U.S. Army, 1958-66. Mem. ABA, Ga. Bar Assn., Atlanta Bar Assn., Am. Jud. Soc., World Trade Club, Atlanta Lawyers Club (pres. 1976-77). Club: Ansley Golf (Atlanta) (pres., bd. dirs. 1976—). Federal civil litigation, State civil litigation, Private international. Home: 160 The Prado NE Atlanta GA 30309 Office: Wildman Harrold Allen et al 2 Midtown Plaza 15th Floor 1360 Peachtree St NE Atlanta GA 30309-3209

BRANCH, TURNER WILLIAMSON, lawyer; b. Houston, Aug. 22, 1938; s. James Alexander and Juanita (Wilson) B.; m. Margaret Moses; children—Brian Kern, Rebecca Claire. B.A., U. N.Mex., 1960; J.D., Baylor U., 1965. Bar: N.Mex. 1966, U.S. Dist. Ct. Dist. N.Mex. 1966, U.S. Ct. Appeals (5th and 10th cir.) 1968, U.S. Supreme Ct. 1972. sole practice, Branch Law Firm, Albuquerque, 1966—, sr. ptnr., 1966—; dir. Alcoholic Beverage Control for State N.Mex., 1966-68; mem. N.Mex. Ho. Reps., 1968-74. Bd. dirs. Albuquerque Little Theatre. Served with USMC, 1960-63. Mem. ABA, Albuquerque Bar Assn., State Bar N.Mex., N.Mex. Trial Lawyers Assn. (dir. 1969-73), Assn. Trial Lawyers Am. (state committeeman 1970-74), Nat. Inst. Trial Advocates, Am. Bd. Trial Advocates (cert. civil trial diplomate Nat. Bd. Adv.), Am. Soc. Law and Medicine, Omicron Delta Kappa, Pi Sigma Alpha, Phi Delta Phi. Republican. Episcopalian. Clubs: Kiwanis, Albuquerque Country, Elks, Masons, Shriner. Contbr. articles to profl. jours. Federal civil litigation, State civil litigation, General practice. Office: 2025 Rio Grande Blvd NW Albuquerque NM 87107

BRAND, JOSEPH LYON, lawyer; b. Urbana, Ohio, Aug. 11, 1936; s. Vance and Katherine (Lyon) B.; children: Elizabeth Brand Schell, Stephanie Lyon, Joseph Howard (dec. 1983). A.B., U. Mich., 1958; M.A., Ohio State U., 1959; J.D. with honors, George Washington U., 1963. Bar: Ohio and D.C. 1963. Ptnr. Patton, Boggs & Blow (and predecessor), 1967—; professorial lectr. George Washington U. Nat. Law Ctr., 1983—; mem. adv. bd. Internat. and Comparative Law Ctr., Southwestern Legal Found. Trustee Urbana Coll., 1981-83. Mem. ABA (chmn. com. banking and fin. sect. internat. law 1971ú72), Washington Inst. Fgn. Affairs, Washington Fgn. Law Soc., Internat. Bar Assn., D.C. Bar Assn., Am. Soc. Internat. Law, George Washington Law Sch. Alumni Assn. (sec.), Order of Coif (chpt. pres. 1970-71). General corporate, Private international, Public international. Home: PO Box 540 Great Falls VA 22066 Office: Patton Boggs & Blow 2550 M St NW Washington DC 20037

BRAND, MALCOLM LEIGH, lawyer; b. Inglewood, Calif., Mar. 5, 1935; s. Robert L. and Jeannette E. (Schureman) B.; m. Myra Jean Friesen, Sept. 19, 1958; children: Martin L., Janice E. BA in Econs., Willamette U., 1957, JD, 1964. Bar: Oreg. 1964. Atty. examiner Salem (Oreg.) Title Co., 1964-68; asst. city atty. City of Salem (Oreg.), 1968-69; ptnr. Rhoten, Rhoten et al, Salem, 1969-84; sole practice Salem, 1984—. Served with USAF, 1960-61. Mem. ABA, Oreg. Bar Assn., Marion County Bar Assn. (pres. 1976), Am. Trial Lawyers Assn., Oreg. Trial Lawyers Assn., Oreg. Assn. Def. Counsel. Republican. Presbyterian. Avocations: woodworking, golfing, tennis. General corporate, Real property, Probate. Home: 720 McGilchrist SE Salem OR 97302 Office: 100 High SE Box 183 Salem OR 97308

BRAND, MICHAEL EDWARD, lawyer; b. New Haven, Jan. 20, 1950; s. Jerome and Sylvia P. (Katz) B.; m. Lois S. Frieman, Dec. 29, 1974; 1 child Jason B. BA, U. Rochester, 1971; cert. law, U. Notre Dame, Uxbridge, Eng., 1972; JD, Cath. U., 1974. Bar: D.C. 1975, Conn. 1976, Md. 1977. Atty., advisor ICC, Washington, 1974-75; assoc. Collins & Lawrence, Washington, 1975-76, Miller, Loewinger & Assocs., Washington, 1977; ptnr. Loewinger, Brand & Kappstatter, Washington, 1980—. V.p. Snoudens Mill Homeowners Assn., Silver Spring, Md., 1981-84, pres. 1983, 87—. Mem. ABA, Am. Trial Lawyers Assn., D.C. Bar Assn., Md. Bar Assn. Avocation: skiing. Real property, State civil litigation, Landlord-tenant. Office: Loewinger Brand & Kappstatter Ch 471 H St NW Washington DC 20001

BRAND, RAY MANNING, lawyer; b. N.Y.C., May 6, 1922; s. David and Mary (Honigman) B.; m. Edythe Bernstein, Sept. 17, 1928; children—Clifford, David, Patrice, Allison. LL.B., St. John's U., 1946. Bar: N.Y. 1946, U.S. Dist. Ct. (ea. and so. dists.) N.Y. 1947, U.S. Supreme Ct. 1961. Sr. ptnr. Brand & Brand, Garden City, N.Y., 1949—; lectr. criminal law Nassau County Bar Assn. Mem. exec. com. Nassau County Democratic County Com., 1960—; chmn. Democratic Town Com., 1955-58. Served as capt. USAF, 1943-46. Decorated Air medal with 5 oak leaf clusters. Mem. N.Y. State Bar Assn., Nassau County Bar Assn., Am. Trial Lawyers Assn., N.Y. State Trial Lawyers Assn., Nassau County Criminal Bar Assn. (past pres.), Nat. Assn. Criminal Def. Attys., Internat. Platform Assn. Clubs: Pine Hollow Country (East Norwich, N.Y.); Frenchmens Creek (North Palm Beach, Fla.); Masons. Criminal, Personal injury, Insurance. Office: 300 Garden City Plaza Garden City NY 11530

BRAND, ROBERT JOSEPH, engineering executive; b. Louisville, Mar. 8, 1947; s. Fred Bernard and Mary Francis (Moran) B. BME, U. Louisville, 1970, MEngring., 1974, MBA, 1975, JD, 1978. Bar: Ky. 1978, U.S. Dist. Ct. (we. dist.) Ky. 1979. Engr. Gen. Electric, Louisville, 1970-75; assoc. Taustine, Post, Berman, Fineman & Kohn, Louisville, 1979-81; engr., supr., legal specialist Amerock Corp., Rockford, Ill., 1981-83, mgr. window hardware engring., 1983-86, dir. window products engring., 1986—; instr. mgrs. course Inter Mgt. Council, Rockford, 1985-87, 1st v.p., 1985—. Instr. Jr. Achievement, Rockford, 1982; bd. dirs. Boys Club, Rockford, 1985—. Recipient Am. Jurisprudence award Am. Jurisprudence Publishers, Louisville, 1977. Mem. ABA (patent and tort sects.), Internat. Mgt. Council (1st v.p. 1985—), Ky. Bar Assn., Louisville Bar Assn., Kentuckiana Delta Epsilon (v.p. 1980-81), ODK. Personal injury, Patent, Trademark and copyright. Home: 715 Garfield Ave Rockford IL 61103 Office: Amerock Corp 4000 Auburn St Rockford IL 61125-7018

BRAND, RONALD ALVAH, lawyer; b. McCook, Nebr., Sept. 19, 1952; s. Marvin Ray and LaVaughn R. (Nelson) B.; m. Mary M. Schmitz, June 5, 1976; children: Joshua, Megan. Lindsey. BA, U. Nebr., 1974; JD, Cornell U., 1977. Bar: Wis. 1977, U.S. Dist. Ct. (ea. and we. dists.) Wis. 1980, U.S. Ct. Appeals 1985. Assoc. Godfrey & Kahn S.C., Milw., 1977-79, Godfrey, Pfeil & Neshek, Elkhorn, Wis., 1979-82; asst. prof. law U. Pitts., 1982-87, assoc. prof., 1987—. Contbr. articles to profl. jours. Chmn. com. pastor-parrish relations U. Meth. Ch., 1984—; bd. dirs. com. Interfaith Housing, Inc., 1985—. Mem. Wis. Bar Assn., Pa. Bar Assn., Am. Soc. Internat. Law (vice chmn. internat. econ. law group 1985-87, chmn. 1987—), U. Pitts. Faculty Social Responsibility (steering com.). Democrat. Avocations: camping, basketball. Private international, Estate planning, Probate. Home: 2611 Gaywood Dr Pittsburgh PA 15235 Office: U Pitts Sch Law 3900 Forbes Ave Pittsburgh PA 15260

BRAND, STEVE AARON, lawyer; b. St. Paul, Sept. 5, 1948; s. Allen A. and Shirley Mae (Mintz) B.; m. Gail Idele Greenspoon, Oct. 9, 1977. BA, U. Minn., 1970; JD, U. Chgo., 1973. Bar: Minn. Supreme Ct. 1973, U.S. Dist. Ct. Minn. 1974, U.S. Supreme Ct. 1977. Assoc. Briggs & Morgan, St. Paul, 1973-78. Pres., Jewish Vocat. Service, 1981-84; pres. Mt. Zion Hebrew Congregation, 1985-87. Mem. ABA, Minn. Bar Assn. (chmn. probate and trust law sect. 1984-85), Am. Coll. Probate Counsel, Phi Beta Kappa. Democrat. Club: Minnesota. Lodge: B'nai B'rith. Estate planning, Probate, Estate taxation. Home: 1907 Hampshire Ave Saint Paul MN 55116 Office: Briggs & Morgan 2200 1st Nat Bank Bldg Saint Paul MN 55101

BRANDENBURG, ROBERT FAIRCHILD, JR., lawyer, business executive; b. Oklahoma City, Mar. 6, 1938; s. Robert Fairchild and Lorraine (Harkey) B.; m. Heidi Harper, Sept. 28, 1962; children—Robert Fairchild III, John Harper, Adam Charles. B.A., U. Okla., 1961, J.D., 1966. Bar: Okla. 1966, U.S. Dist. Ct. (we. dist.) Okla. 1968, U.S. Tax Ct. 1969, U.S. Ct. Appeals (10th cir.) 1972, U.S. Ct. Claims 1977. Sole practice, Norman, Okla., 1968-75; ptnr. Floyd & Brandenburg and predecessors, Norman, 1975—; pres. Brandenburg Enterprises, 1970—, also dir.; pres., dir. Cumberland Heights, Inc., 1973-77, Robert F. Brandenburg, Jr. Atty. at Law P.C., 1979—; instr. dept. continuing edn. U. Okla., 1978; co-trustee John B. Brandenburg Trust, 1971—. Bd. dirs., mem. exec. com. Norman Alcohol Info. Ctr., Inc., 1972—, past pres., sec.; trustee Okla. Resource Found. for Alcoholism & Chem. Dependency, 1975—, vice chmn., chmn.; mem. vestry St. Michael's Episcopal Ch., Norman, 1976-78, 83-85; pres., dir. Southwest Inst. Human Relations, Inc., 1978—; dir. Phi Delta Theta Ednl. Found., Inc., 1982—, Phi Delta Theta Endowment Fund, 1982—. Served to lt. USNR, 1961-70. Mem. ABA, Okla. Bar Assn., Cleveland County Bar Assn., Nat. Assn. Bond Lawyers, Phi Alpha Delta. Republican. Episcopalian. Municipal bonds. Address: 116 E Main St Norman OK 73069

BRANDER, REYNOLDS A., JR., lawyer; b. Grand Rapids, Mich., Nov. 22, 1937; s. Reynolds A. and Gertrude (Boot) B.; m. Janice Ann Lusk, June 29, 1963; children—Gregory, Sara. B.A., U. Mich., 1960; LL.B., Wayne State U., 1966. Bar: Mich. 1966, U.S. Dist. Ct. (we. dist.) Mich. 1966. Asst. pros. atty. Kent County (Mich.), 1966-67; ptnr. Cholette, Perkins and Buchanan, Grand Rapids, Mich., 1967—; instr. bus. law Davenport Coll., 1967-69; assoc. prof. bus. law Acquinas Coll., 1969-70. Served to lt (j.g.) USN, 1960-63. Mem. ABA, Mich. Bar Assn., Grand Rapids County Bar Assn. (trustee), Internat. Assn. Ins. Counsel, (chmn. workers compensation com. 1982-83). Federal civil litigation, Personal injury, Insurance. Office: Suite 600 Old Kent Bank Bldg Grand Rapids MI 40503

BRANDING, FREDERICK H., lawyer, pharmacist; b. Elgin, Ill., Apr. 30, 1944; s. Harry F. and Maxine L. (Van de Vere) B.; m. Suzanne K. Luerssen, Aug. 16, 1969; children—Katherine, John. B.A., Drake U., 1966, B.S., 1968; J.D., Chgo.-Kent Coll. Law, Ill. Inst. Tech., 1973. Bar: Ill. 1973, U.S. Ct. Appeals (7th cir.) 1973, U.S. Dist. Ct. (no. dist.) Ill. 1973; U.S. Supreme Ct. 1981; registered pharmacist, Ill. Lab. analyst Jewel Foods, Barrington, Ill., 1967; assoc. Stansell and Rahn, Chgo., 1973; asst. U.S. atty. U.S. Atty.'s Office, Chgo., 1973-83, chief civil div., 1979-83; chief psychotropics control unit Internat. Narcotics Control Bd., UN, Vienna, Austria, 1983—; instr., lectr. Atty. Gen.'s Adv. Inst., Washington, 1976—; lectr., panalist Food and Drug Law Inst., 1978-82 Recipient Spl. Achievement award Dept. Justice, 1978, 79, 80, Commr.'s Spl. Citation award FDA, 1978, Dir.'s award Dept. Justice, 1982. Federal civil litigation, Food and drug, Public international. Home: 1311 E Clarendon St Arlington Heights IL 60004

BRANDON, DOUGLAS COLLIVER, lawyer; b. Ashland, Ky., Sept. 9, 1941; s. George Elmer and Dorothy Adams (Colliver) B.; m. Judith Ann Compton, July 5, 1969; children: Emily, John, Matthew. BA, Vanderbilt U., 1964; JD, U. Louisville, 1970. Bar: Ky. 1970, U.S. Dist. Ct. (we. dist.) Ky. 1970, U.S. Dist. Ct. (ea. dist.) Ky. 1975, U.S. Ct. Appeals (10th cir.) 1979. Atty., claims investigator Louisville Transit Co., 1968-73; ptnr. Cary & Brandon, Louisville, 1973-75; assoc. counsel, corp. litigation Ashland Oil, Inc., Ashland and Lexington, Ky., 1975-86; sole practice Lexington, 1986—. Mem. ABA, Am. Arbitration Assn. (arbitrator Cin. region 1984—). Republican. Federal civil litigation, State civil litigation, Insurance. Home and Office: 906 Granville Ct Lexington KY 40503

BRANDON, MARK EDWARD, lawyer; b. Augusta, Ga., July 14, 1954; s. Frank Thomas Jr. and Patricia (Alexander) B. BA, U. Montevallo, 1975; JD, U. Ala., 1978; AM, U. Mich., 1986. Bar: Ala. 1978, U.S. Dist. Ct. (mid. dist.) Ala. 1978, U.S. Dist. Ct. (no. and so. dists.) Ala. 1980, U.S. Ct. Appeals (11th cir.) 1981, Mich. 1985. Asst. atty. gen. State of Ala., Montgomery, 1978-80; coordinator consumer unit Legal Services Corp. Ala., Montgomery, 1980-81; ptnr. Cohen & Brandon, Birmingham, Ala., 1981-84; assoc. Davis & Fajen P.C., Ann Arbor, Mich., 1985-86; adj. prof. law U. Ala., University, 1983; v.p. environ. law sect. Ala. State Bar, 1982-84. Legal advisor to bd. dirs. Ala. Conservancy, Birmingham, 1982-84, bd. dirs. 1980-84; advisor Legal Environ. Assistance Found., Birmingham, 1982-84. Gerald R. Ford Regents fellow U. Mich., 1984; Princeton U. fellow, 1986; named one of Outstanding Young Men of Am., 1982, 85. Mem. ABA, Mich. Bar Assn., Am. Polit. Sci. Assn. Jurisprudence, Legal history, Constitutional Interpretation. Office: Princeton Univ The Grad Coll Princeton NJ 08544

BRANDRUP, DOUGLAS WARREN, lawyer; b. Mitchel, S.D., July 11, 1940; s. Clair L. and Ruth M. (Wolverton) B.; m. Patricia R. Tuck, Dec. 20, 1986; children—Kendra, Monika, Peter. A.B. in Econs., Middlebury Coll., 1963; J.D., Boston U., 1966. Bar: N.Y. 1969, U.S. Dist. Ct. (so. dist.) N.Y. 1970, U.S. Ct. Appeals (2d cir.) 1970. Assoc. Donovan, Leisure, Newton & Irvine, N.Y.C., 1968-72; ptnr. Griggs, Baldwin & Baldwin, N.Y.C., 1972—, sr. ptnr., 1980—; dir. Equity Oil Co., Am. Techs., Inc. Mem. Govs. Security Adv. Com., State of N.J., 1975—. Served to capt. U.S. Army, 1966-68. Mem. N.Y. County Bar Assn., N.Y. State Bar Assn., ABA. Republican. Episcopalian. Clubs: World Trade Ctr., Met. (bd. govs.) (N.Y.C.); Club de Mar (Palma, Majorca Spain). General corporate, Estate planning, General practice. Office: Griggs Baldwin & Baldwin 1 Wall St New York NY 10005

BRANDT, CHARLES, lawyer; b. S.I., N.Y., Mar. 13, 1942; s. Charles P. and Caroline (DeMarco) B.; m. Kathleen A. Brandt, July 6, 1963; m. 2d, Nancy Poole, July 8, 1977; children—Tripp, Mimi, Jenny. B.A., U. Del., 1963; J.D., Bklyn. Law Sch., 1969. Bar: Del. 1971. Instr., Del. Law Sch., 1974; dep. atty. gen. Del., 1971-74, chief dep atty. gen., 1974-76; sole practice, Wilmington, Del., 1976-79; ptnr. Brandt & Benson, Wilmington, 1979-83; sole dir. Charles Brandt, P.A., 1983-87; ptnr. Brandt & Dalton, 1987—; mem. bd. profl. responsibility Del. Supreme Ct. 1980—. Mem. ABA, Del. State Bar Assn. (treas. 1982-83), Del. Trial Lawyers Assn. (pres.-elect 1987—), Assn. Trial Lawyers Am., Am. Judicature Soc., Democrat. Roman Catholic. Editor, Del. Trial Lawyers Update. Personal injury, Criminal, Plantiff's personal injury and criminal defense. Home: 117 Polly Drummond Rd Newark DE 19711 Office: 1020 Bancroft Pkwy Wilmington DE 19899

BRANDT, STEPHEN DENNIS, lawyer; b. Wauseon, Ohio, Dec. 29, 1946; s. Edward Albert and Wilhelmina (Plassmann) B.; m. Jeanne Marie Smith, June 22, 1968; children: Gretchen Marie, Christian Edward, Wilfred Marvin. BA, Bowling Green State U., 1968; postgrad., U. Amherst, 1972; JD summa cum laude, Ohio State U., 1975. Bar: Ohio 1976, U.S. Dist. Ct. (no. dist.) Ohio, 1975. Atty. Fuller & Henry, Toledo, 1976-79; gen. counsel, sec. Schindler Elevator Corp., Toledo, 1979-84, v.p., gen. counsel, sec., 1984—. Served to capt. USAF, 1968-72, Vietnam. Mem. ABA, Ohio Bar Assn., Toledo Bar Assn., Order of Coif. Lutheran. Avocations: guitar, sailing, motorcycle, gardening. General corporate, Personal injury, Construction. Home: 7537 Bonniebrook Sylvania OH 43560 Office: Schindler Elevator Corp 671 Spencer St Toledo OH 43609

BRANDVEEN, ANTONIO ISADORE, judge, lawyer; b. N.Y.C., May 19, 1946; s. Antonius A. and Louisa E. (Topping) B.; m. Fern Fisher, Mar. 8, 1980; 1 child, Sean Antonius. BBA, Fordham U., 1969; JD, NYU, 1972. Bar: N.Y. 1974, U.S. Ct. Appeals (2d cir.) 1974, U.S. Ct. Internat. Trade 1975, U.S. Supreme Ct. 1979. Staff atty. N.Y.C. Health and Hosp. Corp., 1972-74, Harlem Legal Services, Inc., N.Y.C., 1974; sr. law clk. N.Y. State Supreme Ct., N.Y.C., 1975-80; judge Housing Ct., N.Y.C., 1980-85, Bronx (N.Y.) Criminal Ct., 1985—. Bd. dirs. Cen. Harlem Sr. Citizens Coalition, Inc., 1974—. Mem. Assn. of Bar of City of N.Y., Met. Black Bar Assn. (v.p. 1985—). Jurisprudence, Criminal, Landlord-tenant. Office: Bronx Criminal Court 215 E 161 St Bronx NY 10451

BRANHAGEN, DARREL RAYMOND, lawyer; b. Decorah, Iowa, Oct. 23, 1949; s. Arthur Theodore and Elsie Clarisa (Winger) B.; m. Betty Anne McKibben, July 2, 1983. BS in Physics, U. Wis., 1972, MA in Pub. Adminstrn., 1974; JD, Drake U., 1977. Bar: Tex. 1983, Iowa 1977, U.S. Dist. Ct. (no. and so. dists.) Iowa 1980, U.S. Ct. Appeals (8th cir.) 1980. Sole practice Decorah, 1977-83; county atty. Winneshiek County, Iowa, 1982-83; asst. gen. counsel Tracor, Inc., Austin, Tex., 1983—; bd. dirs. PC Station Inc., Austin. Councilman City of Decorah, 1982-83. Served to capt. U.S. Army, 1977, with USNG. Democrat. Lutheran. Avocations: sailing, military history, aviation. General corporate, Environment, Government contracts. Home: 12605 Terra Nova Austin TX 78727 Office: Tracor Inc 1-1 6500 Tracor Ln Austin TX 78725-2000

BRANNEY, JOSEPH JOHN, lawyer; b. Casper, Wyo., Aug. 22, 1938; s. John J. and Frances M. (Stanko) B.; children: Scott W., John J., Sean W. BA, U. Colo., 1960; JD, U. Denver, 1962. Bar: Colo. 1963, Wyo. 1963. Assoc. Myrick, Criswell & Branney, Englewood, Colo., 1963-69; sole practice Englewood, 1969-72; ptnr. Branney, Hillyard, Ewing & Barnes, Englewood, 1972-85, Branney, Hillyard, Kudla & Lee, Englewood, 1986—; prof. law U. Denver, 1964—. Mem. Wyo. Bar Assn., Arapahoe County Bar Assn., Assn. Trial Lawyers Am., Colo. Trial Lawyers Assn. (pres. 1966-67), Nat. Bd. Trial Advocacy (cert. civil trial adv. 1983), Internat. Soc. of Barristers. Republican. Personal injury, Federal civil litigation, State civil litiga-

tion. Home: 1717 E Stanford Englewood CO 80110 Office: Branney Hilyard Kudla & Lee 3333 S Bannock #1000 Englewood CO 80110

BRANNON, WILLIAM EARL, lawyer; b. Rome, Ga., Oct. 8, 1936; s. Clifford Charles and Grace Beatrice (Cargle) B.; m. Linda Cook, Oct. 3, 1958. BA, Shorter Coll., 1967; JD, Atlanta Law Sch., 1979. Bar: Ga. 1980. Foreman Brannon Bros. Roofing, Rome, 1954-68, 76-80; counsellor Ga. Dept. Human Resources, Rome, 1968-76; sole practice Rome, 1980—. Mem. ABA, Ga. Bar Assn., N.Y. State Trial Lawyers Assn., Rome Bar Assn., Assn. Trial Lawyers Am., Comml. Law League Am. Avocation: photography. Consumer commercial, General practice, Real property. Home: PO Box 2931 West End Br Rome GA 30161 Office: 413 E 1st St Rome GA 30161

BRANSCOMB, ANNE WELLS (MRS. LEWIS MCADORY BRANSCOMB), lawyer, communications consultant; b. Statesboro, Ga., Nov. 22, 1928; d. Guy Herbert and Ruby Mae (Hammond) Wells; m. Lewis McAdory Branscomb, Oct. 13, 1951; children: Harvie Hammond, Katharine Capers. B.A., Ga. State Coll. Women, 1949, U. N.C., 1949; postgrad., London Sch. Econs., 1950; M.A., Harvard U., 1951; J.D. with honors, George Washington, 1962. Bar: D.C. 1962, Colo. 1963, N.Y. 1973, U.S. Supreme Ct. 1972. Research assoc. Pierson, Ball and Dowd, Washington, 1962; law clk. to presiding judge U.S. Dist. Ct., Denver, 1962-63; assoc. Williams & Zook, 1963-66; sole practice Boulder, 1963-69; assoc. Arnold and Porter, Washington, 1969-72; communications counsel Teleprompter Corp., N.Y.C., 1973; v.p. Kalba-Bowen Assocs. Inc., communication cons., Cambridge, Mass., 1974-77, chmn. bd., 1977-80, sr. assoc. dir., 1980-82; pres. The Raven Group, 1985—; trustee Pacific Telecommunications Council, 1981-83, 86—; Inaugural fellow Gannett Ctr. Media Studies, Columbia U., 1985; mem. tech. adv. bd. Dept. Commerce, 1977-81; WARC adv. com. Dept. State, 1978-79; mem. Carnegie Corp. Task Force on Pub. Broadcasting, 1976-77; mem. overseers, vis. com. Harvard U. Office of Info. Tech., 1977-83; vis. scholar Yale U. Law, 1981-82; mem. program on information resources and pub. policy Harvard U., 1986—; chmn. program com. Legal Symposium Telecom '87, Internat. Telecommunications Union, 1986-87; bd. dirs. Pub. Interest Radio, 1986—. Contbr. articles to profl. jours.; mem. editorial bd.: Info. Soc.; editor: Toward a Law of Global Communications Networks; contbg. editor: Jour. Communications, 1980—. Housing commr. Boulder Pub. Housing Authority, 1969-70; bd. dirs. Nat. Pub. Radio, 1975-78; trustee EDUCOM, Interuniv. Communications Council Inc., 1975-78; vice chmn. Colo. Dem. State Central Com., 1967-69; del., mem. permanent orgn. com. Dem. Nat. Conv., 1968; trustee, exec. com. Rensselaer Poly. Inst., 1980—. Recipient Alumni Achievement award Ga. Coll., 1980; recipient Rotary Found. fellowship, 1950-51. Mem. ABA (Nat. Conf. Lawyers and Scientists ABA/AAAS 1985—, chmn. communications com. sci. and tech. sect. 1980-82, chmn. communications law div. 1982-84, mem. council sci. and tech. sect. 1981-85), Am. Polit. Sci. Assn., Internat. Communications Assn., Internat. Inst. Communications, Soc. Preservation of First Wives and First Husbands (nat. pres. 1981—), Order of Coif, Valkyries, Phi Beta Kappa, Alpha Psi Omega, Chi Delta Phi, Pi Gamma Mu. Communications, Private international, Public international.

BRANSDORFER, STEPHEN CHRISTIE, lawyer; b. Lansing, Mich., Sept. 18, 1929; s. Henry and Sadie (Kohane) B.; m. Peggy Ruth Deisig, May 24, 1952; children: Mark, David, Amy, Jill. A.B. with honors, Mich. State U., 1951; J.D. with distinction, U. Mich., 1956; LL.M., Georgetown U., 1958. Bar: Mich. 1956, U.S. Supreme Ct. 1959. Trial atty. Dept. Justice, Washington, 1956-58; atty., editor Office of Public Info., Office of Atty. Gen., 1958-59; spl. asst. U.S. Atty. for D.C., 1958-59; assoc. firm Miller, Johnson, Snell & Cummiskey, Grand Rapids, Mich., 1959-63; partner Miller, Johnson, Snell & Cummiskey, 1963—; pres. State Bar of Mich., 1974-75, commr., 1968-75; chmn. Mich. Civil Service Commn., 1977-78, mem., 1975-78; adv. com. 6th Circuit Jud. Conf., 1984—. Asst. editor: U. Mich. Law Rev, 1956. Pres. Grand Rapids Child Guidance Clinic, 1969-71; chmn. Kent County Coms., Griffin for Senator, 1972, Lenore Romney for Senator, 1966; mem. council legal advisers Rep. Nat. Com., 1981—; Rep. candidate for atty. gen., Mich., 1978; trustee, v.p. Mich. State Bar Found., 1985—; chmn. Mich. State Bd. Canvassers, 1985-87. Served with U.S. Army, 1951-53. Fellow Am. Bar Found.; mem. 6th Cir. Jud. Conf. (life), Am. Bar Assn., Grand Rapids Bar Assn., Fed. Bar Assn. (pres. West Mich. chpt. 1984), Phi Kappa Phi. Presbyterian. Clubs: Grand Rapids Athletic, Cascade Hills Country. Lodge: Rotary. Federal civil litigation, State civil litigation, General corporate. Home: 7250 Bradfield Rd SE Ada MI 49301 Office: 800 Calder Plaza Bldg Grand Rapids MI 49503

BRANSON, ALBERT HAROLD, lawyer; b. Chgo., May 20, 1935; s. Fred Brooks and Marie (Vowell) B.; m. Siri-Anne Gundrun Lindberg, Nov. 2, 1963; children: Gunnar John, Gulliver Dean, Hanna Marie, Siri Elizabeth. B.A., Northwestern U., 1957; J.D., U. Chgo., 1963. Bar: Pa. 1965, Alaska 1972, U.S. Dist. Ct. Alaska 1972. Staff atty. Alaska Legal Services, Anchorage, 1971-72; ptnr. McVeigh & Branson, Anchorage, 1972-73, Jacobs, Branson & Guetschow, Anchorage, 1973-76, Branson & Guetschow, Anchorage, 1976-82, Branson, Bazeley & Chisolm, 1984-86; sole practice, Anchorage, 1982-84, 86—; U.S. magistrate U.S. Dist. Ct., Anchorage, 1975-76; instr. litigation U. Alaska, Anchorage, 1980-86. Editor Alaska Bar Rag, 1978-84. Served with U.S. Army, 1957-59. Mem. Alaska Bar Assn. (bd. dirs. 1977-80, 83-865, pres. 1985-86), Anchorage Acad. Trial Lawyers, Assn. Trial Lawyers Am.), Anchorage Bar Assn. (bd. dirs. 1983-84). Democrat. State civil litigation, Criminal, Family and matrimonial. Office: 601 W 5th Ave Suite 920 Anchorage AK 99501

BRANSON, DAVID JOHN, lawyer; b. Washington, Nov. 30, 1943; s. Albert Edward and Ellen Dorothea (Cochrane) B.; m. Meredith Elizabeth Pounds, Mar. 7, 1970; children: Kate, John. AB, Cath. U., 1966; JD, Georgetown U., 1973; LLB, Cambridge U., Eng., 1975. Bar: Ill. 1973, N.Y. 1976, D.C. 1979. Assoc. Cravath Swaine & Moore, N.Y.C., 1975-78; assoc. White & Case, Washington, 1978-82, ptnr., 1982-85; ptnr. Kaye, Scholer, Fierman, Hays & Handler, Washington, 1985—; adj. prof. Georgetown U. Law Ctr., 1979-85. Please note we do not list individual articles by title for creative works section. Sr. v.p. Asthma and Allery Found. Am., 1985—. Served to capt. USAF, 1966-70, Korea. Mem. ABA (vice-chmn. com. on internat. arbitration internat. law sect. 1984-85), Internat. Bar Assn. (vice-chmn. com. on settlement of disputes, vice-chmn.internat. arbitration com. 1985—). Private international, Public international. Office: Kaye Scholer Fierman Hays & Handler 1575 Eye St NW Washington DC 20005

BRANSON, FRANK LESLIE, III, law corporation executive; b. Deport, Tex., Feb. 10, 1945; s. Frank Leslie B. Jr.; m. Debbie D. Branson; children: Frank IV, Jennifer. BA, Tex. Christian U., 1967; JD, So. Meth. U., 1969, LLM, 1974. Bar: Tex. 1969. Assoc. Watson & Parkhill, Grand Prairie, Tex., 1969; assoc. Bader, Wilson, Menaker, Cox & Branson, Dallas, 1970-75, ptnr., 1975-77; ptnr. Wilson, Menaker & Branson, Dallas, 1977-79; ptnr., pres. Branson & Misko, Dallas, 1980-83; sole practice Dallas, 1983—; lectr. personal injury topics State Bar Tex., Am. Trial Lawyers Assn.; mem. adv. com. Tex. Supreme Ct., 1985-86. Contbr. over 20 articles on personal injury litigation to profl. jours.; five arguments to Million Dollar Argument tapes, (with Matthew Bender) Malpractice video tape series, 1982. Mem. Dallas Dem. Fin. Council, 1985-86; bd. dirs. Garland (Tex.) Community Hosp., 1981, 82-84. Mem. Am. Bd. Trial Advs. (pres. Dallas chpt. 1982), Dallas Trial Lawyers Assn. (pres. 1976-77), Tex. Trial Lawyers Assn. (bd. dirs. 1972—, lectr.), Am. Trial Lawyers Coll. Med. Malpractice (dean 1985), Med. Malpractice Com. (chmn. 1974-75, 79). Clubs: Royal Oaks Country, Chapparal, 2001 (Dallas). Federal civil litigation, State civil litigation, Personal injury. Office: 2178 N Tower Plaza of Americas Dallas TX 75201

BRANSON, HARLEY KENNETH, lawyer; b. Ukiah, Calif., June 10, 1942; s. Harley Edward and Clara Lucile (Slocum) B.; m. Carole Ann Barnette, Aug. 25, 1963; 1 child, Erik Jordan. AA, San Francisco City Coll., 1963; BS in Acctg. and Fin., San Jose State U., 1965; JD, Santa Clara U., 1968. Bar: Calif. 1969, U.S. Dist. Ct. (so. dist.) Calif. 1969, U.S. Ct. Appeals (9th cir.) 1969, U.S. Tax Ct. 1969, U.S. Ct. Customs and Patent Appeals 1970, U.S. Supreme Ct. 1973. Law clk. to presiding judge U.S. Ct. Appeals (9th cir.), San Diego, 1968-69; ptnr. Klitgaard & Branson, Inc., San Diego, 1969-72; assoc. Jennings, Engstrand & Henrikson, San Diego, 1972-78; div. counsel Ralston Purina Co., San Diego, 1978-83; group gen. counsel Castle & Cooke, Inc., San Diego, 1983-85; gen. counsel, corp. sec. Bumble Bee Seafoods, Inc., San Diego, 1985—, also bd. dirs., exec. v.p. Editor Santa Clara Law Rev., 1967-68. Mem. Mission Valley Unified Planning com., 1978; bd. dirs. Mission Valley Council, San Diego, 1977-78; coach Peninsula YMCA Soccer, San Diego, 1978-79. James B. Emery scholar and Farmers Ins. Group scholar Santa Clara U., 1966-68. Mem. ABA (corp., banking and bus. law, and internat. law sects.), Calif. Bar Assn. (corp. law depts. com.), Am. Soc. Corp. Secs., Nat. Food Processors Assn. (lawyer com., claims com.), Am. Corp. Council Assn. Republican. Club: San Diego Tennis and Racquet. Avocations: racquetball, cycling, reading. General corporate, Private international. Office: Bumble Bee Seafoods Inc 5775 Roscoe Ct San Diego CA 92123

BRANT, CHARLES ENSIGN, lawyer; b. Dayton, Ohio, Mar. 6, 1930; s. Charles William and Lucile Catherine (Deger) B.; m. Nancy Henderson Ashe, Sept. 29, 1962; children: Julie Anne, David Alan. BA, U. Dayton, 1952; JD, Ohio State U., 1959; LLM, Northwestern U., 1960. Bar: Ohio 1959, U.S. Dist. Ct. (so. dist.) Ohio 1960, U.S. Ct. Appeals (6th cir.) 1962, U.S. Supreme Ct. 1973, U.S. Ct. Mil. Appeals, 1978. Commd. 2d lt. U.S. Army, 1952, advanced through grades to col., 1973, ret., 1982; ptnr. Isaac, Brant, Ledman and Becker, Columbus, Ohio, 1982—. Scoutmaster Cen. Ohio council Boy Scouts Am.; pres. Cen. Ohio Planned Parenthood, Columbus, 1964-76. Ford Found. fellow, 1959; Silver Beaver award Boy Scouts Am., 1986. Mem. ABA, Ohio State Bar Assn., Columbus Bar Assn., Fed. Bar Assn. (pres. 1966-67), Assn. Trial Lawyers Am. Democrat. Roman Catholic. Avocations: camping, music. Federal civil litigation, State civil litigation, Insurance. Home: 2251 Oxford Rd Columbus OH 43221 Office: Isaac Brant Ledman and Becker 250 E Broad St Columbus OH 43215

BRANT, JOHN GETTY, lawyer; b. Apr. 13, 1946. BBA, U. Okla., 1968; JD, U. Tex., 1972. Bar: Tex. 1972, Colo. 1974, U.S. Dist. Ct. Colo. 1974, U.S. Tax Ct. 1974. Atty. IRS, Houston, 1972-74; ptnr. Bradley, Campbell & Carney, Golden, Colo., 1975-83, Doussard, Brant, Hodel & Markman, Lakewood, Colo., 1983-86; sole practice Wheat Ridge, Colo., 1986—. Bd. dirs. U. Tex. Law Sch. Assn., Austin, 1983-86; bd. dirs. Nat. Multiple Sclerosis Soc., Denver, 1975—. Mem. Tex. Bar Assn., Colo. Bar Assn., Centennial Estate Planning Council (pres. 1976), Denver Estate Planning Council. Estate taxation, Probate, Estate planning. Office: 4251 Kipling St Suite 585 Wheat Ridge CO 80033

BRANT, KIRBY ENSIGN, lawyer; b. Milw., Dec. 5, 1937; s. Paul Swint and Elsie Ottilie (Pfeiffer) B.; m. Judith Carolyn Ford, Dec. 14, 1974; children: Pamela, Peter, Katherine. BS in Zoology, U. Wis., 1959, JD, 1962; LLM, So. Meth. U., 1970. Bar: Wis. 1962, U.S. Ct. Customs and Patent Appeals 1970, U.S. Ct. Claims 1970, U.S. Ct. Mil. Appeals 1970, U.S. Supreme Ct. 1970. Commmd. lt. (j.g.) JAGC USN, 1962, advanced through grades to lt. comdr., 1968, resigned, 1974; policy analyst GAO, Washington, 1974-79; staff subcom. U.S. Ho. of Reps., Washington, 1979-81; sole practice Watertown, Wis., 1981—; cons. imported crude oil prices Dept. Consumer and Corp. Affairs, Ottawa, Ont., Can., 1982-84. Mem. Watertown Hist. Soc., 1981. Mem. Wis. Bar Assn., Assn. Trial Lawyers Am., Am. Legion. Republican. Avocation: sailing. State civil litigation, Personal injury, Administrative and regulatory. Home: 908 County Ln Watertown WI 53094 Office: 218 S 1st St PO Box 93 Watertown WI 53094

BRANTL, ROBERT FRANCIS, lawyer; b. Bronx, N.Y., June 30, 1953; s. George Edward and Ruth Winafred (Parrish) B.; m. Debra Ann Pelo, June 23, 1984. BA magna cum laude, Williams Coll., 1975; JD cum laude, Harvard U., 1979. Bar: Mass. 1979, N.Y. 1980, N.J. 1983. Assoc. Bressler, Amery & Rothenberg, N.Y.C., 1980—. Securities, General corporate, Contracts commercial. Home: 240 8th St Apt 2N Brooklyn NY 11215 Office: Bressler Amery & Rothenberg 90 Broad St New York NY 10004

BRANTON, WILEY A., legal educator, lawyer; b. 1923. B.S., U. Ark.-Pine Bluff, 1950, LL.D., 1978; J.D., U. Ark.-Fayetteville, 1953. Bar: Ark. 1952, Ga. 1962, D.C. 1967. Sole practice law, Pine Bluff, 1952-62; dir. Voter Edn. Project, So. Regional Council, Atlanta, 1962-65; exec. dir. Council United Civil Rights Leadership, N.Y., 1963-65; spl. asst. to atty. gen. U.S. Dept. Justice, Washington, 1965-67; exec. dir. United Planning Orgn., Washington, 1967-69; dir. Community and Social Action, Alliance for Labor Action, Washington, 1969-71; ptnr. Dolphin, Branton, Stafford & Webber, Washington, 1971-77; dean, prof. Howard U., 1978-83; of counsel Sidley & Austin, Washington, 1983-85, ptnr., 1985—; dir. consol. Rail Corp., Columbia First Fed. Savs. & Loan Assn.; chmn. D.C. Jud. Nomination Commn. Bd. dirs. Africare. Served with AUS, 1943-46. Fellow Am. Bar Found.; mem. NAACP Legal Def. and Edn. Fund Inc., (dir.) Lawyers Com. for Civil Rights Under Law. Office: Sidley & Austin 1722 Eye St NW Washington DC 20006

BRASFIELD, EVANS BOOKER, lawyer; b. Richmond, Va., Sept. 21, 1932; s. George Frederick and Minna (Booker) B.; children: Evans Booker, John McDonald, Elizabeth Lee; m. Anne Dobbins Heilig, June 28, 1980; stepchildren: J. Randall Heilig, Mollie A. Heilig. B.A., U. Va., 1954, LL.B., 1959. Bar: Va. 1959. Since practiced in Richmond; partner firm Hunton & Williams, 1965—; gen. counsel Va. Electric & Power Co., Richmond, 1976—, Dominion Resources, 1983—; mem. Richmond adv. bd. Sovran Bank; lectr. Ga. Inst. Tech., 1968-75. Pres. Children's Home Soc. Va., 1972-73, bd. dirs., 1965—; chmn. Central Va. Ednl. TV Corp., 1978-84, bd. dirs., 1965—; bd. dirs. Richmond Community Action Program, 1974-76, Richmond Area Community Council, 1973-75, Big Bros. Richmond, 1970-75; vestryman St. Paul's Episcopal Ch., Richmond, 1972-75. Served with USNR, 1954-56. Fellow Am. Bar Found.; mem. ABA, Va. Bar Assn. (exec. com. 1981-86, pres. 1985), Richmond Bar Assn., Fed. Energy Bar Assn., Va. State Bar, Phi Beta Kappa (pres. Richmond chpt. 1982-83). Clubs: Country of Va., Commonwealth, Bull and Bear (Richmond); Rappahannock River Yacht (Irvington, Va.); Knickerbocker (N.Y.C.). Home: 9 Maxwell Rd Richmond VA 23226 Office: 707 E Main St Richmond VA 23212

BRATTEN, THOMAS ARNOLD, lawyer, cons. engr.; b. Dayton, Ohio, Sept. 11, 1934; s. Samuel Arnold and Helen Jeannette (Wonderly) B.; m. Glenna Mary Bratten, Apr. 20, 1963; children—Charles, Christina, Thomas. M.E., U. Cin., 1957; J.D., Chase Coll., Cin., 1968. Bar: Ohio, 1968, Fla., 1968, U.S. Supreme Ct., 1972; cert. civil trial lawyer Fla. Bar, Nat. Bd. Trial Advocacy; Engr. in tng. Gen. Motors Corp., 1953-57, test engr., 1957-59, project engr., 1963-68, sr. project engr., 1968; design engr. Pratt & Whitney Aircraft, 1959-61; gen. mgr. Auto-Technia, Inc., 1961-63; with Pub. Defender's Office, 1968-75, chief trial atty., 1970-72, chief Capital div., 1972-75; ptnr. Campbell, Colbath, Kapner & Bratten, West Palm Beach, Fla., 1969-72; prin. Bratten & Harris, P.A., West Palm Beach, 1973-86; of counsel Easley, Massa & Willits, P.A., West Palm Beach, Fla., 1986—; spl. master, 1973-85 ; faculty Nat. Inst. Trial Advocacy, U. Fla., 1978—; nat. panel arbitrators Am. Arbitration Assn., 1970-78. Mem. Palm Beach County Republican Exec. Com., 1971-80, county campaign chmn., 1974. Mem. Fla. Bar Assn. (exec. com. criminal law sect. 1978-81), Acad. Fla. Trial Lawyers, Assn. Trial Lawyers Am., Palm Beach County Bar Assn., Fla. Engring. Soc., Soc. Automotive Engrs., Nat. Acad. Forensic Engrs. (diplomate), Pi Tau Sigma. Author: Criminal Lawyers Trial Notebook, 1977; Florida Criminal Procedure, 1981. Inventor, 6 U.S. and 9 fgn. patents. State civil litigation, Criminal, General corporate. Home: 8623 Thousand Pines Ct West Palm Beach FL 33411 Office: Forum III 1655 Palm Beach Lakes Blvd West Palm Beach FL 33401

BRATTON, HOWARD CALVIN, judge; b. Clovis, N.Mex., Feb. 4, 1922; s. Sam Gilbert and Vivian (Rogers) B. B.A., U. N.Mex., 1941, LL.D., 1971; LL.B., Yale U., 1947. Bar: N.Mex. 1948. Law clk. U.S. Circuit Ct. Appeals, 1948; mem. Grantham & Bratton, Albuquerque, 1949-52; spl. asst. U.S. atty. charge litigation OPS, 1951-52; assoc., then ptnr. Hervy, Dow & Hinkle, Roswell, N.Mex., 1952-64; judge U.S. Dist. Ct. N.Mex., 1964—, chief judge, 1978-87, sr. judge, 1987—; chmn. N.Mex. Jr. Bar Assn., 1952; pres. Chaves County (N.Mex.) Bar Assn., 1962; chmn. pub. lands com. N.Mex. Oil and Gas Assn., 1961-64, Interstate Oil Compact Commn., 1963-64; mem. N.Mex. Commn. Higher Edn., 1962-64, Jud. Conf. of U.S. Com. on operation of jury system, 1966-72, 79—. Bd. regents U. N.Mex., 1958-68, pres., 1963-64; bd. dirs. Fed. Jud. Ctr., 1983-87. Served to capt. AUS, 1942-45. Mem. Trial Judges Assn. 10th Circuit (pres. 1976-78), Nat. Conf. Fed. Trial Judges (exec. com. 1977-79), Sigma Chi. Home: 1117 Salamanca NW Albuquerque NM 87107 Office: PO Box 38 Albuquerque NM 87103

BRATTON, JAMES HENRY, JR., lawyer; b. Pulaski, Tenn., Oct. 9, 1931; s. James Henry and Mabel (Shelley) B.; m. Alleen Sharp Davis, Oct. 15, 1960; children: Susan Shelley, James Henry III, Margaret Alleen. B.A. optime merens, U. South, 1952; B.A., Oxford (Eng.) U., 1954, M.A., 1978; LL.B., Yale U., 1956. Bar: Tenn. 1956, Ga. 1957. With antitrust div. Dept. Justice, summer 1955; since practiced in Atlanta; partner firm Smith, Gambrell & Russell; vis. lectr. U. Ga. Law Sch., 1967; adj. prof. law Emory U., 1984—. Editor Yale Law Jour.; contbr. articles to profl. jours. Mem. Gov.'s Citizens Adv. Council on Environ. Affairs, 1970-74; trustee Trust Fund for Sibley Park, Ga. chpt. Multiple Sclerosis Soc., U. of the South, 1984—; bd. dirs. Christian Council Met. Atlanta, Protestant Welfare and Social Services, Chs. Home for Bus. Girls.; pres. Peachtree Heights West Civic Assn., 1984—. Mem. ABA (standing com. on aero. law 1962-84, chmn. 1977-80), Ga. Bar Assn. (founding chmn. environ. law sect. 1970-73), Ga. Bar Found. (trustee), Fed. Bar Assn., Atlanta Bar Assn., Lawyers Club Atlanta, Old Warhorse Lawyers Club, Am. Acad. Polit. and Social Scis., Am. Judicature Soc., Am. Law Inst., Yale Law Alumni Assn. (exec. com. 1976-79), Phi Beta Kappa, Phi Delta Phi, Pi Gamma Mu, Gridiron. Democrat. Methodist. Antitrust, Federal civil litigation, Contracts commercial. Home: 63 N Muscogee Ave NW Atlanta GA 30305 Office: First Atlanta Tower Atlanta GA 30383

BRATTON, ROBERT MILTON, legal educator; b. Cin., Aug. 1, 1937; s. Robert M. and Dorothy L. Bratton; m. Judy L. Schulz, Mar. 14, 1980. B.A., Ohio Wesleyan U., 1959; J.D., Chase Coll. Law, No. Ky. U., 1964; M.A., U. Cin., 1984. Bar: Ohio 1964, Ky. 1967. Assoc. Smith and Latimer, Cin., 1964-69; asst. atty. gen. State of Ohio, 1969-71; ptnr. French, Short, Valleau & Bratton, Cin., 1971-78; prof. law Chase Coll. Law, No. Ky. U., 1978—, adj. prof., 1974-78. Mem. ABA, Ohio State Bar Assn., Cin. Bar Assn., Ky. State Bar Assn., Ohio Acad. Trial Lawyers, Assn. Trial Lawyers Am., Nat. Inst. Trial Advocacy, Am. Arbitration Assn. Club: Masons. Family and matrimonial, Legal history, Federal civil litigation. Home: 4126 Sherel Ln Cincinnati OH 45209 Office: Chase Coll Law 528 Nunn Hall Highland Heights KY 41076

BRAUDE, HERMAN MARTIN, lawyer; b. N.Y.C., Oct. 16, 1939; m. Marcey Suzanne Braude; children—Sherrie, Brett, Darren. B.S. in Civil Engring., Cooper Union, 1961; J.D., Georgetown U., 1964. Bar: D.C. 1965, U.S. Supreme Ct. 1970. Law clk. to sr. judge U.S. Ct. Claims, 1964-65; ptnr. Sadur, Pelland & Braude, Washington, 1966-77; sr. ptnr. Braude, Margulies, Sacks & Rephan, Washington, 1977—, now pres. Mem. ABA (vice chmn. com. constrn. 1975-78), Fed. Bar Assn., Md. Bar Assn. (com. chmn.), Am. Arbitration Assn. (comml. panel arbitrator), D.C. Bar Assn. Editor Georgetown Law Jour.; contbr. articles to legal jours. Government contracts and claims, Construction. Office: 1828 L St NW Suite 900 Washington DC 20036

BRAUN, GLENN ROBERT, lawyer; b. Hays, Kans., July 16, 1956; s. Lelyn J. and Gladys M. (Werth) B. BS, Kans. State U., 1981. Bar: Kans. 1981, U.S. Dist. Ct. Kans. 1981. Assoc. Robert F. Glassman P.A., Hays, 1981-85; ptnr. Glassman, Bird & Braun, Hays, 1986—; spl. prosecuter Ellis County Atty.'s Office, Hays, 1981—. Sec., treas. Ellis County Dem. coms., Hays, 1981—, chmn. 1986—; bd. dirs. Big Bros./Big Sisters, 1985—. Mem. ABA, Kans. Bar Assn., Ellis County Bar Assn. (sec., treas. 1986—), Assn. Trial Lawyers Am., Kans. Trial Lawyers Assn. Lodge: KC. Bankruptcy, Criminal, Family and matrimonial. Home: 2504 Timber Dr Hays KS 67601 Office: Glassman Bird & Braun 113 W 13th Hays KS 67601

BRAUN, JEFFREY LOUIS, lawyer; b. N.Y.C., Oct. 2, 1946; s. Arthur and Berta (Freimark) B.; m. Beth Essig, June 6, 1982. BA, Rutgers U., 1968; JD, Yale U., 1971. Bar: N.Y. 1974, U.S. Dist. Ct. (so. and ea. dists.) N.Y., U.S. Tax Ct., U.S. Ct. Appeals (2d cir.). Law clk. to judge U.S. Dist. Ct. (cen. dist.) Calif., Los Angeles, 1971-72; assoc. Paul, Weiss, Rifkind, Wharton & Garrison, N.Y.C., 1972-74; assoc. Rosenman & Colin, N.Y.C., 1974-80, ptnr., 1980—. Mem. Assn. of Bar of City of N.Y. (com. on internat. human rights). Federal civil litigation, State civil litigation. Home: 55 East End Ave #8H New York NY 10028 Office: Rosenman & Colin 575 Madison Ave New York NY 10022

BRAUN, JEROME IRWIN, lawyer; b. St. Joseph, Mo., Dec. 16, 1929; s. Martin H. and Bess (Donsker) B.; children: Aaron Hugh, Susan Lori, Daniel Victor. AB with distinction, Stanford U., 1951, LLB, 1953. Bar: Calif., Mo., U.S. Tax Ct., U.S. Ct. Mil. Appeals, U.S. Ct. Appeals (9th cir.). Assoc. Long & Levit, San Francisco, 1957-58, Law Offices of Jefferson Peyser, 1958-62; ptnr. Farella, Braun & Martel (and predecessor firms), San Francisco, 1962—; instr. San Francisco Law Sch., 1958-69; lectr. in field; speaker various State Bar Conventions in Calif., Ill., Nev., Mont. Editor: Stanford U. Law Rev.; contbr. articles to profl. jours. Past pres. Jewish Welfare Fedn. of San Francisco; pres. Marin County and Peninsula Jewish Welfare Fedn., 1979-80; past pres. San Francisco United Jewish Community Ctrs. Served to 1st lt. JAGC, U.S. Army, 1954-57. Recipient Lloyd W. Dinkelspiel award Jewish Welfare Fedn., 1967. Mem. ABA, Calif. Bar Assn. (chmn. adminstrv. justice com. 1977, chmn. lawyer reps. to 9th cir. jud. conf. 1982, frequent moderator continuing edn. of the bar programs), Bar Assn. San Francisco (past chmn. spl. com. on lawyers malpractice and malpractice ins.), Mo. Bar Assn., San Francisco Bar Found. (past trustee), Calif. Acad. Appellate Lawyers (past pres.), Am. Judicature Soc., Am. Coll. Trial Lawyers, Order of Coif. Antitrust, Securities, Federal civil litigation.

BRAUN, N. BARRETT, lawyer; b. St. Louis, Mar. 27, 1946; s. William L. and Jayne (Shellabarger) B.; m. Carolyn Jane Schmidt, Aug. 15, 1970; 1 child, Whitney L. BA, Washington U., 1968, JD, 1971. Bar: Mo. 1971, U.S. Dist. Ct. (ea. dist.) Mo. 1972, Calif. 1974, U.S. Supreme Ct. 1976, U.S. Ct. Appeals (8th cir.) 1977. Managing atty. Legal Aid Soc., St. Louis, 1971-75; assoc. Thoits, Lehman, Hanna & Love, Palo Alto, Calif., 1975-76; ptnr. Braun & Stewart Inc., St. Louis, 1976-86, Braun, Stewart & Anderson, St. Louis, 1986—; pres., bd. dirs. Legal Services of Eastern Mo., St. Louis, 1980—. Mem. ABA, Mo. State Bar Assn. (bd. govs. 1979-80), Calif. Bar Assn., Metro St. Louis Bar Assn., St. Louis County Bar Assn. Club: Sports Car Am. (St. Louis). Avocation: road racing. Federal civil litigation, State civil litigation, General corporate. Office: Braun Stewart & Anderson Inc 120 S Central Clayton MO 63105

BRAUN, ROBERT ALAN, lawyer; b. Bronx, N.Y., Mar. 6, 1950; s. George and Sylvia (Feuerstein) B.; m. Roberta Ellen Shlofmitz, Aug. 29, 1970; children—Alison, Scott. B.A., Queens Coll., 1972; J.D., St. Johns U., 1976. Bar: N.Y. 1977, U.S. Dist. Ct. (ea. and so. dists.) N.Y. 1977, U.S. Ct. Appeals (2d cir.) 1978, U.S. Supreme Ct. 1982. Asst. dist. atty. Kings County Dist. Atty., Bklyn., 1976-80; assoc. Robert Rivers, P.C., Hempstead, N.Y., 1980, Singer & Braun, P.C., 1980-82; assoc. Sarisohn, Sarisohn, et al., Commack, N.Y., 1982-85, ptnr., 1985—; counsel E. Elwood Neighborhood Watch, E. Northport, N.Y., 1982—. Committeeman Huntington Town Democrat. Com., 1982—; councilman E. Northport council Cub Scouts Am. Pack 471, 1984—. Served to staff sgt. USNG, 1970-76. Mem. ABA, N.Y. State Bar Assn., Nassau County Bar Assn., Suffolk County Bar Assn., Suffolk County Crim. Bar Assn. Democrat. Jewish. Clubs: E. Northport Jewish Ctr. Mens (trustee 1983—), Soc. Am. Magicians Assembly #1 (pres. 1981-82). Real property, General corporate, Criminal. Office: Sarisohn Sarisohn et al 350 Veterans Hwy Commack NY 11725

BRAUN, STEPHEN JOHN, lawyer; b. St. Petersburg, Fla., July 14, 1951; s. Robert Marion and Wilma Francis (Lycett) B.; children: S. Stewart, Robert D. BA in Polit. Sci., Wake Forest U., 1973; JD, 1975. Bar: Md. 1975, U.S. Dist. Ct. Md., 1983. Assoc. Briscoe, Kenney & Kaminetz, P.A., Lexington Park, Md., 1976-77, Mudd & Mudd, P.A., La Plata, Md., 1977-79; sole practice, La Plata, 1979-80, 85—; state's atty. Charles County (Md.), La Plata, 1980-85. Pres. Charles County Young Dems., 1977, mem. Charles County Dem. Cen. Com., 1978; chmn. Charles County Children's Aid Soc., 1979; bd. dirs. Charles County Sexual Assault Ctr., Waldorf, Md., 1983—, Charles County Crime Solvers, Inc., Waldorf, 1982-84. Assoc. editor Wake Forest Law Rev., 1974. Named 1 of 5 Outstanding Young Marylanders, Md. Jaycees, 1982. Mem. Assn. Trial Lawyers Am., Md. State's Attys.' Assn. (sec. 1981, 1st v.p. 1983, pres. 1985), Md. Bar Assn., Charles County Bar Assn. (sec. 1984), ABA. Episcopalian. Lodges: Rotary (bd. dirs. 1978), Elks. Criminal, State civil litigation, General practice. Office: Office of State's Atty 101 St Mary's Ave PO Box 2534 La Plata MD 20646

BRAUN, WILLIAM DAVID, lawyer; b. Chgo., June 25, 1950; s. William Norman and Jean Evelyn (Pearson) B. AB, U. Ill., 1972; JD, U. Notre Dame, 1975; cert., U. Munich, 1979. Bar: Ill. 1975, D.C. 1984. Trial atty. antitrust div. U.S. Dept. Justice, Chgo., 1975-78; atty. antitrust div. U.S. Dept. Justice, Washington, 1979-84; assoc. Gardner, Carton & Douglas, Chgo., 1984-86, ptnr., 1987—. Mem. ABA, Chgo. Bar Assn. (chmn. subcom. on fgn. and internat. antitrust law, antitrust law com. 1984—). Antitrust, Private international, General corporate. Home: 2650 Lakeview Ave Apt 2602 Chicago IL 60614 Office: Gardner Carton & Douglas 321 N Clark St Suite 3400 Quaker Tower Chicago IL 60610-4795

BRAVERMAN, HERBERT LESLIE, lawyer; b. Buffalo, Apr. 24, 1947; s. David and Miriam P. (Cohen) B.; m. Janet Marx, June 11, 1972; 1 child, Becca Danielle. BS in Econs., U. Pa., 1969; JD, Harvard U., 1972. Bar: Ohio 1972, U.S. Dist. Ct. (no. dist.) Ohio 1972, U.S. Supreme Ct. 1975, U.S. Ct. Appeals (6th cir.) 1980, U.S. Ct. Claims 1980. Assoc. Hahn, Loeser & Freedheim, Cleve., 1972-75; sole practice Cleve., 1975—. Served to capt. USAR, 1970-82. Mem. Ohio Bar Assn., Bar Assn. Greater Cleve., Suburban East Bar Assn. (pres. 1978-80). Democrat. Jewish. Lodges: Rotary (Cleve. pres. 1980), B'nai B'rith (local pres. 1978-84). Avocations: golf, symphony, reading. Probate, Family and matrimonial, General corporate. Home: 3950 Orangewood Dr Orange OH 44122 Office: 23200 Chagrin Blvd Beachwood OH 44122

BRAWNER, GERALD THEODORE, lawyer; b. Phila., Jan. 15, 1941; s. John Theodore and Gladys Mary (Herbert) B.; m. Linda Ann Debnam, July 1, 1967. B.A., Pa. State U., 1966; J.D., Villanova U., 1969. Bar: Pa. 1970, D.C. 1982. Atty., HUD, 1969-70; assoc. Ballard, Spahr, Andrew & Ingersoll, Phila., 1970-72, 1973-76, ptnr., 1976-84; regional counsel Econ. Devel. Adminstrn., Dept. Commerce, 1972-73; 1st v.p., mgr. pub. fin. Phila. Group, Advest, Inc., 1984-85; ptnr. Morgan, Lewis & Bockius, Phila., 1985—; lectr. on export trading cos. U.S. Internat. Trade Adminstrn. Bd. mgrs. Children's Hosp. of Phila., 1982—; bd. dirs. Phila. Port Corp., Penns Landing Corp.; trustee Pa. Ballet, 1983-85; bd. dirs. Phila. Urban League, 1974-80, gen. counsel 1976-80; bd. dirs. Adoption Ctr. Delaware Valley, 1984—; active Community Leadership Assocs. Wharton Sch. of U. Pa., 1978—. Served with USAF, 1959-63. Mem. Internat. Bar Assn., ABA, Inter-Am. Bar Assn., Nat. Bar Assn., Fed. Bar Assn., Pa. Bar Assn., Barristers Assn. Phila., D.C. Bar Assn., Phila. Bar Assn. Clubs: Union League of Phila., Peale of Pa. Acad. Fine Arts. Real property, Private international, Municipal bonds. Office: Morgan Lewis & Bockius 2000 One Logan Sq Philadelphia PA 19103

BRAY, ABSALOM FRANCIS, JR., lawyer; b. San Francisco, Nov. 24, 1918; s. Absalom Francis and Leila Elizabeth (Veale) B.; m. Lorraine Cerena Paule, June 25, 1949; children—Oliver, Brian, Margot. B.A., Stanford U., 1940; J.D., U. So. Calif., 1949. Bar: Calif. 1949, U.S. Supreme Ct. 1960. Sr. ptnr. Bray & Baldwin and successive firms to Bray, Egan, Breitwieser & Costanza, Martinez, Walnut Creek & Moraga, Calif., 1949—, now pres. Bray, Egan, Breitwieser & Costanza, P.C., Martinez, Walnut Creek & Moraga; founder, dir. John Muir Nat. Bank, Martinez, 1983—. Chmn. Martinez Recreation Commn., 1949-54; chmn. nat. bd. dirs. Camp Fire Girls, 1959-61, 1969-71; pres. Contra Costa County (Calif.) Devel. Assn., 1959-60. Mem. State Bar Calif. (chmn. adoption com. 1955-56), Martinez Hist. Soc. (pres. 1894), Navy League U.S. (pres. Contra Costa Council 1981-83). Republican. Episcopalian. Served to lt. USNR, 1942-46. Club: Masons. General practice, Probate. Home: 600 Flora St Martinez CA 94553 Office: Ward & Ferry Sts Martinez CA 94553

BREAKSTONE, JAY L.T., lawyer; b. Bklyn., Apr. 11, 1951; s. Allen S. and Sarah M. (Cohen) B.; m. Rhonda Wiener, Oct. 31, 1982. BA, Long Island U., 1972; JD, Bklyn. Law Sch., 1976. Bar: N.Y. 1977, U.S. Dist. Ct. (so. and ea. dists.) N.Y. 1977, U.S. Ct. Appeals (2d cir.) 1977, U.S. Ct. Appeals (3d cir.) 1982, U.S. Supreme Ct. 1985. Sr. assoc. Barry Ivan Slotnick P.C., N.Y.C., 1977-82; Ptnr. Zane, Rudofsky & Hynes, N.Y.C., 1982-84, Slater, Vanderpool & Breakstone, Garden City, N.Y., 1984—. Mem. nat. adv. com. Project HOPE, N.Y.C., 1986—; counsel Teamster's Lodge B'nai B'rith, N.Y.C., 1986—; counsel, trustee Bellmore (N.Y.) Jewish Ctr., 1986—. Mem. ABA, N.Y. State Bar Assn. (criminal justice sect. ethics com.), Fed. Bar Council, N.Y. County Lawyers Assn., Nat. Assn. Criminal Def. Lawyers. Avocation: kite flying. General practice, Criminal, Federal and state civil litigation. Office: Slater Vanderpool & Breakstone 200 Garden City Plaza Garden City NY 11530

BREARTON, JAMES JOSEPH, lawyer; b. Troy, N.Y., Aug. 12, 1950; s. James Edward and Lois Marie (Mesnig) B.; m. Margaret Anne Cassidy, Aug. 27, 1977. BA, Coll. Holy Cross, 1972; JD, Albany Law Sch., 1975. Bar: N.Y. 1976, U.S. Dist. Ct. (no. dist.) N.Y. 1976. Sole practice Latham, N.Y., 1976—. Mem. ABA, N.Y. State Bar Assn., Rensselaer County Bar Assn. Personal injury, Probate, Personal income taxation. Office: 849 New Loudon Rd PO Box 889 Latham NY 12110

BRECHER, HOWARD ARTHUR, lawyer; b. N.Y.C., Oct. 18, 1953; s. Milton and Dorothy (Zahler) B. AB magna cum laude, Harvard U., 1975, MBA, 1979, JD cum laude, 1979; LLM, NYU, 1984. Bar: N.Y. 1980, U.S. Dist. Ct. (so. dist.) N.Y. 1982, U.S. Tax Ct. 1984. Assoc. Roberts & Holland, N.Y.C., 1979-82, Chadbourne, Parke, Whiteside & Wolff, N.Y.C., 1982-84; atty. legal dept. N.Y. Telephone Co., N.Y.C., 1984—; mem. tax com. Bus. Council of N.Y. State, Albany, 1984—. Mem. ABA (tax sect., pub. utility law sect.), N.Y. State Bar Assn. (tax sect., trusts and estates sect.), Harvard Bus. Sch. Club of Greater N.Y. Democrat. Jewish. Clubs: Harvard (N.Y.C. and Boston). Corporate taxation, State and local taxation, Public utilities. Home: 40 Spruce St Roslyn Harbor NY 11576 Office: NY Telephone Co 1095 Ave of the Americas Rm 3707 New York NY 10036

BRECHER, MITCHELL FREDRICK, lawyer; b. Washington, July 29, 1948; s. Sam W. and Roslyn P. (Block) B.; m. Sandra L. Levinson, June 10, 1973; children—Reid Scott, Todd Loren. B.A., Franklin and Marshall Coll., 1970; J.D. with honors, George Washington U., 1973. Bar: Md. 1973, D.C. 1975, U.S. Supreme Ct. 1978, U.S. Dist. Ct. D.C. 1981, U.S. Ct. Appeals (D.C. cir.) 1981. Law clk. 5th Jud. Circuit Ct., Annapolis, Md., 1973-74; atty.-advisor FCC, Washington, 1974-81; sr. atty. GTE Sprint Communications Corp., Washington, 1981-84; asst. gen. counsel, dir. regulatory affairs Lexitel Corp., Washington, 1984-85, ALC Communications Corp., 1985—. Mem. Md. Bar Assn., D.C. Bar Assn., Fed Communications Bar Assn. Democrat. Jewish. Communications, Administrative and regulatory, Public utilities. Home: 31 Hollyberry Ct Rockville MD 20852 Office: ALC Communication Corp 1990 M St NW Washington DC 20036

BRECHER, STUART GARY, lawyer; b. Newark, May 18, 1955; s. David and Rita (Feldman) B. AB, Rutgers U., New Brunswick, N.J, 1977; JD, Rutgers U., Newark, 1980. Bar: N.J. 1980, U.S. Dist. Ct. N.J 1980, U.S. Ct. Appeals (3d cir.) 1985. Law sec. N.J. Superior Ct., Elizabeth, 1980-81; assoc. Ravin, Davis & Sweet, P.A., Woodbridge, N.J., 1981-83, Brach, Eichler, Rosenberg, Silver, Bernstein, Hammer & Gladstone, P.A., Roseland, N.J., 1983—. Mem. ABA, N.J. Bar Assn., Essex County Bar Assn. State civil litigation, Contracts commercial, Consumer commercial. Home: 182 Evergreen Rd Apt 7B Edison NJ 08837 Office: Brach Eichler Rosenberg et al 101 Eisenhower Pkwy Roseland NJ 07068

BRECKENRIDGE, BRYAN CRAIG, lawyer; b. Nevada, Mo., Dec. 7, 1951; s. Keith Lorraine and Elizabeth Jane (Osborn) B.; m. Patricia Ann Russell, May 15, 1976. BBA, U. Mo., 1974, JD, 1977. Bar: Mo. 1977, U.S. Dist. Ct. (we. dist.) Mo. 1978. Assoc. Russell, Brown & Bickel, Nevada, Mo., 1977-78; ptnr. Russell, Brown, Bickel & Breckenridge, Nevada, 1978—; asst. pros. atty. Vernon County Mo., Nevada, 1979-82; bd. dirs. Boatmen's Bank Nev. Mem. Home Rule Charter Commn., Nevada, 1978, Nevada Planning Commn., 1980—; vice chmn. Nevada Area Econ. Devel. Com., 1985—. Mem. ABA, Mo. Bar Assn., Vernon County Bar Assn., Assn. Trial Lawyers Am., Mo. Assn. Trial Attys., Nev. C. of C. Lodges: Rotary (bd. dirs. 1982-84), Elks. Avocations: golf, fishing, hunting. Personal injury, Banking, Probate. Home: 816 W Maple Nevada MO 64772 Office: Russell Brown Bickel et al 108 W Walnut Nevada MO 64772

BRECKENRIDGE, JAMES RICHARD, lawyer; b. Manhattan, Kans., Nov. 5, 1950; s. Richard H. and Meda Gae (Litton) B.; m. Suzanne Thoben Marquard, July 13, 1983; 1 child, Cynthia. BA cum laude, Harvard U., 1973; JD with honors, U. Tex., 1979. Bar: N.Y. 1980, D.C. 1981. Assoc. Yamada Condemi Thomas & Dean, N.Y.C., 1979-86; ptnr. Thomas & Breckenridge, N.Y.C., 1986—. Banking, Private international, Personal income taxation. Office: Thomas & Breckenridge 84 William St Suite 600 New York NY 10038

BRECZINSKI, MICHAEL JOSEPH, lawyer; b. El Paso, Tex., Mar. 16, 1953; s. Julius W. and Rosemarie (Kelly) B.; m. Arlene Ann Szafranski, Apr. 20, 1979; children: Emily, Nathan. AA, Oakland Community Coll., 1973; BA, Mich. State U., 1976; JD, Thomas M. Cooley Law Sch., Lansing, Mich., 1981. Bar: Mich. 1982, Minn. 1983. Sole practice Lansing, 1982-83, Flint, Mich., 1983-85, Mt. Morris, Mich., 1985—. Mem. Mich. Bar Assn., Minn. Bar Assn., Genesee County Bar Assn, Assn. Trial Lawyers Am., Cath. Attys. Guild. Republican. Club: Flint Rogues Rugby. Criminal, General practice, Personal injury. Office: 5005 Lapeer Rd Burton MI 48509

BREED, E(RNEST) MARK, III, lawyer; b. Jacksonville, Fla., Dec. 5, 1955; s. Ernest M. and Nancy Charlotte (Naylor) B.; m. Brook Allison Burgess, Mar. 21, 1981; 1 child, David Mark. BS in Econs., U. Fla., 1978, JD, 1981. Bar: Fla. 1982, U.S. Dist. Ct. (middle dist.) Fla. 1982, U.S. Ct. Appeals (11th cir.) 1982. Jud. aide U.S. Ct. Appeals (2d dist.), Lakeland, Fla., 1981-85; assoc. Tilden R. Schofield, Sebring, Fla., 1985—. Elder Covenant Presbyn. Ch., Sebring, 1986. Mem. ABA, Highlands County Bar Assn. (treas.-sec. 1985-86), Christian Legal Soc. Republican. Lodge: Rotary. Avocations: water skiing, photography, golf, racquetball. General practice, Probate, Real property. Home: 209 Revson Ave Sebring FL 33870 Office: Tilden R. Schofield PA 335 S Commerce Sebring FL 33870

BREEDING, EARNIE ROWE, lawyer; b. Hartselle, Ala., Aug. 8, 1939; s. Melvin Leon and W. Marie (Webster) B.; m. Caroline Kay Jones, Nov. 14, 1963; children: Jennifer McLean, Leah Marie. BA, U. Mich., 1963; MBA, U. So. Miss., 1975; JD, John Marshall Sch. Law, Atlanta, 1980. Bar: Ga. 1980, U.S. Dist. Ct. (no. and mid. dist.) Ga. 1980, U.S. Ct. Appeals (5th and 11th cir.) 1981, U.S. Dist. Ct. (mid. dist.) 1986. Enlisted USN, 1959, advanced through grades to commdr., 1978, resigned, 1972; logistics engr. Ingalls Shipbldg., Pascagoula, Miss., 1972-75; sr. buyer Metro Atlanta Rapid Transit, 1975-82; sole practice Decatur, Ga., 1980—; adjunct prof. Brenau Coll., Gainesville, Ga., 1980-84. Mem. St. Johns Luth. Ch., youth chmn., 1982-85; pres. Hickory Hills Civic Assn., Stone Mountain, Ga., 1982-85. Served with USNR, 1972-85. Mem. ABA (spl. task force for gen. practice 1984), Decatur-Dekalb Bar Assn., Ga. Trial Lawyers Assn. (mem. com. 1980—), State Bar Assn. Ga. Avocation: stamp collecting. Personal injury, State civil litigation, Family and matrimonial. Office: 116 E Howard Ave Decatur GA 30030-3345

BREEN, JAMES JOSEPH, insurance company executive; b. Indpls., June 7, 1932; s. James Joseph and Beatrice Alice (Bloye) B.; m. Maureen Frances Pleak, Jan. 30, 1934; children—Elise M., Melissa A. B.A., Butler U., 1955; J.D., Ind. U., 1960. Bar: Ind. 1961, U.S. Dist. Ct. (so. dist.) Ind. 1961, U.S. Supreme Ct. 1968, Ill. 1970, U.S. Dist. Ct. (no. dist.) Ill. 1970, U.S. Ct. Appeals (7th cir.) 1974. Dep. atty. gen. State of Ind., 1961-65; v.p., gen. counsel, sec., dir. Coll./U. Corp., Indpls., 1965-70; exec. v.p., gen. counsel, sec., dir., Fed. Life Cos. Group, 1970—. Mem. Chgo. Estate Planning Council (chmn. Ill. ins. investment code com.). Served to capt. USAF, 1955-57. Mem. ABA, Ill. Bar Assn., Ind. Bar Assn., Indpls. Bar Assn., Chgo. Bar Assn. Republican. Roman Catholic. Club: Rotary Internat. Administrative and regulatory, General corporate, Estate planning. Address: 515 S Valley Rd Lake Forest IL 60045

BREEN, JAMES PATRICK, JR., lawyer; b. Bridgeport, Conn., Aug. 15, 1946; s. James Patrick and Angela Anne (Perrini) B.; m. Geraldine Collier Breen, Aug. 24, 1968; children: Elizabeth Anne, Catherine Collier. BA, U. Pa., 1968; MBA, U. Chgo., 1971; JD, U. Conn., 1974. Bar: Conn. 1974. Assoc. Wiggins & Dana, 1974-78; atty. Stauffer Chem. Co., Westport, Conn., 1978-82, dir. real estate, 1982-85; dir. real estate Chesebrough Pond's Inc., Westport, 1985—. Chmn. bd. trustees Ind. Day Sch., Middlefield, Conn., 1982—. Real property, General corporate, Landlord-tenant.

BREEN, JEAN MARIE, lawyer, educator; b. Neosho, Mo., Oct. 5, 1954; d. John David Breen and Joan Kirkpatrick. BA summa cum laude, Creighton U., 1976, JD, 1980. Bar: Nebr. 1980, Ill. 1984, Mo. 1985, U.S. Dist. Ct. (no. dist.) Ill. 1984. Law clk. to presiding justice Neb. Supreme Ct., Lincoln, 1980-81; adj. prof. Creighton U. Law Sch., Omaha, 1981-82; lectr. U. Nebr., Omaha, 1981-82; law clk. to presiding judge U.S. Dist. Ct. (no. dist.) Ill., Chgo., 1982-84; assoc. Thurman, Smith, Howald, Weber & Bowles, Hillsboro, Mo., 1984—; adj. prof. Washington U. Law Sch., St. Louis, 1985. Editorial bd. Creighton U. Law Rev. Review, 1979-80. Mem. ABA, Nebr. Bar Assn., Mo. Bar Assn., Chgo. Bar Assn., Bar Assn. of Greater St. Louis. Roman Catholic. Federal civil litigation, State civil litigation, Employment law. Office: Thurman Smith et al One Thurman Ct PO Box 277 Hillsboro MO 63050

BREGA, CHARLES FRANKLIN, lawyer; b. Callaway, Nebr., Feb. 5, 1933; s. Richard E. and Bessie (King) B.; m. Betty Jean Witherspoon, Sept. 17, 1960; children: Kerry E., Charles D., Angie G. B.A., The Citadel, 1954; LL.M., U. Colo., 1960. Bar: Colo. 1960. Assoc. firm Hindry & Meyer, Denver, 1960-62; partner Hindry & Meyer, 1962-75, dir., 1975; dir. firm Roath & Brega, Denver, 1975—; lectr. in field; guest prof. U. Colo., U. Denver, U. Nev. (numerous states and), Can. Trustee Pres.'s Leadership Class, U. Colo., 1977—. Served with USAF, 1954-57. Mem. Colo. Trial Lawyers Assn. (pres. 1972-73), Am. Trial Lawyers Assn. (gov. 1972-79), ABA, Internat. Acad. Trial Lawyers, Internat. Soc. Barristers. Episcopalian. Clubs: Cherry Hills Country, Denver Athletic. Criminal, Personal injury, Family and matrimonial. Home: 4501 S Vine Way Englewood CO 80110 Office: Roath & Brega PC PO Box 5560 TA Denver CO 80217

BREGGIN, JANIS ANN, lawyer; b. Rochester, N.Y., Mar. 5, 1955; d. Arnold H. and Eleanor (Wingo) B.; m. Bruce A. Gomez, May 14, 1983; children: Rachel Tyler, Cadiz Safira, Theo Socrates. BA, U. Denver, 1976, JD, 1980. Bar: Colo. 1980, U.S. Ct. Appeals (10th cir.) 1980. Assoc. Sherman & Howard, Denver, 1980-82, Jeffrey M. Nobel & Assocs., Denver, 1982-84; assoc., in house counsel Bill L. Walters Cos., Englewood, Colo., 1984-85; assoc. Deutsch & Sheldon, Englewood, 1985-87; ptnr. Forhan & Breggin, P.C., Englewood, 1987—. Mem. ABA, Colo. Bar Assn., Denver Bar Assn., Colo. Women's Bar Assn. Real property. Office: Forhan & Breggin PC 7951 E Maplewood Ave #326 Englewood CO 80111

BREGLIO, JOHN F., lawyer; b. N.Y.C., June 5, 1946; s. John N. and Sylvia V. (Calucci) B.; m. Nan K. Proctor, May 22, 1976; children: Eliza Mason, Nola Keene. BA, Yale U., 1968; JD, Harvard U., 1971. Bar: N.Y. 1972, U.S. Dist. Ct. (ea. and so. dists.) 1974, U.S. Ct. Appeals (2d cir.) 1975. Ptnr. Paul, Weiss, Rifkind, Wharton & Garrison, N.Y.C., 1971—; chmn., lectr. on entertainment industry N.Y. Law Journal seminars, N.Y.C., 1984—. Bd. dirs. The Acting Co., N.Y.C., 1982—, Theatre Devel. Fund, N.Y.C., 1983—. Mem. ABA, N.Y. State Bar Assn., Assn. of Bar of City of N.Y. Clubs: Yale, Waccabuc Country (N.Y.C.). Entertainment, Copyright. Home: 115 E 82d St #9B New York NY 10028 Office: Paul Weiss Rifkind Wharton & Garrison 1285 Avenue of the Americas New York NY 10019

BREGMAN, JUDY ELLEN, lawyer; b. N.Y.C., Oct. 4, 1949; d. Walter W. and Miriam (Levenkron) B.; m. Mark Howard Welch, Oct. 26, 1985. BA in Psychology, Carnegie-Mellon U., 1971; JD, Thomas M. Cooley Sch. Law, 1980. Bar: Mich. 1981, U.S. Dist. Ct. (ea. and we. dists.) Mich. 1981, U.S. Ct. Appeals (6th cir.) 1983, U.S. Supreme Ct. 1986. Law clk. to presiding judge U.S. Dist. Ct. (we. dist.) Mich., Grand Rapids, 1980-82; assoc. Varnum, Riddering, Schmidt & Howlett, Grand Rapids, 1982—. Mem. ABA, Mich. Bar Assn. (constl. law com., med.-legal problems com.), Fed. Bar Assn., Grand Rapids Bar Assn. Avocations: rock collecting, cooking, antiques. Federal civil litigation, State civil litigation, Criminal. Office: Varnum Riddering et al 171 Monroe NW Grand Rapids MI 49503

BREIBART, RICHARD JEROME, lawyer; b. N.Y.C., Nov. 12, 1950; s. Harold R. and Martha (Killerman) B.; m. Leslie Israel, Aug. 6, 1972 (div. Dec. 1980). BA in Govt., Cornell U., 1971; JD, U. S.C., 1979. Bar: S.C. 1979, U.S. Dist. Ct. S.C. 1981, U.S. Ct. Appeals (4th cir.) 1981. Law clk. to presiding justice S.C. Cir. Ct., 1979-81; ptnr. Coleman, Sawyer, Breibart & McCauley, Lexington, S.C., 1981—; atty. Saluda County, S.C., 1983—, Town of Batesburg, S.C., 1985—. Mem. ABA, S.C. Bar Assn., Assn. Trial Lawyers Am., S.C. Trial Lawyers Assn. (polit. asst.). Criminal, Federal civil litigation, State civil litigation. Office: Coleman Sawyer Breibart & McCauley 129 E Main St Lexington SC 29072

BREIDENBACH, CHERIE ELIZABETH, lawyer; b. Aberdeen, S.D., Aug. 20, 1952; d. Neil Allen and Portia Elizabeth (Bradner) Johnson; m. Steven Theodore Breidenbach, Aug. 9, 1975. BS, U. S.D., 1975, JD, 1979. Bar: S.D. 1979, Calif. 1981. Sole practice La Jolla, Calif., 1982-84; assoc., acct. Law Offices of Larry Siegel, San Diego, 1984-86; ptnr. Fout, Breidenbach & Chin, San Diego, 1986—. Mem. ABA, Calif. Bar Assn., S.D. Bar Assn., Phi Delta Phi. Republican. Methodist. Avocations: antique restoration, interior decoration, piano, horses. General corporate, Probate, Personal income taxation.

BREITENBERG, JOHN FRANCIS, awyer; b. Chgo., May 17, 1948; s. Ronald Francis and Anne Marie (Kastigar) B. B.A., U. Md., 1970; J.D., Georgetown U., 1973. Bar: Md. 1973, D.C. 1975. Adminstrv. asst. Senator George E. Snyder, Md. Senate, Annapolis, 1974; law clk. Hon. Ridgely P. Melvin, Md. State Ct. Spl. Appeals, Annapolis, 1974-75; legis. asst. Hon. Benjamin A. Gilman, U.S. Ho. of Reps., Washington, 1975; asst. counsel Com. on Post Office and Civil Service, U.S. Ho. of Reps., Washington, 1975-79; counsel Hon. James Clark, Jr., Pres. Md. Senate, Annapolis, 1979-82; sole practice, Washington, 1982—. Mem. commn. on future of Montgomery county. Served to capt. USAFR, 1970-80. Mem. Md. Bar Assn., D.C. Bar Assn. Real property, Local government, Legislative. Home: 5225 Pooks Hill Rd 1808N Bethesda MD 20814 Office: 1725 De Sales St NW Suite 900 Washington DC 20036

BRELAND, NORMAN LEROY, lawyer; b. Picayune, Miss., Sept. 25, 1937; s. John Talmadge and Ophelia Leigh (Burdette) B.; m. Kathleen Hirston Carroll, Oct. 22, 1977 (div. June 1981). BS in Chem. Engring., Miss. State U., 1959; MS in Chem. Engring., U. Miss., 1962, JD, 1967. Bar: Miss. 1967, U.S. Dist. Ct. (so. and no. dists.) Miss. 1967, U.S. Ct. Appeals (5th and 11th cirs.) 1967, U.S. Supreme Ct. 1967. Assoc. Holleman & Necaise, Gulfport, Miss., 1967-71; ptnr. Breland & Barnett, Gulfport, 1971-81, Mize, Thompson & Blass, Gulfport, 1982-83; sole practice Gulfport, 1983—; asst. dist. atty. Harrison, Hancock and Stone Counties, 1971-73. Composer songs Do Me A Favor, 1970, Silver Thread of Rain, 1970. Commr. law library Harrison County Bd. Suprs., Gulfport, 1978—; chmn. crusade Am. Cancer Soc., Harrison County, Miss., 1980. Served to lt. USNR, 1968-74. Crosby scholar, 1955; recipient Citizenship award City of Picayune, 1950. Fellow Miss. Bar Assn.; mem. ABA, Miss. Bar Assn. (bd. of commrs. 1969-76), Harrison County Bar Assn. (pres. 1973-74), Am. Judicature Soc., Fifth Cir. Bar Assn., Fed. Bar Assn., Phi Alpha Delta. Democrat. Baptist. Clubs: Gulfport Yacht, Bayou Bluff Tennis, Pass Christian Isles Golf, (Picayune). Lodges: Masons, Rotary. Federal civil litigation, Personal injury, Admiralty. Home: 16th and Church #41 Tally Arms Gulfport MS 39501 Office: 1919 23d Ave Gulfport MS 39501

BREMER, THOMAS FRANCIS, lawyer; b. Cleve., Dec. 16, 1922; s. Herman Albert and Alice Marie (Sinnott) B.; m. Anne Murphy, June 6, 1953; children: T. Christopher, Patty Iwaoka, Peggy Bremer Norris, Janet Gamboa, Judy. BBA, U. Notre Dame, 1944, JD, 1946. Assoc. Frost & Bremer, Cleve., 1946-56; ptnr. Bremer, Thompson, Morhard & Coyne, Cleve., 1956-82; assoc. Roudebush, Brown & Ulrich, Cleve., 1982-87, Zellmer & Gruber, Cleve., 1987—; bd. dirs., sec. Interlake Industries, Willoughby, Ohio, 1956—, Metal Marker Mfg. Co., Cleve., 1971—, Trimline Tool Co., Cleve., 1956—, Ohio Bldg. Products, Willoughby, 1970—. Pres. Montessori Spl. Edn. Sch., Cleveland Heights, 1966-76. Mem. Ohio Bar Assn. Democrat. Roman Catholic. Clubs: Cleve. Athletic, Cleve. Playhouse (pres. 1982-84). General corporate, Pension, profit-sharing, and employee benefits, Probate. Home: 10134 Surfside Circle N Aurora OH 44202 Office: Zellmer & Gruber 1400 Leader Bldg Cleveland OH 44114

BRENDZEL, MICHAEL L., lawyer; b. Breslau, Poland, June 2, 1948; s. Israel and Regina (Nijaki) B.; m. Helane Beth Cohen, Apr. 20, 1985. BA, Rutgers U., 1969; JD, Columbia U., 1973. Bar: N.Y. 1973, U.S. Dist. Ct. (so. dist.) N.Y. 1973. Assoc. Kelley, Drye & Warren, N.Y.C., 1973-75; ptnr. Delson & Gordon, N.Y.C., 1975-85; counsel Nissho Iwai Am. Corp., N.Y.C., 1985—. Avocations: tennis, sailing, golf, chess. Contracts commercial, Private international, Antitrust. Home: 311 E 23d St New York NY 10010 Office: Nissho Iwai Am Corp 1211 Ave of the Americas New York NY 10036

BRENEMAN, WILLIAM DUDLEY, lawyer, educator; b. Chelsea, Mass., July 9, 1943; s. William and Alice M. (Coblin) B.; student Thiel Coll., 1961-62, Case Western Res. U., 1962; B.A., Tex. A&M U., 1967; J.D., John Marshall U., 1967-70; postgrad. Harvard U., 1980-82. Bar: Mass. 1971, U.S. Patent Office 1973, D.C. 1976, U.S. Ct. Appeals (D.C. cir.) 1976, D.C. 1976, U.S. Supreme Ct. 1977. Atty., Watson, Leavenworth, Kelton & Taggart, N.Y.C., 1970-73; patent atty. Cushman, Darby & Cushman, Washington, 1978-80; prof. George Washington U., 1980-83; patent atty. Breneman, Kane & Georges, Washington, 1980—, sr. ptnr., 1980—; asst. prof. George Washington U., 1980—. Mem. Assn. Trial Lawyers Am., Am. Chem. Soc., Am. Patent Law Assn., ABA. Author: Business Law Casebook, 1981. Patent, Federal civil litigation, Trademark and copyright. Home: 2400 Virginia Ave NW Washington DC 20037 Office: Breneman Kane & Georges 1001 Connecticut Ave NW Washington DC 20036

BRENNAN, DANIEL EDWARD, JR., lawyer, educator; b. Houston, Oct. 21, 1942; s. Daniel E. and Emily (Tabor) B.; m. Ruth Miriam Gonchar, Nov. 16, 1973; children—Danna Julie, Benjamin Tabor. A.S., SUNY-Albany, 1974, B.S., 1976; J.D., U. Bridgeport, 1981; I.E.M., Harvard U., 1974. Bar: Conn. 1981, U.S. Dist. Ct. Conn. 1981. Exec. asst. to pres. Hunter Coll., N.Y.C., 1970-77; pres. S&B Mgmt. Systems, N.Y.C., 1977-80; ptnr. Brennan, McNamara & Brennan, P.C., Bridgeport, Conn., 1981—; trial referee Superior Ct., State of Conn.; chief legal advisor Bridgeport Police Dept., 1983-85. Chief labor counsel City of Bridgeport, 1981-85, Town of Trumbull, Conn., 1982—. Mem. ABA, Assn. Trial Lawyers Am., Conn. Trial Lawyers Assn., Conn. Bar Assn. Republican. Labor, State civil litigation, General practice. Home: 471 Beechwood Ave Bridgeport CT 06604 Office: Brennan McNamara & Brennan PC 600 Brooklawn Ave Bridgeport CT 06604

BRENNAN, DANOLDA JEAN, lawyer, insurance agent; b. Omaha, July 22, 1941; d. William Joseph and Danolda Iowala (Perkins) B. grad. Duquesne Coll., 1966; M.B.A., Notre Dame U., 1970; J.D., John Marshall Law Sch., 1974. Bar: Ill. Sr. v.p. Diversified Citigroup, Inc., Lombard, Ill. Patron, Lyric Opera of Chgo. Mem. Am. Soc. Corp. Secs., Chgo. Council Fgn. Relations, ABA, Chgo. Bar Assn., Women's Bar Assn. Ill. Contbr. articles on law to profl. jours. Insurance, General corporate, Labor. Home: 336 Wellington Ave Apt 1605 Chicago IL 60657 Office: Diversified Citigroup Inc 1920 Highland Ave Lombard IL 60148

BRENNAN, DIANTHA GARRETT, lawyer; b. Kansas City, Mo., Mar. 23, 1956; d. Hywell D. and Wynelle (Moxley) Garrett; m. John Christopher Brennan, Dec. 30, 1982. BA in History with honors, U. Tex., 1977, postgrad., 1977-78; JD, South Tex. Coll. Law, 1981. Bar: Tex. 1982, U.S. Dist. Ct. (so. dist.) Tex. 1984. Briefing atty. Tex. Ct. Criminal Appeals, Austin, 1981-82; assoc. Guiberson Law Offices, Houston, 1982-85, Law Offices of Ray J. McQuary, Houston, 1986—. Precinct coordinator Kingwood (Tex.) Dem. Party, 1984; del. regional precinct conv., Houston, 1984. Mem. ABA (Outstanding Speaker in Nation 1981), State Bar Tex., Tex. Young Lawyers Assn., Assn. Trial Lawyers Am., Lawyers' Alliance on Nuclear Arms Control. Democrat. Mem. Christian Ch. Personal injury, State civil litigation, Criminal. Home: 5403 Haven Oaks Kingwood TX 77339 Office: Law Offices of Ray J McQuary 2 Kingwood Place Suite 170 700 Rockmead Dr Kingwood TX 77339

BRENNAN, JAMES JOSEPH, mechanical engineering educator; b. Hot Springs, Ark., Apr. 2, 1924; s. James J. and Cynthia Anne (Straw) B.; m.

Lolan S. Schroeder, June 25, 1949; children—Juli A. Brennan Davis, Cynthia A. Brennan Becker, James Joseph. B.S.E.E., Iowa State Coll., 1945; postgrad. Columbia U., 1949-52; M.S.I.E., U. Ark., 1963; Ph.D., U. Tex., 1972; postgrad. Tex. A&M U., 1980. Diplomate Nat. Acad. Forensic Engrs. Patent examiner U.S. Patent Office, Washington, 1947-48; engr. U.S. Naval Supply Research and Devel. Facility, Bayonne, N.J., 1948-53; dir. indsl. devel. Hot Springs C. of C., 1954-56; indsl. engr. Ark. Indsl. Devel. Commn., Little Rock, 1956-58; plant engr. elec. organ div. Baldwin Piano Co., Fayetteville, Ark., 1958-60; asst. prof. indsl. engring. U. Ark., Fayetteville, 1960-65; research assoc. U. Ark. Med. Ctr., Little Rock, 1962-64; instr. mech. engring. U. Tex., Austin, 1966-68; assoc. prof. Lamar U., Beaumont, Tex., 1968-73, prof., 1974—, head indsl. engring. dept., 1979-80; pres. Brennan Engring. Co., Beaumont, 1977—; cons. Nat. Clay Pipe Mfrs. Assn., 1953-54, Cherokee Molded Products Co., Ft. Smith, Ark., 1960-63, Levingston Shipbuilding Co., Orange, Tex., 1969-73, Beaumont Refinery, Mobil Oil Corp., 1974-76. Served as ensign USN, 1943-46. NSF faculty fellow, 1965-66. Mem. Nat. Soc. Profl. Engrs., Tex. Soc. Profl. Engrs., ASME, Am. Soc. for Quality Control (pres. Sabine subsect. East Tex. chpt. 1976), ASTM (sec. com. on tech. aspects of product liability litigation 1981-82, chmn. statis. group 1950, mem. various coms.), Nat. Safety Council, Am. Inst. Indsl. Engrs. (dir. Austin chpt. 1967), Am. Soc. Safety Engrs., Sigma Xi, Alpha Pi Mu, Pi Tau Sigma. Home: 2441 Liberty St Beaumont TX 77702 Office: PO Box 10032 Lamar U Beaumont TX 77710

BRENNAN, JAMES JOSEPH, lawyer; b. San Francisco, Apr. 13, 1936; s. Joseph Bernard and Dorothy Ann (Smith) B.; m. Sarah Anne Cahill, Aug. 29, 1959; children: Mary, Joseph, Michael, Catherine. BS, Marquette U., 1957; LLB magna cum laude, Harvard U., 1963. Bar: Ill. 1963. Assoc. Sidley & Austin, Chgo., 1963-69, ptnr., 1970—. Served to lt. (j.g.) USN, 1957-60. Mem. Chgo. Bar Assn., Legal Club Chgo. Republican. Clubs: Tavern, Saddle and Cycle (Chgo.). Avocations: tennis, bridge. Securities, General corporate, Private international. Home: 1430 N Lake Shore Dr Chicago IL 60610 Office: Sidley & Austin 1 First Nat Plaza Chicago IL 60603

BRENNAN, JAMES JOSEPH, lawyer; b. Chgo., July 17, 1950; s. John Michael and Rosemary (Rickard) B.; m. Donna Jean Blessing, June 2, 1973; 1 child, Michael James. BS, Purdue U., 1972; JD, Indiana U., 1975. Bar: Ind. 1975, Ill. 1978, U.S. Dist. Ct. (so. dist.) Ind., U.S. Dist. Ct. (no. dist.) Ill., U.S. Tax Ct., U.S. Ct. Appeals (4th, 6th and 7th cirs.), U.S. Supreme Ct. 1981. Law clk. to presiding justice U.S. Dist. Ct., Knoxville, Tenn., 1975-77; assoc. Pope, Ballard, Shepard & Fowle, Ltd., Chgo., 1977-81, ptnr., 1981—; chmn. legal affairs com. Ill. Bankers Assn., Chgo., 1986. Contbr. articles to profl. jours. Mem. ABA, Ill. Bar Assn., Chgo. Bar Assn. Club: Union League (Chgo.). Banking, Contracts commercial, Federal civil litigation. Home: 87 Lawton Rd Riverside IL 60546 Office: Pope Ballard Shepard & Fowle Ltd 69 W Washington St Chicago IL 60602-3069

BRENNAN, JOSEPH VINCENT, lawyer; b. Detroit, Dec. 1, 1954; s. Michael James and Rita Ruth Brennan; m. Margaret Mary Koueiter, July 1, 1977; children: Joseph, John, James. PhB, Wayne State U., Detroit, 1972-76; JD, Detroit Coll. Law, 1977-80. Bar: Mich. 1981, U.S. Dist. Ct. (ea. dist.) Mich. 1981. Assoc. prosecutor Wayne County, Detroit, 1981-83; assoc. Sullivan, Ward & Bone P.C., Detroit, 1983-85, Bockoff & Zamler P.C., Southfield, Mich., 1985—; moderator Inst. Continuing Legal Edn., Detroit, 1986—. Mem. ABA, Mich. Bar Assn., Detroit Bar Assn. Roman Catholic. Avocations: sailing, bike riding, jogging, woodworking, family activities. Personal injury, Insurance, Criminal. Office: Bockoff & Zamler PC 20755 Greenfield Suite 700 Southfield MI 48075

BRENNAN, MARY KATHRYN GONYA, lawyer; b. Millinocket, Maine, Aug. 7, 1946. BA, U. Maine, Orono, 1968; JD, U. Maine, Portland, 1971; MPH, Harvard U., 1975. Bar: Maine 1972, N.J. 1976, N.Y. 1982. Founder, mng. ptnr. Brennan & Brennan, Portland, 1972-75; gen. counsel Ctr. Health Affairs, Princeton, N.J., 1975-85; counsel Stryker, Tams & Dill, Princeton, 1985-86; assoc. Brener, Wallack & Hill, Princeton, 1986-87; sole practice Princeton, 1987—; lectr. U. Medicine and Dentistry N.J., Newark, 1982—. Mem. Am. Acad. Hosp. Attys., Nat. Health Lawyers Assn., Healthcare Fin. Mgmt. Assn., N.J. Soc. Hosp. Attys. (pres. 1985-86). Health. Office: 103 Carnegie Ctr Suite 107 Princeton NJ 08543

BRENNAN, RICHARD SNYDER, banker, lawyer; b. St. Louis, Mar. 18, 1938; s. Clarence Rosso and Anna (Snyder) B.; m. Jill Wilson, July 27, 1963; children—George Mason, Joseph Bicknell, Sophie Scott. A.B., Princeton U.; J.D., U. Mich. Bar: Ill., N.Y. Assoc. Shearman & Sterling, N.Y.C., 1963-64; assoc. Mayer, Brown & Platt, Chgo., 1964-71, ptnr., 1971-82; exec. v.p., gen. counsel, sec. Continental Ill. Corp., Chgo., 1982—. General corporate. Office: Continental Ill Corp 231 S La Salle St Chicago IL 60697 *

BRENNAN, THOMAS EMMETT, JR., lawyer, judge; b. Detroit, Mar. 20, 1952; s. Thomas Emmett and Pauline Mary (Weinberger) B.; m. Julie Schafer, Apr. 23, 1977; children—Thomas Emmett III, Patrick Joseph. B.S., Mich. State U., 1974; J.D., Thomas M. Cooley Law Sch., 1978. Bar: Mich. 1978. Assoc. McGinty, Brown & Jakubiak, P.C., East Lansing, Mich., 1978-79; ptnr. Klug & Brennan, P.C., East Lansing, 1979-81; dist. judge 55th Dist. Ct., Mason, Mich., 1981—; 9th Dist. commr. Ingham County Bd., Mason, 1979-81; bd. dirs. Thomas M. Cooley Law Sch. Lansing, 1980—, adj. prof., 1983—; adj. prof. Mich. State U., 1983—. Mem. Ingham County Bar Assn., ABA, Am. Judges Assn., Ingham County Trial Judges Assn., Mich. Dist. Judges Assn., Thomas M. Cooley Law Sch. Alumni Assn. (Disting. Alumnus award 1983). Clubs: Mich. State U., Downtown Coaches (Lansing) (bd. dirs.). Lodge: Rotary (East Lansing). Criminal, Landlord-tenant, Judicial administration. Office: 55th Dist Ct 700 Buhl Mason MI 48854

BRENNAN, WILLIAM JOSEPH, JR., justice U.S. Supreme Ct.; b. Newark, Apr. 25, 1906; s. William J. and Agnes (McDermott) B.; m. Marjorie Leonard, May 5, 1928 (dec.); children—William Joseph, Hugh Leonard, Nancy; m. Mary Fowler, Mar. 9, 1983. B.S., U. Pa., 1928; LL.B., Harvard, 1931; LL.D., U. Notre Dame, 1968; LLB, Princeton, 1986, Columbia U., 1986, Brandeis U., 1986, N.Y. Law Sch., 1986, John Marshall Law Sch., 1986. Bar: N.J. bar 1931. Practiced Newark, 1931-49; mem. firm Pitney, Hardin, Ward & Brennan; superior ct. judge 1949-50, appellate div. judge, 1950-52; justice Supreme Ct. N.J., 1952-56; asso. justice U.S. Supreme Ct., 1956—. Served to col. with gen. staff corps AUS, World War II. Decorated Legion of Merit. Jurisprudence. Address: Supreme Ct US Washington DC 20543

BRENNECKE, ALLEN EUGENE, lawyer; b. Marshalltown, Iowa, Jan. 8, 1937; s. Arthur Lynn and Julia Alice (Allen) B; m. Billie Jean Johnstone, June 12, 1958; children—Scott, Stephen, Beth, Gregory, Kristen. B.B.A., U. Iowa, 1959, J.D., 1961. Bar: Iowa. Law clk. U.S. Dist. Judge, Des Moines, 1961-62; assoc. Mote, Wilson & Welp, Marshalltown, Iowa, 1962-66; ptnr. Welp, Harrison, Brennecke & Moore, Marshalltown, 1966—. Contr. articles to profl. jours. Fin. chmn. Republican party, 4th Congl. Dist., Iowa, 1970-73, Marshall County Rep. Party, Iowa, 1967-70; bd. trustees United Meth. Ch., Marshalltown, 1978-81, 87—; bd. dirs. Marshalltown YMCA, 1966-71; bd. trustees Iowa Law Sch. Found., 1973-86. Recipient Award of Merit, Young Lawyers sect. Iowa State Bar Assn., 1974. Fellow Am. Coll. Probate Counsel, Am. Coll. Tax Counsel, ABA (chmn. ho. of dels.), Am. Bar Found. Republican. Methodist. Lodges: Elks, Masons. Avocations: golf; travel; sports. Home: 703 Circle Dr Marshalltown IA 50158 Office: Welp Harrison Brennecke and Moore 302 Masonic Temple Bldg Marshalltown IA 50158

BRENNEMAN, DELBERT JAY, lawyer; b. Albany, Oreg., Feb. 4, 1950; s. Calvin M. and Velma Barbara (Whitaker) B.; m. Caroline Yorke Allen, May 29, 1976; children: Mark Stuart, Thomas Allen. BS magna cum laude, Oreg. State U., 1972; JD, U. Oreg., 1976. Bar: Oreg. 1976, U.S. Dist. Ct. Oreg. 1977, U.S. Ct. Appeals (9th cir.) 1977. Assoc. Schwabe, Williamson, Wyatt, Moore & Roberts, Portland, Oreg., 1976-83, ptnr., 1984—; speaker Oreg. Self-Ins., Newport, 1978; seminar instr. U. Oreg. Law Sch., Eugene, 1980. Mem. ABA, Oreg. State Bar Assn., Multnomah County Bar Assn. (speaker 1983-84), Order of Coif, Phi Kappa Phi, Beta Gamma Sigma. Clubs: University, Multnomah Athletic, Propeller Club of U.S. (bd. dirs. 1983-85). Workers' compensation, Administrative and regulatory, Insurance. Office: Schwabe Williamson Wyatt Moore & Roberts Parkwest Ctr Suites 1600-1800 1211 SW 5th Ave Portland OR 97204

BRENNEMAN, FLEET B., lawyer; b. Canton, Ohio, Feb. 14, 1932; s. Fleetus Ingram Brenneman and Maxine (Wollam) O'Mara; m. Carol E. Perlowski, Nov. 13, 1954; children—Kathryn, Paula, Lisa, Laura, Peggy. B.A., Ohio No. U., 1954, J.D., 1959. Bar: Ohio 1959. Dep. clk. Juvenile Ct., Cuyahoga County Cleve., 1959-61; sole practice, Orrville, Ohio, 1961-65; ptnr. Brenneman & Waltman, Orrville, 1966—; corporate atty. First Savings and Loan, Orrville, 1964—; gen. counsel Orrville Community Centennial Com. Inc., 1963-64. Trustee, Orrville United Way, 1968-74, 80-85, pres., 1968-70, 80-82; trustee, gen. counsel Orrville Area Devel. Found., Inc., 1985—. Served with U.S. Army, 1954-56. Mem. Orrville C. of C. (trustee 1975-79), Wayne County Bar Assn. (pres. 1982), Nat. Rifle Assn., Ohio Rifle and Pistol Assn. Republican. Roman Catholic. Lodge: Rotary (pres. 1971-72). Avocations: hunting, fishing, rifle marksmanship, photography. Probate, Real property, Estate planning. Office: Brenneman & Waltman 144 N Main St Orrville OH 44667

BRENNEMAN, HUGH WARREN, JR., federal magistrate; b. Lansing, Mich., July 4, 1945; s. Hugh Warren and Irma June (Redman) B.; m. Katrina Cup Kindel, Apr. 30, 1977; children: Justin Scott, Ross Edward. B.A., Alma Coll., 1967; J.D., U. Mich., 1970. Bar: Mich. 1970, D.C. 1975, U.S. Dist. Ct. (we. dist.) Mich. 1974, U.S. Dist. Ct. Md. 1973, U.S. Ct. Mil. Appeals 1971, U.S. Ct. Appeals (6th cir.) 1976, U.S. Ct. Appeals (D.C. cir.) 1981, U.S. Supreme Ct. 1980. Law clk. Mich. 30th Jud. Cir., Lansing, 1970-71; asst. U.S. atty. Dept. Justice, Grand Rapids, Mich., 1974-77; assoc. Bergstrom, Slykhouse & Shaw, P.C., Grand Rapids, 1977-80; U.S. magistrate U.S. Dist. Ct. (we. dist.) Mich., Grand Rapids, 1980—. Mem. exec. bd. West Michigan Shores council Boy Scouts Am., 1984—. Served to capt. JAGC, U.S. Army, 1971-74. Mem. State Bar Mich. (rep. assembly 1984—), D.C. Bar, Fed. Bar Assn. (pres. Western Mich. chpt. 1979-80, nat. del. 1980-84), Grand Rapids Bar Assn. (chmn. U.S. Constn. Bicentennial com.), Nat. Council U.S. Magistrates, ABA, Phi Delta Phi, Omicron Delta Kappa. Congregationalist. Clubs: Peninsular, Rotary (dir., pres. elect), Econ. of Grand Rapids (past dir.). Federal civil litigation, Criminal, Jurisprudence. Office: 240 Fed Bldg Grand Rapids MI 49503

BRENNER, ANITA SUSAN, lawyer; b. Los Angeles, Aug. 18, 1949; d. Morris I. and Lillian F. (Burten) B.; m. Leonard E. Torres, Aug. 19, 1973; children—Andrew Jacob, Rachel Elizabeth. B.A., UCLA, 1970, J.D., 1973. Bar: Calif. 1974, U.S. Dist. Ct. (cen. dist.) Calif. 1974. Atty. Greater Watts Justice Ctr., Los Angeles, 1974-75; sole practice, Los Angeles, 1975; dep. pub. defender Los Angeles County, 1975-84; assoc. Tyre and Kamins, Los Angeles, 1979; ptnr. Torres-Brenner, Pasadena, Calif., 1984—; lectr. criminal law. Mem., assoc. editor UCLA Law Rev., 1971-73. Editor FORUM mag., 1980-83. Contbr. articles to profl. jours. Bd. dirs. One Stop Immigration; vol. Los Angeles Area Council on Child Passenger Safety, 1981; mem. Los Angeles County Med. Assn. joint com. on med.-legal issues, 1983. Mable Wilson Richards scholar, 1971-72. Mem. Calif. Attys. for Criminal Justice (bd. govs. 1980-86), Los Angeles County Bar (bioethics com.), Barristers Task Force on Jails, Calif. Continuing Edn. of Bar (criminal law sub-com.). Criminal, Federal civil litigation, State civil litigation. Office: Torres-Brenner 301 E Colorado St Suite 614 Pasadena CA 91101

BRENNER, DANIEL LEON, lawyer; b. Kansas City, Mo., Sept. 9, 1904; s. Adolph and Tillie (Brenner) B. A.B., U. Mo., 1925; J.D., U. Mich., 1927. Bar: Mo. 1926. With Borders & Borders, 1927; mem. Roach, Brenner & Wimmell, Kansas City, 1947-51; sr. mem. Brenner, Van Valkenburgh & Wimmell, 1951-59; now Brenner, Lockwood & Peterson; judge Circuit Ct. Jackson County, Mo., 1943-44. Contbr. articles to legal jours. Mem. nat. council Am. Jewish Distbn. Com.; nat. panel Am. Arbitration Assn., 1964—; nat. commr. B'nai B'rith Hillel Founds.; pres. Kansas City Jewish Welfare Fedn. and Council.; Trustee U. Mo. Hillel Found. (charter), Leo N. Levi Meml. Hosp., Bellefarie, Rockhurst Coll.; bd. dirs., v.p., counsel Heart of Am. United Way Greater Kansas City; bd. dirs., counsel United Way; bd. dirs., v.p. Heart of Am. United campaign; bd. dirs. NCCJ, Jewish Vocat. Service Bur.; trustee, mem. investment adv. com. Rockhurst Coll. Endowment Fund, 1969—; pres., bd. curators U. Mo.; chmn., trustee Employees Retirement System, Kansas City, 1973—; bd. curators U. Mo., 1977—; bd. visitors U. Mich. Law Sch. Recipient Brotherhood citation NCCJ, 1956, citation State of Israel, 1961, Non-alumni Achievement award U. Mo. Sch. Law, 1982; named Man of Yr. Jewish Theol. Sem. Am., 1967. Mem. Legion of Honor Order de Molay, ABA, Kansas City Bar Assn., Mo. Bar, Am. Judicature Soc., Native Sons of Kansas City, Order of Coif.; mem. B'nai B'rith (dist. pres. grand lodge 1950-51, v.p. supreme lodge). Jewish (bd. dirs. synagogue). Clubs: Mason; Oakwood Country, Kansas City. General practice, Personal injury, Probate. Home: 333 W Meyer Blvd Apt 713 Kansas City MO 64113 Office: Brenner Lockwood & Peterson 1125 Grand Ave Suite 915 Kansas City MO 64106

BRENNER, DAVID (MERLE), lawyer; b. Rapid City, S.D., Nov. 25, 1954; s. Merle E. and Miriam A. (Frederich) B.; m. Madeleine Ann Fremont, June 4, 1983. BA, Stanford U., 1976; JD, U. Calif., Berkeley, 1980. Bar: Calif. 1980, D.C. 1982, Wash. 1984. Law clk. to presiding judge U.S. Dist. Ct. Calif., San Francisco, 1980-81; assoc. Shea & Gardner, Washington, 1981-84, Riddell, Williams, Bullitt & Walkinshaw, Seattle, 1984—. Editor in chief Calif. Law Rev., 1979-80. Mem. ABA, Seattle/King County Bar Assn., Order of Coif. Avocations: art and archtl. history, hist. preservation. Antitrust, Securities, Federal civil litigation. Office: Riddell Williams Bullitt & Walkinshaw 1001 4th Ave Plaza Seattle WA 98154

BRENNER, EDGAR H., lawyer; b. N.Y.C., Jan. 4, 1930; s. Louis and Bertha B. (Guttman) B.; m. Janet Maybin, Aug. 4, 1979; children from previous marriage—Charles S., David M., Paul R. B.A., Carleton Coll., 1951; J.D., Yale U., 1954. Bar: D.C. 1954, U.S. Ct. Claims 1957, U.S. Supreme Ct. 1957. Mem. 2d Hoover Commn. Legal Task Force, Washington, 1954; trial atty. U.S. Dept. Justice, Washington, 1954-57; assoc. Arnold & Porter, Washington, 1957-62, ptnr., 1962—. Contbr. articles to profl. jours. Commr. Fairfax County Econ. Devel. Corp., Va., 1963-78; v.p., bd. dirs. Stella and Charles Guttman Found., N.Y.C. Mem. ABA (chmn. arbitration com. litigation sect. 1984—), D.C. Bar Assn. Democrat. Clubs: Yale, Explorers (N.Y.C.). Private international, Federal civil litigation. Home: PO Box 145 Route 1 Washington VA 22747 Office: Arnold & Porter 1200 New Hampshire Ave NW Washington DC 20036

BRENNER, FRANK, lawyer; b. N.Y.C., Oct. 26, 1927; s. Jack and Betty (Teifer) B.; children: Jay Marlow, Matthew Adam, Amy Rebecca, Diane Rachel. B.A. cum laude, Lehigh U., 1948; J.D., Harvard U., 1951. Bar: N.Y. 1951, U.S. Supreme Ct. 1955, U.S. Tax Ct. 1975. Asst. dist. atty. N.Y. County, 1951-55; sole practice N.Y.C., 1955-83, 85—; judge N.Y.C. Criminal Ct., 1983-84. Contbr. articles to legal jours. Served with USNR, 1945-46. Recipient commendation Brit. Royal Commn. on Capital Punishment, 1950. Fellow Am. Acad. Matrimonial Lawyers; mem. ABA (litigation sect. com. on trial complex crimes 1977—, criminal justice sect. com. on def. function and services 1979—, RICO subcom. of com. on white collar crime 1982-84), N.Y. State Bar Assn. (ho. dels. 1978-83, 85—, conf. bar leaders 1978-83, 85—, com. on unlawful practice law 1984—, criminal justice sect. com. on criminal discovery 1985—), Assn. Bar City N.Y. (spl. com. on legal aid inquiry 1971-72, com. on penology 1972-77, com. on profl. discipline 1982-85), N.Y. County Lawyers Assn. (chmn. com. criminal law 1952-70, 80-83, com. on matrimonial law 1975—, sec. spl. com. on selection and tenure of judges 1975-77, dir. 1977-83, mem. com. public hearings in pub. interest 1979-80, spl. com. to rev. jud. discipline 1979-80), Fund for Modern Cts. (com. on ct. facilities 1985—), N.Y. State Dist. Attys. Assn. Club: Harvard (N.Y.C.). Criminal, Family and matrimonial, General practice. Home: 470 Park Ave New York NY 10022 Office: 55 E 52d St New York NY 10050

BRENNER, JONATHAN SCOTT, lawyer; b. Passaic, N.J., Oct. 20, 1955; s. Lewis R. and Marilyn (Horowitz) B.; m. Barbara Diane Roslyn, Jan. 7, 1984. AB, Hamilton Coll., 1977; JD magna cum laude, U. Mich., 1980; LLM in Taxation, NYU, 1984. Bar: N.Y. 1981, U.S. Dist. Ct. (so. and ea. dists.) N.Y. 1981, U.S. Tax Ct. 1981. Assoc. Skadden, Arps, Slate, Meagher & Flom, N.Y.C., 1980-84, Weil, Gotshal & Manges, N.Y.C., 1984—. Mem. ABA (tax sect.), N.Y. State Bar Assn. (tax sect.), Order of Coif. Corporate taxation. Office: Weil Gotshal & Manges 767 Fifth Ave New York NY 10153

BRENNER, MARK B., lawyer; b. Revere, Mass., Dec. 20, 1949. B.A. cum laude, U. Mass., 1971; J.D., Boston Coll., 1974. Bar: Mass. 1974, U.S. Dist. Ct. Mass. 1975, N.Y. 1977, U.S. Dist. Ct. (ea. and so. dists.) N.Y. 1978. Sole practice, N.Y.C. Mem. Assn. of Bar of City of N.Y., N.Y. County Lawyers Assn., Westchester County Bar Assn., Assn. Trial Lawyers Am., Phi Beta Kappa. General practice, State civil litigation, Federal civil litigation. Office: 415 Madison Ave New York NY 10017

BRENNER, MARSHALL LEIB, lawyer; b. N.Y.C., Aug. 8, 1933; s. Samuel and Ruth (Novak) B.; m. Gwen A. Krakower, Aug. 9, 1959; children: Scott David, Louri Ann, Robin Lynn. BA, St Lawrence U., Canton, N.Y., 1955; JD, Bklyn. Law Sch., 1959. Bar: N.Y. 1960, U.S. Dist. Ct. (no. and ea. dists.) N.Y. 1960, U.S. Ct. Claims 1964, U.S. Supreme Ct. 1964, U.S. Dist. Ct. (so. dist.) N.Y. 1969. Assoc. Spitz & Levine, Poughkeepsie, N.Y., 1960-62; sr. ptnr. Brenner, Gordon & Lane, Poughkeepsie, 1977—; chief appeals sect. Dutchess County Pub. Defenders Office, Poughkeepsie, 1966-78; tchr. law Marks Realtors/Appraisors, Poughkeepsie and Fishkill, N.Y., 1968-72, Robert-Mark Realtors, Hopewell Junction, N.Y., 1979—; lectr. Dutchess County Realty Bd. for Sales/Broker Lic. Applicants, 1985—. Contbr. articles to profl. jours. Pres., bd. dirs. Sloper-Willen Community Ambulance, Wappingers Falls, N.Y., 1966-79; bd. dirs. Poughkeepsie Jewish Community Ctr., 1980-82. Served to capt. U.S. Army, 1956-63. Mem. N.Y. State Bar Assn., Dutchess County Bar Assn., N.Y. State Trial Lawyers Assn. Republican. Jewish. Clubs: Harding (Poughkeepsie) (pres. 1968-69); County Players (Wappingers Falls) (bd. dirs. 1963-74). Lodges: Masons, Rotary (pres. 1973-74, 78-79, Govs. Trophy 1978). Avocations: golf, tennis, swimming, reading, chess. Real property, General practice, Contracts commercial. Home: 30 Robin Rd Poughkeepsie NY 12601 Office: Brenner Gordon & Lane 35 Market St Poughkeepsie NY 12601

BRENNER, THOMAS EDWARD, lawyer; b. Hanover, Pa., Apr. 30, 1955; s. Philip F. and Ruth H. (Hoke) B.; m. Mary Small, May 26, 1979; children: Matthew D., Rebecca M., John Phillip, Donald Thomas. BA, Villanova U., 1977, JD, 1980. Bar: Pa. 1980, U.S. Dist. Ct. (cen. dist.) Pa. 1980, U.S. Ct. Appeals (3d cir.) 1980, U.S. Ct. Appeals (4th cir.) 1985, U.S. Supreme Ct. 1985. Assoc. Goldberg, Katzman & Shipman, P.C., Harrisburg, Pa., 1980—, also bd. dirs. Bd. dirs. Dauphin County Victim/Witness Assistance Program, Harrisburg, 1984—. Mem. ABA (com. chmn. 1984, rep. young lawyers div. 1985-86), Pa. Bar Assn. (com. chmn. 1985-86), Dauphin County Bar Assn. (sec. 1980, chmn. elect young lawyers sect. 1986—, bd. dirs.), Pa. Def. Inst., Def. Research Inst., Jaycees. Democrat. Roman Catholic. Lodge: KC. Insurance, State civil litigation, Federal civil litigation. Office: Goldberg Katzman & Shipman PC 319 Market St Harrisburg PA 17108-1268

BRENT, ANDREW JACKSON, lawyer; b. Richmond, Va., Nov. 25, 1918; s. Andrew Jackson and Gussie Millhiser (Reinhardt) B.; m. Virginia Armistead McGuire, Nov. 1, 1941; children: Virginia Armistead (Mrs. Roger P. Hailes), Roberta Harper Peek Elizabeth Marshall McGuire (Mrs. Peter F. Nostrand), Andrew Mason, Maria Meade (Mrs. W. Brady Jones). LL.B., U. Va., 1941. Bar: Va. 1940. Practice in Richmond, 1946—; ptnr. Christian, Barton, Epps, Brent & Chappell, 1949—; v.p., gen. counsel, dir. Security Fed. Savs. & Loan Assn.; gen. counsel, sec., dir. Media Gen., Inc.; past chmn., dir. Central Va. Ednl. TV Corp.; sec., dir. Garden State Paper Co., Inc., Richmond Newspapers, Inc., Southeast Media, Inc., Beacon Press, Inc., Piedmont Pub. Co., Inc., Winston-Salem, N.C., Tribune Co., Tampa, Fla.; sec., dir. WFLA Inc., Tampa; dir. Cliggott Pub. Co., Greenwich, Conn., Productora Nacional de Papel Destintado S.A. de C.V., Mexico City. Past pres., bd. dirs. Richmond Area Community Council, 1963-66, Richmond Eye Hosp.; gen. counsel, sec. Richmond Met. Authority; bd. dirs., past chmn. Va. Pub. Telecommunications Council; past sec., visitor Va. Commonwealth U.; pres., trustee Va. Law Found., Collegiate Schs., also past pres., Va. Commonwealth U. Fund, Mary Baldwin Coll., also chmn. bd. Served to lt. comdr. USNR, 1941-46. Recipient Annual Good Govt. award Richmond First Club, 1965, Disting. Service award Va. State C. of C., 1981. Fellow ABA, Va. Law Found.; Mem. Va. Bar Assn., Richmond Bar Assn., Am. Judicature Soc., S.A.R., Richmond C. of C. (past pres., dir.), Omicron Delta Kappa, Phi Alpha Delta, Phi Kappa Psi, Pi Delta Epsilon. Episcopalian (warden, vestryman). Clubs: Commonwealth (past pres., gov.), Country of Va. Downtown (past pres., dir.). General corporate, General practice. Office: 12th Floor Mut Bldg Richmond VA 23219

BRENT, NANCY JEAN, lawyer; b. Erie, Pa., June 28, 1947; d. Edward William and Marian (Maloney) Weiss; m. George William Brent, July 1979. BS in Nursing, Villa Maria Coll., 1969; MS in Psychiat. Nursing, U. Conn., 1975; JD, Loyola U., Chgo., 1981. Bar: Ill. 1981, U.S. Dist. Ct. (no. dist.) Ill. 1981, U.S. Ct. Appeals (7th cir.) 1981. Assoc. Law Offices T.J. Keevers, Chgo., 1981-82; ptnr. Nye, Brent & Shoenberger, Chgo., 1982-85; sole practice Chgo., 1985—; assoc. prof. nursing grad. program St. Xavier Coll., Chgo., 1984—; cons., lectr. to numerous orgns., 1982—. Contbr. articles to profl. jours.; also chpts. Mem. Sch. Nurse Adv. Bd., Chgo. Pub. Schs., 1985-86. Mem. ABA, Ill. Bar Assn., Chgo. Bar Assn., Womens Bar Assn. Ill., Am. Nurses Assn., Ill. Nurses Assn. (human rights and ethics commn. 1985—), Nat. League for Nursing, Am. Assn. Nurse Attys., Sigma Theta Tau. Health, Personal injury, Representation of health professionals. Office: 5445 N Sheridan Rd Suite 2415 Chicago IL 60640

BRENT, STEPHEN M., lawyer; b. Bklyn., June 7, 1941; s. Robert I. and Lea (Tabakowitz) B.; m. Claudia L. Dobbins, June 19, 1967; children: Malinda R., Robert Joshua. BA in Polit. Sci., Bklyn. Coll., 1965; JD, U. Detroit, 1973. Assoc. editor Lawyers Coop. Pub., Rochester, N.Y., 1974-75; assoc. Vogt & Hensel, Rochester, 1975-76; asst. dist. atty. Monroe County, Rochester, 1976-82; sole practice Rochester, 1982-83; ptnr. Brent & Drexler, Rochester, 1983—; spl. prosecutor Monroe County, 1986-87. Co-author Handling Drunk Driving Cases, 1985; mem. editorial bd. DWI Jour. Law & Sci., 1986—. Recipient Pub. Service Medallion Detroit Press Found., 1971; 2d Pl. Alaska Press Club, 1969, Best Singles Pub. Alaska Press Club, 1970. Republican. Jewish. Avocations: sailing, marathoning, weight lifting. Criminal, State civil litigation, Immigration, naturalization, and customs. Home: 84 Hillcrest Dr Penfield NY 14526 Office: Brent & Drexler 30 W Broad Suite 301 Rochester NY 14614

BRENTON, MICHAEL SCOTT, lawyer; b. Elkhorn, Wis., Apr. 18, 1952; s. J. Harris Fleming and Beatrice Aileen (White) Brenton; m. Michele Lee Cormier, Mar 11, 1986. BA with high honors, Mich. State U., 1973; JD, U. Notre Dame, 1976. Bar: Mich. 1976. Assoc. Foster, Swift, Collins & Coey, Lansing, Mich., 1976-84; ptnr. McKay, Murphy, Brenton & Spagnuolo, P.C., Lansing, 1984—. Bd. dirs. Arthritis Found., Lansing, 1982-83. Mem. ABA, Mich. Bar Assn. (mem. adv. bd. Bar Jour. 1983-84), Ingham County Bar Assn. Avocations: water and snowskiing, hunting, snowmobiling, football, volleyball. Workers' compensation, Insurance, Personal injury. Home: 3617 E Meadows Ct Okemos MI 48864 Office: McKay Murphy Brenton & Spagnuolo 2213 E Grand River Ave Lansing MI 48912

BRESLER, MARTIN I., lawyer; b. Bklyn., Feb. 25, 1931; s. Eli and Sylvia (Hinitz) B.; m. Shirley Bauer, Apr. 27, 1960; children: Laura E., Ellen. Student, NYU, 1948-49; B.B.A. CUM LAUDE, CCNY, 1952; J.D., Harvard U., 1955. Bar: N.Y. 1956. Assoc. firm Ungar & Liben, N.Y.C., 1957-59, firm Golenbock & Barell, N.Y.C., 1959-66; gen. counsel Caldor, Inc., Norwalk, Conn., 1966-67; ptnr. firm Stein & Rosen, N.Y.C., 1967-71, firm Krause, Hirsch & Gross, N.Y.C., 1971-80, firm Stroock & Stroock & Lavan, N.Y.C., 1980—. Pres. Lexington Democratic Club, N.Y.C., 1965-66; v.p., dir. Fedn. Employment and Guidance Service, 1976—; chmn. Joint Task Force on Exec. Suite, Am. Jewish Com., 1981, bd. dirs. N.Y. chpt., 1982—, v.p., 1986—; trustee Sam and Esther Minskoff Park East Cultural Ctr., 1976—. Served with U.S. Army, 1955-57. Mem. Assn. Bar City N.Y., Beta Gamma Sigma, Phi Sigma Delta. Jewish. Home: 910 Park Ave New York NY 10021 Office: Stroock & Stroock & Lavan 7 Hanover Sq New York NY 10004-2594

BRESLIN, JOHN JOSEPH, III, lawyer; b. Orange, N.J., Apr. 17, 1947; s. Roger W. and Alice (McKean) B.; m. Margaret Pierce, July 21, 1973; children: Colleen, Rory, Molly, Luke. BA, Boston Coll., 1969; LLB, Seton Hall

U., 1972. Assoc. Breslin & Breslin, Hackensack, N.J., 1972-79; ptnr. Breslin & Breslin, Hackensack, 1980-83, Breslin & Auty, Hackensack, 1983—; prosecutor Wallington (N.J.) County, 1973-86, Ramsey (N.J.) County, 1979-81, 83-86; pub. defender , 1978. Mem. ABA, N.Y. State Bar Assn., N.J. Bar Assn., Bergen County Bar Assn (trustee 1986—). Democrat. Roman Catholic. Avocations: basketball, sailing. State civil litigation, Personal injury, General practice. Office: Breslin & Auty 126 State St Hackensack NJ 07601

BRESNAHAN, ARTHUR STEPHEN, lawyer; b. Chgo., Dec. 26, 1944; s. Arthur Patrick and Margaret Genevieve (Gleason) B.; m. Patricia Margaret Wetz, June 29, 1968; children: Arthur Patrick, Maureen Justina, Brian Michael, Brendan Robert, Sean Matthew. BA in Psychology, Loras Coll., 1967; JD, Ill. Inst. Tech., 1975. Bar: Ill. 1975, U.S. Dist. Ct. (no. dist.) Ill. 1975, U.S. Ct. Appeals (7th cir.) 1978, U.S. Supreme Ct. 1986, U.S Ct. Claims 1986. Assoc. Garbutt, Jacobson & Lee, Chgo., 1975-77; sr. assoc. atty. Purcell & Wardrope, Chgo., 1977-83; ptnr. Bresnahan, Garvey, O'Halloran & Coleman, Chgo., 1983—; speaker in field. Asst. scoutmaster Troop 904 Boy Scouts Am., Chgo., 1980—, Webelos Den leader. Served to capt. USMC, 1967-72. Mem. ABA, Am. Trial Lawyers Assn., Fed. Bar Assn., Ill. Bar Assn., Ill. Trial Lawyers Assn., Chgo. Bar Assn., Def. Research Inst., Trial Lawyers Club, Vietnam Vets. Am., Am. Legion. Democrat. Roman Catholic. Lodge: KC. Avocations: golf, choir singing, coaching little league. State civil litigation, Federal civil litigation, Insurance. Home: 4715 N Kenneth Ave Chicago IL 60630 Office: Bresnahan Garvey O'Halloran & Coleman 188 W Randolph St Suite 3415 Chicago IL 60601

BRESNAHAN, PAMELA ANNE, lawyer, educator; b. Washington, Nov. 21, 1954; d. Harry Anthony and Marilyn (Thompson) B. B.A. magna cum laude, U. Md., 1976, postgrad. 1976-77, J.D. with honors, 1980. Bar: Md. 1980, U.S. Dist. Ct. Md., 1980, U.S. Ct. Appeals (4th cir.) 1981, D.C. 1982, U.S. Dist. Ct. D.C., 1983, U.S. Supreme Ct., 1984. Teaching asst. U. Md., College Park, 1976-77; law clk. Dept. Interior, Washington, 1977-78, Seidenman & Dugan, Balt., 1978-80; ptnr. Seidenman & Bresnahan, Balt., 1980-82; assoc. Finley, Kumble & Wagner, Washington, 1982—; lectr. honors program U. Md., 1976-83; counsel Alpha Omicron Pi, College Park, 1980—; mem. faculty Nat. Coll. of Advocacy, Washington, 1984, 86. Vol. William Donald Schaefer for mayor campaign, Balt., 1983, for Sen. Charles Mac Mathias campaign, College Park, 1975. Fellow Md. Bar Found. (mem.-at-large, jud. appointments com. 1987—); mem. ABA (mem. trial evidence com. 1982—), Am. Trial Lawyers Assn., Young Lawyers Md. State Bar Assn. (chmn. edn. com., 1983—, sec., treas. 1983-84, chmn.-elect 1985-86, chmn. 1986-87), Women's Bar Assn. Md. (chmn. long range planning com. 1983-85, v.p. 1985-86, pres.-elect 1986-87, pres. 1987—), Md. State Bar Assn. (rules adv. com. 1984, search com. 1984, exec. com., bd. govs. 1986-87), Bar Assn. of Balt. City (young lawyers program com. 1982-84, membership com. 1984), Phi Beta Kappa. Democrat. Lutheran. Lodge: Soroptimist. State civil litigation, Federal civil litigation, Personal injury. Home: 1706-H Mount Washington Ct Baltimore MD 21209 Office: Finley Kumble Wagner et al 2852 World Trade Ctr 401 E Pratt St Baltimore MD 21202

BRESS, JOSEPH MICHAEL, lawyer; b. Troy, N.Y., Apr. 26, 1944; s. Leon N. and Shirley (Fox) B.; m. Helena Binder; 1 child, Jonathan W. BA, SUNY-Binghamton, 1966; JD, SUNY-Buffalo, 1969. Bar: N.Y. 1969, U.S. Dist. Ct. (no. dist.) N.Y. 1969, U.S. Supreme Ct., 1976. Assoc. counsel SUNY-Albany, 1969-76; asst. counsel Gov.'s Office Employee Relations, Albany, 1976-77, assoc. counsel, acting counsel, 1977, gen. counsel, 1977—; adj. prof. Albany Law Sch., 1978-79; part-time mem. N.Y. State Deferred Compensation Bd., 1982—. Mem. ABA (mem. state and local subcom. labor law sect. 1980—), Nat. Assn. Coll. and Univ. Attys., N.Y. State Bar Assn. (labor and employment law sect.), Assn. of Bar of City of N.Y. (mem. labor and employment law sect. 1978-80). Administrative and regulatory, Labor, Legislative. Home: 743 Hampshire Seat Schenectady NY 12309 Office: Agy Bldg No 2 12th Floor Albany NY 12223

BRESSAN, PAUL LOUIS, lawyer; b. Rockville Centre, N.Y., June 15, 1947; s. Louis Charles Bressan and Nance Elizabeth Batteley. BA cum laude, Fordham Coll., 1969; JD, Columbia U., 1975. Bar: N.Y 1976, U.S. Dist. Ct. (so., ea. and no. dists.) N.Y. 1976, U.S. Ct. Appeals (2d cir.) 1980, U.S. Supreme Ct. 1980, U.S. Ct. Appeals (1st and 4th cirs.) 1981, U.S. Ct. Appeals (11th cir.) 1982. Assoc. Kelley, Drye & Warren, N.Y.C., 1975-84; ptnr. Kelley, Drye & Warren, N.Y.C. and Los Angeles, 1984—. Served to lt. USNR, 1971-72. Named one of Outstanding Coll. Athletes of Am., 1969; Harlan Fiske Stone scholar. Mem. ABA, N.Y. Bar Assn., Assn. of Bar Of City of N.Y., Fed. Bar Counsel. Republican. Roman Catholic. Labor, Federal civil litigation, State civil litigation. Office: Kelley Drye & Warren 624 S Grand Ave Los Angeles CA 90017

BRESSLER, H.J., lawyer, judge; b. Balt., Dec. 31, 1939; s. Sam Bressler and Rose Cohen; m. Elizabeth Ann Woodward, Dec. 20, 1959; children: Scott, Erika, Jason. Student, U.S. Army Lang. Sch., 1959; BA, Miami U., Oxford, Ohio, 1964; JD, Salmon P. Chase Law Sch., 1968. Regional credit mgr. Procter & Gamble, Cin., 1964-65, U.S. Shoe Co., Cin., 1965-68; ptnr. Holbrock, Jonson, Bressler and Houser, 1972-85, Bressler, Shanks & Gedling Co. L.P.A., Hamilton, Ohio, 1985—; judge Butler County Ct., Ohio, 1981—; lectr. Ohio Jud. Coll., Ohio Bar Assn. Served with U.S. Army, 1958-61. Mem. Ohio Bar Assn., Butler County Bar Assn. (pres. 1981), Am. Acad. Trial Lawyers, Ohio Acad. Trial Lawyers, Greater Hamilton Trial Lawyers Assn. (pres. 1978). Republican. Methodist. State civil litigation, Family and matrimonial, Personal injury. Office: Bressler Shanks & Gelding Co LPA 304 N 2d St Hamilton OH 45011

BRESSMAN, MARC IRA, insurance company executive, lawyer; b. Glen Ridge, N.J., June 18, 1946; s. Lawrence B. and Frances (Donenfeld) B.; m. Anne S., Aug. 28, 1969; 1 son, David Benjamin. B.A., Rutgers U., 1968; J.D., Seton Hall U., 1971. Bar: N.J. 1971, Ariz. 1977, Wis. 1982. Assoc. Budd, Larner, Kent, Gross & Picillo, Newark, 1971-77, Harrison, Myers & Singer, Phoenix, 1977-79; assoc. counsel Sentry Ins. Co., Scottsdale, Ariz., 1979-82, asst. gen. counsel, Stevens Point, Wis., 1982-86, Reliance Ins. Co., Phila., 1986—. Mem. ABA, Ariz. Bar Assn., State Bar Wis. Jewish. Notes editor Seton Hall U. Law Rev., 1970-71. Administrative and regulatory, General corporate, Insurance. Office: Reliance Ins Co 4 Penn Center Plaza Philadelphia PA 19103

BREST, PAUL ANDREW, law educator; b. Jacksonville, Fla., Aug. 9, 1940; s. Alexander and Mia (Deutsch) B.; m. Iris Lang, June 17, 1962; children: Hilary, Jeremy. A.B., Swarthmore Coll., 1962; J.D., Harvard U., 1965; LL.D., Northeastern U., 1980. Bar: N.Y. 1966. Law clk. to judge U.S. Ct. Appeals (1st cir.), Boston, 1965-66; atty. NAACP Legal Def. Fund, Jackson, Miss., 1966-68; law clk. Justice John Harlan, U.S. Supreme Ct., 1968-69; prof. law Stanford U., 1969—, Kenneth and Harle Montgomery Prof. clin. legal edn., Richard E. Lang prof. and dean, 1987—. Author: Processes of Constitutional Decisionmaking, 1965. Mem. Am. Acad. Arts and Scis. Home: 814 Tolman Dr Stanford CA 94305 Office: Stanford Law Sch Stanford CA 94305

BRETT, THOMAS RUTHERFORD, judge; b. Oklahoma City, Oct. 2, 1931; s. John A. and Norma (Dougherty) B.; m. Mary Jean James, Aug. 26, 1952; children: Laura Elizabeth Brett Tribble, James Ford, Susan Marie Brett Crump, Maricarolyn. B.B.A., U. Okla., 1952, LL.B., 1957, J.D., 1971. Bar: Okla. 1957. Asst. county atty. Tulsa, 1957; mem. firm Hudson, Hudson, Wheaton, Kyle & Brett, Tulsa, 1958-59, Jomes, Givens, Brett, Gotcher, Doyle & Bogan, 1969-79; U.S. dist. judge No. Dist. Okla., Tulsa, 1979—. Bd. regents U. Okla., 1971-78; mem. adv. bd. Salvation Army; trustee Okla. Bar Found. Served to col. JAG USAR, 1953-81. Fellow Am. Coll. Trial Lawyers, Am. Bar Found.; mem. Am. Bar Assn., Okla. Bar Assn., Tulsa County Bar Assn., Am. Judicature Soc., U. Okla. Coll. Law Alumni Assn. (dir.), Phi Alpha Delta, Order Coif. Democrat. Federal civil litigation, State civil litigation. Office: U S Courthouse 333 W 4th St Room 4-508 Tulsa OK 74103 *

BRETT, TYBE ANN, law educator; b. Johnstown, Pa., May 6, 1954; d. Leon Solomon and Sarah (Luel) B.; m. Mervin Hayman, Aug. 12, 1979. BA, Barnard Coll., 1977; JD, Columbia U., 1979. Bar: Pa. 1979, U.S. Dist. Ct. (ea. dist.) Pa. 1979, U.S. Ct. Appeals (3d cir.) 1982, U.S. Supreme Ct. 1983. Assoc. Drinker, Biddle & Reath, Phila., 1979-83; assoc. prof. law U. Maine, Portland, 1983—. Contbr. articles to legal jours. Founder, officer, bd. dirs. Cape Elizabeth Land Trust, Maine, 1985—. Mem. ABA. Avocations: music, cross country skiing, hiking. Contracts commercial, Environment, Insurance. Office: U Maine Sch Law 246 Deering Ave Portland ME 04102

BRETT-MAJOR, LIN, lawyer; b. N.Y.C., Sept. 21, 1943; d. Brett Major and Edith H. Brett; children from previous marriage: Dania S., David M. BA, U. Mich., 1965; JD cum laude, Nova Law Ctr., 1978. Bar: Fla. 1978, U.S. Dist. Ct. (so. dist.) Fla. 1978, U.S. Ct. Appeals (5th and 11th cirs.) 1981, U.S. Tax Ct. 1981, U.S. Dist. Ct. (middle and no. dists.) Fla. 1982, U.S. Supreme Ct. 1984. Internat. communications asst. Mitsui and Co., Ltd., N.Y.C., 1962; with dept. pub. relations and devel. St. Rita's Hosp., Lima, Ohio, 1965-66; reporter The Lima News, 1969-70; intern U.S. Atty.'s Office, Miami, 1977; sole practice Ft. Lauderdale, Fla., 1980—; participant Gov.'s Conf. on World Trade, Mia and Jacksonville, Fla., 1984—; speaker Bus. Owners Conf., Hollywood, Fla., 1986. Mem. Ft. Lauderdale Opera Soc., 1985—, Ft. Lauderdale Mus. of Art, 1985—. Recipient Silver Key award ABA, 1977. Mem. Assn. Trial Lawyers Am., Fed. Bar Assn., Fla. Bar Assn., Broward County Bar Assn., Univ. Mich. Alumni Assn.. Club: Propeller of U.S. (Port Everglades, Fla.) (nat. del. 1981—). Avocations: fencing, skeet and trap shooting, tennis, boating. Federal civil litigation, General corporate, Criminal. Office: Galleria Professional Bldg 915 Middle River Dr Fort Lauderdale FL 33304

BRETTSCHNEIDER, RITA ROBERTA, lawyer; b. Bklyn., Nov. 12, 1931; d. Isidore and Augusta (Singer) Fischman; m. Bertram D. Brettschneider, May 7, 1924 (dec. Nov. 1986); children: Jane Brettschneider King, Joseph. BA, Bklyn. Coll., 1953; JD, City Coll. of N.Y., 1956. Bar: N.Y. 1961, U.S. Dist. Ct. 1971, U.S. Supreme Ct. 1979. Sole practice Huntington, N.Y., 1961—; spl. assoc. prof. philosophy of law Hofstra U.; legal counsel Nassau County (N.Y.) Psychological Assn.; adj. prof. C.W. Post Coll.; arbitrator Night Small Claims Ct., 1978. Contbr. to profl. jours. Mem. N.Y. State Bar Assn. (faculty mem. 1981-83, family law sect. 1984—), Nassau County Bar Assn., Suffolk County Bar Assn., Nassau-Suffolk Trial Lawyers Assn., Am. Judge's Assn., Nassau-Suffolk Women's Bar Assn. (pres. 1980-81, bd. dirs. 1980, 82, 84), Women's Bar Assn. of N.Y. State. Jewish. Family and matrimonial. Home: 2 Crosby Pl Huntington NY 11743 Office: 83 Prospect St Huntington NY 11743

BREWER, ANDREA BORDIGA, lawyer; b. Hoboken, N.J., Nov. 22, 1953; d. Arthur Andrew and Rose Mary (Brusco) Bordiga; m. David Madison Brewer, May 20, 1978; children: James D.M. , Caroline E. BA, Fordham U., 1975; JD, Yale U., 1978. Bar: N.Y. 1979. Assoc. Davis, Polk & Wardwell, N.Y.C., 1978-85; asst. gen. counsel Dun & Bradstreet, Inc., Murray Hill, N.J., 1985—. Mem. ABA, N.Y. State Bar Assn., Phi Beta Kappa, Pi Sigma Alpha. Republican. Episcopalian. Avocations: reading, travel. General corporate, Computer, Trademark and copyright. Home: 33 Plymouth Rd Summit NJ 07901 Office: Dun & Bradstreet Inc One Diamond Hill Rd Murray Hill NJ 07974-0027

BREWER, CHARLES ROBINSON, United States attorney; b. Holly Springs, N.C., Oct. 23, 1948; s. Harold Lee and Clara Belle (Robinson) B.; m. Susan Elaine Guest, June 20, 1971; children: Emily Marie, Sarah Elizabeth, Melissa Anne. B.A., Wake Forest U., 1971, J.D., 1974. Bar: N.C. 1974. County atty. Caldwell County, Lenoir, N.C., 1980-81; U.S. atty. Dept. Justice, Asheville, N.C., 1981—. Mem. exec. com. Caldwell County Republican Party, Lenoir, 1976-81; pres. Caldwell County Young Reps., 1976-78. Mary Reynolds Babcock Found. grantee, 1975; recipient Am. Jurisprudence award Lawyers Co-Op Pub. Co., 1976. Mem. N.C. Bar Assn. Republican. Baptist. Home: 83 Gracelyn Rd Asheville NC 28804 Office: US Attorneys Office PO Box 132 Post and Otis St Asheville NC 28802 *

BREWER, CURTIS, lawyer, consultant; b. Cambridge, Mass., Sept. 18, 1925; s. Nathaniel Albert and Ethel Myra (Whittaker) B.; m. Cora Ernestine Clark, Sept. 16, 1945 (div. Aug. 1947); 1 child, Phyllis Carol; m. Bettie Anne Foster, Sept. 17, 1955; 1 child, Scott. BA, New Sch. for Social Research, 1955; postgrad., NYU, 1957-60; JD, Bklyn. Law Sch., 1974. Bar: N.Y. 1974, U.S. Dist. Ct. (ea. and so. dists.) N.Y. 1976, U.S. Supreme Ct. 1980. Dir. Community Service Assocs., N.Y.C., 1955-67; asst. dir. neuropsychol. lab. N.Y. Med. Coll., N.Y.C., 1968-70; exec. dir., gen. counsel Untapped Resources Inc., N.Y.C., 1974—; mem. Nat. Adv. Com. Accessible Environment, Archtl. and Transp. Barriers Compliance Bd., HEW, 1976-78; bd. tech. advisors M.S. Quarterly, 1979-83; mem. EEO/Handicapped Adv. Bd., 1981-82, Citizens Adv. Council, 1981—, Manhattan Borough Pres.'s Adv. Com. on the Disabled, 1986—; bd. dirs. Nat. Ctr. Law and Handicapped, 1975-77. Contbr. articles to profl. jours. Recipient R.W. Morgenthau Meml. award Inst. Crippled and Disabled, 1968, Thurgood Marshall award N.Y. Trial Lawyers Assn., 1972, Humanitarian award Ruth Kirzon Group for Handicapped Children, 1976, Com. to Aid Psychiat. Services in Bronx award, 1978, Teen Entertainment Network award, 1981, Apple Polisher award Assn. Greater N.Y. and WOR-TV, 1981,; named Handicapped Am. Yr., Pres.'s Com. Employment Handicapped, 1980; inducted into Hall of Fame, Persons with Disabilities, 1983. Mem. ABA, Assn. Bar of City of N.Y., N.Y. State Bar Assn. (com. mental and phys.disability), N.Y. County Lawyers Assn., Plaintiff Employment Lawyers Assn., Nat. Rehab. Assn. (Rehabilitant of Yr. award 1975), NAACP (Lifetime Mem. award 1974), New Sch. Social Research Alumni Assn., Bklyn. Law Sch. Alumni Assn. Republican. Administrative and regulatory, Civil rights, Disability law. Home and Office: 60 1st Ave New York NY 10009

BREWER, DANA, lawyer, educator; b. Concordia, Kans., Jan. 25, 1952; s. Dean Decker and Irma Elaine (Ames) B. B.S. cum laude, Kans. State U., 1974; J.D., Washburn U., 1976. Bar: Kans. 1977, U.S. Dist. Ct. Kans. 1977. Assoc. Baldwin, Paulsen & Buechel, Chartered, Concordia, 1977-82; ptnr. Paulsen, Buechel, Swenson, Uri & Brewer, Chartered, Concordia, 1982—; educator Cloud County Community Coll., Concordia, 1979—. Chmn. United Lutheran Ministries, N. Central Kans., 1981-83; commr. Indsl. Devel. Adv. Commn., Concordia, 1982—; bd. dirs. Pan-Am. Hwy. Assn., 1984—. Mem. Cloud County Bar Assn. (sec. 1977-79), Kans. Bar Assn. (com. on legal issues affecting elderly 1985—), ABA (probate and trust div., com. post-mortem tax problems and fed. death tax problems of estates and trusts), Kans. Sch. Attys. Assn. (bd. dirs. 1984—), Concordia C. of C. (bd. dirs. 1984—, chmn. 1986—), Jaycees (community devel. v.p. 1983-84). Republican. Lutheran. Lodges: Moose, Lions. Probate, Estate taxation, Real property. Home: RR 2 Concordia KS 66901 Office: Paulsen Buechel Swenson Uri & Brewer 613 Washington St PO Box 327 Concordia KS 66901

BREWER, EDWARD CAGE, III, lawyer; b. Clarkdale, Miss., Jan. 20, 1953; s. William G. III and Elizabeth (Alford) Little; children: Katherine Martin, Julia Blair. BA, U. of South, 1975; JD, Vanderbilt U., 1979. Bar: Ala. 1980, U.S. Dist. Ct. (so. dist.) Ala. 1981, U.S. Ct. Appeals (5th and 11th cirs) 1981, Ga. 1982, U.S. Dist. Ct. (no. dist.) Ga. 1982, U.S. Ct. Appeals(3d and 8th cirs.) 1983. Law clk. to chief judge U.S. Dist. Ct. (so. dist.) Ala., Mobile, 1979-81; law clk. to judge U.S. Ct. Appeals (5th and 11th cirs.), Atlanta, 1981-82; assoc. Ford & Harrison, Atlanta, 1982-85, Smith, Gambrell & Russell, Atlanta, 1985—; coach moot ct. team Emory U., Atlanta, 1985—. Contbr. articles to profl. jours. Mem. St. Philip's and Evensong Choirs, Cathedral of St. Philip, Atlanta, 1984—. Mem. ABA (labor and employment law sect., project editor com. on railway and labor law, 1984—), State Bar of Ga. (labor and employment, young lawyers sects., treas. internat. law com. 1985—), U. of South Alumni Fund (decade chmn.), Phi Beta Kappa, Omicron Delta Kappa. Episcopalian. Avocations: whitewater canoeing, hiking, guitar, choral music. Labor, Federal civil litigation, Securities. Home: 1435 Benning Pl NE Atlanta GA 30307 Office: Smith Gambrell & Russell 2400 1st Atlanta Tower Atlanta GA 30383

BREWER, LEWIS GORDON, lawyer, educator; b. New Martinsville, W.Va., Sept. 6, 1946; s. Harvey Lee and Ruth Carolyn (Zimmerman) B; m. Kathryn Anne Yunker, May 25, 1985. B.A., W.Va. U., 1968, J.D., 1971; LL.M., George Washington U., 1979. Bar: W.Va. 1971, Calif. 1978. Commd. 2d lt. U.S. Air Force, 1968, advanced through grades to lt. col., 1983; dep. staff judge adv., Travis AFB, Calif., 1976-78, chief civil law San Antonio Air Logistics Center, Kelly AFB, Tex., 1979-83, staff judge adv., MacDill AFB, Fla., 1983-86; chief Air Force Cen. Labor Law Office, Randolph AFB, Tex., 1987—; instr. bus. law No. Mich. U., Marquette, 1972, Solano Coll., Suisun City, Calif., 1978; instr. labor law Webster U., Ft. Sam Houston, 1983. Decorated Air Force Commendation medal, Meritorious Service medal. Mem. W.Va. Bar Assn., State Bar Calif., ABA, Fed. Bar Assn., W.Va. U. Alumni Assn. Methodist. Labor, Civil rights, Military. Home: 21119 Malibu Colony San Antonio TX 78259 Office: HQ USAF/CLLO Randolph AFB TX 78150

BREWER, MARION ALYCE, lawyer; b. Brownfield, Tex., Dec. 28, 1949; d. Deral Henry and Marion Thomas (Magee) B. BA, Stanford U., 1972; JD, Georgetown U., 1980. Bar: Colo. 1982, D.C. 1983, U.S. Dist. Ct. (Colo.), 1982, U.S. Ct. Appeals (10th cir.), U.S. Tax Ct., 1984. Reporter, anchor woman Sta. KMGH-TV CBS, Denver, 1972-76; TV corr. Ind. TV News Assn., Washington, 1976-78; asst. dir. Law Sch. Admission Council, Washington, 1978-79; asst. dean admissions Georgetown U. Law Ctr., Washington, 1979-80; law clk. to judge U.S. Dist. Ct. D.C., 1981-83; assoc. Ireland, Stapleton, Pryor & Pascoe, Washington, 1983-87; gen. counsel Colo. Counties, Inc., Denver, 1987—; mem. coms. Women in Communications, Inc., Denver, 1972-76. Mem. fin. com. Schoettler for Treas., Denver, 1986; co-chmn. Lawyers for Wirth Com., Denver, 1986; mem. Big Sisters Support Group, Denver, 1986—. Recipient Outstanding Service award United Vets. Council Colo., 1976, Outstanding Service award Optimists, Aurora, Colo., 1975. Mem. ABA, Colo. Trial Lawyers Assn., Alliance Profl. Women, Colo. Women's Bar Assn. (bd. dirs. 1984-86), Colo. Bar Assn. (bd. govs. 1985-87), Denver Bar Assn. (mem. coms. 1980—), Stanford Alumni Assn., Georgetown Law Alumni Assn. (inaugural nat. bd. dirs. 1986—), Am. Trial Lawyers Assn. Episcopalian. Clubs: Denver Press, Rocky Mountain Stanford (Denver) (pres., chmn. bd. dirs. 1973-75, treas. 1983—); Nat. Press (Washington). Insurance, General corporate, Legislative. Office: Colo Counties Inc 1177 Grant Denver CO 80202

BREWSTER, CLARK OTTO, lawyer; b. Marlette, Mich., Nov. 5, 1956; s. Charles W. and June V. (Hoff) B.; m. Deborah K. Trowhill, Aug. 3, 1974; m. Cassie Mae, Corbin Clark. BA cum laude, Cen. Mich. U., 1977; JD with honor, Tulsa U., 1980. Bar: Okla. 1981, U.S. Dist. Ct. (no. and ea. dists.) Okla. 1982. Assoc. Riddle and Assocs., Tulsa, 1981, Braly and McEachin, Tulsa, 1981-82; ptnr. Brewster, Shallcross & Rizley, Tulsa, 1982—; officer, bd. dirs. Redy Corp., Tulsa, Cottontail Oil Corp., Tulsa; trustee Travis Kerr Magana Trust, Tulsa, 1985—. Mem. ABA, Assn. Trial Lawyers Am., Okla. Bar Assn., Okla. Trial Lawyers Assn., Tulsa County Bar Assn, Order of Curule Chair, Order of Barristers. Avocations: golf, hunting, horseback riding. State civil litigation, Federal civil litigation, Criminal. Home: 4111 E 131st St Bixby OK 74008 Office: Brewster Shallcross and Rizley 5314 S Yale Suite 600 Tulsa OK 74135

BREWSTER, RUDI MILTON, judge; b. Sioux Falls, S.D., May 18, 1932; s. Charles Edwin and Wilhemina Therese (Rud) B.; m. Gloria Jane Nanson, June 27, 1954; children: Scot Alan, Lauri Diane, Alan Lee, Julie Lynn. AB in Pub. Affairs, Princeton U., 1954; JD, Stanford U., 1960. Bar: Calif. 1960. From assoc. to ptnr. Gray, Cary, Ames & Frye, San Diego, 1960-84; judge U.S. Dist. Ct. (so. dist.) Calif., San Diego, 1984—. Served to capt. USNR, 1954-82. Fellow Am. Coll. Trial Lawyers; mem. Am. Bd. Trial Advs., Internat. Assn. Ins. Counsel. Republican. Lutheran. Lodge: Rotary (pres. San Diego club 1980-81). Avocations: skiing, hunting, gardening. Judicial administration. Office: US Dist Ct 940 Front St San Diego CA 92189

BREYER, STEPHEN GERALD, lawyer, educator, judge; b. San Francisco, Aug. 15, 1938; s. Irving G. and Anne R. B.; m. Joanna Hare, Sept. 4, 1967; children: Chloe, Nell, Michael. A.B., Stanford U., 1959; B.A. (Marshall scholar), Oxford U., 1961; LL.B., Harvard U., 1964; LL.D. (hon.), U. Rochester, 1983. Bar: Calif. 1966, D.C. 1966, Mass. 1971. Law clk. Justice Goldberg, U.S. Supreme Ct., 1964-65; spl. asst. to asst. atty. gen. U.S. Dept. Justice, 1965-67; asst. prof. law Harvard U., 1967-70, prof., 1970-81, lectr., 1981—, prof. govt. J.F. Kennedy Sch., 1978-81; asst. spl. prosecutor Watergate Spl. Prosecution Force, 1973; spl. counsel U.S. Senate Judiciary Com., 1974-75, chief counsel, 1979-81; judge U.S. Ct. of Appeals for 1st Circuit, 1981—; mem. U.S. Sentencing commn., 1985—; vis. lectr. Coll. Law, Sydney, Australia, 1975, Salzburg (Austria) Seminar, 1978; Jud. Conf. rep. to Adminstrv. Conf. U.S. Author: (with Paul MacAvoy) The Federal Power Commission and the Regulation of Energy, 1974, (with Richard Stewart) Adminstrative Law and Regulatory Policy, 1979, 2d edit., 1985, Regulation and its Reform, 1982; Contbr. articles to profl. jours. Trustee U. Mass., 1974-81; bd. overseers Dana Farber Cancer Inst., Boston, 1977—. Mem. Am. Bar Found., Am. Bar Assn., Am. Law Inst., Am. Acad. Arts and Scis., Council on Fgn. Relations. Jurisprudence. Home: 12 Dunstable Rd Cambridge MA 02138 Office: US Ct of Appeals US Courthouse and Post Office Bldg Boston MA 02109

BREZINA, DAVID CHARLES, lawyer, educator; b. Berwyn, Ill., Sept. 11, 1953; s. John Charles and Virginia (Nelson) B.; married, Jan. 4, 1980. J.D. with honors, Chgo.-Kent Law Sch., 1978; student John Marshall Law Sch., 1978-84. Bars: Ill. 1978, U.S. Dist. Ct. (no. dist.) Ill. 1978, Trial Bar (no. dist.) Ill. 1982, U.S. Ct. Appeals (7th cir.) 1978, U.S. Ct. Customs and Patent Appeals 1980, U.S. Ct. Appeals (fed. cir.) 1982, U.S. Supreme Ct. 1981. Assoc. Brezina & Buckingham, P.C., Chgo., 1978—; instr. Columbia Coll., Chgo., 1983—. Author: Cases and Materials on Intellectual Property Law for AEMMP, 1984. Editor: Antitrust and Misuse Aspects of Intellectual Property Law, 1985. Intellectual property cons. Ill. Inst. Tech./Chgo. Kent Law Rev., 1979-83; guest commentator Columbia Coll. Chronicle, 1984; patentee composite vehicle manufacture, 1985; contbr. articles on trademarks to profl. publs. Mem. staff Dick Clark Senate Campaign, Marion, Iowa, 1972; intern 66th Iowa Gen. Assembly, Des Moines, 1975; incorporator Concerned Citizens of Brookfield, Ill., 1976; election troubleshooter Project LEAP, Chgo., 1977—. Mem. ABA, Ill. State Bar Assn., Chgo. Bar Assn., Lawyers Pilots Bar Assn. Clubs: Chgo. Area Rugby Football Union (discipline chmn. 1980-81), Lincoln Park Rugby Football (asst. coach 1981-82). Trademark and copyright, Patent, Antitrust. Office: Brezina & Buckingham PC 135 S LaSalle St #1946 Chicago IL 60603 Office: Brezina & Buckingham PC 111 W Jackson Blvd Chicago IL 60604

BREZINSKY, HELENE, lawyer; b. N.Y.C., July 2, 1950. BA, SUNY, Stony Brook, 1972; JD, NYU, 1975. Bar: N.J., U.S. Dist. Ct. (so. and ea. dists.) N.Y. Assoc. Marshall, Bratter et al, N.Y.C., 1975-82; assoc. Rosenman, Colin, Freund, Lewis & Cohen, N.Y.C., 1982-85, ptnr., 1985—; seminar moderator Columbia U. Law Sch., N.Y.C., 1984. Fellow Am. Acad. Matrimonial Lawyers; mem. N.Y. State Bar Assn. (legis. com. family law sect., lectr. 1986), N.J. Bar Assn. (family law sect.), Practicing Law Inst. (lectr. 1985). Family and matrimonial. Home: 44 Bonn Pl Weehawken NJ 07087 Office: Rosenman Colin Freund Lewis & Cohen 575 Madison Ave New York NY 10022

BRIAN, A(LEXIS) MORGAN, JR., lawyer; b. New Orleans, Oct. 4, 1928; s. Alexis Morgan and Evelyn (Thibaut) B.; m. Elizabeth Louise Graham, 1951; children—Robert Morgan, Ellen Graham. B.A., La. State U., 1949, J.D., 1956; M.S., Trinity U., 1954. Bar: La. 1956, U.S. Supreme Ct. 1971. Assoc. Deutsch, Kerrigan & Stiles, New Orleans, 1956-60, ptnr., 1961-79; sr. ptnr. Brian, Simon, Peragine, Smith & Redfearn, New Orleans, 1979-80; of counsel Simon, Peragine, Smith & Redfearn, New Orleans, 1981-82; sr. ptnr. Fawer, Brian, Hardy & Zatzkis, New Orleans, 1982-86; sole practice, New Orleans, 1986—; spl. asst. to La. Atty. Gen., 1982-86, sole practice, 1986—; speaker profl. seminars; lectr. Inst. Continuing Legal Edn., La. State U. Law Ctr., 1972—. Local merit badge counselor Boy Scouts Am., 1963—; bd. dirs. Goodwill Industries New Orleans, 1968—, v.p. and mem. exec. com., 1975-77, mem. adv. bd., 1978, 86; deacon, trustee, lay preacher, Bible tchr., mem. coms. First Baptist Ch. New Orleans; speaker at convs., confs. So. Bapt. Conv., 1956—, La. Bapt. Conv., 1956—; past pres. bd. trustees New Orleans Bapt. Theol. Sem.; bd. dirs. Inter-Varsity Christian Fellowship, 1974—; mem. nat. legal adv. council Ams. United for Separation of Ch. and State, 1977—. Served with USAF, 1951-55. Recipient Boss of Yr. award New Orleans Legal Secs. Assn., 1966. Mem. ABA (TIPS fidelity and surety com., forum com. contstrn. industry), La. Bar Assn., New Orleans Bar Assn., Internat. Assn. Def. Counsel (vice chmn. fidelity and surety com. 1978-79), La. Assn. Def. Counsel, Def. Research Inst., Am. Arbitration Assn. (arbitrator 1970—), La. Civil Service League, Internat. House, La. State U. Alumni Fedn. (life), Trinity U. Alumni Assn., La. State U. Law Ctr. Alumni Assn. (life), Upper Carrollton Neighborhood Assn. (v.p. 1976), Christian

Legal Soc., Theta Xi, Phi Delta Phi. Democrat. Contbr. articles to legal jours. Construction, Government contracts and claims, Insurance. Home: 1738 S Carrollton Ave New Orleans LA 70118 Office: 700 Camp St New Orleans LA 70130

BRICK, ANN VETA, lawyer; b. Cheyenne, Wyo., Mar. 17, 1947; d. Gerald John and Margaret (Pasternack) Veta; m. Steven Alexander Brick, Dec. 29, 1968; children: Kate Elizabeth, Rachel Suzanne. B.A., Newcomb Coll., Tulane U., 1969; J.D., U. Calif.-Berkeley, 1975. Bar: Calif. 1975, U.S. Dist. Ct. (no. dist.) Calif. 1975, U.S. Ct. Appeals (5th cir.) 1978, U.S. Ct. Appeals (7th cir.) 1981. Law clk. to judge U.S. Dist. Ct. (no. dist.) Calif., San Francisco, 1975-76; assoc. Howard, Rice, Nemerovski, Canady, Robertson & Falk, San Francisco, 1977-81, dir., 1981-84, of counsel, 1984—; dir. Legal Aid Soc. of San Francisco, 1982—, Equal Rights Advocates, San Francisco, 1984—. Contbr. article to legal jour. Mem. Bar. Assn. Calif. (panelist Continuing Edn. of Bar 1983), Lawyers Com. for Urban Affairs, San Francisco Bar Assn. (judiciary com. 1982-84, com. on women in the law 1987—), ACLU (cooperating atty. 1978—), Order of Coif, Phi Beta Kappa. Democrat. Jewish. Antitrust, Federal civil litigation, State civil litigation. Office: Three Embarcadero Ctr 7th Floor San Francisco CA 94705

BRICK, BARRETT LEE, lawyer; b. Middletown, N.Y., Jan. 12, 1954; s. Michael and Barbara Lilian (Rosen) B. BA, Columbia U., 1976, JD, 1979. Bar: N.Y. 1980, U.S. Ct. Appeals (D.C. cir.) 1981, U.S. Supreme Ct. 1984. Atty.-adviser FCC, Washington, 1980—. Contbr. to book, Positively Gay, 1979; book review columnist Washington Blade newspaper, 1982-83; editor National Gay Task Force Action Report, 1975-76. Active Community Board Nine, N.Y.C., 1978-80; mem. Gay Mens' Chorus, Washington, 1984—; bd. dirs. Congregation Bet Mishpachah, Washington, 1980-84, pres., 1984-85. Recipient Advocate 400 award, The Advocate, San Francisco, 1984; named one of Outstanding Young Men of Am. U.S. Jaycees, 1983, 84. Mem. ABA, N.Y. State Bar Assn., Bar Assn. for Human Rights Greater N.Y., Nat. Gay Rights Advocates. Democrat. Jewish. Club: Capital (Washington). Administrative and regulatory, Legal history. Home: 1901 Wyoming Ave NW Washington DC 20009 Office: FCC 1919 M St NW Washington DC 20554

BRICKLEY, JAMES H., judge; b. Flint, Mich., Nov. 15, 1928; s. J. Harry and Marie E. (Fischer) B.; 6 children. B.A., U. Detroit, 1951, LL.B., 1954, Ph.D. (hon.), 1977; LL.M., NYU, 1957; Ph.D. (hon.), Spring Arbor Coll., 1975, Detroit Coll. Bus., 1975, Ferris State Coll., Big Rapids, Mich., 1980, Saginaw Valley State Coll., University Center, Mich., 1980, Detroit Coll. Law, 1981. Bar: Mich. 1954. Spl. agent FBI, Washington, 1954-58; sole practice law Detroit, 1959-62; mem. Detroit City Council, 1962-67, pres. pro tem, 1966-67; chief asst. prosecutor Wayne County, Detroit, 1967-69; U.S. atty. U.S. Dist. Ct. (ea. dist.), Detroit, 1969-70; lt. gov. State of Mich., Lansing, 1971-74, 79-82; justice Supreme Ct. of Mich., Lansing, 1982—; pres. Eastern Mich. U., Ypsilanti, 1975-78; lectr., adj. prof. U. Detroit, Wayne State U., U. Mich., Ann Arbor, Cooley Law Sch., 1958-73. Mem. Mich. Bar Assn., ABA, Inst. Jud. Administrn. Republican. Roman Catholic. Office: Mich Supreme Ct PO Box 30052 Lansing MI 48909

BRICKLIN, LOUIS E., lawyer; b. Phila., Nov. 8, 1949; s. Albert L. and Regina (Edelman) B.; m. Susan Dein, June 17, 1973; children: Evelyn, Carolyn. BA, U. Va., 1971; JD, U. Pa., 1974. Bar: Pa. 1974, U.S. Dist. Ct. (ea. dist.) Pa. 1974, U.S. Ct. Appeals (3d cir.) 1975, U.S. Supreme Ct. 1983. Law clk. to presiding judge U.S. Dist. Ct. (ea. dist.) Pa., Phila., 1974-75; assoc. Bennett, Bricklin & Saltzburg, Phila., 1975-79; ptnr. Bennett, Bricklin, Saltzburg & Fullem, Phila., 1979—. Mem. ABA, Pa. Bar Assn., Phila. Bar Assn. (state civil procedures rules com.), Def. Research Inst., Phila. Assn. Def. Counsel, Phi Beta Kappa. Democrat. Jewish. Insurance, State civil litigation, Federal civil litigation. Home: 718 Braeburn Ln Penn Valley PA 19072 Office: Bennett Bricklin & Saltzburg 1700 Market St Room 1800 Philadelphia PA 19103-3882

BRICKNER, JED WALTER, lawyer; b. N.Y.C., Sept. 27, 1954; s. Philip Walter and Alice (Rinenberg) B.; m. Lynne Michiko Oshita, Feb. 20, 1982. BA, Swarthmore Coll., 1976; JD, Columbia U., 1980. Bar: Calif. 1980, U.S. Dist. Ct. (cen. dist.) Calif. 1980. Assoc. Latham & Watkins, Los Angeles, 1980—. Author: (ann.) World Records for Days of the Week, 1979—. Harlan Fiske Stone scholar, 1977-80. Mem. ABA, Calif. Bar Assn. (tax sect.), Los Angeles County Bar Assn. (employee benefits sect.), Phi Beta Kappa. Avocation: keeping track and field stats. Pension, profit-sharing, and employee benefits, Labor, Corporate taxation. Office: Latham & Watkins 555 S Flower St Los Angeles CA 90017

BRICKWEDDE, RICHARD JAMES, lawyer; b. Bklyn., Dec. 12, 1944; s. George L. and Rose M. (McCarthy) B.; m. June Minsch Gamber, Sept. 2, 1978; stepchildren—Stephanie, Karen, Frances A.B., Syracuse U., 1966; J.D., Fordham U., 1969. Bars: N.Y. 1970, D.C. 1971; staff asst. Syracuse (N.Y.) office Senator Robert F. Kennedy, 1965-66; adminstrv. asst. U.S. P.O. and OEO/VISTA, Washington, 1966; mgmt. cons., Washington, 1969-71; gen. counsel The Student Vote, Washington, 1971; pvt. practice law, Syracuse, 1971-80; regional counsel N.Y. State Dept. Environ. Conservation, Liverpool, 1980, acting regional dir., 1984; assoc. counsel to majority leader N.Y. State Assembly, 1975, asst. counsel to speaker N.Y. State Assembly, 1976-77. Chmn. voting Rights Task Force, Dem. Nat. Com., 1970-71; bd. dirs. N.Y. Alpha Tau Omega Student Aid Fund, Inc., Syracuse, 1972—, Huntington Family Centers, Inc., Syracuse, 1972—, v.p. 1980, Onondaga County (N.Y.) Child Care Council, Inc., 1978-80; mem. Onondaga Neighborhood Legal Services, Inc. (now Legal Services of Central N.Y.) 1978-83, treas. 1980-81, pres., 1981-82. Named Hon. Citizen, State of Tex., 1976; recipient Pub. Citizenship award, N.Y. Pub. Interest Research Group, 1980. Mem. ABA, N.Y. Bar Assn., Onondaga County Bar Assn. Democrat. Author: The Student's Right to Vote, 1971; contbg. editor Network, 1975-76. Environment, Administrative and regulatory. Home: 1115 Euclid Ave Syracuse NY 13210 Office: 7481 Henry Clay Blvd Liverpool NY 13088

BRIDEWELL, SHERRY HAZELWOOD, lawyer; b. Williamsburg, Va., June 3, 1956; d. Howell Percell, Jr. and Mary (Courtney) Hazelwood; m. Travis Arthur Bridewell, May 14, 1977. B.A., Coll. William and Mary, 1978, J.D., 1981. Bar: Va. 1981, U.S. Ct. Appeals (4th cir.) 1983. Reporter, Daily Report, Inc., Newport News, Va., 1978-80; dep. clk. of ct. Williamsburg-James City County Circuit Ct. Clk's. Office, Williamsburg, 1979-80; atty. Office Gen. Counsel, State Corp. Commn., Richmond, Va., 1981—, mem. Task Force for Telecommunications, 1981-84; adj. instr. Sch. Bus., Coll. William and Mary. Author: Resolution for Nat. Assn. of Regulatory Utility Commns., 1983; co-author rules and legis. in field. Clk. Liberty Baptist Ch., Lanexa, Va., 1981-82. Abby Aldrich Rockefeller scholar, 1974. Mem. ABA, Va. Bar Assn., Richmond Bar Assn., Women's Richmond Bar Assn., Phi Beta Kappa. Utility law, General corporate, Administrative and regulatory. Office: 1220 Bank St Office of Gen Counsel Va State Corp Commn PO Box 1197 Richmond VA 23219

BRIDGE, JONATHAN JOSEPH, lawyer, retail executive; b. Seattle, Mar. 19, 1950; s. Herbert Marvin and Shirley Geraldine (Selesnick) B.; m. Bobbe Jean Chaback, May 20, 1978; children: Donald, Rebecca. BA with honors, U. Wash., 1972, JD, 1976. Bar: Wash. 1976, U.S. Dist. Ct. (we. dist.) Wash. 1976, U.S. Ct. Mil. Appeals 1977, U.S. Ct. Appeals (9th cir.) 1979, U.S. Supreme Ct. 1980. Legal service officer USN, Oak Harbor, Wash., 1976-79; staff judge adv. USN, Bremerton, Wash., 1979-81; v.p., corp. counsel Ben Bridge Jeweler, Inc., Seattle, 1981—; bd. dirs. Ben Bridge Corp., Seattle. Bd. dirs. King County Mental Health Bd., Seattle, 1984; mem. exec. bd. Washington Retail Counsel, 1985—; vice chmn. Seattle Urban League, 1986—; pres. Am. Jewish Com., Seattle, 1986—. Served to lt. comdr. USN, 1972-81, Vietnam. Mem. ABA, Wash. State Bar Assn., Seattle/King County Bar Assn., Judge Advs. Assn., U. Wash. Alumni Assn. (bd. dirs. 1986—, Pres.' Club). Democrat. Jewish. Club: Wash. Athletic (Seattle), Columbia Tower (Seattle), City (Seattle), Seattle Chamber Pres.'s. General corporate, Military. Home: 2440 Montavista Pl W Seattle WA 98199 Office: Ben Bridge Jeweler Inc PO Box 1908 Seattle WA 98111

BRIDGE, WINSTON JAY, lawyer; b. Laconia, N.H., Jan. 18, 1935; s. Harold Ellsworth and Althea Shirley (Keezer) B.; m. Martha Ann Hayes, Aug. 10, 1979. AB, Dartmouth Coll., 1956; JD, Suffolk U., 1967. Bar: Mass. 1968, U.S. Dist. Ct. Mass. 1970, U.S. Ct. Appeals (1st cir.) 1972, U.S. Supreme Ct. 1978. Mgr. Paul Revere Life Ins. Co., Worcester, Mass., 1963-65; trust officer State St. Bank and Trust Co., Boston, 1965-69; pres. Bridge, Dyson & Kilmartin P.C., Bedford, Mass., 1969-85, Bridge & Turner P.C., Lexington, Mass., 1985—; bd. dirs. Valley Sports Inc., Concord, Mass. Mem. Bedford sch. com., 1967-70, adv. bd. Middlesex Community Coll., Bedford, 1970-76; chmn. Rep. town com., Bedford, 1968-73. Served to comdr. USNR, 1956-78. Mem. Boston Bar Assn., Middlesex Bar Assn., Cen. Middlesex Bar Assn., Mass. Bankers Assn. (bd. dirs. trust div., 1969-71), Soc. Colonial Wars. Congregationalist. Club: Wardroom (Boston). Lodge: Rotary (pres. Bedford 1978). Real property, Probate, General practice. Home: 4 Summit Dr 601 Reading MA 01867 Office: Bridge & Turner PC 33 Bedford St Suite 11 Lexington MA 02173

BRIDGELAND, JAMES RALPH, JR., lawyer; b. Cleve., Feb. 16, 1929; s. James Ralph and Alice Laura (Huth) B.; m. Margaret Louise Bates, March 24, 1950; children—Deborah, Cynthia, Rebekah, Alicia, John. B.A., U. Akron, 1951; M.A., Harvard U., 1955, J.D., 1957. Bar: Ohio 1957. Mem. internat. staff Goodyear Tire & Rubber Co., Akron, Ohio, 1953-56; ptnr. Taft, Stettinius & Hollister, Cin., 1957—; dir. and mem. exec. com. First Nat. Bank Cin.; dir. Consol. Biscuit Co., SHV N.Am., Inc., Robert A. Cline Co., Art Stamping, Inc., Seinau-Fisher Studios, Inc.; sec. Vortec, Inc. Trustee of Cin. Symphony Orchestra (mem. exec. com.), Louise Taft Semple Found. (sec.), Hillside Trust Co., Jobs for Cin. Grads.; past dir. Cin. Legal Aid Soc.; mem. council City of Indian Hill, Ohio, 1986—. Served to 1st lt. USAF, 1951-53, Korea. Fellow Aspen Inst.; mem. ABA, Ohio Bar Assn., Cin. Bar Assn., Am. Arbitration Assn., Harvard Law Sch. Assn. (past pres. Cin. chpt.), Harvard Alumni Assn. (nat. v.p. 1978-85). Republican. Episcopalian. Clubs: Harvard (pres. 1983-84), Queen City, Commonwealth (treas. 1984-86). General corporate, Banking, Private international. Home: 8175 Brill Rd Cincinnati OH 45243

BRIDGES, B. RIED, lawyer; b. Kansas City, Mo., Oct. 20, 1927; s. Brady R. and Mary H. (Nieuwenhuis) B.; m. Lou George, Feb. 9, 1955; 1 son, Ried George. B.A., U. So. Calif., 1951, LL.B., 1954. Bar: Calif. 1954. Assoc. Overton, Lyman & Prince, Los Angeles, 1956-58, ptnr., 1958-63; partner Bonne, Jones & Bridges, Los Angeles, 1962-74; ptnr. Bonne, Jones, Bridges, Mueller & O'Keefe, Los Angeles, 1974—; referee State Bar Ct., 1980—, judge Calif. State Bar Ct., 1978—. Served with U.S. Army, 1954-56. Fellow Am. Coll. Trial Lawyers, Internat. Acad. Trial Lawyers, Am. Acad. Forensic Sci.; mem. ABA, Calif. Bar Assn., Assn. So. Calif. Def. Counsel, Los Angeles County Bar Assn.; diplomate Am. Bd. Trial Advs. Republican. Clubs: Univ. (Los Angeles); California Yacht; Balboa of Mazatlan (Sinaloa, Mex.). Avocation: sailing. Personal injury, Federal civil litigation, State civil litigation. Home: 4460 Wilshire Blvd #406 Los Angeles CA 90010 Office: Bonne Jones et al 600 S Commonwealth 17th Floor Los Angeles CA 90005

BRIDGES, RUSSELL BRIAN, lawyer; b. Temple, Tex., Mar. 19, 1955; s. Bobby Donald And Edna Louise (Penny) B. BBA, Baylor U., 1977, JD, 1979. Bar: Tex. 1980. Gen. counsel Office Treas. State Tex., Austin, 1981-83; legis. liaison Office of Gov. State Tex., Austin, 1983-84; govt. relations atty. 3M Co., Austin, 1984—. Del. State Dem. Conv., Houston, 1984; mem. exec. com. Baylor Devel. Council Assocs., Waco, Tex., 1985-86. Mem. ABA, Tex. State Bar Assn., Travis County Bar Assn., Tex. Young Lawyers Assn., Tex. Safety Assn. (bd. dirs. 1985-86), Baylor U. Alumni Assn. (bd. dirs. 1977-79), Delta Theta Phi. Baptist. Avocation: travel. Legislative, Administrative and regulatory, General corporate. Home: 4002 Sinclair Austin TX 78756 Office: 3M Co PO Box 2963 Austin TX 78769

BRIDGESMITH, LARRY W., lawyer; b. Pontiac, Mich., July 4, 1948; s. Kenneth Clyde Smith and Charlene (Keith) Parks; m. Linda Sue Bridges, Aug. 24, 1968; children: Lara Elisa, Lance Preston. AA with honors, Mich. Christian Coll., 1968; BA, Oakland U., 1972, postgrad., 1972-73; JD with honors, Wayne State U., 1978. Bar: Mich. 1979, Tenn. 1981, U.S. Dist. Ct. (ea. dist.) Mich., U.S. Dist. Ct. (mid. and we. dists.) Tenn., U.S. Ct. Appeals (5th, 6th and 11th cirs.), U.S. Supreme Ct. Law clk. to presiding justice Oakland County Probate Ct., Pontiac, 1975-77, legal asst., 1977-78; assoc. Cox & Hooth, P.C., Troy, Mich., 1978-80; mng. ptnr. Constangy, Brooks & Smith, Nashville, 1980—. Mem. recruitment com. ARC, Nashville, 1984—. Named one of Outstanding Young Men Am., 1981. Mem. ABA (labor and litigation sects.), Mich. Bar Assn. (labor and litigation sects.), Tenn. Bar Assn. (labor sect., continuing legal edn. com.), Nashville Bar Assn. (community relations com.). Avocations: reading, water sports, racket sports, travel. Labor, Federal civil litigation, State civil litigation. Home: 916 Cynthia Trail Goodlettsville TN 37072 Office: Constangy Brooks & Smith 1080 Vanderbilt Plaza 2100 West End Ave Nashville TN 37203

BRIDGMAN, THOMAS FRANCIS, lawyer; b. Chgo., Dec. 30, 1933; s. Thomas Joseph and Angeline (Gorman) B.; m. Patricia A. McCormick, May 16, 1959; children: Thomas, Kathleen Ann, Ann Marie, Jane T., Molly. B.S. cum laude, John Carroll U., 1955; J.D. cum laude, Loyola U., Chgo., 1958. Bar: Ill. 1958, U.S. Dist. Ct. 1959. Assoc. McCarthy & Levin, Chgo., 1958; assoc. Baker & McKenzie, Chgo., 1958-62, ptnr., 1962—. Trustee John Carroll U., 1982—. Recipient Medal of Excellence Loyola U., 1978. Fellow Am. Coll. Trial Lawyers, Internat. Acad. Trial Lawyers (past pres.). Democrat. Roman Catholic. Clubs: Union League; Beverly Country (Chgo.) (pres. 1983). Federal civil litigation, State civil litigation. Home: 9400 S Pleasant Ave Chicago IL 60620 Office: Baker & McKenzie 130 E Randolph Dr Chicago IL 60601

BRIEANT, CHARLES LA MONTE, JR., judge; b. Ossining, N.Y., Mar. 13, 1923; s. Charles La Monte and Marjorie (Hall) B.; m. Virginia Elizabeth Warfield, Sept. 10, 1948; children: Cynthia W. Brieant Hendricks, Charles La Monte III, Victoria E. Brieant Dunaif, Julia W. Brieant Clavette. B.A., Columbia U., 1947, LL.B., 1949. Bar: N.Y. 1949. Mem. firm Bleakley, Platt, Schmidt & Fritz, White Plains, 1949-71; water commr. Village of Ossining, 1948-51; town justice 1952-58, town supr., 1960-63; village atty. Briarcliff Manor, N.Y.; also spl. asst. dist. atty. Westchester County, 1958-59; asst. counsel N.Y. State Joint Legis. Com. Fire Ins., 1968; U.S. dist. judge So. Dist. N.Y., N.Y.C., 1971-86, chief judge, 1986—; adj. prof. Bklyn. Law Sch. Mem. Westchester County Republican Com., 1957-71; mem. Westchester County Legislature from 2d Dist., 1970-71. Served with AUS, World War II. Mem. ABA, N.Y. State Bar Assn., Westchester County Bar Assn., Ossining Bar Assn. Episcopalian (past vestryman). Club: S.A.R. Jurisprudence. Office: US Courthouse 101 E Post Rd White Plains NY 10601

BRIER, BONNIE SUSAN, lawyer; b. Oct. 19, 1950; d. Jerome W. and Barbara (Srenco) B.; m. Bruce A. Rosenfield, Aug. 15, 1976; children: Rebecca, Elizabeth, Benjamin. AB in Econs. magna cum laude, Cornell U., 1972; JD, Stanford U., 1976. Bar: Pa. 1976, U.S. Dist. Ct. (ea. dist.) Pa., U.S. Tax Ct., U.S. Ct. Appeals (3d cir.), U.S. Supreme Ct. Law clk. to chief judge U.S. Dist. Ct. Pa. (ea. dist.), Phila., 1976-77, asst. U.S. atty. criminal prosecutor, 1977-79; from assoc. to ptnr. Ballard, Spahr, Andrews & Ingersoll, Phila., 1979; lectr., speaker various orgns. and sems.; legal counsel Womens Way, 1979—. Editor Stanford U. Law Rev., 1975-76. Mem. ABA (exempt orgn. tax sect.), Pa. Bar Assn. (tax sect.), Phila. Bar Assn. (tax sect.), Nat. Health Lawyers Assn., Order of Coif. Corporate taxation, Health, Personal income taxation. Home: 620 Spruce St Philadelphia PA 19106 Office: Ballard Spahr Andrews & Ingersoll 30 S 17th St Philadelphia PA 19103

BRIGGS, GEORGE SCOTT, lawyer; b. Amesbury, Mass., Jan. 10, 1944; s. Richard Clark and Marjorie (Lloyd) B.; m. Karen Lee Henry, Aug. 24, 1968; children: Amy Christine and Richard Clark. AB, Brown U., 1966; JD, Vanderbilt U., 1969. Bar: Colo. 1971, U.S. Dist. Ct. Colo. 1971, U.S. Ct. Appeals (10th cir.) 1974, U.S. Supreme Ct. 1975. Assoc. Evans, Peterson & Torbet, Colorado Springs, Colo., 1971; ptnr. Evans, Peterson, Torbet & Briggs, Colorado Springs, 1972-75, Evans & Briggs, Colorado Springs, 1975—. Organizer North Am. Def. Command Cans. Media Hockey Game, Colo. Springs, 1982. Served with U.S. Army, 1969-71. Mem. ABA, Assn. Trial Lawyers Am., Colo. Trial Lawyers Assn., Colo. Bar Assn., El Paso County Bar Assn. (trustee 1978-79, pres. elect 1986-87), Hort. Art Soc. (pres. 1983-84). Republican. Lodge: Lions (pres. 1978-79). General practice, General corporate, Consumer commercial. Home: 1415 N Nevada Ave Colorado Springs CO 80907-7430 Office: Evans & Briggs 532 S Weber St Colorado Springs CO 80903-3906

BRIGGS, MARJORIE CROWDER, lawyer; b. Shreveport, La., Mar. 26, 1946; d. Rowland Edmund and Marjorie Ernestine (Biles) Crowder; m. Ronald J. Briggs, July 11, 1970; children—Sarah, Andrew. B.A., Carson-Newman Coll., 1968; M.A., Ohio State U., 1969, J.D., 1975. Bar: Ohio 1975, U.S. Dist. Ct. (so. dist.) Ohio 1975, U.S. Ct. Appeals (6th cir.) 1983. Asst. dean of women Albion Coll., Mich., 1969-70; dir. residence hall Ohio State U., Columbus, 1970-71, acad. counselor, 1971-72; assoc. Porter, Wright, Morris, Arthur, Columbus, 1975-83, ptnr., 1983—; legal aide Community Law Office, Columbus, 1973-74. Trustee, pres. Epilepsy Assn. Central Ohio, Columbus, 1977-84; bd. dirs. Columbus Speech & Hearing, 1977-82; mem. allocation com. United Way Franklin County, 1984—. Mem. ABA, Ohio Bar Assn., Columbus Bar Assn. (com. chmn. 1979-83, editor 1981-83), Am. Arbitration Assn., Nat. Assn. Women Lawyers, Women Lawyers Franklin County, Columbus Def. Assn. Club: Capital. Federal civil litigation, State civil litigation, Insurance. Home: 4260 Woodhall Rd Columbus OH 43220 Office: Porter Wright Morris & Arthur 41 S High St Columbus OH 43215

BRIGGS, RANDY ROBERT, lawyer; b. Mineola, N.Y., Jan. 23, 1948; s. Robert Oren Briggs and Elizabeth (Pasteur) Keeney; m. Diana Joy Allen; children—Robert Cullen, Allison Elizabeth. B.S.A., U. Fla., 1970, J.D., 1975. Bar: Fla. 1975, U.S. Dist. Ct. (mid. dist.) Fla. 1976; cert. civil trial adv. Nat. Bd. Trial Advocacy, Fla. Bar. Assoc. Maguire, Voorhis & Wells, P.A., Orlando, Fla., 1975-77; ptnr. Ayers, Cluster, Curry, McCall & Briggs, P.A., Ocala, Fla., 1977—. Served to 1st lt. U.S. Army, 1970-72. Mem. Fla. Bar (bd. govs. young lawyers sect. 1980-83, bd. of cert.), Acad. Fla. Trial Lawyers, Assn. Trial Lawyers Am., Order of Coif, Phi Kappa Phi. Episcopalian. Personal injury, State civil litigation, Federal civil litigation. Home: 3385 SW 17th Ave Ocala FL 32674 Office: Ayres Cluster Curry et al 21 NE First Ave PO Box 1148 Ocala FL 32670

BRIGGS, STEVEN ERNEST, lawyer; b. San Diego, Aug. 18, 1942; s. Gordon Ernest and Rena Louise (Lane) B.; m. Linda Lee Holz, May 31, 1975. BSBA, U. San Diego, 1964, JD magna cum laude, 1970. Bar: Calif. 1971, U.S. Dist. Ct. (cen. dist.) Calif. 1971, U.S. Supreme Ct. 1973. Ptnr. Lawton, Christen, Fazio, McDonnell, Briggs & Ward, La Habra, Calif., 1971-82; sole practice La Habra, 1982—; bd. dirs. Surety Ins. Co. of Calif. Served to capt. USMC, 1964-67. Fellow Am. Acad. Matrimonial Lawyers; mem. ABA, Calif. State Bar Assn., Orange County Bar Assn. Republican. Family and matrimonial. Office: 440 E La Habra Blvd La Habra CA 90631

BRIGGS, TAYLOR RASTRICK, lawyer; b. Buffalo, June 5, 1933; s. Ernest Rastrick and Althea (Taylor) B.; m. Jane Genske, Sept. 15, 1956; children—Cynthia B. Kittredge, Jennifer B., Pamela, Taylor Rastrick. A.B., Williams Coll., 1954; LL.B., Columbia U., 1957. Bar: N.Y., U.S. Supreme Ct. Assoc. Simpson Thacher & Bartlett, N.Y.C., 1957-59; counsel N.Y. Com. on Govtl. Ops. of City of N.Y., 1959-60; asst. chief counsel N.Y. State Com. of Investigation, Special Unit, 1960-61; ptnr. LeBoeuf, Lamb, Leiby & MacRae, N.Y.C., 1961—. Chmn. Zoning Bd. Appeals, Tuxedo Park, N.Y., 1972—; pres. Tuxedo Park Library, 1971-79; trustee N.Y. Law Sch., N.Y.C., 1984—; mem. adv. council Trinity Ctr. for Ethics and Corp. Policy, N.Y.C., 1982—. Fellow Am. Bar Found., Am. Coll. Trial Lawyers; mem. ABA (ho. of del. 1985—), Assn. of Bar of City of N.Y., N.Y. State Bar Assn., Phi Delta Phi, Delta Upsilon. Republican. Episcopalian. Clubs: Racquet and Tennis, Tuxedo (sec.), Royal Tennis (Hampton Court, Eng.); Mid-Ocean (Bermuda); New England Soc. Lodge: Masons. Antitrust, Federal civil litigation, General corporate. Home: W Lake Rd Tuxedo Park NY 10987 Office: LeBoeuf Lamb Leiby & MacRae 520 Madison Ave New York NY 10022

BRIGGS, TOM PEERY, lawyer; b. Meridean, Miss., Oct. 20, 1943; s. Marguerite (Peery) Briggs. BBA, So. Meth. U., 1965; JD, U. Tex., 1968. Bar: Tex. 1968, U.S. Dist. Ct. (no. dist.) Tex. 1968. Assoc. Law Offices of Kearby Peery, Wichita Falls, Tex., 1969-72, Bean, Francis, Ford, Francis & Wills, Dallas, 1972-74; ptnr. Briggs, Brown & Berkley, Dallas, 1975—. Mem. Tex. Trial Lawyers Assn. (assoc. bd. dirs. 1973-76), Dallas Trial Lawyers Assn. (bd. dirs. 1976-86). Republican. Methodist. State civil litigation, Personal injury, Probate. Home: 5336 Southern Dallas TX 75209 Office: Berry Briggs Brown & Berkley 4315 W Lovers Ln Dallas TX 75209

BRIGHAM, SAMUEL TOWNSEND JACK, III, lawyer; b. Honolulu, Oct. 8, 1939; s. Samuel Townsend Jack, Jr. and Betty Elizabeth (McNeil) B.; m. Judith Catherine Johnson, Sept. 3, 1960; children: Robert Jack, Bradley Lund, Lori Ann, Lisa Katherine. B.S. in Bus. magna cum laude, Menlo Coll., 1963; J.D., U. Utah, 1966. Bar: Calif. 1967. Asso. firm Petty, Andrews, Olsen & Tufts, San Francisco, 1966-67; accounting mgr. Western sales region Hewlett-Packard Co., North Hollywood, Calif., 1967-68; atty. Hewlett-Packard Co., Palo Alto, Calif., 1968-70; asst. gen. counsel Hewlett-Packard Co., 1971-73, gen. atty., asst. sec., 1974-75, sec., gen. counsel, 1975-82, v.p., gen. counsel, 1982-85, v.p. adminstrn., gen. counsel, 1985—; lectr. law Menlo Coll.; speaker profl. assn. seminars. Bd. dirs. Palo Alto Area YMCA, 1974-81, pres., 1978; bd. govs. Santa Clara County region NCCJ. Served with USMC, 1957-59. Mem. Am. Bar Assn., Calif. Bar Assn., Peninsula Assn. Gen. Counsel, MAPI Law Council, Am. Corp. Counsel Assn. (chmn. 1985, bd. dirs. 1983—), Am. Soc. Corp. Secs. (pres. No. Calif. Chpt. 1983—). Home: 920 Oxford Dr Los Altos CA 94022 Office: 3000 Hanover St Palo Alto CA 94304 •

BRIGHT, FRANCIS EDWARD, lawyer; b. Franklin, N.J., Aug. 1, 1917; s. Frank Edward and Anastasia Mary (Madden) B.; m. Joan Bernice Thompson, Apr. 2, 1943; children: Patrick, Lawrence, Mark, Frank, Joan, Ellyn. BCS magna cum laude, U. Notre Dame, 1939, LLB magna cum laude, 1940. Bar: N.J. 1941, U.S. Dist. Ct. N.J. 1941, U.S. Supreme Ct. 1966. Spl. agt. FBI, Washington, 1941-46; ptnr. Dolan & Dolan, Newton, N.J., 1946-67, v.p., 1967-84, pres., 1984—, also bd. dirs.; bd. dirs. Midantic Nat. Bank, Newton, N.J. Telephone Co., Clinton, N.J., United Telephone Co., Newton. Editor U. Notre Dame Law Rev., 1939-40. Atty. Sparta (N.J.) Twp. Council, 1948-81. Mem. ABA, N.J. Bar Assn., Sussex County Bar Assn. (pres. 1952-53). Republican. Roman Catholic. Club: Lake Nohawk Golf (Sparta, N.J.) (gov. 1976-79). Avocation: golf. Public utilities, Personal injury. Home: 23 S Shore Trail Sparta NJ 07871 Office: Dolan & Dolan PA 53 Spring St Box D Newton NJ 07860

BRIGHT, GERALD, manufacturing company executive; b. Detroit, Feb. 17, 1923; s. Harry B. and Jessie (Vidaver) Bright; m. Marceline Douger, Dec. 28, 1952; children: Russell, Ethan. A.B., U. Mich., 1947, LL.B., 1950. Bar: Mich. 1950. Law clk. presiding justice Mich. Supreme Ct., Lansing, 1950-51; assoc. Travis & Warren, Detroit, 1951-52, Bizer & Sommers, Detroit, 1952-60; ptnr. Derderian, Guidot & Bright, Detroit, 1960-66; gen. counsel Masco Corp., Taylor, Mich., 1966—, v.p., gen. counsel, 1970—, sec., 1983—. Mem. state central com. Republican Party, Lansing, Mich., 1953-55. Served with USAAF, 1943-46. Mem. Detroit Bar Assn., Mich. State Bar Assn., ABA. Jewish. Office: Masco Corp 21001 Van Born Rd Taylor MI 48180

BRIGHT, JOSEPH CONVERSE, lawyer; b. Richmond, Va., July 28, 1940; s. Joseph Elliott and Marion Peeples (Converse) B.; m. Lucia Duval Chase, Nov. 29, 1963; children: Thomas Converse, Elizabeth Chase. BA, U. Va., 1962; LLB, U. Ga., 1965. Bar: Ga. 1964, U.S. Dist. Ct. (so. dist.) Ga. 1965, U.S. Dist. Ct. (mid. dist.) Ga. 1967, U.S. Dist. Ct. (no. dist.) Ga. 1983, U.S. Ct. Appeals (5th cir.) 1965, Fla. 1976, U.S. Dist. Ct. (mid. dist.) Fla. 1982, U.S. Supreme Ct. 1976, U.S. Ct. Appeals (11th cir.) 1981. Assoc. Joseph B. Bergen, Savannah, Ga., 1965-67; sole practice Valdosta, Ga., 1967-69; ptnr. Blackburn & Bright, Valdosta, 1969—; instr. part time Valdosta State Coll., 1967-81. Fellow Am. Bd. Criminal Lawyers, Am. Coll. Trial Lawyers, Assn. Trial Lawyers Am.; mem. Nat. Assn. Criminal Def. Lawyers, Ga. Trial Lawyers Assn. Episcopalian. Avocations: hunting, automobile restoration. Personal injury, Criminal. Office: Blackburn & Bright PO Box 579 Valdosta GA 31603

BRIGHTMAN, RICHARD STEPHEN, lawyer; b. New Bedford, Mass., Sept. 22, 1949; s. Bradford Jr. and Cynthia Sarah (Church) B.; m. Shelley Nathans, June 12, 1975 (div. Aug. 1978). AA, Indian River Jr. Coll., 1969; BS, Fla. State U., 1971; MS, U. Fla., 1976, JD with honors, 1979. Bar: Calif.

1980, U.S. Ct. Appeals (9th cir.) 1980, U.S. Dist. Ct. (no. dist.) Calif. 1980, Fla. 1982, U.S. Ct. Appeals (11th cir.). Grad. research assoc. Ctr. for Wetlands Research, Gainesville, Fla., 1975-76; research assoc. Eastern Water Law Research Ctr., Gainesville, 1976-79, interim dir., 1979; environ. counsel HDR Scis., Santa Barbara, Calif., 1979-82; assoc. Hopping, Boyd, Green & Sams, Tallahassee, 1982-86, ptnr., 1986—; field study team mem. U.S. Agy. for Internat. Devel., Belize City, Belize, 1983. Author: Aspects of Environmental Protection, 1984. Chmn. legal panel Tallahassee chpt. ACLU, 1985—. Served with USN, 1972-73. Mem. ABA (natural resources law sect.), Fla. Bar Assn. (environ. and land use law, and adminstrv. and govtl. law sects.), Tallahassee Soccer Assn. (founding mem. 1983). Democrat. Avocations: soccer, reading, skiing. Environment, Administrative and regulatory, Real property. Office: Hopping Boyd Green & Sams PO Box 6526 Tallahassee FL 32314

BRILL, DAVID ALAN, lawyer; b. Louisville, May 24, 1954. BA, Ohio U., 1976; postgrad., U. Tulsa, 1978; JD, U. Ky., 1980. Bar: Ky. 1980, U.S. Dist. Ct. (we. dist.) Ky. 1980, U.S. Ct. Appeals (6th cir.) 1981, U.S. Dist. Ct. (ea. dist.) Mich. 1986. Assoc. Goldberg & Simpson P.S.C., Louisville, 1980—. Mem. ABA, Ky. Bar Assn., Louisville Bar Assn., Phi Delta Phi. Labor, Federal civil litigation, State civil litigation. Office: Goldberg & Simpson PSC 2800 1st Nat Tower Louisville KY 40202

BRILL, LAWRENCE JOEL, lawyer; b. Washington, Sept. 11, 1945; s. Robert Melvin and Elaine (Friedman) B.; m. Rita Joan Kopit, June 14, 1969; children: Matthew Jason. BS in Bus., Syracuse U., 1968; JD, U. Balt., 1974. Bar: Md. 1975, D.C. 1976. Legis. officer U.S. Dept. Commerce, Washington, 1972-78, spl. asst. to dep. asst. sec. textiles and apparel, 1978-79, sr. program analyst textiles and apparel, 1979—; atty. Pres.' Task Force on Regulatory Reform, Occupational Safety and Health, 1976; bd. dirs. Mero-King, Inc., Columbia, Md. Counsel Harpers Choice Village Assn., Columbia, 1976-79, Kings Contrivance Village Assn., Columbia, 1981-83. Served with USAR, 1969-75. U.S. Dpet. Commerce Sci. and Tech. fellow, 1979-80. Mem. ABA, Fed. Bar Assn., Md. Bar Assn., Assn. Trial Lawyers Am. General practice, Legislative, Personal injury. Home: 9630 W Window Way Columbia MD 21046 Office: 10716 Little Patuxent Pkwy Suite 220 Columbia MD 21044

BRILLIANT, SHALOM, lawyer; b. Bklyn., Apr. 19, 1947; s. Leslie and Mina B.; m. Cynthia Duke Gitelman, Aug. 29, 1976; children: Isaac, Anne. B Hebrew Lit., BA, Yeshiva U., 1969; MA, NYU, 1971; JD, Bklyn. Law Sch., 1975. Bar: N.Y. 1977, U.S. Dist. Ct. (ea. dist.) N.Y. 1977, U.S. Supreme Ct. 1980, U.S. Ct. Appeals (9th cir.) 1981, U.S. Ct. Appeals (10th cir.) 1983, D.C. 1986. Trial atty. U.S. Dept. Justice, Washington, 1975-76, 78—; assoc. Schoengold & Sporn, N.Y.C., 1977. Editor Bklyn. Law Rev., 1974-75. Bd. trustees Woodside Synagogue, Silver Spring, Md., 1980-82, sec., 1984. Mem. ABA (litigation sect. 1982—). Federal civil litigation. Office: US Dept Justice 10th and Pennsylvania Ave NW Washington DC 20530

BRIM, JEFFERSON KEARNEY, III, lawyer; b. Sulphur Springs, Tex., July 15, 1945; s. J. Kearney and June Marie (Wester) B.; m. Jeanine Eloise Clymer, July 3, 1971; children—Cari Christen, Brandon Taylor, Jessica Merrill. B.A., U. Tex., 1971, J.D., 1975. Bar: Tex. 1974, U.S. Dist. Ct. (no. and ea. dists.) Tex. 1976, U.S. Dist. Ct. (we. dist.) Tex. 1978, U.S. Dist. Ct. (so. dist.) Tex. 1981. Ptnr. Carter & Brim, Commerce, Tex., 1974-77; staff atty. Tex. Edn. Agy., Austin, 1977-79; state pres. Tex. Jaycees, Austin, 1979-80; assoc. Davis & Davis, Austin, 1981-83; ptnr. Brim, Tingley & Arnett, Austin, 1983-86; ptnr. Brim & Arnett, Austin, 1986—; counsel Assn. Tex. Profl. Educators, 1980—; state com. chmn. State Bar Tex., 1982-84. Served as staff sgt. USAF, 1967-70: Greece. Decorated Air medal; recipient Clayton Frost Meml. award U.S. Jaycees, 1979-80. Mem. U.S. Jaycees (nat. v.p. 1980-81), Kappa Delta Pi. Democrat. Methodist. Administrative and regulatory, Civil rights. Home: 4906 Timberline Austin TX 78746 Office: Brim & Arnett 1012 Mopac Circle Suite 100 Austin TX 78746

BRIMMER, CLARENCE ADDISON, judge; b. Rawlins, Wyo., July 11, 1922; s. Clarence Addison and Geraldine (Zingsheim) B.; m. Emily O. Docken, Aug. 2, 1953; children: Geraldine Ann, Philip Andrew, Andrew Howard, Elizabeth Ann. B.A., U. Mich., 1944, J.D., 1947. Bar: Wyo. 1948. Practice in Rawlins, 1948-71, mcpl. judge, 1948-54; U.S. commr., magistrate 1963-71; atty. gen. Wyo. Cheyenne, 1971-74; U.S. atty. 1975; chief U.S. dist. judge Wyo. Dist. Cheyenne, 1975—. Sec. Rawlins Bd. Pub. Utilities, 1954-66, Gov.'s Com. on Wyo. Water, 1963-65; del. Rep. Nat. Conv., 1956; chmn. Wyo. Rep. Platform Com., 1966; sec. Wyo. Rep. Com., 1966, chmn., 1967-71, Rep. gubernatorial candidate, 1974; Trustee Rocky Mountain Mineral Law Found., 1963-75. Served with USAAF, 1945-46. Mem. ABA, Wyo. Bar Assn., Am. Judicature Soc., Laramie County Bar Assn., Carbon County Bar Assn. Episcopalian. Clubs: Masons, Shriners. Jurisprudence. Office: US District Court PO Box 985 Cheyenne WY 82003 *

BRINCEFIELD, JAMES CLIFFORD, JR., lawyer; b. Washington, Mar. 6, 1941; s. James Clifford and Rita (Spiess) B.; divorced; 1 child, James Clifford III. AB, Georgetown U., 1963, JD, 1966; MBA, Am. U., 1976. Bar: Va. 1966, D.C. 1966. Sole practice Alexandria, Va., 1966—. Contbr. articles to profl. jours. Mem. Mayor's Task Force on Performing Arts, Alexandria, 1984-85; pres. Va. Young Dems., 1976-77. Named one of Outstanding Young Men Am., U.S. Jaycees, 1977, Outstanding Young Dem., Va. Young Dems., 1976. Mem. Va. Bar Assn. (chmn. real estate sect. 1984-85), D.C. Bar Assn. (chmn. real estate sect. 1980-81), Alexandria Bar Assn., Alexandria C. of C. (chmn. performing arts com. 1984-86). Avocation: acting. Real property, Consumer commercial, Contracts commercial. Home: 501 Slaters Ln Unit 1023 Alexandria VA 22314 Office: 526 King St Suite 423 Alexandria VA 22314

BRIND, DAVID HUTCHISON, lawyer, judge; b. Albany, N.Y., Feb. 4, 1930; s. Charles Albert and Laura Stuart (Hutchison) B.; m. Shirley Jean, Mar. 6, 1954; children—Susan, Charles. A.B., Union Coll., 1951; LL.B., Albany Law Sch., 1954, J.D., 1968. Bar: N.Y. 1954, U.S. Supreme Ct. 1970. Atty. law div. N.Y. State Dep. Edn., Albany, 1954-55; ptnr. Chacchia & Brind, Geneva, N.Y., 1957-64; sole practice, Geneva, 1964—; judge Geneva City Ct., 1974—; counsel real estate N.Y. State Dormitory Authority, 1960—; gen. counsel Geneva Gen. Hosp., 1966—; local counsel Conrail. Bd. dirs. Geneva United Way, 1965—; campaign chmn. United Way of Greater Rochester (N.Y.), 1966-69, pres., 1969-71, bd. dirs., 1979—; trustee Geneva Gen. Hosp., 1962-73, pres., 1969-71; trustee Geneva Hist. Soc., 1963—; chmn. Geneva Hist. Comnn., 1969—; mem. exec. bd. Finger Lakes council Boy Scouts Am., 1968—; bd. dirs. Seven Lakes council Girl Scouts U.S.A., 1966-73; bd. dirs. Geneva Gen. Hosp. Nursing Home, 1969-71; v.p. Geneva Bd. Edn., 1962-67; mem. pres.'s council Eisenhower Coll., 1972—, Hobart & William Smith Colls., 1967—. Recipient Geneva Community Chest Service citation, 1969, named Man of Yr., 1971. Mem. Am. Assn. of Homes for Aging, N.Y. State Sch. Bds. Assn. (law revisions com. and constl. conv. com. 1964-68), Monroe County Judiciary Com., 1976—, Ontario County Bar Assn., N.Y. State Bar Assn., N.Y. Land Title Assn., Am. Arbitration Assn., Am. Hosp. Assn., Soc. Hosp. Attys. Republican. Presbyterian. Club: Rotary (Geneva). Probate, Real property, Judicial administration. Home: 43 DeLancey Dr Geneva NY 14456 Office: 17 Seneca St PO Box 409 Geneva NY 14456

BRINEY, ROGER ALBERT, lawyer; b. Radford, Va., Aug. 9, 1949; s. Gerald S. and Helen M. (Hardesty) B.; m. Jenny B. Oliver, Dec. 22, 1973; children: Matthew K., Sarah M., John W. BA, U. Va., 1971; JD, U. Ga., 1975; cert. pvt. internat. law, Hague Acad. Internat. Law, The Netherlands, 1974. Bar: Ga. 1975, N.J. 1976, N.Y. 1984, U.S. Dist. Ct. N.J. 1976. Atty. AT&T Long Lines, Bedminster, N.J., 1978-80, AT&T Gen. Depts., N.Y.C., 1980-83; atty. AT&T Communications, Basking Ridge, N.J., 1983-85, Fairfax, Va., 1985—. Mem. ABA (vice chmn. young lawyers div. pub. utility law com. 1985-86, exec. bd. young lawyers div. pub. utility law com. 1986—), Ga. Bar Assn., Assn. Corp. Counsel N.J. Methodist. Club: Oakton (Va.); Swim and Racquet. Administrative and regulatory, Antitrust, Private international. Office: AT & T 3201 Jermantown Rd Suite 3A2 Fairfax VA 22030

BRINGLE, WILLIAM TIMOTHY, lawyer; b. Elkhart, Ind., Feb. 19, 1947; s. William Vern and Frances (Temple) B. BA, Ind. U., 1974; JD, Tulane U., 1977. Bar: Ind. 1977, U.S. Dist. Ct. (so. dist.) Ind. 1977, La. 1979, U.S. Dist. Ct. (ea. dist.) La. 1979. Sole practice Indpls., 1977-78, New Orleans, 1979—. Mem. Tulane U. Booster Club, New Orleans. Mem. ABA, La. State Bar Assn., Ind. State Bar Assn., Assn. Trial Lawyers Am., La. Trial Lawyers Assn., Phi Delta Phi. Personal injury, Probate, State civil litigation. Home: 2401 Division St Metairie LA 70001 Office: 921 Canal St Suite 826 New Orleans LA 70112

BRINK, RICHARD EDWARD, lawyer; b. Renwick, Iowa, Apr. 27, 1923; s. John Allyn and Sylvia Lonella (Warman) B.; m. Helen M. Ladwig, Nov. 2, 1946 (dec. Feb. 1987); children—Thomas W., Gretchen K., Sara Jane (dec.), Paul E. (dec.). B.S. in Chem. Engring. with distinction, State U. Iowa, 1944, B.A. in Chemistry with high distinction, 1944; J.D. cum laude, William Mitchell Coll., 1952. Bar: Minn. 1952, U.S. Ct. Appeals (Fed. cir.) 1966, U.S. Dist. Ct. Mich. 1971, U.S. Ct. Appeals (6th cir.) 1973. With Minn. Mining and Mfg. Co., St. Paul, 1946-59; mgr. Minn. Mining and Mfg. Co., 1955-59; mem. firm Carpenter, Abbott, Kinney & Coulter, St. Paul, 1959-70; ptnr. Alexander, Sell, Steldt & DeLaHunt, St. Paul, 1970-76; sr. patent atty. 3M Co., St. Paul, 1976-78; assoc. patent counsel 3M Co., 1978-84, sr. assoc. patent counsel, 1984—. Author: (with others) An Outline of U.S. Patent Law, 1959. Mem. White Bear Lake United Meth. Ch. (charter), White Bear Lake Sch. Bd., 1960-75, chmn., 1969-75; leader People to People tour, China and Russia, 1985. Served with USNR, 1944-46. Mem. ABA (chmn. pub. info. com. patent, trademark and copyright sect. 1983-84), Minn. Bar Assn., Minn. Intellectual Property Law Assn. (chmn. pub. info. com., bd. 1980, bd. dirs., rep. to Nat. Council of Patent Law Assns., pres. 1984), Am. Intellectual Property Law Assn., Minn. Intellectual Property Law Assn., Assn. Protection Indsl. Property, Am. Contract Bridge League, Sons of Norway, Phi Beta Kappa, Tau Beta Pi, Phi Lambda Upsilon, Phi Beta Gamma. Methodist. Patent. Home: 1940 Oak Knoll Dr White Bear Lake MN 55110

BRINKMAN, HERBERT CHARLES, lawyer; b. Cin., Mar. 2, 1926; s. Herbert Charles and Myrtle Louise (Cassity) B.; m. Susan Barbara, Dec. 5, 1955; children: Herbert Charles III, Susan, David Henry. BS MechE, Princeton U., 1947; LLB, U. Cin., 1950. Assoc. Wood, Herron & Evans, Cin., 1950-57, ptnr., 1958—; lectr. on patent law U. Cin., 1953-56, on bus. law, 1958-63. Fund raiser various groups including United Appeal, United Fine Arts Fund. Served as ensign USN, 1944-47. Mem. ABA, Cin. Bar Assn., Cin. Patent Law Assn., Am. Patent Law Assn. Republican. Presbyterian. Clubs: University (Cin.); Camargo (Indian Hill). Avocations: tennis, golf, bridge. Patent, Trademark and copyright, Federal civil litigation. Home: 8130 Indian Hill Rd Cincinnati OH 45243 Office: Wood Herron & Evans 2700 Carew Tower Cincinnati OH 45202

BRINKMANN, ROBERT JOSEPH, lawyer; b. Cin., Dec. 25, 1950; s. Robert Harry and Helen R. (Streuwing) B.; m. Claire Jeanne LeFreche, July 28, 1976; children: Christopher, Julia. BA, U. Notre Dame, 1972; postgrad., Alliance Française, 1974-75; AM, Brown U., 1977; JD, Loyola U., Los Angeles, 1980. Bar: Calif. 1980, D.C. 1981, U.S. Ct. Appeals (D.C. and 9th cirs.) 1981, U.S. Supreme Ct. 1984, U.S. Ct. Appeals (6th cir.) 1987. Tchr. secondary schs., Los Angeles and Paris, 1974-77; assoc. Hedrick & Lane, Washington, 1980-82; gen. counsel Nat. Newspaper Assn., Washington, 1982—; mem. faculty Am. Press Inst., Reston, Va., 1982—. Mem. ABA, Fed. Communications Bar Assn. Roman Catholic. Avocations: sports, gardening, reading. Administrative and regulatory, Legislative, Communications and media law. Home: 4521 Cheltenham Dr Bethesda MD 20814 Office: Nat Newspaper Assn 1627 K St NW Washi..gton DC 20006

BRINKS, SHARON RAE, lawyer; b. Grand Rapids, Mich., Nov. 5, 1955; s. Marvin H. and Helen K. (VanderPloeg) B. BA, Calvin Coll., 1976; JD, Wayne State U., 1980. Bar: Mich. 1980, U.S. Ct. Appeals (6th cir.) 1981, U.S. Supreme Ct. 1986. Law clk. to presiding justice 48th Cir. Ct., Allegan, Mich., 1980-81; assoc. Smith & Quinn P.C., Detroit, 1981-82, Tolley, Fisher & Verwys P.C., Grand Rapids, 1982—; bd. dirs. PWN Inc., Grand Rapids. Presbyterian. Office: Tolley Fisher & Verwys PC 5650 Foremost Dr SE Grand Rapids MI 49506-7081

BRINSON, BENJAMIN PIERCE, lawyer; b. Honolulu, Aug. 24, 1954; s. Remer Young and Shirley (Blitch) B. BBA, U. Ga., 1976, JD, 1979. Bar: Ga. 1979, U.S. Dist. Ct. (so. dist.) Ga. 1982. Law clk. to presiding judge Ga. Superior Ct., Pembroke, 1979-81; assoc. Callaway & Hallman, Claxton, Ga., 1981-85; ptnr. Callaway, Neville & Brinson, Claxton, 1986—. Mem. ABA, Ga. Bar Assn., Atlantic Jud. Bar Assn., Mid. Jud. Cir. Bar Assn., Phi Delta Phi, Claxton Jaycees (pres. 1985). Family and matrimonial, General practice, Real property. Office: PO Box 667 Claxton GA 30417

BRINSON, GAY CRESWELL, JR., lawyer; b. Kingsville, Tex., June 13, 1925; s. Gay Creswell and Lelia (Wendelkin) B.; children from former marriage: Thomas Wade, Mary Kaye; m. Bette Lee Butter, June 17, 1979. Student, U. Ill.-Chgo., 1947-48; B.S., U. Houston, 1953, J.D., 1957; cert. civil trial law, personal injury trial law and family law, Tex. Bd. Legal Splzn. Bar: Tex. 1956, U.S. Dist. Ct. (so. dist.) Tex. 1957, U.S. Dist. Ct. (ea. dist.) Tex. 1959, U.S. Dist. Ct. (we. dist.) Tex. 1965, U.S. Ct. Appeals (5th cir.) 1962, U.S. Supreme Ct. 1974; diplomate: Am. Bd. Trial Advocates. Spl. agt. FBI, Washington and Salt Lake City, 1957-59; trial atty. Liberty Mut. Ins. Co., Houston, 1959-62; assoc. Horace Brown, Houston, 1962-64; assoc. Vinson & Elkins, Houston, 1964-67, ptnr., 1967—; lectr. U. Houston Coll. Law, 1964-65, Tex. Coll. Trial Advocacy, Houston, 1978-86; prosecutor Harris County Grievance Com.-State Bar Tex., Houston, 1965-70. Served with AUS, 1943-46, ETO. Fellow Tex Bar Found. (life); mem. Tex. Acad. Family Law Specialists (cert. trial specialist), Tex. Assn. Def. Counsel, Fedn. Ins. Counsel, Nat. Assn. R.R. Trial Counsel, Phi Delta Phi. Clubs: Houston Center, Beaumont (Tex.). Federal civil litigation, State civil litigation. Home: 2938 San Felipe Houston TX 77019 Office: Vinson & Elkins 2935 First City Tower Houston TX 77002

BRINTON, BRADFORD HICKMAN, lawyer; b. Queens, N.Y., Jan. 26, 1935; s. Bradford Hickman and Eva (LeDuc) B.; m. Marilyn Long, June 8, 1963; children—Bradford T., Sara C., Marcia E. B.A., Union Coll., 1958; J.D., Albany Law Sch., 1961. Bar: N.Y. 1961, U.S. Supreme Ct. 1967. Sole practice, Keeseville, N.Y., 1961—; local counsel Am. Title Ins. Co., 1967—, Prudential Ins. Co. Am., 1986—; atty. AuSable Valley Central Sch., 1968—, Town of Chesterfield, 1973—; state tax atty. Essex County, 1975—; asso. prof. bus. Clinton Community Coll., Plattsburgh, N.Y., 1971-75; dir. North Country Legal Services, 1978-81. Mem. Keeseville Youth Commn., 1970—; mem. Essex County Youth Bus., 1981—; pres. Com. for Econ. Improvement Essex County, 1966-68; active Keeseville Library Assn., 1970—. Mem. Essex County Bar Assn. (past pres.), N.Y. State Bar Assn. Democrat. (state committeeman Essex County). Roman Catholic. General practice. Office: 12-A Front St Keeseville NY 12944

BRISCOE, JACK CLAYTON, lawyer; b. Bradford, Pa., July 23, 1920; s. Park Harry and Elsie Gertrude (Woodward) B.; m. Dorothy Lillian Shaw, Sept. 3, 1949; children—Jacqueline Kamp, Jeffrey S., Joan Ryd. B.S. in Econs. U. Pa., 1943; LL.B. Harvard U., 1948. Bar: Pa. 1950. Assoc. Robert C. Duffy, Phila., 1950-66; ptnr. Briscoe, Haggerty & Howard, Phila., 1966-85, Briscoe & Howard, Phila., 1985—; instr. U. Pa., 1950-56; bd. dirs. SonMark Books and Gifts Inc. Treas. Phila. Flag Day Assn.; bd. dirs. Pa. Bible Soc.; chmn. bd. Community Christian Fellowship Ctr. Inc.; elder United Presbyn. Ch. Manoa; active Fellowship Christian Athletes. Served with USAAF, 1943-46. Branch Ricky Assocs. award; Cert Achievement award compulsory arbitration div. Phila. County Ct. Fellow Harry S. Truman Library Inst.; mem. ABA, Pa. Bar Assn., Phila. Bar Assn., Pa. Trial Lawyers Assn., Am. Arbitration Assn. (panel), Internat. Platform Assn. (Pa Soc.), Harvard Law Sch. Assn., Friendly Sons of St. Patrick, Chapel of Four Chaplains (legion hon. mem.). Clubs: Harvard, Lawyers (Phila.), Union League. General corporate, Probate, Estate planning. Office: Briscoe & Howard 1608 Walnut St Suite 1700 Philadelphia PA 19103

BRISSON, CLAUDIA WISNER, lawyer; b. White Plains, N.Y., Aug. 13, 1953; d. Robert Pierre and Elizabeth Alh (Phillips) B. BA cum laude, SUNY, Buffalo, 1975; JD, Hofstra U., 1979. Bar: N.Y. 1980, U.S. Dist. Ct. (ea. and so. dists.) N.Y. 1980, Calif. 1983, U.S. Dist. Ct. (no. dist.) Calif. 1983, U.S. Ct. Appeals (7th cir.) 1983. Assoc. Richard S. Scanlan, White Plains, 1979-81, Wilson, Elser, Edelman & Dicker, N.Y.C., 1981-84; sole practice San Francisco, 1985—; legal advisor Humanist Polit. Party, San Francisco, 1985—. Mem. San Francisco Bar Assn., Nat. Lawyer's Guild. Democrat. Club: Garfield Pool (San Francisco). Avocations: bicycle touring, wine tasting, discussing politics. Personal injury, Contracts commercial, Civil rights. Home: 1242 Sanchez St San Francisco CA 94114 Office: 66 Mint St San Francisco CA 94103

BRISSON, LLOYD CLIFFORD, JR., lawyer; b. Fayetteville, N.C., July 9, 1953; s. Lloyd Clifford Sr. and Doris (Clark) B.; m. Toni JoAnne Cessna, Oct. 22, 1983. BBA, U. N.C., 1975; JD, N.C. Cen. U., 1978. Bar: N.C. 1978, U.S. Dist. Ct. (ea. dist.) N.C. 1978. Assoc. Faircloth & Taylor, Fayetteville, 1978; asst. dist. atty. Office of Dist. Atty., Fayetteville, 1979; assoc. Blackwell, Thompson & Swaringen, Fayetteville, 1980; sole practice Fayetteville, 1981-84; assoc. Brady & Brady, Fayetteville, 1984-86, David B. Craig & Assocs., Fayetteville, 1986—; lectr. paralegal program Fayetteville Tech. Inst., Fayetteville, 1984-86; bd. dirs. 700 Haymount Assocs., Fayetteville, 1986—. Mem. Young Dems., Fayetteville, 1985—, United Way, Fayetteville, 1985. Mem. ABA, N.C. Bar Assn., Cumberland County Bar Assn., N.C. Acad. Trial Lawyers. Democrat. Presbyterian. Lodge: Kiwanis (treas. 1979—). Avocations: photography, music, camping, running. Bankruptcy, State civil litigation, Workers' compensation. Home: 747 Victorian Pl Fayetteville NC 28301 Office: David B Craig & Assocs 2543 Ravenhill Rd Fayetteville NC 28304

BRISTER, BILL H., lawyer, former bankruptcy judge; b. Sieper, La., Mar. 5, 1930; s. Clayton Houston and Era (Price) B.; m. Carolyn Lee McDowell, June 11, 1955; children—Jeff, Julie. B.S. in Chemistry, Northwestern State U. Natchitoches, La., 1948; J.D., U. Tex., 1958. Bar: Tex. 1957, U.S. Dist. Ct. (no. dist.) Tex. 1959, U.S. Ct. Appeals (5th cir.) 1971, U.S. Supreme Ct. 1971. Sole practice, Lubbock, Tex., 1958-79; bankrupcy judge U.S. Dist. Ct. (no. dist.) Tex., 1979-85; ptnr. Winstead McGuire Sechrest and Minit, 1986—. Served to col. USMCR, 1951-52. Bankruptcy. Office: Winstead McGuire Sechrest & Minick 1700 Merchantile Bldg Dallas TX 75204

BRISTER, SCOTT ANDREW, lawyer; b. Waco, Tex., Jan. 8, 1955; s. Miller Robbins and Annette Josephine (Scott) B. BA summa cum laude, Duke U., 1977; JD cum laude, Harvard U., 1980. Bar: Tex. 1980, U.S. Dist. Ct. (so. dist.) Tex. 1981, U.S. Ct. Appeals 1981 (5th cir.), U.S. Supreme Ct. 1986. Briefing atty. to presiding justice Tex. Supreme Ct., Austin, 1980-81; assoc. Andrews & Kurth, Houston, 1981—. Mem. Phi Beta Kappa. State civil litigation, Personal injury, Federal civil litigation. Office: Andrews & Kurth 4200 Texas Commerce Tower Houston TX 77002

BRISTOW, BILL WAYNE, lawyer; b. Strawberry, Ark., Dec. 7, 1950; s. Bill and Irene Bristow; m. Mary Rutledge, Aug. 5, 1972; children: Melissa, Benjamin. BA, Ark. Coll., 1972; JD, Harvard U., 1975. Bar: Ark. 1975, U.S. Ct. Appeals (8th cir.) 1977, U.S. Supreme Ct. 1980. Sole practice Jonesboro, Ark., 1975—; examiner Ark. Bar, 1982—. Federal civil litigation, State civil litigation, Personal injury. Office: 216 E Washington Jonesboro AR 72401

BRISTOW, WALTER JAMES, JR., judge; b. Columbia, S.C., Oct. 14, 1924; s. Walter James and Caroline Belser (Melton) B.; m. Katherine Stewart Mullins, Sept. 12, 1952; children—Walter James III, Katherine Mullins (dec.). Student Va. Mil. Inst., 1941-43; A.B., U. N.C., 1947; LL.B. cum laude, U. S.C., 1947-49; LL.M., Harvard U., 1950. Mem. Marchant, Bristow & Bates, 1953-76; mem. S.C. Ho. of Reps., 1956-58; mem. S.C. Senate, 1958-76; resident judge 5th Jud. Cir. Ct. S.C., 1976—; nat. pres. Conf. Ins. Legislators, 1974-75. Trustee Elvira Wright Fund for Crippled Children. Served with AUS, 1943-45; ETO, NATOUSA; served to brig. gen. Army N.G. Decorated Meritorious Service medal. Mem. ABA, Wig and Robe, Alpha Tau Omega. Democrat. Clubs: Sertoma, Cotillion, Forest Lake, Palmetto, Columbia Ball, Elks. Jurisprudence. Office: PO Box 1147 Columbia SC 29202

BRITAIN, JAMES EDWARD, lawyer; b. Seattle, Jan. 31, 1950; s. Fred Walter and Maryalice (Schneider) B.; m. Linda Jeanne Peltier, June 23, 1979; m. Carol Elaine Kometz, Dec. 27, 1972 (div. 1977). B.A., Wash. State U.-Pullman, 1972; J.D., Duke U., 1975; LL.M., Temple U., 1977. Bar: Wash. 1975, Ohio 1983, U.S. Dist. Ct. (so. dist.) Ohio 1984. Fellow, instr. law Temple U., Phila., 1975-77; asst. prof. U. Dayton, 1977-79; asst. prof. New Eng. Sch. Law, Boston, 1979-81, assoc. prof., 1981-82; law clk. U.S. Ct. Appeals (6th cir.), Cin., 1982-83; assoc. Taft, Stettinius & Hollister, Cin., 1983—; adj. prof. U. Cin., 1983; participant profl. symposia. Contbr. articles and revs. to profl. publs. Named Best Writer of Yr., Legal Research on Writing Orgn., Duke U. Sch. Law, 1974. Mem. ABA, Fed. Bar Assn., Ohio Bar Assn., Cin. Bar Assn., Montgomery County ACLU (bd. dirs. 1977-78), Phi Beta Kappa, Phi Kappa Phi. Federal civil litigation, State civil litigation, Personal injury. Home: 37 Forest Ave Cincinnati OH 45215 Office: Taft Stettinius & Hollister 1800 First National Bank Ctr Cincinnati OH 45202

BRITT, HENRY MIDDLETON, retired judge; b. Olmsted, Ill., June 9, 1919; s. Henry Middleton and Sarah Theodosia (Roach) B.; m. Barbara Jean Holmes, Oct. 29, 1942; children: Nancy Marsh, Sarah Barbara, Melissa Middleton. A.B., U. Ill., 1941, J.D., 1947. Bar: Ill. 1947, Ark. 1948, U.S. Supreme Ct. 1954. Pvt. practice law Hot Springs, Ark., 1948-67; asst. U.S. atty. Western Dist. Ark., 1953-58; circuit judge 18th Jud. Circuit Ark., Hot Springs, 1967-83; pres. Ark. Jud. Council, 1982-83; mem. Ark.-Fed. Jud. Council, 1973-74; fellow Nat. Coll. Advocacy, Harvard U., 1974; faculty adviser Nat. Coll. State Judiciary, 1973, Nat. Coll. Dist. Attys., U. Houston, 1976, Am. Acad. Jud. Edn., U. Va., 1976; mem. Midwestern Tng. Conf. Organized Crime and Law Enforcement at U. Notre Dame, 1972, Ark. Coll. Juvenile Justice, 1972; mem. exec. com. Ark. Commn. Crime and Law Enforcement, 1968-71; mem. central planning council Ark. Crime Commn. Republican candidate for Gov. of Ark., 1960; gen. counsel Rep. Party of Ark., 1962-64; permanent mem. Ark. State Rep. Com.; alt. del. Rep. Nat. Conv., 1968; mem. Garland County Bd. Election, 1962-64; chmn. Garland County Rep. Com., 1962-64; bd. dirs. United Fund, 1951-52; bd. trustees The Coll. of Ozarks; exec. bd. Boy Scouts Am., Ouachita Area Council, Boy Scouts Am.; pres. Garland County Community Coll. Found. Served to capt. JAGC AUS, 1941-46. Recipient Service to Mankind award Sertoma Club, 1973. Fellow Nat. Coll. State Trial Judges; mem. ABA (ex-officio mem. ho. dels., exec. council 1982-83, award of merit 1983), Ill. Bar Assn., Ark. Bar Assn. (future of judiciary study group), Garland County Bar Assn. (pres. 1961-62), Am. Legion, VFW, U.S. Navy League (pres. Hot Springs council 1966-68, state pres. 1968-70), Hot Springs Jr. C. of C. (life, pres. 1951-52), Delta Phi, Phi Alpha Delta, Am. Judicature Soc., Am. Judges Assn., Hot Springs C. of C. Presbyterian (elder, deacon, trustee). Clubs: Masons (32 deg.), Shriners, Elks, Kiwanis (pres. 1969-70). Probate, General corporate, General practice. Home: 126 Trivista Hot Springs AR 71901 Office: 824 Central Ave Hot Springs AR 71901

BRITT, W. EARL, judge; b. McDonald, N.C., Dec. 7, 1932; s. Dudley H. and Martha Mae (Hall) B.; m. Judith Moore, Apr. 17, 1976; children: Clifford P., Mark E., Elizabeth C. Student, Campbell Jr. Coll., 1952; B.S., Wake Forest U., 1956, J.D., 1958. Bar: N.C. 1958. Practiced law Fairmont, N.C., 1959-72, Lumberton, N.C., 1972-80; judge U.S. Dist. Ct. Eastern Dist. N.C., 1980—, now chief judge. Trustee Southeastern Community Coll., 1965-70, Southeastern Gen. Hosp., Lumberton, 1965-69, Pembroke State U., 1967-72; bd. govs. U. N.C. Served with U.S. Army, 1953-55. Mem. Am. Bar Assn., N.C. Bar Assn. Baptist. Jurisprudence. Office: US Courthouse US Dist Ct PO Box 27504 Raleigh NC 27611 *

BRITTAIN, JOHN SHERRARD, III, lawyer; b. St. Joseph, Mo., May 18, 1922; s. John S. and Vella Griffith (Schmidt) B.; m. Anne Brewster, Aug. 22, 1957; 1 son, John Sherrard. B.A., Yale U., 1943; LL.B., Columbia U., 1949. Bar: N.Y. 1950, Pa. 1961. Assoc. Breed, Abbott & Morgan, N.Y.C., 1949-58, ptnr., 1958-61; ptnr. Morgan, Lewis & Bockius, Phila., 1961—; dir. Lease Financing Corp., Radnor, Pa., 1963—. Served to capt. F.A. AUS, 1943-46, ETO. Mem. ABA, Pa. Bar Assn. Clubs: Philadelphia; Gulph Mills Golf (King of Prussia, Pa.). Home: 8400 Prospect Ave Philadelphia PA 19118 Office: Morgan Lewis & Bockius 2000 One Logan Sq Philadelphia PA 19103

BRITTIGAN, ROBERT LEE, lawyer; b. Columbus, Ohio, Aug. 24, 1942; s. Virgil Devan and Ruth (Clark) B.; m. Sharon Lynn Amore, Aug. 22, 1964; children—Eric Clark, Robert Lee II. B.S. in Bus. Adminstrn. cum laude,

Ohio State U., 1964, J.D. summa cum laude, 1967. Bar: Ohio 1967, U.S. Ct. Mil. Appeals 1974, U.S. Ct. Claims 1977, U.S. Ct. Appeals (5th cir.) 1978, U.S. Supreme Ct. 1974. Commd. 2d lt. U.S. Army, 1968, advanced through grades to maj., 1977; chief mil. justice, Ft. Gordon, Ga., 1972-73; dep. staff judge adv. 5th Inf. Div. (Mech.) and Ft. Polk, Ft. Polk, La., 1974-76; action atty. litigation div. Office of JAG, U.S. Army, Washington, 1976-80; ret., 1980; gen. counsel Def. Nuclear Agy., Washington, 1980—. Decorated Bronze Star medal, Meritorious Service medal with oak leaf cluster, Army Commendation medal. General practice, Federal civil litigation, Public international. Office: Dept Def Def Nuclear Agy 6801 Telegraph Rd Alexandria VA 22310

BRITTON, CLAROLD LAWRENCE, lawyer; b. Soldier, Iowa, Nov. 1, 1932; s. Arnold Olaf and Florence Ruth (Gardner) B.; m. Joyce Helene Hamlett, Feb. 1, 1958; children—Laura, Eric, Val, Martha. B.S. in Engring., U. Mich., Ann Arbor, 1958, J.D., 1961. Bar: Ill. 1961, U.S. Dist. Ct. (no. dist.) Ill. 1962 U.S. Ct. Appeals (7th cir.) 1963, U.S. Supreme Ct. 1970. Assoc., Jenner & Block, Chgo., 1961-70, ptnr., 1970—. Served with USNR, 1952-72. Fellow Am. Coll. Trial Lawyers; mem. Chgo. Bar Assn. (past chmn. fed. civil procedure, judiciary and computer law coms., civil practice com.), Ill. Bar Assn. (chmn. Allerton House Conf. 1984, 86, chmn. rule 23 com. 1985—, vice chmn. civil practice and procedure council 1986—, antitrust com.), ABA (litigation sect., antitrust com., discovery com., past regional chmn. 7th cir.), 7th Cir. Bar Assn., Def. Research Inst. (com. on aerospace 1984), Ill. Soc. Trial Lawyers, Order of Coif, Alpha Phi Mu, Tau Beta Pi. Republican. Lutheran. Clubs: Law (Chgo.), Masons. Asst. editor Mich. Law Rev., 1960. Antitrust, Federal civil litigation, State civil litigation. Office: Jenner & Block 1 IBM Plaza Chicago IL 60611

BRITTON, JAMES EDWARD, lawyer; b. Roswell, N.Mex., June 9, 1946; s. Thomas Warren and Helen Viola (Haynes) B.; m. Sherry Ann Sheehan, May 17, 1969; children: Christa Lynn, Jason Edward. BS, Okla. State U., 1968; postgrad., Iowa State U., 1968, 70-71; JD, U. Okla., 1974. Bar: Okla. 1974, U.S. Dist. Ct. (we., no. and ea. dists.) Okla. 1974, U.S. Ct. Appeals (10th cir.) 1974. Ptnr., sec. McClelland, Collins, Sheehan, Bailey & Bailey, Oklahoma City, 1974-79; v.p., bd. dirs. Hastie and Kirschner, Oklahoma City, 1979—, also bd. dirs.; bd. dirs. Guaranty Bank & Trust Co., Oklahoma City; adminstrv. law judge Dept. of Edn., 1978—. Research editor U. Okla. Law Rev., 1973. Served with U.S. Army, 1968-70, Vietnam. Mem. ABA, Okla. Bar Assn., Oklahoma County Bar Assn. (law day chmn. 1978, ethics and grievance com. 1986), Order of Coif. Democrat. Methodist. Avocations: running, sailing, tennis, bicycling. Banking, Contracts commercial, Franchise law. Home: 6209 Beaver Creek Rd Oklahoma City OK 73132 Office: Hastie and Kirschner 210 W Park Ave Oklahoma City OK 73102

BRITTON, LOUIS FRANKLIN, lawyer; b. Terre Haute, Ind., Mar. 5, 1953; s. Charles J. and Deneta (Reichert) B.; m. Debra Lynne Brown, May 15, 1977; children: Louis J., Laura Elizabeth. B.A. cum laude, Ind. U., 1974, J.D. magna cum laude, 1977. Bar: Ind. 1977, U.S. Dist. Ct. (so. dist.) Ind. 1977. Assoc., Cox, Zwerner, Gambill & Sullivan, Terre Haute, 1977-81, ptnr., 1981—. Vice pres. agy. relations, bd. dirs. United Way, 1981-84; v.p., bd. dirs. Terre Haute Humane Soc., 1982-84; pres., bd. dirs. Leadership Terre Haute Alumni Assn., 1984-85. Ira C. Batman fellow, 1976-77; named one of Outstanding Young Men in Am., 1982. Mem. ABA, Ind. Bar Assn., Terre Haute Bar Assn., Order of Coif, Terre Haute YMCA (bd. dirs. 1985—), Phi Beta Kappa. State civil litigation, General practice, Real property. Home: 2206 N 7th St Terre Haute IN 47804 Office: Cox Zwerner Gambill & Sullivan PO Box 1625 Terre Haute IN 47808

BRIZEL, MICHAEL ALAN, lawyer; b. Monticello, N.Y., Jan. 6, 1957; s. Irving and Ruth (Marcus) B.; m. Amy Frey, Aug. 19, 1979. BS in Indsl. and Labor Relations, Cornell U., 1977, JD, 1980. Bar: N.Y. 1981, U.S. Dist. Ct. (ea. and so. dists.) N.Y., U.S. Ct. Appeals (6th cir.). Assoc. Burns, Summit, Rovins & Feldesman, N.Y.C., 1980-83; labor atty. Gen. Foods Corp., White Plains, N.Y., 1983-84, sr. labor atty., 1984-86, labor counsel, 1986—; arbitrator small claims ct. City of White Plains, 1985—. Bd. dirs., pres. 510 E 86th St. Owners, Inc., 1985-86. Mem. ABA, N.Y. State Bar Assn. Labor, Federal civil litigation. Home: 510 E 86th St #7E New York NY 10028 Office: Gen Foods Corp 250 N St RA 6N White Plains NY 10625

BROADBENT, PETER EDWIN, JR., lawyer; b. Richmond, Va., May 16, 1951; s. Peter Edwin and Nancy Talbot (Norris) B.; m. Mary Anna Toms, June 5, 1976; children: Peter Edwin III, Christopher Toms, Elizabeth Talbot. BA, Duke U., 1973; JD, U. Va., 1976. Bar: Va. 1976, U.S. Dist. Ct. (ea. dist.) Va. 1976, U.S. Ct. Appeals (4th cir.) 1976. Assoc. Christian, Barton, Epps, Brent & Chappell, Richmond, Va., 1976-84; ptnr. Christian, Barton, Epps, Brent & Chapell, Richmond, Va., 1984—. Vice chmn. N.C. Coll. Young Rep. Fedn., Raleigh, N.C., 1971; Dep. Press Sec. Helms for U.S. Senate Campaign, Raleigh, N.C., 1972; mem. Richmond City Rep. Com., 1973—; nat. committeeman Young Rep. Nat. Com., Washington, 1974-75. Mem. ABA, Va. State Bar Assn. (pub. info. com. 1977-82, chmn. 1982-85), Va. Bar Assn., Richmond Bar Assn., Geneal. Research Inst. Va. (v.p., dir. 1984—). Republican. Episcopalian. Avocation: genealogy, politics. General corporate, Entertainment, Communications. Home: 5307 Matoaka Rd Richmond VA 23226 Office: Christian Barton Epps Brent & Chappell 1200 Mutual Bldg Richmond VA 23219

BROADWIN, JOSEPH LOUIS, lawyer; b. Nice, France, July 12, 1930; s. Samuel and Lillian Ruth (Messing) B.; m. Maria Antonia Eligio de la Puente, June 1, 1949 (div. 1974); children—David Anthony, Charles Anthony; m. Susan Elizabeth Podufaly, Oct. 24, 1980; children: Elizabeth Antonia, Samuel Edward. A.B., Columbia U., 1949; LL.B., Yale U., 1952. Bar: N.Y. Assoc. Chadbourne Parke Whiteside Wolff & Brophy, N.Y.C., 1954-59; assoc. Proskauer Rose Goetz & Mendelsohn, N.Y.C., 1959-67, ptnr., 1967-70; ptnr. Willkie Farr & Gallagher, N.Y.C., 1970—. Regent L.I. Coll. Hosp., Bklyn., 1971—, vice chmn. 1985—; bd. dirs. Cobble Hill Nursing Home, Bklyn., 1979—; exec. com. W. Bklyn. Ind. Democrats, 1957-84. Served with U.S. Army, 1952-54. Mem. Assn. Bar City N.Y. Club: Yale (N.Y.C.). Real property. Home: 143 Henry St Brooklyn NY 11201 Office: Willkie Farr & Gallagher 153 E 53d St New York NY 10022

BROADY, TOLLY RUPERT, lawyer, judge; b. Low Moor, Va., Sept. 20, 1917; s. William Henry and Christian Ann (Robinson) B.; m. Eloise Carlotta Rinsland, May 21, 1944; 1 child, Tolly Rupert. B.S. summa cum laude, Tuskegee Inst., 1940; J.D., Fordham U., 1949; M.A., NYU, 1953, LL.M., 1954. Bar: N.Y. 1950, U.S. Supreme Ct. 1959. With Wage Stblzn. Bd., 1951-53; assoc. Weaver Waters & Evans, N.Y.C., 1953-55; spl. prosecutor, appellate atty. Village of Hempstead (N.Y.), 1955-71; pvt. practice, Queens City, N.Y., 1955—, adminstrv. law judge, N.Y.C., 1970—; counsel State Conf. branches NAACP, 1974; gen. counsel Met. N.Y. Synod of the Luth. Ch. Am.; arbitrator Am. Arbitration Assn.; counsel Luth. Community Services, Seamans Internat. House; corps. involved in internat. trade. Past pres. East Elmhurst (N.Y.) Civic Assn., Hempstead Lakes (N.Y.) Civic Assn. Served to lt. adj. gen.'s dept. U.S. Army 1942-46. Mem. ABA (jud. sect.), N.Y. County Lawyers Assn., Queens County Bar Assn., Am. Arbitration Assn., Alpha Kappa Mu, Alpha Phi Alpha, Sigma Pi Phi. Club: NYU. Contbr. articles to profl. jours. Real property, Administrative and regulatory, Private international. Office: 131 Fulton Ave Hempstead NY 11550

BROCHES, ARON, international lawyer, arbitrator; b. Amsterdam, Netherlands, Mar. 22, 1914; s. Abraham and Chaja (Person) B.; m. Catherina J. Pothast, May 2, 1939 (dec. Sept. 1982); children: Ida Alexandra, Paul Elias. LL.M., U. Amsterdam, 1936, LL.D., 1939; J.D., Fordham U., 1942. Bar: N.Y. 1980. Legal adviser Netherlands embassy, also Netherlands Econ. Mission, Washington and N.Y.C., 1942-46; with World Bank, 1946-79, gen. counsel, 1959-79, v.p., 1972-79; mem. Pres.'s Council, 1965-79; sec. gen. Internat. Centre for Settlement Investment Disputes, 1967-80, mem. panel arbitrators, 1980—; mem. Internat. Panel Arbitrators, Am. Arbitration Assn.; mem. panels arbitration ctrs. Asian-African Legal Consultative Com., Kuala Lumpur and Cairo; sec. Netherlands del. UN Monetary and Fin. Conf., Bretton Woods, N.H., 1944; sec., legal adviser Netherlands del. inaugural meeting bd. govs. IMF and IBRD, Savannah, Ga., 1946; chief Internat. Bank gen. survey mission, Nigeria, 1953-54; mem. Internat. Council for Comml. Arbitration, 1971—. Writer and lectr. on legal aspects of econ. devel. Trustee Internat. Legal Ctr., 1970-77. Decorated comdr. Order Orange Nassau. Mem. Am. Arbitration Assn. (internat. law com.). Clubs: Cosmos (Washington). Private international, Public international, International arbitration. Home: 2600 Tilden Pl NW Washington DC 20008 Office: 1919 Pennsylvania Ave NW Washington DC 20006

BROCK, CHARLES MARQUIS, lawyer; b. Watseka, Ill., Oct. 8, 1941; s. Glen Westgate and Muriel Lucile (Bubeck) B.; m. Elizabeth Bonilla, Dec. 17, 1966; children—Henry Christopher, Anna Melissa. A.B. cum laude, Princeton U., 1963; J.D., Georgetown U., 1968; M.B.A., U. Chgo., 1974. Bar: Ill. 1969, U.S. Dist. Ct. (no. dist.) Ill. 1969. Asst. trust counsel Continental Ill. Nat. Bank, Chgo., 1968-74; regional counsel Latin Am., Can. Abbott Labs., Abbott Park, Ill., 1974-77, regional counsel, Europe, Africa and Middle East, 1977-81, div. counsel, 1981—; sec. mgmt. com. TAP Pharms., 1985—. Served with Inter-Am. Def. Coll., U.S. Army, 1964-66. Mem. ABA, Chgo. Bar Assn., Phi Beta Kappa. Republican. Clubs: Princeton (Chgo.); Princeton (N.Y.C.), Mich. Shores (Wilmette, Ill.) General corporate, Contracts commercial, Antitrust. Home: 1473 Asbury Ave Winnetka IL 60093 Office: Abbott Labs Abbott Park IL 60064

BROCK, DAVID ALLEN, chief justice New Hampshire Supreme Court; b. Stoneham, Mass., July 6, 1936; s. Herbert and Margaret B.; m. Sandra Ford, 1960; 6 children. A.B., Dartmouth Coll., 1958; LL.B., U. Mich., 1963; postgrad., Nat. Jud. Coll., Reno, 1977. Bar: N.H. 1963. Assoc. Devine, Millimet, McDonough, Stahl & Branch, Manchester, N.H., 1963-69; U.S. atty. N.H., 1969-72; ptnr. Perkins, Douglas and Brock, Concord, N.H., 1972-74, Perkins & Brock, 1974-76; spl. counsel to Gov. and Exec. Council N.H. 1974-76, legal counsel to Gov. N.H., 1976; assoc. justice N.H. Superior Ct., 1976-78; assoc. justice N.H. Supreme Ct., 1978-86, chief justice, 1986—; chmn. State of N.H. Legal Services Adv. Commn., 1977-79; chmn. dist. ct. reform subcom. Gov.'s commn. for Ct. System Improvement, 1974-75; chmn. N.H. Commn. Ct. Accreditation, 1986—; mem. Select Commn. on Unified Ct. System, 1980-84; chmn. N.H. Supreme Ct. com. on Jud. Conduct, 1981—, com. on Ct. Accreditation, 1986—, rules adv. com., 1985—; mem. State N.H. Jud. Council, 1979—; del. N.H. Constl. Constn., 1974. Del. N.H. Constl. Conv., 1974; Republican candidate for U.S. Senate, 1972; vice chmn. N.H. Rep. State Com., 1968-69; chmn. Manchester Rep. Com., 1967-69; bd. dirs. Manchester Community Guidance Ctr., 1966-72, pres.l, 1969-72; mem. Gov.'s Commn. for Handicapped, 1978-79. Mem. N.H. Bar Assn. (chmn. constl. revision com. 1976-77), ABA (edn. appellate judges conf. 1981—, appellate advocacy com. 1982—), N.H. Jud. Council. Jurisprudence. Office: New Hampshire Supreme Ct Supreme Ct Bldg Concord NH 03301

BROCK, DAVID GEORGE, lawyer; b. Buffalo, Oct. 13, 1986; s. Joseph Louis and Julia Strauss (Amram) B.; m. Marilyn Sandra Katz, May 25, 1969; children: Lauren, Joel. BA in English, Union Coll., 1967; JD, SUNY, Buffalo, 1972. Bar: N.Y. 1973, U.S. Dist. Ct. (we. dist.) 1973. Atty. Liberty Mut. Ins. Co., Buffalo, 1973-77; assoc. Jaeckle, Fleischmann & Mugel, Buffalo, 1977-79, ptnr., 1980—. Mem. ABA, N.Y. State Bar Assn., Erie County Bar Assn., Western N.Y. Trial Lawyers Assn., Def. Research Inst., Inc., Am. Arbitration Assn., Internat. Assn. Def. Counsel, Nat. Inst. Trial Adv. Democrat. Jewish. Avocations: reading, photography. Insurance, Personal injury, State civil litigation. Home: 49 Northington Dr East Amherst NY 14051 Office: Jaeckle Fleischmann & Mugel 12 Fountain Plaza Buffalo NY 14202

BROCK, JOHN TABOR, lawyer; b. Mocksville, N.C., May 30, 1928; s. Burr C. and Laura M. (Tabor) B.; m. Mary M. Brock, July 6, 1957; children—Jennifer D., Robin N., Martin N. A.B., U. N.C., Chapel Hill, 1949, J.D., 1953. Bar: N.C. 1954, U.S. dist. ct. (mid. dist.) N.C. 1963. Ptnr. Brock & McClamrock, Mocksville, N.C., 1979-82, 82—; atty. County of Davie (N.C.), 1961—, ct. solicitor, 1962-66, judge, 1966-70; dir. Branch Banking and Trust Co. Served with U.S. Army, 1950-52. Named Outstanding County Atty., State of N.C., 1981. Mem. N.C. Bar Assn., Am. Judicature Soc., N.C. Assn. Country Attys. (pres. 1980-81). Republican. Methodist. General practice, Local government, Probate.

BROCK, MITCHELL, lawyer; b. Wyncote, Pa., Nov. 10, 1927; s. John W. and Mildred A. (Mitchell) B.; m. Gioia Connell, June 21, 1952; children: Felicity, Marina, Mitchell Hovey, Laura. AB, Princeton U., 1950; LLB, U. Pa., 1953. Assoc. firm Sullivan & Cromwell, N.Y.C., 1953-59; ptnr. Sullivan & Cormwell, N.Y.C., 1960—, Sullivan & Cromwell, Paris, 1965-68; assoc. Sullivan & Cromwell, Tokyo, 1987—. Bd. dirs. Frost Valley YMCA, Oliverea, N.Y., 1980-87, Am. Found. Blind, 1967-87; trustee Helen Keller Internat., N.Y.C., 1970-87. Served with USN, 1945-46. Mem. Council on Fgn. Relations, ABA, N.Y. Bar Assn., Asssn. Bar City N.Y., Union Internat. des Avocats. Republican. Episcopalian. Clubs: Anglers, Down Town Assn, River, Princeton, Ivy. General corporate, Private international. Home: 120 East End Ave New York NY 10028 Office: 250 Park Ave New York NY 10177

BROCK, NEWMAN DEMPSEY, lawyer; b. Lake City, Fla., Nov. 18, 1940; s. Conway and Newell E. (Brackin) B.; m. Sandra Hamilton, Dec. 22, 1969; children—Rebecca Leigh, David Mitchell. B.S.B.A., U. Fla., 1962, J.D., Samford, U., 1970. Bar: Fla. 1970, U.S. Supreme Ct. 1973; cert. civil trial lawyer, cert. arbitrator, cert. civil trial advocate. Chief asst. state's atty. 18th Jud. Cir., Sanford, Fla., 1971-74; practice Altamonte Springs, Fla. 1974—; judge Winter Springs (Fla.) city ct. 1974; city atty. City of Winter Springs, 1975. Pres. bd. dirs. Central Fla. Zool. Soc. 1982. Served as capt. U.S. Army Res. mem. ABA, Fla. Bar, Seminole County Bar Assn. (pres. 1979), Orange County Bar Assn., Assn. Trial Lawyers, Am., Acad. Fla. Trial Lawyers (cert. trial lawyer), Kappa Alpha. Republican. Methodist. Lodges: Masons, Shriners, Rotary. Personal injury, Criminal, Family and matrimonial. Home: 1201 Waverly Way Longwood FL 32701 Office: 620 Jasmine Rd Altamonte Springs FL 32701

BROCK, PAUL WARRINGTON, lawyer; b. Mobile, Ala., Feb. 23, 1928; s. Glen Porter and Esther (Goodwin) B.; m. Grace Leigh Blasingame, Sept. 4, 1948 (dec. June 1960); children—Paul W., Bette Leigh, Valerie Grace; m. Louise Morris Shearer, July 6, 1962; children—Louise Shearer, Richard Goodwin. Student, Ala. Poly. Inst., 1944; B.S., U. Ala., 1948, J.D., 1950. Bar: Ala. 1950. Practiced in Mobile, 1953—; mem. Hand, Arendall & Bedsole, 1953-56, Hand, Arendall, Bedsole, Greaves & Johnston, 1956—; mem. faculty continuing legal edn. program Ala. Bar Assn. Served to 2d lt. USAF, 1952-53. Recipient Nat. Balfour award Sigma Chi, 1946-47. Mem. Am., Ala., Mobile bar assns., Am. Coll. Trial Lawyers, Internat. Assn. Ins. Counsel, Ala. Def. Lawyers Assn. (past pres.), Ala. Law Inst., Def. Research Inst. (past pres.), Fedn. Ins. Counsel, Assn. Ins. Attys., Am. Coll. Mortgage Attys., Nat. Assn. R.R. Trial Counsel, Omicron Delta Kappa, Beta Gamma Sigma. Republican. Episcopalian. Home: 30 Hillwood Rd Mobile AL 36608 Office: PO Box 123 Mobile AL 36601

BROCK, RAY LEONARD, JR., state justice; b. McDonald, Tenn., Sept. 21, 1922; s. Ray Leonard and Ila Venore (Bailey) B.; m. Juanita Addabelle Barker, Sept. 18, 1944; children—Ila Raye, Elaine Rose, Karen Denise. Student, U. Tenn., 1940-43, U. Colo., 1945-46; LL.B., Duke U., 1948. Bar: Tenn. bar 1948. Practiced in Chattanooga, 1948-63; judge Chancery Ct. of Tenn., 1963-74; justice Supreme Ct. Tenn., 1974—. Served with U.S. Army, 1943-44. Mem. Tenn., Chattanooga bar assns., Am. Judicature Soc., Tenn. Trial Lawyers Assn. Democrat. Mem. Congl. United Ch. Christ. Club: Big Orange. Office: 311 Supreme Ct Bldg Nashville TN 37219

BROCK, ROY C., lawyer; b. Haskell, Tex., Aug. 13, 1925; s. Roy and Ruby B.; children—Roy C., James G., Maeghan D. LL.B. cum laude, Baylor U., 1953. Bar: Tex. 1953, U.S. Dist. Ct. (we. dist.) Tex. 1957, U.S. Dist. Ct. (so. dist.) Tex, 1976, U.S. Dist. Ct. (no. dist.) Tex. 1977, U.S. Ct. Appeals (5th cir.) 1977, U.S. Supreme Ct. 1972. Sr. ptnr. Brock & Kelfer, San Antonio. Mem. ABA, San Antonio Bar Assn., State Bar Tex., Internat. Assn. Ins. Counsel, Fedn. Ins. Counsel, Tex. Assn. Def. Counsel, Am. Bd. Trial Advocates. Contbr. articles to legal publs. State civil litigation, Insurance, Personal injury. Office: 1 Riverwalk Pl Suite 1700 700 N St Mary's St San Antonio TX 78205

BROCK, WARREN RICHARD, lawyer; b. Buffalo, Mar. 30, 1919; m. Kathryn Brock; children: Rick (dec.), Jeff, Bonnie. BA, U. Mich., 1940; JD, U.Ariz., 1952. Bar: Ariz. 1952, N.Y. 1952. Sole practice, Tucson, 1952—; spl. ct. commr., Tucson, 1975; chmn. law sch. brief contest U. Ariz., 1966. Active Anti-Defamation Council; del. Democratic Nat. Conv., 1976; mem. character guidance com. Tucson YMCA. Named Tucson Community Leader, Tucson Sun newspaper, 1954. Mem. Am. Arbitration Assn. (panel arbitrators 1972-84), So. Ariz. Claimants compensation Attys. Assn. (cofounder, treas. 1959-63), Nat. Assn. Claimant's Counsel Assn. (former treas. local chpt.), ABA, Ariz. Bar Assn., N.Y. State Bar Assn., Assn. Trial Lawyers Am., Ariz. Trial Lawyers Assn., Calif. Trial Lawyers Assn., Pima County Trial Lawyers Assn., Am. Judicature Soc., Phi Alpha Delta. Contbr. weekly sports column to Green Valley News; editor Pleasure Mag., 1946-48. Personal injury, Probate. Home: 5242 N Genematas St Tucson AZ 85704 Office: 244 W Drachman St Tucson AZ 85705

BROCKMAN, EUGENE E., lawyer; b. Mills, N.Mex., Apr. 7, 1931; s. William D. and Lucile I. (Pursell) B.; m. Jo Ann Bagby, June 15, 1957; children: Patti, Donny, Kirk, Clint. Student, Eastern N.Mex. U., 1954-57; JD, U. N.Mex., 1960. Bar: N.Mex. 1960, U.S. Dist. Ct. N.Mex. 1960, U.S. Ct. Appeals (10th cir.). Ptnr. Hart & Brockman, Tucumcari, N.Mex., 1960-64; sole practice Tucumcari, 1964-73, 75-77; ptnr. Brockman & Villani, Tucumcari, 1973-75, Brockman & Cihak, Tucumcari, 1977—. Bd. regents Eastern N.Mex., Portales, 1962-70; bd. dirs. N.Mex. Bapt. Children'sHome, Portales, 1985—; chmn. Quay County Reps., Tucumcari; Exec. com. N.Mex. Reps., 1968, cen. com. Served with U.S. Army, 1952-54, Korea. Lodge: Kiwanis (pres. Tucumcari 1979). Avocations: hiking, fishing, hunting, ranching. Criminal, Family and matrimonial, Probate. Home: 2101 S 10th Tucumcari NM 88401 Office: Brockman & Cihak 201 S 2d St PO Box 984 Tucumcari NM 88401

BROCKMAN, TERRY JAMES, lawyer; b. Wisconsin Rapids, Wis., July 10, 1955; s. Wilbert Francis and Angeline Catherine (Huser) B.; m. Mary Jane Amdor, Oct. 2, 1982; 1 child, John. BBA, Creighton U., 1977, JD, 1980. Bar: Nebr. 1981, U.S. Dist. Ct. Nebr. 1981, U.S. Tax Ct. 1981. Tax cons. Touche Ross, Omaha, Nebr., 1980-83, tax supr., 1983-85; tax mgr. Grant Thornton, Omaha, 1985-86; sr. tax mgr. Peat Marwick Main, Omaha, 1986—. Mem. ABA, Nebr. Bar Assn., Omaha Bar Assn., Am. Inst. CPA's, Nebr. Soc. CPA's. Republican. Roman Catholic. Lodge: Rotary. Personal income taxation, Corporate taxation, State and local taxation. Home: 1010 S 36th St Omaha NE 68105 Office: Peat Marwick Main 600 Kiewit Plaza Omaha NE 68131

BRODBECK, CHARLES RICHARD, lawyer; b. Pitts., Apr. 8, 1949; s. Joseph Morand and Dorothy Brodbeck; m. Jill Mockrud, Apr. 19, 1980; children: Scott Richard, Christine Lee. AB, Princeton, 1971; JD, Northwestern U., Chgo., 1974. Bar: Pa. 1974. From assoc. to ptnr. Berkman, Ruslander, Pohl, Lieber & Engel, Pitts., 1974-86; ptnr. Karlowitz, Sherman & Picadio and predecessor firm Karlowitz, Hoffman & Brodbeck, Pitts., 1986—. Pres. Outreach South Hills, Inc., Mt. Lebanon, Pa., 1986—. Mem. Nat. Assn. Bond Lawyers (chmn. com. on opinions 1984—), Princeton Alumni Assn. (pres. western Pa. chpt. 1984-86). Republican. Episcopalian. Avocations: reading, running, gardening. Municipal bonds, Real property, Health. Home: 820 Ella St Pittsburgh PA 15243 Office: 600 Grant St Suite 800 Pittsburgh PA 15219

BRODER, JAMES NELSON, lawyer; b. Hartford, Conn., Oct. 2, 1946; s. Jacob and Ruth Naomi (Horowitz) B.; m. Lee Beth Ravitch, June 9, 1968; children—Jacob, Joshua. B.A. magna cum laude, U. Va. 1968; J.D., Georgetown U., 1975. Bar: Md. 1975, D.C. 1976, Maine 1983. Staff dir. U.S. Ho. of Reps. Rep. Task Force on Aging, 1973-75; assoc., then ptnr. Millman, Broder & Curtis, Washington, 1975-79; ptnr. Curtis Thaxter Stevens Broder & Micoleau and Portland, Maine, 1979—; del., vice chmn. housing com. White House Conf. on Aging, 1981; mem. Fed. Council on Aging, 1982-86, chmn. housing com.; cons. Nat. Inst. Aging. Served with USN, 1968-72. Mem. ABA, Phi Beta Kappa. Contbr. articles to profl. jours. Legislative, General corporate, Real property. Office: 1 Canal Plaza Portland ME 04112

BRODERICK, DANIEL THOMAS, III, lawyer; b. Duluth, Minn., Nov. 22, 1944; s. Daniel Thomas Jr. and Yolande (Gordon) B. BS, U. Notre Dame, 1966; MD, Cornell U., 1970; JD, Harvard U., 1973. Bar: Calif. 1973. Assoc. Gray, Cary, Ames & Frye, San Diego, 1973-78; sole practice San Diego, 1978—; lectr. Continuing Edn. of the Bar, San Diego, 1981—, Rutter Group, San Diego, 1981—. Mem. Am. Coll. Legal Medicine, Calif. Trial Lawyers Assn., San Diego County Bar Assn. (bd. dirs. 1983—, pres. 1987), San Diego County Trial Lawyers Assn. (bd. dirs. 1979-83). Republican. Roman Catholic. Club: Friendly Sons of St. Patrick (San Diego). Avocation: Skiing. Personal injury, Federal civil litigation, State civil litigation. Home: 1041 Cypress Ave San Diego CA 92103 Office: 401 West A St Suite 1200 San Diego CA 92101

BRODERICK, VINCENT LYONS, judge; b. N.Y.C., Apr. 26, 1920; s. Joseph A. and Mary Rose (Lyons) B.; m. Sally Brine, Apr. 15, 1950; children: Kathleen, Vincent, Mary, Ellen, Joan, Justin. A.B., Princeton U., 1941; LL.B., Harvard U., 1948. Bar: N.Y. 1948. Assoc. Barrett, Smith, Schapiro, Simon & Armstrong, N.Y.C., 1948-54; dep. commr. charge legal matters N.Y.C. Police Dept., 1954-56; gen. counsel Nat. Assn. Investment Cos., N.Y.C., 1956-61; chief asst. to U.S. atty. U.S. Dist. Ct. (so. dist.) N.Y., 1961-62, 62-65, U.S. atty., 1962; judge U.S. Dist. Ct. (so. dist.) N.Y., N.Y.C., 1976—; police commr. N.Y.C., 1965-66; mem. firm Phillips, Nizer, Benjamin, Krim & Ballon, 1966-71, Forsyth, Decker, Murray & Broderick, 1971-76. Home: 1424 Park Ln Pelham Manor NY 10803 Office: US District Court US Courthouse Foley Sq New York NY 10007 *

BRODHEAD, DAVID CRAWMER, lawyer; b. Madison, Wis., Sept. 16, 1934; s. Richard Jacob and Irma (Crawmer) B.; m. Nancie Christensen, Aug. 17, 1963; children: Compton, Peter, Christoffer. B.S., U. Wis., 1956, LL.B., 1959. Bar: N.Y. 1960, Wis. 1959, D.C. 1979. Asoc. firm Paul, Weiss, Rifkind, Wharton & Garrison, N.Y.C., 1959-68, ptnr., 1969—; dir. Centennial Industries, Inc., N.Y.C. Editor-in-chief: Wis. Law Rev, 1958-59. Trustee Collegiate Sch., N.Y.C., 1978-85; vestryman Christ and St. Stephen's Episcopal Ch., 1972-82. Mem. N.Y. State Bar, Assn. Bar City N.Y., Wis. Bar. Assn., Westside C. of C. of City of N.Y. (dir. 1970-83), Order of Coif, Delta Theta Phi. Clubs: Washington (Conn.); Marco Polo (N.Y.C.), Holland Soc. of N.Y. General corporate, Contracts commercial, Securities.

BRODHEAD, WILLIAM MCNULTY, lawyer, former congressman; b. Cleve., Sept. 12, 1941; s. William McNulty and Agnes Marie (Franz) B.; m. Kathleen Garlock, Jan. 16, 1965; children: Michael, Paul. A.B., Wayne State U., 1965; J.D., U. Mich., 1967. Bar: Mich. 1968. Tchr. Detroit, 1964-66, practiced in, 1968; atty. City of Detroit, 1969-70; mem. Mich. Ho. Reps., 1971-74; mem. 94th-97th Congresses from 17th Dist., mem. com. on ways and means, 1977-82, mem. budget com., 1979-80; chmn. Democratic Study Group, 1981-82; now ptnr. firm Plunkett & Cooney, Washington. Legislative, Government contracts and claims, Administrative and regulatory. Home: 1017 Gelston Circle McLean VA 22102 Office: 2715 M St NW Suite 300 Washington DC 20007

BRODHURST, ALBERT EDWARD, executive, lawyer; b. St. Petersburg, Fla., Sept. 26, 1934; s. George Henry and Olive Agnes (Padget) B. BS in Civil Engring., Tri-State Coll., 1960; LLB, John Marshall Law Sch., 1965; BS in Logistics Engring., Army-Navy Sch., Washington, 1969. Bar: Ill. 1966. Cadastrial surveyor U.S. Coast and Geodetic Survey, Menlo Park, Calif., 1956-59; design engr. Boeing Corp., New Orleans, 1965-67; pres. The Brodhurst Corp., Owings Mills, Md., 1974—; mgr. Staff Builders Tech. Services, Columbia, Md., 1981—. Alderman Chgo., 1963. Served to commdr. U.S. Army, 1952-54, Korea. Mem. ABA, Am. Preparedness Assn., Soc. Logistics Engrs. Democrat. Roman Catholic. Lodge: Elks. Military, Contracts law, Immigration, naturalization, and customs. Home and Office: The Brodhurst Corp Rt 140 Box 183 Owings Mills MD 21117

BRODIE, HARLOW KEITH HAMMOND, university president; b. Stamford, Conn., Aug. 24, 1939; s. Lawrence Sheldon and Elizabeth White (Hammond) B.; m. Brenda Ann Barrowclough, Jan. 26, 1967; children: Melissa Verduin, Cameron Keith, Tyler Hammond, Bryson Barrowclough. AB, Princeton U., 1961; MD, Columbia U., 1965; LLD hon., U. Richmond, 1987. Diplomate Am. Bd. Psychiatry and Neurology. Intern

Ochsner Found. Hosp., New Orleans, 1965-66; resident in psychiatry Columbia-Presbyn. Med. Center, N.Y.C., 1966-68; clin. assoc. intramural research program NIMH, 1968-70; asst. prof. psychiatry, dir. gen. clin. research center Stanford U. Med. Sch., 1970-74; prof. psychiatry, chmn. dept. Duke U. Med. Sch., 1974-82, James B. Duke prof. psychiatry and law, 1981—, adj. prof. psychology, 1980—; psychiatrist-in-chief Duke U. Med. Center, 1974-82; chancellor Duke U., 1982-85, pres., 1985—; adj. prof. psychology, Duke U. Med. Sch., 1980—. Co-author: The Importance of Mental Health Services to General Health Care, 1979, Modern Clinical Psychiatry, 1981; co-editor: American Handbook of Psychiatry, vols. 6, 7 and 8, 1975, 81, 86, Controversy in Psychiatry, 1978; assoc. editor: Am. Jour. Psychiatry, 1973-81. Chmn. Durham Area Mental Health, Mental Retardation and Substance Abuse Bd., 1981-82; pres., trustee Durham Acad., 1985-87. Recipient Disting. Med. Alumni award Columbia U., 1985; Disting. Alumnus award Ochsner Found. Hosp., 1984, Strecker award Inst. of Pa. Hosp., 1980. Mem. Am. Psychiat. Assn. (sec. 1977-81, pres. 1982-83), Inst. Medicine, Royal Coll. Psychiatrists, Soc. Biol. Psychiatry (A.E. Bennet research award 1970). Home: 63 Beverly Dr Durham NC 27707 Office: Duke Univ Office of the Pres 207 Allen Bldg Durham NC 27706

BRODSKY, ARTHUR JAMES, lawyer; b. N.Y.C., Aug. 29, 1946; s. Samuel William and Ruth Lila (Stolzer) B.; m. Marcia Jean Karadbil, Jan. 10, 1971 (div. Feb. 1985); 1 child, Alexandra. AB with honors, Franklin & Marshall Coll., 1967; JD, NYU, 1972. Bar: N.Y. 1972, U.S. Dist. Ct. (ea. dist.) N.Y. 1975, U.S. Ct. Appeals (2d cir.)1975. Atty. Dime Savs. Bank, N.Y.C., 1972-75; counsel Am. Ins. Assn., N.Y.C., 1975-82, corp. sec., counsel, 1982—; sec. Am. Ins. Services Group, Inc., N.Y.C., 1984—; sec., treas. Ctr. for Office Tech.Washington, 1984—. Editor: Survey of State Laws on Lobbying and PACs, 1986. Mem. ABA (labor law, tort and ins. practice sects.). Democrat. Pension, profit-sharing, and employee benefits, Insurance, General corporate. Home: 4401 Ambler Dr Kensington MD 20895 Office: Am Ins Assn 1025 Connecticut Ave NW Washington DC 20036

BRODSKY, DAVID M., lawyer; b. Providence, Oct. 16, 1943; s. Irving and Naomi (Richman) B.; m. Barbara Banks, Aug. 22, 1967; children: Katherine (dec.), Peter. AB cum laude, Brown U., 1964; LLB, Harvard U., 1967. Bar: N.Y. 1968, U.S. Dist. Ct. (so. dist.) N.Y. 1969, U.S. Dist. Ct. (ea. dist.) N.Y. 1977, U.S. Dist. Ct. (no. dist.) Tex. 1986, U.S. Ct. Appeals (2d cir.) 1974, U.S. Ct. Appeals (3d cir.) 1984,U.S. Ct. Appeals (D.C. cir.) 1981, U.S. Supreme Ct. 1977. Law clk. to U.S. Dist. Judge Dudley B. Bonsal, U.S. dist. ct. (so. dist.) N.Y., 1967-69; asst. U.S. atty. So. Dist. N.Y., 1969-73; assoc. Guggenheimer & Untermyer, N.Y.C., 1973-75, ptnr., 1976-80; ptnr. Schulte Roth & Zabel, N.Y.C., 1980—; lectr. ABA, Practising Law Inst., Law and Bus. Securities Enforcement Inst.; Securities Industry Assn. legal and compliance div. Mem. ABA Task Force on Insider Trading Controls; bd. dirs. N.Y. Lawyers for Pub. Interest, Inc. Mem. ABA (chmn. subcom. on SEC enforcement procedures of securities litigation com.), N.Y. County Lawyers Assn., Assn. Bar City of N.Y., Fed. Bar Council. Democrat. Jewish. Clubs: Brown of N.Y.; Heights Casino (Brooklyn Heights, N.Y.). Federal civil litigation, State civil litigation, Criminal.

BRODY, ANITA BLUMSTEIN, judge; b. N.Y.C., May 25, 1935; d. David Theodore and Rita (Sondheim) Blumstein; m. Jerome I. Brody, Oct. 25, 1959; children—Lisa, Marion, Timothy. A.B., Wellesley Coll., 1955; J.D., Columbia U., 1958. Bar: N.Y. 1958, Fla. 1960, Pa. 1972. Asst. atty. gen. State N.Y., 1958-60; sole practice, Ardmore, Pa., 1972-79; ptnr. Brody, Brown & Hepburn, Ardmore, 1979-81; judge Pa. Ct. Common Pleas 38th Jud. Dist., Norristown, 1981—. Mem. Montgomery Bar Assn. (dir.). Republican. Jewish. Jurisprudence. Office: Court House Swede St and Airy St Norristown PA 19404

BRODY, DAVID A., lawyer; b. Bklyn., June 24, 1916; s. Samuel and Lily (Robinson) B.; m. Beatrice K. Brody, Mar. 11, 1943; children—Ann, Michael. B.S.S., CCNY, 1936; LL.B., Columbia U., 1940. Bar: N.Y. 1940, D.C. 1951, U.S. Supreme Ct. 1969. Atty., Office of Solicitor, U.S. Dept. Agr., 1940-49; Washington counsel Anti Defamation League of B'nai B'rith, 1949—; sole practice, Washington, 1953—; mem. rules adv. com. D.C. Ct. Appeals, 1978—, Bicentennial Commn. of U.S. CLaims Ct., 1986—; voting del. Jud. Conf. D.C., 1978—. Served with USN, 1943-46. Mem. Bar Assn. D.C. (chmn. com. trademarks 1975-76), ABA, U.S. Trademark Assn. (mem. internat. trademark com. 1981—), Fed. Cir. Bar Assn., Fed. Bar Assn., Fed. Cir. Bar Assn., Phi Beta Kappa. Jewish. Club: Nat. Lawyers (Washington). Legis. editor Columbia Law Rev., 1939-40; mem. adv. bd. BNA Patent, Trademark and Copyright Jour., 1970—. Trademark and copyright, Legislative, Civil rights. Home: 3001 Veazey Terr NW #202 Washington DC 20008 Office: 1050 17th St NW Washington DC 20036 Office: 1640 Rhode Island Ave NW Washington DC 20036

BRODY, LITA HELEN, lawyer; b. Chgo., May 18, 1932; d. Harry and Emma (Bernstein) Gray; m. Arnold W. Brody, June 27, 1954 (dec. Aug. 1958); 1 child, Jennifer. BA, U. Chgo., 1952; BS, Roosevelt U., 1954; JD, John Marshall Law Sch., 1978. Bar: Ill. 1978, U.S. Dist. Ct. (no. dist.) Ill. 1978. Asst. title officer Chgo. Title Co., 1979-82; sole practice Chgo., 1982-86; assoc. Marshall N. Dickler, Ltd., Arlington Heights, Ill., 1986—. Bd. dirs., clinic dir. Chgo. Vol. Legal Services Found., 1979-83; atty. Wheaton (Ill.) Hist. Preservation Counsel, 1985—. Mem. ABA (assn. insts. com. 1977—, community assn. matters subcom. 1985—, chmn. arbitration subcom. 1985—), Chgo. Bar Assn. (real property com. 1982—, condominium subcom. 1982—, chmn. sci., tech. and law com. 1985-86). Real property, State civil litigation, Construction. Office: Marshall N Dickler Ltd 2045 S Arlington Heights Rd Arlington Heights IL 60005

BRODY, NANCY LOUISE, lawyer; b. Chgo., Nov. 17, 1954; d. Mitchell and Grace Yaden (Williams) Block; m. Daniel Matthew Brody, Oct. 28, 1979. B.A., U. Mich., 1975; J.D., Loyola U., Chgo., 1979. Bar: Ill. 1979, Pa. 1980, Ariz. 1981. Sole practice, Indiana, Pa., 1980—; sec., gen. counsel Block & Co., Inc., Indiana, 1981—, also bd. dirs. Bd. dirs. Ind. YMCA, 1986-87. Named one of Outstanding Young Women Am., 1983. Fellow Pa. Bar Found (dir. 1984—); mem. Ill. State Bar Assn., ABA (mem. ho. of dels. 1987—, state membership chmn. Pa. 1986—), Pa. Bar Assn. (bd. govs. 1984-87, chairperson Young Lawyers Div. 1985-86, treas. Young Lawyers Div. 1983-84), Zonta (parliamentarian Indiana chpt. 1985-86), Pi Beta Phi. Republican. General corporate, Real property. Office: 39 N 7th St Indiana PA 15701

BRODY, NEIL, lawyer; b. N.Y.C., Jan. 21, 1947; s. William and Ann (Goldstein) B.; m. Nanci Jane Rosenberg, Aug. 14, 1982. B.A., C.W. Post Coll., 1968; postgrad. New Sch. Social Research, 1968-70; J.D., Bklyn. Law Sch., 1974. Bar: N.Y. 1975, U.S. Dist. Ct. (ea. dist.) N.Y. 1976, U.S. Dist. Ct. (so. dist.) N.Y. 1978. Assoc. Langen & Levy, N.Y.C., 1975-81, Kroll, Killarney, Pomerantz & Cameron, N.Y.C., 1981-82; ptnr. Killarney, Fabiani & Brody, N.Y.C., 1982—. Cons. editor: Legal Terms and Concepts, 1983. Mem. Moot Ct. Honor Soc., Bklyn. Law Sch., 1974. Mem. N.Y. State Trial Lawyers Assn., N.Y. State Bar Assn., ABA, Assn. Trial Lawyers Am. Personal injury, Insurance, Federal civil litigation. Office: Killarney Fabiani & Brody 747 Third Ave New York NY 10017

BROEKER, BERNARD DREHER, lawyer; b. Natoma, Kans., May 30, 1909; s. Felix and Ruth (Dreher) B.; m. Katherine Oostdyke, Apr. 15, 1934 (dec. Dec. 1960); children—Katherine Anne Cundey, Bernard D.; m. Frances Walker Mills, Sept. 30, 1961. A.B., U. Notre Dame, 1930; J.D. cum laude, Harvard U., 1933. Bar: N.Y. 1934, Pa. 1972. Assoc., Cravath, De Gersdorff, Swaine & Wood, N.Y.C., 1933-40; atty. Bethlehem Steel Co. (Pa.), 1940-53; asst. sec. Bethlehem Steel Corp. (Pa.), 1953-57, dir., 1957-65, 67-77, sec., 1957-63, gen. counsel, 1963-70, chmn. fin. com., 1967-70, exec. v.p., 1970-74; counsel Kolb and Florenz, P.C. Bethlehem, Pa., 1974—. Chmn., Lehigh County (Pa.) Gen. Purpose Authority, 1977—. Recipient DeSales medal Allentown Coll. St. Francis de Sales, 1980—. Mem. ABA, Assn. Gen. Counsel, Am. Law Inst. (hon. life), Pa. Bar Assn. Republican. Roman Catholic. Club: Sancon Valley Country (Bethlehem, Pa.). Probate. Home: RD 4 Weyhill Crescent Bethlehem PA 18015 Office: 437 Main St Suite 310 Bethlehem PA 18018

BROEKER, JOHN MILTON, lawyer; b. Berwyn, Ill., May 27, 1940; s. Milton Monroe and Marjorie Grace (Wilson) B.; m. Linda J. Broeker, Dec. 9, 1983; children—Sara Elizabeth, Ross Goddard; stepchildren: Terrance Mercil Jr., Johnny Mercil, Veronica Mercil. B.A., Grinnell Coll., 1962; J.D. cum laude, U. Minn., 1965. Bar: Minn. 1965, Wis. 1982, U.S. Ct. Appeals (8th cir.) 1966, U.S. Dist. Ct. Minn. 1967, U.S. Tax Ct. 1969, U.S. Ct. Appeals (5th cir.) 1971, U.S. Dist. Ct. (we. dist.) Wis. 1982, U.S. Supreme Ct., 1984. Law clk. to presiding justice U.S. Ct. Appeals, 8th Circuit, 1965-66; ptnr. Gray, Plant, Mooty, Mooty & Bennett, Mpls., 1966-71; ptnr. Broeker, Geer, Fletcher & LaFond and predecessor firm, Mpls., 1971—; instr. U. Minn. Law Sch., 1967-72; lectr. U. Minn. Ctr. for Long Term Care Edn., 1972-77, Gt. Lakes Health Congress, 1972, Sister Kenny Inst., 1972; legal counsel Care Providersof Minn., 1967—, lectr. convs. and seminars, 1969—. Bd. dirs. Minn. Environ. Scis. Found., Inc., 1971-73; bd. dirs. Project Environ. Found., 1977-83, chmn., 1980-82; mem. alumni bd. Grinnell Coll., 1968-71; chmn. Minnetonka Environ. Quality and Natural Resources Commn., 1971-72. Recipient Oustanding Alumni award Grinnell Coll., 1973. Mem. ABA (forum com. on health law 1978—), Minn. Bar Assn. (chmn. environ. law com. 1970-72), State Bar Wis., Hennepin County Bar Assn. (chmn. environ. law com., 1976-77, legis. com. 1972-76, health law com. 1977-79), Am. Soc. Hosp. Attys., Minn. Soc. Hosp. Attys., Am. Health Care Assn. (legal coordinating com. 1970-75, labor com. 1973-74), Nat. Health Lawyers Assn., Sierra Club (nat. dir. 1974-76, chmn. chpt. 1971-72, regional v.p. 1973-74). Contbr. articles to legal jours. Administrative and regulatory, Health, Labor. Home: 11402 Burr Ridge Ln Eden Prairie MN 55344 Office: Broeker Geer Fletcher & LaFond 2850 Metro Dr Suite 800 Minneapolis MN 55420

BROGAN, JAMES MARTIN, lawyer, educator; b. Detroit, June 3, 1952; s. James and Joan Claire (Sullivan) B.; m. Doris Del Tosto, June 26, 1982; 1 child, Daniel Nickerson. BA, Ind. U., 1974; JD, Villanova U., 1981. Bar: Pa. 1981, U.S. Dist. Ct. (ea. dist.) Pa. 1981. Assoc. Harvey, Pennington, Herting & Renneisen Ltd., Phila., 1981—; adj. prof. Immaculata (Pa.) Coll., 1986. Class rep. Villanova Alumni Assn., 1981—; mem. Immaculata Coll. Deferred Giving Com., 1984—. Served to capt. U.S. Army, 1974-78. Mem. ABA, Pa. Bar Assn., Phila. Bar Assn. (mem. jud. retention sect., fed. rules and arbitration coms.). Republican. Roman Catholic. Club: Radnor (Pa.) Rugby (sec. 1981—). Avocations: carpentry, tennis, running, swimming. Federal civil litigation, State civil litigation, Contracts commercial. Home: 165 G Fairview Rd Glenmoore PA 19343 Office: Harvey Pennington et al 1600 Market St 12th Fl Philadelphia PA 19103

BROIDA, PETER BARRY, lawyer; b. Long Island, N.Y., Apr. 2, 1948; m. Patricia M. Goldsmid; 1 child, Lisa Felicity. BA, Dickinson Coll., 1970; JD, NYU, 1973. Bar: Pa. 1973, D.C. 1977, Va. 1980, U.S. Ct. Appeals (3d, 4th, D.C. and Fed. cirs.), U.S. Supreme Ct. Assoc. Montgomery, McCracken, Phila., 1973-75, Winkler, Danoff, Lubin & Toole, Phila., 1975-77; asst. gen. counsel Am. Fedn. Govt. Employees, Washington, 1977-80; ptnr. Passman & Broida, Washington, 1980—; pres. Dewey Pub. Inc., Washington, 1983—; chmn. Merit Systems Protection Bd. com. U.S. Ct. Appeals (Fed. cir.). Author: A Guide to Merit Systems Protection Board Law and Practice, 1984-87, A Guide to Federal Labor Relations Authority Law and Practice, 1979-87; moderator and participant lectures and continuing legal edn. programs. Mem. ABA, D.C. Bar Assn. Avocations: electronics, photography. Labor, Federal civil litigation, Administrative and regulatory. Home: 353 N Edison St Arlington VA 22203 Office: Passman & Broida 1717 K St NW Suite 1102 Washington DC 20006

BROIHIER, JEFFREY T., lawyer; b. LaCrosse, Wis., Nov. 6, 1950; s. Earl Francis and Florence S. (Craigo) B. BA, Mich. State U., 1975; JD, U. Mich., 1978. Bar: Wash. 1979, U.S. Dist. Ct. (we. dist.) Wash. 1979, U.S. Ct. Appeals (9th cir.) 1985, U.S. Supreme Ct. 1985. Mng. ptnr. Broihier & Wotipka, Seattle, 1985—. Sec. conservation div. Seattle Mountaineers, 1985-86. Served to ensign 3d class U.S. Army, 1971-73. Mem. Wash. State Bar Assn., Seattle-King County Bar Assn., Assn. Trial Lawyers Am., Wash. State Trial Lawyers Assn. State civil litigation, Personal injury, Real property. Office: Broihier & Wotipka 506 2d Ave 2600 Smith Tower Seattle WA 98104

BROKATE, BRIAN WILLIAM, lawyer; b. New Rochelle, N.Y., May 14, 1954; s. William Henry and Janet Rhoda (Kaeufer) B.; m. Mary Pamela Grant, June 3, 1978; children: Grant William, Erin Agnes. Student, Gettysburg Coll., 1972-75; BA summa cum laude, Pace U., 1976; JD, Capital U., 1979. Bar: N.Y. 1980, U.S. Dist. Ct. (so. and ea. dists.) N.Y. 1983, U.S. Ct. Appeals (2d cir.)1983, U.S. Ct. Appeals (11th cir.) 1986. Assoc. Gibney, Anthony and Flaherty, N.Y.C., 1979—. Mem. ABA, N.Y. State Bar Assn. Congregationalist. Avocation: golf. Federal civil litigation, State civil litigation, Trademark and copyright. Office: Gibney Anthony and Flaherty 420 Lexington Ave New York NY 10170

BROMBERG, ALAN ROBERT, lawyer, educator, writer; b. Dallas, Nov. 24, 1928; s. Alfred L. and Juanita (Kramer) B.; m. Anne Ruggles, July 26, 1959. A.B., Harvard U., 1949; J.D., Yale U., 1952. Bar: Tex. 1952. Assoc. firm Carrington, Gowan, Johnson, Bromberg and Leeds, Dallas, 1952-56; atty. and cons 1956-76; of counsel firm Jenkens & Gilchrist, 1976—; asst. prof. law So. Meth. U., 1956-58, assoc. prof., 1958-62, prof., 1962-83, Univ. Disting. prof., 1983—, mem. presdl. search group, 1971-72; faculty adviser Southwestern Law Jour., 1958-65; sr. fellow Yale U. Law Faculty, 1966-67; vis. prof. Stanford U., 1972-73; mem. adv. bd. U. Calif. Securities Regulation Inst., 1973-78, 79—; counsel Internat. Data Systems, Inc., 1961-65, sec., dir., 1963-65; mem. Tex. Legis. Council Bus. and Commerce Code Adv. Com., 1966-67. Author: Supplementary Materials on Texas Corporations, 3d edit, 1971, Partnership Primer-Problems and Planning, 1961, Materials on Corporate Securities and Finance—A Growing Company's Search for Funds, 2d edit, 1965, Securities Fraud and Commodities Fraud, Vols. 1-5, 1967-86, Crane and Bromberg on Partnership, 1968; mem. ednl. publs. adv. bd., Matthew Bender & Co., 1977—, chmn., 1981—; contbr. articles and revs. to law and bar jours.; adv. editor: Rev. Securities Regulation, 1969—, Securities Regulation Law Jour., 1973—, Jour. Corp. Law, 1976—. Sec., bd. dirs. Community Arts Fund, 1963-73; gen. atty. Dallas Mus. Contemporary Arts, 1956-63; bd. dirs. Dallas Theater Center, 1955-73, sec., 1957-66, fin. com., 1957-65, mem. exec. com., 1957-70, 79-85, life, 1973—, v.p., trustee endowment fund, 1974-85. Served as cpl. U.S. Army, 1952-54. Mem. Am. Bar Assn. (coms. commodities, partnerships, fed. regulation securities), Dallas Bar Assn. (chmn. com. uniform partnership act 1959-61, library com. 1981-83), State Bar Tex. (chmn. sect. corp. banking and bus. law 1967-68, vice-chmn. 1965-67, com. corp. law revision 1957—, mem. com. securities and investment banking 1965-69, chmn. 1965-69, mem. com. partnership 1957—, chmn. 1979-81), Am. Law Inst., Southwestern Legal Found. (co-chmn. securities com. 1982—), AAUP (exec. com. chpt. 1962-63, chmn. acad. freedom and tenure com. 1968-70, 71-72), Nat. Assn. Corp. Dirs. General corporate, Securities. Office: So Meth U Law Sch 3200 Allied Bank Tower Dallas TX 75202-2711

BROMFIELD, WAYNE ALLAN, judge; b. Kingston, Pa., May 16, 1947; s. Malcolm Poad and Edna Louise (Price) B.; m. Kathleen Joyce Butler, Aug. 29, 1970; children: Kelly Nicole, James Malcolm, Devon Butler. AB in Econs., Duke U., 1969; JD magna cum laude, Dickinson U., 1974. Bar: Pa. 1974, U.S. Dist. Ct. (mid. dist.) Pa. 1975, U.S. Ct. Appeals (3d cir.) 1981. Assoc. Fetter & Kessler, Lewisburg, Pa., 1974-75; ptnr. Matson, Brann & Bromfield, Lewisburg, 1976-78, Brann & Bromfield, Lewisburg, 1979-85; solicitor Union County Commrs., Lewisburg, 1976-86; judge ct. common pleas 17th jud. dist., Snyder and Union Counties, Pa., 1987—; bd. dirs. JPM Co., Lewisburg; adj. asst. prof. Bucknell U., Lewisburg, 1976-77. Bd. dirs. Union County Cancer Soc., Lewisburg, 1975-78, Ea. Union County United Fund, Lewisburg, 1981-85; active Union County Econ. Devel. Council, Lewisburg, 1983-83. Recipient Walter Harrison Hitchler award Dickinson Sch. Law, 1974, Woolsack Soc. award, 1974. Mem. Union County Bar Assn. (pres. 1980-82), Snyder County Bar Assn. Republican. Lutheran. Lodge: Lions (v.p. New Berlin club 1980-85). Home: PO Box 415 New Berlin PA 17855 Office: Snyder County Courthouse PO Box 217 Middleburg PA 17842

BROMM, FREDERICK WHITTEMORE, lawyer; b. Roanoke, Va., Nov. 19, 1953; s. Frederick Thornton and Anne Lee (Cassell) B. BA cum laude, Furman U., 1976; JD cum laude, Washington & Lee U., 1979. Bar: Va. 1979. Assoc. Place, Prillman & Barnett, Roanoke, 1979-81; assoc. Jolly, Place, Fralin & Prillman P.C., Roanoke, 1981-83, ptnr., 1983-86; sole practice Roanoke, 1986—. Treas. Roanoke Reps., 1984—. Mem. ABA, Va. Bar Assn., Roanoke Bar Assn. (chmn. conflicts com. 1986-87), Roanoke Jaycees (bd. dirs. 1980, v.p. 1981, legal counsel 1981, 82). Episcopalian. Bankruptcy, State civil litigation, Contracts commercial. Home: 1801 Greenwood Rd SW Roanoke VA 24015 Office: 305 First St Roanoke VA 24011

BRONFIN, FRED, lawyer; b. New Orleans, Nov. 30, 1918; s. Philip and Edith M. B.; m. Carolyn Pick; children by previous marriage—Daniel R., Kenneth A. B.A., Tulane U., 1938, J.D., 1941. Bar: La. 1941, U.S. Dist. Ct. (ea. dist.) La. 1941, U.S. Ct. Appeals (5th cir.) 1951, U.S. Supreme Ct. 1973. Assoc. Rittenberg & Rittenberg, New Orleans, 1946-48; ptnr. Rittenberg, Weinstein & Bronfin, New Orleans, 1948-56; ptnr. Weinstein & Bronfin, New Orleans, 1956-62; ptnr. Bronfin, Heller, Steinberg & Berins and predecessor Bronfin, Heller, Feldman & Steinberg, New Orleans, 1962—; dist. counsel B'nai B'rith. Mem. Internat. House, New Orleans. Served with USN, 1942-46. Mem. New Orleans Bar Assn., La. Bar Assn., ABA, Estate Planning Council, Order of Coif, Phi Beta Kappa. Mem. editorial bd. Tulane Law Rev., 1939-41. Probate, General corporate, Real property. Office: Bronfin Heller Steinberg & Berins 650 Poydras St 2500 Poydras Ctr New Orleans LA 70130

BRONIS, STEPHEN J., lawyer; b. Miami, Fla., Feb. 23, 1947; s. Larry and Thelma (Berger) B.; m. Jan Louise Wall, Jan. 1, 1984; children: Jason Michael, Tyler Adam. B.S. in Bus. Adminstrn., U. Fla., 1969; J.D., Duke U., 1972. Bar: Fla. 1972, D.C. 1973, U.S. Dist. Ct. (so. dist.) Fla. 1973, U.S. Ct. Appeals (5th cir.) 1977, U.S. Supreme Ct. 1978, U.S. Ct. Appeals (11th cir.) 1981. Asst. pub. defender 11th Jud. Cir. Fla., Miami, 1972-75; ptnr. Rosen & Bronis, P.A., Miami, 1975-77, Rosen, Portela, Bronis, et al., Miami, 1977-82, Bronis & Potela, P.A., Miami, 1982—. mem. faculty Nat. Inst. of Trial Adv., U. N.C., Yeshiva U. Contbr. articles to profl. jours. Recipient Am. Jurisprudence award Bancroft-Whitney Co., 1972; cert. of Appreciation Fla. Shorthand Reporters Assn., 1984; Outstanding Service award Fla. Criminal Def. Attys. Assn., 1981. Mem. Fla. Criminal Def. Attys. Assn. (pres. 1980-81), Am. Bd. Criminal Lawyers (v.p. 1981-82), Assn. Trial Lawyers Am. Nat. Criminal Def. Attys. Assn., Calif. Attys. Criminal Justice, Acad. Fla. Trial Lawyers (criminal law sect. dir.). Democrat. Criminal, national security cases, Personal injury. Home: 9201 SW 69th Ct Miami FL 33156 Office: Bronis & Portela PA 1395 Coral Way Miami FL 33145

BRONNER, WILLIAM ROCHE, lawyer; b. N.Y.C., Mar. 13, 1946; s. Leonard and Gloria (Roche) Bronner; m. Nancy L. Bloomgarden, Oct. 14, 1973; children: Gregory R.B., Caitlin L.B. BA, Dartmouth Coll., 1967; JD, Columbia U., 1970. Bar: N.Y. 1971, U.S. Dist. Ct. (so. and ea. dists.) N.Y. 1972, U.S. Ct. Appeals (2d cir.) 1973, U.S. Ct. Appeals (9th cir.) 1986. Law clk. to presiding judge U.S. Dist. Ct. (so. dist.) N.Y., N.Y.C., 1970-72; asst. U.S. atty. State of N.Y., N.Y.C., 1972-76; assoc. Burns & Jacoby, N.Y.C., 1977; counsel div. NL Industries, N.Y.C., 1978-80, counsel govt. affairs, 1980-82, group counsel, 1982-84, assoc. gen. counsel, 1984-87; gen. counsel NL Chems., Inc., N.Y.C., 1987—. General corporate, Environment, Federal civil litigation. Office: NL Industries 1230 Ave of Americas New York NY 10020

BRONSKY, A.J., lawyer; b. Lafayette, Ind., Dec. 27, 1956; s. Albert J. and Betty Hope (O'Neill) B. BA, St. Louis U., 1978; JD, Washington U., St. Louis, 1981. Bar: Mo. 1981, Ill. 1981, U.S. Dist. Ct. (so. dist.) Ill. 1984, U.S. Ct. Appeals (7th cir.) 1985. Assoc. Evans & Dixon, St. Louis, 1981-82, Brown, James & Rabbitt, St. Louis, 1982—. Mem. ABA, Ill. Bar Assn., Mo. Bar Assn., St. Louis Bar Assn., Assn. Trial Lawyers Am. Avocations: running, swimming, cycling. Personal injury, Workers' compensation, State civil litigation. Home: 1803 Kennett Pl Saint Louis MO 63104 Office: Brown James & Rabbitt PC 705 Olive Suite 1100 Saint Louis MO 63101

BRONSON, BARBARA JUNE, lawyer; b. Malta, Ohio, June 12, 1949; d. Henry and Ilse (Rosenfeld) Bachman; m. Neal Barry Bronson, Aug. 14, 1971; children: Michael J., Alison A. BA, Lake Erie Coll., 1970; JD, U. Cin., 1973. Bar: Ohio 1973. Assoc. James D. Ruppert & Assoc., Franklin, Ohio, 1973-78; ptnr., officer Ruppert, Bronson & Chicarelli Co., L.P.A., Franklin, 1978—; law librarian Warren County Law Library Assn., Lebanon, Ohio, 1979—. V.p. Warren County Women's Dem. Club, Lebanon, 1984; county coordinator Anthony J. Celebrezze for State Atty. Gen., Warren County, 1986; chmn. Civil Service Commn., Lebanon, 1987. Named one of Outstanding Young Women in Am., 1982-83, 85. Mem. Warren County Bar Assn. (v.p. 1985-86, pres. 1986-87). Probate, Real property, General practice. Home: 120 Wright Ave Lebanon OH 45036 Office: Ruppert Bronson & Chicarelli Co LPA 1063 E Second St PO Box 369 Franklin OH 45005

BRONSTEIN, RICHARD J., lawyer; b. Chgo., May 11, 1949; s. Jack and Elaine (Abrams) B.; m. Nancy E. Katz, June 6, 1971; children: Andrew, Grace. AB, U. Pa., 1970; JD, U. Chgo., 1974. Bar: Ill. 1974, N.Y. 1977, U.S. Tax Ct., D.C. 1984. Law clk. to presiding justice U.S. Ct. Appeals, Washington, 1974-75, U.S. Supreme Ct., Washington, 1975-76; assoc. Paul, Weiss, Rifkind, Wharton & Garrison, N.Y.C., 1976-82, ptnr., 1982—; lectr. Practising Law Inst., N.Y.C., 1981—, NYU, N.Y.C., 1985. Mem. ABA (tax sect.), N.Y. State Bar Assn. (com. on depreciation and investment credit tax sect.), Assn. of Bar of City of N.Y. (com. on taxation). Corporate taxation, Personal income taxation, State and local taxation. Office: Paul Weiss Rifkind Wharton & Garrison 345 Park Ave New York NY 10154

BROOKES, VALENTINE, lawyer; b. Red Bluff, Calif., May 30, 1913; s. Langley and Ethel (Valentine) B.; m. Virginia Stovall Cunningham, Feb. 11, 1939; children—Langley (Mrs. Jerrold B. Brandt), Lawrence Valentine, Alan Cunningham. A.B., U. Calif., Berkeley, 1934, J.D., 1937. Bar: Calif. bar 1937, U.S. Supreme Ct. bar 1942. Asst. franchise tax counsel State of Calif., 1937-40; dep. atty. gen. Calif., 1940-42; spl. asst. to U.S. atty. gen., asst. to solicitor gen. U.S., 1942-44; partner firm Kent & Brookes, San Francisco, 1944-70, Alvord & Alvord, Washington, 1944-50, Lee, Toomey & Kent, Washington, 1950-79, Brookes and Brookes, San Francisco, 1971—; lectr. Hastings Coll. Law, U. Calif., 1941-48, U. Calif. Law Sch., Berkeley, 1948-70. Author: The Continuity of Interest Test in Reorganizations, 1946, The Partnership Under the Income Tax Laws, 1949, The Tax Consequences of Widows Elections in Community Property States, 1951, Corporate Trasactions Involving Its Own Stock, 1954, Litigation Expenses and the Income Tax, 1957. Bd. dirs. Childrens Hosp. Med. Center of N.Calif., 1963-74, v.p., 1968-70; trustee Oakes Found., 1957-70; regent St. Mary's Coll., Calif., 1968—, pres. bd., 1970-72. Fellow Am. Bar Found. (life); mem. Am. Law Inst., ABA (chmn. com. on statute of limitations 1954-57, mem. council, tax sect. 1960-63), Calif. Bar Assn. (chmn. com. on taxation 1950-52, 60-61), Soc. Calif. Pioneers (v.p. 1964, 1975-86), Am. Coll. Tax Lawyers, Phi Kappa Sigma, Phi Delta Phi. Republican. Clubs: Pacific Union, Orinda Country, Bankers, World Trade. Corporate taxation, State and local taxation, Personal income taxation. Home: 7 Sycamore Rd Orinda CA 94563 Office: Brookes and Brookes 300 Montgomery St San Francisco CA 94104

BROOKHART, WALTER RAY, lawyer; b. Carlisle, Pa., Sept. 13, 1949; s. Norman Albert and Arlene Audrey (Bell) B.; m. Catherine Hutchins Tulloss, Mar. 6, 1971; 1 child, Daniel Carroll. BS in Chemistry with distinction, U. Va., 1971, MS, 1978, JD, 1979. Bar: Va. 1979, Tex. 1979, U.S. Patent Office 1979, U.S. Ct. Appeals (4th cir.) 1979, U.S. Dist. Ct. (so. dist.) Tex. 1980, U.S. Ct. Appeals (5th cir.) 1980, U.S. Ct. Appeals (11th cir.) 1981, U.S. Ct. Appeals (Fed. cir.) 1986. Assoc. Arnold, White & Durkee, Houston, 1979-82; assoc. Browning, Bushman, Zamecki & Anderson, Houston, 1982-86, ptnr., 1986—. Editor: Current International Legal Aspects of Licensing and Intellectual Property, 1980. Bd. dirs. Royal Oaks Civic Assn., 1981—, treas. 1982, pres. 1982-83, 1985—. Mem. ABA, State Bar Tex., Houston Bar Assn., State Bar Va., Sigma Xi (assoc.), Alpha Chi Sigma, Delta Upsilon. Republican. Methodist. Patent, Trademark and copyright, Trade secret and unfair competition. Home: 1515 Buckman Houston TX 77043 Office: Browning Bushman Zamecki & Anderson 5718 Westheimer Suite 1800 Houston TX 77057

BROOKMAN, ANTHONY RAYMOND, lawyer; b. Chgo., Mar. 23, 1922; s. Raymond Charles and Marie Clara (Alberg) B.; m. Marilyn Joyce Brookman, June 5, 1982; children—Meribeth Brookman Patrick, Anthony Raymond, Lindsay Logan. Student Ripon Coll., 1940-41; B.S., Northwestern U., 1947; J.D., U. Calif.-San Francisco, 1953. Bar: Calif. 1954. Law clk.

Calif. Supreme Ct., 1953-54; ptnr. Nichols, Williams, Morgan, Digardi & Brookman, 1954-68; sr. ptnr. Brookman & Hoffman, Inc., San Francisco, 1968—. Pres., Young Republicans Calif., San Mateo County, 1953-54. Served to 1st lt. USAF. Mem. ABA, Alameda County Bar Assn., State Bar Calif., Lawyers Club Alameda County, Alameda-Contra Costa County Trial Lawyers Assn., Assn. Trial Lawyers Am., Calif. Trial Lawyers Assn. Republican. Clubs: Masons, Athenian Nile, Crow Canyon Country, Shriners. Pub. Contra Costa New Register. Personal injury, State civil litigation. Office: Brookman and Hoffman 901 H St Suite 200 Sacramento CA 95814 Office: 1990 N California Blvd Walnut Creek CA 94596 Office: Court Plaza Bldg Sacramento CA 95814

BROOKS, CLAUDIA MARIE, lawyer; b. Oakland, Calif., Aug. 2, 1952; d. Rex E. and Colleen M. (Walker) Brooks; m. James A. Smith. A.B., U. Calif.-Berkeley, 1974; J.D., U. Calif. Hastings Coll. of Law San Francisco, 1979; postgrad. Monterey Inst. Fgn. Studies (Calif.), 1974, Institut de Francais, Villefranche-sur-Mer, France, 1979, 84, Oxford U. (Eng.), 1973, Hague Acad. Internat. Law (Netherlands), 1980. Bar: Calif. 1979, U.S. Dist. Ct. (no. dist.) Calif. 1979, U.S. Ct. Appeals (9th cir.) 1979. Extern for justice William P. Clark Calif. Supreme Ct., San Francisco, 1978; assoc. Smith & Brooks, Attys. at Law, Redlands, Calif., 1979-82, ptnr., 1982—. Editor-in-chief Hastings Internat. and Comparative Law Rev., 1978-79; contbr. article to law rev. Pub. mem. Fgn. Service selection bds. U.S. Dept. State, Washington, 1983; bd. dirs. Redlands Community Music Assn. Mem. San Bernardino County Bar Assn. (mem. jud. selection com. 1982-83). Clubs: San Francisco Press, Zonta. Probate. Office: Smith & Brooks 130 W Vine St PO Box 672 Redlands CA 92373

BROOKS, DANIEL TOWNLEY, lawyer, electrical engineer; b. N.Y.C., Apr. 15, 1941; s. Robert Daniel and Mary (Lee) B.; m. Barbara Ann Badertscher, June 16, 1973; 1 child, Daniel Townley, Jr. BS in Engring. cum laude, Princeton U., 1963; LLB, Stanford U., 1967, MS in Engring., 1968. Bar: Calif. 1968, U.S. Dist. Ct. (no. dist.) Calif. 1968, U.S. Ct. Appeals (9th cir.) 1968, N.Y. 1970, U.S. Ct. Appeals (2d cir.) 1972, Va. 1982. Assoc., Cadwalader, Wickersham & Taft, N.Y.C., 1968-79, ptnr., Washington, 1985—; atty., fellow U.S. SEC, Washington, 1979-81; with Computer Law Advisers, Springfield, Va., 1981-85; cons. and lectr. in computer law. Vice chmn. Commn. on Software Issues in the 80's. Mem. ABA, Calif. Bar Assn., N.Y. State Bar Assn., Va. Bar Assn., Computer Law Assn. Inc. (bd. dirs., v.p.), Assn. Computing Machinery, D.C. Computer Law Forum, IEEE, Assn. Data Processing Service Orgns., Software Pubs. Assn. Clubs: Princeton (N.Y.C., Washington). Administrative and regulatory, General corporate, Computer. Address: Cadwalader Wickersham & Taft 1333 New Hampshire Ave NW Washington DC 20036

BROOKS, DEXTER, lawyer; b. Pembroke, N.C., May 15, 1943; s. John J. and Lela (Hammond) B. BSE, N.C. State U., 1965, M in Math., 1971; JD, U. N.C., 1976. Bar: N.C. 1976, U.S. Dist. Ct. (ea. dist.) N.C. 1977, U.S. Ct. Appeals (4th cir.) 1979, U.S. Supreme Ct. 1979. Ptnr. Locklear, Brooks, Jacobs & Sutton, Pembroke, 1976—; bd. dirs. Lumbee River Legal Services, Pembroke, 1979—. Mem. ACLU, Common Cause Group, Pub. Citizen Orgn. Served with U.S. Army, 1966-68, Vietnam. Mem. ABA, N.C. Bar Assn., N.C. Acad. Trial Lawyers, Assn. Trial Lawyers Am., Am. Indian Bar Assn., Nat. Congress Am. Indians, Phi Kappa Phi, Eta Kappa Nu, Pi Mu Espilon, Mensa, Smithsonian, VFW, Am. Legion. Democrat. Baptist. Avocations: history, religion, Am. Indian culture. Personal injury, Civil litigation, General practice. Home: PO Box 730 Pembroke NC 28372 Office: Locklear Brooks Jacobs & Sutton 203 S Vance St Pembroke NC 28372

BROOKS, DOUGLAS MICHAEL, lawyer, state official; b. Jefferson City, Mo., May 24, 1954; s. Charles P. and Winifred Dale (Johnson) B.; m. Diana Phyllis Hopkins; children—Christopher, Dale, Douglas Michael. B.A., Northwestern U., 1975; J.D., St. Louis U., 1978. Bar: Mo. 1978. Asst. pros. atty. Office St. Louis County Pros. Atty., Clayton, Mo., 1978; adminstrv. asst. Mo. Ho. of Reps., Jefferson City, 1979; pvt. practice law Clayton, 1979-82; asst. gen. counsel Pub. Service Commn., Jefferson City, 1982-84; pub. counsel Mo. Office Pub. Counsel, Jefferson City, 1984—. alderman City of Manchester, Mo., 1977. Mem. Mo. Bar Assn. Public utilities, Administrative and regulatory. Office: Mo Office Pub Counsel 301 W High St PO Box 7800 Jefferson City MO 65102

BROOKS, GENE EDWARD, federal judge; b. Griffin, Ind., June 21, 1931; s. Claude Romelia and Martha Margaret (Crawford) B.;divorced; children: Marc, Gregory, Penny; m. Jan D. Gibson, Oct. 16, 1982; 1 child, Gene E. Jr. Bar: Ind. Pros. atty. Posey County, Ind., 1959-68; bankruptcy judge So. Dist. Ind., 1968-79, U.S. dist. judge, 1979-87, chief judge, 1987—; mem. faculty Fed. Jud. Ctr., apptd. to bankruptcy edn. com., 1987—; pres. Nat. Conf. Bankruptcy Judges. Contbr. articles to legal jours. Served with USMCR, 1953-55. Recipient Disting. Alumni award Ind. State U., Disting. Service cert. Fed. Bar Assn., Outstanding Service award Nat. Conf. Bankruptcy Judges. Mem. Ind. Bar Assn., Posey County Bar Assn., Vanderburgh County Bar Assn., VFW, Am. Legion. Democrat. Episcopalian. Clubs: Elks, Kiwanis. Office: U S Dist Ct 310 Federal Bldg 101 NW 7th St Evansville IN 47708

BROOKS, GEORGE ANDREW, lawyer, educator; b. N.Y.C., May 11, 1900; s. George H. and Mary Agnes (Winifred (O'Hara) B. A.B., Fordham U., 1924, J.D. (LL.B.) cum laude, 1927, LL.D. (hon.), 1952; LL.M., NYU, 1951; LL.D. (hon.), Scranton U., 1953. Bar: N.Y. 1928, U.S. Dist. Ct. (so. and no. dists.) N.Y. 1938, U.S. Dist. Ct. (no. dist.) Ind. 1939, U.S. Ct. Appeals (2d cir.) 1941, U.S. Dist. Ct. (ea. dist.) N.Y. 1946, U.S. Tax Ct. 1947, U.S. Ct. Appeals (3d cir.) 1949, U.S. Supreme Ct. 1958. Tchr. Regis High Sch., N.Y.C., 1924-27; Seton Hall High Sch., South Orange, N.J., 1924-30; practice, N.Y.C. and Tuckahoe, N.Y., 1928-34; with Gen. Motors Corp., N.Y.C., 1934-65, dir. N.Y. legal staff, 1941-65, corp. sec., 1947-65, sec. fin. policy com., 1947-58, sec. fin. com., 1958-65; lectr. law Fordham U., N.Y.C., 1929-35, adj. asst. prof., 1965-70, adj. assoc. prof., 1970-72, adj. prof. law, 1972—; prof. Seton Hall Coll., South Orange, N.J., 1924-34; atty. Union Free Sch. Dist. 1, Town of Eastchester, Westchester County, N.Y., 1930-56; legal cons., prodn. div. Nat. Def. Adv. Commn., Washington, 1940; arbitrator Nat. Assn. Securities Dealers, Inc. Bd. dirs. Legal Aid Soc. Westchester County, 1964-75, sec., 1965-72, pres., 1972-74; bd. dirs. Lavelle Sch. for Blind, N.Y.C., 1956—, v.p. 1971-78, pres., 1978-80, pres. emeritus; trustee emeritus Fordham U.; bd. dirs. Westchester Legal Services, Inc., 1967-85, N.Y. County Lawyers Assn., 1965-71, Rose Hill Housing Devel. Fund Corp.; trustee St. Agnes Hosp.1982-87, White Plains, N.Y., 1982-87. Served with U.S. Army, 1918. Created knight of Malta; recipient Alumni Achievement award Fordham U., 1959, Encaenia award Fordham Coll., 1959, medal of Achievement Fordham Law Alumni Assn., 1968, Bene Merenti medal Fordham U., 1979, Law Sch. award Fordham U., 1984. Fellow N.Y. Bar Found.; mem. U.S. Cath. Hist. Soc. (bd. dirs. 1958-84, v.p. 1964-66, pres. 1966-68), ABA, Fed. Bar Assn., Westchester County Bar Assn., Cath. Lawyers Guild (bd. dirs. 1958-61), N.Y. State Bar Assn. (ho. of dels. 1972-77), Fordham U. Alumni Fedn. (bd. dirs. 1955-64), Fordham Law Alumni Assn. (bd. dirs. 1960-75), N.Y. County Lawyers Assn. (bd. dirs. 1965-71), Assn. Bar City N.Y., Fordham Coll. Alumni Assn. (pres. 1948-52). Republican. Clubs: University, N.Y. Athletic (N.Y.C.). Legal education. Home: Eton Hall 127 Garth Rd Apt 5A Scarsdale NY 10583

BROOKS, JULIE ANNE, lawyer; b. Portland, Oreg., Nov. 4, 1945; d. Ralph M. and Jessie (Aukema) B.; m. Michael K. Murray, June 9, 1973 (div. 1979); m. George E. Diehr, Sept. 12, 1981. Student, U. Grenoble, France, 1969; BA, U. Wash., 1971; JD, U. Santa Clara, 1974; LLM, Georgetown U., 1981. Bar: Wash., U.S. Dist. Ct. (we. dist.) Wash., U.S. Ct. Claims, U.S. Tax Ct., U.S. Ct. Appeals (9th cir.), U.S. Supreme Ct. Assoc. Lane, Powell et al, Seattle, 1976-81; v.p., gen. counsel, asst. sec. Thousand Trails, Inc., Bellevue, Wash., 1981-86; v.p., gen. counsel, sec. Westmark Internat., Inc., 1986—. Vice chmn. Bus. Vol. for Arts, Seattle, Pike Pl. Market PDA Council, Seattle; active Seattle Opera Assn., Seattle Opera Guild, Seattle Children's Home, Jr. League. Mem. ABA, Wash. State Bar Assn., Seattle King County Bar Assn., Wash. Women Lawyers Assn., Am. Resort and Restaurant Devel. Assn. (legis. com. adv. bd. 1985-86, co-chmn. fed. tax task force 1985—, others). Clubs: Seattle Tennis, Seattle Athletic, Wash. Athletic. General corporate, Real property, Legislative. Home: 1500 38th Ave Seattle WA 98122 Office: Westmark Internat Inc Columbia Center 701 Fifth Ave Suite 6800 Seattle WA 98104

BROOKS, KEEFE ALAN, lawyer, educator; b. Detroit, June 4, 1954; s. Lee and Susan (Benyas) B.; m. Bonnie Leona Gill, Dec. 18, 1976; children: Ryan, Aleea. BA with high distinction, U. Mich., 1977, JD magna cum laude, 1980. Bar: Mich. 1980, U.S. Dist. Ct. (ea. dist.) Mich. 1980, U.S. Ct. Appeals (6th cir.) 1984, U.S. Supreme Ct. 1984. Ptnr. Butzel, Long, Gust, Klein & Van Zile, Detroit, 1980—; adj. prof. U. Detroit, 1983-86; Mem. Mich. State Bar Com. on Pub. Interest Law, 1985—. Mem. ABA, Detroit Bar Assn. Democrat. Jewish. Avocations: sports, theater, music. Libel, Federal civil litigation, State civil litigation. Office: Butzel Long Gust Klein et al 1881 First Nat Bldg Detroit MI 48226

BROOKS, PATRICK WILLIAM, lawyer; b. Grinnell, Iowa, May 11, 1943; s. Mark Dana and Madge Ellen (Walker) B.; m. Mary Jane Davey, Dec. 17, 1966; children—Carolyn Walker, Mark William. B.A., State Coll. Iowa, 1966; J.D., U. Iowa, 1971. Bar: Iowa 1971, U.S. Dist. Ct. (so. dist.) Iowa 1972, U.S. dist. ct. (no. dist.) Iowa 1971, U.S. Sup. Ct. 1974, U.S. Ct. Apls. (8th cir.) 1979. Tchr., Waterloo (Iowa) Community Schs., 1966-68; mem. staff Donahue & Brooks, West Union, Iowa, 1971-72; ptnr., Mowry, Irvine, Brooks & Ward, Marshalltown, Iowa, 1972-84, Brooks, Ward & Trout, Marshalltown, 1984—. Mem. Fayette County (Iowa) Republican Central Com., chmn. platform resolutions com., 1971-72; pres. Marshall County (Iowa) Young Reps., 1974; trustee Iowa Law Sch. Found., 1970-71. mem. Am. Judicature Soc., ABA, Iowa Bar Assn., Marshall County Bar Assn. (pres. 1985-86), Iowa Trial Lawyers Assn., Iowa Def. Counsel Assn. Lutheran. Clubs: Buick Am., Elks. Personal injury, Federal civil litigation, Insurance.

BROOKS, REX DWAIN, lawyer; b. Blanchard, Okla., Feb. 2, 1937; s. Berry Wilson and Edith Bane (Byers) B.; m. Norma Newton, May 16, 1964; 1 dau., Elizabeth Ann. B.B.A., U. Okla., 1965, J.D., 1967. Bar: Okla. 1967, U.S. Dist. Ct. (we. dist.) Okla. 1974, U.S. Sup. Ct. 1977, U.S. Ct. Apls. (10th cir.) 1978. Assoc., Elliot, Woodard and Rolston, 1967-68; atty. Md. Casualty Co., Oklahoma City, 1968-74; sole practice, Oklahoma City, 1974—. Served with U.S. Army, 1960-62. Mem. ABA, Oklahoma County Bar Assn., Okla. Bar Assn., Okla. Heritage Assn., Assn. Trial Lawyers Am., Okla. Trial Lawyers Assn. Democrat. Baptist. Workers' compensation, General practice, Personal injury. Address: 2323 N Indiana St Oklahoma City OK 73106

BROOKS, ROBERT FRANKLIN, lawyer; b. Richmond, Va., July 13, 1939; s. Robert Noel Brooks and Annie Mae (Edwards) Miles; m. Patricia Wilson, May 6, 1972; children: Robert Franklin Jr., Thomas Noel. BA, U. Richmond, 1961, LLB, 1964. Bar: Va. 1964, U.S. Dist. Ct. (ea. and we. dists.) Va. 1964, U.S. Ct. Appeals (4th cir.) 1965, U.S. Ct. Appeals (5th cir.) 1972, D.C. 1977, U.S. Ct. Appeals (2d cir.) 1979, U.S. Supreme Ct. 1979, U.S. Ct. Appeals (11th cir.) 1981. Assoc. Hunton & Williams, Richmond, 1964-71, ptnr., 1971—; chmn. set. II 3d Dist. Com., 1983; mem. rules evidence com. Supreme Ct. Va., 1984-85. Mem. ABA, D.C. Bar Assn., Va. State Bar (council 1986-87, bd. govs. litigation sect., sec. 1984-85, chmn. 1986—), Richmond Bar Assn. (chmn. judiciary com. 1985—), Am. Judicature Soc., Am. Coll. Trial Lawyers, Va. Bar Assn., Richmond Trial Lawyers Assn. Baptist. Clubs: Commonwealth, Va. Country (Richmond). Federal civil litigation, State civil litigation. Home: 500 Kilmarnock Dr Richmond VA 23229 Office: Hunton & Williams PO Box 1535 707 E Main St Richmond VA 23212

BROOKS, ROY HOWARD, JR., lawyer; b. Columbus, Ga., Feb. 10, 1923; s. Roy Howard and Marie Elizabeth (Stubbs) B.; m. Lois Jestine Maddox, Sept. 2, 1923; children—Roy Howard III, Terrell Wayne, Richard Bruce, Diane Susan. J.D., U. Miami-Coral Gables, 1954. Bar: Fla. 1954. Ptnr., Kelly & Brooks, 1955-80; sole practice, Coral Gables, Fla., 1980—; chmn. Fla. Gov. Adv. Council on Veterans Affairs, commr. Fla. Commn. Vets. Affairs. Mem. Dade County Speech and Hearing Ctr. Served with Signal Corps U.S. Army, 1942-46. Recipient VFW Disting. Service award 1956, Outstanding Service award, 1956; DAR medal of Honor, 1977; Fla. Gov.'s Outstanding Service award, 1977; Book of Golden Deeds award Exchange Club, 1984. Mem. Fla. Bar Assn., Coral Gables Bar Assn., Com. of 100. Democrat. Methodist. Clubs: Coral Gables Country, Century. Contbr. articles to veterans orgns. periodicals. Administrative and regulatory, General practice, Probate. Home: 8751 SW 85th St Miami FL 33173 Office: 2625 Ponce De Leon Blvd Coral Gables FL 33134

BROOKS, ROY LAVON, law educator; b. New Haven; s. Freeman and Ruth (Andersen) B.; m. Penny Feller, May 9, 1970; 1 child, Whitney Alison. BA, U. Conn., 1972; JD, Yale U., 1975. Bar: Pa. 1976, U.S. Dist. Ct. (ea. dist.) Pa. 1976, U.S. Ct. Appeals (3d cir.) 1976. Law clk. to presiding justice U.S. Dist. Ct. (ea. dist.) Pa., Phila., 1975-77; assoc. Cravath, Swaine & Moore, N.Y.C., 1977-79; prof. law U. San Diego, 1979—. Contbr. articles to profl. jours. Mem. ABA, Nat. Bar Assn., Fed. Bar Assn., Phi Kappa Phi, Heartland Human Rights Assn. (bd. dirs. 1985—). Avocations: tennis, chess, reading. Civil rights, Federal civil litigation. Office: U San Diego Alcala Park San Diego CA 92110

BROOKS, RUSSELL EDWIN, lawyer; b. Centerport, N.Y., Oct. 25, 1938; s. Edwin F. and Alice (Lucretia) B.; m. Patricia A. Brooks, Sept. 7, 1963; children: Sarah T., Samuel R. BA, Dartmouth Coll., 1960; LLB, Columbia U., 1963, LLM, 1965. Bar: N.Y. 1963, U.S. Dist. Ct. (so. and ea. dists.) N.Y. 1967, U.S. Ct. Appeals (2d cir.) 1967, U.S. Supreme Ct. 1973, U.S. Dist. Ct. D.C. 1976, U.S. Ct. Appeals (5th and D.C. cirs.) 1976, U.S. Ct. Appeals (9th cir.) 1979, U.S. Ct. Appeals (3d cir.) 1982. Instr. law Columbia U., N.Y.C., 1963-65; assoc. Milbank, Tweed, Hadley & McCloy, N.Y.C., 1965-72, ptnr., 1973—. Mem. ABA, N.Y. State Bar Assn., Fed. Bar Council. Federal civil litigation, State civil litigation. Office: Milbank Tweed Hadley & McCloy 1 Chase Manhattan Plaza New York NY 10005

BROOKS, SHEILA DURANT, lawyer, commissioner; b. Atlanta, Nov. 7, 1946; m. Craig Stephe Brooks, June 27, 1968; 1 child, Robert Craig. Bar: Md. 1980, U.S. Ct. Appeals (4th cir.) 1981, U.S. Bankruptcy Ct. 1981. Asst. staff counsel NFL Players Assn., Washington, 1977-80; asst. city solicitor Balt. City Solicitors Office, 1980-84; ptnr. Opara & Brooks P.A., Balt., 1984-86; sole practice Balt., 1986—; commr. Criminal Injury Compensation Bd., 1985—; pres. Sheila Brooks and Assocs., 1986—; v.p. Statewide Janitorial Service, 1985—. v.p. Blews Black-Jewish Coalition, Balt., 1985—; bd. dirs. Symphony Condo Assn., Balt., 1986—. Mem. ABA, Monumental Bar Assn., U. Balt. Alumni Assn. (bd. dirs. 1981—). Democrat. Baptist. Avocations: poetry, music. Family and matrimonial, Bankruptcy, Personal injury. Office: Opara & Brooks PA 13 W Biddle St Baltimore MD 21201

BROOKS, WILLIAM JAMES, III, lawyer; b. West Palm Beach, Fla., Aug. 5, 1953; s. William James and Mary Helen (Olson) B; m. Anna Marie Frances Bourgeois, Sept. 29, 1979; children: William James IV, James Andrew. BA, Mt. Union Coll., 1974; JD, U. Notre Dame, 1977; LLM in Taxation, Emory U., 1985. Bar: Minn. 1977, U.S. Dist. Ct. Minn., 1977. Asst. revisor Revisor of Statutes, St. Paul, 1977-78; assoc. counsel Investors Diversified, Inc., Mpls., 1978-80; ptnr. Brooks & Moehn, P.A., Mpls., 1981-84; asst. gen. counsel Farm Credit Services, St. Paul, 1985-86; ptnr. Brooks & Brooks, P.A., Bloomington, Minn., 1986—. Mem. ABA, Minn. Bar Assn., Hennepin County Bar Assn. Democrat. Roman Catholic. Personal income taxation, General corporate, Securities. Home: 6950 W 83rd St Bloomington MN 55438

BROOKSHIRE, JAMES EARL, lawyer; b. Statesville, N.C., Feb. 16, 1951; s. Earl and Opal (Isenhour) B.; m. Peggy Anne Price, July 31, 1971; children: Jonathan David, Mary Elizabeth. BA in History with honors, N.C. State U., 1973; JD, U. S.C., 1976. Bar: S.C. 1976, D.C. 1979, U.S. Ct. Appeals (4th cir.) 1979, U.S. Ct. Appeals (D.C. cir.) 1980, U.S. Supreme Ct. 1980, U.S. Claims Ct. 1982, U.S. Ct. Appeals (Fed. cir.) 1982. Trial atty. gen. litigation sect. U.S. Dept. Justice Land and Natural Resources Div., Washington, 1976-83, chief, Indian claims sect., 1983-85, dep. chief gen. litigation sect., 1985—; mem. dept. performance standard rev. bd., 1986, Atty. Gen. Advocacy Inst., 1978-81, jud. conf. planning com. Fed. cir., Washington, 1983—, adv. council Claims Ct., Washington, 1983—, vice chmn., 1986—, mem. alternative dispute resolution com., pres.-elect Claims Ct. Bar Assn.; mem. Claims Ct. Constitution Bicentennial com., 1987—. Contbg. author: Claims Court and Federal Circuit Practice Handbook, 1986; co-author: Hospital Franchising Law and Regulation, 1979; editor: Environmental Quality Law, 1976. Councilman Luth. Ch. of Abiding Presence, Springfield, Va., 1981-82, council chmn., 1982. Wig and Robe scholar U. S.C., 1975. Mem. ABA (nat. resources sect.), S.C. Bar Assn., D.C. Bar Assn., Fed. Cir. Bar Assn. (constn. com., govt. contract appeals com., Indian claims com.), Ct. of Claims Bar Assn. Club: Orange Hunt (Springfield). Avocations: astronomy, computer applications. Government contracts and claims, Condemnation, Environment. Office: US Dept Justice 10th and Constitution Room 2133 Washington DC 22530

BROOME, THOMAS JEFFERSON, lawyer; b. Learned, Miss., Jan. 1, 1938; s. James Ector and Ruth Elizabeth (Kimble) B.; m. Paula Ellentine Benjamin, Apr. 12, 1961; children: Clifford Errol, Angela Rachelle. AA, Oakland Jr. Coll., 1958; BA, San Jose State Coll., 1960, postgrad., 1960-61; JD, San Francisco Law Sch., 1973. Bar: Calif., U.S. Dist. Ct. (no. dist.) Calif., U.S. Supreme Ct. Dep. probation officer County of Alameda, Oakland, Calif., 1962-75; ptnr. Broome, Cooper & Assocs., Oakland, 1975—. Recipient Outstanding Service to Edn. award Coll. Bounders, 1982. Mem. Nat. Bar Assn. (region dir. 1980-83, v.p. 1983-84, pres. 1986-87, Presdl. award 1982, 84), Charles Houston Bar Assn. (pres. 1979-80, Service award 1980), Alameda County Bar Assn. (bd. dirs. 1979-81), Phi Beta Sigma (Notable Citizen award 1980). Avocations: bowling, basketball. Criminal, Family and matrimonial, Personal injury. Office: Broome Cooper & Assocs 145 E 14th St Oakland CA 94606

BROOMFIELD, ROBERT CAMERON, judge; b. Detroit, June 18, 1933; s. David Campbell and Mabel Margaret (Van Deventer) B.; m. Cuma Lorena Cecil, Aug. 3, 1958; children: Robert Cameron Jr., Alyson Paige, Scott McKinley. BS, Pa. State U., 1955; LLB, U. Ariz., 1961. Bar: Ariz. 1961, U.S. Dist. Ct. Ariz. 1961. Assoc. Carson, Messinger, Elliot, Laughlin & Ragan, Phoenix, 1962-65, ptnr., 1966-70; judge Ariz. Superior Ct., Phoenix, 1971-85, U.S. Dist. Ct. Ariz., Phoenix, 1985—; faculty Nat. Jud. Coll., Reno, 1975-82. Contbr. articles to profl. jours. Avd. bd. Boy Scouts Am., Phoenix, 1968-75; training com. Ariz. Acad., Phoenix, 1980—; pres. bd. trustees Paradise Valley Sch. Bd., Phoenix, 1965-70, 69—; bd. dirs. Phoenix Together, 1982—, Crisis Nursery, Phoenix, 1976-81. Served to capt. USAFR, 1955-72. Recipient Faculty award Nat. Jud. Coll., 1979, Disting. Jurist award Miss. State U., 1986. Mem. ABA (chmn. Nat. Conf. State Trial Judges 1983-84, pres. Nat. Conf. Met. Cts. 1978-79, chmn. bd. dirs. 1980-82, Justice Tom Clark award 1980, bd. dirs. Nat. Ctr. for State Cts. 1980-85, Disting. Service award 1986), Ariz. Bar Assn., Maricopa County Bar Assn. (Disting. Pub. Service award 1980), Ariz. Judges Assn. (pres. 1981-82), Am. Judicature Soc. (spl. citation 1985), Maricopa County Med. Soc. (Disting. Service medal 1979). Lodge: Rotary. Judicial administration. Office: US Ct House 230 N 1st Ave Room 3077 Phoenix AZ 85025

BROOTEN, KENNETH EDWARD, JR., lawyer; b. Kirkland, Wash., Oct. 17, 1942; s. Kenneth Edward Sr. and Sadie Josephine (Assad) B.; m. Patricia Anne Folsom, Aug. 29, 1965 (div. April 1986); children: Michelle Catherine, Justin Kenneth. Diploma, Lewis Sch. Hotel, Restaurant and Club Mgmt., Washington, 1963; student, U. Md., 1964-66; AA, Sante Fe Community Coll., Gainesville, Fla., 1969; BS in Journalism with highest honors, U. Fla., 1971, MA in Journalism and Communications with highest honors, 1972, JD with honors, 1975; law student, U. Idaho, 1972-73; diploma, Inst. Legal Scis., Polish Acad. Scis., Warsaw, 1974; student, U. Cambridge, England, 1974. Bar: Fla., D.C., U.S. Dist. Ct. (no., mid. and so. dists.) Fla., U.S. Dist. Ct. D.C., U.S. Tax Ct., U.S. Ct. Appeals (5th, 9th, 11th and D.C. circs.), U.S. Supreme Ct. Asst. to several Congressmen U.S. Ho. of Reps., Washington, 1962-67; adminstrv. asst. VA Cen. Office, Washington, 1967; adminstrv. officer VA Hosp., Gainesville, Fla., 1967-72; ptnr. Carter & Brooten, P.A., Gainesville, Fla., 1975-78, Brooten & Fleisher, Chartered, Washington and Gainesville, Fla., 1978-80; sole practice Washington and Gainesville, 1980-86, Washington, 1987—; permanent spl. counsel, acting chief counsel, dir. Select Com. Assassinations U.S. Ho. of Reps., 1976-77. Writer episode Simon & Simon (TV); contbr. articles to profl. jours. Served with USCGR, 1960-68. Named one of Outstanding Young Men Am., U.S. Jaycees, 1977. Mem. ABA, Fla. Bar Assn., D.C. Bar Assn., Am. Coll. Legal Medicine, Sigma Delta Chi. Roman Catholic. Avocations: writing, ranching, yachting, piloting. Legislative, Medical malpractice—personal counsel for physicians, Federal civil litigation. Office: 1817 19th St NW Washington DC 20009

BROPHEY, ALICIA TRACY, lawyer; b. Boston, Oct. 1, 1947; d. Paul Francis and Margaret (Tracy) B.; m. Donald Laffert, Jan. 4, 1985. BA, Newton Coll., 1969; JD, Boston Coll., 1972. Bar: Mass. 1972. Legal advisor GTE, Needham, Mass., 1974-80; regional counsel Wang Labs., Lowell, Mass., 1980-85; corp. counsel Wang Labs. Inc., Lowell, 1986—. Mem. ABA, Mass. Bar Assn., Nat. Contract Mgmt. Assn. General corporate, Government contracts and claims. Home: 67 Bond St Needham MA 02192 Office: Wang Labs Inc 1 Industrial Ave Lowell MA 01887

BROPHY, GILBERT THOMAS, lawyer; b. Southampton, N.Y., July 15, 1926; s. Joseph Lester and Helen Veronica (Scholtz) B.; m. Canora Woodham Brophy, Sept. 3, 1957; m. Isabel Blair Porter; children—Laure Porter Thompson, Erin Woodham Brophy. B.S. with high honors, U. Fla., 1949; LL.B., George Washington U., 1960; postgrad. Grad. Law Sch., U. Miami, 1970-73. Bar: Fla. 1960, U.S. Dist. Ct. D.C., 1970. Title examiner Jesse Phillips Klinge & Kendrick, Arlington, Va., 1959-60; ptnr. Beall, Beall & Brophy, Palm Beach, Fla., 1962-65; asst. city atty. West Palm Beach (Fla.), 1965-67; ptnr. Brophy & Skrandel, Palm Beach, 1968-70, Brophy & Aksomitas, Tequesta, Fla., 1974-75, Brophy, Genovese & Sayler, Jupiter, Fla., 1977-78, Brophy & Genovese, 1978-83; town atty. Lantana (Fla.), 1967-70; judge ad litem Village of Tequesta, 1970-72; town atty. Jupiter, 1974-75. Bd. dirs., disaster chmn. ARC, Palm Beach; past corr. sec. Palm Beach County Hist. Soc. Served with AUS, 1951-54; Korea. Recipent Dedicated Service plaque Town of Jupiter, 1975. Mem. Attys. Title Guaranty Fund, Assn. Trial Lawyers Am., Palm Beach County Bar Assn., Nat. Mil. Intelligence Assn., Nat. CIC Assn., Assn. Former Intelligence Officers, NRA (life), Kappa Sigma Alumni Assn. Mem. exec. com. Republican Com. Martin County. Clubs: Rotary (pres. 1977-78), University (Washington); Elks, River Edge, Everglades Rifle and Pistol (hon. life). State civil litigation, Family and matrimonial, General practice. Home: Villas on Green #504 717 S US Hwy 1 Jupiter FL 33477 Office: 810 Saturn St Parkway Plaza Suite 15 Jupiter FL 33477

BROSKY, JOHN G., judge; b. Scott Twp., Pa., Aug. 4, 1920; m. Rose F. Brosky, June 24, 1950; children—John C., Carol Ann, David J. B.A., U. Pitts., 1942, LL.B., 1949, J.D., 1968. Bar: Pa. 1950. Asst. county solicitor, Allegheny County, Pa., 1951-56; judge County Ct. Allegheny County, 1956-61; adminstrv. judge family div. Common Pleas Ct. Allegheny County, 1961-80; judge Superior Ct. Pa., 1980—; mem. faculty Pa. Coll. Judiciary. Chmn. Operation Patrick Henry, Boy Scouts Am.; pres. Scott Twp. Sch. Bd., 1946-56; 1st pres. Chartiers Valley Joint Sch. Dist., Allegheny County, Pa.; pres. Greater Pitts. Guild for Blind. Served with U.S. Army, 1942-46; maj. gen. (ret.) USAF-PaNG. Recipient Disting. Jud. Service award Pa., Mason Juvenile Ct. Inst., Man of Yr. award in law Pitts. Jr. C. of C., 1960, Humanitarian award New Light Men's Club, 1960, Loyalty Day award VFW, 1960, Four Chaplains award, 1965; Man of Yr. award Cath. War Vets., 1960, 62; Service award Alliance Coll.; ; Disting. Citation, Mil. Order World Wars; Humanitarian award Variety Club, 1974; Jimmy Doolittle fellow award Aerospace Edn. Found., 1975; Pa. Meritorious Service medal Pa. N.G., 1976; State Humanitarian award Domestic Relations Assn. Pa., 1978; Man of Yr. award Am. Legion, 1978; Pa. Disting. Service medal; Disting. Service award Pa. N.G. Assn., 1980; Exceptional Service award USAF, 1982; General Ira Eaker fellow, 1981. Mem. Am. Judicature Soc., ABA, Assn. Trial Lawyers Am., Inst. Jud. Adminstrn., Inc., Internat. Platform Assn., Air Force Assn. (nat. dir., nat. pres., chmn. bd., presidential citation 1974, 80, 81), Am. Acad. Matrimonial Lawyers, N.G. Assn. of Pa. (pres.), Pa. Conf. State Trial Judges (past pres.), Pa. Joint Family Law Council. Clubs: Press, Variety, Aero (past pres.) (Pitts.). State civil litigation, Criminal, Family and matrimonial. Home: 29 Greenview Dr Carnegie PA 15106 Office: 2703 Grant Bldg Pittsburgh PA 15219

BROSNAHAN, JAMES JEROME, lawyer; b. Boston, Jan. 12, 1934; s. James Jerome and Alice B. (Larkin) B.; m. Carol Simon, Nov. 8, 1958; children: Amy Rebecca, James Jerome III, Lisa Katherine. BBA, Boston Coll., 1956; LLB, Harvard U., 1959. Bar: Ariz. 1960, U.S. Ct. Appeals (9th cir.) 1961, Calif. 1963 (chmn. fed. courts commn. 1974-75), U.S. Dist. Ct.

(no. dist.) Calif. 1964, U.S. Supreme Ct. 1970, U.S. Dist. Ct. (cen. dist.) Calif. 1974. Asst. U.S. atty. U.S. Dist. Ct. Ariz., Phoenix, 1961-63, U.S. Dist. Ct. (no. dist.) Calif., San Francisco, 1963-66; from assoc. to ptnr. Cooper, White & Cooper, San Francisco, 1966-75; ptnr. Morrison & Foerster, San Francisco, 1975—; spl. counsel Calif. Legislature Joint Sub-Com. Crude Oil Pricing, 1973-74; chmn. Fed. Cts. com. State Bar Calif., 1974; chmn. del. U.S. Ct. Appeals (9th cir.) Jud. Conf., 1977-78, lawyer rep., 1977-79; mem. jud. council Calif. Adv. Com. on Gender Bias in the Cts., 1987—; frequent lectr., panelist continuing legal edn. programs, various orgns., schs., pub. interest groups. Author: Trial Handbook for California Trial Lawyers, 1974; contbr. articles to profl. jours. Treas. Mexican-Am. Legal Def. Fund, San Francisco, 1981-83, nat. bd. dirs. 1980-84; bd. dirs. ACLU, keynote speaker 1987; bd. dirs. Sierra Club Legal Def. Fund, 1974-77; bd. dirs. Legal Services for Children, Inc., 1984—; civil adv. bd. Raketeer-Influenced and Corrupt Orgns., 1985—. Served with USAF, 1960. Named one of five best attys. in San Francisco, San Francisco Examiner, 1980. Fellow Am. Coll. Trial Lawyers, Internat. Acad. Trial Lawyers, Internat. Soc. Barristers, ABA Found.; mem. ABA (adv. com. to pres.-elect program on competency and contg. legal edn. 1979, active numerous panels, programs, convs.), Calif. Bar Assn. (chmn. panel on cross-exam 1981), Am. Law Inst., Am. Bd. Trial Advs., Bar Assn. San Francisco (past pres. 1977), Practicing Law Inst. (bd. dirs. 1975-77), Calif. Attys. for Criminal Justice (bd. dirs. 1981-83), Harvard Law Sch. Alumni Assn. (panelist 1986). Club: Barristers (San Francisco) (pres. 1968). Federal civil litigation, Criminal, Libel. Home: 2808 Oak Knoll Terr Berkeley CA 94705 Office: Morrison & Foerster 345 California St San Francisco CA 94104

BROSNAHAN, ROGER PAUL, lawyer; b. Kansas City, Mo., Aug. 9, 1935; s. Earl and Helen (Mottin) B.; m. Jill Farley, Aug. 2, 1958; children: Paul, Connor, Helen, Farley, Tracy, Hugh, Lee. BS, St. Louis U., 1956; LLB, Mich. U., 1959. Bar: Mo. 1959, Minn. 1959, U.S. Supreme Ct. 1971, U.S. Ct. Appeals (8th cir.) 1975. Ptnr. Streater, Murphy, Brosnahan & Langford, Winona, Minn., 1959-78, Kutak, Rock & Huie, Mpls., 1979-82, Robins, Zelle, Larson & Kaplan, Mpls., 1982—. Mem. ABA (state del. 1976—), Minn. Bar Assn. (pres. 1974-75), Ramsey County Bar Assn., Hennepin County Bar Assn., Nat. Conf. Bar Pres. (pres. 1980-81). Democrat. Roman Catholic. Federal civil litigation, State civil litigation, Personal injury. Home: 2509 Manitou Island White Bear Lake MN 55110 Office: Robins Zelle Larson & Kaplan 900 2d Ave S 1800 International Ctr Minneapolis MN 55402

BROSSMAN, MARK EDWARD, lawyer; b. N.Y.C., Aug. 13, 1953; s. Isadore Jack and Blanche Brossman. BS, Cornell U., 1975; JD, NYU, 1978, LLM in Labor Law, 1981. Bar: N.Y. 1979, U.S. Dist. Ct. (so. and ea. dists.) N.Y. 1979, U.S. Dist. Ct. (no. and we. dists.) N.Y. 1981, U.S. Ct. Appeals (6th cir.) 1981, U.S. Ct. Appeals (2d cir.) 1983, U.S. Supreme Ct. 1983. Assoc. Morgan, Lewis and Bockius, N.Y.C., 1978-83; assoc. Grutman, Miller et al, N.Y.C., 1984-85, ptnr., 1985-86; counsel Chadbourne and Parke, N.Y.C., 1986-87, ptnr., 1987—; lectr. Cornell U., 1983—; adj. asst. prof. NYU, 1983—. Author: Social Investing for Pension Funds, 1982; contbr. articles to profl. jours. Mem. ABA, Assn. of Bar of City of N.Y., N.Y. State Bar Assn., Indsl. Relations Research Assn., Phi Kappa Phi. Labor, Pension, profit-sharing, and employee benefits. Office: Chadbourne and Parke 30 Rockefeller Plaza New York NY 10112

BROTHERS, THOMAS WHITE, lawyer; b. Nashville, July 16, 1951; s. Mack Prator and Sarah White (Cunningham) B.; m. Karen Roberts, Dec. 11, 1977. BA with honors, U. Tenn., 1973; JD, Vanderbilt U., 1977. Bar: Tenn. 1977, U.S. Dist. Ct. (mid. dist.) Tenn. 1978, U.S. Ct. Appeals (6th cir.) 1985. Chief warrant officer Met. Sheriff's Dept., Nashville, 1977; sole practice Nashville, 1978—. State atty. re-election campaign Pres. Jimmy Carter, Tenn., 1980; state coordinator presdl. campaign Gary Hart, Tenn., 1984; candidate Tenn. Ho. Reps., Nashville, 1976; mem. exec. com. Ned McWherter gubernatorial campaign, Tenn., 1986. Mem. ABA, Tenn. Bar Assn., Nashville Bar Assn., Nat. Assn. Criminal Def. Lawyers, Tenn. Assn. Criminal Def. Lawyers, Assn. Trial Lawyers Am., Tenn. Trial Lawyers Assn. Democrat. Avocations: photography, sailing, outdoor sports. State civil litigation, Federal civil litigation, Criminal. Office: 213 3d Ave N Nashville TN 37201

BROTHERTON, W. T., JR., Justice, W.Va. Supreme Ct., Charleston. Judicial administration. Office: W Va Supreme Ct Office of the Supreme Ct Charleston WV 25305 *

BROTMAN, STANLEY SEYMOUR, judge; b. Vineland, N.J., July 27, 1924; s. Herman Nathaniel and Fanny (Melletz) B.; m. Suzanne M. Simon, Sept. 9, 1951; children: Richard A., Alison B. B.A., Yale U., 1947; LL.B., Harvard U., 1950. Bar: N.J. Sole practitioner Vineland, 1952-57; partner firm Shapiro, Brotman, Eisenstat & Capizola, Vineland, 1957-75; judge U.S. Dist. Ct. for Dist. of N.J., Camden, 1975—; mem. N.J. Bd. Bar Examiners, 1970-74. Chmn. editorial bd. N.J. State Bar Jour, 1969-74; contbr. articles to profl. jours. Trustee Newcomb Hosp., Vineland, 1953-68. Served with U.S. Army, 1943-45, 51-52. Winner Ames competition Harvard Law Sch., 1950. Fellow Am. Bar Found.; mem. ABA (ho. of dels. 1975-80, state del. 83—), Nat. Conf. Fed. Trial Judges (exec. com. 1984-87, chmn. elect 1986-87, chmn. 1987—), Am. Judicature Soc., Fed. Bar Assn., N.J. State Bar Assn. (pres. 1974-75), Cumberland County Bar Assn. (pres. 1969-70), Harvard Law Sch. Assn. N.J. (pres. 1974-75), Yale Alumni Assn., Am. Legion, Jewish War Vets. Clubs: Yale (Phila.); Harvard of N.J, B'nai B'rith, Masons, Shriners. Judicial administration. Office: 230 US Courthouse PO Box 1029 4th and Market Sts Camden NJ 08101

BROTMAN, STUART NEIL, management consultant, lawyer; b. Passaic, N.J., Dec. 5, 1952; s. William and Edith (Berkowitz) B.; m. Gloria Z. Greenfield, June 9, 1985; 1 child, Daniel Greenfield. BS, Northwestern U., 1974; MA, U. Wis., 1975; JD, U. Calif.-Berkeley, 1978. Bar: Calif. 1978. Spl. asst. to the asst. sec. of commerce for communications and info. Nat. Telecommunications and Info. Adminstrn., Washington, 1978-81; pres. Communication Strategies Inc., Cambridge, Mass., 1981-84, sr. mgmt. adv. communications, Lexington, Mass., 1984—; spl. counsel Verner, Liipfert, Bernhard, McPherson & Hand, Washington, 1985-86. Contbr. articles to profl. jours; contbg. editor Cable Communications, Kitchener, Ont., Can., 1983—. Mem. ABA, Fed. Communications Bar Assn., Cable TV Pub. Affairs Assn., Northwestern U. Alumni Assn. Democrat. Jewish. Communications, Computer, Entertainment.

BROUDE, RICHARD FREDERICK, lawyer, educator; b. Los Angeles, June 6, 1936; s. Leo Martin and Frances (Goldman) B.; m. Paula Louise Galnick, June 8, 1958; children: Julie Sue, James Matthew, Mark Allen. BS, Washington U., St Louis, 1957; JD, U. Chgo., 1961. Bar: Ill. 1961, Calif. 1971. Prof. law U. Nebr., Lincoln, 1966-69, Georgetown U., Washington, 1969-71; ptnr. Commons & Broude, Los Angeles, 1974-77, Irell & Manella, Los Angeles, 1977-80, Sidley & Austin, Los Angeles, 1980—; adj. prof. law U. So. Calif., Los Angeles, 1978—. Author: Reorganizations Under Chapter 11, 1986. Mem. ABA, American Law Institute, Calif. Bar Assn., Los Angeles County Bar Assn., Nat. Bankruptcy Conf. (conferee). Bankruptcy, Contracts commercial. Office: Sidley & Austin 2049 Century Park East Los Angeles CA 90067

BROUILLARD, PHILIP ANDRÉ, lawyer; b. Shirley, Mass., Feb. 18, 1956; s. Richard P. and Carmen H. (Houle) B. BA, U. N.H., 1978; JD, Georgetown U., 1981; LLM in Taxation, Boston U., 1986. Bar: N.H. 1984, U.S. Dist. Ct. N.H. 1984, U.S. Ct. Appeals (1st cir.) 1984. Ptnr. Brouillard & Brouillard, Laconia, N.H., 1981—. Mem. ABA (tax sect.), N.H. Bar Assn., Belknap County Bar Assn. Republican. Roman Catholic. Avocations: skiing, boating, running. General practice, Real property, Estate planning. Office: Brouillard & Brouillard 16 Academy St Laconia NH 03247

BROUILLETTE, GARY JOSEPH, lawyer; b. Hastings, Nebr., Oct. 28, 1940; s. Oscar O. and Frances E. (Jurgensmeier) B.; m. Connie M. Spelts, Sept. 2, 1963; children: Michelle M., Scott J. BA, U. Nebr., 1963, JD, 1966. Bar: Nebr. 1966, U.S. Dist. Ct. Nebr. 1966, Mo. 1970, U.S. Dist. Ct. (we. dist.) Mo. 1970, U.S. Supreme Ct. 1976. Assoc. Morrison, Hecker & Cozad, Kansas City, Mo., 1969-72; gen. counsel Mo. Pub. Service Co., Kansas City, 1972-75; ptnr. Jackson, Brouillette, Pohl & Kirley, P.C., Kansas City, 1975—; bd. dirs. 1st Nat. Bank Shawnee Mission, Fairway, Kans., Multiple Client Corps., Kansas City, Spelts of Nebr., Inc., Grand Island. Ward leader Jackson County (Mo.) Rep. Com., 1976, 80. Served to capt. USAF, 1966-69. Mem. Mo. Bar Assn., Nebr. Bar Assn., Kansas City Bar Assn., Kansas City Lawyers Assn. Presbyterian. Clubs: Carriage (bd. dirs. 1978-79), Univ. (Kansas City). Avocations: sailing, flying, tennis. General corporate, Probate, Personal income taxation. Home: 2208 Tomahawk Rd Mission Hills KS 66208 Office: Jackson Brouillette Pohl & Kirley PC 801 W 47th St Suite 400 Kansas City MO 64112

BROUSSARD, ALLEN E., state supreme court justice; b. Lake Charles, La., Apr. 13, 1929; m. Odessa Broussard; children: Eric, Craig, Keith. A.B. in Polit. Sci., U. Calif.-Berkeley, 1950, J.D., 1953. Bar: Calif. 1954. Sole practice San Francisco and Oakland, Calif., 1954-56; research atty. for presiding justice Dist. Ct. Appeals 1st Appellate Dist., 1st Div., 1953-54; sole practice 1956-59; assoc. Wilson, Metoyer & Sweeney, 1959-61; mem. firm Metoyer, Sweeney & Broussard, 1961-64; judge Oakland-Piedmont dist. Mcpl. Ct., 1964-75, Alameda County Superior Ct., Oakland, 1975-81; justice Calif. Supreme Ct., San Francisco, 1981—; mem. faculty Golden Gate Coll., San Francisco, 1971, U. San Francisco, 1972, Calif. Coll. Trial Judges, 1969-72, 74; advisor to exec. com. Jud. Council Calif.; v.p. governing com. Ctr. Jud. Edn. and Research; mem. council judges Nat. Council Crime and Delinquency. Vice pres. East Bay Big Bros. Am.; bd. dirs. Alameda County Community Found.; bd. dirs., past chmn. Oakland Men of Tomorrow, Black Bus. and Profl. Men's Service Orgn. Served with U.S. Army, 1954-56. Arthur Newhouse, Arthur Gold Tashiera scholar. Mem. Conf. Calif. Judges (exec. bd. 1970-71, pres. 1972-73), Nat. Bar Assn. (exec. bd. jud. council), Alameda County Bar Assn. (v.p.), Alameda County Criminal Cts. Bar Assn., Boalt Hall Alumni Assn. (past dir.), State Bar Calif., Phi Alpha Delta. Club: Charles Houston Law. Jurisprudence. Office: Calif Supreme Ct 4050 State Bldg 350 McAllister St San Francisco CA 94102 *

BROUSSARD, RICHARD C., lawyer; b. Lafayette, La., Apr. 1, 1949; s. Charles E. and Rose (Ashy) B.; m. Kathleen Alexis David, May 30, 1970; children: Rebecca, David, John. BS, U. Southwestern La., 1971; JD, La. State U., 1974. Law clk. to presiding justice La. Dist. Ct., Abbeville, 1974-75; from assoc. to ptnr. Domengeaux & Wright, Lafayette, La., 1975—; magistrate Youngsville (La.) Mcpl. Ct., 1982—. Mem. La. Intrastate Air Carrier Bd., 1977—; chmn. Lafayette Regional Airport Commn., 1985; bd. dirs. St. Cecelia Sch. Bd., Broussard, 1980-83, Acadiana Med. Research Found., Lafayette, 1981-86. Served to 1st lt. USAFR, 1972-78. Mem. La. Bar Assn. (ho. of dels. 1980), Lafayette Parish Bar Assn. (v.p. 1985-86, pres. 1986-87), La. Trial Lawyers Assn. (bd. dirs. 1984—). Democrat. Roman Catholic. Lodge: Lions. Avocations: aviation, hunting, skiing, scuba diving. Personal injury, Admiralty, Federal civil litigation. Home: Sky Ranch Youngsville LA 70592 Office: Domengeaux & Wright PO Box 3668 Lafayette LA 70502

BROVITZ, RICHARD STUART, lawyer; b. Rochester, N.Y., Aug. 20, 1951; s. Murray H. and Rifka R. (Rotenberg) B.; m. Joan F. Zarkower, Aug. 11, 1974; children—Justin, Jessica. B.S. cum laude with honors in Acctg., Sch. Mgmt., Syracuse U., 1973, M.S., 1973, J.D. cum laude, Coll. Law, 1976. Bar: N.Y. 1977, U.S. Dist. Ct. (we. dist.) N.Y. 1977, U.S. Tax Ct. 1979. Assoc. Wegman, Mayberry, Burgess & Feldstein, Rochester, 1976-78, Arnold R. Petralia, Rochester, 1978-79; assoc. Fix Spindelman, Turk, Himelein & Shukoff, Rochester, 1979-81, ptnr., 1982—. Pi Mu Epsilon math. scholar Syracuse U. Mem. ABA, N.Y. State Bar Assn., Monroe County Bar Assn. (chmn. Rochester life underwriters com.), Justinian Hon. Law Soc., Beta Gamma Sigma, Beta Alpha Psi, Phi Kappa Phi. Estate planning, Real property, General corporate. Office: Fix Spindelman Turk Himelein & Shukoff Two State St Rochester NY 14614

BROWER, CHARLES HARRY, lawyer; b. Jersey City, Feb. 1, 1948. BA, Rutgers U., 1970; JD, N.Y. Law Sch., 1975. Bar: N.J. 1975, N.Y. 1976, Hawaii 1977. Assoc. Fuchsberg & Fuchsberg, N.Y.C., 1975-77; sole practice Honolulu, 1977-85; ptnr. Brower & Brower, Honolulu, 1985—. Mem. ABA, Hawaii Bar Assn., Assn. Trial Lawyers Am., Hawaii C. of C. Office: Brower & Brower 1088 Bishop St #804 Honolulu HI 96813

BROWER, CHARLES NELSON, lawyer; b. Plainfield, N.J., June 5, 1935; s. Charles Hendrickson and Mary Elizabeth (Nelson) B.; children—Frederica Anne, Charles Hendrickson, II. B.A. cum laude, Harvard U., 1957, J.D., 1961; Fulbright scholar Rheinische Friedrich-Wilhelms-Universitaet, Bonn and Hochschule fuer Politik, Berlin, 1957-58; cert. Parker Sch. Comparative and Internat. Law, Columbia U., 1962. Bars: N.Y. 1962, D.C. 1970, U.S. Supreme Ct. 1967, U.S. Ct. Appeals (D.C. cir., 2d, 5th, 6th, 7th, 9th and 11th cirs.), U.S. Dist. Ct. (so. and ea. dists.) N.Y., U.S. Dist. Ct. (D.C. dist.). Assoc., ptnr. firm White & Case, N.Y.C., 1961-69; asst. legal adviser European Affairs, Dept. State, Washington, 1969-71, dep. legal adviser, 1971-73, acting legal adviser, 1973; ptnr. firm White & Case, Washington, 1973-84; mem. Iran-U.S. Claims Tribunal, The Hague, 1984-87, dep. spl. counsellor to the Pres., Washington, 1987—. Mem. Reagan Adminstrn. State Dept. Transition Team, 1980-81; mem. Republican Nat. Com. Adv. Council on Nat. Security and Internat. Affairs, 1977-80. Mem. Am. Soc. Internat. Law, ABA (chmn. sect. internat. law 1981-82, mem. ho. of. dels. 1982, 84—; bd. govs. 1985—), Assn. Bar City N.Y., Internat. Law Assn. (exec. com. Am. br.), Internat. Bar Assn., Am. Law Inst., German-Am. Lawyers Assn. Republican. Episcopalian. Clubs: Metropolitan, Chevy Chase. Private international, Public international, Federal civil litigation. Office: Office of The President 1600 Pennsylvania Ave NW Washington DC 20500

BROWN, ALBERT JACOB, lawyer; b. San Francisco, May 6, 1914; s. Charles and Rose (Lape) B.; m. Sylvia Esther Kotok, June 16, 1940; children: Katherine Ruth, David Julian. AB, U. Calif., Berkeley, 1937, JD, 1940. Bar: Calif. 1940, U.S. Dist. Ct. (no. dist.) Calif. 1940, U.S. Ct. Appeals (9th cir.) 1940. Sole practice Jackson, Calif., 1941-42; assoc. Pillsbury, Madison & Sutro, San Francisco, 1942-51, ptnr., 1951—. Bar: ABA, Calif. Bar Assn., San Francisco Bar Assn. Clubs: San Francisco Yacht, San Franciso Exchange. Securities, General corporate. Office: Pillsbury Madison & Sutro 225 Bush St San Francisco CA 94104 Home: 665 Sky-Hy Circle Lafayette CA 94549

BROWN, ANNA JAEGER, lawyer; b. Portland, Oreg., July 26, 1952; d. Adalbert and Margarete (Kriegs) Jaeger; m. Paul Brown, Dec. 22, 1977. Student, Lewis & Clark Coll., 1970-72, JD, 1980; BS in Adminsrtn. Justice, Portland State U., 1975. Bar: Oreg. 1980, U.S. Dist. Ct. Oreg. 1980. Police dispatcher City of Portland, 1975-77; assoc. Bullivant, Houser, Bailey, Pendergrass & Hoffman, Portland, 1980-86; ptnr. Bullivnat, Houser, Bailey, Hanna, Pendergrass, Hoffman, O'Connell & Goyak, Portland, 1986—; speaker ins. law presentations, 1983—. Bd. regents St. Mary's Acad., Portland, 1985—. Mem. ABA (chmn. state membership com. 1985—, vice chmn. govt. liability 1986—), Oreg. Bar Assn. (function com. 1982-86, chmn. com. 1985-86), Multnomah Bar Assn. (cir. ct. liaison 1986—, arbitrator and hearings officer 1985—), Oreg. Assn. Def. Counsel. Democrat. Roman Catholic. Avocations: skiing, travel. Civil rights, Insurance, State civil litigation. Home: 37 Walking Woods Dr Lake Oswego OR 97034 Office: Bullivant Houser Bailey et al 1211 SW 5th Ave Suite 1400 POrtland OR 97204

BROWN, BONNIE MARYETTA, lawyer; b. North Plainfield, N.J., Oct. 31, 1953; d. Robert Jeffrey and Diana (Parket) B. AB, Washington U., St. Louis, 1975; JD, U. Louisville, 1978. Bar: Ky. 1978, U.S. Dist. Ct. (we. dist.) Ky. 1979. Sole practice Louisville, Ky., 1978—; lectr. various profl., ednl., governmental and civic groups; cons. marital rape. Editor Ky. Appellate Handbook, 1985; contbr. articles to profl. jours. Vol. legal panel Ky. Civil Liberties Union, Louisville, 1984—; legis. coordinator marital rape, mem. steering com. Ky. Coalition Against Rape and Sexual Assault, 1982—, adv. bd., vol. adv. Louisville RAPE Relief Ctr., 1975—. Recipient Cert. Spl. Recognition RAPE Relief Ctr., 1980, Cert. Outstanding Contbn. Louisville YWCA, 1983, Cert. Appreciation James Graham Brown Cancer Ctr., 1984, Decade of Service award YWCA/RAPE Relief Ctr., 1985. Fellow Louisville Ballet Guild; mem. ABA (family law sect.), Ky. Bar Assn. (family law sect., Continuing Legal Edn. award 1981), Louisville Bar Assn. (liaison to mental health sect., organizer marital rape seminar, chmn. family law sect.), Nat. Health Lawyers Assn. Republican. Club: Jaguar Drivers (Louisville) (chmn. membership 1985-86). Avocations: art, basketball fan, tennis. Family and matrimonial, State civil litigation, Health. Office: 100 N 6th St Burdorf Bldg Suite 400 Louisville KY 40202

BROWN, BOYCE REID, JR., lawyer; b. Shelby, N.C., Sept. 27, 1942; s. Boyce Reid and Ola Elizabeth (Flynn) B.; Boyce R. III, Nicholas Montgomery. BA in Internat. Studies, U. N.C., 1966; JD, Harvard U., 1969. Bar: Hawaii 1970, U.S. Dist. Ct. Hawaii 1970, U.S. Ct. Appeals (9th cir.) 1975, U.S. Supreme Ct. 1976. Assoc. Moore, Torkildson & Schulze, Honolulu, 1969-72; ptnr. Mattoch, Kemper & Brown, Honolulu, 1972-75, Brown & Bettencourt, Honolulu, 1975-82, Brown & Johnston, Honolulu, 1982-86, Brown, Johnston and Day, Honolulu, 1986—; adj. prof. U. Hawaii, Honolulu. Mem. ABA, Hawaii Bar Assn. (Justice award), Phi Beta Kappa. Avocation: sailing. Federal civil litigation, State civil litigation, Real property. Office: Brown Johnston and Day 222 Merchant St Honolulu HI 96813

BROWN, BRUCE ALLEN, lawyer; b. Chgo., Oct. 10, 1946; s. Raymond A. and Anne (Stevenson) B.; m. Carol Anfinson, Nov. 17, 1979. BA, U. Ill., 1968, JD, 1973. Bar: Ill. 1973, U.S. Dist. Ct. (no. dist.) Ill. 1973, U.S. Dist. Ct. (ea. dist.) Wis. 1983. Assoc. Brady, McQueen, et al, Elgin, Ill., 1973-75; from assoc. to ptnr. Goldsmith, Thelin, Schiller & Dickson, Aurora, Ill., 1975—. Mem. com. United Way, Aurora, 1978—. Served to sgt. U.S. Army, 1968-70. Mem. ABA, Ill. Bar Assn., Kane County Bar Assn., Aurora C. of C. (com. 1978—). Republican. Lodge: Kiwanis (local v.p., local pres. 1984—). Consumer commercial, Real property, Contracts commercial. Office: Goldsmith Thelin Schiller & Dickson PO Box 1485 Aurora IL 60507

BROWN, C. HAROLD, lawyer; b. Mendenhall, Ms., July 28, 1931; children: Tracey Gwen, Terry Lynne, Allison Anne, Harold Allen. BA, Vanderbilt U., 1957; LLB, U. Tex., 1960. Bar: Tex. 1960. Sr. ptnr. Wynn, Brown, Mack, Renfro & Thompson, Ft. Worth, 1960—; pres. A.J. and Jessie Duncan Found.; bd. dirs. State Auto and Casualty Underwriters, Inc. Chmn. Ft. Worth Civil Service Commn.; chmn. bd. dirs. Tarrant County Conv. Ctr., 1980; mem. Com. for Greater Tarrant County; past bd. dirs. Ft. Worth Council Camp Fire Girls; bd. dirs. Nat. Com. for Adoption, Tex. Assn. Licensed Children's Services, sec., Edna Gladney Home, exec. com.; mgr. campaign R.M. Stovall for Mayor of Ft. Worth, 1969, 71, 73, Richard T. Andersen for Tarrant County Commr., 1972, 76, 80, 84; former deacon Univ. Christian Ch., Ft. Worth. Served with U.S. Army, 1953-55. Recipient Carnegie Hero Cert. Carnegie Hero Fund Commn., 1972; named Outstanding Young Texan, 1976. Fellow Tex. Bar Found., Southwestern Legal Found.; mem. ABA, Tex. Bar Assn., Ft. Worth-Tarrant County Bar Assn. (bd. dirs. family law sect. 1978-80, family law sect.), Ft. Worth Jr. Bar Assn. (pres. 1963), Am. Acad. Hosp. Attys., Nat. Health Lawyers Assn., Badge and Shield, Vanderbilt U. Alumni Assn. (pres. 1966-67), Alpha Tau Omega, Phi Delta Phi. Clubs: Ridotto (pres. 1974), Petroleum, River Crest Country, City, Steeplechase, Headliners, Nat. Commodore (admiral). Lodges: Rotary, Masons, Shriners, Jesters. General corporate, General practice, Probate. Office: Wynn Brown Mack Renfro & Thompson 201 Main St #1800 Fort Worth TX 76102-6976

BROWN, CHARLES ALAN, lawyer; b. Denver, Aug. 11, 1952; s. Claerence Charles and Thelma May (Campbell) B.;. BS, Lewis-Clark State Coll., 1974; JD, U. Idaho, 1977. Bar: Idaho 1977, U.S. Dist. Ct. Idaho 1977, U.S. Supreme Ct. 1981. Assoc. Aherin & Rice, Lewiston, Idaho, 1977-80; ptnr. Ahcrin, Rice & Brown, Lewiston, 1980—; lectr. on libel and 1st Amendment. Mem. ABA, Idaho Bar Assn., Clearwater Bar Assn., Assn. Trial Lawyers Am., Idaho Trial Lawyers Assn., Nat. Coll. Advocacy, Ct. Practice Inst., Nat. Inst. Trial Advocacy, Lewis-Clark State Coll. Alumni Assn. (pres. 1984-85). Avocations: skiing, reading, piano, writing. Libel, State civil litigation, Criminal. Home: 821 Grelle Dr Lewiston ID 83501 Office: Aherin Rice & Brown PO Drawer 698 Lewiston ID 83501

BROWN, CHARLES GAILEY, state attorney general; b. Mansfield, Ohio, June 6, 1950; s. Charles Gailey and Emily (Campbell) B.; m. Alice Hypes, Sept. 12, 1981 (div. May 1985); 1 child, Tara Jeanne. B.A., Denison U., 1971; J.D., Yale U., 1975. Bar: W.Va. Staff atty. FTC, Washington, 1975-78; dep. atty. gen. State of W.Va., Charleston, 1978-82, atty. gen., 1985—; sole practice law Charleston, 1982-85. Named Democrat of Yr., W.Va. Young Dems., 1985. Mem. Assn. Trial Lawyers Am., W.Va. State Bar, Phi Beta Kappa. Episcopalian. Avocations: jogging; baseball; reading. Criminal. Home: 4110 Venable Ave Charleston WV 25304 Office: Atty Gen's Office State Capitol Charleston WV 25305 *

BROWN, CHARLES STUART, state supreme court justice; b. Freedom, Wyo., June 30, 1918; s. Charles William and Julia Teola (Rainey) B.; m. Jane Hurst, Aug. 6, 1941; children: Ann (Mrs. Paul Christensen), Julia (Mrs. Dan Gibson), James Stuart, Colleen (Mrs. Rick Perkins), Patricia (Mrs. John Evans), Robert William, Helen (Mrs. Timothy Curry), Virginia (Mrs. John Evans). B.S., Utah State U., 1943; J.D., U. Utah, 1950. Bar: Wyo. 1950, Utah 1950. Prin. Freedom Elem. Sch., 1946-47; individual practice law Kemmerer, Wyo., 1950-59; pros. atty. Lincoln County, 1959-65; judge 3d Jud. Dist. Wyo. Dist. Ct., Kemmerer, 1965-81; chief justice Wyo. State Supreme Ct., Cheyenne, 1981—; asso. solicitor Dept. Interior, Washington, 1961-62. Author: Wyoming Ranch and Farm Law, 1959. Served to col. AUS, 1942-46. Office: Supreme Ct Bldg Cheyenne WY 82001 *

BROWN, CLIFFORD F., state supreme ct. justice; b. Bronson Twp. Norwalk, Ohio, Jan. 21, 1916; s. Ignatius A. B.; m. Katherine Brown; adopted children—Charles, Margaret (Mrs. David Kramb), Sheila, Ann (Mrs. Leonard Playko, Jr.). A.B. magna cum laude, U. Notre Dame, 1936, LL.B. cum laude, 1938. Bar: Ohio bar 1938, Mich. bar 1938. Practice law Norwalk, Ohio, 1938-64; judge Huron County Ct., 1958-65, Ohio Ct. Appeals, 1965-81; asso. justice Ohio State Supreme Ct., Columbus, 1981-87. Served with U.S. Army, World War II. Mem. Am. Bar Assn., Ohio State Bar Assn., Lucas County Bar Assn. Democrat. Clubs: Kiwanis, KC, Torch. Jurisprudence. Home: 135 State Rt 61 E Norwalk OH 44857

BROWN, COLIN W(EGAND), diversified company executive, lawyer; b. Port Jefferson, N.Y., Mar. 26, 1949; s. Keirn C. and Jane (Schuhl) B.; m. Cynthia Porter, Aug. 21, 1971; children—Courtney, Alec. B.A., Williams Coll., 1971; J.D., Duke U., 1974. Bar: N.Y. 1975, N.C. 1983. Assoc. Simpson Thacher & Bartlett, N.Y.C., 1974-81; sr. v.p.-gen. counsel Cannon Mills Co., Kannapolis, N.C., 1981-82; v.p., gen. counsel Fuqua Industries, Inc., Atlanta, 1982—. Mem. ABA, Am. Corp. Counsel Assn. (pres. Ga. chpt.). General corporate, Securities, Mergers and acquisitions. Home: 400 King Rd NW Atlanta GA 30342 Office: 4900 Georgia-Pacific Ctr Atlanta GA 30303

BROWN, DAVID EDWARD, lawyer; b. Hyannis, Mass., Dec. 28, 1945; s. Edward Lansing and Barbara (Benjamin) B.; m. Virginia Colby Robinson, Sept. 12, 1964; children—Rebecca, Christopher. B.A., U. N.C., 1967; J.D., Syracuse U., 1970. Bar: N.Y. 1971, U.S. Dist. Ct. (we. dist.) N.Y. 1972, U.S. Dist. Ct. (no. dist.) N.Y. 1982, Mass. 1986. Assoc. Woods, Oviatt, Gilman, Sturman & Clarke, Rochester, N.Y., 1970-73, Martin, Clearwater & Bell, Syracuse, 1973-75; ptnr. Martin, Ganotis & Brown, P.C., Syracuse, 1975-78, mem., v.p., 1979—. Mem. Internat. Assn. Ins. Counsel, Am. Bd. Profl. Liability Attys., ABA, N.Y. State Bar Assn. Republican. Episcopalian. State civil litigation, Personal injury, Federal civil litigation. Office: Martin Ganotis & Brown 499 S Warren St Syracuse NY 13202

BROWN, DON C., lawyer; b. Los Angeles, June 25, 1927; s. Marvin C. and Vera C. (Snyder) B.; m. Veda Matney, Dec. 6, 1935. J.D., Southwestern U., 1954. Bar: Calif. 1955, U.S. Supreme Ct. 1979. Assoc. Spray, Gould & Bowers, Los Angeles, 1956-60; sr. ptnr. Thompson & Colgate, Riverside, Calif., 1960—; mem. faculty Hastings Coll. Law, San Francisco, 1978. Served with USNR, 1944-45. Fellow Am. Coll. Trial Lawyers, Internat. Acad. Trial Lawyers (pres. 1981-82), Am. Bd. Trial Advocates (diplomate), Calif. Trial Lawyers Assn. (Lawyer of Yr. 1981); mem. Internat. Soc. Barristers. Clubs: Victoria; Catalina Island Yacht; Balboa Bay. State civil litigation, Personal injury. Office: PO Box 1299 Riverside CA 92502

BROWN, DONALD, lawyer; b. Phila., Aug. 22, 1932; s. Paul and Sarah (Magil) B.; m. Bernice Katz, May 15, 1960; children: Harold Mordechai, Louis Joseph, Seth Michael. B.A., Antioch Coll., 1954; J.D., Yale U., 1957.

Bar: Pa. 1958. Assoc. mem. firm Fox, Rothschild, O'Brien & Frankel, Phila., 1958-62; ptnr. Fox, Rothschild, O'Brien & Frankel, 1963—, mng. ptnr., 1979-85. Bd. dirs. Am. Technion Soc., Phila., Bezalel Acad. Arts and Design. Served with AUS, 1957-58. Mem. Am. Arbitration Assn. (nat. bd. 1966-67), ABA (sect. draftsman com. supplement atty. gen.'s report on antitrust laws), Pa. Bar Assn., Phila. Bar Assn., Am. Judicature Soc. Clubs: Radnor Country, Peale, Yale, B'nai B'rith. Contracts commercial, General corporate, Antitrust. Home: 523 Howe Rd Merion PA 19066 Office: 2000 Market St 10th Floor Philadelphia PA 19103

BROWN, DONALD ARTHUR, lawyer; b. Washington, Feb. 1, 1929; s. Louis S. and Rose (Kliban) B.; m. Ann Winkelman, July 13, 1959; children: Cathy, Laura. B.A. in Econs., George Washington U., 1949, LL.B. (Case Club oral argument competition winner), 1952, LL.M., 1958. Bar: D.C. 1952. Sr. partner Brown, Gildenhorn & Jacobs (and predecessor), Washington, 1955—; mem. faculty Practising Law Inst.; faculty Harvard U. Sch. Bus., 1984-87, Yale U. Sch. Mgmt., 1986; guest lectr. Am. U., Nat. Assn. Real Estate Counselors, Nat. Assn. Real Estate Investors; pres., sec. JBG Constrn., Inc.; partner JBG Assos.; v.p., treas. JBG Properties, Inc.; trustee, gen. counsel Nat. Bank Rosslyn, Arlington, Va.; mem. minority enterprises com. SBA; finance com. Housing Devel. Corp.; mem. Model Cities Com. D.C. Co-author: Understanding Real Estate Investments, 1967; Contbr. articles to profl. jours. Exec. bd. Forest Hills Citizens Assn.; bd. dirs. D.C. Jr. C. of C.; mem. Friends Kennedy Center, Friends Corcoran Gallery, Big Bros. Orgn. D.C.; bd. dirs. Washington Area Tennis Patrons Found., 1964—, pres., 1973-75, Fed. city council; trustee Woodley House, psychiat. half-way house, Washington, 1973—, pres. bd. dirs., 1975—; trustee U. D.C., Sidwell Friends Sch.; mem. art adv. council Washington Conv. Ctr. com. D.C. Conv. Ctr. Served as officer USNR, 1952-55. Mem. ABA, Fed. Bar Assn., D.C. Bar Assn., Washington Bd. Realtors (chmn. lawyer-realtor liaison com. 1972, chmn. investment property com. 1970), Economics Club of Washington. Jewish (bd. mgrs. congregation 1962, treas. 1965). Club: Georgetown (Washington). Real property. Home: 3005 Audubon Terr NW Washington DC 20008 Office: Brown Gildenhorn & Jacobs 1250 Connecticut Ave NW Washington DC 20036

BROWN, DONALD WESLEY, lawyer; b. Cleve., Jan. 2, 1953; s. Lloyd Elton Brown and Nancy Jeanne Hudson. AB summa cum laude, Ohio U., 1975; JD, Yale U., 1978. Bar: Calif. 1978, U.S. Dist. Ct. (no. dist.) Calif. 1978. Assoc. Brobeck, Phleger & Harrison, San Francisco, 1978-85, ptnr., 1985—. Democrat. Federal civil litigation, State civil litigation. Office: Brobeck Phleger & Harrison Spear St Tower One Market Plaza San Francisco CA 94105 Home: 1 Roble Rd Berkeley CA 94705

BROWN, EARL TERRY, lawyer; b. Birmingham, Ala., Apr. 29, 1953; s. Earl T. and Betty Ann (Shaffield) B.; m. Jean Williams, Oct. 1, 1977; children: Meredith Patricia, Caroline Townson. BA, U. Ala., 1975, JD, 1978. Bar: Ala. 1978, U.S. Dist. Ct. (no., mid. and so. dists.) Ala. 1978, U.S. Supreme Ct. 1982, U.S. Ct. Appeals (11th cir.). Law clk. to presiding justice Ala. Supreme Ct., Montgomery, 1978-79; from assoc. to ptnr. Copeland, Franco, Screws & Gill, Montgomery, 1979—. Contbr. articles to profl. jours. Mem. First Bapt. Ch. of Montgomery, 1978—; advisor Safeplace for Children, Montgomery, 1986—; bd. dirs. Group Homes, Inc., Montgomery, 1985—. Mem. Fed. Bar Assn., Ala. Bar Assn. (exec. bd. 1985-86, sec. bankruptcy and comml. law sect. 1986—), Montgomery County Bar Assn., Supreme Ct. Hist. Soc., Young Mens Bus. Club. Baptist. Bankruptcy, State civil litigation, Federal civil litigation. Office: Copeland Franco Screws & Gill 444 S Perry Montgomery AL 36101

BROWN, EDWARD GEORGE, bank executive, lawyer; b. Wilkinsburg, Pa., Feb. 18, 1947; s. George Edward and Cora Rose (Ricci) B.; m. Jean Stewart, Feb. 27, 1970; 1 child, Jason. BS, U. Pitts., 1969, JD, 1977. Bar: Pa. 1977, U.S. Dist. Ct. (we. dist.) Pa. 1977. Atty. Dollar Bank, Pitts., 1977-78, asst. v.p., 1978-80, v.p., 1980-85, sr. v.p., 1985—. Chmn. Oakmont Reps., Pa. Mem. ABA, Pa. Bar Assn., Allegheny County Bar Assn. Banking, General corporate, Computer. Office: Dollar Bank 3 Gateway Ctr 9W Pittsburgh PA 15222

BROWN, EDWIN LEWIS, JR., lawyer; b. Parker, S.D., Mar. 15, 1903; s. Edwin Lewis and Lucy Elizabeth (Lowenberg) B.; m. Faye Hulbert, May 8, 1926; children—Betty Lou Brown Trainer, Lewis Charles. J.D., U. Nebr., 1926. Bar: Nebr. bar 1926, Ill. bar 1933, U.S. Supreme Ct. bar 1960. Practiced in Chgo., 1933-85; partner firm Brown, Cook, Hanson, 1950-85; Mem. Nat. Conf. Lawyers and Collection Agys., 1964-74. Mem. wills and bequests com. Shriners Crippled Children's Hosp., Chgo.; pres. H.P. & S. Crowell Found. Named Time mag.-NADRA Man of Year, 1974. Mem. ABA, Ill. Bar Assn. (sr. counsellor 1976), Chgo. Bar Assn., Am. Judicature Soc., Comml. Law League Am. (pres. 1963-64), Comml. Law Found. (treas. 1969-74), Nat. Conf. Bar Presidents, Phi Alpha Delta. Republican. Presbyterian. Lodges: Masons (32 deg.), K.T, Shriners. Clubs: Union League (Chgo.); Westmoreland Country (Wilmette, Ill.); Lighthouse Point (Fla.) Yacht and Racquet. Home: 2617 Hurd Ave Evanston IL 60201 Office: 135 S LaSalle St Chicago IL 60603 Office: 2530 Crawford Ave Evanston IL 60201

BROWN, ELAINE MARIE BECHER, judge; b. Huntingburg, Ind., Feb. 8, 1954; d. Edwin Leo and Valeria Emma (Senninger) Becher; m. William Marshall Brown, May 10, 1975; 1 child, Marissa Liane. BS, Ind. U., 1976, JD, 1982. Bar: Ind. 1982, U.S. Dist. Ct. (so. dist.) Ind. 1982. Tchr. Greater Jasper (Ind.) Sch. Corp., 1976-79; assoc. Thom and DeMotte, Jasper, 1982-86; judge Dubois Superior Ct., Jasper, 1986—; tchr. Vincennes U., Jasper, 1983—. Life mem. Ferdinand (Ind.) Community Ctr.; mem. adv. bd. Dubois County Jail, 1986. Mem. ABA, Ind. State Bar Assn., Dubois County Bar Assn (pres. 1985, v.p. 1984, sec. 1983), Dubois County Rep. Women's Club. Roman Catholic. Avocations: water sports, running. Judicial administration, Family and matrimonial, Criminal. Home: Rural Rt 3 Box 254 Ferdinand IN 47532 Office: Dubois Superior Ct Courthouse Jasper IN 47546

BROWN, ERIC STEVEN, lawyer; b. Cleve., Aug. 21, 1953; s. Carl Jacob and Nita Lois (Bloom) B.; m. Marilyn Sue Epstein, Aug. 26, 1973; children: Beryl Judith, Daryn Michele. Student, Denison U., 1971-72; BA, Cleve. State U., 1975; JD, Cleve.-Marshall Law Sch., 1979. Bar: Ohio 1979, U.S. Dist. Ct. (no. dist.) Ohio 1979. Assoc. Yulish, Twohig & Assocs. Co. L.P.A., Cleve., 1979-85; sole practice Beachwood, Ohio, 1985—; gen. counsel Max Inc., Cleve., 1979—, Rivco Realty and Mgmt. Co. Inc., 1979—; impartial hearing officer Cuyahoga Spl. Edn. Services Ctr., Cleve., 1979—. Mem. Bd. Edn. Mayfield City (Ohio) Sch. Dist., pres. 1983-85, v.p. 1980-82; mem. Mayfield Area Recreation Council, Mayfield Ednl. Excellence Found., 1986—, Mayfield Sch. Acad. Boosters Club (charter) 1986; pres. Assn. of Sch. Bds. in Cuyahoga County, 1984. Named to All-Ohio Sch. Bd., Ohio Sch. Bds. Assn., 1986, All- Region Sch. Bd., 1986. Mem. ABA, Ohio Bar Assn., Cleve. Bar Assn., Cuyahoga County Bar Assn. (chmn. young lawyer sect. 1980-83, trustee 1983—, treas. 1986—), Cuyahoga Criminal Def. Lawyers Assn., Ohio Council of Sch. Bd. Attys., Nat. Sch. Bds. Assn. (council of attys.). Democrat. Jewish. Club: The Citizens League (Cleve.). Small business consulting and litigation, Real property, Education and schools. Home: 6565 Ridgebury Blvd Mayfield Heights OH 44124 Office: 24200 Chagrin Blvd Suite 60 Beachwood OH 44122

BROWN, FRANCIS CABELL, JR., lawyer; b. Washington, Jan. 6, 1936; s. Francis Cabell and Helen Montrose (Howes) B.; m. Nancy Adeline Leitzow, June 18, 1960; children—Caroline Montrose, Francis Cabell III, James Herman Loughborough, Jennifer Nancy. B.A., Princeton, 1958; LL.B., Harvard, 1961. Bar: N.Y. bar 1962, D.C. bar 1964. Assoc. firm White & Case, N.Y.C., 1961-64, 67, Paris, 1964-65, Brussels, 1966; spl. asst. to asst. atty. gen. U.S. Dept. Justice, Washington, 1968; practice law N.Y.C., 1969—. Bd. regents (emeritus) Georgetown U. Clubs: Union League (N.Y.C.), University (N.Y.C.); Travellers (Paris). General corporate, Private international. Home: 520 E 86th St New York NY 10028 Office: 315 Park Ave S New York NY 10010-3607

BROWN, FRANK EUGENE, JR., lawyer; b. Okemah, Okla., May 30, 1941; s. Frank Eugene and Mary Lois (Knie) B.; m. Gail Hart, Sept. 30, 1967; children—Christopher Matthew, Meredith Claire. B.A. in Physics Engring., Washington and Lee U., 1963. J.D. summa cum laude, 1965. Bar: Va. 1965, U.S. Dist. Ct. (ea. and we. dists.) Va. 1965, U.S. Supreme Ct. 1971, U.S. Ct. Appeals (4th cir.) 1976, U.S. Ct. Appeals (D.C. cir.) 1978. Law clk. to chief judge U.S. Dist. Ct. (we. dist.) Va., Roanoke, 1965-66; teaching asst. Washington and Lee Sch. Law, Lexington, Va., 1965-66; ptnr. Adams, Porter, Radigan & Mays, Arlington, Va., 1970-74, Barham, Radigan, Suiters & Brown, P.C., Arlington, 1974-86, ptnr. Tolbert, Smith, Fitzgerald & Stackhouse, 1986—; adj. prof. Potomac Sch. Law, Washington, 1974-75. Mem. Christian social relations com. St. Paul's Episc. Ch., Alexandria, Va., 1981-82; trustee Randolph-Macon Acad., Front Royal, Va., Served to capt. USAF, 1966-70. Mem. Va. State Bar (10th dist. grievance com. 1976-79), Va. Bar Assn. (profl. responsibility com. 1981—), Phi Beta Kappa, Order of Coif, Omicron Delta Kappa, Sigma Phi Epsilon, Phi Alpha Delta. Republican. State civil litigation, Federal civil litigation, Contracts commercial. Home: 504 Woodland Terr Alexandria VA 22302 Office: Tolbert Smith Fitzgerald & Stackhouse 2300 9th St S Arlington VA 22204

BROWN, FRED GRANT, lawyer; b. Klamath Falls, Oreg., June 3, 1953; s. Grant Fred and Lois May (Hunt) B.; m. Ann Stoloff, Nov. 30, 1985. BS, Northwest Christian Coll., 1976, U. Oreg., 1976; JD, U. Oreg., 1980. Bar: Oreg. 1981, U.S. Dist. Ct. Oreg. 1982, Alaska 1985. Sole practice Oregon, Alaska, 1981—; hearing officer worker compensation Alaska Dept. Labor, Fairbanks, 1984—; v.p. bd. dirs. Nu-Health Inc., Klamath Falls; pres. bd. dirs. No. Alaska Health Resources Assn., Fairbanks. Campaign cons. various Rep. Candidates, Oregon, Alaska, 1976—; precinct chmn. Rep. Com., Klamath Falls, 1982-84. Mem. ABA, Oreg. Bar Assn., Alaska Bar Assn., Nat. Trial Lawyers Assn., Alaska Pub. Employees Assn. (negotiation), local C. of C. Baptist. Labor, Personal injury, Workers' compensation. Office: Alaska Dept of Labor 675 7th Ave Sta J Fairbanks AK 99701

BROWN, GARRETT E., JR., lawyer; b. Orange, N.J. B.A., Lafayette Coll.; J.D., Duke U. Bar: D.C., N.J. Law clk. N.J. Supreme Ct.; asst. U.S. atty. Dist. of N.J., exec. asst. U.S. atty.; ptnr. Stryker, Tams & Dill; mem. faculty Practicing Law Inst., N.Y.C.; gen. counsel U.S. Govt. Printing Office, Washington, 1981-84; chief legal officer Maritime Adminstrn., U.S. Dept. Transp., Washington, 1984-85, acting dep. maritime adminstr. 1985-86; judge U.S. Dist. Ct. N.J., Trenton, 1986— mem. Maritime Subsidy Bd.; lectr. in field. Issue editor Antitrust Law Jour.; editor: (handbook) Institute of Continuing Legal Education. Recipient Meritorious Service award U.S. Atty. Gen., Pub. Printer's Disting. Service medal. Mem. Am. Arbitration Assn. (panel of arbitrators), ABA, Fed. Bar Assn., N.J. State Bar Assn., D.C. Bar Assn., Union County Bar Assn. (N.J.). Government contracts and claims. Office: US Dist Ct NJ 402 E State St PO Box 515 Trenton NJ 08603

BROWN, GARY ROSS, lawyer, magistrate; b. Denver, Nov. 11, 1947; s. F. Ross and Leona R. (Temple) B.; m. Kelly Ann Simms, May 31, 1969; children—Julie Marie, Phillip Ross. B.A., Lewis and Clark Coll., 1969; J.D., U. Denver, 1973. Bar: Colo. 1973, U.S. Dist. Ct. Colo. 1973. Assoc. Clarence L. Bartholic, Denver, 1973-75; sole practice, Denver and Estes Park, Colo., 1975—; U.S. magistrate U.S. Dist. Ct. Colo. with specific jurisdiction over Rocky Mountain Nat. Park, 1980—; judge adv. gen. Colo. Dept. Military Affairs. Served with Army N.G., 1969—. Named Soldier of Yr., Army N.G., 1975. Mem. ABA, Colo. Bar Assn., Denver County Bar Assn., Larimer County Bar Assn. Presbyterian. Club: Masons (presiding officer Rocky Mountain Consistory). Real property, Probate, Judicial administration.

BROWN, GENE L., lawyer; b. Hillsboro, Oreg., Feb. 2, 1921; s. Richard D. Brown and Lelia L. (VanKirk) Richey; m. Roberta Jean Horton, Dec. 10, 1943; children: Becky, Bonnie, Dana. BA, U. Oreg., 1942, LLB, 1948. Bar: Oreg. 1948, U.S. Dist. Ct. Oreg. 1949, U.S. Ct. Appeals (9th cir.) 1965, U.S. Tax Ct. 1969. Ptnr. Brown & Myrick, Grants Pass, Oreg., 1948-52, Brown, Coulter & Myrick, Grants Pass, 1952-56, Brown & Smith, Grants Pass, 1956-62, Brown, Smith & Robinson, Grants Pass, 1962-70, Brown, Hughes, Bird & Lane, Grants Pass, 1970—; sec., bd. dirs. Rogue Valley Physicians Service, Medford, Oreg., 1954—, Richard's Food Ctrs. Inc., Grant Pass, 1975—; pres. Oreg.-Can. Mining Co., Grants Pass, 1970—. Senator Oreg. Senate, Salem, 1952-56; past pres., trustee Southern Oreg. Coll. Found., Ashland, 1955-85. Served to maj. U.S. Army, 1943-46, ETO. Fellow Am. Coll. Probate Counsel; mem. Oreg. Bar Assn. Republican. Presbyterian. Probate, Health, General mining law. Home: 304 NW Savage St Grants Pass OR 97526 Office: Brown Hughes Bird & Lane 612 NW Fifth St Grants Pass OR 97526

BROWN, GERALDINE REED, lawyer; b. Los Angeles, Feb. 18, 1947; d. William Penn and Alberta Vernice (Coleman) Reed; m. Ronald Wellington Brown, Aug. 20, 1972; children—Kimberly Diana, Michael David. B.A. summa cum laude, Fisk U., 1968; J.D., Harvard U., 1971, M.B.A., 1973. Bar: N.Y. 1974, U.S. Dist. Ct. (so. and ea. dists.) N.Y. 1974, U.S. Ct. Appeals (2d cir.) 1974, U.S. Supreme Ct. 1977. Assoc. firm White & Case, N.Y.C., 1973-78; atty. J.C. Penney Co., Inc., N.Y.C., 1978—. Bd. dirs. Council Concerned Black Execs., N.Y.C., 1977—, Studio Mus. in Harlem, N.Y.C., 1980-81; mem. Montclair Devel. Bd., ad hoc com. on Montclair Econ. Devel. Corp. Mem. Women's Econ. Roundtable, Harvard Bus. Sch. Club, Harvard Law Sch. Assn., Coalition 100 Black Women, ABA (several coms. sect. corp., banking and bus. law, sect. internat. law and practice), Assn. Bar City N.Y. (corp. law com. 1978-81), N.Y. County Lawyers Assn. (corp. law com.), N.Y. State Bar Assn. (exec. com. of corp. counsel sect., chmn. com. on SEC, fin., corp. law and governance), Harvard Bus. Sch. Black Alumni Assn., Harvard Law Sch. Black Alumni Assn., Phi Beta Kappa, Delta Sigma Theta (chair social action com. Montclair alumnae chpt., chair bylaw com., parlimentarian). Club: Harvard (N.Y.C.). General corporate, Securities, Contracts commercial. Home: 180 Union St Montclair NJ 07042 Office: JC Penney Co Inc 1301 Ave of Americas New York NY 10019

BROWN, G(LENN) WILLIAM, JR., lawyer; b. Waynesville, N.C., June 9, 1955; s. Glenn William Sr. and Evelyn Myralyn (Davis) B.; m. Amy Margaret Moss, Apr. 14, 1984. BS in Biology and Polit. Sci., MIT, 1977; JD, Duke U., 1980. Bar: N.Y. 1981. Assoc. Donovan Leisure Newton & Irvine, N.Y.C., 1980-84, Sidley & Austin, N.Y.C., 1984—. Mem. ABA, Assn. of Bar of City of N.Y. (uniform state laws com.). Democrat. Mem. Dutch Reform Ch. General corporate, Private international, Securities. Home: 171 State St Brooklyn Heights NY 11201 Office: Sidley & Austin 520 Madison Ave New York NY 10022

BROWN, HANK, congressman; b. Denver, Feb. 12, 1940; s. Harry W. and Anna M. (Hanks) B.; m. Nana Morrison, Aug. 27, 1967; children: Harry, Christy, Lori. BS, U. Colo., 1961, JD, 1969; LLM, George Washington U., 1986, M in Tax Law, 1986. Bar: Colo. 1969. Tax acct. Arthur Andersen, 1967-68; asst. pres. Monfort of Colo., Inc., Greeley, 1969-70; corp. counsel Monfort of Colo., Inc., 1970-71; v.p. Monfort Food Distbg., 1971-72, v.p. corp. devel., 1973-75, v.p. internat. ops., 1975-78, v.p. lamb div., 1978-80; mem. 97th-100th Congresses from Colo. 4th dist.; mem. Colo. State Senate, 1972-76, asst. majority leader, 1974-76. Served with U.S. Navy, 1962-66. Decorated Air Medal. Mem. Colo. Bar Assn. Republican. Congregationalist. Corporate taxation, Estate taxation, Personal income taxation. Office: US Ho of Reps 1424 Longworth Washington DC 20515

BROWN, HAROLD JENSEN, lawyer; b. Newark, Dec. 2, 1905; s. William Henry and Nellie (West) B.; m. Ruth Bouquet, Mar. 22, 1930; 1 dau., Janice Brown Downey; m. 2d, Catherine Gardner, Apr. 25, 1971. Litt.B., Rutgers U., 1926, LL.B., 1931, J.D., 1970. Bar: N.J. 1931. Assoc. Boyd and Dodd, Montclair, N.J., 1931-41; ptnr. Joyce & Brown, Bloomfield, N.J., 1945-74, Joyce, Brown and Connolly, 1974, Brown, Cass & Connolly, 1974-76, Brown, Connolly & Karosen, 1976-78, Brown, Connolly & Karosen, Bloomfield, 1978—; judge Mcpl. Ct. Glen Ridge (N.J.), 1964-79. Chmn., Glen Ridge Bd. Adjustment, Jud. Conf. Com.; pres. Pub. Health Nursing Assn. Bloomfield and Glen Ridge, League for Family Service. Served to maj. AUS, 1941-45. Mem. ABA, N.J. Bar Assn., Essex County Bar Assn., Bloomfield Lawyers Club. Mem. Reformed Ch. Lodge: Masons. Probate, General practice, Real property. Home: 52 Woodland Ave Glen Ridge NJ 07028 Office: 112 Broad St Bloomfield NJ 07003

BROWN, HARVEY R., lawyer; b. Bklyn., May 10, 1945; s. Bernard and Ruth (Boxer) B.; m. Bernice Weisinger, June 16, 1973; children—Erika, Michael. B.A., Hofstra U., 1967; J.D., Bklyn. Law Sch., 1974. Bar: N.Y. 1975, U.S. Dist. Ct. (so. dist.) N.Y. 1975, U.S. Ct. Appeals (2d cir.) 1975, Fla. 1976, U.S. Dist. Ct. (no. dist.) N.Y. 1977, U.S. Supreme Ct. 1978, U.S. Dist. Ct. (we. dist.) N.Y. 1983. Sr. assoc. Harry H. Lipsig, N.Y.C., 1974-81; sr. assoc. Clune, White & Nelson, Harrison, N.Y., 1981-83; sole practice, White Plains, N.Y., 1983—; dep. village atty. Village of Larchmont, 1984. Mem. ABA, Assn. Trial Lawyers Am., N.Y. State Bar Assn., N.Y. State Trial Lawyers Assn., Westchester County Bar Assn. Personal injury, Family and matrimonial, General practice. Home: 21 Forest Park Ave Larchmont NY 10538 Office: 202 Mamaroneck Ave White Plains NY 10601

BROWN, HENRY OTIS, business educator, lawyer; b. Sandston, Va., July 29, 1949; s. Roy Otis and Mary Irene (Christian) B. BS in Math., Va. State U., petersburg, 1971; JD, N.C. Cen. U., 1975; Postgrad., Cen. Mich. U. Bar: Va. 1980, U.S. Dist. Ct. 1980, U.S. Ct. Appeals (4th cir.) 1980, U.S. Tax Ct. 1985. Interim chmn. bus. adminstrn. dept. Va. State U., 1979-81; sole practice Petersburg, 1980—; asst. prof. Va. State U., Petersburg, 1975—. Mem. bd. deacons Union Bapt. Ch., Quinton, Va., 1979; bd. dirs. south side Va. Legal Service, Petersburg, 1980. Mem. ABA, Petersburg Bar Assn., Old Dominion Bar Assn., Va. Trial Lawyers Assn., Petersburg Jaycees, Phi Alpha Delta. Democrat. Lodge: Masons. Bankruptcy, Personal injury, Criminal. Home: 907 E Wythe St Petersburg VA 23803 Office: 618 E Washington St Petersburg VA 23803

BROWN, HERBERT RUSSELL, justice, lawyer; b. Columbus, Ohio, Sept. 27, 1931; s. Thomas Newton and Irene (Hankinson) B.; m. Beverly Ann Jenkins, Dec. 2, 1967; children: David Herbert, Andrew Jenkins. BA, Denison U., 1953; JD, U. Mich., 1956. Assoc. Vorys, Sater, Seymour and Pease, Columbus, Ohio, 1956, 60-64, ptnr., 1965-82; treas. Sunday Creek Coal Co., Columbus, 1970-86; assoc. justice Ohio Supreme Ct., Columbus, 1987—; examiner Ohio Bar, 1967-72, Multi-State Bar, 1971-76, Dist. Ct. Bar, 1968-71; commnr. Fed. Lands, Columbus, 1967-68, Lake Lands, Columbus, 1981. Mem. editorial bd. U. Mich. Law Rev., 1955-56. bd. dirs. Cen. Community House Columbus, 1967-75; deacon, mem. governing bd. 1st Community Ch., 1966-80; candidate Ohio State Legis., 1966. Served to capt. JAGC, U.S. Army, 1956-57. Fellow Am. Coll. Trial Lawyers; mem. Ohio Bar Assn., Columbus Bar Assn. Democrat. Office: Ohio Supreme Ct 30 E Broad St Columbus OH 43215 *

BROWN, IAN ALEXANDER, lawyer; b. St. Marie, Ont., Can., Mar. 23, 1951; came to U.S., 1977; s. Hugh John and Charlotte Marie (Gregg) B.; m. Deborah Lynn Gordon, Aug. 27, 1977; children: Flora Gordon, Lucy Gordon. AA, Sheridan Coll., Oakville, Ont., 1971; JD, Southwestern U., Los Angeles, 1981. Bar: Calif. 1981, U.S. Dist. Ct. (mid. dist.) Calif. 1981, Colo. 1982, U.S. Dist. Ct. Colo. 1982, U.S. Ct. Appeals (10th cir.) 1982, U.S. Ct. Appeals (10th cir.) 1986. Assoc. Frascona McClow & Joiner, Boulder, Colo., 1982-84; sole practice Boulder, 1984-85; assoc. Law Offices of Stephen H. Cook, Boulder, 1985—. pres. Los Angeles Student Trial Lawyers, 1980-81. Recipient: Bur. Nat. Affairs Inc. award, Los Angeles, 1981. Mem. ABA, Colo. Bar Assn., Calif. Bar Assn., Boulder Bar Assn. , Colo. Trial Layers Assn. State civil litigation, Federal civil litigation, Personal injury. Home: 345 17th St Boulder CO 80302 Office: Law Offices of Stephen H Cook 100 Arapahoe St Suite 9 Boulder CO 80302

BROWN, JAMES B., JR., lawyer; b. Utica, N.Y., June 25, 1939; s. James B. and Dolores R. (Schwink) B.; m. Anne Marie Downes, Feb. 14, 1972 (div.); children—Richard M., Denis E.; m. Alison L. Cioffi, Jan. 22, 1983. A.B., Hamilton Coll., 1961; LL.B., Cornell U., 1964. Bar: N.J. 1965, U.S. Dist. Ct. N.J. 1965, U.S. Supreme Ct. 1968, U.S. Tax Ct. 1983. Assoc. Daniel L. Golden, South River, N.J., 1965-68; sole practice, Old Bridge and East Brunswick, N.J., 1968—; panelist Middlesex County Matrimonial Early Settlement Program, 1978—; bd. adjustment atty. Jamesburg, N.J., 1966-67. Mem. ABA, N.J. State Bar Assn., Middlesex County Bar Assn., Middlesex County Trial Lawyers Assn. Baptist. Lodge: South River-East Brunswick Rotary. Real property, Family and matrimonial, Personal injury. Office: 350 Cranbury Rd PO Box L East Brunswick NJ 08816

BROWN, JAMES BENTON, lawyer; b. Pitts., Jan. 18, 1945; s. Sidney J. and Marian R. (Bailiss) B.; m. Susan M. Brenner, Aug. 6, 1967; children—Jessica Lynn, Joshua David. B.A., U. Louisville, 1967; J.D., Duquesne U., 1971. Bar admittee Pa. 1971, U.S. dist. ct. (we. dist.) Pa. 1971, U.S. Ct. Apls. (3d cir.) 1974, U.S. Sup. Ct. 1982. Assoc. Rothman, Gordon, Foreman & Groudine, Pitts., 1971-75; shareholder Baskin, Flaherty, Elliott & Mannino, P.C., Pitts., 1975—. Mem. Pitts. Histadrut Council. Mem. ABA, Pa. Bar Assn. (treas. labor and employment law sect.) , Allegheny County Bar Assn. Author: An Overview of the Dual Shop Concept (Is It Possible for an Employer to Have Both a Union and Non-Union Shop?), 1980. Democrat. Club: Club One. Labor. Home: 6739 Wilkins Ave Pittsburgh PA 15217 Office: One Mellon Bank Ctr 29th Floor Pittsburgh PA 15219

BROWN, JAMES EARLE, lawyer; b. San Antonio, Aug. 13, 1945; s. Melville Marshall and Hazel Maurine (Byran) B.; m. Camille Ashby Newsom, June 10, 1967; children: Kristen Bryan, Kasey Margaret. BBA, So. Meth. U., 1968, JD, 1972. Bar: U.S. Dist. Ct. (no. and ea. dists.) Tex. 1972. Assoc. Bean, Francis, Ford, Francis & Wills, Dallas, 1972-74; ptnr. Briggs, Brown & Berkley, Dallas, 1975-86; sole practice Dallas, 1986—. Ruling elder Preston Hollow Presbyn. Ch., Dallas, 1981; v.p. Wilcox Endowment, Dallas, 1984. Served with U.S. Army, 1968-69. Mem. Tex. Bar Assn., Dallas Bar Assn., Assn. Trial Lawyers Am., Dallas Trial Lawyers Assn., Tex. Trial Lawyers Assn., Tex. Bd. Legal Specialization (cert. 1978, 83). Republican. Clubs: Trophy (Roanoke, Tex.); Park City (Dallas). Avocations: golf, snow skiing. Personal injury, Workers' compensation, Insurance. Office: 4315 W Lovers Ln Dallas TX 75209

BROWN, JAMES ELLIOTT, lawyer; b. Mt. Vernon, NY, Sept. 5, 1947; s. Gilbert E. and Doris (Elias) B.; m. Elizabeth Ferber, Nov. 16, 1970 (div. Jan. 1977); m. Virginia Linney Freeland, Nov. 26, 1977; children: Elias F., Benjamin J. BA, Cornell U., 1969; JD, U. Denver, 1974. Bar: Colo. 1974, U.S. Dist. Ct. Colo. 1974, U.S. Ct. Appeals (10th cir.) 1976. Assoc. Grant, McHendrie, Hanes and Crouse, P.C., Denver, 1974-81, mng. ptnr. north office, 1984—, also bd. dirs.; bd. dirs. Avimage, Inc., Denver, Omnicom, Inc., Turin Bicylces of Denver; guest lectr. U. Denver Coll. Law, 1984. Bd. govs. Adams County (Colo.) Econ. Devel., 1983—. Mem. ABA, Colo. Bar Assn., Adams County Bar Assn., Denver Bar Assn., MetroNorth C. of C. (chmn. bd. 1986, bd. dirs. 1983—, Econ. Developer of Yr. 1984). Democrat. Jewish. Club: Rocky Mountain Rd. (pres. 1972-76), Rocky Mountain Radio League (Denver). Avocations: ham radio, running, bicycle riding, motor sports. Real property, Bankruptcy, Contracts commercial. Office: Grand McHendrie Haines & Crouse 11990 Grant St Suite 414 Northglenn CO 80233

BROWN, JAMES MILTON, legal educator; b. Streator, Ill., July 16, 1921. BA, U. Ill., 1943; JD, U. Fla., 1963. Bar: Fla. 1963. Pres., gen. mgr. J.C. Ames Lumber Co., Streator, 1947-61, Brown-Vissering Constrn. Co., Streator, 1956-61; Sterling fellow Yale Law Sch., 1964-65; assoc. prof. law U. Miss., 1964-65; prof. law George Washington U., 1965—, dir. land use mgmt. and control program Nat. Law Ctr., 1965—, sr. staff scientist Program of Policy Studies, 1965-82; mem. various panels Nat. Acad. Scis.; cons. in field. Contbr. articles to legal jours. Mem. ABA, D.C. Bar Assn., Fla. Bar Assn., Order of Coif, Phi Delta Phi, Lambda Alpha. Legal education, Land use and zoning, Real property. Home: 7206 Westchester Dr Temple Hills MD 20748 Office: 720 20th St NW Washington DC 20052

BROWN, JAMES SCOTT, lawyer; b. Fayetteville, Ark., Mar. 15, 1945; s. James Truman and Maude Marie (Scott) B.; m. Amy Lee Arnold, July 17, 1971; 1 son, James Justin. B.A., U. Louisville, 1967; J.D., U. Ark., 1970; LL.M., U. Mo.-Kansas City, 1971. Bar: Ark. 1970, U.S. Ct. Mil. Appeals 1971, D.C. 1978, U.S. Ct. Appeals (D.C. cir.) 1982, U.S. Ct. Appeals (8th cir.) 1982. Contracts negotiator, cons./counsel Ryan Cons. GmbH, Koenigstein, W.Ger., 1975; ptnr., sr. atty. Crane & Hawkins, solicitors, London, 1975-80; ptnr., Crane & Hawkins, Gould & Davis, N.Y.C., 1977-80; v.p., legal dir. Gulf & Gt. Plains Legal Found., Kansas City, 1981-82; sr. ptnr. Law Office J. Scott Brown, Shawnee Mission, Kans., 1981-83; chmn. bd. Century Savs. Assn. Kans., Shawnee Mission, 1981-83, adv. dir. 1983-86. Bd. govs. Kansas City Philharm. Orch., 1981-83; mem. Internat. Relations Council and Acad., Kansas City, Mo. Served to capt. JAGC, U.S. Army, 1971-74. Mem. ABA (mem. subcom. on internat. recognition and enforcement of judgements), Law Soc. Eng. (overseas mem.), Ark. Bar Assn., D.C. Bar Assn., Greater Kansas City C. of C. (mem. environ. com. 1981-83), Am.

C. of C. (U.K.), German Chamber of Industry and Commerce in the U.K., London C. of C. and Industry. Republican. Club: American (London). Private international, Contracts commercial. Home: Clive House, The Chase Knott Park, Oxshott KT22 OHR, England Office: Pavia and Harcourt, Indigo House 29 Bedford St, Covent Garden WC2E 9RT, England

BROWN, JAMES WILCOX, lawyer; b. Phila., July 16, 1948; s. Louis James and Genevieve Elizabeth (McDermott) B.; m. Peggy Williams, June 6, 1970; children: Genevieve, Hilary, William, Mary Ellen. BA, U. Del., 1970; JD, Washington & Lee U., 1973. Bar: Del. 1973, U.S. Ct. Mil. Appeals 1974, U.S. Dist. Ct. Del. 1977. Assoc. Terry & Terry, Dover, Del., 1973-74; atty. W.L. Gore and Assoc., Inc., Newark, Del., 1977—, gen. counsel, 1983—; gen. counsel W.L. Gore and Assoc., Inc., Newark, 1983—. Trustee Union Hosp. of Cecil County, Elkton, Md., 1985—, treas., 1986—; bd. dirs., treas. Oaklands Pool Assn., Newark, Del., 1986—. Served to capt. U.S. Army, 1974-77. Mem. Del. Bar Assn., Am. Corp. Counsels Assn. (bd. dirs. Del. Valley chpt. 1985—), Health Industry Mfrs. Assn. (legal and regulatory steering com. 1981-84). Republican. Roman Catholic. General corporate, Contracts commercial, Government contracts and claims. Home: 188 W Main St Newark DE 19711 Office: WL Gore and Assocs Inc 551 Paper Mill Rd PO Box 9206 Newark DE 19714-9206

BROWN, JERROLD STANLEY, lawyer; b. Little Falls, N.Y., Nov. 8, 1953; s. Stanley Clayton and Ruth Jane (Greenlee) B.; m. Catherine M. Agnello, Aug. 2, 1980; 1 child, Nora M. BA, SUNY, Albany, 1975; JD, Union U., 1979. Bar: N.Y. 1980, U.S. Dist. Ct. (no. dist.) N.Y. 1980, U.S. Dist. Ct. (we. dist.) N.Y. 1982, U.S. Ct. Appeals (2d cir.) 1983. Law clk. to judge N.Y. Ct. Appeals, Albany, 1979-81; assoc. Hodgson, Russ, Andrews, Woods & Goodyear, Buffalo, 1981-85, mem., 1986—. Note and comment editor Albany Law Rev., 1978-79. Trustee Westminster Presbyn. Ch., Buffalo, 1986. Federal civil litigation, State civil litigation, Personal injury. Office: Hodgson Russ Andrews Woods & Goodyear 1800 One M&T Plaza Buffalo NY 14203

BROWN, J(OAN) DEVON, lawyer; b. Stockton, Calif., Nov. 12, 1953; d. Nat and Laurie (Edwards) B. B.A. in Psychology, U. Calif.-Santa Cruz, 1975; M.A. in Criminal Justice, Calif. State U.-Sacramento, 1977; cert. in legal investigation Calif. Western Sch. Law, San Diego, 1978, J.D., 1979; postgrad. in bus. Bar: Calif. 1979, U.S. Dist. Ct. (so. dist.) Calif. 1979, U.S. Dist. Ct. (no. dist.) Calif. 1984; U.S. Ct. Appeals 1984. lic. in real estate, Calif. Legal intern Legal Services Project, San Diego, 1978, San Diego County Bd. Suprs., 1978; law clk. Office of G. Randolph Wright, San Diego, 1979, assoc., 1979; environ.-legal research atty. ballistic missile div. TRW, Inc., San Bernardino, Calif., 1980-81, subcontracts specialist space systems div., Redondo Beach, Calif., 1981-82; atty. Todd Shipyards Corp., San Francisco, 1982-85; gen. counsel Phone-Master Communications Corp., Walnut Creek, 1985-87; atty. adv. Shipbuilders Council Am., Washington, 1982-83. Mem. ABA, AAUW, San Francisco County Bar Assn., Contra Costa Bar Assn., Barristers Soc. San Francisco, Attys. for Animal Rights, Maritime Law Assn. U.S. Phi Alpha Delta. Club: Commonwealth of Calif. General corporate, General practice. Office: PO Box 4929 Walnut Creek CA 94596

BROWN, JOE BLACKBURN, lawyer; b. Louisville, Dec. 9, 1940; s. Knox and Miriam (Blackburn) B.; m. Marilyn McGowen, Aug. 10, 1963; children: Jennifer Knox, Michael McGowen. B.A., Vanderbilt U., 1962, J.D., 1965. Bar: Ky. 1965, Tenn. 1972, U.S. Supreme Ct. 1979. Asst. U.S. atty. Dept. Justice, Nashville, 1971-73, 1st asst. U.S. atty., 1974-81, U.S. atty., 1981—; vice chmn. atty. gen.'s adv. com.; instr. math. and bus. law Augusta (Ga.) Coll., 1966-69. Contbr. articles to legal jours. Bd. dirs. Mid Cumberland Durg Abuse Council, Nashville, 1977-86; asst. scoutmaster Boy Scouts Am.; mem. vestry St. David's Episcopal Ch. Served to maj. U.S. Army, 1965-71, col. USAR. Recipient Owens prize in math. Vanderbilt U., 1962. Mem. Nashville Bar Assn., Fed. Bar Assn. (treas. 1978), Ky. Bar Assn., Tenn. Bar Assn., Order of Coif, Phi Beta Kappa. Republican. Criminal. Home: 858 Rodney Dr Nashville TN 37205 Office: US Atty Room 879 US Courthouse Nashville TN 37205

BROWN, JOHN CLARK, JR., lawyer; b. Montclair, N.J., Aug. 11, 1943; s. John Clark and Lois (Svenzrud) B.; m. Marie Elizabeth Stansbury, Dec. 30, 1948; children: Steven Clark, Daniel Johnson. BA, Stanford U., 1966; JD, UCLA, 1971. Bar: Calif. 1972, U.S. Dist. Ct. (cen. dist.) Calif. 1972, Nev. 1981, U.S. Ct. Appeals (9th circuit), 1981. Law clk. to presiding justice Calif. Ct. Appeals, Los Angeles, 1971-72; assoc. Richards, Watson, Dreyfuss & Gerson, Los Angeles, 1972-75, Dickson, Brown & Bonesteel, Los Angeles, 1975-78, Cohen & Freeman, Los Angeles, 1978-80, ptnr., 1980-82; sole practice, Los Angeles, 1982—; arbitrator Los Angeles Superior Ct., Am. Arbitration Assn.; instr. Calif. Continuing Edn. of the Bar Programs on Arbitration, Damages and Breach of Contract Remedies, trial preparation; instr. U. So. Calif. Contbr. articles to profl. jours. Active, Friends of the Ballona Wetlands, 1979-85; bd. dirs. Apt. Assn. Greater Los Angeles, 1982-85; sec. Town Hall Community Affairs sect. Western Los Angeles Regional C. of C. Legislative Activity Com., 1979-85. Mem. State Bar of Calif., ABA, Los Angeles County Bar Assn., Apt. Owners Assn. Greater Los Angeles (bd. dirs., sec.). Democrat. Club: Stanford of Los Angeles County (dir., v.p.). Federal civil litigation, State civil litigation, Contracts commercial. Address: 19th Floor 10880 Wilshire Blvd Los Angeles CA 90024

BROWN, JOHN LEWIS, lawyer; b. Galesburg, Ill., July 2, 1955; s. Charles Lewis and Lois Maria (Nelson) B.; m. Cynthia Sue Bowen, Aug. 31, 1980; 1 child, Whitney Rose. BA, Northwestern U., 1977; JD, U. Iowa, 1980. Bar: Iowa 1980, Ill. 1980, Minn. 1984. Assoc. Lucas, Brown & McDonald, Galesburg, 1980-83; staff atty. ITT Consumer Fin. Corp., Mpls., 1983—. Mem. ABA, Ill. Bar Assn., Iowa Bar Assn., Minn. Bar Assn., Hennepin Bar Assn. Consumer commercial, Computer, Real property. Home: 1440 Angelo Dr Golden Valley MN 55422

BROWN, JOSEPH MORRIS, JR., lawyer; b. Birmingham, Ala., Aug. 29, 1950; s. Joseph M. Sr. and Eula Mae (Pope) B.; divorced; children: Joseph Allan, William Brett, David Tyler. BA, Samford U., 1972; JD, Cumberland Sch. Law, 1977. Bar: Ala. 1977, U.S. Dist. Ct. (no. and so. dists.) Ala. 1978, U.S. Ct. Appeals (5th and 11th cirs.) 1978, U.S. Supreme Ct. 1985. Ptnr. Cunningham, Bounds, Yance,Crowder & Brown, Mobile, Ala., 1978—. Served to capt. USAF, 1973-79. Mem. Ala. Trial Lawyers, Assn. Trial Lawyers Am., Lawyers-Pilots Bar Assn. Baptist. Avocations: snow skiing, handball, softball. State civil litigation, Insurance, Personal injury. Home: 1508 Ridgeland Rd W Mobile AL 36609 Office: Cunningham Bounds et al 1601 Dauphin St Mobile AL 36604

BROWN, JOSEPH WENTLING, lawyer; b. Norfolk, Va., July 31, 1941; s. Edwin Wallace and Nancy Jack (Wentling) B.; m. Pamela Jones, Aug. 18, 1966; children—Tyree, Palmer, Jeffrey, Hunter. B.A., U. Va., 1965; LL.B., Washington and Lee U., 1968. Bar: Nev. 1969, D.C. 1976, U.S. Dist. Ct. Nev. 1969. Assoc. Laxalt, Bell, Berry, Allison & LeBaron, Las Vegas, Nev., 1969; ptnr. Jones, Jones, Bell, Close & Brown, Las Vegas, 1973—; commr. Nev. Dept. of Wildlife, 1979-85; mem. U.S. Fgn. Claims Settlement Commn., 1981—; mem. Bd. of Litigation, Mountain States Legal Found., 1978-82. Bd. dirs. United Way, Nev. Devel. Authority, Clark County Boys Club, Nev. Catholic Community Services, Voluntary Action Ctr.; dep. counsel Rep. Nat. Conv., 1984. Served with USMCR, 1963-69. Editor Washington and Lee Lawyer, 1967-68. Mem. ABA, Nev. Bar Assn., Clark County Bar Assn., Assn. Trial Lawyers Am. Republican. Roman Catholic. Club: Rotary. General practice, General corporate, Administrative and regulatory. Home: 3138 S Redwood St Las Vegas NV 89102 Office: 300 S 4th St Suite 700 Las Vegas NV 89101

BROWN, JUDITH RENZI, lawyer; b. Balt., May 21, 1938; d. William and Olga (Plawin) Renzi. Student, Union Meml. Hosp. Sch. Nursing, 1955-58, Loyola Coll., Balt., 1972-75; BA, York Coll. of Pa., 1976; JD, U. Balt., 1978. Bar: Pa. 1979. With emergency dept. Johns Hopkins Hosp., Balt., 1958-61, supr., 1961-65, clin. nurse III, 1966-75; head nurse Lincoln (Nebr.) State Hosp., 1965-66; v.p. risk mgmt and loss prevention Pa. Med. Soc. Liability Ins. Co., Lemoyne, 1979—; cons. med-legal Springhouse Corp., Springhouse, Pa., 1980—. contbr. articles to profl. jours. Mem. Am. Assn. of Nurse Attys., Am. Coll. Legal Medicine, Am. Soc. Law and Medicine, Nurses Assn. of Am. Coll. of Obs-Gyn., Phila. Horticulture Soc. Personal injury, Health. Home: 306 Maple Ave Hershey PA 17033 Office: Pa Med Soc Liability Ins Co PO Box 303 20-A Erford Rd Lemoyne PA 17043

BROWN, KAREN KENNEDY, magistrate, lawyer; b. Houston, May 23, 1947; d. Edwin Bland and Muriel Elizabeth (Dupuy) Kennedy; m. David Hurst Brown, Mar. 11, 1978; children—Terence, Elizabeth. B.A., U. Pa., 1970; J.D., U. Houston, 1973. Bar: Tex. 1974, U.S. Dist. Ct. (so. and we. dists.) Tex. 1975, U.S. Ct. Appeals (5th cir.) 1974, U.S. Ct. Appeals (11th cir.) 1981. Law clk. Judge John R. Brown, Houston, 1973-75, Judge Woodrow Seals, Houston, 1975-76; asst. fed. pub. defender So. Dist. Tex., Houston, 1976-82; pvt. practice, Houston, 1982-83; U.S. magistrate U.S. Cts. So. Dist. Tex., Houston, 1984—. Mem. LWV. Episcopalian. Criminal, Federal civil litigation, Jurisprudence. Office: PO Box 61252 US Courthouse 515 Rusk Ave Houston TX 77208

BROWN, KENNETH MACKINNON, lawyer; b. Honolulu, Oct. 28, 1946; s. Kenneth Stirling and Chandler (Darden) B.; m. Janet Gail Davis, Feb. 3, 1968; children: Jennifer Darden, Matthew Chapin MacKinnon. BA, U. N.H., 1968; JD, Washington U., 1973. Bar: N.H. 1973, U.S. Dist. Ct. N.H. 1973, U.S. Ct. Appeals (1st cir.) 1974. Assoc. Winer, Lynch & Pillsbury, Nashua, N.H., 1973-76; ptnr. Kahn & Brown, Nashua, 1976—. Pres. bd. trustees N.H. Legal Assistance, Concord, 1978-80; chmn. bd. trustees Rivier Coll. Paralegal Adv. Bd., Nashua, 1984—; trustee N.H. Assn. for Mental Health, Concord, 1978-81, N.H. Soc. Protection of Forests, Concord, 1983—. Mem. N.H. Bar Assn., Assn. Trial Lawyers Am., N.H. Trial Lawyers Assn. Club: Nashua Country (N.H.). Avocations: golf, family. State civil litigation, Workers' compensation, Real property. Home: 29 Baxter Rd Hollis NH 03049 Office: Kahn & Brown 127 Main St Nashua NH 03060

BROWN, LAWRENCE, lawyer; b. N.Y.C., July 30, 1945; s. Harold and Doris (Malach) B.; m. Judith Kristine Gondjian, Oct. 28, 1972; children—Darin Adams, Melissa Lynn. J.D., U. Pacific, 1971. Bar: Calif. 1971, U.S. Dist. Ct. (cen. dist.) Calif. 1971, U.S. Supreme Ct. 1974, U.S. Ct. Appeals (9th cir.) 1983. Prof. law Mid-Valley Coll. Law, Van Nuys, Calif., 1974-80; sole practice, Encino, Calif. Pres. We Hope chpt. City of Hope, 1983-85. Mem. Calif. Bar Assn., San Fernando Valley Bar Assn., Los Angeles County Bar Assn. State civil litigation, Criminal, Family and matrimonial. Office: 16311 Ventura Blvd Suite 990 Encino CA 91436

BROWN, LAWRENCE CHARLES, lawyer; b. Johnson City, N.Y., Apr. 5, 1951; s. Charles Hugh and Cora Rose (O'Connor) B.; m. Constance Angela Grimes, July 28, 1973; children: Jason P., Christina M. BS, Cornell U., 1973; MA, SUNY, Albany, 1974; JD, Syracuse U., 1977. Bar: N.Y. 1978, U.S. Dist. Ct. (so. dist.) N.Y. 1986. Assoc. Phillips, Lytle, Hitchcock, Blaine & Huber, Buffalo, N.Y., 1977-78, Hodgson, Russ, Andrews, Woods & Goodyear, Buffalo, 1978-82; ptnr. Lipsitz, Green, Fahringer, Roll, Schuller & James, Buffalo, 1982—. Research editor Syracuse U. Law Rev., 1976-77. Mem. ABA, N.Y. State Bar Assn., Comml. Law League Am. Methodist. Avocation: public speaking. Contracts commercial, State civil litigation, Bankruptcy. Office: Lipsitz Green Fahringer Roll Schuller & James One Niagara Sq Buffalo NY 14221

BROWN, LAWRENCE RAYMOND, JR., lawyer; b. Rochester, Pa., Apr. 25, 1928; s. Lawrence Raymond and Eva Louisa (Oliver) B.; m. Carol Lucille Vanderford, June 29, 1957; children: Lawrence Raymond III, Carolyn Grier. AB in Econs., Princeton U., 1951; LLB, U. Pa., 1956. Bar: Pa. 1957, U.S. Dist. Ct. (ea. dist.) Pa. 1957, U.S. Ct. Appeals (3d cir.) 1957. Assoc. Duane, Morris & Heckscher, Phila., 1956-58; atty. Provident Mut. Life Ins. Co., Phila., 1958-60, sr. v.p., gen. counsel, 1982—; v.p. Provident Mut. Holding Co., Phila., 1984—, also bd. dirs.; bd. dirs. W.H. Newbold's Son & Co. Inc., Phila., Continental Am. Life Ins. Co., Newark, Del., Washington Sq. Life Ins. Co., Phila. Served to capt. U.S. Army, 1951-53. Mem. ABA, Phila. Bar Assn., Am. Council Life Ins. (chmn. legal sect. 1985-86), Assn. Life Ins. Counsel (gov. 1983-86), Union League of Phila. Republican. Presbyterian. Club: Merion Cricket (Haverford, Pa.). Lodge: Masons. Avocation: golf. General corporate, Insurance, Corporate taxation. Home: 129 Wooded Ln Villanova PA 19085 Office: Provident Mut Life Ins Co 1600 Market St Philadelphia PA 19103

BROWN, LISA CLAIRE, lawyer; b. Salt Lake City, May 28, 1954; d. Robert M. and M. Elise (Wallace) B.; m. Douglas R. Andres, Aug. 8, 1981. Student, Swarthmore Coll., 1972; BA, Northwestern U., 1976; JD, George Washington U. Bar: Oreg. 1979. Asst. atty. gen. Oreg. Dept. Justice, Salem, 1979-81; atty. Kell, Alterman & Runstein, Portland, 1985—. Mem. Oreg. Trial Lawyers Assn., Multnomah Bar Assn., Phi Beta Kappa. Avocations: hiking, skiing. State civil litigation, Insurance, Contracts commercial. Office: Kell Alterman & Runstein 707 SW Washington Suite 1330 Bank Calif Tower Portland OR 97205

BROWN, LORNE JAMES, lawyer; b. Regina, Sask., Can., Nov. 26, 1937; s. Charles Mervyn and Anne Vera (Frohlick) B.; m. Ursula Theresa Grebe, Sept. 8, 1962; children—Nadine, Matthew. B.A., San Jose State U., 1961; LL.B., U. Calif.-San Francisco, 1964. Bar: Calif. 1965, U.S. Dist. Ct. (cen. dist.) Calif. 1965, U.S. Tax Ct. 1981. Assoc. Holmes, Ross, Woodson, Millard & Ryburn, Pasadena, Calif., 1964-67, ptnr., 1967-74; ptnr. Brown & Reed, Pasadena, 1974-78; pres. Brown & Reed, Inc., Pasadena, 1978-81; ptnr. Brown, Reed, & Gibson, Pasadena, 1981—; treas., dir. Legal Services Program, Pasadena. V.p. La Canada Flintridge Ednl. Found.; active Pasadena Tournament of Roses Assn. Mem. ABA, Calif. State Bar, Los Angeles County Bar Assn., Pasadena Bar Assn. (pres. 1985-86). Clubs: Rotary, Optimists, University (Pasadena). Estate planning, Probate, Estate taxation. Home: 3769 Berwick Dr Flintridge CA 91011 Office: 600 S Lake Ave Suite 300 Pasadena CA 91106

BROWN, LOUIS DANIEL, lawyer, corporation executive; b. San Francisco, Aug. 31, 1908; s. Louis Thomas and Rose Ella (Kelly) B.; m. Felice Stamper, Sept. 9, 1932; children—Lawrence Louis, Ronald Stamper, Carol Felice. A.A., U. San Francisco, 1929; A.B., Stanford U., 1931; postgrad. U. Calif.-Hastings Coll. Law, San Francisco, 1934-36; J.D., Southwestern U., 1944. Bar: Calif. 1944, U.S. Supreme Ct. 1950, U.S. Ct. Claims 1950. Ptnr., Romer, Brown, San Francisco and Los Angeles, 1944-72; sole practice, Los Angeles, 1972—; judge pro tem Mcpl. Ct., 1980, 82, 83, 84. Active Boy Scouts Am., La. Zool. Assn., Republican Nat. Com. Mem. Calif. State Guard. Mem. Calif. Bar Assn., Los Angeles County Bar Assn., Los Angeles Bar Assn., Lawyers Club Los Angeles, Am. Judicature Soc., U. San Francisco Alumni (past pres.), U. San Francisco Law Soc., Stanford Alumni (life), Stanford Law Soc., Southwestern U. Alumni Assn. Roman Catholic. Lodges: Lions, Elks, Friars and Friarettes. Contbr. articles to profl. jours. General corporate, Probate, Real property. Address: 3030 Temple St Los Angeles CA 90026

BROWN, MANNY S., lawyer, labor arbitrator; b. Chgo., Nov. 2, 1917; s. Soloman J. and Mona A. (Streicher) B.; m. Jeanne Levin, Feb. 22, 1945; children—Richard S., Charles E. B.A., U. Wis., 1940; J.D., Marquette U., 1952. Bar: Wis. 1952, U.S. Ct. Appeals (7th cir.) 1978, U.S. Supreme Ct. 1972. Sole practice Racine, Wis., 1952—; mem. asst. dist. atty. Racine County, Racine, 1973-74; bankruptcy trustee, 1954—; arbitrator Chgo. Tchrs. Union and Chgo. Sch. Bd., 1980—. Mem. Racine Unified Sch. Bd., 1953-69, pres., 1958-59; mem. Wis. Ho. of Reps., 1964-72; mem. steering com. Edn. Commn. of States, 1970-72; bd. dirs. Goodwill Industries S.E. Wis., 1975-81; mem. Racine County Democratic Com., 1955—; former mem. bd. Beth Israel Sinai Congregation. Served to lt. (s.g.) USN, 1941-46; mem. Res. (ret.); PTO. Recipient honor award Racine Edn. Assn., 1969, disting. spl. award Wis. Secondary Schs. Assn., 1972. Mem. Am. Judicature Soc., Nat. Council Juvenile Judges, Assn. Trial Lawyers Am., Nat. Orgn. Legal Problems of Educators (pres. 1970-71), Am. Arbitration Assn. (arbitration panel 1975—), Nat. Orgn. Social Security Reps., Res. Officers Assn., Am. Legion, VFW, 40 and 8. Clubs: Rotary, B'nai B'rith (Racine). Workers' compensation, Family and matrimonial, Bankruptcy.

BROWN, MARC LAURENCE, lawyer; b. Dallas, Sept. 24, 1951; s. Melvin Bernard and Mary Louise (Burchett) B. BA, U. Wis., 1973; JD, Yale U., 1976. Bar: Calif. 1978, U.S. Ct. Appeals (9th cir.) 1979. Law clk. to judge U.S. Ct. Appeals (9th cir.), Phoenix, 1976-77, U.S. Dist. Ct. (no. dist.) Calif., San Francisco, 1978-79; assoc. Tuttle & Taylor, Los Angeles, 1979-84, ptnr., 1984—. Articles editor Yale U. Law Rev., 1975-76. Mem. ABA, Phi Beta Kappa. Clubs: Riviera Country, University. Avocations: golf, squash. General corporate, Entertainment. Home: 10990 Wellworth Ave Los Angeles CA 90024 Office: Tuttle & Taylor Inc 355 S Grand Ave Los Angeles CA 90071-3101

BROWN, MATTHEW, lawyer; b. N.Y.C., Mar. 26, 1905; s. Jack Goddard and Pauline B. (Roth) B.; m. Edna Goodrich, Nov. 8, 1932; 1 child, Patricia Brown Specter. BS, NYU, 1925; LLB, Harvard U., 1928; LLD (hon.), Suffolk U., 1983. Bar: Mass. 1928, U.S. Supreme Ct. 1935. Sr. ptnr. Brown, Rudnick, Freed & Gesmer, Boston, 1940—; spl. justice Boston Mcpl. Ct., 1962-72; chmn. Boston Broadcasters, 1972-81. Selectman Town of Brookline, Mass., 1953-64; trustee New Eng. Aquarium, Boston, 1981—; chmn. Nat. Jewish Coalition, Boston, 1984. Fellow Brandeis U., Waltham, Mass., 1985 (hon.). Mem. ABA, Mass. Bar Assn., Boston Bar Assn., Am. Jewish Com. (hon. pres., life), Combined Jewish Philanthropies (hon. trustee, life). Club: Harvard (Boston), Boston Racquet; Belmont (Mass.) Country; The Breakers (Palm Beach, Fla.). Home: 180 Beacon St Apt 11-G Boston MA 02116 Office: Brown Rudnick Freed Gesmer 1 Federal St Boston MA 02110

BROWN, MEREDITH M., lawyer; b. N.Y.C., Oct. 18, 1940; s. John Mason Brown and Catherine (Screven) Meredith; m. Sylvia Lawrence Barnard, July 17, 1965; 1 child, Mason Barnard. AB, Harvard U., 1962, JD, 1965. Bar: N.Y. 1965, U.S. Ct. Appeals (2d cir.) 1966, U.S. Dist. Ct. (so. dist.) N.Y. Law clk. to presiding justice U.S. Ct. Appeals (2d cir.), N.Y.C., 1965-66; assoc. Debevoise & Plimpton, N.Y.C., 1966-72, ptnr., 1973—. Mem. ABA (fed. regulation securities com., corp. banking and bus. law sect.). Securities, General corporate. Home: 1021 Park Ave New York NY 10028 Office: Debevoise & Plimpton 875 3d Ave New York NY 10022

BROWN, MICHAEL DEWAYNE, lawyer; b. Guymon, Okla., Nov. 11, 1954; s. Wayne E. and R. Eloise (Ferguson) B.; m. Tamara Ann Oxley, July 19, 1973; children: Jared Michael, Amy Aryann. Student, Southeastern State U., Durant, Okla., 1973-75; BA in Polit. Sci. and English, Cen. State U., Edmond, Okla., 1978; JD, Oklahoma City U., 1981. Bar: Okla. 1982, U.S. Dist. Ct. (no. and we. dists.) Okla. 1982, U.S. Ct. Appeals (10th cir.) 1982. Assoc. Long, Ford, Lester & Brown, Enid, Okla., 1982—; cons. No. Okla. Devel. Assn., Enid, 1983—; gen. counsel Alpha Oil Co., Duncan, Okla., 1985—, Physicians Mgmt. Service Corps., 1985—, Physicians of Okla., Inc., Physicians Med. Plan Okla., Inc.; chmn. bd. dirs. Okla. Mcpl. Power Authority, Edmond. Councilman, City of Edmond, 1981; cons. Okla. Reps., Oklahoma City, 1983; bd. dirs. Okla. Christian Home, Edmond, 1985. Mem. Okla. Bar Assn. (assoc. bar examiner 1984—), MD Physicians Okla., Ariz. and La., MD Physicians of Tulsa. Mem. Christian Ch. (Disciples of Christ). Avocations: travel, photography, reading, wilderness adventures, swimming. Legislative, General corporate, Health. Home: 2826 Haystack Ln Enid OK 73703 Office: PO Box 1731 Enid OK 73702 also: Long Ford Lester & Brown 224 N Independence Suite 723 Enid OK 73701

BROWN, MICHAEL LANCE, lawyer; b. Pearsall, Tex., Jan. 3, 1950; s. Alanson Wesley and Ruth (Gillis) B.; m. Nela Laura Thomas, May 12, 1971; 1 child, Robert Allen. B.A., U. Tex., 1972, J.D., 1975. Bar: Tex. 1975, La. 1981, U.S. Ct. Appeals (5th and 11th cirs.) 1981, U.S. Dist. Ct. (so. dist.) Tex. 1982, U.S. Dist. Ct. (we. dist.) Tex. 1984, U.S. Supreme Ct. 1984, U.S. Dist. Ct. (no. dist.) Tex. 1986. Lease analyst Exxon Co. U.S.A., Houston, 1975-77; staff atty. land dept. Coastal Corp., Houston, 1977-79, law dept. Getty Oil Co., Houston, 1979-81; ptnr. firm Dohoney & Collier and predecessor firm, Houston, 1981-86. Mem. ABA, Houston Bar Assn., Houston Young Lawyers' Assn., Am. Assn. Petroleum Landmen, Houston Assn. Petroleum Landmen, Phi Beta Kappa. Methodist. Clubs: Downtown Optimist (bd. dirs. 1983—), Houston. Oil and gas leasing, General corporate, Probate. Home: 11815 Gladewood Ln Houston TX 77071 Office: 712 Main Suite 2120 Houston TX 77002

BROWN, PAUL EDMONDSON, lawyer, insurance association executive; b. Van Buren County, Iowa, Dec. 24, 1915; s. William Allen and Margaret (Edmondson) B.; m. Lorraine Hill, Jan. 9, 1944; 1 son, Scott. B.A., U. Iowa, 1938, J.D., 1941. Bar: Iowa 1941, U.S. Sup. Ct. 1966. Ptnr., Mahoney, Brown, Mahoney, Boone, Iowa, 1946-52; v.p., counsel Bankers Life Co., Des Moines, 1952-80; pres. Iowa Life Ins. Assn., Des Moines, 1980-85 ; of counsel Grefe & Sidney, Des Moines, 1980-84, Davis, Hockensberg, Wine, Brown & Koehn, Des Moines, 1984—; atty. County of Boone, Iowa, 1948-52. Served with U.S. Army, 1942-46, to col. USAR, 1945-70. Named Outstanding Young Man of Iowa, Iowa State Jr. C. of C. 1948. Mem. ABA, Fed. Bar Assn., Iowa Bar Assn., Polk County Bar Assn. Republican. Congregationalist. Club: Kiwanis. Insurance, Legislative, General corporate. Home: 5804 Harwood Dr Des Moines IA 50312 Office: 2300 Financial Ctr Des Moines IA 50309

BROWN, PAUL M., lawyer; b. N.Y.C., Jan. 10, 1938; s. I. Harry and Rose L. (Kresge) B.; m. Helga J. Fischer, Aug. 4, 1962 (div. 1977); children: Stephanie J., William A.; m. Ruth Reiter, June 28, 1986. Student, Williams Coll., 1955-57; BS in Econs., U. Pa., 1959; LLB, Columbia U., 1962. Bar: N.Y. 1963, U.S. Ct. Appeals (2d cir.) 1963, U.S. Dist. Ct. (so. and ea. dists.) N.Y. 1964, U.S. Dist. Ct. Mass. 1981, U.S. Ct. Appeals (3d cir.)., U.S. Ct. Appeals (1st cir.) 1982, U.S. Dist. Ct. (we. dist.) N.Y. 1983, U.S. Ct. Appeals (6th cir.) 1983, U.S. Dist. Ct. R.I. 1985, U.S. Dist. Ct. (ea. dist.) Mich. 1986. Assoc. Berman & Frost, N.Y.C., 1963-66; ptnr. Havens, Wandless, Stitt & Tighe, N.Y.C., 1966-76, Whitman & Ransom, N.Y.C., 1976—. Councilman, Closter, N.J., 1970-74; police commr. Closter, 1970-73; trustee Northern Valley Regional High Sch., Demarest, N.J., 1972. Served with USAR, 1962-68. Mem. Assn. of Bar of City N.Y., N.Y. State Bar Assn., Fed. Bar Council. Democrat. Club: University (N.Y.). Federal civil litigation, State civil litigation, Construction. Office: Whitman & Ransom 200 Park Ave New York NY 10166

BROWN, PAUL SHERMAN, lawyer; b. St. Louis, June 26, 1921; s. Paul Michael and Norma (Sherman) B.; m. Ann Wilson, Feb. 7, 1959; 1 son, Paul S. B.S. in Commerce, St. Louis U., 1943, J.D. cum laude, 1951. Bar: Mo. 1951, U.S. Dist. Ct. (ea. dist.) Mo. 1951, U.S. Ct. Appeals (8th cir.) 1951, U.S. Supreme Ct. 1966. Shareholder, Brown James & Rabbitt, P.C., St. Louis, 1980—; instr. St. Louis U. Night Law Sch., 1978—; lectr. in field. Mem. St. Louis Amateur Athletic Assn. (dir. 1974-76, pres. 1976-78). Fellow Am. Coll. Trial Lawyers, Internat. Acad. Trial Lawyers, Internat. Soc. Barristers; mem. ABA (vice-chmn. com. consumer products liability 1977-78), Mo. Bar Assn. (bd. govs. 1963-67), Am. Bd. Trial Advs. (adv.), Lawyers Assn. St. Louis, Bar Assn. Met. St. Louis (pres. 1970-71), Am. Judicature Soc., Order of Woolsack, Alpha Sigma Nu. Roman Catholic. Contbr. numerous articles to profl. jours. Federal civil litigation, State civil litigation, Insurance. Home: 7331 Kingsbury Saint Louis MO 63130 Office: 11th Floor 705 Olive St Saint Louis MO 63101

BROWN, PETER MEGARGEE, lawyer; b. Cleve., Mar. 15, 1922; s. George Estabrook and Miriam (Megargee) B.; m. Alexandra Green Johns, May 18, 1974; children: Peter, Blair Tillyer, Andree, Nathaniel; stepchildren—Alexandra, Brooke Stoddard. B.A., Yale U., 1945 (class of 1944), J.D., 1948. Bar: N.Y. 1949. Spl. asst. atty. gen. State N.Y. and asst. counsel N.Y. State Crime Commn., 1951-53; asst. U.S. atty. So. Dist. N.Y., 1953-55, spl. asst., 1956; partner firm Cadwalader, Wickersham & Taft, N.Y.C., 1959-82, Brown & Seymour, N.Y.C., 1983—; mem. Mayor's Com. on Judiciary, 1965-72, vice chmn., 1972-74. Author: The Art of Questioning: Thirty Maxims of Cross-Examination, 1987; author, essays, articles on law profession, pub. nationally. Mem. N.Y. County Rep. Com., 1958—; chmn. and co-founder Design and Art Soc., Ltd., N.Y.C.; pres. Riot Relief Fund; bd. dirs., sec. Episcopal Ch. Found.; bd. dirs. Yale Alumni Fund, 1979-84. Served in AUS, 1943-46. Decorated knight Order St. John of Hosp. of Jerusalem; Recipient award for service to profession Fed. Bar. Assn. (N.Y., N.J., Conn.), 1962; Chmn.'s award Yale Alumni Fund, 1979; Disting. Service award Class of 1944 Yale U., 1983. Fellow Am. Coll. Trial Lawyers, Am. Bar Found., N.Y. State Bar Found.; mem. World Assn. Lawyers (founding), Am. Judicature Soc., Soc. Colonial Wars, Internat., ABA, N.Y. State, N.Y. County bar assns., Assn. Bar City N.Y., Fed. Bar Council (pres. 1961-62, chmn. bd. 1962-64, chmn. judiciary com. 1960-85), St. Nicholas Soc. (past pres.), Design and Art Soc. Ltd. (founder, chmn. 1987), Delta Kappa Epsilon, Phi Delta Phi (magister Waite Inn 1947, pres. province I 1950-55).

Episcopalian (vestryman, sr. warden 1961-77). Clubs: Down Town Assn. (N.Y.C.), Union (N.Y.C.); Mill Reef (Antigua); Coral Beach (Bermuda). General practice, Federal civil litigation, State civil litigation. Home: 1125 Park Ave New York NY 10128 Office: 100 Park Ave New York NY 10017

BROWN, PHILLIP EDWARD, lawyer; b. Portland, Oreg., July 22, 1927; s. Rowland Seth and Bernice Edna (Soule) B.; m. Patricia Diane Flood, June 28, 1952; children: Deborah Anne Brown Robinson, Christopher A., Michael A., Timothy A., Emily A. Student, Oreg. State Coll., 1944-46, George Washington U., 1945, Fu Jen U., 1945; BA, Stanford U., 1949, JD, 1952. Bar: Calif. 1953, U.S. Dist. Ct. (no. dist.) Calif. 1953, U.S. Ct. Appeals (9th cir.) 1953. Assoc. Hoberg & Finger, San Francisco, 1952-58; ptnr. Hoberg, Finger, Brown & Abramson, San Francisco, 1958-75, Hoberg, Finger, Brown, Cox & Molligan P.C., San Francisco, 1975—; lectr. Stanford U., U. Calif. San Francisco, 1965—. Served with USMC, 1945-46, CBI. Fellow Internat. Acad. Trial Lawyers, Am. Coll. Trial Lawyers; mem. Am. Bd. Trial Advocates (pres. San Francisco chpt. 1980-81), San Francisco Trial Lawyers Assn. (pres. 1970-71). Democrat. Methodist. Avocations: carpentry, electrical, plumbing, tile setting. State civil litigation, Personal injury. Home: 45 Reed Ranch Rd Tiburon CA 94920 Office: Hoberg Finger Brown Cox & Molligan PC 703 Market San Francisco CA 94103

BROWN, R. EDWIN, lawyer; b. Dickerson, Md., July 16, 1920; s. J. Herbert and Elizabeth (Oxley) B.; m. Winsome S. Brown; June 22, 1946; children: Malcolm E.D., Herbert O., Richard N., Phyllis W. LLB, So. U., 1941. Bar: Md., U.S. Ct. Appeals (4th cir.), U.S. Supreme Ct. Ptnr. Brown & Sturm P.A., Rockville, Md. Served to sgt. USAF, 1942-45, ETO. Mem. ABA, Md. Bar Assn., Montgomery County Bar Assn. Democrat. Episcopalian. Lodge: Lions. Avocation: yachting. Condemnation, Real property, General practice. Office: Brown & Sturm PA 260 E Jefferson Rockville MD 20850

BROWN, RALPH EVAN, lawyer; b. Parker, Pa., Oct. 6, 1920; s. Millard Edward and Virginia Florence (Glass) B.; m. Jeanne Margaret Jones, July 14, 1951; children: Caroline J., Ralph Evan, Roxane Lee. BA in History and Polit. Sci., Grove City Coll., 1941; LLB, Harvard U., 1948. Bar: Calif. 1954, U.S. Dist. Ct. (no. dist.) Calif. 1954, U.S. Dist. Ct. (cen. dist.) Calif. 1954, U.S. Ct. Appeals (9th cir.) 1954. Ptnr. Brown & Adler, Riverside, Calif., 1979—. Served to 1st lt. USAAF, 1943-45, capt. USAF, 1951-53. Mem. Calif. Bar Assn., Riverside County Bar Assn. (pres. 1981), Assn. Trial Lawyers Am. Democrat. Methodist. State civil litigation, Family and matrimonial, Probate. Office: Brown & Adler 3903 10th St Riverside CA 92501

BROWN, RALPH SAWYER, JR., bus. exec., lawyer; b. Cohasset, Mass., July 21, 1931; s. Ralph Sawyer and Rosemary (Wyman) B.; m. Elizabeth Atkinson Rash, June 12, 1953; children—Lucy Victoria Phillips, Alexander Sawyer Batson. B.A., Swarthmore Coll., 1954; LL.B., Harvard, 1957. Bar: Mass. bar 1957, N.Y. State bar 1963. Asso. Hutchins & Wheeler, Boston, 1957-62, Carter, Ledyard & Milburn, N.Y.C., 1962-68; ptnr. Janklow & Traum, N.Y.C., 1968-71; sec., asst. gen. counsel Indian Head, Inc., N.Y.C., 1971-76; v.p., treas. Indian Head, Inc., 1976-79; v.p., gen. counsel, sec. Esquire, Inc., 1979-83, sr. v.p., counsel, sec., 1983-84; assoc. counsel Gulf&Western, Inc., N.Y.C., 1984—. Bd. mgrs. West Side YMCA, N.Y.C. Mem. Phi Beta Kappa. General corporate. Home: 390 West End Ave New York NY 10024 Office: Gulf&Western Inc One Gulf & Western Plaza New York NY 10023

BROWN, RICHARD LAWRENCE, lawyer; b. Evansville, Ind., Dec. 8, 1932; s. William S. and Mildred (Tenbarge) B.; m. Alice Rae Costello, June 14, 1957; children—Richard Barton, James, Catherine, Vanessa, Mary. A.A., Vincennes U., 1953; A.B., Ind. State U., 1957; J.D., Ind. U., 1960. Bar: Ind., 1960, U.S. dist. ct. (so. dist.) Ind., 1961, U.S. Ct. Apls. (7th cir.), 1972, U.S. Sup. Ct., 1972. Mng. ptnr. Butler, Brown, Hahn & Little and predecessors, Indpls., 1961-84; city atty. City of Beech Grove, Ind., 1967—; dir. Gen. Aviation Electronics, Inc. Bd. dirs. Internat. Trade Inst., Inc.; parish chmn. St. Jude's Ch. Served with AUS, 1953-55. Mem. ABA, Ind. Bar Assn., Ind. Mcpls. Lawyers Assn. (co-editor newsletter, bd. dirs.), Indpls. Bar Assn., Delta Theta Phi. Club: K.C. State civil litigation, Federal civil litigation, Local government. Office: 155 E Market St Suite 301 Indianapolis IN 46204

BROWN, RICHARD P., JR., lawyer; b. Phila., Dec. 21, 1920; s. Richard P. and Edith (Gillette) B.; m. Virginia M. Hanavan Curtin, Nov. 12, 1965. A.B., Princeton U., 1942; LL.B., U. Pa., 1948. Bar: Pa. 1949, U.S. Supreme Ct. 1957. Assoc. Morgan, Lewis & Bockius, Phila., 1948-56, ptnr., 1956—; dir. Fidelity Bank, Phila.; bd. dirs. Fidelity Bank. Pres. Phila. Council for Internat. Visitors, 1966-67; chmn. World Affairs Council, Phila., 1968-70; mem. Council Fgn. Relations, N.Y.C., 1975—; bd. dirs. Internat. Peace Acad., 1977—, Greater Phila. Partnership (now Urban Affairs Partnership), 1968—; bd. overseers U. Pa. Law Sch., 1969—, William Penn Charter Sch., Phila., 1969—; trustee U. Pa., 1979—; bd. mgrs. U. Pa. Mus., 1967-82, St. Christopher's Hosp. for Children, Phila., 1977-80; vice chmn. United Hosp., 1980—; trustee Eisenhower Exchange Fellowships, 1982—. Fellow Am. Coll. Trial Lawyers, Am. Bar Found.; mem. ABA (chmn. sect. internat. law 1975-76), Internat. Bar Assn., Phila. Bar Assn., Am. Soc. Internat. Law, Internat. Law Assn. (Am. br.), Order of Coif. Federal civil litigation, State civil litigation, Private international. Home: 8800 Towanda St Philadelphia PA 19118 Office: Morgan Lewis & Bockius 2000 One Logan Sq Philadelphia PA 19103

BROWN, ROBERT CHARLES, lawyer; b. Mitchell, S.D., June 16, 1949; s. Charles DeWayne and Helen Louise (Alsene) B.; m. Lynne Boyce, Mar. 31, 1977; children: Erik John Gustaf, Elizabeth Patricia. BS, Iowa State U., 1971; MA, Ohio U., 1976; JD, Baylor U., 1982. Bar: Tex. 1982, U.S. Dist. Ct. (no. dist.) Tex. 1982. Tchr. quality assurance Telemedia, Inc., Isfahan, Iran, 1976-79; dir. lang. inst. Transemantics, Inc., Abilene, Tex., 1979-80; assoc. Fanning, Harper et al, Dallas, 1982-84, Calhoun, Gump, Spillman & Stacy, Dallas, 1984—. Vol. Peace Corps Action, Mahasarakam, Thailand, 1972-75; mem. Dallas Symphony Chorus, 1985—. Mem. ABA, Tex. Bar Assn. (unauthorized practice law com.), Dallas Bar Assn. Episcopalian. Avocation: music. Insurance, State civil litigation, Personal injury. Home: 3234 Norcross Ln Dallas TX 75229 Office: Calhoun Gump Spillman & Stacy 500 N Akard Dallas TX 75201

BROWN, ROBERT HOWARD, lawyer; b. Chgo., Feb. 18, 1947; s. Daniel M. and Elaine (Lazar) G.; children: Michele, Byron. BS in Journalism, Northwestern U., 1969; JD, U. Mich., 1972. Bar: Ill. 1972, U.S. Dist. Ct. (no. dist.) Ill. 1972, Conn. 1977, U.S. Ct. Appeals (9th cir.) 1980, U.S. Supreme Ct. 1980, U.S. Ct. Appeals (10th cir.) 1981, U.S. Ct. Appeals (7th cir.) 1983, Fla. 1986. Trial atty. U.S. Dept. Labor, Chgo., 1972-79, United Airlines, Chgo., 1979-85; assoc. Laner, Muchin, Dombrow & Becker, Chgo., 1985—. Mem. ABA, Chgo. Bar Assn. Avocations: running, skiing, cooking. Federal civil litigation, State civil litigation, Labor. Office: Laner Muchin Dombrow & Becker 350 N Clark St Chicago IL 60610

BROWN, ROBERT WAYNE, lawyer; b. Allentown, Pa., July 6, 1942; s. P.P. and Rose (Ferrara) B.; m. Rochelle Kaplan, Oct. 23, 1977; m. Shelley Sherman, Mar. 3, 1973; children—Courtney Sherman, Robin Thea, Ryan Palmer. A.B., Franklin and Marshall Coll., 1964; J.D., Cornell U., 1967. Bar: Ill. 1969, Pa. 1971. VISTA atty. Community Legal Services, Detroit, 1967-68; asst. prof. law U. Ill., 1968-70; court adminstr., law clk. Lehigh County Ct. Common Pleas, 1971-72; ptnr. Gross & Brown, Allentown, Pa., 1972-76; sole practice, 1976-77; sr. ptnr. Brown & Brown, Allentown, Pa., 1977-82, Brown, Brown & Solt, 1982-85; sr. ptnr. Brown, Brown, Solt, Wiener & Krouse, 1985—; instr. bus. law Muhlenburg Coll., 1973-76; pub. defender Lehigh County, 1973-74. Mem. Rape Crisis Council Lehigh Valley, 1978-84, Lehigh County Pre-trial Services, 1975-82; bd. dirs. Hispanic Am. Orgn., 1982—, treas., 1983-86 ; bd. dirs. Lehigh County Sr. Citizens, 1980—, pres., 1984-86 ; bd. dirs. Lehigh County Legal Services, 1973-77. Lindback scholar Franklin and Marshall Coll., 1963-64. Mem. ABA, Pa. Bar Assn., Lehigh County Bar Assn., Order Coif. Democrat. Contracts commercial, Real property, Banking. Home: 225 Parkview Ave Allentown PA 18104 Office: 513 Linden St PO Box 789 Allentown PA 18105

BROWN, RONALD LEE, lawyer; b. Ft. Worth, July 21, 1946; s. Jack L. and Mary Elizabeth (Batton) B.; m. Sharon Haralson, Aug. 31, 1968; children: Grant, Nathan. BA, Tex. Tech U., 1968; JD, So. Meth. U., 1975. Bar: Tex. 1975, U.S. Dist. Ct. (no. dist) Tex. 1976, U.S. Tax Ct., U.S. Ct. Appeals (5th cir.) 1976. Ptnr. Baker, Smith, Mills, Dallas, 1975-80, Riddle & Brown, Dallas, 1980—; bd. dirs. SMB Air Corp, Dallas, Benedict Investment, Inc., Dallas. Sr. warden St. Michael Episc. Ch., Dallas, 1985; mem. chief exec. roundtable, Episcopal Diocese of Dallas, chmn. cen. convocation. Served to lt. USN, 1968-72. Democrat. General corporate, Securities. Office: Riddle & Brown 1999 Bryan Suite 2100 Dallas TX 75201

BROWN, RONALD WELLINGTON, lawyer, business executive; b. Elizabeth, N.J., Oct. 17, 1945; s. Leroy Harry and Mollie (Fitch) B.; m. Geraldine Reed, Aug. 20, 1972; children—Kimberly Diana, Michael David. B.A., Rutgers U., 1967; J.D., Harvard U., 1971, M.B.A., 1973; postgrad. Parker Sch. Fgn. and Comparative Law, Columbia U., summer 1975. Bar: N.Y. 1975, U.S. Dist. Ct. (so. and ea. dists.) N.Y. 1975, U.S. Ct. Appeals (2d cir.) 1975, U.S. Supreme Ct. 1978. Atty. legal dept. ITT, N.Y.C., 1973-74, assoc., 1974-75, staff counsel N.Am. mfg. ops., 1975-80, staff counsel regulatory affairs, 1980-81, staff counsel consumer products and services, 1981-84, staff counsel litigation, 1984-85; dirs. N.A. Commonwealth Antipiracy Ops., Motion Picture Assn. Am.; vis. prof. Huston-Tillotson Coll., Austin, Tex., 1978. Sec., dir., mem. exec. com. Studio Mus. in Harlem, N.Y.C., 1979-81; mem. Bd. of Edn., Montclair, N.J. 1986—, v.p., 1987; bd. dirs. One Hundred Black Men, N.Y.C., 1982—, 1st v.p., 1985-87; dir. Operation Crossroads Africa, Inc., N.Y.C., 1976—, v.p., 1981-86; pres., bd. dirs. Friends of the Davis Ctr. for the Performing Arts, 1987—, Leonard Davis Ctr. For the Performing Arts, N.Y.C., 1984—. Author: Economic and Trade Related Aspects of Transborder Flow: Elements of A Code for Transnational Commerce, 1986, Legal Aspects of Doing Business in the Middle East, 1975, also articles. Bd. editors Harvard Civil Rights-Civil Liberties Law Rev., 1969-71, articles editor, 1970. Named Black Achiever in Industry, Harlem YMCA, 1984. Mem. ABA (mem. council, chmn. European law com., sect. internat. law and practice 1984-86, assoc. editor Internat. Law News 1983-86), Am. Arbitration Assn., Assn. Bar City N.Y. (chmn. subcom. on fed. legislation of com. on art law 1983-86), N.Y. State Bar Assn., Internat. Law Assn., Internat. Bar Assn., Am. Soc. Internat. Law, Union Internationale des Avocats. Democrat. Baptist. Entertainment, Private international, Federal civil litigation. Home: 180 Union St Montclair NJ 07042 Office: Motion Picture Assn of Am 1133 Ave of the Americas New York NY 10036

BROWN, SEYMOUR R., lawyer; b. Cleve., Oct. 24, 1924; s. Leonard and Ella (Rubinstein) B.; m. Madeline Kusevich, July 8, 1956; children: Frederic M., Thomas R., Barbara L. N. B.A., Case-Western Res. U., 1948; J.D., Cleve. State U., 1953. Bar: Ohio 1953. Partner firm Brown & Assocs., Cleve.; pres. Carnegie Fin. Corp., Cleve., 1961—; sole practice Cleve., 1982—; dir. numerous small Ohio cos.; spl. counsel to atty. gen. State of Ohio, 1963-70; chmn. civil service commn., 1978—. Editor, pub.: Gt. Lakes Architecture, 1955-59. Chmn. CSC, University Heights, Ohio, 1978-82; mem. exec. com. Cuyahoga County Republican Orgn., 1966—. Served with AUS, 1943-45. Decorated Purple Heart, Bronze Star. Mem. Am. Bar Assn., Am. Arbitration Assn. (comml. arbitration com.), Zeta Beta Tau (nat. dir., nat. pres. 1978-80). Lodge: Mason. Real property, Contracts commercial, State civil litigation. Home: 3718 Meadowbrook Blvd University Heights OH 44118 Office: 1127 Euclid Ave Cleveland OH 44115

BROWN, STANLEY MELVIN, lawyer; b. Derry, N.H., May 29, 1916; s. Norman Chandler and Ethel Violet (Hodgkins) B.; m. Thalia May Ryder, Nov. 10, 1942; 1 child, Kenneth Chad. A.B., Dartmouth Coll., 1939; J.D., Cornell U., 1942. Bar: N.Y. 1942, N.H. 1945, U.S. Ct. Appeals (1st cir.) 1947, U.S. Supreme Ct. 1948. Ptnr. McLane, Graf, Greene & Brown, Manchester, N.H., 1946-74, Brown & Nixon, P.A., Manchester, 1975—. Chmn., mem. planning bd. Bradford, N.H., 1948-58, town counsel, 1953-65, selectman, 1986—; mem. N.H. Senate, 1951-53; del. Republican nat. conv., 1952, 72. Served to lt. (s.g.) USNR, 1942-46, PTO. Mem. Manchester Bar Assn., Merrimack County Bar Assn., N.H. Bar Assn. (pres. 1968-69), ABA (ho. of dels. 1968-83, chmn. ho. of dels. 1976-78, bd. govs. 1969-72), Am. Coll. Trial Lawyers, Internat. Soc. Barristers, Assn. Trial Lawyers Am., N.H. Bar Found. (treas. 1973-83). General practice, Federal civil litigation, State civil litigation. Office: Brown & Nixon PA 80 Merrimack St Manchester NH 03101

BROWN, STEPHEN PHILLIP, lawyer; b. Birmingham, Ala., June 29, 1941; s. William P. and Milledge (Anderson) B.; m. Dorothy Louise Ogden, Aug. 6, 1967; children: Katherine, Phillip, Steven. BSCE, Auburn U., 1963; LLB, Walter F. George Sch. Law, 1967. Bar: Ga. 1967, U.S. Dist. Ct. (mid. dist.) Ga. 1967, U.S. Ct. Appeals (11th cir.) Ga. 1967, U.S. Supreme Ct. 1967. Atty., regional counsel IRS, N.Y.C., 1967-69; ptnr. Brown, Katz, Flatau & Hasty, Macon, Ga., 1969—. Rep. Ga. House of Reps., Atlanta, 1971-74. Democrat. Methodist. Avocations: organic gardening, woodworking. General practice, Personal injury, State civil litigation. Home: 2434 Wesleyan Dr Macon GA 31210 Office: Brown Katz Flatau & Hasty 355 Cotton Ave Macon GA 31201

BROWN, STEPHEN SMILEY, lawyer; b. Little Rock, May 8, 1952; s. Jefferson Calhoun and Wanda June (Smiley) Peckham; m. Lydia Bunker Hunt, May 28, 1978 (div). BBA in Fin., So. Meth. U., 1974; cert. in Internat. Studies, U. San Diego Internat. Inst., Paris, 1977; JD, So. Meth. U., 1978. Bar: Tex. 1978, U.S. Dist. Ct. (so. dist.) Tex. 1983, U.S. Ct. Appeals (5th cir.) 1984, U.S. Ct. Internat. Trade 1985, U.S. Supreme Ct. 1985. Atty. Hunt Energy Corp., Dallas, 1976, Hunt-Stephens Co., Dallas, 1977, Hughes Tool Co., Houston, 1978-79, U.S. Presdl. Inauguration Com., Washington, 1981, U.S. Dept. Energy, Washington, 1981, Codus Corp., Washington, 1982-83; ptnr. Stephen S. Brown & Assocs., Houston, 1983—. Mem. staff Tex. Constl. Conv., 1974, staff State Rep Ray Hutchinson, 1975; active Reagan and Bush campaign, 1980, 84; bd. dirs. Very Spl. Arts Tex. Mem. ABA, Fed. Bar Assn., Tex. Bar Assn., Houston Bar Assn., Assn. Trial Lawyers Am. Republican. Episcopalian. Avocations: skiing, travel, running, weight lifting. Federal civil litigation, Private international, Labor. Home: 5000 Montrose Blvd #150 Houston TX 77006 Office: Stephen S Brown & Assocs 1001 Texas Ave #500 Houston TX 77002

BROWN, STEVEN JAY, lawyer; b. Phoenix, Apr. 18, 1953; s. Edward and Lillian Rae (Perlman) B. BA, Occidental Coll., 1975; JD, Ariz. State U., 1978. Bar: Ariz. 1978, U.S. Dist. Ct. Ariz. 1978, Calif. 1979, U.S. Ct. Appeals (9th cir.) 1979, U.S. Dist. Ct. (cen. dist.) Calif. 1980, U.S. Tax Ct. 1982, U.S. Supreme Ct. 1986. Ptnr. Eldridge & Brown, Phoenix, 1979-81; sole practice Phoenix, 1981—; of counsel Mori & Welch, 1981-86; facilitator Pres.'s Exhange, Phoenix, 1984—; bd. dirs. Valley Celebrity Sports, Inc., Phoenix. Producer Bert Convy Celebrity Tournament Spina Bifida, Scottsdale, Ariz., 1983—; trustee Ariz. Spina Bifida Charitable Trust, Phoenix, 1985—. Mem. ABA, Ariz. Bar Assn. (counsel), Assn. Trial Lawyers Am., Phoenix C. of C. (bd. dirs. small bus. com. 1985), Profl. Rodeo Cowboys Assn. Republican. Avocations: bull riding, semi-profl. photography, art collecting, snow skiing, equestrian activities. State civil litigation, Securities, Corporate taxation. Home: 4731 E Marston Dr Paradise Valley AZ 85253 Office: 1833 N 3d St Phoenix AZ 85004

BROWN, STEVEN SPENCER, lawyer; b. Manhattan, Kans., Feb. 26, 1948; s. Gerald James and Buelah Marie (Spencer) B. BBA, U. Mo., 1970, JD, 1973. Bar: Mo. 1973, U.S. Tax Ct. 1974, Ill. 1977, U.S. Dist. Ct. (no. dist.) Ill. 1979, U.S. Ct. Appeals (7th cir.) 1980, U.S. Ct. Claims 1986. Trial atty. IRS Regional Counsel, Chgo., 1973-78; sr. trial atty. IRS Dist. Counsel, Chgo., 1978-79; assoc. Silets & Martin Ltd., Chgo., 1979-85, ptnr., 1985—; adj. prof. John Marshall, Chgo., 1985—. Republican. Presbyterian. Avocations: golf, tennis. Personal income taxation, Federal civil litigation, Administrative and regulatory. Home: 1340 N Astor Apt 2805 Chicago IL 60610 Office: Silets and Martin Ltd 140 S Dearborn Suite 1500 Chicago IL 60603

BROWN, STUART MELVILLE, lawyer; b. Portland, Oreg., July 3, 1945; s. Melville Brodie and Elizabeth (Wolfe) B; m. Mary Jennifer Martin, Aug. 23, 1968; children: Stephen, Andrew. BS, Oreg. State U., 1974; JD, U. Oreg., 1976. Bar: Oreg. 1976, U.S. Dist. Ct. Oreg. 1976, U.S. Ct. Appeals (9th cir.) 1976. From assoc. to ptnr. Cass, Scott, Woods & Smith, Eugene, Oreg., 1976-82, Tonkon, Torp, Galen, Marmaduke & Booth, Portland, 1982—. Served to capt. U.S. Army, 1968-73. Republican. Avocations: rowing, running, gardening. Federal civil litigation, State civil litigation, Contracts commercial. Home: 5325 SW Westdale Dr Portland OR 97221 Office: Tonkon Torp Galen et al 1001 SW 5th St Suite 1800 Portland OR 97204

BROWN, THOMAS PHILIP, III, lawyer; b. Washington, Dec. 18, 1931; s. Raymond T. and Beatrice (Cullen) B.; m. Alicia A. Sexton, July 28, 1955; children: Thomas, Mark, Alicia, Maria, Beatrice. B.S., Georgetown U., 1953, LL.B., 1956. Bar: D.C., Md. Practice law Washington, 1958—. Author books and articles on legal malpractice. Pres. Cath. Youth Orgn. of Washington, 1972. Served to lt. USMCR, 1955-58. Mem. Bar Assn. D.C. (pres. 1986, bd. dirs. 1987), ABA (council sect. on econs. law practice). Clubs: Barristers (treas., exec. com. 1976), University, Columbia Country. FERC practice, Real property, Personal injury. Home: 5210 Norway Dr Chevy Chase MD 20815 Office: 5247 Wisconsin Ave NW Suite 4 Washington DC 20015

BROWN, (ROBERT) WENDELL, lawyer; b. Mpls., Feb. 26, 1902; s. Robert and Jane Amanda (Anderson) B.; m. Barbara Ann Fisher, Oct. 20, 1934; children: Barbara Ann (Mrs. Neil Maurice Travis), Mary Alice (Mrs. Alfred Lee Fletcher). A.B., U. Hawaii, 1924; J.D., U. Mich., 1926. Bar: Mich. 1926, U.S. Supreme Ct 1934, U.S. Ct. Appeals (6th cir.) 1952, U.S. Dist. Ct (ea. dist.) Mich. 1927, U.S. Dist. Ct. (we. dist.) Mich. 1931, U.S. Bd. Immigration Appeals 1944, U.S. Tax Ct 1973. Lawyer firm Routier, Nichols & Fildew, Detroit, 1926, Nichols & Fildew, 1927-28, Frank C. Sibley, 1929, Ferguson & Ferguson, 1929-31; asst. atty. gen. Mich., 1931-32; with legal dept. Union Guardian Trust Co., Detroit, 1933-34; sole practice law Detroit, 1934-81, Farmington Hills, Mich., 1981—; Legal adviser Wayne County (Mich.) Graft Grand Jury, 1939-40; asst. pros. atty. civil matters Wayne County, 1940; spl. asst. city atty. to investigate Police Dept. Highland Park, Mich., 1951-52. Chmn. citizens com. to form Oakland County (Mich.) Community Coll., 1962-63; Pres. Farmington (Mich.) Sch. Bd., 1952-56; chmn. Oakland County Republican County Conv., 1952; trustee Farmington Twp., Oakland County, 1957-61; pres. Oakland County Lincoln Rep. Club, 1958; Treas., bd. dirs. Friends of Detroit Library, 1943-44; bd. dirs. Farmington Friends of Library, Inc., 1952-58, pres., 1956-57; Hon. mem. Farmington Hist. Soc., 1966, St. Anthonys Guild, Franciscan Friars, 1975. Mem. Am. Bar Assn., State Bar Mich. (chmn. or mem. various coms. 1935-52, 77-80), Oakland County Bar Assn., Detroit Bar Assn. (bd. dirs. 1939-49, pres. 1948-49). Presbyn. (elder). Probate, Estate taxation, Real property. Home: 29921 Ardmore St Farmington Hills MI 48018 Office: Quakertown Plaza 32969 Hamilton Ct Suite 115 Farmington Hills MI 48018

BROWN, WESLEY ERNEST, U.S. judge; b. Hutchinson, Kans., June 22, 1907; s. Morrison H.H. and Julia (Wesley) B.; m. Mary A. Miller, Nov. 30, 1934; children: Wesley Miller, Loy B. (Mrs. John K. Wiley). Student, Kans. U., 1925-28; LL.B., Kansas City Law Sch., 1933. Bar: Kans. 1933, Mo. 1933. Practiced in Hutchinson, 1933-58; county atty. Reno County, Kans., 1935-39; referee in bankruptcy U.S. Dist. Ct. Kans., 1958-62, judge, 1962-79, sr. judge, 1979—; chief judge, 1971-77; appointee Temporary Emergency Ct. of Appeals of U.S., 1980—; Dir. Nat. Assn. Referees in Bankruptcy, 1959-62; mem. bankruptcy div. Jud. Conf., 1963-70; mem. Jud. Conf., U.S., 1976-79. Served with USNR, 1944-46. Mem. ABA, Kans. Bar Assn. (exec. council 1950-62, pres. 1964-65), Reno County Bar Assn. (pres. 1947), Wichita Bar Assn., S.W. Bar Kan., Delta Theta Phi. Office: U S Dist Ct 423 U S Courthouse 401 N Market St Wichita KS 67202

BROWN, WILLIAM ALLEY, law educator; b. La Grange, Tex., Sept. 5, 1921; s. Leon Dancy and Mary (Alley) B.; m. Ann Dyke Shafer, June 27, 1953; children—Ann Lenora, William Alley. B.B.A., U. Tex., 1942; Indsl. Adminstr., Harvard Bus. Sch., 1943; J.D., U. Tex., 1948. Bar: Tex. 1948, U.S. Dist. Ct. (we. dist.) Tex. 1950, U.S. Dist. Ct. (so. dist.) Tex. 1959, U.S. Ct. Appeals (5th cir.) 1950, U.S. Ct. Appeals (11th cir.) 1983. Assoc., ptnr. Powell, Wirtz Rauhut, Austin, Tex., 1950-58; ptnr. Powell, Rauhut, McGinnis, Reavley & Brown, Houston, 1958-61; assoc. gen. counsel Brown & Root, Inc., Houston, 1961-76, v.p., gen. atty., 1976-83; prof. constrn. law Tex. A&M U., College Station, 1983—. Served to 1st lt. U.S. Army, 1942-46, ETO. Mem. Sons of Rep. of Tex., Alpha Tau Omega. Republican. Episcopalian. Clubs: Frisch Auf Country (La Grange, Tex.), Plaza (Bryan, Tex.). Legal education, Construction, Labor. Home: 2710 Pinehurst St Bryan TX 77802 Office: Tex A & M Univ Construction Sci Dept College Station TX 77843

BROWN, WILLIAM HILL, III, lawyer; b. Phila., Jan. 19, 1928; s. William H. Jr. and Ethel L. (Washington) B.; m. Sonya M. Bell, Aug. 29, 1952 (div. 1974); 1 child, Michele D.; m. D. June Hairston, July 29, 1975; 1 child, Jeanne-Marie. B.S., Temple U., 1952; J.D., U. Pa., 1955. Bar: Pa. 1956, U.S. Ct. Appeals (3d cir.) 1959, U.S. Supreme Ct. 1960, D.C. 1972, U.S. Dist. Ct. (D.C.) 1972, U.S. Ct. Appeals (4th cir.) 1978, U.S. Ct. Appeals (10th cir.) 1986. Assoc. Norris, Schmidt, Phila., 1955-62; ptnr. Norris, Brown, Hall, Phila., 1962-68, Schnader, Harrison, Segal & Lewis, Phila., 1974—; also mem. exec. com; chief of frauds Dist. Atty.'s Office, 1968, dep. dist. atty., 1968; commr. EEOC, Washington, 1968-69; chmn. EEOC, 1969-73; lectr. S.W. Legal Found., Practising Law Inst., Nat. Inst. Trial Advocacy; dir. United Parcel Service, Inc.; dir. Lawyers Com. Civil Rights Under Law, Pub. Interest Law Ctr.; chmn. Phila. Spl. Investigation Commn. MOVE; pres. Nat. Black Child Child Devel., Inc. Contbr. articles to profl. jours. Bd. dirs. Middle State Assn. Colls. and Secondary Schs.; bd. govs. Am. Heart Assn. (southeastern Pa. chpt.); life mem. NAACP. Served with USAF, 1946-48. Recipient award of merit Fed. Bar Assn., Columbus, 1971, J. Austin Norris award Barristers' Assn., 1987. Mem. Phila. Bar Assn., D.C. Bar Assn., Pa. Bar Assn., ABA, Fed. Bar Assn., Inter-Am. Bar Assn., Assn. Trial Lawyers Am., World Assn. Lawyers (founding mem.), Am. Law Inst., Am. Arbitration Assn. (bd. dirs.), Barristers' Assn. Phila. Inc. (J. Austin Norris award 1987), Citizens Commn. Civil Rights, Alpha Phi Alpha (award of recognition 1969). Republican. Episcopalian. Federal civil litigation, State civil litigation, Labor. Office: Schnader Harrison Segal & Lewis 1600 Market St Philadelphia PA 19103

BROWN, WILLIAM HOUSTON, lawyer; b. Union City, Tenn., Apr. 14, 1941; s. George Leon and Hattie Lou (Stubblefield) B.; m. Deborah Kay Wallace, Dec. 10, 1982; children: Shaun Alan, Ward Houston. BA, Union U., Jackson, Tenn., 1963; MA, Middle Tenn. State U., 1976; JD, U. Tenn., 1972. Bar: Tenn. 1972, U.S. Dist. Ct. (we. dist.) Tenn. 1973, U.S. Ct. Appeals (6th cir.) 1973. Asst. dean U. Tenn. Coll. Law, Knoxville, 1972-73; sole practice, Jackson, 1973-79; sr. ptnr. Brown, Holmes & Rich, Jackson, 1979-83; sr. ptnr. Brown & Larson, Jackson, 1983-85; assoc. prof. law Coll. Law U. Wyo., Laramie, 1984-85, Coll. Law U. Miss., 1985—; dir. Western Trial Advocacy Inst., Laramie, 1984-85. Contbg. author: Legal Aspects of Underground Utilities, 1973. Bd. dirs. West Tenn. Legal Services, Inc., Jackson, 1975-80; pres. Jackson Theatre Guild, 1982. Woodrow Wilson fellow, 1963. Fellow Tenn. Bar Found.; mem. Tenn. Bar Assn., Tenn. Trial Lawyers Assn., Assn. Trial Lawyers Am., Tenn. Criminal Def. Lawyers, ABA, Am. Judicature Soc., Order Coif. Democrat. Baptist. Federal civil litigation, State civil litigation, Bankruptcy. Office: Univ Miss Coll of Law University MS 38677

BROWN, WILLIAM TED, lawyer; b. Ruthven, Iowa, June 22, 1953; s. Richard Michael and Bernadine Margaret (Gappa) B.; s. Carolyn Sue Rosacker, June 15, 1974; children: Scott, Tim. BA in Hist., Psychology, U. Iowa, 1975, JD, 1978. Bar: Iowa 1978, U.S. Dist. Ct. (no. dist.) Iowa 1979, U.S. Dist. Ct. (so. dist.) 1981. Assoc. Pendleton & Pendleton, Storm Lake, Iowa, 1979-81; officer Pendleton Law Firm P.C., Storm Lake, 1981-83; ptnr. Pendleton & Brown, Storm Lake, 1983-85; sole practice Storm Lake, 1985—. Trustee Storm Lake Pub. Library, 1984; bd. dirs. Faith Hope & Charity Inc., Storm Lake, 1986—. Mem. ABA, Iowa Bar Assn., Assn. Trial Lawyers Am., Iowa Trial Lawyers Assn., Iowa Defense Counsel Assn. Roman Catholic. Club: Lake Creek Country (Storm Lake) (bd. dirs. 1985—). Avocations: running, basketball, golf. Personal injury, State civil litigation, General practice. Office: 601 Cayuga St Storm Lake IA 50588

BROWNE, C. WILLING, III, lawyer; b. Balt., Oct. 30, 1939; s. C. Willing Jr. and Julia (Williams) B.; m. Mary Wetzel, Aug. 19, 1961; children: C. Willing IV, Marie Louise. BS, U. N.C., 1962; JD, U. Denver, 1966. Bar: Colo. 1968, U.S. Ct. Appeals (10th cir.). Assoc. Vegge, Hall & Evans,

Denver, 1969-74; ptnr. Gorsuch & Kirgis, Denver, 1974-84, Hall & Evans, Denver, 1984—. Mem. planning bd. Columbine Village, Littleton, Colo., 1985—; bd. dirs. S.E. Englewood (Colo.) Water Dist., 1982-83. Mem. ABA, Colo. Bar Assn., Denver Bar Assn. (litigation bd.), Nat. Assn. R.R. Trial Counsel, Am. Bd. Trial Advs. (pres. Colo. chpt. 1983), Def. Research Inst. Republican. Episcopalian. Club: Columbine Country. Avocations: golf, running. Personal injury, Federal civil litigation, State civil litigation. Office: Hall & Evans 1200 17th St Denver CO 80202

BROWNE, JEFFREY FRANCIS, lawyer; b. Clare, South Australia, Australia, Mar. 1, 1944; came to U.S., 1975; s. Patrick Joseph and Irene Kathleen (Cormack) B.; m. Deborah Mary Christine West, Aug. 28, 1971; children: Veronique Namur Irene, Jeffrey James, Nicholas Patrick, Sophie Christina, Amy Elizabeth. LLB, Adelaide U., South Australia, 1966; LLM, Sydney U., Australia, 1968, Harvard U., 1976. Bar: South Australia 1969, Australian Capital Territory 1973, N.Y. 1978, Victoria 1982, New South Wales 1983, Western Australia 1983. Assoc. High Ct. Australia, Canberra, Australian Capital Territory, 1967-68; diplomat Dept. Fgn. Affairs, Canberra, 1969; 2d sec. Australian High Commn., London and Malaysia, 1970-71; acting high commr. Australian High Commn., Ghana, 1972; counsel nuclear tests case Internat. Ct. Justice, 1973-74; assoc. Sullivan & Cromwell, N.Y.C., 1976-81, ptnr., 1983—; gen. counsel Alcoa of Australia, Melbourne, 1981-82. Mem. BNY Australia Ltd. (bd. dirs.), Law Inst. Victoria, Australian Mining and Petroleum Law Assn. (Victorian com.), Law Council Australia (trade law com.), Inst. Dirs. of Australia, Internat. Bar Assn. (sect. on energy and natural resources), Am. Soc. Internat. Law. Clubs: N.Y. Yacht, Australia (Melbourne). General corporate, Securities, Contracts commercial. Home: 13 Albany Rd, Toorak Victoria 3142, Australia

BROWNE, JOHN PATRICK, legal educator; b. East Cleveland, Ohio, Dec. 17, 1935; s. Patrick Joseph and Margaret Anne (O'Grady) B. BS in Social Sci., John Carroll U., 1957; JD, U. Detroit, 1960; MLS, Case Western Res. U., 1965. Bar: Ohio 1960, Mich. 1960, U.S. Dist. Ct. (no. dist.) Ohio 1966, U.S. Dist. Ct. (ea. dist.) Mich. 1966. Assoc. Gallagher, Sharp, Fulton & Norman, Cleve., 1965-69; prof. law Cleve.-Marshall Coll. Law, 1969—. Contbr. articles to profl. jours. Served to capt. JAGC, U.S. Army, 1960-64. Mem. ABA, Ohio Bar Assn., Mich. Bar Assn., Cleve. Bar Assn., Def. Research Assn., Delta Theta Phi. Democrat. Roman Catholic. State civil litigation, Legal education, Personal injury. Home: 17200 Clifton Blvd Lakewood OH 44107-2364 Office: Cleve U Marshall Coll Law 1801 Euclid Ave Cleveland OH 44115

BROWNE, MICHAEL L., lawyer; b. Beaumont, Tex., Sept. 2, 1946; s. Ernest Jewell and Marjorie Jane (Heisig) B.; m. Elizabeth Oswald, Feb. 22, 1969; 1 child, Sarah Skelton. AB, Princeton U., 1968; JD, U. Pa., 1974. Law clk. to presiding justice U.S. Dist. Ct. (ea. dist.) Pa., 1974; assoc. Dilworth, Paxson, Kalish, Levy & Coleman, Phila., 1974-75; spl. asst. to U.S. Sec. of Transp., 1975-77; assoc. Dilworth, Paxson, Kalish, Levy & Kauffman, Phila., 1977-78, ptnr., 1979-80; commr. ins. Commonwealth of Pa., 1980-83; ptnr. Reed, Smith. Shaw & McCaly, Phila. and Pitts., 1983—; bd. dirs. Harleysville Ins. Co. Del. Rep. Nat. Conv., 1984. Served to capt. USMC, 1968-71, Vietnam. Decorated Bronze Star, 1969. Mem. Phila. Bar Assn. (chmn. ins. law com. corps. banking and bus. law sect.). Insurance, Transportaion, Public utilities. Home: 840 Carpenter Ln Philadelphia PA 19119 Office: Reed Smith Shaw & McClay 1600 Ave of Arts Bldg Broad and Chestnut Sts Philadelphia PA 19107

BROWNE, RICHARD CULLEN, lawyer; b. Akron, Ohio, Nov. 21, 1938; s. Francis Cedric and Elizabeth Ann (Cullen) B.; m. Patricia Anne Winkler, Apr. 23, 1962; children—Richard Cullen, Catherine Anne, Paulette Elizabeth, Maureen Frances, Colleen Marie. B.S. in Econs., Holy Cross Coll., 1960; J.D. Catholic U. Am., 1963. Bar: Va. 1963, U.S. Ct. Claims 1963, U.S. Ct. Customs and Patent Appeals 1963, D.C. 1964, U.S. Ct. Mil. Appeals, 1963, U.S. Ct. Appeals (D.C. cir.) 1964, U.S. Supreme Ct. 1966, U.S. Ct. Appeals (fed. cir.) 1982, U.S. Ct. Appeals (9th cir.) 1983. Assoc. Browne, Beveridge, DeGrandi & Kline, Washington, 1963-68, ptnr., 1968-72; ptnr. Shaffert, Miller & Browne, Washington, 1972-74; sr. counsel Office of Enforcement, EPA, Washington, 1974-76; asst. chief hearing counsel U.S. Nuclear Regulatory Commn., Washington, 1976-78; sole practice, Washington, 1978-80; ptnr. Bishop, Liberman, Cook, Purcell & Reynolds and predecessor firms, Washington, 1980—; lectr. U. R.I., 1975, Washburn U., 1978, Legal Inst., CSC, 1975-78. Del., Montgomery County Civic Fedn., 1970-74; chmn. Citizens Adv. Com. on Rockville Corridor, 1972-77; mem. Montgomery County Potomac River Basin Adv. Com., 1972-74. Served to capt. USAF, 1963-66. Named Disting. Mil. grad. Holy Cross Coll., 1960. Mem. ABA, Fed. Bar Assn., D.C. Bar Assn., Va. State Bar, Coll. Holy Cross Alumni Assn. (bd. dirs. 1971-78). Republican. Roman Catholic. Clubs: Holy Cross (pres. Washington 1968-69, 1973-74), Rotary, Nat. Lawyers, Advt., Capitol Hill. Bd. editors Cath. U. Law Rev., 1962-63. General corporate, Environment, Trademark and copyright. Home: 7203 Old Stage Rd Rockville MD 20852 Office: 1200 17th St NW Washington DC 20036

BROWNE, WILLIAM BITNER, lawyer; b. Springfield, Ohio, Nov. 23, 1914; s. John Franklin and Etta Blanche (Bitner) B.; m. Dorothy Ruth Gilbert, Aug. 31, 1939; children: Franklin G., Dale Ann Browne Compton. A.B., Wittenberg U., 1935, LL.D. (hon.), 1970; postgrad., U. Bordeaux, 1935-36; LL.B. cum laude, Harvard U., 1939. Bar: Ohio 1939, U.S. Dist. Ct. (so. dist.) Ohio 1941, U.S. Ct. Appeals (6th cir.) 1950, U.S. Supreme Ct. 1970. Assoc. Donovan, Leisure, Newton & Lumbard, N.Y.C., 1939-40; assoc. Corry, Durfey & Martin, Springfield, Ohio, 1940-48; ptnr. Corry, Durfey, Martin & Browne and successors, Springfield, Ohio, 1948—; dir. Ohio Bar Title Ins. Co. Contbr. (articles to legal jours.). Bd. dirs. Wittenberg U., 1955—; pres. Greater Springfield & Clark Assn., Ohio, 1948-49; vice chmn. Clark County Republican Central and Exec. coms., 1948-52; mem. Springfield City Bd. Edn., 1950-53; mem. exec. com. United Appeals Clark County, 1956-62. Served to capt. OSS Signal Corps, U.S. Army, 1942-46. Decorated Bronze Star; decorated Croix de Guerre with palm, medaille de Reconnaissance Francaise. Fellow Am. Coll. Trial Lawyers, Am. Bar Found., Am. Coll. Probate Counsel, Ohio Bar Found. (pres. 1979 Fellows award research and service); mem. ABA (del. 1971-76), Ohio Bar Assn. (pres. 1969-70 medal of honor 1973), Springfield Bar Assn. (pres. 1967), Springfield C. of C. (pres. 1961-62). Episcopalian. Clubs: Zanesfield Rod and Gun, Springfield Country. Lodges: Rotary; Masons. General practice, Probate. Office: Martin Browne Hull & Harper 203 First Nat Bank Bldg Springfield OH 45501

BROWNELL, CARLTON KEARNS, lawyer, author; b. Geneva, N.Y., May 20, 1937; s. Carlton Kearns and Mildred Ruth (Kennedy) B.; m. Nancy Lee Smith, Aug. 4, 1962; children: Carlton Kearns, Susan Lee, Jennifer Elizabeth. BA, Colgate U., 1959; JD, Syracuse U., 1962. Bar: N.Y. 1966, U.S. Dist. Ct. (we. dist.) N.Y. 1975. Assoc. James S. Fitzgerald, Geneva, N.Y., 1966-68; trust officer Lincoln 1st Bank, N.A., Geneva, 1968-71; ptnr. McGowan & Brownell, Geneva, 1971—; asst. dist. atty. Ontario County, N.Y., Geneva, 1971-75, 1st asst. dist. atty., 1975-79. Author: Criminal Procedure in N.Y., rev. edit., 2 vols., 1982. Scoutleader Boy Scouts Am., Geneva, 1966—; chpt. chmn. ARC, Geneva, 1984-86, mem. Eastern Ops. Adv. Com., 1986—, mem. Nat. Group IV and V Adv. Coms., 1986—. Served to 1st lt. USAF, 1962-65. Mem. N.Y. Bar Assn., Ontario County Bar Assn. (pres. 1982). Lodge: Rotary (pres. 1975-76). Criminal, State civil litigation, Probate. Home: 87 Hillcrest Ave Geneva NY 14456 Office: McGowan and Brownell 37 Seneca St Geneva NY 14456

BROWNING, CHARLES W., lawyer; b. Mt. Clemens, Mich., Feb. 10, 1956; s. Wilbur Brady and Helen Ethelda (Harvey) B.; m. Stacy Elizabeth Skiff, May 17, 1985. BA, Mich. State U., 1978; JD, U. Detroit, 1981. Bar: Mich. 1981, U.S. Dist. Ct. (ea. dist.) Mich. 1982. Assoc. Vandeveer, Garzia, Tonkin, Kerr, Heaphy, Moore, Sills & Poling, P.C., Detroit, 1981—. Mem. ABA, Mich. State Bar Assn. State civil litigation, Federal civil litigation. Office: Vandeveer Garzia Tonkin et al 333 W Fort St Suite 1600 Detroit MI 48226

BROWNING, DAVID STUART, lawyer; b. Amarillo, Tex., June 6, 1939; s. Stuart W. and Pauline (Rogers) B.; m. Judith Helen Jackson, July 31, 1958; 1 son, Mark. B.A., U. Tex., 1960, J.D., 1962; M.A., Johns Hopkins U., 1964. Bar: D.C. bar 1963, Tex. bar 1964, N.Y. bar 1970. Atty. firm Fulbright & Jaworski, Houston, 1964-70; asst. counsel Schlumberger Ltd., N.Y.C., 1970-75; sec., gen. counsel Schlumberger Ltd., 1976—. Contbr. articles to legal jours. Mem. Am., N.Y. State, Tex., Houston bar assns., Assn. Bar City N.Y., Am. Soc. Internat. Law, Southwestern Legal Found. (adv. bd.), Am. Soc. Corporate Secs. General corporate, Private international. Office: Schlumberger Ltd 277 Park Ave New York NY 10172

BROWNING, JAMES ROBERT, U.S. judge; b. Great Falls, Mont., Oct. 1, 1918; s. Nicholas Henry and Minnie Sally (Foley) B.; m. Marie Rose Chapell, Aug. 14, 1941. LL.B. with honors, Mont. State U., 1941; LL.D. (hon.), U. Mont., 1978. Bar: Mont. bar 1941, D.C. bar 1950, U.S. Supreme Ct. bar 1952. Spl. atty. antitrust div. Dept. Justice, 1941-46; chief Dept. Justice (N.W. regional office), 1948-49, asst. chief gen. litigation sect. antitrust div., 1949-51, 1st asst. civil div., 1951-52; exec. asst. to atty. gen. U.S., 1952-53; chief U.S. (Exec. Office for U.S. Attys.), 1953; pvt. practice Washington, 1953-58; lectr. N.Y.U. Sch. Law, 1953, Georgetown U. Law Center, 1957-58; clk. Supreme Ct. U.S., 1958-61; judge U.S. Ct. Appeals 9th Circuit, 1961—, chief judge, 1976—. Mem. Am. Law Inst., Am., Mont., Fed. bar assns., Inst. Jud. Adminstrn., Am. Judicature Soc., Am. Soc. Legal History (adv. bd. jour.). Office: US Court of Appeals and Post Office Bldg San Francisco CA 94101

BROWNING, JOHN RAUM, lawyer; b. St. Louis, Sept. 5, 1946; s. John Roy and Mary Cornelia (Ingersoll) B.; m. Jan Louise Downing, Oct. 7, 1972; 1 child, Jeffrey Roy. BA, Yale U., 1968; JD cum laude, Tex. Tech U., 1980. Bar: Tex. 1980, U.S. Dist. Ct. (no. dist) Tex. 1980, U.S. Dist. Ct. (so. dist.) Tex. 1982, U.S. Dist. Ct. (we. dist.) Tex. 1983, U.S. Dist. Ct. (ea. dist.) Tex. 1984, U.S. Dist. Ct. (ea. dist.) Mich. 1984, U.S. Ct. Appeals (5th cir.) 1985, U.S. Supreme Ct. 1985. Commd. 2d lt. USAF, 1968, advanced through grades to capt., 1972, res., 1977; assoc. Strasburger & Price, Dallas, 1980-83, Shank, Irwin & Conant, Dallas, 1983-85; gen. counsel, sec. Jet East Internat., Inc., Dallas, 1985—, also bd. dirs.; sec. WSE Inc., Dallas, 1985—, Wesael Corp., Dallas, 1985—; bd. dirs., sec. Jet East Internat. Sales and Leasing Inc., Dallas. Contbg. editor Tex. Tech U. Law Rev. Gen. mem. The 500 Inc., Dallas. Decorated D.F.C. with three oak leaf clusters, Air medal with twelve oak leaf clusters; Vietnamese Cross of Gallantry. Mem. ABA, Tex. Bar Assn., Dallas Bar Assn., Phi Delta Phi, Phi Kappa Phi. Republican. Episcopalian. Club: Exchange (Dallas). Avocation: flying. Aviation, General corporate, Insurance. Home: 1403 Chickasaw Richardson TX 75080 Office: Jet East Internat Inc 7363 Cedar Springs Dallas TX 75235

BROWNING, RICHARD EDWARD, lawyer; b. Mobile, Ala., Sept. 7, 1955; s. James Patrick and Elizabeth Joan (Balthrop) B.; m. Rosemary Teresa Steely, June 25, 1977; children: Virginia Marie, Katherine Michele, Andrew Jude. BA, Spring Hill Coll., 1977; JD, U. Ala., 1980. Bar: Ala. 1980, U.S. Dist. Ct. (so. dist.) Ala. 1984, U.S. Ct. Appeals (11th cir.) 1985, U.S. Dist. Ct. (mid. dist.) Ala. 1986, U.S. Supreme Ct. 1986. Assoc. Cunningham, Bounds, Yance, Crowder & Brown, Mobile, 1984—. Served to lt. JAGC, USN, 1980-84. Mem. Assn. Trial Lawyers Am., Ala. Bar Assn., Ala. Trial Lawyers Assn., Mobile Bar Assn. Roman Catholic. Personal injury, State civil litigation. Home: 154 Roberts St Mobile AL 36604 Office: Cunningham Bounds et al 1601 Dauphin St Mobile AL 36604

BROWNING, ROBERT R., state judge. Judge N.C. Supreme Ct., Raleigh, 1986—. Office: NC Supreme Ct PO Box 1841 Raleigh NC 27602 *

BROWNING, WILLIAM DOCKER, judge; b. Tucson, May 19, 1931; s. Horace Benjamin and Mary Louise (Docker) B.; m. Courteny Browning (div.); children: Christopher, Logan, Courtenay; m. Zerilda Sinclair, Dec. 17, 1974; 1 child, Benjamin. BBA, U. Ariz., 1954, LLB, 1960. Bar: Ariz., U.S. Dist. Ct. Ariz., U.S. Ct. Appeals (9th cir.), U.S. Supreme Ct. Sole practice Tucson, 1960-84; judge U.S. Dist. Ct., Tucson, 1984—; mem. jud. nominating comm. appellate ct. appointments, 1975-79. Del. 9th Cir. Jud. Conf., 1968-77, 79-82. Served to 1st lt. USAF, 1954-57, capt. USNG, 1958-61. Fellow Am. Coll. Trial Lawyers, Am. Bar Found.; mem. ABA (spl. com. housing andurban devel. law 1973-78, com. urban problems and human affairs 1978-80), State Bar Ariz. (securities regulation com. 1964-66, chmn. uniform jury instructions com. 1962-66, chmn. merit selection of judges com. 1973-76, bd. govs., 1968-74, pres.-elect 1971-72, pres. 1972-73, named Outstanding Mem. 1980), Pima County Bar Assn. (exec. com. 1964-68, med.-legal screening panel 1965-75, pres. 1967-68), Am. Bd. Trial Advocates, Am. Judicature Soc. (bd. dirs. 1975-77, Herbert Lincoln Harley award 1978), Inst. Ct. Mgmt. (trustee 1978—). Judicial administration. Office: US Dist Ct 55 E Broadway #301 Tucson AZ 85701

BRUCE, E(STEL) EDWARD, lawyer; b. Hutchison, Kans., Nov. 23, 1938; s. Kenneth Dean and Josephine (Vigna) B.; m. Marnell Elaine Higley, Aug. 9, 1960; children—Anthony Dean, Caroline Summers. B.A. summa cum laude, Yale U., 1960, LL.B. magna cum laude, 1966. Bar: D.C. bar 1967. Law clk. U.S. Supreme Ct., Washington, 1966-67; asso. firm Covington & Burling, Washington, 1967-73; partner Covington & Burling, 1973—; adj. prof. constitutional law Georgetown U. Law Center, 1970-75. Served to lt. (j.g.) USN, 1960-63. Mem. Am. Law Inst., Am. Bar Assn., D.C. Bar, Audubon Naturalist Soc. Middle Atlantic States (bd. dirs.), Order of Coif, Phi Beta Kappa. Clubs: Met. (Washington); Chevy Chase. Administrative and regulatory, Federal civil litigation, Environment. Home: 2701 Foxhall Rd Washington DC 20007 Office: Covington & Burling 1201 Pennsylvania Ave NW Washington DC 20044

BRUCE, NEIL CURTIS, lawyer; b. Colorado Springs, Colo., Sept. 3, 1953; s. James Franklin and Lorraine (Crowther) B.; m. Barbara Ann Bruening, May 24, 1975; children: Benjamin, Matthew. BA in Govt., Adams State Coll., 1975; JD, U. Tulsa, 1978. Bar: Colo. 1979, U.S. Dist. Ct. Colo. 1979, U.S. Ct. Appeals (10th cir.) 1979. Assoc. Rector, Retherford, Mullen & Johnson, Colorado Springs, 1979-83, ptnr., 1983—. Notes and comments editor Tulsa Law Jour., 1978. Mem. ABA, Colo. Bar Assn., El Paso City Bar Assn., Colo. Def. Lawyers Assn. Democrat. Methodist. Avocations: backpacking, skiing. State civil litigation, Probate, Real property. Home: 15 W Cimarron Colorado Springs CO 80903 Office: Rector Retherford et al 415 S Sahwatch Colorado Springs CO 80903

BRUCE, PETER WAYNE, insurance company executive; b. Rome, N.Y., July 12, 1945; s. G. Wayne and Helen A. (Hibling) B.; m. Joan M. McCabe, Sept. 20, 1969; children: Allison, Steven. B.A., U. Wis., 1967; J.D., U. Chgo., 1970; postgrad., Harvard Bus. Sch., 1986. Bar: Wis. 1970. Atty. Northwestern Mut. Life Ins. Co., Milw., 1970-74, asst. gen. counsel, 1974-80, gen. counsel, sec., 1980—; v.p. Northwestern Mut. Life Ins. Co., 1983—. Bd. dirs. Alverno Coll., Milw., Children's Service Soc. of Wis., Shorewood Civic Found., Badger Meter Found.; bd. dirs., treas. Curative Rehab. Ctr. Mem. ABA (com. corp. law depts.), Associated Life Ins. Counsel, Am. Council Life Ins., Wis. Bar Assn., Milw. Bar Assn. General corporate, Insurance. Office: Northwestern Mut Life Ins Co 720 E Wisconsin Ave Milwaukee WI 53202

BRUCE, ROBERT ROCKWELL, lawyer; b. Mt. Kisco, N.Y., Mar. 8, 1944; s. Robert R. and Nona (Burtch) B.; m. Collot Guerard, Aug. 30, 1969 (div. Sept. 1983); 1 child, Benjamin. B.A. magna cum laude, Harvard U., 1966, J.D., 1970; M.P.A., Kennedy Sch. Govt., 1970. Bar: D.C. bar 1972. Dir. communications planning Public Broadcasting Service, 1970-72; asso. firm Hogan & Hartson, Washington, 1972-77; gen. counsel FCC, Washington, 1977-81; partner firm Leva, Hawes, Symington, Martin & Oppenheimer, Washington, 1981-83, Debevoise & Plimpton, 1983—. Office: Debevoise & Plimpton 555 13th St NW Suite 1100E Washington DC 20004

BRUCE, WILLIAM ROLAND, lawyer; b. Portsmouth, Va., July 13, 1935; s. William Roland Sr. and Elizabeth (Jack) B.; m. Katherine Martin, Sept. 1, 1956 (div. Apr. 1980); m. Rita Kay Glisson, Jan. 3, 1981; children: Kate, William, Elizabeth, Margaret, Andrew, Alexander. BA, U. Va., 1956, LLB, 1959. Bar: Va. 1959, Tenn. 1960, U.S. Supreme Ct. 1964. Assoc. Martin, Tate & Morrow, Memphis, 1959-62; sole practice Memphis, 1963-65; ptnr. Bruce & Southern, Memphis, 1965-72; chmn. Bruce, Southern, Brandon & Regan, P.C., Memphis, 1972—; lectr. Vanderbilt U. Sch. Law, Nashville, 1972-79. Rep. Tenn. Ho. of Reps., Nashville, 1966-68; senator Tenn. Senate, Nashville, 1968-72; chmn. Health Edn. and Housing Facility Bd. of Memphis, 1984—. Served to capt. U.S. Army, 1957-58. Named Tenn. Outstanding Young Man, Jaycees, 1969, Conservationist of Yr., Tenn. Conservation League, 1972. Fellow Am. Coll. Mortgage Attys., Tenn. Bar Found.; mem. ABA, Tenn. Bar Assn., Va. State Bar Assn. Democrat. Episcopalian. Avocation: sailing. Real property, Legislative, Banking. Home: 1668 Forrest Ave Memphis TN 38112 Office: Bruce Southern et al 696 Oakleaf Office Ln Memphis TN 38117 Address: Bruce Southern et al 500 Church St Nashville TN 37219

BRUCKEN, ROBERT MATTHEW, lawyer; b. Akron, Ohio, Sept. 15, 1934; s. Harold M. and Eunice B. (Boesel) B.; m. Lois R. Gilbert, June 30, 1960; children—Nancy, Elizabeth, Rowland, Gilbert. A.B., Marietta Coll., 1956; J.D., U. Mich., 1959. Bar: Ohio 1960. Assoc., Baker & Hostetler, Cleve., 1960-69, ptnr., 1970—. Trustee Lakeside Assn., 1979—, Marietta Coll., 1983—. Served with AUS, 1959-60. Mem. ABA, Ohio State Bar Assn. (chmn. probate and trust law sect. 1981-83), Bar Assn. Greater Cleve. (chmn. probate ct. com. 1973-75), Am. Coll. Probate Counsel, Phi Beta Kappa. Congregationalist. Estate planning, Probate, Estate taxation. Office: Baker & Hostetler Suite 3200 National City Ctr Cleveland OH 44114

BRUCKNER, WILLIAM H., lawyer; b. Parkersburg, W.Va., Sept. 10, 1938; s. Frank Lewis and Mildred (Horner) B.; m. Wendy Schroeder, July 1, 1961; children: Elizabeth, Anne, Caroline. Student, Yale U., 1956-58; BS in Chem. Engring., U. Tulsa, 1961, LLB, 1964. Bar: Okla. 1964, Tex. 1972, Nebr. 1972. Atty. NLRB, Kansas City, Mo., 1964-67, Borden, Inc., Houston, 1969-70; gen. atty. Cooper Industries, Houston, 1970-72; ptnr. Nelson & Harding, Lincoln, Nebr., 1972-78; mng. ptnr. Bruckner & Sykes, Houston, 1978—. Mem. ABA. Episcopalian. Labor. Office: Bruckner & Sykes 2200 Post Oak Blvd Suite 555 Houston TX 77056

BRUDER, GEORGE FREDERICK, lawyer; b. Ann Arbor, Mich., June 4, 1938; s. George G. and Mary Louise (Pfisterer) B.; m. Jean Riley, July 10, 1965; children—Roxanne, Stephanie. A.B., Dartmouth Coll., 1960; J.D., U. Chgo., 1963. Bar: D.C. 1964. Atty. FPC, Washington, 1964-67; atty. long lines dept. AT&T, Washington, 1967-68; assoc. Debevoise & Liberman, Washington, 1968-70, ptnr., 1971-75; ptnr. Bruder & Gentile, Washington, 1976—. Mem. Fed. Energy Bar Assn. (exec. com. 1980—, pres. 1984—), ABA. Democrat. Episcopalian. FERC practice, Public utilities, Administrative and regulatory. Home: 3213 Morrison St NW Washington DC 20015 Office: 1350 New York Ave NW Washington DC 20005

BRUECKNER, KURT MALCOLM, lawyer; b. Peoria, Ill., Nov. 22, 1954; s. Leonard James and Marian (Johnson) B.; m. Suzanne Gale Brueckner, Feb. 28, 1983; 1 child, Ryan Conrad. BBA, Ariz. State U., 1977; JD, U. Ariz., 1980. Bar: Ariz., U.S. Dist. Ct. Ariz., U.S. Ct. Appeals (9th cir.). Atty. Greyhound Leasing and Fin. Corp., Phoenix, 1980-83; assoc. Furth, Fahrner, Bluemle & Mason, Scottsdale, Ariz., 1983—. Legal counsel Carefree Improvement Assn., Ariz., 1985—, Foothills Community Found., Carefree, 1986—; sec., bd. dirs. Heritage Found. Ariz., 1984—. Continental Oil scholar, 1977, Alan duBois Found. scholar, 1977; named one of Outstanding Young Men Am., 1986. Mem. ABA (subcom. rules and regulations, securities council, sect. corp. banking and bus law, antitrust sect., sect. securities law), Beta Gamma Sigma. Republican. Methodist. Avocation: sports. Securities, Real property. Home: 5026 E Monte Cristo Scottsdale AZ 85254 Office: Furth Fahrner Bluemle & Mason 7373 N Scottsdale Rd Scottsdale AZ 85253

BRUEMMER, RUSSELL JOHN, lawyer; b. Decorah, Iowa, Apr. 23, 1952; s. John William and Marion Jean (Wartinbee) B. BA, Luther Coll., 1974; JD, U. Mich., 1977. Bar: Minn. 1978, D.C. 1980, U.S. Dist. Ct. D.C. 1981. Law clk. to judge U.S. Ct. Appeals (8th cir.), 1977-78; spl. asst. to the dir. FBI, Washington, 1978-80, chief counsel congl. affairs, 1980-81; assoc. Wilmer, Cutler & Pickering, Washington, 1981-84, ptnr., 1985—; speaker numerous profl. seminars. Editor-in-chief U. Mich. Jour. of Law Rev.; contbr. articles to law and banking jours. Mem. adv. group Washington Work Assn., 1981—. Mem. ABA (banking law com. 1982—, subcom. on bank holding cos. and nonbanking activities, chmn. 1982—, com. on devels. in investment services 1985—), Order of the Coif. Republican. Lutheran. Banking, Contracts commercial. Home: 4623 S 30th Rd Arlington VA 22206 Office: Wilmer Cutler & Pickering 2445 M St NW Washington DC 20037

BRUENING, RICHARD PATRICK, lawyer; b. Kansas City, Mo., Mar. 17, 1939; s. Arthur Louis, Jr. and Lorraine Elizebeth (Gamble) B.; m. Jane Marie Egender, Aug. 25, 1962; children—Christiana G., Paul R., Erin E. A.B., Rockhurst Coll., 1960; J.D., U. Mo. at Kansas City, 1963. Bar: Mo. bar 1963. Since practiced in Kansas City; law clk. U.S. Dist. Judge R.M., Duncan, 1963-65; assoc. firm Houts, James, McCanse & Larison, 1965-68; gen. atty. Kansas City So. Ry. Co., 1969; asst. gen. counsel Kansas City So. Industries, Inc., 1970-76, gen. counsel, 1976-82, v.p., gen. counsel, 1982—; mem. Mo. Press-Bar Commn., 1981-85, Mo. Rail Improvement Authority, 1984-86, chmn., 1984-85. Bd. dirs. Kansas City Met. chpt. Nat. Found. March of Dimes, 1969-73, treas., 1971; trustee Livestock Mktg. Inst., 1978—; bd. dirs. Performing Arts Found./Folly Theatre, 1983—, sec., 1984—; mem. bd. trustees conservatory of music UMKC. Mem. ABA, Mo., Kansas City bar assns., Lawyers Assn. Kansas City, Nat. Assn. R.R. Trial Counsel, Practising Law Inst., Phi Delta Phi, Omicron Delta Kappa. Roman Catholic. Clubs: Kansas City Country, Kansas City. Federal civil litigation, Securities, General corporate. Home: 606 W Meyer Blvd Kansas City MO 64113 Office: 301 W 11th St Kansas City MO 64105

BRUESTLE, ERIC GEORGE, lawyer; b. Cin., Apr. 23, 1953; s. George O. and Carol (Roettger) B.; m. Wendy Waggoner, June 5, 1976; children: Amy, Matthew, David. MusB, U. Cin., 1974, JD, 1977. Bar: Ohio 1977. Assoc. Law Office of Robert Tatgenhorst, Cin., 1977-85; ptnr. Tatgenhorst & Bruestle, Cin., 1986—. mem. mgmt. com. Cen. YMCA, Cin., 1980—; v.p. Cin. Community Orch., 1982—; bd. dirs. Gen. Protestant Orphan's Home, Cin. 1986—. Mem. ABA, Ohio Bar Assn., Ohio Acad. Trial Lawyers, Cin. Bar Assn. (chmn. workers' compensation com. 1986—). Avocations: music, sailing, backpacking. Workers' compensation, Probate. Office: Tatgenhorst & Bruestle 524 Walnut Suite 600 Cincinnati OH 45202

BRUGGER, GEORGE ALBERT, lawyer; b. Erie, Pa., Jan. 19, 1941; s. Albert F. and Georgia V. (Bach) B.; m. Elayne Bernadette McCarthy, Aug. 26, 1962; children: Laura, Linda, Mark. BA, Gannon Coll., 1963; JD, Georgetown U., 1967. Bar: Md. 1968, U.S. Dist. Ct. Md. 1972, U.S. Supreme Ct. 1972. Law clk. to U.S. asst. atty. gen. U.S. Dept. of Justice, Washington, 1963-66; mgr. pub. affairs Air Transport Assn. of Am., Washington, 1966-68; ptnr. Beatty & McNamee, Hyattsville, Md., 1968-75; sr. ptnr., pres. Fossett & Brugger, Seabrook, Md., 1975—; bd. dirs. Prince George's County Fin. Services Corp. bd. dirs. Ardmore Devel. Ctr., Cath. Youth Orgn.; mem. Prince George's Econ. Devel. Adv. Com. Fellow Md. Bar Found.; mem. ABA, Md. Bar Assn. (bd. dirs.), Prince George's County Bar Assn. (pres. 1982), Prince George's C. of C. (Disting. Service award 1980, 83, 85). Roman Catholic. Avocations: collecting classic sports cars, marine tropical fish. Real property, Condemnation, Administrative and regulatory. Home: 8805 Belmart Rd Potomac MD 20854 Office: Fossett & Brugger 10210 Greenbelt Rd Suite 900 Seabrook MD 20706

BRUHN, SOREN FREDERICK, insurance company executive; b. Enumclaw, Wash., May 24, 1928; s. Soren Frederik and Helen Mae (Schumacher) B.; m. Nola Katherine Hansen, Sept. 9, 1951; children—Tracy Lee, Rebecca Helen, Robin Margaret, Amy Katherine. B.A., U. Wash., Seattle, 1952, tchrs. cert., 1953, J.D. (asso. editor law rev. 1958-59), 1959. Bar: Wash. bar 1959. Asst. atty. gen. State of Wash., 1959-61; chief dep. ins. commnr. 1961-67; with Safeco Corp., Seattle, 1967—; asso. gen. counsel Safeco Corp., 1972—, gen. counsel, 1974—, v.p., 1979—; dir. Safeco Ins. Co. Am. and affiliates. Chmn. Safeco Polit. Action Com. Served with AUS, 1946-47. Mem. Am. Bar Assn., Nat. Com. Ins. Guaranty Funds, Wash. Bar Assn., Wash. Ins. Council, Seattle-King County Bar Assn. Club: Sand Point Country. General corporate. Home: 1508 9th Ave W Seattle WA 98119 Office: Safeco Plaza Seattle WA 98185 *

BRUIN, LINDA LOU, lawyer; b. Grandville, Mich., June 7, 1938; d. John and Tena (Groeneveld) B. A.A., Grand Rapids Jr. Coll., 1958; A.B., Hope

Coll., 1961; postgrad. U. Stockholm, Sweden, 1963-64; A.M., U. Mich., 1967; J.D., Wayne State U., 1973. Bar: Mich. 1973, U.S. Dist. Ct. (we. dist.) Mich. 1980, U.S. Ct. Appeals (6th cir.) 1984. Tchr. Georgetown Pub. Sch., Jenison, Mich., 1959-63, Bullock Creek Area Sch., Midland, Mich., 1964-70; legal supr. Legis. Service Bur., Mich. State Legis., Lansing, 1973-79; legal counsel Mich. Assn. Sch. Bds., Lansing, 1979—. Monthly columnist Mich. Sch. Bd. Jour., 1981—. Mem. Citizen's Commn. to Improve Mich. Courts, 1986. Fellow Inst. Ednl. Leadership, 1982. Mem. ABA (com. mem. 1983—), Women Lawyers Assn. Mich. (pres. 1984-85), Mich. State Bar Assn. (com. chmn. 1982-87 , State Bar Rep. Assembly 1985—), LWV. Democrat. Education and schools, Legislative, Local government. Office: Mich Assn Sch Bds 421 W Kalamazoo Lansing MI 48933

BRULE, THOMAS RAYMOND, lawyer; b. Rochester, N.Y., Feb. 18, 1954; s. Raymond and Barbara (Ann) B.; m. Sonia Doll, Feb. 12, 1983; children: Adam, Ryan. BS, Ind. U., Pa., 1976; MBA, U. Ky., 1977; JD, U. Louisville, 1980. Bar: Ky. 1980, U.S. Dist. Ct. (we. dist.) Ky. 1980, U.S. Ct. Appeals (6th cir.) 1985, U.S. Dist. Ct. (cen. dist.) Ill. 1983. Sole practice Louisville, 1980-83; franchise counsel Kentucky Fried Chicken Corp., Louisville, 1983-85, dir. franchising, 1985—; lectr. U. Louisville, 1980-85. Trustee Ind. U., Pa., 1975-76. Mem. ABA, Ky. Bar Assn., Louisville Bar Assn. Republican. Avocation: racquetball. Franchise law, Contracts commercial. Home: 14201 Oak Branch Ct Louisville KY 40223 Office: Kentucky Fried Chicken Corp PO Box 32070 Louisville KY 40232

BRUMBAUGH, JOHN MOORE, lawyer; b. Lima, Peru, Aug. 3, 1945; s. John Granville and Annie Lee (Moore) B.; m. Caroline Patterson, Aug. 12, 1967; children: John Patterson, David Elliott, Katherine Anne, Caroline Moore. BA, Wabash Coll., 1967; JD, U. Fla., 1970. Bar: Fla. 1970, U.S. Ct. Appeals (5th and 11th cirs.), U.S. Dist. Ct. (so. dist.) Fla., U.S. Supreme Ct. Law clk. to presiding justice U.S. Dist. Ct. (so. dist.) Fla., Miami, Fla., 1970-72; assoc. Frates, Floyd, Pearson, Miami, 1972-76; ptnr. Frates, Floyd, Pearson, Miami, Fla., 1976-84; sr. ptnr. Floyd, Pearson, Richman, Greer, Weil, Zack & Brumbaugh, P.A., Miami, 1984—. Trustee Trinity Episcopal Sch., Miami, 1985—, chmn. bd. dirs., 1987—. Mem. Fla. Bar Assn. (bd. cert. civil trial lawyer 1984-85), Dade County Bar Assn. (chmn. fed. ct. com. 1984-85), Blue Key, Acad. Fla. Trial Lawyers (diplomate), Phi Kappa Phi. Federal civil litigation, State civil litigation, Personal injury. Office: Floyd Pearson et al 1 Biscayne Tower 25th Floor Miami FL 33131

BRUMER, MICHAEL, lawyer; b. Kingston, N.Y., Oct. 7, 1924; s. Saul and Frieda (Altman) B.; m. Dorothy Dweres, June 8, 1952; children: Pamela Brumer Duboff, Marc L. BS in Econs., Syracuse U., 1949; LLB, 1951, JD, 1968. Bar: N.Y. 1951, Fla. 1952, U.S. Dist. Ct. (so. dist.) Fla. 1953, U.S. Supreme Ct. 1978. Claims mgr. Allstate Ins. Co., Miami, Fla., 1952-57; ptnr. Fuller & Brumer, P.A., and successor firms, Miami, 1957-80; pres. Brumer, Cohen, Logan & Kendall, P.A., Miami, 1980—; tchr. Para-Legal Inst. Served with USAAF, 1943-46. Recipient Syracuse U. Meritorious Service award, 1976. Fellow Acad. Fla. Trial Lawyers; mem. Am. Arbitration Assn. (panel of arbitrators), ABA, Fed. Bar Assn., N.Y. Bar Assn. Fla. Bar Assn. (chmn grievance com. 1976-78) Miami Beach Bar Assn., Dade County Bar Assn., Assn. Trial Lawyers Am. Republican. Jewish. Clubs: Jockey, Cricket, Bankers. Lodges: B'nai B'rith, Elks. State civil litigation, Personal injury, Workers' compensation. Home: 1560 NE Quay Terr Miami Beach FL 33138 Office: Brumer Cohen Logan Kandell Museum Tower Suite 2600 150 W Flagler St Miami FL 33130

BRUMMER, BENNETT H., lawyer; b. Apr. 16, 1941; m. Arlene Brummer, Aug. 25, 1962. A.B., U. Miami, Coral Gables, Fla., 1962, J.D., 1965; postgrad. Harvard U. Sch. Law, 1972, 78. Bar: Fla. 1965, N.Y. 1965, U.S. Dist. Ct. (so. dist.) Fla. 1965, U.S. Dist. Ct. (so. dist.) N.Y. 1968, U.S. Ct. Appeals (5th cir.) 1969, U.S. Supreme Ct. 1970. Vol., U.S. Peace Corps., 1966-68; staff atty. Legal Services of Greater Miami, Inc., 1968-71; sr. atty. Edison-Little River Office, 1969-71; adj. prof. law U. Miami Sch. Law, Coral Gables, Fla., 1977—; asst. pub. defender appellate div. 11th Jud. Cir., Dade County, Fla., 1971-77, chief appellate div., 1973-77, exec. asst., 1975-77, pub. defender, 1976—; mem. Parole and Probation Commn. Qualification Com., 1979-81; mem. cts. task force Fla. Council on Criminal Justice, 1978-82; mem. Gov.'s Commn. on Criminal Justice Standards and Goals, 1977; mem. Dade-Miami Criminal Justice Council, 1977—; mem. Supreme Ct.'s Com. on Standard Jury Instructions, 1977-86, Fla. Fed. Jud. Council, 1986—; mem. Supreme Ct. Appellate Adv. com.; dir. Voters Inc., Transition, Inc. Bd. dirs. Health Systems Agy. S. Fla., Inc.; mem. Drug Abuse Task Force; mem. legal panel ACLU; bd. dirs., defender com. Nat. Legal Aid and Defender Assn.; mem. Am. Jewish Com.; mem. exec. com. of regional bd., chmn. community affairs com., discriminations com. Anti-Defamation League; mem. Spanish-Am. League Against Discrimination; mem. Cuban Nat. Planning Council, Inc.; trustee Greater Miami United; bd. dirs. Haitian Am. Voter Edn. Ctr., Biscayne Democrats; mem. adv. council S.E. Fla. Inst. Criminal Justice, Miami-Dade Community Coll.; mem. adv. council Project Stoppp, Inc. Reginald Heber Smith Community Lawyer fellow U. Pa. Mem. ABA (def. function com.), Nat. Legal Aid and Defender Assn. (bd. dirs. 1983—), Fla. Pub. Defender Assn. (treas. 1976-77, v.p. 1978-79, 82-83, exec. com. 1975-83, pres. elect 1979-80, 86—, pres. 1980-81), Fla. Criminal Def. Attys. Assn. (bd. dirs.), The Fla. Bar (appellate ct. rules com., code and rules of evidence com., criminal law com., prison reform com.), Fla. Justice Inst. (indigent def. services project adv. council), Dade County Bar Assn. (pub. interest law bank adv. bd.), Fla. Assn. Women Lawyers, Am. Judicature Soc. Office: 800 Met Justice Bldg 1351 NW 12th St Miami FL 33125

BRUNDRETT, GEORGE L(EE), JR., lawyer; b. Rockport, Tex., Mar. 17, 1921; s. George L. and Sara Thomas (Drake) B.; m. Jonell Rodgers, July 25, 1957; children—Jan, George L. B.B.A., U. Tex.-Austin, 1946, LL.B., 1950. Bar: Tex. 1949. Assoc. Fischer, Wood & Burney, Corpus Christi, Tex., 1950-54, ptnr., 1954-64; with Coastal States Gas Producing Co. (now The Coastal Corp.), Houston, 1964—, v.p., sr. v.p., sec., gen. counsel, dir., 1973-85, sole practice, 1985—; dir. subs. including Colo. Interstate Gas Co. Served with U.S. Army, 1942-46. Mem. ABA, Tex. Bar Assn., Nueces County Bar Assn., Houston Bar Assn., Corp. Secs. Assn., U. Tex. Alumni Assn., Inns. of Ct. Club. Republican. Presbyterian. Clubs: Houston City, Am. Contract Bridge League (life). General corporate, Oil and gas leasing, Contracts commercial. Home: 11815 Wink Rd Houston TX 77024 Office: Refining & Marketing Inc 9 Greenway Plaza Houston TX 77046

BRUNELL, NORMAN ELIOT, patent lawyer; b. Worcester, Mass., Apr. 18, 1946; s. Henry and Bessie (Saltzman) B.; m. Leslie Jean Brothers, Sept. 13, 1967 (div. Sept. 1971); m. Susan Lynne Fancher, May 26, 1985. BEE, Wocester Poly. Inst., 1968; JD, Suffolk U., 1973. Bar: Mass. 1973, U.S. Patent Office 1973, Calif. 1975, U.S. Dist. Ct. (cen. dist.) Calif. 1975, U.S. Ct. Appeals (fed. cir.) 1984. Engr. Gen. Dynamics, San Diego, 1968-69; patent atty. Foxboro Co., Foxborough, Mass., 1969-74, Beckman Insts., Fullerton, Calif., 1974-75; div. patent counsel Litton Industries, Inc., Beverly Hills, Calif., 1976-79; counsel Litton Energy Systems, Houston, 1979-81; sole practice Los Angeles, 1981—. Mem. ABA, Los Angeles Patent Lawyers Assn. Jewish. Computer, Private international, Patent.

BRUNER, PHILIP LANE, lawyer; b. Chgo., Sept. 26, 1939; s. Henry Pfeiffer and Marjorie (Williamson) B.; A.B., Princeton U., 1961; J.D., U. Mich., 1964; M.B.A., Syracuse U., 1967; m. Ellen Carole Germann, Mar. 21, 1964; children—Philip Richard, Stephen Reed, Carolyn Anne. Admitted to Wis. bar, 1964, Minn. bar, 1968. Ptnr. Briggs and Morgan P.A., Mpls., St. Paul, 1967-83; sr. ptnr. Hart, Bruner, O'Brien & Thorton, P.A., Mpls., 1983— ; mem. firm Briggs & Morgan, St. Paul, 1968-83; adj. prof. William Mitchell Coll. Law, St. Paul, 1970-78, 81; lectr. law seminars univs.; bar assns. and industry. Mem. Bd. Edn., Mahtomedi Ind. Sch. Dist. 832, 1978-86. Served to capt. USAF, 1964-67. Recipient Disting. Service award St. Paul Jaycees, 1974; named One of Ten Outstanding Young Minnesotans, Minn. Jaycees, 1975. Fellow Nat. Contract Mgmt. Assn.; mem. Internat. Am., Fed., Minn., Wis., Ramsey, Hennepin bar assns., Internat. Assn. Ins. Counsel, Am. Arbitration Assn. (nat. panel arbitrators). Club: Mpls. Athletic. Contbr. articles to profl. jours. State civil litigation, Federal civil litigation, Government contracts and claims. Home: 8432 80th St N Stillwater MN 55082 Office: 1221 Nicollet Mall Minneapolis MN 55403

BRUNETTE, STEVEN EDWARD, lawyer, food company executive; b. Grand Junction, Colo., Dec. 6, 1949; s. Terrence Patrick and Lorraine Marlyss (Toppen) B.; m. Janet Lou Wells, June 6, 1981; children: Meggan Marie, Janelle Lorayne. BS, Loyola U., Los Angeles, 1972, JD, 1976. Bar: Calif. 1976. Asst. to gen. counsel City Investing Co., Beverly Hills, Calif., 1974-76; gen. counsel, sec. Franklin Fin. Corp., Los Angeles, 1977-78; assoc. gen. counsel Beatrice/Hunt Wesson, Inc., Fullerton, Calif., 1978—. Mem. ABA, Los Angeles Bar Assn., Orange County Bar Assn., Calif. Bar Assn. General corporate, Labor, Contracts commercial. Home: 1739 Fairford Dr Fullerton CA 92633 Office: Beatrice/Hunt Wesson Inc 1645 W Valencia Dr Fullerton CA 92634

BRUNETTI, JOHN JOSEPH, lawyer; b. Maywood, N.J., Sept. 10, 1948; s. Ferdinand Richard Brunetti and Edith (Dupignac) Murray; m. Rockette S. Pirro, July 11, 1970. AB, Franklin & Marshall Coll., 1970; JD cum laude, N.Y. Law Sch., 1974; LLM, So. Meth. U., 1975. Bar: N.Y. 1975, Tex. 1976, U.S. Dist. Ct. (no. dist.) Tex. 1976, U.S. Dist. Ct. (so. dist.) N.Y. 1976, U.S. Ct. Appeals (5th cir.) 1976, U.S. Dist. Ct. (ea., we. and no. dists.) N.Y. 1978, U.S. Ct. Appeals (2d cir.) 1978, U.S. Supreme Ct. 1978. Asst. prof. Vt. Law Sch., South Royalton, 1975-76; assoc. May & Herridge, Dallas, 1976-77; ptnr. Gordon & Brunetti, Syracuse, N.Y., 1977-80; assoc. Nottingham Law Firm, Syracuse, 1980-84; ptnr. DeFrancisco, Menkin & Brunetti, Syracuse, 1984-87; asst. U.S. atty., no. dist. N.Y. Organized Crime Drug Enforcement Task Force, Syracuse, 1987—; adj. prof. Syracuse U. Coll. Law, 1977—, Syracuse U. Legal Assistant Program, 1979—; instr. Onondaga County Police Acad., Syracuse, 1984—; reporter Fed. Speedy Trial Act. Dist. Vt., Rutland, 1975-76; lectr. various orgns. Mem. ABA, N.Y. State Bar Assn., N.Y. State Trial Lawyers Assn., N.Y. State Defenders Assn., Onondaga County Bar Assn. (coordinator criminal continuing legal edn.). Criminal, Labor. Home: 1681 Channelside Trail Baldwinsville NY 13027 Office: c/o US Attys Office Federal Bldg 100 S Clinton St Rm 369 Syracuse NY 13260

BRUNETTI, MELVIN T., federal judge; b. 1933. Student, U. Nev., 1960; JD, U. Calif., San Francisco, 1964. Sole practice 1964-85; judge U.S. Ct. Appeals (9th cir.), Reno, 1985—. Served with U.S. Army N.G., 1954-56. Office: US Ct Appeals 50 W Liberty St Suite 610 Reno NV 89501 *

BRUNO, GARY ROBERT, lawyer; b. Green Bay, Wis., Oct. 7, 1951; s. Robert John and Mary Lois (Eparviar) B.; m. Terry Lynn Ott, Oct. 22, 1977. BBA in Fin. and Regional Planning, U. Wis., Green Bay, 1973; JD, John Marshall Law Sch., 1977. Bar: Wis. 1977, U.S. Dist. Ct. Wis. 1978. Sole practice Green Bay and Shawano, Wis., 1977-78; prosecutor Code of Fed. Regulation Ct., Keshena, Wis., 1978; asst. dist. atty. Menominee and Shawano Counties, Shawano, 1978-82, dist. atty., corp. counsel, adminstr. child support agy., 1982—; mem. exec. com. Fed. Law Enforcement Coordinating Com. Ea. Dist. Wis., Milw., 1985—. V.p. Big Bros./Big Sisters, Shawano, 1981-83, bd. dirs. 1980—; bd. dirs. Alcohol and Drug Ctr. Shawano, 1979-82; mem. exec. bd. Reps., Shawano, 1985—. Mem. ABA, Wis. Bar Assn., Shawano County Bar Assn. (sec., treas. 1982, v.p. 1983, pres. 1984), Nat. Dist. Atty. Assn., Wis. Dist. Atty. Assn. Club: Shawano. Lodge: Optimists (2d v.p. Shawano 1985—, bd. dirs. 1979-85, optimist of yr. award 1984). Avocations: community service, scuba diving, hunting. Criminal, Juvenile. Home: 1413 E Lieg Ave Shawano WI 54166 Office: Dist Atty Office 311 N Main St Shawano WI 54166

BRUNO, KEVIN ROBERT, lawyer; b. Newark, June 9, 1953; s. Angelo Joseph and Rita Theresa (Klein) B.; m. Lura Current, Apr. 25, 1981; 1 child, Kevin Robert II. BA with honors, Rutgers U., 1975; JD, Union U., 1978. Bar: N.J. 1979, U.S. Dist. Ct. N.J. 1979, N.Y. 1980, N.H. 1980, U.S. Dist. Ct. N.H. 1980. Assoc. Freeman & Bass, Newark, 1979, Bennett & Bennett, West Orange, N.J., 1979-80, Office of Luigi J. Castello, Woodsville, N.H., 1980-83; ptnr., officer Castello & Bruno, P.A., Woodsville, 1983-85; sole practice Woodsville, 1986—. Mem. ABA, N.H. Bar Assn., Grafton County Bar Assn., Phi Beta Kappa, Pi Sigma Alpha. Democrat. Roman Catholic. Avocations: hiking, camping, skiing, snow shoeing, gardening. General practice, Probate, Real property. Home: Rural Rt 1 Box 80 Groton VT 05046 Office: 37 Court St Woodsville NH 03785

BRUNO, RICHARD THOMAS, lawyer; b. Summit, N.J., May 31, 1955; s. Anthony Thomas and Violet Henrietta (Andersen) B.; m. Anne Lee Griffiths, Aug. 8, 1981; 1 child, David Thomas. AB, Dartmouth Coll., 1977; JD, Vanderbilt U., 1981. Bar: N.Y. 1982, U.S. Dist. Ct. (no. dist.) N.Y. 1982, Ohio 1983, U.S. Tax Ct. 1983. Adminstrv. asst. Dem. Com. of Onondaga County, Syracuse, N.Y., 1977-78; assoc. Davoli, McMahon & Kublick, Syracuse, 1981-83; gen. counsel Pat Bombard Buick, Syracuse, 1983-84; sole practice Fayetteville, N.Y., 1984; assoc. O'Hara & Crough, Syracuse, 1984—; mem. local rules com. for no. dist. N.Y. U.S. Bankruptcy Ct., Utica, 1985—; legal counsel Fayetteville-Manlius (N.Y.) A Better Chance Program, 1985—. Mem. N.Y. State Dem. Com., Albany, 1982-86, Onondaga County Dem. Com., Syracuse, 1982-86; enrollment liaison officer Dartmouth Club Cen. N.Y., Syracuse, 1985—, mem. exec. com., 1981; agt. Dartmouth Coll. Class of 1977. Mem. ABA (bus. and corp. law and tax sects.), N.Y. State Bar Assn. (bus. and corp. law and tax sects.), Onondaga County Bar Assn. Roman Catholic. Avocations: downhill skiing, sailing, running, racquetball, nautilus. Contracts commercial, Bankruptcy, General corporate. Home: 122 Edwards Dr Fayetteville NY 13066 Office: O'Hara & Crough 1304 Buckley Rd Syracuse NY 13212

BRUNO, THOMAS ANTHONY, lawyer; b. Berwyn, Ill., Feb. 8, 1954; s. Alexander Nicholas and Mildred Mary (Biciste) B.; m. Elizabeth Ann Matthias, June 12, 1976; children: Anthony Alexander, Evan Stanley. B.A., U. Ill. 1976, J.D., 1979. Bars: Ill. 1980, U.S. Dist. Ct. (cen. dist.) Ill. 1980, U.S. Supreme Ct. 1985. Prin. Thomas A. Bruno and Assocs., Urbana, Ill., 1980—; lectr. U. Ill. Law Sch., Urbana, 1981—; host TV show "Ask A Lawyer". Author (newspaper column) Honest Lawyer, 1983. Bd. dirs. Devel. Services Ctr., Champaign, Ill., 1979-82; vice chmn. bd. Disabled Citizens Found., Champaign, 1982—; mem. Humane Soc. Champaign County, 1984, Chgo. Zool. Soc. Ill. Legis. scholar, 1972-76. Mem. ABA, Ill. Bar Assn., Champaign County Bar Assn., Assn. Trial Lawyers Am., Champaign County Assn. Criminal Defense Lawyers (past pres. Champaign chpt. 1982—), Nat. Assn. for Prevention Child Abuse (v.p. Champaign county chpt.), Phi Eta Sigma. Democrat. Roman Catholic. Clubs: U. Ill. Quarterback, U. Ill. Rebounder. Lodges: K.P., Kiwanis. Criminal, Family and matrimonial, State civil litigation. Home: 1109 W Park Ave Champaign IL 61821 Office: Thomas A Bruno and Assocs 303 W Green St Urbana IL 61801

BRUNSON, HUGH ELLIS, judge; b. Crowley, La., June 7, 1927; s. Hugh Gordon and Martha Elizabeth (Ellis) B.; m. Margaret Elizabeth McNair, Aug. 26, 1950; children—Lauren Kathleen, Jeffery Lane. BBA, La. State U., JD, 1951. Bar: La. 1951, U.S. Dist. Ct. (ea., mid. and we. dists.) La. 1951, U.S. Supreme Ct. 1951. Sole practice, Baton Rouge, La., 1954, Crowley, La., 1954-76; dist. judge 15th Jud. Dist., Parishes of Acadia, Lafayette and Vermillion, La., 1976—; judge U.S. Ct. Appeals (3d cir.); research specialist La. Legis. Council; judge ad hoc Crowley City Ct.; dir. Indigent Defender Program for Acadia Parish; chmn. Notarial Commn. Acadia Parish; Acadia Parish police jury jud. coordinator to dist. atty., spl. asst. dist. atty. 15th Jud. Dist.; gen. counsel La. Rice Promotion and Rice Research Bds.; spl. guest lectr. Lafayette Police Acad., Acadia Parish Sheriff's Aux., La. Dist. Attys. Assn. Active Boy Scouts Am., Campfire Girls, Civil Club, PTA, Little Theatre. Served with USN, World War II, USAF. Mem. ABA, Am. Judges Assn., Nat. Conf. State Trial Judges, Nat. Council Juvenile and Family Ct. Judges, La. Bar Assn., La. Dist. Judges Assn.(exec. com., treas. 1984-85, sec. 1985-86, v.p. 1986-87), La. Council Juvenile Ct. Judges, 15th Jud. Dist. Bar Assn. (past v.p., sec.), Acadia Parish Bar Assn. (past pres., v.p., sec.), Am. Legion, Phi Delta Phi. Democrat. Methodist. Lodge: Rotary. State civil litigation, Criminal, Jurisprudence. Home: 307 E 8th St Crowley LA 70526 Office: Acadia Parish Courthouse Crowley LA 70526

BRUNSON, NOLEN LANDFORD, lawyer; b. Allendale, S.C., Dec. 25, 1928; s. Whewell Wemyss and Lula Grace (Tinsley) B.; m. Margaret Anne Barnette, Sept. 12, 1952; children: David Wesley, Charles Edwin. AA, North Greenville Jr. Coll., 1948; BA, Furman U., 1950; LLB, Tulane U., 1953, LLM, 1954. Bar: La. 1953, S.C. 1954, U.S. Ct. Mil. Appeals 1954, U.S. Ct. Appeals (4th cir.) 1962. Ptnr. Hayes, Brunson & Gatlin, Rock Hill, S.C. Tchr. Sunday Sch., deacon, trustee First Baptist Ch., Rock Hill. Real property, General practice, Estate planning. Home: 2948 Shandon Rd Rock Hill SC 29730 Office: Hayes Brunson & Gatlin PO Box 964 Rock Hill SC 29730

BRUSH, LOUIS FREDERICK, lawyer; b. Amityville, N.Y., Dec. 7, 1946; s. Frederick and Frances (Annunziata) B.; m. Eileen Forsyth, Aug. 13, 1972; children: Christopher, Brian, Stephen. BS in Acctg. and Bus. Adminstrn., L.I. U., 1971; MBA in Taxation, CCNY, 1975; JD, N.Y. Law Sch., 1980. Bar: N.Y. 1980, U.S. Dist. Ct. (so. and ea. dists.) N.Y. 1980, U.S. Tax Ct. 1980, U.S. Ct. Appeals (2d cir.) 1980. Agt. IRS, Mineola, N.Y., 1971-76; appellate conferee IRS, Carle Place, N.Y., 1976-80; sole practice Mineola, 1980—; lectr. 5th Annual Estate Planning Conf. Am. Inst. CPA's, San Francisco, 1982; dept. chmn. Bramson Tech. Coll., N.Y.C., 1980-81; part-time prof. acctg. and tax law SUNY, Farmingdale, 1974-75, Suffolk County Community Coll., Selden, N.Y., 1975-76, CUNY, Queens, 1980-81. Contbr. articles to profl. jours. Mem. N.Y. State Bar Assn. (award 1980), Nassau County Bar Assn., N.Y. State Trial Laywers Assn., N.Y. County Trial Lawyers Assn. Estate taxation, Personal income taxation, State and local taxation. Office: 101 Front St Mineola NY 11501

BRUSHWOOD, DAVID BENSON, pharmacy educator, lawyer; b. Columbia, Mo., Sept. 26, 1948; s. John Stubbs and Carolyn (Norton) B.; m. Mary Christine Parks; children: Charles, Paul, John. BA, U. Kans., 1970, BS in Pharmacy, 1975, JD, 1981. Bar: Kans. 1981, U.S. Dist. Ct. Kans. 1981. Pharmacist Gessler Drug Co., Wichita, Kans., 1975-78; atty. Fisher, Patterson, Sayler & Smith, Topeka, 1981-82; asst. prof. Phila. Coll. Pharmacy, 1982-85; assoc. prof. W.Va. U., Morgantown, 1985—. Recipient Nat. Assn. Retail Druggists award, 1975; Kanehl scholar 1979; Outstanding Tchr. award Sch. of Pharmacy, W. Va. U., 1986. Health, Personal injury. Home: 411 Rotary Ave Morgantown WV 26505 Office: W Va Univ Sch of Pharmacy Morgantown WV 26506

BRUTLAG, MICHAEL LOWELL, lawyer; b. Denver, Aug. 21, 1955; s. Lowell C. and Audrey J. (Grefe) B.; m. Anne Kessler, Oct. 4, 1980; children: Katherine, Daniel, Kevin. BS in Psychology magna cum laude, Western Ill. U., 1977; JD cum laude, U. Minn., 1980. Bar: Minn. 1980, U.S. Dist. Ct. Minn. 1980, Wis. 1984. Assoc. Brenner, Workinger & Thompson P.A., Mpls., 1980-86; ptnr. Brutlag & Okoneski, Mpls., 1986—. Mem. ABA, Wis. Bar Assn., Minn. Bar Assn., Hennepin County Bar Assn., Forum Constrn. Industry, Minn. Assn. Racing Enthusiasts (bd. dirs. 1984—). Lodge: Optimists. Consumer commercial, State civil litigation, Real property. Office: Brutlag & Okoneski 1208 First Bank Pl W Minneapolis MN 55402

BRUZGA, PAUL WHEELER, lawyer; b. Lawrence, Mass., Oct. 15, 1952; s. Peter Paul and Mary Louise (Wheeler) B. BS, U. Colo., 1974; JD, Franklin Pierce Coll., 1978. Bar: N.H. 1978, U.S. Dist. Ct. N.H. 1978. Sole practice Manchester, N.H., 1978—. Mem. Assn. Trial Lawyers Am. Republican. Roman Catholic. General practice. Office: 573 Maple St Manchester NH 03104

BRYAN, ARTHUR ELDRIDGE, JR., lawyer; b. Webster City, Iowa, July 28, 1924; s. Arthur Eldridge and Grace Lillian (Glassburner) B.; B.A., State U. Iowa, 1949, J.D., 1951; m. Elizabeth Ann Stubbings, Oct. 18, 1958; children—Elizabeth Grace, Arthur Eldridge III, John Milner, Daniel Franklin. With U.P. R.R. Co., Omaha, 1942-54; capital ptnr., mem. mgmt. com., chmn. tax dept. McDermott, Will & Emery, Chgo., 1954—; dir. Gits Bros. Mfg., Chgo., 1967-68; dir., v.p., sec. Yuma Mesa Devel. Co., Yuma, Ariz., 1967-79; chmn. bd. dirs., chief exec. officer Lake Arrowhead Devel. Co. (Calif.), 1971-80. Lectr. taxation U. Chgo., Marquette U., No. Ill. U. Mem. com. on legis. action New Trier (Ill.) High Sch., 1974-78; active Boy Scouts Am., Glencoe, Ill., 1968-74; mem. adv. bd. United Settlement Appeal, Chgo., 1962. Bd. dirs., treas., pres. chmn. fin. com. Erie Neighborhood House, Chgo., 1958—; trustee N. Cen. Coll., Naperville, Ill., 1974-79; sec., chmn. bd. trustees, sec. prudential bd. Glencoe Union Ch., 1969-79. Served with inf. AUS, 1942-46; ETO, PTO. Decorated Bronze Star, Combat Inf. badge. Fellow Am. Tax Counsel; mem. ABA. (chmn., spl. adviser sect. taxation com. on comml. banks and financials 1966-74), Ill. Bar Assn., Iowa Bar Assn., Chgo. Bar Assn., Chgo. Fed. Tax Forum., Ill. C. of C. (chmn. fed. tech. tax com. 1970), Chgo. Assn. Commerce and Industry (fed. appropriations and expenditures com. 1968—), Nat. Council Farmer Coops. (LTA com. 1974—, chmn. net operating loss, netting, tracing, tax controversies, patronage v. non-patronage subcoms. 1976—), Am. Soc. of Accts. for Coops. (tax. com. 1976—). Clubs: Chgo., Mid-Day, Monroe, Executive (Chgo.); Skokie Country (Glencoe, Ill.); Quail Creek Country (Naples, Fla.). Contbr. articles to profl. jours. Corporate taxation, Personal income taxation, State and local taxation. Home: 1004 Pine Tree Ln Winnetka IL 60093 Office: McDermott Will & Emery 111 W Monroe St Chicago IL 60603

BRYAN, BARRY RICHARD, lawyer; b. Orange, N.J., Sept. 5, 1930; s. Lloyd Thomas and Amy Rufe (Swank) B.; m. Margaret Susannah Elliot, July 24, 1953; children—Elliot Christopher, Peter George (dec.), Susannah Margaret, Sallie Catharine. B.A., Yale U., 1952, J.D. cum laude, 1955; diploma in comparative legal studies, Cambridge U., Eng., 1956. Bar: N.Y. 1959. Legal advisor to gen. counsel Sec. of U.S. Air Force, Washington, 1956-58; assoc. Debevoise & Plimpton, N.Y.C., 1958-62; ptnr. Debevoise & Plimpton, 1963—. Served to 1st lt. USAF, 1956-58. Fulbright scholar Trinity Coll., Cambridge U., 1956. Mem. ABA, Assn. of Bar of City of N.Y., Union Internationale des Avocats, Phi Beta Kappa, Order of Coif. Republican. Episcopalian. Clubs: Country of New Canaan (Conn.); Polo de Paris (Paris). General corporate, Private international, Securities. Home: 543 Cascade Rd New Canaan CT 06840 Office: Debevoise & Plimpton 875 Third Ave New York NY 10022

BRYAN, HENRY C(LARK), JR., lawyer; b. St. Louis, Dec. 8, 1930; s. Henry Clark and Faith (Young) B.; m. Sarah Ann McCarthy, July 28, 1956; children—Mark Pendleton, Thomas Clark, Sarah Christy. A.B., Washington U., St. Louis, 1952, LL.B., 1956. Bar: Mo. 1956. Law clk. to fed. judge 1956; assoc. McDonald & Wright, St. Louis, 1956-60; ptnr. McDonald, Bernard, Wright & Timm, St. Louis, 1961-64, McDonald, Wright & Bryan, St. Louis, 1964-81, Wright, Bryan & Walsh, St. Louis, 1981-84; v.p., dir. Harbor Point Boat & Dock Co., St. Charles, Mo., 1966-80, Merrell Inst. Agy., 1966-80; dir. Stanley Hanks Painting Co., 1983-84. Served to 1st lt. AUS, 1952-54. Mem. ABA, Mo. Bar Assn., St. Louis Bar Assn. (past chmn. probate and trust sect., marriage and divorce law com.), Kappa Sigma, Phi Delta Phi. Republican. Episcopalian. Lodge: Elks. Probate, General corporate, Family and matrimonial. Home: 41 Ladue Terr Ladue MO 63124 Office: 11 S Meramec Ave Saint Louis MO 63105

BRYAN, MILDRED GOTT, lawyer, real estate broker; b. Washington, Oct. 20; d. Howard Seymour and Cora Elizabeth (Norris) Gott; m. Ernest R. Bryan, Sept. 15, 1952; (dec.); 1 dau., Carolyn Bryan Goodrich. Student Mt. Holyoke Coll., 1924-26; A.B. magna cum laude, Trinity Coll., 1928; J.D. cum laude, George Washington U., 1932. Bar: D.C. 1932. Atty. real estate div. War Dept., Dept. Def., Washington, 1942-46; sole practice, Washington, 1952—; pres. Eastland Gardens, Inc. Mem. women's com. Nat. Symphony Orch.; trustee World's Christian Endeavor Union, Met. Meml., Nat. Meth. Ch., Washington; patron Met. Opera Assn. Mem. ABA, Inter Am. Bar Assn., D.C. Bar Assn., English Speaking Union, Internat. Bar Assn., Nat. Trust for Historic Preservation, World Peace Through Law Assn., Smithsonian Assn., Friend of Nat. Zoo. Democrat. Methodist. Clubs: Columbia Country, Army-Navy, Spring Valley Garden. Real property, Condemnation. Home: 4840 Quebec St NW Washington DC 20016 Office: 1819 H St NW Suite 440 Washington DC 20006

BRYAN, ROBERT J., judge; b. Bremerton, Wash., Oct. 29, 1934; s. James W. and Vena Gladys (Jensen) B.; m. Cathy Ann Welander, June 14, 1958; children: Robert James, Ted Lorin, Ronald Terence. BA, U. Wash., 1956, JD, 1958. Bar: Wash. 1959, U.S. Dist. Ct. (we. dist.) Wash. 1959, U.S. Tax Ct. 1965, U.S. Ct. Appeals (9th cir.) 1985. Assoc., then ptnr. Bryan & Bryan, Bremerton, 1959-67; judge Superior Ct., Port Orchard, Wash., 1967-84; ptnr. Riddell, Williams, Bullitt & Walkinshaw, Seattle, 1984-86; judge U.S. Dist. Ct. (we. dist.) Wash., Tacoma, 1986—; mem. State Jail Comm., Olympia, Wash., 1974-76, Criminal Justice Tng. Com., Olympia, 1978-81, State Bd. on Continuing Legal Edn., Seattle, 1984-86; mem., sec. Jud. Qualifications Commn., Olympia, 1982-83. Author: (with others) Washington Pattern Jury Instructions (civil and criminal vols. and supplements),

1970-85. Served to maj. USAR. Judicial administration. Office: US Dist Ct PO Box 1494 1102 A St Room 314 Tacoma WA 98401

BRYAN, ROBERT RUSSELL, lawyer; b. Shelbyville, Tenn., Mar. 14, 1943; s. Russell Duval and Auda Mai (Ellis) B. Student U. So. Miss., 1961-62; student Samford U., 1962-63, J.D., 1967; student George Washington U., 1964. Bar: Ala. 1967, U.S. Dist. Ct. (no. dist.) Ala. 1967, U.S. Supreme Ct., 1971, U.S. Tax Ct. 1972, U.S. Dist. Ct. S.D. 1973, U.S. Dist. Ct. (ea. dist.) Wis. 1975, Calif. 1978, U.S. Dist. Ct. (no. dist.) Calif. 1978, U.S. Ct. Appeals (5th and 9th cirs.) 1979, U.S. Ct. Appeals (4th cir.) 1980, U.S. Ct. Appeals (3d cir.) 1982, N.Y. 1983. Asst. to v.p. DeHavilland Aircraft of Can., Ltd., Toronto, Ont., Can., 1967; ptnr. Lindbergh, Lindbergh, Leach & Bryan, Birmingham, Ala., 1968-73; sr. counsel Law Offices of R.R. Bryan, Birmingham, 1973-75; ptnr. Bryan, Wiggins, Quinn & Appell, Birmingham, 1975-77; sr. ptnr. Law Offices of Robert R. Bryan, San Francisco, 1978—. Mem. exec. bd. Nat. Coalition Against the Death Penalty, 1984—; bd. dirs. Mill Valley Community Ctr., Calif., 1984-85, No. Calif. Coalition Against Death Penalty. Recipient Presdl. award Assn. to Advance Ethical Hypnosis, 1984. Fellow Am. Bd. Criminal Lawyers; mem. Nat. Assn. Criminal Def. Attys. (death penalty com.), Assn. Trial Lawyers Am., Calif. Trial Lawyers Assn., Criminal Trial Lawyers Assn., Calif. Bar (criminal law sect.), San Francisco Bar Assn., Nat. Lawyers Guild, Am. Acad. Forensic Scis., Calif. Attys. for Criminal Justice (death penalty com.), Amnesty Internat., NAACP (life), ACLU. Democrat. Baptist. Clubs: Press, Commonwealth (San Francisco). Criminal, Civil rights, Federal civil litigation. Office: 2020 Union St San Francisco CA 94123

BRYAN, THOMAS LYNN, lawyer; b. Wichita, Kans., June 10, 1935; s. Herbert Thomas and Ruth Marjorie (Williams) B.; m. Virginia Alice Cooper, June 13, 1981; children by previous marriage—Victoria Lynne, Douglas Edward. B.A., U. Kans., 1957; LL.B., Columbia Law Sch., 1960. Bar: N.Y. Assoc. Willkie Farr & Gallagher, N.Y.C., 1960-66, ptnr., 1967—. Contbg. author: Business Acquisitions, 1971, 2d edit. 1981. Fellow Am. Coll. Investment Counsel; mem. ABA, N.Y. State Bar Assn., Assn. Bar City of N.Y., Conf. of Rwy. Counsel, Phi Beta Kappa. Republican. Clubs: Upper Ridgewood Tennis, Club at Citicorp Center. Avocations: tennis; platform tennis; sports; theatre. General corporate, Bankruptcy. Home: 202 Mountain Ave Ridgewood NJ 07450 Office: Willkie Farr & Gallagher One Citicorp Center 153 E 53d St New York NY 10022

BRYAN, TREVOR GEORGE, lawyer; b. Kingston, Jamaica, Feb. 2, 1946; came to U.S., 1955; s. Clifford Randall and Viola Eugenie (Edwards) B.; m. Violet Demetria Harrington, June 10, 1969; children: Amy, Alma, Courtney. BA, Amherst Coll., 1967; JD, Harvard U., 1971. Bar: Mass. 1971, U.S. Dist. Ct. (ea. dist.) La. 1971, U.S. Ct. Appeals (5th cir.) 1972, La. 1976, U.S. Supreme Ct. 1978. Assoc. Lemle & Kelleher, New Orleans, 1974-76; ptnr. Jefferson, Bryan & Gray (later Jefferson, Bryan, Gray & Jupiter), New Orleans, 1976—; mem. vis. com. Loyola Law Sch., New Orleans, 1984—; mem. La. State Mineral Bd., Baton Rouge, 1979-82. Mem. New Orleans Civil Service Commn., 1977-79; sr. warden St. Luke's Episcopal Ch., New Orleans, 1985—. Served to lt. USN, 1969-74. John Woodruff Simpson fellow, Amherst coll., 1967; recipient cert. merit Mayor City of New Orleans, 1979, Monte M. LeMann award La. Civil Service League, 1980. Mem. La. Bar Assn., Assn. Trial Lawyers Am., Louis Martinet Legal Soc. (pres. 1977-79). Democrat. Avocations: drama, pen and pencil sketching, politics. Personal injury, Medical malpractice. Home: 7127 Parkside Ct New Orleans LA 70217

BRYANS, RICHARD W., lawyer; b. Denver, May 29, 1931; s. William A. and Ruth W. (Waldron) B.; m. Carol Jean, Feb. 17, 1955; children—Richard W., Bridget Ann. B.S., Denver U., 1954, J.D., 1955. Bar: Colo., U.S. Supreme Ct. 1971. Sole practice, Boulder, Colo., 1958-63; ptnr. Kelly, Stansfield & O'Donnell, Denver, 1963—. Served to lt. (j.g.) USNR, 1955-58. Mem. ABA, Colo. Bar Assn., Denver Bar Assn. General corporate, State civil litigation, Condemnation. Office: 550 15th St Suite 900 Denver CO 80202

BRYANT, GEORGE MCEWAN, lawyer, insurance executive; b. N.Y.C., Nov. 24, 1941; s. Sydney James and Ruth Cutter (McEwan) B.; m. Barbara Ann Phyfe, Sept. 10, 1966; children—Meredith Lee, Scott McEwan. B.A., Brown U., 1963; LL.B., Columbia U., 1966. Bar: N.J. 1966, U.S. Dist. Ct. N.J., 1966, N.Y. 1969. Assoc. firm Cravath Swaine & Moore, N.Y.C., 1968-72, Marshall Bratter Greene Allison & Tucker, N.Y.C., 1972-74, Davies Hardy Ives & Lawther, N.Y.C., 1974-77; assoc. counsel N.Y. Life Ins. Co., N.Y.C., 1977—. Vice-pres., bd. dirs. United Way of Ridgewood, Glen Rock and Ho-Ho-Kus, 1978-80; vice chmn. Ridgewood Republican Mcpl. Com., 1979-82. Mem. ABA, Bergen County Bar Assn. Republican. Mem. Ref. Ch. in Am. Clubs: The Moorings Country, Sawgrass Country, Upper Ridgewood Tennis, Ramapo Hunt and Polo Club Estates (bd. dirs., treas. 1983—). General corporate, Probate, Real property. Home: 207 Phelps Rd Ridgewood NJ 07450 Office: N Y Life Ins Co 51 Madison Ave New York NY 10010

BRYANT, IRA HOUSTON, III, lawyer; b. San Antonio, Aug. 30, 1942; s. Ira Houston and Florence (Kimberlin) B.; m. Judith Ann Bryant, Mar. 13, 1971; children—Ira Houston IV, Andrew Nelson, Jennifer Ann. B.A., Oklahoma City U., 1965, J.D., 1973. Bar: Okla., 1973. Physicist, White Sands Missile Range, N.Mex., 1965-70; ins. adjuster U.S. Fidelity & Guaranty Co., Oklahoma City, 1971-72; assoc. Robert Leyton Wheeler, Inc., Oklahoma City, 1973-77, Kerr, Davis, Irvine, Krasnow, Rhodes & Semtner, Oklahoma City, 1977-79; ptnr. Bryant & Scribner, Oklahoma City, 1979-83, Claunch, Bryant & Scribner, 1983—. Mem. Oklahoma City Mineral Lawyers Soc., Oklahoma City Title Attys. Assn., Rocky Mountain Mineral Law Found., Phi Delta Phi. Republican. Methodist. Club: Sportsman's Country (Oklahoma City). Oil and gas leasing, Real property, General corporate. Home: 6001 N State Oklahoma City OK 73122 Office: 710 Union Plaza 3030 Northwest Expressway Oklahoma City OK 73112

BRYANT, SANFORD BENJAMIN, lawyer; b. Huntington, W.Va., May 12, 1951; s. William W. and Martha L. (Smith) B.; m. Loretta G. Hall, Apr. 1, 1972; children: William W., Jesse Daniel, Brooks David. AB, Marshall U., 1973; JD, W.Va. U., 1978. Bar: W.Va. 1978, U.S. Dist. Ct. (so. and no. dists.) W.Va. 1978, U.S. Ct. Appeals (4th cir.) 1981. Law clk. to presiding justice U.S. Dist. Ct., Parkersburg, W.Va., 1978-80; asst. U.S. atty. U.S. Atty.'s Office, Huntington, W.Va., 1980-84; from assoc. to ptnr. Schaub & Bryant L.C., Huntington, 1984—; instr. criminal procedure Marshall U., Huntington, 1985. Mem. W.Va. State Elections Com., Charleston, 1986—. Recipient Spl. Achievement award U.S. Dept. Justice, Washington, 1982. Mem. ABA, W.Va. Bar Assn., Cabell County Bar Assn., Am. Judicature Soc. Democrat. Criminal, Federal civil litigation, State civil litigation. Home: 331 12th Ave W Huntington WV 25701 Office: Schaub & Bryant LC 1111 West Virginia Bldg Huntington WV 25701

BRYANT, THOMAS EARLE, JR., lawyer; b. Lebanon, Tenn., Aug. 10, 1934; s. Thomas Earle and Margaret (Turner) B.; m. Mary Ellen Stapp, Nov. 7, 1957; chidlren: Mary Melissa Lassiter, Thomas III, Mary Kate. BS, U. Ala., 1956, LLB, 1965. Bar: Ala. 1965, N.Y., U.S. Ct. Appeals (5th and 11th cirs.). Assoc. McDermott & Slepian, Mobile, Ala., 1965-69; ptnr. Gaston, Bryant & Gaston, Mobile, 1969-82, Bryant & McKnight, Mobile, 1982-85, Bryant, House, Ulmer & de Juan, Mobile, 1986—; bd. dirs. Govt. Street Lumber Co., Mobile, 1986—, FSF Fin. Corp., Mobile, 1985—. Chmn. Mobile Mcpl. Auditorium, 1971-85. Served to capt. U.S. Army, 1956-63. Mem. ABA, Assn. Trial Lawyers Am., Mobile Bar Assn. (sec. 1975-76), Farrah Law Soc. Republican. Presbyterian. Probate, Estate planning, General practice. Office: Bryant House Ulmer & de Juan 1107 Riverview Plaza Box 1465 Mobile AL 36633

BRYCE, WILLIAM DELF, lawyer; b. Georgetown, Tex., Aug. 7, 1932; s. D. A. Bryce and Frances Maxine (Wilson) Bryce Bakke; m. Sarah Alice Riley, Dec. 20, 1954; children—Douglas Delf, David Dickson. B.A., U. Tex., 1955; LL.B., Yale U., 1960. Bar: Tex. 1960, U.S. Dist. Ct. (we. dist.) Tex. 1963, U.S. Ct. Claims 1964, U.S. Supreme Ct. 1971. Briefing atty. Tex. Supreme Ct., Austin, 1960-61; sole practice, Austin, 1961—; lectr. U. Tex., 1965-66. Served to 1st lt. USAF, 1955-57. Fellow Tex. Bar Found. (sustaning, life); mem. Travis County Bar Assn., State Bar Tex., ABA. Clubs: Argyle (San Antonio); Headliners, Met. (Austin). General corporate, Probate, General practice. Home: 308 E University Ave Georgetown TX 78626 Office: 709 Brown Bldg Austin TX 78701

BRYSH, PAUL JOHN, lawyer; b. New Castle, Pa., Apr. 30, 1949; s. Walter Stanley and Matilda (Gorski) B. B.A., U. Pitts., 1971, J.D., 1974. Bar: Pa. 1974, U.S. Supreme Ct. 1977, U.S. Ct. Appeals (3d cir.) 1981. Law clk. Pa. Supreme Ct., Pitts., 1974-76; atty. U.S. Dept. Justice, Washington, 1976-79; chief appellate sect. western dist. Pa., U.S. Atty.'s Office, Pitts., 1979—. Mem. ABA, Allegheny County Bar Assn. Criminal. Office: US Atty's Office 633 US Post Office and Courthouse Pittsburgh PA 15219

BRYSON, DAVID C., lawyer; b. Hartford, Conn., Oct. 26, 1952; s. Edward F. and Dorothy (M.) B.; m. Kathleen Carroll, Dec. 29, 1979; children: David Dillon, Emily Carroll. BA, St. Anselm Coll., 1974; JD, Suffolk U., 1977. Atty. SBA, Boston, 1978-80; sr. counsel Bank of Boston, 1980—. Mem. ABA, Mass. Bar Assn., Boston Bar Assn. Banking, Consumer commercial, Contracts commercial. Office: Bank of Boston Law Office 100 Federal St Boston MA 02110

BSCHORR, PAUL JOSEPH, lawyer; b. N.Y.C., Jan. 3, 1941; s. Joseph J. and Helen (Sheerin) B.; m. Anne Leventritt, Apr. 12, 1969; children—Sharon, Mary (Molly), Katherine. B.A., Yale U., 1962; LL.B., U. Pa. 1965. Bar: N.Y. 1965, U.S. Dist. Ct. (so. and ea. dist.) N.Y. 1967, U.S. Ct. Appeals (2nd cir.), 1967, U.S. Ct. Appeals (5th cir.) 1970, U.S. Supreme Ct. 1974, D.C. 1976, U.S. Ct. Appeals (D.C. cir.) 1976, U.S. Ct. Appeals (9th cir.) 1977, U.S. Ct. Appeals (11th cir.) 1981. Assoc. law firm White & Case, N.Y.C., 1965-71, ptnr., 1972—. Chmn., City of Rye (N.Y.) Bd. Tax Assessment Rev., 1981—. Mem. ABA (council litigation sect. 1983-86, chmn. litigation sect. discovery com. 1978-82, mem. spl. com. for study of discovery abuse), N.Y. State Bar Assn., D.C. Bar Assn., Bar Assn. City N.Y. (mem. ethics com. 1980-83). Republican. Roman Catholic. Clubs: Apawamis, Manursing Island, Yale of N.Y. Federal civil litigation, State civil litigation. Office: White & Case 1155 Ave of Americas New York NY 10036

BUA, NICHOLAS JOHN, judge; b. Chgo., Feb. 9, 1925; s. Frank and Lena (Marino) B.; m. Camille F. Scordato, Nov. 20, 1943; 1 dau., Lisa Annette. J.D., DePaul U., 1953. Bar: Ill. 1953. Trial atty. Chgo., 1953-63; judge Village Ct., Melrose Park, Ill., 1963-64; asso. judge Circuit Ct. Cook County, Chgo., 1964-71; circuit judge Circuit Ct. Cook County, 1971-76; justice Appellate Ct. Ill., 1st Dist., 1976-77; judge U.S. Dist. Ct., Chgo., 1977—; Mem. exec. com. Jud. Conf. Ill., also mem. supreme ct. rules com., 1970-77; lectr. DePaul U.; mem. faculty Def. Tactics Seminar, Ill. Def. Counsel Seminar, 1971; Fellow Nat. Coll. State Trial Judges, U. Nev., 1966. Contbr. articles to legal publs. Bd. govs. Gottlieb Meml. Hosp., 1978—; trustee Schwab Rehab. Hosp., 1977—. Served with AUS, World War II. Named Man of Yr. Justinian Soc. Lawyers, 1977; recipient Alumni award DePaul U., 1977. Mem. Am. Justinian Soc. Jurists (pres. 1978). Clubs: Nat. Lawyers (Chgo.), Legal (Chgo.), Union League (Chgo.), Lex Legio DePaul U. (Chgo.). Judicial administration. Office: US Dist Ct 219 S Dearborn St Chicago IL 60604

BUCALOS, DEAN WALTER, lawyer; b. Bklyn., Feb. 8, 1952; s. Walter F. and Bernice (Silverton) B.; m. Anne Fowler Browne, May 18, 1974; children: Rebecca Anne, Benjamin Browne. BA cum laude, Vanderbilt U., 1974; JD, U. Ky., 1978. Bar: Ky. 1978, U.S. Dist. Ct. (ea. dist.) Ky. 1978, U.S. Ct. Appeals (fed. cir.) 1985. Staff atty. Northeast Ky. Legal Services, Inc., Ashland, 1978-80; ptnr. Brown, Bucalos & Gardner, Lexington, Ky., 1980-85, Brown, Bucalos, Santana & Bratt, PSC, Lexington, 1985—. Staff mem. Ky. Law Jour., Lexington, 1976-78, editorial assoc., 1978. Chief hearing office natural resources and environ. protection cabinet Commonwealth Ky., Frankfort, 1982-84; mem. Ky. Coalition Against the Death Penalty, Lexington, 1984-86; chmn. Cen. Ky. Fellowship of Reconciliation, 1984-86; cons. atty. Lexington chpt. Ky. Civil Liberties Union 1985—. Mem. ABA, Assn. Trial Lawyers Am., Ky. Bar Assn., Fayette Couty Bar Assn. Democrat. Mem. Disciples of Christ. Bankruptcy, Personal injury, General practice. Home: 3508 Arden Pl Lexington KY 40502 Office: Brown Bucalos Santana & Bratt PSC 201 W Short St Lexington KY 40507

BUCCI, EARL MICHAEL, lawyer; b. Schenectady, N.Y., Nov. 15, 1926; s. Michael A. and Caroline (Vorse) B.; m. Jane Lucas, Apr. 11, 1955 (div. Jan. 1978); children: Gwendolyn, Michael A. II, Catherine. AB, Brown U., 1948; JD, NYU, 1954. Bar: N.Y. 1954, U.S. Supreme Ct. 1961. Staff N.Y. Times, N.Y.C., 1948-51; sole practice Schenectady, 1954—. Mem. N.Y. State Senate, Albany, 1965, assoc. counsel, pres. pro tem.; pres. Torch Club of Schenectady, 1974-76; pres., bd. dirs. Schenectady Symphony Orch. Assn., 1965-68, Schenectady Sr. Citizens Ctr., 1966-68. Mem. ABA (chmn. com. on adminstrn. and distbn. decedents estates, real property probate and trust law sect. 1975-80, contbr. articles to Real Property Probate and Trust Law Jour.), N.Y. State Bar Assn. (exec. com. trusts and estates sect. 1975-80), Estate Planning Council Eastern N.Y. (pres. 1982-83), N.Y. Supreme Ct. (character and fitness com. 1980—), Nature Conservancy (hon. life), Adirondack Mountain Club, Phi Delta Phi. Democrat. Clubs: N.Y. Athletic, Brown (pres. 1967-69). Avocations: hiking, running. Probate, Estate taxation. Home: 1539 Dean St Schenectady NY 12309 Office: 302 State St Schenectady NY 12305

BUCCINO, ERNEST JOHN, JR., lawyer; b. Phila., Oct. 29, 1945; s. Ernest J. and Rachel (Talarico) B.; m. Martha Mollinedo, Dec. 27, 1968; children—Tasha. B.S., Temple U., 1967, M.Ed., 1969, J.D., 1973. Bar: Pa. 1973, U.S. Dist. Ct. (ea. dist.) Pa. 1973, U.S. Ct. Appeals (3d cir.) 1973, N.J. 1974, U.S. Supreme Ct. 1978. Officer, counsel Blue Cross Greater Phila., 1973-74; law clk. Supreme Ct. Pa., Phila., 1974; mem. Gross & Buccino, P.A., Phila., 1975—; lectr. Trial Advocacy Found. Pa., Phila., 1984. Chmn. eastern dist. LAWPAC, Harrisburg, Pa., 1983—. Mem. ABA, Assn. Trial Lawyers Am., Pa. Bar Assn., Pa. Trial Lawyers Assn. (bd. dirs. 1982—), Phila. Trial Lawyers Assn. (bd. dirs. 1982—), Justinian Soc. (bd. dirs. 1982—), Phila. Bar Assn. (chmn. econs. of law practice 1983, nominating com. 1982-83). Lodge: Sons of Italy. Personal injury. Office: 1211 Chestnut St Suite 503 Philadelphia PA 19107

BUCHANAN, ALEXANDER BLACKMAN, lawyer; b. Nashville, Dec. 21, 1953; s. Robert Norman Jr. and Rachel (Blackman) B. BA cum laude, Vanderbilt U., 1975, JD, 1978. Bar: Tenn. 1978, U.S. Dist. Ct. (mid. dist.) Tenn. 1978. From assoc. to ptnr. Waller, Lansden, Dortch & Davis, Nashville, 1978—. Mem. ABA, Tenn. Bar Assn., Nashville Bar Assn. Presbyterian. Club: Exchange (Nashville). Municipal bonds, Real property, Securities. Home: 1212 Nichol Ln Nashville TN 37205 Office: Waller Lansden Dortch & Davis 2100 One Commerce Place Nashville TN 37239

BUCHANAN, J. VINCENT MARINO, lawyer, businessman; b. Ft. Knox, Ky., Feb. 15, 1951; s. Robert Samuel and Jeanice (Moran) B.; children—Thomas S., Maria Antonia. Student U.S. Mil. Acad., 1969-71; B.A., Bowling Green State U., Ohio, 1972; J.D., U. Toledo, 1975. Bar: Ohio 1976, U.S. Dist. Ct. (no. dist.) Ohio 1977, U.S. Ct. Appeals (6th cir.). Mng. atty., ptnr. Buchanan & Stotzer, Risingsun, Ohio, 1976—; sec.-treas. George Palmiter River Cons. Co., Risingsun, 1981—. Bd. dirs. A.B.L.E., Toledo, 1981—; sec., bd. dirs. Ohio Hispanic Inst., Bowling Green, 1983—. Mem ABA (exec. mem. family law div.), Am. Legion. Roman Catholic. Lodges: Elks, Lions. Environment. Home: US 23 N Risingsun OH 43457 Office: Buchanan & Stotzer 8500 US 23 N Risingsun OH 43457

BUCHANAN, JAMES DOUGLAS, lawyer; b. Modesto, Calif., Aug. 7, 1941; s. James Monroe and Gladys Marian (Crowell) B.; m. Claudia Anne Dukes, May 26, 1963; children—Sarah, Jennifer, Amy, Andrew. B.A. in Journalism, U. Nev., 1963; J.D., U. of Pacific, Sacramento, 1975. Bar: Calif. 1975, U.S. Dist. Ct. (ea. dist.) Calif. 1976. Dep. dist. atty. Inyo County, Independence, Calif., 1976-77, pub. defender, 1977-78; ptnr. Smith & Buchanan, Bishop, Calif., 1978-86; legal counsel No. Inyo Hosp. Dist., Bishop, 1980—. Pipe major Loch Ness Scots Pipe Band, Bishop, 1982—; chmn. Selective Service Bd. 87, Bishop, 1983-84. Served to 1st lt. USAR, 1963-65. Mem. Inyo-Mono Bar Assn. (pres. 1980). Episcopalian. Lodge: Masons. Consumer commercial, Criminal, General practice. Office: 459 W Line St Bishop CA 93514

BUCHANAN, JAMES WILLIAM, III, lawyer; b. Denver, Apr. 5, 1948; s. James W. and Miriam L. (Brooks) B. BA, U. Denver, 1971, JD, 1975, LLM in Taxation, 1985. Bar: Colo. 1975, U.S. Dist. Ct. Colo. 1975. Ptnr. Thomas & Esperti P.C., Denver, 1973-79, Buchanan, Thomas & Johnson P.C., Lakewood, Colo., 1979—. Contbr. articles to profl. jours. V.p. Babi Yar Park Found., Denver, 1979-86; pres. Consortium for Community Centered Comprehensive Child Care, Denver, 1983—. Mem. ABA (taxation, real property, probate and trust law sect.), Denver Estate Planning Council, Centennial Estate Planning Council. Estate planning, Probate, Estate taxation. Office: Buchanan Thomas & Johnson 141 Union Blvd Suite 300 Lakewood CO 80228

BUCHANAN, JOHN COWAN, lawyer; b. Detroit, July 16, 1936; s. William D. and Elizabeth L. (Dwyer) B.; m. Sheila K. Olman, June 24, 1961; children—John C., Robert James, Jane Marie. A.B., Mich. State U., 1959; J.D., U. Mich., 1962. Bar: Mich. 1963, U.S. Dist. Ct. (ea. and we. dists.) Mich. 1963, U.S. Ct. Appeals (6th cir.) 1982. Ptnr. Cholette, Perkins & Buchanan, Grand Rapids, 1963-82, Hecht, Buchanan & Cheney, Grand Rapids, 1982-84, Buchanan and Bos, 1984—; mem. faculty Inst. Continuing Legal Edn., Mich.; lectr. in field. Mem. Internat. Acad. Trial Lawyers, Am. Coll. Trial Lawyers, ABA, Mich. Bar Assn., Lawyer-Pilot's Bar Assn., Am. Judicature Soc. Republican. Roman Catholic. Club: Penninsular of Grand Rapids. Personal injury, Federal civil litigation, State civil litigation. Home: 1585 River Oaks Dr SE Ada MI 49301 Office: Buchanan & Bos 600 Frey Bldg Grand Rapids MI 49503

BUCHANAN, PHILLIP GERALD, lawyer; b. Lincolnton, N.C., May 27, 1943; s. Gerald Clifford Buchanan and Ruth (Finger) Hester; m. Loretta Marie Stanton, July 19, 1985; 1 child, Phillip Gerald Jr. BS, U. Md., 1974; JD, U. Md., Balt., 1978. Bar: Md. 1978, U.S. Dist. Ct. Md. 1978, U.S. Ct. Appeals (4th cir.) 1981, U.S. Supreme Ct. 1981. Atty. office of gen. counsel Nat. Security Agy., Ft. Meade, Md., 1978—. Founder, gen. counsel RECA (civic assn.), Glen Burnie, Md., 1968—. Mem. ABA, Fed. Bar Assn., Md. Bar Assn., ACLU, Am. Soc. Internat. Law. Avocations: boating, fishing. General practice, Administrative and regulatory, Criminal. Home: 548 Crest Park Dr Glen Burnie MD 21061 Office: Nat Security Agy Office of Gen Counsel Fort George G Meade MD 21061

BUCHANAN, ROBERT LEE, JR., lawyer; b. Aiken, S.C., May 22, 1951; s. Robert Lee and Ruth (Nicholson) B.; m. Clara Bailey Robeson, May 18, 1974; chiodren: Robert Lee III, William Tarrant, Mary Bailey. AB, Erskine Coll., 1973; JD, U. S.C., 1976. Bar: S.C. 1976, U.S. Dist. Ct. S.C. 1976. Assoc. Williams & Johnson, Aiken, S.C., 1976-80; ptnr. Williams, Johnson, Buchanan & Beasley, Aiken, 1980—; part-time magistrate U.S. Dist. Ct. S.C., Aiken Div., 1979—. Mem. minimum housing Bd. Adjustments and Appeals, City of Aiken, 1978; chmn. edn. funds crusade Am. Cancer Soc., Aiken, 1978; coach football Aiken Elem. Sch., 1976-81. Mem. Aiken County Bar Assn. (sec. 1978-79, treas. 1985—), Assn. Trial Lawyers Am., S.C. Trial Lawyers Assn., Am. Judicature Soc., Omicron Delta Kappa. Presbyterian. Federal civil litigation, State civil litigation, Real property. Home: 1057 Highland Park Ave SW Aiken SC 29801 Office: Williams Johnson Buchanan & Beasley 526 Richland Ave W Aiken SC 29802-0463

BUCHANAN, WILLIAM D., lawyer; b. Ont., Can., Feb. 23, 1909; came to U.S., 1919; s. Robert George and Mary Rodina (Henry) B.; children: John, William, Thomas; m. P. Joyce Mooney, Dec. 14, 1964; 1 child, Daniel. LLB, Detroit Coll. Law, 1933. Bar: Mich. 1933, U.S. Dist. Ct. (ea. and we. dists.) Mich. 1933, U.S. Ct. Appeals (6th cir.) 1933. Ptnr. Lacey, Scrogee, Lacey & Buchanan, Detroit, 1933-50; sr. ptnr. Cholette, Perkins & Buchanan, Grand Rapids, Mich., 1950—. Fellow Am. Coll. Trial Lawyers; mem. ABA, Mich. Bar Assn., Internat. Acad. TrialLawyers (bd. dirs. 1972-78), Internat. Assn. Ins. Counsel, Fedn. Ins. Counsel, 6th Cir. Jud. Conf. Baptist. Clubs: Blythefield Country, University, Peninsular (Grand Rapids). Avocations: golf, boating. Federal civil litigation, State civil litigation, Insurance. Home: 680 Cascade Hills Hollow SE Grand Rapids MI 49506 Office: Cholette Perkins & Buchanan 600 Old Kent Bldg Grand Rapids MI 49503

BUCHBINDER, DARRELL BRUCE, lawyer, b. N.Y.C., Oct. 17, 1946; s. Julian and Bernice (Levy) B.; m. Janet Grey McLean, Jan. 22, 1977; children—Julian Bradford, Andrew Grey. B.A. in Politics with honors, NYU, 1968, J.D., 1971. Bar: N.Y. 1972, U.S. Dist. Ct. (so. and ea. dists.) N.Y. 1973. Sole practice, N.Y.C., 1972-79; atty. Port Authority of N.Y. and N.J., N.Y.C., 1979-83, prin. atty., 1983-86, dep. chief fin. div. Law Dept., 1986—. Served with USNR, 1968-70. Mem. Bar Assn. of City of N.Y., Pi Sigma Alpha. Republican. Club: Larchmont Shore. Municipal bonds. Office: Port Authority of NY and NJ 1 World Trade Ctr New York NY 10048

BUCHENROTH, STEPHEN RICHARD, lawyer; b. Bellefontaine, Ohio, Feb. 8, 1948; s. Richard G. and Patricia (Muller) B.; m. Vicki Anderson, June 6, 1974; children: Matthew Brian, Sarah Elizabeth. BA, Wittenburg U., Springfield, Ohio, 1970; JD, U. Chgo., 1974. Bar: Ohio 1974, U.S. Dist. Ct. (so. and no. dists.) Ohio 1974, U.S. Ct. Appeals (6th cir.) 1974. Ptnr. Vorys, Sater, Seymour & Pease, Columbus, Ohio, 1974—. Author: Ohio Mortgage Foreclosures, 1986; also chpts. in books. Trustee, v.p. Godman Guild Assn., Columbus, 1977-83; trustee, sec. Neighborhood Homes, Inc., Columbus, 1977-85. mem. ABA (forum com. franchising), Ohio State Bar Assn. (council dels., vice chmn. legal assts. com.), Columbus Bar Assn. (bd. govs.), Am. Coll. Real Estate Lawyers. Republican. Lutheran. Club: Columbus Athletic. Real property, Contracts commercial, Franchise law.. Home: 2342 Collins Dr Worthington OH 43085 Office: Vorys Sater Seymore & Pease 52 E Gay St Columbus OH 43215

BUCHIGNANI, LEO JOSEPH, lawyer; b. Memphis, Nov. 4, 1922; s. Joseph Richard and Leonora B. (Shea) B.; m. Grace Elisabeth Crisler, Nov. 23, 1950; children—Leo, Crisler Buchignani Quick, Joan. B.A., Notre Dame U., 1944; LL.B., Harvard U., 1948. Bar: Tenn., 1948, U.S. Sup. Ct., 1960, U.S. Dist. Ct., 1950. Assoc., Chandler, Shepherd, Heiskill & Williams, Memphis, 1948-50; ptnr. Buchignani & Greener, Memphis, 1950-53; ptnr. Quick, Buchignani & Greener, Memphis, 1953-58; ptnr. Buchignani & Greener, Memphis, 1958-80; ptnr. Buchignani & Neal, Memphis, 1981—; comm. Tenn. Jud. Standards Commn., 1971-74; commr. Tenn. Law Revision Commn., 1971-74. Mem. Tenn. Republican State Exec. Com., 1960-62. Served with USN, 1942-45. Mem. ABA, Tenn. Bar Assn., Memphis and Shelby County Bar Assn. (dir. 1959-61, sec.-treas. 1964-65, v.p. 1965-66, pres. 1966-67), Fedn. Ins. Csl., Am. Judicature Soc., Tenn. Def. Lawyers Assn. Republican. Roman Catholic. Clubs: Harvard, Notre Dame, Memphis Country, Colonial Country, Univ. Insurance, Personal injury, Probate. Home: 315 Kenilworth Pl Memphis TN 38112 Office: 100 N Main Bldg Suite 1601 Memphis TN 38103

BUCHLER, PETER ROBERT, lawyer; b. New Orleans, Mar. 31, 1946; s. Peter P. and Alice Buchler; Deborah Tribou, Feb. 8, 1969; children: Suzette, Kelly, Katherine. BA, St. Edward's U., 1968; JD, Loyola U., New Orleans, 1978. Bar: La. 1979, U.S. Dist. Ct. (ea. dist.) La., U.S. Ct. Appeals (5th cir.). Adminstrv. asst. McDermott, New Orleans, 1974-79, asst. sec., 1979—. Pres. St. James Mjr. Sch. Bd., New Orleans, 1980, bd. dirs. 1978—. Served to capt. USAF, 1968-74; judge advocate air La. Air Nat. Guard, 1975—. Recipient Civic Achievement award City of New Orleans, 1979. Mem. ABA, La. Bar Assn., New Orleans Bar Assn. Republican. Roman Catholic. Securities, Pension, profit-sharing, and employee benefits, Military. Home: 11030 S Hardy St New Orleans LA 70127 Office: McDermott 1010 Common St New Orleans LA 70112

BUCHMAN, KENNETH WILLIAM, lawyer; b. Plant City, Fla., Nov. 20, 1956; s. Paul Sidney and Beryle (Solomon) B.; m. MarDee H. Buchman, May 9, 1985. AA, U. Fla., 1976, BBA, 1978, JD, 1981. Bar: Fla. 1981, U.S. Dist. Ct. (mid. dist.) Fla. 1981, U.S. Ct. Appeals (11th cir.) 1986. Ptnr. Buchman and Buchman, Plant City, 1981-85, Buchman and Buchman, P.A., Plant City, 1985—. Mem. ABA, Hillsborough County Bar Assn. (local chmn. 1983-85, cir. ct. family law rules, edn. and liaison com. 1984-86), Fla. Mcpl. Attys. Assn. (steering com. 1984-85), Attys. Title Ins. Fund. Democrat. Jewish. Club: Olin S. Wright (Plant City) (sr. steward 1984, jr. deacon 1985). Lodge: Kiwanis (local sec. 1983-84, 1st v.p. 1985-86, pres. 1986—). Family and matrimonial, Local government, State civil litigation. Office: 212 N Collins St Plant City FL 33566

BUCHMAN, PAUL SIDNEY, lawyer; b. Tampa, Fla., June 5, 1923; s. Julius M. and Lillian (Neuwirth) B.; m. Beryle Solomon, Feb. 7, 1950; children—J. Miles, Kenneth W. Student Univ. Coll., U. Fla., 1941-43; J.D., U. Fla., 1948. Bar: Fla. 1948, U.S. Dist. Ct. (so. and mid. dists.) Fla. 1949, U.S. Supreme Ct. 1960. Practice law, Plant City, Fla., 1948—; ptnr. Buchman and Buchman, 1979—; city atty. City of Plant City, 1949—; mem. Fla. Adv. Council in Intergovtl. Relations, 1977—. Served with U.S. Army, 1943-45. Decorated Bronze Star, Purple Heart. Recipient Disting. Service award, U.S. Jr. C. of C., 1961, Good Govt. award, Plant City Jaycees, 1978; named Plant City's Citizen of Yr., 1982. Mem. ABA, Fla. Bar (Ralph A. Marsicano award local govt. law sect. 1977), Hillsborough County Bar Assn., Nat. Inst. Mcpl. Law Officers, Am. Judicature Soc., Am. Legion (post adj. 1950, vice comdr. 1951). Democrat. Jewish. Clubs: Elks, B'nai B'rith, Lions (sec. Plant City 1949), Masons, Scottish Rite, York Rite, Shriners. Contbr. articles to profl. publs. Local government, General corporate, Probate. Office: PO Box 5 Plant City FL 33566

BUCHMANN, ALAN PAUL, lawyer; b. Yonkers, N.Y., Sept. 5, 1934; s. Paul John and Jessie Gow (Perkins) B.; m. Lizabeth Ann Moody, Sept. 5, 1959. B.A., Yale U., 1956; postgrad. (Fulbright fellow), U. Munich, 1956-57; LL.B., Yale U., 1960. Bar: Ohio 1960, U.S. Dist. Ct. (no. dist.) Ohio 1963, U.S. Ct. Appeals (6th cir.) 1968, U.S. Supreme Ct. 1977. Assoc., Squire, Sanders & Dempsey, Cleve., 1960-70, ptnr., 1970—. State chmn. Ohio Young Republicans, 1970-71, nat. committeeman, 1971-74; mem. exec. com. Cuyahoga County Republicans, 1969—; mem. Selective Service Bd., 1967-75; trustee Cleve. Internat. Program, 1979-82; pres. English Speaking Union, 1981-83. Recipient Robert A. Taft award Young Republicans, 1969, Outstanding State Chmn. award, 1971, James A. Rhodes award, 1974. Mem. ABA, Ohio State Bar Assn., Cleve. Bar Assn., Cuyahoga Bar Assn. Republican. Episcopalian. Clubs: Union, Mid-Day, Play House (Cleve.), Capitol Hill (Washington), Yale (N.Y.C.). Contbr. articles to legal jours. Public utilities, Federal civil litigation, State civil litigation. Office: Squire Sanders & Dempsey Suite 1800 Huntington Bldg Cleveland OH 44115

BUCHMEYER, JERRY, U.S. district court judge; b. Overton, Tex., Sept. 5, 1933. Student, Kilgore Jr. Coll., 1953; B.A., U. Tex., 1955, LL.B., 1957. Bar: Tex. 1957. Assoc. firm Thompson, Knight, Simmons & Bullion, Dallas, 1958-63; partner 1963-66, sr. ptnr., 1968-79; judge U.S. Dist. Ct., No. Dist. Tex., Dallas, 1979—. Mem. Am. Bar Assn., Dallas Bar Assn. (pres. 1979), State Bar Tex. (chmn. com. 1978-79, dir. 1982-84). Office: US District Court US Courthouse 1100 Commerce St Room 15-E-6 Dallas TX 75242 *

BUCHOLTZ, HAROLD RONALD, lawyer; b. Newark, Jan. 24, 1952; s. Samuel and Dorothy (Sorren) B. BBA, Rutgers U., 1973; JD, U. Va., 1976; LLM in Taxation, Georgetown U., 1980. Bar: Va. 1976, D.C. 1980, U.S. Tax Ct. 1980, U.S. Supreme Ct. 1980, U.S. Ct. Appeals (fed. cir.) 1981, U.S. Ct. Appeals (D.C. cir.) 1982, U.S. Ct. Appeals (11th cir.) 1983. Atty. office of the chief counsel IRS, Washington, 1976-81; assoc. Pope, Ballard & Loos, Washington, 1981; assoc. Holland & Knight, Washington, 1982-84, ptnr., 1985—. Mem. ABA (taxation sect.), Va. Bar Assn., D.C. Bar Assn. Corporate taxation, Estate taxation, Municipal bonds. Home: 1304 N Meade St #9 Arlington VA 22209 Office: Holland & Knight 888 17th St NW Suite 400 Washington DC 20006

BUCHSBAUM, NORMAN ROBERT, lawyer; b. Mt. Vernon, N.Y., Sept. 25, 1941; s. Abraham and Sophie (Forrest) B.; m. Roxanne Layton, Jan. 1, 1967; children—Jeffrey, Emily. A.B., Dartmouth Coll., 1963; LL.B., Yale U., 1966; cert. Uppsala (Sweden) U., 1967. Bar: Ga. 1966, Md. 1968, U.S. Dist. Ct. (no. dist.) Ga. 1966, U.S. Dist. Ct. Md. 1968, U.S. Ct. Appeals (4th cir.) 1968, U.S. Ct. Appeals (3d cir.) 1981, U.S. Ct. Appeals (5th cir.) 1966, U.S. Ct. Appeals (8th cir.) 1976, U.S. Ct. Appeals (7th cir.) 1982, U.S. Ct. Appeals (D.C. cir.) 1986, U.S. Supreme Ct. 1974. Mem. Shawe & Rosenthal, Balt., 1968-75; ptnr. Weinberg & Green, Balt., 1975-80, Jackson, Lewis Schnitzler & Krupman, Balt., 1981-84; instr. Indsl. Relations Labor Studies Ctr., U. Balt.; served with Am. embassy, Stockholm, 1967. Mem. ABA, Ga. Bar Assn., Md. Bar Assn. Republican. Jewish. Clubs: Dartmouth of Md., Merchants, Center, Yale of Maryland. Contbg. editor The Developing Labor Law, Mercer Law Rev. Labor. Office: 400 E Pratt St Suite 600 Baltimore MD 21202

BUCHWALD, DON DAVID, lawyer; b. Bklyn., May 10, 1944; m. Naomi Reice, Jan. 19, 1974; children: David, Jennifer. BA, Cornell U., 1961-65, JD, 1965-68. Assoc. Marshall, Bratter, Greene, Allison & Tucker, N.Y.C., 1970-73; asst. U.S. atty. So. Dist. of N.Y., N.Y.C., 1973-80; ptnr. Buchwald & Kaufman, N.Y.C., 1980—. Served to sgt. U.S. Army, 1968-70. Mem. ABA, Fed. Bar Council, Assn. of the Bar of the City of N.Y., N.Y. State Bar Assn., Westchester County Bar Assn. Criminal, Federal civil litigation, State civil litigation. Office: Buchwald & Kaufman 600 Third Ave New York NY 10016

BUCK, DAVID PATRICK, lawyer; b. Rossville, Ga., Mar. 17, 1940; m. Maureen Nenno, May 11, 1968; children—David, Jr., Teresa. B.S. in Acctg., U. Tenn., 1961, J.D., 1964; LL.M. in Internat. Law, U. Mich., 1972; student Air Command and Staff Coll., Air U., 1977. Bar: Tenn. 1965, U.S. Tax Ct. 1977, U.S. Ct. Claims 1977, U.S. Ct. Appeals (D.C. cir.) 1978, U.S. Supreme Ct. 1978, U.S. Ct. Appeals (fed. cir.) 1982, U.S. Ct. Appeals (4th cir.) 1982, U.S. Ct. Appeals (9th and 11th 1984. C.P.A., Md. 1984. Mem. staff law dept. USAF, 1965-85, U.S. Postal Service, 1985—; legal advisor Wilford Hall Med. Ctr., San Antonio, 1968-70; chief civil and internat. law, Torrejon Air Base, Madrid, 1972-76; trial atty. Gen. Litigation div. Office JAG, Washington, 1977-78; spl. atty. Office of Fgn. Litigation, Dept. Justice, Washington, 1978-80; chief civilian personnel and labor law br. Gen. Litigation div. Office JAG, Washington, 1980-85. Decorated Merit Service Medals USAF, 1971, 80, 85; recipient spl. commendation award for Outstanding Service, Dept. Justice, 1980, Meritorious Service Honor award for Outstanding Profl. Performance U.S. Postal Service, 1986. Mem. Am. Soc. Internat. Law, Fed. Bar Assn., Beta Alpha Psi. Contbr. articles to internat. law jours., profl. jours. Government contracts and claims, Labor, Public international. Home: 405 Rexburg Ave Fort Washington MD 20744 Office: HQ USAF/JACL Bolling AFB Washington DC 20332

BUCK, GURDON HALL, lawyer, real estate broker; b. Hartford, Conn., Apr. 10, 1936; s. Richard Saltonstall and Aloha Frances (Hall) B.; m. Sharon Smith, Dec. 27, 1958; children—Keith Saltonstall, Frances Josephine, Daniel Winthrop. B.A. in English, Lehigh U., 1958; J.D., U. Pa., 1965. Bar: Conn. 1965, U.S. Dist. Ct. 1966, U.S. Ct. Appeals (2d cir.) 1966. Assoc. Shipman & Goodwin, Hartford, 1965-67; v.p./counsel R. F. Broderick & Assocs., Hartford, 1968-69; ptnr. Pelgrift, Byrne, Buck & Connolly, Hartford and Farmington, Conn., 1969-75, Byrne, Buck, & Steiner and predecessor Byrne & Buck, Farmington, 1975-79; chmn. real estate dept. Robinson & Cole, Farmington and Hartford, 1980—. Served to lt. (s.g.) USCGR, 1958-62. Recipient Disting. Service award Glastonbury (Conn.) Jaycees, 1968. Mem. ABA (chmn. condominium com. Sect. Real Property and Probate, adv. Uniform Planned Community Act, Model Real Estate Coop. Act and Uniform Common Interest Ownership Act), Conn. Bar Assn., Hartford County Bar Assn., Hartford Bd. Realtors, Am. Coll. Real Estate Lawyers (bd. govs., chmn. common ownership com.), Am. Land Devel. Assn., Community Assns. Inst. (nat. trustee; chmn. lawyers council, pres. Conn. chpt. 1980-83, sec. 1984—, pres. Research Found. 1980-82). Club: Hartford, Prin. co-author: The Connecticut Condominium Manual, 1972; Real Estate Brokers Community Associations Handbook, rev. edit., 1982; Connecticut Common Interest Ownership Manual, 1984; The Alaska Common Interest Ownership Manual, 1985; contbr. numerous articles on zoning, condominiums, planned unit devels. to profl. jours.; Condo Sense columnist Stamford Adv. and Greenwich Time. Real property, Environment. Office: 1 Commercial Plaza Hartford CT 06103

BUCK, THOMAS RANDOLPH, lawyer; b. Washington, Feb. 5, 1930; s. James Charles Francis and Mary Elizabeth (Marshall) B.; m. Alice Armistead James, June 20, 1953; children: Kathryn James, Thomas Randolph, Douglas Marshall, David Andrew; m. Sunny Clark, Sept. 15, 1971; 1 dau., Carey Virginia.; m. Yvonne Brackett, Nov. 27, 1981. B.A. summa cum laude, Am. U., 1951; LL.B., U. Va., 1954. Bar: Va. 1954, Ky. 1964, Fla. 1974. Asst. gen. atty. Seaboard Air Line R.R. Co., 1958-63; sec., gen. counsel Am. Comml. Lines. Inc., Houston, 1963-68; asst. gen. counsel Tex. Gas Transmission Corp., 1968-72; sec., gen. counsel Leadership Housing Inc., 1972-77; pres. law firm Buck and Golden, P.A., 1975—; dir. Hanover Bank of Fla., Plantation, Computer Resources Inc., Ft. Lauderdale, Fla., So. Aviation Inc., Opa Locka, Fla. Bd. dirs. Sheridan House for Youth. Served to capt. USMCR, 1954-58. Mem. Assn. ICC Practitioners (nat. v.p., mem. exec. com.), Am., Va., Ky., Fla. bar assns., Maritime Law Assn. U.S., Am. Judicature Soc., Omicron Delta Kappa, Alpha Sigma Phi, Delta Theta Phi. Clubs: Kiwanian, Propeller of U.S. Banking, General corporate, Real property. Home: 7061 NW 8th Ct Plantation FL 33317 Office: 499 NW 70th Ave Suite 220 Fort Lauderdale FL 33317

BUCKLEY, CHARLES ROBINSON, III, lawyer; b. Richmond, Va., Oct. 9, 1942; s. Charles Robinson and Eleanor (Small) B.; m. Virginia Lee, Apr. 17, 1971; children—Richard, Rebecca. B.S., U. N.C., 1965, J.D., 1969. Bars: N.C. 1969, U.S. Supreme Ct., 1979. Asst. city atty. City of Charlotte (N.C.), 1969-78; ptnr. Constangy, Goines, Buckley & Boyd, 1978-81, Taylor & Buckley, Charlotte, 1981-85; town atty. Town of Matthew (N.C.), 1978—; faculty Central Piedmont Community Coll., 1970. Bd. dirs. Charlotte City Employees Credit Union, 1974-78; pres. PTA, 1980-82. Recipient Certificate of Merit, City of Charlotte, 1982. Mem. Charlotte C. of C., N.C. Bar Assn., N.C. Assn. Mun. Attys. (dir. 1979-81), ABA, Phi Alpha Delta. Democrat. Lutheran. Club: Optimist (pres. 1982-83). Local government, Consumer commercial, General practice. Home: 6813 Linda Lake Dr Charlotte NC 28215

BUCKLEY, DANIEL JEROME, lawyer, educator; b. Ann Arbor, Mich., Jan. 20, 1949; s. Frederick Jean and Josephine Ruth (Kinzer) B.; m. Anne Hackett, Aug. 21, 1976; children: Katherine Anna, Ellen Caroline, Margaret Jean. Student, Aberdeen U., 1969-70; BA, Ohio Wesleyan U., 1971; postgrad., Exeter (Eng.) U., 1973; JD, U. Cin., 1974. Bar: Ohio 1974, U.S. Dist. Ct. (so. dist.) Ohio 1976, U.S. Supreme Ct. 1982. Law clk. to sr. judge U.S. Dist. Ct., Chgo., 1974-76; assoc. Buckley, Miller & Wright, Wilmington, Ohio, 1976-78, ptnr., 1978—; asst. prosecutor City of Wilmington, 1976-78; asst. prof. Wilmington Coll., 1982-86, assoc. prof., 1987—; acting judge Wilmington Mcpl. Ct., 1985—; bd. dirs. Aviation Fuel, Inc., Wilmington, Sound Supression, Inc., Wilmington. Pres. Clinton County Mental Health Ctr., Wilmington, 1979, Clinton County YMCA, 1982; mem. instl. rev. bd. intro-ocular lenses Highland Dist. Hosp., Hillsboro, Ohio, 1985—. Mem. ABA, Ohio Bar Assn., Clinton County Bar Assn. (pres. 1985—), Ohio Assn. Civil Trial Attys., Am. Acad. Hosp. Attys., Def. Research Inst., Omicron Delta Kappa, Pi Sigma Alpha. Republican. Presbyterian. Avocations: reading, squash, cross country skiing, Celtic traditional music. State civil litigation, Health, Insurance. Home: 841 W Truesdell St Wilmington OH 45177 Office: Buckley Miller & Wright 145 N South St Wilmington OH 45177

BUCKLEY, FREDERICK JEAN, lawyer; b. Wilmington, Ohio, Nov. 5, 1923; s. William Millard and Martha (Bright) B.; m. Josephine K. Buckley, Dec. 4, 1945; children—Daniel J., Fredrica Buckley Elder, Matthew J. Student Wilmington Coll., 1941-42, Ohio State U., 1942-43; A.B., U. Mich., 1948, LL.B., 1949. Bar: Ohio 1950, U.S. Dist. Ct. (so. dist.) Ohio, 1952, U.S. Supreme Ct. 1978, U.S. Ct. Appeals (6th cir.) 1981, Fla. 1982. Assoc. G.L. Schilling, Sr., Wilmington, 1951-52; ptnr. Schilling & Buckley, Wilmington, 1953-56; sole practice, Wilmington, 1956-62; sr. ptnr. Buckley, Miller & Wright, Wilmington, 1962—; chmn., counsel The Wilmington Savs. Assn., 1971—, also dir.; solicitor City of Wilmington, 1954-63. Served with AUS, 1943-46; ETO. Joint program Mich. Dept. Revenue and U. Mich. Inst. Pub. Adminstrn. fellow, 1948. Fellow Am. Coll. Trial Lawyers; mem. ABA, Ohio Bar Assn., Clinton County Bar Assn., Internat. Assn. Def. Counsel, Am. Judicature Soc., Selden Soc., Fla. Bar, Collier County Bar Assn., Ohio State Bar Found. Republican. Methodist. Contbr. articles in field. State civil litigation, Insurance, Probate. Office: 145 N South St Wilmington OH 45177 Office: 997 N Collier Blvd Marco Island FL 33937

BUCKLEY, SAMUEL OLLIPHANT, III, lawyer; b. Union, Miss., May 20, 1947; s. Samuel Olliphant Jr. and Mary Lou (Vance) B.; m. Karen Elaine Thompson, Sept. 9, 1967; children: William Paul, Mary Beth. BS in Chemistry, La. State U., 1969; JD, Loyola U., New Orleans, 1977. Bar: La. 1977, U.S. Dist. Ct. (ea. dist.) La. 1977, U.S. Dist. Ct. (mid. dist.) La. 1978, U.S. Ct. Appeals (5th cir.) 1979, U.S. Ct. Appeals (11th cir.) 1981. Dir. environ. Witco Chem. Corp., Gretna, La., 1970-77; assoc. Jones, Walker, Waechter, Poitevent, Carrere & Denegre, New Orleans, 1977-82, ptnr., 1982—; asst. prof. environ. law Loyola U. Law Sch., 1984—. Lead article editor Loyola U. Law Rev., 1976-77. Mem. Friends of New Orleans Symphony, Friends of Audubon Zoo, New Orleans. Mem. ABA (vice chmn. urban law com. 1980-81, solid and hazardous waste com. 1981-85), La. Bar Assn. (vice chmn. environ. law sect. 1980-82, chmn. 1982—), La. Assn. Def. Counsel, New Orleans Bar Assn., Am. Chem. Soc., Loyola U. Law Alumni Assn. (bd. dirs. 1979-80), Nat. Audubon Soc. Democrat. Episcopalian. Avocations: skiing, golf, tennis. Environment, Federal civil litigation, State civil litigation. Home: 844 E Lexington Ave Gretna LA 70056 Office: Jones Walker Waechter Poitevent Carrere & Denegre 201 St Charles Ave New Orleans LA 70170

BUCKLIN, LEONARD HERBERT, lawyer; b. Mpls., Apr. 17, 1933; s. Leonard A. and Lilah B. (Nordland) B.; m. Charla Lee Bucklin; children—Karen, Anne, David, Douglas, Lea, Gregory. B.S. in Law, U. Minn., 1955, J.D., 1957. Bar: Minn. 1957, N.D. 1960, U.S. Dist. Ct. Minn., U.S. Dist. Ct. N.D., U.S. Ct. Appeals (8th cir.), U.S. Supreme Ct. Ptnr. Larson, Loevinger, Lindquist, Freeman & Fraser, Mpls., 1957-60, Zuger & Bucklin, Bismarck, N.D., 1960—; lectr. on product liability to various groups; mem. Joint Trial Procedure Com. N.D. Jud. Council, 1977—; mem. N.D. Supreme Ct. Camera in Courtroom Com., 1980—. Elder First Presbyterian Ch., 1974—; mem. Dakota West Arts Council. Mem. ABA (litigation sect.), Burleigh County Bar Assn. (pres. 1973), 4th Jud. Dist. Bar Assn., N.D. Bar Assn. , Assn. Trial Lawyers Am., Internat. Acad. Trial Lawyers, Am. Council on Transplantation (membership com. 1986—), Order of Coif, Phi Delta Phi, Delta Sigma Rho. Author: Civil Practice of North Dakota, 1975, Products Litigation, Dakota, 1987. Personal injury, Federal civil litigation, Products liability litigation. Home: 225 Juniper Dr Bismarck ND 58501 Office: PO Box 7276 Bismarck ND 58501

BUCKSTEIN, MARK AARON, lawyer; b. N.Y.C., July 1, 1939; s. Henry Al and Minnie Sarah (Russ) B.; m. Rochelle Joan Buchman, Sept. 11, 1960; children: Robin Beth, Michael Alan. BS, CCNY, 1960; JD, NYU, 1963. Bar: N.Y. 1963, U.S. Dist. Ct. (so. and ea. dists.) N.Y. 1965, U.S. Supreme Ct. 1981. Assoc., Russ, Weyl & Levitt, Massapequa, N.Y., 1963-64; assoc. counsel Mut Life Ins. Co. N.Y., N.Y.C., 1964-65; assoc. Moses & Singer, N.Y.C., 1965-67, Leinwand, Maron & Hendler, N.Y.C., 1967-68; sr. ptnr. Baer Marks & Upham, N.Y.C., 1968-86, sr. v.p., gen. counsel Trans World Airlines, Inc. N.Y.C., 1986—, also bd. dirs.; spl. prof. law Hofstra U. Law Sch., Hempstead, N.Y., 1980—; dir. Bayswater Realty & Capital Corp., N.Y.C., 1978—; mem. exec. com. Herzfeld & Stern, N.Y.C., 1981-84. Trustee, Bronx High Sch. Sci. Found., 1984—. Mem. ABA, N.Y. Bar Assn., Am. Arbitration Assn., Internat. Bar Assn. Democrat. Jewish. Lodge: KP (past dep. grand chancellor 1977). Securities, General corporate, Commodities. Office: Trans World Airlines 605 Third Ave New York NY 10158

BUCZKOWSKI, DAVID JOHN, lawyer; b. Springfield, Mass., Apr. 10, 1954. BA in Polit. Sci., U. Conn., 1976; JD, New Eng. Sch. of Law, 1979. Bar: Mass. 1979, U.S. Dist. Ct. Mass. 1980, U.S. Ct. Appeals (1st cir.) 1981, U.S. Tax Ct. 1981, U.S. Supreme Ct. 1984. Bond claims atty. Hartford (Conn.) Ins. Group, 1980-81; sr. bond claims atty. Comml. Union Ins. Group, Boston, 1981-83; assoc. Lecomte, Barber, Emanuelson, Tick & Doyle, Boston, 1983—. Mem. ABA (tort and ins. practices sect., fidelity and surety com.), Mass. Bar Assn., Adjusters Round Table of Boston, Phi Alpha Delta (chpt. justice 1978-79). Avocations: mass transit, bicycling. Construction, Insurance, General practice. Office: Lecomte Barber Emanuelson et al 1 Boston Pl Boston MA 02108

BUDDEN, HARRY EDWARD, JR., lawyer; b. Saginaw, Mich., Dec. 28, 1945; s. Harry Edward and Ann Mary (Sosnowski) B.; m. Jennie A. Scales, Aug. 3, 1983; 1 child by previous marriage, Priscilla Jean. A.B., Marshall U., 1968; J.D., U. Ky., 1973. Bar: Ky. 1973, U.S. Dist. Ct. Ky., U.S. Ct. Appeals (6th cir.), U.S. Supreme Ct. sole practice,Paris, Ky., 1973—. Served to capt. U.S. Army, 1969-71; Vietnam. Decorated Bronze star. Mem. Ky. Bar Assn., Acad. Ky. Trial Lawyers, Omicron Delta Kappa, Sigma Alpha Epsilon. Democrat. Episcopalian. Lodge: Masons. General practice, Family and matrimonial, State civil litigation. Home: 4 Horseshoe Dr Paris KY 40361 Office: 218 Main St Courthouse Sq Paris KY 40361

BUDER, EUGENE HAUCK, lawyer, consul of Netherlands; b. St. Louis, Mar. 3, 1917; s. Oscar Edward and Eugenia Antonia (Hauck) B.; m. Jutta Zelle, June 9, 1956; children—Eugene, Annette Sanburn, Beatrice, Stella. A.B. cum laude, Harvard U., 1938, J.D., 1941. Bar: Mo. 1941, U.S. Dist. Ct. (ea. dist.) Mo. 1941, U.S. Ct. Appeals (8th cir.) 1954, U.S. Supreme Ct. 1948. Assoc. Oscar Edward Buder, St. Louis, 1945-50; ptnr. Stockham, Roth, Buder & Martin, St. Louis, 1953-60, Buder and Martin, St. Louis, 1960-63; assoc. Harold C. Hanke and Benjamin Roth, St. Louis, 1964-85; assoc. Benjamin Roth and Green, Hennings & Henry, 1985—; consul of Netherlands, St. Louis; gen. counsel Urban League Met. St. Louis, 1964-87. Active St. Louis br. ACLU, 1946—. Served with Q.M.C., AUS, 1941-45, to maj. USAF, 1950-52. Decorated D.F.C., officer Order Orange-Nassau (Netherlands); recipient Civil Liberties award ACLU of Eastern Mo., 1972, Urban League St. Louis award, 1972. Mem. ABA, Mo. Bar, Bar Assn. Met. St. Louis. Democrat. Clubs: Mo. Athletic, Noonday, University (St. Louis). Civil rights, General practice, Probate. Office: 314 N Broadway Suite 1830 Saint Louis MO 63102

BUDISH, ARMOND DAVID, lawyer; b. Cleve., June 2, 1953; s. Irving I. and Janice (Ziev) B.; m. Amy Jacoby, Aug. 26, 1979; 1 child, Ryan. BA, Swarthmore Coll., 1974; JD, NYU, 1977. Bar: Ohio, Md., D.C., U.S. Dist. (no. dist.) Ohio, U.S. Dist. Ct. D.C., U.S. Ct. Appeals (6th and D.C. cirs.), U.S. Supreme Ct. Law clk. to presiding justice U.S. Dist. Ct. D.C., 1977-79; assoc. Hahn, Loeser, Freedheim, Dean & Wellham, Cleve., 1979—. Author: (syndicated newspaper column) You and the Law (OSBA Media award 1985), 1982—; (weekly real estate column) Law of the Land (Communicator award 1986), Cleve. Plain Dealer, 1985—. Campaign chmn. numerous polit. candidates, 1979—; mem. exec. com. Cuyahoga County Dem. Party, 1980—; v.p. Hillel Found. N.E. Ohio, Cleve., 1980—; treas. Am. Jewish Congress, Cleve., 1980—; mem. allocations com. Cleve. area United Way, 1986. Mem. ABA (exec. council young lawyers div. 1985—), Ohio Bar Assn. (exec council young lawyers sect. 1985—), Cleve. Bar Assn. (trustee 1983-84, chmn. young lawyers sect. 1983-84), Order of Coif. Federal civil litigation, State civil litigation, Consumer law. Home: 1856 Winchester Lyndhurst OH 44124

BUDLONG, JOHN, lawyer; b. Seattle, Oct. 2, 1953; s. John Edward and Helen May (Griffin) B. BA, U. Wash., 1976, MA, 1980, JD, 1982. Bar: Wash. 1982. Assoc. Safford, Frey & Mertel, Seattle, 1982—. Mem. ABA, Wash. State Bar Assn., Seattle-King County Bar Assn. Presbyterian. Federal civil litigation, State civil litigation, Admiralty. Home: 317 W Prospect Seattle WA 98119 Office: Stafford Frey & Mertel 88 Spring St Seattle WA 98104

BUDNITZ, ARRON EDWARD, lawyer; b. Hanover, N.H., Feb. 27, 1949; s. Harry and Frieda Sara (Altscitz) B. AB, Dartmouth Coll., 1971; MBA, Boston U., 1973, LLM in Taxation, 1981; JD, Suffolk U., 1979. Bar: Fla. 1979, Mass. 1979, N.H. 1980, U.S. Dist. Ct. Mass. 1979, U.S. Dist. Ct. N.H. 1980, U.S. Tax Ct. 1979, U.S. Ct. Appeals (1st cir.) 1979, Maine 1987, U.S. Dist. Ct. Maine 1987; cert. fin. planner. Sole practice Newport, N.H. and Winthrop, Mass., 1979—; adj. faculty N.H. Coll., Manchester, 1984—. Mem. ABA, Fla. Bar Assn., Mass. Bar Assn., N.H. Bar Assn., Maine Bar Assn., Dartmouth Lawyers Assn., Inst. Cert. Fin. Planners, Internat. Assn. Fin. Planning, N.H. Estate Planning Council, Phi Delta Phi. General corporate, Probate, Personal income taxation. Home: 1 Pond St #1-F Winthrop MA 02152-1023 Office: PO Box #508 Newport NH 03773-0508

BUE, CARL OLAF, JR., judge; b. Chgo., Mar. 27, 1922; s. Carl Olaf and Mabel Port (Shollar) B.; m. Mary Kathryn Waring, Dec. 27, 1948; children—Kathryn Anne, Richard Charles. A.A., U. Chgo., 1942; student, U. Rome, Italy, 1945; Ph.B., Northwestern U., 1951; LL.B., U. Tex., 1954. Bar: Tex. bar 1954. Asso. firm Royston, Rayzor & Cook, Houston, 1954-58; mem. firm Royston, Rayzor & Cook, 1958-70; U.S. dist. judge So. Dist. Tex. (Houston div.), 1970—; lectr. various law schs. and admiralty seminars in Tex. and other states. Contbr. articles to profl. jours. Served to capt., Adj. Gen. Dept. AUS, 1942-46, MTO. Recipient Good Citizenship medal Houston chpt. SAR, 1975, Joe R. Greenhill award Tex. Municipal Cts. Assn., 1976-77. Mem. Am., Fed., Tex., Houston bar assns., Maritime Law Assn. of U.S., Am. Judicature Soc., English Speaking Union, Houston Philos. Soc. at Rice U., Alpha Delta Phi, Phi Alpha Delta. Republican. Lutheran. Home: 338 Knipp Rd Houston TX 77024 Office: US Courthouse 515 Rusk Ave Room 11535 Houston TX 77002

BUECHEL, WILLIAM BENJAMIN, lawyer; b. Wichita, Kans., July 27, 1926; s. Donald William and Bonnie S. (Priddy) B.; m. Theresa Marie Girard, Nov. 3, 1955; children—Sarah Ann, Julia Elaine. Student U. Wichita, 1947-49; B.S., U. Kans., 1951, LL.B., 1954. Bar: Kans., 1954, U.S. dist. ct. (Kans.), 1954. Sole practice, Concordia, Kans., 1954-56; stockholder Paulsen, Buechel, Swenson, Uri & Brewer, Chartered, and predecessors, Concordia, 1971-75, sec.-treas., 1975-77, pres., 1977—; dir. Cloud County Bank & Trust, Concordia, 1971—. Bd. dirs. Cloud County Community Coll. Endowment and Scholarship Assn., 1983—. Mem. ABA, Kan. Bar Assn. (exec. council 1966-68, chmn. adv. sect. profl. ethics com. 1974-76), Cloud County Bar Assn. (pres. 1984-86). Republican. Methodist. Clubs: Concordia Country, Elks, Moose, Rotary (pres. 1969-70). Probate, Estate taxation, Estate planning. Home: 325 W 10th St Concordia KS 66901 Office: Paulsen Buechel et al 613 Washington St PO Box 327 Concordia KS 66901

BUECHNER, JACK W., lawyer; b. St. Louis, June 4, 1940; s. John Edw. and Gertrude Emily (Richardson) B.; m. Marietta Rose Conn, Aug. 7, 1965; children: Patrick John, Terrance J. BA, Benedictine Coll., 1962; JD, St. Louis U., 1965. Bar: Mo. 1965, U.S. Dist. Ct. (ea. dist.) Mo. 1965, U.S. Ct. Appeals (8th cir.) 19865. Ptnr. Buechner, McCarthy, Leonard, Kaemmerer, Owen & Laderman, Manchester, Mo., 1965—; mem. 100th Congress from 2d Mo. dist., 1986—; state rep. 94th dist., Mo. Gen. Assembly, 1972-82. Mem. Mo. Tourism Commn., 1976, 82, 85. Recipient Meritorious Service award St. Louis Globe-Democrat, 1973, Legis. Achievement award St. Louis Police Officers, 1982, Pub. Service award Women's Polit., Mo., Distinguished Service award Cardinal Glennon Hosp., Mo., 1982. Mem. ABA, Mo. Bar Assn., Met. Bar Assn. Republican. Roman Catholic. Club: John Marshal (Outstanding Atty. 1986). Avocations: softball, reading, travel. Real property, Legislative, General practice. Home: 14 Ponca Tr Saint Louis MO 63122 Office: Room 502 Cannon House Office Bldg Washington DC 20515

BUECHNER, ROBERT WILLIAM, lawyer, educator; b. Syracuse, N.Y., Oct. 29, 1947; s. Donald F. and Barbara (Northrup) B.; m. Angela Marian Hoetker, May 28, 1978; children: Julie Marie, Robert Jr., Leslie Ann. BSE, Princeton U., 1969; JD, U. Mich., 1974. Bar: Ohio, 1974, Fla. 1974, U.S. Dist. Ct. (so. dist.) Ohio 1974, U.S. Tax Ct. 1974. Assoc. Frost & Jacobs, Cin., 1974-79; pres. Buechner, Haffer, O'Connell & Meyers Co., L.P.A., Cin., 1979—; adj. prof. Salmon P. Chase Coll. Law, No. Ky., 1975-82; instr. Cin. chpt. Charterd Life Underwiters, 1976—; lectr. Million Dollar Roundtable, Atlanta, 1981. Author: (with others) Why Universal Life, 1982, Prosper Through Tax Planning, 1982, Living Gangbusters, 1986, The 8 Pathways to Financial Success, 1987. Mem. planning div. Cin. Community Chest, 1978-84; trustee Cin. Country Day Sch., 1984—. Served to capt. USPHS, 1970-72. Recipient Alumnus of Yr. award Cin. Country Day Sch., 1985. Mem. Cin. Bar Assn. (chmn. taxation sect. 1984-85), Southwest Ohio Tax Inst. (chmn. 1981-82). Republican. Methodist. Clubs: Gyro (Cin.) (sec. 1982-83), Princeton (Cin.) (pres. 1982-84). Avocations: golf, tennis, bridge. Pension, profit-sharing, and employee benefits, Estate planning, Personal income taxation. Office: Buechner Haffner O'Connell & Meyers Co LPA 105 E 4th St Suite 1405 Cincinnati OH 45202

BUEHLER, JAMES CARROLL, lawyer, pilot, educator; b. Columbus, Ind., Apr. 16, 1955; s. James Backsman and K. LeJean (Stinger) B. BA, Ind. U., 1977, JD, 1980. Bar: Ind. 1980, Ill. 1986, U.S. Dist. Ct. (so. dist.) Ind. 1980, U.S. Ct. Appeals (7th cir.) 1986. Assoc. Lewis & Bowman, Indpls., 1980-83, Rocap Law Firm, Indpls., 1983-85; sole practioner Indpls., 1985—; pilot Am. Transair, Indpls., 1985—; adj. prof. Ind. Cen. U., Indpls., 1980-83, Ind. U. Indpls., 1982—; judge pro tem Marion County Mcpl. Ct., Indpls, 1980—. Dem. committeeman Marion County, 1983. Mem. ABA,

Lawyer-Pilots Bar Assn., Ind. Bar Assn. (vice chmn. aviation law com. 1982-84), Phi Delta Phi. Democrat. Avocations: flying, skiing, rugby. Insurance, Contracts commercial, Personal injury. Home: 5429 Winthrop Ave Indianapolis IN 46220 Office: 109 Conrad Bldg 5555 Tacoma Ave Indianapolis IN 46220

BUEHLER, JOHN WILSON, lawyer; b. Fresno, Calif., Aug. 16, 1950; s. John A. and Elizabeth (Wilson) B.; m. Carol M. Davidson, Sept. 9, 1972; children: Nathaniel J., Christopher J. BA, U. Calif., Santa Cruz, 1973; JD magna cum laude, Willamette U., 1977. Bar: Oreg. 1977, U.S. Dist. Ct. Oreg. 1978, U.S. Ct. Appeals (9th. cir.) 1981. Law clk. to presiding justice U.S. Dist. Ct., Portland, Oreg., 1977-79; assoc. Bullivant, Wright et al, Portland, 1979-83; ptnr. Bullivant, Houser, Bailey, Pendergrass & Hoffman, Portland, 1984—; bar examiner Bd. of Bar Examiners, Portland, Oreg., 1985—. Vol. atty. sr. law project City of Portland, 1980—. Mem. ABA, Oreg. Bar Assn., Multnomah Bar Assn, Def. Research Inst., Oreg. Assn. Def. Counsel,. Democrat. Insurance, Federal civil litigation, State civil litigation. Office: Bullivant Houser Bailey et al 1211 SW 5th Ave Suite 1400 Portland OR 97204

BUEHLER, THOMAS LEE, lawyer; b. Highland, Ill., Jan. 9, 1948; s. Leo Thomas and Jeanne H. Buehler; m. Marsha Anne Centner, June 12, 1970; children: Jennifer Lee, Camilla Jeanne. AB, Xavier U., 1970; JD, U. Ky., 1975. Bar: Ohio 1975, U.S. Dist. Ct. (so. dist.) Ohio 1975. Atty. U.S. Shoe Corp., Cin., 1975-77, asst. sec., 1977-83, asst. sec., assoc. gen. counsel, 1983—; adj. assoc. prof. econs. and indsl. relations Xavier U., Cin., 1975—. Author: Selected Cases on Labor Problems, 1977, Selected Cases on Business Regulations, 1982, Selected Cases on Collective Bargaining, 1983. Served to 1st lt., U.S. Army, 1971-73. Mem. Ohio Bar Assn., Cin. Bar Assn., Am. Corp. Counsel Assn. (bd. dirs., sec. Cin. chpt. 1983—, pres. 1985). Republican. Roman Catholic. General corporate, Labor, Administrative and regulatory. Home: 1248 Michigan Ave Cincinnati OH 45208 Office: US Shoe Corp 1 Eastwood Dr Cincinnati OH 45227

BUELL, EUGENE F(RANKLIN), lawyer; b. Elrama, Pa., Dec. 3, 1916; s. Frank Currey and Altina (Ecklund) B.; m. Elizabeth Ellen Foster, Dec. 28, 1940; children: Ellen E. (dec.), Erik Foster. B.S., St. Vincent's Coll., 1938; grad., Carnegie Inst. Tech., 1938-40, U. Pitts., 1941, Johns Hopkins U., 1942; J.D., Duquesne U., 1944. Bar: D.C. 1949, Canadian Patent Office 1949, U.S. Supreme Ct. 1952. Chemist U.S. Steel Corp., 1938-42; chief chemist Homestead works, 1942-45; with Stebbins, Blenko & Webb, 1945-48; partner firm Blenko, Hoopes, Leonard & Glenn, 1949-52; Blenko, Hoopes, Leonard & Buell Pitts., 1953-66; Blenko, Leonard & Buell 1966-72; partner firm Blenko, Buell, Ziesenheim & Beck (P.C.), 1973-79; pres., chmn. Buell, Blenko, Ziesenheim & Beck, P.C., 1979-84, Tartan Industries Inc.; chmn., pres. Buell, Ziesenheim, Beck & Alstadt, P.C., 1984—; treas. Pitts. Performance Products, Inc.; instr. Law Sch. U., Pitts., 1954-59, adj. prof. law, 1959—. Past pres. Richland Com. for Better Govt., Babcock Sch. Dist. Dirs.; chmn. Richland Sch. Authority; mem. Sch. Bd. Richland Twp. Mem. Am. Bar Assn., Am. Patent Law Assn., Engrs. Soc. Western Pa., Pa. Soc., Assn. Bar City N.Y., Licensing Exec. Soc., Am. Arbitration Assn., Am. Soc. Metals, Interam. Bar Assn., Am. Judicature Soc., Pa. Bar Assn., Allegheny County Bar Assn., Assn. Internationale pour la Protection de la Propriete Industrielle, Order of Coif. Clubs: Duquesne, Elks, Masons, Press, Allegheny, Rivers, Amen Corner. Patent, Federal civil litigation, Trademark and copyright. Home: RD 2 Box 418 Gibsonia PA 15044 Office: 322 Blvd of the Allies Pittsburgh PA 15222

BUERGENTHAL, THOMAS, lawyer, educator, international judge; b. Lubochna, Czechoslovakia, May 11, 1934; came to U.S., 1951, naturalized, 1957; s. Mundek and Gerda (Silbergleit) B.; m. Marjorie J. Bell, 1983; children by previous marriage. Robert, John, Alan. B.A., Bethany Coll., 1957, LL.D., 1981; J.D., N.Y. U., 1960; LL.M., Harvard U., 1961, S.J.D., 1968; Dr. Jur. (hon.), U. Heidelberg, 1986. Bar: N.Y. State 1961, D.C. 1983, U.S. Supreme Ct. 1982. Instr. law U. Pa., 1961-62; asst. prof. SUNY, Buffalo, 1962-64; assoc. prof. SUNY, 1964-67, prof., 1967-75; vis. prof. U. Tex.-Austin, 1975-76, prof., 1976-77, Fulbright and Jaworski prof., 1977-80; judge Inter-Am. Ct. Human Rights, 1979—, pres., 1985—; dean, prof. law Am. U., Washington, 1980-85; disting. prof. law and human rights Emory U. Sch. Law, 1985-86, I.T. Cohen prof. of human rights, 1987—; assoc. reporter, mem. adv. com. Restatement of the Fgn. Relations Law of the U.S.; chmn. human rights com. U.S. Nat. Commn. for UNESCO, 1976-79; U.S. rep. UNESCO Human Rights Working Group, 1977-78; U.S. expert UN Interregional Expert Meeting on Crime Prevention and Control, 1978; mem. adv. bd. Pres. Holocaust Commn., 1978-80; v.p. UNESCO Congress on Teaching of Human Rights, 1978; pres. Inter-Am. Inst. Human Rights, 1980—. Author: Law-Making in the International Civil Aviation Organization, 1969, (with L.B. Sohn) International Protection of Human Rights, 1973, (with J.V. Torney) International Human Rights and International Education, 1976, Human Rights, International Law and the Helsinki Accord, 1977, (with R.E. Norris) Human rights: The Inter-Am. System, 1982; (with Norris and Shelton) Protecting Human Rights in the Americas, 1982, 2d edit. 1986; (with H. Maier) Public International Law in a Nutshell, 1985. Contbr. articles to profl. jours. Recipient Pro-Humanitas Ring, West-Ost Kulturwerk, Fed. Republic of Germany, 1978. Mem. Am. Law Inst., Am. Soc. Internat. Law (v.p. 1980-82), Internat. Law Assn. Legal education. Office: Emory U Law Sch Gambrell Hall Atlanta GA 30322

BUESING, KAREN MEYER, lawyer; b. San Jose, Calif., Oct. 27, 1953; d. George Clifton and Marjorie Helen (Woodruff) Meyer; m. Robert Henry Buesing, Apr. 26, 1986. BJ, U. Fla., 1975, JD, 1982. Bar: Fla. 1982, U.S. Dist. Ct. (mid. dist.) Fla. 1982, U.S. Ct. Appeals (11th cir.) 1982. News reporter, editor Fla. Today, Cocoa, 1975-79; assoc. Trenam, Simmons et al, Tampa, Fla., 1982-86, Rudnick & Wolfe, Tampa, 1986—; adj. lectr. Stetson Coll. Law, St. Petersburg, Fla., 1986, U. Fla., Gainesville, 1979-81; founder, dir. Fed. Trial Vols. Project, Tampa, 1985—. Mem. Fla. Bar Assn., Hillsborough County Bar Assn. (chmn. availability of legal services com. 1985—, pro bono service award 1985). Democrat. Methodist. Federal civil litigation, State civil litigation. Office: Rudnick & Wolfe 201 E Kennedy Blvd Suite 1600 Tampa FL 33602

BUETHER, ERIC W., lawyer; b. Denver, Apr. 8, 1956; s. William H. and Julie L. Buether; m. Lee Thao Le; children: Lily, Easther, Deborah. AB, U. Chgo., 1978, JD, 1981. Bar: Tex. 1981, U.S. Dist. Ct. (no. dist.) Tex. 1981, U.S. Ct. Appeals (5th cir.) 1985, U.S. Supreme Ct. 1985. Assoc. Johnson & Swanson, Dallas, 1981-84, Gibson, Dunn & Crutcher, Dallas, 1984—. Asst. mgr. Reagan presdl. campaign, Chgo., 1980. Mem. ABA (litigation sect., antitrust law sect.), Tex. Bar Assn., Dallas Bar Assn., 5th Cir. Bar Assn. Avocations: photography, baseball, music. Federal civil litigation, State civil litigation, Antitrust. Office: Gibson Dunn & Crutcher 1700 Pacific Ave Suite 4400 Dallas TX 75201

BUFFINGTON, JOHN VICTOR, lawyer; b. Arlington, Va., July 23, 1947; s. John V. Sr. and Patricia (Messer) B.; m. Cynthia Davis, June 13, 1970. BA, U. Va., 1969, JD, 1972. Bar: D.C. 1973, Va. 1973, U.S. Ct. Appeals (3d cir.) 1976, Pa. 1979. Staff atty. U.S. EPA, Phila., 1973-77; regional counsel U.S. Dept. Energy, Phila., 1977-79; chief counsel Pa. Gov.'s Energy Council, Harrisburg, 1979-82; research fellow U. Del., Newark, 1982-84; sole practice Phila., 1985—; lectr. Del. Humanities Forum, Wilmington, 1984—. Contbr. articles to profl. jours. Mem. ABA, Law and Humanities Inst., Phila. Bar Assn. Public utilities, Nuclear power, Real property.

BUFFMIRE, ANDREW WALLACE, lawyer, investment banker; b. Los Angeles, Mar. 21, 1947; s. Wallace Ray and Martha Frances (Irvine) B.; m. Lisa Karen Fundigsland, Mar. 10, 1974; children: Corine, Robert, Jameson. BA, U. So. Calif., 1969; JD, U. Utah, 1973; LLM, London Sch. Econs., 1975. Asst. dean coll. law U. Utah, Salt Lake City, 1974; atty. legal advisor's office European Econ. Community, Brussels, 1975-76; staff trial atty. FTC, Washington, 1976-77; chief antiturst div. Utah Atty. Gen.'s Office, Salt Lake City, 1977-79; ptnr. Jones, Waldo, Holbrook & McDonough, Salt Lake City, 1979-85; mng. dir. McOmber, Travis & Buffmire Inc., Salt Lake City, 1985—; bd. dirs. Gavilan Petroleum Co., Salt Lake City. Bd. dirs. Salt Lake City Housing Authority, 1979—, Presbyn. Utah, Salt Lake City, 1986—; chmn. bd. of trustees Presbytery of Utah. Mem. ABA, Utah Bar Assn. Democrat. Lodge: Masons (sr. warden Mt. Moriah lodge 1985-86). Avocations: skiing, mountaineering, tai chi. Securities, General corporate, Oil and gas leasing. Office: McOmber Travis & Buffmire Inc 175 S Main 1110 Walker Ctr Salt Lake City UT 84111

BUFFON, CHARLES EDWARD, lawyer; b. Topeka, Sept. 8, 1939; s. Merritt Woodbridge and Clare Marie (Waterfall) B.; m. Kathleen Craig Vreeland, June 6, 1964; children—Alexandra, Nathaniel Edward. A.B. magna cum laude with highest distinction in Internat. Relations, Dartmouth Coll., 1961; LL.B. cum laude, Harvard U., 1964. Bar: D.C. 1965, U.S. Ct. Appeals (D.C. cir.) 1965, U.S. Dist. Ct. D.C. 1965, U.S. Ct. Appeals (6th cir.) 1968, U.S. Supreme Ct. 1971, U.S. Ct. Appeals (9th cir.) 1975, U.S. Ct. Appeals (2d cir.) 1980, U.S. Ct. Appeals (4th cir.) 1980, U.S. Ct. Appeals (3d cir.) 1981, U.S. Ct. Claims and Patent Appeals 1982. Assoc. Covington & Burling, Washington, 1964-73, ptnr., 1973—; adj. faculty Law Sch., U. Va., 1968—; faculty Continuing Legal Edn. Columbia Law Sch., State Bar Tex., Fed. Bar Assn., Washington Bar Assn. Chmn. Class 1961 Fellowship Com. Dartmouth Coll.; chmn. Aircraft Overflight Com., Chevy Chase, Md. Class of 1926 Pub. Service fellow Dartmouth Coll., recipient Daniel Webster Debate Prize, Woodbury Law Prize, Alfred P. Sloan Found. Nat. Scholar, 1957-61. Mem. ABA (litigation and antitrust sects.), D.C. Bar (chmn. legal ethics com., steering com. div. on lawyers, cts. and adminstrn. of justice, chmn. spl. com. on legal specialization, mem. special com. on model rules of profl. conduct, long range planning com.), Phi Beta Kappa. Contbr. writings to profl. publs. Antitrust, Jurisprudence, Administrative and regulatory. Office: 1201 Pennsylvania Ave NW PO Box 7566 Washington DC 20044

BUFORD, ROBERT PEGRAM, lawyer; b. Roanoke Rapids, N.C., Sept. 7, 1925; s. Robert Pegram and Edith (Rawlings) B.; m. Anne Bliss Whitehead, June 26, 1948; children—Robert, Bliss, Peyton. LL.B., U. Va., 1950. Bar: Va. 1949. Assoc., Florance, Florance & Moore, Richmond, Va., 1950-51; assoc. Hunton & Williams, Richmond, 1952-58, ptnr., 1958—; dir. Tultex Corp., Martinsville, Va., So. Furniture Exposition Bldg. Inc., High Point, N.C. United Va. Bankshares Inc., Richmond, First Colony Life Ins. Co., Lynchburg, Va., United Dominion Realty Trust, Inc., Richmond. Pres., Richmond First Club, 1960; bd. visitors U. Va., Charlottesville, 1972-80; chmn. Met. Richmond C. of C., 1973; vice chmn., bd. trustees St. Paul's Coll., Lawrenceville, Va., 1977-85. Served to lt. (j.g.) USNR, 1943-46. Recipient Disting. Service award Jr. C. of C., 1961, Va. Profl. Assn., 1965, Good Govt. award Richmond First Club, 1967. Fellow Am. Bar Found., Va. Law Found.; mem. ABA, Va. Bar Found. Clubs: Country of Va., Commonwealth (Richmond). Banking, General corporate, Securities. Home: 506 Kilmarnock Dr Richmond VA 23229 Office: Hunton & Williams 707 E Main St PO Box 1535 Richmond VA 23219

BUGDANOWITZ, ROBERT, lawyer; b. Denver, May 28, 1922; s. Abraham and Sadie (Rosenberg) B.; m. Mildred Rae Blecker, Sept. 18, 1959; children—Marcia Lynne, Linda Susan. B.A., U. Denver, 1948, J.D., 1948. Bar: Colo. 1948, U.S. dist. ct. Colo., 1948, U.S. Ct. Apls. (10th cir.), 1948, U.S. Sup. Ct. 1957. Asst. Colo. atty. gen., 1948-50; dist. trial atty. Office Price Stabilization, 1951-52; asst. U.S. atty. Dist. Colo., 1952; sole practice, Denver, 1948—; tchr. family law U. Denver Sch. Social Work, 1965; master domestic relations div. Denver Dist. Ct., 1970. Served with USAAF, 1942-45; ETO. Fellow Am. Acad. Matrimonial Lawyers; mem. Assn. Trial Lawyers Am., ABA, Colo. Trial Lawyers Assn. (lectr. 1st jud. dist. domestic relation seminar 1981), Colo. Bar Assn. (lectr. domestic relations seminar 1983), Denver Bar Assn. Democrat. Jewish. Clubs: City, Masons, Shriners (Denver); Press; Mount Vernon Country. Family and matrimonial. Home and Office: 2968 S Dallas Way Denver CO 80210 Office: 1385 S Colorado Blvd Suite 622 Denver CO 80222

BUIE, DONALD RAY, lawyer; b. Red Springs, N.C., Feb. 4, 1956; m. Becky Jo Peterson, Dec. 26, 1981. AA, Wingate Coll., 1976; BA, Elon Coll., 1978; JD, N.C. Cen. U., 1981. Bar: N.C. 1981, U.S. Dist. Ct. (mid. dist.) N.C. 1981. Assoc. Law Firm of Billy D. Friende, Jr., Winston-Salem, N.C., 1981-87; sole practice Winston-Salem, 1987—. Mem. ABA, N.C. Bar Assn., N.C. Acad. Trial Lawyers, N.C. Assn. Black Lawyers, Forsyth County Bar Assn., Winston-Salem Bar Assn. Democrat. Baptist. Lodge: Masons (sr. deacon 1985—). State civil litigation, General practice, Personal injury. Home: 444 Linville Rd Kernersville NC 27284 Office: PO Box 33o 301 S Liberty St Old Town Hall Bldg Winston-Salem NC 27102

BUJOLD, TYRONE PATRICK, lawyer; b. Duluth, Minn., Dec. 4, 1937; s. Dewey J. and Lucille C. (Donahue) B.; m. Delia H. Goulet, Sept. 17, 1960; children: Christopher Andrew, Anne Elizabeth, Lara Suzanne. BS, Marquette U., 1959; JD, U. Minn., 1962. Bar: Minn. 1962, U.S. Dist. Ct. Minn. 1963, U.S. Ct. Appeals (8th cir.) 1964, U.S. Dist. Ct. (ea. dist.) Wis. 1985, Wis. 1983. Assoc. Furuseth & Bujold, International Falls, Minn., 1962-63; assoc. Sullivan, MacMillan, Hanft & Hastings, Duluth, 1963-68, ptnr., 1968-85; ptnr. Robins, Zelle, Larson & Kaplan, Mpls., 1985—; faculty continuing legal edn. program, Minn., 1965—, Inst. Continuing Legal Edn., Ann Arbor, Mich., 1975—, Nat. Inst. Trial Advocacy, 1983-86. Mem. commn. Fair Housing and Employment Practices, Duluth, 1970-78, City Charter COmmn., Duluth, 1983-85. Roman Catholic. Club: Mpls. Athletic. Avocations: reading, theatre, guitar, swimming. Federal civil litigation, State civil litigation, Personal injury. Office: Robins Zelle Larson & Kaplan 1800 International Centre Minneapolis MN 55402

BUKATY, STEVE A.J., lawyer; b. Kansas City, June 19, 1947; s. Andrew Joseph and Josephine (Egnatic) B.; m. Frances Regina Pringle, June 21, 1970 (div. Dec. 1985); children: Molly Frances, Nathaniel Dylan. AA, Donnelly Coll., 1967; BA, Kans. State Coll., 1969; JD, U. Kans., 1975. Bar: Kans. 1975, U.S. Dist. Ct. Kans. 1975, U.S. Ct. Appeals (5th, 8th, 10th and 11th cirs.) 1975. Assoc. Fisher, Patterson, Sayler & Smith, Topeka, 1975-76; ptnr. Blake & Uhlig P.A., Kansas City, 1976—. Sec., treas., bd. dirs. YMCA, Kansas City, 1977-80. Served to sgt. U.S. Army, 1970-71. Mem. ABA, Wyandotte County Bar Assn. Clubs: Terrace, Dub's Dread Country Club (Kansas City). Avocation: golf. Labor. Home: 4526 N 123d Terr Kansas City KS 66109 Office: Blake & Uhlig PA 475 New Brotherhood Bldg Kansas City KS 66101

BULDRINI, GEORGE JAMES, lawyer; b. N.Y.C.; s. Frederick Paul and Emily Geraldine (Bewick) B. BA, St. Johns U., Jamaica, N.Y., 1969; JD, St. Johns U., 1972; LLM, NYU, 1976. Bar: N.Y. 1973, U.S. Dist. Ct. (no. dist.) N.Y. 1975, U.S. Supreme Ct. 1976. Sr. atty. N.Y. State Dept. Health, Albany, 1974—; shop steward Pub. Employees Fedn., 1982—. Mem. ABA, N.Y. State Bar Assn., Fed. Bar Assn. Republican. Avocations: golf, chess, reading, gardening, photography. Health, Administrative and regulatory. Office: NY Dept Health Legal Affairs Empire State Plaza Tower Bldg Albany NY 12237

BULINSKI, GREGORY PAUL, lawyer; b. Chgo., Aug. 6, 1953; s. Emery S. and Dolores P. (Costello) B.; m. Judith Lucille Hannigan, Sept. 14, 1979. BA, Macalester Coll., 1976; JD cum laude, U. Minn., 1979. Bar: Minn. 1979. Assoc. Richards, Montgomery, Cobb & Bassord, P.A., Mpls., 1979; assoc. Bassford, Heckt, Lockhart & Millin, P.A., Mpls., 1980-84, ptnr., 1985—. Mem. ABA, Minn. Bar Assn., Hennepin County Bar Assn. State civil litigation, Federal civil litigation, Insurance. Home: 1012 E Minnehaha Pkwy Minneapolis MN 55417 Office: Bassford Heckt Lockhart & Mullin PA 3550 Multifoods Tower Minneapolis MN 55402

BULL, HOWARD LIVINGSTON, lawyer; b. Binghamton, N.Y., Oct. 7, 1942; s. Glen Chapel Bull and Martha Gertrade (Mott) Skinner; m. Sheila Kay Settle, Apr. 22, 1977; children: John, Jason. AB, DePauw U., 1964; JD, U. Va., 1967. Bar: Calif. 1973, U.S. Dist. Ct. (no. dist.) Calif. 1973, U.S. Ct. Appeals (9th cir.) 1973. Assoc. Owen, Melbye & Rohlff, Redwood City, Calif., 1973-74; atty. Varian Assocs., Inc., Palo Alto, Calif., 1974—. Pres. Midpeninsula chpt. UN Assn.-USA, Northern Calif. div., Palo Alto, 1987—; trustee Ben Lomond (Calif.) Quaker Ctr., 1975-80. Served to capt. USAF, 1968-72. Mem. ABA, Santa Clara County Bar Assn. (steering com. corp. counsel sect. 1984—), DePauw Alumni Club (pres. 1975). Republican. Mem. Soc. of Friends. Avocations: sports, camping, bicycling, woodworking. Contracts commercial, Environment, Computer. Home: 1457 Isabelle Ave Mountain View CA 94040 Office: Varian Assocs Inc Legal Dept 611 Hansen Way Palo Alto CA 94303

BULLARD, ROCKWOOD WILDE, III, lawyer; b. Chgo., May 20, 1944; s. Rockwood Wilde, Jr. and Maryetta Moylen (Fitts) B.; m. Donna Rae Boles, Oct. 29, 1983; children—Elizabeth Ryan, Cathleen Stickney. B.A., Wayne State U., 1971; J.D., New Eng. Sch. Law, 1974. Bar: D.C. 1974, Mich. 1976, U.S. Dist. Ct. (ea. dist.) Mich. 1976, U.S. Dist. Ct. (we. dist.) Mich. 1977, U.S. Ct. Appeals (6th cir.) 1978, U.S. Supreme Ct. 1979. Atty. advisor HUD, Washington, 1974-76; assoc. Patterson & Patterson, Bloomfield Hills, Mich., 1976-82, Goodenough, Smith, Bloomfield Hills, 1982-84; ptnr. Lyon C. & Bullard, Rochester, Mich., 1984—; panel chmn. Atty. Discipline Bd. State Bar Mich., 1984—; dir. Water St. Bridge Corp., Pontiac, Mich., 1984—. Mem. instl. rev. com. Pontiac Gen. Hosp., 1976-83; chmn. attys.' div. United Way Oakland, Pontiac, 1983. Served as spl. agt. M.I., U.S. Army, 1967-69. Recipient Amos L. Taylor award New Eng. Law Sch., 1974. Mem. Oakland County C. of C. (bd. dirs. 1984-87), Oakland County Bar Assn., D.C. Bar Assn., Nat. Lawyers Club, Fed. Bar Assn. Republican. Episcopalian. Club: Otsego (Gaylord, Mich.). Federal civil litigation, General corporate, Trademark and copyright. Office: Lyon Colbert & Bullard 431 6th St Rochester MI 48063

BULLITT, JOHN C., lawyer; b. Phila., June 6, 1925; s. Orville H. and Susan B. (Ingersoll) B.; m. Lelia M. Wardwell, Nov. 20, 1954 (div.); children: Thomas W., Clarissa W.; m. Judith Ogden Cabot, May 15, 1976; stepchildren: Elizabeth, Edward, Timothy. B.A., Harvard, 1950; LL.B., U. Pa., 1953. Bar: N.Y. 1956. Asso. Shearman & Sterling, N.Y.C., 1953-60; dep. asst. sec. internat. affairs U.S. Treasury, Washington, 1961-62; asst. sec. internat. affairs U.S. Treasury, 1962-64; U.S. exec. dir. Internat. Bank Reconstrn. and Devel., 1962-65; dir. N.J. Office Econ. Opportunity, 1964-67; asst. adminstr. for East Asia AID, Dept. State, 1967-69; partner Shearman & Sterling, 1969—, partner in charge Hong Kong office, 1978-81. Served with inf. AUS, World War II. Mem. Council Fgn. Relations. Clubs: N.Y. Yacht, Century Assn. (N.Y.C.); Fed. City (Washington); Philadelphia; Royal Hong Kong Yacht, Shanghai Frat. Assn. (Hong Kong). Home: RD 1 Princeton NJ 08540

BULLIVANT, RUPERT REID, lawyer; b. Portland, Oreg., Nov. 29, 1903; s. Joe and Ethel Cecelia (Rupert) B.; m. Norma Jean Wilson, July 6, 1926 (dissolved); 1 child, Diane Carter; m. Louise S. Storla, Jan. 1980. JD, U. Oreg., 1926. Bar: Oreg. 1926, U.S. Dist. Ct. Oreg. 1926, U.S. Ct. Appeals, U.S. Supreme Ct. 1979. Sole practice Portland, 1926-28; assoc. Clark & Clark, Portland, 1928-37; ptnr. Bullivant, Houser, Bailey, Hanna and predecessor firms, Portland, 1938—; mem. Oreg. Conf. Uniform Law Commrs., 1948—. Mem. Portland Planning Commn., 1935-45. Mem. Am. Bar Found. (Oreg. chpt.), Oreg. Bar Assn. (pres. 1937-38, bd. govs. 1936-39), Am. Judicature Soc., Phi Beta Kappa. Republican. Clubs: Arlington (v.p.), Waverly, Multnomah Athletic (Portland). Federal civil litigation, State civil litigation, General corporate. Home: 56 Condolea Terr Lake Oswego OR 97034 Office: Bullivant Houser Bailey Hanna Pacwest Ctr Portland OR 97204

BULLOCK, FRANK WILLIAM, JR., federal judge; b. Oxford, N.C., Nov. 3, 1938; s. Frank William and Wilma Jackson (Long) B.; m. Frances Dockery Haywood, May 5, 1984; 1 child, Frank William III. B.S. in Bus. Adminstrn., U. N.C., 1961, LL.B., 1963. Bar: N.C. 1963. Assoc. Maupin, Taylor & Ellis, Raleigh, N.C., 1964-68; asst. dir. Adminstrv. Office of Cts. of N.C., Raleigh, 1968-73; ptnr. Douglas, Ravenel, Hardy, Crihfield & Bullock, Greensboro, N.C., 1973-82; judge U.S. Dist. Ct. N.C., Durham, 1982—. Mem. bd. editors N.C. Law Rev., 1962-63; contbr. articles to profl. jours. Mem. ABA, N.C. Bar Assn., Greensboro Bar Assn., N.C. Soc. of Cincinnati. Republican. Presbyterian. Clubs: Greensboro Country. Avocations: golf; tennis; running; history. Judicial administration. Office: US Dist Ct 323 E Chapel Hill St PO Box 3807 Durham NC 27702 *

BULLOCK, JIM, lawyer; b. Sioux City, Iowa, July 29, 1947; s. Joe Ragland and Margaret (Killeen) B.; m. Velma E. Mason, Nov. 5, 1968 (div. 1980); 1 child, Jonathon Lee. BA, Miss. Coll., 1970, JD, 1980. Bar: Miss. 1980. Ptnr. Shell, Buford, Bufkin, Callicutt & Perry, Jackson, Miss., 1980—. Served to 1st lt. USAF, 1970-73; served to maj. USNG, 1973—. Mem. ABA, Miss. Bar Assn., N.G. Assn. U.S., N.G. Assn. Miss. Republican. Baptist. Avocations: racquetball, swimming, civil aviation. Federal civil litigation, State civil litigation, Insurance. Home: 405 Oakhurst Dr Jackson MS 39204

BULLOCK, ROBERT D., lawyer, state official; b. Hillsboro, Tex., July 10, 1929; s. Thomas A. and Ruth (Mitchell) B.; m. Jan. Felts Bullock; children—Lindy Bullock Ward, Robert DOuglas Jr. B.A., Tex. Tech U., 1955; LL.B., Baylor U., 1958. Bar: Tex. 1958, U.S. Dist. Ct. (so. and ea. dists.) Tex. 1960, U.S. Dist. Ct. (we. dist.) Tex. 1961, U.S. Ct. Appeals (5th cir.) 1972. Sole practice, Hillsboro, Tex., 1957-59, Tyler, Tex., 1960-61, Austin, Tex., 1961-67; asst. atty. gen. State of Tex., Austin, 1967-68, legal counsel, office of gov., 1969-71, sec. of state, 1971-73, comptroller of public accounts, 1975—. Mem. Tex. Ho. of Reps., 1956-59. Served with USAF, 1951-54, Korea. Recipient Louisville Gold Medal award Mcpl. Fin. Officers Assn., 1978. Mem. State Bar Tex., Tex. Trial Lawyers Assn., Travis County Bar Assn., Am. Legion, Tex. State Hist. Assn. Democrat. Home and Office: PO Box 2243 Austin TX 78768

BULLOCK, THOMAS FRANCIS, lawyer; b. Atlantic City, Mar. 28, 1947; s. Henry Thomas and Irene Anna (Kish) B.; m. Lucy Scott Lockhart Amerman, June 25, 1977; children: Ethan H.T., Anna L.L. BA, LaSalle U., 1973; JD, Widener U., 1976. Bar: N.J. 1976, U.S. Dist. Ct. N.J. 1976, U.S. Supreme Ct. 1981. Sole practice Milmay, N.J., 1977—; bd. dirs. Cape-Atlantic Legal Services, Atlantic City. Mem. N.J. Bar Assn., Atlantic City Bar Assn., Cape May City Bar Assn., Assn. Trial Lawyers Am. Republican. Episcopalian. Clubs: Racquet (Phila.), Atlantic County (sec.), Game Preserve (N.J.) (sec. 1972—). General corporate, Environment, Real property. Office: Tuckahoe Rd Box 10 Milmay NJ 08340

BULTJE, RONALD ALAN, lawyer; b. Kalamazoo, Mich., Oct. 26, 1953; s. John Henry and Helen Wilma (Bonselaar) B.; m. Marjorie Jo Bolt, May 17, 1980; 1 child, Crystal Jo. BA, Calvin Coll., 1976; JD, U. Mich., 1978. Bar: Mich. 1979. Assoc. Scholten, Fant & Marquis, Grand Haven, Mich., 1979—. Deacon Ferrysburg (Mich.) Ch., 1981-84; bd. dirs. Am. Cancer Soc., Ottawa County, Mich., 1981—, Grand Haven (Mich.) Christian Sch., 1983—. Mem. ABA, Mich. Bar Assn., Ottawa County Bar Assn. Republican. Club: Gideons (Grand Haven). Avocations: running, sports, reading. Labor, Pension, profit-sharing, and employee benefits, Local government. Office: Scholten Fant & Marquis 233 Washington Grand Haven MI 49417

BUMP, WILBUR NEIL, lawyer; b. Peoria, Ill., July 12, 1929; s. Wilbur Earl and Mae (Nelson) B.; m. Elaine Bonneval, Nov. 24, 1951; children—William Earl, Jeffrey Neil, Steven Bonneval. B.S., State U. Iowa, 1951, J.D., 1958. Bar: Iowa 1958. Solicitor gen. Iowa Atty. Gen.'s Office, Des Moines, 1961-64; practice in Des Moines, 1964—; gen. counsel Iowa Luth. Hosp. Served with USAF, 1951-54. Mem. ABA, Iowa Bar Assn. (bd. govs. 1976-81, chmn. agrl. law com. 1982—), Polk County Bar Assn. (pres. 1976-77). Presbyterian. Club: Kiwanis (pres. 1974-75). General corporate, Health. Home: Route 2 Winterset IA 50273 Office: 2829 Westown Pkwy Suite 100 West Des Moines IA 50265

BUMPAS, STUART MARYMAN, lawyer; b. Little Rock, Oct. 7, 1944; s. Hubert Wayne Bumpas and Martha Conway (Maryman) Gaylord; m. Diane Ellen DeWare, Oct. 1, 1977. BA, Brown U., 1966; JD, U. Tex., 1969; LLM, George Washington U., 1973. Bar: Tex. 1969, D.C. 1972. Atty.-advisor Office of Chief Counsel, Washington, 1969-72; asst. to commr. IRS, Washington, 1973-74; ptnr. Locke, Purnell, Boren, Laney & Neely, Dallas, 1974—; adj. prof. employee benefits So. Meth. U., Dallas, 1975; lectr. Washington Non-Profit Tax Conf., Am. Law Inst. Contbr. articles to profl. jours. Mem. exec. com. Meadows Sch. of Arts, So. Meth. U., Dallas; bd. dirs. Callier Ctr. for Communications Disorders, Dallas, 1984—, Tex. Arts Alliance; bd. dirs., v.p. Dallas Grand Opera Assn., 1984—; nat. counsel Am. Heart Assn., Dallas, 1979—; trustee, gen. counsel Dallas Mus. Art, 1979—. Mem. ABA (mem. exempt orgns. com.), Tex. Bar Assn. (mem. legal aspects of arts com.), Dallas Bar Assn. Episcopalian. Clubs: Dallas, Idlewild (Dallas); Soc. Cin. (Washington). Pension, profit-sharing, and employee benefits, Non-profit organizations, Corporate taxation. Home: 5306 Surrey

Circle Dallas TX 75209 Office: Locke Purnell Boren Laney & Neely 3600 Republic Bank Tower Dallas TX 75201

BUNCH, W. EDWARD, lawyer; b. Asheboro, N.C., July 5, 1955; s. John C. Bunch and Claudine (Cox) Maddux; m. Nancy E. Hord, Mar. 8, 1980; children: Mary Eoline, Rebekah Hord. Student, Wake Forest U., 1973-74, N.C. State U., 1974-75; BA in English, U. N.C., Chapel Hill, 1976; JD, Wake Forest U., 1980. Assoc. Bell & Browne, P.A., Asheboro, 1980-82; sole practice Asheboro, 1982-85; ptnr. Beck, O'Briant, O'Briant & Bunch, Asheboro, 1985—. Chmn. Randolph County Dems., Asheboro, 1983-85. Mem. ABA, N.C. Bar Assn., Randolph County Bar Assn., N.C. Acad. Trial Lawyers, Phi Alpha Delta. Democrat. Methodist. Criminal, Personal injury, General practice. Home: 1201 Timberlane Rd Asheboro NC 27203 Office: Beck O'Briant O'Briant & Bunch 115 S Fayetteville St Asheboro NC 27203

BUNDA, ROBERT ALAN, lawyer; b. McKeesport, Pa., Aug. 2, 1951; s. Edward Francis and Helen (Wichman) B.; m. Linda Mortell, Apr. 25, 1976; children: Matthew, Anne. AB magna cum laude, U. Notre Dame, 1973; JD, U. Mich., 1976. Bar: Mich. 1977, U.S. Dist. Ct. (we. dist.) Mich. 1977, Ohio 1979, U.S. Dist. Ct. (ea. dist.) Mich. 1982, U.S. Dist. Ct. (no. dist.) Calif. 1982. Law clk. to judge U.S. Dist. Ct. (we. dist.) Mich., Grand Rapids, 1976-79; assoc. Fuller & Henry, Toledo, 1979-85, ptnr., 1985—; Wellington counsel for N.W. Ohio, The Asbestos Claims Facility, Princeton, N.J., 1985—. Bd. dirs. Found. for Life, Toledo, 1982—, The Godparents, Toledo, 1984—; pres. Notre Dame Club of Toledo, 1985-86. Mem. ABA, Ohio State Bar Assn., Mich. Bar Assn., Toledo Bar Assn. Roman Catholic. Club: Toledo. Avocations: skiing, swimming, squash, music. Federal civil litigation, State civil litigation, Insurance. Office: Fuller & Henry 300 Madison Ave PO Box 2088 Toledo OH 43603

BUNDERSON, JON J., lawyer; b. Brigham City, Utah, Sept. 14, 1947; s. Dean L. and Velma L. (Straub) B.; m. Peggy L. Howlett, Dec. 14, 1971; children: Eric, Lisa, Adam. BS, Utah State U., 1971; JD, U. Utah, 1974. Bar: Utah 1974, U.S. Dist Ct. Utah. 1974. Assoc. Brandt, Miller & Nelson, Salt Lake City, 1974-75; sole practice Brigham City, 1975-80; ptnr. Bunderson & Baron, Brigham City, 1980—; pros. atty. Box Elder County, Brigham City, 1982—. Pres., bd. dirs. Greater Brigham City C. of C., 1980-84; precinct chmn. cen. com. Box Elder County Reps., 1978-83. Served with USN, 1967-69. Mem. ABA, Utah State Bar Assn. Mormon. Club: Brigham City Golf and Country. Avocations: fly fishing, scouting. General practice. Home: 257 N Sycamore Brigham City UT 84302 Office: Bunderson & Baron Attys at Law 45 N 1st E Brigham City UT 84302

BUNGE, JONATHAN GUNN, lawyer; b. La Crosse, Wis., Oct. 20, 1936; s. Jonathan Clement and Anne Liddell (Gunn) B.; m. Gertrude Shoemaker Bunge, June 18, 1961; children—Jonathan C., William H., Katherine E. A.B. cum laude, Princeton U., 1958; J.D., Harvard U., 1961. Bar: Ill. 1961, U.S. Supreme Ct. 1968. Assoc. Lees & Bunge, Chgo., 1961-62; assoc. Keck, Mahin & Cate, Chgo., 1964-71, ptnr., 1971—; instr. John Marshall Law Sch., 1968-73; mem. adv. panel East-West Trade, U.S. Dept. Commerce, 1977-78. Bd. dirs. Division St. YMCA 1970—; bd. dirs. Mid-Am. chpt. ARC 1975—, vice chmn. 1982—, bd. dirs. Chgo. dist., 1981—, vice chmn., 1981-82, chmn., 1983-86; vestryman Holy Comforter Ch., Kenilworth, Ill. 1979-84. Served with U.S. Army 1962-64. Mem. ABA, Chgo. Bar Assn., Internat. Bar Assn., Ill. State Bar Assn., Bar Assn. 7th Cir., Maritime Law Assn. Episcopalian. Clubs: Economic, Union League, Metropolitan, River (Chgo.); Kenilworth; Princeton (N.Y.C.). Antitrust, Federal civil litigation, General corporate. Home: 306 Oxford Rd Kenilworth IL 60043 Office: 8300 Sears Tower Chicago IL 60606

BUNGER, LEN EDWARD, JR, lawyer; b. Bloomington, Ind., June 1, 1921; s. Len E. and Nellie Evelyn (Swearingen) B.; m. Marianne H. Wiseman, Apr. 17, 1943; children: Susanne, Thomas. BS, Ind. U., 1943, JD, 1949. Bar: Ind. 1949, U.S. Dist. Ct. (so. dist.) Ind. 1949. Ptnr. Bunger, Robertson, Kelley & Steger and predecessor firms, Bloomington, 1949-72, sr. ptnr., 1972—. Judge City of Bloomington, 1951-53; pros. atty. 10th Jud. Circuit, 1953-55. Served to lt U.S. Army, 1942-46. Fellow Am. Coll. Trial Lawyers (state chmn. 1978-80), Ind. Bar Found. (exec. com.); mem. ABA, Ind. Bar Assn. (bd. mgrs. 1980-82), Am. Soc. Hosp. Attys., Monroe County Bar Assn. (past pres.), Def. Research Inst., Assn. Ins. Attys. Republican. Methodist. Clubs: Columbia, Quail Ridge Golf and Tennis (Indpls.). Lodge: Elks. General practice, State civil litigation, Probate. Office: Bunger Harrell & Robertson 226 S College Sq Bloomington IN 47401

BUNNER, PATRICIA ANDREA, lawyer; b. Fairmont, W.Va., Sept. 16, 1953; d. Scott Randolph and Virginia Lenore (Keck) B. AB in History and English, W.Va. U., 1975, JD, 1978. Bar: W.Va. 1978, U.S. Dist. Ct. (so. dist.) W.Va. 1978, U.S. Dist. Ct. (no. dist.) W.Va. 1985, U.S. Supreme Ct. 1987. Staff Dem. Nat. Com., Washington, 1979; assoc. Gailer, Elias & Matz, Washington, 1979-81, John F. Snyder, Washington, 1981; legis. and appellate counsel N.Y. State Bankers Assn., N.Y.C., 1981-83; ptnr. Bunner & Bunner, Fairview and Morgantown, W.Va., 1984—; exec. dir. N.Y. State Consumer Mortgage Rev. Bd.; chmn. dist. VIII Consumer Mortgage Rev. Com., 1982-83; cons. atty. Energy Cons. Assocs., Spring Harbor, N.Y., 1981; Middletown Urban Devel. Corp., 1986—. Author: (jour.) Legis.-Legal Update, 1981-82, also poems, fiction; editor: N.Y. State Bankers Assn. Legis. Directory, 1983. Sec., treas. Monongalia County Dem. Women, Morgantown, 1983—; sec. Monongalia County Devel. Authority, Morgantown, 1984—; pres. United Taxpayers Assn., Inc., 1985—. Rilla Moran Woods fellow Nat. Fedn. Dem. Women, Washington, 1978. Mem. ABA (vice chmn. legal econs. and new lawyers coms., 1986—, litigation sect., 1st amendment rights and media law com., gen. practice com., corps. and banking com.), Assn. Trial Lawyers Am., N.Y. State Bar Assn., Monongalia County Bar Assn., Marion County Bar Assn., Women's Info. Ctr. (founding), LWV (local govt. chmn.), W.Va. Alliance for Women's Studies (founding), Bus. and Profl. Women, Climates, Inc., Monongalia County Hist. Soc., Clay-Batelle Alumni Assn., W.Va. Coll. Law Alumni Assn., Nat. Rifle Assn. (life), Nature Conservancy, Nat. Arbor Day Found., World Wildlife Fund, Am. Assn. Univ. Women, Sierra Club, Audobon Soc., Young Dems. Club W.Va. (sec. 1976), Phi Alpha Theta (chpt. pres. 1974-75), Phi Beta Kappa, Zeta Phi Eta, Alpha Rho. Mem. Ch. of Christ. Clubs: Woman's (bd. dirs. Morgantown, 1986—). Avocations: politics, writing poetry and fiction. Criminal, Libel, Banking. Home: Rt 2 Box 341 Fairview WV 26570 Office: 818 Monongahela Bldg Morgantown WV 26505

BUNNER, WILLIAM KECK, lawyer; b. Fairmont, W.Va., Sept. 2, 1949; s. Scott Randolph and Virginia Lenore (Keck) B. BS in Secondary Edn., W.Va. U., 1970, MA in History, 1973, JD, 1978. Bar: W.Va. 1978, U.S. Dist. Ct. (so. dist.) W.Va. 1978, U.S. Dist. Ct. (no. dist.) W.Va. 1985. Tchr. Monongalia County Bd. Edn., Morgantown, W.Va., 1970-78; adminstr. dept. fin. and adminstrn. State of W.Va., Charleston, 1978-79; sole practice Fairview, W.Va., 1979-84; pres. Farm Home Service, Inc., 1983—; ptnr. Bunner & Bunner, Morgantown and Fairview, 1984—. Pres. Monongalia County Young Dems., 1974, parliamentarian Monongalia County exec. com., 1982—; counsel, parliamentarian Young Dem. Clubs W.Va., 1974-77; bd. dirs., supr. dist. Monongahela Soil Conservation, 1982—; advisor dist. West Run Watershed Improvement, 1983—; mem. W.Va. Commn. on Rural Abandoned Mines, Rural Alliance. Mem. ABA, Monongalia County Bar Assn., Assn. Rural Conservation, Soil Conservation Soc. Am., United Taxpayers' Assn. (counsel), Monongalia County Hist. Soc., Marion County Hist. Soc., Phi Alpha Delta, Phi Alpha Theta. Democrat. Avocations: music, politics, farming. General practice, Environment, Real property. Home: Rt 2 Box 341 Fairview WV 26570 Office: Bunner & Bunner 235 High St Suite 818 Morgantown WV 26505

BUNTAIN, DAVID ROBERT, lawyer; b. Newport, R.I., Feb. 22, 1948; s. Robert E. and Martha Elizabeth (Deane) B.; m. Lucy Hayden Madden, Mar. 25, 1972; children: Bill C., Anne S. BA, U. Nebr., 1970, JD, 1974; M in Pub. Affairs, Princeton U., 1972. Bar: Nebr. 1975, U.S. Ct. Appeals (8th cir.) 1978. Assoc. Cline, Williams, Wright, Johnson & Oldfather, Lincoln, Nebr., 1975-79; ptnr. Cline, Williams, Wright, Johnson & Oldfather, Lincoln, 1980—; instr. U. Nebr. Coll. Law, Lincoln, 1976-79; bd. dirs. Nebr. Continuing Legal Edn. Inc. Pres. Pinewood Bowl Com., Lincoln, 1980-82; vice chmn. Gov.'s Commn. for Study Higher Edn., Nebr., 1984; v.p. Leadership Lincoln Inc., 1986. Named Outstanding Young Individual, Lincoln Jaycees, 1981. Mem. Nebr. Bar Assn. (ho. dels. 1984—, v.p. young lawyers sect. 1980-81), Order of Coif, Order of Barristers, Phi Beta Kappa. Democrat. Lodge: Rotary. Avocations: running, sailing, musical theatre, reading. Legislative, Health, Labor. Home: 6201 Andrew Ct Lincoln NE 68512 Office: Cline Williams Wright et al 1900 First Tier Bank Lincoln NE 68508

BUNTON, LUCIUS DESHA, federal judge; b. Del Rio, Tex., Dec. 1, 1924; s. Lucius Desha and Avis Maurine (Fisher) B.; m. Mary Jane Carsey, June 18, 1947; children:Cathryne Avis Bunton Warner, Lucius Desha. Student, U. Chgo., 1943-44; B.A., U. Tex., Austin, 1947, J.D., 1950. Bar: Tex. 1949. Individual practice law Uvalde, Tex., 1950; asso. firm. H.O. Metcalfe, Marfa, Tex., 1951-54; dist. atty. 83d Jud. Dist. Tex., 1954-59; mem. firm Shafer, Gilliland, Davis, Bunton & McCollum, Odessa, Tex., 1959-79; judge U.S. Dist. Ct. for Western Dist. Tex., Midland, 1979—. Trustee Ector County (Tex.) Ind. Sch. Dist., 1967-76. Served with inf. U.S. Army, 1943-46. Mem. Tex. Bar Found. (charter), Am. Bar Assn., Am. Bar Found., Am. Coll. Probate Counsel, Am. Acad. Matrimonial Lawyers, State Bar Tex. (chmn. 1971-72, v.p. 1973-74, pres.-elect 1979). Baptist. Club: Masons (Marfa).

BUONPANE, GUERIN, lawyer; consultant; b. New Castle, Pa., Jan. 17, 1905; s. Elpidio and Mary Jane (Rizzuto) B.; m. Grace Marie Ross, Aug. 17, 1948; children—Anita Buonpane Hartmann, Elissa, James. B.A., Ohio No. U., 1927; student law pvt. attys., 1922-28. Bar: Ohio 1928, U.S. Dist. Ct. (no. dist.) Ohio 1929. Practice, Cleve., 1928—; mem. Buonpane & Buonpane, 1928-36; sole practice, 1936—; trial referee Ohio Indsl. Commn., 1936-42; gov.'s appointee Cleve. dist. Ohio Workers' Compensation Dist. Bd. Claims, 1942-55; gov.'s appointee, chmn. Ohio Workers' Compensation Bd. Rev., 1955-79; lectr. law Case-Western Res. U., 1961-67; legal cons. Indsl. Advisors Bur., Cleve., 1979—; lectr. in field. Contbr. numerous articles to profl. publs. Govt. appeal agt. World War II, U.S. Govt., Cleve., 1942-45; mem. Beachwood Zoning Bd. Appeals, Ohio, 1954-55, Beachwood Zoning and Planning Commn., 1956-57. Recipient 50-Yr. Meritorious Service award Cleve. Assn. Compensation Attys., 1978; Outstanding Pub. Service award Ohio Acad. Trial Lawyers, 1979; honoree Cleve. Assn. Trial Attys., 1979; Outstanding Profl. Service award Employers Self Insurers Group of Ohio Inc., 1979. Democrat. Workers' compensation. Home: 3283 Somerset Dr Beachwood OH 44122 Office: Indsl Advisors Bur Superior Bldg Room 714 Cleveland OH 44114

BURCH, DAVID RYAN, lawyer, consultant; b. Hughes, Ark., Apr. 5, 1950; s. James William and Mary Lou (Ryan) B. BA, La. State U., 1972, JD, 1975; LLM, U. Mo., 1976, MA, 1976. Bar: La. 1975, Mo. 1977. Legal specialist U. Mo., Columbia, 1977-86; sole practice Columbia, 1986—; cons. City of Independence, Mo., 1982-83, Mo. Mcpl. League, Jefferson City, 1982—. Author: A Guide to Personal Tort Liability, 1980, County Road Administration, 1981, Energy Conservation, 1982; asst. editor Govtl. Affairs Newsletter, 1977-85. Mem. fin. com. Meml. Bapt. Ch., Columbia, 1981—. Mem. ABA (land use planning and zoning com. urban, state and local govt. sect.), Mo. Bar Assn. Democrat. Club: Columbia Ski (pres. 1982-83). Avocation: downhill skiing. Local government, Real property, Librarianship. Home: 4422 Germantown Dr Columbia MO 65203 Office: PO Box 291 Columbia MO 65205

BURCH, JOHN THOMAS, JR., lawyer; b. Balt.; s. John T. and Katheryn Estella (Peregoy) B.; m. Linda Anne Shearer, Nov. 1, 1969; children: John Thomas, Richard James. B.A., U. Richmond, 1964, J.D., 1966; LL.M., George Washington U., 1971. Bar: Va. 1966, D.C. 1974, U.S. Supreme Ct. 1969, Mich. 1983. Pvt. practice Richmond, 1966, Washington, 1974—; pres. firm Burch, Kerns and Klimek, 1977—, Burch & Assocs., P.C., 1982-83, Burch & Bennett, P.C., 1983-85; ptnr. Barnett & Alagia, 1985—; pres. Internat. Procurement Cons. Ltd., Washington, 1977-85; Republican committeeman, City of Alexandria, Va., 1975—, a.d.c. to gov., State of Va., 1976—; chmn. Nat. Vietnam Vets. Coalition. Served to maj. JAGC, U.S. Army, 1966-74, Vietnam. Decorated Bronze Star, Meritorious Service medal, others; named Ky. Col. Mem. ABA (sec. public contract law sect. 1976-77), Fed. Bar Assn. (nat. council, dep. sec. 1982-83), Am. Arbitration Assn., Am. Legion, VFW, Spl. Forces Assn., Va. Soc. SAR (pres. 1975-76, Patriots medal 1978, Good Citizenship medal 1970), Sons Confederate Vets., Scabbard and Blade, Phi Alpha Delta, Phi Sigma Alpha. Republican. Episcopalian. Government contracts and claims, State civil litigation, General practice. Home: 1015 N Pelham St Alexandria VA 22304 Office: 1000 Thomas Jefferson Pl Suite 600 Washington DC 20007

BURCH, MELVIN EARL, lawyer, bank executive; b. El Reno, Okla., July 24, 1949; s. Joy Wayne and Altia Marie (Clevenger) B.; m. Patricia Rae Smith, Apr. 3, 1971 (div. Aug. 1983); children: Justin Earl, Angela Rae. BBA, Cen. State U., 1973; JD, Oklahoma City U., 1978. Bar: Okla. 1978. Air traffic controller FAA, Albuquerque, 1973-74; asst. v.p. 1st Nat. Bank, Oklahoma City, 1975-80; 2d v.p. Northern Trust Co., Phoenix, 1980; sr. v.p. Liberty Nat. Bank, Oklahoma City, 1980—; adj. prof. Oklahoma City Community Coll., 1979-82; lectr. Cen. State U., Edmond, Okla., 1982—, Southwestern Grad. Sch. Banking, Dallas, 1984. Regent Okla. Bankers Assn. Intermediate Trust Sch., Norman, 1982—, lectr., 1983; bd. dirs., v.p. Big Bros./Big Sisters of Greater Oklahoma City, 1985-86, pres. elect, 1986—. Mem. ABA, Okla. Bar Assn., Oklahoma County Bar Assn. Republican. Probate, Real property, General practice. Home: 3500 Jim Robison Dr Edmond OK 73013 Office: Liberty Nat Bank Trust Co 100 Broadway Oklahoma City OK 73125

BURCH, ROBERT DALE, lawyer; b. Washington, Jan. 30, 1928; s. Dallas Stockwell and Hepsy (Berry) B.; m. Joann D. Hansen, Dec. 9, 1966; children—Berkeley, Robert Brett, Barrett Bradley. Student, Va. Mil. Inst., 1945-46; B.S., U. Calif. at Berkeley, 1950, J.D., 1953. Bar: Calif. bar 1954. Since practiced in Los Angeles and Beverly Hills; partner firm Gibson, Dunn & Crutcher, 1961—; lectr. U. So. Calif. Inst. Fed. Taxation, 1960, 62, 65, 75; guest lectr. U. Calif. at Los Angeles Law Sch., 1959; lectr. C.E.B. seminars U. Calif. Author: Federal Tax Procedures for General Practitioners; Contbr. profl. jours., textbooks. Bd. dirs. charitable founds. Served with AUS, 1945-47. Mem. Beverly Hills Bar Assn., bd. govs., chmn. probate and trust com., Law Trust, Tax and Ins. Council (past czar), Los Angeles World Affairs Council, Beverly Hills C. of C. Home: 1301 Delresto Dr Beverly Hills CA 90210 Office: 2029 Century Park E Los Angeles CA 90067

BURCH, VORIS REAGAN, lawyer; b. Liberty, Tex., Feb. 10, 1930; s. Voris Reagan and Jessamae (Coffey) B.; m. Claudia Ramsland, Dec. 30, 1978; children: Melissa Burch Lively, Voris Reagan. B.B.A., Tex. A&M U., 1952; J.D., U. Tex.-Austin, 1957. Bar: Tex. 1957. Ptnr., chmn. employment litigation dept. Baker & Botts, Houston, 1957—. Served to 1st lt. USAF, 1952-54. Mem. ABA, State Bar Tex. (chmn. labor law sect. 1972-73), Houston Bar Assn., Phi Delta Phi. Republican. Methodist. Federal civil litigation, State civil litigation, Labor. Home: 5761 Indian Circle Houston TX 77057 Office: Baker & Botts 3000 One Sell Plaza Houston TX 77057

BURCHAM, RANDALL PARKS, lawyer, farmer; b. Union City, Tenn., July 20, 1917; s. John Simps and Myrtle Caldwell (Howard) B.; m. Hellon Owens, Sept. 30, 1945; children—Randall Parks Jr., Susan. Student Murray State Coll. (Ky.), 1934-38, U. Miss., 1938-39; LL.B., Cumberland U., Lebanon, Tenn., 1940; J.D., Samford U., Birmingham, 1969. Bar: Tenn. 1941. Sole practice, Union City, 1941; atty. U.S. Govt., Nashville, 1945-49; owner Interstate Oil Co., Fulton, Ky., 1949-53; ptnr. Burcham & Fox, Union City, 1953—. Del., Tenn. Constitutional Conv., Nashville, 1971. Served to comdr. U.S. Navy, 1941-45. Fellow Am. Coll. Probate Counsel; mem. ABA, Tenn. Bar Assn. (bd. govs. 1969-72). Democrat. Methodist. State and federal litigation, General corporate, Real estate and probate. Home: 1130 Ethridge Ln PO Box 188 Union City TN 38261 Office: Burcham & Fox 505 S 3d St Union City TN 38261

BURCHILL, WILLIAM ROBERTS, JR., lawyer; b. N.Y.C., Dec. 6, 1947; s. William Roberts and Marion (Eisenhower) B. BA, U. Pa., 1969; JD, George Washington U., 1972. Bar: D.C. 1973, U.S. Dist. Ct. D.C. 1976, U.S. Ct. Appeals (D.C. cir.) 1976, U.S. Supreme Ct. 1978. Atty. magistrates div. Adminstrn. Office U.S. Cts., Washington, 1973-74, atty. office gen. counsel, 1974-76, assoc. gen. counsel, 1976-82, dep. gen. counsel, 1982-85, gen. counsel, 1985—. Mem. ABA, Fed. Bar Assn., Nat. Lawyers Club, Phi Delta Phi. Club: Regency Racquet (McLean, Va.). Judicial administration. Home: 3228 Ravensworth Pl Alexandria VA 22302 Office: Adminstrn Office US Cts 811 Vermont Ave NW Washington DC 20544

BURCIAGA, JUAN GUERRERO, U.S. dist. judge; b. Roswell, N.Mex., Aug. 17, 1929; s. Melesio Antonio and Juana (Guerrero) B.; m. Carolyn Jacoby, Oct. 28, 1958 (dec.); children—Lisa Anne, Lora Anne, Amy Virginia, Carlos Antonio, Pamela. B.S., U.S. Mil. Acad., 1952; J.D., U. N.Mex., 1963. Bar: N.Mex. bar 1964. Asso., then partner firms in Albuquerque, 1964-79; U.S. dist. judge Dist. N.Mex., 1979—; lectr. U. N.Mex. Sch. Law, 1970-71. Bd. dirs. Albuquerque YMCA, 1964-74, NCCJ, Albuquerque, 1969-73; urban renewal commnr. City of Albuquerque, 1972-76. Served as officer USAF, 1952-60. Mem. Am. Bar Assn., Am. Judicature Soc. (dir.), Def. Research Inst., Am. Bd. Arbitration, Am. Trial Lawyers Assn., Am. Bd. Trial Advocates, Albuquerque Bar Assn. Democrat. Roman Catholic. Jurisprudence. Office: US Dist Courthouse 5th and Gold Sts Albuquerque NM 87103

BURCK, CYRIL B., JR., lawyer; b. New Orleans, Dec. 9, 1950; s. Cyril B. and Sarah (Marlette) B; m. Pamela D. Richmond, July 19, 1974; children: Christian, Robin. BS, La. State U., 1972; JD, Tulane U., 1975. Bar: La. 1975, U.S. Dist. Ct. (ea. dist.) La., U.S. Ct. Appeals (5th and 11th cirs.). Assoc. Hailey, McNamara, Hall, Larmann & Papale, New Orleans, 1978—. Contracts commercial, Real property, Bankruptcy. Address: 3121 21st St Metairie LA 70002

BURD, CHARLES LESLIE, lawyer; b. Huntington, W.Va., July 20, 1947; s. Leslie L. and Patricia C. (Holderby) B.; m. JoAnn Renfroe, Jan. 27, 1968 (div. Feb. 1973); 1 child, Lisa Michele; m. Tamara Lynn Wood, Dec. 21, 1979. BA, Ohio State U., 1969, JD, 1972. Bar: Ohio 1973; U.S. Dist. Ct. (so. dist.) Ohio 1975; U.S. Ct. Appeals (4th cir.) 1973; U.S. Supreme Ct. 1979. Legal aide to atty. gen. State of Ohio, Columbus, 1971-72; ptnr. Kaiser & Burd, Chesapeake, Ohio, 1973-78; sole practice Chesapeake, 1978-83; ptnr. Burd & Cooper, Chesapeake, 1984—; acting judge Lawrence County Ct., Chesapeake, 1975-78; judge, Lawrence County Mcpl. Ct., Chesapeake, 1982—. Served to 1st lt. U.S. Army, 1971-76. Recipient Disting. Grad. award Ohio State U., Columbus, 1983. Mem. ABA, Am. Trial Lawyers Assn., Ohio Bar Assn. (family law com. 1974-77), Ohio Acad. Trial Lawyers, Ohio Mcpl. Judges Assn., Lawrence County Bar Assn. (sec. 1974-76, v.p. 1976-77, pres. 1981-82), Lawrence County C. of C. Republican. Lodge: Elks. Avocations: traveling, boating, scuba diving, horses. Personal injury, State civil litigation, Real property. Home: Lakeland Estates Proctorville OH 45669 Office: Burd & Cooper 431 Rockwood Ave Chesapeake OH 45619

BURDEN, JAMES EWERS, lawyer; b. Sacramento, Oct. 24, 1939; s. Herbert Spencer and Ida Elizabeth (Brosemer) B.; m. Kathryn Lee Gardner, Aug. 21, 1965; children—Kara Elizabeth, Justin Gardner. B.S., U. Calif.-Berkeley, 1961; J.D., U. Calif.-Hastings Coll. Law, 1964; postgrad. U. So. Calif., 1964-65. Bar: Calif. 1965, Tax Ct. U.S. 1969, U.S. Supreme Ct. 1970. Assoc. Elliott and Aune, Santa Ana, Calif., 1965, White, Harbor, Fort & Schei, Sacramento, 1965-67; assoc. Miller, Starr & Regalia, Oakland, Calif., 1967-69, ptnr., 1969-73; ptnr. Burden, Aiken, Mansuy & Stein, San Francisco, 1973-82; ptnr. James E. Burden, Inc., San Francisco, 1982—; ptnr. Austex Oil & Gas Co., Luling, Tex., Judgment Oil and Gas Co., Lockhart, Tex., Northpoint Investment Co., San Francisco; mem. exec. com., corp. sec. Doric Devel., Inc., Alameda, Calif.; sec. Harbor Bay Isle Assocs., Alameda; instr. U. Calif.-Berkeley, 1968-75, also Merritt Coll. Mem. ABA, Am. Judicature Soc. Clubs: Claremont Country (Oakland); San Francisco Grid, San Francisco Comml., Commonwealth of Calif. Contbr. articles to profl. jours. Real property, Oil and gas leasing. Office: 451 Jackson St 2d Floor San Francisco CA 94111

BURDGE, MICHAEL JOSEPH, lawyer; b. Dayton, Ohio, Apr. 16, 1950; s. Owen Dale and Nancy Lee (Gabbard) B.; m. Anne Upton Barch; children: Jennifer, Allison, Michael. Student, Miami U., 1969-70; AB, Earlham Coll., 1973; JD, U. Dayton, 1978. Bar: Ohio 1978, U.S. Dist. Ct. (so. dist.) Ohio 1979, U.S. Ct. Appeals (6th cir.) 1981, U.S. Supreme Ct. 1984. Asso. Young, Pryor, Lynn & Jerardi, Dayton, 1978-86, ptnr., 1986—. Mem. ABA, Ohio Bar Assn., Dayton Bar Assn., Assn. Trial Lawyers Am. Republican. Avocations: chess, tennis, golf. Labor, Personal injury, State civil litigation. Office: Young Pryor Lynn & Jerardi 120 W 3d St Suite 350 Old Post Office Dayton OH 45402

BURDITT, GEORGE MILLER, JR., lawyer; b. Chgo., Sept. 21, 1922; s. George Miller and Flora Winifred (Hardie) B.; m. Barbara Helen Stenger, Feb. 17, 1945; children—Betsey Burditt Blessing, George M., Deborah Burditt Norton, Barbara Burditt Perry. B.A., Harvard U., 1944, LL.B., 1948. Bar: Ill. 1949, U.S. Dist. Ct. (no. dist.) Ill. 1952, U.S. Ct. Appeals (7th cir.) 1961, U.S. Ct. Appeals D.C. 1962, U.S. Ct. Appeals (4th cir.) 1974, U.S. Supreme Ct. 1974, U.S. Ct. Appeals (2d cir.) 1978. With law dept. Swift & Co., Chgo., 1948-54; assoc. Chadwell & Kayser and predecessors, Chgo., 1955-69; ptnr. Burditt, Bowles & Radzius, Ltd., Chgo., 1969—; dir. Gerber Products Co.; adj. prof. Northwestern U. Sch. Law; gen. counsel Food and Drug Law Inst.; mem. Ill. State Ho. of Reps., 1965-72, asst. majority leader, 1971-72; Republican candidate U.S. Senate, 1974. Served as 2d lt. USAAF, 1943-45. Named Outstanding Legislator, Better Govt. Assn., 1969, 71; recipient Presdl. award Cook County Bar Assn., 1981. Mem. ABA, Ill. State Bar Assn., D.C. Bar Assn., Chgo. Bar Assn. (pres. 1980-81), N.Y. Bar Assn., Fed. Bar Assn., Met. Bar Leaders Caucus (pres. 1981-82), Harvard Law Sch. Assn. (1st v.p.), Harvard Law Soc. of Ill. (pres. 1980-81). Clubs: Union League, Econ., Mid-Day (Chgo.); Crystal Downs Country (Mich.). Contbr. articles on food and drug laws to profl. jours. Administrative and regulatory, Federal civil litigation, State civil litigation. Office: 333 W Wacker Dr Chicago IL 60606

BURGCHARDT, KATHRYN DEE, lawyer; b. Denver, Nov. 13, 1956; d. Carl Robert and Elva Lucy (Reynolds) B.; m. Lawrence E. Letchford, Aug. 19, 1978 (div. Apr. 1986). BA, Pa. State U., 1978; JD, U. Pitts., 1981. Bar: Pa. 1981, Tex. 1982, U.S. Dist. Ct. (we. dist.) Pa. 1983, U.S. Dist. Ct. (we. dist.) Tex. 1983, U.S. Ct. Appeals (5th cir.) 1983. Assoc. Pytel & Assocs., San Antonio, 1982—. Mem. San Antonio Conservation Soc. Mem. ABA, Tex. Bar Assn., Pa. Bar Assn., Bexar County Women's Bar Assn., San Antonio Young Lawyers Assn., San Antonio Bar Assn., Phi Kappa Phi. Bankruptcy, Consumer commercial. Home: 2122 W Magnolia San Antonio TX 78201 Office: Pytel & Assocs PC 630 Broadway San Antonio TX 78215

BURGER, LEWIS STEPHEN, legal services company executive; b. Bklyn., Aug. 6, 1941; s. Julius Sidney Burger and Eve (Gordon) Tucker; m. Pamela Enid Burger, Dec. 23, 1964 (div.); children: Michael, Allison; m. Judith Friedberg, July 31, 1983; 1 child, Amy Rachel. BA, L.I. U., 1963; JD, Bklyn. Law Sch., 1968. Bar: N.Y. 1968, U.S. Supreme Ct. 1974, D.C. 1983. Asst. dist. atty. Nassau County, 1969-70; sr. ptnr. Burger & LaVallee, Freeport, N.Y., 1970-80; sole practice Hauppauge, N.Y., 1980-81; sr. ptnr. Burger, Kramer, Feldman & Kirschner, Hauppauge, 1981-83; chmn., chief exec. officer group and prepaid legal service plans Nationwide Legal Services Inc., Hartsdale, N.Y., 1983—; bd. dirs. Nat. Resource Ctr. for Consumers of Legal Services; moderator conv. panel on entrepreneurial legal plans Am. Prepaid Legal Services Inst., 1983, mem. pub. edn. com. Appearances on radio and tv programs including Sta. WCBS-TV, Take Two Sta. WQXR-FM, Long Island Spotlight, Dialogue 101 Sta. WCBS Radio, Barry Gray Show Sta. WMCA Radio, Good Morning San Antonio, Sta. WNBC Radio; editor Long Beach (N.Y.) Rep. Paper; contbr. articles to profl. jours. Mem. U.S. Congl. Adv. Bd. Mem. Former Asst. Dist. Atty.'s Assn. Nassau County, Nat. Dist. Atty.'s Assn., Nat. Assn. Criminal Def. Lawyers. Jewish. Criminal, Family and matrimonial, General practice. Home: 19 Junard Dr Roslyn NY 11576 Office: Nationwide Legal Services Inc 141 Central Park Ave S Hartsdale NY 10530

BURGER, WARREN EARL, former chief justice U.S., government official; b. St. Paul, Sept. 17, 1907; s. Charles Joseph and Katharine (Schnittger) B.; m. Elvera Stromberg, Nov. 8, 1933; children: Wade Allan, Margaret Mary Elizabeth. Student, U. Minn., 1925-27; LL.B. magna cum laude, St. Paul Coll. Law (now Mitchell Coll. Law), 1931; LL.D., William Mitchell Coll. Law, Macalester Coll., U. Minn., NYU, Columbia U., U. Pa., N.Y. Coll. Law, Georgetown U., Am. U., Coll. William and Mary, Mercer U., Yeshiva U., Howard U., Ripon Coll., Washington Coll., Brigham Young U., George

Washington U., W.Va. U., Pace U. Bar: Minn. 1931. Ptnr. Faricy, Burger, Moore & Costello (and predecessors firms), 1931-53; faculty Mitchell Coll. Law, 1931-46; asst. atty. gen. U.S., 1953-56; judge U.S. Ct. Appeals, Washington, 1956-69; Chief Justice U.S. Supreme Ct., 1969-86; chairman Commn. on the Bicentennial of the U.S. Constn., Washington, DC, 1986—; Hon. master bencher Middle Temple, 1969; pres. Bentham Club, U. Coll. London, 1972-73; hon. chmn. Inst. Jud. Adminstrn.; criminal justice project ABA Chancellor; chmn. Jud. Conf. of U.S., 1969—. Bd. regents Smithsonian Instn.; ex-officio mem. bd. trustees Nat. Gallery Art, Washington; trustee emeritus Mitchell Coll. Law, Macalester Coll., St. Paul, Mayo Found., Rochester, Minn.; trustee Nat. Geog. Soc. Office: Supreme Ct Bldg Washington DC 20543 *

BURGESS, BENJAMIN L., JR., lawyer; b. Salina, Kans., July 20, 1943; s. Benjamin L. Burgess and Evalena E. Lohman; m. Jolene K. Bellerive, Aug. 20, 1966; children: Matisha, Brett. BA, Kans. Wesleyan U., 1966; JD, Washburn U., 1971. Bar: Kans. 1972, U.S. Dist. Ct. Kans. 1972, U.S. Ct. Appeals (10th cir.) 1973. Asst. county atty. Reno County, Hutchinson, Kans., 1972; asst. U.S. atty. U.S. Dept. of Justice, Wichita, Kans., 1973-78, 80-84, U.S. atty., 1984—; ptnr. Rock, Smith & Burgess, Arkansas City, Kans., 1978-80. Cubmaster Boy Scouts Am., Wichita, 1983-85. Mem. Wichita Bar Assn. Roman Catholic. Lodge: Kiwanis, KC. Avocations: tennis, racquetball, running. Criminal, Federal civil litigation. Office: U S Atty's Office 401 N Market St Room 306 Wichita KS 67202

BURGESS, HAYDEN FERN, lawyer; b. Honolulu, May 5, 1946; s. Ned E. and Nora (Lee) b.; m. Puanani Sonoda, Aug. 28, 1968. JD, U. Hawaii, 1976. Bar: Hawaii, U.S. Tax Ct., U.S. Ct. Appeals (9th cir.). Sole practice Waianae, Hawaii, 1976—; v.p. World Counsel of Indigenous Peoples, 1984—; cons. on indegenous affairs, 1984—, indigenous expert to Internat. Labor Orgn. Conv. Trustee Office of Hawaiian Affairs, Honolulu, 1982-86; mem. Swedish Nat. Commn. on Museums. Mem. Law Assn. Asia and Western Pacific (steering com. on human rights). Public international. Office: 85-791A Farrington Hwy Waianae HI 96792

BURGESS, JACK THOMPSON, lawyer; b. Savannah, Ga., Mar. 23, 1952; s. Cicero Jackson and Sarah (Thompson) B.; m. Teresa Keogh, Mar. 8, 1980; 1 child, Sarah Thompson. BA, Am. U., 1974; JD, Cath. U., 1980. Bar: Va. 1980, U.S. Ct. Appeals (4th cir.) 1980, D.C. 1984. Sole practice Fairfax, Va., 1980—. Mem. Assn. Trial Lawyers Am., Nat. Orgn. Soc. Sec. Claimant's Reps., Fairfax County Bar Assn. Democrat. Methodist. Avocations: golf, fishing, travel. Personal injury, Workers' compensation, Insurance. Home: 3206 Gemstone Ct Oakton VA 22124 Office: 10605-A2 Judicial Dr Fairfax VA 22030

BURGESS, JOHN ALL, lawyer; b. Bennington, Vt., Apr. 8, 1934; s. Albert All and Julia (Connolly) B.; m. Virginia Grey, Aug. 22, 1959; children—John All, Matthew, Barbara, Brian, Timothy, Peter. B.A., U. Vt., 1957; J.D., Boston U., 1960. Bar: Vt. 1960, Calif. 1981; U.S. Dist. Ct. Vt. 1964, U.S. Dist. Ct. R.I. 1978, U.S Dist. Ct. Conn. 1979, U.S. Dist. Ct. (no. dist.) Calif. 1981, U.S. Ct. Appeals (2d cir.) 1965, U.S. Ct. Appeals (1st cir.) 1970, U.S. Ct. Appeals (9th cir.) 1972, U.S. Ct. Appeals (3d cir.) 1973, U.S. Ct. Appeals (5th cir.) 1979. State's atty. County of Bennington (Vt.), 1961-62; legis. draftsman State of Vt., 1962-64; acting judge Mcpl. Ct., Barre, Vt., 1963-65; spl. counsel to Gov. Vt., 1973; commr. Vt. Pub. Service Bd., 1974; sole practice, Berkeley, Calif., 1981—; lectr. in field. Fellow Roscoe Pound Am. Trial Lawyers Found. (pres. 1979-82); mem. Vt. Bar Assn., Calif. State Bar, D.C. Bar. Democrat. Roman Catholic. Author: Courtroom Persuasion, 1982. Federal civil litigation, State civil litigation, Criminal. Office: 2000 Powell St Suite 1680 Emeryville CA 94608

BURGESS, JOHN RICHARD, lawyer; b. Cranston, R.I., Aug. 21, 1949; s. Edgar H. and Edna Marie (Shadden) B.; m. Norma Jane Paolini, June 17, 1972; children: Tyler, Tonia. BBA, Roger Williams Coll., 1972; JD, New Eng. Sch. of Law, 1976. Bar: N.Y. 1980. Sr. ptnr. Burgess & Wojtan, Buffalo, 1980—. Mem. ABA, N.Y. State Bar Assn., Erie County Bar Assn. (mediator, arbitrator, speaker), Buffalo Lawyers Club. Lodge: Kiwanis. Avocations: sports, reading. Family and matrimonial, Criminal. Office: Burgess & Wojtan 2956 Union Rd Buffalo NY 14227

BURGESS, JULIA EDITH, lawyer; b. Kingston, Ont., Can., Jan. 31, 1952; d. Charles Robert and Edith R. (Roselund) B.; m. Egidijus Kazimirus Marcinkevicius, Dec. 22, 1979; 1 child, Emily Victoria. BA with honors, U. Western Ont., 1976, LLB, 1979. Bar: Ohio 1980, U.S. Dist. Ct. (no. dist.) Ohio 1981. Asst. prosecutor Geauga County, Chardon, Ohio, 1979-83; atty. Nat. City Bank, Cleve., 1983—. Mem. Ohio Bar Assn., Cleve. Bar Assn. Banking, Consumer commercial. Office: Nat City Bank 1900 E 9th St Cleveland OH 44114

BURGESS, KENNETH JOHN, lawyer; b. Detroit, June 8, 1953; s. Kenneth Joseph and Kathryn Alice (O'Toole) B. BBA magna cum laude, Western Mich. U., 1974; JD, Wayne State U., 1977, LLM, 1984. Bar: Mich. 1977, U.S. Dist. Ct. (ea. dist.) Mich. 1977, U.S. Ct. Appeals (6th cir.) 1979. Regulation officer corp. and securities bur. State of Mich., Lansing, 1978-82, atty. pub. service commn., 1982—. Public utilities. Office: Mich Pub Service Commn 6545 Mercantile PO Box 30221 Lansing MI 48909

BURGESS, ROBERT KYLE, lawyer; b. Fairfield, Iowa, Sept. 5, 1948; s. Charles and Eleanor Pearl (Morris) B.; children: Alyssa, Kristen. BS, Northwestern U., 1970, JD, 1973. Bar: Calif. 1973, U.S. Dist. Ct. (cen. dist.) Calif. 1974, U.S. Tax Ct. 1975, U.S. Ct. Appeals (9th cir.) 1976, U.S. Ct. Appeals (5th cir.) 1977, U.S. Supreme Ct. 1977, D.C. 1980, U.S. Dist. Ct. Md. 1980, U.S. Ct. Appeals (D.C. cir.) 1981, Ill. 1982. Assoc. Latham & Watkins, Los Angeles, 1973-78; assoc. Latham & Watkins, Washington, 1978-81, ptnr., 1981-82; ptnr. Latham & Watkins, Chgo., 1982—. Mem. ABA, Calif. Bar Assn., Ill. Bar Assn., D.C. Bar Assn., Chgo. Bar Assn. Republican. General corporate, Securities. Office: Latham & Watkins 233 S Wacker Dr Chicago IL 60606

BURGET, MARK EDWARD, lawyer; b. Wiesbaden, Fed. Republic Germany, Feb. 11, 1954; came to U.S., 1955; s. Carl Edward and Mary Sue (McMinimy) B.; m. Elaine Pasque, May 17, 1975; children: Bradley, Brian, Blake. BBA, U. Okla., 1976, JD, 1979; LLM in Taxation, NYU, 1982. Bar: Okla. 1979, U.S. Dist. Ct. (we. dist.) Okla., U.S. Tax Ct., U.S. Ct. Appeals (10th cir.). Assoc. McAfee & Taft, Oklahoma City, 1979-85, ptnr., 1985—. Mem. ABA, Okla. Bar Assn., Okla. County Bar Assn., Am. Inst. CPA's, Okla. Soc. CPA's. Republican. Avocations: young life leader. Corporate taxation, Taxation partnership. Office: McAfee & Taft 2 Leadership Sq 10th Floor Oklahoma City OK 73102

BURGETT, DAVID WALLACE, lawyer; b. Lansing, Mich., June 10, 1955; s. Glenn Alan and Grace (Ashby) B.; m. Brigitte Klink, Sept. 5, 1986. BA summa cum laude, U. Mich., 1977; JD cum laude, M in Pub. Policy, Harvard U., 1981. Bar: D.C. 1981, U.S. Dist. Ct. D.C. 1981, U.S. Ct. Appeals (D.C. cir.) 1981, U.S. Supreme Ct. 1986. Law clk. to judge U.S. Ct. Appeals (D.C. cir.), Washington, 1981-82; assoc. Hogan & Hartson, Washington, 1982—. Coordinator blood drive ARC. Angell scholar U. Mich., 1976. Mem. ABA, Fed. Bar Assn., Jud. Conf. of D.C., Washington Council of Lawyers. Avocations: skiing, tennis, photography. Computer, Government contracts and claims. Office: Hogan & Hartson 555 13th St NW Washington DC 20004

BURGMAN, DIERDRE ANN, lawyer; b. Logansport, Ind., Mar. 25, 1948; d. Ferdinand William Jr. and Doreen Yvonne (Walsh) B. BA, Valparaiso U., 1970, JD, 1979; LLM, Yale U., 1985. Bar: Ind. 1979, U.S. Dist. Ct. (so. dist.) Ind. 1979, N.Y. 1982, U.S. Dist. Ct. (so. dist.) N.Y. 1982, U.S. Ct. Appeals (7th cir.) 1982, U.S. Ct. Appeals (D.C. cir.) 1984, U.S. Ct. Appeals (2d cir.) 1984, U.S. Supreme Ct. 1985. Law clk. to chief judge Ind. Ct. Appeals, Indpls., 1979-80; prof. law Valparaiso (Ind.) U., 1980-81; assoc. Dewey, Ballantine, Bushby, Palmer & Wood, N.Y.C., 1981-84, Cahill Gordon & Reindel, N.Y.C., 1985—. Note editor Valparaiso U. law rev., 1978-79; contbr. articles to law jours. Mem. bd. visitors Valparaiso U. Sch. Law, 1986—. Ind. Bar Found. scholar, 1978. Mem. ABA (trial evidence com.), Assn. Bar of the City of N.Y., N.Y. County Lawyers Assn. Lutheran. Federal civil litigation, State civil litigation, General corporate. Home: 164 E 61st St New York NY 10021 Office: Cahill Gordon & Reindel 80 Pine St Suite 1700 New York NY 10005

BURGON, BARRE GLADE, lawyer; b. Salt Lake City, May 14, 1950; s. Glade Lynn and Laura (Palmer) B.; m. Karen Manning, Oct. 9, 1974; children: Robert, Richard, Rebecca, Stephanie. BS in Polit. Sci., Utah State U., 1976; JD magna cum laude, U. Puget Sound, 1979. Bar: Utah 1979, U.S. Dist. Ct. Utah 1979, U.S. Ct. Claims 1984. Law clk. sr. judge U.S. Ct. Appeals (10th cir.), Salt Lake City, 1979-80; assoc. Watkins & Faber, Salt Lake City, 1980; corp. counsel Flying J Inc., Brigham City, Utah, 1980-86; v.p., corp. counsel Flying J Inc., Brigham City, 1986—. Mem. ABA, Utah Bar Assn., Box Elder County Bar Assn. Republican. Mormon. Avocations: skiing, golf. General corporate, Real property, Labor. Office: Flying J Inc 50 W 990 S Brigham City UT 84302

BURGOYNE, BERT, lawyer; b. Detroit, Aug. 8, 1930; s. Bertram and Margaret Robertson B.; m. Shirley Jean Cox, Apr. 22, 1955; children—Deborah, David, Douglas; m. 2d, Rosemary Kuras, Aug. 25, 1979. B.A., Wayne State U., 1951; J.D. with distinction, U. Mich., 1956. Bar: Oreg. 1956, Mich. 1959. Law clk. Oreg. Supreme Ct., Salem, 1956-57; dep. dist. atty. Douglas County (Oreg.), Roseburg, 1957-58; prof. Akron (Ohio) Law Sch., 1958-59; asst. atty. gen., Lansing, Mich., 1959-63; spl. asst. atty. gen., Detroit, 1963-64; assoc. Travis, Warren & Nayer, Detroit, 1963-66; ptnr. Travis, Warren, Nayer & Burgoyne, Detroit, 1966-73, 74-77, Travis, Warren, Hammond, Ziegelman & Burgoyne, Detroit, 1973-74; v.p. Travis, Warren, Nayer & Burgoyne, P.C., Detroit, 1977-78; pres. Burgoyne, Kaufman, Roche & Ward, P.C., Detroit, 1978-80; v.p., asst. sec. Bromberg, Robinson, Shapero, Cohn & Burgoyne, P.C., Southfield, Mich., 1980-82; pres. Bert Burgoyne, P.C., Birmingham, Mich., 1982—. Mem. ABA, State Bar Mich. (mem. com. on condemnation procedure 1960-80, chmn. 1970-76), Oreg. State Bar, Am. Right of Way Assn. Contbg. author: Mich. Law of Damages, 1979; Mich. Municipal Law, 1980; contbr. articles to profl. jours. Condemnation, Real property, Environment. Office: 32270 Telegraph Rd Suite 200 Birmingham MI 48010

BURGOYNE, JOHN ALBERT, lawyer, management consultant; b. Malden, Mass., May 4, 1914; s. Albert M. and Anna M. (Bagley) B.; m. Juliet M. Moran, Oct. 12, 1940; children—J. Albert, Robert F. A.B., Boston Coll., 1936; J.D., Georgetown U., 1946; postgrad. advanced mgmt. program Harvard U. Grad. Sch. Bus. Adminstrn., 1965. Bar: Mass. 1946, D.C. 1946, U.S. Dist. Ct. Mass. 1950, U.S. Supreme Ct. 1961. Vice pres. Liberty Mut. Ins. Cos., 1936-68, State Farm Ins. Cos., 1968-72, Met. Life Ins. Co., 1972-79; chmn., chief exec. officer Met. Property and Liability Ins. Co., 1972-79; of counsel Coombs and Ryan, Boston, 1980—; instr. law Boston Coll. Law Sch., 1958-68. Served to lt. USNR, 1943-46. Mem. ABA. Clubs: Rockport Golf, Sandy Bay Yacht. General corporate, Insurance, Probate. Home: 15 Prospect St Rockport MA 01966

BURGUM, BRADLEY JOSEPH, lawyer; b. Fargo, N.D., Jan. 3, 1952; s. Joseph B. and Katherine K. (Kilbourne) B.; m. Julie Ann Kay Opp, July 31, 1976; children: James Bradley, Benjamin Lee. BS, N.D. State U., 1974; JD, U. N.D., 1977. Bar: N.D. 1977, U.S. Dist. Ct. N.D. 1977; CPA, N.D. Assoc. Woell & Woell, Casselton, N.D., 1977; ptnr. Woell, Woell & Burgum, Casselton, 1977-81; sole practice Casselton, 1981-85; ptnr. Burgum & Irby P.C., Casselton, 1986—; mng. ptnr. Burgum Farms, Arthur, 1970—; atty. City of Casselton, 1981—; bd. dirs. Farmers Elevators Co., Arthur, N.D., Great Plains Software Inc., Fargo, Dempster Industries, Beatrice, Neb. Mem. Casselton Econ. Devel. Commn., 1985—; pres. Casselton Community Club, 1985—; sec. Casselton Vol. Ambulance, 1978—; bd. dirs. Casselton Community Med. Ctr. Inc., 1983—. Mem. ABA, N.D. Bar Assn. (fee arbitration panel 1986), Cass County Bar Assn., N.D. Soc. CPAs, Nat. Registry Emergency Med. Techs., Sigma Alpha Epsilon Alumni Assn. (treas. 1982—), Cass County Twp. Officers Assn. (sec., treas. 1978—). Club: Pelican Lake (Minn.) Yacht (treas. 1985—). Probate, Personal income taxation, Real property. Home: Box 886 Casselton ND 58012 Office: Burgum & Irby PC Box 308 Casselton ND 58012

BURKARD, PETER HUBERT, lawyer; b. Ottobeuren, Germany, Mar. 26, 1940; s. Peter and Ruth (Klein) B.; m. Barbara A. Sadowski, June 24, 1966; children—Melissa, Elizabeth, Amy. A.B., Harvard U., 1962; J.D., U. Mich., 1965; Dr. Jur., U. Heidelberg (W.Ger.), 1969. Bar: Mich. 1968, N.Y. 1971, Conn. 1979. Atty., Dow Chem. Co., Midland, Mich., 1968-70, Gen. Foods Corp., White Plains, N.Y., 1970-72; counsel Xerox Corp., Stamford, Conn., 1972-80, Rank Xerox Ltd., London, 1975; assoc. gen. counsel Burndy Corp., Norwalk, Conn., 1981; counsel European and Japanese region Eastman Kodak Co., Rochester, N.Y., 1982—. Clubs: U. Rochester; Harvard of N.Y.C. Private international, Antitrust. Home: 208 Allens Creek Rd Rochester NY 14618 Office: Eastman Kodak Co 343 State St Rochester NY 14650

BURKE, CAROL ELIZABETH, lawyer, educator; b. Great Bend, Kans., June 23, 1946; d. Robert Merle and Virginia Mae (Jaworski) Burke; m. Harry Gottesfeld; 1 adopted child, Gina Faye. B.A. in Communications with highest distinction, SUNY-Buffalo, 1971; J.D., 1974; postgrad. in children's lit. Vassar U., 1984. Bar: Tex. 1974, Hawaii 1981, N.Y. 1984, U.S. Tax Ct. 1974, U.S. Dist. Ct. (so. dist.) Tex. 1975, U.S. Supreme Ct. 1985, U.S. Ct. Internat. Trade 1985, U.S. Ct. Appeals (D.C. cir.) 1975, U.S. Dist. Ct. Hawaii 1981, U.S. Ct. Appeals (2nd cir.) 1985, U.S. Ct. Appeals (5th cir.) 1984, U.S. Ct. Appeals (9th cir.) 1981, U.S. Dist. Ct. (so. dist.) N.Y. 1985. sole practice, Houston, 1974-81, N.Y.C., 1984—, dir. research and devel., Honolulu, 1981-83; educator Preventtive Legal Edn. and Awareness Program, N.Y.C., 1984—; speaker at seminars and on video and audio tapes; instr. Nat. Inst. Trial Advocacy, Hemphill, N.Y., 1979—; producer and hostess TV prodn. Legal Trends, Sta. KHOU-TV, Houston, 1978-81. Author: The Rose and the Sunflower, 1984, The Hidden Advantage, 1986, Smarts: Making Things Work for You; Contbr. articles to profl. jours. Bd. dirs. Westchester chpt. Am. Cancer Soc., 1984—; lobbyist Nat. Writers Union, N.Y.C., 1983—. Oratorical scholar Am. Legion, 1964; Jacckle Abrams fellow, 1974. Mem. ABA (chmn., vice chmn. family law sect. 1975-81), Assn. Bar City of N.Y., N.Y. State Trial Lawyers Assn., Tex. Trial Lawyers Assn. (chmn. family law sect. 1978-81), Nat. Acad. Radio and TV Scis., Nat. Women's Polit. Caucus, LWV (legis. mem.). Roman Catholic. Family and matrimonial, Trademark and copyright, Legislative. Office: Burke & Co 10 Waterside Plaza New York NY 10010

BURKE, CHRISTOPHER MARK, law clerk; b. Springfield, Mass., Mar. 6, 1948; s. John Edward and Dorothy May (Laferty) B. AS, Holyoke Community Coll., 1968; BA in Math., Doane Coll., 1973; JD, Western New Eng. Sch. of Law, 1980. Bar: Conn. 1980, U.S. Dist. Ct. Conn. 1980. Asst. clk. Superior Ct., Danielson, Conn., 1980-83; sole practice Danielson, 1980-83; clk. Superior Ct., 1983—; cons. in data processing, Springfield, 1977-80. Served to specialist grade 4 U.S. Army, 1970-72. Mem. ABA, Conn. Bar Assn., Windham County Bar Assn. Democrat. Roman Catholic. Judicial administration. Home: 22 Francis St Danielson CT 06239 Office: Superior Ct 127 Main St Danielson CT 06239

BURKE, DENNIS J., lawyer; b. Evergreen Park, Ill., July 25, 1949; s. John and Catherine N. (Barrett) B.; m. Carol A. Burke, Nov. 17, 1973; children—Dennis, Kathryn, Mary Ellen. Student Univ. Coll., Dublin, 1969-70; B.A., St. Mary's Coll., Winona, Minn., 1971; J.D., John Marshall Law Sch., 1975. Bar: Ill. 1975, U.S. dist. ct. (no. dist.) Ill. 1975. Mem. firm Burke & Burke, Ltd., Chgo., 1975—; moot ct. judge Loyola Law Sch.; guest lectr. Moraine Valley Jr. Coll., Evang. Sch. Nursing. Fellow Ill. Bar Found.; mem. ABA, Ill. Bar Assn. (sec. 1982-83, vice chmn. civil practice and procedure sect. 1983-85, chmn. 1985-86, bd. of govs. 1986—), Chgo. Bar Assn., Assn. Trial Lawyers Am., Ill. Trial Lawyers Assn. Issue editor Trial Briefs, vol. XXV, No. 5, 1979, vol. XXVII, No. 1, 1981. Personal injury, State civil litigation, Federal civil litigation. Office: 200 W Madison Chicago IL 60606

BURKE, E. JAMES, lawyer; b. Wilmington, Del., June 26, 1949; s. Earl J. Burke and Elizabeth M. (Glenn) Jones; m. Michele C. Haney, Aug. 16, 1975 (div. May 1981); 1 child, Erick; m. Linda G. Matthew, Apr. 15, 1982; children: Matthew, Leanna. BS in Psychology, St. Joseph's U., Phila., 1971; JD, U. Wyo., 1977. Bar: Wyo. 1977, U.S. Dist. Ct. Wyo. 1977, U.S. Ct. Appeals (10th cir.) 1981. Ptnr. Hanes & Burke P.C., Cheyenne, Wyo., 1977—. Served to 1st lt. USAF, 1971-74. Mem. Wyo. Bar Assn., Laramie County Bar Assn., Assn. Trial Lawyers Am. (state del. 1985—), Wyo. Trial Lawyers Assn. (bd. dirs. 1977—, pres. 1980), Western Trial Lawyers Assn. (bd. dirs. 1979—, pres. 1986—), Cheyenne C. of C. (leadership award 1986). Personal injury, Federal civil litigation, State civil litigation. Home: 7032 Valley View Pl Cheyenne WY 82009 Office: Hanes & Burke PC 1720 Carey Ave Cheyenne WY 82001

BURKE, EDMOND WAYNE, judge; b. Ukiah, Calif., Sept. 7, 1935; s. Wayne P. and Opal K. B.; m. Sharon E. Halverson, Jan. 25, 1977; children: Kathleen R., Jennifer E. A.B., Humboldt State Coll., 1957, M.A., 1958; J.D., U. Calif., 1964. Bar: Calif., Alaska. Individual practice law Calif. and Alaska, 1965-67; asst. atty. gen. State of Alaska, 1967; asst. dist. atty. Anchorage, Alaska, 1968-69; judge Superior Ct., Alaska, 1970-75; justice Supreme Ct. State of Alaska, Anchorage, 1975—, chief justice, 1981-84. Mem. Alaska Bar Assn., Am. Judicature Soc. Republican. Presbyterian. Office: 1303 K St Anchorage AK 99501

BURKE, EDMUND, lawyer; b. Bozeman, Mont., Sept. 22, 1934; s. Edmund Jr. and Dorothy (Hirschman) B.; m. Martha Benge, Feb. 14, 1959; children: Anna, Thomas, John. BS, U.S. Naval Acad., 1956; LLB, U. Calif., Berkeley, 1963. Bar: Calif. 1964, U.S. Dist. Ct. (no. dist.) Calif. 1964, U.S. Ct. Appeals (9th cir.) 1964, Hawaii 1966, U.S. Dist. Ct. Hawaii 1966. Commd. ensign USN, 1956, advanced through grades to lt., resigned, 1960; assoc. Benton, Orr & Buckingham, Ventura, Calif., 1963-66; ptnr. Conroy, Hamilton et al, Honolulu, 1966-80, Burke, Sakai, McPheeters et al, Honolulu, 1980—. Bd. dirs. Hawaii Med. Library, Honolulu, 1978-84. Fellow Am. Coll. Trial Lawyers; mem. ABA, Calif. Bar Assn., Hawaii Bar Assn., Am. Inns of Ct. (bencher 1981—), Am. Judicature Soc. Democrat. Clubs: Pacific, Waikiki Yacht (Honolulu). Avocations: sailing, swimming. Federal civil litigation, State civil litigation, Personal injury. Home: 17 Kailuana Pl Kailua HI 96734 Office: Burke Sakai McPheeters et al 737 Bishop St Suite 3100 Honolulu HI 96813

BURKE, EDMUND JAMES, lawyer; b. N.Y.C., May 10, 1949; s. Edmund James Burke Jr. and Mary Virginia Hahn. BA, Bates Coll., 1971; postgrad., U. Glasgow, Scotland, 1970; JD, Western New Eng. Coll., 1976. Bar: Maine 1976, U.S. Dist. Ct. Maine, 1977. Ptnr. Burke, Meyer & Bates, Lewiston, Maine, 1977-82, Burke & Gauvreau, Lewiston, 1982-84; pres. Longley, Whalen & Burke, Lewiston, 1984-86, Whalen & Burke, Lewiston, 1986—; complaint justice 8th Jud. Dist., Lewiston, 1982-85. Bd. dirs. Maine Civil Liberties Union, Portland, 1986—, Lewiston-Auburn Children's Home, 1982—, also dir.; trustee and clk. Anproscoggin County Law Library, Auburn, 1978—. Mem. ABA, Maine Trial Lawyers Assn., Androscoggin County Bar Assn. (treas. 1978—). State civil litigation, Personal injury, Trademark and copyright. Office: Whalen & Burke 4 Park St PO Box 1230 Lewiston ME 04240

BURKE, FREDERICK AUGUSTINE, lawyer; b. Buffalo, Aug. 1, 1939; s. William F. and Lucile (Mitchell) B.; m. Mary Rodgers, June 2, 1962; children: Lynn, Patrick, Michael, Matthew, Martin. Student, Manhattan Coll., 1957-59; BA, SUNY, Buffalo, 1962, JD, 1963. Bar: N.Y. 1964, U.S. Supreme Ct. 1970, Ohio 1976, Tenn. 1979, N.C. 1984. Sole practice Buffalo, 1964-67; sec., house counsel Servotronics, Inc., Buffalo, 1967-75; sec., corp. counsel North Electric Co., Galion, Ohio, 1975-78; gen. counsel, sec. ITT North Electric Co. (merger ITT and North Electric Co.), Johnson City, Tenn., 1978-82; gen. counsel telecom internat. div. ITT, Cape Canaveral, Fla., 1982-83; sec., group gen. counsel ITT Telecom Products Corp., Raleigh, N.C., 1983—. Mem. ABA, N.Y. State Bar Assn., Ohio Bar Assn., Tenn. Bar Assn., N.C. Bar Assn., Am. Corp. Counsel Assn. Republican. Roman Catholic. Contracts commercial, General corporate, Private international. Office: ITT Telecom Products Corp 3128 Smoketree Ct Raleigh NC 27604

BURKE, JOHN BARRETT, JR., lawyer; b. St. Paul, Dec. 31, 1939; s. John Burdette and Margaret Mary (Barrett) B.; m. Helen Virginia Peterson, Dec. 26, 1951; children: Michael, Anne, Lisa, Patrick, Mary, Kathleen, Diane. BSL, William Mitchell Coll. of Law, 1954, JD, 1955. Bar: Minn. 1956, U.S. Dist. Ct. Minn. 1965. Commd. sgt. USAR, 1948, advanced through grades to 2d lt., 1957, retired, 1959; adj. prof. William Mitchell Coll. of Law, St. Paul, 1977—; exec. council Ramsey County Bar Assn., St. Paul, 1980-83. Author: Burke & Burton on Mortgage Foreclosures, 1981. Mem. ABA, Minn. State Bar Assn. Real property, Probate. Office: O'Neill Burke & O'Neill 800 Norwest Ctr Saint Paul MN 55101

BURKE, JOHN MICHAEL, lawyer; b. Chgo., Oct. 9, 1941; s. John and Catherine Mary (Barrett) B.; m. Maureen Kay Fox, Oct. 5, 1968; children: Brian, Timothy, Michael. BBA, Loyola U., 1964, JD, 1965. Bar: Ill. 1965, U.S. Dist. Ct. (no. dist.) Ind. 1965, U.S. Ct. Appeals (7th cir.) 1968. Assoc. Pretzel & Stouffer, Chgo., 1965-69, Shaheen, Lundberg & Callahan, Chgo., 1969-70; ptnr. Burke & Burke, Ltd., Chgo., 1970—. Served to sgt. U.S. Army, 1965-68. Mem. ABA, Ill. Bar Assn. (chmn. tort council, service award 1984), Assn. Trial Lawyers Am., Ill. Trial Lawyers, Appellate Lawyers Ill. Club: Westmoreland Country (Wilmette, Ill.). Personal injury, State civil litigation, Federal civil litigation. Home: 2241 Kenilworth Wilmette IL 60090 Office: Burke & Burke Ltd 200 W Madison St Suite 3880 Chicago IL 60606

BURKE, KIM KENNETH, lawyer; b. Pitts., Sept. 13, 1955; s. John Francis and Mildred Antoinette (Jeletic) B.; m. Linda Ann Leasure, Aug. 9, 1980; 1 child, Ryan. BS in Edn., Ind. U., Pa., 1977; JD, U. Pitts., 1980. Bar: Pa. 1980, Ohio 1981, U.S. Dist. Ct. (so. dist.) Ohio 1981, U.S. Dist. Ct. (we. dist.) Pa. 1981, U.S. Ct. Appeals (3d cir.) 1981, U.S. Ct. Appeals (6th cir.) 1986. Assoc. Rose, Schmidt, Dixon, Hasley, Whyte & Hardesty, Pitts., 1980-81, Taft, Stettinius & Hollister, Cin., 1981—. Mem. corp. solicitaion team Am. Heart Assn., Cin., 1983—, Cin. Regatta, 1984—, appellate panel Cin. Met. Sewer Dist., 1985—; legal rep. materials adv. com. City of Cin., 1985—. Named one of Outstanding Young Men in Am., 1985. Mem. ABA (litigation sect., natural resources sect.), Cin. Bar Assn. (vice chmn. environ. law com. 1984—), Greater Cin. C. of C. (vice chmn. emerging issues subcom. 1987, occupational health safety com., energy environment com.). Republican. Roman Catholic. Club: Cin. Athletic. Avocations: running, cycling. Environment, Federal civil litigation, State civil litigation. Home: 3725 Andrew Ave Cincinnati OH 45209 Office: Taft Stettinius & Hollister 1800 First National Bank Ctr Cincinnati OH 45202

BURKE, LINDA BEERBOWER, lawyer; b. Huntington, W.Va., June 19, 1948; d. William Bert and Betty Jane (Weddle) Beerbower; m. Timothy Francis Burke, Jr., Aug. 26, 1972; children—Ryan Timothy, Hannah Elizabeth. B.A., Coll. William and Mary, 1970; J.D., U. Pitts., 1973; postgrad. acctg. U. Pitts., 1976. Bar: Pa. 1973, U.S. Claims Ct. 1982. Tax atty. ALCOA, Pitts., 1973-77, gen. tax atty., 1977-80, mgr. legal and planning taxes, 1980-86, tax counsel, 1987—. Industry coordinator Allegheny Conf. Partnerships in Edn., Pitts. pub. schs., 1981—; mem. United Way adv. com. for Vol. Action Ctr., Pitts.; trustee St. Edmund's Acad.; bd. dirs. YWCA Greater Pitts. Recipient salute Triangle Corner, Pitts., 1983. Mem. Tax Execs. Inst. (pres., bd. dirs., inst. dir.), Pitts. Internat. Taxation Soc., Pitts. Tax Club, ABA, Pa. Bar Assn., Allegheny County Bar Assn. Clubs: Pitts. Athletic Assn., Longue Vue, Rivers. Corporate taxation, Pension, profit-sharing, and employee benefits. Office: Aluminum Co Am 1501 Alcoa Bldg Pittsburgh PA 15219

BURKE, LLOYD HUDSON, judge; b. Oakland, Calif., Apr. 1, 1916; s. James H. and Edna L. (Taylor) B.; m. Virginia Joan Kerchum, Apr. 27, 1941; children—Brian Hudson, Bruce Thomas. A.B., St. Mary's Coll., 1937; LL.B., U. Calif., 1940, J.D., 1972; LL.D., St. Mary's Coll. of Calif. Dep. dist. atty. Alameda County, Calif., 1940-53; sr. criminal trial dep. 1950-53, U.S. atty., 1953-58; U.S. dist. judge Northern Dist. Calif., 1958—. Served with U.S. Army, 1942-46; capt. Res., to 1951. Mem. Phi Delta Phi. Office: US Court House 450 Golden Gate Ave San Francisco CA 94102

BURKE, PAUL BRADFORD, lawyer; b. Detroit, Mar. 3, 1956; s. Donald Joseph and Janet Cottrell (Davis) B.; m. Shannon Louise Egan, Aug. 12, 1978; 1 child, Kelly Marie. BA, Yale U., 1978; JD, U. Mich., 1981. Bar: Minn. 1981. Assoc. Oppenheimer Wolff et al, Mpls., 1981-83, Delaney & Solum, Mpls., 1983; assoc. gen. counsel BMC Industries, Inc., St. Paul, 1983-85, v.p., sec., gen. counsel, 1985—; lectr. Minn. Inst. Legal Edn., Mpls.,

1986, Advanced Legal Edn., St. Paul, 1983. Mem. ABA (fed. regulation of securities com. 1983—), Minn. Bar Assn., Hennepin County Bar Assn., Am. Soc. Corp. Secs., Midwest Corp. Counsel Ctr. Methodist. Club: Mpls. Golf; St. Paul Athletic. General corporate, Securities. Office: BMC Industries Inc 1100 Am Nat Bank Bldg Saint Paul MN 55101

BURKE, RAYMOND DANIEL, lawyer; b. Balt., Apr. 27, 1952; s. Raymond Francis and Eleanor Mildred (Schultz) B.; m. Vickey Lee Stevens, May 2, 1982. BA, Johns Hopkins U., 1974; JD, U. Md., 1978. Bars: Md. 1978, U.S. Dist. Ct. Md. 1979, U.S. Ct. Appeals (4th cir.) 1986, U.S. Supreme Ct. 1986. Legal asst. Baltimore County, Towson, 1975-78, asst. county atty., 1978-79; corp. house counsel McCormick & Co., Inc., Hunt Valley, Md., 1979; assoc. Freishtat & Sandler, Balt., 1980-86, ptnr., 1986—; cons. Towson Devel. Corp., 1980—, legis. com. chmn., exec. com. Towson Devel. Corp., 1986—, bd. dirs. Com. mem. Towson bus. Assn., 1985—; alumni meme. Leadership Assn. Baltimore County, Towson, 1984—; bd. dirs. Knollwood-Donnybrook Improvement Assn., Towson, 1986; bd. dirs., treas. Human Resources Devel. Agy., Balt., 1986—. Mem. ABA, Md. Bar Assn. Democrat. Roman Catholic. Avocations: Lacrosse, history. Federal civil litigation, State civil litigation, General corporate. Home: 608 Fairway Dr Towson MD 21204 Office: Freishtat & Sandler 201 E Baltimore St Baltimore MD 21202

BURKE, RAYMOND F., corporate lawyer. V.p., gen. counsel NYNEX Corp., White Plains, N.Y., 1983—. Office: Nynex Corp 335 Madison Ave New York NY 10017 *

BURKE, RICHARD WILLIAM, lawyer; b. Chgo., Oct. 3, 1933; s. James William and Helen (Creed) B.; m. Maryjeanne Ryan, Feb. 11, 1961; children: Mary, Richard, Sarah, Will. BA cum laude, U. Notre Dame, 1955; JD, U. Chgo., 1958. Bar: Ill. 1959, U.S. Dist. Ct. (no. dist.) Ill. 1959, U.S. Ct. Appeals (7th cir.) 1965, U.S. Supreme Ct. 1977. Assoc. William T. Kirby & Assocs., Chgo., 1958-65; assoc. Hubachek, Kelly, Rauch & Kirby, Chgo., 1965-67, ptnr., 1967-80; ptnr. Burke, Griffin, Chomicz & Wienke, Chgo., 1980—; bd. dirs. various community banks. Mem. ABA, Ill. Bar Assn., Chgo. Bar Assn. Roman Catholic. Avocations: skiing, sailing, reading, travel. Banking, General corporate, Estate planning. Office: Burke Griffin Chomicz & Wienke 303 E Wacker Chicago IL 60305

BURKE, ROBERT ANTHONY, lawyer; b. Scranton, Pa., Mar. 23, 1952; s. Robert James and Mary Rose (Ford) B. BS, U. Scranton, 1974; student, U. Akron, 1975; JD, U. Dayton, 1978. Bar: Ohio 1979, Pa. 1981, U.S. Ct. of Appeals (6th cir.) 1983, U.S. Ct. Appeals (3rd cir.) 1985, U.S. Supreme Ct. 1983, N.Y. 1986. Legal advisor Dayton (Ohio) Police Dept., 1976-78; local counselor Chgo. Title Ins., Dayton, 1979-80; asst. city prosecutor City of Dayton div. Law, 1980-83, asst. city atty., 1980—. Urban fellow City of Dayton, 1986. Mem. ABA, Nat. Dist. Atty. Assn., Pa. Bar Assn., Lackawanna, Pa. Bar Assn., Pi Gamma Mu. Roman Catholic. Home: 3467 Zephyr Dr Dayton OH 45420 Office: City of Dayton Dept Law 101 W Third St Rm 609 Dayton OH 45420

BURKE, ROBERT BERTRAM, lawyer, political consultant; b. Cleve., July 9, 1942; s. Max and Eve (Miller) B.; m. Helen Choate Hall, May 5, 1979 (div. Oct. 1983). B.A., UCLA, 1963, J.D., 1966; LL.M., London Sch. Econs., 1967. Bar: D.C. 1972, Calif. 1978, U.S. Supreme Ct. 1977. Exec. dir. Lawyer's Com. Civil Rts. under Law, Washington, 1968-69; ptnr. Fisk, Wolfe & Burke, Paris, 1969-71; assoc. O'Connor & Hannan, Washington, 1972-74; sole practice, Washington, 1974-79, Los Angeles, 1978—; cons. Commonwealth Pa., Harrisburg, 1973. Chmn. So. Calif. Hollings for Pres., 1984; commr. Bldg. and Appeals Bd. City of Los Angeles, State Adv. Bd. on Alcohol Related Problems. Mem. ABA, Am. Inst. Architects (profl. affiliate). Jewish. Municipal bonds, Administrative and regulatory, Private international. Home: 429 S Arnaz Dr Los Angeles CA 90048 Office: Rosen Wachtell & Gilbert 1888 Century Park E #2100 Los Angeles CA 90067

BURKE, THOMAS EDMUND, lawyer; b. Bklyn., July 2, 1932; s. Richard and Anne (Corcoran) B.; m. Joan Elizabeth Markey, Nov. 12, 1966; children—Patrick Joseph, Elizabeth Ann. A.B., Niagara U., 1953; J.D., Columbia U., 1958. Bar: N.Y. 1958. Assoc. Mendes & Mount, N.Y.C., 1958-64; assoc. LeBoeuf, Lamb, Leiby & MacRae, N.Y.C., 1965-68; v.p., sec. Am. Internat. Ltd., Hamilton, Bermuda, 1968-72; asst. gen. counsel Am. Internat. Ltd., N.Y.C., 1972-75; v.p., gen. counsel Howden Swann, Ltd., Cranford, N.J., 1975-77; ptnr. LeBoeuf, Lamb, Leiby & MacRae, N.Y.C., 1977—; dir. Southwest Internat. Reins. Co., N.Y.C., 1986—. Served to 1st lt. U.S. Army, 1953-55. Mem. ABA, N.Y. State Bar Assn., Internat. Assn. Ins. Counsel. Democrat. Roman Catholic. Lodge: Friendly Sons St. Patrick (N.Y.C.). Avocations: fishing, hiking. Insurance, Private international, Legislative. Office: LeBoeuf Lamb Leiby & MacRae 520 Madison Ave New York NY 10022

BURKE, THOMAS GERALD, lawyer; b. Seattle, June 15, 1947; s. Thomas J. and Eleanor P. (Spencer) B.; m. Susan Kay Burke (dec. 1970). BA, U. Wash., 1971; JD, U. Puget Sound, 1975. Bar: Wash. 1976, U.S. Dist. Ct. (we. dist.) Wash. 1976. Sgt. Seattle Police Dept., 1972-77; sole practice Seattle, 1976—; litigation atty. King County Guardian ad Litem Program, Seattle, 1981—; atty. King County Ct. Appointed Spl. Adv./Family Ct., Seattle, 1985—; adv. Renton Voc-Tech. Inst., Wash., 1981—. Patentee equipment design. Sec., treas. Pacific Northwest AAU Assn., Kirkland, Wash., 1985—; bd. dirs. Eastside Children's Sexual Assault Ctr., Kirkland, 1986—, U.S. Sports Found., Kirkland. Mem. ABA, Assn. Trial Lawyers Am. Republican. Club: Coll. (Seattle). AAU Sr. Men's Karate Champion, 1985. Family and matrimonial, Juvenile, Personal injury. Office: 1715 Market St #103 Kirkland WA 98003

BURKE, THOMAS JOSEPH, JR., lawyer; b. Chgo., Oct. 23, 1941; s. Thomas Joseph and Violet (Green) B.; m. Sharon Lynne Forke, Aug. 29, 1964; children—Lisa Lynne, Heather Ann. B.A., Elmhurst Coll., 1963; J.D., Chgo.-Kent Coll. Law, 1966. Bar: Ill. 1966, U.S. Dist. Ct. (no. dist.) Ill. 1967, U.S. Ct. Appeals (7th cir.) 1972, U.S. Supreme Ct. 1972. Assoc., Lord, Bissell & Brook, Chgo., 1966-74, ptnr., 1974—; faculty Ill. Trial Lawyers Assn., Chgo., 1983; lectr. Ill. Def. Counsel, Chgo., 1983. Mem. ABA, Ill. State Bar Assn., Chgo. Bar Assn. (chmn. mock jury trials com. 1971-72), Assn. Trial Lawyers Am., Soc. Trial Lawyers, Trial Lawyers Club Chgo., Def. Research Inst., Ill. Assn. Def. Trial Counsel, Soc. Automotive Engrs., Am. Assn. Automotive Medicine, Pi Kappa Delta, Phi Delta Phi. Republican. Roman Catholic. Club: Mid-Day (Chgo.). Personal injury, State civil litigation, Federal civil litigation. Office: Lord Bissell & Brook 115 S LaSalle St Chicago IL 60608

BURKE, TIMOTHY JOHN, lawyer; b. Syracuse, N.Y., June 5, 1946; s. Francis Joseph and Alice Marie Burke; 1 child, Ryan Alexander; m. 2d, Denise Kay Blied, Mar. 18, 1978; 1 child, Aimee Noel. B.A. with distinction, Ariz. State U., 1967, J.D. cum laude, 1970. Bar: Ariz. 1970, U.S. Dist. Ct. Ariz. 1970, U.S. Ct. Appeals (9th cir.) 1974. Trial atty. Antitrust div. U.S. Dept. Justice, Washington, 1970-72, asst. to dir. ops., 1972-74; assoc. Fennemore, Craig, von Ammon, Udall & Powers, Phoenix, 1974—, dir., 1978—; part-time instr. in legal writing Ariz. State U., 1974-75. Mem. panel rev. bd. Phoenix United Way, 1975-76; bd. dirs. Florence Crittenton Services, Phoenix, 1980—, pres 1985—. Recipient Spl. Commendation award U.S. Dept. Justice, 1973. Mem. ABA (antitrust and litigation sects.), State Bar Ariz. (council antitrust sect., chmn. 1985-87), Fed. Bar Assn., Maricopa County Bar Assn. Club: Arizona (Phoenix). Antitrust. Office: 100 W Washington St Suite 1700 Phoenix AZ 85003 Office: 2 N Central Ave Suite 2200 Phoenix AZ 85004-2390

BURKE, TIMOTHY MICHAEL, lawyer, educator; b. Cleve., Feb. 10, 1948; s. Ralph and Frances (Dilley) B.; m. Patricia Kathleen LaGrange, June 6, 1970; children—Nora Frances, Tara Kathleen, Michael Ralph. A.B., Xavier U., Cin., 1970; J.D., U. Cin., 1973. Bar: Ohio 1973, U.S. Dist. Ct. (so. dist.) Ohio 1979, U.S. Ct. Appeals (6th cir.) 1978, U.S. Supreme Ct. 1979. Legis. asst. to council mem. Cin. City Council, 1971-74; spl. asst. to Congressman Tom Luken, Cin., 1974, 76-77; exec. dir. Little Miami, Inc., Cin., 1975-76; prin. Manley, Burke & Fischer and predecessor, Cin., 1977—; spl. counsel to atty. gen. State of Ohio, 1978—; law dir. Village of Lockland, Ohio, 1982—; lectr. Xavier U., 1975-78, 81, 82—, adj. asst. prof., 1983—; adj. assoc. prof. U. Cin., 1977-78, 79, dir. law enforcement tech. program, 1977-78. Bd. dirs. Tri State Air Com., 1972-80, chmn., 1976-78; chmn. land use subcom. water quality adv. com. Ohio-Ky.-Ind. Regional Council Govts., 1975-76; bd. dirs. Lower Council of Little Miami, Inc., 1976-82; mem. alumni bd. govs. Xavier U., 1970-76, 78-79, v.p., 1980-81, pres., 1981-82; candidate for U.S. Ho. of Reps. from 1st dist. Ohio, 1978; chmn. legal com. Cin. Zoo, bd. dirs., 1980—; co-chmn. Zoo Tax Levy Campaign, 1982, 86; participant Fgn. Policy Conf. for Young Am. Polit. Leaders, U.S. Dept. State, 1980; exec. co-chmn. Hamilton County Democratic Com., 1982-86; co-chmn. Cin. Dem. Com., 1983-86. Served to 1st lt. U.S. Army, 1974. Recipient service award Ohio River Valley Com. for Occupational Safety and Health, 1983; leadership award Xavier U., 1984. Mem. ABA, Am. Planning Assn. (legal sect.). Roman Catholic. Local government, Environment, Real property. Home: 3560 McGuffey St Cincinnati OH 45226

BURKE, WILLIAM TEMPLE, JR., lawyer; b. San Antonio, Oct. 30, 1935; s. William Temple and Adelaide H. (Raba) B.; m. Mary Sue Johnson, June 8, 1957; children: William Patrick, Michael Edmond, Karen Elizabeth. B.B.A., St. Mary's U., San Antonio, J.D., 1961. Bar: Tex. Practice law Dallas; dir. Phil Ross Realtors, Inc., MB Valuation Systems, Inc. Pres., founder Dallas Assn. KC, 1968-69; v.p., co-founder Dallas KC Credit Union, 1966-69; grand knight, trustee Dallas Council 799 KC, 1964-69; dist. exemplar 4th degree KC, 1968—; pres., dir. Dallas County Small Bus. Devel. Center, 1965-66; v.p. Dallas County Hist. Survey Com., 1966; pres. Dallas Mil. Govt. Assn., 1962-63; pres. men's club St. Patrick's Parish Roman Catholic Ch., 1963, prin. jr. high sch. Christian devel. program, 1970, chmn. scout troop com., 1976-78, chmn. fin. com., 1976-77, 84-86, mem. bldg. com., 1978-87, chmn. bd. consultors, 1978-81; bd. dirs. Dallas County War on Poverty, 1965-66. Served to 1st lt. AUS, 1958-60; capt. Res. ret. Recipient Man of Yr. award Dallas Assn. KC, 1969-70. Mem. ABA, Tex. Bar Assn., Dallas Bar Assn. (chmn. bankruptcy and comml. law sect. 1977-78, lectr. 1985-86), Phi Delta Phi (magister 1960-61), Tau Delta Sigma (pres. 1956). Clubs: Seroco-Empire Toastmasters (past pres.), Dallas Optimist (past v.p., President's award 1968), 2001, Park Cities, Internat. Order Alhambra (dist. exemplar 1980-85). Bankruptcy, General corporate, General practice. Home: 9751 Larchcrest St Dallas TX 75238 Office: Suite 1201 Sherry Lane National Bank Bldg Dallas TX 75225

BURKETT, DAVID INGRAM, lawyer; b. Orange, Tex., July 1, 1948; s. Jack Edward Burkett and LaVern (Ingram) Schmidt; m. Sharon Roberts, Mar. 27, 1970; children: Matthew Howard, Ashley Colleen. BA, No. La. U., 1971; JD, La. State U., 1974. Bar: La. 1975. Ptnr. Dimos, Brown, Erskine, Burkett & Smith, Monroe, La., 1975—; instr. in real estate. Bd. dirs. St. Francis Med. Ctr. Instl. Rev. Bd.; bd. dirs., mem. exec. com. Ronald McDonald House of N.E. La.; bd. dirs. Monroe YWCA; sec. La. Lions Eye Found. Inc., 1986-87; past bd. dirs. La. Lions League for Crippled Children; mem. Monroe Flood Plain Mgmt. Bd., N.E. La. Cen. Corridor Com.; past pres. North La. Mental Health Assn., N.E. La. Arthritis Found.; minister of edn. Forsythe Ave Ch. of Christ. Recipient Outstanding Community Service award Monroe Jaycees, 1984, 100% Dist. Gov.'s award Lions Internat. Assn. Lions Clubs, 1984. Mem. La. State Bar Assn., La. Trial Lawyers Assn., 4th Dist. Bar Assn., Monroe C. of C. (past bd. dirs.), Sigma Tau Gamma (past pres.), Beta Nu. Democrat. Mem. Ch. of Christ. Club: Downtown Lions (bd. dirs.). Real property, Probate, General corporate. Home: 2413 Emerson Monroe LA 71201 Office: Dimos Brown Erskine et al 1216 Stubbs Ave Monroe LA 71207

BURKETT, JOE WYLIE, lawyer, corporate executive; b. Dallas, Aug. 24, 1945; s. Joe Wylie and Marguerite (Barnes) B.; B.A., Vanderbilt U., 1967; J.D., U. Tex., 1971. Bar: Tex. 1971, D.C. 1977. Legis. aide Tex. Ho. of Reps., 1971; briefing atty. Tex. Ct. Criminal Appeals, 1971-72; law clk. U.S. Dist. Ct. (no. dist.) Tex., 1972-74; trial atty. tax div. U.S. Dept. Justice, 1974-77; with Goins & Underkofler, Dallas, 1977-80; pres., chief exec. officer JJS Inc. and Cord Enterprises, Texarkana (Ark.) and Dallas, 1980—; sole practice, Dallas, 1980—. Ford Found. grantee 1970. Mem. ABA, D.C. Bar Assn., Tex. Bar Assn., Assn. Trial Lawyers Am., Tex. Trial Lawyers Assn., Ark. Wholesale Beer Distributers Assn. (chmn. bd. dirs. 1986—), Nat. Beer Wholesalers Assn. (bd. dirs. 1982—, mem. mgmt. com. 1986—, officer, 1987—), Phi Delta Phi. Federal civil litigation, State civil litigation. Home: 4525 Livingston Dallas TX 75205

BURKEY, LEE MELVILLE, lawyer; b. Beach, N.D., Mar. 21, 1914; s. Levi Melville and Mina Lou (Horner) B.; m. Lorraine Lillian Burghardt, June 11, 1938; 1 child, Lee Melville, III. B.A., U. Ill., 1936, M.A., 1938; J.D. with honor, John Marshall Law Sch., 1943. Bar: Ill., 1944, U.S. Dist. Ct., 1947, U.S. Ct. Appeals, 1954, U.S. Supreme Ct.; 1983; cert. secondary tchr., Ill. Tchr. Princeton Twp. Sch., Princeton, Ill., 1937-38; tchr. Thornton Twp. High Sch., Harvey, Ill., 1938-43; atty. Office of Solicitor, U.S. Dept. Labor, Chgo., 1944-51; ptnr. Asher, Gubbins & Segall and predecessor firms, Chgo., 1951—. Contbr. numerous articles on lie detector evidence. Trustee, Village of La Grange, Ill., 1962-68, mayor, 1968-73, village atty., 1973-87; commr., pres. Northeastern Ill. Planning Commn., Chgo., 1969-73; mem. bd. dirs. United Ch. Christ, Bd. of Homeland Ministries, N.Y.C., 1981—. Served to 2d lt. Ill. N.G., 1932. Recipient Disting. Alumnus award John Marshall Law Sch., 1973; Good Citizenship medal S.A.R., 1973, Patriot medal, 1977; meritorious Service award Am. legion Post 1941, 1974. Mem. Chgo. Bar Assn. (substaining mem.), Ill. State Bar Assn., ABA (mem. council, sect. labor and employment law 1982—), SAR (state pres. 1977). Democrat. Mem. United Ch. of Christ. Club: La Grange Country Lodge: Masons, Order of John Marshall. Labor, Local government. Office: Asher Pavalon Gittler and Greenfield Ltd 2 North La Salle St Chicago IL 60602

BURLESON, KAREN TRIPP, lawyer; b. Rocky Mount, N.C., Sept. 2, 1955; d. Bryant and Katherine Rebecca (Watkins) Tripp; m. Robert Mark Burleson, June 25, 1977. B.A., U. N.C., 1976; J.D., U. Ala., 1981. Bar: Tex. 1981, U.S. Dist. Ct. (so. dist.) Tex. 1982, U.S. Ct. Appeals (fed. cir.) 1983. Law clerk Tucker, Gray & Espy, Tuscaloosa, Ala., 1978-81, to presiding justice Ala. Supreme Ct., Montgomery, summer 1980; atty. Exxon Prodn. Research Co., Houston, 1981-86, coordinator tech. transfer, 1986—. Contbr. articles to profl. jours. Recipient Am. Jurisprudence award U. Ala., 1980, Dean's award, 1981. Mem. Houston Bar Assn. (internat. transfer tech. com. 1983-84), Houston Intellectual Property Lawyers Assn. (outstanding inventor com. 1982-84, chmn. student edn. com. 1986), Tex. Bar Assn. (antitrust law com. 1984-85), ABA, Am. Intellectual Property Lawyers Assn., Phi Alpha Delta (clerk 1980). Republican. Methodist. Patent, Private international, Contracts and general corporate consulting. Office: Exxon Prodn Research Co PO Box 2189 Houston TX 77252-2189

BURLESON, LYNN PIERCE, judge, legal educator, lawyer; b. Albemarle, N.C., July 19, 1948; s. Ira Pierce and Hazel (Austin) B.; m. Bunny Joyce Hinkle, June 6, 1978; 1 child, Jennifer Hinkle. BA, U. N.C., 1970, MPA, 1974; JD, Wake Forest U., 1980. Bar: N.C. 1980. Asst. personnel dir. City of Charlotte, N.C., 1971-75; dir. personnel adv. service to govt. State of N.C., Raleigh, 1975-77; assoc. Yokley & Teeter, Winston-Salem, N.C., 1980-81; asst. dist. atty. State of N.C., Winston-Salem, 1981-84, dist. ct. judge, 1984-87; assoc. Petree, Stockton & Robinson, Winston-Salem, 1987—; adj. prof. law Wake Forest U., Winston-Salem, N.C.; vis. lectr. bus. law High Point (N.C.) Coll. Mem. Winston-Salem Human Relations Commn., Winston-Salem Fair Housing Com., civil module adv. com. Adminstrv. Office of Cts., Ct. Information System; vol. ARC; trustee Knollwood Bapt. Ch.; chairperson rev. and comment com. Forsyth County Juvenile Justice Council; bd. dirs. Mental Health Assn. of Forsyth County, v.p. Neighborhood Justice Ctr., N.C. State Spl. Olympics, Theater in the Park, YMCA. Mem. ABA, N.C. Bar Assn., Forsyth County Bar Assn., Criminal Def. Trial Lawyers Assn. Forsyth County Young Lawyers Assn., Juvenile Justice Cert., Adminstrv. Office of Cts., Nat. Council Juvenile and Family Ct. Judges, N.C. Acad. Trial Lawyers, N.C. Coll. of Adv., N.C. Dist. Attys. Assn. Democrat. Family and matrimonial, Juvenile, Criminal. Home: 2451 Greenbrier Rd Winston-Salem NC 27104 Office: Dist Ct PO Box 1411 Winston-Salem NC 27102

BURLESON, WILLIAM ANDERSON, lawyer; b. Bakersville, N.C., Apr. 25, 1929; student Mars Hill Jr. Coll., Western Carolina U., Denver U.; J.D., U. N.C., 1960; postdoctoral, Am. U. Bar: D.C. 1960, U.S. Dist. Ct., D.C. Ct. Appeals, U.S. Ct. Appeals (D.C. cir.), U.S. Supreme Ct. Dep. clk. presiding justice D.C. Mcpl. Ct., 1956-57, law clk., 1958-60; Congressional aide, Washington, 1956; commr. of human rights, Washington, 1971-74; sole practice, Washington, 1960—; 1st dir. Legal Aid Agy. D.C. Superior Ct., 1961. Founder, bd. dirs. Mcpl. Ct. Pub. Defender's Office, 1961; mem. Human Rights Commn., Washington, 1971-74. Served with USAF, 1950-54. Recipient Hon. Lifetime Membership Nat. Found. Consumer Credit, Letter of Superior Performance by bd. judges of mcpl. cts., 1961; certificate of appreciation D.C. Govt. Mem. D.C. Bar Assn., ABA, Superior Ct. Trial Lawyers Assn. of D.C., Supreme Ct. Hist. Soc., Superior Ct. house Com., Animal Rights Soc. (life mem.). Author: "If You Are Unable to Get Out of Jail on Bond, The Court Will Appoint a Lawyer to Represent You", 1961; Laying It On The Line, 1975; White Paper of a Human Rights Commissioner, 1974, What is an Indigent?, What is Legal Prime?; Judicial Regulation of Collection Agencies in the District of Columbia and Maryland, 1974, 77. Legal services in aid. Office: 1000 Pennsylvania Ave SE Washington DC 20003

BURLINGAME, JAMES MONTGOMERY, lawyer; b. Great Falls, Mont., Dec. 25, 1926; s. James Montgomery Jr. and Eloise (Corbin) B.; m. Joella Claire Blache; children: James Montgomery IV, Ann Blache, John Marshall. BA, Tulane U., 1949, JD, 1950. Bar: La. 1950, U.S. Dist. Ct. (ea. dist.) La. 1953, U.S. Dist. Ct. (we. dist.) La. 1959, U.S. Ct. Appeals (5th cir.) 1964, U.S. Ct. Appeals (11th cir.) 1981, U.S. Supreme Ct. 1961. Assoc. Jones, Walker, Waechter, Poitevent, Carrere & Denegre, New Orleans, 1953-56, ptnr., 1956-72, sr. ptnr., 1972-85; sr. ptnr. Burlingame & Burlingame, 1985—. Mem. Tulane Energy Adv. Bd., 1980—; trustee St. Martin's Protestant Episcopal Sch., 1968—, pres., 1976-79. Served to lt. (j.g.) USMS, 1944-46, capt. U.S. Army, 1950-52. Mem. ABA, Fed. Bar Assn., La. Bar Assn., Internat. Bar Assn., Orleans Parish Bar Assn., Interam. Bar Assn., Am. Judicature Soc. Republican. Episcopalian. Clubs: Pickwick, Stratford, New Orleans Country, Petroleum, Plimsoll. FERC practice, Nuclear power, Oil and gas leasing. Home: 433 Iona St Metairie LA 70005 Office: Burlingame & Burlingame 900 Royal St New Orleans LA 70116

BURLINGAME, JOHN HUNTER, lawyer; b. Milw., Apr. 27, 1933; s. Leroy James and Mary Janet (Burchard) B.; m. Carolyn Elizabeth Beachley, Aug. 27, 1960 (div. Feb. 1981); children: Carolyn, Janet, Amy, Alexander; m. Dorcas Hodges, June 5, 1982. BS, U. Wis., 1960, LLB, 1963. Bar: Ohio 1863. From assoc. to ptnr. Baker & Hostetler, Cleve., 1963—. Served to lt. USN, 1955-59. Mem. ABA, Cleve. Bar Assn. Republican. Presbyterian. Clubs: Pepper Pike, Union (Cleve.); Metropolitan (Washington). Avocations: skiing, outdoor life. General corporate, Securities, Administrative and regulatory. Office: Baker & Hostetler 3200 Nat City Ctr Cleveland OH 44114

BURMAN, DAVID JOHN, lawyer; b. Burlington, Iowa, Apr. 29, 1952; s. Keith Roland and Janet Black (Thomason) B.; m. DeeAnn Schaumberg, Aug. 10, 1974; children: Kendall, Blaire. BA, U. Wyo., 1974; JD, Georgetown U., 1977. Bar: Va. 1977, D.C. 1979, U.S. Ct. Appeals (D.C. cir.) 1979, Wash. 1980, U.S. Dist. Ct. (we. dist.) Wash. 1980, U.S. Ct. Appeals (9th cir.) 1980, U.S. Dist. Ct. (ea. dist.) Wash. 1982, U.S. Ct. Appeals (fed. cir.) 1982, U.S. Supreme Ct. 1982, U.S. Ct. Appeals (8th cir.) 1985. Law clk. to presiding judge U.S. Ct. Appeals (D.C. cir.), Washington, 1977-78; law clk. to assoc. justice Byron R. White U.S. Supreme Ct., Washington, 1978-79; ptnr. Perkins Coie, Seattle, 1979—. Editor Georgetown U. Law Jour., 1976-77. Mem. legal, freedom of expression, privacy and tech. coms. ACLU, Wash., 1979—, exec. bd. Today's Constn. and You Project, Seattle, 1983-85; sec., counsel Pub. Initiatives in Pvt. Edn. Mem. ABA (Wash. chmn. commn. on pub. understanding about the law, freedom of press/Zenger project 1985-85, litigation, antitrust, criminal law, communications law sects.), Wash. State Bar Assn. (exec. bd. antitrust sect.), Seattle-King County Bar Assn., N.W. Communications Law Group, Wash. Council Sch. Attys. Democrat. Federal civil litigation, Antitrust, General practice. Office: Perkins Coie 1900 Washington Blvd Seattle WA 98101

BURNAMAN, PHILLIP R., corporation executive, lawyer; A.B., Harvard U., 1956; LL.B., U. Pa., 1962. Counsel, Scott Paper Co., 1962-69; asst. sec., corp. counsel Brockway, Inc. (Pa.), 1970-73, sec., corp. counsel, 1973-79, sec., gen. counsel, 1979-81, v.p., sec., gen. counsel, 1981-84, sr. v.p., sec., gen. counsel, 1984—. Served to 1st lt. USMC, 1956-59. General corporate. Office: Brockway Inc 255 Water St Box 44058 Jacksonville FL 32202

BURNBAUM, MICHAEL WILLIAM, lawyer; b. Boston, Sept. 19, 1949; s. Jack and Remar Burnbaum. Student, U. Denver, 1967-69; BA in Internat. Studies, U. S.C., 1971; JD, Suffolk U., 1976. Bar: Mass. 1977, U.S. Dist. Ct. Mass. 1977, Fla. 1981, U.S. Ct. Appeals (5th and 11th cir.) 1981, U.S. Dist. Ct. (so. dist.) Fla. 1984, U.S. Ct. Appeals (4th cir.) 1985. House counsel Bradford Novelty Co. Inc., Boston, 1976-79; asst. dist. atty. Norfolk County, Mass., 1979-81; asst. atty. U.S. Dept. Justice, Miami, Fla., 1981-85; ptnr. Bronis & Portela P.A., Miami, 1985—. Creator TV program Eye on the Law, 1976. Pres. Key Colony Phase III Condominium Assn., Miami, 1983-85; chmn. com. to elect Shawn M. Harvey to Boston City Council, 1976. Mem. ABA, Fla. Bar Assn., Fed. Bar Assn., Nat. Assn. Criminal Def. Lawyers. Republican. Lodge: Rotary. Avocations: tennis, travel. Criminal, Federal civil litigation, State civil litigation. Home: 151 Crandon Blvd Key Biscayne FL 33149 Office: Bronis & Portela PA 1395 Coral Way 3d Floor Miami FL 33145

BURNETT, (CHARLES) DAVID, circuit court judge; b. Blytheville, Ark., Aug. 18, 1941; s. John David and Marjorie Flo (Wood) B.; m. Sonja Doris Harvey, Oct. 10, 1969; children: Jonathan David, Amanda Karen. BA, U. Ark., 1963, JD, 1966. Bar: Ark. 1966, U.S. Dist. Ct. (ea. dist.) Ark. 1966, U.S. Supreme Ct. 1970. Ptnr. Swift, Alexander & Burnett, Osceola, Ark., 1969-74; pros. atty. 2d Cir., State of Ark., Osceola, 1974-82, cir. ct. judge, 1982—. Active Osceola Boys Club, Northeast Ark. Area council Boy Scouts Am.; mem. Ark. Judical Council; sec., atty. Osceola Riverport Authority; mem. Miss. River Pkwy. Commn., 1972-77; mem. Dem. Cen. Com., Ark.; bd. dirs. 1st Christian Ch.; bd. dirs., bd. govs. Presbyn. Christian Day Sch.; mem. Criminal Detention Facilities Study Commn., Gov.'s Task Force on DWI, Gov.'s Task Force on Child Abuse. Served to capt. U.S. Army; Vietnam. Decorated Bronze Star, Army Commendation award, Vietnam Campaign Ribbon with 4 stars, Vietnamese Govt. Medal of Honor 1st class. Mem. ABA, Ark. Bar Assn., Northeast Ark. Bar Assn., Osceola Bar Assn. (past pres., sec.-treas.), Assn. Trial Lawyers Am., Ark. Pros. Attys. Assn. (sec. 1975, bd. dirs. 1976—, v.p. 1980-81, pres. 1981-82), Nat. Dist. Attys. Assn., Christian Legal Soc., Am. Legion, Osceola C. of C., Jr. C. of C., VFW, Gidions Soc., Phi Alpha Delta. Lodge: Kiwanis. Home: 618 Semmes St Osceola AR 72370 Office: PO Box 704 Suite 4 Professional Bldg Osceola AR 72370

BURNETT, DONALD LEE, JR., judge; b. Pocatello, Idaho, Oct. 1, 1946; s. Donald Lee and Susy Doris (McDermott) B.; m. Karen Trujillo, Dec. 29, 1969; children: Jason, David. BA magna cum laude, Harvard U., 1968; JD, U. Chgo., 1971. Bar: Idaho 1972, U.S. Dist. Ct. Idaho 1972. Law clk. to chief justice Idaho Supreme Ct., Boise, 1971-72; asst. atty. gen. State of Idaho, Pocatello, 1972-75; ptnr. Burnett, Woodland & Hawkes, Pocatello, 1975-77, Burnett & Winmill, Pocatello, 1977-82; judge Idaho Ct. Appeals, Boise, 1982—; adj. prof. U. Idaho Coll. Law, 1987—. Editor: Idaho Appellate Handbook, 1985. Served to capt. JAGC, USAR, 1969—. Mem. ABA (appellate judges conf. 1982—, nat. editor periodical Appellate Judges Conf. News, 1986—), Am. Judicature Soc., Idaho State Bar and Law Found. (pres., commr., 1979-82, chmn. profl. standards com. 1981-82, chmn. Idaho appellate practice com. 1983—). Avocations: hunting, skiing, camping. Judicial administration, Military. Office: Idaho Ct Appeals 537 W Bannock St Boise ID 83720

BURNETTE, GUY ELLINGTON, JR., lawyer; b. Orlando, Fla., May 26, 1952; s. Guy E. Sr. and Celestina (McKay) B.; m. Susan Vass, Mar. 25, 1975; 1 child, George Robert. Student, U. South, 1970-71; BA, Vanderbilt U., 1974; JD, Fla. State U., 1977. Bar: Fla. 1977, U.S. Dist. Ct. (no., mid. and so. dists.) Fla. 1981, U.S. Ct. Appeals (11th cir.) 1981, U.S. Ct. Appeals (5th cir.), 1985. Asst. states atty. State of Fla., Tallahassee, 1977-80, legal counsel div. of state fire marshall, 1980-81; ptnr. Butler & Burnette, Tampa, Fla., 1981—; legal advisor Fla. Arson Control Council, Tallahassee, 1980-81; instr. Lively Law Enforcement Ctr., Tallahassee, 1978-81, Fla. Arson Seminar, Orlando, 1980—; mem. Fla. Adv. Com. on Arson Prevention. Author: Florida Arson Prosecution, 1980. Mem. Def. Research Inst., Fla.

Def. Lawyers Assn., Internat. Assn. Arson Investigators, ABA (torts and ins. practice sect.). Democrat. Roman Catholic. Club: University (Tampa), Yacht. Lodge: Ye Mystic Krewe of Gasparilla. Avocations: golf, fishing. Insurance, Personal injury, Construction. Home: 4615 Sylvan Ramble Tampa FL 33609 Office: Butler & Burnette Suite 1100 6200 Courtney Campbell Causeway Bayport Plaza Tampa FL 33607

BURNETTE, RALPH EDWIN, JR., lawyer; b. Lynchburg, Va., Sept. 25, 1953; s. Ralph Edwin and Carlease (Samuels) B.; m. Patricia Lee Dougan, June 1, 1984. BA, Coll. William & Mary, 1975, JD, 1978. Bar: Va. 1978, U.S. Dist. Ct. (we. dist.) Va., U.S. Ct. Appeals (4th cir.). Assoc. Edmunds & Williams, Lynchburg, 1978-83, ptnr., 1983—. Deacon Peakland Bapt. Ch., Lynchburg, 1983-86; pres. Kaleidoscope Festival, Lynchburg, 1985; bd. dirs. Va. Bapt. Hosp., Lynchburg, 1983—. Mem. Va. Bar Assn., Va. State Bar Assn. (pres. young lawyers conf. 1985—, chmn. com. on alternative dispute resolution 1985—, mem. BAR council 1986—, standing com. on regal ethics 1986—) Lynchburg Bar Assn., Va. Trial Lawyers Assn., Va. Assn. Def. Attys., Def. Research Inst. Avocations: golf, jazz. Federal civil litigation, State civil litigation, Insurance. Home: Rt 4 Box 325-B Lynchburg VA 24503 Office: Edmunds & Williams 800 Main St Suite 400 Lynchburg VA 24505

BURNEY, CECIL EDWARD, lawyer; b. Riesel, Tex., Oct. 6, 1914; s. Frank Edward and Allye Stacye (Goodman) B.; m. Kara Hunsucker, Jan. 15, 1949 (dec. Feb. 1973); children: Cecil Edward (dec.), Kara Lisa, Frank Burleson. B.A., U. Tex., 1936, J.D., 1937; LL.D., U. Corpus Christi, 1975. Bar: Tex. 1938. Since practiced in Corpus Christi; ptnr. Wood & Burney and predecessors, 1941—; pres. Merc. Nat. Bank, 1955-56; past chmn. bd. 1st Nat. Bank, Ingleside; formerly chmn. bd. First City Bank, Aransas Pass; former dir. Kingsville Bank & Trust, Nueces Nat. Bank, Corpus Christi, First City Bank of Aransas Pass; sec. Corpus Christi Broadcasting Co., K-SIX TV Inc.; Spl. asst. atty. gen., Tex., 1956. Mem. exec. bd. Gulf Coast council Boy Scouts Am., 1948-77; chmn. Gov.'s Traffic Safety Com., 1956; past chmn. Corpus Christi Housing Authority, Nueces County Red Cross; past pres. Jr. C. of C., Corpus Christi C. of C. Served to lt. comdr. USNR, 1942-45. Recipient St. Thomas More award St. Mary's U., 1964; Arthur Von Briesen award Nat. Legal Aid and Defender Assn., 1963, Humanitarian award NCCJ, 1981, Outstanding Civic Salesman of Yr. award 1987; named Outstanding Alumnus Tex. A&I U., 1978, Jaycees Hall of Fame, 1983. Fellow Am. Bar Found.; mem. State Bar Tex. (pres. 1951-52), ABA (bd. govs. 1965-68), Am. Judicature Soc. (pres. 1960-62), Nat. Legal Aid Assn. (dir. 1955-65), Nat. Conf. Bar Presidents (chmn. 1955-56), Tex. Hist. Found. (pres. 1970-74), Tex. Hist. Commn. (chmn. 1977-81). Presbyn. Clubs: Rotarian. (Corpus Christi), Town (Corpus Christi); Nueces. Banking, General corporate, Real property. Home: 4500 Ocean Dr Corpus Christi TX 78412 Office: 1700 First City Tower II Corpus Christi TX 78403

BURNEY, FRANK BURLESON, lawyer; b. Corpus Christi, Tex., Dec. 16, 1954; s. Cecil Edward and Kara Belle (Hunsucker) B.; m. Laura Hedges, May 24, 1980; 1 child, Christopher Holland. AB, Duke U., 1976; JD, St. Mary's Sch. Law, 1979. Bar: Tex. 1979, U.S. Dist. Ct. (we. and so. dists.) Tex. 1981, U.S. Ct. Appeals (5th cir.) 1981. Briefing atty. Tex. Ct. Appeals (13th cir.), Corpus Christi, 1979-81; clk. of court U.S. Ct. Appeals (13th cir.), Corpus Christi, 1981; ptnr. Martin, Shannon & Drought, Inc., San Antonio, 1981—, also bd. dirs.; Bd. dirs. Encore, Inc., 1983—, v.p. 1984-85, exec. com. 1986—; outside bd. dirs. Ray West Warehouse, Inc., Corpus Christi Broadcasting Co., Inc.. Vice chmn. bd. Coastal Bend chpt. ARC, 1979-81; bd. dirs. San Antonio chpt. ARC 1981—, Young Arts Patrons-San Antonio Mus. Assn., 1981—, Southwest Craft Ctr, 1982—, v.p. 1983-84; mem. Loop 410 Assn., 1983—, v.p. 1985, pres. 1986; , chmn.-elect San Antonio Dem. Forum, 1985—; active Leadership San Antonio, 1983—. Fellow San Antonio Bar Found.; mem. ABA (young lawyers div. Nat. Law Week com., bd. dirs. 1985, exec. com. 1986), Tex. Bar Assn., San Antonio Bar Assn. (Bar Found. com. 1984-85, co-chmn. Law Day com. 1986, pub. relations com. 1984-85), San Antonio Young Lawyers Assn. (pres. elect 1985-86, pres. 1986—, chmn. Law Day com. 1984-85, bd. dirs. 1983-84), So. Tex. C. of C. (bd. dirs. 1987—), Tex. Assn. Bank Counsel, Mortgage Bankers Assn., Coll. Mortgage Attys., Tex. Savs. and Loan League, U.S. Savs. and Loan League, Greater San Antonio C. of C. Methodist. Banking, Real property. Home: 225 W Granercy San Antonio TX 78212 Office: Martin Shannon & Drought Inc 300 Convent #2500 San Antonio TX 78205

BURNHAM, CARL VON HOFFMANN, JR., lawyer; b. Berkeley, Calif., July 13, 1939; s. Carl Sr. and Margaret (Barber) B.; m. Patricia Brewer, Sept. 2, 1961; children: Carl III, Barbara. BS, U. Oreg., 1961, LLB, 1964. Bar: Oreg. 1984. Sr. ptnr. Yturri, Rose, Burnham, Ebert & Bentz, Ontario, Oreg., 1964—. Counsel on ct. procedure U. Oreg. Law Sch., 1979-83; mem. bd. of visitors, 1980-85. Fellow Am. Coll. Trial Lawyers; mem. Oreg. Bar Assn. (procedure and practice com. 1974-77, bd. of govs. 1974-78, treas. 1978, fed. practice and procedure com. 1984-85), Malheur County Bar Assn., Oreg. Assn. Def. Counsel, Am. Bd. Trial Advs., Phi Delta Phi. Republican. Lodge: Elks. Insurance, Personal injury, Federal civil litigation. Office: Yturri Rose Burnham Ebert & Bentz 89 SW 3d Ave Ontario OR 97914

BURNIM, IRA ABRAHAM, lawyer; b. Bloomington, Ind., May 21, 1951; s. Kalman Aaron and Verna Ruth (Lesser) B.; m. Elizabeth J. Samuels, Apr. 3, 1982; children: Jacob Samuels, Michael Samuels. AB, Harvard U., 1973, JD, 1977. Bar: Ill. 1978, Ala. 1980. Law clk. to presiding justice Ala. State Ct., Montgomery, 1977-78; atty. Legal Assistance Found., Chgo., 1978-79; atty. Southern Poverty Law Ctr., Montgomery, 1979-85, sr. atty., 1985-86; legal dir. Children's Def. Fund, Washington, 1986—. Bd. dirs. ACLU, Montgomery, 1982—, pres. 1985—. Mem. Ala. Bar Assn. (vice chmn. task force on legal services to the poor 1983—). Civil rights, Federal civil litigation, State civil litigation. Office: Children's Def Fund 122 C St NW Washington DC 20001

BURNISON, BOYD EDWARD, lawyer; b. Arnolds Park, Iowa, Dec. 12, 1934; s. Boyd William and Lucile (Harnden) B.; m. Mari Amaral; children—Erica Lafore, Alison Katherine. B.S., Iowa State U., 1957; J.D., U. Calif.-Berkeley, 1961. Bar: Calif. 1962, U.S. Supreme Ct. 1971, U.S. Dist. Ct. (no. dist.) Calif. 1962, U.S. Dist. Ct. (ea. dist.) Calif. 1970, U.S. Ct. Appeals (9th cir.) 1962. Dep. country counsel Yolo County, Calif., 1962-65; counsel Davis and Woodland (Calif.) Unified Sch. Dists., 1962-65; assoc. Steel & Arostegui, Marysville, Calif., 1965-66, St. Sure, Moore & Hoyt, Oakland, 1966-70; ptnr. St. Sure, Moore, Hoyt & Sizoo, Oakland and San Francisco, 1970-75; v.p., dir. Crosby, Heafey, Roach & May, P.C., Oakland, 1975—; mem. labor and employment law sect. State Bar Calif., 1982—, spl. labor counsel, 1981-84. Adviser Berkeley YMCA, 1971—, Yolo County YMCA, 1962-65; bd. dirs. Easter Seal Soc. Crippled Children and Adults of Alameda County, Calif., 1972-75, Yolo County YMCA, 1965, Moot Ct. Bd., U. Calif., 1960-61; trustee, sec., legal counsel Easter Seal Found., Alameda County, 1974-79, hon. trustee, 1979—. Fellow ABA Found.; mem. ABA (labor relations and employment law sect.; equal employment law con. 1972—), Alameda County Bar Assn. (chmn. memberships and directory com. 1973-74, 80, chmn. law office econs. com. 1975-77, assn. dir. 1981-85, pres.-elect, 1983, pres., 1984, vice chmn. bench bar liaison com. 1983, chmn. 1984, Disting. Service award 1987), Yolo County Bar Assn. (sec. 1965), Yuba Sutter Bar Assn., Bar Assn. San Francisco (labor law sect.), Sproul Assoc. Boalt Hall Law Sch. U. Calif. Berkeley, Iowa State Alumni Assn., Order Knoll, Pi Kappa Alpha, Phi Delta Phi. Democrat. Club: Round Hill Country. Lodge: Rotary. Home: 2500 Caballo Ranchero Dr PO Box 743 Diablo CA 94528 Office: Crosby Heafey Roach and May 2300 Lake Merritt Plaza Bldg 1999 Harrison St Oakland CA 94612

BURNS, ARNOLD IRWIN, deputy attorney general U.S.; b. N.Y.C., Apr. 14, 1930; s. Herman Leon and Rose (Lauterstein) B.; m. Felice Bernstein, June 17, 1951; children: Linda Susan, Douglas Todd. A.B., Union Coll., Schenectady, 1950; LL.B., Cornell U., 1953; postgrad., Parker Sch. Internat. Law, 1960; JD, Hofstra U., 1986. Bar: N.Y. 1953, D.C. 1977. Ptnr. Burns Summit Rovins & Feldesman (and predecessors), N.Y.C., 1960-86; from dep. to assoc. atty. gen. U.S. Govt., Washington, 1986—; dep. atty. gen. U.S. Dept. Justice, Washington, 1986—; former dir., vice chmn. bd. Cook United, Inc.; counsel N.Y. State Joint Legis. Com. on Ethics, 1964. Note editor: Cornell Law Quar, 1952-53. Life trustee Union Coll., Schenectady; chmn., bd. dirs. Freedoms Found., Valley Forge, Pa.; nat. bd. dirs., v.p. Boys Clubs Am.; mem. Council Governing Bds.; mem. adv. council Cornell U. Law Sch., Ithaca, N.Y.; former nat. chmn. Cornell Law Sch. Fund; mem. adv. council Hofstra Sch. Law. Served to capt. AUS, 1953-57. Mem. Am., Fed., N.Y. State bar assns., Fed. Bar Council, Assn. Bar City N.Y., Cornell Law Assn., Am. Arbitration Assn. (nat. panel arbitrators), Order of Coif, Phi Kappa Phi, Kappa Nu, Alpha Phi Omega. Republican. Jewish. Clubs: Westhampton Country; Army and Navy (Washington). General practice, Public international, General corporate. Home: 2700 Virginia Ave NW Washington DC 20037 Office: US Justice Dept 10th and Constitution Ave NW Room 4109 Washington DC 20530 Home: 338 Dune Rd Westhampton Beach NY 11978 Other: 25 Sutton Pl S New York NY 10022

BURNS, BRUCE WILLIAM, lawyer; b. San Francisco, May 6, 1950; s. Calvin Paul and Beverly Dorothy (Coll) B.; m. Joanne Elizabeth Cop, Aug. 24, 1969; children: Christopher, Jeffrey, Jessica. BA in History, San Jose State U., 1976; JD, U. Santa Clara, 1979. Bar: Calif. 1981, U.S. Dist. Ct. (no. dist.) Calif. 1981. Assoc. Campbell, Warburton, et al, San Jose, Calif., 1981-87; sole practice San Jose, 1987—. Editor case notes and comments Santa Clara Law Rev. Active in numerous Vietnamese and SE Asian civic and support orgns; commr. Santa Clara Housing Authority, San Jose. Served as sgt. USAF, 1968-72, Vietnam. Mem. ABA, Calif. Bar Assn., Santa Clara County Bar Assn., Am. Trial Lawyers Assn., Calif. Trial lawyers Assn. Democrat. Roman Catholic. Avocations: skiing, model railroading, bicycling. Contracts commercial, State civil litigation, Personal injury. Home: 1743 Fabian Dr San Jose CA 95125 Office: 95 S Market St #300 San Jose CA 95113

BURNS, BYRON BERNARD, JR., lawyer; b. Greenwood, S.C., June 28, 1948; s. Byron Bernard and Dora (Curry) B.; m. Patsy Love, Dec. 19, 1970; children: Byron, Ann. BA, Furman U., 1970; JD, Duke U., 1973. Bar: N.C. 1973. Assoc. Smith, Helms, Mulliss & Moore, Charlotte, N.C., 1973-78, ptnr., 1978—; bd. dirs. Metrolina Entrepreneurial Council, Charlotte. Mem. Sick Child Care Mayor's Com., Charlotte, 1985; bd. dirs. United Way Allocations and Rev. Bd., Charlotte, 1986. Served capt. U.S. Army, 1970-78. Mem. ABA, N.C. Bar Assn. Democrat. Presbyterian. Clubs: Charlotte Country, Charlotte City. Avocations: gardening, golf, walking. General corporate, Venture capital. Home: 1605 Myers Park Dr Charlotte NC 28207 Office: Smith Helms Mulliss & Moore 227 N Tryon St Charlotte NC 28202

BURNS, DONALD ANDREW, lawyer; b. Jan. 2, 1941; m. Katherine I. Snider, June 13, 1970. BS, U.S. Mil. Acad., 1962; JD, Harvard U., 1972. Bar: Ohio, U.S. Dist. Ct. (no. dist.) Ohio, U.S. Ct. Appeals (6th cir.). Commd. 2d lt. U.S. Army, 1962, advances through grades to maj., res., 1969; assoc. Baker & Hostetler, Cleve., 1972-80, ptnr., 1981—. Mem. ABA, Ohio Bar Assn., Cleve. Bar Assn. Bankruptcy, Federal civil litigation, State civil litigation. Home: 16131 Cleviden Rd East Cleveland OH 44112 Office: Baker & Hostetler 3200 Nat City Ctr Cleveland OH 44114

BURNS, DOUGLAS FOSTER, lawyer, mining company executive; b. Indpls., Mar. 9, 1940; s. Douglas Sterling and Nellie May (Foster) B.; m. Jo Carolyn Charles Anzalone, June 7, 1965 (div. Jan. 1979); children: Allan Douglas, Evan Clifford, Laura Alayne. AB, Wabash Coll., 1961; diplome, U. Strasborg, France, 1962; JD, Harvard U., 1965. Bar: Ind. 1965, U.S. Dist. Ct. (so. dist.) Ind. 1965, Pa. 1979. Assoc. Barnes, Hickam, Pantzer & Boyd, Indpls., 1965-70; atty. U.S. Dept. of State, Washington, 1970-72, dep. asst. legal adviser, 1970-72; internat. atty. Westinghouse Electric Corp., Pitts., 1974-76; v.p., gen. counsel Halco Mining Inc., Pitts., 1976—; Bd. dirs. Boke Trading, Inc., Pitts.; adminstr. Boke Service Co., S.A., Brussels, Belgium, 1977—. Trustee Town of Fishers, Ind., 1967-70. Mem. ABA, Ind. Bar Assn., Pa. Bar Assn., Am. Corp. Counsel Assn. Republican. Clubs: Allegheny, City (Pitts.). Avocations: map collecting, sailing. Private international, General corporate. Home: 1013 Thornberry Dr Pittsburgh PA 15237 Office: Halco Mining Inc 900 Two Allegheny Ctr Pittsburgh PA 15212

BURNS, ELLEN BREE, judge; b. New Haven, Conn., Dec. 13, 1923; d. Vincent Thomas and Mildred Bridget (Bannon) Bree; m. Joseph Patrick Burns, Oct. 8, 1955 (dec.); children: Mary Ellen, Joseph Bree, Kevin James. BA, Albertus Magnus Coll., 1944, LLD (hon.), 1974; LLB, Yale U., 1947; LLD (hon.), U. New Haven, 1981, Sacred Heart U., 1986. Bar: Conn. 1947. Dir. legis. legal services State of Conn., 1949-73; judge Conn. Circuit Ct., 1973-74, Conn. Ct. of Common Pleas, 1974-76, Conn. Superior Ct., 1976-78, U.S. Dist. Ct. Conn., New Haven, 1978—. Trustee Fairfield U., 1978—, Albertus Magnus Coll., 1985—. Recipient John Carroll of Carrollton award John Barry Council K.C., 1973, Judiciary award Conn. Trial Lawyers Assn., 1978, Cross Pro Ecclesia et Pontifice, 1981, Law Rev. award U. Conn. Law Rev., 1987. Mem. ABA, Am. Bar Found., Conn. Bar Assn. (Judiciary award 1987), New Haven County Bar Assn. Roman Catholic. Office: US District Court 141 Church St New Haven CT 06510

BURNS, JAMES, lawyer; b. Burlington, Iowa, Feb. 19, 1948; s. Wayne W. and Edna Frances (Taylor) B.; m. Kari E. Onerheim, July 31, 1976; children: Morgan Leigh, Thomas Taylor. BA, Cornell Coll., Mt. Vernon, Iowa, 1970; JD, U. Iowa, 1973. Bar: Iowa 1974, U.S. Dist. Ct. (no. dist.) Iowa. Ptnr. Miller, Pearson, Gloe, Burns, Beatty & Cowie, P.C., Decorah, Iowa, 1973—. Pres. Winneshiek County Heart Assn., Decorah, 1984—, Winneshiek County Devel. Ctr., Decorah, 1978-84, Decorah Luth. Ch., 1985; coordinator Decorah Town Meeting, 1976, War & Peace Iowa, Decorah, 1982, campaign of Tom Tauke Winneshiek County, Decorah, 1978-80, campaign of Cooper Evans Winneshiek County, Decorah, 1982-84, George Bush for Pres. campaign Winneshiek County, Decorah, 1980, Reagan-Bush campaign Winneshiek County, Decorah, 1984; mem. Winneshiek County Assn. for Retarded Citizens, Decorah, 1974—, Winneshiek County Rep. Cen. Com., Decorah, 1974—. Served to capt. USAF, 1974. Mem. ABA, Iowa Bar Assn. (speaker young lawyer sects. 1983, 85), Winneshiek County Bar Assn., Assn. Trial Lawyers Iowa (continuing legal edn. com.), Nat. Orgn. for Legal Problems and Edn., Decorah C. of C., Jaycees (past pres. Decorah). Lodge: Lions (past pres. Decorah). General practice, State civil litigation, Family and matrimonial. Home: 1202 Skyline Dr Decorah IA 52101 Office: Miller Pearson Gloe Burns Beatty & Cowie PC 301 W Broadway PO Box 28 Decorah IA 52101

BURNS, JAMES M., judge; b. Nov. 24, 1924. BA in Bus. Adminstrn., U. Portland, 1947; JD cum laude, Loyola U., Chgo., 1950. Sole pracitce Portland, 1950-52; dist. atty. Harney County, Oreg., 1952-56; ptnr. Black, Kendall, Tremaine, Booth & Higgins, Portland, 1956-66; judge Oreg. Cir. Ct., Multnomah County, 1966-72; mem. faculty Nat. Jud. Coll., 1972—; judge U.S. Dist. Ct. Oreg., Portland, 1972—, chief judge, 1979-84; Mem. Oreg. Criminal Law Revision Commn., 1967-72; chmn. continuing legal edn. com. Oreg. State Bar, 1965-66; faculty advisor Nat. Jud. Coll., 1971. Mem. Oreg. Cir. Judges Assn. (pre. 1969-70), U.S. Jud. Conf. (com. on adminstrn. of probation system 1978—). Office: US Dist Ct 702 US Courthouse 620 SW Main St Portland OR 97205 *

BURNS, JEFFREY ROBERT, lawyer; b. Waltham, Mass., June 13, 1956; s. R. Emerson and Marion I. (Salta) B.; m. Lucinda Frost Wilson, Oct. 6, 1984; children: Kevin Robert, Alison Vail. BA cum laude, U. Mass., 1978; JD, Am. U., 1981. Bar: D.C. 1982, U.S. Dist. Ct. D.C. 1983, U.S. Ct. Appeals (D.C. cir.) 1983, Md. 1984, Maine 1986, Colo. 1987, U.S. Dist. Ct. Maine 1987. Assoc. Law Offices of Joseph F. Cunnningham & Assocs., Washington, 1983-85; atty., advisor D.C. Benefits Rev. Bd., Washington, 1985-86; assoc. Preti, Flaherty, Beliveau & Pachios, Rumford, Maine, 1986—. Mem. ABA, D.C. Bar Assn., Md. Bar Assn., Maine Bar Assn., Oxford County Trial Lawyers Assn. Democrat. Avocations: skiing, softball, tennis. Personal injury, Real property, Workers' compensation. Home: PO Box 491 Rumford ME 04276 Office: Preti Flaherty Beliveau & Pachios 150 Congress St Rumford ME 04276

BURNS, JOHN MACDOUGAL, III, lawyer; b. Ft. Worth, Aug. 23, 1933; s. John MacDougal and Mary Tabitha (Kenney) B.; m. Lorraine Lovell, Aug. 31, 1957; 1 son (dec.). A.B., Columbia U., 1955, M.A., 1960, LL.B., 1961. Bar: N.Y. 1961, U.S. Dist. Ct. (so., ea. and no. dists.) N.Y. 1962, U.S. Ct. Appeals (2d cir.) 1963, U.S. Ct. Appeals (3d cir.) 1980. Assoc. Hughes, Hubbard, Blair & Reed, N.Y.C., 1961-68; legis. counsel to State Senator Whitney North Seymour, Jr., N.Y.C., 1965-68; ptnr. Spear & Hill, N.Y.C., 1969-70, 71-74; exec. asst. U.S. atty. So. Dist. N.Y., 1970-71; ptnr. Alexander, Katz & Rosenberg, N.Y.C., 1974-76; sole practice, N.Y.C., 1976-81; ptnr. Burns & Fox, N.Y.C., 1981-86; sole practice, 1986— . Mem. ABA, Assn. Bar City N.Y. Democrat. Club: Gipsy Tr. (Carmel, N.Y.). Federal civil litigation, State civil litigation, General corporate. Home: 33 Greenwich Ave Apt 7-H New York NY 10014 Office: 360 Lexington Ave Suite 2300 New York NY 10017

BURNS, KATHERINE MILLS, lawyer; b. Wilmington, Del., Sept. 25, 1952; d. Richard Charles and Martha (Wynn) Mills; m. Augustus M. Burns III, Mar. 22, 1980; 1 child, Jane Katherine. BS, U. Fla., 1974, JD, 1977. Bar: Ohio 1978, Fla. 1979, U.S. Dist. Ct. (mid. dist.) Fla. 1982. Atty. products liability dept. Leblond, Inc., Cin., 1979-80; assoc. Law Offices of Mary B. Steddom P.A., Ocala, Fla., 1980-85; ptnr. Steddom & Burns P.A., Ocala, 1985-86; sole practice Ocala, 1986—. Bd. dirs. Marion County Sr. Services, Ocala, 1981—. Mem. Marion County Bar Assn., Marion County Estate Planning Council. Consumer commercial, Probate. Office: 1701 SE Fort King St Ocala FL 32671

BURNS, KENNETH JONES, JR., lawyer, natural resources company executive; b. Cleve., Oct. 3, 1926; s. Kenneth Jones and Isabel (Nanson) B.; m. Edith Louise Mitten, June 23, 1949; children: Deborah, Kenneth Jones III, Sarah, Elizabeth, Nancy, Andrew. B.S., Northwestern U., 1948, J.D., 1951. Bar: Ill. 1951, Ohio 1972. Assoc. Jenner & Block, Chgo., 1951-60; partner Jenner & Block, 1961-72; sr. v.p., gen. counsel, sec. Anchor Hocking Corp., Lancaster, Ohio, 1972-79; v.p., gen. counsel Internat. Minerals & Chem. Corp., Northbrook, Ill., 1979—; legal counsel Chgo. Jr. Assn. Commerce and Industry, 1955-58; lectr. Northwestern U. Sch. Law, 1955. Pres. Wilmette Civic Improvement Assn., 1958-62; v.p., dir. Citizens of Greater Chgo., 1961-64; mem. Chgo. Crime Commn.; bd. dirs. Am. Bar Endowment, 1975—, v.p., 1981-83, pres., 1983-85. Served with USNR, 1945-46, 51-52. Recipient Key award Chgo. Jr. Assn. Commerce, 1956. Fellow Am. Bar Found. (dir. 1983-85); mem. ABA (chmn. jr. bar conf. 1961-62, ho. of dels. 1962-64, 71—, asst. sec. 1967-71, sec., gov. 1971-75), Ill. Bar Assn., Chgo. Bar Assn. (bd. mgrs. 1961-63), Am. Bar Retirement Assn. (bd. dirs. 1982-86), Assn. Gen. Counsel, Chgo. Barrister Inn (pres. 1966-67), Legal Club Chgo. (exec. com. 1981-82), Law Club Chgo., Order of Coif, Sigma Chi, Phi Delta Phi. Club: Skokie (Ill.) Country. General corporate, Administrative and regulatory, Contracts commercial. Home: 15 Warrington Dr Lake Bluff IL 60044 Office: IMC Corp 2315 Sanders Rd Northbrook IL 60062

BURNS, MARK GARDNER, lawyer; b. Aug. 13, 1952; s. Robert H. and Helen Pauline (Childers) B.; m. Jane Clarke Hobbs, May 18, 1985. BA, U. Vt., 1975; JD, Gonzaga U., 1979. Bar: Mo. 1979, Ill. 1980, U.S. Dist. Ct. (ea. and we. dist.) Mo. Ptnr. Burns, Marshall & Burns, Clayton, Mo., 1979—. Mem. ABA, Mo. Bar Assn. Avocations: flying, skiing, backpacking. Insurance, Personal injury, State civil litigation. Home: 1003 Pawtucket Ballwin MO 63011 Office: Burns Marshall & Burns 7710 Carondelet Ave Clayton MO 63105

BURNS, MARSHALL SHELBY, JR., judge; b. Cleve., Jan. 29, 1931; s. Marshall Shelby and Fairybelle (Moses) B.; m. Blanche Marie Coleman, Jan. 28, 1953; children: William M., Brian M. AA, Flint (Mich.) Jr. Coll., 1957; BA, U. Mich., Flint, 1972; JD, Thomas M. Cooley Law Sch., 1979; LLM, Wayne State U., 1984. Bar: Mich. 1980, U.S. Dist. Ct. (ea. and we. dists.) Mich. 1980, U.S. Tax Ct. 1980, U.S. Supreme Ct. 1980. Tax supr. City of Flint, 1965-69; indsl. recreation adminstr. IMA, Flint, 1969-75; dir. personnel and labor relations Flint Gen. Hosp., 1975-76; asst. dir. personnel dept. pub. health State of Mich., Lansing, 1976-78, judge adminstrv. law, 1978—; gen. counsel Greater Lansing Urban League, 1983—; arbitrator Fed. Mediation and Conciliation Service, Washington, 1983—, Better Bus. Bur., 1983—, Am. Arbitration Assn., 1983—. Mem. exec. bd. Tall Pine Counsel Boy Scouts Am., Flint, 1970-75; bd. dirs. Greater Lansing Urban League, 1982-84, Vol. Action Ctr. of Greater Lansing, 1982-84. Served to pvt. 1st class U.S. Army, 1953-55. Mem. Am. Arbitration Assn. (arbitrator), Indsl. Relations Research Assn., Phi Alpha Delta (justice, treas. 1978-80), Alpha Phi Alpha. Baptist. Lodges: Masons, Rotary (bd. dirs. East Lansing chpt. 1983-85). Labor, Administrative and regulatory, General practice. Office: Mich Dept Civil Service Hearings Div Lewis Cass Bldg 320 S Walnut St PO Box 30002 Lansing MI 48909

BURNS, MARY ELIZABETH, lawyer; b. Vermillion, S.D., July 30, 1946; d. Phillips Barton and Mary Elizabeth (Beasom) Crew; m. William Mason Burns, May 12, 1978 (div. 1986); 1 child, Amy Jennifer. BA in English, Mills Coll., 1968; MA in History, U. S.D., 1977, JD, 1980. Bar: S.D. 1980, Idaho 1981, U.S. Dist. Ct. Idaho 1981. Assoc. atty. Dial, Looze & May, Pocatello, Id., 1981-83; ptnr. Crew Law Offices, Vermillion, 1985—. Troop leader Girl Scouts U.S., Vermillion, Pocatello, Idaho, 1978-83; bd. dirs. Vermillion Day Care Ctr., Vermillion, 1978-80, Girl Scouts U.S. Silver Sage council, 1983, Frontier council, 1984-85, chmn. personnel com., 1984-85. Mem. P.E.O. (chaplain 1981-82, treas. 1982-83 Pocatello chpt.). Democrat. Methodist. Family and matrimonial, Probate, Real property. Office: Crew Law Offices 11 E Main St Vermillion SD 57069

BURNS, MICHAEL WILLIAM, lawyer; b. Pitts., May 25, 1947; s. William M. and Jeanne (Smith) B.; m. Nancy Hillgartner, Nov. 22, 1980; children: Michael William, Brandon Cassidy. BA, Princeton U., 1969; JD, U. Pitts., 1972. Bar: Pa. 1972, U.S. Dist. Ct. (we. dist.) Pa. 1972, U.S. Ct. Appeals (3d cir.) 1973, U.S. Supreme Ct. 1978. Assoc. Dickie, McCamey & Chilcote, P.C., Pitts., 1972-76, ptnr., 1977-86, also bd. dirs.; ptnr. Burns, WHite & Hickton, Pitts., 1987—. Mem. ABA, Pa. Bar Assn., Def. Research Inst., Pa. Def. Inst., Pa. Assn. Trial Lawyers, Fedn. Ins. Counsel, Nat. Assn. R.R. Trial Counsel (mem. ad hoc asbestos com. with Assn. Am. R.R.s 1981—). Republican. Roman Catholic. Club: Valleybrook Country (Pitts.). Avocation: sports. Federal civil litigation, State civil litigation, Personal injury. Home: 2654 Gloucester Dr Pittsburgh PA 15241 Office: Burns White & Hickton 700 One Riverfront Ctr Pittsburgh PA 15222

BURNS, PETER FRANCIS, lawyer; b. Ft. Dix, N.J.; s. Frederick Michael and Naomi (Kerschner) B.; m. Kathryn Renea Park, Aug. 19, 1976; children: Kathryn Erin, Peter Francis Jr. BA, Centre Coll., 1971; JD, Samford U., 1975. Bar: Ala. 1975, U.S. Dist. Ct. (so. dist.) Ala. 1975, U.S. Ct. Appeals (5th cir.) 1977, U.S. Supreme Ct. 1983, U.S. Ct. Appeals (11th cir.) 1984. Law clk. to assoc. justice Ala. Supreme Ct., 1975-76; from assoc. to ptnr. Gaston, Bryant, Gaston & Burns, Mobile, Ala., 1976-81; ptnr. Morgan & Burns, Mobile, 1981—. Mem. editorial bd. Cumberland Samford U. Law Rev., 1973-75. Bd. dirs. YMCA, Mobile, 1985—. Named one of Outstanding Young Men in Am., 1981. Mem. ABA, Ala. Bar Assn., Mobile Bar Assn. (chmn. courthouse com. 1985, chmn. speakers com. 1986, exec. bd. dirs. 1984-85), Assn. Trial Lawyers Am., Ala. Trial Lawyers Assn., Am. Arbitration Assn. (panel of arbitrators), Order of Barristers. Club: Athlestan (Mobile). Avocations: handball, scuba diving. Federal civil litigation, State civil litigation. Home: 600 E Chelsea Dr Mobile AL 36608 Office: Morgan & Burns PO Box 1583 Mobile AL 36633

BURNS, PREMILA IRENE, lawyer; b. N.Y.C., Sept. 3, 1949; d. Lee Irving and Florence Helen (Hohn) B.; m. Robert Emmett Chumbley III, Aug. 15, 1970 (div. Nov. 1982). BA in French Lang. and Lit. magna cum laude, Wheaton Coll., 1971; JD, La. State U., 1974. Bar: La. 1974, U.S. Supreme Ct. 1982, U.S. Dist. Ct. (mid. dist.) La. 1983. Supervisory atty. Legal Aid Soc., Baton Rouge, 1974-75; asst. dist. atty., chief prosecutor criminal trial div. City of Baton Rouge, 1975-83, 85—; asst. U.S. atty. Mid. Dist. La., Baton Rouge, 1983-84; asst. adj. prof. law La. State U., 1985—. Named one of Outstanding Young Women in Am., 1983, 85. Mem. ABA, La. Bar Assn., Baton Rouge Bar Assn. (family ct. rules com., vice chmn. criminal ct. rules com. 1986—), Phi Beta Kappa. Republican. Presbyterian. Avocations: aerobics, dancing, travel. Criminal, Legal education. Home: 8155 Jefferson Hwy # 103 Baton Rouge LA 70809 Office: East Baton Rouge Parish Dist Atty 222 Saint Louis St Baton Rouge LA 70801

BURNS, RICHARD OWEN, lawyer; b. Bklyn., Nov. 16, 1942; S. James I. and Ida (Shore) B.; m. Lynda Gail Birnbaum, Dec. 24, 1967; children—Marc Adam, Lisa Ann, Susan Danielle. B.S., Wilkes Coll., 1964; J.D., Bklyn. Law Sch., 1967. Bar: N.Y. 1967, U.S. Dist. Ct. (so. dist.) N.Y. 1969, U.S. Dist. Ct. (ea. dist.) N.Y. 1979. Assoc. Clune & O'Brien, Mineola, N.Y., 1967-73, Clune, Burns, White & Nelson, Harrison, N.Y., 1973-78; ptnr. Schurr & Burns, P.C., Spring Valley, N.Y., 1978—. Bd. dirs. Rockland County unit Am. Cancer Soc., West Nyack, N.Y., 1979-85, 86—, pres., 1981-83; bd. dirs.

Hudson Valley Health System Agy., Sterling Park, N.Y., 1979, Vets. Meml. Assn., Congers, N.Y., 1980-86. Recipient Reese D. Jones award Wilkes Coll. Jr. C. of C., 1964. Mem. Rockland County Bar Assn., N.Y. State Bar Assn., N.Y. State Trial Lawyers Assn. Democrat. Jewish. Personal injury, Labor, State civil litigation. Home: 140 Waters Edge Congers NY 10920 Office: Schurr & Burns PC 4 N Main St PO Box 202 Spring Valley NY 10977

BURNS, RICHARD RAMSEY, lawyer; b. Duluth, Minn., May 3, 1946; s. Herbert Morgan and Janet (Strobel) B.; m. Gail Ann Gonska, Aug. 2, 1969 (div. May 1984); children: Jenny, Brian; m. Elizabeth Murphy, June 14, 1984. BA with distinction, U. Mich., 1968, JD magna cum laude, 1971. Bar: Calif. 1972, U.S. Dist. Ct. (no. dist.) Calif. 1972, U.S. Ct. Appeals (9th cir.) 1972, Minn. 1976, U.S. Dist. Ct. Minn. 1976, Wis. 1983, U.S. Tax. Ct. 1983. Assoc. Orrick, Herrington, Rowley & Sutcliffe, San Francisco, 1971-76; ptnr. Hanft, Fride, O'Brien, Harries, Swelbar & Burns P.A., Duluth, 1976—; gen. counsel Evening Telegram Co., Superior, Wis., 1982—, Murphy TV Stas., Madison, Wis., 1982—. Pres.-elect Duluth-Superior Area Community Found., 1983-86. Named Outstanding Young Man of Am., Duluth Jr. C. of C., 1980. Fellow Am. Coll. Probate Counsel; mem. Calif. Bar Assn., Wis. Bar Assn., Minn. Bar Assn., 11th Dist. Bar Assn., Arrowhead Estate Planning Council (pres. 1980). Republican. Clubs: Northland Country (pres. 1982-84), Kitchi Gammi. Avocations: travel, golf, tennis, fishing. Estate planning, Pension, profit-sharing, and employee benefits, Broadcast law. Home: 180 Paine Farm Rd Duluth MN 55804 Office: Hanft Fride O'Brien Harries Swelbar & Burns PA 1000 First Bank Pl Duluth MN 55802

BURNS, ROBERT PATRICK, law educator; b. N.Y.C., Mar. 23, 1947; s. Frances William and Helen (Moskol) B.; m. Mary Elizabeth Griffin, June 7, 1975; children: Matthew, Elizabeth. AB, Fordham U., 1969; JD, U. Chgo., 1974, PhD, 1982. Bar: Ill. 1974, U.S. Dist. Ct. (no. dist.) Ill. 1974, U.S. Ct. Appeals (7th cir.) 1977, U.S. SUpreme Ct. 1978. Litigation atty. Legal Assistance Found., Chgo., 1974-79, dir. atty. training, 1979; gen. counsel Ill. Legis. Commn., Springfield, 1979-80; prof. law Northwestern U., Chgo., 1980—; tchr. Nat. Inst. Trial Advocacy, South Bend, Ind., 1981—. Contbr. articles to profl. jours. Mediator Neighborhood Justice Ctr., Chgo., 1985—; bd. dirs. Evanston Dems., Ill., 1984. Kent fellow Danforth Found., 1974, NSF fellow, 1970. Mem. ABA, Soc. for Values in Higher Edn. Roman Catholic. Jurisprudence, Civil rights, Criminal. Office: Northwestern U Sch Law 357 E Chicago Ave Chicago IL 60611

BURNS, SANDRA K., lawyer, educator; b. Bryan, Tex., Aug. 9, 1949; d. Clyde W. and Bert (Rychlik) B.; 1 son, Scott. B.S., U. Houston, 1970; M.A., U. Tex.-Austin, 1972, Ph.D., 1975; J.D., St. Mary's U., 1978. Bar: Tex. 1978; cert. tchr., adminstr., supr. instrn., Tex. Tchr. Austin (Tex.) Ind. Sch. Dist., 1970-71; prof. child devel./family life and home econs. edn. Coll. Nutrition, Textiles and Human Devel. Tex. Woman's U., Denton, 1974-75; instrnl. devel. asst. Office of Ednl. Resources div. instrnl. devel. U. Tex. Health Sci. San Antonio, 1976-77; legis. aide William T. Moore, Tex. Senate, Austin, fall, 1978, com. clk.-counsel, spring, 1979; legal cons. Colombotti & Assocs., Aberdeen, Scotland, 1980; corporate counsel First Internat. Oil and Gas, Inc., 1983; atty. Humble Exploration Co., Inc., Dallas, 1984; assoc. Smith, Underwood, Dallas, 1986— ; atty. contracted to Republic Energy Inc., Bryan, Tex., 1981-82, ARCO, Dallas, 1985; vis. lectr. Tex. A&M U., fall 1981, summer, 1981; lectr. home econ. Our Lady of the Lake Coll., San Antonio, fall, 1975. Mem. State Bar of Tex., ABA, Phi Delta Kappa. Methodist. Contbr. articles on law and edn. to profl. jours. General corporate, Contracts commercial, Private international. Office: 12126 Forestwood Circle Dallas TX 75244

BURNS, STEPHEN GILBERT, lawyer; b. N.Y.C., Apr. 29, 1953; s. Gilbert Leo and Ellen (Scully) B.; m. Joan Louise Wallace, Aug. 6, 1977; children: Christopher, Allison. Student, U. Vienna, Austria, 1974; BA, Colgate U., 1975; JD, George Washington U., 1978. Bar: D.C. 1978, U.S. Dist. Ct. D.C. 1979, U.S. Ct. Appeals (D.C. cir.) 1980. Atty. Nuclear Regulatory Commn., Washington, 1978-83, dep. chief counsel regional ops. and enforcement, 1983-86, legal asst. to commr., 1986—. Mem. ABA, Fed. Bar Assn. Presbyterian. Administrative and regulatory, Nuclear power. Home: 242 Whitmoor Terr Silver Spring MD 20901 Office: US Nuclear Regulatory Commn Washington DC 20555

BURNS, STEVEN DWIGHT, lawyer; b. Marshalltown, Iowa, Mar. 20, 1948; s. Dwight Harry and Cleo Maxine (England) B.; m. Mary Lou Stone, Jan. 29, 1971; 1 child, Natalie Stone. BArch, U. Nebr., 1971, JD, 1973. Bar: Nebr. 1973, U.S. Dist. Ct. Nebr. 1973, U.S. Ct. Appeals (8th cir.) 1980, U.S. Supreme Ct. 1985. Sole practice Lincoln, Nebr., 1973-78, 82—; assoc. Luedtke, Radcliffe, Burns, Lincoln, Nebr., 1974-77; ptnr. Noren & Burns, Lincoln, Nebr., 1978-82; village atty. Eagle, Nebr., 1973—, Ceresco, Nebr., 1974—, Hallam, Nebr., 1975—. Hon. dir. Cedars Home for Children, 1978—; Dem. congl. candidate First Dist. Nebr., 1986. Recipient Outstanding Service award Nebr. Assn. Pub. Employees, 1983. Club: Exec. (pres. 1985). Labor, Local government, Business. Office: 605 S 14th St Suite 405 Lincoln NE 68508

BURNS, THOMAS DAVID, lawyer; b. Andover, Mass., Apr. 4, 1921; s. Joseph Lawrence and Catherine (Horne) B.; m. Sylvia Lansing, Sept. 14, 1946 (div. 1982); children—Wendy Tilghman, Lansing, Diane Longley, Lisa; m. Marjorie Andrew Brown, Mar. 12, 1983. Student, Brown U., 1938-41; LL.B., Boston U., 1943. Bar: Mass. 1944, U.S. Dist. Ct. 1948, U.S. Ct. Appeals 1951, U.S. Supreme Ct. 1957. Assoc. Friedman, Atherton, King & Turner, Boston, 1946-51, ptnr., 1950-60; sr. ptnr. Burns & Levinson, Boston, 1960—; mem. Jud. Council Com. of Mass., 1973-77, mem. Mass. Jud. Nominating Commn., 1979-83; mem. Mass. Spl. Legis. Commn. on Med. Malpractice, 1975—. Contbr. articles to profl. jours. Chmn. Planning Bd. Appeals, Andover, 1956-57; trustee Stratton Mountain Vt. Civic Assn.; chmn. Andover Republican Fin. Com., 1953-57; trustee, clk., mem. exec. com. Pike Sch., Andover; mem. alumni council Phillips Andover Acad, Boston U. Law Sch. Served to lt. USNR, 1942-46; ETO, PTO. Fellow Am. Coll. Trial Lawyers, (bd. regents 1970-76, treas. 1974-77), Am. Coll. Trial Lawyers Found. (dir.), Mass. Bar Found (trustee), Mass. Bar Assn., Am. Bar Found., ABA, Boston Bar Assn. (exec. council), Fedn. Ins. Counsel, Internat. Assn. Ins. Counsel, Nat. Assn. R.R. Trial Counsel, Mass. Def. Lawyers Assn. (dir.), Mass. Acad. Trial Lawyers, Delta Kappa Upsilon. Republican. Clubs: North Andover country, The Country (Brookline), Union of Boston, Coral Beach (Bermuda), Windermere Island (Bahamas), Duxbury Yacht. General practice, Medical, Insurance. Home: 5 Union Wharf Boston MA 02109 Office: 50 Milk St Boston MA 02109

BURNS, THOMAS MARTIN, lawyer; b. Yerington, Nev., Nov. 30, 1942; s. John Hugh and Frances (Millar) B.; m. Judy Ann Abbott, Nov. 4, 1967; children: Mitchell Thomas, Jennifer Mikel. BS, U. Nev., 1965; JD, U. Calif., San Francisco, 1973. Bar: Calif. 1973, Nev. 1974, U.S. Dist. Ct. Nev. 1974. Law. clk., atty. Pub. Defender's Office, Clark County, Nev., 1973-76; ptnr. Bell, Leavitt & Green, Las Vegas, Nev., 1976-79; sole practice Las Vegas, 1979—. Chmn. Com. to Reelect Judge Bonaventure, Las Vegas, 1982, 84. Served to capt. U.S. Army, 1965-70, Vietnam. Decorated Bronze Star. Republican. Roman Catholic. Bankruptcy, Criminal, Family and matrimonial. Office: 912 N Eastern Ave Las Vegas NV 89101

BURNS, WILLIAM GLENN, lawyer; b. Shreveport, La., Jan. 13, 1949; s. Carrol and Doris Yvonne (Broadway) B.; m. Linda Roach Aug. 14, 1971 (div. 1981); m. Marilyn Jeanne Waites, Oct. 28, 1982; 1 child, Brandon Nicholas. BS, La. State U., 1971, JD, 1973. Bar: La. 1973, U.S. Ct. Appeals (5th cir.) 1974, U.S. Dist. Ct. (ea. dist.) La. 1976, U.S. Ct. Appeals (11th cir.) 1981, U.S. Dist. Ct. (mid. dist.) La. 1985, U.S. Supreme Ct. 1986. Asst. atty. gen. La. Dept. Justice, New Orleans, 1973-76; assoc. Murray & Murray, New Orleans, 1976-80; asst. U.S. atty. U.S. Dept. Justice, New Orleans, 1980-85; assoc. Monroe & Lemann, New Orleans, 1985—; fellow Inst. of Politics Loyola U., 1978. Editor: Seminar-Consumer Relations and Bank Holding Companies, 1972. Del. Nat. Dem. Mid-Term Conf., La., 1978; mem. bd. devel. Mercy Hosp., New Orleans, 1979. Mem. ABA, Fed. Bar Assn., La. Bar Assn., Assn. Trial Lawyers Am., La. Trial Lawyers Assn. Republican. Baptist. Clubs: World Trade, Plimsoll (New Orleans). Avocations: raquetball, Am. history, La. polit. history. Federal civil litigation, Criminal, Public utilities. Office: Monroe & Lemaun 201 St Charles Ave New Orleans LA 70170-3300

BURNSTEIN, DANIEL, lawyer; b. Hartford, Conn., Oct. 12, 1946; s. Lawrence J. and Margaret (Le Vien) B. A.B., U. Calif.-Berkeley, 1968; J.D. cum laude, New Eng. Sch. Law, 1975. Bar: Mass. 1975, U.S. Dist. Ct. Mass. 1976, U.S. Ct. Appeals (1st cir.) 1976. Exec. dir., tchr. Advocacy Tng. Inst., Boston, 1982—; sole practice, Boston, 1982—; dir. interactive video project Harvard Law Sch., Cambridge, 1985—, trial advisor, 1983—, clin. instr., 1978; cir., counsel Ctr. for Atomic Radiation Studies, Acton, Mass., 1982—, Boston Urban Gardens, 1980—; counsel Citywide Parents Council, Boston, 1977-84; Co-author: (handbook) Filing Requirements for Non-Profits, 1981, Veterans Guide for Obtaining Records, 1983; contbr. chpts. to books. Bd. dirs. Roxbury Action Program, Inc., Mass., 1977—. Mem. Mass. Bar Assn., Boston Bar Assn., Nat. Lawyers Guild (Mass. chpt. bd. dirs. 1976-84). Personal injury, Non-Profit orgns, Freedom of information. Home: 452 Weston Rd Wellesley MA 02181

BURR, CHARLES BENTLEY, II, lawyer; b. Pitts., Mar. 21, 1940; s. Charles Robert and Helen Louise (Felber) B.; m. Mary Ray Peck, Aug. 28, 1965; children: Julia Burr Stuyvesant, Elizabeth Burr Crawford. BS, Yale U., 1962; LLB, U. Pa., 1966. Bar: Pa. 1968, U.S. Ct. Appeals (3d cir.) 1969, U.S. Supreme Ct. 1975, U.S. Ct. Claims 1976. Assoc. Morgan, Lewis & Bockius, Phila., 1966-69; asst. U.S. atty. U.S. Dept. Justice, Phila., 1969-72; assoc. Obermayer, Rebmann, Maxwell & Hippel, Phila., 1972-79; sr. ptnr. Griffith & Burr P.C., Phila., 1979—; trustee Citizens Crime Commn. Phila., 1976—. Solicitor Radnor (Pa.) Twp. Zoning Hearing Bd., 1975—. Mem. ABA (litigation and criminal law sects.), Pa. Bar Assn., Phila. Bar Assn., Union League Phila. Republican. Episcopalian. Club: Martins Dam Swim. Avocations: jogging, paddle tennis, reading, writing. Personal injury, Health, State civil litigation. Home: 425 Huston Rd Radnor PA 19087 Office: Griffith & Burr PC 1608 Walnut St Philadelphia PA 19103

BURR, FRANCIS HARDON, lawyer; b. Nahant, Mass., July 21, 1914. A.B. cum laude, Harvard U., 1935, LL.B, 1938, LL.D., 1982. Bar: Mass. 1938. Assoc. Ropes & Gray, Boston, 1938-47, ptnr., 1947—; bd. dirs. Am. Airlines, Inc., Corning Glass Works, State St. Exchange Fund, State St. Growth Fund, Raytheon Co., Harvard Mgmt. Co., State St. Investment Corp.; mem. com. fin. advisers Comml. Union Corp. Chmn. bd. dirs. Mass. Gen. Hosp. Fellow Harvard Coll., 1954-82; sr. fellow Harvard Coll., 1971-82. Fellow Am. Acad. Arts and Scis., Am. Bar Found; mem. ABA, Boston Bar Assn., Am. Law Inst. General corporate. Office: Ropes & Gray 225 Franklin St Boston MA 02110

BURRASCA, RAYMOND PETER, lawyer; b. N.Y.C., May 26, 1951; s. Dominic and Ellen Veronica (Nocher) B.; m. Harriet Rubin, Oct. 21, 1973; 1 child, Leah Aimée. BA in Am. Studies, Union Coll., 1973; JD, Pace U., 1980. Bar: N.Y. 1981, U.S. Dist. Ct. (ea. and so. dists.) N.Y. 1981, U.S. Ct. Claims 1981, U.S. Ct. Internat. Trade 1981. Atty. Ipco Corp., White Plains, N.Y., 1980-81, Grey Advt., N.Y.C., 1981-83, Great N. Nekoosa Corp., Stamford, Conn., 1984—. Mem. ABA, N.Y. State Bar Assn., Westchester-Fairfield Corp. Counsel Assn. (chmn. young lawyers com. 1985—). General corporate, Private international, Securities. Home: Valeria Circle PO Box 71 Goldens Bridge NY 10526 Office: Great No Nekoosa Corp 75 Prospect St Stamford CT 06904

BURRELL, LIZABETH LORIE, lawyer; b. Bklyn., Feb. 1, 1952; s. George A. and Ione E. (Smith) B.; m. Michael F. Cataldo, Dec. 31, 1977; 1 child, Alexis C. Burrell. BA cum laude, Swarthmore Coll., 1973; MA with honors, Columbia U., 1974, postgrad. degree in English Lit. with distinction, 1976; JD, NYU, 1980. Bar: N.Y. 1981, U.S. Dist. Ct. (so. dist.) N.Y. 1981. Assoc. Burlingham, Underwood & Lord, N.Y.C., 1980—. Alumni rep. Swarthmore Coll., 1980—. Mem. ABA, N.Y. State Bar Assn., Assn. of Bar of City of N.Y. (admiralty com.), N.Y. Womens Bar Assn., Maritime Law Assn. of U.S. (sec. uniformity of U.S. Maritime law com. 1985—, author briefs 1985). Avocation: sailing. Admiralty, Federal civil litigation, Private international. Office: Burlingham Underwood & Lord One Battery Park Plaza New York NY 10004

BURRILL, JANICE HILARY, lawyer; b. San Mateo, Calif., Feb. 15, 1957; d. Robert E. Burrill and Margaret Kathryn (Hansen) Nugent. BS in Acctg. magna cum laude, Loyola Marymount U., Los Angeles, 1979, JD cum laude, 1982. Bar: Calif. 1982, U.S. Dist. Ct. (cen., ea., so., and no. dists.) 1983 Calif., U.S. Ct. Appeals (9th cir.). Assoc. Graham & James, Los Angeles, 1982-86, Shearman & Sterling, Los Angeles, 1986—; exchange atty. Field, Fisher & Martineau, London, 1985-86. Participant Pub. Counsel. Mem. ABA, Calif. Bar Assn., Los Angeles Bar Assn., Fin. Lawyers Conf., Los Angeles C. of C. Democrat. Avocations: calligraphy, horseback riding, travel, fgn. languages. Private international, Banking, General corporate. Office: Shearman & Sterling 725 S Figueroa St 21st Floor Los Angeles CA 90017-5421

BURRIS, JOHNNY CLARK, law educator; b. Paris, Ky., May 21, 1953; s. John Curtis and Ada (Sargent) B.; m. Jane Wright, July 1975 (div. Sept. 1980); m. Cathy Jackson, Mar. 1981 (div. Feb. 1984); m. Nancy Nevius, Aug. 6, 1985. BA, U. Ky., 1975; JD, No. Ky. U., 1978; LLM, Columbia U., 1984. Bar: Ky. 1978, U.S. Ct. Appeals (6th cir.) 1978, Ohio 1979, U.S. Dist. Ct. (ea. dist.) Ky. 1979, U.S. Ct. Appeals (11th cir.) 1987. Law clk. to presiding justice Supreme Ct., Frankfort, Ky., 1978-79; asst. atty. Commonwealth Atty. Kenton County, Covington, Ky., 1979; asst. dean Nova U. Ctr. Study of Law, Ft. Lauderdale, Fla., 1979-84, asst. prof. law, 1981—. Mem. No. Ky. Law Rev., 1978-79. Mem. ABA, Ky. Bar Assn., Fed. Bar Assn., ACLU, Fla. Bar Assn. (affiliate), Omicron Delta Kappa. Administrative and regulatory, Legal education, Contracts commercial. Office: Nova U Ctr for Study of Law 3100 SW 9th Ave Fort Lauderdale FL 33315

BURROUGHS, CHARLES EDWARD, lawyer; b. Milw., June 9, 1939; s. Edward Albert and Ann Monica (Bussman) B.; m. Kathleen Walton, Jan. 30, 1965; children—James, Michael, Lauri, Stephanie. B.S., U. Wis.-Madison, 1962, LL.B., 1965; LL.M., George Washington U., 1968. Bar: Wis. 1965, U.S. Dist. Ct. (ea. and we. dists.) Wis. 1965, U.S. Ct. Clms. 1967, U.S. Ct. Mil. Apls. 1967, U.S. Ct. Apls. (7th cir.) 1969, U.S. Supreme Ct. 1968. Assoc., Porter & Porter, Milw., 1969-71; ptnr. von Briesen and Purtell, S.C. (formerly Purtell, Purcell, Wilmot & Burroughs, S.C.), Milw., 1971—; dir. Reise Corp., Milw. Served to capt. U.S. Army, 1965-69. Mem. ABA. Roman Catholic. Club: Milw. Athletic. Health, Construction, Antitrust. Home: 10937 N Hedgewood Ln Mequon WI 53092 Office: von Briesen and Purtell SC 111 E Wis Ave Milwaukee WI 53202

BURROUGHS, JOHN TOWNSEND, lawyer; b. Akron, Ohio, May 27, 1926; s. Ralph and Helen (Townsend) B.; m. Laverne Casey, Nov. 23, 1966; 1 child, Brien C. BA cum laude, Brown U., 1946; MD, Harvard U., 1950; JD with honors, Calif. Western Sch. Law, 1978. Bar: Calif. 1979, U.S. Ct. Claims 1979, U.S. Dist. Ct. (ea. dist.) Wis. 1981, Wis. 1982, U.S. Dist. Ct. (cen. dist.) Calif. 1982; diplomate Am. Bd. Surgery, Am. Bd. Thoracic Surgery; lic. surgeon Calif., Wis. 1982, Colo. 1986, La. Intern, then resident Johns Hopkins Hosp., Balt., 1950-52; fellow Mayo Clinic, Rochester, Minn., 1954-56; resident in surgery UCLA Med. Ctr., 1956-58, asst. in surgery, 1958-59; asst. prof. dept. surgery UCLA Med. Sch., 1959-63; practice medicine specializing in thoracic and cardiovascular surgery Los Angeles, 1961-72; practice medicine specializing in thoracic, cardiovascular and coronary bypass surgery Milw., 1972-75, Baton Rouge, 1975-76; staff, chief med. legal research div. dept. legal medicine Armed Forces Inst. Pathology, Washington, 1979-82; ptnr. Joling, Rizzo, Willems, Oleniewski, Stern & Burroughs, S.C., Kenosha, Wis., 1982-85; sole practice Salem, Wis., 1985—; vis. surgeon in cardiovascular surgery U. Free Berlin, 1959; asst. prof. dept. surgery UCLA Med. Sch., 1960-63; clin. assoc. prof. U. Calif., Irvine, 1963-72; adj. prof. law Antioch Sch., Washington, 1980; chief sect. thoracic surgery VA Hosp., Los Angeles, 1959-63; lectr. on law and medicine, 1979—. Contbr. articles to profl. jours. Chmn. Edn. com. Inglewood C. of C., 1968-69, chmn. drug com., 1969-71, bd. dirs. 1970-72; chmn. CPR Tng. Milw. Heart Assn., 1972-74, Community Programs Council, Inglewood, 1970-72, southwestern br. Los Angeles County Heart Assn., 1968-70, CPR Tng. Progam, Los Angeles Heart Assn., 1969-72; med. dir. Program in Inglewood Unified Sch. Dist. on Narcotics and Smoking, 1968-72, Narcotics edn. dist atty.'s advisory council, Los Angeles, 1968-70; trustee Centinela Valley Community Hosp., 1971-72; bd. dirs. Associated Centinela Services, 1971-72. Served to lt. M.C., USNR, 1952-54. Recipient Award of Merit Los Angeles County Heart Assn., 1967-70, Heart Recognition award Los Angeles County Heart Assn., 1971, Disting. Service award Los Angeles County Heart Assn., 1972, Cert. Commendation Los Angeles County, 1972, Cert. Merit Inglewood Unified Sch. Dist., 1969. Fellow Am. Coll. Surgeons, Am. Coll. Cardiology, Am. Coll. Legal Medicine, Am. Acad. Forensic Scis.; mem. ABA, Calif. Bar Assn., Wis. Bar Assn., Assn. Trial Lawyers Am., Soc. Thoracic Surgeons (founding), Am. Coll. Chest Physicians, Am. Bd. Law in Medicine (diplomate), Am. Bd. Profl. Liability Attys. (diplomate), Am. Trauma Soc. (founding), Sigma Xi. Federal civil litigation, State civil litigation, Medical malpractice. Office: 21916 84th St Salem WI 53168

BURROUGHS, RICHARD RAY, lawyer; b. Goose Creek, Tex., Aug. 13, 1946; s. Charles Howard Royce and Lillie Adeline (Schultz) B.; m. Nancy Margene Schaeffer, July 12, 1968; children: Rory Schaeffer, Jared Dale. BA, Baylor U., 1968, JD, 1973. Ptnr. Price & Burroughs, Trinity, Tex., 1973; sole practice Cleveland, Tex., 1973—. Mem. sch. bd. New Caney, Tex., 1974-75. Served with U.S. Army, 1969-71. Mem. ABA, State Bar Assn., Houston Bar Assn., Liberty County Bar Assn., Montgomery County Bar Assn., Tex. Trial Lawyer Assn. General practice. Home: Cape Royale Box 71 Coldspring TX 77331 Office: 112 S Bonham PO Box 1676 Cleveland TX 77327

BURROW, RHEA MORGAN, administrative law judge, lawyer; b. Ballard County Ky., Feb. 28, 1916; s. Gupton Burns and Mary (Northington) B.; m. Barbara Ann Perecinic, Dec. 31, 1945; children—Rhea Jr., Gary Stephen. A.B., Tansylvania Coll., Lexington, Ky., 1937; student Cumberland U., Lebanon, Tenn., 1938-39; J.D., Georgetown U., 1950; postgrad. George Washington U., 1951. Bar: Tenn. 1939, U.S. Dist. Ct. (mid. dist.) Tenn. 1940, U.S. Supreme Ct. 1960. Legal cons. VA, Washington, 1946-56; mem. Bd. Vets. Appeals, 1956-70, chief supervisory mem., 1958-70, adminstrv. law judge, 1970—; mem. bd. Contract Appeals, 1972—; with firm Dorsey and Sprouse, Springfield, Tenn., 1939-42. Served in USAF, 1942-45. Recipient Disting. Career award VA, 1970. Mem. ABA, Fed. Bar Assn. Baptist. Labor, Administrative and regulatory, Government contracts and claims. Home: 3300 N Trinidad St Falls Church VA 22043 Office: US Dept Labor Adminsrv Law Judges Vanguard Bldg 1111 20th St NW Washington DC 20036

BURROWS, CECIL J., lawyer, judge; b. Schuyler County, Ill., Mar. 21, 1922; s. Amos R. and Florence M. (Krohe) B.; m. Virginia Pearson, June 27, 1949; children—Sandra, Carol, Deborah. B.S., Western Mich. U., 1944; J.D., Northwestern U., 1952. Bar: Ill. 1952. City atty. Pittsfield, Ill., 1957-64; state's atty. Pike County, Ill., 1964-70; sole practice, Pittsfield, to 1970; cir. judge 8th cir. Ill., 1970—. Served as officer USMC, 1943-46. Mem. ABA, Ill. State Bar Assn., Pike County Bar Assn. Clubs: Masons, Shriners. Jurisprudence. Home: 437 W Washington Pittsfield IL 62363 Office: Pike County Courthouse Pittsfield IL 62363

BURROWS, JON HANES, lawyer; b. Frederick, Okla., July 12, 1946; s. John Henry and Eula Elizabeth (Trull) B.; m. Katie Lea Royal, July 13, 1969; children—Justin Hanes, Kelly Elizabeth. B.M.E., U. Okla., 1968. M.M.E., 1969; J.D., U. Tex., 1976. Bar: Tex. 1976, U.S. Dist. Ct. (we. dist.) Tex. 1978; cert. residential and comml. real estate law Tex. Bd. Legal Specialization. Ptnr., Burrows & Cure, Temple, Tex., 1976-78, Burrows & Baird, Temple, 1982-85; pres. Burrows, Baird, Miller & Crews, P.C., 1985—; sole practice, Temple, 1978-81; mem. faculty in real estate law Temple Jr. Coll., 1980—. Treas., bd. govs. Temple Civic Theatre, 1980; pres. Western Hills Elem. PTO, 1982; mem. human studies subcom. VA Hosp., 1983-86; bd. dirs. Temple United Way, 1983—. Served to capt. USAF, 1969-73, maj. Res. Named Outstanding Young Man of Yr., Temple Jaycees, 1980; decorated Meritorious Service medal. Mem. State Bar Tex., ABA, Bell-Lampasas-Mills Counties Bar Assn., USAF Res. Officers Assn., Phi Alpha Delta. Democrat. Baptist. Lodge: Lions (dir. 1980-86, pres. 1986-87). General practice, Real property, Probate. Home: 2429 Canyon Creek Dr Temple TX 76502 Office: Burrows Baird Miller & Crews 3513 SW HK Dodgen Loop Suite 103 Temple TX 76502

BURROWS, KENNETH DAVID, lawyer; b. Bklyn., Mar. 26, 1941; s. Selig S. and Gladys (Spatt) B.; B.A., Brown U., 1967, J.D., Fordham U., 1971. Bar: N.Y. 1971, U.S. Dist. Ct. (so. dist.) N.Y. 1972, U.S. Dist. Ct. (ea. dist.) N.Y. 1972, U.S. Supreme Ct. 1973. Assoc., Phillips, Nizer, Benjamin, Krim, & Ballon, N.Y.C., 1970-77; ptnr. Kleinberg, Kaplan, Wolff, Cohen & Burrows, N.Y.C., 1977-79, Burrows & Poster, N.Y.C., 1980—; arbitrator small claims ct. City of N.Y., 1975—, compulsory arbitration program, 1980-82; spl. master Sup. Ct. of State of N.Y., N.Y. County, 1980—; arbitrator U.S. Dist. Ct. (ea. dist.) N.Y., 1986—. Served with USCGR, 1960-68. Mem. Assn. of Bar City of N.Y., N.Y. County Lawyers Assn., N.Y. State Bar Assn., ABA, Am. Arbitration Assn. (mem. nat. arbitrators panel 1973—). Federal civil litigation, State civil litigation, Family and matrimonial. Office: 750 3d Ave 16th Floor New York NY 10017

BURRUS, ROBERT LEWIS, JR., lawyer; b. Richmond, Va., Sept. 16, 1934; s. Robert Lewis and Bessie (Hart) B.; m. Ann Williams, Aug. 1, 1964; children—David Curran, Peter Tandy, Lewis Graves. B.A., U. Richmond, 1955; LL.B., Duke U., 1958. Bar: Va. 1958. Assoc. McGuire, Woods & Battle & Boothe, Richmond, Va., 1959-63, ptnr., 1963—; dir. Capitol Cement Corp., W.Va., Best Products Co., Inc., Richmond, Heilig-Meyers Co., Richmond, S&K Famous Brands, Inc., Richmond, Riverton Corp., Va., Wiland Services, Inc., Boulder, Colo., sec. Genicom Corp., Waynesboro, Va., 1983—. Mem. Council Higher Edn. for Va.; chmn. bd. assocs. U. Richmond, 1984—, planning com. law sch.; dir., chmn. exec. com. Richmond Renaissance, Inc., 1982—; v.p. Hist. Richmond Found., 1985-87, v.p., 1985—; mem. nat. council for law sch. Duke U., Durham, N.C., 1984—; past pres. Found. St. Christopher's Sch., Richmond, 1975-77; past del. to state and nat. convs. Democratic Party; bd. dirs. Cir. City Found.; mem. planning and search com. U. Richmond Law Sch. Served to capt. USAR, 1960-68. Fellow Am. Bar Found.; mem. ABA, Va. Bar Assn. (chmn. corp. law com. 1975-77, chmn. bus. sect. 1976-77), Richmond Bar Assn., Omicron Delta Kappa. Episcopalian. Clubs: Commonwealth, Country of Va., Bull and Bear, Forum. Corporate finance and taxation. Home: 220 Ampthill Rd Richmond VA 23226 Office: McGuire Woods Battle & Boothe One James Ctr Richmond VA 23219

BURSLEY, KATHLEEN A., lawyer; b. Washington, Mar. 20, 1954; d. G.H. Patrick and Claire (Mulvany) B. BA, Pomona Coll., 1976; JD, Cornell U., 1979. Bar: N.Y. 1980, U.S. Dist. Ct. (ea. and so. dists.) N.Y. 1980, U.S. Ct. Appeals (5th and 11th cirs.) 1981, Fla. 1984, U.S. Dist. Ct. (middle dist.) Fla. 1984., Tex. 1985. Assoc. Haight, Gardner, Poor & Havens, N.Y.C., 1979-81; counsel Harcourt Brace Jovanovich, Inc., N.Y.C. and Orlando, Fla., 1981-85, San Antonio, 1985—. Mem. Target 90, San Antonio, 1985—. Mem. Maritime Law Assn. (proctor). General corporate, Contracts commercial, Trademark and copyright. Office: Harcourt Brace Jovanovich Inc 555 Academic Ct San Antonio TX 78204

BURSTEIN, BEATRICE S., justice N.Y. Supreme Ct.; b. Bklyn., May 18, 1915; d. Joseph and Tillie (Star) Sobel; m. Herbert Burstein, June 17, 1937; children: Karen, Patricia, Ellen, Jessica, John, Judd. Bar: N.Y. 1940, U.S. Supreme Ct. 1957. LLB, St. John's U.; LLD (hon.), Hofstra U., 1983. Assoc. Zelby & Burstein, N.Y.C.; ptnr. Burstein & Agata, Mineola, N.Y.; commr. corrections State N.Y., 1956-61; dist. ct. judge, N.Y., 1962-68; family ct. judge, N.Y., 1968-73; justice N.Y. Supreme Ct., Mineola, 1973—. Mem. adv. council to dean Hofstra Law Sch.; hon. mem. Legal Aid Soc. Nassau County; former bd. dirs. Mental Health Assn. Nassau County, Nassau County Council Girl Scouts U.S.A., NCCJ, Rehab. Inst., Tempo, Health and Welfare Council Nassau County, LWV, Nat. Council Crime and Delinquency, Nat. Council Jewish Women; hon. life mem. Dist. 15 PTA; mem. N.Y. State Commn. on Bicentennial of U.S. Constitution. Named Woman of Year, Horizon chpt. B'nai B'rith, 1965, Assn. for Help Retarded Children, 1965; recipient Judge Norman Lent award Nassau County Criminal Cts. Bar Assn., 1968, Americanism award Jewish War Vets., 1971, Meritorious Service cert. N.E. region Nat. Rehab. Assn., 1972, Human Relations award Am. Jewish Congress, 1973, Outstanding Woman of Year award N.Y. Inst. Tech., 1973, Boss of Year award L.I. chpt. Nat. Secs. Assn., 1975, Myrtle Wreath Achievement award Hadassah, 1975, Disting. Service award C.W. Post Ctr. Dept. Criminal Justice, L.I. U., 1979, many others. Mem. ABA, Am. Judicature Soc., Am. Trial Lawyers Assn., Assn. Judges Family Ct. State of N.Y., Internat. Fedn. Women Lawyers (v.p. for U.S., rep. to UN

Social Commn. 1953, 55, 56, 61), Assn. Justices Sup. Ct. State N.Y., Bar Assn. Nassau County, Nat. Assn. Women Judges, Assn. Women Judges of State N.Y., Nassau-Suffolk Women's Bar Assn. (pres., chmn. legal clinic), Nat. Assn. Women Lawyers, Nat. Conf. State Trial Judges, Nat. Council Juvenile Ct. Judges, Nat. Leagal Aid and Defender Assn., N.Y. State Bar Assn., Am. Assn. UN, Iota Tau Tau. Contbr. articles to profl. lit. Jurisprudence, Family and matrimonial, Juvenile. Office: NY Supreme Ct Mineola NY 11501

BURSTEIN, MERWYN JEROME, lawyer; b. Springfield, Mass., Apr. 6, 1938; s. Rubin Meyer and Sylvia (Burke) B.; m. Ruth B. Burstein, July 31, 1966; children—David, Judith, Jeffrey. B.A. in Psychology, Am. Internat. Coll., 1959; LL.B., Boston Coll., 1960; J.D., New Eng. Sch. Law, 1962. Bar: Mass. 1963, U.S. Dist. Ct. Mass. 1963, U.S. Dist. Ct. Conn. 1979, U.S. Tax Ct., 1981. Ptnr., Michelman & Burstein, Springfield, 1963-70; sole practice, Springfield, 1970-73; sr. ptnr. Burstein & Dupont, Springfield, 1973—; pres., treas. Springfield Investment Assocs., 1963—. Class chmn. Alumni Fund Raising Drive Am. Internat. Coll., 1969-76, life/mem. Alumni Varsity Club; vice chmn. Longmeadow (Mass.) Dem. Com.; active Beth El Temple and Jewish Community Ctr., both Springfield. Mem. Mass. Bar Assn., Hampden County Bar Assn. Clubs: Masons, Shriners. Author pamphlet: You and the Law, 1963. Personal injury, Probate, Family and matrimonial. Home: 29 Willett Dr Longmeadow MA 01106 Office: 1331 E Columbus Ave Springfield MA 01105

BURSTEIN, NEIL ALAN, lawyer; b. N.Y.C., June 24, 1951; s. Edward Stuart and Pauline (Linksman) B. B.S., Union Coll., Schenectady, 1973; J.D., Albany Law Sch., 1976; LL.M., NYU, 1983. Bar: N.Y. 1977, U.S. Dist. Ct. (so. dist.) N.Y. 1981. Assoc. Clayman, Mead & Gallo, Schenectady, 1976-78; gen. atty. Waldes Kohinour, Inc., Long Island City, N.Y., 1978-81; assoc. counsel Saks Fifth Ave., N.Y.C., 1981-86; mng. atty. Trans World Airlines Inc., 1986—; legis. counsel to N.Y. state senator A. Frederick Meyerson, Albany, 1973-76. Contbr. chpt. to Entertainment Law (Selz & Simensky), 1983, articles to profl. jours. William C. Saxton scholar Albany Law Sch., 1973. Mem. Assn. Bar City N.Y., ABA, N.Y. State Bar Assn. General corporate, Trademark and copyright, Labor. Home: 305 E 86th St New York NY 10028 Office: Trans World Airlines 605 3d Ave New York NY 10158

BURT, BARRY WAKEFIELD, lawyer; b. Atlanta, Feb. 12, 1956; s. William Sineath and Harriet Watt (Allen) B. BSBA, U. N.C., 1978; JD, MBA, U. Ga., 1981. Bar: Ga. 1981, U.S. Dist. Ct. (no. dist.) Ga. 1982. Assoc. Powell, Goldstein, Frazer and Murphy, Atlanta, 1982-85; v.p., sec., legal counsel Johnstown Properties, Inc., Atlanta, 1985—, also bd. dirs. Castellow scholar U. Ga. Sch. Law, 1978-79. Mem. ABA, Atlanta Bar Assn., Corp. Counsel Assn. of Greater Atlanta, Phi Beta Kappa, Beta Gamma Sigma. Presbyterian. General corporate, Landlord-tenant, Real property. Home: 2955 Crosswyeke Forest Circle Atlanta GA 30319 Office: Johnstown Properties Inc 5775 A Peachtree Dunwoody Rd Atlanta GA 30342

BURT, EARL DANIEL, JR., lawyer; b. Shreveport, La., Sept. 29, 1948; s. Earl Daniel Sr. and Lois Gwendolyn (Cassel) B.; m. Jo Linn Whitsell, May 31, 1970; children: Christopher Mark, Jessica Lynn. BS in Mgmt., La. State U., 1971, JD, 1982; MBA in Mgmt., La. Tech. U., 1976. Bar: La. 1982, U.S. Dist. Ct. (we. dist.) La. 1984, U.S. Ct. Appeals (5th cir.) 1985. Law clk. to presiding justice U.S. Dist. Ct. (we. dist.) La., Shreveport, 1982-84; ptnr. Bain & Burt, Shreveport, 1984—. Served to capt. USAF, 1972-79. Mem. ABA, Assn. Trial Lawyers Am., La. Assn. Criminal Def. Lawyers, La. Trial Lawyers Assn., Delta Theta Phi, Phi Kappa Phi, Order of Coif. Democrat. Lodge: Lions. Avocation: running. Criminal, Personal injury, Federal civil litigation. Office: Bain & Burt 1540 Irving Pl Shreveport LA 71101

BURT, JEFFREY AMSTERDAM, lawyer; b. Phila., Apr. 27, 1944; s. Samuel Matthew and Esther (Amsterdam) B.; m. Sandra Cass, Dec. 17, 1967; children—Stephen, Daniel, Jonathan, Andrew. B.A., Princeton U., 1966; LL.B., Yale U., 1970, M.A. in Econs., 1970. Bar: Md. 1971, D.C. 1971. Law clk. to judge U.S. Ct. Appeals (4th cir.), Balt., 1970-71; assoc. firm Arnold & Porter, Washington, 1971-77, ptnr., 1978—; faculty Internat. Law Inst.; frequent lectr. Pres., Green Acres, Inc., Ind. Sch., Rockville, Md., 1984. Author: (with others) International Joint Ventures, 1986. Federal civil litigation, Administrative and regulatory, Private international. Office: Arnold & Porter 1200 New Hampshire Ave NW Washington DC 20036

BURT, RICHARD MAX, lawyer; b. Phila., Dec. 8, 1944; s. Joseph Frank and Louise Esther (Kevitch) B.; m. Katherine Anne Hedrick, Apr. 25, 1965 (div.); children: Corinne, Julie. BA, Gettysburg (Pa.) Coll., 1965; JD, Dickinson U., 1969. Bar: N.Y. 1970, U.S. Dist. Ct. (so. dist.) N.Y. 1972, U.S. Ct. Appeals (2d cir.) 1972. Assoc. Donovan, Leisure, Newton & Irvine, N.Y.C., 1969-73; asst. counsel Sandoz, Inc., East Hanover, N.J., 1974-78; gen. counsel, v.p., sec. Sandoz Corp., N.Y.C., 1978—; sec. Sandoz Nutrition Corp., Mpls., 1983—, Master Builders Inc., 1985—. Mem. ABA, Westchester-Fairfield Corp. Counsel Assn., Internat. Bar Assn., Am. Corp. Counsel Assn. General corporate, Corporate taxation, Private international. Office: Sandoz Corp 608 Fifth Ave New York NY 10020

BURT, ROBERT AMSTERDAM, lawyer, educator; b. Phila., Feb. 3, 1939; s. Samuel Matthew and Esther (Amsterdam) B.; m. Linda Gordon Rose, June 14, 1964; children—Anne Elizabeth, Jessica Ellen. A.B., Princeton U., 1960; B.A. in Jurisprudence, Oxford (Eng.) U., 1962, M.A., 1968; J.D., Yale U., 1964, M.A. (hon.), 1976. Bar: D.C. 1966, Mich. 1973, U.S. Supreme Ct. 1971. Law clk. to chief judge U.S. Ct. Appeals D.C., 1964-65; asst. gen. counsel Office President's Spl. Rep. Trade Negotiations, 1965-66; senatorial legis. asst. 1966-68; assoc. prof. law U. Chgo. Law Sch., 1968-70; assoc. prof., then prof. law U. Mich. Law Sch., 1970-76; prof. law in psychiatry U. Mich. Med. Sch., 1973-76; prof., then Southmayd prof. law Yale U. Law Sch., 1976—. Bd. dirs. Benhaven Sch. Autistic Persons, New Haven, 1977—, chmn., 1983—, Mental Health Law Project, 1985—. Rockefeller fellow, 1976. Mem. Inst. Medicine. Democrat. Jewish. Legal education. Home: 66 Dogwood Circle Woodbridge CT 06525 Office: Yale U Law Sch 127 Wall St New Haven CT 06520

BURT, ROBERT GENE, lawyer, educator; b. Tucson, Sept. 7, 1944; s. Jack A. and Eva Grace (Colton) B.; m. Stasia Payne, June 7, 1968; children—Jason R., Ashley A. A.A., N.Mex. Mil. Inst., Roswell, 1964; B.A., U. Ariz., 1965, J.D., 1972; LL.M. in Taxation, Georgetown U., 1973. Bar: Ariz. 1972, D.C. 1973, Oreg. 1977. Appeals atty., spl. asst. to asst. atty. gen. tax div. U.S. Dept. Justice, 1973-75, trial atty., 1975-77; sole practice, Portland, Oreg., 1978; ptnr. Robert G. Burt, P.C., Portland, 1978-80, Burt & Hagen, P.C., Portland, 1980-85, Burt & Day, P.C., Portland, 1985-86, Burt, Childs & Gordon P.C., Portland, 1986—; adj. prof. Lewis and Clark Coll. Served to capt. U.S. Army, 1967-71. Decorated Silver Star, Bronze Star with two oak leaf clusters, Purple Heart with one oak leaf cluster, Army Commendation medal with 4 oak leaf clusters, Air Medal with oak leaf cluster. Recipient Spl. Meritous award U.S. Dept. Justice, Washington, 1975. Mem. ABA, Oreg. Bar Assn. (chmn. taxation sect.), Multnomah County Bar Assn., Oreg. Trial Lawyers Assn. Episcopalian. Clubs: University, Multnomah Athletic (Portland). Personal income taxation, Corporate taxation, Securities. Office: Suite 1600 101 SW Main St Portland OR 97204

BURTH, JOHN HAMRICK, lawyer; b. Columbus, Ohio, Aug. 14, 1948; s. James Michael and Jeanne (Hamrick) B.; m. Nancy McNeal, Aug. 10, 1974; children: Kelly, Anne, Molly, Maggie. BA, Denison U., 1970; JD summa cum laude, Ohio State U., 1974. Bar: Ohio, U.S. Dist. Ct. (so. dist.) Ohio 1974, u.S. Dist. Ct. (no. dist.) Ohio 1978, U.S. Ct. Appeals (6th cir) 1982, U.S. Supreme Ct. 1985. Ptnr. Baker & Hostetler and predecessor firm George, Greek, King, McMahon & McConnaughey, Columbus, 1974—. Served with USAR, 1970-76. Mem. ABA, Ohio Bar Assn., Columbus Bar Assn., Columbus Jaycees (bd. dirs. 1974-77), Order of Coif. Republican. Lutheran. Clubs: Athletic, Scioto (Columbus). Avocation: sports. Federal civil litigation, State civil litigation. Office: Baker & Hostetler 65 E State St Columbus OH 43215

BURTI, CHRISTOPHER LOUIS, lawyer; b. Muroc, Calif., Oct. 15, 1950; s. Louis Burti and Johanna Renate (Schmidt) Landa; m. Linda Carol Pipkin, Sept. 15, 1973; children: Christopher Louis Jr., Erika Pipkin. BSBA, East Carolina U., 1976; JD, U. N.C., 1979. Bar: N.C. 1979, U.S. Dist. Ct. (ea. dist.) N.C. 1983. Assoc. Lewis, Lewis & Lewis, Farmville, N.C., 1979-82; ptnr. Lewis, Lewis, Burti & Cummings, Farmville, 1982—; mem. college of advocacy N.C. Bar Found., 1983. Atty. Town of Farmville, N.C., 1982—, Town of Hookerton, N.C., 1981—; pres., bd. dirs. Farmville Child Devel. Ctr., 1983-84; Farmville Community Arts Council, 1983-84, Farmville Charitable Services. Served with U.S. Army, 1970-72. Mem. ABA (real property probate and trust law sect.), N.C. Bar Assn. (arts com. young lawyers div.), N.C. Acad. Trial Lawyers, N.C. Mcpl. Attys. Assn., Pitt County Bar Assn., Nat. Inst. Mcpl. Law Officers (municipality owned utilities com.), Phi Kappa Phi, Beta Gamma Sigma, Phi Sigma Pi, Farmville C. of C. (bd. dirs. 1982-83), Farmville Jaycees. Democrat. Episcopalian. Club: Farmville Country. Lodge: Masons. Avocations: sailing, skiing, woodworking, photography. Real property, Contracts commercial, Local government. Office: Lewis Lewis Burti & Cummings 131 N Main St Farmville NC 27828

BURTON, CLAYTON B., SR., lawyer; b. Rock Island, Ill., Dec. 8, 1932; s. Benjamin Clayton and Beatrice (Harpole) B.; m. Joan Hubbel, Sept. 6, 1956; children—Clayton B., Joan Lowell. B.A., U. Md., 1957, J.D., 1960. Bar: Md. 1960, U.S. Ct. Mil. Appeals 1962, Fla. 1967, U.S. Supreme Ct. 1975. Vice pres. Am. Internat. Land Corp., Miami, Fla., 1962-63; corp. counsel Jack Eckerd Corp., Clearwater, Fla., 1963-64, Li'l Gen. Stores, Tampa, Fla., 1964-67; pres. Burton Profl. Assn., and predecessor firms, Clearwater, 1968—. Author: Estate Planning Understood, 1985, Before You Invest, 1985, Before (and After) You Invest, 1986, new edit., 1987; author videotapes. Served with JAGC, USAF, 1960-62. Recipient USAF Res. Lawyer of Yr. award, 1981, Reservist of Yr. award, 1981, Lawyer of Yr. award Tactical Air Command, USAF, 1980, 81; hon. mem. staff and faculty JAG's Sch. U.S. Army, 1985—. Mem. ABA (standing com. on legal assistance for mil. personnel 1981—, chmn. 1984—, vice chmn. mil. law com. gen. practice sect. 1981—, mem. consortium on legal services and the pub. 1984—, vice chmn. estate planning com. gen. practice sect. 1985—), Res. Officers Assn. (life), Air Force Assn. (life), Scabbard and Blade (past nat. v.p.), Fla. Bar Assn. (chmn. mil. law com. 1979-81), Sigma Nu, Phi Alpha Delta. Republican. Episcopalian. General business, Estate taxation, Living trusts. Home: 1441 Maple Forest Dr Clearwater FL 33546 Office: Burton Profl Assn 2233 Nursery Rd Clearwater FL 33546

BURTON, JOHN PAUL, lawyer; b. New Orleans, Feb. 26, 1943; s. John Paul and Nancy (Key) B.; children: Jennifer, Susanna, Derek, Catherine. BBA magna cum laude, La. Tech. U., 1965; LLB, Harvard U., 1968. Bar: N.Mex. 1968, U.S. Dist. Ct. N.Mex. 1968, U.S. Ct. Appeals (10th cir.) 1973, U.S. Supreme Ct. 1979. Assoc., Rodey, Dickason, Sloan, Akin & Robb, Albuquerque, 1968-74, dir., 1974—, chmn. comml. dept., 1980-81; lectr. workshops, seminars. Contbr. articles to legal publs. Packleader, Greater Southwest council Boy Scouts Am., 1976-77; mem. Mus. N.Mex. Found., N.Mex. Mus. Natural History Found.; fellow State Bar Found., Santa Fe Symphony Assn.; vice chmn. St. Simeon's Retirement Complex; chmn. com. N.Mex. Harvard Law Sch. Fund; bd. dirs. Brunn Sch. Mem. N.Mex. State Bar Assn. (dir., budget officer 1983, chmn. uniform comml. code study and legis. com., sect. corp. bus. and banking 1984), Albuquerque Bar Assn., Santa Fe Bar Assn., Am. Arbitration Assn. (panel arbitrators, regional adv. com.). Republican. Episcopalian (vestry 1977-80; lay reader 1982-84, chmn. evaluation commn., mem. constn. and canons com. Diocese of Rio Grande). Club: Harvard-Radcliffe of N.Mex. (dir. 1981-84). Antitrust, Federal civil litigation, Real property. Office: Rodey Dickason Sloan Akin & Robb PA PO Box 1888 Albuquerque NM 87103 Office: PO Box 1357 Santa Fe NM 87504

BURTON, OSMOND ALEXANDER, JR., lawyer; b. Tucson, Feb. 20, 1934; s. Osmond Alexander and Mattie Lee (Handley) B.; m. Virginia Lee, Apr. 20, 1957; children—Lee Walker, Susan Rachelle, Bethanne; m. 2d, Susan Finnell, Dec. 24, 1981. LL.B., U. Ariz., 1960. Bar: Ariz. 1960, U.S. Dist. Ct. Ariz. 1963. City atty., Scottsdale, Ariz., 1961-65, city mgr., 1965; assoc. Bellamak, Zepp & Mitchell, Scottsdale, 1965-67; ptnr. Burton & Weeks, Scottsdale, 1967-70, Burton, Morgan, Phelps & Clark, Scottsdale, 1971-74, Burton, Phelps, McMahon & Weideman, Scottsdale, 1975-80, sole practice, Scottsdale, 1980-85, Tucson, 1982—. Mem. Scottsdale Bd. Edn., 1970-74. Served with Air N.G., 1957-60. Republican. Methodist. Club: Scottsdale Charros. General corporate, Real property, General practice. Office: 80 S Stone St Tucson AZ 85701

BURTON, RANDALL JAMES, lawyer; b. Sacramento, Feb. 4, 1950; s. Edward Jay and Bernice Mae (Overton) B.; m. Joan Ellen Mather, June 16, 1979; children—Kelly Jacquelyn, Andrew Jameson. B.A., Rutgers U., 1972; J.D., Southwestern U., 1975. Bar: Calif. 1976, U.S. Dist. Ct. (ea. dist.) Calif. 1976. Assoc., Brekke & Mathews, Citrus Heights, Calif., 1976; sole practice, North Highlands Calif., 1976-84, Sacramento, 1985—. Bd. dirs. North Highlands Recreation and Park Dist.; chmn. Local Bd. 22, Selective Service, 1982-86; pres. Active 20-30 Club of Sacramento, 1987. Recipient Disting. Citizen award, Golden Empire Council, Boy Scouts Am. Mem. Sacramento Bar Assn., Sacramento Young Lawyers Assn., North Highlands C. of C. (past pres., dir.). Presbyterian. Lodge: Rotary (pres. Foothill-Highlands club 1980-81). General practice, Personal injury, Probate. Address: 3009 O St Sacramento CA 95816

BURTON, RICHARD JAY, lawyer; b. N.Y.C., May 4, 1949; s. Melvin F. Burton and Shirley (Burton) Silber; m. Truly Burton, June 11, 1972; 1 child, Marc Aaron. BA, George Washington U., 1971; JD, U. Miami, 1974. Bar: Fla. 1974, D.C. 1976, U.S. Supreme Ct. 1979. Adminstrv. aide Fla. Legis., 1973-74; gov. affairs liaison Dade County Fla. Legis., 1974; assoc. Richard H.W. Maloy and Assocs., Coral Gables, Fla., 1974-76; atty., advisor FAA, Washington, 1976-77; assoc. Pompan, Rumizen & Reynolds, Washington, 1978-79, Donald M. Murtha and Assocs., Washington, 1978-79; ptnr. Schoninger, Siegfried, Kipnis, Burton & Sussman PA, Miami, Fla., 1979-82; sole practice Miami, 1982—; guest lectr. U. Miami Sch. of Law, Coral Gables, 1982. Mem. Am. Arbitration Assn. Constr. law panel, 1974—, Builders Assn. S. Fla., legis. com. 1980—, Builder Industry Polit. action com. Mem. ABA, D.C. Bar Assn., Fed. Bar Assn., Fla. Bar Assn. (constr. law com.). Democrat. Jewish. Avocations: skiing, scuba diving, tennis. Federal civil litigation, State civil litigation, Construction. Office: 13899 Biscayne Blvd North Miami Beach FL 33181

BURY, JOHN R., electric utility executive; b. Los Angeles, Nov. 24, 1927; s. John Cecil and Keith Edna (Cameron) B.; m. Eleanor Jeanne Piper, Dec. 16, 1949; children—Bruce, Janice, Elaine, Paul. B.S., U. So. Calif., 1950, B.Laws, 1953. Bar: Calif. With So. Calif. Edison Co., Rosemead, 1954—, sr. counsel, then asst. gen. counsel, until 1978, gen. counsel, 1978-81, v.p., gen. counsel, 1982—. Bd. dirs., Vis. Nurses Assn. San Gabriel Valley, Covina, Calif., 1971-86, past pres.; mem. Inter-Community Med. Ctr. Assn., Covina, 1971—; v.p., bd. dirs. Water Edn. Found., Sacramento, 1978-86. Served with USN, 1946-48. Mem. Los Angeles Area C. of C., ABA, State Bar of Calif., Los Angeles County Bar Assn. (exec. com.), Conf. of Calif. Pub. Utility Counsel (chmn. 1972), Edison Electric Inst. (vice chmn. legal com. 1985). Republican. Avocations: golfing; cooking; poker. Office: So Calif Edison Co 2244 Walnut Grove Ave Rosemead CA 91770

BUSBEE, KLINE DANIEL, JR., lawyer; b. Macon, Ga., Mar. 14, 1933; s. Kline Daniel and Bernice (Anderson) B.; children—Rodgers Christopher, Jon Edward. B.B.A., So. Meth. U., 1961, J.D. 1962. Bar: Tex. 1962. Ptnr. Worsham, Forsythe, Sampels & Busbee, Dallas, 1962-70; shareholder, Locke, Purnell, Rain & Harrell, P.C., Dallas, 1970—; adj. prof. law So. Meth. U. Sch. Law, 1974-83. Mem. ABA, Tex. Bar Assn. Clubs: Dallas, Pinnacle (Dallas). General corporate, Private international, Public international. Home: 4360 San Carlos Dr Dallas TX 75205 Office: 3600 Republic Bank Tower Dallas TX 75201

BUSCH, BENJAMIN, lawyer, educator; b. N.Y.C., June 12, 1912; s. S. Henry and Dorothy (Busch) B.; m. Phyllis Toby Schnell, Nov. 8, 1935; children: Frederick Matthew, Eric Edwin. Student, CCNY, 1928-30; LL.B., St. Lawrence U., 1933. Bar: N.Y. 1934. Partner firm Katz & Sommerich, 1946-76; counsel firm Hamburger, Weinschenk, Molnar & Busch, 1976—; Adj. prof. comparative and internat. law N.Y. Law Sch., 1973—; appointed to Arbitration Panel for the U.S. Dist. Ct. (ea. dist.) N.Y., 1986. Author: (with Otto C. Sommerich) Foreign Law-A Guide to Pleading and Proof, 1959; also articles. Explorer, adviser Boy Scouts Am. Served with AUS, 1944-45. Decorated Bronze Star medal, Purple Heart. Mem. ABA (chmn. sect. internat. law 1972-73, observer to UN 1974-79), N.Y.C. Bar Assn. (mem. internat. law com. 1973-76, fgn. law com. 1978-79), N.Y. State Bar Assn., Am. Judicature Soc., Am. Fgn. Law Assn. (pres. 1969-70, Ann. award 1981), Consular Law Soc., Am. Soc. Internat. Law. Club: Appalachian Mountain (life mem.). Private international, Public international. Office: 36 W 44th St New York NY 10036

BUSCH, DAVID JOHN, lawyer; b. Rochester, N.Y., Mar. 23, 1946; s. Fredrick William and Helen Frances (McNamara) B.; m. Susan McLean, July 23, 1977; children: Christopher, Matthew, Andrew. BS, Xavier U., 1968; JD, Boston Coll., 1971. Bar: Fla. 1972, U.S. Dist. Ct. (no. dist.) Fla. 1974, Ohio 1975, U.S. Supreme Ct. 1975, U.S. Ct. Appeals (11th cir.) 1981. Atty. Fla. Dept. Commerce, Tallahassee, 1972-73; research aide Fla. Supreme Ct., Tallahassee, 1973, chief asst. pub. defender, 1973-79; ptnr. Busch & White, Tallahassee, 1979-84; sole practice Tallahassee, 1984—. Bd. govs. Fla. State Union Legal Services, Tallahassee, 1984—, TAPPS, 1982-84. Served to capt. U.S. Army, 1971-72. Recipient Community Service award Legal Services North Fla., 1985. Mem. Fla. Bar Assn. (cert. of appreciation 1985), Tallahassee Bar Assn. (bd. govs. legal services 1985—), Assn. Trial Lawyers Am., Acad. Fla. Trial Lawyers, Nat. Assn. Criminal Def. Lawyers. Democrat. Roman Catholic. Clubs: Serra (pres. 1984-85), Legion of Mary (Tallahassee) (v.p. 1985—). State civil litigation, Criminal, Personal injury. Home: 3428 Robinhood Rd Tallahassee FL 32312 Office: 245 E Virginia Tallahassee FL 32301

BUSCH, GARY M(ITCHELL), lawyer; b. Detroit, Aug. 14, 1956. BA in Philosophy, U. Mich., 1978; JD, Detroit Coll. of Law, 1981. Bar: Mich. 1981, U.S. Dist. Ct. (ea. dist.) Mich. 1981, U.S. Ct. Appeals (6th cir.) 1982. Ptnr. Grant & Busch, Southfield, Mich., 1979—. Labor, Personal injury, Workers' compensation. Office: Grant & Busch 24700 Northwestern Hwy Suite 410 Southfield MI 48075

BUSCH, H. DONALD, lawyer; b. Phila., Sept. 21, 1935; s. Louis J. and Ethel K. (Fels) B.; m. Judith C. Snyder, May 15, 1960; children—Jon, Amy, Lauren, Hillary; m. Sondra B. Schlomchik, Aug. 26, 1979; stepchildren—Janice, Wendy, Cindy, Adam. A.B. in Physics and Math., U. Pa., 1956, LL.B., 1959. Bar: N.Y. 1960, Pa. 1961, U.S. Supreme Ct., U.S. Ct. Appeals (2d, 3d and 9th cirs.), U.S. Dist. Ct. (ea. dist.) Pa., U.S. Dist. Ct. (so. and ea. dists.) N.Y., U.S. Tax Ct. Pres., Busch, Grafman & Von Dreusche, P.C., Bala Cynwyd, Pa. Bd. dirs. Phila. All-Star Forum, Rainbow Fund, Suburban Gen. Hosp., Nat. Assn. of Theatre Owners; pres. Budco Theatres, Inc. Recipient Nat. Math. award Pi Mu Epsilon. Mem. ABA, Pa. Bar Assn., Phila. Bar Assn., Montgomery County Bar Assn. (bd. dirs.), U.S. Dist. Ct. Lawyers Adv. Com. General corporate, Antitrust, Entertainment. Address: 555 City Line Ave Bala Cynwyd PA 19004

BUSCH, JOHN ARTHUR, lawyer; b. Indpls., Mar. 23, 1951; s. John L. and Betty (Thomas) B.; m. Barbara Ann Holt, June 23, 1973; children: Abigail, Elizabeth, Amanda, Rachel. BA, Wabash Coll., 1973; JD, Duke U., 1976. Bar: Wis. 1976, U.S. Dist. Ct. (ea. we. dists.) Wis., U.S. Ct. Appeals (5th and 7th cirs.) 1976. Assoc. Michael, Best & Friedrich, Milw., 1976-83, ptnr., 1983—; counsel Wis. Vision Service Plan, Milw., 1985—. Treas. North Shore Rep. Club, Milw., 1984—, vice chmn., 1985-86, chmn., 1987—; del. Rep. State Conv., Milw., 1986; mem. local rules adv. com., Eastern Dist., Wis. Mem. ABA, Wis. Bar Assn., Milw. Bar Assn. Federal civil litigation, State civil litigation, Health. Home: 4426 N Prospect Ave Shorewood WI 53211 Office: Michael Best & Friedrich 250 E Wisconsin Ave Milwaukee WI 53202

BUSCH, PETER JONATHAN, lawyer; b. Evanston, Ill., June 24, 1952; s. Albert Eliot and Vera (Ellman) B.; m. Catharine S. Barnes, June 6, 1982; 1 child, Frank. BA magna cum laude, Yale Coll., 1974; JD, U. Va., 1977. Bar: Calif. 1981, U.S. Dist. Ct. (no. dist.) Calif. 1981, U.S. Ct. Appeals (9th cir.) 1981. Law clk. U.S. Ct. Appeals (1st cir.), 1977-79; law clk. to Justice William J. Brennan U.S. Supreme Ct., Washington, 1979-80; assoc. Howard, Rice, Nemerovski, Canady, Robertson & Falk, San Francisco, 1980-84, ptnr., 1984—, also bd. dirs. Mem. ABA (litigation, urban, state and local govt. law sections), Bar Assn. Calif., Bar Assn. San Francisco. Federal civil litigation, State civil litigation, Local government. Office: Howard Rice Nemerovski Canady Three Embarcadero Ctr 7th Floor San Francisco CA 94111

BUSH, EDWARD PHILIP, lawyer; b. Nassawadox, Va., May 6, 1953; s. Edward P. Bush and Anne B. (Brewer) Miller; m. Pamela Slaughter, June 12, 1976; children: Elizabeth, Emily. BA, Southwestern U., 1975; JD, So. Meth. U., 1978, LLM in Taxation, 1985. Bar: Tex. 1978, U.S. Dist. Ct. (no. dist.) Tex. 1979, U.S. Tax Ct. 1979, U.S. Ct. Claims 1979, U.S. Ct. Appeals (5th cir.) 1979, U.S. Supreme Ct. 1981. Ptnr. Taylor & Mizell, Dallas, 1978—. Trustee Univ. Park United Meth. Ch. Found., Dallas, 1982—, Southwestern U., Georgetown, Tex., 1975-77. Mem. ABA (taxation sect.), Tex. Bar Assn. (taxation sect.), Dallas Bar Assn. (taxation sect.), Tex. Bd. Legal Specialization (cert.). Republican. Pension, profit-sharing, and employee benefits, Corporate taxation, Personal income taxation. Office: Taylor & Mizell 3000 Lincoln Plaza Dallas TX 75201

BUSH, EDWIN FRANKLIN, JR., lawyer; b. Hartford City, Ind., July 30, 1944; s. Edwin Franklin and Estella Marie (Burklo) B.; children: Edwin F. III, Susan Marie. BS, Ball State U., 1966; JD, Ind. U., Indpls., 1972. Bar: Wis. 1973, Ind. 1973, U.S. Dist. Ct. (so. dist.) Ind. 1973, U.S. Dist. Ct. (ea. and we. dist.) Wis. 1973. Law clk. to presiding justice Ind. Supreme Ct., Indpls., 1972-73; assoc. Gibbs, Roper, Loots & Williams, Milw., 1973-78; legal counsel Johnson Controls Inc., Milw., 1978-80; sr. legal counsel Appleton (Wis.) Papers Inc., 1980-86, asst. gen. counsel, asst. sec., 1986—. Chmn. Parking Transit Commn., Appleton, 1982—; bd. dirs. Friends Mosquito Hill Nature Ctr., Appleton, 1980-84. Mem. ABA, Wis. Bar Assn., Outagamie County BAr Assn., Am. Corp. Counsel Assn. General corporate, Labor, Contracts commercial. Home: 1504 N Nicholas Appleton WI 54914 Office: Appleton Papers Inc PO Box 359 Appleton WI 54912

BUSH, FRED MARSHALL, JR., lawyer; b. Newhebron, Miss., Jan. 25, 1917; s. Frederick Marshall Sr. and Elizabeth Stewart (Buck) B.; m. Katie Ruth Field, May 8, 1942; children: Frederick Marshall III, Carl J., Richard S. AA, Hinds Jr. Coll., 1935; BS, U.S. Naval Acad., 1939; LLB, U. Miss., 1950. Bar: Miss. 1948, U.S. Dist. Ct. Miss. 1948, U.S. Ct. Appeals (5th and 11th cirs.) 1948, U.S. Supreme Ct. 1948. Commd. ensign USN, 1939, advanced through grades to capt., 1948, resigned, 1948, with Res., 1948-60; ptnr. Fant & Bush, Holly Springs, Miss., 1950-60, Mitchell, McNutt, Bush, Lagrone & Sams, Tupelo, Miss., 1962—. Bd. dirs. Miss. Bd. Econ. Devel., Jackson, Miss., 1960-68, Tenn.-Tombigbee Waterway Devel. Authority, Columbus, Miss., 1980-84. Fellow Miss. Bar Found. (chmn. 1978); mem. ABA (ho. of dels. 1986—), Miss. Bar Assn. (pres. 1986-87, various coms. and offices), Miss. Def. Lawyers Assn. (pres. 1973-74). Episcopalian. Lodge: Rotary (pres. local club 1954-55). General corporate, Insurance, Municipal bonds. Office: Mitchell McNutt Bush Lagrone & Sams PO Box 466 Tupelo MS 38802

BUSH, GRANVILLE MCCUTCHEON, III, lawyer; b. Kansas City, Mo., July 15, 1920; s. Granville McCutcheon and Helen Almarine (DeFord) B.; m. Letha Virginia Bush, Jan. 31, 1943; children—Helen Louise Frick, Granville McCutcheon IV, John Stuart. B.S., U. Kans., 1942, J.D., 1948. Bar: Kans. 1948, U.S. dist. ct. Kans. 1948. Assoc. Morrison, Nugent, Berger, Hecker & Buck, Kansas City, Mo., 1948, Woleslagel, Gaston & Bush, Lyons, Kans., 1949-52; county atty. Rice County (Kans.), 1948-50, 53-58; sole practice Lyons, Kans., 1958-77; ptnr. Bush, Bush & Shanelec (formerly Bush and Bush, Lyons and Sterling), Kans., 1978—. Chmn. 5th Congl. Dist. Young Republicans. Served to lt. USN, 1942-46. Fellow Coll. Probate Counsel; mem. Kans. Bar Assn. (chmn. client security fund), S.W. Kans. Bar Assn. (pres. 1975-76), Rice County Bar Assn. (pres.), Phi Delta Phi. Republican. Presbyterian. Probate, Real property, Local government. Home: 904 East Ave S Lyons KS 67554 Office: 111 East Ave S Lyons KS 67554

BUSH, JULIAN S., lawyer, law educator; b. N.Y.C., Aug. 26, 1915; s. Joachim F. and Isabelle (Rosenthal) B.; m. Irma Rhoda Terr, Nov. 7, 1936;

children—Dorothy Isabel, Jacqueline Leslie, Kathryn Debra; m. 2d, Bette Verner Bain Roe, Oct. 31, 1980. A.B., Columbia U., 1934, J.D., 1936. Bar: N.Y. 1937, U.S. Dist. Ct. (so. dist.) N.Y., U.S. Dist. Ct. (ea. dist.) N.Y., U.S. Ct. Appeals (2d cir.), U.S. Ct. Claims, U.S. Tax Ct. Assoc. T. Roland Berner, N.Y.C., 1946-61; ptnr. Leventritt, Bush, Lewittes & Bender, N.Y.C., 1961-68, Bush & Schlesinger, N.Y.C., 1968-73, Roberts & Holland, N.Y.C., 1973-76, Shea & Gould, N.Y.C., 1976—; adj. prof. law Columbia U., 1958-82, NYU, 1982—. Served with AUS, 1945. James Kent scholar Columbia Law Sch., 1936. Mem. ABA, N.Y. State Bar Assn., N.Y.C. Lawyers Assn., Am. Coll. Probate Counsel, Internat. Acad. Estate and Trust Law, N.Y.C. Estate Planning Council. Contbr. numerous articles to profl. jours. Estate planning, Probate, Estate taxation. Office: Shea & Gould 330 Madison Ave New York NY 10017

BUSH, ROBERT G., III, lawyer, state legislator; b. Kansas City, Mo., Jan. 15, 1936; s. Robert G. and Margaret Irene (Woolard) B.; m. Wanda Lou Baker, Jan. 20, 1962; 1 dau., Sherry O'Shea. B.A., Kans. U., 1957; J.D., So. Meth. U., 1963. Bar: Tex. 1963, U.S. Dist. Ct. (ea. dist.) Tex. 1964, U.S. Ct. Appeals (5th cir.) 1974, U.S. Supreme Ct. 1974. Assoc. Nance & Caston, Sherman, Tex., 1963-65; assoc. Slagle & Kennedy, Sherman, 1965-67; sole practice, Sherman, 1967—; mem. Tex. Ho. of Reps., 1977—, majority leader House Democratic Caucus, 1981—, chmn. judiciary com., 1981—; instr. Grayson County Jr. Coll., 1968-72. Served with U.S. Army, 1958-59. Fellow Tex. Bar Found.; mem. Tex. Trial Lawyers Assn. (past assoc. dir.). Episcopalian. State civil litigation, Family and matrimonial, Workers' compensation.

BUSH, WENDELL EARL, lawyer; b. Little Rock, Dec. 10, 1943; s. David J. and Anne (Hampton) B. A.B., Philander South Coll., 1965; postgrad. Atlanta U., 1966; J.D., Emory U., 1969. Bar: Ga. 1971, Ind., Tenn. Atty., Emory U. Law Ctr., Atlanta, 1969-71, Indpls. Legal Aid Soc., 1969-72, EEOC, Memphis, 1973—. Bd. dirs. Boy Scouts Am., Memphis. Hal S. Clark fellow, 1968; Reginald Hebersmitt fellow, 1969-71. Mem. ABA, Nat. Bar Assn., Omega Psi Phi, Phi Alpha Delta (treas.). Methodist. Labor, Federal civil litigation, Administrative and regulatory. Home: 3685 Winchester Park Ctr #8 Memphis TN 38118

BUSH, WILLIAM, lawyer; b. Ft. Bragg, N.C., Feb. 13, 1954; s. Harry Leonard and Mary Olive (Strozier) B.; 1 child, William. AB, Princeton U., 1975; JD, Case Western Res. U., 1978. Bar: Tenn. 1978, U.S. Dist. Ct. (ea. dist.) Tenn. 1979, U.S. Dist. Ct. Mass. 1981, U.S. Ct. Appeals (6th cir.) 1981, U.S. Dist. Ct. (mid. dist.) Tenn. 1982. Atty. Southeast Tenn. Legal Services, Chattanooga, 1978-81, Edn./Instruction, Roxbury, Mass., 1981-82; atty. Rural Legal Services Tenn., Inc., Cookeville, 1982-83, mng. atty., 1983—. Mem. Assn. Trial Lawyers Am. Federal civil litigation, Civil rights, Health. Office: Rural Legal Services Tenn Inc Courthouse Sq Arcade Bldg Cookeville TN 38501

BUSHNELL, GEORGE EDWARD, JR., lawyer; b. Detroit, Nov. 15, 1924; s. George E. and Mary (Bland) B.; m. Elizabeth McLeod Whelden, June 17, 1950; children: George Edward III, Christopher Gilbert Whelden, Robina McLeod. Mil. student, U. Kans., 1943; BA, Amherst Coll., 1948; LLB, U. Mich., 1951. From assoc. to sr. ptnr. Miller, Canfield, Paddock and Stone, Detroit, 1953-77; sr. ptnr. Bushnell, Gage & Reizen, Detroit and Southfield, Mich., 1977—; commr. Mich. Jud. Tenure Commn., 1969-83, chmn., 1979-80; pres. State Bar Mich., 1975-76; bd. dirs. Nat. Jud. Coll.; lectr. in field. Elder Grosse Pointe Meml. Ch.; moderator Detroit Presbytery, United Presbyn. Ch. U.S.A., 1972, pres. program agy. bd., 1972-76; bd. dirs. Econ. Devel. Corp. of Detroit, 1976—, Econ. Growth Corp. of Detroit, 1978—; trustee New Detroit, Inc., 1972—, chmn., 1974-75. Served with USAR, 1943-46, 51-53. Decorated Bronze Star. Mem. ABA (Ho. of Dels. 1976—, bd. govs. 1985—), Detroit Bar Assn. (pres. 1964-65), Nat. Conf. Bar Pres. (pres. 1984-85), 6th Jud. Cir. Conf. (life), Am. Law Inst., Am. Arbitration Assn. (dir. 1970-82), Am. Coll. Trial Lawyers, Am. Bar Found. (life), Am. Judicature Soc. (dir. 1977-82), Internat. Soc. Barristers, Fed. Bar Assn., Trial Attys. Am., Def. Research Inst., Indsl. Relations Research Assn., NAACP (life), Phi Delta Phi, Psi Upsilon. Democrat. Clubs: Detroit, Country of Detroit, The Players (Detroit); Metropolitan (N.Y.C.). Lodge: Masons (33 degree). Federal civil litigation, State civil litigation, General corporate. Home: 262 Vendome Ct Grosse Pointe Farms MI 48236 Office: Bushnell Gage Doctoroff & Reizen 500 Buhl Bldg Detroit MI 48226 Office: 3000 Town Center Bldg Suite 1500 Southfield MI 48075

BUSHNELL, RODERICK P., lawyer; b. Buffalo, Mar. 6, 1944; s. Paul H. and Martha A. Bushnell; m. Suzann Y. Kaiser, Aug. 27, 1966; 1 son, Arlo P. B.A., Rutgers U., 1966; J.D., Georgetown U., 1969. Bar: Calif. 1970, U.S. Supreme Ct. 1980. Atty. dept. water resources Sacramento, 1969-71; ptnr. Bushnell, Caplan & Fielding, San Francisco, 1971—; chmn. bd. dirs. Bread & Roses, Inc., 1983-86. Bd. dirs. Bay Area Lawyers for the Arts. Mem. Bar Assn. of San Francisco, Calif. Bar Assn., Lawyers Club of San Francisco, Calif. Trial Lawyers Assn., San Francisco Trial Lawyers Assn., No. Calif. Criminal Trial Lawyers Assn. Democrat. Presbyterian. Clubs: San Francisco Bay, Commonwealth (San Francisco). Federal civil litigation, State civil litigation, Labor. Home: 86 Montezuma San Francisco CA 94110 Office: Bushnell Caplan & Fielding 901 Market St Suite 230 San Francisco CA 94103

BUSICK, DENZEL REX, lawyer; b. Council Bluffs, Iowa, Oct. 16, 1945; s. Guy Henry and Selma Ardith (Woods) B.; m. Cheryl Ann Callahan, June 17, 1967; children—Elizabeth Colleen, Guy William. B.S. in Bus. Adminstrn., U. Nebr.-Omaha, 1969; J.D., Creighton U., 1971. Bar: Nebr. 1971, U.S. Dist. Ct. Nebr. 1971, U.S. Ct. Apls. (8th cir.) 1975, U.S. Sup. Ct. 1974; civil diplomate Nat. Bd. Trial Advocacy. Law clk., U.S. Dist. Ct. Nebr., 1970-72; mem. Fraser, Stryker, Veach, Vaughn, Meusey, Olsen & Boyer, Omaha, 1972-78; assoc. Kay & Satterfield, North Platte, Nebr., 1979-80; ptnr. Luebs, Dowding, Beltzer, Leininger, Smith & Busick, Grand Island, Nebr., 1980—. Mem. ABA, Assn. Trial Lawyers Am., Nat. Inst. Trial Advocacy, Am. Judicature Soc., Nebr. State Bar Assn., Nebr. Assn. Trial Attys., Mensa, Phi Alpha Delta. Republican. Club: Kiwanis (Grand Island). Contbr. to publs. in field. State civil litigation, Federal civil litigation, Insurance. Home: 3027 Brentwood Pl Grand Island NE 68801 Office: Wheeler at First St PO Box 790 Grand Island NE 68802

BUSNER, PHILIP H., lawyer; b. Bklyn., Mar. 26, 1927; s. Joseph and Ray (Grajewer) B.; m. Naomi Marcia Greenfield, June 24, 1951; children—Joan Alexandra, Carey Elizabeth. B.A. cum laude, NYU, 1949; LL.B., Harvard U., 1952. Bar: N.Y. 1953, U.S. Dist. Ct. (so. dist.) N.Y. 1956, U.S. Dist. Ct. (ea. dist.) N.Y. 1958, U.S. Ct. Appeals (2d cir.) 1956 U.S. Supreme Ct. 1974. Assoc., Hess, Mela, Segall, Popkin & Guterman, N.Y.C., Rein, Mound & Cotton, N.Y.C., Carroad & Carroad, N.Y.C.; now ptnr. Sonnenfeld, Busner & Richman, N.Y.C. Trustee Asthmatic Children's Found. of N.Y., 1978-87. Served with USAAF, 1945-47. Mem. ABA, N.Y. State Bar, Assn. of Bar City of N.Y., Phi Beta Kappa. General practice, Federal civil litigation, State civil litigation. Office: Sonnenfeld Busner & Richman 360 Lexington Ave New York NY 10017

BUSSEWITZ, ROY JON, lawyer; b. Hartford, Wis., Mar. 19, 1944; s. Reginald Max and Bernice (Kadolph) B.; m. Joyce Ann O'Donnell, Aug. 24, 1980; 1 child, Kathleen Ann. BS in Pharmacy, U. Wis., 1967; JD, Valparaiso U., 1973. Bar: Wis. 1973. Legal cons. State of Wis., Madison, 1979; legis. asst., health U.S. Senator Gaylord Nelson, Washington, 1979-81; legis. counsel Am. Health Care Assn., Washington, 1981; exec. dir. Nat. Assn. Med. Equipment Suppliers, Alexandria, Va., 1982-84; dir. govt. relations Nat. Assn. Pvt. Psychiat. Hosps., Washington, 1984-85; dir. fed. govt. affairs Glaxo Inc., Alexandria, 1985—. Mem. Am. Pharm. Assn., Am. Soc. Hosp. Pharmacists, Nat. Assn. Retail Druggists, Am. Soc. Pharmacy Law, Wis. Bar Assn. Club: North Carolina Society (Washington). Avocations: tennis, golf, gardening, photography. Legislative, Health, Administrative and regulatory. Home: 8403 Brewster Dr Alexandria VA 22308 Office: Glaxo Inc 1800 Diagonal Rd Suite 140 Alexandria VA 22314

BUTCHER, BRUCE CAMERON, lawyer; b. N.Y.C., Feb. 17, 1947; s. John Richard and Dorothy Helen (Wehner) B.; m. Kathryn Ann Fiddler, Oct. 12, 1979; 1 child, Kristen Ann. BS, Belknap Coll., 1969; JD, St.John's U., N.Y.C., 1972. Bar: N.Y. 1973, U.S. Dist. Ct. (so. dist.) N.Y. 1974, La. 1980, U.S. Dist. Ct. (ea. dist.) La. 1980, U.S. Ct. Appeals (5th and 11th cirs.) 1981. Assoc. Laporte and Meyers, N.Y.C., 1972-73; asst. chief contract div. Corp. Counsel's Office City of N.Y., 1973-79; ptnr. Chaffe, McCall, Phillips, Toler & Sarpy, New Orleans, 1980-84; prin. Bruce C. Butcher, P.C., Metairie, La., 1985—. Mem. ABA (regional chmn. pub. report 1975, cert. of performance 1975, litigation sect. 1977, state chmn. pub. contracts sect. 1984—), La. Bar Assn., Am. Arbitration Assn. Federal civil litigation, State civil litigation, Construction. Home: 344 Homestead Metairie LA 70005 Office: 1 Lakeway Ctr Suite 1300 Metairie LA 70002

BUTLER, A(RTHUR) BATES, III, lawyer; b. N.Y.C., Aug. 17, 1944; s. A. Bates Jr. and Mary Katherine (Wiley) B.; m. Ann Kathleen Johnson, Nov. 29, 1974; children: Robert Bates, Elizabeth Ann. BA, Trinity U., 1966; JD, George Washington U., 1969. Bar: Ariz. 1969, U.S. Dist. Ct. Ariz. 1969, U.S. Ct. Appeals (9th cir.) 1974, U.S. Supreme Ct. 1977. Dep. atty. Pima County Atty., Tucson, 1970-77; 1st asst. U.S. atty. Dept. Justice, Tucson, 1977-80, U.S. atty., 1980-81; ptnr. Butler & King, Tucson, 1981-84; sole practice Tucson, 1984-85; ptnr. Butler & Stein P.C., Tucson, 1985—. Bd. dirs. Community Orgn. for Drug Abuse Control, Tucson, 1977-81, chmn., 1981-82. Named one of Outstanding Young Men Am., 1979. Founding fellow Ariz. Bar Found.; mem. Ariz. Bar Assn., Pima County Bar Assn., Ariz. Trial Lawyers Assn., Ariz. Criminal Def. Assn. (founding), Assn. Former U.S. Attys. Democrat. Presbyterian. Club: Ducks Unltd. Avocations: hunting, fishing, skiing, scuba diving. General practice, Family and matrimonial, Criminal. Home: 2702 E 4th St Tucson AZ 85716 Office: Butler & Stein PC 110 S Church Suite 420 Tucson AZ 85701

BUTLER, DAVID DOUGLAS, lawyer; b. San Mateo, Calif., Dec. 17, 1945; s. Ernest Porter and Leura Kathryn (Regan) B.; m. Karen Leigh Wendt, July 5, 1975. BA in History, San Francisco State U., 1973; postgrad., Stanford U. Sch. Law, 1976; JD, Willamette U., 1978. Bar: Iowa, 1978, U.S. Dist. Ct. (no. and so. dists.) Iowa 1978, U.S. Ct. Appeals (8th cir.) 1979, U.S. Supreme Ct. 1981. Law clk. to justice Iowa Supreme Ct., Des Moines, 1978-79; assoc. Davis, Hockenberg, Wine, Brown & Koehn, Des Moines, 1979-81; ptnr. Martell & Butler, Des Moines, 1981-85; sole practice Des Moines, 1985—. Author: But We Were Born Free: The Racial and Sexual Quota as a Constitutional Bill of Attainder, 1983. Mem. ABA, Iowa State Bar Assn., Polk County Bar Assn., Assn. Trial Lawyers of Iowa. Republican. Episcopalian. Clubs: Moingona Hunt, Des Moines Polo. Avocations: fox hunting, dressage, reading, writing. Criminal, Personal injury, Family and matrimonial. Office: 600 Fifth Ave Plaza Des Moines IA 50309

BUTLER, EDWARD FRANKLYN, lawyer; b. Memphis, Tenn., July 1, 1937; s. Oliver John and Arlene (Lovelace) B.; m. Donnay Gay Cox, Jan. 29, 1965 (div. Feb. 1975); children: Edward F. (Rhett) II, Jeffrey Darrell. BA, U. Miss., 1958; JD, Vanderbilt U., 1961; MA, Memphis State U., 1984. Bar: Tenn. 1961, Tex. 1962, U.S. Supreme Ct. 1985. Sole practice Memphis, 1961—; practice law South Padre Island, Tex.; prof. law Pan Am. U., Edingburg, Tex., 1985—. Contbr. articles to profl. jours. Served to comdr. USNR. Recipient U.S. Congress Community Service award. Mem. South Padre Island Merchant's Assn. (pres. 1985-86), Port Isabel-South Padre Island C. of C. (pres.), SAR. Republican. Episcopalian. Banking, State civil litigation, General practice. Home: 2800 Gulf Blvd #1104 South Padre Island TX 78597 Office: 100 N Main Bldg Memphisville TN 38103 Office: 2009 A Padre Blvd South Padre Island TX 78597

BUTLER, FELICITA THERESE, lawyer; b. Los Angeles, Jan. 30, 1950; d. James Girard and Eugenia (Jefferson) B. BA, U. Calif., Berkeley, 1977, JD, 1982. Assoc. Butler, Dan, Allis & Reback, Los Angeles, 1982—. Mem. Los Angeles County Bar Assn., Assn. Trial Lawyers Am., Calif. Trial Lawyers Assn., Los Angeles Trial Lawyers Assn., Calif. Women Lawyers. Democrat. State civil litigation, Probate. Office: Butler Dan Allis & Reback 626 Wilshire Blvd Los Angeles CA 90017

BUTLER, GARY FRANK, lawyer; b. Beaumont, Tex., May 12, 1954; s. Archie Frank and Billie Mae (Leatherwood) B.; m. Judith Mills, June 25, 1983; children: Christian Michael, Stewart Madison. BA, Baylor U., 1974; M Pub. Adminstrn., North Tex. State U., 1977; JD, South Tex. State U., 1982. Bar: Tex. 1982, U.S. Dist. Ct. (we. dist.) Tex. 1986, U.S. Ct. Appeals (5th cir.) 1986. Planner Heart of Tex. Council of Govts., Waco, 1974-76; adminstr. Greater East Tex. Health Systems Agy., Beaumont, 1977-80; assoc. Waldman & Smallwood, Beaumont, 1982-84; prosecutor McLennan County Dist. Atty. Office, Waco, 1984-85; sole practice Waco, 1985—; instr. criminal law McLennan Community Coll., 1984-85. Mem. ABA, Tex. Bar Assn., McLennan County Bar Assn., Assn. Trial Lawyers Am., Tex. Trial Lawyers Assn., Waco Jaycees, Order of Lytae, Delta Theta Phi. Democrat. Baptist. Home: 2800 Austin Ave Waco TX 76710 Office: 700 S University Parks Dr Waco TX 76701

BUTLER, GEOFFREY JOHN BUTLER, lawyer; b. Melbourne, Australia, Aug. 18, 1930; s. Arthur Harold and Edith (Moon) B. B.A., U. Utah, 1961; J.D., Golden Gate U., 1973. Bar: Utah. 1975. Clk., Utah Supreme Ct., Salt Lake City, 1976—. Served with U.S. Army, 1954-56. Public international, Judicial administration, Labor. Office: Utah Supreme Ct 332 State Capitol Salt Lake City UT 84114

BUTLER, JOHN EDWARD, lawyer; b. Teaneck N.J., Dec. 8, 1946; s. John Edward and Alice Mary (Knorr) B.; m. Joan Marie Watson, Jan. 18, 1969; children—Jennifer, Kathryn, John Michael. B.S., St. Peter's Coll., 1968; J.D. cum laude, Syracuse U., 1974. Bar: N.Y. 1974, U.S. Dist. Ct. (no. dist.) N.Y. 1974. Assoc. firm Ali & Gerber, Syracuse, N.Y., 1972-77, firm Ali, Gerber, Pappas & Cox, Syracuse, 1977-79; sole practice, Syracuse, 1979—. Mem. Onondaga County Bar Assn. (trial lawyers com. 1981—), N.Y. State Bar Assn., U.S. Res. Officers Assn. Republican. Roman Catholic. Criminal, State civil litigation, Personal injury. Home: 8642 Greybirch St Baldwinsville NY 13027 Office: 601 University Bldg Syracuse NY 13202

BUTLER, PAUL B., lawyer; b. Charleston, S.C., Nov. 27, 1947; s. Paul B. and Mary Anna (Tisdale) B.; m. Virginia Eldridge, June 14, 1969; children: Jeffrey Bryan, Robert Paul. BA, Emory U., 1969, MDiv cum laude, 1972, JD with distinction, 1976. Bar: Ga. 1976, Fla. 1977; ordained minister Meth. Ch. Assoc. minister United Meth. Ch., 1969-73; assoc. Swift, Currie, McGhee and Hiers, Atlanta, 1976-79; ptnr. Butler & Burnette, Tampa, Fla., 1979—; speaker Property Loss Mgr.'s Conf. Property Loss Research Bur., 1981—, Def. Research Inst., ABA Nat. Inst. Contbr. articles to profl. jours. Mem. ABA (chmn. property ins. law com. 1985-86, editor so. region Annotated Homeowner's Policy), Fla. Bar Assn., Ga. Bar Assn., Internat. Assn. Ins. Counsel, Def. Research Inst., Fla. Def. Lawyers Assn., Hillsborough County Bar Assn, Internat. Assn. Def. Counsel. Democrat. Clubs: Temple Terr. (Fla.) Golf and Country; Tampa. Avocation: golf. Insurance, Federal civil litigation, State civil litigation. Home: 807 Ben Lomond Dr Temple Terrace FL 33617 Office: Butler & Burnette 6200 Courtney Campbell Causeway Bayport Plaza Suite 1100 Tampa FL 33607-1458

BUTLER, SAMUEL COLES, lawyer; b. Logansport, Ind., Mar. 10, 1930; s. Melvin Linwood and Jane Lavina (Flynn) B.; m. Sally Eugenia Thackston, June 28, 1952; children: Samuel Coles, Leigh F., Elizabeth J. B.A. magna cum laude, Harvard U., 1951, LL.B. magna cum laude, 1954. Bar: D.C. 1954, Ind. 1954, N.Y. 1957. Law clk. to Justice Minton U.S. Supreme Ct., 1954; assoc. Cravath, Swaine & Moore, N.Y.C., 1956-60, ptnr., 1961—; dir. Ashland Oil, Inc., Geico Corp.; trustee U.S. Trust Co. N.Y. Trustee Vassar Coll., 1969-77; trustee N.Y. Pub. Library, 1979—; chmn. Harvard Coll. Fund., 1977-85; bd. overseers Harvard U., 1982—; bd. dirs. Culver Ednl. Found., 1981—. Served with U.S. Army, 1954-56. Mem. Council Fgn. Relations. General corporate, Securities, Private international. Home: 1220 Park Ave New York NY 10128 Office: Cravath Swaine & Moore 1 Chase Manhattan Plaza New York NY 10005

BUTLER, WALLACE WEBB, lawyer; b. Sibley, Iowa, Apr. 6, 1920; s. Benjamin Franklin and Alice Annice (Webb) B.; m. Marjorie Ann Van Hoesen, Nov. 9, 1946; children: Madelyn Ann Butler Kaufman, Barbara Lorraine, Joan Alice Butler McGee. BSEE, U. Iowa, 1942, JD, 1948. Bar: Iowa 1948. Ptnr. Clark, Butler et al, Waterloo, Iowa. Served to capt. USAF, 1942-45, ETO, PTO. Mem. Black Hawk County Bar Assn. Probate, Real property. Home: 1824 Winter Ridge Rd Cedar Falls IA 50613 Office: Clark Butler et al PO Box 596 Waterloo IA 50704

BUTNER, BLAIN BYERLY, lawyer; b. Winston-Salem, N.C., Oct. 15, 1953; s. Fred Washington Jr. and Martha (Hinkle) B.; m. Peggy Tentinger, Sept. 15, 1984; 1 child, Sarah Thiel. AB, Davidson Coll., 1975; JD, Duke U., 1980. Bar: D.C. 1980, N.C. 1981, U.S. Dist. Ct. D.C. 1981, U.S. Ct. Appeals (D.C. cir.) 1981. Legis. asst. govtl. affairs com. U.S. Senate, Washington, 1975-77; assoc. Dow, Lohnes & Albertson, Washington, 1980—. Chmn. Buckingham Village Housing Corp., Arlington, Va. Mem. Fed. Bar Assn. (bd. dirs. younger lawyers div. 1984—, treas. 1986—), Phi Beta Kappa, Omicron Delta Kappa. Avocations: theater, swimming, travel. Administrative and regulatory, Legislative, Higher education. Home: 4733 S 6th St Arlington VA 22204-1368 Office: Dow Lohnes & Albertson 1255 23d St NW #500 Washington DC 20037

BUTOWSKY, DAVID MARTIN, lawyer; b. Phila., Aug. 14, 1936; s. Hyman and Pearl (Berks) B.; divorced; children: Michael, Ellen, Edward, Erica; m. Fredda Butowsky. A.B., Temple U., 1958; LL.B., George Washington U., 1962. Bar: Md. 1962, N.Y. 1971. Practice law N.Y.C., 1971—; chief enforcement atty. SEC, Washington, 1962-70; assoc. Breed Abbott & Morgan, N.Y.C., 1970-71; ptnr. Butowsky Schwenke & Devine, N.Y.C., 1971-75, Gordon Hurwitz Butowsky Weitzen Shalov & Wein, N.Y.C., 1975—; lectr. to orgns. Contbr. articles to profl. publs. Mem. Am., Fed., N.Y. County bar assns., City Bar Assn. N.Y. Securities. Home: 320 E 46th St Apt 8(e) New York NY 10017 Office: 101 Park Ave New York NY 10178

BUTT, THOMAS FRANKLIN, judge; b. Eureka Springs, Ark., Mar. 26, 1917; s. Festus Orestes and Esther Mae (Cox) B.; m. Cecilia King, Apr. 25, 1942; children: Thomas King, Martin Andrew (dec.), William Jackson II. LLB, U. Ark., 1938, JD, 1967. Bar: Ark. 1938, U.S. Dist. Ct. (we. dist.) Ark. 1940, U.S. Supreme Ct. 1955, U.S. Ct. Mil. Appeals 1969. Chancellor, probate judge 4th Chancery Cir. Ct., Fayetteville, Ark., 1951—; chief judge USAR, 1969-72; del. State Constl. Convention, Washington County, Ark., 1979-80; instr. law U. Ark., 1939-40. Served as brig. gen. USAR, 1969—. Decorated D.S.M., Legion of Merit. Mem. Ark. Bar Assn. (Golden Gavel award 1982), Washington County Bar Assn., Ark. Jud. Council (v.p. 1955-56, pres. 1956-57). Democrat. Club: Fayetteville Country. Lodge: Masons. State civil litigation, Family and matrimonial, Probate. Home: 1004 Rebecca Fayetteville AR 72701 Office: County Ct House PO Box 135 Fayetteville AR 72702

BUTTENWIESER, LAWRENCE BENJAMIN, lawyer; b. N.Y.C., Jan. 11, 1932; s. Benjamin Joseph and Helen (Lehman) B.; m. Ann Harriet Lubin, July 13, 1956; children—William Lawrence, Carol Helen, Jill Ann, Peter Lubin. B.A., U. Chgo., 1951, M.A., 1955; J.D., Yale U., 1956; D.H.L. (hon.), Yeshiva U., 1974. Bar: N.Y. 1956. Assoc. Rosenman & Colin, N.Y.C., 1956-66, ptnr., 1966—; dir. Warner Communications Inc., N.Y.C., Gen. Am. Investors Co., Inc., N.Y.C. Past pres., trustee Associated YM-YWHAs of Greater N.Y.; past v.p., dir. Citizens Housing and Planning Council of N.Y.; past treas., dir. City Ctr. of Music and Drama, Inc.; past dir. Council on Social Work. Edn.; past trustee Dalton Sch., past. hon. chmn. bd., trustee, past pres. Fedn. Jewish Philanthropies N.Y.; past chmn. bd., trustee Montefiore Med. Ctr.; past pres., bd. dirs., past gen. campaign chmn. United Neighborhood Houses N.Y.; trustee U. Chgo. Mem. Assn. Bar City of N.Y., N.Y. County Lawyers' Assn. Probate. Office: Rosenman & Colin 575 Madison Ave New York NY 10022

BUTTERWORTH, ALAN RANDOLPH, lawyer; b. Detroit, June 30, 1952; s. Eric W. Butterworth and Catherine M. (Jones) Knight; m. Pamela J. Meyers, Dec. 28, 1978; children: Joshua Kristopher, Jessica Kelly. BA in Environ. Design magna cum laude, SUNY, Buffalo, 1977, JD, 1980; LLM in Taxation, U. Fla., 1985. Bar: Fla. 1981, N.Y. 1981, U.S. Tax Ct. 1986. Legis. aide common council City of Buffalo, N.Y., 1975-77; assoc. Davis, Downing, Williams & Foster, P.A., Orlando, Fla., 1985-86, Gray, Harris & Robinson, P.A., Orlando, 1986—; lectr. U. Md. 1982-83. Bd. dirs. Mid Fla. Council for Internat. Visitors, Orlando, 1986—. Served to capt. JAGC, U.S. Army, 1981-84. Mem. ABA (taxation and internat. law sects.), Internat. Bar Assn., Fla. Bar Assn., N.Y. State Bar Assn. (taxation and internat. law sects.), Orange County Bar Assn. (tax com. 1986—), Internat. Fiscal Assn., Orlando C. of C. (internat. bus. adv. com. 1985), Winter Park C. of C. (cultural affairs com. 1986—). Lutheran. Club: Windermere. Lodge: Rotary. Avocations: basketball, team handball, volleyball. Corporate taxation, General corporate, Private international. Home: 4109 Winderlakes Dr Orlando FL 32811 Office: Gray Harris & Robinson 201 E Pine St Orlando FL 32802

BUTTERWORTH, ROBERT, state official. Atty. gen. State of Fla., Tallahassee, 1987—. Office: Legal Affairs Dept The Capitol Tallahassee FL 32301 *

BUTTS, SAMUEL ARTHUR, III, lawyer; b. Nashville, Mar. 3, 1949; s. Samuel Arthur Jr. and Virginia Nelle (Bates) B.; m. Linda Ann Ross, Nov. 22, 1973 (div. Dec. 1983). BA with honors, U. N.C., 1971, JD, 1975. Bar: N.C. 1975, Tenn. 1976. Asst. gen. counsel Genesco Inc., Nashville, 1975-78, assoc. gen. counsel, 1978-80; assoc. Brown & Williamson Tobacco Inc., Louisville, Ky., 1980; regional counsel William M. Mercer Inc., Nashville, 1981-82; gen. counsel Bryan, Pendleton, Swats and McAllister, Nashville, 1982—; mem. legis. com. So. Pension Conf., Atlanta, 1982; exec. com. Middle Tenn. Employee Benefit Council, Nashville, 1983-87, bd. dirs. 1983-87. Pres. Nashville Mental Health Assn., 1979; mem. Ptnr. of the Ams., Nashville, 1986. Mem. ABA, Tenn. Bar Assn., Nashville Bar Assn., Middle Tenn. Employee Benefits Council (pres. 1985-86, founder 1981), Southern Pension Conf., Phi Beta Kappa. Club: Nashville City. Avocations: travel, languages, gardening. Pension, profit-sharing, and employee benefits. Home: 432 Lynwood Blvd Nashville TN 37205 Office: Bryan et al One Burton Hills Nashville TN 37215

BUX, WILLIAM JOHN, lawyer; b. Wadsworth, Ohio, Nov. 10, 1946; s. William J. and Helen M. (Sybelnik) B.; m. Linda Alice Zenar, Feb. 13, 1971. BSME, Ohio State U., 1969, MS, 1970; JD, So. Meth. U., 1977. Bar: Tex. 1977, U.S. Dist. Ct. (so. dist.) Tex. 1978, U.S. Ct. Appeals (5th cir.) 1978, U.S. Dist. Ct. (no. dist.) Tex. 1980, U.S. Dist. Ct. (ea. and we. dists.) Tex. 1981, U.S. Ct. Appeals (11th cir.) 1981, U.S. Supreme Ct. 1982. Assoc. Vinson & Elkins, Houston, 1977-85; ptnr. Hughes & Luce, Dallas, 1985—. Author: Developing and Enforcing Drug and Alcohol Abuse Work Rules: A Primer for Texas Employers, 1984. Sec. So. Meth. U. Law Sch. Alumni Council, Dallas, 1986. Served to capt. USAF, 1971-74. Mem. ABA, Tex. Bar Assn., Dallas Bar Assn., 5th Cir. Bar Assn. Republican. Roman Catholic. Labor, Federal civil litigation, State civil litigation. Home: 2860 University Blvd Dallas TX 75205 Office: Hughes & Luce 1000 Dallas Bldg Dallas TX 75201

BUXBAUM, RICHARD M., legal educator, lawyer; b. 1930. A.B., Cornell U., 1950, LL.B., 1952; LL.M., U. Calif.-Berkeley, 1953. Bar: Calif. 1953, N.Y. 1953. Practice law, pvt. firm, Rochester, N.Y., 1957-61; acting assoc. prof. U. Calif.-Berkeley, 1961-64, prof., 1964—. Bd. dirs. Earl Warren Legal Inst., 1970-74. Order of Coif. Office: U Calif Law Sch 225 Boalt Hall Berkeley CA 94720

BUZAID, LAURENCE EDWIN, lawyer; b. Honolulu, Oct. 5, 1948; s. Louis Laurence and Bertha Grace (Record) B.; m. Doris Magdalene Ilk, July 24, 1976. AB, U. So. Calif., 1970, JD, 1973. Bar: Calif. 1974, U.S. Dist. Ct. (cen. dist.) Calif. 1974, Ariz. 1983, U.S. Dist. Ct. Ariz. 1983. Assoc. V.E. Murray, Los Angeles, 1974-75; asst. counsel Beneficial Standard Life Ins. Co., Los Angeles, 1976-83; v.p., gen. counsel Old Equity Mut. Life Ins. Co., Scottsdale, Ariz., 1983-84; counsel Avco Fin. Services, Newport Beach, Calif., 1984-85; v.p., gen. counsel Comml. Bankers Life Ins. Co., Newport Beach, 1985—. Mem. ABA. Insurance, General corporate. Office: Comml Bankers Life Ins Co 2301 Dupont Dr Irvine CA 92715

BUZZARD, STEVEN RAY, lawyer; b. Centralia, Wash., May 22, 1946; s. Richard James and Phylis Margaret (Bevington) B.; m. Joan Elizabeth Merrow, Nov. 11, 1967; children: Elizabeth Jane, Richard Wolcott, James Merrow. BA, Cen. Wash. State Coll., 1971; postgrad., U. Wash., 1973; JD, U. Puget Sound, 1975. Bar: Wash. 1975, U.S. Dist. Ct. (we. dist.) Wash. 1975, U.S. Supreme Ct. 1979, U.S. Tax Ct. 1983. Assoc. Shires, Kruse, Wallace, Roper & Kamps, Port Orchard, Wash., 1975-77; ptnr. Buzzard &

O'Connell, Centralia, 1978-80, Buzzard & Tripp, Centralia, 1980—; city atty. Mossyrock, Wash., 1979—; judge Centralia, 1979-80, Winlock, Wash., 1982—; sec. Consolidated Enterprizes Inc., Centralia, 1986—; instr. Centralia Coll., 1986—. Chmn. bd. dirs. Lewis County Community Services, Chehalis, Wash., 1981-84. Served with USCG, 1967-71. Mem. ABA (rural judges com. 1986—), Wash. State Bar Assn., Lewis County Bar Assn., Assn. Trial Lawyers Am., Wash. State Trial Lawyers Assn. Lodges: Elks (trustee Centralia 1981—), Kiwanis. Avocations: running, boating, hiking, fishing. Personal injury, State civil litigation, General practice. Office: Buzzard & Tripp 314 Harrison Ave Centralia WA 98531

BYBEE, JAY SCOTT, lawyer; b. Oakland, Calif., Oct. 27, 1953; s. Rowan Scott and Joan (Hickman) B.; m. Dianna Jean Greer, Feb. 15, 1986. BA, Brigham Young U., 1977, JD, 1980. Bar: D.C. 1981, U.S. Ct. Appeals (4th cir.) 1983, U.S. Supreme Ct. 1985, U.S. Ct. Appeals (5th cir.) 1986, U.S. Ct. Appeals (10th and D.C. cirs.) 1987. Law clk. to judge U.S. Ct. Appeals (4th cir.), 1980-81; assoc. Sidley & Austin, Washington, 1981-84; atty., advisor U.S. Dept. Justice, Washington, 1984—. Contbr. articles to profl. jours. Missionary Mormon Ch., Santiago, Chile, 1973-75. Edwin S. Hinckley scholar, Brigham Young U., 1976-77. Mem. Phi Kappa Phi. Avocations: piano, all sports, reading. Constitutional law. Home: 2213 N Dearing St Alexandria VA 22302

BYCZYNSKI, EDWARD FRANK, lawyer, financial executive; b. Chgo., Mar. 17, 1946; s. Edward James and Ann (Ruskey) B.; m. Nancy Louise Thompson, Aug. 3, 1968; children—Stefan, Suzanne. B.A., U. Wis., 1968; J.D., U. Ill., 1972; Certificat de Droit, U. Caen, France, 1971. Bar: Ill. 1972, U.S. Dist. Ct. (no. dist.) Ill. 1972, U.S. Supreme Ct. 1976. Title officer Chgo. Title Ins. Co., 1972-73; asst. regional counsel SBA, Chgo., 1973-76; pres. Alderstreet Investments, Portland, Oreg., 1976-82; pres. Nat. Tenant Network, Portland, 1981—, Bay Venture Corp., Portland, 1984—; ptnr. Haley, Pirok, Byczynski. Chgo., 1973-76. Contbr. articles to profl. jours. Mem. ABA, Ill. Bar Assn. Democrat. Roman Catholic. Real property, Personal income taxation, Banking. Home: 17359 SW Wren Ct Lake Oswego OR 97034

BYERS, DONALD CHARLES, home appliances manufacturing company executive, lawyer; b. Fargo, N.D., July 10, 1925; s. Charley Klebert and Agnes Evelyn (Nyhra) B.; m. Doris Kathleen Morrow, Nov. 28, 1947; children—Kathleen Ann Savit, Karen Sue Bonte, Alan Michael, Annette Marie. B.A., Iowa Wesleyan Coll., 1949; J.D., Drake U., 1951. Bar: Iowa 1951. Ptnr., Byers and Girdner, Newton, Iowa, 1951-53; atty. Maytag Co., Newton, 1953—, corp. atty. 1953-67, asst. sec., asst. gen. counsel, 1967-73, gen. counsel, asst. sec., 1973-74, gen. counsel, sec., 1974—. Trustee, Drake U.; bd. counselors, class agt. Drake U. Law Sch., nat. chmn. scholarship campaign; mem. Newton Community Sch. Bd., 1964-73, pres.; chmn. fundraising campaign Ctr. for Performance, 1980-84; Ch. Sch. supt., tchr., lay leader, chmn. long range planning com. 1st United Methodist Ch., Newton; mem. Iowa Conf. Council Meth. Ministries; precinct committeeman Republican Party. Served with U.S. Army, 1943-46, Europe. Recipient Friend of Edn. award Newton Edn. Assn., 1981, Disting. Service award Drake U., 1985. Mem. ABA, Iowa Bar Assn. (coms'.), Iowa Def. Counsel Assn., Internat. Assn. Indsl. Accidents Bds. and Comms., Iowa Mfrs. Assn. (chmn. 1982—), Maytag Mgmt. Club (past pres.), Am. Soc. Corporate Secs., Newton C. of C. (past chmn. Community Betterment Com., Key award 1981, chmn. Project Awake), Order of Coif. Club: Newton Country. General corporate, Legislative, Antitrust. Home: 720 W 11th St S Newton IA 50208 Office: Maytag Co 403 W 4th St N One Dependability Sq Newton IA 50208

BYERS, RONALD GREGORY, lawyer; b. Kansas City, Mo., May 18, 1948; s. Roy Jack and Patricia Mary (Lubbers) B.; m. Linda K. Short, Aug. 23, 1968 (div. Feb. 1986); 1 child, Bradley Wayne. BA, U. Mo., Kansas City, 1970, JD, 1974. Bar: Mo. 1974, U.S. Dist. Ct. (we. dist.) Mo. 1974. Law clk. Mo. Ct. Appeals, Kansas City, 1974-75, research atty., 1975-76; assoc. Rosenwald Jacob, Kansas City, 1976-82; sole practice Independence, Mo., 1982—. Pres. Citizens for Effective Leadership, Independence, 1984; mem. Storm Water Adv. Bd., Independence, 1984-86; unit commr. Blue Elk Dist., Boy Scouts Am., Independence, 1986, com. chmn. 1986. Recipient Disting. Service award Kansas City Bar Young Lawyers, 1982, 83. Mem. Eastern Jackson County Bar Assn., Independence C. of C. (bd. dirs. 1985—, div. vice chmn. legis. affairs 1985). Democrat. Roman Catholic. Lodge: Kiwanis (bd. dirs Independence chpt. 1985-86). Avocations: flying, hunting, hiking. General corporate, Probate, Landlord-tenant. Home: 4312 Canterbury Apt 4 Independence MO 64055 Office: 304 W Walnut Suite 210 Independence MO 64050

BYERS, STEPHEN MICHAEL, lawyer; b. Green Bay, Wis., Mar. 19, 1957; s. James Walsh and Nancy Claire (Marek) B. BA in Sociology, St. Norbert Coll., 1979; JD, Marquette U., 1982. Bar: Wis. 1982, U.S. Dist. Ct. (ea. and we. dists.) Wis. 1982. Staff atty. Legal Aid Soc. of Milw., Inc., 1987—. dir. legal services Milw. AIDS Project, 1985—; pres., legal counsel Brady East STD Clinic Inc., Milw., 1985-87. Mem. Wis. Bar Assn., Milw. Bar Assn., Milw. Young Lawyers Assn. (Outstanding Service award vol. lawyers project 1983), Cream City Bus. Assn. (treas. 1985). Democrat. Roman Catholic. Criminal, Probate, Ge:eral practice. Home: 1937 N Bartlett Ave Milwaukee WI 53202

BYINGTON, ROBERT LEE, lawyer; b. Owosso, Mich., May 28, 1951; s. Rex Elwood and Betty Lou (Brockway) B.; m. Martha Louise Matzkanin, Dec. 18, 1971; children: Sarah Nichole, Eric Alexander. BA, Mich. State U., 1973; JD, Thomas M. Cooley Law Sch, 1977. Bar: Mich. 1977, U.S. Dist. (we. dist.) Mich. 1982. Assoc. Shuster & Wilbur, Hastings, Mich., 1977-82; ptnr. Wilbur & Byington, Hastings, 1983—. Dist. chmn. Boy Scouts Am., Hastings, 1983-84. Mem. ABA, Barry County Bar Assn. (treas. 1982-84, sec. 1984-86, v.p. 1986—). Republican. Baptist. Lodges: Rotary (asst. sec. Hastings chpt. 1980—), Elks. Avocations: reading. woodworking. General practice, Banking, Probate. Home: 722 W Green St Hastings MI 49058 Office: Wilbur & Byington 222 W Apple St PO Box 248 Hastings MI 49058

BYINGTON, S. JOHN, lawyer; b. Grand Rapids, Mich.; m. Sally Ruth Meyer; children: Nancy, Barbra. B.Phar., Ferris State Coll., Big Rapids, Mich.; hon. doctorate, Ferris State Coll.; postgrad., U. Mich. Law Sch.; J.D., Georgetown U., 1963; hon. doctorate, Albany Sch. Pharmacy. Dir. pub. relations Am. Pharm. Assn., 1961-64; asst. pros. atty. Kent County, Grand Rapids, 1964-65; mem. gov.'s staff State of Mich., 1965-68; practice law Oakland County, Mich., 1968-72; dir. Detroit Office Dept. Commerce, from 1972; dep. dir., nat. export mktg. dir. Washington, until 1974; dep. dir. Office Consumer Affairs HEW, Washington, from 1974; dep. spl. asst. for consumer affairs to Pres. Ford White House, Washington; chmn. U.S. Consumer Product Safety Commn., 1976-78; partner firm Bushnell, Gage, Reizen & Byington, Detroit, 1978-81, Rogers Hoge & Hills, N.Y.C. and Washington, 1981-83, Pillsbury Madison & Sutro, San Francisco and Washington, 1983—; co-founder, mem. Interagy. Regulatory Liaison Group, Washington, 1976-78; dir. Control Laser Corp.; guest lectr. on product liability George Washington U. Mem. adv. council Ctr. for Study of Presidency; mem. nat. adv. bd. Citizen's Choice, Inc. Mem. ABA, Fed. Bar Assn., D.C. Bar Assn., Mich. Bar Assn., Am. Soc. Law and Medicine, Nat. Health Lawyers Assn., Am. Soc. for Pharmacy Law, Am. Pharmacists Assn., Mich. Pharmacists Assn., U.S. C. of C. (nat. bus. council on injury compensation, govt. and regulatory affairs, adminstrv. law council), Chemists Club. Administrative and regulatory, General corporate, Health. Office: Pillsbury Madison & Sutro 1667 K St NW Suite 1100 Washington DC 20006

BYKOFSKY, SETH DARRYL, lawyer; b. N.Y.C., June 28, 1956; S. Irving R. and Frances (Kaufman) B.; m. Joan S. Silverblatt, June 24, 1978; 1 child, Francyne Rose. BA, Queens Coll., 1978; JD, Yeshiva U., 1981. Bar: N.Y. 1982, U.S. Dist. Ct. (so. and ea. dists.) N.Y. 1983, D.C. 1985, U.S. Supreme Ct. 1985. Asst. corp. counsel City of N.Y., 1981-83; assoc. Lipsig, Sullivan & Liapakis, P.C., N.Y.C., 1983-86, McCabe & Cozzens, Mineola, N.Y., 1986—. Contbr. articles to N.Y. Law Jour. Recipient Advocacy award World Peace Through Law Ctr., Washington, 1985. Mem. ABA, Assn. Trial Lawyers Am., N.Y. State Bar Assn., N.Y. State Trial Lawyers Assn., Nassau County Bar Assn., Phi Beta Kappa. Democrat. Avocations: travel, photography. Personal injury, State civil litigation, General practice. Home: 254 Meredith Ln West Hempstead NY 11552 Office: McCabe & Cozzens 131 Mineola Blvd Mineola NY 11501

BYLER, M. ELVIN, lawyer; b. Lancaster County, Pa., June 8, 1939; s. Marcus E. and Verda E. (Fisher) B.; m. Barbara Le Fever; children—Marcus Elvin III, W. Bryan, Stephen R. Student, Eastern Mennonite Coll., Harrisonburg, Va., 1958-61; B.A., Coll. of William and Mary, J.D., 1965. Bar: Pa. 1966, U.S. Sup. Ct. 1971. Ptnr., Blakinger, Byler, Grove, Thomas & Chillas, P.C., Lancaster, Pa., 1966-73. Pres., Brooklane Psychiat. Ctr., 1967-73; bd. dirs. Mennonite Mental Health Services, 1967-73; pres. Menno Housing Soc., 1967-76; pres. Tabor Community Services Inc., 1972-76, Mennonite Econ. Devel. Assos., 1978. Mem. ABA, Lawyer Pilots Bar Assn. Republican. Clubs: Conestoga Country (Lancaster), Sea Pines Golf (Hilton Head, S.C.). Contracts commercial, Probate, Real property. Office: Blakinger Byler Grove Thomas & Chillas PC 8 N Queen St 9th Floor Lancaster PA 17603

BYRAM, JAMES ASBERRY, JR., lawyer; b. Gadsden, Ala., July 27, 1954; s. James Asberry Sr. and Barbara Anne (Ryals) B.; m. Virginia Elisabeth Nicholas, Apr. 17, 1982. BS, U. Ala., 1976, JD, 1979. Bar: Ala. 1979, U.S. Dist. Ct. (mid. and no. dists.) Ala. 1980, U.S. Ct. Appeals (11th cir.) 1981, U.S. Supreme Ct. 1985. Assoc. Steiner, Crum & Baker, Montgomery, Ala., 1979-83, ptnr., 1984—. Hugo Black scholar U. Ala., 1978. Mem. Montgomery County Bar Assn. (grievance com. 1984—), Bench and Bar Soc. Presbyterian. Lodge: Kiwanis. Banking, Federal civil litigation, State civil litigation. Home: 1749 Pine Needle Rd Montgomery AL 36106 Office: Steiner Crum & Baker 809 1st Ala Bank Bldg Box 668 Montgomery AL 36101

BYRD, ISAAC KENITH, JR., lawyer; b. Shaw, Miss., Feb. 3, 1952; s. Isaac K. Sr. and Hattie (Isaac) B.; m. Stephanie McMullen, Oct. 12, 1974 (div. Feb. 1984); 1 child, Isaac K. III. BA, Tougaloo Coll., 1973; JD, Northwestern U., 1976. Bar: Ill. 1977, Miss. 1978. Atty. Swift & Co., Chgo., 1976-78; assoc. Bank & Nichols, Jackson, Miss., 1978-82; ptnr. Owens & Byrd, Jackson, 1982-86, Byrd & Assocs., Jackson, 1986—. Bd. dirs. Miss. Econ. Devel. Corp., Jackson, 1980-83, Miss. Dept. Corrections, Jackson, 1984—. Mem. Assn. Trial Lawyers Am., Miss. Trial Lawyers Assn., Nat. Bar Assn., Hinds County Bar Assn., NAACP (gen. counsel 1985—, recipient humanitarian award 1983, Vernon Dahmer award 1985). Democrat. Baptist. Avocations: jogging, reading, antique collecting. Personal injury. Home: 449 W Northside Jackson MS 39206 Office: Owens & Byrd 403 S State Jackson MS 39201

BYRD, LINWARD TONNETT, lawyer, rancher; b. Hamburg, Ark., June 25, 1921; s. Charley E. and Arrie (Montgomery) B.; m. Reba Ann Rowe, Dec. 22, 1965; 1 child, Jana Lynn. LL.B., U. Tex., 1950. Bar: Tex. 1950, U.S. Dist. Ct. (we. dist.) Tex. 1956, U.S. Ct. Appeals (5th cir.) 1965, U.S. Ct. Appeals (11th cir.) 1981. Sr. ptnr. Byrd, Davis & Eisenberg, Austin, Tex., 1959—. Served with USN, 1942-43. Fellow Am. Trial Lawyers Found., Tex. Bar Found., Am. Coll. Trial Lawyers; mem. Assn. Trial Lawyers Am., Am. Bd. Trial Advs. (adv.), Tex. Trial Lawyers Assn., Travis County Bar Assn., State Bar Tex. Baptist. Personal injury, Aviation, Workers' compensation. Home: 3110 Maywood Ave Austin TX 78703 Office: Byrd Davis & Eisenberg 707 W 34th St Austin TX 78705

BYRNE, BARBARA, lawyer; b. Abington, Pa., May 27, 1953; d. Patrick Joseph and Marie Day B. BA, Franklin and Marshall Coll., 1975; JD, Boston U., 1978. Bar: Mass. 1978, Nev. 1980. Sole practice Winthrop, Mass., 1978-80; dep. dist. atty. Elko County, Nev., 1980-81, pub. defender, 1983—; dep. pub. defender State of Nev., Carson City, 1981-82. Democrat. Roman Catholic. Criminal. Home: Carroll's Ranch Lamoille NV 89828 Office: 405 Henderson Bank Bldg 4th and Railroad Elko NV 89801

BYRNE, BRADLEY ROBERTS, lawyer; b. Mobile, Ala., Feb. 16, 1955; s. Arthur LaCoste and Elizabeth Patricia (Langsdale) B.; m. Rebecca Dow Dukes, May 16, 1981; 1 child, Patrick MacGuire. BA, Duke U., 1977; JD, U. Ala., 1980. Bar: Ala. 1980, U.S. Dist. Ct. (so. dist.) Ala. 1980, U.S. Ct. Appeals (5th and 11th cirs.) 1981, U.S. Dist. Ct. (mid. dist.) Ala. 1985, U.S. Ct. Appeals (8th cir.) 1985, U.S. Dist. Ct. (no. dist.) Ala. 1986. Assoc. Miller, Hamilton, Snider & Odom, Mobile, 1980-85, ptnr., 1985—. Mem. Ala. Election Law Commn., Montgomery, 1980—, Mobile County Dem. Exec. Com., 1982—; sr. warden Christ Episc. Ch., Mobile, 1985—. Named one of Outstanding Young Men of Am., 1981, 82. Mem. ABA (litigation sect.), Ala. Bar Assn., Mobile Bar Assn., Am. Judicature Soc. Episcopalian. Federal civil litigation, State civil litigation, Contracts commercial. Office: Miller Hamilton Snider & Odom 254-256 State St Mobile AL 36603

BYRNE, EDWARD MARK, lawyer; b. Watertown, Wis., Sept. 10, 1935; s. Edward Joseph and Rosalie Antoinette (Bell) B.; m. Dorothy Jane Byrne, Sept. 19, 1958; children—Kathryn Ann, Edward Mark. Student Coll. Wooster (Ohio), 1953-55; J.D., Syracuse U., 1959; LL.M., George Washington U., 1971. Bar: N.Y. 1963, U.S. Ct. Mil. Apls., 1969, U.S. Sup. Ct. 1969. Commd. ensign U.S. Navy, 1961; advanced through grades to capt., 1982; course coordinator U.S. Naval Acad., 1968-70; staff judge adv. Iceland Def., 1972-73; dir. tng. Naval Justice Sch., 1974-77; dep. asst. JAG, 1978-81, appellate judge, U.S. Navy Marine Corps Ct. of Mil. Rev., Washington, 1981-84; chief judge Navy/Marine Corps Trial Judiciary, Washington, 1984—. Mem. ABA, N.Y. State Bar Assn. Methodist. Author: Military Law, 1982. Military, Criminal, Public international. Home: 5114 Althea Dr Annandale VA 22003 Office: US Navy/Marine Corps Trial Judiciary Office of Judge Advocate General Washington Navy Yard Washington D C 20374

BYRNE, JEROME CAMILLUS, lawyer; b. Grand Rapids, Mich., Oct. 3, 1925; s. Camillus Abraham and Katherine Blanche (Kelly) B. B.A., Aquinas Coll., 1948; J.D. magna cum laude, Harvard U., 1951. Bar: Calif. 1952. Assoc. firm Gibson Dunn & Crutcher, Los Angeles, 1952-59; partner Gibson Dunn & Crutcher, 1960—, mem. exec. com., 1981—; spl. counsel to regents U. Calif., 1965. Bd. dirs. Constl. Rights Found., 1967—, pres., 1971-72; bd. regents Mt. St. Mary's Coll., 1979—; trustee Aquinas Coll., 1983—, Kolb Found., 1984—. Mem. Am. Bar Assn., Calif. Bar Assn., Los Angeles County Bar Assn. Office: 2029 Century Park East Suite 4000 Los Angeles CA 90067

BYRNE, JOSEPH AHERN, JR., lawyer; b. Kalamazoo, Mich., Dec. 19, 1953; s. Joseph Ahern and Shirley Anne (Hill) B.; m. Patricia Lynn Kamaneck, Aug. 6, 1977; children: Anne Elizabeth, Joseph Ahern III. BBA with distinction, U. Mich., 1976; JD cum laude, Detroit Coll. Law, 1979. Bar: Mich. 1979, U.S. Dist. Ct. (we. dist.) Mich. 1981. Assoc. Lilly & Domeny, P.C., Kalamazoo, 1979-83; ptnr. Lilly, Domeny, Durant, Byrne & Schanz, P.C., Kalamazoo, 1983—. Mem. ABA, Mich. Bar Assn., Kalamazoo County Bar Assn., Def. Research Inst. State civil litigation, Insurance, Workers' compensation. Office: Lilly Domeny Durant Byrne & Schanz PC 505 S Park St Kalamazoo MI 49007

BYRNE, MARGARET MARY, lawyer; b. Glascow, Scotland, Sept. 3, 1951; came to U.S., 1959; d. Charles and Mary (O'Neil) B. BA cum laude, St. John's U., 1973; JD, Fordham U., 1980. Bar: N.Y. 1981. Claims adminstr. Teachers Ins. and Annuity Assn. Coll. Retirement Equities Fund, N.Y.C., 1981-84, atty., 1984-87; asst. counsel TIAA-CREF, N.Y.C., 1987—; vol. atty. Legal Services Corp., N.Y.C., 1981-83. Bd. dirs. Inwood House, N.Y.C., 1984-86, South St. Theater, N.Y.C., 1986. Roman Catholic. Avocations: sailing, tennis, biking, running. Insurance, Pension, profit-sharing, and employee benefits, State civil litigation. Office: Teachers Ins and Annuity Assn Coll Retirement Equities Fund 730 3d Ave New York NY 10017

BYRNE, MAURICE ANDREW, JR., lawyer; b. Louisville, May 23, 1943; s. Maurice Andrew Sr. and Mary Augusta (Ulsh) B.; m. Catherine Ann Seabold, Sept. 11, 1971. Student, St. Thomas Jr. Coll., Louisville, 1961-63, Holy Trinity Coll., 1963-66, Holy Trinity Theology Coll., 1966-67; BA in Philosophy and Sociology, Cath. U. of Am., 1968, JD, 1974. Bar: Ky. 1974, U.S. Dist. Ct. (ea. dist.) Ky. 1975, U.S. Dist. Ct. (we. dist.) Ky. 1976, Ind. 1981, U.S. Dist. Ct. (so. dist.) Ind. 1981. Legis. asst. congressman R.L. Mazzoli, Washington, 1972-74; state consumer protection div. Office of Atty. Gen., State of Ky., Louisville, 1974-76, 79-81; econ. crime dir. Ky. Commonwealth Atty., Louisville, 1977-79; assoc. Barnett & Alagia, Louisville, Frankfort, Ky. and Washington, 1981-84, Fox & Smith, Jeffersonville, Ind. and Louisville, 1984—. Author various procedures guides. Program dir. Fides Settlement House, Washington, 1966-68, Vietnam Christian Service, 1968-70; field coordinator Robert F. Kennedy presdl. campaign, Washington, 1968; coordinator David L. Armstrong for Ky. Atty. Gen. campaign, 1982-83. Mem. ABA (banking and bus. law sects.), Ky. Bar Assn. (mem. corps. com. 1981-86), Ind. Bar Assn., Clark County Bar Assn., Floyd County Bar Assn., Louisville Bar Assn. (mem. profl. responsibility com. 1978-86). Democrat. Roman Catholic. Lodge: Rotary (sec. and pres. Buechel, Ky. 1978-81). Avocations: softball, tennis, volleyball, woodworking, cabinet making. Federal civil litigation, Contracts commercial, Real property. Home: 2231 Richland Dr Louisville KY 40218 Office: Fox & Smith PO Box 98 209 E Chestnut St Jeffersonville IN 47130 Office: 100 N 6th St Louisville KY 40202

BYRNE, WILLIAM MATTHEW, JR., federal judge; b. Los Angeles, Sept. 3, 1930; s. William Matthew and Julia Ann (Lamb) B. B.S., U. So. Calif., 1953, LL.B., 1956; LL.D., Loyola U., 1971. Bar: Calif. 1956. Mem. firm Dryden, Harrington & Schwartz, 1960-67; asst. U.S. atty So. (now Cen. Dist. Calif., 1958-60; U.S. atty. Cen. Dist. Calif., 1967-70; exec. dir. Pres. Nixon's Commn. Campus Unrest, 1970; judge U.S. Dist. Ct. (cen. dist.) Calif., Los Angeles, 1971—; instr. Loyola Law Sch., Harvard U., Whittier Coll. Served with USAF, 1956-58. Mem. ABA, Fed. Bar Assn., Calif. Bar Assn., Los Angeles County Bar Assn. (vice chmn. human rights sect.), Am. Judicature Soc. Jurisprudence. Address: US District Court US Courthouse 312 N Spring St Los Angeles CA 90012 *

BYRNES, JOHN ROBERT, U.S. attorney; b. Washington, Jan. 18, 1948; s. John W. and Barbara (Preston) B.; m. Monica Prueher, Jan. 7, 1977; children: Amy Preston, John Michael. BA, U. Wis.-Madison, 1970—, JD, 1973. Bar: Wis. 1973, U.S. Surpeme Ct. 1982. Asst. U.S. atty. U.S. Dept. Justice, Madison, Wis., 1973-76; U.S. atty. U.S. Dept. Justice, 1981—; sole practice law Green Bay, Wis., 1976-79; adminstr. Worker Compensation div., Madison, 1979-81. Republican. Roman Catholic. Criminal.

BYROM, ROBERT MILTON, lawyer; b. Atlanta, Nov. 26, 1928; s. Alfred Martin and Helen (Tuggle) B.; m. Patricia Anne; children: Robert, Laura, James, Susan, Douglas, Christopher. BA in Edn., U. Nebr., Omaha, 1968; JD, Cath. U., 1976; Diploma in Air Law, McGill U., Montreal, Can., 1982. Bar: D.C. 1976, Va. 1977. Commd. 2d lt. USAF, 1950, advanced through grades to col., 1970, ret., 1975; assoc. with George H. Dygert and William Lee Anderson, Charlottesville, Va., 1976—. Author: Product Liability of the General Aviation Manufacturer, 1982; (contbr.) Defending Criminal Cases in Virginia. Chmn. U. Va. Student Legal Services, Charlottesville, 1976-80; Liason officer USAF Acad., Colorado Springs, Colo., 1976-81. Decorated Bronze Star. Mem. Air Force Assn. Club: Daedalians (San Antonio), USA JAG (Charlottesville). Avocation: aircraft owner and pilot (FAA rated). Federal civil litigation, State civil litigation, Personal injury. Home: Cottonwood Rt 2 Box 432 Crozet VA 22932 Office: Robert M Byrom Esq 609 E High St Suite 2 Charlottesville VA 22901

BYRON, THOMAS WILLIAM, lawyer; b. Gardner, Mass., Jan. 18, 1947; s. Walter Rudolph and Elna (Okker) B.; m. Deborah Lynn Mayfield, Dec. 23, 1979. BA, U. Mass., 1969; JD, Hastings Coll., 1980. Bar: Calif. 1980, U.S. Dist. Ct. (no. and so. dists.) Calif. 1980. Dep. atty. City Atty.'s Office, San Diego, 1980-83; ptnr. Edwards, White & Sooy, San Diego, 1983—. Mem. ABA, Calif. State Bar Assn., San Diego County Bar Assn., San Diego Barristers Club. Avocations: philopsophy, water sports, travel, cooking. Insurance, Personal injury, Construction. Office: Edwards White & Sooy 5030 Camino de la Siesta 204 San Diego CA 92104

BYSSHE, FREDERICK HERBERT, JR., lawyer; b. Long Beach, Calif., Sept. 16, 1937; s. Frederick H. and Virginia (Sterzing) B.; m. Judith Reaves, Feb. 13, 1982; children: Michael Adams, Kelly Rains, Mark Rains, Christopher Ernest. BA, U. Redlands, 1959; JD, U. Calif., San Francisco, 1962. Bar: Calif. 1963, U.S. Ct. Appeals (9th cir.) 1963. Dep. dist. atty. Riverside (Calif.) County, 1963-66, chief trial dep., 1966-68, chief dep. dist. atty., 1968-70; ptnr. Lucking, Bertelsen, Bysshe & Kuttler, Ventura, Calif., 1970—; lectr. U. Calif., 1968-69. Contbg. editor U. Calif. San Francisco Law Rev., 1961-62. Pres. Riverside County Peace Officers Assn., 1968; mem. Ventura County Cancer Soc., 1978-80, Archeol. Soc. Ventura County; trustee Ventura County Law Library, 1974-79, v.p.; bd. dirs. Boys & Girls Clubs Ventura County, Ventura County YMCA, 1972-75. Served with USAR, 1963-69. Mem. ABA, Ventura County Bar Assn. (exec. com. 1973-74, pres. 1982), Ventura County Criminal Bar Assn. (pres. 1973), Ventura County Trial Lawyers Assn. (pres. 1978-79). Republican. Lodge: Rotary (pres. Ventura 1976). State civil litigation, Personal injury. Home: 1187 Norwich Ln Ventura CA 93003 Office: Lucking Bertelsen Bysshe et al 10 S California St Ventura CA 93001

CABANISS, THOMAS EDWARD, lawyer; b. Farmville, Va., Oct. 16, 1949; s. Frank Edward and Myrtle (Stembridge) C.; m. Chrystene Taylor, Aug. 26, 1972; 1 child, Clara Louisa. BS, N.C. State U., 1972; JD, U. Va., 1975. Bar: Va. 1975, U.S. Dist. Ct. (we. and ea. dists.) Va. 1975, U.S. Ct. Appeals (4th cir.) 1975, U.S. Supreme Ct. 1975. Ptnr. Kaufman & Oberndorfer, Norfolk, Va., 1975-81; mem. Kaufman & Canoles P.C., Norfolk, 1982-85; ptnr. McGuire, Woods, Battle & Boothe, Norfolk, 1985—. Alt. del. Rep. Nat. Convention, Miami, Fla., 1972; del. Va. Rep. Conventions, 1969-72. Mem. ABA, Va. Bar Assn. Club: Harbor (Norfolk), Town Point (Norfolk). Banking, Bankruptcy, Federal civil litigation. Home: 806 E Riverview Dr Suffolk VA 23434 Office: McGuire Woods Battle & Boothe 9000 World Trade Ctr Norfolk VA 23510

CABELL, ROBERT GAMBLE, JR., lawyer; b. Richmond, Va., Feb. 12, 1932; s. Robert G. and Jeanne Hunton (Witt) C.; m. Jacqueline Faye Tant, Jan. 30, 1970; children—Robert, Temple Witt, Carrington, Anne, Lynne, Virginia, Angela. B.A., U. Va., 1954, LL.B., 1957. Bar: Va. 1957, U.S. Ct. Appeals (4th cir.) 1957, U.S. Supreme Ct. 1962. Sr. ptnr. Cabell Paris, Lowenstein & Bareford, Richmond, Va., 1963-86, dir. Sands, Anderson, Marks & Miller, 1987—; substitute judge 11th Jud. Cir., 1986—; pres. Richmond Criminal Bar, 1970-72; chmn. criminal law sect. Va. State Bar (lectr., mem. ethics com., 1978-82, jud. ethics com., 1982—, mem. Va. State Bar Council, 1980—. Mem. Richmond Bar Assn., Va. Bar Assn., Va. Trial Lawyers Assn. Episcopalian. Club: Country of Va., Richmond Fed. Hill, Powhatan. Contbr. articles to profl. jours. Criminal. Address: The Ross Bldg 801 E Main St Suite 1400 PO Box 1998 Richmond VA 23219

CABRAL, BERNARDO JOSEPH, lawyer; b. Furnas, Azores, Portugal, May 20, 1944; s. Antonio and Maria (Andrade) C.; m. Sandra Marie Morrow, June 16, 1966; 1 child, Douglas Mark. BA, U. Mass., 1966; JD cum laude, Suffolk U., 1977. Bar: Mass. 1977, U.S. Dist. Ct. Mass. 1978. Assoc. Desmarais & Carey, New Bedford, Mass., 1977-79, Law Offices of Armand Fernandes, New Bedford, 1979-81; sole practice New Bedford, 1981-82; ptnr. Sobral & Cabral, New Bedford, 1982—. Served to capt. U.S. Army, 1966-70, Vietnam. Mem. ABA, Mass. Bar Assn., New Bedford Bar Assn., Bristol County Bar Assn., Assn. Trial Lawyers Am., Am. Arbitration Assn. (arbitrator 1985—), Prince Henry Soc. Roman Catholic. Avocation: gardening. Personal injury, State civil litigation, Workers' compensation. Home: 31 Garrison Rd New Bedford MA 02745 Office: Sobral & Cabral 414 County St New Bedford MA 02740

CABRANES, JOSÉ ALBERTO, federal judge; b. Mayaguez, P.R., Dec. 22, 1940; s. Manuel and Carmen (Lópex) C.; m. Kate Stith, Sept. 15, 1984; 1 child, Alexander Richard Stith; children from previous marriage: Jennifer Ann, Amy Alexandra. AB, Columbia U., 1961; JD, Yale U., 1965; MLitt in Internat. Law, (Kellett research fellowship, Columbia College, Humanitarian Trust Studentship, Faculty Bd. of Law, Cambridge), Queens' Coll., Cambridge (Eng.) U., 1967. Bar: N.Y. 1968, D.C. 1975, Conn. Fed. 1976. Asso. Casey, Lane & Mittendorf, N.Y.C., 1967-71; asso. prof. law Rutgers U. Law Sch., 1971-73; spl. counsel to gov. P.R., also adminstr. Office Commonwealth P.R., Washington, 1973-75; gen. counsel and dir. govt. relations Yale U., 1975-79; judge U.S. Dist. Ct. Dist. Conn. New Haven, 1979—; mem. Pres.'s Commn. Mental Health, 1977-78; founding mem. P.R. Legal Def. and Edn. Fund, 1972, chmn. bd. dirs., 1977-80; counsel Internat. League for Human Rights, 1971-77, v.p., 1977-80; cons. to sec. Dept. State, 1978; mem. U.S. del. Conf. Security and Cooperation in Europe, Belgrade, 1977-78. Author: Citizenship and the American Empire, 1979; also articles on law and internat. affairs. trustee Yale-New Haven Hosp., 1978-80, 84—, Colgate U., 1981—; bd. dirs. Aspira of N.Y., 1970-74, chmn., 1971-73;

trustee 20th Century Fund, 1983—. Mem. Am. Law Inst., ABA, Conn. Bar Assn., Assn. Bar City N.Y., Council Fgn. Relations. Roman Catholic. Judicial administration. Office: US Courthouse 141 Church St New Haven CT 06510 *

CACACE, MICHAEL JOSEPH, lawyer; b. Mt. Vernon, N.Y., Apr. 20, 1952; s. Jerry F. and Margaret F. (Pesditsch) C.; m. Maureen R. Brown, May 24, 1975; children—Joseph M., Christine M. B.A., Fordham U., 1974; J.D., N.Y. Law Sch., 1978. Bar: Conn. 1978, N.Y. 1979, U.S. Dist. Ct. Conn. 1979, U.S. Ct. Appeals (2nd cir.) 1981, U.S. Dist. Ct. (so. dist.) N.Y. 1982. Law clk. Saxe, Bacon & Bolan, N.Y.C., 1976-78, atty., 1978-79; atty. Abate, Fox & Farrell, Stamford, Conn., 1979-82, sole practice, Stamford, 1982—; pres. The Vol. Ctr., Stamford, 1980-86; co.-chmn. 13th Charter Revision Com., Stamford, 1982-83; v.p. Gateway Communities, Inc., Stamford, 1981—; chmn. Stamford Commn. on Aging, 1975-80; instr. adminstrv. law Norwalk Community Coll., Conn., 1980-82. Author book chpt. Age Discrimination Law, 1981. Bd. dirs. Vis. Nurses Assn., Stamford, 1982—, Shippan Point Assn., Stamford, 1980-83, Stamford Ctr. for the Arts, 1986—. Named Outstanding Young Man of Am., 1977, Community Leader of Yr., The Stamford Adv., 1986; recipient Dr. Max Reich award N.Y. Law Sch. Alumni Assn., 1978, Lawyers Co-op Book award Lawyers Co-op Book Co., 1977. Mem. Stamford/Darien Bar Assn. (mem. exec. com. 1980—, treas. 1986-87), Conn. Bar Assn., N.Y. Bar Assn., Conn. Trial Lawyers Assn., Am. Trial Lawyers Assn., State St. Debating Soc. Democrat. Roman Catholic. Club: Roasters (Stamford). General practice, Real property, State civil litigation. Home: 316 Scofieldtown Rd Stamford CT 06903 Office: 1887 Summer St Stamford CT 06905

CACCIATORE, RONALD KEITH, lawyer; b. Donalsonville, Ga., Feb. 5, 1937; s. Angelo D. and Myrtice E. (Williams) C.; m. Jean Jewell, Jan. 12, 1973; children—Rhonda, Cynthia, Sabina, Donna, Rex. Student Spring Hill Coll., 1955-56; B.A., U. Fla., 1960, J.D., 1963. Bar: Fla. 1963, U.S. Supreme Ct. 1969. Asst. state atty. 13th Jud. Cir., 1963-65; sole practice, Tampa, Fla., 1967—; lectr. criminal law; mem. 13th Jud. Cir. Jud. Nominating Commn., 1976-80, chmn., 1980. Trustee, Hillsborough Community Coll., 1979-83, chmn., 1982-83. Fellow Am. Coll. Trial Lawyers; mem. Hillsborough County Bar Assn. (pres. 1975-76, chmn. trial lawyers sect. 1983-85), Fla. Bar Assn. (chmn. criminal law sect. 1977-78), Fla. Council Bar Pres.'s (chmn. 1979-80), Fed. Bar Assn. (pres. Tampa Bay chpt. 1985-86). Clubs: Palma Ceia Golf and Country, Tampa. Criminal.

CACCIATORE, S. SAMMY, JR., lawyer; b. Tampa, Fla., Aug. 2, 1942; s. Sam and Margarita C.; m. Carolyn Michels, Aug. 10, 1963; children: Elaine Michel, Sammy Michel. B.A., Stetson U., DeLand, Fla., 1966, J.D., 1966. Bar: Fla. 1966, U.S. Ct. Appeals (5th cir.) 1967, U.S. Supreme Ct. 1971, U.S. Ct. Appeals (11th cir.) 1981. Asst. public defender 9th jud. circuit State of Fla., 1966; assoc. firm Orlando, Fla., 1966-67; practice in Melbourne, Fla., 1967—; ptnr Nance, Cacciatore & Sisserson (and predecessors), 1970—; mem. 5th Dist. Appellate Nominating Commn., 1979-83, State of Fla. Med. Malpractice Adv. Com., 1982; Fla. Bar Supreme Ct. Jud. Nominating Commn., 1986-90; lectr. in field, 1971—. Contbr. articles to profl. jours., chpts. to books. Trustee A. Max Brewer Meml. Law Library, Brevard County, Fla., 1972—, chmn., 1972-76; mem. sch. bd. Central Catholic High Sch. Mem. ABA, Am. Law Inst., Am. Trial Lawyers Assn., Fla. Bar (exec. council trial sect. 1975), Acad. Fla. Trial Lawyers (dir. 1970-76, 76—, pres.-elect 1983-84, pres. 1984-85, pres.'s award 1983), Brevard County Bar Assn. (dir., President's award 1975), Melbourne Area Com. of 100. Democrat. Roman Catholic. Club: Eau Gallie Yacht (gov., vice commodore 1981-82, commodore 1983-84). Admiralty, State civil litigation, Personal injury. Office: 525 N Harbour City Blvd Melbourne FL 32935

CACHERIS, JAMES C., judge; b. Pitts., Mar. 30, 1933. B.S. in Econs., U. Pa., 1955; J.D. cum laude, George Washington U., 1960. Bar: D.C. 1960, Va. 1962. Asst. corp. counsel Washington, 1960-62; pvt. practice Washington and Alexandria, Va., 1962-71; judge 19th Jud. Circuit Ct. Va., Fairfax, 1971-81, U.S. Dist. Ct., Alexandria, 1981—. Mem. ABA, Va. Bar Assn., Fairfax County Bar Assn. Office: US Dist Ct 200 S Washington St Alexandria VA 22313 *

CADA, JAMES ALDEN, lawyer; b. Columbus, Nebr., Mar. 1, 1944; s. Frank Joseph and Marcelline Ann (Porkorny) C.; m. Judy Ann Cada, Nov. 11, 1945; children—Sarah Anne, Carrie Marie. B.S., U. Nebr., 1967, M.A., 1976, J.D., 1971. Bar: Nebr. 1972, U.S. Dist. Ct. Nebr. 1972, U.S. Ct. Claims 1981, U.S. Ct. Appeals 1977, U.S. Supreme Ct. 1981. With City Atty.'s Office, Lincoln, Nebr., 1971-74; ptnr. Bailey Polsky Cada, Todd, and Cope, Lincoln, 1974—; asst. prof. criminal justice U. Nebr.-Lincoln, 1974-77. Bd. dirs. Combined Health Agy., pres. elect 1987, campaign chmn. 1985-86. Served with U.S. Army, 1968-70; Vietnam. Decorated Purple Heart, Army Commendation medal. Mem. ABA, Nebr. Bar Assn. (del.), Gov's. Health Promotion Coordinating Council, Nebr. Trial Lawyers Assn., Assn. Trial Lawyers Am., Lincoln Bar Assn., Nebr. Bar Found (dir., jud. nominating comm. 1983-85), Arabian Horse Assn. Nebr. (pres. 1985-87), Phi Alpha Delta. Republican. Roman Catholic. Contbr. articles to legal publs. Personal injury, Consumer commercial, Bankruptcy. Home: Route 1 Lincoln NE 68502 Office: 400 Cooper Plaza Suite 211N12 Lincoln NE 68508

CADE, DANIEL STEVEN, lawyer; b. Ravenna, Ohio, Sept. 15, 1955; s. Rodney Murray and Genevieve (Yaros) C.; m. Bonnie Symes, Aug. 11, 1979; children: Melanie Susan, Andrew Steven. BA, Hiram Coll., 1978; JD, Ohio No. U., 1982. Bar: Ohio 1982, U.S. Dist. Ct. (no. dist.) Ohio 1984. Sole practice Ada, Ohio, 1982-83; asst. prosecutor dept. of human services Allen County, Lima, Ohio, 1983-86, adminstr., asst. prosecutor dept. of human services, 1986—. Mem. ABA, Ohio Bar Assn. (family law com. 1985—), Allen County Bar Assn. Republican. Lodge: Kiwanis (bd. dirs. 1986—). Family and matrimonial, Labor, General practice. Home: 4781 A State Rt 235 Ada OH 45810 Office: Allen County Dept of Human Services 550 W Elm St Lima OH 45807

CADENHEAD, ALFRED PAUL, lawyer; b. LaGrange, Ga., Oct. 14, 1926; s. Roy E. and Omie (Bishop) C.; m. Sara Davenport, Oct. 14, 1945; children: Steven Paul, David James. Jr. coll. certificate, W. Ga. Coll., 1944; LL.B., Emory U., 1949. Bar: Ga. 1949. Ptnr. firm Hurt, Richardson, Garner, Todd & Cadenhead, Atlanta; dir. various corps.; pres. Atlanta Legal Aid Soc., 1958. Pres. Met. Atlanta Mental Health Assn., 1964-65, Ga. Assn. Mental Health, 1968; past trustee Queens Coll., Charlotte, N.C. Served with paratroops U.S. Army, 1944-46. Fellow Am. Acad. Matrimonial Lawyers, Am. Coll. Trial Lawyers, Internat. Soc. Barristers; mem. Atlanta Bar Assn. (pres. 1970-71), State Bar Ga. (bd. govs.), Atlanta Estate Planning Council (pres. 1976). Presbyterian. General practice. Home: 6305 Riverside Dr NW Atlanta GA 30328 Office: 1100 Peachtree Center Harris Tower 233 Peachtree St NE Atlanta GA 30343

CADES, JULIUS RUSSELL, lawyer; b. Phila., Oct. 30, 1904; s. Isaac and Ida Frieda (Russell) C.; m. Charlotte Leah McLean, Nov. 28, 1938; 1 son, Russell McLean. A.B., U. Pa., 1925, LL.B. cum laude, 1928, LL.M. (Gowan research fellow corp. law), 1930. Bar: Pa. 1928, Hawaii 1930, U.S. Supreme Ct. 1936. Practice in Honolulu, 1929—; partner firm Cades Schutte Fleming & Wright (and predecessor), 1934—; chmn. com. to promote uniformity of legislation of U.S. for Hawaii, 1949-60, mem., 1962-66; mem. Jud. Council State Hawaii, 1966-71; bd. dirs. Universal Corp., Pacific Devel. Co., Ltd. Writer on taxation, gen. semantics, jurisprudence. Chmn. bd. commrs. Hawaii Bd. Pub. Instrn., 1945; bd. govs., violin and viola player Honolulu Symphony Orch., 1930-65; Chmn. bd. regents U. Hawaii, 1941-43; trustee, bd. dirs. Honolulu Acad. Arts, 1950-51, Watumull Found., 1955—; treas., bd. dirs. Honolulu Art Soc., 1936-50; bd. dirs. Contemporary Art Center of Hawaii, 1967—, chmn., 1980—. Decorated Order Brit. Empire; Order of Distinction for Cultural Leadership Hawaii. Fellow Am. Bar Found. (life); mem. Am. Bar Assn. (del. Hawaii 1950-53), Bar Assn. Hawaii (pres. 1946-48), Am. Law Inst. (life), Am. Judicature Soc. (dir. 1969-73), Order of Coif. General corporate, General practice, Legal history. Home: PO Box 939 Honolulu HI 96808 Office: Bishop Trust Bldg PO Box 939 Honolulu HI 96808

CADLE, JERRY NEAL, lawyer; b. Swainsboro, Ga., June 3, 1951; s. F.H. and Eugenia (Baker) C.; m. Paula Kay Ferre, Dec. 27, 1971; children—Ivy Neal, Donald Jacob, Jean Marie. Student Middle Ga. Coll., 1969-70, Ga. So. Coll., 1970-71; B.B.A., U. Ga., 1972, J.D., 1975. Bar: Ga. 1975, U.S. Dist. Ct. (so. dist.) Ga. 1975, U.S. Tax Ct. 1976, U.S. Ct. Appeals (11th cir.) 1981. Assoc. Rountree & Rountree, Swainsboro, Ga., 1975-76; ptnr. Rountree & Cadle, 1977—. Bd. dirs. Emanuel County 4-H Found., 1975—, v.p., 1979—; pres. Swainsboro Devel. Corp., 1977—; deacon First Bapt. Ch., 1983-85, chmn. bd. trustees, 1984-85. Mem. Ga. Sch. Bd. Attys. Assn., Middle Judicial Cir. Bar Assn. (sec.-treas. 1978, 83). Club: Swainsboro Country (dir. 1981-85, pres. 1984). Contracts commercial, Probate, Real property. Home: W Main St Swainsboro GA 30401 Office: Rountree & Cadle 130 S Main St Swainsboro GA 30401

CADWELL, DAVID ROBERT, lawyer; b. Hartford, Conn., June 7, 1934; s. Robert M. and Esther (Pinsky) C.; m. Carolle Cramer, 1964 (div. 1970); children—David, Kimberly; m. Sumiko Hashigiwa, Dec. 28, 1974; children—Kenneth, Daniel. B.A. magna cum laude, U. Minn., 1956; J.D., UCLA, 1959. Bar: Calif. 1960, U.S. Dist. Ct. (cen. and so. dists.) Calif. 1960, U.S. Supreme Ct. 1968. Dep. atty. gen. Calif. Atty. Gen., Los Angeles, 1960-61; sole practice, Santa Ana, Calif., 1961-70; adminstr. Jacoby & Meyers, Los Angeles, 1972-74, assoc., 1974-82; sole practice, Los Angeles, 1982-84; mng. ptnr. Cadwell & Glenn, Los Angeles, 1984—; lectr. Practical Law Course, Los Angeles, 1975-80. Author: How to Take a Case to Court, 1975; How to Handle Personal Injury Cases, 1976; How to Evaluate a Personal Injury Case, 1978, 80. Nat. committeeman Calif. Young Democrats, Los Angeles, 1959-60; mem. host com. Dem. Nat. Conv., Los Angeles, 1960, county com. Dem. Party, Orange County, Calif., 1962-64; exec. com. Fox Hills Dem. Club, Los Angeles, 1973-78. Recipient Outstanding Legal Services award NAACP, 1963. Mem. Assn. Trial Lawyers Am. Calif. Trial Lawyers Assn., Los Angeles Trial Lawyers Assn. Jewish. Personal injury, State civil litigation. Home: 3575 Green Vista Dr Encino CA 91436 Office: Cadwell & Glenn 9744 Wilshire Blvd Suite 440 Beverly Hills CA 90212

CAFARELLA, JOAN MARIE COURSOLLE, lawyer; b. Mpls., May 25, 1926; d. Nazard M. and Rocena L. (Weissert) Coursolle; m. Vernon W. Cafarella, June 19, 1954; children—John, Paul, Joe, Tom. LL.B., U. Minn., 1949. Bar: Minn. 1949. Assoc. Coursolle, Preus & Maag, Mpls., 1949-56; sole practice, Wayzata, Minn., 1956-59, 1977-80, Excelsior, Minn., 1959-77, 81—; gen. counsel Ben Franklin Fed. Savs. and Loan Assn., 1956-65; exam. atty. Midwest Fed. Savs. & Loan Assn., 1965-77. Mem. Minn. Bar Assn., Hennepin County Bar Assn. Real property, Family and matrimonial, Probate. Home and Office: 603 Lake St Excelsior MN 55331

CAFCAS, THOMAS HENRY, JR., lawyer; b. Evergreen Park, Ill., Oct. 31, 1948; s. Thomas H. and Constance (Gustafson) C.; m. Maria Hooper; children: Alicia, Lara, Thomas H. V. BA, Syracuse U., 1970; JD, Ill. Inst. Tech., 1973. Bar: Ill. 1973, U.S. Dist. Ct (no. dist.) Ill. 1973. Assoc. DeHaan and Stronberg, P.C., Chgo., 1974-78; ptnr. Fohrman, Lurie, Sklar & Simon, Chgo., 1978-82, DeHaan and Richter, P.C., Chgo., 1982-85; gen. counsel Health and Tennis Corp., Los Angeles, 1985—. Mem. ABA, Ill. Bar Assn.

CAFFREY, ANDREW AUGUSTINE, U.S. district judge; b. Lawrence, Mass., Oct. 2, 1920; s. Augustine J. and Monica A. (Regan) C.; m. Evelyn F. White, June 26, 1946; children: Augustine J., Andrew A., James E., Mary L., Francis J., Joseph H. A.B. cum laude, Holy Cross Coll., 1941; LL.B. cum laude, Boston Coll., 1948; LL.M., Harvard U., 1948. Bar: Mass. 1948, U.S. Supreme Ct. 1958. Assoc. prof. law Boston Coll. Law Sch., 1948-55; asst. U.S. atty., chief civil div. Dist. Mass., 1955-59, 1st asst. U.S. atty., 1959-60, U.S. dist. judge, 1960—, chief judge, 1972-86, sr. dist. ct. judge, 1986—; Mem. Jud. Panel on Multidist. Litigation, 1975—, chmn., 1980. Served with AUS, World War II, ETO. Named Alumnus of Yr. Boston Coll. Law Sch., 1986. Mem. Jud. Conf. U.S. (exec. com. 1973-79), Am., Fed., Mass. Boston bar assns., Am. Law Inst., Harvard Law Sch. Assn. Mass., Order of Coif (hon.), Alpha Sigma Nu, Delta Epsilon Sigma. Clubs: Merrimack Valley, Holy Cross Alumni (past pres., dir.). Address: 1629 Post Office Bldg Boston MA 02109

CAGNEY, JOSEPH BERT, lawyer; b. Chgo., Oct. 15, 1945; s. James Edward and Helen (Gast) C.; m. Barbara J. Wojtkiewicz, Apr. 20, 1976; 1 child, Travis James. BBA in Acctg., U. Wis., 1968; JD, Loyola U., Chgo., 1975; LLM in Taxation, John Marshall Law Sch., 1980. CPA, Ill. Assoc. Gorhom, Merge, Bowman & Hourigan, Chgo., 1976-80; ptnr. Goschi & Cagney, Chgo., 1980-85; pres. Maher & Newman, Chgo., 1985—. Served to 1st lt. U.S. Army, 1968-70, Vietnam. Mem. ABA, Am. Inst. CPA's, Chgo. Bar Assn. Personal income taxation, Corporate taxation, Estate taxation. Home: 28 S Mitchell Arlington Heights IL 60005 Office: Maher & Newman 230 W Monroe Chicago IL 60606

CAGNEY, WILLIAM PATRICK, III, lawyer; b. Chgo., Feb. 25, 1942; s. William Patrick, Jr., and Patricia Cuneo (Crowe) C.; m. Bonnie Beth Brown, Nov. 13, 1973 (div.); m. Cynthia N. Sharp, Nov. 5, 1983; children: Catherine Cuneo, Quinn Longstreth. B.A., Georgetown U., 1963, J.D., 1967. Bar: Ill. 1967, U.S. Ct. Appeals (7th cir.) 1970, Fla. 1972, U.S. Supreme Ct. 1973, U.S. Ct. Appeals (D.C. cir.) 1978, U.S. Ct. Appeals (11th cir.) 1981. Asst. U.S. atty., Chgo., 1967-71; dep. chief Miami Strike Force, Dept. Justice, 1971-72; ptnr. Tew, Tew, Murray & Freeman, 1972-73; sole practice, Miami, Fla., 1974—. Mem. ABA, Ill. Bar Assn., Fla. Bar Assn., Chgo. Bar Assn., Dade County Bar Assn., Am. Trial Lawyers Assn., Fla. Trial Lawyers Assn. Republican. Roman Catholic. Clubs: Univ. (Chgo.); Palm Bay, Miami, Surf, City (Miami); Bob o'Link (Highland Park, Ill.); Barrington Hills Country; LaGorce Country (Miami Beach, Fla.). Assoc. editor in criminal law Barrister, 1978-79. Federal civil litigation, State civil litigation, Criminal. Office: 3400 SE Fin Plaza 200 S Biscayne Blvd Miami FL 33131

CAHAN, JUDITH E., lawyer; b. N.Y.C., May 3, 1951; d. Morris Leo and Anne (Stoller) Kaplan; m. Steven Lee Cahan, Mar. 11, 1983 (div. Feb. 1985). BS, Cornell U., 1972; JD cum laude, Yeshiva U., 1979. Bar: N.Y. 1980, Colo. 1981, U.S. Dist. Ct. Colo. 1981, U.S. Ct. Appeals (10th cir.) 1981. Law clk. appellate div. N.Y. State Supreme Ct., N.Y.C., 1980-81; staff atty. 10th Cir. Ct. Appeals, Denver, 1981-82; assoc. Brownstein Hyatt Farber & Madden, Denver, 1982-84; ptnr. Sherman & Howard, Denver, 1984—. Author: (with others) The Unmarried Couples Legal Handbook, 1981. Mem. ABA, Colo. Bar Assn., Denver Bar Assn. Democrat. Jewish. Avocations: skiing, jazz dancing, reading, bicycling, hiking. Banking, Real property, General corporate. Home: 1020 15th St Apt 13H Denver CO 80202 Office: Sherman & Howard 633 17th St 2900 1st Interstate Tower N Denver CO 80202

CAHERIS, JAMES C., judge. m. Sally Caheris, July 9, 1960. BS in Econs., U. Pa., 1955; JD with honors, George Washington U., 1960. Bar: D.C. 1960, Va. 1962. Asst. corp. counsel D.C., 1960-62; sole practice 1962-71; judge 19th Jud. Cir. Va., 1971-81, U.S. Dist. Ct. (ea. dist.) Va., Alexandria, 1981—. Served to 1st lt. U.S. Army, 1955-57. Mem. ABA, Fairfax Bar Assn. Republican. Greek Orthodox. Office: US Dist Ct PO Box 709 Alexandria VA 22313

CAHILL, CLYDE S., U.S. judge; b. St. Louis, Apr. 9, 1923; s. Clyde and Effie (Taylor) C.; m. Thelma Newsom, Apr. 29, 1951; children: Linda Diggs, Marina, Valerian, Randall, Kevin, Myron. B.S., St. Louis U., 1949, J.D., 1951. Bar: Mo. Sole practice 1951-56; asst. circuit atty. City of St. Louis, 1956-64; regional atty. OEO, Kansas City, 1966-68; gen. mgr. Human Devel. Corp., 1968-72; gen. counsel, exec. dir. Legal Aid Soc., St. Louis, 1972-75; circuit judge State of Mo., 1975-80; U.S. dist. judge Eastern Dist. Mo., 1980—; lectr. St. Louis U. Law Sch., 1974-79; counsel to Mo. NAACP, 1958-65. Bd. dirs. St. Louis Urban League, 1974, Met. YMCA, St. Louis, 1975—, Comprehensive Health Center, 1975, Cardinal Ritter High Sch., 1978. Served with USAAF, World War II. Recipient NAACP Disting. Service award, St. Louis Argus award. Mem. Am. Bar Assn., Nat. Bar Assn., Am. Judicature Soc., Mo. Bar Assn., Met. St. Louis Bar Assn., St. Louis Lawyers Assn., Mound City Bar Assn. Jurisprudence. Office: U S Dist Ct US Court and Custom House 1114 Market St Saint Louis MO 63101

CAHILL, MICHAEL EDWARD, lawyer; b. Montreal, Quebec, Can., Feb. 22, 1951. BA, Bishop's U., 1972; LLB, Osgoode Hall, Toronto, 1975; LLM, Harvard U., 1978. Bar: Can. 1977, Calif. 1978, U.S. Dist. Ct. (so. dist.) Calif. 1978, U.S. Supreme Ct. 1983. Assoc. Shenas & Robbins, San Diego, 1978-83, O'Melveny & Myers, Los Angeles, 1983—. Barlow scholarship, 1976. Mem. ABA, Los Angeles Bar Assn., Canadian-Am. Bar Assn. (bd. dirs. 1985—), World Trade Assn. of San Diego (bd. dirs. 1982-83). Securities, Private international, General corporate. Office: O'Melveny & Myers 1800 Century Park E Los Angeles CA 90067

CAHN, EDWARD N., federal judge; b. Allentown, Pa., June 29, 1933; s. Norman A. and Miriam H. C.; m. Alice W.; Dec. 7, 1963; children: Melissa, Jessica. B.A. magna cum laude, Lehigh U., 1955; LL.B., Yale U., 1958. Atty. Cahn & Roberts, 1971-75; judge U.S. Dist. Ct. (ea. dist.) Pa., 1974—. Judicial administration. Office: US District Court 3809 US Courthouse Independence Mall W 601 Market St Philadelphia PA 19106 *

CAHN, RICHARD CALEB, lawyer; b. Bklyn., June 11, 1932; s. Irving and Pearl (Abel) C.; m. Vivian Isabel Meksin, Dec. 24, 1961; children—Michael, Lisa, Daniel, Sara. A.B., Dartmouth Coll., 1953; LL.B., Yale U., 1956. Bar: N.Y. 1956, Fla. 1966, U.S. Supreme Ct. 1960. Student asst. U.S. atty. So. Dist. N.Y., N.Y.C., 1955; atty. U.S. Dept. Justice, Washington 1956-57; ptnr. Cahn, Wishod, Wishod & Lamb, Melville, N.Y.; prin. asst. dist. atty. Suffolk County (N.Y.), 1965-66; dep. atty. Town of Huntington (N.Y.), 1966-68; spl. counsel towns of Smithtown, Islip, Brookhaven, Babylon (N.Y.), 1967-68, Islip, N.Y., 1976-83, Huntington, N.Y., 1981—; counsel Brentwood Sch. Dist., 1977-82, 86—; spl. counsel Amityville Sch. Dist., 1978-79, Village of North Hills, 1978-79, Merrick Pub. Library; adj. prof. Touro Coll., Sch. Law, 1986—; hearing officer N.Y. State Edn. Dept., Nassau and Suffolk Counties, 1971-77; spl. dist. atty. Suffolk County, 1972; participant World Peace Through Law Conf., 1967, Malpractice Mediation Panel, 2d dept., 1974-84, Gov.'s Jud. Nominating Com. 2d dept., 1975-81; mem. screening com. bankruptcy judges U.S. Dist. Ct. Dist. N.Y., 1976-81, mem. screening com. U.S. magistrates, 1977-81; regional counsel SUNY-Stony Brook, 1972—. Bd. dirs. Stony Brook Found., 1974—, Ea. Dist. Civil Litigation Fund, 1982—. Fellow Soc. Values in Higher Edn., 1984—; mem. ABA, N.Y. Bar Assn. (ho. of dels. 1981-83), Suffolk County Bar Assn. (pres. 1981-82), Fed. Bar Assn., Am. Judicature Soc., Fed. Bar Council (v.p. 1982-84, trustee 1984—), Huntington Lawyers Club. Contbr. articles to profl. jours.; bd. editors Yale Law Jour., 1954. Federal civil litigation, State civil litigation, Criminal. Office: 534 Broadhollow Rd CB 179 Melville NY 11747

CAILLAT, CHARLES VICTOR, lawyer; b. Portland, Oreg., May 22, 1920; s. Emil Adam and Beulah Frances (Tinner) C.; m. Wilma Genevieve Kamph, Oct. 24, 1942; children—Charles Gregory, Suzanne Marie. Student, U. Portland, 1938-40; A.B., Stanford U., 1949; LL.B., U. Santa Clara, 1954. Bar: Calif. 1955, U.S. Ct. Appeals (9th cir.) 1955. Adminstrv. sec. Preston Sch. of Industry, Ione, Calif., 1946-51; ptnr. Miller Morton Caillat & Nevis, San Jose, Calif., 1955—. Pres. Santa Clara County Estate Planning Council, 1965-66. Served to 1st lt. USAAF, 1941-46. U. Portland scholar, 1938. Mem. ABA, Calif. Bar Assn., Santa Clara County Bar Assn. (trustee 1966-68). Republican. Roman Catholic. Clubs: Sainte Claire, University pres.). 1979-80) (San Jose). Probate. Office: Suite 500 777 N First St San Jose CA 95112

CAIN, KENNETH JEFFERSON, lawyer, judicial administrator; b. Kansas City, Mo., May 18, 1952; s. Robert Cain and Dorothy Mae (Rall) C. BA, U. Mo., Kansas City, 1974, MA, 1976, JD, 1980. Bar: Mo. 1980, U.S. Dist. Ct. (we. dist.) Mo. 1980, U.S. Ct. Appeals (8th cir.) 1981. Atty. HHS, Kansas City, 1980-83; sole practice Kansas City, 1983-84; asst. atty. gen. State of Mo., Kansas City, 1984-85; legal advisor, assoc. adminstrv. law judge Mo. Div. Workers' Compensation, Kansas City, 1985—; lectr. U. Mo., Kansas City, 1977-78. Fellow Kansas City Bd. Trustees U. Mo., 1975. Mem. ABA, Mo. Bar Assn., Jackson County Bar Assn., Omicron Delta Kappa. Workers' compensation, Labor. Office: Mo Div Workers Compensation 405 E 13th St 7th Floor Kansas City MO 64106

CAIN, MAY LYDIA, lawyer; b. Chgo., Feb. 13, 1956; d. William A. and Audrey (Rosin) C. Student, U. Ill., 1973-74; BA, Northwestern U., 1977; postgrad., U. Miami, Coral Gables, Fla., 1979-80; JD, DePaul U., 1980. Bar: Fla. 1980, U.S. Dist. Ct. (so. dist.) Fla. 1980, U.S. Ct. Appeals (5th and 11th cirs.) 1981, U.S. Supreme Ct. 1986. Ptnr. Cain and Cain, North Miami, Fla., 1980—; adj. prof. Barry U., Miami Shores, Fla., 1986; atty. Pub. Interest Law Bank, Miami, 1982-83. Editor The Fla. Bar Gen. Practice Sect. newsletter, 1984-86, vice chmn. editorial bd. Fla. Bar Jour. and News, 1986, 87-88; contbr. articles to profl. jours. Mem. ABA, Dade County Bar Assn., North Dade Bar Assn., Fla. Bar Gen. Practice Sect. (exec. council 1984—), Fla. Assn. Women Lawyers (v.p. 1982-83, pub. relations dir. 1984-85, sec. 1984-86, pres. Dade County chpt. 1983-84, bd. dirs. 1986—). General practice, State civil litigation, Criminal. Office: 11755 Biscayne Blvd 401 North Miami FL 33181

CAIN, WILLIAM ALLEN, lawyer; b. Chgo., Nov. 9, 1924; s. Albert Paul and May (Gainer) C.; m. Audrey R. Cain, Nov. 28, 1953; children—May L., Jordan S. J.D., DePaul U., 1946. Bar: Ill. 1947, Fla. 1978, U.S. dist. ct. (no. dist.) Ill. 1947, U.S. dist. ct. (so. dist.) Fla. 1979, U.S. Ct. Apls. (5th and 11th cirs.) 1981, U.S. Supreme Ct. 1961. Ptnr. Cain & Cernek, Chgo., 1955-78; sr. ptnr. Cain & Cain, North Miami, Fla., 1978—; adj. prof. U. Miami Law Sch., Coral Gables; hearing officer Dade County Pub. Schs. Bd. Edn., 1983—. Host Legal talk program on local ednl. TV sta., 1986—; past chmn. Am. Guild Variety Artists, Chgo. Mem. Assn. Trial Lawyers Am., Am. Judicature Soc., ABA, Ill. Bar Assn., Chgo. Bar Assn., North Dade Bar Assn., Fla. Assn. Women Lawyers (chmn. com. wills for elderly Dade County), Fla. Bar Assn. (pvt. practitioner com., entertainment and arts law com.; chmn. com. representation of indigents; liaison mem. com. family law sect. to law schs.; also gen. practice sect. to continuing legal edn. com., mem. VPL grievance com. exec. council gen. practice sect.), Dade County Bar Assn. (dir., lawyer referral com.), Acad. Fla. Trial Lawyers. State civil litigation, Criminal, General practice. Office: 11755 Biscayne Blvd Suite 401 North Miami FL 33181

CAIRNS, JAMES DONALD, lawyer; b. Chesea, Mass., Aug. 7, 1931; s. Stewart Scott and Kathleen (Hand) C.; m. Davida Kahrl Steinbrink, June 27, 1953; children: Douglas S., Timothy H., Pamela S., Heather M.; m. Lydia Smithers, Nov. 13, 1982. A.B., Harvard U., 1952; J.D., Ohio State U., 1958. Bar: Fla. 1974, Ohio 1958, U.S. Dist. Ct. (no. dist.) Ohio 1975, U.S. Tax Ct. 1963. Ptnr. Squire, Sanders & Dempsey, Cleve., 1958—. Served to lt. (j.g.) USNR, 1952-55. Mem. ABA, Fla. Bar Assn., Ohio State Bar Assn., Bar Assn. Greater Cleve. Democrat. Episcopalian. Clubs: Union, Lakeside Yacht. Probate. Office: Squire Sanders & Dempsey Suite 1800 Huntington Commerce Bldg Cleveland OH 44115

CALABRESE, MICHAEL RAPHAEL, lawyer; b. Atlantic City, N.J., May 28, 1956; s. Angelo William and Sally (Snyder) C. BS in Fgn. Service, Georgetown U., 1978; JD, U. Va., 1982. Bar: D.C. 1982. Law clk. to cir. judge U.S. Ct. Appeals (4th cir.), Washington, 1982-83; assoc. Mudge, Rose et al, Washington, 1983-84, Finley, Kumble et al, Washington, 1984-86, Morgan, Lewis & Bockius, Washington, 1986—. Mem. Phi Beta Kappa. Republican. Roman Catholic. Clubs: Army, Navy. Private international, Public international. Home: 1024 N Royal St Alexandria VA 22314 Office: Morgan Lewis & Bockius 1800 M St NW Washington DC 20036

CALABRESI, GUIDO, legal educator; b. Milan, Italy, Oct. 19, 1932; s. Massimo and Bianca Maria (Finzi Contini) C.; m. Anne Gordon Audubon Tyler, May 20, 1961; children—Bianca Contini, Anne Gordon Audubon, Massimo Franklin Tyler. B.S. in Analytical Econs., Yale U., 1953, LL.B., 1958, M.A. (hon.), 1962; B.A. in Politics, Philosophy and Econs., Oxford U., 1955, M.A. in Politics, Philosophy and Econs., 1959; LL.D. (hon.), Notre Dame U., 1979; Dott. Ius S.D. (hon.), U. Torino, Italy, 1982; LL.D. (hon.), Villanova U., 1984, U. Toronto, 1985. Bar: Conn. 1958. Asst. instr. dept. econs. Yale U., New Haven, Conn., 1955-56; law clk. to justice Hugo Black U.S. Supreme Ct., Washington, 1958-59; asst. prof. Yale U. Law Sch., 1959-61, assoc. prof., 1961-62, prof., 1962-70, John Thomas Smith prof. law, 1970-78, Sterling prof. law, 1978—, dean, 1985—; fellow Timothy Dwight Coll., 1960—; vis. prof. Harvard U. Law Sch., 1969-70, Japan Am. Studies Seminar, Kyoto-Doshisha Univs., summer 1972, European U. Inst., Florence, Italy, 1979; Arthur L. Goodhart prof. legal sci. Cambridge U., also fellow St. John's Coll., 1980-81; pres. Crosby Co.; dir. First Bancorp, New Haven. Author: The Costs of Acidents: A Legal and Economic Analysis, 1970; (with P. Bobbitt) Tragic Choices, 1978; A Common Law for the Age of Statutes (ABA citation of merit), 1983; Ideals, Beliefs, Attitudes and the

Law: Private Law Perspectives on a Public Law Problem, 1985; contbr. articles to legal jours. Trustee Hopkins Grammar Sch., pres. 1976-80; trustee St. Thomas More Chapel, Yale U., Cath. U. Am., Carolyn Found., Minn.; mem. adv. bd. Joseph and Rose Kennedy Inst. Study of Human Bioethics, Georgetown U.; mem. Democratic Town Com., Woodbridge, Conn. Rhodes scholar, 1953; named one of Ten Outstanding Young Men Am., U.S. Jaycees, 1962; recipient Laetare Medal, U. Notre Dame, 1985. Fellow Am. Acad. Arts and Scis. (council), Associazione Italiana di Diritto Comparato, Brit. Acad. (corr.); mem. Conn. Bar Assn. Personal injury, Jurisprudence, Estate taxation. Home: 639 Amity Rd Woodbridge CT 06525 Office: Yale U Law Sch 401 A Yale Station New Haven CT 06520

CALABRO, MICHAEL JAMES, lawyer; b. Washington, Pa., Aug. 21, 1951; s. A. J. and Tillie (Skowronski) C.; m. Debra M. L. Nocery, Dec. 15, 1973; children: Niccolo Gian, Gina Teraesa. BS, USCG Acad., 1973; JD, Duquesne U., 1981. Bar: Mass. 1981, U.S. Dist. Ct. Mass. 1982, U.S. Ct. Mil. Appeals 1982, U.S. Ct. Appeals (1st cir.) 1982. Commd. ensign USCG, 1973, advanced through grades to lt., 1977, retired, 1979; assoc. Flanagan & Hunter, Boston, 1981-86. Editor-in-chief Juris Mag., 1980-81. Served with USCGR, 1979-83. Mem. ABA, Mass. Bar Assn., Ret. Officers Assn., USCG Acad. Alumni Assn., Duquesne U. Law Alumni Assn. Avocations: computer ops., chess. Admiralty, Military, Personal injury. Home: 200 Sawtelle Ave Brockton MA 02402 Office: Flanagan & Hunter PC 211 Congress St Boston MA 02110

CALAMARI, JOSEPH AUGUST, legal educator; b. N.Y.C., Feb. 20, 1919; s. August Alexander and Margaret Elizabeth (Casella) C.; m. Marie Jean Sileo, June 30, 1951; children—Betty Jo, Ann-Marie, Maryellen, James. B.A., Fordham U., 1939, LL.B., 1942; M.Law, NYU, 1949. Bar: N.Y. 1942, U.S. Dist. Ct. (so. dist.) N.Y. 1946, (ea. dist.) N.Y. 1947, U.S. Ct. Apls. (2d cir.) 1947, Va. 1952, U.S. Supreme Ct. 1951, U.S. Ct. Mil. Apls. 1951. Assoc. counsel Alexander Ash & Schwartz, N.Y.C., 1946-50; post judge adv. Post Headquarters, Ft. Myer, Va., 1950-52; dep. gen. counsel/gen. counsel Mil. Sealift Command Atlantic, Bklyn., 1952-73; prof. law St. John's U. Sch. Law, Jamaica, N.Y., 1973—; hearing officer U.S. EEO, Washington, 1979—. Contbr. articles to profl. jours. Mem. Western Property Owners of Garden City, N.Y., 1956—; sponsor Nat. Republican. Congl. Com., 1984; mem. Republican Nat. Com., 1983. Served to col., USAR, 1972-77. Decorated Bronze Star, Army Commendation medal. Mem. Fed. Bar Assn., ABA, Martime Law Assn. U.S., Bar Assn. Nassau County (arbitrator), Res. Officers Assn., Am. Judicature Soc. Roman Catholic. Clubs: Garden City Country, Mast Hope Lodge. Admiralty, Legal education, Government contracts and claims. Home: 14 Glen Rd Garden City NY 11530 Office: Saint Johns Univ Sch Law Utopia and Grand Central Pkwy Jamaica NY 11439

CALDERWOOD, JAMES ALBERT, lawyer; b. Washington, Dec. 4, 1941; s. Charles Howard and Hilda Pauline (Dull) C. B.S., U. Md., 1964; J.D. cum laude, George Washington U., 1970; postgrad. Oxford Center Mgmt. Studies, Oxford U., 1977. Bar: Md. 1970, D.C. 1973, U.S. Supreme Ct. 1974. Trial atty. antitrust div. U.S. Dept. Justice, Washington, 1970-73, spl. asst. U.S. atty., Washington, 1973, trial atty. antitrust div., 1973-79; ptnr. Grove, Jaskiewicz, Gilliam & Cobert, Washington, 1979—; mem. faculty Transp. Law Inst. U. Denver; adj. prof. Washington Coll. Law, Am. U., 1983; gen. counsel Soc. Govt. Economists. Served to capt. USAF, 1964-68. George Washington U. Law Ctr. scholar, 1969. Mem. ABA (Achievement award 1973), Fed. Bar Assn. (nat. co chmn. council young lawyers 1972-73, chmn. regulated industries com. 1976-79), Fed. Energy Bar Assn. (chmn. antitrust com. 1985-86), Md. Bar Assn., D.C. Bar Assn., U. Md. Alumni Assn. (pres. elect 1984-85, pres. 1985-86), Coll. Bus. Alumni Club (pres. 1980-81), Pi Sigma Alpha, Delta Sigma Pi, Delta Theta Phi, English Speaking Union. Lutheran. Contbr. articles to profl. jours. Antitrust, Federal civil litigation, FERC practice. Home: 5518 Western Ave Chevy Chase MD 20815 Office: 1730 M St NW Suite 501 Washington DC 20036

CALDWELL, CAROL GRAY, lawyer; b. Gadsden, Ala., Mar. 23, 1954; d. Jack E. and Jean Carol (Gillespie) Gray; m. Harry E. Caldwell Jr., Jan. 7, 1984. AB, U. Ala., 1976; JD with distinction, Duke U., 1979. Bar: N.Y. 1980, Ala. 1984. Assoc. Dewey, Ballantine, Bushby, Palmer & Wood, N.Y.C., 1979-83; ptnr. Sirote, Permutt, McDermott, Slepian, Friend, Friedman, Held & Apolinsky, P.C., Birmingham, Ala., 1983—; mem. dean's adv. council Duke U. Sch. Law, Durham, N.C., 1986. Editor Duke U. Law Jour., 1978. Mem. ABA, Ala. Bar Assn., Birmingham Bar Assn., Nat. Assn. Bond Lawyers, Phi Beta Kappa. Municipal bonds, Securities. Home: 2525 Brookwater Circle Birmingham AL 35243 Office: Sirote Permutt et al 2222 Arlington Ave S Birmingham AL 35205

CALDWELL, GILBERT RAYMOND, III, lawyer; b. Newton, Iowa, June 14, 1952; s. Gilbert Raymond and Frances Elizabeth (Ellingsworth) C.; m. Jeanne Sharon Myerscough, Dec. 23, 1974; 1 son, Kyle Myerscough. B.A., U. Tulsa, 1974, J.D., 1977. Bar: Iowa 1978, U.S. Dist Ct. (no. and so. dists.) Iowa 1978. Asst. city prosecutor, legal intern City of Tulsa, 1976-77; asst. county atty. Jasper County, Iowa, 1978; ptnr. Caldwell, Caldwell & Caldwell, Newton, 1979—. Rep. precinct chmn. Fairview Twp, Iowa, 1982-83. Mem. Am. Judicature Soc., ABA (child advocacy and protection com. young lawyers div., juvenile law update), Iowa Bar Assn. (mem. young lawyers sect., mem. juvenile law com. 1982—, chmn. juvenile law com. 1985—, jud. dist. exec. council), Jasper County Bar Assn., Assn. Trial Laywers Iowa, Assn. Trial Lawyers Am., Newton Jaycees (sec. 1978-79, pres. 1979-80), Newton C. of C., Iowa Jaycees (state legal council 1979-80). Clubs: Monroe Community (Iowa); Jasper County Farm Bur. (Newton). Lodge: Kiwanis. General practice. Home: RFD 2 Monroe IA 50170 Office: Caldwell Caldwell & Caldwell Midtown Bldg Suite 203 Newton IA 50208

CALDWELL, JAMES WILEY, lawyer; b. Arkadelphia, Ark., Dec. 14, 1923; s. Joseph Allison and Beulah (Wright) C.; m. Marie Cole, July 11, 1947; children: Susan, Carolyn, James Wiley. B.A., Ouachita Bapt. Coll., 1947; J.D. with honors, U. Tex., 1950. Bar: Tex. Assoc. McGregor & Sewell, Houston, 1950-51; atty. City of Houston, 1951-52; sr. ptnr. Fulbright & Jaworski, Houston. Trustee, gen. counsel Baylor Coll. Medicine; chmn. Houston Tax Research Assn.; originator program for state med. edn. funds Baylor Med., 1969; financing for control of pollution on Houston Ship Channel, 1971. Served to 1st lt. inf. AUS, 1943-46, ETO. Named Ouachita Bapt. U. Disting. Alumnus, 1975. Mem. Houston Bar Assn., ABA, Nat. Assn. Bond Lawyers, State Bar of Tex. Baptist. Clubs: River Oaks Country (pres. 1983); Coronado (Houston) (pres. 1975). Administrative and regulatory, Real property, Municipal bonds. Office: Fulbright & Jaworski 1301 McKinney Ave 51st Floor Houston TX 77010

CALDWELL, JOHN WARWICK, lawyer; b. Dayton, Ohio, May 19, 1949; s. Curtis Philip and Elizabeth L. (Warwick) C.; m. Janet Hudson, June 14, 1975; children: Philip E., Katherine E., Sarah A. BA, Rice U., 1971; MA, Johns Hopkins U., 1975; JD, Villanova U., 1978. Bar: Pa. 1978, U.S. Dist. Ct. (ea. dist.) Pa. 1978, U.S. Ct. Appeals (3d cir.) 1980, U.S. Ct. Appeals (fed. cirs.) 1983, U.S. Supreme Ct. 1986. From assoc. to ptnr. Woodcock, Washburn, Kurtz, Mackiewicz & Norris, Phila., 1978—. Author: Artists' Guide to Copyrights, Patents and Trade Secrets, 1985. Mem. adv. bd. Phila. Vol. Lawyers for Arts. Robert Welch Found. scholar, 1968-71. Mem. ABA, Pa. Bar Assn., Phila. Bar Assn. (fed. cts. com.), Phila. Patent Law Assn. (chmn. antitrust com. 1983-85). Republican. Presbyterian. Patent, Trademark and copyright. Home: 5 Dale Ln Wallingford PA 19086 Office: Woodcock Washburn Kurtz et al 30 S 17th St Philadelphia PA 19103

CALDWELL, PAUL RAYMOND, lawyer; b. Englewood, N.J., July 15, 1942; s. Raymond Charles and Mildred Ruth (Peterson)C.; m. Lynn Paschak, Dec. 28, 1968; children: Charles, Daniel, Joshua. Bar: Mich. 1971, N.Mex. 1978. Staff atty. Ford Motor Co., Dearborn, Mich., 1971-73, 76-78; sr. trial atty. U.S. Dept. Justice, Detroit, 1973-76; assoc. Campbell & Black, Santa Fe, 1978-80; ptnr. Caldwell, Lenssen & Mandel, Santa Fe, 1980—. Deacon First Bapt. Ch., Santa Fe, 1986. Served to maj. USMC, 1964-68, Vietnam. Mem. ABA, Am. Trial Lawyers Assn., N.Mex. Trial Lawyers Assn., Am. Arbitration Assn. Republican. Civil rights, Federal civil litigation, State civil litigation. Home: Rt 9 Box 68B Santa Fe NM 87505 Office: CLM & J 316 E Marcy Santa Fe NM 87504-1904

CALDWELL, WILLIAM W., federal judge; b. Harrisburg, Pa., Nov. 10, 1925; s. Thomas D. and Martha B. C.; m. Janet W. Garber. A.B., Dickinson Coll., 1948, LL.B., 1951. Ptnr. Caldwell, Fox & Stoner, Harrisburg, 1951-70; 1st asst. dist. Atty. Dauphin County, 1960-62; counsel, chmn. Bd. Arbitration of Claims State of Pa., 1963-70; judge Common Pleas Ct., Dauphin County, 1970-82, U.S. Dist. Ct. (mid. dist.) Pa., 1982—. Judicial administration. Office: PO Box 11877 Fed Bldg Harrisburg PA 17108 *

CALFEE, WILLIAM LEWIS, lawyer; b. Cleveland Heights, Ohio, July 12, 1917; s. Robert Martin and Alwine (Haas) C.; m. Eleanor Elizabeth Bliss, Dec. 6, 1941; children: William R., Bruce K., Cynthia B. B.A., Harvard Coll., 1939; LL.D., Yale U., 1946. Bar: Ohio 1946. Assoc. Baker & Hostetler, Cleve., 1946-56, ptnr., 1957—. Bd. dirs. Growth Assn. Greater Cleve., 1979—; trustee Greater Cleve. United Appeal; pres. Health Fund Greater Cleve. Served to lt. col. M.I. U.S. Army, 1941-45. Decorated Legion of Merit; decorated Order of Brit. Empire. Mem. ABA (ho. dels. 1980—), Ohio Bar Assn., Bar Assn. Greater Cleve. (truste, pres. 1979-80), Nat. Conf. Bar Pres. (exec. council 1982-85), Ohio C. of C. (dir. 1983). Republican. Episcopalian. Clubs: Mayfield Country (pres.), Union, Pepper Pike; Fiddlesticks (Ft. Myers, Fla.). Home: 21200 Claythorne Rd Shaker Heights OH 44122 Office: Baker & Hostetler 3200 National City Center Cleveland OH 44114

CALHOUN, CAROL VICTORIA, lawyer; b. Frankfurt, Fed. Republic Germany, Oct. 6, 1953; came to U.S., 1954; d. Daniel Fairchild and Janet Stuart Blair Montgomery (McGovern) C.; m. Paul Martin Rosenberg, June 26, 1977; children: Joshua Micah, Miriam Nehama. Student, St. John's Coll., 1970-72; BA, Johns Hopkins U., 1976; JD, Georgetown U., 1980. Bar: D.C. 1980. Assoc. Morgan, Lewis & Bockius, Washington, 1980—; speaker on employee benefits issues. Mem. Bd. Editors Legal-Legiislative-Regulatory Update, Benefits Quarterly, 1985—; contbr. articles on pension and tax law to profl. jours. Mem. ABA (chair subcom. on distbns., employee benefits com. taxation sect. 1986—), Women's Bar Assn., Washington Employee Benefits Forum, Women in Employee Benefits. Democrat. Jewish. Pension, profit-sharing, and employee benefits, Corporate taxation, Labor. Home: 9112 Lindale Dr Bethesda MD 20817 Office: Morgan Lewis & Bockius 1800 M St NW Washington DC 20036

CALHOUN, CLAYNE MARSH, law librarian; b. Orange, N.J., July 22, 1950; d. John Clayton and Anne (Jack) Marsh; m. Thomas Sidney Calhoun, Aug. 26, 1972; 1 child, Samuel Clayton. BA, Stratford Coll., 1972; MSLS, Cath. U. Am., 1976. Asst. librarian Caplin & Drysdale, Washington, 1975-77; librarian Roanoke (Va.) Law Library, 1977—. Mem. Am. Assn. Law Libraries (southeastern chpt.). Librarianship, Personal income taxation. Office: Roanoke Law Library 315 Church Ave SW Roanoke VA 24016

CALHOUN, FRANK WAYNE, lawyer, former state legislator; b. Houston, Apr. 15, 1933; s. Wilmer Cecil and Ruby Edith (Willis) C.; m. Suzanne Paden Davis, Dec. 14, 1985; children: Michael Lee, Frank David. B.A. in History, Tex. Tech U., 1956; J.D., U. Tex., 1959. Bar: Tex. 1959, U.S. Supreme Ct. 1965. Ptnr. Byrd, Shaw, Weeks & Calhoun, Abilene, Tex., 1959-73, Liddell, Sapp & Zivley, Houston, 1974—; mem. Tex. Ho. of Reps., 1966-75; del. Tex. Constl. Conv., 1974; mem. exec. com. Tex. Film Commn., 1979-83. Contbg. editor Tex. Lawyers Weekly Letter, 1964. Bd. dirs. Tex. Assoc. Bank Counsel, 1982-85; chmn. San Jacinto Hist. Adv. Bd., 1984—; trustee, fellow Tex. Tech Law Sch. Found., 1975—; trustee Colo. Outward Bound Sch., 1982—; past bd. dirs. Abilene YMCA. Served with USN, 1951-53. Named Outstanding Young Man Abilene Jaycees, 1968; recipient Disting. Service award Tex. Bar Assn., 1969, 71, 73. Mem. ABA, Tex. Bar Assn., Travis County Bar Assn., Tex. Tech U. Ex-Students Assn. (past pres.), Tex. Archeol. Soc., Nat. Audubon Soc., Sierra Club, Nat. Trust for Hist. Preservation, Houston Fine Arts Mus., Tex. State Hist. Assn., Sons Confederate Vets., St. Andrews Soc. Tex., Sigma Alpha Epsilon, Alpha Kappa Psi. Democrat. Methodist. Clubs: Houston, Austin, Plaza (dir.). Lodge: Rotary (past pres.). Administrative and regulatory, Legislative. Home: 3040 Locke Ln Houston TX 77019 Office: Liddell Sapp & Zivley 3400 Tex Commerce Tower Houston TX 77002

CALHOUN, GORDON JAMES, lawyer; b. Pitts., Sept. 3, 1953; s. Bertram Allen and Dorothy Mae (Brown) C.; m. Jane Ann Walchli, May 7, 1982; 1 child, Andrew Michael. BA, John Hopkins U., 1975; JD, Stanford U., 1978. Bar: Calif. 1978, U.S. Dist. Ct. (no., cen., ea. and so. dists.) Calif. 1979, U.S. Ct. Appeals (9th cir.) 1980. Ptnr. Parkinson, Wolf, Lazar & Leo, Los Angeles, 1978—. Office: Parkinson Wolf Lazar & Leo 1900 Ave of The Stars Los Angeles CA 90067

CALHOUN, JOHN HENRY, JR., lawyer, educator; b. Pensacola, Fla., May 8, 1932; s. John Henry Sr. and Annie M. (Bethea) C.; m. Shirley M. Bitar, Nov. 12, 1960; children: Kristen Lynn, John Henry III, David Brian. BSEE, Duke U., 1955; MBA, U. Pitts., 1965; JD, Ind. U., 1972. Bar: Ind. 1972, U.S. Dist. Ct. (so. dist.) Ind., U.S. Tax Ct. 1975, U.S. Patent and Trademark Office 1975, U.S. Ct. Appeals (7th cir.) 1979, U.S. Supreme Ct. 1979. Engr. Alcoa, New Kensington, Pa., 1958-66; bus. ventures analyst RCA, Indpls., 1966-68, quality control mgr., 1968-72, mgr. test systems devel., 1972-77; sole practice Indpls., 1977—; lectr. Ind. U., Indpls., 1972—. Served to lt. (j.g.) USN, 1955-58. Mem. ABA, Ind. Bar Assn., Indpls. Bar Assn. Republican. Presbyterian. Avocations: family activities. General practice, Real property, Patent. Home: 9941 Culpepper Dr Carmel IN 46032 Office: 6100 N Keystone Ave Suite 333 Indianapolis IN 46220

CALHOUN, JOHN L., lawyer; b. Balt., Feb. 3, 1948; s. John H. and Evelyn G. (Dennis) C.; m. Trudy Calhoun, July 3, 1976; children—Alison, Michael. B.A. in History, Randolph-Macon Coll., 1970; J.D., U. Miami, 1973. Bar: Fla., 1973, Md., 1974, Pa., 1974, D.C., 1977, various fed. cts. Practice, Balt., 1974-81; asst. pub. defender State of Md., 1981—; ptnr. Calhoun & Henderson, Towson, Md., 1981—; lectr. criminal law Community Coll. Balt., wills and estates Coll. Notre Dame, Md. Mem. Fla. Bar, D.C. Bar, Baltimore County Bar Assn., Am. Paralegal Inst. Personal injury, Consumer commercial, Criminal. Home: 5900 Smith Ave Baltimore MD 21209

CALHOUN, MARILYN JEAN, lawyer; b. San Antonio, June 2, 1952; d. W.W. Calhoun and Polly (Vann) McKnight. BA, U. N.C., 1974; JD, Campbell U., 1980. Bar: N.C. 1980, U.S. Ct. Appeals (4th cir.) 1980, U.S. Dist. Ct. N.C. 1981, U.S. Supreme Ct. 1986,. Assoc. Barringer, Allen & Pinnix, Raleigh, N.C., 1980-81, ptnr., 1981-82; sole practice Raleigh, 1982-84; sr. atty., owner Law Offices of M. Jean Calhoun, Raleigh, 1984-87; ptnr. Everett, Hancock, Nichols & Calhoun, Raleigh, 1987—. Mem. ABA, N.C. Bar Assn., Assn. Trial Lawyers Am., N.C. Acad. Trial Lawyers (bd. govs. 1985—), Wake County Family Law Attys. (chmn. 1985), Wake COunty Real Property Attys., N.C. Assn. Women Bus. Owners (pres. 1986—). Democrat. Avocation: real estate investment. Family and matrimonial, Real property, Personal injury. Office: Everett Hancock Nichols & Calhoun 4038 Barrett Dr Raleigh NC 27609

CALHOUN, MONICA DODD, lawyer; b. Astoria, N.Y., June 3, 1953; d. Enda Aloysius and Christina (McGrath) Dodd; m. Charles H. Calhoun, Feb. 4, 1983. BA, SUNY, Albany, 1975; JD, SUNY, Buffalo, 1978; LLM, NYU, 1983. Bar: N.Y. 1979, U.S. Dist. Ct. (so. dist.) N.Y., 1982. Atty. Windsor Life Ins. Co., N.Y.C., 1978-79; assoc. gen. counsel Manhatten Life Ins. Co., N.Y.C., 1979-84; assoc. counsel Tchrs. Ins. Annuity Assn.-Coll. Retirement Equities Fund, N.Y.C., 1984—. Mem. Am. Life Ins. Counsel, N.Y. State Bar Assn. Pension, profit-sharing, and employee benefits, Insurance, Corporate taxation. Office: Teachers Ins & Ann Assn Am 730 3rd Ave New York NY 10017

CALIENDO, GENNARO D., corporate lawyer; b. 1941. BA, NYU, 1962; JD, Fordham U., 1965. Atty. FCC, N.Y.C., 1965; sole practice Washington, 1966-68; atty. Pa. Power & Light Co., Allentown, 1968-75, asst. counsel, 1975-78, chief counsel regulatory affairs, 1981-85, v.p. gen. counsel, 1985—. Office: Pa Power & Light Co 2 N 9th St Allentown PA 18101 *

CALIFANO, JOSEPH ANTHONY, JR., former sec. HEW; b. Bklyn., May 15, 1931; s. Joseph Anthony and Katherine (Gill) C.; m. Hilary Paley Byers, 1983; children by previous marriage: Mark Gerard, Joseph Anthony III, Claudia Frances; stepchildren: Brooke A. Byers, John Frederick Byers. A.B., Holy Cross Coll., 1952; LL.B., Harvard U., 1955. Bar: N.Y 1955, U.S. Supreme Ct. 1966. With firm Dewey, Ballantine, Bushby, Palmer & Wood, N.Y.C., 1958-61; spl. asst. to gen. counsel Dept. Def., 1961-62; spl. asst. to sec. army 1962-63; gen. counsel Dept. Army, 1963-64; spl. asst. to sec. and dep. sec. def. 1964-65, spl. asst. to Pres., 1965-69; mem. firm Arnold & Porter, Washington, 1969-71; partner firm Williams, Connolly & Califano, Washington, 1971-76; sec. HEW, 1977-79; partner firm Califano, Ross & Heineman, Washington, 1980-82, Dewey, Ballantine, Bushby, Palmer & Wood, 1983—; dir. Chrysler Corp., Am. Can Co., Automatic Data Processing, Inc; Gen. counsel Democratic Nat. Com., 1970-72. Author: The Student Revolution: A Global Confrontation, 1969, A Presidential Nation, 1975, (with Howard Simons) The Media and the Law, 1976, (with Howard Simons) The Media and Business, 1978, Governing America: An Insiders Report from the White House and the Cabinet, 1981, The 1982 Report on Drug Abuse and Alcoholism, 1982; America's Health Care Revolution—Who Lives? Who Dies? Who Pays?, 1985. Trustee Urban Inst., NYU, Kaiser Family Found., chmn. Twentieth Century fund. Ctr. for Social Policy in the Middle East; hon. chmn. Children of Alcoholics Found.; bd. dirs. seminars on media and soc. Columbia U., Georgetown U. Served to lt. USNR, 1955-58. Recipient Distinguished Civilian Service award Dept. Army, 1964; Man of Year award Justinian Soc. Lawyers, 1966; Distinguished Service medal Dept. Def., 1967; named One of Ten Outstanding Young Men of America, 1966. Mem. ABA, Fed. Bar Assn., D.C. Bar Assn., N.Y. State Bar Assn., Am. Judicature Soc. Club: Federal City (dir.).

CALIMAFDE, PAULA ANNETTE, lawyer; b. N.Y.C., Oct. 14, 1951; d. John Michael and Annette (Walicki) C.; m. Alan S. Mark, Oct. 14, 1978; children—Ilana, Clifford. B.A., Swarthmore Coll., 1973; J.D., Cath. U. Am., 1976. Bar: Md. 1976, D.C. 1977. Prin., Paley, Rothman & Cooper, Bethesda, Md., 1976—; chmn., lectr. Practising Law Inst., 1983, 84. Lectr. Montgomery-Prince George's Continuing Legal Edn. Inst., Profl. Bus. Mgmt. Inst.; bd. dirs., v.p. Small Bus. Council Am., Inc., Washington; nat. commr. on payroll costs White House Conf. on Small Bus., 1986. Author: Professional Corporations, 1981-84, Flexible Compensation Plans, 1983; contbr. articles to profl. jours., co-editor Ann. Rev. Montgomery-Prince George's Continuing Legal Edn. Inst., Inc., 1982-86. Mem. ABA (vice chair small bus. com. taxation sect., lectr. tax sect.), Md. Bar Assn., Montgomery County Bar Assn. Corporate taxation, Pension, profit-sharing, and employee benefits, Estate planning. Office: Paley Rothman & Cooper 4800 Hampden Ln 7th Floor Bethesda MD 20814

CALKINS, BENJAMIN, lawyer; b. Boston, Jan. 20, 1956; s. Evan and Virginia (Brady) C.; m. Lindsay Noble, July 4, 1981; children: Sarah Noble, Bradley Phillips. AB, Harvard U., 1978; JD, U. Mich., 1981. Bar: D.C. 1982, U.S. Dist. Ct. (ea. dist.) Mich. 1982, Ohio 1983, U.S. Dist. Ct. (no. dist.) Ohio 1983, U.S. Ct. Appeals (6th cir.) 1986. Law clk. to presiding justice U.S. Dist. Ct. (ea. dist.), Detroit, 1981-83; assoc. Squire, Sanders & Dempsey, Cleve., 1983—. Sr. editor U. Mich. Law Rev., 1979-81; contbr. articles to profl. jours. Sustaining mem. Rep. Nat. Com., Washington, 1985—. Mem. ABA (corp., banking and bus. law sect., fed. regulation of securities com., antitrust law sect., young lawyers sect.), Ohio Bar Assn. (corp. counsel sect., corp. law com.), Cleve. Bar Assn. (securities law sect., corp., banking and bus. law sect., real property sect., young lawyers sect.), D.C. Bar Assn., Rep. Nat. Lawyers Assn., Order of Coif. Presbyterian. Club: Harvard (Cleve.) (trustee 1985—). Avocations: sports, animal husbandry, photography. General corporate, Securities, Contracts commercial. Home: 3219 E Fairfax Cleveland Heights OH 44118 Office: Squire Sanders & Dempsey 1800 Huntington Bldg Cleveland OH 44115

CALKINS, GARY NATHAN, lawyer; b. N.Y.C., Mar. 1, 1911; s. Gary Nathan and Helen R. (Williston) C.; m. Constantia H. Hommann, June 22, 1940 (div. Dec. 1948); m. Susannah Eby, Nov. 19, 1949; children: Helen (dec.), Margaret Calkins Van Auken, Sarah, Abigail. Student, Ecole Internationale, Geneva, Switzerland, 1926-27, Storm King Sch., 1927-29; A.B., Columbia U., 1933; LL.B., Harvard U., 1936. Bar: N.Y. 1936, D.C. 1955, U.S. Supreme Ct. 1965, Va. 1982. Assoc. Beekman & Bogue, N.Y.C., 1936-41; staff CAB, 1941-56, chief internat. and rules div., 1947-56; mem. Galland, Kharasch, Calkins & Morse, P.C. (and predecessor firms), Washington, 1956-81, N.Y.C., 1966-77; mng. partner Galland, Kharasch, Calkins & Morse, P.C. (and predecessor firms), 1969-80, pres., 1980-81, of counsel, 1981-85; sole practice Washington, 1981-86; of counsel to county atty. Fairfax County (Va.), 1982-87; mem. U.S. sect. Comité Internat. Tecnique d' Experts Juridiques Aériens, 1946-47; Mem. U.S. dels. legal com. Internat. Civil Aviation Orgn., 1947-55; delegation chmn. 1st, 3d, 5th, 9th and 10th meetings; chief U.S. negotiator and draftsman Mortgage Conv., Geneva, Switzerland, 1948, mem. drafting com. Rome Conv. on Surface Damage, 1952; chmn. U.S. delegation internat. Diplomatic Conf. for Revision of Warsaw Conv., The Hague, 1955; chmn. legal div. U.S. Air Coordinating Com., 1955-56; industry observer U.S.-U.K. bilateral air transport talks, London, 1956; asst. sec. Philippine Airlines, 1974-86. Asso. editor: United States and Canadian Aviation Reports, 1956-61; asso. editor: Jour. Air Law and Commerce, 1956-58; editor-in-chief, 1958-63; Contbr. articles to profl. jours. Served as lt. USNR, 1943-45. Mem. ABA, D.C., Va., Fairfax County Bar Assns., Am. Judicature Soc., Internat. Platform Assn., Soc. Quiet Birdmen, Psi Upsilon. Clubs: Cosmos, Georgetown (Washington), Nacoms (Columbia U.). Administrative and regulatory, Private international, Air. Home: 6504 Dearborn Dr Falls Church VA 22044 also: Canal Sq 1054 31st St NW Washington DC 20007 Office: County Atty's Office 4100 Chain Bridge Rd. Fairfax VA 20007

CALKINS, HUGH, lawyer; b. Newton, Mass., Feb. 20, 1924; s. Grosvenor and Patty (Phillips) C.; m. Ann Clark, June 14, 1955; children: Peter, Andrew, Margaret, Elizabeth. AB, LLB, Harvard U., 1949. Bar: D.C. 1949, Ohio 1950. Law clk. to presiding justice U.S. Ct. Appeals (2d cir.), N.Y.C., 1949-50; law clk. to justice Felix Frankfurter U.S. Supreme Ct., Washington, 1950-51; from assoc. to ptnr. Jones, Day, Reavis & Pogue, Cleve., 1951—; bd. dirs. Premier Indsl. Corp., Cleve., Brown & Sharpe Mfg. Co., Providence, Am. Greetings Corp., Cleve., Jeffrey Co., Columbus, Ohio. Contbr. articles on fed. income tax to profl. jours. Mem. Bd. Edn., Cleve., 1965-69; assoc. dir. Pres.'s Commn. on Nat. Goals, Washington, 1960, chmn., 1985-86. Served with USAF. Mem. ABA (tax sect.), Am. Law Inst. (council), Phi Beta Kappa. Democrat. Unitarian. Clubs: Union, Cleve. Skating (Cleve.); Metropolitan (Washington); Harvard (N.Y.). Office: Jones Day Reavis & Pogue 901 North Point Bldg Cleveland OH 44114 Home: 2477 Guilford Rd Cleveland Heights OH 44118

CALKINS, STEPHEN, law educator; b. Balt., Mar. 20, 1950; s. Evan and Virginia (Brady) C.; m. Joan Wadsworth, Oct. 18, 1981; children: Timothy and Geoffrey. BA, Yale U., 1972; JD, Harvard U., 1975. Bar: N.Y. 1976, D.C. 1977, U.S. Dist. Ct. D.C. 1979. Law clk. to FTC commr. S. Nye, Washington, 1975-76; assoc. Covington & Burling, Washington, 1976-83; assoc. law prof. Wayne State U., Detroit, 1983—; vis. assoc. prof. law U. Mich., Ann Arbor, 1985, U. Pa., Phila., 1987. Editor: Antitrust Law Developments, 1984; editor legal book revs. The Antitrust Bulletin, 1986. Counsel Ind. Commn. on Admissions Practices in Cranbrook Sch., Detroit, 1984-85. Research fellow Wayne State U., 1984. Mem. ABA, Am. Assn. Law Schs. (sec. antitrust sect.). Presbyterian. Clubs: Harvard, Yale (Detroit); Northville Swim. Avocations: reading, skiing, tennis. Antitrust, General corporate, Legal education. Home: 317 W Dunlap Northville MI 48167 Office: Wayne State U Law Sch Detroit MI 48202

CALKINS, STEVEN POTTER, lawyer; b. Cortland, N.Y., Apr. 5, 1948; s. Robert Neal and Eugenia (Potter) C.; m. Rhea Bel-Jon, Nov. 8, 1980. BA, Boston U., 1971; JD, Hofstra U., 1976. Bar: N.Y. 1977, U.S. Dist. Ct. (so. and ea. dists.) N.Y. 1977, U.S. Ct. Appeals (2d cir.) 1982. Assoc. Cichanowicz & Callan, N.Y.C., 1976-78, Walker & Corsa, N.Y.C., 1979-85; ptnr. Wilson & Calkins, N.Y.C., 1985-86, Halley, Calkins & Avallone, N.Y.C., 1986—. Mem. ABA, Maritime Law Assn., N.Y. County Lawyers Assn., Maritime Assn. of Port of N.Y./N.J. Republican. Presbyterian. Admiralty, Insurance. Office: Halley Calkins & Avallone 300 E 42d St New York NY 10017

CALLAHAN, CARROLL BERNARD, lawyer; b. Montello, Wis., June 14, 1908; s. John and Rose (Reardon) C.; m. Phyllis Luchsinger, Sept. 27, 1939; 1 child, Timothy Sean. LLB, U. Wis., 1931. Bar: Wis. 1931. Sole practice Columbus, Wis., 1931—; pres. First Nat. Bank of Columbus, 1960—; bd. dirs. Rio-Fall River Union Bank. Served to 1st lt. AUS, 1943-46. Fellow

Am. Coll. Trial Lawyers; mem. ABA, State Bar Wis. (pres. 1960-61), Am. Legion, Phi Alpha Delta. Lodge: KC (4th deg.). State civil litigation, Condemnation, Personal injury. Home: 856 S Charles St Columbus WI 53925 Office: Law Bldg 159 S Ludington St PO Box 152 Columbus WI 53925

CALLAHAN, DENNIS JOHN, lawyer; b. Chgo., Oct. 3, 1953; s. John Blyer and Kathleen Agnes (Hudson) C.; m. Mari Carol Barth, July 17, 1976; 1 child Amanda Barth. BS, Ill. Benedictine Coll., 1975; JD, DePaul U., 1978. Bar: Ill. U.S. Dist. Ct. (no. dist.) Ill. Assoc. Shaheen, Lundberg & Callahan, Chgo., 1979-81, Erde & Chaconas, Chgo., 1982—. State civil litigation, Personal injury, Workers' compensation. Office: Erde & Chaconas 4801 W Peterson Chicago IL 60646

CALLAHAN, GARY BRENT, lawyer; b. Ashland, Oreg., Apr. 24, 1942; s. Donald Burr and Joyce Valeri (Powers) C.; m. Nancy Kay King, Feb. 1967 (div. 1978); children: Shawn, Christopher; m. Sally Kornblight, Jan. 18, 1983; 1 child, Zachary. Student, Sacramento State U.; JD, U. of Pacific, 1970. Bar: Calif. 1971, U.S. Dist. Ct. (ea. dist.) Calif. 1971. Assoc. Rust & Mills, Sacramento, Calif., 1971-73, Barrett, Matheny & Newlon, Sacramento, 1973-77; ptnr. Westley & Callahan, Sacramento, 1977-80, Wilcoxen & Callahan, Sacramento, 1980—; instr., lectr. Continuing Edn. Bar, Berkeley, Calif., 1978—; faculty Hastings COll. Trial Advocacy U. Calif., San Francisco, 1983—. Served with USN, 1960-63. Mem. Calif. Bar Assn., Assn. Trial Lawyers Am. (sustaining), Calif. Trial Lawyers Assn., Capitol City Trial Lawyers Assn. (pres. 1984-85), Nat. Bd. Trial Advs. Democrat. Avocations: lecturing, instructing on trial advocacy. State civil litigation, Insurance, Personal injury. Office: Wilcoxen & Callahan 2114 K St Sacramento CA 95816

CALLAHAN, JAMES CARROLL, lawyer, bus. exec.; b. Longview, Tex., June 7, 1923; s. Lehren Dewey and Frances Gladys (Gibson) C.; m. Melba Elaine Shaw, May 14, 1949; children—James Kim, Jan Elaine Callahan Anderson. LL.B., LaSalle U., Chgo., 1963; J.D., Blackstone Coll. Law, 1964. Bar: Mont. 1963, Tex. 1975, U.S. Dist. Ct. Mont. 1963, U.S. Dist. Ct. (ea. dist.) Tex. 1965, U.S. Ct. Appeals (8th cir.) 1964, U.S. Ct. Appeals (5th cir.) 1981, U.S. Ct. Appeals (11th cir.) 1981, U.S. Supreme Ct. 1969. Bus. exec., Longview, 1940—; sole practice, Helena, Mont., 1963—; ptnr. Nichols, Bailey & Watson, Longview, 1975—; pres., owner Carolane Co., Jewelers, Longview, 1953—; pres., owner, gen. counsel Carolane Investment Co., Longview, 1963—; mgr. stocks, bonds investments, 1953—. Precinct del. Gregg County Democratic Conv., 1980; vice chmn. ofcl. bd. Founders Christian Ch., Longview, 1975-76. Served with AUS, 1943-46; PTO. Cert. master watchmaker Am. Watchmakers Assn. 1969. Mem. ABA, Mont. Bar Assn., Tex. Bar Assn., Gregg County Bar Assn., 1st Dist. Mont. Bar Assn., Am. Judicature Soc. Clubs: Rotary (Paul Harris fellow 1975), Masons (32 deg.), Shriners. General practice, Probate, Contracts commercial. Home and Office: Callahan Rd PO Box 1428 Longview TX 75606

CALLAHAN, JAMES CHRISTOPHER, lawyer; b. Rutherfordton, N.C., Dec. 17, 1951; s. James Arthur and Janie Evelyn (Gray) C.; m. Donna Hines, June 6, 1985; 1 child, Tristan Elliott. B.A., U. N.C., 1974; J.D., Wake Forest U., 1977. Bar: N.C. 1977, U.S. Dist. Ct. N.C. 1978, U.S. Ct. Appeals (4th cir.) 1979. Ptnr. Arledge-Callahan, Rutherfordton, N.C., 1977—. Mem. N.C. Bar Assn., Rutherford County Bar Assn., 29th Jud. Dist. Bar Assn. Republican. Methodist. Home: 102 Cedar Ln Rutherfordton NC 28139 Office: Arledge-Callahan 200 E Court St Rutherfordton NC 28139

CALLAHAN, JOHN JOSEPH, lawyer; b. Toledo, Feb. 5, 1922; s. Hugh and Anna (Mackin) C.; m. Joyce Teague, Apr. 18, 1953. BA, John Carroll U., 1949; LLB, U. Mich., 1952. Bar: Ohio 1952, U.S. Supreme Ct. 1966, U.S. Mil. Ct. Appeals 1966, U.S. Ct. Appeals (6th cir.) 1973. Assoc. Burgess & Callahan, Toledo, 1952-72, Openlander, Callahan & Connelly, Toledo, 1972-77; ptnr. Secor, Ide & Callahan, Toledo, 1977—. Served to maj. USAF, 1942-46. Fellow Am. Coll. Trial Lawyers, Ohio State Bar Assn., Toledo Bar Assn. (pres. 1969-70). Democrat. Roman Catholic. Club: Toledo (Ohio). Criminal. Home: 4203 Eaglehurst Dr Sylvania OH 43560 Office: Secor Ide & Callahan 1400 Nat Bank Bldg Toledo OH 43604

CALLAHAN, JOHN WILLIAM, lawyer; b. Rockville Centre, N.Y., Feb. 8, 1947; s. Peter Felix and Catherine Lucille (Walbroehle) C.; m. Janet Gay Pascoe, Aug. 7, 1971. BA, Mich. State U., 1971; JD cum laude, Detroit Coll. Law, 1974. Bar: Mich. 1974, U.S. Dist. Ct. (ea. dist.) Mich. 1974, U.S. Tax Ct. 1976, U.S. Ct. Appeals (6th cir.) 1977. Atty. Bank of Commonwealth, Detroit, 1974-76; assoc. Hoops & Hudson, P.C., Detroit, 1976-79, Tyler & Canham, P.C., Detroit, 1979-80, Stark & Reagan, P.C., Troy, Mich., 1980-81; sole practice Farmington Hills, Mich., 1981-86; ptnr. Plunkett, Cooney, Rutt, Waters, Stancyck & Pedersen P.C., Detroit, 1986—. Bd. dirs. Vietnam Vets. Am. Chpt. 9, Detroit, 1981-85. Served with USMC, 1967-69, Vietnam. Mem. ABA, Oakland County Bar Assn. Avocations: tennis, golf. Bankruptcy, Federal civil litigation, Banking. Office: Plunkett Cooney Rutt et al 900 Marquette Bldg Detroit MI 48226-3260

CALLAHAN, JOSEPH PATRICK, lawyer; b. N.Y.C., Mar. 19, 1945; s. Parnell J.T. and Jane M. (Tubridy) C. B.A., Columbia, 1966; J.D., Albany Law Sch., Union U., Albany, N.Y., 1969. Bar: N.Y. 1969. Ptnr. law firm Callahan & Wolkoff, N.Y.C., 1972—; Chmn., pres. Mackran Assocs., Inc., mortgage brokers, N.Y.C., 1973—; Arbitrator compulsory arbitration program N.Y.C. Civil Ct., 1972—. Mem. Bronx County Bar Assn. Roman Catholic. Club: N.Y. Athletic. State civil litigation, Federal civil litigation, Probate. Office: Callahan & Wolkoff PC 90 Broad St New York NY 10004

CALLAHAN, MICHAEL SEAN, lawyer; b. Hammond, Ind., Nov. 26, 1956; s. Henry Gilpen and Mary Maureen (Shaw) C. BS, Ind. U., 1979, JD, 1982. Bar: Mich. 1982, U.S. Dist. Ct. (we. dist.) Mich. 1982, U.S. Ct. Appeals (6th cir.) 1984. Assoc. Miller, Johnson, Snell and Cummiskey, Grand Rapids, Mich., 1982-86; in-house counsel Amway Corp., Ada, Mich., 1986—. Recipient Am. Jurisprudence award Ind. U., 1981. Mem. ABA, Mich. Bar Assn., Grand Rapids Bar Assn. (treas. Young Lawyers Sect. 1983—). Republican. Roman Catholic. General corporate, Computer, Real property. Home: 2780-6 Woodlake Rd Wyoming MI 49509 Office: Amway Corp Legal Div 7575 E Fulton Ada MI 49355

CALLAHAN, MICHAEL THOMAS, construction consultant, lawyer; b. Kansas City, Mo., Oct. 7, 1948; s. Harry Leslie and Venita June (Yohn) C.; B.A., U. Kans., 1970; J.D., U. Mo., 1973, LL.M., 1979; postgrad. Temple U., 1976-77; m. Stella Sue Paffenbach, Mar. 21, 1970; children—Molly Leigh, Michael Kroh. Admitted to Kans. bar, 1973, N.J. bar, 1975, Mo. bar, 1977; v.p. T.J. Constrn., Inc., Lenexa, Kans., 1973-74; sr. cons. Wagner-Hohns-Inglis, Inc., Mt. Holly, N.J., 1974-77, v.p., Kansas City, Mo., 1977-86; exec. v.p. CCL Constrn. Cons., Overland Park, Kans., 1986—; adj. prof. U. Kans.; arbitrator, lectr. in field; mem. Bldg. Industry Adv. Bd. Mem. Am. Bar Assn., N.J. Bar Assn., Mo. Bar Assn., Am. Arbitration Assn., Internat. Wine and Food Soc. Congregationalist. Clubs: Saddle & Sirloin , Indian Hills Country. Lodge: Rotary Internat. Author: Desk Book of Construction Law, 1981; Discovery in Construction Litigation, 1983; Construction Schedules, 1983, Construction Law, 1986, Delay Claims, 1987; contbr. articles to profl. jours. Government contracts and claims, Construction. Home: 9011 Delmar St Prairie Village KS 66207 Office: CCL Constrn Cons 4400 College Blvd Suite 150 Overland Park KS 66211

CALLAHAN, NANCY KAY, lawyer; b. Sioux Falls, S.D., Sept. 17, 1950; d. Gardiner Bouton and Kathleen (Orr) Jones; m. Joseph Patrick Callahan, June 14, 1980; children: Jane Kathleen, Clare Eileen, Timothy Parnell. BA, U. Hawaii, 1973, JD, 1976. Bar: N.Y. 1977, U.S. Dist. Ct. (so. dist.) N.Y. 1978. Assoc. Haight, Gardner, Poor and Havens, N.Y.C., 1976-84; v.p., sr. assoc. counsel The Chase Manhattan Bank, N.Y.C., 1984—. Roman Catholic. Avocations: pvt. piloting, scuba diving. Admiralty, Banking, Contracts commercial. Home: 593 7th St Brooklyn NY 11215 Office: The Chase Manhattan Bank 140 Broadway New York NY 10005

CALLAHAN, ROBERT JOHN, JR., lawyer, arbitrator; b. St. Louis, July 3, 1923; s. Robert John and Elizabeth Mae Deck (Gentner) C.; m. Dorothy Foley, Apr. 18, 1958 (dec. Nov. 1980); m. Barbara Kelsall Couture, May 22, 1982. Grad. Chaminade Coll., 1941; B.S. in Bus. Adminstrn., Washington U., 1944; J.D. cum laude, Notre Dame U., 1948. Bar: Mo. 1948, U.S. Ct. Appeals (fed. cir.) 1951, U.S. Supreme Ct. 1955, U.S. Ct. Mil. Appeals. Ptnr. Callahan and Callahan, St. Louis, 1948-56; sole practice, St. Louis, 1956—. Contbr. articles to legal jours. Candidate for judge St. Louis County Cir. Ct., 1960. Coro fellow. Served with FBI and USCGR, 1944-45; served to capt. JAGC, USAFR. Mem. ABA, Lawyers Assn. of St. Louis, St. Louis Bar Assn., Am. Assn. Trial Lawyers Notre Dame U. Law Assn., U. Notre Dame Alumni Assn., Nat. Panel Consumer Arbitrators, Ret. Air Force Officers Assn. Phi Delta Theta. Republican. Roman Catholic. Personal injury, Civil rights, Probate. Office: 161 W Jefferson Saint Louis MO 63122

CALLAHAN, ROGER J., state judge. Judge Conn. Supreme Ct., Hartford, 1985—. Office: Conn Supreme Ct Drawer N Station A Hartford CT 06106 *

CALLAN, TERRENCE A., lawyer; b. San Francisco, Sept. 20, 1939; s. Harold A. and Viola A. (Briese) C.; m. Gail R. Raine, Apr. 20, 1968; 1 son, Ryan T. A.B., U. San Francisco, 1961; J.D., U. Calif.-San Francisco, 1964. Bar: Calif. 1965, U.S. Dist. Ct. (no. dist.) Calif. 1965, U.S. Ct. Appeals (9th cir.) 1965, U.S. Dist. Ct. (cen. dist.) Calif. 1970, U.S. Supreme Ct. 1975, U.S. Dist. Ct. (so. dist.) Calif. 1981. Research asst. Pillsbury, Madison & Sutro, San Francisco, 1964-65, assoc., 1965-72, ptnr., 1973—. Sec., gen. counsel Presidio Soc., 1981—, dir., sec., legal counsel Ft. Point and Army Mus. Assn., 1984, U. San Francisco, 1957-61. Recipient various law sch. awards. Mem. ABA, Calif. State Bar Assn. (v.p. antitrust sect.), San Francisco Bar Assn. (mem. judiciary com., exec. com. mem., antitrust and trade regulation sect., mem. No. Dist. merit screening com. bankruptcy judgeships), U. Calif. Alumni Assn., U. San Francisco Alumni Assn., Order of Coif, Phi Alpha Delta. Roman Catholic. Clubs: Green and Gold, 1066, Univ. of Calif. (Hastings). Antitrust, Federal civil litigation, State civil litigation. Office: Pillsbury Madison & Sutro Standard Oil Bldg 225 Bush St San Francisco CA 94104

CALLENDER, JOHN FRANCIS, lawyer; b. Jacksonville, Fla., May 3, 1944; s. Francis Louis and Ethel (McLean) C.; m. Susan Carithers, June 13, 1969; children: John Francis Jr., Susanna McLean. AB cum laude, Davidson Coll., 1966; MA, U. N.C., 1969; JD with distinction, Duke U., 1976. Bar: Fla. 1976, U.S. Supreme Ct. 1982. Asst. states atty. State of Fla., Jacksonville, 1980-81; ptnr. Turner, Ford & Callender, P.A., Jacksonville, 1981-83; sole practice Jacksonville, 1983—. Pres. Mental Health Clinic Jacksonville, Inc., 1985; bd. dirs. Vol. Jacksonville, Inc., 1981-84. Served with U.S. Army, 1970-73. Fellow Am. Soc. Papyrologists, 1969. Fellow Acad. Fla. Trial Lawyers (civil rules com. 1985—); mem. ABA, Fla. Bar Assn., Fed. Bar Assn., Jacksonville Bar Assn. (ethics com. 1981-83, media com. 1983-85), Assn. Trial Lawyers Am. Democrat. Episcopalian. Clubs: Fla. Yacht (Jacksonville), Ye Mystic Revellers (Jacksonville). Avocations: sailing, windsurfing, fishing, golf, squash. State civil litigation, Federal civil litigation, Personal injury. Home: 1745 Woodmere Dr Jacksonville FL 32205 Office: 2105 Gulf Life Tower Jacksonville FL 32207

CALLENDER, WILLIAM LACEY, savings and loan executive, lawyer; b. Oakland, Calif., Feb. 1, 1933; s. William Clarence and Doris (Lacey) C.; m. Joan Ingram, Dec. 14, 1968; 1 child, William Ingram; 1 child from previous marriage, Suzanne. AA, Hartnell Jr. Coll., Salinas, Calif., 1952-53; student, U. Calif., Berkeley, 1953-54; BA in Econs., Fresno State Coll., 1955; JD, U. So. Calif., 1960. Bar: Calif. 1960, U.S. Dist. Ct. (so. dist.) Calif. 1960. V.p., sr. atty. Calif. Fed. Savs. & Loan Co., Los Angeles, 1975-81, v.p., asst. gen. counsel, 1981-82, sr. v.p., gen. counsel, sec., 1982-83, exec. v.p. adminstrn., sec., 1985—; exec. v.p. , gen. counsel, sec. CalFed Inc., Los Angeles, 1983-87; pres. and chief exec. officer Calif. Fed. Savs. and Loan Assn., Los Angeles, 1987—. Served as spl. agt. CIC, U.S. Army, 1955-57. Mem. Order of the Coif. Republican. Episcopalian. Avocations: boating, gardening, reading, spectator sports. General corporate, Banking, Real property. Office: Calif Fed Savs & Loan Assn 5670 Wilshire Blvd Los Angeles CA 90036

CALLETON, THEODORE EDWARD, lawyer; b. Newark, Dec. 13, 1934; s. Edward James and Dorothy (Dewey) C.; m. Elizabeth Bennett Brown, Feb. 4, 1961; children: Susan Bennett, Pamela Barritt, Christopher Dewey.; m. Kathy E'Beth Conkle, Feb. 22, 1983; 1 child, James Frederick. B.A., Yale U., 1956; LL.B., Columbia U., 1962. Bar: Calif. 1963, U.S. Dist. Ct. (so. dist.) Calif. 1963, U.S. Tax Ct. 1977. Asso. firm O'Melveny & Myers, Los Angeles, 1962-69, Agnew, Miller & Carlson, Los Angeles, 1969; ptnr. Agnew, Miller & Carlson, 1970-79; individual practice law Los Angeles, 1979-83; ptnr. Kindel & Anderson, 1983—; academician Internat. Acad. Estate and Trust Law, 1974—; lectr. Calif. Continuing Edn. bar, 1970—, U. So. Calif. Tax Inst., 1972—, Calif. State U., Los Angeles, 1975—, Practising Law Inst., 1976—, Am. Law Inst., 1985—; bd. dirs. UCLA/CEB Continuing Edn. of Bar Estate Planning Inst. Author: A Life Insurance Primer, 1978; co-author: The Short Term Trust, 1977, California Will Drafting Practice, 1982, Tax Planning for Professionals, 1985; contbr. articles to legal jours. Chmn. Arroyo Seco Master Planning Commn., Pasadena, Calif., 1970-71; bd. dirs. Montessori Sch., Inc., 1964-68, chmn., 1966-68; bd. dirs. Am. Montessori Soc., N.Y.C., 1967-72, chmn., 1969-72; trustee Walden Sch. of Calif., 1970-86, chmn., 1980-86; trustee Episcopal Children's Home of Los Angeles, 1971-75. Served as lt. USMC, 1956-59. Fellow Am. Coll. Probate Counsel; mem. ABA, Los Angeles County Bar Assn. (chmn. taxation sect. 1980-81, chmn. probate and trust law sect. 1981-82), Aurelian Honor Soc., Beta Theta Pi, Phi Delta Phi. Unitarian. Clubs: Elihu, University. Estate planning, Probate, Estate taxation. Home: 301 Churchill Rd Sierra Madre CA 91024 Office: 555 S Flower St Suite 2600 Los Angeles CA 90071 also: 1301 Dove St Suite 1050 Newport Beach CA 92660

CALLIES, DAVID LEE, lawyer, educator; b. Chgo., Apr. 21, 1943; s. Gustav E. and Ann D. C.; divorced; 1 child, Sarah Anne; m. Jane Ryburn Starn, June 7, 1987. A.B., DePauw U., 1965; J.D., U. Mich., 1968; LL.M.; Mich.-Ford Found. fellow, Nottingham U., 1969. Bar: Ill. 1969, Hawaii 1978. Spl. asst. states atty. McHenry County, Ill., 1969; assoc. firm Ross, Hardies, O'Keefe, Babcock & Parsons, Chgo., 1969-75; partner Ross, Hardies, O'Keefe, Babcock & Parsons, 1975-78; prof. law Sch. Law, U. Hawaii, Honolulu, 1978—; mem., transp. adv. com. Oahu Devel. Conf., 1978-84, vice chmn., 1985-86; mem. adv. com. on planning and growth mgmt. City and County of Honolulu Council, 1978—, citiens adv. com. on State Functional Plan for Conservation Lands, 1979-84. Author: (with Fred P. Bosselman) The Quiet Revolution in Land Use Control, 1971, (with Fred P. Bosselman and John S. Banta) The Taking Issue, 1973, Regulating Paradise: Land Use Controls in Hawaii, 1984; (with Robert Freilich) Cases and Materials on Land Use, 1986. Mem. Am. Bar Assn. (chmn. com. on land use, planning and zoning 1980-82, council, sect. on urban, state and local govt. 1981-85, exec. com. 1986—, sec. 1986-87, vice chmn., 1987-88), Am. Inst. Cert. Planners, Am. Planning Assn. (exec. com. Hawaii chpt.), Hawaii Bar Assn., Ill. Bar Assn., Internat. Bar Assn., Nat. Trust Hist. Preservation, Royal Oak Soc., Sierra Club. Land use and planning, Local government, Real property. Home: 4621 Aukai Ave Honolulu HI 96816 Office: Richardson Sch Law 2515 Dole St Honolulu HI 96822

CALLIS, FELIX L., lawyer; b. Norfolk, Va., Aug. 12, 1935; s. Felix L. and Nora T. (O'Halleran) C.; m. Joan M. Wegrzyn, Nov. 29, 1963; children—Mona, Elizabeth, Melissa, Philip. B.S., St. Louis U., 1956, J. D., 1959. Bar: Mo. 1959, Ill. 1959, U.S. Supreme Ct. 1968. Assoc. Haley and Frederickson, St. Louis, 1959-63; sole practice, Granite City, Ill., 1963-78; ptnr. Callis & Hartman, Granite City, 1978-86, Pratt & Callis P.C., 1986—; Fellow Ill. Bar Found.; mem. Tri-City Bar Assn. (pres. 1964-65), Madison County Bar Assn. (pres. 1976-77), Ill. State Bar Assn., ABA, Mo. Bar Assn., Ill. Trial Lawyers Assn. (bd. mgrs. 1982—), Assn. Trial Lawyers Am. Labor, Local government, Personal injury. Home: 3136 Harvard Pl Granite City IL 62040 Office: Pratt & Callis PC 1326 Niedringhaus Ave Granite City IL 62040 also: Rt 111 at Airline Dr PO Box 179 East Alton IL 62024

CALLISON, JAMES W., airline executive, lawyer; b. Jamestown, N.Y., Sept. 8, 1928; s. J. Waldo and Gladys A. C.; m. Gladys I. Robinson, Oct. 3, 1959; children: Sharon Elizabeth, Maria Judith, Christopher James. A.B. with honors, U. Mich., 1950, J.D. with honors (Overbeck award 1952, Jerome S. Freud Meml. award 1953), 1953. Bar: D.C. 1954, Ga. 1960. Atty. firm Pogue & Neal, Washington, 1953-57; with Delta Air Lines, Inc., Atlanta, 1957—, v.p. law and regulatory affairs, 1974-78, sr. v.p., gen. counsel, 1978-81, sr. v.p., gen. counsel, corp. sec., 1981—. Contbr. articles to legal jours.; asst. editor: Mich. Law Rev, 1952-53. Bd. dirs. Southeast Region NCCJ, Georgians for Better Transp. Recipient Papal Pro Ecclesia Et Pontifice award, 1966. Mem. ABA (vice chmn. internat. law sect. 1980-81m corp. law depts. com.), State Bar Ga. (sec.-treas. corp. counsel sect. 1987—), Atlanta Bar Assn., Am. Corp. Counsel Assn., Corp. Counsel Assn. Greater Atlanta, Am. Soc. Corp. Secs. (v.p. southeast region 1986—), Order of Coif. Clubs: Atlanta Athletic, Lawyers; Nat. Aviation (Washington). General corporate. Home: 130 Blenheim Place Atlanta GA 30338 Office: Delta Air Lines Hartsfield Atlanta Internat Airport Atlanta GA 30320

CALLISON, JAMES WILLIAM, lawyer; b. Albemarle County, Va., Dec. 24, 1955; s. James Crofts and Jan (Richelsen) C. AB, Oberlin Coll., 1977; JD, U. Colo., 1982. Law clk. to judge Dist. Ct. Colo., Boulder, 1982; assoc. Moye, Giles, O'Keefe, Vermeire & Gorrell, Denver, 1982—. Contbr. articles to profl. jours. Mem. ABA (tax sect.), Colo. Bar Assn. (tax and internat. law sects.), Denver Bar Assn. Democrat. Corporate taxation, General corporate, General practice. Home: 2067 Ogden St Denver CO 80205 Office: Moye Giles O'Keefe et al 730 17th St #600 Denver CO 80202

CALLISON, RUSSELL JAMES, lawyer, small business owner; b. Redding, Calif., Sept. 4, 1954; s. Walter M. and Norma A. (Bruce) C. BA in Polit. Sci., U. of Pacific, 1977, JD with distinction, 1980. Bar: Calif. 1980, U.S. Dist. Ct. (ea. dist.) Calif. 1981, U.S. Dist. Ct. Nev. 1984, U.S. Dist. Ct. (no. dist.) Calif. 1986. Assoc. Memering & DeMers, Sacramento, Calif., 1980-85; ptnr. DeMers, Ferris & Callison, Sacramento, 1985—; judge moot ct. McGeorge Sch. Law, Sacramento, 1982, Lincoln Sch. Law, Sacramento, 1983—; arbitrator Sacramento County Superior Ct., 1986—; co-owner The Merchant of Venice Co. Capt. fund raising Met. YMCA, Sacramento, 1986—. Mem. ABA (litigation sect.), Sacramento County Bar Assn., Assn. Def. Counsel Northern Calif., Calif. Trial Lawyers Assn., SAR, Phi Alpha Delta. Republican. Episcopalian. Clubs: Commonwealth (San Francisco); 20/30 (Sacramento). Avocations: golf, hunting, fishing, antique restoration. State civil litigation, Personal injury, Insurance. Home: 1301 41st St Sacramento CA 95819 Office: DeMers Ferris & Callison 7919 Folsom Blvd Suite 250 Sacramento CA 95826

CALLISTER, MARION JONES, federal judge; b. Moreland, Idaho, June 6, 1921; m. Nina Lynn Hayes, June 7, 1946; children—Nona Lynn Callister Haddock, Lana Sue Callister Meredith, Jenny Ann Callister Thomas, Tamara Callister Banks, Idonna Ruth Callister Andersen, Betty Patricia Callister Jacobs, Deborah Jean Hansen, Mary Clarice Fowler, David Marion, Nancy Irene, Michelle, Kimberly Jane. Student, Utah State U., 1940-41; B.S.L., U. Utah, 1950, J.D., 1951. Bar: Idaho 1951. Dep. pros. atty. Bingham County, Utah, 1951-52; asst. U.S. atty. Dist. of Idaho, 1953-57, U.S. atty., 1975-76; sole practice 1958-69; judge Idaho Dist. Ct. 4th Jud. Dist., 1970-75, U.S. Dist. Ct. Idaho, Boise, 1976—; now chief judge U.S. Dist. Ct. Idaho. Served with U.S. Army, 1944-46. Decorated Purple Heart. Republican. Mormon. Office: US Courthouse PO Box 040 550 W Fort St Boise ID 83724

CALLNER, BRUCE WARREN, lawyer; b. Camden, N.J., Sept. 20, 1948; s. Phillip David and Miriam June (Caplan) C.; m. Janet Adams, Apr. 25, 1970 (div. Dec. 1982); children: David, Michelle; m. Kathy Lyne Portnoy, Mar. 9, 1983; 1 child, Samantha. BS in Psychology, Western Mich. U., 1970; JD, U. Notre Dame, 1974. Bar: Ga. 1974, U.S. Dist. Ct. (no. dist.) Ga. 1975, U.S. Ct. Appeals (5th cir.) 1975, U.S. Ct. Appeals (11th cir.) 1981. Ptnr. Nall & Miller, Atlanta, 1974-81, Alembik, Fine & Callner, P.A., Atlanta, 1981—; lectr. law Emory U., Atlanta. Vol. numerous legal orgns. Mem. ABA (family law and litigation sects.). Ga. Bar Assn. (family law and litigation sects.), Atlanta Bar Assn. (family law, litigation and sects., speaker's bur.); fellow Am. Acad. Matrimonial Lawyers, Nat. Council Family Relations, Southeastern Council Family Relations, NOW, Assn. Family Conciliation Cts. Democrat. Jewish. Family and matrimonial. Home: 956 Heritage Hills Decatur GA 30033 Office: Alembik Fine & Callner PA Fourth Floor Marquis One Tower 245 Peachtree Center Ave Atlanta GA 30303

CALLOW, KEITH MCLEAN, judge; b. Seattle, Jan. 11, 1925; s. Russell Stanley and Dollie (McLean) C.; m. Evelyn Case, July 9, 1949; children: Andrea, Douglas, Kerry. Student, Alfred U., 1943, CCNY, 1944, Biarritz Am. U., 1945; B.A., U. Wash., 1949, J.D., 1952. Bar: Wash. 1952. Asst. atty. gen. Wash., 1952; law clk. Wash. Supreme Ct., 1953; dep. pros. atty. King County, 1954-56; partner firm Little, LeSourd, Palmer, Scott & Slemmons, Seattle, 1957-62, Barker, Day, Callow & Taylor, 1964-68; judge King County Superior Ct., 1969-71, Wash. State Ct. of Appeals, Seattle, 1972-84; presiding chief judge Wash. State Ct. of Appeals, 1980; justice Wash. State Supreme Ct., Olympia, 1985—; lectr. bus. law U. Wash., 1956-62; faculty Nat. Jud. Coll., 1980; co-organizer, sec. Council of Chief Judges, 1980. Editor works in field. Bd. dirs. Evergreen Safety Council; pres. Young Men's Republican Club, 1957, chief Seattle Council Boy Scouts Am. Served with AUS, 1943-46. Decorated Purple Heart.; recipient Brandeis award Wash. State Trial Lawyers Assn., 1981. Mem. ABA (chmn. com. on judiciary 1984—), Wash. State Bar Assn., D.C. Bar Assn., Seattle-King County Bar Assn., Estate Planning Council, Navy League , Psi Upsilon, Phi Delta Phi. Clubs: Rainier (sec. 1978), Harbor, Forty Nine (pres. 1972); Harbor. Lodges: Masons, Rotary. Jurisprudence. Office: Temple of Justice Olympia WA 98504

CALLOW, WILLIAM GRANT, state supreme court justice; b. Waukesha, Wis., Apr. 9, 1921; s. Curtis Grant and Mildred G. C.; m. Jean A. Zilavy, Apr. 15, 1950; children: William G., Christine S., Katherine H. Ph.B. in Econs, U. Wis., 1943, J.D., 1948. Bar: Wis. Asst. city atty. Waukesha, 1948-52; city atty. 1952-60; county judge Waukesha, 1961-77; justice Supreme Ct. Wis., Madison, 1978—; mem. faculty Wis. Jud. Coll., 1968-75; asst. prof. U. Minn., 1951-52; Wis. commr. Nat. Conf. Commrs. on Uniform State Laws, 1967—. Served with USMC, 1943-45; Served with USAF, 1948-52. Recipient Outstanding Alumnus award U. Wis., 1973. Fellow Am. Bar Found.; mem. Am. Bar Assn., Dane County Bar Assn. Episcopalian. Judicial administration. Office: PO Box 1688 State Capitol Madison WI 53701

CALVARUSO, JOSEPH A., lawyer; b. N.Y.C., Oct. 9, 1949. BEE, Manhattan Coll.; JD, Fordham U. Bar: N.Y. 1975, U.S. Dist. Ct. (so. and ea. dists.) N.Y. 1975, U.S. Ct. Appeals (3d cir.) 1982, U.S. Ct. Appeals (Fed. cir.) 1984. Atty. N.Y. City Corp. Counsel, N.Y.C., 1974-76; assoc. Law Office of Anthony J. Casella, N.Y.C., 1976-78; ptnr. Morgan & Finnegan, N.Y.C., 1978—. Mem. ABA, Assn. of Bar of City of N.Y., N.U. Patent Trademark Corp., Am. Intellectual Property Assn., N.Y. Patent, Trademark and Copyright Assn. Federal civil litigation, Patent, Trademark and copyright. Office: Morgan & Finnegan 345 Park Ave New York NY 10154

CALVERT, NADIA RAE VENABLE, lawyer; b. Hope Hull, Ala., Aug. 7, 1930; d. Nathaniel Julian and Clara Gerald (Owen) Venable; m. Robert Wood Calvert, Dec. 15, 1956; children—Nadja Neuman, Winter Owen, Chadwell Spencer, Eric Brittain, Camille. B.A., Huntington Coll., 1953; M.A., Tulane U., 1958; J.D., S. Tex. Coll. Law, 1979. Bar: Tex. 1979, U.S. Dist. Ct. (so. dist.) Tex. 1979, U.S. Ct. Appeals (5th cir.) 1981, U.S. Supreme Ct. 1984. Instr. history Spring Hill Coll., Mobile, Ala., 1959-61, U. Ala., Huntsville, 1965-67, Coll. of the Mainland, Texas City, Tex., 1970-73; legal asst. Able & Coleman, Houston, 1973-79; assoc. Able, Barrow & Able Law Offices, Houston, 1979—. Contbr. articles in field to profl. jours. Tulane U. fellow, 1953-55; Huntington Coll. scholar, 1950; recipient Am. Jurisprudence award Bancroft-Whitney Pubs., 1977. Mem. ABA, Am. Trial Lawyers Assn., Tex. Trial Lawyers Assn., State Bar Tex. (mem. dist. com. on admissions 1983—), Houston Bar Assn., Houston Trial Lawyers Assn. Democrat. Family and matrimonial, Probate. Home: PO Box 52681 Houston TX 77052 Office: Able Barrow & Able 909 Fannin #3450 Houston TX 77010

CALVETTI, FREDERICK F., lawyer, chemical engineer. m. Barbara Calvetti; 1 child, Ashley Marie. BSCE, Mich. Technol. U., MSCE; JD, U. Balt.; LLM, George Washington U. Bar: N.Y., D.C., Va., Mich. Law clk. to presiding justice U.S. Ct. Appeals (D.C. cir.), Washington D.C.; chem. engr. Fisher Body Div. Gen. Motors Corp., Warren, Mich.; assoc. Pennie & Edmonds, N.Y.C.; ptnr. Craig & Burns, Washington, Stevens, Davis, Miller & Mosher, Alexandria, Va.; asst. professorial lectr. George Washington U., Washington; examiner U.S. Patent and Trademark Office, Washington; lectr. and speaker in field. Contbr. articles to profl. jours. Mem. ABA, Assn.

Trial Lawyers Am., Licensing Execs. Soc., Am. Intellectual Property Law Assn. Patent, Trademark and copyright, Antitrust. Office: Stevens Davis Miller & Mosher 515 N Washington St Alexandria VA 22313

CALVIN, EDWARD EUGENE, lawyer; b. Burlington, Colo., Jan. 13, 1931; s. Asa Everette and Helen M. (Evans) C.; m. Barbara Ellen Nichols, June 14, 1953; children: Jennifer Helen, Gregory Edward, Whitney Nichols. BSC, U. Iowa, 1953; LLB, U. Kansas City, 1956. Bar: Mo. 1956, U.S. Dist. Ct. (ea. dist.) Mo. 1961. Ptnr. Kearby & Calvin, Poplar Bluff, Mo., 1960-62; project atty. U.S. Corps of Engrs., Bay St. Louis, Miss., 1962-64; ptnr. McCalley & Calvin, Richmond, Mo., 1964-73; sole practice Cape Girardeau, Mo., 1973—; mcpl. judge Cape Girardeau, 1983—, Scott City, Mo., 1986—. Mem. Cape Girardeau Charter Com., 1981. Served to lt. USN, 1956-60. Democrat. Presbyterian. Lodge: Kiwanis (local pres. 1985, div. lt. gov. 1986). Avocations: camping, golf. Family and matrimonial, Probate, Real property. Home: 348 N Park Ave Cape Girardeau MO 63701 Office: 1707 Mt Auburn Rd Cape Girardeau MO 63701

CALZARETTA, VICTOR, lawyer, educator; b. Chgo., May 8, 1942; s. Victor Anthony Calzaretta and Lucille Alma (Moisant) Schechla. BS, City U., Seattle, 1977; MS, U. Portland, 1978, MEd, 1979; JD, Northwestern U., 1982. Bar: Oreg. 1982, U.S. Dist. Ct. Oreg. 1982, U.S. Ct. Appeals (9th cir.) 1982, U.S. Tax Ct. 1982, U.S. Claims Ct. 1983, U.S. Ct. Mil. Appeals 1983, U.S. Supreme Ct. 1986. Police officer Chgo. Police Dept., 1967-70; chief criminal dep. Clark County Sheriff's Dept., Vancouver, Wash., 1970-79; law clk. to justice Oreg. Supreme Ct., Salem, 1982-83; assoc. Pozzi, Wilson et al, Portland, Oreg., 1983-84; sole practice Portland, 1984—; instr. Am. Acad. Jud. Edn., Washington, 1983—, City U., Portland, 1978—. Pres. City Univ. Adv. Com., Portland, 1985—. Served with U.S. Army, 1961-64. Mem. ABA, Assn. Trial Lawyers Am., Oreg. State Bar Assn. (legal aid com.), Oreg. Trial Lawyers Assn., AAUP, Am. Legion, Phi Alpha Delta. Republican. Roman Catholic. Workers' compensation, Personal injury, State civil litigation. Office: 621 SW Morrison St 440 Am Bank Bldg Portland OR 97205

CAMBRICE, ROBERT LOUIS, lawyer; b. Houston, Nov. 23, 1947; s. Eugene and Edna Bertha (Jackson) C.; m. Christine Jackson, Jan. 7, 1972; children—Bryan, Graham. B.A. cum laude, Tex. So. U., 1969; J.D., U. Tex.-Austin, 1972. Bar: Tex. 1973, U.S. Dist. Ct. (so. dist.) Tex. 1975, U.S. Ct. Apls. (5th cir.) 1975, U.S. Ct. Apls. (11th cir.) 1981, U.S. Sup. Ct. 1981. Asst. atty. City of Houston, 1974-76; sole practice, Houston, 1976-86; asst. atty. Harris County, Tex., 1981-85, City of Houston, 1986—; trial atty. City of Houston Legal Dept., 1986—. Earl Warren fellow, 1969-72. Mem. Nat. Bar Assn., ABA, NAACP, Alpha Kappa Mu. Democrat. Roman Catholic. Health, Insurance, Consumer commercial. Address: 4391 Harvest Ln Houston TX 77004

CAMBRIDGE, ROBERT MATTHEW, lawyer; b. Lakewood, Ohio, July 26, 1945; s. Robert Neil and Jean Decker (Crowley) C.; m. Mary Louise Ellison, Nov. 16, 1973; children: Heather Mary, Robert Matthew Jr. BS, Am. U., 1975, MS, 1976; JD, George Washington U., 1979. Bar: Va. 1979, Calif. 1980, D.C. 1984, U.S. Supreme Ct. 1984. Assoc. Fenwick, Stone, Davis & West, Palo Alto, Calif., 1979-82; mgr. contracts CACI Inc., Arlington, Va., 1982-85; gen. counsel XMCO Inc., Reston, Va., 1985, Am. Systems Corp., Annadale, Va., 1985—. Served to capt. U.S. Army, 1968-75. Mem. ABA (sci. and tech. sect. 1976—), D.C. Computer Law Forum (sec., treas. 1985-86, pres. 1986-87), Computer Law Assn., Nat. Contract Mgmt. Assn. Lodge: Rotary. Computer, Government contracts and claims, General corporate. Home: 3806 N 23d St Arlington VA 22207 Office: Am Systems Corp 7535 Little River Turnpike Annandale VA 22003

CAMEN, TOBY PAUL, lawyer; b. Phila., Nov. 20, 1936; d. Abraham and Celia Paul; m. Richard Sol Camen, Dec. 24, 1955 (div. July 1965); 1 child, Carole Lynn; m. Clyde H. Cutner, Jan. 19, 1985. BA cum laude, Temple U., 1968, MEd, 1974, JD cum laude, 1981. Bar: Pa. 1981, D.C. 1985, U.S. Dist. Ct. (ea. dist.) Pa. 1985, U.S. Ct. Appeals (3d cir.) 1986. Reading specialist Phila. Sch. Dist., 1968-81; sr. trial atty. FAA, Washington, 1981-85; litigation atty. Schnader, Harrison, Segal, Lewis, Phila., 1985—; mem. Bd. for Correction Mil. Appeals, 1984-85. Committeeperson Montgomery County Dems., 1975-77. Mem. ABA (spl. task force on impact of airline deregulation on passenger safety), Fed. Bar Assn. (program counsel air transp. law com. 1984), Pa. Bar Assn., Lawyers Pilot's Bar Lawyers, Alpha Sigma Lamda. Federal civil litigation, State civil litigation, Aviation. Office: Schnader Harrison et al 1600 Market St Suite 3600 Philadelphia PA 19103

CAMERON, CLARENCE ARNOLD, lawyer; b. Cookeville, Tenn., Apr. 5, 1916; s. Orren Edward and Bessie Alberta (Arnold) C.; m. Billie Scott, June 26, 1938; children—William A., Anne E. B.S. in Bus. Adminstrn., Tenn. Technol. U., 1937; LL.B., Andrew Jackson U., 1940; M.A. in Econs. and Bus. Adminstrn., Vanderbilt U., 1953. Bar: Tenn. 1940; U.S. Dist. Ct. (mid. dist.) Tenn. 1946, U.S. Ct. Appeals (6th cir.) 1982. Sole practice, Cookeville, 1946-51; ptnr. Maddux & Cameron, 1951-56, Maddux, Cameron & Poteet, 1956-60, Maddux, Cameron & Jared, 1960-68, Cameron & Jared, 1969-71, 75-77, Cameron, Oakley & Jared, 1971-75, Cameron & Madewell, 1977-83, Cameron & Cameron, 1983— (all Cookeville); prof. bus. adminstrn. Tenn. Technol. U., 1940-41, part-time 1946-59; judge Cookeville City Ct., 1947-50; atty. Putnam County, 1948-49. Pres. Middle Tenn. council Boy Scouts Am., 1978, 79. Served with USN, 1943-45. Recipient Silver Beaver award Middle Tenn. council Boy Scouts Am., 1963. Mem. ABA, Putnam County Bar Assn., Tenn. Bar Assn., Am. Judicature Soc., Def. Research Inst., Assn. Ins. Attys., Tenn. Def. Lawyers Assn. (pres. 1981-82), Am. Legion, VFW. Democrat. Presbyterian. Club: Cookeville Country. General corporate, Personal injury, Workers' compensation. Office: Box 529 Cookeville TN 38501

CAMERON, DUNCAN HUME, lawyer; b. Brandon, Man., Can., May 26, 1934; s. Donald Ewen and Jean Carruthers (Rankine) C.; m. Caroline I. Gilbert, 1975; children—Sarah, Anne. B.A. cum laude, Harvard, 1956; LL.B., Columbia, 1959, Ph.D., 1965. Asso. firm Paul, Weiss, Rifkind, Wharton & Garrison, 1959-62; atty. office gen. counsel AID U.S. Dept. State, 1963-67, legal advisor mission to Dominican Republic, 1966; partner firms Appleton, Rice & Perrin, 1967-71, Cameron, Hornbostel & Butterman, Washington, 1972—; Adj. prof. law Georgetown U. Law Center, 1970-80; lectr. Sch. Fgn. Service, 1973—. Contbr. articles to profl. jours. Trustee Pan Am. Sch. Agriculture, 1986. Mem. Am., Fed., Inter-Am. bar assns. Club: Cosmos. Private international, Public international. Home: 3616 Davenport St NW Washington DC 20008 Office: 1707 H St NW Washington DC 20006

CAMERON, JAMES DUKE, state justice; b. Richmond, Calif., Mar. 25, 1925; s. Charles Lee and Ruth M. (Mabry) C.; m. Suzanne Jane Pratt, Aug. 16, 1952 (div. 1982); children: Alison Valerie, Craig Charles, Jennifer Elaine. A.B., U. Calif. at Berkeley, 1950; J.D., U. Ariz., 1954; LL.M., U. Va., 1982. Bar: Ariz. 1954. Practice in Yuma, 1954-60, 61-65; judge Superior Ct. Yuma County, 1960, Ariz. Ct. Appeals, 1965-70; justice Ariz. Supreme Ct., 1970—, vice chief justice, 1971-75, chief justice, 1975-80; mem. faculty appellate judges seminar Inst. Jud. Adminstrn., 1968-80; bd. dirs. Ariz. State Justice Inst., 1986—. Author: Arizona Appellate Forms and Procedures, 1968, also article. Mem. Ariz. Bd. Pub. Welfare, 1961-64, chmn., 1963-64; Mem. Eagle Scout bd. rev. Theodore Roosevelt council Boy Scouts Am., 1968—; Alternate del. Republican Nat. Conv., 1952; state Ariz. Rep. Party, 1958-60; Trustee Yuma City-County Library, 1958-67. Served with AUS, World War II. Mem. ABA (chmn. appellate judges conf. Judicial Adminstrn. div. 1977-78, jud. mem.-at-large 1986-88), Yuma County Bar Assn. (past pres.), State Bar Ariz., Ariz. Acad., Inst. Jud. Adminstrn., Nat. Inst. Justice (adv. com. 1984-86), Conf. Chief Justices U.S. (chmn. 1978-79), Am. Judicature Soc., Am. Law Inst., Lambda Chi Alpha, Phi Alpha Delta, Delta Theta Phi. Clubs: Mason, Shriner, Arizona. Jurisprudence, State civil litigation. Home: 5812 N 12th St #20 Phoenix AZ 85014 Office: State Capitol Bldg Phoenix AZ 85007

CAMERON, JOHN CLIFFORD, lawyer, health science facility administrator; b. Phila., Sept. 17, 1946; m. Eileen Duffy, July 12, 1975; children: Christopher, Meghan. BA, U. Pitts., 1969; MBA, Temple U., 1972; JD, Widener U., 1976; LLM, NYU, 1980. Bar: Pa. 1977, N.J. 1977. Asst. adminstr. Phila. Psychiatric Ctr., 1972-76; jud. clk. to presiding justice N.J. Superior Ct., Newark, 1976-77; asst. adminstr. St. Elizabeth Hosp., Elizabeth, N.J., 1977; v.p. corp. legal affairs Methodist Hosp., Phila., 1978—; sec. Suthbreit Properties, Ltd., Phila., 1981—, Asbury Corp., Wilmington, Del., 1982—, Healthmark, Inc., Moorsetown, N.J., 1982—, Walt Whitman Convalescent Ctr., Phila., 1983—. Contbr. articles to profl. jours. Mem. United Way campaign, Phila., 1979—, United Meth. Eastern Pa. Conf. health and welfare commn., Phila., 1978—, Partners in Ministry Fund Program, Phila., 1983, steering com. Golden Cross, Phila., 1984—; alumni rep. Widener U. Fellow Am. Coll. Hosp. Adminstrs.; mem. ABA (forum com. health law), N.J. Bar Assn., Pa. Bar Assn., Phila. Bar Assn., Am. Hosp. Assn., Hosp. Assn. Pa., Am. Coll. Healthcare Execs., Am. Coll. Law and Medicine, Am. Corp. Counsel Assn. Avocations: swimming, music. Health, General corporate. Home: 1410 Church Rd Malvern PA 19355 Office: Meth Hosp 2301 S Broad St Philadelphia PA 19148

CAMERON, JOHN GRAY, JR., lawyer; b. Detroit, July 28, 1949; s. John Gray and Helen Jane (Schueler) C.; m. Ann Elizabeth Dargus, June 19, 1976; children—Clara Katherine. A.B., Albion Coll., 1971; J.D. cum laude, Wayne State U., 1974. Bar: Ill. 1974, Mich. 1978, U.S. Ct. Appeals (8th cir.) 1975, U.S. Dist. Ct. (ea. dist.) Mo. 1975, U.S. Dist. Ct. (no. dist.) Ill. 1975, U.S. Dist. Ct. (we. dist.) Mich. 1978, U.S. Ct. Appeals (6th cir.) 1980. Law clk. U.S. Ct. Appeals, St. Louis, 1974-75; assoc. Isham, Lincoln & Beale, Chgo., 1975-78; ptnr. Warner, Norcross & Judd, Grand Rapids, Mich., 1978—; instr. Seidman Sch. Bus., Grand Valley State Coll., Allendale, Mich., 1979—, Mich. Inst. Continuing Legal Edn., 1980-82; lectr. Mich. Bar, 1983. Author: Michigan Real Property Law: Principles and Commentary, 1984; contbg. author: Michigan Real Estate Form Book, 1982-83. Bd. dirs. Urban Inst. Contemporary Art, Grand Rapids, 1980-82; trustee East Congregational Ch., Grand Rapids, 1985—. Mem. ABA, Mich. Bar Assn., Grand Rapids Bar Assn., Grand Rapids Bar Found., Am. Land Title Assn., Omicron Delta Epsilon. Republican. Club: Athletic, Peninsular (Grand Rapids). Real property, Legal education. Home: 2731 Elmwood Dr SE Grand Rapids MI 49506 Office: Warner Norcross & Judd 900 Old Kent Bldg Grand Rapids MI 49503

CAMERON, MARK ALAN, lawyer; b. Boston, Aug. 20, 1954; s. Alan Bruce and Marilyn Ruth (Waldron) C.; m. Sandra Karen Bakko, June 18, 1983. Student, Calif. State, Chico, 1972-74; BA in Econ., U. Calif., Davis, 1976, MA in Econ., 1978; JD, U. Calif., Hastings, 1981. Bar: Calif. 1981, U.S. Dist. Ct. (no. and cen. dists.) Calif. 1982, U.S. Ct. Appeals (9th cir.) 1983, U.S. Supreme Ct. 1985. Atty. Kindel & Anderson, Los Angeles, 1981-83, Miller, Starr & Regalia, Oakland, Calif., 1983—. Mem. ABA, Calif. Bar Assn., San Francisco Bar Assn. Republican. Avocations: tennis, skiing, volleyball. State civil litigation, Antitrust, Real property. Office: Miller Starr & Regalia One Kaiser Plaza Suite 1650 Oakland CA 94612

CAMP, JAMES CARROLL, lawyer; b. Greenville, S.C., Jan. 7, 1951; s. Willard Alford and Joy (Mills) C.; m. Jeanne Esther Katz, May 27, 1979. BA, Duke U., 1973; JD, Emory U., 1976. Bar: Ga. 1976, Calif. 1977, U.S. Dist. Ct. (cen. dist.) Calif. 1977, U.S. Tax Ct. 1981. Assoc. Strother, Weiner & Dwyer, Atlanta, 1976; atty. Pacific Lighting Corp., Los Angeles, 1977-78; ptnr. Greenberg, Bernhard, Weiss & Rosin, Los Angeles, 1978-84, Brown, Winfield & Canzoneri, Los Angeles, 1984—; bd. dirs. A-Mark Fin. Corp., Beverly Hills, Calif. Editorial bd. Los Angeles Lawyer, 1984—, chmn. 1986—. Mem. ABA (real estate fin. subcom.), Los Angeles County Bar Assn. (chmn. lawyer and arts com. 1982-83), Century City Bar Assn. (chmn. real property com. 1983-84). Avocations: music, travel, wine, food, bicycling. Contracts commercial, General corporate, Real property. Office: Brown Winfield & Canzoneri 300 S Grand Ave Suite 1500 Los Angeles CA 90071-3125

CAMP, RANDY COLEMAN, lawyer; b. Alamo, Tenn., Nov. 15, 1952; s. W.L. and Ara (Coleman) C.; m. Lisa Roland, Oct. 27, 1984. AA, Jackson State Coll., 1972; BS, U. Tenn., 1975; JD, Memphis State U., 1980. Bar: Tenn. 1980, U.S. Dist. Ct. (ea., mid., we. dists) Tenn. 1982. Sole practice Alamo, 1980—; exec. asst. to lt. gov. State of Tenn., Nashville, 1984—; county atty. Crockett County, Alamo, 1981—; bank atty. People's Bank, Alamo, 1981—, Bells (Tenn.) Banking Co., 1981—. Chmn. Crockett County Dem. Party, Alamo, 1980—, Crockett County Election Commn., Alamo, 1981—. Mem. ABA, Am. Trial Lawyers Assn., Tenn. Trial Lawyers Assn., Tenn. Bar Assn. (house of dels.). Democrat. Baptist. Banking, Real property, General practice. Office: 117 N Bells Court Sq Alamo TN 38001

CAMPANIE, SAMUEL JOHN, lawyer, consultant; b. Oneida, N.Y., May 30, 1952; s. Samuel G. Campanie and Kathryn A. McCarthy Warner, stepson George A. Warner; m. Susan Noyes Garner, June 14, 1975; children: Joseph Warner, Abigail Noyes. AB cum laude, Colgate U., 1974; JD, Albany Law Sch., 1978; postgrad., Syracuse U., 1982—. Bar: N.Y. 1979, U.S. Dist. Ct. (no. dist.) N.Y. 1979. Assoc. Kiley, Feldman, Whalen, Devine & Patane, Oneida, 1977-81; mgr. Mid-east and African divs. Oneida (N.Y.) Ltd. Silversmiths, 1981-83, mgr. export div., 1982-85, mgr. export and mil. divs., 1985; ptnr. Kohn, Moseman & Campanie, Oneida and Remsen, 1986—; accredited rep. Service Core of Retired Execs./Active Core Execs., Utica, N.Y., 1979—; cons. to various firms, 1985—; pvt. cons. practice Kenwood Assocs. Internat., Oneida, 1986—. Commr. City of Oneida Planning Commn., 1979—; legislator Madison County Bd. Supervisors, 1986—; bd. dirs. Madison County Indsl. Devel. Agy. 1986—; bd. dirs. Oneida-Madison Red Cross, 1979—; mem. platform com. N.Y. State Rep. Com., Albany, 1986; mem. exec. com. Madison County Rep. Com., 1979—; chmn. City of Oneida Rep. Com.; mem. N.Y. State Oneida Lake Adv. Com., 1986—. Named one of Outstanding Young Men in Am., 1985. Mem. ABA, N.Y. State Bar Assn., Madison County Bar Assn., Oneida Jaycees. Republican. Roman Catholic. Avocations: sailing, tennis, skiing, reading, computers. General practice, Private international, Contracts commercial. Home: 209 Kenwood Ave Oneida NY 13421 Office: Kohn Moseman & Campanie 112 Farrier Ave PO Box 643 Oneida NY 13421-0643

CAMPBELL, ANITA PELI, lawyer; b. New Kensington, Pa., Nov. 11, 1956; d. Harry and Anna Marie Peli; m. Kevin R. Campbell, Jan. 5, 1980. Student, Pa. State U., 1974-76; BA, Duquesne U., 1978; JD, U. Akron, 1982. Bar: Ohio 1982, U.S. Dist. Ct. (no. dist.) Ohio 1983. Jud. clk. Summit County Cts., Akron, Ohio, 1980-83; sole practice Akron, 1983-84; regional counsel Transohio Savs. Bank, Akron, 1984—; chmn. Transohio Savs. Polit. Action Com., Cleve. 1985-86. Mem. Jr. League, Akron, 1985—. Mem. Ohio State Bar Assn., Akron Bar Assn. (inquiry com.), Fin. Atty's. (sec. 1986—). Consumer commercial, Real property, Banking. Office: Transohio Savs Bank 1250 Superior Ave NE Cleveland OH 44114

CAMPBELL, BRIAN THOMAS, judge; b. Denver, May 15, 1948; s. Leonard Martin and Dot Jo (Baker) C.; m. Patricia Sue Adams, May 8, 1982; children—Rebecca Mae, Robert Michael. B.A., Knox Coll., 1970; J.D., U. Colo., 1972. Bar: Colo. 1973, U.S. Dist. Ct. Colo. 1973, U.S. Ct. Appeals (10th cir.) 1976. Law clk. U.S. Dist. Ct. Colo., Denver, 1973; assoc. Gorsuch, Kirgis, Denver, 1974-80; judge Denver County Ct., 1980—. Mem. Colo. Bar Assn. (bd. govs), Denver Bar Assn. (young lawyers exec. council), Colo. Women's Bar Assn., Catholic Lawyers Guild, County Ct. Judges Assn. (exec. council). Democrat. Roman Catholic. Environment. Home: 2986 S Whiting Way Denver CO 80231 Office: City and County Court 1437 Bannock St Denver CO 80202

CAMPBELL, BRUCE IRVING, lawyer; b. Mason City, Iowa, July 7, 1947; s. E. Riley Jr. and Donna Mae (Andresen) C.; m. Beverly Ann Clemens, Dec. 27, 1970; children: Anne, John. BA, Upper Iowa U., 1969; JD, Harvard U., 1973. Bar: Iowa 1973, U.S. Dist. Ct. (so. dist.) Iowa 1973, U.S. Dist. Ct. (no. dist.) Iowa 1974, U.S. Tax Ct. 1976, U.S. Ct. Appeals (8th cir.) 1977, U.S. Ct. Claims 1982. Ptnr. Davis, HOckenberg, Wine, Brown, Koehn & Shors, Des Moines, 1973—; adj. prof. law Drake U., Des Moines, 1974—. vice. chmn. bd. trustees Upper Iowa U., Fayette, Iowa, 1978—. Mem. ABA, Iowa Bar Assn., Polk County Bar Assn. Republican. Club: Embassy (Des Moines). Estate planning, Estate taxation, Personal income taxation. Home: 2804 Ridge Rd Des Moines IA 50312 Office: Davis Hockenberg Et Al 2300 Financial Ctr Des Moines IA 50309

CAMPBELL, CAROL NOWELL, lawyer; b. Phoenix, Dec. 16, 1944; d. Richard Converse Nowell and Nancy (Newcomb) Olson; m. Robert Norman Campbell, Jan. 2, 1965 (div. 1968); 1 child, Kelly Christine; m. Harding Briggs Cure, June 28, 1984. B.A., Ariz. State U.-Tempe, 1972, J.D., 1978. Bar: Ariz. 1979, Calif. 1979, U.S. Dist. Ct. Ariz. 1979, U.S. Dist. Ct. (cen. dist.) Calif. 1984, U.S. Ct. Apls. (9th cir.) 1981. Ptnr. O'Connor, Cavanagh, Anderson, Westover, Killingsworth & Beshears, Phoenix, 1978—; faculty mem. Pacific regional chpt. Nat. Inst. Trial Advocacy, 1985-86. Bd. dirs. Ariz. Council of the Blind, Social Services and Rehab. Inc., 1980-85, sec., 1980-82, v.p. ops. 1983-84; bd. dirs. Phoenix Childrens Theatre, 1981-83, v.p. ops., 1982-83; bd. dirs. Ariz. Cen. Credit Union, 1985-87; judge pro tem Ariz. Ct. Appeals. 1985. Mem. ABA (vice-chmn. rules and procedures com. 1983-87, chair-elect, 1987, co-chmn. long range planning subcom. 1984-85, chmn. ann. mtg. arrangements TIPS rules and procedures com. 1986-87, chmn.-elect rules and procedure com. 1987, publ. subcom. for The Brief 1987, chmn. use of expert witness subcom. of com. trial practice), State Bar Ariz. (com. on rules of civil practice and procedure), Maricopa County Bar Assn. (bd. dirs. 1983—), Maricopa County Bar Found. (trustee 1984—, sec. 1986—), Nucleus (chmn. membership com. 1984-85, chmn. 1986-87), AAUW (parliamentarian, bd. dirs. Ariz. State div. 1980-82), Ariz. State U. Alumni Assn. (bd. dirs. 1980-83), Kappa Delta Pi, Assn. Trial Lawyers Am., Phoenix Assn. Def. Counsel, Ariz. Women Lawyers Assn., Def. Research Inst. (practice and procedure com.). Democrat. Episcopalian. State civil litigation, Insurance, Personal injury. Office: O'Connor Cavanagh et al 1 E Camelback Rd Phoenix AZ 85012

CAMPBELL, CAROLYN CLARK, lawyer; b. Washington, May 9, 1941; d. John Gary and Jewell Rochelle (Hill) C.; m. Joungwon A. Kim, July 1, 1960; 1 child, Elizabeth Campbell Kim Mannion. B.A., Barnard Coll., 1970; J.D., Harvard U., 1973. Bar: N.Y. 1974, Pa. 1978, N.J. 1978, D.C. 1978; U.S. Dist. Ct. (ea. dist.) Pa. 1978, U.S. Dist. Ct. N.J. 1978, U.S. Ct. Appeals (3d cir.) 1978, U.S. Dist. Ct. (so. dist.) N.Y. 1984. Assoc., Mudge Rose Guthrie & Alexander, N.Y.C., 1973-77; staff atty. U.S. Ct. Appeals (2d cir.), N.Y.C., 1978-79; ptnr. Campbell & Kim, N.Y.C., 1980—. Mem. ABA, N.Y. State Bar Assn., D.C. Bar Assn., Pa. Bar Assn. General practice, General corporate, Corporate taxation. Home: 969 Park Ave New York NY 10028 Office: Campbell & Kim 489 Fifth Ave New York NY 10017

CAMPBELL, CHARLES PHILIP, JR., lawyer; b. Boulder, Colo., Feb. 18, 1948; s. Charles Philip and Mary (Hart) C.; m. Lucille Siddons, May 31, 1971. Student, Notre Dame Internat., Rome, 1964-66; BA, Rutgers U., 1970; JD, Stetson U., 1973. Bar: Fla. 1973, U.S. Dist. Ct. (mid. dist.) Fla. 1974, U.S. Ct. Appeals (5th and 11th cirs.) 1981. Assoc. Jacobs, Robbins et al, St. Petersburg, Fla., 1974-78; ptnr. Battaglia, Ross et al, St. Petersburg, 1978-82; ptnr., pres. Whittemore & Campbell P.A., St. Petersburg, 1982—. Mem. task force Pinellas County (Fla.) Sch. Bd., 1977; bd. dirs. John Knox Presbyn. Housing Found., St. Petersburg, 1977-81, Leadership St. Petersburg, 1978. Served to capt. USAF, 1974-80. Named one of Outstanding Young Men in Am., 1982. Mem. ABA, Assn. Trial Lawyers Am., Acad. Fla. Trial Attys., Am. Judicature Soc. (communications law com., chmn. subcom. media law, corp. and banking law com.), St. Petersburg C. of C. Clubs: Tiger Bay, Pres.'s, Univ. (St. Petersburg). Avocation: snow skiing. Libel, State civil litigation, Contracts commercial. Office: Whittemore & Campbell PA One Tampa City Ctr Suite 2470 Tampa FL 33602

CAMPBELL, CHRISTIAN LARSEN, lawyer; b. Chgo., Nov. 21, 1950; s. William Joseph and Marie Agnes (Cloherty) C.; m. Mildred Ann Garvy, Oct. 2, 1976 (div. Jan. 1986); children: Christian Jr., Brent; m. Heather Gilcrest, Mar. 7, 1987. BA, MA in Econs., Northwestern U., 1972; JD, Harvard U., 1975. Bar: Ill. 1975, U.S. Dist. Ct. (no. dist.) Ill. 1975, U.S. Ct. Appeals (7th cir.) 1975, U.S. Ct. Appeals (5th cir.) 1980, U.S. Supreme Ct. 1980. Assoc. Sidley & Austin, Chgo., 1975-83, ptnr., 1983—. Mem. ABA, Chgo. Bar Assn., Am. Mgmt. Assn. (lectr.1976—). Roman Catholic. Club: Barclay (Chgo.). Avocations: tennis, jogging. Antitrust, Federal civil litigation. Home: 360 E Randolph Chicago IL 60601 Office: Sidley & Austin 1 First National Plaza Chicago IL 60603

CAMPBELL, EDWARD ADOLPH, judge, electrical engineer; b. Boonville, Ind., Jan. 16, 1936; s. Revis Allen and Sarah Gertrude (Hunsaker) C.; m. Nancy Colleen Keys, July 26, 1957; children—Susan Elizabeth Campbell Frisse, Stephen Edward, Sara Lynne. B.S. in Elec. Engring., U. Evansville, 1959; J.D. Ind. U. Sch. Law, 1965; grad. Nat. Coll. Dist. Attys., U. Houston, 1972, Nat. Jud. Coll. U. Nev., 1978. Bar: Ind. 1965, U.S. Dist. Ct. (so. dist.) Ind. 1965, U.S. Ct. Customs and Patent Appeals 1967, U.S. Supreme Ct. 1973. Patent examiner U.S. Patent Office, Washington, 1959-60; patent adv. U.S. Naval Avionics, Indpls., 1960-65; patent atty. Gen. Elec. Co., Fort Wayne, Ind., 1965-66; ptnr. Weyerbacher & Campbell, attys., Boonville, Ind., 1966-71; pros. atty. 2nd Jud. Cir., Warrick County, Ind., 1971-77; judge Warrick Superior Ct., 1977—. Mem. Ind. State Bar Assn., Ind. Judges Assn., Nat. Council Juvenile and Family Ct. Judges, Ind. Council of Juvenile and Family Ct. Judges, Warrick County C. of C. (bd. dirs. 1978-84), Sigma Pi Sigma, Phi Delta Phi. Democrat. Methodist. Club: Rolling Hills Country (Newburgh, Ind.). Lodges: Lions, Kiwanis. Judicial administration, Local government, Patent. Home: 911 Julian Dr Boonville IN 47601 Office: Warrick Superior Ct PO Box 428 Boonville IN 47601

CAMPBELL, FRANK ANDREW SCOTT, lawyer; b. Paterson, N.J., July 19, 1955; s. Donald and Frances (Terhorst) C. BA, Lafayette Coll., 1977; JD, George Washington U., 1980. Bar: D.C. 1980, U.S. Dist. Ct. D.C. 1981, U.S. Ct. Appeals (D.C. cir.) 1981, U.S. Supreme Ct. 1984. Ptnr. Hemsley & Campbell, Washington, 1980-83; sole practice, Washington, 1984—. Mem. ABA, Assn. Trial Lawyers Am. General practice, Federal civil litigation, Administrative and regulatory. Home: 2312 20th St NW Washington DC 20009 Office: 1607 New Hampshire Ave NW Washington DC 20009

CAMPBELL, FREMONT LEE, lawyer; b. Tacoma, Aug. 24, 1923; s. Fremont C. and Dora B. (Payn) C.; m. Helen Veatch, July 28, 1950; children—Susan L., Scott F., David P. B.A., U. Wash., 1947, J.D., 1950. Bar: Wash. 1950. Atty. Md. Casualty Co., Seattle, 1950-51; ptnr. Karr, Tuttle, Koch, Campbell, Mawer, Morrow & Sax, Seattle, 1951—, pres., mng. dir., 1973-84; chmn. Wash. State Jud. Qualifications Commn., 1981-82. Author: Annotated Aviation Policy, 1972. Active in local politics, Clyde Hill, Wash., 1951-73. Served to 1st lt. U.S. Army, 1943-46. Mem. ABA, Wash. State Bar Assn. (award of merit 1980, bd. govs. 1979-82, pres. 1984-85), Seattle-King County Bar Assn. (pres. 1977-78), Am. Coll. Trial Lawyers (bd. regents 1986—), Internat. Acad. Trial Lawyers. Republican. Clubs: Rainier (Seattle), Seattle Yacht; Overlake Golf and Country (Bellevue, Wash.). Federal civil litigation, State civil litigation, Insurance. Home: 7871 NE 21st St Bellevue WA 98004 Office: Karr Tuttle Koch Campbell Mawer Morrow & Sax PS 1111 3d Ave Bldg Seattle WA 98101

CAMPBELL, GEORGE EMERSON, lawyer; b. Piggott, Ark., Sept. 23, 1932; s. Sid and Mae (Harris) C.; m. Joan Stafford Rule; children: Dianne, Carole. J.D., U. Ark., Fayetteville, 1955. Bar: Ark. bar 1955, U.S. Supreme Ct. bar 1971. Law clk. to judge Ark. Supreme Ct., 1959-60; assoc. Kirsch, Cathey & Brown, Paragould, Ark., 1955; mem. Rose Law Firm (P.A.), Little Rock, 1960—; Del. 7th Ark. Constl. Conv., 1969-70; regional v.p. Nat. Mcpl. League, 1974-86; mem. Ark. Ednl. TV Commn., chmn. 1980-82; bd. dirs. Ark. Ednl. TV Found. Chmn. Pulaski County Law Library Bd., 1980—; bd. dirs. Ark. Symphony Orch. Soc., 1982—, Ark. Capital Corp., The Downtown Partnership. Mem. ABA, Ark. Bar Assn., Pulaski County Bar Assn., Am. Law Inst., Am. Judicature Soc. General corporate, Banking, Local government. Office: 120 E 4th St Little Rock AR 72201

CAMPBELL, GEORGE WENDAL, JR., lawyer; b. Norfolk, Va., Apr. 6, 1947; s. George W. and Betty Ann (Weekley) C.; children: Kevin L., Lauren G. BA, U. Richmond, 1969; JD, Coll. William and Mary, 1974. Bar: Va. 1974, U.S. Supreme Ct. 1978, D.C. 1983. Assoc. Simmonds, Coleburn, Towner, Carman & Evans, Arlington, Va., 1974-78, ptnr., 1978-79; ptnr. Carman, Evans & Campbell, Arlington, 1979-85; prin. Law Offices of George W. Campbell, Jr., P.C., Arlington, 1985—; cert. player rep. NFL Players Assn., Washington, 1983—; agt. NFL; approved player rep. Nat. Collegiate Athletic Assn., 1985; del. Va. State Bar Council, 1985—. Editor-in-Chief Law Sch. Newspaper Coll. William and Mary, 1973-74. Chmn. opening day ceremonies Metro Orange Line, Courthouse Station. Mem. ABA, Va. Bar Assn., Va. Assn. Def. Attys., Va. Trial Lawyers Assn., No. Va. Young Lawyers Assn. (pres. 1977), Arlington County Bar Assn. (pres. 1983-84), D.C. Bar Assn., Greater Rosslyn (Va.) & Bus. Profl. Assn., Coll. William & Mary Law Sch. Alumni Assn. (pres. 1981-83), Arlington County Bar Found. (vice chmn. 1985—), Arlington C. of C. Democrat. Avocations: long-distance running, marathons, weight-lifting. Insurance, Corporate and

Business law, Personal injury. Office: 1515 N Courthouse Rd #502 Arlington VA 22201

CAMPBELL, JOHN A., federal government official. Chief adminstrv. law judge USDA, Washington, 1985—. Office: USDA 14th and Independence Ave SW Washington DC 20250 *

CAMPBELL, JOHN TIMOTHY, oil co. exec., lawyer, petroleum and indsl. cons.; b. Lake Charles, La., July 8, 1945; s. Aubrey Dorriss and Helen Teresa (Wilson) C.; m. Carol Osherenko, May 1, 1971 (dec. Apr. 1986); m. Pamela A. Johnston, Apr. 18, 1987. B.A. in Econs., B.A. in Polit. Sci., Principia Coll., 1967; J.D., So. Meth. U., 1970. Bar: Tex. 1970. Landman, Amoco Prodn. Co., Houston, 1970; internat. negotiator Amoco Internat. Oil Co., Chgo., 1971; v.p. Amoco Tunisia Oil Co., 1972; pres. Campbell Energy Corp., Santa Barbara, Calif. and Dallas, 1975—; chmn. Alaska Pacific Refining Anchorage, Alaska, 1986—. Mem. ABA (Silver Key Award law student div. 1970), Am. Soc. Internat. Law, Inter-Am. Bar Assn., State Bar Tex., Phi Alpha Delta. Republican. Christian Scientist. Club: Birnam Wood Golf (Montecito, Calif.). Private international, Oil and gas leasing.

CAMPBELL, JOSEPH H(OWARD), JR., lawyer; b. Shreveport, La., May 3, 1952; s. Joseph H. Sr. and Olga A. (Maroun) C.; m. Elizabeth Ann Clay, May 8, 1982. BS in Acctg., La. State U., 1973, JD, 1976. Bar: La. 1977. Internal auditor Associated Grocers, Baton Rouge, 1976—, legal counsel, 1977—, also bd. dirs., adminstrv. asst. to pres., 1985—; sole practice Baton Rouge, 1981; bd. dirs. Southeast Mchts., Baton Rouge, Horizon Fed. Savs. and Loan, Baton Rouge. Mem. ABA, La. Bar Assn., Baton Rouge Bar Assn. Democrat. Roman Catholic. Lodge: K.C. Avocations: golf, fishing, bicycling, jogging. General corporate, Probate, Personal income taxation. Office: Associated Grocers PO Box 1748 Baton Rouge LA 70821

CAMPBELL, LEONARD MARTIN, lawyer; b. Denver, Apr. 12, 1918; s. Bernard Francis and May (Moran) C.; m. Dot J. Baker, Sept. 23, 1944; children: Brian T., Teri Pat, Thomas P. A.B., U. Colo., 1941, LL.B., 1943. Bar: Colo. 1943. Since practiced in Denver; mem. firm Gorsuch, Kirgis, Campbell, Walker & Grover, 1946; cons. pub. utility matters City and County Denver, also Colo. Mcpl. League, 1953—; city atty. Denver, 1951-53. Mem. Denver Charter Com., 1947; mgr. Safety and Excise for Denver, 1947-48; chmn. Denver Com. Human Relations, 1954; mem. Denver Planning Bd., 1950-51; mem. Bd. Water Commrs., Denver, 1965-70, pres., 1968-69; mem. Gov.'s Com. on Jud. Compensation, 1972; chmn. U. Colo. Law Alumni Devel. Fund, 1962. Served with USAAF, 1943-46. Mem. ABA, Colo. Bar Assn. (pres. 1978-79), Denver Bar Assn. (pres. 1969), Am. Coll. Trial Lawyers, Cath. Lawyers Guild Denver (pres. 1962), Nat. Inst. Mcpl. Law Officers (v.p. 1952). Democrat. Roman Catholic. Clubs: KC (Denver), Denver Athletic (Denver) (sec. 1960-61, pres. 1962), Cherry Hills Country (Denver). Public utilities, State civil litigation, Municipal law. Home: 3447 S Birch St Denver CO 80222 Office: Gorsuch Kirgis Campbell Walker & Grover 1401 17th St Suite 1100 PO Box 17180 Denver CO 80202

CAMPBELL, LEVIN HICKS, judge; b. Summit, N.J., Jan. 2, 1927; s. Worthington and Louise (Hooper) C.; m. Eleanor Saltonstall Lewis, June 1, 1957; children—Eleanor S., Levin H., Sarah H. A.B. cum laude, Harvard U., 1948, LL.B., 1951; postgrad., Nat. Coll. State Judiciary, 1970; LL.D. (hon.), Suffolk U., 1975. Bar: D.C. 1951, Mass. 1954. Assoc. firm Ropes & Gray, Boston, 1954-64; mem. Mass. Ho. of Reps., 1963-64; asst. atty. gen. State of Mass., 1965-66, spl. asst. atty. gen., 1966-67, 1st asst. atty. gen., 1967-68; assoc. justice Superior Ct. of Mass., 1969-72; judge U.S. Dist. Ct. Mass., Boston, 1972; judge U.S. Ct. Appeals (1st cir.), Boston, 1972—, chief judge, 1983—; fellow Inst. of Politics J.F. Kennedy Sch. Govt. Harvard U., 1968-69, study group leader 1980; faculty chmn. law session Salzburg Seminar in Am. Studies, 1981. Pres. Cambridge 9 Neighborhood Assn., 1960-62; treas. Cambridge Center for Adult Edn., 1961-64; campaign chmn. Cambridge United Fund, 1965; mem. bd. overseers Boston Symphony Orch., 1969-75, 77-80; pres. bd. overseers Shady Hill Sch., 1969-70; mem. vis. com. Harvard U. Press, 1958-64; v.p. Cambridge Community Services; corp. mem. SEA Ednl. Assn., 1982—; trustee Colby Coll., Waterville, Maine, 1982—. Served to 1st lt. JAGC, U.S. Army, 1951-54, Korea. Mem. ABA, Mass. Bar Assn., Boston Bar Assn, U.S. Jud. Conf. (ct. adminstrn. com. 1975-83, chmn. subcom. on supporting personnel 1980-83, exec. com. 1985—), Salzburg Seminar Alumni Assn. (bd. dirs. 1983—). Office: US Post Office and Courthouse Room 1618 Boston MA 02109

CAMPBELL, MARIA BOUCHELLE, banker, lawyer; b. Mullins, S.C., Jan. 23, 1944; d. Colin Reid and Margaret Minor (Perry) C.;. Student, Agnes Scott Coll., 1961-63; A.B., U. Ga., 1965, J.D., 1967. Bar: Ga. 1967, Fla. 1968, Ala. 1969. Practiced in Birmingham, Ala., 1968; law clk. U.S. Circuit Ct. Appeals, Miami, Fla., 1967-68; assoc. Cabaniss, Johnston and Gardner, 1968-73; sec. counsel Ala. Bancorp., Birmingham, 1973-79; sr. v.p., sec., gen. counsel counsel AmSouth Bancorp., 1979-84, exec. v.p., gen. counsel, 1984—; exec. v.p., gen. counsel AmSouth Bank, 1984—; lectr. continuing legal edn. programs; cons. to charitable orgns. Exec. editor Ga. Law Rev, 1966-67. Bd. dirs. St. Anne's Home, Birmingham, 1969-74, chancellor, 1969-74; bd. dirs. Children's Aid Soc., Birmingham, 1970—, Positive Maturity, 1976-78, Mental Health Assn., 1978-81, YWCA, 1979-80, NCCJ, 1985—, Operation New Birmingham, 1985—, Soc. for the Fine Arts U. Ala., 1986—; commr. Housing Authority, Birmingham Dist., 1980-85, Birmingham Partnership, 1986-87; trustee Leadership Birmingham, 1986—Ala. Diocese Episcopal Ch., 1971-72, 74-75, mem. canonical revision com., 1973-75, liturg. commn., 1976-78, treas., chmn. dept. fin., 1979-83, mem. council, 1983-87, chancellor, 1987—, cons. on stewardship edn., 1981—, dep. to gen. conv., 1985. Mem. Am. Corp. Counsel Assn. (bd. dirs. Ala. 1984—), State Bar Ga., Fla. Bar, Am., Ala., Birmingham bar assns., Assn. Bank Holding Cos. (chmn. lawyers com. 1986-87), Women's Network. Club: Mountain Brook, Downtown. Banking, Consumer commercial, General corporate. Home: 141 Camellia Circle Birmingham AL 35213 Office: AmSouth Bank PO Box 11007 Birmingham AL 35288

CAMPBELL, PAUL, III, lawyer; b. Chattanooga, Feb. 1, 1946; m. Martha B. McFall; children: Paul IV, Kolter M. B.A., Vanderbilt U., 1968; M.A., Middlebury Coll., 1972; postgrad. So. Meth. U., 1971-72, Emory U., 1972-73; J.D., U. Tenn., 1975. Bar: Tenn. 1976, Ga. 1977. Ptnr. Campbell & Campbell, Chattanooga, 1976—; adj. prof. English, U. Tenn., Chattanooga, 1976, adj. prof. law Sch. Bus., 1979-81. Co-author: Tennessee Automobile Liability Insurance, 1986, Tennessee Admissibility of Evidence in Civil Cases, 1987; editor-in-chief Tenn. Law Rev., 1975; contbr. articles to profl. jours. Bd. mgrs. YMCA Youth Residential Ctr., 1977-80; mem. McCallie Sch. Alumni Council, 1987—. Mem. ABA, Tenn. Bar Assn. (dir. Young Lawyers conf. 1978-81, bd. govs. 1985—), Chattanooga Bar Assn. (gov. 1983-85), State Bar Ga., Fed. Bar Assn. (dir. chpt. 1983—), Tenn. Def. Lawyers Assn., Def. Research Inst., Order of Coif, Phi Kappa Phi. Federal civil litigation, Insurance, State civil litigation. Home: 200 Robin Hood Trail Lookout Mountain TN 37350 Office: 1200 James Bldg Chattanooga TN 37402

CAMPBELL, PAUL BARTON, lawyer; b. Owosso, Mich., Feb. 24, 1930; s. George Wiley and Louise Marian (Pletke) C.; children: Jane, Paul Barton, James. B.B.A., U. Mich., 1951, M.B.A., 1954, J.D., 1954. Bar: Ohio 1955, Mich 1955, Fla. 1978. Assoc. mem. firm Squire, Sanders & Dempsey, Cleve., 1954-66; ptnr. Squire, Sanders & Dempsey, 1966—; sec. Ferro Corp., Cleve., 1970—; dir. Huntington Nat. Bank, Cleve. Bd., Cleve., 1975-86; sec. Midwest Forge Corp., Cleve., 1979-87; sec., dir. Shelby Paper Box Corp., Cleve., 1980—. Democrat. General corporate, Securities, Banking. Home: 12700 Lake Ave Apt 1306 Lakewood OH 44107 Office: 1800 Huntington Bldg Cleveland OH 44115

CAMPBELL, RICHARD BRUCE, lawyer; b. Phila., Jan. 5, 1947; s. George B. and Edith (Neithammer) C.; m. Patricia Ann James, Mar. 7, 1981; 1 child, Ron Martin. BA, U. S.C., 1968, JD, 1974. Bar: S.C. 1975, U.S. Dist. Ct. S.C. 1975, U.S. Ct. Appeals (4th cir.) 1976, U.S. Ct. Appeals (5th cir.) 1983, Colo. 1985, U.S. Dist. Ct. Colo. 1986. Law clk. to presiding justice U.S. Dist. Ct., Columbia, S.C., 1975; ptnr. Henderson & Salley, Aiken, S.C., 1975-80; atty. TVA, Knoxville, 1980-85; assoc. Wells, Love & Scoby, Boulder, Colo., 1986—. Contbr. articles to profl. jours. Served to capt. USAF, 1968-72. Mem. ABA, Am. Arbitration Assn. (panelist), S.C. Bar Assn., Assoc. Gen. Contractors Am. (legal adv. panel). Avocations: skiing, photography. Construction, Federal civil litigation, State civil litigation. Home: 7425 Mount Sherman Rd Longmont CO 80501 Office: Wells Love & Scoby 225 Canyon Blvd Boulder CO 80302

CAMPBELL, RICHARD P., lawyer; b. Boston, June 17, 1947; s. William Thomas and Mary Patricia (O'Brien) C.; children—Richard, Sean, Lauren. B.A., U. Mass., 1970; J.D. cum laude, Boston Coll., 1974. Bar: N.J. 1974, U.S. Dist. Ct. N.J. 1974, Mass. 1977, U.S. Dist. Ct. Mass. 1977, U.S. Dist. Ct. R.I. 1979, U.S. Ct. Appeals (1st cir.) 1980, Fla., 1984, Maine, 1986. Assoc., Shanley & Fisher, Newark, 1974-77, Nutter, McClennen & Fish, Boston, 1977-79; assoc. Craig & Macauley, Boston, 1979-81, shareholder, 1981-83; pres. Campbell & Assocs., Boston, 1983—. Mem. ABA (vice chmn. products liability com., tort and ins. practice sect. 1980—), Mass. Bar Assn., Def. Research Inst. (product liability com. 1984—), Am. Assn. Automotive Medicine, Product Liability Adv. Council. Clubs: University, Bay (Boston). Federal civil litigation, State civil litigation, Personal injury. Office: Campbell & Assocs PC 83 Atlantic Ave Boston MA 02110

CAMPBELL, ROBERT HEDGCOCK, brokerage executive; lawyer; b. Ann Arbor, Mich., Jan. 16, 1948; s. Robert Miller and Ruth Adele (Hedgcock) C.; m. Katherine Dean Kettering, June 17, 1972; children—Mollie DuPlan, Katherine Elizabeth, Anne Kettering. B.A., U. Wash., 1970, J.D., 1973. Bar: Wash. 1973, U.S. Dist. Ct. (we. dist.) Wash. 1973, U.S. Ct. Appeals (9th cir.) 1981. Assoc., Roberts & Shefelman, Seattle, 1973-79, ptnr., 1979-85; sr. v.p. Shearson Lehman Bros., Inc., 1985-87, mng. dir., 1987—. Author: The Deficit Reduction Act of 1984 and Other Recent Developments Affecting Municipal Borrowing, 1984; also articles in profl. jours. Mem. financing com. U. Wash. Swim Team, 1982—; trustee Wash. Phikeia Found., 1983—; nation chief YMCA Indian Princesses, Bellevue, Wash., 1983—. Mem. Fed. Energy Bar Assn., Seattle-King County Bar Assn. (chmn. com. 1974-75), Wash. State Soc. Hosp. Attys. (pres. 1982-84), Northwest Small Hydroelectric Assn. (dir. 1980-85), Nat. Assn. Bond Lawyers (vice chmn. com. 1981-82, treas. 1982-84, bd. dirs. 1982-85), ABA (vice chmn. com. 1981-82), Phi Delta Theta. Republican. Clubs: Seattle Tennis (membership com.), Bellevue Athletic, Columbia Tower (Wash.). Municipal bonds, FERC practice, Public utilities. Home: 8604 NE 10th St Bellevue WA 98004 Office: Shearson & Lehman Bros Inc Foster & Marshall div 999 3d Ave Suite 4000 Seattle WA 98104

CAMPBELL, ROBERT M., state supreme ct. justice; b. Mar. 1, 1935. B.A., Tex. Wesleyan Coll.; J.D., Baylor U. Practice law Waco, Tex.; justice Tex. Supreme Ct., 1979—. Office: Supreme Ct Bldg Austin TX 78711

CAMPBELL, SCOTT ROBERT, food company executive, lawyer; b. Burbank, Calif., June 7, 1946; s. Robert Clyde and Genevieve Anne (Olsen) C.; m. Thersa Melanie Mack, Oct. 23, 1965; 1 son, Donald Steven. B.A., Claremont Men's Coll., 1970; J.D., Cornell U., 1973. Bar: Ohio 1973, Minn. 1976. Assoc. atty. Taft, Stettinius & Hollister, Cin., 1973-76; atty. Mpls. Star & Tribune, 1976-77; sr. v.p., gen. counsel, sec. Kellogg Co., Battle Creek, Mich., 1977—; U.S. del. ILO Food and Beverage Conf., Geneva, 1984. Mem. ABA, Ohio Bar Assn., Minn. Bar Assn., Grocery Mfrs. Assn. (exec. steering com.), Am. Soc. Corp. Secs. General corporate, Antitrust, Securities. Office: One Kellogg Sq PO Box 3599 Battle Creek MI 49016-3599

CAMPBELL, THOMAS DOUGLAS, lawyer, government affairs and public relations consultant; b. N.Y.C., Jan. 5, 1951; s. Edward Thomas and Dorothy Alice (Moore) C.; m. Mary Anne Campbell, Dec. 22, 1978; 1 dau., Kristen Anne. B.A., U. Del., 1972; J.D., U. Pa., 1976. Bar: Del. 1977. Law clk. Law Offices Bayard Brill & Handleman, Wilmington, Del., 1974-77; Washington rep. Standard Oil Co. (Ind.), 1978-85; pres. Thomas D. Campbell and Assocs., Inc., 1985— ; govt. affairs rep. Northeastern U.S., Standard Oil Co. Ind., 1977-78 . Served with U.S. Army, 1968-69, USAF, 1969-77. Mem. ABA, Del. Bar Assn., World Affairs Council, Nat. Trust for Historic Preservation, Phi Beta Kappa, Phi Kappa Phi, Omicron Delta Epsilon, Omicron Delta Kappa. Republican. Episcopalian. Legislative, Local government. Home: 517 Queen St Alexandria VA 22314

CAMPBELL, WILLIAM COOLIDGE, lawyer; b. Portland, Oreg., Mar. 5, 1954; s. William Douglas and Mary Humphreys (Coolidge) C.; m. Jane Rachel Levy, June 19, 1974; children: Anna Rachel, Elizabeth Mary. BA magna cum laude, Yale U., 1975, JD, 1979. Bar: Oreg. 1979, U.S. Dist. Ct. Oreg. 1979, U.S. Ct. Appeals (9th cir.) 1979, U.S. Ct. Internat. Trade 1983. Assoc. Lindsay, Hart, Neil & Weigler, Portland, 1979-84, ptnr., 1985—. Contbr. articles to profl. jours. Chmn. mayor's internat. task force, Portland, 1985; mem. Oreg. China Commn., Portland, 1986—; trustee World Affairs Council Oreg., Portland, 1984—; bd. dirs. Northwest Regional China Council, Portland, 1981—. Mem. ABA, Oreg. Bar Assn. (chmn. fgn. and internat. law. com. 1982-83), Internat. Bar Assn. Jewish. Avocations: hiking, skiing, mountaineering, reading. Private international, Computer. Office: Lindsay Hart Neil & Weigler 222 SW Columbia Suite 1800 Portland OR 97201

CAMPBELL, W(ILLIAM) DOUGLAS, lawyer; b. Pensacola, Fla., May 18, 1948; m. Carol A. Montegar, July 16, 1980. BA in History cum laude, Brigham Young U., 1973, JD cum laude, 1976. Bar: Fla. 1976, U.S. Dist. Ct. (mid. dist.) 1980. Assoc. Douglas, Davey & Cooper P.A., Tallahassee, 1976-80; counsel labor and human resources com. U.S. Senate, Washington, 1981-83, majority health counsel labor and human resources, 1983—. Republican. Mormon. Legislative, Health. Office: Labor and Human Resources SD-428 Dirksen Senate Office Bldg Washington DC 20510

CAMPBELL, WILLIAM GANT, lawyer, consultant; b. Atlantic City, Aug. 31, 1941; s. Edward T. and Dorothy (Moore) C.; m. Roberta A. Taylor, Nov. 20, 1964; children—Beth, Heather. B.A., U. Del., 1963; J.D., Temple U., 1966. Bar: Del. 1967. With Bayard, Handelman & Murdoch, P.A. and predecessor, Wilmington, Del., 1966—, ptnr., 1971—, mng. dir., 1976-82; counsel Del. Workmen's Compensation Study Commn., 1980; mem. Gov.'s Med. Malpractice Commn., 1975-76; chmn. Del. Ann. Bench and Bar Conf., 1981; counsel Workers' Compensation Coalition, 1980-82. Mem. Republican State Exec. Com., 1976-77; media chmn. counsel Del. Nixon-Agnew Com., 1968. Mem. ABA (chmn. membership com. Del. 1972-80), Del. Bar Assn. Clubs: Capital Hill (Washington); Rodney Square (Wilmington); Masons. General corporate, Legislative, Administrative and regulatory. Office: PO Box 25130 Delaware Trust Bldg Wilmington DE 19899

CAMPBELL, WILLIAM J., judge; b. Chgo., Mar. 19, 1905; s. John and Christina (Larsen) C.; m. Marie Agnes Cloherty, 1937; children—Marie Agnes (Mrs. Walter J. Cummings), Karen Christina (Mrs. James T. Reid), Heather Therese (Mrs. Patrick Henry), Patti Ann (Mrs. Peter V. Fazio, Jr.), Roxane (Mrs. Wesley Sedlacek), William J., Christian Larsen, Thomas John. J.D., Loyola U., 1926, LL.M., 1928, LL.D., 1955; LL.D., Lincoln Coll., 1960; Litt.D., Duchesne Coll., 1965; J.C.D., Barat Coll., 1966. Bar: Ill. 1927. Partner Campbell and Burns, Chgo., 1927-40; Ill. adminstr. Nat. Youth Adminstrn., 1935-39; U.S. dist atty. No. Dist. Ill., 1938-40; judge U.S. Dist. Ct., 1940—; chief judge No. Dist. Ill., 1959-70; Mem. Jud. Conf. U.S., 1958-62; chmn. Jud. Conf. Commn. Budget, 1960-70; asst. dir., chmn. seminars Fed. Jud. Center, 1971—. Mem. nat. exec. bd. Boy Scouts Am., 1934—, mem. regional exec. com., 1937—; mem. exec. bd. Chgo. council, 1930—; Trustee Barat Coll., Lake Forest, Ill.; mem. citizens bd. U. Chgo., Loyola U., Chgo.; bd. dirs. Catholic Charities Chgo. Recipient award of merit Citizens of Greater Chgo., 1966; named Chicagoan of Year, 1965; Lincoln laureate in law State of Ill., 1970; Devitt Disting. Service to Justice award, 1986. Clubs: Ill. Athletic (Chgo.), Union League (Chgo.), Standard (Chgo.), Mid-America (Chgo.); La Coquille (Palm Beach, Fla.). Home: 400 S Ocean Blvd Manalapan FL 33462 Office: U S Dist Ct 401 Fed Bldg 701 Clematis St West Palm Beach FL 33401

CAMPBELL, WOODROW WILSON, lawyer; b. Salt Lake City, Apr. 30, 1944; s. Woodrow W. Campbell and Doris (Tolin) Whittaker; m. Maria Barra, Sept. 29, 1973; children: Alexander Lawrence, Francesca Sara. BA, Yale U., 1966; LLB, Columbia U., 1973. Bar: N.Y. 1974, U.S. Dist. Ct. (so. dist.) N.Y. 1974, U.S. Ct. Appeals (2d cir.) 1974. Trainee Fed. Res. Bank, N.Y.C., 1966-67; law clk. to judge Paul R. Hays U.S. Ct. Appeals (2d. cir.), N.Y.C., 1973-74; assoc. Debevoise & Plimpton, N.Y.C., 1974-81, ptnr., 1982—. Served to capt. USMC, 1967-70, Vietnam. Mem. ABA (investment cos. and investment advisers subcom. corps. com.), N.Y. State Bar Assn., Assn. of Bar of City of N.Y. Presbyterian. Club: Racquet and Tennis (N.Y.C.). General corporate, Securities, Banking. Home: 1185 Park Ave New York NY 10128 Office: Debevoise & Plimpton 875 3d Ave New York NY 10022

CAMPBELL-BELL, DOROTHY KATHRYN, lawyer; b. Mt. Clemens, Mich., Oct. 6, 1955; d. Bruce Hicks and Helen Joyce (Bailey) Campbell; m. Mark Joseph Bell, July 23, 1977. A.B. cum laude, Duke U., 1976; J.D., Vanderbilt U., 1980; student New Coll., Oxford (Eng.) U., 1976. Bar: Tenn. 1980, U.S. Dist. Ct. (mid. dist.) Tenn. 1981, U.S. Ct. Appeals (6th cir.) 1982. Inventory specialist Va. State Dept. Corrections, Richmond, Va., 1977; referral asst. Va. Lawyer Referral Service, Richmond, 1977; law clk. Chambers, Johnson, Brooks & Beckner, Nashville, 1979, Cross & Stiles, Nashville, 1979; clk. Ingraham, Corbett & Zinn, Nashville, 1978-79, 79-80, assoc., 1980-85, ptnr., 1986—. Vol., Friends of Children's Hosp., Nashville, 1981-83; tchr. St. George's Episcopal Ch., 1984-86, sponsor EYC, 1986—; dir. Georgetown Homeowners Assn., Nashville, 1983-86; campaign vol. United Way, Nashville, 1981, 83; vol. instr. ARC Adapted Aquatics Program, 1981—; vol. ARC Safety Services Com., 1985—, bd. dirs., 1986—; coordinator ARC Cert. Merit Program, 1986—; vice chair adv. com. ARC Health Services, 1986—. Angier B. Duke Meml. scholar, 1973. Mem. ABA, Tenn. Bar Assn. (task force on drug and alcohol abuse 1984-87, Tenn. lawyers concerned for lawyers com. 1987—), Nashville Bar Assn. (participant pro-bono program 1980—, coordinator Bridge the Gap Seminar, treas. young lawyers div., 1987—). Contbr. articles to profl. publ. General corporate, Entertainment, Real property. Office: Ingraham Corbett & Zinn 2114 Parkway Towers Nashville TN 37219

CAMPILONGO, MICHAEL, lawyer; b. Bethesda, Md., Nov. 4, 1946; s. Salvatore John and Ella Mae (Smith) C. B.S., Georgetown U., 1968; J.D., Washington and Lee U., 1973. Bar: Va. 1973, D.C. 1978, U.S. Supreme Ct. 1980. Staff dir. Legal Aid Soc., Alexandria, Va., 1973-74; asst. atty. gen. of Va., Richmond, 1974-76; assoc. Landis, Cohen et al, Fairfax, Va., 1977-78; asst. gen. counsel Nat. Paint & Coatings Assn., Washington, 1979—; mem. gov.'s adv. council to Nat. Legal Services Corp., 1985—, Commn. on Women and Minorities in the Legal System, 1986—, Va. Bar Council, 1986—, Va. Conf. of Local Bar Assns., pres., 1986—. Chmn. Alexandria Charter Rev. Commn., 1980-81. Mem. Va. State Bar (chmn. environ. law sect. 1985-86), Va. State Bar Council, Va. Conf. Local Bus. Assns. (pres. 1986—), Alexandria Bar Assn. (pres. 1984-85). Democrat. Roman Catholic. Environment, General corporate, Administrative and regulatory. Home: 1205 N Pitt St Alexandria VA 22314 Office: 1500 Rhode Island Ave NW Washington DC 20005

CAMPION, EILEEN, lawyer; b. Great River, N.Y.; d. Patrick Thomas and Mary Agnes (Gaughan) C. Grad. U. Miami, 1956, J.D., 1961. Bar: Fla. 1962. Sole practice, Miami, Fla., 1962-64, 81—; law editor Lawyers Coop. Pub. Co., Rochester, N.Y., 1964-65; tax atty. U.S. Treasury Dept., Miami, 1965-80. Founder Women's Com. of 100, 1970, pres., 1970-73. Recipient awards for writing, 1963, 82; award Women's Com. of 100, 1973, AAUW, 1976; named one of outstanding women grads. over past five decades U. Miami Law Sch., 1982. Mem. Fed. Bar Assn. (Outstanding Service award 1968, 69), Dade County Bar Assn., Nat. Women's Lawyers Assn. Roman Catholic. Immigration, naturalization, and customs, Probate. Office: 453 Brickell Ave Suite 2C Miami FL 33131

CAMPOLUCCI, ROGER LOUIS, lawyer; b. Bridgeport, Conn., Jan. 28, 1940; s. Louis and Jennie (Spisto) C.; m. Cecilia Stapleton, June 22, 1963; children: Mary E., Laura J. BA, Brown U., 1961; JD, Georgetown U., 1965. Bar: N.J. 1966. From counsel to sr. counsel various divs. RCA Corp., Princeton, Moorestown, and Camden, N.J., and Van Nuys, Calif., 1968-78; staff v.p., group counsel aerospace and def. divs. RCA Corp., Cherry Hill, N.J., 1978—. Mem. ABA (pub. contracts sect.), N.J. Bar Assn., Fed. Bar Assn., Nat. Security and Indsl. Assn. (vice chmn. legal and spl. task subcom. 1981-83, 86—). Government contracts and claims, Contracts commercial. Office: RCA Corp 401 Parry Dr Moorestown NJ 08057

CAMPOS, DAVID NELSON, lawyer; b. Miami, Fla., May 28, 1954; s. Felino and Wilma Jo (Cooper) C. BA, Ind. U., 1977, JD, 1980. Bar: Mich. 1981. Trial lawyer Smith, Haughey, Rice & Roegge, Grand Rapids, Mich., 1980—. Mem. ABA, Mich. Bar Assn., Grand Rapids Bar Assn., Mich. Def. Trail Assn. Insurance, State civil litigation, Personal injury. Home: 4930 Leonard St Coopersville MI 49404 Office: Smith Haughey et al 200 Calder Plaza Grand Rapids MI 49503

CAMPOS, SANTIAGO E., federal judge; b. Santa Rosa, N.Mex., Dec. 25, 1926; s. Ramon and Miquela Campos; m. Patsy Campos, Jan. 27, 1947; children: Teresa, Rebecca, Christina, Miquela Feliz. J.D., U. N.Mex., 1953. Bar: N.Mex. 1953. Asst., 1st asst. atty gen. State of N.Mex., 1955-57; judge N.Mex. Dist. Ct.; 1st Jud. Dist., 1971-78; now judge U.S. Dist. Ct. for Dist. N.Mex. Served as seaman USN, 1944-46. Mem. State Bar N.Mex., First Jud. Dist. Bar Assn., Order of Coif. Office: US Dist Ct PO Box 2244 Santa Fe NM 87504

CANADY, RICHARD WARREN, lawyer; b. Boone, Iowa., Dec. 7, 1934; s. Cecil M. and Myra N. (Shurtz) C.; m. Carol Jean Canady, Feb. 1, 1960; children—Michael Warren, Kelly Lynn. B.S.C., Iowa U., 1956, J.D. with distinction, 1959; LL.M., Georgetown U., 1962. Bar: Iowa 1959, Calif. 1962. Legal specialist Office of Navy JAG, 1960-62; law clk. to judge U.S. Ct. Appeals 9th Cir., 1962-63; assoc. White, Froehlich & Peterson, San Diego, 1963-64; ptnr. Howard, Rice, Nemerovski, Canady, Robertson & Falk, San Francisco, 1965-86, mng. ptnr., 1986—. Trustee Iowa Law Sch. Found. Served with USN, 1959-62. Mem. ABA, State Bar Calif., Iowa Bar Assn., San Francisco Bar Assn., Order of Coif. Presbyterian. Clubs: Olympic, San Francisco Golf; Monterey Country (Palm Desert, Calif.). Corporate taxation, General corporate. Home: 8 St Bernard Ln Tiburon CA 94920 Office: 3 Embarcadero Ctr San Francisco CA 94108

CANBY, WILLIAM CAMERON, JR., U.S. judge; b. St. Paul, May 22, 1931; s. William Cameron and Margaret Leah (Lewis) C.; m. Jane Adams, June 18, 1954; children—William Nathan, John Adams, Margaret Lewis. A.B., Yale U., 1953; LL.B., U. Minn., 1956. Bar: Minn. bar 1956, Ariz. bar 1972. Law clk. U.S. Supreme Ct. Justice Charles E. Whittaker, 1958-59; assoc. firm Oppenheimer, Hodgson, Brown, Baer & Wolff, St. Paul, 1959-62; asso., then dep. dir. Peace Corps, Ethiopia, 1962-64; dir. Peace Corps, Uganda, 1964-66; asst. to U.S. Senator Walter Mondale, 1966; asst. to pres. SUNY, 1967; prof. law Ariz. State U., 1967-80; judge U.S. Ct. Appeals 9th Circuit, Phoenix, 1980—; bd. dirs. Ariz. Center Law in Public Interest, 1974-80, Maricopa County Legal Aid Soc., 1972-78, D.N.A.-People's Legal Services, 1978-80; Fulbright prof. Makerere U. Faculty Law, Kampala, Uganda, 1970-71. Author: American Indian Law, 1981; also articles.; Note editor: Minn. Law Rev, 1955-56. Precinct and state committeeman Democratic Party Ariz., 1972-80; bd. dirs. Central Ariz. Coalition for Right to Choose, 1976-80. Served with USAF, 1956-58. Mem. State Bar Ariz., Minn. Bar Assn., Maricopa County Bar Assn., Phi Beta Kappa, Order of Coif. Office: US Courthouse 1st Ave Phoenix AZ 85025

CANCELLI, DANTE ANTONIO, lawyer; b. Peckville, Pa., Sept. 7, 1954; s. Dante Ernesto and Alyce Helen (Newcott) C.; m. Luciana Luciani, Oct. 8, 1983; 1 child, Anna Maria. BA, Pa. State U., 1976; JD, Temple U., 1979; LLM, George Washington U., 1981. Bar: Pa. 1979, U.S. Dist. Ct. (mid. dist.) Pa. 1979, D.C. 1980, U.S. Tax Ct. 1981, Ohio 1983, U.S. Ct. Claims 1986, U.S. Supreme Ct. 1986. Advisor Fed. Govt., Washington, 1980-81; assoc. Nogi & O'Malley, Scranton, Pa., 1981-83, Gottlieb & Johnston, Zanesville, Ohio, 1983-85, Sachs & Greenebaum, Washington, 1985-86; sole practice Scranton, Pa. and Washington, 1986—; instr. Pa. State U., Dunmore, 1986—. George Washington U. fellow, 1979-81. Mem. ABA, Fed. Bar Assn., Pa. Bar Assn., D.C. Bar Assn., Northeastern Pa. Estate Planning Council, Ohio Bar Assn., Phi Alpha Delta. Republican. Roman Catholic. Avocations: computers, reading. General practice, Corporate taxation, Estate planning. Home: 305 Erie St Dunmore PA 18510 Office: United Penn Bank Bldg 401 Spruce St Suite 402 Scranton PA 18503

CANCELMO, WILLIAM WEINERT, lawyer; b. Phila., June 6, 1932; s. A. Victor and Marie Estelle (Weinert) C. AB magna cum laude, Harvard U., 1954; JD, U. Pa., 1957. Bar: Pa. 1958, U.S. Dist. Ct. (ea. dist.) Pa., 1958, U.S. Supreme Ct., 1963. Assoc. Norris, Lex, Hart & Ross, Phila., 1957-62; ptnr. Cancelmo & McLaughlin, Phila., 1962-65; sole practice Phila., 1965—; lectr. Am. History St. Joseph's U., Phila., 1963-70. Mem. ABA, Pa. Bar Assn., Phila. Bar Assn., Phila. Estate Planning Council, Justinian Soc., Hasty Pudding Inst. 1770. Republican. Roman Catholic. Clubs: Rittenhouse, (sec. 1979-85), Union League, Phila.; DU (Cambrdige, Mass.); Harvard (N.Y.C.). Probate, Estate taxation, Personal income taxation. Home: 1901 Walnut St Philadelphia PA 19103 Office: 2500 Two Mellon Bank Ctr Philadelphia PA 19102

CANCIO, PABLO RAMÓN, lawyer; b. San Sebastian, P.R., Mar. 22, 1931; s. Jose Luis and Narcisa Maria (Rodriguez) C.; m. Haydé e E. Reichard, July 17, 1960; children—Pablo G., Juan Carlos. B.A., U. P.R., 1952; J.D., Mich. U., 1955; postgrad. Middlebury U., 1975. Bar: P.R., 1956, U.S. dist. ct. P.R., 1956. Assoc. firm Brown, Newsom & Cordova, San Juan, 1956-60; partner charge of litigation McConnell, Valdes & Kelley, San Juan, 1960-67; partner Cancio & Cancio, Aguadilla, P.R., 1967—; hon. magistrate Commonwealth of P.R., 1976-80; mem. com. on rules of evidence Judicial Conf. P.R., 1973-79; bd. bar examiners P.R., 1965-66. Mem. Aguadilla Indsl. Com., 1971-78, Ramey Community Council, 1970-75; founder Corporacion pro Defensa Ambiental del Oeste; dir. Concilio de Organizaciones Civicas de Aguadilla, 1982; mem. adv. council Aguadilla Regional Coll., U. P.R., 1984—; trustee U. P.R. Sch. of Law Trust, 1986—. Recipient awards, Ramey Community Council, 1973, Mcpl. Govt. Aguadilla, 1981, Concilio de Organizaciones Civicas, 1981. Mem. Colegio de Abogados de P.R., Am. Coll. Trial Lawyers, P.R. Bar Assn. (bd. govs. 1959-61, 72-74, pres. character of applicants to the bar 1983—), Delta Theta Phi. Roman Catholic. Clubs: Lions, Bankers. State civil litigation, Personal injury, Probate.

CANDLAND, D. STUART, lawyer; b. Madison, Wis., Sept. 6, 1942; s. Don Charles and Dorothy Jane (Nelson) C.; m. Evelyn McComber, Dec. 3, 1982; children: Ashley, Tara Lynn. BA with honors, Brigham Young U., 1967; JD, U. Calif., Berkeley, 1970. Bar: Calif. 1971, U.S. Dist. Ct. (no. dist.) Calif. 1971, U.S. Ct. Appeals (9th cir.) 1971. Dep. atty. gen. State of Calif., San Francisco, 1970-73; dep. dist. atty. Solano County Dist. Atty.'s Office, Fairfield, Calif., 1973-75; assoc. Law Offices of M. Craddick, Walnut Creek, Calif., 1976-78; ptnr. Craddick, Candland & Conti, Alamo, Calif., 1979—; asst. prof. law Armstrong Sch. Law, Berkeley, 1971-77. Mem. Assn. Def. Counsel, Contra Costa County Bar Assn. State civil litigation, Federal civil litigation, Insurance. Office: Craddick Candland & Conti 915 San Ramon Valley Blvd Danville CA 94526

CANDLER, JOHN SLAUGHTER, II, lawyer; b. Atlanta, Nov. 30, 1908; s. Asa Warren and Harriet Lee (West) C.; m. Dorothy Bruce Warthen, June 13, 1933; children: Dorothy Warthen (Mrs. Joseph W. Hamilton, Jr.), John Slaughter, Jr. A.B. magna cum laude, U. Ga., 1929; J.D., Emory U., 1931. Bar: Ga. bar 1931. Sole practice Atlanta, 1931—; ptnr. Candler, Cox & Andrews and predecessor firms, Atlanta, 1931—; dep. asst. atty. gen. Ga. Atty. Gen.'s Office, 1951-68; gen. counsel, sec., dir. The D.M. Weatherly Co.; also dir., officer others; chmn. sect. fiduciary law State Bar Ga., 1964-65. Trustee Ga. Student Ednl. Fund, 1950—; trustee Kappa Alpha Scholarship Fund, 1955-86, pres., 1970-72; trustee Lovett Sch., 1953-59; mem. USO Council Greater Atlanta, 1969—, pres., 1974-75; cathedral chpt. vestry Episc. Ch., 1953-56, sr. warden, 1955, cathedral trustee, 1957-67, lay reader, 1971—. Served to col. USAR, 1941-46. Decorated Army Commendation Ribbon. Fellow Am. Coll. Probate Counsel (bd. regents 1968-74), Ga. Bar Found., Internat. Acad. Law and Sci.; mem. ABA, Atlanta Bar Assn., Lawyers Club Atlanta, Nat. Tax Assn.-Tax Inst. Am. (adv. council Tax Inst. Am. 1969-72), Atlanta Estate Planning Council (pres. 1963-64), Am. Legion (post comdr. 1949-50), Res. Officers Assn. U.S. (state pres. 1946), Am. Judicature Soc., Newcomen Soc., Internat. Platform Assn., Mil. Order World Wars, English Speaking Union, U.S. Power Squadrons, Phi Beta Kappa, Phi Kappa Phi, Phi Delta Phi, Kappa Alpha Order, Sigma Delta Chi. Clubs: Atlanta Touchdown, Piedmont Driving, Capital City, Commerce, Peachtree Racket, Ft. McPherson Officers, Oglethorpe (Savannah), Army-Navy (Washington). Lodges: Kiwanis, Masons. Probate, General corporate, Estate taxation. Home: 413 Manor Ridge Dr NW Atlanta GA 30305 Office: Candler Cox & Andrews 610 Eight Piedmont Ctr Atlanta GA 30305

CANDRIS, LAURA A., lawyer; b. Frankfort, Ky., Apr. 5, 1955; d. Charles M. and Dorothy (King) Sutton; m. Aris S. Candris, Dec. 22, 1974. BA with distinction, Transylvania Coll., 1975; postgrad., U. Fla., 1977-78; JD, U. Pitts., 1978. Bar: Fla. 1978, U.S. Dist. Ct. (mid. dist.) Fla. 1978, U.S. Ct. Appeals (4th and 5th cirs.) 1980, Pa. 1981, U.S. Dist. Ct. (we. dist.) Pa. 1982, U.S. Ct. Appeals (3d cir.) 1983. Assoc. Coffman, Coleman, Andrews & Grogan, Jacksonville, Fla., 1978-80, Manion, Alder & Cohen, Pitts., 1981-85; assoc. Eckert, Seamans, Cherin & Mellott, Pitts., 1985-86, ptnr., 1987—; counsel Nat. Assn. of Women in Constrn. (chpt. 161), Pitts., 1985—. Council mem. O'Hara Twp., Allegheny, Pa., 1986—. Named one of Outstanding Young Women of Am., 1984; named Ky. Col., 1974; Nat. Merit Found. scholar, 1973. Mem. ABA (labor and litigation sects.), Fla. Bar Assn., Pa. Bar Assn. (labor sect.), Allegheny County Bar Assn. (labor sect.), Soc. Hosp. Attys. Western Pa., Nat. Health Lawyers Assn. Republican. Avocations: traveling, bicycling, gardening, reading. Labor, Employment law and contracts, wrongful discharge, Pension, profit-sharing, and employee benefits. Office: Eckert Seamans Cherin & Mellott 600 Grant St 42d Floor Pittsburgh PA 15219

CANE, MARILYN BLUMBERG, lawyer, educator; b. Rockville Center, N.Y., Feb. 26, 1949; d. Howard Godfrey and Lily Ruth (Goldberg) B.; m. Edward Michael Cane, Dec. 24, 1970; children—Daniel Eric, Jonathan Marc Howard. B.A. magna cum laude, Cornell U., 1971; J.D. cum laude, Boston Coll., 1974. Bar: N.Y. 1975, U.S. Dist. Ct. (so. dist.) N.Y. 1975, U.S. Ct. Appeals (2d cir.) 1976, Conn. 1977, Fla. 1981. With Reavis & McGrath, N.Y.C., 1974-76, Badger, Fisher & Assocs., Greenwich, Conn., 1977-80; counsel Corp Components. div. Gen. Electric Co., Fairfield, Conn., 1980-81; with Gunster, Yoakley & Assocs., Palm Beach, Fla., 1981-83; asst. prof. law Nova U., Fort Lauderdale, Fla., 1983-85, assoc. prof. law, 1985—. Contbr. articles to profl. jours. Dir. Jewish Community Day Sch. Palm Beach County, West Palm Beach, Fla., 1983—; mem. adv. com. Conn. Banking Commn., Hartford, 1979-81. Woodrow Wilson fellow designate, 1971. Mem. ABA, Fla. Bar Assn., Order of Coif. Securities, General corporate, Banking. Home: 398 Knotty Wood Ln West Palm Beach FL 33414 Office: Nova Univ Law Ctr 3100 SW 9th Ave Fort Lauderdale FL 33315

CANEL, JAMES HARRISON, lawyer; b. Chgo., Feb. 26, 1944; s. David A. and Pearl (Litowich) C.; m. Judith Marilyn Forman, July 31, 1966; children: Stacey Erin, Jason Joshua, Evan Douglas. Student, Washington U., 1963-65; JD, DePaul U., 1968. Bar: Ill. 1968, U.S. Dist. Ct. (no. dist.) Ill. 1969, U.S. Ct. Appeals (7th cir.) 1973, U.S. Supreme Ct. 1974. Assoc. Canel & Canel, Chgo., 1968-70, ptnr., 1970-75; sole practice Chgo., 1975-78; pres. James H. Canel Ltd., Chgo., 1978—. Mem. ABA, Assn. Trial Lawyers Am., Am. Coll. Legal Medicine (assoc. in law), Chgo. Bar Assn. (chmn. med. legal relations com. 1980-81), Ill. Bar Assn. (ho. of dels. 1978-81), Ill. Trial Lawyers (bd. mgrs. 1985—), Soc. Trial Lawyers. Jewish. Clubs: Chgo. Athletic, Macatawa Yacht. Personal injury, State civil litigation, Federal civil litigation. Office: James H Canel Ltd 20 N Clark Chicago IL 60602

CANERDAY, JON JACKSON, lawyer; b. Russellville, Ark., Mar. 10, 1956; s. Don B. Canerday and Shirley A. (Jackson) Pickle; 1 child, Jon J. Jr. BS in Acctg., Ark. Tech. U., 1978; JD, U. Ark., 1981. Bar: Ark. 1981, U.S. Ct. Mil. Appeals 1981, U.S. Dist. Ct. (we. dist.) Okla. 1983. Commd. JAGC, U.S. Army, 1981, advanced through grades to capt., present; prosecutor JAGC, U.S. Army, Ft. Sill, Okla., 1981-86, spl. asst. U.S. atty., 1983-86; chief adminstrv. law JAGC, U.S. Army, Camp Casey, Republic of Korea, 1986—. Mem. Ark. Bar Assn., Phi Alpha Delta. Mem. Ch. of Christ. Avocations: running, tennis, golf. Administrative and regulatory, Criminal. Home: 202 Skyhill Rd #4 Alexandria VA 22314 Office: HQDA Office of Judge Adv Gen Criminal Law Div (DAJA-CL) Pentagon Washington DC 22310-2200

CANFIELD, PETER CRANE, lawyer; b. Bryn Mawr, Pa., Mar. 6, 1954. BA, Amherst Coll., 1976; JD, Yale U., 1979. Bar: Calif. 1980, U.S. Dist. Ct. (mid. dist.) Ala. 1980, U.S. Ct. Appeals (5th cir.) 1980, U.S. Ct. Appeals (11th cir.) 1981, Ala. 1982, U.S. Ct. Appeals (1st and 9th cirs.) 1982, Wis. 1985, U.S. Dist. Ct. (we. dist.) Wis. 1985, U.S. Ct. Appeals (7th cir.) 1985. Law clk. to presiding justice U.S. Ct. Appeals (5th cir.), Montgomery, Ala., 1979-80; law clk. to Hon. Frank M. Johnson Jr. U.S. Dist. Ct. (mid. dist.) Ala., Montgomery, 1980-81; atty. civil rights div. Dept. Justice, Washington, 1981-83; spl. asst. atty. U.S. Atty.'s office, Washington, 1982-83; dep. dist. atty. State of Ala., Montgomery, 1983-84; assoc. Ross & Stevens, S.C., Madison, Wis., 1985-86, ptnr., 1986; assoc. Dow, Lohnes & Albertson, Atlanta, 1986—; adj. prof. Jones Law Inst., Montgomery, 1984. Mem. ABA, Am. Trial Lawyers Assn., Phi Beta Kappa. Federal civil litigation, Libel, Civil rights. Office: Dow Lohnes & Albertson 1 Ravinia Dr Suite 1300 Atlanta GA 30346

CANGANELLI, MICHAEL ANTONIO, lawyer, emergency management program specialist; b. Indpls., Dec. 1, 1951; s. Vincent G. and Beverly Janice (Neal) C.; m. Debra Ellen Krulik, Feb. 9, 1982; children—William, Joseph, Michael, Anastasia, Eli, Robert, Alexandra. B.A., Ind. U.-Bloomington, 1974; J.D., Ill. Inst. Tech./Chgo.-Kent Coll., 1978. Bar: Ill. 1982, U.S. Ct. Appeals (7th cir.) 1982, U.S. Dist. Ct. (no. dist.) Ill. 1982, U.S. Dist. Ct. (ea. dist.) Wis. 1986, U.S. Dist. Ct. (no. dist.) Ind. 1986. With Fed. Emergency Mgmt. Agy., Chgo., 1981—; sole practice, Chgo., 1982—; assoc. Klimek & Richiardi, Ltd., Chgo., 1984—. Recipient Founders' Day Acad. Achievement award Ind. U., 1974, Outstanding Performance award, 1983, Quality Step Increase award, 1987, Fed. Emergency Mgmt. Agy.; named one of nominees for Congrl. Excalibur award, 1984; Gladys Isaacs Meml. scholar, 1970. Mem. Am. Fedn. Govt. Employees (former chief steward), Kent Coll. Law Alumni Assn., Ind. U. Coll. Arts and Scis Alumni Assn., Justinian Soc. Lawyers, Nat. Geographic Soc., 7th Cir. Bar Assn. Democrat. Roman Catholic. Club: Sierra. Lodge: K.C. General practice. Home: 1401 119th St Apt F Whiting IN 46394-1754 Office: PO Box 7510 Chicago IL 60680-7510

CANGELOSI, CARL J., lawyer; b. Anniston, Ala., Oct. 25, 1942; s. Neri and Elena (Beltramo) C.; m. Mary P. Ralston, Aug. 1, 1964 (div. 1982); children: Lisa, Craig; m. Margaret Gail Heagen, Mar. 6, 1983. Georgetown U., 1964, Boston Coll., 1967. Bar: D.C. Atty. FCC, Washington, 1967-71; counsel RCA Globcom, Washington, 1971-75; gen. atty. RCA Globcom, N.Y.C., 1975-76; v.p., gen. counsel RCA Americom, Princeton, N.J., 1976—; speaker various orgns. Author: Teleports and The Intelligent City, 1985, Electronic Communications Handbook, 1985. Mem. Am. Corp. Counsel Assn., Satellite Law Compendium (edit. adv. bd. 1985). Roman Catholic. Avocations: reading, scuba diving, cross-country skiing. Administrative and regulatory, General corporate. Office: RCA Am Communications Four Research Way Princeton NJ 08540-6684

CANNON, BENJAMIN WINTON, lawyer, business executive; b. Muncie, Ind., Sept. 17, 1944; s. Zane William and Gloria Gene (Phillips) C.; B.A., Western Mich. U., 1965; postgrad. Notre Dame Law Sch., 1966-67; J.D., Wayne State U., 1969; M.B.A., Mich. State U., 1979; m. Diane Joan Koenig, June 24, 1967; children—Matthew Zane, Christine Elizabeth, Leslie Joan, Todd Graham. Admitted to Mich. bar, 1970; law clk. labor relations staff Gen. Motors Corp., Detroit, 1966-69; tax atty. Plante & Moran, C.P.A.s, Southfield, Mich., 1969-71; atty. Burroughs Corp., Detroit, 1971-72; assoc. Nine and Maister, Attys., Bloomfield Hills, Mich., 1972-73; atty. Chrysler Fin. Corp., Troy, Mich., 1973-78, sr. atty., 1978-80; corp. counsel CF Industries Inc., Long Grove, Ill., 1980-81; asst. gen. counsel, asst. sec. COMDISCO, Inc., Rosemont, Ill., 1981-82, asst. v.p. and gen. mgr. internat., 1983-86, pres. COMDISCO Internat. Sales Corp., 1983-86; asst. v.p., dir. capital equipment fin., 1987—; asst. sec., gen. counsel Microtron, Inc., Barrington, Ill.; instr. law Oakland U., Rochester, Mich., 1980. Mem. ABA, Mich. Bar Assn., Ill. Bar Assn., Gray's Inn Legal Soc., Omicron Delta Kappa, Kappa Delta Pi. Republican. Presbyterian. Computer, General corporate, Private international. Home: 21265 N Pheasant Trail Barrington IL 60010 Office: 6400 Shafer Ct Rosemont IL 60018

CANNON, DANIEL WILLARD, lawyer; b. Pitts., Sept. 3, 1920; s. Edgar Carl and Violet Jessie (Burke) C.; m. Ann Marshall Price, Sept. 30, 1942; children—Susan Melchior, David, Judith Lillie, Barbara, Ann Finch. A.B., U. Pitts., 1941, J.D., 1968. Bar: Pa. 1948, D.C. 1952, U.S. Supreme Ct. 1952. Atty., U.S. Steel Corp., Pitts., 1947-50; sec., gen. counsel Bituminous Coal Operators Assn., Washington, 1951-58; dir. Indsl. Devel. and Natural Resources, NAM, N.Y.C., 1958-74, dir. environ. affairs, Washington, 1974-84, dir. program devel., 1984—; lectr. in field. Served to 1st lt. USAAF, 1942-46. Recipient Moot Ct. award, U. Pitts. Law Sch., 1947; Award of Appreciation, Water Quality Research Council, 1974. Mem. ABA, Fed. Bar Assn., Bar Assn. D.C., Allegheny County Bar Assn., Air Pollution Control Assn., Water Pollution Control Fedn., Order of the Coif. Republican. Episcopalian. Clubs: Univ., Army and Navy, Pa. Soc., Masons. Editorial adv. bd. Indsl. Wastes Mag., Air Quality Control, 1975; editor, Hazardous Waste Mgmt. Under RCRA: A Primer for Small Business, 1980; A Pollution Tax Won't Help Control Pollution, 1977; National Strength and the National Environmental Policy Act, 1972; Staying Out of Trouble: What You Should Know About the New Hazardous Waste Law, 1985; Preparing for Emergency Planning, 1987. Environment, Administrative and regulatory, Probate. Home: 637 E Capitol St SE Washington DC 20003 Office: 1331 Pennsylvania Ave NW Suite 1500 N Washington DC 20004-1703

CANNON, THOMAS ROBERTS, lawyer; b. Durham, N.C., May 22, 1940; s. Edward Lee and Elizabeth Hendren (Roberts) C.; m. Martha Craig White, Feb. 19, 1966; children: Caroline Craig, Thomas Roberts Jr. AB, U. N.C., 1962, JD, 1965; postgrad., U. Va., 1962-63. Bar: N.C. 1965, U.S. Dist. Ct. (we. dist.) N.C. 1969. Ptnr. Hamel, Helms, Cannon, Hamel & Pearce P.A., Charlotte, N.C., 1981—. Served with USNR, 1968—. Mem. ABA, Am. Trial Lawyers Assn., N.C. Bar Assn. (chmn. family law sect. 1982-83), N.C. Trial Lawyers Assn. Presbyterian. Clubs: Charlotte Country, Charlotte City, Tower. Family and matrimonial, State civil litigation. Home: 2611 Beretania Circle Charlotte NC 28211 Office: Hamel Helms et al 2300 First Union Plaza Charlotte NC 28282

CANO, MARIO STEPHEN, lawyer; b. Miami, Fla., Sept. 2, 1953; s. Mario Arturo Cano and Irene H. Moreno; m. Johanna Marie Van Rossum, Oct. 13, 1979. AA, Miami Dade Jr. Coll., 1973; BA, Fla. Internat. U., 1975; JD, U. Santa Clara, 1978. Bar: Fla. 1979, U.S. Dist. Ct. (so. dist.) Fla. 1979, U.S. Ct. Claims 1979, U.S. Tax Ct. 1979, U.S. Ct. Mil. Appeals 1979, U.S. Ct. Appeals (9th cir.) 1979, U.S. Dist. Ct. (no. and mid. dists.) Fla. 1980, U.S. Dist. Ct. (no. dist.) Calif. 1980, U.S. Ct. Appeals (3d cir.) 1980, U.S. Ct. Internat. Trade 1981, U.S. Ct. Appeals (11th cir.) 1981, U.S. Ct. Appeals (6th and 10th cirs.) 1983, U.S. Supreme Ct. 1983, Nebr. 1984, U.S. Dist. Ct. Nebr. 1984, U.S. Dist. Ct. Okla. 1984, U.S. Dist. Ct. Hawaii 1984, U.S. Ct. Appeals (2d, 4th, 5th, 7th 8th and D.C. cirs.) 1984, N.Y. 1985, U.S. Dist. Ct. (no., we., ea. and so. dists.) N.Y. 1985, U.S. Ct. Appeals (1st cir.) 1987. Assoc. Orta and Assocs., Miami, 1979-80, Law Office of J. Ramirez, Coral Gables, Fla., 1980—, Law Office of I.G. Lichter, Miami, 1980-82, Gelb & Spatz, Miami, 1982; sole practice Coral Gables, 1982—. Mem. ABA, Coral Gables Bar Assn., Cuban Am. Bar Assn., InterAm. Bar Assn., Nat. Assn. Criminal Def. Lawyers, Alliance Francaise de Miami. Democrat. Criminal, Immigration, naturalization, and customs, Family and matrimonial. Office: 2121 Ponce de Leon Blvd Suite 1035 Coral Gables FL 33134-5218

CANON, JACK ARTHUR, lawyer; b. Quincy, Ill., May 7, 1949; s. Max A. and Clara Daphine (Crocker) C.; m. Pegeen Anne Seger, June 12, 1971; 1 child, Patrick. BS in Acctg., Quincy Coll., 1971; JD, U. Tulsa, 1976. Bar: Okla. 1977, U.S. Dist. Ct. (no. dist.) Okla. 1977. Assoc. Dyer, Powers & Marsh, Tulsa, 1976-82; atty. Terra Resources, Inc., Tulsa, 1982-83; sr. atty. Samson Resources Co., Tulsa, 1983-86, v.p., gen. counsel, 1986—; mcpl. judge Collinsville, Okla., 1980-81. Webelos leader Boy Scouts Am., Tulsa, 1985-86. Served to comdr. USNR. Mem. ABA, Okla. Bar Assn., Tulsa County Bar Assn. General corporate, Oil and gas leasing. Office: Samson Resources Co Two W Second St Tulsa OK 74103

CANONI, JOHN DAVID, lawyer; b. Newton, Mass., May 11, 1939; s. John Joseph and Olga Elizabeth (Mangini) C.; m. Katherine Ariadna Bryant, Aug. 18, 1962; children: Lisa Ann, Peter Christopher, John Charles, Scott Francis. BA, Amherst Coll., 1960; LLB, Yale U., 1963. Bar: N.Y. 1964, U.S. Ct. Appeals (2d cir.) 1966, U.S. Ct. Appeals (3d cir.) 1967, U.S. Ct. Appeals (4th cir.) 1968, U.S. Ct. Appeals (1st cir.) 1969, U.S. Supreme Ct. 1971, U.S. Ct. Appeals (7th cir.) 1972. Assoc. Townley & Updike, N.Y.C., 1963-71, ptnr., 1971—; mem. Lt. Gov.'s Task Force on Plant Closings, N.Y., 1984-85. Mem. N.Y. State Bar Assn. (chmn. labor & employment law sect. 1983-84). Republican. Roman Catholic. Club: Yale (N.Y.C.). Labor, Pension, profit-sharing, and employee benefits. Home: 6 Legget Rd Bronxville NY 10708 Office: Townley & Updike 405 Lexington Ave New York NY 10174

CANOVA, LEO PHILLIP, JR., lawyer; b. Plaquemine, La., Mar. 24, 1954; s. Leo Phillip and Dorothy Ann (Daigle) C.; m. Rita Lynn D'Albor, Aug. 6, 1976; children: Abbie Lynn, Phillip Lee. BA, La. State U., 1976; JD, Loyola U., New Orleans, 1979. Bar: La. 1979, U.S. Dist. Ct. La. 1979, U.S. Ct. Appeals (5th cir.) 1979. Assoc. Freeman & Pendley Ltd., Plaquemine, 1979-82; ptnr. Freeman, Pendley & Canova Ltd., Plaquemine, 1983-84; sole practice Plaquemine, 1984—; atty., prosecutor City of Plaquemine, 1985—. Bd. dirs. Gulf Coast Teaching Family Services, Inc., New Orleans, 1984—. Democrat. Roman Catholic. State civil litigation, Federal civil litigation, Criminal.

CANTER, BRAM D. E., lawyer; b. Louisville, July 25, 1951; s. Nathan Canter and Bette Lou (Miller) Fernandez; m. Susan Wheatley, Jan. 20, 1970 (div. Nov. 1977); 1 child: Brett. BA summa cum laude, U. South Fla., 1974; JD, U. Fla., 1977; LLM in Environ. Law, George Washington U., 1981 summa cum laude. Bar: Fla. 1978, U.S. Ct. Appeals (5th and 11th cirs.) 1982. Legal research asst. U. Fla. Coll. Law, Gainesville, 1976-77; dir. Eastern Water Law Ctr., U. Fla. Sch. Law, Gainesville, 1978-80; asst. gen. counsel Fla. Dept. Environ. Regulation, Tallahassee, 1981-84; assoc. atty. Gunster, Yoakley, Criser and Stewart P.A., West Palm Beach, Fla., 1984—. Co-author: Florida Water Law, 1980; contbr. articles to profl. jours. Served with U.S. Army, 1971-72. Mem. ABA (natural resources sect.), Fla. Bar. Assn. (environ. law sect.), Palm Beach County Bar Assn., Palm Beach Planning Congress. Avocations: camping, backpacking, guitar. Environment, Administrative and regulatory, Land use and planning. Home: 437 Chilian Ave Palm Beach FL 33480 Office: Gunster Yoakley Criser & Stewart 777 S Flagler Dr Suite 500 West Palm Beach FL 33401

CANTILO, PATRICK HERRERA, lawyer; b. Santiago, Chile, Mar. 19, 1954; came to U.S., 1965; s. Luis M. and Yvonne (Cantilo) Herrera-Cantilo; m. Kathryn Gail Goltra, June 18, 1977; 1 child, Michael. BA, U. Tex., 1977, JD, 1980. Bar: Tex. 1980, U.S. Dist. Ct. (we. dist.) Tex. 1983. Counsel to receiver Tex. Bd. Ins., Austin, 1980-83; assoc. Davis & Davis P.C., Austin, 1983-85; ptnr. Davis, Cantilo, Welch & Ewbank, Austin, 1985-86; of counsel Freytag, Perry, LaForce, Rubinstein & Teofan, Austin, 1986-87, ptnr., 1987—. Mem. ABA (litigation sect.), Tex. Bar Assn. (litigation sect.), Travis County Bar Assn. (litigation sect.), Austin Young Lawyers Assn., Nat. Assn. Ins. Commrs. (liquidators task force 1982-83, adv. com. 1985—, chmn. fin. subcom., adv. com. health maintenance orgn. 1986). Democrat. Roman Catholic. State civil litigation, Insurance, Administrative and regulatory. Home: 7213 Hartnell Austin TX 78723 Office: Freytag Perry LaForce Rubinstein & Teofan 100 Congress Suite 900 Austin TX 78701

CANTOR, ALENA, lawyer; b. Prague, Czechoslovakia, June 13, 1927; d. Kamil and Sona Kleiner; m. Irwin Cantor, Dec. 19, 1948; children: Michael Lee, Garry Paul, Kim Abbie. BA, U. Ill., 1949; JD, U. Ariz., 1952. Bar: Ariz. 1952, U.S. Dist. Ct. Ariz. 1962, U.S. Supreme Ct. 1966, U.S. Tax Ct. 1975, U.S. Ct. Appeals (9th cir.) 1979. Ptnr. Hash, Cantor & Tomanek, Phoenix, 1952—. Mem. Ariz. Bar Assn., Maricopa County Bar Assn. Jewish. Family and matrimonial, Probate, General practice. Home: 1808 Palmcroft Way NW Phoenix AZ 85007 Office: Hash Cantor & Tomanek 111 W Monroe Suite 1200 Phoenix AZ 85003

CANTOR, LOUIS, lawyer; b. Atlantic City, N.J., Sept. 17, 1921; s. Joseph B. and Miryl (Ginsberg) C.; m. Olga Yovu, Sept. 12, 1947; children—Diana Louise Dorman, David Joseph. B.S. in Social Scis., CCNY, 1942; J.D., Columbia U., 1949. Bar: N.Y. 1949, D.C. 1967, U.S. Dist. Ct. (so. and ea. dists.) N.Y. 1951. Assoc. Sol A. Herzog, N.Y.C., 1949-53, Max E. Greenberg, N.Y.C., 1953-67; sr. ptnr. Greenberg, Cantor & Reiss, N.Y.C., 1968—; bd. dirs. CCNY Alumni Fund, N.Y.C., 1980—; bd. dirs., v.p. Am. Red Mogen David for Israel, N.Y.C., 1980—. Served to cpl. U.S. Army, 1943-46, CBI. Mem. N.Y. County Lawyers Assn., N.Y. State Bar Assn., ABA. Jewish. Club: Robert F. Wagner, Sr. Democratic (pres. 1959-62). Construction, Government contracts and claims, Contracts commercial. Office: Greenberg Cantor & Reiss 100 Church St New York NY 10007

CANTOR, SAMUEL C., lawyer; b. Phila., Mar. 11, 1919; s. Joseph and Miryl (Ginzberg) C.; m. Dorothy Van Brink, Apr. 9, 1943; children: Judith Ann Stone, Barbara Ann Palm. B.S.S., CCNY, 1940; J.D., Columbia, 1943. Bar: N.Y. 1943, U.S. Dist. Ct. (so. and ea. dists.) N.Y. 1951, U.S. Supreme Ct 1969, D.C. 1971. Asst. dist. atty. N.Y.C., 1943-48; legislative counsel N.Y. State Senate; counsel N.Y.C. Affairs Com. N.Y. State Senate, 1949-59; mem. firm Newcomb, Woolsey & Cantor, Newcomb & Cantor, N.Y.C., 1951-59; 1st dep. supt. ins. State of N.Y., 1959-64, acting supt. ins., 1963-64; 2d v.p., gen. solicitor Mut. Life Ins. Co. N.Y., 1964-66, v.p., gen. counsel, 1967-72, sr. v.p., gen. counsel, 1973-74, sr. v.p. law and external affairs, 1974-75, sr. v.p. law and corporate affairs, 1975-78, exec. v.p. law and corp. affairs, 1978-84; counsel Rogers & Wells, 1984—; dir. Mut. Life Ins. Co N.Y., Mony Reins. Corp., Monyco, Inc., Key Resources, Inc., Mony Advisors, Inc., Mony Sales, Inc.; chmn. exec. com. N.Y. Life Ins. Guaranty Corp., 1974-84; Mem. spl. com. on ins. holding holding cos. N.Y. Supt. Ins., 1967, N.Y. State select com. pub. employee pensions, 1973. Contbr. to various legal and ins. publs. Fellow Am. Bar Found.; mem. Ins. Fedn. N.Y. (pres. 1967-68), Am. Bar Assn., N.Y. State Bar Assn., Am. Life Conv. (v.p. N.Y. State 1965-70), Am. Council Life Ins. (chmn. legal sect. 1977, chmn. legis. com. 1977-78, N.Y. State v.p. 1977-84), Health Ins. Assn. Am. (chmn. govt. relations com. 1975, chmn. health care com. N.Y. State 1974-80), Assn. Life Ins. Counsel (dir.), Am. Judicature Soc., Bar Assn. City N.Y., N.Y. Law Inst., Nat., N.Y. State dist. attys. assns., Union Internationale des Avocats, Columbia Law Sch. Alumni Assn. (dir.). Clubs: Mason. (N.Y.C.), University (N.Y.C.); Metropolitan, University (Washington); Fort Orange (Albany, N.Y.); Sawgrass Country, Marsh Landing, Ponte Vedra (Fla.); La Costa Country (Carlsbad, Calif.); Confrérie des Chevaliers du Tastevin; Fairview Country (Greenwich, Conn.); Royal Dornoch (Scotland) Golf. Administrative and regulatory, General corporate. Home: Audubon Ln Greenwich CT 06830 Office: c/o Rogers & Wells 200 Park Ave New York NY 10166

CANTWELL, ROBERT, consumer products mfg. co. exec.; b. Buffalo, Sept. 12, 1931; s. Thomas and Helen (Robinson) C.; m. Barbara Hurlbert, Oct. 19, 1963; children—Robert, Helen Virginia, Sara Elizabeth. A.B., Cornell U., 1953, J.D., 1956; LL.M., N.Y. U., 1959. Bar: N.Y. State bar 1956. Asso. firm Jaeckle, Fleischmann & Mugel (and predecessor firm), Buffalo, 1956-62; mem. legal dept. Colgate-Palmolive Co., N.Y.C., 1962-68, London, dep. gen. counsel, 1972-73; v.p., gen. counsel Colgate-Palmolive Co., 1973-86, sec., 1974-86; v.p., sec., gen. counsel Roblin Industries, Inc., Buffalo, 1968-72; ptnr. Serchuk, Wolfe and Zelermyer, White Plains, N.Y., 1986—. Mem. Am.,N.Y. State, Erie County bar assns., Assn. Bar City N.Y., Am. Soc. Corp. Secs., Brit. Inst. Internat. and Comparative Law. Clubs: Metropolitan (N.Y.); Saturn (Buffalo); Belle Haven, Exchange (Greenwich, Conn.). General corporate, Securities, Private international. Home: 5 Meadow Dr Greenwich CT 06830 Office: 235 Main St White Plains NY 10601

CAPE, BILLIE JEAN, lawyer; b. Okemah, Okla., Oct. 26, 1931; d. Reuben Robert Cape and Iva Mae (Taylor) Cape Birt; m. Richard K. Abrahams (div.). B.Music, U. Okla., 1953; LL.B., Oklahoma City U., 1958; LL.M., NYU, 1963. Bar: Okla. 1958, N.Y. 1965. Law clk. U.S. Dist. Ct. Oklahoma City, 1958-62; atty. Port Authority of N.Y. and N.J., N.Y.C., 1964-67; asst. counsel N.Y. State Atomic and Space Devel. Authority, N.Y.C., 1969-72; asst. counsel Met. Transp. Authority, N.Y.C., 1973-81; dep. gen. counsel, 1981-84; asst. chief contract div. Port Authority of N.Y. and N.J., N.Y.C., 1984—. Mem. ABA. Democrat. Presbyterian. General corporate, Government contracts and claims, Labor. Office: Port Authority NY and NJ One World Trade Ctr New York NY 10048

CAPECELATRO, MARK JOHN, lawyer; b. New Haven, June 2, 1948; s. Ralph Ettore and Elaine (Scialla) C.; m. Jane Beals, June 19, 1971; children: Christopher Beals, Kate Rowley, Jonathan Mark. BA, Colgate U., 1970; JD, U. Conn., 1973. Bar: Conn. 1973. Assoc. Ells, Quinlan, Eddy & Robinson, Canaan, Conn., 1973-77; ptnr. Ells, Quinlan & Robinson, Canaan, 1977—; bd. of advisors Canaan Nat. Bank, 1982—; mortgage counsel People's Bank, Canaan and Hartford, Conn., 1983—; bd. of trustees Sharon (Conn.) Hosp., 1984—. Bd. dirs. Housatonic Homemaker Health Aide, West Cornwall, Conn., 1977-80, Housatonic Day Care Ctr., Inc., Lakeville, Conn., 1981—, Salisbury Pub. Health Nursing, Lakeville, 1983-85, Salisbury Winter Sports Assn., 1983—. Mem. ABA, Conn. Bar Assn., Litchfield County Bar Assn., Assn. Trial Lawyers Am., Conn. Assn. Trial Lawyers, Nat. Assn. Criminal Def. Lawyers. Republican. Avocations: gardening, fishing. General practice, Probate, Real property. Home: Belgo Rd Box 73A Lakeville CT 06039 Office: Ells Quinlan & Robinson Main St Canaan CT 06018

CAPEL, GUY B., lawyer, banker; b. Brussels, Belgium, Mar. 26, 1938; came to U.S., 1941; s. Maurice and Lola (Low) C.; m. Anna J. Krakowski, July 15, 1974; 1 child, Abigale Julia. A.B., Columbia U., 1962, J.D., 1964. Bar: N.Y. 1965, Vt. 1987. Assoc. Milbank Tweed, Hadley & McCloy, N.Y.C., 1969-71; assoc. gen. counsel N.Y. State Banking Dept., N.Y.C., 1971-74; v.p., gen. counsel Savs. Banks Assn. of N.Y. State, N.Y.C., 1974-77; sr. v.p., gen. counsel Apple Bank, N.Y.C., 1977-86; counsel Downs, Rachlin and Martin, Burlington, Vt., 1986—; chmn. Banking Roundtable, Vail, Colo., 1983—; bd. dirs. N.Y. League for Hard of Hearing, 1982—. Mem. ABA, Vt. Bar Assn. Clubs: Yale (N.Y.); Burlington Tennis. Avocations: music, tennis; skiing. Banking, Contracts commercial, General corporate. Office: Downs Rachlin and Martin 100 Dorset St Burlington VT 05402

CAPELL, WALTER RICHARD, lawyer; b. Bklyn., Feb. 3, 1949; s. Moses and Ruth (Reich) C.; m. Elyse M. Gordon, July 5, 1970; children: Jesse, Adam, Marissa. BA, SUNY, Buffalo; JD, N.Y Law Sch. bar: N.Y. 1974, U.S. Dist. Ct. (we. dist) N.Y. 1975. Ptnr. Culley, Marks, Corbett, Tanenbaum, Leifsteck & Potter, Rochester, N.Y., 1975—; adj. faculty Rochester Inst. Tech., 1977-84. Mem. ABA, N.Y. State Bar Assn., Monroe County Bar Assn. Democrat. Jewish. Bankruptcy, Family and matrimonial, General corporate. Office: Culley Marks et al 36 W Main St Rochester NY 14614

CAPENER, COLE R., lawyer, consultant; b. Seattle, Oct. 28, 1955; s. Ronald LeGrand Capener and Rosemary (Pantone) Reed. BA in Polit. Sci. magna cum laude, U. Utah, 1978; JD with honors, George Washington U., 1981. Bar: N.Y. 1982, D.C. 1982, Utah 1984. Assoc. Shearman and Sterling, N.Y.C., 1981-84, Berman and Anderson, Salt Lake City, 1984; sole practice Salt Lake City, 1985; assoc. Baker and McKenzie, Beijing, 1986—. Contbr. articles to profl. jours. State Dem. del., Salt Lake City, 1984; cons. Wayne Owens for Gov. campaign com., Salt Lake City, 1984. Mem. ABA. Mormon. Avocations: Chinese studies, skiing, basketball. Private international, Contracts commercial, Federal civil litigation. Home: Beijing Hotel, Suite 5036, Beijing Peoples Republic of China Office: Baker and McKenzie, CITIC Bldg Suite 1801, Beijing Peoples Republic of China

CAPETOLA, ANTHONY ADAM, lawyer; b. Jersey City, Oct. 4, 1945; s. Anthony and Anna Rose (Le Fante) C.; dovorced; children—Lauren, Michele, Jean. B.S., Wagner Coll., N.Y., 1967; J.D., N.Y. Law Sch., 1970. Bar: N.Y. 1971. Staff atty. Nassau Dist. Atty., Mineola, N.Y., 1971-73; assoc. Richard Hartmann, Mineola, 1973-76; ptnr. D'Amato, Forchell & Capetola, Mineola, 1976-83; ptnr. Axelrod, Cornachio, Famighetti & Capetola, Mineola, 1983-84; owner law office Anthony A. Capetola, Williston Park, N.Y., 1984—; assoc. village justice Bayville Village Ct., N.Y., 1973-75; dir. Willow Ridge Devel. Corp., Bayville. Mem. ABA, Assn. Trial Lawyers Am., Former Dist. Attys. Assn., Magistrates Assocs. of State of N.Y., N.Y. State Bar Assn., Columbian Lawyers Nassau County (past pres., dir.). Republican. Roman Catholic. Criminal, Family and matrimonial, General practice. Office: 2C Hillside Ave Williston Park NY 11596

CAPIZZI, ANTHONY, lawyer; b. Rochester, N.Y., June 22, 1954; s. Patsy Peter and Amelia Mary (DiBiase) C.; Virginia Mary Doucas, Sept. 2, 1978; 1 child, Daniel Patrick. BA in History, St. Bonaventure U., 1976; JD, U. Dayton, 1979. Bar: Ohio 1979, U.S. Dist. Ct. (so. dist.) 1979. Assoc. Robert L. Abrahamson Co. LPA, Dayton, Ohio, 1979-83, Zarka, Karas & Allen, Dayton, 1983-84; ptnr. Capizzi, Cousineau & Susser, Dayton, 1985—; bd. dirs. Advance Mgmt. Concept, Dayton, Telesaver Inc., Dayton, Ray Brown Architects, Dayton, Michel Resources, Inc., D.A.E. Homes Services, Cassette Recording Co., Neighborhoods, U.S.A. chmn. Southeast Dayton Priority Bd., 1981-85; treas. Mark Henry for City Commn., Dayton, 1983—; trustee Second Shelf, Dayton, 1984—; city commn., Dayton, 1986—. Named One of Outstanding Young Men of Am., Dayton, 1984. Mem. Assn. Trial Lawyers Am., Ohio Bar Assn., Ohio Trial Lawyers Assn., Dayton Bar Assn., Priority Bd. Chmns. Council (chmn. 1985, Outstanding Service award 1985). Democrat. Roman Catholic. Lodges: Optimist (pres. Dayton club 1983-85), Sons of Italy. Avocation: soccer. Personal injury, Family and matrimonial, State civil litigation. Home: 105 Stonemill Rd Dayton OH 45409 Office: Capizzi Cousineau & Susser 1110 First National Plaza Dayton OH 45402 Office: City of Dayton 101 W Third St Dayton OH 45402

CAPLAN, GERALD A., lawyer; b. Passaic, N.J., Oct. 15, 1931; s. Herman A. and Mina (Harrop) C.; m. Elizabeth Starr Bruning, Sept. 1, 1956; children—Lindsay, Jeffrey. B.A., Syracuse U., 1955, J.D., 1957. Bar: N.Y. 1957, Colo. 1961. Sr. ptnr. Caplan and Earnest, Boulder, Colo., 1961—; guest lectr. U. Colo., Colo. State U., U. No. Colo., Regis Coll. Mcpl. judge City of Boulder, 1962-67; pub. trustee Boulder County, 1967-77; mem. jud. nominating commn., 1971-75; chmn. bd. trustees U. No. Colo., 1973-80; spl. asst. atty. gen., 1974-75. Served to 1st lt. JAGC, U.S. Army, 1957-60. Fellow Am. Coll. Trial Lawyers; mem. ABA, Colo. Bar Assn., Nat. Council Sch. Attys. (bd. dirs. 1978—). Episcopalian. Contbr. articles on law to profl. jours. Federal civil litigation, State civil litigation, Legal education. Home: 400 Ord Dr Boulder CO 80303 Office: 1301 Spruce St Suite 300 Boulder CO 80302

CAPLAN, MORTON LAWRENCE, lawyer; b. N.Y.C., July 12, 1932; s. Lewis and Belle (Silverman) C; m. Annette Brofman, Nov. 12, 1959 (div. July 1986); children: Lisa, Joshua, Jonathan. BSME, U. Maine, 1955; JD, Southwestern U., Los Angeles, 1972. Assoc. Brill, Hunt, De Buys & Burby, Los Angeles, 1972-74; ptnr. Caplan and Overlander, Los Angeles, 1977-85, M.L. Caplan and Assocs., Los Angeles, 1974-77, 1985—; judge pro tem Los Angeles Mcpl. Ct., 1980—; arbitrator Calif. Superior Ct., County of Los Angeles, 1981—; conv. del. Calif State Bar Assn., 1974, 77. Recipient Colwell award, Soc. Automotive Engrs., 1968. Mem. Am. Bd. Trial Advocates, Assn. So. Calif. Def. Counsel (bd. dirs. 1982-85), South Bay Bar Assn., Los Angeles County Bar Assn. (arbitrator 1982—). Clubs: Los Angeles Athletic, Cabrillo Beach Yacht (San Pedro, Calif.). Avocations: flying, sailing, skiing. State civil litigation, Personal injury. Office: ML Caplan & Assocs 800 S Hope St Suite 602 Los Angeles CA 90017

CAPLAN, RUSSELL L., lawyer; b. N.Y.C., Apr. 24, 1952; s. Alfred Joseph and June (Schultz) C. AB, Dartmouth Coll., 1972; MA, Oxford U., 1974; JD, Yale U., 1977. Bar: Pa., D.C. Law clk. to presiding judge U.S. Dist. Ct. (ea. dist.) Mich., Detroit, 1977-79; trial atty. Dept. Justice, Washington, 1979—. Author: Amending the Constitution by National Convention, 1987. Fulbright scholar, England, 1972. Mem. ABA. Administrative and regulatory, Legal history, Jurisprudence. Home: 1701 N Kent St Arlington VA 22209 Office: Dept Justice Washington DC 20530

CAPLES, MICHAEL EDWARD, lawyer; b. Glendale, Calif., Oct. 1, 1951; s. Edward Warren and Frances Maude (Bulla) C.; m. Therese Ann Mueller, Oct. 8, 1983. BA, Calif. State U., 1973; JD, Whittier Coll. of Law, 1980; LLM in Labor Law, NYU, 1981. Bar: Calif. 1980, N.J. 1981, U.S. Dist. Ct. N.J. 1981, U.S. Ct. Appeals (3d cir.) 1981, U.S. Dist. Ct. (no., so. and cen. dists.) Calif. 1983, U.S. Ct. Appeals (9th cir.) 1983, U.S. Supreme Ct. 1986. Assoc. Pitney, Hardin, Kipp & Szuch, Morristown, N.J., 1981-82, Barlow & Attaway, Los Angeles, 1982-86; ptnr. Barlow, Kobata & Caples, Los Angeles, 1986-87; assoc. Jackson, Lewis, Schnitzler & Krupman, Los Angeles, 1987—. Contbr. articles to profl. jours. Mem. ABA (labor sect.), Calif. Bar Assn. (labor sect., trademark sect.), Los Angeles County Bar Assn. (labor sect.). Labor, Federal civil litigation, State civil litigation. Office: Jackson Lewis Schnitzler & Krupman 1925 Century Park E #1100 Los Angeles CA 90067

CAPLICKI, DENNIS P., lawyer; b. Warwick, N.Y., Mar. 17, 1947; s. Edmund V. and Pauline (Kamrowski) C.; m. Janet P. Caplicki, Oct. 12, 1969; children: Kimberly, Kelly, Matthew. BSBA, Georgetown U., 1969; JD, Cornell U., 1972. Sole practice Goshen, N.Y., 1975—; gen. counsel Nat. Bank of Florida, N.Y., 1975—; atty. Town of Goshen, 1978—, Village of Florida, 1981—. Chmn. Town of Goshen Rep. Com., 1978—. Mem. N.Y. State Bar Assn., Orange County Bar Assn., Goshen Bar Assn. Roman Catholic. Real property, Probate, General practice. Office: 158 N. Main St Florida NY 10921

CAPORALE, D. NICK, state supreme court judge; b. Omaha, Sept. 13, 1928; s. Michele and Lucia (DeLuca) C.; m. Margaret Nilson, Aug. 5, 1950; children: Laura Diane Caporale Stevenson, Leland Alan. B.A., U. Nebr.-Omaha, 1949, M.Sc., 1954; J.D. with distinction, U. Nebr.-Lincoln, 1957. Bar: Nebr. 1957, U.S. Dist. Ct. Nebr. 1957, U.S. Ct. Appeals 8th cir. 1958, U.S. Supreme Ct. 1970. Mem. firm Stoehr, Rickerson, Sodoro & Caporale, Omaha, 1957-66; ptnr. Schmid, Ford, Mooney, Frederick & Caporale, Omaha, 1966-79; judge Nebr. Dist. Ct., Omaha, 1979-81, Nebr. Supreme Ct., Lincoln, 1982—; lectr. U. Nebr., Lincoln, 1982-84. Pres. Omaha Community Playhouse, 1976. Served to 1st lt. U.S. Army, 1952-54, Korea. Decorated Bronze Star; recipient Alumni Achievement U. Nebr.-Omaha, 1972. Fellow Am. Coll. Trial Lawyers, Internat. Soc. Barristers. Federal civil litigation. Office: Room 2222 State House 1445 K St Lincoln NE 68509

CAPP, ALVIN, lawyer; b. St. Louis, Feb. 23, 1939. B.A. in Polit. Sci. and History, George Washington U., 1961, J.D. with honors, 1964. Bar: Fla. 1964, U.S. Dist. Ct. (so. dist.) Fla. 1964, U.S. Ct. Appeals (5th cir.) 1965, U.S. Ct. Appeals (11th cir.) 1983, U.S. Supreme Ct. 1968. City prosecutor, Plantation, Fla., 1974-76; pres. Capp, Reinstein, Kopelowitz & Atlas, Ft. Lauderdale, Fla., 1975-85. Book rev. editor George Washington Law Rev., 1963-64. Served with USAR, 1956-64. Mem. ABA, Fla. Bar Assn., Broward County Bar Assn. State civil litigation, General corporate, Real property. Office: 800 E Broward Blvd Cumberland Bldg Suite 608 Fort Lauderdale FL 33301

CAPPALLI, RICHARD ANTHONY, lawyer; b. Providence, R.I., Sept. 14, 1940; s. Americo Saverio and Anna (DiNola) C.; m. Regina Martha Love, June 10, 1978; children: Maria, Debra, Susan. AB, Brown U., 1962; JD, Georgetown U., 1965. Bar: R.I. 1965, U.S. Dist. Ct. R.I. 1966. Assoc., ptnr. Gelfuso & Cappalli, Cranston, R.I., 1965-74; sole practice Woonsocket, R.I., 1975—; legal counsel to Gov. of R.I., 1967-68, senate minority leaders, 1969-75; judge Probate Ct., Burrillville, R.I., 1983—; guest lectr. bar assn. seminars, 1978—; liaison counsel Providence Asbestos Litigation, 1980—. Legal advisor youth and law program R.I. High Sch. System, 1974—. Mem. R.I. Bar Assn., Assn. Trial Lawyers Am., R.I. Trial Lawyers Assn. (pres. 1977-78), Am. Soc. Medicine and Law, Am. Judicature Soc. Republican. Roman Catholic. Avocations: hunting, skiing,. Federal civil litigation, Personal injury, Probate. Home: 149 Douglas Pike Burrillville RI 02895 Office: Two Main St Woonsocket RI 02895

CAPPELLETTI, MAURO, legal educator, lawyer; b. 1927. Djur, U. Florence (Italy), 1952, Libero Docente, 1957; Drhc, U. Aix-Marseille (France), 1977, U. Ghent (Belgium), 1979. Bar: Italy 1952. Clk. to pres. Italian Bar, 1952-54; research fellow U. Freiburg (Fed. Republic Germany), 1955-57; prof. U. Macerata (Italy), 1957-62; prof. U. Florence, 1962—; dir. Inst. Comparative Law, Florence, 1962-76; Fulbright vis. prof. Stanford (Calif.) U., 1968, prof. law, 1970-86, L. Shelton prof. internat. legal studies, 1986—; pres. Ctr. Comparative Jud. Studies, Florence, 1968-80; vis. prof. Harvard U., 1969, U. Calif.-Berkeley, 1970; Cooley lectr. U. Mich., 1970; co-dir. Ford Found. com. research project on access to justice, 1973-79; Mitchell lectr. U. Buffalo, 1975; prof. European U. Inst., Florence, 1976-87, chmn. law dept., 1977-79, 83, 85-86; dir. Ford Found. research project on European integration and Am. fed. experience, 1979—. Bd. advisors Max-Planck-Inst. für AuslÄndisches und Internationales Privatrecht. Recipient Premio Linceo for Law, Italian Accademia Nazionale dei Lincei, 1981; Premio Europeo Lorenzo il Magnifico, Accademia Internazionale Medicea, 1981. Mem. Internat. Acad. Comparative Law, Brit. Acad. (corr. fellow), Royal Acad. of Scis., Letters and Arts, Belgium (fgn. mem.), Internat. Assn. Legal Sci. (v.p. 1979-82, pres. 1983-84), Institut de France (corr. mem.), Accademia dei Lincei, Italian Assn. Comparative Law (pres. 1970-77), Instituto Latinoamericano de Derecho Procesal (hon.), Internat. Assn. Procedural Law (pres. 1983—), Am. Fgn. Law Assn., Société de Législation Comparée, Accademia Toscana di Scienze e Lettere La Colombaria. Author: (with others) The Italian Legal System, 1967; Judicial Review in the Comparative World, 1971; Toward Equal Justice, 1975; Access to Justice, 4 vols., 1978-79; Comparative Constitutional Law, 1979; editor, co-author: New Perspectives for a Common Law of Europe, 1979; Access to Justice and the Welfare State, 1981; Integration Through Law: Europe and the American Federal Experience, 6 vols., 1985—; editor-in-chief Internat. Ency. Comparative Law, Vol. XVI, 1965—. Legal education. Office: Stanford U Law Sch Stanford CA 94305

CAPPS, GEORGE HALL, lawyer; b. Kansas City, Mo., June 14, 1950; s. Joe Hall and Roberta Lou (Casteel) C.; m. Suzanne Walsh, July 15, 1972; children: John Curtis, Michael, Jessica. BA, Drake U., 1971, JD, 1975. Bar: Iowa 1975, U.S. Dist. Ct. (so. dist.) Iowa 1975, U.S. Ct. Appeals (8th cir.) 1977. Assoc. Comito, Roehrick & Vincent, Des Moines, 1975-77; ptnr. Comito & Capps, Des Moines, 1977—. Mem. ABA, Iowa Bar Assn., Polk County Bar Assn., Assn. Trial Lawyers Am., Assn. Trial Lawyers Iowa (pub. relations com. 1986—). Baptist. Avocations: softball, fishing, biking, golf, water skiing. Insurance, Consumer commercial, Real property. Office: Comito & Capps 1441 29th St 310 Continental Bldg West Des Moines IA 50265

CAPPUCCIO, RONALD JOSEPH, lawyer; b. Phila., Mar. 3, 1954; s. Anthony R. and Marie A. (Rigolizzo) C.; m. Sondra J. Lippi, Aug. 2, 1980; 1 dau., Sondra Nicole. B.S.F.S. in Internat. Econs., Georgetown U., 1974, LL.M. in Taxation, 1977; J.D., U. Kans., 1976. Bar: N.J. 1976, U.S. Dist. Ct. N.J. 1976, D.C. 1977, U.S. Tax Ct. 1977, U.S. Ct. Appeals, (3d cir.) 1984. Chief law clk. to judge, 1977-78; assoc. Lario & Nardi, Haddonfield, N.J., 1978-80; sole practice 1980—; solicitor Gloucester Twp. Planning Bd., 1981-82, Evesham Twp Planning Bd., 1982-83; adj. instr. dept. govtl. services Rutgers U., 1977-80. Mem. ABA, N.J. Bar Assn., Camden County Bar Assn. Corporate taxation, Estate planning, Real property. Address: 212 Haddon Ave Westmont NJ 08108

CAPRA, DANIEL JOSEPH, law educator, lawyer; b. Cumberland, Wis., July 20, 1953; s. Joseph John and MaryJane (Knowlton) C.; m. Anne Hope Tresser, June 8, 1980. BA summa cum laude, Rockhurst Coll., 1974; JD, U. Calif.-Berkeley, 1977. Bar: N.Y. 1978. Assoc. Lord, Day & Lord, N.Y.C., 1977-79; asst. prof. law Tulane U. Law Sch., New Orleans, 1979-81; vis. prof. U. Grenoble, France, summers, 1980-81; assoc. prof. law Fordham U. Law Sch., N.Y.C., 1981-86, prof. law, 1986—; cons. Marx Realty Co., N.Y.C., 1983-84. Contbr. articles to law revs. Unico scholar, 1970. Mem. ABA, Assn. Bar City N.Y., Maritime Law Assn. (marine fin. com.), Order of Coif, Alpha Sigma Nu. Jewish. Federal civil litigation, State civil litigation, Criminal. Home: 239 E 79th St New York NY 10021 Office: Fordham U Sch Law 140 W 62d St New York NY 10023

CAPRITTO, ANTHONY JOSEPH, lawyer; b. New Orleans, July 11, 1931; s. Philip Joseph and Marie Virginia (Longo) C.; m. Eileen Mary Frisbee, June 6, 1964; children—Ann, Jane, Michael, Margaret, Elizabeth, Alice, Judith, David, Mary. B.B.A., Loyola U., New Orleans, 1953, J.D., 1959. Bar: La. 1959, U.S. Dist. Ct. (ea. dist.) La. 1959, U.S. Ct. Appeals (5th cir.) 1965, U.S. Supreme Ct. 1971. Sole practice law, New Orleans, 1959—; gen. counsel Bank of La., New Orleans, 1979—. Mem. legal com., bd. dirs. New Orleans Opera Assn., 1975—; commr. La. Civil Service Commn., Baton Rouge, 1979—; pres. Cath. Charities, New Orleans, 1980, La. Cystic Fibrosis Found., 1976-78; pres. Christian Bros. Found., New Orleans, 1985-87. Served to capt. U.S. Army, 1953-55. Mem. La. Bar Assn., Assn. Trial Lawyers Am., Am. Arbitration Assn. (arbitrator), Am. Judicature Soc., La. Trial Lawyers Assn., St. Thomas More Cath. Law Assn. (pres. 1980-84). Democrat. Roman Catholic. Club: Semreh (bd. dirs.). State civil litigation, Contracts commercial, Real property. Home: 500 Turquoise St New Orleans LA 70124 Office: Suite 811 234 Loyola Bldg 234 Loyola Ave New Orleans LA 70112

CAPSHAW, TOM DEAN, administrative law judge; b. Oklahoma City, Sept. 20, 1936; m. Dian Shipp; 1 child, Charles W. BS in Bus., Oklahoma City U., 1958; student U. Ark. Coll. Law, Fayetteville, 1958-59; JD, U. Okla.-Norman, 1961. Bar: Okla. 1961, Wyo. 1971, Ind. 1975. Assoc. Looney, Watts, Looney, Nichols and Johnson, Oklahoma City, 1961-63, Pierce, Duncan, Couch and Hendrickson, Oklahoma City, 1963-70; trial atty., v.p. Capshaw Well Service Co., Liberty Pipe and Supply Co., Casper, Wyo., judge HUD, adminstrv. law judge, Evansville, Ind., 1973-75, judge in charge, 1975—; acting regional chief adminstrv. law judge, Chgo., 1977-78; acting appeals council mem., Arlington, Va., 1980, acting chief adminstrv. law judge, 1984; mem. faculty U. Evansville, 1977; lectr. in field. Author: A Manual for Continuing Judicial Education, 1981, Practical Aspects of Handling Social Security Disability Claims, 1982; contbr. numerous articles to profl. jours., chpts. to textbooks. Mem. exec. council Boy Scouts Am., scoutmaster, den leader, 1969—; bd. dirs. Casper Symphony, 1972-73, Casper United Fund, 1972-73, Midget Football Assn., Casper, 1972-73, German Twp. Water Dist., 1982; pres. Unitarian Universalist Ch., 1984-86. Recipient Kappa Alpha Order Ct. of Honor award, 1962, Silver Beaver award Boy Scouts Am., 1980; named Ky. Col., 1984; Unitarian Universalist fellowship. Mem. ABA (chmn. edn. com. Conf. Adminstrv. law judges 1979-81), Okla. Bar Assn., Okla. County Bar Assn. (v.p. 1967),81), Wyo. Bar Assn., Evansville Bar Assn. (jud. rep. 1986-87), Young Lawyers Conf. of Okla. County (pres. 1966), Okla. Assn. Def. Council, Okla. City Trial Lawyers Assn., Assn. Adminstrv. Law Judges HHS (bd. dirs. 1979-82), Fed. Adminstrv. Law Judges Assn., Nat. Jud. Coll. U. Nev., Oklahoma City U. Alumni Assn. (bd. dirs. 1965). Administrative and regulatory, Judicial administration, Pension, profit-sharing, and employee benefits. Home: 6105 School Rd #6 Evansville IN 47712

CARASIK, KAREN SUE, lawyer, educator; b. Jacksonville, Fla., May 11, 1955; d. Howard H. and Shirley Ruth (Rubin) C. BS magna cum laude, U. Wis., Green Bay, 1977; JD, Ill. Inst. Tech., 1980. Bar: Ill. 1980, U.S. Dist. Ct. (no. dist.) Ill. 1981. Atty. Chgo. Bd. Trade, Chgo., 1980-81; ptnr. Fishman & Merrick P.C., Chgo., 1981—; lectr. law Ill. Inst. Tech., Chgo., 1981—; bd. dirs. 1st Personal Ltd., Highland Park, Ill., Gaffrig Precision Instruments, Chgo. Mem. ABA, Chgo. Bar Assn., Chgo. Acad. Scis., CEO Club Chgo. Democrat. Jewish. Avocation: off shore power boat racing. General corporate, Securities, Commodities. Office: Fishman & Merrick PC 30 N LaSalle #3600 Chicago IL 60602

CARBO, MICHAEL JAMES, county court official, lawyer; b. Port Jefferson, N.Y., June 23, 1951; s. Michael and Grace Theresa (Depaolo) C.; m. Roseanne Marie Crincoli, Sept. 12, 1976; 1 dau., Kimberly Ann. B.A. in English, Rutgers U., 1973, J.D. cum laude, 1976. Bar: Fla. 1976, U.S. Dist. Ct. (so. dist.) Fla. 1977, U.S. Ct. Appeals (5th cir.) 1979. Law clk. U.S. Attys. Office, Camden, N.J., 1975-76; assoc. Schlichte, Carbo and Platt, P.A., Ft. Lauderdale, Fla., 1976-77, ptnr., 1978-80; sole practice, Ft. Lauderdale, 1981; gen. master, 17th Jud. Circuit Broward County, Fla., Ft. Lauderdale, 1981—; lectr. Nova Law Ctr., Ft. Lauderdale, 1983-84, U. Miami, Coral Gables, 1984. Mem. Hollywood Jaycees (Fla.), 1976, Columbus Civic Club of Broward County, Hollywood, 1981-84. Recipient Corpus Juris Secundum award Rutgers Sch. Law, 1976. Mem. Fla. Bar (chmn. grievance com. 1982-85, guardian ad litem task force 1984—, jud. nominating procedures com. 1984—, com. for spl. needs of children 1984—, exec. council family law sect. 1985—, student edn. and admissions to bar com. 1986—, young lawyers sect., trial lawyers sect.), Broward County Bar Assn., Nat. Child Support Enforcement Assn., Acad. Fla. Trial Lawyers, Assn. Trial Lawyers Am., ABA, Lawyers Title Guaranty Fund, Phi Eta Sigma. Roman Catholic. Family and matrimonial, Judicial administration, General practice. Office: Broward County Courthouse 201 Southeast Sixth St Fort Lauderdale FL 33301

CARBON, SUSAN BERKSON, lawyer, consultant; b. Richland, Wash., Oct. 1, 1953; d. Max William and Phyllis Camile (Myers) C.; m. Larry Charles Berkson, Nov. 26, 1977; 1 child, Quintin Barnes Berkson. BA, U. Wis., 1974; JD, DePaul U., 1980. Bar: N.H., Ill., U.S. Dist. Ct. N.H., U.S. Dist. Ct. (no. dist.) Ill. Ptnr. Wescott, Millham & Dyer, Laconia, N.H., 1982—; cons. freelance in Chgo., and N.H., 1981—. Author: Court Unification: History, Politics and Implementation, 1978, The U.S. Circuit Judge Nominating Commission, 1980; editor: Managing the State Courts: Text and Readings, 1977. Mem. ABA (jud. qualification and selection com.), N.H. Bar Assn. (legis. and adminstrv. law com.), Ill. Bar Assn., Am. Judicature Soc. Real property, General corporate. Home: RFD 3 Upper City Rd Pittsfield NH 03263 Office: Wescott Millham & Dyer 28 Bowman St PO Box 1700 Laconia NH 03247

CARDALI, RICHARD JAMES, lawyer; b. N.Y.C., Jan. 14, 1931; s. Salvatore and Gladys (Wynn) C.; m. Josephine Gabriel; children: Richard, Karen, Robert, Joanne, David. BA cum laude, Bklyn. Coll., 1964; JD, St. John's U., 1964. Bar: N.Y. 1965, U.S. Dist. Ct. (so. and ea. dists.) N.Y. 1966, U.S. Ct. Appeals (2d cir.) 1966, U.S. Supreme Ct. 1967. Prin. Law Offices of Richard J. Cardali Assocs. P.C., N.Y.C., 1965—; Lectr. on basic trial techniques and jury selection. Profl. mem. Legal Aid Soc. N.Y., 1973. Recipient Humanitarian award Inst. Jewish Humanities, 1985. Mem. ABA (litigation sect.), N.Y. State Bar Assn., Queens County Bar Assn., Fed. Bar Council, Pa. Trial Lawyers Assn., Assn. Trial Lawyers Am. (sustaining 1973—), N.Y. State Trial Lawyers Assn. (bd. dirs. 1984—), N.Y. City Trial Lawyers Assn., N.Y. County Lawyers Assn., N.J. Trial Lawyers Assn., Tex. Trial Lawyers Assn., N.Y. State Trial Lawyers Assn. (chmn. ethics and procedures com.), Nat. Inst. Trial Advocacy (fac. mem., trial techniques lectr. 1981—), Bklyn. Coll. Alumni Assn., St. John's Law Sch. Alumni Assn., Life Camps Trail Blazers Alumni Assn. Democrat. Roman Catholic. Avocations: reading, outdoor activities. Personal injury, Workers' compensation. Office: Law Offices Richard J Cardali 233 Broadway Woolworth Bldg New York NY 10279

CARDAMONE, RICHARD J., federal judge; b. Utica, N.Y., Oct. 10, 1925; s. Joseph J. and Josephine (Scala) C.; m. Catherine Baker Clarke, Aug. 28, 1946; 10 children. B.A., Harvard U., 1948; LL.B., Syracuse U., 1952. Bar: N.Y. 1952. Practice law Utica, 1952-62; justice N.Y. State Supreme Ct., 1963-71, N.Y. State Supreme Ct. Appellate Div., 4th Dept., 1971-81; judge U.S. Ct. Appeals for 2d Circuit, Utica, 1981—. Trustee Syracuse U. Coll. Law; trustee Slocum Dickson Found., Utica, St. Luke Hosp. Ctr., New Hartford, N.Y. Served as lt. (j.g.) USNR, 1943-46. Mem. Am. Law Inst., N.Y. State Bar Assn., Oneida County Bar Assn. Roman Catholic. Office: US Ct Appeals 2d Circuit US Courthouse 10 Broad St Utica NY 13503

CARDILLO, JOHN POLLARA, lawyer; b. Ft. Lee, N.J., July 1, 1942; s. John E. and Margaret (Pollara) C.; m. Linda Bantey, Sept. 25, 1976; children: John Thomas, Joseph Pollara, Margaret Celia, Mark Luigi. BA, Furman U., 1964; postgrad., W.Va. U., 1965; JD, U. S.C., 1968. Bar: S.C. 1968, N.Y. 1971, Fla. 1972, U.S. Ct. Appeals (2d cir., 4th cir. 5th cir. 11th cir.) 1972, U.S. Dist. Ct. (ea. and so. dists.) N.Y. 1972, U.S. Dist. Ct. S.C. 1972, U.S. Dist. Ct. (so. and mid. dists.) Fla. 1972, U.S. Tax Ct. 1972, U.S. Supreme Ct. 1972. Assoc. Cardillo & Corbett, N.Y.C., 1968-71, Mays & McLellan, Columbia, S.C., 1971-72, Sorokoty, Monaco & Cervelli, Naples, Fla., 1972-75; ptnr. Monaco, Cardillo & Keith, P.A., Naples, 1975—. Chmn. Environ. Adv. Council, Collier County, Fla., 1983, 87—; mem. Dem. Exec. Council, Collier County, Fine Arts Soc. of Collier County; bd. dirs. YMCA, Collier County (past pres.). Mem. Assn. Trial Lawyers Am., ABA (trial lawyers sect.), Am. Judicature Soc., Am. Arbitration Assn. (arbitrator), Acad. Fla. Trial Lawyers, Fla. Bar Jud. Adminstrn. (selection, tenure and cir. legis. coms.), Collier County Bar Assn. (past pres.), Fla. Bar Assn. (grievance com., jud. adminstrn., selection and tenure com., pres. bar council, cir. legis. com. fee arbitration com.), Furman U. Alumni Bd., Maritime Law Assn., Melvin Belli Soc. (trustee), Collier County Bar Assn. (past pres.), Furman U. Alumni Assn. Home: 395 Ridge Dr Naples FL 33963 Office: Monaco Cardillo & Keith PA 3550 S Tamiami Trail Naples FL 33962-4999

CARDINE, GODFREY JOSEPH, state supreme court justice; b. Prairie Du Chien, Wis., July 6, 1924; s. Joseph Frederick and Mary (Kasparek) C.; m. Janice Irene Brown, Sept. 14, 1946; children—Susan, John, Lisa. B.S. in Engring., U. Ill., 1948; J.D. with honors, U. Wyo., 1954. Bar: Wyo. 1954, U.S. Dist. Ct. Wyo. 1954, U.S. Ct. Appeals (10th cir.) 1954. Assoc. Schwartz, Bon & McCrary, Casper, Wyo., 1954-66; dist. atty. Natrona County, Wyo., 1966-70; ptnr. Cardine, Vlastos & Reeves, Casper, 1966-77; prof. law U. Wyo., Laramie, 1977-83; justice Wyo. Supreme Ct., Cheyenne, 1983—; mem. Wyo. State Bd. Law Examiners, 1973-77; faculty, dir. Western Trial Advocacy Inst., Laramie, 1981—; bd. advisors Land and Water Law Rev., 1985—. Contbr. articles to profl. jours. Active Little League Baseball, Casper, 1960-62; mem. Gov.'s Com. on Dangerous Drugs, 1968-69. Served to 1st lt. USAF, 1943-46, PTO. Fellow Internat. Soc. Barristers; mem. Assn. Trial Lawyers Am., Wyo. State Bar (pres. 1977-78), Chi Epsilon, Phi Alpha Delta. Club: Potter Law (pres. 1953-54). Lodge: Rotary. Judicial administration, State civil litigation. Home: PO Box 223 Cheyenne WY 82003 Office: Wyo Supreme Ct Supreme Ct Bldg Cheyenne WY 82002

CARDOZO, BENJAMIN MORDECAI, lawyer; b. N.Y.C., May 15, 1915; s. Sidney Benjamin and Eva Cecile (Mordecai) C.; m. Barbara Ruth Schaffer, Sept. 21, 1941; children—Enid Cardozo Lamcn, Ellen Cardozo Sonsino. B.A., Dartmouth Coll., 1937; postgrad., Columbia U., 1938; J.D., N.Y. U., 1941. Bar: N.Y. State bar 1942, U.S. Supreme Ct. bar 1947, Conn. bar 1954. Mem. staff Moreland Commn. Workmen's Compensation Investigation, N.Y. State, 1941, Office Alien Property, U.S. Dept. Justice, Washington, 1946-49; asso. firm Cardozo & Nathan, N.Y.C., 1949-51, Cardozo & Cardozo, N.Y.C., 1952—. Mem. Assn. Bar City N.Y., N.Y. County Lawyers Assn., Conn. Fed., Am. bar assns., N.Y. State Assn., Trial Lawyers, Nat. Arts Club. Estate planning, Probate, Estate taxation. Home: 325 E 79th St New York NY 10021 Office: 11 E 44th St New York NY 10017

CARDWELL, DAVID EARL, lawyer; b. Bowling Green, Ky., Dec. 14, 1951; s. Emery Earl and Vera Mae (Reed) C.; m. Dagmar Reece Larsen, Sept. 8, 1973; children: Reece Elizabeth, Patrick John. BA with honors, U. Fla., 1973, JD, 1975. Bar: Fla. 1975, U.S. Dist. Ct. (no., so. and mid. dists.) Fla. 1977, D.C. 1978, U.S. Ct. Appeals (11th cir.) 1980. Dir. staff Fla. Ho. of Reps., Tallahassee, 1979; assoc. Hahn, Breathitt & Roberts, Lakeland, Fla., 1979-82; ptnr. Holland & Knight, Lakeland, 1982—. Author: Elections and Ethics, 1980. Mem. ABA (urban state and local govt. sect. council; chmn. adminstrv. law sect., com. chmn.), Fla. Bar Assn. (chmn. local govt. law sect. 1982, continuing legal edn. com.), U. Fla. Nat. Alumni Assn. (pres.), Nat. Assn. Bond Lawyers (lectr.). Municipal bonds, Local government, Administrative and regulatory. Office: Holland & Knight 92 Lake Wire Dr Lakeland FL 33802

CARELLA, EUGENE JOHN, lawyer; b. Stamford, Conn., Apr. 27, 1943; s. Richard L. and Theresa (Uva) C.; m. Paula E. Pfister, 1987. BA in Polit. Sci., Denison U., 1965; JD, U. Toledo, 1968. Bar: Colo. 1968, U.S. Dist. Ct. Colo. 1968, U.S. Ct. Appeals (5th and D.C. cirs.) 1977, U.S. Supreme Ct. 1977. Cons. advanced underwriting Mut. Life Ins. Co. N.Y., N.Y.C., 1968-69; fin. planner U.S. Trust Co., N.Y.C., 1969-70; sr. v.p. corp. div. Groesbeck Fin. Advisors Inc., Century City, Calif., 1970-73; dir. mktg. Edward N. Hay Assocs., Phila., 1973-74; v.p. Inverness Planning Corp., N.Y.C., 1974-75; sole practice Century City, 1975—. Active support groups Boy's Club, Los Angeles, 1960-85. Fellow Assn. Trial Lawyers Am., Am. Mgmt. Assn.; mem. ABA (corp. banking and bus. sect.), Am. Compensation Assn. (hon., award of distinction 1970), Smithsonian Inst., Phi Gamma Delta. Roman Catholic. Avocations: tennis, swimming, boating, hiking, travel. Federal civil litigation, Pension, profit-sharing, and employee benefits, Labor. Office: PO Box 67292 Century City Los Angeles CA 90067

CARETTI, RICHARD LOUIS, lawyer; b. Grosse Pointe, Mich., Dec. 17, 1953; s. Richard John and Doris Eleanor (Evans) C.; m. Nancy Louise Matouk, Oct. 14, 1983; 1 child, Katherine Lynn. BA, Wayne State U., 1975; JD magna cum laude, Detroit Coll. Law, 1980. Bar: Mich. 1980, U.S. Dist. Ct. (ea dist.) Mich. 1980, U.S. Ct. Appeals (6th cir.) 1982. Assoc. Dickinson, Wright, Moon, Van Dusen & Freeman, Detroit, 1979-84, ptnr., 1985—. Mem. ABA, Detroit Bar Assn., Mich. Def. Trial Counsel, Assn. Def. Trial Counsel. Delta Theta Phi. Roman Catholic. Club: Detroit Athletic (club open raquetball champion). Avocations: raquetball, softball, golf, boating. Product liability defense, Personal injury, Insurance. Home: 1380 Devonshire Grosse Pointe Park MI 48230 Office: Dickinson Wright Moon et al 800 First Nat Bldg Detroit MI 48226

CAREY, HUGH L., lawyer, former governor of New York; b. Bklyn.; s. Dennis and Margaret C.; m. Owen Twohy, Feb. 27, 1947 (dec. Mar. 1974); children—Christopher, Susan, Peter (dec.), Hugh (dec.), Michael, Donald, Marianne, Nancy, Helen, Bryan, Paul, Kevin, Thomas; 1 stepchild, Alexandria; m. Evangeline Gouletas, Apr. 11, 1981; 1 stepchild, Maria. J.D., St. John's U. Mem. N.Y. Ho. of Reps., 1960-74, dep. whip; gov. N.Y., 1974-82; ptnr., mem. mgmt. com. Finley, Kumble, Wagner, Heine, Underberg, Manley, Myerson & Casey, N.Y.C., 1982—. Bd. dirs. Am. Blood Pressure Ctrs., Inc., Rooney, Pace, Inc. Chmn. N.Y. State World Trade Council, 1984—. Served with N.Y. N.G. Decorated Bronze Star Medal, Croix de Guerre. Office: Finley Kumble Wagner Heine Underberg Manley Myerson & Casey 425 Park Ave New York NY 10022

CAREY, J. EDWIN, lawyer; b. N.Y.C., Aug. 29, 1923; s. Edwin J. and Nora L. (Greene) C.; m. Marian G. Burke, May 23, 1954; children—Brianne, Christopher. Student, Manhattan Coll., 1941-43; LL.B., St. John's U., 1951. Bar: N.Y. bar 1951. Since practiced in N.Y.C.; sr. partner firm Hill, Rivkins, Carey, Loesberg, O'Brien & Mulroy (and predecessors), 1961—; Lectr. admiralty law Practicing Law Inst., 1959—. Served with inf. AUS, 1943-46, ETO. Mem. ABA, N.Y. State Bar Assn., Maritime Law Assn. U.S. (chmn. membership com. 1958-60, membership sec. 1960-66, sec. 1966-69, 1st v.p. 1970-72, pres. 1972-74, U.S. del. internat. confs. UN), Comité Maritime International (titular mem.), Union Internationale des Avocats, Am. Judicature Soc., Assn. Average Adjusters, Ins. Soc. N.Y., St. Thomas More Soc. (pres. 1948-49), Phi Delta Phi. Clubs: India House (N.Y.C.), Arcola Country (Paramus, N.J.). Home: 393 Carriage Ln Wyckoff NJ 07481 Office: 21 West St New York NY 10006

CAREY, JANA HOWARD, lawyer; b. Huntsville, Ala., Apr. 20, 1945; d. Ernest Randall and Mary Regna (Baites) Howard; m. James Johnston Hale Carey, Jan. 15, 1983. BS in Home Econs., Auburn U., 1967; MS in Audiovisual Communications, Towson State U., 1973; JD, U. Balt., 1976. Tchr. Hampton High Sch., Melbourne, Australia, 1967; home economist U. Ga., Athens, 1967-70, devel. specialist state youth program, 1970-72; devel. specialist state youth program U. Md., College Park, 1972-73; clk. appellate div. Pub. Defender's Office, Balt., 1974; assoc. Venable, Baetjer & Howard, Balt., 1975, 76-84, ptnr., 1984—. Co-author: Legal Aspects of the Employment Relationship—An Introduction for the General Practitioner, 1978, Recent Developments on the Rights of the Handicapped, Disabled or Injured Worker, 1985; profl. articles editor U. Balt. Law Rev., 1974; contbr. articles to legal jours. Bd. dirs. Mcpl. Mus. Balt. City, 1984—, Balt. New Directions for Women, 1979-84, also past pres.; active women's mgmt. devel. program Goucher Coll., Balt., 1982-84; mem. affirmative action com. United Way Cen. Md., Balt., 1983-84.,. Mem. ABA (labor law sect., equal employment opportunity com., chair program div. of the com. on equal employment opportunity law), Fed. Bar Assn. (dep. chmn. labor relations 1978), Md. Bar Assn., Bar Assn. Balt. City, Md. C. of C. (small bus. adv. com., labor relations adv. com.), Gtr. Balt. Com. (chamber council, small bus. edn. com.), Balt. Women's Forum, Balt. Women's Law Ctr., Mortar Bd., CWENS, Alpha Gamma Delta (past chpt. pres.), Alpha Lambda Delta, Omicron Delta Kappa, Omicron Nu. Club: Loophole Law (Balt.). Labor. Office: Venable Baetjer & Howard 1800 Mercantile Bank & Trust Bldg Two Hopkins Plaza Baltimore MD 21201

CAREY, JOHN LEO, lawyer; b. Morris, Ill., Oct. 1, 1920; s. John Leo and Loretta (Conley) C.; m. Rhea M. White, July 15, 1950; children: John Leo III, Daniel Hobart, Deborah M. B.S., St. Ambrose Coll., Davenport, Ia., 1941; J.D., Georgetown U., 1947, LL.B., 1949. Bar: Ind. 1954. Legislative asst. Sen. Scott W. Lucas, 1945-47; spl. atty. IRS, Washington, 1947-54; since practiced in South Bend; partner firm Barnes & Thornburg, 1954—; law prof. taxation Notre Dame Law Sch., 1968—. Trustee LaLumire Prep. Sch., Laporte, Ind. Served with USAAF, World War II; to lt. col. USAF, Korean War. Decorated D.F.C., Air medal. Mem. ABA (bd. govs. 1985—), Ind. Bar Assn. (pres. 1976-77), St. Joseph County Bar Assn. Club: Signal Point Country. General corporate, Corporate taxation. Home: 1326 Ridgedale Rd South Bend IN 46614 Office: 1st Source Center South Bend IN 46601

CAREY, JOSEPH PATRICK, lawyer; b. Poughkeepsie, N.Y., Sept. 22, 1930; s. Thomas and Margaret (Havens) C.; m. Jean Marie Ouellette, Sept. 21, 1957; children: Thomas, Daniel, Anne-Marie, Ruth-Anne, John, Mark. Student, St. John's U., Bklyn., LLB, 1955; LLM in Labor Law, NYU, 1961. Bar: N.Y. 1955, U.S. Dist. Ct. (so. and ea. dists.) N.Y. 1956, U.S. Ct. Appeals (3d, 6th and 8th cirs.) 1980, U.S. Ct. Appeals (5th and 11th cirs.) 1981. Sole practice White Plains, N.Y., 1955—. Mem. ABA (equal employment opportunity com. labor and employment law sect.), Def. Research Inst. (equal employment opportunity com.). Labor, Employment law. Home: 32 Gold Rd Wappingers Falls NY 12590 Office: 34 S Broadway White Plains NY 10601

CAREY, MARCUS STEPHEN, lawyer; b. Covington, Ky., Mar. 5, 1953; s. Granville Orear and Shirley Mae (Stanfill) C.; m. Harriet Elizabeth Kirk, Oct. 26, 1973; children: Daniel Marcus, Andrew Stephen. BA, No. Ky. U., 1976, JD, 1980. Bar: Ky. 1980, U.S. Dist. Ct. (ea. dist.) Ky. 1980, U.S. Ct. Appeals (6th cir.) 1983. Assoc. Jolly, Johnson, Blau, Parry, Newport, Ky., 1980-81; sole practice Ft. Mitchell, Ky., 1982—. Bd. dirs. Kenton County Rep. Exec. Com., Ft. Mitchell, 1983-85; treas. Kenton County Rep. Men's Club, Ft. Mitchell, 1985—; chmn. Lou Defalaise campaign for state rep., Doug Stephens campaign for circuit judge. Mem. ABA, Ky. Bar Assn., Cin. Bar Assn., Louisville Bar Assn., Assn. Trial Lawyers Am., Ky. Acad. Trial Lawyers, Jaycees. Republican. Presbyterian. Lodges: Lions (scholarship chmn. Erlanger, Ky. club 1986). Avocation: white tail deer hunting. General practice, Personal injury, Federal civil litigation. Office: 211 Grandview Dr Suite 213 PO Box 17416 Fort Mitchell KY 41017

CAREY, MICHAEL W., lawyer. U.S. atty. State of W.Va., Charleston. Office: Post Office Box 3234 Charleston WV 25332 *

CAREY, RICHARD PETER, lawyer; b. Rockville Centre, N.Y., Sept. 4, 1948; s. Richard John and Ruth Mary (Brown) C.; m. Lois Jean Lipton, May 30, 1978; 1 child, Sara. Student, Emory U., 1966-68; AB, U. Ill., 1970, JD, 1973. Bar: Ill. 1973, U.S. Dist. Ct. (no. dist.) Ill. 1973, U.S. Ct. Appeals (7th cir.) 1978, U.S. Supreme Ct. 1978. Assoc. Kirkland & Ellis, Chgo., 1973-75, Fox & Grove, Chgo., 1975-76; assoc. Mandel, Lipton and Stevenson, Ltd., Chgo., 1976-80, ptnr., 1980—; cooperating atty. Roger Baldwin Found. ACLU, Inc. Bd. dirs. Chinese Am. Service League, Chgo., 1978-80, Mental Health Assn. Evanston (Ill.), 1980—. Mem. ABA, Ill. Bar Assn., Chgo. Council Lawyers. Federal civil litigation, State civil litigation, Labor. Office: Mandel Lipton and Stevenson Ltd 33 N Dearborn Chicago IL 60602

CAREY, SARAH COLLINS, lawyer; b. N.Y.C., Aug. 12, 1938; d. Jerome Joseph and Susan (Atlee) Collins; m. James J. Carey, Aug. 28, 1962 (div. 1977); 1 child, Sasha; m. 2d John D. Reilly, Jan. 27, 1979; children—Sarah, Katherine. B.A., Radcliffe Coll., 1960; LL.B., Georgetown U., 1965. Bar: D.C. 1966, U.S. Supreme Ct. 1977. Soviet specialist USIA/U.S. Dept. State, 1961-65; asso. Arnold & Porter, Washington, 1965-68; asst. dir. Lawyers Com. for Civil Rights, Washington, 1968-73; ptnr. Adams Duque & Hazeltine and predecessor cos., Washington, 1973-87, Heron, Burchette, Ruckert & Rothwell, Washington, 1987—; dir. HSB Internat.; cons. Ford Found., 1975-83, Carnegie Corp., 1984, Kettering Found., 1982—. Contbr. articles to profl. jours. Bd. dirs. New Transcentury Found., Washington, 1982—, Overseas Edn. Fund., 1982—, Inst. for Soviet-Am. Relations, 1983—, Georgetown U. Sch. Law Inst. for Pub. Representation, 1971-85, Am. Arbitration Assn., 1975-82, Vis. Nurses Assn., 1976-81. Mem. ABA (internat. law com.), D.C. Bar Assn. (sect. internat. law), Womens Bar Assn., Washington Internat. Trade Assn., others. Democrat. Administrative and regulatory, Private international, Legislative. Office: Heron Burchette Ruckert & Rothwell 1025 Thomas Jefferson St NW #700 Washington DC 20007

CARGERMAN, ALAN WILLIAM, circuit court judge; b. Chgo., Jan. 17, 1945; s. Harry and Bertha (Snider) C.(div.); children—Jack Marshall, Jill Faith. Student. U. Ill., 1961-64; LL.B., DePaul U., 1970. Bar: Ill. 1970. Editorial writer Commerce Clearing House, Inc., Chgo., 1969-70; asst. state's atty. Ogle County, Oregon, Ill., 1970-72; assoc. judge 15th Jud. Cir. Ill., Oregon, 1972—; lectr. Ill. Jud. Conf., 1981—, Nat. Jud. Coll., 1982; vice chmn. Northwest Ill. Criminal Justice Commn., 1971. Author Ill. Judges Assn. Manual History of the Illinois Judicial System, 1984. Mem. Ill. Commn. on Am. Constn. Bicentennial, 1985-87; chmn. Ogle County Commn. on Bicentennial, Oreg., 1987. Fellow Ill. Bar Found.; mem. Ill. State Bar Assn. (sec. criminal law sect. 1971), Ogle County Bar Assn. (sec. 1971), Am. Judicature Soc., ABA, Ill. Judges Assn. (dir. Chgo. 1977-83, 86—), Ill. Jud. Conf. (chmn. study com. Chgo. 1979-81), Conf. Chief Cir. Judges (rules com. Chgo. 1981—, coor. com. 1986—), Ill. Judges Assn. (jud. selection and retention com. 1981—, spl. task force on dispute resolution 1985—). Judicial administration, Jurisprudence, Legal history. Office: Assoc Judge 15th Cir Ogle County Courthouse Oregon IL 61061

CARGO, DAVID FRANCIS, lawyer; b. Dowagiac, Mich., Jan. 13, 1929; s. Francis Clair and Mary E. (Harton) C.; children—Veronica Ann, David Joseph, Patrick Michael, Maria Elena Christina, Eamon Francis. A.B., U. Mich., 1951, M.Pub. Adminstrn., 1953, LL.B., 1957. Bar: Mich., N.Mex. bars 1957, Oreg. bar 1974. Practice in Albuquerque, 1957, asst. dist. atty., 1958-59; mem. N.Mex. Ho. of Reps., 1962; gov. N.Mex., 1967-71; practice law Santa Fe, 1970-73, Portland, Oreg., 1973-84. Chmn. Four Corners Regional Commn., 1967-71, Oil and Gas Conservation Commn.; chmn. N.Mex. Young Republicans, 1959-61, Clackamas County Rep. Central Com.; mem. Israel Bond Com. Served with AUS, 1953-55. Named Man of Year Albuquerque Jr. C. of C., 1964; recipient Outstanding Conservationist award N.Mex. Wildlife Assn., 1969, 70. Mem. Mich., N.Mex., Albuquerque bar assns., Issac Walton League (past v.p. N.Mex.), World Affairs Council Oreg. (pres.), Interstate Oil and Gas Compact, Izaak Walton League Oreg. General corporate, Criminal, Family and matrimonial. Home: 6422 Concordia St NE Albuquerque NM 87111 Office: 708 Marquette St NW Albuquerque NM 87102

CARLEN, LEON C., lawyer; b. N.Y.C., Oct. 22, 1915; s. Eisig and Fanny (Lazarus) C.; m. Esta Seligman, June 27, 1948; children—Elliot Cardozo, Frances A. B.A., Bklyn. Coll., 1936, LL.B., 1939. Bar: N.Y. 1940, U.S. Dist. Ct. (so. dist.) N.Y. 1948, U.S. Dist. Ct. (ea. dist.) N.Y. 1957, U.S. Supreme Ct. 1960, U.S. Ct. Appeals (2d cir.) 1966. Assoc. Fuchsberg & Fuchsberg, N.Y.C., 1950-54; ptnr. Jaffe, Carlen & Stern, Mineola, N.Y., 1972-82. Served with USAF, 1942-45; CBI. Mem. Nassau County Bar Assn., N.Y. State Bar Assn., Bklyn. Coll. Law Assn. Democrat. Jewish. State civil litigation, Personal injury. Home: 2 Caffrey Ave Bethpage NY 11714

CARLENO, HARRY EUGENE, lawyer; b. Denver, Mar. 3, 1928; s. Benjamin Edward and Elizabeth Bess (De Rose) C.; m. Ann Marie Kraft, Sept. 14, 1957; children: Gregory S., Paul C., Jennifer A., Machelle L. BBA, U. Denver, 1951, LLB, 1955, JD, 1970. Bar: Colo. 1955, U.S. Dist. Ct. Colo. 1955, U.S. Ct. Appeals (10th cir.) 1959, U.S. Supreme Ct. 1959. Pres., atty. H.E. Carleno & Assoc., P.C., Englewood, Colo., 1955-79, Littleton, Colo., 1979—; mcpl. judge City of Wheat Ridge, Colo., 1971-78; dep. dist. atty. Arapahoe County, Letttleton, 1958-68. Chmn. Dem. Com., Arapahoe County, 1964-65; chmn. Career Service Commn., Englewood, 1961-64; pres. Inter Faith Task Force Found., Englewood, 1986—. Served as col. USAF, 1947-53. Recipient St. Geroge award Denver Area council Boy Scouts Am., 1980. Mem. ABA, Colo. Bar Assn., Arapahoe County Bar Assn. (trustee 1968-70), Res. Officers Assn. of U.S. Roman Catholic. Lodge: Kiwanis (local pres. 1966-67). Probate, Family and matrimonial, State civil litigation. Home: 5471 S Sherman St Littleton CO 80121 Office: 1800 West Littleton Blvd Littleton CO 80120

CARLILE, CRAIG, lawyer; b. Heber, Utah, May 16, 1955; s. Rulon George and Jennie (Broadbent) C.; m. (Lucy) Jane Levanger, Sept. 8, 1977; children: Chelsea, Chase. BA, Utah State U., 1978; JD, Brigham Young U., 1981. Bar: U.S. Dist. Ct. Utah 1981, Utah 1981. Assoc. Parsons, Behle & Latimer, Salt Lake City, 1981; law clk. to presiding judge U.S. Dist. Ct. Utah, Salt Lake City, 1982; assoc. Ray, Quinney & Nebeker, Provo, Utah, 1983-87, ptnr., 1987—; bd. dirs. Ins. Concepts, Inc., Salt Lake City, P.U.P. Inc., Provo, Mazuma Corp., Provo. Mem. exec com. to Elect Wayne Owens for Gov., Salt Lake City, 1984. Mem. ABA, Utah Bar Assn., Cen. Utah Bar Assn., Order of the Barristers. Democrat. Mormon. Avocations: golf, water skiing, basketball, racquetball. Contracts commercial, Banking, State civil litigation. Home: 771 N 1200 E Provo UT 84601 Office: Ray Quinney & Nebeker 92 N University Ave Suite 210 Provo UT 84601

CARLILE, ROBERT TOY, lawyer; b. Phila., July 27, 1926; s. Robert and Eva (MacQueen) C.; m. Doris A. Arnold, Aug. 10, 1948; children—Robert A., Regan J. B.B.A., U. Miami, 1949; J.D., U. Fla., 1958. Bar: Fla. 1958. Assoc., Grimditch & Smith, Deerfield Beach, Fla., 1958-60; sole practice Deerfield Beach, 1960-65, 73—; ptnr. Carlile & Pulskamp, Deerfield Beach, 1965-69, Carlile, Pulskamp & Fletcher, 1969-72, Carlile & Fletcher, 1972-73; city atty., Deerfield Beach, 1963-68; mcpl. judge, 1971-77. Served with U.S. Army, 1944-46, USAF, 1951-53. Mem. Fla. Bar Assn., North Broward County Bar Assn. (pres. 1966), Broward County Bar Assn., Broward County Mcpl. Judges Assn. (v.p. 1975), Deerfield Beach C. of C. (pres. 1966), Phi Alpha Delta. Democrat. Clubs: Kiwanis (pres.), Billiken (pres.), Gold Coast Shriners, Jesters. Probate, Real property, General corporate. Office: 1215 E Hillsboro Blvd Deerfield Beach FL 33441

CARLIN, CLAIR MYRON, lawyer; b. Sharon, Pa., Apr. 20, 1947; s. Charles William and Carolyn L. (Vukasich) C.; m. Cecilia Julia Reis, Sept. 21, 1971 (div. Mar. 1982); children—Elizabeth Marie, Alexander Myron; m. Pamela Ann Roshon, Sept. 30, 1982; 1 son, Eric Richard. B.S. in Econs., Ohio State U., 1969, J.D., 1972. Bar: Ohio 1973, Pa. 1973, U.S. Dist. Ct. (so. dist.) Ohio 1973, U.S. Dist. Ct. (no. dist.) Ohio 1975, U.S. Supreme Ct. 1976, U.S. Ct. Claims 1983, U.S. Ct. Appeals (6th cir.) 1983, U.S. Tax Ct. 1985. Staff atty. Ohio Dept. Taxation, Columbus, 1972-73; asst. city atty. City of Warren, Ohio, 1973-75; assoc. McLaughlin, DiBlasio & Harshman, Youngstown, Ohio, 1975-80; ptnr. McLaughlin, McNally & Carlin, Youngstown, 1980—. Mem. Trumbull County Bicentennial Commn., Ohio, 1976; v.p. Services for the Aging, Trumbull County, 1976-77; mem. Pres.' Club Ohio State U. Served to maj. Ohio NG, 1972-84. Mem. ABA, Ohio State Bar Assn., Ohio State Bar Coll., Mahoning County Bar Assn. (chmn. legal edn. com. 1985-86), Am. Acad. Trial Lawyers, Ohio Acad. Trial Lawyers, Ohio State U. Alumni Assn. (pres. Trumbull County chpt. 1985—), Cath. War Vets. (judge advocate). Democrat. Roman Catholic. Club: Tippecanoe Country (Canfield, Ohio). Lodge: Rotary. Contracts commercial, Federal civil litigation, Personal injury. Home: 5510 W Boulevard Youngstown OH 44512 Office: McLaughlin McNally & Carlin 500 City Centre One Youngstown OH 44503

CARLIN, DONALD WALTER, lawyer, food company executive; b. Gary, Ind., Aug. 27, 1934; s. Walter Joseph and Mabel (Ebert) C.; m. Kathleen Susan McCone, Jan. 21, 1961; children: Michael Scott, Karen Mary, Mark Steven. B.S. in Engring, U. Notre Dame, 1956; LL.B., U. Mich., 1959; student, Advanced Mgmt. Program, Harvard U., 1978. Bar: Ind. 1959, Ill. 1960. Sole practice Chgo., 1960—; mem. firm Anderson, Luedeka, Fitch, Even and Tabin, 1965-72; sr. atty. Kraft Inc., Glenview, Ill, 1972-73, asst. v.p., asst. gen. counsel, 1973-74, v.p., asst. gen. counsel, 1974-79, sr. v.p., gen. counsel, 1979-86, v.p., assoc. gen. counsel, 1986—; Bd. dirs. Food and Drug Law Inst., 1977—, Food Update, 1978-80. Served with USAFR, 1959-63; 1960-65. Mem. ABA, Chgo. Bar Assn. (mem. exec. com. 1981-83) Grocery Mfrs. Am. (mem. legal exec. com. 1981—), Assn. Gen. Counsel, Assn. Corp. Patent Counsel, Patent Law Assn. Chgo., Am. Soc. Corp. Secs. Clubs: Westmoreland Country (Wilmette, Ill.); Notre Dame (Chgo.). General corporate. Home: 3020 Normandy Pl Evanston IL 60201 Office: Kraft Inc Glenview IL 60025

CARLIN, JOHN BERNARD, JR., lawyer; b. Detroit, July 28, 1939; s. John B. and Marjorie A. (Brunner) C.; m. Mary Jane Gaertner, Nov. 27, 1971; children: Judith, Debra, John, Brian, Kevin. AB, St. Joseph's Coll., Rensselaer, Ind., 1962; JD, U. Detroit, 1965. Bar: Mich. 1966, Fla. 1972. Asst. atty. City of Detroit, 1966-68; sole practice Southfield and Birmingham, Mich., 1968-70, 72-85; exec. sec., dir. Detroit Fire Dept., 1970-72; prin. Barbier, Petersmark, Tolleson, Mead, Paige & Carlin P.C., Birmingham, 1985—. Contbr. articles on legal aspects of restaurants to profl. jours. Councilman City of Orchard Lake, Mich., 1981—, former Mayor; vice chmn. Mich. week com. Greater West Bloomfield, chmn. 1986—; trustee St. mary's Prep. High Sch., Orchard Lake, 1985—. Mem. Mich. Bar Assn., Fla. Bar Assn., Oakland County Bar Assn. Administrative and regulatory, Contracts commercial, Retaurants and liquor licenses. Home: 3670 Erie Dr Orchard Lake MI 48003 Office: Barbier Petersmark et al 300 Park Suite 485 Birmingham MI 48009

CARLIN, PAUL V., bar association executive; b. McKeesport, Pa., Nov. 11, 1945. B.A., Grove City Coll., 1967; J.D., Dickinson Law Sch., 1970. Bar: Pa. 1971, D.C. 1978, U.S. Dist. Ct. (we. dist.) Pa. 1971, U.S. Dist. Ct. D.C. 1978, U.S. Supreme Ct. 1979. Exec. dir. Balt. City Bar Assn., 1981-84, Conn. Bar Assn., Rocky Hill, 1984—, Md. Bar Assn., Balt., 1985-85 . Office: Md State Bar Assn 520 W Fayette St Baltimore MD 21201 *

CARLINER, DAVID, lawyer; b. Washington, Aug. 13, 1918; s. Louis and Cassie (Brooks) C.; m. Miriam Kalter, Jan. 24, 1944; children: Geoffrey Owen, Deborah Joan (Mrs. Robert Remes). Student, Am. U., 1935-36, U. Va., 1936-38; student in law, U. Va., 1938-40; LL.B., Nat. U., 1941. Bar: D.C., Va. Atty. JAG Office Army Dept., Washington, 1946; Washington rep. New Council Am. Bus., Washington, 1946-48; practice law David Carliner and Remes P.C., Washington.; vis. lectr. Fgn. Service Inst., Dept. State, USIA, Harvard U. Law Sch., 1985. Author: Rights of Aliens. Nat. bd. dirs. ACLU, 1965-83, gen. counsel, 1976-79; chmn. Internat. Human Rights Law Group, 1978-86, Washington Home Rule Com., 1966-70; co-chmn. D.C. Com. for Re-Orgn. Plan, 1967-68; chmn. Washington chpt., mem. nat. exec. council Am. Jewish Com., 1969-71; mem. nat. adv. council Amnesty Internat., 1969—; hon. chmn. Am. Haitian Com., 1976—; Bd. dirs. Am. Council for Nationalities Services, 1977—, Internat. League for Human Rights; trustee Washington Inst. Values in Pub. Policy, 1984—. Served with AUS, 1941-45. Recipient Oliver Wendell Holmes award, 1966. Mem. Am. Bar Assn. (chmn. immigration and nationality com. adminstrv. law sect. 1979-83, mem. council administrv. law sect. 1983-87), Am. Law Inst., Assn. Immigration, Nationality Lawyers (gov.), Fed. Bar Assn. (chmn. com. immigration and naturalization 1961-62), D.C. Bar (vice chmn. opinions com. ethics 1974-76, dir. 1980-83), Va. State Bar, Nat. Lawyers Club. Immigration, naturalization, and customs. Home: 2941 Chesapeake St NW Washington DC 20008 Office: 931 Investment Bldg 1511 K St NW Washington DC 20005

CARLINI, LAWRENCE J., corporate lawyer. Sr. v.p. gen. counsel, sec. Soc. Corp., Cleve. Office: Soc Corp 127 Public Sq Cleveland OH 44114 *

CARLISLE, JAY CHARLES, II, lawyer, educator; b. Washington, Apr. 8, 1942; s. Jay C. and Opal Fiske C.; m. Frances Bell, Nov. 22, 1970 (div.); 1 dau., Marie Bell; m. Janessa C. Nisley, June 22, 1984. A.B., UCLA, 1965; J.D., U. Calif.-Davis, 1969; postgrad. Columbia U., 1969-70. Bar: N.Y. 1970, N.Mex. 1972, U.S. Dist. Ct. (so., ea. and we. dists.) N.Y. 1975, U.S. Ct. Appeals (2d cir.) 1975, U.S. Supreme Ct. 1971. Asst. trial counsel ITT, Hartford, 1970-71; assoc. Bigbee, Bryd, Carpenter & Crout, Santa Fe, 1971-73; sole practice, 1973-75; asst. dean SUNY-AB Law Sch., 1975-78; counsel Nierenberg, Zeif & Weinstein, 1977-80, Olsen & So-rentino, 1981-83; sole practice, N.Y.C., 1980—; lectr. Pace U., 1978-80, prof. civil procedure, N.Y. practice, criminal procedure and ethics, Pace U., 1980—; adj. prof. Fordham U., 1987—; commr. N.Y. Task Force on Women and Cts., 1984-86. Co-author: CPLR Manual; contbr. articles to profl. jours. Recipient SUNY-Buffalo Law Sch. Alumni award, 1978, Erie County Bar Assn. Commendation award 1978, cert. of Appreciation N.Y. Sup. Ct. for Spl. Master Service 1982. Mem. N.Y. State Bar Assn., Assn. Bar City N.Y. Republican. Episcopalian. Civil rights, Federal civil litigation, Legal education. Office: Pace Univ School of Law White Plains NY 10603

CARLSEN, CHRIS JEFFREY, lawyer; b. Sioux Falls, S.D., Nov. 26, 1956; s. Ernest George and Bonnie Jean (Brammer) C. BA, Augustana Coll., 1978; JD, U. So. Calif., Los Angeles, 1981. Bar: S.D. 1981, Calif. 1982.

Atty. Burbank (Calif.) Studios, 1982-83; ptnr. Delbridge, Hanson & Carlsen, Sioux Falls, 1983-84, Swanson, Carlsen et al, Sioux Falls, 1984—. Pres. Handi-Riders, Inc., Sioux Falls, 1984. Mem. ABA, Calif. Bar Assn., S.D. Bar Assn., Internat. Bar Assn. (chmn. sports law div.), C. of C. Lutheran. Lodge: Rotary. General corporate, Real property, Sports law. Home: Penmarch Pl Sioux Falls SD 57106 Office: Swanson Carlsen Carter Hoy & Anderson 101 S Main 5th Floor Sioux Falls SD 57102

CARLSON, ALAN DOUGLAS, lawyer; b. Omaha, May 24, 1951; s. John Peter and Elizabeth Jean (Pflasterer) C.; m. Sarah Louise Ware, June 28, 1975; children: Elizabeth, Anne, Sally. AB, Augustana Coll., Rock Island, Ill., 1973; postgrad., Luth. Sch. Theology, 1974-75; JD, Creighton U., 1978. Bar: Nebr. 1978, U.S. Dist. Ct. Nebr. 1978, Colo. 1981, U.S. Dist. Ct. Colo. 1981. Staff asst. govt. relations Luth. Council USA, Washington, 1973-74; assoc. Holtorf, Kovarik & Nuttleman, Gering, Nebr., 1978-80; sales assoc. Van Schaak Real Estate, Boulder, Colo., 1981; ptnr. Hopp, Carlson & Beckmann, Longmont, Colo., 1981—. Del. County Rep. Conv. and Nebr. Rep. Conv., 1976; sec. Gering Jaycees, 1979-80; mem. subcom. social ministry Rocky Mountain Synod, Denver, 1984—, adv. bd. Luth. Office Govt. Ministry, Denver, 1984—. Mem. ABA, Nebr. Bar Assn., Colo. Bar Assn., Assn. Trial Lawyers Am., Colo. Trial Lawyers Assn., Christian Legal Soc. Republican. Lodge: Optimists. Avocations: horseback riding, swimming, tennis, mountain hiking. State civil litigation, Personal injury, Real property. Office: Hopp Carlson & Beckmann PC 2130 Mountain View Suite A Longmont CO 80501

CARLSON, DAVID BRET, lawyer; b. Jamestown, N.Y., Aug. 16, 1918; s. David Albert and Gertrude (Johnson) C.; m. Jane Tapley, Apr. 12, 1947; children: Chistopher Tapley, David Kurt, Nancy. A.B., Brown U., 1940; LL.B., Harvard U., 1947. Bar: N.Y. 1947, U.S. Supreme Ct. 1972. Assoc. firm Debevoise & Plimpton, N.Y.C., 1947-53, ptnr., 1953—. Contbr. articles to profl. publs. Mem. ABA, N.Y. State Bar Assn., Bar Assn. City N.Y., Am. Law Inst., Tax Forum. Corporate taxation, Pension, profit-sharing, and employee benefits, Personal income taxation. Home: 2700 Redding Rd Fairfield CT 06430 Office: 875 3d Ave New York NY 10022

CARLSON, JEFFERY JOHN, lawyer; b. Mpls., May 23, 1947; s. John Joseph and Sylvia Lorraine (Sandberg) C.; m. Adrienne M. Cunha; children—Erik John, Bryan Jeffery, Kimberly Anne. Student Augsburg Coll., 1965-66; B.A. summa cum laude, U. Minn., 1969, postgrad., 1970-71; J.D., UCLA, 1974. Bar: Calif. 1974, U.S. Dist. Ct. (cen. dist.) Calif. 1974, U.S. Ct. Appeals (9th cir.) 1976. Teaching asst., research asst. U. Minn., Mpls., 1970-71; assoc. Harwood & Adkinson, Newport Beach, Calif., 1974-77; assoc. Haight, Dickson, Brown & Bonesteel, Santa Monica, Calif., 1977-81, ptnr., 1981—; judge pro tem West Los Angeles Mcpl. Ct., 1981-83; arbitrator Panel of Arbitrators, Los Angeles, Orange, and Ventura counties, 1980—; lectr. bus. law Calif. State U., Northridge, 1978; lectr. Calif. Continuing Edn. of the Bar, 1984—. Mem. So. Calif. Def. Counsel, Def. Research Inst., Phi Beta Kappa (James Hartley Beal award 1987). Lutheran. Personal injury, State civil litigation, Insurance. Office: Haight Dickson Brown & Bonesteel 201 Santa Monica Blvd Santa Monica CA 90401

CARLSON, J(OHN) PHILIP, lawyer; b. Shickley, Nebr., Apr. 16, 1915; s. Christopher Theodore and Klara Louise (Blomquist) C.; m. Maryjo Suverkrup, Oct. 14, 1950. Student Luther Coll., 1931-33; A.B., Wayne State Coll., 1935; M.A., Columbia U., 1967; J.D., Georgetown U., 1951. Bar: D.C. 1952, U.S. Dist. Ct. D.C. 1952, U.S. Ct. Appeals D.C. cir. 1952, U.S. Supreme Ct. 1957, U.S. Ct. Mil. Appeals 1970, D.C. Ct. Appeals 1972. Tchr., athletic coach high schs. of Bristow, Nebr., 1935-37, Carroll, Nebr., 1937-38, Ashland, Nebr., 1938-42; vets. relations advisor OPA, Washington, 1946-47; tng. specialist Dept. Navy, 1947-56; minority counsel House Com. on Govt. Ops., 1956-80; sole practice law, Washington, 1980—. Bd. dirs. Fellowship Sq. Found., Reston, Va., 1961-86, Peter Muehlenberg Meml. Assn., 1972—. Served to capt. USAAF, 1942-45; ETO. Congl. Staff fellow Am. Polit. Sci. Assn., 1964-65, 66-67; Decorated D.F.C., Air medal with oak leaf cluster; recipient Meritorious Service award Am. Nat. Standards Inst., 1980, Meritorious Service award Fellowship Square Found., 1986. Mem. ABA, Fed. Bar Assn., D.C. Bar Assn., Am. Econ. Assn., Air Force Assn., Res. Officers Assn. Republican. Lutheran. Clubs: Metropolitan, Capitol Hill, Nat. Econs. (Washington); Belle Haven County (Alexandria, Va.). Home: 2206 Belle Haven Rd Alexandria VA 22307

CARLSON, MARY SUSAN, lawyer; b. Lincoln, Nebr., Nov. 2, 1949; d. Arnold Emil and Mary (Lloyd) C.; m. Gerald Philip Greiman, May 2, 1982; children: David Carlson, Nora Carlson. AA, Cottey Coll., 1970; BFA in Edn., U. Nebr., 1972; postgrad., Notre Dame Law Sch., Tokyo, 1974; JD, U. Nebr., 1976. Bar: Nebr. 1977, D.C. 1979, U.S. Supreme Ct. 1986. Staff law clk. to presiding justice U.S. Ct. Appeals (8th cir.), St. Louis, 1976-78; assoc. Kilcullen, Smith & Heenan, Washington, 1978-79; trial atty. Guam land claims litigation U.S. Dept. Justice, Agana, 1981; trial atty. civil div. U.S. Dept. Justice, Washington, 1980-86; vis. asst. prof. law Washington U., St. Louis, 1987—. Mem. ABA, Nebr. Bar Assn., D.C. Bar Assn. Federal civil litigation, Private international, Public international. Office: Washington U Sch Law Washington U Campus Box 1120 One Brookings Dr Saint Louis MO 63130

CARLSON, ROBERT JAMES, lawyer; b. Grand Junction, Colo., May 22, 1955; s. John Perry and Betty Anne (Glassburn) C. BSEE, U. Colo., 1977, JD, 1982. Bar: Colo. 1982, U.S. Dist. Ct. Colo. 1982. Assoc. Madden & Strate P.C., Wheat Ridge, Colo., 1982—. Mem. Colo. Bar Assn., Phi Delta Phi. State civil litigation, Federal civil litigation, Insurance. Office: Madden & Strate PC 4465 Kipling Wheat Ridge CO 80033

CARLSON, STEPHEN CURTIS, lawyer; b. Mpls., Mar. 22, 1951; s. Curtis Harvey and Edna Mae (Pfunder) C.; m. Patricia Jane Brown, Aug. 21, 1976; children: Elizabeth Buckley, Susan Pfunder. AB magna cum laude, Princeton U., 1973; JD, Yale U., 1976. Bar: Minn. 1977, Ill. 1977, U.S. Dist. Ct. Minn. 1977, U.S. Dist. Ct. (no. dist.) Ill. 1977, U.S. Ct. Appeals (7th and 8th cirs.) 1977. Law clk. to presiding justice Minn. Supreme Ct., St. Paul, 1976-77; assoc. Sidley & Austin, Chgo., 1977-83, ptnr., 1983—. Capt. 1st Ward 11th precinct Reps., Chgo., 1985—; pres. Dearborn Park Unit One Townhomes Condominium Assn., 1987—. Mem. ABA, Ill. Bar Assn., Chgo. Bar Assn., Am. Judicature Soc., Legal Club, Phi Beta Kappa. Presbyterian. Club: Princeton, Yale (Chgo.). Avocations: theater, opera, symphony. Federal civil litigation, State civil litigation. Home: 1132 S Plymouth Ct Chicago IL 60605 Office: Sidley & Austin One First National Plaza Chicago IL 60603

CARLSON, TIMOTHY JOHN, lawyer; b. Rhinelander, Wis., Dec. 29, 1952; s. Carl B. and Mabel M. Carlson; m. Karin Christine Larsen, Aug. 20, 1977; children: Katherine, Brian, Elizabeth. BA in Chemistry, St. Olaf Coll., 1975; JD with honors, Gonzaga U., 1980. Bar: Wash. 1980, U.S. Dist. Ct. (we. and ea. dists.) Wash. 1980, U.S. Bankruptcy Ct. 1981, U.S. Ct. Appeals (9th cir.) 1985. From assoc. to ptnr. Halverson & Applegate, P.S., Yakima, Wash., 1980—; mem. rules com. U.S. Bankruptcy Ct. (ea. dist.) Wash., Spokane, 1982—. Symposium editor Gonzaga U. Law Rev. Mem. Civil Service Commn., Yakima; bd. dirs. Boy Scouts Am., Yakima. Mem. ABA (debtor-creditor, real property probate and trusts sects.), Wash. State Bar Assn. (trustee young lawyers div., debtor-creditor, real property probate and trust sects., continuing legal edn. com.), Yakima County Bar Assn., Yakima C. of C., Order of Barristers. Club: YMCA (Yakima). Consumer commercial, Bankruptcy, Computer. Home: 1416 S 30th Ave Yakima WA 98902 Office: Halverson & Applegate PS 311 N 4th St PO Box 526 Yakima WA 98907

CARLTON, DIANE MICHELE, lawyer, judge; b. Los Angeles, Sept. 26, 1950; d. Thomas Neal and Fanny Jean (Crawford) Moon; m. Gregory Carlton, Sept. 12, 1969; children: Brendan, Dylan. BA in Spanish and Criminal Justice, U. Calif., Irvine, 1972; JD, U. Denver, 1976. Bar: Colo. 1977, U.S. Dist. Ct. Colo. 1977, U.S. Ct. Appeals (10th cir.) 1977. Pub. defender State of Colo., Denver, 1978-82; ptnr. Carlton & Jacobi, Denver, 1983—; judge, City of Aurora, Colo., 1983—. Mem. ABA, Colo. Bar Assn., Colo. Criminal Def. Bar Assn., Colo. Women's Bar Assn., Colo. Mcpl. Judge's Assn. Democrat. Avocations: reading, hiking, gardening, skiing. Criminal, Family and matrimonial, Personal injury. Office: Carlton & Jacobi 300 S Jackson #320 Denver CO 80209

CARLUCCI, JOSEPH PAUL, lawyer; b. Port Chester, N.Y., Aug. 21, 1942; m. Barbara Keenan; children—Susan Elizabeth, Kathleen Ann. B.A. in Econs., Georgetown U., 1964; J.D., Fordham U., 1967. Bar: N.Y. 1969. Ptnr. Pierro & Carlucci, Port Chester, N.Y., 1969-76; sole practice, Rye, N.Y., 1977-78; ptnr. Cuddy & Feder, White Plains, N.Y., 1979—; chief legis. counsel to N.Y. senator from New Rochelle, 1971-73; chief counsel N.Y. State Select Com. on State's Economy, 1973-74; mem. co. adv. bd. Security Title-Guarantee, 1986—. Trustee Village of Port Chester, 1975-77; chmn. Port Chester Indsl. Devel. Agy., 1974-76; mem. Westchester County Econ. Devel. Council, 1976—, Narcotics Guidance Council of Port Chester, 1970-74; bd. dirs. Port Chester YMCA, 1970-79, sec., 1972-77, v.p., 1978; mem. Port Chester Govt. Study Commn., 1971-73; commr. of appraisal White Plains and Greenburgh Urban Renewal; counsel to Sound Shore Hotline, 1973-74; mem. Port Chester Pub. Employees Relations Bd., 1971-73; mem. adv. bd. dirs. Salvation Army, 1973-77; adv. bd. Security Title and Guarantee Co., 1986—; bd. dirs. Rye YMCA, 1979—, pres., 1982-85, recipient Gold Man award, 1985; trustee Rye Hist. Soc., 1979-83, sec., 1980-81, v.p., 1982-83. Recipient Golden R award Rennaissance Project, Inc. Mem. ABA (vice chmn. econs. of law practice com. on lawyering skills 1984-85), NY State Bar Assn., Westchester County Bar Assn. (real property com. 1978-81), Port Chester-Rye Bar Assn. (sec. 1970-75, pres. 1976, 77). Clubs: Coveleigh (bd. govs. 1978-85, sec. 1979, v.p. 1980, pres. 1981-84) (Rye); Georgetown U. Met. (bd. dirs. 1980-82). General corporate, Probate, Real property. Office: Cuddy & Feder 90 Maple Ave White Plains NY 10601

CARLUCCIO, ROBERT JAMES, lawyer; b. Hoboken, N.J., Feb. 18, 1930; s. Charles G. and Elsie (Visconti) C.; m. Concetta Tortorella, Sept. 15, 1956; children: Elizabeth Ann, Maria Rose, Robert J., John F., Paul C. BS, St. Peters Coll., 1951; LLD, Fordham U., 1955. Bar: N.J. 1957, U.S. Dist. Ct. N.J. 1957, U.S. Dist. Ct. (ea. dist.) N.Y. 1957, U.S. Ct. Appeals (3d cir.) 1960, U.S. Supreme Ct. 1961. Ptnr. Carluccio & Carluccio, Hoboken, 1955—; tchr. Inst. Continuing Legal Edn., 1970-75; trial atty. N.J. State Supreme Ct., 1983; condemnation commr. Superior Ct. of Bergen County; arbitrator N.J. Superior Ct. of Hudson County, Am. Arbitration Assn.; commr. Teaneck Redevelopment Bd. Co-author: Landlord & Tenant, Real Property Law, 1960. Pres. Teaneck (N.J.) Dems., 1968; campaign mgr. Albert Burstien Dem. Assembly, 1970. Mem. N.J. Bar Assn., N.Y. County Bar Assn., Hudson County Bar Assn., Bergen County Bar Assn., Assn. Trial Lawyers Am., N.J. Trial Lawyers Assn., Nat. Assn. Criminal Def. Attys., N.J. Assn. Criminal Def. Attys., UNICO (legal advisor 1979), Holy Name Soc. (sec. 1968-69). General practice, Personal injury, Criminal. Home: 1297 Sussex Rd Teaneck NJ 07666 Office: Carluccio & Carluccio 96 Hudson St Hoboken NJ 07030

CARMAN, GREGORY WRIGHT, judge; b. Farmingdale, N.Y., Jan. 31, 1937; s. Willis B. and Marjorie (Sosa) C. Exchange student, U. Paris, 1956; B.A., St. Lawrence U., 1958; J.D., St. John's U., 1961; Judge Adv. Gen. honors grad., U. Va. Law Sch., 1962. Bar: N.Y. 1961. Councilman Town of Oyster Bay, N.Y., 1972-81; mem. 97th Congress from 3d Dist. N.Y.; judge U.S. Ct. Internat. Trade, N.Y.C. Served to capt. AUS, 1962-64. Mem. Am. Bar Assn., Nassau County Bar Assn., Nassau Lawyers Assn., Criminal Cts. Bar Assn., N.Y. State Defenders Assn., N.Y. State Bar Assn. Republican. Episcopalian. Club: Rotary. Office: 280 Main St Farmingdale NY 11735

CARMEL, ALAN STUART, lawyer, educator; b. Balt., July 24, 1944; s. Isaac and Sylvia (Sirulnik) C.; m. Ellen Freda Hobman, June 29, 1969; children: Shana Miriam, Jason Mark, Jarre Paige. A.A. magna cum laude, U. Balt., 1963, J.D., 1966. Bar: Md. bar 1966. Sec., asst. counsel 1st Federated Life Ins. Co., Balt., 1966-69; dir. equity mktg. U.S. counsel Mfrs. Life Ins. Co., Toronto, Ont., Can., 1970-75; v.p., dir. ManEquity, Inc., Denver, 1970-75; pres., dir. ManuLife Holding Corp., 1970-75; v.p., gen. counsel, sec., dir. Atlantic Internat. Corp., Balt., 1975-80, Atlantic Internat. Mktg. Corp., Balt., 1975-80, Atlantic Mfg. Corp., Balt., 1975-80; dir. Atlantic Industries, Inc.; gen. counsel AI Services (A.G.), Zug, Switzerland, 1976-80; sole practice 1981-84; prin. McGrow, Pridgeon & Co., P.A., 1984—; exec. v.p., dir. Imperial Group (N.A.) Ltd., 1982—; prof. tax law No. Va. Law Sch.; gen. counsel Brooks Shoe Mfg. Co., Inc., Hanover, Pa., Turner Shoe Co., Aguadilla, P.R., Carmen Athletic Industries, Aguadilla, Romana Athletic Industries, Dominican Republic, Century Shoe Co., St. Kitts, W.I.; exec. mgr. Atliran, P.J.S.C., Tehran, Iran, to 1980; U.S. arbitrator Internat. C. of C. Ct. Arbitration; mem. Inst. Bus. Appriasers Inc.; arbitrator Mcpl. Securities Rulemaking Bd., Nat. Assn. Securities Dealers Inc., N.Y. Stock Exchange Inc., Am. Stock Exchange, Chgo. Bd. Options Exchange, Ins. Arbitration Forums Inc.; mem. exec. com. Citizenship Law Related Edn. Program for Schs. Md. Author: Business Entities and Their Taxation in Liechtenstein; co-author: No Count Accounting, 1986. Fellow Life Mgmt. Inst.; mem. ABA, Md. Bar Assn., Am. Arbitration Assn. (comml. panel), Internat. Soc. Appraisers (affiliate). General corporate, Private international, Estate taxation. Home: 2425 Diana Rd Baltimore MD 21209 Office: McGrow Pridgeon & Co PA 1100 Investment Bldg Towson MD 21204

CARMEL, FRANK JOSEPH, lawyer; b. Hampton, Va., May 11, 1954; s. Melvin M. and Sylvia G. (Garfinkel) C.; m. Debra Ellen Chertok, Sept. 15, 1984. BS in Econs., Va. Polytech. Inst., 1976; JD, U. Va., 1979. Bar: D.C. 1979, Va. 1980, U.S. Ct. Appeals (4th and D.C. cirs.) 1980. Assoc. Ingersoll & Bloch, Washington, 1980-84; ptnr. Carmel & Carmel, Washington, 1984—; bd. dirs. Met. Builders Mortgage Corp. Named one of Outstanding Young Men of Am., 1980. Mem. ABA, D.C. Bar Assn., Fed. Bar Assn. (sustaining), Va. Bar Assn., Am. Resort Assn. and Residential Devel. Assn., Nat. Assn. Mortgage Brokers (cons. 1985-86). Jewish. Avocations: tennis, golf, skiing, water sports, rehabilitation of hist. property. Real property, Banking, Administrative and regulatory. Home: 4111 Emery Place NW Washington DC 20016 Office: Carmel & Carmel 1747 Pennsylvania Ave NW Suite 1100 Washington DC 20006

CARMICHAEL, CARSON, III, lawyer; b. Abingdon, Va., Sept. 29, 1954; s. Carson Jr. and Frances Rosemary (Clarkston) C.; m. Deborah Nell Murray, May 19, 1984. BSChemE, BS in Pulp, Paper Sci. and Tech., N.C. State U., 1976; JD, Wake Forest U., 1980. Bar: N.C. 1981, U.S. Dist. Ct. (ea. dist.) N.C. 1981, U.S. Ct. Appeals (4th cir.) 1981. Project engr. Fed. Paper Bd., Riegelwood, N.C., 1977; assoc. Bailey, Dixon, Wooten, McDonald, Fountain & Walker, Raleigh, N.C., 1981-85, ptnr., 1985—; mem. legal com. Gov.'s Waste Mgmt. Bd., Raleigh, 1986—. Mem. ABA, N.C. Bar Assn. (environ. law com. 1984—), Wake County Bar Assn. Democrat. Presbyterian. Administrative and regulatory, Environment, Legislative. Office: Bailey Dixon Wooten McDonald Fountain 601 St Marys St PO Box 12865 Raleigh NC 27605-2865

CARMIEN, DONALD CHARLES, lawyer, transportation consultant; b. Peoria, Ill., July 20, 1932; s. Enest Donald and Helen Elizabeth (Tench) C.; m. Janice Farwell Carmien, Sept. 4, 1954; children—Nancy Carmien Francis, Carol, Michael, Mark. B.A., Albion (Mich.) Coll., 1954; LL.B., Syracuse U., 1958. Bar: N.Y. 1958, U.S. Dist. Ct. (no. dist.) N.Y., 1960, U.S. Supreme Ct. 1964. Ptnr. Chernin & Gold, Binghamton, N.Y., 1958-70; ptnr. Carmien & Young, Binghamton, 1970-79; sole practice Binghamton, 1979—; transp. cons. Pres. Broome County (N.Y.) Heart Assn., 1976-78. Served to lt. USNR, 1954-56. Mem. ABA, N.Y. State Bar Assn. (recipient Disting. Service award young lawyers sect. 1967), Broome County Bar Assn., Assn. ICC Practitioners, Motor Carrier Lawyers Assn. Republican. Presbyterian. Clubs: Elks (Vestal, N.Y.); Shriners (Binghamton). Transportation, State civil litigation, Environment. Home: 416 W Benita Blvd Vestal NY 13850 Office: 408 Press Bldg Binghamton NY 13901

CARMODY, JAMES ALBERT, lawyer; b. St. Louis, Nov. 21, 1945; s. Lawrence C. and Anna Louise (Hanes) C.; m. Helen Louise Valin, Mar. 22, 1969; children: Paul Valin, Leigh Christin. BA, Vanderbilt U., 1967; JD, U. Ark., 1973. Bar: Tex. 1974, U.S. Dist. Ct. (so. dist.) Tex. 1974, U.S. Ct. Appeals (5th cir.) 1975. Assoc. Mabry & Gunn, Texas City, Tex., 1974-75; mcpl. ct. judge Texas City, Tex., 1975; assoc. Chamberlain & Hrdlicka, Houston, 1975-78, ptnr., 1978—. Assoc. editor U. Ark. Law Rev., 1973. Incorporator, Gulf Coast Big Bros. and Sisters, Inc., Galveston County, Tex., 1975; mem. St. Maximillian Cath. Community Bldg. Com., Houston, 1985—. Served to lt. USN, 1967-71. Named Outstanding Young Lawyer, Galveston County Bar Assn., 1985. Mem. Fed. Bar Assn., Delta Theta Phi (placement coordinator 1979-83, master inspector 1983-85, dep. vice chancellor 1985—). Republican. Roman Catholic. Club: Houston Met. Racquet Club. Avocations: ham radio, jogging, traveling. Antitrust, Bankruptcy, Business litigation. Home: 15910 Congo Houston TX 77040 Office: Chamberlain Hrdlicka et al 1400 Citicorp Ctr 1200 Smith St Houston TX 77002

CARNAHAN, ROBERT NARVELL, lawyer; b. Littlefield, Tex., Nov. 22, 1928; s. C.D. and Wilma L. (Hartness) C.; m. Betty L. Stewart, Mar. 25, 1951; children—Cynthia, Michael, Christopher. B.B.A., Tex. Tech. Coll., 1950; J.D., U. Tex.-Austin, 1957. Bar. Tex. 1956. Asst. atty. Potter County, Tex., Amarillo; assoc. Underwood, Wilson, Sutton, Heare & Boise, Amarillo; ptnr. Stokes, Carnahan & Fields, Amarillo; sole practice, Corpus Christi, Tex. Served to 1st lt. USAF, 1954. Mem. State Bar Tex., Nueces County Bar Assn., Tex. Trial Lawyers Assn., Tex. Assn. Criminal Def. Lawyers, Am. Judicature Assn. Contbr. article to Tex. Bar Jour. Insurance, Criminal, Personal injury. Office: 800 Petroleum Tower Corpus Christi TX 78574

CARNALL, GEORGE HURSEY, II, lawyer, business executive; b. Ft. Smith, Ark., Feb. 19, 1947; s. George and Kathleen (Browne) C.; m. Janet Spaulding, Aug. 28, 1971; children—Clayton Wilson, Abigail Browne, Kevin Joseph. B.S. in Econs., Bus. Adminstrn., Millikin U., Decatur, Ill., 1969; J.D., Vanderbilt U., 1974. Bar: Tenn. 1974, U.S. Dist. Ct. (we. dist.) Tenn. 1974. Assoc., Arnoult & May, Memphis, 1974-76, Watson Cox & Arnoult, Memphis, 1976-79; gen. counsel S.M.R. Enterprises, Memphis, 1980—. Contbr. articles to legal jours. Bd. dirs. Teen Challenge, Memphis, 1983, First Assembly Christian Sch., Memphis, 1982. Served with U.S. Army, 1969-71. Mem. ABA, Tenn. Bar Assn., Memphis Bar Assn., Shelby Bar Assn. Mem. Assembly of God Ch. Franchising. Home: 6870 Wytham St Memphis TN 38119 Office: Enterprise Inc PO Box 18845 Memphis TN 38181-0845

CARNECCHIA, BALDO M., JR, lawyer; b. Hackensack, N.J., Sept. 2, 1947; s. Baldo M. Carnecchia and Cleo (Gerhart) Harper; m. Barbara Wolf, Mar. 1, 1969; children: Brian B., Justin W., Laura A. BS, Pa. State U., 1969; JD, Villanova U., 1972; LLM, Harvard U., 1973. Bar: Pa. 1972, U.S. Dist. Ct. (ea. dist.) Pa., U.S. Ct. Appeals (3d cir.) 1973. Legal writing asst. Boston U., 1973; assoc. Montgomery, McCracken, Walker & Rhoads, Phila., 1973-79, ptnr., 1979—. Editor Villanova U. Law Rev., 1971-72. Mem. ABA, Pa. Bar Assn., Phila. Bar Assn. Clubs: Harvard, The Union League. Bankruptcy, General corporate, Municipal bonds. Home: 220 N Ithan Ave Villanova PA 19085 Office: Montgomery McCracken et al 3 Parkway 20th Fl Philadelphia PA 19102

CARNEGIE, CHRISTA LEW, lawyer, urban planner; b. Kansas City, Mo., Feb. 12, 1945; d. Lew James and Lucile (Parkins) C.; m. Thomas A. Reppetto, Jan. 30, 1975. BA, Mt. Holyoke Coll., 1968; M in City Planning, MIT, 1971; JD, Suffolk U., 1975. Bar: N.Y. 1976, U.S. Dist. Ct. (so. dist.) N.Y. 1976, U.S. Dist. Ct. (ea. dist.) N.Y. 1981. Editorial asst. Christian Sci. Monitor, 1971-72; project dir. Urban Systems Research and Engring., Cambridge, Mass., 1972-74; atty., prin. atty. Port Authority of N.Y. and N.J., N.Y.C., 1975—. State civil litigation, Federal civil litigation. Office: Port Authority NY and NJ 1 World Trade Ctr Suite 66 S New York NY 10048

CARNES, LAMAR, lawyer; b. Beaumont, Tex., Aug. 19, 1923; s. Garland and Hattie (Butler) C. B.A., Cornell U., 1941, M.B.A., 1942; J.D., So. Meth. U., 1948. Bar: Tex. 1948, U.S. Supreme Ct. 1954, U.S. Dist. Ct. (so. dist.) Tex. 1954, U.S. Dist. Ct. (no. dist.) Tex. 1971, U.S. Ct. Appeals (5th cir) 1954. Sole practice, Houston, 1948-53; v.p., gen. counsel ADA Oil Co., Houston, 1953-58; sole practice, Houston, 1958-68, Dallas, 1969—. Served to lt. col. USAF, 1942-46, ETO. Mem. ABA, Tex. Bar Assn., Dallas Bar Assn., Delta Theta Phi. Republican. Federal civil litigation, State civil litigation, Oil and gas leasing. Office: 401 Capital Bank Bldg Dallas TX 75206

CARNEY, BRADFORD GEORGE YOST, lawyer, educator; b. Balt., Oct. 25, 1950; s. Blanchard Donald and Anne Carolyn (Yost) C.; m. Gail Elaine Hasson, Jan. 6, 1973; children—Jason Bradford, Brandon Burroughs. B.A., Washington Coll., 1972; J.D., U. Balt., 1976. Bar: Md. 1977, U.S. Dist. Ct. Md. 1978, U.S. Supreme Ct. 1982. Ptnr. Callahan, Calwell, Laudeman, Balt., 1975-82 ; asst. prof. law Villa Julie Coll., Stevenson, Md., 1983—. Pres. Stone Oaks Condominium Assn., Balt., 1980. Mem. Md. State Bar Assn., Balt. City Bar Assn., Md. Trial Lawyers Assn., Md. Criminal Def. Attys. Assn., Assn. Trial Lawyers Am., U. Balt. Alumni Assn. (bd. govs. 1984—), Boys' Latin Sch. Alumni Assn. (bd. dirs. 1983—, pres. 1986—). State civil litigation, Real property, General practice. Home: 474 Five Farms Ln Timonium MD 21093 Office: Callahan Calwell & Laudeman 17 Commerce St Baltimore MD 21202

CARNEY, DEBORAH LEAH TURNER, lawyer; b. Great Bend, Kans., Aug. 19, 1952; d. Harold Lee and Elizabeth Lura (Dillon) T.; m. Thomas J.T. Carney, Mar. 20, 1976; children: Amber Blythe, Sonia Briana, Ross Dillon. BA in Human Biology, Stanford U., 1974; JD, U. Denver, 1976. Bar: Kans. 1977, U.S. Dist. Ct. Kans. 1977, U.S. Ct. Appeals (10th cir.) 1982, Colo. 1984, U.S. Dist. Ct. Colo. 1984. With Turner & Boisseau, Great Bend, 1976-84, of counsel, 1984—; assoc. Lutz & Oliver, Arvada, Colo., 1984-85; sole practice Golden, Colo., 1985—. Author (newsletter) Profl. Solutions, 1984; editor Apple Law newsletter, 1984-86; contbr. articles ot law jours. Mem. ABA (computer div.), Colo. Bar Assn., Kans. Bar Assn., Assn. Trial Lawyers Am. Republican. Avocations: horses, computers. Personal injury, Federal civil litigation, State civil litigation. Office: 23876 Currant Dr Golden CO 80401

CARNEY, DONALD F., JR., lawyer; b. Detroit, July 30, 1948; s. Donald F. and Kathryn (Lucas) C.; m. Jacqueline Anne Miller, Aug. 28, 1971; children: Jennifer Suzanne, Julianne, Rebecca Anne. BA, Mich. State U., 1970; JD, Detroit Coll. Law, 1976. Assoc. Dinan & Schenden, P.C., Troy, Mich., 1977-79, Joslyn & Keydel, Detroit, 1979-83; ptnr. Joslyn, Keydel, Wallace & Joslyn, Detroit, 1983—. Mem. ABA, Oakland County Bar Assn., Detroit Bar Assn., Fin. and Estate Planning Council Detroit, Sigm Chi Detroit Alumni Assn. (pres. 1984), Gamma Psi Alumni House Corp. (bd. dirs. 1970-86, pres. 1975-76). Roman Catholic. Clubs: Detroit Athletic, Orchard Lake Country. Probate, Estate planning, State civil litigation. Home: 295 Fairfax Birmingham MI 48009 Office: Joslyn Keydel Wallace & Joslyn 2211 Comerica Bldg Detroit MI 48226

CARNEY, THOMAS T.J., lawyer; b. Denver, July 18, 1952; s. Thomas Joseph Carney and Patricia Lee (Amack) Calkins; m. Deborah Leah Turner, Mar. 20, 1976; children: Amber Blythe Turner Carney, Sonia Briana Turner Carney, Ross Dillon Turner Carney. BA in Econs., U. Notre Dame, 1974; JD, U. Denver, 1976. Bar: Colo. 1977, Kans. 1977, U.S. Dist. Ct. Colo. 1977, U.S. Dist. Ct. Kans. 1977, U.S. Ct. Appeals (10th cir.) 1983. Paralegal Turner, Hensley & Boisseau Chartered, Great Bend, Kans., 1977, assoc., 1977-78; ptnr., bd. dirs. Turner & Boisseau Chartered, Great Bend, 1978-84; assoc. Bradley, Campbell & Carney, Golden, Colo., 1984—. Mem. ABA, Colo. Bar Assn., Kans. Bar Assn., Assn. Trial Lawyers Am., Colo. Trial Lawyers Assn., Phi Delta Phi. Republican. Avocations: lacrosse, horses. Personal injury, Federal civil litigation, State civil litigation. Home: 23876 Currant Dr Golden CO 80401 Office: Bradley Campbell & Carney 1717 Washington Ave Golden CO 80401

CARON, WILFRED RENE, lawyer; b. N.Y.C., July 23, 1931; s. Joseph Wilfred and Eva (Berube) C.; m. Anne Theresa Flanagan, Aug. 2, 1958. JD, St. John's U., 1956. Bar: N.Y. 1956, D.C. 1977, U.S. Dist. Ct. D.C. 1977, U.S. Dist. Ct. (no. dist.) N.Y. 1957, U.S. Dist. Ct. (so.and ea. dists.) N.Y. 1961, U.S. Ct. Appeals (2d cir.) 1965, U.S. Ct. Appeals (3d cir.) 1973, U.S. Ct. Appeals (5th cir.) 1977, U.S. Ct. Appeals (6th cir.) 1973, U.S. Ct. Appeals (8th cir.) 1975, U.S. Ct. Appeals (9th cir.) 1976, U.S. Ct. Appeals (D.C. cir.) 1975, U.S. Supreme Ct. 1961. Law clk. to chief judge N.Y. State Ct. Appeals 1956-59; spl. asst. atty. gen. N.Y., 1959-60; assoc. Goldman & Drazen, 1960-64, Corner, Finn, Cuomo & Charles, N.Y.C., 1964-69; asst. gen. counsel Ronson Corp., Woodbridge, N.J., 1969-71; assoc. gen. counsel Securities Investor Protection Corp., Washington, 1972-80; gen. counsel U.S. Cath. Conf., Inc., Washington, 1980-87, Nat. Conf. Cath. Bishops, 1980-87, Cath. Telecommunications Network Am., Inc., N.Y.C., 1981—; ptnr. O'Connor & Hannan, Washington, 1987—. Adv. bd. St. Thomas More Inst. Legal Research, St. John's U. Sch. Law, N.Y.C., 1981—; exec. bd. Ctr. for

Ch.-State Studies, DePaul U. Law Coll., Chgo., 1982—. Served to 1st lt. U.S. Army, 1952-54, Korea. Mem. ABA, D.C. Bar Assn., Fed. Bar Council, Canon Law Soc. Am., Supreme Ct. Hist. Soc., Washington Performing Arts Soc., Met. Opera Guild, Friends of Kennedy Center, Am. Film Inst., St. Thomas More Soc. Am., John Carroll Soc., VFW, Am. Legion. Roman Catholic. Clubs: University (Washington): K.C. (N.Y.C.). Contbr. articles to profl. jours. Federal civil litigation, General corporate, Legislative. Home: 560 N St SW Apt N901 Washington DC 20024

CARPENTER, CHARLES L., lawyer; b. Hope, Ark., Mar. 24, 1917; s. Ray E. and Willise E. (Ford) C.; m. Elaine M. McDonald, Sept. 9, 1921; children—Charles L., Thomas M. Student Little Rock Jr. Coll., 1935-38; J.D., U. Ark., 1941. Bar: Ark. 1941, U.S. Dist. Ct. (ea. dist.) Ark. 1946, U.S. Dist. Ct. (we. dist.) Ark. 1962, U.S. Ct. Appeals (8th cir.) 1976, U.S. Supreme Ct. 1950, U.S. Ct. Mil. Appeals 1953. Asst. city atty., North Little Rock, Ark., 1946-48, 64-66; city atty., Sherwood, Ark., 1948-70; sole practice, North Little Rock, 1941, 46-51, 53—. Served to capt., AUS, 1941-46, to col. JAGD, 1951-56. Fellow Ark. Bar Found.; mem. Internat. Bar Assn., Ark. Bar Assn. (ho. of dels. 1973-76, 77-78, 81-83, tenured mem. ho. of dels. 1982—; Golden Gavel award 1982, E.J. Ransick Award 1985), Ark. Jud. Council (hon. life), Pulaski County Bar Assn., North Pulaski Bar Assn., Internat. Bar Assn., Air Force Ret. Judge Advs. Assn., Am. Judicature Soc. Democrat. Methodist. Clubs: North Little Rock Elks, Woodmen of World, Little Rock AFB Officers. Family and matrimonial, General practice, Military. Home: 203 W B St North Little Rock AR 72116 Office: 1405 Main St North Little Rock AR 72114

CARPENTER, DARRELL FRANKLIN, lawyer; b. Jacksonville, Fla., Oct. 22, 1955; s. Rufus F. and Gwendolyn L. (Voss) C.; m. Rita Regina Rose Pierson, June 17, 1978; children: Darrell Jr., Kimsey, Bryant Russell. BBA, U. Fla, 1977, JD, 1980. Bar: Fla. 1980, U.S. Dist. Ct. (mid. dist.) Fla. 1980. Assoc. Wells, Gattis & Hallowes, Orlando, Fla., 1980-82, Wells, Gattis, Hallowes & Carpenter, Orlando, 1983—. Bd. dirs. Fellowship of Christian Athletes, Orlando, 1983. Nat. Collegiate Athletic Assn. scholar, 1977. Mem. ABA, Am. Trial Lawyers Assn., Fla. Bar Assn., Acad. Fla. Trial Lawyers. Republican. Presbyterian. Clubs: Country of Orlando, Downtown Athletic of Orlando, Univ. Avocations: golf, fishing. Personal injury. Office: Wells Gattis Hallowes & Carpenter 130 Hillcrest St Orlando FL 32801

CARPENTER, DAVID WILLIAM, lawyer; b. Chgo., Aug. 26, 1950; s. William Warren and Dorothy Susan (Jacobs) C.; m. Jane Ellen French, Aug. 18, 1973; children: Johanna Lindsay, Julie Rachel. BA, Yale U., 1972; JD, Boston U., 1975. Bar: Mass. 1975, U.S. Ct. Appeals (1st Cir.) 1977, D.C. 1979, Ill. 1979, U.S. Dist. Ct. (no. dist.) Ill.1979, U.S. Ct. Appeals (D.C. cir.) 1980, U.S. Ct. Appeals (3d and 7th cirs.) 1981, U.S. Supreme Ct. 1981, U.S. Ct. Appeals (10th cir.) 1985, U.S. Ct. Appeals (8th cir.) 1986. Law clk. to presiding justice U.S. Ct. Appeals (1st cir.), Portland, Maine, 1975-77, U.S. Supreme Ct., Washington, 1977-78; assoc. Sidley & Austin, Chgo., 1978-82, ptnr., 1982—; lectr. Ill. Inst. Tech., Chgo., 1980-82. Democrat. Mem. United Ch. Christ. Antitrust, Federal civil litigation, State civil litigation. Home: 1660 N Burling Chicago IL 60614 Office: Sidley & Austin One First National Plaza Chicago IL 60603

CARPENTER, DONALD ALFRED, senior judge; b. Greeley, Colo., Jan. 2, 1907. J.D., George Washington U., 1931. Bar: Tex. 1931, Colo. 1949. Sole practice, El Paso, 1931-34; dir. Colo. Use Tax Div., Denver, 1938-40; adminstrv. asst. to Hon. William S. Hill, mem. U.S. Congress, 1940-43; judge Weld County (Colo.) Ct., 1946-52, Colo. Dist. Ct. 8th Jud. Dist., 1952-64; chief judge 19th Jud. Dist., 1964-79; adminstrv. judge No. Colo. Water Conservancy Dist., Greeley, 1965-79, Central Colo. Water Conservancy Dist., Greeley, 1965-79; water judge South Platte River System, 1969-79; master Colo. Supreme Ct., 1960-61; mem. Gov.'s Jud. Conf. Colo., 1957, 58, Colo. Jud. Council, 1958, chmn. com. appellate practice, 1958; mem. jud. council Chief Justice Colo. Supreme Ct., 1973-79. Mem. ABA, Colo. Bar Assn., Tex. Bar Assn., Weld County Bar Assn., Colo. Dist. Judges Assn., Nat. Coll. Probate Judges, Am. Judicature Soc., Nat. Conf. State Trial Judges, World Assn. Judges, Am. Acad. Polit. and Social Scis. Administrative and regulatory. Home and Office: 14953 Weld County Rd 70 Greeley CO 80631

CARPENTER, EDMUND NELSON, II, lawyer; b. Phila., Jan. 27, 1921; s. Walter S. and Mary (Wootten) C.; m. Carroll Morgan, July 18, 1970; children: Mary W., Edmund Nelson III, Katherine R.R., Elizabeth Lea; stepchildren: John D. Gates, Ashley du Pont Gates. A.B., Princeton U., 1943; LL.B., Harvard U., 1948. Bar: Del. 1949, U.S. Supreme Ct. 1957. Assoc. firm Richards, Layton & Finger, Wilmington, Del., 1949-53; partner Richards, Layton & Finger, 1953-78, dir., 1978—, pres., 1982-85; dep. atty. gen. State of Del., 1953-54, spl. dep. atty., 1960-62; chmn. Del. Superior Ct. Jury Study Com., 1963-66, Del. Supreme Ct. Cts. Consolidation Com., 1985-87; mem. Del. Gov.'s Commn. Law Enforcement and Adminstrn. Justice, 1969; chmn. Del. Agy. to Reduce Crime, 1970-71, chmn. Del. Supreme Ct. Adv. Com. on Profl. Fin. Accountability, 1974-75; mem. Long Range Cts. Planning Com., 1976—; dir. Bank Del. Trustee Wilmington Med. Center, 1965-82, U. Del., 1971-77, Princeton U., 1974-84, 86—, World Affairs Council of Wilmington, 1968-80, Woodrow Wilson Found., 1985—; trustee Lawrenceville Sch., 1953-74, trustee emeritus, 1974—; bd. dirs. Good Samaritan Inc., 1973—; chmn. lawyers adv. com. U.S. Ct. Appeals 3d Circuit, 1975-77; mem. Del Health Care Injury Ins. Study Commn., 1976—. Fellow Am. Coll. Trial Lawyers, Am. Bar Found.; mem. ABA (ho. of dels. 1979-86), Del. State Bar Assn., Am. Judicature Soc. (dir. 1974—, exec. com. 1978-80, v.p. 1980-81, pres. 1981-83), Am. Trial Lawyers Assn. Federal civil litigation, State civil litigation, General corporate. Home: 600 Center Mill Rd Wilmington DE 19807 Office: PO Box 551 One Rodney Sq Wilmington DE 19899

CARPENTER, GORDON RUSSELL, lawyer, banker; b. Denton, Tex., Feb. 6, 1920; s. Solomon Lafayette and Grace L. (Fowler) C.; m. Muriel E. James, Sept. 18, 1943 (dec.); m. 2d, Mary Alice Borah, Aug. 4, 1962. B.S., North Tex. State U., 1940; postgrad. Georgetown U. Law Sch., 1941-42; LL.B., So. Meth. U., 1948. Bar: Tex. 1947, U.S. Supreme Ct. 1960. Announcer radio sta. KDNT, Denton, 1940-41; spl. agt. FBI, 1941-46; exec. sec. Southwestern Legal Found., Dallas, 1947-56, exec. dir., 1956-58; adminstrv. asst. to dean So. Meth. U. Law Sch., 1951-58, asst. prof. law, 1956-58; trust officer 1st Nat. Bank, Dallas, 1958-60, v.p., 1960-79; v.p., sr. fin. planning officer InterFirst Bank Dallas, 1979—. Bd. regents Tex. Sch. Trust Banking, 1981-82; bd. trustees Hatton W. Sumners Found., 1959-85, exec. dir. 1985—; chmn. North Tex. State U. Ednl. Found.; chmn. Luth. Med. System of Tex. Found., 1980-83; vice chmn. Farmers Br. Hosp. Authority, 1976-77. Recipient Pres.'s award State Bar Tex., 1963, Bd. Dirs. award, 1971. Fellow Tex. Bar Found.; mem. ABA (chmn. publs. com. mineral and natural resources law sect. 1958-64, chmn. membership com. 1963-64), State Bar Tex. (chmn. continuing legal edn. com. 1952-54, 58-66, chmn. real estate, probate and trust law sect. 1964-65), Dallas Bar Assn. (dir. 1960-61, 65-66, chmn. centennial com. 1972-73), Dallas Bar Found. (trustee, sec.-treas.), Tex. Bankers Assn. (chmn. trust div. 1980-81), Soc. Former Spl. Agts. FBI (pres. 1963), Delta Theta Phi. Republican. Presbyterian. Clubs: Brookhaven Country, Masons. Estate planning, Probate. Office: 3333 Republic Bank Tower Dallas TX 75201

CARPENTER, JAMES CRAIG, lawyer; b. Louisville, Ky., Nov. 20, 1949; s. Errett Larue and Edna Margaret (Lausman) C.; m. Deborah Elizabeth Fergus, Aug. 26, 1972; children: Katheryn Elizabeth, Elizabeth Anne. BA summa cum laude, Ohio U., 1972; JD, Ohio State U., 1974. Bar: Ohio 1975, U.S. Dist. Ct. (so. dist.) Ohio 1975, U.S. Dist. Ct. (no. dist.) Ohio 1977, U.S. Tax Ct. 1977, U.S. Ct. Claims 1980, U.S. Supreme Ct. 1980, U.S. Ct. Appeals (6th cir.) 1982, U.S. Ct. Appeals (3d cir.) 1984. Assoc. Knepper, White, Arter & Hadden, Columbus, Ohio, 1975-80; adminstrv. asst. U.S. rep. Robert Shamansky, Washington, 1981-82; ptnr. Carlile, Patchen, Murphy & Allison, Columbus, 1982—. Trustee League Against Child Abuse, Columbus, 1980-81, Columbus Area Leadership Program, 1985—. Mem. ABA, Ohio Bar Assn., Columbus Bar Assn., Def. Research Inst., Assn. Trial Lawyers Am., Phi Beta Kappa. Democrat. Lutheran. Personal injury, Insurance, Legislative. Home: 2695 Sandover Rd Columbus OH 43220 Office: Carlile Patchen Murphy & Allison 366 E Broad St Columbus OH 43215

CARPENTER, JAMES WILLARD, lawyer; b. Columbus, Ohio, Feb. 28, 1935; s. Clare Milton Carpenter and Laura Belle (Bass) Hyde; m. Rose Ellen Levitsky, Apr. 2, 1955; children: James, John, Matthew, Elizabeth, Mary, Rebecca, Robert. BA, Ohio State U., 1961, JD summa cum laude, 1964. Bar: Calif. 1965, Ohio 1966. Assoc. McCutcheon, Black, Verleger & Shea, Los Angeles, 1964-65; from asst. prof. to prof. Ohio State U. Law Sch., Columbus, 1965-71; from assoc. counsel to sr. counsel Western-So. Life Ins. Co., Cin., 1971—; sole practice Cin., 1975-84; adj. prof. Chase Law Sch., Ft. Wright, Ky., 1974-76. Editor Ohio State U. Law Rev., 1962-64; contbr. articles to profl. jours. Served to 1st lt. USMCR, 1956-58. Mershon fellow, 1963-64. Mem. Ohio Bar Assn., Cin. Bar Assn., Order of Coif. Democrat. Presbyterian. Avocations: golf, movies, reading. Real property, Insurance, State civil litigation. Home: 1188 Beverly Hill Dr Cincinnati OH 45226 Office: Western So Life Ins Co 400 Broadway Cincinnati OH 45202

CARPENTER, RAYMOND PRINCE, lawyer; b. Little Rock, Apr. 2, 1944; s. Reuben Alvin and Ellen Helen (Turner) C.; m. Barbara Joyce Pearson, Sept. 2, 1971; 1 child, Raymond Prince Jr. BA, U. Ark., 1966; JD, Emory U., 1975. Bar: Ga. 1975. Assoc. counsel Lockheed Ga. Co., Atlanta, 1975-76, Ward & Wyatt, Atlanta, 1976-78; sr. tax counsel Sears, Roebuck and Co., Atlanta, 1978—; vice chmn. Met. Atlanta Rapid Transit Authority, 1978—. Bd. pres. Child Service and Family Counseling Ctr., Atlanta, 1985—. Served to corp. USMC, 1969-70, Vietnam. Recipient Leadership award City of Atlanta, 1983. Mem. ABA (state and local tax com.), Ga. Bar Assn. (childrens law com.). Republican. Mem. Christian Church. State and local taxation, General corporate, Corporate taxation. Home: 3360 Old Fairburn Rd Atlanta GA 30331 Office: Sears Roebuck and Co 675 Ponce de Leon Ave Atlanta GA 30395

CARPENTER, RICHARD NORRIS, lawyer; b. Cortland, N.Y., Feb. 14, 1937; s. Robert P. and Sylvia (Norris) C.; m. Elizabeth Bigbee, Aug. 1961 (div. June 1975); 1 child, Andrew Norris. BA magna cum laude, Syracuse U., 1958; LLB, Yale U., 1962. Bar: N.Y. 1962, N.Mex. 1963, U.S. Dist. Ct. (no. dist.) N.Y., U.S. Dist. Ct. N.Mex., U.S. Ct. Appeals (D.C. and 10th cirs.), U.S. Supreme Ct. Assoc. Breed, Abbott & Morgan, N.Y.C., 1962-63, Bigbee & Byrd, Santa Fe, 1963-67; ptnr. Stephenson, Carpenter, Crout & Olmsted, Santa Fe, 1967—; spl. asst. atty. gen., State of N.Mex., 1963-74; bd. dirs. Bigbee Bros. Cattle Co., Encino, N.Mex. Mem. adv. bd. Interstate Mining Compact, N.Mex., 1981—; elder 1st Presbyn. Ch., Santa Fe, 1978-80, 86—, trustee, 1975-77, pres., 1977; bd. dirs. Santa Fe Community Council, 1965-67, St. Vincent Hosp. Found., Santa Fe, 1980-84; trustee Santa Fe Prep. Sch., 1981-84, pres. 1982-84; trustee St. Vincent Hosp., 1980-86, chmn. 1985-86; bd. dirs. Santa Fe YMCA, 1964-69, pres., 1969; trustee Santa Fe Prep. Permanent Endowment Fund., 1987—. Rotary Found. fellow, Panjab U., Pakistan, 1959-60. Mem. ABA, N.Mex. Bar Assn., 1st Jud. Bar Assn., N.Y. State Bar Assn., Phi Beta Kappa, Pi Sigma Alpha, Phi Beta Phi. Public utilities, Legislative, Natural resources. Home: 1048 Bishops Lodge Rd Santa Fe NM 87501 Office: Stephenson Carpenter et al 141 E Palace Ave Santa Fe NM 87501

CARPENTER, ROBERT BRENT, lawyer; b. Newton, Mass., Feb. 2, 1949; s. Edward N. and Charlotte F. (Grant) C.; m. L. Deborah Gorchov, Mar. 25, 1978; children: Stephen Michael, Matthew Jeremy, Meredith Anne. A.B., Bowdoin Coll., 1971; J.D., Boston Coll., 1975; LL.M., Temple U., 1977. Bar: Mass. 1975, U.S. Dist. Ct. Mass. 1977, U.S. Ct. Appeals (1st cir.) 1977, U.S. Supreme Ct. 1980. Teaching fellow, lectr. Temple U., Phila., 1975-77; ptnr. Goldstein & Manello, Boston, 1977—. Contbr. articles to profl. jours. Mem. ABA, Mass. Bar Assn., Boston Bar Assn. Federal civil litigation, State civil litigation, Construction. Home: 1 Commonwealth Park Wellesley MA 02181 Office: Goldstein & Manello 265 Franklin St Boston MA 02110

CARPENTER, SUSAN KAREN, lawyer; b. New Orleans, May 6, 1951; d. Donald Jack and Elise Ann (Diehl) C. B.A. magna cum laude with honors in English, Smith Coll., 1973; J.D., Ind. U., 1976. Bar: Ind. 1976. Dep. pub. defender of Ind. State of Ind., Indpls., 1976-81, pub. defender, 1981—; chief pub. defender Wayne County, Richmond, Ind., 1981; bd. dirs. Ind. Pub. Defender Council, Indpls., 1981—, Ind. Lawyer's Commn., Indpls., 1984—; trustee Ind. Criminal Justice Inst., Indpls., 1983—. Mem. Criminal Code Study Commn., Indpls., 1981—, Supreme Ct. Records Mgmt. Com., Indpls., 1983—. Mem. Ind. State Bar Assn. (criminal justice sect.), Nat. Legal Aid and Defender Assn. (mem. Amicus com. 1984—), Nat. Assn. Defense Lawyers, Phi Beta Kappa. Criminal, Juvenile. Office: Office of State Pub Defender 309 W Washington St Suite 501 Indianapolis IN 46204

CARPENTER, THOMAS MILTON, lawyer; b. Lubbock, Tex., Feb. 15, 1952; s. Charles Loren and Mildred Elaine (McDonald) C.; m. Betty Kathryn Wilkins, Mar. 26, 1983. B.A., Hendrix Coll., 1974; J.D., U. Ark.-Fayetteville, 1977. Bar: Ark. 1977, U.S. Dist. Ct. (ea. dist.) Ark. 1978, U.S. Ct. Appeals (8th cir.) 1980, U.S. Supreme Ct. 1981, U.S. Ct. Mil. Appeals 1985; cert.criminal trial specialist. Law clk. Ark. Supreme Ct., Little Rock, 1977-78; ptnr. Lessenberry & Carpenter, Little Rock, 1978-84; asst. city atty., Little Rock, 1984—, chief comml. litigation div.; coordinator Ark. Coalition Against the Death Penalty, 1978-83. Dist. commr. Boy Scouts Am., 1979; adminstrv. council Pulaski Heights Meth. Ch., Little Rock, 1982-85. Fellow Ark. Bar Assn.; mem. ABA, Ark. Bar Assn. (del. 1979-81, 83-85, tenured del., Golden Gate award 1982), Assn. Trial Lawyers Am., Pulaski County Bar Assn. Democrat. Contbr. articles to profl. jours. Government contracts and claims, Federal civil litigation, Criminal. Office: Little Rock City Atty City Hall Romm 102 Little Rock AR 72201

CARPENTER, WILLIAM C., lawyer; b. 1951. BS, U. Del. Bar: Del. 1976. U.S. atty. State of Del., Wilmington. Office: J Caleb Boggs Fed Bldg 844 King St Room 5001 Wilmington DE 19801 *

CARPONELLI, STEPHEN PETER, lawyer; b. Chgo., Dec. 11, 1947; s. Peter J. and Diana M. (Cappelletti) C.; m. Andrea Mann, July 19, 1969; children: Lisa Beth, Ross Stephen. BS, Drake U., 1969; JD with honors, John Marshall Sch. of Law, 1972. Bar: Ill. 1972, U.S. Dist. Ct. (no. dist.) Ill. 1972, U.S. Ct. Appeals (7th cir.) 1976, U.S. Supreme Ct. 1979, U.S. Tax Ct. 1980. Ptnr. Carponelli, Krug & Adamski and predecessor firms, Chgo., 1972—; bd. dirs. Putman Pub. Co., Chgo.; instr. trial practice Ill. Inst. Continuing Legal Edn., Chgo., 1984—. Mem. ABA, Ill. Bar Assn., Chgo. Bar Assn., Assn. Trial Lawyers Am., Ill. Trial Lawyers Assn. Roman Catholic. Club: Union League (Chgo.). Avocations: baseball, tennis, fishing. Federal civil litigation, State civil litigation, Libel. Home: 80 Meadow Hill Barrington Hills IL 60010 Office: Carponelli Krug & Adamski 55 W Monore 2350 Xerox Centre Chicago IL 60602

CARR, DAVIS, lawyer; b. Elmhurst, Ill., Apr. 1, 1956; s. Harold Dewane and Molly (Wade) C.; m. Gwen Chappelle, Mar. 20, 1976; children: Whitney, Griffin, Jordan. BA summa cum laude, U. S. Ala., 1976; JD, U. Ala., 1979. Bar: Ala. 1979, U.S. Ct. Appeals (5th cir.) 1980, U.S. Ct. Appeals (11th cir.) 1982, U.S. Supreme Ct. 1984. Ptnr. Hand, Arendall, Bedsole, Greaves & Johnston, Mobile, Ala., 1979—. Research editor Ala. Law Rev., 1978-79; contbr. articles to profl. jours. Recipient M. Leigh Harrison award; Hugo Black scholar. Mem. ABA (litigation sect.), Ala. Bar Assn., Mobile County Bar Assn., Ala. Def. Lawyers Assn. (editor journal 1986—), Def. Research Inst., Order of Coif. Republican. Baptist. Personal injury. Home: 103 Levert Mobile AL 36607 Office: Hand Arendall et al 2900 1st Nat Bank Bldg PO Box 123 Mobile AL 36601

CARR, FRANCIS THOMAS, lawyer; b. Mahanoy City, Pa., Dec. 9, 1923; s. James Francis and Anne Loretta (Durkin) C.; m. Cora Virginia Gay (div.); children: Gay Margaret, David Francis; m. Collette Loretta Stohn, 1974; children: Tracey, Francis Thomas, Zino John. BSCE, Lehigh U., 1944; LLB, U. Va., 1948. Bar: N.Y. 1949, U.S. Dist. Ct. (so. dist.) N.Y. 1950, U.S. Dist. Ct. (ea. dist.) N.Y. 1952, U.S. Ct. Claims 1969, U.S. Ct. Appeals (fed. cir.) 1963, U.S. Ct. Appeals (6th cir.) 1965, U.S. Ct. Appeals (7th cir.) 1966, U.S. Ct. Appeals (9th and 4th cirs.) 1973, U.S. Ct. Appeals (2d cir.) 1976, U.S. Ct. Appeals (5th cir.) 1977,U.S. Supreme Ct. 1986. Assoc. Kenyon & Kenyon, N.Y.C., 1948-56, mem., 1956—, sr. ptnr., 1969— . Served with USNR, 1944-46. Fellow Am. Coll. Trial Lawyers; mem. ABA, Assn. Bar City N.Y., N.Y. Patent Law Assn., Am. Patent Law Assn., Internat. Patent and Trademark Assn., Fed. Bar Council, Lehigh U. Alumni Assn., U. Va. Alumni Assn., Delta Theta Phi, Phi Delta Theta. Clubs: Winged Foot Golf, Confrerie des Chevaliers du Tastevin. Patent, Trademark and copyright. Office: Kenyon & Kenyon 1 Broadway New York NY 10004

CARR, GEORGE C., judge; b. 1929. B.S., B.A., U. Fla., 1951, LL.B., 1954. Bar: Fla. bar 1954. Sole practice 1954-51; mem. firm Carr, Chiles & Ellsworth, 1957-63, firm Bently, Miller, Sinder, Carr, Chiles & Ellsworth, 1963-67, firm Carr & Chiles, 1967-69, firm Peterson, Carr & Harris, 1969-77; Polk County atty. 1973-78; U.S. dist. judge Dist. of Middle Fla., Tampa., 1977—. Mem. Am. Bar Assn. Office: US Dist Ct US Courthouse Tampa FL 33602 *

CARR, HUBERT FRANKLIN, lawyer; b. Pitts., Nov. 20, 1920; s. Peter John and Grace Marie (Franklin) C.; m. Barbara Patricia Madory, Aug. 23, 1980; children: John Peter, Peter John. BS, NYU, 1946; LLB, Bklyn. Law Sch., 1952. Bar: N.Y. 1953, U.S. Dist. Ct. (ea. and so. dists.) N.Y. 1956. Clk. L.C. Smith Typewriter Co., Newark, 1939-40, Mason-Dixon Lines, Newark, 1940-41; v.p., sec., gen. counsel Moore McCormack Lines Inc., N.Y.C., 1941-83; counsel U.S. Lines Inc., Cranford, N.J., 1983—; mem. U.S. del. to UN Conf. of Carriage of Goods by Sea UN Council Internat. Trade Law, Hamburg, Fed. Republic Germany, 1978; mem. adv. com. law of sea U.S. Dept. State, 1979-82; bd. dirs. Marine Index Bur., N.Y.C. Pres. Pearl River (N.Y.) Civic Assn., 1952. Mem. N.Y. County Lawyers Assn., Maritime Law Assn. (bill of landing com.). Republican. Roman Catholic. Club: Propellor N.Y. (bd. dirs. 1968—). Admiralty, General corporate, Insurance. Home: 116 Matthews Rd Colts Neck NJ 07722 Office: US Lines Inc 27 Commerce Dr Cranford NJ 07016

CARR, JAMES FRANCIS, lawyer; b. Buffalo, May 7, 1946; s. Maurice Kilner and Cecelia Francis (Harmon) C.; children: James Robert, Marguerite Louise. BS, USAF Acad., 1968; JD, George Washington U., 1971. Bar: D.C. 1972, Mich. 1972, Pa. 1972, U.S. Dist. Ct. D.C. 1972, U.S. Ct. Appeals (D.C. cir.) 1972, U.S. Supreme Ct. 1975, Colo. 1979, U.S. Dist. Ct. Colo. 1979, U.S. Ct. Appeals (10th cir.) 1979. Atty. Unity Ctr., Meadville, Pa., 1971-73; asst. pros. atty. Genesee County, Flint, Mich., 1973-79; asst. atty. gen. State of Colo., Denver, 1979-82, 85—; assoc. Sumners, Miller & Clark, Denver, 1982-83, Miles & McManus, Denver, 1983-85. Contbr. articles to profl. jours. Mem. Mich. Pub. Consultation Panel of Internat. Joint Commn., 1976-78, West Univ. Community Assn., Denver, 1984—; chmn. com. Boy Scout Troop 195, Denver, 1985—. Mem. ABA (tort and ins. practice sect., vice chmn. environ. law , communications and pub. relations coms. 1981—, editor in chief tips sect. The Brief, 1981—), Denver Bar Assn. (law day com.), Colo. Bar Assn. (council mem. gen. small firm sect. 1985-86), Assn. Trial Lawyers Am. Democrat. Roman Catholic. Environment, Federal civil litigation, Labor. Home: 1801 S Fillmore Denver CO 80210 Office: CERCLA Litigation Sect 1560 Broadway Suite 250 Denver CO 80202

CARR, JAMES PATRICK, lawyer; b. Cheverly, Md., Apr. 13, 1950; s. Lawrence Edward Jr. and Agnes (Dyer) C.; children: James P. Jr., Kristin, Kevin; m. Mona L. Kyle, May 28, 1986. BA, U. Notre Dame, 1972, JD, 1976. Bar: Md. 1976, Calif. 1977, U.S. Dist. Ct. (cen. dist.) Calif. 1977, U.S. Dist. Ct. (so. dist.) Calif. 1986. Assoc. Carr, Jordan et al, Washington, 1976-77; ptnr. Breidenbach, Swainston et al, Los Angeles, 1977-84, Harney, Wolfe, Pagliuso, Shaller & Carr, Los Angeles, 1984—. Mem. Am. Bd. Trial Advs., Assn. Trial Lawyers Am., Calif. Trial Lawyers Assn. Democrat. Roman Catholic. Club: Los Angeles Athletic. Personal injury. Office: Harney Wolfe Pagliuso Shaller & Carr 201 N Figueroa St Suite 1300 Los Angeles CA 90012-2636

CARR, JOHN L., corporate lawyer; b. 1932. BS, Loyola U., 1954, LLB, 1958. With First Nationwide Savs., San Francisco, 1959—, vice chmn., gen. counsel; vice chmn. First Nationwide Fin. Corp., San Francisco. Office: First Nationwide Savings 700 Market St San Francisco CA 94102 *

CARR, JOSEPH B., lawyer; b. Albany, N.Y., Aug. 27, 1944; s. Benjamin D. And Edythe (Garber) C.; m. Roxanne M. Carr, Aug. 19, 1967; children: Aaron M., John T. AB, U. Rochester, 1966; JD cum laude, Albany Law Sch., 1975. Bar: N.Y. 1976, U.S. Dist. Ct. (no. dist.) N.Y. 1976. Assoc. John H. Dennis, Albany, 1975-76; ptnr. Carr & Rowlands, Albany, 1977-79, McClung, Peters & Simon, Albany, 1979—. Assoc. editor, Albany Law Rev., 1973-74, notes editor, 1974-75. Served with U.S. Army, 1969-70, Vietnam. Mem. ABA, N.Y. State Bar Assn., Albany County Bar Assn., Justinian Soc., Siasconset Casino Assn. Clubs: Hudson River (Albany); Schuyler Meadows (Loudonville). Lodge: KP (prelate). Contracts commercial, Real property, General corporate. Office: McClung Peters & Simon 41 State St Albany NY 12207

CARR, LAWRENCE EDWARD, JR., lawyer; b. Colorado Springs, Colo., Aug. 10, 1923; s. Lawrence Edward and Lelah R. (Rubert) C.; m. Agnes Isabel Dyer, Dec. 26, 1946; children—Mary Lee, James Patrick, Lawrence Edward III, Eileen Louise, Thomas Vincent. B.S., U. Notre Dame, 1948, LL.B., 1949; LL.M., George Washington U., 1954. Bar: Colo. bar 1949, D.C. bar 1952, Md. bar 1961. With Travelers Ins. Co., 1949-51; practiced in Washington, 1952—; sr. partner firm Carr, Goodson & Lee. Served with USMCR, 1943-46, 51-52; col. Res.; ret.). Mem. Am. Bar Assn. (ho. of dels. 1973-75), Bar Assn. D.C. (dir. 1969-71, pres. 1974-75), Internat. Assn. Ins. Counsel, D.C. Def. Lawyers Assn. (pres. 1978-79), Bar Assn. D.C. Research Found. (pres. 1985-86). Federal civil litigation, Insurance, Environment. Home: 12001 Piney Glen Ln Potomac MD 20854 Office: 1919 Pennsylvania Ave NW #700 Washington DC 20006

CARR, MARY JO, lawyer, judge; b. Newton, Mass., Sept. 26, 1950; d. Howell Coleman and Anne (Kerr) C.; m. William J. Larson, Nov. 14, 1981. BA, Swarthmore Coll., 1972; JD, Rutgers U., 1978. Bar: Pa. 1978, U.S. Dist. Ct. (ea. dist.) Pa. 1978, N.J. 1979, U.S. Dist. Ct. (so. dist.) N.J. 1979, R.I. 1981, U.S. Dist. Ct. (so. dist.) R.I. 1984. Sole practice Phila., 1978-81, Warwick, R.I., 1981-83; probate judge City of Newport, R.I., 1983—, city solicitor, 1986—; incorporator Bank of Newport, 1986—; pres. bd. dirs. Island Moving Co., Newport, 1986—. Local government, Probate, General practice. Home and Office: 25 Cranston Ave Newport RI 02840

CARR, OSCAR CLARK, III, lawyer; b. Memphis, Apr. 9, 1951; s. Oscar Clark Carr Jr. and Billie (Fisher) Carr Houghton; m. Mary Leatherman, Aug. 4, 1973; children—Camilla Fisher, Oscar Clark V. B.A. in English with distinction, U. Va., 1973; J.D., Emory U., 1976. Bar: Tenn. 1976, U.S. Dist. Ct. (we. dist.) Tenn. 1976, U.S. Dist. Ct. (no. dist.) Miss. 1977, U.S. Ct. Appeals (6th cir.) 1985. Assoc. firm Glankler, Brown, Gilliland, Chase, Robinson & Raines, Memphis, 1976-82, ptnr., 1982—. Bd. dirs. Memphis Ballet Soc., 1980, Memphis-Shelby County Unit Am. Cancer Soc., 1985—. Mem. ABA, Tenn. Bar Assn., Memphis and Shelby County Bar Assn. (bd. dirs. 1985—), U. Va. Alumni Assn. Episcopalian. Clubs: Memphis Country, Memphis Hunt and Polo. Federal civil litigation, State civil litigation, General corporate. Office: Glankler Brown Et Al 1700 One Commerce Sq Memphis TN 38103

CARR, PATRICK E., U.S. judge; b. Jasper County, Miss., Oct. 2, 1922; s. Eugene A. and Sarah (Finnegan) C.; m. Jean Massey, Dec. 20, 1947; children: Karen, Stanley, Judy Janice, Pat, Mary, Brian. Grad., St. Bernard Jr. Coll.; LL.B., Loyola U. Bar: La. 1950. Pvt. practice Metaire, La., 1950-75; judge La. Dist. Ct., 24th Jud. Dist., 1975-79, U.S. Dist. Ct. (ea. dist.) La., New Orleans, 1979—. Served with A.C. U.S. Army, 1942-45. Mem. Am. Bar Assn., Jefferson Parish Bar Assn., La. State Bar Assn., VFW (nat. comdr.). Democrat. Jurisprudence. Office: US District Court Chambers C-376 U S Courthouse 500 Camp St New Orleans LA 70130 *

CARR, ROBERT STUART, U.S. magistrate; b. Atlanta, Jan. 25, 1946; s. James Stuart and Emily Rita (Gruntz) C.; m. Diane Barnett, June 27, 1970; children—Laura Barnett, John Patrick. B.S., Furman U., 1967; J.D., U. S.C., 1971. Bar: S.C. 1971, U.S. Dist. Ct. S.C. 1972, U.S. Ct. Appeals (4th cir.) 1974. Asst. legis. asst. to U.S. Senator Strom Thurmond, Washington, 1971; law clk. to judge U.S. Dist. Ct. S.C., 1971-72; assoc. Easterling & Brantley, P.A., Columbia, S.C., 1972-75; U.S. magistrate U.S. Dist. Ct. S.C., Charleston, 1975—; adj. prof. adminstrv. law Coll. Charleston; legal counsel S.C. Jaycees, 1976; supporting personnel subcom. of Court Adminstrn. Com. Jud. Conf. U.S., 1986. Chmn. S.C. Young Reps., 1975; trustee Inst. for Ct. Mgmt., 1985, Hibben United Meth. Ch., Mt. Pleasant, S.C. Served to maj.

JAGC, USAR, 1968—. Named Outstanding Young Man, Charleston (S.C.) Jaycees, 1982. Mem. Nat. Council U.S. Magistrates (past pres.), ABA, Nat. Conf. Spl. Ct. Judges, (chmn. elect 1986-87), S.C. Bar Assn., Furman U. Alumni Assn. (dir. 1980-85). Club: Snee Farm Country (Mt. Pleasant, S.C.). Pension, profit-sharing, and employee benefits, Criminal, Civil rights. Office: PO Box 835 Charleston SC 29402

CARR, ROKKI KNEE, lawyer; b. Bronx, N.Y.; d. Benjamin and Elsie (Uhrman) B.; m. David I. Knee, Aug. 16, 1959 (div. 1974); children—Adam J., Jonathan A.; m. Edward Q. Carr, Jr., Nov. 25, 1981 (dec.). B.A., CCNY, 1958; J.D., Hofstra U., 1973. Bar: N.Y. 1974, Calif. 1977, U.S. Dist. Ct. (ea. and so. dists.) N.Y. 1975, U.S. Supreme Ct. 1985. Mng. atty. Legal Services, Inland Co., San Bernardino, Calif., 1977-78; sr. atty. So. Calif. Ctr. Law & Deaf, Los Angeles, 1978; staff atty. Legal Aid Soc., N.Y.C., 1972-77, 78-79, hearing examiner Family Ct., 1985—; sole practice, Bklyn., 1979-85 . Dem. candidate for N.Y. State Assembly, Nassau County, 1972; mem. Visitation Ch., Bklyn., 1985—. Mem. Kings County Criminal Bar, Nat. Assn. Criminal Def. Lawyers, Bklyn. Bar Assn. (chmn. criminal law sect.) Roman Catholic. Criminal. Office: Family Ct 283 Adams St Brooklyn NY 11201

CARR, RONALD GENE, lawyer, government official; b. Chgo., Jan. 19, 1946; s. Harry Bertram and Marion Esther (Adlam) C.; m. Mary Laurie Azcuenaga, Aug. 24, 1968. A.B., Stanford U., 1968; M.A., U. Calif.-Berkeley, 1970; J.D., U. Chgo., 1973. Law clk. to chief judge U.S. Ct. Appeals (D.C. cir.), Washington, 1973-74; law clk. to Justice Lewis F. Powell U.S. Supreme Ct., Washington, 1974-75; spl. asst. to Atty. Gen. Edward H. Levi U.S. Dept. Justice, Washington, 1975-76; assoc. ptnr. Morrison & Foerster, San Francisco, 1977-81, ptnr., 1983—; dep. asst. atty. gen. antitrust div. U.S. Dept. Justice, Washington, 1981-83; lectr. fed. jurisdiction Law Sch., U. Calif.-Berkeley, 1978; vis. prof. law Boston U., 1985. Editor-in-chief: U. Chgo. Law Rev., 1972-73. Mem. ABA, Order of Coif, Phi Beta Kappa. Antitrust, Administrative and regulatory, Federal civil litigation. Home: 5100 Manning Pl NW Washington DC 20016 Office: Morrison & Foerster 2000 Pennsylvania Ave NW Suite 5500 Washington DC 20006

CARR, THOMAS ELDRIDGE, lawyer; b. Austin, Tex., Aug. 16, 1953; s. Peter Gordon and Margaret (Johnson) C.; m. Cathy Diane Franson, Dec. 18, 1977; 1 child, Christopher Allen. BA, Tex. Tech U., 1975, JD, 1977. Bar: Tex. 1978, U.S. Dist. Ct. (no. dist.) Tex. 1978, U.S. Ct. Appeals (5th cir.) 1981, U.S. Supreme Ct. 1982. Assoc. Morgan, Gambill & Owen, Ft. Worth, 1978-81; ptnr. Morgan, Owen, & Carr, Ft. Worth, 1981-85, Quillin, Owen & Thompson, Ft. Worth, 1985—. Co-author: Of Counsel to Classrooms: A Resource Guide to Assist Attorneys and Teachers in Law Focused Education. Active Benbrook City Council, Tex., 1984-86, Park and Recreation Bd., Benbrook, 1981-84; mem. exec. bd. Longhorn council Boy Scouts Am., 1983-86; mem. devel. bd. Western Nat. Bank Tex., Ft. Worth, 1983—; mem. Home Rule Charter Commn., Benbrook, 1983. Named one of Outstanding Young Men of Am. Mem. ABA (chmn. com), Ft. Worth Tarrant County Young Lawyers Assn. (pres. 1983), Tex. Young Lawyers Assn. (bd. dirs. 1984-86). Clubs: Petroleum, Lost Creek Country (Ft. Worth). School law, General corporate, Probate. Office: Quillin Owen & Thompson 550 Bailey Suite 530 Fort Worth TX 76107

CARR, WALTER STANLEY, lawyer; b. Chgo., May 5, 1945; s. Robert Adams and Margaret (Wiley) C.; m. Mary Baine, Sept. 20, 1969. BS, U. Pa., 1967; JD, U. Chgo., 1970. Bar: Ill. 1970. From assoc. to ptnr. McDermott, Will & Emery, Chgo., 1970-86; atty. Miami Corp., Chgo., 1987—. V.p. Hull House Assn., Chgo., 1985; bd. dirs. Planned Parenthood Assn. Chgo. Area, 1980—. Mem. ABA, Ill. Bar Assn., Chgo. Bar Assn., Chgo. Council Lawyers, Chgo. Estate Planning Council. Club: Univ. (Chgo.). Estate planning, Estate taxation, Probate. Home: 507 W Briar Pl Chicago IL 60657 Office: Miami Corp 410 N Michigan Ave Chicago IL 60611

CARR, WILLARD ZELLER, JR., lawyer; b. Richmond, Ind., Dec. 18, 1927; s. Willard Zeller and Susan (Brownell) C.; m. Margaret Paterson, Feb. 15, 1952; children: Clayton Paterson, Jeffrey Westcott. BS, Purdue U., 1948; JD, Ind. U., 1951. Bar: Calif. 1951, U.S. Supreme Ct. 1963. Ptnr. Gibson, Dunn & Crutcher, Los Angeles, 1952—; mem. nat. panel arbitrators Am. Arbitration Assn.; former labor relations cons. State of Alaska; lectr. bd. visitors Southwestern U. Law Sch.; mem. adv. council Southwestern Legal Found., Internat. and Comparative Law Ctr. Trustee Calif. Adminstrv. Law Coll.; bd. dirs. Hollywood Presbyn. Med. Ctr., Greater Los Angeles Visitors and Conv. Bur., Mchts. and Mfrs. Assn., Greater Los Angeles Zoo Assn., Los Angeles council Boy Scouts Am.; mem. Mayor's Econ. Devel. Policies Com.; mem. adv. com. Econ. Literacy Council of Calif. State Univ. and Colls. Found.; trustee, chmn. Pacific Legal Found.; past chmn. men's adv. com. Los Angeles County-USC Med. Ctr. Aux. for Recuitment, Edn. and Service; past chmn. bd. Wilshire Republican Club; past mem. Rep. State Central Com.; past mem. pres.'s council Calif. Mus. Sci. and Industry; mem. Nat. Def. Exec. Res., Los Angeles World Affairs Council; bd. dirs., sec. Los Angeles Police Meml. Found.; past chmn. Los Angeles sect. United Way; mem. adv. com. Los Angeles County Human Relations Commn.; Los Angeles chpt. ARC; mem. Fellow Am. Bar Found.; mem. ABA (co-chmn. com. benefits to unemployed persons, past chmn. econ. and resources controls com. of corp., banking and bus. law sect.; internat. labor relations law com. of labor and employment law sect., also com. devel. of law under Nat. Labor Relations Act), Internat. Bar Assn. (past chmn. labor law com. of bus. law sect.), Calif. State Bar, Los Angeles County Bar Assn., Los Angeles C. of C. (chmn. 1980). Administrative and regulatory, Labor. Home: 123 N McCadden Pl Los Angeles CA 90004 Office: Gibson Dunn & Crutcher 333 S Grand Ave 49th Floor Los Angeles CA 90071

CARR, WILLIAM ORVILLE, judge; b. Havre De Grace, Md., Oct. 27, 1948; s. Walter Orville and Eleanor (Pippin) C.; m. Judith Ann Coleman, Aug. 31, 1984; children: Megan Ann, Alison Elizabeth. BS, Towson State U., 1970; JD, U. Md., 1973. Bar: Md. 1973, U.S. Dist. Ct. Md. 1977, U.S. Supreme Ct. 1981. Asst. county atty. Harford County, Md., 1974-76; master in chancery Harford County Cir. Ct., 1979-84, judge, 1984—. Commr. Town of Bel Air, Md., 1977-84. Mem. ABA, Md. Bar Assn. (bd. govs. 1981-82), Harford County Bar Assn. (sec. 1973), Am. Judges Assn., Md. Soc. SAR (law enforcement medal 1986). Democrat. Lutheran. Lodge: Rotary. Judicial administration. Home: 208 Northview Rd Bel Air MD 21014

CARRAD, DAVID CLAYTON, lawyer; b. Englewood, N.J., May 19, 1944; s. Anthony Landon and Sara Kathryn (Harris) C.; m. Karen Alice Kristoff, Dec. 20, 1966 (div. 1973); 1 child, Christina E.M.; m. Lynda Lee Johnson, July 23, 1977; children: Carey Elizabeth, David Grier. BA in English, Trinity Coll., 1965; MS in Journalism, Columbia U., 1966; JD, Harvard U., 1972. Bar: N.Y. 1974, U.S. Dist. Ct. (so. and ea. dists.) N.Y. 1974, U.S. Ct. Appeals (2d cir.) 1974, Del. 1975, U.S. Dist. Ct. Del. 1977, U.S. Ct. Appeals (3d cir.) 1977, U.S. Supreme Ct. 1978. Assoc. Sullivan & Cromwell, N.Y.C., 1972-74, Morris, Nichols, Arshy & Tunnell, Wilmington, Del., 1974-75; sole practice Wilmington, 1976-85; assoc. W.L. Gore & Assocs. Inc., Newark, Del., 1985—; pres. Oxford Assocs. Inc., Wilmington, 1984-85. Contbr. articles to profl. jours. Mem., v.p. bd. student advisors Harvard Law Sch., 1970-72; lay reader Christ Ch. Christiana Hundred, Greenville, Del., 1981—; pres. Wilmington Friends Sch. Home and Sch. Assn., 1984-86. Served to 1st lt. U.S. Army, 1966-69, Vietnam. Mem. ABA, Del. Bar Assn. (sect. chmn. 1981-83), Am. Corp. Counsel Assn. Republican. Episcoapl. Club: Wilmington Country. General corporate, Contracts commercial, Securities. Home: 112 School Rd Alapocas Wilmington DE 19803 Office: WL Gore & Assocs Inc 551 Paper Mill Rd PO Box 9206 Newark DE 19714

CARRANO, FRANK ANTHONY, lawyer; b. New Haven, Sept. 20, 1957; s. James Joseph and Evelyn Eleanor (Carbone) C. BA in Psychology with honors, Southern Conn. State U., 1979; JD with honors, Washburn U., 1982. Bar: Conn. 1982. Sole practice Branford, Conn., 1982-85, North Haven, Conn., 1986—. Mem. ABA, New Haven County Bar Assn., Assn. Trial Lawyers Am., Conn. Trial Lawyers Assn., Internat. Acad. Trial Lawyers (award). Personal injury, Family and matrimonial, Criminal. Office: 270 Quinnipiac Ave North Haven CT 06473

CARRELL, DANIEL ALLAN, lawyer; b. Louisville, Jan. 2, 1941; s. Elmer N. and Mary F. (Pfingst) C.; m. Janis M. Wilhelm, July 3, 1976; children: Mary Monroe, Courtney Adele. AB, Davidson Coll., 1963; BA, Oxford U., 1965, MA, 1969; JD, Stanford U., 1968. Bar: Va. 1972, U.S. Dist. Ct. (ea. dist.) Va. 1972, U.S. Ct. Appeals (4th cir.) 1975, U.S. Dist. Ct. (we. dist.) Va. 1985. Asst. prof. U.S. Mil. Acad., West Point, N.Y., 1968-71; assoc. Hunton & Williams, Richmond, Va., 1971-79, ptnr., 1979—. Mem. Richmond Rep. Com., 1974—; co-counsel Dalton for Gov. campaign, Richmond, 1977; counsel Obenshain for Senate campaign, Richmond, 1978; v.p., bd. dirs. Southampton Citizens Assn., 1985—; pres.-elect Davidson Coll Alumni Assn., 1986—; trustee Davidson Coll. Served to capt. U.S. Army, 1968-71. Rhodes scholar, 1962; recipient Award of Merit Sports Illustrated Mag., 1963. Mem. ABA (chmn. exemptions com. 1984-86, state action exemption and Noerr Doctrine com. 1986—, antitrust sect.), Va. Bar Assn. (chmn. young lawyers joint law-related edn. com. 1978-79, young lawyers fellow award 1980), Va. State Bar (chmn. com. on legal edn. and admission to bar), Richmond Bar Assn., Christian Legal Soc. Presbyterian. Clubs: Westwood Racquet, Downtown (Richmond). Avocations: tennis, basketball, theatre, concerts. Antitrust, Federal civil litigation, General corporate. Home: 3724 Custis Rd Richmond VA 23225 Office: Hunton & Williams PO Box 1535 Richmond VA 23212

CARRERE, CHARLES SCOTT, judge; b. Dublin, Ga., Sept. 26, 1937; 1 son, Daniel Austin. B.A., U. Ga., 1959; LL.B., Stetson U., 1961. Bar: Fla. 1961, Ga. 1960. Law clk. U.S. Dist. Judge, Orlando, Fla., 1962-63; asst. U.S. atty. Middle Dist. Fla., 1963-66, 68-69, chief trial atty., 1965-66, 68-69; ptnr. Harrison, Greene, Mann, Rowe & Stanton, 1970-80; judge Pinellas County, Fla., 1980—. Mem. State Bar Ga., Fla. Bar, Phi Beta Kappa. Presbyterian. Jurisprudence. Mailing: PO Box 22034 Gateway Mall Station Saint Petersburg FL 33742 Office: 150 Fifth St N 254 County Bldg Saint Petersburg FL 33701

CARRES, LOUIS GEORGE, lawyer; b. Miami Beach, Fla., Aug. 14, 1943; s. Louis John and Helen (Davis) C.; m. Margaret Craig Good, July 10, 1983; children: Michele, Elliot. B.A., Fla. Atlantic U., Boca Raton, 1965; J.D., Stetson U., 1969. Bar: Fla. 1969, U.S. Dist. Ct. (so. dist.) Fla. 1971, U.S. Dist. Ct. (mid. dist.) Fla. 1974, U.S. Dist. Ct. (no. dist.) Fla. 1975, U.S. Ct. Appeals (5th cir.) 1973, U.S. Ct. Appeals (11th cir.) 1982, U.S. Supreme Ct. 1976. Staff atty. South Fla. Migrant Legal Services, Delray Beach, 1969-71; mng. atty. Fla. Rural Legal Services Delray Beach, 1971-73; chief appellate asst. Office of Pub. Defender, Tallahassee, Fla., 1977-80, asst., West Palm Beach, Fla., 1980—; instr. bus. law Hillsborough Community Coll., Tampa, 1974. Mem. The Fla. Bar, ABA, Palm Beach County Bar Assn. (mem. law reform com. 1971-72), Palm Beach Criminal Def. Assn., Am. Judicature Soc., Robert Bullington Law Soc. Democrat. Greek Orthodox. Criminal. Home: 830 Palmetto St West Palm Beach FL 33405 Office: Office of Pub Defender 301 N Olive Ave 9th Floor West Palm Beach FL 33401

CARREY, NEIL, lawyer, educator; b. Bronx, N.Y., Nov. 19, 1942; s. David L. and Betty (Kurtzburg) C.; m. Karen Krysher, Apr. 9, 1980; children—Jana, Christopher; children by previous marriage—Scott, Douglas, Dana. B.S. in Econs., U. Pa., 1964; J.D., Stanford U., 1967. Bar: Calif. 1968. Mem. firm, v.p. corp. DeCastro, West, Chodorow & Burns, Inc., Los Angeles, 1967—; instr. program for legal paraprofls. U. So. Calif., 1977—. Author: Nonqualified Deffered Compensation Plans-The Wave of the Future, 1985. Officer, Vista Del Mar Child Care Center, Los Angeles, 1968-84; treas. Nat. Little League of Santa Monica, 1984-85, pres., 1985-86, coach Bobby Sox Team, Santa Monica, 1987—; curriculum com. Santa Monica Sch. Dist., 1983-84. Mem. ABA, Western Pension Conf., U. Pa. Alumni Soc. So. Calif. (pres. 1971-79, dir. 1979—), The Group, Alpha Kappa Psi (disting. life). Republican. Jewish. Club: Mountaingate Tennis Los Angeles). Pension, profit-sharing, and employee benefits, General corporate, Personal income taxation. Home: 616 23d St Santa Monica CA 90402 Office: 10960 Wilshire Blvd Suite 1800 Los Angeles CA 90024

CARRICO, HARRY LEE, state chief justice; b. Washington, Sept. 4, 1916; s. William Temple and Nellie Nadalia (Willett) C.; m. Betty Lou Peck, May 18, 1940; 1 child, Lucretia Ann. Jr. cert., George Washington U., 1938, J.D., 1942, LL.D., 1987; LL.D., U. Richmond, Va., 1973. Bar: Va. 1941. With firm Rust & Rust, Fairfax, 1941-43; trial justice Fairfax County, Va., 1943-51; pvt. practice Fairfax, 1951-56; judge 16th Jud. Circuit Va., 1956-61; justice Supreme Ct. Va., 1961-81, chief justice, 1981—. Served to ensign USNR, 1945-46. Recipient Alumni Profl. Achievement award George Washington U., 1981. Mem. McNeill Law Soc., Conf. Chief Justices (bd. dirs. 1985—), Order of Coif, Phi Delta Phi., Omicron Delta Kappa. Episcopalian. Jurisprudence. Office: Supreme Ct Bldg 100 N 9th St Richmond VA 23219

CARRIGAN, JIM RICHARD, judge; b. Mobridge, S.D., Aug. 24, 1929; s. Leo Michael and Mildred Ione (Jaycox) C.; m. Beverly Jean Halpin, June 2, 1956; children: Sheila, Maura, Patrick, Kathleen, Andrew, Michael. Ph.B., J.D., U. N.D., 1953; LL.M. in Taxation, NYU, 1956. Bar: N.D. 1953, Colo. 1956. Assoc. firm Long & Smart, Denver, 1956; asst. prof. law U. Denver, 1956-59; vis. assoc. prof. NYU Law Sch., 1958, U. Wash. Law Sch., 1959-60; jud. adminstr. State of Colo., 1960-61; individual practice law Denver, 1961-62; prof. law U. Colo., 1961-67; partner firm Carrigan & Bragg (and predecessors); (predecessors), Boulder, Colo., Denver, 1967-76; justice Colo. Supreme Ct., 1976-79; judge U.S. Dist. Ct. for Colo., 1979—; mem. Colo. Bd. Bar Examiners, 1969-71; lectr. Nat. Coll. State Judiciary, 1964-77; bd. dirs., mem. exec. com. Nat. Bd. Trial Advocacy, 1978—; bd. dirs., mem. faculty, mem. exec. com. Nat. Inst. Trial Advocacy. Editor-in-chief: N.D. Law Rev., 1952-53; editor: DICTA, 1957-59, Internat. Soc. Barristers Quar, 1972-79; contbr. numerous articles to profl. jours. Chmn. Boulder County Democratic Party, 1967-68; bd. regents U. Colo., 1975-76; bd. visitors U. N.D. Coll. Law, 1983—. Recipient Disting. Service award Nat. Coll. State Judiciary, 1969, Outstanding Alumnus award U. N.D., 1973, Regent Emeritus award U. Colo., 1977. Fellow Colo. Bar Found., Boulder County Bar Found.; mem. ABA (action com. on tort system improvement 1985—, TIPS sect. long range planning council 1986—), Colo., Boulder, Denver County bar assns., Cath. Lawyers Guild, Internat. Soc. Barristers, Internat. Acad. Trial Lawyers, Fed. Judges Assn. (bd. dirs. 1985—), Am. Judicature Soc. (bd. dirs. 1985—), Order of Coif, Phi Beta Kappa. Roman Catholic. Club: Denver Athletic. Lodge: Rotary. Jurisprudence. Office: US Dist Ct C-236 1929 Stout St Denver CO 80294

CARRIGAN, STEPHEN PAUL, lawyer; b. Houston, Feb. 8, 1955; s. Ralph S. and Lilly (Gatzke) C.; m. Catherine Stewart, July 11, 1980; children: Lauren, Leslie. BBA in Acctg., U. Tex., Austin, 1976, JD, 1980. Bar: Tex. 1980. Assoc. Fulbright & Jaworski, Houston, 1980-85; ptnr. Kirk & Carrigan P.C., Houston, 1985—. Fellow Houston Bar Found.; mem. ABA, Tex. Bar Assn., Houston Bar Assn., Houston Young Lawyers Assn. Republican. Baptist. Club: Plaza. Federal civil litigation, State civil litigation, Contracts commercial. Office: Kirk & Carrigan PC 910 Louisiana 4025 1 Shell Plaza Houston TX 77002

CARRINGTON, FRANK GAMBLE, JR., lawyer; b. Paris, May 11, 1936; s. Frank Gamble and Edith (Rule) C.; m. Mary Olson, May 11, 1968; children—Christine, Claire. B.A., Hampden Sydney Coll., 1956; LL.B., U. Mich., 1960; LL.M., Northwestern U., 1970. Bar: Ohio 1966, Colo. 1969, Ill. 1976, U.S. Supreme Ct. 1970, Va. 1979. Spl. agt. Intelligence Div., IRS, Cin., 1960-67; legal advisor Narcotics Squad, Chgo. Police Dept., 1967-68, Denver, 1968-70; exec. dir. Ams. for Effective Law Enforcement, Inc., Evanston, Ill., 1970-79; exec. dir. Victim's Assistance Legal Orgn., Virginia Beach Va., 1979—; legal cons. Sunny Von Bülow Nat. Victim Advocacy Ctr., Ft. Worth, 1986—; mem. adv. task forces on victims, law enforcement and criminal justice for Ronald Reagan, Presdl. Campaign, 1980; mem. U.S. Atty. Gen.'s Task Force on Violent Crime, 1981; mem. Pres.'s Task Force on Victims of Crime, 1982; mem., then vice chmn. adv. bd. Nat. Inst. Justice, 1982-84; bd. dirs. Nat. Assn. Victims' Assistance, 1975-82; lectr. U. Mich, U. Houston, 1981. Served to lance cpl. USMC. Recipient Law Enforcement Medal, SAR, 1978; appreciation award Nat. Criminal Justice Assn. Mem. ABA (mem., vice chmn., then chmn. victims com. 1976-84), Va. Bar Assn., Ill. Bar Assn., Internat. Assn. Chiefs of Police, Nat. Law Enforcement Council. Republican. Episcopalian. Author: The Victims, 1975, The Defenseless Society, 1976, Neither Cruel Nor Unusual, 1978; (with others) Evidence Law for Police, 1972, School Crime and Victims and Victims' Rights, 1986; contbr. numerous articles to profl. jours. Criminal, Civil rights, State civil litigation. Home: 4530 Ocean Front Rd Virginia Beach VA 23451 Office: 4530 Oceanfront Virginia Beach VA 23451

CARRINGTON, MORRIS CLIFFORD, lawyer; b. Marshall, Tex., July 1, 1957; s. Emory John and Sybill Charlean (Witherspoon) C.; m. Sandra Sparr, July 16, 1983. BBA in Acctg., Tex. Tech U., 1979, JD, 1982. Bar: Tex. 1982, U.S. Tax Ct. 1983, U.S. Dist. Ct. (ea. dist.) Tex. 1984, U.S. Dist. Ct. (so. dist.) Tex. 1985. Assoc. Mehaffy, Weber, Keith & Gonsoulin, Beaumont, Tex., 1982—. Mem. ABA, Tex. Bar Assn., Am. Inst. CPA's, Tex. Assn. Def. Counsel, Tex. Soc. CPA's, Jefferson County Young Lawyers Assn. (bd. dirs. 1985-86), Def. Research Inst., Order of Barristers. Admiralty, Federal civil litigation, Insurance.

CARRINGTON, PAUL DEWITT, lawyer, educator; b. Dallas, June 12, 1931; s. Paul and Frances Ellen (DeWitt) C.; m. Bessie Meek, Aug., 1952; children: Clark DeWitt, Mary, William James, Emily. BA, U. Tex., 1952; LLB, Harvard U., 1955. Bar: Tex. 1955, Ohio 1962, Mich. 1967. Sole practice Dallas, 1955; teaching fellow Harvard U., 1957-58; asst. prof. law U. Wyo., 1958-60, Ind. U., 1960-62; assoc. prof. Ohio State U., 1962-65; prof. U. Mich., 1965-78; dean, prof. Duke U. Sch. Law, 1978—; reporter civil rules adv. com. Jud. Conf. of U.S., 1985—. Author: (with Meador and Rosenberg) Justice on Appeal, 1977, (with Babcock) Civil Procedure, 1977, 3d edit., 1983. Mem. Ann Arbor (Mich.) Bd. Edn., 1970-73. Served with U.S. Army, 1955-57. Fellow Am. Bar Found.; mem. ABA, Am. Law Inst. Episcopalian. Club: Cosmos. Office: Duke U Sch Law Durham NC 27706

CARRO, JORGE LUIS, law educator, consultant; b. Havana, Cuba, Nov. 27, 1924; came to U.S., 1967, naturalized, 1973; s. Luis and Maria G. (Gonzalez) C.; m. Edy Jimenez; 1 dau., Edy C. B.A., Havana Inst., 1945; J.D., U. Havana, 1950; M.L.S., Kans. State Tchrs. Coll., 1969. Bar: Havana, Cuba 1950. Practice, Havana, 1950-67; legal cons. Swiss embassy, Havana and legal adv. Apostolic Nuncio, Havana, 1963-67; asst. librarian U. Wis.-Milw., 1969; asst. librarian, instr. U. Wis.-Whitewater, 1969-72; librarian, asst. prof. Ohio No. U., 1972-75, assoc. prof., 1975-76; assoc. prof. law, librarian U. Cin., 1976-78, acting dean, 1978-79, prof., librarian 1979-86, prof., 1986—; Mem. ABA, Cin. Bar Assn. Republican. Roman Catholic. Author: Government Regulation of Business Ethics, 3 vols., 1981-82; contbr. articles, books revs. to profl. jours.; reviewer Law Books in Rev. Legal ethics, Public international, Immigration, naturalization, and customs. Office: U Cin College of Law Cincinnati OH 45221

CARROL, ROBERT KELTON, lawyer; b. Washington, Ind., Sept. 28, 1952; s. Louis Leon and Beatrice (Colbert) C. BA with distinction, So. Meth. U., 1974, JD, 1977. Bar: Tex. 1977, Calif. 1978, U.S. Dist. Ct. (no. and ea. dists.) Calif. 1978, U.S. Dist. Ct. (cen. and so. dists.) Calif. 1984, U.S. Ct. Appeals (9th cir.) 1978, U.S. Ct. Appeals (D.C. cir.) 1983, U.S. Supreme Ct. 1983. Assoc. Littler, Mendelson, Fastiff & Tichy, San Francisco, 1977-82, ptnr., 1982—. Contbr. articles to profl. publs. Vestry mem. St. Mary the Virgin Episc. Ch., San Francisco, 1982—. Mem. ABA (labor law sect. 1977—, entertainment com. on devel. and sports law 1977—), State Bar Calif., State Bar Tex., Bar Assn. San Francisco, Phi Beta Kappa, Phi Delta Phi. Clubs: Lawyers' of San Francisco, Barristers of San Francisco. Labor, Entertainment, State civil litigation.

CARROLL, CATHERINE NORTH, lawyer; b. LaJolla, Calif., Aug. 11, 1948; d. Philip Frederick and Virginia Catherine (North) W. BA, St. John's Coll., Santa Fe, 1971; JD, U. N.Mex., 1975. Bar: N.Mex. 1975, Oreg. 1977. Sole practice Portland, Oreg., 1980—; sec. NW Oreg. Health Systems, Portland, 1980-81. Mem. ABA (family law sect.), LWV (bd. dirs. 1985—), Oreg. Bar Assn. (family and juvenile law sect.). Family and matrimonial, State civil litigation. Home: 12375 Mount Jefferson Terr Apt 11E Lake Oswego OR 97034 Office: 700 Crown Plaza 1500 SW 1st Ave Portland OR 97201

CARROLL, DONALD R., trust company executive, lawyer; b. Toledo, May 31, 1950; s. Frank L. and Anne M. (Smith) C.; m. Linda M. KaSavage, June 22, 1974; 1 child, John F. BA in History, Philosophy, and Psychology, U. Toledo, 1973, JD, 1979. Bar: Ohio 1979, U.S. Dist. Ct. (no. dist.) Ohio 1980, U.S. Dist. Ct. (no. dist.) Calif. 1982. Mktg. rep. Libbey-Owens Ford Co., N.Y.C., 1973-74; retail mgr. Russell's, Inc., Toledo, 1974-76; v.p., trust probate mgr. Ohio Citizens Bank, Toledo, 1979-82, v.p., trust legal counsel, 1982-84, v.p., mgr., trust co. benefits dir., 1984-86; atty. fin. mgmt. dept. Equibank, Pitts., 1986—. Asst. sec. Edward Drummond Libbey Endowment, Toledo, 1982—; trustee and chmn. planning and devel. com. Zepf Community Mental Health Ctr., Toledo, 1984—; bd. dirs. bus., industry, labor adv. bd. Merit Inc., Toledo, 1986—; vice-chmn. Jamie Farr Toledo Classic, Ladies Profl. Golf Assn. tournament, 1985. Mem. ABA, Ohio State Bar Assn., Toledo Bar Assn., Lucas County Bar Assn., Toledo Estate Planning Council. Club: Toledo. Avocations: golf, art. Pension, profit-sharing, and employee benefits, Estate planning, Personal income taxation. Office: Equibank Fin Mgmt Dept Oliver Plaza Pittsburgh PA 15222-2705

CARROLL, EARL HAMBLIN, judge; b. Tucson, Mar. 26, 1925; s. John Vernon and Ruby (Wood) C.; m. Louise Rowlands, Nov. 1, 1952; children—Katherine Carroll Pearson, Margaret Anne. B.S. in Bus. Adminstrn., U. Ariz., 1948, LL.B., 1951. Bar: Ariz., U.S. Ct. Appeals (9th and 10th cirs.), U.S. Ct. of Claims, U.S. Supreme Ct. Law clk. Ariz. Supreme Ct., Phoenix, 1951-52; assoc. Evans, Kitchel & Jenckes, Phoenix, 1952-56, ptnr., 1956-80; judge U.S. Dist. Ct. Ariz., Phoenix, 1980—; spl. counsel City of Tombstone, Ariz., 1962-65, Maricopa County, Phoenix, 1968-75, City of Tucson, 1974, City of Phoenix, 1979. Mem. City of Phoenix Bd. of Adjustment, 1955-58; trustee Phoenix Elem. Sch. Bd., 1961-72; mem. Gov.'s Council on Intergovtl. Relations, Phoenix, 1970-73; mem. Ariz. Bd. Regents, 1978-80. Served with USNR, 1943-46; PTO. Recipient Nat. Service awards Campfire, 1973, 75, Alumni Service award U. Ariz., 1980, Disting. Citizen award No. Ariz. U., Flagstaff, 1983. Fellow Am. Coll. Trial Lawyers, Am. Bar Found.; mem. ABA, Ariz. Bar Assn., U. Ariz. Law Coll. Assn. (pres. 1975), Sigma Chi, Phi Delta Phi. Democrat. Club: Phoenix Country. Judicial administration. Office: US Dist Ct Federal Bldg Room 6000 230 N 1st Ave Phoenix AZ 85025 *

CARROLL, JAMES JOSEPH, corporation executive; b. Cin., Aug. 1, 1946; s. John Daniel and Virgeal Catherine (Grever) C.; m. Marie Gemelli, May 7, 1977; children: Katharine, Emily. BBA, U. Cin., 1969; JD, No. Ky. U., 1978. Bar: Ohio 1978, U.S. Dist. Ct. (so. dist.) Ohio 1978, U.S. Tax Ct. 1979, U.S. Supreme Ct. 1979. Tax mgr. Main LaFrantz, Cin., 1974-77; sec., treas. R.E.S.C.O., Inc., Cin., 1977-80, Sterling-Mead, Inc., Cin., 1980-87; sole practice Cin., 1987—. Candidate Hamilton County auditor, 1974; treas. for various polit. candidates, Hamilton County, 1980, 82, 84; bd. dirs., past pres. Hyde Park Neighborhood Council, Cin., 1980—; pres., trustee Neighborhood Improvement Corp., 1986—. Served with USAR, 1969-75. Mem. Cin. Bar Assn., Ohio Soc. CPA's, Cin. C. of C. (trustee Leadership Cin. Alumni 1986—). Democrat. Roman Catholic. Club: Bankers (Cin.). General corporate, Real property, Personal income taxation. Office: 1100 Gwynne Bldg 602 Main St Cincinnati OH 45202

CARROLL, JAMES MICHAEL, lawyer; b. Cin., Feb. 23, 1950; s. James Matthew and Elizabeth (Sanders) C.; m. Sandra Ann Blake, May 16, 1982; children: Nicole, James, Sean. BA, U. Cin., 1972; JD, No. Ky. State U., 1976. Sole practice Cin., 1976—; adjunct prof. Mt. St. Joseph's Coll., Cin., 1981-84; lectr. Practical Law Inst., 1986. V.p. Clifton Heights Bus. Assn., Cin., 1978-80. Recipient scholarship U. Cin. 1968-72. Mem. ABA, Assn. Trial Lawyers Am., Ohio Assn. Trial Lawyers, Ohio State Bar Assn., Cin. Bar Assn. (chmn. young lawyers sect. 1983-84, chair-elect, 1982-83, sec. 1981-82). Avocations: sports. Criminal, State civil litigation, Personal injury. Office: 3101 Carew Tower 441 Vine St Cincinnati OH 45202

CARROLL, JAMES VINCENT, III, lawyer; b. Houston, Sept. 21, 1940; s. James Vincent and Adoline (Easley) C.; children—Mary Latham, David Carter, James Vincent IV. B.B.A., U. Tex., 1962, J.D., 1964. Bar: Tex. 1965, D.C. 1983. Mem. Andrews & Kurth and predecessors, 1965—, mng. ptnr., Washington, 1981-83; mem. U.S. del. 2d UN Conf. on Exploration and Peaceful Uses of Outer Space, 1982. Served with USCG, 1964-65. Mem. NAM (labor law adv. com.), ABA (vice-chmn. oil com. natural resources sect. 1980-85, chmn. energy and natural resources litigation com. 1985-86,

council mem. 1986—), Tex. Bar Assn. (dir. labor law sect. 1974-76, chmn. fed. and state agy. subcom. com. on coordination with other state and fed. groups 1975-77), Tex. Assn. of Bus. (bd. dirs. 1986—), U.S. C. of C. (labor law adv. com.), East Tex. C. of C. (bd. dirs. 1984—), U. Tex. Law Sch. Assn. (dir. 1980-83). Clubs: Houston Country, Texas, Met. Club of Washington (D.C.). Contbr. articles in field to profl. jours. Labor, Oil and gas leasing. Home: 5936 Deerwood Houston TX 77057 Office: Andrews & Kurth 4200 Texas Commerce Tower Houston TX 77002

CARROLL, JAMES WALTER, JR., lawyer; b. Phila., Mar. 28, 1950; s. James Walter and Catherine Marie (Flaherty) C.; m. Lisette Margaret McCormick, Sept. 24, 1983. BS in Fgn. Service, Georgetown U., 1972; JD, Villanova U., 1975. Bar: Pa. 1975, U.S. Dist. Ct. (we. dist.) Pa. 1975, U.S. Dist. Ct. (mid. dist.) Pa. 1977, U.S. Ct. Appeals (3d cir.) 1980, U.S. Ct. Appeals (4th cir.) 1985, U.S. Supreme Ct. 1986. Staff atty. Neighborhood Legal Services, Pitts., 1975-77, consumer specialist, 1977-80, consumer unit coordinator, 1980-82; assoc. Strassburger & McKenna, Pitts., 1982-83; ptnr. Tabakin, Carroll & Curtin, Pitts., 1983—; mem. exec. council Neighborhood Legal Services Assn., Pitts., 1980-85, also bd. dirs. 1984—, asst. treas. 1986—. Mem. Zoning Bd. of Adjustment, Swissvale, Pa., 1986. Mem. ABA, Assn. Trial Lawyers Am., Pa. Bar Assn., Pa. Trial Lawyers Assn., Allegheny County Bar Assn. (chairperson young lawyers sect., bd. govs. 1985—, asst. sec.-treas. 1987—). Democrat. Roman Catholic. Club: City (Pitts.). Personal injury, Civil rights, Criminal. Home: 7511 Hutchinson Ave Pittsburgh PA 15218 Office: Tabakin Carroll & Curtin 1430 Grant Bldg Pittsburgh PA 15219

CARROLL, JOHN HAWKINS, lawyer; b. N.Y.C., Nov. 16, 1921; s. Charles J. and Mary H. (Hawkins) C.; m. Marie G. Tobin, Feb. 4, 1950; children: Charles S., Paul V., Christina M., John D., Denise M. BA, Fordham U., 1947, JD, 1951. Bar: N.Y. 1951, Del. 1962. Law clk. U.S. Dist. Ct. (so. dist.) N.Y., N.Y.C., 1951-54, asst. U.S. atty., 1954-57; trial atty. N.Y. Life Ins. Co., N.Y.C., 1957-58; sr. atty. Atlas Chem. Industries, Wilmington, Del., 1958-60, asst. gen. counsel, 1960-68, gen. counsel, sec., 1968-79; v.p., gen. counsel ICI Ams. Inc. (name changed from Atlas Chem. Industries 1972), Wilmington, 1979-86; ret. Mem. bd. overseers Del. Law Sch., Wilmington, 1977-86; bd. dirs. Del. Symphony, Wilmington, 1982-86; Served with USAF, 1943-46. Roman Catholic. Antitrust, General corporate. Office: ICI Ams Inc Wilmington DE 19897

CARROLL, JOHN LEO, lawyer; b. Chgo., Apr. 6, 1922; s. Leo and Mary (Howe) C.; m. Patricia A. Kennell, Feb. 18, 1950; children—Barbara Carroll Rogers, Timothy, Patrick, Brian, Cezanne, John Leo. B.A., Ind. U., 1948, J.D., 1948. Bar: Ind. 1948, U.S. Dist. Ct. (so. and no. dists.) Ind. 1948, U.S. Ct. Appeals (6th cir.) 1979, U.S. Ct. Appeals (7th cir.) 1960, U.S. Supreme Ct. 1961. Ptnr., Johnson, Carroll & Griffith, P.C., Evansville, Ind., 1952—, now pres.; pres. Ind. Continuing Legal Edn. Forum, 1983. lectr. in field, 1960-72. Bd. overseers St. Meinrad Coll., 1968-83, chmn., 1970-72; pres. Ind. Pub. TV Soc., 1978. Served with inf. AUS, 1942-45. Decorated Bronze Star medal, Combat Inf. Badge. Fellow ABA, Ind. Bar Found.; mem. Ind. State Bar Assn. (pres. 1983-84; Presdl. citation 1976), Evansville Bar Assn. (James Bethel Gresham Freedom award 1962). Roman Catholic. Club: Evansville Country. Author: Primer of Indiana Procedure, 1977; Avoiding the Will Contest, 1979. General practice, Probate, Condemnation. Office: Johnson Carroll & Griffith PC 2230 W Franklin St Evansville IN 47712

CARROLL, JOHN THOMAS, lawyer; b. Freeport, N.Y., May 3, 1955; s. Edward Thomas and Margaret (MacDermid) C. AB, Dartmouth Coll., 1977; JD, U. Mich., 1980. Bar: Mass. 1980, U.S. Dist. Ct. Mass. 1980. Assoc. Rackemann, Sawyer & Brewster, Boston, 1980—. Mem. ABA, Boston Bar Assn., Mass. Bar Assn. Republican. Roman Catholic. Avocation: sports. Real property, Construction, Landlord-tenant. Home: 20 Dartmouth Pl Boston MA 02116 Office: Rackemann Sawyer & Brewster One Financial Ctr Boston MA 02111

CARROLL, JOSEPH J., lawyer; b. N.Y.C., Sept. 18, 1936; s. James J. and M. Catherine (Molloy) C.; m. Barbara Ann Lediger, May 16, 1959; 1 child, Barbara Ann. B.S., Manhattan Coll., 1958; LL.B., St. John's U., 1963; LL.M., NYU, 1968. Bar: N.Y. 1964, U.S. Supreme Ct. 1967, D.C. 1978. Ins. underwriter Atlantic Mut. Ins. Co., N.Y.C., 1959-63; pub. adminstrn. intern N.Y. State Housing Fin. Agy., N.Y.C., 1963-64, adminstv. asst., 1964-67; assoc. Mudge Rose Guthrie Alexander & Ferdon, N.Y.C., 1967-77, ptnr., 1977—. Mem. ABA, N.Y. State Bar Assn., D.C. Bar Assn., Nat. Health Lawyers Assn. Health, Municipal bonds. Office: Mudge Rose Guthrie Alexander & Ferdon 180 Maiden Ln New York NY 10038

CARROLL, MARK THOMAS, lawyer; b. Queens, N.Y., May 12, 1956; s. Bernard James and Thalia (Antypas) C.; m. Joanne Mary Grinnell, Aug. 4, 1979; children: Stephen, Thomas. BA, Columbia U., 1977; JD, Harvard U., 1980. Bar: Pa. 1980, U.S. Ct. Appeals (3d cir.) 1980, U.S. Dist. Ct. (ea. dist.) Pa. 1980. Assoc. Duane, Morris & Heckscher, Phila., 1980-82; asst. dir. ALI-ABA, Phila., 1982-85, dir. office of periodicals, 1985—. Mem. ABA. Republican. Roman Catholic. Legal history, Libel. Home: 1402 Ashcom Dr Downingtown PA 19335 Office: ALI-ABA 4025 Chestnut Philadelphia PA 19104

CARROLL, MICHAEL DENNIS, lawyer; b. Phila., June 24, 1955; s. Henry Michael and Joan Marie (Burke) C. BS in Polit. Sci., U. Scranton, 1977; JD, Temple U., 1980. Bar: Pa. 1980, U.S. Dist. Ct. (ea. dist.) Pa. 1980, N.J. 1981, U.S. Dist. Ct. N.J. 1981. ABA, N.J. Bar Assn. Avocations: sports, ice hockey, skiing, softball. Real property, General practice, Personal injury. Home: 1113 Bay Ave Ocean City NJ 08226 Office: 1200 Atlantic Ave Suite 301 Atlantic City NJ 08401

CARROLL, RAOUL LORD, lawyer; b. Washington, Mar. 16, 1950; s. John Thomas and Gertrude Barbara (Jenkins) C.; m. Elizabeth Jane Coleman, Mar. 22, 1980; 1 dau., Alexandria Nicole. B.S., Morgan State U., 1972; J.D., St. Johns U., Jamaica, N.Y., 1975; postgrad. Georgetown U., 1980-81. Bar: N.Y. 1976, D.C. 1979, U.S. Dist. Ct. D.C. 1979, U.S. Supreme Ct. 1979, U.S. Dist. Ct. (so. and ea. dist.) N.Y. 1982. Asst. U.S. atty. Office U.S. Atty., Dept. Justice, Washington, 1979-80; assoc. mem. U.S. Bd. Vets. Appeals, Washington, 1980-81; ptnr. Hart, Carroll & Chavers, Washington, 1981-85, Bishop, Cook, Purcell & Reynolds, Washington, 1986—; dir., treas. Conwest-USA, Washington; vice chmn. Am. Ctr. for Internat. Leadership, Columbus, Ind. Pres. Black Asst. U.S. Attys. Assn., Washington, 1980-83; counsel D.C. Democratic State Com., 1982-84; gen. counsel Md./D.C. Minority Supplier Devel. Council, Columbia, Md., 1984—. Served to capt. U.S. Army, 1975-79. Decorated Joint Service Commendation medal, Army Commendation medal; named Outstanding Young Man Am., U.S. Jaycees, 1979. Mem. D.C. Bar Assn., Washington Bar Assn., Nat. Assn. Bond Lawyers, Omega Psi Phi. Baptist. Administrative and regulatory, Municipal bonds. Home: 1226 Kirby St NW Washington DC 20001 Office: Bishop Liberman et al 1200 17th St NW Washington DC 20036

CARROLL, SEAVY ALEXANDER, lawyer, former judge; b. Lumberton, N.C., Feb. 4, 1918; s. Samuel Willard and Berta (Butler) C.; m. Virginia Brooks Corbett, Nov. 16, 1956; children—Carrie, Catherine, Wesley, Martha, Ernest. B.A., Wake Forest U., 1940, LL.B., 1946, J.D., 1970; postgrad. St. Andrews Coll., Eng., 1959, Ind. U., 1965, Nat. Coll. State Judiciary, 1973. Bar: N.C. 1947, U.S. Dist. Ct. (ea. dist.) N.C. 1948. Adviser Duke Legal Aid Clinic, 1946-47; sole practice, Fayetteville, N.C., 1947-58; ptnr. Carroll & Herring, Fayetteville, 1958-59; missionary United Methodist Ch., Rhodesia, 1959-70; supt. schs. Nyadiri, Rhodesia, 1960; dir. publicity and promotion, Salisbury, Rhodesia, 1961-69; judge Cumberland County Recorders Ct., 1952-56, 12th Jud. Dist., 1970-74; sole practice, Fayetteville, 1974—; atty. Town of Spring Lake, N.C., 1974-78; adviser Duke Legal Aid Clinic. Chmn., United Fund, 1949; mem. N.C. Senate, 1957-59. Mem. ABA, N.C. Bar Assn., 12th Jud. Dist. Bar Assn., Cumberland County Bar Assn. Democrat. Contbr. articles to religious jours. State civil litigation, Criminal, Family and matrimonial. Home: 2404 Morganton Rd Fayetteville NC 28303 Office: 115 S Cool Spring St Fayetteville NC 28301

CARROLL, THOMAS CHARLES, lawyer; b. Louisville, Sept. 1, 1921; s. Tarlton Combs and Irene (Crutcher) C.; m. Julianne Kirk, Apr. 23, 1959. B.A., Harvard U., 1942; J.D., U. Ky., 1948. Bar: Ky. 1948, U.S. Dist. Ct. (we. dist.) Ky. 1950, U.S. Ct. Appeals (6th cir.) 1969, U.S. Supreme Ct. 1971. Since practiced in Louisville, 1949—; ptnr. firm Carroll, Steinfeld & Longmeyer, 1983—; dir. Brokerage, Inc., Service Erection & Machine Co., Inc., Roads and Rivers Transp., Inc.; legal counsel Ky. Democratic Com., 1964-75, spl. counsel, 1975-79; parliamentarian Dem. Nat. Com., 1973-75; mem. Dem. Charter Com., 1973-75, Ky. Dem. Exec. Com., 1964-75. Served to capt. U.S. Army, 1942-46. Mem. ABA, Ky. Bar Assn., Louisville Bar Assn., Assn. Trial Lawyers Am. (Ky. outstanding service award 1957), Ky. Acad. Trial Attys., Phi Delta Phi. Clubs: Pendennis, Jefferson (Louisville); Hasty Pudding (Harvard U.); Harvard (N.Y.C.); Nat. Democratic (Washington). General corporate, Probate, State civil litigation. Home: 1603 Evergreen Rd Anchorage KY 40223 Office: Carroll Steinfeld & Longmeyer 310 W Liberty St Suite 600 Louisville KY 40202

CARROLL, THOMAS PHILLIP, lawyer; b. Trenton, N.J., Oct. 2, 1955; s. Robert B. and Margaret (Heslin) C. AB, Georgetown U., 1977; JD, U. Chgo., 1981. Bar: N.J. 1982, U.S. Dist. Ct. N.J. 1982, N.Y. 1983, U.S. Dist. Ct. (ea. and. so. dists.) N.Y. 1983, Pa. 1985, DC 1985, U.S. Dist. Ct. D.C. 1986, U.S. Ct. Appeals (D.C. cir.) 1986. Law clk. to Chief Justice Robert N. Wilentz Supreme Ct. N.J., Perth Amboy, 1981-82; assoc. Debevoise & Plimpton, N.Y.C., 1982-84, Washington, 1984—. Mem. ABA, Fed. Bar. Assn., D.C. Bar Assn. Roman Catholic. Federal civil litigation, Securities, Antitrust. Office: Debevoise & Plimpton 555 13th St NW Washington DC 20004

CARROLL, TIMOTHY WAYNE, lawyer; b. Ft. Worth, Oct. 8, 1951; s. Wayne Charles and Ragnild Berlyl (Holland) C.; m. M. Bridget Kinerk, Nov. 26, 1982; children: Patrick Timothy, Ryan Robert, Molly Bridget. BA in History, Creighton U., 1973, JD, 1976. Bar: Nebr. 1976, U.S. Dist. Ct. Nebr. 1976. Re. casualty claims Allstate Ins. Co., Omaha, 1977-79; supr. casualty claims Allstate Ins. Co., Kansas City, Mo., 1979-80; mgr. unit claims Allstate Ins. Co., Tulsa, 1980-84; asst. counsel Iowa Nat. Ins. Group, Cedar Rapids, 1984-85; claims counsel Employers Reins. Corp., Overland Park, Kans., 1985—. Served to 1st lt. U.S. Army, 1974. Insurance, Personal injury, Workers' compensation. Office: Employers Reins Corp 5200 Metcalf PO Box 2991 Overland Park KS 66201

CARROLL, WILLIAM KENNETH, law educator, psychologist, theologian; b. Oak Park, Ill., May 8, 1927; s. Ralph Thomas and Edith (Fay) C.; m. Frances Louise Forgue; children: Michele, Brian. B.S. in Edn., Quincy Coll., Ill., 1950, B.A. in Philosophy, 1950; M.A., Duquesne U., 1964; S.T.L., Catholic U., 1965; Ph.D., U. Strasbourg, France, 1968; J.D., Northwestern U., 1972. Bar: Ill. 1972, U.S. Dist. Ct. (no. dist.) Ill 1972, U.S. Ct. Appeals (7th cir.) 1973; registered psychologist. Asst/ editor Franciscan Press, Chgo., 1955-60; asst. prof. psychology and religion Carlow Coll., Pitts., 1962-65, Loyola U., Chgo., 1968-70; staff atty. Fed. Defender Program, Chgo., 1972-75; prof. law John Marshall Law Sch., Chgo., 1975—; bd. dirs. Am. Inst. Adlerian Studies, 1982—; law reporter ABA Criminal Justice Mental Health Standards Project, 1981-83. Author: (with Kosnik et al.) Human Sexuality, 1977; Eyewitness Testimony, Strategies and Tactics, 1984; contbg. author: By Reason of Insanity, 1983, Law for Illinois Psychologists, 1985. Bd. dirs. Chgo. Sch. Profl. Psychology, 1978-82; mem. bd. advisors Ill. Sch. Profl. Psychology, 1985. Recipient Am. Juris award, 1970. Fellow Inst. Social and Behavioral Pathology; mem. ABA, Catholic Theol. Soc. Am., Ill. Psychol. Assn. (ethics com. 1979—), Am. Psychol. Assn., AAUP. Avocation: pvt. pilot. Federal civil litigation, Criminal, Jurisprudence. Office: John Marshall Law School 315 S Plymouth Ct Chicago IL 60604

CARROW, HARVEY HILL, JR., lawyer; b. Washington, Jan. 3, 1955; s. Harvey Hill Sr. and Senora Wilson (Lindsey) C.; m. Susan Champion Swindell, Aug. 8, 1981. AB, U. N.C., 1977; JD, Columbia U., 190. Bar: N.C. 1980, U.S. Dist. Ct. (ea. dist.) N.C. 1980. Assoc. Manning, Fulton & Skinner, Raleigh, N.C., 1980-82; atty. Carolina Power and Light Co., Raleigh, 1982-85; exec. dir. N.C. Amateur Sports/U.S. Olympic Festival, Research Triangle Park, 1985—, also bd. dirs., pres. Mem. exec. com. Coliseum com. City of Raleigh, 1984—; vice chmn. Raleigh Transit Authority; founder, bd. dirs. N.C. Swimming Hall of Fame, Raleigh; bd. dirs. Boys Club of Wake County, Raleigh, 1985—. Recipient Gov. Hunt's Vol. award State of N.C., 1985, Gov. Martin's Vol. award State of N.C., 1985, Disting. Service award Raleigh Jaycees, 1987. Mem. ABA, N.C. Bar Assn., Wake County Bar Assn., Assn. Trial Lawyers Am., N.C. Acad. Trial Lawyers. Club: Raleigh Area Masters (v.p. 1984-85). Avocation: swimming. Public utilities, Environment, Nuclear power. Home: 2901 Sandia Dr Raleigh NC 27607 Office: NC Amateur Sports PO Box 12727 Research Triangle Park NC 27709

CARROW, ROBERT DUANE, lawyer, barrister; b. Marshall, Minn., Feb. 5, 1934; s. Meddie Joseph and Estelle Marie (Kough) C.; m. Jacqueline Mary Givens, Sept. 3, 1960; children: Leslie, Tamara, Amelia, Vanessa, Creighton, Jessica, Ramsey. Student, U. Colo., 1952; BA, U. Minn., 1956; JD, Stanford U., 1958. Bar: Calif. 1959, N.Y. 1983; barrister: Eng. 1981. Sole practice Calif., 1959—; barrister London, 1981—. Mayor City of Novato, Calif., 1962-64. Mem. ABA, Assn. Trial Lawyers Am., San Francisco Bar Assn., Honourable Soc. Middle Temple, Honourable Soc. Gray's Inn, Nat. Assn. Criminal Def. Lawyers. Federal civil litigation, State civil litigation, Criminal. Office: Three Embarcadero Ctr Suite 2280 San Francisco CA 94111 Chambers: 3 Gray's Inn Sq, London England WC1

CARRUBA, SALVATORE JOHN, retired lawyer, consultant; b. Maynard, Mass., Mar. 28, 1914; s. John and Geraldine (Carruba) C.; m. Helen Germaine, June 15, 1941; children—Richard John, Maryann Carruba Aprile. B.B.A., St. John's U., 1953; M.B.A., NYU, 1955; LL.B., Bklyn. Law Sch., 1966, J.D., 1967. Bar: N.Y. 1966, U.S. Dist. Ct. (ea. dist.) N.Y. 1968, U.S. Dist. Ct. (so. dist.) N.Y. 1968, U.S. Tax Ct. 1969. Field enforcement agt. Treasury Dept. IRS, Bklyn., 1945-54, mgr., br. chief, 1955-66, asst. div. chief audit, 1967, sr. atty. estate and gift tax, 1968, ret., 1969; sole practice, N.Y.C., 1969-79; cons., N.Y.C., 1980—; dir. Andrea Radio Corp., L.I., N.Y., 1974—. Served with U.S. Army, 1943. Recipient award of honor scholastic achievement N.Y. State Soc. C.P.A.s, 1955, Outstanding Achievement award Sec. Treasury Dept., Washington, 1963, Albert Gallatin award Sec. Treasury, Washington, 1969. Mem. Am. Legion, Catholic Lawyers Guild, Delta Mu Delta. Democrat. Roman Catholic. Probate, Corporate taxation, Estate taxation. Office: Lapatin Lewis Green & Kitzes PC 989 Ave of the America s New York NY 10018

CARSON, MICHAEL JAY, lawyer; b. Denver, Mar. 29, 1944; s. Harry C. and Dorothy Ruth (Dunievitz) C.; m. Claudia Ruth Carson, June 23, 1968; children—Douglas Richard, Adam Harry; m. 2d, Judy Ann Carson, Aug. 14, 1981. B.A., U. Colo., 1966, J.D., 1969. Bar: Colo. 1969, Okla. 1973. Trial atty. FTC, Washington, 1969-73; assoc. Rosenstein, Fist, Ringold, Tulsa, 1973-75; judge Mcpl. Ct., Tulsa, 1975-80; gen. atty. Bigheart Pipeline Corp., 1980-81; ptnr. Gann & Carson, Tulsa, 1985—; instr. criminal justice Tulsa Jr. Coll., 1977—. Recipient Book award Rothgerger Appellate Competition U. Colo., 1968; Meritorious Service award FTC, 1972. Mem. ABA, Okla. Bar Assn., Tulsa County Bar Assn., Am. Judicature Soc. Democrat. Jewish. State civil litigation, Bankruptcy, Administrative and regulatory. Home: 2525 W 78th St Tulsa OK 74132 Office: Gann & Carson 2121 S Columbia #600 Tulsa OK 74114

CARSON, ROBERT WILLIAM, lawyer; b. Port Huron, Mich., Nov. 26, 1948; s. Robert Y. and Cecilia E. (DeMars) C.; m. Pamela Jean French, May 3, 1974; children: Shayna, Keeley, Robbie. AA, St. Clair County Community Coll., 1968; BA, U. Mich., 1970; JD, U. Detroit, 1973. Bar: Mich. 1973. Assoc. Raymond L. Krell, Detroit, 1973-74; assoc. McIntosh, McColl, Allen, Carson, McNamee & Strickler and predecessor firms, Port Huron, 1975-77, ptnr., 1977-79, sr. ptnr., 1979—; bd. dirs. Guaranteed Tires, Inc., Port Huron. Campaign dir. St. Clair County March Dimes, Port Huron, 1978-80, chmn., 1980-82, bd. dirs. 1982—, legal liaison, 1984-85. Republican. Roman Catholic. Club: Port Huron Golf. Avocations: golf, basketball. Personal injury, Workers' compensation, Federal civil litigation. Home: 3672 Old Farm Ln Port Huron MI 48060 Office: McIntosh McColl Allen Carson McNamee & Strickler 333 Pine St Port Huron MI 48060

CARSON, TIMOTHY JOSEPH, lawyer; b. Darby, Pa., Feb. 17, 1949; s. Joseph Timothy and Marian (Maloney) C.; m. Janet Louise Duffy, May 30, 1975; children—Lindsey, Anne. B.S. in Econs., U.Pa., 1970; J.D., Villanova Sch. Law, 1975. Bar: Pa. 1975, U.S. Ct. Claims 1976, U.S. Tax Ct. 1976. Assoc. Lentz, Riley, Cantor, Kilgore & Massey, Paoli, Pa., 1975-77, Townsend, Elliott & Munson, Phila., 1977; assoc. Saul, Ewing, Remick & Saul, Phila., 1977-81, ptnr. 1981—; counsel, asst. sec. Pa. Local Govt. Investment Trust, Valley Forge, Pa., 1981—. Mng. editor Villanova Law Rev., 1974-75; contbr. articles to profl. jours. and newsletters. Chmn. Tri-State Republican Alliance, 1984—; mem. SBA Adv. Council, Phila., 1982-85 ; chmn. fin. com. Rep. State Com. Pa., 1986—, mem. leadership com. Recipient Spl. commendations U. Pa. Bd. Trustees, U.S. Navy and NASA, 1971. Fellow Phila. Bar Found.; mem. Phila. Bar Assn. (exec. com. young lawyers sect. 1981-84), Pa. Bar Assn. (bd. govs. 1979-82, chmn. young lawyers sect. 1980-81, ho. of dels. 1979—, del. 3d cir. jud. conf. 1979, chmn. commn. mcpl. fin. mcpl. law sect. 1984—, chmn.'s award young lawyers sect. 1981), ABA, Nat. Assn. Bond Lawyers, Mcpl. Bond Club Phila. Republican. Roman Catholic. Clubs: St. David's Golf (Wayne, Pa.); Racquet (Phila.). Office: Saul Ewing Remick & Saul 3800 Centre Sq W Philadelphia PA 19102

CARSON, WALLACE PRESTON, JR., state supreme court justice; b. Salem, Oreg., June 10, 1934; s. Wallace Preston and Edith (Bragg) C.; m. Gloria Stolk, June 24, 1956; children: Scott, Carol, Steven (dec. 1981). B.A. in Politics, Stanford U., 1956; J.D., Willamette U., 1962. Bar: Oreg. 1962, U.S. Dist. Ct. Oreg. 1963, U.S. Ct. Appeals (9th cir.) 1968, U.S. Supreme Ct. 1971, U.S. Cit. Mil. Appeals 1977; lic. comml. pilot FAA. Sole practice Salem, Oreg., 1962-77; judge Marion County Circuit Ct., Salem, 1977-82; assoc. justice Oreg. Supreme Ct., Salem, 1982—. Mem. Oreg. Ho. of Reps., 1967-71, maj. leader, 1969-71; mem. Oreg. State Senate, 1971-77, minority floor leader, 1971-77; dir. Salem Area Community Council, 1967-70, pres., 1969-70; mem. Salem Planning Commn., 1966-72, pres., 1970-71; co-chmn. Marion County Mental Health Planning Com., 1965-69; mem. Salem Community Goals Com., 1965; Republican precinct commiteeman, 1963-66; mem. Marion County Rep. Central Exec. Com., 1963-66; com. predinct edn. Oreg. Rep. Central Com., 1965; vestryman, acolyte, Sunday Sch. tchr., youth coach St. Paul's Episcopal Ch., 1935—; task force on cts. Oreg. Council Crime and Delinquency, 1968-69; trustee Willamette U., 1970—; adv. bd. Cath. Ctr. Community Services, 1976-77; mem. comporehensive planning com. Mid-Willamette Valley Council of Govts., 1970-71; adv. com. Oreg. Coll. Edn. Tchr. Edn., 1971-75; pres. Willamette regional Oreg. Lung Assn., 1974-75, state dir., exec. com., 1975-77; pub. relations com. Williamette council Campfire Girls, 1976-77; criminal justice adv. bd. Chemeketa Community Coll., 1977-79; mem. Oreg. Mental Health Com., 1979-80; mem. subcom. Gov's Task Force Mental Health, 1980; you and govt. adv. com. Oreg. YMCA, 1981—. Served to col. USAFR, 1956-59. Recipient Salem Disting. Service award, 1968; recipient Good Fellow award Marion County Fire Service, 1974, Minuteman award Oreg. N.G. Assn., 1980; fellow Eagleton Inst. Politics, Rutgers U., 1971. Mem. Marion County Bar Assn. (sec.-treas. 1965-67, dir. 1968-70), Oreg. Bar Assn., ABA, Willamette U. Coll. Law Alumni Assn. (v.p. 1968-70), Salem Art Assn., Oreg. Hist. Soc., Marion County Hist. Soc., Delta Theta Phi. Club: Salem Stanford (pres. 1963-64). Home: 1309 Hillendale Dr SE Salem OR 97302 Office: Oregon Supreme Court Supreme Court Bldg Salem OR 97310 •

CARSON, WILLIAM SCOTT, lawyer; b. Buffalo, Mar. 13, 1946; s. William Dana and Barbara Brenneman (Powell) C.; m. Elizabeth Karin Ellis, June 28, 1977; children—Bradley Robert, Karen Elizabeth. B.S., Brown U., 1969, A.B., 1969; J.D. with honors, George Washington U., 1973. Bar: Va. 1974, D.C. 1974, U.S. Patent and Trademark Office 1974, Colo. 1977, U.S. Ct. Appeals (D.C. cir.) 1982. Examiner, U.S. Patent Office, Arlington, Va., 1969-74; ptnr. Burton, Dorr and Carson, Denver, 1980-86, Dorr, Carson, Sloan & Peterson, 1987—. Mem. ABA, Colo. Bar Assn., Denver Bar Assn., Licensing Execs. Soc. Patent, Trademark and copyright, Franchising. Home: 101 Hudson Denver CO 80220 Office: Dorr Carson Sloan & Peterson 720 S Colorado Blvd Suite 1240 Denver CO 80222

CARSTETTER, DAVID WILSON, lawyer; b. Lewistown, Pa., Dec. 5, 1937; s. Fred R. and Ruth M. C.; m. Joy Ann Thompson, Jan. 28, 1961; children—David, Mary, John, Laura. B.A., Pa. State U., 1960; J.D., Duke U., 1968. Bar: Fla. 1968, U.S. Dist. Ct. (mid. dist.) Fla. 1969, U.S. Ct. Appeals (11th cir.) 1982. Assoc., Mahoney, Hadlow & Adams, 1968-70; ptnr. Sears, Dunlap & Sears, 1970-73, Kent, Watts, Durden, Kent, Nichols & Mickler, Jacksonville, Fla., 1973—, also dir. Served to lt. comdr., USN, 1960-65. Mem. Lawyer Pilots Bar Assn. Federal civil litigation, State civil litigation, General corporate. Office: Suite 850 Florida 1st National Bank Bldg Jacksonville FL 32202

CARSWELL, ROBERT, lawyer; b. Bklyn., Nov. 25, 1928; s. William Brown and Charlotte Edna (Riegger) C.; m. Mary Killeen Wilde, Dec. 28, 1957; children—Kate, William. A.B. magna cum laude, Harvard U., 1949, LL.B. cum laude, 1952. Bar: N.Y. 1952, Calif. 1954. With firm Shearman & Sterling, N.Y.C., 1955-62; ptnr. Shearman & Sterling, 1965-77, 81—; spl. asst. to sec. treasury 1962-65, dep. sec. treasury, 1977-81. Served to lt. (j.g.) USNR, 1952-55. Mem. ABA, Bar Assn. City N.Y., Calif. State Bar Assn., Am. Law Inst., Am. Soc. Internat. Law, Council Fgn. Relations, Harvard Law Sch. Alumni Assn. N.Y. (pres. 1985), St. Andrews Soc. N.Y., Phi Beta Kappa. Clubs: Century Assn., Links (N.Y.C.); Metropolitan (Washington). Banking, Private international, General corporate. Home: 40 E 88th St New York NY 10128 Office: Shearman & Sterling 153 E 53d St New York NY 10022

CARTA, JOHN JAMES, JR., lawyer; b. Middletown, Conn., Oct. 22, 1944; m. Shirley J. Levine, June 26, 1965; children: Jonathan, Jennifer, Justin. BA, Wesleyan U., 1966; JD, U. Conn., 1968. Bar: Conn. 1969, U.S. Dist. Ct. Conn. 1969, U.S. Tax Ct. 1987. Sole practice Middletown and Essex., Conn., 1969-80; ptnr. Copp, Berall & Hempstead, Essex, 1981—; asst. atty. City of Middletown, 1969-73; fact finder, arbitrator State of Conn. Superior Ct., 1984—, magistrate, 1985—. Legal counsel Middletown Housing Authority, 1972-77; town chmn. Essex Reps., 1978-82. Mem. ABA, Conn. Bar Assn. (family law sect.), Middlesex County Bar Assn., Assn. Trial Lawyers Am., Conn. Trial Laweyrs Assn., Acad. Continuing Profl. Devel. Roman Catholic. Avocations: private piloting, sailing, jogging. Personal injury, Criminal, Family and matrimonial. Office: Copp Berall & Hempstead PO Box 267 Essex CT 06426

CARTEN, FRANCIS NOEL, lawyer; b. Bryn Mawr, Pa., Dec. 25, 1935; s. Francis Patrick and Louise Cathleen (Leach) C. B.S., U. Notre Dame, 1960; J.D., Villanova U., 1964. Bar: Pa. 1967, N.Y. 1967, Conn. 1976. Assoc. Eyre, Mann & Lucas, N.Y.C., 1966-74; sole practice, Danbury and Stamford, Conn., 1975-78; patent counsel TIE/communications, Inc., Shelton, Conn., 1978-79, Automation Industries, Inc., Greenwich, 1979-85; sole practice, Stamford, 1985—. Served with U.S. Army, 1954-56. Mem. ABA, Am. Intellectual Property Law Assn., N.Y. State Bar Assn., N.Y. Patent Trademark and Copyright Law Assn., Conn. Bar Assn., Conn. Patent Law Assn., Lic. Execs. Soc., Westchester-Fairfield Corp. Counsel Assn. Republican. Club: Seawanhaka Corinthian Yacht (Oyster Bay, N.Y.). Patent, Trademark and copyright, Antitrust. Office: 19 Old Kings Hwy Darien CT 06820

CARTENUTO, DAVID J., lawyer; b. N.Y.C., Sept. 9, 1942; s. David Joseph and Madeline (Roehm) C.; m. Christina Lassen, July 10, 1971; children: David, Alicia. BA, Cathedral Coll., 1964; B in Theology, Gregorian U., Rome, 1966; JD, Fordham U., 1972. Bar: N.Y. 1973. Systems engr. IBM, N.Y.C., 1967-72; atty. IBM, Poughkeepsie, N.Y., 1972-76; regional counsel IBM, Montevideo, Uruguay, 1977-80; staff counsel IBM, White Plains, N.Y., 1980-81, Paris, 1981-83; counsel IBM, Montvale, N.J., 1983-86; asst. group counsel IS & IG IBM, White Plains, N.Y., 1986—. V.p. Transfiguration Parents Guild, Tarrytown, N.J., 1986. Mem. Am. Assn. Uruguay (pres. 1979). Antitrust, Contracts commercial, General corporate. Office: IBM Corp 1000 Westchester Ave White Plains NY 10604

CARTER, BARRY EDWARD, lawyer, educator; b. Los Angeles, Oct. 14, 1942; s. Byron Edward and Ethel Catherine (Turner) C.; m. Kathleen Anne Ambrose, May 17, 1987. A.B. with great distinction, Stanford U., 1964; M.P.A., Princeton U., 1966; J.D., Yale U., 1969. Bar: Calif. 1970, D.C. 1972. Program analyst Office of Sec. Def., Washington, 1969-70; mem. staff NSC, Washington, 1970-72; research fellow Kennedy Sch., Harvard U., Cambridge, Mass., 1972; internat. affairs fellow Council on Fgn. Relations, 1972; pvt. practice law Washington, 1973-75; sr. counsel Select Com. on Intelligence Activities, U.S. Senate, Washington, 1975; assoc. Morrison &

Foerster, San Francisco, 1976-79; assoc. prof. law Georgetown U. Law Ctr., Washington, 1979—; Bd. dir. Arms Control Assn., 1973—; mem. UN Assn. Soviet-Am. Parallel Studies Project.; trustee No. Calif. World Affairs Council, 1978-80; sr. fgn. policy adviser Mondale-Ferraro presdl. campaign, Washington, 1984. Contbr. articles to profl. jours. Served with AUS, 1969-71. Mem. Council on Fgn. Relations, Am., Calif., D.C. bar assns., Phi Beta Kappa, Phi Delta Phi. Democrat. Private international, Public international, Antitrust. Home: 2922 45th St NW Washington DC 20016 Office: 600 New Jersey Ave NW Washington DC 20001

CARTER, CHARLES MICHAEL, lawyer; b. Boston, Apr. 18, 1943; s. Charles and Florence Carter; m. Janis Maryanne Freeman June 15, 1968 (div.); children: Brandon H., Chad F., Courtney C.; m. Jocelyne Hinfray, Dec. 31, 1985. BS, U. Calif., Berkeley, 1967; JD, George Washington U., 1973. Bar: N.Y. 1974, Conn. 1978. Assoc. Winthrop, Stimson, Putnam & Roberts, N.Y.C., 1973-81; div. counsel, fin. staff and investment counsel The Singer Co., Stamford, Conn., 1981-83; sr. counsel RJR Nabisco Inc., Winston-Salem, N.C., 1983—. Mem. ABA, N.C. Bar Assn. Contracts commercial, General corporate, Securities. Home: 3001 Lake Shore Dr Winston-Salem NC 27106 Office: RJR Nabisco Inc 1100 Reynolds Blvd Winston-Salem NC 27105

CARTER, DANIEL PAUL, lawyer, educator; b. Massillon, Ohio, Mar. 22, 1948; s. Harry A. and Anna Jean (Steiner) C.; m. Regina Ranieri, July 9, 1983; 1 child, Emily Hedges. BS, St. Joseph's Coll., Phila., 1971; JD, Villanova U., 1974. Bar: Pa. 1974, U.S. Dist. Ct. (ea. dist.) Pa. 1980, U.S. Ct. Appeals (3d cir.) 1981, U.S. Dist. Ct. (mid. dist.) Pa. 1985, U.S. Ct. Claims 1986. Asst. prof. of law, dir. admissions Widener U., Wilmington, Del., 1974-79; ptnr. LaBrum & Doak, Phila., 1979-86, Shaffer, Palma, Dougherty & Carter, West Chester, Pa., 1986—; counsel jury study Delaware County, Media, Pa., 1976; adj. prof. law Widener U., 1984—. legal counsel Pa. Young Reps., 1977-78; regional legal counsel Young Rep. Nat. Fedn., 1978-79. Named One of Outstanding Young Men of Am., Jaycees, 1979. Mem. ABA, Del. County Bar Assn., Chester County Bar Assn., Phila. Bar Assn., Pa. Bar Assn. (vice chmn. law sch. liaison 1981-82). Republican. Episcopalian. State civil litigation, Federal civil litigation, Legal education. Office: Shaffer Palma Dougherty & Carter 107 S Church St West Chester PA 19382

CARTER, GENE, judge; b. Milbridge, Maine, Nov. 1, 1935; s. K.W. and S. Loreta (Beal) C.; m. Judith Ann Kittredge, June 24, 1961; children: Matthew G., Mark G. B.A., U. Maine, 1958, LL.D. (hon.), 1985; LL.B., NYU, 1961. Bar: Maine 1962. Ptnr. Rudman, Winchell, Carter & Buckley (and predecessors), Bangor, Maine, 1965-80; assoc. justice Maine Supreme Jud. Ct., 1980-83; judge U.S. Dist. Ct. Maine, 1983—; chmn. adv. com. on rules of civil procedure Maine Supreme Jud. Ct., 1976-80. Chmn. Bangor Housing Authority, 1970-77. Mem. Am. Trial Lawyers Assn., Internat. Soc. Barristers, Am. Coll. Trial Lawyers. Office: 156 Federal St Portland ME 04101

CARTER, GEORGE RICHARD, lawyer; b. Shreveport, La., Mar. 21, 1947; s. George Wilson and Gloria Arland (Jones) C.; divorced; children: Thomas George, Kent Lamond, Mark Brinley. BA in Social Sci., U. Nev., 1975, BS in Acctg., 1986; JD, U. Miami, Coral Gables, Fla., 1979. Bar: Nev. 1979, U.S. Dist. Ct. Nev. 1980, U.S. Tax Ct. 1982. Assoc. Mills, Galliher et al, Las Vegas, Nev., 1980, Gibson & Schwartzer, Las Vegas, 1980-81, James B. Gibson P.C., Las Vegas, 1981-85; ptnr. Mills, Gibson & Carter, Las Vegas, 1985—. Mem. Clark County Bd. Law Library Trustees, Las Vegas, 1982-86, pres. 1984-86; mem. Henderson (Nev.) Planning Commn., 1982-84, Citizens Adv. Com. Master Plan, Henderson, 1983-85. Served with USAR, 1974-80. Mem. ABA, Assn. Trial Lawyers Am., Clark County Bar Assn. Democrat. Mem. Ch. of Christ. Bankruptcy, State civil litigation, Family and matrimonial. Office: 825 Clark Ave Las Vegas NV 89101

CARTER, GLENN THOMAS, lawyer, clergyman; b. Beaumont, Tex., July 20, 1934; s. Glenmore Rust and Sarah Elizabeth (Woods) C.; m. Janette Lucile Mullikin, Aug. 1, 1954; children—Penny Lucile Loucks, Sylvia Lee De Vries. B.A., Union Coll., 1956; J.D., Emory U., 1967. Bar: Ga. 1968, Tex. 1969, D.C. 1976, Md. 1976, Calif. 1984, U.S. Dist. Ct. (no. dist.) Tex. 1981, Md. 1984. Ordained to ministry Seventh-day Adventist Chs., 1960; pastor chs. in Tex., Wyo., Ga., 1956-1965; spl. legal advisor Ga.-Cumberland Conf. Seventh-day Adventists, Decatur, 1968-69; dir. trust services and pub. affairs Texico and Tex. Conf. Seventh-day Adventists, Amarillo and Ft. Worth, Tex., 1969-1976; assoc. dir. trust services Gen. Conf. Seventh-day Adventists, Washington, 1976-1980; dir. pub. affairs assoc. dir. trust services Southwestern Union Conf. Seventh-day Adventists, Burleson, Tex., 1980-82; dir. trust services Pacific Union Conf. Seventh-day Adventists, Westlake Village, Calif., 1982-85; dir. Trust Services Gen. Conf. of Seventh-day Adventists, Washington, 1985—. Contbr. articles to ch. pubs. Recipient Am. Jurisprudence prize for Litigation Emory U. Sch. Law and Lawyers Co-op., 1967. Mem. Supreme Ct. Hist. Soc. Lodge: Rotary. Estate planning, Civil rights. Office: PO Box 5005 Westlake Village CA 91359

CARTER, GORDON THOMAS, lawyer; b. Birmingham, Ala., Sept. 20, 1956; s. George Gordon and Mildred Orene (Davis) C. BA, U. Ala.; JD, Cumberland Sch. of Law. Law clk. Ala. Civil Appeals Ct., Montgomery, 1981-82; asst. gen. counsel Ala. Farm Bur. Ins., Montgomery, 1982—. Mem. ABA, Ala. State Bar, Montgomery County Bar Assn., Sons. of Conf. Vets., Phi Alpha Theta, Phi Alpha Delta, Phi Kappa Psi. Republican. Presbyterian. Club: Toastmasters (Montgomery) (treas. 1986). Avocations: reading, biking, swimming, geneaology. Insurance, Securities. Home: 1750 Sylvan Dr Montgomery AL 36106 Office: Ala Farm Bur 2108 E South Blvd Montgomery AL 36198

CARTER, JAMES H., justice state supreme court; b. Waverly, Iowa, Jan. 18, 1935; s. Harvey J. and Althea (Dominick) C.; m. Jeanne E. Carter, Mar. 1959; children: Carol, James. B.A., U. Iowa, 1956, J.D., 1960. Law clk. to judge U.S. Dist. Ct, 1960-62; assoc. Shuttleworth & Ingersoll, Cedar Rapids, Iowa, 1962-73; judge 6th Jud. Dist., 1973-76, Iowa Ct. Appeals, 1976-82; justice Iowa Supreme Ct., Des Moines, 1982—. Office: Supreme Ct State Capitol Des Moines IA 50319

CARTER, JAMES HAL, JR., lawyer; b. Ames, Iowa, Sept. 25, 1943; s. James H. and Louise (Benge) C.; m. Sara N. Meeker, July 27, 1974; children: Janet, Faith, Katherine. B.A., Yale U., 1965, LL.B., 1969. Bar: N.Y. 1971, U.S. Dist. Ct. (so. dist.) N.Y. 1972, U.S. Dist. Ct. (ea. dist.) N.Y. 1975, U.S. Dist. Ct. Conn. 1981, U.S. Ct. Internat. Trade 1980, U.S. Ct. Appeals (2d cir.) 1971, U.S. Ct. Appeals (1st and 5th cirs.) 1984, U.S. Supreme Ct. 1976. Fulbright scholar Cambridge U., Eng., 1965-66; law clk. U.S. Ct. Appeals (2d cir.), 1969-70; with Sullivan & Cromwell, N.Y.C., 1970, ptnr., 1977; lectr. internat. comml. arbitration Practicing Law Inst. Corr. editor: Internat. Legal Materials; contbr. articles in field to publs. Mem. adv. bd. Southwestern Legal Found. Internat. and Comparative Law Ctr. Mem. ABA, N.Y. State Bar Assn. (former chmn. internat. law com.), Assn. Bar CitY N.Y., U.S. Council Internat. Bus. (com. on arbitration), Am. Soc Internat. Law. International commercial arbitration, Antitrust, Federal civil litigation. Office: Sullivan & Cromwell 125 Broad St New York NY 10004

CARTER, JOHN TILTON, JR., lawyer; b. Bennettsville, S.C., Nov. 16, 1950; s. John Tilton Sr. and Jessie (Tucker) C.; m. Faye Keene, Sept. 2, 1977; children: John Tilton III, Karianne. AA, Wingate Coll., 1971; BA, U. N.C., Charlotte, 1973; JD, U. N.C., Chapel Hill, 1976. Bar: N.C. 1976, U.S. Dist. Ct. (ea. dist.) N.C. 1980. Instr. paralegal law Fayetteville (N.C.) Tech. Inst., 1976-77; asst. dist. atty. State of N.C., Jacksonville, 1977-80; ptnr. Warlick, Milsted, Dotson & Carter, Jacksonville, 1980—. Sr. warden St. Anne's Episc. Ch., Jacksonville, 1986—. Mem. N.C. Acad. Trial Lawyers, N.C. Bar Assn. Democrat. Avocation: crafting stained glass. Family and matrimonial, Real property, Criminal. Office: Warlick Milsted Dotson & Carter 320 New Bridge St PO Drawer 766 Jacksonville NC 28541-0766

CARTER, JOSEPH CARLYLE, JR., lawyer; b. Mayfield, Ky., June 3, 1927; s. Joseph Carlyle and Cynthia Elizabeth (Stokes) C.; m. Dianne C. Dinwiddie, July 15, 1949; children: Joseph Carlyle, Hugh D., William H., Henry S., Dianne C. B.A., U. Va., 1948, LL.B., 1951. Bar: Va. 1951. Since practiced in Richmond; assoc. firm Hunton & Williams, 1951-58, ptnr., 1958—, mng. ptnr., 1972-82; dir. Va. Fed. Savs. and Loan Assn., Ethyl Corp. Active elder 2d Presbyn. Ch., Richmond, 1962—; chmn. Richmond Pub. Library Bd., 1967-77, mem., 1980-85; trustee Colonial Williamsburg Found., 1977—; trustee Med. Coll. Va. Found., 1976—, pres., 1984—; trustee U. Va. Patent Found., 1975—, trustee, v.p. U. Va. Law Sch. Found., 1985—. Recipient Algernon Sidney Sullivan award, 1948. Mem. Am. Bar Assn., Va. Bar Assn., Richmond Bar Assn., Am. Law Inst., Am. Judicature Soc., Newcomen Soc. Presbyterian. Clubs: Commonwealth (Richmond), Country of Va. (Richmond), Bull & Bear. General corporate, Contracts commercial, Banking. Home: 6102 St Andrew Ln Richmond VA 23226 Office: Hunton & Williams PO Box 1535 Richmond VA 23212

CARTER, MELANIE SUE, lawyer; b. White Plains, N.Y., Jan. 2, 1957; d. Selden Booker and Shirley Emma (Abbott) C. A.B. with honors, Randolph-Macon Woman's Coll., 1978; J.D., Northwestern U., 1981. Bar: Ill. 1981. Assoc. Hoellen, Lukes & Halper, Chgo., 1981-86, ptnr., 1986—; mem. Chgo. Vol. Legal Services, 1985—. Vol. tchr., adviser Chgo. Coalition for Legal Edn., 1984. Mem. ABA, Ill. Bar Assn., Chgo. Bar Assn. (legal com. for disabled 1983-84, 86-87, probate com. 1984-85), Womens' Bar Assn. Ill., Chgo. Council Fgn. Relations, Phi Beta Kappa. Baptist. Banking, Probate, Real property. Office: Hoellen Lukes & Halper 1940 W Irving Park Rd Chicago IL 60613

CARTER, PAUL STANLEY, lawyer; b. Hempstead, N.Y., Jan. 23, 1950; s. Stanley Ray and Gertrude Mary (Welch) C.; m. Constance Daniele, Sept. 1, 1979; children: Sarah Anne, Burton J. BA in History, Boston Coll., 1971; JD, Suffolk law Sch., 1975. Bar: Mass. 1975, U.S. Dist. Ct. Mass. 1980, U.S. Supreme Ct., 1980. Assoc. Law Offices of Martin S. Cosgrove, Quincy, Mass., 1975-77; sole practice Dedham and Boston, Mass., 1977—. Bd. dirs. Personel Bd., Town of Norfolk, Mass., 1984. Mem. Am. Trial Lawyers Assn., Mass. Bar Assn., Norfolk County Bar Assn., Western Norfolk Bar Assn. Democrat. Roman Catholic. Avocation: painting, gentleman farmer. Criminal, State civil litigation, Personal injury. Home: 114 Anawan Ave. West Roxbury MA 02132 Office: 300 VFW Pkwy Box 151 Dedham MA 02026

CARTER, RICHARD WAYNE, judge; b. Dallas, Nov. 15, 1948; s. George Hubert and Ilona (Grossman) C.; m. Mavis Lee Stamets, Oct. 12, 1974; children—Tanya Marie, Richard Wayne. B.A., E. Tex. State U., 1970; J.D., Tex. Tech. U., 1973. Bar: Tex., U.S. dist. ct. (no. dist.) Tex. 1974, U.S. Ct. Appeals (5th cir.) 1976, U.S. Supreme Ct. 1976, U.S. Ct. Appeals (11th cir.) 1981. Sole practice, Commerce, Tex., 1973-74; asst. atty. Hunt County, Greenville, Tex., 1974-75, atty., 1975-76; sr. ptnr. Carter and Brim, Commerce, 1974-77; police legal advisor, Waco, Tex., 1977-83; judge Mcpl. Ct., Arlington, Tex., 1983—; chmn. Gov.'s Tex. Crime Stoppers Adv. Council, 1983—; lectr. Baylor U., Waco, 1981-82, also Southwestern Law Enforcement Inst., Richardson, Tex., Tex. Crime Prevention Inst., San Marcos. Bd. dirs. Nat. Hispanics Arts Endowment, 1982-83; sec., gen. counsel Crime Stoppers Internat., Inc. Recipient Cert. of merit MedicAlert, 1982. Mem. Internat. Assn. Chiefs of Police (gen. chmn. legal officers sect. 1981-82), Tex. Assn. Police Attys. (gen. chmn. 1981-82), State Bar Tex. (legis. in pub. interest com. 1982-85, dir. mcpl. judges sect. 1984—), Tex. Police Assn. (chmn. legis. com. 1982-83), Arlington Bar Assn., Tarrant County Bar Assn., Tex. Mcpl. Cts. Assn., Ar,.ngton C. of C. (law, order and justice com. chmn. 1986). Contbg. author: Tex. Prosecutor's Trial Manual, 1978, 83; Crime Stoppers Operations Manual, 1983; author: Crime Stoppers Case Digest, 1986. Office: 200 W Abram PO Box 231 Arlington TX 76010

CARTER, ROBERT LEE, judge; b. Caryville, Fla., Mar. 11, 1917; s. Robert and Annie (Martin) C.; m. Gloria Spencer, Dec. 4, 1946 (dec. Nov. 1971); children: John Walton, David Christopher. A.B. magna cum laude, Lincoln U., 1937, D.C.L., 1964; LL.B. magna cum laude, Howard U., 1940; LL.M., Columbia U., 1941. Bar: N.Y. 1945. Assp. spl. counsel NAACP, N.Y.C., 1944-56; gen. counsel NAACP, 1956-68; mem. firm Poletti, Freidin, Prashker, Feldman & Gartner, N.Y.C., 1969-72; judge U.S. Dist. Ct. So. Dist. N.Y., N.Y.C., 1972—; dir. vets. affairs Am. Vets. Com., Washington, 1948-49; adj. prof. Law Sch., NYU, 1966-70; spl. asst. U.S. atty. So. Dist. N.Y., 1968; mem. N.Y.C. Mayor's Jud. Com., 1968-72. Editorial bd.: N.Y. Law Jour., 1969-72; contbr. articles to profl. jours. Pres. Nat. Com. Against Discrimination in Housing, 1966-72; mem. N.Y. State Spl. Commn. on Attica, N.Y. State Temp. Commn. on Ct. Reform, 1970-72, Am. del. UN Third World Conf. on Crime and the Treatment of Offenders, Stockholm, 1965; bd. dirs. Northside Center Child Devel. Served to 2d lt. USAAF, 1941-44. Rosenwald fellow, 1940-41; Columbia Urban Center fellow, 1968-69; recipient Howard U. Disting. Alumni award, 1980. Mem. Nat. Conf. Black Lawyers (co-chmn. 1968-72), Assn. Bar City N.Y. (exec. com.). Office: US Dist Ct 2903 US Courthouse Foley Sq New York NY 10007 *

CARTER, ROBERT PHILIP, lawyer; b. Lexington, Ky., Sept. 4, 1946; s. George Philip and Alice Joy (Scott) C.; m. Carol Sharon Hall, Aug. 23, 1969 (div. Feb. 1976); 1 child, Robert Philip Jr.; m. Marsha Gayle Colley, June 6, 1981. BS, Morehead State U., 1971; JD, Emory U., 1973. Bar: Ky. 1974, W.Va. 1986, U.S. Dist. Ct. (ea. dist.) Ky., U.S. Dist. Ct. (so. dist.) W.Va. 1986. Sole practice Louisa, Ky., 1974-75; gen. counsel Black Diamond Coal Co., Lexington, 1975-76, Ky. Mortgage Co., Lexington, 1976-78; sole practice Louisa, 1978—; approved atty. Chgo. Title Ins. Co., 1976—, Commonwealth Land Title Ins. Co., Louisville, 1974—, Title Ins. Co. Minn., 1976—; cons. Louisa Med. Ctr., Inc., 1974—. Mem. at large adminstrv. bd. Louisa United Meth. Ch., 1986—. Mem. Mensa, Phi Delta Phi. Democrat. General practice, Real property, General corporate. Office: PO Box 336 Louisa KY 41230

CARTER, SAMUEL HEBARD, lawyer; b. Phila., Dec. 21, 1941; s. Frederic Phillips Jr. and Laura Jane (Hebard) C.; children: Deborah Marie, Matthew Wolf. BA, U. Mich., 1963; M in Pub. Adminstrn., U. S.C., 1973, JD, 1976. Bar: S.C. 1977, U.S. Dist. Ct. S.C. 1977, U.S. Ct. Appeals (4th cir.) 1981, U.S. Supreme Ct. 1981. Dir. community relations Alexandria (Va.) C. of C., 1967-69; dir. govt. affairs Columbia (S.C.) C. of C., 1969-76; sole practice Columbia, 1977-83; exec. dir. research S.C. Ho. of Reps., Columbia, 1983—; legal counsel S.C. Press Assn., Columbia, 1977-83; adj. prof. polit. sci. U. S.C., Columbia, 1972-83. Bd. dirs. Midlands Human Resources Devel. Commn., Columbia, 1981-87, chmn., 1983-85. Served with USN, 1964-67. Mem. S.C. Bar Assn., Am. Soc. Pub. Adminstrn. (exec. com. S.C. chpt.), Southern Legis. Conf. (legis. service agy. dirs. group 1983—, chmn. 1983—). Legislative. Home: 1436 Sunbury Ln Columbia SC 29205 Office: SC Ho Reps PO Box 11867 Columbia SC 29211

CARTER, T. BARTON, law educator; b. Dallas, Aug. 6, 1949; s. Sydney Hobart and Josephine (Wren) C.; m. Eleonore Dorothy Alexander, June 3, 1978; 1 child, Richard Alexander. BA in Psychology, Yale U., 1971; JD, U. Pa., 1974; MS in Mass Communication, Boston U., 1978. Bar: Mass. 1974, U.S. Dist. Ct. Mass. 1975, U.S. Ct. Appeals (1st cir.) 1975. Asst. prof. law Boston U., 1979-85, assoc. prof., 1985—; sole practice, Boston, 1974—; pres. Tanist Broadcasting Corp., Augusta, Maine, 1981—. Co-author: The First Amendment and the Fourth Estate, 1985, The First Amendment and the Fifth Estate, 1986. Mem. ABA, Assn. for Edn. in Journalism and Mass Communication (clk. 1981-82, asst. head 1982-83, head 1983-84). Club: University (Boston). Avocation: bridge. Communications law. Home: 31 Lime St Boston MA 02108 Office: Boston U 640 Commonwealth Ave Boston MA 02215

CARTIER, RUDOLPH HENRI, JR., lawyer, legal educator; b. Yonkers, N.Y., Oct. 8, 1947; s. Rudolph Henri and Edith Edna (Hartling) C.; m. Linda Clair Truzzolino, Jan. 24, 1970 (div. July 1980); m. Mary Anne Lavorata, Aug. 16, 1980; children—Laura Anne, Stephen Robert. B.A., LaSalle Coll., 1969; J.D., St. John's U., Jamaica, N.Y., 1975. Bar: N.Y. 1976, U.S. Dist. Ct. (ea. and so. dists.) N.Y. 1976, U.S. Supreme Ct. 1982. Asst. dist. atty. Suffolk County Dist. Atty.'s Office, Riverhead, N.Y., 1975-77; sole practice, Selden, N.Y., 1977-82; ptnr. Rogers & Cartier, P.C., Patchogue, N.Y., 1982—; gen. counsel Suffolk County Assn. Mcpl. Employees; asst. prof. Suffolk County Community Coll., Selden, N.Y., 1978-84, paralegal adv. bd.; spl. asst. dist. atty., Village of Head of the Harbor, 1985—. Atty., mem. steering com. Smithtown Citizens for Edn., N.Y., 1983—. Mem. N.Y. State Bar Assn. (criminal discovery and correctional services coms.), Suffolk County Bar Assn. (fee dispute resolution and criminal law coms.), Suffolk County Criminal Assn., L.I. Indsl. Relations Research Assn. Republican. Roman Catholic. Criminal, Family and matrimonial, State civil litigation. Home: 59 Neil Dr Smithtown NY 11787 Office: Rogers and Cartier PC 180 E Main St Patchogue NY 11772 also Office: 1205 Franklin Ave Garden City NY 11530

CARTO, DAVID DRAFFAN, lawyer; b. St. Paul, Jan. 10, 1956; s. David Lawrence and Frances Eleanor (Draffan) C.; m. Carolyn Elizabeth Malkis, Sept. 6, 1981; 1 child, David Willis. BA, Ohio Wesleyan U., 1978; JD, Case Western Res. U., 1981. Bar: Ohio 1981, U.S. Dist. Ct. (no. dist.) Ohio 1981. Assoc. Weldon, Huston & Keyser, Mansfield, Ohio, 1981-86, ptnr., 1986—. Bd. dirs. Richland County Heart Assn., Mansfield, 1983-84, Mansfield Art Ctr., 1986—. Mem. ABA, Assn. Trial Lawyers Am., Ohio Acad. Trial Lawyers, Ohio Bar Assn., Richland County Bar Assn. Republican. Congregationalist. Clubs: University, Our (Mansfield). Lodge: Kiwanis (bd. dirs. Mansfield club, 1983-84). Avocations: skiing, tennis, hunting, golf. State civil litigation, Personal injury, Criminal. Office: Weldon Huston & Keyser 28 Park Ave W Mansfield OH 44902

CARTON, LAURENCE ALFRED, lawyer; b. Chgo., Oct. 11, 1918; s. Alfred Thomas and Mildred (Wells) C.; m. Ann Fontaine Schmidt, July 2, 1949; children—Katherine Lynch, Ellen, John Laurence, Mary, Evelyn. Grad., Hotchkiss Sch., Lakeville, Conn., 1936; A.B., Princeton, 1940; J.D., U. Chgo., 1947. Bar: Ill. 1947. Practiced with Gardner, Carton & Douglas and predecessors, Chgo., 1947—; mem. firm Gardner, Carton & Douglas and predecessors, 1952—. Trustee Morton Arboretum, Lake Forest Acad.-Ferry Hall, John G. Shedd Aquarium, Chgo. Sunday Evening Club; trustee, chmn. Presbyn. Home. Served as lt. comdr. USNR, 1942-46. Mem. Am., Ill., Lake County, Chgo. bar assns., Chgo. Zool. Soc., Art Inst. Chgo. (gov.), Orchestral Assn., Chgo. Com. Council Fgn. Relations. Clubs: Chicago, University, Onwentsia. Labor, Federal civil litigation. Home: 285 W Laurel Ave Lake Forest IL 60045 Office: Gardner Carton & Douglas 1 First National Plaza Chicago IL 60603

CARVER, KEVIN SCOTT, lawyer; b. Kansas City, Mo., July 3, 1953; s. Ray Fuller and Georgia Arlene (Saylor) C.; m. Francie L. Williams, June 30, 1984; 1 stepchild, David Davis Jr. BS, U. Kans., 1975; JD, Washburn U., 1978. Bar: Kans. 1978, U.S. Dist. Ct. Kans. 1978, U.S. Ct. Appeals (10th cir.) 1982. Assoc. Thomas Brooks Chartered, Shawnee Mission, Kans., 1978-79, Laurence Jarvis Chartered, Kansas City, Kans., 1979—. Mem. ABA, Kans. Bar Assn., Wyandotte County Bar Assn., Kansas Trial Lawyers Assn., Greater Kansas City (Mo.) Jaycees. Democrat. Episcopalian. Avocations: music, electronics. Bankruptcy, Criminal, Workers' compensation. Home: 8020 Canterbury Prairie Village KS 66106-1128 Office: Laurence M Jarvis Chartered 2100 Silver Ave Kansas City KS 66106

CARY, CHARLES MUSE, lawyer; b. Salina, Kans., May 23, 1948; s. Charles Muse and Carolyn Elizabeth (Blalock) C. BS, U. Tenn., 1969, JD, 1972. Bar: Tenn. 1972, U.S. Dist. Ct. (mid. dist.) Tenn. 1972, U.S. Dist. Ct. (we. dist.) Tenn. 1974, U.S. Ct. Mil. Appeals 1980, U.S. Supreme Ct. 1984. Staff atty. Div. Water Quality Control, Nashville, 1972-74; assoc. H. Morris Denton, Bolivar, Tenn., 1974-75; ptnr. Denton and Cary, Bolivar, 1975—; atty. Hardeman County, Bolivar, 1976—; atty. City of Middleton, Tenn., 1976—, City of Grand Junction, Tenn., 1981—. Mayor Town of Whiteville, Tenn., 1976-79. Served to maj. USNG, 1979—. Mem. ABA, Tenn. Bar Assn. (House of Dels. 1982—), Hardeman County Bar Assn. Presbyterian. Avocations: piloting, tennis, traveling. General practice, State civil litigation, Real property. Home: Oak St Whiteville TN 38075 Office: Denton and Cary 118 Warren St Bolivar TN 38008

CASAGRANDE, DANIEL EUGENE, lawyer; b. New Haven, June 7, 1954; s. Eugene B. and Anne P. (Heron) C.; m. Mary E. Rodarmer, May 8, 1981. BA, Fairfield U., 1976; JD, Fordham U., 1979. Bar: N.Y. 1980, U.S. Dist. Ct. (so. and ea. dists.) N.Y. 1980, Conn. 1986, U.S. Dist. Ct. Conn. 1987. Law clk. to presiding justice U.S. Ct. Appeals (2d cir.), N.Y.C., 1979-81; assoc. Stillman, Friedman & Shaw, N.Y.C., 1981-86, Secor, Cassidy & McPartland, Danbury, Conn., 1986—. Mem. ABA, Fed. Bar Council, Assn. of Bar of City of N.Y., Fordham U. Alumni Assn. Democrat. Roman Catholic. State civil litigation, Federal civil litigation, Personal injury. Home: 31 Sterling Dr New Milford CT 06776 Office: Secor Cassidy & McPartland 301 Main St Danbury CT 06810

CASCINO, ANTHONY ELMO, JR., lawyer; b. South Bend, Ind., Aug. 21, 1948; s. Anthony E. and Lorayne (Allegretti) C.; m. Mary Anne Dory, July 28, 1973; children—Anthony Elmo, III, Christine Ann, Caroline Stephanie. B.A., Loyola U., Chgo., 1970; J.D., Ill. Inst. Tech., 1974; MBA Northwestern U., 1987. Bar: Ill. 1974, U.S. Dist. Ct. (no. dist.) Ill. 1974, U.S. Supreme Ct. 1986. Div. counsel CF Industries Inc., Long Grove, Ill., 1974-79; sec., gen. counsel Energy Coop., Inc., Rosemont, Ill., 1979-83; v.p., gen. counsel GHR Energy Corp., Good Hope, La., 1983; dep. gen. counsel AM Internat., Inc., Chgo., 1983-86; v.p. bus. devel. Multigraphics div. AM Internat., Rolling Meadows, Ill., 1986—; lectr. Ill. Inst. Continuing Edn., 1986, mem. adv. com. on postgrad. programs, 1983-86; v.p. Bus. Devel., Multigraphics, Mount Prospect, 1986—. Contbg. author: Commercial Damage, 1984. Mem. ABA, Fed. Energy Bar Assn., Ill. State Bar Assn., Chgo. Bar Assn., Bar and Gavel Soc. Democrat. Roman Catholic. Clubs: Union League (Chgo.); Meadow (Rolling Meadows, Ill.). General corporate, Bankruptcy, Oil and gas leasing. Home: 385 Lincoln Ave Glencoe IL 60022 Office: Multigraphics 1800 W Central Rd Mount Prospect IL 60056

CASE, CHARLES DIXON, lawyer; b. Manning, S.C., Mar. 23, 1952; s. James E. and Jennie (Stout) C.; m. Margie Toy, Aug. 26, 1982; 1 child, J. Everett II. BS in Physics, N.C. State U., 1973; JD, Harvard U., 1977. Bar: N.C. 1977, D.C., U.S. Dist. Ct. (ea. and mid. dists.) N.C., U.S. Supreme Ct. Ptnr. Moore & Van Allen, Raleigh, N.C., 1977—; adj. prof. law Campbell U., Bries Creek, N.C, 1981-84; hearing officer N.C. Safety and Health Rev. Bd., Raleigh, 1981-84; chmn. Wake County Bd. Adjustment, Raleigh, 1979-83. Contbr. articles to profl. jours. Environment, Administrative and regulatory, Computer. Home: 1540 Carr St Raleigh NC 27608 Office: Moore & Van Allen PO Box 26507 Raleigh NC 27611

CASE, DAVID LEON, lawyer; b. Lansing, Mich., Sept. 22, 1948; s. Harlow Hoyt and Barbara Jean (Denman) C.; m. Cynthia Lou Rhinehart, Jan. 28, 1968; children: Beau, Ryan, Kimberly, Darren, Stephanie. BS with distinction, Ariz. State U., 1970, JD cum laude, 1973. Bar: Calif. 1973, U.S. Dist. Ct. (cen. dist.) Calif. 1973, U.S. Tax Ct. 1974, Ariz. 1976. Assoc. Willis, Butler & Scheifly, Los Angeles, 1973-75; from assoc. to ptnr. Ryley, Carlock & Applewhite, Phoenix, 1975—. Mem. ABA (tax sect., corp. sect.), Ariz. Bar Assn. (tax sect.), Calif. Bar Assn. (tax sect.), Cen. Ariz. Estate Planning Council (bd. dirs.), Beta Gamma Sigma. Republican. Presbyterian. Avocations: running, guitar, sports. Corporate taxation, Real property, General corporate. Office: Ryley Carlock & Applewhite 101 N 1st Ave Phoenix AZ 85003

CASE, DOUGLAS MANNING, lawyer; b. Cleve., Jan. 3, 1947; s. Manning Eugene and Ernestine (Bryan) C.; m. Marilyn Cooper, Aug. 23, 1969. BA, U. Pa., 1969; JD, MBA, Columbia U., 1973. Bar: N.Y. 1974, N.J. 1975, Calif. 1980. Assoc. Brown & Wood, N.Y.C., 1973-77; corp. counsel PepsiCo Inc., Purchase, N.Y. and Irvine, Calif., 1977-83, Nabisco Brands Inc., N.Y.C. and East Hanover, N.J., 1983—. Chmn. Olde Colonial Dist., Morris-Sussex Area Council Boy Scouts Am., 1986—; Sec., trustee Marble Scholarship Com., N.Y.C., 1983—. Mem. ABA, N.Y. State Bar Assn. Republican. Clubs: Morris County Golf (Convent Station, N.J.); Columbia Bus. Sch. (N.Y.C.) (pres. and bd. dirs. 1974-79). Avocations: golf, tennis. Private international, Mergers and acquisitions, General corporate. Office: Nabisco Brands Inc 100 DeForest Ave PO Box 1937 East Hanover NJ 07936

CASE, EDWARD HAILE, lawyer; b. Albany, N.Y., Oct. 9, 1908; s. Floyd Randolph and Louise Helen (Haile) C.; m. Neeltje VanBergen, Apr. 20, 1935; children: Penelope Jane Case Hennenam, Judith Ann. AB, Cornell U., 1929, JD, 1931. Bar: N.Y. 1932, U.S. Dist. Ct. (no. dist.) N.Y. 1933, U.S. Ct. Appeals (2d cir.) 1933. Assoc. Bond, Schoenick & King, Syracuse, N.Y., 1931-36; corp. counsel Village of Gouverneur, N.Y., 1936-73; sole practice Gouverneur, 1936-66; ptnr. Case & Leader, Gouverneur, 1966—; bd. dirs. St. Lawrence Nat. Bank. Chmn. St. Lawrence County Rep. Com., Canton, N.Y., 1955-56; bd. dirs. N.Y. State Power Authority, Massena, 1957-59.

Served to lt. USN, 1944-46, PTO. Mem. ABA, N.Y. State Bar Assn., St. Lawrence County Bar Assn. (pres. 1960-61). Presbyterian. Club: Luncheon. Probate, Estate planning, Real property. Home: 28 Barney St Gouverneur NY 13642 Office: Case & Leader 107 E Main Box 13 Gouverneur NY 13642-0013

CASE, IRVIN VINCENT, JR., lawyer, municipal judge; b. Walsenburg, Colo., June 17, 1950; s. Irvin Vincent and Annette Marie (Gasperetti) C.; m. Marcia Ann Feterl, June 5, 1976; 1 child, Carmelle Ann. BS, U. Wyo., 1972, JD, 1975. Bar: Wyo. 1975, U.S. Dist. Ct. Wyo. 1975. Assoc. Hand, Hand & Hand, P.C., Douglas, Wyo., 1975-77; sole practice, Doulgas, 1977—; city atty. Town of Glenrock, Wyo., 1976-82; mcpl. judge Town of Douglas, 1977—; dep. atty. Converse County, Wyo., 1978-79; instr. Ea. Wyo. Coll., Douglas, 1984, 86, 87; apptd. County Ct. Commr., 1987. Mem. Converse County Bar Assn. (pres. 1979-80, sec. 1984—), Wyo. Trial Lawyers Assn., Wyo. Bar Assn., ABA, Wyo. Assn. Judges, U. Wyo. Alumni Assn., Douglas C. of C. Republican. Roman Catholic. Club: Community (Douglas). Lodges: Moose, Kiwanis (past pres.). General practice, Probate, General corporate. Home: 706 Harrison St Douglas WY 82633 Office: 309 E Center St PO Box 528 Douglas WY 82633

CASE, JAMES HEBARD, lawyer; b. Lihue, Hawaii, Apr. 10, 1920; s. Adrial Hebard and Elizabeth (McConnell) C.; m. Suzanne Catherine Espenett, Sept. 18, 1948; children: Edward E., John H., Suzanne D., Russell L., Elisabeth D. Bradford Case. AB, Williams Coll., 1941; JD, Harvard U., 1949. Bar: Hawaii 1949, U.S. Supreme Ct. 1985. Assoc. Pratt, Tavares & Cassidy, Honolulu, 1949-51, Carlsmith & Carsmith, Honolulu, 1951-59; ptnr. Carlsmith, Carlsmith, Wichman & Case, Honolulu, 1959-84, Carlsmith, Wichman, Case, Mukai & Ichiki, Honolulu, 1984—; bd. dirs. Hamakua Sugar Co., Honolulu, Mauna Loa Resources, Honolulu, InterIsland Resorts, Honolulu. Trustee Hanahauoli Sch., Honolulu, 1970-82, Cen. Union Ch., Honolulu, 1985—. Served to lt. comdr. USNR, 1943-46, PTO. Mem. ABA, Hawaii Bar Assn. Republican. Congregationalist. Clubs: Pacific (bd. dirs. 1978-82); Kaneone Yacht (fleet capt. 1982-84) (Honolulu). Avocations: sailing, tennis. General corporate, Public utilities, Securities. Home: 3757 Round Top Dr Honolulu HI 96822 Office: Carlsmith Wichman Case et al PO Box 656 Honolulu HI 96809

CASE, KAREN ANN, lawyer; b. Milw., Apr. 7, 1944; d. Alfred F. and Hilda M. (Tomich) Case. B.S., Marquette U., 1963, J.D. 1966; LL.M., N.Y.U., 1973. Bar: Wis. 1966, U.S. Ct. Claims, 1973, U.S. Tax Ct. 1973. Ptnr. Meldman, Case & Weine, Milw., 1973-85; ptnr. Meldman, Case & Weine div. Mulcahy & Wherry, S.C., 1985-87; Sec. of Revenue State of Wis., 1987—; lectr. U. Wis., Milw., 1974-78; guest lectr. Marquette U. Law Sch., 1975-78. Fellow Wis. Bar Found. (dir. 1977—, treas. 1980—); mem. Milw. Assn. Women Lawyers (bd. dirs. 1975-78, 81-82), Milw. Bar Assn. (bd. dirs. 1985-87), State Bar Wis. (bd. govs. 1981-85, 87—, dir. taxation sect. 1981-87, vice chmn. 1986-87), Am. Acad. Matrimonial Lawyers, Nat. Assn. Women Lawyers (Wis. del. 1982-83), Milw. Rose Soc. (pres. 1981, dir. 1981-83), Friends of Boerner Bat. Gardens (pres. 1984—), Clubs: Professional Dimensions (dir. 1985-87), Tempo (sec. 1984-85). Contbr. articles to legal jours. Corporate taxation, Personal income taxation, State and local taxation. Home: 9803 W Meadow Park Dr Hales Corners WI 53130 Office: 125 S Webster Madison WI 53708

CASE, MATTHEW ALAN, lawyer; b. Detroit, Nov. 11, 1957; s. Alan Henry and Timi (Faulmann) C. BA, U. Mich., Dearborn, 1979; JD, Wayne State U., 1982. Bar: Mich. 1982, U.S. Dist. Ct. (ea. dist.) Mich. 1984. Clk. Mich. Supreme Ct., Farmington Hills, 1982-83; assoc. Dykema, Gossett, Spencer, Goodnow & Trigg, Bloomfield Hills, Mich., 1983—. James B. Angell scholar U. Mich., 1979; Arthur B. Lederle scholar Wayne State U., 1979, Max Smitt scholar, 1980; recipient Bronze, Silver and Gold Key Cert., Wayne State U., 1980-82. Mem. ABA, State Bar Mich., Oakland County Bar Assn. Avocations: softball, racquetball. General corporate, Securities, Contracts commercial. Office: Dykema Gossett Spencer et al 505 N Woodward Ave Suite 3000 Bloomfield Hills MI 48013

CASEBOLT, JAMES STANTON, lawyer; b. Denver, Apr. 27, 1950; s. Stanton Taylor and Josephine Almira (Cole) C.; m. Joanne Ruth Tuthill, June 10, 1972; children—Matthew, Zachary. B.A. magna cum laude, Colo. Coll., 1972; J.D., U. Colo., 1975. Bar: Colo. 1975, U.S. Dist. Ct. Colo. 1975, U.S. Ct. Appeals (10th cir.) 1983. Assoc. Younge & Hockensmith, P.C., Grand Junction, Colo., 1975-78, dir., sec., 1978—, sr. litigation ptnr., 1984—. Author: Civil Jury Selection Procedure and Pattern Voir Dire. Mem. adv. bd. Salvation Army Grand Junction; trustee Presbytery Western Colo., 1982-85, chmn., 1984-85; cubmaster Boy Scouts Am., Grand Junction, 1984—. Mem. ABA, Colo. Bar Assn. (litigation council 1982-85), Mesa County Bar Assn. (sec.-treas. 1980-83, bd. dirs.), Colo. Def. Lawyers, Phi Beta Kappa. State civil litigation, Insurance, Personal injury. Home: 3350 Music Ln Grand Junction CO 81506 Office: Younge & Hockensmith PC Box 1768 200 Grand Ave Grand Junction CO 81502

CASELLA, PETER F(IORE), patent and licensing executive, consultant; b. N.Y.C., June 5, 1922; s. Fiore Peter and Lucy (Grimaldi) C.; m. Marjorie Eloise Enos, Mar. 9, 1946; children—William Peter, Susan Elaine, Richard Mark. B.Ch.E., Poly. Inst. Bklyn. (Now Poly. U. N.Y.), 1943; student in chemistry St. John's U., N.Y.C., 1940. Registered to practice by U.S. Patent and Trademark Office, Can. Patent and Trade Mark Offices. Head patent sect. Hooker Electrochem. Co., Niagara Falls, N.Y., 1943-54; mgr. patent dept. Hooker Chem. Corp. (named changed to Occidental Chem. Corp. 1981), Niagara Falls, 1954-64, dir. patents and licensing, 1964-81, asst. sec., 1966-81, ret., 1981; pres., chief exec. officer Intra Gene Internat., Inc., Niagara Falls, 1981—; chmn. bd., chief exec. officer In Vitro Internat., Inc., Ann Arbor, Mich., 1983—; cons. patents and licensing, Lewiston, N.Y., 1981—; Dept. Commerce del. on patents and licensing exchange, USSR, 1973, Poland and German Democratic Republic, 1976. Editor: Drafting the Patent Application, 1957. Mem. Lewiston Bd. Edn., 1968-70. Served with AUS, 1944-46; MTO. Recipient Centennial citation Poly. Inst. Bklyn., 1955. Mem. Assn. Corp. Patent Counsel (emeritus, mem. exec. com. 1974-77, charter mem.), N.Y. Patent Law Assn., Niagara Frontier Patent Law Assn. (pres. 1973-74, Founder award 1974), Licensing Execs. Soc. (v.p. 1976-77, Trustees award 1977), Chartered Inst. Patent Agts. Gt. Britain, Patent and Trademark Inst. Can., Internat. Patent and Trademark Assn., U.S. Trademark Assn., Nat. Assn. Mfrs. (patent com.), Mfg. Chemists Assn., Pacific Indsl. Property Assn., U.S. Patent Office Soc. (assoc.), U.S. Trade Mark Office Soc. (assoc.), Am. Chem. Soc., Am. Inst. Chem. Engrs. Clubs: Chemists (N.Y.C.); Niagara (pres. 1973-74) (Niagara Falls). Patent, Trademark and copyright, Environment.

CASEY, BERNARD JOSEPH, lawyer; b. Pawtucket, R.I., June 4, 1942; s. Andrew J. and Theresa (Lennon) C.; m. Kathleen A. Wall; children—Brendan, B. John. A.B., Providence Coll., 1964; J.D., Catholic U., 1967. Bar: R.I. Supreme Ct. 1967, D.C. 1971, U.S. Supreme Ct. 1972, U.S. Cir. Ct. (D.C. cir., 4th cir., 6th cir.). Assoc., Gall, Lane & Powell, Washington, 1971-76, ptnr., 1976; ptnr. Reed Smith Shaw & McClay, Washington, 1976—, co-mng. ptnr., 1982—. Served to capt. AUS, 1967-71. Decorated Bronze Star medal. Mem. ABA (mem. litigation com., labor relations com.), D.C. Bar Assn. Roman Catholic. Clubs: University, Chevy Chase Country Club. Labor, Product liability, Administrative and regulatory. Home: 3257 Worthington St NW Washington DC 20015 Office: Suite 900 1150 Connecticut Ave NW Washington DC 20036

CASEY, GERALDINE HOLLAND, lawyer, military officer; b. Plainfield, N.J., Dec. 22, 1952; d. Earl Lee and Barbara (Shockley) Holland; m. Ronald Levoid Casey, July 20, 1975; children: Lauren Dan, Kevin Michael. BA, Howard U., 1974; JD, Rutgers U., 1981. Bar: Pa. 1981, N.J. 1984, U.S. Dist. Ct. N.J. 1984. Commd. lt. USN, Phila., 1981, atty. JAGC, 1981-85; atty. JAGC USN, Washington, 1985—. Mem. ABA, Pa. Bar Assn., N.J. Bar Assn., Assn. Trial Lawyers Am., Nat. Naval Officers Assn. (judge adv., bd. dirs. 1984—). Military, Federal civil litigation, Admiralty. Home: 2700 Advent Ct S Bowie MD 20716 Office: Navy Marine Corps Appellate Rev Activity Office of Judge Adv Gen Bldg 200 Washington Navy Yard Washington DC 20374-2002

CASEY, JOHN L., lawyer; b. Medford, Mass., Jan. 13, 1924; s. John L. and Ruth (Jones) C. AB, Harvard U., 1944, JD, 1948. Bar: N.Y. 1949, U.S. Dist. Ct. (so. and we. dists.) N.Y. 1949, U.S. Ct. Appeals (2d cir.) 1951, Mass. 1969, U.S. Supreme Ct. 1978. Assoc. Simpson, Thacher & Bartlett, N.Y.C., 1948-54; law asst. N.Y. County Surrogates Ct., 1954-56, 56-61; chief counsel Joint Legis. Counsel on Housing, N.Y.C., 1957-59; assoc. Scudder, Stevens & Clark, N.Y.C., 1961-70, sr. v.p., 1969-85, gen. ptnr., 1970-85, mng. dir., 1985—; bd. dirs. Scudder Devel. Fund, Scudder Duo-Vest Inc., Scudder Internat. Fund, Scudder, Stevens & Clark of Can., Ltd., of Ill., of Del.; registered rep., v.p., bd. dirs. Scudder Fund Distbrs.; mem. adv. council on pensions to U.S. Sec. Labor, 1981-83. Author: Destroyer 697, 1945; (poems) This Just Man, 1948, Ethics in the Financial Marketplace, 1987; contbr. articles to profl. jours. Pres., trustee St. David's Sch., N.Y.C.; mem. adv. com. Inst. Ethics in Mgmt., Cambridge, Mass., Ctr. for Study of World Religion, Divinity Sch., Harvard U.; nat. chmn. Youth for Eisenhower, 1956. Served to lt. (j.g.) USNR, 1944-45. Mem. ABA, Fed. Bar Assn., Mass. Bar Assn., N.Y. State Bar Assn., Assn. of Bar of City of N.Y., Investment Counsel Assn. Am. (chmn. legal and regulatory com., hon. gov.). Office: Scudder Stevens & Clark 345 Park Ave New York NY 10154

CASEY, KATHLEEN HEIRICH, lawyer, educator; b. Chgo., Mar. 10, 1937; d. Bruneau Ernest and Kathleen Brennan (Grogan) Heirich; m. John M. Casey, Nov. 18, 1959 (div. 1974); children—Sean M., Kyle L., Siobhan C. A.B., Radcliffe Coll., 1959; J.D., St. John's U., 1974. Bar: N.Y. 1975, U.S. Dist. Ct. (so. and ea. dists.) N.Y. 1975, U.S. Ct. Appeals (2d cir.) 1975, U.S. Supreme Ct. 1976. Asst. corp. counsel N.Y.C. Law Dept., 1974-76; appellate counsel Div. Criminal Justice, N.Y.C., 1976-77; asst. atty. gen. N.Y. Law Dept., 1977-78; prin. law clk. N.Y. State Supreme Ct., N.Y.C., 1978-81; assoc. Colton, Weissberg, Hartnick, Yamin & Sheresky, N.Y.C., 1981-83, Milbank, Tweed, Hadley & McCloy, N.Y.C., 1983—; adj. faculty N.Y. Law Sch., N.Y.C., 1983—; mem. family dispute resolution and comml. panels Am. Arbitration Assn., N.Y.C., 1984—. Contbr. articles to profl. jours. Nassau County committeewoman, 1972-79, 81—; mem. law com. Nassau County Democratic Party, 1977-81, Navy League of U.S., N.Y. Council, 1980. Fellow Am. Acad. Matrimonial Law; mem. N.Y. Women's Bar Assn. (officer 1985—), ABA, N.Y. State Bar Assn., Assn. Bar City N.Y., N.Y.C. Lawyers Assn. Family and matrimonial. Office: Milbank Tweed Hadley & McCloy 1 Chase Manhattan Plaza New York NY 10005

CASEY, PATRICK ANTHONY, lawyer; b. Santa Fe, Apr. 20, 1944; s. Ivanhoe and Eutimia (Casados) C.; m. Gail Marie Johns, Aug. 1, 1970; children—Christopher Gaelen, Matthew Colin. B.A., N.Mex. State U., 1970; J.D., U. Ariz., 1973. Bar: N.Mex. 1973, U.S. Dist. Ct. N.Mex. 1973, Ariz. 1973, U.S. Ct. Appeals (10th cir.) 1979, U.S. Supreme Ct. 1980. Assoc. firm Bachicha & Corlett, Santa Fe, 1973-75; assoc. firm Bachicha & Casey, Santa Fe, 1975-77; sole practice, Santa Fe, 1977—. Bd. dirs. Santa Fe Sch. Arts and Crafts, 1974, Santa Fe Animal Shelter, 1975-81, Cath. Charities of Santa Fe, 1979-82, Old Santa Fe Assn., 1979—. Served with USN, 1961-65; Vietnam. Mem. Assn. Trial Lawyers Am., ABA, N.Mex. Trial Lawyers Assn. (dir. 1977-79, treas. 1979-83, pres. 1983-84), Bar Assn. 1st Jud. Dist. (pres. 1980), Am. Legion, VFW, Vietnam Vets. of Am. Lodges: Elks, Rotary. Federal civil litigation, State civil litigation, Personal injury. Office: 1421 Luisa St Suite Q Santa Fe NM 87501

CASEY, PATRICK JON, lawyer; b. Elk City, Okla., July 5, 1943; s. A. Harold and Bernice (Brooks) C.; m. Ellen Kay Webster, Feb. 24, 1967; children: Kimberly, Julia Ann. BBA, U. Okla., 1967; JD, Oklahoma City U., 1974. Bar: Okla. 1974, U.S. Dist. Ct. (we. dist.) Okla. 1974, U.S. Tax Ct. 1975, U.S. Ct. Claims 1977, U.S. Ct. Appeals (10th cir.) 1977, U.S. Supreme Ct. 1977. Ptnr. McDivitt & Casey, Oklahoma City, 1974—; speaker various seminars on taxes, real estate and syndications, 1975—. Contbr. articles on tax to mags., 1976—. Chmn. devel. campaign Oklahoma City U., 1974-79. Mem. ABA, Okla. Bar Assn., Oklahoma County Bar Assn., Oklahoma City Lawyers Tax Group, Nat. Assn. Home Builders (nat. dir., trustee 1980—), Cen. Okla. Home Builders Assn. (exec. com., legal counsel 1978—). Mem. Christian Ch. Real property, Personal income taxation, Corporate taxation. Office: McDivitt & Casey 623 N Harvey Oklahoma City OK 73102

CASEY, ROBERT FITZGERALD, lawyer, educator; b. Chgo., Sept. 28, 1943; s. John Francis and Gertrude Bernice (Fitzgerald) C. B.A., Notre Dame U., 1964; M.S. in Edn., No. Ill. U., 1968; J.D., DePaul U., 1974, LL.M., 1980; MBA, Notre Dame U., 1987. Bar: Ill. 1975, Ind. 1976, Fla. 1977, U.S. Tax Ct. 1981, U.S. Ct. Claims 1982, U.S. Ct. Mil. Appeals 1982, U.S. Supreme Ct. 1982. Mem. James J. Conlon & Assocs., Chgo., 1976—; educator Amos Alonzo Stagg High Sch., Palos Hills, Ill., 1969—. Served to lt. JAGC USNR, 1981—. Mem. Ill. Bar Assn., Ind. Bar Assn., ABA, The Fla. Bar, Chgo. Bar Assn., Phi Alpha Delta. Roman Catholic. Club: Notre Dame of Chgo. General practice, Real property, Military. Home: 403 N Country Club Dr McHenry IL 60050 Office: 205 W Randolph St Suite 1220 Chicago IL 60606

CASHEL, THOMAS WILLIAM, lawyer; b. N.Y.C., Feb. 12, 1930; s. Thomas Leo and Vera Lucia (Blattmacher) C.; m. Sarah Ann Strife, Oct. 11, 1958; children: Thomas W. Jr., Michael S., Alison K., Colin M. A.B., Cornell U., 1952, LL.B., 1956; diploma in internat. law, Cambridge U., Eng., 1958. Bar: N.Y. 1957, U.S. Supreme Ct. 1963. Assoc. law firm Simpson Thacher & Bartlett, N.Y.C., 1958-65; ptnr. Simpson Thacher & Bartlett, 1965—; sr. vis. fellow Queen Mary Coll., U. London, 1984—. Trustee Practising Law Inst., N.Y.C., 1978-81. Served to lt. U.S. Army, 1952-54. Fellow Am. Bar Found.; mem. Am. Soc. Internat. Law, Internat. Bar Assn., ABA, Assn. Bar City N.Y., Order of the Coif, Phi Kappa Phi. Roman Catholic. Clubs: Racquet and Tennis, N.Y. Yacht, Fishers Island Country, Oxford-Cambridge. Banking, Private international. Office: Simpson Thacher & Bartlett 270 Park Ave New York NY 10017

CASHION, SHELLEY JEAN, lawyer, educator; b. Bryan, Tex., June 29, 1955; d. Mason L. and Lou (Burgess) C. BJ, U. Tex., Austin, 1975; JD, Tex. Tech U., 1978; LLM in Taxation, NYU, 1981. Bar: Tex. 1978, U.S. Dist. Ct. (no. dist.) Tex. 1979, U.S. Dist. Ct. (so. dist.) Tex. 1981, U.S. Tax Ct. 1981, U.S. Ct. Claims 1981, U.S. Ct. Appeals (5th cir.) 1982, U.S. Ct. Appeals (fed. cir.) 1983, U.S. Ct. Appeals (8th, 9th and 10th cirs.) 1984. Assoc. Geary, Stahl & Spencer, Dallas, 1976; assoc. Chamberlain, Hrdlicka, White, Johnson & Williams, Houston, 1981-83, ptnr., 1983—; adjunct prof. law U. Houston Sch. Law, 1984—. Author: Advanced Planning Techniques with S Corporations, 1983. Mem. ABA, Houston Bar Assn. (sec. tax section 1986—, treas. 1985-86), Order of Coif, Phi Delta Phi, Phi Delta Theta. Personal income taxation, Corporate taxation, Federal civil litigation. Office: Chamberlain Hrdlicka White Johnson & Williams 1200 Smith St Houston TX 77002

CASHMAN, GIDEON, lawyer; b. N.Y.C., Sept. 10, 1929; s. Abba Morris and Rachel (Cashman) C.; m. Ruth Lucinda Parker, Sept. 8, 1956 (div.); married, 1985; children—Adam Parker, Lindsey Avril. A.B., NYU, 1951; J.D., Columbia U., 1954. Bar: D.C. 1954, N.Y. 1954. Asst. counsel Waterfront Commn. of N.Y., 1954-55; asst. U.S. atty. criminal div. U.S. Dist. Ct. So. Dist. N.Y., 1958-61, chief criminal apls., 1959-61; assoc. Christy Perkins & Christy, N.Y.C., 1961-63; ptnr. Pryor Cashman Sherman & Flynn, N.Y.C., 1963-82, sr. ptnr., 1973—; lectr. trial tactics Practicing Law Inst. Bd. dirs. Irvington House Inst. for Med. Research, 1982—; trustee Friars Found., Heart Research Found., Eugene O'Neill Theatre Ctr. Mem. ABA, N.Y. State Bar Assn., Assn. Bar City N.Y., N.Y. County Lawyers Assn. Jewish. Club: Friars (N.Y.C.). Federal civil litigation, State civil litigation, General corporate. Home: 812 Park Ave New York NY 10021 Office: 410 Park Ave New York NY 10022

CASHOUR, MARY CATHERINE, lawyer; b. Balt., July 30, 1947; d. Paul Everett and Mary Margaret (Cadden) C. BA in Social Sci., U. Balt., 1971, JD, 1976. Bar: Md. 1982. Operator directory assistance C&P Telephone Co. Md., Balt., 1965-70, summarization clk., 1970-73; examiner ins. claims Social Security Adminstrn., Balt., 1973-79, govt. rep., 1982-84, project leader, legal asst., 1984—; hearings analyst Social Security Adminstrn., Arlington, Va., 1979-82. Mem. ABA, Md. Bar Assn., Exec. Women's Network, Seton High Sch. Alumnae Assn. (bd. dirs. 1985—). Democrat. Roman Catholic. Avocations: stuffed bear collecting, reading, sports. Administrative and regulatory, Pension, profit-sharing, and employee benefits. Home: 2510 N Calvert St Baltimore MD 21218 Office: Social Security Adminstrn 6400 Security Blvd Baltimore MD 21235

CASIELLO, NICHOLAS, JR., lawyer; b. Passaic, N.J., May 7, 1953; s. Nicholas Sr. and Jeanette (Passaretti) C. BA, Drew U., 1975; JD, Seton Hall U., 1978. Bar: N.J. 1979, U.S. Dist. Ct. N.J. 1979, U.S. Supreme Ct. 1985. Law clk. to presiding judge N.J. Superior Ct., Atlantic City, 1978-79; assoc. Horn, Kaplan, Goldberg, Gorny & Daniels, P.A., Atlantic City, 1979-82, ptnr., 1982—; lectr. casino law Del. Law Sch., 1984, Public Gaming Research Inst. Conf., Atlantic City, 1984, Laventhol & Horwath Gaming Conf., Atlantic City, 1985; mem com. on civil case mgmt. and procedures N.J. Supreme Ct., Trenton, N.J., 1983-84. Mem. ABA (gaming law com.), N.J. Bar Assn. (sec. casino law sect. 1985—); Internat. Assn. Gaming Attys. (charter), Am. Mensa Ltd. Administrative and regulatory, Contracts commercial, General corporate. Office: Horn Kaplan et al 1300 Atlantic Ave Suite 500 Atlantic City NJ 08401

CASPER, GERHARD, lawyer, university dean; b. Hamburg, Germany, Dec. 25, 1937; s. Heinrich and Hertha C.; m. Regina Koschel, Dec. 26, 1964; 1 child, Hanna. Legal state exam., Hamburg, 1961; LL.M., Yale U., 1962; Dr.iur.utr., U. Freiburg, Germany, 1964; LL.D. (hon.), John Marshall Law Sch., 1982, Ill. Inst. Tech., 1987. Asst. prof. polit. sci. U. Calif., Berkeley, 1964-66; assoc. prof. law and polit. sci. U. Chgo., 1966-69, prof., 1969-76, Max Pam prof. law, 1976-80, William B. Graham prof. law, 1980—; dean (Law Sch.), 1979-87; vis. prof. law Cath. U., Louvain, Belgium, 1970. Author: Realism and Political Theory in American Legal Thought, 1967, (with Richard A. Posner) The Workload of the Supreme Court, 1976; Co-editor: The Supreme Court Rev., 1977—. Fellow Am. Acad. Arts and Scis.; mem. Council on Fgn. Relations, Am. Law Inst. (council 1980—), Oliver Wendell Holmes Devise (permanent com. 1985—), Chgo. Bar Assn., Chgo. Council Lawyers (bd. govs. 1973-75), Am. Council on Germany. Constitutional, Legal history.

CASPER, PAUL WILLIAM, JR., lawyer; b. Greensburg, Pa., Nov. 14, 1946; s. Paul William Sr. and Julia Lee (Safran) C.; m. Michele Katherine Casper, Nov. 12, 1976. BA in Biology and Chemistry, St. Vincent Coll., 1968; MS in Physiology, U. Dayton, 1975, JD, 1981. Bar: Ohio 1981, U.S. Dist. Ct. (so. dist.) Ohio 1981. Research chemist U.S. Steel, Monroeville, Pa., 1968; clin. biologist, chemist Jeannette (Pa.) Dist. Meml. Hosp., 1972-73; health and safety officer Occupational Safety and Health Adminstrn., Cin., 1976-77; physiologist and tech. writer SRL Med., Inc., Dayton, Ohio, 1977-78; assoc. Smith & Schnacke, LPA, Dayton, 1981—. Served with Med. Service Corps, U.S. Army, 1969-72. St. Vincent Coll. scholar, 1964. Mem. ABA, Ohio Bar Assn., Dayton Bar Assn., Am. Trial Lawyers Assn., Air Pollution Control Assn., Dayton Area C. of C. (legisl. and govtl. affairs com. 1983—, steering com. 1985—, chmn. energy and environ. subcom. 1985—, water resources com. 1986—), Phi Alpha Delta. Avocations: tennis, golf, swimming, sports cars. Environment, Administrative and regulatory, Legislative. Office: Smith & Schnacke LPA 2000 Courthouse Plaza NE PO Box 1817 Dayton OH 45401

CASS, NEIL EARL, lawyer; b. Carthage, Ill., Jan. 8, 1952; s. Earl and Katheryn Louise (Lovell) C.; m. Marilyn Kay Schell, Nov. 14, 1970; children: Brian, Sara, Amy. BBA with honors, U. Puget Sound, 1974; MBA, JD with high distinction, U. Iowa, 1977; LLM in Estate Planning, U. Miami, 1980. Bar: Iowa 1977, Wis. 1977, Ill. 1980; CPA Ill. Tax staff. Touche Ross, Milw., 1977, Den, Hartog & Hogan, Waterloo, Iowa, 1977-78; assoc. Strand & Anderson, Decorah, Iowa, 1978-79; ptnr. Kirkland & Ellis, Chgo., 1980—. Trustee Village of Flossmoor, Ill., 1985—. Served to staff sgt. USAF, 1970-74. Mem. ABA, Ill. Bar Assn., Iowa Bar Assn., Wis. Bar Assn., Chgo. Estate Planning Council. Republican. Club: MidAm. (Chgo.). Probate, Personal income taxation, General corporate. Office: Kirkland & Ellis 200 E Randolph Dr Chicago IL 60601

CASS, ROBERT MICHAEL, lawyer, reinsurance executive; b. Carlisle, Pa., July 5, 1945; s. Robert Lau and Norma Jean (McCaleb) C.; BA, Pa. State U., 1967; JD, Temple U., 1971; m. Patricia Ann Garber, Aug. 12, 1967; children: Charles McCaleb, David Lau. Benefit examiner Social Security Adminstrn., Phila., 1967-68; mktg. rep. Employers Comml. Union Ins. Co., Phila., 1968-70; asst. sec. Nat. Reins. Corp., N.Y.C., 1970-77; admitted to N.Y. bar, 1974; asst. v.p. Skandia Am. Reins. Corp., N.Y.C., 1977-80; mgr. Allstate Reins. div., South Barrington, Ill., 1980-86; mgr. R.K. Carvill, Inc., Chgo., 1986—. Mem. Am. Bar Assn. (com. on internat. ins. law, profl. dir. & officers ins. law, excess, surplus lines and reins. law, vice chmn. elect), N.Y. State Bar Assn., Soc. CPCU's, Soc. Ins. Research. Insurance. Home: 325 Old Mill Rd Barrington IL 60010

CASSAN, VITO J., lawyer; b. Rochester, N.Y., Aug. 30, 1929; s. Vincenzo and Giovanna (Bufano) Casamassima; m. Dagmar A. Zahm, Nov. 9, 1972; children—James, Donna, Wendy, David, Matthew. B.A., Ohio State U., 1952; J.D., Cornell U., 1955. Bar: N.Y. 1955, U.S. Dist. Ct. (we. dist.) N.Y. 1955, U.S. Dist. Ct. (so. and ea. dists.) N.Y. 1971, U.S. Ct. Appeals (2d and D.C. cirs.) 1975. Assoc. MacFarlane, Harris, Dankoff & Martin, Rochester, 1955-57; ptnr. Whitbeck & Holloran, Rochester, 1957-71, Wolf Popper Ross Wolf & Jones, N.Y.C., 1971-76; asst. gen. counsel Power Authority N.Y. State, N.Y.C., 1976-81; of counsel Reid & Priest, N.Y.C., 1981-84, Galpeer Altus & Beckerman, 1984-85; ptnr. Sullivan, Donovan, Hanrahan & Silliere, N.Y.C., 1985-86, cons. Nivon, Hargrave, Devans, Doyle, 1986—; adj. prof. environ. law Fordham U. Law Sch., N.Y.C., 1982—. Mem. ABA (com. on anti-trust competition and trade regulation and com. on environ. matters sect. adminstrv. law 1982), Lawyers Conf. Jud. Adminstrn., N.Y. State Bar Assn. (com. on utility law 1983), Assn. Bar City of N.Y. (com. on adminstrv. law 1980-83, com. on nuclear tech. and law 1983—), Atomic Indsl. Forum (subcom. on decommissioning of nuclear power stas. 1979—, lawyers com. 1983—), Am. Arbitration Assn. (arbitrator 1962—). Roman Catholic. Public utilities, Nuclear power, Private international. Home: 301 E 66th St New York NY 10021

CASSARINO, JOSEPH FRANCIS, lawyer; b. McKeesport, Pa., Dec. 13, 1948; s. Francis F. Cassarino and Elizabeth S. (Kundman) Banaszak; m. Mary Kay Plumb, Apr. 3, 1971; children—Joseph M., Gina M., Elizabeth D. B.A., California U. (Pa.), 1974; J.D., U. Notre Dame, 1977. Bar: Pa. 1977, U.S. Dist. Ct. Pa. 1977, U.S. Ct. Appeals (3d cir.) 1978, U.S. Tax Ct. 1984, U.S. Supreme Ct. 1981. Assoc. Catalano & Catalano, 1977-78; ptnr. Duffy, Austin & Cassarino, 1978-80; prin. Joseph F. Cassarino and Assocs., P.C., Greensburg, Pa., 1980—. Assoc. Jour. Legis. Research, Law Rev., 1976-77. Served with U.S. Army, 1967-70; Vietnam; PTO. Pres., Immaculate Conception Parish Council; coach Norwin Soccer Club, Immaculate Conception Basketball; bd. dirs. United Way, Irwin, Pa.; pres. Norwin chpt. United Way; chmn. bd. Pvt. Industry Council of Westmoreland/Fayette; bd. dirs. Norwin Jaycees. Mem. ABA, Pa. Bar Assn., Allegheny County Bar Assn., Westmoreland County Bar Assn., Assn. Trial Lawyers Am., Pa. Trial Lawyers Assn., Western Pa. Trial Lawyers Assn., Irwin C. of C., VFW (sr. vice comdr., chmn. Voice of Democracy Program; chmn. Poppy Day), Am. Legion, AMVETS, Pi Gamma Mu, Gamma Theta Epsilon. Lodges: Elks, K.C. Democrat. Roman Catholic. Criminal, Family and matrimonial, General practice. Home: 1219 10th Ave Irwin PA 15642 Office: Joseph F Cassarino and Assocs PC 301 Law & Finance Bldg Greensburg PA 15601

CASSEB, ROBERT MICHAEL, lawyer; b. Alpine, Tex., June 25, 1951; s. Paul Ernest and Mary Margaret (Mullins) C.; m. Diana Candace Mathews, Aug. 4, 1978. B.A., U. Tex., 1973; J.D., St. Mary's U., San Antonio, 1976. Bar: Tex. 1977, U.S. Supreme Ct. 1983. Assoc. Lang, Cross, San Antonio, 1976-81; ptnr. Brite, Drought, Bobbitt & Halter, San Antonio, 1981—; dir., chmn. exec. com. InterCon Bank-Starcrest, San Antonio, 1983—. Bd. dirs. Classical Broadcasting Soc., San Antonio, 1984. Mem. San Antonio Bar Assn. Republican. Roman Catholic. Club: Bachelors (bd. dirs. 1980). Real property, Private international, Banking. Home: 1001 Canterbury Hill San Antonio TX 78209 Office: Brite Drought Bobbitt & Halter 2400 InterFirst Plaza San Antonio TX 78205

CASSEL, MARWIN SHEPARD, lawyer; b. N.Y.C., July 4, 1925; s. Irwin M. and Mana-Zucca Cassel; children by a previous marriage: Bradley William, James Scott, Thomas Drew; m. Leslie Stein, Nov. 24, 1983; 1 child, Michael Alan. JD, U. Fla., 1949. Bar: Fla. 1949, D.C. 1980. Sr. ptnr. Broad and Cassel, Miami, Fla., 1985—; chmn. bd., pres. Internat. Savs. and Loan Assn., Miami, 1980-83. Vice chmn. Miami Beach Redevel. Authority, 1978-82; mem. nat. jud. council Dem. Nat. Com., 1976-80; mem. State Fla. Containment Bd., 1986—; bd. dirs., v.p. corp. affairs Friends of the Art,

Lowe Gallery, Coral Gables, Fla., 1985—. Served with USAAF, 1943-45. Named Outstanding Alumni U. Fla., 1979. Mem. ABA, Fla. Bar Assn. Jewish. Club: Bankers, Jockey, City (Miami). Office: 2 S Biscayne Blvd Miami FL 33131

CASSELL, RICHARD EMMETT, lawyer; b. N.Y.C., Jan. 3, 1949; s. Max and Sylvia (Cohen) Cassell; m. Madeline Gail Erdman, June 13, 1970; children: Lori Faith, Marc Joshua. BA cum laude, SUNY, Buffalo, 1971; JD, Georgetown U., 1974. Bar: D.C. 1974, Va. 1974, Md. 1985. Assoc. Ira Lechner, Washington, 1974-75, Benson, Stien & Braunstien, Washington, 1975-85; sole practice Alexandria, Va., 1986—; Mem. Landlord-Tenant Commn., Arlington, 1974-76. Committeeperson Arlington Dems., 1973-76, Arlingtonians for Better County, 1973-76. Mem. ABA, Va. Bar Assn., D.C. Bar Assn., Md. Bar Assn. Personal injury, Workers' compensation, Family and matrimonial. Home: 7497 Covent Woods Ct Annandale VA 22003 Office: 1513 King St Alexandria VA 22314

CASSIDY, FRANK JOSEPH, lawyer; b. Stuttgart, Fed. Republic of Germany, June 15, 1958; came to U.S., 1959; s. John Patrick and Helen Irene (Remski) C.; m. Renee Marcia Johnson, Aug. 30, 1980; children: Brett, Megan, Kristin. BA in History, U. Ariz., 1979, JD, 1982. Bar: Ariz. 1982, U.S. Dist. Ct. Ariz. 1982. Spl. dep. Pima County Atty., Tucson, 1982; assoc. Basinger and Assocs. P.C., Scottsdale, Ariz., 1982-83; dep. Pima County Atty., Tucson, 1983-86; assoc. Winston & Strawn, Tucson, 1986—. Advisor Pima County Planning and Zoning Commn., Tucson, 1983-86, Pima County Bd. of Suprs., Tucson, 1985-86; choir dir. Holy Trinity Parish, Tucson, 1986—. Mem. ABA, Ariz. Bar Assn., Pima County Bar Assn. (chmn. speaker com. 1986—), Phi Delta Phi. Democrat. Roman Catholic. Avocations: vocalist, guitarist, runner. Real property, Government contracts and claims, Administrative and regulatory. Office: Winston & Strawn 5210 E Williams Circle Suite 600 Tucson AZ 85711

CASSIDY, PAUL DAVID, lawyer; b. Portsmouth, Ohio, Oct. 1, 1930; s. James A. and Ethel Cassidy; divorced; children: James P., Heather Fawn. Student, U. Cin., 1948, Marshall Coll., 1950; BS, Ohio State U., 1956, JD, 1958. Bar: Ohio 1958, Calif. 1974, U.S. Dist. Ct. (so. dist.) Ohio 1959, U.S. Supreme Ct. 1973, U.S. Ct. Appeals (6th cir.) 1974. Sole practice Columbus, Ohio, 1958—; commr. Ohio Pub. Defender, Columbus, 1977-83; spl. counsel Ohio Atty. Gen., Columbus, 1971-74. Served with USAF, 1950-51, 1st lt. U.S. Army, 1951-53. Mem. ABA, Calif. Bar Assn., Ohio Bar Assn., Columbus Bar Assn., Franklin County Trial Lawyers Assn., Nat. Assn. Criminal Def. Lawyers. Criminal. Home: 1000 Urlin Ave Columbus OH 43212 Office: 503 S High St Columbus OH 43215

CASSIDY, RICHARD THOMAS, lawyer; b. Rutland, Vt., July 13, 1953; s. Paul Patrick Cassidy and Sarah Hellen Jackson; m. Rebecca Hellen Burr, Dec. 21, 1974. BA, U. Vt., 1975; JD, Albany Law Sch., 1978. Bar: N.Y. 1979, Vt. 1979, U.S. Dist. Ct. (no. dist.) N.Y. 1979, U.S. Dist. Ct. Vt. 1979. Law clk. to assoc. justice Vt. Supreme Ct., Montpelier, 1978-79, chief law clk., 1979-80; com. counsel Vt. Supreme Ct.'s spl. study on bar admissions and continuing legal edn., Montpelier, 1982, standing adv. com. bar admissions and continuing legal competence 1982-84. Mem. ABA, Vt. Bar Assn., Chittenden County Bar Assn. Democrat. Avocations: swimming, windsurfing, skiing. State civil litigation, Personal injury, Federal civil litigation. Home: 39 Laurel Hill Dr South Burlington VT 05401 Office: Hoff Wilson Powell and Lang PO Box 567 Burlington VT 05402-0567

CASSIDY, WILLIAM ANTHONY, lawyer; b. Cleve., June 13, 1953; s. James Thomas and Ruth Ann (Von Franzke) C.; m. Bonnie Szymoniak, Sept. 8, 1984. BS in Polit. Sci., Kenyon Coll., 1975; JD, Cleve. State U., 1980. Bar: Ohio 1981, U.S. Dist. Ct. (no. dist.) Ohio 1983, U.S. Ct. Appeals (6th cir.) 1984, U.S. Supreme Ct. 1984. From caseworker to dept. head Cuyahoga County Welfare Dept., Cleve., 1975-80; congl. aide Congressman Charles A. Vanik, Washington, 1980-81; adult services coordinator United Steelworkers Am., Cleve., 1981; asst. county prosecutor criminal div. Cuyahoga County, 1981-84, 86—; law dir., pros. Cuyahoga County, North Ridgeville, Ohio, 1984-86; asst. county pros. Cuyahoga County, North Ridgeville, 1986—. Contbr. polit. satire articles to newspapers. Coach youth swimming, baseball, softball; mem. subcom. on child abuse and child pornography Law Enforcement Coordinating Com. for No. Dist. Ohio. Mem. ABA, Ohio Bar Assn., Assn. Trial Lawyers Am. Democrat. Roman Catholic. Avocations: acting, swimming. Child pornography, State civil litigation, Federal civil litigation. Home: 32749 Brookstone Ln North Ridgeville OH 44039 Office: Cuyahoga County Prosecutor's Office 1200 Ontario 9th Floor Cleveland OH 44113

CASSIMATIS, EMANUEL ANDREW, county court judge; b. Pottsville, Pa., Dec. 2, 1926; s. Andrew Emanuel and Mary H. (Calopedis) C.; m. Thecla Karambelas, June 2, 1952; children—Mary Ann Maza, John E., Gregory E. B.A., Dickinson Coll., 1949, LL.B., 1951. Bar: Pa. 1951. Sole practice law, York, Pa., 1951-53, 55-57; assoc. Kain, Kain & Kain, York, Pa., 1953-55; ptnr. Stock & Leader, York, 1957-78; judge Ct. Common Pleas, York, Pa., 1978—; solicitor Springettsbury Twp., York, Pa., 1960-66, Sewer Authority, 1965-66; solicitor Wrightsville Borough, Pa., 1966-71, Municipal Authority, 1968-78, York Suburban Sch. Dist., 1970-77; faculty Pa. Coll. Judiciary, 1981, 82, 83; 2d v.p. Pa. Conf. State Trial Judges, 1986—. Pres. United Way of York County, 1964-65; co-chmn. steering com. York Community Audit for Human Rights, 1959; pres. Children's Growth and Devel. Clinic, 1974; trustee Meml. Osteopathic Hosp., 1963-80; bd. dirs. Capital Blue Cross, Harrisburg, Pa., 1970-79, Historic York, 1977-82. Served with U.S. Army, 1945-46. Named Young Man of Yr., York Jr. C. of C., 1960; Vol. of Yr., Pilot Club, 1965; Mem. Hall of Fame, William Penn Sr. High Sch., York, 1981. Mem. Pa. Conf. State Trial Judges (chmn. spl. projects com. 1980-82, ann. meeting com. 1984-85, 1st v.p. Juvenile Ct. sect. 1986—. Republican. Greek Orthodox. Lodges: Masons (hon. mem. supreme council), K.T., Tall Cedars of Lebanon, Shriners, Royal Order Jesters. Juvenile, Judicial administration. Home: 176 Rathton Rd York PA 17403

CASSIN, WILLIAM BOURKE, lawyer; b. Mexico City, Mexico, Sept. 11, 1931; s. William Michael and Elouise (Hall) C.; m. Kristi Shipnes, July 15, 1961; children: Clay Brian, Michael Bourke, Macy Armstrong. A.B., Princeton U., 1953; J.D., U. Tex., 1959. Bar: Tex. 1959. Law clk. Judge Warren L. Jones, Fifth Circuit U.S., 1959-60; atty. Baker & Botts, Houston, 1960-70; v.p., gen. atty. United Gas Pipe Line Co., Houston, 1970-73; sr. v.p., gen. atty. United Gas Pipe Line Co., 1973, group v.p., gen. counsel, dir., mem. exec. com., 1974-76; exec. v.p., gen. counsel, mem. exec. com. United Energy Resources, Inc., Houston, 1976-84, dir., 1976-86; of counsel Mayer, Brown & Platt, Houston, 1985—; Gen. counsel Houston Grand Opera Assn., 1961-70, mem. governing council, 1977—, also bd. dirs. Contbr. articles to profl. jours.; editor-in-chief Tex. Law Rev, 1959. Gen. counsel Harris County Republican Exec. Com., 1963-64, 67-68; exec. vp. Tex. Bill Rights Found., 1967-68; mem. exec. com. Associated Reps. of Tex., 1976—, Landmark Legal Found., 1985—, Armand Bayou Nature Ctr., 1986—; bd. dirs. Houston Ballet Found., Legal Found. Am.; trustee Tex. Mil. Inst., Atwill Meml. Chapel; mem. vestry Christ Ch. Cathedral, 1970-72, 80-82. Served to lt. Airborne Arty. AUS, 1953-57; capt. Res. ret. Fellow Tex. Bar Found. (life); mem. Am., Tex., Houston, Fed. Energy, Fed. bar assns., Order of Coif, Phi Delta Phi. Republican. Episcopalian. Clubs: Houston Country, Houston Met. Racquet, Bayou, Ramada, Houston Polo, Texas, Allegro, Garwood Hunting; Argyle (San Antonio); Army and Navy (Washington); Northport Point (Mich.); Princeton (N.Y.C.); Princeton Terrace. Administrative and regulatory, General corporate, FERC practice. Home: 1 S Wynden Dr Houston TX 77056 Office: Suite 3600 Republic Bank Center Houston TX 77002

CASSITY, JAMES JUNIOR, lawyer; b. Ogden, Utah, Nov. 3, 1953; s. Junior Thatcher and Phyllis (Wilson) C.; m. Sherri Lynne Taylor, May 21, 1976; children: Jamie, Robert, Shelly, Tammy. BA, Weber State Coll., 1978; JD, U. Idaho, 1981. Bar: Utah 1981, U.S. Dist. Ct. Utah 1981, U.S. Ct. Appeals (10th cir.) 1984. Bus. communication instr. Stevens-Henager Jr. Coll. Bus., Ogden, 1981-82; bus. law instr. Weber State Coll., Ogden, 1981-83; asst. atty. gen. Utah Atty. Gens. Office, Salt Lake City, 1982-83; litigation atty. Kirton, McConkie & Bushnell, Salt Lake City, 1983—; gen. counsel Utah Ind. Telephone Assn., Salt Lake City, 1984-86, Exchange Carriers of Utah, Salt Lake City, 1986—. Editor notes and comments Idaho Law Rev., 1980-81. Named one of Outstanding Young Men in Am., 1983. Mem. ABA, Utah Bar Assn., Am. Soc. Writers of Legal Subjects (SCRIBES award 1981). Mormon. Avocations: fishing, camping, reading, writing, collections. Administrative and regulatory, Contracts commercial, State civil litigation. Home: 574 S 250 East Kaysville UT 84037 Office: Kirton McConkie & Bushnell 330 S Third East Salt Lake City UT 84111

CASSON, JOSEPH EDWARD, lawyer; b. N.Y.C., May 24, 1943; s. Joseph Raymond and Dorothy Patricia (Kearney) C.; m. Susan Jane Greenberg, July 25, 1970; 1 dau., Jessica Kendall. B.A. in history, Fairfield U., 1965; J.D., Georgetown U., 1968, LL.M., 1969. Bar: D.C. 1969. Spl. asst. to undersec. U.S. Dept. Commerce, 1969-70, exec. asst. to sec., 1970-72; cons. Cost of Living Council, Washington, 1972; alt. U.S. Pay Bd., Washington, 1972; assoc. Arent, Fox, Kintner, Plotkin & Kahn, Washington, 1972-74, ptnr. 1974-78; adj. prof. Georgetown Law Center, 1970-71, 77-78; sr. ptnr. Casson, Calligaro & Mutryn, Washington, 1978—. Pres. Woods Homeowners Assn. 1980-85. Fegan fellow 1968-69. Mem. ABA, Sup. Ct. Bar Assn. Republican. Contbr. in field. Health, Antitrust, Oil and gas leasing. Home: 9425 Wooden Bridge Rd Potomac MD 20854 Office: 1233 20th St NW Suite 800 Washington DC 20036

CASSON, RICHARD FREDERICK, corporation executive, travel bureau executive; b. Boston, Apr. 11, 1939; s. Louis H. and Beatrix S. C. A.B., Colby Coll., 1960; J.D., U. Chgo., 1963. Bar: Ill. 1963, Mass. 1964. Ptnr., Casson & Casson, Boston, 1967-68; assoc. counsel, corporate sec. Bankers Leasing Corp., 1968-75; asst. gen. counsel, corporate sec. Commonwealth Planning Corp., 1975-76; assoc. gen. counsel, asst. sec. Pru Capital, Inc., 1976—; ptnr. Cities of Sea Cruise Cen., Travel Agency . Bd. dirs. Children's Speech and Hearing Found., Temple Ahavath Achim, Gloucester, Mass. Served to capt. JAGC U.S. Army, 1964-67. Decorated Bronze Star. Jewish. Club: B'nai B'rith (Gloucester) (v.p.). Contracts commercial, General corporate, Nuclear power. Address: Off Lowe Dr Magnolia MA 01930

CASTAGNA, WILLIAM JOHN, U.S. district judge; b. Phila., June 25, 1924; s. Charles and Ninetta C.; m. Carolyn Ann Spoto, Sept. 1, 1954; children—Charles N., William D., Lisa Ann, Catherine Alice. Student, U. Pa., 1941-43; LL.B., J.D., U. Fla., 1949. Bar: Fla. 1949. Practice in Morehead, Pallot & Forrest, Miami, 1949-50; practice in Clearwater, 1951-53, 54-65, 69; mem. Castagna, Satterfield & Stamathis, 1951-53, Castagna & Korones, 1965-68; ptnr. firm MacKenzie, Castagna, Bennison & Gardner, 1970-79; U.S. dist. judge Middle Dist. Fla., 1979—. Served with USAAF, 1943-45. Mem. ABA, Fed. Bar Assn., Am. Trial Lawyers Assn., Am. Judicature Soc., Fla. State Bar (bd. govs., seminar lectr.), Acad. Fla. Trial Lawyers, Clearwater Bar Assn. (pres. 1965). Democrat. Lodge: Masons. Jurisprudence. Office: PO Box 3424 Tampa FL 33601

CASTAÑO, SYLVIA ELIZABETH, lawyer; b. Bakersfield, Calif., Feb. 2, 1953; d. John R. and Loretta M. (McCutcheon) C.; m. Kenneth R. Cox, June 17, 1979. BA, U. Redlands, 1975; MLS, U. Ill., 1976; JD, U. Houston, 1982. Bar: Tex. 1982, U.S. Dist. Ct. (so. dist.) Tex. 1984, U.S. Ct. Appeals (5th cir.) 1984. Law clk. to presiding justice U.S. Dist. Ct. (so. dist.) Tex., Houston, 1982-84; reference librarian U. Houston Law Ctr., 1980-82, dir. communications, 1984-86. Mem. ABA, ALA, Am. Library Assn., Southwestern Assn. Law Libraries, Tex. Bar Assn. Lutheran. Legal education, Librarianship. Office: U Houston Law Ctr Houston TX 77004

CASTEL, P. KEVIN, lawyer; b. N.Y.C., Aug. 5, 1950; s. Peter A. and Mildred (Cronin) C.; m. Patricia A. McLernon; 1 child, Jeanne Margaret. BS, St. John's U., Jamaica, N.Y., 1972, JD, 1975. Bar: N.Y. 1976, U.S. Dist. Ct. (so. and ea. dists.) N.Y. 1976, U.S. Ct. Appeals (2d cir.) 1979, U.S. Ct. Appeals (fed. cir.) 1985, U.S. Supreme Ct. 1986. Law clk. to judge U.S. Dist. Ct. (so. dist.) N.Y., 1975-77; assoc. Cahill Gordon & Reindel, N.Y.C., 1977-83; ptnr. Cahill, Gordon & Reindel, N.Y.C., 1983—. Mem. N.Y. State Bar Assn. (com. on cts. of appellate jurisdiction 1979-86, com. fed. cts. 1986—), Fed. Bar Council (sec. 1983-85, trustee 1985—, chmn. publs. com. 1984—), Assn. of Bar of City of N.Y., N.Y. County Lawyers Assn. Federal civil litigation, State civil litigation. Office: Cahill Gordon & Reindel 80 Pine St New York NY 10005

CASTELLO, RAYMOND VINCENT, lawyer; b. San Jose, Calif., Apr. 25, 1939; s. Joseph V. and Josephine M. (Gallina) C.; m. W. Karla Grusonik, July 29, 1963; children: Joseph W., Julie A. BS, Calif. State U., San Jose, 1961; JD, Stanford U., 1964. Bar: Calif. 1965, U.S. Dist. Ct. (no. dist.) Calif. 1965, U.S. Ct. Appeals (9th cir.) 1965, U.S. Supreme Ct. 1976. Sole practice Campbell, Calif., 1965-68; ptnr. Finch, Castello & Tennant, Campbell, 1968-78, Castello, Daily & Gerbino, Campbell, 1978—; gen. ptnr. Castello, Marino & Orr, Tracy, Calif., 1963—, Castello Farms, Tracy, 1963—, Castello Properties, San Jose, 1975—, Teresi & Castello, San Jose, 1985—. Coach Police Athletic League, San Jose, 1973-83; pres. Dry Creek Community Assn., San Jose, 1975—. Mem. Calif. Bar Assn., Santa Clara County Bar Assn. (trustee 1973-80), West Valley Bar Assn. (pres. 1973), Am. Arbitrary Assn., Phi Alpha Delta. Club: Civic of Santa Clara County (San Jose) (pres. 1982-84). Lodge: Rotary (bd. dirs. Campbell club 1966-74). State civil litigation, Personal injury, Probate. Office: Castello Daily & Gerbino 1790 Winchester Blvd #1 Campbell CA 95008

CASTERLINE, CECIL W., lawyer; b. Rockport, Tex., Dec. 31, 1938; s. Cecil Weber and Mildred (Olney) C.; children—Cheryl, Scott. B.A. in English, Baylor U., 1961, LL.B., 1966. Bar: Tex. 1967, U.S. Supreme Ct. 1976. Atty. Kleberg-Mobley, Corpus Christi, 1967-69, Lee, Douglass, Pletcher & Casterline, Dallas, 1969-75; ptnr. Shank, Irwin, Conant, Lipshy & Casterline, Dallas, 1975—; briefing atty. Tex. Supreme Ct., 1966-67; lectr. Wills and Probate Inst., Southwestern Legal Found. Mem. Assn. Trial Lawyers Am. Republican. Methodist. Club: Baylor Bear (pres. 1975-76). Editor-in-chief Baylor Law Rev., 1965-66. Federal civil litigation, State civil litigation, Antitrust. Office: 4100 Thanksgiving Tower Dallas TX 75202

CASTILLO, HAL STEPHEN, lawyer; b. Jacksonville, Fla., July 21, 1947; s. Cleveland and Gladys C. (Wood) C.; children: Laurie L., Hal Stephen Jr. BBA, Ga. State U., 1969; JD, Emory U., 1974. Bar: Ga. 1974, Fla. 1974, U.S. Dist. Ct. (mid. dist.) Fla. 1974, U.S. Supreme Ct. 1979. Asst. pub. defender 4th Jud. Cir., Jacksonville, 1974-75; assoc. Blalock, Holbrook, Lewis, Paul & Isaac P.A., Jacksonville, 1975-77; ptnr. Lewis, Paul, Isaac & Castillo P.A., Jacksonville, 1977—. Mem. ABA, Jacksonville Bar Assn., Am. Acad. Trial Lawyers, Fla. Acad. Trial Lawyers, Jacksonville Trial Lawyers Assn. Lodge: Sertoma (pres. South Jacksonville dist. 1978-79, lt. gov. Northeast Jacksonville dist. 1984-86). State civil litigation, Personal injury, Criminal. Office: Lewis Paul Isaac & Castillo PA 2468 Atlantic Blvd Jacksonville FL 32207

CASTLE, JOHN RAYMOND, JR., lawyer; b. Longview, Tex., Jan. 6, 1943; s. John R. Sr. and Laverne (Luna) C.; m. Dorothy Renshaw, Sept. 4, 1965; 1 child, Amy Elizabeth. Student, So. Meth. U., 1961-62; BA, U. Tex., 1964, LLB, 1967. Bar: Tex. 1967. Ptnr. Geary, Brice, Barron & Stahl, Dallas, 1967-73, Hughes & Luce, Dallas, 1974—. Mem. ABA, Tex. Bar Assn., Dallas Bar Assn., U. Tex. Law Sch. Assn. (pres. 1983-84, bd. dirs.). Democrat. Methodist. General corporate, Real property, Banking. Home: 10474 Epping Ln Dallas TX 75229 Office: Hughes & Luce 1500 United Bank Tower Austin TX 78701

CASTO, KEITH MICHAEL, lawyer; b. Columbus, Ohio, Aug. 5, 1947; s. David Russell and Evelyn Ruth (Dunlap) C.; m. Kristen Copes, June 7, 1969; children: Kristopher Michael, Timothy Lucas. BA, Stetson U., 1969, JD, 1973. Bar: Fla. 1973, U.S. Dist. Ct. (mid. dist.) Fla. 1973, U.S. Ct. Appeals (5th cir.) 1973, Ga. 1976, U.S. Dist. Ct. (no. dist.) Ga. 1976, U.S. Ct. Appeals (11th cir.) 1983. Law clk. to presiding justice U.S. Dist. Ct. (mid. dist.) Fla., Jacksonville, 1973-75; atty. Office of Regional Counsel U.S. EPA, Atlanta, 1975-85; assoc. Troutman, Sanders, Lockerman & Ashmore, Atlanta, 1985—; asst. prof. law Stetson U., St. Petersburg, 1978-79; adj. prof. law Emory U., 1987—. Co-author: Environmental Health, 1985. Fellow Environ. Law Inst.; mem. ABA. Environment, Administrative and regulatory. Home: 3920 Garfield Dr Stone Mountain GA 30083 Office: Troutman Sanders Lockerman & Ashmore 1400 Candler Bldg 127 Peachtree St NE Atlanta GA 30043

CASTRO, LEONARD EDWARD, lawyer; b. Los Angeles, Mar. 18, 1934; s. Emil Galvez and Lily (Meyers) C.; 1 son, Stephen Paul. A.B., UCLA, 1959, J.D., 1962. Bar: Calif. 1963, U.S. Supreme Ct. 1970. Assoc. Musick, Peeler & Garrett, Los Angeles, 1962-68, ptnr., 1968—. Mem. ABA, Internat. Bar Assn., Los Angeles County Bar Assn. Banking, General corporate, Private international. Office: Musick Peeler & Garrett 1 Wilshire Blvd Suite 2000 Los Angeles CA 90017

CASTRO, RAUL HECTOR, lawyer, former ambassador, former governor of Arizona; b. Cananea, Mexico, June 12, 1916; came to U.S., 1926, naturalized, 1939; s. Francisco D. and Rosario (Acosta) C.; m. Patricia M. Norris, Nov. 13, 1954; children—Mary Pat, Beth. B.A., Ariz. State Coll., 1939; J.D., U. Ariz., 1949; LL.D. (hon.), No. Ariz. U., 1966, Ariz. State U., 1972, U. Autonoma de Guadalajara, Mex. Bar: Ariz. bar 1949. Fgn. service clk. Dept. State, Agua Prieta, Mexico, 1941-46; instr. Spanish U. Ariz., 1946-49; practiced in Tucson, 1949-51; dep. county atty. Pima County, Ariz., 1951-54; county atty. 1954-58; judge Superior Ct., Tucson, 1958-64, Juvenile Ct., Tucson, 1961-64; U.S. ambassador to El Salvador, San Salvador, 1964-68, to Bolivia, La Paz, 1968-69; practice internat. law Tucson, 1969-74, Phoenix, 1980—; gov. Ariz., 1975-77; U.S. ambassador to Argentina, 1977-80; operator Castro Pony Farm, 1954-64. Pres. Pima County Tb and Health Assn., Tucson Youth Bd., Ariz. Horseman's Assn.; Bd. dirs. Tucson chpt. A.R.C., Tucson council Boy Scouts Am., Tucson YMCA, Nat. Council Christians and Jews, YWCA Camp; Bd. Mem. Ariz. N.G., 1935-39. Recipient Outstanding Naturalized Citizen award Pima County Bar Assn., 1964, Outstanding Am. Citizen award D.A.R., 1964; Pub. Service award U. Ariz., 1966; John F. Kennedy medal Kennedy U., Buenos Aires. Mem. Am. Fgn. Service Assn., Am. Judicature Soc., Inter-Am. Bar Assn., Ariz. Bar Assn., Pima County Bar Assn., Nat. Council Crime and Deliquency (bd. dirs.), Assn. Trial Lawyers Am., Council Am. Ambassadors, Nat. Assn. Trial Judges, Nat. Council Juvenile Ct. Judges, Fed. Bar Assn., Nat. Lawyers Club, Phi Alpha Delta. Democrat. Roman Catholic. Club: Rotarian. Immigration, naturalization, and customs, Private international, Public international. Office: 3030 E Camelback Rd Suite 250 Phoenix AZ 85016

CASTRO, ROBERT C., lawyer; b. Oak Park, Ill., June 4, 1956; s. Anthony J. Castro and Barbara Ann (Clark) Hayes; m. Anita Jo Billow, Aug. 19, 1978; children: Rebekah Nancy, Timothy Michael. BA, Wittenberg U., 1978; JD, U. Wis., 1981. Bar: Wis. 1981, U.S. Dist. Ct. (we. dist.) Wis. 1981, U.S. Dist. Ct. (ea. dist.) Wis. 1982. Assoc. Callahan & Arnold, Columbus, Wis., 1981-86, John J. McLario, Menomonee Falls, Wis., 1986—. Vol. track coach Columbus High Sch., 1979-86; chmn. St. Jude's Bike-a-thon, 1985. Named Man of Yr., Columbus High Sch., 1985. Mem. Am. Assn. Trial Lawyers, Wis. Acad. Trial Lawyers. Lutheran. Avocations: triathalons, hunting, fishing. Family and matrimonial, Juvenile, Personal injury. Home: N 90 W 17087 Appleton Ave Menomonee Falls WI 53051 Home: 413 Parkview Dr Columbus WI 53925 Office: Law Offices of John J. McLario Main St Menomonee Falls WI 53051

CASWELL, PAULETTE REVA, lawyer; b. Chgo., June 8, 1951; d. Ben and Lillian (Cohen) Watstein; m. Michael Evidson, May 15, 1975 (div. Mar. 1979); 1 child, David Allan Philip; m. Charles Frank Caswell, III, Jan. 8, 1983. A.A., West Los Angeles Community Coll., 1971; B.A., Calif. State U.-Los Angeles, 1975; J.D., Whittier Coll., 1982; D.D. (hon.), St. Alban's Coll., San Francisco, 1974. Bar: Calif. 1982, U.S. Dist. Ct. (cen. dist.) Calif., 1983. Dir., Mensa of Los Angeles, 1977-83; sole practice, Los Angeles, 1982—; dir., founder Amicus, Los Angeles Area Ctr. Law and the Deaf; cons. Editor: Consumer Rights, 1982; author legal articles pamphlets, booklets. Legal adv. Ind. Living Ctrs.; adv. for deaf and visually-impaired. Mem. ABA, Los Angeles County Bar Assn., Legal Assistance Assn. Calif., State Bar Calif., Arts. Democrat. Jewish. General practice, Legal services pro bono, Administrative and regulatory. Home: 645 N Gardner St Los Angeles CA 90036-5712

CASWELL, ROGER LEE, lawyer; b. Cheboygan, Mich., Mar. 9, 1947; s. Merle Lee and Catherine C. (Peppler) C.; m. Carol Marie Leffler, May 10, 1975. BS, Cen. Mich. U., Mt. Pleasant, 1969; JD, Ohio No. U., Ada, 1975. Bar: Mich. 1975, U.S. Dist. Ct. (ea. and we. dists.) Mich. 1977. Asst. pros. atty., chief civil counsel Calhoun County, Marshall, Mich., 1975-78; sole practice Caswell, Moore & Marsh, Albion, 1978—. Guest columnist for Albion newspaper, 1981—. V.p. Albion Pub. Schs. Bd. Edn., 1979—; bd. dirs. Southcentral Mich. Legal Services Orgn., 1982—; Albion Econ. Devel. Corp., 1983—. Served to sgt. U.S. Army, 1969-71. Mem. State Bar of Mich., Calhoun County Bar Assn., Am. Legion. Roman Catholic. Club: Leisure Hour (Albion) (pres. 1979, 84). Lodge: Elks. Avocations: reading, music, golf, fishing. General practice, State civil litigation, Criminal. Home: 208 E North St Albion MI 49224 Office: Caswell Moore & Marsh 1601 E Michigan Ave Albion MI 49224

CATALANO, MICHAEL WILLIAM, lawyer; b. Jackson, Miss., Apr. 6, 1954; s. Paul John and Doris Maxine (Windham) C.; m. Peggy Jean Nance, Mar. 19, 1978. BA, Memphis State U., 1976; JD, U. Tenn., 1978. Bar: Tenn. 1979. Atty. for exec. sec. Tenn. Supreme Ct., Nashville, 1979-80; asst. atty. gen. State of Tenn., Nashville, 1980-85, dep. atty. gen., 1985—. Mem. Nat. Bar Assn., Tenn. Bar Assn., Nashville Bar Assn. Democrat. Methodist. Personal injury, State civil litigation, Legislative reapportionment. Home: 1505 Grandview Dr Nashville TN 37215 Office: Tenn Atty Gen 450 James Robertson Pkwy Nashville TN 37219

CATALFO, ALFRED (ALFIO), JR., lawyer; b. Lawrence, Mass., Jan. 31, 1920; s. Alfio and Viencenza (Amato) C.; m. Caroline Joanne Mosca (dec. Apr. 1968); children—Alfred Thomas, Carol Joanne, Gina Marie. B.A., U. N.H., 1945, M.A. in History, 1952; LL.B., Boston U., 1947, J.D. (hon.), 1969; postgrad., Suffolk U. Sch. Law, 1955-56, Am. Law Inst., N.Y.C., 1959. Bar: N.H. 1947, U.S. Dist. Ct. 1948, U.S. Ct. Appeals 1978, U.S. Supreme Ct. 1979. Sole practice law Dover, N.H., 1948—; county atty. Strafford County, Dover, N.H., 1949-50, 55-56; mem. bd. Immigration Appeals, U.S. Dept. Justice, 1953—; football coach Berwick Acad., South Berwick, Maine, 1944, Mission Catholic High Sch., Roxbury, Mass., 1945-46. Author: Laws of Divorces, Marriages, and Separations in New Hampshire, 1962, History of the Town of Rollinsford, 1623-1973, 1973. Pres. Young Democrats of Dover, 1953-55; 1st vice-chmn. Young Dems., N.H., 1954-56; mem. Strafford County Dem. com., 1948-75; vice chmn. N.H. Dem. com., 1954-56, 1st chmn., 1956-58, chmn. spl. activities, 1958-60; del. Dem. Nat. Conv., 1956, 60, 76; chmn. N.H. Dem. Conv., 1958, conv. dir., 1960; mem. Dem. state exec. com., 1960-70; Dem. nominee for US Senate, 1962; vice chmn. Dover Cath. Sch. Com., 1969-71; mem. Dover Bd. Adjustment, 1960-65. Served as pilot AC, USN, 1942-44; lt. comdr. USNR. Recipient keys to cities of Dover, Somersworth, Concord, Berlin and Manchester, N.H.; 4 nat. plaques DAV; 3 disting. service awards Am. Legion; Am. Legion Life Membership award; spl. recognition award Berwick Acad., 1985. Mem. ABA, N.H. Bar Assn., Strafford County Bar Assn. (v.p. 1966-69, pres. 1968-69), Assn. Trial Lawyers Assn., N.Y. State Trial Lawyers Assn., Mass. Trial Lawyers Assn., Tex. Trial Lawyers Assn., Nat. Assn. Criminal Def. Lawyers, Am. Judicature Soc., Phi Delta Phi, DAV (judge adv. N.H. dept. 1950-56, 57-68, 72—; comdr. chpt. 1953-54, comdr. N.H. 1956-57), Am. Legion (chmn. state conv. 1967, 77, 84), Navy League, N.H. Hist. Soc., Dover Hist. Soc., Rollinsford Hist. Soc. Clubs: Eagles (Somersworth, N.H.); Sons of Italy (Portsmouth, N.H.). Lodges: Lions, Elks, K.C. (grand knight 1975-77), Moose, Lebanese (Dover). Criminal, Personal injury, General practice. Home: 20 Arch St Dover NH 03820 Office: 450 Central Ave Dover NH 03820

CATANZANO, RAYMOND AUGUSTINE, lawyer; b. Bklyn., Sept. 16, 1946; s. Raymond E. and Ruth M. (Powers) C.; m. Lucille M. Rotondo, Mar. 29, 1970; children—Kimberly, Tara. BS St. Johns U., 1968, JD, 1973; LLM London Sch. Econs. 1985. Bar: N.Y. 1974, U.S. Dist. Ct. (ea. dist.) N.Y. 1974, U.S. Ct. Appeals (2d cir.) 1975, U.S. Supreme Ct. 1978. Prof. law Nassau Community Coll., Garden City, N.Y., 1973—; sole practice Elmont, N.Y., 1974—. Dir. real estate studies Nassau Community Coll., 1981—; referee Med. Malpractice Panel Supreme Ct. N.Y., 1983. Author: Student Course Mastery Guide, 1984. Recipient Holt Rinehart and Winston Honorarium award, 1979; named to Men of Achievement, Cambridge, Eng., 1986. Mem. ABA, N.Y. State Bar Assn., Bar Assn. Nassau County, Roman Catholic. Committeeman, Elmont North Republican Club, 1974-76. Contracts commercial, General corporate, Real property. Office: Raymond A Catanzano 220 Litchfield Ave Elmont NY 11003

CATES, C. BRAD, lawyer; b. Mt. Vernon, Ill., Apr. 20, 1950; s. Charles R. Lane and Jean (Starwalt) C.; m. Nancy Wright, June 26, 1981. BBA in Mgmt., N.Mex. State U., 1972; JD, U. N.Mex., 1975. Bar: N.Mex. 1975, U.S. Supreme Ct. 1980. Legislator N.Mex. Ho. of Reps., Santa Fe, 1975-82; sole practice Albuquerque, 1978-79; atty. Ranchers Exploration Corp., Albuquerque, 1979-80; spl. counsel to adminstr. EPA, Washington, 1981-83; dir. asset forfeitures U.S. Dept. of Justice, Washington, 1983—; mem. law and justice com. Nat. Conf. State Legislators, Washington, 1978-81; bd. dirs. Am. Legis. Exchange Council, Washington, 1979-84. Nat. committeeman N.Mex. Young Reps., 1975-79, mem. exec. com., 1979-80; vice chmn. judiciary com. N.Mex. Ho. of Reps., 1979-81. Mem. Sigma Chi. Criminal, Environment, Real property. Home: Box 16002 Station G Albuquerque NM 87191 Office: US Dept of Justice Dir Asset Forfeiture Office Washington DC 20530

CATES, JENNIFER ANN, lawyer; b. Providence, Feb. 22, 1956; d. John Stephen McKnight and Mary Morrison; m. Howard Claran Cates, June 8, 1980. BA in Polit. Sci., Oakland U., 1976; JD, U. Okla., 1980. Bar: Okla. 1980, U.S. Ct. Appeals (5th, 10th, 11th and D.C. cirs.) 1981, U.S. Supreme Ct. 1983, U.S. Ct. Appeals (8th cir.) 1985, U.S. Dist. Ct. (no. dist.) Okla. 1986. Atty. Phillips Petroleum Co., Bartlesville, Okla., 1980—; Mem. legal subcom. Offshore Operators, 1983—. Editor U. Okla. Law Rev., 1978-80. Pres., adv. council Retired Sr. Vol. Program, Bartlesville, 1982—; bd. dirs. Bluestem Girl Scout Council, Bartlesville, 1982—, SunFest, Inc., Bartlesville, 1984—. Named one of Outstanding Young Women in Am., 1984. Mem. ABA (royalty task force 1983), Okla. Bar Assn., Washington County Bar Assn., Fed. Energy Bar Assn., Am. Petroleum Inst. (royalty task force 1983—), Phi Alpha Delta, Pilot Internat. (coordinator 1985—). Avocations: French, art history, tennis, weaving. Administrative and regulatory, FERC practice, Oil and gas leasing. Home: 630 Kenwood Dr Bartlesville OK 74006-8222 Office: Phillips Petroleum Co 1254 Adams Bldg Bartlesville OK 74004

CATES, RONALD DEAN, lawyer; b. Tulsa, Aug. 25, 1955; s. Medwin Adams and Bessie Jane (Dykes) C.; m. Nancy Haven Howe, May 8, 1982. BS, Okla. State U., 1977; JD, Tulsa U., 1980. Bar: Okla. 1980, U.S. Dist. (no. dist.) Okla. 1980, U.S. Dist. Ct. (we. dist.) Okla. 1983. Assoc. Boyd & Parks, Tulsa, 1980-81, ptnr., 1981-82; sole practice Tulsa, 1982-84; ptnr. Boyd, Nichols & Cates, Tulsa, 1985—. Mem. ABA, Assn. Trial Lawyers Am., Okla. Bar Assn., Okla. Trial Lawyers Assn., Phi Delta Phi, Pi Sigma Alpha. Democrat. Baptist. Avocations: gardening, fishing, swimming. Local government, Labor, Contracts commercial. Home and Office: 111 W 5th St Suite 800 Tulsa OK 74102

CATHCART, PATRICK ALAN, lawyer; b. Palo Alto, Calif., Sept. 28, 1945; s. Arthur James and Martelle Henrietta (Leeper) C.; m. Ruth Winifred, Nov. 9, 1968 (div. 1980); 1 child, Alice Marie; m. Joan Fisher Fornaciari, May 16, 1981; children: Robert William, Anne Louise. AB, Stanford U., 1968; JD, U. Calif., San Francisco, 1975. Bar: Calif. 1975, U.S. Dist. Ct. (no. dist.) Calif. 1975, U.S. Ct. Appeals (9th cir.) 1975, U.S. Supreme Ct. 1980. Law clk. to presiding judge U.S. Dist. Ct. Calif., San Francisco, 1975-77; assoc. Morrison & Foerster, San Francisco, 1977-79; ptnr. Hancock, Rothert & Bunshoft, San Francisco, 1979—. Trustee French-Am. Sch., Berkeley, Calif., 1984-86. Mem. ABA (fed. cts. com. 1978-83), Calif. Bar Assn. (fed. cts. com. 1978-81). Club: St. Francis Yacht (San Francisco). State civil litigation, Federal civil litigation, Private international. Home: 5844 Margarido Dr Oakland CA 94618 Office: Hancock Rothert & Bunshoft 4 Embarcadero Ctr 10th Floor San Francisco CA 94111

CATLIN, HAROLD HARVEY, lawyer; b. Jacksonville, Fla., Apr. 29, 1949; s. Sam Marshall and Marcy Jean (Harvey) C.; m. Juliana Claire Mikulas, Apr. 1, 1978; children: Hampton Harvey, Davis Marshall. BA, Washington and Lee U., 1972; MBA, U. North Fla., 1973; JD, Mercer U., 1976. Bar: Ga. 1976, Fla. 1976, U.S. Dist. Ct. (no. and mid. dists.) Fla. 1976, U.S. Dist. Ct. (no. and mid. dists.) Ga. 1976, U.S. Dist. Ct. (so. dist.) Ga. 1979, U.S. Ct. Appeals (5th and 11th cirs.) 1981. Assoc. Marks, Gray, Conroy & Gibbs, Jacksonville, 1976-77; from assoc. to ptnr. Howell, Liles, Braddock & Milton, Jacksonville, 1977—. Mem. citizens com. Downtown People Mover, Jacksonville, 1980; chmn. com. Cummer Art Gallery Ball and Auction, Jacksonville, 1986—. Mem. Fla. Bar Assn., Jacksonville Bar Assn. (bd. govs. 1984—, pres. young lawyers sect. 1984), Jacksonville Assn. Def. Counsel (treas. 1985, sec. 1986—). Republican. Methodist. Clubs: Timuquana Country, The River (Jacksonville). Avocations: golf, swimming, gardening. Insurance, Personal injury, State civil litigation. Office: Howell Liles Braddock & Milton 901 Blackstone Bldg Jacksonville FL 32202

CATRON, GARY WAYNE, lawyer; b. Hamilton, Ohio, Sept. 19, 1944; m. Mary Hamilton Brown, Sept. 5, 1964; children: Nancy, Galileo. BA, Miami U., Oxford, Ohio, 1965; PhD, Harvard U., 1971; JD, U. Tex., 1976. Bar: Tex. 1976, U.S. Ct. Appeals (10th cir.) 1980, Okla. 1981, U.S. Dist. Ct. (we. dist.) Okla. 1981, U.S. Supreme Ct. 1984, U.S. Dist. Ct. (no. dist.) Okla. 1985. Assoc. Pannill & Hooper, Houston, 1979-80; assoc. McAfee & Taft, Oklahoma City, 1980-85, ptnr., 1985—. Federal civil litigation, State civil litigation, Oil and gas leasing. Home: 2417 NW 111th Oklahoma City OK 73120 Office: McAfee & Taft 2 Leadership Sq Oklahoma City OK 73102

CATTANACH, ROBERT EDWARD, JR., lawyer; b. Thorp, Wis., Jan. 14, 1949; s. Robert Edmund Sr. and Irene Louise (Papierniak) C.; m. Terry Theirl, June 9, 1972; children: Philip, Sarah. BS, U.S. Naval Acad., 1972; JD, U. Wis., 1975. Bar: U.S. Supreme Ct. 1980. Spl. counsel, sec. USN Dept., Washington, 1976-78; trial atty. U.S. Dept. of Justice, Washington, 1978-80; assoc. Reinhart, Boerner et al, Milw., 1981-82; ptnr. Oppenheimer, Wolff & Donnelly, St. Paul, 1983—. Articles editor U. Wis. Law Rev., 1974-75. Mem. Summit Ave. Preservation, St. Paul, 1983—. Mem. ABA, Wis. Bar Assn. (bd. dirs. non-resident div. 1984—), Minn. Bar Assn. Avocations: running, cross-country and downhill skiing, bicycling. Environment, Federal civil litigation, Insurance. Home: 1737 Summit Ave Saint Paul MN 55105 Office: Oppenheimer Wolff & Donnelly 1700 First Bank Saint Paul MN 55101

CATTANI, MARYELLEN BILLETTE, financial services company executive, lawyer; b. Bakersfield, Calif., Dec. 1, 1943; d. Arnold Theodore and Corinne Marilyn (Kovacevich) C.; m. Bernard Joseph Mikell, Apr. 1, 1978; 1 child, Sarah Cattani Mikele. A.B., Vassar Coll., 1965; J.D., U. Calif.-Berkeley, 1968. Bar: N.Y. 1969, Calif. 1969. Assoc. Davis Polk & Wardwell, N.Y.C., 1968-69; assoc. Orrick, Herrington & Sutcliffe, San Francisco, 1970-74; ptnr. Orrick, Herrington & Sutcliffe, 1975-81; v.p., gen. counsel Transam. Corp., San Francisco, 1981-83; sr. v.p., gen. counsel Transam. Corp., 1983—; mem. adv. com. U. San Francisco Inst. on Fin. Services, 1984-86; mem. vis. com. Golden Gate U. Sch. Law, San Francisco, 1983—. Mem. pvt. sector task force on juvenile justice Nat. Council on Crime and Delinquency, San Francisco, 1985-87; trustee Vassar Coll., 1985—; bd. regents St. Mary's Coll. Calif., 1985—. Named Outstanding Woman, Equal Rights Advocates, 1984. Mem. ABA, State Bar Calif. (chmn. bus. law sect. 1979-80), Bar Assn. San Francisco, Calif. Women Lawyers, San Francisco C. of C. (bd. dirs. 1987—), Am. Corp. Counsel Assn. (bd. dirs. 1982—), Women's Forum West (bd. dirs. 1984-87). Democrat. Roman Catholic. General corporate. Office: Transamerica Corp 600 Montgomery St San Francisco CA 94111

CATUZZI, J.P., JR., lawyer; b. N.Y.C., Aug. 23, 1938; s. J.P. Sr. and Ida (Ghezzi) C.; m. Chantal Mauricette Marais, Nov. 2, 1979; children: Daniella Firenze, Vanessa Carmen, Vanessita Lee. BA, Columbia U., 1958; JD, Georgetown U., 1961; LLM in Internat. Law, NYU, 1963. Bar: N.Y., D.C. Assoc. Baker & McKenzie, N.Y.C. and Chgo., 1963-65; gen. counsel, exec. v.p. Royal Bus. Fund Corp., N.Y.C., 1965-72; internat. counsel, mng. dir. Occidental S.A., Madrid and Geneva, 1972-84; U.S. gen. counsel Soparind S.A., N.Y.C. and Paris, 1984-86; resident U.S. ptnr. Berlioz, Ferry, David, Lutz & Rochefort, N.Y.C., 1986—; adj. prof. law and fin. C.W. Post campus Long Island U., N.Y.C., 1985—; nat. lectr. Internat. Bus. Network, N.Y.C. and Santa Monica, Calif., 1980-84. Legis. cons. to Gov. Rockefeller div. human rights State of N.Y., Albany, 1968-70; mem. legal com. N.Y. County Reps., 1967-72. Roman Catholic. Club: Confrerie des Chevalier Du Tastevin (N.Y.C.) (chevalier 1985—). Lodge: Knights of Malta (bailif 1982—). Private international, General corporate, Mergers and acquisitions. Home: 6 Luquer Rd Plandome Manor NY 11030 Office: Berlioz Ferry David Lutz & Rochefort 1 Rockefeller Plaza New York NY 10020

CAUDILL, DAVID STANLEY, lawyer; b. Hazard, Ky., Mar. 12, 1951; s. Everett Lee and Rudell (Caudill) C.; m. Nancy Burch, June 29, 1976. BA with honors, Mich. State U., 1973; Doctorandus, Vrije U., Amsterdam, The Netherlands, 1978; JD, U. Houston, 1981. Bar: Tex. 1981, Calif. 1982, U.S. Dist. Ct. (so. dist.) Tex. 1981, U.S. Dist. Ct. (so. dist.) Calif. 1982, U.S. Ct. Appeals (5th cir.) 1981. Law clk. to judge U.S. Ct. Appeals (5th cir.), Houston, 1981-82; assoc. Gray, Cary, Ames & Frye, San Diego, 1982-85, Graves, Dougherty, Hearon & Moody, Austin, Tex., 1985—; adj. prof. law U. Houston, 1986, U. Tex., 1987; lectr. law U. Houston, 1986. Editor-in-chief U. Houston Law Review, 1980-81; contbr. articles to profl. jours. Served to capt. USAF, 1973-76. Judge Wood fellow, 1981. Mem. ABA, Calif. Bar Assn., Tex. Bar Assn., Fellowship Christian Athletes (bd. dirs. 1985—). Club: Metropolitian (Austin). Real property, Legal education, Jurisprudence. Home: 1955 Westlake Dr Austin TX 78746 Office: Graves Dougherty Hearon & Moody 2200 Interfirst Tower Austin TX 78701

CAUGHLAN, DEIRDRE, lawyer; b. Bozeman, Mont., Dec. 16, 1950; d. Charles Norris and Georgeanne (Robertson) C. BA, U. Wash., 1971; JD, U. Mont., 1978. Bar: Mont., U.S. Dist. Ct. Mont. Dep. county atty. Butte-Silver Bow, Butte, Mont., 1978-80; ptnr. Dunlap & Caughlan, Butte, 1980—. Mem. Mont. Bar Assn. Bankruptcy, Criminal, Family and matrimonial. Office: Dunlap & Caughlan 27 W Broadway Butte MT 59701

CAVANAGH, EDWARD DEAN, law educator; b. Oneida, N.Y., Apr. 23, 1949; s. Joseph F. and and Anne (Rauschenberg) C.; m. Janet E. Guenkel, Aug. 17, 1974; 1 child, Christopher. AB, U. Notre Dame, 1971; JD, Cornell U., 1974; LLM, Columbia U., 1986. Bar: N.Y., U.S. Dist. Ct. (so. and ea. dists.) N.Y., U.S. Ct. Appeals (2d cir.), U.S. Supreme Ct. Assoc. Bond, Schoeneck and King, Syracuse, N.Y., 1974-76, Donovan, Leisure, Newton and Irvine, N.Y.C., 1976-80, Kelley, Drye and Warren, N.Y.C., 1980-81; prof. law St. John's U., Jamaica, N.Y., 1982—. Contbr. articles to profl. jours. Democrat. Roman Catholic. Antitrust, Federal civil litigation. Office: St Johns U Sch Law Fromkes Hall Jamaica NY 11439

CAVANAGH, MICHAEL F., judge; b. Detroit, Oct. 21, 1940; s. Sylvester J. and Mary Irene (Timmins) C.; m. Patricia E. Ferriss, Apr. 30, 1966; children—Jane Elizabeth, Michael F., Megan Kathleen. B.A., U. Detroit, 1962, J.D., 1966. Law clk. Ct. Appeals, Detroit, 1966-67; atty. City of Lansing, Mich., 1967-69; ptnr. Farhat, Story, et al., Lansing, Mich., 1969-73; judge 54-A Dist. Ct., Lansing, Mich., 1973-75, Mich. Ct. Appeals, Lansing, 1975-82; justice Mich. Supreme Ct., Lansing, 1983—; supervising justice Sentencing Guidelines Com., Lansing, 1983—, Mich. Jud. Inst., Lansing, 1986—. Chmn. bd. Am. Heart Assn. Mich., Lathrup Village, 1985; bd. dirs. YMCA, Lansing, 1978. Mem. ABA, Ingham County Bar Assn., Inst. Jud. Adminstrn. (hon.), Thomas M. Cooley Law Sch. (bd. dirs.). Democrat. Roman Catholic. Avocations: jogging; racquetball; fishing. Judicial administration. Home: 234 Kensington St East Lansing MI 48823 Office: Mich Supreme Ct Law Bldg PO Box 30052 Lansing MI 48909

CAVANAUGH, MICHAEL FLYNN, lawyer; b. Biloxi, Miss., Nov. 13, 1949; s. John August and Claudia (McKenzie) C.; m. Cynthia Marie Cook, June 12, 1971 (div. Aug. 1984); children: Kerry Catherine, Patrick Flynn. BS in Polit. Sci., U. So. Miss., 1972; JD, Miss. Coll., 1976. Assoc. Law Offices of Robert M. Acevedo, Biloxi, 1977-79; ptnr. Blessey & Cavanaugh, Biloxi, 1980-82; sole practice Biloxi, 1982-84, 86—; ptnr. Cavanaugh & Pisarich, Biloxi, 1984-86; mcpl. judge City of Biloxi, 1979-81; bd. dirs. Gulf Nat. Investment, Biloxi. Rep. Biloxi Harrison County Jail Adv. Commn., 1980-83; chmn. Mayor Blessey Re-election Com., Biloxi, 1981-85, Biloxi CSC, 1984—; mem. Harrison County Devel. Commn., 1985—. Served with USNG, 1971-76. Mem. ABA, Miss. Bar Assn., Harrison County Bar Assn., Biloxi Bar Assn. (pres. 1980-81). Democrat. Roman Catholic. General corporate, Insurance, Real property. Home: 101 Fred Haise Blvd #305 Biloxi MS 39530 Office: PO Box 1911 Biloxi MS 39530

CAVANAUGH, PATRICK JAMES, JR., lawyer; b. Hoosick Falls, N.Y., Oct. 4, 1924; s. Patrick F. and Mary (Ladden) C.; m. Joyce Ann Hammill, Sept. 21, 1957; children: Patrick III, Albert H., Peter F. BSBA, St. Michael's Coll., 1951; JD, Georgetown U., 1958. Time study specialist Gen. Electric, Schenectady, N.Y., 1951-55; ins. investigator AllState Ins. Co., Syracuse, N.Y., 1961-75; assoc. county atty. State of Iowa, Ottumwa, 1979-84; sole practice Norwood, N.Y., 1984—. Organizer, mem. com. Flood Control Project, Hoosick Falls, 1949-51; pres., bd. dirs. Norfolk-Norwood Minor Hoc Assn., 1975-77; asst. coach, Potsdam (N.Y.) Jr. Football, 1955-77, publicity dir. 1985—; coach Babe Ruth Baseball League, Norfolk, N.Y., 1967-70. Served with AC, U.S. Army, 1943-46. Mem. ABA, N.Y. Bar Assn., Iowa Bar Assn., Nat. Dist. Attys. Assn., St. Lawrence County Bar Assn., Am. Legion. Roman Catholic. General practice, State civil litigation. Home and Office: 26 Spring St Norwood NY 13668

CAVELL, DANIEL A., lawyer; b. Lafayette, La., July 5, 1954; s. Leo A. and Lina K. (Coyne) C.; m. Belinda J. Hymel, Aug. 10, 1979; children: Alaina, Carolyn, Benjamin. BA, Nicholls State U., Thibodaux, La., 1977; JD, La. State U., 1980. Bar: La. 1980, U.S. Dist. Ct. (ea. and mid. dists.) La., U.S. Ct. Appeals (5th cir.). Law clk. to presiding judge U.S. Ct. Appeals (1st cir.), Thibodaux, 1980-81; assoc. Law Offices of Johnny X. Allemand, Thibodaux, 1981-86; sole practice Thibodaux, 1986—. Named Outstanding Young Man of Am., Jaycees, 1985. Mem. ABA, Lafourche Bar Assn. (pres. 1985), Nicholls State Alumni Fedn. (pres. 1985—). Roman Catholic. State civil litigation, Consumer commercial, Family and matrimonial. Office: PO Box 1103 Thibodaux LA 70302

CAVENDISH, THOMAS EDGAR, lawyer; b. Columbus, Ohio, June 11, 1929; s. Charles Henry and Alma R. (Wolf) C.; m. Joanna L. Lawyer, June 28, 1958; children—Elizabeth Ann, Sara Joan, Martha Jean. B.S., Ohio State U., 1951, J.D. summa cum laude, 1953. Bar: Ohio 1953, U.S. Dist. Ct. (so. dist.), 1954. Chief bill drafter Ohio Legislative Reference Bur., 1952-53; adj. prof. Franklin Law Sch., Capital U., 1965-70, Ohio State U. Coll. Law, 1972-74; ptnr. Porter, Wright, Morris & Arthur, Columbus, Ohio, 1953—; commr. Ohio to Nat. Conf. Commrs. on Uniform State Laws, 1975, treas., mem. exec. com. 1984—; legis. rep. Ohio Bd. Uniform State Laws, 1977—. Mem. founding sponsors assn., bd. trustees Columbus Internat. Coll., Seville, Spain, 1974-79; mem. nat. council Ohio State U. Coll. Law, 1962—, chmn., 1981-86. Mem. ABA, Am. Judicature Soc., Ohio State Bar Assn. (mem. council dels., chmn. joint com. bankers and lawyers, chmn. banking and comml. law com.), Columbus Bar Assn. (bd. govs., pres. 1970-71), Lawyers Club Columbus (pres. 1969-70), Ohio State U. Law Alumni Assn. (past pres. 1973-74). Banking, Contracts commercial, General corporate. Office: Porter Wright Morris & Arthur 41 S High St Columbus OH 43215

CAVIN, RHONDA LYNN, lawyer; b. Loma Linda, Calif., Aug. 29, 1955; d. William James and M. Janece (Ridenhour) Cavin, Jr.; m. John Alexander Stewart, Aug. 29, 1981 (div. 1983). B.S., Loma Linda U., 1977; J.D., U. San Diego, 1980. Bar: Calif. 1982, Nev. 1983. Pvt. practice, San Diego, 1982; legal asst. Beckley, Singleton, DeLanoy & Jemison, Las Vegas, Nev., 1982-83; pvt. practice Hilbrecht & Assocs., Las Vegas, 1983—. Mem. ABA, Calif. Bar Assn., Nev. Bar Assn., Nev. Trial Lawyers Assn., So. Nev. Assn. Women Attys., Am. Trial Lawyers Assn., Las Vegas Bus. Women's Network, Phi Delta Phi. Democrat. Club: Renaissance Women (Las Vegas). Administrative and regulatory, State civil litigation, General corporate. Office: Hilbrecht & Assocs 723 S Casino Ctr Blvd Las Vegas NV 89101

CAYEA, DONALD JOSEPH, lawyer; b. Bklyn., Mar. 3, 1948; s. Glendon Vernon and Marie Nicola (Gesualdo) C.; m. Elizabeth Mary Peck, Jan. 27, 1973 (div. Sept. 1975); m. Yvonne Karen Kemeny, Sept. 11, 1983. BA, L.I. U., 1969; JD, Western New Eng. Coll., 1975. Bar: N.Y. 1976, U.S. Dist. Ct. (so. and ea. dists.) N.Y. 1978, U.S. Dist. Ct. D.C. 1979, U.S. Supreme Ct. 1979. Prin. N.Y.C., 1976—; lectr. Paralegal Inst., NYU, 1984—, adult edn. program Nassau County (N.Y.) Bar Assn., Mineola, 1978-79; panelist Trial Advocacy Program, Cardozo Law Sch. Yeshiva U., N.Y.C., 1984—. Pres. Seascape Condominium, Westhampton Beach, N.Y., 1986—; sponsor Richmond Roller Hockey Assn., Staten Island, N.Y., 1984—. Served with U.S. Army, 1970-71. Mem. ABA, Assn. Trial Lawyers Am., N.Y. State Bar Assn., Assn. of Bar of City of N.Y., New York County Lawyers Assn., Phi Epsilon Pi. Federal civil litigation, Insurance, Libel. Home: 200 Winston Dr Cliffside Park NJ 07010 Office: Donald J Cayea & Assocs 1180 Ave of Americas New York NY 10036

CAYWOOD, WARREN GUSTAVE, JR., lawyer; b. Abington, Pa., Nov. 30, 1951; s. Warren Gustave and Lorraine (Clayton) C. B.A., Yale U., 1973; J.D., Columbia U., 1976. Bar: N.Y. 1977, U.S. Dist. Ct. (so. dist.) N.Y. 1983. Assoc. firm Sullivan & Cromwell, N.Y.C., 1976-83; ptnr. firm Howard, Darby & Levin, N.Y.C., 1983—. Fin. editor Columbia Jour. Transnat. Law, 1975-76. Harlan Fiske Stone scholar Columbia Law Sch., 1973-74, 75-76; James Kent scholar, 1974-75. Mem. ABA. General corporate, Securities, Banking. Home: 131 W 78th St New York NY 10024 Office: Howard Darby & Levin 10 E 53d St New York NY 10022

CAZALAS, MARY REBECCA WILLIAMS, lawyer, nurse; b. Atlanta, Nov. 11, 1927; d. George Edgar and Mary Annie (Slappey) Williams; m. Albert Joseph Cazalas (dec.). R.N., St. Joseph's Infirmary Sch. Nursing, Atlanta, 1948; B.S. in Pre-medicine, Oglethorpe U., 1954; M.S. in Anatomy, Emory U., 1960; J.D., Loyola U., 1967. Gen. duty nurse, 1948-68; instr. maternity nursing St. Joseph's Infirmary Sch. Nursing, 1954-59; med. researcher in urology Tulane U. Sch. Medicine, 1961-65; legal researcher for presiding judge La. Ct. Appeals (4th cir.), 1965-71; sole practice, 1967-71; asst. U.S. atty., New Orleans, 1971-79; sr. trial atty. EEOC, New Orleans, 1979-84; owner Cazalas Apts., New Orleans, 1962—; lectr. in field. Contbr. articles to med. and legal publs. Bd. advisors Loyola U. Sch. Law, New Orleans, 1974, v.p. adv. bd., 1975; mem. New Orleans Drug Abuse Adv. Com., 1976-80, task force Area Agy. on Aging, 1976-80, pres.'s council Loyola U., 1978—, adv. bd. Odyssey House, Inc., New Orleans, 1973; chmn. women's com. Fed. Exec. Bd., 1974; bd. dirs. Bethlehem House of Bread, 1975-79. Named Hon. La. State Senator, 1974; recipient Superior Performance award U.S. Dept. Justice, 1974, Cert. Appreciation Fed. Exec. Bd., 1975, 76, 77, 78, Rev. E.A. Doyle award, 1976, commendation for teaching Guam Legislature, 1977. Mem. Am. Judicature Soc., La. State Bar Assn., Fed. Bus. Assn. (v.p. 1976—, pres. 1976-78, bd. dirs. 1972-75), Fed. Bar Assn. (1st v.p. 1973, pres. New Orleans chpt. 1974-75, nat. council 1974-79), Assn. Women Lawyers, Nat. Health Lawyers Assn., DAR, Bus. and Profl. Women's Club, Am. Heart Assn., Emory Alumni Assn., Oglethorpe U. Alumni Assn., Loyola U. Alumni Assn. (bd. dirs. 1974-75, 1977, v.p. 1976), Jefferson Parish Hist. Soc., Phi Delta Delta (merged with Phi Alpha Delta, pres. 1970-72, bd. dirs., vice justice 1974-75), Sierra Club, Alpha Epsilon Delta, Phi Sigma, Leconte Hon. Sci. Soc. Democrat. Real property, Health.

CECCHINI, GARRETT LEE, lawyer; b. McKeesport, Pa., Mar. 7, 1948; s. Dominic A. Cecchini and Hannah (Rosner) Anderson; m. Carol A. Esser, Nov. 18, 1984. BA, Duquesne U., 1970; M in Polit. and Instl. Adminstrn., U. Pitts., 1972; MBA, Golden Gate U., 1976; JD, Lincoln U., 1978. Bar: Calif. 1980, U.S. Dist. Ct. (no. dist.) Calif. 1980, U.S. Tax Ct. 1981, U.S. Ct. Appeals (9th cir.) 1981. Pres. Transcom Data Systems, Inc., Pitts., 1970-71, Legal Resources, Inc., San Francisco, 1974-77; assoc. Law Offices of Max Cline, San Francisco, 1981-85; ptnr. Niesar & Wickersham, San Francisco, 1985—. Author: (with others) Sanctions, 1985, California Securities Institute, 1986. Trustee Lincoln U., San Francisco, 1981—; mem. Save the River, Inc., San Francisco, 1986. Recipient Evidence award West's Pub., San Francisco, 1977, Labor Law award West's Pub., San Francisco, 1978, Attorney Service award Calif. State Bar, San Francisco, 1985. Mem. ABA (fed. rules com. 1985—), San Francisco Bar Assn., Am. Trial Lawyers Assn., Barristers Club, Sigma Nu. Democrat. Bankruptcy, Contracts commercial. Office: Niesar & Wickersham 214 Grant Ave 4th Fl San Francisco CA 94108

CECI, LOUIS J., justice state supreme court; b. N.Y.C., Sept. 10, 1927; s. Louis and Filomena C.; m. Shirley; children—Joseph, Geraldine, David; children by previous marriage: Kristin, Remy, Louis. Ph.B., Marquette U., 1951, J.D., 1954. Bar: Wis. 1954, U.S. Dist. Ct. (ea. dist.) Wis. 1954. Sole practice Milw., 1954-58, 63-68; asst. city atty. City of Milw., 1958-63; mem. Wis. Assembly, Madison, 1965-66; judge Milw. County Ct., 1968-73, Milw. Circuit Ct., 1973-82; justice Wis. Supreme Ct., Madison, 1982—; lectr. Wis. Jud. Confs., 1970-79. Lectr. Badger Boys State, Ripon, Wis., 1961, 1982-84; asst. dist. commr. Boy Scouts Am., 1962. Recipient Wis. Civic Recognition PLAV, Milw., 1970; recipient Community Improvement Pompeii Men's Club, Milw., 1971, Good Govt. Milw Jaycees, 1973, Community-Judiciary Pompeii Men's Club, 1982. Mem. ABA, Wis. Bar Assn., Dane County Bar Assn., Am. Legion (comdr. 1962-63). Office: Wisconsin Supreme Court PO Box 1688 Madison WI 53701

CEDARBAUM, MIRIAM GOLDMAN, lawyer; b. N.Y.C., Sept. 16, 1929; d. Louis Albert and Sarah (Shapiro) Goldman; m. Bernard Cedarbaum, Aug. 25, 1957; children—Daniel Goldman, Jonathan Goldman. B.A., Barnard Coll., 1950; LL.B., Columbia U., 1953. Bar: N.Y. 1954, U.S. Dist. Ct. (so. dist.) N.Y. 1956 U.S. Ct. Appeals (2d cir.) 1956, U.S. Ct. Claims 1958, U.S. Supreme Ct. 1958, U.S. Dist. Ct. (ea. dist.) N.Y. 1980, U.S. Ct. Appeals (5th and 11th cirs.) 1980. Law clk. to judge U.S. Dist. Ct. (so. dist.) N.Y., 1953-54, asst. U.S. atty., 1954-57; atty. Dept. Justice, Washington, 1958-59; cons. to law firms in litigation matters, part-time 1959-62; 1st asst. counsel N.Y. State Moreland Act Commn., 1963-64; assoc. counsel Mus. Modern Art, N.Y.C., 1965-79; assoc. litigation dept. Davis, Polk & Wardwell, N.Y.C., 1979-83, sr. atty., 1983-86; judge U.S. Dist. Ct. (so. dist.) N.Y., 1986—; co-counsel Scarsdale Open Soc. Assn., 1969-86; acting justice Village of Scarsdale, 1978-82, justice, 1982-86. Mem. adv. com. on labor relations Scarsdale (N.Y.) Bd. Edn., 1976-77; mem. Scarsdale Bd. Archtl. Rev., 1977-79. Mem. Am. Law Inst., ABA (chmn. com. on pictorial graphic sculptural and choreographic works 1979-81), N.Y. State Bar Assn. (chmn. com. on fed. legislation 1978-80), Assn. Bar City of N.Y., Fed. Bar Council, Copyright Soc. U.S.A. (trustee 1979-82), N.Y. State Assn. Magistrates, Westchester County Magistrates Assn. Jewish. Club: Town (Scarsdale), Merchants (N.Y.C.). Federal civil litigation, State civil litigation. Home: 125 Brewster Rd Scarsdale NY 10583 Office: U S Courthouse 40 Foley Sq New York NY 10007-1581

CEDERBAUM, EUGENE E., lawyer; b. Bklyn., Apr. 16, 1942; s. Kiva and Zelda (Brieff) C.; m. Carol Ellen Winograd, Mar. 3, 1968; children: Mark, Deborah. BS, NYU, 1964; JD, Columbia U., 1967. Bar: U.S. Dist. Ct. D.C. 1968, U.S. Ct. Appeals (D.C. cir.) 1969, U.S. Ct. Mil. Appeals 1969, Conn. 1974, U.S. Dist. Ct. Conn. 1975, U.S. Tax Ct. 1978. Assoc. Constantikes & Schlossberg, Westport, Conn., 1973-75, Nevas, Nevas & Rubin, Westport, 1975-79; ptnr. Rubenstein & Cederbaum, Westport, 1979-83; sole practice Westport, 1983-87; assoc. Goldstein & Peck, P.C., Bridgeport and Westport, Conn., 1987—. Bd. dirs. United Way, Westport, 1982—; mem. Westport Representative Town Meeting, 1981-85, Selectmen's Art Ctr. Task Force, Westport, 1983, Selectmen's Ethics Com., Westport, 1983-86; Fair Housing agent, Westport, 1985—; bd. dirs. Ctr. for Arts, Westport, 1985—. Served to capt. U.S. Army, 1968-73. Mem. Am. Trial Lawyers Assn., Conn. Bar Assn. (ho. dels. 1980-83), Westport Bar Assn. (pres. 1986-87), Beta Gamma Sigma. Democrat. Lodge: Masons. Avocations: photography. General practice, Contracts commercial, Real property. Home: 57 Patrick Rd Westport CT 06880 Office: Goldstein & Peck PC 1900 Main St PO Box 5031 Westport CT 06881

CEGAVSKE, WALLACE DUANE, lawyer; b. Albany, Oreg., July 21, 1940; s. Raymond Emil and Hester Leona (Goin) C.; m. Janet Elizabeth Fisher, July 8, 1962; children: Carisa Ann, Christiane Amy. BS, Oreg. State U., 1962; MS, Air Force Inst. Tech., 1968; JD, U. Oreg., 1974. Bar: Oreg. 1974, U.S. Dist. Ct. Oreg. 1985.. Ecologist Bur. Land Mgmt. Dist. 13, Burns, Oreg., 1962-63; enlisted USAF, 1963, advanced through grades to capt., 1963-71, resigned, 1971; sole practice law Roseburg, Oreg., 1974—; bd. dirs. Douglas County Museum Found., Roseburg, 1982—. Pres. Umpqua Council Campfire Girls, Douglas County, Oreg., 1976-77. Served with Oreg. Air Guard, 1971-74. Mem. ABA, Oreg. Bar Assn., Oreg. Estate Planning Council, Roseburg C. of C. Republican. Lodges: Optimists (bd. dirs. Douglas County chpt. 1976-81), Rotary. Avocations: fishing, hiking, farming. Probate, Real property, General corporate. Office: Cegavske & Seitz 420 SE Jackson St Roseburg OR 97470

CELEBREZZE, ANTHONY J., JR., attorney general Ohio; b. Cleve., Sept. 8, 1941; s. Anthony J. and Anne M. C.; m. Louisa Godwin, June 19, 1965; children: Anthony J. III, Catherine, Charles, David, Maria. BS, U.S. Naval Acad., 1963; MS, George Washington U., 1966; JD, Cleve. State U., 1973. Bar: Ohio 1973. Ptnr. Celebrezze and Marco, Cleve., 1975-79; mem. Ohio State Senate, 1975-79; sec. of state State of Ohio, Columbus, 1979-83, atty. gen., 1983—. Pres. Joint Vets. Commn. of Cuyahoga County, Ohio, from 1977; v.p. Lake Erie Regional Transp. Authority, 1972-74; mem. Gt. Lakes Commn., 1975-78, vice chmn., 1977-78. Served with USN, 1963-68. Decorated Navy Commendation medal; recipient Jeffersonian Lodge award, 1977, Man of Yr. award Delta Theta Phi, Freedoms Found. Honor medal, 1980, 86; named 1 of 5 Outstanding Legislators by 2 Ohio mags., 1978. Democrat. Roman Catholic. Office: State Office Tower 30 E Broad St Columbus OH 43215

CELEBREZZE, FRANK D., chief justice Ohio Supreme Court; b. Cleve., Nov. 13, 1928; s. Frank D. and Mary (Delsander) C.; m. Mary Ann Armstrong, Jan. 20, 1949; children: Judith, Frank, Laura, David, Brian, Steven, Jeffrey, Keith, Matthew. Student, Ohio State U., 1948-50; BS, Baldwin-Wallace Coll., 1952; LLB, Cleve.-Marshall Coll. Law, 1956; LLD (hon.), Capital U., 1980, Ohio Coll. Podiatric Medicine, 1985. Bar: Ohio 1957. Began legal practice Cleve., 1957; judge Ohio Ct. Common Pleas Cuyahoga County, 1964-72; justice Ohio Supreme Ct., 1972-78, chief justice, 1978—; mem. Ohio Senate, 1956-58. Served with U.S. Army, 1946-47. Recipient Jud. Service award Ohio Supreme Ct., 1972, Outstanding Alumnus award Cleve.-Marshall Coll. Law, 1973, Community Service award AFL-CIO, 1973, Disting. Citizen of Parma award, 1976, Unita Civic award of Youngstown, 1976, Man of Yr. award Greater Cin. UAW-CAP Council, 1986; named Man of Yr., Delta Theta Phi Law Frat., 1986. Mem. ABA, Inst. Jud. Adminstrn. of Bar Assn. Greater Cleve., Cuyahoga County Bar Assn., Cuyahoga County Joint Vets. Adminstrn. (past pres., past trustee), Cleve. YMCA, Catholic War Vets. Democrat. Roman Catholic. Office: Supreme Ct Ohio State Office Tower 30 E Broad St Columbus OH 43215

CENTENO, DOUGLAS JOSEPH, lawyer; b. N.Y.C., Nov. 22, 1957; s. Joseph Frederick and Faith Elanor (Woicicki) C.; m. Jeanie Parker, Dec. 19, 1981. BA, Fla. State U., 1979; JD, Cumberland U., 1982. Bar: Ala. 1982, U.S. Dist. Ct. (no. dist.) Ala. 1982, Fla. 1983, U.S. Ct. Appeals (11th cir.) 1983. Assoc. Denaburg, Schoel et al, Birmingham, Ala., 1982-85, Najjar, Denaburg et al, Birmingham, 1985-86, Schoel, Ogle & Benton, Birmingham, 1986—. Big brother Big Bros./Big Sisters, Birmingham, 1985—, adv. com. 1986—. Named one of Outstanding Young Men of Am., Birmingham, 1984. Mem. ABA, Birmingham Bar Assn. (grievance com. 1984), Am. Trial Lawyers Assn., Ala. Trial Lawyers Assn. Republican. Avocation: raquetball. Construction, Consumer commercial, Federal civil litigation. Home: 1016 C 42d St S Birmingham AL 35222 Office: Schoel Ogle & Benton 2008 3d Ave N Birmingham AL 35203

CENTER, TONY, lawyer; b. Savannah, Ga., Aug. 7, 1949; s. Leo E. and Miriam (Kantsiper) C.; m. Donna Goldman, Dec. 26, 1976; children: Kristy, Jeffrey. BS, U. Fla., 1971; JD, U. Ga., 1975. Sole practice Atlanta, 1975—. Producer Larry Bartley Story, 1986. Mem. Ga. Bar Assn., Tau Epsilon Phi (treas. 1969-70, pres. 1970-71). Democrat. Clubs: Gate City (trustee 1985—), Standard (Atlanta) (golf champion 1980, 84, 86). Lodge: B'nai B'rith (parliamentarian 1979—, trustee 1980-83). Avocation: golf. General corporate, General practice, Sports law. Office: 3400 Peachtree Rd NE Suite 1701 Atlanta GA 30326

CENTERS, LOUISE CLAUDENA, clinical psychologist, lawyer; b. Huntington Park, Calif.. BA, U. So. Calif., 1953, PhD in Psychology, 1958; JD, Detroit Coll. Law, 1979. Bar: Mich. 1979, Fla. 1980; diplomate Am. Bd. Profl. Psychology. Pvt. practice psychology specializing in forensic assessment Southfield, Mich., 1959—; chief, clin. psychology sect. Sinai Hosp., Detroit, 1970—. Contbr. 9 articles to profl. jours. Fellow Am. Orthopsychiat. Assn., Mich. Psychol. Assn. (pres. 1981, Disting. Psychologist award 1984); mem. Am. Psychol. Assn., Mich. Soc. Clin. Psychologists (pres. 1975), Mich. Interprofl. Assn. (pres. 1985). Clubs: Fairlane (Dearborn, Mich.), Women's Econ. (Detroit), Econ. of Detroit. Forensic evaluation, Personal injury, Family and matrimonial. Home: 25052 Sherwood Circle Southfield MI 48075 Office: Sinai Hosp Dept Psychiatry 14800 W McNichols Detroit MI 48235

CENTNER, CHARLES WILLIAM, lawyer; b. Battle Creek, Mich., July 4, 1915; s. Charles William and Lucy Irene (Patterson); m. Evi Rohr, Dec. 22, 1956; children—Charles Patterson, David William, Geoffrey Christopher. A.B., U. Chgo., 1936, A.M., 1936, A.M., 1939, Ph.D., 1941; J.D., Detroit Coll. Law, 1970; LL.B., LaSalle Extension U., 1965. Bar: Mich. 1970. Asst. prof. U. N.D., 1940-41, Tulane U., New Orleans, 1941-42; liaison officer for Latin Am., Lend-Lease Adminstrn., 1942; assoc. dir. Western Hemisphere div. Nat. Fgn Trade Council, 1946-52; exec. Ford Motor Co., Detroit, 1952-57, Chrysler Corp. and Chrysler Internat. S.A., Detroit and Geneva, Switzerland, 1957-70; adj. prof. Wayne State U., U. Detroit, Wayne County Community Coll., 1970—. Served to lt. comdr. USNR, 1942-45. Mem. State Bar of Mich., ABA, Detroit Bar Assn., Oakland County Bar Assn. Republican. Episcopalian. Club: Masons. Author: Great Britain and Chile, 1810-1914, 1941. Contracts commercial, General corporate, State civil litigation. Home: 936 Harcourt Rd Grosse Pointe Park MI 48230 Office: 100 Renassance Ctr Suite 1575 Detroit MI 48243-1075

CENTOLA, LAWRENCE JOSEPH, lawyer; b. New Orleans, Aug. 31, 1946; s. Lawrence Joseph and Mona (Francis) C.; m. Denise Villere, July 31, 1971; children: Lawrence, Denise, Deborah. BS in Govt., La. State U., 1968, JD, 1971. Bar: La. 1972, U.S. Dist. Ct. (ea., mid. and we. dists.) La. 1972, U.S. Ct. Appeals (5th cir.) 1972. Asst. dist. atty. Orleans Parish, New Orleans, 1972-77; dir. Carmouche, Gray & Hoffman, New Orleans, 1981—. Mem. La. Assn. Def. Counsel, Maritime Law Assn. Democrat. Roman Catholic. Federal civil litigation, State civil litigation, Personal injury. Home: 3921 S Post Oak New Orleans LA 70114 Office: Carmouche Gray & Hoffman 650 Poydras Suite 2100 New Orleans LA 70130-6121

CERAR, JEFFREY O'DELL, lawyer; b. West Point, N.Y., Mar. 28, 1946; s. Paul Robert and Vivian Eileen (Womack) C.; m. Luisa Diaz-Soltero, Nov. 7, 1969 (div. Sept. 1982); children: Katya Melissa, Heather Anne. BA in Econs., U. Utah, 1967; JD, Columbia U., 1972. Bar: N.Y. 1972, U.S. Ct. Appeals (1st cir.) 76, U.S. Ct. Appeals (D.C. cir.) 1977, D.C. 1978, U.S. Ct. Appeals (5th cir.) 1982, U.S. Dist. Ct. (D.C. dist.) 1983, U.S. Ct. Appeals (3d cir.) 1986. Assoc. Milbank, Tweed, Hadley & McCloy, N.Y.C., 1972-74; counsel U.S. EPA, Washington, 1974-77, dep. assoc. gen. counsel, 1977-79; assoc. Squire, Sanders & Dempsey, Washington, 1979-83, ptnr., 1983—; bd. dirs. Kenning Corp., Kensington, Md., 1985—. mem. environ. com. Greater Washington Bd. Trade, 1985—. Served to 1st lt. U.S. Army, 1969-71. Constitutional Law Fellow NEH, 1978. Mem. Am. Soc. for Testing and Materials (chmn. environ. issues in biotechnology subcom. 1985—), Waterview Cluster Assn. (pres. 1979), Phi Beta Kappa. Democrat. Roman Catholic. Club: The Writers Ctr. Avocations: tennis, skiing, writing poetry, woodworking, music. Administrative and regulatory, Environment, Labor. Office: Squire Sanders & Dempsey 1201 Pennsylvania Ave NW Washington DC 20004

CERAUL, DAVID JAMES, lawyer; b. Easton, Pa., Dec. 8, 1955; s. David A. Ceraul and Josephine (Ruggiero) Barczynski; m. Jacqueline A. Onjack, May 17, 1986. BS in Polit. Sci., U. Scranton, 1977; JD, U. Pitts., 1980. Bar: Pa. 1980. Law clk. to presiding justice Ct. of Common Pleas, Stroudsburg, Pa., 1980-81; sole practice Bangor, Pa., 1981—; solicitor Wind Gap (Pa.) Borough, 1981—, State Belt Mcpl. Assn., Bangor, 1981—. Bd. dirs. Salvation Army, Pen Argyl, Pa., 1982—, Unico Nat., Roseto, Pa., 1983-84, United Way, Lehigh Valley, Pa., 1985-86. Mem. Northampton County Bar Assn., Monroe County Bar Assn. Democrat. Roman Catholic. Lodge: K.C. Family and matrimonial, Real property, Local government. Office: 22 Market St Bangor PA 18013

CERMINARO, ANTHONY RICHARD, lawyer; b. Scranton, Pa., Feb. 28, 1954; s. Samuel Patrick and Doris Mary (Veglia) C.; m. Christine Johanna Walter, Jun 25, 1983; 1 child, Deidre. BA in Econs., Princeton U., 1976; JD, U. Pitts., 1980. Bar: Pa. 1981. Atty. PPG Industries Inc., Pitts., 1981-85, sr. atty., 1985—. Mem. ABA, Pa. Bar Assn., Allegheny County Bar Assn., Am. Corp. Counsel Assn. Contracts commercial, Computer, Private international. Office: PPG Industries Inc 1 PPG Pl Pittsburgh PA 15272

CERNIGLIARO, MICHAEL J., lawyer; b. Englewood, N.J., Mar. 31, 1938; s. Sebastian and Marie (Bivone) C.; m. Patricia Goy, June 8, 1963; children: Allison, Nicole. BA, Rutgers U., 1960, JD, 1963. Bar: N.J. 1963, D.C. 1963, U.S. Dist. Ct. N.J. 1963, U.S. Supreme Ct. 1969. Assoc., ptnr. Campbell, Foley, Lee, Murphy & Cernigliaro, Asbury Park, N.J., 1963—; mcpl. ct. judge Twp. of Ocean, N.J., 1972-80; atty. Bd. of Adjustment, Eatontown, N.J., 1966—; vice-chmn. Ethics Com. Monmouth County, N.J. 1981-82. Bd. govs. Jersey Shore Med. Ctr., Neptune, N.J., 1974-85. Served as cpl. USMC, 1956-62. Mem. ABA, N.J. Bar Assn., Trial Lawyers of N.J., N.J. Def. Assn. (pres. 1976), Monmouth Mcpl. Judges Assn. (pres. 1975). Republican. Roman Catholic. Insurance, Personal injury. Home: 412 Windermere Interlaken NJ 07712-4321 Office: 601 Bangs Ave Asbury Park NJ 07712

CERNY, EDWARD CHARLES, III, lawyer; b. St. Louis, Aug. 18, 1943; s. Edward Charles Jr. and Martha Patricia (Pearcy); m. Sarah Leota Parr, Sept. 4, 1965; children: Edward Charles IV, Grant Pearcy, Ward Van Siclen. BA magna cum laude, Wesleyan U., 1965; cert. cultural studies, U. Madrid, 1964; JD, Columbia U., 1968. Bar: N.Y. 1968, U.S. Dist. Ct. (so. and ea. dists.) N.Y. 1971, U.S. Dist. Ct. N.J. 1974, U.S. Ct. Appeals (2d, 8th and 9th cirs.) 1974, U.S. Supreme Ct. 1974, N.J. 1974, U.S. Tax Ct. 1975, U.S. Dist. Ct. (we. dist.) N.Y. 1980, U.S. Ct. Appeals (3d cir.) 1980, U.S. Ct. Appeals (5th cir.) 1986, U.S. Temporary Emergency Ct. Appeals 1986. Assoc. Lane & Mittendorf, N.Y.C., 1968-77, ptnr., 1977—; ptnr. Cerny & Mochary (N.J. affiliate of Lane & Mittendorf), 1982-85. Packmaster Boy Scouts Am., Summit, N.J., 1979-84. Served to sgt. USAR, 1968-70. Mem. ABA, N.Y. Bar Assn., N.J. Bar Assn., Assn. of Bar of City of N.Y., Phi Beta Kappa, Alpha Delta Phi. Republican. Episcopalian. Clubs: Univ. (N.Y.C.), Beacon Hill (Summit). Federal civil litigation, State civil litigation, Insurance. Home: 2 Sherman Ave Summit NJ 07901 Office: Lane & Mittendorf 120 Wood Ave S Metro Park NJ 08830

CERTILMAN, MORTON LAWRENCE, lawyer; b. N.Y.C., Jan. 26, 1932; s. Philip and Anna (Rosinsky) C.; m. Joyce Haiken, July 4, 1955; children—Andrea, Patrice, Debbie, Alyssa. Student N.Y. U., 1950-51, Hofstra U., 1951-53; LL.B. cum laude, Bklyn. Law Sch., 1956. Bar: N.Y. 1956, U.S. Dist. Ct. (so. dist.) N.Y. 1956, U.S. Ct. Apls. (2d cir.) 1956. Asst. atty. gen. N.Y. State, 1956-59; mem. firm Rutenberg and Certilman, N.Y.C., 1959-65; ptnr. Certilman, Haft, Lebow, Buckley & Kremer, N.Y.C., Mitchell Field and Mineola, N.Y., Boca Raton, Fla., Hackensack, N.J., 1965—; lectr. Am. Law Inst./ABA Practising Law Inst., U. Miami Law Center, Hofstra Law Sch., assoc. prof. N.Y.U. Real Estate Inst. Mem. ABA, N.Y. State Bar Assn., Nassau County Bar Assn. Contbr. articles to profl. jours. Real property, General corporate, Legislative. Office: 805 3d Ave New York NY 10022

CESINGER, JOHN ROBERT, human resources consultant, lawyer; b. Chgo., June 29, 1934; s. John Michael and Katherine Elizabeth (Mankel) C.; m. Joan Wagner, July 7, 1956; children—Michael, Richard, Steven. B.S. in Indsl. Econs., Iowa State U., 1956; J.D., John Marshall Law Sch., 1963. Bar: Ill. 1966. Vice pres. adminstrn., gen. counsel Beloit Foundry Co., South Beloit, Ill., 1972-74; cons. Towers, Perrin, Forster & Crosby, Atlanta, 1974-78; v.p. Meidinger & Assocs., Louisville, 1978-79; ptnr. in charge actuarial, benefits and compensation cons. Los Angeles office Coopers & Lybrand, 1979-84; v.p. R. Wald & Assocs., 1984-85; chmn. bd. dirs., treas. Caco Pacific Corp., Covina, Calif., 1985—; pres. Dynamic Resources, Inc. La Verne, Calif., 1980—. Div. chmn. United Fund, 1981-82. Mem. Los Angeles County Bar Assn., Ill. Bar Assn., ABA, Am. Compensation Assn., Am. Soc. Personnel Adminstrn., Am. Mgmt. Assn., Western Pension Conf. Clubs: Jonathan (Los Angeles); Via Verde (San Dimas). Pension, profit-sharing, and employee benefits, Labor. Office: 2159 Base Line Rd La Verne CA 91750

CHABOT, ELLIOT CHARLES, federal lawyer; b. Anniston, Ala., Mar. 29, 1955; s. Herbert L. and Aleen (Kerwin) C. BA with honors, U. Md., 1977; JD, George Washington U., 1980. Bar: D.C. 1980, U.S. Dist. Ct. D.C. 1981, U.S. Claims Ct. 1981, U.S. Ct. Internat. Trade 1981, U.S. Tax Ct. 1981, U.S. Ct. Mil. Appeals 1981, U.S. Emergency Ct. Appeals 1981, U.S. Ct. Appeals (4th, 5th, 8th, 9th, 10th, 11th, D.C. cirs.) 1982, U.S. Ct. Appeals (7th and Fed. cirs.) 1983. Application analyst, atty. Com. on Ho. Adminstrn., House Info. Systems U.S. Congress, Washington, 1980-81, mgr. integrated law revision and retrieval project, 1981—; bd. dirs. Am. Revenue Assn., Rockford, Iowa, Threshold Services, Inc., Silver Spring, Md. Pres. Aspen Hill (Md.) Civic Assn., 1985—; council pres. Parkland Jr. High Community Sch., Aspen Hill, 1983—, v.p., 1971-73; chmn. Services to People com. Wheaton Citizens Adv. Bd., Montgomery County, Md.,1986—, chmn. Community Edn. Devel. subcom. of Citizens Adv. com. to the Interagency Coordinating Bd. for Community Use of Ednl. Facilities and Services, 1985—; exec. com. Robert E. Peary High Sch. PTA, Aspen Hill, 1972-73; Montgomery County gov. com. on re-use of Peary High Sch., 1986—; corr. sec. Area 2 adv. council Montgomery County Pub. Schs, 1972-74, adv. com. spl. edn. programs, 1974; commr. Gov.'s Commn. on Student Affairs, Md., 1976-77; adv. com. Aspen Hill Library, 1977; alt. Montgomery County Youth Services Commn., 1972; rec. sec. Dist. 19 Dem. Club, Montgomery County, 1983—, precinct treas., Aspen Hill, 1978-85; legal and acctg. div. steering com. Washington Israel Bonds, 1984—. Recipient George Washington award, George Washington U., 1980; named One of Outstanding Young Men, U.S. C. of C., 1982. Mem. ABA, Fed. Bar. Assn., D.C. Bar Assn., George Washington U. Law Alumni Assn. (sec. Capitol Hill chpt. 1985—), Phi Alpha Delta (clk. Jay chpt. 1979-80), Omicron Delta Kappa. Computer, Local government, Legislative. Home: 12929 Magellan Ave Rockville MD 20853 Office: Com on House Adminstrn House Info Systems US Congress H2-693 House Office Bldg Annex #2 Washington DC 20515

CHABOT, HERBERT L., judge; b. N.Y.C., July 17, 1931; s. Meyer and Esther (Mogilansky) C.; m. Aleen Carol Kerwin, Jun. 16, 1951; children—Elliot C., Donald J., Lewis A., Nancy Jo. B.A., CCNY, 1952; LL.B., Columbia U., 1957; LL.M., Georgetown U., 1964. Bar: N.Y. 1958. Staff counsel Am. Jewish Congress, 1957-60; law clk. U.S. Tax Ct., Washington, 1961-65, judge, 1978—; atty. Joint Congl. Com. Taxation, 1965-78. Del. Md. Constl. Conv., 1967-68. Served with U.S. Army, 1953-55. Mem. ABA, Fed. Bar Assn. Judicial administration, Corporate taxation, Estate taxation. Home: 14104 Bauer Dr Rockville MD 20853 Office: 400 2d St NW Washington DC 20217

CHABOT, PHILIP LOUIS, JR., lawyer; b. Coaldale, Pa., Mar. 23, 1951; s. Philip Louis and Dorothy Louise (Casselberry) C.; m. Karen Sue Pirko, June 6, 1970 (div. 1981); m. Lynne Marx, Nov. 23, 1985; 1 child, Alexander. B.A. with high honors, U. Va., 1973, J.D., 1976. Bar: Va. 1976, D.C. 1976, U.S. Ct. Claims 1978, U.S. Dist. Ct. D.C. 1976, U.S. Dist. Ct. (ea. dist.) Va. 1984, U.S. Ct. Appeals (1st, 2d, 4th, 5th, 8th, 9th and 10th cirs.), U.S. Ct. Appeals (D.C. cir.) 1976, U.S. Supreme Ct. 1979. Assoc. Northcutt Ely, Washington, 1976-77; prin. Duncan, Weinberg & Miller, P.C., Washington, 1978-84; pres. Philip Chabot, Chartered, Washington and Alexandria, Va., 1984—; aide U.S. Senator John V. Tunney, 1973, U.S. Senator William V. Roth, 1974-75; adj. prof. law Am. U., Washington, 1977-81; asst. to dir. com. on tech. transfer and utilization Nat. Acad. Engring., Washington, 1973-74; bd. dirs. Route One Corridor Housing, Inc., 1985—. Editor: (newsletter) Stateline, 1983—. Democratic candidate Va. Ho. of Dels., 44th House Dist., Va., 1983; bd. dirs., sec. Mt. Vernon-Lee Cultural Ctr. Found., Inc., Fairfax, Va., 1984-86; state coordinator Youth Coalition for Muskie, Va., 1972; mem. Fairfax Com. 100, 1983—; mem. Mt. Vernon Dem. Com., 1982-86 ; mem. Fairfax County Dem. Com., 1982-86 ; mem. citizens adv. bd. Mt. Vernon Nursing Ctr., Fairfax, 1982—; bd. dirs. Gum Springs Hist. Soc., Inc., 1985—, Rt. 1 Corridor Housing, Inc., 1985— ; trustee Va. Outdoors Found., 1982-86; trustee, vice chmn. Fairfax County Uniformed Retirement System Bd., 1982-86; nat. vice chief Order of Arrow Boy Scouts Am., 1968-70. Recipient Eagle Scout award Boy Scouts Am., 1964. Mem. ABA, Va. State Bar Assn., Va. Trial Lawyers' Assn., D.C. Bar Assn., Mt. Vernon-Lee C. of C., Fairfax C. of C., Alexandria C. of C., Phi Beta Kappa. Avocation: sailing. Federal civil litigation, FERC practice, Legislative. Home: 2201 Sherwood Hall Ln Alexandria VA 22306 Office: 1990 M St NW #800 Washington DC 20036 Office: 600 Cameron St #200 Alexandria VA 22314

CHABROW, PENN BENJAMIN, lawyer; b. Phila., Feb. 16, 1939; s. Benjamin Penn and Annette (Shapiro) C.; m. Sheila Sue Steinberg, June 18, 1961; children—Michael Penn, Carolyn Debra, Frederick Penn. B.S., Muhlenberg Coll., Allentown, Pa., 1960; J.D., George Washington U., 1962, LL.M. in Taxation, 1968; postgrad. in econs. Harvard U. Bar: Va. 1963, D.C. 1964, U.S. Ct. Appeals (D.C. cir.) 1964, U.S. Tax Ct. 1964, U.S. Supreme Ct. 1966, Fla. 1972, U.S. Ct. Claims 1974, U.S. Ct. Appeals (5th and 11th cirs.) 1981; bd. cert. tax atty., Fla. Tax law specialist IRS, Washington, 1961-67; tax counsel C. of C. U.S., Washington, 1967-74; sole practice, Miami, Fla., 1974—; pres. Forum Realty Co., Phila.; lectr. fed. taxation Barry U. Grad. Sch. of Bus., 1977-81. Mem. ABA, Fla. Bar Assn., Fed. Bar Assn., Va. Bar Assn., D.C. Bar Assn., Greater Miami Estate Planning Council, Collier County Estate Planning Council, Phi Alpha Delta, Phi Sigma Tau. Contbr. articles profl. jours. Corporate taxation, General corporate, Probate. Office: 2222 Ponce De Leon Blvd 3d Floor Coral Gables FL 33134

CHACKES, KENNETH MICHAEL, lawyer, legal educator; b. St. Louis, Sept. 12, 1949; s. Alex and Shirlee (Radloff) C.; m. Carole Gail Breen, June 14, 1970; children: Laura Michelle, Andrew Scott, Brian Carl. BA in Psychology, Tulane U., 1971; JD cum laude, St. Louis U., 1976. Bar: Mo. 1976, U.S. Dist. Ct. (ea. and we. dists.) Mo. 1976, U.S. Ct. Appeals (8th cir.) 1976, U.S. Ct. Appeals (D.C. cir.) 1979, U.S. Ct. Appeals (7th cir.) 1981. Ptnr. Chackes & Hoare, St. Louis, 1976-84; vis. asst. prof. law Washington U., St. Louis, 1984—; adj. prof. law Washington U., 1982-83, supr. clin. students, 1981-84; lectr. various orgns.; appearances on TV show Law Talk, 1985-86; judge Fed. Practice Training Inst., St. Louis, 1983, trial training program Legal Services Atty. Training Programs, St. Louis, 1986, instr., 1984-85; mem. fed. practice com. U.S. Dist. Ct. (ea. dist.) Mo., chmn. subcom. on appointment of counsel in civil rights cases; mem. discovery abuse and civil jury instructions subcom. Mem. editorial bd. St. Louis U. Law Jour. Mem. ABA (labor and employment law and litigation sects.), Mo. Bar Assn. (lectr. seminars 1979, 86), St. Louis Met. Bar Assn. (consumer affairs, conservation and environ. law and pro bono coms.), Am. Assn. Law Schs. (clin. edn. sect.), Order of Woolsack. Legal education, Civil rights, Federal civil litigation. Home: 8100 Gannon Ave University City MO 63130 Office: Washington U Sch Law Campus Box 1120 Saint Louis MO 63130

CHADSEY, PHILLIP DUKE, lawyer; b. Klamath Falls, Oreg., July 23, 1936; s. Milton E. and Mildred L. (Duke) C.; m. Helen Van Dyke, June 26, 1962; children—Phillip Duke II, Dana Lea, Jeffrey Dyke. B.S., U. Oreg., 1958; J.D., Willamette U., 1966. Bar: Oreg. 1966, U.S. Dist. Ct. Oreg. 1966, U.S. Ct. Appeals (9th cir.) 1966, U.S. Ct. Claims 1982. Ptnr. Stoel, Rives, Boley, Fraser and Wyse (formerly Davies, Biggs, Strayer, Stoel and Boley), Portland, Oreg., 1966—; lectr. med. dental legal matters U. Oreg. Health Scis. Ctr., 1972-82. Bd. dirs. Carl V. Morrison Ctr. for Youth and Family Counseling, 1973-79, pres. 1977; trustee First Unitarian Ch., 1972-75, moderator, 1975; bd. visitors Willamette U. Coll. Law, 1982—. Served to capt. USAF, 1959-63. Fellow Am. Coll. Trial Lawyers, Am. Bar Found., Oreg. Bar Found. (charter); mem. Oreg. Commn. on Jud. Fitness (chmn. 1985), Oreg. State Bar (bd. govs. 1979-82, sec. 1981-82), Oreg. State Bd. Bar Examiners (chmn. 1977-78), Oreg. Assn. Def. Counsel, Multnomah County Bar, ABA, Internat. Assn. Ins. Counsel. Clubs: Multnomah Athletic, City (Portland). Federal civil litigation, State civil litigation. Home: 2705 SW Summit Dr Portland OR 97201 Office: 900 SW 5th Ave Portland OR 97204

CHADWICK, H. BEATTY, lawyer; b. Phila., June 21, 1936; s. Herbert Crawford and Eleanor (Beatty) C.; m. Elizabeth Palmer, Mar. 3, 1962 (div. Feb. 1977); children—William, John A.; m. Barbara Crowther, Mar. 31, 1977. A.B., U. Pa., 1957, J.D., 1960. Bar: Pa. 1961, D.C. 1961. Assoc. Morgan, Lewis & Bockius, Phila., 1960-61; assoc. Biester & Ludwig, Doylestown, Pa., 1964-66; asst. counsel, asst. sec. Fidelity Bank, Phila., 1966-69; asst. gen. counsel IU Internat. Corp., Phila., 1969-85; v.p., gen. counsel IU Internat. Corp., 1985—, sec., 1982—. Served as capt. JAGC, USAF, 1961-64. Mem. ABA, Pa. Bar Assn., Phila. Bar Assn., Phi Beta Kappa, Pi Gamma Mu, Pi Sigma Alpha. Republican. Presbyterian. General corporate, Federal civil litigation, Securities. Home: 3728 Darby Rd Bryn Mawr PA 19010 Office: IU Internat Corp 1500 Walnut St Philadelphia PA 19102

CHAE, DON BAIRD, lawyer; b. Kwangju, Korea, Aug. 27, 1934; came to U.S., 1969; s. Hebyong and Woo-Ae Chae; m. Margaret Ann Ferguson, Feb. 14, 1970; 1 child, Donald. BA, Chonnam Nat. U., Kwangju, 1958; MA, U. Pa., 1962; PhD, U. Tex., 1972; JD, So. Meth. U., 1980. Bar: Tex. 1980. Assoc. prof. Chonnam Nat. U., Kwangju, 1962-69; prof. Tarrant County Jr. Coll., Ft. Worth, 1974-79; sole practice Dallas, 1980—. Elder First Korean United Meth. Ch., Dallas, 1983—. Mem. ABA, Tex. Bar Assn., Am. Immigration Lawyers Assn., Korean Assn. Ft. Worth, Tex. (pres. 1978-81), Korean-Am. Citizens League (pres. 1984—), Korean Honam Assn. Dallas (pres. 1986-87). Family and matrimonial, General practice, Immigration, naturalization, and customs. Home: 12518 Pleasant Valley Dallas TX 75243 Office: 2828 Forest Ln Suite 1100 Dallas TX 75234

CHAFETZ, MARC EDWARD, lawyer; b. Boston, Apr. 21, 1953; s. Morris Edward and Marion (Donovan) C.; m. Andrea Laurie Barkan, Aug. 20, 1977; children: Drew Edward, Maria Caitlin. BA, Oberlin Coll., 1975; JD, U. Va., 1979. Bar: D.C. Ct. Appeals 1980, U.S. Dist. Ct. D.C. 1980, U.S. Ct. Appeals (D.C. cir.) 1982. Law clk. to presiding justice U.S. Dist. Ct., Bryan, Va., 1979-80; assoc. Fulbright & Jaworski, Washington, 1980-82; sr. counsel SEC, Washington, 1982-84; gen. counsel Health Communications Inc., Washington, 1984—, also bd. dirs.; assoc. Ballard, Spahr, Andrews & Ingersoll, Washington, 1984-87; pres. Health Communications, Inc., Washington, 1987—. Contbr. articles to profl. jours. Mem. ABA, Fed. Bar Assn., D.C. Bar Assn. Federal civil litigation, Securities, Criminal. Home: 5105 Chevy Chase Pkwy Washington DC 20008 Office: Health Communications Inc 600 New Hampshire Ave NW Suite 100 Washington DC 20037

CHAFFIN, WILLIAM MICHAEL, lawyer; b. Memphis, Jan. 27, 1947; s. William Emmett and Mary (DeWeese) C.; m. Paula Gayle Young, Apr. 5, 1969; children: Katherine Young, Courtney DeWeese. BBA, U. Miss., 1969, JD, 1972. Bar: Miss. 1972, U.S. Dist. Ct. (no. dist.) Miss. 1972. Assoc. Maynard, Fitzgerald & Bradley, Clarksdale, Miss., 1972-73; ptnr. Maynard, Fitzgerald, Bradley & Chaffin, Clarksdale, 1973-74; assoc. Holcomb, Dunbar, Connell, Merkel & Tollison, Clarksdale, 1975-78; ptnr. Holcomb, Dunbar, Connell, Chaffin & Willard, Clarksdale, 1978—; counsel to bd. dirs. United Southern Bank, Clarksdale, 1982—. Mem. Dem. exec. com., Coahoma County, Miss., 1976—; counsel to Coahoma County bd. suprs., 1984—. Mem. Miss. Bar Found., Miss. State Bar Assn., Miss. Trial Lawyers Assn., Assn. Trial Lawyers Am., Assn. County Bd. Attys. Episcopalian. Avocations: hunting, scuba diving. Insurance, Real property, Banking. Home: 516 W 2d St Clarksdale MS 38614 Office: Holcomb Dunbar Connell Chaffin et al 152 Delta Ave Clarksdale MS 38614

CHAITMAN, HELEN DAVIS, lawyer; b. N.Y.C., July 5, 1941; d. Philip and Miriam (Pfeffer) D.; m. Edmund Chaitman, Feb. 29, 1964 (div. 1978); children: Jennifer, Alison; m. George B. Gelman, Oct. 21, 1979. AB cum laude, Bryn Mawr Coll., 1963; JD, Rutgers U., 1976. Bar: N.Y., N.J., U.S. Dist. Ct. N.Y., U.S. Dist. Ct. N.J., U.S. Supreme Ct. Assoc. Paul, Weiss, Rifkind, Wharton & Garrison, N.Y.C., 1977-82; ptnr. Wilentz, Goldman & Spitzer, Woodbridge, N.J., 1983—. Contbg. author Commercial Damages, 1985; editor Emerging Theories of Lender Liability, 1985. Mem. ABA (litigation, chmn. comml. fin. services com.'s subcom. on creditor's liabilities), PLI. Bankruptcy, Contracts commercial. Home: Gus' Farm RD 1 Box 457 Frenchtown NJ 08825 Office: Wilentz Goldman & Spitzer 900 Rt 9 PO Box 10 Woodbridge NJ 07095

CHALAT, JAMES HAROLD, lawyer; b. Livermore, Calif., Apr. 9, 1953; s. Ned Ira and Joann (Steinberg) C.; m. Nancy Swain, Aug. 20, 1981 (div. Nov. 1985); 1 child, Alexandra Sarah. BS with distinction, U. Mich., 1974; JD, U. Denver, 1977. Bar: Colo. 1977, U.S. Dist. Ct. Colo. 1977, U.S. Supreme Ct. 1981, U.S. Ct. Appeals (10th cir.) 1981, Mich. 1983. Pres. Atty.'s Research, Inc., Denver; ptnr. Chalat & Kram, Denver, Kritzer & Chalat, Denver; sole practice Denver, 1983—; adj. prof. law U. Denver, 1979, 85; instr. ski law various profl. orgns. Contbr. articles on ski law to profl. jours. Co-founder, bd. dirs. Ayrie Corp. Mem. ABA (litigation sect.), Colo. Bar Assn., Mich. Bar Assn., Denver Bar Assn., Jefferson County Bar Assn.,

Assn. Trial Lawyers Am., Colo. Trial Lawyers Assn., Mich. Trial Lawyers Assn., Nat. Inst. Trial Advocacy (diplomate), Thursday Night Bar (vol., Pro Bono award 1985). Democrat. Jewish. Avocations: sports, vol. work. Personal injury, Federal civil litigation, State civil litigation. Office: 1535 Grant Suite 360 Denver CO 80203

CHALEFF, GERALD LAWRENCE, lawyer; b. Detroit, Nov. 24, 1941; s. Jules and Anne (Melick) C. B.S., UCLA, 1963; LL.B., Harvard U., 1966. Bar: Calif. 1966. Assoc. Lemaire & Mohi, Los Angeles, 1966-68; dist. atty. Los Angeles County, 1967-68, pub. defender, 1968-77; ptnr. Lafaille, Chaleff & English, Los Angeles, 1978-83; ptnr. Chaleff & English, Los Angeles, 1982—; guest lectr. in field. Mem. Los Angeles County Bar Assn. (jud. appts. com.). Criminal, Juvenile. Office: 1337 Ocean Ave Garden Suite Santa Monica CA 90401

CHALIF, SEYMOUR H., lawyer; b. N.Y.C., Feb. 27, 1927; s. Hyman and Sarah (Short) C.; m. Ronnie Stern, June 13, 1954; children: John, Peter. B.S., NYU, 1948; M.S. in Bus. Adminstrn., Columbia U., 1949, LL.B., 1952. Bar: N.Y. 1953, U.S. Dist. Ct. (so. dist.) N.Y. 1954, U.S. Supreme Ct. 1959, U.S. Ct. Appeals (2d cir.) 1960. Assoc. firm Hale, Kay & Brennan, N.Y.C., 1952-59, Beer, Richards, Lane, Haller & Buttenwieser, N.Y.C., 1959-60; ptnr. firm London, Buttenwieser & Chalif, N.Y.C., 1960-75, Kaye, Scholer, Fierman, Hays & Handler, N.Y.C., 1975—. Served with USN, 1945-46. Mem. ABA, N.Y. State Bar Assn., Assn. Bar City N.Y. Club: University (N.Y.C.). Office: Kaye Scholer Fierman Hays & Handler 425 Park Ave New York NY 10022

CHALK, JOHN ALLEN, lawyer; b. Lexington, Tenn., Jan. 16, 1937. A.A., Freed-Hardeman Coll., 1956; B.S., Tenn. Tech. U., 1962, M.A., 1967; J.D., U. Tex., 1973. Bar: Tex. 1973, D.C. 1977; ordained to ministry Ch. of Christ, 1956. Pastor chs. Dayton, Ohio, 1956-60, Cookeville, Tenn., 1960-66, Abilene, Tex., 1966-71; assoc. Rhodes and Seamster, Abilene, 1973-74, Rhodes and Doscher, Abilene, 1974; ptnr. Rhodes, Doscher, Chalk and Heatherly,, Abilene, 1975-78; gen. counsel La Jet, Inc., Abilene, 1978-84, also v.p., sec; exec. v.p. Dabney Corp., 1984-86; pres. Dabney Capital, 1984-86; ptnr. Gandy, Michener, Swindle, Whitaker & Pratt, Ft. Worth, 1986—; pres. Equity, Inc., 1982—, Trustcorp., Inc., 1980—. Author: The Praying Christ, 1964, Three American Revolutions, 1970, Jesus' Church, 1970, The Christian Family, 1973, Great Biblical Doctrines, 1973, The Devil, You Say!, 1974; contbr. articles to religious jours. Trustee Abilene Regional Mental Health Retardation Ctr., 1978-80; chmn. Abilene Bicentennial Com., 1975-76; nat. adv. council Ams. United for Separation of Ch. and State, 1979-82, pres. bd. trustees, 1981-82; nat. devel. council Abilene Christian U.; featured speaker Herald of Truth radio and TV programs, 1966-69. Mem. ABA (acting assoc. editor, editorial bd. Family Advocate 1977-78), Tex. Bar Assn., Ft. Worth Bar Assn., Fed. Bar Assn., Tex. Criminal Def. Lawyers Assn., Assn. Trial Lawyers Am., Tex. Trial Lawyers Assn. General corporate, Personal injury, Banking. Home: 3706 W 6th ST Fort Worth TX 76107 Office: Gandy Michener Swindle Whittaker & Pratt 2501 Parkview Dr Suite 600 Fort Worth TX 76102

CHAMBERLAIN, DOUGLAS REGINALD, lawyer; b. Burlington, Vt., Sept. 8, 1951; s. Reginald B. and Ethelda B. (Towle) C.; m. Linda J. Canfield, Sept. 11, 1982. A.B., Harvard Coll., 1973; J.D., Columbia U., 1976. Bar: N.H. 1976, U.S. Dist. Ct. N.H. 1976. Assoc. Wiggin & Nourie, Manchester, N.H., 1976-81, ptnr., 1982—. Bd. dirs. N.H. Performing Arts Ctr., Manchester, 1981—. Mem. N.H. Employee Benefits Council (pres. 1983-84), N.H. Bar Assn. (com. on ethics 1981-86, chmn., 1986—, chmn. group ins. pension plan com. 1984-85), ABA (employee benefits com. 1982—). Republican. General corporate, Pension, profit-sharing, and employee benefits, Corporate taxation. Office: Wiggin & Nourie PO Box 808 Franklin & Market Sts Manchester NH 03105

CHAMBERLAIN, GERARD ALFRED, lawyer; b. Methuen, Mass., Sept. 11, 1955; s. Gerard Joseph and Catherine Theresa (Lynch) C.; m. Margaret Ann Bacheson, Sept. 10, 1983. BA, MA, U. Pa., 1977, JD, 1981. Bar: Pa. 1981, U.S. Ct. Appeals (3d cir.) 1982. Law clk. to presiding justice Pa. Supreme Ct., Phila., 1981-82; assoc. Wolf, Block, Schorr & Solis-Cohen, Phila., 1982-85; assoc. counsel Franklin Realty Group, Blue Bell, Pa., 1985—. Mem. Ctr. City Residents Assn., 1985—. Mem. ABA, Pa. Bar Assn., Phila. Bar Assn., ACLU, U.S. Weightlifting Fedn. (athlete's rep. 1986—). Democrat. Roman Catholic. Avocations: olympic weightlifting, jazz music, jogging. General corporate, Securities, Banking. Home: 225 S 18th St Philadelphia PA 19103 Office: Franklin Realty Group 4 Sentry Pkwy Blue Bell PA 19422

CHAMBERLAIN, JAMES ROBERT, lawyer; b. Cedar Rapids, Iowa, Nov. 13, 1949; s. Robert Glenn and Jane Helen (Newlin) C.; m. Marsha Lois Gurland, June 23, 1971; children: Jonathan James, Zachary Todd, Seth Andrew. BA, U. Wis., 1971, MS, 1973; JD, So. Meth. U., 1976. Bar: Tex. 1976, U.S. Dist. Ct. (no. dist.) Tex. 1978, Wis. 1980. Atty. trade regulation div. FTC, Dallas, 1976-80; sr. counsel antitrust div. Westinghouse Electric Corp., Pitts., 1980-86; adj. prof. antitrust law Duquesne U. Law Sch., 1986-87. Editor Human Rights Jour., 1975-76. Mem. ABA (antitrust sect.), Christian Legal Soc. Antitrust, General corporate. Home: 519 Longridge Dr Pittsburgh PA 15243 Office: Westinghouse Electric Corp 6 Gateway Ctr Pittsburgh PA 15222

CHAMBERLAIN, JOHN, lawyer; b. N.Y.C., Jan. 21, 1930; s. Simon and Mary (Sdonas) C.; m. Eileen Brown; children—Claudia Chamberlain Zohorsky, Eileen, Matthew. B.A., U. S.C., 1951; J.D., Columbia U., 1957. Bar: N.Y. 1958, U.S. Supreme Ct. 1969. Assoc. Hall, Casey, Brady & Dickler, N.Y.C., 1958-59; assoc. James Blake, Esq., Garden City, N.Y., 1959-62; ptnr. Blake & Chamberlain, 1962-68; sole practice, Garden City, 1968—. Served to lt. USN, 1951-57. Mem. Nassau County Bar Assn. (vice chmn. criminal law and procedure com. 1977-78, chmn. criminal law and procedure com. 1979-81, dir. 1982—), N.Y. State Bar Assn., Criminal Cts. Bar Assn. Nassau County (pres. 1968-69, dir. 1969—), Nassau Lawyers Assn., Phi Alpha Delta. Club: Seawanhaka Corinthian Yacht (Centre Island, N.Y.). Criminal, Environment, Family and matrimonial. Home: 58 RyeField Rd Locust Valley NY 11560 Office: 1205 Franklin Ave Garden City NY 11530

CHAMBERLIN, C. RICK, lawyer; b. San Diego, July 8, 1947; s. Don L. and Lauralee (Brewer) C. BA, U. Calif., Berkeley, 1969; JD, U. Calif., Hastings, 1972. Bar: Calif. 1973, U.S. Dist. Ct. (no. dist.) Calif. 1973, U.S. Ct. Appeals (9th cir.) 1973, U.S. Supreme Ct. 1983. Dir. domestic relations dept. San Francisco Neighborhood Legal Assistance, 1973-78; ptnr. Picardo & Chamberlin, San Francisco, 1978-81; from assoc. to ptnr. Stotter, Samuels & Chamberlin, San Francisco, 1981—. Author: Marital Termination Settlement Agreements, 1986, California Family Law Services, 1986. Fellow Am. Acad. Matrimonial Lawyers (sec. 1985-86, treas. 1986—); mem. ABA (family law sect., chmn. specialization com. 1986-87, co-chair nat. mtg. host com., 1987—), Calif. Bar Assn. (cert. specialist 1981—, commr. family law adv. commn. 1986—), Assn. Family Law Specialists (pres. 1985-86). Family and matrimonial. Office: Stotter Samuels & Chamberlin 1735 Franklin San Francisco CA 94109-3526

CHAMBERLIN, MICHAEL MEADE, lawyer; b. Omaha; s. C. Meade and Helen Gail (Russell) C. AB in Econs., Princeton U., 1972; JD, George Washington U., 1975. Bar: N.Y. 1976. Assoc. Shearman & Sterling, N.Y.C., 1975-83, ptnr., 1983—. Episcopalian. Avocations: running, music. Banking, Private international. Home: 30 E 10th St New York NY 10003

CHAMBERS, CHARLES MACKAY, science administrator lawyer, consultant; b. Hampton, Va., June 22, 1941; s. Charles MacKay and Ruth Ellanora (Wallach) C.; m. Barbara Mae Fromm, June 9, 1962; children: Charles M., Catherine M., Christina M., Carleton M. BS, U. Ala., 1962, MS, 1963, PhD, 1964; JD, George Washington U., 1976. Bar: Va. 1977, D.C. 1978, U.S. Patent Office 1978, U.S. Supreme Ct. 1980, U.S. Dist. Ct. D.C. 1985. Research fellow Harvard U., Cambridge, Mass., 1964-65; assoc. prof. U. Ala., Tuscaloosa, 1965-69; mng. dir. Univ. Assocs., Washington, 1969-72; prof., assoc. dean George Washington U., Washington, 1972-77; v.p., gen. counsel Council on Postsecondary Accreditation, Washington, 1977-83; exec. dir. Am. Inst. Biol. Sci., Washington, 1983—. Author: (with others) Understanding Accreditation, 1983; contbr. chptrs. to books. Mem. Diocesan Adv. Council, Arlington, Va., 1978-84, Fairfax County (Va.) Dem. Com., 1979—; trustee, sec. Southeastern U., Washington, 1983—. Recipient Olive Branch award Editors and Writers Com., N.Y.C., 1986, Citizenship award Am. Legion, 1959. Mem. ABA, AAUP, Am. Assn. of Univ. Adminstrs. (pres. 1983-84), Phi Beta Kappa, Sigma Xi, Tau Beta Pi. Roman Catholic. Avocation: sailing. Administrative and regulatory, General corporate, Legal education. Home: 4220 Dandridge Terr Alexandria VA 22309-2807 Offices: Am Inst Biol Scis 730 11th St NW Washington DC 20001-4584

CHAMBERS, DAVID L., III, legal educator; b. Indpls., Sept. 24, 1940; s. David L. and Estelle (Burpee) C.; m. Mary Wales Blanton, June 6, 1962; children: Lucy, Abbot, Liza. A.B., Princeton U., 1962; LL.B., Harvard U., 1965. Bar: D.C. 1966, Mich. 1971. Assoc. Wilmer, Cutter & Pickering, Washington, 1965-67; spl. asst. to exec. dir. Nat. Adv. Com. on Civil Disorders, Washington, 1967-68; mem. faculty Sch. Law, U. Mich., Ann Arbor, now prof. law; chmn. bd. Mich. Legal Services, Inc., Detroit, 1975-80. Author: Making Fathers Pay: The Enforcement of Child Support, 1979. Mem. Soc. Am. Law Tchrs. (pres. 1977-79). Democrat. Family and matrimonial, Criminal. Home: 1055 Ferdon Rd Ann Arbor MI 48104 Office: Univ Mich Law Sch Ann Arbor MI 48109 *

CHAMBERS, DOROTHY J., lawyer; b. St. Louis, Dec. 27, 1950; d. Philip and Dorothy M. (Hollenbach) Helfrich; m. Gerald T. Chambers, Jan. 26, 1973; children: Stephen M., Daniel P. BA summa cum laude, St. Louis U., 1972; JD magna cum laude, Georgetown U., 1979. Bar: Ky., U.S. Dist. Ct. (we. dist.) Ky., U.S. Ct. Appeals (5th and 6th cirs.). Personnel mgmt. specialist CSC, St. Louis, 1972-76; law clk. to presiding justice U.S. Dist. Ct. (we. dist.) Ky., Louisville, 1979-81; assoc. Stites & Harbison, Louisville, 1981-85; atty. South Cen. Bell Telephone Co., Louisville, 1986—. Editorial staff Georgetown U. Law Rev., 1978-79. Mem. ABA, Ky. Bar Assn., Louisville Bar Assn. (sub-com. economical litigation), Women Lawyers Assn. of Jefferson County, Phi Beta Kappa. Federal civil litigation, Labor, Public utilities. Office: South Cen Bell Telephone Co PO Box 32410 Louisville KY 40232

CHAMBERS, K.W. MICHAEL, lawyer; b. Anniston, Ala., July 18, 1954; s. James Michael and Dorothy N. (Bailey) C. BA, U. Ala., 1975, JD, 1979; postgrad., U. Geneva, 1980—. Bar: Ala. 1979. Ptnr. Johnstone, Adams et al, Mobile, Ala., 1982—. Bd. dirs. Alliance Francaise, Mobile, 1985—. Fellow Rotary Internat., 1979-80, Fulbright Swiss Confederation scholar, 1980-82. Fellow Am. Acad. Hosp. Attys.; mem. ABA, Ala. Bar Assn., Am. Arbitration Assn. (cert. arbitrator), Southeastern Admiralty Law Inst., U.S. Maritime Law Assn. Avocation: French and Spanish langs. spoken fluently. Admiralty, Federal civil litigation, Health. Office: 104 St Francis Annex PO Box 1988 Mobile AL 36633

CHAMBERS, THOMAS JEFFERSON, lawyer; b. Yakima, Wash., Oct. 11, 1943; s. Thomas J. and Doris May (Ellyson) C.; m. Judy Larene Cable, June 11, 1967; children: Joli, Jana, Tommy. BA in Polit. Sci., Wash. State U., 1966; JD, U. Wash., 1969. Bar: Wash., U.S. Dist. Ct. (we. and ea. dists.) Wash. 1969. Assoc. Lycette, Diamond & Sylvester, Seattle, 1969-71, Barokas & Martin, Seattle, 1972; sole practice Seattle, 1972—; mem. congestion com. Wash. State Cts., 1984, King County Mandatory Arbitration Council, 1981-86, Damages Atty. Roundtable, 1983-86. Contbr. articles to profl. jours. Mem. jud. evaluation com. Mcpl. League, 1982. Mem. Wash. State Trial Lawyers Assn. (pres. 1985-86, pres.-elect 1984-85, bd. govs. 1976—, various coms.), Am. Bd. Trial Advs. Avocation: flying airplanes. Personal injury. Home: 4514 193d Pl SE Issaquah WA 98027 Office: 1400 Broadway Seattle WA 98122

CHAMBLIN, SPENCER DIEHL, lawyer; b. Columbus, Ohio, Dec. 7, 1941; s. George H. and Anne (Diehl) C.; B.A., Union Coll., 1965; J.D., U. Cin., 1968. Bar: Ohio 1968, U.S. Dist. Ct. (so. dist.) Ohio 1970. Asst. city solicitor City of Cin., 1968-72; assoc. Chamblin & Snyder, Columbus, 1972-75, 78-83. Mem. Cin. Bar Assn., ABA, Am. Judicature Soc., Ohio Legal Ctr. Inst. (recipient award of merit 1974), Phi Delta Phi. Episcopalian. Clubs: Athletic of Columbus, Columbus Country, University of Cin. Real property. Home: 723 E Capitol St SE Washington DC 20003

CHAMBLISS, LINDA CHRISTINE, lawyer, educator; b. Miami, Fla., Nov. 26, 1949; d. Claude Franklin Chambliss Jr. and Dorothea Malinda (Bailey) Ross; m. Franklin J. Lindsay, Dec. 28, 1978. BBA, Fla. Atlantic U., 1971, MBA, 1972; JD summa cum laude, Nova U., 1978; LLM summa cum laude, U. Miami, 1979. Bar: Fla. 1978, U.S. Dist. Ct. (so. dist.) Fla. 1981, U.S. Tax Ct. 1981. Assoc. MacLean, Amato & Arlen P.A., Pompano Beach, Fla., 1979-80; ptnr. Copeland & Chambliss P.A., Ft. Lauderdale, Fla., 1980—; adj. prof. Nova U., Ft. Lauderdale, 1981—. Mem. Broward County Human Rights Bd., Ft. Lauderdale, 1985—. Mem. Fla. Bar Assn. (grievance com. 1985—), Broward County Bar Assn. (chmn. continuing legal edn. com. 1985—), Nova Law Alumni Assn. (treas. 1979—). Democrat. Estate planning, Probate, Estate taxation. Office: Copeland & Chambliss 707 SE 3d Ave Fort Lauderdale FL 33316

CHAMBLISS, PRINCE CAESAR, JR., lawyer; b. Birmingham, Ala., Oct. 3, 1948; s. Prince Caesar and Marguerite (Pearson) C.; m. Patricia Toney, Dec. 26, 1971; 1 dau., Patience Brandyn. Student Wesleyan U., Middletown, Conn., 1966-68; B.A., U. Ala., Birmingham, 1969-71; J.D., Harvard U., 1974. Bar: Ala. 1974, Tenn. 1976. Spl. asst. to pres. U. Ala., Birmingham, 1974-75; law clk. to judge U.S. Dist. Ct. (no. dist.) Ala., Birmingham, 1975-76; assoc. firm Armstrong, Allen, Braden, Goodman, McBride & Prewitt, Memphis, 1976-81, ptnr., 1981—. Bd. dirs. Girls Club of Memphis, 1982—; trustee Miles Coll. Sch. Law, Birmingham, 1982—. Recipient Community Service award Jud. Council Nat. Bar Assn., 1982; named Boss of Yr., Memphis Legal Secs. Assn., 1984. Mem. Memphis-Shelby County Bar Assn. (dir. 1983-85), Fed. Bar Assn. (pres. Mid-South chpt. 1984-85), ABA, Nat. Bar Assn., Tenn. Bar Assn., Ala. Bar Assn, Memphis Council for Internat. Visitors (bd. dirs. 1983—). Federal civil litigation, State civil litigation, General corporate. Home: 1917 Miller Farms Rd Germantown TN 38138 Office: Armstrong Allen Braden Goodman McBride & Prewitt 1900 One Commerce Sq Memphis TN 38103

CHAMPION, FORREST LEE, JR., lawyer; b. Pine Mountain, Ga., Aug. 17, 1921; s. Forrest Lee and Sallie Irene (Babb) C.; m. Irene Mae Spencer, June 6, 1948; children—Forrest Lee, Spencer, Grace Irene. B.A. in Polit. Sci. with spl. departmental honors, Emory U., 1942; LL.B. summa cum laude, U. Ga., 1945. Bar: Ga. 1945, U.S. Dist. Ct. (mid. dist.) Ga. 1945, U.S. Ct. Appeals (5th cir.), U.S. Ct. Appeals (11th cir.) 1982, U.S. Supreme Ct. 1963. Assoc. Foley, Chappell, Kelley & Champion, Columbus, Ga., 1945-61; ptnr. Kelly, Champion, Denney & Pease and predecessor, Columbus, 1961-76, Champion & Champion, Columbus, 1976—; speaker seminars on condemnation, banking, estates and other fields of law Ctr. Continuing Legal Edn., U. Ga.; legal cons. Commn. for Consol. Govts. of City of Columbus and Muscogee County. Fellow Am. Coll. Trial Lawyers; mem. Ga. Bar Assn. (chmn. com. trustees and their adminstrn.), Columbus Lawyers Club (pres. 1950), Ga. State Bar (bd. govs.), ABA. Baptist. Club: Columbus Country. General civil practice, Condemnation, Probate. Office: PO Box 2525 1030 2nd Ave Columbus GA 31902

CHAMPION, ROGER CORNELIUS, food products executive, lawyer; b. Selma, Ala., Mar. 6, 1944; s. Dacey C. and Sarah C. (Warren) C.; m. Donna Sue Blow, Sept. 6, 1969; children: Hunter, Spencer. BS, Auburn U., 1966, MBA, 1971; JD, U. Ala., 1979. Bar: Ga. 1979, U.S. Dist. Ct. (so. dist.) Ga. 1981; CPA, Ga. Project controller Rust Internat., Birmingham, 1972-78; chief fin. officer Frye Copy Systems, Des Moines, 1978-79, Sinclair & Valentine Inc., Des Moines, 1979-80; v.p. Sunnyland Foods Inc., Thomasville, Ga., 1980-86; pres. C&W Food Services, Inc., Tallahassee, 1987—. Bd. dirs. United Way, Thomasville, 1984-86; mem. Parks and Recreation Commn., Thomasville, 1985. Served to capt. USAF, 1967-71. Mem. ABA, Ga. Bar Assn., Am. Inst. CPA's, Ga. Soc. CPA's. Club: Glen Arven Country (Thomasville) (bd. dirs. 1984). Avocations: hunting, fishing. General corporate, Pension, profit-sharing, and employee benefits, Corporate taxation. Home: PO Box 2011 Thomasville GA 31799 Office: C&W Food Services Inc PO Box 5074 Tallahassee FL 32304

CHAMPION, WALTER THOMAS, JR., law librarian; b. Phila., Nov. 22, 1950; s. Walter Thomas and Elizabeth Mary (Eagles) C.; m. Linda Christine Lawson, Jan. 18, 1975 (div. Nov. 1984); 1 child, Walter Thomas III. BA, St. Joseph's U., 1973; MA, Western Ill. U., 1975; MLS, Drexel U., 1977; JD, Temple U., 1982. Bar: Pa. 1982, U.S. Dist. Ct. (ea. dist.) Pa. 1982, U.S. Ct. Appeals (3d cir.) 1982, U.S. Tax Ct. 1982. Librarian Office of Aging, Phila., 1977, Villanova (Pa.) U. Law Sch., 1981-84; editor Am. Law Inst., Phila., 1977-80; law clk. Ct. Common Pleas, Phila., 1983-84; dir. library, asst. prof. Thurgood Marshall Law Sch., Houston, 1984—; legal cons. Sports Services Unltd., Inc., Phila., 1984—. Assoc. editor Packard Law Reports, Phila., 1981-83; contbg. editor Pa. Law Jour., 1981-84; columnist The Tex. Lawyer, 1985; contbr. articles to legal and hist. jours. Mem. ABA, Assn. Trial Lawyers Am., Am. Assn. Law Librarians (Houston chpt., southwest area chpt.), Pa. Bar Assn., Phila. Bar Assn. Democrat. Lutheran. Office: Thurgood Marshall Sch Law 3100 Cleburne Ave Houston TX 77004

CHAMPLIN, PHILIP ALDEN, judge; b. Annapolis, Md., Sept. 1, 1939; s. Jackson Selover and Betty (Trotter) C.; m. Lynne Barbara McWilliams, Nov. 3, 1966; children—Christopher, Catherine. B.A., Yale U., 1961; LL.B., U. Calif.-Berkeley, 1964. Bar: Calif. 1965, U.S. Supreme Ct. 1971. Assoc. Coombs & Dunlap, Napa, Calif., 1965-66; ptnr. Coombs, Dunlap, Dunlap & Champlin, Napa, 1966-77; judge Napa County (Calif.) Mcpl. Ct., 1977-79; judge Napa County Superior Ct., 1979—; city atty. City of Yountville (Calif.), 1967-77; dep. city atty. City of Napa, 1967-77; chmn. Napa County Criminal Justice Planning Com., 1978—. Trustee Napa Community Coll., 1967-77, pres. bd., 1970-72, 75-76; pres. Silverado council Boy Scouts Am., 1983. Mem. Calif. Judges Assn., Napa County Bar Assn. (pres. 1973-74). Club: Rotary (pres. club 1983-84) (Napa). Jurisprudence. Office: 825 Brown St Napa CA 94556

CHAN, THOMAS TAK-WAH, lawyer; b. Kowloon, Hong Kong, June 5, 1950; s. Frank L. and Suit-Chun (Luk) C.; m. Wai-Sing Chow, Apr. 27, 1986. BA magna cum laude, U. Wis., Whitewater, 1973; JD, U. Wis., 1979. Bar: Wis. 1979, U.S. Dist. Ct. (ea. dist.) Wis. 1979, Minn. 1983. Atty. Wasau (Wis.) Ins., 1979-82; staff atty. CPT Corp., Eden Prairie, Minn., 1982-84; gen. counsel Lee Data Corp., Eden Prairie, 1984-85; dep. gen. counsel Ashton-Tate Corp., Torrance, Calif., 1985—; founder Coalition Against Internat. Software Pirates, Torrance, 1986—. Mem. Minn. Bar Assn. (lectr. computer law com. 1985), Wis. Bar Assn., Computer Law Assn., Phi Kappa Phi. Avocations: marathon cross-country skiing, hiking, poetry. Computer, Private international, General corporate. Office: Ashton-Tate Corp 20101 Hamilton Ave Torrance CA 90025

CHANCELLOR, THOMAS HARVEY, lawyer, educator; b. Dallas, Oct. 21, 1936; s. Thomas Harvey and Josephine Louise (Staton) C.; m. Diane Kay Williams, Dec. 26, 1959; children—Robin Leigh, Christopher Thomas; m. Denise J. Nolan, Aug. 30, 1976. B.A. in Econs. with highest honors, North Tex. State, 1961; J.D. cum laude, Harvard U., 1964. Bar: Calif. 1965, U.S. Dist. Ct. (so. dist.) Calif. 1965, U.S. Ct. Appeals (9th cir.) 1965, Tex. 1981. Assoc., Gibson, Dunn & Crutcher, Los Angeles and Paris, 1964-71, ptnr., 1971-78; adj. prof. law U. Utah, Salt Lake City, 1979-80, assoc. prof., 1982—; assoc. prof. Tex. Tech. U., 1980-82; prof., program dir. London Law Consortium Univ. Coll. of London, 1985; lectr. on continuing edn. programs for attys. Mem. ABA taxation, internat. law and bus. coms.), Internat. Bar Assn., Internat. Fiscal Assn. Contbr. numerous articles to profl. jours. Private international, Personal income taxation, General corporate. Office: U Utah Coll Law Salt Lake City UT 84112

CHANDLER, JOHN BRANDON, JR., lawyer; b. Boston, Sept. 25, 1939; s. John Brandon and Juliette (Blackburn) C.; m. Helen Elizabeth Demski, Mar. 22, 1986; 1 son, John Brandon III. B.A., Vanderbilt U., 1961, J.D., 1964. Bar: Tenn. 1964, Fla. 1967, U.S. Supreme Ct. 1971. Assoc. Rogers Towers Bailey Jones & Gay, Jacksonville, Fla., 1967-72, ptnr., 1973—. Served to capt. U.S. Army, 1964-66. Mem. ABA (regional chmn. discovery com., litigation sect.), Fla. Bar, Am. Arbitration Assn. (mem. panel), Jacksonville Bar Assn. (bd. govs. 1975-80), Phi Delta Phi. Clubs: Fla. Yacht, Seminole, Ponte Vedra, Ye Mystic Revellers, Friars, Sawgrass, University, Jacksonville Vanderbilt (pres. 1973-84). Contbr. articles to legal jours. Labor, Federal civil litigation, Trademark and copyright. Home: 2025 Oceanfront Atlantic Beach FL 32233 Office: 1300 Gulf Life Dr Jacksonville FL 32207

CHANDLER, KENT, JR., lawyer; b. Chgo., Jan. 10, 1920; s. Kent and Grace Emeret (Tuttle) C.; m. Frances Robertson, June 19, 1948; children—Gail, Robertson Kent. B.A., Yale U., 1942; J.D., U. Mich., 1949. Bar: Ill. 1949, U.S. Dist. Ct. (no. dist.) Ill. 1949, U.S. Ct. Claims 1958, U.S. Ct. Appeals (7th cir.) 1955. Assoc. Wilson & McIlvaine, Chgo., 1949-56, ptnr., 1957—; dir. First Nat. Bank Lake Forest, 1969—. Mem. zoning bd. appeals City Lake Forest (Ill.), 1953-63, chmn., 1963-67, mem. plan commn., 1955-69, chmn., 1969-70, pres. bd. local improvements, 1970-73, mem., 1973-78, mayor, 1970-73, mem. bd. fire and police commn., 1975-82, chmn., 1982-84. Served to maj. USMCR, 1941-46. Mem. ABA, Chgo. Bar Assn., Ill. State Bar Assn., Lake County Bar Assn., Legal Club Chgo., Law Club. Republican. Presbyterian. Clubs: Comml. of Chgo., Univ. of Chgo., Onwentsia (Lake Forest), Old Elm (Fort Sheridan, Ill.). Banking, Pension, profit-sharing, and employee benefits, Personal income taxation. Office: 135 S LaSalle St Room 2300 Chicago IL 60603

CHANDLER, LAWRENCE BRADFORD, JR., lawyer; b. New Bedford, Mass., June 20, 1942; s. Lawrence Bradford and Anne (Crane) C.; m. Madeleine Bibeau, Sept. 7, 1963 (div. June 1984); children: Dawn, Colleen, Brad; m. Cynthia Korn Howe, May 11, 1985. BS in Bus. Adminstrn., Boston Coll., 1963; LLB, U. Va., 1966, JD, 1970. Bar: Mass. 1966, U.S. Supreme Ct. 1967, Va. 1970. Assoc. Chandler, Franklin & O'Bryan, Charlottesville, Va., 1971—. Served to cpt. U.S. Army, 1967-71. Mem. ABA, Charlottesville Bar Assn., Assn. Trial Lawyers Am., Va. Trial Lawyers Assn. (pres. 1985-86), Assn. U.S. Army. Roman Catholic. Lodges: Elks, K.C. Personal injury. Home: 1445 Old Ballard Rd Charlottesville VA 22901 Office: Chandler Franklin & O'Bryan PO Box 6747 Charlottesville VA 22906

CHANEN, FRANKLIN ALLEN, lawyer; b. Burlington, Iowa, Mar. 12, 1933; s. Sam and Sonia C.; m. Doralu Kohlman, Sept. 9, 1956; children: Gregory, Stuart, Bruce. B.B.A., Northwestern U., 1954, J.D., 1957. Bar: Ill. 1957; C.P.A., Ill. Assoc. Leibman, Williams, Bennett, Baird & Minow, Chgo., 1957-64, ptnr., 1964-72; consol. with Sidley & Austin, 1972, ptnr., 1972—. Contbr. articles to profl. jours. Pres. Ill. Soc. Prevention of Blindness, 1983-85. Mem. Chgo. Bar Assn., Order of Coif, Beta Gamma Sigma. Corporate taxation, Personal income taxation, General corporate. Office: Sidley & Austin One 1st National Plaza Chicago IL 60603

CHANEN, STEVEN ROBERT, lawyer; b. Phoenix, May 15, 1953; s. Herman and Lois Marion (Boshes) C. Student, UCLA, 1971-73; BS in Mass Communications, Ariz. State U., 1975, JD, 1979. Bar: Ariz. 1980, U.S. Dist. Ct. Ariz. 1980, U.S. Ct. Appeals (9th cir.) 1980, Calif. 1981, U.S. Dist. Ct. (no. dist.) Calif. 1982. Assoc. Eldridge & Brown, Phoenix, 1979-80; ptnr. Wentworth & Lundin, Phoenix, 1980-86, of counsel, 1986—; ptnr. Cen. Ariz. Sun Homes, Phoenix, 1982—; pres., FMR Capital Corp., Phoenix, 1983—, bd. dirs.; appointed mem. Ariz. Gov.'s Commn. on Motion Pictures and TV, 1986; chmn. bd. dirs. S.R. Chanen and Co., Inc., Phoenix; bd. dirs. Norcap Fin. Corp., Phoenix. Bd. dirs. Anytown, Am., Phoenix, 1986—, COMPAS, Inc., Phoenix, 1986—. Mem. ABA (form com. entertainment and sports industries 1981—), Ariz. Bar Assn., Calif. Bar Assn., Maricopa County Bar Assn., Assn. Trial Lawyers Am. Republican. Jewish. General corporate, Securities, Administrative and regulatory. Office: Wentworth & Lundin 201 N Central Ave 3500 Valley Bank Ctr Phoenix AZ 85073

CHANEY, JOHN LESTER, JR., lawyer; b. Washington, Sept. 20, 1926; s. John Lester and Gertrude Frances (Dunn) C.; m. Joan Theresa Muren, Sept. 10, 1955; children—John Robert, Catherine Ann, Donald Jeffrey, Ann Margaret. B.A., George Washington U., 1953, LL.B., 1957. Bar: Md. 1961. Tax law specialist IRS, Washington, 1957-61; atty. ICC, Washington, 1961-74, asst. chief atty., 1969-74, chief atty., interpretations, office of compliance and consumer assistance, 1975—. Pres. Seabrook Park Citizens Assn., Lanham, Md., 1961-63, St. Matthias PTA, Lanham, 1971-72. Served to lt. USN, 1953-55. Recipient Disting. Service award George Washington U. Gen.

Alumni Assn., 1984. Mem. Md. Bar Assn., Nat. Law Assn. of George Washington U. Nat. Law Ctr., Gen. Alumni Assn. George Washington U. (sec. governing bd. 1982-84). Roman Catholic. Club: George Washington U. (dir. 1983-84) (Washington). Administrative and regulatory. Home: 6315 Barrs Ln Lanham MD 20706 Office: ICC 12th and Constitution Ave NW Washington DC 20423

CHANEY, MARK JAMES, JR., lawyer; b. Durant, Miss., May 10, 1952; s. Mark J. and Kathryn (Montgomery) C.; m. Karen Heern, June 1977; children: Mark James III, Sarah Kathryn. BA, U. Miss., 1974, JD, 1976. Bar: Miss. 1977, U.S. Dist. Ct. (no. and so. dists.) Miss. 1977, U.S. Ct. Appeals (5th cir.) 1977. Spl. asst. atty. gen. Miss. Atty. Gen.'s Office, Jackson, 1976-77; ptnr. Teller, Chaney & Rector, Vicksburg, Miss., 1977—. Mem. exec. com. Warren County Reps., Vicksburg, 1976-80; pres., bd. dirs. Vicksburg Area Chpt. ARC, 1980-83. Mem. ABA, Assn. Trial Lawyers Am., Miss. Bar Assn., Miss. Council Sch. Bd. Attys. (bd. dirs. 1980-82, 1984—), Warren County Young Lawyers (v.p. 1979), Vicksburg Jaycees (bd. dirs. 1977). Baptist. Lodge: Kiwanis (pres. Vicksburg club 1981). Avocations: hunting, fishing. General practice, Personal injury, Contracts commercial. Home: 707 Newit Vick Dr Vicksburg MS 39180 Office: Teller Chaney & Rector 1201 Cherry St Vicksburg MS 39180

CHANEY, MICHAEL THOMAS, lawyer; b. Charleston, W.Va., Feb. 4, 1948; s. Vincent V. and Caroline (O'Neale) C.; m. Nancy Jane Bierley, May 25, 1974; children: Matthew Thomas, Megan O'Neale, Christopher Michael. BA, Duke U., 1970; JD magna cum laude, U. Mich., 1973. Bar: W.Va. 1973, U.S. Dist. Ct. (so. dist.) W.Va. 1973, U.S. Dist. Ct. (no. dist.) W.Va. 1974, U.S. Ct. Appeals (4th cir.) 1982. Assoc. Kay, Casto & Chaney, Charleston, 1973-76, ptnr., 1976—. Mem. ABA, W.Va. Bar Assn. (exec. com. young law sect. 1981-84), Kanawha County Bar Assn., Order of Coif. Bankruptcy, General corporate, energy, coal, oil and gas. Office: Kay Casto & Chaney 1600 Charleston Nat Plaza Charleston WV 25301

CHANEY, WILLIAM CALVIN, lawyer; b. Abilene, Tex., Dec. 31, 1952; s. William W. and Carolyn (Cowden) C.; m. Clare Buie, Feb. 16, 1980; children: Brent Buie, William Clarkson. BA with high honors, U. Tex., 1975, JD, 1978. Bar: Tex. 1978. Assoc. Mahon, Fitzgerald & Winston, Dallas, 1978-82; ptnr. Mahon, Winston & Chaney, Dallas, 1983; 2d v.p. legal dept. Lomas & Nettleton Co., Dallas, 1983—. Pres. Winnetka Heights Hist. Dist., Dallas, 1981-82, The 500 Inc., Dallas, 1984-85, Shakespeare Fest. of Dallas, 1986-87; bd. dirs. Dallas Housing Fin. Corp., 1984—; bd. govs. Tex. Arts Alliance, Austin, Tex., 1985—. Recipient Commendation, TEx. Hist. Commn., 1983. Mem. ABA, Mortgage Bankers Assn. (regulatory compliance commn.), Tex. Bar Assn., Dallas Bar Assn. Presbyterian. Avocations: sailing, running, tennis. Banking, Real property, Bankruptcy. Home: 228 S Windomere Dallas TX 75208 Office: The Lomas & Nettleton Co PO Box 660723 Dallas TX 75266-0723

CHANG, DONALD MARK, law and economics educator, consultant; b. Honolulu, Nov. 30, 1927; s. Y.K. and L.K. (Leong) C.; m. Mildred Sachiko Matsunaga, July 6, 1957. B.A. cum laude, U. Nebr., 1950; J.D., Yale U., 1953; Ph.D. in Econs. and Ethics and Law, U. Chgo. and Claremont Sch. Theology, U. So. Calif., 1961; student U. Hawaii, 1945-46, 47-48. Jr. exec. Castle & Cooke Co., Honolulu, 1953-54; gen. counsel Hawaii AFL-CIO, Honolulu, 1954-56; spl. asst. to chmn. NLRB, Washington, 1961-62; minority, gen. counsel Com. on Judiciary, U.S. Senate, Washington, 1962-71; prof. law and econs. U. Hawaii, Honolulu, 1971—; cons. Calif. Western Sch. Law, San Diego, 1978-81, Patton, Boggs & Blow, Washington, 1978-80. Bd. dirs. Honolulu Symphony Soc., 1973-78; chmn. United Charities, Honolulu, 1976; chmn. Gubernatorial Candidacy Com., Honolulu, 1972; pres. Waialee Nui Assn., Honolulu, 1972-79. Recipient Outstanding Accomplishment award Moot Ct. Program, U. Hawaii, 1983. Fellow Ethics and Society Colloquium (dir. 1976-85; gold award 1984); mem. Am. Bus. Law Assn., Am. Econ. Assn., Am. Indsl. and Labor Relations Assn., Am. Immigration and Nationality Conf. Democrat. Methodist. Mem. Phi Alpha Delta (pres. 1972-73), Acacia. Lodge: Lancers (pres. 1972-76). Contracts commercial, Labor, Legislative. Home: 1803 Halekoa Dr Honolulu HI 96821 Office: U of Hawaii 96-045 Ala Ike Pearl City HI 96782

CHANG, LEO, lawyer; b. San Francisco, Dec. 21, 1952; s. Chen-Chi and Yu Nien-Tze (Yu) C. BA in History and Asian Studies, Pa. State U., 1973; JD, Columbia U., 1978. Bar: N.Y. 1979, U.S. Dist. Ct. (so. and ea. dists.) N.Y. 1979. Assoc. Burlingham, Underwood & Lord, N.Y.C., 1978-85, ptnr., 1985—; of counsel Law Offices Hassan Mahassni, Jeddah, Saudi Arabia, 1986—. Mem. ABA, Internat. Bar Assn., Maritime Bar Assn. Admiralty, Private international, Banking. Home: c/o Burlingham Underwood & Lord 1 Battery Park Plaza New York NY 10004 Office: Law Office Hassan Mahassni, PO BOx 2256, Jeddah 21451, Saudi Arabia

CHANG, PETER ASHA, JR., lawyer; b. Honolulu, Feb. 1, 1937; s. Peter Asha and Helen (Lee) C.; m. Mayselle Ching, Sept. 3, 1955 (div. Aug. 1982); m. Denise Marie Knoblock, Sept. 30, 1985; children: Catherine, Peter III, Christopher. AB, Stanford U., 1958, JD, 1961. Bar: Calif. 1962, U.S. Dist. Ct. (no. and cen. dists.) Calif. 1962, U.S. Ct. Appeals (9th cir.) 1962, U.S. Supreme Ct. 1964. Asst. dist. atty. Monterey, Calif., 1961-63, chief asst. dist. atty., 1963-66; dist. atty. Santa Cruz, Calif., 1966-75; sole practice Santa Cruz, 1975—; instr., cons. Calif. Dist. Atty.'s Assn., Sacramento, Calif., 1967-74, Nat. Coll. Dist. Atty., 1968-72, Stanford Law Sch., Palo Alto, Calif., 1969-71. Recipient Disting. Achievement award Calif. Dist. Atty.'s Assn., 1971, Morton Advocacy award Nat. Dist. Atty.'s Assn., 1973. Mem. ABA, Nat. Assn. Criminal Def. Lawyers, Calif. Trial Lawyers Assn., Calif. Atty. for Criminal Justice. Democrat. Criminal, Personal injury. Home: 53 Pasatiempo Dr Santa Cruz CA 95060 Office: 331 Soquel Ave Santa Cruz CA 95062

CHANG, SAM HSIEN-CHENG, lawyer; b. Nanking, Peoples Republic of China, Sept. 6, 1946; came to U.S., 1973; s. Tien-Yi and Ju-Jen (Wang) C.; m. Susie Hsi-Ling, July 12, 1970; children: Richard, Edward. LLB, Taiwan U., 1968; M of Comparative Laws, Howard U., 1975. Bar: D.C. 1981. Assoc. Wasserman, Orlow, Washington, 1981-83; ptnr. Wasserman, Mancini & Chang, Washington, 1983—. Gen. counsel Asian Am. Voters' Coalition, Washington, 1986—; prin. Gaithersburg (Md.) Chinese Sch., 1983-84. Mem. ABA, Am. Immigration Lawyers Assn. Avocations: swimming, tennis. Immigration, naturalization, and customs. Office: Wasserman Mancini & Chang 1724 H St NW Washington DC 20006

CHANIN, BERNARD, lawyer; b. Phila., Oct. 12, 1932; s. Benjamin and Irene (Holutin) C.; children—Heidi, Susan, Gary, Eve. B.A., U. PA., 1962, LL.B. cum laude, 1965. Bar: Pa. 1965, U.S. Supreme Ct. 1976. Law clk. Assoc. Justice Supreme Ct. Pa., Phila., 1965-66; ptnr. Wolf, Block, Schorr, & Solis-Cohen, Phila., 1966—. Served with USMC, 1951-54, Korea. Mem. ABA, Pa. Bar Assn., Phila. Bar Assn., Order of the Coif. Republican. Jewish. Federal civil litigation, State civil litigation. Home: 15A5 The Philadelphian Philadelphia PA 19130 Office: 12th floor Packard Bldg 15th and Chestnut Sts Philadelphia PA 19102

CHANIN, MICHAEL HENRY, lawyer; b. Atlanta, Nov. 11, 1943; s. Henry and Herma Irene (Blumenthal) C.; m. Margaret L. Jennings, June 15, 1968; children: Herma Louise, Richard Henry, Patrick Jennings. A.B., U. N.C., 1965; J.D., Emory U., 1968. Bar: Ga. 1968, D.C. 1981. Dir. So. Ctr. for Studies in Pub. Policy, Atlanta, 1968-69; asst. and acting legal officer 1st Coast Guard Dist., Boston, 1969-72; atty. Powell, Goldstein Frazer & Murphy, Atlanta, 1972-77; spl. asst. sec. U.S. Dept. Commerce, Washington, 1977-78; dep. asst. to pres. The White House, Washington, 1978-81; ptnr. Powell, Goldstein, Frazer & Murphy, Washington, 1981—. Served to lt. USCGR, 1969-72. Mem. ABA, D.C. Bar Assn., State Bar Ga. Democrat. General corporate, Corporate taxation. Office: 6th Floor S 1001 Pennsylvania Ave NW Washington DC 20004

CHANNING, STACEY LISA, lawyer; b. Detroit, Nov. 29, 1957; d. Mark G. and Lila (Lang) C.; m. Robert B. Portney, Apr. 8, 1984. BA, Brown U., 1978; JD, Boston U., 1981. Bar: Mass. 1981, U.S. Dist. Ct. Mass. 1981, U.S. Ct. Appeals (1st cir.) 1982, U.S. Patent Office 1983, U.S. Ct. Appeals (D.C. cir.) 1984. Patent atty. Kenway and Jenney, Boston, 1981-83, W.R. Grace & Co., Lexington, Mass., 1983—. Violinist North Shore Philharmonic, Marblehead, Mass., 1981—. Mem. ABA, Boston Patent Law Assn., Am. Intellectual Property Law Assn., Brown Univ. Club. Patent, Trademark and copyright. Office: WR Grace and Co 55 Hayden Ave Lexington MA 02173

CHANNON, PATRICIA SUGRUE, lawyer; b. N.Y.C., Jan. 14, 1938; d. Thomas Joseph and Mary Margaret (Ganey) Sugrue; m. A. Bertrand Channon, Apr. 15, 1961 (div. 1982); children: Thomas Sugrue, Aengus Brian. AB, Bryn Mawr Coll., 1958; JD, William and Mary Coll., 1980. Bar: Va. 1980, U.S. Ct. Appeals (4th cir.) 1980, D.C. 1981, U.S. Dist. Ct. (ea. dist.) Va. 1983, U.S. Dist. Ct. (D.C. dist.) 1983. Atty. benefits rev. bd. U.S. Dept. of Labor, Washington, 1980-81; law clk. to presiding justice U.S. Bankruptcy Ct., Alexandria, Va., 1981-83; assoc. Docter, Docter & Salus, P.C., Washington, 1983-85; atty. Adminstrv. Office of The U.S. Cts., Washington, 1985—. Mem. ABA, Va. State Bar Assn., D.C. Bar Assn., Alexandria Bar Assn. Bankruptcy, Consumer commercial, Judicial administration. Home: 3930 Taney Ave Alexandria VA 22304 Office: Adminstrv Office US Courts Washington DC 20544

CHAPEKIS, NICHOLAS PETER, lawyer; b. Escanaba, Mich., Feb. 9, 1921; s. Anthony Nicholas and Alice (Petropolis) C.; m. Marina Sitaras, Feb. 4, 1950; children: Nick A., Phrosolisa M. AB, U. Mich., 1942, MBA, 1943, JD, 1949. Bar: Mich. 1949, Fla. 1980. Prosecuting atty. Delta County, Escanaba, 1952-70; asst. atty. gen. Escanaba and Lansing, Mich., 1972-79; ptnr. Chapekis, Chapekis & Pearson, Escanaba, 1979—. Author: Prosecuting Attorney's Handbook, 1965. Chmn. charitable orgn. Unites Fund, Delta County, 1952-53; del. Dem. Nat. Convention, Chgo., 1968; bd. dirs. Delta County (Mich.) Cancer Soc., Salvation Army, Delta County. Served to 1st lt. U.S. Army, 1943-46. U. Mich. scholar, 1938-46. Mem. Mich. Bar Assn. (pres. 1958-61), Nat. Dist. Attys. Assn. (chmn. scholarship com. 1964-66), Mich. Dist. Attys. Assn. (bd. dirs., v.p. 1968-70). Lodge: Rotary (chmn. Escanaba com. 1982-85). Avocations: golf, investing in stock market. Probate, Personal injury, Estate planning. home: 1601 S 16th St Escanaba MI 49829 Office: Chapekis Chapekis & Pearson PC 808 Ludington St Escanaba MI 49829

CHAPIN, DAVID CHESTER, lawyer; b. Holyoke, Mass., Apr. 14, 1954; s. Hugh A. and Judith Anne (Kinne) C.; m. Sheeran Phelps Howard, May 30, 1981. BA, Lafayette Coll., 1972-76; JD, Harvard U., 1980. Bar: Mass. 1980. Assoc. Ropes & Gray, Boston, 1980—. Mem. ABA, Mass. Bar Assn., Boston Bar Assn. Democrat. Episcopalian. Avocations: tennis, golf, skiing. Securities, General corporate. Office: Ropes & Gray 225 Franklin St Boston MA 02110

CHAPIN, EDWARD WHITING, lawyer; b. Springfield, Mass., Oct. 22, 1931; s. Neil Chapin and Ruth (Whiting) Green; m. Ethel D. Stout, June 14, 1957; children: Edward W. Jr., Bayard S., Bruce B. BA, Yale U., 1954; LLB, U. Va., 1957. Bar: N.Y. 1959, U.S. Dist. Ct. (so. dist.) N.Y. 1960, U.S. Supreme Ct. 1979. Assoc. Lord, Day & Lord, N.Y.C., 1957-61; sec., counsel Wheelabrator-Frye, N.Y.C., 1961-71; ptnr. Palmer, Serles & Baar, N.Y.C., 1971-74; v.p., sec., gen. counsel Broadcast Music Inc., N.Y.C., 1974—. Mem. Assn. of Bar of City of N.Y., Country Music Assn., Copyright Soc. USA. General practice, General corporate, Federal civil litigation. Office: Broadcast Music Inc 320 W 57th St New York NY 10019

CHAPIN, MELVILLE, lawyer; b. Boston, Dec. 14, 1918; s. Edward Barton and Jeannette (Thomas) C.; m. Elizabeth Ann Parker, Sept. 6, 1940; children: Allan M., Elizabeth M. B.A., Yale U., 1940; J.D., Harvard U., 1943. Bar: Mass. 1943. Sr. ptnr. Warner & Stackpole, Boston, 1954—; dir. H.B. Smith Co., Inc.; chmn. Security Capital Corp; pres., trustee Phillips Acad.; bd. mgr., chmn. Mass. Eye and Ear Infirmary Found. Served to lt. USNR, World War II. Fellow Am. Bar Found., Mass. Bar Found.; mem. ABA, Boston Bar Assn., Mass. Bar Assn., Internat. Bar Assn. General corporate, Probate, General practice. Home: 15 Traill St Cambridge MA 02138 Office: Security Capital Corp 1290 Ave of the Americas New York NY 10104

CHAPLIN, PEGGY FANNON, lawyer; b. Guantanamo Bay Naval Base, Cuba, Nov. 22, 1940; d. Raymond Gerard Fannon and Joan Marie (Carguil) Boyce; m. Walter V. Chaplin, Nov. 7, 1959. BS, Johns Hopkins U., 1971; JD, U. Md., 1973; LLM, Georgetown U., 1983. Bar: Md. 1973, U.S. Dist. Ct. Md. 1973, U.S. Ct. Internat. Trade 1975. V.p. Vanguard Shipping & Import, Balt., 1972-77, F.W. Myers & Co., Inc., Balt., 1977-84; assoc. Ober, Kaler, Grimes & Shriver, Balt., 1984—; bd. dirs. Internat. Visitors Ctr., Balt. Contbr. articles to bar jours. Mem. Gov.'s Commn. World Trade Efforts, 1984, Balt. City Wage Commn., 1986—, Md. Trade Policy Com., 1986. Mem. ABA, Md. State Bar Assn., Women's Bar Assn. Md. (pres. 1977-79), Md. Internat. Trade Assn. (bd. dirs. 1981—, pres. 1984-86), Balt./Washington Dist. Export Council, Md. C. of C. (chmn. internat. trade com.). Administrative and regulatory, Immigration, naturalization, and customs, Private international. Office: Ober Kaler et al Ten Light St Baltimore MD 21217

CHAPMAN, ALEX DAVID, JR., lawyer; b. Ville Platte, La., Oct. 28, 1954; s. Alexon Sr. and Winnie (Soileau) C.; m. Janita Ann Fontenot, Apr. 29, 1983; children: Korey Matthew, Meghann Marie. BA, La. State U., 1976, JD, 1979. Bar: La. 1979, U.S. Dist. Ct. (we. dist.) La. 1979, U.S. Dist. Ct. (ea. dist.) La. 1980, U.S. Ct. Appeals (5th cir.) 1980. Assoc. Law Offices of J. Wendeal Fusilier, Ville Platte, 1979-83; sole practice Ville Platte, 1983—. Mem. La. Jaycees, 1979-83. Mem. Assn. Trial Lawyers Am., La. Trial Lawyers Assn., Evangeline Parish Bar Assn. (sec., treas. 1984-86, v.p. 1986—), Ville Platte C. of C. Democrat. Roman Catholic. Avocations: hunting, fishing, camping, golf, snow skiing. Admiralty, Personal injury, Workers' compensation. Home: Rt 1 Box 605-A Ville Platte LA 70586 Office: 305 W Magnolia PO Box 528 Ville Platte LA 70586

CHAPMAN, BARRY RYAN, lawyer; b. Ft. Stewart, Ga., Dec. 9, 1952; s. Clyde Paris Chapman and Jean (Gilreath) Frasso; m. Mary Pam Boone, Aug. 17, 1974; children—Ryan Andrew, Casey Leigh. B.A., Emory U., 1974; J.D., Samford U., 1977. Bar: Ga. 1977, U.S. Dist. Ct. (mid. dist.) Ga. 1977, Fla. 1981, U.S. Ct. Appeals (11th cir.) 1981. Assoc., Bennett, Wisenbaker, Bennett, Valdosta, Ga., 1977-78; ptnr. Bennett, Wisenbaker, Bennett and Chapman, Valdosta, 1978-82, Langdale, Vallotton, Hickman and Chapman, Valdosta, 1984—; sole practice, Valdosta, 1982-84; judge Recorder's Ct., Valdosta, 1983—. Bd. dirs. Valdosta-Lowndes County Family YMCA, Valdosta, 1981—, treas., 1982, 83, pres., 1985; bd. dirs. United Way of Lowndes County, 1986—. Recipient Am. Jurisprudence Book award-Bankruptcy, Lawyer's Co-Op. Pub. Co., 1977. Mem. ABA, Am. Judicature Soc., Ga. Bar Assn., Fla. Bar Assn., Valdosta C. of C., SAE Alumni Assn. (pres. Valdostachpt. 1987). Club: North Valdosta Rotary (bd. dirs. 1983—, pres.-elect 1986). Lodge: Masons. Bankruptcy, Real property, General practice. Home: 1106 Cloverhill Dr Valdosta Ga 31602 Office: 1007 N Patterson St PO Box 1547 Valdosta GA 31603

CHAPMAN, CHARLES ALAN, lawyer; b. Gadsden, Ala., Feb. 5, 1949; s. Charles Clebron and Betty (Mackey) C.; m. Kay Dugins, Dec. 20, 1975; children: Clark McCoy, Charles Clayton. Student, U. Paris, France, 1969-70; BA, U. Ala., 1971; postgrad., U. London, Eng., 1972; JD, U. Ala., 1974. Bar: Tenn. 1975, S.C. 1977, U.S. Dist. Ct. S.C. 1981, U.S. Ct. Appeals (4th cir.) 1981, U.S. Supreme Ct. 1981. Atty. Provident Life and Accident Ins. Co., Chattanooga, 1974-75; atty. Liberty Corp. and Liberty Life Ins. Co., 1976-80, asst. sec., 1976—, assoc. counsel, 1980-82; counsel Liberty Corp. and Liberty Life Ins. Co., Greenville, S.C., 1982—; bd. dirs. N.C. Life Ins. Guaranty Assn., Raleigh, 1982—. Author: The Practical Lawyer mag., 1983—. Mem. Leadership S.C., Columbia, 1981-82; treas. Greenville County Dems., 1980-82. Fellow Life Office Mgmt. Assn.; mem. ABA, Tenn. Bar Assn., Greenville County Bar Assn., S.C. Bar Assn., N.C. Life Ins. Guaranty Assn. (bd. dirs. 1982—), S.C. Life Ins. Guaranty Assn. (bd. dirs. 1982—), Soc. CLU's, Greater Greenville C. of C. (chmn. local govt. commn. 1982-83), Phi Delta Phi. Democrat. Presbyterian. Clubs: Green Valley Country (Greenville); Palmetto (Columbia). Lodge: Rotary. General corporate, Insurance, Legislative. Home: 8 Scotland Circle Greenville SC 29615 Office: The Liberty Corp 2000 Wade Hampton Blvd PO Box 789 Greenville SC 29602

CHAPMAN, CONRAD DANIEL, lawyer; b. Detroit, July 31, 1933; s. Conrad F. and Alexandrine C. (Baranski) C.; m. Carol Lynn DeBash, Sept. 1, 1956; children: Stephen Daniel, Richard Thomas, Suzanne Marie. BA, U. Detroit, 1954, JD summa cum laude, 1957; LLM in Taxation, Wayne State U., 1964. Bar: Mich. 1957, U.S. Dist. Ct. (so. dist.) Mich. 1957. Ptnr. Powers, Chapman, DeAgostino, Meyers, McTigue & Milia and predecessor firms, Troy, Mich., 1964—. Mem. ABA, Detroit Bar Assn., Oakland Bar Assn., Am. Arbitration Assn., Detroit Estate Planning Council, Oakland Estate Planning Council. Clubs: Detroit Athletic, Detroit Golf. Lodge: Elks. Estate planning, General corporate, Corporate taxation. Office: Powers Chapman DeAgostino Meyers McTigue & Milia 3001 W Big Beaver Rd Suite 704 Troy MI 48084

CHAPMAN, DAVID RALPH, lawyer; b. Portland, Oreg., July 21, 1947; s. Herman and Virginia (Johnston) C.; m. Sharon Marie Meagher, Dec. 27, 1969; children: Christopher, Jessica. BA, Reed Coll., 1969; LLB, U. B.C., Can., 1973. Bar: Calif. 1977, U.S. Dist. Ct. (so. dist.) Calif. 1977, U.S. Supreme Ct. 1984. Assoc. Cumming, Richards & Co., Vancouver, B.C., Can., 1973-76; dep. city atty. City of Escondido, Calif., 1977-78, asst. city atty., 1978-81, city atty., 1981—. Mem. State Legis. Analysis Com. Mem. ABA (urban law sect.), San Diego-Imperial County City Attys. Assn. (pres. 1983, league of Calif. cities city attys. sect. 1978—, chmn. legis. adv. com 1983-84), Escondido C. of C. Democrat. Congregationalist. Office: City of Escondido 100 Valley Blvd Escondido CA 92025

CHAPMAN, DUDLEY HARRY, lawyer; b. Omaha, Oct. 23, 1934; m. Nancy Greg, Dec. 28, 1957; children: Karen, Sharon, Dwight. JD, U. Mich., 1959. Bar: D.C. 1959, Mich. 1960, U.S. Supreme Ct. 1963, N.Y. 1964. Instr. U. Mich., Ann Arbor, 1959-60; assoc. Cleary, Gottlieb, Steen & Hamilton, Washington, N.Y.C. and Brussels, 1963-67; staff atty., asst. chief fgn. commerce antitrust div. Washington, 1967-73; assoc. counsel to pres. White House, Washington, 1973-76; ptnr. Chapman & Clearwaters, Washington, 1977-81, Ward, Lazarus, Grow & Cihlar, Washington, 1982-87. Pres., editor newsletter Mid County Citizens Assn., Montgomery County, Md., 1968—; mem. adv. com. Cable TV, Montgomery County, 1985. Served to capt. U.S. Army, 1960-63. Republican. Club: University (Washington). Antitrust, Federal civil litigation, State civil litigation. Office: Ward Lazarus Grow & Cihlar 1711 N St NW Washington DC 20036

CHAPMAN, JOHN SHERWOOD, lawyer; b. Twin Falls, Idaho, July 6, 1936; s. Marshall Byron and Dorothy (Parsons) C.; m. Judith June Day, May 28, 1966 (div. July 1982); children: Christina Jean, Heidi Suzanne, Elizabeth June. BA, U. Idaho, 1958; JD, Stanford U., 1961. Bar: Idaho 1962, U.S. Dist. Ct. Idaho 1962, U.S. Supreme Ct. 1975, U.S. Ct. Appeals (9th cir.) 1982. Assoc. Hawley, Troxell, Boise, Idaho, 1961-64; ptnr. Martin, Chapman, Park & Burkett, Boise, 1965—. Precinct committeeman Ada County Cen. Com.; mem. Idaho State Cen. Com., treas., 1947-75; former chmn. State Dem. Pledge Fund; mem. state exec. com. Idaho Dem. Party, 1974-84; treas. Gov. John V. Evans' re-election campaign; del. Nat. Dem. Conv., N.Y., 1976, 80; state fin. chmn. Carter/Mondale Campaign, 1980; active United Way of Ada County; bd. dirs., former state chmn. Idaho Ptnrs. of the Alliance; bd. dirs., mem. exec. com. Boise chpt. ARC, chmn., 1985-86; trustee Boise State U. Found.; former bd. dirs. Boise YMCA; chmn. Idaho Commn. on Arts, 1986; mem., past pres. Boise Estate Planning Council. Named Boise's Young Man of Yr., Boise Jaycees, 1965, One of Outstanding Young Men of Am., U.S. Jaycees, 1966, Disting. Citizen of Idaho, Idaho Statesman, 1976. Democrat. Episcopalian. Estate planning, General corporate. Home: 2990 Holl Dr Eagle ID 83616 Office: Martin Chapman Park & Burkett 775 8th St Suite 200 Statehouse Center Bldg Boise ID 83702

CHAPMAN, JOHN WENDELL, lawyer; b. Louisville, Miss., May 20, 1946; s. Joseph Leo and Katherine Hall (Callahan) C.; m. Karen Lynn Forster, June 13, 1970; 1 child, Philip Joseph. B.S., Miss. State U., Starkville, 1969; student Delta State U., 1967-68; J.D., U. Miss., 1974. Bar: Miss. 1974. Assoc., Deramus & Strickland, Louiville, Miss., 1974-76; assoc., ptnr. Bryan, Nelson, Allen & Schroeder, Pascagoula, Miss., 1976-81; assoc., ptnr. Bryant, Stennis & Colingo, Pascagoula, 1981-83; ptnr. Robertson & Chapman, Moss Point, Miss., 1983-84, Pritchard & Chapman, Pascagoula, 1984—. Mem. ABA, Am. Trial Lawyers Assn., Miss. Bar Assn., Miss. Trial Lawyers Assn., Gulf Coast Football Ofcls. Assn. (pres. 1982-85). Personal injury, State civil litigation, Admiralty. Office: Pritchard & Chapman 712 Watts Ave Pascagoula MS 39567

CHAPMAN, KAREN LOUISE, lawyer; b. Denver, Apr. 1, 1954; s. Arthur Alec and Kathleen Joan (Weiss) C.; m. Stuart Donovan Jenkins, June 30, 1984. BS, U. Colo., 1976; JD, Stanford U., 1979. Bar: Colo. 1979, D.C. 1980. Atty. bur. competition FTC, Washington, 1972-82; assoc. Morrison & Foerster, Denver, 1982-84; assoc. Kirkland & Ellis, Denver, 1984-85, ptnr., 1985—. Pres. Stanford Pub. Interest Law Found., Calif., 1978-79. Regents scholar, 1972-73, Boettcher scholar, 1972-76; recipient Wall Street Journal award, 1976. Mem. ABA (com. on significant lit. real property and probate sect.), D.C. Bar Assn., Colo. Bar Assn. Avocations: skiing, hiking, bicycling. Real property, Contracts commercial, Bankruptcy. Office: Kirkland & Ellis 1999 Broadway 40th Floor Denver CO 80202

CHAPMAN, MATTHEW WILLIAM, lawyer; b. Portland, Oreg., Aug. 7, 1950; s. James Don and Regan Mary (McCoy) C.; m. Lillian Louise Richards, Sept. 21, 1985. BA in Econs., U. Portland, 1971; JD, U. Oreg., 1974. Bar: Oreg. 1974, U.S. Dist. Ct. Oreg. 1974, Wash. 1985. Assoc. Stoel, Rives, Boley, Fraser & Wyse, Portland, 1974-80; ptnr. Martin, Bischoff, Templeton, Biggs & Ericsson, Portland, 1980-81, Waggoner, Chapman, Farleigh, Wada & Bogrand, Portland, 1981—; Lectr. numerous bus. assn. seminars. Editor Oreg. Law Rev., 1973-74; contbr. articles to profl. jours. Paul Patterson fellow. Mem. ABA (subcom. credit unions, comml. fin. services com. sect. corp. banking and bus.), Oreg. Bar Assn., Wash. State Bar Assn., Multnomah Bar Assn., Order of Coif, Oreg. Mortgage Bankers Assn. Republican. Roman Catholic. Clubs: Arlington, Multnomah Athletic. Lodge: Rotary. Banking, Bankruptcy, Computer. Home: 615 Burlingame Terr Portland OR 97201 Office: Waggoner Chapman Farleigh et al 1515 SW 5th Suite 770 Portland OR 97201

CHAPMAN, ROBERT FOSTER, federal judge; b. Inman, S.C., Apr. 24, 1926; s. James Alfred and Martha (Marshall) C.; m. Mary Winston Gwathmey, Dec. 21, 1951; children: Edward, Foster, Winston. B.S., U. S.C., 1945, LL.B., 1949, LLD, 1986. Bar: S.C. 1949. Asso. firm Butler & Moore, Spartanburg, 1949-51; partner firm Butler, Chapman & Morgan, Spartanburg, 1953-71; U.S. dist. judge for S.C. 1971-81, U.S. cir. judge, 1981—. Chmn. S.C. Republican Party, 1961-63. Served to lt. USNR, 1943-46, 51-53. Recipient Nat. Patriot's award Congl. Medal of Honor Soc., 1985. Fellow Am. Coll. Trial Lawyers. Presbyn. (ruling elder). Jurisprudence. Home: 1822 Fair St Camden SC 29020 Office: US Court Appeals PO Box 7097 Columbia SC 29202

CHAPMAN, RUSSELL DALE, lawyer; b. Altus, Okla., Mar. 21, 1951; s. Dale Barkley Chapman and Doris Quay (Saunders) Weddle; m. Joan Elizabeth Decker, Sept. 3, 1977; children: Katherine Elaine, Emily Christine. BA, U. Okla., 1975; JD with honors, U. Tulsa, 1978; ML in Taxation, So. Meth. U., 1983. Bar: Okla. 1978, U.S. Tax Ct. 1980. Staff tax atty. Phillips Petroleum Co., Bartlesville, Okla., 1978-80, sr. tax atty., 1984; sr. tax atty. Phillips Coal Co., Dallas, 1980-84; assoc. Wright & Johnson Inc., Oklahoma City, 1984, Speck, Philbin, Fleig, Trudgeon & Lutz P.C., Oklahoma City, 1984—; adj. prof. law Oklahoma City U., 1986 (spring semester). Served to sgt. USAF, 1972-74. Mem. ABA (tax sect.), Oklahoma City Tax Lawyer's Group, Oklahoma City Estate Planning Counsel, Oklahoma City Employee Benefit Conf. Lodge: Lions. Corporate taxation, Pension, profit-sharing, and employee benefits, Probate. Home: 2408 N Brookside Ave Edmond OK 73034 Office: Speck Philbin et al 800 First City Pl Oklahoma City OK 73102

CHAPMAN, STEPHEN SPERRY, lawyer; b. Dallas, Jan. 8, 1948; s. Lloyd Sperry and Lela Avanell (Mayfield) C.; m. Penny Lee Irene Carl, Apr. 23, 1984; children: Matthew, Lee. BBA, U. Tex., Arlington, 1969; JD, U. Houston, 1973. Bar: Tex. 1973, U.S. Dist. Ct. (no. dist.) Tex. 1977, U.S. Ct. Appeals (5th cir.) 1981. Atty. Fidelity and Deposit Co. of Md., Balt., 1973-74, Detroit, 1974-75; sole practice Irving, Tex., 1975-76, Dallas, 1976-80, Plano, Tex., 1980—. Mem. City of Plano Human Relations Com., 1984—; bd. dirs. Pat O'Connor Workshop for Retarded, Collin County, Tex., 1981-83. Mem. ABA, Tex. Trial Lawyers Assn., Collin County Bar Assn., Plano

Bar Assn. (pres. 1984-85). Democrat. Unitarian. Lodge: Kiwanis, Lions. General practice, Personal injury, Criminal. Office: 2305 W Parker Plano TX 75023

CHAPPELEAR, CLAUDE KEPLAR, data systems corporation executive; b. Macomb, Ill., Mar. 1, 1937; s. Claude S. and Fannie Virginia (McCall) C.; m. Carol Charlene Pearson. B.A., Northwestern U., 1959, J.D., 1965. Bar: Tex. With Breed, Abbott & Morgan, N.Y.C., 1965-69, LTV Corp., Dallas, 1969-70; sec., v.p., gen. counsel Ramada Europe, Inc., Brussels, 1971-73; gen. counsel, v.p., sec. Ramada Inns, Inc., Phoenix, 1973-78; v.p., gen. counsel, sec. Electronic Data Systems Corp., Dallas, 1978—. Served to lt. USNR, 1955-73. Mem. ABA, N.Y. State Bar Assn., Am. Assn. Corp. Secs., Pi Kappa Alpha. Republican. Methodist. Office: Electronic Data Systems Corp 7171 Forest Ln Dallas TX 75230

CHAPPELL, CLOVIS GILLHAM, JR., lawyer; b. Waverly, Tenn., Sept. 13, 1911; s. Clovis Gillham and Cecil (Hart) C.; m. Pauline Mikell LaRoche, Oct. 28, 1938; children: Carolyn (Mrs. D.W. Light III), Polly (Mrs. F. Ferrell Davis), Marian (Mrs. David Scott Miles). Student, Southwestern at Memphis, 1929-30; B.A., So. Methodist U., 1934, LL.B., 1936. Bar: Tex. 1936. Landman Humble Oil & Refining Co., 1938-44; atty. Baker & Botts, Houston, 1944-50; partner firm Stubbeman, McRae, Sealy & Laughlin, Midland, 1950-59, Lynch, Chappell, Allday & Alsup, 1959—; Past sec., dir. Tex. Am. Oil Corp., Midland. Contbr. articles to profl. jours. Past mem. bd. visitors So. Methodist U. Law Sch. Fellow Am. Coll. Probate Counsel; mem. Am., Tex., Midland County bar assns., Pi Kappa Alpha. Methodist. Oil and gas leasing, Real property. Home: 1605 Bedford Dr Midland TX 79701 Office: Lynch Chappell Allday & Alsup Summit Bldg Midland TX 79701

CHAPPELL, DAVID FRANKLIN, lawyer; b. St. Louis, Apr. 18, 1943; married; children: Libbey Paige, Wade Garrett. BA in Polit. Sci., U. Tex., 1964, JD with honors, 1968. Bar: Tex., U.S. Ct. Appeals (5th, 9th, and 11th cirs.); cert. civil trial law, Tex. Bd. Legal Specialization, 1978. Ptnr. Chappell & Handy, P.C., FT. Worth, Tex.; appointed to Tarrant County CSC, 1975, task force on delay Supreme Ct. Tex., 1985, spl. master U.S. Dist. Ct. (no. dist.) Tex., Ft. Worth. Editorial bd. The Texas Lawyer, 1985-86. V.p., gen. counsel Tarrant County Arts Council, 1980-86; vice chmn. City of Ft. Worth Human Relations Com.; coordinator Tarrant County Lt. Gov. William P. Hobby, 1971—; mem. jud. rev. com. U.S. Senator Lloyd Bentsen's no. dist., 1976-80; mem. Ft. Worth Mayor's Adv. Com., 1975-76; bd. dirs. Ft. Worth Community Theatre, Tex. Boys Choir. Named Outstanding Young Man, Ft. Worth Jaycees, 1975. Fellow Tex. Bar Found. (program coordinator symposium on solicitation and legal advt. 1985, sec. bd. trustees 1985-86, chmn. bd. trustees 1987—); mem. Am. Bar Found., Tex. Bar Assn. (bd. dirs. 1982-86, chmn. bd. 1984-85, health law sect. 1985-86, spl. com. to revise grievance process), ABA (editor Practice TIPS 1980, sec., exec. council of tort and ins. practice sect. 1983-87, chmn. young lawyers div. 1978), Am. Judicature Soc. (exec. com, bd. dirs. 1979), Tex. Young Lawyers Assn. (sec. 1976), Ft. Worth and Tarrant County Young Lawyers Assn. (pres. 1974, Outstanding Young Lawyer award 1979), Am. Arbitration Assn. (arbitrator). Federal civil litigation, State civil litigation, Personal injury. Office: Chappell & Handy PC 1800 City Center Tower II 301 Commerce St Fort Worth TX 76102-4118

CHAPPELL, JOHN CHARLES, lawyer; b. Minden, Nebr., Jan. 28, 1935; s. Charles Arthur and Eletta Hope (Pattison) C.; m. Joyce Joan Dawson, Sept. 1, 1957; children: Laura, Pamela, James, Allegra. B.S. in Edn., U. Nebr., 1956; LL.B., NYU, 1960. Bar: N.Y. 1960. Summer assoc. firm Dewey, Ballantine, Bushby, Palmer & Wood, N.Y.C., 1959, assoc., 1960-68, ptnr., 1968—. Served to 1st lt. U.S. Army, 1957. Root-Tilden scholar NYU, 1956. Mem. ABA, N.Y. State Bar Assn., Assn. Bar City N.Y. Club: Down Town Assn. (N.Y.C.). Lodge: Masons. Home: 2 Galloping Hill Circle Holmdel NJ 07733 Office: Dewey Ballantine Bushby Palmer & Wood 140 Broadway New York NY 10005

CHAPPELL, MILTON LEROY, lawyer; b. Accra, Ghana, Mar. 25, 1951; (parents Am. citizens); s. Derwood Lee and Helen Jean (Freeman) C.; m. Margot Cecelia Shields, Dec. 18, 1972; children: Marton Gerald, Monet Louise. BA summa cum laude, Columbia Union Coll., 1973; JD, Cath. U., 1976; diploma, Nat. Inst. Trial Advocacy, Boulder, Colo., 1978; cert., U. Miami, 1982. Bar: Md. 1976, D.C. 1977, U.S. Ct. Appeals (4th, 5th, 9th and D.C. cirs.) 1977, U.S. Dist. Ct. D.C. 1978, U.S. Ct. Appeals (6th cir.) 1979, U.S. Supreme Ct. 1980, U.S. Ct. Appeals (11th cir.) 1981, U.S. Dist. Ct. Md. 1982. Sole practice Silver Spring, Md., 1976—; staff atty. Nat. Right to Work Legal Def. Found., Springfield, Va., 1976—; lectr. Columbia Union Coll., Takoma Park, Md., 1976-77; legal cons. JNA Elem. Sch., Takoma Park, 1980-83. Mem. Hillandale Civic Assn., Silver Spring, 1980—; legal cons., bd. dirs. Silver Spring Seventh-Day Adventist Ch., 1976-84. Mem. ABA, Md. Bar Assn., D.C. Bar Assn. Labor, Federal civil litigation, General practice. Home: 10321 Royal Rd Silver Spring MD 20903 Office: Nat Right to Work Legal Def Found 8001 Braddock Rd #600 Springfield VA 22160

CHAPPELL, ROBERT HARVEY, JR., lawyer; b. Clarksville, Va., Nov. 28, 1926; s. Robert Harvey and Edna Kathryn (Lumpkin) C.; m. Ann Marie Callahan, Nov. 25, 1950; 1 son, Robert Harvey III. BA, Coll. William and Mary, 1948, B.C.L., 1950, LL.D. (hon.), 1984. Bar: Va. 1949. Partner firm Christian, Barton, Epps, Brent & Chappell, Richmond, Va., 1950—; dir., gen. counsel Thalhimer Bros., Richmond. Mem. Richmond Independence Bicentennial Commn., 1971-80; bd. dirs. Children's Hosp., pres., 1974-76; bd. dirs. Richmond Eye Hosp.; trustee Westminster-Canterbury, 1979—; rector Coll. William and Mary, 1972-76, bd. visitors, 1968-76. Served with USAAF, 1944-46. Recipient Alumni Medallion Soc. of Alumni of Coll. of William and Mary, 1968. Mem. Va. Bar Assn. (exec. council 1972-79, pres. 1977-78), Am. Bar Assn. (gov. 1978-81, chmn. standing com. on fed. judiciary 1977-78), Richmond Bar Assn. (pres. 1969-70), Am. Law Inst., Am. Bar Found., Am. Coll. Trial Lawyers (bd. regents 1979—, pres. 1986-87), Soc. of Alumni Coll. of William and Mary (pres. 1963-64), William and Mary Law Sch. Assn. (pres. 1951-52), SAR (pres. Va. chpt. 1970-72), Order of Coif, Phi Beta Kappa (pres. chpt. 1978-81), Omicron Delta Kappa, Pi Kappa Alpha. Clubs: Country, Commonwealth, Downtown (pres. 1976-77). Federal civil litigation, State civil litigation, General corporate. Home: 4607 Menokin Rd Richmond VA 23225 Office: 1200 Mutual Bldg Richmond VA 23219

CHAPPELL, THOMAS TYE, lawyer; b. Jersey City, Nov. 15, 1926; s. William Nelson and Florence De Chantel (Ryan) C.; m. Laurel Reichert, Oct. 1, 1949. A.B. in Econs., Duke U., 1947, J.D., 1951. Bar: N.J. 1952, U.S. Dist. Ct. N.J. 1952, U.S. Supreme Ct. 1961. Assoc., Emory, Langan & Lamb, 1952-58; ptnr. Lamb, Chappell, Hartung, Gallipoli & Coughlin and predecessors, Jersey City, 1958-85; of counsel DeGonge, Garrity & Fitzpatrick, Bloomfield, N.J., 1986—; lectr. handling complicated litigation. Served with USNR, 1944-46. Fellow Am. Coll. Trial Lawyers, Internat. Soc. Barristers; mem. Am. Soc. Law and Medicine, Am. Soc. Hosp. Lawyers, Trial Attys. N.J., ABA, N.J. State Bar Assn., Pitts. Inst. Legal Medicine, Nat. Assn. R.R. Trial Counsel, Def. Research Inst., N.J. Def. Assn., Hudson County Bar Assn., Morris County Bar Assn., Am. Arbitration Assn., Am. Judicature Soc. Club: Springbrook Country. Personal injury, State civil litigation, Insurance. Office: DeGonge Garrity & Fitzpatrick 430 Broad St Bloomfield NJ 07003

CHAPPLE, THOMAS LESLIE, lawyer; b. Canandaigua, N.Y., Nov. 28, 1947; s. Howard Leslie and Elizabeth (Stearns) C.; m. Shelly Smith, July 17, 1982; children: Adam Roger, Hannah Elizabeth. B.A., Cornell U., 1970; J.D., Albany Law Sch., 1973. Bar: N.Y. 1974, U.S. Supreme Ct. 1981. Atty assoc. Nixon, Hargrave, Devans & Doyle, Rochester, N.Y., 1973-76; sec., asst. gen. counsel Gannett Co., Inc., Rochester, N.Y., 1977-79, assoc. gen. counsel., sec., 1979-81, v.p., assoc. gen. counsel, sec., 1981—; sec. The Gannett Found., 1983—. Mem. ABA, Assn. Corp. Counsel, N.Y. State Bar Assn., Sigma Pi. Republican. Methodist. General corporate. Office: Gannett Co Inc 1100 Wilson Blvd Arlington VA 22209

CHAPUK, THOMAS CHRISTOPHER, lawyer; b. Darby, Pa., Dec. 5, 1953; s. Joseph Michael and Bernice Anne (Miller) C. BA in Philosophy and English, Williams Coll., 1975; JD, U. Ky., 1979. Bar: Ky. 1979, U.S. Dist. Ct. (ea. dist.) Ky. 1982, U.S. Ct. Appeals (6th cir.) 1986. Sole practice Lexington, Ky., 1979-82; assoc. Rouse, Rouse, Combs & Pierce, Versailles, Ky., 1982-84; pub. defender Fayette County Legal Aide, Inc., Lexington, Ky., 1985—. Mem. Ky. Bar Assn. Democrat. Roman Catholic. Clubs: Ky. Sportsman, YMCA (Lexington). Avocations: hunting with bow and gun, softball, karate. Criminal. Office: Fayette County Legal Aide Inc 317 W Short St Lexington KY 40507

CHAPURAN, RONALD FRANCIS, lawyer; b. Omaha, Mar. 14, 1938; s. John Joseph and Alice Claire (Kopecky) C.; m. Nancy Ann Eastman, Aug. 20, 1960; children: Jean Ann, Jennifer, Matthew. BSEE, Marquette U., 1960; MS, U. Wis., 1962; JD, George Washington U., 1972. Bar: Va. 1972, Ind. 1973, U.S. Ct. Appeals (Fed. cir.) 1983, N.Y. 1984. Atty. CTS Corp., Elkhart, Ind., 1972-75; internat. patent atty. Xerox Corp., Rochester, N.Y., 1975-77; counsel patent ops. Xerox Corp., Rochester, 1977—; arbitrator Nat. Consumer Arbitration Program, Rochester, 1983—. Mem. Environ. Bd., Pittsford, N.Y., 1984—; vol. Legal Services Project, Inc., Rochester, 1983—; mem. exec. com. Pittsford Reps., 1983—; vice chmn. adv. bd. Montgomery Neighborhood, Rochester, 1985—; pres. adv. council Rochester Psychiatric Ctr., 1983-85; bd. dirs. Better Bus. Bur., Rochester, 1979—. Served to 1st lt. Signal Corps U.S. Army, 1962-64. Recipient Cert. of Appreciation Rochester Psychiatric Ctr., 1983, 84, 85, Vol. Service award Vol. Legal Services Project, Inc., 1986. Mem. ABA, N.Y. State Bar Assn. (pro bono service award 1986), Monroe County Bar Assn., Rochester Patent Law Assn. (pres. 1985-86). Roman Catholic. Club: St. Louis Parish Mens (Pittsford) (pres. 1985-86). Computer, Patent, Trademark and copyright. Home: 2 Rustic Pines Pittsford NY 14534 Office: Xerox Corp Xerox Sq Rochester NY 14644

CHAR, RANDALL YAU KUNN, lawyer; b. Honolulu, Jan. 2, 1952; s. Arthur T. and Audrey (Leong) C.; m. Soon Im Choe, Aug. 31, 1979; children: Sandra, Ramona, Tara. BA, U. Hawaii, 1973; JD, U. Calif., San Francisco, 1976. Bar: Hawaii 1976. Assoc. Robert A. Smith, Honolulu, 1976-77, Schutter, O'Brien & Walnberg, Honolulu, 1977-79; ptnr. O'Brien & Char, Honolulu, 1979-84; sole practice Honolulu, 1984—. Mem. ABA, Assn. Trial Lawyers Am. General corporate, Contracts commercial. Office: 745 Fort St Suite 300-D Honolulu HI 96813

CHAR, VERNON FOOK LEONG, lawyer; b. Honolulu, Dec. 15, 1934; s. Charles A. and Annie (Ching) C.; m. Evelyn Lau, June 14, 1958; children—Richard, Daniel, Douglas, Jeffrey, Elizabeth. B.A., U. Hawaii, 1956; LL.B., Harvard U., 1959. Bar: Hawaii 1959, U.S. Dist. Ct. Hawaii 1959, U.S. Ct. Appeals (9th cir.) 1962. Dep. atty. gen. State of Hawaii, Honolulu, 1959-65; ptnr. Damon, Key, Char & Bocken, Honolulu, 1966—; chmn. State of Hawaii Ethics Com., 1968-75, Hawaii Bicentennial Commn., 1986—. Mem. ABA (state del. 1986), Hawaii State Bar Assn. (pres. 1985). Antitrust. Home: 351 Anonia St Honolulu HI 96821 Office: Damon Key Char & Bocken 1001 Bishop St 1600 Pauahi Tower Honolulu HI 96813

CHARBONEAU, BRIAN PAIGE, lawyer; b. Wichita, Kans., Nov. 18, 1949; s. Jesse Lyneol and Dorothy Mary (Shaw) C.; children: Tifanie Wind, Jesse Valentine. BA, Tulane U., 1970; MS in Pub. Adminstrn., Troy State U., 1976; JD, Loyola U., New Orleans, 1980; M in Civil Law, Tulane U., 1981. Bar: La. 1981, U.S. Dist. Ct. (ea. dist.) La. 1981. Law clk. to presiding justice La. Ct. Appeal, New Orleans, 1980-81; sole practice New Orleans, 1981-82; law clk. to presiding justice Criminal Dist. Ct., New Orleans, 1982-86; assoc. Mmahat, Duffy, Opotowsky & Walker, New Orleans, 1986-87, Middleberg & Riddle, New Orleans, 1987—. Served to 1st lt. La. Air N.G., 1987. Mem. La. Bar Assn. Avocation: photography. Banking, Pension, profit-sharing, and employee benefits. Office: Middleberg & Riddle 3131 I-10 Service Rd Metairie LA 70002

CHAREN, STEVEN CRAIG, lawyer; b. Maplewood, N.J., July 11, 1949; s. Milton and Dorothy (Friedman) C. A.B. magna cum (Univ. scholar, Caine scholar) Princeton U., 1971, M.P.A., 1974; student London Sch. Econs., 1970; J.D. (Root-Tilden scholar), N.Y.U., 1977. Bar: N.Y. 1978, U.S. Sup. Ct. 1981. Congressional intern to Rep. Peter Rodino, Washington, 1968; jud. intern U.S. Sup. Ct., Washington, 1972; research assoc., criminal justice planning specialist Vera Inst. Justice, N.Y.C., 1974; law clk. U.S. Dept. Justice, U.S. Atty.'s Office Dist. N.J., 1975; assoc. Patterson, Belknap, Webb & Tyler, N.Y.C., 1977-85, counsel, 1985—; mem. Com. of Jud. Conf. of U.S. to Consider Standards for Admission to Practice in Fed. Cts., 1976-79. Mem. ABA (chmn. N.Y. state young lawyers membership 1979-84, ho. of dels. 1976-77), N.Y. State Bar Assn., Assn. Bar City N.Y., young lawyers com. 1980-83), N.Y. County Lawyers Assn. Club: Princeton (N.Y.C.). Federal civil litigation, Antitrust, State civil litigation. Office: 30 Rockefeller Plaza Suite 3500 New York NY 10112

CHARLA, LEONARD FRANCIS, auto manufacturing company executive, lawyer; b. New Rochelle, N.Y., May 4, 1940; s. Leonard A. and Mary L. Charla; m. Kathleen Gerace, Feb. 3, 1968; children—Larisa, Christopher. B.A., Iona Coll., 1962; J.D., Cath. U., 1965; LL.M., George Washington U., 1971. Bar: D.C. 1967, N.J. 1970, Mich. 1971. Tech. writer IRS, Washington, 1966-67; atty. adv. ICC, Washington, 1967, atty., 1968-69; mgmt. intern HEW, Washington, 1967-68; atty. Bowes & Millner, Transp. Cons., Roseland, N.J., 1969-71; atty. legal staff Gen. Motors Corp., Detroit, 1971-85, sr. counsel, 1985-87, asst. gen. counsel, 1987—; faculty Center for Creative Studies, Coll. Art and Design, Detroit, 1978—, adj. asst. prof., 1982—; faculty art U. Mich., 1980, 84, 85, 86, 87. Bd. dirs. Gt. Lakes Performing Artists Assocs., 1983—, Mich. Assn. Community Arts Agys., 1983—; bd. govs. Cath. U. Am. Alumni, 1982—. N.Y. State Regents teaching fellow, 1962; Cath. U. Law Sch. scholar, 1962-65. Mem. ABA, Mich. State Bar Assn. (chmn. arts sect. 1980-81), Assn. ICC Practitioners (pres. Gt. Lakes chpt. 1974-75, v.p. region VIII 1976-77). Environment, Art Law. Office: Gen Motors Legal Staff New Center One Bldg 3031 W Grand Blvd Suite 7104 Detroit MI 48232

CHARLES, BEVERLY M.M., law educator; b. Jersey City, Aug. 10, 1947; d. Raymond and Grace (Herbert) McQueary; 1 child, Walter. BA, Jersey City State Coll., 1970; MA, Rutgers U., 1974; JD, NYU, 1977. Bar: D.C. 1978, W.Va. 1981, Tex. 1981. Legis. asst. U.S. Senate, Washington, 1977-79; law clk. to presiding judge U.S. Dist. Ct. (ea. dist.) Mich., Detroit, 1979-80; program advisor and atty. advisor FTC, Washington, 1980-82; atty., advisor U.S. Dept. Interior, Washington, 1982-84; assoc. prof. law S. Tex. Coll. of Law, Houston, 1984—. bd. dirs. Nat. Kidney Found., Houston, 1985—. Mem. ABA, Nat. Bar Assn., Am. Trial Lawyers Assn., Houston Lawyers Assn. Bankruptcy, Contracts commercial, Consumer commercial. Office: S Tex Coll Law 1303 San Jacinto Houston TX 77002

CHARLES, ROBERT MARSHALL, JR., lawyer; b. Phoenix, May 20, 1957; s. Robert Marshall and Margaret (Babbitt) C.; m. Ann Hardy, May 23, 1982; 1 child, Rachael Ann. BA, U. Ariz., 1979, JD, 1982. Bar: Ariz. 1982, U.S. Dist. Ct. Ariz. 1982, U.S. Ct. Appeals (9th cir.) 1984. Law clk. U.S. Dist. Ct. Ariz., Phoenix, 1982-84; assoc. Lewis & Roca, Phoenix, 1984—. Mem. ABA, Ariz. Bar Assn. Bankruptcy, Federal civil litigation, Contracts commercial. Home: 127 E Myrtle Phoenix AZ 85020 Office: Lewis & Roca 100 W Washington St Phoenix AZ 85003-1899

CHARNEY, JONATHAN ISA, legal educator, lawyer; b. N.Y.C., Oct. 29, 1943; s. Wolfe R. and Rita Dorothy (Greenfield) C.; m. Sharon Renee Lehman, June 12, 1966; children—Tamar, Adam, Noah. B.A., NYU, 1965; J.D., U. Wis., 1968. Bar: Wis. 1968, Tenn. 1974, N.Y. 1980, U.S. Supreme Ct. 1971. Atty. Land and Natural Resources div. Dept. Justice, Washington, 1968-71, chief marine resources sect., 1972; asst. prof. law Vanderbilt U., Nashville, 1972-75, assoc. prof., 1975-78, prof., 1978—; cons. in field. Mem. ABA, Am. Br. Internat. Law Assn., Woods Hole Oceanographic Inst. (sr. adv. com.), Am. Law Inst., Marine Policy Ctr., Am. Soc. Internat. Law (exec. council 1982-85, bd. editors Ocean Devel. and Internat. Law 1985—), Assn. Am. Law Schs. (chmn. internat. law sect. 1985), Order of Coif. Contbr. numerous articles to profl. jours. Public international, Federal civil litigation, Private international. Office: Vanderbilt U Sch Law Nashville TN 37240

CHARNEY, MITCHELL A., lawyer; b. Bklyn., Nov. 20, 1944. BA, U. Louisville, 1966, JD, 1969, MS in Social Work, 1978. Office: Goldberg & Simpson 2800 1st Nat Tower Louisville KY 40202

CHARTRAND, DOUGLAS ARTHUR, lawyer; b. Detroit, Feb. 22, 1940; s. Edgar J. Chartrand and Mildred (Altland) Forbes: m. Janet Ormsby, June 22, 1963 (div. Dec. 1964); m. Anne Marie Stevenson, Dec. 13, 1970; children: Maria Glenn, Thomas L. BA, Mich. State U., 1962; JD, Wayne State U., 1967. Bar: Mich. 1968, U.S. Dist. Ct. (ea. dist.) Mich. 1976, Fla. 1984. Sr. ptnr., v.p. Smith, Magnusson, Chartrand, Adkison P.C., Bloomfield Hills, Mich., 1968—; panel mem. Atty. Discipline Bd., Detroit, 1977—. Trustee Oakland County Law Library, Pontiac, Mich., 1980—. Mem. Fla. Bar Assn., Mich. Bar Assn. (prosecutor grievance bd. 1970-77), Oakland County Bar Assn., Assn. Trial Lawyers Am., Mich. Trial Lawyers Assn. Personal injury, Probate, Family and matrimonial. Home: 2750 Lola Ct Pontiac MI 48055 Office: Smith Magnusson Chartrand Adkison PC 2550 S Telegraph Rd Suite 108 Bloomfield Hills MI 48103

CHASE, JONATHON B., law school dean, educator; b. Orange, N.J., June 6, 1939; s. David Boyd and Lillian (Reuben) C.; m. Nancy Markey, June 25, 1961; children—Tamara, Adam, Rebecca, Eli. B.A., Williams Coll., Williamstown, Mass., 1961; LL.B., Columbia U., 1964. Bar: N.Y. 1964, Colo. 1969, U.S. Dist. Ct. (D.C. dist.), U.S. Ct. Appeals (10th cir.), U.S. Supreme Ct. Asst. prof. law Boston U., 1965-66; prof. law U. Colo., Boulder, 1966-82; exec. dir. Colo. Rural Legal Services, 1969-72; dean, prof. Sch. of Law, Vt. Law Sch., South Royalton, 1982—. Contbr. articles to profl. jours. Bd. dirs. Colo. br. ACLU, 1975-82, ACLU, Vt., 1982—, Vt. Planned Parenthood, 1982-84, Vt. Legal Aid, 1984—. Mem. ABA, Vt. Bar Assn. Democrat. Jewish. Civil rights, Federal civil litigation, Legal education. Home: PO Box 684 Norwich VT 05055 Office: Vt Law Sch South Royalton VT 05068

CHASE, SAM J., lawyer; b. Abilene, Tex., July 3, 1947; s. George Edward Chase and Marietta (Council) Mills; m. Linda Lea Patterson, July 29, 1967; children—Heather Brooke, Hunter Bryan. B.B.A., Tex. Tech. U., 1969, J.D., 1972. Bar: Tex. 1972. Prin. Law Offices of Sam J. Chase, Abilene, 1975—. Active Boys Club of Abilene, 1974—; chmn. lawyer div. United Way, Abilene, 1980-81; bd. dirs. Taylor County Am. Cancer Soc., 1974-81, v.p., 1977-78, 78-79; asst. coach Big Country Soccer Assn., 1981-82, YMCA T-Ball Sluggers, 1980-81; sec. Key City Little League, 1984-86, coach, 1986. Mem. Abilene Bar Assn. (bd. dirs. 1980-81), Abilene Young Lawyers Assn. (pres. 1978-79, award of achievement 1978-79), Tex. Young Lawyers Assn. (bd. dirs. 1979-81, Outstanding Young Lawyers award, 1984), Tex. Trial Lawyers Assn., Jaycees (pres. Tex. 1983-84, legal counsel 1979-81), Abilene C. of C., Sigma Chi, Delta Theta Phi. Baptist. Contracts commercial, General corporate, Workers' compensation. Home: 650 Meander St Abilene TX 79602 Office: 400 Oak St Suite 105 Abilene TX 79602

CHASE, SEYMOUR M., lawyer; b. N.Y.C., Apr. 14, 1924; s. Harold Chase and Rhoda (Oshrin) Chase Singer; m. Janet Schwartz, Nov. 12, 1960; 1 child, Neil. A.B., U. Mich., 1947; M.A., Columbia U., 1949, LL.B., Columbus U., 1951. Bar: D.C. 1952, N.Y. 1953, U.S. Ct. Appeals (D.C. cir.) 1952, U.S. Supreme Ct. 1956. Atty.-adviser FCC, Washington, 1952-53; assoc. Segal, Smith & Hennessey, Washington, 1953-57; sole practice, Washington, 1958-62, 72—; ptnr. Lyon & Chase, Washington, 1962-63, Philipson, Lyon & Chase, Washington, 1963-67, Smith & Pepper, Washington, 1967-72; mem. D.C. securities adv. com. D.C. Pub. Service Commn., 1965-66. Author: Candidate's Checklist, the Law on Using Radio and Television, 1972, 2d rev. edit., 1976, 3d rev. edit., 1980. Bd. dirs. Washington Home Rule Com., 1963-69, v.p., 1965, chmn. legis. com., 1965; del. Democratic Nat. Conv., 1956, alt. del., 1964; mem. Dem. Central Com., Washington, 1961-68, vice chmn., 1968; field adviser Dem. Nat. Com. Presdl. Campaign, 1968; campaign dir. Dems. United for Johnson, later Dems. United, Washington Primary, 1968. Served with U.S. Army, 1943-45; ETO. Mem. ABA, D.C. Bar Assn., Fed. Communications Bar Assn., Broadcast Pioneers, Clubs: U. Mich. of Washington, Nat. Broadcasters, Nat. Lawyers, Nat. Capital Dem. Administrative and regulatory. Office: Seymour M Chase PC 4201 Connecticut Ave Washington DC 20008

CHASSAING, J. PATRICK, lawyer; b. St. Louis, May 8, 1952; s. Joseph Edward Chassaing and Roberta (Dooley) Torrence; m. Lisa Ann Howe, Aug. 2, 1980. BBA, St. Louis U., 1975; JD, U. Mo., 1978. Bar: Mo. 1978, U.S. Dist. Ct. (ea. and we. dists.) Mo. 1978, Il.. 1979. Assoc. Law Offices of Anthony J. Sestric, St. Louis, 1978-79; assoc. house counsel Liberty Mut. Ins. Co., St. Louis, 1979-81; mng. house counsel Home Ins. Co., St. Louis, 1981-85; ptnr. Cooper & Duggan, St. Louis, 1985-87, Steinberg & Crotzer, St. Louis, 1987—; pros. atty. City of Brentwood, St. Louis County, 1982—. Mem. Mo. Bar Assn., Bar Assn. Met. St. Louis. Avocations: general aviation, commercial pilot, participatory athletics. Personal injury, State civil litigation, Federal civil litigation. Office: Steinberg & Crotzer 230 S Bemiston Ave Suite 1010 Saint Louis MO 63105

CHASTAIN, DAVID JESSE, lawyer; b. Birmingham, Ala., Aug. 16, 1952; s. Solomon Jesse and Louise (Hamilton) C.; m. Wanda Elaine Coats, June 24, 1972; children: Amanda Elaine, Jessica Louise. BA, U. Ala., Birmingham, 1973; JD with honors, Samford U., 1978; LLM in Taxation, U. Ala., University, 1985. Bar: Ala. 1978, U.S. Dist. Ct. (no. dist.) Ala. 1978. Counselor Ala. Dept. Vocat. Rehab., Birmingham, 1973-75; assoc. Law Office of W.A. Jenkins Jr., Birmingham, 1978-85; ptnr. Jenkins, Chastain & Smith, Birmingham, 1986—. Mem. ABA, Birmingham Bar Assn., Greater Birmingham Assn. Home Builders, U. Ala. Birmingham Nat. Alumni Soc. (charter). Democrat. Episcopalian. Club: Birmingham Track. Lodges: Masons, Shriners. General practice, Consumer commercial, Landlord-tenant. Home: 6407 Glenview Circle Gardendale AL 35071 Office: Jenkins Chastain & Smith 227 Frank Nelson Bldg Birmingham AL 35203

CHASTAIN, MERRITT BANNING, JR., lawyer; b. Shreveport, La., Jan. 28, 1940; s. Merritt Banning and Lydia (Spock) C.; m. Virginia Anne Ferguson, July 21, 1962; children—Merritt Banning III, Grayson Anne. B.S., U. Okla., 1962; J.D., La. State U., 1967. Bar: La. 1967, U.S. Dist. Ct. (we. dist.) La. 1968, U.S. Dist. Ct. (ea. dist.) La. 1972, U.S. Ct. Appeals (5th cir.) 1972, U.S. Supreme Ct. 1979. Law clk. La. Ct. Appeals (2d cir.), Shreveport, 1967-68; assoc. Smitherman, Lunn, Chastain & Hill Shreveport, 1968-72, ptnr., 1972—; mng. dir. Nat. Assn. Pipe Coating Applicators, 1979—; spl. counsel La. Pub. Facilities Authority, 1985—; bd. dirs., sec. bd. dirs. United Mercantile Bank; bd. dirs., sec. United Mercantile Bancshares, Inc. Chmn. United Way of Shreveport/Bossier City, 1975; pres. Vols. Am., 1976, Norwela council Boy Scouts Am., 1977-78, Ark.-La.-Tex. Tax Inst., 1977; exec. v.p. Shreveport Symphony Soc., 1981; bd. dirs. Shreveport Opera, 1981—, sec., 1981; trustee Loyola Coll. Prep. Sch., 1984—, exec. com., 1985—, v.p. bd. of trustees, 1986-87; chmn. bd. Loyola Found. Shreveport, 1987—. Served to 1st lt. U.S. Army, 1962-64. Named Outstanding Young Man of La., La. Jaycees, 1975, Outstanding Young Man of Shreveport, Shreveport Jaycees, 1975. Mem. ABA (La. mem. chmn. 1976-82), La. State Bar Assn. (spl. com. 1974-75), Shreveport Bar Assn., (exec. council 1971-75, sec.-treas. 1972, bd. govs. young lawyer's sect. 1967-74, pres. young lawyer's sect. 1974). Democrat. Episcopalian. Clubs: Cambridge, University, Pierremont Oaks Tennis, Ambassador (Shreveport) (bd. dirs.). Contracts commercial, Banking, Real property. Home: 330 Corinne Circle Shreveport LA 71106 Office: Smitherman Lunn Chastain & HIll 333 Texas St Comml Nat Bank Bldg 8th Floor Shreveport LA 71101

CHATROO, ARTHUR JAY, lawyer; b. N.Y.C., July 1, 1946; s. George and Lillian (Leibowitz) C. BChemE, CCNY, 1968; JD cum laude, New York Law Sch., 1979; MBA with distinction, NYU, 1982. Bar: N.Y. 1980. Process engr. Standard Oil Co. of Ohio, various locations, 1968-73; process specialist BP Oil, Inc., Marcus Hook, Pa., 1974-75; sr. process engr. Sci. Design Co., Inc., N.Y.C., 1975-78; mgr. spl. projects The Halcon SD Group, N.Y.C., 1978-82; corp. counsel, tax and fin. The Lubrizol Corp., Wickliffe, Ohio, 1982-85; gen. counsel Lubrizol Enterprises, Inc., Wickliffe, 1985. Mem. Met. Parks Adv. com., Allen County, Ohio, 1973. Mem. ABA, Am. Chem. Soc., Am. Inst. Chem. Engrs., N.Y. State Bar Assn., Cleve. Bar Assn., Jaycees (personnel dir. Lima, Ohio chpt. 1972-73), Omega Chi Epsilon, Beta Gamma Sigma. Club: Toastmasters. Avocations: photography, skiing. General corporate, Corporate taxation, High technology venture capital. Home: 1 Bratenahl Pl Suite 705 Bratenahl OH 44108 Office: Lubrizol Enterprises Inc 29400 Lakeland Blvd Wickliffe OH 29400

CHATTERTON, ALFRED F., federal government official. Chief adminstrv. law judge USCG, Washington, 1985—. Office: Dept Transp USCG 2100 2d St Sw Washington DC 20590 *

CHATZKY, MICHAEL GARY, lawyer. BS in Acctg., U. Md., 1966, JD, 1969. Bar: Calif. 1970, U.S. Dist. Ct. (no. dist.) Calif., U.S. Tax Ct., U.S. Ct. Appeals (9th cir.), U.S. Supreme Ct. Ptnr. Margolis, Chatzky, Dunnett & Muelienbeck P.C., Los Gatos, Calif., 1970-80; sole practice San Jose, Calif.; ptnr. Chatzky, Fong & Fong, San Jose; lectr. on fgn. trusts, internat. and domestic taxation subjects for various orgns.; instr. West Valley Coll., Saratoga, Calif., Cabrillo Coll., Aptos, Calif. Contbr. articles to profl. jours. Mem. ABA (fgn. activities of U.S. taxpayers com., U.S. activities foreigners and tax treaties com.), Santa Clara County Bar Assn. (exec. tax com.), Asian Law Alliance (adv. bd.), Internat. Common Law Exchange Soc. (instr. continuing legal edn. programs, mng. editor publ.). Corporate taxation, Estate taxation, Personal income taxation. Office: Chatzky Fong & Fong 762 El Paseo de Saratoga San Jose CA 95130

CHAUNCEY, TOM WEBSTER, II, lawyer; b. Phoenix, May 30, 1947; s. Tom Webster and Kathryn (Geare) C.; m. Mary Kathleen LaCroix, Dec. 28, 1972. BA with departmental honors in Sociology, Northwestern U., 1970; JD, Ariz. State U., 1973. Bar: Ariz. 1973, U.S. Dist. Ct. Ariz. 1973. Assoc. Gust, Rosenfeld, Divelbess & Henderson, Phoenix, 1972-76; exec. v.p., counsel KOOL Radio-TV, Inc., Phoenix, 1972-82; gen. counsel, sta. mgr. KOOL-AM-FM, Phoenix, 1982-86; chmn. Cameras in the Courtroom Com., 1979-86; mem. bd. CBS RadioRadio Network Affiliates, 1984-86. V.p. 1st Amendment Coalition, 1981-83, pres., 1984-85; bd. dirs. Park Found. of Phoenix, 1980-84, NCCJ, 1978—, nat. exec. bd. 1986—; bd. dirs. Ariz. Bus.-Industry-Edn. Council, Inc., 1979-83, Friendly House, 1983-84, Ariz. Community Found., 1981-85, Sands North Townhouse Homeowners Assn., 1973-77; mem. met. fin. com. YMCA Phoenix and Valley of Sun, 1974-80, mem. camp com., 1978-80; bd. dirs., mem. Project Pool It, Valley Forward Assn., 1977-83; mem. media adv. bd. Traffic Accident Reduction Task Force, 1980; bd. dirs. Meml. Hosp. Found., 1978-83, planning com., 1980-83, community relations com., 1982-83; bd. dirs. Barrow Neurol. Found., 1979—, mem. exec. com., 1980—, v.p., 1983-85, pres., 1986—, mem. investment com. 1985—; bd. dirs. Ariz. Hist. Soc., 1982-84, mem. bldg. com., 1983, bylaws com., 1983, bd. dirs. Central Ariz. Mus. chpt., 1979-84; mem. Walter Cronkite Found. for Journalism and Telecommunications, Ariz. State U., 1982—; mem. Maricopa City voter awareness com. 1986—. Fellow Ariz. State Bar Found.; mem. ABA, Ariz. Bar Assn. (pub. relations com. 1975-86, fee arbitration com. 1976-86), FCC Bar Assn., Maricopa County Bar Assn. (past dir. Young Lawyers sect.), Ariz. Trial Lawyers Assn., Assn. Trial Lawyers Am., Phoenix Assn. Def. Counsel, Orme Sch. Alumni Assn., Northwestern U. Alumni Assn. Phoenix (pres. 1975-76), Ariz. State U. Alumni Assn., Ariz. State U. Law Alumni Assn., Phoenix Press Club, Nat. Assn. Broadcasters, Ariz. Broadcasters Assn. (bd. dirs. 1985-86), Met. Phoenix Broadcasters (bd. dirs. 1976-86, pres. 1985-86), Phi Delta Phi, Phi Gamma Delta. Libel, General corporate, Real property. Office: Gust Rosenfeld Divelbess & Henderson 3300 Valley Bank Ctr Phoenix AZ 85073

CHAUVIN, LEONARD STANLEY, JR., lawyer; b. Franklin, Ky., Feb. 13, 1935; s. Leonard Stanley Sr. C.; m. Cecilia McKay; children: Leonard Stanley III, Jacqueline, McKay. Student, Castle Heights Mil. Acad., 1953; AB in Polit. Sci., U. Ky., 1957; JD, U. Louisville, 1961. Bar: Ky. 1961, U.S. Dist. Ct. (we. dist.) Ky. 1962, U.S. Ct. Appeals (6th cir.) 1964, U.S. Ct. Mil. Appeals 1966, U.S. Ct. Claims 1966, U.S. Supreme Ct. 1966, N.Y. 1983, Ind. 1983, Tenn. 1983, D.C. 1983, U.S. Dist. Ct. (so. and na. dists.) Ind. 1983, U.S. Dist. Ct. D.C. 1983, U.S. Ct. Appeals (7th, D.C. and Fed. cirs.) 1983, U.S. Tax Ct. 1983, U.S. Ct. Internat. Trade 1983, Wis. 1984, U.S. Dist. Ct. (so.and ea. dist.) 1984, U.S. Ct. Appeals (2d cir.) 1984, Fla. 1985, Nebr. 1985, Minn. 1985, Mass. 1986, W.Va. 1986. Assoc. Daniel B. Boone, Louisville, 1962-63, Laurence E. Higgins, Louisville, 1963-68; ptnr. Brown & Chauvin, Louisville, 1968-78, Carroll, Chauvin, Miller & Conliffe, Louisville, 1978-82; sole practice Louisville, 1982-83; ptnr. Barnett & Alagia, Louisville, 1983—; asst. Commonwealth atty. Jefferson County Commonwealth Attys. Office, Louisville, 1962-63; asst. gen. counsel dept. of hwys. Commonwealth of Ky., Louisville; judge pro tem Louisville Police Ct.; dep. master commr. Jefferson Cir. Ct., Louisville, 1972-78; research asst. to county atty. of Jefferson County. Chmn. Registry; mem. Ky. jud. retirement form system Old Ky. Home Boy Scouts, Frankfort, Ky. Fellow Am. Bar Found. (chmn.); mem. ABA (chmn. Ho. of Dels.), Ky. Bar Assn. (Lawyer of Yr.), Louisville Bar Assn. (pres., Lawyer of Yr.), Am. Arbitration Assn., Am. Coll. Real Estate Lawyers, Nat. Jud. Coll., Am. Judicature Soc. (pres. 1986—, Harley award). Federal civil litigation, State civil litigation, Probate. Home: 1648 Cherokee Rd Louisville KY 40205 Office: Barnett & Alagia 444 S 5th St Louisville KY 40202

CHAVEZ, RUDOLPH BEN, lawyer; b. Albuquerque, June 19, 1955; s. Benito I. and Consuelo (Velarde) C. BA, U. N.Mex., 1977; JD, U. Mich., 1981. Bar: N.Mex. 1981, U.S. Ct. Appeals (10th cir.) 1982. City atty. City of Albuquerque, 1981; gen. counsel Mut. Oil of Am., Santa Fe, 1982-83; assoc. Nordhaus, Haltom & Taylor, Albuquerque, 1983; sole practice Albuquerque, 1983-84; ptnr. Tapia, Montes & Chavez, Albuquerque, 1984-86, Chavez, Montes & Assocs., Albuquerque, 1986. Fund raiser U. N.Mex. Lobo Club, Albuquerque, 1985-86. Mem. ABA, N.Mex. Trial Lawyers Assn., U. Mich. Alumni Assn. (organizer), Sigma Alpha Epsilon. Republican. Roman Catholic. Avocations: sports, water skiing, snow skiing. Personal injury, General practice, Federal civil litigation. Office: Chavez Montes & Assocs PC 4520 Montgomery NE Suite 2B Albuquerque NM 87109

CHAYES, ABRAM, educator, lawyer; b. Chgo., July 18, 1922; s. Edward and Kitty (Torch) C.; m. Antonia Handler, Dec. 24, 1947; children: Eve, Abigail, Lincoln, Sarah Prudence, Angelica. AB magna cum laude, Harvard U., 1943, LLB magna cum laude, 1949. Bar: D.C. 1953, Conn. 1950, Mass. 1958. Legal adviser to Gov. of Conn., 1949-51; assoc. gen. counsel Pres.'s Materials Policy Commn., 1951; law clk. to Justice Felix Frankfurter, 1951-52; assoc. Covington & Burling, Washington, 1952-55; asst. prof. law Harvard U., 1955-58, prof., 1958-61, 65—; legal adv. U.S. Dept. State, Washington, 1961-64; with Ginsburg & Feldman, Washington, 1964-65; guest scholar Brookings Inst., 1977-78; chmn. coordinating com. Internat. Nuclear Fuel Cycle Evaluation, 1977-80; dir. fgn. policy task forces McGovern campaign, 1972; mem. fgn. policy and def. task force Carter Presdl. campaign, 1976, nuclear energy policy study, 1976-77; chmn. Georgetown U. Law Ctr. Inst. for Pub. Representation, 1979—; vis. scholar Kistiakowsky Visiting Scholar program Am. Acad. Arts and Scis., 1985-86. Author: (with others) The International Legal Process, 2 vols, 1968, ABM, An Evaluation of the Decision to Deploy an Antiballistic Missile System, 1969, The Cuban Missiles Crisis: International Crises and the Role of Law, 1974; note editor and pres. Harvard U. Law Review; contbr. numerous articles to law jours. Staff dir. Dem. Platform Com., 1960; dir. fgn. policy task forces Dem. campaign, 1972; trustee World Peace Found., 1977; adv. bd. Lawyers Alliance for Nuclear Arms Control, 1982—; v.p. Albert Einstein Peace Prize Found., 1980—. Served to capt. F.A. AUS, 1943-46. Decorated Bronze Star. Named Felix Frankfurter Prof. Law Harvard U., 1976; Rubin fellow Columbia U. Law Sch., 1985. Fellow Am. Acad. Arts and Scis.; mem. U.S. Nat. Group Permanent Ct. Arbitration. Civil rights, Private international. Home: 3 Hubbard Park Rd Cambridge MA 02138 Office: Harvard Law Sch G-404 Cambridge MA 02138

CHAZEN, HARTLEY JAMES, lawyer; b. N.Y.C., Feb. 14, 1932; s. Joseph and Helen (Jacobson) C.; m. Lois Audry, Dec. 12, 1967; 1 dau., Nicole Joanna. A.B., CCNY, 1953; LL.B., Harvard U., 1958; LL.M., NYU, 1959. Bar: N.Y. 1959. Assoc., Hays, St. John, Abramson & Heibron, 1959-65, Shea, Gallop, Climenko & Gould, N.Y.C., 1965-68, Rosenman, Colin, Kay, Petselek & Emil, N.Y.C., 1968-70; ptnr. Monasch Chazen & Stream, N.Y.C., 1970-82; sole practice, N.Y.C., 1982—; lectr. in field. Served to capt. USAR, 1958-68. Mem. Assn. Bar City N.Y. (com. on trademark and unfair competition 1977-80), ABA (subcom. depreciation and investment tax credit 1975—). Unitarian. Club: Harvard (N.Y.C.). General practice, Corporate taxation, Contracts commercial. Home: 75 Perkins Rd Greenwich CT 06830 Office: 777 3d Ave New York NY 10017

CHEATHAM, ROBERT WILLIAM, lawyer; b. St. Paul, June 4, 1938; s. Robert William and Hildegard Frances (Kromer) C.; m. Kay C. Sarnecki, Mar. 20, 1964; children: Ann Marie, Lynn Marie, Paul William. BCE, U. Minn., 1961, JD, 1966. Bar: Calif. 1967. Assoc. Brobeck, Phleger & Harrison, San Francisco, 1967-74, ptnr., 1974—; speaker on continuing legal edn., San Francisco. Co-author: Calif. Attorneys Guide to Real Estate Syndicates, 1970, Cheatham and Merritt California Real Estate Forms and Commentaries, 1984. Pres. Piedmont (Calif.) Campfire Girls, 1979; treas. Piedmont Parents Together, 1986. Mem. ABA, Calif. Bar Assn., San Francisco Bar Assn., Am. Arbitration Assn., (arbitrator on real estate disputes). Democrat. Real property, Securities. Office: Brobeck Phleger & Harrison One Market Plaza Spear St Tower San Francisco CA 94105

CHEATHAM, ROBIN BRYAN, lawyer; b. Lewisville, Ark., Feb. 16, 1954; s. Robert T. and Portia (Dew) C.; m. Leslie Marie Held, Dec. 4, 1976; children: Erin, Scott, Cory. BBA, U. New Orleans, 1976; JD, Loyola U., New Orleans, 1979. Bar: La. 1979, U.S. Dist. Ct. (ea., we. and mid. dists.) La., U.S. Ct. Appeals (5th cir.). Ptnr. Satterlee, Mestayer & Freeman, New Orleans, 1975—. Author: Louisiana Collection Law for Creditors, Creditors Practices and Techniques. Consumer commercial, Bankruptcy, Banking. Office: Satterlee Mestayer & Freeman One Poydras Plaza Suite 2700 639 Loyola Ave New Orleans LA 70113

CHEATWOOD, ROY CLIFTON, lawyer; b. Rome, Ga., Aug. 27, 1946; s. Herman Arthur and Dorothy Mary (Griffin) C.; m. Cynthia Morrison, June 27, 1969; children: Clifton, Scott. BA, U. South Fla., 1968; JD, Tulane U., 1974. Bar: La., U.S. Dist. Ct. (ea., mid. and we. dists.) La., U.S. Ct. Appeals (5th and 11th cirs.), U.S. Supreme Ct. Assoc. Jones, Walker, Waechter, Poitevent, Carrere & Denegre, New Orleans, 1974-78, ptnr., 1978—; adj. prof. La. State U., Baton Rouge, 1980, Loyola U., New Orleans, 1981, Tulane U., New Orleans, 1981, 84, 85, 86. Firm rep. United Way campaign, New Orleans, 1982, recruiter, 1983, 84, 85, 86. Served to lt. U.S. Army, 1968-71, Vietnam. Mem. ABA (vice chmn. 5th cir. trial practice com. 1975-76, co-chmn. 1976-78; judge regional nat. appellate adv. com. 1978; co-chmn. annual litigation meeting 1981; judge nat. appellate adv. competition 1978; membership chmn. gen. litigation sect. 1983-86), La. State Bar Assn., New Orleans Assn. Def. Counsel. Federal civil litigation, State civil litigation, Construction. Office: Jones Walker Waechter Poitevent Carrere & Denegre 201 Saint Charles Ave 49th Fl New Orleans LA 70170

CHEAVENS, JOSEPH D., lawyer; b. Dallas, Aug. 27, 1940; s. David A. and Alice (Dawson) C.; m. Georgine Roberts, Aug. 15, 1964; children: Mark, Joseph, Elizabeth, Sarah. BA, Baylor U., 1962; JD, Harvard U., 1965. Assoc. Baker & Botts, Houston, 1965-72, ptnr., 1973—. Gen. counsel Concert Chorale Houston, bd. dirs.; pres. Houston Internat. Seaman's Ctr., bd. dirs. Mem. ABA, Tex. Bar Assn., Houston Bar Assn., Maritime Law Assn. (chmn. com. on maritime legislation). Admiralty, Federal civil litigation, State civil litigation. Office: Baker & Botts One Shell Plaza Houston TX 77002

CHEEK, JAMES HOWE, III, lawyer; b. Nashville, Nov. 28, 1942; s. James H. and Anne H. C.; m. Sigourney Woods, June 1, 1968; children—James Howe, IV, Daniel W., Matthew H. A.B., Duke U., 1964; J.D., Vanderbilt U., 1967; LL.M., Harvard U., 1968. Bar: Tenn. bar 1967. Assoc. firm Shearman & Sterling, N.Y.C., 1967; asst. dean, asst. prof. law Vanderbilt U. Law Sch., 1968-70, mem. adj. faculty, 1970—; ptnr. firm Bass, Berry & Sims, Nashville, 1970—; vis. fellow Jesus Coll. Cambridge U., London, 1985-86, cons. Securities and Investments Bd U.K., 1985-86; cons. comml. crime unit Commonwealth Secretariat, 1985-86. Lectr. on continuing legal edn. at seminars, insts; trustee Elliott E. Cheatham Fund.; pres. dean's council Vanderbilt U. Law Sch., 1986—. Contbr. articles to law jours. Mem. Am. Law Inst., ABA (chmn. subcom. on 1933 Act 1978-85, vice chmn. fed. regulation of securities com. 1986—, sec. com. on corp. law 1980-85), Tenn. Bar Assn. (chmn. com. on corp. law rev. 1984-86), Nashville Bar Assn., Order of Coif. Clubs: Belle Meade Country, Cumberland, Queen's. General corporate, Securities. Home: 4404 Honeywood Dr Nashville TN 37205 Office: First American Center Nashville TN 37238

CHEEK, JO FRANCES, lawyer; b. Norfolk, Va., Aug. 22, 1954; d. Joseph Cranfield and Lossie Alice (Bradley) C.; m. David Berel Kaplan, June 28, 1981; 1 child, Elizabeth Price. BS in Jour. cum laude, Boston U., 1976; JD cum laude, Suffolk U., 1982. Bar: Mass. 1982, U.S. Dist. Ct. Mass. 1984, U.S. Ct. Appeals (1st cir.) 1985. Law clk. to presiding justice U.S. Dist. Ct. R.I., Providence, 1982-83; assoc. Haussermann, Dawson & Shattuck, Boston, 1983-84, McCabe/Gordon P.C., Boston, 1984—. Mem. ABA, Women's Bar Assn., Mass. Bar Assn., Boston Bar Assn., Mass. Assn. of Women Lawyers. Democrat. Avocations: travel, skiing. Federal civil litigation, State civil litigation, Bankruptcy. Office: McCabe/Gordon PC 200 State St Boston MA 02109

CHEEK, LOUIS EUGENE, lawyer; b. East Liverpool, Ohio, Apr. 4, 1951; s. Eugene Edwin and Tobias Ester (Lebman) C.; m. Robin Sue Sparks, May 25, 1984. BA, U. Del., 1972; JD, New Eng. Sch. Law, 1977. Bar: Pa. 1977, U.S. Dist. Ct. (ea. dist.) Pa. 1977, Mich. 1983, U.S. Dist. Ct. (ea. dist.) Mich. 1983, U.S. Ct. Appeals (6th cir.) 1984, U.S. Dist. Ct. (we. dist.) Mich. 1986. Pub. defender Dover, Del., 1978-79; assoc. Law Office L. M. Sullivan, Wilmington, Del., 1979-80; staff counsel Reliance Ins., Phila., 1980-81; sole practice Secane, Pa., 1981-84; assoc. Bacalis & Assocs., Detroit, 1984—. Mem. ABA, Mich. Bar Assn., Detroit Bar Assn. Avocations: music, photography, travel, writing. Federal civil litigation, Insurance, Personal injury.

CHEELY, DANIEL JOSEPH, lawyer; b. Melrose Park, Ill., Oct. 24, 1949; s. Walter Hubbard and Edith Arlene (Orlandino) C.; m. Patricia Elizabeth Dorsey, May 14, 1977; children: Mary Elizabeth, Daniel, Katherine, Laura, Anne-Marie. AB, Princeton U., 1971; JD, Harvard U., 1974. Bar: Ill. 1974, U.S. Dist. Ct (no. dist.) Ill. 1975, U.S. Ct. Appeals (7th cir.) 1975. Assoc. Baker & McKenzie, Chgo., 1974-81, ptnr. litigation, 1981-85, capital ptnr. litigation, 1985—; liaison counsel Asbestes Claims Facility, Chgo., 1985—. Advisor Midtown Sports and Cultural Ctr., Chgo., 1974—; mem. River Forest Regular Reps., Ill., 1980—, Ill. Rep. Assembly, Chgo., 1984—; bd. dirs. River Forest Young Reps., 1983—. Mem. ABA, Ill. Bar Assn., Chgo. Bar Assn., Trial Lawyers Club Chgo., Phi Beta Kappa. Roman Catholic. Club: Chgo. Athletic. Avocations: hist., parent effectiveness tng., edn. State civil litigation, Federal civil litigation, Personal injury. Office: Baker & McKenzie 130 E Randolph Dr Chicago IL 60601

CHEEVER, GEORGE MARTIN, lawyer; b. Boston, Jan. 13, 1947; s. Francis Sargent and Julia Whitney (Martin) C.; m. Mary Margaret Duplain, Apr. 10, 1979; children: Charles Duplain, Frances Sargent. AB, Harvard U., 1969; JD, U. Pa., 1973. Bar: Pa. 1973, U.S. Dist. Ct. (we. dist.) Pa. 1973, U.S. Ct. Appeals (3d cir.) 1978, U.S. Ct. Appeals (4th cir.) 1985. Law clk. to assoc. justice Pa. Supreme Ct., Pitts., 1973-74; assoc. Kirkpatrick & Lockhart, Pitts., 1974-82, ptnr., 1982—. Mem. ABA, Pa. Bar Assn. Allegheny County Bar Assn. Bankruptcy, Contracts commercial, Federal civil litigation. Office: Kirkpatrick & Lockhart 1500 Oliver Bldg Pittsburgh PA 15222

CHEFFY, EDWARD KEFGEN, lawyer; b. Barnesville, Ohio, July 25, 1953; s. George W. and Louise (Kefgen) C.; m. Jane Yeager, July 31, 1978; children: Emily, Sarah. BA cum laude, Harvard U., 1975; JD with honors, Ohio State U., 1978. Bar: Ohio 1978, U.S. Dist. Ct. (so. dist.) Ohio 1980, U.S. Dist. Ct. (no. dist.) Ohio 1981, U.S. Ct. Appeals (4th cir.) 1981, Fla. 1984, U.S. Dist. Ct. (so. dist.) Fla. 1986. From assoc. to ptnr. Kinder, Kinder & Hanlon, St. Clairsville, Ohio, 1978-84; ptnr. Frost & Jacobs, Naples, Fla., 1984—. Asst. to editor: Older Americans Act Project Management: Legal Duties and Responsibilities, 1978. County chmn. Taft for Gov. of Ohio, Clairsville, 1983. Mem. ABA, Fla. Bar Assn., Ohio Bar Assn., Collier County Bar Assn. Republican. Unitarian. Avocations: racquetball, reading. State civil litigation, Federal civil litigation, General corporate. Home: 74 Center St Naples FL 33963 Office: Frost & Jacobs 1300 3d St S Naples FL 33940

CHEIFETZ, CARY BENNET, lawyer; b. Bklyn., June 25, 1954; s. Michael and Gloria (Mendel) C.; m. Judy L. Greenstein, Aug. 24, 1980. BA, George Washington U., 1976; JD, N.Y. Law Sch., 1979. Bar: N.J. 1980, N.Y. 1980. Law clk. Superior Ct. of N.J., Newark, 1979-80; atty. Skoloff and Wolfe, Newark and Morristown, N.J., 1981—; lectr. family law Inst. Continuing Legal Edn. Contbr. articles and book revs. to various law jours. Chmn. Essex County Early Settlement Program, Newark, 1982-85. Mem. ABA (family law sect.), N.J. Bar Assn. (family law sect.). Avocation: hiking. Family and matrimonial. Office: 17 Academy St Newark NJ 97102 Office: 10 Park Pl Morristown NJ 07960

CHELEN, JOHN CAS, lawyer; b. Monessen, Pa., Jan. 22, 1948; s. John Joseph and Jane B. (Zywicki) C.; m. Gloria Charlene Cohen, June 28, 1980; children: Michael, Julia. B.S., Carnegie-Mellon U., 1970; J.D., U. Pitts., 1973. Bar: N.Y. 1973, D.C. 1982, U.S. Dist. Ct. (so. dist.) N.Y. 1974, U.S. Dist. Ct. D.C. 1982. Legis. analyst Seneca Corp., Washington, 1973-75; legis. analyst Mott-McDonald Assocs., Washington, 1975-79; corp. mgr. Genesis Corp., Rockville, Md., 1979-80; dir. regulations, systems engring. U.S. Dept. Energy, Washington, 1980-81; exec. dir. Systems, Inc., Washington, 1982-85; dir. legal affairs, expert systems CACI, Inc., 1985-86; gen. counsel, exec. v.p. Unison Corp., Washington, 1986—; sole practice, Washington, 1973—; cons. Informatics Corp., Washington, 1979, Planning Research Corp., Washington, 1978, Inst. for Info. and Systems, Washington, 1982. Author: Legal Implications of Intelligent Autonomous Systems; co-author: International Information Flows, 1984. Patentee in field. Mem. Nat. Child Research Ctr.; bd. dirs. Jazz Arts Soc., Washington, New Democratic Forum, Washington, Community Advocates, Alexandria, Va., 1981-83. Mem. ABA, Assn. Bar City N.Y., D.C. Bar. Democrat. Administrative and regulatory, Computer. Home: 3411 30th St NW Washington DC 20008 Office: CACI Inc 1815 N Fort Myer Dr Arlington VA 22209

CHELLIS, EUGENE CLIFTON, lawyer; b. San Antonio, Jan. 10, 1954; s. Allen Golden and Lenella Marion (Hitchman) C.; m. LaNelle Rhondda Rees; 1 child, Aubrie Heather. BA with honors, Walla Walla Coll., 1976; JD, Yale U., 1980. Bar: Wash. 1980, U.S. Dist. Ct. (we. dist.) Wash. 1980, U.S. Ct. Appeals (9th cir.) 1981, U.S. Dist. Ct. (ea. dist) Wash. 1983, U.S. Dist. Ct. (no. dist.) Calif. 1984, U.S. Ct. Appeals (D.C. cir.) 1985, U.S. Supreme Ct. 1985, D.C. 1986, U.S. Ct. Appeals (fed. cir.) 1986. Assoc. Perkins Coie and predecessor firm Perkins, Coie, Stone, Olson & Williams, Seattle and Washington, D.C., 1980—. Cooperating atty. ACLU, Seattle, 1982—, bd. dirs. 1984-85; trustee Puget Sound Cooperative Federation, Seattle, 1981-82. Mem. ABA, Seattle-King County Bar Assn. (judiciary and cts. com. 1984-85). Civil litigation, Environment, Civil rights. Office: Perkins Coie 1900 Washington Bldg Seattle WA 98101

CHEMERS, ROBERT MARC, lawyer; b. Chgo., July 24, 1951; s. Donald and Florence (Weinberg) C.; m. Lenore Ziemann, Aug. 16, 1975; children—Brandon J., Derek M. B.A., U. So. Calif., 1973; J.D., Ind. U.-Indpls., 1976. Bar: Ind. 1976, Ill. 1976, U.S. Dist. Ct. (so. dist.) Ind. 1976, U.S. Dist. Ct. (no. and so. dists.) Ill. 1977, U.S. Ct. Appeals 7th cir.) 1977, U.S. Ct. Appeals (5th cir.) 1985. Assoc. Pretzel & Stouffer, Chgo., 1976-79, officer, 1979-81, dir., 1981—. Author: IICLE - Civil Practice, 1978, rev. edit. 1982; IICLE Settlements, 1984. Mem. ABA, Ill. State Bar Assn., Chgo. Bar Assn., Def. Research Inst., Ill. Def. Counsel, Appellate Lawyers Assn. Democrat. State civil litigation, Federal civil litigation, Insurance. Office: Pretzel & Stouffer One S Wacker Dr Chicago IL 60606

CHENEY, HUDDIE LEE, III, investment consulting executive; b. Augusta, Ga., Oct. 6, 1953; s. Huddie Lee Jr. and Anne (Connelly) C.; m. Nancy Watson Singletary, Aug. 5, 1978. BA, Emory U., 1975, JD, 1978, LLM in Taxation, 1983. Bar: Ga. 1978, U.S. Dist. Ct. (so. dist.) Ga. 1978. Assoc. McCollum & Rawlins, Thomasville, Ga., 1978-82; v.p., gen. counsel H.L. Cheney & Co., Thomasville, 1982-83; sr. fin. planner Peterson Wealth Planning, Atlanta, 1984-85; v.p., tax counsel Consol. Planning Corp., Atlanta, 1985—. Mem. ABA, Internat. Assn. Fin. Planning, Inst. Cert. Fin. Planners. Presbyterian. Lodge: Kiwanis. Avocations: tennis, golf, hunting. Corporate taxation, Estate taxation, Personal income taxation. Home: 303 Noble Creek Dr NW Atlanta GA 30327 Office: Consol Planning Corp 400 Colony Sq Suite 525 Atlanta GA 30361

CHENEY, KIMBERLY BUNCE, lawyer; b. Manchester, Conn., Nov. 25, 1935; s. Kimberly and Margreta (Swenson) C.; m. Dorthy Tod, Feb. 7, 1977; children: Alison, Margreta, Benjamin. BA, Yale U., 1957, LLB, 1964. Bar: Conn. 1964, U.S. Ct. Appeals (2d cir.) 1965, Vt. 1968. Assoc. Gumbart, Corbin, New Haven, 1964-67; asst. atty. gen. State of Vt., Montpelier, 1967-68, atty. gen., 1972-75; state's atty. Washington County, Montpelier, 1968-72; ptnr. Cheney, Brock and Saudek, Montpelier, 1975—; chmn. Vt. Labor Relations Bd., Montpelier, 1978—; mem. Vt. adv. com. US Civil Rights Commn., 1982—. Bd. dirs. ARC, Montpelier, 1976; mem. Montpelier Sch. Bd., 1978-81. Served to lt. USNR, 1959-61. Mem. Assn. Trial Lawyers Am., Vt. Bar Assn. (del. family proceedings com., Montpelier, 1985), Am. Arbitration Assn. (arbitrator). Republican. State civil litigation, Family and matrimonial, Administrative and regulatory. Home: 20 Bailey Ave Montpelier VT 05602

CHERAMIE, CARLTON JOSEPH, lawyer, business consultant; b. Raceland, La., Sept. 29, 1952; s. Antoine Joseph and Gladys Marie (Plaisance) C.; m. Myra Joan Diaz, July 15, 1973; 1 child, Andrea Ragan. B.A., Nicholls State U., Thibodaux, La., 1973; J.D., La. State U., 1976. Bar: La. 1976, U.S. Dist. Ct. (ea. dist.) La. 1977, U.S. Dist. Ct. (we. dist.) La. 1977, U.S. Ct. Appeals (5th cir.) 1982, U.S. Ct. Appeals (10th cir.) 1984, U.S. Supreme Ct. 1984. Law clk. Dist. Ct. 19th Jud. dist., Baton Rouge, 1975-76; assoc. Diaz & Herrin, Golden Meadow, La., 1976-77; assoc. Law Office of Ed Diaz, Golden Meadow, 1977-79; ptnr. Diaz & Cheramie, Golden Meadow, 1979-83, Cheramie & Smith, Cut Off, La., 1983—; pres., dir. Tradewinds Marine, Cut Off, 1982—; corp. cons. First Am. Investments, Dallas; atty. Town of Golden Meadow, 1980-83; dir. Westwind Capital, Cut Off. State advisor U.S. Congl. Adv. Bd., Cut Off, 1980. Mem. Fed. Bar Assn., Assn. Trial Lawyers Am., La. Trial Lawyers Assn., ABA, Phi Alpha Theta, Phi Delta Phi. Republican. Roman Catholic. Federal civil litigation, State civil litigation, General corporate. Home: 134 W 47th St Cut Off LA 70345 Office: Cheramie & Smith 2024 W Main St Cut Off LA 70345

CHEREWKA, MICHAEL, lawyer; b. Taylor, Pa., July 3, 1955; s. Michael Jr. and Anne (Regan) C.; m. Michele Mary Robinson, Aug. 2, 1980; 1 child, Michael Colin. Student, U. Bristol, Eng., 1976-77; BSBA cum laude, Bucknell U., 1978; JD cum laude, Dickinson Sch. Law, 1981. Bar: Pa. 1981, U.S. Dist. Ct. (mid. dist.) Pa. 1983, U.S. Tax Ct. 1983, U.S. Ct. Appeals (3d cir.) 1983, U.S. Supreme Ct. 1985. Sr. mem. tax staff Ernst & Whinney, Harrisburg, Pa., 1981-83; assoc. Ball & Skelly, Harrisburg, 1983—. Contbg. editor (legal column) Strictly Business, 1985—. Adviser Law Explorers Post Boy Scouts Am., 1982—; mem. Country Club Park Civic Assn., 1983—, pres., 1987—; mem. Hist. Harrisburg Assn., 1982—; active Tri-County United Way, 1985—; bd. dirs. Tri-County council Am. Heart Assn., 1986—. Named Outstanding Young Man Am., U.S. Jaycees, 1983. Mem. ABA (taxation sect.), Pa. Bar Assn. (tax sect. 1981—, real estate, probate and trust law sect. 1981—, com. state taxation 1984—, chmn. subcom. on compromise tax 1986—), Dauphin County Bar Assn. (interprofl. relations com. 1984—), Dauphin County Young Lawyers Assn. (social com. 1985—), Estate Planning Council Cen. Pa. (chmn. CPA subcom. 1982-83), Polit. Info. Com. of CPA's, Pa. (treas. 1982-83), Greater Harrisburg Area C. of C. (bus. liaison com. 1984—), Delta Mu Delta, Omicron Delta Kappa. Republican. Orthodox Greek Catholic. Club: Range End Country (Dillsburg, Pa.). Avocations: coin collecting, golf, basketball. General corporate, Probate, Corporate taxation. Home: 64 Little Run Rd Camp Hill PA 17011 Office: Ball & Skelly 511 N 2d St Harrisburg PA 17101

CHERKEN, HARRY SARKIS, JR., lawyer; b. Phila., Dec. 8, 1949; s. Harry Sarkis and Lorna G. (Demurjian) C. BA, Lafayette Coll., 1971; JD, Villanova U., 1976. Bar: Pa. 1976, U.S. Dist. Ct. (ea. dist.) Pa. 1976, U.S. Supreme Ct. 1983. Assoc. counsel Albert M. Greenfield & Co., Inc. (name now Helmsey-Greenfield, Inc.), Phila., 1976-79; assoc. Drinker, Biddle & Reath, Phila., 1979-84, ptnr., 1984—; Mem. Phila. adv. bd. Chgo. Title Ins. Co., 1986—. Trustee The Kulicke Fund, Phila., 1985—; fellow trustee The Armenian Assembly Charitable Trust, 1986—. Fellow Armenian Assembly Am. (trustee 1986—); mem. ABA, Am. Arbitration Assn. (panel arbitrators), Pa. Bar Assn., Phila. Bar Assn., Pa. Land Title Assn. (affiliate). Armenian Apostolic. Club: Racquet. Real property. Home: 106-B N 21st St Philadelphia PA 19103 Office: Drinker Biddle & Reath 1100 PNB Bldg Philadelphia PA 19107

CHERNEY, JAMES ALAN, lawyer; b. Boston, Mar. 19, 1948; s. Alvin George and Janice (Elaine) C. BA, Tufts U., 1969; JD, Columbia U., 1973. Bar: Ill. 1973, U.S. Ct. Appeals (3d, 7th and 10th cir.), U.S. Supreme Ct. Assoc. Kirkland & Ellis, Chgo., 1973-76; assoc. Hedlund, Hunter & Lynch, Chgo., 1976-79, ptnr., 1979-82; ptnr. Latham & Watkins, Chgo., 1982—. Mem. ABA, Chgo. Bar Assn. Federal civil litigation, State civil litigation, Antitrust. Office: Latham & Watkins Sears Tower Suite 6900 Chicago IL 60606

CHERNOFF, CARL G., lawyer, personnel executive; b. N.Y.C., Jan. 30, 1943; s. George and Sara (Leitch) C.; m. Rosalind Rivin, Apr. 4, 1982; children: Jason, Samuel. BA, NYU, 1963, LLB, 1966. Bar: N.Y. 1966. Assoc. Poletti, Freidin et al., N.Y.C., 1972-73; labor relations atty. NBC, N.Y.C., 1973-75; with personnel dept. employee relations Hertz Corp., N.Y.C., 1975-83, staff v.p., 1983—. Served to capt. JAGC U.S. Army, 1967-72. Mem. Assn. Bar of City of N.Y. Avocations: high fidelity recordings, reading. Labor, Civil rights, Workers' compensation. Home: 12 Soundview Dr Larchmont NY 10538 Office: The Hertz Corp 660 Madison Ave New York NY 10538

CHERNOFF, DANIEL PAREGOL, patent lawyer; b. Washington, Jan. 24, 1935; s. Bernard M. and Goldie S. (Paregol) C.; m. Nancy M. Kuehner, June 17, 1965; children: Scott, Graham. B.E.E. with distinction, Cornell U., 1957, LL.B., 1959. Bar: N.Y. 1959, D.C. 1959, Oreg. 1968. Instr. Cornell U., 1957-59, Oreg. Bd. Higher Edn., Portland, Oreg., 1970-72; practiced in N.Y.C., 1959-67, Portland, 1967—; patent counsel Polarad Electronics Corp., Long Island City, N.Y., 1959-61; assoc. firm Fish, Richardson & Neave, N.Y.C., 1961-67, Davies, Biggs, Strayer, Stoel & Boley, Portland, 1967-70; patent atty., sr. mem. Chernoff, Vilhauer, McClung & Stenzel, Portland, 1970—, gen. counsel. Bd. dirs. Cardio-Pulmonary Research Inst., Pacific Ballet Theatre, 1985—; gen. counsel, bd. dirs. Learning Resource Ctr., Inc., chmn., 1975-79; mem. adv. council Cornell Law Sch., 1981—. Mem. Oreg. Bar Assn., N.Y. Bar Assn., D.C. Bar Assn., Am. Patent Law Assn., N.Y. Patent Law Assn., Oreg. Patent Law Assn. (pres. 1973-74), U.S. Trademark Assn., Cornell U. Law Assn., Cornell U. Council, Order of Coif, Tau Beta Pi, Eta Kappa Nu. Club: Multnomah Athletic. Patent, Trademark and copyright, Computer. Home: 600 Benjamin Franklin Plaza 1 SW Columbia Portland OR 97258 Office: Chernoff Vilhauer McClung & Stenzel 600 Benjamin Franklin Plaza One SW Columbia Portland OR 97258

CHERNOW, JEFFREY SCOTT, lawyer, educator; b. Phila., Mar. 8, 1951; s. William and Sylvia Ann (Rosenberg) C.; m. Debra Sharon Shapiro, Dec. 29, 1974; children: William Ross, Stephanie Lynne. BS, Pa. State U., 1972; JD, U. Balt., 1976. Bar: Md. 1976, U.S. Dist. Ct. Md. 1977, U.S. Supreme Ct. 1980. Assoc. Goodman, Meagher & Enoch, Balt., 1977-79; asst. atty. gen. State of Md., Balt., 1980-85; assoc. Cardin & Cardin, P.A., Balt., 1985-86; sole practice Balt., 1986—; asst. prof. Towson (Md.) State U., 1978-83, assoc. prof., 1983-86; panel chmn. Md. Health Claims Arbitration Office, 1983-84; lectr. Md. Inst. for Continuing Profl. Edn. of Lawyers, Inc., 1986. Chmn. bldg. com. Congregation Adat Chaim, 1985-86, trustee, 1986—. Mem. ABA, Md. Bar Assn., Bar Assn. Balt. City, N.Am. Securities Administrs. Assn. (mem. various coms. 1980-85, chmn. franchise and bus. opportunites com. 1984-85.). Securities, General corporate, Franchise law. Home: 24 Baroness Ct Owings Mills MD 21117 Office: 6615 Reisterstown Rd Suite 301 Baltimore MD 21215

CHERNY, DAVID EDWARD, lawyer; b. Brookline, Mass., Jan. 21, 1957; s. Jacob and Anne (Gray) C.; m. Elise Joan Sallen, June 4, 1978; children: Michael Aaron, Allyson Jill. BSBA cum laude, Boston U., 1978; JD cum laude, Suffolk U., 1981. Bar: Mass. 1981, U.S. Dist. Ct. Mass. 1982, U.S. Tax Ct. 1982, U.S. Ct. Appeals (1st cir.) 1982, U.S. Supreme Ct. 1985. Assoc. Atwood & Wright, Boston, 1981-84, Jacob M. Atwood P.C., Boston, 1984-86; ptnr. Atwood & Cherny, Boston, 1986—; prin., gen. ptnr. Brolaw Assocs., Newton, Mass., 1984—, Algonquin Assocs., Boston, 1986—. Mem. ABA, Mass. Bar Assn. (author article 1983), Boston Bar Assn. (author article 1983), Assn. Trial Lawyers Am., Mass. Acad. Trial Attys. (lectr. family law 1983), Phi Delta Phi. Club: Blue Hill Country (Canton, Mass.); Algonguin (Boston). Family and matrimonial, State civil litigation, Probate. Office: Atwood & Cherny 211 Commonwealth Ave Boston MA 02116

CHEROVSKY, ERWIN LOUIS, lawyer; b. Dover, N.J., Dec. 31, 1933; s. Sam and Ida (Bluestein) C.; m. Edith Mayer, June 26, 1966; children—Kim, Karen; children by previous marriage—Debra, Jill. A.B., U. Rochester, 1955; LL.B., Harvard U., 1958. Bar: N.Y. 1958, U.S. Dist. Ct. (so. dist.) N.Y. 1964, U.S. Ct. Appeals (2d cir.) 1964. Assoc., Stamer & Haft, N.Y.C., 1958-63; assoc. Summit Rovins & Feldesman, N.Y.C., 1963-68, ptnr., 1968—; sec. Space & Leisure Time, Ltd., N.Y.C., 1972-80, Ghiordian Knot, Ltd., N.Y.C., 1978—, ORS Automation, Inc., Princeton, N.J., 1983-86, Cook United, Inc., Cleve., 1986. Contbr. articles to profl. jours. Mem. house com. 1185 Tenants Corp, N.Y.C. Mem. N.Y. State Bar Assn., Bar Assn. of City of N.Y., Fed. Bar Council (chmn. winter meeting 1980, mem. alternative dispute resolution com. 1984—), Phi Beta Kappa. Democrat. Jewish. Club: Canadian (N.Y.C.) (editor The Maple Leaf 1984—). Securities, General corporate. Home: 1185 Park Ave New York NY 10128 Office: Summit Rovins & Feldesman 445 Park Ave New York NY 10022

CHERPAS, CHRISTOPHER THEODORE, lawyer; b. Toledo, Mar. 23, 1924; s. Theodore C. and Mary (Veronie) C.; m. Ortha N. Mollis, June 23, 1946; children—Maria Glatt, Patricia, Christopher T. B.S. in Polit. Sci., Akron U., 1949; postgrad. Akron Law Sch., 1949-50, Western Res. U., 1951; J.D., Cleveland Marshall U., 1951. Bar: Ohio 1952, U.S. Dist. Ct. (no. dist.) Ohio 1954, U.S. Ct. Appeals (6th cir.) 1966. Counsel United Rubber Workers, Akron, Ohio, 1954-57; ptnr. Cherpas, Manos & Syracopoulos, Akron, 1957-74, Cherpas and Manos, Akron, 1974-79, Teodosio, Cherpas and Manos, Akron, 1979—. Served to capt. U.S. Army, ETO, PTO, Korea, 1942-46, 51-53. Mem. ABA, Ohio Bar Assn., Summit County Bar Assn. Democrat. Greek Orthodox. Clubs: Pan Arcadian Fedn. (Chgo.) (supreme pres. 1957-58); Am. Hellenic Edn. Progressive Assn. (chpt. pres. 1979-80). Lodges: Masons, Shriners, Jesters, K.T. Federal civil litigation, State civil litigation, Personal injury. Home: 1594 Alton Dr Akron OH 44313 Office: Teodosio Cherpas and Manos 907 Akron Savs Bldg Akron OH 44308

CHERRY, BARBARA ANN, lawyer; b. Mpls., Jan. 20, 1954; d. Clifford Daniel and Ruby Evelyn (Norman) C.; m. Gary Steven Was, Aug. 26, 1976 (div. May 1980). BS, U. Mich., 1976; AM in Econs., JD, Harvard U., 1980. Bar: Ill. 1980, U.S. Dist. Ct. (no. dist.) Ill. 1980. Assoc. Schiff, Hardin & Waite, Chgo., 1980-83; regulatory atty. AT&T Corp., Chgo., 1983-85, regional atty. govt. relations, 1985—. Rep. Harvard Law Sch. Fund, Cambridge, Mass., 1980—. NSF fellow, 1976. Mem. ABA, Ill. Bar Assn., Chgo. Bar Assn., Harvard Law Soc. Ill. (bd. dirs. 1980—, v.p. 1986—). Avocation: equestrian sports. Legislative, Public utilities. Home: 575 W Madison St Apt 2407 Chicago IL 60606 Office: AT & T 11 S LaSalle St 12th Floor Chicago IL 60603

CHERRY, DANIEL RONALD, lawyer; b. Mpls., Dec. 31, 1948; s. Clifford D. and Ruby E. (Norman) C.; s. Dianne Brown, Jan. 24, 1971; 1 child, Matthew A. SB, MIT, 1970; JD, Harvard U., 1976. Bar: Ohio 1976, U.S. Dist. Ct. (no. dist.) Ohio 1976, U.S. Ct. Patent Office 1978, U.S. Ct. Appeals (6th and Fed. cirs.) 1982. Assoc. Squire, Sanders & Dempsey, Cleve., 1976-85, ptnr., 1985-87; ptnr. Welsh & Katz, Ltd., Chgo., 1987—. Served with USCGR, 1970-73. Mem. ABA, Ohio Bar Assn., Am. Intellectual Property Law Assn., Licensing Execs. Soc. Patent, Trademark and copyright, Federal civil litigation. Home: 284 Columbine Claredon Hills IL 60514 Office: Welsh & Katz Ltd 135 S LaSalle St Suite 1625 Chicago IL 60603

CHERRY, DAVID EARL, lawyer; b. Ft. Worth, Sept. 10, 1944; s. Leonard Earl and Dorothy Hazel (Brown) C.; m. Katherine Ann Yarborough, Dec. 23, 1967; children: Lisa, Craig. BBA, Tex. Christian U., 1967; JD, Baylor U., 1968. Bar: Tex. 1968, U.S. Dist. Ct. (we. dist.) Tex. 1970, U.S. Dist. Ct. (so. dist.) Tex. 1977, U.S. Ct. Appeals (5th cir.) 1977, U.S. Supreme Ct. 1978, U.S. Ct. Appeals (11th cir.) 1981, U.S. Ct. Claims 1985. Ptnr. Pakis, Cherry, Beard & Giotes, Inc., Waco, Tex., 1968—. Mem. Charter Commn., Woodway, Tex., 1973; chmn. Planning and Zoning Commn., Woodway, 1976-79. Fellow Tex. Bar Found.; mem. ABA, Assn. Trial Lawyers Am., Am. Judicature Soc., Tex. Bar Assn., Tex. Trial Lawyers Assn., Waco-McLennan County Bar Assn., Waco-McLennan County Legal Aid Soc. (dir. 1971-73), Waco-McLennan County Young Lawyers Assn.(pres. 1974-75, namedOutstanding Young Lawyer, 1977). Avocations: running, camping, fishing, photography, hunting. Federal civil litigation, State civil litigation. Office: Pakis Cherry Beard & Giotes Inc 800 M Bank Tower Waco TX 76701

CHERRY, MACK HENRY, judge; b. Memphis, Tenn., Jan. 1, 1947; s. Ned M. and Gladys Eleanor (Parker) C.; m. Sumalee Soponsri, Feb. 21, 1976; children: Mark Sopon, Malee Ann, Martin Boone. BS, Memphis State U., 1969; JD, U. Tenn., 1972. Bar: Tenn. 1973, U.S. Dist. Ct. Tenn. (we. and mid. dists.) Tenn., U.S. Ct. Mil. Appeals, U.S. Ct. Appeals (6th cir.). Asst. pub. defender Shelby County Pub. Defender's Office, Memphis, 1976-77; sole practice Memphis, 1977-79; asst. gen. counsel Tenn. Pub. Service Commn., Nashville, 1979-81, adminstrv. judge, 1981—. Served to capt. JAGC, U.S. Army 1973-76. Mem. ABA. Presbyterian. Administrative and regulatory, Public utilities. Home: 307 Walton Ln Madison TN 37115 Office: Tenn Pub Service Commn Nashville TN 37219

CHERUNDOLO, JOHN CHARLES, lawyer; b. Pitts., Nov. 24, 1948; s. John Charles and Margaret E. (Whitehead) C.; m. Elizabeth Flack, July 26, 1980; children: Allison Belle, Leane Elizabeth. BA in Polit. Sci., Syracuse U., 1970, M Pub Adminstrn., 1972, JD, 1973. Bar: Ill. 1974, N.Y. 1974, U.S. Dist. Ct. (ea. dist.) Ill. 1974. Asst. gen. atty. Roper Corp., Kankakee, Ill., 1974-75; assoc. Hancock Law Firm, Syracuse, N.Y., 1975-80, Banbaum & Manaker, Syracuse, 1980-83; sr. ptnr. Cherundolo, Bottar & Delduchetto, P.C., Syracuse, 1983—. Bd. dirs. Syracuse Friends of Amateur Boxing, 1980—. Named All-Am. UPI, AP, Syracuse, 1970, Acad. All-Am., U.S. Coaches, Syracuse, 1970. Mem. ABA, Assn. Trial Lawyers Am., N.Y. State Bar Assn., N.Y. State Trial Lawyers Assn., Upstate Trial Lawyers Assn. (bd. dirs.), Onondaga County Bar Assn., Syracuse U. Varsity Club (bd. dirs. 1976—), Order of Coif. Roman Catholic. Avocations: sports, real estate. State civil litigation, Federal civil litigation, Personal injury. Home: 4775 Country Club Dr Syracuse NY 13215 Office: Cherundolo Bottar & Delduchetto 407 S Warren St Syracuse NY 13202

CHERWIN, JOEL IRA, lawyer; b. Winthrop, Mass., Apr. 29, 1942; s. Melvin Arthur and Martha (Baer) C.; m. Sherry Lenore Cherwin, July 5, 1970; children: Alison, Matthew, Joshua. BS in Econs., U. Pa., 1963; JD, Boston U., 1966. Bar: Mass. 1966, U.S.. Dist. Ct. Mass. 1968, U.S. Tax Ct. 1969. Ptnr. Cherwin & Glazier, Boston, 1967-77, Cherwin & Glickman, Boston, 1977—; mem. gov.'s entrepreneurial counsel, Boston, 1985—; bd. dirs. New Eng. Fed. Savs. Bank, Wellesley, Mass. Mem. ABA, Mass. Bar Assn. Democrat. Jewish. General corporate, Finance, Real property. Office: Cherwin & Glickman One Post Office Sq Boston MA 02109

CHESHIRE, LUCIUS MCGEHEE, lawyer; b. Raleigh, N.C., Mar. 29, 1925; s. James Webb and Anne Ludlow (McGehee) C.; m. Nellie David, Nov. 16, 1946; children—Lucius McGehee, Carl Davis. Student U. N.C., 1946, cert. in law, 1965. Bar: N.C. Sup. Ct. 1965, U.S. dist. ct. (mid. dist.) N.C. 1969, U.S. Sup. Ct. 1971. Assoc., Graham and Levings, Hillsborough, N.C., 1965; ptnr. Graham, Levings & Cheshire, 1966-67; ptnr. Graham & Cheshire, 1967-81; sr. ptnr. Cheshire & Parker, 1981—; pres. 15 Jud. Dist. Bar, 1971-72, chmn. Dist. 15 B Bar Candidate Com. Active Hist. Hillsborough Commn.; trustee N.C. State Employees Retirement System. Served with USMC, 1943-46. Mem. N.C. State Bar, N.C. Bar Assn., N.C. Acad. Trial Lawyers, Orange County Bar Assn. (pres. 1969-70). Democrat. Anglican Orthodox. Club: Sphinx (Raleigh). Contbr. article to legal review. State civil litigation, General practice. Home: Barracks Rd Hillsborough NC 27278 Office: 100 N Churton St Hillsborough NC 27278

CHESLEY, STANLEY MORRIS, lawyer; b. Cin., Mar. 26, 1936; s. Frank and Rachel (Kinsburg) C.; m. Suellen Kaufman (div.); children—Richard A., Lauren B. B.A., U. Cin., 1958, LL.B., 1960. Bar: Ohio 1960, Ky. 1978, W.Va., Tex., Nev. 1981. Ptnr. Waite, Schneider, Bayless & Chesley Co., Cin., 1960; adj. prof. No. Ky. U., 1973—. Contbr. articles to profl. jours. Mem. Jewish Welfare Fund Bd., Bonds for Israel Bd.; past pres. Camp Livingstone; past chmn. Isaac Wise Temple Religious Sch. Com.; mem. exec. com. Jewish Fedn.; bd. dirs. Friends of the Plum Street Temple. Mem. ABA, Fed. Bar Assn., Maritime Law Assn., Assn. Trial Lawyers Am., Melvin M. Belli Soc., Ohio Bar Assn., Ky. Bar Assn., W.Va. Bar Assn., Tex. Bar Assn., Nev. Bar Assn., Cin. Bar Assn. Personal injury. Office: Waite Schneider Bayless & Chesley Co 1513 Central Trust Tower Cincinnati OH 45202

CHESNUT, CHARLES CALDWELL, lawyer; b. Salem, Ark., May 2, 1912; s. William Royal and Laura Angeline (Caldwell) C.; m. Mary Elizabeth Bush, July 15, 1939; children: Elizabeth, Susan, Linda, Charles W. AB, George Washington U., 1934, LLB, 1938. Bar: Okla. 1940, U.S. Dist. Ct. (no. dist.) Okla. 1942, U.S. Supreme Ct. 1950, U.S. Dist. Ct. (we. dist.) Okla. 1956. County atty. Ottawa County, Miami, Okla., 1941-43; councilman City of Miami, Okla., 1947-49; mem. or chmn. pardon and parole bd. State of Okla., 1955-83. Chmn. Ottawa County Dem. Cen. Com., Miami, 1948-62, 1st United Meth. Ch., Miami, pres., bd. trustees 1st United Meth. Ch., pres. Bd. of Edn., Miami, 1955-62. Served to lt. USNR, 1943-46, PTO. Mem. Okla. Bar Assn. (bd. govs. 1977-80, v.p. 1982), Ottawa County Bar Assn. (pres. 1941-42), Okla. Trial Lawyers Assn. (pres. 1977-78), VFW (post advocate), Am. Legion (vice comdr.). Democrat. Methodist. Lodges: Rotary (pres., Paul Harris fellow), Masons. General practice, Probate, Personal injury. Home: 1805 Lincoln Blvd Miami OK 74354 Office: Chesnut & Chesnut 300 Professi[illegible]l Bldg Miami OK 74354

CHESNUTT, CHARL[illegible] RAPHAEL, lawyer; b. Little Rock, Feb. 25, 1947; s. C.R. and Katherine (Fulk) C.; m. Carolyn Lydia Aiken, Apr. 23, 1977; children—Christy, Charles, Caroline, Catherine. B.A., U. of South, 1969; J.D., La. State U., 1973; Th.M., Dallas Theol. Sem., 1983. Bar: La. 1974 (ret.), U.S. Dist. Ct. (ea. dist.) La. 1974, Texas 1981, U.S. Dist. Ct. (no. dist.) Tex. 1981, U.S. Ct. Appeals (5th cir.) 1983. Sole practice, New Orleans, 1974-79, Dallas, 1981—; speaker on 1st amendment rights and home schs. Author: The Pastor and The Criminal Law, 1983. Mem. Tex. Bar Assn. Republican. Bankruptcy.

CHESSER, DAVID MICHAEL, lawyer; b. Pensacola, Fla., Aug. 12, 1947; s. Julian Edward and Arabelle (Martin) C.; m. Carolyn Anne Miller, Aug. 31, 1968; children: Patrick, Lanie, Anna, Matthew. BA in Psychology, U. Fla., 1969, JD, 1971. Bar: Fla. 1972, U.S. Dist. Ct. (no. dist.) Fla. 1972, U.S. Ct. Appeals (5th and 11th cirs.) 1972, U.S. Tax Ct. 1974, U.S. Supreme Ct. 1976. Ptnr. Chesser, Wingard, Barr & Townsend, Ft. Walton Beach, Fla., 1971—; city atty. Shalimar, Fla., 1972-86, Ft. Walton Beach, 1982-84. Chmn. Zoning Revision Panel, Okaloosa County, Fla., 1982; pres. Okaloosa Guidance Clinic, Ft. Walton Beach, 1978, Okaloosa Guidance Found., Ft. Walton Beach, 1978—. Served to capt. U.S. Army, 1971-78. Mem. Fla. Bar Assn. (continuing edn. com.), Okaloosa-Walton Bar Assn. (pres. 1978), Niceville C. of C. (bd. dirs. 1980-82). Democrat. Methodist. Lodge: Kiwanis. Avocations: tennis, books, music, sports. Real property, General corporate, Contracts commercial. Office: Chesser Wingard Barr & Townsend 838 N Elgin Pkwy Suite 601 Fort Walton Beach FL 32548

CHESTER, JOHN JONAS, lawyer; b. Columbus, Ohio, July 13, 1920; s. John J. and Harriet Bonnadine (Rice) C.; m. Cynthia Johnson, Apr. 18, 1959; children—John, James, Joel, Cecily. A.B. cum laude, Amherst Coll., 1942; J.D., Yale U., 1948. Bar: Ohio, 1948. Ptnr., Chester & Chester, Columbus, 1948-57; ptnr. Chester & Rose, Columbus, 1958-70; ptnr. Chester, Hoffman & Willcox, Columbus, 1971—. Trustee Columbus Sch. for Girls, Riverside Meth. Hosp., Shepherd Hill Hosp., Ohio Hist. Found. mem. Ohio Gen. Assembly, 1953-58; spl. counsel Pres. U.S., 1974. Served to lt. USNR, 1942-46. Mem. ABA, Ohio State Bar Assn., Columbus Bar Assn., Am. Coll. Trial Lawyers. Republican. Episcopalian. Clubs: Columbus, Columbus Athletic, Scioto Country, Rocky Fork Hunt & Country, Mason (Columbus). General practice, Federal civil litigation, State civil litigation. Home: 4906 Riverside Dr Columbus OH 43220 Office: 8 E Broad St Columbus OH 43215

CHESTER, MARK VINCENT, lawyer; b. Chgo., Apr. 22, 1952; s. Alvin L. and Barbara (Segal) C.; m. Shelly L. Beeber, May 20, 1979; children: Jonathan Harry, Michael Steven. B.A., Emory U., 1974, M.A., 1974; postgrad. Victoria U. of Manchester, 1972-73; J.D., Northwestern U., 1977. Bar: Ill. 1977, U.S. Dist. Ct. (no. dist.) Ill. 1977, Ga. 1979, U.S. Ct. Appeals (7th, 11th and 5th cirs.) 1981, U.S. Supreme Ct. 1981. Asst. state's atty. Cook County (Ill.), 1977-81, spl. asst. state's atty., 1981—; spl. asst. atty. gen. Ill., 1981-83; assoc. Butler, Rubin, Newcomer & Saltarelli, Chgo., 1981-83; ptnr. Johnson and Colmar, Chgo., 1983—. Bd. dirs. Project LEAP, 1976—. Mem. ABA, Ill. Bar Assn., Ga. Bar Assn., Chgo. Bar Assn. State and local taxation, State civil litigation, Federal civil litigation. Home: 1017 Prairie Ave Deerfield IL 60015 Office: Johnson and Colmar 75 E Wacker Dr Suite 1000 Chicago IL 60601

CHESTER, STEPHANIE ANN, lawyer, banker; b. Mpls., Oct. 8, 1951; d. Alden Runge and Nina Lavina (Hanson) C.; divorced. B.A. magna cum laude, Augustana Coll., 1973; J.D., U. S.D., 1977; postgrad. C.F.S.C., ABA Nat. Grad. Trust Sch., Evanston, Ill., 1984. Bar: S.D. 1977, Minn. 1979. Asst. counselor Minnehaha County Juvenile Ct. Ctr., Sioux Falls, S.D., 1972-73; child care worker Project Threshold, Sioux Falls, 1973-74; legal intern Davenport, Evans, Hurwitz & Smith, Sioux Falls, 1976; law clk. S.D. Supreme Ct., Pierre, 1977-78; originations dept. buyer Dain Bosworth, Inc., Mpls., 1978-79; v.p., trust officer 1st Bank of S.D., N.A., Sioux Falls, 1979-86; v.p., First Trust Co., Inc., St. Paul, 1986—; bd. dirs., mem. program com. Sioux Falls Estate Planning Council, 1983-85; Projects and research editor S.D. Law Rev., 1977; author law rev. comment. Mem. fund raising com. S.D. Symphony, Sioux Falls Community Playhouse, Augustana Coll., 1982-83; mem. S.D. div. Nat. Women's Polit. Caucus; mem. events com. Augustana Coll. Fellows, Sioux Falls, 1984; bd. dirs. YWCA, Sioux Falls, 1984, Sioux Falls Arena/Coliseum, 1985; mem. Sioux Falls Jr. Service League, 1984. Augustana Coll. scholar, 1969-73; Augustana Coll. Bd. Regents scholar, 1973. Mem. S.D. Bar Assn., Minn. Bar Assn., ABA, 2d S.D. Jud. Circuit Bar Assn., Nat. Assn. Bank Women (state conv. com. 1983-85), Phi Delta Phi, Chi Epsilon. Republican. Lutheran. Clubs: Network, Portia (Sioux Falls). Pension, profit-sharing, and employee benefits. Office: First Trust Co Inc 180 E 5th St Saint Paul MN 55102

CHESTNUTT, ELLEN JOANNE, state official; b. Milw., May 15, 1928; d. Arthur Herman and Lydia Boaz (Groff) Ziemann; m. William John Chestnutt, Sept. 3, 1954; children—David William C., Douglas John C., Gregory Mark C., Timothy Eric C. B.S., U. Wis., 1950, J.D., 1952. Bar: Wis. 1952, U.S. Dist. Ct. Wis. 1952, Colo. 1964, U.S. Dist. Ct. Colo. 1964. Editor Shepard's Citations, Colorado Springs, Colo., 1952-54; sole practice, Colorado Springs, 1964-68; staff dist. atty's office, Colorado Springs, 1966-85; appeal referee Colo. Dept. Labor, 1985—; instr. law Pikes Peak Community Coll., Colorado Springs, 1978—, also Chapman Coll. Mem. Task Force on Child Support, HEW, 1974, Adv. com. Fed. Child Support Law Regulations, 1975; speaker Secs. Nat. Conf. on Fraud, Abuse, and Error, 1978; judge regional sci. fair, 1978-87; v.p. Longfellow Sch. PTA, Colorado Springs; active Cub Scouts, Colorado Springs; vol. instr. swimming YMCA; bd. dirs. Salvation Army. Recipient Disting. Faculty award Nat. Dist. Attys. Coll. Law, 1976. Mem. ABA, Wis. Bar Assn., Colo. Bar Assn., El Paso County Bar Assn. (past sec., trustee), Colo. Women's Bar Assn. (Silver honoree), Nat. Dist. Attys. Assn., Colo. Family Support Council (past pres.), Nat. Welfare Fraud Assn., (past. pres.), Colo. Welfare Fraud Council (pres.), Nat. Reciprocal Family Support Enforcement Assn. (past pres.), Alpha Gamma Delta (past v.p. alumni assn.). Republican. Methodist. Club: Pikes Peak Geneal. Soc. (Colorado Springs). Contbr. articles to profl. jours. Criminal, Family and matrimonial, Legal education. Home: 718 Pioneer Ln Colorado Springs CO 80904

CHESWICK, PHILLIP THOMAS, lawyer; b. Mesa, Ariz., Jan. 23, 1943; s. Thomas F. and May (Reick) C.; m. Cherie L., Apr. 20, 1968; 1 child, Thomas. BA, U. Pitts., 1974; JD, Duquesne U., 1979. Bar: Pa. 1979, U.S. Dist. Ct. Pa. 1979, U.S. Supreme Ct. 1984. Police officer City of Pitts., 1966—; assoc. Markovitz & Vitt., Pitts., 1979-80; sole practice Pitts., 1980—; bd. dirs. Elder-Ado, City of Pitts., 1985-86. Bd. dirs. Mt. Oliver C. of C., 1984-85; solicitor Western Pa. Crime Prevention Officers, Pitts. Served with U.S. Army, 1961-64. Mem. ABA, Pa. Bar Assn., Allegheny Bar Assn., Pa. Trial Lawyers Assn., Fraternal Order Police. Democrat. Presbyterian. Lodge: Masons. Personal injury, General practice, State civil litigation. Home: 2433 Rose Garden Rd Pittsburgh PA 15220 Office: 502 Brownsville Rd Pittsburgh PA 15210

CHEVIS, CHERYL ANN, lawyer; b. Ann Arbor, Mich., Nov. 9, 1947; d. Peter Paul and Antoinette (Slapinski) C.; m. Edwin Mahaffey Gerow, Nov. 18, 1976. BA, U. Wash., 1969, MA, 1974; postgrad. in Sanskrit, U. Chgo., 1974-77, JD, 1980. Bar: Ill. 1980, U.S. Dist. Ct. (no. dist.) Ill. 1980, U.S. Ct. Appeals (7th cir.) 1982, U.S. Tax Ct. 1982, Oreg. 1986. Tax assoc. Sidley and Austin, Chgo., 1979-80, Mayer Brown and Platt, Chgo., 1981-85; sr. tax atty. Perkins Coie, Portland, 1985-87, tax ptnr., 1987—; faculty mem. Ill. Continuing Legal Edn., Chgo., 1982; vis. lectr. U. B.C., Vancouver, Can., 1982; lectr. Chgo. Tax Club, 1983; lectr. Oreg. Securities Lawyers Bar, Bend, 1986. Contbr. articles to Jour. Taxation. Vol. atty. Com. Civil Rights Under Law, Chgo., 1982-85. Smithsonian Inst. grantee, 1981. Mem. ABA (tax sect., com. capital recovery and leasing), Oreg. State Bar. Avocations: music, theater, outdoor sports. Corporate taxation, State and local taxation, Real property. Home: 4260 SW Council Crest Dr Portland OR 97201 Office: Perkins Coie 111 SW 5th Ave Portland OR 97204

CHICKERING, JOHN BRADLEY, lawyer, judge; b. Washington, Oct. 5, 1924; B.S., U.S. Mil. Acad., 1945; M.S., Purdue U., 1950; J.D., George Washington U., 1966; Ph.D., U. Ariz., 1976. Bar: Va. 1966, D.C. 1967, U.S. Supreme Ct. 1970, Ariz. 1974; registered profl. engr., Vt. Commd. 2nd lt., pilot U.S. Army Air Corps, 1945, advanced through grades to lt. col., USAF, 1963, ret. 1965; practice law, Leesburg, Va., 1966-67; assoc. Browne, Schuyler & Beveridge, Washington, 1967-69; nat. fellow, teaching assoc. U. Ariz., 1969-72; instr. U. Ariz., 1972-75; adminstrv. law judge State of Ariz. Indsl. Commn., Tucson, 1975-85; trial lawyer, counsel Ariz. State Compensation Fund, Tucson, 1985—. Mem. Assn. Grads. U.S. Mil. Acad., Ariz. Bar Assn., D.C. Bar Assn., Va. Bar Assn., Gamma Alpha Rho, Phi Delta Phi. Administrative and regulatory, State civil litigation, Workers' compensation. Home: 6675 N Los Leones Dr Tucson AZ 85718 Office: Ariz State Compensation Fund Bldg 55 E Helen St Tucson AZ 85705

CHIDNESE, PATRICK N., lawyer; b. Neptune, N.J., May 26, 1940; s. Louis and Helen C.; m. Rene E. Chidnese, Aug. 19, 1968; 1 child, Krista; m. Kathy J. Chidnese, Feb. 16, 1985; 1 child, Patrick. B.A., U. Miami, 1964, J.D., 1968. Assoc. Sinclair, Louis & Huttoe, Miami, 1968-69; assoc. Stephens, Demos, Magil & Thornton, Miami, 1969-70; assoc. Howell, Kirby, Montgomery, D'Aiuto, Dean & Hallowes, Fort Lauderdale, Fla., 1970-71; sole practice, Fort Lauderdale, 1971—; county atty. Broward County Juvenile Ct., 1971-72. Mem. Fla. Bar Assn. (chmn. auto ins. com. 1977-78, chmn. 17th jud. circuit legis. com. 1977-80), Broward County Bar Assn., Acad. Fla. Trial Lawyers, Broward County Trial Lawyers Assn. (bd. dirs. 1974-80). Insurance, Personal injury, Workers' compensation. Office: 201 SE 12th St Fort Lauderdale FL 33316

CHIERICHELLA, JOHN W., lawyer; b. N.Y.C., Mar. 26, 1947; s. Pasquale Joseph and Ruth Cecilia (White) C.; m. Susan R. Hahn, Aug. 23, 1969; children—Amy Beth, Rebecca A., Michael H. A.B., Cornell U., 1969; J.D., Columbia U., 1972. Bar: N.Y. 1973, D.C., 1975. Assoc., Cravath, Swaine & Moore, N.Y.C. 1972-73; assoc., then ptnr. Jones, Day, Reavis & Pogue, Washington, 1975-79, 87—; ptnr. Crowell & Moring, Washington, 1979-84, Gibson, Dunn & Crutcher, Washington, 1984-87. Contbr. articles to profl. jours. Served to capt. USAF, 1973-75. Harlan Fiske Stone scholar, 1971, James Kent scholar, 1972. Mem. ABA (past chmn. contracts com., contracts clauses and forms com., pub. contracts law sect.), Nat. Contract. Mgmt. Assn., Nat. Security Indsl. Assn. Government contracts and claims, Federal civil litigation, State civil litigation. Office: Jones Day Reavis & Pogue 655 15th St NW Washington DC 20005-5701

CHILD, JOHN SOWDEN, JR., lawyer; b. Lansdale, Pa., July 22, 1944; s. John Sowden and Beatrice Thelma (Landes) C. B.S. in Polit. Sci., MIT, 1967; B.S. in Chem. Engring., 1967; J.D., U. Pa., 1973; B.Lit. in Politics, Oxford U., 1974. Bar: Pa. 1974, N.Y. 1977, U.S. Dist. Ct. (ea. dist.) Pa. 1978, U.S. Dist. Ct. (ea. dist.) N.Y. 1978, U.S. Patent and Trademark Office 1978, U.S. Ct. Appeals (2d cir.) 1978, U.S. Ct. Appeals (fed. cir.) 1981, U.S. Ct.Appeals (3d cir.) 1986. Assoc. Davis Hoxie Faithfull & Hapgood, N.Y.C., 1974-78; assoc. Synnestvedt & Lechner, Phila., 1978—; arbitrator Pa. Ct. Common

Pleas, Phila., 1979, U.S. Dist. Ct., Ea. Dist.) Pa., Phila., 1983. Firm coordinator United Way Southeastern Pa., 1983—. Mem. Am. Intellectual Property Law Assn., N.Y. Patent, Trademark and Copyright Law Assn., Phila. Bar Assn., Phila. Patent Law Assn. (chmn. program com. 1981-85, editor, co-editor newsletter 1980—, gov. 1985-87, sec. 1987—), Mil. Order Fgn. Wars, Com. of Seventy, Soc. Colonial Wars, English Speaking Union, Colonial Soc. Pa., Phila. Oxford and Cambridge Soc. (sec. 1985—). Republican. Mem. Soc. of Friends. Clubs: Union League, Cricket (Phila.). Patent, Trademark and copyright. Home: 8221 Seminole Ave Philadelphia PA 19118 Office: Synnestvedt & Lechner 2600 One Reading Ctr 1101 Market St Philadelphia PA 19107

CHILDERS, ROBERT LAWSON, state judge; b. Memphis, Mar. 12, 1948; s. Howard Lawson and Velma Pearl (Baker) C.; m. Donna Kay Tapper, Dec. 15, 1969 (div. Feb. 1983); 1 child, Lisa Kay. BBA, Memphis State U., 1971, JD, 1974. Bar: Tenn. 1975, U.S. Dist. Ct. (we. dist.) Tenn. 1975, U.S. Supreme Ct. 1985. Of counsel Law offices of James F. Schaefer, Memphis, 1975-78; sole practice Memphis, 1978-84; judge cir. ct. 30th jud. dist. State of Tenn., Memphis, 1984—; guest lectr. Cecil C. Humphreys Sch. Law, Memphis State U. Mem. Tenn. Young Dems., Memphis, 1978-83. Mem. Memphis-Shelby County Bar Assn. (bd. dirs. 1979-81, Best Participant award 1986, Outstanding Judge of Yr. award 1986), Memphis Trial Lawyers Assn. (pres. 1983-84), Tenn. Trial Lawyers Assn. (bd. govs. 1980-82), Cecil C. Humphreys Sch. Law Alumni Assn. (pres. nat. council 1983), Delta Theta Phi. Methodist. Avocations: sports, music. Home: 273 N Angelus Memphis TN 38112-5201 Office: Tenn Cir Ct 30th Jud Dist 140 Adams Ave Memphis TN 38103

CHILDS, ALAN D., lawyer, corporate executive; b. 1930. B.A., Mich. State U., 1952; John Marshall Law Sch., 1963. Atty., Sherwin Williams Co., Cleve., 1954—, asst. dir. indsl. relations, 1963-65, asst. gen. counsel, 1965-66, asst. sec., 1966-67, gen. counsel, 1967—, sec., 1968-71, asst. v.p., 1971-74, v.p., 1974—, v.p., sec., gen. counsel, 1978—. General corporate. Office: Sherwin-Williams Co 101 Prospect Ave NW Cleveland OH 44115 *

CHILDS, JULIE, lawyer; b. Atlanta, Oct. 5, 1950; d. Otis Lee Jr. and Eloise (Wilson) C. BA, U. Ga., 1971, JD magna cum laude, 1978. Bar: Ga. 1978, U.S. Dist. Ct. (no. dist.) Ga. 1978, U.S. Ct. Appeals (5th and llth cirs.) 1978. Assoc. Cofer, Beauchamp & Hawes, Atlanta, 1978-85; sole practice Atlanta, 1985-86; assoc. McLain & Merritt, P.C., Atlanta, 1986—. State chmn. Ga. Jr. Leagues, 1985-86; bd. dirs. Dekalb Jr. League, Dekalb County, Ga., 1982—, community v.p. 1986—. Mem. Ga. State Bar Assn. (young lawyers sect.), Atlanta Bar Assn., Ga. Assn. Women Lawyers, Order of the Coif, De Kalb County C. of C. (adv. bd. adopt-a-sch. program 1982—). Democrat. Methodist. Avocations: golf, vol. activities. Estate planning, State civil litigation, Contracts commercial. Office: McLain & Merritt PC 1250 Tower Pl Atlanta GA 30026

CHILDS, LARRY BRITTAIN, lawyer; b. Feb. 26, 1952; s. Don and Mattie Frances (Brittain) C.; m. Julie Truss; children: Lucy, Elizabeth, George. BA, U. Ala., 1974; JD, U. Va., 1977. Bar: Ala. 1977. Law clk. to presiding sr. judge U.S. Dist. Ct. (no. dist.) Ala., Birmingham, 1977-78; assoc. Cabaniss, Johnston, Gardner, Dumas & O'Neal, Birmingham, 1978-83, ptnr., 1984—. Mem. ABA, Ala. Bar Assn., Birmingham Bar Assn. Presbyterian. Banking, Construction, Securities. Home: 1537 Camden Ave Birmingham AL 35226 Office: Cabaniss Johnston Gardner Dumas & O'Neal 1900 1st Nat So Natural Bldg Birmingham AL 35226

CHILDS, MARJORIE M., lawyer; b. N.Y.C., July 13, 1918; d. Charles W. and Eva M. (Tarrant) C. Student Hunter Coll., 1942-46; BA in Econs., U. Calif., Berkeley, 1948; JD, U. San Francisco, 1956; LLD (hon.), Iowa Wesleyan Coll., 1973. Bar: Calif. 1957, U.S. Supreme Ct. 1969. With Office of Regional Counsel, U.S. Navy, Ft. Mason, Calif., 1957-60; asst. county counsel Humboldt County, Calif., 1960-62; sole practice, San Francisco, 1962-64, 79—; referee, commr. Juvenile dept. Superior Ct., San Francisco, 1964-79. Pres. Diamond Heights Community Assn., 1983-84. Recipient James A. Harlan award Iowa Wesleyan Coll., 1969. Fellow Am. Bar Found.; mem. ABA, Internat. Bar Assn., Lawyers Club San Francisco, Queen's Bench (pres. 1967), Bar Assn. San Francisco, Internat. Fedn. Women Lawyers (pres. 1974-75), Nat. Assn. Women Lawyers (pres. 1974-75). Democrat. Episcopalian. Club: Metropolitan (San Francisco). Contbr. articles to profl. jours. Private international, Family and matrimonial, Probate. Address: 64 Turquoise Way San Francisco CA 94131 Office: 301 Junipero Serra Blvd #260 San Francisco CA 94127

CHILES, STEPHEN MICHAEL, lawyer; b. Chillicothe, Ohio, July 15, 1942; s. Daniel Duncan and Helen Virginia (Hayes) C.; m. Deborah E. Nash, June 13, 1964; children—Stephen, Abigail. B.A., Davidson Coll., 1964; J.D., Duke U., 1967. Bars: N.Y. 1970, Pa. 1978, Wis. 1981, U.S. Supreme Ct. 1978, U.S. Ct. Appeals (3d cir.) 1978, U.S. Dist. Ct. (ea. dist.) Pa. 1978, U.S. Tax Ct. 1978, Ill. 1986. Officer trust dept. Irving Trust Co., N.Y.C., 1970-75, v.p., 1975-77; assoc. atty. Stassen Kostos & Mason, Phila., 1978-79, mem., shareholder, 1979-85; ptnr. McDermott, Will & Emery, Chgo., 1986—. Contbr. articles to profl. jours. Served to capt. U.S. Army, 1967-69. Decorated Bronze Star, Army Commendation medal. Mem. ABA, Wis. Bar Assn. Republican. Episcopalian. Clubs: Monroe (Chgo.); Aronimink Golf, Newtown Sq. Estate planning, General corporate, Estate taxation. Office: McDermott Will & Emery 111 W Monroe St Chicago IL 60603

CHILLERI, GINO AMERIGO, lawyer; b. Chgo., Oct. 25, 1956. MBA, U. Calif., Berkeley, 1978; JD, U. Calif., San Francisco, 1981. Bar: Calif. 1982. Auditor regulatory compliance Crocker Nat. Bank, San Francisco, 1982-84; assoc. Union Bank, Los Angeles, 1984—. Mem. ABA, Los Angeles Lawyers County Bar Assn. Banking, Consumer commercial, Contracts commercial. Office: Union Bank Legal Dept 445 S Figueroa St Los Angeles CA 90071

CHILVERS, ROBERT MERRITT, lawyer; b. Long Beach, Calif., Oct. 23, 1942; s. James Merritt and Elizabeth Louise (Blackburn) C.; m. Sandra Lee Rigg, Sept. 5, 1969; children: Jeremy Merritt, Jessica Rigg. AB, U. Calif., Berkeley, 1972; JD, Harvard U., 1975. Bar: Calif. 1975, U.S. Dist. Ct. (no. dist.) Calif. 1975, U.S. Ct. Appeals (9th cir.) 1980, U.S. Supreme Ct. 1980, U.S. Dist. Ct. (cen. dist.) Calif. 1981, U.S. Ct. Claims 1984, U.S. Ct. Appeals (Fed. cir.) 1987. Assoc. Brobeck, Phleger & Harrison, San Francisco, 1975-82, ptnr., 1982—; faculty U. Calif., San Francisco, 1983—, Emory U., Atlanta, 1984—, fed. practice program U.S. Dist. Ct. (no. dist.) Calif., 1984—, Nat. Inst. for Trial Advocacy, 1986—. Mem. Calif. Sch. Bds. Assn., 1985—; trustee Mill Valley Sch. Dist., Calif., 1985—; bd. dirs. Marin County Sch. Bds. Assn., Calif., 1985-86. Mem. ABA (litigation and sci. and tech. sects.), Calif. Bar Assn. (commendation for Outstanding Contributions to the delivery of vol. legal services. 1984), San Francisco Bar Assn., Tau Beta Pi, Sigma Tau. Republican. Federal civil litigation, State civil litigation, Antitrust. Office: Brobeck Phleger & Harrison 1 Market Plaza Spear St Tower San Francisco CA 94105 Home: 830 Chamberlain Ct Mill Valley CA 94941

CHIN, SHERRY (LYNN), lawyer; b. Highland Park, Mich., July 15, 1951; d. Nick Boyd and Elizabeth Royer; m. John Alden Chin, Dec. 30, 1973; children: Jonathan, Stacey. BBA, U. Mich., 1973, JD, 1975. Bar: Mich. 1976, U.S. Dist. Ct. (ea. dist.) Mich. 1976. Ptnr. Laird, Chin & Schwartz, Ann Arbor, Mich., 1976—. Bd. dirs. Ann Arbor Symphony, 1987-88; treas. Glacier Area Home Owners Assn., 1985-87. Mem. ABA, State Bar Assn. Mich. (character and fitness sub com.), Asian Am. Bar Assn. Mich., Washtenaw County Bar Assn. (chmn. friend of ct. com. 1986-87, treas. 1987-88), Ann Arbor Area C. of C., Ann Arbor Apt. Assn. General practice, Real property, Family and matrimonial. Home: 3648 Middleton Ann Arbor MI 48105 Office: Laird Chin & Schwartz 220 E Huron Suite 250 Ann Arbor MI 48104

CHING, ANTHONY, lawyer; b. Lin Pao, Honan, Peoples Republic of China, Feb. 3, 1947; came to U.S., 1956; s. Eugene and Jean (Su) C. BA, Calif. State U., San Jose, 1971; JD, U. Pa., 1975. Bar: Calif. 1976. Trial atty. EEOC, San Francisco, 1975-77; dep. dist. atty. Martinez, Calif., 1977-79; gen. atty. Western Pacific R.R., San Francisco, 1979-84; sr. litigation counsel Litton Industries, Inc., Los Angeles, 1984—. Mem. Los Angeles County Bar Assn., San Francisco Bar Assn., Nat. R.R. Trial Atty. Assn., Asian Bus. League. Avocations: skiing, tennis, sailing. State civil litigation, Personal injury, General corporate. Office: Litton Industries Inc 360 N Crescent Dr Beverly Hills CA 90210

CHING, ANTHONY BARTHOLOMEW, lawyer, educator, consultant; b. Shanghai, China, Nov. 18, 1935; came to U.S., 1956; s. William L.K. and Christina Ching; m. Nancy Ann Prigge, Apr. 10, 1961; children—Anthony, Alice, Alexander, Andrew, Ann, Audrey, Anastasia, Albert. Student Universite Catholique de L'ouest, 1953-54, Cambridgeshire Tech. Coll., 1954-55; matriculated Cambridge U., 1955, St. John's Coll., 1956; B.S. in Geology, U. Ariz., 1959, postgrad., 1959-60, LL.B., 1965; LL.M., Harvard U., 1971. Bar: Ariz. 1965, U.S. Dist. Ct. Ariz. 1965, U.S. Ct. Appeals (9th cir.) 1969, U.S. Supreme Ct. 1969, U.S. Ct. Appeals (5th cir.) 1972. Geologist, Duval Sulphur and Potash, Kingman, Ariz. and Tucson, 1959-60, Am. Smelting and Refining Co., Tucson, part-time 1960-61; engr. Marum and Marum Cons. Engrs., Tucson, 1961-65; sole practice, Tucson, 1965-66; atty., chief trial counsel Pima County Legal Aid Soc., Tucson, 1966-70; fellow clin. legal edn. Harvard Law Sch., Cambridge, Mass., 1970-71, acting prof. Law Sch., Loyola U., Los Angeles, 1971-73, 74-75, adj. prof., 1982; dir. litigation, acting project dir. Hawaii Legal Aid Soc., Honolulu, 1973-74; chief counsel Econ. Protection div. Atty. Gen.'s Office, State of Ariz., Phoenix, 1975-79; solicitor gen. Ariz. Dept. Law, Phoenix, 1979—; chmn. Western Attys. Gen. Litigation Action Com., 1983-86; pres. Nat. Consumer Law Ctr., Boston, 1979—; judge pro tem Maricopa County Superior Ct., 1984—. Mem. Pima County Democratic Com., 1966-70, Tucson Community Council, 1968-70, Pio Decimo Ctr., 1968-70; bd. dirs. Ariz. Consumer Council, 1968-70; pres. Young Dems. Greater Tucson, 1969-70. Mem. ABA, State Bar Ariz., Maricopa County Bar Assn., Nat. Legal Aid and Defender Assn. (treas. 1973-74, Reginald Heber Smith award 1969), Harvard Law Sch. Assn. Ariz. (pres. 1980-83). Roman Catholic. Federal civil litigation, Civil rights, Administrative and regulatory. Home: 2632 S Fairfield St Tempe AZ 85282 Office: 1275 W Washington Phoenix AZ 85007

CHING, GALE LIN FONG, lawyer; b. Honolulu, Nov. 27, 1954; s. Richard L. and Helen Y.C. (Wong) C. BA in Psychology with distinction, U. Hawaii, 1976; JD, Gonzaga U., 1980. Dep. pros. atty. Hawaii County Ct., Hilo, 1981-86; dep. atty. gen. State of Hawaii, Honolulu, 1986—. Mem. ABA, Hawaii Bar Assn. Criminal, State civil litigation. Home: 2315 Auhuhu St Pearl City HI 96782 Office: Atty Gens Office State Capitol Bldg Honolulu HI 96813

CHINITZ, STEPHEN SOLOMON, lawyer; b. Hartford, Conn., Jan. 13, 1953; s. Martin Irving and Harriet Sylvia (Wallace) C. B.A., U. Conn., 1975; J.D., John Marshall Law Sch., 1979. Bar: Conn. 1979, U.S. Dist. Ct. Conn. 1979. Lawyer, DiPietro, Kantrovitz and Brownstein, New Haven, 1979-82, Berman & Sable, Hartford, Conn., 1982-84, Green & Kleinman, P.C., Hartford, 1984—; lectr. secured trans. Conn. Bar Assn. Young Lawyers, Hartford, 1982-84; speaker consumer rights Conn. Bar Assn. WPOP Radio, 1984—. Mem. Conn. Bar Assn., ABA, Assn. Trial Lawyers Am., Conn. Trial Lawyers Assn., Comml. Law League of Am., State of Connecticut membership chmn. Jewish. Consumer commercial, Contracts commercial, Federal civil litigation. Home: 190 Brewster Rd West Hartford CT 06117 Office: Green and Kleinman PC One Corporate Center Hartford CT 06103

CHIP, WILLIAM WADDINGTON, lawyer; b. Evansville, Ind., Dec. 9, 1948; s. William Charles and Jean (Waddington) C.; m. Sylvia Martin Moreno, July 1, 1974; children: Francine, Alexander. BA, Yale U., 1971, JD, 1979; MA, Cambridge U., 1973. Bar: D.C. 1979, U.S. Dist. Ct. (D.C. dist.) 1981, U.S. Claims Ct. 1981, U.S. Tax Ct. 1981, U.S. Ct. Appeals (Fed. cir.) 1983. Assoc. Ivins, Phillips & Barker, Washington, 1979-84, ptnr., 1985-86; counsel Cadwalader, Wickersham & Taft, Washington, 1986—. Editor Yale U. Law Jour., 1978-79; contbr. articles to profl. jours. Mem. nat. adv. bd. Fedn. Am. Immigration Reform, Washington, 1980—. Served to capt. USMC, 1973-76. Mem. ABA, NFL Alumni (exec. com. 1982—). Republican. Roman Catholic. Corporate taxation, Pension, profit-sharing, and employee benefits, Legislative. Office: Cadwalader Wickersham & Taft 1333 New Hampshire Ave NW Washington DC 20036

CHIRRA, JOSEPH, lawyer; b. Pottstown, Pa., Aug. 17, 1946; s. James and Mary (Makarevitz) Cirafesi; m. Gloria Floren, Dec. 8, 1979. B.A. in Polit. Sci., Pa. State U., 1968; J.D., U. San Diego, 1974. Bar: Calif. 1974, U.S. Dist. Ct. (so. dist.) Calif. 1974. Sole practice, Vista, Calif., 1974-78; staff atty. Defenders, Inc., San Diego, 1979-82; ptnr. Saunders, Chirra, Orlansky & Judd, Vista, 1982-84, Chirra, Margolis & Hubbard, and predecessor firm, Vista, 1984—. Author short story, theatrical plays, poetry. Pres. Miracosta Coll. Theater Arts Found., Oceanside, Calif., 1983—; Dem. nominee for Congress 43d Dist. Calif., 1986. Mem. State Bar Calif., N. County Bar Assn. Democrat. Criminal, Personal injury.

CHIUMENTO, GARY C., lawyer; b. Camden, N.J., Mar. 29, 1954; s. Carl E. and Rosemarie (Giordano) C.; m. Deborah S. Wolfe, Jan. 12, 1979; children: Peter, Katherine. BA, U. Pa., 1976; JD, Rutgers U., 1979. Bar: N.J. 1979, U.S. Dist. Ct. N.J. 1979, U.S. Ct. Appeals (3d cir.) 1981, Pa. 1984, U.S. Dist. Ct. (ea. dist.) Pa. 1984. Law sec. to presiding justice appelleate div. N.J. Superior Ct., Asbury Park, 1979-80; assoc. Parker, McCay & Crisruolo, Mt. Holly, N.J., 1980-83, Jackson & Crow, Princeton, N.J., 1983-84, Pennington & Thompson, Haddonfield, N.J., 1984—; adj. prof. Glassboro (N.J.) State Coll., 1984-85, St. Joseph's U., Phila., 1985—; mcpl. prosecutor Southampton twp., Vincentown, N.J., 1980-83; mcpl. pub. defender Oaklyn (N.J.) twp., 1985—. Mem. Am. Arbitration Assn. (arbitrator), Am. Assn. Trial Attys., Trial Attys. of N.J. State civil litigation, Federal civil litigation, General practice. Office: Pennington & Thompson One Centennial Sq Haddonfield NJ 08033

CHIZMADIA, STEPHEN MARK, lawyer; b. Perth Amboy, N.J., June 19, 1950; s. Stephen Thomas and Madeline Cecilia (Vojack) C. B.A. in Econs., U. Pa., 1971; M.S. in Mgmt., N.J. Inst. Tech., 1975; J.D. with honors, N.Y. Law Sch., 1977. Bar: N.J. 1977, Fla. 1978, N.Y. 1980, U.S. dist. ct. (so. and ea. dists.) N.Y. 1981, U.S. dist. ct. N.J. 1977. Assoc., Hampson & Millet, P.C., Somerset, N.J., 1978, sole practice, New Brunswick, N.J., 1979-80; counsel Home Ins. Co., Short Hills, N.J., 1980-81; assoc. John M. Downing, P.C., N.Y.C., 1981-84, Schneider, Kleinick & Weitz, P.C., N.Y.C., 1984—; arbitrator Small Claims, N.Y.C. Civil Ct., 1986—; lectr. legal topics profl. seminars; adj. instr. law and bus. mgmt. Middlesex County Coll., 1978-80. Dir. Raritan Bay (N.J.) Area YMCA, 1980-86 . Recipient Am. Jurisprudence award, 1977, several community service awards. Mem. N.J. Bar Assn., N.Y. State Bar Assn., Fla. Bar Assn., Am. Judicature Soc. Insurance, Federal civil litigation, State civil litigation. Home: 599 Amboy Ave Perth Amboy NJ 08861 Office: 11 Park Pl New York NY 10007

CHO, TAI YONG, lawyer; b. Seoul, Republic of Korea, May 27, 1943; came to U.S., 1966; s. Nam Suck and Sun Yeo (Yoon) C; m. Hea Sun Cho, July 14, 1973; children: Robert, Richard, Susan. BS, Seoul U., 1965; MS, Cooper Union, 1971; CE, Columbia U., 1971; JD, Fordham U., 1981. Bar: N.Y. 1982; registered profl. engr., N.Y. Engr. Ministry of Constrn., Seoul, 1965-66, Andrews & Clark, N.Y.C., 1967-68, Parsons, Brinckerhoff, Quade & Douglas, N.Y.C., 1969-71; v.p. John R. McCarthy Corp., N.Y.C., 1972-80; pres., owner Tai CPM Corp., N.Y.C., 1980—; sole practice N.Y.C., 1982—. Mem. ASCE, ABA, N.Y. State Bar Assn., Am. Arbitration Assn. (panel of arbitrators). Contracts commercial, General corporate, Private international. Home: 56 Tuttle Rd Briarcliff Manor NY 10510 Office: 1 Penn Plaza New York NY 10001

CHOATE, ALAN G., lawyer; b. Detroit, Oct. 16, 1939; m. Lynne MacCallum, Sept. 17, 1977; children: Bradford Alden, Victoria Ross. BA in Philosophy, Harvard U., 1961; LLB, U. Mich., 1964; diplome d'Etudes Superieures, U. Genoble, France, 1965. Bar: D.C. 1965, Pa. 1966, U.S. Ct. Appeals (3d cir.) 1968, U.S. Supreme Ct. 1968. Assoc. Pepper, Hamilton & Sheetz, Phila., 1965-72, ptnr., 1972-84; v.p. law Am. Trading and Prodn. Corp., Balt., 1984—. Author: Foreign Operations-Base Companies, Bureau of National Affairs, 1968; contbr. articles to profl. jours. Trustee Nat. Maritime Hist. Soc., 1968—, vice-chmn., 1986—. Contracts commercial, General corporate, Corporate taxation. Office: Am Trading and Prodn Corp PO Box 238 Baltimore MD 21203

CHOATE, DENNIS JEFFREY, judge; b. Albany, Ky., Sept. 11, 1956; s. Maurice Higginbotham and Estell (Snow) C.; m. Robin McCollum, Aug. 20, 1977; 1 child, Matthew. BA, Berea Coll., 1978; JD, U. Ky., 1981. Bar: Ky. 1981, U.S. Dist. Ct. (we. dist.) Ky. 1981, U.S. Dist. Ct. (we. dist.) Ky. 1987, U.S. Ct. Appeals (6th cir.) 1987. Advisor City of Albany, 1981-82; sole practice Albany, 1982-83; asst. atty. Commonwealth of Ky., Albany, 1981-82, trial commr., 1982-83, judge 40th jud. dist., 1983-86, chief judge 40th dist., 1986—. Mem. Ky. Bar Assn., Ky. Acad. Trial Lawyers, Assn. Trial Lawyers of Am. Republican. Lodge: Masons. Avocations: water and snow skiing, boating, golf. Judicial administration, State civil litigation, Criminal. Home: 901 Rainbow Dr Albany KY 42602 Office: Courthouse PO Box 213 Albany KY 42602

CHOATE, EDWARD L., lawyer, educator; b. Carbondale, Ill., Jan. 8, 1951; s. Loree and Geraldine Louise (Minton) C.; m. Lenetta Kay Blackburn, Sept. 10, 1983. B.A. with honors in History (President's scholar), So. Ill. U., 1972; J.D., U. Notre Dame, 1975. Bar: Ill., 1975, U.S. Dist. Ct. (so. dist.) Ill., 1981, U.S. Ct. Appeals (7th cir.), 1981. Sole practice, Carterville, Ill., 1975—; asst. state's atty. Williamson County, Ill., 1982-84; asst. vis. prof. aviation law Sch. Tech. Careers, So. Ill. U., Carbondale, 1981, 82. Precinct committeeman Carterville Republican Com., 1982—. Mem. ABA, Ill. Bar Assn., Williamson County Bar Assn., Phi Alpha Theta. Baptist. Clubs: Masons (32 degree, numerous offices in various local and state divs.), Shriners, KT (past comdr.), Order Eastern Star (past patron), Rotary. General practice, Probate, Real property. Home: 32 Meadowlark Dr Carterville IL 62918 Office: 1st Federal Bldg Route 13 W Carterville IL 62918

CHOATE, JOHN LEE, lawyer; b. Waterville, Maine, Sept. 6, 1946; s. C. Randall and Margaret (Applebee) C.; m. Mary Pless Wyatt, Aug. 1, 1970; 1 child, Andrew. BA, Duke u., 1968; JD, U. S.C., 1974. Asst. atty gen. State of S.C., Columbia, 1974-76; ptnr. Nelson, Mullins, Riley & Scarborough, Columbia, 1976—. Served with U.S. Army, 1968-70, Vietnam. Mem. ABA, S.C. Bar Assn., Richland County Bar Assn., S.C. Def. Trial Attys. Assn., Fedn. Ins. and Corp. Counsel, Def. Research Inst. Roman Catholic. Club: Wildewood Country (Columbia). Lodge: Optimists. Avocation: golf. Federal civil litigation, State civil litigation, Personal injury. Office: Nelson Mullins Riley & Scarborough 1330 Lady St Columbia SC 29201

CHOATE, MURRAY RICKLIFFE, II, lawyer; b. Anna, Ill., Jan. 27, 1954; s. Murray R. and Frances C. (Waller) C. BA cum laude, Dartmouth Coll., 1976; JD, Vanderbilt U., 1979. Bar: Ind. 1979, U.S. Dist. Ct. (so. dist.) Ind. 1979, Ill. 1982, Ark. 1985, U.S. Dist. Ct. (ea. and we. dists.) Ark. 1986. Assoc. Cadick, Burns, Duck & Peterson, Indpls., 1979-80, Barnes & Thornburg, Indpls., 1980-82; corp. counsel, sec. Resort Condominiums Internat., Inc., Indpls., 1982-84; atty. Fairfield Communities, Inc., Little Rock, 1984—. Coll. coordinator Reagan for Pres., Hanover, N.H. 1976, Bush for Pres. Ind., 1980; mem. Ark. Children's Hosp. Found., Inc., Little Rock, 1986—. Named one of Outstanding Young Men Am., 1977. Republican. Methodist. Lodge: Masons. Avocations: golf, squash, jogging. Real property, General corporate, Inter/intra-state sale of real property litigation. Office: Fairfield Communities Inc legal dept 2800 Cantrell Rd Little Rock AR 72203

CHOBOT, JOHN CHARLES, lawyer; b. N.Y.C., Feb. 14, 1948; s. Arthur E. and Eleanore L. (Lotito) C.; m. Catherine Ann Moran, Aug. 24, 1974; children: Christine, Keith. BA, Cornell U., 1969; MS in Edn., CCNY, 1971; JD, Fordham U., 1975. Bar: N.Y. 1976, U.S. Dist. Ct. (we. dist.) N.Y. 1976, N.J. 1985, U.S. Dist. Ct. N.J. 1985. Assoc. Phillips, Lytle, Hitchcock, Blaine & Huber, Buffalo, 1975-85; v.p., atty. The CIT Group/Sales Financing, Inc., Livingston, N.J., 1985—. Mem. ABA,. Kappa Alpha Soc. Bankruptcy, Commercial, Secured transactions. Home: 53 Ann Rd Long Valley NJ 07853 Office: The CIT Group 650 CIT Dr Livingston NJ 07039

CHOCKLEY, FREDERICK WILSON, JR., lawyer; b. Joliet, Ill., Jan. 23, 1923; s. Frederick Wilson Sr. and Vera B. (Barrowman) C.; m. Jean Schilling; children from a previous marriage: Nancy D. Seelbach, Beth Chockley Dee, F.W. III, Laurel Y. Student, Duke U., 1941-42; BS in Econs., U. Pa., 1942-43, 45-47; LLB, Case Western Res. U., 1949. Bar: Ohio, U.S. Dist. Ct. (no. dist.) Ohio, U.S. Ct. Appeals (3d, 4th, 6th and 11th cirs.), U.S. Tax Ct., U.S. Supreme Ct. Ptnr. Walter, Haverfield, Buescher & Chockley, Cleve., 1949—; spl. counsel to atty. gen. Ohio, 1953; mem. bd. examiners Supreme Ct. Ohio, 1960-65; acting judge Lakewood (Ohio) Mcpl. Ct., 1968-69. Mem. Lakewood City Council, 1953-61, pres. 1960-61; mem. Lakewood Library Bd., 1967-69; pres. Lakewood Hosp. Found., 1981—. Served as cpl. U.S. Army, 1943-45, ETO. Mem. ABA (labor law sect.), Ohio State Bar Assn., Cleve. Bar Assn. (exec com. 1964-66, domestic relations sect. 1982—, labor law sect.), Am. Arbitration Assn. Republican. Presbyterian. Clubs: Westwood Country (bd. dirs.), Union (Ohio); Royal Poinciana Golf (Naples, Fla.). Lodge: Masons. Federal civil litigation, State civil litigation. Office: 1215 Terminal Tower Cleveland OH 44113

CHOMAS, JAMES LOUIS, JR., lawyer; b. McKeesport, Pa., Jan. 10, 1952; s. James Louis and Ruth Ann (Pigford) C.; children: Louis Caley, Gretchen Hannah, Jacob Alan. BA, Pa. State U., 1973; JD, U. Pitts., 1977. Sole practice Pitts., 1977—. Mem. ABA, Pa. Bar Assn., Allegheny County Bar Assn., Elizabeth (Pa.) C. of C. (sec. 1986). Real property, Family and matrimonial, Probate. Office: 200 Standard Life Bldg 345 4th Ave Pittsburgh PA 15222

CHONG, CLAYTON ELLIOTT, lawyer; b. Hilo, Hawaii, July 6, 1950; s. Wing Kong and Ethel (Ishii) C. BS in Bus., Miami U., Oxford, Ohio, 1972, MBA, 1973; JD, Ohio No. U., 1977. Bar: U.S. Dist. Ct. Hawaii 1978, U.S. Ct. Appeals (9th cir.) 1978. Sole practice Hilo, 1978-79; ptnr. Chong & Chong, Hilo, 1979—. Mem. ABA, Hawaii State Bar Assn., Hawaii County Bar Assn., Assn. Trial Lawyers Am., Lehua Jaycees, Kuilima Jaycees, Delta Theta Phi (dist. chancellor 1983—, Clarence W. Pierce award 1983), Delta Sigma Pi. Club: Lions (pres. Hilo club 1986-87). Avocation: rock collecting. General practice. Home and Office: PO Box 1483 Hilo HI 96721-1483

CHONG, DEBRA ANN, lawyer; b. Houston, Dec. 13, 1953; d. Ai Fook and Lan Sen (Hom) Wong; m. Martin D. Chong, Apr. 7, 1973; 1 child, Michael William. BA, Boston U., 1975; JD, Georgetown U., 1978. Bar: D.C. 1978, Calif. 1981. Sr. atty. Comptroller of Currency, Washington and San Francisco, 1978-85; assoc. Lillick, McHose & Charles, San Francisco, 1985—. Recipient Cert. Award Dept. Justice, 1980, Cert. Appreciation Dept. Treas., 1985. Mem. ABA, San Francisco Bar Assn., Asian Am. Bar Assn., Asian Bus. League. Democrat. Club: Commonwealth (San Francisco). Banking, Securities. Office: Lillick McHose & Charles Two Embarcadero Ctr #2600 San Francisco CA 94111

CHOO, YEOW MING, lawyer; b. Johore Bahru, Malaysia, Aug. 1, 1953; s. Far Tong and Kim Fong (Wong) C.; LL.B. with honors (first in class), U. Malaya, 1977; LL.M., Harvard U., 1979; J.D., Chgo.-Kent Coll., 1980. Admitted to Malaysia bar, 1977, Ill. bar, 1980; lectr. law U. Malaya Law Sch., Kuala Lumpur, Malaysia, 1977-78, Monash U. Law Sch., Melbourne, Australia, 1978; internat. atty. Standard Oil Co. (Ind.), Chgo., 1979-82; partner firm Anderson, Liu and Choo, Chgo., 1982-84; ptnr. Baer Marks and Upham, N.Y.C., 1984-85; ptnr. Winston and Strawn, Chgo., 1985—; dir. Harvard Bros. Internat. Corp.; Boston; chmn. tax subcom. Nat. Council for US-China Trade, 1980—. Mem. Am. Mining Congress (alt. mem. com. on law of sea 1980-82), ABA, Ill. Bar Assn., Chgo. Bar Assn., Malayan Bar Council, U.S. Chess Fedn., Harvard Law Sch. Alumni Assn. Club: Harvard. Private international, General corporate. Home: 1181 Father Capodanno Blvd Staten Island NY 10306 Office: Winston & Strawn One First National Plaza Chicago IL 60603

CHOPER, JESSE HERBERT, law educator, university dean; b. Wilkes-Barre, Pa., Sept. 19, 1935; s. Edward and Dorothy (Resnick) C.; m. Sonya Rae Schwartz, June 27, 1961; children: Marc Steven, Edward Nathaniel. B.S., Wilkes Coll., 1957, D.H.L., 1967; LL.B., U. Pa., 1960. Bar: D.C. 1961. Instr. Wharton Sch., U. Pa., 1957-60; law clk. Chief Justice Earl Warren, U.S. Supreme Ct., 1960-61; asst. prof. U. Minn. Law Sch., 1961-62, asso. prof., 1962-65; prof. U. Calif. Law Sch. at Berkeley, 1965—, dean, 1982—; vis. prof. Cath. U. Law Sch., 1967, Harvard U., 1970-71. Author: Constitutional Law: Cases-Comments-Questions, 6th edit., 1986,

The American Constitution, Cases and Materials, 6th edit., 1986, Constitutional Rights and Liberties, Cases and Materials, 6th edit., 1986, Corporations, Cases and Materials, 2d edit., 1977, Judicial Review and the National Political Process, 1980; contbr. articles to profl. jours. Mem. AAUP, Am. Law Inst., Am. Acad. Arts and Scis., Order of Coif. Democrat. Jewish. Legal education. Home: 118 Alvarado Rd Berkeley CA 94705 *

CHOPIN, L. FRANK, lawyer; b. New Orleans, Apr. 29, 1942; s. Alton Francis and Floretta (Thensted) C.; m. Susan Gardiner, Sept. 4, 1964; children: Philip, Alexandra, Christopher. BBA, Loyola U., New Orleans, 1964, JD, 1966; diploma in mil. law, Judge Adv. Gen.'s Sch., U. Va. Sch. Law, 1966; postgrad., Nat. Law Ctr., George Wash. U., 1967-68; LLM in Taxation, U. Miami, Fla., 1976; PhD in Law, Cambridge U., Eng., 1986. Bar: La. 1966, Fla. 1968, Iowa 1980, U.S. Dist. Ct. (so. dist.) Fla. 1968, U.S. Ct. Appeals (5th cir.) 1968. Ptnr. Chopin & Chopin, Miami, 1969-77; assoc. prof. law Drake U., Des Moines, 1979-80; ptnr. Cadwalader, Wickersham & Taft, Palm Beach, Fla., 1980—; adj. prof. law U. Miami, 1982—, U. Sherbrooke, Can., 1982—. Author: The New Residency Rules for Canadian Tax Considerations, 1985; also numerous articles in legal jours. Mem. Housing Fin. Authority; trustee Preservation Found., Palm Beach Community Chest, Inc. Served to capt. U.S. Army, 1966-68. Mem. ABA, Internat. Bar Assn., Fed. Bar Assn., Fla. Bar (tax sect.), Loyola U. Alumni Assn., U. Miami Alumni Assn., St. Thomas More Law Soc., Phi Alpha Delta (charter). Republican. Roman Catholic. Estate taxation, Personal income taxation, International taxation. Home: 465 Glenbrook Dr Atlantis FL 33462 Office: Cadwalader Wickersham & Taft 440 Royal Palm Way Palm Beach FL 33480

CHOPIN, SUSAN GARDINER, lawyer; b. Miami, Fla., Feb. 23, 1947; d. Maurice and Judith (Warden) Gardiner; m. L. Frank Chopin, Sept. 4, 1964; children: Philip, Alexandra, Christopher. BBA, Loyola U., New Orleans, 1966; JD cum laude, U. Miami, 1972; MLitt (Law), Oxford U., Eng., 1983. Bar: Fla. 1972, Iowa 1979. Sr. law clk. to presiding judge U.S. Dist. Ct. (so. dist.) Fla., Miami, 1972-73; ptnr. Chopin & Chopin, Miami, 1973-77; assoc. prof. Drake U. Law Sch., Des Moines, 1979-80; sole practice Palm Beach, Fla., 1981—. Mem. editorial bd. Fla. Bar Jour., 1975—; contbr. articles to profl. jours., legal revs. Mem. ABA, Fla. Bar Assn., Iowa Bar Assn., Fed. Bar Assn., Internat. Bar Assn., Fla. Assn. Women Lawyers, Soc. Wig and Robe, Phi Kappa Phi, Phi Alpha Delta. Democrat. State civil litigation, Family and matrimonial, Personal injury. Office: 1st National Bank Ctr 2875 S Ocean Blvd Suite 200 Palm Beach FL 33480

CHOPLIN, JOHN MAX, II, lawyer; b. Cedar Rapids, Iowa, Nov. 10, 1945; s. John M. Sr. and Joyce G. (Mickelson) C.; m. Linda H. Kutchen, Feb. 14, 1969; children: Julie, John, James. BA, Drake U., 1967; JD, U. Mich., 1974. Bar: Ind. 1974, U.S. Dist. Ct. (so. dist.) Ind. 1974, U.S. Ct. Appeals (7th cir.) 1976, U.S. Supreme Ct. 1977, U.S. Ct. Appeals (6th cir.) 1983. Assoc. Wilson, Tabor & Holland, Indpls., 1974-80; ptnr. Norris, Choplin & Johnson, Indpls., 1980—. Committeeman precinct Carmel Reps., Ind., 1982-84. Served to capt. USAF, 1969-73. Mem. ABA, Ind. Bar Assn., Indpls. Bar Assn., 7th Fed. Cir. Bar Assn., Lawyers-Pilots Bar Assn., Ind. Trial Lawyers Assn., Assn. Trial Lawyers Am., Phi Beta Kappa, Omicron Delta Kappa. Baptist. Avocations: water sports, tennis. Federal civil litigation, State civil litigation, Personal injury. Home: 3407 Tahoe Rd Carmel IN 46032 Office: Norris Choplin & Johnson 1 Virginia Ave 3d Floor Indianapolis IN 46204

CHOTINER, KENNETH LEE, judge; b. Los Angeles, Aug. 14, 1937; s. Murray M. and Phyllis Sylvia (Levenson) C.; m. Florence Helene Penney, May 29, 1964; children—Dana Lynne, Cara Lee. B.A. in Polit. Sci. with honors, UCLA, 1959; J.D. with honors, Loyola U., Los Angeles, 1969; grad. Hastings Coll. Law Coll. Criminal Advocacy, San Francisco, 1980, Calif. Jud. Coll., U. Calif.-Berkeley, 1981. Bar: Calif. 1970, U.S. Ct. Customs and Patent Appeals 1971, U.S. Ct. Mil. Appeals 1974, U.S. Sup. Ct. 1975. Instr. Am. govt. U. Alaska, 1962; dep. city atty., Los Angeles, 1970-71; sole practice, Santa Monica, Calif., 1971-81; spl. counsel City of Hawthorne (Calif.), 1973-80; judge pro tem Los Angeles Mcpl. Ct., 1975-81, Santa Monica Mcpl. Ct., 1977-81; judge Los Angeles Mcpl. Ct., 1981—, supervising judge valley div., 1983, Van Nuys-Encino br., 1983-84; justice pro tem Calif. Ct. Appeal, 1982; adj. prof. U. West Los Angeles Sch. Law, 1981-82; faculty Calif. Jud. Coll., Earl Warren Legal Inst., U. Calif., Berkeley, 1982, Calif. Ctr. Jud. Edn. and Research, Berkeley, 1982—, Media Workshop on Calif. Cts., 1982—; chmn. Media Conf. on Calif. Cts., 1986; conf. del. State Bar Calif., 1972, 73, 76-80. Mem. exec. com. Los Angeles Mcpl. Ct., 1975. Bd. dirs. So. Calif. ACLU, 1972-81, v.p., 1978-81; dir. ex-officio Legal Aid Soc. Santa Monica, 1979-80; bd. dirs. Friends of the Santa Monica Mountains, Parks and Seashore, 1979-81; mem. dean's council UCLA Coll. Letters and Sci.; mem. wildlife adv. com. Los Angeles County Fish and Game Commn., 1973-75, chmn., 1974; mem. Los Angeles County Interdepartmental Drinking Driver Program, Task Force, 1985—; mem. PTA, 1973-81, Los Angeles Olympic Organizing Com. Criminal Justice System Subcom., 1983-84. Served to capt. USAF, 1961-66. Recipient recognition awards Calif. Trial Lawyers Assn. (trial lawyer and criminal def.), 1980, U. W. Los Angeles Sch. Law award for Outstanding Service, 1984, Nat. Council on Alcoholism award of Appreciation, 1984, Eagle Scout award Boy Scouts Am., Order of the Arrow. Mem. Nat. Conf. State Trial Judges, Nat. Conf. Spl. Ct. Judges (del. 1985), Calif. Judges Assn., Nat. Conf. Bar Pres., ABA (presdl. showcase program, Washington 1985), Am. Arbitration Assn. (panel 1970-81), Santa Monica Bay Dist. Bar Assn. (pres. 1979), Assn. Trial Lawyers Am., Women's Lawyers Assn. Los Angeles, Criminal Ct. Bar Assn., Los Angeles County Bar Assn., St. Thomas More Law Soc., UCLA Alumni Assn. (Blue and Gold Circle), U. Calif. Santa Cruz Fiat Lux Soc., Am. Judicature Soc., Ephebian Soc., Quill and Scroll Soc., Sealbearer Soc., Phi Alpha Delta. Lodge: Lions (zone chmn. 1975-76). Author: Restricting Handguns, 1979; contbr. articles to legal jours. Judicial administration. Office: Los Angeles Mcpl Ct 110 N Grand Ave Los Angeles CA 90012-3055

CHOVANES, EUGENE, lawyer; b. Hazleton, Penn., Jan. 1, 1926; s. Michael and Anna (Watro) C.; m. Claire Amelia Puhak, Mar. 27, 1952; children: Michael, George, Nicholas, Joseph, John. BS Engring., Lehigh U., 1950; JD, Villanova U., 1960. Bar: Pa. 1961. Assoc. William Steell Jackson & Sons, Phila., 1957-63; ptnr. Jackson & Chovanes, Phila. and Bala-Cynwyd, Pa., 1963—; lectr. in patent law Villanova U., 1957-80. Served to sgt. U.S. Army, 1943-46, to 1st lt. Ordnance Corps, 1951-52. Mem. ABA, Phila. Patent Law Assn., Phila. Bar Assn., Soc. Registered Profl. Engrs., Am. Intellectual Property Law Assn. Patent, Trademark and copyright. Office: One Bala Plaza Suite 319 Bala-Cynwyd PA 19004

CHRISMAN, PERRY OSWIN, lawyer; b. Port Arthur, Tex., Aug. 5, 1935; s. Leo Erroll and Doratha Odelia (Wright) C.; m. Marilyn Jo Barron, Mar. 27, 1959; children—Lori Paige, David Keith. B.A., Baylor U., 1957, J.D., 1959. Bar: Tex. 1960, U.S. Supreme Ct. 1964, U.S. Dist. Ct. (no., we., and ea. dists.) Tex. 1982, U.S. Ct. Appeals (5th cir.) 1982. Asst. city atty., Ft. Worth, 1960-61; house counsel Bapt. Gen. Conv. Tex., 1961-65; ptnr. Green, Gilmore, Chrisman, Rothpletz, 1965-69; judge Dallas County Probate Ct., 1969-73; judge Dallas County Domestic Relations Ct., 1973-76, Dallas County Family Dist. Ct., 1976-78, 44th Jud. Dist. Ct., 1978-82; ptnr. Vial, Hamilton, Koch & Knox, 1982—; lectr. in field. Pres. Mental Health Assn. Tex., past pres. Mental Health Assn. Dallas County, Dallas County Council on Alcoholism; past chmn. Juvenile Bd. Dallas County; chmn. bd. dirs. Southwestern Bapt. Theol. Sem., Ft. Worth; chmn. joint com. on pub. affairs, mem. exec. bd. Bapt. Gen. Conv. Tex.; treas. United Way. Mem. ABA, State Bar Tex., Dallas Bar Assn., Baylor U. Alumni Assn. (pres.). Democrat. Clubs: Lions, Masons. Contbr. articles to legal and profl. jours. Federal civil litigation, State civil litigation, Estate planning. Office: 1500 Republic Bank Tower Dallas TX 75201

CHRIST, DONALD C., lawyer; b. Mineola, N.Y., Aug. 17, 1935; s. Marcus G. and Marion (Hallsted) C.; m. Iris Smith, Sept. 18, 1976; children: Margaret C., Timothy C., Sarah N. BA, Yale U., 1958, LLB, 1964. Bar: N.Y. 1964, U.S. Ct. Appeals (2d cir.) 1965, U.S. Dist. Ct. (so. and ea. dists.) N.Y. 1966, U.S. Supreme Ct. 1969, U.S. Tax Ct. 1976. Assoc. Sullivan & Cromwell, N.Y.C., 1964-72, ptnr., 1972%. Acting justice, zoning bd. appeals Village of Mill Neck. Served to capt. USMCR,1958-61. Fellow Am. Coll. Probate Counsel, N.Y. State Found.; mem. ABA, N.Y. State Bar Assn., Assn. of Bar of Bar of City of N.Y., Nassau County Bar Assn., N.Y. County Lawyers Assn., Am. Judicature Soc. Club: Yale (N.Y.C.). Avocations: fishing, golf. Probate, Estate planning. Home: Cleft Rd Mill Neck NY 11765 Office: Sullivan & Cromwell 125 Broad St New York NY 10004

CHRISTENSEN, ALBERT SHERMAN, judge; b. Manti, Utah, June 9, 1905; s. Albert H. and Jennie (Snow) C.; m. Lois Bowen, Apr. 4, 1927; children: A. Kent, Karen D., Krege B. Student, Brigham Young U., intermittently 1923-27; J.D., Nat. U., 1931. Bar: D.C. 1932, Utah 1933. Asst. bus. specialist U.S. Dept. Commerce, 1930-32; practiced in Provo, Utah, 1933-42, 45-54; U.S. dist. judge Salt Lake City, 1954—; mem. com. on revision laws Jud. Conf. U.S., 1960-68, com. on ct. adminstrn., 1968-75, mem. adv. com. rules of civil procedure, 1972-82, mem. rev. com., 1977-78, jud. ethics com., 1978-82; mem. Temporary Emergency Ct. Appeals, 1972—; mem. bd. Utah Bar Examiners, 1939-42. Republican congressional candidate, 1939. Served from lt. to lt. comdr. USNR, 1942-45. Mem. ABA, Utah Bar Assn. (pres. 1951-52), Utah Jr. Bar Assn. (pres. 1937-38), Utah County Bar Assn. (pres. 1936-37, 47-48). Mem. Ch. Jesus Christ of Latter-day Saints. Jurisprudence.

CHRISTENSEN, CRAIG WANE, university dean, legal educator; b. Lehi, Utah, Mar. 11, 1939. B.S., Brigham Young U., 1961; J.D. magna cum laude, Northwestern U., 1964. Bar: Ill. 1965, U.S. Supreme Ct. 1973. Assoc. Kirkland, Ellis, Hodson, Chaffetz & Masters, Chgo., 1964-66; exec. asst. to chmn. and pres. C & N.W. Ry. Co., Chgo., 1966-67; dir. Nat. Inst. for Edn. in Law and Poverty, Chgo., 1967-70; assoc. prof. law, legal adviser to pres. U. Mich., 1970-71; dean, prof. law Cleve. State U., 1971-75, Syracuse U., 1975—. Trustee Law Sch. Admission Council, 1979—, pres.-elect, 1987—, pres. 1988—; asst. to chmn. White House Civil Rights Conf., 1966; mem. legal services nat. adv. com. OEO, 1968-70. Mem. ABA (vice chmn. div. state adminstrv. law 1977-81, mem. Right to Legal Services Com. 1970-71), N.Y. State Bar Assn., Order of Coif. Legal education. Home: Peninsula Rd Tully NY 13159 Office: Syracuse U Coll Law Syracuse NY 13244

CHRISTENSEN, CURTIS LEE, lawyer; b. Ithaca, N.Y., Aug. 16, 1950; s. George Curtis and Janeth Margaret (Reid) C.; m. Susan Frances McClusky, Aug. 9, 1977; 1 child, Elizabeth Ann. AB, Cornell U., 1972; JD, U. Mich., 1978. Bar: Nebr. 1978, U.S. Dist. Ct. Nebr. 1978. Assoc. Kutak, Rock & Campbell, Omaha, 1978-84; ptnr. Kutak Rock & Campbell, Omaha, 1984—. Served with U.S. Army, 1972-75. Mem. ABA, Nebr. Bar Assn., Omaha Bar Assn., Phi Beta Kappa. Lutheran. Avocation: photography. Municipal bonds. Home: 816 S 94th St Omaha NE 68114 Office: Kutak Rock & Campbell 1650 Farnam St Omaha NE 68102

CHRISTENSEN, DONN DOUGLAS, lawyer; b. St. Paul, June 30, 1929; s. Jonas Jergen and Hildur Minerva (Lundeen) C.; m. Renee E. Pinet, Aug. 31, 1970; children—Keith, Catherine, Eric. B.S., U. Minn., 1950, J.D., 1952. Bar: Minn. 1952, U.S. Fed. Ct. 1955, U.S. Supreme Ct. 1981. Practiced in St. Paul, 1954-68, 70—; dep. atty. gen. State of Minn., 1968-70; justice of peace, City of Mendota Heights, Minn., 1961-66; instr. bus. law Macalester Coll., St. Paul, 1960-67; mediator Minn. Farm Mediation Program, 1986—. Served with U.S. Army, 1952-54. Mem. ABA, Minn. Bar Assn. (chmn. environ. law sect. 1972-73), Ramsey County Bar Assn., Execs. Assn. St. Paul (pres. 1966), Mendota Heights C. of C. (sec. 1965), Delta Theta Phi. Clubs: Athletic, Torch (pres. 1982-83) (St. Paul). Probate, Real property, Environment. Home: 676 Schifsky Rd Saint Paul MN 55126 Office: 3585 N Lexington Ave Suite 155 Saint Paul MN 55126 also: North Branch MN 55056

CHRISTENSEN, GORDON EDWARD, lawyer; b. Takoma Park, Md., July 7, 1948; s. Merton Aubrey and Florence Mabel (Senger) C.; m. Barbara Lee Parrish, Dec. 29, 1972; children: Jennifer Colleen, Lisa Kathleen. BA, U. Del., 1970; JD, U. Md., 1974. Bar: Md. 1975. Sole practice Columbia, Md., 1976-82; assoc. Clements & Nutt, Balt., 1982—; instr. labor studies Dundalk (Md.) Community Coll. Pres. Cinnamon Tree Community Assn., Columbia, 1979; mem. vestry Christ Episcopal Ch., 1986—, registrar, 1986-87. Mem. ABA, Md. Bar Assn., U. Del. Student Alumni Assn. (v.p. 1985—). Episcopalian. Club: Civitan (Columbia) (v.p. 1984). Consumer commercial, General practice, Real property. Home: 6482 Barchink Pl Columbia MD 21045 Office: Clements & Nutt 1023 Cathedral St Baltimore MD 21045

CHRISTENSEN, HENRY, III, lawyer; b. Jersey City, Nov. 8, 1944; s. Henry Jr. and M. Louise (Brooke) C.; m. Constance L. Cumpton, July 1, 1967; children: Alexander, Gustavus, Elizabeth, Katherine. BA, Yale U., 1966; JD, Harvard U., 1969. Bar: N.Y. 1970, U.S. Tax Ct. 1973, U.S. Ct. Appeals (2d. cir.) 1973, U.S. Supreme Ct. 1975. Assoc. Sullivan & Cromwell, N.Y.C., 1969-77, ptnr., 1977—; adj. assoc. prof. NYU, N.Y.C., 1985—. Contbr. articles to profl. jours. Chmn. Prospect Park Alliance, Bklyn., 1985—; trustee Peddie Sch., Hightstown, N.J., 1986—; dir., sec. Freedom Inst., N.Y.C., 1980—. Fellow Am. Coll. Probate Counsel; mem. N.Y. State Bar Assn. (chmn. estate and gift tax com. 1983-84, chmn. income taxation of trusts com. 1984-85, 87—, exec. com. tax sect. 1983—, exempt orgns. com. 1986), Internat. Acad. Estate and Trust Law (academician). Probate, Estate taxation, Personal income taxation. Home: 61 Prospect Park W Brooklyn NY 11215 Office: Sullivan & Cromwell 125 Broad St New York NY 10004

CHRISTENSEN, JON ALEXANDER, lawyer; b. Bridgetown, Barbados, Dec. 21, 1940; s. William Harold and Flora (McRae) C.; m. Karen L. Wolfe, Apr. 19, 1960 (div. Nov. 1983); 1 child, Kerry A. BA, Ohio State U., 1961, JD, 1981. Bar: Ohio 1981, U.S. Dist. Ct. (so. dist.) Ohio 1981. Producer news WBNS-TV, Columbus, Ohio, 1966-72; asst. to dir. Ohio Dept. Commerce, Columbus, 1972-75; chief communications div. Ohio Dept. Health, Columbus, 1975-79; assoc. Jones, Day, Reavis & Pogue, Columbus, 1981—; bd. dirs. Perfecto Dist. Co., Columbus. Contbr. articles on legal issues to profl. jours. and on food and wine to mags.; photographer documentary film Vietnam: War Comes Home, 1970. Chmn. Cert. of Need/Urgent Care Ctrs. Task Force, Columbus, 1984-85; treas. com. Jackson for Congress, Columbus, 1986. Mem. ABA, Ohio Bar Assn., Columbus Bar Assn. Democrat. Mem. Unitarian Ch. Avocations: photography, music, wine, food. Administrative and regulatory, General corporate, Banking. Home: 1112 E Cooke Rd Columbus OH 43224 Office: Jones Day Reavis & Pogue 1900 Huntington Ctr Columbus OH 43215

CHRISTENSEN, KAREN KAY, lawyer; b. Ann Arbor, Mich., Mar. 9, 1947; s. Jack Edward and Evangeline (Pitsch) C.; m. Kenneth Robert Kay, Sept. 2, 1977; children: Jeffrey Smithson, Braden, Bergen. BS, U. Mich., 1969; JD, U. Denver, 1975. Bar: Colo. 1975, D.C. 1976, U.S. Supreme Ct. 1979. Atty., advisor office of dep. atty. gen. U.S. Dept. of Justice, Washington, 1975-76, trial atty. civil rights div., 1976-79; legis. counsel ACLU, Washington, 1979-80; staff atty. D.C. Pub. Defender Service, Washington, 1980-85; asst. gen. counsel Nat. Pub. Radio, Washington, 1985—. Mem. D.C. Bar Assn., ACLU (exec. bd. 1986—), Phi Beta Kappa. Communications, Civil rights, Criminal. Office: Nat Pub Radio 2025 M St NW Washington DC 20036

CHRISTENSEN, KREGE BOWEN, lawyer; b. Provo, Utah, Oct. 28, 1942; s. Albert Sherman and Lois (Bowen) C.; m. Judith Lynne Brown, Nov. 11, 1942; children—Daniel, Adam, Mindy, Tami, Megan, Marin. B.S. in Acctg., U. Utah, 1965, M.B.A., 1967; J.D. with honors, George Washington U., 1973. Bar: Utah 1973, U.S. Dist. Ct. Utah; C.P.A., Utah. Acct., SEC, Washington, 1969-73; assoc. Parson, Behle & Latimer, Salt Lake City, 1973-75, ptnr., 1975-85, sole practice, 1985-86, of counsel, Salt Lake City, 1986—. Named All-Am. Track and Field, NCAA, 1963. Mem. Utah State Bar, ABA, Salt Lake County Bar Assn., Utah Assn. C.P.A.s, Am. Inst. C.P.A.s, Sigma Chi. Republican. Mormon. Clubs: Salt Lake Swimming and Tennis, Timpanogos (Salt Lake City). Securities, Contracts commercial, General corporate. Address: 19 W S Temple Suite 700 Salt Lake City UT 84101

CHRISTENSEN, PATRICIA ANNE WATKINS, lawyer; b. Corpus Christi, Tex., June 24, 1947; d. Owen Milton Jr. and Margaret (McFarland) Watkins; m. Steven Ray Christensen, May 28, 1977 (dec. 1985); children: Geoffrey Holland, Jeremy Ladd. BS, North Tex. State U., 1971; JD, U. Houston, 1977. Bar: Utah 1977, Tex. 1977, U.S. Dist. Ct. Utah 1977, U.S. Ct. Appeals (10th cir.) 1977, U.S. Supreme Ct. 1977. Assoc. Berman & Giauque, Salt Lake City, 1977-80; ptnr. Kimball, Parr, Crockett & Waddoups, Salt Lake City, 1980—; adj. prof. law U. Utah Law Sch., Salt Lake City, 1979-81. Vision screener Nat. Soc. to Prevent Blindness, Utah affiliate, 1985—, sec. exec. com., 1986—, bd. of trustees, 1985—; mem. home and sch. bd. exec. auction com. Rowland Hall St. Mark's Sch., 1985—. Mem. Utah Bar Assn. (bar examiner, litigation sect., legal specialization com.), Tex. Bar Assn., Salt Lake County Bar Assn. (exec. com., author, editor Utah Lawyers Practice Manual 1986), Assn. Trial Lawyers Am., Phi Delta Phi, Delta Gamma, Alpha Lambda Delta. Methodist. Avocations: golf, cross-country skiing, writing, travel, performing arts. Federal civil litigation, State civil litigation. Office: Kimball Parr Crockett & Waddoups 185 S State St Suite 1300 PO Box 11019 Salt Lake City UT 84147

CHRISTENSON, GORDON A., legal educator; b. Salt Lake City, June 22, 1932; s. Gordon B. and Ruth Arzella (Anderson) C.; m. Katherine Joy deMik, Nov. 2, 1951 (div. 1977); children: Gordon Scott, Marjorie Lynne, Ruth Ann, Nanette; m. Fabienne Fadeley, Sept. 16, 1979. B.S. in Law, U. Utah, 1955, J.D., 1956; S.J.D., George Washington U., 1961. Bar: Utah 1956, U.S. Supreme Ct. 1971, D.C. 1978. Practiced in Salt Lake City, 1957-58; law clk. to chief justice Utah Supreme Ct., 1956-57; assoc. firm Christenson & Callister, Salt Lake City, 1956-58; atty. Dept. of Army, Nat. Guard Bur., Washington, 1957-58; atty., acting asst. legal adviser Office of Legal Adviser, U.S. Dept. State, Washington, 1958-62; asst. gen. counsel for sci. and tech. U.S. Dept. Commerce, 1962-67, spl. asst. to undersec. of commerce, 1967, counsel to commerce tech. adv. bd., 1962-67, chmn. task force on telecommunications missions and orgn., 1967, counsel to panel on engring. and commodity standards, tech. adv. bd., 1963-65; assoc. prof. law U. Okla., Norman, 1967-70; exec. asst. to pres. U. Okla., 1967-70; univ. dean for ednl. devel., central adminstrn. State U. N.Y., Albany, 1970-71; prof. law Am. U. Law Sch., Washington, 1971-79; dean Am. U. Law Sch., 1971-77; on leave 1977-79; Charles H. Stockton prof. internat. law U.S. Naval War Coll., Newport, R.I., 1977-79; dean, Nippert prof. law U. Cin. Coll. Law, 1979-85, univ. prof. law, 1985—; assoc. professorial lectr. in internat. affairs George Washington U., 1961-67; vis. scholar Harvard U. Law Sch., 1977-78; vis. scholar Yale Law Sch., 1985-86; participant summer confs. on internat. law Cornell Law Sch., Ithaca, N.Y., 1962, 64; cons. in internat. law U.S. Naval War Coll., Newport, R.I., 1969; faculty mem., reporter seminars for experienced fed. dist. judges Fed. Jud. Center, Washington, 1972-77. Author: (with Richard B. Lillich) International Claims: Their Preparation and Presentation, 1962, The Future of the University, 1969; Contbr. articles to legal jours. Cons. to Center for Policy Alternatives Mass. Inst. Tech., Cambridge, 1970-81; mem. intergovtl. com. on Internat. Policy on Weather Modification, 1967; Vice pres. Procedural Aspects of Internat. Law Inst., N.Y.C., 1962—. Served with intelligence sect. USAF, 1951-52, Japan. Recipient Silver Medal award Dept. Commerce, 1967; fellow Grad. Sch. U. Cin. Mem. Am. Soc. Internat. Law (mem. panel on state responsibility), D.C. Bar Assn., Am. Bar Assn., Utah Bar Assn., Cin. Bar Assn., Order of Coif, Phi Delta Phi, Kappa Sigma. Clubs: Literary (Cin.); Cosmos (Washington). Public international, Jurisprudence, Constitutional. Home: 3465 Principio Ave Cincinnati OH 45226 Office: U Cin Coll Law Cincinnati OH 45221

CHRISTENSON, JEFFREY ROBERT, lawyer; b. Bedford, Ohio, Aug. 15, 1950; s. Chris and Eunice (McAdoo) C.; m. Teresa Wigdor, Aug. 20, 1973; 1 child, Adam S. BS in Journalism cum laude, Ohio U., 1972; JD, Ohio No. U., 1976. Bar: Idaho 1976, U.S. Dist. Ct. Idaho 1976. Assoc. Anderson, Kaufman, Ringert & Clark, Boise, Idaho, 1976-83, ptnr., 1983-84; ptnr. Ringert, Clark, Harrington, Reid, Christenson & Kaufman, Boise, 1984—. Mem. design rev. com. City of Boise, 1980—, chmn. 1984; mem. cen. dist. Health Family Planning Bd. Govs., Boise, 1982-87. Mem. ABA, Idaho Bar Assn., Boise Bar Assn., Delta Theta Phi. Republican. Avocations: snow skiing, water skiing, aerobic exercise, hunting. State civil litigation, Federal civil litigation, Family and matrimonial. Home: 5498 Collister Dr Boise ID 83703 Office: Ringert Clark Harrington et al 599 W Bannock St PO Box 2773 Boise ID 83701

CHRISTIAN, ALMERIC LEANDER, chief judge; b. Christiansted, St. Croix, V.I., Nov. 23, 1919; s. Adam Emmanuel and Elena (Davis) C.; m. Virginia Cecilia Sterling, Sept. 13, 1943 (div. Sept. 1962); 1 dau., Donna Marie; m. Shirley Camille Frorup, Aug. 31, 1963; children: Adam, Rebecca. Student, U. P.R., 1937-38; A.B., Columbia, 1941, J.D., 1947. Bar: V.I. bar 1947. Practiced law V.I., 1947-62; U.S. dist. atty. for V.I., St. Thomas, 1962-69; chief judge U.S. Dist. Ct. for V.I., St. Thomas., 1962—. Dist. commr. Boy Scouts Am., V.I., from 1962; adv. bd. St. Dunstan's Episcopal Sch., St. Croix.; Mem. V.I. Bd. Edn., from 1961; Bd. visitors Columbia Law Sch. Served to 1st lt. AUS, 1942-46, ETO; Served to 1st lt. AUS, PTO. Mem. V.I. Bar Assn., Am. Judicature Soc., Fed. Bar Assn. Democrat. Office: US Dist Court PO Box 720 Charlotte Amalie Saint Thomas VI 00801 *

CHRISTIAN, GARY IRVIN, lawyer; b. Albany, Ga., July 7, 1951; s. Rupert Irvin and Alice Amelia (Smith) C.; m. Katie Beaty, Dec. 22, 1973. BA in History, Polit. Sci., David Lipscomb Coll., 1973; MPA, U. Tenn., 1974; JD, Vanderbilt U., 1979. Bar: Fla. 1979, U.S. Dist. Ct. (no. and mid. dists.) Fla 1979. Research dir. Ala. League of Mcpls., Montgomery, 1974-76; instr. in pub. adminstrn. David Lipscomb Coll., Nashville, 1977-79; assoc. Rogers, Towers, Bailey, Jones & Gay, Jacksonville, Fla., 1979-83, Foley & Lardner, Jacksonville, 1983-86; ptnr. Christian, Prom & Korn, Jacksonville, 1986—. Editor-in-chief Vanderbilt U. Law Rev., 1978-79. Pres., bd. dirs. PACE Ctr. for Girls, Inc., Jacksonville, 1984—; mem. Leadership Jacksonville, 1986-87. Mem. ABA (planned devels. com.), Fla. Bar Assn. (condominiums and planned devels. com.), Jacksonville Bar Assn. (coordinator continuing edn. 1984-85, vice chmn. real property sect. 1986-87). Democrat. Mem. Ch. of Christ. Club: Wavemasters Soc. (Neptune Beach, Fla.) (pres. 1986-87). Avocations: golf, tennis, racquetball, stamp collecting. Real property, Contracts commercial, Banking. Home: 1018 Main St Atlantic Beach FL 32233 Office: Christian Prom & Korn 6620 Southpoint Dr Southpoint Bldg Suite 6620 Jacksonville FL 32216

CHRISTIAN, WARREN HAROLD, JR., lawyer; b. Greenville, S.C., June 11, 1949; s. Warren Harold Sr. and Doris Marie (Hopkins) C.; m. Connie Sue Collett, June 19, 1971; children: Matthew, Joshua, Jill. BA, Carson Newman Coll., 1971; JD, U. S.C., 1975. Bar: S.C. 1975, U.S. Dist. Ct. S.C. 1977, U.S. Ct. Appeals (4th cir.) 1982. Assoc. Law Offices of John Bolt Culbertson, Greenville, 1975-80; ptnr. Culbertson, Christian & Moorhead, Greenville, 1980—. Coach youth soccer teams YMCA; v.p. Dem. precinct, 1978. Named one of Outstanding Young Men of Am., U.S. Jaycees, 1978. Sustaining mem. S.C. Trial Lawyers Assn.; mem. ABA, Assn. Trial Lawyers Am., S.C. Bar Assn. (speaker S.C. Workers Compensation Seminar 1984, 87), Greenville County Bar Assn. Baptist. Avocations: basketball, tennis. Workers' compensation, Personal injury. Home: Rt 5 #7 Bateswood Dr Greer SC 29651 Office: Culbertson Christian & Moorhead PO Box 332 1007 E Washington St Greenville SC 29602

CHRISTIANSEN, ERIC ROBERT, lawyer; b. Milw., Dec. 29, 1953; s. Robert L. and Annemarie (Gabor) C.; m. Jeanne E. Erdevig, May 28, 1983; children: Samantha M., W. Brett. Student, Williams Coll., 1972-74, Conn. Coll., 1974; student in speech, Northwestern U., 1974-75, Hartman Theatre Conservatory, 1975-77; BA in Philosophy, Marquette U., 1979; JD, U. Wis., 1982. Bar: Wis. 1982, U.S. Dist. Ct. (ea. dist.) Wis. 1982, Mich. 1983. Assoc. Michael, Best & Friedrich, Milw., 1982—; mem. adminstrv. rules adv. com., Securities Commn., 1985, citizens adv. com. on Wis. corp. takeover law, 1984-86. Mem. U. Wis. Law Sch. Bd. Visitors, Madison, 1985; bd. dirs. Friends of Art Milw. Art Mus., 1985—, Red Bus, Milw., 1985—, Wis. chpt. Nat. Soc. to Prevent Blindness, Milw., 1985—, Next Generation Theater, Milw., 1986—. AFS Internat. Scholarship, Belgium, 1971-72. Securities, General corporate. Office: Michael Best & Friedrich 250 E Wisconsin Ave Milwaukee WI 53202

CHRISTIANSEN, JON PETER, lawyer; b. Sprit Lake, Ia., June 12, 1950; s. Holger Klock and Dagny (Fjelstad) C.; m. Nancy Jane Renner, Dec. 30, 1971; children: Emily, Marie, Daniel Max. BA, St. Olaf Coll., 1972; JD, Vanderbilt U., 1975. Bar: Ga. 1975, U.S. Ct. Appeals (5th cir.) 1975, Wis. 1976, U.S. Dist. Ct. (ea. dist.) Wis. 1976, U.S. Ct. Appeals (7th cir.) 1981. Law clk. to presiding justice U.S. Ct. Appeals (5th cir.), Atlanta, 1975-76;

assoc. Foley and Lardner, Milw., 1976-82, ptnr., 1982—. Sec. Lakeside Child and Family Ctr., Inc., Milw., 1985—; bd. dirs. Milw. Council on Alcoholism, 1984-86. Mem. Milw. Bar Assn. (bd. dirs. 1984-87), Milw. Young Lawyers Assn. (bd. dirs. 1978-79, 81-82). Lutheran. Federal civil litigation, State civil litigation, Personal injury. Office: Foley and Lardner 777 E Wisconsin Ave Milwaukee WI 53702

CHRISTIANSEN, STEVEN ALLAN, lawyer; b. St. Louis, Apr. 11, 1947; s. Allan Peter and Ellen Kay (Nelson) C.; m. Julie Zierenberg, June 6, 1969; children: Tara, Tamara, Aaron. BA, U. Mo., 1969; JD, U. Mo., Kansas City, 1974. Bar: U.S. Dist. Ct. (we. dist.) Mo. 1974. Asst. prosecutor Jackson County Juvenile Ct., Kansas City, Mo., 1974-75; asst. gen. counsel Empire Gas Corp., Lebanon, Mo., 1975-77; asst. corp. counsel H&R Block, Kansas City, 1977—. Counsel Queens of Kansas City, Independence, Mo., 1982; vol. Republicans for Reagan, Prairie Village, Kansas, 1984; mediator Christian Conciliation Service, Kansas City, 1983-84; bd. dirs. New Life Covenant Ch., Kansas City, 1981-82. Served to lt. (j.g.) USN, 1969-71. General corporate, Legislative, Administrative and regulatory. Home: 5408 W 80th St Prairie Village KS 66208 Office: H&R Block Inc 4410 Main St Kansas City MO 64111

CHRISTIANSON, JAMES MILTON, lawyer, accountant; b. Austin, Feb. 5, 1951; s. E. Quinton and Ruby (Johnson) C. BA, U. Tex., 1973, JD, 1975. Bar: Tex. 1976; CPA, Tex. Atty. Tex. Real Estate Commn., Austin, 1976-78, IRS, Austin, 1978—; instr. Austin Community Coll., 1979—; chmn. bd. dirs. Govt. Employee Credit Union, Austin. Mem. City of Austin Hist. Landmark, 1975—. Named one of Outstanding Young Men of Am., Jaycees, 1975, 76; recipient Distinguished Service award Austin City Council, 1980. Mem. Tex. Bar Assn., Travis County Bar Assn., Austin Jaycees. Democrat. Mem. Evangelical Ch. Estate taxation, Legal education, Personal income taxation. Home: 3205 Bridle Path Austin TX 78703

CHRISTIE, ANDREW DOBBIE, judge; b. Cin., Feb. 11, 1922; s. John W. and Ruth (Bigelow) C.; m. Carol Graves, July 20, 1946; children: Anne Waugh, Andrew D. Jr., George D., Elizabeth M. AB, Princeton U., 1946; LLB, U. Pa., 1949. Bar: Del. 1949. Sole practice Wilmington, Del., 1949-57; chief atty. Del. Gen. Assembly, Dover, 1953-57; judge Del. Superior Ct., Wilmington, 1957-83; justice Del. Supreme Ct., Wilmington, 1983-85, chief justice, 1985—; instr. Nat. Coll. State Trial Judges, 1967, Nat. Coll. State Judiciary, 1969, 72, 73, 74; pres. Legal Aid Soc., Wilmington, 1957-67. Former trustee Westminster Presbyn. Ch., Family Ct. Assn., Child Guidance Clinic, Florence Crittendon Home. Served with USAAF, 1943-46. Mem. ABA, Am. Judicature Soc., Del. Bar Assn. Republican. Clubs: Wilmington, Greenville Country, Nassau (Princeton). Avocations: gardening, stamp collecting, ornithology. Judicial administration. Home: 114 Brook Valley Rd Wilmington DE 19807 Office: Del Supreme Ct State Office Bldg 820 French St Wilmington DE 19801

CHRISTIE, GEORGE CUSTIS, legal educator, author; b. N.Y.C., Mar. 3, 1934. A.B., Columbia U., 1955, J.D., 1957; diploma in internat. law (Fulbright scholar), Cambridge (Eng.) U., 1962; S.J.D., Harvard U., 1966. Bar: N.Y. 1957, D.C. 1958. Assoc. Covington & Burling, Washington, 1958-60; Ford Found. fellow in law teaching Harvard U., 1960-61; asso. prof. law U. Minn., Mpls., 1962-65; prof. U. Minn., 1965-66; asst. gen. counsel for Near E. and S. Asia, AID, Dept. State, 1966-67; prof. law Duke U., 1967-79, James B. Duke prof. law, 1979—; vis. lectr. U. Witwatersrand, South Africa, 1980, Fudan U., China, U. Otago, New Zealand, 1985; fellow Nat. Humanities Center, 1980-81; scholar-in-residence McGuire, Woods & Battle, Richmond, Va., 1983. Author: Jurisprudence: Text and Readings on the Philosophy of Law, 1973, The Sum and Substance of the Law of Torts, 1980, Law, Norms & Authority, 1982; Cases and Materials on the Law of Torts, 1983; contbr. articles to legal jours.; mem. bd. editors Am. Jour. Legal History, 1971-76, Law and Philosophy, 1982—. Served with U.S. Army, 1957. Mem. ABA, Am. Law Inst., Am. Soc. Internat. Law, Phi Beta Kappa. Legal education, Jurisprudence, Personal injury. Office: Duke U Sch Law Durham NC 27706

CHRISTOPHER, M. RONALD, lawyer; b. Cairo, Ill., May 17, 1941; s. Maurice Parker and Julietta (Eaker) C.; m. Eleanor Tate Potter, May 5, 1973; children: Shannon, Kelsey, Carroll Lane, Courtney. AB, U. Ky., 1964, JD, 1967. Bar: Ky. 1967, U.S. Supreme Ct. 1976. Ptnr. Christopher & Hutchens, Murray, Ky.; judge pro tem Murray, Ky., 1970-72; pres. 42d Jud. Dist., 1973-74; commonwealth atty. Calloway and Marshall Counties, 1974—. Regent Nat. Boy Scout Mus., 1981-82; chmn. Bd. of Regents Murray State U., 1977-83. Named one of Outstanding Young Men of Yr., 1975. Mem. ABA, Fed. Bar Assn., Ky. Bar Assn., Calloway County Bar Assn. Democrat. Methodist. Lodge: Rotary. State civil litigation, Criminal, General practice.

CHRISTOPHER, WARREN MINOR, lawyer, govt. ofcl.; b. Scranton, N.D., Oct. 27, 1925; s. Ernest W. and Catharine Anna (Lemen) C.; m. Marie Josephine Wyllis, Dec. 21, 1956; children—Lynn, Scott, Thomas, Kristen. Student, U. Redlands, 1942-43; B.S. magna cum laude, U. So. Calif., 1945; LL.B., Stanford, 1949; LL.D. (hon.), Occidental U., 1977, Bates Coll., 1981, Brown U., 1981, Claremont Coll., 1981. Bar: Calif. bar 1949, U.S. Supreme Ct. bar 1949. Law clk. U.S. Supreme Ct. Justice William O. Douglas, Washington, 1949-50; practice in Los Angeles, 1950-67, 69-76, 81—; mem. firm O'Melveny & Myers, 1950-67, 69, partner, 1958-67, 69-76, 81—; dep. atty. gen. U.S., Washington, 1967-69; dep. sec. of state Dept. State, Washington, 1977-81; spl. counsel to Gov. Calif., 1959; cons. Office Under Sec. State, 1961-65; mem. bd. bar examiners State Bar Calif., 1966-67; dir. So. Calif. Edison Co., First Interstate Bancorp; Mem. Calif. Coordinating Council for Higher Edn., 1960-67, pres., 1963-65; vice chmn. Gov.'s Commn. on Los Angeles Riots, 1965-66; chmn. U.S. delegations to U.S.-Japan Cotton Textile Negotiations, 1961, Geneva Conf. on Cotton Textiles, 1961; spl. rep. sec. state for Wool Textile Meetings, London, Rome, Tokyo, 1964-65; mem. Trilateral Commn., 1975-77, 81—. Trustee Stanford U., 1973-77, 81—, pres. bd. trustees 1985—, bd. dirs. council on fgn. relations. Served to lt. (j.g.) USNR, 1943-46. Decorated Medal of Freedom; recipient Harold Weill award N.Y. U., 1981; Louis Stein award Fordham U., 1981. Fellow Am. Bar Found., Am. Coll. Trial Lawyers; mem. ABA (ho. of dels. 1975-77, chmn. standing com. fed. judiciary 1975-77), Calif. Bar Assn. (gov. 1975-77), Los Angeles County Bar Assn. (pres. 1974-75), Am. Law Inst., Order of Coif, Phi Kappa Phi. Clubs: Calif, Chancery, Bohemian. Office: O'Melveny & Myers 400 S Hope St Los Angeles CA 90071-2899

CHRISTOPHER, WILLIAM GARTH, lawyer; b. Beaumont, Tex., Oct. 14, 1940; s. Garth Daugherty and Ollye Mittie (Harkness) C.; m. Elizabeth O'Hara, June 9, 1962; children—John William, David Noah, Michael O'Hara. B.S. in Engring., U.S. Mil. Acad., 1962; J.D., U. Va., 1970. Bar: Va. 1970, D.C. 1970, U.S. Supreme Ct. 1975, Mich. 1977. Assoc. Steptoe & Johnson, Washington, 1970-77; ptnr. Honigman Miller Schwartz & Cohn, Detroit, 1977—. Pres. Birmingham (Mich.) Hockey Assn., 1982-84; mem. Episcopal Diocese of Mich. Commn. on Ministry, 1983—, co-chmn. 1987—. Served to capt. C.E. U.S. Army, 1962-67. Elected to Raven Soc., U. Va., 1970. Mem. ABA, Fed. Bar Assn., Va. Bar Assn., D.C. Bar Assn., Mich. Bar Assn., Detroit Bar Assn. (trustee 1984—, sec. 1986-87, Order of Coif, Phi Delta Phi. Episcopalian. Contbr. article to legal publ. Federal civil litigation, State civil litigation, Condemnation. Home: 7290 Parkhurst Dr Birmingham MI 48010 Office: Suite 2290 First Nat Bldg Detroit MI 48226

CHRISTY, GARY CHRISTOPHER, lawyer; b. Los Angeles, July 23, 1948; s. Harry Voorhees and Theresa (Wolff) C.; m. Debra Deiter, June 29, 1984; 1 child, Casey. B.A., U. Tampa, 1971; J.D., Woodrow Wilson Coll. Law, Atlanta, 1976. Bar: Ga., U.S. Ct. Appeals (11th cir.), U.S. Dist. Ct. (no. and mid. dists.) Ga. Asst. dist. atty. Cordele Jud. Cir., Ga., 1976-79, dist. atty., 1979-85; ptnr. Davis, Pridgen, Jones & Christy, Vienna, Ga., 1985-86, Rainwater & Christy, Cordele, Ga., 1986—; mem. Organized Crime Prevention Council Ga., 1981-85. Bd. dirs. Crisp Area YMCA, Cordele, 1984. Recipient Disting. Service award Ga. Bur. Investigation, 1983. Mem. Nat. Dist. Attys. Assn., Assn. Trial Lawyers Am., Ga. Trial Lawyers Assn. (lectr. cross examination and closing argument 1986), Dist. Attys. Assn. Ga. (pres. 1984-85). Democrat. Roman Catholic. Criminal, Federal civil litigation, State civil litigation. Home: Hwy 41 N PO Box 444 Vienna GA 31092 Office: Rainwater & Christy PO Box 5230 Cordele GA 31015

CHU, MORGAN, lawyer; b. N.Y.C., Dec. 27, 1950; m. Helen M. Wong, Dec. 29, 1970. AB, UCLA, 1971, MA, 1972, PhD, 1973; postdoctoral studies in library sci., Yale U., 1974; JD, Harvard U., 1976. Bar: Calif. 1976, U.S. Dist. Ct. (cen. dist.) Calif. 1977, U.S. Ct. Appeals (9th cir.) 1976, 77, U.S. Dist. Ct. (no. dist.) Calif. 1980, U.S. Dist. Ct. (so dist.) Calif. 1984, U.S. Dist. Ct. (ea. dist.) Calif. 1986. Law clk. to presiding judge U.S. Ct. Appeals (9th cir.) Calif., San Francisco, 1976-77; assoc. Irell & Manella, Los Angeles, 1977-82, ptnr., 1982—; adj. prof. UCLA Sch. Law, 1979-82; judge pro tem Los Angeles Mcpl. Ct., 1980—. Assoc. editor Litigation News, 1981-84. Fellow, Yale U., 1974. Mem. ABA (chmn. high tech. intellectual property and patent trials subcom. 1986—, trial practice com., litigation sect.), Calif. Bar Assn., Los Angeles County Bar Assn. (judiciary com.). Federal civil litigation, State civil litigation, Libel. Office: Irell & Manella 1800 Ave of Stars Suite 900 Los Angeles CA 90067

CHUCK, WALTER G(OONSUN), lawyer; b. Wailuku, Maui, Hawaii, Sept. 10, 1920; s. Hong Yee and Aoe (Ting) C.; m. Marian Chun, Sept. 11, 1943; children: Jamie Allison, Walter Gregory, Meredith Jayne. Ed.B., U. Hawaii, 1941; J.D., Harvard U., 1948. Bar: Hawaii 1948. Navy auditor Pearl Harbor, 1941; field agt. Social Security Bd., 1942; labor law insp. Terr. Dept. Labor, 1943; law clk. firm Ropes, Gray, Best, Coolidge & Rugg, 1948; asst. pub. prosecutor City and County of Honolulu, 1949; with Fong, Miho & Choy, 1950-53; ptnr. Fong, Miho, Choy & Chuck, 1953-58; pvt. practice law Honolulu, 1958-65; ptnr. Chuck & Fujiyama, Honolulu, 1965-74; ptnr. firm Chuck, Wong & Tonaki, Honolulu, 1974-76, Chuck & Pai, Honolulu, 1976-78; sole practice Honolulu, 1978-80; pres. Walter G. Chuck Law Corp., Honolulu, 1980—; dist. magistrate Dist. Ct. Honolulu, 1956-63; mem. ad hoc specialization of lawyers com. Superior Ct. Hawaii; treas., dir. M & W, Inc.; gen. ptnr. Tripler Warehousing Co., Kapalama Investment Co.; dir. Pacific Resources, Inc., Gasco, Inc., Aloha Airlines, Inc., Hawaiian Ind. Refinery, Inc., Honolulu Painting Co., Ltd., Enerco, Inc. Chmn. Hawaii Employment Relations Bd., 1955-59; bd. dirs. Nat. Assn. State Labor Relations Bd., 1957-58, Honolulu Theatre for Youth, 1977-80; chief clk. Ho. of Reps., 1951, 53; chief clk. Hawaii senate, 1959-61; govt. appeal agt. SSS, 1953-72; mem. jud. council, State of Hawaii; exec. com. Hawaiian Open; mem. Friends of Judiciary Mus., ad hoc com. for Supreme Ct. of Hawaii on Specialization of Lawyers; former bd. dirs. YMCA. Served as capt. inf. Hawaii Territorial Guard. Fellow Internat. Acad. Trial Lawyers (dir.); mem. ABA (chmn. Hawaii sr. lawyers div.), Hawaii Bar Assn. (pres. 1963), Am. Trial Lawyers Assn. (editor), U. Hawaii Alumni Assn. (Distinguished Service award 1967, dir., bd. govs.), Law Sci. Inst., Assoc. Students U. Hawaii, Am. Judicature Soc., Internat. Soc. Barristers, Am. Inst. Banking, Chinese C. of C. Republican. Clubs: Harvard of Hawaii, Waialae Country (pres. 1975), Pacific, Oahu Country. Federal civil litigation, State civil litigation, General practice. Home: 2691 Aaliamanu Pl Honolulu HI 96813 Office: Suite 1814 745 Fort St Honolulu HI 96813

CHUMAN, FRANK FUJIO, lawyer; b. Montecito, Calif., Apr. 29, 1917; s. Hitsuji Henry and Kiyo (Yamamoto) C.; m. Ruby Ryoko Dewa, June 22, 1948 (div. Oct. 1968); children: Daniel Christopher, Paul Randolph; m. Donna Daungvipar Karschamroon, Apr. 17, 1983; 1 child, Diana. BA in Polit. Sci., UCLA, 1938; postgrad., U. So. Calif., 1940-42, U. Toledo, 1943-44; JD, U. Md., 1945. Bar: Md. 1945, Calif. 1947. Clk. with probation dept. County of Los Angeles, 1939-42; adminstr. Base Hosp., Manzanar, Calif., 1942-43; acct. Goodyear Tire and Rubber Co., Balt., 1945; sole practice Los Angeles, 1947—; arbitrator Los Angeles County Superior Ct., 1968—; judge pro tem Los Angeles Dist. Mcpl. Ct., 1968—; gen. ptnr. Japanese Village Plaza Shopping Ctr., Los Angeles, 1976-85; chmn. Founders Savs. and Loan. Author: "Bamboo People" Law and Japanese Americans, 1976. Pres. Japanese Am. Dem. Club, Los Angeles, 1950-60; chmn. 63d Assembly dist. Los Angeles Dems., 1960-62, vice chmn. 15th Congl. dist., 1960-62; mem. Japanese Am. Citizens League (nat. pres. 1960-62). Recipient Bishop's Merit award Episc. Diocese of Los Angeles, 1963, Eagle Scout award Boy Scouts Am. 1939, Silver Beavers award, 1974, Disting. Eagle Scout award, 1979. Mem. ABA, Japanese Am. Bar Assn., Assn. Immigration Lawyers (chmn. Los Angeles chpt. 1958-59). Avocations: golf, music. Immigration, naturalization, and customs, General corporate. Office: 5306 Angeles Crest Hwy La Canada Flintridge CA 91011

CHUMBRIS, STEPHEN CLAUDE, lawyer; b. Washington, July 5, 1950; s. Milton Stephen and Ann (Rhodes) C.; m. Valerie Muller, June 4, 1977; children: Stephen Claude Jr., Tara Elizabeth. BA cum laude, U. Md., 1972; JD cum laude, Stetson U., 1976. Bar: Fla. 1976, U.S. Dist. Ct. (mid. dist.) Fla. 1977, U.S. Ct. Appeals (11th cir.) 1981, U.S. Supreme Ct. 1981. Assoc. Greene, Mann, Rowe, Stanton, Mastry & Burton, St. Petersburg, Fla., 1976-81, ptnr., 1981-84; ptnr. Greene & Mastry, P.A., St. Petersburg, 1984—; v.p., bd. dirs. Alpha A Beginning, Inc., 1987—. Mem. ABA, St. Petersburg Bar Assn., St. Petersburg C. of C., Pinellas County Contractors & Builders Assn., Nat. Assn. Home Builders, Phi Beta Kappa, Phi Kappa Phi, Pi Sigma Alpha. Democrat. Roman Catholic. Club: St. Petersburg Yacht. Administrative and regulatory, State civil litigation, Environment. Home: 8022 Stimie Ave N Saint Petersburg FL 33710 Office: Greene & Mastry PA 360 Central Ave Saint Petersburg FL 33701

CHUNG, HARRISON PAUL, lawyer; b. Honolulu, Aug. 13, 1951; m. Lisa Clare Lee; children: Ashlee Clare, Bryce Paul. BBA cum laude, U. Notre Dame, 1973; MBA, Golden Gate U., 1977; JD, U. Calif., San Francisco, 1980. Bar: Hawaii 1980, U.S. Dist. Ct. Hawaii 1980, U.S. Ct. Appeals (9th cir) 1985. Assoc. Carlsmith, Wichman, Case, Mukai & Ichiki, Honolulu, 1980-87, ptnr., 1987—; mem. local rules com. U.S. Bankruptcy Ct., Honolulu, 1984—. Served to 1st lt. U.S. Army, 1973-77. Mem. ABA, Hawaii Bar Assn. Bankruptcy, Banking, Consumer commercial. Home: 954 Honokahua Pl Honolulu HI 96825 Office: Carlsmith Wichman Case et al 1001 Bishop St Pacific Tower Suite 2200 Honolulu HI 96813

CHUNG, STEVEN KAMSEIN, lawyer; b. Honolulu, Oct. 13, 1947; s. Edward K.O. and Amy B.J. (Chun) C.; m. Evelyn Reiko, July 5, 1980; children: Chanelle Mari, Tiffany Rei. BA in Acctg., U. Hawaii, 1972; JD, U. Calif.-San Francisco, 1976. Bar: Hawaii 1976, U.S. Dist. Ct. Hawaii 1976, U.S. Ct. Appeals (9th cir.) 1978, U.S. Supreme Ct. 1983. Assoc. firm Frank D. Padgett, Atty. at Law, Honolulu, 1976-80, ptnr. firm Chung, Lau, MacLaren & Lau, Honolulu, 1980-81, firm Walter G. Chuck and Assocs., Honolulu, 1981-86; sole practice, Honolulu, 1987—. Served to 1st lt. U.S. Army, 1966-69, Vietnam. Mem. Assn. Trial Lawyers Am., ABA, Hawaii Bar Assn. Roman Catholic. Federal civil litigation, State civil litigation, Bankruptcy. Home: 1127 Kahului St Honolulu HI 96825 Office: 841 Bishop St Suite 488 Honolulu HI 96813

CHUN-HOON, LOWELL KOON YING, lawyer; b. Honolulu, Aug. 23, 1949; s. Kenneth Chew Ming and Alice Mee Chan (Yee) Chun-H. BA, Yale U., 1971; MA, UCLA, 1974; JD, U. Calif., Berkeley, 1977. Bar: Hi. 1977, U.S. Dist. Ct. Hi. 1977, U.S. Ct. Appeals (9th cir.) 1980, U.S. Ct. Appeals (fed. cir.) 1985. Assoc. Bouslog & Symonds, Honolulu, 1977-79; ptnr. King, Nakamura & Chun-Hoon, Honolulu, 1979—; v.p. Na Loio No Na Kanaka, Honolulu, 1984-86, bd. dirs. Named one of Outstanding Young Men of Am., U.S. Jaycees, 1984. Mem. ABA, Hi. Bar Assn. Labor, Workers' compensation, Personal injury. Home: 1140-D Alewa Dr Honolulu HI 96813 Office: King Nakamura & Chun-Hoon 900 Ft St Mall Suite 300 Honolulu HI 96813

CHURCH, GLENN J., lawyer; b. Grand Island, Nebr., Aug. 20, 1932; s. Glenn Jennings and Rachel Frances (Cochran) C.; m. Norma Ann Ray; children: Susan Jo, Zackary William. AB, U. Ill., 1954, JD, 1959. Bar: Ill. 1959, U.S. Dist. Ct. (cen. dist.) Ill. 1960, U.S. Ct. Appeals (7th cir.) 1967, U.S. Supreme Ct. 1971, Ohio 1983. Assoc. Kavanaugh, Bond, Scully, Sudow & White, Peoria, Ill., 1959-62; ptnr. Smith, Whitney & Church, Peoria, 1962-66; sole practice Peoria, 1966-70; prin. Glenn J. Church Ltd., Peoria, 1970-86; spl. asst. atty. gen. water pollution div. State of Ill. , 1960-61; hearing officer Am. Arbitration Assn., Chgo., 1966—; mem. Ill. Fair Employment Practice Commn., 1974-79. Liasion officer Air Force Acad., Colorado Springs, Colo., 1968-82; bd. dirs. W.D. Boyce council Boy Scouts Am., 1970-86, Heart of Ill. Fair and Exposition Gardens, Peoria, 1978-84; exec. bd. chmn. eagle rev. com. Boy Scouts Am. , Peoria, 1977-86. Served to lt. col. USAF, 1954-82. Mem. Ill. Bar Assn., Ohio Bar Assn., Peoria Bar Assn., Assn. Trial Lawyers Am., Phi Alpha Delta. Republican. Methodist. Lodge: Sertoma. Personal injury, Workers' compensation, Family and matrimonial. Home: 4709 N War Meml Dr Peoria IL 61615 Office: 1000 Savings Ctr Tower Peoria IL 61602

CHURCH, RANDOLPH WARNER, JR., lawyer; b. Richmond, Va., Nov. 6, 1934; s. Randolph Warner and Elizabeth Lewis (Gochnauer) C.; m. Lucy Ann Canary, July 4, 1970; children: Leslie R. Pennell, Lucy W. Ringle. BA with honors, U. Va., 1957, LLB, 1960. Bar: Va. 1960, U.S. Dist. Ct. (ea. dist.) Va. 1962, U.S. Ct. Appeals (4th cir.) 1981. Assoc. McCandlish, Lillard & Marsh, Fairfax, Va., 1960-63; ptnr. McCandlish, Lillard, Rust & Church, Fairfax, 1963-84, Hunton & Williams, Fairfax, 1984—. Author: Appellate Civil Litigation, 1984. Bd. visitors George Mason U., Fairfax, 1982—, rector, 1983-86; nat. com. Young Dems. Clubs Va., 1966-67. Named Outstanding Alumnus Sigma Phi Epsilon, 1986. Mem. ABA, Va. Bar Assn., Phi Beta Kappa. Episcopalian. Club: Country of Fairfax County. General corporate, State civil litigation. Home: 5114 Forsgate Pl Fairfax VA 22030 Office: Hunton & Williams 3050 Chain St Bridge Rd Fairfax VA 22030

CHURCHILL, ALLEN DELOS, lawyer; b. Sioux Falls, S.D., June 5, 1921; s. Edward Delos and Iva Edna (Allen) C.; m. Melva Fein, Jan. 16, 1925; 1 dau., Victoria Ann. B.A., Washington U.-St. Louis, 1948, J.D., 1950. Bar: Mo. 1950, U.S. Dist. Ct. (ea. dist.) Mo. 1950, Ill. 1965, U.S. Dist. Ct. (so. dist.) Ill. 1965, U.S. Ct. Appeals (7th cir.) 1974. Trial atty. Mo. Pacific R.R., St. Louis, 1952-62; sole practice, St. Louis, 1962-65, Belleville, Ill., 1965-67; ptnr. Dunham, Boman, Leskera & Churchill, Belleville, 1967-77, Churchill, Nester & McDonnell, Belleville, 1977-85, Churchill & McDonnell, 1985—. Served with U.S. Army AC, 1942-45. Fellow Internat. Soc. Barristers, Am. coll. Trial Lawyers, Ill. Bar Found.; mem. Ill. Trial Lawyers Assn., Ill. State Bar Assn. (econs. com. 1970-72), Assn. Trial Lawyers Am., Def. Research Inst., Ill. Def. Counsel Assn., Mo. Bar Assn., St. Louis Met. Bar Assn., St. Clair (Ill.) County Bar Assn. (pres. 1974-75), Am. Bd. Trial Advs. (adv.). Clubs: Mo. Athletic (St. Louis), Media. Insurance, Federal civil litigation, State civil litigation. Office: Churchill & McDonnell 10 E Washington St Belleville IL 62220

CHURCHILL, DAVID JAMES, lawyer; b. Saginaw, Mich., Oct. 22, 1953; s. James P. and Annabel (Muir) C.; m. Kathy Marie Stamey, Sept. 17, 1983. BA with honors, Mich. State U., 1975; JD, Wayne State U., 1978. Bar: Mich. 1978, U.S. Dist. Ct. (ea. dist.) Mich. 1981. Asst. pros. atty. Antrim County, Bellaire, Mich., 1978-79; atty. Taylor, Carter, Butterfield, Riseman, Clark, & Howell, Lapeer, Mich., 1979—. Treas. Lapeer County Dem. Party, 1982. Mem. Lapeer County Bar Assn. (pres. 1985-86), Lapeer Area C. of C. (pres. 1984). Lutheran. Avocations: photography, fly-fishing, sailing. State civil litigation, General practice, Contracts commercial. Home: 135 Daley Lapeer MI 48446 Office: Taylor Clark et al 407 Clay St Lapeer MI 48446

CHURCHILL, JAMES PAUL, judge; b. Imlay City, Mich., Apr. 10, 1924; s. Howard and Faye (Shurte) C.; m. Ann Muir, Aug. 30, 1950; children: Nancy Ann Churchill Nyquist, David James, Sally Jo. B.A., U. Mich., 1947, J.D., 1950. Bar: Mich. Sole practice Vassar, Mich., 1950-65; circuit judge 40th Jud. Circuit Mich., 1965-74; U.S. dist. judge Eastern Dist. Mich., Detroit, 1974—; ct. commr. Tuscola County Cir., 1963-65; adj. prof. Detroit Coll. Law, 1980-81. Served with U.S. Army, 1943-46. Mem. Fed. Judges Assn., Fed. Bar Assn., 40th Jud. Cir. Bar Assn. Office: US Dist Ct 214 Fed Bldg Bay City MI 48707

CHURUTI, SUSAN HAMILTON, lawyer; b. Houston, Nov. 28, 1954; d. John McFarland and Imogene (Nicholson) Hamilton; m. Robert Edward Churuti, Oct. 2, 1982. BA with honors, Coll. of William & Mary, 1976; JD, Washington & Lee U., 1979. Bar: U.S. Ct. Appeals (D.C. cir.) 1980, U.S. Dist. Ct. (mid. dist.) Fla. 1981, U.S. Ct. Appeals (11th cir.) 1981. County atty. Pinellas County, Clearwater, Fla., 1981—. Mem. ABA, Fla. Bar Assn. (vice chmn. eminent domain com.), Clearwater Bar Assn. (bd. dirs. 1986—, chmn. eminent domain com. 1986—). Republican. Episcopalian. Condemnation, State and local taxation. Office: County Attys Office 315 Court St Clearwater FL 33516

CHUTE, ALAN DALE, military lawyer; b. International Falls, Minn.; s. Lester Robert and Florence Adele (Jensen) C.; m. Sharon Marie McHenry, June 9, 1979; children: Andrew Alan, Anthony Lee. BS, U.S. Mil. Acad., 1977; JD, U. Minn., 1982. Bar: Minn., U.S. Ct. Mil. Appeals, Army Ct. Mil. Rev. Commd. 2d lt. U.S. Army, 1977, advanced through grades to capt., 1981; signal officer U.S. Army, Charlottesville, Va. and Korea, 1977-79; claims judge adv. Office of Staff Judge Adv., Ft. Lewis, Wash., 1982-83, prosecutor, 1983-85; atty. U.S. Army Trial Def. Service, Ft. Lewis, Wash., 1985-86; sr. def. counsel 2d inf. div. U.S. Army Trial Def. Service, Korea, 1986—. Editor-in-chief U. Minn. Law Rev., 1981-82. Mem. ABA, Minn. Bar Assn., Assn. Trail Lawyers Am. Roman Catholic. Lodge: KC. Criminal, Military, General practice. Home: 1701 Easy Ln Charlottesville VA 22901 Address: Judge Adv Gen's Sch TJAGSA Charlottesville VA 22903

CHYTEN, EDWIN RICHARD, lawyer; b. Boston, May 15, 1925; s. William and Elizabeth (Carpenter) C.; m. Helen Siegal, Apr. 26, 1949 (div. Feb. 1981); children—Leslie. Kenneth, Neil; m. Rosalyn Levine, May 11, 1983. A.B., Harvard Coll., 1947; J.D., Boston Coll., 1971. Bar: Mass. 1971, U.S. Dist. Ct. Mass. 1971. Atty., legal counsel, v.p. Purity Supreme, Inc., North Billerica, Mass., 1974-79; ptnr. Meyers, Goldstein & Chyten, Chestnut Hill, Mass., 1979—. Served to lt. (j.g.) USN, 1943-46; PTO. Fellow Mass. Bar Assn., Mass. Acad. Trial Attys. Club: Newton Tennis (pres., 1978-80) (Mass.). State civil litigation, General corporate, General practice. Home: 250 Hammond Pond Pkwy Chestnut Hill MA 02167 Office: Meyers Goldstein & Chyten 850 Boylston St Chestnut Hill MA 02167

CIACCIO, KARIN MCLAUGHLIN, lawyer; b. Galesburg, Ill., Feb. 9, 1947; d. Cleo Edward and Kathryn Louise (Payton) McLaughlin; m. Frederick Steven Ciaccio, May 4, 1968; children: John, Jennifer. BS, So. Ill. U., 1969; postgrad., Temple U. Law Sch., 1971-72; JD, DePaul U., 1975. Bar: Ill. 1975, U.S. Dist. Ct. (no. dist.) Ill. 1975. Tchr. French Sherrard (Ill.) High Sch., 1969-70; prof. law U. Wis., Racine, 1975, Coll. DuPage, Glen Ellyn, Ill., 1976; sole practice Chgo. and Lombard, Ill., 1975-80, Galesburg and Woodhull, Ill., 1980—; lectr. on consumer law, various orgns., 1976—; city atty. Woodhull, 1983—. Ofcl. Lombard Zoning Bd., 1978-80; mem. Alpha (Ill.) Cemetary Bd., 1980—, St. John's Cemetary Bd., Woodhull, 1983—; legis. chmn. Rep. Women Henry County, 1981-83; bd. dirs. Alwood Bus. Assn., 1984—. Mem. ABA, Ill. Bar Assn., Henry County Bar Assn., Phi Alpha Delta. Lodge: Altrusa. Avocation: photography. General practice. Office: 147 N Division Woodhull IL 61490

CIAMBELLA, CORY JOSEPH, lawyer; b. Buffalo, Nov. 2, 1956; s. Peter Donald and Jeanette Ann (Reisch) C.; m. Carla Marie Giardina, July 6, 1985. BA in Econs., SUNY, Buffalo, 1978, MBA, 1979, JD, 1982. Bar: N.Y. 1983, Calif. 1983, U.S. Ct. Appeals (6th cir.) 1985. Assoc. Clifford N. Barry, Beverly Hills, Calif., 1982-83, Rand & Goodchild, Santa Ana, Calif., 1983-84, Jerrold Wolf, Inc., Santa Ana, 1984-85; sole practice Beverly Hills, 1985-86, Long Beach, Calif., 1986—. Mem. ABA, Beverly Hills Bar Assn., Assn. Trial Lawyers Am., Calif. Trial Lawyers Assn., Calif. Applicant Atty's. Assn. Democrat. Roman Catholic. Workers' compensation, Personal injury. Office: 400 Oceangate Suite 218 Long Beach CA 90802

CICERO, FRANK, JR., lawyer; b. Chgo., Nov. 30, 1935; s. Frank and Mary (Balma) C.; m. Janice Pickett, July 11, 1959; children—Erica, Caroline. Student Amherst Coll., 1953-54; A.B. with honors, Wheaton Coll., 1957; M in Pub. Affairs, Woodrow Wilson Sch. of Pub. and Internat. Affairs, 1962; J.D., U. Chgo. Law Sch., 1965. Bar; Ill., U.S. Dist. Ct. (no. dist.) Ill., 1965, U.S. Ct. Appeals (7th cir.), U.S. Ct. Appeals (5th cir.), U.S. Supreme Ct. Polit. sci. instr. Wheaton Coll., Ill., 1957-58; spl. asst. Gov. Richard J. Hughes of N.J., 1962; assoc. Kirkland & Ellis, Chgo., 1965—, ptnr., 1970—; mem. vis. com. U. Chgo. Law Sch., 1971-74; del. to 6th Ill. Constl. Conv., 1969-70. Bd. editors U. Chgo. Law Rev., also author articles, 1963-64. Recipient Joseph Henry Beale prize U. Chgo., 1963, Outstanding Young Man award Evanston Jaycees, 1970. Fellow Am. Coll. Trial Lawyers, Internat. Acad. Trial Lawyers; mem. ABA, Ill. State Bar Assn., Bar Assn. 7th Fed. Circuit, Am. Polit. Sci. Assn., Am. Acad. Polit. and Social Sci. Clubs: Chicago, Mid-Am. (gov. 1981-84), Saddle and Cycle (gov. 1984). Federal

civil litigation, State civil litigation, Private international. Office: Kirkland & Ellis 200 E Randolph Dr Chicago IL 60601

CICET, DONALD JAMES, lawyer; b. New Orleans, May 24, 1940; s. Arthur Alphonse and Myrtle (Ress) C. B.A., Nicholls State U., 1963; J.D., Loyola U., New Orleans, 1969. Bar: La. 1969, U.S. Dist. Ct. (ea. dist.) La. 1972, U.S. Ct. Appeals (5th cir.) 1972, U.S. Supreme Ct. 1972, U.S. Dist. Ct. (mid. dist.) La. 1978, U.S. Dist. Ct. (we. dist.) La. 1979. Sole practice, Reserve, La., 1969—; staff atty. La. Legis. Council, 1972-73; legal counsel Nicholls State U. Alumni Fedn., 1974-76, 78-80; spl. counsel Pontchartrain Levee Dist., 1976—; administrv. law judge La. Dept. Civil Service, 1981—. Served with AUS, 1964, USNG, 1964-70. Recipient Am. Jurisprudence award Loyola U., 1968. Mem. 40th Jud. Dist. Bar Assn., (pres. 1985-87), La. Bar Assn. (ho. dels. 1973-77, 79-85), ABA, La. Trial Lawyers Assn., Assn. Trial Lawyers Am., Nicholls State U. Alumni Fedn. (exec. council 1972-76, 77-85, pres. 1982, James Lynn Powell award 1980), Am. Judicature Soc., Am. Legion (post comdr. 1976-77, dist. judge advocate, 1975—, mem. La. dept. comn. on nat. security and govtl. affairs, 1974—, chmn. 1977-78, 79-81, 85—, M.C. "Mike" Gehr Blue Cap award 1983). Roman Catholic. Administrative and regulatory, Local government, Juvenile. Home: 124 W 1st St Reserve LA 70084 Office: 2810 W Airline Hwy Suite 100 PO Box 442 Reserve LA 70084

CICIO, ANTHONY LEE, lawyer; b. Birmingham, Ala., July 8, 1926; s. Joseph and Rosa (Tombrello) C.; m. Yvonne Antonio, Nov. 4, 1959; children: Valerie, Anthony Jr., Mark. BS, Samford U., 1951; LLB, Birmingham Sch. Law, 1955. Bar: Ala. 1956, U.S. Dist. Ct. Ala. 1956, U.S. Supreme Ct. 1961, U.S. Ct. Appeals (11th cir.) 1968. Ptnr. Cicio & Nolen, Birmingham, 1976—. Served with USAF, 1944-46, PTO. Mem. ABA, Ala. Bar Assn. (chmn. pub. relations com.), Birmingham Bar Assn. (ethics com., ch. com. on media and pub. relations), Am. Trial Lawyers Assn., Ala. Trial Lawyers Assn. (exec. com. 1983—). Democrat. Roman Catholic. Clubs: The Club, Roma Country, Vestavia Country (Birmingham). Personal injury, Probate, General practice. Home: 3128 N Woodridge Rd Birmingham AL 35223 Office: Cicio & Gleissner Cicio Profl Bldg 2153 14th Ave S Birmingham AL 35205

CICONTE, EDWARD THOMAS, lawyer; b. Wilmington, Del., Dec. 14, 1948; s. Joseph John and Josephine E. (Roda) C.; m. Diane Marie Penza, Mar. 3, 1973; children—Andrea, Michele, Jacklyn. B.S., St. Joseph's U., Phila., 1970; J.D., Villanova (Pa.) U., 1973. Bar: Del. 1973, U.S. Dist. Ct. Del. 1973. Ptnr. Ciconte and Roseman (formerly D'Angelo, Ciconte & Roseman), Wilmington, 1973—. Co-author: Delaware Collection Law, 1982. Served as capt. USAF, 1974. Mem. Del. Bar Assn., ABA, Am. Trial Lawyers Assn., Del. Trial Lawyers Assn., Comml. Law League Am. Democrat. Roman Catholic. Consumer commercial, Personal injury, Workers' compensation. Home: 1402 Ivy Dr Wilmington DE 19803 Office: Ciconte and Roseman 1300 King St Wilmington DE 19801

CICOTTE, LYNN JOSEPH, lawyer, physicist; b. River Rouge, Mich., Mar. 2, 1935; s. Edward Albert and Marie Ida (Meyers) C.; m. Lorraine Annette Gasiewski, Jan. 4, 1958; children: Kerry Jean Carden, Kimberly Marie. Cert. in electronics, Rets Sch., 1957; BS in Physics, Cen. Mich. U., 1964; MS in Physics, Wayne State U., 1970; JD, Loyola U., Los Angeles, 1976. Bar: Calif. 1977, U.S. Dist. Ct. (cen. dist.) Calif. 1977, U.S. Patent Office 1977. Research physicist Ford Sci. Labs., Dearborn, Mich., 1964-68; sr. physicist Ovonic Memories, Los Angeles, 1968-72; physicist Hughes Aircraft, Torrance, Calif., 1972-73; engr., cons. Chase, Rotchford, Drukker & Bogust, Los Angeles, 1973-77; ptnr. Parker, Stanbury, McGee, Babcock & Combs, Los Angeles, 1977—. Author 2 short stories; patentee gas laser starting device, 1973. Mem. Selective Service Bd., Detroit and Los Angeles. Served with U.S. Army, 1958-60. Mem. So. Calif. Def. Counsel, Lawyers in Mensa, U.S. Chess Fedn. Republican. Club: South Bay Archery (Palos Verdes, Calif.). Home: 25447 Basswood Ave Rancho Palos Verdes CA 90274 Office: Parker Stanbury McGee Babcock & Combs 611 W 6th St Suite 3360 Los Angeles CA 90017

CIFELLI, ARMAND, lawyer; b. Newark, Apr. 2, 1924; s. Thomas and Joanna (Duva) C.; m. Irene Echelman, June 24, 1945; children—Donna G. Cifelli Bisson, James C., Laura B. Cifelli Reynolds. Student Newark Coll. Engring., 1943, Yale U., 1943-44, Ga. Inst. Tech., 1944-45; J.D. with honors, George Washington U., 1950. Bar: Conn. 1963, U.S. Dist. Ct. D.C. 1951. Patent examiner U.S. Patent Office, 1946-50; patent atty. Dept. Def., 1950-53; atty. legal dept. Gen. Electric Co., Bridgeport, Conn., 1953-59; ptnr. Wooster, Davis & Cifelli, 1959-79; sr. ptnr. Cifelli and Frederick, 1979-81; sr. ptnr. Cifelli, Frederick & Tully, Bridgeport, Conn., 1981-87, ptnr. Kramer, Brufsky & Cifelli, P.C., Southport and Bridgeport, 1987—; adj. prof. intellectual property law U. Bridgeport, 1977—. Served to lt. (j.g.) USN, 1943-46. Mem. Bridgeport Bar Assn., Conn. Bar Assn., ABA, Conn. Pat. Law Assn., N.Y. Patent Law Assn., Am. Intellectual Property Law Assn. Republican. Unitarian-Universalist. Club: Patterson (Fairfield, Conn.). Patent, Trademark and copyright, Federal civil litigation. Home: 27 Wedgewood Dr Easton CT 06612 Home: 1600 SE St Lucie Blvd Stuart FL 33494 Office: One Lafayette Circle PO Box 1180 Bridgeport CT 06601

CIFELLI, JOHN LOUIS, lawyer; b. Chicago Heights, Ill., Aug. 19, 1923; s. Antonio and Domenica (Liberatore) C.; m. Irene Romandine, Jan. 4, 1948; children—Carla, David, John L., Bruce, Thomas, Carol. Student, Bowdoin Coll., 1943, Norwich Mil. Acad., 1943, Mt. Piliar Acad., 1943, U. Ill. Extension Center, 1946-47; LL.B., DePaul U., 1950, J.D. (hon.), 1975. Bar: Ill. 1950, U.S. Supreme Ct. 1960. Partner firm Piacenti, Cifelli & Sims and (predecessor firms), Chicago Heights, 1950—; spl. counsel City of Chicago Heights, 1961-72; village atty. Village of Richton Park, Ill., 1962-77; counsel Maj. League Umpires Assn., 1973-78, Ill. High Sch. Baseball Coaches Assn., 1975—; atty. Village of Ford Heights, Ill., 1984—. Sec. Bd. Fire and Police, Chicago Heights, 1959-65; co-founder Small Fry Internat. Basketball, 1969, pres., 1969—; coach, baseball coordinator Chicago Heights Park Dist., 1970-75; coach Babe Ruth League Baseball, 1972, 74, 75, asst. Ill. dir., 1973; dir. Ill. tournament, 1973. Served to 2d lt. USAAF, 1942-45, ETO. Mem. Ill. Bar Assn., ABA, South Suburban Bar Assn., Ill. Trial Lawyers Assn., Assn. Trial Lawyers Am., Am. Soc. Ecol. Edn., Justinian Soc. Lawyers, Am. Judicature Soc., Roscoe Pound/Am. Trial Lawyers Found., Chicago Heights C. of C., DePaul U. Devel. Program, Isaac Walton League, Italo Am. Vets. Group, VFW (judge adv. 1951-72), Cath. War Vets. (judge adv. 1951-70), Am. Legion, Delta Theta Phi. Clubs: Chicago Heights Country, Pike Lake Fishing and Gun, U. N.Mex. Lobo, Moose, DeMolay. General practice, Criminal, Personal injury. Home: 879 D'Amico Dr Chicago Heights IL 60411 Office: Cifelli Baczynski & Scrementi 450 W 14th St Chicago Heights IL 60411

CIMINI, JOSEPH FEDELE, law educator, lawyer, magistrate; b. Scranton, Pa., Sept. 8, 1948; s. Frank Anthony and Dorothy Theresa (Musso) C. A.B. in German and Polit. Sci., U. Scranton, 1970; J.D., Columbus Sch. Law, Cath. U. Am., 1973. Bar: Pa. 1973, U.S. Dist. Ct. (mid. dist.) Pa. 1973, D.C. 1976, U.S. Ct. Appeals (3d cir.) 1978, U.S. Supreme Ct. 1978. Law clk. to judge Ct. Common Pleas Lackawanna County (Pa.), 1973-75; asst. U.S. atty. Middle Dist. Pa., Dept. Justice, 1975-80, spl. asst. to U.S. Atty. Middle Dist. Pa., 1980-81; asst. prof. sociology/criminal justice U. Scranton, 1980—; U.S. magistrate U.S. Dist. Ct. (mid. dist.) Pa., 1981—. First v.p. Lackawanna Hist. Soc.; mem. adv. bd. Holy Family Residence, Scranton, Pa. Recipient Meritorious award Dept. Justice; German Acad. Exchange Service fgn. study travel grantee, W.Ger., 1981. Mem. ABA, Pa. Bar Assn., Northeastern Assn. Criminal Justice Scis. (1st v.p.), Lackawanna Bar Assn., Fed. Bar Assn., Nat. Dist. Attys. Assn., U. Scranton Alumni (past chpt. pres.), Cath. U. Law Alumni (sec. chpt.). Republican. Roman Catholic. Clubs: Nat. Lawyers; Purple (Scranton). Legal education, Federal civil litigation, Criminal. Address: PO Box 443 Scranton PA 18501

CINABRO, ROBERT HENRY, lawyer; b. Kalamazoo, Mich., June 10, 1948; s. Louis and Maria (Breviglieri) C.; m. Pamela Mae Eschenburg, Aug. 19, 1972; 1 child, Jennifer Elise. BA cum laude, Kalamazoo Coll., 1970; JD, Cornell U., 1973. Bar: Mich. 1973, U.S. Dist. Ct. (we. dist.) Mich., 1975, U.S. Supreme Ct. 1979, U.S. Ct. Appeals (6th cir.) 1983. Law clk. to presiding judge 9th Judicial Ct., Kalamazoo, 1973-74; asst. city atty. City of Kalamazoo, 1974-77, dep. city atty., 1977—; civil mediator N. Judicial Cir. Ct., Kalamazoo, 1985—; civil arbitrator U.S. Dist. Ct. (we. dist.) Mich., Grand Rapids, 1986—, legal counsel Kalamazoo Met. Transit Authority, 1985—. Mem. Kalamazoo Criminal Justice Commn., 1982-83, Kalamazoo Safety Council, Drunk Driving Task Force, 1983—; bd. dirs. Kalamazoo County Humane Soc., 1983-85. Mem. ABA, Kalamazoo County Bar Assn., Fed. Bar Assn., Phi Beta Kappa. Roman Catholic. Lodge: Optimists (bd. dirs. 1981-82). Avocations: civil war history, travel, animal welfare. Local government, Federal civil litigation, State and local taxation. Home: 2525 Frederick Ave Kalamazoo MI 49008 Office: Office of City Atty 241 W South St Kalamazoo MI 49007

CINO, VINCENT ALPHONSE, lawyer; b. Newark, Sept. 27, 1951; s. Alphonse P. and Rose (Caruso) C.; m. Julia M. De Araujo, Nov. 1, 1975; children: Robert, Christopher. BA, Rutgers U., 1973, MA, 1974, JD, 1979. Bar: N.J. 1979, U.S. Dist. Ct. N.J. 1979, U.S. Ct. Appeals (3d cir.) 1983, N.Y. 1985, U.S. Supreme Ct. 1985. Law sec. to presiding judge Superior Ct. of N.J., Union County, 1979-80; asst. prosecutor Union County, Elizabeth, N.J., 1980-81; assoc. Goodman, Stoldt, Breslin & Horan, Hackensack, N.J., 1981-84; ptnr. Stoldt, Horan & Cino, Hackensack, 1984-87; chief counsel claims div. Essex County, Newark, 1987—. Mem. ABA, N.J. Bar Assn., Bergen County Bar Assn. (environ. law com., hazardous waste com.), Assn. Trial Lawyers Am. Roman Catholic. Avocations: reading, tennis. State civil litigation, Environment, Nuclear power. Office: Essex County Counsel Hall of Records Newark NJ 17102

CIOVACCO, ROBERT JOHN, lawyer; b. Bklyn., June 23, 1941; s. Frank and Frances (Grieci) C.; m. Phyllis Marie Russo, Aug. 14, 1966; children—Jennifer Jude, Lauren Marie. B.A., Adelphi U., 1963; LL.B., St. John's U., Bklyn., 1967 Bar: N.Y. 1967, U.S. Dist. Ct. (so. and ea. dists.) N.Y. 1975. Assoc., Roth Carlson Kwit Spengler & Mallin, N.Y.C., 1966-68; asst. counsel Celanese Corp., N.Y.C., 1968-71; ptnr., officer Lawrence Ciovacco & Walsh, P.C., Hempstead, N.Y., 1971—; bd. dirs., sec., mem. exec. com. L.I. Forum for Tech., Farmingdale, N.Y., 1980-84. Bd. dirs. Community Program Ctrs. of L.I., Inc., Deer Park, N.Y., 1983—. Republican. Roman Catholic. Club: Nassau (Glen Cove, N.Y.). Securities, General corporate, Real property. Office: Lawrence Ciovacco & Walsh PC 215 Hilton Ave Hempstead NY 11550

CIPOLLA, THOMAS ALPHONSE, lawyer; b. St. Louis, Mar. 14, 1950; s. Alphonse Anthony and Marie (Herminghaus) C. AB magna cum laude, St. Louis U., 1972; JD, So. Meth. U., 1975. Bar: Tex. 1975, Mo. 1975, Ill. 1976, U.S. Dist. Ct. (no. dist.) Tex. 1976, U.S. Supreme Ct., 1980, U.S. Dist. Ct. (ea. dist.) Mo. 1985. Atty. office of regional counsel Fed. Energy Adminstrn., Dallas, 1975-76; asst. corp. counsel Am. Bakeries Co., Chgo., 1976-83; sr. mgr. indsl. relations Anheuser-Busch, Inc., St. Louis, 1983-84; sole practice St. Louis, 1985; of counsel Danis, Reid, Murphy, Garvin, Tobben, Schreiber and Mohan, St. Louis, 1985-86; assoc. Anthony J. Sestric and Assocs., St. Louis, 1986; arbitrator Mo. Arbitration Services, St. Louis, 1985—. Recipient Best Meml. award Phillip C. Jessup Internat. Moot Ct., Dallas, 1974. Mem. ABA, Dallas Bar Assn., Bar Assn. Met. St. Louis, Am. Arbitration Assn. (arbitrator labor panel 1986). Roman Catholic. Labor, Local government, Federal civil litigation. Office: Anthony J Sestric & Assocs 1015 Locust Suite 1110 Saint Louis MO 63101

CIPOLLA, VINCENT CHARLES, lawyer; b. Chgo., Nov. 6, 1943; s. Joseph John and Florence M. (Mistretta) C.; m. Marcella Ruth Ashland, June 11, 1967; children: Joseph A., Raena Lynn. BS in Humanities, Loyola U., Chgo., 1965; JD, John Marshall Law Sch., 1974. Bar: Ill. 1974, U.S. Dist. Ct. (no. dist.) Ill. 1974, U.S. Ct. Appeals (7th cir.) 1978. Assoc. Judge & Schirot, Park Ridge, Ill., 1974-78; ptnr. Judge, Drew, Cipolla & Kurnik, Park Ridge, 1978-82; of counsel Judge, Kurnik & Knight, Park Ridge, 1982-83; ptnr. Kurnik & Cipolla Ltd., Arlington Heights, Ill., 1983—; instr. John Marshall Law Sch., Chgo., 1974-80. Served to capt. U.S. Army, 1965-70, Vietnam. Decorated Bronze Star. Mem. ABA, Ill. Bar Assn., Chgo. Bar Assn., Assn. Trial Lawyers Am., Ill. Trial Lawyers Assn., Am. Judicature Soc., Justinian Soc. Lawyers, Northwest Suburban Bar Assn., Am. Arbitration Assn. (arbitrator 1978—). Roman Catholic. Lodge: Vince Lombardi. Avocation: amateur radio. Civil rights, Personal injury, Federal civil litigation. Home: 1416 S Belmont Arlington Heights IL 60005 Office: Kurnick & Cipolla Ltd 120 W Eastman Arlington Heights IL 60004

CIPOLLONE, ANTHONY DOMINIC, judge; b. N.Y.C., Mar. 15, 1939; s. Domencio and Caterina (Brancazio) C.; m. Eileen Mary Patricia Kelly, Sept. 14, 1963; children: Catherine Mary, Kelly Ann, Mary Rose. BA, CCNY, 1961, MA, 1968; JD, Seton Hall U., 1978. Bar: N.J. 1978, Pa. 1978, U.S. Patent Office 1978, Fla. 1980, N.Y. 1984, D.C. 1985. Chemist Am. Chicle Co., Long Island City, N.Y., 1961-65; research chemist Denver Chem. Mfg. Co., Stamford, Conn., 1965-66; chem. sales engr. GAF Corp., N.Y.C., 1966-68; nat. acct. rep. Stauffer Chem., N.Y.C., 1968-72; sales mgr. Rhone-Poulenc Inc., South Brunswick, N.J., 1972; prosecutor Town of Elmwood Park, N.J., 1981-84, Town of Paramus, N.J., 1983-84; mcpl. ct. judge Town of Paramus (N.J.), N.J., 1985—, Town of Little Ferry (N.J.), 1986—; atty. Twp. Saddle Brook, 1986—; adj. faculty MBA program for chem. and pharm. mgrs., Farleigh Dickinson U. Served to sgt. USMC, 1961-66. Mem. ABA, Bergen Bar Assn., N.J. Bar Assn., Pa. Bar Assn., N.Y. Bar Assn., Fed. Bar Assn., D.C. Bar Assn., Am. Chem. Soc., Mensa. Roman Catholic. General practice, Patent, Trademark and copyright. Home: 115 Lincoln Ave Ridgewood NJ 07450 Office: 49 Market St Saddle Brook NJ 07662

CIRESI, MICHAEL VINCENT, lawyer; b. St. Paul, Apr. 18, 1946; s. Samuel Vincent and Selena Marie (Bloom) C.; m. Nathalia Catherine Faribault, June 21, 1969; children: Dominic, Adam. BBA, St. Thomas Coll.; JD, U. Minn. Bar: Minn. 1971, U.S. Dist. Ct. Minn. 1971, U.S. Ct. Appeals (8th cir.) 1971, U.S. Supreme Ct. 1981, U.S. Ct. Appeals (2d cir.) 1986. Assoc. Robins, Zelle, Larson & Kaplan, Mpls., 1971-78, ptnr., 1978—, also exec. council, 1983—. Mem. ABA, Hennepin County Bar Assn., Ramsey County Bar Assn., Assn. Trial Lawyers Am., Minn. Trial Lawyers Assn. Roman Catholic. Avocation: sports. Federal civil litigation, State civil litigation, Personal injury. Home: 1654 Pinehurst Ave Saint Paul MN 55116 Office: Robins Zelle Larson & Kaplan 900 2d Ave S Minneapolis MN 55402

CIRILLO, RICHARD ALLAN, lawyer; b. N.Y.C., Feb. 7, 1951; s. Paul F. and Edith A. (Flanagan) C.; m. Kathleen V. Rossi, Aug. 23, 1975; children: Benjamin F., Theodore T. BA, Yale U., 1972; JD cum laude, Fordham U., 1975. Bar: N.Y. 1976, U.S. Dist. Ct. (so. dist.) N.Y. 1977, U.S. Ct. Appeals (5th and 10th cirs.) 1978, U.S. Ct. Appeals (2d cir.) 1982, U.S. Supreme Ct. 1983, U.S. Tax Ct. 1984, U.S. Ct. Appeals (9th cir.) 1984. Assoc. Rogers & Wells, N.Y.C., 1975-83, ptnr., 1983—. Contbr. articles to profl. jours. Trustee Colony Found., New Haven, 1982-84. Republican. Presbyterian. Antitrust, Securities, Federal civil litigation. Home: 7 Peter Cooper Rd Apt 2F New York NY 10010 Office: Rogers & Wells 200 Park Ave Suite 5200 New York NY 10166

CISSELL, JAMES CHARLES, lawyer; b. Cleve., May 29, 1940; s. Robert Francis and Helen Cecelia (Freeman) C.; children: Denise, Helen-Marie, Suzanne, James. A.B., Xavier U., 1962; postgrad., Sophia U., Tokyo, summer 1961; J.D., U. Cin., 1966; postgrad. (Ford Found. fellow), Ohio State U., 1973-74; DTL hon. degree, Cin. Tech. Coll., 1979. Bar: Ohio 1966, U.S. Dist. Ct. (so. dist.) Ohio 1967, U.S. Ct. Appeals (6th cir.) 1978, U.S. Supreme Ct. 1980, U.S. Dist. Ct. (ea. dist.) Ky. 1981. Ptnr. Cissell, Smith & Farrish, Cin., 1966-78, 82—; U.S. atty. So. Dist. Ohio, Cin., 1978-82; first v.p. Cin. Bd. Park Commrs., 1973-74; mem. council City of Cin., 1974-78, 85—, vice mayor, 1976-77; mem. Cin. Recreation Commn., 1974, Cin. Planning Commn., 1977; asst. atty. gen. State of Ohio, 1971-74; adj. instr. law Chase Coll. of Law, 1982—. Editor, contbr.: Proving Federal Crimes; author: Federal Criminal Trials. Gen. chmn. Amateur Pub. Links Championship, U.S. Golf Assn., 1987. Mem. ABA, Ohio Bar Assn., Cin. Bar Assn., Fed. Bar Assn., Lawyers Club Cin. General corporate, State civil litigation, Criminal. Home: 3900 Rose Hill Cincinnati OH 45229 Office: Cissell Smith & Farrish 602 Main St 1100 Gwynne Bldg Cincinnati OH 45202

CITRIN, PHILLIP MARSHALL, lawyer; b. Chgo., Nov. 1, 1931; s. Mandel Hirsch and Birdie (Gulman) C.; m. Judith Goldfeder, Dec. 23, 1967 (div. 1984); 1 child, Jeffrey Scott Levin. B.S., Northwestern U., 1953, J.D., 1956. Bar: Ill. 1957. Ptnr. Davis, Jones & Baer, Chgo., 1961-80; sole practice law specializing in domestic relations Chgo., 1980—. Republican candidate for judge circuit ct., Cook County, Ill., 1976, 78. Served with USNR, 1956-58. Fellow Am. Acad. Matrimonial Lawyers (founding); mem. Chgo. Bar Assn. (bd. mgrs. 1974-76, chmn. entertainment com. 1971, co-author ann. satire program 1963—, matrimonial law com. 1963—), Ill. Bar Assn. (mem. assembly of dels. 1972-73, family law com. 1964—), ABA (gavel awards com.), Internat. Soc. Family Law (exec. com. of domestic relations mgmt., adv. com. Cir. Ct. Cook County, chmn. ct. facilities security subcom. 1986—), Phi Delta Phi. Family and matrimonial. Office: 30 N LaSalle St Chicago IL 60602

CLAASSEN, SHARON ELAINE, lawyer; b. Beatrice, Nebr., Jan. 23, 1953; d. Alfred H. and Valois M. (Penner) C.; m. Robert Michael Still, Sept. 10, 1983. BA, U. Nebr., 1975; JD, U. Okla., 1980. Bar: Okla. 1980, Nev. 1982, U.S. Dist. Ct. Nev. 1982, U.S. Ct. Appeals (9th cir.) 1983. Paralegal Legal Services, Ft. Wayne, Ind., 1976-77; intern Legal Services Western Okla., Oklahoma City, 1979-80; atty. Nev. Indian-Rural Legal Services, Carson City, Nev., 1980-84, legal dir., 1984-86; ptnr. Claassen & Olson, Carson City, 1986—. Mng. editor Am. Indian Law Rev., 1978-79, editor-in-chief, 1979-80. Bd. dirs. Advocates to End Domestic Violence, Carson City, 1981—, co-chairperson, 1984—; bd. dirs. Nev. Network Against Domestic Violence, 1986. Recipient John B. Cheadle Meml. award, U. Okla., 1979. Silver Key award law student div. ABA, 1979. Mem. Young Lawyers div. ABA, Nev. Bar Assn., Okla. Bar Assn., 1st Jud. Dist. Bar Assn., Womens Polit. Caucus (coordinator law student div. ABA 1978), Phi Delta Phi. Democrat. Mennonite. Indian law, Family and matrimonial, Federal civil litigation. Home: PO Box 209 Carson City NV 89702 Office: Claassen & Olson 108 W Telegraph PO Box 2101 Carson City NV 89702

CLABAUGH, ELMER EUGENE, JR., lawyer; b. Anaheim, Calif., Sept. 18, 1927; s. Elmer Eugene and Eleanor Margaret (Heitshusen) C.; m. Donna Marie Organ, Dec. 19, 1960 (div.); children—Christopher C., Matthew M. B.B.A. cum laude, Woodbury U.; B.A. Summa Cum Laude, Claremont McKenna Coll., 1958; J.D., Stanford U., 1961. Bar: Calif. 1961, U.S. Dist. Ct. (cen. dist.) Calif., U.S. Ct. Apls. (9th cir.) 1961, U.S. Sup. Ct. 1971. Fgn. service staff U.S. Dept. State, Jerusalem and Tel Aviv, 1951-53; field staff Pub. Adminstrn. Service, El Salvador, Ethiopia, U.S., 1953-57; dep. dist. atty. Ventura County, Calif., 1961-62; practiced in Ventura, Calif., 1962—; mem. Hathaway, Clabaugh, Perrett and Webster and predecessors, 1962-79, Clabaugh & Perloff, Ventura, 1979—; state inheritance tax referee, 1968-78. Bd. dirs. San Antonio Water Conservation Dist., Ventura Community Meml. Hosp., 1964-80; trustee Ojai Unified Sch. Dist., 1974-79; mem. pres.'s adv. council Claremont Mckenna Coll. Served with USCGR, 1944-46, USMCR, 1946-48. Mem. Calif. Bar Assn., Am. Arbitration Assn., Phi Alpha Delta. Republican. Methodist. Clubs: Mason, Shriners. Real property, Contracts commercial, General corporate. Home: 241 Highland Dr Channel Island Harbor CA 93035 Office: 1st Nationwide Savs Bldg 1190 S Victoria Rd Suite 3 05 Ventura CA 93003

CLAGETT, BRICE MCADOO, lawyer, writer; b. Washington, July 6, 1933; s. Brice and Sarah Fleming (McAdoo) C.; m. Virginia Lawrence Parker, Sept. 18, 1965; children—John Brice, Ann Calvert Brooke. A.B. summa cum laude, Princeton U., 1954; postgrad. U. Allahabad (India), 1954-55; J.D. magna cum laude, Harvard U., 1958. Bar: D.C. 1958, U.S. Supreme Ct. 1962. Assoc., Covington & Burling, Washington, 1958-67, ptnr., 1967—; juridical counsellor Cambodian delegation to Internat. Ct. Justice, 1960-62; mem. nat. steering com. U.S. Iran Claimants Com., 1982—. Bd. advisors Nat. Trust for Hist. Preservationm 1878-81; Clagett family com. Chesapeake Bay Found., 1982—; trustee Md. Hist. Trust, 1971-78, chmn., 1972-78, Md. State House Trust, 1972-76 Md. Environ. Trust, 1978—, vice chmn., 1981-85, chmn. 1985—; legal advisor Transition Team U.S. Dept. State, 1980-81; bd. dirs. Chester-Sassafras Found., 1985—. Commdr. Royal Order Cambodia, 1962. Recipient Cert. Disting. Citizens, State of Md., 1978. Mem. ABA, Am. Soc. Internat. Law, Am. Law Inst., Internat. Law Assn., Washington Inst. Fgn. Affairs, Sons Confederate Vets., Phi Beta Kappa. Episcopalian. Clubs: Met., City (Washington); Chevy Chase; Harvard (N.Y.C.); Soc. Cin. Md., Marlborough Hunt (Upper Marlboro, Md.). Co-author: The Valuation of Property in International Law, vol. 4, 1987; bd. editors: Harvard Law Review, 1956-58; contbr. numerous articles to legal, genealogical and hist. jours. Federal civil litigation, Private international, Public international. Home: Holly Hill Friendship MD 20758 also Home: 3331 O St NW Washington DC 20007 Office: Covington & Burling PO Box 7566 1201 Pennsylvania Ave NW Washington DC 20044

CLAGGETT, DANIEL ELLIOT, lawyer; b. St. Louis, Dec. 14, 1951; s. Charles Evans and Blanche (Fischel) C.; m. Marilyn Derby Smith; children: Elizabeth, Ellen, Robert, John. BA, U. Pa., 1974; JD cum laude, St. Louis U., 1978. Bar: Mo. 1979, U.S. Dist. Ct. (ea. and we. dists.) Mo. 1979, Ill. 1982. Assoc. Boyce & Mersman, St. Louis, 1978-80, Sumner, Hanlon, Sumner, MacDonald & Nouss, St. Louis, 1981-84, Brown, James, Rabbitt, P.C., St. Louis, 1981-84, Lewis & Rice, St. Louis, 1984—. Mem. ABA, Mo. Bar Assn., Ill. Bar Assn., St. Louis Met. Bar Assn. Federal civil litigation, State civil litigation. Home: 16 Hillard Rd Glendale MO 63122 Office: Lewis & Rice 611 Olive St Saint Louis MO 63101

CLAIR, IRA S., lawyer, educator; b. Phila., Feb. 27, 1953; s. Herbert O. Clair and Harriet (Brockman) Cooper; m. Rita Lynn Mondelli, June 15, 1975; children—John Michael, Lisa Rafaela, Sara Elizabeth. B.A. in History and Govt., Fairleigh Dickinson U., 1975; J.D., Case Western Res. U., 1978. Bar: Pa. 1978, N.Y. 1979, U.S. Dist. Ct. (so. and ea. dists.) N.Y. 1979, U.S. Ct. Appeals (2d cir.) 1985, U.S. Supreme Ct. 1985. Assoc. Goldstein & Anderman, P.C., N.Y.C., 1979-81, Lauterbach & Lauterbach, Esqs., Yonkers, N.Y., 1981-83; sole practice, Yonkers, 1983—; adj. prof. Pace U., N.Y.C., 1979—, Mercy Coll., Dobbs Ferry, N.Y., 1983—. State dir. The Student Vote, Inc., N.J., 1972. Mennen Corp. scholar, 1975. Mem. Yonkers Lawyers Assn., Westchester County Bar Assn., Phi Omega Epsilon. Club: Creta Columba (Yonkers) (pres. 1984—). Real property, Consumer commercial, Contracts commercial. Home: 161 Elk Ave New Rochelle NY 10804 Office: 20 S Broadway Yonkers NY 10701

CLAIRE, JUDITH SUSAN, lawyer; b. Phila., Dec. 29, 1950; d. Martin and Barbara Gantshar; m. Robert Walter Van Every, June 20, 1976; children: Alison Beth, Benjamin Harris. BA, U. Mass., 1972; JD, SUNY, Buffalo, 1975. Bar: N.Y. 1976, U.S. Dist. Ct. (we. dist.) N.Y. 1978. Health planning counsel N.Y. Govs. Commn. Health Planning, Albany, 1975-76; atty. Mental Health Info. Service, Ogdensburg, N.Y., 1976-78; ptnr. Van Every & Claire, Falconer, N.Y., 1978—. Bd. dirs., v.p. Palace Civic Ctr.; co-chmn. Route 60 Orgn. Named Outstanding Young Woman of Am., 1980. Mem. N.Y. Bar Assn., Jamestown Bar Assn., Jamestown Bus. and Profl. Womens Club (pres. 1983-85), LWV. Democrat. Lodge: Zonta. General practice, State civil litigation, Personal injury. Office: Van Every & Claire 19 N Work St Falconer NY 14733

CLAMAGE, BRETT D., lawyer; b. Chgo., Apr. 26, 1955; s. Herbert Maxwell and Vicki M. (Miles) C.; m. Cynthia Rose Schmidt, Nov. 30, 1980; children: Chad Matthew, Ashley Brooke. BS, U. Ill., 1977, CPA, 1978; JD, Ill. Inst. Tech., 1980. Bar: Ill. 1980, Fla. 1980, U.S. Dist. Ct. (no. dist.) Ill. 1980; CPA, Ill. Pres. C & C Florists Supplies Inc., Chgo.; sole practice Chgo. Mem. ABA, Ill. Bar Assn., Fla. Bar Assn., Am. Inst. CPA's. Corporate taxation, Consumer commercial, Immigration, naturalization, and customs. Office: C & C Florists Supplies Inc 1245 W Washington Blvd Chicago IL 60607

CLANCY, JOSEPH PATRICK, lawyer; b. Washington, July 10, 1931; s. Patrick J. and Esther M. (Crowley) C.; m. Margaret E. Kennedy, May 22, 1965; children—Susan, Kevin, Kathleen, Megan. A.B., U. Notre Dame, 1953, LL.B., 1959; LL.M., Georgetown U., 1962. Bar: D.C. 1960, Md. 1966, U.S. Ct. Appeals (4th cir.) 1970, U.S. Supreme Ct. 1964. Law clk. to chief judge U.S. Dist. Ct. D.C., 1959; assoc. McCarthy & McDermott, Washington, 1960-63; ptnr. Richey & Clancy, Washington, 1964-72, Clancy & Pfeifer, Chevy Chase, Md., 1972—. Trustee Montgomery County (Md.) Heart Assn., Catholic Youth Orgn. Served to capt. USMC, 1954-56. Mem. Am., D.C., Montgomery County bar assns., Jud. Conf. for D.C. Circuit. Republican. Roman Catholic. Clubs: K.C. (Washington), Notre Dame (Washington) (pres.); Kenwood Country. Insurance, Personal injury, General corporate. Home: 5004 Overlea Ct Sumner MD 20816 Office: 5454 Wisconsin Ave Chevy Chase MD 20815

CLANN, MICHAEL KAMMER, lawyer; b. New Orleans, Sept. 3, 1942; s. James Maltby and Mary Phister (Kammer) C.; m. Linda L. Hudson; children—Melissa Gomila, Michael Kammer. B.S., U. So. Miss., 1965; J.D., Tulane U., 1969. Bar: La. 1969, U.S. Dist. Ct. (ea., mid. and we. dists.) La. 1969, Tex. 1976, U.S. Dist. Ct. (so. and ea. dists.) Tex. 1976, U.S. Ct. Appeals (5th cir.). Ptnr. Chaffe, McCall, Phillips, Toler & Sarpy, New Orleans, 1969-74; maritime counsel Zapata Corp., Houston, 1974-76; assoc. Vinson & Elkins, Houston, 1976-78; ptnr. Clann, Bill & Murphy, Houston, 1978—. Mem. speakers com. Houston Livestock Show and Rodeo. Mem. Maritime Law Assn. (coms. transp. of hazardous substance and ship constn. contracts). Republican. Admiralty. Office: 1300 Post Oak Blvd Houston TX 77056

CLAPP, ALFRED C., lawyer; b. N.Y.C., June 8, 1903; s. Alfred C. and Anna (Roth) C.; m. Catharine Shotwell, June 11, 1932; children—Alfred C. Jr., Edward S., John W., Roger S. Ph.B., U. Vt., 1919; J.D., Harvard U., 1923; LL.D., U. Vt., 1957. Bar: N.J. 1929, N.Y. 1931. Dean, Rutgers Law Sch., 1951-53; presiding judge Appelate Div. N.J. Superior Ct., 1953-59; ptnr. Clapp and Eisenberg, Newark, 1959—; counsel to Legislature on drafting N.J. Constn., 1944; chmn. N.J. Real Property, Probate and Trust Sect., 1975; chmn. N.J. Supreme Ct. Civil Practice Com., 1948—, Inst. Continuing Legal Edn., 1932—; draftsman Jud. article N.J. Constn., 1947, 66; mem. N.J. Senate, 1948-53. Mem. Am. Coll. Probate Counsel. Author: Wills and Administration-N.J. (7 vols.), 1982; Post Mortem Tax Planning, 1982. Antitrust, Estate planning, Probate. Office: Clapp and Eisenberg 80 Park Plaza Newark NJ 07102

CLAREMON, GLENDA RUTH, lawyer; b. Beacon, N.Y., Aug. 13, 1951; d. Louis David and Sarah (Smith) Friedman; m. Robert Nolan Claremon, June 23, 1974; children: Michael, Scott, Rachel, Steven. Student, Stern Coll., 1969-70, Hebrew U., Jerusalem, 1970-71; AB, Douglass Coll., 1972; JD, Georgetown U., 1976. Bar: Md. 1976, D.C. 1977, Calif. 1981. Sole practice Silver Spring, Md., 1978-81, Sacramento, 1984-86; assoc. Waits, Britt & Wallace, Sacramento, 1981-84, Weintraub, Genshlea, Hardy, Erich & Brown, Sacramento, 1986—. Pres. Shalom Sch. PTA, Sacramento, 1983-86. Mem. Calif. Bar Assn., D.C. Bar Assn. Avocations: tennis, running, bridge. Personal income taxation, Corporate taxation. Home: 4144 Crondall Dr Sacramento CA 95864 Office: Weintraub Genshlea Hardy Erich & Brown 2535 Capitol Oaks Dr Sacramento CA 95833

CLAREY, ROBERT LOUIS, lawyer; b. Albany, N.Y., Nov. 18, 1942; s. Marvin Louis and Mary Rose (Dolan) C.; m. Barbara Pagano, July 29, 1967; children—Ellen, Brian, Carolyn. B.B.A. in Acctg., Siena Coll., Loudonville, N.Y., 1964; J.D., Villanova U., 1967. Bar: N.Y. 1967, U.S. Dist. Ct. (no. dist.) N.Y. 1967, U.S. Dist. Ct. (ea. and so. dists.) N.Y. 1972, U.S. Ct. Appeals (2d cir.) 1972. Atty. State of N.Y. Comptroller's office, Albany, 1967-68; asst. U.S. atty Eastern Dist. N.Y., Bklyn., 1971-75; chief comml. fraud bur. Nassau County Dist. Atty., Mineola, N.Y., 1975-81; ptnr. firm Reisch, Clarey, Simoni & Gleason, Mineola, 1981—. Author numerous articles on white-collar crime. Bd. dirs. Eastern Property Owners Assn., Garden City, N.Y., 1983—. Served to lt. JAGC, USNR, 1968-71. Mem. N.Y. County Lawyers Guild, Nassau County Bar Assn. Roman Catholic. Club: Atlantic Beach (N.Y.). Criminal, Federal civil litigation, Probate. Home: 24 Avalon Rd Garden City NY 11530 Office: Reisch Clarey & Kent 1501 Franklin Ave Mineola NY 11501

CLARK, ALAN BENJAMIN, lawyer; b. Anniston, Ala., Oct. 14, 1946; s. Edward Wilson and Elsie Louise (Rhodes) C.; m. Anna Margarita Ortiz, Jan. 25, 1967; children; Bradford Scott, Sydney Katherine. BS, U. Ala., 1968; JD, U. Va., 1974; DCLS, Cambridge U., 1975. Bar: Calif. 1975. Assoc. Latham & Watkins, Los Angeles, 1974—. Served to capt. U.S. Army, 1968-71. Mem. ABA, Los Angeles County Bar Assn. Republican. Episcopalian. Club: Jonathon (Los Angeles). Antitrust, Federal civil litigation, State civil litigation. Office: Latham & Watkins 555 S Flower St Los Angeles CA 90071

CLARK, ANJA MARIA, lawyer; b. Vienna, Austria, Mar. 31, 1942; came to U.S., 1966, naturalized, 1982; d. Joseph and Josephine (Mokesch) Rernboeck; m. Robert Eugene Smith, Jan. 26, 1969 (div.); m. Donald Otis Clark, Nov. 5, 1983. B.A. summa cum laude in Sociology, Oglethorpe U., 1974; M.A. cum laude in Sociology, Ga. State U., 1977; J.D., John Marshall Law Sch., 1977. Bar: Ga. 1978, D.C. 1984. Paralegal asst., Atlanta, 1976-78; sole practice, Atlanta, 1978-84; trial atty. oil and gas litigation Fed. Energy Regulatory Commn., Washington, 1985—. Recipient Benjamin Parker Law award Oglethorpe U., 1974. Mem. Ga. Assn. Women Lawyers (sec.-treas. 1981-83), State Bar Ga., ABA, Bus. Council Ga. (internat. subcom. 1981-83), Women's Bar Assn. D.C. (dir. career opportunities 1984-85). Republican. Roman Catholic. FERC practice.

CLARK, BEVERLY ANN, lawyer; b. Davenport, Iowa, Dec. 9, 1944; d. F. Henry and Arlene F. (Meyer) C.; m. Richard Floss; children—Amy and Barry (twins). Student, Mich. State U., 1963-65; B.A., Calif. State U.-Fullerton, 1967; M.S.W., U. Iowa, 1975, J.D., 1980. Bar: Iowa 1980. Probation officer County of San Bernardino, San Bernardino, Calif., 1968, County of Riverside, Riverside, Calif., 1968-69; social worker Skiff Hosp., Newton, Iowa, 1971-73; social worker State of Iowa, Mitchellville, 1973-74, planner, Des Moines, 1976-77, law clk., Des Moines, 1980-81; instr. Des Moines Area Community Coll., Ankeny, Iowa, 1974-75; gen. counsel Pioneer Hi-Bred Internat., Inc., Des Moines, 1981—. Editor: Proceedings: Bicentennial Symposium on New Directions in Juvenile Justice, 1975. Founder Mothers of Twins Club, Newton, Iowa, 1971; co-chmn. Juvenile Justice Symposium, Des Moines, 1974-75; mem. Juvenile Justice Com., Des Moines, 1974-75; mem. Nat. Offender Based State Corrections Info. System Com., Ia. rep., 1976-78; incorporator, dir. Iowa Dance Theatre, Des Moines, 1981; mem. Pesticide User's Adv. Com., Fort Collins, Colo., 1981—. Mem. ABA (subcom. on devel. individual rights in work place, termination-at-will subcom.), Iowa Bar Assn., Polk County Bar Assn., Polk County Women Atty.'s Assn., Am. Trial Lawyers Assn., Am. Assn. Agrl. Lawyers, Am. Corp. Counsel Assn. (litigation subcommittee). Antitrust, General corporate, Environment. Home: Rural Rt 1 Box 80 Baxter IA 50028 Office: Pioneer Hi-Bred Internat Inc 400 Locust St 700 Capital Sq Des Moines IA 50309

CLARK, BRUCE ARLINGTON, JR., lawyer; b. Hopewell, Va., Nov. 17, 1951; s. Bruce Arlington Sr. and Thelma (Givens) C.; m. Catherine Mary Lambert, Aug. 11, 1973; children: Andrew, David, Caryn. BA, Coll. William and Mary, 1973; JD, U. Richmond, 1979. Bar: Va. 1979, U.S. Dist. Ct. (ea. dist.) Va. 1979, U.S. Ct. Appeals (4th cir.) 1979. Law clk. to presiding justice U.S. Bankruptcy Ct., Richmond, Va., 1979-80; assoc. Marks, Stokes & Harrison, Hopewell, 1980-82; sole practice Hopewell, 1982—; asst. commonwealth atty. City of Hopewell, 1986—. Pres. PTO, Hopewell, 1985; chmn. Hopewell chpt. Am. Heart Soc., 1986—; mem. Hopewell chpt. Am. Cancer Soc., 1985—; bd. dirs. Hopewell Youth Soccer League, 1984. Served with U.S. Army, 1973-77. Mem. ABA, Va. Bar Assn., Hopewell Bar Assn. (pres. 1986—), Va. Trial Lawyers Assn., Hopewell-Prince George C. of C. (vice chmn. 1986—, chmn. bd. dirs. 1987—, pres. 1987), Ducks Unltd. (chmn. 1986—). Methodist. Club: Jordan Point Country (Prince George, Va.). Lodge: Moose. Avocations: golf, fishing, youth soccer. Bankruptcy, General practice. Home: 2703 Princess Anne St Hopewell VA 23860 Office: 105 N 2d Ave Hopewell VA 23860

CLARK, CAMERON, lawyer; b. Boston, June 5, 1944; s. Blair Clark and Jesse Holladay (Philbin) James; m. Sheila Macdonald Watson, June 25, 1966; children: Elizabeth Blair, W. Simon C. BA, Harvard U., 1966; JD, U. Minn., 1969. Bar: N.Y. 1969, U.S. Ct. Appeals (2d cir.) 1970, U.S. Dist. Ct. (so. dist.) N.Y. 1971, U.S. Dist. Ct. (ea. dist.) N.Y. 1975, U.S. Supreme Ct. 1978, D.C. 1982. Instr. law U. Chgo., 1969-70; assoc. Paul, Weiss, Rifkind, Wharton & Garrison, N.Y.C., 1970-77, ptnr., 1977—. Mem. Assn. of Bar of City of N.Y., Internat. Bar Assn., Union Internat. des Avocats. Democrat. Federal civil litigation, State civil litigation, Private international. Office: Paul Weiss Rifkind Wharton & Garrison 1285 Ave of the Americas New York NY 10019

CLARK, CAROLYN COCHRAN, lawyer; b. Kansas City, Mo., Oct. 30, 1941; d. John Rogers and Betty Charleton (Holmes) Cochran; m. L. David Clark, Jr., Dec. 29, 1967; children: Gregory David, Timothy Rogers. B.A., U. Mo., 1963; LL.B., Harvard U., 1968. Bar: N.Y. 1968, Fla. 1979. Assoc. Milbank, Tweed, Hadley & McCloy, N.Y.C., 1968-76, ptnr., 1977—. Mem. deferred giving com. regional chmn. major gifts com. Harvard Law Sch. Fund; mem. vis. com. Harvard Law Sch., 1982—; mem. com. on trust and estate gift plans Rockefeller U.; trustee Madison Ave. Presbyn. Ch., 1984-86. Fellow Am. Coll. Probate Counsel, N.Y. Bar Found.; mem. Assn. Bar City N.Y. (chmn. com. on non-profit orgns. 1986—, sec. com. philanthropic orgns. 1976-82, mem. com. trusts, estates and surrogates cts. 1977-80, 85-86), N.Y. State Bar Assn. (com. estate planning, trusts and estates sect. 1978—), ABA (chmn. subcom. income taxation of charitable trusts 1976-78, vice chmn. com. charitable instns.), Am. Law Inst., Practising Law Inst. (lectr.), Harvard Law Sch., Assn. Greater N.Y. (trustee 1978-80, v.p. 1980-81, pres. 1981-82), Nat. Harvard Law Sch. Assn. (exec. com. 1978-80, v.p. 1986—), Soc. Colonial Dames Am. in Mo. Clubs: Wall Street, Cosmopolitan (N.Y.C.); Maidstone (East Hampton, N.Y.). Estate planning, Probate, Estate taxation. Home: 161 E 79th St New York NY 10021 Office: 1 Chase Manhattan Plaza New York NY 10005

CLARK, CHARLES, judge; b. Memphis, Sept. 12, 1925; s. Charles and Anita (Massengill) C. Student, Millsaps Coll., 1943-44, Tulane U., 1944; LL.B., U. Miss., 1948. Bar: Miss. bar 1948. Mem. firm Wells, Thomas & Wells, Jackson, Miss., 1948-61, Cox, Dunn & Clark, Jackson, 1961-69; spl. asst. to atty. gen. State of Miss., 1961-66; judge U.S. Ct. Appeals, 5th Circuit, Jackson, 1969—; chief judge U.S. Ct. Appeals, 5th Circuit, 1981—. Served to lt. USNR, 1943-46, 51-52. Mem. ABA, Miss. Bar Assn., Am. Coll. Trial Lawyers, Jud. Conf. U.S. (chmn. budget com. 1981—). Episcopalian. Federal civil litigation, Criminal, Jurisprudence. Office: US Courthouse PO Drawer 2219 Jackson MS 39205 *

CLARK, CHARLES EDWARD, arbitrator; b. Cleve., Feb. 27, 1921; s. Douglas John and Mae (Egermayer) C.; student Berea Coll., 1939-41, King Coll., 1945; LLB, U. Tex., 1948; m. Nancy Jane Hilt, Mar. 11, 1942; children: Annette S. (Mrs. Paul Gernhardt), Charles Edward, John A., Nancy P., Paul R., Stephen C., David G. Bar: Tex. 1948, Mass. 1956, U.S. Supreme Ct. 1959. sole practice, San Antonio, 1948-55; writer legal articles, editor NACCA Law Jour., Boston, 1955-58; legal asst. to vice chmn., chief voting sect. U.S. Commn. on Civil Rights, Washington, 1958-61; spl. counsel Pres.'s Com. on Equal Employment Opportunity, 1961-65; sr. compliance officer Office Fed. Contract Compliance, 1965-66; regional dir. Equal Employment Opportunity Commn., Kansas City, Mo., 1966-79; arbitrator, 1979—; prof. law, asst. dean St. Mary's U. Sch. Law, 1948-55; lectr. Rockhurst Coll., 1980—. Active Boy Scouts Am. Served with AUS, 1943-44. Mem. Soc. Profls. in Dispute Resolution, State Bar Tex., Nat. Acad. Concillators, Am. GI Forum (D.C. vice chmn. 1962-63), Indsl. Relations Research Assn. (exec. bd. Kansas City 1976—, pres. chpt. 1986), Phi Delta Phi (province pres. 1951-55). Contbr. articles to legal jours. Labor, Workers' compensation, Arbitration. Home and Office: 6418 Washington St Kansas City MO 64113

CLARK, CHARLES EDWARD, lawyer; b. Los Angles, Sept. 10, 1949; s. Charles Albert and Sara (Rodriguez) C. BA, U. So. Calif., 1971; JD, Georgetown U., 1974. Bar: Calif. 1977, Fla. 1979. Sole practice Pasadena, Calif., 1980—; vol atty. Legal Aid Found. Los Angeles, 1979. contbr. articles to profl. jours. Mem. Comision Femenil Mexicana national, Inc., 1980—; bd. dirs. Foothill Apartent Assn. Mem. ABA (sports and entertainment forum 1978-80, real property, probate and trust law sect. 1978—, real estate financing com. 1981—), Calif. Bar Assn., Los Angeles County Bar Assn. (exec. com. real property sect. 1985-86, chmn. gen. real estate law subsect. real property sect. 1985-86), Assn. Real Estate Attys. (edit. bd. real estate securities jour. 1983-85), Real Estate Securities and Syndication Inst., Nat. Lawyers Club, Georgetown U. Alumni, Phi Sigma Alpha. Real property, State civil litigation. Office: 301 E Colorado Blvd #600 Pasadena CA 91101

CLARK, DAVID KEITH, lawyer, real estate developer; b. Lakewood, Ohio, July 28, 1952; s. Don Roger and Patricia Ann (Hunt) C.; m. Beth Moore Malone, June 14, 1980; children: Blaire Megan, Shannon Elizabeth. BArch, U. Ariz., 1977, BSBA, 1977; JD, U. Houston, 1980. Bar: Tex. 1980, U.S. Dist. Ct. (no., so. and ea. dists.) Tex. 1980, U.S. Ct. Appeals (5th cir.) 1980. Law librarian, clk. Baker & Botts & Vinson & Elkins, Houston, 1977-78; assoc. Baker, Brown, Sharman et al, Houston, 1980-82; asst. gen. counsel Cadillac Fairview, Dallas, 1982-85; devel. officer, asst. sec. Cadillac Fairview Urban Devel., Dallas, 1985—; bd. dirs. Don R. Clark M.D., P.C., Roswell, N.Mex., 1972—. Sec. Highlands West Homeowners Assn., Dallas, 1984, pres. 1985. Mem. ABA (real estate, probate and trust sects.), Tex. Bar Assn. (real estate, probate and trust sects.), Houston Bar Assn., Dallas Bar Assn., Dallas Real Estate Lawyers Group, North Dallas C. of C., Farmers Branch C. of C., Phi Delta Phi. Republican. Methodist. Real property, Landlord-tenant, Contracts commercial. Home: 9129 Drumcliffe Dallas TX 75231 Office: Cadillac Fairview Urban Devel 1910 Pacific Suite 400 Dallas TX 75201

CLARK, DAVID LEWIS, lawyer; b. Forest Grove, Oreg., Mar. 11, 1946; s. Virgil James and Lovina (Culbertson) C.; m. Karen Dianne McClelland, July 26, 1968; children: Emily Janis, Bradley David. BS in Sociology, U. Oreg., 1968, JD, 1975. Bar: Oreg. 1975, U.S. Dist. Ct. Oreg. 1976. Ptnr. Nicholson & Clark, Florence, 1978-86; sole practice Florence, 1986—; atty. City of Florence, 1975-81, Port of Siuslaw, Florence, 1975—. Bd. dirs. Western Ln. County Found., Florence, 1982—; justice of peace, Florence, 1983—. Served with USAF, 1968-72. Mem. U. Oreg. Law Sch. Alumni Assn. (bd. dirs. 1982-83). Roman Catholic. Lodges: Rotary (pres., bd. dirs. 1982—), Elks (justice 1976—). Avocations: family activities, reading. General practice, Local government, Judicial administration. Office: PO Box 146 Florence OR 97439

CLARK, DONALD OTIS, lawyer; b. Charlotte, N.C., May 30, 1934; s. Erwin and Ruby Lee (Church) C.; m. Jo Ann Hager, June 15, 1957 (div. 1980); children: Deborah Elise, Stephen Merritt; m. Anja Maria Smith, Nov. 5, 1983. A.B., U. S.C., 1956, J.D. cum laude, 1963; M.A., U. Ill., 1957. Bar: S.C. 1963, Ga. 1964. Practice law Atlanta, 1963-83; mem. Candler, Cox, McClain & Andrews, 1968-70, McClain, Mellen, Bowling & Hickman, 1970-75; ptnr. King & Spalding, 1975-78; sr. ptnr. Hurt, Richardson, Garner, Todd & Cadenhead, 1978-83; ptnr. Bishop, Liberman, Cook, Purcell & Reynolds,, Washington, 1983-86, Kaplan Russin & Vecchi, Washington, 1986—; mem. dist. export council U.S. Dept Commerce, 1974—; adj. prof. law Emory U., 1970—, U.S.C., 1974; lectr. Ga. State U., 1972; lectr. numerous internat. trade seminars and workshops. Author: German govt. study on doing bus. in Southeastern U.S., 1974; editor-in-chief: S.C. Law Rev., 1963; contbr. articles to profl. jours. Served to capt. USAF, 1957-60. Decorated knight Order St. John of Jerusalem; knight and minister of justice Order of New Aragon, Sungrye medal Korea; recipient Nat. Leadership medal Air Force Assn., 1956, Coll. award Am. Legion, Outstanding Sr. award U. S.C., 1956, hon. consul Republic of Korea, 1972—. Mem. Atlanta Bar Assn., ABA, S.C. Bar Assn., Ga. Bar Assn., Lawyers Club Atlanta, Am. Judicature Soc., Am. Soc. Internat. Law, Atlanta C. of C., Ga. C. of C. (exec. com. Internat. Councils), Inst. Internat. Edn. (chmn. Southeastern regional adv. bd. 1974—, nat. trustee), So. Consortium Internat. Edn. Inc. (dir.), Wig & Robe, Sigma Chi (pres. 1956 Province Balfour award), Omicron Delta Kappa, Kappa Sigma Kappa, Phi Delta Phi (pres. 1963 Province Grad. of Yr. award). Private international, Public international, Corporate taxation. Home: 3010 Ellicott St NW Washington DC Office: Kaplan Russin & Vecchi 1215 17th St NW Washington DC 20036

CLARK, DWIGHT WILLIAM, public administrator, lawyer; b. Gothenburg, Nebr., Sept. 24, 1944; s. William Elwood Clark and Christina Antina Koster; m. Sharon Louise Anderson, Aug. 31, 1968; children: Andrea Christine, Nathan William. BBA, U. Nebr., 1967; JD, Calif. Western Law Sch., 1974; MPA, U. So. Calif., 1976. Bar: Calif. 1975; cert. specialist in jud. adminstrn. Adminstrv. intern U.S. Probation Office, Los Angeles, 1975-76; exec. asst. San Francisco Mcpl. Ct., 1976-84, clk.-adminstr., 1984—; moot ct. judge U. San Francisco Sch. Anthropology, 1977; dir. Corp. Bus. Brokers No. Calif., Inc.; user rep. EDP priority com. City and County San Francisco, 1979, electronic info. steering com., 1983—; assoc. faculty Nat. Judges Coll., Reno, 1985—; lectr. in law and computer related fields. Mem. adv. bd. Coll. Bus. Adminstrn. U. Nebr., Lincoln, 1966, 67, chmn. placement bd. program, 1967; chmn. honor code revision com. Calif. Western Law Sch., San Diego, 1968, 69; trustee San Mateo Elem. Sch. Dist. (Calif.), 1983—; San Mateo PTA. Recipient Am. Jurisprudence Scholastic award, 1969, Tech. Achievement award Fin., Pub. Tech., Inc., Washington, 1984, Hon. Service award PTA, 1986. Mem. ABA, Am. Judicature Soc., Calif. State Bar, Calif. Mcpl. Ct. Clks. Assn., San Mateo County Bar Assn., Nat. Assn. Ct. Mgrs., Western Internat. Law Soc. (founding mem.), Calif. Western Law Sch. Alumni Club, U. So. Calif. Alumni Club, Phi Delta Phi, Delta Sigma Pi (life, sec. 1965, v.p. 1966, pres. 1967). Democrat. Lutheran. Club: Lawyers. Judicial administration, Local government. Home: 312 Cupertino Way San Mateo CA 94403 Office: San Francisco Mcpl Ct City Hall Room 301 San Francisco CA 94102

CLARK, EDWARD AUBREY, lawyer, banker, former ambassador; b. San Augustine, Tex., July 15, 1906; s. John David and Leila (Downs) C.; m. Anne Metcalfe, Dec. 28, 1927; 1 child, Leila Clark Wynn. Student Southwestern U., Tulane U.; J.D., U. Tex.; LL.D., Southwestern U.; D. Sc. (hon.) Cleary Coll., Ypsilanti, Mich. Bar: Tex. 1928, U.S. Dist. Ct. (no., so., ea. and we. dists.) Tex., U.S. Ct. Appeals (5th cir.) U.S. Supreme Ct. Sr. Ptnr. Clark, Thomas, Winter & Newton, Austin; chmn. First Nat. Bank, San Augustine; sr. chmn. bd. Tex. Commerce Bank-Austin; dir. Tex. Commerce Bank and Tec. Commerce Bancshares, Inc., Houston, Employers Nat. Life and Employers Casualty Cos., Dallas, San Benito Bank & Trust Tex.; asst. atty. gen. of Tex., 1932-35; asst. to Gov. Jimmy Allred, 1935-37; sec. of State of Tex., 1937-39; U.S. Ambassador to Australia, 1965-68; fed. commr. to HemisFair, San Antonio, 1968; exec. dir. Inter-Am. Devel. Bank, Washington, 1968-69. Served to capt. AUS, 1942. Bd. dirs. Lady Bird Endowment Fund, Friends of LBJ Library, Austin; U. Tex. Law Sch. Found., Austin; trustee Southwestern U., Georgetown; bd. regents U. Tex. System, Austin, 1973-79. Fellow Am. Bar Assn. Found., Southwestern Legal Found.; mem. Tex. Philos. Soc., Tex. State Hist. Assn., Sons of the Republic of Tex., SAR, Knights of San Jacinto, Phi Delta Phi. Democrat. Episcopalian. Clubs: Capital, Citadel, Headliners (Austin). General practice. Office: Tex Commerce Bank Bldg 12th Floor Austin TX 78701 Office: PO Box 1148 Austin TX 78767

CLARK, ELIAS, law educator; b. New Haven, Aug. 19, 1921. B.A., Yale U., 1943, LL.B., 1947, M.A., 1957. Bar: N.Y. 1948, Conn. 1950. Assoc. Cleary, Gottlieb, Friendly & Cox, N.Y.C., 1947-49; mem. faculty Law Sch., Yale U., New Haven, 1949—, prof., 1958—, Lafayette S. Foster prof., 1968—; master Stillman Coll., 1962-81. Co-author: Gratuitous Transfers, 1977, Cases and Materials on Federal Estate and Gift Taxation, 1984; contbr. articles to legal jours. Bd. dirs. Mental Health Conn., 1957-67; bd. dirs. New Haven Found., 1969-76. Mem. Conn. Bar Assn. (Disting. Pub. Service 1959). Legal education. Home: 155 Bradley St New Haven CT 06511 Office: Yale U Law Sch New Haven CT 06520 *

CLARK, ERIC ODEN, lawyer; b. St. Louis, Nov. 2, 1955; s. Euell F. Jr. and Kathryn (Clayborne) C.; m. Lisa V. Porter, Oct. 26, 1985. BA, Valparaiso U., 1978, JD, 1981. Bar: Ind. 1982, U.S. Tax Ct. 1983. Sole practice Gary, Ind., 1982—; atty. Lake County Pub. Defender, Crown Point, Ind., 1983—, Hammond (Ind.) Housing Authority, 1985—. Treas. Luth. Family Services, Merrillville, Ind., 1985—. Mem. ABA, Nat. Assoc. Criminal Def. Lawyers, Thurgood Marshall Law Assn. Republican. Personal injury, Criminal, Labor. Office: 4746 Broadway Gary IN 46408

CLARK, H. SOL, lawyer; b. Savannah, Ga., Dec. 29, 1906; s. Sam and Ella (Raskin) C.; m. Matilda Shapiro, May 14, 1933; children: Fred Stephen, Janet (dec.). A.B., Cornell U., 1928, LL.B., 1930. Bar: Ga. 1929. Practice law Savannah, 1930-72; mem. Brannen Clark & Hester, 1945-70, Brannen & Clark, 1970-72; judge Ct. Appeals Ga., Atlanta, 1972-77; mem. firm Lee & Clark, 1977—; asst. city atty. Savannah, 1944-47. Mem. Ga. Indsl. Loan Adv. Bd., 1955-59; founder Savannah Legal Aid Office, 1946; mem. Chatham County Civil Service Bd., 1968-70, Ga. State Jud. Council, 1974-75; founder Authors Ct., Ga. State Bar. Compiler: Ga. Masonic Code, 1954; co-author: Settlements-Law and Strategies. Trustee Telfair Art Acad., 1959-62, v.p., 1983-84. Recipient Reginald Heber Smith Legal Aid award, 1961, Arthur von Briesen Legal Aid award, 1970, plaque Harvard Law Sch. Assn. Ga., 1971; Ga. State Bar created H. Sol Clark award in his honor, 1983. Fellow Am. Bar Found. (50 Yr. award 1982), Internat. Acad. Trial Lawyers (dean 1969-70, dir. 1967-71, 78-82), Am. Coll. Probate Counsel, Internat. Soc. Barristers; mem. Am. Judicature Soc. (dir. 1960-64), Savannah Bar Assn. (pres. 1952), Nat. Legal Aid Assn. (dir. 1960-64), Scribes (pres. 1979). Jewish. Club: Mason (33 deg.). Home: PO Box 8205 Savannah GA 31412

CLARK, HAROLD ROBINSON, judge (retired); b. Jacksonville, Fla., Sept. 10, 1918; s. Edwin Thomas and Rose Elizabeth (Woodward) C.; m. Vivian E. Armington, Nov. 26, 1947; children—Harold Robinson, Christine Armington. J.D., Stetson U., 1942. Bar: Fla. 1942. Ptnr. firm, Jacksonville, 1942-71; judge County Judges Ct., Duval County, 1971-72, 4th Jud. Cir. Ct. Fla., Jacksonville, 1972—. Chmn., Fla. Conf. Cir. Judges, 1977-78. Trustee, People to People Internat., 1980—; vice chmn., 1983, chmn. trustees, 1986, pres., 1987—; bd. dirs. Jacksonville Sister Cities Assn., 1982—. Served with USNR, World War II. Recipient Distinguished Eagle Scout award, 1975, William Treat award, Nat. Coll. Probate Judges, 1980. Jud. fellow Am. Coll. Probate Counsel; mem. Nat. Coll. Probate Judges (dir. 1974-77), ABA, Jacksonville Bar Assn. (past pres.), Fla. Bar (dir. 1959-64), Am. Judicature Soc., Stetson U. Alumni Assn. (pres. 1973-74). Club: Rotary. Jurisprudence, Probate. Home: 1213 Mapleton Rd Jacksonville FL 32207

CLARK, HERMAN, lawyer, corporate counsel; b. Walland, Tenn., May 24, 1942; s. David Edgar and Helen Lee (Caincross) C.; m. Shirlee Sharber, Aug. 24, 1964 (div. Mar. 1972); m. Charlotte Jean Chamness, Dec. 23, 1972; children: David, Dawn, Daniel, Daryl & Dana. BS, Brenau Coll., 1973; JD, Woodrow Wilson Coll. Law, 1978. Bar: Ga. 1979, U.S. Dist. Ct. (no. dist.) Ga. 1979, U.S. Ct. Appeals (5th and 11th cirs.) 1979, U.S. Tax Ct. 1982, U.S. Ct. Claims 1983, U.S. Supreme Ct. 1983. Dir. constrn. and engrng. First Am. (Days Inn), Atlanta, 1972-75; chief constrn. specifications PB/T (MARTA), Atlanta, 1976-78; contract adminstr. Stone & Webster, Atlanta, 1978-80; corp. counsel Law Engrng. Testing Co., Atlanta, 1980—. Contbr. articles to profl. jours. Scouter Boy Scouts Am., Atlanta, 1980-84, scoutmaster, Acworth, Ga., 1984—; bd. dirs. Kennesaw (Ga.) Baseball Assn., 1981-83. Served to lt. col. USAF Air N.G., 1963—. Named to Hon. Order Ky. Cols., Gov. of Ky., 1970; recipient Deans award Woodrow Wilson Coll. Law, Atlanta, 1978, Contbn. to Engring. Profession award Assn. Soil & Found. Engrs., Washington, 1983. Mem. ABA, State Bar Ga., Nat. Contract Mgmt. Assn., Constrn. Specifications Inst., Cobb County Bar Assn., Sigma Delta Kappa. Republican. Baptist. Lodge: Kiwanis. General corporate, Construction, Environment. Home: 3708 Summit Dr Acworth GA 30101 Office: Law Engring Testing Co PO Box 888013 Atlanta GA 30356-0013

CLARK, JAMES FRANCIS, lawyer; b. Madison, Wis., Aug. 28, 1920; s. Richard Francis and Adele Rose (Garvoille) C.; m. Gloria J. Sardeson, Oct. 7, 1944; children: James Richard, John Thomas, Jeffrey Paul, Cynthia Ann. Student, Platteville (Wis.) Tchrs. Coll., 1938-41; LLB, U. Wis., 1947. Bar: Wis. 1947, U.S. Dist.Ct. (we. dist.) Wis. 1950, U.S. Dist. Ct. (ea. dist.) Wis. 1969, U.S. Ct. Appeals (7th cir.) 1969, U.S. Supreme Ct. 1975. Assoc. Els, Christianson, Esch, Hart & Clark and predecessor firms, Madison, 1948-53; ptnr. Ela, Christianson, Esch, Hart & Clark and predecessor firms, Madison, 1953-78, Isaksen, Lathrop, Esch, Hart & Clark, Madison, 1978—; lectr., prof. gen. practice course U. Wis., 1960—. Contbr. numerous legal articles to sch. publs. Gen. counsel Wis. Assn. Sch. Bds., 1961—; bd. dirs. Am. Cancer Soc., Columbia County, Wis., 1967—, Nat. Assn. Sch. Bds., 1982-83. Served with USAAF, 1943-45. Mem. ABA, Wis. Bar Assn. (bd. govs. 1967-68, chmn. real estate trust and probat sect. 1983-85, past pres. Columbia County), Dane County Bar Assn., Nat. Council Sch. Attys. (bd. dirs. 1976-80, chmn. 1982-83), Wis. Sch. Attys. Assn. (recognition of service 1981), Order of Coif, Phi Alpha Delta, Poynette C. of C., Madison C. of C. Roman Catholic. Lodges: KC, Lions, Elks. Local government, Probate. Home: 208 Old Settlers Trail Poynette WI 53955 Office: Isaksen Lathrop Esch Hart & Clark 122 W Washington Ave Madison WI 53703

CLARK, JOHN FOSTER, lawyer; b. Charlotte, N.C., Mar. 2, 1950; s. Robert Foster and Ellen Jane (Ziglar) C.; m. Elizabeth Jayne Currie, June 21, 1975. BS in Indls. Mgmt., Ga. Inst. Tech., 1972; JD, U. Ga., 1975. Bar: Ala. 1975, Ga. 1975, U.S. Dist. Ct. (no. dist.) Ala. 1975. Ptnr. Balch & Bingham, Birmingham, Ala., 1975—; bond counsel Ala. Housing Fin. Authority, Montgomery, 1983—, Ala. Hwy. Authority, Montgomery,

1984—, Ala. Pub. Sch. and Coll. Authority, Montgomery, 1985—, Ala. Supreme Ct., Montgomery, 1985—. Articles editor U. Ga. Law Rev., 1974-75. Lawyers fund raising chmn. United Way, Birmingham, 1983; bd. dirs. Ala. Kidney Found., Birmingham, 1976-79. Mem. ABA, Ga. Bar Assn., Ala. Bar Assn., Birmingham Bar Assn., Nat. Assn. Bond Lawyers, Govt. Fin. Officers Assn. Ala. Presbyterian. Club: Shoal Creek (Birmingham). Avocations: golf, tennis. Municipal bonds, Banking, General corporate. Home: 834B Dunnavant Valley Rd Leeds AL 35094 Office: Balch & Bingham 700 Financial Ctr Birmingham AL 35203

CLARK, JOHN HOLLEY, III, lawyer; b. N.Y.C., May 31, 1918; s. John Holley, Jr. and Mary (Angus) C.; m. Eleanor Jackson, June 4, 1964; children—Benjamin Hayden, Christopher Angus. B.A. with high honors, Princeton U., 1939; J.D., Columbia U., 1942; M.A., NYU, 1965. Bar: N.Y. 1942, U.S. Dist. Ct. (so. dist.) N.Y. 1949, U.S. Ct. Appeals (2d cir.) 1952, U.S. Ct. Mil. Appeals 1986. Assoc. Cahill, Gordon, Reindel & Ohl, N.Y.C., 1946-54; atty. Antitrust div. U.S. Dept. Justice, N.Y.C., 1954—. Vice pres. N.Y. Young Republican Club, 1953-54; mem. sch. com. Cathedral Ch. St. John the Divine, N.Y.C., 1979-81. Mem. NYU Grad Sch. Arts & Sci. Alumni Assn. (pres. 1983-85), NYU Alumni Council, Assn. Bar City N.Y., Am. Sociol. Assn., Am. Anthropol. Assn., Law and Soc. Assn. Democrat. Episcopalian. Antitrust. Home: 375 Riverside Dr Apt 9C New York NY 10025 Office: US Dept Justice Antitrust div 26 Federal Plaza Room 3630 New York NY 10278

CLARK, JOHN SCOTT, lawyer; b. Bad Axe, Mich., Jan. 27, 1912; s. George M. and Eva (Scott) C.; m. Sally S. Clark, Sept. 8, 1934. BA, U. Mich., 1933, LLB, 1936. Bar: Mich. 1936. Sole practice Petoskey, Mich., 1936—; chmn. adv. council Nat. Ctr. for State Cts., 1977-78, vice chmn. independence support fund com., 1980-84; chmn. Coordinating Council Nat. Ct. Orgns., 1978-79; bd. dirs. Foremost Corp. Am., Grand Rapids, Mich., Detroit & Mackinac Ry., Tawas City, Mich. Pres. Little Traverse Hosp., Petoskey, 1970-77, Greenwood Cemetery, Petoskey, 1953, Mich. Rep. Assembly, 1972-74; chmn. State Officers Compensation Com., 1978; chmn. bd. dirs. No. Mich. Hosps., Petoskey, 1977-78. Served to lt. USNR, 1941-45, PTO. Mem. ABA (ho. dels. 1968-75), Mich. Bar Assn. (pres. 1965-66), Am. Judicature Soc. (pres. 1973-75, Herbert Harley award 1984), Mich. Assn. Professions (most disting. award 1974). Republican. Methodist. Club: Little Harbor (Harbor Springs, Mich.). General corporate, Estate planning, Probate. Home: 1128 Valley View Petoskey MI 49770 Office: 1st Nat Bank Bldg Petoskey MI 49770

CLARK, JOHN STEVEN, state attorney general; b. Leachville, Ark., Mar. 21, 1947; s. John Willis and Elizabeth Jean (Bearden) C.; m. Kathryn Marie Fairchild, Dec. 20, 1968; children—Donna Marie, Anna Kathryn. B.A. in Polit. Sci, Ark. State U., 1968; J.D., U. Ark., 1971. Bar: Ark. 1971, U.S. Supreme Ct. 1978. Assoc. firm Sharp & Sharp, Brinkley, Ark., 1971-73; asst. prof., asst. dean of Sch. of Law, U. Ark., Fayetteville, 1973-76; exec. sec. to Gov. David Pryor, State of Ark., 1976-78; partner firm Clark & Nichols, Little Rock, 1978-79; atty. gen. State of Ark., Little Rock, from 1979. State chmn. Multiple Sclerosis campaign, 1979—. Recipient Employer of Year award Ark. Council Blind, 1979; named Ark. Outstanding Young Man, 1979. Mem. Nat. Assn. Attys. Gen., Ark. Bar Assn., Am. Bar Assn. Democrat. Methodist. Local government. Office: Atty Gens Office 201 E Markham St Little Rock AR 72201

CLARK, JOHN W., JR., lawyer; b. Dallas, Nov. 7, 1938; s. John W. and Grace L. (Hobgood) C.; m. Anna B. Clark, Feb. 16, 1962; children: Catherine, Sue. Student Washington and Lee U.; B.A., J.D., So. Meth. U. Bar: Tex. 1963. Ptnr., Johnson, Blakeley, Johnson, Smith & Clark, Dallas. Mem. State Bar Assn. Tex., Dallas Bar Assn., ABA. Club: Royal Bars Country. (Dallas). Office: 2100 Republic Bank Bldg Dallas TX 75201 *

CLARK, JULIE ANN, lawyer; b. Miami, Fla.; d. Chester W. and Viola (Bernard) C. BA, Western State Coll., 1961; JD, U. Ark., 1975. Assoc. Nangle & Clark, Anchorage, 1975-82; sole practice Anchorage, 1982—. Mem. Alaska Acad. Trial Lawyers. Construction, Personal injury, General practice. Home and Office: 1111 Oceanview Anchorage AK 99515-3906

CLARK, LARRY ALLEN, trust analyst; b. Kansas City, Mo., Jan. 12, 1948; s. Ralph Eugene and Helen Louise (Osenburg) C.; m. Judy Dawn Jennings, Jan. 1, 1978. BA in Polit. Sci., U. Kans., 1970, MBA, JD, 1974. Bar: Kans. 1974. Sr. trust examiner Fed. Res. Bank, Kansas City, 1975-78; sr. trust analyst Fed. Res. Bd., Washington, 1978—. Mem. ABA, Kans. Bar Assn. Democrat. Avocations: hiking, skiing. Administrative and regulatory, Banking. Home: 2524 Brofferton Ct Herndon VA 22071 Office: Fed Res Bd 20th & C NW Washington DC 20551

CLARK, LYNNE NUBER, lawyer; b. Wilmington, Del., Aug. 26, 1953; d. Donald Franklin and Elizabeth (Persing) Nuber; m. Daniel Martin Clark, Oct. 23, 1982; 1 child, Daniel M. Jr. BA, Grinnell (Iowa) Coll., 1975; JD, U. Toledo, 1978; MLT, Georgetown U., 1985. Bar: D.C. 1981, Va. 1982, U.S. Tax Ct. 1982. Assoc. Katz, From & Slan, Kensington, Md., 1982; mktg. counsel Acacia Mut. Life Ins., Washington, 1983-85; assoc. Clary, Lawrence, Lickstein & Moore, Springfield, Va., 1985—. Research editor U. Toledo Law Rev. 1978. Mem. Women's Bar Assn. of D.C., AAUW (community rep. 1985). Corporate taxation, Probate, Personal income taxation. Home: 8113 Winter Blue Ct Springfield VA 22153 Office: Clary Lawrence Lickstein & Moore 6501 Loisdale Ct Springfield VA 22150

CLARK, MARK LEE, lawyer; b. Muskegon, Mich., July 13, 1953; s. Alva Lee and Esther Luella (Bellinger) C.; m. Jane Ellen Lyons, Sept. 3, 1983; 1 child, Zachary. BA with high honors, Mich. State U., 1975; JD with honors, Wayne State U., 1978. Bar: Mich. 1978, U.S. Dist. Ct. (ea. dist.) Mich. 1982. Assoc. McLean & Mijak, Romeo, Mich., 1978-82; ptnr. McLean, Mijak & Clark, Romeo, 1982—; mcpl. atty. Village of Romeo, 1985—. Pres. bd. trustees, bd. dirs. Romeo Dist. Library, 1981-85. Mem. Mich. Bar Assn., Macomb County Bar Assn. Lodge: Rotary. Avocations: snow skiing, softball, golf. General practice, State civil litigation, Local government. Home: 268 W St Clair St Romeo MI 48065 Office: McLean Mijak & Clark 137 W St Clair St Romeo MI 48065

CLARK, MERLYN WESLEY, lawyer; b. Grand Forks, British Columbia, Can., Oct. 27, 1937; came to U.S., 1938; s. Robert Wesley and Lilia Ann (Frechette) C.; m. Sandra Sue Bolan, Mar. 15, 1969. JD, U. Idaho, 1964. Bar: Idaho 1964, U.S. Dist. Ct. Idaho 1964. Assoc. Blake, Givens & Feeney, Lewiston, Idaho, 1964-66; ptnr. Blake, Givens, Feeney & Clark, Lewiston, 1966-68; sole practice 1968-74, 78-79; ptnr. Clark, Curtin & Creason, Lewiston, 1974-78, Hawley, Troxell, Ennis & Hawley, Boise, Idaho, 1979—; pros. atty. Nez Perce County, Lewiston, 1974-77; mem. Idaho Supreme Ct. Civil Rules Adv. com., Boise, 1975—86; mem. Idaho Supreme Ct. Evidence Rules com., Boise, 1986—. Mem. ABA, Idaho Bar Assn. (commr. 1977-79, cert. appreciation 1984), Boise Bar Assn., Assn. Trial Lawyers Am., Idaho Assn. Def. Counsel, Idaho Law Found (pres. 1984-86). Federal civil litigation, State civil litigation, Real property. Home: 2931 Raindrop Dr Boise ID 83706 Office: Hawley Troxell Ennis & Hawley #1 Capital Ctr Boise ID 83701

CLARK, NATALIE LODER, law educator; b. Potsdam, N.Y., Mar. 15, 1941; d. Richard Ivan and Jeanne Harnish (Loder) C.; m. David G. Gillette, Apr. 28, 1962 (div. Jan. 1969); children: Richard, Rosemary, Amy; m. E. Blythe Stason, May 11, 1974 (div. June 1986). BA, SUNY, Albany, 1963; JD, William and Mary Coll., 1972; LLM, Columbia U., 1973. Bar: Ill. 1979. Tchr. Colonie (N.Y.) Pub. Schs., 1964-65, Schenectady (N.Y.) Pub. Schs., 1965-66; asst. prof. law U. Cin., 1973-75; assoc. prof. Lewis U., Glen Ellyn, Ill., 1975-79; prof. Northern Ill. U., DeKalb, 1979—; legal advisor Family Service, Glen Ellyn, 1978-79. Pres. bd. dirs. Safe Passage, DeKalb, 1983-86; Libertarian atty. gen. candidate, Ill., 1982, 86; soprano Laudate Dominum, Wheaton, Ill., 1979-82, DeKalb Festival Chorus, 1982—; mem. St. Peter's Episcopal Ch., Sycamore, Ill., 1982—. Mem. Phi Delta Phi, Kappa Delta Epsilon. Avocations: singing, playing guitar, writing poetry, studying theology. Family and matrimonial, Legal education. Home: 653 N 11th St DeKalb IL 60115 Office: No Ill U Coll Law DeKalb IL 60115

CLARK, PAT ENGLISH, lawyer; b. Austin, Tex., Feb. 26, 1940; s. Pat Wheeler and Jennie Bell (Lagrone) C.; m. Maren Louise Westerfeldt, June 1, 1961; 1 child, Susan Louise. BA, U. Tex., JD. Bar: Tex. 1963, U.S. Ct. Mil. Appeals 1964, U.S. Dist. Ct. (so. and no. dists.) Tex. Staff atty. Phillips Petroleum Co., Houston, 1967-69; atty. Amoco Production Co., Houston, 1969-75; ptnr. Vinson & Elkins, Houston, 1975—. Served to capt. JAGC, U.S. Army, 1964-67. Democrat. Methodist. Oil and gas leasing, Real property. Office: Vinson & Elkins 3300 First City Tower 1001 Fannin Houston TX 77002-6760

CLARK, RAMSEY, lawyer; b. Dallas, Dec. 18, 1927; s. Tom C. and Mary (Ramsey) C.; m. Georgia Welch, Apr. 16, 1949; children: Ronda Kathleen, Thomas Campbell. B.A., U. Tex., 1949; A.M., J.D., U. Chgo., 1950. Bar: Tex. 1951, U.S. Supreme Ct. 1956, D.C. 1969, N.Y. 1970. Practiced law Dallas, 1951-61, N.Y.C., 1970—; asst. atty. gen. U.S. Dept. Justice, 1961-65, dep. atty. gen., 1965-67, atty. gen. U.S., 1967-69; Adj. prof. Howard U., 1969-72, Bklyn. Law Sch., 1973-81. Author: Crime in America. Served with USMCR, 1945-46. Civil rights, Criminal, General practice. Home: 37 W 12th St New York NY 10011 Office: 36 E 12th St 6th Floor New York NY 10003

CLARK, RICHARD EDWARD, lawyer; b. Geneva, N.Y., Jan. 4, 1947; s. Henry F. and Leona (Naughton) C.; m. Sherilyn Johns, Dec. 30, 1972; children: Robert F., Jennifer P. AB summa cum laude, Syracuse U., 1972; JD, Union U., Albany, N.Y., 1976. Bar: N.Y. 1977, U.S. Dist. Ct. (no. dist.) N.Y. 1977, Ariz. 1983, U.S. Dist. Ct. Ariz. 1983. Assoc. Carey, LaRocque & Piasecki, Malone, N.Y., 1977-78, ptnr., 1978-83; sole practice Scottsdale, Ariz., 1983—. Mem. council Our Lady Perpetual Help Ch., Scottsdale, 1985—. Served with USAF, 1967-71, Vietnam. Mem. ABA, N.Y. State Bar Assn., Ariz. Bar Assn., Scottsdale Bar Assn., Am. Arbitration Assn. (assocs. comml. panel), Comml. Law League, Scottsdale C. of C., Phi Kappa Phi. Democrat. Roman Catholic. Lodge: KC (chancellor 1985—). Probate, Personal injury, Commercial and mediation. Office: 6040 E Thomas Rd Scottsdale AZ 85251

CLARK, ROBERT CHARLES, lawyer, educator; b. New Orleans, Feb. 26, 1944; s. William Vernon and Edwina Ellen (Nuessly) C.; m. Kathleen Margaret Tighe, June 1, 1968; children—Alexander Ian, Matthew Tighe. B.A., Maryknoll Sem., 1966; Ph.D., Columbia U., 1971; J.D., Harvard U., 1972. Bar: Mass. bar 1972. Asso. firm Ropes & Gray, Boston, 1972-74; asst. prof. Yale U. Law Sch., New Haven, 1974-76; asso. prof. Yale U. Law Sch., 1976-77, prof., 1977-78; prof. law Harvard U., Cambridge, Mass., 1978—. Contbr. articles to profl. jours. Mem. Am. Bar Assn. Legal education. Office: Harvard Law Sch Cambridge MA 02138

CLARK, ROBERT FRANCIS, lawyer; b. Rochester, N.Y., Sept. 25, 1938; s. Arthur Harry and Cora Ann (Rossiter) C.; m. Katherine Marie Poncauage, Oct. 10, 1964 (dec. 1986); children: Katherine Ann, Susan Elizabeth, David Michael. BA, Bklyn. Coll., 1968; JD, Boston Coll., 1971. Bar: N.Y. 1972. Assoc. Fix., Spindleman, Turk & Himeline, Rochester, 1971-73; counsel Monroe County Dept. Social Services, Rochester, 1973-79; asst. dist. atty. Monroe County Dist. Atty.'s Office, Rochester, 1979—; guest lectr. Geneseo (N.Y.) State Coll., 1975-77; cons. family ct. practice and procedure Cornell U., Ithica, N.Y., 1980—. Author: Child Sexual Abuse, 1984. Trainer against child abuse N.Y. State Social Services, Albany, 1981—; cons. task force on sexual abuse N.Y. State Commr. of Social Services, Albany, 1981-82; bd. dirs. Sch. of Holy Childhood, Rochester, 1981—; dir. Parent Anoymous N.Y. State Resource Office, Rochester, 1983—. Mem. ABA (criminal law com., family law com.), N.Y. State Bar Assn. (criminal law com., family law com.), Monroe County Bar Assn. (criminal law com., juvenile justice com.), Nat. Assn. Counsel for Children, N.Y. State Dist. Atty.'s Assn. Criminal, Family and matrimonial, Juvenile. Office: 201 Hall of Justice Exchange Blvd Rochester NY 14614

CLARK, ROGER ARTHUR, lawyer; b. Chgo., May 23, 1932; s. Frank Arthur and Alice Rita (Mahoney) C.; m. Kate Dawson, June 24, 1961; children: Alice Anne, John, Michael. B.S., U. Ill., 1954, LL.B., 1958. Bar: Ill. 1958, N.Y. 1961, D.C. 1962, U.S. Supreme Ct. 1967. Trial atty. Antitrust div. U.S. Dept. Justice, Washington, 1958-60; assoc. Donovan, Leisure, Newton & Irvine, N.Y.C., 1960-61; sr. ptnr. Rogers & Wells, Washington, 1961—; adj. prof. law Georgetown U., Washington, 1961-67; dir. Cafritz Cos., Washington; spl. counsel U.S. Architect of the Capitol, 1963-64; trustee, gen. counsel Fed. City Council, Washington, 1969—; dir., gen. counsel Fed. City Housing Corp., Washington, 1972—; gen. counsel Presdl. Inaugural Com., 980-81. Nationalities coordinator Citizens for Nixon-Agnew, Washington, 1968; inaugural com., 1980-81. Served to 1st lt. U.S. Army, 1955-57. Mem. ABA, D.C. Bar Assn., Order of the Coif. Republican. Clubs: Chevy Chase, Metropolitan. Home: 4 E Kirke St Chevy Chase MD 20815 Office: Rogers & Wells 1737 H St NW Washington DC 20006

CLARK, ROGER EARL, lawyer; b. New Orleans, Oct. 23, 1946; s. Earl B. and Erma Le (Chambers) C.; m. Barbara Jo Columbus, Dec. 23, 1971; 1 dau., Kelly Elizabeth. B.A., Rice U., 1968; J.D., Harvard U., 1971. Bar: Ill. 1971, Colo. 1973. Assoc. Pope, Ballard, Shepard and Fowle, Chgo., 1971-73, Hammond and Chilson, Loveland, Colo., 1973-76; assoc. Lynn A. Hammond Law Offices, Loveland, Colo., 1976-80, ptnr. Hammond, Clark and White, 1980—. Bd. dirs. Loveland Community YMCA, 1979—, pres. 1985-86; bd. dirs. Jr. Achievement of Loveland, 1977-82, pres., 1980. Mem. ABA, Colo. Bar Assn. (exec. council young lawyers sect. 1977-83, chmn. 1982-83, bd. of govs. 1985—, v.p. 1986-87), Larimer County Bar Assn. (pres. 1984-85), Colo. Trial Lawyers Assn., Loveland C. of C. (bd. dirs. 1983—, pres.-elect 1987). Democrat. Methodist. Club: Loveland Sertoma (pres. 1980-81). General practice, State civil litigation, Real property. Office: Hammond Clark & White PO Box 701 Loveland CO 80539 Home: 1220 W 6th Loveland CO 80537

CLARK, RONALD HURLEY, lawyer; b. Venezuela, Jan. 5, 1953. BA, U. Conn., 1974, MA, 1974; JD, U. Tex., 1979. Bar: Tex. 1979, U.S. Dist. Ct. (no. dist.) Tex. 1980, U.S. Ct. Appeals (5th and 11th cirs.) 1981, U.S. Supreme Ct. 1982, U.S. Dist. Ct. (ea. dist.) Tex. 1983; cert. trial specialist. Trial atty. City of Abilene, Tex., 1979-82; ptnr. Henderson, Bryant & Wolfe, Sherman, Tex., 1983—. Mem. Eagle Bd. Rev. Boy Scouts Am., Sherman, 1983—. Served to 2d lt. U.S. Army, 1974-76, with Res. 1976-82. Named one of Outstanding Young Men of Yr., 1984. Mem. 5th Cir. Bar Assn., Grayson County Bar Assn., Tex. City Attys. Assn., Tex. Assn. Def. Counsel, Sherman Jaycees (bd. dirs. 1985), Phi Beta Kappa. Roman Catholic. Lodges: Kiwanis (bd. dirs. 1984-85, v.p. 1985-86, pres. elect 1986—), KC (Knight of Yr. 1982). Federal civil litigation, State civil litigation, Local government. Home and Office: Henderson Bryant & Wolfe PO Box 239 Sherman TX 75090

CLARK, ROSS TOWNSEND, lawyer; b. Jacksonville, Fla., Nov. 21, 1956; s. William George and Isabel (Blanc) C. BA, U. Fla., 1977, JD, 1981. Bar: Fla. 1981, U.S. Dist. Ct. (no. and mid. dists.) Fla. 1981, U.S. Ct. Appeals (5th and 11th cirs.) 1981. Assoc. Boyer, Tanzler, Blackburn, Boyer & Nichols P.A., Jacksonville, 1981-83, Fowler & Clark P.A., Jacksonville, 1983—. Mem. Jacksonville Bar Assn., Assn. Trial Lawyer Am., Acad. Fla. Trial Lawyers. Democrat. Family and matrimonial, Criminal, State civil litigation. Home: 2057 Huntsford Rd Jacksonville FL 32207 Office: Fowler & Clark PA 5915 Cedar Hills Blvd Jacksonville FL 32210

CLARK, R(UFUS) BRADBURY, lawyer; b. Des Moines, May 11, 1924; s. Rufus Bradbury and Gertrude Martha (Burns) C.; m. Polly Ann King, Sept. 6, 1949; children: Cynthia Clark Maxwell, Rufus Bradbury, John Atherton. B.A., Harvard U., 1948, J.D., 1951; diploma in law, Oxford U., Eng., 1952; D.H.L., Ch. Div. Sch. Pacific, San Francisco, 1983. Bar: Calif. Assoc. firm O'Melveny & Myers, Los Angeles, 1952-62, sr. ptnr., 1961—, mem. mgmt. com., 1983—; dir. So. Calif. Water Co., Econ. Resources Corp., Brown Internat. Corp., Automatic Machinery & Electronics Corp. Editor: California Corporation Laws, 6 vols, 1976—. Pres. John Tracy Clinic, Los Angeles; chancellor Episcopal Diocese of Los Angeles, 1967—, hon. canon, 1983—. Served to capt. U.S. Army, 1943-46. Decorated Bronze star with oak leaf cluster; decorated Purple Heart with oak leaf cluster; Fulbright grantee, 1952. Mem. ABA (subcom. on audit letter responses, com. on law and acctg.), State Bar Calif. (chmn. drafting com. on gen. corp. law 1973-81, chmn. drafting com. on nonprofit corp. law 1980-84, mem. exec. com. bus. law sect. 1984-87, sec. 1986-87), Los Angeles County Bar Assn. Republican. Clubs: California (Los Angeles), Harvard (Los Angeles), Chancery (Los Angeles); Alamitos Bay Yacht (Long Beach). General corporate, Public utilities, Banking. Office: O'Melveny & Myers 400 S Hope St Los Angeles CA 90071

CLARK, RUSSELL GENTRY, U.S. dist. judge; b. Myrtle, Mo., July 27, 1925; s. William B. and Grace Frances (Jenkins) C.; m. Jerry Elaine Burrows, Apr. 30, 1959; children: Vincent A., Viki F. LL.B., U. Mo., 1952. Bar: Mo. 1952. Mem. firm Woolsey, Fisher, Clark, Whiteaker & Stenger, Springfield, Mo., 1952-77; U.S. dist. judge Western Dist. of Mo., Kansas City, 1977—. Served to 2d lt. U.S. Army, 1944-46. Mem. ABA, Mo. Bar Assn. (continuing legal edn. com. 1969), Greene County bar assn. (dir. 1968-71). Democrat. Methodist. Club: Kiwanis (past pres. Springfield chpt.). Office: US Dist Ct 654 US Courthouse 811 Grand Ave Kansas City MO 64106 also: 320 US Courthouse 870 Booneville St Springfield MO 65801 *

CLARK, THOMAS ALONZO, judge; b. Atlanta, Dec. 20, 1920; s. Fred and Prudence (Sprayberry) C.; m. Betty Medlock, July 16, 1978; children: Thomas Alonzo, Christopher S., Julia M.; stepchildren: Allen L. Carter, Rosalyn Lackey Howell. B.S., Washington and Lee U., 1942; LL.B., U. Ga., 1949. Sole practice Bainbridge, Ga., 1949-55; ptnr. Dykes, Marshall & Clark, Americus, Ga., 1955-57, Fowler, White et al, Tampa, Fla., 1957-61; sr. ptnr. Carlton, Fields, et al, Tampa, 1961-79; judge U.S. Ct. Appeals (5th cir.), 1979-81, U.S. Ct. of Appeals (11th cir.), Atlanta, 1981—. Mem. Ga. Ho. of Reps., 1951-52; pres. Fla. Assn. for Retarded Citizens, 1974-75, Served to lt. comdr. USN, 1942-46. Fellow Am. Coll. Trial Lawyers; mem. ABA, Ga. Bar Assn., Fla. Bar Assn., Am. Judicature Soc. Jurisprudence. Office: US Court Apeals 50 Spring St SW Atlanta GA 30303 *

CLARK, WILLIAM GEORGE, judge; b. Chgo., July 16, 1924; s. John S. and Ita (Kennedy) C.; m. Rosalie Locatis, Nov. 28, 1946; children: Merrilee, William George, Donald, John Steven, Robert. Student, Loyola U., Chgo., 1942-43, 44; J.D., DePaul U., 1946; J.D. (hon.), John Marshall Law Sch., Chgo., 1962. Bar: Ill. 1947. Mem. firm Crane, Kearney, Korzen, Phelan & Clark (and predecessor), Chgo., 1947-56; atty. for Pub. Adminstr. Ill., 1949-53; mem. Ill. Ho. of Reps. from Austin Dist. of Chgo., 1952-54, 56-60; mem. Senate, 1954-56, majority leader, 1959; atty. gen. Ill., 1960-69; partner firm Arvey, Hodes & Mantynband, Chgo., 1968-76; justice Supreme Ct. Ill., 1976—, chief justice, 1984—. Served with AUS, 1942-44. Mem. Ill., Chgo., bar assns., AMVETS, Celtic Legal Soc., Am. Legion, Irish Fellowship Club (pres. 1961-62), Catholic Lawyers Guild Chgo., Delta Theta Phi. Jurisprudence. Office: Supreme Court Office Ill Supreme Ct Richard J Daley Center Chicago IL 60602 *

CLARKE, CHARLES FENTON, lawyer; b. Hillsboro, Ohio, July 25, 1916; s. Charles F. and Margaret (Patton) C.; m. Virginia Schoppenhorst, Apr. 3, 1945; children: Elizabeth, Margaret, Jane, Charles Fenton, IV. A.B. summa cum laude, Washington and Lee U., Lexington, Va., 1938; LL.B., U. Mich., 1940; LL.D. (hon.), Cleve. State U., 1971. Bar: Mich. 1940, Ohio 1946. Pvt. practice Detroit, 1942, Cleve., 1946—; ptnr. firm Squire, Sanders & Dempsey, 1957—, adminstr. litigation dept., 1979-85; trustee Cleve. Legal Aid Soc., 1959-67; pres. Nat. Assn. R.R. Trial Counsel, 1966-68; life mem. 6th Circuit Jud. Conf.; chmn. legis. com. Cleve. Welfare Fedn., 1961-68; bd. dirs. W.M. Brode Co., Park Mfg. Co. Pres. alumni bd. dirs. Washington and Lee U., 1970-72; pres. bd. dirs. Free Med. Clinic Greater Cleve., 1970-87; trustee Cleve. Citizens League, 1956-62; bd. dirs. citizens adv. bd. Cuyahoga County (Ohio) Juvenile Ct., 1970-73; bd. dirs. George Jr. Republic, Greenville, Pa., 1970-73, Bowman Tech. Sch., Cleve., 1970—; vice chmn. Cleve. Crime Commn., 1973-75; exec. com. Cuyahoga County Republican Orgn., 1950—; councilman Bay Village, Ohio, 1948-53; pres., trustee Cleve. Hearing and Speech Center, 1957-62; Laurel Sch., 1962-72, Fedn. Community Progress, 1984—; trustee Cleve. chpt. ACLU, 1986—. Served to 1st lt. AUS, World War II. Fellow Am. Coll. Trial Lawyers; mem. Greater Cleve. Bar Assn. (trustee 1983-86), Cleve. Civil War Round Table (pres. 1968), Cleve. Zool. Soc. (dir. 1970), Phi Beta Kappa. Presbyterian. Clubs: Skating, Union (Cleve.); Tavern. Home: 2262 Tudor Dr Cleveland Heights OH 44106 Office: Huntington Bldg Cleveland OH 44115

CLARKE, DENNIS PERSON, lawyer; b. Helena, Mont., Nov. 27, 1947; s. William Howard and Thelma (Person) C.; m. Sandra Jean Hatfield, Nov. 26, 1969 (div. Feb. 1984); 1 child, Aleksandra; m. Melinda Lee Dahlquist, May 11, 1984; 1 child, Jeffrey. Bar: Mont. 1974, U.S. Dist. Ct. Mont. 1974. Research dir. rules evidence Supreme Ct. Commn., Missoula, Mont., 1974-76; ptnr. Smith, Baillie & Walsh, Great Falls, Mont., 1977—; lectr. cts. ltd. jurisdiction State Mont., Helena, 1977; cons. bill drafting legis. council State Mont., 1977; mem. Supreme Com. Rules Evidence, Helena, 1977—. Bd. dirs. Cascade County Housing for Developmentally Disabled, Great Falls, 1978-80. Served with USNG, 1966-72. Mem. ABA, Mont. Bar Assn., Cascade County Bar Assn. (sec. 1978-79). Democrat. Presbyterian. Club: Meadowlark Country (Great Falls). Avocations: outdoor sports, golf. Insurance, Personal injury, Federal civil litigation. Home: 1529 Meadowlark Dr Great Falls MT 59404 Office: Smith Baillie & Walsh 121 4th St N Great Falls MT 59401

CLARKE, EDWARD OWEN, JR., lawyer; b. Balt., Dec. 19, 1929; s. Edward Owen and Agnes Oakford C.; m. P. Rhea Parker, Dec. 18, 1954; children—Deborah Jeanne, Catherine Ann, Carolyn Agnes, Edward Owen III. A.B. magna cum laude, Loyola Coll., Balt., 1950; LL.B. with honors, U. Md., 1956. Bar: Md. 1956, U.S. Dist. Ct. Md. 1956. Law clk. U.S. Dist. Ct. Md., 1956-57; assoc. Smith, Somerville & Case, Balt., 1957-62; ptnr. Smith, Somerville & Case, Balt., 1962-71; ptnr. Piper & Marbury, Balt., 1971-87, mem. policy and mgmt. com. 1981—, mng. ptnr., 1987—; mem. Gov.'s Com. to Study Blue Sky Law, 1961, Dir. Pittsburgh Child Guidance Ctr. Found., 1987-90; mem. Md. Commn. on Revision Corp. Law, 1965-66. Bd. dirs. Bon Secours Hosp., 1964-73, sec., 1968-73; bd. dirs. Hosp. Cost Analysis Service, 1966-81; bd. pres. mem. exec. council Md. Hosp. Assn., 1968-74, chmn. com. on legislation, 1971-73, treas., 1973; trustee St. Mary's Coll. Md., 1983—, St. Mary's Sem., U. Balt., 1986—, Loyola High Sch., Balt., 1984—. Served with USNR, 1952-55. Mem. ABA, Md. State Bar Assn. (mem. sect. council corp., banking and bus. law sect. 1968-71, chmn. 1970-71), Balt. City Bar Assn., Alpha Sigma Nu, Tau Kappa Alpha, Order of Coif. Clubs: Wednesday Law, Center (Balt.). Municipal bonds, General corporate, Tax exempt financing and Local government. Office: 1100 Charles Center South 36 S Charles St Baltimore MD 21201

CLARKE, HAROLD G., justice Supreme Ct. Ga.; b. Forsyth, Ga., Sept. 28, 1927. J.D., U. Ga., 1950. Bar: Ga. 1950. Mem. Ga. State Legislature, 1961-71; chmn. Ga. Inst. for Continuing Legal Edn.; justice Ga. Supreme Ct., 1979—. Fellow Am. Coll. Trial Lawyers, Am. Bar Found.; mem. ABA, Flint Circuit Bar Assn. (pres. 1960-61), Am. Judicature Soc. (bd. dirs.), State Bar Ga. (gov. 1971—, exec. com. 1973—, pres. 1976-77), Omicron Delta Kappa. Office: Supreme Ct Judicial Bldg Atlanta GA 30334 *

CLARKE, J. CALVITT, JR., federal judge; b. Harrisburg, Pa., Aug. 9, 1920; s. Joseph Calvitt and Helen Caroline (Mattson) C.; m. Mary Jane Cromer, Feb. 1, 1943 (dec.1985); children: Joseph Calvitt III, Martha Tiffany; m. Betty Ann Holladay, May 29, 1986. B.S. in Commerce, U. Va., 1944, LL.B., 1944. Bar: Va. 1944. Practiced in Richmond, Va., 1944-74; partner firm Bowles, Anderson, Boyd, Clarke & Herod, 1944-60; firm Sands Anderson, Marks and Clarke, 1960-74; judge U.S. Dist. Ct. Eastern dist. of Va., 1975—; mem. 4th Circuit Judicial Conf., 1963; hon. consul for Republic of Bolivia, 1959-75. Chmn. Citizen's Advisory Com. on Joint Water System for Henrico and Hanover counties, Va., 1968-69; mem. Mayor's Freedom Train Com., 1948-50; del. Young Republican Nat. Conv., Salt Lake City, 1949, Boston, 1951; chmn. Richmond (Va.) Republican Com., 1952-54; candidate for Congress, 1954; chmn. Va. 3d Dist. Rep. Com., 1955-58, 74—, Va. State Rep. Conv., 1958—; co-founder Young Rep. Fedn. of Va., 1950, nat. committeeman, 1950-54; chmn. Speakers Bur., Nixon-Lodge campaign, 1960, mem. fin. com., 1960-74; chmn. Henrico County Republican Com., 1956-58; fin. chmn. 1956; pres. Couples Sunday Sch. class Second Presbyn. Ch., Richmond, Va., 1948-50, mem. bd. deacons, 1948-61, elder, 1964—; bd. dirs. Family Service Children's Aid Soc., 1948-61, Gambles Hill Community Center, 1950-60, Christian Children's Fund, Inc., 1960-67, Children, Inc., 1967-75, Norfolk Forum, 1978—; mem. bd. of chancellors Internat. Consular Acad., 1965-75; trustee Henrico County Pub. Library, chmn., 1971-73.

Mem. Va. State Bar (mem. 3rd dist. com. 1967-70, chmn. 1969-70), Am. Judicature Soc., ABA, Va. Bar Assn. (vice chmn. com. on cooperation with fgn. bars 1960-61), Richmond Jr. C. of C. (dir. 1946-50), Delta Theta Phi. Clubs: Windmill Point Yacht, Westwood Racquet (pres. 1961-62), Commonwealth. Jurisprudence. Office: 358 US Courthouse 600 Granby St Norfolk VA 23510

CLARKE, MARILEE MILLER, lawyer; b. Aurora, Ill., Apr. 1, 1953; d. Darvin Lowell and Marge (Mitchell) M.; m. David A. Clarke; 1 child, Douglas. BA in English, Ind. U., 1974; JD, U. Wis., 1977. Bar: Wis. 1977, Ariz. 1979, U.S. Dist. Ct. Ariz. 1979. Law clk. to presiding justice Idaho Supreme Ct., Boise, 1977-78; assoc. Rawlins, Ellis, Burrus & Kiewit, Phoenix, 1978-81; counsel Wells Fargo Credit Corp., Scottsdale, Ariz., 1981-82, sr. counsel, v.p., 1982-83, asst. v.p., asst. gen. counsel, 1983-85, v.p. legal, 1985-86, v.p., gen. counsel, 1986—. Author, editor: Arizona Civil Remedies, 1983; mng. editor U. Wis. Law Rev., 1976-77. Mem. Ariz. Bar Assn. (continuing legal edn. com., chmn. basic skills subcom. 1983—), Maricopa County Bar Assn. (corp. counsel sect.). Methodist. Banking, Consumer commercial, Contracts commercial. Home: 8204 N 53d St Paradise Valley AZ 85253 Office: Wells Fargo Credit Corp 6991 E Camelback Rd C-309 Scottsdale AZ 85251

CLARKE, MILTON CHARLES, lawyer; b. Chgo., Jan. 31, 1929; s. Gordon Robert and Senoria Josephine (Carlisa) C.; m. Dorothy Jane Brodie, Feb. 19, 1955; children: Laura, Virginia, Senoria K. BS, Northwestern U., 1950, JD, 1953. Bar: Ill. 1953, Mo. 1956, U.S. Dist. Ct. (we. dist.) Mo. 1961, U.S. Ct. Appeals (8th cir.) 1961. Assoc. Swanson, Midgley, Gangwere, Clarke & Kitchin, Kansas City, Mo., 1955-61, ptnr., 1961—; bd. dirs. W.C. Tingle Co., Kansas City. Served with U.S. Army, 1953-55. Mem. Kansas City Met. Bar Assn., Lawyers Assn., Estate Planning Soc. Club: University (Kansas City). Lodge: Rotary (chmn. legal affairs com. Kansas City). Federal civil litigation, State civil litigation, Probate. Office: Swanson Midgley Gangwere Clarke & Kitchin 1500 Commerce Trust Bldg 922 Walnut St Kansas City MO 64106

CLARKE, THOMAS HAL, lawyer; b. Atlanta, Aug. 10, 1914; s. James Caleb and Mary Cox (DeSaussure) C.; m. Mary Louise Hastings, July 12, 1951; children: Thomas Hal, Mary Katherine, Rebecca DeSaussure. LL.B., Washington and Lee U., 1938. Bar: Ga. 1939. Practiced law Atlanta, 1946-69, 73—; mem. firm Mitchell, Clarke, Pate, Anderson & Wimberly, 1948-69, 73-85; counsel Gambell, Clarke, Anderson & Stolz, 1985—. Mem. Fed. Home Loan Bank Bd., Washington, 1969-73; past pres., bd. dirs. Atlanta Hist. Soc.; past bd. visitors Emory U.; trustee emeritus Washington and Lee U.; mem. Hibernian United Service Club, Dublin, Ireland. Served with USNR, 1942-46, ETO. Mem. Internat. Bar Assn. (vice chmn. savs. and bldg. socs. com.), ABA (past chmn. sect. corp., banking and bus. law, mem. ho. of dels. 1974-80), Ga. Bar Assn., Atlanta Bar Assn., Am. Law Inst., Atlanta Lawyers Club (past pres.), Selden Soc., English Speaking Union (past pres., chmn. bd.). Clubs: Piedmont Driving, Commerce (Atlanta); Metropolitan (Washington). Banking, General corporate, Real property. Home: 186 15th St NE Atlanta GA 30309 Office: Gambrell Clarke Anderson & Stolz 3600 First National Tower 2 Peachtree St NW Atlanta GA 30338

CLARKE, WILLIAM ANTHONY LEE, III, lawyer; b. Balt., May 7, 1949; s. William Anthony Jr. and Eileen Shiela (Walsh) C. Student, John Carroll U., 1969-72; JD magna cum laude, U. Balt., 1975. Bar: Md. 1975, U.S. Dist. Ct. Md. 1975, U.S. Supreme Ct. 1979, U.S. Ct. Appeals (4th cir.) 1981. Trial atty. Tenn. Valley Authority, Knoxville, 1975-76; sole practice Salisbury, Md., 1977—. Pres. Wicomico County Dems., Salisbury, 1981-83; commr. Md. Human Relations Commn., Balt., 1983-85. Served to cpl. USMC, 1967-69, Vietnam. Mem. ABA, Md. Bar Assn., Wicomico County Bar Assn., Md. Criminal Def. Attys. Assn. (bd. dirs. 1984—), Nat. Assn. Criminal Def. Attys., Salisbury Jaycees (legal counsel 1977-79), Nat. Bd. Trial Adv. (cert. criminal trial advocate). Criminal, State civil litigation, Federal civil litigation. Home: 1707 Ocean Pines Berlin MD 21811 Office: 111 W Main St PO Box 669 Salisbury MD 21801

CLARKSON, JULIAN DERIEUX, lawyer; b. Coral Gables, Fla., Mar. 12, 1929; s. Julian Livingston and Hazel (Lamar) C.; m. Joan Combs, Dec. 24, 1950, children—James L., Julian L., Joanna D., Melinda C.; m. 2d, Shirley Lazonby, Nov. 8, 1979; children—George Allen, Shirley Lamar. B.A., U. Fla., 1950, LL.B., 1955, J.D., 1967. Bar: Fla. 1955, U.S. Ct. Appeals (5th cir.) 1961, U.S. Supreme Ct. 1964, U.S. Ct. Appeals (11th cir.) 1981, D.C. 1983. Ptnr., Henderson, Franklin, Starnes & Holt, Ft. Myers, Fla., 1955-76; sole practice, Ft. Myers, 1976-77; ptnr. Holland & Knight, Ft. Myers, 1977-79, Tampa, 1979-82, Tallahassee, 1982—; lectr. in field. Chmn. Fla. Supreme Ct. Jud. Nominating Commn., 1976-78. Served to 1st lt. U.S. Army, 1950-53. Decorated Purple Heart, 1951; named Outstanding Grad. Province V Phi Delta Phi, 1955. Mem. Am. Coll. Trial Lawyers, Am. Law Inst., Fla. Blue Key, Order of Coif, Phi Beta Kappa. Democrat. Episcopalian. Author: Let No Man Put Asunder—Story of a Football Rivalry, 1968. Federal civil litigation, State civil litigation. Address: 1002 Kenilworth Rd Tallahassee FL

CLARKSON, STEPHEN BATCHELDER, lawyer; b. Hartford, Conn., July 1, 1937; s. Albert Batchelder and Elsie (Eden) C.; m. Nancy Lee Michelmore, Oct. 16, 1965; children—Janet, Leigh. B.A., Yale U., 1959; LL.B., U. Va. Law Sch., 1962. Bar: N.Y. 1963, D.C. 1969, U.S. Supreme Ct. 1967. Spl. asst. to gen. counsel and under-sec. U.S. Dept. Commerce, 1968-69; ptrs. Pierson, Ball & Dowd, Washington, 1982—; mem. adv. bd. Bur. Nat. Affairs Fed. Contracts Report, 1974-76; editorial cons., 1976—. Mem. ABA (antitrust, litigation, corp. banking and bus. law, pub. contract law, ct. of claims com. sects.), Fed. Bar Assn., D.C. Bar Assn., Assn. Bar City N.Y. Antitrust, Government contracts and claims. Home: 7101 Heatherhill Rd Bethesda MD 20817 Office: 1200 18th St NW Washington DC 20036

CLARY, EVERETT BURTON, lawyer; b. San Francisco, Dec. 1, 1921; s. William Webb and Elizabeth Augusta (Foss) C.; m. Mary Marjorie DeFriest, May 6, 1944; children—Ann Clary Judy, Carter DeFriest. B.A., Stanford U., 1943, LL.B., 1949. Bar: Calif. 1949. Practiced in Los Angeles; partner firm O'Melveny & Myers, 1960—, adminstrv. head litigation dept., 1977-85, mem. mgmt. com., 1977-86. Contbr. articles to legal jours. Bd. visitors Stanford U. Law Sch.; trustee Pacific Oaks Coll. and Children's Sch., Pasadena, Calif.; bd. fellows Claremont U. Center; vestryman Episcopal Ch. of Angels, Pasadena. Served with USNR, 1943-46. Fellow Am. Bar Found., Am. Coll. Trial Lawyers; mem. Am. Bar Assn., Los Angeles County Bar Assn. Clubs: Calif., Stock Exchange (Los Angeles); Annandale (Calif.), Golf; Valley Hunt (Pasadena). Office: 400 S Hope St Los Angeles CA 90071

CLARY, RICHARD WAYLAND, lawyer; b. Tarboro, N.C., Oct. 10, 1953; s. S. Grayson and Jean (Beazley) C.; m. Claudia Anne Stone, Oct. 18, 1980. BA magna cum laude, Amherst Coll., 1975; JD magna cum laude, Harvard U., 1978. Bar: N.Y. 1981, U.S. Dist. Ct. (so. and ea. dists.) N.Y. 1981, U.S. Tax. Ct. 1981, U.S. Dist. Ct. (no. dist.) Calif. 1982, U.S. Ct. Appeals (9th cir.) 1983. Law clk. to judge U.S. Ct. Appeals (2d cir.), N.Y.C., 1978-79; law clk. to Justice Thurgood Marshall U.S. Supreme Ct., Washington, 1979-80; assoc. Cravath, Swaine & Moore, N.Y.C., 1980-85, ptnr., 1985—. John Woodruff Simpson fellow Amherst Coll., 1975-76. Mem. ABA, N.Y. State Bar Assn., Assn. of Bar of City of N.Y., Phi Beta Kappa. Episcopalian. Clubs: Harvard, Wall St. (N.Y.C.). Federal civil litigation, State civil litigation, Computer. Office: Cravath Swaine & Moore One Chase Manhattan Plaza New York NY 10005

CLAUSS, C. DAVID, lawyer; b. Louisville, Sept. 22, 1948. BS, Ohio State U., 1970; JD, U. Louisville, 1973. Bar: Ky. 1973, U.S. Supreme Ct. 1978, Wyo. 1981, U.S. Dist. Ct. (ea. and we. dists.) Ky., U.S. Dist. Ct. Wyo. 1982, U.S. Ct. Appeals (6th cir.). Law clk. to presiding justice Ky. Supreme Ct., Frankfort, 1973-74; asst. atty. gen. Commonwealth of Ky., Frankfort, 1977-80; sole practice Jackson, Wyo., 1980-81, 82—, Lander, Wyo., 1981. Served to capt. USAR. Mem. ABA, Wyo. Bar Assn., Ky. Bar Assn., Louisville Bar Assn., Teton County Bar Assn., Wyo. Trial Lawyers Assn., Wyo. State Soccer Assn. (pres. 1985). Lodge: Rotary (bd. dirs. Jackson Hole club 1985-87, v.p. 1987—). State civil litigation, Family and matrimonial, Personal injury. Office: PO Box 1172 Jackson WY 83001

CLAUSS, PETER OTTO, lawyer; b. Knoxville, Tenn., Sept. 23, 1936; s. Alfred and Jane (West) C.; m. Elizabeth Mary Lou Percival, Apr. 28, 1962; children—Andrew Bradford, Victoria Johns. AB, U. Chgo., 1955; LLB, Yale U., 1958. Bar: Pa. 1959, U.S. Dist. Ct. (ea. dist.) Pa. 1959, U.S. Tax Ct. 1959, U.S. Ct. Appeals (3d cir.) 1959, U.S. Supreme Ct. 1963, U.S. Ct. Claims 1960, U.S. Ct. Customs 1962. Assoc. Clark, Ladner, Fortenbaugh & Young, Phila., 1958-65, ptnr., 1966—, mem. exec. com., 1967-76, mng. ptnr., 1968-72, sr. ptnr., chmn. corp. and bus. dept., 1983—; past dir. Norcross, Inc., Nutrion Corp., Helicrane Constrn. Corp., Mannion Co., Henry Cantor, Inc.; dir. Keystone Helicopter Corp., Interactive Graphics, Inc.; asst. sec. C.H. Masland, 1974-86. Past sec., mem. vestry Christ Ch., mem. Outreach Com., stewardship com.; past coach Little League Baseball; past treas. Ithan Sch. PTA; past treas. Boy Scouts Am., Ithan, Pa. Ford Found. fellow, 1952-55. Served with Army N.G., 1959-67. Mem. ABA (past chmn. sales, exchanges and basis com. tax sect.), Phila. Bar Assn. (past chmn. unpopular causes com., past vice chmn. pub. service com.). Pa. Bar Assn., Juristic Soc. of Phila. (past bd. govs.), Yale Law Sch. Assn. for Eastern Pa. (pres. 1974-82), Assn. Yale Alumni (Phila. del. 1982-84), Phi Gamma Delta (nat. sec., bd. dirs., past gen. counsel), Phi Delta Phi. Republican. Episcopalian. Clubs: Yale of Phila. (past pres.), Racquet of Phila., First Troop Phila. City Calvary, University Barge; Merion Cricket, Orpheus; First Monday (past pres.); Ocean Point Golf (Fripp Island, S.C.) Contbr. articles to legal jours. Corporate taxation, General corporate, Pension, profit-sharing, and employee benefits. Home: 758 Darby-Paoli Rd Newtown Square PA 19073 Office: 1818 Market St 32d Floor Philadelphia PA 19103

CLAXTON, EDWARD BURTON, III, lawyer; b. Macon, Ga., Apr. 15, 1956; s. Edward Burton Jr. and Harriet Maroy (Jones) C. BS in Biology, U. Ga., 1979; JD, Mercer U., 1982. Bar: Ga., U.S. Dist. Ct. (mid. and so. dists.) Ga., U.S. Ct. Appeals. Assoc. Jones, Jones & Hilburn, Dublin, Ga., 1982-85, ptnr., 1986—. chmn. dignitaries com. Dublin-Laurens County St. Patrick's Festival, 1983-84; pres. Friends of Laurens County Library, Inc., 1986-88; mem. Dublin Community Band, 1984—, Ga. Power Consumer Adv. Council, 1986—; exec. bd. dirs. Laurens County Chapter Am. Cancer Soc., 1984—, v.p., 1987-88; bd. dirs. Dublin Clean Community Assn., Inc., 1984—; bd. dirs. Laurens County Hist. Soc., 1984—, pres. 1987—. Mem. ABA, Ga. Bar Assn., Dublin Cir. Bar Assn. (sec./treas. 1985-86, v.p. 1986-87), Assn. Trial Lawyers Am., Ga. Trial Lawyers Assn., Phi Delta Phi, Pi Kappa Phi (warden 1978-79). Lodge: Elks, Rotary. Avocations: golf, jogging, racquetball, hunting, fishing. General practice, Bankruptcy, Insurance. Office: Jones Jones & Hilburn 205 N Franklin St Dublin GA 31021

CLAY, AARON RICHARD, lawyer; b. Delta, Colo., Aug. 11, 1953; s. Neil K. and Willetta B. (Thornberry) C.; m. Gayla D. King, Aug. 17, 1974; children: Nathan, Andrea. BA, U. Colo., 1975, JD, 1979. Bar: Colo. 1979, U.S. Dist. Ct. Colo. 1979. Ptnr. Briscoe, Stanway, Clay, Dodson & Harper P.C., Hotchkiss, Colo., 1979—; water referee 7th judicial dist., Montrose, Colo., 1982—. Mem. ABA, Assn. Trial Lawyers Am., Colo. Trial Lawyers Assn., Internat. Assn. Approved Basketball Officials (state bd. dirs. 1984—). Methodist. Avocations: tennis, basketball officiating. Water and natural resources law, Personal injury, Real property. Home: 890 Sharpe Circle Delta CO 81416 Office: Briscoe Stanway Clay et al PO Box 38 Delta CO 81416

CLAY, JASPER R., federal government official; b. Fairmont, W.Va., Nov. 26, 1933. BS, Morgan State U., 1954. Staff specialist Md. div. Parole and Probation, 1966-68, dist. supr. Balt. div., 1968; assoc. mem. Md. Parole Bd., 1969-76; commr. Md. Parole Commn., 1976-84, U.S. Parole Commn., Washington, 1985—. Office: Dept of Justice US Parole Commn 5550 Friendship Blvd Chevy Chase MD 20815 *

CLAY, JOHN ERNEST, lawyer; b. Kansas City, Mo., Nov. 27, 1921; s. Ernest Worman and Gertrude Marie (Turfler) C.; m. Theodora Summerfield Buchman, Mar. 11, 1944 (div. Aug. 1973); children: Peter Worman, Robert Scott; m. Mary A. Dailey, Oct.20,1973. B.A., Carleton Coll., 1943; J.D., Harvard U., 1948. Bar: Ill. 1948. With Taylor, Miller, Busch & Magner, Chgo., 1948-51; with Mayer, Brown & Platt, Chgo.; pres. Pub. Interest Law Internship, Chgo., 1985—. Chmn. Ill. Com. for Eugene McCarthy, Chgo., 1976, vice presdl. running mate in Ill., 1976; chmn. Glencoe Bd. Edn., Ill., 1966-68; treas. 1st Nat. Conf. Optimum Population and Environ., Chgo., 1970. Served to 2d lt. U.S. Army, 1945-46. Mem. Chgo. Bar Assn., Chgo. Council Lawyers, Phi Beta Kappa. Clubs: Law (Chgo.) (sec.-treas. 1986-87), Monroe. Banking, General corporate. Home: 229 6th St Wilmette IL 60091 Office: Mayer Brown & Platt 190 S LaSalle St Chicago IL 60603

CLAYMAN, CHARLES ELLIOTT, lawyer; b. Quincy, Mass., Nov. 26, 1944; s. Benjamin and Lillian Josephine (Fleischman) C.; m. Dee A. Lesser, May 19, 1968; children—Gregory, Thomas. A.B., Harvard Coll., 1966; J.D., U. Pa., 1969. Bar: N.Y. 1970, U.S. Dist. Ct. (so. and ea. dists.) N.Y. 1973, U.S. Ct. Appeals (2d cir.) 1973. Asst. dist. atty. N.Y. County, 1969-73; asst. U.S. atty. Eastern Dist. N.Y., 1973-77; gen. counsel N.Y.C. Dept. Investigation, 1977-78; ptnr. Gallop, Dawson & Clayman, N.Y.C., 1977—. Mem. ABA, N.Y. State Bar Assn., N.Y. Criminal Bar Assn. Club: Harvard of N.Y. Criminal. Office: 305 Madison Ave Suite 1301 New York NY 10165

CLAYTON, HUGH NEWTON, lawyer; b. Ripley, Miss., Aug. 22, 1907; s. Ira L. and Nancy (McCord) C.; m. Cathryn Rose Carter, June 26, 1939; children: Rose Clayton Cochran, Hugh Carter. A.B., U. Miss., 1929, J.D., 1931. Bar: Miss. 1931, Tenn. 1931. Practiced in Memphis, 1931-33; practiced in Ripley, 1933-36, city atty., 1933-36; city atty. New Albany, Miss., 1937-75, 76-82; atty. New Albany Sch. Bd., 1937-85; dir. Bank of New Albany. Editor: Miss. Law Jour, 1931; asso. editor: New Orleans Christian Advocate, 1941-42; contbr. articles to profl. jours. Chmn. Union County chpt. ARC, 1945-51, nat. com. on internat. ops., 1946-47, chmn. nat. conv., 1959, mem. nat. exec. com. and chmn. nat. chpt. relations com., 1954-56, vice chmn. and parliamentarian, 1948; nat. conv.; chmn. area adv. com. Southeastern U.S., 1949-51, nat. bd. govs., 1950-56, vol. field cons., 1956—, chmn. nat. conv., 1959, chmn. state conv., 1961, mem. state div. council, 1979—; mem. exec. bd. Yocona Area council Boy Scouts Am., 1955—, pres., 1963-65, chmn. com. on advancements, 1956-57, chmn. com. on orgn. and extension, 1958-60; chmn. com. on trust fund promotion Region 5, 1968-72, chmn. fin. com., 1972-73, mem. nat. council, 1959-81, mem. regional exec. com., 1966—, mem. nat. ann. meeting com., 1970-72, mem. nat. com. on local council fin., 1973—, chmn. trust fund com. S.E. region, 1974-80, vice chmn. adminstrn. com. S.E. region, 1973-75; chmn. adminstrn. com. 1975-77; pres. Union County Tb Assn., 1937-40, New Albany Planning Com., 1945-49; mem. nat. conf. Commrs. on Uniform State Laws, 1956—; mem. Miss. Democratic Exec. Com., 1952-56; mem. Nat. Dem. Com., 1956-60, mem. exec. com., 1958-60; mem. Dem. Nat. Adv. Council, 1959-60; Founder, 1st pres. Miss. Jr. Bar, 1936. Served from lt. to lt. comdr. USNR, 1942-45; served as acting comdg. officer Naval Air Sta., 1945, New Orleans. Recipient Silver Beaver award Boy Scouts Am., 1962, Silver Antelope award, 1968; Paul Harris award Rotary Internat., 1976; Disting. Alumnus award U. Miss., 1983; named Outstanding Law Alumnus U. Miss., 1977-78. Fellow Am. Coll. Trial Lawyers, Miss. Bar Found. (trustee), Am. Bar Found. (State chmn. fellows 1980—), Am. Coll. Probate Counsel, Internat. Acad. Law and Sci.; mem. Am. Judicature Soc. (dir. 1962-65), Internat. Platform Assn., Internat. Bar Assn. (patron), Fed. Bar Assn., Am. Counsel Assn. (bd. dirs. 1980-83), ABA (mem. various coms., mem. ho. dels. 1966-86, state del. 1974-80, chmn. communications com. 1967-68, chmn. standing com. on membership 1973-78, chmn. standing com. on jurisprudence, tenure and compensation 1980-81, gov. 1981-84, bd. govs. fin. com. 1981-84, chmn. bd. govs. fin. com. 1983-84, bd. coms. long range fin. planning, planning and mgmt. systems, relocation 1983-84, mem. exec. com. 1983-84, mem. standing com. on scope and correlation of work 1984—, sec. 1986), Miss. Bar Found. (trustee 1963-65, pres. 1965-66), Miss. Def. Lawyers Assn. (bd. dirs. 1980-83), Miss. State Bar (1st v.p. 1958-59, pres. 1959-60), Miss. Law Jour. Assn. (bd. dirs. 1978-84), 3d Miss. Circuit Bar Assn. (pres. 1963-68), Jud. Conf. U.S. 5th Circuit, U. Miss. Alumni Assn. (dir. 1962-65, founder, 1st pres. law alumni chpt. 1964-65), Am. Acad. Polit. and Social Sci., Miss. Assn. Meth. Ministers and Laymen (pres. 1958), Am. Bar Retirement Assn. (bd. dirs. 1981-82), Inst. Jud. Adminstrn., Am. Legion, Scribes (dir. 1969-73), Omicron Delta Kappa, Phi Delta Theta, Phi Alpha Delta, Tau Kappa Alpha, Sigma Upsilon. Methodist (treas. North Miss. Conf. bd. missions 1938-60, trustee North Miss. Conf. 1960—, chmn. bd. trustees Miss. Conf. 1973—, treas. Lewis Meml. Hosp. Fund Miss. 1938-49, nat. emergency com. 1940). Clubs: Masons (New Albany, Miss.), Rotary (New Albany, Miss.) (dist. gov. 1965-66), Oaks Country (New Albany, Miss.). General practice, Insurance. Office: Clayton Bldg PO Box 157 New Albany MS 38652

CLEAR, JOHN MICHAEL, lawyer; b. St. Louis, Dec. 16, 1948; s. Raymond H. and Marian (Clark) C.; m. Isabel Marie Bone, May 10, 1980. BA summa cum laude, Washington U., St. Louis, 1971; JD with honors, U. Chgo., 1974. Bar: Mo. 1974, D.C. 1975, U.S. Ct. Appeals (5th and D.C. cirs.) 1975, U.S. Supreme Ct. 1977, U.S. Ct. Appeals (3d cir.) 1978, U.S. Ct. Appeals (8th cir.) 1980. Law clk. to judge U.S. Ct. Appeals (5th cir.), Atlanta, 1974-75; assoc. Covington & Burling, Washington, 1975-80; jr. ptnr. Bryan, Cave, McPheeters & McRoberts, St. Louis, 1980-81, ptnr., 1982—. Mem. ABA, Mo. Bar Assn., D.C. Bar Assn., St. Louis Met. Bar Assn., Order of Coif, Phi Beta Kappa. Club: Racquet, Noonday, Mo. Athletic (St. Louis). Antitrust, Federal civil litigation, Securities. Office: Bryan Cave et al 500 N Broadway Saint Louis MO 63102

CLEARY, EDWARD JOSEPH, lawyer; b. St. Paul, Dec. 31, 1952; s. Edward Emmet and Eleanor (Donlin) C. Student econs. Stanford U., 1972; B.A. magna cum laude, U. Minn., 1974, J.D., 1977. Bar: Minn. 1977, U.S. Dist. Ct. Minn. 1977, U.S. Ct. Appeals (8th cir.) 1981, U.S. Supreme Ct. 1981. Assoc. with Judge D.D. Wozniak, St. Paul, 1978-80; assoc. Ramsey County Pub. Defender's Office, St. Paul, 1980—; sole practice, St. Paul, 1980—. Author: Ramsey County Court Bench Book, 1982. Mem. Minn. Bar Assn. (bench and bar com. 1986—), Ramsey County Bar Assn. (ct. rules and procedures com. 1986—). Criminal, Personal injury, Real property. Office: 409 Midwest Federal Bldg Saint Paul MN 55101

CLEARY, PHILIP EDWARD, lawyer, educator; b. Boston, Dec. 27, 1947; s. Philip Clement and Eleanor Dorothy (Duggan) C.; m. Lila Catherine Stacey, July 31, 1982; children: Anne Marie, Gregory Philip, Elizabeth Mary. A.B., Boston Coll., 1969, J.D., 1980; A.M., Harvard U., 1971, postgrad., 1971-75. Bar: Mass. 1980, U.S. Dist. Ct. Mass. 1981, U.S. Ct. Appeals (1st cir.) 1981, U.S. Tax Ct. 1982. Assoc. Murphy & Beane, Boston, 1980-81, Freeley & Freeley, Boston, 1982—; law clk. to presiding justice Brockton Dist. Ct., Mass., 1981-82; instr. So. New Eng. Sch. Law, New Bedford, Mass., 1983—; corporator Lincoln Savs. Bank, Boston, 1972-86 . Mem. Mass. Bar Assn., Boston Bar Assn., Assn. Trial Lawyers Am. Roman Catholic. State civil litigation, General practice, Legal education. Home: 35 Fernwood Rd West Roxbury MA 02132 Office: Freeley & Freeley One McKinley Sq Boston MA 02109

CLEARY, RICHARD SIMON, lawyer; b. Yonkers, N.Y., May 18, 1956; s. Timothy Finbar and Patricia Agnes (Hanley) C.; m. Helen Bragg Curtin, June 4, 1983. BA cum laude, Washington and Lee U., 1978; JD, Georgetown U., 1981. Bar: Ky. 1981, U.S. Dist. Ct. (we. dist.) Ky. 1981, U.S. Ct. Appeals (6th cir.) 1983. With Greenebaum Doll & McDonald, Louisville, Ky., 1981—. Co-author: Volume 1A West Federal Practice Manual, 1986; contbg. editor: The Developing Labor Law, 1987; topic editor How Arbitration Works, 5th edit., 1987; mem. editorial bd. Human Resources Mgmt. Reporter, 1987—. Mem. adv. bd. U. Louisville Mgmt. Ctr., 1986—, steering com. U. Louisville Labor and Employment Law Inst., 1984—, advanced gift com. St. Catharine Dominican Sisters, Louisville, 1986. Gov. scholar State of Md., 1974. Mem. ABA (com. on devel. of law under nat. labor relations act sect. of labor and employment law). Roman Catholic. Labor. Home: 268 St Matthews Ave Louisville KY 40207 Office: Greenebaum Doll & McDonald 3300 First Nat Tower Louisville KY 40207

CLEARY, WILLIAM JOSEPH, JR., lawyer; b. Wilmington, N.C., Aug. 14, 1942; s. William Joseph and Eileen Ada (Gannon) C.; A.B. in History, St. Joseph's U., 1964; J.D., Villanova U., 1967. Bar: N.J. 1967, U.S. Ct. Appeals (3d cir.) 1969, Calif. 1982, U.S. Ct. Appeals (9th cir.) 1983. Law clk. to judge N.J. Superior Ct. Jersey City, 1967-68; assoc. Lamb, Blake, H&D, Jersey City, 1968-72; dep. pub. defender State of N.J., Newark, 1972-73; 1st asst. city corp. counsel, Jersey City, 1973-76; assoc. Robert Wassewald, Inc., Hollywood, Calif., 1984-86, Gould & Burke, Los Angeles, 1986—. Mem. ABA, N.J. State Bar, Calif. Bar Assn., Los Angeles County Bar. Democrat. Roman Catholic. State civil litigation, Family and matrimonial, Personal injury. Office: Gould & Burke 1900 Ave of Stars Suite 250 Los Angeles CA 90067 also: Robert Wassewald Inc 6922 Hollywood Blvd Hollywood CA 90028

CLEAVER, DAVID CHARLES, lawyer, educator; b. Sunbury, Pa., Dec. 26, 1941; s. C. Perry and Gertrude Lillian (Clarke) C.; m. Patricia Arlene Caputo, Aug. 23, 1974; children—David Clarke, Christopher Perry. Bar: Pa. 1967, U.S. Supreme Ct. 1971. Ptnr. Sharpe Cleaver, Wenger & Townsend, Chambersburg, Pa., 1967-84; sole practice, Chambersburg, 1985—; adj. prof. law Dickinson Sch. Law, Carlisle, Pa., 1971—. Past pres., bd. dirs. Chambersburg YMCA; chmn. Franklin County (Pa.) Reps., 1986—. Mem. ABA, Assn. Trial Lawyers Am., Pa. Trial Lawyers Assn. Lodges: Chambersburg Rotary, Elks, Moose. Author: Cases and Materials on Wills and Decedent's Estates, 1976; Probate and Estate Administration, The Law in Pennsylvania, 1983. State civil litigation. Home: 455 Overhill Dr Chambersburg PA 17201 Office: 1035 Wayne Ave Chambersburg PA 17201

CLEAVER, WILLIAM LEHN, lawyer; b. Harrisburg, Pa., Dec. 7, 1949; s. Gene Franklin and Goldie Jean (Haldeman) C.; m. Susan Kay Neville, Aug. 17, 1974; children: Benjamin Neville, Valerie Anne. BA, Augustana Coll., 1971; JD, U. Iowa, 1974. Bar: Iowa 1974, Ill. 1975, U.S. Dist. Ct. (so. dist.) Iowa 1975, U.S. Dist. Ct. (so. dist.) Ill. 1975. Assoc. Van Der Kamp & Crampton, Rock Island, Ill., 1975-79; ptnr. Van Der Kamp, Cleaver & Stojan, P.C., Rock Island, 1980—. Mem. adv. council Luth. Social Services of Ill. Adult Day Care Ctr., Rock Island; bd. dirs. United Way of Quad Cities, Rock Island; pres. adv. council Ret. Sr. Vol. Program, Moline; bd. govs. Rock Island Community Found.; assoc. mem. Rock Island Preservation Commn. Mem. ABA, Ill. State Bar Assn., Iowa State Bar Assn., Rock Island County Bar Assn., Scott County Bar Assn. Lutheran. Lodge: Kiwanis (pres., bd. dirs.). Avocations: fine arts, racquet sports. Contracts commercial, Consumer commercial, Real property. Home: 4412-39th Ave Rock Island IL 61201 Office: Van Der Kamp Cleaver & Stojan PC 1600-4th Ave Rock Island IL 61201

CLEGG, KAREN KOHLER, lawyer; b. Junction City, Kans., Jan. 7, 1949; d. John Emil and Delores Maxine (Letkeman) Kohler; m. Stephen J. Clegg Jr., Mar. 28, 1970. BS, Emporia State U., 1970; JD, U. Kans., 1975. Bar: Kans. 1975, U.S. Dist. Ct. Kans. 1975, Mo. 1977, U.S. Dist. Ct. (we. dist.) Mo. 1977. Asst. atty. gen. State of Kans., Topeka, 1975-77; atty. The Bendix Corp., Kansas City, Mo., 1977-81, sr. atty., 1981-84; counsel Allied Corp., Kansas City, 1984—; mem. council human resources mgmt. adv. bd. Commerce Clearing House, Chgo., 1985—. Sec. Assn. Greater Devel. Coll. Blvd., Shawnee Mission, Kans., 1986—; bd. dirs. adv. council Avila Coll. Bus., Kansas City, 1984—, Dimensions Unltd., Kansas City, 1985-86. Mem. ABA, Mo. Bar Assn., Am. Soc. Personnel Adminstrn. (v.p., bd. dirs. EEO 1985, profl. services 1986—), Greater Kansas City C. of C. (centurian leadership program). Avocations: music, theatre, art, reading, travel. Government contracts and claims, Labor, Environment. Home: 11501 Lowell Overland Park KS 66210 Office: Allied Corp 2000 E 95th Kansas City MO 64131

CLEM, GARY SMITH, lawyer; b. Yellville, Ark., June 18, 1940; s. Leslie G. and Mary Frances (Smith) C. Jr.; m. Judith Ann Koenigsberg, Mar. 25, 1967; children—Deborah Lynn, Lauren Beth. Grad., Washington U., St. Louis, 1962; J.D., U. Mo., 1966. Bar: Mo. 1966, Ill. 1970. Assoc. firm Davis & Morgan, Peoria, Ill., 1969-72, ptnr., 1985—; assoc. Kavanagh, Scully, Sudow, White & Frederick, Peoria, Ill., 1972-76; pres. Clem & Triggs, P.C., Peoria, Ill., 1976-85. Vice pres., bd. dirs. Sr. Citizens Found., Inc., 1971-75; bd. dirs. Ill. Valley Pub. Telecommunications, Inc., 1976-78, Community Workshop and Tng. Ctr. Served with U.S. Army, 1967-69. Mem. ABA, Mo. Bar Assn., Ill. Bar Assn., Peoria County Bar Assn. (dir. 1982—), Nat. Council Sch. Attys., U. Mo. Columbia Alumni Assn. (pres. Peoria chpt. 1985—). Republican. Jewish. Clubs: Creve Coeur, Willow Knolls Country, Arrowhead Country. Labor, Local government. Office: 1125 1st Nat Bank Bldg Peoria IL 61602

CLEM, ROBERT CHARLES, lawyer; b. Sioux City, Iowa, Oct. 15, 1935; s. A.D. and Wilma Margaret (Heath) C.; m. Helen Jean Smith, Aug. 23, 1959; children: David, James, Steven. BA, Grinnell Coll., 1957; JD, U. Iowa, 1960. Bar: Iowa 1960, U.S. Dist. Ct. (no. dist.) Iowa 1960. Ptnr. Clem & Clem, Sioux City, 1960-63, Clem & Adams, Sioux City, 1963-72; city atty. Sioux City, 1968-73; ptnr. Crary, Huff, Clem, Raby & Inkster P.C., Sioux City, 1972—. Bd. dirs. Morningside Coll., Sioux City, 1981—. Served with USAR, 1960-66. Mem. ABA, Iowa Bar Assn., Woodbury County Bar Assn. (pres.), Estate Planning Council Greater Siouxland. Republican. Methodist. Club: Cosmopolitan (Sioux City). Lodges: Masons, Shriners. Probate. Home: 3708 Seger Sioux City IA 51106 Office: Crary Huff Clem Raby & Inkster PC 614 Pierce St PO Box 27 Sioux City IA 51102

CLEMEN, JOHN DOUGLAS, lawyer; b. Mineola, N.Y., Dec. 18, 1944; s. John Douglas and Amy Gertrude (Ackerson) C.; m. Judith Anne Davis, June 3, 1967; children: Elizabeth, Jennifer. BA, Hobart Coll., 1966; JD, Seton Hall U., 1974. Bar: N.J. 1974, U.S. Dist. Ct. N.J. 1974, U.S. Ct. Appeals (3d cir.) 1980, U.S. Supreme Ct. 1982, N.Y. 1985, U.S. Dist. Ct. (so. dist.) N.Y. 1985. Law sec. to assoc. justice N.J. Supreme Ct., Trenton, 1974-75; assoc. Shanley & Fisher, Newark, 1975-83; ptnr. Shanley & Fisher, P.C., Newark, 1983—; arbitrator U.S. Dist. Ct. N.J., 1985—, N.J. Superior Ct., Morristown, 1986—; guest lectr. Acad. Medicine N.J., 1980-82. Contbg. editor Seton Hall Rev., 1973-74. Served to capt. USAF, 1966-71, Vietnam. Decorated Air medal. Mem. ABA, N.J. Bar Assn., N.Y. State Bar Assn., Trial Attys. N.J., Bergen County Bar Assn., Morris County Bar Assn., Commerce & Industry Assn. of N.J. (bd. dirs.). Clubs: Essex (Newark); Morristown. Federal civil litigation, State civil litigation, Personal injury. Home: 574 Colonial Rd River Vale NJ 07675 Office: Shanley & Fisher PC 131 Madison Ave Morristown NJ 07960

CLEMENS, RICHARD GLENN, lawyer; b. Chgo., Oct. 8, 1940; s. James Ralston and Jeanette Louise (Moellering) C.; m. Judith B. Clemens, Aug. 19, 1967; 1 dau., Kathleen. B.A., U. Va., 1962, J.D., 1965. Bar: Ill. 1965. Assoc. Sidley & Austin, Chgo., 1965-66, Washington, 1968-71, Brussels, Belgium, 1972-73, ptnr., Chgo., 1973—. Served to capt. U.S. Army, 1966-68. Mem. ABA, Ill. Bar Assn., Chgo. Bar Assn. Clubs: Legal, Monroe (Chgo.). General corporate, Private international, Securities. Home: 2928 Iroquois Rd Wilmette IL 60091 Office: 1 First National Plaza Suite 4800 Chicago IL 60603

CLEMENT, LESLIE JOSEPH, JR., lawyer; b. Thibodaux, La., June 26, 1948; s. Leslie Joseph and Shirley Marie (Picou) C.; m. Sandra Ann Rome, June 18, 1971; children: Paul, Philip, Rebecca. BA, Nicholls State Coll., 1970; JD, La. State U., 1974. Assoc. Porteous, Toledano, Hainkel & Johnson, Thibodaux, 1974-76; ptnr. Boudreaux & Clement, Thibodaux, 1976-78; sole practice Thibodaux, 1978—. Served to 1st lt. La. N.G., 1970-76. Mem. ABA, La. Bar Assn., Lafourche Parish Bar Assn., La. Trial Lawyers Assn. Democrat. Roman Catholic. State civil litigation, Family and matrimonial, General practice. Office: 409 Canal Blvd Thibodaux LA 70301

CLEMENT, ROBERT LEBBY, JR., lawyer; b. Charleston, S.C., Dec. 14, 1928; s. Robert Lebby and Julia Axson (Thayer) C.; m. Helen Mathilda Lewis, Nov. 26, 1954; children: Jeanne Marie, Robert Lebby III, Thomas L.T. AB, The Citadel, 1948; JD, Duke U., 1951. Bar: N.C. 1951, S.C. 1954. Practiced in Charlotte, N.C., 1951-53; ptnr. Cornish, Clement & Horlbeck, Charleston, S.C., 1955-60, Hagood, Rivers & Young, 1960-65, Young, Clement, Rivers & Tisdale, 1965—; pres. Charleston Automotive Parts, Inc., 1969-84; bd. dirs. Am. Mut. Fire Ins. Co., William M. Bird & Co., Inc., WCSC, Inc., C & S Nat. Bank; asst. city atty., Charleston, 1960; judge Mcpl. Ct., Charleston, 1961-63. Mem. adv. bd., pres. bd. trustees Charleston Mus., 1980-83; mem. Charleston County Council, 1983-86, chmn., 1985-86. Served with JAGC, USAF, 1953-55. Mem. ABA, N.C. Bar Assn., S.C. Bar Assn. Democrat. Presbyterian. Lodge: Rotary. Banking, General corporate, Estate planning. Office: Young Clement Rivers & Tisdale PO Box 993 Charleston SC 29402

CLEMENTS, ALLEN, JR., lawyer; b. Macon, Ga., Jan. 15, 1924; s. Allen C. and Mamie F. (Vinson) C.; children—Mary, Jill, Byng, Allen. B.B.A., U. Miami, 1948, J.D., 1951. Bar: Fla. 1951, U.S. Tax Ct. 1951, U.S. Dist. Ct. (so. dist.) Fla. 1951, U.S. Ct. Appeals (5th cir.) 1952, U.S. Ct. Appeals (11th cir.) 1981. Sr. assoc. Claude Pepper Law Offices, Miami Beach, Fla., 1953-72; ptnr. Pepper, Clements, Hopkins & Weaver, Miami Beach, 1972-79; of counsel Tew, Critchlow, Sonberg, Traum & Friedbauer, Miami, Fla., 1979-82, Finley, Kumble, Wagner, Heinz, Underberg & Casey, Miami, 1982—; pros. atty. City of West Miami, Fla., 1954-56, city atty., 1956-83; legal advisor Dade County Council Mayors, 1964-72; cons. atty. Dade County League of Cities, 1966-77; atty. Miami Beach Tourist Devel. Authority, 1970-78, Village of Biscayne Park, 1972-75. Mem. West Miami (Fla.) Town Council, 1952-53. Served in U.S. Army, 1943-45. Decorated Bronze Star. Mem. Dade County Bar Assn. (bd. dirs. 1984-86). Democrat. Methodist. Local government, Real property. Home: 134 NE 90 St El Portal FL 33138 Office: 777 Brickell Ave Suite 1000 Miami FL 33131

CLEMENTS, JAMIE HAGER, lawyer; b. Crockett, Tex., Dec. 9, 1930; s. Neal William and Alberta (Hager) C.; m. Ann Trigg, Apr. 28, 1962; children—Susan Clements Negley, Jamie Hager, Cynthia. B.A. with honors, U. Tex., 1952, J.D., 1955. Bar: Tex. 1956. Gen. counsel Scott and White Med. Center, Temple, Tex., 1960—; dir. Interfirst Bank, Temple. Mem. Tex. Ho. of Reps., 1953-60; chmn. Tex. State Bd. Human Resources, 1977-78; chmn. Planning commn. City of Temple, 1969, mayor, 1970-74; pres. Temple United Fund, 1969; bd. dirs. Temple Boy Choir; trustee, pres. Ralph Wilson Pub. Trust, Temple, 1980, 85; pres. Cultural Activities Ctr., Temple, 1981-82; mem. Tex. Bd. of Mental Health and Mental Retardation, 1986—. Served with USMC, 1956-58. Mem. ABA, Am. Soc. Hosp. Attys., Nat. Health Lawyers Assn. (pres. 1980-81), State Bar Tex. (chmn. com. on liaison with med. profession 1966-69), Bell-Lampasas-Mills Counties Bar Assn. (pres. 1966), Temple C. of C., East Tex. C. of C. (dir.). Democrat. Presbyterian. Health. Home: 2644 Marland Wood Circle Temple TX 76502

CLEMON, U. W., federal judge; b. Birmingham, Ala., Apr. 9, 1943; m. Barbara Lang; children: Herman Issac, Addine Michele. Bar: Ala. Partner firm Adams and Clemon and predecessor, Birmingham, 1969-80; fed. judge U.S. Dist. Ct., No. Dist. Ala., Birmingham, 1980—. Mem. Ala. Senate, 1974-80. Recipient Law and Justice award SCLC, 1980. Mem. Am. Bar Assn. (exec. council 1976-79, C. Francis Stratford award 1986), Alpha Phi Alpha. Jurisprudence. Office: US Dist Ct 305 Fed Courthouse Birmingham AL 35203 *

CLEMONS, ALPHA OTTIS, JR., systems corporation executive, lawyer; b. Yakima, Wash., Aug. 11, 1948; s. Alpha Ottis and Edna Ann (Chisum) C.; m. Patricia Ann Young, June 12, 1971; children: Hilary, Sarah, Alexis, Emily. BA in Econs., Wash. State U., 1970; JD, Gonzaga U., 1976. Bar: Wash. 1977, U.S. Dist. Ct. (ea. dist.) Wash. 1978, U.S. Supreme Ct. 1979. Bailiff Superior Ct., Spokane, Wash., 1974-77; ptnr. Murphy, Bantz, Spokane, 1977-81; assoc. Underwood, Campbell, Spokane, 1981-82; dir. legal affairs ISC Systems Corp., Spokane, 1982-84, v.p., gen. counsel, sec., 1985-86, v.p., sec., H. Rand corp. adminstr., 1986—; adj. prof. Nat. Moot Ct., Gonzaga U., Spokane, 1979. Articles editor Gonzaga Law Rev., 1979. Mem. ABA, Wash. State Bar Assn., Spokane County Bar Assn., Spokane County Young Lawyers (trustee 1979-81, v.p. 1981-82), Delta Sigma Rho, Tau Kappa Alpha. General corporate, Computer, Contracts commercial. Home: 2109 W Johansen Rd Spokane WA 99208 Office: ISC Systems Corp 22425 Appleway Spokane WA 99019

CLENDENEN, WILLIAM HERBERT, JR., lawyer; b. New London, Conn., Dec. 2, 1942; s. William H. and Ethel L. (Clifford) C.; m. Sandra Allaire, Sept. 12, 1964; children: William, Patrick. BA, Providence Coll., 1964; JD, Cath. U. Am., 1967. Bar: Conn. 1967, U.S. dist. ct. Conn. 1971, U.S. dist. ct. (so. dist.) N.Y. 1977, U.S. dist. ct. R.I. 1977, U.S. ct. clms., 1977, U.S. Ct. Apls. (2d cir.) 1971, U.S. Sup. Ct. 1976. Reginald Heber Smith Community Lawyer fellow U. Pa. 1967-68; staff atty. New Haven Legal Assistance Assn., Inc., 1968-73; ptnr. Clendenen and Lesser, P.C., New Haven, 1973—; supervising atty. Yale Law Sch., 1981; alt. pub. mem. Conn. State Bd. Mediation and Arbitration, 1976-78. Pres. Greater New Haven Pee Wee Hockey Assn., 1980, 81. Mem. ABA, Conn. Bar Assn. (chmn. consumer law sect. 1974-78), New Haven County Bar Assn. (sec. 1986—), Conn. Trial Lawyers Assn., Assn. Trial Lawyers Am. Federal civil litigation, State civil litigation, Consumer commercial. Home: 35 W Park Ave New Haven CT 06511 Office: 400 Orange St New Haven CT 06511

CLENNAN, JOHN FRANCIS, lawyer; b. Long Island City, N.Y., Jan. 1, 1952; s. John and Esther (McCarthy) C.; m. Susan E. Clennan, Dec. 19, 1978; 1 child, John. BA, St. John's U., Jamaica, N.Y., 1972, JD, 1975. Bar: N.Y. 1976, U.S. Dist. Ct. (ea. and so. dists.) N.Y. 1976, U.S. Supreme Ct. 1979, U.S. Dist. Ct. (no. dist.) N.Y. 1981. Law clk. to presiding justice Appellate Ct., Bklyn., 1975-77, N.Y. Ct. Appeals, Albany, N.Y., 1977; asst. dist. atty. Dist. Atty.'s Office, Bronx County, N.Y., 1978; sole practice Centereach, N.Y., 1982—. V.p. Rockaway Park Philosophical Soc., Shoreham, N.Y., 1971-86. Served to U.S. Army, 1978-82. Mem. N.Y. State Bar Assn. (mil. affairs com.), Suffolk County Bar Assn. (appellate practice com.). Lodge: Lions. State civil litigation, Criminal. Home: 28 Selden Blvd Centereach NY 11720 Office: 2206 Ocean Ave Ronkonkoma NY 11779

CLERMONT, KEVIN MICHAEL, legal educator; b. N.Y.C., Oct. 25, 1945; s. William Theodore and Rita Ruth (Healy) C.; m. Pamela Anne Cummings, Sept. 15, 1979; 1 child, Adrienne Shaine. A.B. summa cum laude, Princeton U., 1967; postgrad. U. Nancy (France), 1967-68; J.D. magna cum laude, Harvard U., 1971. Bar: Mass. 1971, N.Y. 1974, U.S. Dist. Ct. (so. and ea. dists.) N.Y. 1974, U.S. Ct. Appeals (2d cir.) 1974. Law clk. to judge U.S. Dist. Ct. (so. dist.) N.Y., 1971-72; assoc. Cleary, Gottlieb, Steen & Hamilton, N.Y.C., 1972-74; asst. prof. Sch. Law, Cornell U., Ithaca, N.Y., 1974-77, assoc. prof., 1977-80, prof., 1980—. Fulbright scholar, 1967-68. Mem. ABA, Assn. Am. Law Schs., Order of Coif, Phi Beta Kappa, Sigma Xi. Author: (with others) Materials for a Basic Course in Civil Procedure, 5th edit., 1984; Civil Procedure, 1982; (with others) Law: Its Nature, Functions, and Limits, 3d edit., 1986; editor Harvard Law Rev., 1969-71. Legal education, Federal civil litigation. Home: 916 Steam Mill Rd Ithaca NY 14850 Office: Cornell U Law Sch Myron Taylor Hall Ithaca NY 14853

CLEVELAND, LESLIE CLICK, lawyer; b. Corpus Christi, Tex., May 21, 1951; d. LaVar Donald and Patricia (McIlvaine) Click; m. Clement Cleveland, June, 1978 (div. May, 1985); 1 child Elizabeth W. BA with distinction, U. Colo., 1973, JD, 1976. Bar: Colo. 1976, U.S. Dist. Ct. Colo. 1976. Assoc. Clanahan, Tanner, Downing & Knowlton, Denver, 1975-78, Martin, Knapple, Humphrey & Tharp, Boulder, Colo., 1978-80; atty. J.C. Penney Co., Denver, 1980-82; assoc. Bourke & Jacobs P.C., Denver, 1982—; dir., sec. Click & Geddes Lumber Co., Denver, 1981—; grader Colo. Bar Exam, Denver, 1982—; panel trustee bankruptcy U.S. Justice Dept., Denver, 1986—. Bd. dirs. Jr. League of Denver, 1981-82; cons. Tech. Assistance Ctr., Denver, 1985-86. Mem. ABA, Colo. Bar Assn. (corps. sect.), Colo. Women's Bar Assn., Denver Bar Assn. (real estate sect.), Denver Law Club. Republican. Episcopalian. Avocations: gardening, running, tennis, skiing. Bankruptcy, General corporate, General practice. Home: 3245 Race St Englewood CO 80110 Office: Bourke & Jacobs, PC 4100 E Mississippi Ave Denver CO 80222

CLEVELAND, PETER DEVINE, lawyer; b. Chgo., Dec. 20, 1955; s. John A. and Patricia (Devine) C.; m. Rebecca Reasner, Sept. 18, 1982. BA, U. N.C., 1978; JD, Ind. U., 1981. Bar: Ind. 1981, U.S. Dist. Ct. (so. dist.) Ind. 1981. Assoc. Rocap, Rocap, Reese & Young, Indpls., 1981-84; ptnr. Lawrence, Carter, Gresk, Leerkamp & Walsh, Indpls., 1984—. Bd. dirs. Fall Creek YMCA, Indpls., 1984—. Mem. ABA, Ind. Bar Assn., Indpls. Bar Assn., Beta Theta Pi Alumni Assn. (pres. Indpls. chpt. 1983). Republican. Roman Catholic. General corporate, Federal civil litigation, State civil litigation. Home: 8415 Spring Mill Ct Indianapolis IN 46204 Office: Lawrence Carter et al 1145 Market Square Ctr 151 N Delaware Indianapolis IN 46204

CLICK, DAVID FORREST, lawyer; b. Miami Beach, Fla., Dec. 17, 1947; s. David Gorman and Helen Margaret (McPhail) C.; m. Helaine London, June 2, 1974; children: Kenneth Randall, Adam Elliott. BA, Yale U., 1969, JD, 1973, MA, 1974. Bar: Conn. 1973, Md. 1983, U.S. Supreme Ct. 1983, Fla. 1984, Maine 1984. Asst. prof. Western New England Sch. Law, Springfield, Mass., 1974-77; assoc. prof. Ind. U., Bloomington, 1977-78, U. Md., Balt., 1978-84; assoc. Nixon, Hargrave, Devans & Doyle, Jupiter, Fla., 1984-86; sole practice 1986—; bd. dirs. Click Farms, Inc., Clewiston, Fla. Contbr. articles to profl. jours. Mem. Christmas Cove (Maine) Improvement Assn., adv. bd. Sun Bank South Fla., N.A.; bd. dirs. Palm Beach-Martin County Estate Planning council. Mem. ABA, Fla. Bar Assn., Palm Beach County Bar Assn. (editorial bd. bar bulletin). Presbyterian. Estate planning, Probate, Real property. Home: 19216 Pine Tree Dr Tequesta FL 33469 Office: 1001 US One Suite 503 Jupiter FL 33477

CLIFF, JOHN WILLIAM, JR., lawyer; b. Bonham, Tex., Mar. 25, 1949; s. John William and Betty Lou (Wheeler) C.; m. Brenda Reneé Garrison, Aug. 21, 1976; children: Jason, Jacob, Heidi, Jordan, Hillary, Holli. BS, U. Houston, 1971, JD, 1974. Bar: Tex. 1974, U.S. Dist. Ct. (we. dist.) Tex. 1975, U.S. Ct. Appeals (5th cir.) 1977, U.S. Dist. Ct. (no. dist.) Tex. 1982, U.S. Dist. Ct. (ea. and we. dist.) Ark. 1983. Ptnr. Kenworthy & Cliff, Odessa, Tex., 1974-76; assoc. Childs & Bishop, Odessa, 1976-77, Ater & Hirsch, Odessa, 1977-79; ptnr. Moore & Cliff, Odessa, 1979-81, Smith & Cliff, P.C., Odessa, 1981—; instr. legal research Odessa Coll., 1985. Mem. ABA, Tex. Criminal Def. Lawyers Assn. Democrat. Methodist. Lodges: Order of Barrister, Order of Barons, Masons. Family and matrimonial, Criminal, General practice. Home: 3721 Oakridge Odessa TX 79762 Office: Smith & Cliff PC 323 N Grant Odessa TX 79761

CLIFF, WALTER CONWAY, lawyer; b. Detroit, Jan. 2, 1932; s. Frank V. and Virginia L. (Conway) C.; m. Ursula McHugh, Nov. 5, 1960; children: Walter C., Mary F., Catherine C. B.S., U. Detroit, 1955, LL.B., 1955; LL.M., NYU, 1956. Bar: Mich. 1956, N.Y. 1958. Assoc. firm Cahill Gordon & Reindel, N.Y.C., 1958-66, ptnr., 1966-82; pres. Walter C. Cliff, P.C. (ptnr. in Cahill Gordon & Reindel), N.Y.C., 1982—. Bd. dirs. Florence Gould Found., N.Y.C., 1983—; bd. dirs. Austen Riggs Center, Stockbridge, Mass., 1983—. Served with U.S. Army, 1956-58. J.K. Lasser fellow NYU, 1955-56. Mem. ABA, N.Y. Bar Assn., Assn. Bar City N.Y. Democrat. Roman Catholic. Clubs: Down Town, Stockbridge Golf. Corporate taxation. Office: Cahill Gordon & Reindel 80 Pine St New York NY 10005

CLIFFORD, CLARK MCADAMS, lawyer; b. Fort Scott, Kans., Dec. 25, 1906; s. Frank Andrew and Georgia (McAdams) C.; m. Margery Pepperell Kimball, Oct. 3, 1931; children—Margery Pepperell Clifford Lanagan, Joyce Carter Clifford Burland, Randall Clifford Wight. LL.B., Washington U., St. Louis, 1928. Assoc. firm Holland, Lashly & Donnell, St. Louis, 1928-33; with Holland, Lashly & Lashly, 1933-37; ptnr. Lashly, Lashly, Miller & Clifford, 1938-43; sr. ptnr. Clifford & Miller, Washington, 1950-68; sec. Dept. Def., Washington, 1968-69; sr. ptnr. Clifford & Warnke, Washington, 1969—; chmn. bd. First Am. Bankshares, Inc.; dir. Knight-Ridder Newspapers; spl. counsel to Pres. U.S., 1946-50. Served from lt. (j.g.) to capt. USNR, 1944-46; naval aide to Pres. U.S. 1946. Recipient medal of Freedom. Mem. Fed., Am., Mo., D.C., St. Louis bar assns., Kappa Alpha. Clubs: Burning Tree (Washington), Metropolitan (Washington), Chevy Chase (Washington). General corporate. Home: 9421 Rockville Pike Bethesda MD 20814 Office: First Am Bankshares Inc 740 15th St Washington DC 20005

CLIFFORD, ROBERT L., supreme ct. justice N.J.; b. Passaic, N.J., Dec. 17, 1924; s. John P. and Elizabeth E. C.; m. Joan Sieben, Oct. 20, 1951; children: Robert L., John P. II, Michael A. B.A., Lehigh U., 1947; LL.B., Duke U., 1950. Bar: N.J. bar 1950. Law sec. to Hon. William A. Wachenfeld, N.J. Supreme Ct., 1953-54; practice law Newark, 1954-62, Morristown, N.J., 1962-70; commr. of banking and ins. State of N.J., 1970-72, commr. of instns. and agys., 1972-73; assoc. justice N.J. Supreme Ct., 1973—. Served with USNR, 1943-46. Recipient Trial Bar award Trial Attys. N.J., 1970. Fellow Am. Coll. Trial Lawyers, Am. Bar Found.; mem. Am. Judicature Soc., Morris County Bar Assn., N.J. State Bar Assn. (officer 1968-70), Am. Bar Assn. Democrat. Office: Morris County Courthouse Washington St Morristown NJ 07960 *

CLIFFORD, ROBERT WILLIAM, judge; b. Lewiston, Maine, May 2, 1937; s. William H. and Alice (Sughrue) C.; m. Clementina Radillo, Jan. 18, 1964; children: Laurence M., Matthew P. BA, Bowdoin Coll., 1959; LLB, Boston Coll., 1962. Bar: Maine 1962, U.S. Dist. Ct. Maine 1965. Ptnr. Clifford & Clifford, Lewiston, 1964-79; justice Maine Superior Ct., Auburn, 1979-83; chief justice Maine Superior Ct., 1984-86; assoc. justice Maine Supreme Jud. Ct., Portland, 1986—. Mem. Lewiston City Council, 1968-70, mayor, 1971-72; mem. Maine State Senate, 1973-76; chmn. Lewiston Charter Commn., 1978-79. Mem. ABA, Maine Bar Assn., Androscoggin County Bar Assn., Am. Judicature Soc. Democrat. Roman Catholic. Home: 14 Nelke Pl Lewiston ME 04240 Office: Maine Supreme Jud Ct Androscoggin County Bldg Turner St Portland ME 04210

CLIFTON, HENRY, JR., lawyer; b. Bklyn., May 8, 1909; s. Henry and Adele Rollins (Miller) C.; m. Elizabeth Mihalka, July 31, 1936 (div.); children—Jane Elizabeth Clifton Dockery, Henry Stephen; m. 2d, Loretta Marguerite Hoard. A.B., Princeton U., 1931; J.D., Harvard, 1934. Bar: N.Y. 1935, U.S. Dist. Ct. (so. and ea. dists.) N.Y. 1936, U.S. Ct. Appeals (2d and 6th cirs.) 1938, U.S. Supreme Ct. 1942. Ptnr. McLanahan, Merritt & Ingraham, N.Y.C., 1942-59, Buell Clifton & Turner, N.Y.C., 1959-69; Clifton Budd & Burke, N.Y.C., 1970-75; Clifton Budd Burke & DeMaria, N.Y.C., 1975-81, of counsel, 1981—; past bd. dirs., exec. com. Am. Arbitration Assn. Served as comdr. USNR, 1942-46. Recipient Whitney North Seymour, Sr. Arbitration medal, 1976. Mem. ABA, Assn. Bar City N.Y. Clubs: Westhampton Country (Westhampton Beach, N.Y.); Ponte Vedra (Fla.); Pinehurst (N.C.) Country. Labor, Pension, profit-sharing, and employee benefits. Address: 420 Lexington Ave New York NY 10170

CLIFTON, RICHARD RANDALL, lawyer, legal educator; b. Framingham, Mass., Nov. 13, 1950; s. Arthur Calvin and Vivian Juanita (Himes) C. AB, Princeton U., 1972; JD, Yale U., 1975. Bar: Ill. 1975, Hawaii 1976, U.S. Dist. Ct. Hawaii 1976, U.S. Ct. Appeals (9th cir.) 1976, U.S. Ct. Appeals (2d cir.) 1979, U.S. Supreme Ct. 1982. Law clk. to judge U.S. Ct. Appeals (9th cir.), Honolulu, 1975-76; from assoc. to ptnr. Cades, Schutte, Fleming & Wright, Honolulu, 1977—; adj. prof. law U. Hawaii, Honolulu, 1979—. Co-author: The Shreveport Plan: An Experiment in the Delivery of Legal Services, 1974. Mem. dist. com. Nancy J. Stivers Meml. Fund, Honolulu, 1984—, fin. com. Hawaii Pub. Radio, Honolulu, 1985—. Mem. ABA, Hawaii Bar Assn., Hawaii Women Lawyers Found. Club: Plaza (Honolulu). Federal civil litigation, State civil litigation. Home: 3683 Woodlawn Dr Honolulu HI 96822 Office: Cades Schutte Fleming & Wright PO Box 939 Honolulu HI 96808

CLIMAN, RICHARD ELLIOT, lawyer; b. N.Y.C., July 19, 1953; s. David Arthur and Mary (Vitale) C. AB cum laude, Harvard U., 1974, JD cum laude, 1977. Bar: Calif. 1977. Assoc. Pettit & Martin, San Francisco, 1977-83, ptnr., 1984—. Mem. ABA, San Francisco Bar Assn. General corporate, Securities. Home: 2355 Jones St Apt 5 San Francisco CA 94133 Office: Pettit & Martin 101 California St San Francisco CA 94111

CLIMER, JAMES ALAN, lawyer; b. Chillicothe, Ohio, Dec. 17, 1954; s. James Parker and Jane Louise (Halsey) C.; m. Mary Ellen Murray, Oct. 17, 1981. BA in Polit. Sci., Miami U., Ohio, 1977; JD, U. Toledo, 1980. Bar: Ohio 1980, U.S. Dist. Ct. (no. and so. dists.) Ohio 1981. Assoc. Jones, Schell & Schaefer Co., Toledo, 1980-81; sole practice W. Carrollton, Ohio, 1981-83; asst. law dir. City of Parma, Ohio, 1984—; sole practice Cleve., 1983—. Mem. ABA, Ohio State Bar Assn., Cleve. Bar Assn., Greater Cleve. Bldg. Industry Assn., Jaycees (sec. 1984-85, v.p. 1985-86). Democrat. Presbyterian. Avocations: golf, skiing, reading. State civil litigation, Construction, Local government. Office: James Alan Climer 916 Engrs Bldg 1365 Ontario St Cleveland OH 44114

CLINARD, ROBERT NOEL, lawyer; b. Welch, W.Va., Nov. 1, 1946; s. Vernon Carlos and Mary Elizabeth (Noel) C.; m. Margaret Hawthorne Higgins, May 21, 1977; children: Elizabeth Kercheval, Edward Noel. BA, Washington & Lee U., 1968, JD, 1975. Bar: N.Y. 1977, U.S. Dist. Ct. (so. dist.) N.Y. 1977, Va. 1978, U.S. Dist. Ct. (ea. dist.) Va. 1978, U.S. Ct. Appeals (4th cir.) 1986. Assoc. Winthrop, Stimson, Putnam & Roberts, N.Y.C., 1976-78; assoc. Hunton & Williams, Richmond, Va., 1978-86, ptnr., 1986—. Sec. Va. Cultural Laureate Soc., Richmond, 1981-86, bd. dirs., 1981—. Served to lt. USNR, 1969-72. Mem. ABA (antitrust sect., franchising and healthcare coms.), Va. Bar Assn. (vice chmn. antitrust com. health law sect. 1985—, vice chmn. 1986-87), Order of Coif, Phi Beta Kappa, Omicrom Delta Kappa. Republican. Episcopalian. Club: Westwood Racquet (Richmond). Avocations: boating, saltwater fishing, house renovation. Antitrust, Federal civil litigation, Franchise law. Home: 1710 Grove Ave Richmond VA 23220 Office: Hunton & Williams PO Box 1535 Richmond VA 23212

CLINCH, H(ENRI) CARLETON, lawyer, legal educator; b. Hackensack, N.J., Aug. 9, 1950; s. H. Courtenay and Dorothy E (Scheffold) C.; m. Jonel Bartlett, Sept. 14, 1974; children—H. Courtenay, Justine Julia. A.B., Brown U., 1972; J.D., Rutgers U., 1975. Bar: N.J. 1975. Law clk. to superior ct. judge, Jersey City, 1975-76; asst. prosecutor Bergen County, Hackensack, 1976-79; ptnr. Clinch & Clinch, Hackensack, 1979-84, Kohler & Clinch, Hackensack, 1984—; chief Bergen County Narcotics Task Force, 1978-79; adj. prof. Rutgers U. Law Sch., Newark, 1980—. Vice pres., bd. atty. Northwest Bergen ARC, Ridgewood, N.J., 1979—; bd. atty. West Bergen Mental Health Ctr., Ridgewood, 1980—. Mem. ABA, N.J. State Bar Assn., Bergen County Bar Assn., Order of Barristers. Republican. Episcopalian. Clubs: Ridgewood Country; Brown (N.J.). Lodge: Masons. Estate planning, Personal injury, Real property. Home: 377 Bevenidge Rd Ridgewood NJ 07450 Office: Kohler & Clinch 241 Main St Hackensack NJ 07601

CLINE, DANIEL JAMES, lawyer; b. Saginaw, Mich., Dec. 2, 1955; s. Lenwell A. and Jean (Hegler) C.; m. Linda Nichols, May 16, 1981. BA, Yale U., 1978; JD, U. Mich., 1981. Bar: Mich. 1981, U.S. Dist. Ct. (ea. dist.) Mich. 1981. Assoc. Braun, Kendrick et al, Saginaw, 1981-84; mem. Currie & Kendall, P.C., Midland, Mich., 1984—. Bd. dirs. Midland Community Cancer Services, Midland, 1986—. Mem. Mich. Bar Assn. (legal econs. sect. 1983—). Real property, Bankruptcy, General practice. Home: 1885 W Tranquil Trail Midland MI 48640 Office: Currie & Kendall PC PO Box 1846 Midland MI 48640-1846

CLINE, LANCE DOUGLAS, lawyer; b. Columbus, Ind., Oct. 8, 1951; s. Leon Dale and Jo Ann Alice (Fauser) C.; m. Mary Margaret Nagle, Oct. 8, 1977; children—Rachel Ann, Natalie Brooke, Kathleen Nagle. B.A., Ind. U., 1973, J.D., 1980. Bar: Ind. 1980, U.S. Dist. Ct. (so. dist.) Ind. 1980. Ptnr. Townsend, Yosha & Cline, Indpls., 1980—. Contbr. articles to profl. jours. Mem. Ind. Trial Lawyers Assn. (bd. dirs. 1984—), Am. Trial Lawyers Assn., ABA, Ind. State Bar Assn., Indpls. Bar Assn., Phi Beta Kappa. Personal injury. Home: 8800 Moore Rd Indianapolis IN 46278 Office: Townsend Yosha & Cline 2220 N Meridian St Indianapolis IN 46208

CLINE, LEE WILLIAMSON, lawyer; b. Ft. Sill, Okla., June 19, 1944; s. Harvey V. Jr. and Virginia Jo (McCarter) Marmon; m. Mary Jane Fairweather , June 18, 1982 (div.); children: Christopher, Andrew, April, Meghan. AB in Polit. Economy, Wabash Coll., 1966; JD, Miss. Coll., 1979. Bar: La. 1985. Sole practice Bay St. Louis, Miss., 1979-86; with Delta Pipeline Co., Houston, 1986—. Mem. ABA, Am. Trial Lawyers Assn., Ind. Petroleum Assn. Am., Am. Assn. Petroleum Landmen, C. of C., La. Bar Assn., New Orleans Natural Gas Assn. Republican. Lutheran. Oil and gas leasing, Probate, Real property. Home: Rt 3 Box 394B Bay Saint Louis MS 39520 Office: Delta Pipeline Co 4250 Republic Bank Ctr Houston TX 77002

CLINE, MICHAEL ROBERT, lawyer; b. Parkersburg, W.Va., Oct. 13, 1949; s. Robert Rader and Hazel Mae (Boice) C.; m. Carole R. Davis, Aug. 28, 1972. A.B., Morris Harvey Coll., 1972; J.D., Wake Forest U., 1975. Project coordinator Gov.'s Office Fed.-State Relations, Charleston, W.Va., 1970-72; spl. asst. W.Va. Office Econ. Opportunity, 1973; spl. asst. W.Va. Dept. Labor, Charleston, 1974; staff asst., hearing officer, 1975-77; sole practice, Charleston, 1977—. Mem. ABA, Assn. Trial Lawyers Am., Comml. Law League Am., Nat. Assn. Criminal Defense Lawyers, W.Va. Trial Lawyers Assn. (treas. 1984, v.p. 1985-86, outstanding mem. 1983), W.Va. Bar Assn. (chmn. com. on econs. of law practice 1986), Pi Kappa Delta, Phi Alpha Delta. Republican. Methodist. Lodge: Kiwanis, Elks, Rotary. Con-

sumer commercial, Personal injury, Criminal. Home: 1531 Dixie St Charleston WV 25301 Office: 323 Morrison Bldg Charleston WV 25301

CLINE, RICHARD ALLEN, lawyer; b. Columbus, Ohio, Oct. 1, 1955; s. Ralph S. and Myrtle O. (Harrison) C.; m. Nora Jean Arth, Oct. 2. 1982; children: Caitlin, Patrick. BA in Polit. Sci., Kent State U., 1977, BS in Criminal Justice, 1977; JD, Ohio State U., 1981. Bar: Ohio 1981, U.S. Dist. Ct. (so. dist.) Ohio 1981, U.S. Ct. Appeals (6th cir.) 1983, U.S. Supreme Ct. 1985. Assoc. David Riebel, Columbus, 1981-84; ptnr. Riebel & Cline, Columbus, 1984-85; ptnr., pres. Durkin, Cline and Co. L.P.A., Columbus, 1985—; prosecutor City of Whitehall, Ohio, 1980-81, Village of Powell, Ohio, 1983—; instr. Ohio Peace Officers Tng. Counsel, Columbus, 1985. Bd. dirs. Woodbridge Village Assn., Columbus, 1983—. Served with JAGC, Ohio Nat. Guard, 1983—. Mem. Ohio Bar Assn., Jaycees (named one of Outstanding Young Men of Am., 1979), Phi Alpha Delta, Omicron Delta Kappa. Republican. Baptist. Avocations: martial arts, military history. Criminal, State civil litigation, General practice. Home: 6858 Worthington-Galena Rd Worthington OH 43085 Office: Durkin Cline and Co LPA 580 S High St Suite 316 Columbus OH 43215

CLINE, THOMAS FARRELL, lawyer; b. Columbus, Ind., May 25, 1953; s. Leon Dale and Jo Ann Cline. AB cum laude, Harvard U., 1975; MA in Sociology, U. Wash., 1978, JD, 1981. Bar: Wash. 1981, U.S. Dist. Ct. (we. dist.) Wash. 1981. Sole practice Seattle, 1981—. Fellow NSF, 1975. Mem. Assn. Trial Lawyers Am., Wash. State Trial Lawyers Assn., Wash. State Bar Assn. Federal civil litigation, State civil litigation, Personal injury. Office: 5308 Ballard Ave NW Seattle WA 98107

CLINK, STEPHEN HENRY, lawyer; b. Muskegon, Mich., Jan. 26, 1911; s. Stephen H. and Lena (Haan) C.; m. Susan Parker. A.B., U. Mich., 1933, J.D., 1936; LL.M. in Taxation, N.Y.U., 1949. Bar: Mich. bar 1936. Pros. atty. Muskegon County, 1939-41, judge of probate, 1941-48; now sr. ptnr. firm Landman, Latimer, Clink & Robb, Muskegon, 1950—; Teaching fellow in drafting wills and trust agreements NYU 1948-49. Contbr. articles to profl. jours. Pres. Muskegon Area Child Guidance Clinic, 1942; chmn. Mich. Juvenile Inst. Commn., 1945-47, bd. deacons Congl. Ch., endowment com.; pres. Mich. Welfare League, 1951-53; pres. Timber Trails council Boy Scouts Am., 1965-66, chmn. bd. trustees, 1962-74; pres. Muskegon County Community Found., 1972-74; sec. Fremont Area Found., 1970-76; chmn. United Appeal Planning and Research Council, 1968-69; pres. Muskegon County United Appeal, 1970-71; Mem. com. of visitors U. Mich. Law Sch., 1963-64; bd. dirs. numerous charitable founds. Named Young Man of Year Jr. C. of C., 1940, Muskegon's Outstanding Citizen, 1978; recipient Silver Beaver award, Disting. Eagle Scout award Boy Scouts Am. Fellow Am. Coll. Probate Counsel (regent 1967-76); mem. ABA (chmn. probate judges com. 1946), Muskegon County Bar Assn. (pres. 1952-53), State Bar Mich. (chmn. taxation sect. 1958-59, chmn. probate and trust law sect. 1968-69, ethics com. 1958-70). Lodge: Kiwanis (pres. Muskegon club 1958, Legion of Honor). Estate planning, Probate, Estate taxation. Office: 400 Terrace Plaza Muskegon MI 49443

CLINKSCALES, J(AMES) RANDALL, lawyer; b. Hillsboro, Tex., Mar. 12, 1954; s. Ronald Orr Clinkscales and Vallee (Wafer) Hefner; m. Barbara Jean Stucky, Sept. 28, 1980; 1 child, Joshua Lane. BS in Polit. Sci., Howard Payne U., 1976; JD, Washburn U., 1980. Bar: Kans. 1980, U.S. Dist. Ct. Kans. 1980. Assoc. Hiatt & Carpenter, Topeka, 1980-83, Ken Havner, Hays, Kans., 1983-85; sole practice Hays, 1985—. Mem. ABA, Kans. Bar Assn., Ellis County Bar Assn. Lodge: Kiwanis (pres. elect 1986). Banking, Contracts commercial, General practice. Office: 2604 General Hays Rd Hays KS 67601 Home: 323 W 32d Hays KS 67601

CLODFELTER, DANIEL GARY, lawyer; b. Thomasville, N.C., June 2, 1950; s. Billy G. and Marie Lorene (Wells) C.; m. Elizabeth Kay Bevan, Aug. 20, 1974; children: Julia Elizabeth, Catherine Gray. BA, Davidson Coll., 1972; AB, MA, Oxford U., Eng., 1974; JD, Yale U., 1977. Bar: N.C. 1977, U.S. Dist. Ct. (we. dist.) N.C. 1977, U.S. Dist. Ct. (ea. dist.) N.C. 1979, U.S. Ct. Appeals (4th cir.) 1984, U.S. Dist. Ct. (mid. dist.) N.C. 1985. Law clk. to presiding justice U.S. Dist. Ct., Charlotte, N.C., 1977-78; assoc. Moore & Van Allen, Charlotte, 1978-82, ptnr., 1983—. Chmn. Charlotte-Mecklenburg Planning Commn., 1986—; state sec. Rhodes Scholarship Trust, N.C., 1986—; trustee Z. Smith Reynolds Found., Inc., Winston-Salem, N.C., 1983—. Rhodes scholar, 1972. Mem. N.C. Bar Assn. (environ. law com.). Bankruptcy, Environment, Antitrust. Office: Moore & Van Allen 3000 NCNB Plaza Charlotte NC 28280

CLOGG, RICHARD BRUCE, lawyer; b. Oklahoma City, Sept. 6, 1949; s. Maurice and Mary E. (Horstmeier) C.; m. Christine Jane Sieff, June 19, 1970; children: Carrie, Emily, Johnathan. BA, Simpson Coll., 1971; JD, Drake U., 1974. Bar: Iowa 1974, U.S. Dist. Ct. (so. dist.) Iowa 1974, U.S. Supreme Ct. 1980, U.S. Ct. Appeals (8th cir.) 1985. Ptnr. Elgin, Hoyman, Clogg & Patin, Indianola, Iowa, 1974—. Mem. ABA, Iowa Bar Assn., Warren County Bar Assn. (pres. 1978-80), Assn. Trial Lawyers Iowa. Republican. Presbyterian. Lodge: Rotary. General practice, State civil litigation, Personal injury. Home: 1010 Scott Felten Indianola IA 50125 Office: Elgin Hoyman Clogg & Patin 106 E Salem PO Box 215 Indianola IA 50125

CLONTZ, STANFORD KENT, lawyer; b. Asheville, N.C., Oct. 8, 1950; s. Homer Asbury and Dora Marie (Watkins) C.; m. Janice Lynn Hunter, Feb. 15, 1986. BA, Western Carolina U., 1972; MS, George Washington U., 1977; JD, U. Tenn., 1979. Bar: N.C. 1980, U.S. Dist. Ct. (we. dist.) N.C. 1981, U.S. Ct. Appeals (4th cir.) 1984. Asst. atty. Buncombe County, Asheville, 1980-82; sole practice Asheville, 1982-84; ptnr. Baley, Baley & Clontz P.A., Asheville, 1984—. V.p. Buncombe County Young Dems., Asheville, 1981-82; trustee Woodfin (N.C.) San. Water And Sewer Dist., 1984-85. Served to lt. USN, 1972-77. Mem. ABA, N.C. Bar Assn. (appellate rules study commn.), Assn. Trial Lawyers Am., N.C. Acad. Trial Lawyers, Western Carolina U. Alumni Assn. (bd. dirs. 1985—). Presbyterian. Lodge: Kiwanis (pres. West Asheville chpt. 1983-84). State civil litigation, Personal injury, Workers' compensation. Home: 107E Manor Ridge Apts Asheville NC 28804 Office: Baley Baley & Clontz PA 510 Northwestern Plaza Asheville NC 28801

CLOON, WILLIAM GRAHAM, JR., judge; b. Bessemer Twp., Mich., Apr. 11, 1931; s. William Gabriel and Mary Louisa (King) C.; m. Leonora Scales, June 28, 1958; 1 child, William Gregory. AB, U. Mich., 1952, JD with distinction, 1955. Bar: Mich. 1955, U.S. Dist. Ct. (we. dist.) Mich. 1960, U.S. Ct. Mil. Appeals 1956, U.S. Ct. Appeals (6th cir.) 1969. Sole practice Ironwood, Mich., 1955-56, 59-82; judge 98th Jud. Dist. Ct., Bessemer and Ontonagon, Mich., 1982, 32d Jud. Cir. Ct., Bessemer and Ontonagon, Mich., 1982—. Asst. editor U. Mich. Law Rev., 1954-55. Served to 1st lt. JAGC, U.S. Army, 1956-59. Mem. Mich. Bar Assn., Gogebic-Ontonagon County Bar Assn. (past pres.), Am. Judicature Soc., Mich. Judges Assn., Judge Advocates Assn., Delta Theta Phi. Presbyterian. Lodges: Kiwanis, Elks, Shriners. Avocations: hunting, fishing, snowmobiling, power boat racing. Criminal, Federal civil litigation, State civil litigation. Home: 125 Francis St Ironwood MI 49938 Office: 32d Jud Cir Ct Courthouse Bessemer MI 49911

CLORAN, WILLIAM FRANCIS, lawyer; b. Lynn, Mass., Sept. 19, 1947; s. Francis Joseph and Anne Marie (Scanlon) C.; m. Martha Allison Messner, July 31, 1971; children: Francis Joseph, Timothy John. BA, U. Portland, 1969; JD, Willamette U., 1972. Bar: Oreg. 1972, U.S. Ct. Mil. Appeals 1973, U.S. Supreme Ct. 1979, U.S. Dist. Ct. Oreg. 1986. Commd. 2d lt. USAF, 1969, advanced through grades to capt. JAGC, 1972; asst. staff judge adv. USAF, Hill AFB, Utah, 1972-74, Udorn Royal Thai AFB, Thailand, 1974-75; dep. staff judge adv. USAF, McChord AFB, Wash., 1975-78; trial atty. USAF, Wright-Patterson AFB, Ohio, 1978-80; asst. staff judge adv. USAFR, Wright-Patterson AFB, Ohio, 1980-82, Travis AFB, Calif., 1982—; atty. City of The Dalles, Oreg., 1980-84; asst. atty. gen. State of Oreg., Salem, 1984—. Bd. dirs. Mid Columbia Vietnam Vet. Meml. Com., The Dalles. Recipient 2 meritorious service awards Oreg. Atty. Gen., 1984, 85. Mem. ABA, Oreg. Bar Assn. (bd. dirs. govt. and constrn. sects.). Republican. Roman Catholic. Clubs: Mazamas (Portland), Oreg. Nordic (Salem) (pres. and state rep. 1982-84). Lodge: Rotary (airshow com. 1982-84). Avocations: skiing, mountaineering, canoeing, bicycling. State civil litigation, Construction, Military. Home: 3394 Augusta Nat Dr Salem OR 97302 Office: Dept Justice Trial Div 450 Justice Bldg Salem OR 97302

CLOSE, DAVID PALMER, lawyer; b. N.Y.C., Mar. 16, 1915; s. Walter Harvey and Louise De Arango (Palmer) C.; m. Margaret Howell Gordon, June 26, 1954; children: Louise, Peter, Katharine, Barbara. B.A., Williams Coll., 1938; J.D., Columbia U., 1942. Bar: N.Y. State bar 1942. Practice law Washington, 1946—; partner Dahlgren & Close; dir. Nat. Savs. and Trust Co., Washington. Mem. adv. council Nat. Capital area Boy Scouts Am., 1961—; bd. dirs. Nat. Soc. Prevention Blindness, 1961-63, Internat. Humanities, Inc., 1960—, Internat. Eye Found., 1965-85, chmn., 1985—; bd. dirs. D.C. Soc. Prevention of Blindness, 1957-63, pres., 1961-63; bd. dirs. Marjorie Merriweather Post Found., 1974—, sec.-treas., 1974-76; trustee Williams Coll., 1963-68; trustee Hill Sch., 1965—, chmn., 1974-85 ; trustee Mount Vernon Coll., 1963-75 , pres., 1971-74. Served with USN, (intelligence) 1942-46. Mem. Am., Inter-Am., D.C. bar assns., Assn. Bar City N.Y., Assn. Trial Lawyers Am., World Assn. Lawyers for World Peace Through Law, Pilgrims, Order of St. John. Clubs: Chevy Chase (Md.), Fauquier Srgs. CE (Warrenton, Va.), University (Washington). General practice, Administrative and regulatory, Probate. Home: Hungry Run Farm Route 1 PO Box 600 Amissville VA 22002 Office: 1000 Connecticut Ave NW Washington DC 20036

CLOSEN, MICHAEL LEE, law educator, lawyer; b. Peoria, Ill., Jan. 25, 1949; s. Stanley Paul and Dorothy Mae (Kendall) C.; B.S., Bradley U., 1971, M.A., 1971; J.D., U. Ill., 1974. Bar: Ill. 1974. Instr. U. Ill., Champaign, 1974; jud. clk. Ill. Appellate Ct., Springfield, 1974-76, 77-78; asst. states atty. Cook County, Chgo., 1978; prof. law John Marshall Law Sch., Chgo., 1976—vis. prof. No. Ill. U., 1985-86; reporter Ill. Jud. Conf., Chgo., 1981—; arbitrator Am. Arbitration Assn., Chgo., 1981—; lectr. Ill. Inst. Continuing Legal Edn., Chgo., 1981—. Author casebook Agency, Employment and Partnership Law, 1984, (with others) Contracts, 1984; co-author: The Shopping Bag: Portable Art, 1986; contbr. articles to profl. jours. Recipient Service award Am. Arbitration Assn. 1984; named one of Outstanding Young Men in Am., 1981. Mem. ABA, Ill. Bar Assn., Appellate Lawyers Assn. Legal education, Contracts commercial, Agency and partnership. Home: 1247 N State #204 Chicago IL 60610 Office: John Marshall Law Sch 315 S Plymouth Ct Chicago IL 60604

CLOUGH, JOHN F., III, lawyer; b. Westchester, Pa., Dec. 12, 1953; s. John F. Jr. and Suzanne D. Clough; m. Lisa Rollin, Aug. 4, 1979; 1 child, Megan Elizabeth. BA, Franklin Marshall Coll., 1975; JD, Dickinson Sch. of Law, 1979. Bar: Pa. 1979, U.S. Dist. Ct. (ea. dist.) Pa. 1979, Alaska 1981, U.S. Dist. Ct. Alaska 1981, U.S. Ct. Appeals (9th cir.) 1981. Assoc. Weglarz, Tryon & Friedman, Lancaster, Pa., 1979-81; assoc. Faulkner, Banfield, Doogan & Holmes, Juneau, Alaska, 1981-85, ptnr., 1985—; prof. law U. Alaska, Juneau, 1981—. Bd. dirs. Reach, Inc., Juneau, Alaska, 1982—. Mem. Alaska Bar Assn. (chmn. adminstrv. law sect. 1984—), Juneau Bar Assn. (pres. 1984). Democrat. State civil litigation, Environment, Corporate taxation. Home: 1703 Willow Dr Juneau AK 99801 Office: Faulkner Banfield Doogan & Holmes 302 Gold St Juneau AK 99801-1150

CLOUSE, JOHN DANIEL, lawyer; b. Evansville, Ind., Sept. 4, 1925; s. Frank Paul and Anna Lucille (Frank) C.; m. Georgia L. Ross, Dec. 7, 1978; 1 child, George Chauncey. AB, U. Evansville, 1950; JD, Ind. U., 1952. Bar: Ind. 1952, U.S. Supreme Ct. 1962, U.S. Ct. Appeals (7th cir.) 1965. Assoc. firm James D. Lopp, Evansville, 1952-56; pvt. practice law, Evansville, 1956—; guest editorialist Viewpoint, Evansville Courier, 1978-86, Evansville Press, 1986—, Focus, Radio Sta. WGBF, 1978-84; 2d asst. city atty. Evansville, 1954-55; mem. appellate rules sub-com. Ind. Supreme Ct. Com. on Rules of Practice and Procedure, 1980. Pres. Civil Service Commn. of Evansville Police Dept., 1961-62, Ind. War Memls. Com., 1963-69; mem. jud. nominating com. Vanderburgh County, Ind., 1976-80. Served with inf. U.S. Army, 1943-46. Decorated Bronze Star. Fellow Ind. Bar Found.; mem. Evansville Bar Assn. (v.p. 1972), Ind. Bar Assn., Selden Soc., Pi Gamma Mu. Republican. Methodist. Club: Travelers Century (Los Angeles). Criminal, Family and matrimonial, State civil litigation. Home: 819 S Hebron Ave Evansville IN 47715 Office: 1010 Hulman Bldg Evansville IN 47708

CLOUTIER, RAYMOND ARTHUR, lawyer, probate judge; b. Manchester, N.H., Aug. 11, 1938; s. Ernest J. and Jeannette J. (Marion) C.; m. Theresa A. Maheu, June 3, 1961; children—Elise, Celeste, Raymond, Ernest. B.A., Assumption Coll., 1960; LL.B., Boston U., 1963. Bar: N.H. 1963, U.S. Dist. Ct. N.H. 1963. Atty. Hillsborough County (N.H.), 1976-81; now probate judge. Chmn., Hillsborough County Democratic Party, 1975. Mem. Am. Judicature Soc., Assn. Trial Lawyers Am., ABA. Roman Catholic. Club: Jolliet, KC. Banking, Consumer commercial, Contracts commercial. Address: 1415 Elm St PO Box 3150 Manchester NH 03105

CLUBB, BRUCE EDWIN, lawyer; b. Blackduck, Minn., Feb. 6, 1931; s. Ernest and Abigail (Gordy) C.; m. Martha Lucia Trapp, Dec. 19, 1954; children: Bruce Allen, Christopher Wade. B.B.A., U. Minn., 1955, LL.B. cum laude, 1958. Bar: D.C. 1959. Atty. Covington & Burling, 1958-61, Devel. Loan Fund, 1961-62, Chapman, DiSalle and Friedman, 1962-67; commr. U.S. Tariff Commn., 1967-71; ptnr. firm Baker & McKenzie, Washington, 1971—; disting. lawyer in residence U. Minn. Law Sch., 1981-82. Contbr. law revs. Served with AUS, 1952-54. Mem. D.C. Bar Assn., Am. Judicature Soc., Order of Coif. Republican. Clubs: Cosmos (pres. 1986), Metropolitan, Army Navy. International trade, Contracts commercial, Public international. Home: 100 Quay St Alexandria VA 22314 Office: Baker & McKenzie 815 Connecticut Ave NW Washington DC 20006

CLUGSTON, SCOTT, judge; b. Denver, June 1, 1932; s. Chester Roscoe Clugston and Addie Gertrude (McKenny) Ware; m. Karen Katherine Gilbert, June 12, 1960; children: Becky Lynn, Katia Lisanne, Andrea Carroll. BA, U. Utah, 1953; JD, U. Denver, 1958. Bar: Colo. 1958, U.S. Dist. Ct. Colo. 1958. Dist. claims mgr. Allstate Ins. Co., Denver and Salt Lake City, 1958-63; dep. dist. atty. 8th Jud. dist., Greeley, Colo., 1963-64; asst. atty. City of Greeley, 1865-72; sole practice Greeley, 1963-73; judge Weld County Ct., Greeley, 1973—. Served with USNR, 1953-55. Mem. Colo. Bar Assn., Colo. Assn. County Judges (pres. 1978-79). Home: 1844 26th Ave Greeley CO 80631 Office: Weld County Ct PO Box C Greeley CO 80632

CLUTE, JOHN E, lawyer, manufacturing company executive; b. Kooskia, Idaho, Oct. 28, 1934; s. J.L. and Elsie (Moore) C.; B.A. magna cum laude, Gonzaga U., 1960, J.D. summa cum laude, 1963; children: Jody Bernadette, Molly Anne. Bar: Idaho 1972. Asst. trust officer Seattle 1st Nat. Bank, 1960-63; atty. AEC, Richland, Wash., 1963-65; assoc. gen. counsel Boise Cascade Corp., Idaho, 1965-67, gen. counsel, 1967-70, v.p., gen. counsel, 1970-72, sr. v.p., gen. counsel, 1972—; mem. Paper Industry Counsel Group, 1972—; dir. Hecla Mining Co. Chmn. bd. dirs. Idaho Assn. Commerce and Industry, 1976-79; mem. Ivory 500, 1976—; chmn. Boise Cascade's Polit. Action Fund, 1978—; vice chmn. bd. trustees Gonzaga U., 1975—, mem. law council, 1970—; bd. dirs. United Way of Ada County, Inc.; chmn. leadership devel. com. Kellog-Found.-United Way S.W. Idaho, 1979—; bd. dirs. Nat. Fgn. Trade Council, 1969—. Served with U.S. Army, 1953-56. Decorated Army Commendation medal. Mem. NAM (dir.), ABA, Idaho Bar Assn., Wash. Bar Assn., Fed. Bar Assn., Internat. Bar Assn. Roman Catholic. Clubs: Arid, Hillcrest Country. Union League, Spokane. General corporate. Office: Boise Cascade Corp 1 Jefferson Sq Boise ID 83728 *

COADY, MICHAEL FRANCIS, construction company executive; b. Columbus, Oct. 21, 1957; s. Richard Joseph and Sally Ann (Baker) C. BBA, Ohio State U., 1979, BA, 1979, JD, 1982. Bar: Ohio 1982, U.S. Dist. Ct. (so. dist.) Ohio, 1984. V.p. Coady Contracting Co., Columbus, 1971—. Mem. Franklin County Young Reps., Columbus, 1983—; vol. Mothers March of Dimes, Columbus, 1971—. Mem. ABA, Ohio State Bar Assn., Columbus Bar Assn., Thomas More Soc., Assn. Trial Lawyers Am., Am. Soc. Hwy. Engrs. Republican. Roman Catholic. Club: Athletic of Columbus. Avocations: stamp collecting, short wave listening. Construction, Contracts commercial, Probate. Home: 1420 Haddon Rd Columbus OH 43209 Office: Coady Contracting Co 1455 E Fifth Ave Columbus OH 43219

COAKLEY, CHARLES, lawyer; b. Cambridge, Mass., Aug. 20, 1933; s. Timothy and Anne (Spillane) C.; m. Trudi Novina, Apr. 27, 1968; children—Lyssa, Gregory. A.B., Bowdoin Coll., 1954; J.D., N.Y. Law Sch., 1974. Bar: N.Y. 1975. Hearing rep. Travelers Ins. Co., N.Y.C., 1960-75; sr. counsel Am. Ins. Assn., N.Y.C., 1975—; cons. Internat. Assn. Indsl. Accident Bds. and Commns., Jackson, Miss., 1982—; mem. adv. Spl. Funds Conservation Com., N.Y.C., 1975—, Nat. Assn. Ins. Commrs.(task force on group self ins., draftsman model bill for group ins. 1983, adv. com. on occupational disease 1983-85), N.Y. Workers Compensation Bds. (recodification of the N.Y. workers compensation law adv. com. 1985—). Served with AUS, 1954-56. Mem. N.Y. Workers Compensation Bar Assn., U.S. C. of C. Workers' compensation, Insurance, Labor. Home: Beach Walk Saltaire NY 11706 Mailing Address: 34 W 89th St New York NY 10024

COAN, RICHARD MORTON, lawyer; b. N.Y.C., Sept. 17, 1948; s. Nelson W. and Phyllis (Tomashoff) C.; m. Kathleen M. Mitcheom, Sept. 5, 1983; children: Benjamin, Spencer. AB, U. Rochester, 1969; JD, Yale U., 1974. Bar: Conn. 1974, U.S. Dist. Ct. Conn. 1981, U.S. Ct. Appeals (2d cir.) 1982. Ptnr. Belford, Belford & Coan, New Haven, Conn., 1977-81, Coan, Lewendon and Royston, New Haven, 1981—. Mem. ABA (family law, corp. banking and bus. law sects.), Conn. Bar Assn. (family law, real estate, comml. law sects.). Bankruptcy, Family and matrimonial, Real property. Home: 69 Seaview Ave Branford CT 06405 Office: Coan Lewendon and Royston 18 Trumbull St New Haven CT 06511

COANE, BRUCE A., lawyer; b. Phila., Sept. 1, 1958; m. Rhia Centeno, Aug. 26, 1983; children: Sara; William. BA with honors, Pa. State U., 1979; JD, U. Houston, 1981. Bar: Tex. 1982, U.S. Dist. Ct. (so. dist.) Tex. 1982, U.S. Ct. Appeals (5th cir.) 1983, U.S. Ct. Appeals (3d cir.) 1984, U.S. Supreme Ct. 1985. Ptnr. Coane & Assocs., Houston, 1982—. Instr. U.S. citizenship ARC, Houston, 1982-85; radio talk show host S. Asian Info. Network, Houston, 1986. Mem. ABA, Am. Immigration Lawyers Assn., Tagalog Assn. Tex. (legal advisor 1985-86). Consumer commercial, Immigration, naturalization, and customs, Labor. Home: 4212 San Felipe Houston TX 77027 Office: Coane & Assocs 1900 W Loop S Suite 820 Houston TX 77027

COATES, BRADLEY ALLEN, lawyer, realtor; b. Los Angeles, Mar. 27, 1951; s. Mark Edmund and Elizabeth (Allen) C.; m. Margaret Fife Bentley, Apr. 17, 1977 (div. Dec. 1980). BA, U. So. Calif., 1973; JD, UCLA, 1976. Bar: Calif. 1977, Hawaii 1978, No. Marianas Islands 1978, Marshall Islands 1979, Federated States Micronesia 1981. Staff atty. Congress of Micronesia, Saipan, 1976-78; mng. ptnr. Rohlfing, Smith & Coates, Honolulu, 1978-85; prin. ptnr. Law Offices Bradley A. Coates, Honolulu, 1985—; pres., exec. dir. Pacific Arbitration and Mediation, Honolulu, 1985—. Chief counsel Hawaii State Rep. Party, Honolulu, 1981; founder, pres. Divorce with Decency Mediation Assn., Honolulu, 1985. Mem. Hawaii Bar Assn. (family law sect.). Clubs: Outdigger Canoe, Honolulu. Avocations: all water sports, skiing, hiking. Family and matrimonial, Probate, General corporate. Home: 941 Kului Pl Honolulu HI 96821 Office: 900 Fort St Mall Honolulu HI 96813

COATES, CHARLES ELTING, III, lawyer; b. West Point, N.Y., June 27, 1948; s. Charles E. Jr. and Beverly (Cohill) C.; m. Elizabeth L. R., June 10, 1972; children: Susanna H., Margaret L., Catherine A. BA, Harvard U., 1970, JD, 1974. Bar: Conn. 1974, U.S. Dist. Ct. Conn. 1974, U.S. Ct. Appeals (2d cir.) 1974. Assoc. Hirschberg, Pettengill, Strong & Nagle, Greenwich, Conn., 1974-78, Whitman & Ransom, Greenwich, 1978—; lectr. U. Conn. 1983-85. Pres. Community Ctrs. Inc., Greenwich, 1982-84; v.p. adminstrn. United Way of Greenwich, 1984-87. Served to capt. USAR, 1970. Mem. Greenwich Bar Assn. (pres. 1986—), Conn. Bar Assn. (mem. House of Dels. 1985—, exec. com. estates and probate sect. 1982-84), ABA. Republican. Presbyterian. Clubs: Belle Haven (Greenwich), Harvard of Fairfield County (sec. 1975-80). Probate, Real property. Home: 303 Old Norwalk Rd New Canaan CT 06840 Office: Whitman & Ranson 100 Field Point Rd Greenwich CT 06830

COATES, WILLIAM ALEXANDER, lawyer; b. Newberry, S.C., Oct. 8, 1949; s. William Floyd and Clara Monette (Alexander). B.S. in Bus. Administrn., U. S.C., 1971, J.D., 1974. Bar: S.C. 1974, U.S. Dist. Ct. S.C. 1976, U.S. Ct. Appeals (4th cir.) 1977. Asst. legis. asst. to senator Strom Thurmond, Washington, 1974-75; counsel to minority subcom. adminstrv. practice and procedure Com. on Judiciary U.S. Senate, 1975-76; asst. U.S. atty. Dept. of Justice, Greenville, S.C., 1976-80; ptnr. Love, Thornton, Arnold & Thomason, Greenville, 1980—; instr. Atty. Gen. Adv. Inst. U.S. Dept. of Justice, Washington, 1979. Chmn. Citizens Adv. Council, Greenville Gen. Hosp., Greenville County Heart Fund, Easter Seal Soc. Greenville County. Served with Air N.G., 1970-76. Mem. ABA, S.C. Bar, S.C. Def. Trial Attys. Assn., S.C. Trial Lawyers Assn., Phi Delta Phi (magister 1973-74). Republican. Baptist. Clubs: Commerce, Heritage Sertoma Federal civil litigation, Personal injury, Criminal. Office: Love Thornton Arnold & Thomason PO Box 10045 410 E Washington St Greenville SC 29603

COATS, WILLIAM SLOAN, III, lawyer; b. Fresno, Calif., Mar. 31, 1950; s. William Sloan Jr. and Willa (Macdonell) C.; m. Sherri Lee Young, Aug. 3, 1980; children: Devin Roseanne, Allyn Elizabeth. AB, U. San Francisco, 1972; JD, U. Calif., San Francisco, 1980. Bar: Calif. 1980, U.S. Dist. Ct. (no. dist.) Calif. 1980, U.S. Dist. Ct. (cen. and so. dists.) Calif. 1982. Assoc. Bancroft, Avery & McAlister, San Francisco, 1980-82, Hopkins, Mitchell & Carley, San Jose, Calif., 1982-84, Gibson, Dunn & Crutcher, San Jose and San Francisco, 1984—. Nat. Merit scholar, 1968. Mem. ABA, Calif. Bar Assn. Republican. Roman Catholic. Clubs: Green and Gold (San Francisco); Churchill (Palo Alto, Calif.). Federal civil litigation, State civil litigation, Bankruptcy. Office: Gibson Dunn & Crutcher One Montgomery St San Francisco CA 94104

COBAU, CHARLES DUFFY, JR., lawyer; b. Phila., Aug. 14, 1954; s. Charles Duffy Sr. and Edna (Nunn) C.; m. Gene Penelope Karabedian, July 2, 1983. BA, Amherst Coll., 1976; JD, Case Western Res. U., 1979. Bar: Ohio 1979, U.S. Dist. Ct. (no. dist.) Ohio 1980, U.S. Ct. Appeals (6th cir.) 1984. Ptnr. Cobau & Lublin, Perrysburg, Ohio, 1980—; arbitrator Perrysburg (Ohio) Mcpl. Ct., 1983—; judge moot ct. U. Toledo, 1983-84; referee Wood County Domestic Relations Ct., 1986. Mem. St. Michael's Choir, Toledo, 1979—; bd. dirs. ACLU Northwest Ohio, 1980—, chmn. 1984-85; v.p. Perrysburg Downtown Bus. Assn., 1981-82. Recipient Employer Support award Clay High Sch., 1986. Mem. ABA, Toledo Bar Assn. (investigator grievance com. 1983—), Lucas County Bar Assn. Episcopalian. Avocations: skiing, furniture making, squash, piano. Civil rights, General practice. Home: 2532 Cheltenham Toledo OH 43606 Office: Cobau & Lublin 108 1/2 W 3d St Perrysburg OH 43551

COBB, CHARLES LOUIS, lawyer; b. Seminole, Tex., July 20, 1913; s. Cleveland Ira and Florence Esther (Walker) C.; m. Margaret Ethel McVeigh, Feb. 3, 1945; children—Carol, Camilla, Shannon, Bronwyn. B.A., Tex. Tech. U., Lubbock, 1933; LL.B., U. Okla., 1937. Bar: Tex. 1938, U.S. Dist. Ct. (no. dist.) Tex. 1940, U.S. Ct. Appeals (5th cir.) 1949, U.S. Supreme Ct. 1957. Assoc. McWhorter & Howard, Lubbock, 1938-40; ptnr. McWhorter, Howard and Cobb, Lubbock, 1940-56, McWhorter, Cobb and Johnson, Lubbock, 1956—; lectr. legal aspects of marriage Tex. Tech. U. Pres. Lubbock council Camp Fire Girls, 1957-59. Served to capt. AUS, 1941-45. Mem. State Bar Tex., ABA, Am. Judicature Soc., Tex. Assn. Bank Counsel, Tex. Assn. Def. Counsel, Nat. Assn. Sch. Bd. Attys., Lubbock County Bar Assn. (pres. 1950), Am. Legion (comdr.). Democrat. Presbyterian. Clubs: Knife and Fork (pres.), University-City, Masons. Banking, General corporate, Probate. Office: PO Box 2547 Lubbock TX 79408

COBB, CHESTER LEE, lawyer; b. N.Y.C., Aug. 16, 1952; s. Chester Alden and Teresa (Cancellier) C.; m. Mary Katherine Campo, Sept. 15, 1984; children: Sarah, Elizabeth. BA, Yale U., 1974, JD, 1977. Bar: N.Y. 1978, Tex. 1985, U.S. Dist. Ct. (ea. and so. dists.) N.Y. 1985. Assoc. Milbank, Tweed, Hadley & McCloy, N.Y.C., 1977-81, Parker, Chapin, Flattau & Klimpl, N.Y.C., 1981-84, Winstead, McGuire, Sechrest & Minick, Dallas, 1984—. Mem. ABA, Tex. Bar Assn., Dallas County Bar Assn. Banking, General corporate, Securities. Office: Winstead McGuire Sechrest & Minick 1700 Dallas Bldg Dallas TX 75201

COBB, HOWELL, federal judge; b. Beaumont, Tex., Dec. 7, 1922; s. Howell and Dorothy (Hart) C.; m. Torrance Chalmers (dec. 1963); children: Catherine Cobb Cook, Howell III, Mary Ann Cobb Walton; m. Amelie Suberbielle, July 3, 1965; children: Caroline T., Thomas H., John L. Student, St. John's Coll., Annapolis, Md., 1940-42; LLB, U. Va., 1948. Assoc. Kelley & Ryan, Houston, 1949-51, Fountain, Cox & Gaines, Houston, 1951-54; assoc. Orgain, Bell & Tucker, Beaumont, 1954-57, ptnr., 1957-85; judge U.S. Dist. Ct. (ea. dist.) Tex., Beaumont, 1985—; mem. adv. com. East Tex. Legal Services, Beaumont. Pres. Beaumont Art Mus., 1969, bd. dirs., 1967-68; mem. vestry St. Stephens Episcopal Ch., Beaumont, 1973; mem. bd. adjustment City of Beaumont, 1972-82; trustee All Saints Episcopal Sch., Beaumont, 1972-76. Served to 1st lt. USMC, 1942-45, PTO. Fellow Tex. Bar Found. (life); mem. ABA, Tex. Bar Assn. (grievance com. 1970-72, chmn. 72, admissions com. 1974—, grievance com. 1970-72), Jefferson County Bar Assn. (sec. 1960, bd. dirs. 1960-61, 67-68), Fed. Judges Assn., Am. Judicature Soc., Am. Bd. Trial Advs., Maritime Law Assn. U.S. Republican. Club: Beaumont Country. Office: US Dist Ct 217 US Courthouse Beaumont TX 77701 *

COBB, SAM BURTON, JR., lawyer; b. Avon Park, Fla., Oct. 24, 1927; s. Sam Burton and Mary Morris (Ott) C.; m. Elizabeth Bollman, Mar. 6, 1954; children—Cynthia, Melissa, Tracy Cobb Mc Gilberry, Wendy, Kristi; m. Beryl Ann Oldeman, Aug. 3, 1977; stepchildren—Jim, Tay. Student U. Southwestern La., 1946-47; LL.B., La. State U., 1950. Bar: La. 1950, Tex. 1961, U.S. Dist. Ct. (we. dist.) Tex. 1964, U.S. Dist. Ct. (ea. dist.) Tex. 1967, U.S. Ct. Appeals (5th cir.) 1982. Sole practice, Lafayette, La., 1950-52; landman Shell Oil Co., Midland, Tex., 1952-62; assoc. Turpin, Kerr, Smith & Dyer, Midland, 1962-65; ptnr. Ramey, Brelsford, Flock & Hutchins, Tyler, Tex., 1965-74; owner Sam B. Cobb, Jr. & Assocs., P.C., Tyler, 1975—; dir. First Nat. Bank of Whitehouse (Tex.), 1979-84; mem. council oil gas and mineral law sect. State Bar Tex., 1980-84. Author, lectr. Advanced Oil and Gas Inst., 1983; (series) Suing, Defending and Negotiating with Oil and Gas Producers, 1985. Chmn. George Bush Senate Campaign, Smith County, Tex., 1970; chmn. N.E. Tex. Rep. Ballot Security, 1972. Served with USN, 1944-46. Mem. ABA, La. Bar Assn. Episcopalian. Clubs: Willow Brook & Holly Tree Country, Plaza (Tyler); Garden of the Gods (Colorado Springs). General corporate, Oil and gas leasing. Office: PO Box 6996 Tyler TX 75711

COBB, TY, lawyer; b. Great Bend, Kans., Aug. 25, 1950; s. Grover Cowling and Elizabeth Anne (McCleary) C.; m. Leigh Elliott Stevenson, Aug. 21, 1976; children: Chance Wyatt, Chelsea Leigh. AB, Harvard U., 1972; JD, Georgetown U., 1978. Bar: D.C. 1979, U.S. Dist. Ct. D.C. 1979, U.S. Dist. Ct. Md. 1979, U.S. Ct. Appeals (4th and D.C. cirs.) 1979, U.S. Ct. Internat. Trade 1980, Md. 1987. Law clk. to presiding justice U.S. Dist. Ct., Balt., 1978-79; assoc. Collier, Shannon, Rill & Scott, Washington, 1979-81; asst. U.S. atty. Office of U.S. Atty., Balt., 1981-86; ptnr. Miles & Stockbridge, Balt., 1986—; legis., adminstrv. asst. U.S. Ho. of Reps., Washington, 1984-85; mid-atlantic regional coordinator Organized Crime Drug Enforcement Task Force, Balt., 1985-86. Counsel Forest Glen Park Civic Assn., Montgomery County, Md., 1984—. Mem. ABA. Republican. Federal civil litigation, Criminal. Office: Miles & Stockbridge 10 Light St Baltimore MD 21202

COBBS, LOUISE BERTRAM, lawyer; b. Miami, Fla., Dec. 7, 1947. Mem. ABA, Fed. Bar Assn., Nat. Transp. Safety Bd. Bar Assn. Clubs: Internat. Aviation of Washington, Aero of Washington. Aviation, Private international, Public international. Office: Finley Kumble Wagner Heine et al 1120 Connecticut Ave NW Washington DC 20036

COBEN, CARL GERALD, lawyer; b. Winthrop, Mass., Aug. 21, 1928; m. Barbara Ann Kronberg, Oct. 23, 1954; children: Lawrence S., Harlan G., Craig B. BA, Boston U., 1950, JD, 1953. Bar: Mass. 1953, U.S. Dist. Ct. Mass. 1953, U.S. Supreme Ct. 1956, N.J. 1967, U.S. Dist. Ct. N.J. 1967, U.S. Ct. Appeals (D.C. cir.) 1973, U.S. Ct. Appeals (3d cir.) 1978. Asst. atty. gen. Commonwealth of Mass., Boston, 1953-54; trial atty. U.S. Dept. Justice, Washington, 1954-57; supervisory trial atty. NLRB, Washington and N.Y.C., 1957-67; gen. counsel Servisco, Hillside, N.J., 1967—. Served to capt. USAF, 1954-57. Mem. ABA, N.J. Bar Assn., Am. Arbitration Assn. (arbitrator 1973—). Lodge: Masons. Labor, Antitrust, General corporate. Home: 3 Downing Pl Livingston NJ 07039 Office: Servisco 470 Mundet Pl Hillside NJ 07205

COBEY, CHRISTOPHER EARLE, lawyer; b. Merced, Calif., Mar. 18, 1949; s. James Alexander and Virginia Joy (Branum) C.; m. Elizabeth Jordan Rantz, Aug. 26, 1972; children—Sarah Elizabeth, Carolyn Branum. Student Pomona Coll., 1967-69; B.A. with distinction and honors, Stanford U., 1971; J.D., U. Calif.-Davis, 1974. Bar: Calif. 1974, U.S. Dist. Ct. (no. dist.) Calif. 1981, U.S. Supreme Ct. 1983, U.S. Ct. Appeals (9th cir.) 1984, U.S. Dist. Ct. (ea. dist.) Calif. 1985. Dep. dist. atty. Los Angeles County, 1974-75, San Mateo County, Redwood City, Calif., 1975-77; assoc. Hession & Creedon, San Mateo, Calif., 1979-85; of counsel, Jackson, Lewis, Schnitzler & Krupman, San Francisco, 1985—. Mem. San Mateo County Democratic Central Com., 1975-84, Calif. Dem. State Central Com., 1978-80; chmn. Town of Atherton Planning Commn, 1985-86; mem. Atherton Town Council, 1986—; bd. dirs. Calif. Common Cause, 1980-81. Mem. ABA, San Mateo County Bar Assn. (bd. dirs. 1982-86; chmn. conf. of dels. delegation 1987), State Bar Calif. (resolutions com., conf. of dels. 1980-85, chmn. 1985), San Francisco Bar Assn. (exec. com., BASF delegation to conf. dels, 1986), Stanford Alumni Assn. Episcopalian. Club: Commonwealth (San Francisco). Labor, State civil litigation, Federal civil litigation. Office: 44 Montgomery St Suite 2666 San Francisco CA 94104

COBEY, JAMES ALEXANDER, law educator; b. Frostburg, Md., Oct. 3, 1913; s. James Carpinter and Elizabeth Kownslar (Earle) C; m. Virginia Joy Branum, Aug. 1, 1942; children—Hope Batey, Christopher E., Lisa. A.B., Princeton U., 1934; J.D., Yale U., 1938; cert. Harvard Grad. Sch. Bus. Adminstrn., 1938. Bar: D.C. 1939, U.S. Supreme Ct. 1946, Calif. 1947. Atty. review, NLRB, Washington, 1938-39, field, Los Angeles, 1940-41, 1946; chief research atty. Calif. Ct. Appeal, Los Angeles, 1946-48; dep. county counsel Los Angeles County, 1948; assoc. C. Ray Robinson, Merced, Calif., 1949-60; ptnr. Cobey & Adams, Merced, 1961-66; prof. law Southwestern U., Los Angeles, 1982—; mem. Calif. State Senate from Merced-Madena Counties, 1955-66; assoc. justice Calif. Ct. Appeal, Los Angeles, 1966-81. Dist. commdr. Am. Legion, Merced, 1952; pres. Constl. Rights Found., Los Angeles, 1976-78; trustee Westridge Sch., Pasadena, 1972-82. Served to lt. USNR, 1942-46. Recipient Golden Gavel award Nat. Assn. Legis. Leaders, 1962, Disting. Alumnus award Mercersburg Acad., 1982. Justice James A Cobey Day proclaimed by Mayor Los Angeles, 1981. Mem. ABA, Democrat. Episcopalian. Club: Valley Hunt (Pasadena). Legislative, Local government, Water law. Home: 645 Westbridge Pl Pasadena CA 91105 Office: Southwestern U Sch Law 675 S Westmoreland Ave Los Angeles CA 90005

COBEY, JOHN GEOFFREY, lawyer; b. Cleve., Aug. 16, 1943; s. Herbert Todd and Phyllis Jean (Weston) C.; m. Jan M. Frankel, 1983; 1 child, David William. BS, Cornell U., 1966; postgrad. U. de Deusto, Balboa, Spain, 1968, Exeter U. (Eng.), 1969; JD, U. Cin., 1969. Bar: Ohio 1969, U.S. Dist. Ct. (so. dist.) Ohio 1969, U.S. Ct. Appeals (6th cir.) 1970, Ky. 1978, U.S. Dist. Ct. (no. dist.) Ky. 1978. Ptnr., Cohen, Todd, Kite and Stanford, 1969—; counsel coop. housing City of Cin. Founder, pres. Young Men's Wing, Mercantile Library, 1971; trustee Ohio chpt. Nature Conservancy, 1974-82; sec. Arts Consortium, Cin., 1975-77, trustee, 1975-78; trustee Am. Jewish Com., 1981—, Hillel House, Better Housing League; chmn. bd. Friends Cin. Parks, 1982-84, pres., 1977-79. Mem. Lawyers Club, Cornell U. Coll. Life Scis. and Agr. Alumni Assn. (dist. dir.), Ohio Apt. Assn. (bd. dirs.), Cin. Apt. Assn. (bd. dirs., v.p. 1986-87), U. Cin. Law Sch. Alumni Assn. (bd. dirs 1973-76). General corporate, Real property. Home: 231 Oliver Cincinnati OH 45215 Office: Cohen Todd Kite and Stanford 525 Vine St 16th Floor Cincinnati OH 45202

COBIA, PAULA IVEY, lawyer; b. Columbus, Ga., Aug. 16, 1957; d. Paul M. and Viria (McCollum) I.; m. Gary W. Cobia, May 15, 1982. BBA, Jacksonville (Ala.) State U., 1978; JD, U. Ala., 1981. Bar: Ala., U.S. Dist. Ct. (no. and so. dists.) Ala., U.S. Ct. Appeals (11th cir.). Law clk. to assoc. justice Ala. Supreme Ct., Anniston, 1981-82; law clk. to presiding justice U.S. Dist. Ct. (no. dist.), Anniston, 1982-83; assoc. Jack S. Wallach P.C., Anniston, 1983-84; ptnr. Bolt, Isom, Jackson & Bailey, P.C., Anniston, 1984—. Mem. Anniston (Ala.) Area Mgmt. Assn.; bd. dirs. Vol. Info. Ctr., Anniston Community Theatre. Mem. ABA, Ala. Bar Assn., Calhoun County Bar Assn. Club: Altrusa. Labor, General corporate. Home: 801 Lynell Ct Oxford AL 36203 Office: Bolt Isom Jackson & Bailey PO Box 2066 Anniston AL 36202

COBURN, DAVID H., lawyer; b. Paterson, N.J., Oct. 25, 1951; s. Perry and Ida (Barnet) C.; m. Phyllis Miriam Brenner, Oct. 28, 1978; children: Avi, Brian. BA, Brandeis U., 1973; JD, Georgetown U., 1976. Bar: D.C. 1976, U.S. Dist. Ct. D.C., 1976, U.S. Ct. Appeals (D.C. cir.) 1977, U.S. Ct. Appeals (4th cir.) 1978, U.S. Ct. Appeals (10th cir.) 1979. Assoc. Rea, Cross & Auchincloss, Washington, 1976-82; ptnr. Short, Klein & Karas P.C., Washington, 1982—. Mem. ABA, D.C. Bar Assn., Maritime Admnstrv. Bar Assn., Brandeis U. Alumni Assn. (v.p. 1978-84), Assn. Transportation Practitioners (seminar com. 1985—), Phi Beta Kappa. Avocations: bicycle riding, hiking. Antitrust, Administrative and regulatory, Federal civil litigation. Office: Short Klein & Karas PC 1101 30th St Washington DC 20007

COCANOWER, DAVID LEHMAN, lawyer; b. Elkhart, Ind., Dec. 3, 1939; s. Glen Merl and Augusta Mae (Lehman) C.; m. Liana Cheryl Miller, Sept. 21, 1983; 1 child, Emily Elizabeth; children by previous marriage: Michael Whitten, Joseph Charles. BS with high distinction, Ind. U., 1967, JD magna cum laude, 1970. Bar: Ariz. 1970, U.S. Dist. Ct. Ariz. 1970, U.S. Ct. Appeals (9th cir.) 1970. Assoc., Lewis and Roca, Phoenix, 1970-73, ptnr., 1973—; chmn. sect. corp. banking and bus. law State Bar Ariz., 1978-79. Articles editor Ind. U. Law Jour., 1969-70. Bd. dirs. Ariz. Kidney Found., 1978-82, Hospice of the Valley, Phoenix, 1977-82, Neighborhood Housing Services of Phoenix, 1976-78, Phoenix Integrated Surgical Residency Program Found., Inc., 1980—. Served with USN, 1961-65. Mem. ABA (Ariz. liaison com. corp. laws 1979—), Maricopa County Bar Assn., Nat. Assn. Bond Lawyers, Indiana U. Alumni Club of Phoenix (pres. 1976-77), Order of Coif, Beta Gamma Sigma, Beta Alpha Psi, Phi Delta Phi, Delta Sigma Pi, Tau Kappa Epsilon. Republican. Presbyterian. Clubs: Ariz., Mansion. Lodge: Rotary (pres. Phoenix East 1981-82, dir. 1979-84, dist. 549 gov. 1987-88). General corporate, Securities, Probate. Office: Lewis and Roca 100 W Washington St 22d Floor Phoenix AZ 85003

COCCIA, MICHEL ANDRE, lawyer; b. Sept. 17, 1922. BS in Indsl. Engring., Ill. Inst. Tech., 1944; JD, John Marshall Law Sch., 1951; docteur, l'Universite de Paris, 1965. Bar: Ill. 1951, U.S. Supreme Ct. 1951. Ptnr. litigation Baker & McKenzie, Chgo., 1951—; author and lectr. in fields of products liability, malpractice and trial procedure. Contbr. articles to profl. jours. Served with USNR. Fellow Am. Bar Found., Am. Coll. Trial Lawyers, Internat. Acad. Trial Lawyers, Internat. Soc. Barristers; mem. ABA (various coms., past ho. of dels.), Ill. Bar Assn. (pres. 1981-82, past bd. govs., various coms.), Chgo. Bar Assn. (various coms.), Am. Judicature Soc., Soc. Trial Lawyers (past pres.), Trial Lawyers Club Chgo., Internat. Assn. Ins. Counsel (sec., treas. 1975-78, products liability com., fed. rules com.), Def. Research Inst. (chmn. products liability com., 1971-77, bd. dirs. 1977-80), Rev. Bd. Atty. Registration and Disiplinary Commn. Ill. Supreme Ct., Ill. Ins.t. Tech. Alumni Assn. (past pres., past trustee, various awards), John Marshall Law Sch. Alumni Assn. (past pres., Citation of Merit 1971), Justinian Soc. (Man of Yr. 1981). Club: Union League, Mid-Am., Burnum Park Yacht. Avocations: French, barbershop chorus, amateur radio, boating. Federal civil litigation, State civil litigation, Personal injury. Office: Baker & McKenzie Prudential Plaza Suite 2700 Chicago IL 60601 Home: 915 Isabella Evanston IL 60201

COCCO, LEONARD M., lawyer; b. Bridgeport, Conn., Aug. 25, 1933; s. Ralph J. and Elvira M. (Fumo) C.; m. Jean Ann Grillo, June 22, 1957. BA, U. Bridgeport, 1955; JD, Boston U., 1958. Bar: Conn. 1958, U.S. Dist. Ct. Conn. 1960. Sole practice Bridgeport, 1958—; atty. trial referee Conn. Superior Ct., 1984—. Republican. Roman Catholic. Avocations: reading, swimming. Juvenile, General practice, Personal injury. Office: 1115 Main St Bridgeport CT 06604

COCHEO, JOHN FRANK, lawyer; b. Hartford, Conn., Jan. 28, 1944; s. Frank and Olga Freida (Zotter) C. B.A., Quinnipiac Coll., 1969; J.D., New Eng. Sch. Law, 1973. Bar: Mass. 1974, Conn. 1975, U.S. Dist. Ct. Conn. 1975, U.S. Ct. Appeals (2d cir.) 1983, U.S. Supreme Ct. 1979; cert. Nat. Bd. Trial Advocacy. With Lach & Barron Research, Hartford, 1973; assoc. Deloreto & Karanian Assocs., New Britain, Conn., 1973-76; dep. asst. state's atty. New Britain, 1976-82, asst. state's atty., New London, 1982—. Rep. Victim-Witness Orgn., 1984. Mem. New Britain Bar Assn., New London Bar Assn. Continuing Legal Edn. Acad. Democrat. Roman Catholic. Lodge: K.C. Criminal. Home: 12 Water St Apt 306 Mystic CT 06355 Office: States Attys Office 302 State St New London CT 06320

COCHRAN, ADAM, lawyer; b. Pitts., Mar. 23, 1941; s. Harry Adam and Helen Hazel (Keck) C.; m. Janette Freeman, Jan. 2, 1980; children: Jennifer, Heather. BA in Chemistry, BBA, Hanover Coll., 1962; MS, Purdue U., 1976; JD, Loyola U., Chgo., 1978. Bar: Ill. 1978, U.S. Patent Office 1979, Calif. 1982, U.S. Dist Ct. (no. dist.) Ill., U.S. Dist. Ct. (cen. dist) Calif., U.S. Ct. Appeals (7th and 9th cirs.). Patent law extern to presiding judge U.S. Ct. Appeals (7th cir.), 1978; assoc. Trexler, Bushnell & Wolters, Chgo., 1978-81; assoc. Nilsson, Robbins, Dalgarn, Berliner, Carson & Wurst, Los Angeles, 1981-85, ptnr., 1986—. Bd. dirs. Pasadena (Calif.) Symphony Orch., 1985-86, v.p. and legal advisor, 1986—. Mem. ABA, Los Angeles County Bar Assn., Los Angeles Patent Law Assn., Chgo. Patent Law Assn., Am. Fedn. Musicians. Patent, Trademark and copyright, Entertainment. Home: 1210 Brookmere Rd Pasadena CA 91105 Office: Nilsson Robbins et al 201 N Figueroa St Los Angeles CA 90012

COCHRAN, GEORGE CALLOWAY, III, banker; b. Dallas, Aug. 29, 1932; s. George Calloway and Miriam (Welty) C.; m. Jerry Bywaters, Dec. 9, 1961; children—Mary, Robert. B.A., So. Meth. U., 1954; J.D., Harvard U., 1957; cert., Sch. Banking, La. State U., 1969. Bar: Tex. 1957. Assoc. Leachman, Gardere, Akin and Porter, Dallas, 1960-62; various positions Fed. Res. Bank of Dallas, 1962-76, sr. v.p., 1976—; mem. adv. com. Bank Ops. Inst., East Tex. State U., Commerce, 1982—; mem. task force on truth in lending regulation Bd. Govs. of FRS, Washington, 1968-69. Mem. hist. landmark survey task force City of Dallas, 1974-78. Served to capt. USAF, 1958-60. Mem. ABA, State Bar Tex., Dallas Bar Assn., Phi Beta Kappa. Methodist. Club: Harvard (Dallas). Banking, Administrative and regulatory. Home: 3541 Villanova Dallas TX 75225 Office: Fed Res Bank of Dallas 400 S Akard St Dallas TX 75222

COCHRAN, GEORGE MOFFETT, lawyer, retired judge; b. Staunton, Va., Apr. 20, 1912; s. Peyton and Susie (Robertson) C.; m. Marion Lee Stuart, May 1, 1948; children—George Moffett, Harry Carter Stuart. Grad., Episcopal High Sch., Alexandria, Va., 1930; B.A., U. Va., 1934, LL.B., 1936. Bar: Md. bar 1936, Va. bar 1935. Asso. law firm Balt., 1936-38; partner firm Peyton Cochran and George M. Cochran, Staunton, 1938-64, Cochran, Lotz & Black, Staunton, 1964-69; justice Supreme Ct., Richmond, Va., 1969-87; sole practice Staunton, Va., 1987—; Pres. Planters Bank & Trust Co., Staunton, 1963-69. Chmn. Woodrow Wilson Centennial Commn. of Va., 1952-58, Va. Cultural Devel. Study Commn., 1966-68; mem. Va. Commn. on Constl. Revision, 1968-69, Jud. Council of Va., 1963-69; mem. Va. Ho. of Dels., 1948-66, Va. Senate, 1966-68; chmn. bd. dirs. Stuart Hall, 1971-86; bd. visitors Va. Poly. Inst., 1960-68; trustee Mary Baldwin Coll., 1967-81, U. Va. Law Sch. Found., 1975—. Served to lt. comdr. USNR, 1942-46. Recipient Algernon Sydney Sullivan award Mary Baldwin Coll., 1981. Mem. ABA, Va. Bar Assn. (pres. 1965-66), Raven Soc., Soc. of Cin., Phi Beta Kappa, Phi Delta Phi, Beta Theta Pi. Episcopalian. Jurisprudence. Office: 13 W Beverley St Staunton VA 24401

COCHRAN, JOHN M., III, lawyer; b. N.Y.C., June 26, 1941; s. John M. Jr. and Mildred Lee (Ford) C. AB, Coll. William and Mary, 1963; JD, George Washington U., 1967; Doctorat de l'Université, Univ. Paris, 1971. Bar: N.Y. 1967, Calif. 1974. Assoc. Rogers & Wells, New York and Paris, 1967-73; ptnr. Gibson, Dunn & Crutcher, Paris, 1973-84, Willkie, Farr & Gallagher, Paris, 1984—. Editor Worldlaw, 1984, Butterworth's Jour. of Internat. Banking and Finance Law, 1986. Mem. ABA, Internat. Bar Assn., Assn. of Bar of City of N.Y., Am. Soc. Internat. Law, Internat. C. of C. (arbitration com. 1983). Clubs: Racing Club de France, Cercle Interalliée, Soc. Sportive du Jeu de Paume et des Raquettes (Paris). Private international, International commercial arbitration, Common market, antitrust. Home: 6 rue du Commandant Marchand, 75116, Paris France Office: Willkie Farr & Gallagher, 16 av Pierre ler de Serbie, 75116 Paris France

COCHRAN, SHIRLEY ANN, assistant attorney general; b. Akron, Ohio, Apr. 18, 1953; d. Harry Blaine and Ruth Shirley (Keifer) Cool; m. Mitchell Stephen Cochran, Dec. 4, 1982. BA, U. Akron, 1974, postgrad., 1974-75, JD, 1979. Bar: Ohio 1979, U.S. Dist. Ct. (so. dist.) Ohio 1980, U.S. Dist. Ct. (no. dist.) Ohio 1981. Rep. Avon Products, Akron, 1972-73; clk. bookstores U. Akron, 1973-74; teaching asst. U. Akron, 1974-75; student dir. Appellate Rev. Office, Akron, 1976-78, legal intern, 1978-79; asst. atty. gen. State of Ohio, Columbus, 1979—. Mem. Ohio State Bar Assn. (chairperson young lawyers sect. 1984-86), ABA, Columbus Bar Assn. (com. chairperson 1982-83), Independence Village Civic Assn., Delta Theta Phi (bailiff local chpt. 1983—). Democrat. Club: Aux. United Fellowship (Barberton, Ohio). Government contracts and claims, Consumer commercial. Home: 2897 Liberty Bell Ln Reynoldsburg OH 43068

COCHRAN-BOND, WALTER C., lawyer; b. Palo Alto, Calif., Feb. 18, 1948; s. George Cline and Winifred Jean (Cammack) Bond; m. Suzanne Cochran, Sept. 5, 1970; children: Jenna Lisl, Kira Lorin, Alan Brent, Brendan Brett. BA, Swarthmore Coll., 1970; JD, UCLA, 1974. Bar: Calif. 1974, U.S. Dist. Ct. (cen. dist.) Calif. 1974, U.S. Ct. Appeals (9th cir.) 1978, U.S. Supreme Ct. 1978, U.S. Dist. Ct. (so. dist.) Calif. 1981, U.S. Dist. Ct. (ea. dist.) Calif. 1983, U.S. Dist. Ct. (no. dist.) Calif. 1984. Computer programmer Sun Oil Co., Phila., 1970-71; sole practice Los Angeles, 1974-78; staff atty. Ctr. for Law in Pub. Interest, Los Angeles, 1979-81; ptnr. Taylor, Roth & Hunt, Los Angeles, 1981-84, Hunt & Cochran-Bond, Los Angeles, 1984—. Pres. Swarthmore Connection, Los Angeles, 1985—; bd. dirs. West Pasadena (Calif.) Residents Assn., 1981-83. Mem. ABA (equal employment opportunity com., labor and employment law sect.), Calif. Bar Assn., Los Angeles County Bar Assn., Swarthmore Coll. Alumni Assn. (western region rep. 1984—). Democrat. Civil rights, Labor, Federal civil litigation. Office: Hunt & Cochran-Bond 617 S Olive St Suite 1100 Los Angeles CA 90014

COCKLIN, KIM ROLAND, lawyer; b. Massillon, Ohio, Apr. 13, 1951; s. Roland nad Jacqueline Lou (Cope) C.; m. Crystal Elaine Chandler; children: Ross, Toben, Brooke. BS, Wichita State U., 1973, M in Adminstrn Justice, 1975; JD, Washburn U., 1981. Bar: Colo. 1981, D.C. 1984, U.S. Appeals Ct. (5th, 8th and 10th cirs.) 1984. Instr. Wichita (Kans.) State U., 1974-81; atty. Colo. Interstate Gas Co., Colorado Springs, 1981-84, Tex. Gas Transmission Corp., Owensboro, Ky., 1984-85; gen. counsel Tex. Gas Transmission Corp., Owensboro, 1985—. Mem. ABA, Fed. Energy Bar Assn., Colo. Bar Assn., Ky. Bar Assn., Davies County Bar Assn., Phi Kappa Phi. Avocations: fishing, golf, family. Administrative and regulatory, General corporate, FERC practice. Home: 801 Maple Ave Owensboro KY 43201 Office: Tex Gas Transmission Corp 3800 Frederica St Owensboro KY 43201

COCKRELL, RICHARD CARTER, lawyer; b. Denver, Oct. 9, 1925; s. Harold Arthur Sweet and Mary Lynne Cockrell. AB, U. Denver, 1949, JD cum laude, 1950. Bar: Colo. 1950, U.S. Supreme Ct. 1954. Supr. real estate, tax and claims Standard Oil, Denver, 1950-52; from assoc. to ptnr. Cockrell, Quinn & Creighton and predecessor firms, Denver, 1952—. Mem. law com. Colo. State Bd. of Examiners, Denver, 1958-79, bd. of mgrs. Nat. Conf. Bar Examiners, Chgo., 1965-69. Served to maj. U.S. Army, 1943-46; USAR, 1946-51; USAFR, 1951-67, ret. 1985. Mem. ABA, Denver Bar Assn., Colo. Bar Assn., Am. Judicature Soc., Law Club of Denver (pres. 1963-64). Republican. Episcopalian. Clubs: University (Denver) (bd. dirs. 1982—); Denver Tennis. Probate, Real property, General corporate. Home: 1155 Ash St Apt 1504 Denver CO 80220 Office: Cockrell Quinn & Creighton 950 S Cherry St Suite 516 Denver CO 80222

CODY, WALTER JAMES MICHAEL, state attorney general; b. Memphis, Mar. 13, 1936; s. Walter James and Bess Lou (Hill) C.; m. Suzanna Marten; children: Jane Barton, Michael. B.A., Southwestern at Memphis, 1958; J.D., U. Va., 1961. Bar: Tenn. 1961. Partner Burch, Porter & Johnson, Memphis, 1961-77, 81-84; U.S. atty. Western Dist. Tenn., Memphis, 1977-81; attorney gen. State of Tenn., 1984—; lectr. LeMoyne-Owen Coll., Memphis State U. Law Sch.; instr. polit. sci. Southwestern U. at Memphis. Contbr. to: You Can't Eat Magnolias, 1972. Pres. L.Q.C. Lamar Soc., 1970-71; chmn. Shelby County Democratic Party, 1972-74; mem.-at-large Memphis City Council, 1975-77; trustee, mem. exec. com. Memphis Acad. Arts. Served to 1st lt. U.S. Army Res., 1961-67. Recipient Sam A. Myer Meml. award, 1976. Mem. ABA, Fed. Bar Assn., Tenn. Bar Assn., Memphis and Shelby County Bar Assn. (co-founder neighborhood legal service project), Nat. Assn. Former U.S. Attys., Memphis and Shelby County Legal Services Assn. (dir.). Democrat. Episcopalian. Criminal. Office: Office of Atty Gen 450 James Robertson Pkwy Nashville TN 37219

COE, JACK MARTIN, lawyer; b. Orange, N.J., Mar. 25, 1945; s. Irving and Evelyn (Phillips) C.; m. Diana Jean Martino, Oct. 24, 1981. B.A., U. Va., 1967; A.M., Brown U., 1969; J.D., U. Fla., 1975. Bar: Fla. 1975, U.S. Ct. Appeals (5th cir.) 1976, U.S. Dist. Ct. (so. dist.) Fla. 1976, D.C. 1978, U.S. Supreme Ct. 1978, U.S. Ct. Appeals (11th cir.) 1981. Assoc. Adams, George, Lee & Schulte, Miami, Fla., 1975-77, Thomas E. Lee Jr., P.A., Miami, 1977-78; ptnr. Lee, Schulte, Murphy & Coe, P.A., Miami, 1978—; alumni dir. Sta. WUVA, U. Va., Charlottesville, 1977—. Active in Tiger Bay Polit. Club, Miami, 1978—. Served to 1st lt. USAF, 1969-72. Mem. ABA, Assn. Trial Lawyers Am., Acad. Fla. Trial Lawyers (rules com. 1985—), Pa. Trial Lawyers Assn., Dade County Bar Assn., Palm Beach County Bar Assn. Democrat. Federal civil litigation, State civil litigation, Appellate. Home: 1546 Catalonia Ave Coral Gables FL 33134 Office: Lee Schulte Murphy & Coe PA 610 Franklyn Internat Plaza 253 Alhambra Circle Coral Gables FL 33134

COEN, GEORGE WEBER, lawyer; b. Lancaster, Ohio, Mar. 26, 1914; s. Noble and Georgia (Weber) C.; m. Dorothy Kirn, Dec. 13, 1941; children: Rush, Andrew. JD, U. Va., 1938; postdoctoral, La. State U., 1946, Ohio State U., 1948. Bar: Ohio 1938. Asst. solicitor City of Lancaster, 1938-40; law clk. to presiding justice eastern div. U.S. Dist. Ct. (so. dist.) Ohio, Columbus, 1945-46; solicitor Village of Bremen, Ohio, 1947-55; sole practice 1955-68; ptnr. Coen & Wexler, Lancaster, 1968—; commr. under Frazier Lempe Act, 1939-40; faculty Columbus Coll. Art and Design, 1955-80, Ohio Sch. Banking, 1966-82; referee juvenile div. Fairfield County Ct. Common Pleas, 1971-73, small claims div. Lancaster Mcpl. Ct., 1973-80; chmn. bd. commrs. on grievance and discipline Supreme Ct. Ohio, 1980; bd. dirs. 1st Bremen Bank, Kingston Bldg. and Loan, treas., Ohio Bar Title Ins. Co. Contbr. articles to profl. jours. Clk., treas. Lancaster-Fairfield County Hosp. bldg. project, 1952-55; law commr. Ohio Commn. on Aging, 1973-76; bd. dirs. Fairfield County Library, Ohio State Library. Served with U.S. Army, 1940-46. Fellow Ohio State Bar Found.; mem. ABA, Fed. Bar Assn., Ohio Bar Assn. (editor Desk Manual 1950-60), Fairfield County Bar Assn., Ohio Bankers Assn. (adv. counsel 1973-75). Democrat. Presbyterian. Clubs: University, Press, Columbus Metro. Lodges: Scribes, Masons. Probate, General practice, Banking. Home: 209 E Mulberry St Lancaster OH 43130 Office: Coen Wexler & Wentz 123 S Broad St Suite 234 PO Box 1028 Lancaster OH 43130-1028

COEN, SETH EZRA, lawyer; b. July 21, 1950. BA in Acctg., Pace U., 1972. Bar: N.Y. 1977, U.S. Dist. Ct. (so. and ea. dists.) N.Y. 1977, U.S. Supreme Ct. 1980. Ptnr. Fetell & Coen, P.C., Bklyn., 1979—; arbitrator N.Y.C. Civil Ct., 1982—, Am. Stock Exchange, Inc., N.Y.C., 1983—. Mem. ABA, N.Y. Bar Assn., Am. Trial Lawyers Assn., N.Y. Trial Lawyers Assn. (legis. com. 1978-82). Personal injury, Insurance, State civil litigation. Home: 1229 Bloomfield St Hoboken NJ 07030 Office: Fetell & Coen PC 44 Court St Brooklyn NY 11201

COENEN, DAN THOMAS, lawyer; b. Dubuque, Iowa, Nov. 10, 1952; s. Clayton John and LaVerne (Tillman) C.; m. Sara McCall Wyche, July 7, 1979; children: Michael Bradford, Amy Wyche. BS, U. Wis., 1974; JD, Cornell U., 1978. Bar: N.C. 1981, S.C. 1981, U.S. Dist. Ct. (we. dist.) N.C. 1981, U.S. Ct. Appeals (4th cir.) 1981, U.S. Supreme Ct. 1986. Law clk. to chief judge U.S. Ct. Appeals, Greenville, S.C., 1978-79; assoc. justice U.S. Supreme Ct., Washington, 1979-80; assoc. Robinson, Bradshaw and Hinson,

Charlotte, N.C., 1981-85, ptnr., 1985—. Bd. dirs. Energy Committed to Offenders, Charlotte. Avocations: bridge, basketball, camping, canoeing. Federal civil litigation, State civil litigation. Office: Robinson Bradshaw and Hinson 1900 Independence Ctr 101 N Tryon St Charlotte NC 28246

COFFEE, JAMES FREDERICK, retired lawyer; b. Decatur, Ind., Mar. 6, 1918; s. Claude M. and Frances N. (Butler) C.; m. Jeanmarie Hackman, Dec. 29, 1945 (dec. 1978); children: James, Carolyn, Susan, Sheila, Kevin, Richard, Elizabeth, Thomas, Claudia; m. Marjorie E. Masterson, Oct. 4, 1980. B.C.E., Purdue U., 1939; J.D., Ind. U., 1947. Bar: Wis. 1947, Ill. 1952. Patent atty. Allis Chalmers Mfg. Co., Milw., 1947-51; mem. firm Anderson, Luedeka, Fitch, Even & Tabin (and predecessors), Chgo., 1951-64; partner Anderson, Luedeka, Fitch, Even & Tabin (and predecessors), 1956-64; individual practice law Chgo., 1964-71; partner law firm Coffee & Sweeney, Chgo., 1971-76; partner, gen. counsel design firm Marvin Glass & Assos., Chgo., from 1973, now ret. Served to capt. AUS, 1941-46. Mem. ABA, Ill. Bar Assn., Chgo. Bar Assn. (chmn. com. patents, trademark and unfair trade practices 1967), Am. Patent Law Assn., Patent Law Assn. Chgo. (chmn. com. copyrights 1969), Am. Judicature Soc. Club: Tower of Chgo. (bd. govs. 1978—, sec. 1982-83, treas. 1983-85). Patent. Home: 320 Earls Ct Deerfield IL 60015

COFFEE, JOHN COLLINS, JR., legal educator; b. Albany, N.Y., Nov. 15, 1944; s. John Collins and Mary E. (Morse) C.; m. Jane Purcell, July 1, 1970; 1 dau., Megan Purcell. B.A., Amherst Coll., 1966; LL.B., Yale U., 1969; LL.M. in Taxation, NYU, 1976. Bar: N.Y. 1970, U.S. Dist. Cts. (so. and ea. dists.) N.Y. 1974, U.S. Ct. Appeals (2d cir.) 1974, D.C. 1980. Assoc. Cravath, Swaine & Moore, N.Y.C., 1970-76; assoc. prof. law Georgetown U. Law Ctr., Washington, 1976-79; vis. prof. U. Va. Law Sch., Charlottesville, 1979; Adolf A. Berle prof. law Columbia U. Law Sch., N.Y.C., 1980—. vis. prof. Stanford U. Law Sch., Palo Alto, Calif., 1987. Mem. panel on sentencing research Nat. Acad. Scis., 1980-83. Reginald Heber Smith fellow, 1969-70. Mem. Am. Law Inst. (reporter project on corp. governance), ABA (reporter minimum standards for criminal justice), Am. Assn. Law Sch. (chmn. sect. on bus. assns. 1981-82, chmn. com. on sects. 1984-85), Assn. Bar City N.Y. (com. on corp. laws 1981—). Author: (with others) Business Organization and Finance 2d edit., 1986. Contbr. articles to legal jours. General corporate, Criminal. Office: Columbia U Law Sch 435 W 116 St NY NY 10027

COFFEE, RICHARD JEROME, II, lawyer; b. Chgo., Nov. 12, 1954; s. James F. and Jean Marie (Hackman) C.; m. Judith Lynn Libby, Feb. 14, 1981; children: David Patrick, Brent William. BS, So. Ill. U., 1975; JD, U. Ill., 1978. Bar: Ill. 1978, U.S. Dist. Ct. (no. dist.) Ill. 1978, U.S. Dist. Ct. (cen. dist.) Ill. 1980. Staff atty. Ill. Dept. Ins., Springfield, 1979-80; counsel Ill. State Employees Assn., Springfield, 1980-84; staff counsel Ill. Bd. Regents, Springfield, 1984—. Mem. ABA, Ill. Bar Assn., Chgo. Bar Assn., Nat. Assn. Coll. and Univ. Attys., Nat. Orgn. Legal Problems in Edn., Ill. Pub. Employer Labor Relations Assn. Avocations: licensed pilot, licensed amateur radio operator. Higher education law, Labor, Administrative and regulatory. Office: Ill Bd Regents One W Old State Capitol Plaza Springfield IL 62701

COFFEY, JOHN LOUIS, judge; b. Milw., Apr. 15, 1922; s. William Leo and Elizabeth Ann (Walsh) C.; m. Marion Kunzelmann, Feb. 3, 1951; children: Peter Lee, Elizabeth Mary Coffey Robbins. B.A., Marquette U., 1943, JD, 1948; M.B.A. (hon.), Spencerian Coll., 1964. Bar: Wis. 1948, U.S. Dist. Ct. 1948, U.S. Supreme Ct. 1980. Asst. city atty. Milw., 1949-54; judge Civil Ct., Milw. County, 1954-60, Milw. Mcpl. Ct., 1960-62; judge Circuit Ct. (criminal div.), Milw. County, 1962-72, sr. judge, 1972-75, chief presiding judge, 1976; circuit ct. judge Circuit Ct. (civil div.), Milw. County, 1976-78; justice Wis. Supreme Ct., Madison, 1978-82; circuit judge U.S. Ct. Appeals (7th cir.), Chgo., 1982—; mem. Wis. Bd. Criminal Ct. Judges, 1960-78, Wis. Bd. Circuit Ct. Judges, 1962-78. Chmn. adv. bd. St. Joseph's Home for Children, 1958-65; mem. adv. bd. St. Mary's Hosp., 1964-70; mem. Milwaukee County council Boy Scouts Am.; chmn. St. Eugene's Sch. Bd., 1967-70, St. Eugene's Parish Council, 1974; mem. vol. services adv. com. Milwaukee County Dept. Public Welfare; bd. govs. Marquette U. High Sch. Served with USNR, 1943-46. Recipient Disting. Service award Cudworth Post Am. Legion, 1973; Alumni Merit award Marquette U., 1985; named Outstanding Law Alumnus of Yr., Marquette U., 1980. Fellow Am. Bar Found.; mem. Alpha Sigma Nu. Roman Catholic.

COFFEY, ROBERT DENNIS, lawyer; b. White Plains, N.Y., July 3, 1950; s. Robert Eugene and Barbara Madeline (Starch) C.; m. Helen Marie Ueberacher, June 10, 1978; children: Jeffrey M., Diane L. BA, Rutgers U., 1972; JD, U. Conn., 1977. Bar: Conn. 1977, U.S. Dist. Ct. Conn. 1982. Counsel Conn. Jud. Dept., Hartford, 1977-81, dir. labor relations, 1981—. Trustee Conn. State Employees Retirement Commn., Hartford, 1985—. Mem. ABA, Conn. Bar Assn., Nat. Pub. Employer Labor Relations Assn. Roman Catholic. Avocation: camping. Labor, Judicial administration. Home: 472 Old Colchester Rd Amston CT 06231 Office: Conn Jud Dept Drawer N Sta A Hartford CT 06106

COFFIELD, CONRAD EUGENE, lawyer; b. Hot Springs, S.D., Nov. 26, 1930; s. Eugene M. and Alice (Hotvet) C.; m. Maggie Lee Murphy, Aug. 1, 1953; children: Conrad Eugene, Michael, Megan, Edward, Philip. Student S.D. Sch. Mines and Tech., 1948-49; BBA, Washington U., St. Louis, 1952; LLB, U. Tex., 1959. Bar: Tex. 1959, N.Mex. 1959. Mem. Hervey, Dow & Hinkle, Roswell, N.Mex., 1959-64; gen. ptnr. Hinkle, Cox, Eaton, Coffield & Hensley, Roswell, 1964-66, resident ptnr., Midland, 1966—. Trustee Petroleum Mus., Library and Hall of Fame; bd. govs. Midland Community Theatre. Served with USCGR, 1952-56. Fellow Tex. Bar Found.; mem. ABA, Tex. Bar Assn., N.Mex. Bar Assn., Midland County Bar Assn., N.Mex. Oil and Gas Assn. Episcopalian. Clubs: Midland Petroleum, Midland Country. Oil and gas leasing, Administrative and regulatory, General practice. Home: 2813 W Dengar St Midland TX 79701 Office: Hinkle Cox Eaton Coffield Hensley 200 Blanks Bldg Midland TX 79701

COFFILL, WILLIAM CHARLES, lawyer; b. Sonora, Calif., Jan. 19, 1908; s. Harris James and Olive Moore (Hampton) C.; m. Marjorie Louise Segerstrom, Jan. 25, 1948; children—William James, Eric John. A.B., U. Calif.-Berkeley, 1933; J.D., Hastings Coll. Law, 1937. Bar: Calif. 1938, U.S. Dist. Ct. (no. dist.) Calif. 1938, U.S. Dist. Ct. (so. dist.) Calif. 1938, U.S. Ct. Appeals (9th cir.) 1938, U.S. Supreme Ct. 1941, U.S. Dist. Ct. (ea. dist.) 1967. Gen. Mgr. Riverbank Water Co., Riverbank and Hughson, Calif., 1948-68; sole practice, Sonora, 1938-41, 45-76; ptnr. Coffill & Coffill, Sonora, 1976—; city atty. City of Sonora, 1952-75. Past mem., chmn. Tuolumne County Republican Central Com., Calif. Served to lt. comdr. USNR, 1941-46. Mem. Tuolumne County Bar Assn. (past pres.), Am. Legion, VFW. Lodges: Lions, Masons (32 degree), Elks. Probate. Office: Coffill and Coffill 23 N Washington St PO Box 1117 Sonora CA 95370

COFFIN, FRANK MOREY, judge; b. Lewiston, Maine, May 11, 1919; s. Herbert Rice and Ruth (Morey) C.; m. Ruth Ulrich, Dec. 19, 1942; children: Nancy, Douglas, Meredith, Susan. A.B., Bates Coll., 1940, LL.D., 1959; postgrad. indsl. adminstrn., Harvard U., 1943, LL.B., 1947; LL.D., U. Maine, 1967, Bowdoin Coll., 1969; degree (hon.), Colby Coll., 1975. Bar: Maine 1947. Law clk. to fed. judge Dist. of Maine 1947-49; engaged in practice Lewiston, 1947-52; Verrill, Dana, Walker, Philbrick & Whitehouse, Portland, Maine, 1952-56; mem. 85th-86th Congresses from 2d Dist. Maine, House Com. Fgn. Affairs; mng. dir. Devel. Loan Fund, Dept. State, Washington, 1961; dep. adminstr. AID, 1961-64; U.S. rep. devel. assistance com. Orgn. Econ. Coop. and Devel., 1964-65; judge 1st circuit U.S. Ct. Appeals, 1965—, chief judge, 1972-83; chmn. com. jud. br. U.S. Jud. Conf., 1984—; adj. prof. U. Maine Sch. Law, 1986—. Author: Witness for Aid, 1964, The Ways of a Judge-Reflections from the Federal Appellate Bench, 1980, A Lexicon of Oral Advocacy, 1984. Trustee Bates Coll.; mem. Overseas Devel. Council, The Examiner. Served from ensign to lt. USNR, 1943-46. Mem. Am. Acad. Arts and Scis. Office: 156 Federal St Portland ME 04112

COFFIN, MARY MCCARTHY, lawyer; b. Syracuse, N.Y., Oct. 15, 1920; m. Louis F. Coffin, Apr. 24, 1943; children—John, Sally, Laurie, Robert, Patricia, Deborah, Louis, Margaret. A.B., Radcliffe Coll., 1942; postgrad. MIT, 1942-43; LL.B., Albany Law Sch., 1967. Bar: N.Y. 1968, U.S. Supreme Ct. 1974. Law clk. County Ct., Schenectady, N.Y., 1968-70; counsel Schenectady Urban Renewal Agy., 1970-72; sole practice, Schenectady, 1972-79; ptnr. Antokol & Coffin, Schenectady. Trustee, YWCA, 1975—; mem. Schenectady Housing Code Commn., 1973—, Hospice of Schenectady, 1982—, Law, Order and Justice, 1975-82, Schenectady Family and Child Service, 1977-82; mem. bd. Schenectady County Legal Aid, 1968-81, pres., 1970; mem. bd. N.E. Legal Aid Soc., 1979-82. Recipient Susan B. Anthony award Schenectady County LWV, 1982; named Schenectady Jr. League Vol. of Yr., 1957; recipient Schenectady Law, Order and Justice award for Service, 1982; Community Service award YWCA, 1982. Mem. Schenectady Bar Assn., N.Y. State Bar Assn., ABA. Republican. Club: Torch Internat. of Schenectady. Family and matrimonial, Criminal, Real property. Home: 1178 Lowell Rd Schenectady NY 12306 Office: 514 State St Schenectady NY 12305

COFFIN, RICHARD KEITH, lawyer; b. St. Louis, Apr. 6, 1940; s. Kenneth and Agnes (Ryan) C.; m. June Springmeyer, Apr. 8, 1972; children—Jennifer, Joanna. B.S., U. Notre Dame, 1962; M.B.A., St. Louis U., 1967, J.D., 1971. Engr., Nooter Corp., St. Louis, 1962-72; spl. prosecutor U.S. Dept. Justice, St. Louis, 1972-74; ptnr. Phelps, Coffin, Andreatta & Lorenz, P.C., St. Louis, 1974—; gen. counsel Southwestern Linen & Indsl. Supply Assn., St. Louis, 1979—. Mem. Citizens Adv. Com., Parkway Sch. Bd., Chesterfield, Mo., 1980-82; treas. PSO Com., Parkway Sch., 1982-83. Mem. ABA, Mo. Bar Assn., Met. Bar Assn. St. Louis, Assn. Trial Lawyers Am., Mo. Assn. Trial Attys., Phi Alpha Delta. Roman Catholic. Club: Optimist (sec. 1981). General corporate, Real property, General practice. Home: 1748 Orchard Hill Dr Chesterfield MO 63017 Office: Phelps Coffin Andreatta & Lorenz PC 230 S Bemiston Ave Suite 1000 Saint Louis MO 63105

COFFMAN, ANNE BLANKENBURG, lawyer; b. New Albany, Ind., Aug. 15, 1948; d. Donald O. and Mary Elizabeth (Wilkinson) B.; divorced; 1 child, Brian A. BS, Ind. U., 1973, MPA, 1978, JD, 1978. Bar: U.S. Dist. Ct. (so. dist.) Ind. 1978. Dep. prosecutor Clark County Dist., Jeffersonville, Ind., 1978-81; sole practice Jeffersonville, 1981—; pub. defender Clark County Dist., Jeffersonville, 1985—. Vol. Clark County Dems., Jeffersonville, 1978—, Clark County Dems. Women's Orgn., Jeffersonville, 1978. Mem. ABA, Ind. State Bar Assn., Clark County Bar Assn. Avocations: theatre, swimming, children. Criminal, Personal injury, Family and matrimonial. Home: 512 Chippewa Dr Jeffersonville IN 47130 Office: Anne B Coffman 424 E Court Ave Jeffersonville IN 47130

COFFMAN, CLAUDE T., law educator, lawyer; b. Robinsonville, Miss., Jan. 20, 1916; s. Tulus Jackson and Addie (Mick) C.; m. Ninna Carr Bailey, July 15, 1940; children—Mary, Margaret. A.B, LL.B., U. Miss., 1938; postgrad. Harvard U., 1939. Bar: Miss. 1938. Atty., U.S. Dept. Agr., Washington, 1939-51, dep. gen counsel, 1968-74; asst. legal counsel Tech. Corp. Adminstrn., Washington, 1951-53; prof. law Memphis State U., 1974-86; prof. emeritus and interim dean, 1986—. Contbr. articles to profl. jours. Mem. ABA. Episcopalian. Legal education. Home: 5439 Glenwild Rd Memphis TN 38119 Office: Dept Law Memphis State U Memphis TN 38152

COFFMAN, DANIEL RAY, JR., lawyer; b. Richmond, Va., Feb. 13, 1933; s. D. Ray and Clara (Noell) C.; m. Blanche Gray Coffman, Oct. 8, 1960; children—Elizabeth, Julia, Virginia, Emily. B.A., Vanderbilt U., 1954, J.D., 1960. Bar: Fla. 1960. Shareholder Coffman, Coleman, Andrews & Grogan, P.A., Jacksonville, Fla., 1971—; labor counsel Fla. Jr. Coll., Jacksonville, 1975-87. Bd. dirs. Childrens Home Soc. Fla., Salvation Army; mem. adv. bd. Learn to Read, Jacksonville. Served to lt USNR, 1954-57. Mem. ABA, Jacksonville Bar Assn., Bar (chmn. labor and employment law com. 1969-70), Jacksonville Area C. of C. (gen. counsel 1985, v.p. 1987). Republican. Presbyterian Club: Exchange (past pres.). Labor. Home: 4061 Timuquana Rd Jacksonville FL 32210 Office: Coffman Coleman Andrews & Grogan 2065 Herschel St Jacksonville FL 32204

COFFRIN, ALBERT WHEELER, judge; b. Burlington, Vt., Dec. 21, 1919; s. Morris Daniel and Florence Belle (Browe) C.; m. Elizabeth Ann MacCornack, May 14, 1943; children—Peter S., Albert W., III, James W., Nancy (Mrs. Michael G. Furlong). A.B., Middlebury Coll., 1941; LL.B., Cornell U., 1947. Bar: Vt. bar 1948. Mem. firm Black & Wilson, Burlington, 1947-51, 52-56, Black, Wilson, Coffrin & Hoff, 1956-60; partner Coffrin & Pierson, 1962-68, Coffrin, Pierson & Affolter, 1968-72; judge U.S. Dist. Ct., Dist. of Vt., 1972—. Trustee Middlebury Coll. Served with USN, 1942-45, 51-52; to comdr. Res. 1952-66. Fellow Am. Bar Found.; mem. Am., Vt., Chittenden County bar assns., Phi Delta Phi, Kappa Delta Rho. Republican. Unitarian. Club: Burlington Tennis. Jurisprudence. Office: Box 522 Burlington VT 05402

COGAN, MICHAEL BARR, lawyer; b. N.Y.C., Oct. 12, 1945; s. Alan D. and Phyllis S. (Shultz) C.; m. Louise Santana, Dec. 17, 1978; children: Benjamin, Sarah. BS, Cornell U., 1967; MBA, JD, UCLA, 1975. Bar: Calif. 1975. Ptnr. Kelly, Knapp, Sanders & Cogan, Santa Monica, Calif., 1976-78, Sklar, Cogan, Stashower, Kelly & Knapp, Santa Monica, 1978-79; pres. Kelly & Cogan, Santa Monica, 1979—; judge pro tem Los Angeles County Mcpl. Ct., Los Angeles, 1984—. Treas. Calif. Dem. voter drive, Los Angeles, 1986; founder El Proyecto Del Barrio, San Fernando, Calif., 1966. Named Young Man of Yr. San Fernando chpt. Jaycees; Regents' scholar UCLA. Mem. ABA, State Bar Calif., Los Angeles County Bar Assn., Italian-Am. Bar Assn., Wilderness Fly Fishers. Avocations: fly fishing, golf. Office: Kelly & Cogan 2632 Lincoln Blvd Santa Monica CA 90405

COGBURN, MAX OLIVER, lawyer; b. Canton, N.C., Mar. 21, 1927; s. Chester Amberg and Ruby Elizabeth (Davis) C.; m. Mary Heidt, Oct. 15, 1949; children: Max O. Jr., Michael David, Steven Douglas, Cynthia Diane. AB, U. N.C., 1948, LLB, 1950; LLM, Harvard U., 1951. Bar; N.C. 1950, U.S. Dist. Ct. (we. dist.) N.C. 1953, U.S. Ct. Appeals (4th cir.) 1984. Asst. dir. Inst. Govt., Chapel-Hill, N.C., 1951-52; staff mem. Atty. Gen. N.C., Raleigh, 1952-54; adminstr. asst. Chief Justice N.C., Raleigh, 1954-55; judge Gen. County Ct. Buncombe County, Asheville, N.C., 1968-70; sole practice Canton, Asheville, N.C., 1968, 1971—; ptnr. Roberts, Stevens & Cogburn, P.A., Asheville, 1986—. Chmn. Buncombe County Dem. Exec. Com., Asheville, 1974-76; mem. State Dem. Exec. Com., Raleigh, 1974-76. Mem. ABA, N.C. State Bar Assn., N.C. Bar Assn., 28th Judicial Dist. Bar State of N.C., Buncombe County Bar Assn. (past pres.). Roman Catholic. Federal civil litigation, State civil litigation, General practice. Home: Rt 1 Pisgah View Ranch Candler NC 28715 Office: Roberts Stevens et al PO Box 7647 Asheville NC 28807

COGDELL, JOE BENNETT, JR., lawyer; b. Duncan, Okla., May 6, 1953; s. Joe Bennett Sr. and Sue (Alexander) C.; m. Margaret Buford, July 29, 1978; children: Joe Bennett III, Brian D. BA, U. Ark., 1975, JD, 1977; LLM in Taxation, So. Meth. U., 1979. Bar: Ark. 1978, Okla. 1979, U.S. Tax Ct. 1979, U.S. Dist. Ct. (we. dist.) Okla. 1980, U.S. Supreme Ct. 1983. Assoc. McIntyre, McDivitt, Oklahoma City, 1979-83, ptnr., 1983-85; ptnr. Albright, Golden & Cogdell, Oklahoma City, 1985—; adj. prof. law Okla. City U., 1982—. Author: Tax Management Portfolio, 147-5th, Practice Before the IRS and Circular 230, Bur. of Nat. Affairs. Adv. dir. Oklahoma City Beautiful, 1984—; bd. dirs. Arthritis Found. Okla., Inc., 1987—. Mem. ABA (taxation sect. 1982—), Okla. Bar Assn., Ark. Bar Assn. Lodge: Kiwanis (bd. dirs. Oklahoma City) 1985. Corporate taxation, Estate taxation, Tax litigation. Home: 3001 Brush Creek Rd Oklahoma City OK 73120 Office: Albright Golden & Cogdell 921 NW 63d St Oklahoma City OK 73116

COGHILL, WILLIAM THOMAS, JR., lawyer; b. St. Louis, July 20, 1927; s. William Thomas and Mildred Mary (Crenshaw) C.; m. Patricia Lee Hughes, Aug. 7, 1948; children—James Prentiss, Victoria Lynn, Cathryn Ann. J.D., U. Mo., 1950. Bar: Mo. 1950, Ill. 1958. Sole practice, Farmington, Mo., 1950-51; spl. agt. FBI, 1951-52; ptnr. Smith, Smith & Coghill, Farmington, 1952-57; assoc. Coburn & Croft, St. Louis, 1957-58; assoc., ptnr. Thompson & Mitchell (formerly Pope & Driemeyer), Belleville, Ill., 1958—. Served with U.S. Navy, 1945-46. Fellow Am. Coll. Trial Lawyers; mem. ABA, Ill. State Bar Assn., Mo. State Bar Assn., St. Clair County (Ill.) Bar Assn., East St. Louis Bar Assn. Clubs: Media, Mo. Athletic (St. Louis). Lodge: Elks. Federal civil litigation, State civil litigation, Insurance. Home: 20 Autumn Ln Belleville IL 62223 Office: 1 S Church St Belleville IL 62220

COGRAVE, JOHN EDWIN, retired lawyer; b. Washington, Dec. 29, 1929; s. John Roscoe Cograve and Eleanor Frances (Reus) Rosenburg; m. Mary Claire Carpenter, Aug. 23, 1952; children: John, Karen, Joan. LLB, U. Va., 1959. Bar: Va. 1959. Mem. office gen. counsel FMC, Washington, 1961-65, dep. gen. counsel, 1965-74, chief adminstrv. law judge, 1974-86, mng. dir., 1986. Served to 1st lt. U.S. Army, 1951-54. Administrative and regulatory. Office: Fed Maritime Commission Office of the Chairman 1100 L St NW Washington DC 20573

COHAN, JOHN ROBERT, lawyer; b. Arnhem, Netherlands, Feb. 10, 1931; came to U.S., 1940, naturalized, 1945; s. Max and Ann (deWinter) C.; m. Joan B. Gollob, Sept. 6, 1954; children: Deborah Joyce, Steven Mark, Judson Seth; m. Patricia S. Cohan, Nov. 8, 1970; m. Roberta Cohan, Nov. 23, 1980. B.S. in Bus. Adminstrn, U. Ariz., 1952; LL.B., Stanford U., 1955. Bar: Calif. 1956; cert. specialist in taxation. Assoc. firm Irell & Manella, Los Angeles, 1955-61, ptnr., 1961—; adj. prof. U. Miami Sch. Law, 1975-85; lectr. fed. income taxation U. So. Calif. Sch. Law, 1961-63; lectr., writer Calif. Continuing Edn. Bar Program, 1959—; Practicing Law Inst., 1968—, also various tax and probate insts. Editor: Drafting California Revocable Trusts, 1972, 2d edit., 1984, Drafting California Irrevocable Trusts, 1973, Inter Vivos Trusts, Shepard's Citations, 1975; Contbr. articles on tax, estate planning, probate law to profl. jours. Pres. Portals House, Inc., 1966-69; chmn. Jewish Big Bros., Los Angeles, 1963-65; bd. dirs. Hope for Hearing Research Found., 1965-77, pres., 1972-74, trustee, 1978—; chmn. charitable founds. com. Big Bros. Big Sisters Am., 1965-67, chmn. internat. expansion, 1967—, pres. western region, 1977-78, also bd. dirs.; bd. dirs. Jewish Community Found., 1979—, v.p., chmn. legal com., 1978—; mem. planning com. U. So. Calif. Tax Inst., 1969—, chmn., 1983—; mem. planning com. U. Miami Estate Planning Inst.; bd. dirs. Los Angeles Campus Hebrew Union Coll., 1974-77. Fellow Am. Coll. Probate Counsel (mem. planning com. 1986—); mem. ABA (chmn. com. on estate planning for closely held bus. 1979-80, vice chmn. estate and gift tax com. of sect. on taxation), Los Angeles Bar Assn. (com. on fed. and Calif. death and gift taxation 1965-67, co-chmn. com. on bioethics 1979-80), Beverly Hills Bar Assn. (past chmn., lawyer placement com. and probate com.), Calif. State Bar (probate and trust com. 1971-74), Internat. Acad. Probate and Trust Law (exec. com.), Town Hall of Los Angeles (exec. com., past pres. Western div.), Beta Gamma Sigma, Alpha Kappa Psi, Phi Alpha Delta. Personal income taxation, Probate, Estate taxation. Home: 4233 Aleman Dr Tarzana CA 91356 Office: Irell & Manella 1800 Ave of Stars Century City Los Angeles CA 90067

COHAN, LEON SUMNER, electric company executive, lawyer; b. Detroit, June 24, 1929; s. Maurice and Lillian (Rosenfeld) C.; m. Heidi Ruth Seelmann, Jan. 22, 1956; children: Nicole, Timothy David, Jonathan Daniel. B.A., Wayne State U., 1949, J.D., 1952. Bar: Mich. 1953. Sole practice Detroit, 1954-58; asst. atty. gen. State of Mich., Lansing, 1958-61, dep. atty. gen., 1961-72; v.p. legal affairs Detroit Edison Co., 1973-75, v.p., 1975-79, sr. v.p., 1979—, gen. counsel, 1975—; bd. dirs. United Savings Bank, FSB. Chmn. State Bd. Ethics; bd. trustees Mich. Cancer Found.; bd. dirs. Orch. Hall; mem. Mich. Council for Arts; bd. govs. Jewish Welfare Fedn.; mem. Arts Commn. adv. com. Detroit Inst. Arts; mem. exec. bd. Friends of Detroit Pub. Library; pres. Jewish Community Council Met. Detroit. Served in U.S. Army, 1952-54. Recipient Disting. Alumni award Wayne State U. Law Sch., 1972, Disting. Service award Bd. Govs., Wayne State U., 1973, Judge Ira W. Jayne award NAACP, 1987, Israel Histadrut Menorah award, 1987. Mem. Am., Detroit bar assns., State Bar Mich., Mich. Gen. Counsel Assn., Am. Arbitration Assn. (mem. comml. panel). Democrat. Jewish. Club: Detroit. Public utilities, General corporate. Home: 5324 Forest Way Bloomfield Hills MI 48013 Office: Detroit Edison 2000 2d Ave Detroit MI 48226

COHEN, ALLAN RICHARD, lawyer; b. Chgo., Feb. 25, 1923; s. Louis and Ruth (Cohen) C.; m. Audrey Doris Levy, Oct. 14, 1960; children: Joseph, David, Gale. B.A., U. Wis., 1947, J.D., 1949; postgrad., Northwestern U., 1953-54. Bar: Ill. 1950. Assoc. Blum, Jacobsen & Shkoler, Chgo., 1950-53; ptnr. Cohen & Cohen, Chgo., 1953—. Served with AUS, 1943-45. Decorated Presdl. citation with oak leaf cluster. Mem. Fed. Bar Assn., Ill. Bar Assn. (vice chmn. comml. banking and bankruptcy sect. 1977—), Chgo. Bar Assn. (vice chmn. com. bankruptcy 1972-73, chmn. 1973-74, panelist bankruptcy seminars 1968, 72, 74, 82, 83), Zeta Beta Tau, Tau Epsilon Rho. Club: Elms Swim Tennis (Highland Park, Ill.). Bankruptcy, Consumer commercial, Contracts commercial. Office: Cohen & Cohen 55 W Monroe Chicago IL 60603

COHEN, ANITA MARILYN, lawyer; b. Pitts., Dec. 4, 1945; d. Leonard and Rosalie (Agger) C. B.A., U. Pitts., 1967; J.D., Duquesne U., 1970. Bar: Pa. 1970, U.S. Dist. Ct. (ea. dist.) Pa. 1978, U.S. Dist. Ct. (we. dist.) Pa. 1970. Law clk. and asst. pub. defender Appellate Div., Office Pub. Defender of Allegheny County, 1968-71; asst. dist. atty. trial div. Office of Dist. Atty. of Phila. County, 1971-78; sole practice, Phila., 1978—; lectr. in field; counsel Phila. Boosters Assn., 1982-86. Bd. dirs. Girls Coalition of Southeastern Pa., 1981-85, counsel 1983-86; bd. dirs. Planned Parenthood Southeastern Pa., 1981-85. Mem. ABA, Pa. Bar Assn. (legal ethics and profl. responsibility com. 1985—), Am. Judicature Soc., Nat. Dist. Atty. Assn. Clubs: Shomrim, F.O.P. Contbr. articles to profl. jours. Criminal, Family and matrimonial, Juvenile. Office: 1216 B Robinson Bldg 42 S 15th St Philadelphia PA 19102

COHEN, ARLENE SWITOW, lawyer; b. Louisville, Jan. 8, 1956; d. Irvin Bloom and Maxine (Rudman) Switow; m. James Harrison Cohen, June 17, 1979. BA, Emory U., 1978; JD, U. Ky., 1981. Bar: Ky. 1981, U.S. Dist. Ct. (no. dist.) Ohio 1982, Ohio 1983, U.S. Ct. Appeals (6th cir.) 1984. Assoc. Kasdan & Baxter Co., Cleve., 1982-85; sole practice Cleve., 1985—. Mem. Am. Trial Lawyers Assn., Ohio Bar Assn., Ky. Bar Assn., Cuyahoga County Bar Assn., Greater Cleve. Bar Assn., Women Bus. Owners Assn. (devel. com. 1985—), WomenSpace (helpline vol., legal cons. 1985—), Kappa Kappa Gamma. Democrat. Jewish. Avocations: swimming, running, weight lifting, biking. Family and matrimonial, Consumer commercial, Personal injury. Home: 20647 Beaconsfield Blvd Rocky River OH 44107 Office: 15400 Madison Ave Lakewood OH 44107

COHEN, ARTHUR ALAN, lawyer; b. N.Y.C., Jan. 15, 1954; s. Walter J. and Marion W. Cohen. BA, Yale U., 1976; JD, Columbia U., 1979. Bar: N.J. 1979, U.S. Dist. Ct. N.J. 1979, N.Y. 1980, U.S. Dist. Ct. (so. and ea. dists.) N.Y. 1980. Assoc. Donovan, Leisure, Newton & Irvine, N.Y.C., 1979-82, Spengler, Carlson & Gubar, N.Y.C., 1982-84; v.p., gen. counsel Microband Corp. Am., N.Y.C., 1984-86; assoc. Skadden, Arps, Slate, Meagher & Flom, N.Y.C., 1986—. Trustee No. Valley Regional High Sch. Dist., Haworth, N.J., 1976-79. Mem. Assn. of Bar of City of N.Y. (young lawyers com. 1986—, judge Nat. Moot Ct. Competition 1986—). Avocations: skiing, golf, windsurfing, reading, theatre. General corporate, Securities, Contracts commercial. Home: 1601 3d Ave #27H New York NY 10128 Office: Skadden Arps Slate Meagher & Flom 919 3d Ave New York NY 10022

COHEN, BARRY DAVID, lawyer; b. Vineland, N.J., Apr. 21, 1952; s. Joseph and Doris (Maier) C.; m. Ronnie Kestenbaum, June 15, 1975; children: Joshua Aaron, Noah Avrum. BA, Rutgers U., 1974; JD, Cath. U., 1979. Bar: N.J., U.S. Dist. Ct. N.J., U.S. Supreme Ct. Assoc. Cooper, Perskie, April, Niedelman, Wagenheim & Weiss, Atlantic City, 1979—, assoc. mem. firm, 1983—. Chmn. Jewish Community Relations Council, Atlantic County, 1986—; bd. dirs. Fedn. Jewish Agencies Atlantic County, 1985—, Beth Judah Synagogue, Ventor, N.J., trustee, 1986—. Mem. ABA, Atlantic County Bar Assn., Def. Research Inst., Assn. Trial Lawyers Am., Construction Specification Inst., Phi Beta Kappa. Avocations: polit. sci., history, song writing. Personal injury, Insurance, State civil litigation. Office: Cooper Perskie April et al 1125 Atlantic Ave Atlantic City NJ 08401

COHEN, BENJAMIN JACK, lawyer; b. New Bedford, Mass., Sept. 20, 1948; s. David H. and Louise R. (Rosen) C.; m. Michele Leslie Kaye, Oct. 4, 1981; children: Raphael Joshua, Ariella Sara, Miriam Hannah. BS, Brown U., 1970; JD, Yale U., 1974. Bar: Mass. 1974, N.Y. 1981. Atty. office of chief counsel IRS, Washington, 1974-77; atty. office of tax legis. counsel Dept. Treasury, Washington, 1977-80; ptnr. Cahill, Gordon & Reindel, N.Y.C., 1980—. Mem. ABA (tax sect.), N.Y. State Bar Assn., Mass. Bar Assn., Assn. of Bar of City of N.Y. (tax com.). Corporate taxation. Office: Cahill Gordon & Reindel 80 Pine St New York NY 10005

COHEN, BENNETT D., lawyer; b. Chgo., Mar. 14, 1953; s. Joseph B. and Susan (Ribniker) C. BA, Harvard U., 1976, postgrad., 1976-77, JD, 1981. Bar: Ill. 1982, Mass. 1982, N.Y. 1986. Assoc. Bingham, Dana & Gould, Boston, 1981-83, Willkie, Farr & Gallager, N.Y.C., 1984—; instr. Internat. Tax Program seminar, Harvard U., Cambridge, Mass., 1982-83. Mem. ABA. Corporate taxation, Personal income taxation, General corporate. Office: Willkie Farr & Gallagher 153 E 53d St New York NY 10022

COHEN, BERNARD BARRIE, lawyer; b. N.Y.C., Jan. 30, 1944; s. Theodore and Helen Cohen; m. Arlene Kay Licht, Aug. 7, 1966; children: Stephanie, Jason, Dara. BA, L.I. U., 1963; JD, Bklyn. Law Sch., 1966; postdoctoral, NYU, 1967. Bar: N.Y. 1966, U.S. Dist. Ct. (so. dist.) N.Y. 1979. Law sec. to presiding justice N.Y. Civil Ct., N.Y.C., 1967-73; assoc. Santangelo, Santangelo & Cohen, N.Y.C., 1972-74, ptnr., 1974-83; mng. ptnr. Santangelo & Cohen, N.Y.C., 1983—; counsel to senator minority leader N.Y. State Senate, Albany, 1978-80, oversight legis. com., 1983-85, adminsrtv. rev. com., 1985—. V.p., counsel Midtown Dem. Assn., N.Y.C., 1966—; counsel N.Y. State Joint Legis. Task Force on Racing Wagering and Breeding; pres., chmn. bd. trustees French Synagouge Am., Manhattan. Mem. ABA, N.Y. State Bar Assn. Democrat. Jewish. Avocations: fishing, reading, hiking. Probate, State civil litigation, General practice. Office: Santangelo & Cohen 225 Broadway New York NY 10007

COHEN, DARRYL BRANDT, lawyer; b. Chgo., Oct. 11, 1944; s. Milton A. and Myrrium Babe (Gurin) C. AB, U. Ga., 1967; JD, Mercer U., 1970. Bar: Fla. 1970, Ga. 1971, U.S. Supreme Ct. 1976. Asst. state's atty. Fla. State Ct., Miami, 1970-71; asst. dist. atty. Ga. State Ct., Atlanta, 1971-74; ptnr. Cohen, Pollock, Cooper & Comolli, Atlanta, 1974—. Mem. ABA, AFTRA (bd. dirs.), Nat. Acad. TV Arts and Scis. (bd. dirs., legal counsel Ga. chpt.), Screen Actors Guild (pres., v.p., governing council), Atlanta Bar Assn., Lawyers Club Atlanta, Assn. Trial Lawyers Am., Criminal Def. Lawyers Assn., Atlanta Models Guild (bd. dirs.), Atlanta Jaycees (legal counsel). Criminal, Entertainment. Home: 4000 Orchard Lake Ct Atlanta GA 30339 Office: Cohen Pollock Cooper & Comolli 401 W Peachtree St NE Suite 1550 Atlanta GA 30308

COHEN, DIANE BERKOWITZ, lawyer; b. Vineland, N.J., June 11, 1938; d. Myer and Ida Mae (Subin) Berkowitz; m. Robert H. Cohen, June 11, 1958 (div. Dec. 1980); children: Ronald Jay, Stuart Daniel, Amy Suzanne; m. Samuel Gerstein, Aug. 5, 1984. AA magna cum laude, Fairleigh Dickinson U., 1958; BA summa cum laude, Glassboro State Coll., 1976; JD, Temple U., 1979. Bar: Pa. 1979, N.J. 1980, U.S. Ct. Appeals (3d cir.) 1981. Assoc. Lewis Katz, Cherry Hill, N.J., 1979-81, Steven D. Weinstein, Cherry Hill, 1981-83; sole practice Collingswood, N.J., 1983-85; ptnr. Gerstein, Cohen & Kurtzman PA, Haddonfield, N.J., 1985—; active ethics com. N.J. Supreme Ct. Vice chmn. Allied Jewish Appeal, Cherry Hill, 1968-72; v.p. Nat. Council Jewish Women, Haddonfield, 1969-71; bd. dirs. Planned Parenthood Assn. Camden County, N.J., 1982—. Mem. ABA, N.J. Bar Assn., Camden County Bar Assn. (chmn. women lawyers com., mem. jud. appointment com.), Assn. Trial Lawyers Am. General practice, Family and matrimonial. Home: 4 Harrowgate Dr Cherry Hill NJ 08003 Office: Gerstein Cohen & Kurtzman PA 20 Kings Hwy W Haddonfield NJ 08033

COHEN, DONNA EDEN, lawyer; b. Harlingen, Tex., Oct. 23, 1956; d. Gerald Myer and Annette Rose (Rodman) C. Student, U. Hawaii, 1976-77; BA, U. Mass., 1978; JD, Suffolk U., 1981. Bar: Mass. 1981, U.S. Dist. Ct. Mass. 1982, U.S. Ct. Appeals (1st cir.) 1982. Assoc. Gilman, McLaughlin & Hanrahan, Boston, 1981—; of counsel Gerald M. Cohen, Andover, Mass., 1986—; counsel Commonwealth Mass. Purchasing Agt., Boston, 1982. Mem. Gov.'s Prepaid Legal Services Com., Boston, 1982—; bd. dirs. Am. Heart Assn. Needham, Mass., 1983—. Mem. ABA, Mass. Bar Assn., Boston Bar Assn., Assn. Trial Lawyers Am. (v.p. Suffolk chpt. 1979-81), Mass. Acad. Trial Attys. (lectr. continuing legal edn .seminar 1982—). Democrat. Jewish. Avocations: sailing, vol. work, fishing. State civil litigation, Landlord-tenant, Family and matrimonial. Office: Gilman McLaughlin & Hanrahan 470 Atlantic Ave Boston MA 02210

COHEN, EARL S., lawyer; b. Pitts., Dec. 18, 1946; m. Susan R. Cohen, Apr. 24, 1969; children: Jill, Andrew. BA, Clemson U., 1968; JD, U. Pitts., 1974; postgrad., Community Coll. of Allegheny, 1975-77. Bar: Pa. 1975, U.S. Dist. Ct. (we. dist.) Pa. 1975. Atty. Juvenile Ct., Pitts., 1975-81; assoc. Law Office of Philip T. Cheswick, Pitts., 1981—. Vice-chmn., sec. O'Hara (Pa.) Twp. Civil Service Commn., 1984—; chmn. Selective Service Bd. 5-17, 1984—; coach Foxchapel Soccer, O'Hara, 1986; mgr. Aspinwall Baseball, O'Hara, 1986. Served with U.S. Army, 1969-70. Mem. Pa. Bar Assn., Allegheny County Bar Assn. Avocations: jogging, sky-diving, skiing. Family and matrimonial, Criminal, State civil litigation. Office: Law Office of Philp T Cheswick 502 Brownsville Rd Pittsburgh PA 15210

COHEN, EDWARD A., lawyer; b. N.Y.C., Feb. 20, 1956; s. Merle and Rita (Borenstein) C. Bar: Ill. 1981, U.S. Dist. Ct. (no. dist.) Ill. 1981, U.S. Ct. Appeals (7th cir.) 1985. Assoc. W.S. Grotfeld & Assocs., Chgo., 1981-85, Vedder, Price, Kaufman & Kammholz, Chgo., 1985—. Mem. ABA, Ill. Bar Assn., Chgo. Bar Assn. Republican. Jewish. Avocations: Politics, soccer. Federal civil litigation, State civil litigation, Insurance. Office: Vedder Price Kaufman & Kammholz 115 S LaSalle #3000 Chicago IL 60603

COHEN, EDWARD HERSCHEL, apparel company executive, lawyer; b. Lewistown, Pa., Sept. 30, 1938; s. Saul Allen and Barbara (Getz) C.; m. Arlene Greenbaum, Aug. 12, 1962; children: Fredrick, James, Paul. AB, U. Mich., 1960; JD, Harvard U., 1963. Bar: N.Y. 1964. Assoc. Rosenman and Colin, N.Y.C., 1963-72, ptnr., 1972-87, counsel, 1982—; v.p., gen. counsel Phillips-Van Heusen Corp., N.Y.C., 1987—. Republican. Jewish. Club: Fenway Golf (Scarsdale, N.Y.). Avocations: golf, travel. General corporate, Securities. Home: 21 Sycamore Rd Scarsdale NY 10583 Office: Phillips-Van Heusen Corp 1290 Ave of Americas New York NY 10104

COHEN, ERIC MARTIN, lawyer; b. Mineola, N.Y., May 22, 1955; s. Emanuel and Irene (Kushner) C. BA, SUNY, Albany, 1977; JD, U. Miami, Fla., 1981. Bar: Fla. 1981, U.S. Ct. Appeals (11th cir.) 1981, U.S. Dist. Ct. (so. dist.) Fla. 1982; instr. cert. State of Fla. Commn. on Criminal Justice Standards and Tng. Jr. ptnr. Blumenfeld & Cohen, Coral Gables, Fla., 1981—. Mem. ABA, Nat. Assn. Criminal Def. Lawyers, Nat. Organization for Reform of Marijuana Laws, Soc. Wig and Robe, Dade County Bar Assn. Democrat. Avocation: running. Criminal. Home: 11912 SW 110th St Circle East Miami FL 33183 Office: Blumenfeld & Cohen 2550 Douglas Rd Coral Gables FL 33134

COHEN, GERRY FARMER, lawyer; b. Hartford, Conn., May 11, 1950; s. Joseph Marshall and Muriel Zelda (Sidrane) C.; m. Pamela Sue Farmer, Mar. 7, 1982; children: Aaron Louis, Zachary Edmond. AB, U. N.C., 1971, JD, 1975. Bar: N.C. 1975. A.P.A. coordinator N.C. Dept. Cultural Resources, Raleigh, 1975-76; staff atty. Nat. Assn. Attys. Gen., Raleigh, 1976-77; staff atty. N.C. Gen. Assembly, Raleigh, 1977-81, dir. bill drafting, 1981—. Mem. Chapel Hill Town Council, N.C., 1973-79, Dem. State Exec. Com., Raleigh, 1975-77, 81-83; chmn. Orange County Jury Commn., Hillsborough, N.C., 1979-84. Mem. ABA, Phi Beta Kappa. Jewish. Lodge: B'nai B'rith. Legislative, Personal income taxation, State and local taxation. Home: 8909 Taymouth Ct Raleigh NC 27612 Office: NC Gen Assembly Legis Office Bldg Raleigh NC 27611

COHEN, HENRY RODGIN, lawyer; b. Charleston, W.Va, May 7, 1944; s. Louis W. and Bertie (Rodgin) C.; m. Barbara Latz, Aug. 31, 1969; 1 child, Sarah Abigail. BA, Harvard U., 1965, LLB, 1968. Bar: W.Va. 1968, N.Y. 1970. Assoc. Sullivan & Cromwell, N.Y.C., 1970-77, ptnr., 1977—. Contbg. editor Financial Services Regulation Newsletter, 1985. Served with U.S. Army, 1968-70. Banking. Office: Sullivan & Cromwell 125 Broad St New York NY 10004

COHEN, HYMAN K., lawyer; b. Balt., July 26, 1925; s. Jacob and Tillie (Greenberg) C.; m. Eileen Ruth Manko, Nov. 7, 1954; children: Jill Leslie, Brent Paul (dec.). AB, U. N.C., 1948; JD, U. Balt., 1954. Bar: Md. 1954, U.S. Dist. Ct. Md. 1955, U. S. Supreme Ct. 1959, D.C. 1979. Sole practice Balt., 1954—; instr. U. Md., Catonsville, 1983—; bd. dirs. Fgn. Motors Ltd., Koren Furniture House, Inc.; v.p., bd. dirs. 7800, Ltd. pres. Liberty Rd. Recreation and Parks Council, Randallstown, Md., 1977-81; pres. Reserve Officers Assn. Balt. Naval Chpt., 1963-67, treas. 1967—; chmn. bd. Cockpit in Ct., Essex Community Coll., Balt. 1983—; vol. Jewish Big Brother League. Named Big Brother of Yr. Jewish Big Brother League, 1983, Vol. of Yr. Liberty Rd. Recreation and Parks Council, 1984. Mem. Md. State Bar Assn. Democrat. Jewish. Avocations: theater, reading, community activities. General practice, Personal injury, Family and matrimonial. Home: 9013 Bruno Rd Randallstown MD 21133 Office: 514 Saint Paul St Baltimore MD 21202

COHEN, JAY LORING, lawyer; b. Erie, Pa., Oct. 26, 1953; s. Harold H. and Adelle (Stein) C.; m. Martha Kaepplein, June 20, 1976; children—Natanel M., Katrielle Z. B.A. cum laude, U. Rochester, 1974; J.D., Georgetown U., 1977. Bar: Pa. 1977, U.S. Claims Ct. 1978, U.S. Ct. Appeals (D.C. cir.) 1978, D.C. 1979, U.S. Supreme Ct. 1981, U.S. Ct. Appeals (fed. cir.) 1982, Md. 1986. Mem. firm Israel, Raley & Cohen, Chartered (formerly Israel & Raley), Washington, 1977—. Editor Am. Criminal Law Rev., 1977. Vice-chmn. Montgomery County Ethics Commn., 1986—; bd. dirs. Hebrew Day Inst., 1984—. Mem. Assn. Trial Lawyers Am. (comml. litigation sect.), ABA (pub. contract law sect.), Fed. Bar Assn. (fed. litigation sect.), Fed. Cir. Bar Assn. (gov. contract appeals sect.). Government contracts and claims, Federal civil litigation. Office: Israel Raley & Cohen Chartered 1513 16th St NW Washington DC 20036

COHEN, JEFFREY, lawyer; b. Bklyn., Jan. 31, 1956; s. Fred and Ann (Piel) C. A.B. in Politics and Philosophy with depart mental honors magna cum laude, Brandeis U., 1977; J.D., Bklyn. Law Sch., 1980. Bar: N.Y. 1981, Colo. 1981. Assoc. Freedman & May, N.Y.C., 1980-81, Alter, Zall & Haligman, Denver, 1981-82; ptnr. Quiat & Dice, Denver, 1982—; dir. Palombo Farms, Henderson, Colo., L-Cat, Inc., Denver. Mem. ABA (bus. bankruptcy com.), Colo. Bar Assn., Denver Bar Assn. Republican. Jewish. Clubs: Colo. Mountain, Internat. Athletic, Denver Chess (bd. dirs., v.p. 1983—) (Denver). Bankruptcy, State civil litigation, General corporate. Home: 1330 Gaylord #1103 Denver CO 80206 Office: Koransky Friedman & Cohen PC 1225 17th St Suite 2500 Denver CO 80203

COHEN, JEFFREY MICHAEL, lawyer; b. Dayton, Ohio, Nov. 13, 1940; s. H. Mort and Evelyn (Friedlob) C.; m. Betsy Z. Zimmerman, July 3, 1966; children—Meredith Sue, Seth Alan. A.B., Colgate U., 1962; J.D., Columbia U., 1965. Bar: Fla. 1965, U.S. Supreme Ct. 1969; cert. civil trial lawyer Fla. Bar Bd. Cert., diplomate Nat. Bd. Trial Advocacy. Asst. pub. defender Dade County (Fla.), 1968-70, asst. state's atty., 1970-72, spl. asst. state's atty., 1973; ptnr. Fromberg Fromberg Gross Cohen Shore & Berke, P.A., 1972-84, Cohen, Berke, Bernstein, Brodie & Kondell, P.A., Miami, Fla., 1984—. Mem. ABA, Dade County Bar Assn., Acad. Fla. Trial Lawyers, Assn. Trial Lawyers Am., Am. Judicature Soc., Fla. Criminal Def. Attys. Assn. Personal injury, Federal civil litigation, State civil litigation. Home: 16725 SW 82 Ct Miami FL 33157 Office: Cohen Berke Bernstein Brodie & Kondell PA 9100 S Dadeland Blvd Suite 1003 Miami FL 33156

COHEN, JULES SIMON, lawyer; b. Orlando, Fla., Nov. 1, 1937; s. Barney Joseph and Dorothy (Collman) C.; m. Elizabeth Ann Wiese, May 21, 1971; children: Lynda Kaye, Laurel Ann, Richard Wiese, Ronald Herman. BA, U. Fla., 1959; JD, Harvard U., 1962. Bar: Fla. 1962. Ptnr. Cohen & Cohen, Orlando, Fla., 1962-67; sole practice Orlando, 1967-72; pres. Jules S. Cohen, P.A., Orlando, 1972—; chmn. bankruptcy com. Fla. Bar, 1973-75, chmn. corp., banking, bus. law sect. 1976-77, lectr continuing legal edn. com. 1974—. Contbr. articles to legal jours. Mem. exec. com. Orange County Dem. Exec. Com., 1972-80; mem. Friends of the Library, Orange County Mental Health Assn., John Young Mus., Nat. Marriage Encounter Cen. Fla. Mem. ABA (bus. bankruptcy com. 1978—), Southeastern Bankruptcy Law Inst. (mem. bd. dirs. 1977—), Am. Arbitration Assn., Orange County Bar Assn., Fed. Bar Assn., Am. Judicature Soc., Comml. Law League Am., Fla. Trial Assn., Fla. Bar Found., Am. Numismatic Assn., Phi Beta Kappa, Phi Eta Sigma. Club: Harvard of Cen. Fla. (past pres.). Bankruptcy, Consumer commercial. Office: 808 N Mills Ave Orlando FL 32803

COHEN, LAURENCE JOEL, lawyer; b. Washington, May 15, 1932; s. Harry Leonard and Ethel (Blaustein) C.; m. Jo R., Dec. 22, 1962; children—Hal, Jill. B.S. in Econs., U. Pa., 1954; LL.B., Yale U., 1959. Bar: D.C. 1959, U.S. Supreme Ct. 1963. Legal asst., supr. atty. NLRB, Washington, 1964-67; ptnr. Sherman, Dunn, Cohen, Leifer & Counts, Washington, 1967—; gen. counsel Internat. Brotherhood Elec. Workers, 1980—; Bldg. and Constrn. Trades Dept. AFL-CIO, 1980—; gen. counsel Internat. Assn. Heat and Frost Insulators and Asbestos Workers, 1977—; alt. mem. chmn.'s task force NLRB, 1976-77. Mem. ABA (sect. labor and employment law, council 1976-84, chmn. 1985-86). Contbr. articles to legal jours.; co-editor The Developing Labor Law, 2d edit., 1983. Labor. Office: 1125-15th St NW Suite 801 Washington DC 20005

COHEN, LAWRENCE GENE, lawyer; b. Newark, May 5, 1946; s. Herman and Bernice (Luber) C.; m. Kathleen Mary Ritter, Jan. 11, 1977; children: Jennifer, Courtenay. AB in History, Beloit Coll., 1968; JD, Washington and Lee U., 1973. Bar: N.Y. 1973, U.S. Dist. Ct. (so. and ea. dists.) N.Y. 1973, U.S. Ct. Appeals (2d cir.) 1974. Ptnr. Kirlin, Campbell & Keating, N.Y.C., 1973-80; maritime counsel Exxon Corp., N.Y.C., 1980—; bd. dirs. Internat. Tanker Owners Pollution Fedn.; mem. faculty Pacific Admiralty Seminar, San Francisco, 1983. Mem. ABA, Maritime Law Assn. (vice-chmn. Marine Ecology com. 1984—), City Bar of N.Y. Republican. Club: N.Y. Yacht. Avocations: yachting, gardening, tennis. Admiralty, Environment, Private international. Office: Exxon Co Internat 200 Park Ave Florham Park NJ 07932-1002

COHEN, LINDA MARKS, lawyer; b. N.Y.C., Oct. 8, 1943; s. Lawrence and Helena (Simons) Marks, m. Steven I. Cohen, Aug. 18, 1973; children: Jennifer, David. BA, Conn. Coll., 1965; JD, Northeastern U., 1980. Bar: R.I. 1980. Dep. counsel Old Stone Bank, Providence, 1979—; assoc. counsel Old Stone Corp. Mem. Employee Stock Ownership Assn. (fin. inst. adv. com. 1986—). Securities, General corporate, Banking. Office: Old State Bank 150 S Main St Providence RI 02903

COHEN, LINDA MERYL, lawyer; b. N.Y.C., Nov. 18, 1948; s. Aaron Solomon and Fae (Kerbel) Bilgrei. BA, SUNY, Stony Brook, 1971; JD, Am. U., 1973; LLM, George Washington U., 1977. Bar: D.C. 1974, Va. 1974. Dir. office of consumer affairs Nat. Credit Union Adminstrn., Washington, 1978-82; v.p. Citicorp Savs., Oakland, Calif., 1983-84; v.p. govt. relations Citicorp, Los Angeles, 1984-86; atty. Citicorp Investment Bank, N.Y.C., 1986-87, v.p., 1987—; lectr. on women and credit and womens legal rights Nat. Orgn. for Women Speakers Bur., 1974-79; mem. consumer adv. council Fed. Res. Bd., 1976-78; project cons. White Ho. Task Force on Women and Bus., 1977. Advisor women career adv. program Georgetown U. Ctr. for Career Planning and Placement, Washington, 1976-81; mem. com. on taxation Pres.'s Interdepartmental Task Force on Women, 1979. Mem. ABA (com. on consumer fin. services 1976—, comml. fin. services 1987). Consumer commercial, Government contracts and claims, Investment banking. Office: Citicorp Investment Bank 55 Water St 44th Floor New York NY 10043

COHEN, MARCY SHARON, lawyer, bank executive; b. N.Y.C., Apr. 29, 1954; d. Morton Gilbert and Sue (Krumstock) C.; m. Lawrence Liebs. AB, Lehman Coll., 1975; JD, NYU, 1978. Bar: N.Y. 1979, U.S. Dist. Ct. (ea. and so. dists.) N.Y. 1979, U.S. Supreme Ct. 1982. Assoc. Marcus & Marcus, N.Y.C., 1978-80; v.p., assoc. gen. counsel Bank Leumi Trust Co. N.Y., N.Y.C., 1980-84; v.p., gen. counsel Atlantic Bank N.Y., N.Y.C., 1984—; mem. faculty Am. Inst. Banking, N.Y.C., 1984—. Mem. ABA (corp. banking and bus. law com.), Assn. Bar of City of N.Y. (banking law com.), Assn. Comml. Fin. Attys. Avocations: sailing, gardening, tennis. Banking, Contracts commercial. Office: Atlantic Bank of NY 960 Ave of the Americas New York NY 10001

COHEN, MARY ANN, judge U.S. Tax Ct.; b. Albuquerque, July 16, 1943; d. Gus R. and Mary Carolyn (Avriette) C. B.S., UCLA, 1964; J.D. U. So. Calif., 1967. Bar: Calif. 1967. Ptnr., Abbott & Cohen P.C. and predecessors, Los Angeles, 1967-82; judge U.S. Tax Ct., Washington 1982—. Mem. ABA (sect. taxation), Legion Lex. Republican. Jurisprudence. Office: US Tax Court 400 2nd St NW Washington DC 20217

COHEN, MEREDITH JOSEPH, lawyer; b. Orlando, Fla., Aug. 3, 1929; s. Barney J. and Dorothy (Collman) C.; m. Audrey E. Mayer, Mar. 11, 1956; children—Robert, Wendy, Jennifer, Arthur. B.S. with honors, U. Fla., 1950, J.D., 1952. Bar: Fla. 1952, U.S. Supreme Ct. 1964; cert. marital and family law Fla. Bar. Asst. pros. atty. State of Fla., 1955-59, 65-69; sole practice, Orlando, Fla., 1960-65, 69—; adj. prof. law office mgmt. Valencia Community Coll., 1978-81. Served to 1st lt. JAGC, AUS, 1952-55. Decorated Bronze Star. Fellow Am. Acad. Matrimonial Lawyers; mem. ABA, Fla. Bar Assn. (chmn. criminal law sect. 1981-82, exec. council family law sect.), Assn. Trial Lawyers Am., Acad. Fla. Trial Lawyers, Nat. Assn. Criminal Def. Lawyers, Orange County Bar Assn. (chmn. family law sect. 1982-83). Jewish. Clubs: Toastmasters Internat., Shriners. Criminal, Family and matrimonial. Office: Suite 455 Landmark Center II 225 E Robinson St Orlando FL 32801

COHEN, MITCHELL HARRY, U.S. judge; b. Phila., Sept. 11, 1904; s. Harry and Minnie (Rubin) C.; children: Margaret, Fredric. Student, Temple U., 1922-24; LL.B., Dickinson Law Sch., 1928; LLD (hon.), Dickinson Sch. Law, 1975. Bar: N.J. 1930. Practiced in Camden, 1930-58, city prosecutor, 1936-42; freeholder Camden County, 1940; judge Camden Mcpl. Ct., 1942-47; county prosecutor Camden County, 1948-58; county judge 1958-61; judge Superior Ct. N.J., New Brunswick, 1961-62; judge U.S. Dist. Ct. N.J., Camden, 1962-73, sr. judge., 1973—. Founder, co-producer Camden County Music Fair, 1955; chmn. Camden County chpt. Sister Kenny Found., Allied Jewish Appeal, Camden; leader Camden Republican Com., 1947-58. Served with AUS, World War II. Recipient Outstanding Alumni award Dickinson Coll., 1972. Mem. Am., N.J., Camden County bar assns., Am. Judicature Soc. Office: US Court House and Post Office Bldg 401 Market St Camden NJ 08101 *

COHEN, MITCHELL ROBERT, lawyer; b. Phila., Nov. 15, 1955; s. Joseph and Carrie (Kramer) C.; m. Sherry L. Suravitz, Aug. 15, 1979; children: Joshua David, Justin Michael. BSBA, Drexel U., 1976; JD, Temple U., 1979. Assoc. Pepper, Hamilton & Scheetz, Phila., 1979-82; ptnr. Segal, Elkind & Cohen, Haddonfield, N.J., 1982-84, Elkind & Cohen, Cherry Hill, N.J., 1984-86, Elkind, Cohen & Dimento, Cherry Hill, 1986—. Bd. dirs. Cherry Hill Swim Club, 1986—, advisor, 1985—; advisor Locker Room Softball League, Cherry Hill, 1985—. Named one of Outstanding Young Men Am., 1985. Mem. ABA, Assn. Trial Lawyers Am., Pa. Bar Assn., Camden County Bar Assn., Burlington County Bar Assn., N.J. Remodelers Assn. (bd. dirs. 1984—, Man of Yr. award 1985), Tau Epsilon Phi. Jewish. Karate instructor, 2d degree black belt. Real property, General corporate, Bankruptcy. Office: Elkind Cohen & Dimento PA 100 Brace Rd Cherry Hill NJ 08034

COHEN, MURRAY, lawyer; b. Union City, N.J., Nov. 2, 1926; s. Harry and Fay Z. (Zimmerman) C.; m. Rita S. Cohen, Sept. 20, 1950; children—Deborah C. Shah, Justin A., Jennifer S. Student, NYU; J.D. magna cum laude, Harvard U., 1948. Bar: N.Y. 1949. Assoc. Rosenman & Colin, N.Y.C., 1948-55, ptnr., 1955-86, mng. sr. ptnr., 1985-86, of counsel, 1986—. Trustee Henry Meinhard Charitable Trusts. Mem. ABA, N.Y. State Bar Assn., Bar Assn. City of N.Y. Democrat. Jewish. Club: University (N.Y.C.). General corporate, Securities. Home: 363 Lydecker St Englewood NJ 07631 Office: Rosenman & Colin 575 Madison Ave New York NY 10022

COHEN, NANCY M., lawyer; b. Boston, July 14, 1941; d. Gerald Murray and Margaret (Callahan) Mahoney; m. William Cohen, Aug. 8, 1976; 1 child, Margaret Emily. AB, Emmanuel Coll., 1963; JD, Stanford U., 1975. Bar: Calif. 1975. Asst. gen. counsel Bendix Forest Products Corp., San Francisco, 1976-81; assoc. Brown & Bain, Phoenix, Ariz., 1981; counsel Syntex Corp., Palo Alto, Calif., 1982-86; sr. counsel Syntex Corp., Palo Alto, 1986—; bd. dirs. Syntex Fed. Credit Union, Palo Alto. Chmn. Rental Housing Mediation Task Force, Palo Alto, 1972-74; mem. All Saints Vestry, Palo Alto, 1985—. Mem. ABA, Am. Corp. Counsel Assn. General corporate, Antitrust. Office: Syntex Corp 3401 Hillview Ave Palo Alto CA 94304

COHEN, NORTON JACOB, lawyer; b. Detroit, Nov. 5, 1935; s. Norman and Molly Rose (Natinsky) C.; m. Lorelei Freda Schuman, June 16, 1957; children—Debrah Anne, Sander Ivan. Student U. Mich., 1953-55, U. Detroit, 1955-56; J.D., Wayne State U., 1959. Bar: Mich. 1959, Tex. 1962, U.S. Dist. Ct. (so. dist.) Mich. 1963, U.S. Ct. Appeals (6th cir.) 1966, U.S. Supreme Ct. 1970. law clk. to presiding justice Mich. Supreme Ct., Lansing, 1959; assoc. Zwerdling, Miller, Klimist & Maurer, Detroit, 1963-68; legal dir. ACLU of Mich., Detroit, 1968-69; sr. ptnr. Miller, Cohen, Martens & Ice, P.C., Southfield, Mich., 1969—. Chmn., Southfield Dem. Party, Mich., 1965-67; co-chair Robert F. Kennedy for Pres., Oakland County, Mich., 1968; exec. bd. Met. Detroit ACLU, 1969—, chmn., 1972-74; vice-chair Equal Justice Council, Detroit, 1970-74; spl. counsel workers compensation Mich. AFL-CIO, 1983—, Mich. Dept. Labor, 1986—. Served to capt. U.S. Army, 1960-63. Recipient Spirit of Detroit award Detroit Common Council, 1982. Mem. ABA, Fed. Bar Assn. Jewish. Lodge: B'nai B'rith. Workers' compensation, Labor. Office: Miller Cohen Martens & Ice PC 17117 W Nine Mile Rd Suite 1400 Southfield MI 48075

COHEN, RICHARD BARTON, lawyer; b. Bklyn., Mar. 13, 1953; s. Ronald and Roslyn (Younger) C. BA, Harpur Coll., 1974; JD, N.Y. Law Sch., 1977. Bar: N.Y. 1978, U.S. Dist. Ct. (so. and ea. dists.) N.Y., U.S. Ct. Appeals (2d cir.), U.S. Supreme Ct. Asst. corp. counsel N.Y.C. Law Dept., 1977-80; assoc. Friedlander, Gaines, Rosenthal et al, N.Y.C., 1981; v.p., counsel Mfr.'s Hanover Trust Co., N.Y.C., 1981—. Mem. Assn. of Bar of City of N.Y. (com. on corrections 1983-86). Avocations: sports, reading. Federal civil litigation, State civil litigation, Banking. Office: Mfr's Hanover Trust 270 Park Ave New York NY 10017

COHEN, RICHARD STOCKMAN, U.S. dist. atty.; b. Boston, Apr. 5, 1937; s. Abram I. and Cele (Stockman) C.; m. Suzanne Thomas Burnett, Aug. 29, 1964; children—Andrew Stockman, Meredith Ware. B.B.A., U. Ga., 1958; J.D., Boston U., 1963. Bar: Maine bar 1963. Asst. atty. gen. and counsel Maine Bur. Taxation, Augusta, 1963-65; with Atty. Gen.'s Dept., State of Maine, Augusta, 1963—; chief criminal div. Atty. Gen.'s Dept., State of Maine, 1966-71, dep. atty. gen. in charge law enforcement and criminal div., 1971-79, atty. gen., 1979-81; U.S. atty. Dist. of Maine, 1981—; chmn. Maine Criminal Justice Planning Assistance Agy., Augusta, 1972-79; mem. Criminal Law Adv. Commn. Mem. Maine-Medico Legal Soc. (pres. 1973). Home: 94 Winthrop St Augusta ME 04330

COHEN, ROBERT (AVRAM), lawyer; b. Pitts., July 23, 1929; s. Max R. and Mollie (Segal) C.; m. Frances H. Steiner, Dec. 24, 1951 (div. Feb. 1974); children: Deborah E., David R.; m. Mary E. Connors, Apr. 11, 1974; children: Deborah A., Charles E., Chrisann. AB magna cum laude, Harvard U., 1951, JD, 1954. Bar: Pa. 1955, U.S. Dist. Ct. (we. dist.) Pa. 1955, U.S. Ct. Appeals (3d cir.) 1961, U.S. Supreme Ct. 1962, Fla. 1974, U.S. Dist. Ct. (so. dist.) Fla. 1974, U.S. Tax Ct. 1983. Assoc. Goldstock, Schwartz, Teitelbaum & Schwartz, Pitts., 1955-60; ptnr. Goldstock, Schwartz, Cohen & Schwartz, Pitts., 1960-67, Fine, Perlow, Stone & Cohen, Pitts., 1967-70, Cohen & Goldstock, Pitts., 1970-73; assoc. Herring, Evans & Fulton, West Palm Beach, Fla., 1974; from assoc. to ptnr. Rothman, Gordon, Foreman and Groudine, P.A., Pitts., 1974-86; sole practice Pitts., 1986—. Mem. ABA, Pa. Bar Assn., Allegheny County Bar Assn., Acad. Trial Lawyers Allegheny County, Am. Judicature Soc., Assn. Trial Lawyers Am. (pres. Western Pa. chpt. 1972-73), Pa. Trial Lawyers Assn., Fla. Bar Assn., Fla. Trial Lawyers Assn. Democrat. Jewish. Lodges: Golden Triangle (v.p. 1966-69), B'nai B'rith. Personal injury, Federal civil litigation, State civil litigation. Home: 205 Oak Heights Dr Oakdale PA 15071 Office: 819 Frick Bldg Pittsburgh PA 15219

COHEN, ROBERT STEPHAN, lawyer; b. N.Y.C., Jan. 14, 1939; s. Abraham and Florence C.; m. Margery H. Cohen, Jan. 17, 1968; children—Christopher, Ian, Nicholas. B.A., Alfred U., 1959; LL.B., Fordham U., 1962. Bar: N.Y. 1963, U.S. Dist. Ct. (so. and ea. dists.) N.Y., U.S. Ct. Appeals (2d cir.). Assoc. Saxe, Bacon & O'Shea, N.Y.C., 1963-68; ptnr. Morrison, Cohen & Singer, and predecessor firms, N.Y.C., 1968—; lectr. in

field; faculty Am Acad. Psychiatry and the Law, 1984—. Bd. dirs. Nat. Council Alcoholism, N.Y.C., 1980—, N.Y. Pops, 1982—; trustee Alfred U., 1984—. Served to 1st lt. JAG, USAR, 1965-67. Mem. ABA, Fed. Bar Assn., N.Y. State Bar Assn., N.Y.C. Bar Assn., Assn. Trial Lawyers Am., N.Y. Acad. Matrimonial Lawyers (bd. govs.). Club: Univ. (N.Y.C.). Contbr. to legal jours. Federal civil litigation, State civil litigation, Family and matrimonial. Home: 1107 Fifth Ave New York NY 10028 Office: 110 E 59th St New York NY 10022

COHEN, ROBERT YALE, II, lawyer; b. Little Rock, Ark., Mar. 14, 1950; s. Robert Yale and Fredona (Forshag) C. BA, Hendrix Coll., 1972; JD, U. Ark., 1975; LLM, So. Methodist U., 1976. Bar: Ark. 1975, U.S. Dist. Ct. Ark. 1977, U.S. Ct. Appeals (8th cir.) 1980, U.S. Tax Ct. 1981. Assoc. Harper, Young, Smith & Maurras, Ft. Smith, Ark., 1977-79, ptnr., 1979—. Pres. Ft. Smith Chorale, 1986; bd. dirs. Community Hospice, Ft. Smith, 1986; trustee South Side Baptist Ch., Ft. Smith, 1986. Mem. ABA, Ark. Bar Assn., Sebastian County Bar Assn., Hendrix Coll. Alumni Assn. (bd. govs. 1986—), Ark. Bd. Legal Specialization (cert.). Club: Ft. Smith Girl's (bd. dirs. 1987). Lodge: Rotary (pres. Ft. Smith Southside 1985-86). Estate taxation, Banking, Corporate taxation.

COHEN, ROBIN ELLEN, lawyer; b. N.Y.C., Aug. 23, 1955; d. Charles Solomon and Evelyn (Sweisky) C.; m. Peter T. Shapiro, June 23, 1985. J.D. cum laude, NYU, 1981; B.S., SUNY-Stony Brook, 1976; postgrad. Sloan Kettering Div. Cornell Grad. Sch. Med. Scis., 1976-77. Bar: N.Y. 1982, U.S. Dist. Ct. (ea. and so. dists.) N.Y. 1983. Assoc. atty. corp. dept. Rosenman Colin Freund Lewis & Cohen, N.Y.C., 1981-84, Kramer Levin Nessen Kamin & Frankel, N.Y.C., 1984-87; clk. to presiding justice appellate div. 2d Dept., N.Y. State Supreme Ct., 1979. Mem. ABA, N.Y. Women's Bar Assn., N.Y. State Bar Assn., New York County Bar Assn., Bar Assn. City N.Y., Order of Coif. Democrat. Jewish. Contracts commercial, General corporate, Securities. Home: 315 E 80th St New York NY 10021

COHEN, SEYMOUR, lawyer; b. Chgo., Sept. 27, 1917; s. Sol and Sophie (Norinsky) C.; m. Marcia Meltzer, Aug. 10, 1952; children—Susan Ruth, James Burton. B.S., Ind. U., 1939, J.D., 1941. Bar: Ind. 1941, Ill. 1948, U.S. Supreme Ct. 1971. Atty. NLRB, Washington, 1946-47; practice law Chgo., 1947—; mem. firm Dorfman, Cohen, Laner & Muchin, Ltd. (and predecessor), 1953-86. Mem. Northbrook (Ill.) Library Bd., 1963-69, pres., 1965-67. Served to lt. comdr. USNR, 1941-45. Mem. Chgo. Bar Assn. (chmn. com. labor law 1961-63), ABA. Labor, Pension, profit-sharing, and employee benefits. Home: 1201 Wendy Dr Northbrook IL 60062 Office: 350 N Clark St Chicago IL 60610

COHEN, SHELDON STANLEY, lawyer; b. Washington, June 28, 1927; s. Herman and Pearl (Jaffe) C.; m. Faye Fram, Feb. 21, 1951; children: Melinda Ann Cohen Goetzl, Laura Eve, Jonathan Adam, Sharon Ruevena. A.B. with spl. honors, George Washington U., 1950, J.D. with highest honors (Charles W. Dorsey scholar), 1952; D.Lit. (hon.), Lincoln Coll. Bar: D.C. 1952, U.S. Supreme Ct. 1956, U.S. Tax Ct. 1956; C.P.A., Md. Acct. 1950-52; legis. atty. Office Chief Counsel, IRS, Dept. Treasury, 1952-56, chief counsel, 1963-65, commr. internal revenue, 1965-69; assoc. Paul, Weiss, Rifkind, Wharton & Garrison, Washington, 1956-60; ptnr. Arnold, Fortas & Porter, Washington, 1960-63; mem. Cohen & Uretz, Washington, 1969-85; ptnr. Morgan, Lewis & Bockius, Washington, 1985—; lectr. Howard U. Law Sch., 1957-58; professorial lectr. George Washington U. Law Sch., 1958-81; adj. prof. U. Miami Law Sch., Fla., 1974-85; mem. adv. com. Inst. Estate Planning, U. Miami Law Center, 1969—; chmn. exec. compensation com. U.S. Pay Bd., 1971-72; mem. Commn. on Founds. and Pvt. Philanthropy, 1969-70; mem. adv. group to commr. IRS, 1969-70; chmn. steering com. Adminstrv. Conf. U.S., 1974-84; mem. exec. com. Washington Lawyer's Com. for Civil Rights Under Law, 1975—; mem. cons. panel to controller gen. U.S., 1980—, Gen. Acctg. Office, 1981—; pres. Am.-Israel Tax Found., 1969-80; mem. council Sch. Govt. and Bus. Adminstrn., George Washington U., 1969-79, mem. commn. on governance, 1970, bd. govs. univ., 1980; pres. Law Assn., 1978-79; bd. dirs. Nat. Found. for Jewish Culture, 1968-72, Am. Joint Distbn. Com.; bd. dirs., v.p. United Jewish Appeal of D.C., 1980-84; past v.p. Jewish Community Center, Greater Washington; bd. dirs., past v.p. Jewish Community Found. Editorial and bus. sec.: George Washington U. Law Rev, 1952; case notes editor, 1951-52; bd. editors Nat. Law Jour. Mem. adv. com. to D.C. Ct. Appeals Admission Com.; past pres. Jewish Social Service Agy., Washington; bd. dirs. Adas Israel Congregation, Jewish Welfare Bd., United Synagogues Am., Common Cause, Nat. Council for a Responsible Firearms Policy, Inc.; bd. regents Omar N. Bradley Found., U.S. Army Hist. Collection, 1970-73; bd. dirs., chmn. devel. com. Washington Community Found., 1982—; trustee B'nai B'rith Found. of U.S.; spl. tax counsel Democratic Nat. Com., 1969-72, gen. counsel, 1972-77; bd. overseers Jewish Theol. Sem. Am., 1972—; trustee United Jewish Endowment Fund, 1980—. Served with USNR, 1945-46. Recipient Alumni Achievement award George Washington U., 1965, Arthur Flemming award, 1966, Alexander Hamilton award U.S. Treasury Dept., 1969, Joseph Ottenstein community service award Jewish Social Agy., 1976. Mem. Nat. Acad. Pub. Adminstrn. (chmn. com. on energy 1978—, trustee, sec.), ABA (chmn. spl. com. on retirement benefits legis. tax sect. 1972-73), Fed. Bar Assn. (council tax sect.), D.C. Bar Assn. (bd. dirs. 1969-72, bd. govs. 1972-75), D.C. Inst. C.P.A.s (hon.), Am.-Israel C. of C. (chmn. tax com. 1980), Order of Coif, Phi Delta Phi, Phi Sigma Delta, Omicron Delta Kappa (hon.), Beta Alpha Psi (hon.). Clubs: Cosmos (tournament players assn. award) (Washington); Golf (Avenel); Internat. (bd. dirs. 1979-85). Lodges: Masons, B'nai B'rith. Corporate taxation, Estate taxation, Personal income taxation. Home: 5518 Trent St Chevy Chase MD 20815 Office: Morgan Lewis & Bockius 1800 M St NW Washington DC 20036

COHEN, STANLEY DALE, lawyer; b. Nassau County, N.Y., Mar. 14, 1952; s. Lester and Eleanor (Mait) C.; m. Janis Wendrow, Sept. 11, 1976; children: Adam Benjamin, Heather Jill. JD, Western New Eng. Coll., 1976. Bar: N.Y. 1977, D.C. 1980, Fla. 1981, U.S. Dist. Ct. (so. and ea. dists.) N.Y. 1977, D.C. 1980, Fla. 1981, U.S. Ct. Appeals (9th cir.) 1982. Mem. firm Reuben, Schwartz & Silverberg, N.Y.C., 1977-78; sole practice, N.Y.C., 1978-83; mem. firm Cohen & Jaeger, 1984—; sec., bd. dirs. Manhattan Mag. Found. Corp. Mem. N.Y. County Lawyers Assn. General corporate, Real property, Contracts commercial. Home: 83 Peachtree Ln Roslyn Heights NY 11577 Office: Cohen & Jaeger 450 7th Ave Suite 3900 New York NY 10123 Office: 250 Old Country Rd Mineola NY 11501

COHEN, STEPHEN BRUCE, lawyer; b. East Chicago, Ind., Mar. 14, 1939; s. Cecil Bernard and Ida Edith (Goldstein) C.; m. Lynn Sneider, Mar. 23, 1969; children—Debra Suzanne, Aaron Eliot, Sabrina Beth. A.B., Harvard Coll., 1961; JD., Vanderbilt U., 1964; LL.B. in Internat. Law, Cambridge U. (Eng.), 1966, diploma, 1972. Bar: Ind. 1965, Ill. 1965, U.S. Dist. Ct. (no. dist.) Ill. 1967, U.S. Dist. Ct. (no. dist.) Ind. 1965, U.S. Dist. Ct. (so. dist.) Ind. 1965, U.S. Ct. Appeals (7th cir.) 1968, U.S. Supreme Ct. 1972. Assoc., Cohen, Foss, Schuman & Drake, and predecessor firms, East Chgo., Foss, Schuhman, Drake & Barnard, Chgo., 1965-69, ptnr., 1969-86; ptnr. Cohen, Starck & Burchett, Northbrook, Ill., and East Chicago, 1986—. Mem. ABA, Ill. Bar Assn., Ind. Bar Assn., Chgo. Bar Assn. (chmn. condominium subcom. 1980-82, exec. council real property law com. 1980—). Jewish. Real property, Personal injury, General practice. Office: Cohen Starck & Burchett 500 Skokie Blvd Suite 535 Northbrook IL 60062 Other office: 3609 Main St East Chicago IN 46312

COHEN, STEPHEN M(ARTIN), lawyer; b. West Palm Beach, Fla., Oct. 15, 1957; s. Joseph R. and Marilyn F. Cohen. BA, U. S.C., 1978; J.D., John Marshall Law Sch., 1981. Bar: Fla. 1981, U.S. Dist. Ct. (mid. and so. dists.) Fla. 1985. Asst. state atty. Office of the State Atty., West Palm Beach, 1981-83; assoc. Alley, Maass, Rogers, Lindsay & Chauncey, Palm Beach, Fla., 1984—; program atty. Guardian ad Litem, West Palm Beach, 1984. Trustee Temple Israel, West Palm Beach, 1985-86. Mem. ABA, Palm Beach County Bar Assn. Avocations: tennis, golf, travel. Consumer commercial, Contracts commercial, State civil litigation. Office: Alley Maass Rogers Lindsay & Chauncey PO Box 431 Palm Beach FL 33480

COHEN, STEVEN, lawyer; b. Boston, June 22, 1954; s. Merrill Michael and Eleanor Barbara (Goldstein) C.; m. Karen Marie Lydiksen, June 1, 1986. BS in Econs., U. Pa., 1976; JD, Boston U., 1981, M in Taxation, 1983. Bar: N.H. 1981, U.S. Dist. Ct. N.H. 1981; CPA, N.H. Tax ptnr. Devine Millimet Stahl and Branch, Manchester, N.H., 1981—. Author: The Internal Revenue Code As a Vehicle to Foster Solar Commercialization, 1979. Mem. N.H. Soc. CPA's (chmn. fed. tax com. 1982-84, bd. dirs. 1986—). Avocations: flyfishing, hunting, surf fishing. Corporate taxation, General corporate, Estate planning. Office: Devine Millimet Stahl & Branch 111 Amherst St PO Box 719 Manchester NH 03105

COHEN, STEVEN ELLIOTT, lawyer; b. Phila., July 4, 1956; s. Herman and Geraldine Frances Cohen; m. Kim Gorre Cantil, Nov. 10, 1984. BS in Mgmt., MIT, 1977; JD, Cornell U., 1981. Bar: Calif. 1981, U.S. Dist. Ct. (ea. dist.) Calif. 1983. Dep. dist. atty. Dist. Atty.'s Office, Sacramento, 1981-84; ptnr. Law Offices Cohen & Hom, Sacramento, 1984—. Criminal, Personal injury. Home: 1303 J St Suite 500 Sacramento CA 95814 Office: Law Office of Cohen & Hom 801 12th st Suite 500 Sacramento CA 95814

COHEN, WALLACE M., lawyer; b. Norton, Va., July 11, 1908; s. Jacob Edward and Annie (Hyman) C.; m. Sylvia J. Stone, Sept. 7, 1932; children: Anne E. (Mrs. Steven A. Winkelman), Edward S., David W. Grad., Lake Forest Acad., 1925; S.B., Harvard U., 1929; postgrad., Law Sch., 1930-31; LL.B., Cornell U., 1932. Bar: Mass. 1932, Md. 1952, D.C. 1946, U.S. Supreme Ct 1946. Practice of law Boston, 1932-38; staff NLRB, Dept. Labor, Shipbldg. Stablzn. Commn., Adv. Commn. Council Nat. Def., OPA, Lend Lease Adminstrn., Fgn. Econ. Adminstrn., 1938-45; dep. administrv. asst. to Pres.; partner Landis, Cohen, Rauh & Zelenko, Washington, 1951—; Former mem. adv. bd. Clinch Valley Coll. of U. Va.; Fellow Brandeis U. Served with USCGR, 1943-45. Mem. Am., Fed., Fed. Communications, D.C., Mass., Md. bar assns. Clubs: Harvard (Boston and Washington) (former dir. Washington); Lonesome Pine Country (Norton, Va.); Federal City (Washington), International, Nat. Press (Washington); Federal Bar. Probate, Corporate taxation, General practice. Home: 2444 Massachusetts Ave NW Washington DC 20008 Office: 1019 19th St NW Washington DC 20036

COHEN, WILLIAM, legal educator; b. Scranton, Pa., June 1, 1933; s. Maurice M. and Nellie (Rubin) C.; m. Betty C. Stein, Sept. 13, 1952 (div. 1976); children: Barbara Jean, David Alan, Rebecca Anne; m. Nancy M. Mahoney, Aug. 8, 1976; 1 dau., Margaret Emily. B.A., UCLA, 1953, LL.B., 1956. Bar: Calif. 1961. Law clk. to U.S. Supreme Ct. Justice William O. Douglas, 1956-57; from asst. prof. to assoc. prof. U. Minn. Law Sch., 1957-60; vis. asso. prof. UCLA Law Sch., 1959-60, mem. faculty, 1960-70, prof., 1962-70; prof. Stanford (Calif.) Law Sch., 1970—, C. Wendell and Edith M. Carlsmith prof. law, 1983—; vis. prof. law European U. Inst., Florence, Italy, fall 1977; Merriam vis. prof. Ariz. State U. Law Sch., Spring 1981. Co-author: The Bill of Rights, a Source Book, 1968, Comparative Constitutional Law, 1978, Constitutional Law Cases and Materials, 1981, 2d edit., 1985, Constitutional Law: The Structure of Government, 1981, Constitutional Law: Civil Liberty and Individual Rights, 1982. Home: 698 Maybell Ave Palo Alto CA 94306

COHEN, WILLIAM J., lawyer; b. Elkhart, Ind., Dec. 31, 1950; s. Henry and Mollie (Zavatsky) C.; m. Christina J. Linder, Dec. 31, 1973; 1 child, Josephine. BA, U. Ariz., 1972; JD, Ind. U., 1978. Bar: Ind. 1978, U.S. Dist. Ct. (no. dist.) Ind. 1978, Mich. 1979, U.S. Ct. Appeals (7th cir.) 1979, U.S. Supreme Ct. 1979. Assoc. Slabaugh, Cosentino et al, Elkhart, 1979-83; sole practice Elkhart, 1983—. Mem. ABA, Ind. Bar Assn., Elkhart County Bar Assn., Elkhart City Bar Assn., Ind. Trial Lawyers Assn., YMCA. Republican. Jewish. Avocations: tennis, racquetball. State civil litigation, Criminal, General practice. Home: 1534 Greenleaf Blvd Elkhart IN 46514 Office: 219 S 4th St Elkhart IN 46516

COHEN, WILLIAM MARK, lawyer; b. N.Y.C., May 22, 1951; s. Martin and Annabelle (Turner) C.; m. Melinda Pauline Salomon, Aug. 3, 1975; children: Jessica, Adam. AB, Rutgers U., 1973; JD, Georgetown U., 1976. Bar: Tenn. 1976, U.S. Dist. Ct. (mid. dist.) Tenn. 1976, U.S. Ct. Appeals (6th cir.) 1977, U.S. Supreme Ct. 1980. Law clk. to chief judge U.S. Dist. Ct. (mid. dist.) Tenn., Nashville, 1976-78; from asst. U.S. atty. 1st asst. U.S. Atty.'s Office, Nashville, 1978—. Criminal. Home: 6021 Foxland Dr Brentwood TN 37027 Office: US Attys Office 879 US Courthouse Nashville TN 37203

COHILL, MAURICE BLANCHARD, JR., judge; b. Pitts., Nov. 26, 1929; s. Maurice Blanchard and Florence (Clarke) C.; m. Suzanne Miller, June 27, 1952 (dec. May 1986); children: Cynthia Cohill Plattner, Jonathan, Jennifer, Victoria. A.B., Princeton U., 1951; LL.B., U. Pitts., 1956. Bar: Pa. 1957. Judge family div. Common Pleas Ct., Allegheny County, Pitts., 1965-76; judge U.S. Dist. Ct. for Western Dist., Pa., 1976-85; chief judge U.S. Dist. Ct. for Western Dist., 1985—; bd. dirs. Pa. George Jr. Republic, Grove City; bd. visitors Grad. Sch. Social Work, U. Pitts.; chmn. bd. fellows Nat. Center for Juvenile Justice. Served to capt. USMCR, 1951-53. Mem. Am., Pa., Allegheny County bar assns., Nat. Council Juvenile Ct. Judges (v.p.), Pa. Council Juvenile Ct. Judges (past pres.), Pa. Conf. State Trial Judges, Phi Delta Phi. Republican. Presbyterian. Judicial administration. Office: US Dist Ct US Post Office and Courthouse Room 803 Pittsburgh PA 15219

COHN, ALBERT LINN, lawyer, educator; b. Paterson, N.J., June 18, 1928; s. David and Rose (Yolken) C.; m. Sylvia J. Jacoby, June 14, 1959; children: Melissa Lynn, Joshua Peter, Priscilla Betsy, Liza-Faith Michaelis, Thaddeus Augustus David. BS, Georgetown U., 1948; JD, Harvard U., 1951. Bar: D.C. 1951, N.J. 1954; cert. civil trial atty. Supreme Ct. N.J. Bd. Trial Atty. Cert. Assoc. David Cohn, Paterson, 1954-59; ptnr. David & Albert L. Cohn, 1959-66; sr. ptnr. Cohn & Lifland, Saddle Brook, N.J., 1967—; mem. faculty Rutgers U. Law Sch., Newark, 1979—, Inst. Continuing Legal Edn., 1980, 82—, chmn. curriculum adv. com., 1984-85; vis. instr. Mass. Continuing Legal Edn., Nat. Inst. Trial Attys., Harvard Law Sch., 1981. Pres. Temple Shomrei Emunah, 1968-70. Served to 1st lt. USAF, 1951-53. Mem. Passaic County Bar Assn. (trustee 1978—), Bergen County Bar Assn., N.J. State Bar Assn., ABA, Soc. Med. Jurisprudence, Trial Attys. of N.J., Saddle Brook C. of C. (past pres., trustee). Clubs: Harvard (N.Y.C.); Hamilton (Paterson). Contbr. articles to profl. jours. State civil litigation, Personal injury, Family and matrimonial. Home: Llewellyn Park West Orange NJ 07052 Office: Cohn & Lifland Park 80 Plaza West-One Saddle Brook NJ 07662

COHN, JANICE MARIE, lawyer; b. San Francisco, Sept. 21, 1957; d. Frederick Cohn and Sondra Lee (Rosenthal) Eastham; m. Dean Merritt Dinner, May 25, 1986. Student, Inst. de Sci. Politique, Paris, 1977-78; BA with distinction, Stanford U., 1979; JD cum laude, U. Mich., 1982. Bar: Colo. 1982, Ariz. 1985. Assoc. Holland & Hart, Denver, 1982-85; corp. atty. SamCor, Phoenix, 1985—. Fellow mgmt. devel. Samaritan Health Service; mem. atty.'s action council Planned Parenthood. Mem. Colo. Bar Assn., Ariz. Bar Assn. (corp. counsel sect.), Ariz. Women's Bar Assn., Am. Health Lawyers Assn., Jewish Bus. and Profl. Women's Assn., Ariz. Hosp. Assn. (council govt. and pub. affairs). Health. Home: 13027 N 1st Ave Phoenix AZ 85029 Office: SamCor PO Box 25489 1410 N 3d St Phoenix AZ 85002

COHN, JEFFREY BROOKS, lawyer; b. Omaha, Sept. 18, 1956; s. Theodore Lloyd and Gwendolyn Yvonne (Kiewit) C.; m. Kathleen Ann Kenney, Sept. 2, 1983. BS, U. Ariz., 1979; JD, U. Nebr., 1982. Bar: Ariz. 1982, U.S. Dist. Ct. Ariz. 1982, Nebr. 1983. Assoc. Allen, McClennen & Fels, Phoenix, 1982-83; tax supr. Coopers & Lybrand, Phoenix, 1983-86; assoc. Furth, Fahrner, Bluemle & Mason, Phoenix, 1986—; mem. Cen. Ariz. Estate Planning Council, Scottsdale Estate Planning Council; fin. advisor Univ. Network Pubs., Phoenix, 1983-84, Marc III, Inc., Phoenix, 1983—; instr. Ariz. State U., 1985. Active John McCain for Senate Com., Phoenix, 1986. Holt Meml. scholar U. Nebr., 1980. Mem. State Bar Ariz. (tax, real estate, trust and probate coms.), Phoenix Met. C. of C., Beta Alpha Psi, Delta Sigma Pi. Republican. Avocations: sports, reading, travel. Estate taxation, Personal income taxation, Corporate taxation. Home: 4702 E Lafayette Blvd Phoenix AZ 85010 Office: Furth Fahrner Bluemle & Mason 7373 N Scottsdale Rd Suite 252 Phoenix AZ 85253

COHN, LAWRENCE WILLIAM, lawyer; b. Palo Alto, Calif., Jan. 12, 1948; s. Melvin Edward and Nita (Waxman) C.; m. Cynthia Berg, Apr. 17, 1981; children—Benjamin Nicholas, Jason Thomas. B.A., U. of Pacific, 1970, J.D., 1973. Bar: Hawaii 1974, U.S. Dist. Ct. Hawaii 1974, U.S. Ct. Appeals (9th cir.) 1975. Assoc., E.D. Crumpacker, Kailua-Kona, Hawaii, 1974-75; sole practice, Kailua-Kona, 1975-79, 1984—; ptnr. Cohn & Smith, Kailua-Kona, 1979-83, Cohn, Smith & Seiter, Kailua-Kona, 1983-84. Per diem judge State of Hawaii, 1983—. Mem. Assn. Trial Lawyers Am. (sustaining). Personal injury. Office: 75-5751 Kuakini Hwy Suite 104 Kailua-Kona HI 96740

COHN, NATHAN, lawyer; b. Charleston, S.C., Jan. 20, 1918; s. Samuel and Rose (Baron) C.; 1 son, Norman; m. Carolyn Venturini, May 18, 1970. J.D., San Francisco Law Sch., 1947. Bar: Calif. 1947, U.S. Supreme Ct. 1957. Sole practice, San Francisco, 1947—;judge pro tem Mcpl. Ct., Superior Ct. Mem. Calif. State Recreation Commn., 1965-68; former mem. Democratic State Central Com. Served to 1st lt. USAF, 1950-55. Fellow Am. Bd. Criminal Lawyers (past pres.); mem. Am. Bd. Trial Advs. (diplomate, chpt. pres. 1984), Assn. Trial Lawyers Am., Calif. Trial Lawyers Assn., San Francisco Trial Lawyers Assn. (past pres.). Jewish. Columnist San Francisco Progress, 1982-86; condr. seminars in field. Criminal, General practice, Personal injury. Office: 1255 Post St San Francisco CA 94109

COHRSSEN, JOHN JOSEPH, lawyer, consultant; b. N.Y.C., Nov. 4, 1939; s. Hans and Alice (Natt) C.; m. Roberta Gross, Aug. 27, 1964; children—James, Noah. B.S. with honors, CCNY, 1961; M.Sc., McGill U., Montreal, Que., Can., 1963; J.D., George Washington U., 1967. Bar: Va. 1968, D.C. 1972, U.S. Dist. Ct. D.C., U.S. Ct. Appeals (D.C. cir.), U.S. Supreme Ct. Sr. asso. Pres.'s Adv. Council Exec. Orgn., 1970; exec. dir. White House Conf. Youth, Drug Task Force, 1971; counsel U.S. Nat. Commn. Diabetes, 1976, White House Conf. Libraries and Info. Services, 1979, U.S. Regulatory Council, 1979-81, office of sci. and tech. policy Exec. office Pres., 1985-86, atty. advisor council on environ. quality, 1986—; mem. drug abuse adv. com. FDA, 1978-80; of counsel Boasberg, Klores, Feldsman & Tucker, Washington, 1977—; pres. John J. Cohrssen, P.C., Washington and Arlington, Va., 1972-86; cons. to various White House and govt. agencies on adminstrv. regulatory and health law, info. systems, 1972—; sr. policy advisor NSF, 1986—; cons. Bur. Justice Statistics, Bur. Narcotics and Dangerous Drugs, Can. Commn. Inquiry into Non-Med. Use of Drugs, Drug Abuse Council, EPA, FDA, Nat. Ctr. Health Statistics, Nat. Commn. Marihuana and Drug Abuse, NIMH, Nat. Inst. Alcohol Abuse and Alcoholism, Nat. Inst. Drug Abuse, Office Mgmt. and Budget, Exec. Office of Pres., White House Office of Planning and Eval., White House Spl. Action Office for Drug Abuse Prevention; mem. drug abuse adv. com. FDA, 1978-80. Served to maj. USPHS, 1967-70. Mem. ABA, Va. Bar Assn., D.C. Bar Assn., Arlington County Bar Assn. Contbr. articles to profl. jours. General practice, Administrative and regulatory, Health. Office: 722 Jackson Pl Washington DC 20503

COIL, HORACE ORCUTT, lawyer; b. Riverside, Calif., Aug. 18, 1934; s. Henry Wilson and Alice Edna (Orcutt) C.; m. Beverly Rae Larson, Mar. 19, 1978; children: Vance, Marne. Student, U. Calif., Berkeley, 1954; LLB, U. Calif., San Francisco, 1957. Bar: Calif. 1957, U.S. Supreme Ct. 1975. Assoc. Best, Best & Krieger, Riverside, 1958-62; sr. ptnr. Reid, Babbage & Coil, Riverside, 1962-85; sr. atty. Reid & Hellyer, Riverside, 1985—; speaker various seminars and confs. Past pres. Hastings Coll. Law Found., San Francisco, 1981-83; bd. dirs. med. research and edn. soc. U. Calif., Irvine, 1983—. Served to sgt. JAGC, USAF, 1957-59. Mem. ABA, Calif. Bar Assn. (disciplinary rev. bd. 1980-83), Orange County Bar Assn., Riverside County Bar Assn. (pres. 1974-75), Calif. Trial Lawyers Assn. (pres. 1969-70), Riverside County Barristers (pres. 1963), Assn. Trial Lawyers Am. Republican. Club: Balboa Bay (Newport Beach, Calif.). Lodges: Lions (pres. 1965), Vikings, Ritz Bros., Confrerie des Vignerons de St. Vincent Macon. Avocations: sailing, travel. State civil litigation, Personal injury, Insurance. Office: Reid & Hellyer 3800 Orange St Riverside CA 92502

COLACCI, IRVING ROGER, lawyer; b. Mpls., June 20, 1953; s. Mario and Maria Concetina (Pizzuto) C.; m. Elizabeth Carol Hoeft, Oct. 7, 1978; children: April Sunshine, Nicholas Mario, Jared Wynton. BA, Augsburg Coll., 1974; JD magna cum laude, William Mitchell Coll. Law, 1982. Bar: Minn. 1982, U.S. Dist. Ct. Minn. 1982, U.S. Ct. Appeals (8th cir.) 1984. Law clk. to presiding justice Minn. Supreme Ct., St. Paul, 1982-83; assoc. Dorsey & Whitney, Mpls., 1983—. Mem. ABA, Minn. Bar Assn. Democrat. Avocations: recreational sports, musician. State civil litigation, Federal civil litigation. Home: 3120 Holmes Ave S Minneapolis MN 55408 Office: Dorsey & Whitney 2200 1st Bank Pl E Minneapolis MN 55402

COLAGIOVANNI, JOSEPH ALFRED, JR., lawyer; b. Providence, Dec. 26, 1956; s. Joseph Alfred Sr. and Rosemarie (Giordano) C.; m. Mary Jo Gagliardo, Aug. 9, 1980. AB in Polit. Sci. and Philosophy, Brown U., 1979; JD, Boston U., 1982. Bar: Mo. 1982, U.S. Dist. Ct. (ea. and we. dists.) Mo. 1982. Asst. atty. gen. State of Mo., Jefferson City, 1982-84; assoc. Bryan, Cave, McPheeters & McRoberts, St. Louis, 1984—. Bd. dirs., legal counsel Vitale Med. Found., St. Louis, 1983—. Mem. ABA, Mo. Bar Assn. Clubs: Mo. Athletic, UNICO (St. Louis). Avocations: tennis, music, collecting matchbooks. Federal civil litigation, Construction, Health. Office: Bryan Cave McPheeters & McRoberts 500 N Broadway Suite 2100 Saint Louis MO 63102

COLAGUORI, LOUIS ALBERT, lawyer; b. Long Branch, N.J., Sept. 6, 1945; s. Anthony and Clara (Bruno) C.; m. Linda N. Lodge, Mar. 15, 1975; 1 child, Jennifer Ivy. B.A., George Washington U., 1967; J.D., Am. U., 1972. Bar: N.J., 1972, U.S. Dist. Ct., 1972, Pa., 1975. Assoc. Sidney W. Bookbinder, Burlington, N.J. 1972-75; ptnr. Bookbinder, Colaguori & Bookbinder, Burlington, 1976-81, Bookbinder & Colaguori, Burlington, 1981-84, Colaguori & Orr, Burlington, 1984—; Gen. counsel, dir. Big Bros. & Big Sisters of Burlington, Riverside, N.J., 1975—; chmn. N.J. Supreme Ct. Fee Arbitration Com., Burlington and Ocean Counties, 1984—; solicitor City of Beverly, N.J., 1976-82. Served in U.S. Army, 1969-71. Mem. ABA, N.J. Bar Assn., Burlington County Bar Assn., Am. Trial Lawyer's Assn., Commercial Law League of Am. Club: Riverton Country. General corporate, State civil litigation. Office: Colaguori & Orr 505 High St Burlington NJ 08016

COLAN, OWEN RICHARD, lawyer, land acquisition consultant; b. Lincoln, Nebr., Dec. 4, 1922; s. Richard Mitchell and Lucille (Pitman) C.; m. Ruth Louise Hilenbrand, July 14, 1944 (dec.); 1 dau., Catherine Colan Muth. B.A., W.Va. U., 1944; LL.B., Georgetown U., 1948. Bar: W.Va. 1948, D.C. 1948. Spl. asst. atty. gen. W.Va. Road Commn., 1948-52, dir. right of way 1962-69; chief right of way agt. W.Va. Turnpike Authority, 1952-57; right of way officer U.S. Bur. Pub. Roads, 1958-62; pres. O.R. Colan Assocs. Inc., South Charleston, W.Va., 1969—, Tenn. Right of Way Assocs. Inc., South Charleston, Lewis-Colan Ltd., South Charleston; land acquisition cons. for airports, hwys., mass transit, rail and pvt. large acquisitions. Served with USNR, 1942-44. Mem. ABA, W.Va. Bar Assn., Internat. Right of Way Assn. Democrat. Mem. Christian Ch. (Disciples of Christ). Contbr. articles to legal jours. Condemnation, Real property. Home: 201 2d Ave South Charleston WV 25303 Office: 205 D St South Charleston WV 25303 Office: 727 NE 3rd Ave Fort Lauderdale FL 33304

COLANTONI, ANTHONY MICHAEL, lawyer; b. Rochester, N.Y., Oct. 4, 1952; s. Anthony C. and Evelyn (Paura) C.; m. Cynthia Kay Schaumberger, Aug. 4, 1978; 1 child, Christina Marie. BA, Villanova U., 1974; JD, John Marshall Law Sch., 1978. Bar: Ill. 1978, U.S. Dist. Ct. (no. dist.) Ill. 1978, U.S. Ct. Appeals (7th cir.) 1986. Assoc. Thomas Baretta & Assocs., Chgo., 1978-79; ptnr. McDowell & Colantoni, Ltd., Chgo., 1979—. Mem. Advs. for a Safe Vaccine, Chgo., 1985—; rep. children injured by various vaccines. Mem. ABA, Assn. Trial Lawyers Am., Ill. Bar Assn., Ill. Trial Lawyers Assn., Chgo. Bar Assn. Democrat. Roman Catholic. Personal injury, Federal civil litigation, State civil litigation. Home: 1202 Barclay Circle Inverness IL 60010 Office: McDowell & Colantoni Ltd 35 E Wacker Dr Suite 1001 Chicago IL 60601

COLBERT, KATHRYN HENDON, lawyer; b. Englewood, N.J., Aug. 26, 1947; d. Charles R. and Rosemary F. (Schrafft) C. AB, Vassar Coll., 1969; JD, Tulane U., 1972. Bar: La. 1972, D.C. 1975, U.S. Dist. Ct. (ea. dist.) La. 1975, U.S. Supreme Ct. 1977, U.S. Dist. Ct. (mid. dist.) La. 1987. Atty. SBA, Harrisburg, Pa., 1972-73; staff mem. for rep. Leonor K. Sullivan Ho. of Reps., Washington, 1973-74; sole practice New Orleans, 1975; atty. office of hearings and appeals Social Security Adminstrn., HHS, New Orleans, 1976-87; trial atty. EEOC, New Orleans, 1987—. Met. Area Com. Leadership Forum, New Orleans, 1976; mem. Alliance For Good Govt., 1975-85, chmn.

ethics com. 1979-80; bd. dirs. LWV, New Orleans, 1982—; vol. Orleans Indigent Defender Program. Fellow Loyola Inst. Politics, 1975-76. Mem. ABA, Fed. Bar Assn. (D.C. and New Orleans chpts.), La. Bar Assn. (sec., treas. labor sect. 1987—), D.C. Bar Assn., Orleans Parish Bar Assn. Democrat. Presbyterian. Avocations: travel, tennis, aerobics, French. Administrative and regulatory, Labor, Civil rights. Office: Office of Hearing & Appeals F Edward Hebert Bldg Room 520 600 S Maestri Pl New Orleans LA 70130

COLBURN, JAMES ALLAN, lawyer; b. Huntington, W.Va., July 5, 1942; s. Ray S. and Edith Abigail (Blood) C.; m. Virginia Ann Carter, June 19, 1965; children—Heather Lara, Sarah Carter. A.B., Davidson (N.C.) Coll., 1964; J.D., Rutgers U., 1967; postgrad. Marshall U., Austin Peay State U. Bar: W.Va. 1970, U.S. Dist. Ct. (no. and so. dists.) W.Va. 1970, U.S. Ct. Appeals (4th cir.) 1973, U.S. Dist. Ct. (ea. dist.) Ky. 1975, U.S. Tax Ct. 1982, U.S. Supreme Ct. 1983, U.S. Ct. Appeals (6th cir.) 1985. Assoc., Levy & Patton, 1970-72; sole practice, Huntington, W.Va., 1973-75; ptnr. Baer, Napier & Colburn, Huntington, 1975-81; ptnr., pres. Baer, Colburn and Morris, L.C., Huntington, 1981—; instr. legal asst. program Marshall U., 1978-82; lectr. in field. Asst. pros. atty. Cabell County, 1977-79, spl. prosecuting atty. 1986-87; Nicholas County, 1985-87, Wayne County, 1987—. Served with U.S. Army, 1968-70. Mem. W.Va. Bar Assn., ABA (vice chmn. mktg. legal services subcom. sect. of econs. practice of law), Assn. Trial Lawyers Am., West. Va. Trial Lawyers Assn. (bd. govs.), Union Internat. des-Advocats, Cabell County Bar Assn. (pres. 1980), Nat. Assn. Dist. Attys., Am. Arbitration Assn. (panel comml. arbitrators). Democrat. Presbyterian. Personal injury, General practice, General corporate. Office: 731 5th Ave Huntington WV 25701

COLBY, RICHARD DEATLEE, lawyer; b. Columbus, Ohio, Aug. 31, 1949; s. Hugh D. and Doris C. (Burris) C. B.A., Ohio State U., 1971; J.D., Capital Law Sch., 1974. Bar: Ohio 1974. Sole practice, Columbus, 1974—; pres. Trust Properties, Inc.; trustee Real Estate Investment Trust II. Chmn., bd. dirs. Touchstone, 1978-82. Mem. Franklin County Bar Assn., Ohio State Bar Assn., ABA, Am. Trial Lawyers Assn. Club: Columbus Ski (bd. dirs. 1982). Criminal, Personal injury, Real property. Home: 6984 Lakebrook Blvd Worthington OH 43085 Office: 50 W Broad St Suite 2620 Columbus OH 43215

COLDREN, IRA BURDETTE, JR., lawyer; b. Uniontown, Pa., June 15, 1924; s. Ira Burdette and Eleanor Clarke (Lincoln) C.; m. Phyllis Miles, Sept. 7 (div. Oct. 1970); children: Kathy, Lee Ellen, Janice, David; m. Frances Thomas, Aug. 27, 1971. BS, U.S. Mil. Acad., 1945; LLB, U. Pa., 1952; LLM in Estate Planning, U. Miami, 1982. Bar: Pa. 1952, U.S. Dist. Ct. (we. dist.) Pa. 1953, U.S. Ct. Appeals (3d cir.) 1983. Commd. 2d lt. U.S. Army, 1945, advanced through grades to lt. col., 1952, ret., 1956; assoc. Ray, Coldren & Buck, Uniontown, Pa., 1956-59; ptnr. Coldren & Coldren, Uniontown, 1959-62, 75-83, Coldren & Adams, Uniontown, 1962-75, Coldren, DeHaas & Radcliffe, Uniontown, 1983—. Pres. Greater Uniontown United Fund, 1962, Fayette County Devel. Council, 1971-75. Fellow Am. Bar Found., Am. Coll. Probate Council; mem. Pa. Bar Assn. (ho. of dels. 1976-79, bd. govs. 1979-82, v.p. 1985-86, pres. 1986—), Pa. Bar Inst. (pres. 1982-83), Fayette County Bar Assn. (pres. 1983), Am. Judicature Soc., Internat. Assn. Ins. Counsel, Pa. Jaycees (pres. 1959). Democrat. Presbyterian. Club: Uniontown Country (pres. 1969-71). Lodges: Rotary (pres. Uniontown club 1964), Masons (master 1964, 69). General practice, Banking, Probate. Home: 117 Belmont Circle Uniontown PA 15401 Office: Coldren DeHaas & Radcliffe PO Box 1327 700 Gallatin Bank Bldg Uniontown PA 15401

COLE, CHARLES DEWEY, JR., lawyer; b. Lower Merion Twp., Pa., Aug. 12, 1952; s. Charles Dewey Sr. and Margaret Ann (Leach) C.; m. Ann Carlton Beattie, Aug. 9. 1979; children: Charles Dewey IV, Thomas Joseph Beattie. BA, Columbia U., 1974; JD, St. John's U., Jamaica, N.Y., 1979; ML Info. Sci., U. Tex., 1982. Bar: N.Y. 1980, Tex. 1980, U.S. Dist. Ct. (we. and ea. dists.) Tex. 1980, U.S. Dist. Ct. (so. and ea. dists.) N.Y. 1980, U.S. Ct. Internat. Trade 1980, U.S. Ct. Appeals (5th and 11th cirs.) 1981, U.S. Dist. Ct. (no. dist.) Tex. 1982, U.S. Ct. Appeals (Fed. cir.) 1982, U.S. Dist. Ct. (no. dist.) N.Y. 1983, U.S. Dist. Ct. (we. dist.) N.Y. 1984, U.S. Ct. Appeals (2d cir.) 1984, U.S. Tax Ct. 1984, U.S. Supreme Ct. 1984, N.J. 1986, U.S. Dist. Ct. N.J. 1986, U.S. Ct. Appeals (D.C. cir.) 1987. Law clk. to chief judge U.S. Dist. Ct. (ea. dist.), Beaumont, Tex., 1979-80, U.S. Ct. Appeals (5th cir.), Austin, Tex., 1981-82; assoc. Moore, Berson, Lifflander & Mewhinney, Garden City and N.Y.C., N.Y., 1982-85, Newman, Schlau, Fitch & Burns P.C., Mineola and N.Y.C., 1985—. Mem. ABA (litigation sect., appellate practice com., Young Lawyers div., litigation com.), N.Y. State Bar Assn., N.J. State Bar Assn., State Bar Tex. (jour. com.), N.Y. County Lawyers Assn., Bar Assn. of 5th Fed. Cir., Assn. of Bar of City of N.Y., Assn. Trial Lawyers Am., N.Y. State Trial Lawyers Assn., Fed. Bar Council, Am. Judicature Soc., Am. Assn. Law Libraries, Law Library Assn. Greater N.Y., British and Irish Assn. of Law Librarians, Osgoode Soc., Am. Soc. for Legal History, Selden Soc., Federalist Soc. for Law and Pub. Policy. Republican. Federal civil litigation, State civil litigation, Librarianship. Home: 277 Brown St Mineola NY 11501 Office: Newman Schlau Fitch & Burns PC 305 Broadway New York NY 10007

COLE, GEORGE THOMAS, lawyer; b. Orlando, Fla., Mar. 14, 1946; s. Robert Bates and Frances (Arnold) C.; m. Peggy Ellen Stimson, May 23, 1981; children—Leslie Elizabeth, Ashley Ellen, Robert Warren. A.B., Yale U., 1968; J.D., U. Mich., 1975. Bar: Ariz. 1975, U.S. Dist Ct. Ariz. 1975, White Mountain Apache Tribal Ct., 1977, U.S. Ct. Appeals (9th cir.) 1978. Assoc., Fennemore, Craig, von Ammon, Udall & Powers, Phoenix, 1975-81; ptnr., Fennemore Craig, Phoenix, 1981—. Mem. funds allocation Panel United Way, 1983. Served to lt. (j.g.) USN, 1968-71. Mem. ABA (com. on condominiums, cooperatives and homeowners assns., 1985—, real property and probate sect.), Ariz. Bar Assn. (council Real Property sect. 1985—, chmn.-elect, 1986-87, chmn., 1987—), Maricopa Bar Assn. Republican. Methodist. Clubs: Yale (pres. 1984), Paradise Valley Country (Phoenix). Real property. Home: 5102 E Desert Park Ln Paradise Valley AZ 85253 Office: Fennemore Craig 6991 E Camelback Suite A-201 Scottsdale AZ 85251-2466

COLE, HAROLD EDWIN, lawyer; b. Cin., Sept. 30, 1937; s. Ernest Lee and Zora (Jones) C.; m. Judith Elizabeth Rosen, Nov. 18, 1967; children: Kristie Lynn, David Michael, Lauren Elizabeth. BS in Chem. Engring., U. Cin., 1960; JD, Georgetown U., 1965. Bar: Va. 1965, N.Y. 1966. Chem. engr. NCR Corp., Dayton, Ohio, 1960-61; patent examiner U.S. Patent and Trademark Office, Washington, 1961-65; sr. patent atty. Eastman Kodak Co., Rochester, N.Y., 1965—. Patentee in field. Mem. Rochester Patent Law Assn. (corr. sec. 1971-72). Republican. Mormon. Patent, Real property, Trademark and copyright. Home: 101 Mountain Rd Rochester NY 14625 Office: Eastman Kodak Co Patent Dept 343 State St Rochester NY 14650

COLE, HARRY A., judge; b. Washington; m. Doris Freeland; children: Susan, Harriette, Stephanie. A.B. magna cum laude, Morgan State Coll., 1943; LL.D., 1975; LL.B., U. Md., 1949. Apptd. justice of peace 1951, substitute magistrate, 1952, asst. atty. gen., 1953; state senator Maryland State Senate, Annapolis, 1954-58; assoc. judge Md. Circuit Ct., 8th Jud. Circuit, Supreme Bench Balt. City, 1968-77; now assoc. judge Md. Ct. Appeals, 1977—. Mem. Md. Adv. Com. on Civil Rights to U.S. Civil Rights Commn.; also 1st chmn. Bd. dirs. Balt. Zool. Soc., Union Meml. Hosp., Camp Fire Girls, Balt. Mus. Art; bd. visitors Morgan State Coll.; also chmn.; bd. mgrs. YMCA; mem. exec. com. U.S. Nat. Com. for UNESCO. Served to 1st lt. U.S. Army, 1943-46, ETO. Named Man of Yr. NAACP, Man of Yr. Md. Beauticians, Man of Yr. A.M.E. Ch. Mem. Am. Judicature Soc., Md. Jud. Conf. (exec. com. 1971), Monumental City Bar Assn., Md. State Bar Assn., Nat. Bar Assn., NAACP (life), U. Md. Law Sch. Alumni Assn. (pres.). Mem. African Methodist Episcopal Ch. Office: Courthouse#634E 111 N Carvert St Baltimore MD 21202 *

COLE, JAMES RAY, lawyer; b. Reedsburg, Wis., Aug. 14, 1944; s. Stanley I. and Dorothy M. (Brandt) C.; children from a previous marriage: Peter, Nathaniel; m. Lauri D. Morris, May 13, 1978; 1 child, Melissa. BS in Am. Instns. Law, U. Wis., 1966, JD, 1969. Bar: Wis. 1969, U.S. Dist. Ct. (ea. and we. dists.) Wis. 1969, U.S. Ct. Appeals (7th cir.) 1973, U.S. Supreme Ct. 1973. Law clk. to presiding justice Wis. Supreme Ct., Madison, 1969-70; staff counsel commn. Calif. rural legal assistance OEO, San Francisco, 1971; ptnr. Ross & Stevens S.C., Madison, 1973—; counsel Wis. Com. on Jud. Reorgn., 1973. Mem. personnel com., commodore marina Village of Shorewood Hills, Madison; chmn. Personnel Bd., Madison, 1975-80. Mem. Wis. Bar Assn. (bd. dirs. litigation sect. 1985—), Wis. Acad. Trial Lawyers, Assn. Trial Lawyers Am., Dane County Bar Assn. Democrat. Congregationalist. Lodge: Rotary. Avocations: skiing, sailing, distance running. State civil litigation, Federal civil litigation, Personal injury. Home: 3547 Topping Rd Madison WI 53705

COLE, JAMES SILAS, JR., lawyer; b. Cheyenne, Wyo., Sept. 8, 1953; s. James Silas and Joyce Jeanne (Pawson) C.; m. Ann Marie Shoemaker, May 24, 1975; children—Jean Louise, Timothy James, Mary Elizabeth, Stephen Vincent. B.A. summa cum laude, St. Louis U., 1975; J.D. cum laude, Harvard U., 1978. Bar: Mo. 1979, U.S. Dist. Ct. (ea. dist.) Mo. 1979, U.S. Bankruptcy Ct. (we. dist.) Mo. 1983. Law clk. Mo. Supreme Ct., Jefferson City, 1978-79; assoc. Mulford & Cole and predecessor Michael W. Mulford, Kirksville, Mo., 1979-80, ptnr., 1980—. Contbr. articles to law jours. Cofounder, officer Birthright of Kirksville, 1980-85; mem. parish council Mary Immaculate Ch., Kirksville, 1980-83; state bd. dirs. Mo. Citizens for Life, 1986—, v.p. 1987—. Mem. ABA, Assn. Trial Lawyers Am., Phi Beta Kappa, Alpha Sigma Nu. Democrat. Roman Catholic. Lodge: K.C. (officer local lodge 1985-86, Mo. State council advocate 1986—). Bankruptcy, State civil litigation, Federal civil litigation. Office: Mulford & Cole PC 113 E Washington St Kirksville MO 63501

COLE, LARRY MICHAEL, lawyer; b. N.Y.C., June 7, 1938; s. Samuel M. and Frances (Lieberman) C.; m. Jean S. Willner, June 12, 1961; children—Jill Hope, Susan Ruth. B.A., U. Pa., 1959; LL.B., Columbia U., 1962. Bar: N.J. 1962. Partner, Cole & Cole, Jersey City, 1963-78, 83—, Cole & Lynch, Jersey City, 1978-83. Served with U.S. Army, 1962-63. Mem. ABA, N.J. State Bar Assn., Hudson County Bar Assn. Jewish. Club: Alpine (N.J.) Country. Labor, General corporate, State civil litigation. Office: 90 Court House Pl Jersey City NJ 07306

COLE, LEWIS GEORGE, lawyer; b. N.Y.C., Mar. 9, 1931; s. Ralph David and Emma (Balterman) C.; m. Sara Livingston, June 22, 1952; children: Elizabeth, Peter. B.S. in Econ., U. Pa., 1951; LL.B, Yale U., 1954. Bar: N.Y. 1954. Ptnr. Stroock & Stroock & Lavan, N.Y.C., 1958—. Served as 1st lt. U.S. Army, 1954-57. Mem. ABA, Assn. Bar City N.Y., N.Y. State Bar Assn., N.Y. County Lawyers Assn. Office: Stroock & Stroock & Lavan 7 Hanover Sq New York NY 10004

COLE, LUTHER FRANCIS, justice; b. Alexandria, La., Oct. 25, 1925; s. Clem and Catherine (Wiley) C.; m. Juanita Barton, Mar. 9, 1945; children: Frances Jeannette, Jeffrey Martin, Christopher Warren. Student, La. Tech. U., 1943-44; JD, La. State U., 1950. Ptnr. Cole, Mengis & Durant, Baton Rouge, 1950-66; judge 19th Jud. Dist., Baton Rouge, 1966-75, chief judge, 1975-79; judge Ct. Appeals, Baton Rouge, 1979-86; assoc. justice Supreme Ct. La., New Orleans, 1986—. Rep. La. Legis., Baton Rouge, 1964-66; v.p. Merchants Assn., Baton Rouge, 1954; chmn. awards Boy Scouts Am., Baton Rouge, 1956; mem. Civic Ctr. com., Baton Rouge, 1971-74; bd. dirs. Blundon Home, Baton Rouge, 1984-86. Served to lt. (j.g.) USN, 1943-46. Mem. ABA, La. Bar Assn., Baton Rouge Bar Assn. (pres. 1966), La. Dist. Judges Assn. (pres. 1972-73). Democrat. Baptist. Club: Exchange (Baton Rouge) (pres. 1954). Avocations: hunting, cooking. State civil litigation, Criminal, Jurisprudence. Home: 9525 Donna Dr Baton Rouge LA 70815 Office: Supreme Court of Louisiana 301 Loyola Ave New Orleans LA 70112

COLE, MICHAEL FREDERICK, lawyer; b. Washington, May 16, 1941; s. Reginald Everett and Mavis Elinor (Strong) C.; m. Linda Ann Collison, Nov. 5, 1967; children: Michael Brian, Brett Hamilton, Blake Alexander. BA with honors magna cum laude, Vanderbilt U., 1963; LLB, NYU, 1966. Bar: N.Y. 1966, U.S. Dist. Ct. (so. and ea. dists.) N.Y. 1966. Assoc. Royall, Koegel, Rogers & Wells, N.Y.C., 1966-69; atty. Johnson & Johnson, New Brunswick, N.J., 1969-79; v.p., gen. counsel Health Industry Mfg. Assn., Washington, 1979-81; assoc. Pento, Duerk & Pinco, Washington, 1981-85; ptnr. Finley, Kumble, Wagner, Heine, Underberg, Manley & Casey, Washington, 1985—. Contbr. articles on med. device legislation and regulation to profl. jours. Served as pvt. U.S. Army, 1966. Mem. ABA. Republican. Methodist. Health, Food and drug. Home: 8610 Lochaven Dr Gaithersburg MD 20879 Office: Finley Kumble Wagner Heine et al 1140 Connecticut Ave Washington DC 20036

COLE, MURRAY L., lawyer; b. Paterson, N.J., Apr. 25, 1922; s. Louis E. and Ida (Glick) C.; m. Miriam Levinsohn, Sept. 19, 1948; children: Jonathan S., Peter B., Matthew H. (dec.). BA, Williams Coll. of Law, 1943; JD, Cornell U., 1948. Bar: N.J. 1949, U.S. Dist. Ct. N.J. 1949, U.S. Supreme Ct. 1949. Ptnr. Cole, Morrill & Berman, Paterson, 1949-56; counsel Bengar Corp., 1956-58; prin. Cole, Geaney, Yamner & Byrne P.C., Paterson, 1958—; sec., bd. dirs. Treadway Cos., Inc., 1961-82; mem. adv. bd. First Nat. Bank of N.J., 1967-73; v.p. United Jersey Bank (Partroy), 1970-72, sec. 1973-79, bd. dirs. Mem. adv. bd. Nat. Council Boy Scouts Am., exec. com. Northeast region Boy Scouts Am.; hon. trustee Passaic Valley Givers Fund; trustee trust fund, mem. exec. bd. Passaic Valley Council Boy Scouts Am.; chmn. bd. trustees Montclair State Coll. Served to comdr. USNR, 1943-65. Mem. ABA, N.J. Bar Assn. (trustee), Passaic County Bar Assn. (trustee), Am. Arbitration Assn. (nat. panel arbitrators). Jewish. Clubs: Williams (N.Y.); Hamilton. Real property, Contracts commercial, Probate. Home: 46 Basswood Terr Wayne NJ 07470 Office: Cole Geaney Yamner & Byrne PC 100 Hamilton Pl PO Box D Paterson NJ 07509

COLE, RICHARD CHARLES, lawyer; b. Albany, N.Y., Apr. 23, 1950; s. Charles Stanley and Doris Jean (Hatch) C. BA, Cornell U., 1972; JD, Harvard U., 1975. Bar: N.Y. 1976, U.S. Dist. Ct. (so. and ea. dists.) N.Y., U.S. Ct. Appeals (2d, 5th and D.C. cirs.). Assoc. LeBoeuf, Lamb, Leiby & MacRae, N.Y.C., 1975-83, ptnr., 1984—. Mem. ABA. Avocations: woodwind music. Federal civil litigation, Insurance, Entertainment. Home: 264 Prospect Pl Brooklyn NY 11238 Office: LeBoeuf Lamb Leiby & MacRae 520 Madison Ave New York NY 10022

COLE, ROBERT ALLEN, lawyer; b. Jacksonville, Fla., June 14, 1952; s. Frank Harris and Julia (Knowles) C.; m. Kathleen Holman, Aug. 17, 1974; children: Brian, Blake, Brett. BS cum laude, Fla. State U., 1974, JD, 1977. Bar: Fla. 1978, U.S. Dist. Ct. (mid. dist.) Fla. 1978, U.S. Ct. Appeals (5th cir.) 1978, U.S. Ct. Appeals (11th cir.) 1981, U.S. Dist. Ct. (no. dist.) Fla. 1984, U.S. Supreme Ct. 1985. Ptnr. Howell, Liles, Braddock & Milton, Jacksonville, 1978-86, Cole, Stone & Whitaker, Jacksonville, 1986—. Mem. council Jacksonville U., 1984-86; bd. dirs. Jacksonville chpt. of March of Dimes, 1984-86. Mem. Fla. Bar Assn. (relation with other professions com., admiralty law com.), Jacksonville Bar Assn. (chmn. law week 1984, chmn. speakers bur. 1981-82), Assn. Trial Lawyers Am., Jacksonville Def. Lawyers Assn., Southeastern Admiralty Law Inst., Maritime Law Assn., Bapt. Health Found., Propeller Club of U.S., Phi Beta Kappa. Democrat. Presbyterian. Personal injury, Admiralty, Federal civil litigation. Home: 3859 Octave Dr Jacksonville FL 32211 Office: Cole Stone & Whitaker 211 Liberty St Suite 3 Jacksonville FL 32202

COLE, ROBERT H., law educator, lawyer; b. 1931. A.B., 1952; LL.B., Harvard U., 1955. Bar: D.C. 1956, Mass. 1960. Law clk. Justice Sherman Minton, U.S. Supreme Ct., 1955-56; acting assoc. prof. U. Calif.-Berkeley Sch. Law, 1961-64, prof., 1964—; vis. prof. Northwestern Spring, 1965, Harvard U., 1966-67, Banaras Hindu U. India, 1971. Past book rev. editor Harvard Law Rev. Legal education. Office: U Calif Law Sch 225 Boalt Hall Berkeley CA 94720 *

COLEMAN, BRYAN DOUGLAS, lawyer, corporate executive, educator; b. Texarkana, Tex., Aug. 16, 1948; s. William Bryan and Armeda (Crawford) C.; m. Tommye Lou Bettis, Jan. 31, 1984; children: Douglas Patrick, Sarah Elizabeth. AS, Texarkana Coll., 1968; BS in Bus. Admistrn., Stephen F. Austin U., 1970; postgrad. Rice U., 1971-73; JD (E.E. Townes award, Am. Jurisprudence award), South Tex. Coll. Law, 1973; grad. JAG Sch., U.S. Army, 1978. Bar: Tex. 1973, U.S. Dist. Ct. (so. dist.) Tex. 1974, U.S. Ct. Appeals (11th cir.) 1982, U.S. Ct. Appeals (5th cir.) 1975; cert. Fellow Life Mgmt. Inst. Quality control insp. Lone Star Ammunition Plant, Texarkana, 1966-68; law clk. Fulbright & Jaworski, Houston, 1970-71, Boswell, O'Toole, Davis & Pickering, Houston, 1971-72, Helm, Pletcher & Hogan, Houston, 1972-73; assoc. Law Office Gus Zgourides, Houston, 1973-76, Ray & Coleman, P.C., Houston, 1976—; dir. Med. Assurance Group, Houston, 1978—; counsel Gt. SW Life Ins. Co., Houston, 1983—; instr. U. Houston, 1979-81. Mem. Republican Nat. Com., 1983—. Served to comdr. Army ROTC, 1972-73, to 1st lt. U.S. Army, 1973-79. Mem. ABA, State Bar Tex. (founder law student div. 1973, chmn. grievance com. 1979-81), Assn. Trial Lawyers Am., Tex. Trial Lawyers Assn., Am. Judicature Soc., Houston Bar Found., Houston Bar Assn., Alpha Kappa Psi (sec. 1969-70), Alpha Phi Omega (pledge trainer 1970) Delta Theta Phi. State civil litigation, Insurance, Personal injury. Home: 3510 Saratoga Ln Houston TX 77088 Office: Ray & Coleman PC 1314 Tex Ave 500 Great SW Bldg Houston TX 77002

COLEMAN, C. RANDOLPH, lawyer; b. Panama City, Fla., June 7, 1950; s. Carl Freeman and Lola M. (Dicks) C.; m. Phyllis Eileen Gallub, July 1, 1972 (div. Aug. 1981); m. Bethany Anne Baldwin, May 27, 1983; 1 child, Carole Jacqueline. BBA, U. Fla., 1972, JD, 1978. CPA, Fla.; bar: Fla. 1978, U.S. Dist. Ct. (so. dist.) Fla. 1978, U.S. Ct. Appeals (5th cir.) 1978, U.S. Tax Ct. 1979, U.S. Ct. Appeals (11th cir.) 1981. Staff acct. Peat, Marwick, Mitchell, Atlanta, 1972-73; ptnr. Budd, Sisler & Co., CPAs, Gainesville, Fla., 1974-78; assoc. Mershon, Sawyer, Johnston, Miami, Fla., 1978-82; ptnr. Finley, Kumble, Wagner, Miami, 1983-85; sole practice Coral Gables, Fla., 1985—. Pres. 1992 Fla. Columbus Expn., Miami, 1982, Big Bros./Big Sisters Greater Miami, 1986; city chmn. United Way Dade County, Miami, 1985; mem. mil. acad. appointments adv. bd. to Senator Paula Hawkins, 1985. Mem. ABA (various coms.), Fla. Bar Assn. (various coms.), Dade County Bar Assn. (various coms.), Am. Inst. CPAs, Fla. Inst. CPAs. Consumer commercial, State civil litigation, Federal civil litigation. Office: 2921 Le Jeune Rd Coral Gables FL 33134

COLEMAN, JAMES HOWARD, JR., lawyer; b. Farmington, W.Va., Aug. 12, 1909; s. James Howard and Laura Furbee (Conway) C.; m. Catherine Chandler Sloan, Feb. 23, 1935. AB, W.Va. U., 1930, LLB, 1933. Bar: W.Va. 1933, U.S. Dist. Ct. (no. dist.) W.Va. 1934, U.S. Ct. Appeals (4th cir.) 1945, U.S. Supreme Ct. 1964. Ptnr. Coleman & Wallace, Buckhannon, W.Va., 1933—. Fellow Am. Coll. Trial Lawyers; mem. ABA, W.Va. Bar Assn. (pres. 1967-68), W.Va. Law Sch. Assn. (pres. 1982-83), Buckhannon C. of C. Republican. Methodist. Lodges: Lions (pres. Buckhannon 1942, 53), Masons. Avocations: golf, camping, travel. General practice, State civil litigation, Probate. Home: 51 Boggess St Buckhannon WV 26201 Office: Coleman & Wallace 11 N Kanawha St PO Box 518 Buckhannon WV 26201

COLEMAN, JAMES JULIAN, lawyer, businessman; b. New Orleans, May 5, 1915; s. William Ballin and Millie (Davis) C.; m. Dorothy Louise Jurisich, July 30, 1940; children: James Julian, Thomas Blaise, Peter Dee, Dian Judith. B.A., Tulane U., 1934, J.D., 1937; LL.D. (hon.), Hampden-Sydney Coll., 1982. Bar: La. 1937. Sr. partner firm Coleman, Dutrey & Thomson, New Orleans; chmn. bd. Internat. MATEX Tank Terminals, Ltd., West Pakistan, Bangladesh, and South Korea, Loving Enterprises; past pres. Internat. Trade Mart, New Orleans Philharmonic Symphony; hon. consul gen. Republic of Korea. Past pres. New Orleans C. of C.; past bd. dirs. U.S. C. of C.; past chmn. New Orleans coordinating com. NASA; past pres. Jr. Achievement New Orleans; founder Peoples League; trustee Principia Coll.; past chmn. bus. council Tulane U.; past pres. Adult Edn. Center; past trustee Cordell Hull Found.; trustee Loving Found.; past bd. dirs. Internat. House, Fed. Relations Assn., La. Civil Service League. Decorated Order Diplomatic Service Merit Republic Korea; recipient Nat. Achievement award Jr. Achievement, Loving Cup award New Orleans Times-Picayune, 1980, Joseph W. Simon, Jr. award, 1981, Disting. Alumnus award Tulane U., 1982, New Orleans Activist award, 1984, C. Alvin Bertel award, 1985; named to Bus. Hall of Fame, 1984. Mem. Am., Internat., La., New Orleans bar assns., Am. Judicature Soc. (past dir.), Beta Gamma Sigma (hon.). Christian Scientist (1st reader 1953-56). General practice, Probate, Real property. Home: 10 Audubon Pl New Orleans LA 70118 Office: 321 St Charles Ave New Orleans LA 70130

COLEMAN, JAMES PLEMON, lawyer, former U.S. judge; b. Ackerman, Miss., Jan. 9, 1914; s. Thomas A. and Jennie Essie (Worrell) C.; m. Margaret Janet Dennis, May 2, 1937; 1 child, Thomas Allen. Student, U. Miss., 1932-35; LL.B., George Washington U., 1939, LL.D., 1960. Bar: Miss. bar 1937. Sec. to Rep. Aaron Lane Ford, Washington, 1935-39; practiced in Ackerman, 1939-40, 84—; dist. atty. 5th circuit Ct., Dist. of Miss., 1940-46, circuit judge, 1946-50; commr. Supreme Ct. of Miss., Sept. 1 to Oct. 23, 1950; atty. gen. Miss., 1950-56, gov., 1956-60; mem. Miss. Ho. Reps. from Choctaw County, 1960-65; judge U.S. Ct. Appeals 5th Circuit, 1965-84, chief judge, 1979-81; publisher Choctaw Plaindealer, weekly, 1949-56. Trustee Miss. Coll., 1952-56. Democrat (presdl. elector 1944). Baptist. Club: Mason (Shriner). Office: 115 E Quinn Ave Ackerman MS 39735

COLEMAN, RICHARD MICHAEL, lawyer; b. Bklyn., Sept. 16, 1935; s. Frank T. and Eileen (Cafferty) C.; m. Bonnie S. Mathews, May 30, 1980; 1 child, Matthew Stephen. A.B. summa cum laude, Georgetown U., 1957, LL.M. (Prettyman fellow), 1961; J.D., Harvard U., 1960; postgrad., U. So. Calif., 1968-70. Bar: D.C. 1960, Calif. 1967, U.S. Supreme Ct. 1964. Asst. U.S. atty., spl. atty. in organized crime racketeering sect. Dept. Justice, Washington, 1961-64; chief organized crime sect. U.S. Atty.'s Office, Washington, 1964-66, chief spl. prosecutions div. So. and Cen. Divs. Calif., 1966-67; assoc. McKeena & Fitting, Los Angeles, 1967-68, ptnr., 1969-70; pvt. practice, Los Angeles, 1971—; moderator, host Law Forum, Sta. KSCI-TV, 1982-83, Sta. KWHY, 1985-86; lectr. Loyola U., Los Angeles, 1971-74, 76, 79-85. Charter mem. Fraternity of Friends of the Music Ctr.; nat. co-chmn. Lawyers for Reagan/Bush, 1984. Fellow Am. Bar Found.; mem. ABA (pres. nat. caucus of met. bar leaders 1982-83, exec. council 1980-85), Calif. Bar Assn. (commn. jud. nominees evaluation 1987—), Nat. Conf. Bar Pres. (exec. council 1985—), Los Angeles County Bar Assn. (pres. 1981-82, trustee 1978-80, exec. com. trial lawyers sect., jud. com., fed. cts. and practice com.), Century City Bar Assn. (pres. 1977-78, bd. govs. 1973—, Outstanding Achievement award 1975, 77, 79), Los Angeles Trial Lawyers Assn. (pres.' award 1981, 82), Assn. Bus. Trial Lawyers (bd. govs. 1976-78, panelist 1977, 79, 82), Assn. Trial Lawyers Am., Calif. Trial Lawyers Assn., Fed. Bar Assn., Century City C. of C. (bd. dirs. 1977—, sec. 1978-79, v.p. 1979-80), Georgetown U. Alumni Assn. (past pres., So. Calif. dir., nat. bd. govs.), Mensa, Rep. Nat. Lawyers Assn. (treas. 1985—, co-chair Calif. chpt. 1985-86). Contracts commercial, Criminal, Entertainment. Office: 1801 Ave of the Stars Suite 810 Los Angeles CA 90067

COLEMAN, ROBERT LEE, lawyer; b. Kansas City, Mo., June 14, 1929; s. William and Edna (Smith) C. B.Mus. Edn., Drake U., 1951, LL.B., U. Mo., 1959. Bar: Mo. 1959, Fla. 1973. Law clk. to judge U.S. dist. ct. (we. dist.) Mo., 1959-60; assoc. Watson, Ess, Marshall & Enggas, Kansas City, Mo., 1960-66; asst. gen. csl. Gas Service Co., Kansas City, Mo., 1966-74; corp. csl. H & R Block, Inc., Kansas City, Mo., 1974—. Served with U.S. Army, 1955-57. Mem. ABA, Kansas City Bar Assn., Lawyers Assn. Kansas City. General corporate.

COLEMAN, THOMAS YOUNG, lawyer; b. Richmond, Va., Jan. 6, 1949; s. Emmet Macadium and Mary Katherine (Gay) C.; m. Janet Clare Norris, Aug. 30, 1980; 1 child, Dana Alicia. BA, U. Va., 1971, JD, 1975. Bar: Va. 1975, U.S. Dist. Ct. (we. dist.) Va. 1975, U.S. Ct. Appeals (4th cir.) 1976, Calif. 1977, U.S. Dist Ct. (no. dist.) Calif. 1977. Law clk. chief judge U.S. Dist. Ct. (we. dist.) Va., Charlottesville, 1975-76; assoc. Morrison & Foerster, San Francisco, 1976-79; v.p., counsel Calif. 1st Bank, San Francisco, 1979-85; of counsel Orrick, Herrington & Sutcliffe, San Francisco, 1985-86, ptnr., 1987—; speaker in field; vis. atty. Clifford-Turner Solicitors, London, 1984. Mem. Calif. Bar Assn. (uniform comml. code com. bus. law sect.). Banking, Contracts financing. Office: Orrick Herrington & Sutcliffe 600 Montgomery St San Francisco CA 94111

COLEMAN, WILLIAM FRANKLIN, state judge; b. West Point, Ms., Sept. 19, 1929; s. David Howard and Susie Marie (Clark) C.; m. Teresa Mathews, Apr. 15, 1956 (div. Feb. 1976); m. Kaye K. Kerr, Nov. 21, 1984; children: Patricia, Thomas, John, Louis. LLB, U. Miss., 1952. Bar: Miss. 1952, U.S. Ct. Appeals (5th cir.) 1969. Assoc. Crisler, Crisler & Bowling, Jackson, Miss., 1959-68; ptnr. Bowling & Coleman, Jackson, 1968-73,

Coleman & Cothran, Jackson, 1973-76; cir. judge State of Miss., Jackson, 1976—. Served with U.S. Army, 1952, col. Res. 1985. Mem. ABA, Miss. Bar Assn. Episcopalian. Club: Jackson Yacht. Judicial administration. Home: 1843 Springridge Dr Jackson MS 39211 Office: PO Box 327 Jackson MS 39205

COLEMAN, WILLIAM THADDEUS, JR., lawyer; b. Germantown, Pa., July 7, 1920; s. William Thaddeus and Laura Beatrice (Mason) C.; m. Lovida Hardin, Feb. 10, 1945; children: William Thaddeus III, Lovida Hardin Jr., Hardin L. A.B. summa cum laude, U. Pa., 1941; LL.B. magna cum laude, Harvard U., 1946. Bar: Pa. 1947, D.C. 1977. Law sec. Judge Herbert F. Goodrich, U.S. Ct. of Appeals, 3d Circuit, 1947-48, Justice Felix Frankfurter (asso. justice Supreme Ct. U.S.), 1948-49; assoc. Paul, Weiss, Rifkind, Wharton & Garrison, N.Y.C., 1949-52, Dilworth, Paxson, Kalish, Levy & Coleman, Phila., 1952-56; partner Dilworth, Paxson, Kalish, Levy & Coleman, 1956-75; sec. Dept. Transp., Washington, 1975-77; sr. partner firm O'Melveny & Myers, Washington, Los Angeles, N.Y.C. and London, 1977—; spl. counsel for transit matters City of Phila., 1952-63; rep. atty. gen. Pa. and Commonwealth of Pa. in litigation to remove racial restrictions at Girard Coll., 1965; bd. dirs. IBM, Chase Manhattan Bank, Chase Manhattan Corp., PepsiCo., AMAX, Inc., Pan Am. World Airways, Inc., Phila. Electric Co., CIGNA Corp.; mem. Pres.'s Com. on Govt. Employment Policy, 1959-61; cons. ACDA, 1963-74; sr. cons., asst. counsel Pres.'s Commn. on Assassination of Pres. Kennedy, 1964; co-chmn. planning sessions White House Conf. to Fulfill These Rights, 1965-66; mem. U.S. del. 24th Session UN Gen. Assembly, 1969; mem. legal adv. com. Council on Environ. Quality, 1970; pub. mem. Pres.'s Nat. Commn. on Productivity, 1970; commr. Price Commn., 1971-72, Phila Fairmount Park Commn., 1967-75; mem. Gov.'s Commn. on Constl. Revision, 1963-65. Contbr. articles to prof. jours. Chmn. bd. NAACP Legal Def. and Ednl. Fund; v.p., trustee, mem. exec. com. Phila. Mus. Art; trustee Brookings Instn.; mem. Trilateral Commn.; mem. exec. com. Lawyers Com. for Civil Rights Under Law; bd. overseers Harvard U., 1975-81. Recipient Joseph E. Beale prize, 1946; Langdell fellow, 1946-47. Fellow Am. Coll. Trial Lawyers; mem. Am. Law Inst. (council), Phila. Bar Assn. (past chmn. judiciary com.), Am. Arbitration Assn. (gov.), Council Fgn. Relations, Phi Beta Kappa, Pi Gamma Mu. Clubs: Harvard Law Sch., Junior Legal (Phila.); Cosmos, Alfalfa, Metropolitan (Washington). Office: O'Melveny & Myers 1800 M St NW Washington DC 20036

COLEMAN, WILLIAM T(HOMAS), lawyer; b. Oak Park, Ill., July 6, 1938; s. John Harlan and Mary Veronica (Schaefer) C.; m. Katherine Theresa Carlson, Dec. 27, 1968; children: Michelle, Michael, Theresa, Elizabeth, Timothy. BA, U. Notre Dame, 1962, JD, 1968. Bar: Ill. 1968, U.S. Dist. Ct. (no. dist.) Ill. 1968, U.S. Ct. Appeals (7th cir.) 1969, U.S. Supreme Ct. 1973. Law clk., 1968-70; trial atty. NLRB, Chgo., 1971-73; supervising trial atty. EEOC, Chgo., 1973-74; ptnr. Coleman & Moenning, Chgo., 1974-76; assoc. Naphin, Banta & Cox, Chgo., 1976-78, ptnr., 1979-86; ptnr. Hedberg, Tobin, Flaherty & Whalen, P.C., Chgo., 1986—; arbitrator CTA, Ill. Bell; guest arbitrator Lake Forest (Ill.) Sch. Mgmt. Served with USNR, 1962-65. Mem. ABA, Chgo. Bar Assn., Am. Arbitration Assn. Roman Catholic. Mng. editor Notre Dame Lawyer, 1967-68, contbr. articles. Labor, Federal civil litigation, State civil litigation. Address: Three First Nat Plaza Suite 1950 Chicago IL 60602

COLER, WILLIAM LEE, lawyer; b. Akron, Ohio, Mar. 24, 1937; s. Virgil Lessley and Margaret Elizabeth (Wagner) C.; m. Donna Imogene Nelson, Jan. 19, 1957; children: Susan, William H., Matthew, Peter, Martha. BA, Kent State U., 1967; JD, U. Akron, 1982. Bar: Ohio 1982. Supr. Goodyear Tire and Rubber Co., Brookpark, Ohio, 1967-72; dir. warehousing and traffic Nobil Shoe Co., Akron, Ohio, 1972-73; sr. mgr. contracts Babcock & Wilcox, Alliance, Ohio, 1973—. Mem. Ch. in Soc. Commn., Wadsworth, Ohio, 1983—, Twp. Zoning Commn., Wadsworth, 1984—. Mem. ABA, Nat. Contract Mgmt. Assn. Democrat. Methodist. Lodges: Masons, Shriners. Contracts commercial, Government contracts and claims. Home: 3278 S Medina Line Rd Wadsworth OH 44281 Office: Babcock & Wilcox Contract Research Div 1562 Beeson St Alliance OH 44601

COLES, KEVIN ANDREW, lawyer; b. Bridgeport, Conn., Aug. 7, 1947; s. Albert Leonard and Eileen Margaret (Pelath) C.; m. Anne Galvin Cotter, Aug. 1, 1970; children: Steven A., Leland G. BS in Bus. Adminstrn., Georgetown U., 1970; JD, U. Houston, 1974. Bar: Conn. 1974, U.S. Dist. Ct. Conn. 1974, U.S. Ct. Appeals (2d cir.) 1975, U.S. Supreme Ct. 1977. Assoc. Coles, O'Connell, Dolan & McDonald, Bridgeport, 1974-79; sole practice Bridgeport, 1979-83; prin. Cotter, Cotter & Sohon P.C., Bridgeport, 1983—. Chmn. pension bd. Town of Trumbull, Conn., 1978—; bd. dirs. St. Thomas More Sch., Colchester, Conn., 1979—. Mem. ABA, Conn Bar Assn., Greater Bridgeport Bar Assn., Assn. Trial Lawyers Am., Conn. Trial Lawyers Assn. Democrat. Roman Catholic. Clubs: Brroklawn Country (Fairfield, Conn.), Fayerweather Yacht (Bridgeport). Avocations: boating, fishing, snow and water skiing. Federal civil litigation, State civil litigation, Insurance. Home: 56 Oldfield Rd Trumbull CT 06611 Office: Cotter Cotter & Sohon PC 195 Brooklawn Ave Bridgeport CT 06604

COLETTA, RALPH JOHN, lawyer; b. Chillicothe, Ill., Dec. 13, 1921; s. Joseph and Assunta Maria (Aromatario) C.; m. Ethel Mary Meyers, Nov. 19, 1949; children—Jean, Marianne, Suzanne, Joseph, Robert, Michele, Renee. B.S., Bradley U., 1943; J.D., U. Chgo., 1949. Bar: Ill. 1949. Practice law, Peoria, Ill., 1949—; pres. White Star Corp.; asst. state's atty. Peoria County. Chmn. United Fund. Served to 1st lt. AUS, 1943-46. Mem. Peoria County Bar Assn., Chgo. Bar Assn., Ill. State Bar Assn. Republican. Roman Catholic. Clubs: Creve Coeur, Mt. Hawley Country, K.C. (Peoria); Union League (Chgo.). Real property, Probate, General corporate. Home: 301 W Crestwood Dr Peoria IL 61614 Office: Suite 1714 Savs Center Tower Peoria IL 61602

COLETTA, RAYMOND ROBERT, law educator; b. Cin., May 31, 1948; s. Armand Victor and Martha Jeanne (Roberts) C.; m. Claudia Sorbal RamalHo, Oct. 11, 1976; 1 child, Sean. AB, Colgate U., 1970; postgrad., Columbia U.; JD, U. Calif., Berkeley, 1981. Bar: Ohio 1981, U.S. Dist. Ct. (no. dist.) Ohio 1983. Assoc. Squire, Sanders & Dempsey, Cleve., 1981-85; prof. sch. law St. Thomas U. Sch. Law, Miami, Fla., 1985. Mem. ABA, Assn. Am. Law Schs., Phi Beta Kappa. Avocations: jogging, backpacking. Real property, Probate, Legal education. Home: 17000 NW 67th Ave 425 Miami FL 33015 Office: St Thomas U Sch Law 16400 NW 32d Ave Miami FL 33054

COLLAS, JUAN GARDUÑO, JR., lawyer; b. Manila, Apr. 25, 1932; s. Juan D. and Soledad (Garduño) C.; m. Maria L. Moreira, Aug. 1, 1959; children—Juan Jose, Elias Lopes, Cristina Maria, Daniel Benjamin. LL.B., U. of Philippines, Quezon City, 1955; LL.M., Yale U., 1958, J.S.D., 1959. Bar: Philippines 1956, Ill. 1960, Calif. 1971, U.S. Supreme Ct. 1967. Assoc., Sy Cip, Salazar & Assocs., Manila, 1956-57; atty. N.Y., N.H. & H. R.R., New Haven, 1959-60; assoc. Baker & McKenzie, Chgo., 1960-63, ptnr., Manila, 1963-70, San Francisco, 1970—. Contbr. articles to profl. jours. Trustee, sec. Friends of U. of Philippines Found. in Am., San Francisco, 1982; co-chmn. San Francisco Lawyers for Better Govt., 1982—; chmn. San Francisco-Manila Sister City Com., 1986—. Recipient Outstanding Filipino Overseas in Law award, Philippine Ministry Tourism Philippines Jaycees, 1979. Mem. ABA, Am. Arbitration Assn. (panelist), Ill. Bar Assn., State Bar Calif., Integrated Bar of Philippines, Filipino-Am. C. of C. (bd. dirs. 1974—, pres. 1985—). Republican. Roman Catholic. Clubs: World Trade, Commercial (San Francisco). Private international, General corporate, Contracts commercial. Office: Baker & McKenzie 580 California St San Francisco CA 94104

COLLAZO, SALVADOR, lawyer; b. Santa Isabel, P.R., Apr. 9, 1948; came to U.S., 1948; s. Carlos Ortiz and Carmen Luz (Melendez) C.; m. Maria D. Lopez, Oct. 19, 1969; 1 child, Salvador Raphael. BA in History, Fordham U., 1973; JD, Seton Hall U., 1977. Bar: N.Y. 1980, U.S. Dist. Ct. (so. dist.) N.Y. 1980. Asst. dist. atty. City of N.Y., Bronx, 1977-83; ptnr. Collazo & Reyes, Bronx, 1983—; of counsel Bronx City Pub. Adminstrn., 1985—; cons. N.Y.C. Transit Authority, Bklyn., 1986—; mem. panel N.Y.C. Mayor's Judiciary Com., 1986—. Counsel North End Dem. Club, Bronx, 1985—. Served to sgt. USMC, 1968-70. Recipient Cert. of Appreciation, N.Y.C. Partnerships, 1983, Merit award N.Y.C. Dept. Correction Hispanic Soc., 1986; Pedro Albizu scholar Spanish Am. Law Students, 1977. Mem. Bronx County Bar Assn., Puerto Rican Bar Assn. (2d v.p. 1985—), Hispanic Nat. Bar Assn. (regional pres. 1986—). Roman Catholic. Avocations: salt water fishing, reading, home repair. Contracts commercial, Criminal, Probate. Home: 3629 Waldo Ave Riverdale NY 10463 Office: Collazo & Reyes 888 Grand Concourse Bronx NY 10451

COLLEN, JOHN OLAF, lawyer; b. Chgo., Dec. 26, 1954; s. Sheldon Orrin and Ann Marie (Blager) C.; m. Lauren Kay Smulyan, Sept. 20, 1986. AB summa cum laude, Dartmouth Coll., 1977; JD, Georgetown U., 1980. Bar: Ill. 1980, U.S. Dist. Ct. (no. dist.) Ill. 1980, U.S. Ct. Appeals (7th cir.) 1984. Assoc. Peterson, Ross, Schloerb & Seidel, Chgo., 1980-82, Nachman, Munitz & Sweig, Chgo., 1982-85; ptnr. Chapman & Cutler, Chgo., 1985—. Mem. ABA, Ill. Bar Assn., Chgo. Bar Assn., Phi Beta Kappa. Club: Union League (Chgo.). Avocations: scuba diving. Bankruptcy, Federal civil litigation, Real property. Office: Chapman & Cutler 111 W Monroe St Chicago IL 60603

COLLEN, SHELDON ORRIN, lawyer; b. Chgo., Feb. 7, 1922; s. Jacob Allen and Ann (Andalman) C.; m. Ann Blager, Apr. 8, 1946; 1 child, John O. B.A. cum laude, Carleton Coll., 1944; J.D., U. Chgo., 1948. Bar: Minn. 1976, Ill. 1949, U.S. Dist. Ct. (no. dist.) Ill. 1949, U.S. Supreme Ct. 1965. Assoc. Adcock, Fink & Day, Chgo., 1948-51; mem. Simon & Collen, Chgo., 1952-57, Friedman & Koven, Chgo., 1958-86, Epton, Mullin & Druth, Ltd., Chgo., 1986—; specialist fed. antitrust litigation; sec. Jupiter Industries, Inc., Chgo., 1961-86. Mem. adv. bd. Antitrust Bull. and Jour. Reprints for Antitrust Law and Econs. Mem. bd. edn. U. Chgo. Law Rev., 1948-49; bd. dirs. Lower Northcenter, Chgo. Youth Ctrs., Union League Found. for Boys, Contemporary Art Workshop, Edward P. Martin Soc., Ctr. for Study of Multiple Births; sec., bd. dirs. 3750 Lake Shore Dr., Inc.; pres. Union League Civic and Arts Found., 1984-86. Served with AUS, 1943-46. Fellow Norwegian Am. Mus., Decorah, Iowa. Mem. Am. Judicature Soc., ABA, Chgo. Bar Assn. (antitrust law and securities law coms., chmn. antitrust 1976-77), Ill. Bar Assn. (council corp. and securities law sect.), Bar Assn. 7th Circuit, Art Inst. Chgo., Mus. Comtemporary Art, Chgo. Council Fgn. Relations. Clubs: Union League (Chgo.); Lafayette (Minnetonka Beach, Minn.). General practice, Federal civil litigation, General corporate. Home: 3750 Lake Shore Dr Chicago IL 60613-4970 also: Meadville Rd Excelsior MN 55331 Office: Epton Mullin & Druth Ltd 140 S Dearborn St Chicago IL 60603

COLLENS, LEWIS MORTON, legal educator; b. Chgo., Feb. 10, 1938. B.S., U. Ill., Urbana, 1960, M.A., 1963; J.D., U. Chgo., 1966. Bar: Ill. 1966. Assoc. Ross, Hardies, Chgo., 1966-67; spl. asst. to gen. counsel EEOC, Washington, 1967-68; asst. prof. Ill. Inst. Tech., Chgo. Kent Coll. Law, 1970-72, assoc. prof., 1972-74, prof., 1975—, dean Coll. Law, 1974—. Chmn. bd. dirs. Bar Rev. Inst., 1967-74; bd. dirs. Ill. Inst. Continuing Legal Edn., 1974—. Mem. ABA, Ill. Bar Assn., Chgo. Bar Assn., Am. Law Inst., Order of Coif. Legal education. Office: 77 S Wacker Dr Chicago IL 60606

COLLER, JULIUS ANTHONY, II, lawyer; b. St. Paul, May 10, 1909; s. Julius Anthony and Cora Elizabeth (Dennis) C.; m. Lorraine Imelda Libby, Nov. 24, 1938; children: Frederick W., Julius E., Lorraine Joan, Cecille Marie. BA, U. Minn., 1932, JD, 1934. Bar: Minn. 1934, U.S. Dist. Ct. Minn. 1939. Sole practice Shakopee, Minn., 1934—; atty. City of Shakopee, 1935—, 1st. Nat. Bank, Shakopee, 1935—, Scott County, 1941; examiner titles Scott County, 1955—. Republican. Roman Catholic. Lodges: K.C., Cath. Order Foresters (bd. dirs. Chgo. 1952-76, v.p. 1976-84). Avocations: hist. research, photography. General practice, Probate, Real property. Home: 434 Lewis St Shakopee MN 55379 Office: 211 W First Ave Shakopee MN 55379

COLLERAN, KEVIN, lawyer; b. Spalding, Nebr., July 16, 1941; s. James Edward and Helen Marcella (Vybiral) C.; m. Karen Ann Rooney, Aug. 1, 1964; children—Mary Jane, Patrick. B.S., U. Nebr., 1964, J.D. with distinction, 1968. Bar: Nebr. 1968, U.S. Dist. Ct. Nebr. 1968, U.S. Dist. Ct. (we. dist.) La. 1975, U.S. Dist. Ct. (no. dist.) Tex. 1978, U.S. Supreme Ct. 1980, U.S. Ct. Appeals (8th cir.) 1981. Law clk. U.S. Dist. Ct. Nebr., 1968-69; assoc. Cline, Williams, Wright, Johnson & Oldfather, Lincoln, Nebr., 1969-74; ptnr., 1975—. Bd. dirs. Lancaster County unit Am. Cancer Soc., 1972-83, pres., 1979. Mem. ABA, Nebr. Bar Assn. (chmn. worker's compensation com. 1980-82), Nat. Assn. Trial Attys., Order of Coif. Democrat. Federal civil litigation, State civil litigation, Litigation state agencies. Office: Cline Williams Wright Johnson & Oldfather Firstier Bank Bldg Lincoln NE 68508

COLLETTE, KEVIN J., lawyer; b. Salt Lake City, Nov. 17, 1952; s. Dale D. and Grace B. (Leatham) C.; m. Vickie J. Collette, Aug. 6, 1977; children: Andrea, Jon, Carrie, Julie. BA cum laude, U. Wash., 1977; JD cum laude, Brigham Young U., 1980. Bar: Wash. 1980, U.S. Dist. Ct. (we. dist.) Wash. 1980. Ptnr. Ryan, Swanson & Cleveland, Seattle, 1980—; bd. dirs. N.W. Venture Group, Seattle, The Investment Quorum, Seattle. Contbr. articles to profl. jours. Mem. ABA (various coms.), Wash. State Bar Assn. (various coms.), Seattle King County Bar Assn. (various coms.), Phi Beta Kappa, Beta Theta Pi. Mormon. Real property, General corporate, Computer. Office: Ryan Swanson & Cleveland Bank of Calif Ctr 32d Floor Seattle WA 98164

COLLEY, NATHANIEL S(EXTUS), JR., lawyer; b. Sacramento, June 8, 1956; s. Nathaniel S. and Jerlean (Jackson) C.; m. Toni D. Conner, Mar. 8, 1975 (div. 1986); children: Jasmine, Aishah, Mazuri. BA, U. Mich., 1977, JD, 1979; postgrad., Golden Gate Bapt. Theol. Sem., 1984—. Bar: Calif. 1980, U.S. Dist. Ct. (ea. dist.) Calif. 1980, U.S. Dist. Ct. (no. dist.) Calif. 1980, U.S. Ct. Appeals (9th cir.) 1980. Pres. Sacramento chpt. NAACP, 1981-82; chmn. evangelism com. Calif. State Bapt. Young Adult Conf., 1985-86. Mem. ABA, Assn. Trial Lawyers Am., Calif. Trial Lawyers Assn., Nat. Bar Assn., Black Entertainment and Sports Lawyers Assn. Democrat. Personal injury, State civil litigation, Federal civil litigation. Office: Colley Lindsey and Colley 1810 S St Sacramento CA 95814 Home: 1100 Alder Tree Way 300 Sacramento CA 95831

COLLIE, MARVIN KEY, lawyer; b. San Antonio, July 16, 1918; s. Marvin K. and Gladys (Stanley) C.; m. Nancy Morriss, Nov. 21, 1942; children: Gwynne Collie Brooks, M. Key III, David Wade. BA, Washington & Lee U., 1939; LLB, U. Tex., 1941. Bar: Tex. 1941. From assoc. to ptnr. Vinson & Elkins, Houston. Corporate taxation, Estate taxation, Personal income taxation. Home: No 9 Shadder Way Houston TX 77109 Office: Vinson & Elkins 3300 1st City Tower 1001 Fannin Houston TX 77002-6760

COLLIER-MAGAR, KENNETH ANTHONY, lawyer; b. Braddock, Pa., Apr. 20, 1948; s. Anthony and Helen (Pavelko) Magar; m. Gaynell Collier-Magar. BA in Polit. Sci., St. Vincent Coll., 1970; JD, U. Pitts., 1973. Pa. 1973, U.S. Dist. Ct. (we. dist.) Pa. 1973, U.S. Ct. Appeals (3d cir.) 1981, Ind. 1984, U.S. Dist. Ct. (so. dist.) Ind. 1984, U.S. Ct. Appeals (7th cir.) 1984. Staff atty. South Alleghenies Legal Aid, Johnstown, Pa., 1973-76; exec. dir. Blair County Legal Services, Altoona, Pa., 1976-84; mng. atty. Legal Services Orgn. Ind., Evansville, 1984—; lectr. Pa. State U., Altoona, 1976-84, St. Francis Coll., Loretto, Pa., 1973-84, U. So. Ind., Evansville, 1984—. Chmn. bd. dirs. Blair County Mental Health/Mental Retardation, Hollidaysburg, Pa., 1980-84. Mem. Ind. Bar Assn. (com. on legal edn. and admissions to bar 1986—), Pa. Bar Assn. (standing com. on merit selection of judges 1982-84). Democrat. Roman Catholic. State civil litigation, Administrative and regulatory, Public utilities. Office: Legal Services Orgn Ind Inc 101 Court St Suite 102 Evansville IN 47708

COLLINS, JAMES FRANCIS, lawyer; b. Neptune, N.J., Feb. 14, 1946; s. James Wesley and Kathryn Veronica (Cooney) C.; m. Susan Irons, Nov. 15, 1969; 1 child, Christopher James. BA, LaSalle Coll., 1968; MA, Rutgers U., 1976; JD, Vt. Law Sch., 1977. Bar: N.J. 1977, U.S. Dist. Ct. N.J. 1977, U.S. Ct. Appeals (3d cir.) 1980, U.S. Supreme Ct. 1982, N.Y. 1983. Ptnr. Marks, Holland, LaRosa & Collins, Freehold, N.J., 1979-82, Lo Murro, Eastman & Collins, Freehold, 1982-85; sole practice Freehold, 1985—. Mem. Assn. Trial Lawyers Am. (panelist lawyer referral service), Monmouth Bar Assn., N.J. Bar Assn., Trial Attys. N.J., Greater Western Monmouth C. of C. Democrat. Roman Catholic. State civil litigation, Criminal, Personal injury. Office: 76 W Main St Freehold NJ 07728

COLLINS, JAMES IGNATIUS, lawyer; b. Washington, Mar. 19, 1949; s. Thomas M. and Dorothy (Clifford) C.; m. Susan Earl Collins, Dec. 22, 1974; children: Katherine, Anne, Maighdlin. BA in History and Philosophy, U. Ariz., 1971, BA in Chemistry, 1976, MA in Chemistry, 1982; JD, U. Pacific, 1981. Bar: Calif. 1981, U. S. Dist. Ct. (eastern dist.) Calif. 1981, U.S. Ct. Appeals (9th cir.) 1981. Atty. Pacific Legal Found., Sacramento, 1981-84; assoc. Kronick, Moskovitz, Tiedemann & Girard, Sacramento, 1984-86; pres. Technos Environ. Compliance, Sacramento, 1984—; v.p. Indsl. Innovations, Inc., 1986—. Author: Hazardous Materials Enforcement and Liability, 1985. Mem. ABA, Am. Chem. Soc. Democrat. Roman Catholic. Avocaitons: sports. Environment. Office: Indsl Innovations Inc 620 S Aurora St Stockton CA 95203

COLLINS, JAMES SLADE, II, lawyer; b. St. Louis, June 9, 1937; s. James Slade and Dolma Ruby (Neilsen) C.; m. Neva Frances Guinn, June 27, 1959; children—Shari, Camala Ann. B.S. in Bus. Adminstrn., Washington U., 1958, J.D., 1961. Bar: Mo. 1961, U.S. Supreme Ct. 1969, U.S. Dist. Ct. (ea. dist.) Mo. 1972, U.S. Ct. Appeals (8th cir.) 1972. Assoc., Whalen, O'Connor, Grauel & Sarkisian, St. Louis, 1961-70, ptnr., 1970-72, Whalen, O'Connor, Collins & Danis, St. Louis, 1972-75; assoc. Hullverson, Hullverson & Frank, Inc., St. Louis, 1975-78; sole practice, St. Louis, 1979—. Trustee, Village of Hanley Hills, Mo., 1966-69, mayor, 1967, mcpl. judge, 1967-68, 1969-70. Mem. ABA, Bar Assn. Met. St. Louis, Lawyers Assn., St. Louis Am. Trial Lawyers Assn., Mo. Trial Lawyers Assn., Phi Delta Phi. Republican. Baptist. Federal civil litigation, State civil litigation, Personal injury. Home: 916 Parkwatch Dr Ballwin MO 63011 Office: 1015 Locust St Suite 528 St Louis MO 63101

COLLINS, JOHN ALBERT, III, lawyer; b. Boston, Jan. 30, 1956; s. John Albert and Catherine Elizabeth (McDermott) C.; m. Katherine Ann Phelan, Aug. 23, 1983. BA, Coll. of Holy Cross, 1978; JD, Case Western Res. U., 1981. Bar: Conn. 1981, U.S. Dist. Ct. Conn. 1981. Ptnr. Suisman, Shapiro, Wool, Brennan & Gray P.C., New London, Conn., 1981—. Mem. ABA, Conn. Bar Assn., New London Bar Assn., Assn. Trial Lawyers Am., Conn. Trial Lawyers Assn., Nat. Assn. Criminal Def. Lawyers. Democrat. Roman Catholic. Club: Holy Cross (pres. Southeast Conn. 1986). Lodges: Lions. Avocations: skiing, carpentry. Personal injury, Criminal, Workers' compensation. Home: 221 Mile Creek Rd Old Lyme CT 06371 Office: Suisman Shapiro Wool Brennan Gray PC PO Box 1591 New London CT 06320

COLLINS, JOHN FRANCIS, lawyer; b. Oakland, Calif., Feb. 28, 1946; s. John Thomas and Mary Margret (Hirsch) C. B.A., Hobart Coll., 1968; J.D., SUNY, Buffalo, 1971; M. Labor and Indsl. Relations, Mich. State U., 1974. Bar: N.Y. 1972, U.S. Dist. Ct. (we. dist.) N.Y., 1972, U.S. Dist. Ct. (no. dist.) 1972, U.S. Ct. Apls. (2d cir.) 1974. Locomotive engr. United Transp. Union; mem. United Transp. Union, 1970—, now csl.; sr. ptnr. Collins, Collins, DiNardo, P.C., Buffalo; instr. Niagara U., Mich. State U.; locomotive engr. Consol. Rail Corp. sec. treas. local 708 United Transp. Union, del. internat. conv. 1979, legis. rep., 1979—, designated counsel Brotherhood Locomotive Engrs., chmn. N.Y. State Legis.; designated counsel Transp. Workers Union of Am.; spl. counsel Laborer's Local #210 and Ironworker's Local #210 and Ironworker's Local #6 and Ironworker's Local #12; developer, instr. Buffalo R.R. studies program Cornell U. Mem. Erie County Bar Assn., N.Y. State Bar Assn., U.S. Trial Lawyers Assn., Am. Arbitration Assn. (labor panel). Democrat. Roman Catholic. Club: Buffalo Athletic. Labor, Personal injury, Workers' compensation. Home: 54 Agassiz Circle Buffalo NY 14202 Office: Collins Collins & Dinardo 415 Franklin St Buffalo NY 14214

COLLINS, KYLE BOYD, lawyer; b. Waco, Tex., Mar. 4, 1954; s. George Howard and Dorothy Faye (Gooden) C.; m. Linda Darlene Conder, Aug. 5, 1975; 1 child, Ian Matthew. BS, Baylor U., 1975; JD, Tex. So. U., 1978. Bar: Tex. 1979, U.S. Dist. Ct. (we. and so. dists.) Tex. 1979, U.S. Ct. Appeals (5th cir.) 1979, U.S. Tax Ct. 1979. Law clk. to presiding justice U.S. Atty.'s Office, Houston, 1978; assoc. Dewberry & Fitch, Houston, 1979; staff atty. dept. community affairs Gov.'s Office, Austin, Tex., 1979-80; sole practice Austin, 1980—. Editor Tex. So. U. Law Rev., 1976-78; contbr. articles to profl. jours. Election insp. State of Tex., 1982, 84. Mem. ABA, Tex. Bar Assn., Tex. Young Lawyers Assn., Austin Young Lawyers Assn. Democrat. Methodist. Avocations: sailing, fencing. Criminal, Probate, Oil and gas leasing. Home and Office: 1605 E 7th St Austin TX 78702

COLLINS, LEON FREDERICK, lawyer; b. Texarkana, Tex., Nov. 24, 1952; s. Leon Frederick Collins and Peggy Jo (Smith) Normile; m. Mary Lee Klein, June 20, 1981; children: Amy Lee, Noel Frederick. BA, Southeastern State U., 1971-75; postgrad., Cumberland Law Sch., 1975-76; JD, Oklahoma City U., 1978. Bar: Okla. 1978, U.S. Dist. Ct. (ea. dist.) Okla. 1980, U.S. Dist. Ct. (we. dist.) Okla. 1986. Atty. Dept. Transp., Oklahoma City, 1979; asst. dist. atty. 20th jud. dist. State of Okla., Ardmore, 1979-85, dist. atty. 20th jud. dist., 1986—. Mem. Ardmore Little Theater; chmn. Carter County (Okla.) Dem. Party, 1983—; deacon Bapt. Ch. Mem. ABA, Okla. Bar Assn., Carter County Bar Assn. (v.p. 1985), Okla. Dist. Atty. Assn. Baptist. Lodge: Optimist (local bd. dirs. 1983-84). Avocations: jogging, chess, reading. Criminal, Federal civil litigation, Jurisprudence. Home: 41 Sandy Ln Ardmore OK 73401 Office: Dist Attys Office Carter County Ct House Ardmore OK 73401

COLLINS, MARVIN, lawyer. U.S. atty. no. dist. State of Tex., Dallas. Office: US Fed Bldg and Courthouse 1100 Commerce St Room 16628 Dallas TX 75242 *

COLLINS, MICHAEL JOHN, lawyer; b. Wausau, Wis., Sept. 22, 1951; s. Donald Edward and Juanita Mae (Pollard) C.; m. Debra Y. Braverman, May 25, 1975 (div. 1977); m. Margaret Ann Phillips, Aug. 12, 1978; children: Alana M., Aaron M., Megan K. BA with honors, U. Wis., 1973, JD, 1977; MA, SUNY, 1974. Bar: Wis. 1977, U.S. Dist. Ct. (we. dist.) Wis. 1977. Assoc. Aagaard, Nichol, Wyngaard & Wilson, Madison, Wis., 1977-78, Wyngaard & Wilson, Madison, 1978-80, Tomlinson, Gilman & Travers, Madison, 1980-82; ptnr. Collins, Beatty & Krekeler, S.C., Madison, 1982—. Bd. dirs. Wis. Chamber Orchestra, 1986—, Meals for Madison (Wis.), Inc., 1986—. Mem. ABA, Wis. Bar Assn., Nat. Transp. Safety Assn. (sec. 1984—), Christian Legal Soc. Republican. Roman Catholic. Avocations: political memorabilia collecting, bicycling, family activities. Family and matrimonial, General corporate, Real property. Home: 233 S Segoe Rd Madison WI 53705 Office: Collins Beatty & Krekeler SC 15 N Pinckney St Madison WI 53703

COLLINS, PHILIP REILLY, lawyer, educator; b. New Orleans, July 26, 1921; s. James Mark and Katherine (Gallaher) C.; m. Mary Catherine O'Leary, Feb. 9, 1946. B.A., Loyola U., New Orleans, 1939, J.D., 1942; M.A. in Govt. and Internat. Law and Relations, Georgetown U., 1948, Ph.D., 1950; LL.M., George Washington U., 1952. Bar: La. 1942, Mass. 1948, D.C. 1953, Md. 1983, Va. 1986. Atty. Bur. Land Mgmt., Dept. Interior, Washington, 1946-47; asst. legis. counsel Office of Solicitor, P.O. Dept., 1947-48; sole practice law Washington and Arlington, Va., 1954-77, 78—; ptnr. MacCracken, Collins & Hawes, 1960-69; chief counsel, staff dir. com. on rules U.S. Ho. of Reps., 1977-78; spl. counsel Fed. Home Loan Bank Bd., 1961-69, Ky. Savs. and Loan League, 1967-68, state of Alaska, 1967-68; vis. prof., spl. asst. to pres. for labor relations Queens Coll., 1969-70; lectr. in pub. adminstrn. sch. social scis. Cath. U. Am., 1954-56; lectr. in law Cath. U. Law Sch., 1954-60. Mem. adv. com. on wills, trusts and other bequests Loyola U., New Orleans, 1966-69; charter mem. bd. visitors Law Sch., 1968-85; mem. Pres.'s Council, 1976-85. Served to capt. USAAF, 1942-46, PTO; maj. USAF, Korean Conflict; col. Res. Mem. ABA, La. Bar Assn., Mass. Bar Assn., D.C. Bar Assn., N.Y. State Bar Assn., Md. Bar Assn., Va. Bar Assn., Delta Theta Phi, Phi Alpha Theta. Democrat. Roman Catholic. Clubs: K.C. (4 degree); University (Washington). Probate, Legislative, Federal civil litigation. Home: 1300 Crystal Dr Apt 209 S Arlington VA 22202

COLLINS, ROBERT FREDERICK, federal judge; b. New Orleans, Jan. 27, 1931; s. Frederick and Irma V. (Anderson) C.; m. Aloha, Dec. 28, 1957; children: Francesca Collins McManus, Lisa Ann, Nanette Collins Martin, Robert A. B.A. cum laude, Dillard U., 1951, LL.D. (hon.), 1979; J.D., La. State U., 1954; grad. spl. summer course, Nat. Jud. Coll., U. Nev., 1973. Bar: La. bar 1954. Mem. firm Augustine, Collins, Smith & Warren, New

Orleans, 1956-59; instr. law So. U., 1959-61, 80-86; sr. ptnr. firm Collins, Douglas & Elie, New Orleans, 1960-72; asst. city atty.-legal adv. New Orleans Police Dept., 1967-69; judge ad-hoc Traffic Ct., New Orleans, 1969-72; atty. Housing Authority, New Orleans, 1971-72; judge magistrate sect. Criminal Dist. Ct., Orleans Parish, La., 1971-78; judge U.S. Dist. Ct., Eastern Dist. La., 1978—; asst. bar examiner, State of La., 1970-78. Bd. dirs. New Orleans Housing Council, 1962-64, Social Welfare Planning Council, New Orleans, 1965-67, Dryades St. YMCA, 1963-65, New Orleans Urban League, 1970-72, 75; trustee Loyola U., New Orleans, 1977-83. Served with U.S. Army, 1954-56. Mem. La. Bar Assn., Nat. Bar Assn. (regional dir. 1964-65), Am. Bar Assn., Louis A. Martinet Legal Soc. (pres. 1959-60), Am. Judicature Soc., 5th Circuit Dist. Judges Assn. Democrat. Roman Catholic. Judicial administration. Office: Chambers C-465 US Courthouse 500 Camp St New Orleans LA 70130

COLLINS, THEODORE JOSEPH, lawyer, educator; b. St. Paul, May 3, 1932; s. Theodore Joseph and Claire (Scanlan) C.; m. Mary Joan Tierney, June 30, 1962 (dec. Apr. 1982); children: Theodore Joseph, Anthony Joseph; m. Jean Marie Dick, Sept. 7, 1985; stepchildren—Nathan, Colin, Phillip, Stacy. B.A., St. Paul Sem., 1954; J.D. cum laude, William Mitchell Coll. Law, 1960. Bar: Minn. 1960, U.S. Dist. Ct. Minn. 1960, U.S. Ct. Appeals (8th cir.) 1961, U.S. Supreme Ct. 1963. Asst. gen. counsel 3M Co., 1960-61; asst. corp. counsel gen. city legal work, chief city prosecutor St. Paul, 1961-63; assoc. Maun, Hazel, Green, Hayes, Simon & Aretz, 1963-66; ptnr. Collins and Abramson, St. Paul, 1966-71, Collins, Buckley, Sauntry and Haugh, St. Paul, 1971—; instr. criminal law St. Paul Police Acad., 1963-78; spl. asst. atty. gen., spl. asst. Washington, Ramsey, Dakota and Sherburne countries; mem. adv. bd. Legal Assistance Ramsey County, So. Minn. Regional Legal Services, Inc. Past pres., chmn. bd. trustees St. Paul-Ramsey Hosp. Med. Edn. and Research Found. Fellow Am. Bar Found.; mem. Ramsey County Bar Assn. (pres. 1976-77), Minn. Bar Assn. (treas. 1978-81, pres. 1982-83), ABA, Am. Judicature Soc. (dir.), Minn. Trial Lawyers Assn., Minn. Def. Lawyers Assn., Minn. Women Lawyers, Washington County Bar Assn. (various coms.). Democrat. Roman Catholic. Club: Rotary. State civil litigation, Criminal, General practice. Office: W-1100 First National Bank Bldg Saint Paul MN 55101

COLLINS, WALLACE EDMUND JAMES, lawyer, manufacturing company executive; b. Huntington, N.Y., May 16, 1923; s. Wallace E.J. and Cecilia Veronica (Bryne) C.; m. Aldona Helen Barr, May 1, 1954 (dec. 1985); children—Wallace Edmund James, III, Kevin F., Anne Marie, Paul Vincent. B.A., Fordham U., 1944, J.D., 1946. Bar: N.Y. bar 1946. Asso., then partner firm Palmer, Serles, Delaney, Shaw & Pomeroy (and predecessor), N.Y.C., 1946-64; with N. Am. Philips Corp. (and predecessor), N.Y.C., 1964—; sec., corp. counsel N. Am. Philips Corp. (and predecessor), 1965—, v.p., gen. counsel, 1969—, also v.p., sec. all subsidiaries; bd. dirs. D.C.F. Internat, Inc. Active local Boy Scouts Am., 1960-80; pres. bd. edn. St. Joseph's Sch., Oradell, N.J., 1967-75. Life mem. Nat. Model R.R. Assn., Delta Theta Phi. Roman Catholic. Club: White Beeches Golf and Country. Lodge: K.C. General corporate, Securities. Home: 167 Country Club Dr Oradell NJ 07649 Office: 100 E 42d St New York NY 10017

COLLINS, WAYNE DALE, lawyer; b. Portsmouth, Va., Dec. 23, 1951; s. Wayne D. Sr. and Mary. L. (Higdon) C.; m. Mary Ann Bradshaw, Aug. 9, 1981; children: Laura, Melissa. BS with honors, Calif. Inst. Tech., 1973, MS, 1974; JD, U. Chgo., 1978. Bar: N.Y. 1979, U.S. Supreme Ct. 1983. Assoc. Shearman & Sterling, N.Y.C., 1978-81, 83-86, ptnr., 1986—; dep. asst. atty. gen. U.S. Dept. Justice, Washington, 1982-83. White House fellow, 1981-82. Mem. ABA (chmn. antitrust sect. subcom. on fin. markets and instns. 1983—), Am. Econ. Assn., Econometric Soc., Am. Polit. Sci., Assn., Lawyers Com. for Human Rights (bd. dirs. 1980-81). Republican. Roman Catholic. Antitrust, Constitutional law. Home: 3 North Terr Maplewood NJ 07040 Office: Shearman & Sterling 53 Wall St New York NY 10005

COLLINSON, DALE STANLEY, lawyer; b. Tulsa, Okla., Sept. 1, 1938; s. Harold Everett and Charlotte Elizabeth (Bonds) C.; m. Susan Waring Smith, June 7, 1969; children—Stuart, Eleanor. A.B. summa cum laude in Politics and Econs., Yale U., 1960; LL.B., Columbia U., 1963. Bar: N.Y. 1963, U.S. Tax Ct. 1977. Law clk. U.S. Ct. Appeals (2d cir.), N.Y.C., 1963-64; law clk. to Justice Byron R. White, U.S. Supreme Ct., Washington, 1964-66; asst. prof. Stanford (Calif.) Law Sch., 1966-68, assoc. prof., 1968-72; atty.-advisor Office of Tax Policy, U.S. Dept. Treasury, Washington, 1972-73, assoc. tax legis. counsel, 1973-74, dep. tax legis. counsel, 1974-75, tax legis. counsel, 1975-76; now tax ptnr. Willkie Farr & Gallagher, N.Y.C.; panel mem. Practising Law Inst. programs, 1981, 82, 84, Am. Law Inst.-ABA program, 1984. Mem. ABA, N.Y. State Bar (chmn. tax sect.), Assn. Bar City N.Y., Nat. Assn. Bond Lawyers. Republican. Contbr. articles to legal jours. Corporate taxation. Home: 357 Quaker Rd Chappaqua NY 10514 Office: Willkie Farr & Gallagher 153 E 53d St New York NY 10022

COLLOFF, MARGERY A., lawyer; b. Cleve., Nov. 8, 1945; d. Thomas Edwards and Margery A. (Vogleson) Bletcher; m. Roger D. Colloff, May 28, 1967; children: Pamela, David Edwards. BA, Brown U., 1967; JD, George Washington U., 1977. Bar: D.C. 1977, N.Y. 1981, U.S. Supreme Ct. 1983. Counsel, staff dir. com. on health and the environment U.S. House of Reps., Washington, 1978-80; sr. assoc. White & Case, N.Y.C., 1982—; bd. dirs. Empire Blue Cross-Blue Shield, N.Y.C. Mem. Phi Beta Kappa. General corporate. Home: 1185 Park Ave New York NY 10128 Office: White & Case 1155 Ave of the Americas New York NY 10036

COLMANT, ANDREW ROBERT, lawyer; b. Bklyn., Oct. 10, 1931; s. Edward J. and Mary Elizabeth (Byrne) C.; m. Anselma DeLuca, Sept. 19, 1959; children—Stephen, Robert, Elizabeth, Carolyn. B.B.A., St. Johns U., 1957, LL.B., 1959. Bar: N.Y. 1959, U.S. Dist. Ct. N.Y. 1959. Assoc. Hill, Rivkins, Carey, Loesberg, O'Brien & Mulroy and predecessor firms, 1959-73, ptnr., 1973—; of counsel Vincent, Berg & Russo, N.Y.C., 1986—. Served as cpl. USMC, 1952-54. Mem. ABA, N.Y. State Bar Assn., N.Y. County Lawyers Assn., Maritime Law Assn. Admiralty, Insurance. Home: 71 Cresci Blvd Hazlet NJ 07730 Office: 21 West St New York NY 10006

COLOGNE, KNOX MASON, III, lawyer; b. Los Angeles, Aug. 7, 1943; s. Knox Mason Jr. and L. Jeanne (Dodge) C.; m. Mary Enlund, Aug. 20, 1966; children: Kyle, Karinn. AB, San Diego State U., 1965; JD, Stanford U., 1968; MBA, U. So. Calif., 1980. Bar: U.S. Dist. Ct. (cen. dist.) Calif. 1969, U.S. Ct. Appeals (9th cir.) 1969, U.S. Supreme Ct. 1974. Atty. Bank of Am., Los Angeles, 1968-69, atty., sr. counsel, 1973-77, asst. gen. counsel, 1977-80, v.p., asst. gen. counsel, 1980-81, v.p., assoc. gen. counsel, 1981-83, sr. v.p., assoc. gen. counsel, 1983—. Served to capt. U.S. Army, 1969-73, Vietnam. Mem. ABA, Inst. Corp. Counsel (bd. govs.), Los Angeles County Bar Assn. (chmn. corp. law depts. sect. 1986—). Clubs: Jonathan (Los Angeles); San Gabriel (Calif.) Country. Banking, Contracts commercial, General corporate. Office: Bank of Am 555 S Flower St 51st Floor Los Angeles CA 90071

COLOMBIK, RICHARD MICHAEL, lawyer; b. Chgo., July 10, 1953; s. S. Robert and Rose Y. (Ziegler) C.; children: Jeremy Paul, Justin Franklin, Samantha Brooke. BS, U. Colo., 1975; CPA, U. Ill., Champaign, 1977; JD with distinction, John Marshall Law Sch., Chgo., 1980. Bar: Ill. 1980. Tax acct. Henry Crown and Co., Chgo., 1977-78, Schur, Yormark & Rabyne, Northfield, Ill., 1978-80; tax cons. Touche Ross and Co., Chgo., 1980-82; sr. ptnr. Colombik & Bell, Palatine, Ill., 1982—; gen. ptnr. United Holsteins, Owosso, Mich., 1982-87; regional dir. Amtax Mgmt., N.Y.C., 1980—; bd. dirs. U.S. Embryo, Inc., Deerfield, Ill., 1984—; chief exec. officer Sports Communication Agy., 1987. Trustee Rep. Presdl. Task Force, 1975. Mem. Internat. Assn. Fin. Planners. Republican. Estate planning, Personal income taxation, Real property. Address: PO Box 1713 Highland Park IL 60035 Office: Colombik & Bell 1530 E Dundee Rd Suite 230 Palatine IL 60067

COLOMBO, FREDERICK J., lawyer; b. Detroit, Dec. 7, 1916; s. Louis J. and Irene Elizabeth (McKinney) C.; m. Frances Elizabeth Fisher, June 12, 1947; children—William, Joan, Richard, John. A.B., U. Mich., 1938, J.D., 1940. Bar: Mich. 1940, U.S. Dist. Ct. (ea. dist.) Mich. 1940, U.S. Ct. Appeals (6th cir.) 1940, U.S. Supreme Ct. 1940. Ptnr., Colombo and Colombo, P.C., Birmingham, Mich., 1945—; of counsel, Birmingham, 1987—. Trustee emeritus Harper Grace Hosp., Detroit; chmn. spl. gifts com. United Found.; mem. exec. com. Mich. Republican Party. Mem. ABA, Mich. State Bar Assn., Am. Judicature Soc., Detroit Bar Assn., Oakland County Bar Assn. Roman Catholic. Club: Cardinal (past pres.) (Detroit). General corporate, Estate planning, Family and matrimonial. Office: Colombo & Colombo 1500 N Woodward Ave Birmingham MI 48011

COLQUITT, JOSEPH ARLINGTON, judge; b. Birmingham, Ala., Nov. 26, 1940; s. Ivey Kelly and Gladys Pauline (Brown) C.; m. Mary Sue Stone, Jan. 21, 1967. B.S., U. Ala., 1967, J.D., 1970; postgrad. Nat. Jud. Coll., 1972. Bar: Ala. 1970. Sole practice, 1970-71; judge Ala. 6th Jud. Cir., Tuscaloosa County, Ala., 1971—; adj. instr. U. Ala. Law Ctr., Ala. Law Enforcement Acad.; past mem. Nat. Task Force to Draft Nat. Standards On Jud. Ed. Bd. dirs., past pres. Ala. Sight Conservation Assn.; bd. dirs. West Central (Ala.) div. Am. Cancer Soc.; commr. Black Warrior council Boy Scouts Am.; bd. of mgrs. Tuscaloosa Boys Club; past chmn. adminstrn. bd. St. Mark United Methodist Ch. Served USAF, 1961-65. Named One of Ala. Four Outstanding Young Men, Jaycees, 1971; Jaycee of the Yr. Tuscaloosa Jaycees, 1972; Founders award, Ala. Sight Conservation Assn. Melvin Jones fellow Lions Clubs Internat. Found. Mem. ABA, Am. Judicature Soc., Ala. Bar Assn., Ala. Cir. Judges Assn. (chmn. jud. edn.), Farrah Law Soc., Tuscaloosa Bar Assn., West Ala. C. of C. (bd. dirs.). Democrat. Clubs: Lions (past dist. gov., Lion of Yr. Ala. 1984-85, Dist. 1984-85, Northport 1979-80), (Northport, Ala.), Masons, Shriners, Am. Legion. Contbr. articles to profl. jours. State civil litigation, Criminal. Office: Courthouse Tuscaloosa AL 35401

COLTON, HERBERT SPENCER, lawyer, corporation consultant; b. Covington, Ga., Oct. 5, 1903; s. Abram and Estelle C.; m. Margaret DeCordova Sanville, May 25, 1933; children: Catherine, Judith. JD, Cornell U., 1927. Bar: Fla. 1928, N.Y. 1929, Md. 1945, D.C. 1947. Assoc. Schlesinger & Schlesinger, N.Y.C., 1930-36; chief counsel FHA, Washington, 1936-40; defense housing coordinator U.S. Govt., Washington, 1940-42; atty. FHA, Washington, 1942-46; sr. ptnr. Colton & Boykin, Washington, 1946—. Named Disting. Citizen of Md., 1978. Mem. D.C. Bar Assn. Democrat. Construction, General corporate, Real property. Home: 7511 Hampden Ln Bethesda MD 20814 Office: Colton & Boykin 1025 Thomas Jefferson St NW Washington DC 20007

COLTON, STERLING DON, lawyer, business executive; b. Vernal, Utah, Apr. 28, 1929; s. Hugh Wilkens and Marguerite (Maughan) C.; m. Eleanor Ricks, Aug. 21, 1954; children—Sterling David, Carolyn, Bradley Hugh, Steven Ricks. B.S. in Banking and Fin., U. Utah, 1951; J.D., Stanford U., 1954. Bar: Calif. 1954, Utah 1954, D.C. 1967. Ptnr., Van Cott, Bagley, Cornwall & McCarthy, Salt Lake City, 1957-66; gen. counsel Marriott Corp., Washington, 1966—, sr. v.p., 1974—; also bd. dirs.; dir. Dynalectron Corp., 1983. Chmn. nat. adv. council U. Utah, Ballet West; nat. adv. counsel. Served to maj. JAG, U.S. Army, 1954-57. Mem. ABA, Calif. Bar Assn., Utah Bar Assn., D.C. Bar Assn., Washington Met. Corp. Counsel Assn. (pres. dir.), Sigma Chi. Republican. Mormon. General corporate, Real property, Corporate taxation. Home: 8005 Greentree Rd Bethesda MD 20817 Office: Marriott Corp 10400 Fernwood Bethesda MD 20058

COLTUN, HARRY, lawyer, consultant; b. Revere, Mass., Sept. 10, 1913; s. Samuel B. Coltun and Mollie Saslavsky. J.D., Northeastern U., 1935; postgrad. Boston U., 1946. Bar: Mass. 1936, U.S. Dist. Ct. Mass. 1937, U.S. Ct. Appeals (1st cir.) 1937, U.S. Supreme Ct. 1940. Assoc., Richard Gottlieb, Boston, 1936-41; ptnr. Flynn, Abrams, Coltun & Schwartz, Boston, 1946-74; sr. ptnr. Coltun, Chapman & Panarese, Boston, 1974-82; ptnr. Coltun & Panarese, Boston, 1982—; counsel Mass. Ho. of Reps., Boston, 1956-72, lectr. U. Mass., 1962, 72, 83-84. Mem. bd. aldermen City of Chelsea, Mass., 1947-52; rep. Gen. Ct., Boston, 1950-57. Served with AUS, 1941-46; ETO. Decorated Legion of Merit. Mem. Mass. Bar Assn., Mass. Bar Found., Mass. Trial Lawyers Assn. Democrat. Jewish. Lodges: Euclid, Mason, Shriners. Legislative, General corporate, Probate. Office: Harry Coltun 14 Beacon St Boston MA 02108

COLUMBUS, R. TIMOTHY, lawyer; b. West Bend, Wis., Mar. 17, 1949; s. Robert M. and Dena (Eggabean) C.; m. Penny G. Baker, June 16, 1979; children: Alexandra Baker, Robert Benjamin. BA, Harvard U., 1971; JD, U. Va., 1974. Bar: Va. 1974, D.C. 1975. Assoc. Collier, Shannon, Rill & Scott, Washington, 1974-80, ptnr., 1980—. Legislative, Administrative and regulatory. Home: 6011 Nevada Ave NW Washington DC 20015 Office: Collier Shannon Rill & Scott 1055 Thomas Jefferson St NW Washington DC 20007

COLVILLE, ROBERT E, county district attorney; b. Pitts., May 23, 1935; s. John and Mary M. (Goldbronn) C.; children—Michael C., Robert J., Molly. B.A. Duquesne U., 1963, J.D., 1969. Bar: Pa. 1969, U.S. Dist. Ct. (we. dist.) Pa. 1969. Tchr., coach North Catholic High Sch., Pitts., 1959-64; patrolman, detective Bur. of Police, Dept. Pub. Safety, Pitts., 1964-68, police legal adviser, 1969-70, asst. dir. Dept. Pub. Safety, 1970-71, supt. Bur. of Police, Pitts., 1971-75; clk., detective Dist. Atty.'s Office of Allegheny County, Pitts., 1968-69, dist. atty., 1976—; adj. prof. law Duquesne U. Sch. of Law, Pitts., 1976-78; instr. in labor law LaRoche Coll., Pitts., 1983—. Contbr. articles to profl. jours. Past chmn. Joint Allegheny County Narcotics Task Force; mem. Pa. Democratic Com. Served with USMC, 1953-56. Recipient Dapper Dan award Pitts. Post Gazette, 1963, named Disting. Service award County Detectives Assn., 1977, Service Recognition award Pitts. Community Crime Prevention Coalition, 1980; Law Enforcement award Dep. Sheriff's Assn. of Pa., 1983; Outstanding Grad., Duquesne U., 1969; Jr. C. of C. Man of Yr. in Law, 1973; Phi Alpha Delta Law Alumni of Yr., 1976; Outstanding Grad., Duquesne U. Century Club, 1978; Outstanding Law Alumnus Duquesne U. Law Alumni Assn., 1985. Mem. Nat. Dist. Attys. Assn. (bd. dirs., met. prosecutors policy subcom.), Internat. Assn. Chiefs of Police, Pa. Commn. on Crime and Delinquency (prison and jail over-crowding task force), Pa. Dist. Attys. Assn. (appeals chmn.), Pa. Bar Assn., Allegheny County Bar Assn., Law Enforcement Coordinating Com. (co-chmn. Western Dist. Pa.). Criminal. Address: Dist Atty 303 Courthouse Pittsburgh PA 15219

COLVIN, CHARLES BRUCE, lawyer; b. Gadsden, Ala., Apr. 5, 1953; s. William Charlie and Nello Ruth (Palmer) C.; m. Elizabeth Louise du Treil, June 20, 1980; children: Amy, Laurie. BA in Geography, La. Tech. U., 1975; JD, La. State U., 1978. Bar: La. 1979, U.S. Dist. Ct. (ea. and mid. dists) La. 1979, U.S. Ct. Appeals (5th cir.) 1980. Assoc. Offices of Walton Barnes, Baton Rouge, La., 1978-79, Hebert, Abbott & Horack, New Orleans, La., 1979-80; ptnr. Abadie, Harang & Colvin, Metairie, La., 1981-86, Law Offices of Jack W. Harang, Metairie, 1987—. Mem. ABA, Assn. Trial Lawyers Am., La. Trial Lawyers Assn. Personal injury. Home: 2113 Guardian Gretna LA 70056 Office: Law Offices of Jack W Harang 210 Veterans Blvd Metairie LA 70005

COMBS, RICHARD ENNIS, magistrate; b. Visalia, Calif., Nov. 3, 1903; s. James Ennis and Maude (Brown) C.; m. Marjorie Muriel Pool, Dec. 23, 1933; children—Richard Ennis, Elizabeth Combs Renzi, John, Mary Combs Powell. A.B., U. Calif., 1926, J.D., 1931. Bar: U.S. Dist. Ct. (ea. dist.) Calif. Ptnr., McClure & Combs, Visalia, 1931-42; counsel Calif. legis. coms. on counter-subversion, 1941-70; U.S. commr., 1970-71; magistrate U.S. Dist. Ct. (ea. dist.) Calif., 1971-86; lectr. on Soviet subversion to armed forces, 1942-70; cons. Commn. on Govt. Security, Washington, 1956-57; Recipient citation of merit Calif. Am. Legion, Am.-Jewish League Against Communism, DAR, U.S. Commn. on Govt. Security. Mem. Nat. Council U.S. Magistrates (dir.-at-large 1976), English Magistrates' Assn. (assoc.), Friends of Bancroft Library, Calif. Hist. Soc., Tulare County Hist. Soc. Clubs: Book of Calif., Masons. Author 14 vols. of reports to Calif. Legislature. Criminal, Legal history. Address: Box 176 Three Rivers CA 93271

COMBS, WILLIAM HENRY, III, lawyer; b. Casper, Wyo., Mar. 18, 1949; s. William Henry and Ruth M. (Wooster) C.; m. Patricia M. Bostwick, Aug. 30, 1970; 1 child, J. Bradley. Student, Northwestern U., 1967-69; BS, U. Wyo., 1972, JD, 1975. Bar: Wyo. 1975, U.S. Dist. Ct. Wyo. 1975. Assoc. Murane & Bostwick, Casper, 1975-77, ptnr., 1978—. Mem. ABA, Am. Judicature Soc., Def. Lawyers Assn. Wyo., U.S. Handball Assn., Am. Water Ski Assn., U.S. Ski Assn. Republican. Episcopalian. Clubs: Casper Boat; Porsche Am. Avocations: handball, waterskiing, snow skiing, driving. Federal civil litigation, State civil litigation, Personal injury. Office: Murane & Bostwick 350 West A Casper WY 82601

COMEAU, MICHAEL GERARD, lawyer; b. Balt., July 13, 1956; s. Joseph Gerard and Irma (Cullison) C.; m. Penny Lee Derrickson, Apr. 14, 1984. BA, Randolph-Macon Coll., 1978; JD, U. Balt., 1981; postgrad., George Washington U., 1982-83. Bar: Md. 1981, U.S. Dist Ct. Md. 1982, U.S. Ct. Appeals (4th and D.C. cirs.) 1982, D.C. 1984, U.S. Dist Ct. D.C. 1984, U.S. Supreme Ct. (1985). Law clk. Balt. County Solicitor's Office, Towson, Md., 1980-81; assoc. county atty. Prince George's County, Upper Marlboro, Md., 1981-84, 86—; assoc. Knight, Manzi, Brennan & Ostrom, Upper Marlboro, 1984-86; chief dep. clk. Ct. Spl. Appeals, Annapolis, Md., 1986; Mem. adv. com. Loyola Coll. Bar Rev., Balt., 1982. Mem. ch. council All Saints Luth. Ch., Bowie, Md., 1986—, pres., 1987—. Mem. ABA, Md. Bar Assn., Prince George's County Bar Assn., Balt. City Bar Assn., Assn. Trial Lawyers Am., Md. Trial Lawyers Assn., Kappa Alpha. Democrat. Avocations: baseball card collecting, softball. Federal civil litigation, Local government, State civil litigation. Home: 3003 Athens Circle Bowie MD 20716 Office: County Atty's Office County Adminstrn Bldg Room 5121 Upper Marlboro MD 20722

COMEGYS, WALKER BROCKTON, lawyer; b. Oklahoma City, July 30, 1929; s. Walker B. and Dorcas (McConnell) C.; m. Adelaide M. Eicks, June 19, 1954; children: Elizabeth Lee Chafee, Catherine. B.A. with honors, U. Tex., 1951; LL.B., Harvard U., 1954. Bar: Mass. 1955, D.C. 1972, U.S. Supreme Ct. 1970. Assoc. Goodwin, Procter & Hoar, Boston, 1954-64; ptnr. Goodwin, Procter & Hoar, 1964-69; dep. asst. atty. gen. antitrust Dept. Justice, Washington, 1969-72; asst. atty. gen. antitrust Dept. Justice, 1972; ptnr. Powers & Hall P.C., Boston, 1975-79; dir. Powers & Hall P.C. (P.C.), 1979-84; practice law offices Walker B. Comegys P.C., Boston, 1984—; lectr. Boston U. Sch. Law, 1984-85; U.S. del. OECD, Paris, 1970, 72; chmn. New Eng. Antitrust Conf., 1967, 68, co-chmn., 1983, 84, 85. Adv. bd. editors: Antitrust Bull., 1967-69; contbr.: ABA Antitrust Section Antitrust Law Developments, 2d edit., 1984; author: "Antitrust Compliance Manual, A Guide for Counsel, Management and Public Officials", Practicing Law Institute, 1986. Mem. Bd. Zoning Appeals, Town of Wenham (Mass.), 1972—; bd. overseers Met. Center Performing Arts, Boston, 1981-84, Wang Center Performing Arts, 1984—. Mem. ABA (chmn. Sherman act com. antitrust sect. 1966-69, mem. council antitrust sect. 1972-76), Internat. Bar Assn. (com. 1984—), Boston Bar Assn. (chmn. antitrust com. 1968-69), N.Y. State Bar Assn., Fed. Bar Assn. Antitrust. Home: 202 Main St Wenham MA 01984 Office: 28 State St 18th Floor Boston MA 02109

COMER, VIVIAN ADELIA, lawyer; b. Oak Ridge, June 11, 1954; d. Evan Philip and Mary Adelia (Blanc) C. Student Pa. State U., 1973-75; A.B., Brown U., 1978; J.D., U. Md.-Balt., 1981. Bar: Md. 1981, U.S. Ct. Appeals (2d cir.) 1982. Law clk. Md. Atty. Gen., Balt., 1979, U.S. atty., Balt., 1979, Commodity Futures Trading Commn., Washington, 1980-81, atty., 1981-82; atty. FDIC, Washington, 1982-84, sr. atty., 1985—, acting chief bankruptcy sect., 1985—; research editor Internat. Trade Law Jour., 1980-81. Mem. ABA, Md. Bar Assn., Democrat. Bankruptcy, Consumer commercial, Administrative and regulatory.

COMERFORD, WALTER THOMPSON, JR., lawyer; b. Bristol, Va., May 27, 1949; s. Walter Thompson, and Mary Lou (Phetteplace) C.; m. Joyce Faye Call; children—Callison Taylor, Erin Elizabeth, Kristen Nicole. Student, U. Tenn., 1968-70; B.A. magna cum laude, Wake Forest U., 1972, J.D. cum laude, 1974. Bar: N.C. 1974, U.S. Dist. Ct. (mid. and we. dists.) N.C. 1974, U.S. Ct. Appeals (4th cir.) 1977. Ptnr., Petree, Stockton, Robinson, Vaughn, Glaze & Maready, Winston-Salem, N.C., 1980—. Contbr. articles to profl. jours. Chmn. profl. div. Forsyth County Arts Council Fund Drive, Winston-Salem, 1977, Wake Forest Law Fund Campaign, 1980. Recipient Disting. Achievement award Internat. Acad. Trial Lawyers, 1974. Mem. Internat. Assn. Def. Counsel, N.C. Assn. Def. Attys., ABA (vice chmn. property ins. com.), N.C. Bar Assn., N.C. State Bar, Forsyth County Bar Assn., Aviation Ins. Assn. State civil litigation, Federal civil litigation, Insurance. Home: 461 Heritage Dr Lewisville NC 27023 Office: Petree Stockton Robinson Vaughn Glaze & Maready 1001 W 4th St Winston-Salem NC 27101

COMLEY, FREDERICK LUQUIENS, lawyer; b. Bridgeport, Conn., Jan. 17, 1916; s. William Henry and Maud Bernice (Skidmore) C.; m. Jane Gilkison, June 7, 1941; children—Lynn Comley Tinker, Mark H.; m. 2d, Henree Hall, July 28, 1977. A.B., Yale U., 1937, LL.B., 1940. Bar: Conn. 1940, U.S. Dist. Ct. Conn. 1946, U.S. Ct. Appeals (2d cir.) 1955. Assoc. Pullman, Comley, Bradley & Reeves, formerly Pullman and Comley, Bridgeport, Conn., 1940-48, ptnr., 1948—, ptnr. companion firm Pullman, Comley, Marshall & Parker, Greenwich, Conn., 1948-50. Mem. Conn. Bar Exam. Com., 1963-78. Active Weston Bd. Edn., 1959-67, Weston Hist. Dist. Commn., 1972-76. Served to lt. comdr. USNR, 1940-45. Recipient Beckwith medal in Astronomy, 1937. Mem. ABA, Conn. Bar Assn., Bridgeport Bar Assn., Am. Judicature Soc, Am. Bar Found., Am. Coll. Trial Lawyers, Internat. Assn. Ins. Counsel, Sigma Xi (assoc.). Republican. Episcopalian. Clubs: Pequot Yacht, Grad. (New Haven). Federal civil litigation, State civil litigation, Probate. Office: Pullman Comley Bradley & Reeves 855 Main St Bridgeport CT 06604

COMPTON, ALLEN T., justice state supreme court; b. Kansas City, Mo., Feb. 25, 1938; m. Sue Ellen Tatter; 3 children. B.A., U. Kans.; LL.B., U. Colo. Staff atty. legal services office in Colo., later entered pvt. practic; supervising atty. Alaska Legal Services, Juneau, 1970-73; sole practice Juneau, 1973-76; judge Superior Ct., Alaska, 1976-80; justice Alaska Supreme Ct., Anchorage, 1980—. Mem. 4 bar assns. including Juneau Bar Assn. (past pres.). Judicial administration. Office: Alaska Supreme Ct 303 K St Anchorage AK 99502 *

COMPTON, ASBURY CHRISTIAN, state justice; b. Portsmouth, Va., Oct. 24, 1929; s. George Pierce and Edyth Gordon (Christian) C.; m. Betty Stephenson, Nov. 17, 1953; children: Leigh Christian, Mary Bryan, Melissa Anne. B.A., Washington and Lee U., 1950, LL.B., 1953, LL.D. (hon.), 1975. Bar: Va. 1957. Mem. firm May, Garrett, Miller, Newman & Compton, Richmond, 1957-66; judge Law and Equity Ct., City of Richmond, 1966-74; justice Supreme Ct. Va., Richmond, 1974—. Trustee Collegiate Schs., Richmond, 1972—, chmn. bd., 1978-80; mem. adminstrv. bd. Trinity United Methodist Ch., Richmond, 1974-78; trustee Washington and Lee U., 1978—. Served as officer USNR, 1953-56. Decorated Letter of Commendation. Mem. Va. Bar Assn., Va. State Bar, Bar Assn. City Richmond, Washington and Lee U. Alumni Assn. (past pres., dir.), Omicron Delta Kappa, Phi Kappa Sigma, Phi Alpha Delta. Club: Country of Va. Jurisprudence. Home: 5508 Queensbury Rd Richmond VA 23226 Office: PO Box 1315 Richmond VA 23210

COMSTOCK, CLYDE NELSON, lawyer; b. Petoskey, Mich., Feb. 26, 1908; s. Roy H. and Dorothea L. C.; m. Adelaide Mason, Oct. 4, 1941; children—Christine Herbruck, Clyde N., Stevens T.M., Elizabeth Humphrey. A.B. cum laude, Harvard U., 1930, J.D., 1933. Bar: Mich. 1933, Ohio 1945. Sole practice, Petoskey, 1933-41; pros. atty. Emmet County, Mich., 1935-39; with firm Andrews, Hadden & Putnam, Cleve., 1945-51; ptnr. Arter & Hadden, Cleve., 1951—, chmn., mng. ptnr. 1966-77, of counsel, 1982—. Served to lt. comdr. USNR, 1942-45. Mem. Greater Cleve. Bar Assn. Clubs: Union, Cleve. Country, Delray Dunes Golf and Country (Boynton Beach, Fla.), Pepper Pike (Ohio). General corporate, Mining and minerals. Home: 5 Bonsai Dr Boynton Beach FL 33436 Office: Arter & Hadden Cleveland OH 44115

COMSTOCK, DAVID COOPER, lawyer; b. Buffalo, Feb. 10, 1932; s. William De Revere and Helen (Peuchen) C.; m. Marjorie Short, June 29, 1975; children: David Cooper, Richard W. BA, Ohio Wesleyan U., 1954; LLB, Case Western Res. U., 1959. Bar: Ohio 1959. Assoc. Pfau & Pfau, Youngstown, Ohio, 1959-64; ptnr. Pfau, Comstock & Springer, Youngstown, 1964-80, Comstock, Springer & Wilson, Youngstown, 1980—. Served with U.S. Army, 1954-56. Mem. ABA, Ohio Bar Assn. (exec. com. 1984-87), Mahoning County Bar Assn., Internat. Assn. Ins. Counsel, Am. Coll. Trial Lawyers. Club: Youngstown. Lodge: Rotary. State civil litigation, Insurance. Home: 4849 Oak Knoll Dr Boardman OH 44512 Office: Comstock Springer & Wilson 926 City Centre One Youngstown OH 44501

CONABOY, RICHARD PAUL, judge; b. Scranton, Pa., June 12, 1925; m. Marion Hartnett; children: Mary Ann, Richard, Judith, Conan, Michele, Kathryn, Patrick, William, Margaret, Janet, John, Nancy. Student, U. Scranton, 1943-45; LL.B., Cath. U. Am., 1950. Bar: Pa. 1951. Ptnr. firm Powell & Conaboy, Scranton, 1951-54; dep. atty. gen. 1953-62; assoc. firm Kennedy O'Brien & O'Brien, 1954-62; judge Pa. Ct. Common Pleas, 1962-80; presiding judge U.S. Dist. Ct. Middle Pa., 1978-80, judge, 1980—; pres. Pa. Joint Council on Criminal Justice System, 1971-79; mem. Nat. Conf. Juvenile Justice, Nat. Conf. Corrections. Contbr. articles to legal jours. Bd. dirs. Marywood Coll., U. Scranton. Served with USAF, 1945-47. Mem. Pa. Conf. State Trial Judges (pres. 1976-77, v.p. 1973-76, sec. 1968-73), ABA, Pa. Bar Assn., Am. Judicature Soc. Office: US District Court US Courthouse PO Box 189 Scranton PA 18501 *

CONARD, JANE REISTER, lawyer; b. Eldora, Iowa, Apr. 10, 1947; d. Eugene Lowell and Lois Sylvia (Reed) Reister; m. William Jarrett Conard, June 12, 1971 (div. 1980); 1 child, Tacy Jane; m. Richard A. Maneval, Apr. 8, 1985. B.A., Macalester Coll., 1969; M.A., U. Iowa, 1971; J.D., U. Calif.-Davis, 1976. Bar: Calif. 1976, Utah 1983. Legal counsel Calif. State Dept. Health, 1976-78; staff counsel Calif. Dept. Mental Health, Sacramento, 1978-82; counsel Intermountain Health Care, Inc., Salt Lake City, 1982—. Trustee Wasatch Canyons Hosp. Mem. Salt Lake County Bar Assn. (exec. bd. 1985—), Nat. Health Lawyers Assn., Am. Acad. Hosp. Attys., Utah Women Lawyers (exec. bd. 1984-86). Democrat. Unitarian. Club: Zonta (sec. 1984-85) (Salt Lake City). Health. Home: 829 N Grandridge Dr Salt Lake City UT 84103 Office: Intermountain Health Care Inc 36 S State St 22d Floor Salt Lake City UT 84111

CONAWAY-RACZKA, NANCY, lawyer; b. Kokomo, Ind., Aug. 20, 1953; s. John Oliver and Rosemary (Burkhardt) Conaway; m. Theodore Vincent Raczka, Mar. 17, 1979; 1 child, Christine. BS, Ind. State U., Terre Haute, 1975; JD, U. Puget Sound, 1980. Bar: Conn., 1980, U.S. Dist. Ct. Conn., 1980. Assoc. Jozus & Milardo, Middletown, Conn., 1980-85; ptnr. Raczka & Raczka, Middletown, 1985—. Mem. Middletown Charter Rev. Commn., 1986-87; chmn. Middletown Commn. on the Arts, 1983-85; corporator Middlesex Meml. Hosp., 1984—; fin. advisor Alpha Xi Delta, U. Hartford, Conn., 1984-86. Mem. Conn. Bar Assn., Middlesex County Bar Assn. (treas. 1983-85), Assn. Trial Lawyers Am., Conn. Trial Lawyers Assn., NOW (pres. Middletown chpt. 1983-85), LWV. Democrat. Methodist. General practice, Probate, State civil litigation. Home: 7 Red Yellow Rd Middletown CT 06457

CONBOY, CAROL ANN, lawyer; b. Jackson Heights, N.Y., July 10, 1947; d. Walter A. and Lucy (LaPlace) Knott; m. Bernard James Conboy, Jan. 9, 1971; children: Mark T., Paul G., David J. BA magna cum laude, U. Conn., 1969; JD, Franklin Pierce Coll., 1978. Bar: N.H. 1978, U.S. Dist. Ct. N.H. 1979. Law clk. to chief judge U.S. Dist. Ct. N.H., Concord, 1978-79; assoc. McLane, Graf, Raulerson & Middleton P.A., Manchester, N.H., 1979-85, ptnr., 1986—. Served to 1st lt. USAF, 1969-71. Mem. ABA, N.H. Bar Assn., Assn. Trial Lawyers Am., N.H. Trial Lawyers Assn., Phi Beta Kappa, Phi Kappa Phi. Labor, State civil litigation, Federal civil litigation. Office: McLane Graf Raulerson & Middleton PA 40 Stark St Manchester NH 03105

CONCANNON, DON OWEN, lawyer; b. Garden City, Kans., Oct. 28, 1927; s. Hugh Christopher and Margaret Elizabeth (McKinley) C.; m. Patricia June Davis, Nov. 23, 1952; children: Chris O., Debra L., Craig A. AA, Garden City Community Coll., 1948; BA, JD, Washburn U., 1952. Bar: Kans. 1952, U.S. Dist. Ct. Kans. 1952, U.S. Ct. Appeals (10th cir.) 1975. Sr. ptnr. Concannon & Concannon, Hugoton, Kans., 1952—; chmn., bd. dirs. Norton Bankshares, Inc., Hugoton; bd. dirs. First State Bank, Norton, 1976—. Chmn. Kans. State Reps., 1968-70; chmn. Kans. for Reagan, Topeka, 1976; Kans. Presdl. Electors, Topeka,1960; Kans. Young GOP state chmn., 1958-60; chmn. Gov.'s Task Force on Rural Communities, 1986; mem. Kans. Commn. for Bi-Centennial for U.S. Constn., 1986. Served with USN, 1945-46. Mem. ABA, Southwest Kans. Bar Assn., Hugoton C. of C. (pres., Man of Yr. 1972). Methodist. Lodges: Masons, Elks. Oil and gas leasing, Federal civil litigation, State civil litigation. Home: 129 N Jackson Hugoton KS 67951 Office: Concannon & Concannon PO Box 1089 120 W 6th St Hugoton KS 67951

CONDIE, ROBERT STEVENS, lawyer; b. Palo Alto, Calif., May 28, 1950; s. Robert S. Condie and Ellen Jean (Wylie) Barthold; m. Margaret Anne Lieferman, Mar. 13, 1982; 1 child, Matthew Robert. BA, U. Calif., Berkeley, 1971, JD, 1974. Bar: Calif. 1974, U.S. Dist. Ct. (no. dist.) Calif. 1975. Ptnr. Condie & Lee, Oakland, Calif., 1975—. Office: Condie & Lee 11 Embarcadero W Suite 140 Oakland CA 94607

CONDLIFFE, DAVID CHARLES, lawyer; b. N.Y.C., July 7, 1948; s. John Charles and Jane Grace Rosenthal C.; m. Jane Falk, July 6, 1974; children: Kate, Barbara. BA, NYU, 1973; MPA, Harvard U., 1974-76; JD, Rutgers U., 1980. Bar: N.Y. 1981. Assoc. Greenbaum, Wolff & Ernst, N.Y.C., 1980-82, Olwine, Conelly, Chase, O'Donnell & Weyher, N.Y.C., 1982-84, Debevoise & Plimpton, N.Y.C., 1984—; pres., bd. dirs. The Dessoff Choirs, N.Y.C., 1983-86. Exec. asst. to 1st Dep. Mayor, N.Y.C., 1971-74; bd. dirs. Vietnam Vets Leadership Program, N.Y.C., 1983-86; trustee North County Sch./Camp Treetops, Lake Placid, N.Y., 1986—. Mem. ABA, N.Y. State Bar Assn., Assn. of Bar of City of N.Y. (sec. com. on mcpl. affairs 1983-86). Club: Harvard (N.Y.C.). General corporate, Securities, Entertainment. Office: Debevoise & Plimpton 875 Third Ave New York NY 10022

CONDO, JAMES ROBERT, lawyer; b. Somerville, N.J., Mar. 2, 1952; s. Ralph Vincent and Betty Louise (MacQuaide) C.; m. Peggy Marie Rader, Oct. 16, 1982. BS in Bus. and Econs., Lehigh U., 1974; JD, Boston Coll., 1979. Bar: Ariz. 1979, U.S. Dist. Ct. Ariz. 1979, U.S. Ct. Appeals (9th cir.) 1982, U.S. Supreme Ct. 1983. Assoc. Snell & Wilmer, Phoenix, 1979-84, ptnr., 1985—. Contbr. articles to profl. jours. Mem. ABA, Ariz. Bar Assn., Maricopa County Bar Assn., Am. Arbitration Assn., Phoenix Assn. Def. Counsel. Construction, State civil litigation, Personal injury. Home: 2939 N Manor Dr W Phoenix AZ 85014 Office: Snell & Wilmer 3100 Valley Bank Ctr Phoenix AZ 85073

CONDON, CHARLES MOLONY, lawyer; b. Charleston, S.C., May 2, 1953; s. James Joseph and Harriet (Molony) C.; m. Emily Yarborough, June 21, 1980; 1 child, Charles Molony Jr. Student, Saltzburg (Austria) Summer Sch., 1972, U. Innsbruck, Austria, 1972-73; BA, U. Notre Dame, 1975; JD, Duke U., 1978. Assoc. Nexsen, Pruet, Jacobs & Pollard, Columbus, S.C., 1978-79; asst. solicitor S.C. 9th Jud. Cir., Charleston, 1979-80, solicitor, 1980—. Mem. ABA, S.C. Bar Assn., Charleston County Bar Assn., Charleston Lawyers Club, S.C. Cir. Solicitors Assn. (v.p.), S.C. Law Enforcement Assn., Hibernian Soc. Criminal. Home: 3204 Marshall Blvd Sullivans Island SC 29482 Office: Solicitors Office Charleston Courthouse Corner Meeting and Broad Sts Charleston SC 29401

CONDON, DAVID BRUCE, lawyer; b. Tacoma, May 20, 1949; s. Lester Milo and Ruby Elizabeth (Elson) C.; m. Constance Lynn Montgomery, Aug. 27, 1971; children: Amy M., Anne E. BA, U. Wash., 1971; JD cum laude, Gonzaga U., 1974. Bar: Wash. 1974, U.S. Dist. Ct. (we. dist.) Wash. 1974, U.S. Ct. Appeals (9th cir.) 1976. Assoc. Griffin & Enslow, Tacoma, 1974-78; ptnr. Welch & Condon, Tacoma, 1978—; examiner Wash. State Higher Edn. Personnel Bd., 1979—. Mem. Fed. Bar Assn., Wash. State Bar Assn., Tacoma-Pierce County Bar Assn., Assn. Trial Lawyers Am., Wash. Trial Lawyers Assn. Avocations: triathlons, swimming. Workers' compensation, Personal injury, Labor. Office: Welch & Condon 1109 Tacoma Ave S Tacoma WA 98407

CONDON, JOHN WILLIAM, JR., lawyer; b. Buffalo, Feb. 3, 1922; s. John W. Sr. and Susan (Nehin) C.; m. Joan C. Borkowski, Nov. 17, 1951; children: Julia Ann, Susan Ann, Sean William, Moira Ann, Matthew William. BA, Canisius Coll., 1947; JD, Albany Law Sch., 1950. Bar: N.Y. 1951, U.S. Supreme Ct. 1957, U.S. Ct. Customs and Patant Appeals 1959, U.S. Ct. Appeals (2d cir.) 1959, U.S. Tax Ct. 1963. Asst. dist. atty. Erie County, Buffalo, 1951-52; ptnr. Condon, LaTona, Pieri & Dillon P.C. and predeccesor firms, Buffalo, 1953—, Condon & Nasca P.C., Buffalo, 1983—. Contbr. articles to profl. jours. Served with U.S. Army, 1942-43, ETO. Mem. ABA, N.Y. State Bar Assn. (criminal justice sect. 1972-73, Outstanding Practitioner 1977), Erie County Bar Assn. (chmn. penal law com.), Erie County Trial Lawyers Assn. (bd. govs.), Am. Coll. Trial Lawyers, Nat. Assn. Criminal Def. Lawyers (bd. dirs. 1958-71). Republican. Roman Catholic. Clubs: Buffalo, Marshall. Criminal, Administrative and regulatory, Taxation - personal and corporate. Home: 4566 Marie Dr Hamburg NY 14075 Office: Condon LaTona Pieri & Dillon PC 300 Statler Towers Buffalo NY 14202

CONDRAY, SCOTT ROBERT, lawyer; b. Concordia, Kans., Oct. 9, 1954; s. Robert Merrill and Judith Suzanne (Ford) C.; married; children: Richard, David, Rebecca. AA, Cloud County Community Coll., 1974; BS, Kans. State U., 1976; JD, Washburn U., 1978. Bar: Kans. 1979. Atty James M. Milliken, St. Francis, Kans., 1979-81, Cheyenne County, St. Francis, 1980—, Milliken & Condray, St. Francis, 1982-85; sole practice St. Francis, 1985—. Vice pres. Peace Luth. Ch., St. Francis, 1982-84. Mem. Kans. Bar Assn., Northwestern Kans. Bar Assn., St. Francis C. of C. (pres. 1985). Republican. Lutheran. Lodge: Lions (St. Francis, Kans.) (v.p. 1982-84, pres. 1984-85). Avocations: golf, running, reading, flying. General practice, Probate, Real property. Office: Scott R Condray 109 E Washington PO Box 845 Saint Francis KS 67756

CONDRELL, WILLIAM KENNETH, lawyer; b. Buffalo, N.Y., Sept. 19, 1926; s. Paul Kenneth and Celia Olga (Schinas) C.; m. Constance A. Katsaros, June 22, 1958 (div. 1978); children—Paul, William, Alexander. B.S., Yale U., 1946; S.M., MIT, 1947; JD, Harvard U., 1950. Bar: N.Y. 1951, D.C. 1964, U.S. Ct. Appeals (4th cir.) 1974, U.S. Ct. Appeals (Fed. cir.) 1982, U.S. Ct. Appeals (D.C. cir.) 1984, U.S. Supreme Ct. 1965. Assoc. econ. adv. Exec. Office Pres., D.C., 1951-54; mgmt. cons. McKinsey and Co., Chgo., 1954-55; mgr. budgets Hotpoint div. Gen. Electric Co., Chgo., 1955-59; sole practice 1959-68; ptnr. Steptoe & Johnson, D.C., 1968—; adj. prof. Duke U., dir. Duke Ctr. Forestry Investment; gen. counsel Coalition for Uniform Product Liability Law, Am. Geophys. Union. Editor: Timber Tax Journal, 1965—. Served to lt.j.g. USNR, 1944-46. Mem. ABA, Am. Inst. C.P.A.s, National Press Club. Clubs: Metropolitan (D.C.); Congressional Country (Bethesda, Md.). Corporate taxation, Estate taxation, Legislative. Home: 6601 Michaels Dr Bethesda MD 20817 Office: Steptoe & Johnson 1330 Connecticut Ave Washington DC 20036

CONE, LORYNN ADDERHOLDT, legal educator; b. Goldsboro, N.C., Jan. 26, 1954; d. Charles H. and Lorynn (Crocker) Adderholdt; m. Thomas Edward Cone, June 4, 1977; children: Bradford, Daniel, Anna. BA cum laude, Mount Holyoke Coll., 1976; JD, Duke U., 1979. Bar: N.C. 1979. Assoc. Powe, Porter & Alpin, Durham, N.C., 1979-81; editor Constn. Law Inst., Greensboro, N.C., 1981-83; lectr. U. N.C., Greensboro, 1984-85, asst. prof., 1986—. Mem. Greensboro (N.C.) Jr. League, 1981-86; bd. dirs. Civic Ballet Theatre, Greensboro, 1981-85, pres., bd. dirs., 1984; bd. dirs. United Arts Council, Greensboro, 1984, Greensboro Jewish Fedn., 1981-86, Hadassah Greensboro chpt., 1984-86. Mem. ABA, N.C. Bar Assn., Am. Bus. Law Assn., Southeastern Regional Bus. Law Assn., N.C. Assn. Women Attys. Democrat. Jewish. Club: Greensboro Country. Avocations: skiing, swimming, travel, reading. Legal education, Labor. Office: U NC Sch of Bus and Econs 1000 Spring Garden St Greensboro NC 27412-5001

CONGALTON, SUSAN TICHENOR, lawyer; b. Mt. Vernon, N.Y., July 12, 1946; d. Arthur George and M. Marjorie (McDermott) Tichenor; m. Christopher William Congalton, May 29, 1971. BA summa cum laude, Loretto Heights Coll., 1968; JD, Georgetown U., 1971. Bar: N.Y. 1972, Ill. 1986. Assoc. Reavis & McGrath, N.Y.C., 1971-78, ptnr., 1978-85; v.p., gen. counsel and sec. Carson Pirie Scott & Co., Chgo., 1985—. Mem. bd. of overseers IIT Chgo.-Kent Coll. of Law, 1985—. Mem. ABA, N.Y. State Bar Assn. (corp. law com., partnership law subcom. 1984-85), Am. Corp. Counsel Assn., Nat. Assn. Corp. Dirs., Am. Soc. Corp. Secs. Clubs: Chicago, Chicago Network, Executives. General corporate. Office: Carson Pirie Scott & Co 36 S Wabash Chicago IL 60603

CONGLETON, JOSEPH PATRICK, lawyer, conservationist; b. Barbourville, Ky., June 8, 1947; s. Isaac and B. (Johnson) C.; m. Rose Willingham Stewart; children: Isaac Tyler, Rosalie Mallary. MA, Centre Coll., 1969; JD, U. Va., 1972. Bar: Tenn. 1972. Ptnr. Fowler & Rowntree, Knoxville, Tenn., 1972-83, Hunton & Williams, Knoxville, 1983—. Adv. editor Jour. Mineral Law and Policy, 1985—. Chmn. atty. div. United Way Knoxville, 1985—; bd. dirs. Nature Conservancy, 1980—, Knoxville Symphony, 1985—, pres.-elect, 1987, Great Smoky Mountain Conservation Assn., Knoxville, 1985—, Webb Sch., Knoxville, 1986—; pres. Knoxville Watersports Festival, 1986-87; mem. Leadership Knoxville, 1986-87. Fellow Tenn. Bar Found.; mem. ABA, Tenn. Bar Assn., Knoxville Bar Assn., Nat. Assn. Bond Lawyers, Eastern Mineral Law Found. (trustee, exec. com. 1970-85), Trout Unltd. (nat. bd. dirs.). Clubs: Appalachian (Elkmont, Tenn.); Old City (bd. dirs. 1984—), Knoxville Racquet (bd. dirs. 1980-82), Cherokee Country. Lodge: Rotary (v.p. Knoxville club 1986-87). Avocations: upland and waterfowl hunting, fly fishing, Appalchian ecology. Municipal bonds, General corporate, Coal. Home: 7004 Sherwood Dr Knoxville TN 37919 Office: Hunton & WIlliams 530 S Gay St 700 1st Tenn Bank Bldg Knoxville TN 37902

CONINE, GARY BAINARD, lawyer; b. Jackson, Miss., Nov. 26, 1947; s. Wallace Bainard and Mary Belle (Thompson) C.; m. Donna Sue Burnett, Sept. 2, 1982; 1 child, Joshua Wallace. B.A. in Econs., So. Meth. U., 1970; J.D., U. Okla., 1977. Bar: Tex. 1977. Assoc. Liddell, Sapp, Zivley & Brown, Houston, 1977-79; asst. prof. law U. Wyo., Laramie, 1979-80; assoc. Liddell, Sapp, Zivley, Brown & LaBoon, Houston, 1980-83; adj. prof. law South Tex. Coll. Law, Houston, 1982; ptnr. Liddell, Sapp & Zivley, Houston, 1984-87; adj. prof. law, advanced energy studies U. Houston Law Ctr., 1985-87. Contbr. articles to profl. jours. Served to 1st lt. USAF, 1970-74. Decorated Air Force Commendation medal; Leon J. York, Jr. scholar U. Okla., 1975, Rayburn L. Foster Meml. scholar 1975, George J. Fagin Mcpl. Law endowment scholar, 1976, William R. Bandy Meml. scholar 1977. Mem. ABA (vice chmn. oil com. 1981-83), Houston Bar Assn., Order of Barristers, Order of Coif, Houston C. of C. (govt. relations council 1983-87). Republican. Mem. Christian Ch. FERC practice, Oil and gas leasing, Real property. Office: Liddell Sapp & Zivley 3400 Tex Commerce Tower Houston TX 77002

CONISON, JAY, lawyer; b. Cin., Oct. 21, 1953; s. Allan Abraham and Theresa (Yudofsky) C.; m. Nancy Jo Kelber, Sept. 7, 1980; 1 child, Alexander. BA, Yale U., 1975; MA, U. Minn., 1978, JD, 1981. Bar: Ill. 1981, U.S. Dist. Ct. (no. dist.) Ill. 1980, U.S. Dist. Ct. (ea. dist.) Wis. 1984, U.S. Dist. Ct. (no. dist. trial) Ill. 1985. Assoc. Sonnenschein, Carlin, Nath & Rosenthal, Chgo., 1981—. Mem. ABA (Sherman Act com., antitrust sect., Forum com. franchising). Antitrust, Federal civil litigation, State civil litigation. Home: 1028 S Clinton Oak Park IL 60304 Office: Sonnenschein Carlin Nath & Rosenthal 8000 Sears Tower Chicago IL 60606

CONKEL, ROBERT DALE, pension consultant, lawyer; b. Martins Ferry, Ohio, Oct. 13, 1936; s. Chester William and Marian Matilda (Ashton) C.; m. Elizabeth A. Cargill, June 15, 1958; children—Debra Lynn Conkel McGlone, Dale William, Douglas Alan; m. 2d, Brenda Jo Myers, Aug. 2, 1980. B.A., Mt. Union Coll., 1958; J.D. cum laude, Cleve. Marshall Law Sch., 1965; LL.M., Case Western Res. U., 1972. Bar: Ohio 1965, U.S. Tax Ct. 1974, U.S. Supreme Ct. 1974, Tex. 1978, U.S. Ct. Appeals (5th cir.) 1979. Supr., Social Security Adminstrn., Cleve., 1958-65; trust officer Harter Bank & Trust Co., Canton, Ohio, 1965-70; exec. v.p. Am. Actuaries, Inc., Grand Rapids, Mich., 1970-73, pension cons., southwest regional dir., Dallas, 1974—; mgr. plans and research A.S. Hansen, Inc., Dallas, 1973-74; sole practice, Dallas, 1973—; mem. devel. bd. Met. Nat. Bank, Richardson, Tex.; instr. Am. Mgmt. Assn., 1975, Am. Coll. Advanced Pension Planning, 1975-76. Sustaining mem. Republican Nat. Com., 1980—. Enrolled actuary, Joint Bd. Enrollment U.S. Depts. Labor and Treasury. Mem. ABA (employee benefit com. sect. taxation), Ohio State Bar Assn., Tex. Bar Assn., Dallas Bar Assn., Am. Soc. Pension Actuaries (dir. 1973-81), Am. Acad. Actuaries. Contbr. articles to legal publs.; editorial adv. bd. Jour. Pension Planning and Compliance, 1974-83. Pension, profit-sharing, and employee benefits, Estate planning, Personal income taxation. Office: PO Box 31481 Dallas TX 75231

CONKLING, DANIEL CHARLES, lawyer; accountant; b. Balt. Aug. 25, 1940; s. William N. and Hazel (Gum) C.; m. Verne Patricia Fuhrer, May 28, 1962 (div. 1975); children—Charles, Bryan; m. Nancy Elizabeth Gruss, June 1, 1979; children—Timothy, Brittany; 1 step-son, James. A.A., Balt. Coll. Commerce, 1962; B.S., U. Balt., 1965, J.D., 1968. C.P.A., Md. Bar: Md. 1970, U.S. Tax Ct. 1971, U.S. Dist. Ct. Md. 1983. Auditor Balt. Gas & Electric Co., 1958-61; ptnr. Naron & Wagner, C.P.A.s, Balt., 1961-69; sole practice, Balt., 1969—. Bd. dirs., coach St. Jones Soccer League, 1980-85. Mem. Anne Arundel County Bar Assn., Md. Assn. C.P.A.s, Glen Burnie Jaycees (bd. dirs. 1970-76, pres. 1973-74), N. Anne Arundel County C. of C. (bd. dirs. 1978-86, pres. 1981), Sigma Delta Kappa (nat. pres. 1985-86, pres. Balt. alumni chpt. 1979). Democrat. Personal income taxation, State and local taxation, Probate. Office: 6 Aquahart Rd Glen Burnie MD 21061

CONLEY, DAVID THOMAS, lawyer; b. Marion, N.C., Sept. 13, 1954; s. William Tate and Mary Lillian (Jonas) C.; m. Stephanie Ilene Simms, May 13, 1979; children: Stephen David, Alexander Thomas. BBA, U. N.C., 1976; JD, Wake Forest U., 1979. Bar: U.S. Dist. Ct. (we. dist.) N.C. 1979, Fla. 1984. Assoc. Raymer, Lewis, Eisele & Patterson, Statesville, N.C., 1979-81; atty. The Babcock & Wilcox Co., Lynchburg, Va., 1981-84; assoc. counsel Racal Data Communications, Inc., Miami, Fla., 1984-85; assoc. gen. counsel Carolina Power & Light Co., Raleigh, N.C., 1985—. Vol. counsel Am. Radio Relay League, Newington, Conn., 1985. Mem. ABA, N.C. Bar Assn., Wake County Bar Assn., Am. Corp. Counsel Assn., Raleigh Amateur Radio Soc., Phi Beta Kappa, Beta Gamma Sigma, Phi Alpha Delta. Republican. Methodist. Avocations: amateur radio, flying, traveling. Contracts commercial, Computer, Private international. Home: 5912 N Hills Dr Raleigh NC 27609 Office: Carolina Power & Light Co 411 Fayetteville St Raleigh NC 27602

CONLEY, MARTHA RICHARDS, lawyer; b. Pitts., Jan. 12, 1947; d. Writt Adam Richards and Mary Jane (Brunges) Jennings; m. Charles Donald Conley, Jan. 20, 1978; children: David, Daniel. BA, Waynesburg Coll., 1968; JD, U. Pittsburgh, 1971. Bar: Pa. 1972, U.S. Dist. Ct. (we. dist.) Pa. 1972, U.S. Supreme Ct. 1977. Asst. solicitor Sch. Dist. of Pitts., 1972-73; ptnr. Brown & Cotton, Pitts., 1973-74; staff asst. U.S. Steel Corp., Pitts., 1974-76, asst. mgr. arbitration, 1976-84, asst. mgr. compliance, 1984-85, mgr. compliance, 1985-87, atty., 1987—; hazard commn. com. mem. Am. Iron and Steel Inst., Washington, 1984—. Mem. resource devel. com. YWCA, Pitts., 1984—. Mem. ABA, Nat. Bar Assn., Allegheny County Bar Assn., Am. Conf. on Chem. Labeling, Christian Legal Soc. Pitts. Democrat. Presbyterian. Club: Aurora Reading (Pitts.) (pres. 1983—). Avocations: gardening, reading, writing. Administrative and regulatory, Workers' compensation. Home: 6439 Navarro St Pittsburgh PA 15206 Office: US Steel Corp 600 Grant St Room 1580 Pittsburgh PA 15230

CONLEY, NED LEROY, lawyer; b. Lovelady, Tex., Dec. 7, 1925; s. Robert Preston and Myrtle Ida (Snell) C.; m. Betty Jean Bailey, June 20, 1948; children—Robert Eugene, Richard Owen. B.S.M.E., Tex. A&M U., College Station, 1947; LL.B., So. Tex. Coll. Law, Houston, 1955. Bar: Tex. 1955. Engr. Mission Mfg. Co., Houston, 1948-55; engr. Hudson Engring. Co., Houston, 1955-56; examiner U.S. Patent Office, 1957; atty. Sun Oil Co., Phila., 1957-59; ptnr. Butler & Binion, Houston, 1959—, adminstrv. ptnr. patent law sect., 1978—. Past pres. Lamar Terr. Civic Club; past pres. Bayou Woods Civic Assn.; mem. Harris County Heritage Soc. Served to lt. comdr. USNR, 1944-68. Recipient Layman of Yr. award Disciples of Christ in Tex., 1971. Mem. ABA, Am. Patent Law Assn., Houston Bar Assn., State Bar Tex. (chmn. intellectual property law sect. 1980-81), Houston Patent Law Assn. (pres. 1972), Alumni Assn. South Tex. Coll. Law (bd. dirs.), Tex. Bar Found. Clubs: Houston, Inns of Court, Century of Tex. A & M U. Federal civil litigation, Patent, Trademark and copyright. Office: Allied Bank Plaza Houston TX 77002

CONLIN, ROXANNE BARTON, lawyer; b. Huron, S.D., June 30, 1944; d. Marion William and Alyce Muraine (Madden) Barton; m. James Clyde Conlin, Mar. 21, 1964; children: Jacalyn Rae, James Barton, Deborah Ann, Douglas Benton. B.A., Drake U., 1964, J.D., 1966, M.P.A., 1979; LL.D. (hon.), U. Dubuque, 1975. Bar: Iowa 1966. Assoc. firm Davis, Huebner, Johnson & Burt, Des Moines, 1966-67; dep. indsl. commr. State of Iowa, 1967-68, asst. atty. gen., 1969-76; U.S. atty. So. Dist. Iowa, 1977-81; assoc. firm James, Galligan & Conlin, P.C., 1983—; gen. counsel Legal Def. and Edn. Fund, NOW, 1985-86, pres., 1986—; adj. prof. law U. Iowa, 1977-79; guest lectr. numerous univs. Chmn. Iowa Women's Polit. Caucus, 1973-75, del. nat. steering com., 1973-77; cons. U.S. Commn. on Internat. Women's Year, 1976-77. Contbr. articles to profl. publs. Nat. committeewoman Iowa Young Democrats; also pres. Polk County Young Dems., 1965-66; del. Iowa Presdl. Conv., 1972; Dem. candidate for gov. of Iowa, 1982; nat. policy chmn. John Glenn for Pres. Com., 1983-84; bd. dirs. Riverhills Day Care Center, YWCA; chmn. Drake U. Law Sch. Endowment Trust, 1985-86 ; bd. counselors Drake U., 1982-86; pres. Civil Justice Found., 1986—. Recipient award Iowa Civil Liberties Union, 1974; named to Iowa Women's Hall of Fame, 1981; other awards.; Fischer Found. scholar, 1965-66; Readers Digest scholar, 1963-64. Mem. Am., Iowa bar assns., ACLU, NAACP, Common Cause, Assn. Children Learning Disabilities, Assn. Trial Lawyers Iowa (bd. dirs.), Assn. Trial Lawyers Am. (chmn. consumer and victims coalition com. 1985—), Women's Equity Action League, NOW (dir. 1969), Phi Beta Kappa, Alpha Lambda Delta, Chi Omega (Social Service award). Federal civil litigation, State civil litigation, Personal injury. Office: 610 Equitable Bldg Des Moines IA 50309-3790

CONLON, DEBERA FRICK, lawyer; b. Washington, Feb. 14, 1956; d. Richard Allen and Clarice Ann (Vance) Frick; m. David Lloyd Conlon, May 24, 1986. BA, U. Md., 1977; JD, Washington and Lee U., 1981. Bar: Va. 1981, U.S. Dist. Ct. (ea. dist.) Va. 1981, U.S. Ct. Appeals (4th cir.) 1981. Law clk. to presiding justice U.S. Bankruptcy Ct., Norfolk, Va., 1981-82; assoc. Harlan, Knight, Dudley & Pincus, Norfolk, 1982-83; asst. trustee Office of U.S. Trustee, Norfolk, 1983—. Mem. ABA. Club: Quota (Norfolk). Bankruptcy. Home: 2005 Sterling Point Dr Portsmouth VA 23703 Office: Office of US Trustee Fed Bldg Room 744 Norfolk VA 23510

CONLON, MICHAEL WILLIAM, lawyer; b. Wilkes Barre, Pa., Nov. 9, 1946; s. William Peter and Dorothy (Stone) C.; m. Alice Cario, June 14, 1969; children: Michele, Stacia. A.B., Cath. U., 1968; J.D., Duke U., 1971. Bar: Tex. 1971. Ptnr. Fulbright & Jaworski, Houston, 1978—. General corporate, Securities, Contracts commercial. Office: 1301 McKinney Suite 5100 Houston TX 77010

CONNALLY, MICHAEL W., lawyer; b. Long Beach, Calif., July 8, 1957; s. Jack Walton and Melba June (Renfro) C.; m. Mary Kathleen Tubbiola, June 11, 1977; children: Steven William, Lisa Marie, Amber Lynn. BA in History, Loyola Marymount U., Los Angeles, 1978; JD, Loyola Law Sch., Los Angeles, 1981. Bar: Calif. 1981. Assoc. Parkinson, Wolf, Lazar & Leo, Los Angeles, 1981—, sr. assoc., 1984—; faculty Calif. Mission Bapt. Inst., Bellflower, 1984—. Youth assoc. Calif. Rep. State Cen. Com., 1976, assoc., 1985-86; deacon Hillcrest Missionary Bapt. Ch., Huntington Beach Calif., 1979-85, Grace Missionary Bapt. Ch., Anaheim, Calif., 1985—. Mem. ABA, Calif. State Bar, Los Angeles Bar Assn., Century City Bar Assn. Republican. Baptist. Avocations: white water rafting, bowling, chess, basketball, cooking. State civil litigation, Federal civil litigation, Insurance. Home: 16737 Olive St Fountain Valley CA 92708 Office: Parkinson Wolf Lazar & Leo 1900 Ave of the Stars 18th Fl Los Angeles CA 90067

CONNALLY, TOM, lawyer; b. Houston, Feb. 11, 1940; s. Ben C. and Sally (Allen) C.; m. Erin Alessandra Connally, May 4, 1968; children: Erin, Dan. BBA, U. Tex., 1961, LLB, 1963. Bar: Tex. 1963, U.S. Dist. Ct. (so. dist.) Tex. 1965, U.S. Ct. Appeals (5th cir.) 1966, U.S. Dist. Ct. (we. dist.) Tex. 1978, U.S. Dist. Ct. (no. dist.) Tex. 1980. Assoc. Fulbright & Jaworski, Houston, 1963-72, ptnr., 1972—. Assoc. editor U. Tex. Law Rev., 1962; contbr. articles to profl. jours. Served to capt. JAG, 1963-69. Mem. Tex. Bar Assn., Houston Bar Assn., Internat. Assn. Ins. Counsel, Order of Coif. Insurance, Construction. Office: Fulbright & Jaworski 1301 McKinney St 51st Floor Houston TX 77010 Home: 651 Shartle Circle Houston TX 77024

CONNELL, JANICE TIMCHAK, lawyer, transportation executive; b. Johnstown, Pa., Mar. 30, 1939; d. Louis John and Edna Ann (Bonistall) Timchak; m. Edward F. Connell, Nov. 24, 1960; children: Elizabeth Ward, Edward F. III, William Troy. BS in Fgn. Service, Georgetown U., 1961; M in Polit. and Internat. Adminstrn., U. Pitts., 1976; JD, Duquesne U., 1979.

Bar: Pa. 1979, U.S. Dist. Ct. (we. dist.) Pa. 1979, U.S. Ct. Appeals (3d cir.) 1979, U.S. Supreme Ct. 1983. Pres. Regency Advertising, Jacksonville, Fla. and Pitts., 1968-74, Connell Leasing of Fla., Jacksonville and Pitts., 1970-80; v.p., sec. Nat. Motor Leasing Inc., Pitts., 1980-86; ptnr. Connell & Connell, Pitts., 1980—; v.p., sec. Transportation Lease Cons. Inc., Pitts., 1986—, also bd. dirs.; pres. Internat. Motor Leasing Inc., Pitts., 1986—; pres., chief exec. officer Power Sources Inc., 1986—; arbitrator N.Y. Stock Exchange, 1981—, Am. Arbitration Assn., 1985—, Nat. Assn. Securities Dealers, 1983—. Bd. dirs. Assn. Jr. Leagues Inc., Wheeling, W.Va., Jacksonville and Pitts., 1964—, Salvation Army, Wheeling, 1967-68, United Way, Jacksonville, 1971, YMCA, Jacksonville, 1972-73, Legal Aid Soc., Pitts., 1985—; bd. dirs. women's adv. bd. Duquesne U., Pitts., 1980—; founding dir. Inst. for World Concern, Duquesne U., 1981—. Mem. ABA (real property sect.), Pa. Bar Assn., Allegheny County Bar Assn. Clubs: Allegheny Country (Sewickley, Pa.); 20th Century (Pitts.). Avocations: boating, golfing, bridge. General corporate, Securities, Real property. Home: Backbone Rd Sewickley PA 15143 Office: Connell & Connell 107 Patton Dr Coraopolis PA 15108

CONNELL, WILLIAM TERRENCE, lawyer; b. Montclair, N.J., July 29, 1949; s. Raymond Charles and Kathryn (Hanley) C.; m. Honor Marilyn McMahon, July 19, 1975; children—Sean William, Heather Erin, Lauren Blythe. A.B., Providence Coll., 1971; J.D., Seton Hall U., 1976. Bar: N.J. 1977, D.C. 1979, U.S. Dist. Ct. N.J. 1977, U.S. Ct. Appeals (3d cir.) 1984. Cert. trial atty. Investigator, Comml. Union Ins. Co., West Orange, N.J., 1971, Essex County Prosecutor, Newark, 1971-77; mem. firm Dwyer, Connell & Lisbona, Montclair, N.J., 1977—; arbitrator Middlesex County Superior Ct., New Brunswick, N.J., 1984—; mem. Lawyers Encouraging Govt. and the Law, N.J., 1978—. Mem. Republican Nat. Com., Washington, 1981—. Mem. ABA, Assn. Trial Lawyers Am., N.J. Bar Assn., D.C. Bar Assn., Essex County Bar Assn., Middlesex County Bar Assn., Middlesex County Trial Lawyers Assn. Roman Catholic. Club: Essex Falls Country (N.J.). Insurance, Federal civil litigation, State civil litigation. Home: 18 Ford Ln Roseland NJ 07068 Office: Dwyer Connell & Lisbona 427 Bloomfield Ave Montclair NJ 07042

CONNELLY, JOHN ROBERT, JR., lawyer; b. Chgo., Mar. 22, 1956; s. John Robert Sr. and Rosemary (Campbell) C. BA, Stanford U., 1978; JD, U. Calif., San Francisco, 1981. Bar: Wash. 1981, U.S. Dist. Ct. (we. dist.) Wash. 1981. Law clk. to presiding justice U.S. Dist. Ct. (no. dist.) Calif., San Francisco, 1981; assoc. Gordon, Thomas, Honeywell, Malanca, Peterson & Daheim, Tacoma, 1981-85, ptnr., 1986—. Coach water polo team Lakes High Sch., Tacoma, 1981—; trustee Pierce County Non Profit Arbitration Service, Tacoma, 1986. Mem. ABA, Wash. State Bar Assn. (bd. govs. young lawyers sect. 1986—), Tacoma-Pierce County Bar Assn. (pres. young lawyers sect. 1984, v.p. young lawyers sect. 1982-83, trustee young lawyers sect. 1985—), Assn. Trial Lawyers Am., Wash. State Trial Lawyers Assn. Democrat. Roman Catholic. Avocations: swimming, boating. Personal injury, Criminal, Federal civil litigation. Office: Gordon Thomas Honeywell et al 2200 1st Interstate Plaza Tacoma WA 98401

CONNELLY, LEWIS BRANCH SUTTON, lawyer; b. St. Louis, Sept. 17, 1950; s. Lewis Branch and Mary Ellen (Henneberger) C.; m. Anna Kristina Cook, Oct. 15, 1977; children—Christopher Sutton, Jeffrey Scott, Sarah Elizabeth. B.A., Vanderbilt U., 1972; J.D., U. Tenn., 1977. Mem. Smith, Cohen, Ringel, Kohler & Martin, Atlanta, 1977-79, Cook & Palmour, Summerville, Ga., 1979—. Staff mem. Tenn. Law Rev., 1975-77. Mem. ABA (complex crime com. litigation sect. 1982—, consumer affairs com. corp. banking sect. 1982—), Assn. Trial Lawyers Am., Ga. Assn. Trial Lawyers, Nat. Assn. Criminal Def. Lawyers, Ga. Assn. Criminal Def. Lawyers. Democrat. Presbyterian. Criminal, Federal civil litigation, State civil litigation. Office: Cook & Palmour 128 S Commerce St Summerville GA 30747

CONNELLY, P. KEVIN, lawyer; b. Chgo., Apr. 29, 1950; s. John J. and Dorothy M. (Day) C.; m. Maureen A. Sheehan, Aug. 23, 1974; children: Sheila S., J. Neil, D. Owen. BS in Fgn. Service, Georgetown U., 1972; JD, Loyola U., Chgo., 1975. Bar: Ill., U.S. Dist. Ct. (no. dist.) Ill., U.S. Ct. Appeals (4th, 5th and 7th cirs.), U.S. Supreme Ct. Assoc. Lederer, Fox & Grove, Chgo., 1975-78; ptnr. Lederer, Reich, Sheldon & Connelly, Chgo., 1978—; lectr. Loyola U. Law Sch., Chgo., 1977-85, adj. prof., 1985—. Contbr. articles to profl. jours. Mem. ABA (litigation, adminstrv. law and labor and employment law sects.), Ill. Bar Assn., Chgo. Bar Assn. Roman Catholic. Labor, Federal civil litigation, Legal education. Home: 666 Revere Rd Glen Ellyn IL 60137 Office: Lederer Reich Sheldon & Connelly 208 S LaSalle St Chicago IL 60604

CONNELLY, SHARON RUDOLPH, lawyer, federal official; b. Kingwood, W.Va., Oct. 16, 1940; d. John E. and Lorene E. Rudolph; m. Francis J. Connelly, June 24, 1969; 1 child, John. BBA, W.Va. State U., 1966; MBA, Ind. U., 1968; JD, Cath. Univ., 1976. Bar: Va. 1977. Mgr. IRS, Washington, 1969-76; asst. controller Mfrs. Hanover, N.Y.C., 1976-77; compliance chief D.C. Dept. Labor, Washington, 1977-79; dir. compliance U.S. Dept. Commerce, Washington, 1979-82; asst. insp. gen. NASA, Washington, 1982-84; auditor, dir. insp. office Nuclear Regulatory Commn., Washington, 1984—; attendee Assn. Govt. Accts., Assn. Fed. Investigators. Contbr. articles to profl. jours. Mem. ABA, Exec. Women in Govt. Personal income taxation, Landlord-tenant, Export control law. Office: PO Box 2074 Merrifield VA 22116

CONNELLY, THOMAS JOSEPH, lawyer; b. Kansas City, Kans., Jan. 31, 1940; s. Edward J. and Mary (McCallum) C.; m. Barbara Helen Marciniak, Aug. 1, 1964; children: Catherine, Jennifer. AB, U. Detroit, 1963, JD, 1968. Bar: Mich. 1969, U.S. Dist. Ct. (so. and ea. dists.) Mich. 1969, U.S. Ct. Appeals (6th cir.) 1969. Sr. ptnr. Connelly, Reilly & Groth, Walled Lake, Mich., 1975—. Exec. bd. dirs. Oakland County (Mich.) Reps., 1979-82. Mem. Mich. Bar Assn. (rep. assembly 1978-87), Oakland County Bar Assn., Mich. Arabian Horse Assn. (pres. 1986—). Roman Catholic. Local government, Personal injury, Real property. Home: 1635 S Garner Rd Milford MI 48042 Office: Connelly Crowley & Groth 2410 S Commerce Walled Lake MI 48088

CONNER, FRED L., lawyer; b. Hutchinson, Kans., Nov. 30, 1909; s. Hugh and Ida (Guldner) C.; m. Helen Opie, Sept. 15, 1940; 1 son, Brian. J.D. U. Kans. 1934. Bar: Kans. 1934. Assoc. Andrew F. Schoeppel, Ness City, Kans., 1934-37; sole practice Great Bend, Kans., 1937-38; ptnr. Conner, Opie & Friedeman and predecessors, Great Bend, 1938—; dir. Insured Titles, Inc. Mem. Faculty Philmont Scout Ranch, 1956; mem. Kans. Jud. Council Com. to Redistrict Dist. Cts. of Kans., 1968. Served to lt. comdr. USN, 1942-45. Fellow Am. Coll. Probate Counsel; mem. ABA, Kans. Bar Assn. (pres. 1980-81), S.W. Kans. Bar Assn., Barton County Bar Assn., Phi Delta Phi. Republican. Methodist. Clubs: Rotary (pres. Great Bend 1948), Masons. Probate, Real property, General practice. Home: 3611-21st St Great Bend KS 67530 Office: 2015 Forest Ave 102 Great Bend KS 67530

CONNER, GEORGE MANION, III, lawyer; b. Tyler, Tex., Dec. 9, 1949; s. George Manion and Louise (Norman) C.; m. Elaine Uzzel, Jan. 5, 1973; children—Bonnie Elaine, Elizabeth Ann. A.B.A., Tyler Jr. Coll., 1970; B.A., U. Tex., 1972; J.D., Tex. Tech U., 1975. Bar: Tex. 1975, U.S. Dist. Ct. (ea. dist.) Tex. 1978, U.S. Ct. Appeals (5th cir.) 1981. Asst. dist. atty. Smith County, Tyler, 1976-78; assoc. to ptnr Lawrence & Lawrence, Tyler, 1978-84; sole practice, Tyler, 1984—. Served to 2d lt. U.S. Army, 1975. Mem. Tex. Bar Assn. (cert. specialist in family law), Smith County Bar Assn., Coll. of State Bar Tex. Methodist. Lodge: Lions (pres. Tyler Evening 1982-83). Family and matrimonial, Bankruptcy, State civil litigation. Home: 2600 Boldt Tyler TX 75701 Office: 909 ESE Loop 323 Suite 210 Tyler TX 75701

CONNER, LESLIE LYNN, JR., lawyer; b. Oklahoma City, July 15, 1939; s. Leslie Lynn and Grace Dorothy (Hartnell) C.; m. Nancy Newblock, Sept. 9, 1960; children: Deborah Lynn, Lauren Elaine, Thomas Hartnell. BA, Okla. U., 1961, LLB, 1963. Bar: Okla. 1963, U.S. Dist. Ct. (we. dist.) Okla. 1963, U.S. Ct. Appeals (10th cir.) 1963, U.S. Dist. Ct. (no. dist.) Okla. 1967, U.S. Supreme Ct. Ptnr. Ungerman, Conner & Little, Oklahoma City, 1966—; bd. dirs. First State Bank, Jones, Okla. Trustee Heritage Hall Sch., Oklahoma City, 1977-83, sec. bd. trustees, 1977-78, pres. bd. trustees, 1979-82; trustee, chmn. various coms., mem. choir United Meth. Ch., Nichols Hills, Okla., 1978—. Served to capt. USAF, 1963-66, lt. col. res. ret. Fellow Am. Coll. Probate Council; mem. ABA (ho. of dels. 1978-81), Okla. Bar Assn. (bd. of govs. 1977-81, pres. 1980, chmn. various coms.), Okla. Trial Lawyers Assn., Comml. Law League Am., Okla. County Bar Assn. (Outstanding Service award 1974). Democrat. Methodist. Avocations: reading fiction, woodworking. Bankruptcy, Probate, Real property. Home: 19 Oakdale Farm Rd Edmond OK 73013 Office: Ungerman Conner & Little 623 W California Oklahoma City OK 73102

CONNER, RICHARD ELWOOD, lawyer; b. Grand Rapids, Mich., Mar. 15, 1924; s. Richard Elwood and Marian (Devoe) C.; m. Jeanne Rizzo, Apr. 14, 1977. BS, U. Wis., 1949, JD, 1950; MS, Nova U., 1978, D. of Pub. Adminstrn., 1985. Bar: Wis. 1950, Fla. 1956, U.S. Dist. Ct. (so. dist.) Fla. 1959, U.S. Dist. Ct. (no. dist.) Fla. 1961, U.S. Supreme Ct. 1961, U.S. Ct. Appeals (5th and 11th cirs.) 1981. Sole practice New Smyrna Beach and Ft. Lauderdale, Fla., 1958-74, Plantation, Fla., 1979—; commr. City of New Smyrna Beach, Fla., 1960-64; asst. solicitor Broward County, Fla., 1969, asst. pub. defender, 1971-74, dir. property div., 1974-79; asst. atty. City of Pompano Beach, Fla., 1973-74; gen. counsel Hollywood (Fla.) Housing Authority, 1980—; contract atty. State of Fla. Dept. Health and Rehab., 1986—. Author: Juvenile Diversion, 1985 (DPA award, 1985). Served with U.S. Air Corps, 1942-45, ETO; USAF, 1951-55, USAFR, 1955-64, ret. Decorated DFC, Purple Heart, Air Medal with 14 oak leaf clusters. Mem. Fla. Bar Assn., Internat. Right of Way Assn., Attys. Title Ins. Fund. Democrat. Lodges: Masons, Shriners, Elks. Real property, State civil litigation, Probate. Office: 410 NW 74th Ave Plantation FL 33317

CONNER, TIMOTHY JAMES, lawyer; b. Panama City, Fla., Jan. 7, 1954; s. James F. Conner and Margie (Scott) Roberts; m. Bonnie A. Berns, June 24, 1983; children: Jessica, Harris, Monica. BA in Polit. Sci., Fla. Tech. U., 1977; JD, U. Fla., 1980. Bar: Fla. 1981, U.S. Dist. Ct. (mid. dist.) Fla. 1982. Legal asst. David M. Lipman, Miami, Fla., 1980-82; staff atty. Cen. Fla. Legal Services, Palatka, 1982-83, mng. atty., 1983-86; ptnr. Berns & Conner, Palm Coast, Fla., 1986—. Pres. Fla. Low Income Housing Coalition, Inc., Tallahassee, 1982-86. Mem. ABA, St. John's County Bar Assn., Putnam County Bar Assn., Flagler County Bar Assn., Assn. Trial Lawyers Am. Democrat. Avocations: electronics, boating, motorcycles, woodworking. General corporate, General practice, Real property. Home: PO Box 208 Flagler Beach FL 32036 Office: Berns & Conner PO Box 2530 Palm Coast FL 32037

CONNER, WARREN WESLEY, lawyer, title insurance executive; b. Cat Spring, Tex., Aug. 14, 1932; s. George William and Frieda Johanna (Kollatschny) C.; m. Suzanne Rosser, Oct. 29, 1955; children—Connie Suzanne, Cathy Lorrane; m. 2d, Sharon Ann Welch, July 28, 1978. B.B.A., So. Meth. U., 1959; J.D., 1963. Bar: Tex. 1963, U.S. Dist. Ct. (so. dist.) Tex. 1971. Ptnr., Sheehan & Conner, Friona, Tex., 1963-65; founder, ptnr. Conner, Odom and Clover, P.C., Sealy, Tex., 1965—; pres. Sealy Title Co.; dir. Citizens State Bank, Sealy, Industry Telephone Co. City atty., Sealy. Served with U.S. Army, 1953-55. Mem. State Bar Tex., Austin County Bar Assn. (past pres.). Presbyterian. Clubs: Safari, Mason, Shriners (past pres.), Rotary (past pres.). Banking, Family and matrimonial, Probate. Office: PO Box 570 Sealy TX 77474

CONNER, WILLIAM CURTIS, judge; b. Wichita Falls, Tex., Mar. 27, 1920; s. D.H. and Mae (Weeks) C.; m. Janice Files, Mar. 22, 1944; children: William Curtis, Stephen, Christopher, Molly. B.B.A., U. Tex., 1941, LL.B., 1942; postgrad., Harvard, 1942-43, Mass. Inst. Tech., 1943. Bar: Tex. bar 1942, N.Y. State bar 1949. Asso., mem. firm Curtis, Morris & Safford (and predecessor firm), N.Y.C., 1946-73; judge U.S. Dist. Ct., So. dist. N.Y., 1973—. Editor Tex. Law Rev. Served to lt. USNR, 1942-45, PTO. Recipient Jefferson medal N.J. Patent Law Assn. Mem. Am. Judicature Soc., N.Y. Patent Law Assn. (pres. 1972-73). Presbyterian (elder). Club: St. Andrews Golf. Patent, Trademark and copyright. Office: US Dist Ct US Courthouse Room 608 Foley Sq New York NY 10007 *

CONNER, WILLIAM HERBERT, lawyer; b. Columbus, Ohio, Jan. 29, 1940; s. Herbert Lee and Beulah Doris (Hammond) C.; m. Julie Ann Katzan, Aug. 13, 1966; children: W. David, Kristen Ann. Student, Purdue U.; AB, Miami U., Oxford, Ohio; JD cum laude, U. Mich. Bar: Ohio 1967, U.S. Dist. Ct. (no. dist.) Ohio. Assoc. Squire, Sanders & Dempsey, Cleve., 1967-77, ptnr., 1977—. Contbr. articles ot profl. jours. Mem. ABA (mem. tax exempt financing com. 1980—), Ohio Bar Assn. (chmn. taxation com. 1981-84), Cleve. Bar Assn. (chmn. gen. tax com. 1983-84). Republican. Methodist. Tax-exempt financing. Home: 3139 Falmouth Rd Shaker Heights OH 44122 Office: Squire Sanders & Dempsey 1800 Huntington Bldg Cleveland OH 44115

CONNER, WILLIAM ROBY, lawyer, judge; b. Gallup, N.Mex., Aug. 14, 1948; s. Roby Douglas and Mary Alline (Williams) C.; m. Susan McDevitt (div.); m. Susan Michelle Pfeiffer, Nov. 21, 1980. B.S., N.Mex. State U., 1971, M.S., 1973; J.D., Baylor U., 1976. Bar: N.Mex. 1977, Tex. 1977, U.S. dist. ct. N.Mex. 1978, U.S. ct. appeals (10th cir.) 1978. Asst. city atty. City of Albuquerque, 1977-82; sole practice, Rio Rancho, N.Mex., 1982-86; ptnr. Wheeler & Conner, 1986—; mcpl. judge City of Rio Rancho, 1980—; probate judge Sandoval County, N.Mex., 1987—. Active Rio Rancho Democratic Club, Friends of Vets., Albuquerque; bd. dirs. Safer N.Mex. Now, 1987—. Mem. N.Mex. Judge's Assn. (bd. dirs. 1985—), Rio Rancho C. of C. Lodges: Elks (exalted ruler 1984-85), Kiwanis. Probate, Real property, General corporate. Home: 95 Summer Winds Rio Rancho NM 87124 Office: 4011 Barbara Loop Suite 203 Rio Rancho NM 87124

CONNOLLY, GEORGE CHARLES, JR., civil district judge; b. New Orleans, La., July 20, 1928; s. George Charles and Clare (Walsh) C.; m. Elinor C. Van Geffen, Apr. 19, 1958. BA, Loyola U.-New Orleans, 1947, JD, 1950, BBA, 1952. Bar: La. 1950, U.S. Dist. Ct. (ea. dist.) La. 1952, U.S. Supreme Ct. 1968. Pvt. practice, New Orleans, 1950-70; commr. and judge ad hoc Civil Dist. Ct., Parish of Orleans, 1960-70, judge, 1970—; chief judge Civil Dist. Ct., 1981-82; judge pro tem U.S. Ct. Appeals (4th cir.), 1973. Pres. Met. Safety Council, New Orleans, 1981-82; Cystic Fibrosis Found. New Orleans, 1975-76. Served to col. USNG, 1948-84. Recipient Disting. Service award New Orleans Jaycees, 1962-63, Exceptional Service and Meritorious Service medal Selective Service System. Mem. 4th & 5th Cir. Judges Assn. (pres. 1980), Young Men's Bus. Club (pres. 1961-62, hon. life mem.), Loyola U. Law Alumni (pres. 1968-69), New Orleans Bar Assn. (hon. mem.), Blue Key Nat. Hon. Soc. (hon. mem.), La. Bar Assn. (hon. mem.). Democrat. Roman Catholic. Clubs: La. Nat. Guard Officers (New Orleans) (pres. 1957-68), Tulane-Newman Alumni (New Orleans) (pres. 1956-57-58). State civil litigation, Personal injury, Probate. Office: Civil Dist Ct Div J 421 Loyola Ave New Orleans LA 70112

CONNOLLY, GERALD EDWARD, lawyer; b. Boston, Oct. 13, 1943; s. Thomas E. and Grace J. (Fitzgerald) C.; m. Elizabeth Heidi Eckert, Jan. 6, 1968; children: Matthew F., Dennis F., David D., Edward F. BS, Coll. of Holy Cross, 1965; JD, U. Va., 1972. Bar: Wis. 1972, U.S. Tax Ct. 1973. From assoc. to ptnr. Whyte & Hirschboeck S.C., Milw., 1972-78; ptnr. Minahan & Peterson S.C., Milw., 1978—; v.p. Reinhart Instl. Foods, Inc.; bd. dirs. Alpha Cellulose Corp., Lumberton, N.C., Hatco Corp., Milw., Infratrol Mfg. Corp., Milw., Sunlite Plastics, Inc., Milw.; bd. dirs., sec. Rainbow Foods, Inc., Hopkins, Minn., Gateway Foods, Inc., LaCrosse, Wis., Lake Markets, Inc., Mpls.; sec. Hometown Inc., Milw. Served to lt. USN, 1966-69. Mem. ABA, Order of Coif. Clubs: University, Milw. General corporate, Real property, Corporate taxation. Home: 860 E Ravine Ln Bayside WI 53217 Office: Minahan & Peterson SC 411 E Wisconsin Ave Suite 2200 Milwaukee WI 53202-4499

CONNOLLY, JOSEPH THOMAS, lawyer, judge; b. Montclair, N.J., Mar. 22, 1938; s. Patrick Joseph and Ethelyn Marie (Dilkes) C.; m. Phyllis Jane Marturano, June 25, 1966; children—James V., Michael J., Victoria L. B.S., St. Peter's Coll., Jersey City, 1959; J.D., Fordham U., 1966. Bar: N.J. 1967, U.S. Dist. Ct. N.J. 1967, U.S. Supreme Ct. 1972. Claim adjuster Md. Am. Gen. Group, East Orange, N.J., 1962-66; jud. clk. Superior Ct. N.J., Newark, 1966-67; assoc. Feuerstein & Sachs, Newark, 1967-68, Donohue & Donohue, Nutley, N.J., 1969-71; trial lawyer Office Pub. Defender N.J., Newark, 1968-69; ptnr. Brown, Connolly & Karosen, Bloomfield, N.J., 1971—; judge Mcpl. Ct., Glen Ridge, N.J., 1980—; instr. William Paterson Coll., Wayne, N.J., 1980; lectr. Inst. for Continuing Legal Edn., Trenton and Newark, 1975—; moot ct. judge Seton Hall U. Sch. Law, Newark, 1980—. Pres. Glen Ridge Community Fund, 1978-79, Bloomfield Jaycees, 1971-72. Served with U.S. Army, 1959-60. Mem. ABA, N.J. Bar Assn. (consultor 1979-84), Essex County Bar Assn. Republican. Roman Catholic. Clubs: Bloomfield Lawyers (pres. 1976-77, Outstanding Service award 1977); Glen Ridge Country. Lodge: Kiwanis (pres. 1979-80, sec., bd. dirs., Disting. Pres. award). General practice, Personal injury, Real property. Home: 13 Winsor Pl Glen Ridge NJ 07028 Office: Brown Connolly and Karosen 112 Broad St Bloomfield NJ 07003

CONNOLLY, L. WILLIAM, lawyer; b. Gary, Ind., June 14, 1923; s. Leo W. and Lauretta E. (Feely) C.; m. Suzanne M. Irving, Sept. 2, 1950; children—Thomas A., Charles D., Alicia M., James J., Charlene Susan, John J., Robert P. Student, Miss. State U., CUNY; Ph.B., Marquette U., 1948, J.D., 1951. Bar: Wis. 1952, U.S. Supreme Ct. 1967. With Am. Automobile Ins. Co., Milw., 1951-52; mem. Rummel & Connolly, Milw., 1952-55, Spence, Rummel & Connolly, Milw., 1955-59, Spence & Connolly, Milw., 1959-64; practice law Spence & Connolly, 1964—. Trustee Village of Thiensville, Wis., 1957-61. Served with AUS, 1943-46. Fellow Internat. Acad. Lex et Scienta; mem. ABA, Wis. Bar Assn., Milw. Bar Assn., Am. Arbitration Assn. (nat. panel arbitrator 1973—), Am. Judicature Soc., Delta Theta Phi. State civil litigation, Criminal. Home: 830 Wood Dr Oconomowoc WI 53066 Office: 3106 W 80th St Milwaukee WI 53222

CONNOLLY, ROBERT MICHAEL, lawyer; b. Honolulu, Aug. 3, 1955; s. Thomas Joseph and Mary Elizabeth (Donegan) C.; m. Theresa Thomas, May 27, 1978; children: Katrina Donegan, Kristen Rebecca, Kelley Kessel, Megan Elisabeth. BA magna cum laude, Dartmouth Coll., 1977; JD, Washington & Lee U., 1980. Bar: Ky. 1980, U.S. Dist. Ct. (we. dist.) Ky. 1981, U.S. Dist. Ct. (ea. dist.) Ky. 1982, U.S. Ct. Appeals (6th cir.) 1982. Assoc. Stites & Harbison, Louisville, 1980-86, ptnr., 1987—. Editor Kentucky Litigation Quarterly, 1985—. Deacon Highland Bapt. Ch., Louisville, 1985; chmn. bd. dirs. Young Life Kentuckiana, Louisville, 1986. Burks scholar Washington & Lee U., 1979-80. Mem. ABA (com. on products liability), Ky. Bar Assn., Def. Research Inst., Ky. Def. Counsel Assn. Democrat. Club: Dartmouth Ky. (v.p. Louisville 1984—). Avocation: handball. Personal injury, Construction, State civil litigation. Home: 1711 Edenside Ave Louisville KY 40204 Office: Stites & Harbison 600 W Main St Louisville KY 40202

CONNOLLY, THOMAS EDWARD, lawyer; b. Boston, Nov. 7, 1942; s. Thomas Francis and Catherine Elizabeth (Skehill) C.; A.B., St. John's Sem., Brighton, Mass., 1964; J.D., Boston Coll., 1969. Admitted to Mass. bar, 1969; assoc. Schneider & Reilly, Boston, 1969-73; ptnr. Schneider, Reilly, Zabin, Connolly & Costello, P.C., Boston, 1973-85, Connolly & Leavis, Boston, 1986—; instr. law Northeastern Law Sch., Boston, 1975-76. Mem. governing council Boston Coll. Law Sch. Alumni Council, 1980—. Mem. Am. Trial Lawyers Assn. (nat. gov. 1977-80), Mass. Acad. Trial Lawyers (gov. 1976—), Am. Bar Assn. (vice chmn. products liability sect. 1978—). Democrat. Roman Catholic. Club: Univ. (Boston). Personal injury, Construction. Home: 15 Vincent Rd Roslindale MA 02131 Office: Connolly & Leavis 168 Milk St Boston MA 02109

CONNOR, JOHN THOMAS, JR., lawyer; b. N.Y.C., June 16, 1941; s. John Thomas and Mary (O'Boyle) C.; B.A. cum laude, Williams Coll., 1963; J.D., Harvard U., 1967; m. Susan Scholle Connor, Dec. 18, 1965; children—Seanna, Marin, John. Admitted to N.Y. State bar, 1968, D.C. bar, 1980; assoc. firm Cravath, Swaine & Moore, N.Y.C., 1967-71; dep. dir. Office Econ. Policy and Case Analysis, Pay Bd., Washington, 1971-72; dep. dir. Bur. E.-W. Trade, U.S. Dept. Commerce, Washington, 1972-73; sr. v.p. U.S.-USSR Trade and Econ. Council, Moscow, 1973-76; assoc. firm Milbank, Tweed, Hadley & McCloy, N.Y.C., 1976-79; ptnr. firm Curtis, Mallet-Prevost, Colt and Mosle, Washington, 1980-82; v.p., gen. counsel PHH Group, Inc., 1982—; dir. Micros Systems, Inc. Exec. dir. Democratic party N.J., 1969-70; trustee Council for Religion in Ind. Schs. Fulbright tutor Ferguson Coll., Poona, India, 1963-64. Mem. ABA, N.Y. State Bar Assn., D.C. Bar Assn., Council Fgn. Relations, Phi Beta Kappa. Clubs: Met. (Washington); Union (N.Y.C.); Chevy Chase (Md.). Home: 12 Primrose St Chevy Chase MD 20815 Office: PHH Group Inc 11333 McCormick Rd Hunt Valley MD 21031

CONNOR, TERENCE GREGORY, lawyer; b. Chelsea, Mass., Dec. 28, 1942; s. Joseph Gerard Sr. and Rosalie Cecilia (Ryan) C.; m. Julie Kaye Berry, Dec. 18, 1971; children: Cormac, Kristin, Etain, Brendan. AB, Georgetown U., 1964; LLB, Seton Hall U., 1967; LLM, Georgetown U., 1975. Bar: D.C. 1968, U.S. Supreme Ct. 1976, Fla. 1980. Trial atty. U.S. Dept. Justice, Washington, 1973-76; labor counsel Nat. Airlines Inc., Miami, Fla., 1976-79; practicing atty. Morgan, Lewis & Bockius, Miami, 1979—. Chmn. Miami: Dade citizen com. for Observance Bicentennial of U.S. Constitution, 1986. Served to capt. JAG, USAF, 1968-73. Mem. Fla. Bar Assn. (exec. council labor sect. 1986—). Roman Catholic. Labor, Civil rights, Federal civil litigation. Home: 1517 San Rafael Ave Coral Gables FL 33134 Office: Morgan Lewis & Bockius 200 S Biscayne Blvd 5300 Southeast Fin Ctr Miami FL 33131-2339

CONNORS, EUGENE KENNETH, lawyer; b. Dobbs Ferry, N.Y., Oct. 3, 1946; s. Edward Micheal and Eileen (Burke) C.; m. Mary Therese Hannan, Nov. 23, 1968; children: Kevin Patrick, Kathryn Margaret. B.A., Holy Cross Coll., 1968; J.D., Columbia U., 1971. Bar: Pa. 1971. Assoc. Reed Smith Shaw & McClay, Pitts., 1971-76, ptnr., 1977—; adj. prof. St. Francis Coll., Loretto, Pa., 1975—; bd. dirs. Green Garden Industries, Inc. Bd. dirs. Sch. Vol. Assn. Pitts., 1973—. Mem. ABA, Pa. Bar Assn., Allegheny County Bar Assn. Persuader U.S. Supreme Ct. to overturn employment discrimination decision adverse to employers, 1979. Labor, Federal civil litigation, State civil litigation. Office: Reed Smith Shaw & McClay 435 6th Ave PO Box 2009 Pittsburgh PA 15230

CONNORS, JAMES PATRICK, lawyer; b. N.Y.C., May 28, 1952; s. Joseph Patrick Connors and Edna Theresa Fitzgerald; m. Gloria Ann Ciccarelli, Jan. 12, 1974; children: Nicholas, Patrick. BA, Herbert H. Lehman Coll., 1974; JD, NYU, 1977, LLM, 1985. Bar: N.Y. 1978, U.S. Dist. Ct. (so. and ea. dists.) N.Y. 1978. Assoc. Bower & Gardner, N.Y.C., 1978-80, Joseph W. Conklin, N.Y.C., 1980-82; ptnr. Jones, Hirsch, Connors & Bull, N.Y.C., 1982—; lectr. NYU Sch. Medicine, 1983, N.Y. Law Jour., 1984, Bellevue Hosp., 1984, Hillcrest Gen. Hosp., 1984, Mt. Sinai Hosp., 1985, Am. Coll. Opthamologists, 1986. Contbr. articles to profl. jours. Recipient Am. Jurisprudence award Lawyers Pub. Coop., 1977. Mem. ABA, N.Y. State Bar Assn., N.Y. County Bar Assn., Def. Assn. of N.Y. State civil litigation, Personal injury, Insurance. Home: 85 Mayflower Dr Yonkers NY 10710

CONNORS, JOSEPH ALOYSIUS, III, lawyer; b. Washington, June 24, 1946; s. Joseph Aloysius Jr. and Charlotte Rita (Fox) C.; m. Mary Louise Bucklin, June 14, 1969; children: John Patrick, Joseph Aloysius IV. BBA, U. Southwestern La., 1970; JD, U. Tex., 1973. Bar: Tex. 1973, U.S. Dist. Ct. (so. dist.) Tex. 1975, U.S. Supreme Ct. 1976, U.S. Ct. Appeals (5th cir.) 1976, U.S. Dist. Ct. (ea., we. and no. dists.) Tex. 1981, U.S. Ct. Appeals (11th cir.) 1981, U.S. Ct. Appeals (3d, 4th, 6th, 7th, 8th, 9th, 10th and D.C. cirs.) 1986. Law clk. to assoc. justice Tex. Ct. Civil Appeals, Amarillo, 1973-74; assoc. Rankin & Kern, McAllen, Tex., 1974-76; asst. criminal dist. atty. Hidalgo County, Tex., 1976-78; sole practice McAllen, 1978—; faculty mem. Criminal Trial Advocacy Inst., Huntsville, Tex., 1981-84; speaker State Bar of Tex. seminars, 1980-81, 84. Contbg. editor Criminal Trial Manual, Tex., 1984—; contbr. articles to legal pubs. Served with USMCR, 1966-71. Mem. Hidalgo County Bar Assn. (bd. dirs. 1981-83), Nat. Assn. Criminal Def. Lawyers, Tex. Assn. Criminal Def. Lawyers (bd. dirs. 1982—, award of excellence 1983, 84), Am. Soc. Writers on Legal Subjects, Tex. Bd. Legal Specialization (cert.). Democrat. Roman Catholic. Criminal. Home: 106 W Fern McAllen TX 78501 Office: 804 Pecan St PO Box 5838 McAllen TX 78502-5838

CONOUR, WILLIAM FREDERICK, lawyer; b. Indpls., June 21, 1947; s. William E. and Marian L. (Smith) C.; m. Melanie Christine Linn; children: Tonja, Andrea, Erin, Rachel. AB in History, Ind. U., 1970, JD cum laude, 1974. Bar: Ind. 1974, U.S. Dist. Ct. (so. dist.) Ind. 1974, U.S. Ct. Appeals (7th cir.) 1975, U.S. Supreme Ct. 1982. Dir. training Ind. Pros. Attys. Council, Indpls., 1974-82; ptnr. Conour & Davis, Indpls., 1974-86; sole

practice Offices of William F. Conour, Indpls., 1986—; assoc. faculty Ind. U. Purdue U. Indpls. Sch. Pub. and Environ. Affairs; lectr. Ind. Law Enforcement Acad.; research analyst Ind. Criminal Law Study Commn., 1973-74. Contbg. author Indiana Criminal Procedure Sourcebook, 1974, Indiana Prosecuting Attorney's Deskbook; editor profl. bulletins; contbr. articles to profl. jours. Guarantor Butler U. Clowes Hall; patron Ind. Repertory Theatre, Indpls. Symphony Orch.; mem. chmn.'s club Marion County Dems., Phoenix Gold club Ind. Dems., Conner Prairie Pioneer Settlement. Recipient commendation Drug Enforcement Adminstrn. U.S. Dept. Justice, 1977. Mem. ABA (litigation sect.), Ind. Bar Assn. (sec. criminal justice sect. 1977-78, treas. criminal justice sect. 1981-82, ad hoc com. on legal cert.), Indpls. Bar Assn. (grievance com. 1983—, litigation sect.), Assn. Trial Lawyers Am. (cert. Nat. Coll. Advocacy 1979, Advanced Coll. Advocacy 1981), Ind. Trial Lawyers Assn., Ind. Lawyers Commn. (ad hoc com. on criminal justice goals and standards), Woodburn Guild, Ind. U. Alumni Assn., Phi Delta Phi. Democrat. Clubs: Inpls. Athletic; Ind. Soc. Chgo., Atla "M". Federal civil litigation, State civil litigation. Home: 114 Heady Ln Noblesville IN 46060 Office: One Indiana Sq Suite 1725 Indianapolis IN 46204

CONOVER, RICHARD CORRILL, lawyer; b. Bridgeport, Nebr., Jan. 12, 1942; s. John Cedric and Mildred (Dunn) C.; m. Cathy Harlan, Dec. 19, 1970; children—William Cedric, Theodore Cyril. B.S., U. Nebr., Lincoln, 1965, M.S., 1966; J.D., Cornell U., 1969. Bar: N.Y. 1970, Mont. 1982, U.S. Dist. Ct. (so. and ea. dists.) N.Y. 1971, U.S. Supreme Ct. 1977, U.S. Ct. Customs and Patent Appeals 1979, U.S. Ct. Claims 1980. Assoc. Brumbaugh, Graves, Donohue & Raymond, N.Y.C., 1969-73; assoc. Townley, Updike, Carter & Rodgers, N.Y.C., 1974-75; assoc. gen. csl. legal office Automatic Data Processing, Inc., Clifton, N.J., 1975-77; assoc. Nims, Howes, Collison & Isner, N.Y.C., 1977-81; sole practice, Mont., 1981—; lectr. indsl. and mech. engring. dept. Mont. State U. Mem. Mont. Gov.'s Bd. Sci. and Tech., 1985—. Mem. ABA (bd. of gov.'s on sci. and tech. 1985—), Assn. Bar City N.Y., Mont. Bar Assn., Am. Pat. Law Assn. Patent, Trademark and copyright, General practice. Home: PO Box 1329 Bozeman MT 59715 Office: 404 1st Nat Bank Bldg PO Box 1329 Bozeman MT 59715

CONRAD, JOHN REGIS, lawyer; b. Bloomington, Ind., Feb. 23, 1955; s. John Francis and Patricia Ann (English) C.; m. Paula Jane Vessels, July 4, 1980; children: William Celestine Vessels, John Paul Vessels. AB cum laude, Harvard U., 1977; MBA, JD, Ind. U., 1981. Bar: Hawaii 1981, U.S. Dist. Ct. Hawaii 1981, U.S. Ct. Claims 1981, U.S. Tax Ct. 1981, U.S. Ct. Appeals (9th cir.) 1981. Assoc. Cades, Schutte, Fleming & Wright, Honolulu, 1981-85, Thompson & Chan, Honolulu, 1985—; lectr. Kapiolani Community Coll., Honolulu, 1984-86. Author: Hawaii Probate Sourcebook, 1985, rev. ed. 1986; co-author: Beyond the Basics: Hawaii Estate Planning & Probate, 1985, Hawaii Wills & Trusts Sourcebook, 1986. Mem. planned giving com. Hawaii Heart Assn., Honolulu, 1983-86. Mem. Hawaii Bar Assn. (chmn. estate and gift tax com. 1984-85), Hawaii Estate Planning Council, Hawaii Bar Found. (bd. dirs. 1985—). Roman Catholic. Avocations: running, geneology. Probate, General corporate, Securities. Home: 60 N Beretania St #1710 Honolulu HI 96817 Office: Thompson & Chan 119 Merchant St #300 Honolulu HI 96813

CONRAD, PAUL EDWARD, lawyer; b. Milw., June 23, 1956; s. Clarence Walter and Joan Therese (Gill) C.; m. Susan Joyce Shedd, June 7, 1980; children: Angela Susan, Conrad. BS in Edn. with distinction, U. Wis., 1978, JD, 1981. Bar: Wis. 1981, U.S Dist. Ct. (we. dist.) Wis. 1981, U.S. Ct. Mil. Appeals 1981, U.S. Army Ct. Mil. Rev. 1983. Gen. counsel, asst. sec. Wis. Housing and Econ. Devel. Authority, Madison, 1985-86; assoc. Brynelson, Herrick, Bucaida, Dorschel & Armstong, Madison, 1986—. Served to capt. JAGC, U.S Army, 1981-85. Recipient Nat. Def. Transp., Am. Minutemen Assn. award, 1978. Mem. ABA, Wis. Bar Assn., Iron Cross Soc., Phi Kappa Phi, Sigma Eta Phi, Phi Alpha Delta (Sgt.-at-Arms 1982-83). Democrat. Roman Catholic. Lodge: KC (Inner Guard 1976-77, adv. 1980-81). Avocations: travel, camping, fishing, history, woodworking. Military, State civil litigation, Real property. Home: 3301 Heatherdell Ln Madison WI 53713

CONRAD, WINTHROP BROWN, JR., lawyer; b. Detroit, May 26, 1945; s. Winthrop Brown and Dolores (Millard) C.; m. Ellen Rouse, May 12, 1973; children: Parker Rouse, Louisa Katherine, Frances Winthrop. AB, Yale U., 1967; JD, Harvard U., 1971. Bar: N.Y. 1972, U.S. Dist. Ct. (so. dist.) N.Y. 1975, U.S. Ct. Appeals (2d cir.) 1975. Ptnr. Davis, Polk & Wardwell, N.Y.C., 1979-85, Paris, 1985—. Bd. dirs. Found. for Joffrey Ballet, N.Y.C., 1985—. General corporate, Contracts commercial, Securities. Home: 6 Ave Emile Deschanel, Paris France 75007 Office: Davis Polk Wardwell, 4 Place de la Concorde, Paris France

CONRAN, JOSEPH PALMER, lawyer; b. St. Louis, Oct. 4, 1945; s. Palmer and Theresa (Bussmann) C.; m. Daria D. Conran, June 8, 1968; children: Andrew, Lisabeth, Theresa. BA, St. Louis U., 1967, JD with honors, 1970. Bar: Mo. 1970, U.S. Ct. Mil. Appeals 1971, U.S. Ct. Appeals (8th cir.) 1974. Assoc. Husch, Eppenberger, Donohue, Elson & Cornfeld, St. Louis, 1974-78, ptnr., 1978—; mem. faculty Trial Practice Inst. Served to capt., JAGC, USAF, 1970-74. Mem. Bar Assn. Met. St. Louis recipient Merit award 1976,77). Roman Catholic. Club: Mo. Athletic (pres. 1986-87). Federal civil litigation, State civil litigation, Antitrust. Home: 2306 E Royal Ct Saint Louis MO 63131 Office: 100 N Broadway #1800 Saint Louis MO 63102

CONROY, JOHN THOMAS, lawyer; b. Columbus, Ohio, Feb. 11, 1937; s. Thomas Joseph and Helen Agnes (Schwartz) C.; m. Rosemary Schirtzinger, Aug. 2, 1969; children: Krista, Sean, Anne. BS in Commerce, Ohio U., 1959; JD, Ohio No. U., 1962. Bar: Ohio 1962, U.S. Dist. Ct. (so. dist.) Ohio 1963, U.S. Supreme Ct. 1980. Atty. legal aid and defender's office State of Ohio, Columbus, 1963-71, asst. atty. gen., 1971-76; hearing officer State Personnel Bd. Rev., Columbus, 1976-77; sole practice Columbus, 1976—. Mem. cen. com. Franklin County Dems., Columbus, 1978—; chmn. Alliance for Coop. Justice, Columbus, 1983—. Mem. Ohio State Bar Assn., Columbus Bar Assn., Assn. Trial Lawyers Am., Ohio Trial Lawyers Assn. Democrat. Roman Catholic. Juvenile, Family and matrimonial, Probate. Office: 150 E Mound St Columbus OH 43215

CONROY, ROBERT J., lawyer; b. Newark, Feb. 17, 1953; s. Michael John and Frances (Goncalves) C.; m. Mary Catherine McGuire, June 7, 1975; children: Caitlin Michaela, Michael Colin. BS, St. Peter's Coll., 1977; M in Pub. Adminstrn., CUNY, 1981; JD, N.Y. Law Sch., 1981; MPH, Harvard U., 1985. Bar: N.Y. 1981, N.J. 1981, U.S. Dist. Ct. N.J. 1981, Calif. 1982, U.S. Dist. Ct. (so. and ea. dists.) N.Y. 1982, U.S. Ct. Appeals (2d and 3d cirs.) 1982, Fla. 1984, D.C. 1984, U.S. Supreme Ct. 1984. Asst. corp. counsel City of N.Y., 1981-83, dep. chief med. malpractice unit, 1983, chief med. malpractice unit, 1984; assoc. Jones, Hirsch, Connors & Bull, N.Y.C., 1985—; spl. counsel pro bono med. malpractice research project, City of N.Y., 1985—. Solomon scholar, N.Y. Law Sch., 1979. Mem. ABA (chmn. govt. mgmt. com. 1984-86, mgr. products media bd. 1985—, chmn. document retrieval com. 1985—, econs. of law practice sect.), N.J. Bar Assn., San Diego County Bar Assn., Assn. of Bar of City of N.Y., Am. Soc. Law and Medicine, Pi Alpha Alpha. Health, Personal injury, Medical legal affairs. Home: 69 Sandy Hill Rd Westfield NJ 07090 Office: Jones Hirsch Connors & Bull 101 E 52d St New York NY 10022

CONSTANT, JOSEPH, lawyer; b. N.Y.C., May 27, 1956; s. Irving and Selma (Yablonick) C.; m. Susan Handelman, Aug. 10, 1985. BA, Columbia U., 1978; JD, Tulane U., 1981. Bar: La. 1982, U.S. Dist. Ct. (ea. dist) La. 1982, Fla. 1983, U.S. Tax Ct. 1983, N.Y. 1985. Staff atty. La. State Law Inst., New Orleans, 1981-82; assoc. Rubin, Baum, Levin, Constant, Friedman & Bilzin, Miami, Fla., 1983-87, McCune, Hiaasen, Crum, Ferris & Gardner, Ft. Lauderdale, Fla., 1987—; teaching asst. legal edn. program Jr. High Sch. Treas. Dade County Young Dems., Miami, 1984, bd. dirs., 1985; mem. South Dade Dem. Club, Kendall, Fla., 1985—, bd. dirs., 1987. Mem. ABA, Am. Judicature Soc. Democrat. Jewish. Lodge: B'nai B'rith (teaching asst. jr. high sch. legal edn. program). Avocation: fencing. Real property, Probate. Office: McCane Hiaasen Crum Ferris & Gardner PA 1 E Broward Blvd Penthouse Fort Lauderdale FL 33302

CONSTANT, PATRICIA REED, lawyer; b. Chandler, Ariz., Mar. 14, 1949; d. Charles William and Patricia (Elliott) Reed; m. Anthony F. Constant, Oct. 12, 1976 (div. 1981); children—Rebecca Kay, Jennifer Leigh. B.A. summa cum laude, Tex. A&I U., 1976; J.D., U. Tex., 1979. Bar: Tex. 1979, U.S. Dist. Ct. (so. dist.) Tex. 1980, U.S. Ct. Appeals (5th cir.) 1984. Assoc. Wood & Burney, Corpus Christi, Tex., 1979-85, ptnr., 1985—. Bd. dirs. Beautify Corpus Christi Assn., 1981-85; mem. Corpus Christi Bldg. Standards Rev. Bd., 1984—. Mem. ABA, Tex. Bar Assn., Nueces County Bar Assn. (sec. 1980-81), Nueces County Young Lawyers Assn. (dir. 1982-84, pres. 1984-85). Democrat. Episcopalian. Bankruptcy, Federal civil litigation. Home: 3335 San Antonio Corpus Christi TX 78411 Office: Wood & Burney 1700 First City Tower II Corpus Christi TX 78478

CONTI, JOY FLOWERS, lawyer; b. Kane, Pa., Dec. 7, 1948; d Bernard A. Flowers and Elizabeth (Tingley) Rodgers; m. Anthony T. Conti, Jan. 16, 1971; children: Andrew, Michael, Gregory. BA, Duquesne U., 1970, JD summa cum laude, 1973. Bar: Pa. 1973, U.S. Dist. Ct. (we. dist.) Pa. 1973, U.S. Ct. Appeals (3d cir.) 1976. Law clk. Supreme Ct. Pa., Monessen, 1973-74; assoc. Kirkpatrick & Lockhart, Pitts., 1974-76, 1982-83, ptnr., 1983—; prof. law Duquense U., Pitts., 1976-82; hearing examiner Pa. Dept. State, Bur. Profl. Occupation and Affairs, 1978-82; chairperson search com. for judge of U.S. Bankruptcy Ct., Western dist. Pa., 1987. Contbr. articles to profl. jours. Mem. hearing com. Supreme Ct. Pa., 1982—; v.p. Com. for Justice Edn., Pitts., 1983-84. Named One of Ten Outstanding Young Women in Am., 1981; recipient Award of Achievement, Pa. Bar Assn., 1982, 87. Mem. ABA (ho. of dels. 1980-86), Pa. Bar Assn. (ho. of dels. 1978—, corp. banking & bus. law sect. council 1983—, chairperson civil rights and responsibilities com. 1986—), Allegheny County Bar Assn. (adminstrv. v.p. 1984-86, chairperson corp. banking and bus. law sect. 1987—). Club: Rivers (Pitts.). Democrat. Roman Catholic. General corporate, Bankruptcy, Contracts commercial. Home: 106 Barnwood Ln Pittsburgh PA 15237 Office: Kirkpatrick & Lockhart 1500 Oliver Bldg Pittsburgh PA 15222

CONTI, SAMUEL, judge; b. Los Angeles, July 16, 1922; s. Fred and Katie C.; m. Dolores Crosby, July 12, 1952; children: Richard, Robert, Cynthia. B.S., U. Santa Clara, 1945; LL.B., Stanford U., 1948, LL.D. Bar: Calif. 1948. Pvt. practice San Francisco and Contra Costa County, 1948-60; city atty. Concord, Calif., 1960-69; judge Superior Ct. Contra Costa County, 1968-70, U.S. Dist. Ct., No. Dist. Calif., San Francisco, 1970—. Mem. Bd. Edn. Pittsburg Unified Sch. Dist., 1952-58; mem. Sch. Redistricting Com. for Contra Costa County, 1956-58. Served with AUS, 1940-44. Mem. Central Contra Costa Bar Assn. (pres.), Concord C. of C. (pres.), Alpha Sigma Nu. Judicial administration. Office: US Dist Court House PO Box 36060 San Francisco CA 94102 *

CONTI, SARA ANGELA, lawyer; b. Miami, Fla., Mar. 2, 1950; d. Ferdinand Nicolas and Sara Elizabeth (Winfree) C.; children: David Michael Smith Jr., Savannah Ashley Smith, Samuel Lister Erwin, Martin Nesbitt Erwin Jr. AB, U. N.C., 1977; JD, Wake Forest U., 1981. Bar: N.C. 1981, U.S. Dist. Ct. (we., mid. and ea. dists.) N.C 1981. Assoc. Falk, Carruthers & Roth, Greensboro, N.C., 1981-84, Mount, White, Hutson & Carden, Durham, N.C., 1984—. Mem. Commn. on the Status of Women, Greensboro, 1975-77, vice chmn., 1977-78; bd. dirs. Young Dems., Guilford County, N.C., 1978. Mem. ABA (corp., banking and bus. sect. bus. bankruptcy subcom. 1986—), N.C. Bar Assn. (councilor bankruptcy sect. 1985—), Am. Bankruptcy Inst. (chmn. continuing legal edn. sect. 1986-87, editor N.C. Bankruptcy Practice Manual). Roman Catholic. Bankruptcy. Home: 420 Waterside Dr Carrboro NC 27510 Office: Mount White Hutson & Carden 201 N Roxboro PO Box 1371 Durham NC 27702

CONTIE, LEROY JOHN, JR., judge; b. Canton, Ohio, Apr. 2, 1920; s. Leroy John and Mary M. (DeSantis) C.; m. Janice M. Zollars, Nov. 28, 1953; children: Ann L., Leroy John III. B.A., U. Mich., 1941, J.D., 1948. Bar: Ohio 1948. Law dir. City of Canton, 1952-60; chmn. Canton City Charter Commn., 1963; mem. Stark County Bd. Elections, Canton, 1964-69; judge Common Pleas Ct., Stark County, 1969-71, U.S. Dist. Ct., No. Dist. Ohio, Cleve., 1971-82, U.S. Ct. Appeals (6th cir.), Cin., 1982—. Trustee Stark County Legal Aid Soc., Canton chpt. ARC; adv. bd. Walsh Coll., Canton, Ohio., U. Akron Law Coll. Served with AUS, 1942-46. Mem. Am., Ohio, Stark County, Summit County, Cuyahoga County, Akron bar assns., Am. Judicature Soc., U.S. Jr. C. of C. (internat. senator), Canton Jr. C. of C. (trustee), Stark County Hist. Soc., Stark County Wilderness Soc., Am. Legion, Sigma Phi Epsilon (Nat. citation award), Phi Alpha Delta., Omicron Delta Kappa. Roman Catholic. Clubs: K.C. (4 deg.), Elks. Judicial administration. Office: US Courthouse Akron OH 44308

CONTINO, RICHARD MARTIN, lawyer, business consultant, equipment leasing company executive; b. Richmond, Va., Mar. 31, 1940; s. Samuel and Theresa C . B.Aero. Engring., Rensselaer Poly. Inst., 1962; J.D., U. Md., 1965; LL.M., NYU, 1972. Bar: Md. 1965, D.C. 1965, N.Y. 1969. Assoc., Winthrop, Stimson, Putnam & Roberts, N.Y.C., 1969-72; assoc. Fried, Frank, Harris, Shriver & Jacobson, N.Y.C., 1972-74; eastern regional counsel Gatx Leasing Corp., N.Y.C., 1974-76, v.p. mktg., 1976-78; ptnr. Contino Ross & Benedict, N.Y.C., 1978-86; cons. equipment lease bus.; lectr. in field, 1987—; chmn., founder ELM Corp. 1986—. Served to capt. USAF, 1966-68. Mem. ABA, N.Y. State Bar Assn., Assn. Bar City N.Y. Author: Legal and Financial Aspects of Equipment Leasing Transactions, 1979. Home: 303 E 49th St New York NY 10017

CONWAY, ANDREW WAYNE, lawyer; b. Rochester, N.Y., Dec. 15, 1954; s. Cyril J. and Bernice Conway. BA in Econs., U. Rochester, 1977; JD, SUNY, Buffalo, 1981. Bar: N.Y. 1982, U.S. Dist. Ct. (we. dist.) N.Y. 1982, D.C. 1986. Acct. exec. EF Hutton, Rochester, 1982-85; sole practice Rochester, 1982-86; promoter, agt. ProSports Mgmt., Rochester, 1985—. Mem. ABA, N.Y. State Bar Assn., Sports Lawyers Assn., D.C. Bar Assn. Avocations: golf, skiing, hockey, music. Entertainment, contracts, General practice. Home: 16 Sturbridge Ln Pittsford NY 14534 Office: 508 Times Sq Bldg Rochester NY 14614

CONWAY, FRANK HARRISON, lawyer, government official; b. Providence, May 2, 1913; s. Frank Harrison and Margaret Mary (Cannon) C.; m. Jean Arthur Watt, Apr. 6, 1940; m. Elizabeth Hoppin Chafee, Feb. 7, 1973; stepchildren—Arthur, William, Sherrill, Henry. Ph.B., Providence Coll., 1935; J.D., Boston U., 1952; spl. student Harvard U. Law Sch., 1952-53. Bar: Mass. 1952, U.S. Dist. Ct. Mass. 1954, U.S. Supreme Ct. 1962. Mgmt. ofcl. New Eng. Tel.&Tel., Boston, 1935-77; pvt. practice law, Boston, 1977-80; mem. Jameson, Locke & Fullerton, Wellesley, Mass., 1980—; mem. Fgn. Claims Settlement Commn., Washington, 1981—; treas., dir. Young Orchard Co., Providence, 1975-81; trustee Young Orchard Trust. Mem. Mass. Republican State Com., 1974-80, treas., 1976-80; del. Nat. Rep. Conv., 1976, 80, 84, also mem. rules com.; mem. bd. Selectmen Wellesley, 1979-82. Served to maj. Signal Corps, U.S. Army, 1942-46. Mem. Norfolk Bar Assn., Boston Bar Assn., Mass. Bar Assn., ABA. Republican. Roman Catholic. Clubs: Harvard of Boston, Wellesley Country; University (Washington). Home: 37 Longmeadow Rd Wellesley MA 02181 Office: 8 Grove St Wellesley MA 02181

CONWAY, JOHN JOSEPH, lawyer; b. Denver, June 24, 1931; s. John M. and Nora V. (Barrett) C.; m. Margaret M. Perko, Dec. 30, 1950; children: John P., Kathleen V., Jean M., Michael J., Ann T., Christine L. BS in History, Regis Coll., 1954; JD, U. Denver, 1956. Bar: Colo. 1957, U.S. Dist. Ct. Colo. 1957, U.S. Supreme Ct. 1963, U.S. Ct. Appeals (10th cir.) 1967. Dep. clk. Denver Superior Ct., 1955-56; atty. U.S. Dept. Interior, Denver, 1956-60; asst. atty. gen. State of Colo., Denver, 1960-64; sole practice Denver, 1964—. Served to sgt. USAF, 1951-53. Named Alumnus of Yr. Regis Coll., 1984; recipient Alumni Service award Regis Coll. Alumni Council, 1986. Mem. ABA, Colo. Bar Assn., Denver Bar Assn. Republican. Roman Catholic. Clubs: North Denver Golf, Wheatridge Men's Garden. Avocations: playing and announcing sports, photography, reading. Administrative and regulatory, Public utilities, Transportation. Home: 4433 Wolff St Denver CO 80212 Office: 4704 Harlan St #500 Denver CO 80212

CONWAY, JOHN MARTIN, lawyer; b. Juneau, Alaska, Sept. 6, 1936; s. John Joseph and Gertrude Mary (McGrath) C.; m. Sally Marcia Pebbles, Aug. 26, 1961; children: Shannon, Lael, Maribeth, Molly. BA, U. Wash., 1958, JD, 1961. Bar: Alaska 1962, U.S. Dist. Ct. Alaska 1962. Sr. ptnr. Atkinson, Conway & Gagnon, Inc., Anchorage, 1962—; counsel to Gov. Alaska Impeachment Proceedings, 1985. Mem. adv. bd. Providence Hosp., Anchorage, 1972—; bd. dirs. Anchorage Symphony, 1968. Mem. ABA, Alaska Bar Assn., Anchorage Bar Assn., Alaska Bar Found. (trustee 1984—), Assn. Trial Lawyers Am., Am. Acad. Hosp. Attys., Maritime Law Assn. (proctor), Admiralty Bar Alaska (founder 1985—), Assn. Ski Def. Attys., Asia-Pacific Lawyers Assn. Lodge: Rotary (pres. Anchorage club 1979-80). Admiralty, Federal civil litigation, Insurance. Office: Atkinson Conway & Gagnon 420 L St Suite 500 Anchorage AK 99501

CONWAY, KEVIN GEORGE, lawyer; b. Teaneck, N.J., Aug. 24, 1948; s. William Joseph and Mildred Claire (Dunn) C.; m. Patricia Rose, Aug. 21, 1971; children: Ryan, Meredith, Colleen, Kaitlyn. BA in Polit. Sci. magna cum laude, Fairleigh Dickinson U., 1970; JD, Rutgers U., 1972; LLM in Taxation, NYU, 1979. Bar: N.J. 1972, U.S. Dist. Ct. N.J. 1972, U.S. Tax Ct. 1979. Assoc. Schiffman & Berger, Carlstadt, N.J., 1973-74; group atty., tax counsel Hoffmann LaRoche, Inc., Nutley, N.J., 1974-83; tax dir. Squibb Corp., Princeton, N.J., 1983-85; sr. v.p. law, fin. and adminstrn. Zenith Labs., Inc., Ramsey, N.J., 1985—. Pres. Community Assn. Northeast Ridgewood, N.J., 1982-83. Mem. ABA, N.J. Bar Assn., Tax Exec. Inst. Corporate taxation, General corporate. Home: 451 E Saddle River Rd Ridgewood NJ 07450 Office: Zenith Labs Inc 50 Williams Dr Ramsey NJ 07446

CONWAY, MARTIN EUGENE, JR., judge; b. Aledo, Ill., Aug. 1, 1942; s. Martin E. Conway and J. Marie Hess; m. Patricia R. Guccione, July 8, 1967; children: Sean Michael, Kelly Martin, William Colin. BA, U. Notre Dame, 1965, JD, 1966. Bar: Ill. 1966, U.S. Ct. Claims 1967, U.S. Tax Ct. 1967, U.S. Ct. Mil. Appeals 1967, U.S. Supreme Ct. 1971. Ptnr. Conway & Shoemaker, Aledo, 1970-83; sole practice Aledo, 1984-85; judge Ill. Circuit Ct. 14th Cir., 1985—; lectr. Ill. Farm Bur., 1984—. Atty. Villages of New Windsor, New Boston, and Joy, Ill., 1970-85; Rep. precinct committeeman, Mercer County, Ill., 1970-72; bd. dirs. YMCA, Aledo, 1975; sec. Mercer County Sheriff's Merit Commn., 1977-83. Served to capt. USMC, 1966-70, Vietnam. Decorated Bronze Star with combat V, 1969; recipient Vietnamese Cross of Galantry Republic of S. Vietnam, 1969. Fellow Ill. Bar Found.; mem. Ill Bar Assn. (chmn. family law sect. 1975, bd. dirs., sec. 1971-76, mem. gen. assembly 1976-82), Mercer County Bar Assn. (pres. 1977-78), Ill. Judge's Assn., Agrl. Law Assn. Roman Catholic. Lodge: Kiwanis (bd. dirs. 1984). Judicial administration, Family and matrimonial, Probate. Home: 905 SE 2d Ave Aledo IL 61231

CONWAY, RICHARD JAMES, JR., lawyer; b. Newark, Sept. 9, 1952; s. Richard J. Sr. and Miriam R. (Noll) C.; m. Velma E. Gebhard, May 22, 1976; 1 child, Megan G. BA with honors, Lehigh U., 1974; JD with honors, Rutgers U., 1979. Bar: N.J. 1979, U.S. Dist. Ct. N.J. 1979, U.S. Ct. Appeals (3d cir.) 1983. Law clk. to judges N.J. Superior Ct., Union and Mercer Counties, N.J., 1979-80; assoc. Hannoch Weisman P.C., Roseland, N.J., 1980-87, dir., 1987—. Mem. ABA, N.J. Bar Assn., Essex County Bar Assn. General corporate, Real property, Environment. Home: 55 Connor Ave Metuchen NJ 08840 Office: Hannoch Weisman PC 4 Becker Farm Rd Roseland NJ 07068

CONWAY, ROBERT GEORGE, JR., judge advocate, military officer; b. Albany, N.Y., Apr. 26, 1951; s. Robert George Sr. and Kathryn Ann (Kelly) C.; m. Lynda Rae Christenson, Dec. 15, 1979. AB, Dartmouth Coll., 1973; JD, Union U., 1976; cert. judge advocate, U.S. Army JAG Sch., 1986. Bar: Pa. 1978, U.S. Ct. Mil. Appeals 1978, N.C. 1983, U.S. Dist. Ct. (ea. dist.) N.C. 1983, U.S. Army Ct. Mil. Rev. 1986, U.S. Supreme Ct. 1986. Commd. 2d lt. USMC, 1975, advanced through grades to maj., 1983; gen. staff sec. USMC, Camp Lejeune, N.C., 1982-83, chief rev. officer, 1983-84, spl. asst. U.S. atty., 1984-85; dir. joint law ctr. Marine Corps Air Sta., Cherry Point, N.C., 1986—. Trustee cath. student ctr. Aquinas House Dartmouth Coll., Hanover, N.H., 1973—. Mem. ABA, Pa. Bar Assn., N.C. Bar Assn., Fed. Bar Assn., Dartmouth Lawyers Assn. Roman Catholic. Lodge: K.C. (adv. 1984-85). Military, Criminal, Administrative and regulatory. Home: 2500 Northwoods Dr Jacksonville NC 28540-4565 Office: Marine Corps Air Sta Joint Law Center Cherry Point NC 28533-5000

CONWAY, SUSAN MARIE, judge; b. Salem, Mass., Sept. 24, 1946; d. Walter Arthur and Marie Isabell (Mullin) C.; m. Robert David Levy, July 13, 1976; 1 child, Jane Conway. BA, Columbia U., 1968; JD, Northeastern U., 1973. Bar: N.Mex. 1974, U.S. Dist. Ct. N.Mex. 1974, U.S. Ct. Appeals (10th cir.) 1984. VISTA atty. Albuquerque Legal Aid Soc., 1974-75; staff atty. N.Mex. Human Services, Albuquerque, 1975-77; sr. ptnr. Conway & Levy, Albuquerque, 1977-85; judge Family Ct. 2d Jud. Dist., Albuquerque, 1985—. Vice chmn. Albuquerque/Bernalillo City Child Abuse Council, 1984-85, N.Mex. Council on Crime and Delinquency, Albuquerque, 1984-85, state chmn., 1985—; bd. dirs. N.Mex. Children's Psychiatric Hosp., Albuquerque, 1981. Named Spl. Friend to Children North Am. Council on Adoptible Children, 1985. Mem. N.Mex. Bar Assn. (chmn. mediation and arbitration com. family law sect. 1984-85, alt. methods dispute resolution com. 1984-85), Am. Assn. Family and Conciliation Cts. Democrat. Club: Albuquerque Bus. and Profl. Women's. Avocations: cooking, gardening, reading, writing. Family and matrimonial, Jurisprudence, Judicial administration. Office: 2d Jud Dist Ct 415 Tijeras Ave NW Albuquerque NM 87102

CONWAY, WILLIAM AUGUSTINE, investment banking executive; b. Queens, N.Y., Apr. 10, 1948; s. William A. Jr. and C. Isabel Conway; m. Ann George Womack, Oct. 1972. BS, Georgetown U., 1970, JD, 1974. Bar: Va. 1975, D.C. 1979, Fla. 1983. Pres. DeRand Investment Corp. Am., Arlington, Va. and Washington, 1970—; adj. prof. law George Mason U., Arlington, 1978-83; chmn. Washington Law Affairs Com., 1983-85. Mem. ABA, Va. Bar Assn., D.C. Bar Assn., Fla. Bar Assn., Internat. Assn. Fin. Planners, Registry of Fin. Planners, Georgetown U. Alumni Club (bd. dirs. 1982—, nat. alumni bd. sch. law ctr. 1986—). Estate planning, Securities, Personal income taxation. Office: DeRand Investment Corp 2201 Wilson Blvd 3d Floor Arlington VA 22201

CONWELL, GARY L., lawyer; b. Manhattan, Kans., Dec. 9, 1954; s. Jerry S. Conwell and Betty A. (Johnson) Webb; m. Debra C. Lintz, June 7, 1980; children: Matthew T. Student, Kans. State U., 1973-74; BA, Washburn U., 1978, JD, 1981. Bar: Kans. 1982, U.S. Dist. Ct. Kans. 1982. Asst. dist. atty. Shawnee County, Topeka, 1981-84; asst. city atty. City of Topeka, 1984-86; assoc. Ochs and Kelly, P.A., Topeka, 1986—. Bd. dirs. Community Youth Homes, Inc., Topeka, 1981—. Mem. ABA, Kans. Bar Assn., Kans. Trial Lawyers Assn., Topeka Bar Assn., Phi Alpha Delta. Republican. Roman Catholic. Lodge: K.C. Avocations: sports, books. Office: Ochs and Kelly PA PO Box 67026 Topeka KS 66667-0026

CONWELL, JOSEPH THOMAS, lawyer; b. Oakman, Ala., Nov. 9, 1914; s. Joe D. and Elma Pettus (Wells) C.; student Transylvania Coll., 1934-35; B.A., U. Ala., 1937, LL.B., 1940; m. Winifred Maxwell, June 25, 1946; 1 son, Joseph Thomas. Admitted to Ala. bar, 1940; pvt. practice law, Jasper, Ala., 1940-42, Birmingham, Ala., 1946-48, Huntsville, Ala., 1955—; atty. ICC, Atlanta, 1948-49; claim and ins. investigator, San Francisco, 1949-54. Mem. nat. honor sec. Walker County High Sch.; mem. Madison County Democratic exec. com. Served with AUS, World War II. Mem. Am., Ala., Huntsville-Madison County (meml. com.) bar assns., Am. Judicature Soc., Ala. Trial Lawyers Assn. (gov.), Farrah Law Soc., Civitan Club, Am. Legion. Episcopalian. Lodge: Woodmen of World. Club: Century of U. Ala. Contbr. articles to profl. pubs. Bankruptcy, State civil litigation, Criminal. Office: Conwell Legal Bldg 607 Madison St Huntsville AL 35801

COOGAN, PATRICK DONLAN, lawyer; b. Yakima, Wash., July 23, 1934; s. Michael Eugene Coogan and Amy Patricia Donlan; m. Patricia Ann Gibbons, Aug. 31, 1957; children: Teresa Hillis, Steven, Timothy, Thomas, Peter, Mary Catherine. Student, Marquette U., 1953-54; BSME, U. Wash., 1957; JD, Georgetown U., 1963. Bar: Wash. 1964. Examiner patents U.S. Patent Office, Washington, 1961-63; patent atty. Weyerhaeuser Co., Tacoma, 1963-67, patent counsel, 1969-86, asst. gen. counsel, corp. patent counsel, asst. sec., 1986—; patent atty. Christenson, Sanborn, Seattle, 1967-69. Chmn. bd. dirs. Cath. Children's Services, Tacoma, 1970, Bellarmine Prep. Sch., Tacoma, 1980; chmn. St. Leo's Parish Ch. Counsel, Tacoma, 1976.

Served to lt. USN, 1957-61. Mem. Wash. State Bar Assn. (chmn. intellectual and indsl. property sect. 1975—), Assn. Corp. Patent Counsel, Am. Patent Law Assn., Wash. State Patent Law Assn. (chmn. 1973). Patent, Trademark and copyright, Environment. Home: 2005 N 29th Apt 1 Tacoma WA 98403 Office: Weyerhaeuser Co Tacoma WA 98477

COOK, AUGUST JOSEPH, lawyer, accountant; b. Devine, Tex., Sept. 25, 1926; s. August E. and Mary H. (Schmidt) C.; m. Matie M. Brangan, July 12, 1952; children—Lisa Ann, Mary Beth, John J. B.S., Trinity U., 1949; B.B.A., U. Tex., 1954; J.D., St. Mary's U., 1960. Bar: Tex. 1960, Tenn. 1975. Bus. mgr., corp. sec. Life Enterprises, Inc. and affiliated cos., San Antonio, 1950-58, also dir.; mgr. Ernst and Whinney, San Antonio, 1960-69, ptnr. Memphis, 1970-84; ptnr. Wildman, Harrold, Allen, Dixon, and McDonnel, Memphis, 1984—. Author newspaper column A.J.'s Tax Fables, 1983—. Author: A.J. $ Tax Court, 1987; contbr. articles to profl. jours. Alderman City of Castle Hills, Tex., 1961-63, mayor, 1963-69; chmn. Bexar County Council Mayors, 1967-69; v.p. Tex Mcpl. League, 1968-69; bd. dirs. San Antonio Met. YMCA. Served with U.S. Army, 1945-46, PTO. Mem. Tex. Soc. CPA's, Tex. Bar Assn., Am. Inst. CPA's, Estate Planning Council San Antonio (pres. 1967), Tenn. Soc. CPA's, Tenn. Bar Assn., Estate Planning Council Memphis (pres. 1983-84), Toastmasters (pres. 1963), Delta Theta Phi, Kappa Pi Sigma. Roman Catholic. Clubs: University (Memphis); Canyon Creek Country (San Antonio) (bd. dirs.). Lodges: Optimists (bd. dirs.), Rotary (treas. bd. dirs. 1978-79). Corporate taxation, Estate taxation, Personal income taxation. Home: 6785 Slash Pine Cove Memphis TN 38119 Office: Wildman Harrold Allen Dixon and McDonnell 6060 Primary Pkwy Memphis TN 38119

COOK, BARBARA ANN, lawyer; b. N.Y.C., Sept. 14, 1947; d. Paul J. and Mary (Doogan) McGuire; m. David S. Cook, Aug. 14, 1971; 1 child, Peter James. AB, Manhattanville Coll., 1968; JD, Columbia U., 1971. Bar: N.Y. 1971, U.S. Dist. Ct. (so. and ea. dists.) N.Y. 1977. Assoc. Lynton, Klein, Opton & Saslow, N.Y.C., 1971-74; atty. McGraw-Hill, Inc., N.Y.C., 1974-85; sr. counsel and asst. sec. Phelps Dodge Corp., N.Y.C., 1986—. Contbr. articles to profl. jours. Mem. Assn. of Bar of City of N.Y. (communications law com., lectures and continuing edn. com.), N.Y. County Lawyers Assn. (corp. law depts. com.), N.Y. Women's Bar Assn. (corp. securities com.). General corporate, Securities, Real property. Home: 2 Stuyvesant Oval MG New York NY 10009 Office: Phelps Dodge Corp 300 Park Ave New York NY 10009

COOK, BRATTEN HALE, II, lawyer; b. Lebanon, tenn., Sept. 9, 1952; s. Bratten Hale and Jo Bill (Murphy) C.; m. Judy Annette Driver, July 28, 1973; children: Megan Ashley, Bratten Hale III, Andrew Stephen. BS, Middle Tenn. State U., 1977; JD, U. Tenn., 1979. Bar: Tenn. 1980, U.S. Dist. Ct. (mid. dist.) Tenn. 1980, U.S. Ct. Appeals (6th cir.) 1984. Ptnr. Buck & Cook, Smithville, Tenn., 1980-86; sole practice Smithville, Tenn., 1986—. Mem. ABA, Fed. Bar Assn., Am. Trial Lawyers Assn., Tenn. Bar Assn., Tenn. Trial Lawyers Assn. Democrat. Baptist. Avocations: golf, travel. State civil litigation, Local government, Personal injury. Home: 615 Maple Ln Smithville TN 37166 Office: 104 N Third St Smithville TN 37166

COOK, CAMERON H., lawyer; b. Madison, Wis., Mar. 27, 1954; s. Harry J. and Louise Betty (Knaack) C. BA, U. Wis., 1976, JD, 1979; postdoctoral, U. Melbourne, Australia. Bar: Wis. 1979, Pa. 1979. Assoc. Alcoa Corp., Pitts., 1979-81, Loeff & Van Der Ploeg, N.Y.C., 1981-83; atty. Westinghouse Electric Corp., Pitts., 1983—. Atty. Pitts. Leadership Found., 1983—. Private international, Custom import and export, Real property. Home: 2034 Swallow Hill Rd Pittsburgh PA 15222 Office: Westinghouse Electric Corp West Bldg Gateway Ctr Pittsburgh PA 15222

COOK, CHARLES ADDISON, gas utility company executive, lawyer; b. N.Y.C., Mar. 31, 1952; s. Hugh F. and Lurana (Higgins) C.; m. Barbara Edgar, June 10, 1973. B.A., U. Conn., 1974; M.Pub. Adminstrn., Northeastern U., 1976; J.D. magna cum laude, New Eng. Sch. Law, 1980. Bar: Mass. 1980., U.S. Dist. Ct. Mass. 1980, U.S. Ct. Appeals (1st cir.) 1980. With Colonial Gas Co., Lowell, Mass., 1978—, v.p., 1982—. Mem. ABA, Mass. Bar Assn. Republican. Club: Bristol Yacht (commodore R.I. 1985-87). Labor, General corporate, Public utilities. Home: 70 Amble Rd Chelmsford MA 01824 Office: Colonial Gas Co 40 Market St Lowell MA 01852

COOK, CHARLOTTE SMALLWOOD, lawyer; b. Union Springs, N.Y., Jan. 24, 1923; d. William H. and Alice (Utter) Licht; m. Edward M. Smallwood, May 22, 1943; children—Edward Christopher, Susan Smallwood Grossman; m. 2d Frederick S. Cook, July 25, 1970. B.A., Cornell U., 1944; LL.B., Columbia U., 1946. Bar: N.Y. 1947, U.S. Supreme Ct. 1958. Ptnr. Smallwood & Smallwood, 1947-52, Smallwood & Ladd, 1970-74, Smallwood, Cook & Stout, 1975-77, 82—, Smallwood, Cook, Stout & Erickson, 1977-82 (all Warsaw, N.Y.); dist. atty. Wyoming County (N.Y.), 1949. Mem. N.Y. State Bar Assn. N.Y. State Bar Found., Am. Bar Found., Western N.Y. Trial Lawyers Assn. (dir. 1987). State civil litigation, Personal injury, Probate. Office: 140 N Main St Warsaw NY 14569

COOK, DANIEL JOHN, lawyer; b. Cleve., Sept. 12, 1952; s. James Conlisk and Margaret Mary (O'Brien) C. AB, Marquette U., 1973, JD, 1977. Bar: Wis. 1977, U.S. Dist. Ct. (ea. and we. dist.) Wis. 1977, U.S. Ct. Appeals (7th cir.) 1977.,. Assoc. Warshafsky Law Firm, Milw., 1977-87; Sole Practice Milw., 1987—. Mem. ABA (dist. rep. young lawyer div. 1984-86), Wis. Bar Assn., Assn. Trial Lawyers Am., Wis. Acad. Trial Lawyers, Milw. Young Lawyers Assn. (pres. 1983-84, service award 1982, pres.'s award 1984), Phi Beta Kappa, Delta Phi Alpha, Phi Alpha Theta. Avocations: running, skiing, reading, home repair. Personal injury, Federal civil litigation, State civil litigation. Home: 2540 N Oakland Milwaukee WI 53211 Office: 744 N 4th St Suite 633 Milwaukee WI 53203

COOK, DAVID SHERMAN, lawyer; b. Alexandria, La., Sept. 30, 1952; s. Sherman Wilson and Patricia Jane (Jeansonne) C.; m. Nanette Clare Simon, Aug. 6, 1982; children: Clare Michelle, Emily Colleen. Student, McNeese State U., 1970-73; JD, La. State U., 1976. Bar: La. 1976, U.S. Dist. Ct. (we., ea. and mid. dists.) La., U.S. Ct. Appeals (5th cir.). Assoc. Devillier & Ardoin, Eunice, La., 1976-78, Mouton & Jeansonne, Lafayette, La., 1978-81; ptnr. Hannah, Cook & Kaufman, Lafayette, 1981-83; sole practice Lafayette, 1983—. Lector St. John's Cathedral, Lafayette, 1981—. Named one of Outstanding Young Men in Am., U.S. Jaycees, 1983. Mem. ABA, La. Bar Assn., Lafayette Parish Bar Assn., La. Assn. Def. Counsel, Lafayette C. of C. Republican. Roman Catholic. Club: Beavers (Lafayette). Avocation: gardening. Insurance, General corporate, General practice. Office: PO Box 5107 Lafayette LA 70502

COOK, EUGENE AUGUSTUS, lawyer; b. Houston, May 2, 1938; s. Eugene A. and Estelle Mary (Stiner) C.; m. Sondra Attaway, Aug. 27, 1968; children—Laurie Ann, Eugene A. B.B.A., U. Houston, 1961, J.D., 1966. Bar: Tex. 1966, U.S. Dist. Ct. (so. dist.) Tex. 1967, U.S. Ct. Appeals (5th cir.) 1969, U.S. Supreme Ct. 1971, U.S. Ct. Claims 1972, U.S. Tax Ct. 1974, U.S. Ct. Appeals (11th cir.) 1982, U.S. Dist. Ct. (no., we. and ea. dists.) Tex. 1983. Ptnr. Butler & Binion, Houston, 1966-85; mng. ptnr. Cook, Davis & McFall, 1985—. adj. asst. prof. law U. Houston, 1971-72, 74. Assoc. editor, contbg. author: Texas Collection Manual, 1980; editor-in-chief, contbg. author: Creditors' Rights in Texas, 2d edit., 1982. Bd. dirs. U. Houston Law Rev., 1978-79; contbr. articles to law jours. Fellow Houston Bar Found., Am. Coll. Trial Lawyers, Am. Acad. Matrimonial Lawyers, Tex. Bar Found.; mem. ABA, Tex. Acad. Family Law Specialists, Houston Law Forum, Am. Acad. Matrimonial Lawyers, State Bar of Tex. (chmn. grievance com. 1971-72, bd. dirs. 1975-80, vice chmn. consumer law sect. 1976-77, chmn. consumer law sect. 1979-80, Presdl. Citation 1979, dir. family law sect. 1984—, Outstanding Atty. 1983, 84, 86, bd. dirs. 1981-85, chmn. pubs. com. 1981-82, Achievement award 1982, chmn. litigation sect. 1982-84), Houston Bar Assn. (seminar com. 1976-77, Chmn. of Yr. award, 1976-77, chmn. insts. com. 1977-78, Outstanding Service award 1977-78, chmn. continuing legal edn. com. 1978-79, Pres.'s award 1978-79, chmn. consumer law sect. 1978-79, vice chmn. family law sect. 1981-82, chmn. family law sect. 1982-83, Officers award 1983, chmn. staff and staffing com. 1985-86, dir. 1984-86, v.p. 1986—), Tex. Bd. Legal Specialization (cert.), Houston Family Law Forum, Tex. Assn. Cert. Family Law Lawyers, Gulf Coast Family Law Specialists Assn., ABA, State Bar Tex., Phi Kappa Phi, Phi Theta Kappa, Omicron Chi Epsilon, Omicron Delta Kappa, Phi Rho Pi. State civil litigation, Family and matrimonial. Home: 8316 Winningham St Houston TX 77055 Office: Cook Davis & McFall 2600 Two Houston Ctr 909 Fanin Houston TX 77010-1003

COOK, FRANK ROBERT, JR., business chance, real estate, and insurance broker, accountant, management consultant, lawyer; b. Washington, Aug. 19, 1923. B.S. in Psychology, Howard U., 1945, postgrad. in psychology, 1946, J.D., 1949; LL.M., Georgetown U., B.C.S. Southeastern U., 1963, M.C.S., 1964; Ph.D., Western U., 1951 Bar: U.S. Ct. Appeals 1949, U.S. Supreme Ct. 1954, D.C. 1967, U.S. Dist. Ct. Md. 1976. Bus. chance broker, Washington, 1944—; real estate broker, Washington, 1945—; ins. broker, Washington, 1946—; pvt. practice acctg., Washington, 1944—; prin. Frank R. Cook, Jr. and Assocs., mgmt. cons., Seat Pleasant, Md. Minister, Ministry of Salvation, Washington. Mem. Washington Bar Assn., D.C. Unified Bar, Nat. Soc. Pub. Accts., Am. Assn. Sex Educators and Counselors. Real property, Family and matrimonial, General practice. Office: 1715 11th St NW Washington DC 20001-5099

COOK, HAROLD DALE, fed. judge; b. Guthrie, Okla., Apr. 14, 1924; s. Harold Payton and Mildred Arvesta (Swanson) C.; divorced; children: Harold Dale II, Caren Irene, Randall Swanson. B.S. in Bus, U. Okla., 1950, LL.B., 1950, J.D., 1970. Bar: Okla. bar 1950. Individual practice law Guthrie, Okla., 1950; county atty. Logan County, Okla., 1951-54; asst. U.S. atty. Oklahoma City, 1954-58; asso. firm Butler, Rinehart and Morrison, Oklahoma City, 1958-61; partner Rinehart, Morrison and Cook, 1961-63; legal counsel and adviser to Gov. State of Okla., 1963-65; partner firm Cook and Ming, Oklahoma City, 1965, Cook, O'Toole, Ming and Tourtellotte, Oklahoma City, 1966-68, Cook, O'Toole and Tourtellotte, 1969-70, Cook and O'Toole, 1971; gen. counsel Shepherd Mall State Bank, Oklahoma City, 1967-71; pres. Shepherd Mall State Bank, 1969-71, chmn. bd., 1969-71; dir. Bur. of Hearings and Appeals, Social Security Adminstrn., HEW, 1971-74; judge U.S. Dist. Ct., Tulsa, 1974-79; chief judge No. Dist. Okla., 1979—; mem. legal adv. council Okla. Hwy. Patrol, 1969-70; mem. magistrates com. Jud. Conf. U.S., 1980—; mem. indsl. adv. council Bur. Bus. and Econ. Research, U. Okla., 1970-71. First v.p. PTA, Sunset Elementary Sch., 1959-60; v.p. Parent-Tchrs. & Students Assn., John Marshall High Sch., Oklahoma City, 1970-71, pres., 1971; mem. Econ. Opportunity Com., Okla., 1963-65; tchr. Sunday sch. classes for coll., high sch. and adult ages Village Methodist Ch., Oklahoma City, 1959-65; mem. bd. of stewards First Meth. Ch., Guthrie, Okla., 1951-54. Served with USAAF, 1943-45. Recipient Secretary's Spl. Citation HEW, 1973. Fellow Am. Bar Found.; mem. ABA, Fed. Bar Assn., Okla. Bar Assn. (del. to state bar convs.), Oklahoma City C. of C. Republican. Clubs: So. Hills Country, Shriners, Masons, Tulsa, Order Eastern Star (past worthy patron Okla.), Scottish Rite (hon. insp. gen.). Jurisprudence. Office: U S Court House 333 W 4th St Tulsa OK 74103 *

COOK, HARRY CLAYTON, JR., lawyer; b. Washington, Mar. 25, 1935; s. Harry Clayton and Lillian June (A'harrah) C.; children—Christianne, Nicole, Harry Clayton III. B.S. in Chem. Engring, Princeton U., 1956; LL.B., U. Va., 1960. Bar: Colo. 1960, N.Y. 1961, Pa. 1966, D.C. 1973. Assoc. firm Sullivan & Cromwell, N.Y.C., 1960-63, Holme Roberts & Owen, Denver, 1964, Pepper Hamilton & Scheetz, Phila., 1965-69; ptnr. Pepper Hamilton & Scheetz, 1969-70, 73; on assignment as sr. tax counsel Sun Oil Co., Phila., 1970; ptnr. Cadwalader Wickersham & Taft, Washington, 1974—; page to U.S. Sen. E.D. Milliken, Colo., 1950-52; gen. counsel Maritime Adminstrn.; mem. Maritime Subs. Bd., U.S. Dept. Commerce, Washington, 1970-73; U.S. del. to Soviet Union for Maritime Agreement between U.S. and USSR, 1971-73; mem. Adminstrv. Conf. U.S., 1980—, chmn. com. on jud. rev., 1982-87; mem. Nat. Def. Exec. Res., U.S. Mil. Sealift Command, 1983—, U.S. Office of Tech. Assessment, also mem. citizens' adv. panel on U.S. Maritime Industry, 1982-85, cargo policy workshop participant, 1984-85; presdl. transition team Fed. Maritime Commn., 1980-81. Contbr. articles to profl. jours. Bd. dirs. Inst. for Fgn. Policy Analysis, Inc., 1980—, Com. on the Present Danger, 1981—. Served to 1st lt. USAR JAGC, 1957-65. Mem. ABA (standing com. on law and nat. security 1987, tax sect. 1965—, adminstr. practice sect. 1974—), D.C. Bar Assn., Fed. Bar Assn. (com. gen. counsels 1970—), Am. Law Inst., Maritime Law Assn. U.S. (marine fin. com. 1981—), Order of Coif, Phi Delta Phi. Clubs: Racquet of Phila; Univ. (N.Y.C.), Univ. (D.C.). Administrative and regulatory, Corporate taxation. Office: Cadwalader Wickersham & Taft 1333 New Hampshire Ave Suite 700 Washington DC 20036

COOK, JAMES CHRISTOPHER, lawyer; b. Quincy, Ill., Oct. 4, 1951; s. Waldo Fuller and Rita Cecilia (Kathmann) C.; m. Bernardeen Mary Kohler, Dec. 30, 1978; children—Christopher Aaron, Erin Leigh. Student Quincy Coll., 1969-71; B.A., U. Ill., 1973; J.D., Loyola U., Chgo., 1976. Bar: Ill. 1976, U.S. Ct. Appeals (D.C. cir.) 1977, U.S. Ct. Appeals (7th cir.) 1978, U.S. Dist. Ct. (cen. dist.) Ill. 1978, U.S. Dist. Ct. (so. dist.) Ill. 1979, U.S. Supreme Ct. 1979, Mo. 1984. clk, to justice Ill. Ct. Appeals (4th dist.), Springfield, 1976-78; assoc. Walker & Williams, P.C., Belleville, Ill., 1978-83, shareholder, 1983—. Pres. bd. trustees St. Clair County Law Library, Belleville, Ill., 1982—. Mem. ABA, Ill. State Bar Assn., Mo. Bar, Bar Assn. Met. St. Louis, Nat. Assn. R.R. Trial Counsel, St. Clair County Bar Assn. (bd. dirs. 1983—). Roman Catholic. Labor, Federal civil litigation, State civil litigation. Office: Walker & Williams PC 4343 W Main St Belleville IL 62223 Office: 1115 Pine St Saint Louis MO 63188

COOK, JOSEPH LEE, lawyer; b. Waukesha, Wis., Sept. 17, 1944; s. Jerome F. and Agnes (Blank) C. BS, U. Wis., 1967; JD, Marquette U., 1975. Bar: Wis. 1975, U.S. Dist. Ct. (ea. and we. diss.) Wis. 1975, U.S. Supreme Ct. 1979, U.S. Ct. Mil. Appeals 1982. Ptnr. Cook & Hickey, Waukesha, Wis., 1975—; commr. Waukesha Cir. Ct., 1979—; bd. dirs. Primary Trend Mutual Fund, Milw. Alderman City of Waukesha, 1965-68; legal counsel Boy Scouts Am., Waukesha, 1980—. Served with USAR, 1964—. Mem. Wis. Bar Assn., Wis. Bar Found. (pro bono publico 1983—), Waukesha County Bar Assn., Phi Delta Phi. Republican. Mem. United Ch. Christ. Avocations: project inquiry, teaching high sch. law. Consumer commercial, General practice, Probate. Home: 420 Prospect Ct Waukesha WI 53186 Office: Cook & Hickey 1220 S Grand Ave Waukesha WI 53186

COOK, JULIAN ABELE, JR., federal judge; b. Washington, June 22, 1930; s. Julian Abele and Ruth Elizabeth (McNeill) C.; m. Carol Annette Dibble, Dec. 22, 1957; children: Julian Abele III, Peter Dibble, Susan Annette. B.A., Pa. State U., 1952; J.D., Georgetown U., 1957. Bar: Mich. 1957. Law clk. to judge Pontiac, Mich., 1957-58; sole practice Detroit, 1958-78; judge U.S. Dist. Ct. (ea. dist.) Mich., Detroit, 1978—; spl. asst. atty. gen. State of Mich., 1968-78; adj. prof. law U. Detroit Sch. Law, 1971-74; gen. counsel Sta. WTVS (Public TV), 1973-78; labor arbitrator Am. Arbitration Assn. and Mich. Employment Relations Commn., 1975-78; mem. Mich. State Bd. Ethics, 1977-78. Contbr. articles to legal jours. Mem. exec. bd. dirs., past pres. Child and Family Services Mich.; bd. dirs. Mich. Heart Assn., Brighton Health Services Corp., Brighton Hosp., Hutzel Hosp., Georgetown U. Law Ctr.; chmn. Mich. Civil Rights Commn., 1968-71; mem. adv. council Ashland Theol. Sem. Served with Signal Corps U.S. Army, 1952-54. Recipient merit citation Pontiac Area Urban League, 1971, Pathfinders award Oakland U., 1977, Service award Todd-Phillips Home, Inc., 1978, Disting. Alumnus award Pa. State U., 1985, Focus and Impact award Oakland U., 1985; resolution Mich. Ho. of Reps., 1971; named Boss of Yr. Oakland County Legal Secs. Assn., 1973-74. Fellow Am. Bar Found.; mem. NAACP (Disting. Citizen of Yr. 1970, mem. state constl. revision and legal redress com. 1963), Mich. Bar Assn. (chmn. constl. law com. 1969, vice-chmn. civil liberties com. 1970, co-chmn. profl. devel. task force 1984—), Oakland County Bar Assn. (chmn. continuing legal edn. com. 1968-69, jud. liaison Dist. Ct. com. 1977, continuing legal edn. com. 1977, unauthorized practice law com. 1977), ABA, Nat. Bar Assn., Fed. Bar Assn., Wolverine Bar Assn., Mich. Assn. Black Judges, Am. Inn of Ct. (pres., master of bench, chmn. 6th cir. com. on standing jury instructions), Georgetown U. Alumni Assn. (bd. dirs.), Pa. State U. Alumni Assn. (bd. dirs.).

COOK, KENNETH TOTMAN, lawyer; b. Bangor, Maine, Feb. 8, 1950; s. Charles Theauphilus and Virginia Louise (Totman) C.; m. Linda Anne McMahan, May 12, 1984. BA, Fla. State U., 1973; JD, Stetson U., 1978. Bar: Colo. 1981, U.S. Dist. Ct. Colo. 1982. Law clk. Colo. Dist. Ct., Colorado Springs, 1979-80; assoc. Trott, Kunstle & Hughes, Colorado Springs, 1981-83, ptnr., 1984—; mediator Neighborhood Justice Ctr., Colorado Springs, 1979—; instr. Street Law Program, Colorado Springs, 1981—. Mem. Citizens Goals Leadership 1980, Colorado Springs, 1985-86, City Council Campaign Com., Colorado Springs, 1985, 87. Served as 2d lt. USAF, 1974-76. Named one of Outstanding Young Men of Am., Jaycees, 1982. Mem. ABA (space law com. 1984—), El Paso County Bar Assn. (chmn. swearing-in com. 1981-82, space law com., 1986), Train Collectors Assn. Avocations: train collecting, running, skiing, racquetball. Bankruptcy, Personal injury, General practice. Office: Trott Kunstle & Hughes 102 S Tejon Suite 750 Colorado Springs CO 80903

COOK, MARTHA JEAN, lawyer; b. Owensboro, Ky., Aug. 13, 1949; d. E.S. and Marjorie Jean (Oberg) C. BA in Psychology magna cum laude, Stetson U., 1970; MA in Psychology cum laude, U. So. Fla., 1971; JD cum laude, U. Fla., 1977. Asst. atty. gen. legal affairs dept. State of Fla., Tallahassee, 1977-78, spl. asst. atty. gen. revenue dept., 1978-81; assoc. Carlton, Fields, Ward, Emmanuel, Smith & Cutler P.A., Tallahassee, 1981-83; ptnr. Guttshall, Cook & Guttshall, Thomasville, Ga., 1984-87; sole practice Thomasville, 1987—. Commr. nominating com. 2d jud. cir. Leon County, 1982-86, Statewide Human Rights Advocacy Commn., Tallahassee, 1983-84. Mem. ABA, Ga. Bar Assn., Fla. Bar Assn., Thomas County Bar Assn. (treas. 1985-86), Fla. Assn. Women Lawyers, Tallahassee Women Lawyers Assn. (pres. 1979-80), Tallahassee Bar Assn. (bd. dirs. 1980-81), Capital Womens Network , Ga. Med. Aux., Thomas County Med. Aux. Avocations: piano, art. Family and matrimonial, General practice, State civil litigation. Office: 419 N Dawson St PO Box 1638 Thomasville GA 31799

COOK, MICHAEL HARRY, lawyer; b. Oshkosh, Wis., June 9, 1947; s. Leonard James and Ethel (Shapiro) C.; m. Michele Anne Reday, Apr. 21, 1979; children—Noah Reday, Megan Rose. Student U. Wis.-Madison, 1965-66; B.A. with honors cum laude, Temple U., 1969; J.D., Villanova U., 1973. Bar: Pa. 1973, D.C. 1979, U.S. Dist. Ct. (no. dist.) Ill. 1977, U.S. Dist. Ct. D.C. 1981, U.S. Ct. Claims 1982, U.S. Ct. Appeals (3d cir.) 1982, U.S. Ct. Appeals (5th cir.) 1981, U.S. Ct. Appeals (9th cir.) 1979, U.S. Ct. Appeals (11th cir.) 1981, U.S. Ct. Appeals (7th cir.) 1984, U.S. Ct. Appeals (10th cir.) 1984, U.S. Ct. Appeals (Fed. cir.) 1984, U.S. Ct. Appeals (D.C. cir.) 1981, U.S. Supreme Ct. 1976. Atty., Gen. Counsel's Office, U.S. Dept. Health and Human Services, Washington, 1973-80; ptnr. Wood, Lucksinger & Epstein, Washington, 1981—; lectr. Nat. Health Lawyers Assn., Washington, Aspen Systems, Inc., various state and nat. hosps. and long term care assns. Contbr. articles to profl. health care jours. Vice pres. Taylor Run Citizens Assn., Alexandria, Va., 1982-84, pres., 1984-85, bd. dirs. 1985—. Pres.'s scholar Temple U., Phila., 1969. Mem. ABA, Nat. Health Lawyers Assn., Am. Soc. Hosp. Attys., Fed. Bar Assn., Healthcare Fin. Mgmt. Assn. (mem. nat. adv. task force on long term care), Sword Soc., Phi Eta Sigma, Tau Epsilon Phi. Democrat. Jewish. Health, Federal civil litigation, Administrative and regulatory. Home: 2724 King St Alexandria VA 22302 Office: Wood Lucksinger & Epstein 2000 M St NWSuite 500 Washington DC 20036

COOK, MICHAEL LEWIS, lawyer; b. Rochester, N.H., Mar. 5, 1944; s. Israel J. and Molly L. C.; m. Stephanie L. Cook, Apr. 11, 1976. A.B. Columbia U., 1965; J.D., NYU, 1968. Bar: N.Y. 1968. Assoc. Weil, Gotshal & Manges, N.Y.C., 1970-75, ptnr., 1975-80; ptnr. Skadden, Arps, Slate, Meagher & Flom, N.Y.C., 1980—; adj. prof. law NYU Sch. Law, 1975—. Co-author: A Practical Guide to the Bankruptcy Reform Act, 1979; Creditors' Rights, Debtors' Protection and Bankruptcy, 1985; contbr.: Collier on Bankruptcy, 1979, Collier Bankruptcy Guide, 1981. Mem. ABA, Assn. Bar City N.Y., Fed. Bar Council. Bankruptcy, Federal civil litigation. Home: 47 East 88th St Apt 6A New York NY 10128 Office: Skadden Arps Slate Meagher & Flom 919 3d Ave New York NY 10022

COOK, REBECCA JOHNSON, lawyer, educator; A.B., Columbia U., 1970; M.A., Tufts U., 1972; M.P.A., Harvard U., 1973; J.D., Georgetown U., 1982. Bar: D.C. 1982. Dir. law program Internat. Planned Parenthood Fedn., London, 1973-78, legal adviser 1982—; assoc. firm Beveridge, Fairbanks and Diamond, 1980; cons. U.S. Congress, 1978-81; mem. legal counsel office The Upjohn Co., 1981-82; asst. prof. faculty of law U. Toronto, 1987—; asst. prof. clin. pub. health Columbia U., N.Y.C., 1983-87, staff atty. devel. law and policy program Ctr. for Population and Family Health, 1983-87. adj. faculty Humphrey Inst. Pub. Affairs, U. Minn., 1985-87; dep. dir. Internat. Women's Rights Action Watch, 1986-87. Contbr. articles to profl. jours. Bd. dirs. Operation Crossroads Africa, 1972-74, Pathfinder Fund, 1978—, Assn. for Vol. Surg. Contraception, 1982—, Internat. Projects Assistance Service, 1982—; mem. adv. com. on depo provera AID, 1978-80; adv. bd. Program for Intro. and Adaptation of Contraceptive Tech., 1982—, standing com. study of ethical aspects of human reproduction Internat. Fedn. Gynecology and Obstetrics, 1986—; U.S. del. 2d World Conf. on Nat. Parks, 1972; mem. Mass. Citizens Com. for Environ. Affairs 1972. Office: Columbia U Ctr for Population & Family Health 60 Haven Ave New York NY 10032

COOK, ROBERT NEVIN, educator, consultant; b. Vicksburg, Pa., Dec. 11, 1912; s. Ralph B. and Mabel Grace (Maurer) C.; m. Frances Katherine Murphy, Mar. 18, 1939; children—Katherine Cook Leith, Robert N., Ann Cook Krebs. A.B. cum laude, Bucknell U., 1933; J.D., Duke U., 1936. Bar: Pa. 1937. Assoc. firm Knight & Kivko, Sunbury, Pa., 1936-37; instr. Mercer U. Sch. Law, 1937-38 asst. prof., law librarian Vanderbilt U., 1938-39; asst. prof. U. Louisville Sch. Law, 1939-41; atty. NLRB, 1941, office Gen. Counsel, Treas. Dept., 1941-45, office Alien Property, 1945, office Small Bus., 1946; assoc. prof. Western Res. U. Sch. Law, 1946-50, prof. 1950-63; prof. U. Cin. Coll. Law, 1963-81, prof. emeritus, 1982—, cons., researcher Nat. Research Council, Nat. Acad. Sci.; prin. organizer N. Am. Inst. for Modernization of Land Data Systems, 1974, dir., 1974-79, cons., 1979—, hon. life dir., 1984—; procs. organizer, participant, editor Tri-State Conf. on Comprehensive Unified Land Data System, Coll. Law U. Cin., 1966. Mem. ABA (chmn. land title records improvement com. Real Property, Probate and Trust Law Sect., 1964-69), Pa. Bar Assn., Cin. Bar Assn., Am. Coll. Real Estate Lawyers, Order of Coif. Democrat. Methodist. Author: Legal Drafting, 1950; contbr. articles in field to law jours.; prin. developer of Comprehensive Unified Land Data System (CULDATA) now known as Compatible Multi-Purpose Land Info. System. Legal education, Environment, Real property. Home: 62 Rawson Woods Circle Cincinnati OH 45220 Office: Cin Coll Law Cincinnati OH 45221

COOK, RONALD WALTER, lawyer; b. Redlands, Calif., Nov. 12, 1943; s. Walter G. and Elizabeth (Ireson) C.; m. Barbara L. Bennett, Sept. 7, 1968; 1 child, Kellie Anne. B.A., U. Calif.-Santa Barbara, 1965; J.D., U. Calif.-Berkeley, 1968. Bar: Calif. 1969. Assoc. Price, Postel & Parma, Santa Barbara, 1968-72, Hatch & Parent, Santa Barbara, 1973-80; ptnr. Cook, Berryhill & Edwards and predecessor firm Cook & Berryhill, Santa Barbara, 1980—. Trustee U. Calif.-Santa Barbara Found., 1980-84. Local government, State civil litigation, Real property. Office: Cook Berryhill & Edwards 120 E De La Guerra Santa Barbara CA 93101

COOK, TERRY LEE, lawyer; b. Grand Junction, Colo., Sept. 15, 1955; s. Calvin Coldiron and Lorraine B. (Blaser) C.; m. Candace Dorothy Sperstad, Aug. 31, 1979. BS, BA summa cum laude, U. Denver, 1977, JD, 1980. Bar: Colo. 1980, U.S. Dist. Ct. Colo. 1980. Assoc. Calkins, Kramer, Grimshaw & Harring, Denver, 1980-85, ptnr., 1985—; bd. dirs. DST, Inc., Denver, Drill Stem Testers, Inc., Denver; speaker OTC small bus. and other various programs. Mem. Colo. Assn. Commerce and Industry, Denver, 1984, Trinity Bapt. Ch., Aurora, Colo., 1979—. Mem. ABA, Colo. Bar Assn., Denver Bar Assn., Beta Gamma Sigma, Phi Theta Kappa (sec. 1975). Republican. Club: Club 20 (Grand Junction). Contracts commercial, General corporate, Securities. Office: Calkins Kramer Grimshaw & Harring 1700 Lincoln St Suite 3800 Denver CO 80203

COOK, WALTER MCQUEEN, lawyer; b. Selma, Ala., Jan. 29, 1915; s. Wlater PItts and Mattie Julia (McQueen) C.; m. Norma Webster Rogers, June 15, 1938; children: Norma McQueen, Julia Cook Melson, Walter, Kathryn Cook Satchfield. LLB, LLM, George Washington U., 1948. Bar: D.C. 1948. Examiner Office of Price Adminstrn., Selma and Mobile, Ala., 1943-47; sr. ptnr. Lyons, Pipes & Cook, Mobile, 1949-82, of counsel, 1982—. Ppres. Mobile Azalea Trail, 1952, Am.'s Jr. Miss Pageant, Mobile, 1962, Mobile County Wildlife Assn., 1964, Ala. Wildlife Fedn., Montgomery, 1968, Ala. Wildlife Endowment, Mobile, 1968—. Mem. ABA, D.C. Bar Assn., Ala. Bar Assn., Mobile Bar Assn., Ala. Judicature Soc., Fedn. Ins. Counsel. Club: Athelstan, Mobile Country, Bienville. State civil litigation.

Home: 2009 Old Shell Rd Mobile AL 36607 Office: Lyons Pipes & Cook PO Drawer 2727 Mobile AL 36652

COOK, WAYNE RALPH, lawyer; b. Danville, Ill., Aug. 13, 1912; s. Charles Alonzo and Grace Mae (Massey) C.; m. Irene Gaston Samuel, Apr. 17, 1976; m. Maryla K. Karpin, June 4, 1934 (dec. Dec. 1969); children—Bonnie Karen Tallitsch. A.B., U. Ill., 1934; J.D., Ind. U., 1944; M.A., Georgetown U., 1946. Bar: Ind. 1944, Ill. 1945, U.S. Supreme Ct. 1960, Ark. 1977. Sole practice, Danville, Ill., 1947-51; asst. atty. gen. Springfield, Ill., 1949-53; assoc. Hubachek & Kelly, Chgo., 1953-59; spl. csl. Bankers Life & Casualty Co., Chgo., 1959-69; asst. U.S. atty. No. Dist. Ill., 1969-70; asst. atty. gen. environ. law Indpls., 1970-73; chief csl. Office Atty. Gen., Indpls., 1973-76; appeals referee Ark. Bd. Rev., Little Rock, 1977-80; chmn., 1980-81; now sole practice, Little Rock; past pres., dir. Okla. Oil Co. Served to lt. col. AUS, 1941-47. Decorated Purple Heart, Bronze Star; medialle de la France Liberé e; named Ark. Traveler, 1970, Ky. Col., 1970, hon. Tex. Citizen, 1971; Disting. Pub. Service award Atty. Gen. Ind., 1976. Mem. ABA, Ill. Bar Assn., Ind. Bar Assn., Ark. Bar Assn., 7th Fed. Cir. Bar Assn., Pulaski County (Ark.) Bar Assn., Chgo. Bar Assn., Indpls. Bar Assn., Am. Soc. Internat. Law, Am. Judicature Soc., Selden Soc., U.S. Armor Assn., 1st Armored Div. Assn., U.S. HOrse Cavalry Assn., Sigma Delta Kappa. Democrat. Clubs: Capital (Little Rock); Army and Navy (Washington). General corporate, General practice, Jurisprudence.

COOK, WILLIAM LESLIE, JR., lawyer; b. Greenwood, Miss., July 1, 1949; s. William Leslie and Mary Elizabeth (Roberts) C.; m. Mary Jo Dorr, July 17, 1976; children—Leslie Patton, William Roberts, Maribeth Dorr. BA, U. Miss., 1971, JD, 1974. Bar: Miss. 1974, U.S Dist. Ct. (no. dist.) Miss. 1974, U.S. Dist. Ct. (we. dist.) Tenn. 1986. Assoc. Bailey & Trusty, Batesville, Miss., 1974-79; ptnr. Bailey, Trusty & Cook, Batesville, 1980—. Chmn., Miss. Coll. Republican Clubs, 1973, Panola County March of Dimes, Batesville, 1976-78; Miss. Chmn. Nat. Orgn. Social Security Claimants Reps., 1981-82; rep. Honor Council, Sch. Law, U. Miss., 1974; mem. Panola County C. of C., Batesville, 1978-84. Mem. ABA (torts and ins. practice sect. 1979—, vice chmn. com. on delivery of legal services to the disabled Young Lawyers Div. 1983-85, gen. practice sect. 1985—), Miss. State Bar, (state bd. bar admissions 1978-79, ethics com. 1980-83, bd. dirs. Young Lawyers Sect. 1980-83, chmn. com. on unauthorized practice of law 1983-86), Panola County Bar Assn. (pres. 1979-80), Assn. Trial Lawyers Am., Miss. Trial Lawyers Assn. (membership com. 1983-84), Ct. Practice Inst. (diplomate), Lawyer-Pilots Bar Assn., Lamar Soc. Internat. Law, Omicron Delta Kappa, Pi Sigma Alpha, Delta Theta Phi. Methodist. Club: Jaycees (legal counsel Batesville 1975-77). Lodges: Shriners, Masons, Rotary. Personal injury, Workers' compensation. Home: 110 Shagbark Dr Batesville MS 38606 Office: Bailey Trusty & Cook 244 Hwy 6 W Batesville MS 38606

COOKE, BRADFORD, lawyer; b. N.Y.C., Feb. 25, 1950; s. George Bradford and Catherine (Lee) C.; m. Marion Mundy, June 30, 1984. BA in History, Hamilton Coll., 1972; JD, Syracuse U., 1978. Bar: N.Y. 1979, U.S. Dist. Ct. (no. dist.) N.Y. 1979. Sole practice Syracuse, N.Y., 1979-80; assoc. Julien Schlesinger & Finz, N.Y.C., 1980-82, Schneider, Kleinick & Weitz, N.Y.C., 1982—. Mem. Assn. of Bar of City of N.Y. (legis. liason com. on product liability 1985—). Personal injury, Civil rights, Federal and state civil litigation. Home: 878 W End Ave New York NY 10025 Office: Schneider Kleinick & Weitz 11 Park Pl New York NY 10007

COOKE, GEORGE ALEXANDER, JR., lawyer; b. Bklyn., Oct. 23, 1947; s. George Alexander Sr. and Eva Maria (Renz) C. AB, Dartmouth Coll., 1969; MA, Cambridge (Eng.) U., 1975; JD, Harvard U., 1978. Bar: Mass. 1978, N.Y. 1985. Assoc. Ropes & Gray, Boston, 1978-83; v.p., sr. counsel film programming Home Box Office, Inc., N.Y.C., 1983—. Served to lt. USN, 1969-73, Vietnam. Danforth Found. fellow, 1973. Mem. Phi Beta Kappa. Mem. Orthodox Ch. Am. Avocations: creative writing, photography, surfing. Entertainment, General corporate, Contracts commercial. Office: Home Box Office Inc 1100 Ave of Americas New York NY 10036

COOKE, MARCIA GAIL, lawyer; b. Sumter, S.C., Oct. 16, 1954; d. Heyward and Ella (Randolph) C.; m. Marc Robert Shelton, June 15, 1985. BS in Fgn. Services, Georgetown U., 1975; JD, Wayne State U., 1977. Bar: Mich. 1978, U.S. Dist. Ct. (ea. dist.) Mich. 1978, U.S. Ct. Appeals (6th cir.) 1983. Staff atty. Wayne County Legal Services, Detroit, 1978-79; asst. defender Detroit Defender's Office, 1979-80; asst. atty. U.S. Atty.'s Office, Detroit, 1980-83; assoc. Miro, Miro & Weiner, Bloomfield Hills, Mich., 1983-84; magistrate U.S. Dist. Ct., Detroit, 1984—. Mem. ABA, Fed. Bar Assn. (bd. dirs. 1986), Wolverine Bar Assn., Nat. Conf. Black Lawyers (bd. dirs. 1979-80), Order of Barristers, NCCJ (Pathfinder award 1986), Women's Econ. Club. Roman Catholic. Avocations: film, lit., race walking. Federal civil litigation. Office: US Dist Ct 231 W Lafayette Blvd Detroit MI 48226

COOKE, MORRIS DAWES, JR., lawyer; b. Beaufort, S.C., July 20, 1954; s. Morris Dawes and Georgianna (McTeer) C.; m. Helen Cecelia Haffey, May 16, 1981; children: Morris Dawes III, George Henry. BA with distinction, U. Va., 1976; JD cum laude, U. S.C., 1979. Bar: S.C. 1979, U.S. Dist. Ct. S.C. 1979, U.S. Ct. Appeals (4th cir.) 1980, U.S. Supreme Ct. 1986. Law clk. to presiding judge U.S. Dist. Ct. S.C., Charleston, 1979-80; assoc. Barnwell, Whaley, Patterson & Helms, Charleston, 1980-82, ptnr., 1982—. Mem. S.C. Bar Assn. (pub. affairs com. 1986), Assn. Trial Lawyers Am., Am. Judicature Soc., Southeastern Admiralty Law Inst., Def. Research Inst. Republican. Episcopalian. Federal civil litigation, General corporate, Insurance. Home: 1132 Park Way Dr Mount Pleasant SC 29464 Office: Barnwell Whaley et al 120 Meeting St Charleston SC 29402

COOLIDGE, DANIEL SCOTT, lawyer; b. Portland, Maine, Sept. 20, 1948; s. John Walter and Mary Louise (Arnold) C.; m. Carolyn Stiles, Nov. 23, 1984; 1 child, Lillian Mae. BS summa cum laude, U. Bridgeport, 1976; JD, Harvard U., 1980. Bar: Conn. 1980, N.H. 1982, U.S. Ct. Appeals (1st cir.) 1983, U.S. Supreme Ct. 1985. Assoc. Cummings & Lockwood, Stamford, Conn., 1980-82; assoc. Sheehan, Phinney, Bass & Green P.A., Manchester, N.H., 1982-87, ptnr., 1987—; chmn. juvenile diversion com. Pittsfield (N.H.) Dist. Ct., 1982-85. Patentee Telephone Test Equipment, 1985. Chmn. Bradford Constitution Bicentennial Com.; mem. Pittsfield Planning Bd., 1984-85; treas., trustee First Congl. Ch., Pittsfield, 1984-85, First Bapt. Ch. Bradford; pres. Pittsfield Arts Council, 1985; del. N.H. Constl. Conv., Concord, 1984—. Mem. ABA (bus. law sect.), N.H. Bar Assn., Manchester Bar Assn. Avocations: computers, farming. General corporate, Computer, Environment. Home: RD 2 Box 123A Warner NH 03278 Office: Sheehan Phinney Bass & Green PA 1000 Elm St Manchester NH 03101

COOMBS, FREDERICK STANLEY, III, lawyer; b. Youngstown, Ohio, Aug. 22, 1950; s. Frederick Stanley Jr. and Alyce Mae (Walker) C.; m. Janice Louise Myers, June 5, 1982. BA, Denison U., 1972; JD, Ohio State U., 1975. Bar: Ohio 1975, U.S. Dist. Ct. (no. dist.) Ohio 1976, U.S. Ct. Appeals (6th cir.) 1981. Assoc. Harrington, Huxley & Smith, Youngstown, 1975-79, ptnr., 1980—. Bd. dirs. Jr. Achievement of Youngstown, 1981—. Mem. ABA, Ohio Bar Assn., Mahoning County Bar Assn., Comml. Law League Am., Internat. Brotherhood of Magicians (pres. Ring 2 1980), Phi Delta Phi. Presbyterian. Club: Torch (Youngstown) (pres. 1979). Avocation: magic. Bankruptcy, Contracts commercial, Libel. Office: Harrington Huxley & Smith 1200 Mahoning Bank Bldg Youngstown OH 44503

COOMBS, RONALD LEE, lawyer; b. Louisville, May 24, 1946; s. Clay T. and Jo Anne (Lytle) C.; m. Sharon Seitz, July 6, 1968; children: Bryan, Leslie, Jason Clay. BSci., U. Louisville, 1968, JD, 1972. Bar: Ky. 1972, U.S. Tax Ct. 1973, U.S. Dist. Ct. (ea. dist.) Ky. 1977, Ind. 1978. Assoc. Eubanks, Gardner & Lorenz, Louisville, 1972-76; ptnr. Lorenz, Coombs & Rankin P.S.C., Louisville, 1976-78; sole practice Louisville, 1978—; past gov. Ind.-Ky. dist. Sertoma Internat., Louisville; bd. dirs. Market Finders Ins. Corp., Louisville. Pres. Louisville Luth. Home, 1981-85; bd. dirs. Meredith-Dunn Learning Ctr., Louisville, 1984. General corporate, Insurance, Probate. Home: 10208 Ledbury Way Louisville KY 40223 Office: 9117 Leesgate Rd Louisville KY 40222

COOMBS, WILLIAM ELMER, accountant, lawyer; b. Keosauqua, Iowa, Jan. 17, 1911; s. Elmer Clyde and Myra Ann (Moon) C.; AB in Econs., U. Calif. at Los Angeles, 1933; JD, Loyola U., Los Angeles, 1954; m. Katheryn Rose Logan, Oct. 20, 1934 (dec. May 1984); children: Katheryn M. Coombs Kirkendoll, Rose Ann (Mrs. Luciano Siracusa); m. Elta Louise Pfister, Feb. 17, 1985. CPA, Calif.; bar: Calif. 1955, U.S. Dist. Ct. (cen. dist.) Calif. 1955, U.S. Dist. Ct. (no. dist.) Calif. 1957, U.S. Supreme Ct. 1960, U.S. Ct. Appeals (9th cir.) 1963, U.S. Dist. Ct. (so. dist.) Calif. 1980. Acct., Shell Oil Co., Los Angeles, 1933-36, So. Calif. Edison Co., Los Angeles, 1936-37; auditor State of Calif., Los Angeles, 1937-41; sr. acct. Arthur Andersen & Co., 1941-43; controller Case Constrn. Co., San Pedro, Calif., 1943-46; C.P.A., Roberts & Coombs, 1946-49, Deloitte, Plender, Griffths & Co., 1949-52; controller Ford J. Twaits Co., Los Angeles, 1952-55; overseas auditor Morrison-Knudsen Internat., San Francisco, 1955-56; asst. prof. bus. Calif. State U., Chico 1956-58; sec.-treas., dir., house counsel Matich Corp., Colton, Calif. 1958-61; practiced in Rialto, 1962—; mem. Calif. Senate, 1967-73, Calif. Adv. Council on Econ. Devel., 1984—; city atty. Rialto, 1977-81, Big Bear Lake, Calif., 1980-82. Mem. Rialto City Planning Commn., 1960-62; councilman, Rialto, 1962-67; bd. dirs. Regional Econ. Devel. Council, 1964-67, pres., 1944—. Mem. Calif. Bar Assn., ABA, Am. Inst. CPAs, Calif. Soc. CPAs, Calif., San Bernardino County Bar Assn. (pres. 1966-67) taxpayers assns. Rotarian. Author reference book: Construction Accounting and Financial Management 1968. Estate taxation, State and local taxation, Construction. Home and Office: 5810 Date Ave Rialto CA 92376

COONEY, BRADLEY KENT, lawyer, writer; b. Cleve., Jan. 10, 1950; s. Robert and Doris (MacAusland) C.; m. Margaret Motte Turner, Sept. 27, 1975; children: Christopher Channing, Caitlin Motte. BA, Oakland U., 1972; JD, Boston U., 1980. Bar: Conn. 1980, U.S. Dist. Ct. Conn. 1981, U.S. Ct. Claims 1985, U.S. Ct. Appeals (2d cir.) 1986. Assoc. Raymond A. Garcia, P.C., New Haven, Conn., 1981-85; ptnr. Garcia, Cooney & Bender, New Haven, 1985—. Editor, researcher: How to Try a Criminal Case, 1980. Sponsor Internat. Ctr. Host Family Program, New Haven, 1984-86. Mem. ABA (litigation sect. 1984—, forum com. on constrn. law 1984—), Conn. Bar Assn., Am. Arbitration Assn. (panel of arbitrators, 1985—), New Haven C. of C. Construction, Government contracts and claims. Office: 44 Trumbull St New Haven CT 06510

COONEY, DAVID FRANCIS, lawyer; b. Chgo., Sept. 21, 1954; s. John Thomas and Margaret (Bonner) C. BBA in Fin. magna cum laude, U. Notre Dame, 1975, JD, 1978. Bar: Fla., U.S. Dist. Ct. (so. dist.) Fla., U.S. Ct. Appeal (5th, 8th and 11th cirs.). Assoc. Grimmett, Scherer & James, Ft. Lauderdale, Fla., 1978-82; ptnr. Conrad, Scherer & James, Ft. Lauderdale, 1982—. Republican. Roman Catholic. Avocation: sports. State civil litigation, Insurance, Personal injury. Home: 1325 Ponce de Leon Dr Fort Lauderdale FL 33316 Office: Conrad Scherer & James 633 S Federal Hwy Fort Lauderdale FL 33301

COONEY, MICHAEL FRANCIS, lawyer; b. Bklyn., Dec. 25, 1942; s. Michael F. Cooney. BA, St. Alphonsus Coll., 1965; MBA, NYU, 1973; JD, Bklyn. Law Sch., 1979. Bar: N.Y. 1980, U.S. Dist. Ct. (so. and ea. dists.) N.Y. 1982, U.S. Tax Ct. 1985. Mgr. various N.Y. Life Ins., N.Y.C., 1966-81; pres. Windsor Life Ins. Co., N.Y.C., 1981-83; v.p., sec., gen. counsel Gamma Reins. Co., N.Y.C., 1983—, also bd. dirs.; group gen. counsel AXA Am. Inc., Chgo., 1984—; sec. Appalachian Nat. Corp., Knoxville, Tenn., 1985—; bd. dirs. Appalachian Nat. Life Ins. Co., Knoxville. Mem. ABA, Assn. of Bar of City of N.Y., N.Y. County Lawyers Assn., Assn. Trial Lawyers Am., Am. Assn. Corp. Secs. General corporate, Insurance, Administrative and regulatory. Home: 145 Nassau St New York NY 10038 Office: Gamma Reins Co 175 Water St New York NY 10038

COONEY, THOMAS EMMETT, lawyer; b. Portland, Oreg., July 16, 1931; s. Thomas M. and Ruth (Clune) C.; children from previous marriage: Jeff, Tom, Paul, Tracy. BA, U. Portland, 1953; JD, Willamette U., 1956. Bar: Oreg. 1956, U.S. Dist. Ct. Oreg. 1956, U.S. Ct. Apls. (9th cir.) 1956, U.S. Supreme Ct. 1980. Assoc., Maguire, Shields, Morrison, Bailey & Kester, Portland, 1956-60, ptnr., 1960-65; ptnr. Morrison & Dunn, Portland, 1965-80, Cooney and Van Hoomissen, Portland, Oreg., 1980-82, Cooney & Crew, Portland, 1982—; adj. instr. Coll. Law Lewis and Clark U., 1978-79. Served with USAF, 1951-52. Fellow Am. Coll. Trial Lawyers, Nat. Health Lawyers Assn., Assn. Med. Soc. Attys., Oreg. Assn. Hosp. Atty's., Am. Acad. Hosp. Atty's; mem. Oreg. Assn. Def. Counsel, Am. Bd. Trial Advocates (diplomate), Internat. Assn. Ins. Counsel, Def. Research Inst. Club: Oswego Lake Country. Lodge: Elks. State civil litigation, Federal civil litigation, Insurance. Address: 1618 SW 1st Ave Suite 205 Portland OR 97201

COONEY, WILLIAM J., lawyer; b. Augusta, Ga., July 31, 1929; s. John F. and Ellen (Joy) C.; m. Martha L. Whaley, May 1, 1971; children: William J., Sarah C., William J. IV. BS, U. Notre Dame, 1951; JD, Georgetown U., 1954, LLM, 1955. Bar: Ga. 1963, Calif. 1961, D.C. 1954. Law clk. U.S. Ct. Appeals, Washington, 1954, U.S. Claims Ct., Washington, 1955; asst. U.S. atty. Washington, 1958-60, San Francisco, 1960-63; sole practice Augusta, 1963—. Served to lt. JAGC, U.S. Army, 1955-58. Mem. ABA. Roman Catholic. Federal civil litigation, Trademark and copyright, Corporate taxation. Office: 1100 First Union Bank Bldg Augusta GA 30901-1450

COONRAD, DOUGLAS V., lawyer; b. Troy, N.Y., June 16, 1945. BA, Dartmouth Coll., 1967; JD cum laude, New Eng. Sch. Law, 1975. Bar: Mass 1975, Iowa 1978, U.S. Dist. Ct. Iowa 1978, U.S. Ct. Appeals (8th cir.) 1978, U.S. Supreme Ct. 1979, U.S. Ct. Mil. Appeals, 1985. With JAGC, USN, 1975-78; sole practice Hudson, Iowa, 1978—; with JAGC, USNR, 1978—; devel. Iowa Computer Law Forms, 1984—. Editor: New England Jour. on Law. Fund drive agt. Dartmouth Alumni Fund., 1967-86; mem. resolutions com. Iowa Ann. Conf. United Meth. Ch., 1986-89. Mem. ABA, Iowa Bar Assn. Lodge: Lions (2d v.p. Hudson 1986). Avocations: skiing, boating, outdoor activities. General practice, Personal injury, Consumer commercial. Home: 109 Ardis St Hudson IA 50643

COONS, JOHN E., legal educator, lawyer; b. 1929. B.A., U. Minn., 1950; J.D., Northwestern U., 1953. Bar: D.C. 1953, Ill. 1953. Trial atty. Army Panel Bd. Contract Appeals, 1953-55; asst. prof. Northwestern U., 1955-58, assoc. prof., 1958-62, prof., 1962-68, asst. dean Sch. Law, 1955-60; vis. prof. U. Calif.-Berkeley Sch. Law, 1967-68; prof. 1968—. Author: (with Clune and Sugarman) Private Wealth and Public Education, 1970, (with Sugarman) Education by Choice, 1978; past mng. editor: Northwestern U. Law Rev. Served with U.S. Army, 1953-55. Mem. Cleve. Conf., Order of Coif. Legal education. Office: U Calif Law Sch 225 Boalt Hall Berkeley CA 94720 *

COONS, STEPHEN MERLE, lawyer; b. Indpls., May 27, 1941; s. Harold M. and Margaret L. (Richman) C.; m. Joan Eleanor Tischer; children: Michael, Tracy, Richard, Lori, Caroline. BA, Wabash Coll., 1963; JD, Ind. U., 1971. Bar: Ind. 1971, U.S. Dist. Ct. (so. dist.) Ind. 1971, U.S. Tax Ct. 191, U.S. Dist. Ct. (no. dist.) Ind. 1980, U.S. Ct. Appeals (7th cir.) 1980, U.S. Supreme Ct. 1978. Ptnr. Bradford & Coons, Indpls., 1971-72; assoc. Yockey & Yockey, Indpls., 1972-73; ptnr. Compton, Coons & Fetta, Indpls., 1973-78, Coons & Saint, Indpls., 1979—; securities commr. State Ind., Indpls., 1978-83. Mem. Indpls. Bar Assn., Ind. State Bar Assn., ABA, Am. Assn. Trial Lawyers , Indpls. C. of C. Republican. Presbyterian. Clubs: Columbia, Athletic (Indpls.). Securities, General corporate, Real property. Home: 7850 Bay Shore Dr Indianapolis IN 46240 Office: Coons & Saint 440 North East St Indianapolis IN 46204-1512

COOPER, ALAN SAMUEL, lawyer; b. Louisville, June 13, 1942; s. Rudey and Rosalie (Schwartz) C.; m. Maxine Jacobs, Aug. 13, 1966 (dec.); children—Lauren K., Jennifer D. B.A., Vanderbilt U., 1964, J.D., 1968. Bar: Tenn. 1968, D.C. 1969, U.S. Dist. Ct. D.C. 1969, U.S. Ct. Appeals (Fed. cir.) 1975, U.S. Supreme Ct. 1980. Law clk. U.S. Dist. Ct. (mid. dist.) Tenn., 1967-68; assoc. Browne, Schuyler & Beveridge and Browne, Beveridge & DeGrandi, Washington, 1968-72; assoc. Schuyler, Birch, Swindler, McKie & Beckett, Washington, 1972-74; ptnr. Schuyler, Banner, Birch, McKie & Beckett and successor firm Banner, Birch, McKie & Beckett, Washington, 1974—; adj. prof. Gerogetown U. Law Ctr., 1985—; adviser on trademark law to U.S. del. to Diplomatic Conf. on Revision of Paris Conv. for Protection of Indsl. Property, Nairobi, Kenya, 1981. Mem. ABA (faculty Nat. Insts. on Trademark Litigation 1978, 79), U.S. Trademark Assn., D.C. Bar, Bar. Assn. D.C., Tenn. Bar Assn. Jewish. Trademark and copyright. Office: One Thomas Circle NW Washington DC 20005

COOPER, CHARLES JUSTIN, lawyer, government official; b. Dayton, Ohio, Mar. 8, 1952; s. Robert Lee and Katherine (Thompson) C.; m. Jill Cole, Feb. 27, 1972; children—Paul Davis, Jay Daniel. B.S. in Fin., U. Ala.-Tuscaloosa, 1974; J.D., U. Ala., Tuscaloosa, 1977. Law clk. U.S. Ct. Appeals (5th cir.), St. Petersburg, Fla., 1977-78, U.S. Supreme Ct., Washington, 1978-79; assoc. Long & Aldridge, Atlanta, 1979-81; spl. asst. Civil Rights Div. U.S. Dept. Justice, Washington, 1981-82, dep. asst., 1982-85; asst. atty. gen. Office Legal Counsel U.S. Dept. Justice, Washington, 1985—. Mem. ABA, Ala. Bar Assn., D.C. Bar Assn., State Bar Ga., Atlanta Bar Assn.

COOPER, CHARLES NEILSON, lawyer; b. Norfolk, Va., July 13, 1935; s. Dudley and Mary (Miller) C.; m. Bettie Minette Switzer, June 22, 1958; children: C. Neilson Jr., Erik Switzer, Jefferson Switzer. BA in History, U. Va., 1957; LLB, Columbia U., 1962. Bar: Va. 1962, U.S. Dist. Ct. (ea. dist.) Va. 1963, U.S. Supreme Ct. 1971. Ptnr. Cooper & Cooper, Norfolk, 1963-72, sr. ptnr., 1972-78; sr. ptnr. Cooper, Kalfus & Nachman, Norfolk, 1978-79, pres., 1979-81; sr. ptnr. Cooper & North, Norfolk, 1981-85; sole practice Norfolk, 1985—. Fund-raiser, gen. counsel Young Audiences Va., Inc., Norfolk, 1970—; commr. Eastern Va. Med. Authority, Norfolk, 1977-79; trustee Norfolk Acad., 1983—; bd. dirs. WHRO, Norfolk, 1985—, Entrepreneurship and Private Enterprise Ctr., 1987; sec. Greater Norfolk Corp., 1986-87. Served to 1st lt. U.S. Army, 1957-65. Recipient Award of Honor, Jr. C. of C., Norfolk, 1965, Life Bravissimo award Citizens of Tidewater, Va., 1980, cert. appreciation of outstanding service Va. Philharm. Orch., Norfolk, 1980. Mem. ABA, Va. Bar Assn., Norfolk and Portsmouth Bar Assn., Tidewater Estate Planning Council. Avocation: yachting. Estate planning, Probate, Estate taxation. Office: Cooper Law Offices 706 Plaza One Bldg Norfolk VA 23510

COOPER, CORINNE, law educator; b. Albuquerque, July 12, 1952; d. David D. and Martha Lucille (Rosenblum) C. BA magna cum laude, U. Ariz., 1975, JD summa cum laude, 1978. Bar: Ariz. 1978, U.S. Dist. Ct. Ariz. 1978, Mo. 1985. Assoc. Streich, Lang, Weeks & Cardon, Phoenix, 1978-82; asst. prof. U. Mo., Kansas City, 1982-86, assoc. prof., 1986—. Contbr. articles to profl. jours. Legal counsel Mo. for Hart campaign, 1984; bd. dirs. Com. for County Progress, Kansas City, 1985—. Mem. ABA (Uniform Commercial Code com., dispute resolution com., corp., bus. and banking membership com., sect. econ. chmn. profs. users group 1986—), Am. Assn. Law Schs. (comml. law 1982—, alternative dispute resolution com.), Am. Arbitration Assn. (arbitrator), Soc. Profls. in Dispute Resolution, Mo. Bar Assn. (commercial law com.), Phi Beta Kappa, Phi Kappa Phi. Democrat. Jewish. Avocations: automobile racing, art collecting. Banking, Contracts commercial, Alternative dispute resolution arbitration. Office: U Mo Sch Law 5100 Rockhill Rd Kansas City MO 64116

COOPER, DAVID JOHN, lawyer; b. Wyandotte, Mich., Sept. 27, 1935; s. John Howard and Kathryn Louise (Cauley) C.; m. Roseann Elizabeth McCarty, Dec. 29, 1962; 1 child, David John, Jr. B.A., U. Mich., 1957, J.D., 1960. Bar: Mich. 1960, U.S. Dist. Ct. (ea. dist.) Mich. 1960, U.S. Ct. Appeals (6th cir.) 1972, U.S. Supreme Ct. 1974. Atty., assoc. Joselyn, Rowe, Jamieson, Detroit, 1961-65; atty., ptnr. Garan, Lucow, Miller, Seward, Cooper & Becker, P.C., Detroit, 1965—; dir., founder Medical-Legal Symposium, Med.-Law Workshop, 1984; speaker cons., seminars. Contbr. articles to prof. jours. Served with U.S. Army, 1960-61. Mem. Assn. Def. Trial Counsel (pres. Mich. chpt. 1971-72), Internat. Assn. of Ins. Counsel, Am. Soc. Hosp. Attys., Am. Bd. Profl. Liability Attys. Roman Catholic. Clubs: Pine Lake Country (Orchard Lake); Renaissance (Detroit). Personal injury, State civil litigation, Insurance. Home: 4648 Brafferton Dr Bloomfield Hills MI 48013 Office: Law Offices 1000 Woodbridge Pl Detroit MI 48207

COOPER, DAVID JOSEPH, lawyer; b. Detroit, Jan. 11, 1944; s. Charles Samuel and Phyllis (Copans) C.; m. Patricia Ann Drozer, Oct. 9, 1973; 1 child, Rachel Adrianna. BA, Wayne State U., 1968; JD, U. Detroit, 1971. Bar: Mich. 1972, U.S. Dist. Ct. (ea. and we. dists.) Mich. 1973, U.S. Ct. Appeals (6th cir.) 1979, U.S. Dist. Ct. (no. dist.) Wis. 1983. Treas. Philo, Cockrel et al, Detroit, 1973-77; v.p. Cockrel, Cooper et al, Detroit, 1977-82; sole practice Tecumseh, Mich., 1982—. Mem. New Detroit, Inc., 1972-73. Recipient Am. Jurisprudence award Bancroft-Whitney Co., 1968. Mem. Mich. Bar Assn. (hearing panel grievance commn. 1983—). Democrat. Jewish. Avocations: tennis, sailing. Workers' compensation, Personal injury, Federal civil litigation. Office: 4153 Occidental Hwy Box 380 Tecumseh MI 49286

COOPER, DOUGLAS KENNETH, lawyer; b. Ithaca, N.Y., June 6, 1947; s. Murray I. and Meta F. Cooper; m. Pamela A. Regan, Aug. 22, 1970; children—James, Sarah. B.A., N.C. State U., 1970; J.D., U. N.C., 1974. Bar: Ohio 1974. Assoc., Shapiro, Persky, Stone & Marken Co., L.P.A., Cleve., 1974-76; of counsel Leaseway Transp. Corp., Cleve., 1976-78, assoc. corp. counsel, 1978-82, corp. counsel, 1982—. Contbr. articles to law reviews. Mem. Cleve. Citizens League, 1974—. Mem. Bar Assn. Greater Cleve., Ohio State Bar Assn., ABA. General corporate, Real property, Securities. Office: Leaseway Transp Corp 3700 Park East Dr Cleveland OH 44122

COOPER, EDWARD HAYES, lawyer, educator; b. Highland Park, Mich., Oct. 13, 1941; s. Frank Edward and Margaret Ellen (Hayes) C.; m. Nancy Carol Wybo, June 29, 1963; children: Lisa, Chandra. A.B., Dartmouth Coll., 1961; LL.B., Harvard U., 1964. Bar: Mich. 1965. Law clk. Hon. Clifford O'Sullivan, U.S. Ct. of Appeals, 1964-65; sole practice Detroit, 1965-67; adj. prof. Wayne State U. Law Sch., 1965-67; assoc. prof. U. Minn. Law Sch., 1967-72; prof. law U. Mich. Law Sch., Ann Arbor, 1972—, assoc. dean for acad. affairs, 1981—; adv. Restatement of the Law, 2d, Judgements, 1976-80. Author: (with C.A. Wright and A.R. Miller) Federal Practice and Procedure: Jurisdiction, Vols. 13-19, 1975-81, 2d edit., 1984-86. Contbr. articles to law revs. Mem. ABA, Mich. Bar Assn., Am. Law Inst. Antitrust, Federal civil litigation, Legal education. Office: 320 Hutchins Hall Law Sch U Mich Ann Arbor MI 48109-1215

COOPER, GARY ALLAN, lawyer; b. Bristol, Va., Feb. 3, 1947; s. Earl Clarence and Reba Evelyn (Jenkins) C.; m. Lynn Ellen Weir, Feb. 17, 1973; chidlren: Drew Kelsey, Gavin Morgan. BS in Journalism, U. Tenn., 1969, JD, 1972. Bar: Tenn. 1972, U.S. Dist. Ct. (ea. dist.) Tenn. 1972, U.S. Supreme Ct. 1979, Fla. 1981,. Assoc. Luther, Anderson & Ruth, Chattanooga, 1972-76; ptnr. Luther, Anderson, Cleary, Luhowiak & Cooper, Chattanooga, 1976-79, Luther, Anderson, Cleary & Cooper, Chattanooga, 1979-80, Anderson, Cleary & Cooper, Chattanooga, 1981, Fleissner & Cooper, Chattanooga, 1982, Fleissner, Cooper & Marcus, Chattanooga, 1983—. Author: Tennessee Forms for Trial Practice, 1977, (rev. ed. 1980), Tennessee Law Office Administration, 1977. Served with USAR, 1972-79. Recipient Herman Hickman Postgrad. scholarship for Athletes U. Tenn., 1969. Mem. ABA, Chattanooga Bar Assn. (bd. dirs. 1984-86), Fla. Bar Assn. (mem. out-of-state practitioners com. 1983-86), Tenn. Bar Assn., Tenn. Def. Lawyers Assn., Phi Delta Phi. Republican. Methodist. Club: Chattanooga Golf and Country. Avocations: golf, reading. State civil litigation, Insurance, Federal civil litigation. Home: 837 Ravine Rd Signal Mountain TN 37377 Office: Fleissner Cooper & Marcus 555 River St Suite 200 Chattanooga TN 37405

COOPER, GEORGE, writer, consultant; b. Balt., May 31, 1937; s. Harry and Hilda C.; m. Jill Zimmerman, June 19, 1960 (div. 1972); 1 child, Amanda; m. Judy Blume, 1987. B.S., U. Pa., 1958; LL.B., Harvard U., 1961; cert. in celestial nav. Hayden Planetarium, 1972. Bar: D.C. 1961, N.Y. 1975, U.S. Supreme Ct. 1966. Assoc. Covington & Burling, Washington, 1963-66; faculty Columbia Law Sch., 1966-85, prof. law, 1969-85; writer, consultant, 1985—; vis. prof. Harvard U. Law Sch., 1975, U. Witwatersrand, Johannesburg, S.Africa, 1979. Author: Voluntary Tax, 1979; (with Rabb and Rubin) Equal Employment Opportunity, 1975; A Voluntary Tax?, 1979. Editor: Law and Poverty, 1972. Civil rights, Personal income taxation. Home: 121 Good Hill Rd Weston CT 06883

COOPER, GEORGE WILSON, lawyer; b. Elizabeth, N.J., Nov. 19, 1927; s. Leon and Lucy Ellen (Price) C.; m. Elaine Anita Jaffe, May 2, 1954; children—Richard M., Julia A.; m. Isolde Kurz, May 27, 1974; 1 son, Daniel R. A.B., Columbia U., 1947, J.D., 1950. Bar: N.Y. 1951, U.S. Dist. Ct. (so. and ea. dists.) N.Y. 1953, U.S. Ct. Customs and Patent Appeals 1979, U.S. Supreme Ct. 1980. Assoc., Langner, Parry, Card & Langner, N.Y.C., 1951-53, Pennie, Edmonds, Morton, Barrows & Taylor, N.Y.C., 1953-60; internat.

atty. Avon Products, Inc., N.Y.C., 1960-63, dir. legal affairs internat., 1963-69, v.p. legal affairs internat., 1969-72, v.p. legal affairs corp., 1972-79; sole practice, N.Y.C., 1979-86; ptnr. Grimes & Battersby, Stamford, Conn., 1986— . Active Am. Jewish Com., 1955—, exec. bd. N.Y. chpt., 1958-84; mem. Stamford Symphony Soc., 1975—. Mem. ABA, Internat. Bar Assn., Inter-Am. Bar Assn., U.S. Trademark Assn. (award merit 1968, Outstanding Service citations 1972, 79, contbg. editor Trademark Mgmt. 1981), Internat. Patent and Trademark Assn., N.Y. Patent Law Assn., Copyright Soc., Direct Selling Assn. (editor Internat. Bull. 1974-76), Columbia U. Alumni Assn., Columbia Law Sch. Alumni Assn. Trademark and copyright, Private international, General corporate. Office: 184 Atlantic St Stamford CT 06904

COOPER, HAL DEAN, lawyer; b. Marshall County, Iowa, Dec. 8, 1934; s. Truman B. and Golda F. (Chadwick) C.; m. Constance B. Simms, Dec. 31, 1960; children: Shannon, Charles, Ellen. Student, Neb. U., 1952-54; B.S. in Mech. Engring., Iowa State U., 1957; J.D. with honors, George Washington U., 1962. Bar: Iowa 1963, Ohio 1963, U.S. Supreme Ct. 1971. Assoc., ptnr. Fay & Fay, Cleve., 1962-67; ptnr. Meyer, Tilberry & Body, Cleve., 1967-69, Yount, Tarolli, Weinshenker & Cooper, Cleve, 1969-72; trial judge U.S. Ct. Claims, Washington, 1972-75; ptnr. Jones, Day, Reavis & Pogue, Cleve., 1975—. Served with AUS, 1957-59. Mem. ABA, Cleve. Pat. Law Assn. Episcopalian. Clubs: Rowfant, Clifton. Lodge: Masons. Federal civil litigation, Patent, Trademark and copyright. Home: 16924 Edgewater Dr Lakewood OH 44107 Office: Jones Day Reavis & Pogue 1700 Huntington Bldg Cleveland OH 44115

COOPER, IRVING BEN, U.S. judge; b. London, Eng., Feb. 7, 1902; came to U.S., 1912, naturalized, 1921; s. Max and Rachel (Shimansky) C.; m. Anita Bennett, Mar. 28, 1929; children—Richard Bennett, Benita H. (Mrs. Theodore Lee Marks). LL.B., Washington U., 1925. Bar: N.Y. bar 1927. Gen. practice civil law N.Y.C., 1927-38; asso. counsel ambulance chasing investigation Appellate div. N.Y. Supreme Ct., 1928; asso. counsel bar assns. disciplinary proc. 1928-30, spl. dep. atty. gen. to investigate improper med. practices, 1929, asso. counsel investigation Magistrates courts, 1930-31; asso. counsel to Judge Samuel Seabury in investigation N.Y.C. Govt., 1932-33; spl. counsel Dept. Investigation, N.Y.C., 1934-37; city magistrate 1938-39; asso. justice Ct. Spl. Sessions, 1939-51, chief justice, 1951-60; U.S. dist. judge So. Dist. N.Y., 1962—, now sr. judge; lectr., cons. program of law and psychiatry Menninger Found., 1960; lectr. criminal law, 1960-61; Hon. pres. Univ. Settlement, N.Y.C.; trustee Nat. Council Crime and Delinquency, chmn. criminal courts sect., adv. counsel of judges, 1954-69. Trustee Reconstructionist Found. Recipient Silver Buffalo award Boy Scouts Am., 1965. Mem. Am. Judicature Soc., Assn. Bar City N.Y., N.Y. County Lawyers Assn., Am. Bar Assn. (chmn. com. on sentencing, probation and parole 1957-61). Jurisprudence. Office: US Courthouse Foley Sq New York NY 10007

COOPER, IVER PETER, lawyer, chemist; b. N.Y.C., Nov. 10, 1953; s. Morris Robert and Lillie Cooper; m. Lee Shpiegelman, May 15, 1983; 1 child, Louise. SB, MIT, 1974; JD, Boston U., 1977; LLM, George Washington U., 1979. Bar: U.S. Patent Office 1976, N.Y. 1978, U.S. Ct. Claims 1978, U.S. Ct. Customs and Patent Appeals 1978, D.C. 1980, U.S. Ct. Appeals (fed. cir.) 1982, Va. 1984. Law clk. to presiding justice U.S. Ct. Claims, Washington, 1977-78; assoc. Weitzman & Rogal, Washington, 1979-80; assoc. litigation Craig & Antonelli, Washington, 1980-83; sole practice Arlington, Va., 1983-85; ptnr. Mackler, Cooper & Gibbs, Washington, 1985—. Author: Biotechnology and the Law, 1982; mem. editorial bd. Biotechnology Law Reports, 1983—, Bio Innovation, 1986—; contbg. editor Medical Devices and Diagnostics Industry mag.; contbr. articles to profl. jours. Recipient 1st Prize Burkan Competition, Boston U., 1976, Ladas award U.S. Patent Assn., 1979; Food and Drug Law Inst. fellow, 1978. Mem. Am. Patent Law Assn. (Watson award 1979), Assn. Biotechnology Cos. (patent and assoc. regulatory counsel). Avocations: nature photography, folk dancing. Patent, Trademark and copyright, Environment. Office: Mackler Cooper & Gibbs 1220 L St NW #615 Washington DC 20005

COOPER, JEAN SARALEE, judge; b. Huntington, N.Y., Mar. 7, 1946; d. Ralph and Henrietta (Halbreich) C. B.A., Sophie Newcomb Coll. of Tulane U., 1968; J.D., Emory U., 1970. Bar: La. 1970, Ga. 1970, U.S. Dist. Ct. (ea. dist.) La. 1970, U.S. Ct. Appeals (5th cir.) 1972, U.S. Ct. Appeals (2d cir.) 1976, U.S. Ct. Appeals (4th cir.) 1979, U.S. Ct. Appeals (fed. cir.) 1982, U.S. Supreme Ct. 1974. Trial atty. Office of Solicitor, U.S. Dept. Labor, Washington, 1970-73, spl. projects asst., 1973, sr. trial atty., 1973-77; adminstrv. judge Bd. Contract Appeals, HUD, Washington, 1977—, acting chmn. and chief judge, 1980-81, vice chmn., 1983; cons., lectr. Contbr. articles to profl. jours. Recipient Moot Court award Tulane Law Sch., 1968. Mem. ABA, Am. Law Inst., La. Bar Assn., Am. Judicature Soc., Inst. Jud. Adminstrn., Bd. of Contract Appeals Judges Assn., Nat. Assn. Women Judges, Exec. Women in Govt., Wolf Trap Assocs., Am. Inst. Wine and Food, L'Acadamie de Cuisine (instr.; chevalier de canardier). Republican. Administrative and regulatory, Federal civil litigation. Address: HUD Bd Contract Appeals 451 7th St SW Suite 2158 Washington DC 20410

COOPER, JOHN JOSEPH, lawyer; b. Vincennes, Ind., Oct. 20, 1924; s. Homer O. and Ruth (House) C.; m. Nathalie Brooke, 1945. A.B., Stanford, 1950, LL.B., 1951; LL.M., U. So. Calif., 1964. Bar: Calif. 1952. Practice in San Francisco, 1951-54, Los Angeles, 1954-61, Palo Alto, 1961—; gen. counsel, v.p. Varian Assos., 1970—; lectr. Am. Law Inst.-Am. Bar Assn., Seattle, 1964, Kansas City, 1965, 66; moderator Trademark and Copyright Inst., George Washington U., 1968; participant Tokyo Conf., U.S.-Japanese Patent Licensing Symposium, U. Wash.-Japanese Inst. Internat. Bus. Law, 1968; speaker Mid-Am. World Trade Conf., Chgo., 1971. Contbr.: chpt. to Patent and Know-How Licensing in Japan and the United States; also law rev. articles and profl. jours. Served with USNR, 1942-45. Mem. ABA, Calif. Bar Assn. (speaker Conf. Corp. Counsel 1969), Am. Corp. Counsel Assn. (pres., bd. dirs. San Francisco chpt.), Bay Area Gen. Counsels Group, Peninsula Assn. Gen. Counsels, Santa Clara Bar Assn. Republican. Home: 191 Ramoso Rd Portola Valley CA 94025 Office: 611 Hansen Way Palo Alto CA 94303

COOPER, JOHN NICHOLAS, lawyer; b. New Brunswick, N.J., Nov. 30, 1910; s. Drury Walls and Esther Stevenson (Nicholas) C.; m. Anna Rose VanCleve, Mar. 20, 1937; children: Jacob N., Peter W., Cary Ann, Nina H.; m. Jocelyn W. Woodworth, Dec. 30, 1961; 1 child, Nicholas Drury. BA, Brown U., 1932; LLB, Yale U., 1935. Bar: N.Y. 1938, U.S. Dist. Ct. (so. dist.) N.Y. 1941, U.S. Ct. Appeals (2d cir.) 1943, U.S. Ct. Appeals (6th cir.) 1955, U.S. Ct. Appeals (7th cir.) 1967. Assoc. Davie, Auerbach & Cornell, N.Y.C., 1935-40, Cooper, Kerr & Dunham, N.Y.C., 1940-46; ptnr. Cooper, Kerr & Dunham and successor firms, N.Y.C., 1946-1986; of counsel Cooper, Dunham, Griffin & Moran, N.Y.C., 1986—. Mem. Morris Township Com., N.J., 1950-60; sec. Bd. Adjustment, Morris Township, 1951-56. Mem. ABA, N.Y. State Bar Assn., Assn. of Bar N.Y.C., N.Y. County Lawyers Assn., N.Y. Patent Lawyers Assn. (v.p. 1962-64, pres. 1964-65), Campfire Club Am. Republican. Episcopalian. Clubs: Yale (N.Y.C.), Brown (N.Y.C.). Patent, Trademark and copyright. Home: 711 Rockrimmon Rd Stamford CT 06903 Office: Cooper Dunham Griffin & Moran 30 Rockefeller Plaza New York NY 10112

COOPER, LAWRENCE ALLEN, lawyer; b. San Antonio, Feb. 1, 1948; s. Elmer E. and Sally (Tempkin) C.; m. Annie Nataf, Aug. 19, 1973; 1 son, Jonathan Alexander. B.A., Tulane U., 1970; J.D., St. Mary's U., San Antonio, 1974; LL.M., Emory U., 1980. Bar: Ga. 1975, Tex. 1975. Ptnr., Cohen, Pollock, Cooper & Comolli, Atlanta, 1979—. Mem. Atlanta Bar Assn., ABA, Ga. Bar Assn., Tex. Bar Assn., Ga. Trial Lawyers Assn., Assn. Trial Lawyers Am., Ga. Assn. Criminal Def. Lawyers. State civil litigation, Criminal, Family and matrimonial. Home: 3985 Randall Mill Rd NW Atlanta GA 30327 Office: 3985 Randall Mill Rd NW Atlanta GA 30327

COOPER, LINDA DAWN, lawyer; b. Cleve., April 30, 1953; d. Robert Boyd and Catherine S. (Powell) C. B.S. in Psychology with honors, Eastern Ky. U., 1975; J.D., Cleve.-Marshall Law Sch., 1977. Bar: Ohio 1978, U.S. Dist. Ct. (no. dist.) Ohio 1980. Law clk. Vanik, Monroe, Zucco and Klein, Cleve., 1976-78; legal intern Cleve.-Marshall Legal Clinic, 1977; assoc. Vanik, Monroe, Zucco, Klein & Scanlon, Cleve. and Chesterland, Ohio, 1978-79; sr. staff atty. Lake County Pub. Defender, Painesville, Ohio, 1979-80; ptnr. Heffernan & Cooper, Painesville, Cleve., 1980-83; sole practice Painesville, 1983—; lectr. criminal justice seminar, Painesville, 1981. Speaker, adv., counselor Cleve. Rape Crisis Center, 1976; appointee Congressman Eckart's Com. on Health, Environment and Energy, Mentor, Ohio, 1983; chmn. juvenile justice com. LWV, Painesville, 1983; councilwoman Willoughby City Council, Ohio, 1984. Mem. Assn. Trial Lawyers Am., ABA, Ohio Bar Assn., Lake County Bar Assn. Democrat. Episcopalian. General practice, Personal injury, Family and matrimonial. Home: 5534 D Wrens Ln Willoughby OH 44094 Office: 174 Main St Painesville OH 44077

COOPER, MARGARET LESLIE, lawyer; b. Geneva, N.Y., Apr. 13, 1950; d. Jack Frederick and Barbara Ann (Hitchings) C. BA in Math., Rollins Coll., 1972; JD, Mercer U., 1976. Bar: Fla. 1976, U.S. Dist. Ct. (so. dist.) Fla. 1977, U.S. Ct. Appeals (5th cir.) 1977, U.S. Ct. Appeals (11th cir.) 1981. Assoc. Jones & Foster P.A., West Palm Beach, Fla., 1976-81, ptnr., 1981—; assoc. prof. Palm Beach Jr. Coll., West Palm Beach, 1985-86. Pres. young people's pres.'s council Norton Gallery Art, West Palm Beach, 1982-84; chmn. campaign Lou Frey for Gov., Palm Beach County, 1986. Named to Sports Hall Fame, Rollins Coll., 1986. Mem. Palm Beach County Bar Assn., Exec. Women Palm Beach, Palm Beach Jr. League, Women's Internat. Tennis Assn. (disciplinary rev. bd. 1985—). Republican. Clubs: The Beach, The Tennis Palm Beach. Avocations: tennis, snow skiing. Commercial state and federal litigation. Home: 317 Cordova Rd West Palm Beach FL 33401 Office: Jones & Foster PA PO Drawer E West Palm Beach FL 33402

COOPER, MICHAEL ANTHONY, lawyer; b. Passaic, N.J., Mar. 29, 1936. B.A., Harvard U., 1957, LL.B., 1960. Bar: N.Y. State 1961, U.S. Supreme Ct. 1969. With firm Sullivan & Cromwell, N.Y.C., 1960—; partner Sullivan & Cromwell, 1968—; Bd. dirs. Legal Aid Soc., pres., 1981-83; Bd. dirs. Lawyers Com. for Civil Rights Under Law. Fellow Am. Coll. Trial Lawyers; mem. Am., N.Y. bar assns., Assn. Bar City N.Y., Am. Law Inst., N.Y. County Lawyers Assn., Am. Judicature Soc. Contracts commercial, Antitrust, Securities. Office: 125 Broad St New York NY 10004

COOPER, MICHAEL DAVID, lawyer; b. Gardener, Maine, Feb. 12, 1949. BA, U. Minn., 1972; JD, U. Maine, 1976. Bar: Maine 1976, U.S. Dist. Ct. Maine 1976. Staff atty. City of Westbrook, Maine, 1973-77, asst. soliciter, 1977-81, solicitor, 1987—; ptnr. Cooper, Manderson & Millet, Westbrook, 1982—. Mem. planning bd. Town of Cumberland, Maine, 1980-82, town counsel, 1982-83. Mem. ABA, Maine Bar Assn., Maine Trial Lawyers Assn., Regional Orgn. Mcpl. Attys. Local government, Contracts commercial, Real property. Home: 41 Deer Hill Circle Westbrook ME 04092 Office: Cooper Manderson & Millett 836 Main St PO Box 309 Westbrook ME 04092

COOPER, PATRICIA JACQUELINE, lawyer; b. Detroit, Feb. 6, 1958; d. Donald and Aileen Cooper. BA, Vassars Coll., 1978; JD, U. San Francisco, Hastings, 1981. Bar: D.C. 1982. Assoc. Costello Assocs., Washington, 1981-82; atty. VA, Washington, 1982-83; sole practice Washington, 1983—; atty. Ground Floors Mgmt., Washington, 1983—. Mem. ABA (entertainment and sports law com.), Songwriters Assn. of Washington, Women in Music, Women's Bar Assn., Am. Women Composers (nat. bd. dirs. 1982—). Entertainment. Office: 3365 18th St NW Washington DC 20010

COOPER, PAUL DOUGLAS, lawyer; b. Kansas City, Mo., July 22, 1941; s. W.W. and Emma Marie (Ringo) C.; m. Elsa B. Shaw, June 15, 1963; children—Richard, Dean. B.A. in English, U. Mich., 1963; LL.B., U. Calif., Hastings Coll. Law, 1966. Bar: Colo. 1966, U.S. Dist. Colo. 1966, U.S. Ct. Appeals (10th cir.) 1967, U.S. Supreme Ct. 1979. Dep. dist. atty. Denver, 1969-71; asst. U.S. atty. Dist. of Colo., 1973-80; ptnr. Yegge, Hall & Evans, Denver, 1973-80; pres., dir. Cooper & Kelley, P.C., Denver, 1980—; mem. faculty trial practice seminar Denver U. Law Sch., 1982; asst. U.S. atty. Dist. of Colo., 1973-75; spl. prosecutor Mar. 1977 term, Garfield County Grand Jury; pres. Bow Mar Owners, Inc., 1976-77. Recipient Spl. Commendation for Outstanding Service, 1972. Mem. ABA, Colo. Bar Assn. (interprofl. com., bd. govs.), Denver Bar Assn. (trustee, 1st v.p. 1982-83), Colo. Med. Soc. (chmn. interprofl. com., Denver bar liaison com.), Internat. Assn. Ins. Counsel. Republican. Club: Denver Athletic. Insurance, Libel, Personal injury. Office: 1660 Wynkoop St Suite 900 Denver CO 80202

COOPER, R. JOHN, III, advertising agency executive, lawyer; b. East Orange, N.J., Mar. 2, 1942; s. Russell John and Cynthia Rhe (Runser) C.; m. Unni Irene Langaanes, June 20, 1964; children—Kirsten Elizabeth, R. John IV. A.B., Amherst Coll., 1964; postgrad., U. Oslo, 1965; J.D., Harvard U., 1968. Chief law clk. Supreme Jud. Ct. Mass., Boston, 1968-69; assoc. Cravath, Swaine & Moore, N.Y.C., 1969-77; ptnr. Casey Lane & Mittendorf, N.Y.C., 1977-82; gen. counsel video group Time Inc., N.Y.C., 1982-84; exec. v.p., gen. counsel, sec. Young & Rubicam, Inc., N.Y.C., 1984—, also bd. dirs.; bd. dirs. HCM, Inc., N.Y. and Paris, DWD, Tokyo. Editor: Cablespeech, 1983. Clk. of vestry Christ Ch., Short Hills, N.J., 1978-82, lay minister, 1980—; trustee N.J. Shakespeare Fest, 1986; chmn. Millburn-Short Hills Cable TV Com., 1986—. Amherst Coll. fellow, Oslo, Norway, 1964-65. Mem. ABA (governing com., forum com. on sports and entertainment industries 1983-86), Assn. Bar City of N.Y. (mem. antitrust and trade regulation com. 1982-84, corp. law depts. com. 1986—), Am. Assn. Advt. Agys. (govt. relations com. 1986—). Republican. Episcopalian. Clubs: Short Hills (N.J.); Union League (N.Y.C.); Boothbay Harbor Yacht (Maine). Administrative and regulatory, Antitrust, General corporate. Home: 9 East Ln Short Hills NJ 07078 Office: Young & Rubicam Inc 285 Madison Ave New York NY 10017

COOPER, RICHARD ALAN, lawyer; b. Hattisburg, Miss., July 19, 1953; s. H. Douglas and Elaine (Reece) C.; m. Margaret Jeanne Luth, May 9, 1981. B.A., B.S., U. Ark.-Little Rock, 1976; J.D., Washington U., St. Louis, 1979. Bar: Mo. 1979, Ill. 1980, U.S. Dist. Ct. (ea. dist.) Mo. 1980. Law clk. U.S. Dist. Ct., St. Louis, 1979-80; assoc. William R. Gartenberg, St. Louis, 1980-81, Danis, Reid, Murphy, Tobben, Schreiber, Mohan & Cooper, St. Louis, 1983-86, ptnr. 1987—; liaison to Washington U. Sch. Law, Mo. Assn. Trial Attys., St. Louis, 1983-85 . Bus. mgr. Urban Law Jour., 1978-79; editor Bankruptcy Law Reporter, 1983—, co-mgr., editor, 1984—. Recipient Milton F. Napier trial award Lawyers Assn. of St. Louis, 1979. Mem. ABA, Mo. Bar Assn., Am. Assn. Trial Attys., Nat. Orgn. Social Security Claimants Reps., Ill. State Bar Assn. Clubs: Clayton, Media (St. Louis). Avocation: basketball. Bankruptcy, Federal civil litigation, Pension, profit-sharing, and employee benefits. Home: 330 Stark Ct Webster Groves MO 63119 Office: Danis Reid Murphy et al 8850 Ladue Rd Ladue MO 63124

COOPER, RICHARD CRAIG, lawyer; b. Pittsfield, Mass., July 9, 1941; s. John Bradley and Agnes Hall (Thomson) C.; m. Laurel Lucy Frisch, Aug. 11, 1962; children—Jeffrey, Scott, Ethan. B.E., Yale U., 1963, LL.B., 1966. Bar: N.J. 1967. Assoc., McCarter & English, Newark, 1966-72, mem. firm, 1972—. Founding mem. bd. dirs. Craig Sch., Rockaway, N.J.; panel of arbitrators Am. Arbitration Assn. Mem. ABA, Am. Judicature Soc., Supreme Ct. Hist. Soc., Essex County Bar Assn., Morris County Bar Assn., N.J. Bar Assn., Soc. Mayflower Descendants. Presbyterian. Clubs: Essex (Newark); Yale of Central N.J. (v.p.), Fiddler's Elbow Country. Federal civil litigation, State civil litigation, Labor. Home: 83 Hilltop Dr Randolph Township NJ 07869 Office: 550 Broad St Newark NJ 07102

COOPER, RICHARD I., judge; b. Reed City, Mich., Dec. 28, 1940; s. Dic I. and Bette Kay (Zimmerman) C.; m. Carol Susan Schneider, Sept. 2, 1978; 1 child, Craig R. BA, Central Mich. U., 1963; MA, Ind. U., 1970; JD, Detroit Coll. Law, 1973. Bar: Mich. 1973. Lang. instr. Brit. Sch. Milan, Italy, 1963-64; tchr. high sch., Greenville, Mich., 1967-68; intern Internat. Affairs, NASA, Washington, summer 1969; city pros. atty. Reed City, 1973-76; probate judge Lake County, Baldwin, Mich., 1977-78; cir. judge 51st Cir., Ludington and Baldwin, Mich., 1979—; vis. judge Mich. Ct. Appeals; instr. bus. law Ferris State Coll., Big Rapids, Mich., 1974-75. Bd. dirs. Mental Health Clinic, Baldwin, 1975-77. Recipient Gideons Ann. Bible award 1983; Rotary fellow U. Vienna, Austria, 1965-66. Mem. Mich. Bar Assn., Mason/Lake Bar Assn., Mich. Judges Assn. Congregationalist. Criminal, Family and matrimonial, General practice. Home: PO Box 416 Ludington MI 49431

COOPER, RICK WILLIAM, lawyer, bank executive; b. Greenfield, Tenn., June 21, 1955; s. Billy Lee and Nellie Sue (Hawkins) C.; m. Jaey Lynn Hutchison, Sept. 2, 1984;. BS in History, U. Tenn., 1977; JD, Memphis State U., 1980. Bar: Tenn. 1980. Sole practice Sharon, Tenn., 1980-82; v.p., trust officer First State Bank, Caruthersville, Mo., 1982-84, Peoples Bank and Trust Co., Mountain Home, Ark., 1984—; mcpl. judge, Sharon, 1981-82. Named one of Outstanding Young Men Am., 1983. Mem. ABA (real property probate and trust law sect.), Tenn. Bar Assn., Baxter County Bar Assn. (sec., treas.). Democrat. Club: Rotary (treas. Caruthersville club 1983). Avocations: golf, fishing, duck hunting, skiing. Probate. Home: 701 Arkansas Ave Mountain Home AR 72653 Office: Peoples Bank and Trust Co PO Drawer B Mountain Home AR 72653

COOPER, ROBERT ELBERT, state supreme court justice; b. Chattanooga, Oct. 14, 1920; s. John Thurman and Susie Inez (Hollingsworth) C.; m. Catherine Pauline Kelly, Nov. 24, 1949; children: Susan Florence Cooper Hodges, Bobbie Cooper Martin, Kelly Ann Smith, Robert Elbert Jr. B.A., U. N.C., 1946; J.D., Vanderbilt U., 1949. Bar: Tenn. 1948. Asso. Kolwyck and Clark, 1949-51; partner Cooper and Barger, 1951-53; asst. atty. gen. 6th Jud. Ct. Tenn., 1951-53; judge 6th Jud. Circuit Tenn., 1953-60; judge Tenn. Ct. Appeals, 1960-70, presiding judge Eastern div., 1970-74; justice Tenn. Supreme Ct., 1974—, chief justice, 1976-77, 84-85; chmn. Tenn. Jud. Council, 1967—; chmn. Tenn. Code Commn., 1976-77, 84-85; mem. Tenn. Jud. Standards Commn., 1971-77. Mem. exec. bd. Cherokee council Boy Scouts Am., 1960-64; bd. dirs. Met. YMCA, 1956-65, St. Barnabas Nursing Home and Apts. for Aged, 1966-69. Served with USNR, 1941-46. Mem. Am., Tenn., Chattanooga bar assns., Conf. Chief Justices, Phi Beta Kappa, Order of Coif, Kappa Sigma, Phi Alpha Delta. Democrat. Presbyterian. Clubs: Signal Mountain Golf and Country, Masons (33 deg.), Shriners. Jurisprudence. Home: 196 Woodcliff Circle Signal Mountain TN 37377 Office: 311 Supreme Ct Bldg Nashville TN 37219

COOPER, ROBERT GORDON, lawyer; b. Roanoke, Va., July 2, 1953; s. Arthur Darrah and C. Jane (Redman) C.; m. Ruth K. Cathcart, June 7, 1975; 1 child, Kimberly Anne. BBA, Furman U., 1974; JD, U. S.C., 1977. Bar: S.C. 1977, U.S. Dist. Ct. S.C. 1977, U.S. Ct. Appeals (4th cir.), U.S. Supreme Ct. Assoc. Robinson, McFadden, Moore & Pope, Columbia, S.C., 1977-80; asst. city atty. City of Columbia, 1980-82; sole practice Columbia, 1982—. Deacon, chmn. bd. deacons, youth worker Cornerstone Presbyn. Ch., Columbia. Mem. ABA, S.C. Bar Assn., Richland County Bar Assn. State civil litigation, Consumer commercial, Personal injury. Home: 107 Maid Stone Circle Irmo SC 29063 Office: 1229 Elmwood Ave Columbia SC 29201

COOPER, SCOTT FRANCIS, lawyer, educator; b. Berwyn, Ill., July 3, 1953; s. Roland M. and Amelia (Razim) C.; m. Jumana H. Jabaji, July 21, 1979. BS, Ill. Inst. Tech., 1975, JD, 1978. Bar: Ill. 1979, U.S. Dist. Ct. (no. dist.) Ill. 1979. Assoc. dean U. Ill. Med. Ctr., Chgo., 1978-86; sole practice Oak Park, Ill., 1979-86; assoc. Fragomen, De Rey, Bernsen & Inman, Chgo., 1986—; cons. Georgetown U., Washington, 1981, Nat. Assn. Fgn. Student Affairs, Washington, 1984—. Fulbright scholar U.S. German Fulbright Commn., 1985. Mem. Chgo. Bar Assn. (chmn. immigration com. 1985-86), Nat. Assn. Fgn. Student Affairs (chmn. region V 1986—), Am. Immigration Lawyers Assn. Immigration, naturalization, and customs. Office: Fragomen De Rey Bernsen & Inman 332 S Mich Ave Suite 1710 Chicago IL 60604

COOPER, STEPHEN HERBERT, lawyer; b. N.Y.C., Mar. 29, 1939; s. Walter S. and Selma (Herbert) C.; m. Linda Cohen, Aug. 29, 1965 (dec.); m. Karen Gross, Sept. 6, 1981; 1 child, Zachary Noel. A.B., Columbia U., 1960, J.D. cum laude, 1965. Bar: N.Y. 1965. Assoc. Breed, Abbott & Morgan, N.Y.C., 1965-66; assoc. Weil, Gotshal & Manges, N.Y.C., 1966-73, ptnr., 1973—; lectr. Nat. Inst. Securities Regulation U. Colo. Boulder 1985. Served to lt. USNR, 1960-62. Mem. ABA (com. fed. regulation securities, subcom. internat. securities matters). Democrat. Jewish. Club: City Athletic (N.Y.C.). General corporate, Private international, Securities. Home: 1125 Park Ave New York NY 10128 Office: Weil Gotshal & Manges 767 Fifth Ave New York NY 10153

COOPER, THOMAS LOUIS, lawyer; b. Pitts., Mar. 16, 1938; s. Louis D. and Gertrude V. (Edmonds) C.; m. Leah Mary Meyers, Aug. 5, 1961; children—Marcia, Jeffrey, Daniel. B.A., Dartmouth Coll., 1959; LL.B., U. Pitts., 1962. Bar: Pa. 1962, U.S. Dist. Ct. (we. dist.) Pa. 1962, U.S. Ct. Appeals (3d cir.), U.S. Supreme Ct. Assoc. McArdle & McLaughlin, Pitts., 1962-69; ptnr. Gilardi, Cooper & Gismondi, Pitts., 1969—. mem. rules of civil procedure com. Pa. Supreme Ct.; adj. prof. U. Pitts. Sch. Law, 1986. Fellow Am. Coll. Trial Lawyers; mem. Pa. Bar Assn. (bd. of govs.), Allegheny County Bar Assn. (pres. 1984), Allegheny County Acad. Trial Lawyers (pres. 1979), Pa. Trial Lawyers Assn. (bd. govs.), Western Pa. Trial Lawyers Assn. (bd. govs.). Contbr. articles to profl. jours. Federal civil litigation, State civil litigation, Criminal. Office: Gilardi Cooper & Gismondi 808 Grant Bldg Pittsburgh PA 15219

COOPERMAN, ROBERT N., lawyer; b. Bklyn., July 9, 1935; s. Albert J. and Edith (Seligman) C.; m. Barbara F. Burger, Mar. 22, 1959; children: M. James, Tod D., Nancy D. BBA, CCNY, 1956; LLB, Columbia U., 1959; LLM in Taxation, NYU, 1964. Bar: N.Y. 1959, U.S. Dist. Ct. (so. and ea. dists.) N.Y. 1959, U.S. Tax Ct. 1968, U.S. Supreme Ct. 1968. Assoc. Arthur Richenthal, N.Y.C., 1960-65; ptnr. Cooperman, Levitt & Winikoff and predecessor firms Goldman, Cooperman & Levitt, Kuh, Goldman, Cooperman & Levitt, and Cooperman & Levitt, N.Y.C., 1966—. Pres. United Community Fund, Great Neck, N.Y., 1969; vice chmn. Great Neck Village Bd. Appeals, 1980-85; v.p. Temple Israel, Great Neck, 1975-81. Mem. ABA, N.Y. State Bar Assn. General corporate, Real property, Corporate taxation. Home: 25 Strathmore Rd Great Neck NY 11023 Office: Cooperman Levitt & Winikoff 800 3d Ave New York NY 10022 Other Office: 98 Cuttermill Rd Great Neck NY 11021

COOTER, DALE A., lawyer; b. Syracuse, N.Y., Aug. 28, 1948; s. Charles Henry and Mavis Elizabeth (Wagner) C.; m. Mary Kathryn Nolan, Oct. 8, 1977; children: John Andrew, Jessica Averie. BA cum laude, SUNY, Fredonia, 1970; JD, Georgetown U., 1975. Bar: Md. 1975, D.C. 1976, Va. 1984, U.S. Dist. Ct. Md. 1976, U.S. Dist. Ct. D.C. 1976, U.S. Ct. Appeals (4th and D.C. cirs.) 1976, U.S. Supreme Ct. 1979. Ptnr. Cooter & Gell, Washington, 1976—; adj. prof. law Georgetown U., Washington, 1985—. Editor Georgetown U. Law Jour., 1973-75. Served with N.G. Mem. ABA, Va. Bar Assn., Md. Bar Assn., D.C. Bar Assn. Federal civil litigation, State civil litigation. Home: 4675 Kenmore Dr NW Washington DC 20007 Office: Cooter & Gell 1333 H Street NW Washington DC 20005

COOTER, ROBERT, law educator; b. 1945. PhD, Harvard U., 1975. Asst. prof. econs. U. Calif., Berkeley, 1975-80, asst. prof. law, 1980-82, acting prof., 1982-83, prof., 1983—. Office: U Calif Berkeley Boalt Law Berkeley CA 94720 *

COPE, JOSEPH ADAMS, lawyer; b. Summit, N.J., Jan. 15, 1945; s. Joseph H. and Eunice (Adams) Cope; m. Michele Zeleny, Sept. 25, 1982. BA, U. Colo., 1967, JD, 1976. Bar: Colo. 1976, U.S. Dist. Ct. Colo. 1976, U.S. Ct. Appeals (10th cir.) 1977, U.S. Claims Ct. 1984, U.S. Supreme Ct. 1984, Calif. 1985. Assoc. Vranesh & Musick, Boulder, Colo., 1976-78; ptnr. Musick and Cope, Boulder, Colo., 1978—. Served to lt. USN, 1967-73. Mem. ABA, Colo. Bar Assn., Boulder County Bar Assn., Calif. Bar Assn. Avocation: raising shire draft horses. Real property, Environment, Water rights. Home: 3880 N 57th St Boulder CO 80301 Office: Musick and Cope 4141 Arapahoe Ave PO Box 4579 Boulder CO 80306

COPENBARGER, LLOYD GAYLORD, lawyer; b. Geary, Okla., Feb. 25, 1941; s. Lloyd G. and Audrey G. C.; m. Laura M. Drinnon, Mar. 6, 1943; children: Gwendolyn Ann, Larry G. BS, U. Okla., 1968, JD, 1971. Bar: Okla. 1971, Ohio 1976, Calif. 1979. Ptnr. Copenbarger & Welch, Norman, Okla., 1971-76; gen. counsel Rex Humbard Found., Akron, Ohio, 1976-79; prin. Lloyd Copenberger & Assocs. (formerly Copenbarger & Copenbarger), Irvine, Calif., 1979—. Bd. dirs., Canyon Acres, Home of Ministering Angel. Non-profit corporations, Estate planning, Probate. Office: Suite 200 2171 Campus Dr Irvine CA 92715

COPENHAVER, JOHN THOMAS, JR., federal judge; b. Charleston, W.Va., Sept. 29, 1925; s. John Thomas and Ruth Cherrington (Roberts) C.;

m. Camille Ruth Smith, Oct. 7, 1950; children—John Thomas III, James Smith, Brent Paul. A.B., W.Va. U., 1947, LL.B., 1950. Bar: W.Va. Law clk. to U.S. dist. judge Ben Moore, So. Dist. of W.Va., 1950-51; mem. firm Copenhaver & Copenhaver, Charleston, 1951-58; U.S. bankruptcy judge So. Dist. W.Va. Charleston, 1958-76; U.S. dist. judge 1976—; adj. prof. law W.Va. U. Coll. Law, 1970-76; mem. faculty Fed. Jud. Center, 1972-76; Pres. Legal Aid. Soc. Charleston, 1954; Chmn. Mcpl. Planning Commn. City of Charleston, 1964; chmn., pres. W.Va. Housing Devel. Fund, 1969-72; chmn. vis. com. W.Va. U. Coll. Law, 1980-83; mem. adv. com. on bankruptcy rules Jud. Conf. U.S., 1978-84. Contbr.: articles in fields of bankruptcy and comml. law to Bus. Lawyer, Am. Bankruptcy Law Jour., Personal Fin. Law Quar., W. Va. Law Rev., others. Served with U.S. Army, 1944-46. Recipient Gavel award W.Va. U. Coll. Law, 1971, Outstanding Judge award W. Va. Trial Lawyers Assn., 1983. Mem. ABA, W.Va., Kanawha County bar assns., Nat. Bankruptcy Conf., Nat. Conf. Bankruptcy Judges (past pres.), Phi Delta Phi, Beta Theta Pi. Republican. Presbyterian. Jurisprudence. Office: US Courthouse Charleston WV 25329

COPILEVITZ, ERROL, lawyer; b. East St. Louis, Ill., Apr. 2, 1943; s. Maurice and Rose (Buxner) C.; m. Cissy L. Cohn, Aug. 15, 1965; children—Clay H., Cori A. B.A., U. Okla., 1965, J.D., 1968. Bar: Mo. 1968, U.S. Dist. Ct. (we. dist.) Mo. 1969, U.S. Supreme Ct. 1977, U.S. Ct. Appeals (4th cir.) 1986. Assoc. Koenigsdorf, Kaplan, Kraft & Fox, Kansas City, Mo., 1968-77; sr. ptnr. Copilevitz, Bryant, Gray & Jennings, P.C., Kansas City, 1977—; keynote speaker Mo. Library Assn., 1977; guest lectr. U. Okla. Sch. Law, 1979; guest speaker Nat. Assn. Atty. Gens., 1984; law day speaker Pasco County Bar Assn., 1985. Vol. to edn. Young Lawyers Assn., Kansas City, 1973; pres. Kansas City chpt. Am. Jewish Congress, 1986. Contbr. articles to profl. jours. Bd. mgrs. Downtown YMCA, Kansas City, 1976-79; mem. Johnson County Adv. Bd. for Senator Robert Dole, 1983-85. Mem. First Amendment Lawyers Assn. (pres. 1983-84), Kansas City Bar Assn. (mcpl. ct. com. 1976-78), Phi Alpha Delta. General corporate, General practice, Constitutional. Home: 4502 W 126th St Leawood KS 66209 Office: Copilevitz Bryant et al 911 Main St Kansas City MO 64105

COPLAN, LARRY MYLES, lawyer; b. Wilkes-Barre, Pa., Dec. 21, 1943; s. Charles and Adele (Green) C.; m. Katherine Yu, Oct. 5, 1980; 1 child, Jaime Tai Ming. BS, Lehigh U., 1965; JD, Georgetown U., 1968; LLM, George Washington U., 1977. Bar: D.C. 1969. Assoc. Craighill, Mayfield & McCally, Washington, 1971-74; staff atty. U.S. Fed. Energy Adminstrn., Washington, 1974-77; assoc. Akin, Gump, Strauss, Hauer & Feld, Washington, 1977-80, ptnr., 1980—. Served to capt. U.S. Army, 1968-70, Vietnam. Mem. ABA, D.C. Bar Assn. Democrat. Jewish. General corporate, Securities. Home: 3925 Georgetown Ct NW Washington DC 20007 Office: Akin Gump Strauss Hauer & Feld 1333 New Hampshire Ave NW Washington DC 20036

COPLEY, EDWARD ALVIN, lawyer; b. Memphis, Jan. 17, 1936; s. Edward Alvin and Ethel Marie (Fooshee) C.; m. Helen Frances Fason, Aug. 17, 1957; children: Julie, Ward, Drew. BA, So. Meth. U., 1957, JD, 1960. Bar: U.S. Dist. Ct. (no. dist.) Tex., U.S. Ct. Claims 1962, U.S. Supreme Ct. 1963, U.S. Tax Ct. 1966, U.S. Ct. Appeals (5th cir.) 1968. Atty. U.S. Dept. Justice, Washington, 1960-64, Ft. Worth, 1964-66; assoc. Akin, Gump, Strauss, Hauer & Feld, Dallas, 1966-67, ptnr., 1968—. Mem. ushering com., benevolence com. Highland Park Presbyn. Ch., Dallas, 1982. Fellow Am. Coll. Probate Counsel; mem. Dallas Bar Assn. (tax sect.), Dallas Estate Council (pres. 1975-76), So. Meth. U. Law Sch. Alumni Assn. (pres. 1978-79), Salesmanship Club (legal counsel 1984), Order of Woolsac, Barristers, Phi Alpha Delta. Clubs: Northwood Country, Dallas (pres.). Avocations: racquetball, photography, hunting, fishing, reading. Corporate taxation, Estate taxation, Personal income taxation. Office: Akin Gump Strauss Hauer & Feld 4100 First City Ctr 1700 Pacific Ave Dallas TX 75201-4618 Home: 3711 Shenandoah Dallas TX 75205

COPLIN, MARK DAVID, lawyer; b. Balt., Dec. 1, 1928; s. Simon and Anna (Sherry) C. B.A., U. Md., 1949, LL.B., 1952. Bar: Md. 1952. Law clk. presiding justice U.S. Ct. Appeals 4th Cir., 1952-53; assoc. Weinberg and Green, Balt., 1953-60, ptnr., 1960—. Pres. Md. chpt., Am. Jewish Congress, 1971-74, Balt. Jewish Council, 1976-78; pres. HIAS of Balt., Inc., 1972-74; mem. adv. com. Md. Blue Sky, 1968—. Mem. ABA, Md. Bar Assn., Balt. City Bar Assn., Order of Coif, Omicron Delta Kappa. Jewish. General corporate, Corporate taxation, Personal income taxation.

COPLIN, WILLIAM THOMAS, JR., lawyer, judge; b. Gadsden, Ala., Nov. 10, 1950; s. William Thomas Coplin and Margie B. Camp; m. Elisabeth Banks, June 19, 1976; children: William Thomas III, Kathryn Elisabeth. BS, Jacksonville State U., 1973; JD, Samford U., 1977. Bar: Ala. 1977, U.S. Ct. Appeals (5th and 11th cirs.), U.S. Supreme Ct. Atty. Ala. Bar Assn., Demopolis, Ala., 1977-86; spl. asst. atty. gen. State of Ala., Demopolis, 1986—; mcpl. judges, City of Demopolis, 1978-80, City of Faunsdale, Ala., 1979—. Trustee Samford U., Birmingham, Ala., 1985—. Mem. Internat. Bar Assn., Ala. Bar Assn., 17th Jud. Cir. Bar Assn. (v.p. 1980), Assn. Trial Lawyers Am., Ala. Trial Lawyers Assn., Am. Judicature Soc., Ala. Sheriff Assn., Demopolis Area C. of C. (pres. 1981), Marengo County Hist. Soc. (pres. 1986). Democrat. Baptist. Lodge: Masons. General practice, State civil litigation, Contracts commercial. Home: 1402 Colony Rd Demopolis AL 36732 Office: 215 S Cedar PO Box 987 Demopolis AL 36732

COPPINGER, JOHN BAMPFIELD, lawyer; b. Edwardsville, Ill., Sept. 3, 1913; s. John Biggins and Clara (Bampfield) C.; m. Glenna Lou Edgington, Aug. 25, 1955 (div. 1979); children—John Brian, Elnora Anne. Student Shurtleff Coll., 1932-34; J.D., St. Louis U., 1937. Bar: Mo. 1937, Ill. 1938, U.S. Dist. Ct. (so. dist.) Ill. 1939, Supreme Ct. Korea 1946, U.S. Ct. Mil. Appeals 1957, U.S. Supreme Ct. 1963. Atty. Travelers Ins. Co., St. Louis, 1937-39; practice, Alton, Ill., 1939—; sole practice, 1949-55; ptnr. various firms, 1939-49, 55-64; ptnr. Coppinger, Carter, Schrempf & Blaine, Alton, 1964—; atty. Village of Hartford, Ill., 1939-71; master in chancery Madison County Cir. Ct., Ill., 1956-60. Served with U.S. Army, 1943-46, lt. col. Res. ret. Mem. ABA, Ill. Bar Assn., Mo. Bar Assn., Met. St. Louis Bar Assn., Judge Advs. Assn., Madison County Bar Assn., Am. Judicature Assn., Alton C. of C. (pres. 1957-58). Republican. Roman Catholic. Local government, Probate, Real property. Home: 1621 Shurtleff Ct Alton IL 62002 Office: Coppinger Carter Schrempf & Blaine 307 Henry St Alton IL 62002

COQUILLETTE, DANIEL ROBERT, lawyer, legal educator; b. Boston, May 23, 1944; s. Robert McTavish and Dagmar Alvida (Bistrup) C.; m. Judith Courtney Rogers, July 5, 1969; children: Anna, Sophia, Julia. A.B., Williams Coll., 1966; M.A. Juris., Univ. Coll., Oxford U., Eng., 1969; J.D., Harvard U., 1971. Bar: Mass. 1974, U.S. Dist. Ct. Mass. 1974, U.S. Ct. Appeals (1st cir.) 1974. Law clk. Mass. Supreme Ct., 1971-72; to Warren E. Burger, chief justice U.S. Supreme Ct., 1972-73; assoc. Palmer & Dodge, Boston, 1973-75, ptnr., 1980-85; assoc. prof. law Boston U., 1975-78; dean, prof. Boston Coll. Law, 1985—; vis. assoc. prof. law Cornell U., Ithaca, N.Y., 1977-78; vis. prof. law Harvard Law Sch., 1978-79, 83-85; reporter com. rules and procedures Jud. Conf. U.S.; vis. assoc. prof. law Cornell U., Ithaca, N.Y., 1977-78; vis. prof. law Harvard U., 1978-79, 83-85. Editor: Law in Colonial Massachusetts, 1985; bd. dirs. New England Quarterly, 1986—; contbr. articles to legal jours. Trustee, sec.-treas. Ames Found., Cambridge Friends Day Sch.; treas. Byron Meml Fund; propr. Boston Athenaeum. Recipient Kaufman prize in English Williams Coll., 1966; recipient Sentinel of the Republic prize in polit. sci. Williams Coll., 1965; Hutchins scholar, 1966-67; Fulbright scholar, 1966-68. Mem. Am. Law Inst., ABA, Mass Bar Assn. (task force on model rules of profl. conduct), Boston Bar Assn., Am. Soc. Legal History (bd. dirs. 1985—), Mass. Soc. Continuing Legal Edn. (dir.), Social Welfare Research Inst. (dir.), Selden Soc. (state corr.), Colonial Soc. Mass. (mem. council), Anglo-Am. Cathedral Soc. (dir.), Mass. Hist. Soc., Am. Antiquarian Soc., Phi Beta Kappa. Democrat. Quaker. Clubs: Curtis, Tavern, Country, Club of Old Volumes. General practice, Legal education, Jurisprudence. Home: 12 Rutland St Cambridge MA 02138 Office: Boston College Law School 885 Centre St Newton Centre MA 02159

COQUILLETTE, WILLIAM HOLLIS, lawyer; b. Boston, Oct. 7, 1949; s. Robert McTauish and Dagmar (Bistrup) C.; m. Mary Katherine Templeton, June 19, 1971 (div. Oct. 1984); 1 child, Carolyn Patricia; m. Janet Marie Weiland, Dec. 8, 1984; 1 child, Benjamin. BA, Yale U., 1971, Oxford U., 1973; JD, Harvard U., 1975. Bar: Ohio 1976, Mass. 1976. Law clk. to presiding justice Mass. Supreme Ct., Boston, 1975-76; assoc. Jones, Day, Reavis & Pogue, Cleve., 1976-83, ptnr., 1984—. Trustee Greater Cleve. Community Foodbank, Marotta Montessori Sch. Clubs: Union, Rowfant (Cleve.). Banking, General corporate, Private international. Office: Jones Day Reavis & Pogue 1700 Huntington Bldg Cleveland OH 44115

CORASH, RICHARD, lawyer; b. N.Y.C., Mar. 31, 1938; s. Paul and Mildred (Spanier) C.; m. Carol A. McKevitt, Dec. 11, 1966; children—Richard Jr., Sharon, Peter, Amy. B.A., Harpur Coll., SUNY, 1959; M.A., Bklyn. Law Sch., 1966; J.D., Rutgers U., 1963. Bar: N.Y. 1964, U.S. Dist. Ct. D.C. 1964, U.S. Sup. Ct. 1972. Sole practice, N.Y.C., 1964-77; sr. ptnr. Corash & Hollender, N.Y.C., 1977—; pres. Kobe Trading Co., N.Y.C.; chmn. North Eastern Fiscal Mgmt. Co., N.Y.C.; counsel Bd. Advisers S.I. Hist. Soc., Caywood Homeowners Assn. Mem. N.Y. State Bar Assn. (real estate sect.), N.Y. Bankruptcy Bar Assn. (chmn. grievance com.), Richmond County Bar Assn. Democrat. Episcopalian. Bankruptcy, Contracts commercial, Construction. Address: RD 1 PO Box 197 Roxiticus Rd Far Hills NJ 07931

CORBER, ROBERT JACK, lawyer; b. Topeka, June 29, 1926; s. Alva Forrest and Katherine (Salzer) C.; m. Joan Irene Tennal, July 16, 1949; children—Janet, Suzanne, Wesley Sean, Robert Jack II. B.S. in Aero. Engring, U. Kans., 1946; J.D. cum laude, Washburn U., 1950; postgrad., U. Mich., 1950-51. Bar: Kans. bar 1950, D.C. bar 1951, U.S. Supreme Ct. bar 1964. Asso. firm Steptoe & Johnson, Washington, 1951-57; partner Steptoe & Johnson, 1957-75, 80—; commr. ICC, Washington, 1975-76; partner firm Conner, Moore & Corber, Washington, 1977-80. Author: Motor Carrier Leasing and Interchange Under the Interstate Commerce Act, 1977; contbr. legal and polit. articles to various pubs. Chmn. Arlington (Va.) Republican Com., 1960-62; chmn. Va. 10th Congl. Dist. Rep. Com., 1962-64; state chmn. Rep. Party of Va., 1964-68. Served to lt. (j.g.) USNR, 1944-47. Mem. ABA (chmn. motor carrier com. pub. utility sect. 1983-86), Bar Assn. D.C. (chmn. adminstrv. law sect. 1978-79, chmn. continuing legal edn. com. 1979-83), Motor Carrier Lawyers Assn., ICC Practitioners Assn. Methodist. Clubs: Met. (Washington), Internat. (Washington), Capitol Hill (Washington), Washington Golf and Country (Washington). Administrative and regulatory, Federal civil litigation, General corporate. Home: 3701 N Harrison St Arlington VA 22207 Office: Steptoe & Johnson 1250 Connecticut Ave NW Washington DC 20036

CORBETT, PETER GERALD, lawyer; b. Shanghai, June 2, 1935; s. Peter Andrew and Martha Laurie (Gilmour) C.; m. Margaret Sacco; 3 children. Student Stonyhurst Coll. Eng., 1948-52; B.A., U. B.C. 1957, LL.B., 1958; LL.M., Harvard U., 1959. Bar: N.Y. 1964, U.S. Dist. Ct. (so. dist.) N.Y. 1966, U.S. Dist. Ct. (ea. dist.) N.Y. 1966, U.S. Ct. Appeals (2d cir.) 1966. Atty., Allied Chem. Corp., N.Y.C., 1959-61; assoc. Olwine Connelly Chase O'Donnell & Weyher, N.Y.C., 1961-66; assoc. Regan Goldfarb Powell & Quinn, N.Y.C., 1966-70, ptnr., 1970-72; atty. Western Electric Co., N.Y.C., 1972-83, AT&T Technologies, Inc., 1984-85, gen. atty. AT&T, 1985-86, AT&T Tech. Systems, 1987—. Mem. Republican Presdl. Task Force, 1981; mem. Rep. Nat. Com., 1980; mem. U.S. Congl. Adv. Bd., 1983; Served with Can. Army, 1954-58. Harvard Law Sch. fellow, 1958-59; U. B.C. scholar. Mem. Am. Arbitration Assn. (nat. panel 1971—), ABA, N.Y. State Bar Assn., Bar Assn. City N.Y. Republican. Roman Catholic. Antitrust, Federal civil litigation, Public international. Home: Hamden Hollow Farm Allerton Rd Annandale NJ 08801 Office: One Oak Way 3 WA 116 Berkeley Heights NJ 07922

CORBIN, ROBERT K., state attorney general; b. 1928; married; 3 daus. B.S., Ind. U., 1952, J.D., 1956. Bar: Ind. 1957, Ariz. 1958. County atty. Maricopa County, 1965-69; chmn. Maricopa County Bd. Suprs., 1974-77; atty. gen. State of Ariz., Phoenix, 1979—; former mem. stats. adv. bd. U.S. Bur. Justice; chmn. Ariz. Criminal Justice Commn. Served with USN, 1946-48. Mem. Ariz. State Bar Assn. (past mem. ethics com.), Ariz. County Attys. Assn., NRA (bd. dirs.), Nat. Assn. Attys. Gen. (chmn. antitrust com. 1981-83), Americans for Effective Law Enforcement (pres. 1974), Conf. Western Attys. Gen. (chmn. 1982). Republican. Club: Masons. Criminal. Home: 1275 W Washington Phoenix AZ 85007 Office: Office of the Attorney General Dept of Law State Capitol 1275 W Washington Phoenix AZ 85007 *

CORBITT, SHARON L., lawyer; b. Prague, Okla., Nov. 13, 1946; d. Harold G. and Lillie B. (Ondrasek) Terry; m. Tom R. Corbitt, Feb. 10, 1968; children: Chad Ray, Blake J. BS, Northeastern State U.; JD, U. Tulsa. Bar: Okla. 1982, U.S. Dist. Ct. (no. and ea. dists.) Okla. Sole practice Tulsa, 1982—. Mem. ABA, Am. Trial Lawyers Assn., Okla. Bar Assn., Okla. Trial Lawyers Assn. (bd. dirs. 1986—), Tulsa County Bar Assn. Republican. Methodist. Avocation: bridge. Family and matrimonial. Office: 2642 E 21st St Suite 251 Tulsa OK 74114

CORCORAN, ANDREW PATRICK, JR., lawyer; b. Fredrick, Md., Nov. 20, 1948; s. Andrew Patrick and Beatrice Josephine (Poletti) C.; m. Margaret Cecila Boyle, July 3, 1971; children: Maureen Meredith, Andrew Patrick III. BA, Villanova U., 1970; JD, Seton Hall U., 1973. Bar: Pa. 1973, U.S Dist. Ct. (ea. dist.) Pa. 1974, U.S. Ct. Appeals (7th cir.) 1976, U.S. Ct. Appeals (3d cir.) 1977, U.S. Supreme Ct. 1982. Atty. Pa. Cen. Transp. Co., Phila., 1973-75, sr. atty., 1975-79; asst. gen. atty. Consol. Rail Corp., Phila., 1979-82, gen. atty., 1982-85, sr. gen. atty., 1985—; counsel Eastern Freight Claim and Damage Prevention Conf. (1985—). Mem. Conf. of R.R. Loss and Damage Counsel (vice chmn. 1986-88), Assn. of Am. R.R.'s (legal affairs com). Democrat. Roman Catholic. Club: Vesper (Phila.). Federal civil litigation, Contracts commercial, Personal injury. Home: 10 Lowrys Ln Rosemont PA 19010 Office: Consol Rail Corp 1138 6 Penn Center Philadelphia PA 19103

CORCORAN, C. TIMOTHY, III, lawyer; b. Kansas City, Mo., Dec. 18, 1945; s. Clement T. and Bette Lou (Hohl) C. B.A., U. N.C.-Chapel Hill, 1967; J.D., U. Va., 1973. Bar: Fla. 1973, U.S. Dist. Ct. (mid. dist.) Fla. 1973, D.C. 1974, U.S. Dist. Ct. (no. and so. dists.) Fla. 1975, U.S. Ct. Appeals (5th cir.) 1979, U.S. Supreme Ct. 1979, U.S. Ct. Appeals (11th cir.) 1981. Law clk. U.S. Dist. Ct., Tampa, 1973-75; assoc., shareholder Carlton, Fields, Ward, Emmanuel, Smith, Cutler & Kent, P.A., Tampa, 1975—; dir. Bay Area Legal Services, Inc., Tampa, 1983—, v.p., 1987—; bd. dirs. Fla. Council Bar Pres., 1982—, pres. 1986-87; arbitrator Ct. Annexed Arbitration Program, U.S. Dist. Ct. (mid. dist.) Fla., 1984—. Fellow U. Tampa, 1986—. Co-author: Conflicts of Interest, 1984; contbr. articles to legal jours. Counselor, U. Tampa, 1981-86. Mem. ABA (assoc. editor Litigations News 1982—), Fla. Bar Assn. (chmn. voluntary bar liaison com. 1985-86, chmn. grievance com. 13-D 1986—, chmn. legal edn. com. 1981-82, Most Prodn. Young Lawyer award 1981), Am. Judicature Soc., Hillsborough County Bar Assn. (Red McEwen award 1980, pres. 1982-83). Democrat. Roman Catholic. Federal civil litigation, State civil litigation. Home: 2530-B Maryland Ave Tampa FL 33629 Office: PO Box 3239 Tampa FL 33601

CORCORAN, SHEILA MARGARET, lawyer; b. Evansville, Ind., Nov. 21, 1950; d. Patrick J.V. and Margaret Alice (Booth) Corcoran. BA cum laude, U. Evansville, 1972; JD cum laude, Ind. U., 1979. Bar: Ind., 1979. Asst. to dir. dept. health ins. AMA, Chgo., 1973-75; assoc. Berger and Berger, Evansville, 1979-83, ptnr., 1984—; Bd. dirs. Legal Aid Soc. Evansville, 1982—, Vanderburgh County CASA, Inc., 1982—, pres., 1987—, Women's Alcoholic Halfway House, Evansville, 1982-85; spl. pub. defender, Vanderburgh Cir. Ct., 1986—; mem. adv. council Vanderburgh County Blood Services Council ARC, Evansville, 1982—; Troopleader Raintree Council Girl Scouts U.S., 1970-72, bd. dirs., 1972-73. Mem. Evansville Bar Assn. (continuing legal edn. com., 1985—, probate com. 1986—), Ind. State Bar Assn., ABA, Chgo. Jaycees, Network Evansville Women, LWV, Samuel Johnson Soc. (U. Evansville chpt.), Jane Austen Soc.Roman Catholic. Club: Irish (Evansville). Avocations: reading, Celtic studies, classical music, jogging, needlework. Probate, Estate planning, Personal injury.

CORDELL, MARTIN LEWIS, lawyer; b. N.Y.C., Apr. 21, 1950. BA cum laude, City Coll. N.Y., 1971; JD, Stetson U., 1975. Bar: Fla. 1975, U.S. Dist. Ct. (mid. dist.) Fla. 1976, U.S. Ct. Appeals (5th cir.) 1977, U.S. Ct. Appeals (11th cir.) 1981. Assoc. Gurney & Handley P.A., Orlando, Fla., 1976-78; sole practice Orlando, 1978—. Mem. ABA, Fla. Bar Assn., Orange County Bar Assn., Assn. Trial Lawyers Am., Acad. Fla. Trial Lawyers, Phi Delta Phi. Avocation: fishing. Personal injury, Insurance, Criminal. Office: 1600 W Colonial Dr Suite 102 Orlando FL 32804

CORDERMAN, JOHN PRINTZ, judge; b. Hagerstown, Md., May 14, 1942; s. John Eader and Gertrude (Printz) C.; m. Ann Bender, Aug. 20, 1966; children—Elizabeth, Robert, Paul. A.A., Hagerstown Jr. Coll., 1963; B.A., U. Md., 1965; J.D. with honors, 1968. Bar: Md. 1968, U.S. Dist. Ct. Md. 1969, U.S. Supreme Ct. 1972. Assoc. Meyers, Wagaman, Corderman & Young, Hagerstown, 1969-77; judge Circuit Ct. of Washington County, Hagerstown, 1977—; dep. states atty. Washington County, 1971-74. Contbr. articles to profl. jours. Mem. Md. State Senate, 1975-77. Named Legislator of Yr., Md. States Atty. Assn., 1976. Fellow Am. Bar Found., Md. Bar Found., ABA (ho. of dels. 1983—); mem. Md. State Bar Assn. (pres. 1984-85), Washington County Bar Assn. (bd. dirs. 1973-74). Democrat. Lutheran. Clubs: Rotary. Judicial administration. Office: Circuit Ct Washington County Courthouse Hagerstown MD 21740

CORDES, CLIFFORD FREDERICK, III, lawyer; b. Washington, May 23, 1946; s. Clifford Frederick Jr. and Mary Maxine (Kautz) C.; m. Christine M. Wyckoff, Apr. 26, 1969 (div. Nov. 1979); 1 child, Wyle. BA, U. Puget Sound, 1968; JD cum laude, Gonzaga U., 1974. Bar: Wash. 1974, U.S. Dist. Ct. (we. dist.) Wash. 1975. Ptnr. Cordes, Cordes & Younglove, Olympia, Wash., 1974-82, Cordes, Younglove & Wyckoff, Olympia, 1982-84, Swanson, Parr, Cordes, Younglove, Peeples & Wyckoff P.S., Olympia, 1984—. Served to sgt. U.S. Army, 1968-71. Mem. ABA, Assn. Trial Lawyers Am., Wash. State Bar Assn., Wash. State Trial Lawyers Assn. (criminal law and family law sects.), Thurston County Bar Assn. (chmn. criminal law com.). Family and matrimonial, Personal injury, Criminal. Office: Swanson Parr Cordes et al 924 E 7th Suite A Olympia WA 98501

CORK, ROBERT LANDER, lawyer; b. Central, S.C., Oct. 27, 1927; s. James Walter and Lila (Mitchell) C.; m. Anne McNeill Ward, Oct. 11, 1952; children—Leah, Robert Jr., Travis, Patrick. A.B., U. Ga., 1952, LL.B., 1953. Bar: Ga. 1951, U.S. Dist. Ct. (mid. dist.) Ga. 1951, Fla. 1958, U.S. Ct. Appeals (11th cir.) 1981, U.S. Dist. Ct. (mid. dist.) Fla. 1983. Ptnr. firm Cork & Gaines, Athens, Ga., 1951-53; sole practice, Valdosta, Ga., 1954-83; ptnr. firm Cork & Cork, Valdosta, 1983—; gen. counsel Warrior Cattle Co., Sylvester, Ga., 1964-70; legal draftsman charter and mcpl. code Town of Dasher, Ga., 1967; gen. counsel Edwards Aircraft, Inc., Dover, Del., 1978—. County co-chmn. campaign Goldwater for Pres., Valdosta, 1964, county chmn. campaign Wallace for pres., Valdosta, 1968; precinct chmn., del. to state Republican convention, Valdosta, 1983, 84. Served with AUS, 1953-54. Mem. Am. Legion, Delta Theta Phi. Republican. Methodist. Lodges: Shriners, Mason, St. John the Baptist, Lions. Real property, Probate, General practice. Home: Sunnyside Lake Francis Lake Park GA 31634 Office: Cork & Cork 700 N Patterson St Valdosta GA 31601

CORLETT, EDWARD STANLEY, III, lawyer; b. Miami, Fla., May 28, 1924; s. Edward Stanley, Jr., and Marjorie (Cook) C.; m. Jeanne Sherouse, Mar. 27, 1948; children—Karen Marie Corlett McCammon, Edward S. A.A., U. Fla., 1946, LL.B., 1949. Bar: Fla. 1949, U.S. Dist. Ct. (so. dist.) Fla. 1949, U.S. Ct. Appeals (5th cir.) 1949, U.S. Ct. Appeals (11th cir.) 1981. Sole practice, 1949-58; sr. ptnr. Sherouse and Corlett, and successor Corlett, Killian, Hardeman, McIntosh and Levi, P.A., Miami, 1958— Fellow Am. Coll. Trial Lawyers; chmn. bd. Internat. Oceanographic Found.; pres. Miami Met. Fishing Tournament, 1973-80. mem. Fed. Jud. Nominating Panel. Served with USN, 1942-44. Recipient Henry Hyman trophy, 1974. Fellow Am. Coll. Trial Lawyers; mem. ABA, Fla. Bar Assn., Dade County Bar Assn., Fedn. Ins. Counsel (pres. 1978-79, testimonial award 1979), Fla. Def. Lawyers Assn. (pres. 1970), Def. Research Inst. (dir. 1978-79, testimonial award 1979), Internat. Assn. Ins. Counsel. Republican. Presbyterian. Clubs: Miami Rod and Reel, Riviera Country, Bankers. Insurance, Personal injury, State civil litigation. Office: 116 W Flagler St Miami FL 33130

CORLEW, JOHN GORDON, lawyer; b. Dyersburg, Tenn., July 13, 1943; s. Emmett Atkins and Margaret Elizabeth (Swann) C.; m. Elizabeth Lee Scott, July 8, 1967; children—John Scott, William Heath, Carey Elizabeth. B.A., U. Miss., 1965; J.D., Vanderbilt U., 1968. Bar: Miss. 1968. Clk. to judge U.S. Dist. Ct. (so. dist.) Miss. 1968-69; assoc., then ptnr. Megehee, Brown, Williams & Corlew, Pascagoula, 1969-74; sole practice Pascagoula, 1975-78; ptnr. Corlew, Krebs & Hammond, Pascagoula, 1978-84; ptnr. Watkins & Eager, Jackson, Miss., 1984—. Mem. Miss. State Senate, 1974-80, chmn. appropriations com. 1979, chmn. constitution com. 1975-79, chmn. legis. audit com. 1978; chmn. Miss. State Bd. Pub. Welfare, 1980-84. Mem. ABA, Miss. Bar Assn., Hinds County Bar Assn., Miss. Bar Found., Order of Coif, Phi Delta Phi. Democrat. Methodist. General practice, General corporate. Home: 212ₐ Eastover Dr Jackson MS 39211 Office: 800 Eastover Bank Bldg Jackson MS 39205

CORLEY, E. TERRILL, lawyer; b. Eufaula, Okla., Oct. 20, 1942; s. O.C. and Grace Marie Corley; m. Elizabeth Ann Cullison, Apr. 24, 1970; children: Elizabeth, Carrie. BA, Cen. State U., Edmond, Okla., 1964, MA, 1966; JD, U. Tulsa, 1970. Bar: Okla. 1972, U.S. Dist. Ct. (no., ea. and we. dists.) Okla. 1972, U.S. Ct. Appeals (10th cir.) 1972. Tchr. Oklahoma City Pub. Schs., 1964-68; rep. claims Travelers Ins. Co., Oklahoma City, 1968-70; pub. defender Tulsa County, 1972-76; sole practice Tulsa, 1976—; dep. chief pub. defender Tulsa County, 1976. Served to capt. N.G., 1966-74. Mem. Assn. Trial Lawyers Am. (sustaining), Okla. Trial Lawyers Assn. (bd. dirs. 1985—), Tulsa County Bar Assn. Democrat. Methodist. Insurance, Personal injury. Office: 1809 E 15th St Tulsa OK 74104

CORNABY, KAY STERLING, lawyer, state senator; b. Spanish Fork, Utah, Jan. 14, 1936; s. Sterling A. and Hilda G. (Stoker) C.; m. Linda Rasmussen, July 23, 1965; children: Alyse, Derek, Tara, Heather, Brandon. AB, Brigham Young U., 1960; postgrad. law Heidelberg (W.Ger.), 1961-63; JD, Harvard U., 1966. Bar: N.Y. 1967, Utah 1969, U.S. Patent and Trademark Office 1967. Assoc. Brumbaugh, Graves, Donahue & Raymond, N.Y.C., 1966-69; ptnr. Mallinckrodt & Cornaby, Salt Lake City, 1969-72; sole practice, Salt Lake City, 1972-85; assoc. Jones, Waldo, Holbrook & McDonough, Salt Lake City, 1985—; mem. Utah State Senate, 1977—, majority leader, 1983-84. Chmn. 2d Congl. Dist., Utah Rep. Party, 1973-77; mem. council legal advisers Rep. Nat. Com., 1981—. chmn. North and East Regional Council of Neighborhoods, 1976-77; mem. Salt Lake County Commn. on Youth, 1979—; mem. Utah Health Cost Found., 1979-86, chmn., 1979-84; mem. Utah State Jud. Conduct Commn., 1983—, chmn. 1984-85; bd. dirs. Friends of KUED, 1982—, chmn. 1985-87; bd. dirs. Salt Lake Conv. and Visitors Bur., 1985—; mem. adv. council Salt Lake dist. Small Bus. Assn.; pres. Utah Opera Co., 1985-86. Mem. Utah Bar Assn., Utah Harvard Alumni Assn. (pres. 1977-79), Harvard U. Law Sch. Alumni Assn. (v.p. 1979—). Mormon. Club: Alta (Salt Lake City). Patent, Trademark and copyright, Real property. Office: Jones Waldo Holbrook & McDonough 1500 First Interstate Plaza 170 S Main St Salt Lake City UT 84101

CORNELISON, ALBERT OTTO, JR., lawyer; b. N.Y.C., Apr. 22, 1949; s. Albert O. and Margaret E. (Adams) C.; m. Diane Snow, Jan. 26, 1980; children: Adam Snow, Brendan Stover. Bar: Calif. 1975, D.C. 1975, U.S. Dist. Ct. D.C. 1975, U.S. Ct. Appeals (D.C. cir.) 1976. Assoc. Howrey & Simon, Washington, 1974-82, ptnr., 1983-84; sr. assoc. counsel litigation Ogden Corp., N.Y.C., 1984-86; v.p. and gen. counsel Ogden Fin. Services, N.Y.C., 1987—. Mem. ABA, N.Y. State Bar Assn., Calif. Bar Assn., D.C. Bar Assn., Assn. of Bar of City of N.Y., Am. Corp. Counsel Assn. Federal civil litigation, Antitrust, Contracts commercial. Office: Ogden Corp 277 Park Ave New York NY 10172

CORNELIUS, ELLEN AUDREY, lawyer; b. Bklyn., Mar. 6, 1958; d. Ronald and Suzanne (Zevator) Westley; m. William T. Cornelius, June 17, 1979; 1 child, Matthew Westley. BA, NYU, 1979; JD, U. Detriot, 1982. Bar: Mich. 1982. Staff atty. Ford Motor Co., Dearborn, Mich., 1982-83; litigation atty. Ford Motor Credit Co., Dearborn, 1983-86, real estate atty., 1986—. Vol. Big Bros./Big Sisters of Mich., Inkster, 1983—. Mem. ABA, State Bar of Mich. Assn. Consumer commercial, Real property, Bankruptcy. Home: 6635 Oakman Blvd Dearborn MI 48126 Office: Ford Motor Credit Co The American Rd PO Box 6044 Dearborn MI 48121

CORNELIUS, MARCUS MARION, III, staff judge advocate; b. Cedartown, Ga., Dec. 30, 1938; s. Marcus Marion II and Edna (Harwell) C.; m. Diana Morris, Sept. 5, 1961; 1 child, Marcus Marion IV. BS in Bus., Stetson U., 1961; MBA, Ga. So. U., 1974; JD, Antioch Coll. of Law, 1977. Bar: Ga. 1977, Fla. 1977, D.C. 1978, U.S. Dist. Ct. (mid. dist.) Ga., U.S. Ct. Appeals (D.C. cir.), U.S. Ct. Mil. Appeals. Comdr. co. U.S. Army, advanced through grades to lt. col.; asst. mgr. for expense acctg. Gen. Electric Co., 1964-66; stockbroker A.G. Edwards and Sons, N.Y.C., 1966-71; pres., chief exec. officer Leon Wood Preserving div. Mark-Ked, Tallahassee, Fla., 1971-73; sole practice 1977-81; asst. pub. defender 7th Jud. Cir., St. Augustine, Fla., 1981-84; staff judge adv. to adj. gen. Fla. Nat. Guard, St. Augustine, 1984—; investigator subcom. fed. spending practices U.S. Senate, Fla., 1976; adj. prof. bus. Truett McConnell Coll., Cleve., Ga., 1977-80; adj. prof. criminal justice Piedmont Coll., Demorest, Ga., 1979-80; adj. prof. bus. and bus. law St. Johns River Jr. Coll., Palatka, Fla., 1983-84; judge City of Clarksville, Ga., 1978-81. Mem. vestry Grace Calvary Episcopal Ch., Clarkesville, Ga., 1978-81. Mem. ABA (gen. practice sect.), Ga. Bar Assn., Fla. Bar Assn., D.C. Bar Assn., Assn. Trial Lawyers Am., Ga. Trial Lawyers Assn., C. of C., Jaycees, Wilderness Soc., Sierra, Scabbard and Blade, Sigma Nu (treas.). Democrat. Lodge: Kiwanis, Lions. Avocations: swimming, skiing, fishing, sailing. Office: Dept Mil Affairs 82 Marine St Saint Augustine FL 32085

CORNELIUS, WALTER FELIX, lawyer; b. Homewood, Ala., Apr. 20, 1922; s. William Felix and Nancy Ann (Cross) C.; m. Virginia Holliman, Jan. 30, 1942, (div. Feb. 1973); children: Nancy Carol, Susan Elanie; m. Lenora Black, May 4, 1974; 1 stepchild, Kristy Ann Wells. AB, Birmingham So. Coll., 1949; JD, U. Ala., 1953. Bar: Ala. 1953, U.S. Dist. Ct. (no. dist.) Ala. 1953, U.S. Tax Ct. 1954. Sole practice Birmingham, Ala., 1953—; bd. dirs. numerous corps., Birmingham. Elder, teacher Presbyn. Ch., Birmingham, 1963—; chmn. bd. dirs. Brother Bryan Mission, Birmingham, 1981—; pres. bd. trustees Cahaba Valley Fire and Medical Res. Dist., Shelby County, Ala., 1984—; mem. Horizon 280 Assn., Birmingham, 1985—. Served to cpl. USAAF, 1943-46, PTO. Mem. ABA, Ala. Bar Assn., Birmingham Bar Assn., Farrah Order Jurisprudence. Avocations: guitar, hunting, hiking, fishing, bird watching. General practice, Contracts commercial, Real property. Home: Rt 1 Box 754 Leeds AL 35094 Office: 200 Frank Nelson Bldg Birmingham AL 35203

CORNELL, JOHN ROBERT, lawyer; b. Boston, Nov. 7, 1943; s. Robert Cole Cornell and Thelma M. (Bassett) Strout; m. Susan L. Jordan, June 11, 1966; children: Jared, Joshua, Alexandra, Margaret. AB, Colby Coll., 1965; JD, Georgetown U., 1968; LLM in Taxation, NYU, 1972. Bar: N.Y. 1969, Maine 1972, U.S. Dist. Ct. Maine 1972, Ohio 1982. Assoc. Dewey, Ballantine, Bushby, Palmer & Wood, N.Y.C., 1968-72; from assoc. to ptnr. Drummond, Woodsum, Plimpton & MacMahon, Portland, Maine, 1972-81; ptnr. Jones, Day, Reavis & Pogue, Cleve., 1981—. Mem. ABA (tax sect.), Maine Bar Assn. (chmn. tax sect. 1980-81), N.Y. State Bar Assn. Republican. Club: Cleve. Yachting (Rocky River, Ohio). Pension, profit-sharing, and employee benefits, Corporate taxation, Personal income taxation. Office: Jones Day Reavis & Pogue 901 Lakeside Ave Cleveland OH 44114

CORNELL, KENNETH LEE, lawyer; b. Palo Alto, Calif., Feb. 23, 1945; s. Clinton Burdette and Mildred Lucy (Sheafer) C.; m. Barbara J. Smith, June 26, 1966; children: Melinda Lee, Geoffery Mark. BBA, BA in Social Sci., Pacific Union Coll., 1966; JD, U. Wash., 1971. Bar: Wash. 1971, U.S. Dist. Ct. (we. dist.) Wash. 1971, U.S. Supreme Ct. 1974. Ptnr. Keller & Rohrback, Seattle, 1971-75, Richard, Rossano & Cornell, Seattle, 1975-77, Moren, Lageschulte, Seattle, 1978—; cons. atty. Town of Clyde Hill, Wash. 1980—. Editor Wash. U. Law Rev., 1970-71. Bd. dirs. Kirkland (Wash.) Seventh Day Adventist Sch., 1972-78, Auburn (Wash.) Acad., 1974-80, Western Wash. Corp. Seventh Day Adventists, Bothell, 1974-80. Mem. ABA, Assn. Trial Lawyers Am., Christian Legal Soc., Wash. State Bar Assn., Wash. State Trial Lawyers Assn., Order of Coif. Republican. Avocations: skiing, jogging, reading, gardening, baseball. State civil litigation, Real property, Personal injury. Office: Moren Lageschulte & Cornell 11320 Roosevelt Way NE Seattle WA 98125

CORNELL, RICHARD FARNHAM, lawyer; b. Pitts., June 9, 1952; s. Paul Watson and Margaret Lucy (Boose) C.; m. Denise Vandevelde, May 24, 1975; children: Jonathan Watson, Julie Elizabeth, Benjamin Dunlap. BA in Polit Sci. and Econs., U. Calif., Irvine, 1974; JD, U. San Francisco, 1977. Bar: Calif. 1977, U.S. Dist. Ct. (no. dist.) Calif. 1977, Nev. 1979, U.S. Dist. Ct. Nev. 1979, U.S. Ct. Appeals (9th cir.) 1981. Law clk. to chief judge U.S. Dist. Ct. Nev., Las Vegas, 1978-80; dep. dist. atty. Washoe County Dist. Atty., Reno, 1980-81; assoc. Raggio, Wooster & Lindell, Reno, 1981-86; sole practice Reno, 1986—. Co-editor Nevada Civil Practice Manual, 1985-86. Bd. dirs. Drunk Drivers Inc. d/b/a Call-a-Ride, Reno, 1984-85, Assn. Excellence in Edn., Reno, 1986. Mem. Nev. Bar Assn. (criminal practice and procedures com. 1986—), Soc. Preservation and Encouragement of Barbershop Quartet Singing in Am. Club: Toastmasters (Reno). State civil litigation, Criminal, Family and matrimonial. Office: 326 W Liberty Reno NV 89501

CORNING, NICHOLAS F., lawyer; b. Seattle, Nov. 8, 1945; s. Frank C. and Jessie D. (Weeks) C.; m. Patricia A. Tomlinson, Dec. 14, 1968; children: Kristen Marie, Lauren Margaret. B in Comm. Sci. cum laude, Seattle U., 1968; JD, U. Wash., 1972. Bar: Wash. 1972, U.S. Ct. Appeals (9th cir.) 1972, U.S. Dist. Ct. (we. dist.) Wash. 1973, U.S. Supreme Ct. 1976, U.S. Ct. of Claims 1981. Assoc. Jennings P. Felix, Seattle, 1972-75; ptnr. Lagerquist, McConnell & Corning, Seattle, 1975-77; pres. Treece, Richdale, Malone & Corning, Inc., P.S., Seattle, 1977—; bd. dirs. Windermere Corp., Seattle. Mem. Ballard tourism task force, Seattle, 1986—. Recipient Am. Jurisprudence award in Criminal Law U. Wash., 1971. Mem. Wash. State Bar Assn., Wash. Trial Lawyers Assn., Assn. Trial Lawyers Am., Seattle-King County Bar Assn. (speakers bur. 1983—), Ballard C. of C. (chmn. Park com. 1982—), Beta Gamma Sigma (local chpt. Key award 1968). Federal civil litigation, State civil litigation, Personal injury. Home: 5640 NE 55th Seattle WA 98105 Office: Treece Richdale Malone & Corning 1718 NW 56th Seattle WA 98107

CORNISH, JEANNETTE CARTER, lawyer; b. Steelton, Pa., Sept. 17, 1946; d. Ellis Pollard and Anna Elizabeth (Stannard) C.; m. Harry L. Cornish; children: Lee Jason, Geoffrey Charles. BA, Howard U., 1968, JD, 1971. Bar: N.J. 1976, U.S. Dist. Ct. N.J. 1976. Atty. Newark-Essex Law Reform, 1971-72; technician EEOC, Newark, 1972-73; atty., asst. sec. Inmont Corp., N.Y.C., 1974-82; sr. atty., asst. sec. Inmont Corp., Clifton, N.J., 1982-85, BASF Corp., Clifton, 1986—; speaker on women in bus. Bd. dirs. YMCA, Paterson, N.J., 1977-1980, Lenni-Lenape council Girl Scouts, 1986—. Mem. ABA, Nat. Bar Assn., Am. Corp. Counsel, Assn. Black Women Lawyers, Nat. Urban League., Alpha Kappa Alpha (scholar 1964), Delta Sigma Theta (scholar). General corporate, Real property, Labor. Home: 614 11th Ave Paterson NJ 07514 Office: BASF Corp 1255 Broad St Clifton NJ 07015-6001

CORNISH, LEBBEUS M., lawyer; b. Honolulu, Apr. 20, 1921; s. Lebbeus M. and Lydia (Herrmann) C.; m. Dorothy L., Nov. 7, 1945; children: Craig, Kent. AB, Washburn U., 1947, JD, 1948. Bar: Kans. 1948. Ptnr. Glenn, Cornish, Hanson & Karns, Chartered, Topeka, 1948—, now mng. ptnr.; lectr. bus. law Washburn U., 1951-75; spl. asst. atty. gen., Kans., 1973-74; spl. legal counsel Kans. Corp. Commn., 1955-57, Kans. Hwy Commn., 1955-57, Kans. Bd. Tax Appeals, 1965-69; chmn. bd. Topeka Bank & Trust; bd. dirs. Kans. Mut. Ins. Co. Bd. dirs. Topeka United Way, 1960-80, pres., 1964-66; bd. regents Washburn U., 1969-73, chmn., 1972-73; trustee Topeka Pub. Library, 1964-68, St. Francis Hosp., 1965-68. Served with AUS, 1942-46. Decorated Air medal, D.F.C. Mem. Topeka Bar Assn., Kans. Bar Assn., ABA (vice chmn. property law com. 1975-85, mem. banking com. 1982—), Am. Judicature Soc., Internat. Assn. Ins. Counsel. Roman Catholic. Clubs: Topeka Country, Topeka, Top of the First (Topeka); Kansas City (Mo.); Garden of the Gods (Colorado Springs, Colo.). Insurance, Banking. Home: 3621 Holly Ln Topeka KS 66603 Office: 900 Merchants Nat Tower Topeka KS 66612

CORNISH, RICHARD POOL, lawyer; b. Evanston, Ill., Sept. 9, 1942; s. William A. and Rita (Pool) C.; m. Suzanne Darby, June 21, 1967 (div.); children—William Darby, Richard Gordon. B.S., Okla. State U., 1964; LL.B., U. Okla., 1966. Bar: Okla. 1966, U.S. Dist. Ct. (ea. dist.) Okla. 1969, U.S. Supreme Ct. 1979. Ptnr., Baumert & Cornish, McAlester, Okla., 1967-71, Cornish & Cornish, Inc., McAlester, Okla., 1971-77; magistrate U.S. Dist. Ct. Eastern Dist. Okla., 1976—; prin. Richard P. Cornish, Inc., McAlester, Okla., 1977—. Bd. dirs. McAlester Boys Club, 1970-80, pres., 1974. Served to capt. JAGC, USAR, 1966-78. Mem. ABA, Okla. Bar Assn. (mem. legal aid to servicemen com., legal specialization com.), Pittsburg County Bar Assn., McAlester C. of C. (dir. 1973-75). Roman Catholic. Probate, General practice. Home: 611 East Creek McAlester OK 74501 Office: PO Box 1106 McAlester OK 74502

CORRALES, MANUEL, JR., lawyer; b. Long Beach, Calif., Aug. 21, 1952; s. Manuel Sr. Corrales and Emma (Amezquita) Lewis; m. Tauna Alexandria Pittard, June 30, 1984; children: Michael John, Chelsea Eva. BA in English, Brigham Young U., 1979, JD, 1982. Bar: Utah 1982, U.S. Dist. Ct. Utah 1983, U.S. Ct. Appeals (10th cir.) 1985, Calif. 1985, U.S. Dist. Ct. (so. dist.) Calif. 1985, U.S. Ct. Appeals (9th cir.) 1986, N.Mex. 1986, U.S. Dist. Ct. N.Mex. 1986, U.S. Supreme Ct. 1986. Law clk. to presiding justice N.Mex. Supreme Ct., Santa Fe, 1982-83; sole practice Salt Lake City, 1983-84; assoc. Roe, Fowler & Moxley, Salt Lake City, 1984-85, McInnis, Fitzgerald et al, San Diego, 1985—. Liaison for ch. Boy Scouts Am., San Diego County, 1986—; missionary Latter Day Saints Ch., Dusseldorf, Fed. Rep. of Germany, 1976-78. Served to sgt. USAF, 1971-75. Mem. ABA, Fed. Bar Assn. (treas. young lawyers div. 1985-86, bd. dirs. young lawyers div. 1984-85), N.Mex. Bar Assn., Calif. Bar Assn., Utah Bar Assn., San Diego Bar Assn., Am. Inn of Ct. Democrat. Personal injury, Federal civil litigation, State civil litigation. Home: 17185 W Bernardo Dr #201 San Diego CA 92127 Office: McInnis Fitzgerald Rees Sharkey & McIntyre 1320 Columbia St San Diego CA 92101

CORSE, CHESTER CLINTON, JR., lawyer; b. Pitts., Feb. 17, 1940; s. Chester Clinton Sr. and Elizabeth (Scanlin) C.; m. Norma Jean Greff, Aug. 7, 1965; children: Daun Lauran, Kerry Lynne. AB, U. Pitts., 1962, JD, 1965. Bar: Pa. 1965, U.S. Dist. Ct. (we. dist.) Pa. 1965. Ptnr. Williamson, Friedberg & Jones, Pottsville, Pa., 1968—; solicitor Borough of Palo Alto, Schuylkill County Govt. Study Commn. Past pres. Schuylkill Unit Am. Cancer Soc., crusade chmn. 1977, spl. gifts chmn. Palo Alto Cancer Crusasde, 1983-84. Served to capt. U.S. Army, 1966-68. Mem. ABA, Pa. Bar Assn. (ho. of dels., legal ethics and profl. responsibility com.), Schuylkill County Bar Assn. (past pres., officer and bd. dirs.), Allegheny County Bar Assn., Pa. Trial Lawyers Assn. (former chmn.), Pa. Mcpl. Solicitors, Am. Judicature Soc. (diplomat), Schuylkill County Swimming Assn. (pres.). Lodge: Elks. Personal injury, Insurance, Family and matrimonial. Office: Williamson Friedberg & Jones One Norwegian Plaza Pottsville PA 17901

CORSO, FRANK MITCHELL, lawyer; b. N.Y.C., July 28, 1928; s. Joseph and Jane (DeBenedetto) C.; m. Dorothy G. McVeety, Apr. 7, 1951; children—Frank, Elaine, Patricia, Dorothy. LL.B., St. John's U., 1952. Bar: N.Y. 1954, D.C. 1981, U.S. ct. mil. apls. 1954, U.S. Sup. Ct. 1960. Ptnr. Corso & Fertig, 1957-61, Corso & Petito, 1966-69, ptnr. Corso & Landa, Jericho, N.Y., 1971-73, Corso & Engelberg, 1973-82;sole practice, Westbury, N.Y., 1982—. Appointed bd. dirs. UN Devel. Corp. by former N.Y. Gov., N.Y. Mcpl. Bond Bank Agy.; trustee WLIW pub. TV channel. Served with U.S. Army 1951-53. Named Man of Yr., Am.-Italians of L.I., 1966. Mem. ABA, N.Y. State Bar Assn., Nassau Bar Assn., Assn. Trial Lawyers Am., Internat. Bar Assn., World Assn. Lawyers (founding mem.), Vatican Knight of Holy Sepulchre. Contbr. articles to legal jours.; TV commentator legal topics. State civil litigation, Personal injury, General corporate. Home: 5 Suncrest Dr Dix Hills NY 11746 Office: 999 Brush Hollow Rd Westbury NY 11590

CORTEZ, HERNAN GLENN, Lawyer; b. Harlingen, Tex., Nov. 12, 1934; s. Hernan and Laura (Howell) C.; m. Carole Elaine DuBois, Jan. 29, 1958 (div. Aug. 1976); children: Vicky Foss, Marta Stephens, Jill Hubach, Ingrid, H. Glenn Jr.; m. Carole Jean Simms, Dec. 31, 1976; 1 child, Troy Dillinger. BA, U. Tex., 1956, JD, 1962. Bar: Tex. 1962, U.S. Dist. Ct. (we. dist.) Tex. 1970, U.S. Ct. Appeals (5th cir.) 1981. Asst. atty. City of Austin, Tex., 1962-69; assoc. atty. City of Austin, 1969, atty., 1969-70; sole practice Austin, 1971—; atty. City of Rollingwood, Tex. 1972-86, City of Pflugerville, Tex., 1974—, City of Manor, Tex., 1972—, City of Granite Shoals, Tex., 1983-86. Served as capt. U.S. Army, 1957-59. Mem. ABA, Tex. Bar Assn., Travis County Bar Assn., Assn. Trial Lawyers Am., Tex. Trial Lawyers Assn., Nat. Inst. Mcpl. Law Officers. Local government, Personal injury, Public utilities. Home: 4701 Fieldstone Dr Austin TX 78735 Office: 1411 West Ave Suite 200 Austin TX 78701

CORTEZ, MILES COGLEY, JR., lawyer; b. Chgo., Dec. 7, 1943; s. Miles and Carol (Sandstrom) C.; m. Janice Lynn Gillespie; children: Miles III, Amy, Jeff Salzenstein, Drew. BA in Econs., Trinity U., San Antonio, 1964; JD, Northwestern U., 1967. Bar: Ill. 1967, Colo. 1970, U.S. Dist. Ct. Colo. 1970, U.S. Ct. Appeals (10th cir.) 1970, U.S. Ct. Appeals (3d cir.) 1974. Ptnr. Welborn, Dufford & Brown, Denver, 1970-84; pres. Cortez & Friedman, P.C., Denver, 1984—; Bd. dirs. The Profl. Bank, Englewood, Colo.; lectr. Continuing Legal Edn. Seminars, Colo., 1978—. Contbr. articles to profl. jours. Bd. dirs. Colo. Youth Tennis Found., Denver, 1982-84. Served to capt. U.S. Army, 1967-69. Fellow Colo. Bar Found.; mem. ABA, Denver Bar Assn. (pres. 1982-83), Colo. Bar Assn. (bd. govs. 1976-78, 81-83), Nat. Conf. Bar Pres., Colo. Supreme Ct. Bd. Law Examiners. Avocation: tennis. Federal civil litigation, State civil litigation, Real property. Home: 7025 E Costilla Dr Englewood CO 80112 Office: Cortez & Friedman P.C. 5251 DTC Pkwy Denver CO 80111

CORTHELL, JON RANDOLPH, lawyer; b. Seattle, Mar. 31, 1955; s. Daniel O. and Jane (Overmann) C.; m. Susan Elizabeth Gamache, Sept. 15, 1977; 1 child, Emilie. BS in Econs., U. Wash., 1977, JD, 1980. Bar: Wash. 1981, N.Y. 1984. Atty. nat. accounts div. IBM Corp., White Plains, N.Y., 1981, sr. atty. telecommunications products div., 1985; staff atty. nat. accounts div. IBM Corp., Los Angeles, 1984; counsel, industry systems products IBM Corp., Milford, Conn., 1986. Antitrust, Computer, Contracts commercial. Office: IBM Corp 472 Wheelers Farms Rd Milford CT 06460

CORUM, JESSE MAXWELL, IV, lawyer; b. Richmond, Va., Dec. 19, 1950; s. Jesse Maxwell and Joy (MacKubbin) C.; m. Lynn Hummel, Aug. 12, 1972; children—Jesse Maxwell V, Scott W. B.A., Guilford Coll., 1973; J.D., Vt. Law Sch., 1977. Bar: Vt. 1977, U.S. Dist. Ct. Vt. 1978. Dep. state's atty. Windham County State's Atty.'s Office, Brattleboro, Vt., 1977-81; assoc. Gale, Gale & Barile, Brattleboro, 1981-82; ptnr. Gale, Gale, Barile & Corum, Brattleboro, 1982-86; ptnr. Gale, Gale & Corum, Brattleboro, 1987—. pres. Windham County Law Library, Brattleboro, 1981-85. Sec.-clk. Youth Services Windham County, Brattleboro, 1981-85, pres., 1985—; mem. Brattleboro Planning Commn., Vt., 1981-85, chmn., 1984-85. Mem. Vt. Bar Assn., Windham County Bar Assn. (sec. 1978). Club: Optimists Investment (Brattleboro, Vt.) (pres. 1982-83). Lodge: Rotary (sec. 1984-86, v.p. 1986-87). Criminal, State civil litigation, Family and matrimonial. Home: 30 Oak St. Brattleboro VT 05301 Office: PO Box 1171 12 Park Pl Brattleboro VT 05301

CORY, BARBARA ELLEN, lawyer; b. Oak Park, Ill., July 26, 1951; d. Paul Russell and Mary Clark (Holbrook) C.; m. Spencer Richard Knapp, Aug. 21, 1976; children: Emily Cory Knapp, Alexandra Cory Knapp. Student, Dartmouth Coll., 1971-72; BA, Wellesley Coll., 1973; JD, Cornell U., 1976. Bar: Vt. 1977, U.S. Dist. Ct. Vt. 1978. Law clk. to presiding justice U.S. Dist. Ct. Vt., Rutland, 1977-78; assoc. Dinse, Erdmann & Clapp, Burlington, Vt., 1976-83; ptnr. Dinse, Erdmann & Clapp, Burlington, 1983—. Chairperson Adult Day Care Ctr. Inc., Burlington, 1981-85; bd. dirs., v.p., sec. Child Care Ctr. Inc. Mem. ABA, Vt. Bar Assn. (young lawyers sect.), Vis. Nurse Assn. (bd. dirs. 1983—). Federal civil litigation, State civil litigation, Personal injury. Home: 7 Heather Ln Shelburne VT 05482 Office: Dinse Endmann & Clapp 209 Battery St Burlington VT 05482

COSCARELLI, DIANNE SMITH, lawyer; b. Tiffin, Ohio, Jan. 17, 1952; d. Ralph Asa and Lucille Lucius Smith; m. Thomas Edward Coscarelli, Jan. 7, 1977; 1 child, Laura Christine. AB summa cum laude, Ohio U., 1974; JD magna cum laude, U. San Francisco, 1978. Bar: Ohio 1978. Assoc. Thompson, Hine & Flory, Cleve., 1978—; trustee Legal Aid Soc. of Cleve., 1980—, sec. 1984—. Mem. ABA, Ohio State Bar Assn., Cleve. Bar Assn., Phi Beta Kappa. Real property. Office: Thompson Hine & Flory 1100 Nat City Bank Bldg Cleveland OH 44114

COSGRAVE, CARMEL M., lawyer, educator; b. Chgo., Feb. 24, 1955; d. Joseph D. and Mary G. (Nowak) C.; m. Daniel J. Roth, Jan. 31, 1981. BA, Roosevelt U., 1977; JD, Loyola U., Chgo., 1980. Bar: Ill., U.S. Dist. Ct. (no. dist.) Ill. Assoc. Querrey, Harrow, Gulanick & Kennedy, Chgo., 1980—; instr. law Loyola U., Chgo., 1982-86, Nat. Inst. Trial Adv., Chgo., 1986—. Mem. Ill. Bar Assn., Chgo. Bar Assn., Ill. Def. Council. Democrat. Roman Catholic. Avocations: golf, gardening. Insurance, Personal injury, Legal education. Home: 9222 S Bell Chicago IL 60620 Office: Querrey Harrow Gulanick & Kennedy 135 S LaSalle Suite 3600 Chicago IL 60603

COSGROVE, RITAMAE GOBER, lawyer; b. New Britain, Conn., Oct. 7, 1950; d. Anthony William and Adele Rita (Akromas) G.; m. Gerald Paul Cosgrove, Sept. 10, 1982; 1 child, Sarah Adele. AS in Acctg., Greater Hartford Community Coll., 1970; BA in Econs., U. Hartford, 1977, MA in Econs., 1978; JD, U. Tulsa, 1981. Bar: Conn. 1981. Dir. prodn. and broadcasting Chirurg & Cairns, Farmington, Conn., 1968-71; dir. media Knudsen & Moore, Stamford, Conn., 1971-72; retail buyer G.Fox and Co., Hartford, Conn., 1972-76; prodn. analyst Conn. Dept. Transp., Wethersfield, 1977-78; hearing examiner Conn. Dept. Pub. Utilities, Hartford, 1979-81; atty., land dept. ARCO Oil and Gas Co., Houston, 1981—; research asst. Nat. Energy Law and Policy Inst., Tulsa, 1979-81; adj. prof. U. Midland, Tex., 1981-82, U. Houston, 1983—; pres. bd. dirs. Mill Ridge Forest, Houston; bd. dirs., pres. Harris County Northwest number 9 Mcpl. utility dist., Houston. Mem. ABA, Conn. Bar Assn., Nat. Soc. for Econs., Am. Petroleum Inst. Democrat. Roman Catholic. Avocations: sailing, reading, snow skiing. Administrative and regulatory, General corporate, Oil and gas leasing. Home: 11406 Skyway Dr Cypress TX 77249 Office: ARCO Oil and Gas Co PO Box 1346 Houston TX 77251

COSLETT, CHARLES REYNOLDS, lawyer; b. Kingston, Pa., July 18, 1952; s. E. Charles and Ruth (Middleton) C.; m. Donna Joan Crawford, Aug. 9, 1980; children: Benjamin C., Bradley M. BA magna cum laude, Dickinson Coll., 1974, JD, 1977. Bar: Pa. 1977, U.S. Dist. Ct. (mid. dist.) Pa., U.S. Ct. Appeals (3d cir.). Mng. ptnr. Coslett and Coslett, Kingston, Pa., 1977—; asst. dist. atty. Luzerne County, Wilkes-Barre, Pa., 1978-87; solicitor West Side Area Vocat.-Tech. Sch., Kingston, 1981—, NW Area Sch. Dist., Shickshinny, Pa., 1986—. Trustee Diocese of Bethlehem, Pa., 1984—, vice-chancellor, 1985—; chmn. Alumni Admissions program Dickinson Coll., 1985—; clk. and mem. of Vestry St. Stephen's Episcopal Ch., Wilkes-Barre, 1980-85. Mem. Assn. Trial Lawyers Am., Pa. Trial Lawyers Assn., Dist. Atty.'s Assn. of Pa., Pa. Bar Assn., Wilkes-Barre Law and Library Assn., Pa. Sch. Bd. Solicitors Assn., Pa. Interscholastic Athletic Assn., Phi Beta Kappa. Republican. Episcopalian. Avocations: high sch., coll. and Am. Legion baseball umpiring. Criminal, Local government, Family and matrimonial. Home: 17 Dorchester Dr Dallas PA 18612 Office: Coslett and Coslett 312 Wyoming Ave Kingston PA 18704

COSNER, CHARLES KINIAN, JR., lawyer; b. Nashville, May 3, 1950; s. Charles Kinian and Margaret (Cash) C.; m. B. Gail Reese, Feb. 24, 1982. BA, Vanderbilt U., 1972; JD, U. Tenn., 1975. Bar: Tenn. 1976, U.S. Dist. Ct. (mid. dist.) Tenn. 1976, U.S. Tax Ct. 1976, U.S. Ct. Appeals (6th cir.) 1977, U.S. Dist. Ct. (we. dist.) Tenn. 1982, U.S. Supreme Ct. 1983, U.S. Ct. Internat. Trade 1985. Ptnr. Cosner & Waldschmidt, Nashville, 1976—. Mem. ABA, Comml. Law League Am., Tenn. Bar Assn., Tenn. Trial Lawyers Assn., Nashville Bar Assn. Methodist. Clubs: Nashville City, Hillwood Country (Nashville). Bankruptcy, Federal civil litigation, General corporate. Home: 6666 Brookmont Terr #1106 Nashville TN 37205 Office: Cosner & Waldschmidt 1st Am Ctr 20th Fl Nashville TN 37238

COSTA, JOHN ANTHONY, lawyer; b. Bklyn., Oct. 6, 1942; s. Salvatore Francis and Ann (Moltisanti) C.; m. Norma Meurer, June 20, 1964; children: Loreen, Cynthia. BA, Fairleigh Dickinson U., 1964; JD, St. John's U., 1970. Bar: N.Y. 1971, U.S. Dist. Ct. (so. and ea. dists.) N.Y. Legal advisor N.Y.C. Police Dept., 1970-73; spl. asst. atty. gen., spl. prosecutor N.Y.C., 1973-74; asst. pub. defender Rock County, N.Y.C., 1978; town atty. Town of Clarkstown, New City, N.Y., 1982—; lectr. Rockland Community Coll., Suffern, N.Y., 1974-81, Dutchess Community Coll., Poughkeepsie, N.Y., 1975-77. Trustee Nyack (N.Y.) Union Free Sch. Dist., 1976-78; bd. dirs. Rock County Legal Aid Soc., N.Y.C., 1980-82. Mem. Rockland County Bar Assn. Democrat. Roman Catholic. Lodge: Lions. Avocations: reading, woodworking. Real property, Contracts commercial, Local government. Home: 351 B Boxberger Rd Valley Cottage NY 10989 Office: Costa & McKay 47 B Rt 303 Valley Cottage NY 10989

COSTANTINO, MARK AMERICUS, judge; b. Staten Island, N.Y., Apr. 9, 1920; s. Anne Marie (Caruselle) C.; m. Dorothy Summers, July 28, 1944; children—Mark, Thomas, Dennis, Richard, Kathryn Ann. Student, Manhattan Coll., 1938-40; LL.B., Bklyn. Law Sch., 1947. Spl. dep. atty. gen. State of N.Y., N.Y.C., 1947-51; sole practice Staten Island, 1951-56; judge City Ct., N.Y.C., 1957-61, Civil Ct., N.Y.C., 1961-71, U.S. Dist. Ct. N.Y., Bklyn., 1971—; acting judge N.Y. State Supreme Ct., 1958-71; nat. chmn. Am. Inns of Ct., Bklyn., 1984—. Contbr. articles to profl. jours. Active Boy Scouts Am.; bd. dirs. Drs. Hosp., Staten Island; planned, developed spl. naturalization proceeding on Ellis Island, 1986. Served with U.S. Army, 1942-46. Recipient Alumnus of Yr. award Bklyn. Law Sch. Alumni Assn., 1978, 1st ann. Warren Burger award Bklyn. Trial Lawyers Assn., 1970, Man of Yr. award Amicus Curiae Columbia Assn., 1984, resolution DAR, 1984. Mem. Fed. Bar Council, Richmond County Bar Assn., Columbian Lawyers, Am. Legion (citation 1982), Phi Delta Phi, Italian-Am. Assn. Republican. Roman Catholic. Immigration, naturalization, and customs, Patent, Criminal. Office: US Dist Ct 225 Cadman Plaza E Brooklyn NY 11201

COSTELLO, DONALD FREDRIC, lawyer; b. Tacoma, Wash., Nov. 8, 1948; s. Bernard Peter and Ada Harriet (Morrill) C.; m. Debra Ann Shaw, Sept. 21, 1969; 1 child, Don Eric. BA, Calif. State U.-San Francisco, 1970; JD, U. Calif.-Hastings Coll., 1974. Bar: Calif. 1974, U.S. Supreme Ct. 1980. Assoc. Frolik-Filley & Schey, San Francisco, 1974-78; mem. Salomon & Costello, 1978-80; mem. law offices Donald F. Costello, Palo Alto, Calif., 1980-84, Santa Cruz, Calif., 1984—; lectr. Stanford U., 1983, U. Santa Clara, 1980. Mem. Planning Commn., City of Belmont (Calif.), 1976. Mem. ABA, Assn. Trial Lawyers Am., Calif. Trial Lawyers Assn. (contbr. articles to Forum), Am. Soc. Law and Medicine. State civil litigation, Personal injury. Office: 331 Soquel Ave Santa Cruz CA 95062

COSTELLO, EDWARD J., JR., lawyer; b. N.Y.C., Apr. 18, 1939; s. Edward J. Sr. and Madeleine (Carroi) C.; m. Karin Bergstrom, Aug. 21, 1981; 1 child, Catharine A. AB, Fordham U., 1961; JD, NYU, 1964. Assoc. Donovan, Leisure, Newton & Irvine, N.Y.C., 1962-64, O'Melveny & Myers, Los Angeles, 1963, 68-72; spl. agt. FBI, Washington, 1964-67; ptnr. Costello & Walcher, Los Angeles, 1972-85, Proskauer, Rose, Goetz & Mendelsohn, Los Angeles, 1985—; adj. assoc. prof. law, evidence and criminal procedure Southwestern U. Sch. Law, Los Angeles, 1970-73, internat. bus. trans. U. So. Calif. Law Ctr., Los Angeles, 1973-75; judge pro tem Los Angeles Mcpl. Ct., 1971—; pres. The Compass Orgn. Inc., Los Angeles, 1985—; chmn. bd. dirs. Year Labs. Inc., Los Angeles; bd. dirs. Nat. Exchange Inc., McLean, Va. Chmn., trustee Brentwood Sch., Los Angeles, 1986-87. Mem. ABA (litigation, internat. law and antitrust law sects.), Calif. Bar Assn. (bar examiners com.), N.Y. State Bar Assn., Fla. Bar Assn., Los Angeles County Bar Assn. (past mem. juvenile ct. and judiciary coms., trial lawyer sect.), Assn. Bus. Trial Lawyers, Western Assn. Venture Capitalists. Federal civil litigation, State civil litigation, Legal education. Home: 11060 Cashmere St Los Angeles CA 90049 Office: Proskauer Rose Goetz & Mendelsohn 2029 Century Park E Suite 1700 Los Angeles CA 90067-3003

COSTELLO, JAMES PAUL, lawyer; b. Elgin, Ill., Nov. 12, 1953; s. John Desmond and Helena (Brennan) C.; m. Kathryn Charlotte Schafer, June 16, 1979; children: James Albert, Robert Francis. BA, U. Ill., 1975; JD, DePaul U., 1978. Bar: Ill. 1978, U.S. Dist. Ct. (no. dist.) Ill. 1978. Assoc. J. Thomas Demos & Assocs., Chgo., 1978-83; ptnr. James Paul Costello Ltd., Des Plaines and Chgo., Ill., 1983—. Contbg. author: Law Enforcement Legal Defense Manual, 1977-78; editor: Jail Law Bulletin, Police Plaintiff,

Law Enforcement Employment Digest, 1977-78. Mem. Ill. Bar Assn., Assn. Trial Lawyers Am., Ill. Trial Lawyers Assn. (amicus curiae com. 1981—). Democrat. Roman Catholic. Personal injury. Home: 3328 Daniels Arlington Heights IL 60004 Office: 205 W Randolph St Chicago IL 60606

COSTELLO, JOHN WILLIAM, lawyer; b. Chgo., Apr. 16, 1947; s. William John and June Ester (O'Neill) C.; m. Maureen Grace Matthews, June 13, 1970; children—Colleen, William, Erin, Owen. B.A., John Carroll U., 1969; J.D., DePaul U., 1972. Bar: U.S. Dist. Ct. (no. dist.) Ill. 1982. Assoc. Arvey, Hodes, Costello & Burman, Chgo., 1972-76; ptnr., 1976—. Co-author: (manual) The Bankrupcy Reform Act of 1978, 1981. Served to capt. U.S. Army, 1972-73. Mem. ABA (bus. bankruptcy com., jurisdiction and venue and secured creditors subcoms.), Comml. Law League Am., Ill. State Bar Assn. (vice chmn., chmn. comml. banking and bankrupcy law sect. 1979-81), Am. Bankruptcy Inst. Democrat. Roman Catholic. Office: Arvey Hodes Costello & Burman 180 N LaSalle St Chicago IL 60601

COSTELLO, MICHAEL JOSEPH, lawyer; b. Milw., Mar. 24, 1952; s. Harold Joseph and Rosemary Francis (Alexander) C.; m. Lindl Wiederholdt, Mar. 22, 1986. BA in Polit. Sci., U. Mo., 1974; JD cum laude, St. Louis U., 1977; LLM in Internat. Law cum laude, Vrije UniversiteitBrussels, 1979. Bar: Mo. 1977, D.C. 1978, U.S. Supreme Ct. 1982. Atty. Nordic Law Cons., Brussels, 1977-80, Commn. European Com., Brussels, 1980; assoc. Gallop, Johnson & Neuman, St. Louis, 1982-84, Thompson & Mitchell, St. Louis, 1984—; adj. prof. Webster U., St. Louis, 1984—, Washington U., St. Louis, 1986—; ednl. leader legal study tour of Soviet Union Profl. Seminar Cons., 1986. Sigma Chi. Roman Catholic. Club: Mo. Athletic. Avocations: skiing, sailing, scuba. Home: 7472 Flora Saint Louis MO 63143 Office: Thompson & Mitchell One Mercantile Ctr 3400 Saint Louis MO 63101

COSTELLO, ROBERT JOSEPH, lawyer; b. N.Y.C., Jan. 4, 1948; s. Peter John and Barbara Theresa (Sheeran) C.; m. Alice Boyle, Aug. 31, 1975; children—Robert Ian, Maura Alison, Megan Ailish. B.A., Fordham U., 1969, J.D., 1972. Bar: N.Y. 1973. Assoc., Dewey, Ballantine et al, N.Y.C., 1972-75; asst. U.S. atty. So. Dist. N.Y., N.Y.C., 1975-80, dep. chief criminal div., 1980-81; ptnr. Lumbard & Phelan, N.Y.C., 1981-82, Phelan & Costello, N.Y.C., 1982—. Mem. ABA, N.Y. State Bar Assn., Assn. Bar City of N.Y. Roman Catholic. Criminal, Federal civil litigation, Securities. Home: 70 Great Oak Rd Manhasset NY 11030 Office: Phelan & Costello PC One Penn Plaza Suite 4310 New York NY 10119

COSTELLO, WALTER ANTHONY, JR., lawyer; b. Boston, June 24, 1946; s. Walter Anthony and Mary Francis (Duggan) C.; m. Carol Ann Sanchez, Apr. 24, 1970; children—Sarah Meredith, Mary Elaina. A.B. in Econs., Boston U., 1969; J.D., Boston Coll., 1973. Bar: Mass. 1973, U.S. Dist. Ct. Mass. 1974, U.S. Ct. Appeals (5th cir.) 1975. Assoc. Kisloff, Hock, Shuman and Flannagan, Boston, 1973-74; ptnr. Costello, Frattaroli, Barrett & Gonthier, Salem, Mass., 1975—; instr. North Shore Community Coll., Beverly, Mass., 1978-80. Bd. editors Mass. Lawyers Weekly, 1987. Chmn. zoning bd. appeal Town of Swampscott, Mass., 1982-83, mem. bd. appeal, 1978-82; bd. govs., co-chmn. Boston Coll. Law Day, 1983, bd. govs. chmn. Boston Coll. Law. Mem. Essex County Bar Assn. (exec. council), Am. Trial Lawyers Assn., Mass. Acad. Trial Attys. (bd. govs.), Mass. Trial Lawyers Edn. Found. (bd. govs., bd. dirs.), Mass. Bar Assn., Boston Coll. Law Sch. Alumni Assn. (exec. council 1976-82). Democrat. Roman Catholic. Admiralty, Federal civil litigation, State civil litigation. Home: 164 Atlantic Ave Swampscott MA 01907 Office: Costello Frattaroli Barrett & Gonthier 314 Essex St Salem MA 01907

COSTIGAN, JOHN MARK, lawyer, consumer products executive; b. Newark, Aug. 2, 1942; s. Dennis Aloysius and Claire (Reilly) C.; m. Emily Anne Lincoln, July 2, 1966; children—Elizabeth Anne, Catherine Lynn, Matthew David, Daniel John. B.A.in English, Fordham U., 1964; LL.B., Columbia U., 1967; M.B.A., U. Chgo., 1978. Bar: N.Y. 1968, Ill. 1973. Atty. Bigham, Englar, Jones & Houston, N.Y.C., 1967-70; atty. Kraft, Inc., Glenview, Ill., 1970-74, gen. atty., 1974-76, sr. atty., 1976-79, v.p., asst. gen. counsel, 1979-81; sr. corp. counsel Dart & Kraft, Inc., Northbrook, Ill., 1981-82, v.p. investor relations, 1982-84, v.p., assoc. gen. counsel, 1985-86; sr. v.p., gen. counsel Premark Internat. Inc., Deerfield, Ill., 1986—. Mem. ABA. Roman Catholic. General corporate, Antitrust. Home: 671 Newcastle Dr Lake Forest IL 60045 Office: Premark Internat Inc 1717 Deerfield Rd Deerfield IL 60045

COSTIKYAN, EDWARD N(AZAR), lawyer; b. Weehawken, N.J., Sept. 14, 1924; s. Mihran Nazar and Berthe (Muller) C.; m. Barbara Fatt, Mar. 5, 1977; children: Gregory John, Emilie Berthe. A.B., Columbia U., 1947, LL.B., 1949. Bar: N.Y. 1949, U.S. Supreme Ct. 1964. Law sec. to judge Harold R. Medina U.S. Dist. Ct., N.Y.C., 1949-51; ptnr. firm Paul, Weiss, Rifkind, Wharton & Garrison, N.Y.C., 1960—; mem. commn. on Integrity in Govt., N.Y.C., 1986, joint com. on Jud. Adminstrn., 1985—. Author: Behind Closed Doors: Politics in the Public Interest, 1966, How to Win Votes: The Politics of 1980, 1980; co-author: Re-Structuring the Government of New York City, 1972, New Strategies for Regional Cooperation, 1973; research editor: Columbia Law Rev.; bd. editors: N.Y. Law Jour., 1976—; contbr. articles of legal, polit. subjects to periodicals and profl. jours. Chmn. N.Y. State Task Force on N.Y.C. Jurisdiction and Structure, 1971-72; vice-chmn. State Charter Revision for N.Y.C., 1972-77; mem. com. character and fitness 1st Jud. Dept. Democratic dist. leader, 1955-65; county leader Dem. County Com. N.Y. County, 1962-64; presdl. elector Dem. Party, 1964; trustee Columbia U.; bd. dirs. 42d St Redevel. Corp. Served to 1st lt. AUS, 1942-46. Fellow Am. Coll. Trial Lawyers; mem. Assn. Bar City N.Y. (mem. exec. com. 1986—), ABA, N.Y. State Bar Assn., Columbia Law Alumni. Unitarian. Club: Century. General practice, State civil litigation. Home: 50 Sutton Pl S New York NY 10022 Office: Paul Weiss Rifkind Wharton & Garrison 1285 Ave Americas New York NY 10019

COSTON, JAMES E., lawyer; b. Chgo., Apr. 21, 1955; s. Sam T. and Demetra P. (Kokoris) C.; m. Carol Ann Patejdl, June 13, 1981. BA, Northwestern U., 1977; JD, DePaul U., 1980. Bar: Ill. 1980, U.S. Dist. Ct. (no. dist.) Ill. 1980, U.S. Ct. Appeals (7th cir.) 1981. Assoc. Hogan, McNulty & Meyer, Chgo., 1980-82; mng. ptnr. Chgo. office Malley, Yelsky, Rosenfeld & Scott, Chgo., 1982-86; mng. ptnr. McNeily, Rosenfeld & Coston, Chgo., 1986—. Mem. ABA, Assn. Trial Lawyers Am., Ill. Bar Assn., Chgo. Bar Assn., Phi Alpha Delta. Democrat. Greek Orthodox. Club: Chgo. Athletic Assn. Avocation: traveling. Consumer commercial, General practice, General corporate. Home: 1168 S Plymouth Ct 1 NW Chicago IL 60605 Office: McNeily Rosenfeld & Coston 100 W Monroe St Suite 2010 Chicago IL 60603

COTCHETT, JOSEPH WINTERS, lawyer; b. Chgo., Jan. 6, 1939; s. Joseph Winters and Jean (Renaud) C.; children—Leslie F., Charles P., Rachael E. B.S. in Engring., Calif. Poly. Coll., 1960; LL.B., U. Calif. Hastings Coll. Law, 1964. Bar: Calif. 1965. Ptnr. Cotchett & Illston, Burlingame, Calif., 1965—; mem. Calif. Jud. Council, 1975-77, Calif. Commn. on Jud. Performance, 1985—. Author: (with R. Cartwright) California Products Liability Actions, 1970, (with F. Haight) California Courtroom Evidence, 1972, (with A. Elkind) Federal Courtroom Evidence, 1976; contbr. articles to profl. jours. Chmn. San Mateo County Heart Assn., 1967, 68; pres. San Mateo Boys Club, 1971; bd. dirs. U. Calif. Hastings Law Sch., 1980—. Served with Intelligence Corps U.S. Army, 1960-61; now col. JAGC, Res. Fellow Am. Bar Found., Am. Bd. Trial Advocates, Internat. Acad. Trial Lawyers; mem. Calif. Trial Lawyers Assn., Am. Trial Lawyers Assn., Nat. Bd. Trial Advocates (diplomate civil trial advocate), State Bar Calif. (gov. 1972-75, v.p. 1975). Clubs: Commonwealth, Press (San Francisco). Federal civil litigation, State civil litigation. Office: 840 Malcolm Rd Burlingame CA 94010 Office: 9454 Wilshire Suite 907 Beverly Hills CA 90212

COTHORN, JOHN ARTHUR, lawyer; b. Des Moines, Dec. 12, 1939; s. John L. and Marguerite (Esters) C.; children: Jeffrey, Judith. BS in Math., Aeronautical Engring., U. Mich., 1961, JD, 1980. Bar: U.S. Dist. Ct. (ea. dist.) Mich. 1981, U.S. Ct. Appeals (6th cir.) 1981. Jr. exec. U.S Govt., 1965-78; asst. prosecutor Washtenaw County, Ann Arbor, Mich., 1981-82; ptnr. Kitch, Saurbier, Drutchas, Wagner & Kenney P.C., Detroit, 1982—. Served to capt. U.S. Army, 1961-65. Mem. ABA (numerous fed. and state coms.), Nat. Bar Assn. (numerous fed. and state coms.), Soc. Automotive Engrs., Assn. Def. Trial Counsel, Phi Alpha Delta. Republican. Avocations: bridge, golf. State civil litigation, Federal civil litigation. Office: 1 Woodward Ave 10th Fl Detroit MI 48226

COTHRAN, JAMES CLARDY, JR., lawyer; b. Battlecreek, Mich., Aug. 25, 1942; s. Mary (Rhodes) C.; m. Elizabeth Gattshall, Nov. 27, 1982; 1 child, Michael Glass. U. S.C., 1965, JD, 1968. Bar: S.C. 1969, U.S. Dist. Ct. S.C. 1969, U.S. Ct. Appeals (4th cir.) 1976. Ptnr. King, Cothran & Hray, Spartanburg, S.C., 1974—. Served to staff sgt. USAFNG, 1968-74. Mem. S.C. Trial Lawyers Assn. State civil litigation, Federal civil litigation, Personal injury. Office: King Cothran & Hray 1451 E Main St Spartanburg SC 29302

COTNER, ROGER GARNER, lawyer; b. Springfield, Ohio, Oct. 3, 1952; s. James Bryan and Winifred (Garner) C.; m. Marlan Winter, Sept. 22, 1984. BA, Wittenberg U., 1974; JD, U. Richmond, 1982. Bar: Va. 1982, U.S. Tax Ct. 1982, Ohio 1983, U.S. Ct. Claims 1983, U.S. Ct. Appeals (4th and 6th cirs.) 1983, Mich. 1984, U.S. Dist. Ct. (so. dist.) Ohio 1984, U.S. Dist. Ct. (we. and ea. dists.) Mich. 1984, U.S. Supreme Ct. 1986. Sole practice West Olive, Mich., 1982—. Mem. ABA, Va. Bar Assn., Ohio Bar Assn., Mich. Bar Assn., Ottawa County Bar Assn. Personal income taxation, State and local taxation, Probate. Office: 9384 Ottawa House Dr West Olive MI 49460

COTTELEER, MICHAEL ALEXANDER, lawyer; b. Chgo., Feb. 4, 1944; s. Alexander Charles and Helen Lucille (Schmitt) C.; B.A., No. Ill. U., 1968; J.D. (Alumni scholar), Loyola U., Chgo., 1971; children—Jennifer, Amy, Kevin. Bar: Ill. 1971. Atty. Chgo. Title & Trust Co., 1971-72; atty. firm Herrick, McNeill, McElroy & Peregrine, Chgo., 1972-74, Daniels, Hancock & Faris, Elmhurst, Ill., 1974-75; asst. dean, assoc. prof. law No. Ill. U. Coll. Law, Glen Ellyn, 1975-78; sole practice, Wheaton, Ill., 1978-81, 82—; ptnr. Borenstein, Cotteleer, Greenberg & Young, Chgo. and Wheaton, 1981-82. Bd. dirs. No. Ill. U. Found., 1979—, mem. pres.'s legis. action com., 1978—; bd. dirs. Festival Theater, Oak Park, Ill., 1981-82. Served with U.S. Army, 1962-65. Recipient award for service Ill. Bd. Regents, 1979. Mem. ABA, Ill. Bar Assn. (vice chmn. sect. council on corps. and securities law 1981-82), Chgo. Bar Assn., DuPage County Bar Assn., No. Ill. U. Alumni Assn. (v.p., bd. dirs. 1977-82, pres. 1985—), Sigma Alpha Epsilon. Roman Catholic. General corporate, Contracts commercial, State civil litigation. Office: 209 N Washington St Wheaton IL 60187

COTTER, DENNIS BLAIR, lawyer; b. Grosse Pointe Farms, Mich., Mar. 4, 1945; s. Raymond Richard and Julia Ann (Skiffington) C.; m. Denise Ann Gieryn, May 25, 1979; children: Brendan Blair, Kevin Richard. BME, U. Mich., 1967, JD, 1973. Bar: Mich. 1973, U.S. Dist. Ct. (ea. dist.) Mich. 1973, U.S. Ct. Appeals (6th cir.) 1974. Assoc. Zeff & Zeff, Detroit, 1973-76, Vandeveer & Garzia, Detroit, 1976—. Vol. U.S. Peace Corps., Honduras, 1968-70; law officer Detroit Power Squadron, 1979—. Mem. ABA (tort and ins. practice). Roman Catholic. Club: Grosse Pointe Sail (various offices 1977—). Personal injury, Insurance, Product liability construction. Home: 1274 Audubon Grosse Pointe Park MI 48230 Office: Vandeveer & Garzia 333 W Fort #1600 Detroit MI 48226

COTTER, FRANK JAMES, lawyer, airline executive; b. N.Y.C., Feb. 21, 1943; s. James Francis and Ruth Antoinette (Nekola) C.; m. Janice Grant Myron, July 29, 1972; children—Francis James (F.J.), Jr., Margaret Carrington (Maggie), Justin Grant. B.A., Notre Dame U., 1965; J.D., So. Methodist U., 1968. Bar: Tex. 1968, Ga. 1971. Briefing atty. U.S. Dist. Ct. No. Dist. Tex., Dallas, 1968-70; atty. Delta Air Lines, Inc., Atlanta, 1970-78; sr. atty. U.S. Air Inc., Washington, 1978—. Active McLean Little League, Va. Recipient Am. Jurisprudence award, 1968. Mem. Washington Met. Corporate Counsel Assn., ABA, Tex. Bar Assn., Ga. Bar Assn., Phi Delta Phi. Roman Catholic. Contbr. articles in field to profl. jours. Administrative and regulatory, Antitrust, Trademark and copyright. Office: US Air Inc National Airport Washington DC 20001

COTTER, JAMES MICHAEL, lawyer; b. Providence, May 12, 1942; s. James Henry and Marguerite Louise (Clark) C.; m. Melinda Irene Tighe, Feb. 6, 1971; children; Elizabeth, Heather, Kathryn. AB, Fairfield U., 1964; LLB, U. Va., 1967. Bar: N.Y. 1967. Assoc. Simpson Thacher & Bartlett, N.Y.C., 1967-75; ptnr. Simpson, Thacher & Bartlett, N.Y.C., 1975—. Served as lt. comdr. USNR, 1968-71. Mem. ABA, N.Y. State Bar Assn., N.Y. Law Inst. (bd. dirs. 1984—), Met. Golf Assn. (sec., bd. dirs. 1972—). Clubs: Greenwich (Conn.) Country; Downtown Athletic (N.Y.C.). General corporate, Securities, Public utilities. Office: Simpson Thacher & Bartlett One Battery Park Plaza New York NY 10004

COTTER, WILLIAM HENRY, III, lawyer; b. Providence, July 8, 1946; s. William Henry, Jr. and Margaret Mary (Barrett) C.; m. Carole-Anne Manella, Aug. 3, 1968; 1 son, Andrew Steere. A.B., Georgetown U., 1968; J.D., U. Calif.-San Francisco, 1971. Bar: R.I. 1971, U.S. Dist. Ct. R.I. 1971, Calif. 1973, U.S. DIst. Ct. (no. dist.) Calif. 1973, U.S. Ct. Appeals (9th cir.) 1973, U.S. Tax Ct. 1974, U.S. Ct. Claims 1974. Assoc. Hinckley, Allen, Salisbury & Parsons, Providence, 1971-72, Pillsbury, Madison & Sutro, San Francisco, 1973-76; assoc. Levy, Goodman, Semonoff & Gorin, Providence, 1976-77, ptnr., 1978-85; ptnr. Licht & Semonoff, Providence, 1985—; former prof. grad. tax program Bryant Coll. Mem. East Greenwich (R.I.) Housing Authority; past chmn. admissions com. United Way of Southeastern New Eng. Served to capt. U.S. Army, 1968-76. Mem. ABA, R.I. Bar Assn. (chmn. tax com. 1986—), Order of Coif. Roman Catholic. Clubs: Warwick Country (R.I.), University (Providence), Olympic (San Francisco). Corporate taxation, Personal income taxation. Home: 25 Bow St East Greenwich RI 02818

COTTON, EUGENE, lawyer; b. N.Y.C., May 20, 1914; s. Jacob and Ida (Fundler) C.; m. Sylvia Glickstein, Jan. 21, 1940; children: Richard, Stephen Eric. B.S.S., CCNY, 1933; LL.B., Columbia U., 1936. Bar: N.Y. 1936, U.S. Supreme Ct. 1942, Ill. 1947, U.S. Ct. Appeals (D.C., 1st, 5th, 7th, and 8th cirs.) 1947. Asso. firm Szold & Brandwen, N.Y.C., 1936-37; atty. N.Y. Labor Relations Bd., N.Y.C., 1937-41; spl. counsel FCC, Washington, 1941-42; asst. gen. counsel CIO, Washington, 1942-48; partner firm Elson & Cotton, Chgo., 1948-50, Cotton, Watt, Jones & King, Chgo., 1951—; Gen. counsel United Packinghouse Workers Am., 1948-68; gen. counsel packinghouse dept. Amalgamated Meat Cutters, Butcher Workmen Am., 1968-79. Served with USNR, 1943-45. Mem. Ill., Chgo. bar assns., Chgo. Council Lawyers. Club: City of Chgo. (gov., pres. 1966-68). Labor, Pension, profit-sharing, and employee benefits. Home: 5050 S Lake Shore Dr Chicago IL 60615 Office: Cotton Watt Jones & King 1 IBM Plaza Chicago IL 60611

COTTON, GREGORY DALE, lawyer; b. Rantoul, Ill., Oct. 4, 1955; s. Van Dale and Barbara Sue (Newsom) C.; m. Julie Jean Cottingham, Aug. 14, 1982. BA, U. Ala., 1978; JD, Cumberland Sch. of Law, 1981. Bar: Ala. 1981, U.S. Dist. Ct. (no. dist.) Ala. 1981, U.S. Ct. Appeals (11th cir.) 1981, U.S. Dist. Ct. Appeals (5th cir.) 1981, U.S. Supreme Ct. 1985. Assoc. Hanes and Hanes, Birmingham, Ala., 1981-84; ptnr. Hanes and Cotton, Birmingham, Ala., 1984—; scoring judge Cumberland Sch. of Law Trial Advocacy Bd., Birmingham, 1981—. Sunday Sch. tchr. Dawson Meml. Bapt. Ch., Birmingham, 1985. Mem. ABA, Ala. Bar Assn. (task force on legal advt. 1983—, task force to index code of profl. responsibility 1985—), Birmingham Bar Assn., Assn. Trial Lawyers Am., Ala. Trial Lawyers Assn., U. Ala. Alumni Assn. Clubs: Red and White, Touchdown (Birmingham). Lodges: Masons, Shriners. Avocations: hunting, fishing, gardening, reading, collecting and restoring antiques. Personal injury, Family and matrimonial, Bankruptcy. Office: 933 Frank Nelson Bldg Birmingham AL 35203

COTTON, JAMES ALEXENDRE, lawyer; b. Ft. Riley, Kans., Nov. 22, 1939; s. James and Myrtle (Lallis) C.; m. Margaret A. Davis, Aug. 15, 1965 (div. Dec. 1978); children: Lallis A., Allison M.; m. Marjorie Evangeline Keene, Mar. 15, 1980; 1 child, William J.K. AA, Mesa Coll., 1961; BA, Colo. Coll., 1963; JD, U. Colo., 1970. Bar: N.Y., U.S. Dist. Ct. (so. dist.) N.Y. Atty. IBM Corp., Armonk, N.Y., 1970-73; staff atty. IBM Corp., Poughkeepsie, N.Y., 1973-75, Boulder, Colo., 1975-78; area counsel IBM Corp., Tucson, 1978-81; sr. atty. IBM Corp., Armonk, 1981—; vis. prof. Thurgood Marshall Sch. Law, Houston, 1981-82, adj. prof., 1982—. Bd. dirs. Nat. Urban League, Tucson, 1978-79, chmn. 1979-80; capt. dist. Yorktown (N.Y.) Dems., 1982—. Served to capt. U.S. Army, 1963-67. Mem. ABA, Westchester-Fairfield Corp. Counsel Assn. Democrat. Baptist. Avocations: chess, tennis. Securities, Antitrust, General corporate. Home: 1257 Judy Rd Mohegan Lake NY 10547 Office: IBM Corp Old Orchard Rd Armonk NY 10504

COUCH, LESLIE FRANKLIN, lawyer; b. Albany, N.Y., July 22, 1930; s. Leslie S. and Mary J. (Owens) C.; m. Joan Dunham, Dec. 29, 1951; children—Sharon DeBonis, Lawrence, Mark, Todd. LL.B., Union U., 1955, J.D., 1968. Bar: N.Y. 1955, U.S. Dist. Ct. (no. dist.) N.Y. 1955, U.S. Dist. Ct. (so. dist.) N.Y. 1979, U.S. Ct. Claims 1963, U.S. Ct. Appeals (2d cir.) 1962, U.S. Supreme Ct. 1979. Sole practice, Albany, 1955-62; ptnr. Medwin & Couch, Albany, 1962-65, DiFabio & Couch, P.C., Albany, 1965-79, Couch & Howard, P.C., Albany, 1979—; lectr. Am. Arbitration Assn., N.Y. State Bar Assn., others. Mem. North Colonie Sch. Dist., 1975-78. Mem. Am. Arbitration Assn. (nat. panel), Albany County Bar Assn. (com. on continuing legal edn. 1983—), N.Y. Bar Assn. (com. unlawful practice 1960-63, com. pub. info. 1969-72, com. media awards 1970-76), ABA, Capital Dist. Trial Lawyers Assn. Clubs: Albany Curling, Fort Orange (Albany); Schuyler Meadows (Loudonville, N.Y.). Construction. Home: 6 Schuyler Meadows Club Rd Loudonville NY 12211 Office: 48 Howard St Albany NY 12207

COUGHENOUR, JOHN CLARE, federal judge; b. Pittsburg, Kans., July 27, 1941; s. Owren M. and Margaret E. (Widner) C.; m. Gwendolyn A. Kieffaber, June 1, 1963; children—Jeffrey, Douglas, Marta. B.S., Kans. State Coll., 1963; J.D., U. Iowa, 1966. Bar: Iowa 1963, D.C. 1963, U.S. Dist. Ct. (we. dist.) Wash. 1966. Ptnr. Bogle & Gates, Seattle, 1966-81; vis. asst. prof. law U. Washington, Seattle, 1970-73; judge U.S. Dist. Ct., Seattle. Mem. Iowa State Bar Assn., Wash. State Bar Assn. Federal civil litigation. Office: U S Dist Ct US Courthouse Seattle WA 98104

COUGHLAN, KENNETH LEWIS, lawyer; b. Chgo., July 8, 1940; s. Edward James and Mary Virginia (Lewis) C.; m. Therese Koziol, Oct. 11, 1981; 1 son, Kevin Edward. BA, U. Notre Dame, 1962; JD, Northwestern U., Chgo., 1966. Bar: Ill. 1967. Trust officer Am. Nat. Bank & Trust Co., Chgo., 1969-72; sec. bd., sr. v.p., gen. counsel, cashier Cen. Nat. Bank, Chgo., 1972-82; sec., gen. counsel Cen. Nat. Chgo. Corp., 1976-82; sr. v.p., gen. counsel Exchange Nat. Bank, Chgo., 1982-83; gen. counsel Exchange Internat. Corp., Chgo., 1982-83; chmn. bd., pres. Union Realty Mortgage Co., Inc., Chgo., 1981-83; ptnr. DeHaan & Richter P.C., 1983—. Mem. aux. bd. North Ave. Day Nursery, 1980-85. Served to capt. U.S. Army, 1966-68. Fellow Ill. Bar Found.; mem. ABA, Ill. Bar Assn. (chmn. sect. on comml., banking and bankruptcy law 1981-82), Chgo. Bar Assn. (chmn. fin. instns. com. 1980-81, comml. law com. 1979-80). Clubs: Law of Chgo., Chgo. Athletic Assn. Contracts commercial, Banking, Bankruptcy. Office: DeHaan & Richter 55 W Monroe St Chicago IL 60603

COUGHLIN, RICHARD EDWARD, lawyer; b. St. Louis, Oct. 4, 1948; s. Thomas Joseph and Virginia Lucille (Cunningham) C.; m. Barbara A. Jaskiewicz, Sept. 18, 1976; children: Anne-Marie, Jeffrey. BA in Polit. Sci., U. Mo., 1970; JD, St. Louis U., 1973; LLM in Taxation, Washington U., St. Louis, 1982. Bar: Mo. 1973, U.S. Dist. Ct. (ea. dist.) Mo. 1974, U.S. Ct. Appeals (8th cir.) 1974, U.S. Dist. Ct. (ea. dist.) Wis. 1981. Asst. atty. U.S. Dist. Ct. (ea. dist.) Mo., St. Louis, 1973-77; assoc. Sumner, Hanlon, Sumner, MacDonald & Nouss P.C., St. Louis, 1977-81; ptnr. Hanlon, Nouss, Inkley & Coughlin P.C., St. Louis, 1981-82; corp. counsel The J.L. Mason Group Inc., St. Louis, 1982—. Pres. Parent's Assn. Childrens Home Soc. Mo., St. Louis, 1986—. Mem. ABA, Met. St. Louis Bar Assn. Roman Catholic. Construction, Real property, State civil litigation. Home: 528 Locust Ct Webster Groves MO 63119 Office: The JL Mason Group Inc 1215 Fern Ridge Suite 200 Saint Louis MO 63141

COUGHLIN, TERRANCE J, lawyer; b. Sioux Falls, S.D., June 11, 1948; s. John William and Blanche (Stekl) C.; m. Suzanne Houghton, June, 27, 1981; children: Michael, Brian. BChemE, S.D. Sch. Mining, 1970; JD with high honors, Ill. Inst. Tech., 1977. Bar: Ill. 1977, U.S. Dist. Ct. (no. dist.) Ill. 1977, U.S. Patent Office 1977, U.S. Ct. Appeals (7th cir.) 1977, U.S. Supreme 1980. Engr. E.I. Dupont, East Chicago, Ind., 1970-74, Container Corp. of Am., Carol Stream, Ill., 1974-77; ptnr. Coughlin and Marutzky, Chgo., 1977-80; sole practice Chgo., 1980—; hearing officer Ill. Poll. Control Bd., 1979—. Editor: IIT Law Review, 1974-77. Mem ABA, Ill. State Bar Assn. (mem. gen. assembly), Chgo. Bar Assn. Republican. Roman Catholic. Lodge: KC (officer 1986—). Avocations: golf, boating, sports. State civil litigation, Personal injury, Probate. Home: 5642 Murray Berkeley IL 60163 Office: 39 S LaSalle St #820 Chicago IL 60603

COUKOS, CAROLYN COOK, lawyer; b. Vinita, Okla., Apr. 15, 1941; d. Lloyd Eugene and Louise (Lester) Cook; m. James Stephen Coukos, June 11, 1966; children: Pamela Sue, Stephen James. BA, U. Kans., 1964; JD, Ind. U., 1976. Bar: Ind. 1976, U.S. Dist. Ct. (so. dist.) Ind. 1976. Asst. v.p., trust officer Am. Fletcher Nat. Bank, Indpls., 1976-84, v.p., trust counsel, 1984—. Contbr. articles to profl. jours. Committee mem. vice precinct Marion County (Ind.) Reps., 1982—; pres. Fairness Coalition, Indpls., 1985—; sec. Indpls. Women's Rep. Club, 1986—; mem. policy council Ind. Women's Polit. Caucus, Indpls., 1986—; bd. dirs. Girls Clubs Indpls., 1986—. Mem. ABA (group editor newsletter tax sect. 1982—, real property, probate and trust law sect., task force on Uniform Marital Property Act and significant current trust and probate legis. com.), Ind. Bar Assn. (best jour. article award 1977, co-chmn. pub. com. probate, trust and real property sect.), Indpls. Bar Assn. (chmn. women lawyer's div. 1986—), Indpls. Bar Found. Methodist. Avocations: golf, tennis, skiing. General corporate, Probate, Pension, profit-sharing, and employee benefits. Office: Am Fletcher Nat Bank 111 Monument Circle Indianapolis IN 46277

COULSON, WILLIAM ROY, lawyer; b. Waukegan, Ill., Oct. 5, 1949; s. Robert E. and Rose (Stone) C.; m. Elizabeth A. Shafernich, Feb. 14, 1986. AB, Dartmouth Coll., 1969; JD, U. Ill., 1972. Bar: Ill. 1972, U.S. Dist. Ct. (no. dist.) Ill. 1974, U.S. Supreme Ct. 1976. Law clk. to judge U.S. Dist. Ct., East St. Louis, Ill., 1972-74; law clk. to presiding judge U.S. Dist. Ct., Chgo., 1975; asst. U.S. atty. U.S. Dept. Justice, Chgo., 1975—, supr. criminal div., 1980—; faculty Atty. Gen.'s Adv. Inst., Washington, 1980—, Ill. Inst. for Continuing Legal Edn., Springfield, Ill., 1983—, Fed. Law Enforcement Tng. Ctr., Glynco, Ga., 1983—. Author: Federal Juvenile Law, 1980. Served to 2d lt. Ill. N.G., 1965-66. Mem. ABA, Chgo. Bar Assn. (jud. evaluation com. 1984—), Fed. Bar Assn. (bd. dirs. Chgo. 1985—). Club: Dartmouth (Chgo.). Federal civil litigation, Criminal. Office: US Dept Justice 219 S Dearbron 1500 Chicago IL 60604

COUNCIL, BRENDA JOYCE, lawyer; b. Omaha, Oct. 3, 1953; s. Willis Lacy and Evelyn Nadine (Harmon) Warren; m. Otha Kenneth Council, Oct. 5, 1985. BS, U. Nebr., 1974; JD, Creighton U., 1977. Bar: Nebr. 1977, U.S. Dist. Ct. Nebr. 1977, U.S. Ct. Appeals (8th cir.) 1985. Dir. Omaha Pre-Trial Release, Omaha, 1975-77; field atty. NLRB, Kansas City, Kans., 1977-80; gen. atty. Union Pacific R.R., Omaha, 1980—. Mem., past pres. Omaha Bd. Edn., 1982—; mem. State Bd. Ednl. Lands & Funds, Lincoln, Nebr., 1986; chair Gov.'s Task Force on Excellence in Edn., State of Nebr., 1983; mem., bd. dirs. Greater Omaha Corp., 1981—. Named One of 50 Young Leaders, Ebony Mag., 1983, One of Nebr.'s Outstanding Young Women, Nebr. Women of Today, 1985; recipient Nat. Prominence award Urban League of Nebr., 1984, Community Role Model award Girl's Clubs of Omaha, 1985. Mem. ABA, Nebr. Bar Assn., Omaha Bar Assn., Midlands Bar Assn. (v.p. 1981-82). Democrat. Mem. Ch. of Living God. Avocations: officiating football and basketball. General corporate. Office: Union Pacific RR Co 1416 Dodge St Room 830 Omaha NE 68179

COUNTRYMAN, VERN, educator; b. Roundup, Mont., May 13, 1917; s. Alexander and Carrie (Harriman) C.; m. Vera Pound, Nov. 9, 1940; children—Kay, Debra. B.A., U. Wash., 1939, LL.B., 1942; student, Yale Law Sch., 1947-48. Bar: Wash. State bar 1942, Md. bar 1955, D.C. bar 1956, Mass. bar 1965. Law clk. to Justice William O. Douglas, 1942- 43; asst. atty. general Wash. State, 1946; instr. U. Wash. Sch. Law, 1946-47; asst., then asso. prof. law Yale Law Sch., 1948-55; practice law with firm Shea, Greenman & Gardner, Washington, 1955-59; dean U. N.Mex. Sch. Law, 1959-64; prof. law Harvard, 1964—. Served with USAAF, 1943-46. Mem.

Am. Bar Assn., Order of Coif, Phi Beta Kappa. Bankruptcy, Contracts commercial, General corporate. Home: 98 Adams St Lexington MA 02173

COURSEN, CHRISTOPHER DENNISON, lawyer; b. Mpls., Dec. 6, 1948; s. Richard Dennison and Helen Wilson (Stevens) C.; m. Pamela Elizabeth Lynch, June 3, 1978; children: Cameron Dennison, Matthew Ashbolt, Madeline Messurier. BA, Washington & Lee U., 1970; JD, The George Washington U., 1975. Bar: D.C. 1975, U.S. Dist. Ct. D.C., 1976, U.S. Ct. Appeals (D.C. Cir.) 1976, U.S. Ct. Mil. Appeals 1976, U.S. Supreme Ct. 1978. Sole practice, Washington, 1975-78; assoc. Dempsey & Koplovitz, Washington, 1978-80; communications counsel U.S. Senate Com. Commerce, Sci., and Transportation, Washington, 1980-83; ptnr. O'Connor & Hannan, Washington, 1983—; adj. prof. law The George Washington U., Washington, 1983. Team mem. Pres.-Elect Reagan's Transition Team, Washington, 1980; atty. adv. Reagan-Bush 1984, Washington. Mem. ABA, Fed. Communications Bar Assn., D.C. Bar Assn. Roman Catholic. Club: Chevy Chase (Md.). Communications, Legislative, Administrative and regulatory. Home: 5006 Nahant St Bethesda MD 20816 Office: O'Connor & Hannan 1919 Pennsylvania Ave NW Washington DC 20006

COURT, LEONARD, lawyer, educator; b. Ardmore, Okla., Jan. 11, 1947; s. Leonard and Margaret Janet (Harvey) C.; m. JoAnn Dilleshaw, Sept. 2, 1967; children—Chris, Todd, Brooke. B.A., Okla. State U., 1969; J.D., Harvard U., 1972. Bar: Okla. 1973, U.S. Dist. Ct. (we. dist.) Okla. 1973, U.S. Dist. Ct. (no. dist.) Okla., 1978, U.S. Dist. Ct. (ea. dist.) Okla. 1983, U.S. Ct. Appeals (10th cir.) 1980, U.S. Ct. Mil. Appeals 1973., Assoc. Crowe & Dunlevy, Oklahoma City, Okla., 1977-81, ptnr., 1981—; adj. prof. Okla. U. Law Sch., Norman, 1984-85; planning com. Annual Inst. Labor Law, S.W. Legal Found., Dallas, 1984—. Contbg. author: (supplement book) The Developing Labor Law, 1978, Corporate Counsel's Annual, 1974. Chmn. bd. elders Meml. Christian Ch., Oklahoma City, 1980; cubmaster Last Frontier council Boy Scouts Am., 1984. Served to capt. USAF, 1973-77. Mem. Okla. State Univ. Bar Assn. (bd. dirs. 1980—), Oklahoma City C. of C. (mem. sports and recreation com. 1982-85, indsl. devel. com. 1986), Okla. State U. Alumni Assn., Harvard Law Sch. Assn., ABA (labor and employment law sect. com. on devel. of law under Nat. Labor Relations Act, com. on EEO law, subcom. on substantive devels involving sex under Title VII, and subcom. of EEOC process Title VII coverage and multiple forums, litigation sect./employment and labor relations law com.), Okla. Bar Assn. (labor and employment law sect. council 1978-83, 85—, chmn. 1986), Okla. County Bar Assn., Fed. Bar Assn., Defence Research Inst. Okla. Assn. Defense Counsel. Labor, Civil rights. Office: Crowe & Dunlevy 20 N Broadway Oklahoma City OK 73102

COURTNEY, THOMAS FRANCES, lawyer; b. Chgo., Aug. 7, 1942; s. John W. and Grayce B. (Comise) C.; m. Barbara E. Lura, Aug. 16, 1967; children: Thomas, Christopher, John. BS, U. Ill., 1965; JD, John Marshall Law Sch., 1973. Bar: Ill. 1973, U.S. Dist. Ct. (no. dist.) Ill. 1973. Sole practice Palos Heights, Ill., 1973—; advisor Southwest Suburban Bd. of Realtors, Palos Heights, Ill., 1982-85. Bd. dirs. Consolidated High Sch. Dist., Palos Heights, 1985; chmn. Am. Cancer Soc., Palos Heights, 1985. Served with USAR, 1967-73. Recipient Dist. Service award Phillipine Med. Assn., Chgo., 1982. Mem. ABA, Ill. State Bar Assn., Chgo. Bar Assn., Phi Alpha Delta. Republican. Lutheran. Avocations: tennis, golf. Federal civil litigation, State civil litigation, Real property. Office: 7000 W 127th St Palos Heights IL 60463

COVATTA, ANTHONY GALLO, JR., lawyer; b. Louisville, July 11, 1944; s. Anthony Gallo and Rosemary (Danenberg) C.; m. Susan Tietig, Dec. 23, 1975; children: Holland, Sybil, Christopher. BA, Bellarmine Coll., 1966; MA, Columbia U., 1967, PhD, 1971; JD, U. Cin., 1979. Bar: Ohio 1979, U.S. Dist. Ct. (so. dist.) Ohio 1980, U.S. Ct. Appeals (6th cir.) 1983. Ptnr. Graydon, Head & Ritchey, Cin., 1979—. Author: Thomas Middleton's City Comedies, 1974; contbr. articles to profl. jours. and law revs. Trustee, sec. Clovernook Home and Sch. for the Blind, Cin., 1984—; trustee Cin. Children's Theatre, 1984—, Sch. for Creative and Performing Arts, Cin., 1985—. Woodrow Wilson Found. fellow, 1967, Folger Library fellow, 1973. Mem. ABA, Ohio Bar Assn., Cin. Bar Assn. Clubs: Cin. Country, Univ. Avocations: reading, tennis, jogging. General corporate, Real property, State civil litigation. Home: 2565 Handasyde Ave Cincinnati OH 45208 Office: Graydon Head & Ritchey 511 Walnut St 1900 5th 3d Ctr Cincinnati OH 45202

COVEL, RICHARD ALLAN, lawyer; b. Springfield, Mass., Feb. 7, 1947; s. Robert Edward and Lillian (James) C.; m. Kathleen Mary Shepard, June 15, 1974; children: Catherine Allison, Clayton James. BS, Mass. Maritime Acad., 1967; JD, New England Sch. Law, 1975. Bar: Mass. 1975, U.S. Dist. Ct. D.C. 1976, U.S. Supreme Ct. 1978. Regulatory atty. Stone and Webster Engrng. Co., Boston, 1970-78; asst. gen. counsel Massachusetts Bay Transp. Authority, Boston, 1978-80, SCA Services, Inc., Boston, 1980-85; counsel Foster-Miller, Inc., Waltham, Mass., 1985—; counsel Norwell (Mass.) Hist. Soc., 1981—; mem. Route 128 Lawyers Corp., 1985—. mem. faculty selection com. Mass. Maritime Acad., Buzzards Bay, Mass., 1977-78. Served as lt. USN, 1967-78, with res. Mem. ABA, Mass. Maritime Alumni Assn. (bd. dirs., treas. 1972-78). Republican. Avocations: participating in sports, racing, sailing, soccer. General corporate, Construction, Environment. Office: Foster Miller Inc 350 Second Ave Waltham MA 02154

COVER, E. MCINTOSH, corporate lawyer; b. 1933. BA, Princeton U., 1955; LLB, Harvard U., 1960. Assoc. Kelley, Drye & Warren, N.Y., 1960-63; corp. counsel Tex. Industries, Inc., 1963-67; asst. sec., assoc. gen. counsel LTV Co., Dallas, 1967-68; v.p., gen. counsel Okonite Co., Ramsey, N.J., 1968-71; corp. counsel Omega-Alpha Inc., 1971-74; v.p., gen. counsel Olin-Am. Inc., Stamford, Conn., 1974-76; group counsel Olin Corp., Stamford, 1976-83, v.p., gen. counsel, 1983—. Office: Olin Corp 120 Long Ridge Rd Stamford CT 06904 *

COVINGTON, ALICE LUCILLE, lawyer; b. Fredericksburg, Va., June 11, 1955; d. James Lomax and Violet Hazel (Herring) C.; m. Anthony H. Rickert, Mar. 9, 1985. BA with high distinction, U. Va., 1977; JD cum laude, Georgetown U., 1981. Bar: D.C. 1982, U.S. Dist. Ct. (D.C.) 1984. Law clk. to presiding justice D.C. Ct. Appeals, 1981-82; assoc. Arent, Fox, Kintner, Plotkin & Kahn, Washington, 1982-85; atty. labor law office U.S. Postal Service, Washington, 1985—. Echols scholar U. Va., 1973-77. Mem. ABA, Bar Assn. of D.C., Phi Beta Kappa. Avocation: literature. Labor, Civil rights, Federal civil litigation. Home: 525 10th St SE Washington DC 20003 Office: US Postal Service 475 L'Enfant Plaza SW Washington DC 20260-1134

COVINGTON, EARL GENE, lawyer; b. St. Louis, Nov. 10, 1939; s. Earl Lloyd and Mary (Johnson) C.; m. Pamela Marquis, Smither, July 28, 1967. B.B.A., U. Tex., 1963; J.D., U. Houston, 1969. Bar: Tex. Supreme Ct. 1967, U.S. Dist. Ct. (so. dist.) Tex. 1967, U.S. Tax Ct. 1976, U.S. Supreme Ct. 1980; cert. in tax law, comml. real estate law Tex. Bd. Legal Specialization. Tax specialist Ernst & Whinney, C.P.A.s, Houston, 1967-72; assoc. Urban Coolidge, Pennington & Scott, Houston, 1973-74; sole practice, Houston, 1974-76; pres. Covington & Reese, P.C., Houston, 1976-85; sole practice, 1985—. Pres., mem. exec. com. Bayou Wood Assn. Property Owners, 1977-78. Served with USMCR, 1962-67. Mem. ABA, Houston Bar Assn., Tex. State Bar Assn., Houston Estate Forum, Tex. Soc. C.P.A.s, Houston Soc. C.P.A.s. Corporate taxation, Estate taxation, Personal income taxation. Office: 1700 W Loop S Suite 257 Houston TX 77027

COVINGTON, ROBERT NEWMAN, lawyer, educator; b. Evansville, Ind., Sept. 9, 1936; s. George Milburn and Roberta (Newman) C.; m. Paula Anne Hattox, July 29, 1972. B.A., Yale U., 1958; J.D., Vanderbilt U., 1961. Bar: Tenn. 1961. Asst. prof. law Vanderbilt U., Nashville, 1961-64; assoc. prof. Vanderbilt U., 1964-69, prof., 1969—; vis. prof. U. Mich., 1971, U. Calif., Davis, 1975-76, U. Tex., 1983; Adminstrv. law officer Calif. Agrl. Labor Relations Bd., 1975-76; cons. Tenn. Dept. Labor, 1972, Tenn. Law Library Commn., 1965-75. Author works in field. Mem. Am. Bar Assn., Tenn. Bar Assn., Am. Arbitration Assn., Order of Coif, Phi Beta Kappa. Democrat. Episcopalian. Club: Univ. (Nashville). Labor, Workers' compensation, Legal education. Home: 907 Estes Rd Nashville TN 37215 Office: Vanderbilt Law Sch Nashville TN 37240

COWAN, CASPAR FRANK, lawyer; b. Calais, Maine, May 7, 1915; s. Frank Irving and Helen Anna (Caspar) C.; m. Nancy Hopkinson Linnell, Oct. 19, 1946; children—Joanna Cowan New, Seth W., June Cowan Roelle. A.B., Bowdoin Coll., 1936; J.D. Harvard U., 1940. Bar: Maine 1940, U.S. Dist. Ct. Maine 1941, U.S. Ct. Appeals (1st cir.) 1946. Assoc. Cowan and Cowan, Portland, Maine, 1940-48; assoc. Perkins, Thompson, Hinckley and Keddy, Portland, 1948-51, ptnr. 1951—. Chmn. Portland Renewal Authority, 1952-64; chmn, Portland Housing Authority, 1958-59. Served to lt. U.S. Army, 1942-46. Decorated Bronze Star. Mem. ABA, Maine State Bar Assn. (probate rules com., title standards com.), Cumberland County Bar Assn., Am. Coll. Real Estate Lawyers, 10th Mt. Div. Alumni Assn., Maine Charitable Mechanics Assn. Clubs: Woodfords, Junto. Lodge: Masons (32d degree). Real property, Probate, Personal income taxation. Home: 99 Vannah Ave Portland ME 04103

COWAN, FREDERIC JOSEPH, JR., lawyer, state representative; b. N.Y.C., Oct. 11, 1945; s. Frederic Joseph Sr. and Mary Virginia (Wesley) C.; m. Linda Marshall Scholle, Apr. 28, 1974; children: Elizabeth, Caroline, Allison. AB, Dartmouth Coll., 1967; JD, Harvard U., 1978. Bar: Ky. 1978, U.S. Dist. Ct. (we. dist.) Ky. 1979. Assoc. Brown, Todd & Heyburn, Louisville, 1979-83; ptnr. Rice, Porter, Seiller & Price, Louisville, 1983—; bd. dirs. Ky. Job Tng. Coordinating Council, Frankfort, Louisville Bar Found., 1986. Vice chmn. judiciary criminal com. Ky. Ho. of Reps., 1985—, 32d Dist. Dems., Louisville, 1980—; chmn. budget com. on justice Judiciary and Corrections Ky. Ho. of Reps., 1985—, Leadership Ky., 1985. Mem. ABA, Ky. Bar Assn., Louisville Bar Assn., Ky. Acad. Trial Attys., Ky. C. of C. (Leadership Ky., chartered). Methodist. Federal civil litigation, State civil litigation. Home: 1747 Sulgrave Rd Louisville KY 40205 Office: Rice Porter Seiller & Price 2200 Meidinger Tower Louisville KY 40202

COWAN, JOHN JOSEPH, lawyer; b. Chester, Pa., Nov. 14, 1932; s. John Joseph and Helen Marie (Frame) C.; m. Hilary Ann Gregory, Dec. 29, 1960; children—Daniel, Patrick, Meg, Jennifer. A.B., LaSalle Coll., 1954; J.D. cum laude, U. Pa., 1959. Bar: D.C. 1960, Ohio 1964, W.Va. 1968, U.S. Supreme Ct. 1971. Teaching fellow Stanford U., Palo Alto, Calif., 1959-60; trial atty. civil div. U.S. Dept. Justice, Washington, 1960-63; assoc. Taft, Stettinius & Hollister, Cin., 1963-67; gen. atty. Chesapeake & Potomac Telephone Co. of W.Va., Charleston, 1968-79; ptnr. Sullivan & Cowan, Charleston, 1979-82; sole practice, Charleston, 1982—. Served to 1st lt. AUS, 1954-56. Mem. ABA. Sr. adv. editor U. Pa. Law Rev., 1958-59. State civil litigation, Federal civil litigation, Criminal. Home: 2326 Windham Rd South Charleston WV 25303 Office: John J Cowan PO Box 152 Charleston WV 25321

COWAN, PHILIP MATTHEW, lawyer; b. N.Y.C., Sept. 8, 1943; s. A. Halsey and Gabrielle C. (Haas) C.; m. Ellen Spritzer, June 24, 1963 (div. Dec. 1980); children: Joshua, Julianne. BS, Cornell U., 1965, JD, 1968. Bar: N.Y. 1968, U.S. Dist. Ct. (no., so. and ea. dists.) N.Y. 1968. Assoc. Halperin, Morris, Granett & Cowan, N.Y.C., 1968-74; ptnr. Cowan & Cowan, N.Y.C., 1974-80, Morris, Berliner, Cowan & Cowan, N.Y.C., 1980-82, Cowan & Bodine, N.Y.C., 1983—. Mem. U.S. Copyright Soc. (trustee 1984—). Avocation: bridge. Entertainment, Trademark and copyright, Probate. Office: Cowan & Bodine 477 Madison Ave New York NY 10022

COWAN, ROBERT CHARLES, JR., lawyer; b. San Antonio, Jan. 20, 1943; s. Robert Charles Cowan and Jeanette (Silcock) Cowan Kaiser; m. Diane D. Mendoza, Feb. 21, 1965; children—Annalisa, Robert Christopher. B.B.A., St. Mary's U., San Antonio, 1965, J.D., 1973. Bar: Tex. 1975, U.S. Supreme Ct. 1979. Supr., Travelers Ins. Co., San Antonio, 1965-76; sole practice Law Office Robert C. Cowan, Jr., Inc., San Antonio, 1976—. Mem. Assn. Trial Lawyers Am., Tex. Trial Lawyers, San Antonio Trial Lawyers (dir. 1982). Roman Catholic. Personal injury, Workers' compensation, Family and matrimonial.

COWAN, WALLACE EDGAR, lawyer; b. Jersey City, Jan. 28, 1924; s. Benjamin and Dorothy (Zunz) C.; m. Ruth Daitzman, June 8, 1947; children: Laurie, Paul, Judith. J.D. cum laude, Harvard U., 1950; B.S. magna cum laude, N.Y.U., 1947. Partner firm Stroock, Stroock & Lavan (attys.), N.Y.C., 1950—; sec., dir. Ametek, Inc.; sec. The Whitlock Corp., Marshall Cavendish Corp. Mem. Teaneck (N.J.) Adv. Bd. on Parks, Playgrounds and Recreation, 1966—, chmn., 1974—; pres. No. Valley Commuters Assn.; v.p., trustee Congregation Beth Sholom, Teaneck. Served to 1st lt. USAF, 1942-45. Decorated Air medal with Silver cluster. Mem. Am. Bar Assn., N.Y. State Bar Assn., Beta Gamma Sigma. Home: 499 Emerson Ave Teaneck NJ 07666 Office: Stroock & Stroock & Lavan 7 Hanover Sq New York NY 10004

COWARD, THOMAS SCOTT, lawyer; b. Johnson County, Ind., Dec. 4, 1954; s. Robert Yeoman and Hester Miriam (Hartman) C.; m. Deborah Jean Firth, Aug. 20, 1978; children: Penelope Leah Firth, Miriam Deborah Firth. Baccalaureate, Coll. de Saint Marie, Saint Chamond, France, 1974; student, Franklin Coll., 1976-77; BA, Ind. U., 1977; JD, U. Maine, 1981. Bar: Maine 1981, U.S. Dist. Ct. Maine 1981. Assoc. Poland and Ketterer, Norridgewock, Maine, 1981-83, Smith and Elliott P.A., Saco, Maine, 1983—; chief exec. officer Saco River Title Co., 1986—. Trustee Woodfords Inc., Portland, Maine, 1985—. Mem. ABA, Assn. Trial Lawyers Am., Maine Bar Assn., Am. Judicature Soc. Real property, General corporate, Contracts commercial. Office: Smith and Elliott PA 199 Main St PO Box 1179 Saco ME 04072

COWART, RICHARD MERRILL, lawyer, state court judge; b. Valdosta, Ga., Oct. 13, 1951; s. Merrill L. and Annabel (Sherman) C.; m. Jeanne C. Hansen, July 13, 1974; children: Zachary Richard, Justin Merrill, Adam Hansen. BA, Valdosta State Coll., 1973; JD, Mercer U., 1976. Bar: Ga. 1976, U.S. Dist. Ct. (mid. dist.) Ga. 1976. Sole practice Valdosta, 1976-79; ptnr. Barham, Elliott, Bennett, Miller, Stone & Cowart, P.C., Valdosta, 1979—; judge Recorder's Ct., City of Valdosta, 1978-83, Lowndes County Ct., State of Ga., Valdosta, 1983—; lectr. Valdosta State Coll., 1978—. Trustee Park Ave. United Meth. Ch., Valdosta, 1985—. Mem. ABA, Ga. State Bar Assn., Valdosta Bar Assn., Valdosta State Coll. Alumni Assn., Phi Delta Phi, Omicron Delta Kappa. Lodge: Rotary (pres.-elect 1986—). State civil litigation, Probate, Real property. Home: 2001 Hammock Dr Valdosta GA 31602 Office: Bartam Elliott Bennett Miller et al 701 N Patterson St Valdosta GA 31601 Mailing: PO Box 729 Valdosta GA 31603

COWART, T(HOMAS) DAVID, lawyer; b. San Benito, Tex., June 12, 1953; s. Thomas W. Jr. and Glenda Claire (Miller) C.; m. Marquita Rea Stearman, May 28, 1983; children: Thomas Kevin, Lauren Michelle. BBA, U. Miss., 1975, JD, 1978; LLM in Taxation, NYU, 1979. Bar: Miss. 1978, Tex. 1979; CPA Tex., Miss. Assoc. Dossett, Magruder and Montgomery, Jackson, Miss., 1978; assoc. Strasburger and Price, Dallas, 1979-84, ptnr., 1985—; lectr. Tex. Soc. CPA's, 1985—, Am. Soc. Pension Actuaries, 1983-84, Tex. Soc. CLU's, 1985, Dallas Bar Assn., 1985, Ali-ABA, 1986—. Mem. adv. com. Goals for Dallas, 1984-85; deacon Ch. of Christ. Mem. ABA (sect. taxation, employee benefits com., fiduciary responsibility subcom.), Tex. Bar Assn. (sect. taxation, com. compensation and employee benefits, fed. legis., regulations and revenue rulings subcom.), Southwest Pension Conf., Phi Delta Phi, Omicron Delta Kappa. Pension, profit-sharing, and employee benefits. Office: Strasburger and Price 4300 InterFirst Plaza 901 Main St Dallas TX 75202

COWDERY, ALLEN CRAIG, lawyer; b. Bartlesville, Okla., July 1, 1943; s. Herman Charles and Jane (Sparr) C.; m. Jane Reed, May 31, 1969; children—Elizabeth, Owen. B.A., Okla. U., 1965, J.D., 1968. Bar: Okla. 1968, Kans. 1973, Tex. 1976. Staff atty. Koch Industries, Inc., Wichita, Kans., 1968-74; sr. assoc. counsel Mitchell Energy & Devel. Corp., Houston, 1974-81; v.p., gen. counsel, sec. Tex. Internat. Petroleum Corp., Oklahoma City, 1981-82; gen. counsel, v.p. Samson Resources Co., Tulsa, 1983-86; sole practice, 1986—. Mem. ABA, Okla. Bar Assn., Kans. Bar Assn., Kansas City Bar Assn., Tex. Bar Assn., Tulsa Bar Assn., Oklahoma City Bar Assn. Republican. Episcopalian. General practice, Bankruptcy, Probate. Home: 6816 E 105th Tulsa OK 74133 Office: PO Box 701583 Suite 510 Tulsa OK 74170-1583

COWELL, MARION AUBREY, JR., lawyer; b. Wilmington, N.C., Dec. 25, 1934; s. Marion Aubrey and Alice Saunders (Hargett) C.; children: Lindsay G., Mark P. B.S. B.A., U. N.C., 1958, LL.B., 1964. Bar: N.C. 1964. Pvt. practice law Durham, N.C., 1964-72; asso. law firm Bryant, Lipton, Bryant and Battle, 1964-69, partner, 1971-72; pvt. practice law Durham, 1969-70; gen. counsel Cameron Brown Co., Raleigh, N.C., 1972-78; sr. v.p., gen. counsel, sec. First Union Corp., Charlotte, N.C., 1978—. Office: First Union Corp One First Union Plaza Charlotte NC 28288

COWEN, EDWARD S., lawyer; b. N.Y.C., Mar. 3, 1936; s. Michael and Edith (Cohen) C.; m. Lesley J. Hoffman, Nov. 16, 1958; children—Adriene, Justine. B.S., Syracuse U., 1957; J.D., N.Y.U., 1961. Bar: N.Y. 1962, U.S. Dist. Ct. (so. dist.) N.Y. 1965, U.S. Dist. Ct. (ea. dist.) N.Y. 1979, U.S. Ct. Appeals (2d cir.) 1965, U.S. Supreme Ct. 1967. Law clk. to judge U.S. Dist. Ct. (so. dist.) N.Y., 1961-62; ptnr. Seligson & Morris, N.Y.C., 1963-69, Kronish, Lieb, Shainswit, Weiner & Helman, N.Y.C., 1969-72, Cowen, Ullman & Shiff, N.Y.C., 1972-75, Robinson, Silverman, Pearce, Aronsohn & Berman, N.Y.C., 1975—; mem. faculty Practicing Law Inst. Author: Bankruptcy in Joint Venture Partnerships. Served in USAF, 1958. Mem. ABA, Assn. of Bar of City of N.Y. (chmn. corp. reorgn.), N.Y. State Bar Assn. Clubs: Les Ambassadeurs (London); Harmonie (N.Y.C.). General corporate, Bankruptcy, Contracts commercial. Home: 993 Park Ave New York NY 10028 Office: 230 Park Ave New York NY 10169

COWEN, MARTIN LINDSEY, III, lawyer; b. Charlottesville, Va., Oct. 31, 1951; s. Martin Lindsey Jr. and Eleanor (Boaz) C.; m. Linda Jean Sharpe, June 26, 1982. BA, U. Ga., 1972, JD, 1975. Bar: Ga. 1975, U.S. Dist. Ct. (no. dist.) Ga. 1975, U.S. Supreme Ct. 1978, U.S. Ct. Appeals (5th and 11th cirs.) 1981. Law clk. to judge Ga. Supreme Ct., Atlanta, 1975-76; sole practice Clayton County, Ga., 1976-85; ptnr. Cowen & Cowen, Clayton County, 1985—; bd. of govs. State Bar of Ga., 1985—; mem. Clayton County Law Library Com. Mem. Clayton County C. of C., Clayton County Toastmasters (past pres.), Clayton County Bar Assn. (past pres.), ABA, Ga. Trial Lawyers Assn., Assn. Criminal Def. Lawyers (v.p. 6th dist.). Family and matrimonial, Probate, Criminal. Office: Cowen & Cowen 148 S Main St PO Box 1195 Jonesboro GA 30237

COWEN, ROBERT E., federal judge; b. Newark, Sept. 4, 1930; s. Saul and Lillie (Selzer) C.; m. Toby Cowen, Dec. 21, 1973; children: Shalie, Eve. BS, Drake U., 1952; LLB, Rutgers U., 1958. Assoc. Schreiber, Lancaster & Demos, Newark, 1959-70; asst. prosecutor Essex County, N.J., 1970-71; dep. atty. gen. organized crime Criminal Justice Dept., N.J., 1971-73; dir. Div. Ethics and Profl. Services, 1973-78; magistrate U.S. Dist. Ct. N.J., Trenton, 1978-85, judge, 1985—; sole practice, Newark, 1961-70. Office: US Dist Ct 402 E State PO Box 1688 Trenton NJ 08608 *

COWLES, FREDERICK OLIVER, lawyer; b. Steubenville, Ohio, Oct. 18, 1937; s. Oliver Howard and Cornelia Blanche (Regal) C.; m. Christina Monica Muller, Sept. 9, 1961; children—Randall, Eric, Gregory, Cornelius. A.B. magna cum laude, Yale U., 1959; J.D., Harvard U., 1962. Bar: R.I. 1963, Mich. 1967, Ill. 1969. Assoc. Hinckley, Allen, Salisbury & Parsons, Providence, 1962-67; internat. atty. Upjohn Co., Kalamazoo, Mich., 1967-69; chief internat. atty. Am. Hosp. Supply Crp., Evanston, Ill., 1969-71; internat. atty. Kendall Co., Boston, 1971-73; chief internat. counsel, assoc. gen. counsel, asst. sec. Colgate Palmolive Co., N.Y.C., 1973—; dir. various cos. Deacon, South Salem Presbyn. Ch.; mem. com. Lewisboro Boy Scouts; co-founder Internat. House R.I. Inc.; group leader Operation Crossroads Africa, Gambia. Mem. ABA, Westchester Fairfield Corp. Csl. Assn., Internat. Lawyers Assn., Phi Beta Kappa. Estate planning, Immigration, naturalization, and customs, Private international. Home: Oscaleta Rd South Salem NY 10590 Office: 300 Park Ave New York NY 10022

COWLING, DAVID EDWARD, lawyer; b. Lubbock, Tex., May 29, 1951; s. Ben Edward and Doris Patricia (Lovelace) C.; m. Amy Bosson Youngquist, Apr. 24, 1982. BA, Tex. Tech U., 1973; JD, U. Tex., 1976; LLM in Taxation, NYU, 1977. Bar: Tex. 1976, D.C. 1977, N.Y. 1979. Tax atty. Kronish, Lieb, Shainswit, Wiener & Hellman, N.Y.C., 1977-82, Jones, Day, Reavis & Pogue, Dallas, 1982—. Mem. ABA. N.Y. State Bar Assn., D.C. Bar Assn., Tex. Bar Assn., Assn. of Bar of City of N.Y. Personal income taxation, Corporate taxation, Municipal bonds. Home: 4630 Edmondson Ave Dallas TX 75209-6010 Office: Jones Day Reavis & Pogue 2001 Ross Ave 2300 LTV Ctr Dallas TX 75201-2916

COWSER, DANNY LEE, lawyer, mental health specialist; b. Canton, Ill., July 7, 1948; s. Albert Paul Cowser and Shirley Mae (Donaldson) Chatten; m. Nancy Lyn Hatch, Nov. 11, 1976; children: Kimberly Katherine Hatch Cowser, Dustin Paul Hatch Cowser. BA, No. Ill. U., 1972, MS, 1975; JD, DePaul U., 1980. Bar: Ill. 1980, Wis. 1981, U.S. Dist. Ct. (no. dist.) Ill. 1981, U.S. Ct. Appeals (7th cir.) 1983, U.S. Dist. Ct. (ea. and we. dists.) Wis. 1984, U.S. Supreme Ct. 1984, Ariz. 1985, U.S. Ct. Appeals (9th cir.) 1987. Adminstr. Ill. Dept. Mental Health, Elgin, 1972-76, psychotherapist, 1976-79; assoc. Slaby, Deda & Henderson, Phillips, Wis., 1982-83; ptnr. Slaby, Deda & Cowser, Phillips, 1983-86; asst. atty. City of Flagstaff, Ariz., 1986—; atty. City of Park Falls, Wis., 1983-86; asst. corp. counsel Price County, 1984-86. Bd. dirs. DeKalb County (Ill.) Drug Council, 1973-75, Counseling and Personal Devel., Phillips, 1985-86. Reginald Heber Smith fellow, 1979-81. Mem. ABA, Wis. Bar Assn., Ill. Bar Assn., Ariz. Bar Assn., Wis. Acad. Trial Lawyers, Am. Bankruptcy Inst. Republican. Lodge: Lions. Avocations: skiing, photography, gardening. Bankruptcy, Contracts commercial, Civil rights. Office: City of Flagstaff 211 E Aspen Flagstaff AZ 86001

COX, C. CHRISTOPHER, lawyer; b. St. Paul, Oct. 16, 1952; s. Charles C. and Marilyn A. (Miller) C. BA, U. So. Calif., 1973; MBA, JD, Harvard U., 1977. Bar: Calif. 1978, D.C. 1980. Law clk. to judge U.S. Ct. Appeals (9th cir.), 1977-78; assoc. Latham & Watkins, Newport Beach, Calif., 1978-85, ptnr., 1985-86; sr. assoc. counsel to the Pres. The White House, Washington, 1986—; prin., founder Associated Publs. Inc., St. Paul, 1984—; lectr. bus. adminstrn. Harvard U., 1982-83. Editor Harvard U. Law Rev., 1975-77. Bd. govs. Rep. Assocs. Orange County, Calif., 1985—. Republican. Roman Catholic. Home: 2812 N 27th St Arlington VA 22207 Office: The White House Washington DC 20500

COX, CHARLES C., federal government official; b. Missoula, Mont., May 8, 1945. BA, U. Wash., 1967; MA, U. Chgo., 1970, PhD, 1975. Asst. prof. econs. Ohio State U., Columbus, 1972-80; asst. prof. mgmt. Tex. A&M U., College Station, 1980-82; chief economist SEC, Washington, 1982-83, commr., 1984—. Nat. fellow Stanford (Calif.) U., 1977-78. Office: SEC 450 5th St NW Washington DC 20549 *

COX, EMMETT RIPLEY, federal judge; b. Cottonwood, Ala., Feb. 13, 1935; s. Emmett M. Cox, Jr. and Myra E. (Ripley) Stewart; m. Ann MacKay Haas, May 16, 1964; children—John Haas, Catherine MacKay. B.A., U. Ala., 1957, J.D., 1959. Bar: Ala. Judge U.S. Dist. Ct., Mobile, Ala. Mem. Ala. Bar Assn., Mobile Bar Assn. Judicial administration. Office: US Dist Ct PO Box 3104 Mobile AL 36652 *

COX, IRVIN EDMOND, law librarian, educator; b. Baltimore, Jan. 29, 1911; s. Jeter Edmond and Mary Eliza (smith) C.; m. Elsie Wilson, May 10, 1933; (div. Aug. 1944); m. Ethel Minerva Glover, May 7, 1944. LLB, Terrell Law Sch., 1948; BA, San Francisco State U., 1950; MA, NYU, 1952; Cert. of Advance Study Edn., Johns Hopkins U. Asst. prof. edn. Wilberforce (Ohio) U., 1954-56; freelance real estate investor Balt., 1957-64; asst. dean students Bowie (Md.) State Coll., 1964-68; vocat. counselor Balt. Job Corps Skill Ctr., 1968-70; asst. prof. edn. Coppin State Coll., Balt., 1971-76; librarian law dept. City of Balt., 1977—. Contbr. articles to profl. jours. Sec. religious liberty Seventh Day Adventist Ch., 1971. Recipient cert. competence Am. Assn. Law Libraries, 1982, citation for excellence Balt. Assoc. City Solicitor, 1986; Professionalism in Library Sci. award Herbert M. Frisby Hist. Soc., Balt., 1984. Librarianship, Legal education. Home: 1809 Eutaw Pl Baltimore MD 21217 Office: Balt City Law Dept Library 100 N Holliday St Baltimore MD 21202

COX, JAMES D., legal educator; b. 1943. J.D., U. Calif. Hastings Sch. Law, 1969; LL.M., Harvard U., 1971. Bar: Calif. 1970. Atty.-adv. Office Gen. Counsel FTC, Washington, 1969-70; teaching fellow Boston U., 1970-71; asst. prof. U. San Francisco, 1971-74; assoc. prof. U. Calif. Hastings Sch. Law, 1974-75; vis. assoc. prof. Stanford U., 1976-77; prof. U. Calif. Hastings

Sch. Law, 1977-79; vis. prof. Duke U. Sch. Law, spring 1979, prof., 1979—; mem. com. on corps. State Bar Calif.; E.T. Bost research prof., fall 1980. Author: Sum and Substance of Corporations, 4th edit., 1980, Financial Information, Accounting and the Law, 1980. Mem. Am. Law Inst., Order of Coif, Phi Kappa Phi. Legal education. Office: Duke U Sch Law Durham NC 27706 *

COX, JAMES DARRELL, lawyer; b. Wilmington, N.C., Nov. 11, 1950; s. Albert Darrell and Christine Elizabeth (Eubank) C.; m. Shearin Leigh Teague, Aug. 10, 1974; children—Amy Elizabeth, Amanda Leigh. B.A. with honors, N.C. State U., 1972; J.D. cum laude, Wake Forest U., 1975; LLM in Taxation, Georgetown U., 1978. Bar: N.C. 1975, U.S. Tax Ct. 1976, U.S. Ct. Claims 1976, U.S. Dist. Ct. (ea. dist.) N.C. 1981. Staff atty. IRS-Chief Counsel, Washington, 1975-78; assoc. Smith, Anderson, Raleigh, N.C., 1978-82; ptnr. Reynolds & Cox, P.A., Raleigh, 1983, Smith, Moore, Smith, Schell & Hunter, Raleigh, 1983-84; sole practice, Raleigh, 1984-86; ptnr. Cox, Carraway & Wilson, Raleigh, 1986—. Author: Farming and Ranching-Tax Accounting-Tax Management Portfolio, 1981. Treas. Cary Jaycees, N.C., 1980-81. Mem. ABA (com. on agr., tax sect.), Wake County Bar Assn., N.C. Bar Assn. (tax sect.), Phi Kappa Phi. Corporate taxation, Estate taxation, Probate.

COX, JOHN COATES, lawyer; b. Evansville, Ind., Nov. 15, 1941; s. Warren M. and Ruby (Diehl) C.; m. Joan Richardson Brown, Dec. 21, 1963; children—Michael John, Kenneth Robert, Heather Leigh, Rebecca Mae. B.A., Johns Hopkins U., 1963; J.D., Ind. U., 1966. Bar: Ind. 1966, U.S. Dist. Ct. (so. dist.) Ind. 1966. Assoc., Sydney L. Berger, Evansville, 1966-69; mem. Ind. Gen. Assembly, Indpls., 1969-71; sr. ptnr. Cox, Mitchell & Staser, Evansville, 1971-79; sole practice, Evansville, 1981—; corp counsel City of Evansville, 1972-79. Mem. Evansville Drug Council, 1971, 72; active Big Brothers Inc., Evansville, 1971; pres. McCutchanville Community Assn., 1971-72. Named Outstanding Freshman Legislator of Yr. by mems. Ind. Gen. Assembly, 1969. Mem. Evansville Bar Assn., Ind. Bar Assn., ABA, Am. Trial Lawyers Assn., Ind. Assn. Trial Lawyers, Am. Judicature Soc., Am. Arbitration Assn. Consumer commercial, Criminal, Family and matrimonial Office: 123 Main St Suite 320 Evansville IN 47708

COX, JOSEPH KING, lawyer; b. Detroit, Oct. 5, 1950; s. Joseph Crane and Helen Marie (King) C.; m. Karlin Ann Tait, Dec. 27, 1976; children: Jessica Susan, Elisabeth Karlin, Joseph Tait, Alexander King. BA, U. Detroit, 1973, JD, 1977. Bar: Mich. 1977, U.S. Dist. Ct. (ea. and we. dists.) Mich. 1977. Ptnr. Cox Law Firm, Fowlerville, Mich., 1976-84; sole practice Webberville, Mich., 1984—; atty. Village of Webberville, 1978—, Village of Dansville, Mich., 1980—, Village of Stockbridge, Mich. 1980—. Mem. Ingham County Bd. Commrs., Mason, Mich., 1980-84, vice-chair pro tem 1984, City of Williamston Econ. Devel. Corp.; chmn. Ingham County Reps., Lansing, 1984-85. Mem. Ingham County Bar Assn., Livingston County Bar Assn. Roman Catholic. Lodge: KC. Avocations: politics, historic restoration, camping, fishing, traveling. General practice, Local government, Family and matrimonial. Home: 180 Noble Rd Williamston MI 48895 Office: 119 W Grand River Webberville MI 48892-0239

COX, LEWIS CALVIN, lawyer; b. Fisher, Ark., Jan. 16, 1924; s. Lewis Calvin and Erma (Smith) C.; m. Sherley Annette Shepard, Aug. 23, 1944; children: Diana Cox Bergman, Lewis Calvin Cox, Annette Cox Russell. Student Abilene Christian Coll., 1941-43, Pittsburg Tchrs. Coll., 1943-44; JD, George Washington U., 1948. Bar: N.Mex. 1948. Assoc. Quinn & Cox, Clovis, N.Mex., 1948-53; sole practice, Clovis, 1953-55; assoc. Hinkle, Cox, Eaton, Coffield & Hensley, and predecessors, Roswell, N.Mex., 1955-58, ptnr., 1958—, now sr. ptnr. Mem. N.Mex. Ho. of Reps., 1951-52; mem. N.Mex. State Senate, 1953-55, chmn. ins. com. and rules com.; mem. N.Mex. Constl. Conv., 1967, 68, 2d v.p., 1969; trustee, past pres. Rocky Mountain Mineral Law Found.; mem. bd. litigation Mountain States Legal Found.; mem. adv. bd. Abilene Christian U. Served with USN, 1943-44. Mem. ABA, N.Mex. Bar Assn., Chaves County Bar Assn., N.Mex. Oil and Gas Assn. (past chmn. pub. lands com.), Am. Coll. Real Estate Lawyers), Roswell (N.Mex.) C. of C. (bd. dirs.). Republican. Mem. Ch. of Christ (elder). Clubs: Roswell Country, Lions. Contbr. articles to profl. jours. Oil and gas leasing, Legislative, Public utilities. Office: Hinkle Cox Eaton Coffield Hensley 1PO Box 10 Roswell NM 88201

COX, MARSHALL, lawyer; b. Cleve., Nov. 17, 1932; s. Marshall H. C. and Mary (Bateman) Mills; m. Nancy Huntley, Aug. 3, 1957; 1 dau., Vanessa. B.A., Vanderbilt U., 1954; J.D., Ohio State U., 1958. Bar: N.Y. 1959. Assoc. Cahill, Gordon & Reindel, N.Y.C., 1959-67, ptnr., 1968—. Served to 1st. lt. U.S. Army, 1955-57, Korea. Mem. N.Y. State Bar Assn. (Ho. of Dels.), N.Y. County Lawyers Assn. (former dir.). Republican. Unitarian. Clubs: Down Town Assn. (N.Y.C.); Nantucket Yacht (Mass.). Antitrust, Federal civil litigation, State civil litigation. Home: 13 Vandam St New York NY 10013 Office: Cahill Gordon & Reindel 80 Pine St New York NY 10005

COX, MARY JANE TRUESDELL, lawyer; b. LeMars, Iowa, Jan. 23, 1945; d. Myrle Edward and Jane (Steele) Truesdell; m. William N. Cox, Oct. 19, 1973; children—(Truman (dec.), Rebecca. stepchildren—Courtland, Kathleen. B.S., Mont State U., 1967, Masters degree, 1970; J.D., U. Denver, 1976. Bar: Colo. 1976. Clk., Office of Edn., Denver, 1967-68; caseworker Nev. State Welfare, Las Vegas, 1968-69; sec. Labor Finance Indsl. Bank, Denver, 1970-71; v.p. Denver Indsl. Bank, 1971-73; legal intern trust dept. Security Nat. Bank, Denver, 1973-74; assoc. Joyce S. Steinhardt, Englewood, Colo., 1976-77; sole practice, Denver, 1977-79, Littleton, Colo., 1979-80, Englewood, Colo., 1983-84, Littleton, Colo., 1984—; assoc. Robert T. Hinds, Littleton, 1980-83; real estate agt. Able & Co., Littleton, 1979-80. Editor Mo. Family Law Newsletter, 1979-81. Sunday sch. tchr., youth leader, Denver, 1978-84. Mem. ABA, Colo. Bar Assn. (chmn. family law sect. 1981-82, bd. govs. 1984-86, v.p. 1986-87), Arapahoe Bar Assn. (dir. 1981-84), Phi Kappa Phi. Family and matrimonial. Office: Cox & Mustain-Wood 6601 S University Blvd Littleton CO 80121

COX, MELVIN MONROE, lawyer, law educator; b. Omaha, Jan. 31, 1947; s. Monroe M. Cox and Wilma Grace (Prickett) McPherson. BA with high honors, U. Wyo., 1969; JD, Harvard U., 1972. Bar: Pa. 1972, U.S. Dist. Ct. (we. dist.) Pa. 1972. Assoc. Rose, Schmidt & Dixon, Pitts., 1972-78; atty. Chgo. Pneumatic Tool Co., N.Y.C., 1978-81, asst. sec., 1981—; adj. prof. engring. law The Cooper Union, N.Y.C., 1984—. Mem. ABA, Phi Beta Kappa, Phi Kappa Phi. General corporate, Private international. Office: Chgo Pneumatic Tool Co 6 E 44th St New York NY 10017

COX, SANFORD CURTIS, JR., lawyer; b. El Paso, Tex., July 31, 1929; s. Sanford Curtis Sr. and Iva M. (Richardson) C.; m. Helen A. Thurston, Sept. 27, 1958; children: Sanford Curtis III, Christopher Thurston. BA, Tex. Western Coll., 1951, MA, 1952; LLB, U. Tex., 1957. Bar: Tex. 1957, U.S. Dist. Ct. (we. dist.) Tex. 1960, U.S. Ct. Appeals (5th cir.) 1964, U.S. Ct. Appeals (D.C. cir.) 1975. Assoc. Andress, Lipscomb, Peticolas & Fisk, El Paso, 1957-61; ptnr. Lipscomb, Fisk & Cox, El Paso, 1961-74, Fisk & Cox, El Paso, 1974-79; sole practice El Paso, 1979—. Mem. bd. editors U. Tex. Law Rev. Mem. adv. bd. Booth Meml. Home, 1963-79, Pleasant View Home, 1979—. Served with U.S. Army, 1952-54. Mem. ABA, Tex. Bar Assn. (admissions com. 17th dist. 1976), El Paso Bar Assn. (ethics com. 1965-69, fee arbitration com. 1973-75), Order of Coif, Phi Delta Phi. Republican. Episcopalian. Probate, Banking, Real property. Office: Coronado Tower Bldg Suite 220 El Paso TX 79912

COX, STEPHEN JEFFREY, lawyer; b. Houston, Aug. 28, 1948; s. Claude Milton Jr. and Frances Emma (Sapp) C. BA, Vanderbilt U., 1970; MBA, Western Mich. U., 1972; JD, Emory U., 1978. Bar: Ga. 1978, Tenn. 1980, U.S. Dist. Ct. (ea. dist.) Tenn. 1980. Sole practice Knoxville, Tenn., 1980—. Served to 1st lt. U.S. Army, 1972-75. Lodge: Elks (scholarship chmn. 1985-86). Avocations: astronomy, bicycling, swimming, hiking. General practice. Home: 7915 W Cliff Dr Knoxville TN 37909 Office: Suite 509 Third Nat Bank Bldg Knoxville TN 37902

COX, STEPHEN TROYCE, lawyer; b. Borger, Tex., Dec. 6, 1941; s. Sidney Thomas and Lois Juanita (Mead) C.; children: Shelby Ann, Stacy. BA, U. Calif., Berkeley, 1963; LLB, U. Calif., San Francisco, 1966. Bar: Calif. 1966, U.S. Dist. Ct. (no. dist.) Calif. 1966, U.S. Supreme Ct. 1975. Mng. ptnr. Hoberg, Finger, Brown, Cox & Molligan, San Francisco, 1969—; lectr. Continuing Legal Edn. of Bar, San Francisco, 1977—, U. San Francisco Law Sch., 1983—; del. Calif. Bar Conv., 1977-79. Commr. Piedmont (Calif.) Recreation Commn., 1978-84; treas. Piedmont Boosters Club, 1984—. Served to capt. USAR, 1967-69. Fellow Am. Bd. Trial Advs., Am. Coll. Trial Lawyers; mem. Calif. Bar Assn. (named by jour. one of top ten lawyers in northern Calif. under 40, 1980). Democrat. Clubs: Olympic (San Francisco); Claremont Country (Oakland). Avocation: musical comedy performer. Antitrust, Personal injury. Office: Hoberg Finger Brown Cox & Molligan 703 Market St San Francisco CA 94103

COX, WILLIAM MARTIN, lawyer, educator; b. Bernardsville, N.J., Dec. 26, 1922; s. Martin John and Nellie (Fotens) C.; m. Julia S., June 14, 1952; children—Janice Cox Walker, William Martin, Joann Cox Meyer, Julieann. A.B., Syracuse U., 1947; J.D., Cornell U., 1950. Bar: N.J., U.S. Dist. Ct. Mem. Dolan & Dolan, Newton, N.J., 1950—; mem. faculty, tchr. zoning adminstrn. Rutgers U.; gen. counsel N.J. Fedn. Planning Ofcls.; bd. dirs. Newton Cemetery Assn.; pres. N.J. Inst. Mcpl. Attys., 1982-84; mem. Land Use Law Drafting Com., 1970—. Recipient Pres.'s Disting. Service award N.J. League Municipalities, 1981. Mem. ABA, N.J. Bar Assn., Sussex County Bar Assn., Am. Planning Assn. Baptist. Clubs: Rotary, Masons (Newton). Author: Zoning and Land Use Administration in New Jersey, 6th edit., 1984. Local government, Land Use and planning. Office: One Legal Ln Newton NJ 07860

COYLE, MARTIN ADOLPHUS, JR., lawyer, electronic and engring. co. exec.; b. Hamilton, Ohio, June 3, 1941; s. Martin Adolphus and Lucille Baird C.; m. Sharon Sullivan, Mar. 29, 1969; children—Cynthia Ann, David Martin, Jennifer Ann. B.A., Ohio Wesleyan U., 1963; J.D. summa cum laude, Ohio State U., 1966. Bar: N.Y. bar 1967. Asso. firm Cravath, Swaine & Moore, N.Y.C., 1966-72; chief counsel securities and fin. TRW Inc., Cleve., 1972-73; sr. counsel, asst. sec. TRW Inc., 1973-75, asst. gen. counsel, asst. sec., 1976, asst. gen. counsel, sec., 1976-80, v.p., gen. counsel, sec., 1980—; sec. TRW Found., 1975-80, trustee, 1980—. Pres., trustee Judson Retirement Community; chmn., sec. Martin A. Coyle Found. Mem. ABA, Am. Soc. Corporate Secs. (pres. Ohio regional group 1978-80, nat. dir. 1981—, nat. chmn. 1985-86), Assn. Gen. Counsel, Ohio Bar Assn., Bar Assn. Greater Cleve., Ohio Wesleyan Assocs. (nat. chmn. 1987). Clubs: Mayfield Country, Union. Co-inventor voting machine. Home: 23175 Laureldale Rd Shaker Heights OH 44122 Office: TRW Inc 1900 Richmond Rd Cleveland OH 44124

COYLE, ROBERT EVERETT, federal judge; b. Fresno, Calif., May 6, 1930; s. Everett LaJoya and Virginia Chandler C.; m. Faye Turnbaugh, June 11, 1953; children—Robert Allen, Richard Lee, Barbara Jean. B.A., Fresno State Coll., 1953; J.D., U. Calif., 1956. Bar: Calif. Ptnr. McCormick, Barstow, Sheppard, Coyle & Wayte, 1958-82; judge U.S. Dist. Ct. (ea. dist.) Calif., 1982—. Mem. Fresno County Bar Assn. Judicial administration. Office: 5116 U S Courthouse Fresno CA 93721 *

COYNE, CHARLES COLE, lawyer; b. Abington, Pa., Dec. 3, 1948; s. James Kitchenman and Pearl (Black) C.; m. Paula J. Latta, May 15, 1976; 1 dau., Anna Elizabeth. B.S. in Econs., U. Pa., 1970; J.D., Temple U., 1973. Bar: Pa. 1973, U.S. Dist. Ct. (ea. dist.) Pa. 1974, U.S. Ct. Appeals (3d cir.) 1982, U.S. Supreme Ct. 1982, N.J. 1985. Assoc. Fell, Spalding, Goff & Rubin, Phila., 1973-78; mng. atty. Charles C. Coyne & Assocs., Phila., 1978-80; mng. ptnr. Coyne & Perry, and predecessor firm Coyne & Moore, Phila., 1980-86; ptnr. Fell & Spalding, Phila., 1987—; dir., sec., mem. mgmt. com. George S. Coyne Chem. Co., Inc., Croydon, Pa. Assoc. editor Temple Law Quar., 1972-73. Chester County (Pa.) rep. Del. Valley Regional Planning Commn., 1982—; bd. dirs. Chester County Hosp. Authority, 1982—, sec., 1984—; bd. suprs. East Fallowfield Twp., Chester County, 1982-83; mem. Chester County Rep. Com., 1980-82, Phila. Rep. City Com., 1974-76; bd. dirs. Pa. Young Reps., 1976-77; chmn. Greater Phila. Young Reps., 1975-76; trustee Doe Run Presbyn. Ch., Chester County, 1981-82. Recipient Disting. Young Rep. award Greater Phila. Young Reps., 1976. Mem. ABA, Pa. Bar Assn., Phila. Bar Assn. (chmn. sub-com. local bankruptcy rules 1974-75), Chester County Bar Assn., Temple Law Sch. Alumni Assn. (chmn. 10th reunion com.). Clubs: Union League (Phila.), Racquet, Right Angle (bd. control 1984-85). Lodge: Masons (master 1982). General corporate, Contracts commercial, Bankruptcy. Home: Sycamore Run Farm Box 454 RD8 Coatesville PA 19320 Office: 211 S Broad St 8th Floor Philadelphia PA 19107

COYNE, LYNN HARRY, lawyer; b. Braddock, Pa., Oct. 21, 1944; s. Harry James and Florence Edna (Mondale) C.; m. Ute M. Fuchs, Dec. 31, 1971; children: Erik C., Bryan C. AB, Ind. U., 1970, JD, 1972. Bar: Ind. 1972. Assoc. Bunger, Harrell & Robertson, Bloomington, Ind., 1972-74, ptnr., 1975-85; ptnr. Harrell, Clendening & Coyne, Bloomington, 1985—; instr. Ind., U., Bloomington, 1984—. Author: Initial Considerations in Corporate Formation, 1985, Basic Real Estate Practice Title Insurance, 1986. Chmn. Monroe County chpt. ARC, Bloomington, 1984—. Served as sgt. USAF, 1965-69. Named Hon. Burgermeister City of Bloomington, 1985; recipient Hospitality award Conv. and Visitors Bur., Bloomington, 1985. Fellow Ind. Bar Found.; mem. ABA, Ind. Bar Assn., Greater Bloomington C. of C. (pres. 1984-85). Presbyterian. General corporate, Real property, Probate. Office: Harrell Clendening & Coyne 205 N College PO Box 5667 Bloomington IN 47402

COYNE, M. JEANNE, state supreme court justice; b. Mpls., Dec. 7, 1926; d. Vincent Mathias and Mae Lucille (Steinmetz) C. B.S. in Law, U. Minn., 1955, J.D., 1957. Bar: Minn. 1957, U.S. Dist. Ct. Minn. 1957, U.S. Ct. Appeals (8th cir.) 1958, U.S. Supreme Ct. 1964. Law clk. Minn. Supreme Ct., St. Paul, 1956-57; assoc. Meagher, Geer & Markham, Mpls., 1957-70, ptnr., 1970-82; assoc. justice Minn. Supreme Ct., St. Paul; mem. Am. Arbitration Assn., 1967-82; mem. bd. conciliation Archdiocese St. Paul and Mpls., 1981-82; instr. U. Minn. Law Sch., Mpls., 1964-68; mem. Lawyers Profl. Responsibility Bd., St. Paul, 1982; chmn. com. rules of civil appellate procedure Minn. Supreme Ct., St. Paul, 1982—. Editor: Women Lawyers Jour., 1971-72. Mem. ABA, Minn. State Bar Assn., Nat. Assn. Women Lawyers, Nat. Assn. Women Judges, Minn. Women Lawyers Assn. (dir.), U. Minn. Law Alumni Assn. Office: Minn Supreme Ct 230 State Capitol Saint Paul MN 55155

COZ, THOMAS ANTHONY, lawyer, educator; b. Ravenna, Ohio, Mar. 20, 1953; s. Frank Joseph and Clara Jean (Flogge) C.; m. Mary Maureen Murphy, May 29, 1982; children: Joseph M., Elizabeth S. Diplôme Annuel, La Sorbonne U., Paris, 1975; BA, Xavier U., 1976; JD, U. Cin., 1979. Bar: Ohio 1979, U.S. Dist. Ct. (so. dist.) Ohio 1980. Atty. ATE Mgmt. and Service Co., Inc., Cin., 1979-83; sr. atty. North Am. Van Lines, Inc., Ft. Wayne, Ind., 1983—; adj. prof. No. Ky. U., Highland Heights, Ky., 1983-84; bd. dirs. Glen Aqua Pool Club, Inc., Ft. Wayne, N.A.V.L. Fed. Employees Credit Union, Ft. Wayne. Fundraiser Boy Scouts Am., Ft. Wayne, 1985—; tchr. Priject Bus. Jr. Achievement , Ft. Wayne, 1986—. Mem. ABA, Ohio Bar Assn., Ind. Bar Assn., Allen County Bar Assn., Xavier U. Alumni Assn. Roman Catholic. Avocations: photography, bicycling, golf. General corporate, Labor, Pension, profit-sharing, and employee benefits. Home: 3616 Delray Dr Fort Wayne IN 46815 Office: North Am Van Lines Inc Law Dept 5001 US Hwy 30 W Fort Wayne IN 46818

CRABB, BARBARA BRANDRIFF, U.S. dist. judge; b. Green Bay, Wis., Mar. 17, 1939; d. Charles Edward and Mary (Forrest) Brandriff; m. Theodore E. Crabb, Jr., Aug. 29, 1959; children: Julia Forrest, Philip Elliott. A.B., U. Wis., 1960, J.D., 1962. Bar: Wis. bar 1963. Asso. firm Roberts, Boardman, Suhr and Curry, Madison, 1968-70; research asst. Law Sch. U. Wis., 1968-70; research asst. Am. Bar Assn., Madison, 1970-71; U.S. magistrate Madison, 1971-79; U.S. dist. judge Western Dist. Wis., 1979—, chief judge, 1980—; mem. Gov. Wis. Task Force Prison Reform, 1971-73. Membership chmn., v.p. Milw. LWV, 1966-68; mem. Milw. Jr. League, 1967-68. Mem. Am. Bar Assn., Nat. Council Fed. Magistrates, Nat. Assn. Women Judges, State Bar Wis., Dane County Bar Assn., U. Wis. Law Alumni Assn. Home: 741 Seneca Pl Madison WI 53711 Office: US District Court Box 591 Madison WI 53701 *

CRABTREE, ROBERT CROSBY, lawyer; b. Atlanta, Feb. 6, 1954; s. James Robert and Carolyn Muriel (Berry) C.; m. Ellen Haselwood, July 25, 1981; 1 child, Rebecca Gray. BA, U. Va., 1976; JD with honors, Fla. State U., 1979. Bar: Fla. 1979, U.S. Dist. Ct. (no. dist.) Fla. 1979, U.S. Ct. Appeals (11th cir.) 1985. Assoc. Holland & Knight, Tallahassee, 1979-81; ptnr. Fuller & Johnson P.A., Tallahassee, 1981—. Contbr. Fla. State U. Law Rev., 1978-79. Mem. Fla. Bar Assn., Tallahassee Bar Assn. (law day dir. 1982), Fla. Def. Lawyers Assn., Phi Delta Phi (treas. 1978-79), Sigma Alpha Epsilon. Republican. Club: Gentry (Tallahassee) (pres. 1985-86). Insurance, Federal civil litigation, State civil litigation. Office: Fuller & Johnson PA 111 N Calhoun St Tallahassee FL 32301

CRACRAFT, BRUCE NOEL, lawyer; b. Indpls., Dec. 24, 1921. Student, Ind. U., 1942, Butler U., 1946; LL.B., Stetson U., 1949. Bar: Fla., Ind. 1949. Assoc. Slaymaker, Locke & Reynolds, Inpls., 1949-54, ptnr., 1955; atty. Ind. Bell Telephone Co., Indpls., 1955-59, gen. atty., 1959-72; v.p., gen. counsel Ind. Bell Telephone Co., 1972-87; of counsel hackman, McClarnon & McTurnan, Indpls., 1987—; dir. Statesman Ins. Co., 1982—. Bd. dirs. Child Guidance Clinic, Marion County, Ind., 1957-65, pres., 1960-61; bd. dirs. Ind. Legal Found., 1982—, chmn. adv. com., 1978—; bd. dirs. Crossroads Rehab. Ctr., 1985—; mem. Gov.'s Task Force on Bus. Tax, 1983—; mem. bd. visitors Ind. U. Sch. Law, Indpls., 1976-80, chmn., 1979-80; mem. Ind. Jud. Council on Legal Edn. and Competence at the Bar; chmn. bd. dirs. Ind. Fiscal Policy Inst., 1985—. Served to 1st lt. USAAF, 1942-45; PTO. Decorated Air medal with oak leaf cluster. Fellow Am. Bar Found., Ind. Bar Found. (chmn. 1984-85); mem. ABA, Ind. Bar Assn. (chmn. adminstrv. law com., del. 1969-73), Indpls. Bar Assn., Am. Judicature Soc., Nat. Tax Assn.-Tax Inst. Am. (dir. 1980), Lawyers Assn. Indpls. (pres. 1960), Lawyers Club (pres. 1981), Am. Right of Way Assn. (pres. 1965), Internat. Assn. Assessing Officers, Ind. Taxpayers Assn. (pres., dir.), Ind. C. of C. (chmn. taxation com. 1961-86), Sigma Delta Kappa, Phi Kappa Psi. Clubs: Columbia, Skyline. Administrative and regulatory, Public utilities, State and local taxation. Home: 5253 Shorewood Dr Indianapolis IN 46220 Office: Hackman McClarnon & McTurnan 1900 One Indiana Sq Indianapolis IN 46204

CRADDOCK, THOMAS WOFFORD, lawyer; b. Dallas, June 18, 1946; s. Dan Murchison Jr. and Arabella (Wofford) C.; m. Jill Reynolds, Aug. 17, 1974; children: Ashley Reynolds, Tenison Elizabeth. BA, U. Tex., 1968, JD, 1972. Bar: U.S. Dist. Ct. (so. dist.) Tex. 1973, U.S. Dist. Ct. (no. dist.) Tex. 1974, U.S. Supreme Ct. 1977, U.S. Dist. Ct. (ea. dist.) Tex. 1980, U.S. Ct. Appeals (5th cir.) 1980, U.S. Dist. Ct. (we. dist.) Tex. 1981, U.S. Ct. Appeals (11th cir.) 1981, U.S. Ct. Appeals (10th cir.) 1985. Law clk. to presiding judge U.S. Dist. Ct. (so. dist.) Tex., 1972-74; assoc. Coke & Coke, Dallas, 1974-84, Gibson, Dunn & Crutcher, Dallas, 1984—. Served to 1st lt. USAFNG, 1968-74. Fellow Tex. Bar Found.; mem. ABA, Dallas Bar Assn. (bd. dirs. 1978-79), Tex. Young Lawyers Assn. (v.p. 1982-83), Dallas Assn. Young Lawyers (pres. 1979). Presbyterian. Avocations: hunting, fishing, wildlife photography. Federal civil litigation, State civil litigation. Office: Gibson Dunn & Crutcher 1700 Pacific Ave Suite 4400 Dallas TX 75201

CRAFT, ALICE MAY, lawyer; b. Washington, Aug. 1, 1947; d. Edward Oliver and Wilma Clare (Williams) C. AB, Duke U., 1969; MLS, Ind. U., 1970, JD, 1973. Bar: Ind. 1973, U.S. Dist. Ct. (so. dist.) Ind. 1973. Ptnr. Thomas & Craft, Bloomington, Ind., 1973-76; dep. city atty. City of Bloomington, 1974-78; staff counsel Ind. Civil Rights Commn., Indpls., 1978-81, chief staff counsel, 1981-83; sr. trial atty. EEOC, Indpls., 1983-86, supervisory trial atty., 1986—. Mem. ABA, Ind. Bar Assn., Fed. Bar Assn. Labor. Home: 2120 Kessler Blvd E Dr Indianapolis IN 46220 Office: EEOC 46 E Ohio St Indianapolis IN 46204

CRAFT, GEORGE SULLIVAN, lawyer; b. N.Y.C., May 2, 1947; s. Robert Homan and Janet (Sullivan) C.; divorced; children: Jennifer M., George Sullivan Jr. BBA, Tex. Christian U., 1970; JD, U. Houston, 1973. Bar: Tex. 1973, U.S. Dist. Ct. (so. dist.) Tex. 1977. Ptnr. Sewell & Riggs, Houston, 1973-81, Holland & Stephenson, Houston, 1981-82, Cochran, Rooke & Craft, Houston, 1982—; bd. dirs. Houston Young Lawyers Assn. Mem. ABA (real estate fin. com.), Tex. Bar Assn., Houston Bar Assn. Clubs: University, Briar, Houstonian. Banking, Real property. Office: Cochran Rooke & Craft 2200 Post Oak Blvd Suite 700 Houston TX 77056

CRAFT, JOSEPH W., corporate lawyer. BS, U. Ky., Knoxville, 1972, JD, 1976. Counsel Falcon Coal Co., 1975-80, Diamond Shamrock, 1980; asst. gen. counsel Mapco Inc., Tulsa, 1980-82, gen. counsel, 1982-85, sr. v.p. legal and fin., 1985—. Office: Mapco Inc 1800 S Baltimore Ave Tulsa OK 74119 *

CRAFT, WINFRED OWENS, JR., lawyer; b. Tampa, Fla., Mar. 23, 1944; s. Winfred Owens and Joyce Roselia (Clark) C.; m. Carol Garnett, July 20, 1950. BA, U. Tex.-El Paso, 1966; JD, Ariz. State U., 1971. Bar: Ariz. 1971, U.S. Sup. Ct. 1976, D.C. 1977. Aide to Gov. Ariz., 1969-71; asst. U.S. atty. Dist. of Ariz., 1971-72; dep. minority counsel Interior and Insular Affairs Com. U.S. Senate, 1973-75; dep. under-sec. Dept. Interior, Washington, 1975-76; minority counsel Energy and Natural Resources Com. U.S. Senate, Washington, 1976-79; mgr. external affairs Sun Energy Devel. Co., Dallas, 1979-82; founding ptnr. Craft & Loesch, P.C., Washington, 1982—; chief of staff, dep. team leader Presdl. transition team Dept. Interior, 1980-81. Commr., Western Interstate Commn. for Higher Edn., 1971-74; mem. U.S. Nat. Com., World Energy Conf. Spl. Com. on Synthetic Fuels. Served to capt. U.S. Army, 1966-68. Mem. ABA, D.C. Bar Assn., Ariz. Bar Assn. Republican. Presbyterian. Club: Army/Navy Country. Legislative, Oil and gas leasing, Environment. Office: 1050 Thomas Jefferson St NW Suite 600 Washington DC 20007

CRAIG, BENJAMIN LAWRENCE, lawyer; b. Great Falls, Mont., Mar. 15, 1931; s. Russell Edgar and Gladys Glenore (Chance) C.; m. Jeanne E. Higgins, Jan. 1, 1984; children—Russell Ivar, Pamela Sue. B.S. in Bus. Adminstrn., U. Mont., 1953; J.D., U. Denver, 1960. Bar: Colo. 1960, U.S. Dist. Ct. Colo. 1960, U.S. Ct. Appeals (10th cir.) 1960, U.S. Supreme Ct. 1966. Assoc. Cockrell, Quinn & Creighton and predecessor firm Henry, Cockrell, Quinn & Creighton and Henry & Adams, Denver, 1960—, ptnr., 1966—. Pres. Pres.'s Roundtable Denver, 1975; bd. dirs. Boys Club Denver, Balarat Council. Served to col. USAFR, 1953—. Mem. Denver Bar Assn., Colo. Bar Assn., ABA, Am. Judicature Soc., The Law Club Denver, Nat. Orgn. Legal Problems Edn., Nat. Sch. Bds. Assn. Council Sch. Attys. (chmn. 1973-75), Order of St. Ives Hon. Soc. Republican. Presbyterian. Clubs: Univ. (Denver), Army-Navy (Washington), Masons. Local government, Real property, Labor. Office: 950 S Cherry St Suite 516 Denver CO 80222

CRAIG, BERNARD DUFFY, lawyer; b. Kansas City, Mo., Nov. 12, 1909; s. John Clarence and Edith Margaret (Duffy) C.; m. Margaret Mary Conrad, June 25, 1938; children: Bernard D. Jr., Jo Anne Craig Fanganello, John E., Kathleen M. Craig Harbert. JD, U. Mo., 1936. Bar: Mo. 1936, U.S. Dist. Ct. (we. dist.) Mo. 1937, U.S. Supreme Ct. 1946, U.S. Tax Ct. 1975. Ptnr. Levy & Kirschner, Kansas City, 1936-50, Granoff, Levy & Craig, Kansas City, 1950-60; ptnr. Levy & Craig, Kansas City, 1961-75, sr. ptnr., 1975—. Gen. chmn. Brotherhood Citation Banquet Nat. Conf. Christians and Jews, 1959; nat. dir. Nat. Conf. Christians and Jews, 1966; trustee Pope John XXIII Found., 1964-67, Law Found. U. Mo. at Kansas City, Legal Aid and Defender Soc. of Greater Kansas City, 1964-70, v.p. 1970; mem. St. Joseph Hosp. Adv. Council, 1978—. Decorated Knight of Holy Sepulchere Pope Paul VI, 1965; named hon. Col. Staff Gov. Warren E. Hearned, 1964-72. Mem. ABA, Mo. Bar Assn., Kansas City Bar Assn., Assn. of Bar of City of N.Y. Roman Catholic. Clubs: Kansas City, Blue Hills Country (Kansas City). General practice, Private international, General corporate. Home: 1019 W 69th St Kansas City MO 64113 Office: Levy and Craig 916 Walnut St Kansas City MO 64106

CRAIG, ROBERT LEE, JR., lawyer; b. Brownfield, Tex., Dec. 6, 1950; s. DeLores (Gillham) C.; m. Dana Gwyn Brookshire, Dec. 16, 1972; children: Robert Lee III, Crystal, Danielle. BA with honors, Tex. Tech U., 1973; JD, So. Meth. U., 1976; postgrad., U. Kent, Eng., 1975. Bar: Tex. 1976, U.S. Dist. Ct. (ea., we. and no. dists.) Tex. 1977, U.S. Ct. Appeals (5th cir.) 1978. Assoc. Carr, Evans, Fouts and Hunt, Lubbock, Tex., 1976-78; ptnr. Carr, Evans, Fouts and Hunt, Lubbock, 1979—; speaker in field, 1982—. Chmn. bd. dirs. Wesley Found., Lubbock, 1984. Served to 1st lt. USAR, 1973-81.

Mem. ABA, Lubbock County Young Lawyers Assn. (pres. 1981-82, named Outstanding Young Lawyer 1983), Lubbock County Bar Assn. (treas. 1981-82, bd. dirs. 1984-87), Tex. Assn. Def. Counsel, State Bar of Tex., Internat. Assn. Ins. Counsel, Leadership Lubbock. Democrat. Methodist. Lodge: Rotary. State civil litigation, Personal injury, Workers' compensation. Home: 4403 88th Pl Lubbock TX 79423 Office: Carr Evans Fouts and Hunt 916 Main PO Box 2585 Lubbock TX 79408

CRAIG, ROBERT MARK, III, lawyer, educator; b. Mpls., Sept. 21, 1948; s. Robert Mark Jr. and Shirley A. (Collier) C.; m. Suzanne Bartlett, Aug. 22, 1970; children: Shannon Michelle, Scott Collier. BA in Journalism, Tex. Christian U., 1970; JD, U. Va., 1973. Bar: Va. 1973, U.S. Ct. Mil. Appeals 1974, Tex. 1975, U.S. Dist. Ct. (no. dist.) Tex. 1976, U.S. Dist. Ct. (so. dist.) Tex. 1980, U.S. Ct. Appeals (5th and 11th cirs.) 1981, U.S. Supreme Ct. 1981, U.S. Ct. Appeals (10th cir.) 1984. Assoc. Judin, Ellis & Barron, McAllen, Tex., 1979-80, ptnr., 1980-81; gen. atty. Tenneco Oil Co., Houston, 1981—; staff atty. Presdl. Clemency Bd., Washington, 1975; adj. prof. U. Houston, Woodlands, 1986—; faculty Vernon Regional Jr. Coll., Sheppard AFB, 1975-76; instr. Paralegal Trg., Houston, 1982-85, USAF Acad., 1976-77, asst. prof. law, 1977-79. V.p. Upper Rio Grande Valley Heart Assn., McAllen, 1980-81; ruling elder Timber Ridge Presbyn. Ch., 1983-85; pres. Montgomery County Assn. for the Gifted/Talented, Conroe, Tex., 1985; clk. of session Timber Ridge Presbyn. Ch., Spring, Tex., 1985—. Served to capt. USAF, 1973-79. Mem. ABA, Va. Bar Assn. (assoc.), Tex. Bar Assn., McAllen Jaycees (sec., bd. dirs. 1979-81). Republican. Avocations: youth coaching, golf, racquetball, softball. Federal civil litigation, State civil litigation, General corporate. Home: 27122 Wells Ln Conroe TX 77385 Office: Tenneco Oil Co 1100 Milam Suite 805 Houston TX 77001

CRAIN, J. LESTER, JR., corporate lawyer; b. 1929. BA, Southwestern U., Georgetown, Tex., 1951; LLB, Harvard U., 1954. Sole practice 1958-77; v.p., gen. counsel Malone & Hyde Inc., Memphis, 1977-79, v.p., sec., gen. counsel, 1979—. Served to lt. comdr. USN, 1954-58. Office: Malone & Hyde Inc 3030 Poplar Ave Memphis TN 38111 *

CRAIN, JAMES MICHAEL, lawyer; b. Martinsville, Ind., May 9, 1942; s. James William and Frances (Utterback) C.; m. Karen Ann Wade, Oct. 9, 1970; children: Erin Leigh, James Eric. BS in History, U. Tenn., 1966, JD, 1973, MA in History, 1980. Bar: Tenn. 1973, U.S. DIst. Ct. (ea. dist.) Tenn. 1973, U.S. Ct. Appeals (6th cir.) 1978. Assoc. Arnett, Draper & Hagood, Knoxville, Tenn., 1973-74; sole practice Knoxville, 1974—. Served to capt. U.S. Army, 1966-70. Consumer commercial, Contracts commercial, General corporate. Office: 608 Main Ave Knoxville TN 37902

CRAIN, WILLIAM EARL, lawyer; b. Bklyn., May 16, 1942; s. Irving Jay and Eleanor (Blum) C.; m. Mary Ellen Broughton, Jan. 24, 1976; children: Sarah, Lisa, Anthony, Sacha. Student, Princeton U., 1960-61; BA, Cornell U., 1964; LLB, NYU, 1966. Bar: N.Y. 1966, U.S. Dist. Ct. N.Y. 1967, Vt. 1971, U.S. Dist. Ct. Vt. 1971, Mass. 1973, U.S. Dist. Ct. Mass. 1973, Ohio 1978. Staff atty. N.Y.C. Legal Aid, 1966-67; assoc. Karpatkin & Ohrenstein, N.Y.C., 1967-68; ptnr. Lefcourt, Garfinkle, Crain & Cohn, N.Y.C., 1968-71; sr. ptnr. Crain & Rones, P.C., Newburgh, N.Y., 1976—; of counsel Drake, Sommers, Loeb, Tarshis & Catania, P.C., Newburgh, 1985—; sole practice 1987—; cons. Regional Legal Services, N.Y.C., 1976; gen. counsel P.O.D.E.R., Newburgh, 1976—. Panelist on child abuse Phil Donahue Show, 1986. Candidate Newburgh City Judge, 1976. Mem. N.Y. State Bar Assn., Assn. Trial Lawyers Am., N.Y. Trial Lawyers Assn. (fed. ct. trial counsel 1980—), Am. Arbitration Assn. (arbitrator 1978—). Democrat. Jewish. Avocations: tennis, cycling. Federal civil litigation, Personal injury, Civil rights. Home: 10 Willow Dr New Paltz NY 12561 Office: Drake Summers Loeb & Tarshis PC 873 Union Ave PO Box 1479 Newburgh NY 12550

CRAMER, HAROLD, lawyer; b. Phila., June 16, 1927; s. Aaron Harry and Blanche (Greenberg) C.; m. Geraldine Hassuk, July 14, 1957; 1 dau., Patricia Gail. A.B., Temple U., 1948; LL.B. cum laude, U. Pa., 1951. Bar: Pa. 1951. Law clk. to judge Common Pleas Ct. No. 2, 1953; mem. law faculty U. Pa., 1954; assoc. firm Shapiro, Rosenfeld, Stalberg & Cook, 1955-56, partner, 1956-67; partner firm Mesirov, Gelman, Jaffe & Cramer, Phila., 1974-77, Mesirov, Gelman, Jaffee, Cramer & Jamieson, 1977—; instr. Nat. Inst. Trial Advocacy, 1970—; pres. Jewish Exponent, Times. Co-author: Trial Advocacy, 1968; contbr. articles to profl. jours. Chmn. bd. Eastern Pa. Psychiat. Hosp., 1974-81, Grad. Hosp., 1975—; trustee Fedn. Jewish Agys., Jewish Publ. Soc. Served to 1st lt. U.S. Army, 1951-53. Decorated Bronze Star. Fellow Am. Bar Found.; mem. Phila. Bar Found. (trustee, pres. elect), ABA, Pa. Bar Assn. (ho. of dels. 1966-75, 78—, bd. govs. 1975-78), Phila. Bar Assn. (bd. govs. 1967-69, chmn. 1969, vice chancellor 1970, chancellor 1972, editor The Shingle 1970—), Am. Law Inst., U. Pa. Law Alumni Soc. (bd. mgrs. 1959-64, pres. 1968-70), Order of Coif (past chpt. pres., nat. exec. com. 1973-76), Tau Epsilon Rho (chancellor Phila. grad. chpt. 1960-62), pres. elect. Phila Bar Found. Clubs: Locust, Philmont Country. Federal civil litigation, General corporate, Health. Home: 728 Pine St Philadelphia PA 19106 Office: Fidelity Bldg 123 S Broad St Philadelphia PA 19109

CRAMER, MARK CLIFTON, lawyer; b. St. Petersburg, Fla., July 20, 1954; s. William Cato and Alice J. Cramer; m. Carol Blankenship, Aug. 6, 1977; children: Ryan Albert, Philip Rogers. B.A., U. N.C., 1976; J.D., U. Va., 1979. Bar: D.C. 1979, Fla. 1982, N.C. 1986. Assoc., Cramer & Lipsen, 1979-80; ptnr. Cramer & Cramer, 1980-81; dir. congl. relations U.S. Govt. Printing Office, Washington, 1981, dep. gen. counsel, 1981-83, gen. counsel, 1983-85; v.p., gen. counsel Blankenship-Cramer Devel. Corp, Charlotte, N.C., 1985—. Editor: Legislative Histories of those Laws Affecting the U.S. Government Printing Office as Codified in Title 44 of the U.S. Code. Liaison mem. Adminstrv. Conf. U.S., 1984-85; mem. Mecklenburg County Zoning Bd. of Adjustment; asst. chmn. fin. Mecklenburg County Reps. Recipient Pub. Printer's Gold medal for disting. service, U.S. GPO. Mem. ABA, Fed. Bar Assn., Nat. Homebuilders Assn., Phi Beta Kappa, Sigma Nu. Government contracts and claims, Real property, Legislative. Office: Blankenship-Cramer Devel Corp 4425 Randolph Rd Suite 219 Charlotte NC 28211

CRAMER, R. NORMAN, JR., lawyer; b. Indpls., Oct. 30, 1954; s. Ralph Norman and Helen Virginia (Peterman) C.; m. Patricia Alice Neil, June 3, 1978 (div. Mar. 1982); m. Susan C. Nance, Mar. 9, 1985; 1 child, Ryan Norman. BA with high honors, Denison U., 1977; JD, U. Denver, 1980. Bar: Colo. 1980, U.S. Dist. Ct. Colo. 1980, U.S. Ct. Appeals (10th cir.) 1981, U.S. Ct. Appeals (9th cir.) 1982, U.S. Ct. Appeals (D.C. cir.) 1983, U.S. Ct. Claims 1985. Atty. Mountain States Legal Found., Denver, 1980-82, 84-85; assoc. Cohen, Brame & Smith, Denver, 1983-84; atty. FTC, Denver, 1985—. Mem. ABA, Colo. Bar Assn., Denver Bar Assn. Avocations: stained glass, jazz. Antitrust, Federal civil litigation, General corporate. Office: FTC 1405 Curtis Suite 2900 Denver CO 80202

CRAMER, WILLIAM DONALD, lawyer; b. Milton, Oreg., Sept. 9, 1924; s. John Francis and Mabel Clare (Oesterling) C.; m. Bennidene Backlund, Mar. 21, 1951; children—Christine, Constance, William Donald, Jackson, Andrew, Joseph. Student Princeton U., 1943-44, McGill U., 1949, U. Oreg., 1942; B.A., U. Oreg., 1947, LL.B., 1949, J.D., 1971. Bar: Oreg. 1949, U.S. Dist. Ct. Oreg. 1955, U.S. Ct. Appeals (9th cir.) 1951. Ptnr., Cramer & Pinkerton, Burns, Oreg., 1977—; city atty. Hines (Oreg.), 1960—, Burns, 1950-67. Mem. Oreg. State Water Policy Rev. Bd., 1981—; former dir. Oreg. Hist. Soc.; sec. Harney County Hist. Soc. Served in U.S. Army, 1943-45. Decorated Purple Heart; named Outstanding Jr. Citizen of Harvey County, 1955. Mem. ABA, Am. Trial Lawyers Assn., Oreg. Bar Assn., Oreg. Water Policy Ry. Bd., Oreg. Sch. Bds. Assn. (pres.), Harney County Bar Assn. (pres.), Oreg. Sch. Attys. Assn. (past dir.), Phi Beta Kappa, Phi Delta Phi. Republican. Presbyterian. Clubs: Kiwanis (past pres.), Masons, Shriners. State civil litigation, Probate, Real property. Office: Cramer & Pinkerton PO Box 646 Burns OR 97720

CRAMER, WILLIAM MITCHELL, lawyer; b. Omaha, Mar. 31, 1948; s. William Alva and Shirley Anne (Eddy) C.; m. Aleda Ann Luna, Sept. 4, 1971; children: Teresa Lynn, James William. BS, U. Oreg., 1970; JD, U. Tenn., 1973. Bar: Tenn. 1974, U.S. Dist. Ct. (ea. dist.) Tenn. 1974, U.S. Ct. Appeals (3d cir.) 1985. Asst. atty. City of Knoxville, Tenn., 1973-76, dep. atty., 1976-83; assoc. Rowland & Rowland P.C., Knoxville, 1983—. Served with U.S. Army N.G., 1970-78. Mem. ABA, Tenn. Bar Assn., Tenn. Trial Lawyers Assn. Republican. Presbyterian. Lodge: Optimist. Avocations: coaching soccer, basketball. Personal injury, Workers' compensation, Local government. Home: 10004 Roxbury Point Knoxville TN 37922 Office: Rowland & Rowland PC 10 Emory Pl PO Box 3308 Knoxville TN 37927-3308

CRAMP, JOHN FRANKLIN, lawyer; b. Ridley Park, Pa., Mar. 14, 1923; s. Alfred Charles and Mildred Frances (Cummins) C.; m. Suzanne Surrick, Sept. 15, 1951 (div.); children—John F., Catherine T., David B., Andrew H., Daniel E.; m. 2d, Gloria C. Maddox, Jan. 29, 1972. B.S. Pa. Mil. Coll. (now Widener U.), 1943; LL.B. Dickinson Sch. Law, 1948. Bar: Pa. 1949, U.S. Dist. Ct. (ea. dist.) Pa. 1951, U.S. Ct. Appeals (3d cir.) 1951. Assoc. Hodge, Hodge & Balderston, Chester, Pa., 1949-53; sr. ptnr. Cramp, D'Iorio, McConchie & Forbes, P.C., Media, Pa., 1954-75, pres., 1975—; gen. counsel, dir., sec., pres. Dixon Ticonderoga, Inc.(formerly Bryn Mawr Group and Phila. Sub. Transp. Co.). Trustee, Williamson Sch.; bd. dirs., chmn. bd. Crozer Chester Med. Ctr.; bd. dirs., chmn. bd. Elwyn Inst.; bd. dirs. Chester Hosp.; chmn. bd. Am. Inst. Mental Studies; county chmn. Republican Party, 1957-61; del. Rep. Nat. Conv., 1960; state chmn. Citizens for Scranton, 1962. Served to capt. AUS, 1943-46. Mem. ABA, Delaware County Bar Assn., Pa. Bar Assn., Internat. Soc. Barristers, Nat. Assn. Coll. and Univ. Attys., Def. Research Inst. Episcopalian. Clubs: Union League (Phila.); Masons, Moose. State civil litigation, General corporate, Insurance. Office: 215 N Olive St Media PA 19063

CRAMTON, ROGER CONANT, lawyer, legal educator; b. Pittsfield, Mass., May 18, 1929; s. Edward Allen and Dorothy Stewart (Conant) C.; m. Harriet Cutler Haseltine, June 29, 1952; children: Ann, Charles, Peter, Cutter. A.B., Harvard U., 1950; J.D., U. Chgo., 1955. Bar: Vt. 1956, Mich. 1964, N.Y. State 1979. Law clk. to presiding judge U.S. Ct. of Appeals (2d cir.), 1955-56; law clk. to assoc. justice Harold H. Burton U.S. Supreme Ct., 1956-57; asst. prof. U. Chgo., 1957-61; assoc. prof. U. Mich. Law Sch., 1961-64, prof., 1964-70; chmn. Adminstrv. Conf. of U.S., 1970-72; asst. atty. gen. Justice Dept., 1972-73; dean Cornell U. Law Sch., Ithaca, N.Y., 1973-80, Robert S. Stevens prof., 1982—; mem. U.S. Commn. on Revision Fed. Ct. Appellate System, 1973-75; bd. dirs. U.S. Legal Services Corp., 1975-79, chmn. bd., 1975-78. Author: (with others) Conflict of Laws, 4th edit., 1987; editor: Jour. Legal Edn., 1981-87; contbr. articles to profl. jours. Mem. ABA, Am. Law Inst. (council mem.), Assn. Am. Law Schs. (pres. 1985), Am. Acad. Arts and Scis., Order of Coif, Phi Beta Kappa. Congregationalist. Legal education, Jurisprudence, Professional responsibility. Home: 49 Highgate Circle Ithaca NY 14850

CRANDALL, GRANT FOTHERINGHAM, lawyer; b. Columbus, Ohio, Aug. 22, 1947; s. Vaughn Joseph and Virginia C. (Fotheringham) C.; m. Penelope Anne Caldwell, June 23, 1971; children: Jesse Scott, Andrew Ross. BS, Grinnell Coll., 1969; PhD, Oxford U., Eng., 1972; JD, UCLA, 1975. Bar: W.Va. 1975, U.S. Dist. Ct. (so. dist.) W.Va. 1975, U.S. Ct. Appeals (4th cir.) 1979, U.S. Dist. Ct. (no. dist.) W.Va. 1986, U.S. Supreme Ct. 1987. Ptnr. Crandall & Pyles (and predecessor firms), Charleston, W.Va., 1975—. Rhodes scholar, 1970-72. Mem. Mountain Bar Assn., Legal Aid Soc. (v.p. 1979-84), Nat. Lawyers Guild (v.p. 1981-82). Democrat. Avocation: athletics. Labor, Workers' compensation. Home: 801 Grant St Charleston WV 25302 Office: Crandall & Pyles PO Box 3465 Charleston WV 25334

CRANDALL, NELSON DAVID, III, lawyer; b. Auburn, Calif., Aug. 8, 1954; s. Nelson David and Alice (Reimer) C.; m. Elizabeth L. Donovan, Aug. 25, 1984. Student, U. Calif., Irvine, 1974-76; AB with high honors, U. Calif., Berkeley, 1976; JD, U. Calif., Davis, 1979. Bar: Calif. 1979, U.S. Dist. Ct. (no. dist.) Calif. 1979, U.S. Dist. Ct. (ea. dist.) Calif. 1980. Ptnr. Hopkins & Carley, San Jose, Calif., 1979—. Contbr. articles to profl. jours. Mediator, arbitrator Santa Clara County Neighborhood Small Claims Project, San Jose, 1980-82; active Santa Clara chpt. ARC, San Jose, 1986—; trustee Jr. Statesman Found., 1986—; bd. dirs. Hope Rehab. Services, San Jose, 1985—. Mem. ABA, Calif. Bar Assn., Santa Clara County Bar Assn., Phi Beta Kappa. Republican. Lodge: Rotary. Avocations: travel, photography, backpacking, reading. General corporate, Securities. Office: Hopkins Mitchell & Carley 150 Almaden Blvd Suite 1500 San Jose CA 95113-2089

CRANDALL, PATRICIA IRENE, lawyer; b. Rhinelander, Wis., Apr. 28, 1945; d. John Edward and Irene Selma (Koskelin) Cerney; m. Thomas Dwane Crandall, Aug. 28, 1965 (div. 1976); m. Jack Donald Brenton, Nov. 23, 1982. BS, Ind. U., 1969; MS, U. Wis., 1973; JD, Gonzaga U., 1977. Bar: Wash. 1977, U.S. Dist. Ct. (ea. dist.) Wash. 1978. Tchr. Notre Dame High Sch., Milw., 1970-71, Holy Rosary Sch., Milw., 1970-73; communications specialist Human Relations Council Greater Harrisburg, Pa., 1973-74; assoc. Shine, Rein, Stiles, Spokane, Wash., 1977-78; assoc. Lukins & Annis, P.S., Spokane, 1978-81, prin., 1981—, mem. exec. com., 1986—; bd. dirs. Wash. Soc. of Hosp. Attys.; adj. faculty Whitworth Coll., Spokane, 1986. Bd. dirs. Profl. Resource Optional, Spokane, 1983—, sec. 1986-87; atty. team capt. United Way Campaign, 1984. Mem. ABA, Am. Acad. Hosp. Attys., Wash. Bar Assn. (chairperson code of profl. responsibility 1981-82, chairperson clients security funds com. 1983-85, spl. dist. counsel 1985—), Spokane County Bar Assn. (trustee 1982-84). Club: Spokane. Bankruptcy, Contracts commercial. Home: S 2424 Magnolia Spokane WA 99204 Office: Lukins & Annis PS 1600 Washington Trust Ctr Spokane WA 99204

CRANDELL, JOHN SMITH, retired judge; b. Howell, Mich., July 17, 1924; s. Alger Buell and Marion Grace (Peters) C.; m. Barbara Lou Eddy, Feb. 27, 1944; children—John Smith, Joan Ellen Elsen. A.B., U. Mich., 1946, J.D., 1949. Bar: Mich. 1949, U.S. Supreme Ct. 1965. Ptnr. Crandell & Crandell, Northville, Mich., 1949-51; mem. staff legal office Detroit Procurement Dist., 1951-65, counsel, 1964-65; counsel Def. Contract Adminstrn., Detroit, 1965-76; U.S. adminstrv. law judge Social Security Adminstrn., Detroit, 1977-78, Southfield, Mich., 1979-85; prof. bus. law Walsh Inst., 1954-68. Elder Presbyn. Ch. Served to lt. USNR, 1943-46. Recipient Meritorious Civilian Service award Def. Supply Agy., 1967, 75; named Outstanding Fed. Profl. Employee of Yr., Fed. Exec. Assn., Detroit, 1969. Mem. Mich. Bar Assn., Fed. Bar Assn. (pres. Detroit chpt. 1971-73, nat. v.p. 1973-75). Club: Appalachian Trail Conf. (Harpers Ferry, W.Va.). Administrative and regulatory, Pension, profit-sharing, and employee benefits, Government contracts and claims.

CRANE, BENJAMIN FIELD, lawyer; b. Holden, Mass., May 5, 1929; s. Frederick Turner and Gertrude (Stange) C.; m. Sarah Anne Molloy, Feb. 8, 1959; children: Michael Turner, Elizabeth Loring, Susan Field. B.A., U. Iowa, 1951; LL.B., NYU, 1954. Bar: N.Y. 1955. Assoc. Cravath, Swaine & Moore, N.Y.C., 1954-63, ptnr., 1963—. Served with U.S. Army, 1946-47. Mem. ABA, Assn. Bar City N.Y., N.Y. State Bar Assn. Clubs: Wall Street (N.Y.C.); Travellers (Paris). Office: Cravath Swaine & Moore 1 Chase Manhattan Plaza New York NY 10005

CRANE, CHARLOTTE, law educator; b. Hanover, N.H., Aug. 30, 1951; d. Henry D. and Emily (Townsend) C.; m. Eric R. Fox, July 5, 1975; children: Hillary, Teresa. AB, Harvard U., 1973; JD, U. Mich., 1976. Bar: N.H. 1976, Ill. 1978. Law clk. to presiding judge U.S. Ct. Appeals (6th cir.), Detroit, 1976-77; law clk. to presiding justice U.S. Supreme Ct., Washington, 1977-78; assoc. Hopkins & Sutter, Chgo., 1978-82; asst. prof. Northwestern U., Chgo., 1982-86, assoc. prof., 1986—. Mem. ABA. Mem. U.S. Women's Nat. Crew Team, 1976. Corporate taxation, Personal income taxation, Legislative. Office: Northwestern U Sch Law 357 E Chicago Chicago IL 60611

CRANE, DONALD RAY, lawyer; b. Eugene, Oreg., Sept. 7, 1940; s. Donald Edwin and Lucile Dorothy (Hedin) C.; m. Carol Ann Merrilees, Sept. 4, 1965; children—Donald Perry, Jason David, Jeffrey Joshua. B.A., U. Oreg., 1962, LL.B., 1964. Bar: Oreg. 1964, U.S. Dist. Ct. Oreg. 1965, U.S. Supreme Ct. 1974. Assoc. Proctor, Puckett & Crane, Klamath Falls, Oreg., 1964-66, Richard C. Beesley, Klamath Falls, 1966-68; dist. atty. Klamath County, 1969-72; ptnr. Crane & Bailey, Klamath Falls, 1972—. Bd. dirs. Klamath Falls Elem. Sch. Bd., 1975-79, Oreg. State Fair Dismissal Apls. Bd., 1976-82; charter pres., bd. dirs. Klamath Child and Family Treatment Ctr., 1977-82; mem. Klamath County Mental Health Adv. Bd., 1979-82; chmn. Klamath County Republican Com., 1973-74. Mem. ABA, Oreg. Bar Assn., Klamath County Bar Assn. (pres. 1970). Club: Yacht (Klamath Falls). Lodge: Rotary. General practice, Consumer commercial, Family and matrimonial. Home: 1171 Lynnewood Blvd Klamath Falls OR 97601 Office: Crane & Bailey 540 Main St Suite 204 Klamath Falls OR 97601

CRANE, EDWARD HOLMAN, lawyer; b. Bklyn., Mar. 26, 1929; s. Edward V. and Eleanor R. (Robinson) C.; m. Sheila G. Gerhart; 4 children. B.S., Yale Sch. Engring., 1951; J.D., Yale U., 1956. Bar: Ohio 1956, U.S. Dist. Ct. (no. dist.) Ohio 1957. Ptnr. Thompson, Hine & Flory, Cleve., 1956-73; v.p., gen. counsel Jacobs, Visconsi & Jacobs Co., Cleve., 1973—. Pres. Citizens Mental Health Assembly, 1985—. Served to 1st lt. USAF, 1951-53. Mem. ABA, Ohio Bar Assn., Am. Coll. Real Estate Lawyers, Internat. Council Shopping Ctrs. Clubs: Catawba Island, Cleve. Yacht. General corporate, Real property, Environment. Home: 17408 Edgewater Dr Lakewood OH 44107 Office: 25425 Center Ridge Rd Cleveland OH 44145

CRANE, JOHN MURDOCH, lawyer; b. N.Y.C., Apr. 10, 1939; s. John Murdoch and Helen Anne (Daly) C.; m. Jacqueline Deidra Burke, Sept. 7, 1965; children: John Murdoch, Kathleen Deidra. BA in Social Studies, St. John's U., Jamiaca, N.Y., 1960, JD, 1963; diploma Turkish lang., Def. Lang. Inst., 1967; LLM, George Washington U., 1971. Bar: N.Y. 1963, U.S. Ct. Mil. Appeals 1965, U.S. Supreme Ct. 1970; cert. tchr., Fla. Commd. 1st lt. USAF, 1964, advanced through grades to col., 1977, retired, 1984; ctr. asst. staff judge adv. contracts armament div. Air Force Systems Command, Eglin AFB, Fla., 1971-74; gen. counsel Army and Air Force Exchange Pacific, Honolulu, 1974-77; dep. staff judge adv., chief contract law div., space div. Air Force Systems Command, Los Angeles Air Force Sta., 1977-81; staff judge adv. electronics systems div. Air Force Systems Command, Hanscom AFB, Mass., 1981-84; counsel Hercules Inc., Wilmington, Del., 1984-86, dir. contract compliance and law Hercules Aerospace Co. div., 1986—. Mem. ABA, Nat. Contract Mgmt. Assn., Air Force Assn., Dover Air Force Club. Republican. Roman Catholic. Avocations: waterfowl hunting, genealogy. Government contracts and claims, General corporate, Military. Home: 116 Old Bury Dr Wilmington DE 19808 Office: Hercules Inc Hercules Plaza Wilmington DE 19894

CRANE, MAIDA ROSENFELD, lawyer; b. Pitts. Mar. 14, 1955; d. David and Lois Jean (Blyler) Rosenfeld; m. Jon Crane, May 17, 1981. B.A. summa cum laude, U. Pa., 1976, J.D. cum laude, 1982. Bar: Pa. 1982. Customer services mgr. Counselor Films, Phila., 1977-79; summer assoc. Schnader, Harrison, Segal & Lewis, Phila., 1981, assoc., 1984—; law clk. U.S. Dist. Ct. for N.J., 1982-84. Mem. ABA, Pa. Bar Assn., Phila. Bar Assn., ACLU, Mortar Bd., Phi Beta Kappa. Democrat. Jewish. Federal civil litigation, State civil litigation, Environment. Office: Schnader Harrison Segal & Lewis 1600 Market St Philadelphia PA 19103

CRANE, MARK, lawyer; b. Chgo., Aug. 27, 1930; s. Martin and Ruth (Bangs) C.; m. Constance Bird Wilson, Aug. 18, 1956; children: Christopher, Katherine, Stephanie. AB, Princeton U., 1952; LLB, Harvard U., 1957. Bar: U.S. Dist. Ct. (so. and no. dists.) Ill. 1957, U.S. Ct. Appeals (7th cir.) 1968, U.S. Ct. Appeals (9th cir.) 1972, U.S. Supreme Ct. 1978, U.S. Ct. Appeals (10th cir.) 1982, U.S. Ct. Appeals (fed. cir.) 1983. Assoc. Hopkins & Sutter, Chgo., 1957-63, ptnr., 1963—. Served to lt. (j.g.) USNR, 1952-54, PTO. Fellow Am. Bar Found., Am. Coll. Trial Lawyers; mem. ABA (chmn. antitrust sect. 1986-87), Ill. Bar Assn. (chmn. fed. jud. appointments com. 1978-79), Chgo. Bar Assn., 7th Cir. Bar Assn. (Pres. 1984-85). Republican. Episcopalian. Antitrust, Federal civil litigation. Home: 300 Woodland Ave Winnetka IL 60093 Office: Hopkins & Sutter 3 First Nat Plaza Suite 4200 Chicago IL 60602

CRANE, STEPHEN JOEL, lawyer, consultant; b. Sonoma, Calif., May 20, 1946; s. David Wynn and Wilma Roof (Crane); 1 child, Christina Anne Elizabeth. BA, San Jose U., 1964; JD, U. Calif., San Francisco, 1972; LLM, U. Wash., 1974. Bar: Wash. 1973, U.S. Dist. (we. dist.) Wash. 1973, U.S. Ct. Appeals (9th cir.) 1973. Dir. Wash. Council on Environ. Policy, Olympia, 1974-76; sole practice Seattle, 1976-78; sr. mng. ptnr. Crane, Stamper, Boese, Dunham & Drury, Seattle, 1978—; pres. STECRA Corp., Seattle, 1982—. Co-author Washington Real Property Desk Book, 1986. Mem. ABA, Wash. State Bar Assn., Seattle-King County Bar Assn., Greater Seattle C. of C. Real property, Environment, Administrative and regulatory. Home: 2030 13th W #201 Seattle WA 98119 Office: Crane & Stamper 5700 Columbia Ctr Seattle WA 98104

CRANFORD, STEVEN LEON, lawyer; b. Oakland, Calif., Aug. 22, 1951; s. Leon B. and Dixie Lee (Hammond) C. AA, Cowley County Community Coll., Arkansas City, Kans., 1971; BS, Pittsburg State U., Kans., 1973; JD, Washburn U., 1977. Bar: Kans. 1977, U.S. Dist. Ct. Kans. 1977, U.S. Supreme Ct. 1987. Assoc. Wheeler and Mitchelson, Pittsburg, Kans., 1977-78; staff counsel S.E. Kans. Community Action Program, Girard, 1978-79; gen. counsel Distbn. Cos. Am. Inc., Houston, 1979-80; sole practice Winfield and Arkansas City, Kans., 1980-83; dep. county atty. Cowley County, Kans., 1981-82; spl. prosecutor Butler County, Kans., 1982-83; asst. sec., asst. gen. counsel Rent-a-Ctr., Inc., Wichita, Kans., 1984—; vis. instr. bus. and comml. law St. Johns Coll., Winfield, 1983. staff aide Don Allegrucci for Congress Com., 1978, state committeeman Kans. Dem. Party, Topeka, 1983. Democrat. General corporate, Labor, Securities. Office: Rent-A-Ctr of Am Inc 9920 E Harry Wichita KS 62707

CRANNEY, MARILYN KANREK, lawyer; b. Bklyn., June 18, 1949; d. Sidney Paul and Aurelia (Valice) Kanrek; m. John William Cranney, Jan. 1, 1970 (div. June 1975); 1 child, David Julian. BA, Brandeis U., 1970; MA in History, Brigham Young U., 1975; JD, U. Utah, 1979; LLM in Tax Law, NYU, 1984. Bar: N.Y. 1980. Assoc. Cravath Swaine & Moore, N.Y.C., 1979-81; v.p., asst. gen. counsel intercapital div. Dean Witter Reynolds Inc., 1981—. Mem. ABA, N.Y. County Lawyers Assn. Democrat. Jewish. Avocations: travel, reading. Securities, Personal income taxation, Probate. Home: 1830 E 23d St Brooklyn NY 11229 Office: Dean Witter Reynolds Inc Intercapital Div One World Trade Ctr New York NY 11229

CRANWELL, C. RICHARD, lawyer; b. CredeKanova, W.Va., July 26, 1942; s. James Edward and Mary Elizabeth (Peters) C.; m. Carol Jean Morris, July 27, 1963; children: C. Richard Jr., Whitney Carol, James Robert, Jean Jarrett. BS, Va. Polytech. Inst., 1965; JD, U. Richmond, 1968. Assoc. Tilley & Pedigo, Roanoke, Va., 1968-70; ptnr. Pedigo & Cranwell, Roanoke, 1970-78, Cranwell, Flora, Selbe & Barbe, Roanoke, 1978-80, Gardner, Rocovich & Cranwell, Roanoke, 1980-82, Cranwell, Flora & Moore, Vinton, Va., 1982—. Del. 14th legis dist. Va. Ho. of Dels., 1972-85, chmn. militia and police com., fin. com., cts. of justice com., counties and towns com.; past pres. Vinton Dogwood Festival, bd. dirs. 1973-75; legal advisor Vinton Rescue Squad, Mt. Pleasant Rescue Squad, Montvale Rescue Squad; bd. dirs. Roanoke Valley Juvenile Diabetes Found. Named one of Outstanding Young Men in Am., U.S. Jaycees, 1970, 72; Selected Influential Young Mem. Gen. Assembly, Capital Press Corps, 1975, 77; Williams scholar. Mem. Phi Delta Phi, Vinton C. of C. (legal advisor). Democrat. Methodist. Lodge: Lions. Avocations: reading, golf, tennis, politics. Federal civil litigation, State civil litigation, Personal injury. Home: 1539 Bali Hai Dr Vinton VA 24179 Office: Cranwell Flora & Moore 111 Virginia Ave Vinton VA 24179

CRAVEN, DAVID LEIGH, lawyer; b. Winston-Salem, N.C., Mar. 23, 1953; s. Charles Henry and Beryl (Atherton) C.; m. Sally Casteel, Oct. 7, 1978; 1 child, David Casteel. BA, Davidson Coll., 1975; JD, Wake Forest U., 1978. Bar: N.C. 1978, U.S. Supreme Ct. 1982, Dist. Ct. (ea. dist.) N.C. 1985. Staff atty. Northwestern Bank, Wilkesboro, N.C., 1978-81, assoc. gen. counsel, 1981-84, asst. v.p., assoc. gen. counsel, 1984-85; v.p., gen. counsel Planters Bank, Wilkesboro, 1985—. Dana Found. scholar, 1972, Carswell scholar Wake Forest U., 1975. Mem. ABA, N.C. Bar Assn. Republican. Episcopalian. Lodge: Kiwanis. Banking, Consumer commercial, General corporate. Office: Planters Bank 131 N Church St Rocky Mount NC 27801

CRAVER, JAMES B., lawyer; b. Morristown, N.J., July 20, 1943; s. Herbert Seward and Anne (Brady) C.; m. Elinor Ladd, Aug. 27, 1966; children: Elisabeth Ladd, Amy Richmond. A.B. cum laude, Harvard U., 1965; J.D., U. Pa., 1970. Bar: N.Y. 1970, Mass. 1974, Ohio 1980. Assoc. firm Sullivan & Cromwell, N.Y.C., 1970-73; asst. counsel, asst. sec. Mass.

Fin. Services Co., Boston, 1973-76; gen. counsel, sec. Anchor Corp., Elizabeth, N.J., 1976-79; sec., sr. corp. counsel B.F. Goodrich Co., Akron, Ohio, 1979-84; ptnr. Baker & Hostetler, Columbus, 1984—. Mem. N.Y. Bar Assn., Mass. Bar Assn., Ohio Bar Assn., Cleve. Bar Assn. Clubs: Sakonnet Golf (Little Compton, R.I.); Harvard (Boston); Harvard (pres.) (Akron). General corporate, Securities. Home: 761 S 3d St Columbus OH 43206 Office: Baker & Hostetler 65 E State St Suite 2200 Columbus OH 43215

CRAWFORD, B(URNETT) HAYDEN, lawyer; b. Tulsa, June 29, 1922; s. Burnett Hayden and Margaret Sara (Stevenson) C.; m. Carolyn McCann Hayes, June 5, 1946 (div.); m. Virginia Baker, July 23, 1970; children: Margaret Louise Crawford Thompson, Robert Hayden. BA, U. Mich., 1944, JD, 1949. Bar: Okla. 1949, U.S. Dist. Ct. (no. dist.) Okla. 1949, U.S. Supreme Ct. 1954, U.S. Ct. Appeals (10th cir.) 1954, U.S. Dist. Ct. (so. dist.) Ill. 1959, U.S. Ct. Mil. Appeals 1959, U.S. Ct. Appeals (fed. cir.) 1959, U.S. Dist. Ct. (we. and ea. dists.) Okla. 1960, U.S. Tax Ct. 1967. Law clk. to presiding justice U.S. Dist. Ct. (no. dist.) Okla., 1950-51, dist. atty., 1954-58; asst. city prosecuter City of Tulsa, 1951-52, alt. mcpl. judge, 1952-54; asst. dep. atty. gen. U.S. Dept. Justice, 1958-60; sole practice Tulsa, 1960-77; sr. ptnr. Crawford, Crowe & Bainbridge, Tulsa, 1978—; lectr. in field. Rep. nominee U.S. Senate from Okla., 1960, 62; active civic and polit. orgns. Served to Rear Adm. USNR, 1942-78. Decorated Legion of Merit, Purple Heart, Disting. Pub. Service medal, Dept. Def. Disting. Service award; recipient Okla. Minute Man award 1974. Fellow Am. Assn. Matrimonial Lawyers; mem. ABA, Okla. Bar Assn., Tulsa County Bar Assn., Assn. Trial Lawyers Am., Okla. Trial Lawyers Assn., U.S. Res. Officers Assn. (nat. pres. 1973-74), Phi Delta Phi. Presbyterian. Clubs: Tulsa, Army and Navy (Washington), Garden of Gods (Colorado Springs. Colo.), So. Hills Country (Tulsa). Lodges: Masons, Kiwanis (pres. 1969). Federal civil litigation, State civil litigation, Criminal. Home: 2300 Riverside Dr Tulsa OK 74114 Office: 1714 1st Nat Bldg Tulsa OK 74103

CRAWFORD, HOWARD ALLEN, lawyer; b. Stafford, Kans., Aug. 4, 1917; s. Perry V. and Kate (Allen) C.; m. Millie Houseworth, Oct. 9, 1948; children—Catherine, Edward. B.S., Kans. State U., 1939; J.D., U. Mich., 1942. Mem. firm Lathrop Koontz & Norquist, Kansas City, MO., 1950—; mng. ptnr. Lathrop Koontz & Norquist, 1970-85; dir. various cos. Mem. City Council, City of Mission Hills, Kans., 1965-70. Mem. Lawyers Assn. Kansas City, Mo. Bar Soc., Estate Planning Council Kansas City. Clubs: Kansas City, Mission Hills Country. Estate taxation, Probate, General corporate. Home: 3103 W 67 Terr Mission Hills KS 66208 Office: Lathrop Koontz & Norquist 2345 Grand Ave 26th Floor Kansas City MO 64108

CRAWFORD, LINDA SIBERY, lawyer, educator; b. Ann Arbor, Mich., Apr. 27, 1947; d. Donald Eugene and Verla Lillian (Schneck) Sibery; m. Leland Allardice Crawford, Apr. 4, 1970; children: Christina, Lillian, Leland. Student, Keele U., 1969; BA, U. Mich., 1969; postgrad., SUNY, Potsdam, 1971; JD, U. Maine, 1977. Bar: Maine 1977, U.S. Dist. Ct. Maine 1982, U.S. Ct. Appeals (1st cir.) 1983. Tchr. Pub. Sch., Tupper Lake, N.Y., 1970-71; asst. dist. atty. State of Maine, Farmington, 1977-79; asst. atty. gen. State of Maine, Augusta, Maine, 1979—; legal advisor U. Maine, Farmington, 1975; legal counsel Fire Marshall's Office, Maine, 1980-83, Warden Service, Maine, 1981-83, Dept. Mental Health, 1983—. Mem. Natural Resources Council, Maine, 1985—; bd. dirs. Diocesan Human Relations Council, Maine, 1977-78, Arthritis Found., Maine, 1983—. Named one of Outstanding Young Women of Yr. Jaycees, 1981. Mem. ABA, Maine Bar Assn., Kennebec County Bar Assn., Assn. Trial Lawyers Am., Maine Trial Lawyers Assn., Nat. Health Lawyers Assn., Nat. Assn. State Mental Health Attys. (treas. 1984-86, vice chmn. 1987—), Bus. and Profl. Womens Club. Health, State civil litigation, Personal injury. Home: 25 Winthrop St Hallowell ME 04347 Office: Dept Atty Gen State of Maine State House Station #6 Augusta ME 04333

CRAWFORD, MURIEL LAURA, lawyer, author, educator; b. Bend, Oreg., Oct. 10, 1931; d. Mason Leland and Pauline Marie (DesIlets) Henderson; m. Barrett Matson Crawford, May 10, 1959; children—Laura Joanne, Janet Muriel, Barbara Elizabeth. Student, U. Calif., Berkeley, 1958-60, 67-69; B.A. with honors, U. Ill., 1973; J.D. with honors, Ill. Inst. Tech./Chgo.-Kent Coll. Law, 1977. Bar: Ill. 1977; C.L.U.; Chartered Fin. Cons. Atty., Washington Nat. Ins. Co., Evanston, Ill., 1977-80, sr. atty., 1980-81, asst. counsel, 1982-83, asst. gen. counsel, 1984-87, assoc. gen. counsel, sec., 1987—. Author: (with Greider and Beadles) Law and the Life Insurance Contract, 1984, also articles. Recipient Am. Jurisprudence award Lawyer's Coop. Pub. Co., 1975; 2d prize Internat. LeTourneau Student Med.-Legal Article contest, 1976; Bar and Gavel Soc. award Ill. Inst. Tech./Chgo.-Kent Student Bar Assn., 1977. Mem. ABA, Ill. Bar Assn., Chgo. Bar Assn., Am. Corporate Counsels Assn., Ill. Inst. Tech./Chgo.-Kent Alumni Assn. (dir. 1981—) Republican. Congregationalist. Labor, Insurance, Pension, profit-sharing, and employee benefits.

CRAWFORD, R(OBERT) GEORGE, lawyer; b. Mpls., Oct. 30, 1943; s. Robert John and Agnes C.; m. M. Holly, May 17, 1980; 1 dau., Katherine Barnes. B.A., Harvard U., 1965, J.D., 1968. Bar: Ohio 1969, D.C. 1971, Calif. 1972. Law clk. to Justice Bryon R. White, U.S. Supreme Ct., 1968-69; assoc. Jones, Day, Reavis, & Pogue, Cleve., 1969-70; staff asst. to Pres., White House, Washington, 1970-72; gen. counsel. v.p. Archon Inc., Beverly Hills, Calif., 1972-75; chmn. pvt. bus. sect., ptnr. Jones, Day, Reavis & Pogue, Los Angeles, 1976—. Pres., Harvard U. Law Rev., 1966-68. Mem. ABA, Calif. Bar Assn., Los Angeles Bar Assn., Phi Beta Kappa. Episcopalian. Club: Harvard (N.Y.C.); California. General corporate, Corporate taxation, Real property.

CRAWFORD, ROY EDGINGTON, lawyer; b. Topeka, Dec. 23, 1938; s. Roy E. and Ethel Trula (Senne) C.; m. Kristy S. Pigeon, June 27, 1981; children: Michael, Jennifer. B.S., U. Pa., 1960; LL.B., Stanford U., 1963. Bar: Calif. 1964, U.S. Ct. Mil. Appeals 1964, U.S. Tax Ct. 1969, U.S. Dist. Ct. (no. dist.) Calif. 1971, U.S. Ct. Claims 1974, U.S. Supreme Ct. 1979. Contbr. chpts. to books; bd. editors: Stanford U. Law Rev., 1962-63. Served to capt. AUS, 1964-67. Recipient award of merit U.S. Ski Assn., 1980. Mem. ABA (chmn. com. on state and local taxes 1979-81), Calif. State Bar Assn., San Francisco Bar Assn., Calif. Trout (bd. dirs. 1970—, v.p. 1975—), Beta Gamma Sigma. State and local taxation, Corporate taxation, Personal income taxation. Office: Brobeck Phleger & Harrison 1 Market Plaza San Francisco CA 94105

CRAWFORD, SANDRA KAY, lawyer; b. Henderson, Tex., Sept 23, 1934; d. Obie Lee and Zilpha Elizabeth (Ash) Stalcup; m. William Walsh Crawford, Dec. 21, 1968; children—Bill, Jonathan, Constance, Amelia, Patrick. B.A., Wellesley Coll., 1957; LL.B., U. Tex., 1960. Bar: Tex. 1960, U.S. Supreme Ct. 1965, Colo. 1967, Ill. 1974. Asst. v.p.-legal Hamilton Mgmt. Corp., Denver, 1966-68; v.p., gen. counsel, sec. Transamerica Fund Mgmt. Corp., Los Angeles, 1968; cons. to law dept. Met. Life Ins. Co., N.Y.C., 1969-71; counsel Touche Ross & Co., Chgo., 1972-75; v.p., assoc. gen. counsel Continental Ill. Bank, Chgo., 1975-83; sr. div. counsel Motorola, Inc., Schaumburg, Ill., 1984; corp. atty. Sears Roebuck & Co., 1985—. Mem. ABA, Ill. State Bar Assn., Colo. Bar Assn., Tex. Bar Assn. Clubs: Saddle & Cycle, Carlton (Chgo.). General corporate, Securities, Federal civil litigation. Home: 3900 S Mission Hills Rd Northbrook IL 60062

CRAWFORD, SUSAN J., federal government official; b. Pitts., Apr. 22, 1947. BA, Bucknell U., 1969; JD, New Eng. Sch. Law, 1977. History tchr. Radnor (Pa.) High Sch., 1969-74; assoc. Burnett & Eiswert, Oakland, Md., 1977-79; asst. states atty. Garrett County, Md., 1978-79; ptnr. Burnett, Eswert and Crawford, Oakland, 1979-81; dep. gen. counsel U.S. Dept. Army, Washington, 1981-83, gen. counsel, 1983—; instr. Garrett County Community Coll., 1979-81. Office: US Dept Army Gen Counsel The Pentagon Washington DC 20310 *

CRAWFORD, WILLIAM WALSH, consumer products company executive; b. Clearwater, Fla., Oct. 7, 1927; s. Francis Marion and Frances Marie (Walsh) C. B.S., Georgetown U., 1950; LL.B., Harvard, 1954. Bar: N.Y. 1955, Ill. 1972. Assoc. firm Sullivan & Cromwell, N.Y.C., 1954-58; counsel Esso Standard Oil, N.Y.C., 1958-60; partner Alexander & Green, N.Y.C., 1960-71; v.p. Internat. Harvester Co., Chgo., 1971-76; v.p., gen. counsel, sec. 1976-80; sr. v.p. gen. counsel Kraft, Inc., Glenview, Ill., 1980-81; sr. v.p., gen. counsel, sec. Dart & Kraft, Inc., 1981—. Mem. ABA, Ill. Bar Assn., Assn. Bar City N.Y., Am. Soc. Corp. Secs., Assn. Gen. Counsel. Clubs: Saddle and Cycle, Chgo.; Chgo. Golf (Wheaton, Ill.). General corporate. Office: Kraft Inc Kraft Ct Glenview IL 60025

CREAN, JOHN ANTHONY, lawyer; b. Orange, N.J., Sept. 8, 1950; s. Anthony Edward and Lorraine Elizabeth (Meister) C.; m. Melinda Sue Palkowitsh, Aug. 11, 1973; children: Kevin, Mary Megan, Leslie. BA, Coll. of the Holy Cross, Worcester, Mass., 1972; JD, U. Denver, 1979, MBA, 1980. Bar: Colo. 1979, U.S. Dist. Ct. Colo. 1979. Assoc. Folkstad & Withers (name changed to Folkstad & Kokish), Castle Rock, Colo., 1979-82; sole practice Castle Rock, 1982-85; ct. referee Douglas County Colo. Jud. Dept., Castle Rock, 1982-85; counsel The Mut. Life Inc. Co. of N.Y., Atlanta, 1985—; judge Mcpl. Ct., Parker, Colo., 1984-85. Mem. parish counsel St. Francis of Assisi Ch., Castle Rock, 1983-85; mem., atty. Douglas County Child Protection Team, Castle Rock, 1982-85. Republican. Roman Catholic. Lodge: Optimist (v.p. Castle Rock club 1984-85, treas. 1983-85). Real property. Home: 4373 Dunriver Dr Lilburn GA 30247 Office: The Mut Life Ins Co of NY 2310 Parklake Dr NE Suite 550 Atlanta GA 30345

CREASMAN, WILLIAM PAUL, lawyer; b. Washington, Dec. 6, 1952; s. Paul and Esther B. (Tucker) C.; m. S. Teresa Deese, Aug. 18, 1973; children: Matthew, Anna. BA, Johns Hopkins U., 1974; JD, Wake Forest U., 1977. Bar: N.C. 1977, U.S. Dist. Ct. (mid. dist.) N.C. 1978. Atty. Blue Bell Inc., Greensboro, N.C. and Brussels, 1978-83; sr. corp. atty. Imasco USA Inc., Rocky Mount, N.C., 1983-84, asst. gen. counsel, 1985-87; gen. counsel Church's Fried Chicken, San Antonio, 1984-85; sr. v.p., gen. counsel TCBY Enterprises, Inc., Little Rock, Ark., 1987—. Antitrust, Contracts commercial, Labor. Home: 12 Barber Dr Maumelle AR 72118

CREATO, ANTHONY EDMUND, lawyer; b. Phila., Aug. 7, 1945; s. Edmund Vincent and Rita Frances Florence (Fiscella) C.; m. Phyllis Mary Grandizio, Sept. 30, 1978; children: Anthony E. Jr., Heather Ashley. BA, Temple U., 1967, JD, 1970. Bar: Pa. 1970, U.S. Dist. Ct. (ea. dist.) Pa. 1971, U.S. Ct. Appeals (3d cir.) 1977, U.S. Supreme Ct. 1982. From assoc. to ptnr. Mesirov, Gelman, Jaffe, Cramer & Jamieson, Phila., 1970—. Fellow ABA. Pa. Bar Assn., Phila Bar Assn. Roman Catholic. State civil litigation, Federal civil litigation, Personal injury. Home: 1021 Edwards Dr Springfield PA 19064 Office: Mesirov Gelman Jaffe et al Fidelity Bldg 15th Floor Philadelphia PA 19109

CREBBIN, ANTHONY MICEK, lawyer, military officer; b. Columbus, Neb., Sept. 10, 1952; s. Harry and Donna Mae (Micek) C. BA, Rockhurst Coll., 1974; JD, St Louis U., 1977. Bar: Mo. 1977, U.S. Ct. Mil. Appeals 1980, Hawaii 1987. Commd. 2d lt. USMC, 1978, advanced through grades to maj., 1986; trial counsel USMC, Cherry Point, N.C., 1979, officer legal assistance, def. counsel, 1980, chief trial counsel, 1982; chief def. counsel USMC, Kaneohe Bay, Hawaii, 1986-87; staff judge adv. marine amphibious unit USMC, 1980-81, 84-85. Mem. ABA, Mo. Bar Assn., Hawaii Bar Assn., Assn. Trial Lawyers Am., Phi Alpha Delta. Democrat. Roman Catholic. Avocations: marathoning, scuba diving, snow skiing. Criminal, Military. Office: 1st Marine Amphibious Brigade Marine Corps Air Sta Legal Services Ctr Kaneohe Bay HI 96863-5501

CREECH, HERBERT, lawyer, educator; b. Harlan, Ky., Mar. 17, 1947; s. Herbert and Delphia (Caudill) C.; m. Jill S. Hobbs, Dec. 21, 1969 (div. Mar. 1979); children: Michelle, Briana, Charlotte, Ransley. BA, U. Ky., 1968, JD, 1973. Bar: Ohio 1973, U.S. Dist. Ct. (so. dist.) Ohio 1974, U.S. Ct. Appeals (6th cir.) 1974, U.S. Supreme Ct. 1982. Law clk. Dayton Fed. Cts., Ohio, 1973-75; asst. prosecutor Montgomery County Prosecutor's Office, Dayton, 1976-78; sole practice Dayton, 1978—; instr. Antioch Coll., Yellow Springs, Ohio, 1977-81; Sinclair Coll., Dayton, 1976-81. Mem. Dayton Dem. Club. Served with U.S. Army, 1969-71, Vietnam. Named to Hon. Order Ky. Col. Mem. ABA, Ohio State Bar Assn., Fed. Bar Assn., Dayton Bar Assn., Assn. Trial Lawyers Am. Democrat. Avocations: sports, politics, writing, travel. General practice, Federal civil litigation, Personal injury. Home: 359 Telford Ave Dayton OH 45419 Office: 7211 Taylorsville Rd Dayton OH 45424

CREECH, JAY HEYWARD, lawyer; b. Richmond, Va., Nov. 26, 1956; s. Cecil Knight and Eleanor Longard (Tinkham) C. BS, U. Md., 1979, JD, 1982. Bar: Md. 1982, U.S. Dist. Ct. Md. 1983, U.S. Ct. Appeals (4th cir.) 1985, U.S. Supreme Ct. 1986. Law clk. to presiding justice Md. Cir. Ct. (7th cir.), Upper Marlboro, 1982-83; asst. state's atty. Prince George's County, Upper Marlboro, 1983—. Mem. ABA, Md. Bar Assn., Prince George's County Bar Assn., Nat. Dist. Atty.'s Assn., Md. State's Atty.'s Assn. Democrat. Methodist. Avocations: skiing, tennis, camping, photography. Criminal. Office: Prince Georges County States Atty Cthouse Suite 410 Upper Marlboro MD 20772

CREEDEN, CARL FRANCIS, legal editor, lawyer; b. Newburyport, Mass., Apr. 21, 1953; s. Frank Elmer and Rita Anne (Poliquin) C.; m. Christine AnnNolan, Aug. 14, 1976; children—Meghan, Patrick, Kelly, Michael. B.S., Northeastern U., 1976, J.D., 1979. Bar: Mass. 1979, U.S. Dist. Ct. Mass. 1980. Sole practice, Malden, Mass., 1979-82; assoc. legal editor Equity Publ. Corp., Orford, N.H., 1982-85; commd. U.S. Army, 1985, advanced through grades to capt., with JAGC Trial Def. Service, Ft. Bliss, Tex., 1985—. Bd. dirs. Tri City Area Community Metal Health and Retardation Bd., Malden, 1982. Mem. Phi Kappa Phi. Democrat. Roman Catholic. Admiralty, Criminal. Home: 272 Shadow Mountain Dr Apt 84 El Paso TX 79912 Office: Trial Def Service Fort Bliss Field Office Fort Bliss TX 79916

CREEDON, MICHAEL PATRICK, lawyer; b. Wilmington, Del., Mar. 4, 1950; s. John Joseph and Cecilia Frances (Shields) C.; m. Regina Anne Ventresca, June 23, 1973; children: Michael Patrick Jr., Julie Marie. BA, St. Joseph's U., Phila., 1972; JD, Temple U., 1976. Bar: Pa. 1976, U.S. Dist. Ct. (ea. dist.) Pa. 1979. Assoc. Sanford Cohen, P.C., Phila., 1976-77; law clk. to presiding judge Ct. Common Pleas, Phila., 1977-80; assoc. Marshall, Dennehey, Warner, Coleman & Goggin, Phila., 1980—. Mem. ABA, Pa. Bar Assn., Phila. Bar Assn., Lawyers Club Phila., Phi Alpha Delta. Democrat. Roman Catholic. Lodges: Sons of Italy (sec., orator, past pres. Cross Keys lodge). Federal civil litigation, State civil litigation, Personal injury. Home: 809 Princeton Ave Philadelphia PA 19111 Office: Marshall Dennehey et al 1515 Locust St Philadelphia PA 19102

CREEKMORE, DAVID DICKASON, lawyer; b. Knoxville, Tenn., Aug. 8, 1942; s. Frank Benson and Betsey (Beeler) C.; 1 child, Walton N.; m. Patricia A. Watkins, Oct., 1984; 1 stepchild, Kelly Levy. J.D., U. Tenn., 1965; grad. Judge Adv. Gen.'s Sch., 1979. Bar: Tenn. 1966, U.S. Supreme Ct. 1970. Law clk. Gen. Session Ct., Knox County, Tenn., 1963-66; asst. county atty. Knox County, 1966-70; ptnr. Creekmore, Thomson & Hollow, Knoxville, 1966-72; judge gen. sessions ct. div. II, Knox County, 1972-82; sole practice law, 1986—; instr. criminal law and evidence Walters State Coll., Morristown, Tenn., 1974-80, U. Tenn., 1982—. Knox County Republican committeeman, 1970—; active Tenn. Hist. Assn., Blount Mansion Assn. Served to maj. JAGC, USAR, 1978. Mem. ABA, Tenn. Bar Assn., Knox Bar Assn., Fed. Bar Assn., Tenn. Judges Conf. (v.p. 1976-78), Res. Officers Assn. Methodist. Clubs: Old City, Masons, Shriners, Elks, Eagles, Lions. State civil litigation, Consumer commercial, General practice. Home: 11824 Midhurst Rd Knoxville TN 37922 Office: 905 Locust St Knoxville TN 37902

CREEL, LUTHER EDWARD, III, lawyer; b. Huntsville, Ala., Sept. 23, 1937; s. Luther Edward and June (Oldacre) C.; m. Nan Dee McHalek, Apr. 11, 1974; children by previous marriage: Scott Mitchell, Todd Oldacre. A.B. in Psychology, George Washington U., 1959; J.D., So. Methodist U., 1963. Bar: Tex. 1963. Since practice in Dallas; ptnr. Creel and Atwood (and predecessors), 1971—; past pres. Am. Bankruptcy Inst.; lectr. in field of bankruptcy and reorgn. law. Contbr. articles to legal jours. Mem. ABA (bus. bankruptcy com., internat. bankruptcy law subcom.), Tex. Bar Assn., Dallas Bar Assn. (chmn. bankruptcy sect. 1972), State Bar Tex. (chmn. bankruptcy com. 1979-81), Am. Bankruptcy Inst. (pres. 1982-87). Republican. Baptist. Clubs: City, University, Lakewood. Bankruptcy. Home: 5750 Swiss Ave Dallas TX 75214 Office: Creel & Atwood 3100 LTV Tower Dallas TX 75201

CREEL, THOMAS LEONARD, lawyer; b. Kansas City, Mo., June 21, 1937; s. Thomas Howard and Elizabeth Alberta (Sharon) C.; m. Frances Ann Martin, Aug. 29, 1959; children—Charles, Andrew, Andrea. B.S., U. Kans., 1960; LL.B., U. Mich., 1963. Bar: Mich. 1963, N.Y. 1967, D.C. 1983, U.S. Supreme Ct. 1973, Ct. Mil. Appeals 1964, U.S. Patent and Trademark Office 1965. Assoc. Kenyon and Kenyon, N.Y.C., 1966-74, ptnr., 1974—; faculty lectr. Columbia U., N.Y.C., 1984—. Editor: Selected Cases and Materials on Intellectual Property Law, 1984. Served to capt. U.S. Army, 1963-66. Mem. N.Y. Patent, Trademark and Copyright Law Assn. (chmn arbitration com. 1982—), Am. Intellectual Property Law Assn., Internat. Trade Commn. Trial Lawyers Assn. Clubs: Scarsdale Golf (gov. 1982-83) (Hartsdale, N.Y.); Graduates (New Haven). Patent, Trademark and copyright, Federal civil litigation. Home: 21 Clubway Hartsdale NY 10530 Office: Kenyon and Kenyon 1 Broadway New York NY 10004

CREHAN, JOSEPH EDWARD, lawyer; b. Detroit, Dec. 8, 1938; s. Owen Thomas and Marguerite (Dunn) C.; m. Sheila Anderson, Nov. 6, 1965; children: Kerry Marie, Christa Ellen. A.B., Wayne State U., Detroit, 1961; J.D., Ind. U., 1965. Bar: Ind. 1965, Mich. 1966, U.S. Supreme Ct. 1984. Practice in Detroit 1966—; assoc. Louisell & Barris (P.C.), 1967-73; partner Fenton, Nederlander, Dodge, Barris & Crehan (P.C.), 1975-77; sole practice 1977—, 1977—. Mem. Am. Trial Lawyers Assn. Roman Catholic. Personal injury, Federal civil litigation, General practice. Home: 827 Bentwood Dr Naples FL 33963 Office: 10 W Square Lake Rd Bloomfield Hills MI 48013

CREME, PAUL DAVID, lawyer; b. Syracuse, N.Y., July 10, 1953; s. Eugene Joseph and Jeanette Anne (Schmoon) C.; m. Alice Smith, June 4, 1979; children: David Matthew, Sarah Elizabeth. BA with honors, U. N.C., 1975; JD, Mercer U., 1979. Bar: Ga. 1979, U.S. Dist. Ct. (mid. dist.) Ga. 1979, Mass. 1984. Assoc. Landau Davis, Albany, Ga., 1979-81; adminstr. contracts Adams-Russell, Amesbury, Mass., 1982-84; negotiator contracts Computervision, Bedford, Mass., 1984-85; dir. contracts Sprague Electric, Lexington, Mass., 1985—. Bd. dirs. United Way, Merrimack Valley, 1983-84. Mem. ABA, Mass. Bar Assn. Contracts commercial, Computer. Office: Sprague Electric 92 Hayden Ave Lexington MA 02173

CRENSHAW, RICHARD N., lawyer; b. Phoenix, Nov. 21, 1950; s. Ralph Norman and Cova (Williams) C.; m. Martha Ann, July 8, 1978; children: Kyle, Nicholas. BA in Philosophy, Ariz. State U., 1976, JD, 1981. Bar: Ariz. 1981, U.S. Dist. Ct. Ariz. 1981. Assoc. Monbleau, Vermeire & Turley, Phoenix, 1981-86; ptnr. Vermeire, Turley & Ryan, Phoenix, 1986—. Democrat. Roman Catholic. Federal civil litigation, State civil litigation, Insurance. Office: Vermeire Turley & Ryan 340 E Palm Ln Suite 340 Phoenix AZ 85004

CREO, ROBERT ANGELO, lawyer, legal educator; b. Pitts., June 23, 1952; s. Robert Harvey and Ana Jean (Constable) C.; m. Brett Elaine Copper, Oct. 15, 1983; 1 child, Benjamin Copper. BA, Brandeis U., 1974; JD, Washington U., St. Louis, 1977. Bar: Pa. 1977, U.S. Supreme Ct. 1981. Atty. Ampco-Pitts. Corp., Pitts., 1977-79; sole practice Pitts., 1979—; adj. prof. Community Coll. of Allegheny County, Pa., 1980—. Mem. ABA, Fed. Bar Assn. (chmn. labor arbitration com. 1983—), Allegheny County Bar Assn. (chmn. alt. dispute resolution com. 1986—, sec. labor law sect. 1985-87, vice chmn. 1987—), Am. Arbitration Assn., Soc. Profl. in Dispute Resolution, Soc. Fed. Labor Relations Profls., Nat. Acad. Arbitrators. Labor. Office: 1807 Jancey St Pittsburgh PA 15206-1065

CREPEAU, DEWEY LEE, lawyer; b. Richmond Heights, Mo., June 3, 1956; s. Dewey Lee and Floy Evelyn (Lacefield) Crapo m. Susan Jane Stonner, July 15, 1978; children—Elizabeth, Courtney. A.B., U. Mo., 1977, J.D., 1980. Bar: Mo. 1980, U.S. Dist. Ct. (we. dist.) Mo. 1980, U.S. Ct. Appeals (8th cir.) 1984. Assoc. William Johnson, P.C., Versailles, Mo. 1980-81; asst. prosecutor Morgan County, Mo., 1980; legal aid atty. Mid-Mo. Legal Services Corp., Columbia, 1982; sole practice, Columbia, 1982—; adj. prof. criminal justice Columbia Coll., 1983-84. Active Christian Fellowship of Columbia. Mem. Assn. Trial Lawyers Am., Mo. Bar Assn., Boone County Bar Assn., Mo. Assn. Trial Attys., Nat. Orgn. Social Security Claimants' Reps., Order Barristers. Workers' compensation, Social security disability, Personal injury. Home: 212 Bright Star Columbia MO 65203 Office: 1705 N Stadium Suite D Columbia MO 65202

CRESPI, MICHAEL ALBERT, lawyer; b. Bridgeport, Conn., Aug. 23, 1946; s. Albert Vincent and Patricia (Pope) C.; m. Dixie Dysart, Apr. 23, 1973. AB, Harvard U., 1968; JD, Samford U., 1973. Bar: Ala. 1973, U.S. Dist. Ct. (no. dist.) Ala. 1973, U.S. Tax Ct. 1973, U.S. Ct. Appeals (5th cir. 1973, U.S. Supreme Ct. 1976, U.S. Dist. Ct. (mid. dist.) Ala. 1977, Fla. 1983, U.S. Dist. Ct. (no. dist.) Fla. 1986. Sole practice Hoover, Ala., 1973-76, Headland, Ala., 1976—; mcpl. judge City of Headland, 1977-80, 85, City of Abbeville, Ala., 1977—. Sec. Henry County Reps., Ala., 1970-72; chmn. Henry County Exec. Com., 1976—; mem. Ala. State Re. Exec.Com., 1982-84. Mem. ABA, Ala. Bar Assn., Fla. Bar Assn., Henry County Bar Assn. (pres. 1980-84). Roman Catholic. Club: Meadowbrook (Headland) (sec. 1976-78). Avocations: photography, flying, sailing, salt-water fishing. Consumer commercial, Criminal, Personal injury. Home: Rt 1 Headland AL 36345 Office: PO Box 245 Headland AL 36345

CRESPO, MANUEL A., lawyer; b. Havana, Cuba, Oct. 2, 1945; came to U.S., 1952; s. Manuel M. and Esther (Morales) C.; m. Aracely Soto, June 22, 1968; children: Manuel L., Elizabeth Ann. BA, Fla. Atlantic U., 1971; JD, Memphis State U., 1975. Bar: Tenn. 1975, Fla. 1977, U.S. Dist. Ct. (so. dist.) Fla. 1978, U.S. Ct. Appeals (5th and 11th cirs.) 1981. Ptnr. Crespo & Lidsky, P.A., Coral Gables, Fla., 1977-79; sole practice Miami, Fla., 1979—; mem. 11th Jud. Nominating Commn., Miami, 1984—. Bd. dirs. Spanish Am. League Against Discrimination, Miami, 1984—; mem. Dade County Dem. Party, Miami, 1985—. Mem. Fla. Bar Assn., Tenn. Bar Assn., Cuban Am. Bar Assn. (pres. 1981-82, bd. dirs. 1986), Dade County Bar Assn., Dade County Trial Lawyers Assn. Lodge: Lions. Personal injury, Criminal. Home: 3916 SW 62nd Ave Miami FL 33155 Office: 780 NW LeJeune Rd #316 Miami FL 33126

CRESSMAN, PAUL RUSSELL, JR., lawyer; b. Seattle, Nov. 14, 1952; s. Paul Russell and Dorothy (Strailman) C.; m. Debra Diane Cooley, Apr. 1, 1978; children: Kyle Tracy, Kimberly Cooley. BBA magna cum laude, U. Wash., 1973, JD, 1976. Bar: Wash. 1976, U.S. Dist. Ct. (we. dist.) Wash. 1976, U.S. Ct. Appeals (9th cir.) 1977, U.S. Supreme Ct. 1980, U.S. Tax Ct. 1984. Assoc. Short & Cressman, Seattle, 1976-81, ptnr., 1982—. Bd. dirs. Silver Skis Chalet Condominium Assn., Crystal Mountain, Wash., 1983—. . Mem. ABA, Assn. Trial Lawyers Am., Wash. State Trial Lawyers Assn., Comml. Law League Am., Assoc. Builders and Contractors (legal rights and strategies com.), Assn. Gen. Contractors Am. (legal affairs com.), Order of the Coif. Club: Overlake Golf and Country (Bellevue, Wash.). Federal civil litigation, State civil litigation, Construction. Home: 12 Tulalip Key Bellevue WA 98006 Office: Short & Cressman First Interstate Ctr 30th Floor 999 3d Ave Seattle WA 98104

CREWE, TRENTON GUY, JR., lawyer; b. Portsmouth, Va., June 22, 1950; s. Trenton Guy Sr. and Celia Lois (Conner) C.; m. Linda JoAnn Grist, Aug. 20, 1970 (div. June 1975). BA, Marshall U., 1972; JD, Washington & Lee U., 1975. Bar: W.Va. 1975, Va. 1976. Assoc. Campbell, Young & Hodges, Wytheville, Va., 1975-78, ptnr., 1978-85; ptnr. Campbell, Young & Crewe, Wytheville, 1985—; substitute judge juvenile and domestic relations Gen. Dist. Ct., Va., 1983—. Mem. Town Council, Wytheville, 1983—; pres. Wytheville Baseball Club, 1985—. Mem. ABA, Va. Bar Assn., 27th Jud. Cir. (v.p. 1983-85, pres. 1985—), Wytheville Jaycees (internal v.p. 1979). Democrat. Presbyterian. Avocations: flying, jogging, fishing, hunting. Criminal, Personal injury, Real property. Home: 165 Meadowlark Dr Wytheville VA 24382 Office: Campbell Young & Crewe 210 W Main St PO Box 320 Wytheville VA 24382

CREWS, KENNETH DONALD, lawyer; b. Fairborn, Ohio, Feb. 14, 1955; s. Ralph Wilson and Betty Jo (Anderson) C.; m. Elizabeth Dellvera St. Clair, July 24, 1982; 1 child, Veronica St. Clair Crews. BA, Northwestern U., 1977; JD, Washington U., 1980; postgrad., UCLA, 1984—. Bar: Calif. 1980. Assoc. Booth, Mitchel, Strange & Smith, Los Angeles, 1980-82; sole practice

Los Angeles, 1982—; exec. dir., co-founder Los Angeles Venture Assn., 1984-85. Author: Edward S. Corwin and the American Constitution, 1985; editor Corwin's Constitution, 1986. Counsel Wesley Found. Serving UCLA, 1983—. Recipient Disting. Scholar award UCLA Alumni Assn., 1986. Mem. ABA, Calif. Bar Assn. (chmn. history of law com. 1985-86), Am. Library Assn., Am. Assn. Law Libraries, Assn. Library Info. Sci. Edn. Democrat. Methodist. Avocations: camping, hiking, bicycling, architecture. General corporate, Librarianship, Trademark and copyright. Home: 3315 Sepulveda Blvd #23 Los Angeles CA 90034

CRIDER, CHARLES JOSEPH, lawyer; b. New Iberia, La., Dec. 2, 1943; s. Robert and Sydalise (Broussard) C.; m. Sharon Maureen Hummer, July 19, 1969; children: Charles Joseph Jr., Meredith Anne. BEE, La. State U., 1967; JD, U. N.Mex., 1974. Bar: N.Mex., U.S. Dist. Ct. N.Mex., U.S. Ct. Appeals (10th cir.). Sole practice Albuquerque, 1975-79; ptnr. Matthews, Crider, Calvert & Bingham PC, Albuquerque, 1979—; bd. dirs. Fiberglass Fabricators, Inc., Albuquerque; 1986—. Served to capt. USAF, 1967-71. Mem. ABA, N.Mex. Bar Assn., Albuquerque Bar Assn. Republican. Avocation: skiing. Federal civil litigation, State civil litigation, General corporate. Office: Matthews Crider Calvert & Bingham 3908 Carlisle Albuquerque NM 87107

CRIGLER, B. WAUGH, magistrate; b. Charlottesville, Va., July 17, 1948; s. Bernard Weaver and Jayne (Waugh) C.; m. Anne Kendall, June 20, 1970; children: C. Kendall, Jason C., Anne Stuart. BA in History, Washington & Lee U., 1970; JD, U. Tenn., 1973. Bar: Tenn. 1973, U.S. Dist. Ct. (ea. dist.) Tenn. 1973, Va. 1974, D.C. 1974, U.S. Dist. Ct. (we. and ea. dists.) Va. 1975, U.S. Ct. Appeals (4th cir.) 1978. Law clk. to presiding judge U.S. Dist. Ct. Tenn., Knoxville, 1973-74; ptnr. Lea & Crigler, Culpeper, Va., 1974-75, Lea, Davies, Crigler & Barrell, Culpeper, 1975-79, Davies, Crigler, Barrell & Will, P.C., Culpeper, 1979-81; magistrate U.S. Dist. Ct., Charlottesville, 1981—; instr. trial practice U. Va. Sch. Law, 1986—. Mem. ABA (chmn. criminal law com. young lawyers div. 1979-80), Va. Bar Assn. (chmn. criminal law corrections young lawyers div. 1979-80), Tenn. Bar Assn., D.C. Bar Assn., Order of Coif, Phi Kappa Phi. Avocations: landscaping, swimming, antiquing. Personal injury, Federal civil litigation, State civil litigation. Office: US Magistrate 255 W Main St Room 328 Charlottesville VA 22901

CRIGLER, SUSAN GUM, lawyer; b. Springfield, Mo., Sept. 8, 1954; d. R.P. and Pauline (Gum) Crigler. B.A., NE Mo. State U., 1976; J.D., U. Mo.-Columbia, 1979. Bar: Mo. 1979, U.S. Dist. Ct. (we. dist.) Mo. 1979. Legis. intern Mo. Ho. of Reps., Jefferson City, 1975-76; legal intern State of Mo. Securities Div., 1978; asst. city counselor City of Columbia, 1979—. Bd. dirs. Mid-Mo. br. Gateway chpt. Multiple Sclerosis Soc. J.J. Pershing scholar N.E. Mo. State U., 1973-76; Law Sch. Found. scholar U. Mo.-Columbia, 1976-79. Mem. Mo. Bar Assn., Boone County Bar Assn., Columbia C. of C. (women's network), Columbia Bus. and Profl. Women's Club. Democrat. Methodist. Local government, Condemnation, Government contracts and claims. Office: City of Columbia Law Dept 701 E Broadway Columbia MO 65201

CRIM, JOSEPH CALVIN, lawyer; b. Winfield, W.Va., Nov. 7, 1926; s. Floyd Dewitt and Stella (Sparks) C.; m. Ann Cook, July 26, 1965; children: Kim E., Joseph F., John C. BS, W.Va. U., 1947, LLB, 1950. Bar: W.Va. 1950. Supt. Columbia Gas Transmission Corp., Charleston, W.Va., 1959-67; supt. land Columbia Gas Transmission Corp., Charleston, 1967-73, dir. land, 1973-80, sr. atty., 1984—; v.p. Appalachian Co., Worthington, Ohio, 1980-84. Served to 1st lt. U.S. Army, 1943-46, 51-53, 61-62, PTO, ETO, with Res., ret. Mem. W.Va. Bar Assn., Eastern Mineral Law Found., Am. Assn. Petroleum Landmen. Oil and gas leasing, Contracts commercial, Real property. Home: 1504 Virginia St E Charleston WV 25311 Office: Columbia Gas Transmission Corp 1700 MacCorkle Ave SE Charleston WV 25314

CRIMMINS, EILEEN MARIE, lawyer; b. N.Y.C., Apr. 22, 1943; d. Michael John and Susan Teresa (Shannon) C. BA, Coll. New Rochelle, 1965; MS, Columbia U., 1967; JD, Fordham U., 1971; LLM in Labor Law, NYU, 1977. Bar: N.Y. 1972, U.S. Dist. Ct.(so. and ea. dists.) N.Y. 1975, Conn. 1979. Assoc. Parker, Chapin & Flattau, N.Y.C., 1971-74; atty., asst. counsel Otis Elevator Co., N.Y.C. and Farmington, Conn., 1974-84; dep. counsel Hamilton Standard div., United Tech. Corp., Windsor Locks, Conn., 1984—; seminar leader Profl. Seminar Assocs., Westfield N.J., 1975, 77-78. Dir., sec. Talcott Glen Assn., Inc., Farmington, Conn., 1981—. Regents scholar N.Y. State Regents Bd., N.Y.C. 1961-65. Mem. ABA. General corporate, Government contracts and claims, Personal injury. Office: United Tech Corp Hamilton Standard Div Bradley Field Rd Windsor Locks CT 06096

CRISPO, LAWRENCE WALTER, lawyer; b. N.Y.C., Mar. 23, 1934; s. Charles A. and Elda Beatrice (D'Orazi) C.; m. Wilhelmina Moore, June 11, 1955; children: Susan, Patricia, Christopher, Therese, Marianne, Thomas. B.S. in Polit. Sci., Loyola U., Los Angeles, 1956, J.D., 1961. Bar: Calif. 1961, U.S. Supreme Ct. 1970. Pros. atty. City of Los Angeles, 1961-62; partner firm Breidenbach, Swainston, Crispo & Way, Los Angeles, 1967—; judge pro tem Los Angeles-Alhambra Mcpl. Ct., 1966—; lectr., mem. faculty U. So. Calif. Law Ctr., Calif. Continuing Edn. of Bar, Calif. Inst. Trial Advocacy, 1978, 79, 80, 82, 83, 86; mem. bench and bar council Los Angeles Superior Ct., 1976-85; civil service commr. City of San Gabriel, Calif., 1974—; pres. bd. govs. Loyola U. Law Sch., 1980-81, sec. bd. govs. student bar, 1958-59; speaker on juvenile delinquency, 1961—. Profl. chmn. United Crusade, Alhambra, 1967; mem. solicitation fund Los Angeles YMCA, 1969; precinct chmn. San Gabriel Republican Com., 1968, 70, 72, 74; alt. del. Rep. County Central Com., 1973-76; past pres. Archdiocesan Holy Name Union. Mem. Am. Judicature Soc., Am. Bd. Trial Advocates (exec. com. 1974-77, 81—), Am. Arbitration Assn. (arbitrator 1966—), Los Angeles County Bar Assn. (chmn. jud. com. 1977-78, mem. law office mgmt. exec. com. 1979-82, exec. com. trial lawyers sect. 1984—), Wilshire Bar Assn. (pres. 1980-81), State Bar Calif. (ethical practices examiner 1971-72, chmn. adminstrv. com. 1972-76, vice chmn. ct. rules and procedures com. 1980-81, mem. Commn. on Jud. Nominee Evaluation 1982-83, exec. com. litigation sect. 1985), San Gabriel C. of C. (dir. 1975—, pres. 1979-80). Clubs: Elks (past state v.p., past dist. dep.), K.C. (past grand knight). Address: 611 W 6th St Suite 1300 Los Angeles CA 90017

CRIST, PAUL GRANT, lawyer; b. Denver, Sept. 9, 1949; s. Max Warren and Marjorie Raymond (Catland) C.; m. Christine Faye Clements, June 4, 1972; children—Susan, Benjamin, John. B.A., U. Nebr.-Lincoln, 1971; J.D. summa cum laude, NYU, 1974; cert. of completion Nat. Inst. Trial Advocacy, Boulder, 1982. Bar: Ohio 1974, U.S. Ct. Mil. Appeals 1975, Calif. 1976, U.S. Dist. Ct. (no. dist.) Ohio 1979, U.S. Ct. Appeals (6th cir.) 1982. Assoc. Jones Day Reavis & Pogue, Cleve., 1974, ptnr., 1984—. Research editor NYU Law Rev., 1972-74. Served as capt. JAGC, USAF, 1974-78. Decorated Meritorious Service medal. Mem. ABA, Cleve. Bar Assn. Democrat. Methodist. Federal civil litigation, State civil litigation. Home: 2265 Chatfield Cleveland Heights OH 44106 Office: Jones Day Reavis & Pogue 1700 Huntington Bldg Cleveland OH 44115

CRITCHLOW, CHARLES HOWARD, lawyer; b. Morristown, NJ, Nov. 23, 1950; s. George F. and Florence Critchlow; m. Mary Ellen Donnelly; children: Katharine F, Mary E.G. BA, Yale U., 1972; JD, Columbia U., 1975. Bar: N.Y. 1976, U.S. Dist. Ct. (so. and ea. dists.) N.Y. 1976, U.S. Ct. Appeals (2d cir.) 1982. Assoc. Lord, Day & Lord, N.Y.C., 1975-85, ptnr., 1985-86; ptnr. Coudert Bros., N.Y.C., 1986—. Mem. ABA. Antitrust, Federal civil litigation, Private international. Office: Coudert Bros 200 Park Ave New York NY 10166

CRITELLI, LYLEA MAY DODSON, lawyer; b. Ottawa, Ill., May 12, 1956; d. Lyle F. and Dorothy M. (Bray) D.; m. Nicholas Critelli, May 27, 1984. BA, Ill. Wesleyan U., 1978; JD, Drake U., 1981. Bar: Iowa 1981, U.S. Dist. Ct. (no. and so. dists.) Iowa 1981, U.S. Ct. Appeals (8th cir.) 1981, U.S. Supreme Ct. 1985. Sole practice Des Moines, 1981-85; assoc. Dreher, Wilson, Simpson, Jensen & Adams, Des Moines, 1985-87, Law Offices of Nick Critelli & Assocs., Des Moines, 1987—; treas. Iowa Legal Services Corp., Des Moines, 1985, bd. dirs. Co-coach mock trial team Lincoln High Sch., Des Moines, 1983—. Mem. ABA (mem. exec. council young lawyers div., dist. 19 rep.), Iowa Bar Assn. (exec. council young lawyers sect. 1983—, sec. 1987—, co-chmn. seminar 1984-86), Polk County Bar Assn., Assn. Trial Lawyers Am. State civil litigation, Criminal, Family and matrimonial. Office: 317 Sixth Ave #500 Des Moines IA 50309

CRITES, D. MICHAEL, lawyer. U.S. atty. so. dist. State of Ohio, Cin. Office: 220 USPO & Courthouse 5th & Walnut Streets Cincinnati OH 45202 *

CRITES, RICHARD DON, lawyer; b. Ft. Worth, Sept. 3, 1943; s. Ewell Barnett Crites and Frances Loretta (Prichard) Castro; m. Annabel Lee Sheilds, June 17, 1964 (div. 1975); children—Amy Lee, Jonathon Peter; m. Judith Jean Gildig, May 30, 1976; children—Kimberly Ann, Kevin John. B.S., Ariz. State U., 1965; J.D., U. Ariz., 1968. Bar: Ariz. Assoc., Knez & Glatz, Tucson, 1968-73; ptnr. Knez, Glatz & Crites, Tucson, 1973-78; chief counsel City Utilities, Springfield, Mo., 1978-79; sole practice, Springfield, 1979—; referee Pima County Juvenile Ct., Tucson, 1972-76. Contbr. articles to law revs. Recipient Excellence in Ins. Law award Bancroft-Whitney Co., 1967, Excellence in Criminal Law award, 1968. Mem. Greene County Bar Assn., Mo. Bar Assn., ABA. Republican. Presbyterian. Lodges: Elks, Shriners, Optomists, Royal Order of Jesters. Personal injury, Workers' compensation, Family and matrimonial. Home: 2268 Thompson Pl Springfield MO 65804 Office: 4139 S Fremont Springfield MO 65807

CROAK, FRANCIS R., lawyer; b. Janesville, Wis., Feb. 19, 1929; s. Francis Joseph and Virginia (Blakey) C.; m. Susan Nolte, Aug. 15, 1953; m. 2d, Judith Torbenson, Apr. 30, 1976; children—Carolyn, Martha, Daniel. B.S., U. Wis., 1950, J.D., 1953. Bar: Wis. 1953, U.S. Ct. Appeals (7th cir.) 1960, U.S. Supreme Ct. 1980. First asst. dist. atty. Milwaukee County, Wis., 1956-69; ptnr. Cook & Franke S.C., Milw., 1960—; lectr. in law Marquette U., 1972-74, U. Wis., 1973-78. Mem. Wis. Jud. Council, 1971-82. Served to lt. U.S. Army, 1953-56; to col. USAR, 1956-80. Fellow Am. Coll. Trial Lawyers; mem. Am. Law Inst. Democrat. Clubs: Milwaukee Athletic, Westmoor Country. Federal civil litigation, Environment, Federal civil litigation. Home: 12555 W Grove Terr Elm Grove WI 53122 Office: 660 E Mason St Milwaukee WI 53202

CROCKER, MICHAEL PUE, lawyer; b. Bel Air, Md., July 23, 1918; s. Henry Trew and Berthenia Stansbury (Pue) C.; m. Rosa Tucker Fletcher, June 11, 1945; children—Forest Fletcher, Berthenia Stansbury, Rosa Tucker. B.A. cum laude, Washington and Lee U., 1940; LL.B., U. Va., 1947. Bar: Md. 1947, U.S. Dist. Ct. Md. 1948, U.S. Ct. Appeals (4th cir.) 1951, U.S. Supreme Ct. 1967, D.C. 1982. Assoc. Marbury, Miller & Evans, Balt., 1947-55; ptnr. Piper & Marbury, Balt., 1955-83; sole practice, Bel Air, Md., 1983—. Trustee, Md. Children's Aid and Family Service Soc., 1967-77. Served with USMC, 1942-45, PTO; to maj. USMCR, 1942-57. Decorated Purple Heart. Mem. Maritime Law Assn. U.S., Jud. Conf. U.S., (4th Jud. Circuit), Internat. Bar Assn., Balt. City Bar Assn., Md. State Bar Assn., Harford County Bar Assn., ABA, Am. Judicature Soc., Internat. Assn. Ins. Counsel, Assn. Trial Lawyers Am., Phi Beta Kappa, Phi Delta Phi. Episcopalian. Club: Merchants (Balt.). Federal civil litigation, Condemnation, Insurance. Home and Office: 1326 Somerville Rd Bel Air MD 21014

CROCKETT, DAVID GIDEON, lawyer; b. Columbus, Ga., Sept. 29, 1943; s. G.P. and Mable (Brookins) C.; m. Amelia Ann Rood, Apr. 7, 1985; children: Elizabeth Ann, Carolyn Rood, David Gideon Jr. BA in History, Yale U., 1966; JD, NYU, 1969. Bar: U.S. Dist Ct. (no., mid. and so. dists.) Ga. 1969, U.S. Ct. Appeals (5th cir.) 1970, U.S. Ct. Appeals (11th cir.), U.S. Supreme Ct. 1977. Assoc. counsel Atlanta Legal Aid Soc., 1969-72; assoc. Nall, Miller & Cadenhead, Atlanta, 1973-77; sole practice Atlanta, 1978—. Contbr. articles to profl. jours. Bd. dirs. Southside Day Care Assn., Atlanta, 1970-84; pres. Neighborhood Justice Ctr. Atlanta, Inc., 1977—; mem. Northwest Presbyn. Ch., Atlanta, 1981, elder, 1987—. Recipient Community Service award WXIA-TV, 1981, Nat. Jefferson award Am. Inst. Pub. Service, 1981. Mem. Ga. Bar Assn., Atlanta Bar Assn. (chmn. indigent program com. 1975-78, 100% membership award 1977—, chmn. spl. projects com. 1986-87), Am. Judicature Soc., Comml. Law League Am., Atlanta Lawyer's Club (election and rules com.). Democrat. Clubs: Atlanta City, Ansley Golf. Bankruptcy, Federal civil litigation, State civil litigation. Home: 422 Blanton Rd NW Atlanta GA 30324 Office: 134 Peachtree St Suite 1000 Atlanta GA 30303

CROCKETT, RICHARD BOYD, lawyer; b. Albuquerque, Aug. 5, 1944; s. Richard Colwell and Janice Adair (Nelson) C.; m. Susan Joan Anderson, Aug. 13, 1966; children: Eric Douglas, Seth David. BA, U. N.D., 1966; JD, Stanford U., 1969. Bar: Calif. 1970, U.S. Dist. Ct. N.D. 1970, N.D. 1972, U.S. Supreme Ct. 1980, U.S. Ct. Appeals (8th cir.) 1986. Cons. legal research N.D. Water Resources Research Inst., Fargo, 1969-72; asst. provost Tri-Coll. U., Fargo, 1972-75; atty. N.D. State U., Fargo, 1969—; ptnr. Crockett & Anderson, Fargo, 1980—. Editor: Guide to Outlines of the National Association of College and University Attorneys, 1986. Chmn., mem. N.D. State Water Pollution Control Bd., Fargo, 1971-77, Cultural Environ. Commn., Fargo, 1975-83; treas., bd. dirs. Tri-Coll. U., 1975—; pres., bd. dirs. Plains Art Mus., Moorhead, Minn., 1973-83; bd. dirs. Fargo-Moorhead Area Found., Fargo, 1986. Mem. ABA, N.D. Bar Assn., Calif. Bar Assn., Cass County Bar Assn., Nat. Assn. Coll. and Univ. Attys. (bd. dirs. 1981-84, 85-86), Phi Beta Kappa. Republican. Presbyterian. Club: Fargo Country. Lodges: Kiwanis, Elks. Real property, Estate planning, Higher education law. Home: 1422 6th St S Fargo ND 58103 Office: Crockett & Anderson 112 Roberts St Fed Sq Suite 300 Fargo ND 58102

CROESSMANN, PHILIP RICHARD, lawyer; b. Buffalo, May 3, 1953; s. Robert William Croessmann and Dewella Jane (Groat) Dobson. BArch, U. Oreg., 1976; JD, Syracuse U., 1980. Bar: N.Y. 1980, D.C. 1981, U.S. Dist. Ct. D.C.; registered architect, Md. Archtl. apprentice Andrew U. Donnelly & Assoc., Bethesda, Md., 1980-82; lobbyist AIA, Washington, 1982-83, dep. gen. counsel, 1983-84; ptnr. Croessmann & Lawrence, Washington, 1984-85; sole practice Washington, 1986—; v.p., bd. dirs. Britten Banners, Washington, 1986—; bd. dirs. Cagley, Riva & Braaksma, Miami, Fla., Wedgco Engrng., Gaithersburg, Md. Author: Recordkeeping Guide for Design Firms, 1985. Recipient Design award Nat. Masonry Inst., 1980, Drafting award AIA Potomac Valley chpt., 1982. Mem. ABA, AIA. Construction. Office: 1921 Sunderland Pl NW Washington DC 20036

CROFT, JOHN W., oil company executive, lawyer; b. Jacksonville, Tex., Nov. 15, 1935; s. John E. and Alty (Durrett) C.; m. Kathryn J. Garlock, Sept. 15, 1962; children—Karen Eileen, John Michael, Allison Lynn. A.A., Lon Morris Coll., Jacksonville, 1955; B.B.A., U. Tex.-Austin, 1957, J.D., 1959. Bar: Tex. 1959, N.Y. 1980. Assoc., Norman Rounsaville & Hassell, Rusk, Tex., 1959; mem. law dept. Exxon Co. and affiliates, 1962-69, 71—, asst. to pres. Exxon Co. U.S.A., 1969-71, gen. counsel Exxon Research & Engng. Co., 1982—; former dir. InteCom, Inc., Dallas. Trustee, Lon Morris Coll., 1975—; v.p., dir., exec. com. Houston Symphony Soc., 1972-76; mem. N.Y. ann. conf. United Methodist Ch., 1980, 81. Served to capt. JAGC, U.S. Army, 1959-62. Decorated Army Commendation Medal. Recipient Disting. Alumnus award Lon Morris Coll., 1972; John and Kay Croft Physics Lab. of Lon Morris Coll. named in his honor, 1981. Life fellow Tex. Bar Found.; mem. Tex. Bar Assn., ABA, Assn. Bar City N.Y., Phi Theta Kappa, Beta Gamma Sigma. Clubs: Meml. Drive Country (Houston); Cherokee Country (Jacksonville). General corporate, Antitrust, Oil and gas leasing. Address: PO Box 390 180 Park Ave Florham Pk NJ 07932

CROFTS, MICHAEL LYNN, lawyer; b. Idaho Falls, Idaho, May 21, 1954; s. William Edward Crofts and Gladys (Barnes) Wilkins; m. Anne Louise Woerner, Sept. 27, 1975; children: Kelli, Brett, Travis. BA, U. Idaho, 1977; JD, Gonzaga U., 1980. Bar: Wash. 1980, U.S. Dist. Ct. (ea. dist.) Wash. 1980. Assoc. Underwood & Campbell, Spokane, Wash., 1980-84, ptnr., 1984-85; corp. atty. ISC Systems Corp., Spokane, 1986—. Bd. dirs. Cannon Hill Boys Home, Spokane, 1983—. Mem. Wash. State Bar Assn., Spokane County Bar Assn., Wash. State Jaycees (legal counsel 1984-85), South Spokane Jaycees (pres. 1985-86). General corporate, Contracts commercial, Computer. Home: S 1220 Stevens Spokane WA 99204 Office: ISC Systems Corp PO Box Taf-C8 Spokane WA 99220

CROMLEY, JON LOWELL, lawyer; b. Riverton, Ill., May 23, 1934; s. John Donald and Naomi M. (Mathews) C.; B.S., U. Ill., 1958; J.D., John Marshall Law Sch., 1966. Real estate title examiner Chgo. Title & Trust Co., 1966-70; admitted to Ill. bar, 1966; practiced in Genoa, Ill., 1970—; mem. firm O'Grady & Cromley, Genoa, 1970—; dir. Genoa State Bank, Kingston Mut. County Fire Ins. Co. Bd. dirs. Genoa Day Care Center, Inc. Mem. Am. Judicature Soc., Am., Ill., Chgo., DeKalb County bar assns. Probate, Real property, General practice. Home: 130 Homewood Dr Genoa IL 60135 Office: 213 W Main St Genoa IL 60135

CROMPTON, CHARLES SENTMAN, JR., lawyer; b. Wilmington, Del., Dec. 30, 1936; s. Charles S. and R. Eugenia (Armstrong) C.; m. Jean W. Ashe, June 15, 1958 (div. Sept. 1976); children: Rebecca Ashe, Charles S. III; m. Milbrey Warner Dean, May 21, 1977. BA, U. Del., 1958; LLB, U. Va., 1961. Bar: Del. 1962. Law clk. to presiding justice U.S. Dist. Ct. Del., Wilmington, 1961-62; ptnr. Potter, Anderson & Corroon, Wilmington, 1962—; bd. dirs. Wilmington Trust Co. Mem. ABA, Del. Bar Assn. (treas. 1968-72, pres. 1985-86), Am. Coll. Trial Lawyers (state chmn. 1986—), Del. Hist. Soc. (pres. 1983-84), Raven Soc., Phi Beta Kappa. Clubs: Wilmington; Vicmead Hunt (Greenville, Del). General corporate, Federal civil litigation, State civil litigation. Office: Potter Anderson & Coroon PO Box 951 Wilmington DE 19899 Home: Campbell Rd Box 3946 Greenville DE 19806

CRON, JENNIFER LYNNE, lawyer; b. N.Y.C., July 27, 1956; d. Charles Michael and Dolores (Rafael) C. BSBA in Acctg. with honors, U. Fla., 1977, JD with honors, 1980, LLM in Taxation, 1981. Bar: Fla. 1980. Assoc. Osborne & Hankins, Boca Raton, Fla., 1981-82; Raymond & Dillon, West Palm Beach, Fla., 1982-84, Smathers & Thompson, Miami, Fla., 1984—. Producer (TV Show) Something for Seniors, 1986. Mem. Fla. Bar Assn. (young lawyers sect.), Dade County Bar Assn. (probate and guardianship com., law week com., bd. dirs. young lawyers sect., chairperson community relations com.). Avocations: swimming, bicycling, photography. Probate, Estate taxation. Office: Smathers & Thompson 1301 AI DuPont Bldg Miami FL 33131

CRONAN, JOHN MICHAEL, lawyer; b. Columbia, Mo., Feb. 20, 1949; s. Patsy Daniel and Jean Wilma (Dearing) C.; m. Kathleen Bernard Manos, Dec. 20, 1970; children: Carolyn Bernard, John Kyle. BA, Westminster Coll., 1971; JD, U. Mo., 1974. Bar: Mo. 1974, U.S. Dist. Ct. (we. dist.) Mo. 1974, U.S. Ct. Appeals (8th cir.) 1980. Assoc. Jackson & Sherman, Kansas City, Mo., 1974-79, ptnr., 1979-81; ptnr. Cronan & Messick, Kansas City, 1981—; part-time faculty mem. Avila Coll., Kansas City, 1986. Mem. ABA (v.p. products gen. liability and consumer law com., torts and ins. practice sect.), Mo. Bar Assn. Democrat. Methodist. Personal injury, Federal civil litigation, State civil litigation. Home: 510 W 123d St Kansas City MO 64145 Office: Cronan & Messick 9200 Ward Pkwy Suite 675 Kansas City MO 64114

CRONAN, KATHLEEN MICHELE, lawyer; b. Denver, Oct. 23, 1953; d. John Forrest and Kathleen Elizabeth (Wade) C.; m. John T. Van Voorhis, May 24, 1980; 1 child, Michael Sean. BA, U. Colo., 1975; JD, U. Denver, 1978. Bar: Colo. 1978, U.S. Dist. Ct. Colo. 1978, U.S. Ct. Appeals (10th cir.) 1985. Ptnr. Ott, Kirkwood & Cronan, Denver, 1982-84; sole practice Denver, 1978-82, 84—. Active St. Michael's Social Justice Com., Aurora, Colo., 1982—, chmn. 1985-86; Committeeperson Arapahoe County Dem. Party, 1982—, sec. house dist. 49, 1985—. Mem. Colo. Bar Assn., Denver Bar Assn., Am. Trial Lawyers Assn., Colo. Trial Lawyers Assn. Roman Catholic. Probate, General practice, Family and matrimonial. Office: 1155 Sherman St Suite 213 Denver CO 80203

CRONER, FRED B., JR., lawyer; b. Indianapolis, Feb. 20, 1929; s. Fred B. and Helen L. (Hubbard) C.; m. Alice Joan Pishan, Nov. 16, 1957; children—Cynthia Lynn, Cathleen Ann. B.S., Butler U., 1952; J.D., Ind. U.-Indpls., 1955. Bar: Ind. 1955. Dep. atty. gen. State Ind., 1958-60; asst. atty. gen. State Ind., 1960-62; atty. Pub. Service Co. Ind., Inc., Plainfield, 1962-63; atty. Eli Lilly and Co., Indpls., 1963-69, sr. counsel, 1969-75, asst. sec., sr. counsel, 1975—. Served with U.S. Army, 1955-57. Mem. ABA, Ind. State Bar Assn. General corporate. Home: 6455 Cornwall Circle Indianapolis IN 46256 Office: Lilly Corp Ctr Indianapolis IN 46285

CRONIG, STEVEN CARLYLE, lawyer; b. New Bedford, Mass., Feb. 5, 1955; s. Carlyle Stevens and E. Phyllis (Kramer) C. BA, U. Vt., 1977; JD, U. Miami, 1980; LLM in Taxation, Boston U., 1983. Bar: Fla. 1980, U.S. Dist. Ct. (so. dist.) Fla. 1980, U.S. Ct. Appeals (11th cir.) 1980, Mass. 1981. Assoc. Pallot, Poppell et al, Miami, Fla., 1980-82, Holland & Knight, Miami, 1983-84; ptnr. Cronig & Dillard, Miami Shores, Fla., 1984—. Mem. ABA, Dade County Bar Assn., Boston Bar Assn., Phi Delta Phi, Alpha Tau Omega. Democrat. Real property, General corporate, Banking. Office: Cronig & Dillard 9999 NE 2d Ave Suite 311 Miami Shores FL 33138

CRONMILLER, THOMAS BERNARD, lawyer; b. Rochester, N.Y., Feb. 21, 1956; s. Michael J. and Hazel C. (Evans) C. BA, SUNY, Geneseo, 1978; JD, Franklin Pierce Coll., 1981. Bar: N.H. 1981, U.S. Dist. Ct. N.H. 1981. Energy coordinator Gov. Council on Energy, Concord, N.H., 1981-83; assoc. Sulloway, Hollis & Soden, Concord, 1984—. Mem. ABA, Granite State Hydro Power Assn. Democrat. Roman Catholic. Avocations: golf, tennis. FERC practice, Administrative and regulatory, General corporate. Office: Sulloway Hollis & Soden 9 Capitol St Concord NH 03301

CROOK, CHARLES DAVID, lawyer; b. Paris, Tex., Dec. 13, 1950; s. Robert Ney and Mary Kathryne (McEwin) C.; m. Rebecca Martin, Dec. 29, 1973. BA, U. Tex., Austin, 1972; JD with honors, U. Tex., 1978. Bar: Tex. 1978, U.S. Dist. Ct. (so. dist.) Tex. 1980. Social worker Tex. Dept. of Welfare, San Antonio, 1974-75; assoc. Atlas & Hall, McAllen, Tex., 1978-83; ptnr. Arnold, Crook & Assocs., Austin, 1983—. Mem. Tex. Bar Assn., Travis County Bar Assn. (continuing legal edn. com.). Lodge: Rotary. Avocations: politics, photography, movies, gardening, woodworking. Probate, Real property, Contracts commercial. Office: Arnold Crook & Assocs 406 Sterzing St Austin TX 78704-1027

CROOK, CHARLES SAMUEL, III, lawyer; b. Des Moines, Iowa, Oct. 24, 1944; s. Charles S. Jr. and Gertrude A. (Nichols) C.; children—Donald, Michael, Brian, Nicole. B.A., Drake U., 1969, J.D., 1971. Bar: Iowa 1971. Law clk. to chief dist. judge U.S. Dist. Ct. (so. dist.) Iowa, 1971-73; pros. atty. Polk County Atty.'s Office, Des Moines, 1973-76; ptnr. Beving, Swanson & Forrest, P.C., Des Moines, 1976-83; sole practice, 1983—; lectr. Des Moines Area Community Coll., 1979, U. Osteo. Health Scis. Leader Cub Scouts Am., Des Moines. Served with U.S. Army, 1963-66. Mem. ABA, Iowa Bar Assn., Nat. Dist. Atty's. Assn., Polk County Bar Assn., Nat. Bd. Trial Advocacy (cert.). Democrat. Roman Catholic. Contbr. articles to profl. jours. State civil litigation, Federal civil litigation, Personal injury. Home: PO Box 721 Des Moines IA 50303 Office: Suite 1100 Fleming Bldg 218 6th Ave Des Moines IA 50309

CROOK, E(DWARD) CARTER, JR., lawyer, law educator; b. Washington, Mar. 30, 1947; s. Edward C. Crook and Barbara (Baker) Washington; m. Jan C. Crook, May 14, 1977. BA, Trinity U., 1969; MBA, So. Meth. U., 1973; JD, St. Mary's U., 1978; LLM, Georgetown U., 1979. Bar: Tex., U.S. Tax Ct. Mng. dir. I.C.H., Dallas and Hong Kong, 1973-75; atty. Cantey Hanger, Ft. Worth, Tex., 1980-82; assoc. Bailey & Williams, Dallas, 1983—; adj. prof. U. Tex., Arlington, 1983—. Mem. adv. bd. C.A.U.S., Dallas, 1984—, Parent Love, Dallas, 1984—, Parents Without Ptnrs., Dallas, 1986—; mem. San Antonio Estate Planning Council, MidCities Estate Planning Council, pres. 1987—; mem. Dallas Estate Planners Council, Dallas Bd. Dirs.; vol. United Way, Dallas-Ft. Worth, 1980—. Served to cpt. U.S. Army, 1969-71. Fellow Southwestern Legal Found.; mem. ABA, Dallas Bar Assn., Summervell County Bar Assn. (treas. 1986—), State Bar Tex. Republican. Episcopalian. Clubs: Calyx (treas 1972-73), Pinnacle (Dallas); Ft. Worth, Dalworth Investment (Dallas-Ft. Worth) (v.p. 1986—). Avocations: hist. socs., geneaology, fishing, travel, photography. Probate, General corporate, Real property. Office: Bailey & Williams 3500 InterFirst Plaza Dallas TX 75202

CROOK, ROBERT LACEY, lawyer; b. Bolton, Miss., Apr. 22, 1929; s. Walter Barber and Louise (Lacey) C.; m. Brigita Nerings, Sept. 20, 1953; children—Robert Lacey II, Hubert William. Student, Delta State U., 1948-50, U. Miss., 1951-52; J.D., Jackson Sch. Law, 1965. Bar: Miss. 1965, U.S. Dist. Ct. (no. and so. dists.) Miss. 1965, U.S. Supreme Ct. 1973. Sole prac-

tice, Ruleville, Miss., 1965—; atty. City of Ruleville, 1973—, City of Moorhead, Miss., 1977—; atty. Miss. Agrl. Aviation Assn., Clarksdale, 1971—, North Sunflower County Hosp., Ruleville. Mem. Miss. Senate, 1964—, sr. mem. senate judiciary com., chmn. subcom. on regulation and licensing. Served to cpl. USMC, 1946-47. Recipient Elected Ofcl. of Yr. award Miss. chpt. Am. Soc. Pub. Administrn., 1981. Fellow Miss. Bar Found.; mem. Miss. Bar Assn. (past mem. worker's compensation com.), Pi Alpha Alpha. Democrat. Episcopalian. General practice, Legislative, Local government. Home: 125 N Ruby St Ruleville MS 38771 Office: 500 N Division St Box 85 Ruleville MS 38771

CROOKHAM, CHARLES SEWELL, judge; b. Portland, Oreg., Mar. 17, 1923; s. Kenneth Robert and Helen Alberta (Dauber) C.; m. Elizabeth Pruden Kelley, Dec. 19, 1950; children: Kelley Fitzcharles, Berkeley Fitzcharles, Whitney Fitzcharles. Student, Oreg. State U., 1941-43, Loyola U., Los Angeles, 1943-44; BA, Stanford U., 1948; JD, Lewis & Clark Coll., 1951. Bar: Oreg. 1952, U.S. Dist. Ct. Oreg. 1952, U.S. Ct. Mil. Appeals 1975, U.S. Supreme Ct. 1980. Atty. Vergeer & Samuels, Portland, 1952-62; judge Cir. Ct. Oreg., Portland, 1963—; presiding judge 4th Dist. Cir. Ct., Portland, 1978—; dir. Nat. Conf. Met. Judges, 1985—. Author and editor: Procedure and Practice, 1964, 69, Insurance, 1967, Evidence, 1970, 86. Served to sgt. U.S. Army, 1943-46, col. Res. Decorated Bronze Star. Mem. Oreg. Bar Assn., Multnomah Bar Assn. Republican. Presbyterian. Club: Multnomah Athletic. Avocation: military history. Jurisprudence, Judicial administration, Military. Home: 3565 SW Council Crest Dr Portland OR 97201 Office: Cir Ct Courthouse 1021 SW 4th Ave Room 206 Portland OR 97204

CROOM, SAM GASTON, JR., lawyer; b. Houston, Mar. 25, 1930; s. Sam Gaston and Lola Mae (Whorton) C.; m. Earlane Baccus, Nov. 28, 1952; children—Curtis B., Carolyn Croom Beatty. B.B.A., U. Tex.-Austin, 1952, LL.B., 1957. Bar: Tex. 1957. Ptnr. law firm Baker & Botts, Houston, 1957—. Served to lt. USNR, 1952-54. Mem. Southwest Pension Conf., Am. Automobile Assn. (mem. adv. bd. dirs., chmn.). Republican. Presbyterian. Clubs: Houston Racquet (past dir.), Athletic of Houston. Pension, profit-sharing, and employee benefits. Home: 511 Hunters Park Ln Houston TX 77024 Office: Baker & Botts 3000 One Shell Plaza Houston TX 77002

CROPPER, STEPHEN WALLACE, lawyer; b. Huntingdon Park, Calif., Dec. 27, 1947; s. Wayne and Bernice Irene (Shively) C.; m. Kathleen Elizabeth Schaaf, Sept. 8, 1979; children: Amanda, Evan. BA, Haverford Coll., 1969; JD, Cornell U., 1972. Bar: N.Y. 1973. Assoc. Jackson and Nash, N.Y.C., 1972-78; assoc. counsel, asst. sec. Gulf and Western, Inc., N.Y.C., 1978—. Mem. ABA, Am. Soc. Corp. Secs., Assn. of Bar of the City of N.Y., Am. Corp. Counsel Assn. General corporate, Securities, Contracts commercial. Office: Gulf and Western Inc One gulf and Western Plaza New York NY 10023

CROSBY, PHILIP, lawyer; b. Strawn, Tex., Oct. 23, 1922; s. James Thomas and Ruth (Holmes) C.; m. Bobby Ruth Hamilton, June 9, 1944; children: John Hamilton, James Philip. BS, U.S. Naval Acad., 1944; MS, Lowell Textile Inst., 1950; JD, So. Meth. U., 1982. Bar: Tex. 1982, U.S. Dist. Ct. (no. dist.) Tex. 1982. Commd. ensign USN, 1944, advanced through grades to rear adm., 1970, ret., 1978; assoc. Murrell & Freeman, Dallas, 1982—. Fellow Soc. Logistics Engrs.; mem. Nat. Security Indsl. Assn. (life hon.). General practice, Family and matrimonial, Probate. Office: Murrell & Freeman 2121 San Jacinto St. 1030 San Jacinto Tower LB60 Dallas TX 75201

CROSBY, ROBERT BERKEY, lawyer; b. North Platte, Nebr., Mar. 26, 1911; s. Mainard E. and Cora M. (Berkey) C.; m. Elizabeth D. Ehler, Nov. 29, 1934; children—Robert M., Susan M. Smith, Mary Bolin, Michael, James Timothy, Frederick; m. 2d, LaVon K. Kehoe Stuart, May 22, 1971. B.A., U. Minn., 1931; LL.B., Harvard U., 1935. Bar: Nebr. 1935, U.S. Dist. Ct. Nebr. 1935, U.S. Ct. Appeals (8th cir.) 1970, U.S. Supreme Ct. 1970. Ptnr. Henry J. Beal, Omaha, 1936; ptnr. Crosby & Baskins, North Platte, Nebr., 1937-47, Crosby & Crosby, North Platte, 1948-54; sr. ptnr. Crosby, Guenzel, Davis, Kessner & Kuester, Lincoln, Nebr., 1955—; bd. dirs. Gulf & Freat Plains Legal Found. speaker State of Nebr. Legislature, 1943; lt. gov. State of Nebr., 1947-49, gov., 1953-55. Acting state chmn. Nebr. Republican Com., 1948, chmn. fin. com., 1972-73; chmn. bd. dirs. Nebr. Heart Assn., 1958-59. Served to lt. USNR, 1944-46. Mem. Am. Coll. Trial Lawyers, Internat. Soc. Barristers, Fedn. Ins. Counsel, ABA, Nebr. Bar Assn., Lincoln Bar Assn., Am. Legion. Roman Catholic. Club: Kiwanis. General corporate, Legislative, General practice. Home: 3440 Hillside Lincoln NE 68506 Office: Crosby Guenzel Davis Kessner & Kuester 400 Lincoln Benefit Bldg Lincoln NE 68508

CROSBY, WILLIAM MARSHALL, lawyer; b. Pasadena, Calif., Jan. 26, 1945; s. Joseph Marshall and Margaret Jane (Aldridge) C.; m. Johanna Sniher, July 12, 1975; children—Mary Beth, Joseph William. A.B., U. Calif.-Berkeley, 1967; J.D., Loyola U., Los Angeles, 1970. Bar: Calif. 1971, U.S. Dist. Ct. (cen. dist.) Calif. 1978, U.S. Ct. Appeals (9th cir.) 1974. Dep. dist. atty. County of Riverside (Calif.), 1971; dep. city atty. City of Anaheim (Calif.), 1971-72; sole practice, Westminster, Calif., 1972-73, San Francisco, 1974-75; staff counsel Monex Internat., Ltd., Newport Beach, Calif., 1975-76; sole practice, Newport Beach, 1976-82, Orange, Calif., 1982—. Trustee Eisenhower Scholarship, 1978—; lectr. Calif. Continuing Edn. of Bar; Dist. chmn. Orange County council Boy Scouts Am.; mem. Calif. Republican State Central Com., 1981-82; candidate for Calif. State Assembly, 1976; bd. dirs. High Hopes Neurol. Recovery Group. Recipient Republican Youth Assn. award 1980. Mem. ABA (litigation sect.), Orange County Bar Assn., Am. Bd. Trial Advs., Assn. Trial Lawyers Am., Calif. Trial Lawyers Assn. (legis. com.), Orange County Trial Lawyers Assn., Rep. Assocs. of Orange County (bd. dirs. 1983—). (bd. dirs. 1983—). Clubs: Irvine Exchange; Lincoln (Orange County, Calif.). Contbr. articles on trial practice and wrongful termination of employement to profl. jours. General practice, State civil litigation, Personal injury. Office: 12800 Von Karman #820 Irvine CA 92715

CROSLAND, EDWARD BURTON, former telephone company executive, lawyer; b. Montgomery, Ala., Jan. 6, 1912; s. David Woolley and Virginia (Burton) C.; m. Helen Burns, Oct. 21, 1939; children: Edward Burton, Lucien Burns. Student, U. of South, 1930-32; J.D., U. Ala., 1935. Bar: Ala. 1935. Practiced in Montgomery 1935-38; asst. atty. gen., chief div. local finance State of Ala., 1938-42; atty. So. Bell Tel. & Tel. Co., Atlanta, 1946; gen. atty. So. Bell Tel. & Tel. Co., 1949; asst. v.p., atty. AT&T, Washington, 1952-55; asst. to pres. AT&T, N.Y.C., 1955-58; v.p. AT&T, 1958-74, sr. v.p., 1974-77; former chmn. bd. Wolftrap Found., 1980-81, Fed. Home Loan Bank of N.Y.; dir. Am. Security Bank N.A. Former trustee Overlook Hosp., Summit, N.J.; trustee U. South. Served as lt. col. JAGC, U.S. Army, 1942-46. Decorated Legion of Merit. Mem. Am., Ala., Ga., D.C. bar assns., Kappa Sigma, Phi Delta Phi, Omicron Delta Kappa. Clubs: Burning Tree (Washington), Metropolitan (Washington); Chevy Chase (Md.). Home: 4412 Chalfont Pl Bethesda MD 20816 Office: 1722 Eye St NW Washington DC 20006 also: 550 Madison Ave New York NY 10022

CROSS, CHESTER JOSEPH, lawyer, acct.; b. Cicero, Ill., June 16, 1931; s. Chester Walter and Stephanie (Nowaczyk) Krzyzaniak. Student Northwestern U., 1950-56, DePaul U., 1958-59; LL.B., U. Ill., 1962. Bar: Ill. 1963, U.S. Dist. Ct. (no. dist.) Ill. 1963. Sr. acct. S.D. Leidesdorf & Co., Chgo. 1954-57, Hall, Penny, Jackson & Co., Chgo. 1957-58; controller Comml. Discount Corp., Chgo. 1958-59; sole practice law, Oak Park, Ill. and Chgo. 1963—. Mem. Ill. State Bar Assn., Chgo. Bar Assn., West Suburban Bar Assn., Am. Inst. C.P.A.s, Ill. C.P.A. Soc. Clubs: East Bank (Chgo.); Elks (Berwyn, Ill.). Probate, Estate taxation, General corporate. Office: 300 W Washington St Suite 907 Chicago IL 60606

CROSS, DAVID BERT, lawyer; b. Steubenville, Ohio, Feb. 27, 1943; s. David B. and Elizabeth (Herman) C.; m. Theresa J. Filberto, Feb. 9, 1964; children: David, Danielle. AB, West Liberty (W.Va.) State Coll., 1965; MS in Speech Pathology, W.Va. U., 1968, JD, 1978. Bars: W.Va. 1978, U.S. Dist. Ct. (no. and so. dists.), W.Va. 1978. Steel co. laborer W.Va., 1964-65; tchr. Follansbee High Sch., W.Va., 1965; speech pathologist Ohio County Schs., Wheeling, W.Va., 1968-69; assoc. prof. speech pathology West Liberty State Coll., W.Va., 1969-75; ptnr. Bell, McMullen & Cross, Wellsburg, W.Va., 1978—; speech pathologist Brooke County Easter Seals, Wellsburg, 1968-75; instr. W.Va. U. Grad. Extension, Wheeling, 1970-72; adj. speech instr. W.Va. No. Community Coll., Weirton, 1972-74; group leader interethnic workshop West Liberty State Coll., 1973; city solicitor City of Wellsburg, 1979-80; asst. pros. atty. Brooke County, Wellsburg, 1979-80, pros. atty., 1981—. Easter Seal scholar Brooke County chpt., 1968; grantee for study in speech pathology U.S. Govt., 1966-68. Mem. ABA, Am. Trial Lawyers Assn., Nat. Dist. Atty.'s Assn., W.Va. State Bar Assn., W.Va. Trial Lawyers Assn., W.Va. Pros. Atty. Assn., Brooke County Bar Assn. Democrat. Methodist. Avocations: fishing, reading, furniture refinishing. Personal injury, General practice, Criminal. Home: 2016 Main St Wellsburg WV 26070 Office: Bell McMullen & Cross 67 Seventh St Wellsburg WV 26070

CROSS, DAVID R., lawyer; b. Madison, Wis., Nov. 18, 1954; s. Robert C. and Hope (Hoffman) C.; m. Joan M. Fagan, Jan. 21, 1983; children: Colleen, Jacqueline. BA in Econs., U. Wis., 1976; JD, U. Chgo., 1980. Bar: Wis. 1980, N.Y. 1980, U.S. Dist. Ct. (ea. and we. dists.) Wis. 1981, U.S. Ct. Appeals (7th cir.) 1983. Adminstrv. asst. Office of Lt. Gov. and Gov., Madison, 1976-77; assoc. Simpson, Thacher & Bartlett, N.Y.C., 1980-81, Quarles & Brady, Milw., 1981—. Bd. dirs. Children's Outing Assn., Milw., 1981—, The Counseling Ctr. Milw., Inc., 1986—. Mem. Phi Beta Kappa. Democrat. Avocation: distance running. Antitrust, Federal civil litigation, State civil litigation. Home: 2679 N Lake Dr Milwaukee WI 53211 Office: Quarles & Brady 780 N Water St Milwaukee WI 53202

CROSS, HARRY MAYBURY, retired law educator, consultant; b. Ritzville, Wash., Aug. 23, 1913; s. James Leman and Mary Rosella (Maybury) C.; m. Mylinn A. Gould, Dec. 25, 1935; children: Harry Maybury, BruceMichael, Kim Judson. B.A., Wash. State U., 1936; J.D., U. Wash., 1940. Bar: Wash. 1941. Reporter Yakima (Wash.) Morning Herald, 1937; abstracter, title examiner Wash. Title Ins. Co., Seattle, 1937-40; Sterling fellow in law Yale U., 1940-41; atty. U.S. Treasury Dept., Washington, 1941-42, TVA, Chattanooga, 1942-43; asst. prof. law U. Wash., Seattle, 1943-45; asso. prof. U. Wash., 1945-49, prof., 1949-84; prof. emeritus U. Wash., Seattle, 1984—; asso. dean U. Wash. (Sch. of Law), 1975-78, acting dean, 1978, 79; vis. prof. Columbia U., 1956-57, NYU, 1964, U. Mich., 1972. Mem. Wash. State Bar Assn. (Honor and Merit award 1984), ABA, Nat. Collegiate Athletic Assn. (pres. 1969-70), Order of Coif, Crimson Circle, Phi Beta Kappa, Phi Kappa Phi, Sigma Delta Chi, Phi Alpha Delta, Kappa Sigma. Club: Oval. Legal education, Real property, Family and matrimonial. Home: 12454 100th Ave NE Kirkland WA 98034 Office: U Wash Law Sch JB 20 Seattle WA 98105

CROSS, JAMES EDWIN, lawyer; b. Fort Dodge, Iowa, Aug. 18, 1921; s. Jim B. and Gladys F. (Bird) C.; m. Jean Steigerwald, Sept. 4, 1945; children: Richard Alan, Susan Lynn, Diane Louise, William James. B.S., State U. Iowa, 1942; LL.B., U. So. Calif., 1949. Assoc. O'Melveny & Myers, Los Angeles, 1949-59, ptnr., 1960—; dir. Am. Capital Mut. Funds Earle M. Jorgensen Co., TICOR Source Capital Inc., Others. Trustee Claremont McKenna Coll.; trustee Calif. Mus. Found., Nat. Multiple Sclerosis Soc., Los Angeles World Affairs Council. Mem. ABA, Calif. Bar Assn., Los Angeles C. of C. (bd. dirs.). Clubs: California (Los Angeles); Center (Costa Mesa). Office: O'Melveny & Myers 400 S Hope St Los Angeles CA 90071

CROSS, JAMES ESTES, JR., lawyer; b. Greensboro, N.C., Nov. 16, 1947; s. James Estes and Pauline Virginia (Owens) C.; m. Deborah Lee Riley, June 6, 1970; 1 child, James Evans. BA, Wake Forest U., 1970, JD, 1973. Bar: N.C. 1973, U.S. Dist. Ct. (ea. dist.) N.C. 1978. From assoc. to ptnr. Currin & Cross, Oxford, N.C., 1973-77; sole practice Oxford, 1977-78; ptnr. Royster, Royster & Cross, Oxford, 1978—; trustee Wake Forest U., Winston-Salem, N.C., 1969-72; bd. dirs. Central Carolina Bank and Trust Co., Oxford. Bd. dirs. N.C. Cen. Orphanage, Oxford, 1985—, Granville County Hist. Soc., Oxford, 1986—, fund raising chmn. 1985-86; bd. dirs. Granville Arts Council, Oxford, 1978-81, Granville County Schs. Endowment Fund Corp., 1987—; bd. deacons Oxford Baptist Ch., 1985—, sec., 1985-86; asst. chmn. fund raising Boy Scouts Am., Granville County, N.C., 1985-86; chmn. Am. Heart Assn., Granville County, 1975; mem. Granville County Bd. Edn. Bus./Industry Adv. Council, 1987—. Mem. ABA, N.C. Bar Assn., N.C. Acad. Trial Lawyers, Ninth Jud. Dist. Bar Assn. (sec., treas. 1977), Granville County Bar Assn. (sec., treas. 1975), Oxford Jaycees (v.p. 1975), Wake Forest U. Alumni Council, Wake Forest U. Pres.'s Club, Granville C. of C. (bd. dirs. 1980-83), Omicron Delta Kappa. Lodge: Kiwanis (pres. Oxford club 1981-82, bd. dirs. 1986—). Real property, Probate, General practice. Home: 219 Devin St Oxford NC 27565 Office: Royster Royster & Cross PO Drawer 1166 Oxford NC 27565

CROSS, JANIS ALEXANDER, lawyer; b. Plainview, Tex., Sept. 8, 1954; d. James Robert Alexander and Virginia May (Etter) Rech; m. Stephen Douglas Cross, Aug. 19, 1978; children: Beau Austin, Katherine Elizabeth. BA, Tex. Tech U., 1976, JD, 1979. Bar: Tex. 1979, U.S. Dist. Ct. (no. dist.) Tex. 1980. Pvt. practice Amarillo, Tex., 1979-81; atty. Pioneer Corp., Amarillo, 1981-84, Cabot Corp., Amarillo, 1983—; instr. West Tex. State U., Amarillo, 1983—. Bd. dirs. March of Dimes, Amarillo, 1980-83, Campfire, Inc., Amarillo, 1980-83, women's programs Amarillo Coll., 1982-85, human relations com. Amarillo City Commn., 1984—. Named one of Outstanding Young Women in Am., 1983. Mem. Tex. Bar Assn., Amarillo Bar Assn., Amarillo Area Young Lawyers Assn., Amarillo Women's Network (bd. dirs. 1980-83), Delta Theta Phi, Gamma Phi Beta. Republican. Baptist. Avocations: bicycling, swimming, reading. FERC practice, General corporate, Federal civil litigation. Home: 5107 Emil Ave Amarillo TX 79106 Office: Cabot Corp 301 S Taylor Amarillo TX 79101

CROSS, JOSEPH RUSSELL, JR., law librarian; b. Bennettsville, S.C., July 29, 1945; s. Joseph Russell and Julia Harrington (Rogers) C.; m. Inez Mary Robinson, May 12, 1973; children: David Sebastian, Sarah Harrington. BA, Wofford Coll., 1967; MLM, Emory U., 1972; JD, U. S.C., 1978. Bar: S.C. 1978. Tchr. Cross (S.C.) Schs., 1967-68, 70-71; reference librarian U. S.C., Columbia, 1972-75; head of pub. services U. S.C. Law Library, Columbia, 1978—. Served as staff sgt. U.S. Army, 1968-70, Vietnam. Mem. ABA, S.C. Bar Assn., Am. Assn. Law Libraries, S.C. Library Assn. Democrat. United Methodist. Librarianship. Home: 608 Saluda Ave Columbia SC 29205 Office: U SC Coleman Karesh Law Library Columbia SC 29208

CROSS, JUNIUS BRACY, JR., lawyer; b. Little Rock, May 19, 1953; s. Junius Bracy Sr. and Sarah Elizabeth (Riley) C.; m. Deborah Elizabeth Davies, Aug. 6, 1977; 1 child, Junius Bracy III. BA in Polit. Sci., History, Hendrix Coll., 1975; JD, U. Ark., 1978. Bar: Ark. 1975, U.S. Dist. Ct. (ea. dist.) Ark. 1975, U.S. Ct. Appeals (8th cir.) 1975. Assoc. Law Offices of Jack Holt Jr., Little Rock, 1978-80, McMath, Leatherman & Woods, Little Rock, 1980-81; sole practice Little Rock, 1981—; gardina ad litem Pulaski County Chancery Cts., Little Rock, 1980—; bd. dirs. Econometric, Inc., Little Rock. Chmn. state Hugh O'Brien Youth Leadership Seminar, Ark. 1985—; bd. dirs. St. Jude Children's Hosp., Little Rock, 1984-85. Mem. Ark. Bar Assn., Pulaski County Bar Assn., Ark. Jaycees (legal counsel 1985, named outstanding state officer Fall 1984). Episcopalian. Club: Little Rock Country. Construction, State civil litigation, Real property. Office: 923 Pyramid Pl Little Rock AR 72201

CROSS, MILTON H., lawyer; b. Phila., July 28, 1942; s. Sidney B. and Edythe Cross; m. Joyce Volchok, June 4, 1966; children—Brian, Jonathon. B.S., U. San Francisco, 1965; J.D., Villanova U., 1968. Bar: Pa. 1968. Asst. corp. counsel AEL, Inc., Phila., 1968-70, corp. counsel, 1970-75; assoc. Cohen, Verlin, Sherzer & Porter, Phila., 1975-78; sole practice, Phila., 1978-79; ptnr. Monteverde, Hemphill, Maschmeyer & Obert, Phila., 1980—; adj. prof. Phila. Coll. Textile & Sci., 1970-73. Chmn. Cheltenham Twp. Sch. Bd. Authority. Mem. ABA (sect. corp., banking and bus. law), Pa. Bar Assn., Phila. Bar Assn. Republican. Jewish. Club: Ashbourne Country (Cheltenham, Pa.). General corporate, Corporate taxation, Real property. Home: 310 Curtis Dr Wyncote PA 19095 Office: Fidelity Bldg 22d Floor 123 S Broad St Philadelphia PA 19109

CROSS, SAMUEL S., lawyer; b. Detroit, Oct. 19, 1919; s. Samuel Stogden and Mildred Lurline (Hay) C.; m. Jodie E. Hecht, Jan. 3, 1947 (div. 1948); 1 child, Edward T.; m. Audrey Brauneck, Nov. 25, 1950; children—Stephen W., Lauren E., Robert A., Wendy A. B.S., Lehigh U., 1941; LL.B., U. Pa., 1949. Bar: N.Y. 1951, Conn. 1953, Pa. 1977. Test engr. Bethlehem Steel Co., Steelton, Pa., 1941-43; assoc. Watson, Johnson, Leavenworth & Blair, N.Y.C., 1949-52; gen. counsel, sec. Perkin-Elmer Corp., Norwalk, Conn., 1952-64; counsel Maguire, Cole & Bentley, Stamford, Conn., 1964-68; ptnr. Cross, Brodrick & Chipman, Stamford, Conn., 1969-79, Kelley Drye & Warren, N.Y.C., 1979—; gen. counsel Southwestern Area Commerce and Industry Assn. of Conn., Inc., Stamford, 1970—. Author: Corporation Law in Connecticut, 1972; editor-in-chief Conn. Bar Jour., 1982-85; contbr. articles to profl. jours. Mem. Legis. Commn. on Revision of Corp. Laws, Hartford, Conn., 1957-62; pres. The Ferguson Library, Stamford, Conn., 1977-78; trustee The Ferguson Library Found., 1987—, Engring. Edn. Found. Inc., 1969—; bd. dirs. Forum for World Affairs Inc., 1987—. Served as lt. (j.g.), USNR, 1943-46. Mem. ABA, Am. Soc. Corp. Secs., Inc., Am. Soc. Internat. Law, Southwestern Legal Found. (adv. bd. Internat. and Comparative Law Ctr.), Tau Beta Pi. Republican. Congregationalist. Clubs: Union League (N.Y.C.); Metropolitan (Washington). Home: 1021 Ridgefield Rd Wilton CT 06897 Office: Kelley Drye & Warren 101 Park Ave New York NY 10178

CROSS, SANDRA LEE, lawyer; b. St. Louis, Oct. 13, 1946; d. Glen Olin and Elinor (Ermes) C.; m. Henry Joseph Crawford, Jan. 22, 1977 (div. Oct. 1985); 1 child, Melissa Fayre. BA, U. Chgo., 1968; JD, U. Calif., San Francisco, 1975. Bar: Calif. 1976, U.S. Dist. Ct. (no. and ea. dists.) Calif. 1976. Assoc. Law Offices Max Cline, Oakland, Calif., 1979-85, Niesar, Kregstein & Cecchini, San Francisco, 1985—; instr. bankruptcy law Armstrong Coll., Berkeley, Calif., 1985. Mem. exec. com. PTA Washington Sch., Berkeley, 1985-86. Mem. ABA, Am. Bankruptcy Inst., ACLU. Avocations: skiing, guitar, tennis. Bankruptcy, General corporate. Home: 1720 Addison St Apt 3 Berkeley CA 94703 Office: Niesar Kregstein & Cecchini 214 Grant Ave San Francisco CA 94108

CROSSMAN, HARLAN JAY, lawyer; b. Bklyn., July 27, 1941; s. Sydney Russell and Mary Lee (Cohen) C.; m. Gayla Glascock, July 1, 1964; children—Monica Ann, Avery Naomi. Student Menlo Coll., 1958-60; B.A., U. N.Mex., 1962, J.D., 1965. Bar: Ariz. 1968. Clk. to presiding judge N.Mex. Ct. Appeals, Santa Fe, 1966-67; atty. Navajo Legal Services Program, Window Rock, Ariz., 1967-69; atty. state compensation fund, Phoenix, 1969-72; pres. Harlan J. Crossman, P.C., 1972—; adj. prof. law Ariz. State U., 1985. Pres., Temple Solel, 1974-76; mem. Ariz. Gov.'s Com. on Workmen's Compensation, 1980-81; vice chmn. YMCA, 1980-84, chmn. youth com., 1981—, mem. nominating com., 1982. Mem. Maricopa County Bar Assn., State Bar Ariz. (sec. workmen's compensation sect. 1979—), ABA, Ariz. Trial Lawyers Assn. Democrat. Jewish. Club: Temple Solel Men's. Contbr. articles to profl. jours. Workers' compensation. Office: Suite 520 11 W Jefferson St Phoenix AZ 85003

CROTTY, EDWARD, lawyer; b. Cleve., Jan. 22, 1951; s. Robert Godfrey and Myra (Witt) C.; m. Daphna Crotty, May 20, 1978; children: Robert Sean, Amanda Elizabeth. BBA, U. Mich., 1973; JD, Columbia U., 1976. Bar: Ill. 1976, D.C. 1985, N.Y. 1985. Assoc. Kirkland & Ellis, Chgo., 1976-79; dep. asst. gen. counsel USAF, Washington, 1979-1984; gen. counsel Occidental Internat. Corp., Washington, 1984—. General corporate, Private international, Contracts commercial. Home: 5316 Moorland Ln Bethesda MD 20814 Office: Occidental Internat Corp 1747 Pennsylvania Ave NW Washington DC 20006

CROTTY, MICHAEL F., lawyer; b. Balt., Sept. 1, 1947; s. Francis N. Sr. and Lois M. (Engels) C.; m. Anne E. Shipley, Aug. 29, 1970; children: Jeanne K., Michael F. II. BA with honors, Loyola U., Chgo., 1969; JD, Northwestern U., 1972. Bar: U.S. Ct. Mil. Appeals 1974, D.C. 1976, U.S. Dist. Ct. 1977, U.S. Ct. Appeals (D.C. cir.) 1978, U.S. Supreme Ct., 1979, U.S. Ct. Appeals (5th cir.) 1982, U.S. Ct. Appeals (4th cir.) 1984, Md. 1986. Assoc. gen. counsel litigation Am. Bankers Assn., Washington, 1976—. Pres. Maryland City Civic Assn., Laurel, 1979-83; del. nominating conv. Anne Arundel County Sch. Bd., 1980-83; mem. Anne Arundel County Transp. Study Group, Annapolis, Md., 1981, Anne Arundel County Sch. Resource Evaluation Com., Annapolis, 1983; chmn. Maryland City Study Group, Laurel, 1981-82. Served to lt. USNR, 1972-76. Named one of Outstanding Young Men of Am., U.S. Jaycees, 1983. Mem. ABA, Md. Bar Assn., D.C. Bar Assn., Fed. Bar Assn., Computer Law Assn. Republican. Roman Catholic. Banking, Federal civil litigation, Administrative and regulatory. Home: 421 Yellow Springs S Laurel MD 20707 Office: Am Bankers Assn 1120 Connecticut Ave NW Washington DC 20036

CROTTY, ROBERT BELL, lawyer; b. Dallas, Aug. 16, 1951; s. Willard and Betty (Bell) C.; m. Sarah Smith, Mar. 8, 1980; children: Robert Edwin, Rebecca Bell. BA, Va. Mil. Inst., 1973; JD, U. Tex., 1976. Bar: Tex. 1976, U.S. Dist. Ct. (no. dist.) Tex. 1977, U.S. Ct. Appeals (5th cir.) 1978, U.S. Ct. Appeals (11th cir.) 1982. Assoc. firm Akin, Gump, Strauss, Hauer & Feld, Dallas, 1976-82, ptnr., 1983—. Note and comment editor Tex. Law Rev. 1975-76. V.p., bd. dirs. Big Bros. and Sisters of Met. Dallas, 1981-87; pres., bd. dirs. Dallas Bus. League, 1981-84. Mem. Tex. Law Rev. Assn., Dallas Bar Assn., ABA, State Bar Tex., Salesmanship Club. Federal civil litigation, State civil litigation. Office: Akin Gump Strauss Hauer & Feld 4100 First City Ctr 1700 Pacific Ave Dallas TX 75201-4618

CROUCH, JAMES MICHAEL, lawyer; b. Birmingham, Ala., Sept. 27, 1949; s. James Claude and Mary Lou (Stack) C.; m. Elizabeth Louise Adams, Dec. 19, 1970; children: Gabe, Kimberly. BS in Acctg., U. Ala., 1971, JD, 1974. Bar: Ala. 1974, U.S. Dist. Ct. (mid. dist.) Ala. 1975, U.S. Ct. Appeals (5th cir.) 1975, U.S. Dist. Ct. (no. dist.) Ala. 1976, U.S. Ct. Appeals (11th cir.) 1981. Asst. atty. gen. State of Ala., Montgomery, 1974-76; atty. Hartford Ins. Group, Birmingham, 1976—, also bd. dirs.; legal rep. and cons. Ala. Dept. Human Resources, Montgomery, 1981—. Asst. coach Midstate Soccer League Am. Soccer Club, Birmingham, 1983—; tchr., catechist Our Lady of Valley Cath. Ch., Birmingham, 1984—. Mem. ABA, Ala. Bar Assn., Def. Research Inst., Nat. Inst. Trial Advs. Republican. Avocations: swimming, woodworking. Insurance, Federal civil litigation, State civil litigation. Home: 5205 Timberline Cove Birmingham AL 35244 Office: Hartford Ins Group PO Box 36988 One Riverchase Plaza Suite 126 Birmingham AL 35244

CROUCH, RICHARD EDELIN, lawyer; b. Arlington, Va., Dec. 3, 1940; s. Howard Fairfax and Helen Nora (Edelin) C.; m. Mary Blake French, Feb. 6, 1965; children: John Howard, Virginia Elizabeth. AB, Coll. William and Mary, 1962, JD, 1964. Bar: Va. 1964, U.S. Ct. Mil. Appeals 1965, U.S. Dist. Ct. (ea. dist.) Va. 1970, U.S. Ct. Appeals (D.C. cir.) 1970, U.S. Supreme Ct. 1970, U.S. Ct. Appeals (4th cir.) 1972. Assoc. Crouch & Crouch, Arlington, 1964; editor U.S. Law Week & Criminal Law Reporter, Washington, 1968-74; sole practice Arlington, 1974—; mng. editor The Family Law Reporter, 1974-81; cons. editor for legal services Bur. Nat. Affairs, Inc., Washington, 1981-84. Author: The Rights of Homemakers in Virginia, 1977, Interstate Custody Litigation, 1981; contbr. articles to profl. jours. Legal dir. ACLU Va., 1972-76, bd. dirs. 1977-80. Served as capt. U.S. Army, 1966-68. Mem. ABA, Acad. Matrimonial Lawyers, Internat. Soc. Family Law, King and Queen County Hist. Soc., Arlington Hist. Soc., Fairfax County Hist. Soc., Loudoun County Preservation Soc. Episcopalian. Family and matrimonial, Civil rights, Military. Home: 2624 N 18th St Arlington VA 22201 Office: 1515 N Court House Rd Arlington VA 22201

CROW, CARL ARNOLD, JR., lawyer; b. Hot Springs, Ark., Aug. 15, 1951; s. Carl A. Sr. and Betty Jo (Hale) C.; m. Lynne Killgore, Dec. 29, 1974; children: Adam Hale, John William. BA, Hendrix Coll., 1973; JD, U. Ark., 1976. Bar: Ark. 1976, U.S. Dist. Ct. (we. dist.) Ark. 1976, U.S. Tax Ct. 1979. Assoc. Glover, Sanders, Parkerson & Hargraves, Hot Springs, 1976-81; ptnr. Callahan, Crow, Bachelor & Newell, P.A., Hot Springs, 1981—; asst. atty. gen. State of Ark., Little Rock, 1979-80, pros. atty. 18th jud. cir. east, 1987—; atty. City of Hot Springs, 1983-86; bd. dirs. Main St. Hot Springs Inc. Bd. dirs. Gov.'s Adv. Commn. on Hot Springs Nat. Park, 1986—. Mem. Ark. Bar Assn. (chmn. pub. info. com. 1985—, chmn. young lawyers sect. 1983-84), Ark. Inst. Continuing Legal Edn. (bd. dirs. 1985—). Lodge: Rotary (bd. dirs. Hot Springs 1982). General corporate, State civil litigation, General practice. Mailing Address: PO Box 1620 Hot Springs AR 71901

CROW, SAM ALFRED, federal judge; b. Topeka, May 5, 1926; s. Samuel Wheadon and Phyllis K. (Brown) C.; m. Ruth M. Rush, Jan. 30, 1948; children—Sam A., Dan W. B.A., U. Kans., 1949; J.D., Washburn U., 1952. Bar: Kans. 1952, U.S. Dist. Ct. Kans. 1952, U.S. Supreme Ct. 1962, U.S. Ct. Appeals (10th cir.) 1963, U.S. Mil. Ct. Appeals 1953. Ptnr. Rooney, Dickinson, Prager & Crow, Topeka, 1953-63; ptnr. Dickinson, Crow, Skoog & Honeyman, Topeka, 1963-70; sr. ptnr. Crow & Skoog, Topeka, 1971-75; part-time U.S. magistrate 1973-75, U.S. magistrate, 1975-81; judge U.S. Dist. Ct. Kans., Wichita, 1981—; lectr. Washburn U. Sch. Law, also assns., convs. Bd. rev. Boy Scouts Am., 1960-70, cubmaster, 1957-60; mem. vestry Grace Episcopal Ch., Topeka, 1960-65; chmn. Kans. March of Dimes, 1959, bd. dirs. 1960-65; bd. dirs. Topeka Council Chs., 1960-70; mem. Mulvane Art Soc., 1965—, Kans. Hist. Soc., 1960—; pres., v.p. PTA. Served to col. JAGC, USAR, ret. Fellow Acad. Internat. Law and Sci.; mem. ABA (del. Nat. Conf. Spl. Ct. Judges 1978, 79), Kans. Bar Assn. (trustee 1970-76, chmn. mil. law sect. 1965, 67, 70, 72, 74, 75), Assn. Trial Lawyers Am., Kans. Trial Lawyers Assn. (sec. 1959-60, pres. 1960-61), Nat. Assn. U.S. Magistrates (com. discovery abuse), Topeka Bar Assn. (chmn. jud. reform com., chmn. bench and bar com., chmn. criminal law com.), Wichita Bar Assn., Wichita Lawyers Club, Topeka Lawyers Club (sec. 1964-65, pres. 1965-66), Res. Officers Assn., Am. Legion, Delta Theta Phi, Sigma Alpha Epsilon. Club: Shawnee Country, Wichita Lawyers. Judicial administration. Office: 401 Market St Suite 322 Wichita KS 67202

CROWE, DANIEL WALSTON, lawyer; b. Visalia, Calif., July 1, 1940; s. J. Thomas and Wanda (Walston) C.; m. Nancy V. Berard, May 10, 1969; children—Daniel W., Karyn Louise, Thomas Dwight. B.A., U. Santa Clara, 1962; J.D., U. Calif. Hastings Coll. Law, 1965. Bar: Calif. 1966, U.S. Dist. Ct. (ea. dist.) Calif. 1969, U.S. Dist. Ct. (cen. dist.) Calif. 1973, U.S. Ct. Appeals (9th cir.) 1973, U.S. Supreme Ct. 1973. Assoc. Crowe, Mitchell & Crowe, and predecessors, Visalia, Calif., 1968-74, ptnr., 1974-83; ptnr. Crowe & Williams, 1983—; sec., treas., dir. The Exeter Devel. Co.; dir., treas. Willson Ranch Co., 1983—. Founding mem., dir. Visalia Balloon Assn., Inc. Served to capt. U.S. Army, 1965-68. Decorated Bronze Star, Air medal, Purple Heart, Nat. Def. Service medal. Mem. ABA, Calif. Bar Assn., Tulare County Bar Assn. Republican. Roman Catholic. Clubs: Visalia Rotary, Elks, Moose, Am. Radio Relay League, DAV. Real property, State civil litigation, Probate. Address: PO Box 1110 Visalia CA 93279

CROWE, GARY ALLEN, lawyer; b. Tampa, Fla., Oct. 27, 1955; s. Donald Allen and Patricia Jewel (Concannon) C. BA in Polit. Sci. with high honors, U. Mont., 1976, JD, 1980. Bar: Mont. 1980, U.S. Dist. Ct. Mont. 1980. Mem. Moore, Doran & Crowe, Kalispell, Mont., 1980-83; sole practice Kalispell, 1983—. Mem. ABA, Mont. Bar Assn., N.W. Mont. Bar Assn., Mont. Bowhunters Assn., Flathead Wildlife Assn., Nat. Rifle Assn., Sigma Alpha Epsilon, Pi Sigma Alpha, Phi Alpha Theta, Phi Delta Phi, Ducks Unltd., (bd. dirs. 1982—). Republican. Methodist. Club: Pope and Young. Avocations: hunting, fishing. Personal injury, State civil litigation, General practice. Office: 30 5th St E Suite 203 PO Box 924 Kalispell MT 59903

CROWE, JAMES JOSEPH, shoe company executive; b. New Castle, Pa., June 9, 1935; s. William J. and Anna M. (Dickson) C.; m. Joan D. Verba, Dec. 26, 1959. B.A., Youngstown State U., 1958; J.D., Georgetown U., 1963. Bar: Va. bar 1963, Ohio bar 1966. Atty. SEC, Washington, 1964-65, Gen. Tire & Rubber Co., Akron, Ohio, 1965-68; sr. atty. Eaton Corp., Cleve., 1968-72; sec., gen. counsel U.S. Shoe Corp., Cin., 1972—; v.p. U.S. Shoe Corp., 1975—. Chmn. div. Fine Arts Fund, 1976; trustee Springer Ednl. Found., 1978-84, Cin. Music Festival Assn., 1980-86; trustee Invest in Neighborhood Inc., 1982—, pres. 1984-86; group chmn. United Appeal, 1980; mem. pres.'s council Coll. Mt. St. Jospeh, 1985—; trustee Tennis for Charity Inc., 1986—. Served to 2d lt. U.S. Army, 1958-59. Mem. Ohio Bar Assn., Va. Bar Assn., Cin. Bar Assn., Am. Soc. Corp. Secs., Cin. C. of C. Clubs: Cin. Country (Cin.), Queen City (Cin.). General corporate. Office: US Shoe Corp One Eastwood Dr Cincinnati OH 45227

CROWE, JOHN T., lawyer; b. Cabin Cove, Calif., Aug. 14, 1938; s. J. Thomas and Wanda (Walston) C.; m. Marina Protopapa, Dec. 28, 1968; 1 dau., Erin Aleka. B.A., U. Santa Clara, 1960, J.D., 1962. Bar: Calif. 1962, U.S. Dist. Ct. (no. dist.) Calif. 1964, U.S. Dist. Ct. (ea. dist.) Calif. 1967. Practiced in Visalia, Calif., 1964—; ptnr. firm Crowe, Mitchell & Crowe, 1971-85; referee State Bar Ct., 1976-82; gen. counsel Sierra Wine, 1986—. Bd. dirs. Mt. Whitney Area council Boy Scouts Am., 1966—, pres., 1971, 72; bd. dirs. Visalia Associated In-Group Donors (AID), 1973-81, pres., 1978-79; mem. Visalia Airport Commn., 1982—. Served to 1st lt. U.S. Army, 1962-64; col. Res. Decorated Meritorious Service Medal, Army Commendation Medal; named Young Man of Yr., Visalia, 1973; Senator, Jr. Chamber Internat., 1970; recipient Silver Beaver award Boy Scouts Am., 1983. Mem. ABA, Tulare County Bar Assn., Nat. Assn. R.R. Trial Counsel, State Bar Calif., Visalia C. of C. (pres. 1979-80). Republican. Roman Catholic. Clubs: Rotary (pres. 1980-81 ; Downtown (Fresno, Calif.). General corporate, General practice. Home: 3939 W School St Visalia CA 93291

CROWE, ROBERT ALAN, lawyer; b. N.Y.C., Feb. 20, 1950; s. John Thomas and Annette (Korall) C.; m. Carolyn Ann Kruse, Apr. 14, 1974; children: Emily, Andrew. AB, St. Louis U., 1971, JD, 1974. Bar: Mo. 1974, U.S. Dist. Ct. Mo. 1975, U.S. Ct. Appeals (8th cir.) 1976, U.S. Ct. Appeals (7th cir.) 1977, U.S. Supreme Ct. 1977. Assoc. Law Office of Harry J. Nichols, St. Louis, 1974-76; sole practice St. Louis, 1976-83; ptnr. Kell, Kell, Custer, Weller & Crowe, St. Louis, 1983-85, Crowe & Shanahan, St. Louis, 1985—; mem. editorial adv. bd. West's Social Security Reporting Service, 1983—; pres. Mo. Arbitration Services Inc., St. Louis, 1985—; midwest regional dir. U.S. Arbitration Inc., St. Louis, 1985—. Mem. ABA, Mo. Bar Assn., Bar Assn. Met. St. Louis, Nat. Orgn. Social Security Claimants Reps. (exec. com. 1984—). Pension, profit-sharing, and employee benefits, Arbitration, Mediation. Home: 5629 Finkman St Saint Louis MO 63109 Office: Crowe & Shanahan 915 Olive St Suite 1001C Saint Louis MO 63101

CROWE, ROBERT DENNING, II, lawyer; b. Oklahoma City, Oct. 15, 1942; s. Robert D. and Ewing (Hardy) C.; m. Beverly Reynolds, June 5, 1965; children: Ewing Elizabeth, Tracy Renee. AB, Cen. Meth. Coll., 1964; JD, U. Okla., 1967. Bar: Okla. 1967, U.S. Ct. Appeals (10th cir.) 1970, U.S. Supreme Ct. 1971. Ptnr. Crowe & Crowe, Inc., Oklahoma City; spl. judge Okla. Ct. Appeals. Vol. atty. Okla. County Children's Ct.; bd. curators Cen. Meth. Coll., Fayette, Mo.; Dem. nominee Okla. Ho. of Reps.; Dem. precinct and dist. chmn. Served to maj. USAFR, 1967-85. Mem. ABA, Okla. Bar Assn. (mem. computer application com., legis. relations com., desk manual revisions com.), Am. Arbitration Assn., Phi Alpha Delta. Methodist. Avocations: computers, travel, cooking, reading. Home: 4319 NW 60th St Oklahoma City OK 73112-1318 Office: Crowe & Crowe Inc Attys 3113 Classen Blvd Suite 8 Oklahoma City OK 73118-3898

CROWE, THOMAS LEONARD, lawyer; b. Amsterdam, N.Y., Aug. 3, 1944; s. Leonard Hoctor and Grace Agnes (O'Malley) C.; m. Barbara Ann Hauck, Aug. 2, 1969; children: Patrick, Brendan. AB, Georgetown U., 1966, JD, 1969. Law clk. to chief judge U.S. Dist. Ct. (no. dist.), Elkins, W.Va., 1969-70; trial atty. U.S. Dept. Justice, Washington, 1970-72; asst. U.S. atty. U.S. Dist. Atty., Balt., 1973-78; chief of criminal div. U.S. Atty.'s Office, Balt., 1977-78; atty Cable, McDaniel, Bowie & Bond, Balt., 1978—. Fellow Md. Bar Found.; mem. ABA, Fed. Bar Assn. (pres. Balt. chpt. 1981-82), Balt. City Bar Assn., Md. Bar Assn., Barristers Club (v.p. 1985-86, sec. 1986-87). Democrat. Roman Catholic. Club: Merchants (Balt.). Federal civil litigation, State civil litigation, Criminal. Home: 11 Osborne Ave Catonsville MD 21228 Office: Cable McDaniel Bowie & Bond 1 North Charles St Baltimore MD 21201

CROWELL, WILLIAM JEFFERSON, lawyer; b. Tucson, Aug. 30, 1913; s. William J. Crowell and Juanita Saralegui; m. Harriet C. Lemson, Nov. 20, 1940; children: William J. Jr., Robert L. BA, U. Nev., 1934; JD, U. Calif., San Francisco, 1937. Bar: Nev. 1937, U.S. Dist. Ct. Nev. 1937, U.S. Ct. Appeals (9th cir.). Dist. atty. Nye County, Tonopah, N.Y., 1947-54; ptnr. Crowell, Crowell, Crowell & Susich, Carson City, Nev., 1964; gen. counsel Nev. Indls. Commn., Carson City, 1959-78. Chmn. Nev. Dems., 1952-54. Rose Sigler Mathews scholar, 1931. Lodges: Masons (Tonopah master 1946), Rotary (Tonopah pres. 1949, Carson City pres. 1961). Office: Crowell Crowell Crowell & Susich 510 W 4th Carson City NV 89701

CROWLEY, DENNIS DANIEL, lawyer; b. Bklyn., Sept. 15, 1940; s. John William and Helen Teresa (McDermott) C; m. Mary Lou Melkun, Aug. 23, 1969; children: Dennis Daniel, Marianne Therese. BA, St. Boniventure U., 1962; MA, Columbia U., 1967; JD, St. John's U., Jamaica, N.Y., 1976. Bar: N.Y. 1977, U.S. Tax Ct. 1977, U.S. Dist. Ct. (ea. and so. dists.) N.Y. 1982, U.S. Ct. Appeals (2d cir.) 1982, U.S. Supreme Ct. 1982. Instr. law studies Nassau County Pub. Schs., N.Y., 1974-79; assoc. Maran & Maran, Malverne, N.Y., 1977-81, Corcoran & Brady, N.Y.C., 1981-83; sole practice Mineola, N.Y., 1983—. Mem. N.Y. State Bar Assn., Nassau County Bar Assn., Nassau County Lawyers Assn. Republican. Roman Catholic. Avocations: travel, boating. Personal injury, Probate, Real property. Home: 27 Deacons Ln Wilton CT 06897 Office: 114 Old Country Rd Suite 620 Mineola NY 11501

CROWLEY, JAMES WORTHINGTON, lawyer; b. Cookville, Tenn., Feb. 18, 1930; s. Worth and Jessie (Officer) C.; m. Laura June Bauserman, Jan. 27, 1951; children—James Kenneth, Laura Cynthia; m. Joyce A. Goode, Jan. 15, 1966; children—John Worthington, Noelle Virginia; m. Carol Golden, Sept. 4, 1981. B.A., George Washington U., 1950, LL.B., 1953. Bar: D.C. bar 1954. Underwriter, spl. agt. Am. Surety Co. of N.Y., Washington, 1953-56; adminstrv. asst., contract adminstr. Atlantic Research Corp., Alexandria, Va., 1956-59; mgr. legal dept., asst. sec., counsel Atlantic Research Corp., 1959-65, sec., legal mgr., counsel, 1965-67; sec., legal mgr., counsel Susquehanna Corp. (merger with Atlantic Research Corp.), 1967-70; pres., dir. Gen. Communication Co., Boston, 1962-70; v.p., gen. counsel E-Systems, Inc., 1970-, sec., 1976—; v.p., asst. sec., dir. Air Asia Co. Ltd., Tainan, Taiwan, Republic China, 1975—; dir. Cemco, Inc., Continental Electronic Systems, Inc.; v.p., dir. TAI, Inc., Serv-air, Inc., Houston; mem. adv. bd. Internat. and Comparative Law Center, Southwestern Legal Found. Mem. Am. Soc. Corp. Secs., Inf. Mus. Assn., Am. Bar Assn., Nat. Security Indsl. Assn., Omicron Delta Kappa, Alpha Chi Sigma, Phi Sigma Kappa. Republican. Baptist. General corporate, Government contracts and claims. Home: 16203 Spring Creek Rd Dallas TX 75248 Office: PO Box 660248 Dallas TX 75266

CROWLEY, RICHARD ALLERTON, lawyer; b. Brockton, Mass., July 28, 1949; s. John Lawrence and Ruth Willemann (Horlick) C. AB, Harvard U., 1971; JD, U. Pa., 1977. Bar: N.Y. 1978, U.S. Dist. Ct. (ea. and so. dists.) N.Y. 1978, U.S. Tax Ct. 1979, U.S. Ct. Claims 1979. Assoc. Sullivan & Cromwell, N.Y.C., 1977-84; assoc. Haight, Gardner, Poor & Havens, N.Y.C., 1984-85, ptnr., 1985—. Served to lt. (j.g.) USNR, 1972-74. Mem. ABA, N.Y. State Bar Assn. Corporate taxation, Personal income taxation, State and local taxation. Home: 111 E 76th St Apt 4D New York NY 10021 Office: Haight Gardner Poor & Havens 195 Broadway New York NY 10007

CROWLEY, THOMAS MICHAEL, lawyer; b. Johnstown, Pa., Sept. 16, 1954; s. Thomas Nathaniel and Dorothy Jean (Dorian) C. BA in Philosophy, U. Notre Dame, 1976, MA in Philosophy, 1979, JD, 1982. Bar: Pa. 1982, U.S. Dist. Ct. (mid. dist.) Pa. 1984, U.S. Ct. Appeals (3d cir.) 1985, U.S. Supreme Ct. 1986. Law clk. to presiding justice Supreme Ct. Pa., Harrisburg, 1982-85; dep. atty. gen. State of Pa., Harrisburg, 1985—. Editorial bd., book rev. editor Am. Jour. Jurisprudence, Notre Dame, Ind., 1982—. V.p. Cen. Pa. Literary Council, Harrisburg, 1986—. Mem. ABA, Pa. Bar Assn., Dauphin County Bar Assn. Republican. Roman Catholic. Lodge: KC. Federal civil litigation, State civil litigation, Jurisprudence. Home: 301 Chestnut St Apt 1708 Harrisburg PA 17101 Office: Office of Atty Gen Strawberry Sq 15th Floor Harrisburg PA 17120

CROWLEY, WILBERT FRANCIS, lawyer; b. Chgo., Sept. 1, 1940; s. Wilbert F. and Mary C. (McDermot) C.; m. Kathleen Stockmar, 1968; children—Brian, Erin. B.S. in Econs. with honors, Coll. Holy Cross, 1962; J.D. cum laude, U. Mich., 1965. Bar: Ill. 1965, U.S. Dist. Ct. (no. dist.) Ill. 1968. Instr. U. Wis. Law Sch., 1965-66; ptnr. Cowen, Crowley & Hager, Chgo., 1966—. committeeman New Trier Democratic Orgn., 1985—. Mem. ABA, Chgo. Bar Assn., Ill. State Bar Assn. (chmn. long range planning com. 1981-82). Club: Union League. General corporate, Federal civil litigation, State civil litigation. Office: Cowen Crowley & Hager Suite 4333 55 E Monroe Chicago IL 60603

CROWNOVER, WALTER PARKER, lawyer; b. Estill Springs, Tenn., Nov. 9, 1934; s. Walter Rosser and Dorothy Williams (Black) C.; m. Ellen Louise Zimmerman, Nov. 2, 1953; children—Jo Ellen, Kenneth Walter. B.A., U. Ala., 1960, J.D., 1962. Bar: Ala. 1962, U.S. Dist. Ct. (no. dist.) Ala. 1962, U.S. Ct. Appeals (5th cir.) 1970, U.S. Supreme Ct. 1971, U.S. Dist. Ct. (mid. and so. dist.) Ala. 1982, U.S. Ct. Appeals (11th cir.) 1982. Practice, Tuscaloosa, Ala., 1962—, ptnr. Crownover & Black, and predecessors, 1982—; bd. commrs. Ala. State Bar, 1971—. Chmn. Tuscaloosa County Dem. Party exec. com., 1976-86. Served with USAF, 1953-57. Mem. ABA, Ala. Bar Assn., Am. Arbitration Assn., Tuscaloosa Trial Lawyers Assn. (pres. 1987—), Am. Judicature Soc. Bankruptcy, Criminal, Personal injury. Office: Box 2507 Tuscaloosa AL 35403

CROZIER, JOHN HUNTINGTON, manufacturing company executive, lawyer; b. Waukegan, Ill., Nov. 10, 1935; s. Ronald Gilpin and Ruth Minerva (Huntington) C.; m. Eleanor Jean Wood, Aug. 20, 1967; 1 child, Julia Lynn; children from previous marriage: Susan Ruth, Jean Louise, Jacqueline Ann, Anne Huntington. BS in Chem. Engring., Northwestern U., 1959; JD, U. Akron, 1974. Bar: Conn. 1975, U.S. Dist. Ct. Conn. 1981, U.S. Patent Office 1981; registered profl. engr., Ohio. Project engr. Union Carbide Corp., Charleston, W.Va., 1959-66; engring. supr. Mobay Chem Co., New Martinsville, W.Va., 1966-68; project mgr., engr. Gen. Tire and Rubber Co., Akron, Ohio, 1968-74; corp. counsel Crawford and Russell, Stamford, Conn., 1974-80; gen. counsel, sec. The Superior Electric Co., Bristol, Conn., 1980—. Active various community orgs. Mem. ABA, Conn. Bar Assn., Westchester/Fairfield Corp. Counsel Assn., Am. Arbitration Assn. (comml. arbitrator). Avocations: sailing, skiing. General corporate, Patent, Contracts commercial. Home: 1934 Huntington Turnpike Trumbull CT 06611 Office: The Superior Electric Co 383 Middle St Bristol CT 06010

CRUIKSHANK, DAVID EARL, lawyer; b. Painesville, Ohio, Apr. 23, 1945; s. Earl W. and Kathryn (Schlender) C.; m. Nancy Kathryn Heine, June 9, 1984. B.A., DePauw U., 1967; J.D., Case West Res. U., 1973. Bar: Ohio 1973, U.S. Dist. Ct. (so. dist.) Ohio 1973, U.S. Supreme Ct. 1980. Assoc. Turner & Badger, Mount Vernon, Ohio, 1973-75, Baker, Byron & Hackenberg, Painesville, 1975-76; assoc., ins. mgr. E.W. Cruikshank, Painesville, 1976-84; assoc. Byron & Ryan, Willoughby, Ohio, 1984—; mem. faculty Ohio Legal Ctr. Inst., 1985, 86, U. Toledo Sch. of Law, CLE div., 1985. Served to 1st lt. USMC, 1968-71, Vietnam. Mem. ABA, Ohio Bar Assn. (chmn. ins. law com. 1984—, vice chmn. 1981-84), Lake County Bar Assn., Def. Research Inst., Ohio Bar Found, Ohio Acad. Civil Trial Attys. (lectr. 1984). Lodge: Masons. Insurance. Home: 2245 Evergeen Dr North Perry Village OH 44081 Office: Byron & Ryan 36100 Euclid Ave Willoughby OH 44094

CRUM, JAMES MERRILL, lawyer; b. Virginia, Ill., Oct. 14, 1912; s. Elton M. and Anna C. (Freitag) C.; m. Thelma Mae Williams, June 28, 1941; children—Suzanne, Deborah, James Frederick. A.B. with honors, Ind. U. (1937), J.D. with distinction, 1939. Bar: Ind. bar 1939, Fla. bar 1947. Practiced in Evansville, 1939-40, Indpls., 1941-47, Ft. Lauderdale, Fla., 1947—; assoc. firm Kahn & Dees, 1939-40; law clk. U.S. Dist. Ct., Indpls., 1941, 46; agt., acting agt. charge U.S. Secret Service, 1941-45; ptnr. firm McCune, Hiaasen, Crum, Ferris & Gardner, 1947—; city atty. Hallandale, Fla., 1949-53, 57-63, Plantation, Fla., 1953-59, Miramar, Fla., 1955-59; Supr. Old Plantation Water Control Dist., 1952-74; mem. Broward County Law Library Com., 1955-65. Mem. City Council, Miramar, 1955-59. Mem. Fedn. Ins. Counsel, Am., Fla., Broward County bar assns., Order of Coif. Clubs: The Drummers (Ft. Lauderdale), One Hundred of Broward County (Ft. Lauderdale). Probate, Real property, General practice. Home: 441 Holly Ln Plantation FL 33313 Office: PO Box 14636 Fort Lauderdale FL 33302

CRUMBLEY, R. ALEX, lawyer; b. McDonough, Ga., Jan. 31, 1942; s. Reuben Alexander and Lucy Margaret (Turner) C.; m. Claire Herd, Nov. 11, 1967; 1 son, Alexander Herd. B.A. in Journalism, U. Ga., 1964, J.D., 1966; student Am. Acad. Jud. Adminstrn., U. Va., 1980. Bar: Ga. 1965, U.S. Dist. Ct. (no. dist.) Ga. 1970, U.S. Supreme Ct. 1976. Asst. atty. gen. State of Ga., 1967-70; ptnr. Weltner, Kidd, Crumbley & Tate, Atlanta, 1970-76; pub. defender Flint Jud. Cir., 1976-77; judge Flint Jud. Circuit Superior Ct., 1978-83; ptnr. Crumbley & Crumbley, McDonough, Ga., 1983—; senator 17th dist. Ga. Senate, 1987—; prof. Woodrow Wilson Coll. Law, Atlanta, 1971-75; counsel to com. on judiciary Ga. State Senate, 1970. Served with Ga. N.G., 1966-72. Mem. ABA, Henry County Bar Assn., State Bar Ga. (mem. disciplinary bd. 1985—). Lawyers Club Atlanta, Atlanta Bar Assn. Democrat. Presbyterian. Club: Henry County Kiwanis (hon.). Contbr. articles to profl. jours. State civil litigation, Criminal, Family and matrimonial. Address: PO Box 775 McDonough GA 30253

CRUMLISH, JOSEPH DOUGHERTY, lawyer; b. Phila., Aug. 19, 1922; s. James Charles and Ruth (Hardy) C.; m. Rebecca Kelley, Sept. 12, 1950 (div. 1979); 1 child, Rebecca Kelley Crumlish Zuver. B.S.S., Georgetown U., 1946, Ph.D., 1954; M.A., Cath. U. Am., 1948, J.D., 1966. Bar: D.C. 1967, U.S. Ct. Appeals (D.C. cir.) 1968, U.S. Supreme Ct. 1975, U.S. Ct. Appeals (Fed. cir.) 1982, U.S. Claims Ct. 1980. Research coordinator Ford Motor Co., Dearborn, Mich., 1953-61; fund dir. Georgetown U. Alumni Assn., Washington, 1961-62; econ. devel. adminstr. U.S. Dept. Commerce, Washington, 1962-64; research program mgr., cons. Nat. Bur. Standards, Washington, 1964-77; counsel Casey, Scott & Canfield, Washington, 1977—; dir., co-founder, former pres. and chmn. Thomas More Soc. Am., Washington, 1980—; adj. faculty Georgetown U., U. Md., George Washington U., 1973-79. Author: A City Finds Itself, 1950; author monographs. Contbr. articles to profl. jours. Co-founder, First Friday Club of Phila., 1959; bd. dirs. Georgetown U. Alumni Assn., 1961-62, Cath. U. Am. Alumni Assn., 1962-65; sec., co-founder Men of Mercy, 1983—. Served with USAAF, 1943-46. Recipient Outstanding Community Service award Ford Motor Co., 1959; High Quality Performance, Nat. Bur. Standards, 1966; Commendation, Presdl. Clemency Bd., 1975. Mem. Found. for Research in Human Behavior (bd. advisors 1959-60), Ctr. for Applied Research in the Apostolate (lay bd. advisors 1978-83), D.C. Bar Assn., Fed. Bar Assn., John Carroll Soc. Clubs: Sharswood Law, Nat. Lawyers, Friendly Sons of St. Patrick. Government contracts and claims, Administrative and regulatory, Civil rights. Home: 10305 Gary Rd Potomac MD 20845 Office: Casey Scott and Canfield 524 National Pl 1331 Pennsylv ania Ave NW Washington DC 20004

CRUMP, BEVERLEY L., lawyer; b. Richmond, Va., Apr. 23, 1941; d. William Wood and Cyane (Bemiss) C.; m. Susanne Brown; children: Cyane B., William T. BA, U. Va., 1963, LLB, 1968; LLM, NYU, 1971. Assoc. Christian, Barton, Parker, Epps & Brent, Richmond, 1968-74; dir., ptnr. McDonald & Crump, Richmond, 1974-82; sole practice Richmond, 1982-85; dir., ptnr. McSweeney, Burtch & Crump, Richmond, 1985—; adj. prof. Va. Commonwealth U., 1981—. Served to lt. USNR, 1963-65. Mem. ABA, Va. State Bar Assn., Richmond Bar Assn. Episcopalian. General corporate, Real property, General practice. Office: McSweeney Burtch & Crump 9 S 12th St Richmond VA 23219

CRUMP, FRANCIS JEFFERSON, III, lawyer; b. Alexandria, Va., Dec. 4, 1942; s. Ross Gault and Pauline (DeVore) C.; BS in Math., Va. Mil. Inst., 1964; JD, Ind. U., 1967; m. Nancy Jo Burkle, Aug. 20, 1966; children: Tom, Laura, Elizabeth. Admitted to Ind. bar, 1967; gen. ptnr. firm Jewell, Crump & Angermeier, Columbus, Ind., 1971—; pres. Bonaventure Corp.; lectr. on estate planning and legal aspects of child abuse and neglect; sec., bd. dirs. Vancorp. Pres., bd. dirs. Columbus Boys' Club; past deacon, elder 1st United Presbyn. Ch. of Columbus, 1972-75, 1977-80; founding bd. dirs. Y Columbus Family Fitness Ctr., YMCA; pres. Dowtown Columbus Antique Mall, Inc. Served with U.S. Army, 1968-70, lt. col. USAR. Mem. Ind. State Bar Assn. (mem. ho. dels.), Bartholomew County Bar Assn. (pres. 1983), Columbus Coin Club, Inc. (pres.), Phi Alpha Delta. Republican. General corporate, Probate, Real property. Home: PO Box 1061 Columbus IN 47202 Office: Jewell Crump & Angermeier PO Box 1061 Columbus IN 47202

CRUMP, GERALD FRANKLIN, lawyer; b. Sacramento, Feb. 16, 1935; s. John Laurin and Ida May (Banta) C.; m. Glenda Roberts Glass, Nov. 21, 1959; children—Sara Elizabeth, Juliane Kathryn, Joseph Stephen. A.B., U. Calif.-Berkeley 1956, J.D., 1959; M.A., Baylor U., 1966. Bar: Calif. 1960. Dep. county counsel Los Angeles County, 1963—, legis. rep., 1970-73; chief pub. works div. Los Angeles County Counsel, 1973-84, sr. asst. county counsel, 1984-85, chief asst. county counsel, 1985—; lectr. Pepperdine U., 1978, U. Calif., 1982. Served to capt. USAF, 1960-63; to col. USAFR, 1963—. Mem. ABA, State Bar of Calif. (del.), Los Angeles County Bar Assn. (chmn. govtl. law sect. 1983-84), Am. Judicature Soc., Am. Acad. Polit. and Social Sci., Res. Officers Assn., Air Force Assn., Phi Alpha Delta, Delta Sigma Phi. Local government, Military, Environment. Home: 4020 Camino de la Cumbre Sherman Oaks CA 91423 Office: 648 Hall of Administration Los Angeles CA 90012

CRUMP, JOHN, Exec. dir. Nat. Bar Assn., Washington. Office: Nat Bar Assn 1225 11th St NW Washington DC 20001§

CRUMP, RONALD CORDELL, lawyer; b. Washington, Nov. 2, 1951; s. Robert Callwell and Marie Evangeline (Green) C. BBA, U. Ariz., 1974; JD, U. Notre Dame, 1979. Bar: D.C. 1980, U.S. Dist Ct. D.C. 1980, U.S. Ct. Appeals 1980, U.S. Ct. Claims 1980, U.S. Tax Ct. 1980, U.S. Ct. Mil. Appeals 1980, U.S. Ct. Appeals (4th cir.) 1981, U.S. Supreme Ct. 1984. Law revision counsel U.S. Ho. of Reps., Washington, 1978; law clk. to presiding justice D.C. Ct. Appeals, Washington, 1979-80; gen atty. VA, Washington, 1980-86; asst. atty. Office of U.S. Atty., Washington, 1986—. Mem. ABA, Fed. Bar Assn. (bd. dirs. 1984—), Washington Bar Assn., D.C. Bar Assn., Sigma Delta Tau. Republican. Roman Catholic. Club: Notre Dame (Washington). Administrative and regulatory, Criminal. Home: 3433 Summit Ct NE Washington DC 20018 Office: VA 555 4th St NW Washington DC 20001

CRUMP, THOMAS RICHARD, lawyer; b. Seguin, Tex., Oct. 24, 1945; s. Tom and Helen Margaret (Smith) C.; m. Theresa Frazier, Dec. 24, 1979; children—Tony, Kim, Wade, Val, Jon. B.S. summa cum laude, St. Mary's U., 1969; J.D., 1971. Bar: Tex. 1972, U.S. Tax Ct. 1976. With Petty Geophys., San Antonio, 1966-73; instr. St. Mary's U., San Antonio, 1967-69; sole practice, Seguin, 1973—. Mem. State Bar Tex., San Antonio Bar Assn., Guadalupe County Bar Assn., South Central Tex. Bar Assn., ABA, Tex. Trial Lawyers Assn., Delta Theta Phi. Oil and gas leasing, Real property. Office: PO Box 1306 108 W Court St Seguin TX 78155

CRUMPTON, CHARLES WHITMARSH, lawyer; b. Shreveport, La., May 29, 1946; s. Charles W. and Frances M. (McInnis) C.; m. Thu-Huong T. Cong-Huyen, Sept. 17, 1971; children: Francesca, Ian. BA, Carleton Coll., 1968; MA, U. Hawaii, 1974, JD, 1978. Bar: Hawaii 1978, U.S. Dist. Ct. Hawaii 1978, U.S. Ct. Appeals (9th cir.) 1982. Tchr. dept. edn. State of Hawaii, Honolulu, 1972-73, 75-77; prof. U. Can Tho, Vietnam, 1973-75; assoc. John S. Edmunds, Honolulu, 1978-80, Ashford & Wriston, Honolulu, 1980-85, David W. Hall, Honolulu, 1985—; barrister Am. Inn of Ct. IV, Honolulu, 1985—. Asst. dir. youth vols. Am. cancer Soc., Honolulu, 1972-73. Fulbright grantee U.S. Dept. State, 1973-75. Mem. ABA (torts and ins. practice sect., litigation sect.), Hawaii Bar Assn., Assn. Trial Lawyers Am. Avocations: water sports, tennis, running, guitar. Personal injury, Federal civil litigation, State civil litigation. Office: David W Hall Law Corp 1280 Grosvenor Ctr 733 Bishop St Honolulu HI 96813

CRUSE, FREDRICH JAMES, lawyer; b. Marysville, Calif., Sept. 7, 1947; s. Monta Parish and Jennie Ruth (Cudworth) C.; m. Nancy Kay Kress, Dec. 30, 1967; 1 child, Jason Alan. AB, William Jewell Coll., 1969; JD, U. Mo., Kansas City, 1973; postdoctoral, U. Va., 1974-75. Bar: Mo. 1974, U.S. Dist. Ct. (we. dist.) Mo. 1974, U.S. Ct. Mil. Appeals 1975, U.S. Dist. Ct. (ea. dist.) Mo. 1977, U.S. Supreme Ct. 1977, Ill. 1982, Utah 1987. Pub. defender 10th Jud. Cir., Hannibal, Mo., 1977-80; sole practice Hannibal, 1981—; ptnr. Cruse & Redington PC, Hannibal, Mo., 1983-84; v.p. Mo. State Pub. Defender's Assn., Jefferson City, 1978-79; bd. dirs. Lakeland Telephone and Tech. Services, Inc.; pres. Mark Twain Area Title Ins. Co., Hannibal, 1986; bd. dirs. Great Plains. Pres., drive chmn. United Way of Hannibal, 1978-80; dist. chmn., scoutmaster, varsity coach Boy Scouts Am., Hannibal, 1979—; atty. City of Hannibal, 1981-85. Served to capt. USMC, 1974-77. Recipient Vigil Honor Order of Arrow, Boy Scouts Am., 1984, Dist. Award of Merit, Mark Twain dist., Boy Scouts Am., 1985. Mem. ABA, Ill. State Bar Assn., Utah Bar Assn., Mo. Bar Assn. (chmn. econs. and methods of practice com.

1984—, chmn. non-urban lawyer com. 1982-84), Mo. Trial Lawyers Assn. Democrat. Mormon. Lodge: Kiwanis (Distinguished Pres. award 1980-81). Avocations: restoring old houses, backpacking. Bankruptcy, Family and matrimonial, General practice. Home: #9 Stillwell Pl Hannibal MO 63401 Office: Hannibal Nat Bank Bldg PO Box 914 Hannibal MO 63401

CRUZ, BENJAMIN JOSEPH FRANQUEZ, judge; b. Agana, Guam, Mar. 3, 1951; s. Juan Quenga Cruz and Antonia (Franquez) Guerrero. BA, Claremont Men's Coll., 1972; JD, U. Santa Clara, 1975. Asst. consumer counsel Office Atty. Gen., Agana, 1975; gov.'s legal counsel Gov. of Guam, Agana, 1975-79; sole practice law Agana, 1979-82; minority legal counsel Guam Legis., Agana, 1979-82; dir. Guam/Wash. Liaison Office, Washington, 1983-84; judge Superior Ct. Guam, Agana, 1984—. Pres. Am. Cancer Soc., 1978-80; committeeman Dem. Nat. Com., Washington, 1984; TV co-host Muscular Dystrophy Assn. Telethon, Agana, 1977-78; exec. dir. Dem. Party Guam, Agana, 1979-83. Mem. Nat. Judges Assn., Nat. Assn. Juvenile and Family Ct. Judges. Avocations: aerobics, weightlifting. Home: PO Box 3326 Agana GU 96910 Office: Superior Ct of Guam 110 W O'Brien Dr Agana GU 96910 *

CRYSTAL, JOEL FROME, lawyer; b. Bklyn., Feb. 3, 1945; s. Aaron and Sophie (Gerschwitz) C.; m. Marilyn Markfeld, Mar. 31, 1968; 1 child, Wendy Elissa. BA, Bklyn. Coll., 1965; JD, Columbia U., 1968. Bar: N.Y. 1969, U.S. Dist. Ct. (so. and ea. dists.) N.Y. 1974. Sr. staff atty., asst. sec. IPCO Corp., White Plains, N.Y., 1976—. Mem. Nat. Assn. Corp. Real Estate Execs. (chpt. sec. 1978-79). Office: IPCO Corp 1025 Westchester Ave White Plains NY 10604

CSANK, PAUL LEWIS, lawyer, financial company executive; b. Cleve., Nov. 14, 1939; s. Frank P. and Marie (Palmer) C.; m. Carole J. Nicholson, Aug. 4, 1965; children—Melissa, Aaron. B.A., Ohio State U., 1963; J.D., Cleve.-Marshall Law Sch., 1967. Bar: Ohio 1967, U.S. Dist. Ct. (no. dist.) Ohio 1969, Fla. 1982. Pres. Csank Csank & Weiner, Cleve., 1967—, ptnr., Palm Beach, Fla., 1983—; sec., gen. counsel, dir. Broadview Fin. Corp., Broadview Savs. and Loan, Cleve., 1974—; Mem. Ohio Bar Assn., Fla. Bar Assn., Cleve. Bar Assn., ABA. Banking, Real property, Securities. Office: Broadview Fin Corp 6000 Rockside Woods Blvd Cleveland OH 44131

CUADRA, DOROTHY ELIZABETH, lawyer; b. Washington County, Kans., Dec. 5, 1932; d. Gilbert H. and Nan Ellen (Smith) Stanbrough; m. Emilio L. Cuadra, 1957 (div. Mar. 1965); 1 child, Dione Catherine. BS in Engring., UCLA, 1959, MS in Engring., 1965; JD, U. Va., 1977. Bar: Alaska, Va., D.C. Research engr. The Marquardt Corp., Van Nuys, Calif., 1959-63, The Boeing Co., Seattle, 1965-66; sr. research engr., cons. Wyle Labs., El Segundo, Calif., 1966-71; dep. program devel. office of noise control U.S. EPA, Washington, 1971-74; assoc. Robertson, Monagle & Eastaugh P.C., Juneau, Alaska, 1977—, also bd. dirs., mgmt. com. Author numerous poems; contbr. articles on noise control to profl. jours. Mem. assembly science and tech. adv. council Calif. Legislature, 1970, science adv. com. Alaska Eskimo Whaling Commn., 1980-82; pres. League Women Voters Juneau, 1981-82; bd. dirs. League Women Voters Alaska, 1984. Amelia Earhart Graduate fellow Zonta Internat., 1963-64, 75-76; recipient pub. service commendations Los Angeles City Council, 1971, Calif. Legislature, 1970-71. Mem. ABA (law student div., Silver Key award com. environ. law 1977), Alaska Bar Assn., Acoustical Soc. Am. (Alaska region coordinator 1977—). Democrat. Jewish. Avocations: skiing, hiking, writing poetry, reading. State civil litigation, General practice, Administrative and regulatory. Home: 9151 Skywood Ln Juneau AK 99801 Office: Robertson Monagle & Eastaugh PC PO Box 1211 Juneau AK 99802

CUBA, BENJAMIN JAMES, lawyer, farmer; b. San Antonio, Dec. 12, 1936; s. Ben and Patricia (Machalek) C.; m. Bernadette Theresa Haney, Sept. 4, 1964; children—Benjamin Courtney, Tristan Konrad. A.A., Temple Jr. Coll., 1957; B.B.A., U. Tex., 1959; J.D., Baylor U., 1963. Bar: Tex. 1964, U.S. Dist. Ct. (we. dist.) Tex. 1970, U.S. Ct. Appeals (5th and 11th cirs.) 1981, U.S. Supreme Ct. 1978. Assoc. Law Offices of Jarrard Secrest, Temple, Tex., 1964-66; ptnr. Secrest & Cuba, Temple, 1966-68; sr. ptnr. Cuba, Simmon & Mayfield and predecessor firms, Temple, 1968—; gen. counsel Lone Star Savings Assn., Temple, 1984—, also dir. Founding trustee, atty. Inst. for Humanities at Salado, Tex., 1980—, founding trustee, legal counsel First House, Inc., Temple, 1981—; v.p. Temple Indsl. Devel. Corp., 1984. Fellow Tex. Bar Found.; mem. Bell-Lampasas-Mills Counties Bar Assn. (pres. 1973-74), State Bar Tex., Tex. Assn. Defense Counsel, Tex. Assn. Bank Counsel, Tex. Assn. Savings and Loan Counsel, U. Tex. Ex Students Assn., Baylor Law Alumni Assn., Phi Delta Phi. Lutheran. Club: Quarterback (dir. 1984, 85). State civil litigation, General corporate, Real property. Office: Cuba Simmon & Mayfield 18-20 S Main St Temple TX 76501

CUDAHY, RICHARD D., judge; b. Milw., Feb. 2, 1926; s. Michael F. and Alice (Dickson) C.; m. Ann Featherson, July 14, 1956 (dec. 1974); m. Janet Stuart, July 17, 1976; children: Richard Dickson, Norma Kathleen, Theresa Ellen, Daniel Michael, Michaela Alice, Marguerite Lois, Patrick George. B.S., U.S. Mil. Acad., 1948; J.D., Yale U., 1955; LL.D. (hon.), Ripon Coll., 1981. Commd. 2d. lt. U.S. Army, 1948, advanced through grades to 1st lt., 1950; law clk. to presiding judge U.S. Ct. Appeals (2d cir.), 1955-56; asst. to legal adv. Dept. State, 1956-57; assoc. firm Isham, Lincoln & Beale, Chgo., 1957-60, ptnr., 1976-79; pres. Patrick Cudahy, Inc., Wis., 1961-71; ptnr. firm Godfrey & Kahn, Milw., 1972; commr., chmn. Wis. Pub. Service Commn., 1972-75; judge U.S. Ct Appeals (7th cir.), Chgo., 1979—; lectr. law Marquette U. Law Sch., 1961-66; vis. prof. law U. Wis., 1966-67; prof. lectr. law George Washington U., Washington, D.C., 1978-79;. Commr. Milw. Harbor, 1964-66; pres. Milw. Urban League, 1965-66; trustee Environ. Def. Fund, 1976-79 chmn. Wis. Democratic party, 1967-68; Dem. candidate for Wis. atty. gen., 1968. Mem. ABA (spl. com. on Energy Law 1978-84, council adminstrv. law sect. 1986—), Am. Law Inst., Wis. Bar Assn., Milw. Bar Assn., Chgo. Bar Assn. Roman Catholic. Jurisprudence. Office: US Courthouse and Fed Office Bldg 219 S Dearborn St Chicago IL 60604

CUDLIPP, KATHERINE YEAMANS, lawyer, public policy formulator; b. Richmond, Va., June 26, 1943; d. William Samuel and Ruth Kennon (Yeamans) C. A.B., Randolph-Macon Woman's Coll., 1964; J.D., Georgetown U., 1976. Bar: D.C. 1976. Staff asst. C & P Telephone Co., Washington, 1966-68; assoc. dir. admissions Webster Coll., St. Louis, 1968-71; profl. staff mem. Senate Com. on Environ. and Pub. Works, Washington, 1971-79, chief counsel, 1981-87, minority chief counsel, 1987—; gen. counsel Nat. Commn. Air Quality, Washington, 1979-81; mem. U.S. environ. del. to USSR, 1983. Fulbright scholar, 1964. Mem. ABA (vice chmn. air quality com. 1981—). Avocation: bicycling. Administrative and regulatory, Environment. Office: Com on Environ and Pub Works US Senate Washington DC 20510

CUELLAR, ENRIQUE ROBERTO, lawyer; b. Laredo, Tex., Sept. 19, 1955; s. Martin and Odilia (Perez) C. AA in Polit. Sci. summa cum laude, Laredo Jr. Coll., 1976; BS in Internat. Relations, Law and Orgn. cum laude, Georgetown U., 1978; postgrad., U. Panamericana, Mexico City, 1980; M in Internat. Trade, Laredo State U., 1982; JD, U. Tex., 1981. Bar: Tex. 1981, U.S. Dist. Ct. (so. dist.) Tex. 1981, U.S. Ct. Internat. Trade, 1981, U.S. Ct. Appeals (5th cir.) 1981. Ptnr. Zaffirini, Cuellar & Castillo, Laredo, 1981—; mem. Tex. Ho. Reps., 1986—; adj. prof. internat. comml. law Laredo State U., 1984—; instr. state and nat. govt. Laredo Jr. Coll., 1982—; speaker in field. Pres. bd. dirs. Laredo Legal Aid Soc. Inc., 1982-84, Laredo Vol. Lawyers Program Inc., 1982-83, Internat. Good Neighbor Council, 1984-85; treas. bd. dirs. Stop Child Abuse and Neglect, 1982-83, adv. bd., 1984—; state legal advisor Am. GI Forum of Tex., 1986—; bd. dirs. United Way. 1982-83. Named one of Outstanding Young Men Am., 1982, 86. Mem. ABA, Tex. Bar Assn., Inter-Am. Bar Assn., Laredo Young Lawyers Assn. (pres. 1983-84). Democrat. Roamn Catholic. Lodge: Kiwanis (bd. dirs. Laredo 1982-83). Avocations: reading, karate, football, weightlifting. General practice, Private international, General corporate. Home: 4800 Marcella #74 Laredo TX 78041 Office: Zaffirini Cuellar & Castillo 1407 Washington St 2d Floor Laredo TX 78042-0627

CULLEN, JAMES D., lawyer; b. St. Louis, May 18, 1925; s. James and Frances C. Cullen; m. Joyce Marie Jackson, Aug. 19, 1950; children—Mary Lynn Cullen Walsh, James D., Michael, Carol Cullen Bernstein. LL.D., St. Louis U., 1948. Bar: Mo. 1948. Mem. firm Thomas, Busse, Goodwin, Cullen, Clooney & Gibbons, St. Louis, 1950—; Bd. dirs. Dismas House, Gen. Protestant Children's Home, Marygrove. Served to 1st lt. USAF, 1943-46. Mem. ABA, Mo. Bar Assn., St. Louis Bar Assn., Lawyers Assn. St. Louis. Democrat. Roman Catholic. Clubs: MAC, Frederick Pl. Farms. General corporate, Real property. Home: 16 Berkshire Saint Louis MO 63117 Office: Thomas Busse Goodwin Cullen Clooney & Gibbons 8631 Delmar Blvd Suite 300 Saint Louis MO 63124

CULLEN, THOMAS FRANCIS, JR., lawyer; b. Scranton, Pa., Mar. 23, 1949; s. Thomas Francis Cullen Sr.; m. Elizabeth Davis, Mar. 2, 1985; children: Elizabeth Mellody, Thomas McDonough. AB, Harvard U., 1971, JD, 1974. Bar: U.S. Dist. Ct. Pa. 1979, U.S. Supreme Ct. 1983, Mass., U.S. Ct. Appeals. Law clk. to presiding justice U.S. Ct. Appeals, Balt., 1974; assoc. Jones, Day, Reavis & Pogue, Washington, 1975-80, ptnr., 1981—. Editor Harvard U. Law Rev. Federal civil litigation, Administrative and regulatory, Public international. Office: Jones Day Reavis & Pogue 655 15th St NW Met Sq Washington DC 20005

CULLINA, WILLIAM MICHAEL, lawyer; b. Hartford, Conn., July 22, 1921; s. Michael Stephen and Margaret (Carroll) C.; m. Gertrude Evelyn Blasig, Apr. 29, 1961; children: William Gregory, Kevin Michael, John Stephen, Susan Margaret. A.B., Catholic U. Am., 1942; LL.B., Yale, 1948. Bar: Conn. bar 1948. Mem. firm Murtha, Cullina, Richter & Pinney, Hartford, 1948—; ptnr. Murtha, Cullina, Richter & Pinney, 1952—. Bd. dirs. St. Francis Hosp. and Med. Ctr., Jr. Achievement; bd. trustees St. Joseph Coll. Served with USNR, 1942-46. Mem. Am., Conn., Hartford County bar assns., Phi Beta Kappa. Roman Catholic. Clubs: Hartford Tennis, University, Hartford (bd. govs., 1st v.p.). Labor, Pension, profit-sharing, and employee benefits, General corporate. Home: 255 Westmont West Hartford CT 06117 Office: City Pl Hartford CT 06103

CULLINANE, PAUL BLAKE, lawyer; b. Beverly, Mass., Feb. 14, 1951; s. John Patrick and Lorraine Winifred (Powers) C.; m. Deborah Ann Black, Jan. 4, 1986. BA, Brandeis U., 1973; JD, George Washington U., 1977. Bar: Mass. 1978. Assoc. Bertram W. Allen Law Office, Manchester, Mass., 1977-81; sole practice Manchester, 1981-82; ptnr. Gilmore & Cullinane, Beverly, 1982—; bd. dirs. Cape Ann Indsl. Services, Inc., Rockport, Mass., L. Rossi Equipment Corp., Beverly. Mem. dem. com. Town of Manchester, 1978—, chmn. 1985-86, select chmn, 1981-84; bd. dirs. Vis. Nurse Assn. of North Shore, Danvers, Mass., 1984—, treas., 1985-86. Mem. Mass. Bar Assn., Salem County Bar Assn., Essex County Bar Assn. (exec. com.). Democrat. Roman Catholic. Avocations: running, theatre, studying history, travel. Consumer commercial, Criminal, Family and matrimonial. Home: 31 Lincoln St Manchester MA 01944 Offfice: Gilmore & Cullinane Three Ellis Sq Beverly MA 01915

CULLITAN, REGINALD KENNETH, lawyer; b. El Paso, Tex., Oct. 3, 1943; s. Kenneth Robert and Evelyn Emily (Boyd) Cullitan; m. Emelita Grajo. AA, Spokane Falls Community Coll., Spokane, Wash., 1965, Assoc. in Applied Sci., 1979; BA, Eastern Wash. State U., Cheney, 1967; JD, Gonzaga U., 1982. Bar: Wash. 1982. Staff atty. U.S. Dist. Ct. (ea. dist.) Wash., Spokane, 1982—. Exec. editor Gonzaga Law Rev., 1981-82. Dem. precinct committeeman, Spokane, 1966-67; polit. advisor Grass Roots Citizens Com., Spokane, 1964-70. Mem. ABA, Spokane County Bar Assn., Phi Delta Phi. General assistant to Chief Judge Robert J. McNichols. Office: US Cts PO Box 1039 Spokane WA 99210

CULP, CHARLES WILLIAM, lawyer; b. Louisville, Nov. 13, 1931; s. Charles Cantrell and Carolyn Marticia (O'Bannon) C.; m. Elisabeth Martha Stoker, Sept. 22, 1962; children—Charles Cantrell, Virginia Sheldon. B.A., Yale U., 1953; J.D., Harvard U., 1958. Bar: Ind. 1958. Ptnr., Cadick, Burns Duck & Peterson, Indpls., 1958-81, Shortridge & Culp, Indpls., 1981—; dir. Indpls. Opera. Clubs: Lawyers, Traders Point Hunt, Woodstock, University, Dramatic. Pension, profit-sharing, and employee benefits, Estate planning, General corporate. Home: 5791 Sunset Ln Indianapolis IN 46208 Office: 1 Indiana Sq Suite 2250 Indianapolis IN 46204

CULP, JAMES DAVID, lawyer; b. Montgomery, Ala., June 12, 1951; s. Delos Poe and Martha Edwardine (Street) C.; m. Gretchen Ina Greene, Aug. 4, 1974; 1 son, James Delos. B.S., East Tenn. State U., 1973, M.A., 1978; J.D., U. Tenn., 1977. Bar: Tenn. 1978, U.S. Dist. Ct. (ea. dist.) Tenn. 1978. Sole practice, Johnson City, Tenn., 1978-79, 83——; ptnr. Culp and Fleming, Johnson City, 1979-81, Thornton, Culp and Fleming, Johnson City, 1981-83; sole practice, Jonesborough, Tenn., 1983—; part-time instr. polit. sci. East Tenn. State U., 1980; part-time instr. bus. law Draughons Jr. Coll., 1983—. Active Johnson City Symphony Orch., 1969-74, Jr. Achievement, 1978-79; pres. Alcohol and Drug Counseling and Prevention Ctr., 1981-82; mem. East Tenn. State U. Wesley Found., 1979—, treas., 1981-82; mem. Upper East Tenn. Council on Alcoholism and Drug Dependence, 1981—; mem. East Tenn. State U. Friends of Music, 1981-82, pres., 1982; mem. Johnson City Bd. Dwelling Standards and Rev., 1983—, Washington County Election Commn., 1986—. Served with USNR, 1971-73. Mem. Washington County Bar Assn., Tenn. Trial Lawyers Assn., Mensa, Internat. Soc. for Philos. Enquiry, Am. Legion (judge adv. 1981-82), Johnson City Jaycees (state dir. 1979, named Spoke of Yr. 1978-79). Democrat. Methodist. General practice, State civil litigation, Criminal. Home: 913 Beech Dr Johnson City TN 37601 Office: 103 Courthouse Sq Jonesborough TN 37659 Office: 205 E Unaka Ave Johnson City TN 37601

CULPEPPER, BOBBY LOYCE, lawyer; b. Jonesboro, La., July 26, 1941; s. Edwin C. and Myrtle (Perry) C.; m. Elizabeth Walker, May 28, 1964; children: Teresa Loyce, William Todd. Student in govt., La. State U., JD, 1965. Bar: La. 1966. Law clk. to presiding justice La. Ct. Appeals, Lake Charles, 1965-66; ptnr. Culpepper, Teat, Caldwell & Avery, Jonesboro, 1968—. Chmn. exec. com. Jackson Parish Dems.; mem. La. Dems. Cen. Com. Served to capt. U.S. Army, 1966-68. Mem. ABA, La. Bar Assn. (ho. dels.), Jackson Parish Bar Assn. (pres.), Assn. Trial Lawyers Am., La. Trial Lawyers Assn. (gov.), Am. Judicature Soc., Phi Alpha Delta, Farm Bur. Assn. Lodge: Kiwanis. Office: Culpepper Teat Caldwell & Avery 525 E Court Ave Jonesboro LA 71251

CULPEPPER, GEORGE BROWN, III, judge; b. Fort Valley, Ga., Dec. 26, 1920; s. George B. Jr. and Mary (Adams) C.; m. Alice Wright, Oct. 23, 1943; children: Bryant, Lewis, Wright, Michele. AA, Mars Hill Jr. Coll., 1940; LLB, Mercer U., 1943. Bar: Ga. 1946. Judge Macon jud. cir. Ga. Superior Cts., 1967-82, sr. judge, 1982—. Served with USNR, 1942-46, PTO. Home: 311 College St Fort Valley GA 31030

CULPEPPER, MINIARD, lawyer; b. Boston, Nov. 3, 1953; s. Gentle Lee and Madeline (Bullock) C. BA, Brandeis U., 1976; JD, Suffolk U., 1981. Bar: Mass. 1982, U.S. Dist. Ct. Mass. 1982, U.S. Ct. Appeals (1st cir) 1982. Assoc. Charles H. Lewis, Roxbury, Mass., 1981-82; sole practice Boston, 1982—. Bd. dirs. Boston br. NAACP, 1980—; campaign aide Andrew Young campaign, 1976, Edward Brooke campaign, 1978; minority coordinator Edward Kennedy Presdl. campaign, 1979-80. Mem. ABA, Mass. Bar Assn., Mass. Black Lawyers Assn., Assn. Trial Lawyers Am., N.Y. Assn. Trial Lawyers, Alpha Phi Alpha. Democrat. Baptist. Avocations: tennis, chess, fishing, hunting, politics. Personal injury, Civil rights, Criminal. Home: 254 Seaver St Roxbury MA 02119 Office: 185 Devonshire St Suite 500 Boston MA 02110

CULVER, ROBERT WINTHROP, lawyer; b. Montclair, N.J., July 26, 1932; s. Winthrop Parker and Beryl Jessie (Gelhaar) C.; m. Carol Jean Nicholson, Mar. 16, 1957; 1 child, Robert Winthrop Jr. AB, Stanford U., 1954; JD, U. Calif., San Francisco, 1961. Bar: Calif. 1961, Mich. 1964, U.S. Supreme Ct. 1965. Trial atty. Antitrust div. U.S. Dept. Justice, Washington, 1960-62; assoc. Hansen & Dolle, Los Angeles, 1962-63; atty. Gen. Motors Corp., Detroit, 1963—, atty.-in-charge, gen. litigation sect., 1982—, asst. gen. counsel, 1983—. Advisor Birmingham, Mich. council Boy Scouts Am., 1974-78; bd. trustees Immanual Presbyn. Ch., Los Angeles. Served with U.S. Army, 1955-57. Mem. ABA (litigation sect., co-chair products liability com. 1984—), Calif. Bar Assn., Mich. Bar Assn., Am. Corp. Counsel Assn. Clubs: The Recess (Detroit), Torrey Pines Golf (La Jolla, Calif.). Avocations: golf, cross-country skiing, hiking. Federal civil litigation, State civil litigation, General corporate.

CULVER, SUE ANN RAY, lawyer; b. Austin, Tex., June 2, 1955; d. C.L. Jr. and Betty (Atkinson) Ray; m. James Harding Culver, May 1, 1982; 1 child, Kathryn Sue. BA in Govt., U. Tex., 1976; JD, S. Tex. Coll. of Law, 1980. Bar: Tex. 1980, U.S. Dist. Ct. (ea. and so. dist.) Tex. 1981. Adminstrv. aide U.S. Rep. Sam Hall, Washington, 1976-77; asst. atty. gen. State of Tex., Austin, 1981-82; legal staff atty. Tex. Bd. Ins., Austin, 1982-84; assoc. Boyd, Viegel & Hance, Austin, 1984-86; sr. staff atty. Tex. A&M Univ. System, College Station, 1986—. Mem. friend of scouting capitol area council exploring div. Boy Scouts Am., Austin, 1985—. Mem. ABA, Tex. Young Lawyers Assn., Travis County Bar Assn., Travis County Women Lawyers Assn. (pres. 1984-85), U. Tex. Longhorn Assocs. Democrat. Methodist. Avocations: piano, photography. Administrative and regulatory, State civil litigation.

CUMBS, CHARLES WILCOX, lawyer; b. San Antonio, Nov. 17, 1948; s. Guy St. Clair and Martha (Wilcox) C.; m. Bonnie Browne, May 27, 1972; children: Matthew David Wilcox, Daniel Browne. BA, Stanford U., 1971; JD, U. Tex., 1974. Bar: Tex. 1974, Hawaii 1979, U.S. Dist. Ct. Hawaii 1979. Assoc. Hooper, Kerry, Chappell & Broiles, Ft. Worth, 1975-78; assoc. Case, Kay & Lynch, Honolulu, 1979-85, ptnr., 1985—. Editor Am. Jour. Criminal Law, 1973-74. Mem. ABA, Hawaii Bar Assn., Tex. Bar Assn., Maui County Bar Assn. (bd. dirs. 1986), Assn. Trial Lawyers Am. Republican. Lodge: Rotary (pres. Kahului 1985-86). Avocations: golf, reading, running, photography. Real property, Workers' compensation, General corporate. Office: Case Kay & Lynch 33 Lono Ave Kahului HI 96732

CUMINALE, JAMES WILLIAM, lawyer; b. Amityville, N.Y., Mar. 10, 1953; s. Richard Paul and Margaret Virginia (Crook) C.; m. Cynthia Anne Conron, Aug. 19, 1978. BA, Trinity Coll., 1975; JD, Vanderbilt U., 1978. Bar: Conn. 1978, U.S. Dist. Ct. Conn. 1978. Assoc. Ivey, Barnum & O'Mara, Greenwich, Conn., 1978-82, ptnr., 1983—. Chmn. Greenwich Bd. Social Services, 1983—; bd. dirs. Greenwich Chpt. ARC, 1986—. Mem. Greenwich Bar Assn. Republican. Club: Riverside (Conn.) Yacht. Lodge: Rotary. Avocations: sailing, skiing. General corporate, Contracts commercial, Real property. Home: 9 Watch Tower Ln Old Greenwich CT 06870 Office: Ivey Barnum & O'Mara 170 Mason St Greenwich CT 06830

CUMMING, GEORGE ANDERSON, JR., lawyer; b. Washington, Apr. 16, 1942; s. George Anderson and Gene (Chapman) C.; m. Linda Lucille Harder, Aug. 25, 1963; children: Mary Elizabeth, Andrew Gordon. AA, Coll. San Mateo, 1962; AB magna cum laude, San Francisco State U., 1963; JD, U. Calif., Berkeley, 1967. Bar: Calif. 1967, U.S. Dist. Ct. (no. dist.) Calif. 1967, U.S. Ct. Appeals (9th cir.) 1967, U.S. Supreme Ct. 1974. Assoc. Brobeck, Phelger & Harrison, San Francisco, 1967-75, ptnr., 1975—. Bd. dirs. Twain Harte Improvement Assn., Calif., 1985—. Mem. ABA, San Francisco Bar Assn., Order of Coif. Avocation: model railroading. Antitrust, Federal civil litigation. Office: Brobeck Phleger & Harrison One Market Plaza San Francisco CA 94105

CUMMINGS, CHARLES ROGERS, lawyer; b. Fall River, Mass., Jan. 17, 1930; s. Joseph William and Ethel (Hudner) C.; m. Ann Hedges, Aug. 27, 1960; children—Carroll Ann, Robert Hudner, Peter Newman. B.A., Hobart Coll., 1953; LL.B., Boston U., 1956. Bar: Vt. 1957, U.S. Dist. Ct. Vt. 1957, U.S. Ct. Appeals (2d cir.) 1961. Ptnr. Kristensen, Cummings, Murtha & Stewart, Brattleboro, Vt.; mem. Vt. Statutory Revision Commn., 1969—; dir. Vt. Mcpl. Bond Bank, 1972-81; chmn. Vt. Bd. Labor Mediation and Arbitration, 1978-81. Trustee U. Vt., 1981-87, chmn. 1986-87. Fellow Am. Bar Found.; mem. ABA (state del. 1979-84, bd. govs. 1984—), Vt. Bar Assn. (bd. mgrs. 1975-78), Windham County Bar Assn. (pres. 1976), New Eng. Bar Assn. (pres. 1975-76). Republican. Roman Catholic. Avocations: skiing; body surfing; snorkling. Probate, General corporate, Family and matrimonial. Home: 8 New England Dr Brattleboro VT 05301 Office: Kristensen Cummings Murtha & Stewart 5 Grove St Brattleboro VT 05301

CUMMINGS, FRANK, lawyer; b. N.Y.C., Dec. 11, 1929; s. Louis and Florence (Levine) C.; m. Jill Schartz, July 6, 1958; children: Peter Jan, Margaret Anne. B.A., Hobart Coll., 1951; M.A., Columbia U., 1955, LL.B., 1958. Bar: N.Y. 1959, D.C. 1963. Adminstrv. asst. to U.S. Senator Javits, 1969-71; minority counsel com. labor and pub. welfare U.S. Senate, 1965-67, 71-72; assoc. firms in N.Y.C. and Washington, 1958-63, 67-68; ptnr. firm Gall, Lane & Powell, Washington, 1972-75, Marshall, Bratter, Greene, Allison & Tucker, Washington, 1976-82, Nossaman, Krueger & Knox, 1982-83, Cummings & Cummings, P.C. and predecessor firm Cummings & Kershaw, P.C., 1983-86, Le Boeuf, Lamb, Leiby & MacRae, Washington, 1986—; lectr. law Columbia U. Law Sch., 1970-74; adj. prof. Georgetown U. Law Sch., 1983-86; mem. pub. adv. council employee welfare and pension benefit plans Dept. Labor, 1972-74; mem. adv. bd. Pension Reporter Bur. Nat. Affairs. Mem. ABA (chmn. com. pension, welfare and related plans 1976-79), Am. Law Inst.; Bar Assn. D.C. (chmn. com. labor relations law 1972-73), Phi Beta Kappa. Author: Capitol Hill Manual, 1976, 2d edit. 1984, Multiemployer Plans, 2d edit., 1986; articles editor Columbia U. Law Rev., 1957-58. Federal civil litigation, Insurance, Labor, Pension, profit-sharing, and employee benefits. Home: 4305 Bradley Ln Chevy Chase MD 20815 Office: LeBoeuf Lamb Leiby & MacRae 1333 New Hampshire Ave NW Washington DC 20036

CUMMINGS, JOHN PATRICK, lawyer; b. Westfield, Mass., June 28, 1933; s. Daniel Thoams and Nora (Brick) C.; m. Dorothy June D'Ingianni, Dec. 27, 1957 (div. May 1978); children: John Patrick, Mary Catherine, Michael Brick, Kevin Andrew, Colleen Elise, Erin Christine, Christopher Gerald; m. Marilyn Ann Welch, May 23, 1980. BS, St. Michael's Coll., 1955; PhD, U. Tex., 1969; JD, U. Toledo, 1973, MCE, 1977. Bar: Ohio 1973, U.S. Mil. Appeals 1974, U.S. Dist. Ct. (no. dist.) Ohio 1979. Instr. U. Tex., Austin, 1962-68; scientist Owens Ill., Toledo, Ohio, 1968-75, atty., 1976-83; legal counsel Ecotherm Ltd., Sacramento, 1982—; pres. Hansa World, Toledo, 1983—; cons. EPA, Washington, 1970-74, Owens Corning Fiberglass, Toledo, 1978-79; bd. dirs., v.p. World Wide Transport, Toledo; bd. dirs. Interport Systems, Houston; adj. prof. U. Toledo, 1978-82. Contbr. articles to profl jours.; patentee in field. Mem. Bay Area Pub. Affairs Council, San Francisco. Served to col. USAFR, 1955-85. USPHS fellow, 1963-66. Fellow The Chem. Soc.; mem. ABA, Am. Chem. Soc., ASTM (chmn. 1979), Am. Ceramic Soc. (chmn. 1973), Res. Officers Assn. (legis. chmn. 1979—), Am. Legion. Roman Catholic. Club: Toledo Press. Lodge: KC. Avocations: reading, traveling, coin and stamp collecting. Environment, Private international, Customs and trade practice. Home: 843 Barcelona Dr Fremont CA 94536 Office: Hansa World 1507 21st St Suite 340 Sacramento CA 95814

CUMMINGS, WALTER DILLON, lawyer; b. Chgo., Sept. 29, 1931; s. Walter A. and Florence Mary (Dillon) C.; m. Madeleine A. Fridenburg, Oct. 20, 1956; children—Christopher, David, Andrew, Peter; m. 2d, Barbara S. Grigsby, Jan. 18, 1981. B.S., DePaul U., Chgo., 1953, LL.B., 1955. Bar: Ill. 1955, U.S. Ct. Clms., U.S. Dist. Ct. (no. dist.) Ill., U.S. Dist. Ct. (so. dist.) Ind., U.S. Ct. Apls. (7th cir.). Trial atty. U.S. Dept. Justice, 1955-56, spl. atty., 1959-61; sole practice, 1961-64; gen. atty. Chgo. & Eastern Ill. R.R., 1964-67; sole practice, Chgo., 1967—; mem. faculty bus. law DePaul U., 1961-64; atty. Village of Homewood, Ill., 1967—; panel mem. Fed. Defender program U.S. Dist. Ct. No. Dist. Ill.; legal advisor Ill. Police. Served to capt. USMCR, 1956-64. Mem. ABA, Ill. Bar Assn., Chgo. Bar Assn. Editor in chief DePaul Law Rev., 1955. Local government, Probate, Criminal. Office: 18027 Harwood Ave Homewood IL 60430

CUMMINGS, WALTER J., U.S. circuit judge; b. Chgo., Sept. 29, 1916; s. Walter J. and Lillian (Garvy) C.; m. Therese Farrell Murray, May 18, 1946 (dec. Nov. 1968); children: Walter J. III, Keith M., Mark F.; m. Marie Campbell Krane, Sept. 6, 1975. A.B., Yale U., 1937; LL.B., Harvard U., 1940. Bar: Ill. 1940. Mem. staff U.S. solicitor gen., Washington, 1940-46; spl. asst. to U.S. atty. gen. 1944-46; ptnr. Sidley, Austin, Burgess & Smith, Chgo., 1946-66; solicitor gen. U.S., 1952-53; judge 7th circuit U.S. Ct. Appeals, Chgo., 1966—; chief judge 7th circuit U.S. Ct. Appeals, 1981-86, sr. judge, 1986—; former mem. Joint Coms. Jud. Articles and Uniform Comml. Code; former grievance commr. Ill. Supreme Ct.; former mem. U.S. Jud. Conf.; chmn. Conf. Chief U.S. Cir. Ct. Judges, 1985-86, also subcom. judicial improvements, chmn. ad hoc com. on disposition of ct. records. Former mem. vis. com. Harvard Law Sch.; former mem. bd. visitors Stanford Law Sch.; past mem. vis. com. Northwestern U. Law Sch., U. Chgo. Law Sch.

Past nat. bd. dirs., vice chmn. Ill. div. Am. Cancer Soc.; past bd. govs. Citizens Greater Chgo.; governing life mem. Art Inst. Chgo. Named knight of Malta, knight of Holy Sepulchre. Mem. ABA (past chmn. spl. com. fed. rules procedure, past chmn. com. jud. center, mem. com. consumer credit, nat. ct. assistance com., Ross essay contest, mem. ad hoc com. on award of litigation costs), Fed. Bar Assn. (bd. dirs. Chgo. chpt.), Ill. Bar Assn. (past chmn. internat. law sect., past chmn. antitrust sect., comml. and bankruptcy law com., com. jud. ethics), Chgo. Bar Assn. (com. on judiciary, past chmn. com. constl. revision, grievance com. div. III A, bd. mgrs., past chmn. com. founds.), Bar Assn. 7th Fed. Cir. (past pres.), Chgo. Bar Found., Am. Bar Found., Harvard Soc. Ill. (past dir.), Thomas More Assn. (dir.), Am. Law Inst., Am. Judicature Soc., Appellate Lawyers Assn., Fed. Judges Assn. (bd. dirs.). Roman Catholic. Clubs: Law, Legal, Racquet, Tavern, Standard, Union League, Saddle and Cycle (Chgo.); Metropolitan (Washington); Yale (N.Y.C.). Office: U S Ct of Appeals Dirksen Fed Bldg 219 S Dearborn St Chicago IL 60604

CUMMINS, ELLIOTT BIRD, lawyer; b. McMinnville, Oreg., Nov. 25, 1910; s. Elmer E. and Kathleen (Bird) C.; m. Florence Elizabeth Pyatt, Sept. 20, 1939; children: Elliott C., Alice J., Carol E., Sarah J. BA, Linfield Coll., 1932; postgrad., U. Wash., 1932-33; JD, U. Oreg., 1935. Bar: Oreg. 1935. Asst. atty. gen. State of Oreg., Salem, 1942-44; rep. Oreg. Legislature, 1951; dist. atty. Yamhill County, Oreg., 1953-57; ptnr. Cummins, Cummins, Brown, Goodman & Fish P.C., McMinnville, 1957—. Chmn. Yamhill Rep. Cen. Com., 1949. Served to lt. (j.g.) USN, 1944-46, PTO. Fellow Oreg. Law Found.; mem. Oreg. Bar Assn. (bar examiner 1952-55). Republican. Presbyterian. General practice, Insurance, Probate. Home: 438 W 18th Pl McMinnville OR 97128 Office: Cummins Cummins Brown & Goodman PC 434 N Evans McMinnville OR 97128

CUMMINS, KENNETH COPELAND, lawyer; b. Cambridge, Mass., Mar. 22, 1943; s. David and Josephine (Copeland) C.; m. Annie Garrignot, Sept. 28, 1980. BA, Colgate U., 1965; JD, Boston U., 1968. Bar: Mass. 1968. Sole practice Canton, Mass., 1969-74; counsel Morse Shoe, Inc., Canton, 1974-75, asst. gen. counsel, asst. sec., asst. v.p., 1975-80, sec., asst. v.p., asst. gen. counsel, 1980-82, v.p., sec., gen. counsel, 1982—. Mem. ABA, Mass. Bar Assn., Boston Bar Assn., Am. Mgmt. Assn., Am. Soc. Corp. Secs., Am. Corp. Counsel Assn., Practising Law Inst. Avocations: sailing, skiing, woodworking, camping, sculpting. General corporate. Office: Morse Shoe Inc 555 Turnpike St Canton MA 02021

CUMMINS, NEIL JOSEPH, JR., land surveyor; b. Oxnard, Calif., Sept. 14, 1945; s. Neil Joseph and Helen Louise (Porter) C.; student Claremont Men's Coll., 1962-64, Calif. State Poly. Coll., 1965-67; JD, Mid Valley Coll. Law, 1978; Bar: Calif. 1978. m. Lynn D. Mealer, Sept. 16, 1967. Designer, Ludwig Engring., San Bernardino, Calif., 1967-69; field supr. Sikand Engring., Van Nuys, Calif., 1969-77; land surveyor, Reseda, Calif., 1977—; lectr. civil engring. Calif. Poly. Coll., Pomona, 1979-80; admitted to Calif. bar, 1978. Registered profl. engr., Ariz., Calif., Nev.; registered land surveyor, Calif., Nev., Ariz. Fellow ASCE; mem. Am. Congress Surveying and Mapping (chmn. So. Calif. sect. 1984), Am. Water Works Assn., ABA, Los Angeles County Bar Assn., Calif. Land Surveyors Assn. Construction, Real property, Malpractice defense; engineers and surveyors. Office: 7122 Reseda Blvd Reseda CA 91335-4210

CUMMINS, ROBERT PATRICK, lawyer; b. Oak Park, Ill., Mar. 17, 1933; s. John Francis and Ruth Elizabeth (Duffy) C.; m. Deborah Bolda; children—Michael, Patrick, Peter, Shannon, Ann, Molly. B.S. with distinction in Elec. Engring., Purdue U., 1958; J.D., DePaul U., 1962. Ptnr. Hume, Clement et al., Chgo., 1963-76; founding ptnr. Cummins, Decker & Webb, Chgo., 1976-81; ptnr. Burditt & Calkins, Chgo., 1981-82; founding ptnr. R.P. Cummins P.C., Chgo., 1982-85; v.p., trial counsel Motorola, Inc., Chgo., 1982-85; ptnr. Katten, Muchin, Zavis, Pearl , Greenberger & Galler, Chgo., 1985—; mem. governing bd. Chgo. Law Enforcement Study Group, 1971-73; mem. performance assistance com. U.S. Dist. Ct., Ill., 1982—; lectr. trial practice John Marshall Law Sch., 1973-74; lectr. Loyola U. Sch. Law, 1979—; mem. dean's vis. com. DePaul U. Law Sch., 1982—; mem. Ill. Jud. Inquiry Bd., 1979—, chmn., 1980—; mem. rev. bd. Atty. Registration and Disciplinary Commn. of Ill. Supreme Ct., 1973-80; mem. performance assistance com. U.S. Dist. Ct., 1982—. Contbr. articles to profl. jours.; mem. editorial bd. DePaul U. Law Rev., 1961-62. Bd. dirs., pres. Gastro-Intestinal Research Found., 1979—; bd. dirs. Lawyers Assistance Program, 1979—, Legal Clinic for Disabled, 1982—, Central States Inst. Addiction, 1983—. Served with USMC, 1952-54. Mem. Chgo. Bar Assn. (bd. mgrs. 1978-80), Ill. Bar Assn. (bd. govs. 1972-77), ABA (standing com. on profl. discipline 1981—, chmn. 1983—, co-chmn. joint com. profl. sanctions 1984—), Bar Assn. Seventh Fed. Cir., Am. Judicature Soc. (bd. dirs. 1985—), Chgo. Council Lawyers (exec. v.p. 1972, dir. 1972-73), Law Club Chgo., Legal Club Chgo., Eta Kappa Nu, Tau Beta Pi. Federal civil litigation, State civil litigation, Criminal. Home: 950 N Michigan Chicago IL 60611 Office: 525 W Monroe St Suite 1600 Chicago IL 60606

CUNDIFF, JAMES NELSON, lawyer; b. Perkins, Okla., Dec. 18, 1954; s. Nelson A. and Meryl E. (Peebles) C. BSBA, Okla. State U., 1976; JD, U. Tulsa, 1979. Bar: Okla. 1979, U.S. Dist. Ct. (we. dist.) Okla. 1979, U.S. Dist. Ct. (no. dist.) Okla. 1980, U.S. Ct. Appeals (10th cir.) 1980. Asst. CLE dir. Okla. Bar Assn., Oklahoma City, 1979-80; contract coordinator Cities Service Co., Tulsa, 1980-81; atty. ETSI Pipeline Project, Tulsa, 1981-85, Mapco Inc., Tulsa, 1985—; mem. CLE resource bd. Tulsa U. Coll. Law, 1983—; bd. dirs. Hyde Park Homeowner Assn., Tulsa, 1984—. Mem. ABA, Okla. State Bar Assn., Tulsa County Bar Assn., Am. Corp. Counsel Assn. (bd. dirs. Okla. chpt. 1986—), Phi Delta Phi (cert. of merit 1977), Phi Kappa Phi, Beta Gamma Sigma. Democrat. Baptist. Avocations: traveling, swimming, oil painting. Contracts commercial, General corporate, Environment. Office: Mapco Inc 1800 S Baltimore Ave Tulsa OK 74119

CUNHA, JOHN HENRY, JR., lawyer; b. Cambridge, Mass., Apr. 1, 1950; s. John Henry Sr. and Dolores Antonia (de Rosas) C.; m. Catherine Rondeau, July 6, 1985; 1 child, Christopher. BA, Boston Coll., 1973, JD, 1977. Bar: Mass. 1977, U.S. Dist. Ct. Mass. 1978, U.S. Ct. Appeals (1st cir.) 1981, N.Y. 1986. Trial atty. Mass. Defenders Com., Boston, 1977-79; pros. atty. State Ethics Commn., Boston, 1979-81; ptnr. Salsberg & Cunha, Boston, 1981—; instr. law Suffolk U., Boston, 1982-85, Harvard U., Cambridge, 1985—. Mem. Mass. Bar Assn., Boston Bar Assn. (co-chmn. indigent criminal def. com. 1985-86), Mass. Assn. Criminal Def. Lawyers, ACLU, Nat. Lawyers Guild. Democrat. Criminal, Personal injury. Office: Salsberg & Cunha 9 Hamilton Place Boston MA 02108

CUNHA, MARK GEOFFREY, lawyer; b. Lexington, Mass., Sept. 26, 1955; s. John Henry and Dolores (de Roses) C. AB magna cum laude, Cornell U., 1977; JD, Stanford U., 1980. Bar: N.Y. 1981, U.S. Dist. Ct. (so. and ea. dists.) N.Y. 1981. Assoc. Simpson, Thacher & Bartlett, N.Y.C., 1980—. Mem. ABA, Assn. of Bar of City of N.Y., Phi Beta Kappa. Democrat. Federal civil litigation, State civil litigation. Home: 322 W 57th St #12S New York NY 10019 Office: Simpson Thacher & Bartlett 1 Battery Park Plaza New York NY 10004

CUNNINGHAM, ALICE WELT, lawyer, legal educator; b. Washington, Aug. 18, 1949; d. Samuel Louis and Beatrice (Boxer) Welt; m. Daniel Paul Cunningham, Aug. 10, 1975; 1 child, Samuel Paul. BA summa cum laude, Yale U., 1971; JD, Harvard U., 1974. Bar: N.Y. 1975, Calif. 1975, U.S. Dist. Ct. (no. dist.) Calif. 1975, U.S. Tax Ct. 1976, U.S. Ct. Claims 1980, U.S. Ct. Appeals (D.C. cir.) 1980. Assoc. Shearman & Sterling, N.Y.C., 1974-75, Heller, Ehrman, White & McAuliffe, San Francisco, 1975-78, Debevoise & Plimpton, N.Y.C., 1978-83; assoc. prof. New York Law Sch., N.Y.C., 1983-86. Contbr. articles to profl. jours. Mem. ABA (subcom. U.S. activities of foreigners and tax treaties 1978—), N.Y. State Bar Assn., Assn. Bar City N.Y., Phi Beta Kappa. Corporate taxation, Personal income taxation, Private international.

CUNNINGHAM, G. KEVIN, lawyer; b. Houston, Oct. 6, 1953; s. Andrew Dent and Tera Francis (Wilborn) C.; m. Tricia L. Cunningham, Apr. 20, 1985. BA, U. Tex., JD. Bar: Tex. Briefing atty. Tex. Ct. Criminal Appeals, Austin, 1979-80; assoc. Haynes & Fullenweider, Houston, 1980-81, Shanks & Svetlik, Houston, 1981-82; atty. Amoco Prdn. Co., Houston, 1982-84, Pennzoil Co., Houston, 1984—. Mem. ABA (energy sect.), Tex. Bar Assn. (oil, gas and mineral law sect.). Clubs: Tex., Post Oak YMCA (Houston). Avocations: hunting, sailing, racquetball, jogging. Oil and gas. Home: 4921 Welford Bellaire TX 77401 Office: Pennzoil Co PO Box 2967 Houston TX 77001

CUNNINGHAM, GEORGE GRAY, lawyer; b. Franklin, N.C., July 15, 1951; s. John Fredrick and Betty Sue (Gray) C.; m. Christine B. Cunningham, Aug. 9, 1981. BA, Wake Forest U., 1973, JD, 1975. Bar: N.C. 1975, U.S. Dist. Ct. (mid. dist.) N.C. 1975. Assoc., v.p. Max F. Ferree P.A., Wilkesboro, N.C., 1975-81; ptnr., v.p. Ferree, Cunningham & Gray P.A., Wilkesboro, 1981—; atty. Wilkes County, Wilkesboro, 1982-84, 421 W Sanitary Dist., Wilkesboro, 1984—. Officer Wilkes Young Dems., Wilkesboro, 1976-79; del. Nat. Dem. Convention, San Francisco, 1984; sponsor Wilkes Little League Assn., Wilkesboro, 1984; commr. Northwestern Regional Housing Authority, Boone, N.C., 1984—; bd. dirs. Northwest N.C. Devel., Winston-Salem, 1982. Mem. N.C. Bar Assn. (family law com.), Wilkes County Bar Assn. (pres. 1982), Assn. Trial Lawyers Am., N.C. Acad. Trial Lawyers (sustaining), Wilkes Young Lawyers Assn. (pres. 1981). Democrat. Lodges: Masons, Elks. State civil litigation, Probate, Family and matrimonial. Home: PO Box 86 Wilkesboro NC 28697 Office: Ferree Cunningham & Gray PA 1 Court Square Wilkesboro NC 28697

CUNNINGHAM, JAMES JOSEPH, lawyer; b. Covington, Ky., Oct. 29, 1949; s. John Francis and Anna Mae (Dusing) C.; m. Patricia Ann Aubke, Aug. 5, 1978; children: Christina Ann, Elizabeth Ann. AB, Thomas More Coll., 1969; JD, U. Notre Dame, 1972; LLM, U. London, 1973. Bar: Ohio 1973, Ky. 1975, U.S Tax Ct. 1975. Assoc. Cors, Hair & Hartsock, Cin., 1973-80, ptnr., 1981; ptnr. Graydon, Head & Ritchey, Cin., 1981—. Mem. ABA (corp. banking and bus. law sect., uniform comml. code com., comml. fin. services com.). Avocation: sailing. Contracts commercial, Bankruptcy, Real property. Office: Graydon Head Ritchey 1900 Fifth Third Ctr Cincinnati OH 45202

CUNNINGHAM, JAMES REYNOLDS, lawyer; b. Schenectady, Apr. 27, 1946; s. James Jay and Kathryn Alice (Walker) C.; m. Jane Martin, Nov. 2, 1980. B.A. with honors, U. South Fla., 1967; J.D., Fla. State U., 1969. Bar: Fla. 1970, U.S. Supreme Ct. 1973, U.S. Ct. Customs and Patent Appeals 1974, U.S. Ct. Appeals (D.C.) 1974, U.S. Ct. Claims 1974, N.Y. 1980. Assoc., Maguire, Voorhis & Wells, P.A., Orlando, Fla., 1970-73; ptnr. Roby, Cunningham & O'Neill, P.A., Orlando, 1973-75, Moreland & Cunningham, P.A., Winter Park, Fla., 1975-80; sole practice James R. Cunningham, P.A., Orlando and Winter Park, 1980—; assoc. mcpl. judge, Winter Park, 1975, 76. Past pres. Maitland Grove Homeowners Assn., Winter Park C. of C., Park Ave. Assn. of Winter Park; mem. Republican Presdl. Task Force, 1981, Republican Nat. Com., Fla. State U. Coll. of Law scholar, 1968-69. Mem. Fla. Bar Assn., N.Y. State Bar Assn., Assn. Trial Lawyers Am., Acad. Fla. Trial Lawyers, ABA, Orange County Bar Assn., Phi Alpha Delta. Club: Masons. Personal injury, Federal civil litigation, State civil litigation. Office: 200 E Robinson St Suite 1220 Orlando FL 32801

CUNNINGHAM, JANIS ANN, lawyer; b. Seattle, May 13, 1952; d. Luvern Victor and Anna Jane (Bierstedt) Rieke; m. D. John Cunningham, June 10, 1972; children: Emily Jane, Laura Christine. BS with honors, U. Wis., Milw., 1973; JD, U. Wash., 1976. Bar: Wash. 1976, U.S. Dist. Ct. (we. dist.) Wash. 1976, U.S. Ct. Appeals (9th cir.) 1976. Law clk. to judge U.S. Ct. Appeals (9th cir.), Seattle, 1976-77; assoc. Karr, Tuttle, Koch, Campbell, Mawer & Sax, Seattle, 1977-84, ptnr., 1984—; lectr. community property law U. Wash., Seattle, 1984. Co-author: Washington Practical Probate, 1982, 4th rev. edit., 1986; editor in chief U. Wash. Law Rev., 1975-76. Mem. estate plnning com. Am. Heart Assn., Seattle, 1978; bd. dirs. Community Services for the Blind, Seattle, 1977-79. Mem. Wash. Bar Assn., Seattle Estate Planning Council (exec. bd. 1986—), U. Wash. Estate Planning Council Adv. Bd. (1984-1985), Order of Coif. Republican. Lutheran. Avocations: family, hiking, canoeing. Estate planning, Probate, Adoptions. Home: 2811 NE 177th Pl Seattle WA 98155 Office: Karr Tuttle Koch Campbell et al 1111 3d #2500 Seattle WA 98101

CUNNINGHAM, M.C., II, lawyer; b. Austin, Tex., Feb. 19, 1942; s. M.C. and Lottie (Dover) C.; m. Judith Greenway, Aug. 10, 1963; children: Amy, Sean, Erin. BA, Westminster Coll., 1964; JD, U. Mich., 1966. Bar: Colo. 1966, U.S. Dist. Ct. Colo. 1966, Okla. 1973. Staff atty. Phillips Petroleum Co., Denver, 1966-72; staff atty. Phillips Petroleum Co., Bartlesville, Okla., 1972-85, sr. counsel, 1986—. Named Outstanding Young Man, Outstanding Ams. 1973. Mem. Okla. Bar Assn., Washington County Bar Assn. Bankruptcy, Contracts commercial, General corporate. Home: 2608 Oakdale Dr Bartlesville OK 74006 Office: Phillips Petroleum Co 1289 Adams Bldg Bartlesville OK 74004

CUNNINGHAM, RALPH EUGENE, JR., lawyer, land developer; b. Hackensack, N.J., May 12, 1927; s. Ralph Eugene and Helen Virginia (Oliver) C.; m. Bonnie Grieser, July 10, 1962; children—Patrick T., Michael E., Candace T. Cunningham Dixon, Christian B.; m. 2d Michele Sleva, Dec. 11, 1982. Student U. Toledo, 1946-49; J.D., U. Miami, 1953. Bar: Fla. 1953, U.S. Dist. Ct. (so. dist.) Fla. 1953. Sole practice, Marathon, Fla., 1953-57, 61-71, ptnr. Cunningham & Jones, Marathon, 1957-59, Cunningham & Lane, Marathon, 1959-61, Cunningham, Albritton & Bee, Marathon, 1971-77, Cunningham, Albritton, Lenzi & Warner and predecessor, Cunningham, Albritton & Lenzi, Marathon, 1977—; chmn. bd. dirs. Marine Bank of Monroe County, Fla.; land developer; justice of the peace, 3d dist. Monroe County, 1955-57; state atty. 16th Jud. Cir. Fla., 1969-71. Mem. Fla. Ho. of Reps., 1959-60. Served with Q.M.C., USN, 1943-45; PTO. Mem. ABA, Marathon C. of C. (pres. 1960-61); Fla. Bar (bd. govs. 1974-77). Democrat. Clubs: Lions (pres. Marathon club 1956-57); Sombrero Country (pres. 1961-64), Elks (exalted ruler 1959-61). Banking. Office: PO Box 938 Marathon FL 33050

CUNNINGHAM, ROBERT JAMES, lawyer; b. Kearney, Nebr., June 27, 1942; m. Sara Jean Dickson, July 22, 1967. BA, U. Nebr., 1964; JD, NYU, 1967, LLM in Taxation, 1969. Bar: N.Y. 1967, Ill. 1969, U.S. Dist. Ct. (no. dist.) Ill. 1969, U.S. Ct. Claims 1970, U.S. Tax Ct. 1970, U.S. Ct. Appeals (D.C. cir.) 1972, U.S. Ct. Appeals (9th cir.) 1975, U.S. Ct. Appeals (7th cir.) 1979, U.S. Ct. Appeals (fed. cir.) 1982. Instr. law NYU, N.Y.C., 1967-69; assoc. Baker & McKenzie, Chgo., 1969-74, ptnr., 1974—; speaker in field. Contbr. articles to profl. jours. Mem. ABA, Ill. Bar Assn., Chgo. Bar Assn. Corporate taxation, Private international. Office: Baker & McKenzie Prudential Plaza Suite 2800 Chicago IL 60601

CUNNINGHAM, ROGER A., legal educator; b. 1921. S.B., Harvard U., 1942, J.D., 1948. Bar: Mass. 1948. Assoc. Nutter, McClennen and Fish, Boston, 1948-49; asst. prof. law George Washington U., 1950-54; assoc. prof. Rutgers U., New Brunswick, N.J., 1954-57; prof. Rutgers U., 1957-59, U. Mich., Ann Arbor, 1959—. Author: (with Browder and Smith) Basic Property Law, 1966, 4th edit. 1984, (with Tischler) Law of Mortgages in New Jersey Practice, 2 vols., 1975, (with Stoebuck and Whitman) Property, 1984, (with Mandeeker) Planning and Control of Land Development, 1979, 85, Cases on Land Financing, 1984. Legal education. Office: U Mich Law Sch 621 S State St Ann Arbor MI 48109 *

CUNNINGHAM, TOM ALAN, lawyer; b. Houston, Nov. 5, 1946; s. Warren Peek and Ellen Ardelle (Benner) C.; m. Jeanne Adrienne Moran, July 21, 1972; 1 child, Christopher Alan. B.A., U. Tex., 1968, J.D., 1974. Bar: Tex. 1974, U.S. Ct. Appeals (5th and 11th cirs.) 1981, U.S. Dist. Ct. (so. dist.) Tex. 1976, U.S. Dist. Ct. (no. dist.) Tex. 1982, U.S. Dist. Ct. (we. dist.) Tex. 1984. Ptnr., Fulbright & Jaworski, Houston, 1974—. Bd. dirs. Childrens Charity Fund, Houston, 1983—. Served to lt. (j.g.) USNR, 1969-72. Mem. Houston Bar Assn., State Bar Tex. (Pres's. award 1983, chmn. dist. 4H grievance com. 1982—, chmn. spl. com. on lawyer advt. and solicitation 1982). Clubs: Houston, Houston Yacht. Lodge: Kiwanis. Federal civil litigation, State civil litigation. Home: 10811 Pine Bayou St Houston TX 77024

CUNNINGHAM, WILLIAM ALLEN, lawyer; b. Oklahoma City, Okla., Aug. 25, 1945; s. John Henry and Jane Ann (Kraft) C.; m. Marsha Kay Wedel, Jan. 2, 1972; children: William Allen Jr., John Ryan, Marshall Trent, Derek Collin. BA, Tex. Tech U., 1973, JD, 1976. Bar: Tex. 1976, U.S. Supreme Ct. 1980. Assoc. Davis & David, Dalhart, Tex., 1976-78; ptnr. Davis, David & Cunningham, Dalhart, 1978-80, Davis & Cunningham, Dalhart, 1980-85, Davis, Cunningham & Enns, Dalhart, 1985—; bd. dirs. Dalhart Fed. Svgs. and Loan, 1985—. Served to staff sgt. USAF, 1967-71. Mem. ABA, 69th Dist. Bar Assn. (pres.), Delta Theta Phi. Methodist. Lodge: Lions (boss lion 1981). Avocation: sports. Contracts commercial, Family and matrimonial, Real property. Home: 1308 Peach Ave Dalhart TX 79022 Office: Davis Cunningham & Enns 513 Denrock Ave PO Box 1110 Dalhart TX 79022

CUNNINGHAM, WILLIAM FRANCIS, lawyer; b. Chgo., Feb. 24, 1945; s. Michael and Catherine B.C.; m. Patricia M. Grant, June 29, 1968; children—Kellie Marie, Kiera Megan, Michael Grant. B.A., DePaul U., 1967, J.D., 1971. Bar: Ill. 1971, U.S. Dist. Ct. (no. dist.) Ill. 1971. Mem. firm Gates W. Clancy, Geneva, Ill., 1971-74, O'Reilly & Quetsch, Wheaton, Ill., 1974-75, Roger K. O'Reilly, Wheaton, 1975-78; ptnr. O'Reilly & Cunningham, Duncan & Norton, 1978—. Mem. ABA, Ill. Bar Assn., DuPage County Bar Assn., Kane County Bar Assn., Assn. Trial Lawyers Am., Ill. Assn. Def. Trial Counsel, Internat. Assn. Ins. Counsel, Soc. Trial Lawyers. Roman Catholic. State civil litigation, Insurance, Personal injury. Home: 1613 Kaneville Rd Geneva IL 60134 Office: 109 N Hale St Wheaton IL 60187

CUNYUS, GEORGE MARVIN, oil company executive; b. Dallas, Jan. 13, 1930; s. George Grady and Ruby Gordon (King) C.; m. Mary Ellen Faust, Apr. 24, 1952; children: Bruce, Stuart, John. B.A., Rice U., 1951; J.D., So. Meth. U., 1956. Bar: Tex. 1956. With Hunt Oil Co., Dallas, 1956—; sr. v.p., gen. counsel Hunt Oil Co., 1962—, corp. sec., 1976—, dir., mem. exec. com.; chmn. bd, exec. com. E. Tex. Salt Water Disposal Co.; chmn. bd. Brooks Well Servicing, Inc. Trustees Disciples Found. of Dallas.; pres. Thai Christian Found. Served with U.S. Army, 1951-53. Mem. Mid-Continent Oil and Gas Assn. (dir. La. div.). Republican. Club: Dallas Petroleum. Oil and gas exploration and production. Home: 5634 Ledgestone Dr Dallas TX 75214 Office: 2900 Interfirst One Bldg Dallas TX 75202

CUOCO, DANIEL ANTHONY, lawyer; b. N.Y.C., Oct. 19, 1937; s. Angelo and Mary (deGeso) C.; m. Joanne C. Colavita, July 8, 1961; children: Dana, Mark, Susan, Victoria. AB summa cum laude, Iona Coll., 1959; JD, Columbia U., 1962. Bar: N.Y. 1962, U.S. Supreme Ct. 1965. Assoc. Dewey Ballantine Bushby Palmer & Wood, N.Y.C., 1962-71; v.p., asst. gen. counsel Squibb Corp., N.Y.C., 1971-82; sr. v.p., gen. counsel Squibb Corp., Princeton, N.J., 1982—, also bd. dirs.; trustee Food and Drug Law Inst., Washington. Mem. ABA, N.Y. State Bar Assn., Bar Assn. City N.Y. Republican. Club: Univ. (N.Y.C.). General corporate. Home: 28 Edgerstoune Rd Princeton NJ 08540 Office: Squibb Corp PO Box 4000 Princeton NJ 08540

CUPPLES, STEPHEN ELLIOT, lawyer; b. St. Louis, Feb. 20, 1955; s. Ronald L. Elisabeth (Pollock) C.; m. Ann McGeehan, Dec. 26, 1976; children: Christina, James, Catherine, Stephanie. AB summa cum laude, U. Mo., 1976, JD summa cum laude, 1979. Bar: Mo. 1979, U.S. Dist. Ct. (ea., we. dists.) Mo. 1979, U.S. Ct. Appeals (8th cir.) 1980, U.S. Tax Ct. 1981. Assoc. Peper, Martin, Jensen, Maichel and Hetlage, St. Louis, 1979-84; ptnr. Cupples, Edwards, Cooper and Singer, St. Louis, 1985—. Mem. ABA, Mo. Bar Assn., Bar Assn. Met. St. Louis (sec. taxation sect. 1986—), St. Louis County Bar Assn., Phi Beta Kappa, Phi Kappa Phi. Club: Young Lawyers Tax (chmn. 1983—). Probate, Estate planning, Personal income taxation. Office: Cupples et al 7733 Forsyth Suite 1000 Saint Louis MO 63105

CUPRILL, CHARLES, legal educator, university dean; b. 1916. J.D., U. P.R., 1947; postgrad. Inst. Fed. Taxation NYU, 1958. Bar: P.R. 1947. Prof. law, dean Sch. Law, Cath. U. P.R., Santa Maria Ponce; counsel Mario Mercado & Hijos, Ponce, 1947-67, Gen. Electric Corp., Ponce, 1952-67, Banco Credito Y Ahorro, Ponce, 1960-67, Ponce TV Corp., 1960-67, Voice of P.R., 1960-67. Pres. P.R. SSS Appeals Bd.; trustee Cath. U. P.R., pres. disciplinary bd., mem. acad. senate. Served to maj. U.S. Army, 1940-46; to lt. col., 1950-52; to col. P.R. NG, 1964; to. brig. gen., 1969. Club: Rotary Internat. (past gov.). Legal education. Office: Cath U PR Sch Law Avenido de las Americas & Avenido San Jorge Santa Maria Ponce PR 00731

CURFISS, ROBERT C., lawyer; b. Cin., June 7, 1946; s. Clinton S. and Jeanette I. (Falquet) C.; m. Jill MacDonald, June 14, 1969; children: David, Randall, Michelle. BSEE, U. Cin., 1969, JD, 1973. Bar: Ohio 1973, Ill. 1976, Tex. 1985. Assoc. Kinney & Schenk, Cin., 1973-76, Lee & Smith, Chgo., 1976-79; gen. patent counsel A.M. Internat., Inc., Chgo., 1979-82; gen. counsel Hydril Co., Houston, 1982—. Mem. ABA, Tex. Bar Assn., Houston Bar Assn., Licensing Exec. Soc., Am. Intellectual Patent Law Assn. Club: Atascocita Country (Humble, Tex.). General corporate, Patent, Trademark and copyright. Office: Hydril Co PO Box 60600 Houston TX 77205

CURFMAN, LAWRENCE EVERETT, lawyer; b. Champaign, Ill., Apr. 13, 1909; s. Lawrence Everett and Winifred (Williams) C.; m. Margaret Sylvia Baldwin, May 1, 1937; children: Lawrence Everett III, Elizabeth Ann (Mrs. Peter Koch), John Edward. A.B., U. Mich., 1930, J.D., 1932. Bar: Kans. 1932. Since practiced in Wichita; ptnr. Curfman, Harris, Stallings & Snow, 1982—. Contbr. articles to legal jours. Pres. Wichita Pub. Library Bd., 1954, 57, 58; Trustee E.A. Watkins Found. Mem. ABA (chmn. sect. local govt. law 1970- 71), Wichita Bar Assn. (pres. 1956), City Attys. Assn. Kan. (pres. 1953). Club: University (Wichita) (pres. 1965-66). Municipal bonds, Probate. Home: 7900 Donegal Wichita KS 67206 Office: 830 First Nat Bldg Wichita KS 67202

CURIONE, CHARLES, lawyer; b. Omaha, Mar. 7, 1922; s. Nunzio Joseph and Lorenza (Bellevia) C.; m. Nora Mae Lawson, Apr. 22, 1944; children—Charles J., Robert G., Lee Ana Curione Dorsett. B.S.C.E., U. Nebr., 1947; M.S.C.E., U. Ill., 1956; LL.B., LaSalle Extension U., 1967; J.D., Baylor U., 1976. Bar: Tex. 1977, U.S. Dist. Ct. (we. dist.) Tex. 1979. Commd. ensign U.S. Navy, 1947, advanced through grades to comdr. 1964; ret. 1966. research mgr. Stanford Research Inst., Menlo Park, Calif., 1966-71; pres. MLS, Inc., Los Altos, Calif., 1971-72; v.p. Success Motivation, Inc., Waco, Tex., 1972-74; sole practice, San Antonio, 1977—; instr. Stanford U., Palo Alto, Calif., 1967-70. Served to 2d lt. USAAF, 1943-45; ETO. Named Engr. of Yr., Architect Assn., Washington, 1958. Mem. San Antonio Bar Assn., Tex. Bar Assn., ABA, Am. Arbitration Assn. (arbitration panel 1980—). Republican. Roman Catholic. Real property, General practice. Home: 14203 Parksite Woods San Antonio TX 78249 Office: 450 GPM Bldg S Tower San Antonio TX 78216

CURLEY, ROBERT AMBROSE, JR., lawyer; b. Boston, June 5, 1949; s. Robert Ambrose and Terese M. (O'Hara) C.; m. Kathleen M. Foley, June 10, 1972; children—Christine, Elizabeth, Margaret. A.B. cum laude, Harvard U., 1971; J.D., Cornell U., 1974. Bar: Mass. 1974, U.S. Dist. Ct. Mass. 1975, U.S. Ct. Appeals (1st cir.) 1976. Ptnr. Curley & Curley, P.C., Boston, 1974—, also officer; lectr. Mass. Acad. Trial Attys. Com. mem. Am. Field Service, Hingham, Mass., 1978-79; counselor Old Colony council Boy Scouts Am., 1979—. Named Man of Yr. Old Colony council troop 52 Boy Scouts Am., 1984. Mem. ABA, Mass. Bar Assn., Def. Research Inst., Assn. Trial Lawyers Am. (assoc.), Charitable Irish Soc. Roman Catholic. Club: Harvard (Hingham) (treas. 1983-84, v.p. 1984-85, pres. 1985-86). Federal civil litigation, State civil litigation, Personal injury. Home: 29 Pioneer Rd Hingham MA 02043 Office: Curley & Curley PC 27 School St Boston MA 02108

CURNIN, THOMAS FRANCIS, lawyer; b. Bklyn., Sept. 16, 1933; s. Thomas Francis and Marion (Wallace) C.; m. Miriam Johnson, Sept. 19, 1959; children: Thomas, Paul, Kevin, Mark. B.S., Mt. St. Mary's, 1955; LL.B., Fordham U., 1958. Bar: N.Y. 1959, U.S. Ct. Appeals (2d cir.) 1959, U.S. Dist. Ct. (so. dist.) N.Y. 1961, U.S. Dist. Ct. ea. dist.) N.Y. 1961, U.S. Ct. Appeals (5th cir.) 1978, U.S. Supreme Ct. 1979, U.S. Ct. Appeals (8th cir.) 1983. Ptnr. firm Cahill Gordon & Reindel, N.Y.C., 1968—; hearing panel chmn. dept. disciplinary com. First Jud. Dept., N.Y., 1980-84. Mem. Bd. Arbitration Archdiocese n.Y., 1978—. Served with USMCR, 1958-64. Fellow Am. Coll. Trial Lawyers; mem. ABA (com. on corp. counsel litigation sect. 1980—), Fordham Law Sch. Alumni Assn. of N.Y.C. Democrat. Roman Catholic. Clubs: University (Larchmont, N.Y.); Down Town Assn.

(N.Y.C.). Federal civil litigation, State civil litigation. Home: 40 Ocean Ave Larchmont NY 10538 Office: Cahill Gordon & Reindel 80 Pine St New York NY 10005

CUROTTO, RICKY JOSEPH, lawyer, corporate executive; b. Lomita Park, Calif., Dec. 22, 1931; s. Enrico and Nora M. (Giusso) C.; m. Lynne Therese Ingram, Dec. 31, 1983; children—Dina L., John F., Alexis J. B.S. cum laude, U. San Francisco, 1953, J.D., 1958. Bar: Calif. 1959. Assoc. Peart, Baraty & Hassard, San Francisco, 1958-60; sr. counsel, asst. sec. Utah Internat. Inc., San Francisco, 1960—; of counsel Curotto Law Offices, San Francisco and Sacramento, Calif., 1984—; counsel, sec. Ross Valley Homes, Inc., Greenbrae, Calif.; dir. First Security Realty Services Corp., Simco Indsl. Mortgage Co., Garden Hotels Investment Co. Trustee, U. San Francisco. Served to 1st lt. U.S. Army, 1954-56. Named to U. San Francisco Athletic Hall of Fame, 1985; recipient Bur. Nat. Affairs award, 1958, Disting. Service award U. San Francisco, 1981. Mem. State Bar Calif., San Francisco Bar Assn., ABA, Am. Arbitration Assn. (nat. panel arbitrators), Am. Corp. Counsel Assn. Republican. Roman Catholic. Club: Commonwealth of Calif. (San Francisco). Contbr. articles to law revs. Real property, Contracts commercial, General corporate. Office: Utah Internat Inc 550 California St Suite 700 San Francisco CA 94104

CURRAN, BARBARA ADELL, research institute executive; b. Washington, Oct. 21, 1928; d. John R. and Beda (Parkins) Curran. B.A., U. Mass., 1950; LL.B., U. Conn., 1953; LL.M., Yale U., 1961. Bar: Conn. 1953. Atty., Conn. Gen. Life Ins. Co., 1953-61; mem. research staff Am. Bar Found., Chgo., 1961—, assoc. exec. dir., 1976—; vis. prof. U. Ill. Law Sch., 1965, Sch. Social Service, U. Chgo., 1966-68, Ariz. State U., 1980; cons. in field. Mem. Ill. Gov.'s Consumer Credit Adv. com., 1962-63; consumer credit adv. com. Nat. Conf. Commns. on Uniform State Laws, 1964-70; credit legis. subcom. Mayor Daley's Com. on New Residents, 1966-69; cons. Pres.'s Commn. on Consumer Interests, 1966-70, others. Fellow Am. Bar Found.; mem. ABA, Pi Beta Phi. Contbr. articles to profl. jours.; author five books in field. Consumer commercial. Address: Am Bar Found 750 N Lake Shore Dr Chicago IL 60611

CURRAN, BILL, lawyer; b. Mpls., Feb. 27, 1946; s. William P. and Margaret (Killoren) C.; m. Jean Lorraine Stabenow, Jan. 1, 1978; children: Patrick, Lisa, John. B.A., U. Minn., 1969; J.D., U. Calif., 1972. Bar: Calif. 1972, Nev. 1974, D.C. 1982. Adminstr. Nev. State Ct., Carson City, 1973-74, clk. Nev. Supreme Ct., 1973-74; assoc. Wiener, Goldwater, Galatz & Waldman, Las Vegas, 1974-75; chief dep. atty. Clark County Dist. Atty.'s Office, Las Vegas, 1975—; mem. Clark County Jud. Task Force, Las Vegas, 1977—; county counsel Clark County, 1979—; head Civil Div., Clark County Dist. Atty.'s Office. Co-author: (manual) Nevada Judicial Orientation Manual, 1974. Mem. ABA, Nat. Dist. Attys. Assn., Am. Trial Lawyers Assn., Nat. Assn. County Civil Attys. (pres. 1984-85), Calif. Bar Assn., Nev. Bar Assn. (gov. 1978—, v.p. 1986-87, pres.-elect 1987—), Nev. Dist. Attys. Assn., Nev. Judges Assn. (hon.). Democrat. Roman Catholic. Local government. Home: 3865 Alice Ln Las Vegas NV 89103 Office: Clark County Dist Atty's Office 200 S 3d St Las Vegas NV 89155

CURRAN, CATHERINE MOORE, lawyer; b. Jersey City, June 25, 1948; d. Harold Joseph and Mary Kathleen (Mindrup) Moore; m. Patrick M. Curran, Jan. 25, 1969; children—Patrick Michael, Mark Andrew. A.B., Douglass Coll., 1973; J.D., Seton Hall U., 1978. Bar: N.J. 1978, U.S. Dist. Ct. N.J. 1978, U.S. Ct. Appeals (3d cir.) 1980. Law clk. to justice Supreme Ct. N.J., Morristown, 1978-79; assoc. Lum, Biunno & Tompkins, Newark, 1979-83, Lum, Hoens, Abeles, Conant & Danzis, Newark, 1984-85; litigation atty. Sea-Land Corp., 1985—; mem. spl. com. on admission to bar Supreme Ct., Newark, 1980-81, adv. com. on admission to bar, 1981—. Mem. ABA, N.J. Bar Assn., Morris County Bar Assn. Federal civil litigation, State civil litigation, Contracts commercial. Home: 4 Jessica Ct Chatham NJ 07928 Office: Sea-Land Corp Law Dept 10 Parsonage Rd Edison NJ 08837

CURRAN, J. JOSEPH, JR., lawyer, state official; b. West Palm Beach, Fla., July 7, 1931; s. J. Joseph and Catherine (Clark) C.; m. Barbara Marie Atkins, 1959; children—Mary Carole, Alice Ann, Catherine Marie, J. Joseph III. LL.B., U. Balt., 1959. Mem. Md. Senate, 1963-83; lt. gov. State of Md., 1983-86; attorney general State of Maryland, Annapolis, 1987—; mem. Md. Regional Planning Council, 1963-82. Office: 216 E Lexington St Baltimore MD 21202

CURRAN, JOHN GERARD, lawyer, city official; b. Rochester, N.Y., Dec. 22, 1934; s. Arthur B. and Evelyn A. (MacDonald) C.; m. Ann Louise Barnett, Nov. 23, 1963; children—Joan, Eileen, Teresa, Kathryn. B.A. cum laude, U. Notre Dame, 1957, J.D., 1958. Bar: N.Y. 1958, U.S. Dist. Ct. (we. dist.) N.Y. 1958, Colo. 1960, U.S. Dist. Ct. Colo. 1960, Sole practice, Rochester, 1961—. Vice mayor City of Rochester, 1977-85 , city councilman, 1974—; bd. dirs. Monroe County Youth Bd., 1973-81; mem. Monroe County Fire Adv. Bd., 1981-86 ; mem. planning com. United Way; bd. dirs. Roches for Econ. Devel. Corp., 1986—. Served with U.S. Army, 1958-60. Mem. ABA, N.Y. State Bar Assn., Monroe County Bar Assn. Democrat. Roman Catholic. Club: Notre Dame (man of year award 1979) (Rochester). General practice, Consumer commercial, Bankruptcy. Office: 310 Exec Office Bldg Rochester NY 14614

CURRAN, JOHN PETER, lawyer; b. Springfield, Mass., May 24, 1956; s. John Peter and Theresa Mary (Lynch) C.; m. Victoria Deborah Tuma, Sept. 13, 1986. BA, Fordham U., 1978, JD, 1981. Bar: N.Y. 1982, D.C. 1985, U.S. Supreme Ct. 1986. Atty. Union Labor Life Ins. Co., Washington, 1982—. Mem. ABA, Assn. Life Ins. Counsel, Nat. Health Lawyers Assn. Democrat. Roman Catholic. Avocations: hunting, fishing. General corporate, Insurance, Pension, profit-sharing, and employee benefits. Home: 810 S Arlington Mill Dr #302 Arlington VA 22204 Office: Union Labor Life Ins Co 111 Massachusetts Ave NW Washington DC 20001

CURRAN, MARK COONEY, lawyer; b. Chgo., Sept. 11, 1924; s. William Thomas and Josephine Mercedes (Cooney) C.; m. Mary Gladys Wholey, May 12, 1962 (dec.); m. 2d Mary Jane McCarthy, Oct. 31, 1964; children: Mark, Mary Jane, Anthony, Nicholas. B.S., St. Ambrose Coll., Davenport, Iowa, 1947; J.D., Northwestern U., 1950. Bar: Ill. 1950, Iowa 1950. Trial atty. NLRB, Washington, 1950-52, Chgo., 1952-55; asst. counsel PPG Industries, Inc., Pitts., 1956-67; assoc. gen. counsel Montgomery Ward & Co., Chgo., 1967-76; ptnr. Sidley & Austin, 1976—. Mem. adv. com. Ill. State Toll Hwy. Com., 1975-80. Served to lt. (j.g.) USN, 1943-46. Mem. ABA, Chgo. Bar Assn. Roman Catholic. Club: MidDay (Chgo.). Labor, Personal injury. Home: 794 S Cherokee Rd Lake Forest IL 60045 Office: One First Nat Plaza 4800 Chicago IL 60603

CURRAN, MAURICE FRANCIS, lawyer; b. Yonkers, N.Y., Feb. 20, 1931; s. James F. and Mary (O'Brien) C.; m. Deborah M., May 7, 1960; children—James, Maurice, Amy, Bridget, Ceara, Sara. Student Cathedral Coll., 1950; B.A. in Philosophy, St. Joseph Coll. and Sem., 1952; LL.B., Fordham U., 1958. Bar: N.Y. 1958, U.S. Dist. Ct. (so. and ea. dists.) N.Y. 1960, U.S. Ct. Appeals (2d cir.) 1982. Assoc. Kelley, Drye, Newhall & Maginnes, N.Y.C., 1958-60; assoc. Wilson & Bave, Yonkers, 1960-65; div. counsel Merck & Co., Rahway, N.J., 1965-67; asst. gen. counsel E. R. Squibb & Sons, Inc., N.Y.C., 1967-70; corp. counsel, chief law dept. City of Yonkers, 1970-72; ptnr. Bleakley, Platt, Schmidt & Fritz, White Plains, N.Y., 1972-83, Anderson, Banks, Moore, Curran & Hollis, Mt. Kisco, N.Y., 1983—; counsel Yonkers Bd. Edn. Trustee, Westchester Community Coll. Served to capt. USMC, 1952-58. Mem. ABA, N.Y. State Bar Assn., City Bar City N.Y. Democrat. Roman Catholic. State civil litigation, Federal civil litigation, Local government. Home: 388 Bronxville Rd Yonkers NY 10708 Office: 61 Smith Ave Mount Kisco NY 10549

CURRAN, RICHARD EMERY, JR., lawyer; b. Portland, Maine, Jan. 31, 1950; s. Richard Emery and Catherine Margaret (Bunker) C.; m. Nancy Bokron, Aug. 16, 1975 (div. May 1982). AB, Dartmouth Coll., 1972, MBA, 1973; JD, Harvard U., 1977; LLM, Boston U., 1983. Bar: Maine 1977, U.S. Dist. Ct. Maine 1977, U.S. Tax Ct. 1984. Assoc. Pierce, Atwood, Scribner, Allen, Smith & Lancaster, Portland, Maine, 1977-82, ptnr., 1983—. Mem. ABA. Republican. Congregationalist. Clubs: Portland Country (Falmouth). Corporate taxation, Estate taxation, General corporate. Home: 77E Park St Portland ME 04101

CURRAN, ROBERT BRUCE, lawyer; b. Charleston, W.Va., July 2, 1948; s. Bruce Frederick and Hazel Viola (Hoy) C.; m. Constance Marie Eggers, Jan. 24, 1970; children: Michael Robert, Laura Elizabeth. BA, U. Del., 1971; JD, U. Md., 1974. Bar: Md. 1974. Ptnr. Frank, Bernstein, Conaway & Goldman, Balt., 1974—. Co-author: Tax Planning Forms for Businesses and Individuals, 1985. Mem. Md. Bar Assn. (sec. and treas. taxation sect. 1985-86, chmn. elect taxation sect. 1987—). Pension, profit-sharing, and employee benefits, General corporate, Corporate taxation. Office: Frank Bernstein Conaway & Goldman 300 E Lombard St Baltimore MD 21202

CURRAN, WILLIAM JAMES, III, lawyer; b. Omaha, Dec. 26, 1940; s. William James Jr. and Blanche Josephine (Lisco) C.; m. Mary Kathryn Notopoulos, Oct. 28, 1967 (dec. Mar. 1987); 1 child, Elizabeth Marie. BS, Creighton U., 1962, JD, 1965. Bar: Nebr., N.Y. Editor in chief The Antitrust Bulletin; contbr. articles on antitrust law to profl. jours. Served as lt. USN, 1966-69. Antitrust, Jurisprudence. Home: 421 Hemlock Ct Pittsburgh PA 15237

CURRER, WILLIAM JOHN, JR., lawyer; b. Alhambra, Calif., Feb. 8, 1912; s. William John and Leah Alice (Bullock) C.; m. Lucie Cecelia Miller, Sept. 28, 1942; children: William John III, Peter Sherman, Paul McNeil. Student, UCLA, 1933-35; LLB, U. So. Calif., 1938. Bar: Calif. 1938, U.S. Dist. Ct. (so. dist.) Calif. 1938, U.S. Ct. Appeals (9th cir.) 1941, U.S. Dist. Ct. (no. dist.) Calif. 1967, U.S. Tax Ct. 1969, U.S. Supreme Ct. 1969. Assoc. Law Offices of Clyde C. Shoemaker, Los Angeles, 1939-40; sole practice Los Angeles, 1940-41, 46-57, 60—; assoc. Newlin & Ashburn, Los Angeles, 1941-43, Law Offices of Forrest A. Betts, Los Angeles, 1943-46; ptnr. Moore, Trinkaus & Currer, Los Angeles, 1957-60. Mem. exec. com. Episcopal Ch. Diocese of Los Angeles, com. on revision of cannons, standing com., legal adv. to bishop, del. to Triennial Conv., former vestryman Parish of Advent; mem Parish St. Stephen, Civil Service com. on Selection of Police Officer Candidates, 1960-70. Mem. ABA, Calif. Bar Assn., Los Angeles County Bar Assn., Am. Judicature Soc., Am. Arbitration Assn. (panel). Federal civil litigation, General corporate, General practice. Office: 417 S Hill St Suite 770 Los Angeles CA 90013

CURREY, CHARLES THOMAS, lawyer; b. Evanston, Ill., Dec. 2, 1944; s. Charles H. and Georganna (Luttrell) C.; m. Marilyn Elizabeth Sands, Oct. 29, 1966; children—Karen Lynn, Charles Thomas, Nancy Anne, Gregory Roy. B.A., Beloit (Wis.) Coll., 1966; J.D., Cornell U., 1969. Bar: N.Y. 1971, U.S. Dist. Ct. (no. dist.) N.Y. 1971, U.S. Dist. Ct. (we. dist.) N.Y. 1985, U.S. Supreme Ct. 1974. Assoc., Richard I Mulvey, Esq., Ithaca, N.Y., 1971-73; sole practice, Ithaca, 1973-84; ptnr. Currey & Smithson, Ithaca, 1984-86, sole practice, 1986—; asst. dist. atty., 1973-79. Bd. dirs. United Way, 1980-87, treas., 1981, 1st v.p., 1984, pres., 1985-87; bd. dirs. Reconstrn. Home, 1980—; bd. dirs. Ballet Guild of Ithaca, 1974-84, treas., 1976-84; chmn. Easter Seal campaign, 1970. Mem. ABA, N.Y. State Bar Assn., Tompkins County Bar Assn., Comml. Law League Am. Federal civil litigation, State civil litigation, Criminal. Office: 109 E Seneca St Ithaca NY 14850

CURRIE, DAVID PARK, lawyer, educator; b. Macon, Ga., May 29, 1936; s. Gillette Brainerd and Elmyr (Park) C.; m. Barbara Suzanne Flynn, Dec. 29, 1959; children—Stephen Francis, Margaret Rose. B.A., U. Chgo., 1957; LL.B., Harvard U., 1960. Bar: Ill. bar 1963. Law clk. to Hon. Henry J. Friendly U.S. Ct. Appeals (2d cir.), N.Y.C., 1960-61; to Hon. Felix Frankfurter U.S. Supreme Ct., Washington, 1961-62; asst. prof. law U. Chgo., 1962-65, assoc. prof., 1965-68, prof. law, 1968—; coordinator environ. quality State of Ill., Chgo., 1970; chmn. Ill. Pollution Control Bd., Chgo., 1970-72; vis. prof. Stanford U. Law Sch., 1965, U. Mich. Law Sch., 1964, 68, U. Hannover, W. Ger., 1981. Author: Cases and Materials on Federal Courts, 1968, 3d edit., 1981, On Pollution, 1975, (with R. Cramton and H. Kay) On Conflict of Laws, 1968, 3d edit., 1981, Federal Jurisdiction in a Nutshell, 1976, 81, Air Pollution: Federal Law and Analysis, 1981, Constitution in the Supreme Ct., 1985. Administrative and regulatory, Environment, Legal history. Office: 1111 E 60th St Chicago IL 60637

CURRIE, EDWARD JONES, JR., lawyer; b. Jackson, Miss., May 23, 1951; s. Edward J. and Nell (Branton) C.; m. Barbara Scott Miller, June 26, 1976; children: Morgan E., Scott E. BA, U. Miss., 1973, JD, 1976. Bar: Miss. 1976, U.S. Dist. Ct. (no. and so. dists.) Miss. 1976, U.S. Ct. Appeals (5th cir.) 1978, U.S. Supreme Ct. 1979. Assoc. Wise, Carter, Child, Steen & Caraway, Jackson, Miss., 1976-80; ptnr. Steen, Reynolds, Dalehite & Currie, Jackson, 1980-86; adj. prof. Miss. Coll. Sch. Law, Jackson, 1977-81, 84-86. Bd. dirs. Miss. chpt. Am. Diabetes Assn., Jackson, 1980-82. Mem. Miss. Bar Assn. (bd. dirs. young lawyers sect. 1981-82), Jackson Young Lawyers (bd. dirs. 1980-81), Fed. Bar Assn. (v.p. cen. dist. Miss.), Miss. Def. Lawyers Assn., Hinds County Bar Assn., Am. Trial Lawyers Assn., Nat. Inst. Trial Advocacy, Phi Delta Phi, Sigma Alpha Epsilon (pres. Central Miss. alumni 1981). Presbyterian. Federal civil litigation, State civil litigation, Insurance. Home: 50 Moss Forest Circle Jackson MS 39211 Office: Steen Reynolds Dalehite & Currie PO Box 900 Jackson MS 39205

CURRIE, MICHAEL ROBERT, lawyer; b. Jersey City, N.J., Nov. 27, 1952; s. Stanley R. and Mildred (Byronas) C.; m. Jennifer M. Goff, June 28, 1975; children: Meredith A., Elizabeth C., Samantha G. BA, Colby Coll., 1974; JD, U. Maine, 1980; LLM in Taxation, Boston U., 1986. Bar: Maine 1980, U.S. Dist. Ct. Maine 1980, U.S. Tax Ct. 1984. Ptnr. Pierce, Atwood, Scribner, Smith & Lancaster, Portland, Maine, 1980—. Chmn. Planned Giving Com. United Way, Portland. Mem. ABA, Maine Bar Assn., Cumberland Bar Assn. Corporate taxation, Personal income taxation, Probate. Office: Pierce Atwood Scribner et al One Monument Sq Portland ME 04101

CURRIE, OVERTON ANDERSON, lawyer; b. Hattiesburg, Miss., Nov. 28, 1926; s. Edward Alexander and Terry (Anderson) C.; m. Lavona Stringer, Dec. 31, 1949; children: Iva Terry, Overton Anderson, Martha Lavona, Lucy Flora, Judy Stringer. Assoc. Sci., Marion Inst., 1944; B.B.A., U. Miss., 1948, LL.B., 1949; B.D., Emory U., 1958, M.Div., 1968; LL.M., Yale U., 1958. Bar: Miss. Bar 1949, Ga. bar 1959. Practice in Hattiesburg, Miss., 1949-55, Atlanta, 1959—; county prosecuting atty. 1952-55, spl. asst. atty. gen. Miss., 1954-55; mem. faculty Yale U. Law Sch., 1958-59; partner Smith, Currie & Hancock, 1959—; adj. prof. Emory U. Law Sch., 1966-73, Fla. State U., 1973; lectr. chpt. seminars on constrn. law Asso. Gen. Contractors, Ga., 1967, 72-74, 76, 80, Fla., 1967-68, 71, 73-75, 78-85, Carolinas, 1968-86, Okla., 1968, 76, Ind., 1969, 71, 75, 77, Pa., 1969, 72, 73, 79, 86, N.Y., 1969-70, Ky., 1972-74, Va., 1973-75, Tenn., 1974-79, Ala., 1974-83; lectr. constrn. law seminars Mech. Contractors Assn., various locations, 1971-77; lectr. numerous other constrn. industry trade assns. Author: Preparing Construction Claims for Settlement, 1968, Subcontracts and Labor Problems, 1969, Differing Site (Changed) Conditions, 1971, Preparing and Settling Construction Claims, 1983, Changed Conditions, 1984, Understanding Construction Contracts: A Myriad of Special Clauses, 1986. Bd. dirs. Ga. Assn. Pastoral Care; mem. profl. adv. com. Pastoral Counseling Service. Served with U.S. Mcht. Marine Corps USNR, 1944-46. Mem. ABA (nat. chmn. sect. on public contract law 1971-72, mem. council ho. of dels. 1972-74, nat. chmn. constrn. cases com. 1978-80), Am. Trial lawyers. (past nat. v.p.), Am. Arbitration Assn. (bd. dirs. 1986—), State Bar Ga., Lawyers Club Atlanta, Phi Delta Theta, Phi Delta Phi, Omicron Delta Kappa, Phi Kappa Phi (nat. pres.), Beta Gamma Sigma, Phi Sigma Alpha. Clubs: Piedmont Driving (Atlanta), Capital City (Atlanta), Commerce (Atlanta). Home: 1055 Nawench Dr NW Atlanta GA 30327 Office: 2600 Peachtree Center Harris Tower Atlanta GA 30043-6601

CURRIER, BARRY ARTHUR, law educator; b. Columbus, Ohio, Apr. 16, 1946; s. Arthur Edmund and Marian Louise (Dunavent) C.; m. Marilyn Joanne Cashion; children: Christine Joanne, Ryan Cashion. AB, UCLA, 1968; JD, U. So. Calif., 1971. Bar: Calif. 1972. Law clk. to presiding justice U.S. Ct. Appeals (D.C. cir.), Washington, 1971-72; assoc. Latham & Watkins, Los Angeles, 1972-73; asst. prof. law U. Ky., Lexington, 1974-77; assoc. prof. law U. Fla., Gainesville, 1977-80, prof. law, 1980—; vis. asst. prof. law Duke U., Durham, N.C., 1976, Monash U., Melbourne, Australia, 1985. Mem. Am. Law Inst., Urban Law Inst., Order of Coif. Real property, Personal income taxation, State and local taxation. Office: U Fla Coll Law Gainesville FL 32611

CURRIER, THOMAS SHOLARS, lawyer; b. Shreveport, La., Aug. 18, 1932; s. Charles Ford and Caroline (Sholars) C.; m. Barbara Ann Dawson, July 3, 1954; children: Charles Ford, II, Thomas Dawson, Henrietta Sholars. Student, Princeton U., 1950-52; LL.B., Tulane U., 1956. Bar: La. 1956, Va 1967, D.C 1970, N.Y 1970. Asso. firm Stone, Pigman & Benjamin, New Orleans, 1957-59; asst. prof. law Tulane U., 1959-62; asso. prof. La. State U., 1962-64; asso. prof. U. Va., 1964-67, prof., 1967-70; partner firm Mudge Rose Guthrie & Alexander, N.Y.C., 1971-77, Dewey, Ballantine, Bushby, Palmer & Wood, N.Y.C., 1977—; lectr. Practicing Law Inst.; mem. labor arbitration panel Fed. Mediation and Conciliation Service, Am. Arbitration Assn.; Trustee South Kent (Conn.) Sch., 1969-74, Davis and Elkins Coll., 1971-83. Author: (with J.W. Moore) Moore's Federal Practice, vol. 1B, 1963, (with Forrester) Federal Jurisdiction and Procedure, 1962; contbr. articles in law revs. Mem. Am. Law Inst., Nat. Assn. Bond Lawyers (dir.), Order of Coif. Club: Downtown Assn. Home: 580 Park Ave New York NY 10021 Office: Dewey Balantine Bushby Palmer & Wood 140 Broadway New York NY 10005 *

CURRIER, TIMOTHY JORDAN, lawyer; b. Detroit, Apr. 18, 1952; s. Vincent James Currier and Jean Enid (Flett) McCann; m. Mary Ellen Minter, May 22, 1976; children: Mary Bridget, Meghan Kathleen, Timothy Jordan Jr. BA, U. Notre Dame, 1975; JD, U. Detroit, 1978. Bar: Mich. 1978, U.S. Dist. Ct. (ea. dist.) Mich. 1978, U.S. Supreme Ct. 1982. Dep. sheriff marine div. Oakland County Sheriff Dept., Pontiac, Mich., 1973-78; assoc. Dell, Shantz, Booker & Schulte, Royal Oak, Mich., 1978-81; ptnr. Shantz, Booker & Currier P.C., Bloomfield Hills, Mich., 1981; lectr. in field. Campaign chmn. For Candidate for County Sheriff, Pontiac, 1972, 76; co-chmn. golf outing Christ Child Soc., 1987. Mem. ABA (probate trust and real property sect.), Assn. Trial Lawyers Am., Nat. Orgn. of Legal Problems of Edn., Mich. Bar Assn., Oakland County Bar Assn. (probate and trust sect.), Oakland County Estate Planning Council, Nat. Sch. Bd. Assn. (council sch. attys.), Brother Rice Alumni Assn. (pres. 1983). Republican. Roman Catholic. Clubs: Notre Dame, Economic (Detroit). Estate planning, Probate, School law. Home: 2437 Chelsea Ln Troy MI 48084 Office: Shantz Booker and Currier PC 525 N Woodward Suite 1100 Bloomfield Hills MI 48013

CURRIN, SAMUEL THOMAS, lawyer; b. Oxford, N.C., Dec. 13, 1948; s. Thomas Benjamin and Lois (Brady) C.; m. Margaret Person, June 24, 1973. B.A. cum laude, Wake Forest U., 1971; J.D., U. N.C., 1974. Bar: N.C. 1974. Asst. U.S. atty. Eastern Dist. N.C., Raleigh, 1976-78; legis. asst. to Sen. Jesse Helms Washington, 1978-81; U.S. atty. Eastern Dist. N.C., Raleigh, 1981—. Chmn. pub. affairs com. So. Bapt. Conv., 1983—. Republican. Lodge: Lions (Raleigh). Federal civil litigation, Criminal, Administrative and regulatory. Home: 1700 Pineview St Raleigh NC 27608 Office: US Atty PO Box 26897 Raleigh NC 27611

CURRY, DANIEL ARTHUR, lawyer, corporation executive; b. Phoenix, Mar. 28, 1937; s. John Joseph and Eva May (Wills) C.; m. Joy M. Shallenberger, Sept. 5, 1959; children: Elizabeth Marie, Catherine Jane, Peter Damien, Jennifer Louise, Julia Maureen, David Gordon. B.S., Loyola U., Los Angeles, 1957, LL.B., 1960; postgrad., U. So. Calif. Law Center, 1964-65; postgrad. exec. program, Grad. Sch. Bus., Stanford U., 1980. Bar: Calif. 1961, Hawaii 1972, U.S. Ct. Appeals (9th cir.) 1972, U.S. Dist. Ct. (cen. and no. dists.) Calif. 1972, U.S. Dist. Ct. Hawaii 1972, U.S. Ct. Mil. Appeals 1963, U.S. Customs Ct. 1968. Assoc. Wolford, Johnson, Pike & Covell, El Monte, Calif., 1964-65, Demetriou & Del Guercio, Los Angeles, 1965-67; counsel, corporate staff divisional asst. Technicolor, Inc., Hollywood, Calif., 1967-70; v.p., sec., gen. counsel Amfac, Inc., Honolulu, 1970-78; sr. v.p., gen. counsel Amfac, Inc., 1978—; bd. dirs. Amfac Found.; bd. regents Loyola Marymount U., Chaminade U. (hon.). Served to capt. USAF, 1961-64. Mem. ABA (com. corp. law depts.), Sigma Rho, Phi Delta Phi. Clubs: Pacific (Honolulu); The Family, St. Francis Yacht (San Francisco); 1925 F Street (Washington), The California (Los Angeles). General corporate, Securities, Antitrust. Office: 44 Montgomery St PO Box 7813 San Francisco CA 94120

CURRY, DONALD ROBERT, lawyer; b. Pampa, Tex., Aug. 7, 1943; s. Robert Ward and Alleith Elizabeth (Elliston) C.; m. Carolyn Sue Boland, Apr. 17, 1965; 1 son, James Ward. B.S., West Tex. State U., 1965; J.D., U. Tex., 1968. Bar: Tex. 1968, U.S. Dist. Ct. (no. dist.) Tex. 1970, U.S. Tax Ct. 1973. Assoc., Day & Gandy, Ft. Worth, 1968-69, ptnr., 1970-72; sole practice, Ft. Worth, 1972—; lectr. in field. Bd. regents West Tex. State U., Canyon, 1969-77, sec., mem. exec. com., 1972-75; mem. exec. bd. Longhorn council Boy Scouts Am., 1970—, dist. chmn., 1970-75; precinct chmn. Tarrant County (Tex.) Democratic Party, 1982—, election judge, 1982—. Mem. State Bar Tex., ABA, Fort Worth-Tarrant County Bar Assn., Ft. Worth Bus. and Estate Council, Tex. Ind. Producers and Royalty Owners Assn., Phi Alpha Delta. Methodist. Clubs: Ft. Worth, Petroleum of Fort Worth. General corporate, Oil and gas leasing. Home: 3800 Tulsa Way Fort Worth TX 76107 Office: 905 Ft Worth Club Bldg Fort Worth TX 76102

CURRY, GEORGE STEVEN, lawyer; b. Dodgeville, Iowa, Oct. 8, 1947; s. Arthur George and Phyllis Iona (Andrews) C.; m. Linda Karen Saunders, Sept. 27, 1975; children: Jeffrey, Nathaniel, Jonathan. BA, Luther Coll., 1969; JD, U. Wis., 1972. Bar: Wis. 1972, U.S. Dist. Ct. (we. dist.) Wis. 1984. Ptnr. Kopp, McKichan, Geyer and McKichan, Curry, Geyer & Clare, Platteville, Wis., 1972-76; sole practice Platteville, 1976—; bus. law lectr. U. Wis., Platteville, 1980-82. Treas. 3d Rep. Congl. Dist. Western Wis., 1976. Served with USAR, 1969-71. Mem. Wis. Bar Assn., Wis. Bar Found., Assn. Trial Lawyers Am., Wis. Trial Lawyers Assn., Civil Trial Counsel Wis., Def. Research Inst., U. Wis. Alumni Assn. (bd. dirs.). State civil litigation, Personal injury, Insurance. Home: Box 322 Platteville WI 53818-0322 Office: Kopp McKichan Geyer et al 44 E Main Platteville WI 53818-0253

CURRY, ROBERT EMMET, JR., lawyer, business executive; b. N.Y.C., Jan. 18, 1946; s. Robert Emmet and Rose Ann (Mooney) C.; m. Margaret Courtney Kennedy, May 6, 1973; 1 child, Robert Emmet III. B.A. with honors, Georgetown U., 1967; J.D., Columbia U., 1970. Bar: N.Y. 1971, U.S. Supreme Ct. 1973. Assoc. Patterson, Belknap, Webb & Tyler, N.Y.C., 1971-73; sr. counsel Rouse Co., Columbia, Md., 1973-75; assoc. counsel Ogden Corp., N.Y.C., 1976-80, v.p., 1981-85, gen. counsel, 1983-87, sr. v.p., 1985-87, ptnr. Dickstein, Shapiro & Morin, 1987—. Mem. Assn. Bar City N.Y. (energy com.), N.Y. State Bar Assn. ABA, Am. Corp. Counsel Assn. (pres. Met. N.Y. chpt.). Roman Catholic. Club: Washington (Conn.). Office: Dickstein Shapiro & Morin 598 Madison Ave New York NY 10022

CURRY, STEPHEN EUREE, lawyer; b. Sandersville, Ga., Aug. 11, 1950; s. J.E. and Lytha (Dixon) C.; m. Valerie Curry; stepchildren: Joshua E. Pinson, Ashley L. Pinson. AB, U. Ga., 1972, JD, 1975. Bar: Ga. 1975. Chief asst. dist. atty. Augusta (Ga.) Jud. Cir., 1975-78; sole practice Augusta, 1978—. Pres. U. Ga. Young Dems., Athens, 1971. Mem. ABA, Am. Trial Lawyers Assn., Ga. Trial Lawyers Assn., Order Barristers. Avocation: aircraft pilot. Personal injury, Federal civil litigation, State civil litigation. Office: PO Box 2494 Augusta GA 30903

CURTIN, CHRISTOPHER JAMES, lawyer; b. Wilmington, Del., July 14, 1951; s. George Morrison and Margaret (Nichols) C.; m. Bonnie Louise Reid, Mar. 31, 1973; children: Laura, Andrew, Kelly. BA, U. Va., 1973; JD, N.Y. Law Sch., 1977. Bar: Del. 1977. Mgr. trainee Wilmington Trust Co., Del., 1973-74; dep. atty. gen. Del. Dept. of Justice, Wilmington, 1977-85; assoc. Sawyer & Akin P.A., Wilmington, 1985-87, ptnr., 1987—; instr. writing Del. Law Sch., 1983-84; spl. asst. U.S. Atty., 1984-85. Mem. ABA, Am. Trial Lawyers Assn., Del. Bar Assn. (state, fed. civil litigation, editor Advocate mag.), Del. Trial Lawyers Assn. State civil litigation, Criminal, Insurance. Office: Sawyer & Akin PA Del Trust Bldg 18th Floor Wilmington DE 19801

CURTIN, JOHN T., judge; b. 1921. B.S., Canisius Coll. Bar: N.Y. bar 1949. Formerly U.S. atty. for Western Dist. N.Y., 1961-67; judge U.S. Dist. Ct. for Western N.Y., Buffalo, 1967—; now chief judge. U.S. Dist. Ct. for Western N.Y. Office: US Dist Ct 624 US Court House Buffalo NY 14202 *

CURTIN, WILLIAM JOSEPH, lawyer; b. Auburn, N.Y., Mar. 9, 1931; s. William Joseph and Edith A. (Murray) C.; m. Helen Bragg White, Aug. 3,

1956; children: Helen Bragg, Caroline Goddard, William Joseph III, Christopher Newport. B.S., Georgetown U., 1953, J.D., 1956, LL.M., 1957. Bar: D.C. bar 1956, U.S. Supreme Ct. bar 1961. Asso. firm Morgan, Lewis & Bockius, Washington, 1960-64; partner Morgan, Lewis & Bockius, 1965—; public mem. Adminstrv. Conf. U.S., 1968-72; editor-in-chief Legal Legis. Reporter, 1968—; Chmn. trustees Norwood Sch., Bethesda, Md., 1976-79. Contbr. articles to legal jours. Recipient Labor Mgmt. Peace award Am. Arbitration Assn., 1966, John Carroll award Georgetown U., 1973. Fellow Am. Bar Found.; mem. Am. Bar Assn. (chmn. spl. com. nat. strikes in transp. industries 1968-70, chmn. labor relations law com., public utility sect. 1967-81, chmn. public utility law sect. 1982), D.C. Bar Assn. (chmn. labor law com. 1968-70). Labor, Public utilities, Administrative and regulatory. Office: Morgan Lewis & Bockius 1800 M St NW Suite 800 Washington DC 20036

CURTIS, DALE JAY, lawyer; b. Stillwater, Okla., Dec. 9, 1942; s. Dale R. and Muriel (Morris) C.; m. Kathryn Hoops, Aug. 6, 1965; children—Dale, Jonathan, Tyler, Bryan, Andrew. B.S., U. Utah, 1968, J.D., 1971. Bar: Utah 1971, U.S. Dist. Ct. Utah 1971, U.S. Tax Ct. 1984. Ptnr., Kesler, Gordon & Curtis, Salt Lake City, 1971-77, Nielsen & Senior, and predecessor, Salt Lake City, 1977—. Mem. adv. bd. China-U.S. Sci. Exchanges, 1983—; mem. deferred gifts com. Primary Children's Med. Ctr., 1980-81; active Amicus Club for LDS Hosp. Expansion Program, 1982—; mem. Mountain States Pension Conf., 1974—, pres., 1979; mem. planned giving com. Holy Cross Found., 1985—. Served with U.S. Army Res., 1961-68. Mem. ABA, Utah State Bar Assn. (chmn. lawyer benefits com. 1980-83), Salt Lake County Bar Assn., Estate Planning Council Salt Lake City. Republican. Mormon. Club: Bonneville Knife and Fork (Salt Lake City). Probate, Pension, profit-sharing, and employee benefits, General corporate. Office: Nielsen & Senior 1100 Beneficial Life Tower 36 S State St Salt Lake City UT 84111

CURTIS, DAVID W., lawyer; b. Montpelier, Vt., Apr. 15, 1938; s. Newell H. and Alice P. Curtis; children: David W. Jr., Julia A., Christopher J. AB, U. Vt., 1960; LLB, Boston Coll., 1963. From assoc. to ptnr. Hoff, Curtis, Bayon, Zwine & Jenkins, Burlington, Vt., 1964-76; dep. defender gen. State of Vt., Montpelier, 1977-80, defender gen., 1985—; sr. counsel Legal Services of So. Cen. Tenn., Columbia, 1980-83; dir. Dakota Plains Legal Services, Mission, S.D., 1983-85. Criminal. Home: PO Box 358 Hinesburg VT 05461 Office: Defender Gen Office State Office Bldg Montpelier VT 05601

CURTIS, DAVID WILLIAM, JR., lawyer; b. Tucson, Dec. 23, 1945; s. David W. Curtis and Wanda (Knight) Merrin; m. Sondra Vitoria, Dec. 10, 1970 (div. June 1975); m. Edna Merisol Estrada, Mar. 4, 1978; children: Jason Carlos, Jonathan Scott. BS in Polit. Sci., No. Ariz. U., 1974; JD, Hamlin U., 1977. Bar: Ariz. 1978, U.S. Dist. Ct. Ariz. 1978, U.S. Ct. Appeals (9th cir.) 1983. Law clk. to judge Maricopa County Superior Ct., Phoenix, 1978; assoc. Brice E. Buehler, Phoenix, 1978-79, Wellever, Smith & Howard, Phoenix, 1979-80; ptnr. Jacobs & Curtis, Phoenix, 1980-81; sole practice Phoenix, 1981-82; ptnr. Smith & Curtis, Phoenix, 1982-86; sole practice Phoenix, 1986-87; ptnr. David W. Curtis, P.C., Phoenix, 1987—; mng. ptnr. Quetzel Rand Inv. Co., Phoenix, 1982—; gen. ptnr. Precision Tools Ariz. Ltd., Tempe, 1985—; chmn. bd. dirs. InterMark Enterprises, Inc., Tempe. Mem. Scottsdale Ctr. for Arts, Ariz., 1984—, Friends of Channel 8, Tempe, 1984—. Mem. Assn. Trial Lawyers Am., Phoenix Trial Lawyers Assn. (pres. 1984-85, bd. dirs.). Democrat. Club: Nucleus (Phoenix). Avocations: camping, hiking, sports. State civil litigation, Real property, Securities. Home: 4430 E Western Star Blvd Phoenix AZ 85044 Office: 2633 E Indian School Rd #300 Phoenix AZ 85016

CURTIS, FRANK R., lawyer; b. Valley Stream, N.Y., Sept. 27, 1946; s. Frank and Rosalind (Vreeland) C.; m. Cynthia Mary Knapik, May 14, 1977; children—Lauren Josephine, Frank Edward, Michael Bennett. A.B. magna cum laude, Harvard Coll., 1968; J.D., Yale U., 1971. Bar: N.Y. 1972, U.S. Dist. Cts. (so. and ea. dists.) N.Y. 1973, U.S. Ct. Appeals (2d cir.) 1975. Assoc. Hellerstein Rosier & Rembar, N.Y.C., 1971-73; ptnr. Rembar Wolf & Curtis, N.Y., 1974-77, Rembar & Curtis, N.Y.C., 1978—; lectr. PLI, N.Y.C., 1980. Trustee, North Salem Free Library, N.Y. Mem. Assn. Bar City N.Y. (sec. com. on copyright 1979-80), Copyright Soc. of the U.S.A., Phi Beta Kappa. Club: Harvard of N.Y.C. Entertainment, Libel, Trademark and copyright. Home: Hillside Ave PO Box 108 Croton Falls NY 10519 Office: Rembar & Curtis 19 W 44th St New York NY 10036

CURTIS, GEORGE WARREN, lawyer; b. Merrill, Wis., Sept. 24, 1936; s. George Gregory and Rose E. (Zimmerman) C.; m. Judith Olson, 1956 (div. 1966); m. Mary Pelman, 1967 (widowed 1973); children: George, Catherine Edwall, Eric, Greg, Paul, David; m. Mary Ruth Kersztyn, Dec. 27, 1973; 1 child, Emily. BA, U. Minn., 1959; JD, U. Wis., 1962. Bar: Wis. 1962, Fla. 1968. Assoc. Russell & Curtis, Merrill, 1962-68; ptnr. Nolan, Engler, Yakes & Curtis, Oshkosh, Wis., 1968-74, Curtis, MacKenzie, Haase & Brown, Oshkosh, 1974-83, Curtis-Wilde Law Offices, Oshkosh, 1984—. Mem. Wis. Acad. Trial Lawyers (bd. dirs. 1978-83, treas. 1984, sec. 1985, v.p. 1986, pres. 1987). Democrat. Avocations: conservationist, dog trainer. Personal injury, Criminal, State civil litigation. Home: Rt 1 PO Box 61 Ripon WI 54971 Office: Curtis Wilde Law Offices 1010 W 20th Ave Oshkosh WI 54903-2845

CURTIS, GREGORY DYER, investment and philanthropic company executive; b. Mechanicsburg, Ohio, Jan. 14, 1947; s. Vernon L. and Jean (Dyer) C.; m. Lynne Everett, June 29, 1968; children: Sarah E., Alice D. AB cum laude, Dartmouth Coll., 1969; JD cum laude, Harvard U., 1974. Bar: Pa. 1974, U.S. Dist. Ct. (we. dist.) Pa. 1974. Assoc. Reed, Smith, Shaw & McClay, Pitts., 1974-79; counsel Roldiva, Inc., Pitts., 1979-81, v.p., bd. dirs., 1981-83; fin. adv. C.S. May Family Interests, Pitts., 1983—; pres. Laurel Found., Pitts., 1983—; pres., bd. govs. Laurel Assets Group, Pitts., 1983—; bd. dirs. Clark Techs., Inc., Boulder, Enrecon, Inc., Golden, Colo., L.C. Holdings, Inc., Boulder, Phoenix Technologies, Inc., Denver, Water Resources Am., Tulsa, Western Water Reserves, Inc., Boulder, Sewickley Heights Estates, Inc., Pitts., Tenir, Inc., Pitts., Winding River Properties, Inc., St. George, Utah. Mem. legal com. ACLU, Pitts., 1974-78; bd. dirs. Neighborhood Legal Services Assn., Pitts., 1976-79, Grantmakers Western Pa., Pitts., 1986—, The Ellis Sch., 1987—. Served to sgt. U.S. Army, 1970-72. Mem. ABA, Allegheny County Bar Assn. Club: Duquesne (Pitts.), Rolling Rock (Ligonier). General corporate, Estate planning, Private international. Home: 1338 Malvern Ave Pittsburgh PA 15217 Office: Laurel Found Three Gateway Ctr-6 North Pittsburgh PA 15222

CURTIS, JEFFREY HUTTON, lawyer; b. Winchester, Va., Oct. 24, 1957; s. William Franklin and Trula (Hutton) C. BA in Econs., Va. Mil. Inst., 1979; JD, U. Richmond, 1982; MBA, Webster U., 1986. Bar: Va. 1982, U.S. Ct. Mil. Appeals 1982, U.S. Ct. Appeals (4th cir.) 1985, U.S. Supreme Ct., 1987, U.S. Dist. Ct. (ea. dist.) Va. 1987. Commd. 2d lt. USAF, 1979, advanced through grades to capt., 1982; asst. staff judge adv. USAF, Chanute AFB, Ill., 1982-83; dep. staff judge adv. USAF, Kunsan AFB, Republic of Korea, 1983-84; dep. staff judge adv. USAF, Myrtle Beach AFB, S.C., 1984-85, area def. counsel, 1985-87; appellate govt. counsel USAF Hdqrs., Bolling AFB, Washington, 1987—. Mem. ABA (recipient younger lawyers award fed. lawyers sect.), Va. Bar Assn., Assn. Trial Lawyers Am. Methodist. Avocations: tennis, golf, jogging. Military, Criminal, Public international. Home: Rt 2 PO Box 498 The Plains VA 22171

CURTIS, KENNETH M., lawyer; b. Leeds, Maine, Feb. 8, 1931; s. Archie M. and Harriet (Turner) C.; m. Pauline B. Curtis, Nov. 17, 1956; children: Susan L. (dec.), Angela Curtis Hall. BS, Maine Maritime Acad., 1952; JD, U. Maine, 1952. Sec. state State of Maine, Augusta, 1965-66, gov., 1967-74; ptnr. Curtis, Thaxter, Stevens, Micholeau & Broder, Portland, Maine, 1975—; ambassador to Can. Ottawa, 1979-81; bd. dirs. Hall Security Inc., Brewer, Maine, New Eng. Telephone Co., Boston. Co-author: Canadian American Relations: The Promise and the Challenge, 1983. Chmn. Dem. Nat. Com., Washington, 1977-78; bd. govs. Common Cause, Washington, 1984—; trustee Susan Curtis Found., Portland, 1973—; mem. Nat. Research Coucil Cystic Fibrosis Found., Washington, 1982—; bd. dirs. Spurwink Found., Portland, 1983—. Served to lt. comdr. USNR, 1953-65. Mem. Maine Bar Assn., Council Former Am. Ambassadors. Avocations: boating, golf. Administrative and regulatory, Private international. Office: Maine Maritime Academy Castine ME 04112

CURTIS, MICHAEL KENT, lawyer; b. Dallas, July 21, 1942; s. Thomas Lisle and Kent (Adams) C.; m. Deborah F. Maury, Sept. 18, 1982; 1 child, Matthew F. Curtis-Maury. BA, U. of South, Sewanee, Tenn., 1964; JD, U. N.C., 1969. Bar: U.S. Dist. Ct. (ea., mid. and we. dists.) N.C. 1969, U.S. Ct. Appeals (4th cir.), U.S. Supreme Ct. 1974. Law clk. to chief justice N.C. Supreme Ct., Raleigh, 1969-70; ptnr. Smith, Patterson, Follin, Curtis, James & Harkavy, Greensboro, N.C., 1970—. Author: No State Shall Abridge, 1986; contbr. articles to law revs., 1979-84. Mem. citizens rev. panel Human Relations Commn., Greensboro, 1980-81, N.C. Safety and Health Rev. Bd., Greensboro, 1979-85. Recipient Frank Porter Graham award N.C. Civil Liberties Union, 1985; named Lawyer in Residence Washington and Lee Law Sch., 1985. Mem. Assn. Trial Lawyers Am., N.C. Acad. Trial Lawyers. Democrat. Mem. Soc. of Friends. Avocations: photography, legal history. Personal injury, State civil litigation, Civil rights. Home: 201 E Avondale Greensboro NC 27403 Office: Smith Patterson et al 700 Southeastern Bldg Greensboro NC 27401

CURTIS, STEPHEN PAUL, lawyer; b. Bklyn., Mar. 2, 1949; s. Paul Arthur and Arleen E. (Bauer) C.; m. Joanne Louise Schreiner (div. 1976); m. Mary Miello, Nov. 27, 1982; 1 child, Kelly. BS, Northwestern U., 1971; JD, U. Va., 1978. Bar: N.Mex. 1978, Ariz. 1981. Programmer, analyst Am. Mgmt. Systems, Arlington, Va., 1973-75; systems analyst Rockwell Internat., Arlington, 1974-75; assoc. Poole, Tinnin & Martin, P.C., Albuquerque, 1978-83; ptnr. Melton & Puccini, P.A., Albuquerque, 1983—. Chmn. N.Mex. Libertarian Party, 1980-82; Libertarian candidate for U.S. Congress, 1984. Mem. ABA, State Bar N.Mex., State Bar Ariz. Republican. Avocations: skiing, windsurfing, hiking, camping, tennis. State civil litigation, Contracts commercial, Bankruptcy. Home: 6029 Redondo Ct NW Albuquerque NM 87107 Office: Melton & Puccini PA PO Box 27690 Albuquerque NM 87125

CURTIS, SUSAN GRACE, lawyer; b. N.Y.C., Apr. 24, 1950; d. Henry G. and Helen Curtis; m. Robert Y. Pelgrift Jr., June 8, 1974; 1 child, Robert III. A.B., Yale Coll., 1971; J.D., Columbia U., 1974. Bar: N.Y. 1975, U.S. Ct. Appeals (2d cir.) 1975. With Lord, Day & Lord, N.Y.C., 1974-79, Shearman & Sterling, N.Y.C., 1979-84, Proskauer, Rose, Goetz & Mendelsohn, N.Y.C., 1984—. Contbr. articles to profl. jours. Mem. ABA (com. employee benefits), N.Y. State Bar Assn. (com. employee benefits), Assn. Bar City N.Y. Clubs: Yale, India House. Pension, profit-sharing, and employee benefits. Home: 55 E 72d St NYC NY 10021 Office: Proskauer Rose Goetz & Mendelsohn 300 Park Ave New York City NY 10022

CURTIS, THOMAS BRADFORD, lawyer; b. St. Louis, May 14, 1911; s. Edward Glion and Isabel (Wallace) C.; m. Susan R. Chivvis, June 28, 1941; children—Elizabeth, Leland, Allan, Charles, Jonathan. A.B., Dartmouth Coll, 1932, M.A. (hon.), 1951; J.D., Washington U., St. Louis, 1935, LL.D., 1969; LL.D., Westminster Coll., 1962. Bar: Mo. 1934. Ptnr. Curtis & Crossen, St. Louis, 1934-69, 74-87, Curtis, Bamburg, Oetting, Brackman & Crossen, 1987—; v.p., gen. counsel Ency. Brit., 1969-74; mem. 82d Congress 12th Dist. Mo., 83d-90th Congresses 2d Dist Mo.; chmn. bd. Lafayette Fed. Savs. & Loan, 1974-82, Brooking Park Geriatrics, Inc., 1974—. Am. Tech. Inst., 1979—; Mem. Pres. Nixon's Task Force on Internat. Devel., Com. on All-Vol. Armed Forces, Nat. Commn. Founds. and Pvt. Philanthropy; chmn. Corp. for Pub. Broadcasting, 1973-74, Fed. Election Commn, 1975-76; chmn. Mo. del. Rep. Nat. Conv., 1964, 76, 80; trustee Dartmouth Coll., 1951-72, William Woods Coll., 1962—; Westminster Coll., 1966-79, Nat. Coll. Edn., 1970-83, Lincoln Found., 1970-80, Lincoln Inst., 1976-80, Dartmouth Inst., 1972-82, Ctr. for Strategic and Internat. Studies, Georgetown U., 1972-82; bd. dirs. Webster U. 1979—, Agri-Energy Roundtable, Inc., 1979—. Served with U.S. Navy 1942-45. Recipient Congl. Disting. Service award Am. Polit. Sci. Assn., 1963-64, Perry award Nat. Fedn. for Blind, 1961, Silver Beaver award Boy Scouts Am., 1964, Disting. Eagle award Boy Scouts Am., 1973. Mem. Comf. Bd. (sr. adv. council 1973-75), ABA, Am. Polit. Sci. Assn., Assn., Order of Coif, Phi Delta Phi, Phi Sigma Kappa. Unitarian. Author: 87 Million Jobs: A Dynamic Solution for Unemployment, 1964; The Kennedy Round: The Future of U.S. Trade, 1970. Legislative, General corporate, Health. Home: 230 S Brentwood Blvd Clayton MO 63105

CURTISS, THOMAS, JR., lawyer, educator; b. Buffalo, Nov. 4, 1941; s. Thomas and Hope (Middleton Plumb) C.; B.A., Yale U., 1963; J.D., Harvard U., 1970. Bar: Calif. 1971. Assoc., Musick, Peeler & Garrett, Los Angeles, 1970-72; assoc. Macdonald, Halsted & Laybourne, Los Angeles, 1972-76, ptnr., 1976—; adj. prof. Loyola U., Los Angeles Law Sch., 1982—. Mem. vestry Trinity Episcopal Ch., Los Angeles, sr. warden, 1982, 84-86; mem. Commn. on Ordained Ministry, Diocese of Los Angeles, 1983-87; mem. Music Center Found. Legal Com. Served to maj. USMCR, 1963-78. Mem. ABA (mem. sect. real property, probate and trust law), Los Angeles County Bar Assn. (probate and trust sect.). Contbr. articles to profl. jours. Probate, Real property. Home: 2250 Micheltorena St Los Angeles CA 90039 Office: Macdonald Halsted & Laybourne 725 S Figueroa St 36th Floor Los Angeles CA 90017

CURTISS, WILLIS DAVID, lawyer, educator; b. Sodus, N.Y., May 31, 1916; s. Willis David and Louise Anna (Shoecraft) C.; m. Mary Melissa Fowler, June 29, 1951; children—David Fowler, Melissa Anne. A.B., Cornell U., 1938, LL.B., 1940. Bar: N.Y. bar 1940. Gen. practice Sodus, 1940-42; dist. atty. Wayne County, N.Y., 1941; asst. prof. law U. Buffalo, 1946-47, Cornell U. Law Sch., Ithaca, N.Y., 1947-51; asso. prof. Cornell U. Law Sch., 1951-56, prof., 1956-86, assoc. dean, 1958-62, prof. emeritus, 1986—; Vis. prof. U. Mich. Law Sch., summer 1950; spl. atty. Dept. Justice, 1954. Research cons. N.Y. State Law Revision Commn., 1952-56, exec. sec., 1956-60; mem. N.Y. Temporary Commn. on State Ct. System, 1970-73; Faculty trustee Cornell U., 1966-71. Served to lt. comdr. USNR, 1942-46. Mem. Tompkins County Bar Assn., Am. Arbitration Assn., Am. Law Inst., Order of Coif, Phi Beta Kappa, Phi Kappa Phi, Delta Sigma Rho, Phi Delta Phi, Sigma Nu. Democrat. Presbyn. Legal education, Local government, Legislative. Home: 108 Hampton Rd Ithaca NY 14850 Office: Cornell Law Sch Ithaca NY 14853

CURVIN, STEVEN P., lawyer; b. Buffalo, Nov. 8, 1954; s. Lowell C. and Prudence M. (DiFranco) C.; m. Claudia L. Batzer, Feb. 3, 1978 (div. Apr. 1981); m. Corinne S. Serwinowski, Sept. 28, 1984; stepchildren: Kimberly Kensy, Wendy Kensy, Jodie Kensy, Ward-Charles L. Mundorff; 1 child, Elizabeth Ann. BA, SUNY, Buffalo, 1975, JD, 1980. Bar: N.Y. 1980, U.S. Dist. Ct. (we., so. and ea. dists.) N.Y. 1980, U.S. Supreme Ct. 1984. Asst. mgr. Tops Market, Inc. and B-Kwik Markets, Inc., Buffalo, 1972-73; service mgr. Buffalo Evening News, 1973-77; law clk Buffalo City Ct., 1974-77; assoc. Rosenthal, Siegel, Muenkel & Wolf, Buffalo, 1980-84; ptnr. Rosenthal, Siegel, Muenkel, Wolf & Curvin, Buffalo, 1985—; instr. criminal justice SUNY U., Buffalo, 1975-77. Recipient Regents scholar N.Y. State Bd. Regents, Albany, 1972. Mem. ABA (vice chmn. products liability com. 1986—), N.Y. State Bar Assn., Erie County Bar Assn. (chmn. com. practice and procedure in state cts. 1987—, Connelly Trial Technique award 1980), Assn. Trial Lawyers Am., N.Y. State Trial Lawyers Assn., Western N.Y. Trial Lawyers Assn. Clubs: Lawyers of Buffalo, Marshall (Buffalo). State civil litigation, Criminal, Federal civil litigation. Home: 255 Lexington Ave Buffalo NY 14222 Office: Rosenthal Siegel Muenkel et al 300 Main St Buffalo NY 14202

CURZAN, MYRON PAUL, lawyer; b. N.Y.C., May 13, 1940; s. Lee and Hannah Rose (Tannenbaum) C.; m. Mary Hannah Curzan; children—Elisabeth, Anne, Katherine. B.A., Columbia U., 1961, LL.B., 1965; M.A., Yale U., 1962. Bar: Calif. 1966, D.C. 1969. Clk. to chief justice Calif. Supreme Ct., 1965-66; legis. asst. to Senator Robert F. Kennedy, Washington, 1966-67; ptnr. Arnold & Porter, Washington, 1967—; pres., chief exec. officer APCO Assocs., The Arnold & Porter Cons. Group, 1984—, MPC & Assocs., Inc., 1984—; dir. Conn. Mut. Life Ins. Co., Nat. Captioning Inst., Greater Washington Telecommunications Assn., Inc.; mem. adv. bd. Bur. Nat. Affairs Housing and Devel. Reporter; exec. in residence Tuck Sch. Bus., Dartmouth Coll., spring 1980. Contbr. articles to profl. jours. Real property, Communications. Address: 5519 Uppingham St Chevy Chase MD 20015

CUSACK, MARY JO, lawyer; A.B., Marquette U., 1957; J.D., Ohio State U., 1959. Bar: Ohio, 1959, U.S. Dist. Ct. Ohio, 1965, U.S. Supreme Ct., 1962. Atty., Indsl. Commn. Ohio, 1960-61, Ohio Dept. Taxation, 1961-65; ptnr. Cotruvo & Cusack, Columbus, Ohio, 1961-79; sole practice, 1979—; spl. counsel to atty. gen., 1971-73; adj. prof. family and probate law Capital U. Law Sch., Columbus, 1971-74. . Mem. legis. com. Ohio Commn. on Status of Women; bd. dirs. Columbus Theater Ballet Assn. Fellow Ohio Bar Found., Columbus Bar Assn. (profl. ethics com., judiciary com., speakers bur. com.), Columbus Bar Found. (charter), Am. Bar Found.; mem. ABA, Ohio Bar Assn. (council of dels.), Ohio Acad. Trial Lawyers (worker's compensation com.), Franklin County Trial Lawyers Assn. (past pres.), Nat. Assn. Women Lawyers (past pres.), Women Lawyers Columbus (past pres.), Ohio Dem. Attys., Franklin County Dem. Attys. (past v.p.), Ohio Assn. Attys. Gen. (past pres.), Nat. Bd. Trial Advocacy, Am. Arbitration Assn. (nat. panel arbitrators), Ohio State U. Alumni Assn., Marquette U. Alumni Assn. (past sec.-treas. Cen. Ohio), Nat. Women's Polit. Caucus, Columbus Women's Polit. Caucus, Press Club of Ohio, Kappa Beta Pi (chmn. bd., 1st assoc. internat. v.p., past internat. pres., past province dean, past province dir. Clubs: Columbus Metropolitan, Pilot Internat. Family and matrimonial, Probate, Workers' compensation. Office: 50 W Broad St Suite 2430 Columbus OH 43215

CUSHING, JAMES ROBERT, lawyer; b. Ithaca, N.Y., June 5, 1947; s. Robert Levaitt and Enid June (Gillett) C. BS, U. Hawaii, 1976; JD, U. Puget Sound, 1980. Bar: Wash. 1980, U.S. Dist. Ct. (we. dist.) Wash. 1981. Assoc. Sinmitt & Sinmitt, Tacoma, 1980-84; ptnr. Williams & Cushing, Tacoma, 1984—. Mem. ABA, Wash. Bar Assn., Tacoma/Pierce County Bar Assn., Wash. Trial Lawyers Assn. Avocations: motorcycles, motorcycle racing. State civil litigation, Insurance, Personal injury. Office: 401 Broadway Tacoma WA 98402

CUSHING, ROBERT HUNTER, government official, lawyer; b. N.Y.C., Feb. 9, 1952; s. Robert Murray and Robin (Fersten) C.; B.A., U. Denver, 1974; J.D., George Mason Law Sch., 1977. Bar: D.C. 1977. With instl. services dept. Colin, Hochstein Co., N.Y.C., 1978; dir. field ops. Com. to Re-elect Congressman Bill Green, N.Y.C., 1978-80; legis. asst. to Congressman Bill Green, Washington, 1979-81; spl. asst. to gen. counsel HUD, Washington, 1981-84, spl. asst. to sec., 1984-86, dep. asst. sec. for multifamily housing, 1986—. Active N.Y. County Republican Com., N.Y.C., 1978-81; del. N.Y. Jud. Conv., 1980; v.p., exec. com. Met. Rep. Club, N.Y.C., 1978-80. Mem. N.Y. Bar Assn., ABA, Fed. Bar Assn., D.C. Bar Assn. Unitarian. Clubs: Capital Hill (Washington); Doubles (N.Y.C.); Avocations: photography (Life mag. award 1970). Real property, Banking, Probate. Home: 1070 Park Ave New York NY 10028 Office: Dept of HUD 451 7th St SW Washington DC 20410

CUSICK, ELIZABETH EMMA, lawyer; b. Westfield, Mass., Aug. 12, 1957; d. Joseph Jr. and Concetta Anna (Silvestri) Emma; m. William Henry Cusick, Aug. 18, 1984. BA, Boston Coll., 1979, JD, 1982. Bar: Mass. 1982, R.I. 1983, U.S. Dist. Ct. Mass. 1985. Spl. counsel City of Providence, 1982-84; assoc. Field & Schultz, Boston, 1985, Mofenson & Nicoletti, Newton, Mass., 1985—. Mem. ABA, Mass. Bar Assn., R.I. Bar Assn., Phi Beta Kappa. Avocations: piano, sewing, needlework. State civil litigation, Personal injury, Family and matrimonial. Office: Mofenson & Nicoletti One Wells Ave Newton MA 02159

CUSTER, LAWRENCE BENJAMIN, lawyer; b. N.Y.C., May 13, 1935; s. Benjamin L. and Marian (Cherkes) C.; m. Mary Arnett Ware, Dec. 26, 1958 (div.); children: George Ware, Jane Crawford, m. Margaret Sharon Simpson Doris, Jan. 27, 1972; 1 dau., Ashley Michelle Doris; BA, Emory U., 1957; LLB, U. Pa., 1960. Bar: Ga. 1960, U.S. Dist. Ct. (no. dist.) Ga. 1961, U.S. Ct. Appeals (5th cir.) 1961, U.S. Supreme Ct. 1964, U.S. Dist Ct. (no. dist.) Tex. 1969, U.S. Ct. Appeals (11th cir.) 1981. Law clk. to presiding justice U.S. Ct. Appeals (5th cir.), 1960-61; assoc. Smith, Kilpatrick, Cody, Rogers & McClatchey, Atlanta, 1961-62; ptnr. Reed, Ingram, Flournoy & Custer, Marietta, Ga., 1962-64; ptnr. Custer, Johnson & Burke and predecessor firms, Marietta, 1964—; dep. asst. atty. gen. Ga., 1962-64; asst. solicitor gen. Cobb Jud. Cir., 1964-66; chmn. Ga. Bd. Determine Fitness of Bar Applicants, 1977—. Pres., Cobb County Youth Mus., 1969-70; chmn. bd. trustees J.T. Walker Sch., 1969-71, Ga. Legal History Found., 1984—; pres. Cobb County Symposium, 1973-74. Recipient Marion Luther Brittain Service award, 1957. Fellow Am. Acad. Matrimonial Lawyers; mem. ABA, Am. Bar Found. (com. on legal history fellowships 1979—), Am. Judicature Soc., Selden Soc., State Bar Ga. (chmn. family law sect. 1985, chancellor, authors ct. 1981-82), Cobb County Bar Assn. (pres. 1974-75), Pi Delta Epsilon, Omicron Delta Kappa, Sigma Nu. Club: Marietta Country. Lodge: Kiwanis (pres. 1974-75). Family and matrimonial, State civil litigation, General practice. Address: PO Box 1224 Marietta GA 30061

CUSTURERI, RICHARD DOMENICK, lawyer; b. Jersey City, Nov. 14, 1957; s. Domenick and Mary (Foca) C.; m. Sherry Lynn Suereth, Aug. 30, 1980. B.S. in Chemistry, U. Fla., 1977, J.D., 1980. Bar: Fla. 1980, U.S. Dist. Ct. (mid. dist.) Fla. 1981, U.S. Ct. Claims 1982, U.S. Tax Ct. 1982, U.S. Ct. Appeals (11th cir.) 1985, U.S. Dist. Ct. (so. dist.) Fla. 1986, U.S. Supreme Ct. 1986. Mem. Congressional staff, Washington, 1978; law clk. Student Legal Services, Gainesville, Fla., 1978-80; ptnr. Blanchard, Custureri & Merriam, Ocala, 1980—. Chmn. Am. Heart Assn., Marion County, Fla., 1983-86; charter bd. mem. Marion County CPR Program, Inc., 1983-86; precinct committeeman Marion County Reps., 1980—; pres. Marion County Young Reps., 1982—; state legal chmn. Fla. Fedn. Young Reps., 1985-86. Inducted into U. Fla. Hall of Fame, 1978. Mem. Acad. Fla. Trial Lawyers, ABA, Assn. Trial Lawyers Am., Am. Judicature Soc., Jaycees (legal counsel 1981—), Fla. Blue Key, Phi Delta Phi, Omicron Delta Kappa. Roman Catholic. Lodges: K.C., Kiwanis, Elks. State civil litigation, Family and matrimonial, Personal injury. Home: 1309 SE 10th Ave Ocala FL 32671 Office: Blanchard Custureri & Merriam PA PO Box 24 Ocala FL 32678

CUTCHIN, JAMES MCKENNEY, IV, lawyer, engineer; b. Whitakers, N.C., Oct. 11, 1933; s. James McKenney III and Helen Christine (Perkins) C.; m. Nancy Lucille Elks, June 12, 1955; children—James McKenney V, John William. B.S., U.S. Mil. Acad., 1955; M.S. in Mech. Engring., N.C. State U., 1962; J.D., George Washington U., 1975. Bar: Va. 1975, D.C. 1976, U.S. Dist. Ct. (ea. dist.) Va. 1976, U.S. Dist. Ct. D.C. 1976, U.S. Ct. Appeals (4th and D.C. cirs.) 1976, U.S. Supreme Ct. 1978. Engr., sr. engr. Babcock & Wilcox Co., Lynchburg, Va., 1962-68; licensing supr., 1968-71; sr. project mgr. U.S. Nuclear Regulatory Commn., Washington, 1971-76, atty., 1976-78, sr. litigation atty., 1978-83, legal adviser to commr., 1983—. Pres. Lynchburg Young Republican Club, 1967-69; v.p. Sandusky Jr. High Sch. PTA, 1970; chmn. Lynchburg City Rep. Com., 1970-71. Served to 1st lt. USAF, 1955-59. Mem. Va. Bar, D.C. Bar, ASME (bd. dirs. Va. sect. 1970), Am. Nuclear Soc. (pres. N.C.-Va. sect. 1968), Lynchburg Jaycees (v.p. 1967-68), Sigma Xi, Tau Beta Pi. Republican. Club: Westwood Country. Nuclear power, Administrative and regulatory. Home: 11000 Devenish Dr Oakton VA 22124 Office: US Nuclear Regulatory Commn 1717 H St NW Washington DC 20555

CUTCHINS, CLIFFORD ARMSTRONG, IV, lawyer; b. Norfolk, Va., May 13, 1948; s. Clifford Armstrong III and Ann (Woods) C.; m. Jane McKenzie, Aug. 14, 1971; children: Sarah Helen, Ann Woods. BA, Princeton U., 1971; JD, MBA, U. Va., 1975. Bar: Va. 1975, U.S. Dist. Ct. (ea. dist.) Va. 1975, U.S. Ct. Appeals (4th cir.) 1975. Ptnr. McGuire, Woods, Battle & Boothe, Richmond, Va., 1975—. Bd. dirs. Arts Council Richmond, 1980-86, Richmond Heart Assn., 1980-83, St. Catherine's Sch., Richmond, 1983-86, Richmond Ballet, 1986—, Richmond Children's Mus., 1986—, Richmond on the James, 1986—, Henrico Drs. Hosp., 1986—. Mem. ABA, Am. Soc. Hosp. Attys., Va. Bar Assn. Republican. Baptist. Clubs: Country of Va. (Richmond), Commonwealth (bd. dirs. 1983-86); Princess Anne Country (Virginia Beach, Va.). Avocations: golf, photography. Securities, General corporate, Health. Home: 118 Tempsford Ln Richmond VA 23226 Office: McGuire Woods Battle & Boothe One James Ctr Richmond VA 23219

CUTLER, ARNOLD R., lawyer; b. New Haven, Mar. 20, 1908; s. Max Nathan and Kate (Harder) C.; m. Hazel Lourie, Apr. 8, 1942; 1 son, David. B.A., Yale U., 1930, J.D., 1932. Bar: Conn. 1932, Mass. 1946. Mem. staff Office of Gen. Counsel, Pub. Works Adminstrn., Washington, 1933-36; chief counsel State of Wash., 1937-38; spl. asst. to chief counsel IRS, 1939-42, trial counsel New Eng. div., 1945-47; ptnr. Lourie & Cutler, Boston, 1947—; lectr. on taxation. Contbr. to books articles to legal jours. Trustee Beth Israel Hosp.; trustee Brandeis U.; trustee, past mem. exec. com.

Combined Jewish Philanthropies Greater Boston; past. bd. dirs. Nat. Jewish Welfare Bd.; past pres. Brookline, Brighton and Newton Jewish Community Center; past. treas. Associated Jewish Community Centers of Greater Boston; past chmn. bd. Yale Law Sch. Fund; chmn. bequest com. Yale Law Sch. Lt. comdr. USCG, 1942-45. Fellow Am. Coll. Tax Counsel, Mass. Bar Found.; mem. ABA (com. on govt. submissions 1987—, past chmn. spl. adv. exempt orgns. com. tax sect.), Mass. Bar Assn., Boston Bar Assn. (past chmn. fed. tax com., past mem. council), Am. Law Inst. Clubs: New Century (past pres.), Greater Boston Brandeis (past pres.), Yale, Harvard, Wightman Tennis, Rotary (past bd. dirs.). Corporate taxation, Estate taxation, Personal income taxation. Office: Lourie & Cutler 60 State St Boston MA 02109

CUTLER, BEVERLY WINSLOW, judge; b. Washington, Sept. 10, 1949; d. Lloyd Norton and Louise Winslow (Howe) Cutler; m. Mark Andrew Weaver, Sept. 22, 1977; children—Lucia Mary, Andrew Thaddeus. B.A., Stanford U., 1971; J.D., Yale U., 1974. Bar: Alaska 1975. Research atty. Alaska Jud. Council, Anchorage, 1974-75; atty. Alaska Pub. Defender Agy., Anchorage, 1975-77; judge Alaska Dist. Ct., Anchorage, 1977-82, Alaska Superior Ct., Palmer, 1982—. Mem. ABA, Alaska Bar Assn., Anchorage Assn. Women Lawyers, Nat. Assn. Women Judges, Nat. Assn. Women in Criminal Justice. Home: Edgerton Park Rd Palmer AK 99645 Office: Alaska Court System 268 E Firewood Ln Palmer AK 99645

CUTLER, CHARLES EDWARD, lawyer; b. Des Moines, Apr. 2, 1956; s. Robert Edward and Joann Mae (Staker) C.; m. Diane Renee Sargent, Aug. 8, 1953; children: John Sargent, Scott Charles. BS, U. Iowa, 1978, JD, 1981. Bar: Iowa 1981, U.S. Dist. Ct. (no. and so. dists.) Iowa 1981, U.S. Ct. Appeals (8th cir.) 1981. Assoc. Patterson, Lorentzen, Duffield, Timmons, Irish, Becker & Ordway, Des Moines, 1981—. Mem. ABA, Iowa Bar Assn., Polk County Bar Assn., Assn. Trial Lawyers Iowa. Personal injury, Insurance, Workers' compensation. Office: Patterson Lorentzen et al 729 Insurance Exchange Bldg Des Moines IA 50309

CUTLER, CHARLES RUSSELL, lawyer; b. Macomb, Ill., July 15, 1924; s. Russell Lowell and Amy (Short) C.; m. Margaret Hughes, Dec. 3, 1949; children—Thomas, Alan, Patricia, Roger. B.S. in Elec. Engring., Calif. Inst. Tech., 1945; J.D. with honors, George Washington U., 1949. Bar: D.C. 1949, Md., 1955, U.S. Ct. Apls. (D.C. cir.) 1949, U.S. Ct. Apls. (4th cir.) 1975, U.S. Ct. Apls. (2d cir.) 1977, U.S. Sup. Ct. 1955. Assoc., Kirkland & Ellis, Washington, 1949-57, ptnr., 1957—; lectr. on devel. computer, communications law, 1965-80. Bd. dirs. Unitarian-Universalist Housing Found., 1978—. Fellow Am. Bar Found.; mem. ABA, Md. State Bar Assn., Bar Assn. D.C. (chmn. jr. bar sect. 1957-58), D.C. Bar (gen. csl. to bd. govs. 1981-83), Computer Law Assn., Fed. Communications Bar Assn., Am. Arbitration Assn. (panel 1966—), Calif. Tech. Inst. Alumni Assn. (pres. D.C. chpt. 1953-54), George Washington U. Law Alumni Assn. (exec. com. 1959-61). Clubs: Cosmos (Washington) . Assoc. editor: George Washington U. Law Rev., 1949. Contbr. articles, papers to profl. lit. General corporate, Administrative and regulatory, General practice. Home: 6828 Millwood Rd Bethesda MD 20817 Office: Kirkland & Ellis 655 15th St NW Washington DC 20005

CUTLER, ELIOT RAPHAEL, lawyer; b. Bangor, Maine, July 29, 1946; s. Lawrence M. and Catherine A. (Epstein) C.; m. Melanie Suzanne Stewart, Dec. 28, 1973; children: Abigail, Zachary. BA, Harvard U., 1968; JD, Georgetown U., 1973. Bar: Maine 1974, N.Y. 1975, D.C. 1980. Legis. asst. to senator Edmund S. Muskie U.S. Senate, Washington, 1968-73; gen. counsel Internat. Council Shopping Ctrs., N.Y.C., 1974-75; assoc. Webster & Sheffield, N.Y.C., 1975-77; ptnr. Webster & Sheffield, Washington, 1980—; assoc. dir. Office Mgmt. & Budget, Washington, 1977-80; trustee Internat. Law Inst., Washington, 1982—; bd. dirs. Ltd. Term Mcpl. Fund, Santa Fe, 1984—. Democrat. Jewish. Environment, Local government, Real property. Office: Webster & Sheffield 1200 New Hampshire Ave NW Washington DC 20036

CUTLER, JOHN ARTHUR, lawyer; b. Tokyo, Mar. 4, 1953; came to U.S., 1953; s. C. L. Jr. and Marjorie (Lamb) C.; m. Linda Kite, June 12, 1976. BA, U. Va., 1975; JD, U. Ga., 1978. Bar: Ga. 1978, D.C. 1982, U.S. Ct. Appeals (5th cir.) 1982. Staff atty. Machinery & Allied Products Inst., Washington, 1979-82; staff counsel No. Mariana Islands Commn. on Fed. Laws, Washington, 1982-85; ptnr. MacMeekin, Cutler & Woodworth, Washington, 1985—. Contbr. articles to profl. jours. Treas. Alexandria (Va.) Dem. Com., 1980-82; commr. Alexandria Human Rights Commn., 1980-82; mem. Alexandria Bd. Zoning Appeals, 1987—; chmn. bd. Alexandria Cable TV Commn., 1983-87, Holmes Run Park Com., Alexandria, 1983-85. Mem. ABA, Fed. Bar Assn., D.C. Bar Assn., Ga. Bar Assn. Democrat. Roman Catholic. Private international, General corporate, Legislative. Home: 5360 Thayer Ave Alexandria VA 22304 Office: MacMeekin Cutler & Woodworth 1331 H St NW Suite 901 Washington DC 20005

CUTLER, MITCHELL S., lawyer; b. Quincy, Mass., Sept. 24, 1933. Grad. in Fgn. Service, Georgetown U., 1955; LLB cum laude with distinction, Georgw Washington U., 1958. Bar: D.C., Md. Assoc. Welch, Mott & Morgan; spl. asst. The White House, Washington; assoc. Klagsburnnm Haynes & Irwin; house counsel Disc Inc.; ptnr. Foreman, Cutler & Diamond, 1964-69, Danzansky, Dickey, Tydings, Quint & Gordon, 1970—; cons. real estate adv. com. SEC, 1972; adj. prof. law Georgetown U. Editor in chief Georgetown U. Law Rev.; contbr. articles to profl. jours. Mem. ABA, Fed. Bar Assn. Home: 13 Darby Ct Bethesda MD 20034 Office: Finley Kumble Wagner Heine et al 1120 Connecticut Ave NW Washington DC 20036

CUTSHAW, JAMES MICHAEL, lawyer; b. New Orleans, May 30, 1950; s. James Arthur and Leila Mays (Obier) Cutshaw Schroeder; m. Becky Lynn Simmons, Aug. 6, 1975; 1 child, Lewis Prentiss. B.A., Tulane U., 1972; J.D., La. State U., 1975. Bar: La. 1975, U.S. Dist. Ct. (we. dist.) La. 1975, U.S. Dist. Ct. (mid. dist.) La. 1977, U.S. Dist. Ct. (ea. dist.) La. 1980, U.S. Ct. Appeals (5th cir.) 1981, U.S. Supreme Ct. 1981. Law clk. La. Ct. Appeals, 3d Cir., Lake Charles, La., summer 1973, U. Dist. Ct. (we. dist.) La., Alexandria, 1975-77; ptnr. Howell, Schroeder & Cutshaw, Baton Rouge, La., 1977-81; gen. counsel La. Bankers Assn., Baton Rouge, 1981—, contbr. legal bulletin, 1982—; lectr. La. Banking Sch., Baton Rouge, 1983-85. Editor: Louisiana Banking Laws, 1983—; contbr. (with Walter Stuart IV) articles to profl. jours. Pres. Baton Rouge Symphony, 1984-85, bd. dirs., 1980—; pres. Garden Dist. Civic Assn., 1979-81; bd. dirs. Old State Capitol Assn., 1983—, Public Radio WRKF, 1981—. Mem. ABA, La. Bar Assn. (co-chmn. consumer credit com. 1982), Baton Rouge Bar Assn. (chmn. law sch. com. 1985), SAR, Baton Rouge C. of C. (chmn. state affairs council 1986—), Phi Beta Kappa, Phi Eta Sigma. Democrat. Episcopalian. Clubs: City, Baton Rouge Country. Banking, Legislative, General corporate. Home: 2231 Cherokee Ave Baton Rouge LA 70806 Office: La Bankers Assn 666 North St PO Box 2871 Baton Rouge LA 70821

CUTSUMPAS, LLOYD, lawyer; b. Danbury, Conn., Oct. 14, 1933; s. John and Pauline (Dalacas) C.; m. Nicolletta Kakavas, July 31, 1960; children: John, Theodore. BBA, U. Conn., 1955; JD, Georgetown U., 1960. Bar: Conn. 1962, U.S. Dist. Ct. Conn. 1963. Sole practice Conn., 1962—; ptnr. Cutsumpas, Collins, Hannafin, Garamella, Jaber and Tuozzolo, P.C., Danbury, 1962—; lectr. law Western Conn. State U., Danbury, 1980—. Contbr. articles on family law to profl. jours. Chmn. March of Dimes; pres. regional YMCA; pres. Parish Council Assumption Greek Orthodox Ch.; vice-chmn. Richter Park Authority. Served with U.S. Army, 1955-57. Named one of Outstanding Men of Am., Danbury Jaycees, 1967. Fellow Am. Acad. Matrimonial Lawyers (bd. mgrs. Conn. chpt.); mem. ABA (family law div.), Conn. Bar Assn. (family law div., jud. com.), Danbury Bar Assn. (pres.). Democrat. Greek Orthodox. Family and matrimonial, State civil litigation. Office: Cutsumpas Collins Hannafin et al 148 Deer Hill Ave PO Box 440 Danbury CT 06810

CUTTER, EDWARD AHERN, consumer products company executive, lawyer; b. Berkeley, Calif., July 17, 1939; s. Edward Ahern and Helen (Westgate) C.; m. Susan Kren Cutter; children: Eric Alan, Spencer Edward. B.A., Stanford U., 1961, postgrad., 1964-65; J.D., Harvard U., 1964. Bar: Calif. 1965. Atty. Thelen, Marrin, Johnson & Bridges, San Francisco, 1965-67; mgr. legal services Cutter Labs. Inc., Berkeley, 1968-70; sec., corp. counsel Cutter Labs. Inc., 1970-78, gen. counsel, sec., 1978-83, v.p. adminstrn., 1983-84; v.p., gen. counsel, sec. Clorox Co., Oakland, Calif., 1984—. Mem. ABA, Calif., San Francisco bar assns. Home: Box 468 Belvedere CA 94920 Office: Clorox Co 1221 Broadway Oakland CA 94623

CUTTLER, H. KAREN, lawyer; b. N.Y.C., May 17, 1956; d. Harry A. and Barbara Schwartzbard; m. Gary S. Cuttler, Aug. 14, 1977; 1 child, Zachary Saul. AB, Rutgers U., 1977, JD with highest honors, 1980. Bar: N.J. 1980, N.Y. 1981. Law clk. to assoc. justice N.J. Supreme Ct., Newark, 1980-81; assoc. Riker, Danzig, Scherer, Hyland & Peretti, Morristown, N.J., 1981-84, Goldberg, Drescher & Cheslow, Cranford, N.J., 1985—. Trustee, sec. Legal Services Found. of Essex County, Inc., Newark, 1981-84. Saul Tischler scholar Rutgers U., 1979-80; Hornbook award West Pubs. Co., 1980. Mem. ABA, N.J. Bar Assn., Rutgers U. Alumni Assn. (trustee 1983—), Phi Beta Kappa. Democrat. Pension, profit-sharing, and employee benefits, Probate, Estate taxation. Home: 1 Donsen Ln Scotch Plains NJ 07076 Office: Goldberg Drescher & Cheslow PA 354 North Ave E Cranford NJ 07016

CUYPERS, CHARLES JAMES, lawyer; b. Jamestown, N.D., Dec. 11, 1949; s. Donald Charles and Hazel Charlotte (Hollingsworth) C.; m. Judy Arlene Stutzman, Dec. 18, 1971; 1 child, Christina Jean. B.S., Kearney State Coll., 1974; J.D., Creighton U., 1976. Bar: Nebr. 1976, U.S. Dist. Ct. Nebr. 1976. Ptnr. Sherwood & Cuypers, Oxford, Cambridge, Nebr., 1976-86; pres. Oxford Devel. Corp., 1979-86; cons. Butler Meml. Library Found., Cambridge, 1983-86; cons., lawyer Cambridge Mus. Found., Inc., 1983-86 , Fairview Cemetary Found., 1983-86; city atty., Cambridge, Nebr., 1982-86; village atty., Oxford, Nebr., 1976-86, Orleans, Nebr., 1976-81; city atty. Grand Island, Nebr., 1986—. Author, narrator Oxford Centennial Radio Series, 1980. Bd. dirs. Oxford Pub. Library Bd., 1978-86; county chmn. Gov. Thone Reelection Com., Oxford, 1982. Mem. ABA, Assn. Trial Lawyers Am., Nebr. Bar Assn., Nebr. Assn. Trial Lawyers, 14th Jud. Dist. Bar Assn. (pres. 1980-81), Oxford C. of C. (pres. 1980-81), Young Lawyers Study Group. Republican. Lutheran. State civil litigation, Bankruptcy, Local government. Home: 1508 Spruce Pl Grand Island NE 68801 Office: City Hall 2nd and Pine St Grand Island NE 68801

CVETANOVICH, DANNY LEE, lawyer; b. Wheeling, W.Va., Oct. 2, 1952; s. Louis J. and Nila J. (Hall) C.; m. Sharon M. Smith, Sept. 8, 1979; 1 child, Gregory L. BA, West Liberty State Coll., 1974; JD, Harvard U., 1977. Bar: Ohio 1977, U.S. Dist. Ct. (so. dist.) Ohio 1978, U.S. Ct. Appeals (6th cir.) 1980, U.S. Dist. Ct. (no. dist.) Ohio 1984, W.Va. 1985, U.S. Dist. Ct. (so. dist.) W.Va. 1985, U.S. Ct. Appeals (4th cir.) 1986. Assoc. Bricker & Eckler, Columbus, Ohio, 1977-82, ptnr., 1983—. Dir. Capital Area Humane Soc., Columbus, 1983—. Mem. ABA, Ohio Bar Assn., W.Va. Bar Assn., Columbus Bar Assn., Columbus Def. Assn., Ducks Unltd. (com. mem. 1981—). Democrat. Roman Catholic. Club: Columbus Athletic. Avocations: hunting, fishing, golf. Federal civil litigation, State civil litigation. Office: Bricker & Eckler 100 S 3d St Columbus OH 43215-4291

CWIRKO, CLARIS KAYE, administrative law judge; b. Highland Park, Mich., Nov. 1, 1944; d. Mitchell and Mary (Lazarecky) Kaye; m. Joseph Anthony Cwirko, Sept. 20, 1975. B.A., Wayne State U., 1966, M.Ed., 1973; J.D. cum laude, Detroit Coll. Law, 1977. Bar: Mich. 1977, U.S. Dist. Ct. (ea. dist.) Mich. 1977, U.S. Supreme Ct., 1986. Tchr., Detroit Pub. Schs., 1966-76; assoc. Canlock & Thumm, Utica, Mich., 1977-78; assoc. Citizens Legal Services, Pontiac, Mich., 1978-79; sole practice, Royal Oak, Mich., 1979; adminstrv. law judge Mich. Tax Tribunal, Detroit, 1979—. Contbr. article to profl. publ. Mem. Republican Nat. Com., 1984. Recipient Criminal Law award Detroit Coll. Law, 1976; Cert. of Appreciation, Oakland U., 1983. Mem. ABA, State Bar Mich., Nat. Conf. Adminstrv. Law Judges, Mich. Assn. Adminstrv. Law Judges, Detroit Econ. Club. State and local taxation, Personal income taxation, Administrative and regulatory. Home: 1212 S Washington Royal Oak MI 48067 Office: Mich Tax Tribunal 1300 Lafayette Bldg 144 W Lafayette Detroit MI 48226

CYR, CONRAD KEEFE, federal judge; b. Limestone, Maine, Dec. 9, 1931; s. Louis Emery and Kathleen Mary (Keefe) C.; m. Judith Ann Pirie, June 23, 1962 (dec. Mar. 1985); children: Keefe Clark, Jeffrey Louis Frederick. B.S. cum laude, Holy Cross Coll., 1953; J.D., Yale U., 1956. Bar: Maine 1956. Sole practice Limestone, 1956-59; asst. U.S. atty., Bangor, Maine, 1959-61; judge U.S. Bankruptcy Court, Bangor, 1961-81; judge U.S. Dist. Ct., Bangor, 1981-83, chief judge, 1983-87; judge U.S. Fgn. Intelligence Surveillance Ct., 1987—; standing spl. master U.S. Dist. Ct., Maine, 1974-76; chief judge Bankruptcy Appellate Panel Dist., Mass., 1980-81. Editor-in-chief Am. Bankruptcy Law Jour., 1970-81; contbg. author, editor: Collier on Bankruptcy, Vol. 10. Treas. Limestone Republican Com., 1958; chmn. Town of Limestone Budget Com., 1959. Recipient cert. of appreciation Kans. Bar Assn., 1979, U. Maine, 1983; Nat. Judge's Recognition award Nat. Conf. Bankruptcy Judges, 1979; Key to Town Limestone, 1983; named one of Outstanding Young Men of Maine, 1963. Mem. ABA, Maine Bar Assn., Penobscot Bar Assn., Nat. Conf. Bankruptcy Judges (pres. 1976-77), Nat. Bankruptcy Conf. (exec. bd. 1974-77), Am. Judicature Soc., Limestone C. of C. (pres.). Roman Catholic. Jurisprudence.

CYR, STEVEN MILES, lawyer; b. Centralia, Wash., Mar. 8, 1948; s. Delbert Lee and Lila M. (Tatro) C.; m. Bonnie R. Lefor Cyr, Sept. 8, 1972, children: Miles Lee, Lindsay Ann. Student, U. S.D.; BS, Oreg. State U., 1970; JD, Lewis & Clark U., 1979. Bar: Oreg. 1979, U.S. Dist. Ct. Oreg. 1979, U.S. Tax Ct. 1979, U.S. Ct. Appeals (9th cir.) 1979. Inheritence tax examiner Oreg. Dept. Revenue, Salem, 1970-74; mgr. trust tax dept. 1st Interstate Bank of Oreg., Portland, 1974-79; ptnr. Cyr, Moe & Benner P.C., Portland, 1979—. Author: Oregon Practical Probate, 1985-86, Oregon Estate Planning, 1985, Oregon Partnership Law, 1986. Mem. Oreg. Bar Assn. (exec. com. taxation sect. 1985-86, treas. 1986—, chmn.-elect 1987). Club: Univ., Riverside Golf and Country (Portland). Avocations: skiing, golf, music. Probate, Corporate taxation, Estate taxation. Office: Cyr Moe & Benner PC 400 SW 6th Ave Suite 1010 Portland OR 97204

CZAJKOWSKI, FRANK HENRY, lawyer; b. Bklyn., Jan. 7, 1936; m. Cecilia J. Artowicz, Sept. 3, 1955. B.A., St. John's U., Bklyn., 1957, J.D., 1959; LL.M., George Washington U., 1966. Bar: N.Y. 1960, Pa. 1970, Conn. 1974, U.S. Supreme Ct. 1964. Claims adjuster Hartford Accident & Indsl. Ins. Co., N.Y.C., 1959-60; agt. Equitable Life Assurance Soc., N.Y.C., 1960; atty. Corp. Counsel's Office, N.Y.C., 1960-62; atty. Fgn. Claims Settlement Commn., Washington, 1962-68; atty. Atlantic-Richfield Co., N.Y.C., 1968-70, Phila., 1970-72; employee relations counsel Cheesebrough Pond's Inc., Westport, Conn., 1972—; instr. Fairfield U. Ctr. Lifetime Learning, 1976, Sacred Heart U., 1983; arbitrator Am. Arbitration Assn. Mem. ABA, Conn. Bar Assn., Westchester-Fairfield Corp. Counsel Assn. Republican. Roman Catholic. Labor, Pension, profit-sharing, and employee benefits, Workers' compensation. Home: 7 Lafayette Dr Trumbull CT 06611 Office: Cheesebrough Ponds Inc Nyala Farms Rd Westport CT 06880

CZARRA, EDGAR F., JR., lawyer; b. Langhorne, Pa., Oct. 4, 1928; s. Edgar F. and Mary Agnes (Copeland) C.; m. Doris Catharine Lane, June 14, 1952; children: Penelope L., Edgar F. III, Jonathan C., Melanie A. BS, Yale U., 1949, LLB, 1952. Bar: U.S. Dist. Ct. D.C. 1954, U.S. Ct. Appeals (D.C. cir.) 1954, U.S. Supreme Ct. 1959. Assoc. Covington & Burling, Washington, 1952, 55-63, ptnr., 1963—. Served to lt. (j.g.) USN, 1952-55. Mem. D.C. Bar Assn., Fed. Communications Bar Assn. Administrative and regulatory, Federal civil litigation, Entertainment. Office: Covington & Burling 1201 Pennsylvania Ave NW PO Box 7566 Washington DC 20044

CZERWONKA, JOSEPH JOHN, lawyer; b. Fall River, Mass., Feb. 14, 1956; s. Joseph Paul and Francis S. (Wojcik) C.; m. Diane Marie Bunk, July 10, 1982. BS, Suffolk U., 1977, JD, 1979. Bar: Mass., U.S. Dist. Ct. Mass., U.S. Supreme Ct. Assoc. Vrana & Cunha, Fall River, 1979-85; sole practice Fall River, 1985—. Counsel Fall River chpt. ARC. Recipient citation Commonwealth of Mass. Ho. Reps., 1983. Mem. ABA, Mass. Bar Assn., Fall River Bar Assn., Bristol County Bar Assn., Assn. Trial Lawyers Am. Roman Catholic. Avocations: fishing, boating, target shooting. Bankruptcy, Personal injury, Real property. Home: 401 Bullock St Fall River MA 02720 Office: 456 Rock St PO Box 1508 Fall River MA 02722

DAAR, DAVID, lawyer; b. Chgo., May 23, 1931. AB, Sacramento State Coll., 1955; JD, Loyola U., Los Angeles, 1956. Bar: Calif. 1956, U.S Tax Ct. 1960, U.S. Supreme Ct. 1960. Ptnr. David Daar and Assocs., Los Angeles, 1956-75, Daar & Newman, P.C., Los Angeles, 1975-78, Miller & Daar, P.C., Los Angeles, 1978—; lectr. in ins. law and regulation, maj. litigation, class actions and trial strategy in securities and commodities cases; mem. faculty 1st Nat. Coll. Advocacy U. Calif, San Francisco. Author: Aviation Insurance, 1986; contbr. articles to profl. jours. Mem. Calif. Bar Assn. (chmn. com. on fed. cts. 1973), Conf. on Ins. Counsel. Insurance, Federal civil litigation, State civil litigation. Office: Miller & Daar 11500 W Olympic Blvd Suite 600 Los Angeles CA 90064

DACCA, FRANKLIN LOUIS, lawyer; b. Tacoma, July 13, 1947; s. Louis Leo and Marion Charlotte (Hanson) D.; m. Terese Mosher, Mar. 16, 1974; children: R. Ryan, Joseph T. BA in Polit. Sci. cum laude, U. Wash., 1969; JD, U. Calif., Davis, 1973. Bar: Wash. 1973, U.S. Ct. Appeals (9th cir.) 1974, U.S. Dist. Ct. (we. dist.) Wash. 1978. Law clk. to presiding justice U.S. Supreme Ct., Wash., 1973-74; asst. U.S. atty. criminal div. U.S. Dist. Ct. (cen. dist.), Los Angeles, 1974-77; assoc. Burgess & Kennedy, Tacoma, 1977-80; ptnr. Dacca & Hickman, Tacoma, 1980—; traffic commr. Pierce County Dist. Ct., Tacoma, 1981—. Mem. ABA, Wash. State Bar Assn., Tacoma Pierce County Bar Assn., Fed. Bar Assn. Lodge: Rotary, Elks. Avocations: gardening, sports, reading, fly fishing. State civil litigation, Personal injury, Criminal. Home: 5414 46th Ave Ct NW Gig Harbor WA 98335 Office: Dacca & Hickman 6010 20th St E Tacoma WA 98424

DACEY, KATHLEEN RYAN, judge; b. Boston; m. William A. Dacey (dec. Aug. 1986); 1 child, Mary Dacey White. A.B. with honors, Emmanuel Coll., 1941; M.S. in L.S., Simmons Coll., 1942; J.D., Northeastern U., 1945; postgrad., Boston U. Law Sch., 1945-46. Bar: Mass. 1945, U.S. Supreme Ct. 1957. Practiced in Boston, 1947-75; asst. atty. gen., chief civil bur. Mass. Dept. Atty. Gen., Boston, 1975-77; law clk. to justices Mass. Supreme Jud. Ct., 1945-47; U.S. adminstrv. law judge Boston, 1977—; auditor, master Commonwealth of Mass., 1972-75, Suffolk and Norfolk Counties, Mass., 1972-75; asst. dist. atty. Suffolk County, Mass., 1971-72; mem. panel def. counsel for indigent persons U.S. Dist. Ct. Dist. Mass.; lectr., speaker in field. Contbr. articles to profl. jours. Bd. dirs. Mission United Neighborhood Improvement Team, Boston; mem. Boston Sch. Com., 1945-46, chmn., 1946-47. Recipient Silver Shingle award Boston U. Sch. Law, 1980; named Alumnae Woman of Yr., Northeastern U. Law Sch. Assn., 1976. Mem. ABA (ho. of dels. 1982—, exec. com. conf. of adminstrv. law judges jud. adminstrn. div. 1987—), Internat. Bar Assn., Mass. Bar Assn., Boston Bar Assn., Norfolk Bar Lawyers Assn., Nat. Assn. Women Lawyers (pres.), Mass. Assn. Women Lawyers, Internat. Fedn. Women Lawyers, Boston U. Law Sch. Alumni Assn. (corr. sec. 1974-76), Boston U. Nat. Alumni Council. Administrative and regulatory, Judicial administration. Office: SSA-OHA 10 Causeway St Room 417 Boston MA 02221-0091

DACK, CHRISTOPHER EDWARD HUGHES, lawyer; b. Huntingdon, Eng., Jan. 12, 1942; s. Edward Harold and Nora Gwendolyn (Hughes) D.; m Gail Frances Hymel, Jan. 20, 1962; 1 child, Hilary Gail. BA, U. Southwestern La., 1964; JD, U. Tex., 1970. Bar: Tex. 1970. Ptnr. Fulbright & Jaworski, Houston, 1970-77, 82—, London, 1977-82. Served to capt. USAF, 1964-68. Mem. ABA, Internat. Bar Assn. General corporate, Private international, Contracts commercial. Office: Fulbright & Jaworski 1301 McKinney Houston TX 77010

DACSO, SHERYL TATAR, lawyer; b. Pasadena, Tex., Aug. 4, 1950; d. Mervin and Ruth (Bieber) Tatar; m. Clifford C. Dacso, Dec. 22, 1974; children: Matthew, Mara, Rebecca. BA, U. Tex., 1972; MPH, U. Tex., Houston, 1974, DrPH, 1979; JD, S. Tex. Coll. Law, Houston, 1979. Bar: Tex. 1979, U.S. Dist. Ct. (so. dist.) Tex. 1979, Ala. 1983. Assoc. Hicks, Hirsch, Glover, Robinson, Houston, 1979-82; counsel Sisters of Charity of Incarnate Word, Houston, 1982; assoc. Hand, Arendall, Mobile, Ala., 1982-83; counsel Providence Hosp., Mobile, 1983-87, John T. Mooresmith, P.C., Mobile, 1987—; Adj. asst. prof. Univ. S. Ala. Coll. of Med., Mobile, 1983—. Sec. Fedn. Jewish Charities, Mobile, 1985. Mem. ABA, Ala. Bar Assn., State Bar Tex. Avocation: swimming. Health, General corporate, Personal injury. Office: John T Mooresmith PC 2970 Cottage Hill Rd Suite 158 Mobile AL 36616

DADDS, HARRY LEON, II, lawyer; b. Louisville, Oct. 28, 1950; s. Harry Leon and Mary K. (Pulliam) D.; m. Brenda Ford, Aug. 9, 1980 (dec. Dec. 1983). BA, U. Ky., 1972, JD, 1975. Bar: Ky. 1975, U.S. Ct. Mil. Appeals 1975, D.C. 1979, Ala. 1984, Tenn. 1985, U.S. Dist. Ct. Tenn. 1986. Commd. 2d lt. U.S. Army, 1975, advanced through grades to maj., resigned, 1985; assoc. Spears, Moore, Rebman and Williams, Chattanooga, 1985—. Served to maj. USAR, 1985—. Mem. ABA, Tenn. Bar Assn., Ky. Bar Assn., Ala. Bar Assn., Phi Beta Kappa, Omicron Delta Kappa. Republican. Pension, profit-sharing, and employee benefits, Government contracts and claims, Environment. Office: Spears Moore Rebman and Williams Blue Cross Bldg Chattanooga TN 37402

DADY, ROBERT EDWARD, lawyer; b. N.Y.C., Nov. 11, 1936; s. Edward Joseph and Florence (Scheidt) D.; m. Mollie D. Richman; children—Michael, Andrew, Rachel. B.A., Queens Coll., 1958; LL.B., Fordham U., 1961. Bar: N.Y. 1962, Fla. 1974. Asst. gen. csl. The Equity Corp., N.Y.C., 1962-66; gen. atty. ITT-Levitt and Sons, Inc., Washington and Lake Success, N.Y., 1966-70; sr. v.p.-legal First Realty Investment Corp., Miami Beach, Fla., 1970-71; v.p.-legal, sec. Cavanagh Communities Corp., Miami, Fla., 1971-75; ptnr. Mann & Dady, P.A., Miami, 1975-80, Mann, Dady, Corrigan & Zelman, P.A., 1980-83, Dady, Siegfried & Kipnis, P.A., 1984-85, sole practice, 1985—; adj. prof. law U. Miami Sch. Law.; bd. dirs. Spectrum Programs, Inc., pres., 1984-86. Mem. Nat. Land Council (pres. 1974-81, bd. dirs. 1973—), ABA (environ. law com.), Fla. Bar Assn. Republican. Author: Land Acquistion and Development, 1975. Administrative and regulatory, General corporate, Real property. Home: 8440 SW 143d St Miami FL 33158 Office: 1570 Madruga Ave 311 Coral Gables FL 33146

DAGGETT, ROBERT SHERMAN, lawyer; b. La Crosse, Wis., Sept. 16, 1930; s. Willard Manning and Vida Naomi (Sherman) D.; m. Lee Sullivan Burton, Sept. 16, 1960; children: Ann Sherman, John Sullivan; m. Helen Ackerman, July 20, 1976. A.B. with honors in Polit. Sci. and Journalism, U. Calif.-Berkeley, 1952, J.D., 1955. Bar: Calif. 1955, U.S. Supreme Ct. 1967. Assoc. firm Brobec, Phleger & Harrison, San Francisco, 1958-66, ptnr., 1966—; counsel Calif. Senate Reapportionment Com., 1972-73; adj. prof. evidence and advocacy Hastings Coll. Law, 1982—; demonstrator-instr. Nat. Inst. for Trial Advocacy, 1981—, Hastings Ctr. for Trial and Appellate Advocacy, 1981—, mem. adv. bd., 1983—; vol. pro tem small claims judge San Francisco Mcpl. Ct., 1981—. Bd. editors: Calif. Law Rev., 1953-55; contbr. articles to profl. jours. Rep. Pacific Assn. AAU, 1973; bd. dirs. San Francisco Legal Aid Soc.; bd. visitors Coll. V U. Calif.-Santa Cruz. Served to 1st lt. JAGC U.S. Army, 1958-62. Walter Perry Johnson scholar, 1953. Mem. ABA, State Bar Calif. (chmn. local adminstrv. com. 1964-65), San Francisco Bar Assn. (past dir.), Am. Judicature Soc., Order of Golden Bear, Phi Delta Phi, Theta Xi. Republican. Club: Bohemian, Commonwealth, Commercial (San Francisco). Antitrust, Federal civil litigation, Trademark and copyright. Office: Brobeck Phleger & Harrison Spear St Tower One Market Plaza San Francisco CA 94105

DAGGETT, WILLIAM ATHERN, lawyer; b. Brunswick, Maine, Oct. 10, 1937; s. William Athern and Catherine (Travis) D.; m. Phyllis Peters, Sept. 20, 1969; children—Catherine, Zoë. B.A., Wesleyan Univ., 1959; LL.B., Yale Univ., 1962. Bar: Mass. 1962. Assoc. Goodwin, Procter & Hoar, Boston, 1966-74; asst. v.p. Bank of New England, Boston, 1974-77, v.p., 1977-80, v.p., sec., corp. counsel, 1980-84, sec., corp. counsel, 1984-87, sr. v.p., sec., assoc. gen. counsel, 1987—. Home: 212 Main St Winchester MA 01890 Office: Bank of New England 28 State St Boston MA 02109

DAHAR, VICTOR WILLIAM, lawyer; b. Nashua, N.H., Jan. 5, 1930; s. Saheed and Mercedes Sacre D.; m. Eleanor M. Mooney, July 2, 1960; children—Eleanor, Victor, Mercedes, Saheed. J.D., Boston Coll., 1958. Bar: N.H. 1958, Mass. 1958. Sole practice, Manchester, N.H., 1958—. Bd. dirs. Info. Ctr. on Immigration, 1963-65; chmn. Manchester March of Dimes, 1964, county chmn., 1968-69, cpt. chmn., 1970-76; bd. dirs. Multiple Sclerosis Soc., 1966-75; mem. Manchester Sch. Bd., 1962-66. Served with U.S.

Army, 1952-55; Korea. Mem. N.H. Bar Assn., Manchester Bar Assn., ABA, Am. Trial Lawyers Assn. Club: Optimists. General practice, Contracts commercial, Personal injury. Home: 100 Esty Ave Manchester NH 03102 Office: 20 Merrimack St Manchester NH 03101

DAHL, HARRY WALDEMAR, lawyer; b. Des Moines, Aug. 7, 1927; s. Harry Waldemar and Helen Gerda (Anderson) D.; m. Bonnie Sorensen, June 14, 1952; children: Harry Waldemar, Lisabeth (dec.), Christina. B.A., U. Iowa, 1950; J.D., Drake U., 1955. Bar: Iowa 1955, Fla. 1970, Nebr., Minn., U.S. Dist. Ct. (no. and so. dists.) Iowa, U.S. Supreme Ct. Practiced in Des Moines, 1955-59, 70—, Miami, Fla., 1972—; mem. firm Steward & Crouch, Des Moines, 1955-59; Iowa dep. indsl. commr. Des Moines, 1959-62; commr. 1962-71; mem. firm Underwood, Gillis and Karcher, Miami, 1972-77; adj. prof. law Drake U., 1972—; Exec. dir. Internat. Assn. Indsl. Accident Bds. and Commns., 1972-77; pres. Workers Compensation Studies, Inc., 1974—, Workers' Compensation Services, Inc., 1978—, Hewitt, Coleman & Assos. Iowa, Inc., 1975-79; mem. adv. com. Second Injury Fund, Fla. Indsl. Relations Commn. Author: Iowa Law on Workmen's Compensation, 1975; Editor: ABC Newsletter, 1964-77. Served with USNR, 1945-46. Recipient Adminstrs. award, 1967. Mem. Am. Trial Lawyers Assn., ABA, Iowa Bar Assn., Fla. Bar Assn., Nebr. Bar Assn., Minn. Bar Assn., Internat. Bar Assn., Am. Soc. Law and Medicine (council 1975-82), Iowa Assn. Workers' Compensation Lawyers (co-founder, past pres.), Def. Research Inst., Coll. of Workers Compensation Inc. (co-founder, regent), Swedish Pioneer Hist. Soc., Am. Swedish Inst., Des Moines Pioneer Club, East High Alumni Assn. (pres. 1975-76), Order of Coif. Lutheran. Clubs: Masons, Shriners, Sertoma (chmn. bd. 1974-75). Workers' compensation, Administrative and regulatory, Insurance. Home: 3005 Sylvania Dr West Des Moines IA 50265 Office: 974 73 St #16 Des Moines IA 50312

DAHL, JEFFREY A(LAN), lawyer; b. Salt Lake City, July 31, 1953; s. Alan Craven and Dorothy (Beckstead) D.; m. Julie Ann Jelte, Jan. 3, 1975; children: Erika, Hillary, Miriam, Katherine. BS magna cum laude, U. Utah, 1976; JD cum laude, Brigham Young U., 1979. Bar: N.Mex. 1979, U.S. Dist. Ct. N.Mex. 1979, U.S. Ct. Appeals (10th cir.) 1985. Assoc. Lamb, Metzgar and Lines, Albuquerque, 1979-84, ptnr., 1984—; mem. faculty U. Phoenix, Albuquerque, 1985—. Com. mem. Boy Scouts Am. Rio Grande dist., Albuquerque, 1983. Recipient Christenson Meml. award Brigham Young U., 1979. Mem. ABA, N.Mex. State Bar Assn., Albuquerque Bar Assn., Phi Beta Kappa, Phi Kappa Phi. Mormon. Avocations: running, biking, swimming, backpacking, skiing. State civil litigation, Federal civil litigation, Bankruptcy. Home: 6216 Dellyne Ct NW Albuquerque NM 87120 Office: Lamb Metzgar and Lines PO Box 987 300 Central SW Albuquerque NM 87103

DAHL, TYRUS VANCE, JR., lawyer; b. Elizabeth City, N.C., July 23, 1949; s. Tyrus Vance and Emerald (Taylor) D.; m. Susan Morrow Fitzgerald, Aug. 7, 1976; children: Katherine Fitzgerald, Elizabeth Sommers. AB, Duke U., 1971; JD, U. Tulsa, 1979. Bar: Tenn. 1979, U.S. Dist. Ct. (mid. dist.) Tenn. 1979, Okla. 1981, U.S. Dist. Ct. (no. and we. dists.) Okla. 1982, U.S. Ct. Appeals (10th cir.) 1982, N.C. 1985, U.S. Dist. Ct. (ea., mid., and we. dists.) N.C. 1985, U.S. Ct. Appeals (4th cir.) 1985, U.S. Supreme Ct. 1985. Law clk. to chief fed. judge Nashville, 1979-81; assoc. Hall, Estill, Tulsa, 1981-84, Womble Carlyle Sandridge & Rice, Winston-Salem, N.C., 1984—. Contbr. articles to law rev. Mem. ABA, Forsyth County Bar Assn. Democrat. Methodist. Avocation: photography, music. Civil rights, Federal civil litigation, Insurance. Office: Womble Carlyle Sandridge & Rice 2400 Wachovia Bldg Winston-Salem NC 27102

DAHLEN, RICHARD LESTER, lawyer; b. Minot, N.D., June 17, 1943; s. Lester and Ragnhild Marie (Dahl) D.; m. Anne Carey Phillips, Feb. 8, 1969; 1 son, Christopher B.R. A.B. magna cum laude, Harvard U., 1965; LL.B., Yale U., 1968. Bar: Minn. 1970, U.S. Dist. Ct. Minn. 1971, U.S. Ct. Appeals (8th cir.) 1971, U.S. Supreme Ct. 1973, Mass. 1976, U.S. Dist. Ct. Mass. 1976, U.S. Ct. Appeals (1st cir.) 1976, U.S. Ct. Appeals (2d cir.) 1981. Law clk. to justice Minn. Supreme Ct., St. Paul, 1968-69; assoc. Johnson, Thompson, Klaverkamp & James, Mpls., 1971-74; litigation atty. E.I. du Pont deNemours & Co., Wilmington, Del., 1974-75; assoc. Chaplin, Casner & Edwards, Boston, 1976-78, ptnr., 1978-81; ptnr. Dahlen & Glovsky, Boston, 1981-86, Gray, Wendell, Chalmers & Dahlen, 1986-87, Haus, Sanderson, Byrnes & Morton, 1987—. Served with U.S. Army, 1969-71; JAGC, USNR, 1972—. Mem. ABA, Boston Bar Assn., Essex County Bar Assn., Maritime Law Assn. U.S. Republican. Episcopalian. Club: Harvard (Boston, N.Y.C.). Admiralty, Federal civil litigation, State civil litigation. Office: 1 Center Plaza Boston MA 02108

DAHLING, GERALD VERNON, lawyer; b. Red Wing, Minn., Jan. 11, 1947; s. Vernon and Lucille Alfrieda (Reuter) D.; m. Edell Marie Villella, July 26, 1969; children: David (dec.), Christopher, Elizabeth, Mary. BS, Winona (Minn.) State Coll., 1968; MS, U. Minn., 1970; PhD, Harvard U., 1974; JD, William Mitchell Coll. of Law, 1980. Bar: U.S. Patent Office 1979, Minn. 1980, Ind. 1980, U.S. Dist. Ct. (so. dist.) Ind. 1980. Patent atty. Eli Lilly and Co., Indpls., 1980-84, mgr. biotech. patents, 1984-86, asst. patent counsel biotech., 1986—. Mem. ABA, Ind. Bar Assn., Am. Intellectual Property Law Assn. (biotech. task force). Democrat. Roman Catholic. Patent, Federal civil litigation, Contracts commercial. Home: 5362 Washington Blvd Indianapolis IN 46220 Office: Eli Lilly and Co Corporate Center Indianapolis IN 46285

DAHLK, THOMAS HARLAN, lawyer; b. Madison, Wis., Aug. 22, 1952; s. Harlan Edward and Ardys (Hanson) D.; m. Janice Kay Larson, Dec. 21, 1973; children: Lesley Anne, Thomas Larson. BA with distinction, U. Wis., 1974; JD magna cum laude, Creighton U., 1977. Bar: Nebr. 1977, U.S. Dist. Ct. Nebr. 1977. Assoc. Fitzgerald and Brown, Omaha, 1977-83, ptnr., 1983—; adj. faculty Creighton Law Sch., Omaha, 1981—. Contbr. articles to legal publs. Mem. ABA (com. fed. securities regulation 1982—), Nebr. Bar Assn., Omaha Bar Assn. Lutheran. Securities, Federal civil litigation, State civil litigation. Home: 330 N 68th St Omaha NE 68132 Office: Fitzgerald and Brown 1000 Woodmen Tower Omaha NE 68102

DAHM, PETER FRANKLIN, lawyer; b. Willmar, Minn., Mar. 14, 1948; s. Peter Francis Sr. and Grace (Monsma) D.; m. Helen Faye Padding, Aug. 24, 1968; children: Elizabeth, Andrea. BA, Calvin Coll., 1970; JD, U. Ill., 1975. Bar: Mich. 1975, U.S. Dist. Ct. (ea. dist.) Mich. 1979, U.S. Ct. Appeals (6th cir.) 1984. Asst. pros. atty. Bay County, Bay City, Mich., 1975-78; ptnr. Lambert, Leser, Dahm, Giunta, Cook & Schmidt P.C., Bay City, 1979—; instr. Delta Coll., Univ. Ctr., Mich., 1984-85. Mgr. campaign com. to elect Kennedy Senator, Bay City, 1978. Mem. Mich. Bar Assn. Club: Bay City Yacht (commodore 1986—). Avocation: sailing. Labor, Federal civil litigation, State civil litigation. Home: 2126 6th St Bay City MI 48708 Office: Lambert Leser Dahm Giunta Cook & Schmidt PC 309 Davidson Bldg Bay City MI 48708

DAIGLE, PATRICK KEITH, lawyer; b. Lafayette, La., Nov. 18, 1949. BA, Nicholls State U., 1971; JD, La. State U., 1979. Bar: La. 1979, U.S. Dist. Ct. (ea. and cen. dists.) La. 1980, U.S. Ct. Appeals (5th cir.) 1980. Assoc. Gordon Arata & McCollam, New Orleans, 1979-81; ptnr. Halpern & Daigle, Metairie, La., 1981—. Served to lt. (j.g.) USN, 1973-76. Mem. ABA (litigation and natural resources sect.), La. Bar Assn. (natural resources sect.), Fed. Energy Bar Assn. Oil and gas leasing, Federal civil litigation, State civil litigation. Office: Halpern and Daigle 3636 N Causeway Blvd Suite 100 Metairie LA 70002

DAILEY, COLEEN HALL, lawyer; b. East Liverpool, Ohio, Aug. 10, 1955; d. David Lawrence and Deloris Mae (Rosensteel) Hall; m. Donald W. Dailey Jr., Aug. 16, 1980. Student, Wittenberg U., 1973-75; BA, Youngstown State U., 1977; JD, U. Cin., 1980. Bar: Ohio 1981, U.S. Dist. Ct. (no. dist.) Ohio 1981. Sr. library assoc. Marx Law Library, Cin., 1979-80; law clk. Kapp Law Office, East Liverpool, 1979, 1980-81, assoc., 1981-85; sole practice East Liverpool, 1985—; spl. counsel Atty. Gen. Ohio, East Liverpool, 1985—. Pres. Columbiana County (Ohio) Young Dems., 1985—; bd. dirs. Big Bros. Big Sisters Columbiana County, Inc., Lisbon, Ohio, 1984—. Mem. ABA, Ohio Bar Assn., Columbiana County Bar Assn., Assn. Trial Lawyers Am., Ohio Trial Lawyers Assn., St. Clair Bus. and Profl. Women Assn. (pres. 1985—), Columbiana County LWV. Democrat. Lutheran. Family and matrimonial, Real property, State civil litigation. Office: 16687 St Clair Ave PO Box 2519 East Liverpool OH 43920

DAILEY, MICHAEL ALAN, lawyer; b. Columbus, Ohio, Sept. 28, 1951; s. Alan Ward and Vivian Louise (Jackson) D. AB, Duke U., 1973; JD, Emory U., 1977. Bar: Ga. 1977, U.S. Dist. Ct. (no. dist.) Ga. 1977, U.S. Ct. Appeals (11th cir.) 1984. Atty. Harman, Asbill, Roach & Nellis, Atlanta, 1977-83, Sumner & Hewes, Atlanta, 1983-85; of counsel Vaughan, Roach, Davis, Birch & Murphy, Atlanta, 1985—; faculty trial techniques sch. law Emory U., Atlanta, 1982—, Atlanta Coll. Trial Advocacy, 1982-85; adj. faculty coll. law Ga. State U., Atlanta, 1984-85. Chmn. precinct Jack Watson for Gov., Atlanta, 1982; big brother United Way, Atlanta, 1982—; bd. dirs. Profls. Offstage Alliance Theatre, Atlanta, 1983-85, Theatrical Outfit, Atlanta, 1983—. Mem. ABA, Ga. Bar Assn., Atlanta Bar Assn., Assn. Trial Lawyers Am. Democrat. Presbyterian. Avocations: running, photography. Federal civil litigation, Private international, Trademark and copyright. Office: Vaughan Roach Davis Birch & Murphy 1 Ravinia Dr Suite 1500 Atlanta GA 30346

DAINGERFIELD, RICHARD PAUL, lawyer; b. Boonton, N.J., Oct. 6, 1953; s. Edward L. and Miriam (Guiton) D.; m. Margaret Ann Farrell, May 20, 1980; children: Kathleen, Laura. BA with highest honors, Rutgers U., 1977; JD, U. Pa., 1980. Bar: N.J. 1980, Pa. 1981, U.S. Dist. Ct. N.J. 1980, U.S. Ct. Appeals (3d cir.) 1983. Assoc. Wilentz, Goldman & Spitzer, Woodbridge, N.J., 1980-86; v.p., counsel Nat. Westminster Bank USA, N.Y.C., 1986—; instr. Am. Inst. Banking, Elizabeth, N.J., 1982-85. Columnist The Jersey Banker mag., 1983-85. Recipient Jason Outstanding Service award MSU chpt. Am. Inst. Banking, 1985. Mem. ABA, N.J. Bar Assn. (charter mem. fin. transactions com.), Omicron Delta Epsilon. Roman Catholic. Avocation: guitar playing. Banking. Home: 118 Nelson Pl Westfield NJ 07090 Office: Nat Westminster Bank USA 175 Water St 18th Floor New York NY 10038

DAITZ, RONALD FREDERICK, lawyer; b. N.Y.C., Sept. 1, 1940; s. Abraham and Anne (Birnbaum) D.; m. Linda Fay Rosenberg, Aug. 2, 1964; children: Paul Bennett, Charles Spencer. AB, Amherst Coll., 1961; LLB, Harvard U., 1964. Bar: N.Y. 1966, Colo. 1964, U.S. Dist. Ct. Colo. 1964, U.S. Ct. Appeals (10th cir.) 1964, U.S. Dist. Ct. (so. dist.) N.Y. 1979. Assoc. Henry & Adams, Denver, 1964-65; from assoc. to ptnr. Weil, Gotshal & Manges, N.Y.C., 1965—. Mem. ABA (fed. regulation of securites com. banking and bus. law sect. 1979—), N.Y. State Bar Assn. (com. securities regulation, banking corp. and bus. law sect. 1984—), Assn. of Bar of City of N.Y. (com. corp. law). Securities, Banking, General corporate. Office: Weil Gotshal & Manges 767 Fifth Ave New York NY 10153

DALAGER, JON KARL, lawyer; b. Morris, Minn., Apr. 30, 1956; s. Vincent F. and Joyce Catherine (Stanley) D.; m. Teresa Marie Mehl, Aug. 2, 1986. Diploma, Brown Inst., 1975; BA, U. Minn., Morris, 1979; JD, U. Minn., Mpls., 1982. Bar: Minn. 1982, U.S. Dist. Ct. Minn. 1982, N.D. 1983. Assoc. Michael J. McCartney, Breckenridge, Minn., 1982-83; ptnr. McCartney & Dalager, Breckenridge, 1983-85; assoc. Fluegel, Anderson, Dalager, Dalager & Seibel, Morris, 1985—. Named one of Outstanding Young Men of Am., 1985. Mem. ABA, Minn. Bar Assn., N.D. Bar Assn., 16th Dist. Bar Assn. (treas. 1985—), Assn. Trial Lawyers Am., Minn. Trial Lawyers Assn., Jaycees (pres. Breckenridge chpt. 1984, pres. Morris chpt. 1987, editor 1985-87), Breckenridge C. of C. (bd. dirs., v.p. 1983-85), Gamma Eta Gamma. Mem. Democratic Farm Labor Party. Lutheran. Lodge: Rotary (bd. dirs. Breckenridge 1983-85). Avocations: softball, volleyball, golf. Personal injury, State civil litigation, General practice. Home: 312 Atlantic Ave Morris MN 56267 Office: Fluegel Anderson Dalager et al PO Box 527 Atlantic Plaza Morris MN 56267

DALE, CANDY WAGAHOFF, lawyer; b. Boise, Idaho, Nov. 7, 1956; d. Fred Olan and Elaine denise (Brekke) Wagahoff; m. James Christopher Dale, June 2, 1984. BS, Coll. of Idaho, 1979; JD, U. Idaho, 1982. Bar: Idaho 1982, U.S. Dist. Ct. Idaho 1982. Assoc. Moffatt, Thomas, Barrett & Blanton Ltd., Boise, 1982—. Editor in chief Idaho U. Law Rev., 1981-82. Mem. Idaho Assn. Affirmative Action, 1985—. Mem. ABA (litigation sect.), Idaho Bar Assn. (continuing legal edn. com.), Boise Bar Assn. Presbyterian. Labor, Personal injury, Insurance. Office: Moffatt Thomas Barnett & Blanton Ltd PO Box 829 Boise ID 83701

DALE, DOUGLAS DON, lawyer; b. Guymon, Okla., Aug. 13, 1950; s. Don and Lavina (Haffner) D.; m. Nancy L. Fajen, Feb. 9, 1980; children: Jennifer Dawn, David Douglas. BBA, Okla. U., 1973; JD, Tulsa U., 1977. Bar: Okla. 1977, U.S. Dist. Ct. (we. dist.) Okla. 1978, U.S. Ct. Appeals (10th cir.) 1982. Ptnr. Wright, Dale & Jett, Guymon, 1980—. Named one of Outstanding Young Men in Am., 1983. Mem. ABA, Okla. Bar Assn. (Outstanding Service to Pub. award 1985), Tex. County Bar Assn. Democrat. Presbyterian. Probate, Family and matrimonial, Oil and gas leasing. Home: #1 Seneca Dr Guymon OK 73942 Office: Wright Dale & Jett 114 E 4th PO Box 591 Guymon OK 73942

DALEIDEN, NORBERT ALFRED, lawyer; b. Evanston, Ill., Sept. 24, 1942; s. Norbert John and Hilda Catherine (Daubenfeld) D.; m. Bonnie Jo Youngren, Aug. 26, 1967; children—Norbert Alfred, Jonna Beth, Timothy John. B.S., Northwestern U., 1964, M.B.A., 1965, J.D. cum laude, 1968. Bar: Ill. 1968, U.S. Dist. Ct. (no. dist.) Ill. 1968, U.S. Sup. Ct. 1977. Ptnr., McDermott, Will & Emery, Chgo., 1968-76; prin. Hosier, Niro & Daleiden, Ltd., Chgo., 1976-84, Daleiden, Thompson & Tremaine, Ltd., 1984—. Mem. ABA, Ill. State Bar Assn., Chgo. Bar Assn. Contbr. articles in field to profl. jours. General corporate, Corporate taxation, Pension, profit-sharing, and employee benefits.

DALENBERG, ROBERT VAN RAALTE, lawyer, utility company executive; b. Chgo., Nov. 1, 1929; s. John R. and Helene (Van Raalte) D.; m. Diane Curtis, June 19, 1954; children: Douglas, Donald, Betsy. Student, Morgan Park Jr. Coll., 1947-49; J.D., U. Chgo., 1953. Bar: Ill. 1956, Calif. 1973. Assoc. firm Essington, McKibben, Beebe & Pratt, Chgo., 1955-58; assoc. firm Schuyler, Stough & Morris, Chgo., 1958-64, ptnr., 1965-67; gen. atty. Ill. Bell Telephone Co., Chgo., 1967-72; assoc. gen. counsel Pacific Tel. & Tel. Co., San Francisco, 1972-76, v.p., gen. counsel, 1976-82; exec. v.p., gen. counsel, sec. Pacific Telesis Group and Pacific Bell, 1983—. Served to lt. USCGR, 1953-55. Mem. Am., Ill., Chgo., Calif. bar assns., Am. Judicature Soc., Phi Kappa Psi, Legal Club Chgo., Law Club Chgo. Office: Pacific Telesis and Pacific Bell 140 New Montgomery St San Francisco CA 94105

D'ALESSANDRO, DANIEL ANTHONY, lawyer, educator; b. Jersey City, Oct. 10, 1949; s. Donato Marino D'Alessandro and Rose Teresa (Casamassimo) Drennan; m. Beth Anne Lill, Sept. 2, 1978; children: Daniel Patrick, Eric Charles. BA, St. Peter's Coll., 1971; JD, Seton Hall U., 1974; LLM in Criminal Justice, NYU, 1981. Bar: N.Y. 1982, N.J. 1985, U.S. Dist. Ct. N.J. 1985, U.S. Supreme Ct. 1985. Law clk. to presiding judge Juvenile and Domestic Relations Ct., Hudson County, N.J., 1974-75; pub. defender City of Jersey City, 1975-76; prosecutor Town of Secaucus, N.J., 1976-77; prin. D'Alessandro & Assocs., Jersey City, 1977-82; ptnr. D' Alessandro & Tutak, Jersey City, 1982—; adj. prof. Middlesex County Coll., Edison, N.J., 1981-83, St. Peter's Prep., 1981-83; arbitrator automobile arbitration program N.J. Supreme Ct. Vol. probation officer Hudson County Probation Dept., 1977; pro bono counsel Anthony R. Cucci Civic Assn., Jersey City, 1981—; pro bono cons. Battered Women's Shelter, Jersey City, 1982; pro bono counsel Mayor's Task Force for the Handicapped, Jersey City, 1985—. Named Prof. of Yr. Secaucus (N.J.) Patrolmen's Benevolent Assn., 1980. Mem. ABA, N.J. State Bar Assn., Hudson County Bar Assn. (past chmn. and participant various coms.). Democrat. Roman Catholic. Avocations: renovating old homes, sports, photography. General practice, Real property, State civil litigation. Office: D'Alessandro & Tutak 3279 Kennedy Blvd Jersey City NJ 07306

DALEY, RICHARD M., state's attorney; b. Chgo., Apr. 24, 1942; s. Richard J. and Eleanor (Guilfoyle) D.; m. Margaret Corbett, Mar. 25, 1972; children: Nora, Patrick, Elizabeth. B.A., Providence Coll., 1964; J.D., DePaul U., Chgo. Practice law Chgo., 1969-80; mem. Ill. State Senate, 1973-80, chmn. Judiciary I Com, 1975, 77; state's atty. Cook County, Ill., 1980—. Bd. dirs. Little City Home; mem. Citizens Bd. U. Chgo.; mem. adv. bd. Mercy Hosp., Chgo.; bd. mgrs. Valentine Boys Club; active Nativity of Our Lord Parish, Chgo. Recipient Golden Rule plaque Chgo. Boys Club Am.; named Outstanding Legislator of Yr., Lt. Gov's. Sr. Legis. Forum, 1979, Outstanding Leader in Revision of Ill. Mental Health Code, Ill. Assn. Retarded Citizens, 1979, Outstanding Leader, Ill. Assn. Social workers, 1978, Pub. Citizen of Yr., Ill. Chpt. Nat. Assn. Social Workers, 1979. Mem. Chgo. Bar Assn., Ill. State Bar Assn., ABA, Cath. Lawyers Guild. Democrat. Roman Catholic. Office: State's Atty Cook County 500 Richard J Daley Ctr Chicago IL 60602 *

DALEY, SUSAN JEAN, lawyer; b. New Britain, Conn., May 27, 1959; s. George Joseph and Norma (Woods) D. BA, U. Conn., 1978; JD, Harvard U., 1981. Bar: Ill. 1981. Assoc. Altheimer & Gray, Chgo., 1981-86, ptnr., 1986—. Mem. Chgo. Council on Fgn. Relations, 1981—. Mem. ABA (real property, probate and trust law sect. plan termination com. 1983—, taxation sect. employee benefits com. 1984—), Ill. Bar Assn. (chmn. employee benefits div. fed. taxation sect. 1984—), Chgo. Bar Assn. (chmn. employee benefits div. fed. taxation com. 1985-86). Avocations: reading, jogging. Pension, profit-sharing, and employee benefits. Home: 1636 N Wells Apt 415 Chicago IL 60614 Office: Altheimer & Gray 333 W Wacker Suite 2600 Chicago IL 60606

D'ALFONSO, MARIO JOSEPH, lawyer, consultant; b. Phila., Nov. 3, 1951; s. Albert Carmine and Yolanda (Zanfrisco) D'A.; m. Rita F. Borrelli, Apr. 26, 1975; 1 child, Mario C. B.A., Villanova U., 1973; J.D., Widener U., 1979. Bar: Pa. 1979, N.J. 1979, U.S. Dist. Ct. (ea. dist.) Pa. 1979, U.S. Dist. Ct. N.J. 1979, U.S. Ct. Appeals (3rd dist.) 1980, U.S. Supreme Ct. 1983. Assoc. Avena, Hendren & Friedman, Camden, N.J., 1979-81; ptnr. Avena, Hendren, Friedman & D'Alfonso, 1981-84; sole practice, Cherry Hill, N.J., 1984—; cons. Marbert Construction, Upper Darby, Pa., 1982—. Mem. Am. Arbitration Assn. (Service award 1984), Am. Criminal Def. League, Camden County Bar Assn., N.J. Trial Lawyers Assn., Phi Delta Phi (pres. 1978), Phi Kappa Phi. Roman Catholic. Criminal, Personal injury, General practice. Home: 64 Lady Diana Circle Marlton NJ 08053 Office: 601 Longwood Ave Cherry Hill NJ 08002

DALLAS, WILLIAM MOFFIT, JR., lawyer; b. Cedar Rapids, Iowa, May 7, 1949; s. William Moffit and Winifred Mae (Lillie) D.; m. Lynne Louise Russo, July 30, 1977 (div. July 1984). A.B., Oberlin Coll., 1971; J.D., Harvard U., 1974. Bar: N.Y. 1975, U.S. Dist. Ct. (so. and ea. dists.) N.Y. 1975, U.S. Ct. Appeals (2d cir.) 1976, U.S. Ct. Appeals (3d cir.) 1983, U.S. Ct. Appeals (8th cir.) 1984. Assoc. Sullivan & Cromwell, N.Y.C., 1974-82, ptnr., 1982—. Contbr. articles on antitrust issues to law revs., 1978—, chpt. to book. Served to lt. USN, 1971-77. Mem. Assn. Bar City N.Y. (sec. judiciary com. 1977-80), N.Y. County Lawyers' Assn. (chmn. com. on trade regulation 1978-81), ABA. Club: India House (N.Y.C.). Federal civil litigation, State civil litigation, Antitrust. Office: Sullivan & Cromwell 125 Broad St New York NY 10004

DALLIMORE, SUZANNE MEREDITH, lawyer; b. Idaho Falls, Idaho, Aug. 7, 1950; d. George Maxwell and Virginia Margaret (Jensen) Meredith; m. John K. Dallimore, May 6, 1976 (div. June 1978); 1 child, Steven Ray; m. James R. Davis, Feb. 8, 1980. BA in Philosophy, U. Utah, 1974, JD, 1977. Bar: Utah 1977, U.S. Dist. Ct. Utah, 1977. Ptnr. Jones, Waldo, Holbrook & McDonough, Salt Lake City, 1976-82; asst. atty. gen. State of Utah, Salt Lake City, 1982-85; sole practice Salt Lake City, 1985—; adj. prof. Westminster Coll., Salt Lake City, 1985—; assoc. instr. U. Utah, Salt Lake City, 1986—. Named one of Outstanding Young Women of Am., Outstanding Young Women Bd., 1978, 85. Mem. ABA, Utah State Bar Assn. (pres. litigation sect. 1984-85), Salt Lake County Bar Assn., Salt Lake City C. of C., Sierra Club (SCCOPE advisor 1983-87), Order of Coif. Avocations: photography, wildlife, camping. Antitrust, Federal civil litigation, State civil litigation. Office: 1025 East 2100 South Suite 205 Salt Lake City UT 84105

DALLY, REBECCA POLSTON, lawyer; b. Columbus, Ga., Dec. 4, 1955; d. James Olon and Lottie Myrl (Woodham) Polston; m. Hal W. Dally, June 28, 1980; children—Patrick William, Melissa Leigh. Student Mercer U., 1973-75; B.A. cum laude, Ga. State U., 1976; J.D., U. Ga., 1979. Bar: Ga. 1979. Asst. loan coordinator Transam. Real Estate Tax Service, Atlanta, 1975-77; sole practice law, Social Circle, Ga., 1981—; spl. asst. dist. atty. Alcovy Jud. Circuit, Monroe and Covington, Ga., 1982-84; spl. asst. atty. gen., 1984—. Bd. dirs. Social Circle Hist. Preservation Soc., 1982—, The Alcove, 1986—; trustee Walton County Arts Council, 1983—, Hist. Soc. Walton County, 1984—; mem. fin. com. Social Circle Pub. Library; vol. ARC, Social Circle Nursing Home, 1980-81. Mem. ABA, Ga. Trial Lawyers Assn., Alcovy Jud. Circuit Bar Assn. (v.p. 1983-84, pres. 1984-85), Walton County Bar Assn. (v.p. 1982-83, pres. 1983-84), State Bar Ga., Social Circle Mcht. and Trade Assn., Walton County C. of C., Phi Alpha Delta. Baptist. Family and matrimonial, Juvenile, Real property. Home: PO Box 745 Social Circle GA 30279 Office: 137 E Hightower Trail PO Box 745 Social Circle GA 30279

DALRYMPLE, DONALD WYLIE, lawyer; b. Bloomington, Ill., June 3, 1947; s. Franklin Wells and Mary June (Endsley) Shearer; m. Marcia Bresee Dalrymple, Sept. 8, 1979; children: Daylen Wells, Lauren Lee. BS, Centre Coll., 1969; postgrad., Stetson U., 1969-72; JD magna cum laude, U. Balt., 1973. Bar: D.C. 1975, Fla. 1974. Counsel subcom. on health and environ., com. on energy commerce U.S. Ho. of Reps., Washington, 1974-79; dir. med. govt. relations Am. Cyanamid Co., Washington, 1979—; bd. dirs. Bresee Warner, Inc., Champaign, Ill. Served to specialist grade 4 USAR, 1970-76. Mem. ABA, Fla. Bar Assn., D.C. Bar Assn., Heiusler Legal Hon. Soc., Sigma Alpha Epsilon, Phi Alpha Delta. Presbyterian. Legislative, Administrative and regulatory. Home: 2801 34th Pl NW Washington DC 20007 Office: Am Cyanamid Co 1575 I St NW #200 Washington DC 20005

DAL SANTO, DIANE, judge; b. East Chicago, Ind., Sept. 20, 1949; d. John Quentin Dal Santo and Helen (Koval) D.; m. Fred O'Cheskey, June 29, 1985. B.A., U. N. Mex., 1971; cert. Inst. Internat. and Comparative Law, Guadalajara, Mex., 1978; J.D., U. San Diego, 1980. Bar: N.Mex. 1980, U.S. Dist. Ct. N.Mex. 1980. Ct. planner Met. Criminal Justice Coordinating Council, Albuquerque, 1973-75; planning coordinator Dist. Atty.'s Office, Albuquerque, 1975-76, exec. asst. to dist. atty., 1976-77, asst dist. atty. for violent crimes, 1980-82; chief dep. city atty. City of Albuquerque, 1983; assoc. firm T.B. Keleher & Assocs., 1983-84; judge Met. Ct., 1985—. Bd. dirs. Nat. Council Alcoholism, 1984, S.W. Ballet Co., Albuquerque, 1982-83; mem. Mayor's Task Force on Alcoholism and Crime. Recipient Woman of Yr. award Duke City Bus. and Profl. Women, 1985; U. San Diego scholar, 1978-79. Mem. ABA, N.Mex. Bar Assn., Albuquerque Bar Assn., Nat. Assn. Women Judges, LWV, N.Mex. Council on Crime and Delinquency, N.Mex. Magistrate Judges Assn. Democrat. Judicial administration, Jurisprudence, Criminal. Home: PO Box 2005 Albuquerque NM 87103 Office: Met Ct 401 Roma NW Albuquerque NM 87103

DALTHORP, GEORGE CARROL, lawyer; b. Wibaux, Mont., Aug. 7, 1929; s. Henry Charles and Clara (Rud) D.; m. Lois Esther Mattson, Aug. 30, 1956; children: David Charles, Kristin Dagny Jones, Beth Helen Dalthorp Johnson, Daniel Henry. BS, Mont. State U., 1951; postgrad., Denver U., 1955-56; JD, U. Mont., 1958. Bar: Mont. 1958, U.S. Dist. Ct. Mont. 1958, U.S. Ct. Appeals (9th cir.) 1969, U.S. Supreme Ct. 1979. Law clk. to presiding justice U.S. Dist. Ct. Mont., Billings, 1958-59; assoc. Crowley, Haughey, Hanson, Toole & Dietrich, Billings, 1959-67, ptnr., 1967—. Co. chmn., drive mem. exec. com., bd. dirs. United Way of Billings, 1970-80. Served to lt. USNR, 1952-55, Korea. Fellow Am. Coll. Trial Lawyers; mem. ABA, Mont. Bar Assn. (pres. 1985-86, bd. trustees 1982—), Yellowstone County Bar Assn., Internat. Assn. Def. Council. Republican. Lutheran. Club: Yellowstone (Billings). Lodge: Kiwanis, Elks. Avocations: backpacking, racquetball, skiing, fishing. Federal civil litigation, State civil litigation, Insurance. Office: Crowley Haughey Hanson Toole & Dietrich PO Box 2529 Billings MT 59103 Home: 2415 Granite Billings MT 59102

DALTON, DOUGLAS, lawyer; b. Astoria, Oreg., Sept. 1, 1929; s. Mervyn Edgar and Julia Margaret (Hitchcock) D.; m. Shirley Kirkpatrick, Aug. 29, 1953; children—Julia M., Douglas C., John D., Matthew J., Bartholomew P. B.A., UCLA, 1951; J.D., U. So. Calif., 1956. Bar: Calif. bar 1956. City prosecutor Long Beach, Calif., 1956-60; partner Ball, Hunt, Hart, Brown & Baerwitz, Los Angeles, 1960-77; prin. Dalton & Godfrey, Inc., Los Angeles,

1977—; adj. prof. law Pepperdine U. Sch. Law, Los Angeles, 1978-80. Counsel Pres. Nixon's Commn. on Campus Unrest, 1970. Served with USN, 1951-53. Fellow Am. Coll. Trial Lawyers; mem. ABA, State Bar Calif. (bd. govs. 1985—), County Bar Los Angeles. Republican. Federal civil litigation, State civil litigation, Criminal. Office: Dalton & Godfrey Inc 4525 Wilshire Blvd 3d Floor Los Angeles CA 90010

DALTON, KENNETH M., lawyer; b. N.Y.C., May 13, 1954; s. John M. and Carolyn (Knief) D.; m. Charlene Wilkinson, Sept. 11, 1982. BA magna cum laude, Brooklyn Coll., 1976; JD, Fordham U., 1980. Bar: N.Y., U.S. Dist. Ct. (ea. and so. dists.) N.Y., U.S. Tax Ct. Ptnr. Sutera, Siracuse & Sutera, N.Y.C., 1981—. Contbr. articles to profl. jours. Mem. N.Y. State Bar Assn., Assn. Trial Lawyers Am. Personal injury, Federal civil litigation, Insurance. Office: Sutera Siracuse & Sutera 111 John St New York NY 10038

DALTON, LEROY LAVERNE, lawyer, state official; b. Lodi, Wis., Feb. 28, 1924; s. Frederick P. and Ella C. (Johnson) D.; m. Virginia Mae Love, Dec. 18, 1954; children—Gregg, Jill. B.S. in Econs., U. Wis.-Madison, 1951, J.D., 1953. Bar: Wis. 1953, U.S. Dist. Ct. (we. dist.) Wis. 1959, U.S. Dist. Ct. (ea. dist.) Wis. 1960, U.S. Ct. Appeals (7th cir.) 1970, U.S. Supreme Ct. 1971. Asst. atty. gen. State of Wis., Madison, 1955-86; chmn. legal affairs com. Motor Vehicle Adminstrs. Assn., Washington, 1964-68; mem. Uniform Traffic Laws Com., Washington, 1967-68; lectr. U. Wis. Sch. Law-Madison, 1966, 81; founder Atty. Gen.'s Law Enforcement Conf., 1965. Founder Prosecutor's Bull. Wis. Dept. Justice, 1966, Wis. Law Enforcement Bull., 1965. Pres. Drum and Bugle Corps, Madison council Boy Scouts Am., 1976-77; pres. Ill.-So. Wis. Exchange Clubs, 1981-82; bd. dirs. Nat. Exchange Club, 1983-87; v.p. Child Abuse Prevention Ctr., 1984-87, also bd. dirs. Served with USN, 1943-46, PTO. Decorated Naval Air medal, Combat Wings, three stars; recipient Disting. Service award Ill.-So. Wis. Dist. Exchange Clubs, 1977, Outstanding Dist. Pres. award Nat. Exchange Club, 1983. Mem. Dane County Bar Assn., State Bar Wis., Madison Zool. Soc. (v.p., bd. dirs. 1975-87), Delta Theta Phi (chmn. 1952-53). Republican. Presbyterian. Club: Blackhawk Country (Madison). Administrative and regulatory, Labor, Civil rights. Home: 5058 Marathon Dr Madison WI 53705

DALTON, VICTORIA CLAYMAN, lawyer; b. Washington, Dec. 11, 1955; d. Lee Heiman and Marjorie Newton (Meade) Clayman. BA, W.Va. U., 1976, JD, 1980. Bar: W.Va. 1980, U.S. Dist. Ct. (no. and so. dists.) W.Va. 1980, U.S. Ct. Appeals (2d cir.) 1984, U.S. Dist. Ct. Conn. 1985. Labor rep. Kaiser Aluminum & Chem., Ravenswood, W.Va., 1980-82; sole practice Parkersburg, W.Va., 1982-83; ops. mgr. U.S. Ct. Appeals (2d cir.), N.Y.C., 1983-85; chief dep. clk. U.S. Dist. Ct. Conn., New Haven, 1985—. Mem. ABA, W.Va. Bar Assn., Fed. Bar Assn., Soc. Fed. Labor Relations Profls., Smithsonian Instn. Avocations: music, golf. Federal civil litigation, Judicial administration, Criminal. Home: 149 Peddlers Dr Branford CT 06405 Office: US Dist Ct Conn 141 Church St New Haven CT 06510

DALY, JOAN CHILTON, lawyer; b. Boston, Aug. 19, 1925; d. Charles Edward and Priscilla (Wicker) Daly. A.B., Vassar Coll., 1945; LL.B., Columbia U., 1960. Bar: N.Y. 1960, N.Y. Ct. Appeals, 1960. With Newsweek, N.Y.C., 1946-48, Esquire, N.Y.C., 1948; writer/researcher Newsweek, 1948-60; assoc. Paul Weiss Rifkind Wharton & Garrison, N.Y.C., 1960—. Editor Coll. Class Jour., 1981. Sec., dir. The New Dramatists, Inc., N.Y.C., 1975—; exec. com. Lexington Democratic Club, 1954-57; vice chmn. Newsweek unit Newspaper Guild, 1952-54; vol. atty. Community Law Offices; mem. Women's City Club. Mem. Assn. Bar City of N.Y. Club: Cosmopolitan (bd. govs.). Entertainment. Home: 315 Riverside Dr New York NY 10025 Office: Paul Weiss Rifkind Wharton & Garrison 1285 Ave of Americas New York NY 10019

DALY, JOHN JOSEPH, judge; b. Hartford, Conn., Nov. 5, 1923; s. Michael J. and Nora (Shea) D.; m. Jane Crosby, Aug. 16, 1952; children: Marianne, Michael C., Noreen. Student, Trinity Coll., 1941-43, BA, MA, 1947; student, Drexel U., 1943-44, U. Paris, 1945, Cambridge U., 1946; JD, U. Conn., 1950. Bar: Conn. 1950. Pros. atty. Hartford Police Ct., 1957-59; judge cir. ct., Hartford, 1961-67, chief judge, 1967-73; judge Superior Ct. Conn., Hartford, 1973-84, Appellate Ct., Hartford, 1984—; mem. Conn. Safety Commn., 1967-73, Conn. Jud. Council, 1967-73, State Drug Adv. Council, Conn., 1969-73, State Alcoholism Council, Conn., 1969-73, Planning Commn. on Criminal Adminstrn., Conn., 1970-73. Author: Conn. Evidence, 1966. Mem. Hartford Bd. Edn., 1951-57, pres. 1953-54. Served with U.S. Army, 1943-46, ETO. Named Knight of St. Gregory by Pope John Paul II, Vatican City, 1981. Mem. Conn. Bar. Assn., Hartford Bar Assn. Democrat. Roman Catholic. Home: 257 Terry Rd Hartford CT 06105 Office: Appellate Ct 95 Washington St Hartford CT 06106

DALY, JOHN PAUL, lawyer; b. Pitts., Aug. 6, 1939; s. John Ambrose and Cora Evelyn (Faye) D.; m. Kathleen Ellen Paul, Dec. 21, 1961. AB, U. Calif., Riverside, 1961; JD, Loyola U., Los Angeles, 1971. Bar: Calif. 1972. Dep. dist. atty. San Luis Obispo, Calif., 1971-78, dep. county counsel, 1978—; law prof. U. Calif. Polytech., 1979-81, lectr. Calif. Jud. Coll., 1982. Speaker Mental Health Dept. Social Services, San Luis Obispo, 1975—. Served to lt. comdr USCGR, 1962—. Mem. San Luis Obispo Govt. Attys. Union (founder, pres. 1977-82, chief negotiator 1977-79). Home: 10650 Colorado Rd Atascadero CA 93422 Office: County Counsel Govt Ctr San Luis Obispo CA 93408

DALY, LEO MICHAEL, lawyer; b. Phila., Apr. 4, 1947; s. Leo Vincent and Genevieve (McGinnis) D.; m. Cynthia Jean Turrentine, June 23, 1973; children: Nicholas, Timothy. BA, U. Minn., 1973; JD, Hamline U., 1977. Mgr. Conn. Gen. Ins. Co., Mpls., 1973-74; tchr. St. Alberts Sch., Mpls., 1974-76; law clk. to presiding justice Ramsey County Dist. Ct., St. Paul, 1976-77; assoc. Schwebel, Goetz et al, Mpls., 1977-82; sole practice St. Paul, 1982—. Editor: Minnesota Real Estate, 1974; author, editor: The Student Lawyer, 1977. Served to sgt. USAF, 1966-70, Vietnam. Mem. Assn. Trial Lawyers Am., Minn. Bar Assn., Am. Arbitration Assn., Ramsey County Bar Assn. Avocations: pvt. pilot, aircraft owner. Personal injury. Home: 24 Eagle Ridge Rd North Oaks MN 55114 Office: 1300 One Capital Ctr Plaza 386 N Wabasha Saint Paul MN 55102

DALY, MICHAEL FRANCIS, lawyer; b. Afton, N.Y., Jan. 2, 1947; s. David Francis and Avelda Marie (Hanssen) D.; m. Ann Carolyn Oberting, June 5, 1971; children: David V., Christopher E., Timothy P. BS, Yale U., 1968; JD, Albany Law Sch., 1972; LLM in Taxation, NYU, 1973. Bar: N.Y. 1973, U.S. Dist. Ct. (no. dist.) N.Y. 1973, U.S. Tax Ct. 1977. Assoc. DeGraff, Fay, Conway, Holt-Harris & Mealey, Albany, N.Y., 1973-77; ptnr. DeGraff, Fay, Conway, Holt-Harris & Mealey, Albany, 1978-83; sole practice Albany, 1984—; lectr. Nat. Bus. Inst., Eau Claire, Wis., 1985—. Editor: Estate Planning and Probate in New York, 1986. Cubmaster Boy Scouts Am., Londonville, N.Y., 1982-85; mem. bd. assocs. CP Ctr. for Disabled, Albany, 1984—; Rep. committeeman, Albany County, Colonie, N.Y., 1984—. Mem. ABA, N.Y. State Bar Assn., Albany County Bar Assn. Episcopalian. Clubs: Yale (N.Y.C.), Steuben Athletic (Albany). Estate taxation, Personal income taxation, Probate. Home: 18 Chestnut Hill S Londonville NY 12211 Office: 123 State St Albany NY 12207

DALY, T(HOMAS) F(RANCIS) GILROY, fed. judge; b. N.Y.C., Feb. 25, 1931; s. Paul Gerard and Madeleine (Mulqueen) D.; m. Stuart Stetson, Jan. 16, 1960; children—Timothy Francis Gilroy, Matthew M., Loan, Anna L. B.A., Georgetown U., 1952; LL.B., Yale U., 1957. Bar: Conn. bar 1957, N.Y. bar 1959. Mem. firm Simpson Thacher and Bartlett, N.Y.C., 1957-61; asst. U.S. atty. U.S. Dept. Justice, So. Dist. of N.Y., 1961-64; dept. atty. gen. State of Conn., 1967-71; spl. asst. to atty. gen. State of Conn., Conn., 1971-75; dep. state treas. State of Conn., 1976-77, ins. commr., 1976-77; U.S. Dist. Ct. judge Conn., 1977—; now chief judge State of Conn., 1983; individual practice law Fairfield, 1964-77. Trustee Leukemia Soc. Am. (chmn. 1971). Served as 1st. lt. U.S. Army, 1952-54. Recipient Distinguished Service award Fairfield Jr. C. of C., 1967. Mem. Am., Conn., Fed. bar assns., Am. Judicature Soc., Fed. Bar Council, Assn. of Bar City of N.Y., Am. Legion, Phi Delta Phi. Democrat. Roman Catholic. Jurisprudence. Office: United States Courthouse 915 Lafayette Blvd Bridgeport CT 06604

DALY, WILLIAM JOSEPH, lawyer; b. Bklyn., Mar. 19, 1928; s. William Bernard and Charlotte Marie (Saunders) D.; m. Barbara A. Longenecker, Nov. 19, 1955; children: Sharon, Nancy, Carol. B.A., St. John's U., 1951, J.D., 1953. Bar: N.Y. 1954, U.S. Dist. Ct. (so. and ea. dists.) N.Y. 1958, U.S. Ct. Mil. Appeals 1969, U.S. Ct. Claims 1969, U.S. Tax Ct. 1969, U.S. Supreme Ct. 1973. Assoc. Garvey & Conway, Esquires, N.Y.C., 1954-55, Wing & Wing, Esquires, N.Y.C., 1955-58; ptnr. Daly & Lavery, Esquires and predecessors, Ossining, N.Y., 1958—; also bd. dirs. Bd. dirs. Legal Aid Soc., Westchester County N.Y., 1980—, v.p., 1983—; mem. 9th Jud. Dist. Grievance Com., 1981—; trustee Supreme Ct. Library at White Plains, 1985—. Served with U.S. Army, 1946-48; col. JAGC USAR, 1978. Fellow Am. Bar Found., N.Y. Bar Found.; mem. ABA, N.Y. State Bar Assn. (ho. dels. 1977—, exec. com. 1983—, v.p. 1985—), Westchester County Bar Assn. (pres. 1979-81), Ossining Bar Assn. (pres. 1966-67), Assn. Trial Lawyers Am., N.Y. State Trial Lawyers Assn., Res. Officers Assn. U.S., Assn. U.S. Army, Skull and Circle, Phi Delta Phi. Roman Catholic. State civil litigation, Family and matrimonial, Personal injury. Home: 232 Hunter Ave North Tarrytown NY 10591 Office: Barclays Bank Bldg Ossining NY 10562

DALZIEL, CHARLES MEREDITH, JR., lawyer; b. Lake City, S.C., July 16, 1956; s. Charles Meredith and Ida Lou (Davis) D.; m. Mary Elizabeth Smith, Feb. 25, 1984. BS cum laude, Ga. So. Coll., 1977; JD magna cum laude, U. Ga., 1980. Bar: Ga. 1980, U.S. Dist. Ct. (no. and mid. dists.) Ga. 1980, U.S. Ct. Appeals (11th cir.) 1980. Assoc. Kilpatrick & Cody, Atlanta, 1980-84, Savell, William, Cox & Angel, Atlanta, 1984-87; ptnr. Savell & Williams, Atlanta, 1987—. Fundraiser Am. Heart Assn., Atlanta, 1985; Ga. Trust for Hist. Preservation, 1987. Mem. ABA, Atlanta Bar Assn. Baptist. Federal civil litigation, Securities, State civil litigation. Office: Savell & Williams 2300 Equitable Bldg Atlanta GA 30043-6201

DAMAS, STANISLAW STEFAN, lawyer; b. Cologne, Fed. Republic Germany, Nov. 1, 1948; came to U.S., 1950;; s. Jan Edward and Rosemarie (Grundman) D. BS, U. Detroit, 1970; JD, Wayne State U., 1974. Bar: Mich. 1974, U.S. Dist. Ct. (ea. dist.) Mich. 1974, Colo. 1975, U.S. Dist. Ct. Colo. 1975, U.S. Ct. Appeals (10th cir.) 1978. Specialist labor relations City of Detroit, 1970-75, City and County of Denver, 1975-76; atty. labor Mulligan & Damas, P.C., Denver, 1976-78; ptnr. Damas & Smith, P.C., Denver, 1978—. Mem. ABA (com. state and local govt. bargaining), Nat. Pub. Employer Relations Assn., Nat. Assn. Ednl. Negotiators. Labor, State civil litigation, School law. Home: 9200 Cherry Creek Dr S #34 Denver CO 80231 Office: Damas & Smith PC 1900 Grant St #730 Denver CO 80203-4307

DAMASHEK, PHILIP MICHAEL, lawyer; b. N.Y.C., May 18, 1940; s. Jacob and Esther (Sassower) D.; m. Judith Ellen Gold, Dec. 3, 1967; children—Alan S., Jonathan S., Harris R. B.B.A., U. Miami, 1964. Bar: N.Y. 1969, U.S. Dist. Ct. (so. and ea. dists.) N.Y. 1977. Lawyer, Cosmopolitan Mut. Ins. Co., N.Y.C., 1969-70, Schneider, Kleinick, Weitz & Damashek, 1971-73; sr. ptnr. Philip M. Damashek, P.C., N.Y.C., 1974—; dir. Tech. Support Services, Inc., Ossining, N.Y. Chmn. Combined Bar Assns. Jud. Screening Panel, N.Y.C., 1983—. Mem. N.Y. State Trial Lawyers Assn. (2d v.p.), Assn. Trial Lawyers City N.Y. (bd. dirs.), Jewish Lawyers Guild (bd. govs.), ABA, N.Y. State Bar Assn., Am. Trial Lawyers Assn., Met. Womens Bar Assn. Jewish. Personal injury, Contracts commercial, State civil litigation. Office: Philip M Damashek PC 35 Worth St New York NY 10013

DAMASKA, MIRJAN RADOVAN, legal educator; b. Brezice, Yugoslavia, Oct. 8, 1931; came to U.S., 1972; s. Radovan and Ljerka (Tkalcic) D.; m. Marija Brkoevic, Aug. 10, 1960. LL.M., U. Zagreb, Yugoslavia, 1956; D.Jurisprudence, Ljubljana Law Sch., 1960. Prof. law U. Zagreb, 1960-72, acting dean Law Sch., 1970-71; prof. law U. Pa. Law Sch., Phila., 1972-76; Ford Found. prof. law Yale U. Law Sch., New Haven, Conn., 1976—; cons. Author: Position of the Criminal Defendant, 1962, Faces of Justice and State Authority, 1986; contbr. articles to profl. jours. Nat. Found. for Study of Humanities fellow, 1978-79. Mem. Societe de Defense Sociale, Am. Assn. for Comparative Study of Law, Internat. Acad. Comparative Law. Republican. Criminal, Legal education, Private international.

D'AMATO, ANTHONY, legal educator; b. N.Y.C., Jan. 10, 1937; s. Anthony A. and Mary (DiNicholas) D'A.; m. Barbara W. Steketee, Sept. 4, 1958; children: Brian, Paul. B.A., Cornell U., 1958; J.D., Harvard U., 1961; Ph.D., Columbia U., 1968. Bar: N.Y. 1963, U.S. Supreme Ct. 1967, U.S. Tax Ct. 1987. Instr. Wellesley Coll., 1963-65; of counsel S.W. Africa Cases, N.Y.C., 1965-66; Woodrow Wilson fellow U. Mich., Ann Arbor, 1966-67; prof. law Northwestern U. Law Sch., Chgo., 1968—, dir. Inst. Advancement of Prosthetics; bd. dirs. Globus Growth Group Inc. Author: The Concept of Custom in International Law, 1971, (with O'Neil) The Judiciary and Vietnam, 1972, (with Hargrove) Environment and the Law of the Sea, 1976, (with Wasby and Metrailer) Desegregation from Brown to Alexander, 1977, (with Weston and Falk) International Law and World Order, 1980, Jurisprudence: A Descriptive and Normative Analysis of Law, 1984, Internat. Law: Process and Prospect, 1987; bd. editors Am. Jour. Internat. Law, 1981—. Recipient Annual Book award Am. Soc. Internat. Law., 1981. Mem. Internat. Law Assn., Am. Soc. Legal and Polit. Philosophy (chair inter-bar study group on ind. of lawyers and judges), ABA (council internat. law and practice, chair), Am. Soc. Internat. Law (chair human rights advocacy group, chair internat. commn. com. on customary law). Public international, Jurisprudence. Home: 716 Greenwood Ave Glencoe IL 60022 Office: Northwestern Law Sch Chicago IL 60611

DAMERON, DEL STILTNER, lawyer; b. Pikeville, Ky., July 12, 1953; d. Billy Arvin Stiltner and Ruby (Charles) Leffler; m. Floyd S. Dameron, Aug. 19, 1984; 1 child, William Charles. BA, Pikeville Coll., 1974; JD, U. Cin., 1977. Bar: Ohio 1977, D.C. 1977, U.S. Ct. Appeals (D.C. cir.) 1978, U.S. Ct. Claims 1979. Assoc. Howrey & Simon, Washington, 1977-79, Sellers, Conner & Cuneo, Washington, 1979-82; ptnr. McKenna, Conner & Cuneo, Washington, 1982—. Contbr. articles to profl. jours. Mem. ABA, Ohio Bar Assn., D.C. Bar Assn., Women's Bar Assn. Republican. Presbyterian. Antitrust, Government contracts and claims. Home: 6814 Delaware St Chevy Chase MD 20815 Office: McKenna Conner & Cuneo 1575 Eye St Washington DC 20005

DAMIANI, LOUIS CARMEN, lawyer; b. Bellaire, Ohio, May 23, 1953; s. Primo Maggio and Angela Rose (Perticarini) D. BA, Ohio State U., 1975; JD, Cleve. Marshall Coll. Law, 1979. Bar: Ohio 1979, U.S. Dist. Ct. (no. dist.) Ohio 1979, U.S. Ct. Appeals (6th cir.) 1980, U.S. Supreme Ct. 1985. Trial referee Cuyahoga County Common Pleas Ct., Cleve., 1980-81; adminstrv. asst. to chief justice Supreme Ct. Ohio, Columbus, 1981-83, asst. dir., 1983, dir., 1983—; sec. bd. commrs. on grievences and discipline, Columbus, 1983—; sec. Ohio Supreme Ct. rules adv. commn., Columbus, 1983—; treas. Ohio Jud. Conf., Columbus, 1983—. Mem. state exec. com. Ohio Dems., 1983—; mem. county exec. com. Cuyahoga Dems., Cleve., 1983—. Mem. ABA, Columbus Bar Assn., Cuyahoga County Bar Assn., Nat. Assn. Ct. Mgmt., Inst. Jud. Adminstrn., Am. Judicature Soc., Conf. State Ct. Adminstrs. Roman Catholic. Judicial administration, Jurisprudence, Legislative. Home: Box 42037 Brook Park OH 44142 Office: The Mall Bldg Suite 900 118 St Claire Ave NE Cleveland OH 44114-1215

D'AMICO, JOHN, JR., lawyer; b. Long Branch, N.J., Jan. 24, 1941; s. John and Elvira (Caravello) D'A.; m. Sandra V. Vaccarelli, Nov. 25, 1967; 1 child, Kimberly Jean. AB cum laude, Harvard U., 1963, JD, 1966. Bar: N.J. 1966. Law clk. to presiding justice Monmouth County Ct., Freehold, N.J., 1966-67; assoc. Drazin, Warshaw, Auerbach & Rudnick, Red Bank, N.J., 1967-70; atty. Mut. Benefit Life Ins. Co., Newark, 1970-72, asst. counsel, 1972-74, assoc. counsel, 1974-77, counsel, 1978-81, 2d v.p., counsel, 1981—. Counsel Nat. Soc. to Prevent Blindness, New Brunswick, 1978—, Partnership for N.J., New Brunswick, 1984—; pres. Oceanport Dems. 1979-80; mem. N. Jersey Transp. Co-ordinating Council, Newark, 1984—, Monmouth County Bd. Social Services, Freehold, 1986; councilman Borough of Oceanport, N.J., 1979-84; freeholder County of Monmouth, 1983—; bd. dirs. Shore Commuter Coalition, Eatontown, N.J. Mem. ABA, N.J. Bar Assn., Monmouth County Bar Assn., Assn. Life Ins. Counsel, Harvard Law Sch. Assn. Avocations: reading, golf, tennis. Insurance, General corporate, Legislative. Home: 53 Wittenburg Ct Oceanport NJ 07757 Office: Mut Benefit Life Ins Co 520 Broad St Newark NJ 07101

DAMICO, NICHOLAS PETER, lawyer; b. Chester, Pa., June 29, 1937; s. Ralph A. and Mary C. (Ametrane) D.; m. Patricia Ann Swatek, Aug. 26, 1967; children—Christine, Gregory. B.S. in Acctg. St. Joseph's U. 1960, LL.B., U. Pa., 1963; LL.M., Georgetown U., 1967. Bar: Pa. 1963, D.C. 1967, Md. 1986. Tax law specialist IRS, Washington, 1963-66; assoc. Silverstein and Mullens, Washington, 1972-76, ptnr. 1972-76; prin. Damico & Assocs., P.C., Washington, 1976-86, of counsel, Sanders, Schnabel & Brandenburg, P.C., 1987—; adj. prof. Georgetown U. Law Ctr., Washington, 1973-75. Mem. ABA, Fed. Bar Assn. Author: Qualified Plans-Taxation of Distributions, Tax Management Portfolio, 1978. Pension, profit-sharing, and employee benefits, Corporate taxation, Estate planning. Office: Sanders Schnabel & Brandenburg PC 1110 Vermont Ave NW Suite 600 Washington DC 20005

DAMON, CLAUDIA CORDS, lawyer; b. Heidelberg, Fed. Republic Germany, Aug. 11, 1946; came to U.S., 1952, naturalized, 1957; d. Helmuth and Jutta (Sorge) Cords; married; children: Caroline, Samuel. BA, Wellesley Coll., 1967; MA, Boston U., 1968, JD, 1974. Bar: N.H. 1974, U.S. Dist. Ct. N.H. 1974, U.S. Tax Ct. 1976. Tchr. history MacDuffie Sch. for Girls, Springfield, Mass., 1968-69; research asst. Princeton (N.J.) U., 1969-71; assoc. Sheehan, Phinney, Bass & Green P.A., Manchester, N.H., 1974-78, mem., 1979—; mem. N.H. Bd. Bar Examiners, Concord, 1980—. Chmn. Boscawen (N.H.) Zoning Bd. Adjustment, 1976—; bd. dirs. Manchester Girls Club, 1975-80, Merrimack Valley Day Care Services, Concord, 1983—, pres., 1987—, Manchester YMCA, 1986—. Mem. ABA, N.H. Bar Assn., Assn. Trial Lawyers Am., N.H. Trial Lawyers Assn., N.H. chpt. Lawyers Alliance for Nuclear Arms Control (exec. bd. mem. 1985—). Democrat. Avocations: skiing, bicycling. Federal civil litigation, State civil litigation, Personal injury. Office: Sheehan Phinney Bass & Green PA 1000 Elm St Manchester NH 03303

DAMSGAARD, KELL MARSH, lawyer; b. Darby, Pa., May 16, 1949; s. Kjeld and Dorothy (Fanck) D.; m. Katherine Elizabeth Stark, June 17, 1972; children: Peter Kjeld, Christopher William, David Zentner. BA cum laude, Yale U., 1971; JD, U. Pa., 1974. Bar: Pa. 1974, U.S. Dist. Ct. (ea. dist.) Pa. 1975, U.S. Ct. Appeals (3d cir.) 1984. Law clk. to judge Superior Ct. of Pa., Phila., 1974-75; assoc. Morgan, Lewis & Bockius, Phila., 1975-81, ptnr., 1981—. Served to lt. USN, 1973-75. Mem. ABA, Phila. Bar Assn., Chester County Hist. Soc. Avocations: skiing, jogging, tennis, reading, antiques. Federal civil litigation, State civil litigation. Home: PO Box 141 Birchrunville PA 19421 Office: Morgan Lewis & Bockius 2000 One Logan Square Philadelphia PA 19103

DANA, RANDALL M., defender; b. San Diego, Aug. 5, 1945; s. David S. and Patrcia P. (Bodiford) D.; m. Sarah Ann Holden, Sept. 6, 1964; children—Christopher Holden, Randall Michael, Allison Marie; m. 2d, Nancy Marie Sheeran, May 21, 1977. Student Denison U., 1964; B.A., Ohio State U., 1968; J.D., Capitol U. Law Sch., 1974. Bar: Ohio 1974, U.S. Dist. Ct. (so. dist.) Ohio 1974, U.S. Supreme Ct. 1982. With city atty.'s office, Columbus, Ohio, 1974-75; sole practice, Columbus, 1975-79; v.p., gen. counsel Am. Bank of Central Ohio, 1979-80; dep. dir. Ohio Pub. Defender Office, Columbus, 1980-81, pub. defender, 1981—. Served to maj. Army N.G., 1975—; with U.S. Army, 1968-71. Mem. Nat. Legal Aid and Defender Assn., Ohio Bar Assn., Nat. Assn. Criminal Def. Lawyers. Republican. Episcopalian. Club: Athletic (Columbus). Criminal. Office: Pub Defender 11th Floor 8 E Long St Columbus OH 43215

DANDO, DAVID FREDERICK, trust administrator; b. Port Huron, Mich., June 29, 1952; s. Robert Earl and Alma Veronica (Brown) D. BS in Acctg., SUNY, Binghampton, 1974; JD, N.Y. Law Sch., 1978. Bar: N.Y. 1979. Asst. v.p. Irving Trust Co., N.Y.C., 1974-82; v.p. City Nat. Bank, Miami, Fla., 1982-84, Sun Bank of South Fla., Ft. Lauderdale, 1984—. Mem. ABA, Internat. Assn. Fin. Planning, Estate Planning Council Broward County. Estate taxation, Probate. Office: Sun Bank South Fla NA 2626 E Oakland Park Blvd Fort Lauderdale FL 33306

DANEKAS, STEVEN ERNEST, lawyer; b. Rochelle, Ill., Nov. 7, 1955; s. Franklin E. and Evelyn L. (Kuemmel) D. BS in Psychology magna cum laude, No. Ill. U., 1977; JD cum laude, U. Ill., 1981. Bar: Ill. 1981, U.S. Dist. Ct. (no. and ea. dists.) Ill. 1981, U.S. Ct. Appeals (7th cir.) 1983, U.S. Claims Ct. 1983. Assoc. Wildman, Harrold, Allen & Dixon., Chgo., 1981—. Mem. ABA, Ill. State Bar Assn., Chgo. Bar Assn., Trial Lawyers Club Chgo., Def./Research Inst. Insurance, Federal civil litigation, State civil litigation. Home: 65 E Scott Apt 17K Chicago IL 60610 Office: Wildman Harrold Allen and Dixon One IBM Plaza Chicago IL 60611

DANELO, PETER ANTHONY, lawyer; b. Spokane, Wash., July 16, 1950; s. Tony and Leona Juliet (Skauge) D.; m. Wendy Lee Paul, Aug. 2, 1980. AB magna cum laude, Harvard U., 1972, JD, 1975. Bar: Wash. 1975, Calif. 1979, U.S. Dist. Ct. (we. dist.) Wash. 1975, U.S. Dist. Ct. (no. dist.) Calif. 1979, U.S. Ct. Appeals (9th cir.) 1979, U.S. Dist. Ct. (cen. dist.) Calif. 1980. Assoc. Preston, Thorgrahmson, Ellis, Holman & Fletcher, Seattle, 1975-78, Petty, Andrews, Tufts & Jackson, San Francisco, 1979-80; ptnr. Syrdal, Danelo, Klein, Myre & Woods, P.S., Seattle, 1980—. Asst. editor Harvard U. Civil Rights Civil Liberties Law Rev., 1973-75. Mem. ABA, Wash. State Bar Assn., Calif. Bar Assn., Seattle-King County Bar Assn., Wash. State Trial Lawyers Assn. (chmn. bus. torts sect. 1985—). Clubs: Seattle, Harvard-Radcliffe Western Wash. (pres. 1983-85). State civil litigation, Federal civil litigation. Office: Syrdal Danelo Klein Myre & Woods PS 2400 4th & Blanchard Bldg Seattle WA 98121

DANENBARGER, W. WRIGHT, lawyer; b. El Paso, Tex., Apr. 24, 1939; s. William Fowler and Winifred (Wright) D.; m. Mary Elizabeth Connor, Aug. 1, 1964 (div. 1973); children: William Wright Jr., Anna Winifred, Margaret Lawrence; m. Kathy Joan Bender, June 13, 1983. BS, Yale U., 1961, LLB, 1964. Bar: N.Y. 1964, N.H. 1968, U.S. Dist. Ct. N.H., U.S. Dist. Ct. (so. dist.) N.Y., U.S. Ct. Appeals (1st. and 2d cirs.). Assoc. Townley & Updike, N.Y.C., 1964-68; from assoc. to ptnr. Wiggin & Nourie, Manchester, N.H., 1968—. Mem. N.H. Trial Lawyers Assn., (pres. 1979-81), N.H. Bar Assn., Med. Malpractice and Products Liability Com. (chmn. 1984-85), Tort Reform Com. (chmn. 1985—). Federal civil litigation, State civil litigation, Construction. Home: 1025 Chestnut St Manchester NH 03104 Office: Wiggin and Nourie Franklin and Market Sts PO Box 808 Manchester NH 03105

DANG, MARVIN S.C., lawyer; b. Honolulu, Feb. 11, 1954; s. Brian K.T. and Flora (Yuen) D. BA with distinction, U. Hawaii, 1974; JD, George Washington U., 1978. Bar: Hawaii 1978, U.S. Dist. Ct. Hawaii 1978, U.S. Ct. Appeals (9th cir.) 1979. Atty. Gerson, Steiner & Anderson and predecessor firms, Honolulu, 1978-81; owner, atty. Law Offices of Marvin S.C. Dang, Honolulu, 1981—; bd. dirs. Foster Equipment Co. Ltd., Honolulu; sr. v.p., bd. dirs. Rainbow Fin. Corp., Honolulu, 1984—. Chmn., vice chmn., mem. Manoa Neighborhood Bd. Honolulu, 1979-82, 84-87; pres., v.p., mem., Hawaii Council on Legal Edn. for Youth, Honolulu, 1979-86; state rep. Hawaii State Legislature, Honolulu, 1982-84; mem. Hawaii Bicentennial Commn., Honolulu, 1986—. Recipient Cert. of Appreciation Hawaii Speech-Language-Hearing Assn., Honolulu, 1984. Mem. ABA (standing com. on law and the electoral process, 1985—, spl. com. on youth edn. for citizenship 1979-85, Hawaii state membership chmn. 1983—), Nat. Assn. Realtors, Hawaii State Bar Assn., Hawaii State Jaycees (one of ten Outstanding Young Persons of Hawaii, 1983), Honolulu. Republican. Club: Plaza of Hawaii (Honolulu). Avocations: tennis, bowling, law, politics, travel. Consumer commercial, General corporate, Real property. Home: 1717 Mott-Smith Dr Honolulu HI 96822 Office: Suite 575 Cen Pacific Plaza 220 s King St Honolulu HI 96813

D'ANGELO, CHRISTOPHER SCOTT, lawyer; b. Phila., Aug. 30, 1953; s. George Anthony and Antonia Scott (Billett) D'A.; m. Betsy Hart Josephs, May 22, 1982; children: John Robert, Christopher Hart, Caroline Colt. Student, Episc. Acad., 1971; BA with honors, U. Va., 1975, JD, 1978. Bar: Pa. 1978, U.S. Dist. Ct. (ea. dist.) Pa. 1978, U.S. Ct. Appeals (3d cir.) 1978, U.S. Supreme Ct. 1981. From assoc. to sr. assoc. Montgomery, McCracken, Walker & Rhoads, Phila., 1978—. Co-founder (U. Va. newsweekly) The Declaration, 1973-75. Counsel for COMPASS, Council for Internat. Visitors, Phila., 1982—; mem. selection com. Jefferson Scholar U. Va., Phila., 1980-84, chmn. 1981-82; fundraiser U.S. Ski Team, Phila.,

1979—, chmn. 1982-83; fundraiser Acad. Natural Scis., Phila., 1979—; chmn. ann. giving fund Episc. Acad., 1983—; bd. mgrs. Episc. Acad. Alumni Soc., Merion, Pa., 1983—, treas. 1984-85, v.p. 1985—; treas., exec. com. Phila. Art Alliance, 1980-85, bd. dirs., 1980-86; bd. dirs. English Speaking Union U.S., 1979-82, chmn. young mem. group, 1980-83; bd. dirs. English Speaking Union Phila., 1980—, chmn. fin. com. 1985—; counsel honor com. and judiciary com. U. Va., 1977-78. Mem. ABA, Pa. Bar Assn. (exec. com. young lawyers div.), Phila. Bar Assn., Acad. Natural Scis., Anthenaeum, Phila. Mus. Art, Phila. Zoo. Republican. Clubs: Merion Cricket (Haverford); Rittenhouse (Phila.) (treas. 1982—, chmn. ho. com. 1980-83, bd. dirs. 1980—), Penn. Avocations: sailing, photography, travel, squash. General corporate, Federal civil litigation, Probate. Office: Montgomery McCracken Walker & Rhoads 3 Pkwy 20th Floor Philadelphia PA 19102

D'ANGELO, GEORGE A., lawyer; b. Phila., Dec. 7, 1926; s. Dominic S. and Lillian (Alessi) D'A.; m. Antonia Scott Billett, Sept. 3, 1949; children—Marc Scott, Christopher Scott, David Steven, Victoria Scott. B.A., U. Pa., 1947, LL.B., 1950. Bar: Pa. 1950. Sr. ptnr. D'Angelo and Eurell, Phila., 1970—; mem. faculty Temple U. Law Sch., 1954-69. Pres., Phila. Art Alliance. Mem. Phila. Bar Assn., ABA, Pa. Bar Assn. Clubs: Rittenhouse, Philobiblon, Phila. Lawyers (dir. 1982—), Merion Cricket. Federal civil litigation, State civil litigation, Personal injury. Office: D'Angelo & Eurell Land Title Bldg 22d Floor Philadelphia PA 19110

DANHOF, ROBERT JOHN, judge; b. Grand Rapids, Mich., Aug. 24, 1925; s. Nicholas J. and Joan G. (Buter) D.; m. Marguerite T. Den Herder, June 28, 1947; children: William J., Kenneth R., Carol M., Linda R. BA, Hope Coll., 1947; JD, U. Mich., 1950. Bar: Mich. 1951, U.S. Dist. (we. dist.) Mich. 1951, U.S. Supreme Ct. 1957. Sole practice Muskegon, 1951-53; asst. atty. U.S. Dept. Justice, Grand Rapids, 1953-60, atty., 1960-61; exec. asst., legal adv. to Gov. State of Mich., Lansing, 1963-68; judge Mich. Ct. Appeals, Lansing, 1969—, chief judge, 1976—; del. to constitutional conv., Lansing, 1961-62; mem. nat. crime info. ctr. adv. policy bd. Dept. Justice. Mem. ABA, Appellate Judges Conf. (past mem. exec. bd.), Mich. Judges Assn., Am. Judicature Soc. (past bd. dirs.), Council of Chief Judges Cts. Appeal (exec. bd.). Judicial administration, Appellate court judge. Home: 710 Pebblebrook Ln East Lansing MI 48823 Office: Mich Ct Appeals PO Box 30022 109 W Michigan Ave Lansing MI 48909

DANIEL, AUBREY MARSHALL, III, lawyer; b. Monks Corner, S.C., May 16, 1941; s. Aubrey Marshall and Laura D.; m. Carolyn H. Williams, June 16, 1984; children—Laura E., Anne Meade. B.A., U. Va., 1963; LL.B., U. Richmond, 1966. Assoc. Atty. Minor, Savage, Richmond, Va., 1966-67; atty. Williams & Connolly, Washington, 1971—. Bd. dirs. Council for Ct. Excellence, Washington, 1982—, chmn. devel. com., 1983-84. Served to capt. JAGC, U.S. Army, 1967-71. Recipient Outstanding Service award Nat. Dist. Attys. Assn., 1971. Mem. Assn. Trial Lawyers Am., Va. Bar Assn., D.C. Bar Assn. Methodist. Clubs: Metropolitan (Washington); Farmington Golf and Country (Charlottesville, Va.); Talbot Golf and Country (Easton, Md.). Federal civil litigation, State civil litigation, Criminal. Office: Williams and Connolly 839 17th St NW Washington DC 20006

DANIEL, JAMES EDWARD, lawyer; b. Danville, Va., Dec. 27, 1955; s. Edward Hudson and Betty Jean (Riddle); m. Patricia Ann Anderson, June 21, 1980; 1 child, William Thomas. BBA, U. N.C., 1978; MBA, Emory U., 1979, JD, 1982. Bar: N.C. 1982, U.S. Dist. Ct. (mid. dist.) N.C. 1983. Atty. Womble, Carlyle, Sandridge & Rice, Winston-Salem, N.C., 1982—. Mem. ABA (employee benefits com. tax sect., employee benefits and exec. compensation com. corp. bus and banking sect., so. pension conf.), N.C. Bar Assn., Forsyth County Bar Assn., Order of Coif, Phi Beta Kappa, Beta Gamma Sigma, Phi Eta Sigma. Pension, profit-sharing, and employee benefits. Office: Womble Carlyle Sandridge & Rice PO Drawer 84 Winston-Salem NC 27102

DANIEL, MARVIN VALERIUS, lawyer; b. Waukesha, Wis., Oct. 19, 1946; s. Rheinhold Bernard and Elizabeth Mary (Valerius) D.; m. Claudette Catherine Williams, Mar. 9, 1974; children: Claire Elizabeth, Bridget Catherine. Student, St. Francis Coll., 1964-67; BA, U. Wis., Milw., 1969; JD, U. Wis., Madison, 1972. Bar: Wis. 1972, U.S. Dist. Ct. (ea. and we. dists.) Wis. 1972. Sole practice Milw., 1972-77; ptnr. Richter & Daniel, Burlington, Wis., 1977—; commr. cir. ct. Racine County, Wis, 1978—. Alderman City of Franklin, Wis., 1970-75. Mem. ABA, Racine County Bar Assn. Roman Catholic. Lodge: Kiwanis. Avocations: running, tennis, biking. Real property, Personal income taxation, Probate. Home: 365 Randolph St Burlington WI 53105 Office: Richter & Daniel 525 Milwaukee Ave Burlington WI 53105

DANIEL, ROYAL, III, lawyer; b. Pitts., Aug. 20, 1945; s. Royal Jr. and Dorothy (Smith) D.; m. Joyce Dorothy Thomas, Feb. 24, 1966; children: Dorothy, Katherine, Justin, Thomas, Robert, Margaret, Hugh. BA in Polit. Sci., Yale U., 1967; LLB, U. Va., 1970, LLM in Pvt. and Internat. Law, 1972, postdoctoral, 1972. Bar: Ba. 1970, D.C. 1976, U.S. Supreme Ct. 1976. Assoc. Tucker, Arensburg & Gerguson, Pitts., 1970, Hogan & Hartson, 1976-78; sole practice 1979-81; of counsel Arter, Hadden & Hemmendinger, Washington, 1981-83; ptnr. Wald, Harkrader & Ross, Washington, 1983-85, Willkie, Farr & Gallagher, Washington, 1985—; adj. prof. law U. Va., 1975, adj. lectr. on mktg. and pub. policy Harvard U., 1977; spl. asst. to gen. counsel for Tariff Policy Planning, U.S. Dept. Treasury, 1978-79; pres. Internat. Trade Research Group Inc., 1979-81. Author: Trade Law and Policy of the United States, 1981, Exporting to the United States: A Guide for the Latin American Exporter, 1983. Served to capt. JAGC, U.S. Army, 1970-75. Mem. ABA, D.C. Bar Assn., Am. Econ. Assn., Am. Soc. Internat. Law, Order of Coif, Omicron Delta Epsilon. Avocations: Portuguese, Spanish, Italian, German. Private international, General corporate, Legislative. Home: 2413 Taylor Ave Alexandria VA 22302 Office: Willkie Farr & Gallagher 818 Connecticut Ave NW Washington DC 20006

DANIELS, DOUGLAS ROBERT, lawyer; b. Chgo., July 11, 1936; s. David and Lydia (Pera) D.; m. Martha Starr, Dec. 28, 1976; children—Timothy, Douglas, B.A., Yale U., 1958, J.D., 1961. Bar: Miss. 1965, Conn. 1967, U.S. Dist. Ct. Conn. 1967, U.S. Ct. Appeals (2d cir.) 1967. Instr., U. Miss., Biloxi, 1963-64; gen. counsel Model Cities Program, New Haven, 1971-74; sole practice, New Haven, 1966—. Treas., New Haven Republican Town Com., 1973-76, chmn., 1977-79. Served to capt. USAF, 1962-66. Mem. ABA, Conn. Bar Assn., Miss. Bar Assn., Assn. Trial Lawyers Am., Am. Judicature Soc. Congregationalist. Lodge: Rotary (bd. dirs. 1973-75) (Woodbridge, Conn.). General practice, Family and matrimonial, State civil litigation. Office: Crown Tower Suite 4 123 York St New Haven CT 06511

DANIELS, GEORGE BENJAMIN, lawyer; b. Allendale, S.C., May 13, 1953; s. Rufus Jacob and Florence (Morten) D. Student, Suffield Acad., 1967-71; BA, Yale U., 1975; JD, U. Calif., Berkeley, 1978. Bar: D.C. 1978, N.Y. 1979, Calif. 1981, N.J. 1983, U.S. Supreme Ct. 1982; notary public, N.Y. Trial atty. criminal def. div. Legal Aid Soc. N.Y., N.Y.C., 1978-80; law clk. to presiding justice Calif. Supreme Ct., San Francisco, 1980-81; litigation atty. Skadden, Arps, Slate, Meagher & Flom, N.Y.C., 1981-83; asst. U.S. atty. U.S. Atty.'s Office, Bklyn., 1983—. Bd. trustees Suffield (Conn.) Acad., 1986—; bd. dirs. Andrew Glover Youth Program, N.Y.C., 1982—. Named one of Outstanding Young Men Am., 1984. Mem. ABA, Assn. Bar City of N.Y. Federal civil litigation, State civil litigation, Criminal. Home: 816 Warwick St Brooklyn NY 11207 Office: US Attys Office 225 Cadman Plaza E Brooklyn NY 11207

DANIELS, JAMES ELIOT, lawyer; b. Bklyn., Feb. 17, 1941; s. Alfred Harvey and Ada May (Schoenberg) D.; m. Alice Jarman, Sept. 12, 1964; children—Justin Jarman, Rebecca Caitlin. A.B., Harvard Coll., 1962; J.D., Harvard U., 1965. Bar: N.Y. 1966, U.S. Dist. Ct. (so. and ea. dists.) N.Y. 1966, U.S. Ct. Appeals (2d cir.) 1966, U.S. Supreme Ct. 1982. Clk. to judge U.S. Dist. Ct. Conn., 1965-66; trial atty. antitrust div. U.S. Dept. Justice, N.Y.C., 1966-68; assoc. Donovan Leisure Newton & Irvine, N.Y.C., 1968-73, ptnr., 1973-83; ptnr. Warshaw Burstein Cohen Schlesinger & Kuh, 1983—. Contbr. articles to profl. jours. Mem. ABA (sects. litigation and antitrust), Am. Arbitration Assn. (panel arbitrators). Clubs: New Canaan (Conn.) Field; Harvard (N.Y.C.). Federal civil litigation, Antitrust, State civil litigation. Office: 11th Floor 555 Fifth Ave New York NY 10017

DANIELS, JAMES WALTER, lawyer; b. Chgo., Oct. 13, 1945; s. Ben George and Delores L. (Wolanin) D. m. Gail Anne Rihacek, June 14, 1969; children—Morgan, Abigail, Rachel. A.B., Brown U., 1967; J.D., U. Chgo., 1970. Bar: Calif. 1970, U.S. Dist. Ct. (cen. dist.) Calif. 1970, U.S. Tax Ct. 1972, U.S. Supreme Ct 1979. Assoc. firm Latham & Watkins, Los Angeles and Newport Beach, Calif., 1970-77, ptnr., 1977—; arbitrator Orange County Superior Ct., Santa Ana, Calif., 1978—, judge pro tem, 1979—. Fin. dir. St. Elizabeth Ann Seton Parish, Irvine, Calif., 1975-82; sec. Turtlerock Tennis Com., Irvine, 1981-83, 86-87, pres. 1985-86; bd. dirs. Turtlerock Terr. Homeowners Assn., 1983-85. Mem. ABA, Internat. Council Shopping Ctrs. Democrat. Roman Catholic. Clubs: Center, Irvine Racquet. General corporate, Real property, Landlord-tenant. Home: 19241 Beckwith Terr Irvine CA 92715 Office: Latham & Watkins 660 Newport Ctr Dr Suite 1400 Newport Beach CA 92660

DANIELS, JOHN HILL, lawyer; b. Albany, N.Y., Oct. 17, 1928; s. David Samuel and Sadie (Davidson) D.; m. Helen R. Marcus, May 24, 1952; children—Marc, Scott, Seth. Grad. L.I. U., 1949; LL.B., Bklyn. Law Sch., 1952; LL.M., NYU, 1958. Bar: N.Y. 1954, U.S. Dist. Ct. (ea. and so. dists) N.Y. 1954, U.S. Supreme Ct. 1958. Assoc., Friedman & Friedman, Bklyn., 1954, Finkelstein, Benton & Soll, N.Y.C., 1955-58, Levy & Kornblum, Bklyn., 1959; ptnr. Kamen & Daniels, Bklyn., 1959-61, Daniels & Daniels, Mineola, N.Y., 1983—; sole practice, Roosevelt, N.Y., 1960—, Mineola, 1975—; lectr. in field. Candidate for judge Nassau County Dist. Ct., Mineola, 1960-63; bd. dirs. Mental Health and Alcohol, Roosevelt, 1980—; past pres. Civic Assn. of Woodbury. Served to sgt. U.S. Army, 1952-54. Mem. N.Y. State Bar Assn., Nassau County Bar Assn., Nassau Lawyers Assn. of L.I. (dir. 1970—, pres. 1984), Jewish Lawyers Assn. Nassau County (pres. 1985—), Epsilon Phi Alpha, Iota Theta. Club: Yankee Sports and Gun (Roosevelt) (past pres). Lodges: Lions (dir. 1960-84), Kiwanis (dir. 1978-84). Criminal, Probate, Real property. Home: 29 Kodiak Dr Woodbury NY 11797 Office: Daniels & Daniels Attys 114 Old Country Rd Mineola NY 11501

DANIELS, JOHN PETER, lawyer; b. N.Y.C., Feb. 5, 1937; s. Jack Brainard and Isabelle (McConachie) D.; m. Lynn Eldridge, Aug. 28, 1978 (div. Jan. 1980); m. Susan Gurley, Apr. 1, 1983. AB, Dartmouth Coll., 1959; JD, U. So. Calif., Los Angeles, 1963. Bar: Calif. 1964; diplomate Am. Bd. Trial Advocates. Assoc. Bolton, Groff and Dunne, Los Angeles, 1964-67, Jones and Daniels, Los Angeles, 1967-70, Acret and Perrochet, Los Angeles, 1971-81; ptnr. Daniels, Baratta and Fine, Los Angeles, 1982—. Mem. Assn. So. Calif. Def. Counsel (bd. dirs. 1975-80), Fedn. Ins and Corp. Counsel. Clubs: Wilshire Country (Los Angeles), Los Angeles Athletic. Avocations: scuba diving, golf, hunting. Federal civil litigation, State civil litigation. Office: Daniels Baratta & Fine 1801 Century Park E 9th Floor Los Angeles CA 90067

DANIELS, MICHAEL ALAN, lawyer; b. Cape Girardeau, Mo., Mar. 6, 1946. B.S. in Speech, Northwestern U., 1968, M.A. in Polit. Sci., 1969; J.D., U. Mo., 1973. Bar: Fla. 1974, U. S. Supreme Ct. 1983. Spl. asst. for polit. sci. research Office Naval Research, Washington, 1969-71; legal aid Edwards, Seigfried, Runge and Hodge, Mexico, Mo., 1972-73; corp. atty. CACI, Inc., Washington, 1974-77; exec. v.p. gen. counsel Datex, Inc., Washington, 1977-78; chmn. bd., pres. Internat. Pub. Policy Research Corp., Falls Church, Va., 1978—; pres. U.S. Global Strategy Council. Mem. Republican Nat. Com., Internat. Affairs Council, Nat. Security Adv. Council; mem. investment policy adv. com. Office U.S. Trade Rep., 1982—. Recipient Outstanding Fed. Securities Law Student award U. Mo., 1973. Mem. ABA (chmn. working group on law, nat. security and tech., standing com. law and nat. security 1984—), Fla. Bar Assn., Fed. Bar Assn. (chmn. internat. law com. 1979-86), Internat. Studies Assn. General corporate, Private international. Office: Internat Pub Policy Research Corp 7297 E Lee Hwy Falls Church VA 22042

DANIELSON, CYNTHIA HOWARD, lawyer; b. Ft. Madison, Iowa, Sept. 29, 1950; d. Lewis Lyle and Shirley (Sanford) Howard; m. Dale Harland Marzolf, Oct. 23, 1982; 1 child, Kathryn Farrell Marzolf. B.A., U. Iowa, 1972, J.D., 1976. Bar: Iowa 1976, U.S. Ct. Appeals (8th cir.) 1976, U.S. Dist. Ct. (no. and so. dists.) Iowa 1976. Dir. student legal services U. Iowa, Iowa City, 1975-76; assoc. Humphreys & Assocs., Cedar Rapids, Iowa, 1976; ptnr. Thompson & Danielson, Mt. Pleasant, 1977-78; sole practice, Mt. Pleasant, 1978—; jud. magistrate Henry County, Iowa, 1981-85; Iowa rep. Nat. Conf. Spl. Ct. Judges, 1984; Iowa rep. Nat. Conf. Judiciary, 1985; mem. grievance commn. Iowa Supreme Ct., 1986—; mem. regional bd. dirs. Legal Services Corp. Iowa. Trustee S.E. Iowa Library Services; bd. dirs. Henry County Jr. Achievement. Mem. ABA, Iowa Bar Assn., Mt. Pleasant C. of C. (bd. dirs., treas. 1986—), Iowa Assn. Judges Ltd. Jurisdiction (v.p.). Methodist. Author: Dissolution Handbook, 1976. Family and matrimonial. Office: 105 E Washington St Mount Pleasant IA 52641

DANILEK, DONALD J., lawyer; b. N.Y.C., Mar. 25, 1937; s. Joseph A. and Mary (Dedina) D.; m. Jane Till, Mar. 26, 1958; children—Christopher, Mary Jane, Gregory, Thomas. A.B., Princeton U., 1958; J.D., U. Va., 1961. Bar: Va. 1961, N.Y. 1961, U.S. Tax Ct. 1983. Asst. prof. law U.S. Mil. Acad., West Point, N.Y., 1961-65; assoc. firm Kirlin, Campbell & Keating, N.Y.C., 1965-70, ptnr., 1970-71, 75—; ptnr. Gasser & Hayes, N.Y.C., 1971-74; dir. Chilean Line, Inc., N.Y.C., Ships Operational Safety, Inc., Port Washington, N.Y., North Am. Fin. and Devel. Co., Inc. Chmn. Boating Pollution Control Com., Port Washington, 1971—. Named Yachtsman of Yr, Port Washington Yacht Club, 1974, 77. Mem. Va. State Bar, N.Y. State Bar Assn. Republican. Roman Catholic. Clubs: N.Y. Yacht (N.Y.C.); Manhasset Bay Yacht (Port Washington). Real property, Probate, General corporate. Office: Kirlin Campbell & Keating 14 Wall St New York NY 10005

DANILSON, DAVID RAY, lawyer; b. Perry, Iowa, Mar. 10, 1954; s. Dale and Edna LaRue (McNorris) D.; m. Kathleen Ann Spenla, Dec. 28, 1979; children: Elizabeth, Sarah. BS, Iowa State U., 1976; JD, Creighton U., 1979. Bar: Nebr. 1979, Iowa 1980, U.S. Dist. Ct. (so. dist.) Iowa 1980. Asst. trust officer Omaha Nat. Bank, 1979-80; sole practice Boone, Iowa, 1980—; jud. hospitalization referee State of Iowa, Boone, 1981; magistrate, 1981—; faculty mem. Iowa Magistrate Conf., Des Moines, 1985—; bd. dirs. Jud. Dist. 2B, Iowa; chmn. Boone Estate and Fin. Planners, 1984. Bd. dirs. Boone County Fair Bd., 1984—, Boone County Prevention and Community Services, 1985—. Mem. ABA, Iowa Bar Assn., Nebr. Bar Assn., Boone County Bar Assn. (pres. 1982-83), Am. Judicature Soc., Boone C. of C. (chmn. legis. com. 1986—, chmn. agril. com. 1984), Boone Jaycees (bd. dirs. 1983), Assn. Ltd. Jurisdiction Judges (bd. dirs. 1985—). Democrat. Lodge: Lions (2d v.p. Boone chpt. 1986—). General practice, Family and matrimonial. Home: 614 Cedar St Boone IA 50036 Office: 817 Keeler St Boone IA 50036

DANKNER, JAY WARREN, lawyer; b. Bklyn., June 15, 1949; s. Morris and Frances Dankner; m. Iris Rose Terens, May 15, 1983; 1 child, Danielle Renee. BA cum laude, Bklyn. Coll., 1970, JD cum laude, 1973. Bar: N.Y. 1974, Fla. 1974, U.S. Dist. Ct. (ea. and so. dists.) N.Y. 1974, U.S. Ct. Appeals (2d cir.) 1974, U.S. Supreme Ct. 1977, U.S. Dist. Ct. (no. dist.) N.Y. 1986. From assoc. to ptnr. Lipsig, Sullivan & Liapakis P.C., N.Y.C., 1974—; lectr. Practicing Law Inst., N.Y.C., 1983-87, continuing legal edn. program Bklyn. Law Sch., 1986—. Mem. ABA, N.Y. State Bar Assn., Fla. Bar Assn., Assn. Trial Lawyers Am., N.Y. State Trial Lawyers Assn. (lectr. 1985), N.Y. Civil and Criminal Bar Assn., N.Y. County Lawyers Assn. Federal civil litigation, State civil litigation, Personal injury. Home: 301 E 79th St New York NY 10021 Office: Lipsig Sullivan & Liapakis PC 100 Church St Room 1500 New York NY 10007

DANKO, STEPHEN GASPAR, lawyer; b. Detroit, July 23, 1942; s. Stephen and Julia (Papp) D.; m. Donna M. Zouyras, Feb. 11, 1983; 1 child, Derek S.; 1 child by previous marriage, Deana L. B.A., Elmhurst Coll., 1963; J.D., Wayne State U., 1966. Bar: Mich. 1967, U.S. Dist. Ct. Mich. 1967, U.S. Ct. Appeals (6th cir.) 1972, U.S. Ct. Appeals (11th cir.) 1984, U.S. Supreme Ct. 1973. Pres. city council City of Southgate, Mich., 1965-72; mem. firm D'Avanzo and Danko, Southgate, 1967—; asst. city atty. City of Southgate, 1972-77, city atty., 1977, 83; chmn. bd. William Penn Assn., Pitts., 1983—. County supr. County of Wayne, Mich., 1967-72. Recipient Disting. Service award, Outstanding Jaycee award Southgate Jaycees, 1965; named Outstanding Young Man, Mich. Jaycees, 1965. Mem. Mich. Bar Assn., Mich. Assn. Professions, Detroit Bar Assn., Downriver Bar Assn. Republican. General practice, Criminal, Local government. Home: 26048 Lancashire Ln Grosse Ile MI 48138 Office: D'Avanzo and Danko 12154 Dix-Toledo Southgate MI 48195

DANNE, WILLIAM HERBERT, JR., legal publishing executive; b. Washington, Aug. 12, 1942; s. William Herbert Sr. and Helen Frances (McNerney) D.; m. Kathryn J. Ligozio, Aug. 30, 1975; children: Yvonne, Justin. BA, Georgetown U., 1964; JD, Villanova U., 1967. Bar: U.S. Dist. Ct. D.C. 1967, U.S. Ct. Appeals (D.C. cir.) 1968. Atty. U.S. Dept. Justice, Washington, 1967-70; sr. editor Lawyers Coop. Publ. Co., Rochester, N.Y., 1970-76; mng. editor Lawyers Coop. Publ. Co., Washington, 1976-79; sr. v.p. publ./ops. Callaghan & Co., Wilmette, Ill., 1979—. Contbr. articles to profl. jours. Served with U.S. Army, 1968-70. Mem. ABA, Assn. Trial Lawyers Am., Am. Assn. Law Librarians, Info. Industry Assn. Republican. Roman Catholic. Legal publishing. Office: Callaghan & Co 3201 Old Glenview Rd Wilmette IL 60091

DANNEHY, JOSEPH F., state supreme court justice. Judge Conn. Circuit Ct., 1961-65; chief judge Conn. Ct. Common Pleas, 1965-68; judge Conn. Superior Ct., 1968-84; chief presiding judge Conn. Appellate Ct., 1984-85; justice Conn. Supreme Ct., Hartford, 1985—. Judicial administration. Office: Conn Supreme Ct PO Drawer D Sta A Hartford CT 06106 *

DANNER, DOUGLAS, lawyer, writer; b. Phila., Oct. 25, 1924; s. Carl F. and Cornelia Joy (Hatmaker) D.; m. Mary Bigelow, Aug. 19, 1950; children—David Bigelow, William Brewster. A.B., Harvard U., 1946; J.D., Boston U., 1949. Bar: Mass. 1949, U.S. Dist. Ct. Mass., U.S. Ct. Apls. (1st cir.), U.S. Sup. Ct. Assoc., Peabody & Arnold, Boston, 1949-55; assoc., ptnr. Powers & Hall, Boston, 1955-79, v.p., 1979—; dir. Eaton Investments Inc. Parliamentarian Mass. Republican State Com., 1962-64; life trustee Rivers Country Day Sch., 1955-74, sec., 1958-64, pres., 1964-67; trustee Mabel Louise Riley Found., 1979—; dir. Jordan Hosp., Plymouth, Mass., 1973—, pres., 1979-81; bd. mgrs. Children's Hosp. Med. Ctr., 1979-81, overseer, 1981-82. Served with USNR, 1942-46. Fellow Am. Coll. Trial Lawyers; mem. Mass. Def. Lawyers Assn. (dir. 1979—, pres. 1983-84), Assn. Trial Lawyer Am. (v.p. 1974—), ABA, Mass. Bar Assn., Boston Bar Assn., Am. Soc. Law and Medicine, Inc. (co-founder, sec. 1972-74, 1st v.p., 1974-78, gen. counsel 1978-82). Clubs: Duxbury Yacht, Fox, Pilgrim Tennis. Author books. Patent, Trademark and copyright, Federal civil litigation. Home: 32 Linden Ln Duxbury MA 02332 Office: 100 Franklin St Boston MA 02110

DANNER, WILLIAM B., lawyer; b. Mobile, Ala., Aug. 18, 1944; s. John J. and Helen T. (Bekurs) D.; m. Eleanor E. Uehlinger; children: William B., Christina T. BS, Spring Hill Coll., 1967; JD, U. Louisville, 1978. Bar: Ky. 1979. Commd. USN, 1967, advanced through grades to lt., ret., 1977; atty. U.S. Ecology Inc., Louisville, 1979-80, assoc. gen. counsel, 1980-81; staff atty. McDermott Internat., New Orleans, 1981-83; counsel Europe and Africa area McDermott Internat., Brussels, 1983—. Vice chmn. parish council, New Albany, Ind., 1980-81; bd. dirs. parish council, Brussels, 1984—. Mem. ABA (internat. law and practice sect.), Ky. Bar Assn., Phi Kappa Phi. Republican. Roman Catholic. Club: Booster (Brussels) (treas. 1984—). Avocations: furniture refinishing, reading. Private international, Contracts commercial, Construction. Home: 207 Driftwood Slidell LA 70458 Office: McDermott Legal Dept 1010 Common St New Orleans LA 70112

DANSBY, HARRY BISHOP, lawyer; b. Ozark, Ala., Dec. 31, 1945; s. John Bishop and Clydie Mae (Whigham) D.; m. Laura Lynn Willis, June 9, 1969; children: Adam Bishop, Jordan Long, Benjamin Whigham. Student, Davidson Coll., 1963-65; BS in Engring. Sci., U. Fla., 1968; JD, Fla. State U., 1974. Bar: Fla. 1975, Va. 1980, U.S. Dist. ct. (no. dist.) Fla., U.S. Dist. Ct. (we. dist.) Va. Engr. Martin Marietta, Orlando, Fla., 1968-72; ptnr. Dansby & Dansby, Perry, Fla., 1975-80; assoc. William Smith Law Office, Harrisonburg, Va., 1980-81; sole practice Harrisonburg, 1981—; pres. 503 Cert. Devel. Co., Va., 1985—. Dist. chmn. Rockingham County Dems., 1984—; chmn. com. Va, Community Certification Program, Harrisonburg, 1985—. Mem. Fla. Bar Assn., Va. Bar Assn., Assn. Trial Lawyers Am., Va. Trial Lawyer Assn., Va. Advanced Tech. Assn., Small Bus. High Tech. Assn. Democrat. Presbyterian. Avocation: jogging. Personal injury, General practice, State civil litigation. Home: Rt 1 Box 118-A Keezletown VA 22832 Office: 501 Sovran Bank Bldg Harrisonburg VA 22801

D'ANTONIO, GREGORY DOUGLAS, lawyer; b. Tucson, Oct. 6, 1951; s. Lawrence Patrick and Rosemary Catherine (Kane) D'A.; m. Judith Ann Furst, Sept. 8, 1979; 1 child, John Lawrence. B.A., U. Ariz., 1973, J.D., 1976. Bar: Ariz. 1976, U.S. Dist. Ct. Ariz. 1976, U.S. Ct. Mil. Appeals 1979. Sole practice, Tucson, 1979—. Served to capt. JAGC, U.S. Army, 1976-79. Mem. ABA, Assn. Trial Lawyers Am., Pima County Bar Assn., State Bar Ariz. Federal civil litigation, State civil litigation, Real property. Address: 70 W Cushing St Tucson AZ 85701

DANTZLER, JOHN WILLIAM, JR., lawyer; b. Orangeburg, S.C., Mar. 14, 1953; s. John William and Dorothy Idonia (Whittle) D.; m. Kathleen Louise Mosack, May 30, 1986. BS with honors, Clemson U., 1974; JD, NYU, 1979. Bar: N.Y. 1980, U.S. Tax Ct. 1984; CPA, N.C. Acct. Peat, Marwick, Mitchell & Co., Charlotte, N.C., 1974-76; assoc. Mudge, Rose, Guthrie, Alexander & Ferdon, N.Y.C., 1979-85, ptnr., 1985—. Mem. ABA, N.Y. State Bar Assn. Corporate taxation. Home: 342 E 67th St New York NY 10021 Office: Mudge Rose Guthrie Alexander & Ferdon 180 Maiden Ln New York NY 10038

DANZIG, RICHARD JEFFREY, lawyer; b. N.Y.C., Sept. 8, 1944; s. Aaron and Elinor (Moskowitz) D.; m. Andrea Auster, June 26, 1966; children: David, Lisa. B.A., Reed Coll., 1965; B.Phil., Magdalen Coll., Oxford U., 1967, D.Phil., 1968; J.D., Yale U., 1971. Bar: Calif. 1973, D.C. 1983. Asst. to pres. Rand Inst., N.Y.C., 1971; law clk. Justice White, U.S. Supreme Ct., Washington, 1971-72; fellow Harvard Soc. Fellows, 1975-77; asst. prof. Stanford Law Sch., 1972-75, assoc. prof., 1975-77; mem. faculty Harvard Program in the Law and Humanities, 1976; dep. asst. sec. of Def. for program devel. Dept. Def., Washington, 1977-79; acting prin. dep. asst. sec. of Def. for manpower, res. affairs and logistics Dept. Def., 1979, prin. dep. asst. sec., 1979-81; now mem. firm Latham, Watkins & Hills, Washington; vis. prof. Georgetown U. Sch. Law, 1980-82; cons. Police Found.; cons. Urban Affairs N.Y. Rand Inst., 1969-74; mem. NRC Com. Mil. Personnel, 1983—; cons. UN Ctr. Transnat. Corps. Author: The Capability Problem in Contract Law, 1978; co-author: National Service: What Would It Mean?, 1986; contbr. articles to profl. jours. Trustee Reed Coll., 1984—. Rockefeller Found. fellow, 1976-77; Rhodes scholar, 1965-68; recipient Harlan Fiske Stone prize Yale Law Sch., 1970; Herbert prize Oxford U., 1967. Mem. Calif. Bar Assn., Phi Beta Kappa. Criminal, Government contracts and claims, Legal history. Home: 3670 Upton St NW Washington DC 20008 Office: Latham Watkins & Hills 1333 New Hampshire Ave NW Suite 1200 Washington DC 20036

DANZIGER, FREDERICK MICHAEL, lawyer; b. N.Y.C., Mar. 12, 1940; s. Frederick Simon and Louise (Paskus) D.; m. Lucy Cullman, July 25, 1963; children: David M., Rebecca B. B.A., Harvard U., 1962; LL.B., Yale U., 1965. Law clk. Nixon Mudge Rose Guthrie & Alexander, N.Y.C., 1964, assoc., 1967-74, ptnr., 1974—; law clk. Kupfer, Silberfeld, Nathan & Danziger, N.Y.C., 1965-67; chmn. exec. com., dir. Culbro Corp., N.Y.C.; dir. B. Bros. Realty Corp., N.Y.C. Mem. ABA. Club: Century Country (Purchase, N.Y.). Home: 2 E 73d St New York NY 10021 Office: Mudge Rose Guthrie Alexander & Ferdon 180 Maiden Lane 34th Floor New York NY 10038

DANZIGER, JOEL BERNARD, lawyer; b. N.Y.C., Oct. 17, 1932; s. Harry and Mildred (Collier) D.; m. Joan Kaufman, June 15, 1958; children—Robert, Marc, Sarah. A.B., Columbia U., 1953; LL.B., Yale U., 1956. Bar: N.Y. 1958, Conn. 1958, U.S. Dist. Ct. (so. and ea. dists.) N.Y. 1963, U.S. Ct. Appeals (2d cir.) 1958, U.S. Supreme Ct. 1964. Ptnr. Danziger & Markhoff, White Plains, N.Y., 1958—; adj. prof. law Bridgeport (N.Y.) Law Sch., 1982—. Mem. ABA, N.Y. Bar Assn., Westchester County Bar Assn. Club: Yale. Pension, profit-sharing, and employee benefits, Estate planning,

Corporate taxation. Office: Danziger & Markhoff 123 Main St Centroplex White Plains NY 10601

DANZIGER, MARTIN BREITEL, lawyer; b. N.Y.C., Apr. 8, 1931; s. Joseph and Ethel (Breitel) D.; m. Joan Schwartz, June 18, 1958. BA, NYU, 1955, LLB, 1958. Bar: N.Y. 1958, Fla. 1959, U.S. Supreme Ct. 1968, D.C. 1978. Assoc. Kommel & Rogers, N.Y.C., 1959-61; sr. trial atty. rackets N.Y. County Dist. Attys. Office, N.Y.C., 1961-67; exec. asst. to spl. asst. to sec. U.S. Treasury Dept., Washington, 1967-69; asst. adminstr. nat. inst. law enforcement and criminal justice U.S. Dept. Justice Law Enforcement Asst. Adminstrn., Washington, 1971-73; assoc. dep. atty. gen. U.S. Dept. Justice, Washington, 1973-74; dir., health and retirement funds United Mine Workers Am., Washington, 1974-80; dep. commr. Immigration and Naturalization Service, Washington, 1980; commr., acting chmn. N.J. Casino Control, Princeton, 1980-82; ptnr. Barst & Mukamal, Washington, 1982—. Served with U.S. Army, 1953-55. Immigration, naturalization, and customs, legal audit. Office: Barst & Mukamal 1819 H St NW Suite 500 Washington DC 20006

D'AQUILA, THOMAS CARL, lawyer; b. Virginia, Minn., Nov. 4, 1949; s. Carl M. and Dolores M. (Casagrande) D'A. BBA in Acctg., U. Notre Dame, 1972; JD, U. Denver, 1974. Bar: Colo. 1975, U.S. Dist. Ct. Colo. 1975, U.S. Ct. Appeals (10th cir.) 1975, Minn. 1977, U.S. Dist. Ct. Minn. 1975, U.S. Ct. Appeals (8th cir.) 1977, U.S. Tax Ct. 1981. Assoc. Yegge, Hall & Evans, Denver, 1974-76; ptnr. Henretta, D'Aquila & Cross, Mpls., 1976-81, Popham, Haik, Schnobrich, Kaufman & Doty Ltd., Mpls., 1981—; lectr. Advanced Legal Edn. Govt. Training Inst., 1986. Mem. adv. com., bd. dirs. Make-a-Wish Minn., Mpls., 1985-86. Mem. ABA, Minn. Bar Assn., Colo. Bar Assn. Club: Notre Dame (Mpls.) (bd. dirs. 1982-85). Personal income taxation, Pension, profit-sharing, and employee benefits. Office: Popham Haik Schnobrich Kaufman & Doty Ltd 4344 IDS Center Minneapolis MN 55402

DARDEN, MARSHALL TAYLOR, lawyer; b. Porstmouth, Va., Dec. 6, 1952; s. Arthur Dandridge and Marian (Mann) D.; m. Claudia Kay Golay, Feb. 11, 1978; 1 child, Brandon Taylor. B.A., La. State U., 1974, J.D., 1977. Bar: La. 1977. Assoc. Milling, Benson, Woodward, Hillyer, Pierson & Miller, New Orleans, 1977-82, ptnr., 1983—; speaker 31st Ann. Mineral Law Inst., Baton Rouge, Mar. 1984. Mem. ABA, La. State Bar Assn., Lambda Chi Alpha. Republican. Episcopalian. Oil and gas leasing, Federal civil litigation, State civil litigation. Home: 3517 Pine Oak Ave New Orleans LA 70114 Office: Milling Benson Woodward Hillyer Pierson & Miller 1100 Whitney Bldg New Orleans LA 70130

DARIOTIS, TERRENCE THEODORE, lawyer; b. Chgo., Feb. 28, 1946; s. Theodore S. and Dorothy Mizzen (Thompson) D.; m. Jeanne Elizabeth Gibbons, Oct. 24, 1970; children—Sara Mizzen, Kristin Elizabeth, Jennifer Ann. B.A. in Philosophy, St. Joseph's Coll., Rensselaer, Ind., 1969; J.D., Loyola U., 1973. Bar: Ill. 1973, Fla. 1975, U.S. Supreme Ct. 1978. Law clk. to presiding justice Appellate Ct. of Ill. (2d dist.), Waukegan, Ill., 1973-74; assoc. Keith Kinderman, Tallahassee, 1975-76; sole practice, Tallahassee, 1976-82; ptnr. Kahn & Dariotis, P.A., Tallahassee, 1982—; adj. prof. Fla. State U. Coll. Bus., 1987—. Mem. Ill. State Bar Assn. Roman Catholic. General practice, Real property, Contracts commercial. Office: Kahn and Dariotis PA 227 E Virginia St Tallahassee FL 32301

DARKE, RICHARD F., corporate lawyer; b. Detroit, June 17, 1943; s. Francis Joseph and Irene Anne (Potts) D.; m. Alice Mary Renger, Feb. 14, 1968; children: Kimberly, Richard, Kelly, Sean, Colin. BBA, U. Notre Dame, 1965; JD, Detroit Coll. Law, 1969. Atty. AAA, Detroit, 1969-72; assoc. Oster & Mollett P.C., Mt. Clemens, Mich., 1972-73; ptnr. Small, Darke, Oakes P.C., Southfield, Mich., 1973-77; v.p., gen. counsel, sec. Fruehauf Corp., Detroit, 1977—. Mem. ABA, Mich. Bar Assn., Detroit Bar Assn., Machinery and Allied Products Inst. (counsel), Mich. Gen. Counsel Group. Roman Catholic. Club: Essex Country (Windsor, Ont., Can.). Avocation: golfing. Home: 1038 Audubon Grosse Pointe Park MI 48230 Office: Fruehauf Corp 10900 Harper Ave Detroit MI 48213 *

DARLING, CHARLES M., IV, lawyer; b. Phoenix, July 19, 1948; s. Charles M. and Dovie A. (Springer) D.; m. Vivian A. Brogan, Sept. 30, 1978; children: Charles V, Christopher B. BA, Columbia U., 1969; JD, U. Pa., 1972. Bar: D.C. 1973, U.S. Dist. Ct. D.C., U.S. Dist. Ct. (ea. dist.) Pa., U.S. Ct. Appeals (1st, 3d, 4th, 5th, 9th, 10th, 11th and D.C. cirs.), U.S. Supreme Ct. Law clk. to presiding justice U.S. Ct. Appeals (3d cir.), Wilmington, Del., 1972-73; staff atty. Adminstrv. Conf. of U.S., Washington, 1973; assoc. Baker & Botts, Washington, 1974-79, ptnr., 1980—. Assoc. editor, officer U. Pa. Law Rev., 1970-72. Mem. Fed. Energy Bar Assn., Fed. Bar Assn. Republican. Avocations: computer interfacing, reading. Federal civil litigation, State civil litigation, FERC practice. Office: Baker & Botts 555 13th St NW Suite 500 E Washington DC 20004-1109

DARLING, ROBERT HOWARD, lawyer; b. Detroit, Oct. 29, 1947; s. George Beatson and Jeanne May (Mainville) D.; m. Cathy Lee Trygstad, Apr. 30, 1970; children—Bradley Howard, Brian Lee, Kara Kristine, Blake Robert. B.S. in Mech. Engring., U. Mich., 1969, M.S. in Mech. Engring., 1971; J.D., Wayne State U., 1975. Bar: Mich. 1975, U.S. Dist. Ct. (ea. dist.) Mich. 1975, U.S. Ct. Appeals (6th cir.) 1975. Engr., Bendix Corp., Ann Arbor, Mich., 1970, Ford Motor Co., Dearborn, Mich., 1972-73; ptnr. Philo, Atkinson, Darling, Steinberg, Harper and Edwards, Detroit, 1975-81; sr. ptnr. Sommers, Schwartz, Silver & Schwartz, Southfield, Mich., 1981—. Author: Michigan Products Liability, 1982; Michigan Premises Liability, 1984. Mem. ABA, Assn. Trial Lawyers Am., Mich. Trial Lawyers Assn. (exec. bd. 1981—, publs. chmn. 1981-85, products liability chmn. 1986—), Met. Detroit Trial Lawyers Assn. (mem. exec. bd. 1981—), Oakland County Trial Lawyers Assn., State Bar Mich., Detroit Bar Assn., Plymouth Hist. Soc., Pi Tau Sigma. Episcopalian. Avocations: numismatics; history; golf. Federal civil litigation, State civil litigation, Personal injury. Home: 12940 Portsmouth Crossing Plymouth MI 48170 Office: Sommers Schwartz Silver Schwartz 1800 Travelers Tower Southfield MI 48076 Office: 747 S Main St Plymouth MI 48170

DARLING, SCOTT EDWARD, lawyer; b. Los Angeles, Dec. 31, 1949; s. Dick R. and Marjorie Helen (Otto) D.; m. Cynthia Diane Harrah, June 1970 (div.); 1 child, Smokie; m. Deborah Lee Cochran, Aug. 22, 1981; children: Ryan, Jacob. BA, U. Redlands, 1972; JD, U.S.C., 1975. Bar: Calif. 1976, U.S. Dist. Ct. (cen. dist.) Calif. 1976. Assoc. atty. Elver, Falsetti, Boone & Crafts, Riverside, 1976-78; ptnr. Falsetti, Crafts, Pritchard & Darling, Riverside, 1978-84; sr. ptnr. Darling, Medof & Miller, Riverside, 1984—; grant reviewer HHS, Washington, 1982—; judge pro tem Riverside County Mcpl. Ct., 1980; bd. dirs. Tel Law Nat. Legal Pub. Info. System, Riverside, 1978-80. Author, editor: Small Law Office Computer Legal System, 1984. Bd. dirs. Youth Adv. Com. to Selective Service, 1968-70; atty. panel Calif. Assn. Realtors, Los Angeles, 1980—; pres. Calif. Young Reps., 1978-80; mem. Govt. Issue Forum, Riverside, 1970—; presdl. del. Nat. Rep. Party; asst. treas. Calif. Rep. Party, 1981-83; Rep. Congl. candidate, Riverside, 1982; treas. Citizen's Univ. Com., Riverside, 1978—, World Affairs Council, Riverside Sickle Cell Orgn., 1980-82, Urban League, Riverside, 1980-82. Named one of Outstanding Young Men in Am., U.S. Jaycees, 1979—. Mem. ABA, Riverside County Bar Assn., Sickle Cell Found. (treas. 1980-82, recipient Eddie D. Smith award), Calif. Scholarship Fedn. (life), Riverside C. of C. Lodge: Native Sons of Golden West. Avocations: skiing, swimming, reading. Real property, Personal injury, Estate taxation. Office: Darling Miller & King 7121 Magnolia Ave Riverside CA 92504

DARLING, STEPHEN EDWARD, lawyer; b. Columbia, S.C., Apr. 12, 1949; s. Norman Rushton and Elizabeth (Clarkson) D.; m. Denise Howell, June 30, 1979; children: Julia Hanley, Edward McCrady. BS in Banking, Fin., Real Estate, Ins., U. S.C., 1971, JD, 1974. Bar: S.C. 1974, U.S. Dist. Ct. S.C. 1975, U.S. Ct. Appeals (4th cir.) 1975, U.S. Ct. Appeals (5th cir.) 1976, U.S. Supreme Ct. 1982. From assoc. to ptnr. Sinkler, Gibbs & Simons, Charleston, S.C., 1974-87; ptnr. Sinkler & Boyd, Charleston, 1987—; bd. dirs. Nat. Kidney Found. of S.C., Columbia. Mem. ABA, S.C. Bar Assn., Def. Research Inst. Episcopalian. Club: Met. Exchange (Charleston, S.C.) (sec. 1980). Federal civil litigation, State civil litigation, Workers' compensation. Home: 171 Broad St Charleston SC 29401 Office: Sinkler & Boyd 160 E Bay St Charleston SC 29401

DARMAN, DINAH LEA, lawyer; b. Greenfield, Ohio, Apr. 10, 1951; d. James David and Helen Ruth (Hudson) Hixon; m. Daniel Martin DeVere, Mar. 25, 1978 (div. Feb. 1985); m. A. David Darman, Jan. 17, 1986 (div. Mar. 1987). BA with distinction, Ohio State U., 1975, JD with honors, 1978. Bar: Calif. 1978, U.S. Dist. Ct. (no. dist.) Calif. 1978. Assoc. Bronson, Bronson & McKinnon, San Francisco, 1978-82; sr. counsel McKesson Corp., San Francisco, 1982—. Mem. San Francisco Bar Assn. (co-chmn. corp. counsel com. 1984—), Am. Corp. Counsel Assn. (chmn. litigation com. Bay Area chpt. 1983-85), Phi Beta Kappa. Jewish. General corporate, Environment. Office: McKesson Corp One Post St San Francisco CA 94104

DARNELL, JAMES ORAL, lawyer; b. Oklahoma City, Apr. 3, 1955; s. Victor Lee and Eileen (Bliss) D.; m. Susan Marie Cheslousky, Aug. 5, 1978; children: James Oral Jr., Jake Morris. AB cum laude, Dartmouth Coll.; JD cum laude, So. Meth. U. Bar: Tex. 1980, U.S. Dist. Ct. (we. dist.) Tex. 1982, U.S. Ct. Appeals (5th cir.) 1986. Ptnr. Grambling & Mounce, El Paso, Tex., 1980-86. Worker Sun Bowl Assn., 1981-82; com. chmn. Southwestern Internat. Livestock Show & Rodeo, Inc., 1982—, bd. dirs., 1987—; mem. steering com. Ralph Scoggins for Dist. Judge Campaign, 1982; bd. dirs. YMCA, 1984—, Crimestoppers, 1985—; participant Leadership El Paso, 1985—; mem. steering com. Kent Hance for Gov. Campaign, 1985—. Mem. ABA, Tex. Bar Assn., Tex. Young Lawyers Assn., Tex. Criminal Def. Lawyers Assn., El Paso Young Lawyers Assn. (bd. dirs. 1983-85, treas. 1985-86). Democrat. Baptist. Avocations: basketball, baseball, horses, football. Criminal, Insurance, Personal injury. Home: 5 Paseo de Paz El Paso TX 79932 Office: Gambling & Mounce Mesa & Main Sts. 7th Floor El Paso TX 79901

DARNELL, RICHARD WAYNE, lawyer; b. Hollis, Okla., June 9, 1942; s. Wayne Hart and Mayrene (Wynn) Darnell; m. Linda Wolf, Mar. 6, 1982; children: S. Rynnea, Valerie L. BS, Eastern N.Mex. U., 1970; MA, PhD, U. Okla., 1971; JD, Tex. Tech. U., 1980. Assoc. Robert Cardin, Farmington, N.Mex., 1980-81, Neal & Neal, Hobbs, N.Mex., 1981-82, Williams, Johnson & Darnell, Hobbs, 1982-84; sole practice Hobbs, 1984—. Mem. rules com. N.Mex. Dems., Albuquerque, 1985-86; precinct chmn. Lea County Dems., Hobbs, 1984—. Mem. ABA, N.Mex. Bar Assn. (chmn. pro bono for Lea County 1986), Lea County Bar Assn., Assn. Trial Lawyers Am., N.Mex. Trial Lawyers Assn. Lodge: Masons (master 1986—). Criminal, Personal injury, Workers' compensation. Home: 1015 N Jefferson Hobbs NM 88240 Office: 206 W Snyder PO Box 5750 Hobbs NM 88241

DAROSA, RONALD ANTHONY, lawyer; b. Joliet, Ill., June 28, 1943; s. Edmund A. and Claire L. (Turner) DaR.; m. Judith A. French, Aug. 1, 1963 (div. Apr. 1985); children: Ronald II, Laurel, Ryan; m. Cynthia E. Ohlenkamp. BS, No. Ill. U., 1965; JD, John Marshall Law Sch., 1970. Bar: Ill. 1970, U.S. Dist. Ct. (no. dist.) Ill. 1970. Asst. state's atty. DuPage County, Wheaton, Ill., 1970-71; ptnr. Mountcastle & DaRosa, P.C., Wheaton, 1971—; co-chmn. DuPage County Criminal Justice Council, 1979-80. Chmn. Zoning Bd. Appeals, Glen Ellyn, Ill., 1975-77; mayor Village of Glen Ellyn (cert. appreciation 1981), 1977-81; pres. Mayors and Mgrs. Conf. (cert. appreciation 1981), DuPage County, 1980-81; commr. Du Page Airport Authority, 1987—. Mem. ABA, Ill. Bar Assn., DuPage County Bar Assn. (chmn. matrimonial law com. 1981-82, bd. dirs. 1984—). Republican. Roman Catholic. Club: Medinah Country. Family and matrimonial. Office: Mountcastle & DaRosa PC 208 N West Wheaton IL 60189-0048

DARRAH, WILLIAM CHARLES, lawyer; b. Providence, Oct. 6, 1948; s. Horace Drane and Drusilla (Ephramison) D.; m. Joan Lucille Columbia, July 10, 1978 (div. Jan. 1984); 1 child, Jennifer Rene. BA, U. N.C., 1970; JD, NYU, 1975. Bar: Hawaii 1976, U.S. Dist. Ct. Hawaii 1976. Law clk. to presiding justice U.S. Dist. Ct., Portland, Oreg., 1975; ptnr. Douthit & Darrah, Honolulu, 1976—. Co-author: Hawaii Divorce Manual, 1982. Co-moderator Hawaii Family Ct. "The Divorce Experience," Honolulu, 1979—; mediator Neighborhood Justice Ctr., Honolulu, 1980—. Fellow Am. Acad. Matrimonial Lawyers; mem. ABA, Hawaii Bar Assn. (vice chmn., 2d chmn. elect 1985—, family law sect.), Chi Psi. Avocations: yachting, bicycling, model railroading. Family and matrimonial. Home: 1433 Mamalu St Honolulu HI 96817 Office: Douthit & Darrah 547 Halekauwila #105 Honolulu HI 96813

DARRELL, NORRIS, JR., lawyer; b. Berlin, Germany, May 10, 1929; s. Norris and Doris Clare (Williams) D. (parents Am. citizens); m. Henriette Maria Haid, July 31, 1962; 1 child, Andrew. A.B., Harvard U., 1951, LL.B. cum laude, 1954. Bar: N.Y. 1955, U.S. Supreme Ct. 1965. Assoc. Sullivan & Cromwell, N.Y.C., 1956-65, ptnr., 1965—; with European office Sullivan & Cromwell, Paris, 1968-71; bd. dirs. J. Henry Schroder Bank & Trust Co. Trustee Cold Spring Harbor Lab., Inc., 1974-81, United Student Aid Funds, Inc., N.Y.C., 1974—, East Woods Sch., Oyster Bay, N.Y., 1974-79, Heckscher Mus., Huntington, N.Y., 1984—. Served with U.S. Army, 1954-56. Fellow Am. Bar Found.; mem. Am. Law Inst., ABA, N.Y. State Bar Assn., Assn. Bar City N.Y. Clubs: Down Town Assn., Harvard of N.Y., Pilgrims, River (bd. govs. 1978—). Home: 44 Walnut Tree Ln Cold Spring Harbor New York NY 11724 Office: 125 Broad St New York NY 10004

DASILVA, WILLARD H., lawyer; b. Freeport, N.Y., Oct. 17, 1923; m. Frances A. DaSilva. B.A., NYU, 1946; LL.B., Columbia U., 1949. Bar: N.Y. 1949, U.S. Supreme Ct. 1969, U.S. Tax Ct. 1969. Sole practice, N.Y.C., 1949-70; ptnr. Goodman & DaSilva, 1970-73; sole practice, Carle Place, N.Y., 1973-76; ptnr. DaSilva & Samuelson, 1977; sole practice, Garden City, N.Y., 1978—; v.p. Marcus Bros. Textile Corp., N.Y.C., 1951-63; pres. Cortley Fabrics subs. Cone Mills Corp., N.Y.C., 1964-65; lectr. Columbia U. Law Sch., Bklyn. Law Sch., St. John's Law Sch., Touro Law Sch; faculty Practising Law Inst., N.Y.C., 1972—; trustee NAFA Found., 1977-85; mem. nat. panel of arbitrators Am. Arbitration Assn., 1965—. Served to lt. USAAF, 1942-46. Mem. Am. Acad. Matrimonial Lawyers (pres. 1982-84, bd. mgrs. 1977—), ABA (mem. family law sect. 1977—), Assn. Trial Lawyers Am., N.Y. State Bar Assn. (continuing legal edn. com. 1980—, program chmn. family law sect. 1978-82), Nassau County Bar Assn., Suffolk County Bar Assn. (chmn. family law sect. 1982-84), Internat. Soc. on Family Law, Am. Soc. Writers on Legal Subjects, Phi Beta Kappa. Editor Family Advocate, 1981—, Matrimonial Law Jour., 1977-85; author N.Y. Matrimonial Practice, 1980—; editor, author Family Law Practice Systems Manual, 1982—; editor FairShare mag., 1985—; contbr. articles to legal jours. Family and matrimonial, Real property. Office: 585 Stewart Ave Garden City NY 11530

DATTILO, JAMES ANTHONY, lawyer; b. Danville, Pa., Apr. 26, 1950; s. James Thomas and Winifred Jean (Appelbe) D.; m. Colleen Marie McDonnell, Apr. 17, 1982; 2 children—Jane Margaret, Julia Maureen. B.A., Fordham U., 1972; J.D. Duquesne U., 1975. Bar: Pa. 1975, U.S. Dist. Ct. (we. dist.) Pa., U.S. Ct. Appeals (3d cir.), U.S. Supreme Ct. Assoc. Wayman, Irvin & McAuley, Pitts., 1977-79; Gilardi & Cooper, Pitts., 1979-83; ptnr. Dattilo, Barry, Fasulo & Cambest, P.C., Pitts., 1983—. Mem. ABA, Pa. Bar Assn., Allegheny County Bar Assn., Assn. Trial Lawyers Am., Acad. Trial Lawyers Allegheny County. Democrat. Roman Catholic. Personal injury, Federal civil litigation, State civil litigation. Home: 215 Main Entrance Dr Pittsburgh PA 15228 Office: Dattilo Barry Fasulo & Cambest PC 3200 Gulf Tower Pittsburgh PA 15219-1913

DAUER, EDWARD ARNOLD, law educator; b. Providence, Sept. 28, 1944; s. Marshall and Shirly (Moverman) D.; m. Carol Jean Egglestone, June 16, 1966; children—E. Craig, Rachel P. A.B., Brown U., 1966; LL.B. cum laude, Yale U., 1969. Bar: Conn. 1978, Colo. 1986. Asst. prof. law U. Toledo, 1969-72; assoc. prof. law U. So. Calif., Los Angeles, 1972-74; prof. law Yale U., New Haven, 1975-85, assoc. dean, 1978-83, dep. dean law sch., 1983-85; dean, prof. law U. Denver, 1985—; cons. Ctr. for Pub. Resources. Bd. dirs. New Haven Community Action Agy., 1978-81, Cerebral Palsy Found. of Fairfield County, 1979—; founder Nat. Ctr. for Preventive Law. Mem. Am. Law Inst., Order of the Coif. Republican. Jewish. Club: Denver. Author: Materials on a Nonadversarial Legal Process, 1978; contbr. articles to profl. jours. Contracts commercial, Jurisprudence, Banking. Address: 5811 S Geneva St Englewood CO 80111

DAUGHERTY, FREDERICK ALVIN, U.S. judge; b. Oklahoma City, Aug. 18, 1914; s. Charles Lemuel and Felicia (Mitchell) D.; m. Marjorie E. Green, Mar. 15, 1947 (dec. Feb. 1964); m. Betsy F. Amis, Dec. 15, 1965. LL.B., Cumberland U., 1933; postgrad., Oklahoma City U., 1934-35, LL.B. (hon.), 1974; postgrad., Okla. U., 1936-37; HHD (hon.), Okla. Christian Coll., 1976. Bar: Okla. 1937. Practiced Oklahoma City, 1937-40; mem. firm Ames, Ames & Daugherty, Oklahoma City, 1946-50; firm Ames, Daugherty, Bynum & Black, Oklahoma City, 1952-55; judge 7th Jud. Dist. Ct., Okla., 1955-61; U.S. dist. judge Western, Eastern and No. Dists., Okla., 1961—, chief judge, 1972-82, sr. judge, 1982—; mem. Fgn. Intelligence Surveillance Ct., 1981—, Temporary Emergency Ct. Appeals, 1983—, Multi dist. Litigation panel, 1980—; mem. codes of conduct com. U.S. Jud. Conf., 1980—. Active local ARC, 1956—, chmn., 1958-60, nat. bd. govs., 1963-69, 3d vice chmn., 1968-69; active United Fund Greater Oklahoma City, 1957—, pres., 1961, trustee, 1963—; pres. Community Council Oklahoma City and County, 1967-69; mem. exec. com. Oklahoma City Council Alcoholism, 1964—; exec. com. Okla. Med. Research Found., 1966-69. Served as officer with AUS, 1940-45, 50-52. Decorated Legion of Merit with 2 oak leaf clusters, Bronze Star with oak leaf cluster; recipient award to mankind Oklahoma City Sertoma Club, 1962, Outstanding Citizen award Oklahoma City Jr. C. of C., 1965, Distinguished Alumni citation Samford U., 1974, Distinguished Service citation Okla. U., 1973; named to Okla. Hall of Fame, 1969. Mem. Fed., Okla. bar assns., Am. Bar Found., Sigma Alpha Epsilon, Phi Delta Phi. Episcopalian (sr. warden 1957). Club: Men's Dinner Oklahoma City (pres. 1968-69) Lodges: Kiwanis (pres. 1957, lt. gov. 1959), Masons (33 deg., sovereign grand insp. gen. in Okla. 1982-86), Shriners, Jesters. Jurisprudence. Office: US Courthouse Room 5102 Oklahoma City OK 73102

DAUGHERTY, MICHAEL DENNIS, lawyer; b. Tyler, Tex., May 27, 1948; s. John Wayne and Frances Mahoney (Reynolds) D.; m. Janet Mary Laird, Oct. 27, 1973; children: Christopher David, Virginia Elizabeth, Jonathan Laird. BA, La. State U., 1970, JD, 1973. Bar: La. 1973, U.S. Dist. Ct. (we. dist.) La. 1974, U.S. Supreme Ct. 1979. Dist. mgr. Bur. of Census, Lake Charles, La., 1970; assoc. Camp, Carmouche & Palmer, Lake Charles, 1973-74; legis. asst. Congressman David Treen, Washington, 1974-80; dir. fed. relations Office of Gov., Baton Rouge, 1980-82; dir. govt. relations, v.p., sec. Legal Services Corp., Washington, 1982-85; legal counsel to chmn. Occupational Safety and Health Rev. Commn., Washington, 1985—. Dir. region VI Young Rep. Nat. Fedn., Washington, 1969-71; 1st v.p. Leadership Inst., Springfield, Va., 1979—; mem. Adminstrv. Conf. U.S., 1985—. Mem. ABA, La. Bar Assn. Presbyterian. Avocation: genealogy. Labor, Administrative and regulatory, Legislative. Home: 10209 Oxfordshire Dr Nokesville VA 22123 Office: Occupational Safety and Health Rev Commn 1825 K St NW Suite 409 Washington DC 20006

DAUGHERTY, RICHARD BERNARD, lawyer; b. Los Angeles, Aug. 30, 1915; s. Edwin Matthew and Mabel (Dunbar) D.; m. Margaret Amey, Nov. 15, 1941; children: Richard Bernard Jr., Patricia Anne Shallenberger. AB in Econs. and Acctg., Stanford U., 1937; LLB, Harvard U., 1940. Bar: Calif. 1940, U.S. Dist. Ct. (no. dist.) Calif. 1940, U.S. Ct. Claims 1964, U.S. Supreme Ct. 1974. Assoc. Pillsbury, Madison & Sutro, San Francisco, 1940-41, 45-55, ptnr., 1955—; gen. atty. Pacific Telephone and Telegraph Co., San Francisco, 1969-79; gen. counsel Presidio Soc., San Francisco, 1978-83. Sec., gen. counsel Ft. Point and Army Museum Assn., San Francisco, 1968-79, pres., 1979-80, bd. dirs., 1979—; v.p., bd. dirs. Irish Beach Improvement Club, Manchester, Calif., 1970-73; pres., bd. dirs. Irish Beach Water Dist., Manchester, 1975-79. Served to lt. col. U.S. Army, 1941-46. Mem. ABA, Calif. Bar Assn., San Francisco Bar Assn., Harvard Law Sch. Alumni Assn., Beta Theta Pi Alumni Assn. (pres. 1945-47). Republican. Roman Catholic. Club: Bohemian (San Francisco). Avocations: swimming, woodworking, gardening. Public utilities, General corporate, Real property. Home: 100 Thorndale Dr #102 San Rafael CA 94903 Office: Pillsbury Madison & Sutro 225 Bush St San Francisco CA 94104

DAUGHTON, DONALD, lawyer; b. Grand River, Iowa, Mar. 11, 1932; s. F.J. and Ethel (Edwards) D.; children by previous marriage—Erin, Thomas, Andrew, J.P. B.S.C., U. Iowa, 1953, J.D., 1956. Bar: Iowa, 1956, Ariz., 1958. Assoc., Snell & Wilmer, Phoenix, 1959-64, Browder & Daughton, Phoenix, 1964-65, Browder, Gillenwater & Daughton, 1967-72; ptnr. Daughton Feinstein & Wilson, Phoenix, 1972-86, Daughton, Hawkins & Beacon P.C., 1986—; judge Super. Ct. Ariz., 1956-67; asst. county atty. Polk County, 1958-59; chmn. Phoenix Employees Relations Bd., 1976; pres. Maricopa County Legal Aid Soc., 1971-73. Served to 1st lt. JAG, USAF, 1956-58. Fellow Am. Bar Found. (founder); mem. ABA (state bar del. ho. of dels., 1984-87, state del. 1987—), State Bar Ariz. (chmn. pub. relations com. 1980-84, chmn. jud. evaluation poll com. 1984—), Iowa State Bar, Maricopa County Bar Assn. (dir. 1962-64), 9th Cir. Jud. Conf. (lawyer rep. 1981-84), Ariz. Acad., Nat. Acad. Arbirtrators. Club: Univs. Phoenix, Paradise Valley Country. Federal civil litigation, State civil litigation. Home: 7214 N 6th Way Phoenix AZ 85020 Office: Daughton Hawkins & Beacon PC 363 N Central Ave 11th Floor Phoenix AZ 85012

DAUM, BRYAN EDWIN, lawyer; b. Granite City, Ill., Sept. 14, 1949; s. Edwin Leo and Melba Louise (King) D.; m. Elizabeth Lanney, May 5, 1974; children: Andrea, Veronica, Benjamin. BA, Tex. Christian U., 1971; JD, U. Tex., 1979. Bar: Fla. 1979, U.S. Ct. Appeals (5th and 11th cirs.) 1981, U.S. Ct. Appeals (9th cir.) 1985, Ariz. 1985, U.S. Dist. Ct. Ariz. 1985. Assoc. Trenam, Simmons et al, Tampa, Fla., 1979-85, Bilby & Shoenhair, P.C., Tucson, 1985—. Served with USN, 1972-76. Mem. ABA, Fla. Bar Assn., Ariz. Bar Assn., Order of Coif, Phi Beta Kappa. Pension, profit-sharing, and employee benefits, Corporate taxation, Personal income taxation. Home: 5735 N Camino del Conde Tucson AZ 85718 Office: Bilby & Shoenhair PC 1 S Carolina Tucson AZ 85701

DAUS, DONALD GEORGE, lawyer, federal government official; b. Melrose Park, Ill., Nov. 17, 1931; s. George A. and Lillian M. (Culham) D.; m. Martha Joanne, Sept. 1, 1957; children—Robert Donald, Frederic George. B.S. in Chem. Engring. with honors, U. Ill., 1953; M.S., Mich. State U., 1954; J.D. with honors, George Washington U., 1966, LL.M. with highest honors, 1973. Bar: D.C. 1967, Va. 1969. Chem. engr. with industry, 1954-64; patent examiner U.S. Patent Office, Washington, 1964-73, supervisory patent examiner, 1973—. Served to comdr. JAG Corps, USNR, 1970—. NIH fellow, 1953. Mem. ABA, Am. Intellectual Property Law Assn., Am. Chem. Soc., Judge Advs. Assn., Patent Office Soc. (chmn. 1981, bd. govs. Jour. 1977-80), Order of Coif, Phi Alpha Delta, Alpha Chi Sigma. Contbr. articles to profl. jours. Patent, Administrative and regulatory, Military. Home: 2230 Primrose Dr Falls Church VA 22046 Office: U S Patent and Trademark Office Washington DC 20231

DAU-SCHMIDT, KENNETH GLENN, lawyer; b. Des Moines, Oct. 12, 1956; s. Glenn Erwin Dau-Schmidt and Barbara Jane Bloom; m. Elizabeth Ross Birch, Aug. 16, 1980; 1 child, Nick. BA, U. Wis., 1978; MA, JD, U. Mich., 1981, PhD, 1984. Bar: Wis. 1982, Minn. 1984, U. Dist. Ct. Minn. 1984, U.S. Ct. Appeals (6th and 7th cirs.) 1985, U.S. Dist. Ct. (ea. and we. dists.) Wis. 1985, U.S. Dist. Ct. (ea. dist.) Mich. 1985. Counsel to labor com. House of Reps., Minn., 1982-85; assoc. Previant, Goldberg and Uelmen, Milw., 1985—. Contbr. articles to profl. jours. Mem. ABA, Am. Econs. Assn., Indsl. Relations Research Assn. Democrat. Mem. Soc. of Friends. Avocations: camping, canoeing. Labor, Workers' compensation, Legislative. Home: 4511 N Newhall Milwaukee WI 53211 Office: Previant Goldberg and Uelmen 788 N Jefferson St Milwaukee WI 53202

DAVENPORT, DAVID STERLING, lawyer, educator; b. Chgo., Aug. 5, 1946; s. John R. and Martha J. (Miller) D.; m. Marilyn Jones (div.); 1 child, Stephen. AB, Amherst Coll., 1968; JD, Harvard U., 1971. Bar: Mass. 1973, U.S. Dist. Ct. Mass. 1984, U.S. Tax Ct. 1984, U.S. Ct. Appeals (1st cir.) 1984. Law clk. to judge U.S. Ct. Appeals (9th cir.), San Francisco, 1971-72; assoc. Ropes & Gray, Boston, 1972-80, ptnr., 1980—; vis. assoc. prof. law Boston Coll., Newton, Mass., 1984-86, lectr., 1986—. Note editor Harvard Law Rev., 1970-71; contbr. articles to profl. jours. Advisor on Mass. taxation Gov. Dukakis' Task Force, Boston, 1983. Mem. ABA (chmn. com. affiliated and related corps. tax sect. 1987—), Boston Bar Assn. (chmn. tax sect. 1984-87, council 1986—). Mem. Unitarian Ch. Avocations: skiing, sailing, camping. Corporate taxation, State and local taxation, General corporate. Office: Ropes & Gray 225 Franklin St Boston MA 02110

DAVENPORT, GEORGE WILLIAM, lawyer, educator; b. Birmingham, Ala., July 26, 1949; s. George Martin and Marjorie Salma (Lee) D.; m. Lisa

Fisher Zammit, Nov. 6, 1982; 1 child, William Matthew. B.A. magna cum laude in History, Philosophy, Polit. Sci., Birmingham So. Coll., 1972; M.A., Duke U., 1974, Ph.D. in Polit. Sci. and Internat. Law, 1976, J.D., 1977. Bar: Ala. 1977, U.S. dist. ct. (no. dist.) Ala. 1977, U.S. Ct. Appeals (5th cir.) 1978, U.S. Ct. Appeals (11th cir.) 1982. Cons. internat. affairs sect., fin. aid dept. U. Ala. in Birmingham, summer 1974; assoc. Dawson & Thomason, Birmingham, 1977-79; trial atty. EEOC, Birmingham, 1979—; instr. U. Ala. and Birmingham So. Coll. Rule of Law Research Center fellow, 1977-79. Mem. ABA, Assn. Trial Lawyers Am., Ala. Trial Lawyers Assn., Phi Beta Kappa, Omicron Delta Kappa, Sigma Xi, Lambda Chi Alpha, MENSA. Methodist. Author: Controlling the Multinational Corporations: A Challenge for International Law and the International Community, 1976; contbr. articles to legal jours. Civil rights, Labor, Federal civil litigation. Address: 2216 Marion St Birmingham AL 35226

DAVENPORT, TERESA JOANNA, lawyer, military officer, educator; b. Knoxville, Tenn., May 4, 1955; d. Jesse W. and Patricia Jo (Wallace) Fox; m. Michael Davenport, Aug. 9, 1980; 1 child, Melissa Jo. BA, U. Tenn., 1977, JD, 1980. Bar: Tenn. 1980, U.S. Ct. Mil. Appeals 1983, U.S. Supreme Ct. 1986. Commd. ensign USN, 1979, advanced through grades to lt., 1981; trial atty. Naval Legal Service Office, Norfolk, Va., 1980-84, asst. U.S. atty., 1983-85; staff judge adv. USS Emory S. Land, Norfolk, 1984-85; instr. criminal law Naval Justice Sch., Newport, R.I., 1985—; instr. Nat. Inst. Trial Advocacy, 1986. Book rev. editor Naval Law Rev., 1986. Mem. ABA, Tenn. Bar Assn., Nat. Assn. Trial Lawyers, Nat. Inst. Trial Advocacy Assn., Judge Advs. Assn. Episcopalian. Avocations: hiking, bicycling, water sports. Criminal, Military, Legal education. Office: Naval Justice Sch NETC Newport RI 02841

DAVEY, GERARD PAUL, lawyer; b. Alton, Ill., May 31, 1949; s. Paul D. and Mary G. (O'Neill) D.; m. Martha Ann Florus, Aug. 13, 1977; children—Brian, Matthew, Kelly. B.S., U. Ill., 1971; J.D., U. Houston, 1974; M.B.A., Golden Gate U., 1982. Bar: Tex. 1974, Calif. 1977, U.S. Supreme Ct. 1978, U.S. Ct. Appeals (5th cir.) 1975, (9th cir.) 1978, U.S. Dist. Ct. (so. dist.) Tex. 1975, U.S. Dist. Ct. (cen. dist.) Calif. 1978. Sec., counsel SW Group Fin., Houston, 1974-77; sole practice, Newport Beach, Calif., 1977-78; v.p., corp. counsel Century 21 Real Estate, Irvine, Calif., 1978-81, also sec., dir. all subsidiaries, 1980-81; prin. Davey Law Corp., Newport Beach, 1981—; lectr. Calif. Continuing Edn. of Bar. Author: Texas Law Institute of Coastal and Marine Resources, 1974; Contbr. articles to profl. jours. Bd. dirs. South Coast Symphony, Costa Mesa, Calif., 1984. Ill. Gen. Assembly scholar U. Ill., 1967-71. Mem. ABA (forum com. on franchising 1980—), Calif. Bar Assn. (franchising legis. com. 1983-86), Tex. Bar Assn., U. Houston Legal Hon. Soc. Club: Kiwanis (Irvine). Franchising, Securities, General corporate. Office: Davey Law Corp 1201 Dove St Suite 600 Newport Beach CA 92660

DAVID, ROBERT JEFFERSON, lawyer; b. Baton Rouge, Aug. 10, 1943; s. Joseph Jefferson and Doris Marie (Olinde) D.; m. Stella Scott, Jan. 21, 1967; children: Robert J. Jr., Richard M. BA, Southeastern La. U., 1966; JD, Loyola U., New Orleans, 1969. Bar: U.S. Dist. Ct. (ea. dist.) La. 1969, U.S. Dist. Ct. (mid. dist.) La. 1969, U.S. Dist. Ct. (we. dist.) La. 1975. Assoc. Kierr, Gainsburgh, Benjamin, Fallon & Lewis, New Orleans, 1969-74, ptnr., 1974—; adj. faculty Tulane U., New Orleans, 1979-81. Staff mem. Loyola U. Law Review, 1967-69. Reader/recorder for La. Blind and Handicapped, 1986—. Mem. ABA, Fed. Bar Assn., La. Bar Assn. (asst. examiner commn. on bar admissions 1974—), La. Bar Found., Assn. Trial Lawyers Am., La. Trial Lawyers Assn. (bd. govs. 1981-83, contbg. editor Civil Trial Tactics manual 1981), Loyola U. Law Alumni Assn. (bd. dirs.), Kappa Sigma, Phi Alpha Delta. Club: Lakewood Country (New Orleans). Avocation: sports. Admiralty, Personal injury, Federal and state civil litigation. Home: 2559 Eton St New Orleans LA 70114 Office: Kierr Gainsburgh et al 1718 1st NBC Bldg New Orleans LA 70112

DAVID, RONALD ALBERT, lawyer; b. Pawtucket, R.I., Mar. 24, 1951; s. Albert S. and Katherine M. David; m. Dona C. Buckner, Nov. 24, 1978; 1 child, Dana. BA in Polit. Sci., U. Fla., 1973, JD, 1975. Bar: Fla. 1975. Assoc. Wagner & Cunningham, Tampa, Fla., 1975-77; ptnr. Kocha, David & Houston, West Palm Beach, Fla., 1977-80, David & French P.A., Boca Raton, Fla., 1982—; liason Fla. Bar, Tallahassee, 1983—. Mem. Fla. Bar Assn., South Palm Beach County Bar Assn., Palm Beach County Bar Assn., Acad. Fla. Trial Lawyers. Club: Bankers (Boca Raton) (bd. dirs.). Lodge: Rotary (sec., bd. dirs., v.p. 1983—, Paul Harris fellow). Personal injury, State civil litigation, Insurance. Office: 855 S Federal Hwy Boca Raton FL 33432

DAVIDOFF, BARRY FREDERICK, lawyer; b. N.Y.C., June 18, 1953; s. Abraham G. and Irma V. (Greeley) D. BA, Manhattanville Coll., 1974; JD, Columbia U., 1977; MBA, NYU, 1985. Bar: N.J. 1978, U.S. Dist. Ct. N.J. 1978, U.S. Ct. Appeals (3d cir.) N.J. 1978. Atty. Allied Chem. Corp., Morristown, N.J., 1977-79; assoc. counsel Olin Corp., Stamford, Conn., 1979-85; dir. corp. and legal affairs Refined Sugar Inc., Yonkers, N.Y., 1985—; corp. sec. Refined Sugar Inc., Yonkers, 1986—. Mem. ABA (banking bus. and corp. law sect. pollution controls com. 1980—), Westchester Fairfield Corp. Counsel Assn. (chmn. computer law com. 1984—), Norwalk Jaycees. Avocations: sailing, photography, curling. Contracts commercial, Computer, Environment. Home: 71 Aiken Rd N-8 Norwalk CT 06851 Office: Refined Sugar Inc 1 Federal St Yonkers NY 10702

DAVIDOFF, E. MARTIN, tax accountant, attorney; b. Suffern, N.Y., Jan. 27, 1952; s. Earle and Estelle (Topper) D.; m. Sheila Temkin, May 30, 1976; children—Sherri, Laura. S.B., MIT, 1974; M.B.A., Boston U., 1975; J.D., Washington U., St. Louis, 1978. Bar: N.J. 1981, N.Y. 1979; CPA, N.J., N.Y. Tax sr. Richard A. Eisner & Co., N.Y.C., 1978-80; tax mgr. Leonard C. Green & Co., Woodbridge, N.J., 1980-81; proprietor E. Martin Davidoff CPA, P.C., Edison, N.J., 1981—; tax counsel Quinn, Cohen, Shields & Bock, Attys. at Law, N.Y.C., 1983—; del. White House Conf. on Small Bus., 1986. Contbr. articles to profl. jours. Mem. Am. Inst. CPAs, N.J. Soc. CPAs, Am. Assn. Attys. and CPAs, ABA, N.J. Bar Assn., U.S. Jaycees. Corporate taxation, Personal income taxation, State and local taxation. Home: 16 Independence Dr East Brunswick NJ 08816 Office: E Martin Davidoff CPA PC 295 Pierson Ave Edison NJ 08837

DAVIDOW, JOEL, lawyer; b. N.J., July 24, 1938; s. Isadore Davidow; m. Katherine Davidow (div.); children: Elizabeth, Judith; m. Debra Lynn Miller; 1 child, Abigail Suzanne. AB, Princeton U., 1960; LLB, Columbia U., 1963; postdoctoral, U. London, Stanford U. Dir. policy planning antitrust div. U.S. Dept. Justice, Washington, 1978-81; ptnr. Mudge, Rose, Guthrie, Alexander & Ferdon, N.Y.C., 1981—; lectr. law Columbia U., N.Y.C., 1983—. Fgn. antitrust editor Antitrust Bulletin, 1981; adv. bd. Bur. Nat. Affairs Antitrust Bulletin, 1981. Mem. ABA. Democrat. Antitrust, Private international. Office: Mudge Rose Guthrie Alexander & Ferdon 180 Maiden Ln New York NY 10038

DAVIDSON, CHARLES E., lawyer; b. Pitts., May 10, 1954; s. Donald and Marilyn (Sparks) D.; m. Karen Guzak, Dec. 22, 1979; 1 child, Benjamin Ross. BA, Carnegie-Mellon U.; JD, U. Pitts. Bar: Tex. 1981, U.S. Dist. Ct. (so. dist.) Tex. 1982. Assoc. Vinson & Elkins, Houston, 1981-85, Winstead, McGuire, Sechrest & Minick, Dallas, 1985—. Author: Consumer Guide to Purchasing a Home, 1985. Mem. ABA (corp., banking and bus. law sect.), Tex. Bar Assn., Dallas Bar Assn., Dallas Young Lawyers Assn. Banking, Real property, Bankruptcy. Office: Winston McGuire Sechrest & Minick 1700 Merc Dallas Bldg Dallas TX 75201

DAVIDSON, DANIEL JOSEPH, administrative law judge; b. Washington, Aug. 27, 1934; s. Abraham I. and Mollie (Mackler) D.; m. Miriam H. Cohen, July 18, 1958; children: Andrew E., Michael W., Tracy C. B.A., U. Md., 1957, J.D., 1958. Bar: Md. 1958. Atty. ICC, 1959-63, counsel to chmn. div. 3, 1963-68, adminstrv. law judge, 1968-75; adminstrv. law judge FDA, Rockville, Md., 1975—. Administrative and regulatory. Office: Food and Drug Adminstrn 5600 Fishers Ln Rockville MD 20857 *

DAVIDSON, DUNCAN MOWBRAY, lawyer, management consultant; b. Houston, Jan. 6, 1953; s. Alexander Norman and Elsie Dorothy (Baumann) D.; m. Jean Ann Kunkel, Feb. 16, 1980; children: James Cameron, Claire Amanda, Julie Logan. BS in Physics, Math with honors, Brown U., 1975; JD magna cum laude, U. Mich., 1978. Bar: N.Y. 1979, Calif. 1980, Colo. 1984. Assoc. Cleary, Gottlieb, Steen & Hamilton, N.Y.C., 1978-80, Irell & Manella, Los Angeles, 1980-83; ptnr. Cambridge Venture Ptnrs., Denver, 1983-85; sr. assoc. Strategic Planning Assocs., Inc., Washington, 1986—; Mem. editorial bd. Computer Law and Practice, London, 1984—, Computer Lawyer, Los Angeles, 1984—. Author: (with others) Advanced Legal Strategies for Buying and Selling Computers and Software, 1986; editor Mich. Law Rev., 1977-78; contbr. articles on software, fin., and computers to profl. jours. Mem. ABA (com. chmn. sci. and tech. sect. 1982—), Computer Law Assn. (bd. dirs. 1984—). Presbyterian. Avocation: chess. Computer, Venture capital. Home: 7731 Huntsman Blvd Springfield VA 22153 Office: Strategic Planning Assocs Inc 2300 N St NW Washington DC 20037

DAVIDSON, FRANK GASSAWAY, III, lawyer; b. Lynchburg, Va., Feb. 25, 1945; s. Frank Gassaway and Katherine (Graves) G.; m. Anne Harvey, May 12, 1973; children—Christian O., Frank G. B.A., Hampden-Sydney Coll., 1969; J.D., Washington and Lee U., 1971; LL.M., NYU, 1975. Bar: Va. 1975. With trust dept. Morgan Guaranty Trust Co., N.Y.C., 1971-72; trust officer The Fiduciary Trust Co., N.Y.C., 1973-75; pres. Davidson & Sakolosky, P.C., Lynchburg, 1975—. Past. pres. Central Va. Speech, Hearing Ctr., Inc. Served to cpl. USMC, 1968-74. Mem. ABA, Va. Bar Assn., Lynchburg Bar Assn. Episcopalian. Club: Boonsboro Country (Lynchburg). General corporate, Estate planning, Pension, profit-sharing, and employee benefits. Home: 3719 Woodside Ave Lynchburg VA 24503 Office: Davidson & Sakolosky PC Box 798 Lynchburg VA 24505

DAVIDSON, FRANK PAUL, macro-engineer, lawyer; b. N.Y.C., May 20, 1918; s. Maurice Philip and Blanche (Reinheimer) D.; m. Izaline Marguerite Doll, May 19, 1951; children—Roger Conrad, Nicholas Henry, Charles Geoffrey. S.B., Harvard U., 1939, J.D., 1948, D.H.L., Hawthorne Coll., 1987. Bar: N.Y. 1953, U.S. Dist. Ct. (so. dist.) N.Y. 1953. Dir. mil. affairs C. of C., Houston, 1948-50; contract analyst U.S. Embassy, Paris, 1950-53; assoc. Carb, Luria, Glassner & Cook, N.Y.C., 1953-54; sole practice, N.Y.C., 1955-70; research assoc. MIT, Cambridge, Mass., 1970—, also chmn. system dynamics steering com. Sloan Sch. Mgmt., coordinator macro-engring. Sch. Engring.; pres. Tech. Studies, Inc., N.Y.C., 1957—; vice chmn. Inst. for Ednl. Services, Bedford, Mass., 1980-84; Nat. Acad. Scis. del. to Renewable Resources Workshop, Katmandu, Nepal, 1981; governing bd. Channel Tunnel Study Group, 1957—. Author: Macro: A Clear Vision of How Science and Technology Will Shape our Future, 1983, Macro: Big Is Beautiful, 1986; editor series of AAAS books on macro-engring., Tunneling and Underground Transportation, 1987; editorial bd. Interdisciplinary Sci. Revs., 1985—; adv. bd. Technology in Society, 1979—, Mountain Research and Development, 1981—, project appraisal, 1986—. Bd. dirs. Internat. Mountain Soc., Boulder, Colo., 1981—; trustee Norwich Ctr. (Vt.), 1980-83. Served to capt. RCAC, 1941-46; ETO. Decorated Bronze Star. Mem. Am. Soc. Macro-Engring. (bd. dirs. 1982—, vice chancellor 1983—), Assn. Bar City N.Y., ABA. Clubs: Knickerbocker (N.Y.C.); St. Botolph (Boston). Construction, Private international, Public international. Home: 140 Walden St Concord MA 01742 Office: E40-294 MIT Cambridge MA 02139

DAVIDSON, GEORGE ALLAN, lawyer; b. N.Y.C., Apr. 6, 1942; s. George Roger and Jean Allan (McKaig) D.; m. Annette L. Richter, Sept. 4, 1965; children—Emily, Charlotte. A.B., Brown U., 1964; LL.B., Columbia U., 1967. Bar: N.Y. 1967, U.S. Dist. Ct. (so. and ea. dists.) N.Y. 1969, U.S. Ct. Appeals (2d cir.) 1970, U.S. Supreme Ct. 1974, U.S. Tax Ct. 1974, U.S. Ct. Appeals (D.C. cir.) 1976, U.S. Dist. Ct. (no. dist.) Calif. 1980, U.S. Ct. Appeals (9th cir.) 1981, U.S. Ct. Appeals (5th cir.) 1982, U.S. Dist. Ct. (no. dist.) N.Y. 1982, U.S. Ct. Appeals (11th cir.) 1983, U.S. Ct. Appeals (1st cir.) 1986. Law clk., 1967-68; assoc. Hughes Hubbard & Reed, N.Y.C., 1968-74, ptnr., 1974—; dir. P.R. Legal Def. and Edn. Fund, Inc., 1980-84, Legal Aid Soc., 1979—, N.Y. Lawyers for Pub. Interest, Inc., 1984-86. Mem. ABA, Fed. Bar Council, Am. Law Inst., N.Y. State Bar Assn., Assn. Bar City N.Y., Am. Judicature Soc., Nat. Assn. Coll. and Univ. Attys., Columbia Law Sch. Alumni Assn., Union Internationale des Avocats. Democrat. Roman Catholic. Club: India House (N.Y.C.). Contbr. writings to legal publs. Federal civil litigation, State civil litigation. Office: Hughes Hubbard & Reed 1 Wall St New York NY 10005

DAVIDSON, GLEN HARRIS, U.S. district judge; b. Pontotoc, Miss., Nov. 20, 1941; s. M. Glen and Lora (Harris) D.; m. Bonnie Payne, Apr. 25, 1973; children: Glen III, Gregory P. B.A., U. Miss, 1962, J.D., 1965. Bar: Miss. 1965, U.S. Ct. Appeals (5th cir.) 1965, U.S. Supreme Ct. 1971. Asst. dist. atty. First Jud. Dist., Tupelo, Miss., 1969-74; dist. atty. First Jud. Dist., 1975; U.S. atty. Dept. Justice No. Dist. 2, Oxford, Miss., 1981-85; U.S. district judge U.S. Ct. House, Aberdeen, Miss., 1985—; atty. Lee County Sch. Bd., Miss., 1974-81. Bd. dirs. Community Devel. Found., Tupelo, 1976-81; mem. exec. bd. Yocona Council Boy Scouts Am., 1972—. Served to maj. USAF, 1966-69. Mem. Fed. Bar Assn. (v.p. 1984), Miss. Bar Found., Lee County Bar Assn. (pres. 1974), Assn. Trial Lawyers Am., Miss. Prosecutors Assn. Presbyterian. Lodge: Kiwanis (pres. Tupelo 1978). Judicial administration.

DAVIDSON, JOSEPH Q., JR., lawyer; b. Columbus, Ga., Aug. 26, 1941; s. Joseph Q. and Maude (Adams) D.; m. Diane Cole, Oct. 29, 1966 (dec. May 1984); children: Joseph Q. III, George Cole; m. Betty Cason, Sept. 7, 1985. AB, Mercer U., 1963, JD cum laude, 1966; LLM in Taxation, NYU, 1967. Assoc. Page, Scranton, Harris, McGlamery, Davidson & Clayman, Columbus, 1967-69, ptnr., 1970-73; ptnr., pres. Davidson & Calhoun, P.C., Columbus, 1973—; bd. dirs. Columbus Bank & Trust Co. Mem. estate planning council, Columbus. Fellow Am. Coll. Tax Counsel; mem. ABA, Ga. Bar Assn. (chmn. tax sect. 1973), Columbus Lawyers Club, Young Lawyers Club of Columbus (pres.). Clubs: Big Eddy (bd. dirs.), Green Island Country, Bachelors II (Columbus) (sec., bd. dirs. 1984—). Securities, Personal income taxation, Corporate taxation. Home: 6613 Waterford Rd Columbus GA 31904 Office: Davidson & Calhoun PC 828 Broadway Columbus GA 31904

DAVIDSON, KEITH L., lawyer; b. Chgo., Il, Oct. 31, 1942; s. Louis G. and Anne Marie (Astley) D.; m. Wendy Sue Ruff, Nov. 22, 1980. A.B., U. Ill., 1965; J.D., Loyola U., 1969. Bar: Ill. 1968, U.S. Dist. Ct. (no. dist.) Ill. 1969, U.S Ct. Appeals (7th cir.) 1971, U.S. Ct. Appeals (4th cir.) 1973, U.S. Supreme Ct. 1978. Ptnr. Louis G. Davidson & Assocs., Ltd., Chgo., 1968—; participating adviser Nat. Ednl. TV Program, 1973; judge Moot Ct. Northwestern U., Chgo., Ill, 1973, 77, 78, Kent Law Sch., 1973, 77, 78, John Marshall Law Sch., 1973, 77, 78; lectr., trial demonstrator (various law sch., assns., seminars). Contbr. articles and book rev. to legal jours. other profl. mags. Fellow Am. Bar Found.; mem. ABA (council 1980-84), Ill. State Bar Assn. (gov. 1980—), Chgo. Bar Assn., Bar Assn. 7th Fed. Cir. Lawyers Am. (mem. com. on adminstrn. of justice 1975-76, 77-78), Assn. Trial Lawyers Am. (mem. internat. law and treaties com. 1980-81), Ill. Trial Lawyers Assn. (mem. bd. mgrs. 1976), Chgo. Council Lawyers (v.p. 1974-76), World Assn Lawyers, Alliance Francaise (bd. dirs. 1975-79, 2d v.p. 1977-79). Club: Literary (Chgo.). Personal injury, Federal civil litigation, State civil litigation. *

DAVIDSON, LAWRENCE IRA, lawyer; b. Chgo., Nov. 6, 1949; s. Robert D. and Marilyn Patricia (Eisenberg) D.; m. Jill Stephens, June 10, 1978; 1 child, Zachary. BA in Acctg., U. Ill., 1972; JD, John Marshall Sch. Law, 1975, LLM in Taxation, 1979. Bar: Ill. 1975, U.S. Dist. Ct. (no. dist.) Ill. 1975, U.S. Ct. Claims 1976, U.S. Tax Ct. 1976, U.S. Ct. Appeals (7th cir.) 1976, U.S. Supreme Ct. 1980. From assoc. to ptnr. Gordon, Glickson, Gordon & Davidson, Chgo., 1975-83; assoc. Aaron, Schimberg, Hess & Gilbert, Chgo., 1983-84; ptnr. Holleb & Coff, Chgo., 1984—. Bd. dirs. Theatre First, Chgo., 1983—. Served with Ill. N.G., 1970-76. Mem. ABA (fed. income taxation com.), Chgo. Bar Assn. (employee benefits com., fed. income tax com.), Ill. Soc. CPA's. Jewish. Avocation: theatre. Pension, profit-sharing, and employee benefits, Estate planning. Office: Holleb & Coff 55 E Monroe St Chicago IL 60603

DAVIDSON, MICHAEL H., lawyer; b. N.Y.C., Nov. 5, 1947; s. Howard C. and Beulah Marie (Williams) D. B.A., U. Fla., 1970, J.D., 1974. Bar: Fla. 1975, U.S. Dist. Ct. (no. dist.) Fla. 1977, U.S. Dist. Ct. (so. dist.) Fla. 1986, U.S. Ct. Appeals (5th and 11th cirs.). Asst. atty. gen. State of Fla., 1975-78; gen. counsel Fla. Parole Commn., 1978-80; assoc. Wattles, Baker & Davidson, Tallahasee, 1981-82; sole practice, Ft. Lauderdale, 1983-85. Republican. Roman Catholic. General practice, State civil litigation, Criminal. Home: 105 Lake Emerald Dr #208 Coral Springs FL 33309 Office: Watson & Clark PO Box 11959 Suite 301 Fort Lauderdale FL 33339

DAVIDSON, ROBERT BRUCE, lawyer; b. N.Y.C., May 6, 1945. BS in Econs. cum laude, U. Pa., 1967; JD, Columbia U., 1972. Bar: N.Y. 1973, U.S. Dist. Ct. (so. and ea. dists.) N.Y. 1973, U.S. Ct. Appeals (2d cir.) 1975, U.S. Ct. Appeals (D.C. cir.) 1981, U.S. Supreme Ct. 1979, U.S. Tax Ct. 1984. Assoc. Baker & McKenzie, N.Y.C., 1972-79, ptnr., 1979—; bd. dirs. The Wall Street Fund, N.Y.C.; mem. adv. bd. World Arbitraion Inst., N.Y.C., 1984—. Author: (with others) Voting Laws and Procedures, 1973; also articles. Vol. U.S. Peace Corps, Philippines, 1968-70. Mem. ABA, Assn. of Bar of City of N.Y. (former chmn. com. on arbitration and alternative dispute resolution), Am. Fgn. Law Assn., Maritime Law Assn. U.S., Fed. Bar Council, Am. Arbitration Assn. (mem. panel of arbitrators 1982—). Commercial arbitration, Private international, Federal civil litigation. Office: Baker & McKenzie 805 Third Ave New York NY 10022

DAVIDSON, ROBERT LEE, III, lawyer, author, consultant; b. Nevada, Mo., May 10, 1923; s. Robert Lee and Nancy Helen (Manker) D.; m. Lorena Elizabeth Turner, children: Roberta Anne, Curtis Lee. BSChemE, U. Mo., 1944, MSChemE, 1947; JD, Fordham U., 1978. Bar: N.J. 1980. Editor in chief Petro/Chem. Engring., Dallas, 1964-66; mng. editor Chem. Engring., N.Y.C., 1966-75; editor-in-chief McGraw Hill Book Co., N.Y.C., 1975-80, dir. book pub. ctr., 1980-82; sole practice, Princeton, N.J., 1980—; editor Attys. Computer Report, Princeton, 1984-85, cons. on publs., 1982—. Author: Sucessful Process Plant Practices, 1958. Editor: Petroleum Processing Handbook, 1967; Handbook of Water Soluble Gums and Resins, 1980. Served to 1st lt. U.S. Army, 1942-46. Mem. ABA, N.J. Bar Assn., Am. Inst. Chem. Engrs., N.Y. Acad. Scis., Sigma XI. General practice. Home: 45 Patton Ave Princeton NJ 08540 Office: 32 Chambers St Princeton NJ 08540

DAVIDSON, TOM WILLIAM, lawyer; b. Madison, Wis., Oct. 10, 1952; s. Alvin William and Louise Elizabeth (Zeratsky) D.; m. Linda Mary Greiber, July 27, 1974; children—Jessica, Heather, Thomas. B.A., U. Wis.-Madison, 1977, J.D., 1974. Bar: U.S. Dist. Ct. (we. dist.) Wis. 1977, Wis. 1977, U.S. Supreme Ct. 1986, U.S. Ct. Appeals (D.C. cir.) 1986. Gen. atty. FCC, Washington, 1977-79, trial atty., 1979; assoc. Sidley & Austin, Washington, 1980-84, ptnr., 1985—. Active Burke Centre Community Assn., Burke, Va., 1977-79, chmn. Bass Pond Cluster Bd., 1977-78. Mem. Fed. Communications Bar Assn., ABA, Fed. Bar Assn., Phi Beta Kappa, Phi Eta Sigma, Phi Kappa Phi. Club: Tournament Players Club at Avenel (Bethesda, Md.). Avocations: golf; softball; racquetball. Administrative and regulatory, Trademark and copyright, Entertainment. Home: 6608 Jill Ct McLean VA 22101 Office: Sidley & Austin 1722 Eye St NW Washington DC 20006

DAVIDSON, VAN MICHAEL, JR., lawyer; b. Baton Rouge, Nov. 26, 1945; s. Van Michael Sr. and Elizabeth Lamoine (Arnold) D.; m. Judith Ann Begue, Aug. 5, 1967; children: Van Michael III, Catherine Annette, Mary Elizabeth. BA in History, La. State U., 1968; JD, U. Miss., 1973. Bar: Miss. 1973, U.S. Dist. Ct. (no. dist.) Miss. 1973, U.S. Ct. Mil. Appeals 1974, U.S. Supreme Ct. 1978, U.S. Ct. Claims 1979, U.S. Tax Ct. 1980, U.S. Ct. Appeals (5th cir.) 1981, La. 1982, U.S. Dist. Ct. (we. and mid. dists.) La. 1982, U.S. Dist. Ct. (no. dist.) Tex. 1982, U.S. Ct. Appeals (Fed. cir.) 1982, U.S. Dist. Ct. (so. dist.) Miss. 1985, U.S. Dist. Ct. (ea. dist.) La. 1985. Commd. 2d lt. U.S. Army, 1968, advanced through grades to maj., 1980, resigned, 1981; forward observer U.S. Army, Ft. Bragg, N.C., 1968; battery battalion officer U.S. Army, Ft. Bliss, Tex., 1968-69, battery comdr., 1969-70; command spokesman IV U.S. Army, Vietnam, 1970-71; trial counsel U.S. Army, New Ulm, Fed. Republic Germany, 1974-77; trial atty. contact appeals div. U.S. Army, Washington, 1978-81; ptnr. Carmouche, Gray & Hoffman, Lake Charles, La., 1981—; chmn. bd. dirs. Southwest Legl Services Agy., Lake Charles. Mem. meml. com. La. Vietnam Vets. Decorated Bronze Star, Vietnamese Gallantry Cross with Palm. Mem. ABA, Fed. Bar Assn., Assn. Trial Lawyers Am., Internat. Right of Way Assn., Indsl. Coll. Armed Forces, Phi Delta Phi. Republican. Presbyterian. Avocations: hunting, fishing, scuba diving, playing piano. Government contracts and claims, Federal civil litigation, Condemnation. Home: 1525 N Greenfield Circle Lake Charles LA 70605 Office: Carmouche Gray & Hoffman One CM Tower Lake Charles LA 70602

DAVIES, BRUCE OWEN, lawyer; b. Rapid City, S.D., Dec. 11, 1950; s. Vessie O. and Marjorie A. (Glenn) D.; m. Sally Templeton, Feb. 14, 1983, children: Alicia, Amanda. BA, Wesleyan U., 1975; JD, U. Denver, 1979. Bar: Colo. 1979, U.S. Dist. Ct. Nebraska 1980, U.S. Dist. Ct. Colo. 1980, Alaska 1981, U.S. Dist. Ct. Alaska 1981, U.S. Ct. of Claims, 1981. Staff atty. Native Am. Rights Fund, Boulder, Colo., 1979-80, Ellis & Whittaker, Ketchikan, Alaska, 1980-82; city mgr. Saxman, Alaska, 1982-84; corp. counsel Klawock-Heenya Corp., Ketchikan, 1984—; sole practice Ketchikan, 1984—. bd. dirs. Rainbird Community Broadcasting, Ketchikan, 1981—. Mem. ABA, Colo. Bar Assn., Alaska Bar Assn. Democrat. General corporate, Bankruptcy, Family and matrimonial. Home: PO Box 5021 Ketchikan AK 99901 Office: 20 Creek St Ketchikan AK 99901

DAVIES, NORLEEN O'SULLIVAN, lawyer; b. Wilton, Conn., Sept. 12, 1946; d. John David and Vesta Ethelwyn (Vandeveer) O'Sullivan; m. George Wilson Davies, June 25, 1978; 1 child, Katharine. Student, Purdue U., 1964-67; BA, Temple U., 1968, JD, 1975. Bar: Pa. 1975. Dir. community affairs World Affairs Counsel, Phila., 1969-71; atty. IU Internat. Corp., Phila., 1975-80, sr. atty., 1980—. Mem. allocation com. YWCA/YMCA, Phila., 1980-82; trustee United Way Southeastern Pa., Phila., 1986—, mem. cen. allocation com., 1982-85, family service allocation com., 1985—; bd. dirs. World Affairs Council, Phila., 1971-75. Mem. ABA, Pa. Bar Assn., Phila. Bar Assn. Democrat. Unitarian. General corporate, Securities, Real property. Office: IU Internat Corp 1500 Walnut St Philadelphia PA 19102

DAVIES, PAUL LEWIS, JR., lawyer; b. San Jose, Calif., July 21, 1930; s. Paul Lewis and Faith (Crummey) D.; m. Barbara Bechtel, Dec. 22, 1955; children: Laura (Mrs. Segundo Mateo), Paul Lewis III. A.B., Stanford U., 1952; J.D., Harvard U., 1957. Bar: Calif. 1957. Assoc. Pillsbury, Madison & Sutro, San Francisco, 1957-63; ptnr. Pillsbury, Madison & Sutro, 1963—; also gen. counsel Chevron Corp., 1984—; dir. FMC Corp., Indsl. Indemnity Co., So. Pacific Transp. Co. Hon. trustee Calif. Acad. Scis., trustee, 1970-83, chmn., 1973-80; pres. Herbert Hoover Found.; bd. overseers Hoover Instn., chmn., 1976-82; bd. regents U. of Pacific; bd. dirs. Merritt Peralta Med. Ctr. Served to 1st lt. U.S. Army, 1952-54. Mem. State Bar Calif., ABA, San Francisco Bar Assn., Phi Beta Kappa, Pi Sigma Alpha. Republican. Clubs: Bankers, Bohemian, Pacific-Union, Stock Exchange, Villa Taverna, World Trade (San Francisco); Claremont Country, Lakeview (Oakland, Calif.); Cypress Point (Pebble Beach, Calif.); Sainte Claire (San Jose, Calif.), Collectors, Explorers, Links (N.Y.C.); Metropolitan, 1925 F St. (Washington); Chicago, Mid-America (Chgo.). General practice. Office: Pillsbury Madison and Sutro 225 Bush St San Francisco CA 94104

DAVIS, ALAN HUGH, lawyer; b. Melrose, Mass., Dec. 8, 1947. BA, St. Lawrence U., 1970; JD, Suffolk U., 1980; LLM in Taxation, Boston U., 1982; LLM in Internat. and Comparative Law, U. Brussels, 1984. Bar: Mass. 1980, U.S. Dist. Ct. Mass. 1980. Asst. dean of students St. Anselm Coll., Manchester, N.H., 1974-79; assoc. Cook & Bell, Melrose, Mass., 1980-82; of counsel McNaught & Moriarty, Melrose, 1982-84; atty., cons. Honeywell Europe, Brussels, 1984-86; assoc. Serafini, Serafini & Darling, Salem, Mass., 1986—. Served to lt. USMC, 1970-74, lt. col. Res. 1974—. Mem. ABA (tax sect., internat. law sect.), Mass. Bar Assn., Phi Delta Phi. General corporate, Private international. Home: 25 Wheeler Ave Melrose MA 02176 Office: Serafini Serafini & Darling 63 Federal St Salem MA 01970

DAVIS, ANDREW HAMBLEY, JR., lawyer; b. Fall River, Mass., Feb. 10, 1937; s. Fall River, Mass., Feb. 10, 1937; s. Andrew Hambley and Doris (Baker) D.; m. Gail D. Perry, July 21, 1962; children—Andrew W., Katherine B., Joshua P. A.B., Brown U., 1960; LL.B., U. Va., 1962. Bar: R.I. 1963, Mass. 1962. Ptnr., Swan, Jenckes, Asquith & Davis, Providence, 1962-79; ptnr. Davis, Jenckes, Kilmarx & Swan, Providence, 1979—; sec., dir. Union Wadding Co. Pres., Bethany Home of R.I., 1966; bd. dirs., exec. com. Bradley Hosp.; bd. dirs. Moses Brown Sch., R.I. Philharmonic Orch., 1967—. Mem. ABA, R.I. Bar Assn., Boston Bar Assn., Estate Planning

Council, Am. Coll. Probate Council. Clubs: University, Acoaxet Golf, Agawam Hunt, Elephant Rock Beach, Art, Hope. Lodge: Masons. General corporate, Probate, Corporate taxation. Home: 9 Harbour Rd Barrington RI 02806 Office: 1420 Hospital Trust Tower 1 Hospital Trust Plaza Providence RI 02903

DAVIS, ANN GOUGER, lawyer; b. New Castle, Pa., Oct. 14, 1939; d. Matthew Martin and Mary Louise (Goehring) Gouger; m. George Humphries Davis, June 17, 1961; children—Matthew Miller, Catherine Powell. A.B., Vassar Coll., 1961; M.A.T., U. Chgo., 1963; J.D. cum laude, Ind. U., Indpls., 1978. Bar: Ind. 1979, U.S. Dist. Ct. (no. and so. dists.) Ind. Tchr., Homewood-Flossmoor High Sch., Flossmoor, Ill., 1962-66, Purdue U., West Lafayette, Ind., 1966-68; atty. Vaughan, Vaughan & Layden, Lafayette, Ind., 1979-83; atty., mgr. Women's Legal Clinic, Indpls., 1983-84; ptnr. Holder & Davis, Lafayette, 1985—. Bd. dirs. LWV Montgomery County, Crawfordsville, Ind., 1968-75, Planned Parenthood, Lafayette; bd. dirs., pres., sec.-treas. Youth Service Bur., Montgomery County, Crawfordsville, 1971-74, 79; pres. Ind. Symphony Soc., Crawfordsville unit, 1972; vestry St. John's Episcopal Ch., Crawfordsville, 1974-75; local chmn. United Fund, Crawfordsville, 1975; chmn. Crawfordsville Commn. on Status of Women, 1979-80. Mem. ABA, Ind. State Bar Assn., Indpls. Bar Assn., Tippecanoe Bar Assn. Episcopalian. Club: The Athenian (membership chmn. 1977) (Crawfordsville). Family and matrimonial, State civil litigation, General practice. Office: Holder & Davis 700 Purdue Nat Bank Bldg Lafayette IN 47902

DAVIS, BARRY LEE, lawyer; b. Miami, Fla., Dec. 29, 1955; s. Edward Arnold and Sandra (Weiner) D.; m. Sheri Shear; 1 child, Aaron Paul. BS, U. Fla., 1976, JD, 1979. Bar: Fla. 1980, U.S. Dist. Ct. (so. and mid. dists.) Fla. 1980, U.S. Ct. Appeals (5th and 11th cirs.) 1981, U.S. Supreme Ct. 1984. Assoc. Howard, Branner & Lovett, Miami, 1980-81; ptnr. Thornton, David & Murray, Miami, 1981—. Recipient Leadership award Fla. Blue Key, 1978. Mem. ABA, Acad. Trial Lawyers Am., Fla. Acad. Trial Lawyers, Dade County Bar Assn. (bd. dirs. 1981-83, Service award 1983), Greater Miami C. of C. (com. co-chmn. 1985). Democrat. Personal injury, Insurance, Federal civil litigation. Home: 7240 SW 117th Terr Miami FL 33156 Office: Thornton David & Murray PA 2950 SW 27th Ave Miami FL 33133

DAVIS, BRADLEY MARK, lawyer; b. San Antonio, Sept. 16, 1955; s. Forrest Lee and Patricia Ann (Kelly) D. BA magna cum laude, Bowling Green State U., 1977; JD, Ohio State U., 1980. Bar: Ohio, U.S. Ct. Mil. Appeals, U.S. Dist. Ct. (no. dist.) Ohio. Assoc. Bendure & Kelbley, Tiffin, Ohio, 1980-83; ptnr. Bendure, Kelbley & Davis, Tiffin, 1984-85, Kelbley & Davis, Tiffin, 1985—. Trustee Seneca County Law Library, Tiffin, 1983—. Mem. ABA, Ohio Bar Assn., Seneca County Bar Assn. (v.p. 1987—), Assn. of Trial Lawyers of Am., Ohio Acad. of Trial Lawyers, Tiffin C. of C. Avocations: golf, tennis, reading. State civil litigation, Criminal, Personal injury. Home: 30 Spayth St Tiffin OH 44883 Office: Kelbley & Davis 38 S Washington St Tiffin OH 44883

DAVIS, CHARLES BISHOP, lawyer; b. El Paso, Tex., Mar. 16, 1942; s. O.C. and Iola B. Davis; m. Ellen Jean Roessler, May 2, 1970; children: Lee Ann, Elizabeth, Cory. BS in Agr., Okla. State U., 1964; JD, U. Okla., 1973. Bar: Okla. 1973. U.S. Dist. Ct. (we. dist.) Okla., U.S. Ct. Appeals (10th cir.). Asst. conservation atty. Okla. Corp. Commn., Oklahoma City, 1974-78; hearing examiner Okla. Corp. Comm., Oklahoma City, 1978-79; assoc. Crabtree, Miller & Musser, Oklahoma City, 1977-78, Brown & Lockhart, Oklahoma City, 1979-81; ptnr. Davis & Fogels, Oklahoma City, 1981-86; sole practice 1986—. Mem. various bds., chmn. edn. com. McFarland Meth. Ch., Norman, Okla., 1973—. Served to maj. USMCR, 1960—. Mem. Oklahoma City Soc. Mineral Lawyers. Club: Tri-City Gun (Oklahoma City) (v.p. for legal affairs 1986). Avocations: hunting, fishing. Oil and gas leasing, Federal civil litigation, State civil litigation. Home: 4009 Stratford Norman OK 73072 Office: Davis & Fogels 1217 Sovereign Row #101 Oklahoma City OK 73108

DAVIS, CHARLES JOSEPH, lawyer; b. Cin., Sept. 29, 1949; s. Robert Joseph and Eileen (Hampe) D.; m. Sherry Louise Short, Sept. 2, 1972; 1 child, Ryan. BS, Coll. Holy Cross, 1971; JD, Salmon P. Chase Coll. Law, 1977. Bar: Ohio 1977, U.S. Dist. Ct. (so. dist.) Ohio 1978. Ptnr. French, Marks, Short, Wiener & Valleau, Cin., 1977—. Mem. Ohio Bar Assn. (negligence and workers compensation coms.), Cin. Bar Assn. (workers compensation and common pleas ct. coms.), Assn. Trial Lawyers Am. Republican. Personal injury, Workers' compensation, State civil litigation. Home: 754 Stout Ave Cincinnati OH 45215 Office: French Marks Short Wiener & Valleau 700 105 E 4th St Cincinnati OH 45202

DAVIS, CHARLES LEROY, lawyer; b. Joplin, Mo., Jan. 16, 1921; s. Charles Leroy and Ruth Eleanor (Daily) D.; m. Helen Darlyne Skeen, Sept. 4, 1981. BA, Washburn U., LLB, JD, 1943. Bar: Kans. 1943, U.S. Dist. Ct. Kans. 1943, U.S. Ct. Appeals (10th cir.) 1948, U.S. Supreme Ct. 1950. Sr. ptnr. Addington, Jones, Davis & Haney, Topeka, 1946-63, Davis, Unrein, Hummer & McCallister, Topeka, 1963—. Pres. Kans. Jaycees, Topeka, 1952-53; state rep. Kans. Ho. of Reps., 1957-59. Served to lt. USN, 1943-46, PTO. Named Outstanding State Pres., U.S. Jaycees, Kansas, 1953. Mem. ABA (chmn. trial techniques com. 1972-75), Kans. Bar Assn. Republican. Presbyterian. Club: Cosmopolitan (Topeka) (internat. judge adv. 1960-61). Avocation: legal research. Federal civil litigation, State civil litigation. Home: 2302 SW 17th St Topeka KS 66604 Office: The Davis Bldg 3715 SW 29 Topeka KS 66614

DAVIS, CHESTER R., JR., lawyer; b. Chgo., Aug. 30, 1930; s. Chester R. and Mead (Scoville) D.; m. Anne Meserve, Mar. 3, 1962; children: John Chester, Julia Snow, Elizabeth Meserve. Grad., Phillips Exeter Acad., 1947; A.B., Princeton, 1951; LL.B., Harvard, 1958. Bar: Ill. 1958, U.S. Dist. Ct. (no. dist.) Ill. 1958. Ptnr. Bell, Boyd & Lloyd and predecessor firms, 1968—. Assoc. Rush-Presbyn.-St. Luke's Med. Center, Chgo., 1964—, Adlai Stevenson Inst. Internat. Affairs, 1968—, Newberry Library, Chgo., 1974—; mem. Winnetka (Ill.) Zoning Commn. and Bd. Appeals, 1974-79; mem. Winnetka Plan Commn., 1976-82, 84—; chmn. Spl. Joint. Com. of Winnetka Zoning Bd. and Plan Commn. to Revise Land Use Ordinances, 1978-83; village trustee Village of Winnetka, 1984—; sec., bd. dirs. Vascular Disease Research Found.; mem. alumni council Phillips Exeter Acad.; chmn. Winnetka Interchurch Council, 1981-84. Served to lt. (j.g.) USNR, 1952-56, now capt. Recipient New Trier Dist. Award of Merit Boy Scouts Am., 1982. Mem. ABA, Ill. Bar Assn., Chgo. Bar Assn. (chmn. com. civil practice 1969-70, chmn. land use and zoning com. 1980-82, chmn. real property law com. 1983-84), Am. Soc. Internat. Law, Am. Judicature Soc., Am. Arbitration Assn. (nat. panel arbitrators), U.S. Naval Inst., Naval Res. Assn., Am. Planning Assn., Urban Land Inst., Chgo. Mortgage Attys. Assn., Harvard Law Soc. Ill. (past pres.), Harvard Law Sch. Assn. (nat. v.p. 1970-71). Episcopalian. Clubs: University (Chgo.), Economic (Chgo.), Law (Chgo.), Legal (Chgo.); Princeton (N.Y.C.), Nassau (Princeton, N.J.). Real property, Land use and planning, Local government. Home: 670 Blackthorn Rd Winnetka IL 60093 Office: Three First Nat Plaza Chicago IL 60602

DAVIS, CHRISTOPHER PATRICK, lawyer; b. Allentown, Pa., July 12, 1954; s. Richard Arthur and Patricia Anne (Henry) D.; m. Carol Hecker, Aug. 19, 1978; children: Gregory Carl, Colin Stuart. AB summa cum laude, Dartmouth Coll., 1976; JD magna cum laude, Harvard U., 1980. Bar: Mass. 1981, U.S. Dist. Ct. Mass. 1981, U.S. Ct. Appeals (1st cir.) 1985, U.S. Dist. Ct. N.H. 1986. Law clk. to judge U.S. Dist. Ct., Boston, 1980-81; assoc. Goodwin, Procter & Hoar, Boston, 1981—. Editor Harvard Law Rev., 1978-80. Mem. ABA, Mass. Bar Assn., Boston Bar Assn., Phi Beta Kappa. Club: Dartmouth Lawyers Assn. (Hanover, N.H.). Avocations: skiing, tennis, running, backpacking, gardening. Environment, Federal civil litigation, State civil litigation. Office: Goodwin Procter & Hoar Exchange Pl Boston MA 02109

DAVIS, CLARENCE CLINTON, JR., lawyer; b. Alexandria, La., Sept. 24, 1956; s. Clarence Clinton Sr. and Julia Isabel (Pace) D.; m. Lisa Cheryl Russell, Aug. 6, 1977 (div. Aug. 1978). BS, Northwestern State U., 1977; JD cum laude, So. Meth. U., 1980. Bar: Fla. 1980, U.S. Tax Ct. 1981, U.S. Ct. Appeals (5th cir.) 1981, Tex. 1982. Assoc. Trenam, Simmons, Kemker, Scharf, Barkin, Frye & O'Neill, Tampa, Fla., 1980-81; assoc. Moore & Peterson, Dallas, 1981-85, mem., 1986—. Mem. ABA (taxation sect.), Tex. Bar Assn. (tax exempt orgn. subcom. taxation sect. 1986—), Fla. Bar Assn., Dallas Bar Assn., Tex. Soc. CPA's, Order of Coif, Phi Kappa Phi. Republican. Episcopalian. Corporate taxation, Personal income taxation, General corporate. Office: Moore & Peterson 2800 1st City Ctr Dallas TX 75201

DAVIS, CLARICE M., lawyer; b. New Orleans, Jan. 20, 1941; d. James A. and Helen J. (Ross) McDonald; m. Pat W. Davis, July 15, 1964. BA, U. Tex., 1962, MA, 1964; JD, So. Meth. U., 1968. Bar: Tex. 1969, U.S. Dist. Ct. (no. dist.) Tex. 1970, U.S. Ct. Appeals (5th cir.) 1971, U.S. Supreme Ct. 1973. Law clk. to presiding justice U.S. Ct. Appeals (5th cir.), Dallas, 1969-71; from assoc. to ptnr. Akin, Gump, Strauss, Hauer & feld, Dallas, 1971—. Bd. visitors So. Meth. U., Dallas, 1979-82. Avocations: photgraphy, swimming, running. Federal civil litigation, State civil litigation, Insurance. Home: 6317 Churchill Way Dallas TX 75230 Office: Akin Gump Strauss Hauer & Feld 1700 Pacific Ave 4100 1st City Ctr Dallas TX 75201

DAVIS, CLAUDE JUNIOR, lawyer; b. St. Augustine, Ill., Jan. 27, 1922; s. Claude Hunter and Lura Mildred (Totten) D.; m. Marguerite Lois Hoffman, Sept. 4, 1948; children—Susan Davis Blevins, Priscilla Davis Rains, Claude Hunter, John Totten. B.A. in Econs. magna cum laude, Princeton U., 1945, J.D., U. Ill., 1948. Bar: Ill. 1948. Assoc. Suddes, Davis and Wittman, P.C., and predecessors, Jerseyville, Ill., 1948-52, ptnr. 1952-76, sr. ptnr. 1976-84; judge 7th Jud. Cir. Ct. of State of Ill., 1984—; city atty. City of Jerseyville 1952; state's atty. Jersey County 1952-65. Pres. Jerseyville Jaycees 1951-52; elder del. Gen. Assembly of United Presbyn. Ch. 1971. Mem. ABA, Ill. Bar Assn., Southwestern Ill. Bar Assn. (pres.), Jersey County Bar Assn. (pres.), Phi Alpha Delta, Phi Beta Chi. Democrat. Club: Quadrangle (Princeton U.). Home: 502 N State St Jerseyville IL 62052 Office: Courthouse Jerseyville IL 62052

DAVIS, CLAUDE-LEONARD, lawyer, educational administrator; b. Augusta, Ga., Feb. 16, 1944; s. James Isaac and Mary Emma (Crawford) D.; m. Margaret Earle Crowley, Dec. 30, 1965; 1 child, Margaret Michelle. BA in Journalism, U. Ga., 1966, JD, 1974. Bar: Ga. 1974. Broadcaster Sta. WKLE Radio, Washington, Ga., 1958-62; realtor Assocs. Realty, Athens, Ga., 1963-66; bus. cons. Palm Beach, Fla., 1970-71; asst. to dir. Ga. Coop. Extension Service, Athens, 1974-81; atty. U. Ga., Athens, 1981—; cons. numerous agrl. chem. industry groups nationwide, 1977—, Congl. Office of Tech. Assessment, Washington, 1978-79, USDA, Washington, 1979-80; del. Kellogg Nat. Leadership Conf., Pullman, Wash., 1980. Editor and contbr. Ga. Jour. of Internat. and Comparative Law, 1972-74; contbr. articles on agr. and fin. planning to profl. jours.; author and editor: DAWGFOOD: The Bulldog Cookbook, 1981, Touchdown Tailgates, 1986. Del. So. Leader Forum, Rock Eagle Ctr., Ga., 1976—; trainer Ga. 4-H Vol. Leader Assn., 1979—; vol. Athens United Way, 1980—; coordinator U. Ga. Equestrian Team, Athens, 1985—; mem. Clarke County Sheriff's Posse. Served to capt. U.S. Army, 1966-70. Chi Psi Scholar, 1965; Recipient Outstanding Alumnus award Chi Psi, 1972, Service to World Community award Chi Psi, 1975. Mem. ABA, Nat. Assn. Coll. Univ. Atty.'s, NRA, Disabled Am. Vets., Chi Psi (advisor and bd. dirs. 1974). Baptist. Clubs: The Pres.'s, City (Athens). Lodge: Gridiron Secret Soc. Avocations: martial arts, physical fitness, creative writing, music. General corporate, Labor, University counsel. Home: 365 Westview Dr Athens GA 30606 Office: Univ Ga Peabody Hall Suite 3 Athens GA 30602

DAVIS, DEAN MARTIN, lawyer; b. Bloomington, Ill., May 9, 1954; s. Dean H. and Geraldine (Martin) D.; m. Ann Costigan, July 11, 1981; children: Erin Frances, Dean William, Vanessa Ann, Shane Martin. BS cum laude, Wesleyan U., Bloomington, Ill., 1976; JD, Drake U., 1979. Bar: Ill. 1979, U.S. Dist. Ct. (cen. dist.) Ill. 1979. Assoc. Strodel & Kingery, Peoria, Ill., 1979-81, Costigan & Wollrab, Bloomington, 1981—. Bd. dirs. McLean County Assn. for Retarded Citizens, Bloomington, 1982-84; mem. Ill. Def. Council. Mem. ABA, Ill. Bar Assn. (practice litigation forum, young lawyers div.), McLean County Bar Assn. Lodge: Masons. Avocations: golf, handball, jogging. State civil litigation, Insurance, Personal injury. Home: 5 Foley Dr Bloomington IL 61701 Office: Costigan & Wollrab 308 E Washington St Bloomington IL 61701

DAVIS, DONALD MARC, lawyer; b. Phila., May 8, 1952; s. Herman S. Davis and Sandra M. (Margolis) Alloy; m. Noel M. Justic, June 9, 1979; children: Scott, Keith. BA, U. Pa., 1974; JD, John Marshall Law Sch., 1978. Bar: Ill. 1978, Pa. 1978, U.S. Dist. Ct. (ea. dist.) Pa. 1978, U.S. Ct. Appeals (3d cir.) 1978. Ptnr. Margolis, Edelstein, Scherlis, Sarowitz & Kraemer, Phila., 1978—. Mem. ABA, Def. Research Inst., Pa. Assn. Def. Counsel, Phila. Bar Assn., Phila. Assn. Def. Counsel. Federal civil litigation, State civil litigation, Insurance. Office: Margolis Edelstein et al 1315 Walnut St Philadelphia PA 19107

DAVIS, DONALD WILLIAM, lawyer; b. Washington, Mar. 6, 1943; s. William Columbus and Vivian (Berry) D.; m. Barbara Cassidy, Aug. 10, 1974; children—Jennifer Alice, Lee William. BA, U. Va., 1964, LLB, 1967. Bar: Ala. 1967. Law clk. U.S. Dist. Ct. No. Dist. Ala., 1969-70; atty. NLRB, Atlanta, 1970-72, Birmingham, Ala., 1972-77; pvt. practice law, Birmingham, Ala., 1977-86; ptnr. Moorer, Davis & Jones, Birmingham, 1986—. Served to capt. AUS, 1967-69. Decorated Bronze Star, Air medal, Combat Infantryman's Badge; Vietnamese Gallantry Cross with bronze star, others. Mem. Ala. Bar Assn., ABA, Fed. Bar Assn., Birmingham Bar Assn. Democrat. Episcopalian. Labor. Home: 3209 Carlisle Rd Birmingham AL 35213 Office: Moorer Davis & Jones 2200 City Fed Bldg Birmingham AL 35203

DAVIS, DOUGLAS WITFIELD, lawyer; b. Richmond, Ill., July 19, 1945; s. Douglas Wingfield and Antionette (Whitfield) D.; m. Ingrid Hook, June 23, 1967; children: Brian, Christopher, Elisabeth. BA, U. Richmond, 1967; MA, Boston U., 1971; JD, Georgetown U., 1974. Bar: Va. 1974, U.S. Dist. Ct. (ea. dist.) Va. 1974, U.S. Dist. Ct. (we. dist.) Va. 1975, U.S. Ct. Appeals (4th cir.) 1976, U.S. Tax Ct. 1978, N.Y. 1986. Assoc. Hunton & Williams, Richmond, 1974-81, ptnr., 1981—; Mem. Va. State Bar Judiciary Com. Served to capt. USAF, 1967-71. Mem. Va. Bar Assn. (litigation com.). Democrat. Presbyterian. Avocations: golf, canoeing, fishing. Federal civil litigation, State civil litigation, Personal injury. Home: 310 Roslyn Rd Richmond VA 23226 Office: Hunton & Williams 707 E Main St PO Box 1535 Richmond VA 23219

DAVIS, E. MARCUS, lawyer; b. Atlanta, Nov. 24, 1951; s. Edward Martin and Marcine (McConnell) D.; 1 child, Edward Clark. AB in Econs., Duke U., 1973; JD, U. Ga., 1976. Bar: U.S. Supreme Ct. 1981. Ptnr. Freeman & Davis, Atlanta, 1976-78, The Garland Firm, Atlanta, 1978-80, Kadish, Davis & Brofman, Atlanta, 1980-83, Davis, Brofman, Zipperman & Kirschenbaum, Atlanta, 1983—. Contbr. articles to profl. jours. Mem. ABA, Assn. Trial Lawyers Am., Nat. Assn. Criminal Def. Lawyers, Ga. Trial Lawyers Assn., Ga. Criminal Def. Lawyers Assn., Nat. Inst. Trial Advocacy. Presbyterian. Avocations: sailing, fishing, running, flying. Personal injury, Criminal, Family and matrimonial. Office: Davis Brofman Zipperman et al 918 Ponce De Leon Ave Atlanta GA 30306

DAVIS, EDWARD BERTRAND, federal judge; b. W. Palm Beach, Fla., Feb. 10, 1933; s. Edward Bertrand and Mattie Mae (Walker) D.; m. Patricia Lee Klein, Apr. 5, 1958; children: Diana Lee Davis, Traci Russell, Edward Bertrand, III. J.D., U. Fla., 1960; LL.M. in Taxation, N.Y. U., 1961. Bar: Fla. bar 1961. Pvt. practice Miami, 1961-79; counsel firm High, Stack, Lazenby & Bender, 1978-79; U.S. dist. judge So. Dist. Fla., 1979—. Served with AUS, 1953-55. Mem. Am. Bar Assn., Fla. Bar Assn., Dade County Bar Assn. Jurisprudence. Home: 6320 SW 50th St Miami FL 33155 Office: U S Courthouse 301 N Miami Ave Miami FL 33128

DAVIS, EVAN ANDERSON, lawyer; b. N.Y.C., Jan. 18, 1944; s. Richard T. and Charlotte (Upham) D. B.A., Harvard U., 1966; J.D., Columbia U., 1969. Bar: N.Y. 1970, U.S. Dist. Ct. (so. dist.) N.Y. 1973, U.S. Ct. Appeals (2d cir.) 1973, U.S. Dist. Ct. (ea. dist.) N.Y., 1978, U.S. Supreme Ct. 1979. Law clk. U.S. Ct. Appeals (D.C. cir.), 1969-70, Justice Potter Stewart, U.S. Supreme Ct., 1970-71; gen. counsel N.Y.C. budget Bur., 1971-72; chief consumer protection div. N.Y.C. Law Dept., 1972-74; task force leader, impeachment inquiry staff U.S. Ho. of Reps., 1974; assoc. Cleary, Gottlieb, Steen & Hamilton, N.Y.C., 1975-78, ptnr., 1978-85; counsel to gov. of N.Y.; vice chmn. bd. dirs. Fund for City N.Y., 1982-85. Editor-in-chief Columbia Law Rev. Mem. Bd. Ethics City of N.Y., 1983-85. Mem. Assn. Bar City N.Y. (chmn. exec. com. 1982-83, v.p. 1983-84), ABA (ho. of dels. 1983-85, chmn. spl. com. youth edn. for citizenship), Legal Aid Soc. (v.p. 1983-85). Home: 70-72 Chestnut St Albany NY 12210 Office: Exec Chamber State Capitol Albany NY 12224

DAVIS, FRANK B., lawyer; b. Richmond, Tex., July 12, 1928; s. Sydney Warren and Elizabeth (Wessendorff) D.; m. Elaine Illig, Oct. 7, 1960; children: Frank Barrett, Doris Elaine. B.B.A., U. Tex., 1949, LL.B., 1958. Asst. dist. atty. Harris County, Houston, 1958-62; ptnr. Andrews & Kurth, Houston, 1970—. Mem adv. bd. Clean Houston, 1982—. Served to lt. (j.g.) USN, 1950-54. Fellow Tex. Bar Found., Houston Bar Found.; mem. State Bar Tex. (bd. dirs. 1986—), Houston Bar Assn. (pres. 1984-85, Pres. award 1985). Clubs: Houston Country, Inns of Ct. (bd. dirs.). Home: 5742 Bayou Glen Houston TX 77057 Office: Andrews & Kurth Texas Commerce Tower Houston TX 77002

DAVIS, FRANK WAYNE, lawyer; b. Ada, Okla., Aug. 24, 1936; s. Roscoe Gladstone and Neva Dell (Peck) D.; m. Kay Diane Higginbotham, Aug. 12, 1961; children: David, Paul. Student, U. Ill., Urbana, 1956-57; BA, East Cen. U., 1958; LLB, U. Okla., Norman, 1959. Bar: Okla. 1959, U.S. Dist. Ct. (we. dist.) Okla. 1959, U.S. Ct. Appeals (10th cir.) 1959. Acting postmaster U.S. Postal Service, Ada, 1959-61; assoc. Denny W. Falkenburg, Medford, Okla., 1961; atty. Logan County, Guthrie, Okla., 1961-65; sole practice Guthrie, 1965-85; ptnr. Davis and Hudson, Guthrie, 1985—; mcpl. judge City of Guthrie, 1974-78; rep. State of Okla., Oklahoma City, 1978—; vice chmn. judiciary com. Okla. Ho. of Reps., 1981-82; minority floor leader, 1982-86. Scoutmaster Boy Scout Troop #850, Guthrie, 1961—; chmn. Logan County Reps., Guthrie, 1964-69. Recipient Silver Beaver award Boy Scouts Am., 1978. Mem. Okla. Bar Assn., Logan County Bar Assn. (pres. 1972-73), Am. Judicature Soc., Gideons. Methodist. Lodges: Lions, Masons. Avocations: fishing, stamp collecting. General practice, Real property, Probate. Home: 2121 N Walnut Guthrie OK 73044 Office: Davis & Hudson 115 N Division Guthrie OK 73044

DAVIS, FREDERICK BENJAMIN, law educator, lawyer, university dean; b. Bklyn., Aug. 21, 1926; s. Clifford Howard and Anne Frances (Forbes) D.; m. Mary Ellen Saecker, Apr. 21, 1956; children—Judith, Robert, James, Mary. A.B., Yale U., 1948; J.D., Cornell U., 1953; LL.M. with honors, Victoria U. of Wellington (N.Z.), 1955. Bar: N.Y. 1953, Mo. 1970, Ohio 1981. Assoc. Engel Judge & Miller, N.Y.C., 1953-54; instr. U. Pa. Law Sch., 1955-56; asst. prof. NYU, 1956-57; asst. prof. U. S.D., 1957-60, assoc. prof., 1960-62; assoc. prof. Emory U., 1962-63, prof., 1963-66; prof. U. Mo.-Columbia, 1966-70, Edward W. Hinton prof. law, 1970-81, Edward W. Hinton prof. emeritus, 1981—; dean, prof. law U. Dayton Sch. Law, 1981-86, prof., 1986-87, dean, prof. Memphis State U., 1987—; cons. adminstrv. procedure Mo. Senate, 1974-77; vis. prof. U. Wis., 1960, George Washington U., 1965, Tulane U., 1966, U. Mo.-Kansas City, 1973, U. Ky., 1977, Wake Forest U., 1980, 1986-87. Served with USNR, 1944-46. Mem. ABA (council sect. adminstrv. law 1969-75), Am. Judicature Soc. Republican. Episcopalian. Clubs: Bicycle of Dayton, Dayton Racquet, Rotary (Dayton, Ohio). Contbr. numerous articles, comments, revs., notes to profl. jours. Legal education, Administrative and regulatory, Personal injury. Office: U Dayton Sch Law 300 College Park Dr Dayton OH 45469

DAVIS, GARY SCOTT, lawyer; b. New Hyde Park, N.Y., July 19, 1957; s. Neil Paul and Sonia (Pomerantz) D.; m. Barbara L. Sheldon, Nov. 4, 1984. BA with honors, SUNY, Binghamton, 1979; JD with honors, George Washington U., 1982. Bar: Fla. 1982, U.S. Dist. Ct. (so. dist.) Fla. 1983. Assoc. Wood, Lucksinger & Epstein, Miami, Fla., 1982—. Congl. intern U.S. Ho. Reps., Washington, 1978. Mem. ABA (forum com. health), Fla. Bar Assn. (health law com.), Group Health Assn. Am., Greater Miami C. of C., Am. Med. Care Rev. Assn., Fla. Assn. Health Maintenace Orgns., Phi Beta Kappa, Pi Sigma Alpha. Health. Office: Wood Lucksinger & Epstein Southeast Fin Ctr Suite 3700 Miami FL 33131-2359

DAVIS, GEORGE THOMAS, lawyer; b. Savannah, Ga., Aug. 6, 1941; s. George W. and Ava Beatrice (Duggar) D.; m. Pamela Jean Cobb, July 11, 1966; children: Jennifer Lynn, Elizabeth, Katherine, Nathaniel, John Ashley. AA, Young Harris Coll., 1961; BS, Ga. So. Coll., 1963; JD, U. Ga., 1971. Bar: Ga. 1971, U.S. Supreme Ct. 1975. Sr. asst. atty. gen. law dept. State of Ga., Atlanta, 1971-76; ptnr. Lawson & Davis, Atlanta, 1976—. Served to lt. USN, 1964-68, PTO. Mem. ABA, Ga. Bar Assn., Lawyers Club of Atlanta. Methodist. Avocations: coaching and playing softball. Federal civil litigation, State civil litigation, Insurance. Home: 1620 Chevron Way Atlanta GA 30350 Office: Lawson & Davis 229 Peachtree St 200 Cain Tower Atlanta GA 30303

DAVIS, GILBERT KENNETH, lawyer, paralegal company executive; b. Waterloo, Iowa, Oct. 2, 1942; s. Dwight M. and Alice (Fredrickson) D.; m. Pamela Sue Saunders, Aug. 29, 1964. B.A., Cornell Coll., 1964; J.D., U. Va. Law Sch., 1969. Bar: Va. 1969, U.S. Dist. Ct. (ea. dist.) Va. 1969, U.S. Ct. Appeals (4th cir.) 1970, D.C. 1973, U.S. Dist. Ct. D.C. 1973, U.S. Dist. Ct. Md. 1973, U.S. Ct. Appeals (D.C. cir.) 1973, U.S. Supreme Ct. 1973, U.S. Dist. Ct. (we. dist.) Va. 1977. Asst. U.S. atty. ea. dist. Va., 1969-73; sr. ptnr. firm Davis, Harris & Herndon, McLean, Va., 1973—; dir. Appalachian Mineral Devel. Corp.; commr. in chancery, judge pro tem Fairfax Circuit Ct. Vice-pres. Cornell Coll. Alumni Bd.; state chmn. Young Republican Fedn. Va., 1973-75; bd. dirs. Profl. Inst. Va.; parliamentarian White House Conf. on Small Bus., 1986. Mem. ABA, Va. State Bar, D.C. Bar, Assn. Trial Lawyers Am., Nat. Assn. Criminal Def. Lawyers, Fed. Bar Assn., Va. Trial Lawyers Assn., McLean Lawyers Assn. (v.p.), Fed. Criminal Investigators Assn. (1st pres., founder D.C. chpt.), Delta Theta Phi. Presbyterian. Clubs: McLean Sporting, Commonwealth, The Counsellors. Lodge: Vienna Optimist. Assoc. editor Va. Lawyer Handbook, revised edit., 1969; author: Criminal Trial Manual. Criminal, Federal civil litigation, Personal injury. Home: 2727 Wrexham Ct Herndon VA 22071 Office: Davis and Gillenwater 2579 John Milton Dr Suite 310 Herndon VA 22071

DAVIS, HAL SCOTT, lawyer; b. N.Y.C., Mar. 11, 1957; s. Joseph Edward and Dianne Eunice (Ellenberg) D. BA, Brandeis U., 1977; JD, Boston U., 1980; MBA, NYU, 1983, LLM, 1987. Bar: N.Y. 1981; CPA, Fla. Tax atty. Ernst & Whinney, N.Y.C., 1982-85; sr. tax atty. Salomon Bros. Inc, N.Y.C., 1985—. Mem. ABA, N.Y. Bar Assn., Am. Inst. CPA's, N.Y. Soc. CPA's. Corporate taxation. Home: 151 W 78th St New York NY 10024 Office: Salomon Bros 1 New York Plaza New York NY 10024

DAVIS, HAROLD CLAYTON, JR., lawyer; b. Ft. Belvoir, Va., Jan. 19, 1956; s. Harold Clayton and Elizabeth (Woods) D. BA, Baylor U., 1977, JD, 1979. Bar: Tex. 1979, U.S. Dist. Ct. (no. dist.) Tex. 1981, U.S. Ct. Mil. Appeals 1981, U.S. Ct. Appeals (5th cir.) 1981, U.S. Dist. Ct. (so. dist.) Miss. 1982, U.S. Ct. Appeals (11th cir.) 1982, U.S. Dist. Ct. (we. dist.) Tex. 1984, U.S. Supreme Ct. 1986. Asst. dist. atty. Tarrant County, Ft. Worth, 1979-81; commd. lt. USAF, 1980, advanced through grades to capt., 1981; asst. staff judge adv. USAF, Keesler AFB, Miss., 1981-82; chief civil and preventive law USAF, Osan AB, Republic of Korea, 1982-83; staff judge adv. USAF, Taegu AB, Republic of Korea, 1983-84; chief mil. justice USAF, Lackland AFB, Tex., 1984-86; med. law cons. USAF Med. Ctr., Lackland AFB, 1986—. Contbr. articles to various newpapers, 1977-85. Legal advisor, scout master local councils, Boy Scouts Am., 1977—. Named one of Outstanding Young Men of Am., 1985, 86. Mem. ABA (outstanding young mil. lawyer award 1984-85), Tex. Bar Assn., Am. Soc. Law and Medicine, Tarrant County Young Lawyers Assn., San Antonio Young Lawyers Assn., Lackland AFB Co. Grade Officers Assn. (pres. 1984—), Air Force Assn. (blue suit award for outstanding performance 1986), Pi Sigma Alpha, Omicron Delta Kappa, Phi Delta Phi, Sigma Tau Gamma (local pres. 1976-77). Methodist. Avocations: flying, sailing, tennis. Military, Health, Government contracts and claims. Home: 5359 Fredericksburg Rd #804 San Antonio TX 78229 Office: USAF Med Ctr Wilford Hall Lackland AFB TX 78236-5300

DAVIS, HARREL LEON, III, lawyer; b. Sheffield, Ala., Dec. 24, 1954; s. Harrel Leon and Lyngene Marie (Taylor) D.; m. Janis Lynn Robertson, Jan. 31, 1981 (div. Sept. 1984). B.S. in Criminal Justice, U. Tex.-El Paso, 1974; J.D., U. Tex., Austin, 1977. Bar: Tex. 1977, U.S. Dist. Ct. (no. dist.) Tex. 1978, U.S. Dist. Ct. (we. dist.) Tex. 1980, U.S. Ct. Appeals (5th cir.) 1980,

U.S. Ct. Appeals (11th cir.) 1983, U.S. Ct. Appeals (10th cir.) 1983. Assoc. James R. Edwards, Lubbock, Tex., 1977-79, Goodman, Hallmark, Akard, Anderson, Villa & Keith, El Paso, 1979; ptnr. Diamond & Davis, P.C., El Paso, 1979-86, assoc. Grambling & Mounce, El Paso, 1986—; Campaign treas. Jack C. Vowell for State Rep. El Paso, 1980—. Mem. El Paso Bar Assn. (fee dispute com. 1983—), Tex. Young Lawyers' Assn. (law focused edn. com. 1982—), Phi Delta Phi, Lambda Alpha Chi. Republican. Baptist. Club: Tex. Exes (Austin). Bankruptcy, General corporate, Federal civil litigation. Home: 136 Calle Olaso El Paso TX 79932 Office: Grambling & Mounce Tex Commerce Bank Bldg 7th Floor El Paso TX 79911

DAVIS, HENRY BARNARD, JR., lawyer; b. East Grand Rapids, Mich., June 3, 1923; s. Henry Barnard and Ethel Margaret (Turnbull) D.; m. Margaret Lees Wilson, Aug. 27, 1947; children—Caroline Dellenbusch, Laura Davis Jackson, George B. B.A., Yale U., 1945; J.D., U. Mich., 1950; LL.D., Olivet Coll., 1983. Bar: Mich. 1951; U.S. Dist. Ct. (we. dist.) Mich. 1956, U.S. Ct. Apls. (6th cir.) 1971, U.S. Supreme Ct. 1978. Assoc. Allaben, Wiarda, Hayes & Hewitt, 1951-52; ptnr. Hayes, Davis & Dellenbusch, Grand Rapids, 1952—. Mem. Kent County Bd. Commrs., 1968-72, Community Mental Health Bd., 1970—, past chmn.; trustee, sec. bd. Olivet Coll., 1965—; pres. Grand Rapids Historic Preservation, 1977-79. Republican. Trustee, East Congregational Ch., 1979-81. Served with USAAF, 1943-46; Philippines. ABA, Mich. Assn. Professions, Mich. Bar Assn., Grand Rapids Round Table (pres. 1969). Clubs: University, Masons. General practice, Probate, Real property. Home: 30 Mayfair Dr NE Grand Rapids MI 49503 Office: 535 Fountain St NE Grand Rapids MI 49503

DAVIS, JAMES CASEY, lawyer; b. Bloomington, Ind., Feb. 23, 1937; s. Frank Vivian and Cornelia Haven (Casey) D.; m. Delores Mae Evans, 1961 (div. 1975); 1 child, Sarah Haven; m. Frances Joyce Budreck, Aug. 21, 1977; 1 child, Felicia Louisa Budreck. B.A., U. Iowa, 1959, J.D., 1962. Bar: Iowa 1962, U.S. Supreme Ct. 1976. Ptnr. law firm France, Nady & Davis, Tipton, Iowa, 1963-65; exec. sec., gen. counsel Iowa Jr. C. of C., Newton, Iowa, 1965-66; assoc. firm Swanson & Davis, Newton, Iowa, 1966-69, ptnr., 1969-70; Justice of Peace, Newton, Iowa, 1967-70; asst. atty. gen. Iowa Dept. Justice, Des Moines, 1970-79; pvt. practice law, Des Moines, 1979-84; ptnr. Woodward, Davis & Rossi, 1984—; assoc. Environmental Law Inst., 1980-86 ; mediator Iowa Pub. Employment Relations Bd., 1980—, arbitrator, 1983—. Bd. dirs. Iowa chpt. Arthritis Found., 1971—, mem. exec. com., 1976-81, mem. govtl. affairs com., 1976—, chmn. 1977-83, mem. adv. com. 1981-84, , mem. nat. bd. 1976-77; Nat. Vol. Service citation 1984; mem. Iowa State Central Com. Young Republicans, 1970-75; mem. Polk County Rep. Central Com., 1984—, exec. com. 1985—, asst, county co-chmn., 1987—; Rep. candidate Iowa Atty. Gen., 1986; bd. dirs. Newton Community Theatre, 1970-73; leader Explorer Scouts Am., 1963-65. Mem. ABA (chmn. interface com. computer div. econs. sect. 1984-85, editor nat. newsletter, 1985—), Fed. Bar Assn. (pres. Iowa chpt. 1982-83, nat. v.p. 1983—, chmn. nat. computer com. 1984-86, chmn. communication & intellectual property sec. 1986—), Iowa Bar Assn. (computer subcom. 1985—), Polk County Bar Assn., Assn. Trial Lawyers Am., Assn. Trial Lawyers Iowa, Iowa Assn. Arbitrators (treas. 1983—), SAR, Sons and Daus. of Pilgrims, Descs. Colonial Clergy, Order of Crown in Am., Trout Unltd. (pres. Iowa chpt. 1974—), Delta Theta Phi. Federal civil litigation, State civil litigation, Administrative and regulatory. Home: 931 32d St West Des Moines IA 50265 Office: Skywalk Suite 203 700 Walnut St Des Moines IA 50309

DAVIS, JAMES EDWARD, lawyer; b. Snohomish, Wash., Apr. 1, 1948; s. Hugh Edward and Lorraine May (Tronsrud) D.; m. Gail Perry Garretson, Aug. 21, 1970; children: Jennifer, Derrin. BS, Cen. Wash. U., 1970; JD, U. Idaho, 1973. Bar: Wash. 1973, U.S. Dist. Ct. (ea. dist.) Wash. 1976, U.S. Ct. Appeals (9th cir.) 1982, U.S. Supreme Ct. 1982. Dep. prosecuting atty. Yakima County, Yakima, Wash., 1974-81; assoc. Brooks and Larson, Yakima, 1981-83, ptnr., 1983—; v.p., bd. dirs. Columbia Empire Broadcasting Corp., Yakima. Pres. bd. dirs. Yakima County Campfire, 1983-84; pres.-elect bd. dirs.Planned Parenthood of Yakima County, 1986. Mem. ABA, Wash. State Bar Assn., Yakima County Bar Assn., Wash. Assn. Def. Counsel, Wash. Assn. of Counties (chmn. jail standards com. 1979-81). Episcopalian. Lodge: Rotary. State civil litigation, Insurance, Personal injury. Home: Naches Heights Rd Yakima WA 98908 Office: Brooks and Larson 105 N 3d St Yakima WA 98902

DAVIS, JAMES EDWIN, lawyer; b. McAlester, Okla., Jan. 10, 1945; s. Lewis Ward and Margaret Jane (Lindblad) D.; m. Sunnye Susan Stegall, Feb. 20, 1946; children—Ward, Alan, Brian. B.A., U. Tex.-Austin, 1967, J.D., 1969. Bar: Tex. 1969, Ark. 1971, U.S. Dist. Ct. (ea. dist.) Tex., U.S. Dist. Ct. (ea. and we. dists.) Ark., U.S. Dist. Ct. (ea. dist.) Okla., U.S. Ct. Apls. (5th and 8th cir.), U.S. Sup. Ct. Sole practice, Texarkana, Ark., 1969—; pub. defender County of Miller, Ark., 1978-80. Vice pres. ACLU of Ark., 1979—. Mem. State Bar Tex., Tex. Criminal Def. Lawyers Assn., Tex. Assn. Bd. Cert. Specialists in Criminal Law, Delta Theta Phi. Criminal, General practice, Civil rights. Address: 711 Pecan St Texarkana AR 75502

DAVIS, JAMES FRANCIS, lawyer; b. Chester, Pa., Mar. 14, 1947; s. Paul Lamoyne and Kathryn Cora (Stump) D.; m. Patricia Ann Hewson, Aug. 7, 1971; children—Michael Brandon, Victoria Ashley. B.A., Columbia Coll., 1969; J.D., Villanova U., 1972. Bar: Del. 1973, Pa. 1973, U.S. Dist. Ct. Del. 1973, U.S. Ct. Appeals (3d cir.) 1983. Jud. law clk. Superior Ct. New Castle County, Wilmington, Del., 1972-73; assoc. Biondi & Babiarz, Wilmington, 1973-79, Morris, Nichols, Arsht & Tunnell, Wilmington, 1979-83; counsel I, Hercules, Inc., Wilmington, 1983—. Mem. ABA, Del. Bar Assn. (sec. comml. law sect. 1983-84). Republican. Roman Catholic. Federal civil litigation, State civil litigation, Product liability. Home: 138 Marcella Rd Wilmington DE 19803 Office: Hercules Inc Hercules Plaza Wilmington DE 19894

DAVIS, JAMES HORNOR, III, lawyer; b. Clarksburg, W.Va., Oct. 9, 1928; s. James Hornor II and Martha (Maxwell) D.; m. Ouida Caldwell, July 1, 1950; children—James Hornor IV, Lewis Caldwell. A.B., Princeton U., 1950; LL.B., U. Va., 1953. Bar: W.Va. 1953. Ptnr. firm Preston & Davis, Charleston, 1953-65, Spilman, Thomas, Battle & Klostermeyer, Charleston, 1965-86; of counsel Campbell, Woods, Bagley, Emerson McNeer & Herndon, Charleston, 1986—; Mem. W.Va. Ho. of Dels., 1961-62, W.Va. Senate, 1963-66; pres. Dingess-Rum Coal Co. Served with USAF, 1953-55. Fellow ABA; mem. Am. Law Inst., Am. Judicature Soc. (dir. 1978-81), W.Va. Jud. Council (chmn. 1973-81), W.Va. Bar Assn. (pres. 1985-86), Kanawha County Bar Assn., Nat. Council Coal Lessors (pres.), W.Va. Mfrs. Assn. (chmn. 1973-75, dir.). Democrat. Episcopalian. Office: Campbell Woods Bagley Emerson McNeer & Herndon PO Box 2393 Charleston WV 25328-2393

DAVIS, JAMES JULIAN, lawyer; b. Boise, Idaho, Dec. 31, 1953; s. Patrick H. and Eleanor G. (Johnson) D.; m. Belinda Kay Henry, June 14, 1975; children: Elly Grace Annabelle, Hallie Rose Kersey. BA, Boise State U., 1975; JD, U. Idaho, 1977. Bar: Idaho 1978, U.S. Dist. Ct. Idaho 1978. Ptnr. Eberle, Berlin, Kading, Turnbow & Gillespie, Boise, 1978—. Mem. ABA, Idaho Bar Assn., Boise Bar Assn. Avocations: softball, tennis, fishing, backpacking, running. Civil rights, Insurance, Federal civil litigation. Home: 2282 Cornhusk Ct Boise ID 83706 Office: Eberle Berlin Kading Turnbow & Gillespie 300 N 6th St Boise ID 83702

DAVIS, JAMES THOMAS, lawyer; b. Uniontown, Pa., Oct. 17, 1951; s. Norman J. and Thelma (Solomon) D.; m. Martha Russin, Sept. 4, 1976; children—Cara Catherine, Jeremy James, Adina Ann. B.A., California State Coll., Pa., 1973; J.D., Duquesne U., 1976. Bar: Pa. 1976, U.S. Dist. Ct. (we. dist.) Pa. 1976, U.S. Supreme Ct. 1984. Asst. dist. atty. Fayette County, Pa., 1977-83; ptnr. firm Davis & Davis, Uniontown, Pa., 1976—. Mem. Pa. Trial Lawyers Assn., Assn. Trial Lawyers Am. Democrat. Eastern Orthodox. Personal injury, Probate, Criminal. Office: Davis & Davis 107 E Main St Uniontown PA 15401

DAVIS, JEFFREY J., lawyer; b. Seattle, May 24, 1947; s. Eugene Howard and Carol June (Archdale) D.; m. Mary Frances Elder, Mar. 2, 1968 (div. Oct. 1983); children: Jennifer, Matthew, Michael; m. Sue Ann Patterson, Nov. 16, 1985; children: Christy, Jennifer. BS in Bus. Adminstrn., U. Ill., 1972, JD, 1975. Bar: N.C., U.S. Dist. Ct. (ea., mid. and we. dists.) N.C., U.S. Ct. Appeals (4th cir.), U.S. Supreme Ct. Law clk. to presiding justice U.S. Dist. Ct., Charlotte, N.C., 1975-76; assoc. Moore, Van Allen et al, Charlotte, 1976-81, ptnr., 1981—. Served to sgt. USMC, 1966-70, Vietnam. Mem. ABA, N.C. Bar Assn., Order of Coif. Avocations: skiing, racquetball, running. Federal civil litigation, State civil litigation, Securities. Home: 3410 Selwyn Ave Charlotte NC 28209 Office: Moore Van Allen et al 3000 NCNB Plaza Charlotte NC 28280

DAVIS, JESSE DUNBAR, lawyer, consultant; b. Burden, Kans., June 19, 1908; s. Jesse Bowman and Hazel (Dunbar) D.; m. Frances Lou Vinson, June 19, 1929; children—Brett Vinson and Sydney Davis Dove (twins). Student U. Okla., Norman, 1926-28; LL.B., U. Tulsa, 1944. Bar: Okla. 1944, U.S. Dist. Ct. (no. dist.) Okla., 1944, U.S. Ct. Apls. (10th cir.) 1946, U.S. Supreme Ct. 1950, Mo. 1959, U.S. Dist. Ct. (we. dist.) Mo. 1959, U.S. Ct. Apls. (8th cir.) 1960. Sole practice, Tulsa, Okla., 1946—, Joplin, Mo., 1959, Kansas City, Mo., 1960-65, Claremore, Okla., 1969-79; asst. mgr. Longbell Lumber Co., Claremore, 1928-29, Clinton, Okla., 1929-30, Muskogee, Okla., 1930-32, mgr., Pauls Valley, Okla., 1932-33, gen. mgr., Tulsa, 1933-48, div. mgr., Kansas City, 1949-57; v.p., dir. Tamko Asphalt Products, Inc., Joplin, 1958-59; gen. counsel Southwestern Lumbermen's Assn., Kansas City, 1960-65, corp. sec., 1962-65; tchr. bus. law U. Mo., 1946-65, real estate law U. Tulsa, 1969-76; lectr. in field. Served to lt. USN, 1944-46, legal officer, 1945-46. Recipient Civic award Tulsa C. of C. 1939, Tulsa YMCA, 1946-47, chartered Assn. Exec. award Am. Soc. Assn. Execs., 1964. Mem. ABA, Okla. Bar Assn., Mo. Bar Assn., Kansas City Bar Assn., Rogers County Bar Assn., Tulsa County Bar Assn., Nat. Assn. Realtors, Met. Tulsa Bd. Realtors (bd. dirs. 1970-72, treas. 1971, corp. sec. 1972), Am. Judicature Soc., Phi Delta Theta, Phi Beta Gamma, Mid Am. Lumbermens Assn., Tulsa Lumbermens Assn. (pres. 1941-42), Okla. Heritage Assn., Okla. Hist. Soc., Tulsa County Hist. Soc., Nat. Lumber and Bldg. Materials Assn. (bd. dirs. 1963-65), Navy League U.S. Soc., SAR, Sons Am. Colonists, Am. Legion, Res. Officers Assn. U.S. Republican. Presbyterian. Club: University (charter). Lodge: Kiwanis Internat. (pres. Tulsa 1941, sect. treas. Tex.-Okla. dist. 1942). Estate planning, General practice, Real property. Address: 3231 S Utica Ave Tulsa OK 74105-2125

DAVIS, JIMMY FRANK, lawyer; b. Lubbock, Tex., June 14, 1945; s. Jack and Fern Lisemby D.; m. Joyce Zelma Hart, Nov. 6, 1976; children: Jayme Leigh, Julee Ellen. B.S. in Edn., Tex. Tech. U., 1968; J.D. U. Tex., 1972. Bar: Tex. 1972, U.S. Supreme Ct. 1975, U.S. Dist. (no. dist.) Tex. 1976, U.S. Ct. Appeals (5th cir.) 1976, U.S. Ct. Appeals (11 cir.) 1981. Asst. criminal dist. atty. Lubbock County, Tex., 1973-76, adminstrv. asst. for office, 1976-77; county and dist. atty. Castro County, Tex., 1977—. Mem. ABA, Nat. Dist. Attys. Assn., Tex. Dist. and County Attys. Assn., Lubbock County Jr. Bar Assn. (pres. 1977), Tex. Tech. Ex Students Assn. (dist. rep. 1981-84, bd. dirs, 1985—), Coll. of State Bar of Tex. (continuing legal edn. 1984—), Delta Theta Phi. Baptist. Club: Kiwanis of Lubbock (pres. 1977), Kiwanis of Dimmitt (pres. 1981). Criminal, Juvenile, State civil litigation. Office: Castro County Courthouse Dimmitt TX 79027

DAVIS, JIMMY KYLE, lawyer, state legislator; b. Knoxville, Tenn., Jan. 31, 1954; s. Jess W. and Elsie (Nelson) D.; m. Susan Cox, June 21, 1974; 1 child, Judson Kyle. BS, U. Tenn., 1976, JD, 1980. Bar: Tenn. 1981, U.S. Dist. Ct. (ea. dist.) Tenn.; cert. tchr. Ptnr. Garrett, Coffee & Davis, Knoxville, 1981-82; dist. atty. gen. Knox County, Knoxville, 1982-84; ptnr. Claiborne, Davis, Buuck & Hurley, Knoxville, 1984—; state rep. 94th and 95th Gen. Assembly Tenn., Nashville, 1985—; owner Lawson's Industries, Morristown, Tenn.; mem. House Judiciary Com., Nashville, 1985—, House State and Local Govt. com., Nashville, 1985—, corrections subcom.; chmn. Internat. Trade and Export Devel. Study Com.; asst. minority floor leader. Mem. Rep. exec. com. Knox County, Knoxville, 1978—; mem. Knox County Young Reps., treas. 1984; pres. 8th Dist. Rep. Club, 1984. Recipient Achievement award Found. for Improvement of Justice, Inc., 1986; named Knox County Young Rep. Yr., 1984, one of Outstanding Young Men Am., Jaycees, 1985. Mem. ABA (sect. on internat. law and practice), Tenn. Bar Assn., Knox County Bar Assn., Assn. Trial Lawyers Am., Assn. Tenn. Trial Lawyers, Tenn. Assn. Criminal Def. Attys. Lodges: Odd Fellows, Optimists, Elks. Avocation: horses. Criminal, Legislative, Personal injury. Office: Claiborne Davis Buuck & Hurley 713 Market St Suite 300 Knoxville TN 37902-2396

DAVIS, JOHN PHILLIPS, JR., lawyer; b. Pitts., June 1, 1925; s. John Phillips and Jean Stout (Miller) D.; m. Mary McCreery Oates, Sept. 13, 1952; children: George B., John P. III, Elizabeth M., Mary O. Student, Williams Coll.; A.B., Harvard U., 1947, J.D., 1950. Bar: Pa. 1951. Since practiced in Pitts; partner Reed Smith Shaw & McClay, 1961—; dir. Firth Stirling Inc., Pitts. Gage and Supply Co., Bloom Engring. Co., Inc. Bd. dirs. Staunton Farm Found., 1964—, pres., 1968-85, Vis. Nurse Assn. Allegheny County, 1955-68, pres., 1962-64, Met. Pitts. Pub. Broadcasting Inc. Sta. WQED, 1984—; trustee Shady Side Acad., Pitts., 1959—, chmn., 1971-74; trustee Ellis Sch., Pitts., 1969-74; bd. dirs. Pitts. Child Guidance Ctr., 1960-63; trustee Robert S. Waters Charitable Trust, 1971—; bd. dirs. Snyder Found., 1979—; trustee Carnegie Inst., 1985—. Served with AUS, 1943-45, ETO. Decorated Bronze Star, Purple Heart. Mem. Am. Law Inst., ABA, Pa. Bar Assn. (chmn. jr. bar conf. 1957), Allegheny County Bar Assn. (pres. jr. bar sect. 1955). Republican. Episcopalian. Clubs: Duquesne, Fox Chapel Golf (bd. dirs., sec. 1985—), Harvard-Yale-Princeton (Pitts.). General practice, Probate. Home: 144 North Dr Pittsburgh PA 15238 Office: 435 6th Ave PO Box 2009 Pittsburgh PA 15230

DAVIS, JOHN WHITTAKER, lawyer, developer; b. Houston, Sept. 19, 1947; s. John W. and Martha (Sneed) D.; m. Algenita Scott, Aug. 21, 1976; 1 child, Marthea. BS, U. Houston, 1972; JD, South Tex. Coll. Law, 1975. Bar: Tex., U.S. Dist. Ct. (so. dist.) Tex., U.S. Ct. Appeals (5th cir.), U.S. Supreme Ct. Programmer Tenneco Inc., Houston, 1967-69; v.p. Judson W. Robinson & Sons, Houston, 1970-80; ptnr. Robinson & Davis, Houston, 1980—. Bd. dirs. Houston Health Facilities Devel. Corp., Houston, 1986. Mem. ABA, Nat. Bar Assn., Houston Bar Assn., Houston Lawyers. Democrat. Real property, Personal injury, Probate. Home: 3340 S MacGregor Houston TX 77021 Office: 2905 Elgin Houston TX 77004

DAVIS, JONATHAN DAVID, lawyer; b. N.Y.C., Oct. 23, 1957; s. Nathan Leon and Dora Rose (Tuchman) D. AB, Franklin and Marshall Coll., 1979; JD, Villanova U., 1982. Bar: N.J. 1982, N.Y. 1983. Assoc. Jaffe & Asher, N.Y.C., 1982-84, Certilman, Haft, Lebow, Balin, Buckley & Kremer, N.Y.C., 1984-87, Gold, Farrell & Marks, N.Y.C., 1987—. Mem. ABA, N.Y. State Bar Assn., N.J. Bar Assn., N.Y. County Lawyers Assn (Profl. ethics com. 1984—). Federal civil litigation, State civil litigation.

DAVIS, JOSLIN, lawyer; b. Raleigh, N.C., Dec. 30, 1951; d. Marion Johnson and Carrie (Chamberlain) D.; m. Fred R. Harwell Jr., Aug. 12, 1980; children: Scott Robinson, Josh Chamberlain. BA, U. Ga., 1974; JD, Wake Forest U., 1977. Bar: N.C. 1977, Fla. 1978, D.C. 1978, U.S. Dist. Ct. (mid. dist.) N.C. 1978. Asst. dist. atty. Cumberland County, Fayetteville, N.C., 1977-78, Wake County, Raleigh, 1978-79; ptnr. Cheshire & Davis, Raleigh, 1980, Davis & Harwell P.A., Winston-Salem, N.C., 1980—. Mem. Jr. League of Winston-Salem, 1975-77, 80-84, Jr. League of Raleigh, 1979-80; pres. elect Planned Parenthood of the Triad, 1985, bd. dirs., 1981-85; bd. of law visitors Wake Forest U., 1980—; advising bd. dirs. Family Services, Inc., 1985; bd. dirs. YWCA of Winston-Salem, 1981-83. Mem. ABA (Ho. of Dels., young lawyers rep. 1980-82), N.C. Bar Assn. (liaison com., ethics com., family law sect., estate and probate sect.), Wake County Bar Assn. (bd. dirs. 1980), Forsyth County Bar Assn. (long range planning com., nominating com., treas. , sec. 1985-86), Fla. Bar Assn., D.C. Bar Assn., N.C. Assn. Women Attys., N.C. Acad. Trial Lawyers (pub. service and information com., membership com.). Democrat. Methodist. State civil litigation, Family and matrimonial, Personal injury. Home: 2760 Old Town Club Rd Winston-Salem NC 27106 Office: 1144 W 4th St Winston-Salem NC 27101

DAVIS, KENNETH BOONE, JR., law educator; b. Louisville, Sept. 1, 1947; s. Kenneth Boone and Doris Edna (Gordon) D. m. Arrietta Evoline Hastings, June 2, 1984; 1 child, Peter Hastings. AB, U. Mich., 1969; JD, Case Western Res. U., 1974. Bar: D.C. 1975, Ohio 1974. Law clk. to chief judge U.S. Ct. Appeals (9th cir.), San Francisco, 1974-75; assoc. Covington & Burling, Washington, 1975-78; prof. law U. Wis., Madison, 1978—. Contbr. numerous articles on corp. and securities law to profl jours. Mem. ABA, Am. Fin. Assn., Wis. Bar Assn. (reporter, corp. and bus. law com.). General corporate, Securities, Legal education. Office: U Wis Law Sch 975 Bascom Mall Madison WI 53706

DAVIS, LOUIS POISSON, JR., lawyer, consultant; b. Washington, July 17, 1919; s. Louis Poisson and Edna (Shethar) D.; m. Emily Elizabeth Carl, Mar. 9, 1922; 1 dau., Cynthia. B.Sc., U.S. Naval Acad., 1941; postgrad. Princeton U., 1947-48; J.D., Rutgers U., 1953. Bar: N.Y. 1954, Ill. 1963, U.S. Supreme Ct. 1964, U.S. Dist. Ct. (so. dist.) N.Y. 1956, U.S. Dist. Ct. (no. dist.) Ill. 1965. Mgr. engring. Esso Standard Oil, Linden, N.J., 1946-57; sr. economist, head econs. and market research dept. Internat. Petroleum Co., Lima, Peru, 1957-60; asst. overseas ops. AMF Internat, N.Y.C., 1961-62; sr. atty. Internat. Abbott Labs., North Chicago, Ill., 1962-65; gen. mgr. Far East ops. Ralston Purina Co., pres. Ralston Purina Eastern, Hong Kong, 1966-71; dir. internat. devel. Archer Daniels Midland Co., v.p. Archer Daniels Midland Internat., Decatur, Ill., 1972-74; lectr., researcher internat. law and mgmt., N.Y.C., 1974-76; corp. rep. Europe, Mid East, Africa, Alexander & Baldwin Agribus., Inc., Abidjan, Ivory Coast, 1976, Madrid, Spain, 1977; internat. atty., cons., Sarasota, Fla., 1978—; mem. ad hoc task force on Extraterritorial Application of Antitrust Laws, 1983; cons. Sarasota County Office of Scientific Advisor, 1985-86; vol. income tax assistance program IRS, 1983—; gen. counsel Manasota Industry Council Inc., bd. dirs. Exxon Annutant Club of Sarasota-Monatee Counties, Inc., 1986—, also v.p. Served to lt. comdr. USN, 1937-46. Recipient Pres. Bonus, Ralston Purina Co., 1969, 70, Mem. Am. Bar Assn. (com. internat. taxation, com. internat. aspects of antitrust laws, com. internat. trade). Republican. Episcopalian. Clubs: Hong Kong Country; Army and Navy (Washington). General corporate, Public international, Personal income taxation. Home and Office: 620 Mangrove Point Rd Sarasota FL 34242

DAVIS, MALLORY DONALD, JR., lawyer; b. Tuscaloosa, Ala., Apr. 10, 1957; s. Mallory Donald Davis and Nell Joan (Allen) Bell; m. Laura Elizabeth Davis, Aug. 2, 1980. BA, U. South Ala., 1978; JD, Samford U., 1981. Bar: Ala. 1981, U.S. Dist. Ct. (so. dist.) Ala. 1981, U.S. Ct. Appeals (11th cir.) 1986. Assoc. McDermott, Slepian, Windom & Reed, Mobile, Ala., 1981-87, Sirote, Permutt, McDermott, Slepiam, Friend, Freidman, Held and Apolinsky. Assoc. editor Am. Jour. Trial Advocacy, 1979-81. Mem. ABA, Ala. Bar Assn., Assn. Trial Lawyers Am., Ala. Trial Lawyers Assn., Am. Bankruptcy Inst., Kappa Alpha (sec. Mobile alumni chpt. 1984—). Methodist. Lodge: Kiwanis. Avocations: sailing, music. Bankruptcy, General corporate, Real property. Home: 4824 Janice Dr Mobile AL 36618 Office: Sirote Permutt McDermott et al PO Drawer 2025 Mobile AL 36652

DAVIS, MARTHA ALGENITA SCOTT, lawyer; b. Houston, Oct. 1, 1950; d. C.B. Scott and Althea (Lewis) Scott Renfro; m. John Whittaker Davis, III, Aug. 21, 1976; 1 child, Marthea. B.B.A., Howard U., 1971, J.D., 1974. Bar: Tex. 1974, U.S. Dist. Ct. (so. dist.) Tex. 1975, U.S. Ct. Appeals (5th cir.) 1976, U.S. Supreme Ct. 1980. Tax atty. Shell Oil Co., Houston, 1974-79; counsel Port of Houston Authority, 1979—; ptnr. Burney, Edwards, Hall, Hartsfield & Scott, Houston, 1975-78; bd. dirs. Unity Nat. Bank. Bd. dirs. Houston Citizens Chamber, 1980-87, Neighborhood Ednl. Ctr., Houston, 1983-87, Peoples' Workshop to Performing Arts; coordinator Operation Big Vote, Washington, 1984-85; mem. planning commn. City of Houston, 1987-89. Recipient Achievement award Greek Council, Houston, 1973; Houston's Most Influential Black Women award Black Experience Mag. Mem. Nat. Bar Assn. (sec. 1983—, chmn. voter edn./registration com. 1985-86, pres. award 1983), Black Women Lawyers Assn. (vice chair 1983-84, profl. achievement award 1984), Houston Lawyers Assn. (bd. dirs. 1977-78, 85-86). Baptist. Club: Links (Houston) (fin. sec. 1982-83). General corporate, Admiralty, Landlord-tenant. Office: Port of Houston Authority PO Box 2562 Houston TX 77252

DAVIS, MICHAEL A., lawyer; b. Bethesda, Md., July 8, 1955; s. Donald Keith Davis and Carrie Leone (ALexander) Hung. BA, Shippensburg State (Pa.) Coll., 1977; JD, Wake Forest U., 1980. Bar: Nev. 1980, Wash. 1984. Atty. Deaner & Deaner, Las Vegas, 1980-82, Dickerson, Miles, et al, Las Vegas, 1982-83, Carney & Stephenson, Seattle, 1983-84; asst. gen. counsel Church's Fried Chicken, Inc., San Antonio, Tex., 1984—; instr. bus. law, real estate U Nev., Las Vegas, 1980-83. Mem. Nat. Right to Work Com., 1977—, Rutherford Inst., 1983—; bd.dirs. Red Cross, Las Vegas, 1982, Woman's Crisis Ctr., 1981-83. Named one of Outstanding Young Men Am., 1984. Mem. ABA, The Federalist Soc., Phi Alpha Theta, Alpha Phi Omega. Republican. Episcopalian. General corporate, Real property, State civil litigation. Home: 11815 Vance Jackson #602 San Antonio TX 78284 Office: church's Fried Chicken PO Box BH001 San Antonio TX 78284

DAVIS, MICHAEL JAMES, university dean, law educator, lawyer; b. Clay Center, Kans., Aug. 31, 1942; s. Maynard James and Florence Mathilda (Steffen) D.; m. Jacqueline Zurat, Dec. 13, 1969; children—Adam Steffen, Ashley Michelle. B.A., magna cum laude, Kans. State U., 1964; J.D. cum laude, U. Mich., 1967. Bar: Mo. 1968, Kans. 1972, U.S. Dist. Ct. Kans. 1972, U.S. Ct. Appeals (10th cir.) 1976. Assoc. Arent, Fox, Kinter, Plotkin & Kahn, Washington, 1967; Reginald Heber Smith fellow, Kansas City, Mo., 1967-68; legis. asst. to Congressman Louis Stokes, Washington, 1969-71; assoc. prof. law U. Kans.-Lawrence, 1971-74, gen. counsel, prof., 1974-80, dean Sch. Law, prof., 1980—. Recipient Rice prize Kans. U. Law Sch., 1975, 84; named Outstanding Young Men Am., U.S. Jaycees, 1976. Fellow Am. Bar Found.; mem. ABA, Kans. Bd. for Admissions of Attys. Editor Mich. Law Rev., 1966-67. Legal education, Real property. Office: Green Hall 1601 High Dr Lawrence KS 66044

DAVIS, MULLER, lawyer; b. Chgo., Apr. 23, 1935; s. Benjamin B. and Janice (Muller) D.; m. Jane Lynn Strauss, Dec. 28, 1963; children: Melissa Jane, Muller, Joseph Jeffrey. Grad. with honors, Phillips Exeter (N.H.) Acad., 1953; B.A. magna cum laude, Yale U., 1957; J.D., Harvard U., 1960. Bar: Ill. 1960, U.S. Dist. Ct. (no. dist.) Ill. 1961. Practice law Chgo., 1960—; assoc. Jenner & Block, 1960-67; ptnr. Davis, Friedman, Zavett, Kane & MacRae, 1967—; lectr. continuing legal edn., matrimonial law and litigation Legal adviser Michael Reese Med. Research Inst. Council, 1967-82. Contbr. articles to law jours.; author (with Sherman C. Feinstein) The Parental Couple in a Successful Divorce; mem. editorial bd. Equitable Distbn. Jour., 1984—. Bd. dirs. Infant Welfare Soc., 1975—, pres., 1978-82. Served to capt. U.S. Army, Ill. N.G., 1960-67. Fellow Am. Acad. Matrimonial Lawyers; mem. Fed. Bar Assn., ABA, Ill. Bar Assn., Chgo. Bar Assn. (matrimonial com., sec. civil practice com. 1979-80, vice chmn. 1980-81, chmn. 1981-82), Chgo. Estate Planning Council, Law Club Chgo. Republican. Jewish. Clubs: Tavern, Lake Shore Country. Family and matrimonial, State civil litigation. Home: 1020 E Westleigh Rd Lake Forest IL 60045 Office: 140 S Dearborn St Chicago IL 60603

DAVIS, OSCAR HIRSH, U.S. judge; b. N.Y.C., Feb. 27, 1914; s. Jacob and Minnie (Robison) D. AB, Harvard U., 1934; LLB, Columbia U., 1937. Bar: N.Y. 1938. Pvt. practice N.Y.C., 1937-39; with Dept. Justice, 1939-42, 46-62, first asst. to solicitor gen., 1954-62; assoc. judge U.S. Ct. Claims, 1962-82, acting chief judge, 1977-78; judge U.S. Ct. Appeals (fed. cir.), 1982—. Served to capt. USAAF, 1942-46. Mem. Am., Fed. bar assns., Am. Law Inst., N.Y. County Lawyers Assn., N.Y. State Bar Assn. Jurisprudence. Home: 1101 3d St SW Washington DC 20024 Office: US Ct Appeals Fed Cir Washington DC 20439

DAVIS, PENELOPE ANN, lawyer; b. Kennedy, Ala., Feb. 14, 1952; d. John William and Mary Evelyn (Keenum) D.; m. Eugene B. Williams, May 10, 1984; 1 child, Lance Christopher. BS, U. Ala., 1973, MA, 1974, JD, 1978. Bar: Ala. 1978, U.S. Ct. Appeals (5th cir.) 1979, U.S. Ct. Appeals (11th cir.) 1981. Law clk. to sr. justice U.S. Ct. Appeals (5th cir.), Tuscaloosa, Ala., 1978-79; assoc. dir. Ala. Law Inst., University, 1979—; adj. faculty law U. Ala., 1984—. Mem. citizen adv. com. State Jail Standard, 1981, Ala. Victim/Witness Resource Task Force, 1981-82, Ala. Domestic Violence Commn., 1981-82. Named one of Outstanding Young Women of Am., 1984. Mem. ABA, Ala. Bar Assn. Baptist. Avocation: sports. Legislative, Legal education, Family and matrimonial. Home: 21 Englewood Dr Tuscaloosa AL 35405 Office: Ala Law Inst PO Box 1425 University AL 35486

DAVIS, PHILIP CARL, lawyer; b. Mansfield, Ohio, Mar. 22, 1949; s. Harry O. and Bernice (Tracy) D. B.A., U. Toledo, 1971; J.D., Ohio No. U., 1976. Bar: Ohio 1977. Assoc. DeMuth & John, Toledo, 1977-80, ptnr.,

1981—; solicitor Village of Whitehouse, Ohio, 1978—. Mem. Wood County Democratic Exec. Com., Ohio, 1977—. Mem. ABA, Toledo Bar Assn., Ohio Bar Assn. Democrat. Lutheran. Club: Ducks Unltd. Lodge: Masons. Avocations: fly fishing, waterfowl hunting, skiing. Contracts commercial, General corporate, Real property. Home: 305 Martindale Rd Bowling Green OH 43402 Office: DeMuth & John 626 Madison Ave Suite 700 Toledo OH 43604

DAVIS, RICHARD JOEL, lawyer, former govt. ofcl.; b. N.Y.C., Mar. 27, 1946; s. Herbert H. and Sylvia (Ginesin) D. B.A., U. Rochester, 1966; J.D., Columbia U., 1969. Bar: N.Y. State bar 1970. Law clk. to Judge Jack B. Weinstein, U.S. Dist. Ct. for Eastern Dist. N.Y., 1969-70; asst. U.S. atty. So. Dist. N.Y., 1970-73; task force leader Watergate Spl. Prosecution Force, Washington, 1973-75; assoc. Weil, Gotshal and Manges, N.Y.C., 1976-77; partner Weil, Gotshal and Manges, 1981—; asst. sec. of the treasury for enforcement and ops. Dept. Treasury, Washington, 1977-81; instr. in trial advocacy Harvard U.; instr. Nat. Inst. Trial Advocacy. Mem. Am. Bar Assn. Federal civil litigation, Private international. Office: Weil Gotshal & Manges 767 Fifth Ave New York NY 10153

DAVIS, RICHARD RALPH, lawyer; b. Houston, July 28, 1936; s. William Ralph and Virginia (Allison) D.; m. Christina R. Zelkoff, June 1, 1974; 1 dau., Virginia Lee Allison. B.A., Yale U., 1962, LL.B., 1965; M.B.A., Columbia U., 1965. Bar: N.Y. 1966. Law clk. FAA, Washington, 1964; assoc. Chadbourne & Parke, N.Y.C., 1965-73, ptnr., 1974-83; sr. v.p., gen. counsel Inspiration Resources Corp., N.Y.C., 1983—, also dir. Served with U.S. Army, 1956-59. Mem. Assn. Bar City N.Y., ABA. General corporate, Antitrust. Home: 1185 Park Ave Apt 6-G New York NY 10128

DAVIS, RICHARD WATERS, lawyer; b. Rocky Mount, Va., July 9, 1931; s. Beverly Andrew and Julia (Waters) D.; m. Mary Alice Woods, Nov. 28, 1957; children: Debra, Julie, Richard Jr., Bob, Bev. B, Hampden-Sydney Coll., 1951; LLB, U. Richmond, 1959. Bar: Va. 1959. Sole practice Radford, Va., 1959—; dist. judge City of Radford, 1962-80. Personal injury, Insurance, State civil litigation. Home: 101 5th St Radford VA 24141 Office: PO Box 3448 Radford VA 24143

DAVIS, ROBERT LAWRENCE, lawyer; b. Cin., Apr. 5, 1928; s. Bryan and Henrietta Elizabeth (Weber) D.; m. Mary Lee Schulte, June 14, 1952; children—Gregory, Randy, Jenny, Bradley. B.A., U. Cin., 1952; J.D., Salmon P. Chase Coll. Law, 1958. Bar: Ohio, 1958, U.S. Supreme Ct. 1966. Assoc. Trabert & Gay, Cin., 1958-62; ptnr. Trabert, Gay & Davis, Cin., 1962-68, Gay, Davis & Kelly, Cin., 1969-71; sole practice, Cin., 1972—; lectr. Mt. St. Joseph Coll, 1972-82; arbitrator Am. Arbitration Assn.; assoc. adj. prof. Salmon P. Chase Coll. Sch. Law, 1969-80; lectr. Good Samaritan Hosp. Sch. Nursing, 1960-71. Pres. bd. trustees Community Ltd. Care Dialysis Ctr., 1978—; mem. Hamilton County Ohio Hosp. Commn., 1986. Served to capt. U.S. Army, 1946-48, 52-53. Decorated Army Commendation medal, Bronze Star medal. Fellow Am. Coll. Trial Lawyers, Ohio Assn. Civil Trial Attys.; mem. ABA, Ohio Bar Assn., Cin. Bar Assn., Assn. Trial Lawyers Am., Am. Assn. R.R. Trial Counsel, Phi Delta Theta, Phi Alpha Delta, Sigma Sigma, Omicron Delta Kappa. Club: Lawyers (pres. 1962-63). Lodges: Order of Curia, K.C. Personal injury, State civil litigation, Probate. Home: 5619 Colerain Ave Cincinnati OH 45239 Office: 3600 Carew Tower Cincinnati OH 45202

DAVIS, ROGER EDWIN, lawyer; b. Lakewood, Ohio, Dec. 29, 1928; s. Russell G. and Irma (Aboline) D.; m. Eva Grace Keeler, July 25, 1953 (div. Feb. 1980); children: Susan Lee, Lisa Ann, Steven Russell; m. Yvonne L. Berich, June 1, 1980. A.B., Harvard U., 1950; LL.B., U. Mich., 1953. Bar: Mich. 1953. Practice in Detroit 1955—; asso. Langs, Molyneaux & Armstrong, 1955-60; counsel Avis Enterprises, 1961-62; with legal dept. S.S. Kresge Co. (now Kmart Corp.), 1963-70, v.p., gen. counsel, sec., 1970-85, sr. v.p., gen. counsel, sec., 1985—. Trustee Arnold Home. Served with AUS, 1953-55. Mem. State Bar Mich., Fla. Bar, ABA, Am. Soc. Corp. Secs. Club: Pine Lake Country. General corporate, Antitrust, Contracts commercial. Home: 3234 Pine Lake Rd Orchard Lake MI 48033 Office: K Mart Corp 3100 W Big Beaver Rd Troy MI 48084

DAVIS, RONALD LEE, lawyer; b. Kennedy, Ala., Apr. 8, 1949; s. John William and Mary Evelyn (Keenum) D. B.S., U. Ala., 1971, J.D., 1976. Bar: Ala. 1976, U.S. Supreme Ct. 1981. Law clk. U.S. Dist. Ct., Birmingham, Ala., 1977; assoc. Hand, Arendell, Bedsole, Greaves & Johnston, Mobile, Ala., 1978-80; ptnr. Roberts, Davidson, Wiggins & Davis, Tuscaloosa, Ala., 1981-83, Hubbard, Waldrop, Reynolds, Davis & McIlwain, Tuscaloosa, 1984—; adj. prof. law U. Ala., Tuscaloosa, 1982—. Articles editor Ala. Law Rev., 1974-76, Mem. Ala. Def. Lawyers Assn., Ala. Trial Lawyers Assn., Jasons, Omicron Delta Kappa. Democrat. Presbyterian. State civil litigation, Insurance, Personal injury. Home: 27 Pinehurst Tuscaloosa AL 35401 Office: Hubbard Waldrop Reynolds Davis & McIlwain 808 Lurleen Wallace Blvd N Tuscaloosa AL 35401

DAVIS, ROY WALTON, JR., lawyer; b. Marion, N.C., Jan. 15, 1930; s. Roy Walton and Mildred Gertrude (Wilson) D.; m. Madeline Burch Combs, Sept. 10, 1955; children: R. Walton III, Madeline Trent, Rebekah Wilson, Sally Fielding. BS, Davidson Coll., 1952; JD with honors, U. N.C., 1955. Bar: N.C. 1955, U.S. Dist. Ct. (we. dist.) N.C. 1960, U.S. Ct. Appeals (4th cir.) 1963. Ptnr. Davis & Davis, Marion, 1959-60; from assoc. to ptnr. Van Winkle, Buck, Wall, Starnes & Davis, Asheville, N.C., 1960—. Chancellor Episc. Diocese of Western N.C., Black Mountain, 1980—; bd. dirs. Meml. Mission Hosp. Western N.C., Asheville, 1981—. Served with U.S. Army, 1956-59. Fellow Am. Bar found., Am. Coll. Trial Lawyers; mem. ABA (tort and ins. practice sect., nat. conf. bar pres.), N.C. Bar Assn. (chmn. young lawyers div. 1965-66), N.C. State Bar (pres. 1985-86), N.C. Assn. Def. Attys., Order of Coif. Democrat. State civil litigation, Federal civil litigation, Insurance. Home: 359 Country Club Rd Asheville NC 28804 Office: Van Winkle Buck Wall Starnes & Davis 11 N Market St Asheville NC 28801

DAVIS, RUSSELL H., lawyer; b. Pikeville, Ky., Aug. 26, 1956; s. Russell H. and Leelah (Robards) D.; m. Mary E. Kandrick, Nov. 4, 1978; children: Kate E., Laura K. BS in Acctg., U. Ky., 1978; JD, No. Ky. U., 1981. Bar: Ky. 1981, U.S. Dist. Ct. (ea. dist.) 1982, U.S. Ct. Appeals (6th cir.) 1983. Acct. Kelley & GFalloway CPA, Ashland, Ky., 1978; assoc. Stratton, May & Hays P.S.C., Pikeville, Ky., 1981—. Mem. ABA, Ky. Bar Assn., Ky. Def. Counsel. Republican. Methodist. Contracts commercial, State civil litigation, Federal civil litigation. Office: Stratton & Hayes PSC 2d St Ward Bldg Pikeville KY 41501

DAVIS, S. P., lawyer; b. Shreveport, La., Nov. 2, 1949; s. Andrew Sr. and Lacy (Harris) D.; m. Sharon Antoinette Dunnings, July 28, 1979; children: Kharmen Kanessa, S. P. Jr. BA, So. U., 1971, JD, 1973. Bar: La. 1974, U.S. Dist. Ct. (we. dist.) La. 1975, U.S. Supreme Ct. 1980, U.S. Ct. Appeals (5th cir.) 1983. Legal specialist Nat. Info. Research and Action, Shreveport, 1974-76; atty. Davis Law Office and Legal Clinic Inc., Shreveport, 1976—; instr. part-time So. U., Shreveport, 1985—. Bd. dirs. Caddo Parish Bond, Shreveport, 1984—, Caddo/Bossier Assn. Retarded Children, Shreveport, 1986—. Serves as maj. USAR, 1971—. Recipient Bigger & Better Bus. award Alpha Xi Sigma, 1985; named one of Outstanding Young Men in Am. U.S. Jaycees, 1982. Mem. ABA, La. Bar Assn., Shreveport Bar Assn., Phi Beta Sigma, Delta Theta Phi. Democrat. Baptist. Club: Martin Luther King Civic (Shreveport) (v.p. 1982—). Lodge: Optimist. Avocations: tennis, jogging, traveling, reading. Personal injury, Bankruptcy, State civil litigation. Home: 1717 Audrey Ln Shreveport LA 71107 Office: Davis Law Office and Legal Clinic Inc 4050 Linwood Ave Shreveport LA 71108

DAVIS, SCOTT JONATHAN, lawyer; b. Chgo., Jan. 8, 1952; s. Oscar and Doris (Koller) D.; m. Anne Megan, Jan. 4, 1981; children: William, James. BA, Yale U., 1972; JD, Harvard U., 1976. Bar: Ill. 1976, U.S. Dist. Ct. (no. dist.) Ill. 1976, U.S. Ct. Appeals (7th cir.) 1977, U.S. Ct. Appeals (8th cir.) 1986. Law clk. to judge U.S. Ct. Appeals (7th cir.), Chgo., 1976-77; assoc. Mayer, Brown & Platt, Chgo., 1977-82, ptnr., 1983—. Bd. editors Harvard Law Rev., 1974-76; contbr. articles to profl. jours. Mem. ABA. General corporate, Federal civil litigation, Securities. Home: 838 W Belden Chicago IL 60614 Office: Mayer Brown & Platt 190 S LaSalle St Chicago IL 60603

DAVIS, SMITH WORMLEY, lawyer; b. West Chester, Pa., Mar. 7, 1948; s. John Aubrey and Mavis Elizabeth (Wormley) D.; m. Wendy Ann Butler, July 14, 1975 (div.). BA, Yale U., 1970, JD, 1974. Bar: D.C. 1978. Assoc. Milbank, Tweed, Hadley & McCloy, N.Y.C., 1974-76; law clk. to presiding justice U.S. Dist. Ct. D.C., 1976-77; counsel judiciary com. Ho. of Reps., Washington, 1978-79; assoc. Akin, Gump, Strauss, Hauer & Feld, Washington, 1979-84, ptnr., 1985—. Republican. Presbyterian. Legislative. Home: 5923 Woodfield Estates Dr Alexandria VA 22310 Office: Akin Gump Strauss Hauer & Feld 1333 New Hampshire Ave NW # 400 Washington DC 20036

DAVIS, STEPHEN ALLEN, lawyer; b. Huntington, W.Va., Jan. 18, 1947; s. Allen Reed and Mary (Richardson) D.; m. Martha Helen Frazier, June 29, 1974; children: Reed Frazier, Andrew Richardson, Jeffrey Allen, Kristin Ann. BA, W.Va. U., 1968, LLD, 1974. Bar: W.Va. 1974, U.S. Dist. Ct. (so. dist.) W.Va. 1974, U.S. Ct. Appeals (4th cir.) 1983. Assoc. Law Office John B. Breckinridge, Summersville, W.Va., 1974-76; ptnr. Breckinridge, Davis, Null & Sproles and predecessor firms Breckinridge & Davis and Breckinridge, Davis & Null, Summersville, 1976—; mcpl. judge Town of Summersville, 1976-79; chmn. bd. dirs. pub. defender corp. 23d Jud. Cir., Summersville, 1980—; asst. sec., bd. dirs. Strouds Creek & Muddlety R.R., Summersville, 1982—. Chmn. exec. com. Nicholas County Dems., Summersville, 1980-86; trustee, past chmn. bd. trustees Summersville Meml. Hosp., 1976-83. Served to 1st lt. U.S. Army, 1969-71, Vietnam. Mem. ABA, W.Va. Bar Assn., Nicholas County Bar Asssn. (pres. 1978), Assn. Trial Lawyers Am., W.Va. Trial Lawyers Assn., Am. Assn. Hosp. Lawyers, Summersville Jaycees (pres. 1976). Episcopalian. Real property, State civil litigation, Contracts commercial. Home: 211 Main St Summersville WV 26651 Office: Breckinridge Davis Null & Sproles 509 Church St Summersville WV 26651

DAVIS, STEPHEN JEFFREY, lawyer; b. Mpls., Sept. 4, 1943; s. Julius E. and Lillian (Kropman) D.; m. Jodi Sue Haas, Aug. 1, 1971; children—Jennifer, Timothy, Jill (dec.), Beth. B.S., Boston U., 1965; J.D., Georgetown U., 1968. Bar: Minn. 1968, U.S. Dist. Ct. Minn. 1968. Assoc., Robins, Davis & Lyons, Mpls., 1968-74, ptnr., 1974-82; sole practice, Mpls., 1982—. Bd. visitors U. Minn. Law Sch.; bd. govs., chmn. bd., chmn. fin. com. Mt. Sinai Hosp., Mpls. Served with AUS, 1968. Mem. ABA, Minn. Bar Assn., Hennepin County Bar Assn. Jewish. Clubs: Minneapolis, Oak Ridge Country. General corporate. Home: 2217 E Lake of Isles Pkwy Minneapolis MN 55405 Office: 33 S 6th St 3910 Multifoods Tower Minneapolis MN 55402

DAVIS, STEVEN H., lawyer; b. New York, NY, May 17, 1953; s. Stanley Robert and Ann (Wald) D.; m. Loretta Knaver, May 22, 1977; 1 child, Lucia. AB, Yale U., 1974, JD, 1977. Bar: N.Y. 1978, U.S. Dist. Ct. (so. dist.) N.Y. 1979. Ptnr. LeBoeuf, Lamb, Leiby & MacRae, N.Y.C., 1977—. Mem. ABA. Administrative and regulatory, Public utilities. Office: LeBoeuf Lamb Leiby & MacRae 520 Madison Ave New York NY 10022

DAVIS, STEVEN RAY, lawyer; b. Little Rock, May 9, 1951; s. Herschel Samuel and Barbara (Fryer) D.; m. S. Diane Dean, July 21, 1979; children: Rachel Amber, Elizabeth Marie. BA, Vanderbilt U., 1973; JD, U. Tex., 1975. Bar: Ark. 1976. Atty. Ark. Legis. Council, Little Rock, 1976-79; dep. pub. defender Pulaski County, Little Rock, 1979-82; sole practice Little Rock, 1982-83; assoc. Wood Law Firm, N. Little Rock, 1983-86; asst. pub. defender City of N. Little Rock, 1986—; sole practice N. Little Rock, 1986—. Mem. ABA, Assn. Trial Lawyers Am., Ark. Bar Assn., Pulaski County Bar Assn., N. Pulaski County Bar Assn. (pres. 1986—). Personal injury, Workers' compensation, Construction. Office: 628 W Broadway Suite 200 PO Box 1801 North Little Rock AR 72115

DAVIS, SUMPTER B., III, lawyer; b. Amite, La., Dec. 18, 1942; s. Sumpter Boyer and Blanche (Thomas) D. BA, La. State U., 1964, J.D., 1968. Bar: La. 1968, U.S. Dist. Ct. (ea. dist.) La. 1968, U.S. Dist. Ct. (mid. dist.) La. 1968, U.S. Ct. Appeals (5th cir.) 1968, U.S. Supreme Ct. 1978. Sole practice law, Baton Rouge, 1968-87; ptnr. Davis & Calmes, Baton Rouge, 1987—. Mem. La. Bar Assn., Baton Rouge Bar Assn., Lawyers in Mensa. Republican. Presbyterian. Personal injury, Criminal, State civil litigation. Office: 2501 Nicholson Dr Baton Rouge LA 70802

DAVIS, SUSAN RAE, lawyer; b. Salem, Oreg., July 15, 1948; d. William Ray and Pearl E. (Lundin) Catlin; m. Donald K. Davis, June 13, 1970. BA, U. Wash., 1969, JD, 1977. Bar: Wash. 1977, U.S. Dist. Ct. (we. dist.) Wash. 1977, U.S. Ct. Appeals (9th cir.) 1977. Writer, editor Associated Press, Seattle, 1969-70; news dir. Sta. KUUU, Seattle, 1970-71; reporter, photographer Sta. KXLY-TV, Spokane, Wash., 1971-73, Sta. KHQ-TV, Spokane, 1973-74; ptnr. Burns, Schneiderman, Davis & Finkle P.S., Seattle, 1977—; instr. journalism Eastern Wash. State Coll., Spokane, 1973-74. Mem. tribunal Wash. State Human Rights Commn., Seattle, 1974-79; arbitrator King County Mandatory Arbitration Panel, Seattle, 1985—. Mem. Wash. State Bar Assn., Seattle-King County Bar Assn., Assn. Trial Lawyers Am., Wash. State Trial Lawyers Assn. (leadership award 1984, bd. dirs. 1980-82, treas. 1982-83, v.p. west 1983-84, v.p. pub. affairs 1984-85, pres. elect 1985-86, pres. 1986—), Wash. Women Lawyers. Democrat. Club: Harbor (Seattle). Avocations: photography, golf. Personal injury. Office: The Davis Firm 5301 Ballard Ave NW Seattle WA 98107

DAVIS, TIMOTHY SCOTT, lawyer; b. Tulsa, Jan. 1, 1954; s. Elliott and Hannah (Foreman) D.; m. Patricia Gail Segall, Mar. 24, 1979; children: Stephanie Allison, Benjamin Segall. BA, Northwestern U., 1976; JD, Am. U., 1981. Bar: D.C. 1981, U.S. Dist. Ct. D.C. 1986, U.S. Ct. Appeals (D.C. cir.) 1986. Spl. asst. White House, Washington, 1978; assoc. Akin, Gump, Strauss, Hauer & Feld, Washington, 1981—; mem. juvenile justice and delinquency prevention adv. com. to Pres. U.S., Washington, 1977-81. Dir. midwest field Carter-Mondale campaign, Atlanta, 1975-76, White House Project Dem. Nat. Com., Washington, 1977; bd. dirs. St. Aidan Sch., Washington, 1986—. Mem. ABA, D.C. Bar Assn., Washington Council Lawyers, ACLU. Jewish. Avocations: tennis, golf, antiques. Legislative. Home: 3106 Leland St Chevy Chase MD 20815 Office: Akin Gump Strauss Hauer & Feld 1333 New Hampshire Ave NW Washington DC 20036

DAVIS, TRIGG THOMAS, lawyer; b. Spokane, Wash., July 28, 1945; B.A. with distinction in Polit. Sci., Wash. State U., 1967; J.D., Stanford U., 1970. Bar: Calif. 1970, Alaska 1971. Law clk. to chief justice Alaska Sup. Ct., 1970-72; ptnr. Owen, Davis, Bartlett, Anchorage, 1972-75; sole practice, Anchorage, 1975; ptnr. Davis & Goerisa Profl. Corp., 1978—; mem. Alaska Com. Bar Examiners, 1974, 75, 76, Alaska Probate Com., 1974-84, chmn., 1980, 85. Fellow Am. Coll. Probate Counsel (state chmn.); mem. ABA, Alaska Bar Assn., Anchorage Bar Assn., Am. Coll. Probate Counsel (state chmn. 1986—). Editor Stanford Law Sch. Jour. Internat. Studies, 1968-69. Probate, Estate planning, Estate taxation. Home: 4812 Wesleyan Dr Anchorage AK 99508 Office: Davis & Goerig PC 405 W 36th Ave Suite 200 Anchorage AK 99503

DAVIS, WALTER STEWART, lawyer; b. Evanston, Ill., Mar. 31, 1924; s. Walter Stewart Sr. and Nina Louise (Nixon) D.; m. Betty May Grede, Apr. 19, 1947; children: Walter Stewart, Susan L. Davis Daigneau, Thomas W., Judith A. Davis Pequet, Robert J. BS, Northwestern U., Evanston, 1947; JD, Northwestern U., Chgo., 1950. Bar: Ill. 1950, Wis. 1953, U.S. Ct. Appeals (4th, 6th, 7th D.C. cirs.) 1964, U.S. Supreme Ct. 1964. Gen. atty. Butler Bros., Chgo., 1950-51; judge adv. USAF, Moody AFB, Ga., 1951-52; ptnr. Davis & Kuelthau, Milw., 1952—; bd. dirs. Grede Foundries, Milw., Park State Bank, Milw., Thomas Industries, Louisville. Trustee Village of Elm Grove, Wis., 1958-64; bd. dirs. YMCA Met. Milw., 1964—. Served to 1st lt. USAF, 1942-45, 51-52, ETO. Mem. ABA, Milw. Bar Assn., Wis. Sch. Atty. Assn. (pres. 1975-77). Republican. Congregationalist. Club: Bluemound (Wauwatosa, Wis.) (pres., bd. dirs. 1968-76). Avocation: golf. Labor, General corporate. Home: 1050 Madera Circle Elm Grove WI 53122 Office: Davis & Kuelthau 250 E Wisconsin Ave Milwaukee WI 53202

DAVIS, WANDA ROSE, lawyer; b. Lampasas, Tex., Oct. 4, 1937; d. Ellis DeWitt and Julia Doris (Rose) Cockrell; m. Richard Andrew Fulcher, May 9, 1959 (div. 1969); 1 son, Greg Ellis; m. Edwin Leon Davis, Jan. 14, 1973 (div. 1985). B.B.A., U. Tex., 1959, J.D., 1971. Bar: Tex. 1971, Colo. 1981, U.S. Dist. Ct. (no. dist.) Tex. 1972, U.S. Dist. Ct. Colo. 1981, U.S. Ct. Appeals (10th cir. 1981, U.S. Supreme Ct. 1976. Atty. Atlantic Richfield Co., Dallas, 1971; assoc. firm Crocker & Murphy, Dallas, 1971-72; prin. Wanda Davis, Atty. at Law, Dallas, 1972-73; ptnr. firm Davis & Davis Inc., Dallas, 1973-75; atty. adviser HUD, Dallas, 1974-75, Air Force Acctg. and Fin. Ctr., Denver, 1976—; co-chmn. regional Profl. Devel. Inst., Am. Soc. Mil. Comptrollers, Colorado Springs, Colo., 1982; chmn. Lowry AFB Noontime Edn. Program, Exercise Program, Denver, 1977-83; mem. speakers bur. Colo. Women's Bar, 1982-83, Lowry AFB, 1981-83; mem. fed. ct. liaison com. U.S. Dist. Ct. Colo., 1983; mem. Leaders of the Fed. Bar Assn. People to People Del. to China, USSR and Finland, 1986. Contbr. numerous articles to profl. jours. Bd. dirs. Pres.'s Council Met. Denver, 1981-83; mem. Lowry AFB Alcohol Abuse Exec. Com., 1981-84. Recipient Spl. Achievement award USAF, 1978; Upward Mobility award Fed. Profl. and Adminstrv. Women, Denver, 1979. Mem. Fed. Bar Assn. (pres. Colo. 1982-83, mem. nat. council 1984—, Earl W. Kintner Disting. Service award 1983, 1st v.p. 10th cir. 1986—), Colo. Trial Lawyers Assn., Bus. and Profl. Women's Club (dist. IV East dir. 1983-84, dist. dir. 1983-84, Colo. 1st v.p. 1986—), Am. Soc. Mil. Comptrollers (pres. 1984-85), Denver South Met. Bus. and Profl. Women's Club (pres. 1982-83), Denver Silver Spruce Am. Bus. Women's Assn. (pres. 1981-82; Woman of Yr. award 1982), Colo. Jud. Inst., Colo. Concerned Lawyers, Profl. Mgrs. Assn., Fed. Women's Program (v.p. Denver 1980), Dallas Bar Assn., Tex. Bar Assn., Denver Bar Assn., Altrusa, Zonta, Denver Nancy Langhorn Federally Employed Women. (pres. 1979-80). Christian. Administrative and regulatory, Government contracts and claims, Legislative. Office: Air Force Acctg and Fin Ctr AFAFC/JAL Denver CO 80279

DAVIS, WILLIAM EUGENE, federal judge; b. Winfield, Ala., Aug. 18, 1936; s. A.L. and Addie Lee (Lenahan) D.; m. Celia Chalaron, Oct. 3, 1963. J.D., Tulane U., 1960. Bar: La. 1960. Assoc. Phelps Dunbar Marks Claverie & Sims, New Orleans, 1960-64; ptnr. Caffery Duhe & Davis, New Iberia, La., 1964-76; judge U.S. Dist. Ct., Lafayette, La., 1976-83, U.S. Ct. Appeals 5th Cir., 1983. Mem. ABA, La. Bar Assn., Maritime Assn. U.S. Republican. Office: 556 Jefferson St Suite 300 Lafayette LA 70501

DAVIS, WILLIAM HOWARD, lawyer; b. Monmouth, Ill., May 24, 1951; s. Orville Francis and Alice Gertrude (Hennenfent) D.; m. Susan Claire Parris, April 11, 1981; children: Benjamin Patrick, Jackson Mitchell. BA with honors, U. South Fla., 1974; JD with high honors, Fla. State U., 1977. Bar: Fla. 1977, U.S. Dist. Ct. (no. dist.) Fla. 1977, U.S. Dist. Ct. (mid. dist.) Fla. 1986, U.S. Ct. Appeals (11th cir.) 1986. Assoc. Thompson, Wadsworth, Messer & Rhodes, Tallahassee, 1977-80; ptnr. Wadsworth & Davis, P.A., Tallahassee, 1980—; instr. law Fla. State U., 1976-77. Editor notes and comments Fla. State U. Law Rev., 1976-77. Del. Council Neighborhood Orgns., Tallahassee, 1984; bd. dirs. Legal Aid Found., Inc., 1980-81. Mem. ABA, Fla. Bar Assn. (2d judicial cir. nominations commn. 1986—, Tallahassee-Leon County U.S. Constl. Bicentennial Commn.), Tallahassee Bar Assn. (sec., bd. dirs. 1982-85, pres. 1986-87), Assn. Trial Lawyers Am., Acad. Fla. Trial Lawyers (mem. Amicus com.), Fla. Lawyers Action Group, Amnesty Internat., Civil Justice Found. (founder), Fla. Spl. Ct. Historical Soc., Nature Conservancy, Omicron Delta Kappa, Phi Sigma Alpha. Democrat. Clubs: Exchange (Tallahassee), Gulf Winds Track (Tallahassee). Personal injury, State civil litigation, Federal civil litigation. Home: 914 Mimosa Dr Tallahassee FL 32312 Office: Wadsworth & Davis PA 203 N Gadsden Suite 1 Tallahassee FL 32302

DAVISON, GEORGE FREDERICK, JR., lawyer; b. Kirksville, Mo., Mar. 23, 1950; s. George Frederick and Wanda Jean (Johnson) D.; m. Patricia Louise Bubke, Oct. 16, 1977; 1 child, Erin Louise. BA in Journalism, Drake U., 1968-71, JD, 1979. Bar: Iowa 1980, U.S. Dist. Ct. (so. and no. dists.) Iowa 1980, U.S. Tax Ct. 1980, U.S. Ct. Appeals (8th cir.) 1980, U.S. Ct. Appeals (7th cir.) 1981, U.S. Ct. Appeals (5th cir.) 1982. Reporter WHO-TV/AM/FM, Des Moines, 1971-74; asst. news dir. Sta. KRNT-KRNQ, Des Moines, 1974-78; assoc. Hawkins & Norris, Des Moines, 1980—; chmn. Iowa Railway Fin. Authority, Ames, 1985—, vice chmn. 1982-85. Mem. bd. visitors Mo. Mil. Acad., Mexico, 1977—; sec. Mt. Olive Luth. Ch., Des Moines, 1984-86. Mem. ABA, Iowa Bar Assn., Polk County Bar Assn., Fed. Communications Bar Assn., Assn. Trial Lawyers Am., Train Collectors Assn., Burlington Rt. Hist. Soc., Rock Island Tech. Soc. Republican. Clubs: Toy Train Collectors (Des Moines) (v.p. 1985—), Lionel Collectors of Am. Avocations: model railroading, r.r. history, Am. history, photography. Antitrust, Federal civil litigation, State civil litigation. Home: 2731 Lynner Dr Des Moines IA 50310 Office: Hawkins & Norris 2801 Fleur Dr Des Moines IA 50321

DAVISON, IRWIN STUART, lawyer; b. Hazelton, Pa., Feb. 17, 1942; s. Julius S. and Gertrude (Kempner) D.; m. Ilene F. Hershinson, Nov. 24, 1966; children—Jill, Joshua. B.A., Lafayette Coll., 1963; J.D., Bklyn. Law Sch., 1966. Bar: N.Y. 1967, U.S. Dist. Ct. (so. and ea. dist.) N.Y. 1969, U.S. Supreme Ct. 1971. Dir. criminal justice projects Addition Services Agy., N.Y.C., 1975, asst. commr., 1975-76, gen. counsel, 1976-77; counsel Office of Substance Abuse Services, City of N.Y., 1977-78; dep. gen. counsel Dept. Health, city of N.Y., 1978-80, gen. counsel, 1980—. Chmn. Zoning Bd. Appeals, Mt. Vernon, 1982—. Mem. N.Y. County Lawyers Bar Assn. Administrative and regulatory, Health, Local government. Home: 92 Frederick Pl Mount Vernon NY 10552 Office: City of NY Dept Health 125 Worth St New York NY 10013

DAVISON, JOHN ARTHUR, lawyer; b. Macon, Ga., Sept. 29, 1956; s. Vincent Mercer Davison Sr. and Mary Lylette (Dunn) Smith; m. Muriam Sue Johnson, Aug. 20, 1983. BBA, U. Ga., 1978, JD, 1981. Bar: Ga. 1981, U.S. Dist. Ct. (so. dist.) Ga. 1981, S.C. 1982, U.S. Ct. Appeals (11th cir.) 1982. Ptnr. Fulcher, Hagler, Reed, Augusta, Ga., 1984—. Contbr. law articles to profl. jours. Mem. ABA, Ga. State Bar Assn., S.C. Bar Assn., Def. Research Inst. State civil litigation, Personal injury, Insurance. Office: Fulcher Hagler Reed 520 Greene St Augusta GA 30902

DAVISON, WARREN MALCOLM, lawyer; b. Boston, July 20, 1933; s. Aaron Rynston and Celia Irene (Bullock) D.; m. Mary Michelson, April 13, 1957; 1 child, Elise Ruth. AB, Harvard U., 1954, LLB, 1957. Bar: Mass. 1957, U.S. Supreme Ct. 1962, U.S. Ct. Appeals (4th cir.) 1964, Md. 1972, U.S. Dist. Ct. Md. 1972. Atty., supr. NLRB, Washington, 1958-65, dep. asst. gen. counsel, 1965-72; ptnr. Shawe & Rosenthal, Balt., 1972-84; resident ptnr. Littler, Mendelson, Fastiff & Tichy, Balt., 1984—. Interviewer schs. and scholarship com. Harvard Club of Md., Balt., 1975—. Recipient Younger Fed. Lawyers award Fed. Bar Assn., 1968. Mem. ABA, Md. Bar Assn., Indsl. Relations Resource Assn. Clubs: Suburban, Harvard (Balt.). Labor, General corporate. Home: 8201 Nina Ct Baltimore MD 21208 Office: Littler Mendelson Fastiff & Tichy World Trade Center Suite 1653 Baltimore MD 21202

DAVLIN, MICHAEL CHARLES, lawyer; b. O'Neill, Nebr., May 15, 1955; s. Charles Patrick and Clare Marie (O'Gorman) D. BA, U. Notre Dame, 1977; JD, Creighton U., 1980. Bar: Nebr. 1980, U.S. Dist. Ct. Nebr. 1980. Assoc. gen. counsel Mut. Omaha, 1980-82; v.p., asst. gen. counsel Cen. Nat. Ins., Omaha, 1982—. Mem. ABA, Omaha Bar Assn. Democrat. Roman Catholic. Administrative and regulatory, Insurance, Legislative. Office: Cen Nat Ins 105 S 17th St Omaha NE 68102

DAVOLI, JOSEPH FELIX, lawyer; b. Syracuse, N.Y., Apr. 28, 1941; s. Felix W. and Ida Marie (Curto) D.; m. Joan Ventre, June 28, 1968; children—Joseph F., David J., Andrew M., Mark S., Christianne A. A.B., Syracuse U., 1967; postgrad. John Marshall Law Sch. 1967-68; J.D., Boston Coll., 1970. Bar: N.Y., 1971. Assoc., Mackenzie, Smith, Lewis, Michell & Hughes, Syracuse, 1970-75; ptnr. VanLengen, Sanford & Davoli, Syracuse, 1975-77, Davoli & McMahon, 1977-82, Davoli, McMahon & Kublick, P.C., 1982—; spl. counsel City of Syracuse, City of Binghampton; lectr. Onondaga (N.Y.) Community Coll., 1972-79; adj. prof. SUNY, 1979-82. Mem. N.Y. State Democratic Law Com.; chmn. Onondaga County Dem. Law Com., 5th Jud. Dist. Conv. Fellow Roscoe Pound Found. of Am. Trial Lawyers Assn.; mem. ABA, N.Y. State Bar Assn., N.Y. State Trial Lawyers Assn., Onondaga County Bar Assn. Am. Trial Lawyers Assn. Roman Catholic. Club: Moose (Syracuse). Personal injury, Real property, State civil litigation. Home: 4535 Broad Rd Syracuse NY 13215 Office: 500 S Salina St Syracuse NY 13202

DAW, HAROLD JOHN, lawyer; b. N.Y.C., July 6, 1926; s. Joseph and Dorothy (Dannenberg) D.; m. Meryl Kann, Sept. 25, 1960. A.B., Union Coll., 1950; LL.B., Columbia U., 1954. Bar: N.Y. 1955. Assoc. Shearman & Sterling, N.Y.C., 1954-62, ptnr., 1962—; dir. Nash Engring. Co., Norwalk, Conn., 1975—. Served with USN, 1944-46, ETO. Mem. ABA, N.Y. State Bar Assn., Bar Assn. City N.Y., Phi Beta Kappa. Clubs: University, Broad Street (gov. 1971-86, pres. 1981, 82). General corporate, Private international, Securities. Home: 15 Buena Vista Dr Westport CT 06880 Office: 53 Wall St New York NY 10005

DAWDA, EDWARD C., lawyer; b. Detroit, June 7, 1952; s. Edward and Anna (Cojocari) D.; m. Alice I. Buckley, May 31, 1980. B.A. with high honors, Mich. State U., 1974; J.D. cum laude, Detroit Coll. Law, 1977. Bar: Mich. 1977, U.S. Dist. Ct. Mich. 1977, U.S. Tax Ct. 1978, U.S. Ct. Appeals (6th cir.) 1979. Assoc. Clark, Klein & Beaumont, Detroit, 1977-84, ptnr. 1984—; lectr. on real property and corp. law. Trustee Mich. chpt. Leukemia Soc. Am. Mem. Detroit Bar Assn., Mich. Bar Assn., ABA, Leukemia Soc. Am. (bd. trustees Mich. chpt.). Clubs: Savoyard (Detroit), Econ. Contbr. articles on law to profl. jours. Real property, General corporate. Office: 1600 First Fed Bldg Detroit MI 48226

DAWKINS, WILLIAM J(AMES), lawyer; b. Gulfport, Miss., July 25, 1948; s. James Otis and Marguerite (Gillespie) D.; m. Susan Lisa Anderson, Aug. 25, 1973; children: Scott William, Jeffrey Eric. BA, Fla. State U., 1970; JD, Emory U., 1974. Bar: Ga. 1974. Assoc. Law Offices of Marvin P. Nodvin, Atlanta, 1974-76; v.p., sec., gen. counsel Selig Enterprises, Inc., Atlanta, 1976—, also bd. dirs.; assoc. broker Selig Realty, Inc.; advisor Ga. Gen. Assembly, Ga. Dept. Community Affairs; instr. Inst. Continuing Jud. Edn. Seminars for Magistrates and State Ct. Judges. Author: Landlord and Tenant, Breach and Remedies, The Law in Georgia, 1979, Landlord and Tenant, Lease Forms and Clauses, The Law in Gerogia, 1979, Landlord and Tenant, Lease-Related Forms, The Law in Georgia, 1980, Georgia Landlord and Tenant-Breach and Remedies- With Forms, 1985; contbr. articles to profl. jours. Mem. Ga. Bar Assn. (lectr. real property law sect., young lawyers sect.), Atlanta Bar Assn. (tv and radio panelist real estate topics), Apt. Owners and Mgrs. Assn., Georgetown U. Alumni Assn. Methodist. Club: Dunwoody (Ga.) Country Club. Avocations: tennis, skiing. Real property. Home: 1725 Lazy River Ln Dunwoody GA 30338 Office: Selig Enterprises Inc 1100 Spring St NW Suite 550 Atlanta GA 30367

DAWSON, EDWARD A., lawyer; b. Prosser, Wash., Feb. 21, 1931; s. Edward J. and Norma (Ryan) D.; m. Patricia P. Pellican, June 26, 1931 (dec. Dec. 1979); children: Edward Joseph, Lisa Marie, Jeannine Marie Martin, Chris Andrew, Jay Scott; m. Marcia M. Meade, Aug. 5, 1983. Student, Yakima Jr. Coll., 1950; LLB, Gonzaga Law Sch., 1956. Sole practice Ellensburg and Wilbur, Wash., 1956-59, 59-76; sr. ptnr. Dawson & Meade P.S., Spokane, Wash., 1976—; pros. atty. Lincoln and Grant Counties, Ritzville and Davenport, Wash. Mem. Wash. State Bar Ass., Spokane County Bar Assn., Assn. Trial Lawyers Am., Wash. State Trial Lawyers Assn. (co-class of sr. com., sustaining), Trial Lawyers for Pub. Justice (founding). Avocation: jogging. Personal injury, Toxic tort, Professional negligence litigation. Office: Dawson & Meade PS W 1300 Dean Spokane WA 99201

DAWSON, JACK STERLING, lawyer; b. Oklahoma City, Dec. 24, 1940; s. Sterling Paul and Mae Elizabeth (Ballard) D.; m. Joan L. Eason, May 18, 1968; children: Clayton, Michael, Jacob. BA, Cen. State U., Oklahoma City, 1968; JD, Oklahoma City U., 1972. Assoc. Hunt & Thomas, Oklahoma City, 1972-75; ptnr. Hunt, Thomas & Dawson, Oklahoma City, 1975-78, Hunt & Dawson, Oklahoma City, 1978-82, Miller, Dollarhide, Dawson & Shaw, Oklahoma City, 1982—. pres. Oklahoma City U. Sch. Law Alumni, 1985-86. Served to comd. USNR, 1970—. Mem. ABA, Okla. Bar Assn., Okla County Bar Assn. (bd. dirs. 1972-75, v.p. 1975-78, pres. elect 1985-86, pres. 1986-87). Democrat. Jewish. Avocations: karate, backpacking, hunting, fishing. Federal civil litigation, State civil litigation, Insurance. Office: Miller Dollarhide Dawson & Shaw 1200 Colcord Bldg Oklahoma City OK 73102

DAWSON, ROBERT KEVIN, lawyer, law educator; b. Seattle, May 16, 1953; s. Robert Jens and Mildred Elizabeth (Hansen) D. BA in Bus. Adminstrn., U. Wash., 1975; JD, Willamette U., 1975-78. Bar: Wash. 1979, U.S. Dist. Ct. (we. dist.) Wash. 1979, U.S. Ct. Appeals (9th cir.) 1979. Sole practice Seattle, 1979-85; ptnr. Pence & Dawson, Seattle, 1985—; lectr. U. Wash., Seattle, 1980—. Pub. speaker U. Wash., Seattle, 1985—; bd. dirs. King City Rape Relief, Renton, Wash., 1978-82. Mem. Wash. State Bar Assn., Seattle/King County Bar Assn., Assn. Trial Lawyers Am., Wash. State Trial Lawyers Assn. Avocations: running, hiking, fishing, bicycling, tennis. Personal injury, Insurance, State civil litigation. Office: Pence & Dawson 3000 Smith Tower Seattle WA 98104

DAWSON, WARREN HOPE, lawyer; b. Mulberry, Fla., Oct. 17, 1939; s. J. Lloyd and Naomi D.; m. Joan Delores Brown; 1 child, Wendy Hope. BA in Polit. Sci., Fla. A & M U., 1961; JD, Howard U., 1966. Bar: Fla., D.C. Sole practice Tampa, Fla., 1967—; adv. bd. dirs. Tampa Bay Buccaneers. Field atty. Tampa regional office NLRB; asst. city atty., city pros. City of Tampa, 1967-72; chmn. Hillsborough County Civil Service Bd.; mem. Hillsborough Criminal Justice Planning Council, Fla. Probation and Parole Qualifications Com., Fla. Supreme Ct. Com. on Specialization Regulation, rules com. 1976 Nat. Dem. Conv., adv. council RAPPIN', nat. adv. bd. Bur. Statistics U.S. Dept. Justice, adv. council Drug Abuse (DACCO), Bi-Racial Adv. Bd.; bd. dirs. Tampa Urban League, Tampa chpt. ARC; chmn. Tampa Unified Construction Trade Bd. (Whitney M. Young, Jr. Mem. award); v.p. Tampa chpt. Frontiers Internat. Served as officer USAR, 1961-63. Named one of 100 Most Influential Blacks in Am., Ebony mag., 1983. Mem. ABA (spl com. to survey legal needs 1980-81, standing com. on legal assts. 1980-83), Fla. Bar Assn. (com. on jud. adminstrn., selection and tenure 1980, co-chmn. ethics com. 1971-72), Nat. Bar Assn. (nat. pres. 1982-83, pres. Fla. chpt. 1979-80), Scabbard and Blade, Sigma Delta Tau, Alpha Phi Alpha. Address: 3556 N 29th St Tampa FL 33605

DAY, BARTLEY FULLER, lawyer; b. Terre Haute, Ind., Dec. 16, 1948; s. David I. Jr. and Mary Isabel (Fuller) D.; m. Pierina Parise, Jan. 1, 1984; 1 child, Barrett Paris. BA, Wabash Coll., 1970; JD, Washington U., St. Louis, 1976. Bar: Hawaii 1977, U.S. Dist. Ct. Hawaii 1978, U.S. Ct. Appeals (9th cir.) 1982, Oreg. 1985, U.S. Dist. Ct. Oreg. 1985, U.S. Supreme Ct. 1985. Assoc. Law Offices James P. Wohl, Hilo, Hawaii, 1977-78; sole practice Hilo, 1978-85; assoc. Law Offices Richard G. Helzer, Portland, Oreg., 1985—. Co-author: Legal Aspects of Hawaii's Coastal Zoning Project, 1975. Named one of Outstanding Young Men in Am., 1985. Mem. ABA (forum com. on entertainment and sports industries). Club: City (Portland) (standing com. on high tech.). Avocations: sports, music. Personal injury, Trademark and copyright, State civil litigation. Office: Law Offices Richard Helzer 621 SW Morrison St Am Bank Bldg Suite 1300 Portland OR 97205

DAY, DAVID FRANKLIN, lawyer; b. Camarillo, Calif., Jan. 13, 1949; s. Leroy Edward and Mary Elizabeth (Hornbuckle) D.; m. Ingrid Korth, Dec. 17, 1971 (div. Dec. 1984); 1 child, Stefan Christopher. BA in Internat. Relations and Polit. Sci. magna cum laude, Tufts U., 1971; JDwith honors, George Washington U., 1974. Assoc. Goodsill et al, Honolulu, 1974-77, Brobeck, Phleger et al, San Francisco, 1977-83; sole practice San Francisco, 1983-84; assoc. Kaplan, Russin et al, San Francisco, 1984-86; ptnr. Day & Wong, Honolulu, 1986—. Mem. ABA, Calif. Bar Assn., Hawaii Bar Assn., Bar Assn. San Francisco, U.S. Council Internat. C. of C. Office: Day & Wong 165 S King St #1100 Honolulu HI 96813

DAY, EDWARD FRANCIS, JR., lawyer; b. Portland, Maine, Nov. 4, 1946; s. Edward Francis and Anne (Rague) D.; m. Claire Ann Nicholson, June 27, 1970; children: Kelley Ann, John Edward. BA, St. Anselm Coll., 1968; JD cum laude, U. Maine, 1973; LLM in Taxation, NYU, 1976. Bar: N.J. 1973, U.S. Dist. Ct. N.J. 1973, U.S. Tax Ct. 1974, N.Y. 1981. Assoc. Hannoch, Weisman, Stern & Besser, Newark, 1973-74; assoc. Carpenter, Bennett & Morrissey, Newark, 1975-78, ptnr., 1979—; inst. employee benefits and taxation The Am. Coll.bd., Valley Forge, Pa., 1981-82; dirs. Weiss-Aug. Co., Inc., East Hanover, N.J., 1986—. Editor Maine Law Rev., 1972-73. Mem. Allenhurst (N.J.) Bd. of Adjustment, 1985-86, vice chmn. planning bd. 1987—; com. mem. troop 76 Boy Scouts Am., Ocean Twp., 1985—; mem. Nat. Ski Patrol, Denver, 1985—. Served as sgt. U.S. Army, 1968-70. Named One of Outstanding Young Men of Am., Montgomery, Ala., 1979. Mem. ABA, N.J. Bar Assn., Essex County Bar Assn., Estate Planning Council of No. N.J. Roman Catholic. Clubs: Deal (N.J.) Golf and Country (bd. dirs. 1985—); Jersey Coast (Red Bank, N.J.) (v.p. 1976-77). Lodge: KC. Avocations: golf, skiing, backpacking, piano. Pension, profit-sharing, and employee benefits, Probate, Real property. Home: 225 Spier Ave Allenhurst NJ 07711 Office: Carpenter Bennett & Morrissey Three Gateway Ctr Newark NJ 07102

DAY, FRANK E., lawyer; b. Omaha, May 21, 1918; s. L.B. and Neva (Grimwood) D.; m. Geraldine Binning, Mar. 6, 1943; children: L.B., Chrisann Deurwarder, Linda Jean. BA, U. Nebr., 1940, JD, 1942; LLD, Western States Coll., Portland, Oreg., 1965. Bar: Oreg. 1942, U.S. Dist. Ct. Oreg., U.S. Ct. Appeals (9th cir.) 1947, U.S. Supreme Ct. 1964. Sole practice Portland, 1945-47; judge Oreg. Dist. Ct., Portland, 1947-51; ptnr. Reiter, Day, Wall & Bricker, Portland, 1951-72; pres. Day, Prohaska & Gregores, Portland, 1972-85; v.p. Burt & Day PC, Portland, 1985-86; pres., ptnr. Day & Gregores P.C., Portland, 1986—. Past bd. dirs. Portland Area Council Boy Scouts Am., Portland, bd. dirs. Vol. lawyers, Portland, 1985. Served to capt. U.S. Army 1942-45. Mem. ABA, Am. Law Inst. (life) Def. Research Inst. Fed. Communications Bar Assn., Oreg. Bar Assn., Oreg. Assn. Def. Counsel, Multnomah County Bar Assn., Washington County Bar Assn., Fedn. Ins. and Corp. Counsel. Club: Multnomah Athletic (Portland). Lodges: Elks, Masons, Shriners. Insurance, Federal civil litigation, State civil litigation. Office: Day & Gregores PC 900 SW 5th Ave 1240 Standard Ins Ctr Portland OR 97204

DAY, GEORGE EVERETTE, lawyer; b. Sioux City, Iowa, Feb. 24, 1925; s. John Edward and Christine Marie (Larson) D.; m. Doris Merlene, May 28, 1949; children—Steven Michael, George Everette Day, Sandra Marie, Sonja Marie. LL.B., U. S.D., 1949; B.S., Morningside Coll., 1950; D.H.L. (hon.), 1975; M.A., St. Louis U., 1964. Bar: S.D. 1949, Fla. 1977, U.S. Dist. Ct. (no. dist.) Fla. 1979, U.S. Ct. Appeals (5th cir.) 1980, U.S. Ct. Appeals (11th cir.) 1982, U.S. Dist. Ct. (mid. dist.) Ala. 1982, U.S. Ct. Claims 1983. Commd. maj. U.S. Air Force, 1961, advanced to col. 1970; flight comdr., ops. officer jet fighters, 1955-59; squadron comdr., Vietnam, 1967-73, prisoner of war; vice wing comdr., wing comdr. fighter wing, Eglin AFB, Fla., 1974-76; asst. judge adv. Eglin Law Ctr., 1976-77; ret., 1977; sr. atty. George E. Day, P.A., Ft. Walton Beach, Fla., 1977—. State committeeman Republican Party Fla., Ft. Walton Beach, Fla., 1979—; chmn. Reagan for Pres. campaign, Okaloosa County, Fla., 1980-84; mem. Okaloosa Library Bd., 1980—; nat. chmn. Vets. for Reagan-Bush, 1984. Served with USMC, 1942-45. Recipient Congl. Medal of Honor, 1976. Decorated Bronze Star with 2 oak leaf clusters, Purple Heart with 3 oak leaf clusters, AFC, DSM, Silver Star, DFC; Air Medal with 9 oak leaf clusters, Legion of Merit. Recipient DAR Medal of Honor, 1980; Americanism award Am. Legion, 1983. Mem. ABA, Fla. Bar Assn., Fla. Trial Lawyers Assn., Assn. Trial Lawyers Am., Nat. Inst. Trial Attys., VFW, Am. Legion. Lodge: Elks. Federal civil litigation, State civil litigation, Family and matrimonial. Office: 32 Beal Parkway SW Fort Walton Beach FL 32548

DAY, GREGG ALAN, lawyer; b. Washington, Dec. 4, 1952; s. Paul James and Violette (Hale) D.; m. Elizabeth Sperry, Dec. 29, 1973; children: Bethany Ruth, Leslie Ann. BA in History, George Mason U., 1976; JD, George Washington U., 1981. Bar: D.C. 1982, U.S. Dist. Ct. D.C. 1982, U.S. Ct. Claims 1982, U.S. Ct. Appeals (D.C. and fed. cirs.) 1982. Adminstrv. asst. Arndt & Day, Washington, 1976-78; dir., v.p./treas. Day & Day Inc., Arlington, Va., 1978-81; assoc. Morgan, Lewis & Bockius, Washington, 1981-84; v.p., gen. counsel Eden Hannon & Co., Alexandria, Va., 1984-86; v.p., fed. bus. mgr. Chase Manhattan Leasing Co., Washington, 1986—; adj. instr. fed. govt. contracts U. Va., 1985-86. Mem. Order of Coif, Alpha Chi. Episcopalian. Government contracts and claims, Contracts commercial, Securities. Home: 607 Knollwood Dr Falls Church VA 22046 Office: Chase Manhattan Leasing Co 1050 Connecticut Ave NW #310 Washington DC 20036

DAY, JAMES MCADAM, JR., lawyer; b. Detroit, Aug. 18, 1948; s. James McAdam and Mary Elizabeth (McGibbon) D.; m. Sally Marie Sterud; children: Cara McAdam, Brenna Marie, Michael James. AB, UCLA, 1970; JD magna cum laude, U. Pacific, 1973. Bar: Calif. 1973, U.S. Dist. Ct. (no. dist.) Calif. 1973, U.S. Ct. Appeals (9th cir.) 1975. Assoc. Downey, Brand, Seymour & Rohwer, Sacramento, 1973-78, ptnr., 1978—, chmn. natural resources dept., 1985—. Contbr. articles to profl. jours. Pres., bd. dirs. Sacramento Soc. for Prevention of Cruelty to Animals, 1976-79, Childrens Home Soc. of Calif., Sacramento, 1979-85; bd. dirs. Sta. KXPR-Radio, Sacramento, 1984—. Mem. ABA (natural resources sect.), Calif. Bar. Assn. (real property law sect., exec. com.), Rocky Mountain Mineral Law Found., No. Calif. Assn. Petroleum Landmen, Calif. Mining Assn., U. Pacific McGeorge Law Sch. Alumni Assn. (bd. dirs. 1980-83). Club: Andreas Cove Yacht (Isleton, Calif.). Avocations: yacht racing and cruising, fishing. Oil and gas leasing, Real property. Office: Downey Brand Seymour & Rohwer 555 Capitol Mall 10th Floor Sacramento CA 95814

DAY, JOHN ARTHUR, lawyer; b. Madison, Wis., Sept. 21, 1956; s. John Donald and Elinor Roletta (Heath) D. BS summa cum laude, U. Wis., Platteville, 1978; JD with honors, U. N.C., 1981. Bar: Tenn. 1981, U.S. Dist. Ct. (mid. dist.) Tenn. 1981, U.S. Ct. Appeals (6th cir.) 1981. Assoc. Boult, Cummings, Conners & Berry, Nashville, 1981-86, ptnr., 1987—; instr. Pearl Cohn High Sch., Nashville, 1982-84. Mem. staff N.C. Law Rev., 1979-80. Mem. ABA, Tenn. Bar Assn., Nashville Bar Assn., Assn. Trial Lawyers Am. (chairperson pub. relations com. 1985—, co-chmn. peoples law sch. com. 1986—), Tenn. Trial Lawyers Assn. (bd. dirs. 1984-85, treas. 1985—, chmn. continuing legal edn. com. 1985-86), Order of Coif. Democrat. Avocations: reading, politics. Personal injury. Office: Boult Cummings Conners & Berry PO Box 198062 Nashville TN 37219

DAY, JOHN BALDWIN, lawyer; b. N.Y.C., Apr. 26, 1951; s. Virgil Baldwin and Eugenia Claire (Brunson) D.; m. Diane Louise Chiodo, July 10, 1975; 1 child, John Edmund. BA, Northwestern U., Evanston, 1973; JD, Cornell U., 1976. Bar: N.Y. 1977. Assoc. Cullen & Dykman, Bklyn., 1976-78; asst. gen. counsel Revere Copper and Brass, N.Y.C., 1978-82; labor counsel Union Carbide Corp., Danbury, Conn., 1982—. Mem. ABA, N.Y. State Bar Assn., Westchester-Fairfield Corp. Counsel Assn. Avocations: fly fishing, skiing, sailing, construction. Labor. Office: Union Carbide Law Dept E2283 Old Ridgebury Rd Danbury CT 06817

DAY, KAREN SPRING, lawyer; b. Brunswick, Ga., Sept. 11, 1958; d. Jarman Glen and Sara Ruth (Brown) D.; m. Thomas Bohn, Sept. 11, 1983; children: Ashley Anne, Jarman Wayne. BA, U. Cen. Fla., 1978; MA, JD, George Washington U., 1981. Bar: D.C. 1981, Fla. 1982, U.S. Ct. Appeals (11th cir.) 1982, U.S. Dist. Ct. (mid. dist.) Fla. 1983. Assoc. Law Offices of Gretchen Vose, Orlando, Fla., 1982-83, Shutts & Bowen, Orlando, 1983-86; sole practice Orlando, 1986—. Named One of Outstanding Young Women of Am., Woman's Network, 1985. Mem. ABA, Assn. Trial Lawyers Am., Cen. Fla. Assn. Women Lawyers, Orange County Bar Assn., Am. Immigration Lawyers Assn., Phi Alpha Delta. Republican. Presbyterian. Immigration, naturalization, and customs, Real property, General corporate. Home: 12038 Agana St Orlando FL 32821 Office: 33 E Robinson St Suite 200 Orlando FL 32801

DAY, RICHARD EARL, lawyer, educator; b. St. Joseph, Mo., Nov. 2, 1929; s. William E. and Geneva C. (Miller) D.; m. Melissa W. Blair, Feb. 2, 1951; children: William E., Thomas E. BS, U. Pa., 1951; JD with distinction, U. Mich., 1957. Bar: Ill. 1957, D.C. 1959, S.C. 1980. Assoc. Kirkland & Ellis, Chgo., 1957-58, Howrey Simon Baker & Murchison, Washington, 1958-61; asst. prof. law U. N.C., Chapel Hill, 1961-64; assoc. prof. Ohio State U., Columbus, 1964-66, prof. 1966-75; prof. U. S.C., Columbia, 1975-76, 80-86, dean, 1977-80, John William Thurmond chair prof. of law, 1986—; cons. U.S. Office Edn., 1964-66; course dir. Ohio Legal Ctr. Inst., Columbus, 1970-75. Author: The Intensified Course in Antitrust Law, 1972, rev. edit., 1974; book rev. editor Antitrust Bull., 1968-71, adv. bd., 1971—; adv. bd. Antitrust and Trade Regulation Report, 1973-76, Jour. Reprints for Antitrust Law and Econs., 1974—. Ohio commr. Nat. Conf. on Uniform State Laws, 1967-75, S.C. commr., 1977-80; mem. Ohio Gov.'s Adv. Council Internat. Trade, 1972-74, S.C. Jud. Council, 1977-80; chmn. S.C. Appellate Def. Council, 1977-80, S.C. Com. Intellectual Property and Unfair Trade Practices Law, 1981—. Named John William Thurmond Disting. Prof. Law. Served to lt. USNR, 1952-55. Mem. ABA, S.C. Bar Assn. (bd. govs. 1977-80), Am. Law Inst., Am. Intellectual Property Law Assn. Methodist. Antitrust, Trademark and copyright. Home: 204 Barnwell St Columbia SC 29205 Office: Law Center USC Main and Green Sts Columbia SC 29208

DAY, ROLAND BERNARD, justice Wis. Supreme Ct.; b. Oshkosh, Wis., June 11, 1919; s. Peter Oliver and Joanna King (Wescott) D.; m. Mary Jane Purcell, Dec. 18, 1948; 1 dau., Sarah Jane. B.A., U. Wis., 1942, J.D., 1947. Bar: Wis. 1947. Trainee Office Wis. Atty. Gen., 1947; asso. mem. firm Maloney & Wheeler, Madison, Wis., 1947-49; 1st asst. dist. atty. Dane County, Wis., 1949-52; partner firm Day, Goodman, Madison, 1953-57; firm Wheeler, Van Sickle, Day & Anderson, Madison, 1959-74; legal counsel mem. staff Sen. William Proxmire, Washington, 1957-58; justice Wis. Supreme Ct., 1974—; Mem. Madison Housing Authority, 1960-64, chmn., 1961-63; regent U. Wis. System, 1972-74. Served with AUS, 1943-46. Mem. Am. Bar Assn., State Bar Wis., Am. Trial Lawyers Assn., Am. Judicature Soc., Ygdrasil Lit. Soc. (pres. 1968). Mem. United Ch. of Christ. Clubs: Madison, Madison Lit. Office: Supreme Ct Chambers 231 E State Capitol Madison WI 53702 and: PO Box 1688 Madison WI 53701 *

DAY, RONALD LILES, lawyer; b. Oklahoma City, July 20, 1947; s. John Q. and Hazel (Liles) D.; m. Diana I. Geddes, Mar. 30, 1985; 1 child, Carson. BBA, U. Okla., 1969, JD, 1972. Bar: Okla. 1972, U.S. Dist. Ct. (we., no. and ea. dists.) 1972, U.S. Ct. Appeals (10th cir.) 1973, U.S. Supreme Ct. 1976. Assoc. Fenton, Fenton, Smith, Reneau & Moon, P.C., Oklahoma City, 1972-76, sr. ptnr., 1976—; legal counsel for coop. council Okla. Sch. Adminstrs., 1978—, legal council Okla. City Pub. Schs., Harrah Pub. Schs., Broken Arrow Pub. Schs., Kiamichi Area Vocat.-Tech. Sch., Okla. Contbr. monthly article on sch. law to Better Schools, pub. coop. council Okla. Sch. Adminstrs., 1978—. Mem. ABA (urban, state, local govt. law sect.), Okla. Bar Assn., Am. Trial Lawyers Assn., Okla. Assn. Def. Council (bd. dirs. 1977-78), Nat. Sch. Bds. Assn., Sch. Attys. Council, Nat. Org. Legal Problems Edn., Okla. Sch. Bd. Attys. Assn. Avocations: writing, water sports. Education law, Civil rights, Personal injury. Office: Fenton Fenton Smith et al One Leadership Sq Suite 800 Oklahoma City OK 73102

DAY, STEPHEN LEO, lawyer; b. Hutchinson, Kans., June 5, 1945; s. Leo s. and Lowella E. (Wharton) D.; 1 child, Heather. BA, U. Denver, 1967; JD, Washburn Coll. of Law, 1973. Bar: Colo., Wash., U.S. Dist. Ct. Colo., U.S. Dist. Ct. (we.and ea. dists.) Wash., U.S. Ct. Appeals (9th cir.), U.S. Supreme Ct. Assoc. Lamm & Young, Denver and Boulder, Colo., 1974; atty., advisor ICC, Washington, 1974-75; trial atty. ICC, Atlanta, 1975-78; regional dir. western region ICC, 1986-87; sr. trial atty. Seattle, 1978—; spl. asst. U.S. Atty., various dists., 1977-85; aux. faculty U. Washington Sch. Law, Seattle, 1981, 82, Nat. Inst. for Trial Advocacy, N.W. Regional, 1982; legal counselor Vietnam Veterans Ctr. and Vietnam Veterans Leadership Project. Served to capt. USMC, 1967-70, Vietnam. Decorated Bronze Star with bronze oak leaf cluster, Purple Heart with bronze oak leaf cluster; Cross of Gallantry (Republic of Vietnam);. Mem. ABA, Wash. Bar. Assn. Avocation: sailing. Federal civil litigation, Criminal, Transportation. Office: ICC Enforcement Br 858 Fed Bldg 915 2d Ave Seattle WA 98174

DAYAN, RODNEY S., lawyer; b. Seattle, May 3, 1933; s. Jesse Charles Dayan and Thelma (Spencer) Dorsey; m. Barbara Heustis, Aug. 27, 1958; children: Christopher, Amanda. AB, Princeton U., 1955; LLB, Columbia U., 1961; LLM, NYU, 1967. Bar: N.Y. 1962. Assoc. Cadwalader, Wickersham & Taft, N.Y.C., 1961-69, ptnr., 1969—; Frequent chmn., panelist on legal or investment banking. Chmn. Bd. Examiners Montclair Dept. Pub. Safety, N.J., 1976-80; mem. Montclair Bd. Edn., 1971-75, Montclair Bd. Sch. Estimate, 1972-75. Keasby fellow New Coll. Oxford U., 1955-56. Mem. ABA (fed. regulation securities com. 1972-78), N.Y. State Bar Assn., Assn. of Bar of City of N.Y. (securities regulations com. 1973-76, commodities regulation com. 1976-77). Clubs: Down Town (N.Y.C.); Montclair Golf; Pennask Lake Fishing and Game (British Columbia, Can.). General corporate, Securities. Office: Cadwalader Wickersham & Taft 100 Maiden Ln New York NY 10038

DAYHOFF, CHARLES SIDNEY, III, lawyer; b. Dayton, Ohio, June 19, 1948; s. Charles S. and Bernice H. (Lawson) D.; m. Patricia C. Sezionale, Mar. 23, 1971 (div. Nov. 1981). AB, Colgate U., 1970; JD, U. Mo., 1977. Bar: Mo. 1978, Fla. 1980. Law clk. to presiding justice U.S. Dist. Ct. Mo., Kansas City, 1978-80; assoc. Battaglia, Ross, Hastings et al, St. Petersburg, Fla., 1980-81; from assoc. to ptnr. DeVito, Colen, Forlizzo & Reese, New Port Richey, Fla., 1981-84; sole practice Palm Harbor, Fla., 1984—. Served with USN, 1970-74. Mem. ABA, Fed. Bar Assn. (pres. young lawyers sect. 1979-80, Young Lawyer award 1980), Fla. Bar Assn., Clearwater Bar Assn., West Pasco Bar Assn., Assn. Trial Lawyers Am. Republican. Methodist. Club: Toastmasters (Clearwater, Fla.). Avocations: jogging, baseball, reading, water sports. State civil litigation, Contracts commercial, Family and matrimonial. Office: 2330 US 19 North Suite 206 Palm Harbor FL 33563

DAZÉ, DAVID TIMOTHY, lawyer, consultant; b. Los Angeles, Aug. 6, 1949; s. David Joseph and Eda Kathleen (Gioia) D.; m. Shareen Louise Parks, Apr. 10, 1976; children: Nicole, Colette, David, Michael. BBA, Loyola U., Los Angeles, 1971; JD, Woodland U., 1976. Bar: Calif. 1977, U.S. Dist. Ct. (cen. dist.) Calif. 1978, U.S. Ct. Appeals (9th cir.) 1978, U.S. Dist. Ct. (no. dist.) Calif. 1980, U.S. Supreme Ct. 1984. Assoc. Law Offices of Robert E. Kayyem, Los Angeles, 1977-78; ptnr. Johnson & Dazé, Los Angeles, 1978-80; sole practice Los Angeles, 1980-82; assoc. Wadsworth, Fraser & Dahl, Los Angeles, 1982—; cons. Goldwater Assocs., Los Angeles, 1976—. Author: See The Man, 1976, The Conspiracy, 1980. Press coordinator Lafollette for Controller, Los Angeles, 1974; fin. dir. Goldwater for Congress, Los Angeles, 1976, 78, 80. Mem. ABA, Los Angeles County Bar Assn., Young Trial Lawyers Assn., Am. Fedn. for Creative Cons. (bd. dirs. 1982—). Avocations: pub. speaking, writing, reading. General corporate, State civil litigation, Federal civil litigation. Office: Wadsworth Fraser & Dahl 3580 Wilshire Blvd Suite 1620 Los Angeles CA 90010-2517

DEACON, JOHN C., lawyer; b. Newport, Ark., Sept. 26, 1920. B.A., U. Ark., 1941, J.D., 1948. Bar: Ark. 1948. Ptnr. Barrett, Wheatley, Smith & Deacon, Jonesboro, Ark.; commr. from Ark. to Nat. Conf. Commrs. on Uniform State Laws, 1966—, chmn. exec. com., 1977-79, pres., 1979-81. Recipient Ark. Outstanding Lawyer-Citizen award, 1973. Fellow Am. Coll. Trial Lawyers, Internat. Acad. Trial Lawyers (bd. dirs. 1978-84), Southwestern Legal Found. (trustee 1975—, chmn. Research Fellows 1983-85); mem. Craighead County Bar Assn. (pres. 1968-69), N.E. Ark. Bar Assn. (pres. 1966-68), Ark. Bar Assn. (pres. 1970-71), ABA (chmn. sect. bar activities 1967-68, Ark. del. 1967-79, bd. govs. 1980-83), Am. Counsel Assn. (pres. 1974-75), Internat. Assn. Ins. Counsel, Fedn. Ins. Counsel, Delta Theta Phi. General practice. Office: Century Ctr PO Box 4057 Washington at Madison Jonesboro AR 72401

DEACY, THOMAS EDWARD, JR., lawyer; b. Kansas City, Mo., Oct. 14, 1918; s. Thomas Edward and Grace (Scales) D.; m. Jean Freeman, July 10, 1943; children: Bennette Kay Deacy Kramer, Carolyn G., Margaret Deacy Vickrey, Thomas, Ann. J.D., U. Mo., 1940; M.B.A., U. Chgo., 1949. Bar: Mo. 1940, Ill. 1946. Practice law Kansas City, 1940-42; partner firm Taylor, Miller, Busch & Magner, Chgo., 1946-55, Deacy & Deacy, Kansas City, 1955—; lectr. Northwestern U., 1949-55, U. Chgo., 1950-55; dir., mem. exec. com. St. L.-S.F. Ry., 1962-80; dir. Burlington No. Inc., 1980—; mem. U.S. team Anglo-Am. Legal Exchange, 1973, 77; mem. com. on problems of discovery Fed. Jud. Center, 1976—. Mem. Juvenile Protective Assn. Chgo., 1947-55, pres., bd. dirs., 1950-53; mem. exec. bd. Chgo. council Boy Scouts Am., 1952-55; pres. Kansas City Philharmonic Orch., 1961-63, chmn. bd. trustees, 1963-65; trustee Sunset Hill Sch., 1963-73; trustee, mem. exec. com. U. Kansas City, 1963—; trustee Mo. Law Sch. Found., pres., 1973—. Served to capt. AUS, 1942-45. Fellow Am. Coll. Trial Lawyers (regent 1968—, treas. 1973-74, pres. 1975-76), Am. Bar Found; mem. Am. Law Inst., Jud. Conf. U.S. (implementation com. on admission of attys. to fed. practice 1979—), ABA (commn. standards jud. adminstrn. 1972-74, standing com. fed. judiciary 1974-80), Ill. Bar Assn., Chgo. Bar Assn., Mo. Bar Assn., Kansas City Bar Assn., Lawyers Assn. Kansas City, Beta Gamma Sigma, Sigma Chi. Clubs: Chgo. (Chgo.); Univ. (Kansas City, Mo.), Kansas City Country (Kansas City, Mo.), River

(Kansas City, Mo.). Federal civil litigation, Insurance, General corporate. Home: 2722 Verona Circle Mission Hills KS 66208 Office: Bryant Bldg Kansas City MO 64106

DEAN, BILL VERLIN, JR., lawyer; b. Oklahoma City, Jan. 11, 1957; s. Bill V. and Mary Lou (Dorman) D.; m. Christine Potter; children: Bill V. III, Mary Megan. BS, Cen. State U., 1978; JD, Oklahoma City U., 1981. Bar: Okla. 1982, U.S. Dist. Ct. (we. dist.) Okla. 1983, U.S. Dist. Ct. (no. dist.) Okla. 1986, U.S. Dist. Ct. (ea. dist.) Okla. 1987. Second dep. assessor Okla. County Assessor, Oklahoma City, 1978-80; atty. Struthers Oil and Gas Corp., Oklahoma City, 1980-82; cons. Bill Dean & Co., Jones, Okla., 1978—; ptnr. Dean & Assocs., Jones, Okla., 1982—. Dem. precinct chmn. Okla. County, Oklahoma City, 1984—; police review bd. Town of Jones City, 1986. Mem. ABA, Okla. Trial Lawyers Assn., Okla. County Bar Assn. Democrat. Methodist. Lodge: Masons. Banking, Consumer commercial, Oil and gas leasing. Home: 200 Cherokee Ave Jones OK 73049-1060 Office: Dean & Assocs PO Box 1060 110 W Main Jones OK 73049-1060

DEAN, DANIEL FRANK, lawyer; b. Tyler, Tex., Sept. 28, 1948; s. Durward Stanton and Susanna Kelley (Glancy) D. BS, U. Tex., 1970; JD, Baylor U., 1978. Bar: Tex., U.S. Dist. Ct. (ea. dist.) Tex., U.S. Supreme Ct. Sole practice Palestine, Tex., 1978—. General practice, Family and matrimonial, State civil litigation. Home: 802 E Neches Palestine TX 75801 Office: 603 E Lacy PO Box 1578 Palestine TX 75801

DEAN, DENIS ALLEN, lawyer; b. Detroit, Jan. 29, 1942; s. Allen and Mildred Ella (Stevens) D.; m. Sherrilynn J. Huerkamp, Mar. 16, 1973; children: Denis Allen, Daron Andrew. B.A., U. Miami (Fla.), 1963, J.D., 1966. Bar: Fla. 1966, U.S. Supreme Ct. 1971. Research asst. State Atty.'s Office, Dade County, Fla., 1964-66; asst. state atty. 11th Jud. Cir. of Fla., 1966-70; assoc. Eugene P. Spellman, Miami, 1970-79; ptnr. Dean & Hartman, P.A., Miami, 1979—; instr. criminal law and procedure Dade Jr. Coll., 1969-71; mem. N.Y.S.E. Bd. Arbitration, 1973—. Mem. ABA, Fed. Bar Assn., Dade County Bar Assn., Assn. Trial Lawyers Am., Acad. Fla. Trial Lawyers. Democrat. Presbyterian. Club: Dade County Police Benevolent Assn. (hon. mem.). Criminal. Home: 12680 Hickory Rd North Miami FL 33181 Office: 2212 Biscayne Blvd Miami FL 33137

DEAN, GEORGE ROSS, lawyer, educator; b. Washington, Jan. 7, 1954; s. John Edward and Priscilla (Ross) D. BA, Emory U., 1976; JD, So. Meth. U., 1979. Bar: Ga. 1979, U.S. Dist. Ct. (no. dist.) Ga. 1979, U.S. Supreme Ct. 1984. Sole practice Atlanta, 1980—; sec. Ga. Small Bus. Counsel, Atlanta, 1984; bd. dirs. Bus. Contacts, Inc., Atlanta; adj. prof. John Marshall Law Sch., Atlanta, 1982—; Ga. Paralegal Inst., Atlanta, 1983—; Brown Coll. Ct. Reporting, Atlanta, 1984; arbitrator Fulton County Superior Ct., 1986—. Sec. St. Charles-Greenwood Neighborhood Assn., Atlanta, 1984-86. Mem. Ga. State Bar Assn., Atlanta Bar Assn., Georgia Trial Lawyers Assn., Assn. Trial Lawyers Am. Avocations: running, reading. Personal injury, Family and matrimonial, General corporate. Home: 823 Greenwood Ave NE Atlanta GA 30306 Office: 320 Peachtree St NW 10th fl Atlanta GA 30303

DEAN, J. THOMAS, lawyer; b. Cleve., Feb. 22, 1933; s. John Ladd and Margaret Caroline (Blakely) D.; m. Patricia Jean Whitmore, Aug. 6, 1960; children—Thomas W., Carol M., Joan G. B.A., Ohio Weslyan U., 1956; J.D., Western Res. U., 1959. Bar: Ohio 1959. Asst. pros. atty. Lake County, Ohio, 1960; assoc. Blakely, Rand, Painesville, Ohio, 1961-67; ptnr. Blakely & Dean, 1967-76, Blakely, Dean, Wilson & Klingenberg, Painesville, 1976—; law dir. North Perry Village, Ohio, 1970—. Mem. Painesville Bd. Zoning Appeals, 1971-76; mem. Planning Commn., 1967-79, chmn., 1970-77; pres. Painesville Sr. Citizens, 1982-84; mem. Lake County Bd. Elections, 1964-84; chmn. Lake County Republican. Com., 1970-74, 82-84; mem. Ohio Rep. Central Com., 1980—; clk. Painesville Twp. Park, 1962—. Mem. Lake County Bar Assn. (pres. 1979-80), Ohio State Bar Assn., ABA, Republican. Methodist. Lodge: Kiwanis (pres. 1980-81). Avocation: swimming. State civil litigation, General corporate, Probate. Office: Blakely Dean Wilson & Klingenberg PO Box 526 Painesville OH 44077

DEAN, JAMES B., lawyer; b. Dodge City, Kans., May 23, 1941; s. James Harvey and Bess (Benwell) D.; m. Sharon Ann Carver, Sept. 1, 1962; children: Cynthia G., James M. Student, Southwestern Coll., 1959-60, U. Colo., 1961; BA, Kans. State U., 1962; JD, Harvard U., 1965. Bar: Colo. 1965, U.S. Dist. Ct. Colo. 1965, U.S. Tax Ct. 1966, Nebr. 1971, U.S. Ct. Appeals (10th cir.) 1971. Assoc. Tweedy & Mosley, Denver, 1965-71; from assoc. to ptnr. Kutak, Rock, Cohen, Campbell, Garfinkle & Woodward, Omaha, 1971-73; ptnr. Mosley, Wells & Dean, Denver, 1973-77, Kutak, Rock & Huie, Denver, 1977-81; sole practice Denver, 1981—; lectr. U. Ark. Law Sch., Fayetteville, 1982-86. Co-editor Agricultural Law Jour., 1979-84; contbr. articles to profl. jours. Mem. ABA, Nebr. Bar Assn., Colo. Bar Assn., Denver Bar Assn., Am. Agrl. Law Assn. (pres. elect 1985-86, pres. 1986—, bd. dirs. 1981-83). Republican. Avocations: photography, woodworking, hiking, piano. General corporate, Contracts commercial, Securities. Office: 600 S Cherry St Suite 640 Denver CO 80222

DEAN, MORRIS JONATHAN, lawyer; b. Phila., Feb. 17, 1931; s. David Justin and Lena G. Dean; m. Beryl S. Richman, Mar. 29, 1958; Ilana, Daniel, Rachel. AB, U. Pa., 1951; LLB, Yale U., 1954. Bar: Pa. 1955, U.S. Supreme Ct. 1962. Dep. atty. gen. Commonwealth of Pa., Harrisburg, 1958-63; from assoc. to ptnr., co-chmn. real estate dept. Blank, Rome, Comisky & McCauley, Phila., 1968—; mem. constrn. loan com. Continental Bank; lectr. in field.. Exec. com. Com. of Seventy, 1982—; bd. dirs. Phila. Port Corp., 1983—. Served to lt. USN, 1955-58. Mem. ABA, Pa. Bar Assn., Phila. Bar Assn., Phi Beta Kappa. Clubs: Yale, Union League (Phila.). Real property. Office: Blank Rome Comisky & McCauley 4 Penn Ctr Plaza Suite 10-13 Philadelphia PA 19103

DEAN, ROBERT SCOTT, U.S. diplomat, lawyer; b. Duluth, Minn., Jan. 28, 1955; s. Robert Thomas and Margaret Jane (Bartness) D. BA cum laude, Carleton Coll., 1977; JD, U. Minn., 1981. Bar: Minn. 1981. U.S. vice consul Am. Embassy, Jeddah, Saudi Arabia, 1982-83, ambassador's aide, 1983-84; arms control analyst Dept. State, Washington, 1984-86; mem. staff European and Soviet affairs Nat. Security Council, Washington, 1986-87; atty. U.S. Dept. of State, Washington, 1987—. Mem. ABA. Public international. Home: 3530 E 2d St Duluth MN 55804 Office: US Dept State 2201 C St NW Washington DC 20520

DEAN, RONALD GLENN, lawyer; b. Milw., Feb. 18, 1944; m. Mary Blumberg, Jan. 25, 1969; children—Elizabeth Lucile, Joshua Henry. B.A., Antioch Coll., 1967; J.D., U. Wis. 1970. Bar: Wis. 1970, Calif. 1971; assoc. Mink & Neiman, Los Angeles, 1971; sole practice, Los Angeles, 1974-77; ptnr. Margolis, McTernan, Scope & Sacks, Los Angeles, 1974-77; sole practice, Pacific Palisades, 1977—; mem. judge pro-tem program Los Angeles County Bar, 1978—; judge pro tem Beverly Hills Mcpl. Ct., 1980—; arbitrator Los Angeles Superior Ct., 1980—, Los Angeles County Fee Dispute Panel, 1979—, Santa Monica Mcpl. Ct., 1980—; referee for disciplinary matters State Bar Ct., 1980—, supervising referee, 1984—. Bd. dirs. Pacific Palisades Residents Assn., 1983—, pres., 1985—; counsel to Pacific Palisades Community Council, 1983—; mem. Councilman's Citizen Adv. Com. to Develop Palisades Specific Plan, 1983-85. Mem. Am. Arbitration Assn. (panel 1974—), ABA, Wis. Bar Assn., Calif. Bar Assn., Calif. State Bar (chmn. pension and trust benefits com. of labor sect. 1984), Los Angeles County Bar Assn. Antioch Alumni Assn. (dir. 1982—). Pension, profit-sharing, and employee benefits, Personal injury. Office: 15135 Sunset Blvd Suite 280 Pacific Palisade CA 90272

DEAN, SHARI LAVOLA, lawyer; b. Vallejo, Calif., Aug. 28, 1948; d. Samuel U. and Lavola Alice (Matot) D. AA, Solano Coll., 1968; BBA, U. Calif., Berkeley, 1969; JD, John F. Kennedy U., 1974. Bar: Calif. 1976, U.S. Dist. Ct. (no. and ea. dists.) Calif. 1977. Supr. atty. Community Law Services, Vallejo, 1977-79; sole practice Fall River Mills, Calif., 1980-83; pub. defender Modoc County, Alturas, Calif., 1983—; lectr. legal seminars for sr. citizens, Napa and Solano Counties, Calif., 1978-80. Mem. Calif. Attys. Criminal Justice, Calif. Pub. Defenders Assn. Democrat. Mem. Christian Sci. Ch. Criminal. Office: Modoc County Pub Defender Office 201 S Court St Suite 28 Alturas CA 96101

DEAN, WILLIAM TUCKER, legal educator; b. Chgo., Aug. 31, 1915; s. William Tucker and Martha (Boldt) D.; m. Ann Coulson, May 15, 1943; children: Jonathan, Robert Coulson, Tobias, Sheila. A.B., Harvard, 1937, M.B.A., 1947; J.D., U. Chgo., 1940. Bar: D.C. bar 1940, N.Y. bar 1949, also U.S. Supreme Ct 1949. Atty. bituminous coal div. Dept. Interior, 1940-41; legal adviser fuel sect. OPA, 1941-42; atty. anti-trust div. Dept. Justice, 1943; asst. prof. law U. Kan. Law Sch., 1946-47; asst., then assoc. prof. law NYU Law Sch., 1947-53; assoc., then prof. law Cornell U., 1953-86; gen. counsel, dir. Geotechnics and Resources, Inc., 1959-63; asso. dir. research N.Y. State Law Revision Commn., 1963-66. Author: (with C.O. Gregory and others) Illinois Annotations to Restatement of Torts, 1942; also numerous articles.; Editor: Annual Survey American Law, 1950-53, Survey of New York Law, 1950-53. Justice Village of Cayuga Heights, N.Y., 1962—; Co-chmn. N.Y. State Citizens Com. for Liquor Law Revision, 1964, Democratic candidate for Supreme Ct. from 6th Jud. Dist., 1982. Served to capt. AUS, 1942-46. Mem. ABA (assoc. editor real property, probate and trust law jour. 1979-86, media/books program of real property and trust law sect. 1986—), Tompkins County Magistrates' Assn. (pres. 1969), N.Y. State Bar Assn., Internat. Acad. Estate and Trust Law, Order of Coif, Phi Beta Kappa, Phi Kappa Phi. Mem. United Ch. Christ. Estate planning, Probate, Real property. Home: 206 Overlook Rd Ithaca NY 14850

DEANDA, JAMES, federal judge; b. Houston, Aug. 21, 1925; s. Javier and Mary Louise DeA.; m. Joyce Anita DeAnda; children: Louis, Christopher. B.A., Tex. A&M U.; LL.B., U. Tex., 1950. Bar: Tex. Pvt. practice Houston, 1951-54, Corpus Christi, 1955-57, 66-68; mem. McDonald, Spann & DeAnda, Corpus Christi, 1957-62, Edwards & DeAnda, 1962-66, 69-74, Flores, Sanchez, DeAnda & Vidaurri,, McAllen, 1974-79; U.S. dist. judge So. Dist. Tex., Houston, 1979—. Mem. ABA, Am. Judicature Soc. Roman Catholic. Jurisprudence. Office: Federal Bldg PO Box 610040 Houston TX 77208 *

DEANE, GEORGE INGRAM, III, lawyer; b. Merced, Calif., June 2, 1951; s. George I. Jr. and Alice (Dewitt) D.; m. Nina Burks, June 27, 1982. BA, U. Calif., Berkeley, 1977; JD, U. San Diego, 1980. Bar: Calif. 1980, U.S. Dist. Ct. (so. dist.) Calif. 1980, U.S. Supreme Ct. 1986. Mem. Defenders Program, San Diego, 1980-82; assoc. McCormick & Royce, San Diego, 1982-86, ptnr., 1986—. Mem. Order of Barristers (bd. dirs. 1986—, pres. 1987). Democrat. Presbyterian. Clubs: San Diego Country, Cuyamaca (San Diego). Insurance, State civil litigation, Personal injury. Home: 476 Alameda Blvd Coronado CA 92118 Office: McCormick & Royce 105 W F St Suite 201 San Diego CA 92101

DE ANGELIS, ARNOLD JOHN, lawyer; b. Rome, Oct. 17, 1925; came to U.S., 1928, naturalized, 1944; s. August and Virginia (Dragone) De A.; m. Marie R. De Angelis, June 26, 1948; children—Arnold, Alan, Virginia. B.E.E., Coll. Applied Sci., Syracuse U., 1950, M.B.A., 1951; J.D., St. John's Sch. Law, Bklyn., 1955. Bar: N.Y. 1955, Ill. 1967, U.S. Supreme Ct. 1960, U.S. Dist. Ct. (so. and ea. dists.) N.Y. 1960, U.S. Ct. Customs and Patent Appeals 1967, U.S. Ct. Appeals (fed. cir.) 1982. Elec. engr. Western Electric, 1951-56; pat. atty. Otis Elevator Co., N.Y.C., 1956-61, Sperry-Rand-Univac, Norwalk, Conn., 1961-64; chief pat. csl. Johnson Control, Milw., 1964-78, dir. product safety, 1978—. Served with USN, 1944-46. Mem. Chg. Pat. Law Assn., N.Y. Pat. Law Assn., ABA (tort sect., anti-trust sect., patent, trademark and copyright sect.), Nat. Elec. Mfrs. Assn. (product liability com.), Lic. Execs. Soc., Battery Council Internat. (co-chmn. product safety com.). Personal injury, Patent, Federal civil litigation.

DEANGELUS, RONALD PATRICK, lawyer; b. Schenectady, N.Y., May 31, 1935; s. Dominick and Edith (Matarazzo) DeA.; m. Arlene L. Blanchard, July 1, 1973. BA, Union Coll., 1957; JD, Albany Law Coll., 1960. Bar: N.Y. 1960, U.S. Dist. Ct. (no. dist.) N.Y. 1960. Law clk. to presiding justice U.S. Dist. Ct. Oreg., Portland, 1960-61; dep. pub. defender Schenectady County, N.Y., 1967-68, asst. county atty., 1968-69; asst. corp. counsel City of Schenectady, 1976-79; ptnr. DeAngelus & DeAngelus, Schenectady, 1979—. Mem. Am. Trial Lawyers Assn., Nat. Assn. Criminal Def. Lawyers, N.Y. State Bar Assn., N.Y. State Defenders Assn., Schenectady County Bar Assn., Capital Dist. Trial Lawyers Assn. Democrat. Criminal, State civil litigation. Office: DeAngelus & DeAngelus 434 Franklin St Schenectady NY 12305

DEANS, THOMAS SEYMOUR, lawyer; b. St. Louis, Mar. 21, 1946; s. Thomas Ellison and Eva May (Seymour) D.; m. Barbara Jean Wilson, Aug. 10, 1974; children: Katherine, Tyler. BA, Northwestern U., 1968; JD cum laude, U. Minn., 1973. Bar: Minn. 1973, U.S. Dist. Ct. Minn. 1978. Senate counsel Minn. State Senate, St. Paul, 1973-78; ptnr. Knutson, Flynn, Hetland & Deans, St. Paul, 1978—. Mem. ABA, Minn. Bar Assn., Ramsey County Bar Assn. (chmn. legis. com. 1984-85), Nat. Assn. Bond Lawyers, Nat. Sch. Bds. Assn. Council Sch. Attys. Lutheran. Local government, Municipal bonds, Legislative. Home: 1401 June Ave S Minneapolis MN 55416 Office: Knutson Flynn Hetland & Deans 345 Cedar Suite 800 Saint Paul MN 55101

DEARIE, HAROLD EMMANUEL, II, lawyer; b. New Orleans, Jan. 9, 1939; s. Harold Emmanuel and Mary Pascaline (Abadie) D.; m. Irma Clara Brown, Oct. 24, 1968; children—Megan Mary, Erin Elizabeth. B.Social Scis., Loyola U., New Orleans, 1961, J.D., 1975. Bar: La. 1976, U.S. dist. Ct. (ea. dist.) La. 1976. Ptnr. Dearie & Killian, Metairie, La., 1976—; legal counsel New Orleans chpt. Am. Sub-Contractors Assn., 1981—; judge ad hoc First Parish Ct., Jefferson Parish, La., 1980, 84. Recipient St. Louis medal Archdiocese New Orleans, 1984. Mem. St. Thomas More Soc., Phi Delta Phi. Republican. Roman Catholic. Construction, Consumer commercial, State civil litigation. Office: Dearie & Killian One Prince Plaza 4523 Prince St Metairie LA 70001

DEATHERAGE, WILLIAM VERNON, lawyer; b. Drumright, Okla., Apr. 17, 1927; s. William Johnson and Pearl Mae (Watson) D.; m. Priscilla Ann Campbell, Sept. 16, 1932; children—Thomas William, Andrea Susan. B.S., U. Oreg., 1952, LL.B. with honors, 1954. Bar: Oreg. 1954, U.S. Dist. Ct. Oreg. 1956. Ptnr. Frohnmayer, Deatherage, deSchweinitz, Pratt & Jamieson, Medford, Oreg., 1954—; bd. dirs. Oreg. Law Inst., U. Oreg. Found. Served with USN, 1945-48. Mem. Am. Coll. Trial Lawyers, Internat. Acad. Trial Lawyers, Delta Theta Phi. Democrat. Episcopalian. Clubs: Rogue Valley Country, Rogue River Valley Univ. (Medford, Oreg.). Federal civil litigation, State civil litigation, Insurance. Address: PO Box 1726 Medford OR 97501

DEATS, PAUL EDWIN, judge; b. Los Angeles, Aug. 20, 1946; s. Wayne Wallace and Della Margaret (Decker) D.; m. Penny Laurel Schuck, Aug. 31, 1968; children: Rebecca Lynne, Wayne Charles, Megan Anne. BA, Whittier Coll., 1968, MAT, 1971; JD, U. Notre Dame, 1974. Bar: Ind. 1974, Mich. 1974, U.S. Dist. Ct. (so. dist.) Ind. 1974, U.S. Dist. Ct. (we. dist.) Mich. 1974, U.S. Supreme Ct. 1977. Asst. prosecutor Cass County, Cassopolis, Mich., 1974-75; assoc. O'Connor & Tushla, Cassopolis, 1975-79; judge 4th Jud. Dist., Cassopolis, 1979—; practice ct. participant U. Notre Dame Law Sch., South Bend, Ind., 1975—. Asst. coach Edwardsburg (Mich.) Soccer Assn., 1985, Edwardsburg (Mich.) Little League, 1985; advisor Girl Scouts of Singing Sands, South Bend, 1984—; bd. dirs. Cass County (Mich.) United Way, 1984—. Mem. ABA, Mich. Bar Assn., Cass County Bar Assn. (pres. 1977-79), Mich. Dist. Judges Assn., Am. Jud. Assn. Republican. Presbyterian. Lodges: Optimists, Masons. Avocations: softball, bowling, reading. Judicial administration, Criminal, State civil litigation. Home: 26050 Driftwood Dr Edwardsburg MI 49112 Office: 4th Dist Ct Courthouse Cassopolis MI 49031

DEAVER, PHILLIP LESTER, lawyer; b. Long Beach, Calif., July 21, 1952; s. Albert Lester and Eva Lucille (Welton) D. Student, USCG Acad., 1970-72; BA, UCLA, 1974; JD, U. So. Calif., 1977. Bar: Hawaii 1977, U.S. Dist. Ct. Hawaii 1977, U.S. Ct. Appeals (9th cir.) 1978, U.S. Supreme Ct. 1981. Assoc. Carlsmith, Wichman, Case, Mukai & Ichiki, Honolulu, 1977-83, ptnr., 1983-86; mng. ptnr. Bays, Deaver, Hiatt, Kawachika & Lezak, Honolulu, 1986. Mem. ABA (forum com. on the Constrn. Industry), AIA (affiliate Hawaii chpt.). Construction, State civil litigation, Federal civil litigation. Home: 2471 Pacific Heights Honolulu HI 96813 Office: Bays Deaver Hiatt Kawachika & Lezak PO Box 1760 Honolulu HI 96806

DEBAETS, TIMOTHY JOSEPH, lawyer, legal educator; b. South Bend, Ind., Aug. 16, 1949; s. Joseph H. and Dorothy (Marshall) DeB. B.A., Columbia U., 1971; J.D., Duke U., 1975. Bar: N.Y. 1976, U.S. Dist. Ct. (so. and ea. dists.) N.Y. 1976. Assoc., Simpson Thacher & Bartlett, N.Y.C., 1975-79, Pavia & Harcourt, N.Y.C., 1979-83; now with Stults & Marshall, N.Y.C.; asst. adj. prof. NYU Sch. of Arts, N.Y.C., 1984. Author: The Concepts of Negotiation (in Cultivating the Wasteland, 1983); Legal Business (in Poor Dancers' Almanac, 1984); lectr., panalist in field. Editorial bd. Duke Law Jour., 1974-75. Bd. dirs. Dance Theatre Workshop, N.Y.C., 1981—. Served with USAR, 1971-77. Mem. N.Y. State Bar Assn. (mem. spl. com. on copyright law 1981—, chmn. 1984—), Assn. Bar City N.Y. (mem. spl. com. on entertainment and sports law 1980-84, art law com. 1986—), ABA (forum com. on entertainment and sports industry 1980—), Copyright Soc. U.S. Democrat. Roman Catholic. Entertainment, Trademark and copyright, General corporate. Home: 321 W 78th St 5F New York NY 10024 Office: Stults & Marshall 1370 Ave of Americas New York NY 10019

DE BARBIERI, ROY LOUIS, lawyer; b. Bklyn., Dec. 22, 1947; s. Edward and Olga (Carpeneto) De B.; m. Patricia Walczak, July 19, 1969; children: Aimee, Edward. BS, Mt. St. Mary's Coll., Emmitsburg, Md., 1969; JD, Cleve. State U., 1972. Bar: Conn. 1973, U.S. Dist. Ct. Conn. 1973, U.S. Supreme Ct. 1976. Atty. VISTA, New Haven, 1972-73; assoc. Schine, Julianelle, Karp & Bozelka, Westport, Conn., 1973-75; sole practice New Haven, 1975-80; ptnr. DeBarbieri & Assocs., New Haven, 1980—; advisor Bank of New Haven, 1983—; bd. dirs. Nova Venture Mgmt., New Haven, Trib Bldg. Corp., St. James, N.Y. Campaign treas. The Leadership Fund, New Haven, 1983-85, Citizens for Moffet/86, New Haven, 1983-85; treas. Moffett for Gov., New Haven, 1985—. Mem. Conn. Bar Assn., New Haven Bar Assn., Sons of Italy. Democrat. Roman Catholic. Clubs: Graduates, Amity (New Haven). Real property, Personal injury, General practice. Home and Office: 560 Saw Mill Rd West Haven CT 06516

DEBERARDINIS, ROBERT ANDREW, JR., lawyer; b. Ossining, N.Y., Feb. 3, 1949; s. Robert Andrew and Patricia A. (Gelardo) DeB.; m. Barbara J. Howard, Dec. 2, 1979. BA, Cath. U. Am., 1971, JD, 1980. Bar D.C. 1980, Md. 1981, U.S. Dist. Ct. D.C. 1981. Law clk. to presiding justice D.C. Superior Ct., 1980-81; ptnr. Scavuzzo & DeBerardinis, Washington, 1981-84, Allen, Sparks & DeBerardinis, Washington, 1984—. Mem. D.C. Trial Lawyers Assn. (v.p. 1985-86). Federal civil litigation, State civil litigation, Criminal. Office: Allen Sparks & DeBerardinis 1939 17th St NW Washington DC 20009

DEBERRY, DENNIS CHARLES, lawyer; b. Denver, May 23, 1932; s. Charles and Irene C. (Politopoulos) DeB.; m. Anastasia Limperis, Nov. 24, 1963; children—Irene Denise, Charles Denis, John Denis. B.S., U. Denver, 1954, LL.B., 1957; LL.M. in Taxation, NYU, 1959. Bar: Colo. 1957, U.S. Dist. Ct. Colo. 1957, U.S. Tax Ct. 1960, U.S. Sup. Ct. 1965, U.S. Ct. Clms. 1966, Pa. 1969, Ariz. 1971, U.S. Dist. Ct. Ariz. 1981. Law clk. U.S. Dist. Ct., Denver, 1957-58; teaching fellow NYU, 1958-59; atty. Chief Counsel Office Mid-Atlantic Region, Phila., 1959-70, asst. regional counsel Office, Phoenix, 1970—, spl. trial atty., 1976-80, asst. dist. counsel, 1980—. Active Theodore Roosevelt council Boy Scouts Am.; mem. Holy Trinity Greek Orthodox Ch. Served to 1st lt. U.S. Army, 1954-56. Mem. ABA, Colo. Bar Assn., Ariz. Bar Assn., Phila. Bar Assn., Am. Judicature Soc. Clubs: Hellenic Univ., Am. Hellenic League (Phila.); Mason (Denver). Corporate taxation, Estate taxation, Personal income taxation. Address: 3225 N Central #1500 Phoenix AZ 85012

DEBEVOISE, DICKINSON RICHARDS, judge; b. Orange, N.J., Apr. 23, 1924; s. Elliott and Josephine (Richards) D.; m. Katrina Stephenson Leeb, Feb. 24, 1951; children: Kate, Josephine Debevoise Davies, Mary Debevoise Rennie, Abigail D. Byrne. B.A., Williams Coll., 1948; LL.B., Columbia U., 1951. Bar: N.J. 1953, U.S. Supreme Ct. 1956. Law clk. to Hon. Phillip Forman, chief judge U.S. Dist. Ct. for Dist. N.J., 1952-53; assoc. firm Riker, Emery & Danzig, Newark, 1953-56; partner firm Riker, Danzig, Scherer, Debevoise & Hyland, Newark, 1957-79; judge U.S. Dist. Ct. for N.J., 1979—; pres. Newark Legal Services Project, 1965-70; chmn. N.J. Gov.'s Workmen's Compensation Study Commn., 1972-73; mem. N.J. Supreme Ct. Adv. Com. on Jud. Conduct, 1974-78; chmn. N.J. Disciplinary Rev. Bd., 1978-79; mem. Lawyers Adv. Com. for 3d Circuit, 1975-79, chmn., 1979; chmn. N.J. Legal Services Adv. Council, 1976-78. Asso. editor: N.J. Law Jour, 1959-79. Trustee Ramapo Coll., N.J., 1969-73, chmn. bd., 1971-73; trustee Williams Coll., 1969-74; trustee Hosp. Center at Orange, N.J., v.p., 1975-79; pres. Democrats for Good Govt., 1956-60, active various presdl., senatorial, gubernatorial campaigns. Served from sgt. to 1st lt. U.S. Army, World War II, Korean War. Decorated Bronze Star. Fellow Am. Bar Found.; mem. Am. Bar Assn., N.J. Bar Assn., Fed. Bar Assn. (v.p. 1976), Assn. Fed. Bar State N.J. (v.p. 1977-79), Essex County Bar Assn. (treas. 1960-64, trustee 1968-71), Am. Law Inst., Judicature Soc. Mem. United Ch. of Christ. Office: US Courthouse Newark NJ 07101

DEBEVOISE, THOMAS MCELRATH, lawyer, educator; b. N.Y.C., Aug. 10, 1929; s. Eli Whitney and Barbara (Clay) D.; m. Ann Taylor, Nov. 1951; children: Eli Whitney II, Albert Clay, Thomas McElrath III, Anne Elizabeth. B.A., Yale U., 1950; LL.B., Columbia U., 1954; LL.D. (hon.), Vt. Law Sch., 1984. Bar: N.Y. 1954, Vt. 1957, D.C. 1963. Asst. U.S. Atty. So. Dist. N.Y., 1954-56; pvt. practice law Woodstock, Vt., 1957-59; dep. atty. gen. State of Vt., 1959-60, atty. gen., 1960-62; asst. gen. counsel Fed. Power Commn., 1962-64; pvt. practice law D.C., 1964; partner Debevoise & Liberman, 1965-74, counsel, 1975-82, partner, 1982-84; dean Vt. Law Sch., South Royalton, 1974-82, dean emeritus, 1982, trustee emeritus, 1983—. Pres. Woodstock Found., 1982—; bd. dirs. Lawyers Com. for Civil Rights Under Law, 1972-85, New Eng. Legal Found., 1976—; mem. Commn. on Instns. Higher Edn. of New Eng. Assn. Schs. and Colls., 1980-84; mem. Woods Hole Oceanographic Instn., 1986—; bd. overseers Dartmouth Med. Sch., 1985—. Fellow Am. Bar Found.; mem. Fed. Energy Bar Assn. (pres. 1973-74), ABA, Vt. Bar Assn., Phi Delta Phi. Republican. Episcopalian. Clubs: Lakota, National Lawyers, Century; University, Yale (N.Y.C.). Lodge: Masons. General corporate, Probate, Public utilities. Home: Woodstock VT 05091 Office: 18 Elm St Woodstock VT 05091

DEBO, VINCENT JOSEPH, lawyer, manufacturing company executive; b. Bklyn., Feb. 14, 1940; s. George and Letitia (Ruggiero) D.; m. Linda Mellucci, June 25, 1966; 1 dau., Jennifer Lynn. B.S., Fordham U., 1961, J.D., 1964. Bar: N.Y. 1965, U.S. Dist. Ct. (so. and ea. dists.) N.Y. 1967, U.S. Tax Ct. 1969, U.S. Ct. Appeals (2d cir.) 1967, U.S. Supreme Ct. 1969. Pvt. practice, 1964-70; corp. counsel Bangor Punta Corp., Greenwich, Conn., 1970-73; asst. gen. counsel, asst. sec. Rheem Mfg. Co., N.Y.C., 1973—, dir., officer various corp. subs. and joint ventures. Mem. ABA (subcoms.). Public international, Antitrust, Corporate taxation. Home: 7 Lee's Ln Westport CT 06880 Office: 350 Park Ave 11th Floor New York NY 10022-6022

DEBOIS, JAMES ADOLPHUS, lawyer; b. Oklahoma City, Dec. 23, 1929; s. James D. and Catherine (Bobo) DeB.; m. Mary Catherine Watkins, Aug. 4, 1951; children—James Adolphus Jr., Catherine Cecile, Annette Marie. B.A. in Liberal Arts, Okla. State U., 1951; LL.B., Okla., U., 1955. Bar: Okla. 1954, U.S. Dist. Ct. (ea. dist.) Okla. 1955, U.S. Dist. Ct. (we. dist.) Okla. 1959, Mo. 1963, N.Y. 1965, U.S. Ct. Appeals (8th cir.) 1969, Calif. 1971, U.S. Ct. Appeals (9th cir.) 1971, U.S. Ct. Appeals (D.C. cir.) 1975, U.S. Supreme Ct. 1976. Atty. Southwestern Bell Telephone Co., Oklahoma City, 1959-63, St. Louis, 1963-64, gen. atty., Oklahoma City, 1965-67, gen. solicitor, St. Louis, 1967-70; atty. Am. Telephone & Telegraph Co., N.Y.C., 1964-65, gen. atty., 1976, gen. atty., Basking Ridge, N.J., 1976-78, assoc. gen. counsel, 1978-83, corp. v.p. law, 1985—; v.p. legal dept. Pacific Telephone and Telegraph Co., San Francisco, 1970-71, v.p., gen. counsel, 1971-76; v.p., gen. counsel, sec. AT&T Info. Systems Inc. (formerly Am. Bell Inc.), Morristown, N.J., 1983-85. Served to lt. USAF, 1951-53, Korea. Mem. ABA (chmn. pub. utility law sect. 1985-86), Calif. Bar Assn., San Francisco Bar Assn. (sect. chmn. corp. law dept. 1975). Episcopalian. Club: Baltusrol (bd. govs. Springfield, N.J. 1982—). General corporate, Administrative and regulatory, General practice. Office: 1 Oak Way Room 4ED118 Berkeley Heights NJ 07922

DEBONIS, SHARON COUCH, lawyer; b. Schenectady, N.Y., July 17, 1952; d. Leslie Franklin and Joan Theresa (Dunham) Couch; m. Victor Michael DeBonis, Aug. 23, 1980; 1 child, John Christian Stanton. BA,

Bennington Coll., 1972; JD, Albany Law Sch., 1981. Bar: N.Y. 1982, U.S. Dist. Ct. (no. and we. dists.) N.Y. 1982, U.S. Ct. Appeals (2d cir.) 1985. Assoc. Couch & Howard P.C., Albany, N.Y., 1981—. Mem. exec. com. St. Peter's Hosp. Assn., Albany, 1986—; v.p. Women of St. Peter's Ch., Albany, 1986—; bd. dirs. Downtown Day Care Ctr. Inc., Albany, 1984—. Democrat. Episcopalian. Club: Steuben Athletic (Albany). Construction, Suretyship. Office: Couch & Howard PC 48 Howard St Albany NY 12207

DE BRIER, DONALD PAUL, lawyer; b. Atlantic City, Mar. 20, 1940; s. Daniel and Ethel de B.; m. Nancy Lee McElroy, Aug. 1, 1964; children: Lesley Anne, Rachel Wynne, Danielle Verne. B.A. in History, Princeton U., 1962; LL.B. with honors, U. Pa., 1967. Bar: Tex. 1977, N.Y. 1967, Utah 1983. Asso. firm Sullivan & Cromwell, N.Y.C., 1967-70, Patterson, Belknap, Webb & Tyler, N.Y.C., 1970-76; v.p., gen. counsel, dir. Gulf Resources & Chem. Corp., Houston, 1976-82; v.p. law Kennecott Corp. (a subs. Standard Oil Co.), Salt Lake City, 1983—; assoc. gen. counsel fin. Standard Oil Co., Cleve., 1987—. Served to lt. USNR, 1962-64. Club: Ft. Douglas. General corporate, General practice, Private international. Home: 22900 Shelburne Rd Shaker Heights OH 44122 Office: The Standard Oil Co 200 Public Sq 39-5300-B Cleveland OH 44114-2375

DE BRUIN, DAVID LEE, lawyer; b. Appleton, Wis., Feb. 15, 1955; s. Eugene J. and Alvina W. (Huss) De B.; m. Lynne Defebaugh, Jan. 30, 1982; children: Erica, Christopher. BS in Physics, MIT, 1977; M in Pub. Policy and JD, U. Mich., 1981. Bar: Wis. 1982, U.S. Dist. Ct. (ea. dist.) Wis. 1982, U.S. Ct. Appeals (7th cir.) 1982, U.S. Dist. Ct. (we. dist.) Wis. 1987. Law clk. to chief judge U.S. Dist. Ct., Milw., 1981-83; assoc. Whyte & Hirschboeck, Milw., 1983-85; ptnr. Kravit, Waisbren & De Bruin S.C., Milw., 1985—. Assoc. editor U. Mich. Law Rev., 1979-80, note editor, 1980-81. Mem. Wis. Dem. platform com., 1983—; nat. del. Wis. Dems., 1984; bd. dirs., pres. Cooperation West Side Assn., Milw., 1984-86, pres., Washington Park Community Devel. Corp., Milw., 1985—. Mem. ABA, Wis. Bar Assn., Milw. Bar Assn., 7th Cir. Bar Assn., Milw. Young Lawyers Assn. (legis. com.). Federal civil litigation, Scientific and technical litigation, Local government. Home: 1836 N Hi Mount Milwaukee WI 53208 Office: Kravit Waisbren & De Bruin SC 757 N Broadway Suite 600 Milwaukee WI 53202

DE BRULER, ROGER O., justice Ind. Supreme Ct.; b. 1934. A.B., LL.B., Ind. U. Bar: Ind. 1960. Dep. city prosecutor City of Indpls., 1960-63; judge Ind. Circuit Ct., Steuben County, 1963-68; Now justice Supreme Ct. of Ind., has also served as chief justice, 1968—. Office: Supreme Court of Indiana 321 State House Indianapolis IN 46204 *

DEBUSK, EDITH M., lawyer; b. Waco, Tex., Apr. 12, 1912; Otto Clifton and Margaret (Hatcher) Mann; m. Manuel C. DeBusk, June 13, 1941. LL.B., Dallas Sch. Law, 1941; Cert., So. Meth. U. Sch. Law, 1941. Atty. Regional Atty.'s Office (O.P.A.), Dallas, 1942; assoc. atty. Office of Karl F. Steinmann, Balt., 1943-46; mem. firm DeBusk & DeBusk, 1946—; Vice pres. Killeen Savs. & Loan Assn., The Teeling Mortgage Co., Inc.; dir. DeBusk Corp.; officer East Town Osteo. Hosp. Corp. Former mem. Gov.'s Com. on Aging; dir. Dallas Citizens Commn. on Action for Aging, Inc.; del. to White House Conf. Children and Youth, 1960, Conf. on Aging, 1961; mem. Dallas Bd. Adjustment, 1963-65; former bd. dirs. Dallas United Cerebral Palsy Assn., Tex. Soc. Aging, Dallas County Community Action Com., Inc.; trustee Found. for Cranio-Facial Deformities, Nina Fay Calhoun Scholarship Fund Trust; former mem. adv. council Sr. Citizens Found., Inc.; former mem. div. aging Council of Social Agys., Citizens Traffic Commn.; former sec., legal adviser Tex. Fedn. Bus. and Profl. Women's Clubs; bd. visitors Freedoms Found. at Valley Forge. Named Woman of the Month Dallas Mag., 1948; Woman of Week Balt., 1945; recipient George Washington honor medal Freedoms Found. Fellow Tex. Bar Found. (life); mem. State Bar Tex., ABA (chmn. com. state and local taxation 1979-81), Dallas Bar Assn. (numerous coms.), Women's Council of Dallas County (legis. com.), Bus. and Profl. Women's Club Dallas (past pres.), Nat. Assn. Women in Constrn. (hon.), Delta Kappa Gamma (hon.), Kappa Beta Pi (past dean province IV). Presbyn. Club: Altrusa (Dallas) (pres. internat. 1963-65). General practice, Landlord-tenant, Real property. Home: 7365 Elmridge Dr Dallas TX 75240 Office: DeBusk & DeBusk 13117 Meandering Way Dallas TX 75240

DECHENE, JAMES CHARLES, lawyer; b. Petaluma, Calif., May 14, 1953; s. Harry George and Domenica Theresa (Cuffia) D.; m. Teresa Marie Caserza, Aug. 2, 1975; children: Michelle, Mark, Sabrina, Diane. BS summa cum laude, Santa Clara U., 1975; JD magna cum laude, U. Mich., 1978, AM in Econs., 1978, PhD in Econs., 1980. Bar: Ill. 1979, U.S. Dist. Ct. (no. dist.) Ill. 1980. Assoc. Sidley & Austin, Chgo., 1980-86, ptnr., 1986—. Contbr. articles to profl. jours. Mem. ABA, Ill. Bar Assn., Chgo. Bar. Assn., Nat. Health Lawyers Assn., Am. Economics. Assn. Democrat. Roman Catholic. Health, Administrative and regulatory, Antitrust. Home: 5510 Cumnor Rd Downers Grove IL 60516 Office: Sidley & Austin One First Nat Plaza Chicago IL 60603

DECKER, FRANK NORTON, JR., lawyer; b. Syracuse, N.Y., July 18, 1930; s. Frank N. Sr. and Helen (Ohlman) D.; m. Carol Sowles, Nov. 23, 1978. AB, Syracuse U., 1952, JD, 1955. Bar: N.Y. 1955, U.S. Dist. Ct. (no. dist.) N.Y. 1955, U.S. Ct. Appeals (fed. cir.) 1978. Asst. patent counsel internat. Carrier Corp., Syracuse, 1959—. Mem. adv. council St. Joseph's Hosp., Syracuse. Mem. ABA. Club: University (Syracuse). Private international, Patent, Trademark and copyright. Home: 1342 Broad St Syracuse NY 13224 Office: Carrier Corp PO Box 4800 Syracuse NY 13221

DECKER, HAROLD JAMES, lawyer, educator; b. Kalamazoo, Feb. 23, 1945; s. Harold and Dena Decker; m. Rosemary Tucker, July 23, 1968; children: Mereke E., Ariane E., Joisan E. BA in Polit. Sci., Kalamazoo Coll., 1967; JD, Southwestern U., Los Angeles, 1973. Bar: Calif. 1974, U.S. Dist. Ct. (cen. dist.) Calif. 1974, U.S. Supreme Ct. 1977, U.S. Ct. Appeals (6th cir.) 1983, Mich. 1985, U.S. Dist. Ct. (no. dist.) Calif. 1985, U.S. Dist. Ct. (we. and ea. dists.) Mich. 1985, U.S. Ct. Appeals (9th cir.) 1985. Assoc. Parker, Stanbury, McGee & Combs, Los Angeles, 1974-75; ptnr. Christensen, Fazio, McDonnell, Briggs & Ward, La Habra, Calif., 1975-80; atty. Upjohn Co., Kalamazoo, 1980—; lectr. Los Angeles Trial Lawyers Assn., 1976-80; prof. T.M. Cooley Law Sch., Lansing, Mich., 1985—; arbitrator U.S. Dist. Ct. (we. dist.) Mich., 1985—. Pres. bd. dirs. Boy's and Girl's Club of Whittier, Calif., 1978-80; v.p. found. Montessori Sch., Kalamazoo, 1981-84. Served to sgt. U.S. Army, 1968-70, Vietnam. Decorated Bronze Star, Air medal. Mem. ABA (discovery com., rules and procedure com.), Def. Research Inst. (duty to warn com.), Kalamazoo County Bar Assn., Internat. Assn. Def. Counsel. Republican. Mem. Ch. Christ. Lodge: Rotary. Federal civil litigation, State civil litigation, Personal injury. Home: 5105 Whippoorwill Kalamazoo MI 49002 Office: Upjohn Co 7000 Portage Rd Kalamazoo MI 49001

DECKER, JENNIFER HENSON, lawyer; b. Somerset, Ky., Jan. 19, 1956; d. Harold Edward and Frances (Hawkins) Henson; m. William Bernard Decker Jr., Sept. 25, 1982; 1 child, Jessica Henson. BA, Eastern Ky. U., 1978, MA, 1979; JD, U. Ky., 1982. Bar: Ky. 1982, U.S. Tax Ct. 1982. Atty. dist. counsel IRS, Cin. and Louisville, 1982—. Mem. ABA, Ky. Bar Assn., Cin. Bar Assn., Women's Lawyers Assn., Order of Coif, Phi Delta Phi, U. Ky. Law Sch. Alumni Assn. Republican. Club: United Meth. Women (Williamstown, Ky.). Avocations: tennis, reading, needlework. Corporate taxation, Estate taxation, Personal income taxation. Home: 117 Cheyenne Rd Shelbyville KY 40065 Office: IRS Dist Counsel 600 Federal Pl 659 Fed Bldg Louisville KY 40202

DECKER, JOHN FRANCIS, lawyer, educator; b. Sherrill, Iowa, May 15, 1944; s. Lawrence and Loretta (Hefel) D.; B.A., U. Iowa, 1967; J.D., Creighton U., 1970; LL.M., NYU, 1971, J.S.D., 1979. Bar: Calif. 1973, U.S. Dist. Ct. (no. dist.) Calif. 1973, Ill. 1978, U.S. Dist. Ct. (no. dist.) Ill. 1980, U.S. Ct. Appeals (7th cir.) 1981. Asst. prof. DePaul U. Coll. Law, Chgo., 1971-73, assoc. prof., 1974-79, prof. law, 1979—, coordinator extern program, 1978—; counsel R.E. Robbins Law Firm, Stockton, Ill., 1978-79; vis. prof. U. San Francisco Sch. Law, 1980; reporter Ill. Jud. Conf., Chgo., 1981—. Author: Prostitution: Regulation and Control, 1979, Illinois Criminal Law: A Survey of Crimes and Defenses, 1986; contbr. articles to profl jours; staff editor Creighton Law Rev., 1969-70. Recipient Faculty Achievement award DePaul U., 1984, Outstanding Teaching award, 1985, Award of Distinction, DePaul Law Rev., 1978. Mem. ABA, Assn. Trial Lawyers Am. Democrat. Roman Catholic. Criminal, Legal education. Home: 306 Maple Elmhurst IL 60126 Office: DePaul Univ Coll of Law 25 E Jackson Blvd Chicago IL 60604

DECKER, JOHN ROBERT, lawyer; b. Milw., Apr. 29, 1952; s. John Anthony and Margaret Eleanor (Cook) D.; m. Sandra Jean Kuelz, May 25, 1974; 1 child: Jennifer. BA, U. Wis., 1974; JD, Marquette U., 1977. Bar: Wis. 1977, U.S. Ct. Appeals (7th cir.) 1978. Assoc. Michael, Best & Friedrich, Madison, Wis., 1977-80; assoc. Michael, Best & Friedrich, Milw., 1980-84, ptnr., 1984—. Co-author: Special Verdict Formulation in Wis., 1977; exec. editor Marquette U. Law Rev., 1976-77. Trustee Mt. Zion Luth. Ch., 1986—. Named one of Outstanding Young Men Am. Mem. ABA (house dels. 1984—, governing com. of the forum com. on constrn. industry, 1987—, achievement award 1985), Wis. Bar Assn. (bd. govs. 1984—, exec. com. 1984-85), Milw. Bar Assn., Milw. Young Lawyers Assn. Federal civil litigation, State civil litigation, Construction. Home: 2611 N 89th St Wauwatosa WI 53226 Office: Michael Best & Friedrich 250 E Wisconsin Ave Milwaukee WI 53202

DECKER, KURT HANS, lawyer, lecturer, researcher; b. Phila., Sept. 23, 1946; s. Hans Emil and Gertrude Elsa (Nestler) D.; m. Hilary McAllister, Aug. 13, 1973; children—Kurt Christian, Allison McAllister. B.A. in History, Thiel Coll., 1968; M.P.A., Pa. State U., 1973; J.D., Vanderbilt U., 1976; LL.M. in Labor, Temple U., 1980. Bar: Pa. 1976, U.S. Tax Ct. 1977, U.S. Ct. Internat. Trade 1977, U.S. Ct. Claims 1979, U.S. Dist. Ct. (mid. dist.) Pa. 1976, U.S. Dist. Ct. (ea. dist.) Pa. 1980, U.S. Ct. Appeals (3d cir.) 1980, U.S. Supreme Ct. 1980. Asst. atty. gen. Gov.'s Office, Pa. Bur. Labor Relations, Harrisburg, 1976-79; counsel Stevens & Lee, Reading, Pa., 1979—; adj. asst. prof. Indsl. Relations St. Francis Coll., Pa., 1985—; seminar speaker Reading/Berks Area C. of C., 1980, Dickinson Sch. Law, 1983, Reading Area Community Coll., 1985—; researcher in field. Author: Employment Privacy: Law and Practice; adminstrv. editor Vanderbilt Jour. Transnat. Law; bd. editors Jour. Collective Negotiations in Pub. Sector, 1982—; contbr. chpts. to books, articles to profl. jours. Served with U.S. Army, 1968-72. Decorated Army Commendation medal. Mem. ABA (sect. labor and employment law), Pa. Bar Assn. (sect. labor and employment law, News Media award 1985), Phila. Bar Assn., Berks County Bar Assn., Am. Soc. Personnel Adminstrn., Am. Soc. Pub. Adminstrn., Internat. Personnel Mgmt. Assn., Sigma Phi Epsilon, Phi Alph Delta. Lutheran. Labor. Office: Stevens & Lee 607 Washington St Reading PA 19601

DECKER, MICHAEL LYNN, lawyer, judge; b. Oklahoma City, May 5, 1953; s. Leroy Melvin and Yvonne (Baird) D.; m. Robin Strom. BA, Oklahoma City U., 1975, JD, 1978. Bar: Okla. 1978, U.S. Ct. Appeals (10th cir.) 1979, U.S. Dist. Ct. (we. dist.) Okla. 1985. Assoc. Bay, Hamilton, Lees, Spears, and Verity, Oklahoma City, 1978-80; assoc. dir. devel. Oklahoma City U., 1980-81, asst. dean, Sch. of Law, 1981-82; oil and gas hearing officer Okla. Corp. Commn., Oklahoma City, 1982—; campaign staff intern U.S. senator Henry Bellmon's Re-election Campaign, 1974; mem. Civil Arbitration Panel, U.S. Dist. Ct. (we. dist.) Okla., 1985; seminar speaker Am. Inst. Profl. Geologists (Okla. sect.), 1985; mem. dean's adv. com. Oklahoma City U. Law Sch., 1986. Named One Outstanding Young Men of Am., U.S. Jaycees, 1985. Mem. ABA (adminstrv. law sect.), Nat. Assn. Adminstrv. Law Judges, Okla. Bar Assn. (exec. com. young lawyers sect. 1978-82), Okla. County Bar Assn. (exec. com. young lawyers sect. 1978-82, mem. law day com. 1979-87, chmn. law day luncheon speaker com. 1985-87), Okla. County Mineral Lawyers Soc., Phi Alpha Delta, Lambda Chi Alpha (treas. bldg. corp. 1984-86, Outstanding Alumnus award 1983). Republican. United Methodist. Administrative and regulatory, Jurisprudence, Oil and gas leasing. Home: 2008 NW 44 St Oklahoma City OK 73118 Office: Okla Corp Commn State Capitol Complex Jim Thorpe Bldg Oklahoma City OK 73116

DECKER, THOMAS ANDREW, manufacturing company executive, lawyer; b. Phila., Feb. 13, 1946; s. Arnold f. and Emma M. (Puhl) D.; m. M. Candace Jaeger; children—Samantha Elizabeth, John Thomas. B.A., U. Pa., 1968; J.D., U. Va., 1971. Bar: Pa. Assoc. Pepper, Hamilton & Scheetz, Phila., 1971-73; counsel Lease Financing Corp., Bryn Mawr, Pa., 1973-74; sr. counsel Certain-Teed Corp., Valley Forge, Pa., 1974-81, gen. counsel, 1981—. Served to capt. U.S. Army, 1972. Address: PO Box 860 Valley Forge PA 19482

DECUYPER, JOSEPH YSIDORE, lawyer; b. Arma, Kans., Aug. 22, 1931; s. Ferdinand Alexander and Beulah (Benda) DeC.; m. Helen Margaret Bishop, July 2, 1960; children—Deborah Ann, Joseph Ysidore, Stephen Bradford. B.B.A., Kansas State U., 1959; J.D., U. Mo., 1961. Bar: Mo. 1961, U.S. Dist. Ct. (we. dist.) Mo. 1963, U.S. Supreme Ct. 1980. Assoc., then sr. ptnr. Linde, Thomson et al., Kansas City, Mo., 1961-71; mng. sr. ptnr. Snowden, Crain & DeCuyper, Kansas City, 1971-76, Snowden & DeCuyper, Kansas City, 1976-84, DeCuyper & Lee, Kansas City, 1984-85, De Cuyper & Assocs., 1985—; mcpl. judge City of Gladstone, Mo., 1967-69; chief trial asst. office of pros. atty. Clay County, Mo., 1968-79. Served with USN, 1950-54. Recipient cert. of service City Council, Gladstone, 1969, cert. of merit Mo. Assn. Counties, 1978. Mem. Kansas City Bar Assn., Lawyers Assn. Kansas City, Clay County Bar Assn., ABA, Am. Judicature Soc., Mo. Assn. Trial Lawyers, Assn. Trial Lawyers Am. Roman Catholic. Lodge Rotary. State civil litigation, Federal civil litigation, General practice. Home: 6219 N Askew St Kansas City MO 64119 Office: De Cuyper & Assocs 6317 NE Antioch Rd Kansas City MO 64119

DEE, DAVID SCOTT, lawyer; b. Hollywood, Fla., Sept. 23, 1952; s. Clarence Everett and Lucille Ella (Frederickson) D.; m. Martha Lou Davis, June 25, 1983. BA, Emory U., 1974; JD with high honors, Fla. State U., 1979. Bar: Fla. 1979, U.S. Dist. Ct. (no. dist.) Fla. 1980, U.S. Dist. Ct. (so. dist.) Fla. 1981, U.S. Dist. Ct. (mid. dist.) Fla. 1982, U.S. Ct. Appeals (11th cir.) 1986. Assoc. Hopping, Boyd, Green & Sams, Tallahassee, 1979-81; sr. atty. Carlton, Fields, Ward, Emmanuel, Smith & Cutler, P.A., Tallahassee, 1981—; lectr. on environ. law, 1985-87. Contbr. articles to profl. jours. Bd. dirs. Goodwill Industries Big Bend Inc., Tallahassee, 1986. Mem. ABA, Fla. Bar Assn. (environ. law com.), Tallahassee Bar Assn., Tallahassee C. of C. Leadership (alumni 1985—), Order of Coif, Phi Beta Kappa, Omicron Delta Kappa. Democrat. Lutheran. Environment, Administrative and regulatory, Real property. Office: Carlton Fields Ward et al PO Drawer 190 Tallahassee FL 32302

DEEGAN, NAN MARIE, lawyer; b. Memphis, Dec. 7, 1952; d. Anthony Francis and Frances (Bremer) D.; m. James Douglas Marr, Mar. 4, 1984 (div. July 1985). AA, DeKalb Coll., 1971-72; BA, Mercer U., 1973-74; JD, Woodrow Wilson U., 1978-80; MEd, Ga. State U., 1977-85. Bar: Ga. 1981, U.S. Dist. Ct. (no. dist.) Ga. 1982, U.S. Ct. Appeals (11th cir.) 1982, U.S. Tax Ct. 1983. Tchr. high sch. Decatur, Ga., 1978-81; mgr. Brantley Group, College Park, Ga., 1982; sole practice Jonesboro, Ga., 1982—. Rotary Club fellow, 1975-76. Mem. ABA, Ga. Assn. Women Attys., Clayton County Bar Assn., Ga. Mineral Soc. Club: Atlanta Ski. Avocations: tennis, skiing, sailing, scuba, golf, photography. Personal injury, Criminal, Consumer commercial. Home: 3812 Parklane Dr Clarkston GA 30021 Office: 108 Courthouse Way Jonesboro GA 30236

DEEHL, DAVID LEE, lawyer; b. Miami, Fla., Sept. 15, 1956; s. Robert Marion and Catherine (Rohe) D. BA in Econs., Vanderbilt U., 1978; JD cum laude, U. Miami, 1982. Bar: Fla. 1982, U.S. Dist Ct. (so. and mid. dists.) Fla. 1983, U.S. Ct. Appeals (11th cir.) 1983, U.S. Supreme Ct. 1987. Assoc. Floyd, Pearson, Stewart, Richman, Greer & Weil, Miami, 1982-84, Anderson, Moss, Russo & Gievers, Miami, 1984-85, Payton & Rachlin, Miami, 1985; ptnr. Wallace, Engels & Pertnoy, Miami, 1985—. Active nat. student recruitment com. Vanderbilt U., Nashville, 1985—. Named one of Outstanding Young Men of Am., 1985. Mem. Assn. Trial Lawyers Am., Acad. Fla. Trial Lawyers, S. Fla. Interprofl. Council (treas. 1986), Fla. Bar Assn. (mem. health law com.), Dade County Bar Assn. (bd. dirs. 1983-86, features editor newsletter 1982-84), Dade County Trial Lawyers Assn. (bd. dirs. 1984—), Greater Miami Running Assn. Democrat. Unitarian. Club: Vanderbilt (Miami)(pres. 1982-84). Avocations: marathon running, snow skiing, scuba diving. State civil litigation, Federal civil litigation, Personal injury. Office: Wallace Engels Pertnoy & Martin 330 Biscayne Blvd 6th Floor Miami FL 33132

DEEMS, NYAL DAVID, lawyer, mayor; b. Cleve., Jan. 24, 1948; s. Nyal Wilbert and Octavia C. (Roush) D.; m. Gretchen Ann Pfleghaar, Dec. 27, 1969; children: Brooke Elizabeth, Nyal Christopher, Holly Jean, Eric Wellington. BA in Internat. Studies, Miami U., 1969; JD, U. Ga., 1976. Bar: Ga. 1976, Mich. 1976, U.S. Dist. Ct. (we. dist.) Mich., U.S. Dist. Ct. (no. dist.) Ga. Assoc. then ptnr. Varnum, Riddering, Wierengo & Christenson now Varnum, Riddering, Schmidt & Howlett, Grand Rapids, Mich., 1976—; mayor City of East Grand Rapids, Mich., 1985—. Coauthor: Mich. Real Estate Sales Transactions, 1983. Commr. City of East Grand Rapids, 1982-85; active various fund-raising orgns. Served to lt. USN, 1969-73. Mem. ABA, Ga. Bar Assn., Mich. Bar Assn. (chmn. water law com. 1984—, real property council 1984—), Grand Rapids Bar Assn. Real property, Oil and gas leasing, Landlord-tenant. Home: 508 Cambridge Blvd SE East Grand Rapids MI 49506 Office: Varnum Riddering Schmidt & Howlett 171 Monroe NW Suite 800 Grand Rapids MI 49503

DEEN, THOMAS JEFFERSON, III, lawyer; b. Jacksonville, Fla., Apr. 4, 1952; s. Thomas Jefferson and Betty Jo (Langston) D.; m. Mary Ann Mitchell, Dec. 30, 1976 (div. Sept. 1980). BA in Econs., Stetson U., 1970-74; JD, Cumberland U., 1974-77. Bar: Ala. 1977, U.S. Dist. Ct. (no. dist.) Ala. 1978, U.S. Dist. Ct. (so. dist.) Ala. 1981, U.S. Ct. Appeals (11th cir.) 1982, U.S. Supreme Ct. 1985. Assoc. Merrill, Merrill & Vardaman, Anniston, Ala., 1977-78; mng. atty. Legal Aid Soc., Tuscaloosa, Ala., 1979-80; asst. dist. atty. Mobile County D.A.'s Office, Ala., 1980-81; sole practice Mobile, 1982-86; ptnr. Clark, Deen & Copeland, Mobile, 1987—. Bd. dirs. Ala. Dance Theatre, Mobile, 1982; pres. Mobile Theatre Guild, 1984—; treas. Second Saturday Poetry Series, Mobile, 1984—; mem. Mobile Arts Council, 1984—. Named one of Outstanding Young Men of Am., 1985. Mem. ABA, Ala. Bar Assn., Assn. Trial Lawyers Am., Ala. Trial Lawyers Assn., Nat. Assn. Criminal Def. Lawyers, Omnicron Delta Kappa. Democrat. Baptist. Club: Port City Pacers (bd. dirs. 1984-85). Criminal, Family and matrimonial, State civil litigation. Home: 206 S Cedar St Mobile AL 36602 Office: 207 Church St Mobile AL 36602

DEER, JAMES WILLIS, lawyer; b. Reading, Pa., Mar. 14, 1917; s. Irvin E. and Rosemary (French) D.; m. Marion M. Hawkinson, July 31, 1943; 1 child, Ann Marie. A.B, Oberlin Coll, 1938; J. D., U. Mich., 1941. Bar: Ohio 1941, N.Y. 1948. Legal staff SEC, 1942-45; practice in N.Y.C., 1945—; mem. firm Holtzmann, Wise & Shepard, 1954—; chmn. bd. Western Auto Supply Corp., 1960; sec. Teleregister Corp., 1953-69, DuBois Chems., Inc., 1960-62; dir. Weigh-tronix Inc., 1979-86, Arts Way Mfg. Co., Inc., Selvac Corp., Am. Diversified Enterprises, Inc., Techsci. Industries. Mem. Am., N.Y. State bar assns., Phi Beta Kappa, Phi Alpha Delta. General corporate, Securities. Home: 611 Shore Acres Dr Mamaroneck NY 10543 also: Barr Terr 50 East Dr Delray Beach FL 33444 Office: 745 Fifth Ave New York NY 10151

DEER, WILLIAM HENRY, lawyer; b. Indpls., Dec. 20, 1930; s. Leon and Mary Jane (Ostheimer) D.; m. Helen Glende, Aug. 4, 1978. B.A., DePauw U., 1953; LL.B., Harvard U., 1956. Bar: Ind. 1956, Ill. 1958. Assoc., Ross, Hardies, O'Keefe & Babcock, Chgo., 1959-76; sole practice, Dolton, Ill., 1977-84; ptnr., William H. Deer and Assocs., 1984— . Vice pres., bd. dirs. Dr. K.F. Luke Found., South Holland, 1981—; cons. Episcopal-Chinese Activities, Chgo. Diocese, Nat. Trust Hist. Preservation, 1979-83; mem. Lyric Opera Chgo., 1966-83. Served with AUS, 1956-58. DePauw U. Rector scholar, 1952. Mem. Ill. Bar Assn., Chgo. Bar Assn., South Suburban Bar Assn., Phi Beta Kappa. Bankruptcy, General corporate, General practice. Office: 1350 E Sibley Blvd Suite 206 Dolton IL 60419

DEERSON, BRUCE ALAN, lawyer; b. N.Y.C., Apr. 8, 1951; s. Nathan and Adele (Shapiro) D.; m. Amy Ellen Rips, Sept. 20, 1981; 1 child, Greta Beth. BA, Johns Hopkins U.; JD, George Washington U., 1975. Bar: Va. 1975, N.Y. 1976, D.C. 1976. Law clk. to presiding justice U.S. Dist. Ct. (ea. dist) N.Y., 1975-77; assoc. Howrey & Simon, Washington, 1977-79; asst. gen. counsel Martin Marietta Corp., Bethesda, Md., 1979-87. Mem. ABA, Am. Corp. Counsel Assn. Republican. Jewish. Antitrust, Contracts commercial, General corporate. Home: 5 Cumbernauld Ct Rockville MD 20850 Office: Martin Marietta 6801 Rockledge Dr Bethesda MD 20817

DEES, RICHARD LEE, lawyer; b. Harrisburg, Pa., Jan. 14, 1955; s. David Lee and Joann (Alvey) D.; m. Christina Marie Cook, Aug. 18, 1979; children: Sarah Elizabeth, Elliott Richard. AS, Southeastern Ill. Jr. Coll., 1975; BS, So. Ill. U., 1977; JD, U. Ill., 1980. Bar: Ill. 1980, U.S. Tax Ct. 1981. Ptnr. McDermott, Will & Emery, Chgo., 1980—. Editor: Agricultural Law and Tax Report, 1984—; topics editor U. Ill. Law Forum, 1979-80; also articles. Mem. ABA, Ill. Bar Assn., Chgo. Bar Assn. (chmn. agri-bus. com.), Am. Agricultural Law Assn. (chmn. membership com. 1986—), Chgo. Estate Planning Council, Chgo. Farmers (chmn. program com.), Order of Coif. Methodist. Probate, Estate taxation, Agriculture. Home: 4436 Howard Western Springs IL 60558 Office: McDermott Will & Emery 111 W Monroe St Chicago IL 60603

DEFALAISE, LOUIS, lawyer; b. Covington, Ky., Apr. 27, 1945; s. James Willard and Mildred Carolyn (Howard) DeF.; m. Susan Jane Court, June 12, 1968 (div.); children: David, Mary. B.A., Thomas More Coll., 1968; J.D., U. Ky., 1971. Bar: Ky. 1971, U.S. Dist. Ct. (eastern dist.) Ky. 1972, U.S. Ct. Appeals (6th cir.) 1972, U.S. Supreme Ct. 1975. Assoc. Adams, Brooking & Stepner, Covington, 1971, 74-81; asst. U.S. atty. Eastern Dist. Ky. Dept. Justice, Lexington, 1972-73, U.S. atty., 1981—; mem. Ky. Ho. of Reps., Frankfort, 1976-81, vice chmn. judiciary com., 1976-81; mem. Ky. gov.'s Select Com. on Implementation of New Jud. Article, 1976-78. Paliamentarian Republican Central Com., Frankfort, 1980-81. Roman Catholic. Criminal, Federal civil litigation, Law enforcement. Home: 129 Deauville Ct Fort Mitchell KY 41017

DEFELICE, DENNIS JOSEPH, lawyer; b. Spokane, Mar. 8, 1945; s. Joseph Albert and Yolanda Edna (Giampietri) DeF.; m. Joyce Henrietta Olson, June 4, 1977. BA, Yale U.; JD, U. Tex. Sole practice Pasco, 1981-86; pros. atty. Franklin County, 1987—; dep. prosecutor Skagit County, Mt. Vernon, Wash., 1975, Whatcom County, Bellingham, Wash., 1976-77; asst. atty. City of Seattle, 1977-78; atty. City of Pasco, Wash., 1978-81. Bd. dirs. Benton-Franklin Community Action Com., Pasco, 1984. Mem. Pasco C. of C. (bd. dirs. 1985-86). Republican. Lodge: Kiwanis (bd. mem. Pasco chpt. 1980-81), Moose. Criminal, Local government, Environment. Home: 4607 Hilltop Dr Pasco WA 99301 Office: PO Box 1160 Pasco WA 99301

DEFFINA, THOMAS VICTOR, lawyer, consultant; b. N.Y.C., Mar. 14, 1942; s. Philip Anthony and Antoinette (Napoli) D. BA, St. John's U., Jamaica, N.Y., 1964, JD, 1967. Bar: N.Y. 1967, U.S. Dist. Ct. (so. and ea. dists.) N.Y. 1968, U.S. Ct. Customs and Patent Appeals 1968. Assoc. Manton, Giaimo, P.C., N.Y.C., 1968-74; Anthony L. Schiavetti Law Practice, N.Y.C., 1974-77; ptnr. Deffina & Blau, P.C., N.Y.C., 1977-86, Deffina, Rosner & Nocera, N.Y.C., 1986—; trial cons. Employers Ins. Wausau, N.Y.C., 1977—, Chubb & Son., N.Y.C., 1986—, Aetna Casualty and Surety, N.Y.C., 1986, The Hartford, N.Y.C., 1986—, Fidelity and Deposit Co. of Md., N.J., 1986—, First Fidelity Bank N.A., N.J., 1986—; group council Mutual Ins. Co., N.Y.C.; talk show panelist Readers Digest Lifeline, Nat. Pub. Service TV, 1982. Contbg. author text on med. malpractice. Mem. ABA, N.Y. State Bar Assn., N.Y. State Trial Lawyers Assn. Republican. Roman Catholic. Club: Downtown Athletic. Fidelity/Surety bond claims, Federal civil litigation, State civil litigation. Home: 8 Mountain Run Boonton Township NJ 07005 Office: Deffina Rosner & Nocera 377 Broadway New York NY 10013

DEFFNER, ROGER L., lawyer, investment counselor; b. Merrill, Wis., Aug. 17, 1945; s. Oscar A. and Elsie E. (Liebers) D.; m. Cynthia S. Petrauskas, Aug. 22, 1982. B.S. in Chem. Engring., U. Wis.-Madison, 1968, J.D., 1973. Bar: Wis. 1973, U.S. Dist. Ct. (we. dist.) Wis. 1973. Chem. engr. prodn. and research, spl. products div. NCR, Portage, Wis., 1968-69; chem. engr. plant modernization Olin Chem., Baraboo, Wis., 1969-70; pres., owner Deffner Law Firm, S. C., Wausau, 1973—; gen. ptnr. D&D Investments, Wausau, 1974—, Embryo Genetics, Wausau, Wis., 1983—; sec.-treas. Legal Systems, Inc., Rhinelander, Wis., 1977—; advisor N. Central Tech. Inst., Wausau, 1977-81. Co-author: Legal Systems Inc., 1977-78. Mem. Wausau C. of C. (agribus. com.), Jaycees (bd. dirs. Portage 1969, pres. 1970, state v.p. Madison 1971, dir. Wausau 1974, chmn. 4th celebration 1975, assoc. mem.

1982—). Republican. Lutheran. Club: Wausau Noon Optimists (internal v.p. 1985-86, pres. 1986-87). Lodge: Elks. Consumer commercial, Real property, General practice. Office: Deffner Law Firm SC 124 Washington St Wausau WI 54401

DE FINO, MICHAEL G., lawyer; b. Phila., Sept. 1, 1945; s. Rocco J. and Violet R. (Bono) De F.; m. Mary Jo Jean Christinzio, Mar. 24, 1973; children—Jennifer, Christian. B.A., La Salle Coll., Phila., 1968; J.D., Widener U., Wilmington, Del., 1975. Bar: Pa. U.S. Dist. Ct. (ea. dist.) Pa. 1976, U.S. Ct. Appeals (3d cir.) 1979, U.S. Supreme Ct. 1981. Ptnr. De Fino, Coppolino & Maiale, Phila., 1976-81, De Fino, De Fino & DeFino, Phila., 1981-84; sole practice, Phila., 1984—. Mem. Republican Lawyers Com., 1980—; bd. overseers Del. Law Sch., Widener U., 1981—; mem. Big Bros.-Big Sisters, Delaware County, Pa., 1982—. Recipient outstanding alumni achievement award Del. Law Sch., 1983. Mem. ABA, Pa. Bar Assn., Phila. Bar Assn., Assn. Trial Lawyers Am., Pa. Trial Lawyers Assn., Phila. Trial Lawyers Assn., Justinian Soc. (chancellor 1984-86). General practice, State civil litigation, Personal injury. Home: 1991 Kimberwick Rd Rose Tree Media PA 19063 Office: 1717 Rittenhouse Sq Philadelphia PA 19103 Office: 111 N Olive St Media PA 19063

DEFOOR, JAMES ALLISON, II, judge; b. Coral Gables, Fla., Dec. 6, 1953; s. James Allison Sr. and Marjorie (Keen) DeF.; m. Terry Ann White, June 24, 1977; children: Melissa Anne, Mary Katherine. BA, U. So. Fla., 1976; JD, Stetson U., 1979; MA, U. So. Fla., 1979. Bar: Fla. 1979, U.S. Dist. Ct. (so. dist.) Fla. 1980, U.S. Ct. Appeals (5th cir.) 1981, U.S. Ct. Appeals (11th cir.) 1982. Asst. state's atty. 16th Cir., Key West, Fla., 1980-83; dir. narcotics task force 16th Cir., Key West, 1981-83; judge Monroe County, Plantation Key, Fla., 1983—; pres. Keen Fruit Corp., Key West, 1979-83; adj. faculty St. Leo Coll., Key West, 1980-81, U. So. Fla., Ft. Myers, Fla., 1981-82, Fla. Internat. U., Miami, 1985, U. Miami Law Sch., 1985—; bd. of trustees U. of South, Sewanee, Tenn., 1983—; faculty Nat. Jud. Coll., Reno, Nev., 1985—. Pres. Fla. Keys Land Trust, Key West, 1985-86. Named one of Five Outstanding Young Men in Fla., Jaycees, 1984, Ten Outstanding Young Men in Am., Jaycees, 1985; Merit award Fla. Crime Prevention Commn., 1982. Mem. ABA, Fla. Bar Assn., Monroe County Bar Assn., Lawyers in Mensa, Fla. Conf. County Cir. Judges (bd. dirs. 1985—). Republican. Episcopalian. Clubs: St. Petersburg (Fla.) Yacht, Ocean Reef (Key Largo, Fla.). Avocations: scuba diving, sailing. Judicial administration, Technology and the courts. Office: Monroe County Judges Chambers 88820 Overseas Hwy Tavernier FL 33070

DEGALLEGOS, RICHARD, lawyer, real estate developer; b. Albuquerque, Oct. 21, 1940; s. Enrique Jorge and Bersebabe June G.; children—Suzette Christina, Lisa Marie, Richard Robert, Anna Suzette, Sarah Noel. B.A. in Chemistry and Math., U. N.Mex., 1966, M.A., 1966; J.D., Western State Coll. Law, 1975. Bar: Calif., 1978, Wyo.; teaching cert. in law Calif. Community Colls. Sole practice, San Diego, 1978—; developer; broker; prof. U.S. Internat. U., San Diego, Nat. U., San Diego; instr. North City Community Coll., San Diego, 1977—. Mem. ABA (real estate and probate div.). Estate planning, Contracts commercial, Real property. Home: 2541 Peet Ln Escondido CA 92025 Office: 12323 Poway Rd Poway CA 92064 Office: R Lawrence Fin & Ins Services Inc Treena and Hibert Sts San Diego CA 92138

DEGENHARDT, HAROLD F., lawyer; b. Utica, N.Y., July 28, 1946; s. Harold J. and Winifred (Flattery) D.; m. Patricia Martin, Dec. 21, 1968; children: Harold W., Meredith, Sara Jane. BA in Hist., Villanova U., 1968; JD, Fordham U., 1973. Bar: N.Y., Tex., U.S. Dist. Ct. (so. and ea. dists.) N.Y., U.S. Dist. Ct. N.J., U.S. Dist. Ct. (ea. and no. dists.) Tex., U.S. Ct. Appeals (2d, 3d and 5th cirs.). Assoc. Mudge, Rose, Guthrie & Alexander, N.Y.C., 1973-77; atty. products liability Dresser Industries, Dallas, 1978-79; ptnr. Coke & Coke, Dallas, 1979-84, Gibson, Dunn & Crutcher, Dallas, 1984—. Federal civil litigation, State civil litigation, Antitrust. Office: Gibson Dunn & Crutcher 1700 Pacific Ave Suite 4400 Dallas TX 75201

DEGNAN, JOHN MICHAEL, lawyer; b. Mpls., Apr. 2, 1948; s. John F. and Lorraine A. D.; m. Maureen McCanna, Nov. 7, 1970; children: John Patrick, Amy Marie, David Charles. BA, U. Minn., 1970; JD, William Mitchell Coll. Law, 1976. Bar: Minn. 1976, U.S. Dist. Ct. Minn. 1976, U.S. Ct. Appeals (8th cir.) Minn. 1976, U.S. Supreme Ct. 1976. Ins. underwriter Marsh & McLennan, Mpls., 1973-76; lawyer Bassford, Heckt, Lockhart & Mullin, P.A., Mpls., 1976—; lectr. various seminars and instns. Bd. dirs. Hennepin County Pub. Libraries, 1980-84, Storefront Youth Action, 1981-83. Served to 1st lt. U.S. Army, 1970-72. Mem. ABA, Minn. Bar Assn. (ins. com, lectr. convs. 1984-85), Hennepin County Bar Assn., Minn. Trial Lawyers Assn. (lectr.), Minn. Def. Lawyers Assn. (bd. dirs. 1986—), Minn. Soc. Hosp. Attys., Def. Research Inst., Am. Soc. Law and Medicine, Richfield Jaycees (past pres.). Avocations: running, tennis, golf, boating, sports. Personal injury, Insurance, Federal and state civil litigation. Home: 4512 Hibiscus Ave Edina MN 55435 Office: Bassford Heckt Lockhart & Mullin PA 33 S 6th St 3350 Multifoods Tower Minneapolis MN 55402

DEGNAN, RONAN E., law educator; b. 1942. BS in Law, U. Minn., LLB. Asst. prof. Drake U., Des Moines, 1951-53, U. Minn., Mpls., 1953-54; from assoc. to full prof. U. Utah, Salt Lake City, 1955-62; prof. U. Calif., Berkeley, 1962—; vis. prof. Harvard U., Cambridge, Mass., 1973-74. Office: U Calif Berkeley Boalt Hall Berkeley CA 94720 *

DEGOLIA, JAMES B., lawyer; b. San Mateo, Calif., Aug. 2, 1949; s. Harold G. and Jean (Sparling) DeG.; m. Terri Hanagan, May 28, 1983. BA, U. Calif., Irvine, 1972; JD, U. Calif., San Francisco, 1976. Bar: Calif. 1976, U.S. Dist. Ct. (no. dist.) Calif. 1976, U.S. Dist. Ct. (cen. dist.) Calif. 1977. Assoc. Thelen, Marrin, Johnson & Bridges, San Francisco, 1976-82, Xerox Printing Systems Div., El Segundo, Calif., 1982-84; counsel Xerox Systems Group, El Segundo, 1984-87, Custom Systems div. Xerox Corp., Arlington, Va., 1987—; adj. prof. San Francisco Law Sch., 1980-82; vice chmn. Xerox Fed. Credit Union, El Segundo, 1985—. Spokesperson, facilitator San Francisco Charter Commn., 1978-79; with legal aid clinic San Francisco Legal Aid Office, 1977-80; advance work Mondale for Pres., So. Calif., 1984. Mem. ABA, Am. Corp. Counsel. Assn. Democrat. Club: Lexington Group (Los Angeles). Government contracts and claims, Computer, Private international. Office: Xerox Corp 1616 N Ft Myer Dr 18th Floor Arlington VA 22209-3109

DEGRANDI, JOSEPH A., lawyer; b. Hartford, Conn., 1927; m. Yolanda Salica; children: Terese, Lisa, Donna. B.S., Trinity Coll., Hartford, 1949; M.S., George Washington U., 1950, LL.B., 1952. Bar: D.C. 1952, U.S. Supreme Ct. 1956. Now mem. firm Beveridge, DeGrandi & Weilacher, Washington.; Mem. adv. bd. Marymount Sch., Arlington, Va., pres., 1969-72; mem. Pres.'s Adv. Com. on Indsl. Innovation, 1978-79; legal advisor U.S. delegation Diplomatic Conf. for Revision of Paris Conv., Nairobi, Kenya, 1981. Recipient Disting. Alumnus award George Washington U., 1982. Fellow Am. Bar Found.; mem. ABA (chmn. sect. patent, trademark and copyright law 1981-82, dep. del. 1986—), Inter-Am. Bar Assn., Fed. Bar Assn., Internat. Bar Assn., Nat. Council Patent Law Assns. (sec. 1971-75, adv. panel 1975-79), Bar Assn. D.C. (dir. 1968-69, chmn. patent, trademark and copyright law sect. 1967-68), D.C. Bar Assn. (chmn. div. patent, trademark and copyright law 1978-79), Am. Patent Law Assn. (bd. mgrs. 1976-79), N.Y. Patent Law Assn., Patent Lawyers Club Washington (pres. 1959), Nat. Lawyers Club (bd. govs. 1984—), Am. Judicature Soc., Am. Intellectual Property Law Assn. (dir., v.p. 1984-86, pres. elect 1986—), Patent and Trademark Inst. Can., Chartered Inst. Patent Agts. (Gt. Britain), Internat. Patent and Trademark Assn. (exec. com. 1978-83, v.p. 1983—), Licensing Execs. Soc., Inter-Am. Assn. Indsl. Property, Assn. of Textile Industry, Inc., Federation Internationale des Conseils en Propriete Industrielle, Thomas More Soc. Am., Nu Beta Epsilon. Lodge: Rotary. Trademark and copyright, Patent. Office: Beveridge DeGrandi & Weilacher Fed Bar Bldg W 1819 H St NW Washington DC 20006

DEGUC, VINCENT ANTHONY, lawyer; b. South Bend, Ind., May 25, 1950; s. Anthony Vincent and Lillian Ann (Zalas) D.; m. Beverly Ann Box, June 10, 1972; children: Elizabeth, Emily. BA, U. Notre Dame, 1972; JD, Lewis & Clark U., 1975. Bar: Oreg. 1975, Ind. 1975, U.S. Dist. Ct. Oreg. 1975, U.S. Dist. Ct. (so. dist.) Ind. 1975, U.S. Ct. Appeals (9th cir.) 1977. Atty. VISTA, Portland, Oreg., 1975-77; sole practice Portland, 1977—; judge pro tem State Dist. Ct., Portland, 1982—, State Cir. Ct., Portland, 1984—. Mem. Justice Com., Portland, 1976-86; commr. Met. Human Relations Commn., Portland, 1976-86, chmn., 1983-86; pres. Prepared Childbirth Assn., Portland, 1980-81, William Walker Parent Club, 1985—. Recipient Citizens award Multnomah County, 1984, Vol. of Yr. Mushaw Ctr., Washington County, 1986. Mem. Oreg. Bar Assn. (debtor, creditor com.), Washington County Bar Assn. (cle com.), Westside Profl. and Bus. Assn. (pres. 1980-81, named tipster of yr. 1986). Democrat. Roman Catholic. Avocations: camping, hiking, reading. General corporate, Contracts commercial, Bankruptcy. Home: 12575 SW Edgewood St Portland OR 97225 Office: 4540 SW 110th Beaverton OR 97005

DEGUERIN, DICK, lawyer; b. Austin, Tex., Feb. 16, 1941; s. E. Mack and Marguerite S. DeGuerin; m. Ann DeGuerin; children: Anna Michele, Ann Carlin; m. Janie Mitchell, Apr. 11, 1986. BA, U. Tex., 1963, LLB, 1965. Bar: Tex. 1965, U.S. Dist. Ct. (so. dist.) Tex. 1968, U.S. Ct. Appeals (5th cir.) 1971, U.S. Supreme Ct. 1971, U.S. Dist. Ct. (ea. dist.) Tex. 1973, U.S. Ct. Appeals (8th cir.) 1974, U.S. Dist. Ct. (no. dist.) Tex. 1979, U.S. Ct. Appeals (11th cir.) 1981, U.S. Dist. Ct. (ea. dist.) Mich. 1982, U.S. Ct. Appeals (6th cir.) 1982, U.S. Dist. Ct. (we. dist.) Tex. 1983, U.S. Ct. Appeals (10th cir.) 1984, U.S. Ct. Appeals (4th cir.) 1985. Asst. dist. atty. Harris County, Houston, 1965-68; assoc. Butler, Binion, Rice, Cook & Knapp, Houston, 1968-71; ptnr. Foreman & DeGuerin, Houston, 1971-82; sr. ptnr. DeGuerin, Dickson & Szekely, Houston, 1982-84, DeGuerin & Dickson, Houston, 1984—. Contbr. articles to profl. jours. Mem. Tex. Bar Assn. (various coms.), Houston Bar Assn. (criminal law sect.), Houston Jr. Bar Assn. (chmn. criminal law com., law day com.), Tex. Criminal Def. Lawyers Assn. (bd. dirs. 1973-76, 80—, co-chmn. indigent defenders com.), Harris County Criminal Lawyers Assn. (bd. dirs. 1976, pres. 1977-78), Tex. Bd. Legal Specialization (cert.), Tex. Trial Lawyers Assn., Houston Trial Lawyers Assn., Nat. Assn. Criminal Def. Lawyers. Criminal, Family and matrimonial, Federal civil litigation. Office: DeGuerin & Dickson 1018 Preston 7th Floor Houston TX 77002

DEHART, BARBARA BOUDREAU, lawyer; b. Woonsocket, R.I., Dec. 6, 1946; d. Louis Maurice and Hazen Montine (Pritchett) B. Student, Trinity Coll., 1964-65; BA, R.I. Coll., 1969; JD, Franklin Pierce Law Ctr., Concord, N.H., 1977; LLM, Boston U., 1982. Assoc. Sheehan, Phinney, Bass & Green, Manchester, N.H., 1979-83, Goldstein & Manello, Boston, 1983-86, Cooper, Hall, Whittum & Shillaber P.C., Rochester, N.H., 1986—. Mem. ABA, Mass. Bar Assn., N.H. Bar Assn., N.H. Estate Planning Council. Probate, Estate taxation, Personal income taxation. Office: Cooper Hall Whittum & Shillaber PC 76 Wakefield Box 1200 Rochester NH 03867

DEHART, JAMES LOUIS, lawyer; b. Laconia, N.H., July 3, 1946; s. Norman Edwin and Lucille Emma (Fecteau) DeH.; m. Barbara Jeanne Boudreau, Apr. 4, 1970 (div. Apr. 1979); m. Sharon Edith Sniger, June 30, 1979. BS, Boston U., 1968; JD, Cath. U. Am., 1974. Bar: N.H. 1974, U.S. Dist. Ct. N.H. 1974. Reporter Providence (R.I.) Journal-Bulletin, 1968-71; ptnr. Ray, Hopkins & DeHart, Plymouth, N.H., 1974-81; atty. Am. Bd. Trade Devel. Corp., Concord, N.H., 1981-83; atty., administrator profl. conduct com., character and fitness com. N.H. Supreme Ct., Concord, 1983—. Chmn. Plymouth Bicentennial Com., 1975-76. Mem. ABA, N.H. Bar Assn. (code of profl. responsibility revision com. 1983-86), N.H. Trial Lawyers Assn. (bd. of govs. 1977-79), Plymouth Area Jaycees (pres. 1978). Democrat. Avocations: hunting, fishing, cross-country skiing, travel. Professional responsibility. Home: PO Box 1102 Concord NH 03301 Office: NH Supreme Ct Profl Conduct Com 18 N Main St Suite 205 Concord NH 03301

DEHAY, JOHN CARLISLE, JR., lawyer; b. Jones Prairie, Tex., Mar. 30, 1922; s. John Carlisle and Valda (Drury) DeH.; m. Barbara Jean Smith, Nov. 30, 1956; 1 dau., Leslie. B.B.A., So. Meth. U., 1949, LL.B., 1949. Bar: Tex. bar 1948. Mem. legal dept. Employers Casualty Co., Dallas, 1949-51; pvt. practice law DeHay & Blanchard, Dallas, 1951—; Dir. Tex. Assn. Def. Counsel, 1968. Served with AUS, 1942-45. Decorated D.S.M. Mem. Am. Coll. Trial Lawyers, Internat. Acad. Trial Lawyers, Am., Dallas bar assns. Baptist. Clubs: Woodvale Fishing (Mineola, Tex.); Dallas (Dallas), Dallas Idlewild (Dallas); Brookhollow Golf. Federal civil litigation, State civil litigation. Home: 3201 Villanova St Dallas TX 75225 Office: Plaza of Americas 2500 South Tower Dallas TX 75201

DE JONG, DAVID JOHN, lawyer, physician; b. Grand Rapids, Mich., July 17, 1951; s. Alexander Cornelius and Joanne Minnie (Vander Baan) De J.; m. Gwen Rachel Prins, May 25, 1974; children: Connor David, Caleb Ijmen, Samuel Nicholas. Student, Trinity Christian Coll., 1969-72; MD, Loyola U., Maywood, Ill., 1975; JD, Northwestern U., 1980. Bar: Ill. 1980, U.S. Dist. Ct. (no. dist.) Ill. 1980. Physician emergency dept. Morris (Ill.) Hosp., 1976-77; assoc. John D. Hayes & Assocs., Ltd., Chgo., 1980-84; prin. David J. De Jong & Assocs., Ltd., Chgo., 1984—. Bd. dirs. Ctr. for Life Skills, Chgo., 1985—. Fellow Am. Coll. Legal Medicine; mem. Chgo. Acad. Legal Medicine, Ill. Trial Lawyers Assn. (med. malpractice com. 1985—), Chgo. Bar Assn. Mem. Christian Reformed Ch. Personal injury, State civil litigation. Home: 9203 S Pleasant Chicago IL 60620 Office: 180 N LaSalle Suite 1220 Chicago IL 60601

DE JONG, DAVID SAMUEL, lawyer, educator; b. Washington, Jan. 8, 1951; s. Samuel and Dorothy (Thomas) De J.; m. Alisa Green, Jan. 5, 1980. BA, U. Md., 1972; JD, Washington and Lee U., 1975; LLM in Taxation, Georgetown U., 1979. Bar: Md. 1975, U.S. Dist. Ct. Md. 1977, U.S. Tax Ct. 1977, U.S. Ct. Appeals (4th cir.) 1978, U.S. Supreme Ct. 1979, D.C. 1980, U.S. Dist. Ct. D.C. 1983, U.S. Ct. Claims, U.S. Ct. Appeals (fed. cir.) 1983; CPA, Md. Atty. Gen. Bus. Services Inc., Rockville, Md., 1975-80; ptnr. Stein, Sperling, Bennett, De Jong, Driscoll, Greenfeig & Metro P.A., Rockville, 1980—; adj. prof. Southeastern U., Washington, 1979-85, Am. U., Washington, 1983—; instr. U. Md., College Park, 1986—, Montgomery Coll., Rockville, 1983. Notes and comments editor Washington and Lee U. Law Rev., 1974-75. V.p. Seneca Whetstone Homeowners Assn., Gaithersburg, Md., 1981-82, pres. 1982-83. Mem. ABA, Md. Bar Assn., Montgomery County Bar Assn., D.C. Bar Assn., Am. Inst. CPA's, Md. Assn. CPA's, D.C. Inst. CPA's, Am. Assn. Atty.-CPA's, Phi Alpha Delta. Corporate taxation, Personal income taxation, Estate taxation. Office: Stein Sperling Bennett De Jong Driscoll, Greenfeig & Metro 25 W Middle Ln Rockville MD 20850

DEKIEFFER, DONALD EULETTE, lawyer; b. Newport, R.I., Nov. 8, 1945; s. Robert and Melissa (Hibberd) deK.; m. Nancy Kishida, June 27, 1970; 1 child, Nathan Hiroyuki. BA, U. Colo., 1968; JD, Georgetown U., 1971. Bar: U.S. Supreme Ct. 1982, U.S. Ct. Appeals (D.C. cir.) 1971, U.S. Dist. Ct. D.C. 1971, U.S. Ct. Claims 1971, U.S. Ct. Internat. Trade 1971. Mem. profl. staff Senate Rep. Policy Com., 1969-71; assoc. Collier, Shannon, Rill & Edwards, 1971-74; ptnr. Collier, Shannon, Rill, Edwards & Scott, 1974-80, deKieffer, Berg & Creskoff, 1980; gen. counsel U.S. Trade Rep., Washington, 1981-83; ptnr. Plaia, Schaumburg & deKieffer, Washington, 1983-84, Pillsbury, Madison & Sutro, Washington, 1984—. Author: How to Lobby Congress, 1981, Doing Business with the USA, 1984, Doing Business with Romania, 1985, Doing Business in the United States, 1985. Mem. Presdl. Transition Team, 1980-81. Mem. ABA, D.C. Bar, Bar Assn. D.C., Fed. Bar Assn., Am. Soc. Internat. Law, Internat. Antitrust Soc. Antitrust, Public international, Private international. Office: 1667 K St NW Washington DC 20006

DE KIRBY, VAUGHAN RANSONE, lawyer; b. San Diego, Apr. 15, 1947; s. Vaughan Walton and Perri Louise (Ransone) deK.; m. Christine Liza Dobrin, Sept. 27, 1971; children: Kenton, Leighen. BA in Speech Communication, U. Calif., Northridge, 1975; JD cum laude, Western State U., 1981. Bar: Calif. 1981, U.S. Dist. Ct. (so. dist.) Calif. 1981, U.S. Supreme Ct. 1985. Pres. Law Office of Vaughn de Kirby, San Diego, 1981—. Contbr. articles to San Diego Chiropractic Bull., 1983—. Bd. dirs. Interfest, San Diego, 1986. Recipient Spl. award for disting. service San Diego Chiropractic Soc., 1986, Community Involvement award Bapt. Ministers Union, San Diego, 1986. Mem. San Diego Bar Assn., San Diego Trial Lawyers Assn., Los Angeles Trial Lawyers Assn., Calif. Trial Lawyers Assn. Club: San Diego Athletic. Avocations: running, fitness. Personal injury. Office: Vaughn de Kirby APC 1520 State St Suite 136 San Diego CA 92101

DEKLE, GEORGE ROBERT, lawyer; b. Gainesville, Fla., May 23, 1948; s. Donald James and Jewell Anne (Coleman) D.; m. Gloria Lane Dicks; children: Laura, George, John. BA, U. Fla., 1970, JD, 1973. Bar: Fla. 1973. Asst. pub. defender Pub. Def. Office 3d Cir., Lake City, Fla., 1973-75; asst. states atty. States Atty.'s Office 3d Cir., Live Oak, Fla., 1975-77, chief asst. states atty., 1977-78, dep.. chief asst. states atty., 1978-85, chief spl. prosecution, 1985. Chmn. adv. council Lake City Community Coll. Emergency Med. Services, 1980-83; mem. Fla. Adv. Council on Emergency Med. Services, Tallahassee, 1984, Columbia County Jail Adv. Com., Lake City, 1984. Co-recipient Gene Barry Meml. award, State of Fla., 1986. Mem. ABA, 3d Cir. Bar Assn. (grievance com. 1982-84), U.S. Chess Fedn., Corr. Chess League Am. Criminal, Local government. Office: Office of State Atty PO Drawer 1546 Live Oak FL 32060

DEKOVEN, RONALD, lawyer; b. Chgo., July 16, 1944; m. Nancy Miller Phillips, Oct. 6, 1968; children—Lauren Anne, Elizabeth Karen. A.B., Stanford U., 1965; J.D., U. Chgo., 1968. Bar: Ill. 1968, N.Y. 1981. Ptnr. firm Shearman & Sterling, N.Y.C., 1980—; lectr. Am. Law Inst./ABA, Practicing Law Inst., N.Y. Law Jour.; U.S. del. for Dept. State to Internat. Inst. for Unification of Pvt. Law; mem. State Dept. Working Group on Can./U.S. bankruptcy treaty; reporter Nat. Conf. Commrs. on Uniform State Laws. Mem. Am. Law Inst. (permanent edit. bd. for uniform comml code), Nat. Bankruptcy Conf. Contbr. articles to profl. publs. Banking, Bankruptcy, Private international. Office: 153 E 53d St New York NY 10022

DE LACHAPELLE, PHILIPPE, lawyer, investment advisor; b. Tours, France, May 1, 1941; s. Gerard and Giselle Lachapelle; m. Doria Lachapelle, Sept. 27, 1975; children: Christian, Justin. BA, Columbia U., 1961; JD, Georgetown U., 1966. Bar: N.Y. 1967. Dir. internat. Warner Communications, N.Y.C., 1982-84; sr. v.p., gen. counsel Mastercard Internat., N.Y.C., 1984-85; exec. v.p., gen. counsel RPM Securities Co., N.Y.C., 1986—. Served to lt. USN, 1961-63. Contracts commercial, General corporate, Private international. Office: RPM Securities Co 20 Broad St New York NY 10005

DE LA GARZA, LUIS ADOLFO, lawyer, energy company executive; b. Mission, Tex., Nov. 22, 1943; s. Adolfo and Carmen (Barrera) de la G.; m. Sherry Lynn Hatcher, Apr. 12, 1974; children: Miguel, Gabriel. BBA, U. Tex., 1966; MBA, U. Hawaii, 1972; JD, U. Tex., 1975. Bar: Tex. 1975. Counsel, El Paso Natural Gas Co., Tex., 1975-78; sr. counsel El Paso Co., Houston, 1978-81; sr. atty., asst. sec. Valero Energy Corp., San Antonio, 1981—. Bd. dirs. Valero Polit. Action Com., San Antonio, 1984—, Valero Fed. Credit Union, 1987—; scout leader Boy Scouts Am., San Antonio, 1984; mem Witte Council, Witte Com., San Antonio Mus. Assn., 1985—. Served to capt. USMC, 1966-72, Vietnam. Decorated Air medal with 15 oak leaf clusters. Mem. ABA, Am. Soc. Corp. Secs., Tex. Bar Assn., San Antonio Bar Assn (chmn. corp. counsel sect. 1986—). Democrat. Methodist. General corporate, Banking, Securities. Home: 14203 Bold Ruler San Antonio TX 78248 Office: Valero Energy Corp Legal Dept 530 McCullough Ave San Antonio TX 78215

DE LA GARZA, ROBERTO EDUARDO, lawyer; b. Edinburg, Tex., Apr. 11, 1952; s. Robert and Gilda (Barron) De La G.; m. Carmen Garcia, July 31, 1976; children: Daniel, Andrew, Erik. BA, Pan Am. U., 1975; JD, St. Mary's U., 1978. Bar: Tex. 1979, U.S. Dist. Ct. (so. dist.) Tex. 1979, U.S. Ct. Appeals (5th cir.) Tex. 1979, Ct. Mil. Appeals 1985, U.S. Supreme Ct. 1985. Dep. county clk. Hidalgo County, Tex., 1971-73; legal asst. Law Office of Leo Alvarado, San Antonio, Tex., 1976-77; assoc. Kelly, Looney, Alexander & Sawyer, Edinburg, Tex., 1979-80; ptnr. Meadows, De La Garza & Hanshaw, McAllen, Tex., 1980-83, Mullin & Delagarza, San Antonio, 1983—; trustee Am. Humanics, Inc.-Pan. Am. U., 1980—, bd. dirs. 1980-84, nat. trustee 1984. Speaker seminar Landlord-Tenant Law, 1983. Active Democratic Orgn.; bd. dirs. Rio Grande Valley council Boy Scouts Am., 1979—; chmn. bd. dirs. Am. Humanics; trustee Curtain Call Players, Inc., 1983—. Served as 1st lt. JAGC, 1983-87, capt. 1987—; with res. Named one of Outstanding Young Men Am., 1979. Mem. ABA, Hidalgo County Bar Assn., Tex. Trial Lawyers Assn., Tex. Young Lawyers Assn. (speaker seminar), Pan Am. U. Alumni Assn. (charter, exec. v.p. 1984—, bd. trustees 1984—, pres. 1986—), Phi Kappa Theta. Democrat. Roman Catholic. Lodge: Kiwanis, KC. Probate, Real property, Military.

DELANCETT, JOHN GERALD, lawyer, educator; b. LaLouviere, Belgium, Nov. 9, 1946; m. Marie Hirth, May 30, 1981; children: Michael, Adam. BA, U. Fla., 1968, JD with honors, 1971. Bar: Fla. 1971, U.S. Dist. Ct. (mid. dist.) Fla. 1971, U.S. Supreme Ct. 1978, U.S. Ct. Appeals (5th cir.) 1980, U.S. Ct. Appeals (11th cir.) 1981, U.S. Tax Ct. 1981, U.S. Dist. Ct. (no. dist.) Fla. 1985. Assoc., then ptnr. Giles, Hedrick & Robinson, Orlando, Fla., 1971-80; ptnr. Davis & DeLancett, Orlando, 1980-81; sole practice Orlando, 1981-85; ptnr. Matthias, DeLancett, Morse & Robb, Orlando, 1985—; instr. legal writing U. Fla., Orlando, 1970-71, U. Cen. Fla., 1982; seminar speaker various locations. Bd. mem. U. Fla. Law Rev., Gainesville, 1971. Served to capt. U.S Army, 1968-76. Mem. ABA, Fed. Bar Assn. (pres. Orlando chpt. 1986—), Fla. Bar Assn., Nat. Assn. Criminal Def. Lawyers, Assn. Trial Lawyers Am. Republican. Roman Catholic. Club: Citrus (Orlando). Administrative and regulatory, Criminal tax law, State civil litigation. Home: 442 Mallard Circle Winter Park FL 32792 Office: Matthias DeLancett Morse & Robb 501 N Magnolia Ave Orlando FL 32801

DELANEY, EDWARD NORMAN, lawyer; b. Chgo., Sept. 16, 1927; s. Frederick E. and Wynifred (Ward) D.; m. Carole P. Walter, May 31, 1950; children: Deborah Delaney Rogers, Kathleen Delaney Langan, Edward Norman II, Dorian A. LLB, Loyola U., Chgo., 1951; LLM, NYU, 1959. Bar: Ill. 1952, Minn. 1961, U.S. Supreme Ct. 1963, Mo. 1974, D.C. 1975. Staff Office Chief Counsel, IRS, N.Y.C., 1955-60; atty. Investors Diversified Services Inc., Mpls., 1960-73; v.p., gen. counsel investment adv. group Investors Diversified Services Inc., 1968-73; sr. v.p., gen. counsel Waddell & Reed and United Investors Life Ins. Co., Kansas City, Mo., 1974; ptnr. firm Bogan & Freeland, Washington, 1975-81; prin. Delaney, and Young, Chartered, Washington, 1981—; chmn. tax com. Investment Co. Inst., 1963-74; bus. adv. com. SEC Inter-Agy. Task Force Offshore Funds, 1970-71. Active fundraiser Ctr. for Performing Arts, Kansas City, Mo., 1974; bd. dirs. Civic Orch., Mpls., 1963-68, pres., 1966-68; mem. lawyers com. Washington Performing Arts Soc. Served with USMCR, 1945-46. Fellow Am. Bar Found.; mem. ABA (council tax sect. 1974-77, vice chmn. tax sect. 1978-81, chmn. tax sect. 1983-84), Fed., Minn., Hennepin County, Mo., D.C. bar assns., Am. Law Inst., Am. Coll. Tax Counsel. Clubs: Congl. Country, Univ., Georgetown (Washington). Corporate taxation, General corporate, Legislative. Home: 9405 Tobin Circle Potomac MD 20854 Office: Delaney & Young 1629 K St NW Washington DC 20006

DELANEY, HERBERT WADE, JR., lawyer; b. Leadville, Colo., Mar. 30, 1925; s. Herbert Wade and Marie Ann (Garbarino) DeL.; m. Ramona Rae Ortiz, Aug. 6, 1953; children—Herbert Wade III, Paula Rae, Bonnie Marie Manshel. B.S., U. Denver, 1949, LL.B., 1951. Bar: Colo. 1951, U.S. Supreme Ct. 1959. Sole practice, Denver, 1953-61; faculty U. Denver, Colo., 1960-61; ptnr. Salazar & DeLaney, Denver, 1961-64, DeLaney & West, Denver, 1964-65; sole practice, Denver, 1965—. Served as capt. JAG's Dept., USAF, 1951-53. Mem. Colo. Trial Lawyers Assn., Assn. Trial Lawyers Am., Colo. Bar Assn., Denver Bar Assn., Am. Legion, Phi Alpha Delta. Club: Footprinters (Denver). Lodges: Masons, Elks. State civil litigation, Bankruptcy, Personal injury. Office: Empire Park Suite 606 1355 S Colo Blvd Denver CO 80222

DELANEY, MICHAEL FRANCIS, lawyer; b. Washington, Jan. 22, 1948; s. Donald J. and Evelyn A. (Edwards) D.; m. Sally E. Jenkins, July 30, 1977 (div. Nov. 1984); 1 child, Patrick Neal; m. Kathleen Lynette Gibbons, Feb. 22, 1986. BA, U. Kans., 1969, JD, 1976. Bar: Mo. 1976, U.S. Dist. Ct. (we. dist.) Mo. 1976, U.S. Ct. Appeals (8th cir.) 1978, U.S. Ct. Appeals (10th cir.) 1979. Assoc. Spencer, Fane, Britt & Browne, Kansas City, Mo., 1976-81, ptnr., 1982—; lectr. law U. Kans., Lawrence, 1977-78. Articles editor U. Kans. Law Rev., 1975. Active Kans. City Tomorrow, 1982; mem. steering com. Kansas City Vets. Meml. Fund, 1984-86; vol. citizen rev. United Way, Kansas City, 1985-86. Served to capt. U.S. Army, 1969-73, Vietnam. Mem. ABA, Mo. Bar Assn., Kansas Bar Assn., Lawyers Assn. of Kansas City. Democrat. Roman Catholic. Club: Kansas City. Labor, Federal civil litigation. Home: 615 E 54th St Kansas City MO 64110 Office: Spencer Fane Britt & Browne 1000 Walnut Kansas City MO 64105

DELANO, STEPHEN JAMES, lawyer; b. St. Louis, Sept. 7, 1940; s. James Greason and Alice Elizabeth (Morgan) D.; m. Kathleen Anna Dwan, Dec. 27, 1962; children: Phillip, Jennifer, Elizabeth. BA, Middlebury Coll., 1962; JD, U. Minn., 1966. Bar: Minn. 1963, U.S. Dist. Ct. Minn. 1980. Assoc. Peterson & Challeen Ltd., Winona, Minn., 1966-70; ptnr. Peterson, Challeen & Delano, Winona, 1970-71, Peterson, Delano & Thompson, Winona, 1971-78; sole practice Winona, 1978-83; ptnr. Darby, Delano & Price, Winona, 1983—; instr. para-legal program Winona State U., 1976-80. Councilman City of Winona, 1974-77; commr. Winona Housing Authority, 1975-77; bd. dirs. Winona County Hist. Soc., 1971-80, pres. 1978-80. Mem. Minn. State Bar Assn., Winona County Bar Assn. (sec., treas. 1978-79, pres. 1980). Democrat. Unitarian. Lodges: Elks, Redmen. Family and matrimonial, Criminal, State civil litigation. Home: 257 W 6th St Winona MN 55987 Office: Darby Delano and Price Box 617 Winona MN 55987

DE LASA, JOSÉ M., lawyer; b. Havana, Cuba, Nov. 28, 1941; came to U.S., 1961; s. Miguel and Conchita de Lasa; m. Maria Teresa Figueroa, Nov. 23, 1963; children: Maria Teresa, José, Andrés, Carlos. BA, Yale U., 1968, JD, 1971. Bar: N.Y. 1973. Assoc. Cleary, Gottleib, Steen & Hamilton, N.Y.C., 1971-76; asst. gen. counsel Bristol-Myers Co., N.Y.C., 1976—; lectr. internat. law, various locations. Chmn. Larchmont (N.Y.) Human Rights Commn., 1985—; bd. dirs. Community Action for Legal Services, N.Y.C., 1984—. Mem. ABA, N.Y. County Bar Assn., Assn. of Bar of City of N.Y. Roman Catholic. Private international, General corporate, Health. Office: Bristol-Myers Co 345 Park Ave New York NY 10154

DELATORRE, PHILLIP EUGENE, law educator; b. Chanute, Kans., July 6, 1953; s. Jose Crespin and Margaret (Alonzo) DeL.; m. Patrice Ann Kutz, Sept. 19, 1981; children: Edward Phillip, Daniel Patrick. BA, U. Kans., 1975; JD, Harvard U., 1978. Bar: Mo. 1978, Kans. 1979. Assoc. Watson, Ess, Marshall & Enggas, Kansas City, Mo., 1978-80; prof. law U. Kans., Lawrence, 1980—. Contbr. articles to profl. jours. (recipient Best Article award 1985). Mem. Mo. Bar Assn. Oil and gas leasing, Probate, Real property. Office: U Kans Sch Law Lawrence KS 66045

DELAUGHTER, JERRY L., lawyer; b. Brookhaven, Miss., Oct. 24, 1944; s. Hardy L. and Eloise (Hayes) Del. AA, Copiah Lincoln Jr. Coll., 1965; BA, U. Miss., 1969, JD, 1978; postgrad., U. Calif., Santa Barbara, 1973-74. Bar: Miss. 1978, U.S. Dist. Ct. (no. and so. dists.) Miss. 1978, U.S. Ct. Appeals (5th and 11th cirs.) 1979, Calif. 1982. Law clk. U.S. Dist. Ct. (so. dist.) Miss., 1978-79; assoc. Eaton, Cottrel et al, Gulfport, Miss., 1979-81, Goux, Romasanta et al, Santa Barbara, 1981-82, Hatch & Parent, Santa Barbara, 1983; sole practice Santa Barbara, 1984—; vol. tchr. legal asst. program U. Calif., Santa Barbara, 1984-85. Editor in chief Jour. of Space Law, 1977-78. Served to capt. USAF, 1969-73. Mem. ABA, Calif. Bar Assn., Miss. Bar Assn., Santa Barbara County Bar Assn., Assn. Trial Lawyers Am., Calif. Trial Lawyers Assn., Phi Gamma Delta, Phi Alpha Delta. Democrat. Avocations: running, triathlons, bicycling. State civil litigation, Government contracts and claims, Personal injury. Home: PO Box 20070 Santa Barbara CA 93120 Office: 101 E Victoria St Santa Barbara CA 93101

DELAURENTIS, MICHAEL JOHN, lawyer; b. Phila., June 24, 1947; s. Michael and Mary (Morelli) DeL.; m. Shelley Alexander, June 26, 1971; children: Micah, Lucy. BA, Amherst Coll., 1969, Oxford U., Eng., 1972; MA, Oxford U., Eng., 1976, Brown U., 1973; JD, Yale U., 1978. Bar: Calif. 1978, U.S. Dist. Ct. (no. dist.) Calif. 1978, Pa. 1981. Assoc. Winikur, Schoenberg, Maier & Zang P.C., San Francisco, 1978-80, Wolf, Block, Schorr & Solis-Cohen, Phila., 1980-82, Drinker, Biddle & Reath, Phila., 1982-84, Lesser & Kaplin, P.C., Blue Bell, Pa., 1984—; adj. prof. Villanova (Pa.) Law Sch., 1983—; bd. dirs. Benjamin Co. Inc., Doylestown, Pa. Mem. ABA (drafter Am. Law Inst.-ABA study on fed. taxation of partnerships 1982), Pa. Bar Assn., Calif. Bar Assn., Phila. Bar Assn., Montgomery County Bar Assn. Corporate taxation, Personal income taxation, General corporate. Home: 7616 Mountain Ave Elkins Park PA 19117 Office: Lesser & Kaplin PC 6 Sentry Pkwy Blue Bell PA 19422

DELEHANTY, JOHN MCDONALD, lawyer; b. Terre Haute, Ind., July 31, 1945; s. John J. and Virginia Patricia (McDonald) D.; m. Judith Wald Prince, Nov. 3, 1968; children—Matthew Prince, Michael Simeon, Adam Victor. A.B., Brown U., 1966; J.D., U. Chgo., 1969. Bar: N.Y. 1971, U.S. Ct. Appeals (3d cir.) 1972, U.S. Dist. Ct. (so. and ea. dists.) N.Y. 1973, U.S. Ct. Appeals (2nd cir.) 1975, U.S. Supreme Ct. 1984. Assoc. Paul Weiss Rifkind Wharton & Garrison, N.Y.C., 1970-77; sr. ptnr. Parker Auspitz Neesemann & Delehanty P.C., N.Y.C., 1977—. Mem. Mamaroneck (N.Y.) Sch. Bd. Selection Com., 1982-83, mem. long-range planning com. 1984-85 . Mem. ABA, N.Y. Bar Assn., Assn. Bar City N.Y. (mem. com. on state cts. superior jurisdiction 1979-82,), Fed. Bar Council (com. profl. and jud. ethics 1985—). Club: Orienta Beach. Federal civil litigation, State civil litigation. Address: 415 Madison Ave New York NY 10017

DELEON, PATRICK HENRY, lawyer; b. Waterbury, Conn., Jan. 6, 1943; s. Patrick and Catherine (Dzubay) D.; m. Jean Louise Murphy; children: Patrick Daniel Nainoa, Katherine Malia Malie. BA, Amherst Coll., 1964; MS, Purdue U., 1966, PhD in Clin. Psychology, 1969; MPH, U. Hawaii, 1973; JD, Catholic U., 1980. Bar: Hawaii 1981, U.S. Dist. Ct. Hawaii 1983, U.S. Ct. Appeals (9th cir.) 1983; diplomate Am. Bd. Profl. Psychology, Am. Bd. Forensic Psychology (bd. dirs. 1985—). Tng. psychologist Peace Corps Tng. Ctr., Hilo, Hawaii, 1969-70; staff psychologist Diamond Head Mental Health Ctr., Hawaii State Hosp., Honolulu and Kaneohe, Hawaii, 1970-73; adminstrv. asst. U.S. Senator Daniel K. Inouye, Washington, 1973—. Mem. editorial adv. bd. Computers in Human Behavior, 1984—; cons. editor Psychotherapy in Pvt. Practice, 1982—; mem. adv. bd. Recorded Psychol. Jours., 1985—; contbr. articles to profl. jours. Fellow Am. Psychol. Assn. (clin. psychology div., pub. service div., psychotherapy div., state assns. div., health psychology div., psychology and law div., legis. pub. policy com., pub. info. com., task force on police role, fin. com., health ins. com.; cons. Am. Psychologist Jour. 1978-81, assoc. editor 1981—; health policy editor Health Psychology 1984—, assoc. editor 1981-84; mem. editorial bd. Perspectives in Law and Psychology 1985—, Newsletter 1986—; cons. editor Profl. Psychology: Research and Practice 1976—, Psychotherapy: Theory, Research, and Practice 1980—; adv. editor Contemporary Psychology 1983-85; columnist Pub. Service Psychology 1984—; Harold M. Hildreth award 1985-86), Hawaii Psychol. Assn. (legis. com. 1972, Disting. Service award 1981), Am. Assn. Biofeedback Clinicians (hon.); mem. ABA, Hawaii Bar Assn., Hawaii Pub. Health Assn. Democrat. Health. Home: 5701 Wilson Ln Bethesda MD 20817 Office: care Senator D K Inouye US Senate Washington DC 20510

DEL GADIO, ROBERT G., lawyer; b. Bklyn., Mar. 23, 1943; s. George and Louise (Provenzano) DelG.; m. Grace Miceli, Aug. 18, 1968; children: Michele, Todd, Nicole. BBA, St. John's U., Jamaica, N.Y., 1964, JD, 1967. Bar: N.Y. .1968, U.S. Dist. Ct. (ea. and so. dists.) N.Y., U.S. Ct. Appeals (2d cir.). Sole practice Garden City, N.Y., 1969—. Mem. ABA, N.Y. State Bar Assn., Nassau Bar Assn. Federal civil litigation, State civil litigation, General corporate. Office: 1010 Franklin Ave Garden City NY 11530

DELGADO, RICHARD, law educator; b. 1939. JD, U. Calif., Berkeley, 1974. Asst. prof. Ariz. State U., Tempe, 1974-75; asst. prof. U. Washington, Seattle, 1976-78, assoc. prof., 1978-79; prof. UCLA, 1979—; vis. prof. UCLA, 1978-79. Fellow Yale U., New Haven, 1975-76. Office: UCLA Sch of Law 405 Hilgard Ave Los Angeles CA 90024 *

DELHOTAL, VAN RUSSELL, lawyer; b. San Diego, Nov. 7, 1945; s. Jack Russell and Ruby (Casey) D.; m. Barbara Lee Waite, June 4, 1966; 1 child, Katherine Casey. BA, Wichita (Kans.) State U., 1970; JD, Washburn U., 1973. Bar: Kans. 1973, U.S. Dist. Ct. Kans. 1973, U.S. Ct. Appeals (10th cir.) 1974. Assoc. Weigand,, Curfman, Brainerd, Harris & Kaufman, Wichita, 1973-76; ptnr. Curfman, Brainerd, Harris & Snow, Wichita, 1976-80; atty. ABKO Properties, Inc., Wichita, 1981-82; atty. Koch Industries, Inc., Wichita, 1982-84, sr. litigation atty., 1984—. Mem. Def. Research Inst., Kans. Bar Assn., Wichita Bar Assn. Federal civil litigation, State civil litigation. Home: 402 S Roosevelt Wichita KS 67218 Office: Koch Industries Inc PO Box 2256 Wichita KS 67201

DE LIO, ANTHONY PETER, lawyer; b. Bklyn., June 29, 1928; s. David F. and Margaret M. (Mascali); children—Anthony P., Donna Marie, Lois Anne. B.S. in Physics, Poly. Inst. Bklyn., 1953; J.D. with honors, George Washington U., 1957. Bar: D.C. 1957, Conn. 1958, U.S. Dist. Ct. Conn. 1958. With patent dept. Bendix Corp., Washington, 1954-56; patent advisor U.S. Navy Dept., Washington, 1957; assoc. Blair & Spencer, Stamford, Conn., 1957-60; ptnr. Spencer, Rockwell & Bartholow, Stamford, 1960-62, Rockwell & De Lio, New Haven, 1962-64, De Lio & Montgomery, New Haven, 1964-81, De Lio and Libert, New Haven, 1981-84, De Lio & Assocs., 1984—; lectr. in field. Chmn. Hamden Planning and Zoning Commn., 1969-81; alt. commr. Hamden Zoning Bd. Appeals, 1981-85. Served with USMC, 1946-48. Mem. Conn., ABA, Conn. Patent Law Assn., Am. Patent Law Assn., Internat. Patent Law Assn. Democrat. Roman Catholic. Clubs: Quinnipiack (New Haven); New Haven Country (Hamden, Conn.). Contbr. articles to legal jours. Patent, Trademark and copyright, Federal civil litigation. Office: 121 Whitney Ave New Haven CT 06510

DE LISIO, STEPHEN SCOTT, lawyer; b. San Diego, Dec. 30, 1937; s. Anthony J. and Emma Irving (Cheney) DeL.; m. Margaret Irene Winter, June 26, 1964; children: Anthony W., Stephen Scott, Heather E. Student, Am. U., 1958-59; B.A., Emory U., 1959; LL.B., Albany Law Sch., 1962; LL.M., Georgetown U., 1963. Bar: N.Y. 1963, D.C. 1963, Alaska 1964. Practice law Fairbanks, 1963-71, Anchorage, 1971—; asst. dist. atty. Fairbanks, 1963-65; asso. McNealy & Merdes, 1965-66; lectr. U. Alaska, 1965-67; partner Staley, DeLisio, Cook and Sherry, 1966—; dir. Woodstock Property Co., Inc., Pasit Inc.; vice chmn. Crosstown CBMC, 1986—; city atty., Fairbanks, 1967-70, Barrow, 1969-72, Ft. Yukon and North Pole, 1970-72; past sec. U. Alaska Heating Corp., Inc.; past sec.-treas. Trans-Alaska Electronics, Inc., Baker Aviation, Inc.; arbitrator, mem. Alaska regional council Am. Arbitration Assn. Author: (with others) Law and Tactics in Federal Criminal Cases, 1964. Rep. precinct committeeman, 1970-76; chmn. Alaska Rep. Rules Com., Anchorage Rep. Com., 1973; v.p. We The People, 1977-79; vice-chmn. Alaska Libertarian party, 1983-84; mem. nat. com. Libertarian party, 1982-85; past pres. Tanana Valley State Fair Assn.; past v.p. Fairbanks Mental Health Assn., Fairbanks United Good Neighbors Fund; deacon Anchorage Bible Fellowship, 1986—; bd. dirs. Fairbanks Montessori Assn.; bd. dirs. Anchorage Community Chorus, 1975-77; former bd. dirs. Greater Fairbanks Community Hosp. Found. Recipient Jaycee Disting. Service award, 1968. Mem. ABA, Alaska Bar Assn., D.C. Bar Assn., Anchorage Bar Assn., Spenard Bar Assn. (pres. 1975-77), Am. Trial Lawyers Assn., Lawyer Pilots Bar Assn., Am. Judicature Soc., U.S. (past dir.), Alaska (past pres.), Fairbanks (past pres.), Jaycees (senator), Chi Phi, Pi Sigma Phi. Mem. Alaska Libertarian Party. Club: Woodstock Golf Inc. ((pres. 1984—). State civil litigation, Federal civil litigation, Construction. Home: 5102 Shorecrest Dr Anchorage AK 99515 Office: Staley DeLisio Cook & Sherry 943 W 6th Ave Anchorage AK 99501

DELK, RUSSELL LOUIS, lawyer; b. Dallas, May 6, 1956; s. Mark L. and Shirley B. (Wiemers) D.; m. Terri L. Smith, Apr. 27. 1985. BA in Polit. Sci., U. Tex., 1978; JD, Baylor U., 1981. Bar: Tex. 1982. Ptnr. Delk & Delk, Dallas, 1982—. Mem. Dallas Bar Assn., Assn. Trial Lawyers Am., Tex. Trial Lawyers Assn. Personal injury, Workers' compensation, State civil litigation. Office: Delk & Delk 8828 Stemmons Freeway # 101 Dallas TX 75247

DELL, DONALD LUNDY, lawyer; b. Savannah, Ga., June 17, 1938; s. Julian Peter and Margaret Julien (Lundy) D.; m. Carole Marie Osche, Mar. 21, 1971; children—Alexandra Lundy and Kristina Osche (twins). B.A., Yale U., 1960; LL.B., U. Va., 1964; D.Comml. Sci. (hon.), St. John's U., 1983. Bar: D.C. 1964, Va. 1964. Assoc. firm Hogan & Hartson, Washington, 1965-67; spl. asst. to dir. OEO, Washington, 1967-68; chmn. ProServ, Inc. and Pro Serv TV, 1969—; sr. ptnr. Dell, Benton & Falk, Washington, 1983—; bd. dirs. Washington Area Tennis Patrons Found., 1970-87. Trustee Robt. F. Kennedy Meml. Found. Named Washingtonian of Yr., 1975; inducted Washington Football Hall of Stars, 1985. Mem. D.C. Bar Assn., Va. Bar Assn., Yale Scroll and Key Honor Soc. Roman Catholic. Clubs: Columbia Country, Metropolitan, Les Ambassadeurs. Mem. U.S. Davis Cup Tennis Team 1961, 62, 63, capt. 1968-69; TV tennis sportscaster, 1974—. General practice. Office: Dell Benton & Falk Suite 1200 Brawner Bldg 888 17th St NW Washington DC 20006

DELL, ERNEST ROBERT, lawyer; b. Vandergrift, Pa., Feb. 6, 1928; m. Karen D. Reed, May 8, 1965; children: Robert W., John D., Jane C. B.S., U. Pitts., 1949, M.Litt., 1953; J.D., Harvard U., 1956. Bar: Pa. 1957, U.S. Supreme Ct. 1961; C.P.A., Pa. Ptnr. firm Reed Smith Shaw & McClay, Pitts., 1956—; adj. prof. law Duquesne U. Law Sch., Pitts., 1960; bd. dirs. Attys. Liability Assurance Soc., Ltd., Bermuda. Mem. ABA, Pa. Bar Assn., Allegheny County Bar Assn., Pa. Inst. C.P.A.'s. Banking, General corporate, Corporate taxation. Home: 119 Riding Trail Lane Pittsburgh PA 15215 Office: Reed Smith Shaw & McClay Mellon Sq 435 6th Ave Pittsburgh PA 15230

DELL, MICHAEL JOHN, lawyer; b. N.Y.C., Aug. 18, 1954; Sidney Samuel and Ethel Rachel (Tannenholtz) D.; m. Lisa Ellen Rothschild, Aug. 24, 1980; children: Benjamin Rubin, Joshua Matthew. BA, Oxford U., 1975; JD magna cum laude, Harvard U., 1978. Bar: N.Y. 1979, U.S. Dist. Ct. (no. so., ea., and we. dists.) N.Y., U.S. Ct. Appeals (2d, 3d, 7th, and 8th cirs.), U.S. Supreme Ct. Law clk. to presiding judge U.S. Dist. Ct. Calif., San Francisco, 1978-79; assoc. Kramer, Levin, Nessen, Kamin & Frankel, N.Y.C., 1979-85, ptnr., 1986—. Editor and assoc. editorial dir. Harvard U. Law Rev., 1976-78. Mem. ABA, Bar Assn. of City of N.Y. Avocations: family, travel, swimming. Federal civil litigation, State civil litigation, Pension, profit-sharing, and employee benefits. Office: Kramer Levin Nessen et al 919 3rd Ave New York NY 10022

DELL, ROBERT MICHAEL, lawyer; b. Chgo., Oct. 4, 1952; s. Michael A. and Bertha Dell; m. Ruth Celia Schiffman, May 29, 1976; children: David, Michael, Jessica. BGS, U. Mich., 1974; JD, U. Ill., 1977. Bar: U.S. Dist. Ct. (no. dist.) Ill. 1977, U.S. Ct. Appeals (7th cir.) 1977. Law clk. to presiding justice U.S. Ct. Appeals (7th cir.), Chgo., 1977-79; assoc. Latham & Watkins, Chgo., 1982-85, ptnr., 1985—. Club: Met. (Chgo.). Antitrust, Federal civil litigation, State civil litigation. Home: 800 Sheridan Rd Wilmette IL 60091 Office: Latham & Watkins Sears Tower # 6900 Chicago IL 60606

DELL'ERGO, ROBERT JAMES, lawyer; b. Berkeley, Calif., Mar. 2, 1918; s. Cosmo A. and Lilian James (Rennie) Dell'E.; divorced; children: Robert, Marilee, Richard. BA with honors, U. Calif., Berkeley, 1939, JD, 1942. Assoc. Brobeck, Phleger & Harrison, San Francisco, 1946; ptnr. Millington & Dell'Ergo, Redwood City, Calif., 1947-57, Dell'Ergo & Tinsley, Redwood City, 1971—; sole practice Redwood City, 1957-71; bd. dirs. Whitevale Inc., Menlo Park, Calif. Chmn. Com. for Ct. Reorganization, San Mateo County, Calif., 1954, Com. to Elect John F. Kennedy, San Mateo County; mem. Redwood City 6 Yr. Plan com.; past chmn. bd. trustees Sequoia Union High Sch. Dist., San Mateo County, trustee, 1951-57. Served to lt. USNR, 1942-46, PTO. Mem. ABA, Calif. Bar Assn., San Mateo County Bar Assn. (pres. 1954, chmn. various coms.), Internat. Platform Assn., Sequoia Club, Redwood City C. of C. (pres. 1958), Am. Legion. Democrat. Club: Redwood City Antlers. Lodges: Elks, Sons of Italy, Redwood City (pres.), Native Sons (chmn. grand lodge law commn.). Avocations: travel, running, photography, music, skiing. State civil litigation, Estate planning, Probate. Office: Dell'Ergo & Tinsley 1900 Broadway Suite 200 Redwood City CA 94063

DELLINGER, WALTER ESTES, III, lawyer; b. Charlotte, N.C., May 15, 1941; s. Walter Estes and Grace Phelan (Lawing) D.; m. Anne Elizabeth Maxwell, June 12, 1965; children—Hampton, Andrew. A.B. with honors, U. N.C., Chapel Hill, 1963; LL.B., Yale U., 1966. Bar: N.C. bar 1970. Asso. prof. law U. Miss., 1966-68; law clk. to Justice Hugo L. Black, U.S. Supreme Ct., 1968-69; asso. prof. law Duke U., 1969-72, prof., 1972—; asso. dean Duke U. (Law Sch.), 1974-76, acting dean, 1976-78; vis. prof. U. So. Calif. Law Center, 1973-74, U. Mich. Law Sch., 1977, Cath. U. Leuven, Belgium, 1985; prof. in residence U.S. Dept. Justice, Washington, 1980-81; cons., draftsman N.C. Criminal Code Commn., 1970-78. Mem. bd. editors: Yale Law Jour, 1965-66. Rockefeller Found. Humanities fellow, 1981-82. Mem. Am. Bar Assn., N.C. State Bar. Democrat. Legal education. Home: 513 E Franklin St Chapel Hill NC 27514 Office: Duke U Law Sch Durham NC 27706

DELLO IACONO, PAUL MICHAEL, real estate executive, lawyer, consultant; b. Brookline, Mass., July 26, 1957; s. John B. Jr. and Marie J.C. (Beaulieu) D.-I.; m. Donna M. Lynch, Jan. 10, 1981; children: Brad Michael, Andrea Marie. BA, St. Anselm Coll., 1979; JD, Suffolk U., 1982. Bar: Mass. 1982. V.p. Housing Dynamics, Boston, 1978-82; counsel DMC Energy Inc., Boston, 1982-85; exec. dir. Brockton (Mass.) Cen., Inc., 1985—; registered lobbyist Market Hill Assocs., Lowell, Mass., 1981. Mem. devel. staff Vt. State Prison, 1978; apptd. mem. Citizens Adv. Commn., Boston, 1986—; bd. dirs. Brockton Area Pvt. Industry Council Mayor's Adv. Com. on Handicapped Affairs. Mem. ABA, Mass. Bar Assn., Delta Sigma Rho, Tau Kappa Alpha, Pi Gamma Mu, Met. South C. of C. (water task force 1986—). Democrat. Roman Catholic. Avocations: golf, gardening. Real property, Local government, General corporate. Home: 15 Southern Ave South Weymouth MA 02190 Office: Brockton Cen Inc 60 Legion Pkwy Brockton MA 02401

DEL NEGRO, JOHN THOMAS, lawyer; b. Springfield, Mass., Oct. 2, 1948; s. Angelo Antonio and Marguerite (Garofalo) Del N.; m. Linda Anne Mayberry, July 6, 1973; children: Peter, Pamela. BA, George Washington U., 1970; JD, Cornell U., 1975. Bar: Conn. 1975, U.S. Dist. Ct. Conn. 1978, U.S. Tax Ct. 1981. Assoc. Murtha, Cullina, Richter & Pinney, Hartford, Conn., 1975-81; ptnr. Murtha, Cullina, Richter & Pinney, Hartford, 1982—. Author: (with Levenson) Depreciation and Investment Tax Credits, 1983. Pres. Windsor Land Trust, Conn., 1983, Windsor Ind. Living Assn. Inc., 1985—. Mem. ABA (capital recovery and leasing com. tax sect. 1983—, vice-chmn. subcom. 1986-87), Windsor Jaycees (pres. 1982-83), U.S. Jaycees (ambassador). Corporate taxation, State and local taxation, General corporate. Home: 71 Nook Farms Rd Windsor CT 06095 Office: Murtha Cullina Richter & Pinney City Pl Hartford CT 06103

DELOACH, DONALD BRIAN, lawyer; b. Augusta, Ga., Oct. 10, 1952; s. Earl Haynie and Eleanor Hill (Jackson) DeL.; m. Rochelle Marie Lord, Aug. 26, 1978; 1 child, Donald Jordan. AB, U. Ga., 1974, postgrad., 1978-79; JD with distinction, Emory U., 1981. Bar: Ga. 1981, U.S. Dist. Ct. (no. dist.) Ga. 1981, U.S. Ct. Appeals (11th cir.)1981, U.S. Tax Ct. 1984. Atty. Webb, Daniel & Betts, Atlanta, 1981-83, Betts & Grant, Atlanta, 1983-84, Frantz & Sanders, Atlanta, 1984—; bd. dirs. Rutherford Inst., Ga. Legal Def. Found. Inc., Atlanta. vol. peacemaker Christian Conciliation Service of Atlanta, Inc., 1985—. Mem. ABA, State Bar of Ga., Order of Coif. General corporate, Estate planning, Tax litigation. Office: Frantz & Sanders 3390 Peachtree Rd NE Suite 222 Atlanta GA 30326

DELOACH, HARRIS E(UGENE), JR., lawyer; b. Columbia, S.C., Aug. 7, 1944; s. Harris Eugene and Julia (Murdock) DeL.; m. Louise Hawes, June 12, 1969; children: Harris Eugene III, John Wilson Malloy, Jeanette Hawes. BBA, U.S.C., 1966; JD, 1969. Bar: S.C. 1969, U. S.Dist. Ct. S.C. 1969, U.S. Ct. Appeals (4th cir.) 1974. Ptnr., Wilmeth & DeLoach, Hartsville, S.C., 1972-85; v.p., gen. counsel Sonoco Products Co., Hartsville, 1986—; bd. dirs. Bank of Hartsville, Coker's Pedigreed Seed Co., Hartsville. Trustee Coker Coll., Hartsville, 1974-79, vice chmn., 1979; chmn. bd. trustees Byerly Hosp., Hartsville, 1976-79; chmn. bd. dirs. Thomas Hart Acad., Hartsville, 1984. Served to capt. USAF, 1969-72. Recipient Algernon Sydney Sullivan award Coker Coll., 1985. Mem. ABA, S.C. Bar Assn., 4th Jud. Cir. Assn. S.C. (v.p. 1974-78), Darlington County Bar Assn. (pres. 1984), Hartsville C. of C. (pres. 1977). Presbyterian. Lodge: Rotary (pres. Hartsville club 1977, Citizen of Yr. of Hartsville club 1980). General corporate, Banking, General practice. Home: 329 Kenwood Hartsville SC 29550 Office: Sonoco Products Co N Second St Hartsville SC 29550

DELONG, DEBORAH, lawyer; b. Louisville, Sept. 5, 1950; d. Henry F. and Lois Jean (Stepp) D.; m. Michael A. Marrero, Jan. 12, 1981; children—Amelie DeLong, Samuel Prentice. B.A., Vanderbilt U., 1972; J.D., U. Cin., 1975. Bar: Ohio 1975, U.S. Dist. Ct. (so dist.) Ohio 1975, U.S. Ct. Appeals (6th cir.) 1975, U.S. Supreme Ct. 1982. Assoc. Paxton & Seasongood, Cin., 1975-82, ptnr., 1982—. Contbr. articles to profl. jours. Fund raiser Jr. League Cin., Ohio, 1979-84; bd. dirs. Childrens Psychiatric Ctr., Cin., 1980-84. Mem. ABA, Ohio State Bar Assn., Cin. Bar Assn., Arbitration Tribunal U.S. Dist. Ct., Ohio, 1984. Republican. Episcopalian. Labor, Federal civil litigation, State civil litigation. Office: Paxton & Seasongood 1700 Central Trust Tower 1 W 4th St Cincinnati OH 45202

DELP, WILBUR CHARLES, JR., lawyer; b. Cedar Rapids, Iowa, Oct. 26, 1934; s. Wilbur Charles and Irene Frances (Flynn) D.; m. Patricia Lynn Vesely, June 22, 1963; children: Marci Lynn, Melissa Kathryn, Derek Charles. B.A., Coe Coll., 1956; LL.B., NYU, 1959. Bar: Ill. 1960, U.S. Supreme Ct. 1962. Assoc. Sidley & Austin, Chgo., 1959-68, ptnr., 1968; lectr. securities law seminars. Trustee Wayne Community Assn., 1975-78. Served with USAF, 1959-65. Mem. ABA (securities com.), Chgo. Bar Assn. (sub-com. chmn.), NYU Law Alumni Club (bd. dirs. 1976—), Phi Beta Kappa, Phi Kappa Phi. Republican. Episcopalian. Club: Mid-Day (Chgo.). General corporate, Public utilities, Administrative and regulatory. Home: Box 97 Wayne IL 60184 Office: Sidley & Austin 1 First National Plaza Chicago IL 60603

DEL PESCO, SUSAN MARIE CARR, lawyer; b. Long Beach, Calif., May 20, 1946; d. Clarence Monroe and Leona (Goings) Carr; m. Thomas W. Del Pesco, Aug. 28, 1965; children: Joseph Thomas, Nicholas Paul. Student, UCLA, 1963-65; BA, U. Calif., Santa Barbara, 1967; JD, Widener U., 1975. Bar: Del. 1975, U.S. Dist. Ct. Del. 1975, U.S. Ct. Appeals (3d cir.) 1982. Assoc. Schnee & Castle, Wilmington, Del., 1976-81; ptnr. Prickett, Jones, Elliott, Kristol & Schnee, Wilmington, 1981—, also bd. dirs.; mem. Del. Supreme Ct. Bd. on Profl. Responsibility, 1979-86, Permanent Lawyers Adv. Com. for U.S. Dist. Ct. Del., 1985—. Recipient Outstanding Alumnae award Del. Law Sch., 1987. Mem. Del. State Bar Assn. (treas. 1978-79, v.p. New Castle 1984-85, v.p. at large 1985-86, pres.-elect 1986-87, pres. 1987—). Republican. Federal civil litigation, Personal injury, Insurance. Office: Prickett Jones Elliott Kristol & Schnee 1310 King St PO Box 1328 Wilmington DE 19899

DEL PICCOLO, SILVANA PANNELLA, lawyer; b. Milan, Apr. 21, 1939; came to U.S., 1965; d. Luigi and Maria (DiSabbato) Pannella; m. Luciano Del Piccolo, Dec. 23, 1966. JD, U. Milan, 1961, U. Colo., 1970. Bar: Italy 1963, Colo. 1971. Gen. counsel SEDRIM, Milan, 1961-63; assoc. Boneschi & Boneschi, Milan, 1963-65; of counsel Pavia & Harcourt, N.Y.C., 1966-68; dep. dist. atty. State of Colo., Denver, 1970-71; internat. counsel The Gates Corp., Denver, 1971-87, U.S. West, Inc., Denver, 1987—. Recipient Women of Achievement award, Denver YWCA, 1984. Mem. Am. Corp. Counsel Assn. (bd. dirs. Colo. chpt. 1985, pres. 1986—), Colo. Bar Assn. (internat. law com.). Avocations: skiing, tennis, classical music. Private international. Home: 6253 S Galena Way Englewood CO 80111 Office: US West Inc 9785 Maroon Circle Suite 210 Englewood CO 80112

DEL RUSSO, ALEXANDER D., lawyer; b. Washington, Aug. 29, 1955; s. Carl Richard and Alessandra (Luini) Del R.; m. Denise A. Del Russo, Aug. 27, 1983. BA, Duke U., 1977; JD, U. Miami, 1980. Bar: D.C. 1980, Fla. 1982. Atty. U.S. Dept. HUD, Washington, 1980-83; assoc. Blackwell, Walker, Fascell & Hoehl, Miami, Fla., 1983-85; ptnr. Blackwell, Walker, Fascell & Hoehl, West Palm Beach, Fla., 1986—; assoc. Wolf, Block, Schorr & Solis-Cohen, West Palm Beach, 1985-86; bd. dirs. Legal Services Greater Miami. Mem. ABA, Assn. Trial Lawyers Am. Roman Catholic. Federal civil litigation, State civil litigation, Contracts commercial. Home: 639 Juniper Pl West Palm Beach FL 33414 Office: Blackwell Walker Fascell & Hoehl 1665 Palm Beach Lakes Blvd Suite 1000 West Palm Beach FL 33401

DEL SESTO, RONALD W., lawyer; b. Providence, Oct. 25, 1940; s. Christopher and Lola E. (Faraone) Del S.; m. Bettina Buonanno, Aug. 3, 1963; children: Cristina, Ronald Jr., Justin. AB, Georgetown U., 1962; JD, Boston Coll., 1965. Bar: R.I. 1965, U.S. Dist. Ct. R.I. 1967, U.S. Tax Ct. 1971. Sole practice Providence, 1965—; gen. counsel Sec. of State, 1983-85, law revision officer, 1983, commn. on Uniform State Laws, 1983—, State of R.I.; lectr. various profl. assns. Contbg. editor Boston Coll. Law Rev., 1963-65; contbr. articles to profl. jours. Mem. legal adv. com. Cath. Found. of

R.I., 1983—. Mem. ABA (econs. of law practice sect., litigation sect., com. fee arrangements 1974—, computer com. user groups 1984—, chmn. New Eng. regional Apple-users group, 1984-85, vice chmn. electronic communications 1985, vice chmn. hardware users group 1986—), R.I. Bar Assn. (com. econ. of profession 1968-73, 75-77, chmn. 1970-72, profl. ethics and responsibility com. 1977-82, environ. law com. 1982—, assoc. editor R.I. Bar Jour. 1969-74), Comml. Law League Am., Assn. Trial Lawyers Am. Republican. Roman Catholic. Clubs: Dunes (Narragansett), Point Judith Country (Narragansett), Turks Head (Providence). Avocations: reading, computers. Computer, General corporate, Probate. Home: 238 Highland Ave Warwick RI 02886 Office: 49 Weybosset St Providence RI 02903

DE LUCA, PETER J., lawyer, corporate executive; b. N.Y.C., Oct. 15, 1927; s. Thomas A. and Madeline (Insard) De L.; m. Marie Joan Macchia, Sept. 18, 1954; 1 child, David Laurence. LL.B. cum laude, N.Y. Law Sch., 1953. Bar: N.Y. Sole practice N.Y.C.; mem. firm Cravath, Swaine & Moore, 1953-59; with Pepsi Co., Inc., N.Y.C., 1959-71; v.p. Pepsi Co., Inc., 1963-65, v.p., gen. counsel, sec., 1965-71; sr. v.p. for corp. affairs, gen. counsel, dir. Revlon, Inc., 1971-73; sr. v.p., gen. counsel Gen. Foods Corp., N.Y.C., 1973; also dir. Gen. Foods Corp. Author short stories under name Stephen Scott. Mem. Gov. Carey's Com. on Appointee Standards; bd. dirs. Heart Found., Burke Rehab. Hosp., NAACP Legal Def. and Ednl. Found., N.Y. Foundling Com.; bd. dirs., vice chmn. Council of Better Bus. Bur.; trustee Food and Drug Law Inst. Served with U.S. Mcht. Marine USNR, 1945-47. Mem. ABA, N.Y. State Bar Assn., Assn. Bar City N.Y., Delta Theta Phi, Sigma Pi Phi. Democrat. Clubs: Univ, Westchester Country. Home: 360 E 72d St New York NY 10021 Office: 250 North St White Plains NY 10625

DE LUCA, THOMAS GEORGE, lawyer; b. Jersey City, Dec. 28, 1950; s. Michael Anthony and Estelle Theresa (Wickiewicz) De L.; m. Annette Catherine Pandolfo, Aug. 16, 1975; children: Michele, Thomas, Rachel. BS in Econs., St. Peters Coll., Jersey City, 1972; JD, Seton Hall U., 1978. Bar: N.J. 1978, U.S. Dist. Ct. N.J. 1978, N.Y. 1981, U.S. Dist. Ct. (so. and ea. dists.) N.Y. 1981, U.S. Ct. Appeals (2d cir.) 1986. Supervising underwriter Fireman's Fund Ins. Cos., Newark, 1972-77; assoc. Sellar, Richardson & Stuart, Newark, 1978-80; assoc. Postner & Rubin, N.Y.C., 1980-84, ptnr., 1985—. Mem. ABA, N.J. Bar Assn., N.Y. County Lawyers Assn. Roman Catholic. Construction, State civil litigation, Federal civil litigation. Home: 14 Kilmer Dr Colonia NJ 07067 Office: Postner & Rubin 17 Battery Pl New York NY 10004

DE LUCIA, JOHN JOSEPH, lawyer; b. N.Y.C., May 6, 1931; s. Joseph and Josephine (Massaro) De L.; m. Amalia Camille Giove, June 16, 1962; children—John J., Jr., Jeffrey A., Marianne M. B.B.A., CCNY, 1954; J.D., St. John's U., 1957. Bar: N.Y. 1957, U.S. Dist. Ct. (so. and ea. dists.) N.Y. 1962, U.S. Supreme Ct. 1964. Trial atty. Allstate Ins. Co., N.Y.C., 1957-59, Ins. Co. of N. Am., N.Y.C., 1959-61; atty. of record Statewide Ins. Co., Great Neck, N.Y., 1962-80; sole practice, N.Y.C., 1980—; counsel, officer, dir. Amtec Enterprises, Inc., Newark, 1972—; ptnr. S.W. Creations, Newark, 1974—; dep; atty. gen., spl. investigator Election Frauds Dept., Dept. Law, N.Y.C., 1960; lectr. Hofstra Sch. Law, Hempstead, N.Y., 1982. Mem. N.Y. State Trial Lawyers Assn., Assn. Trial Lawyers Am., Def. Research Inst., Alpha Phi Delta, Delta Theta Phi. Democrat. Roman Catholic. Personal injury, General practice, Criminal. Home and Office: 190-16 Aberdeen Rd Jamaica Estates New York NY 11423

DEL VALLE, IGNACIO GONZALEZ, lawyer; b. Havana, Cuba, Apr. 7, 1944; came to U.S., 1960, naturalized 1966; s. Ambrosio G. and Silvia (Fonts) del V.; m. Olga Maria Rodriguez-Pajon, June 5, 1965; children: Jorge Ignacio, Beatriz. Student, Villanova U., 1961-62; BSChemE, La. State U., 1965, MSChemE, 1970; postgrad., U. Fla., 1965-66; JD, U. Miami, 1973. Bar: Fla. 1974, U.S. Dist Ct. (so. dist.) Fla., U.S. Ct. Appeals (11th cir.). Research engr. Esso Research Labs., Baton Rouge, 1966-69; cons. engr. Nat. Planning and Constrn. Corp., Coral Gables, Fla., 1969-72; ptnr. Salley, Barns, Pajon, Guttman & del Valle, Miami, Fla., 1973—; bd. dirs. Totalbank, Miami. Patentee fuel process. Mem. Am. Inst. Chem. Engrs., ABA, Fla. Bar Assn., Dade County Bar Assn., Attys. Title Guaranty Fund, Tau Beta Pi, Phi Lambda Upsilon. Democrat. Roman Catholic. Banking, Real property, General corporate. Home: 7955 SW 108th St Miami FL 33156 Office: Salley Barns et al 100 N Biscayne Blvd Suite 700 Miami FL 33132

DEMAHY, PAUL JOSEPH, judge; b. St. Matinville, La., Aug. 11, 1949; s. Bernard Moses and Anne Louise (Hamley) DeM.; m. Marilyn Marie Snoddy, Feb. 22, 1969; children: M. Scott, Brigette, James, Suzanne, Caroline. BA, U. Southwestern La., 1973; JD, La. State U., 1973. Bar: La. 1973, U.S. Dist. Ct. (we. dist.) La. 1975, U.S. Dist. Ct. (ea. dist.) La. 1982, U.S. Ct. Appeals (5th cir.) 1982, U.S. Supreme Ct. 1982. Assoc. Willis & Hardy, St. Martinville, 1973-78; sole practice St. Martinville, 1978-86; judge 16th Judicial Dist. Ct., 1986—; judge ad hoc Breaux Bridge (La.) City Ct., 1980-86; chief defender indigent def. bd. 16th Jud. Dist., St. Martinville, 1986; atty. City of St. Martinville, 1974-86. Officer, bd. dirs. St. Martin Assn. for Retarded Citizens, St. Martinville, 1979—. Named Profl. of Yr. St. Martin Assn. Retarded Citizens, 1984. Mem. ABA, La. Bar Assn., Assn. Trial Lawyers Am., La. Trial Lawyers Assn. (bd. of govs. 1982-85), La. Assn. Criminal Def. Lawyers (chartered), St. Martinville Jaycees (Outstanding Young Man 1978, Outstanding Young Family La. chpt. 1980, v.p. community devel. La. chpt. 1978-79). Democrat. Roman Catholic. Office: PO Box 7 Saint Martinville LA 70582

DEMAIO, ANDREW JOHN, lawyer; b. Red Bank, N.J., Jan. 10, 1956; s. Vincent C. and Jo Anne (Pels) DeM.; m. Deborah Z. Zern, Aug. 15, 1981. BA, Rutgers U., 1978; JD, Cornell U., 1981. Bar: N.J. 1981, U.S. Dist. Ct. N.J. 1981, U.S. Supreme Ct. 1986. Assoc. Vincent C. DeMaio Law Firm, Matawan, N.J., 1981-84; ptnr. DeMaio & DeMaio, Matawan, 1984—. Mem. mgmt. com. YMCA, 1985—. Mem. ABA (real property, probate and trust sect.), N.J. Bar Assn., Estate Planning Council of Cen. N.J. Lodge: Rotary (sec. 1985—). General practice, Probate, Estate taxation. Office: DeMaio & DeMaio 154 Main St Matawan NJ 07747

DEMARCO, ANTHONY J., JR., lawyer; b. Bklyn., June 27, 1928; s. Anthony J. and Clementine (Corazza) D.; (div.) children—Angela J., Jennifer C. B.S., Manhattan Coll., 1952; J.D., St. John's U., 1958; postgrad. NYU, Grad. Sch. Law 1960 Bar: N.Y. 1958. Atty. Hartford Accident and Indemnity Co., 1956-58; sole practice, 1958-76, trial counsel Anthony J. DeMarco Jr., P.C., 1976—. Bd. dirs. and counsel S.I. Hosp. Heart Assn., S.I. Artificial Kidney Fund. Served with USMC, 1946-48. Mem. ABA (com. on litigation, com. on trial evidence 1977—), N.Y. State Bar Assn. (permanent chmn. trial adv. and scholarship com., exec. com. trial lawyers sect., chmn. 1984—, faculty continuing legal edn. div.), Bklyn. Bar Assn., Kings County Defenders Assn., Columbia Lawyers Assn., Fed. Bar Council, Nat. Trial Advocacy Assn. (assoc. dir.). Federal civil litigation, State civil litigation, Criminal. Office: 26 Court St Suite 2803 Brooklyn NY 11242

DEMARCO, JAMES JOSEPH, lawyer; b. Phila., Mar. 29, 1933; s. Camillo and Rose (Lista) DeM.; m. Linda Acchione, June 4, 1966; children: Richard, Lawrence, James. BA, Villanova U., 1954, JD, 1959. Bar: Pa. 1960. labor referee Pa. Labor Relations Bd., Phila., 1972-74. Dem. committeeman, Phila., 1957—; mem. local 130 Draft Bd., Phila., 1970-76. Served to capt. USMCR, 1954-56. Named Man of Yr. NAACP, Phila., 1976. Mem. Pa. Bar Assn., Phila. Bar Assn., Assn. Trial Lawyers Am., Pa. Trial Lawyers Assn., Justinian Soc., Villanova U. Alumni Assn. (class rep. 1980—). Roman Catholic. Lodge: Sons of Italy (pres. 1972-74). Avocations: music, boating, fishing. Personal injury, Workers' compensation, General practice. Home: 1514 S Broad St Philadelphia PA 19146 Office: 1420 Walnut St Suite 1107 Philadelphia PA 19103

DEMAREST, SYLVIA M., lawyer; b. Lake Charles, La., Aug. 16, 1944; d. Edmund and Emily (Meyers) D.; m. James A. Johnston, Jr., Oct. 31, 1975 (div. Dec. 1979). Student U. S.W. La., 1963-66; J.D., U. Tex., 1969. Bar: Tex. 1969, U.S. Supreme Ct. 1973, U.S. Ct. Appeals (5th cir.) 1970, U.S. Ct. Appeals (7th cir.) 1979, U.S. Ct. Appeals (11th cir.) 1980, U.S. Dist. Ct. (no. dist.) Tex. 1970, U.S. Dist. Ct. (ea. dist.) Tex. 1970, U.S. Dist. Ct. (so. dist.) Tex. 1972. Reginald H. Smith Community Lawyer fellow, Corpus Christi and Dallas, 1969-71; house counsel Tex. Inst. Ednl. Devel., San Antonio, 1972-73; staff atty. Dallas Legal Services Found., Inc., 1973, exec. dir., 1973-76; sole practice, Dallas, 1977-78; mgr. product litigation, dir. Windle Turley, P.C., Dallas, 1978-83; sole practice, 1983-85; ptnr. Demarest & Smith, 1985—; mem. faculty trial advocacy program So. Meth. U. Law Sch., 1984; lectr. Contbr. articles to profl. jours. Mem. State Bar Tex., ABA, Assn. Trial Lawyers Am., Dallas Bar Assn., Tex. Trial Lawyers Assn. (bd. dirs.), Dallas Trial Lawyers Assn. (past pres.). Democrat. Roman Catholic. Personal injury. Home: 1812 Atlantic St Dallas TX 75208 Office: 750 N St Paul St Suite 1150 Dallas TX 75201

DE MARIE, ANTHONY JOSEPH, lawyer; b. Buffalo, May 10, 1928; s. Joseph and Josephine (Radice) De M.; m. Rose Galluzzo, July 23, 1955; children—Michael, Janice, Gregory, Lynda. J.D., U. Buffalo, 1955. Bar: N.Y. 1956, U.S. Dist. Ct. (we. dist.) N.Y. 1960, U.S. Ct. Appeals (2d cir.) 1982. Ptnr., Dixon & De Marie, Buffalo, 1956—. Dir., Neighborhood Legal Services of Erie County, Buffalo, 1971-74. Served with AUS, 1946-48, 50-51. Mem. Erie County Bar Assn. (past bd. dirs.), Trial Lawyers Assn. Erie County (past pres., gov.) N.Y. State Bar Assn., Fla. Bar Assn., N.Y. State Trial Lawyers Assn., Assn. Trial Lawyers Am., Western N.Y. Trial Lawyers Assn. Republican. Roman Catholic. Club: Transit Valley Country. Personal injury, State civil litigation, Insurance. Home: 59 Timberlane Dr Williamsville NY 14221 Office: Dixon and De Marie PC 930 Convention Tower Buffalo NY 14202

DEMARIE, JOSEPH, lawyer; b. Buffalo, May 11, 1940; s. Joseph A. and osephine C. (Radice) DeM.; m. Midlred M. Rizzuto, Aug. 8, 1964; children: Valerie Ann, Joseph A., Stephen R. JD, U. Buffalo, 1963. Bar: N.Y. 1963, U.S. Dist. Ct. (we. and ea. dists.) N.Y., U.S. Ct. Appeals (2d cir.). Ptnr. Dixon, DeMarie & Schoenborn P.C., Buffalo, 1963—; bd. dirs. Tech. Advancement Labs. Inc., Buffalo. Editor U. Buffalo, 1962-63. Mem. N.Y. State Bar Assn., Erie County Bar Assn. (bd. dirs. 1978-81), Assn. Trial Lawyers Am., N.Y. State Trial Lawyers Assn., Western N.Y. Trial Lawyers Assn. (bd. dirs. 1977-79), Justinian Legal Soc. Clubs: Niagara on Lake Sail, Island Yacht. Avocations: sailing, golf. Federal civil litigation, Insurance, Personal injury. Home: 193 Greenaway Amherst NY 14226 Office: Dixon DeMarie & Schoenborn 930 Convention Tower Buffalo NY 14202

DE MARINO, THOMAS JOHN, lawyer; b. Greensburg, Pa., Nov. 24, 1937; s. Thomas Camille and Sue Eleanor (Nicholson) de M.; m. Elizabeth Hamilton Bardsley, Aug. 22, 1959 (div. Aug. 1978); children—Jeffrey, Lynn; m. Joyce Hobson Lee, May 18, 1979. B.A., Dickinson Coll., 1959, LL.B., 1962. Bar: Pa. 1963, Colo. 1965, U.S. Dist. Ct. Colo. 1965, U.S. Ct. Appeals (10th cir.) 1965, U.S. Supreme Ct. 1984. Assoc. Hamilton, Darmo, Malloy, Phila., 1963; ptnr. firm Ellison, de Marino & Knapp, Denver, 1965-76, de Marino & Knapp, Denver, 1976-77, Sheldon, Bayer, McLean & Glasman, Denver, 1978; Colo. mng. atty. law dept. litigation div. Travelers Ins. Co., Denver, 1979—. Contbr. articles to legal jours. Pres. Denver Lyric Opera Co., 1973; treas. Colo. Mountain Club Found., Denver, 1984. Mem. Colo. Bar Assn. (bd. govs. 1985—, chmn. workmen's compensation com. 1983), Denver Bar Assn. (chmn. interprofl. com. 1983), Colo. Def. Lawyers Assn. (v.p. 1975, pres. 1976), Def. Research Inst. (exceptional performance citation 1977). Republican. Congregationalist. Club: Colo. Mountain (bd. dirs. Denver 1974). Personal injury, Workers' compensation, State civil litigation. Office: 1720 S Bellaire St Suite 1100 Denver CO 80222

DEMAS, JEAN V., lawyer; b. Oak Park, Ill., Dec. 30, 1940; d. Charles William and Helen Alice (Kyriakopolos) D.; m. Harry T. Dallianis, Dec. 8, 1962 (div. July 1979); children: Irene Lorraine, Thomas Harry; m. Emil Athineos, Apr. 24, 1983. BA, Northwestern U., 1962; JD, DePaul U., 1982. Bar: Ill. 1982, U.S. Dist. Ct. (no. dist.) Ill. 1982. Tchr. Von Steuben High Sch., Chgo., 1962-65; sec., treas. Ideal Real Estate and Ins. Brokerage Inc., Chgo., 1965-72, v.p., exec. dir., 1972-79, dir. corp. relocation, 1975-81; assoc. Kois & McLaughlin P.C., Chgo., 1982-84; sole practice Lincolnwood, Ill., 1984-85; staff counsel The Options Clearing Corp., Chgo., 1985—; bd. dirs. Ideal Real Co. Contbr. articles to profl. jours. Mem. Lincolnwood Community Council, Ill., 1972—, Lincolnwood Friends of Library, Lincolnwood Steering Com., 1978—, Lincolnwood Bicentenial Com., Lincolnwood PTA; treas. Lincolnwood Homeowners Assn., 1974-75; den leader Cub Scouts Am., 1978-79; precinct worker Lincolnwood Citizens Action Party, 1975; coordinator 15th dist. Ill. ERA, 1977-78; bd. dirs. Sts. Peter and Paul Greek Orthodox Ch. Sch., 1977-79. Mem. ABA (banking and bus. law com. young lawyers div.), Ill. Bar Assn., Chgo. Bar Assn. (real property com., corp. law depts. com.), Women's Bar Assn. Ill., Chgo. Real Estate Bd. (chmn. sales council 1980-81), North Suburban Real Estate Bd. (pres. 1976-77, bd. dirs. 1978-80), RELO/Inter-City Relocation Service (chairperson Chgo. met. area 1975-76), LWV, Zeta Tau Alpha. General corporate, Securities, Real property. Home: 6842 N Kostner Lincolnwood IL 60646 Office: The Options Clearing Corp 200 S Wacker Dr Suite 2700 Chicago IL 60606

DEMASCIO, ROBERT EDWARD, judge; b. Coraopolis, Pa., Jan. 11, 1923; s. Peter and Rosa (Baretta) DeM.; m. Margaret Loftus, Aug. 6, 1955; children: Thomas, Robert, Mary. Student, Wayne State U., 1942-43, 47-51, LL.B., 1951; student, U. Ill., 1944. Bar: Mich. bar 1951. Practice law Detroit, 1951-53, 61-66, asst. U.S. atty., chief criminal div., 1954-61; judge Recorders Ct., Detroit, 1967-71; U.S. dist. judge Eastern Dist. Mich., 1971—. Served with USNR, 1943-46. Mem. Am., Fed., Detroit bar assns., State Bar Mich. Jurisprudence. Office: U S Dist Ct U S Courthouse 231 W Lafayette Blvd Room 707 Detroit MI 48226 *

DEMAY, JOHN ANDREW, lawyer; b. Phila., Sept. 5, 1925; s. John Andrew and Anne Elizabeth (Mamaux) DeM.; m. Helen Louise Duffy, Sept. 2, 1950; children—John, Patrick, Ann, Mary, Theresa, Michael, Elizabeth, Stephen, Paul, David, Maureen. B.A. in Econs., U. Pitts., 1949, J.D., 1952. Bar: Pa. 1953, U.S. Dist. Ct. (we. dist.) Pa. 1953, U.S. Ct. Appeals (3d cir.) 1960, U.S. Ct. Appeals (2d cir.) 1965, U.S. Supreme Ct. 1965, U.S. Dist. Ct. (we. dist.) N.Y. 1968, U.S. Dist. Ct. (no. dist.) Ohio 1981. Law clk., Ct. Common Pleas, Pitts., 1952-53; asst. U.S. atty. We. Dist. Pa., 1953-57; ptnr. McArdle, Harrington & McLauglin, Pitts., 1957-67; sole practice, Pitts., 1967-80; ptnr. DeMay, DeMay & Donnelly, P.C., Bethel Park, Pa., 1980—. Served to maj. CE USAR, 1950-70. Mem. ABA, Pa. Bar Assn., Allegheny County Bar Assn., Assn. Trial Lawyers Am., Acad. Trial Lawyers Allegheny County, Order Coif. Republican. Roman Catholic. Author: The Plaintiff's Personal Injury Case: It's Preparation, Trial and Settlement, 1977, Discovery-How To Win Your Case Without Trial, 1982. Personal injury, State civil litigation, Federal civil litigation. Home: 7166 Keith Rd Bethel Park PA 15102 Office: 4880 Library Rd Bethel Park PA 15102

DEMBLING, PAUL GERALD, lawyer, former government official; b. Rahway, N.J., Jan. 11, 1920; s. Simon and Fannie (Ellenbogen) D.; m. Florence Brotman, Nov. 22, 1947; children: Ross Wayne, Douglas Evan, Donna Stacy. B.A., Rutgers U., 1940, M.A., 1942; J.D., George Washington U., 1951. Bar: D.C. 1952. Grad. asst., teaching fellow Rutgers U., 1940-42; economist, salary and wage analyst Office Chief Transp., Dept. Army, 1942-45; since practiced in Washington; indsl. relations NACA, 1945-51, spl. counsel, legal adviser, gen. counsel, 1951-58; asst. gen. counsel NASA, 1958-61, dir. legis. affairs, 1961-63, dep. gen. counsel, 1963-67, gen. counsel, 1967-69, chmn. bd. contract appeals, 1958-61, vice chmn. inventions and contbns. bd., 1959-67; mem. and alt. rep. U.S. del. UN Legal Subcom. Com. on Outer Space, 1964-69; gen. counsel GAO, 1969-78; partner Schnader, Harrison, Segal & Lewis, Washington, 1978—; professorial lectr. George Washington U. Law Sch., 1965—. Editor-in-chief: Fed. Bar Jour., 1962-69; contbr. articles to profl. jours. Recipient Meritorious Civilian Service award War Dept., 1945; Disting. Service award NASA, 1968; Nat. Civil Service League award, 1973. Fellow Nat. Contract Mgmt. Assn. (bd. advisers 1973—), AIAA (chmn. com. law and sociology 1969-71); mem. ABA (council public contract law, sec. 1983-84, vice chmn. 1984-85, chmn. elect 1985-86, chmn. 1986—), D.C. Bar Assn., Fed. Bar Assn. (nat. council 1963—, pres. Capitol Hill chpt. 1977-78, nat. sec. 1978-79, pres.-elect 1981-82, nat. pres. 1983-84), Internat. Inst. Space Law (pres. Am. assn. 1970-72), Nat. Acad. Pub. Adminstrn., Phi Delta Phi. Clubs: Cosmos (Washington), Nat. Lawyers (Washington). Public international. Home: 2131 N St NW Washington DC 20037 Office: Schnader Harrison Segal & Lewis 1111 19th St NW Washington DC 20036

DEMBROW, DANA LEE, lawyer; b. Washington, Sept. 29, 1953; s. Daniel William and Catherine Louise (Carder) D. BA, Duke U., 1975; JD, George Washington U., 1980. Bar: D.C., Md., W.Va. Law clk. D.C. Superior Ct., Washington, 1979-80; assoc. Smink & Scheuermann, Washington, 1980-81, Reback & Parsons, Washington, 1981-82, Howard M. Rensin, Hyattsville, Md., 1984-86; mem. com. on constitutional and adminstrv. law, subcom. transp. Md. Ho. of Dels., 1986—; pres. White Oak Towers Tenants Assn., Silver Spring, Md., 1984-85; platform chair Montgomery Democratic Assembly, Silver Spring, 1985-86; com. chair Young Democrats of Montgomery County, Silver Spring, 1985; bd. dirs. Park Bradford condominium. Sec. Greater Colesville Citizens Assn., Md., 1984, Eastern Montgomery, Kensington, Wheaton Dem. Club, Silver Spring, 1986; vol. Sen. John Glenn's campaign, Manchester, N.H., 1984. Personal injury. Office: 1616 16th St NW #701 Washington DC 20009

DE MENT, IRA, lawyer; b. Birmingham, Ala., Dec. 21, 1931; s. Ira Jr. and Helen (Sparks) DeM.; m. Ruth Lester Posey; 1 child, Charles Posey. AS, Marion Mil. Inst., 1951; AB, U. Ala., 1953, LLB, 1958, JD, 1969. Bar: Ala. 1958, U.S. Dist. Ct. (mid. dist.) Ala. 1958, U.S. Ct. Appeals (5th cir.) 1958, U.S. Supreme Ct. 1966, U.S. Dist. Ct. (so. dist.) Ala. 1967, U.S. Dist. Ct. D.C. 1972, U.S. Ct. Appeals (D.C.) 1972, U.S. Tax Ct. 1972, U.S. Customs and Patents Appeals 1976, U.S. Dist. Ct. (no. dist.) Ala. 1977. U.S. Ct. Appeals (11th cir.), 1981. Law clk. Sup. Ct. Ala., 1958-59; asst. atty. gen. State of Ala., 1959, spl. asst. atty. gen., 1966-69, 81—; asst. U.S. atty., Montgomery, Ala., 1959-61; sole practice Montgomery, 1961-69, 77—; acting U.S. atty. Mid. Dist. Ala. 1969, U.S. atty., 1969-73; asst. atty., legal advisor to police and fire depts. City of Montgomery, 1965-69; instr. Jones Law Sch., 1962-64; instr. Montgomery Police Acad. 1964-77; lectr. constl. law Ala. Police Acad., 1971-75; instr. law enforcement U. Ala., 1967, mem. adj. faculty New Coll., 1974-75, adj. prof. psychology, 1975—; spl. counsel to Gov. State Ala., 1980—, gen. counsel Commn. on Aging, 1980-82. Served to lt. col. USAR, 1953-74; now maj. gen. USAFR. Recipient Disting. Service award Internat. Assn. Firefighters, 1975; Rockefeller Pub. Service award, Woodrow Wilson Sch. Pub. and Internat. Affairs Princeton U., 1976. Mem. Am. Arbitration Assn. (mem. nat. panel arbitrators), Nat. Dist. Attys. Assn., ABA, Fed. Bar Assn., D.C. Bar Assn., Ala. Bar Assn. (mem. editorial adv. bd. The Alabama Lawyer 1966-72), Assn. Trial Lawyers Am., Ala. Trial Lawyers Assn., Montgomery County Trial Lawyers Assn., Am. Judicature Soc., Fraternal Order Police, Ala. Peace Officers Assn., Res. Officers Assn. U.S., Air Force Assn., Nat. Assn. Former U.S. Attys., Phi Alpha Delta. Republican. United Methodist. Clubs: Montgomery Country and Beauvoir, Masons, Shriners. Personal injury, State civil litigation, Federal civil litigation. Address: PO Box 4163 Montgomery AL 36103

DEMENT, KENNETH LEE, lawyer; b. Poplar Bluff, Mo., Feb. 13, 1933; s. Charles Kenneth and Ada (Hudson) D.; m. Terisa K. Dement; children—Kenneth L., Gerald C., Laura A., Randolph S., Mary D., Maureen K., Justin L. B.S., S.E. Mo. State U., 1955; J.S.D., Washington U., St. Louis, 1961. Bar: Mo. 1961, U.S. dist. ct. (ea. dist.) Mo. 1961, U.S. Ct. Appeals (8th cir.) 1962, U.S. Supreme Ct. 1975. Sole practice, Sikeston, Mo., 1961—; lectr. continuing legal edn. Bd. regents S.E. Mo. State U., 1979, pres. bd. regents, 1979-81; commr. S.E. Mo. Regional Port Authority, 1983—. Served as capt. USMC, 1953-61. Mem. Nat. Bd. Trial Advocacy (diplomate), Mo. Assn. Trial Attys. (bd. govs.), Am. Trial Lawyers Assn., Am. Judicature Soc., Mo. Bar Assn., Scott County Bar Assn. Democrat. Mem. Christian Ch. Contbr. numerous articles to legal jours. Federal civil litigation, State civil litigation.

DEMENT, SANDRA HELENE, lawyer; b. Tokyo, Apr. 15, 1949; came to U.S. 1950; d. Russell O. and Charlotte (Krupa) D.; m. Victor S. Sterling, Feb. 12, 1972 (div. Nov. 1978); David Arthur Deuter, Aug. 28, 1982. BA, Whitman Coll., 1970; JD, George Washington U., 1978. Bar: D.C. 1978, Ill. 1981. Program dir. Youth Citizenship Fund, Washington, 1971-72; assoc. Citizen Action Group, Washington, 1972-73; exec. dir. Nat. Resource Ctr., Washington, 1974-79; v.p. ops. Banker Legal Service Corp., Chgo., 1979-80; pres. DeMent & Deuter Assoc., Chgo., 1980-81; dir. legal plans Hyatt Legal Services, Kansas City, Mo., 1981-87; mem. adv. bd. on delivery systems study Legal Service Corp., Washington, 1978-80; bd. dirs. Am. Arbitration Assn., N.Y.C. Editor: Group Legal Service Plans, 1981. Bd. dirs. United Labor Agy., 1978-79; Nat. Consumers League, 1977-83. Mem. ABA (commn. on lawyer advertising 1977-80), D.C. Bar Assn., Ill. Bar Assn. Administrative and regulatory, Prepaid legal service plans. Home: 1401 W 50th Terr Kansas City MO 64112

DEMERS, TIMOTHY FRANCIS, lawyer; b. N.Y.C., Feb. 6, 1954; s. Thomas Martin and Dorothy (Ames) D.; m. Imogene Louise Loness, Oct. 5, 1974; children: Sarah Elizabeth, Deirdre Megan, Timothy Michael. BA in Polit. Sci., Pa. State U., 1975; JD, Temple U., 1979. Bar: Pa. 1979, U.S. Dist. Ct. (ea. dist.) Pa. 1979. Assoc. Stevens & Lee, P.C., Reading, Pa., 1979-84, ptnr., 1985—, also bd. dirs. Mem. ABA, Pa. Bar Assn., Berks County Bar Assn. Democrat. Roman Catholic. Avocations: wine, nature, computers. Banking, Securities, Antitrust. Office: Stevens & Lee 607 Washington St PO Box 679 Reading PA 19603

DEMET, DONAL MOFFATT, lawyer; b. Milw., Aug. 16, 1956; s. Francis J. and Margadette (Moffatt) D.; m. Mary E. Gardner, July 30, 1983; children: Lauren Elizabeth, Sean G. BA in Econs., Marquette U., 1978, JD, 1981; LLM in Taxation, NYU, 1983. ar: Wis. 1981. Assoc. Demet & Demet, Milw., 1981—. Pres. Alzheimers Disease and Related Disorders Assn., Milw., 1985-86. Mem. ABA, Milw. Bar Assn. (chmn. probate com. 1985—, program com.), 7th Cir. Bar Assn., Milw. Young Lawyers Assn. (treas. 1986—), Wis. Bar Assn. Roman Catholic. Club: Milw. Athletic. Avocation: sports. Probate, Estate taxation, General corporate. Office: Demet & Demet 815 N Cass St Milwaukee WI 53202

DEMETRIO, THOMAS A., lawyer; b. Evanston, Ill., Sept. 4, 1947. AB, U. Notre Dame, 1969; JD, Ill. Inst. Tech. Chgo.-Kent Coll. Law, 1973. Bar: Ill. 1973, Fla. 1973. Ptnr. Demetrio and Corboy, P.C., Chgo.; mem. faculty Nat. Inst. for Trial Advocacy, 1978—, Ill. Inst. Continuing Legal Edn., 1978—; ptnr. Corboy & Demetrio, PC, Chgo., 1986—; instr. products liability law Ill. Inst. Tech.-Chgo.-Kent Coll. Law, 1979-80; mem. Ill. Pattern Jury Instrns. Com., 1978—, com. on pattern civil jury instructions Ill. Supreme Ct., 1978—; mem. Ill. Law Found. Implementation Commn. for the Lawyers Trust Fund Ill., 1983-84; speaker profl. seminars and confs. Fellow Ill. Bar Found. (charter), Chgo. Bar Found. (life, charter), Internat. Acad. Trial Lawyers; mem. Chgo. Bar Assn. (law library com. 1974-75, evaluation of jud. candidates com. 1978-82, 83-86, bicentennial of U.S. Constn. com. 1986—, lectr. young lawyers sect. seminar 1980—), Ill. Bar Assn. (elected mem. Gen. Assembly, 1981-84, offer of judgment com. 1983-85), ABA (lectr. cross examination litigation sect. 1977, co-counsel videotape series "Training the Advocate," 1983), Fla. Bar Assn., Fed. Bar Assn., Ill. Trial Lawyers Assn. (bd. mgrs. 1978—, amicus curiae com. 1982—, vice chmn. 1983-85, legis. com. 1985—, 3d v.p. 1985, 2d v.p. 1983, pres.-elect 1987), Assn. Trial Lawyer Am. (chmn. nat. seminar programs 1986-87), Am. Bd. Profl. Liability Attys. (conv. program chmn. 1984), Ill. Inst. Tech. Chgo.-Kent Pres. Council, Ill. Inst. Tech. Chgo.-Kent Alumni Assn. (bd. dirs. 1986—, treas. 1986—), Soc. Trial Lawyers Ill., Fed. Trial Bar (advocacy program 1983—), Delta Theta Phi. Author: Medical Malpractice, 1979; contbr. articles to legal jours. State civil litigation, Federal civil litigation. Office: 33 N Dearborn St Suite 630 Chicago IL 60602

DEMING, WILLIS RILEY, business executive; b. Ada, Ohio, Nov. 28, 1914; s. Cliffe and Okla (Riley) D.; m. Dorothy Arline Hill, 1950 (div. 1971); children: Susan Elizabeth, Deborah Anne, David Riley; m. Constance S. Mori, 1971 (dissolved 1986). B.A., Ohio State U., 1935, J.D., 1938. Bar: Ohio 1938, Calif. 1947, D.C. 1957. Pvt. practice Columbus, Ohio, 1938-39; casualty claim examiner Am. Surety Co., N.Y.C., 1939-41; chief bds. and claims rev. br. San Francisco Port of Embarkation, 1946-47; mem. Treadwell and Laughlin, San Francisco, 1947-54; mem. Brobeck, Phleger & Harrison, San Francisco, 1954-56, Washington, 1956-60; pvt. practice Washington, 1961-62; with Matson Nav. Co., San Francisco, 1962-71, 74—; now sr. v.p., gen. counsel Matson Nav. Co.; v.p., sec., gen. counsel Alexander & Baldwin, Inc., Honolulu, 1968-74. Served to lt. col. AUS, 1941-46; col. U.S. Army, ret. Mem. ABA, Fed. Bar Assn., Hawaii Bar Assn., San Francisco Bar Assn., Maritime Bar Assn. Methodist. Clubs: World Trade (San Francisco); Oahu Country (Honolulu). General corporate. Home: 5649 Country Club Dr Oakland CA 94618 Office: Matson Nav Co PO Box 7452 San Francisco CA 94120

DEMIRDJIAN, JEAN-CLAUDE, lawyer, consultant, airline captain; b. Paris, Apr. 24, 1942; came to U.S., 1956; s. Kevork and Arpine (Tchekmeian) D.; m. Valerie Walker, Nov. 2, 1968 (div. 1973). BA in History, UCLA, 1966; MS in Systems Mgmt., U. So. Calif., 1971; JD, U. West Los Angeles, 1982. Bar: Calif. 1982, U.S. Dist. Ct. (cen. dist.) Calif. 1982; licensed airline transport pilot, Calif. Safety cons. world wide, 1968—. Served to capt. USAF, 1966-73. Named one of Outstanding Citizens of So. Calif. KNX News Sta., 1980. Fellow San Diego County Mus. of Art; mem. ABA, Calif. Bar Assn., Los Angeles County Bar Assn., Airline Pilots Assn. Aviation safety, accidents, Private international, Contracts commercial. Home: 2201 Greenfield Ave Los Angeles CA 90064 Home: 79 Rue du Cardinal Lemoine, Paris 75005, France

DEMKO, JOSEPH NICHOLAS, JR., lawyer; b. Scranton, Pa., Nov. 15, 1956; s. Joseph Nicholas Sr. and Marian (Acculto) D.; m. Kristine Kane, May 28, 1977; 1 child, Katherine Harding. BA, U. Scranton, 1977; JD, Duquesne U., 1980. Bar: Pa. 1980, U.S. Dist. Ct. (we. dist.) Pa. 1980, Calif. 1984, U.S. Dist. Ct. (no. dist.) Calif. 1984, U.S. Dist. Ct. (ea. dist.) Calif. 1985. Assoc. Ronald Heck and Assocs., Pitts., 1980-83, Boornazian & Jensen, San Francisco, 1984-85, Frandzel & Share, San Francisco, 1985—; asst. solicitor Borough of Etna, Pitts., 1980-83. Mem. ABA, Pa. Bar Assn., Calif. Bar Assn., San Francisco Bar Assn., Assn. Trial Lawyers Am., San Francisco Bar Assn. Democrat. Roman Catholic. Avocations: golf, softball. State civil litigation, Banking, Contracts commercial. Office: Frandzel & Share 101 Market St Suite 610 San Francisco CA 94105

DEMMLER, JOHN HENRY, lawyer; b. Pitts., June 20, 1932; s. Ralph Henry and Catherine (Hollinger) D.; m. Janet Rice, July 20, 1957; children—Richard H., Ralph W., Carol L. B.A., Princeton U., 1954; LL.B. cum laude, Harvard U., 1959. Bar: Pa. 1960, U.S. Dist. Ct. (we. dist.) Pa. 1960. Assoc., Reed Smith Shaw & McClay, Pitts., 1959-65, ptnr., 1966—; dir. Duquesne Light Co., Pitts. Trustee Shady Side Acad., Pitts., 1969-75, 77—, vice chmn. 1980-84, chmn., 1984—. Mem. ABA (mem. corp. banking and bus. law sect. 1973—, pub. utility law sect. 1975—), Pa. Bar Assn. (mem. mcpl. law sect. 1972—, pub. utility law sect. 1976—). Republican. Episcopalian. Clubs: Duquesne, Fox Chapel Golf, Fox Chapel Racquet (Pitts.); Rolling Rock (Ligonier, Pa.); Nassau (Princeton, N.J.). General corporate, Public utilities, Municipal bonds. Home: 102 Foxtop Dr Pittsburgh PA 15238 Office: Reed Smith Shaw & McClay James H Reed Bldg 435 6th Ave Pittsburgh PA 15219

DEMOFF, MARVIN ALAN, lawyer; b. Los Angeles, Oct. 28, 1942; s. Max and Mildred (Tweer) D.; m. Patricia Caryn Abelov, June 16, 1968; children: Allison Leigh, Kevin Andrew. BA, UCLA, 1964; JD, Loyola U., Los Angeles, 1967. Bar: Calif. 1969. Asst. pub. defender Los Angeles County, 1968-72; ptnr. Steinberg & Demoff, Los Angeles, 1973-83, Craighill, Fentress & Demoff, Los Angeles and Washington, 1983-86; of counsel Mitchell, Silberberg & Knupp, 1987—; mng. dir. Advantage Internat., Washington. Citizens adv. bd. Olympic Organizing Com., Los Angeles, 1982-84; bd. trustees Curtis Sch., Los Angeles, 1985—; sports adv. bd. Constitution Rights Found., Los Angeles, 1986—. Mem. ABA (mem. forum com. on entertainment and sports), Calif. Bar Assn., UCLA Alumni Assn., Phi Delta Phi. Democrat. Jewish. Avocations: sports, music, art. Entertainment, Sports. Office: Mitchell Silberberg & Knupp 11377 W Olympic Blvd Los Angeles CA 90064

DEMOS, JEFFREY CHARLES, lawyer, marketing professional; b. Bryn Mawr, Pa., Dec. 19, 1954; s. Anthony Charles and Lorraine Theresa (Henneberry) D. BA, Conn. Coll., 1977; JD, Calif. Western Sch. Law, 1981. Bar: Calif. 1981, U.S. Dist. Ct. (so. dist.) Calif. 1981, Pa. 1982, U.S. Ct. Appeals (9th cir.) 1985. Sole practice La Jolla, Calif. and Wayne., Pa., 1982—; marketing rep. Platinum Sales Inc., Bryn Mawr, 1982—. Mem. ABA, San Diego Bar Assn., Montgomery County Bar Assn. Personal injury, Insurance. Office: 8950 Villa La Jolla Dr Suite 1200 La Jolla CA 92037

DEMOTT, DEBORAH ANN, legal educator; b. Collingswood, N.J., July 21, 1948; d. Lyle J. and Frances F. (Cummings) DeMott. B.A., Swarthmore Coll., 1970; J.D., NYU, 1973. Bar: N.Y. 1974. Law clk. U.S. Dist. Ct. (so. dist.) N.Y., 1973; assoc. Simpson, Thacher & Bartlett, N.Y.C., 1974-75; vis. asst. prof. U. Tex., Austin, 1977-78; asst. prof. Duke U., Durham, N.C., 1975-78, assoc. prof., 1978-80, prof. law, 1980—, Bost research prof. law, 1981 ; vis. prof. U. Calif. Hastings Coll. Law, 1986; bd. advisors Jour. Legal Edn., 1983-86. Trustee Law Sch. Admission Council, 1984—. Recipient Pomeroy Prize, NYU Sch. Law, 1971-73; AAUW fellow, 1972-73; Fulbright Sr. scholar Sydney U. and Monash (Australia) U, 1986. Mem. Am. Law Inst., ABA. Author: Shareholders' Derivative Actions, 1987; contbr. articles to profl. jours.; editor: Corporations at the Crossroads: Governance and Reform, 1980. Legal education. Address: Duke U Law Sch Durham NC 27706

DEMPSEY, BERNARD HAYDEN, JR., lawyer; b. Evanston, Ill., Mar. 29, 1942; s. Bernard H. and Margaret C. (Gallagher) D.; m. Cynthia T.; children—Bernard H., Matthew B., Kathleen N., Rose Maureen G., Alexandra C. B.S., Coll. Holy Cross, 1964; J.D., Georgetown U., 1967. Bar: Fla. 1968, D.C. 1979. Law clk. to chief judge U.S. Dist. Ct. (mid. dist.) Fla., 1967-69; asst. U.S. atty. Mid. Dist. Fla., 1969-73; assoc. Dixon, Shear, Brown & Stephenson, Orlando, Fla., 1973-75; sr. ptnr. Dempsey & Kelly, Orlando, 1975-77, Dempsey & Slaughter, P.A., 1977-84, Dempsey & Goldsmith, P.A., 1984—. Recipient John Marshall award U.S. Dept. Justice, 1973, Outstanding Performance award, 1972. Mem. Fla. Bar Found., ABA, Fed. Bar Assn., Acad. Fla. Trial Lawyers, Assn. Trial Lawyers Am., Nat. Health Lawyers Assn., Nat. Assn. of Criminal Def. Lawyers, Delta Theta Phi. Republican. Roman Catholic. Clubs: Internat. (Washington); Univ. (Orlando); Winter Park (Fla.) Racquet. Contbr. articles to legal jours. Federal civil litigation, State civil litigation, Criminal. Home: 1132 Country Club Dr Orlando FL 32804 Office: Dempsey & Goldsmith PA 605 E Robinson St Suite 500 Orlando FL 32802

DEMPSEY, DAVID B., lawyer; b. Washington, June 26, 1949; s. James Raymon and Elizabeth (Barnes) D.; m. Elizabeth Carole Harwick, Oct. 9, 1982. B.A. cum laude, Amherst Coll., 1972; M.P.A., U. Tenn., 1973; J.D., U. S.C., 1977. Bar: S.C. 1977, D.C. 1978, U.S. Dist. Ct. D.C. 1978, U.S. Ct. Appeals (D.C. cir.) 1979, U.S. Ct. Appeals (4th cir.) 1980, U.S. Supreme Ct. 1981, U.S. Claims Ct. 1981. Atty. advisor Def. Logistics Agy., Alexandria, Va., 1977-79, asst. counsel, 1980-82; asst. counsel Def. Fuel Supply Ctr., Alexandria, 1979-80; sole practice, Washington, 1982-84; ptnr. Whitney, Dempsey & Greif, Washington, 1984—. Contbr. articles to legal jours. Mem. ABA, Fed. Bar Assn., D.C. Bar Assn., Washington Internat. Trade Assn. Clubs: Burning Tree, Congl. (Bethesda). Government contracts and claims, Private international. Office: Gardner Carton & Douglas 1875 Eye St NW Suite 1050 Washington DC 20006

DEMPSEY, DAVID GERARD, lawyer; b. St. Louis, Apr. 9, 1930; s. John J. and Martha (Blong) D.; m. Patricia J. Juneau; children: Anne, David, Andrew, Jane, Michael. AB magna cum laude, St. Louis U., 1951, JD magna cum laude, 1956. Bar: Mo. 1956. Ptnr. Shifrin & Treiman, St. Louis, 1974—. Served to capt. USAF, 1951-54. Mem. Am. Coll. Real Estate Lawyers, Assn. Trial Lawyers Am., Lawyers Assn. St. Louis, Metropolitan St. Louis Bar Assn., Mo. Bar Integrated (vice chmn. property com. 1986). Democrat. Roman Catholic. Club: Mo. Athletic. Real property, Federal civil litigation, State civil litigation. Office: Shifrin & Treiman 8182 Maryland 10th floor Saint Louis MO 63105

DEMPSEY, EDWARD JOSEPH, lawyer; b. Lynn, Mass., Mar. 13, 1943; s. Timothy Finbar and Christine Margaret (Callahan) D.; m. Eileen Margaret McManus, Apr. 15, 1967; children—Kristen A., Katherine B., Shelagh E., James P. A.B., Boston Coll., 1964; J.D., Cath. U. Am., 1970. Bar: D.C. 1970, Conn. 1982. Assoc., Arent, Fox, Kintner, Plotkin & Kahn, Washington, 1970-72, Akin, Gump, Strauss, Hauer & Feld, Washington, 1972-75; supervisory trial atty. EEOC, Washington, 1975-79; assoc. Whitman & Ransom, Washington, 1979-81, Farmer, Wells, McGuinn & Sibal, Washington, 1981-82; ptnr. Farmer, Wells, Sibal & Dempsey, Washington and Hartford, Conn., 1983-84; dir. indsl. relations and labor counsel United Technologies Corp., Hartford, 1985—. Served to capt. USNR. Mem. ABA. Labor, Civil rights, Federal civil litigation. Office: United Technologies Bldg Hartford CT 06101

DEMPSEY, JAMES HOWARD, JR., lawyer; b. Cleve., Oct. 18, 1916; s. James Howard and Ada (Hunt) D.; m. Julia C. Bolton, Aug. 2, 1942; children: Julia B. Dempsey Cox, Melissa Hunt Dempsey Gerrity. B.A., Yale U., 1938, LL.B., 1941. Bar: Ohio 1941. Practiced in Cleve. 1945—; gen. ptnr. Squire, Sanders & Dempsey, Cleve., 1958—. Mayor, Hunting Valley Village, 1952-58; trustee Cleve. Mus. Art; Trustee U. Hosps., AMASA Stone House. Served to lt. comdr. USNR, 1941-45. Mem. ABA, Ohio, Cleve., D.C. bar assns. Clubs: Yale (N.Y.C.); Union (Cleve.), Tavern (Cleve.), Kirtland (Cleve.), Chagrin Valley Hunt, Peeper Pike (Cleve.). Home: 2659 River Rd Chagrin Falls OH 44022 Office: Squire, Sanders & Dempsey 1800 Huntington Bldg Cleveland OH 44115

DEMPSEY, MICHAEL DOUGLAS, lawyer; b. Los Angeles, Mar. 21, 1943; s. James William and Allura Mardell (Hawley) D.; m. Adrienne Jeanne Gary, Aug. 20, 1983. BA magna cum laude, Calif. State U., Northridge, 1965; JD, UCLA, 1968. Bar: CAlif., U.S. Dist. Ct. Calif., U.S. Dist. Ct. N.Y., U.S. Ct. Appeals (9th cir.), U.S. Supreme Ct. Assoc. Lillick, McHose & Charles, Los Angeles, 1968-73, ptnr., 1973-77; counsel Hardee Barovick, Beverly Hills, Calif., 1978-79; ptnr. Rogers & Wells, Los Angeles, 1979-82, Finley, Kumble, Wagner, Heine, Underberg, Manley & Casey, Beverly Hills, 1982—; bd. dirs. Brentwood Bank, Los Angeles, La Mer Industries Inc., San Diego. Mem. Order of Coif. Federal civil litigation, Surety bonds, State civil litigation. Home: 1200 Stone Canyon Rd Los Angeles CA 90077 Office: Finley Kumble Wagner Heine et al 9100 Wilshire Blvd Beverly Hills CA 90212

DEMPSEY, THOMAS LAWRENCE, lawyer; b. Tacoma, July 31, 1935; s. James and Helen (Hobi) D.; children from previous marriage—John F., Thomas J., Annette M. B.A., Gonzaga U., 1958, LL.B., 1963. Bar: Wash. 1963, U.S. dist. ct. 1964, U.S. Ct. Mil. Appeals 1972. Law clk., Wash. Supreme Ct. 1963-64; pvt. practice, 1964; asst. atty. gen., 1966-67; asst. city atty. Tacoma, 1968—; instr. Seattle U. Chmn. 26th Dist. Democratic Club, 1974. Served to lt. col. JAGC, AUS, 1958—. Mem. ABA, Wash. Bar Assn. Democrat. Roman Catholic. Club: Optimist. Administrative and regulatory, Public utilities, State and local taxation. Home: 7137 Interlaaken Dr Tacoma WA 98499 Office: 1120 Tacoma Mcpl Bldg Tacoma WA 98402

DEMPSEY, WILLIAM HENRY, association executive; b. New Ulm, Minn., Dec. 1, 1930; s. William Henry and Myra Louise (Seifert) D.; m. Mary Margaret Studer, Aug. 25, 1954; children—William Henry, III, Robert J., Timothy M., Elizabeth A., Thomas E., Mary C. Student, Coll. of St. Thomas, 1951; A.B., U. Notre Dame, 1952; LL.B., Yale U., 1955. Bar: D.C. bar 1955. Law clk. to Judge Charles Fahy, U.S. Ct. of Appeals for D.C. Circuit, 1955-56; chief law clk. to Chief Justice Earl Warren, U.S. Supreme Ct., 1959-60; partner firm Shea & Gardner, Washington, 1960-72; chmn. Nat. Ry. Labor Conf., Washington, 1972-77; pres., chief exec. officer Assn. Am. Railroads, Washington, 1977—. Served as 1st lt., Judge Adv. Gen. Corps U.S. Army, 1956-59. Mem. D.C. Bar Assn. Roman Catholic. Clubs: Met, Internat, Washington Golf and Country, F Street, Chevy Chase. Home: 3311 N Glebe Rd Arlington VA 22207 Office: 50 F St NW Washington DC 20001

DEMUTH, ALAN CORNELIUS, lawyer; b. Boulder, Colo., Apr. 29, 1935; s. Laurence Wheeler and Eugenia Augusta (Roach) DeM.; m. Susan McDermott; children—Scott Lewis, Evan Dale, Joel Millard. B.A. magna cum laude, U. Colo., 1958, LL.B., 1961. Bar: Colo. 1961, U.S. Dist. Ct. Colo. 1961, U.S. Ct. Appeals (10th cir.) 1962. Assoc. Akolt, Turnquist, Shepherd & Dick, Denver, 1961-68; ptnr. Akolt, Dick, Rovira, DeMuth & Eiberger, 1968-73, Rovira, DeMuth & Eiberger, 1973-76, DeMuth, Eiberger, Kemp & Backus, 1976-79, DeMuth, Kemp & Backus, 1979-82, DeMuth & Kemp, 1982—. Conf. atty. Rocky Mountain Conf. United Ch. of Christ, 1970—; bd. dirs. Friends of U. Colo. Library, 1978-86; bd. dirs., sponsor Denver Boys Inc. Mem. ABA, Colo. Bar Assn., Denver Bar Assn., Phi Beta Kappa, Sigma Alpha Epsilon, Phi Delta Phi. Republican. Mem. United Ch. of Christ. Club: Denver Athletic. Lodge: Rotary. Banking, Public utilities, Bankruptcy. Office: DeMuth & Kemp 718 17th St Suite 1600 Denver CO 80202

DEMUTH, CHRISTOPHER CLAY, lawyer, editor, publisher; b. Evanston, Ill., Aug. 5, 1946; s. Harry Clay and Ethel Marie (Schaiell) DeM.; m. Susan Ann Shultis, June 9, 1973; children: Christopher Clay, Elizabeth Ann, Catherine Leas. A.B., Harvard Coll., 1968; J.D., U. Chgo., 1973. Bar: Ill. 1973. Staff asst. to Pres. Richard Nixon Washington, 1969-70; assoc. Sidley & Austin, Chgo., 1973-76; assoc. gen. counsel Consol. Rail Corp., Phila., 1976-77; lectr., dir. regulatory studies Harvard Sch. Govt., Cambridge, Mass., 1977-81; adminstr. info. and regulatory affairs U.S. Office Mgmt. and Budget, Washington, 1981-84, exec. dir. Presdl. Task Force on Regulatory Relief, 1981-83; mng. dir. Lexecon Inc., Washington, 1984-86; pres. Am. Enterprise Inst. for Pub. Policy Research, Washington, 1986—. Editor-in-chief, pub. mag. Regulation, 1986—. Mem. ABA, Am. Econ. Assn. Republican. Episcopalian. Administrative and regulatory, Antitrust, Public utilities. Office: Am Enterprise Inst 1150 17th St NW Washington DC 20006

DEMUTH, LAEL SAUNDERS, lawyer; b. Boulder, Colo., Feb. 18, 1931; s. Laurence W. and Eugenia (Roach) DeM.; m. Carriellen Reeve, Aug. 15, 1954; children: Leslie DeMuth Vickery, Cydney DeMuth Stevens, Sam, Lucy. BA cum laude, U. Colo., 1952, JD, 1955. Bar: Colo. 1955, U.S. Dist. Ct. Colo. 1955, U.S. Ct. Appeals (10th cir.) 1955. Assoc. Akolt, Turnquist, Sheperd & Dick, Denver, 1955-61; ptnr. Akolt, Turnquist, Sheperd & Dick (now known as DeMuth & Kemp), 1961—. Treas. Jefferson County Rep. Com., Colo., 1962. Mem. Denver C. of C. (chmn. bd. 1980-81). Club: Denver. Lodge: Rotary. General corporate, State civil litigation, Federal civil litigation. Home: 20764 Sky Meadow Ln Golden CO 80401 Office: 718 17th St Suite 1600 Denver CO 80202

DEMUTH, LAURENCE WHEELER, JR., lawyer, utility company executive; b. Boulder, Colo., Nov. 22, s. Laurence Wheeler and Eugenia Augusta (Roach) DeM.; m. Margaret Evelyn Glasebrook, Jan. 17, 1956; children: Debra Lynn, Laurence Wheeler, III, Brant Hill. A.B., U. Colo., 1951, LL.B., 1953. Gen atty. Mountain State Telephone & Telegraph Co., Denver, 1968, v.p., gen. counsel, 1968—, sec., 1974—; with US West Inc., Englewood, Colo. Dist. capt. Republican Precinct Com., 1957-70; trustee Lakewood Presbyn. Ch., Colo., 1965-68; bd. dirs. Colo. Epilepsy Assn., 1973-79, pres. bd., 1978-79; bd. dirs. Mountain States Legal Found., 1980—. Served to capt. USAF, 1954-56. Mem. ABA, Colo. Bar Assn. (chmn. ethics com. 1973-74, bd. govs., fellow found.), Denver Bar Assn., Am. Judicature Soc., Colo. Assn. Corp. Counsel (pres.), Order of Coif, Phi Beta Kappa, Pi Gamma Mu. Clubs: University, 26, Lakewood Country, Paradise Valley Country. Office: US West Inc 7800 E Orchard Rd Englewood CO 80111 *

DENARO, GREGORY, lawyer; b. Rochester, N.Y., Dec. 10, 1954; m. Nancy Cardiff; 1 child, Adrienne. BA, U. Rochester, 1976; JD, U. Miami, 1979. Bar: Fla. 1979, N.Y. 1985, U.S. Dist. Ct. (so. dist.) Fla. 1979, U.S. Ct. Appeals (5th and 11th cirs.) 1981, U.S. Supreme Ct. 1984. Pub. defender Dade County, Miami, Fla., 1979-82; sr. ptnr. Gregory C. Denaro P.A., Miami, 1982—; advisor nat. mock trial U. Miami Law Sch., 1984—. Mem. ABA (criminal law sect.), Dade County Bar Assn. Criminal. Office: 2780 Douglas Rd Suite 300 Miami FL 33133

DE NATALE, ANDREW PETER, lawyer; b. Bklyn., July 7, 1950; s. Peter E. and Mary (Tamberino) DeN.; m. Lynn Susan Kennedy, July 28, 1973; children: Andrew, Christopher. BS in Econs., U. Pa., 1972; JD, Fordham U., 1975. Bar: N.Y. 1976, U.S. Dist. Ct. (so. dist.) N.Y. 1976, U.S. Dist. Ct. (ea. dist.) N.Y. 1977, U.S. Ct. Appeals (2d cir.) 1978, U.S. Supreme Ct. 1979, U.S. Dist. Ct. (no. dist.) N.Y. 1982. Assoc. Krause, Hirsch & Gross, N.Y.C., 1975-79; assoc. Stroock & Stroock & Lavan, N.Y.C., 1980-83, ptnr., 1984—. Contbr. articles to profl. jours. Mem. ABA. Bankruptcy, Contracts commercial. Office: Stroock & Stroock & Lavan 7 Hanover Square New York NY 10004

DENBY, PETER, lawyer; b. Phila., Dec. 15, 1929; s. Charles and Rosamond (Reed) D.; m. Peggy Ann O'Hearn, May 19, 1956; children: Charles, Peter, Lee Curtis Marshall. A.B., Princeton U., 1951; J.D., Harvard U., 1954. Bar: N.Y. 1957, Pa. 1960. Assoc. Davis Polk & Wardwell, N.Y.C., 1954-59; assoc. Reed Smith Shaw & McClay, Pitts., 1959-62, ptnr., 1962—. Trustee Pressley Ridge Sch., Pitts., 1962-77, pres., 1965-72; bd. dirs. Western Pa. Sch. for Blind Children, 1965—, pres., 1970-82; term trustee Carnegie Inst. Fine Arts Com., Pitts., 1965-72; trustee Sarah Scaife Found., Pitts, 1969—, Pitts. Plan for Art, 1970-73; mem. exec. com. Western Pa. Golf Assn., 1976—, sec., 1978-86; bd. dirs. Pitts. Regional Planning Commn., 1971—; pres. Pitts Regional Planning Commn., 1974—. Mem. ABA, Allegheny County Bar Assn. General corporate, Banking, Probate. Home: 518 Irwin Dr Sewickley PA 15143 Office: Reed Smith Shaw & McClay James H Reed Bldg 435 6th Ave Pittsburgh PA 15219

DENCH, BRYAN MUNDY, lawyer; b. Westfield, Mass., May 30, 1949; s. Edward Charles and Doris (Dean) D.; m. Mary Jane Mellor, Sept. 4, 1971; children: Elisabeth, Joseph, Charlotte. AB, Harvard U., 1972; JD, U. Maine, 1975. Bar: Maine 1975, U.S. Dist. Ct. Maine 1975, U.S. Tax Ct. 1978. Ptnr. Skelton, Taintor & Abbott, Auburn, Maine, 1975—; lectr. U. Maine Law Sch., Portland, 1978-79. Contbr. articles to profl. jours. Chmn. Auburn (Maine) Bd. Appeals, 1977-79, Lewiston Bd. Appeals, 1980-81. Mem. ABA, Maine Bar Assn., Androscoggin County Bar Assn. Democrat. Roman Catholic. Lodge: KC. Estate planning, Estate taxation, General corporate. Office: Skelton Taintor & Abbott 95 Main St Auburn ME 04210

DENECKE, DAVID R., corporate lawyer; b. Portland, Oreg., May 31, 1949; s Arno Harry and Selma Jane (Rockey) D.; m. Gail Neuburg, June 14, 1974; children: Christl Marcelle, Samantha Jane. Student, Oreg. State U., 1967-69, U. Pavia, Italy, 1969-70; BA in History and Secondary Edn., U. Oreg., 1970-71; LLB, Lewis and Clark U., 1976. Bar: Oreg. 1978, U.S. Dist. Ct. Oreg. 1980, U.S. Ct. Appeals (9th cir.) 1981. Law clk. to presiding justice Multnomah County Dist. Ct., Portland, 1975-76, U.S. Ct. Appeals (9th cir.), Portland, 1977-78; assoc. Thompson, Adams, Beaverton, Oreg., 1978-82; asst. gen. counsel, asst. v.p., asst. sec. Amfac Inc., Beaverton, 1982—. bd. dirs. N.W. Portland Neighborhood Assn., Hillside; mem. City of Portland Towing Bd., 1978-80. Mem. ABA, Oreg. Bar Assn. (continuing legal edn. com. 1980-81, fee arbitration panel 1980—), Multnomah and Washington County Bar Assn., Am. Frozen Food Inst. (atty's com.). Office: Amfac Inc 6600 SW Hampton St PO Box 23564 Portland OR 97223

DENEGRE, STANHOPE BAYNE-JONES, lawyer; b. New Orleans, Feb. 15, 1952; s. George and Gayle Francis (Stocker) D.; m. Julia Nelle Baird, May 18, 1982; 1 child, Amelia Gayle. BA, Tulane U., 1976, JD, 1979. Bar: La. 1979. Assoc. Jones, Walker, Waechter, Poitevent, Carrere & Denegre, New Orleans, 1979-84, ptnr., 1984—. Bd. dirs. Met. Crime Commn., New Orleans, 1986—. Served to sgt. spl. forces U.S. Army, 1971-73. Commercial litigation. Office: Jones Walker Waechter et al 201 St Charles Ave New Orleans LA 70170

DENHAM, EARL LAMAR, lawyer; b. Biloxi, Miss., July 1, 1947; s. Earl Lamar and Ruby (Young) D.; children—Katherine Elizabeth, Rachel Ann, Israel Anderson, Nathan Levi. B.S., U. Miss., 1969, J.D., 1972. Bar: Miss. 1972, U.S. Dist. Ct. (no. and so. dists.) Miss. 1972, U.S. Ct. Appeals (5th cir.) 1978, U.S. Supreme Ct. 1978. Assoc. Hurlbert & O'Barr, Biloxi, 1972-73; ptnr. Levi & Denham, Ltd., Ocean Springs, Miss., 1973—. Served to capt. USAR, 1970-78. Recipient Am. Jurisprudence awards Joint Pubs. Total Client-Service Library, 1971. Mem. ABA, Assn. Trial Lawyers Am., Miss. Trial Lawyers Assn., Miss. Bar Assn. Democrat. Jewish. State civil litigation, Criminal, Federal civil litigation. Office: Levi & Denham Ltd Box 596 Ocean Springs MS 39564

DENHAM, VERNON ROBERT, JR., lawyer; b. Atlanta, Apr. 18, 1948; s. Vernon Robert and Sara Elizabeth (Robertson) D.; m. Susan Elizabeth Wills, Mar. 19, 1974; children: Whitney Willis, Tyler Willis. Student, Rensselaer Poly. Inst., 1966-68; BSE, U. Mich., 1970, MSE, 1972; JD, U. Fla., 1979. Bar: Fla. 1979, Ga. 1979, U.S. Ct. Appeals (11th cir.) 1981, U.S. Dist. Ct. (no. dist.) Ga. Engr. Ford Motor Co., Dearborn, Mich., 1972-73; assoc. Powell, Goldstein, Frazer & Murphy, Atlanta, 1979-86, ptnr., 1986—. Mem. No. Dist. Case Notes Com., Atlanta, 1980—, Magistrate Merit Selection Panel, No. Dist. Ga., 1983. Served to lt. USNR, 1973-76. Mem. ABA, Fla. Bar Assn., State Bar Ga., Atlanta Bar Assn., Order of Coif, Tau Beta Pi. Federal civil litigation, Environment, Libel. Home: 1433 Sheridan Walk NE Atlanta GA 30324 Office: Powell Goldstein Frazer & Murphy 35 Broad St NW 1100 C&S Nat Bank Bldg Atlanta GA 30335

DENHOLLEM, JAMES SCOTT, lawyer; b. Shreveport, La., Nov. 6, 1953; s. John William and Sally Leigh (Becker) D. BA, Loyola U., New Orleans, 1975; JD, La. State U., 1980. Law clk. to presiding justice U.S. Ct. Appeals (3d cir.), Lake Charles, La., 1980-81; assoc. Nelson & Achee Ltd., Shreveport, 1981—; bd. dirs. Northwest La. Legal Services Corp., Shreveport. Mem. ABA, La. Bar Assn., Shreveport Bar Assn. Democrat. Roman Catholic. Avocations: books, racquetball, hunting. Insurance, Personal injury, Probate. Office: Nelson & Achee Ltd 207 Texas St 2d Floor Shreveport LA 71101

DENKER, RANDALL ELIZABETH, lawyer; b. N.Y.C., Feb. 10, 1950; d. Arnold Sheldon and Nina (Simmons) D.; m. Paul Alan Lehrman, Dec. 24, 1977; 1 child, Gaea Jacinthe Denker-Lehrman. BA, Bennington Coll., 1972; JD, U. Fla., 1978. Bar: Fla. 1979, U.S. Dist. Ct. (so. and no. dists.) Fla. 1980, U.S. Dist. Ct. (mid. dist.) Fla. 1986, U.S. Ct. Appeals (5th cir.) 1980, U.S. Ct. Appeals (11th cir.) 1984. Asst. gen. counsel sr. enforcement atty. Dept. Environ. Regulation, Tallahassee, 1979-82; ptnr. Lehrman & Denker, Tallahassee, 1982—; lectr. Fla. Atlantic U., Ft. Lauderdale, 1981; moot ct. judge Fla. State U., Tallahassee, 1985. Bd. dirs. Tree Watch, Inc., Tallahassee, 1982—; mem. commn. on tree protection and landscape ordinances Leon County, Fla., 1982. Recipient award for outstanding achievement for pro bono legal services Fla. Wildlife Fedn., 1984. Democrat. Jewish. Avocations: travel, reading, fgn. langs., chess. Administrative and regulatory, Environment, Personal injury. Home: 1130 Crestview Tallahassee FL 32303 Office: Lehrman & Denker 103 N Gadsden St Tallahassee FL 32301

DENKEWALTER, KIM RICHARD, lawyer, medical-legal law consultant; b. Chgo., May 7, 1948; s. Walter J. and Doris A. (Gast) D. B.A., Loyola U., Chgo., 1971; J.D., Chgo.-Kent Coll. Law, 1974. Bar: Ill. 1974, U.S. Dist. Ct. (no. dist.) Ill. 1974, U.S. Ct. Appeals (7th cir.) 1977, U.S. Supreme Ct. 1979. Ptnr., Abramovic, Denkewalter & Ryan, Northfield, Ill., 1974-79; pres. Denkewalter & Assocs., Northfield, 1979—; real estate broker, Chgo., 1978—; guest lectr. Am. Coll. Emergency Physicians, Rosemont, Ill., 1979-84. Pres. 539 Stratford Condo Assn., Chgo., 1985-86, sec. 1985-86, bd. dirs. 1985-86, treas. 1985-86; mem. Hoopis Fin. Group, Northfield, Ill. Served to staff sgt. USAR, 1970-76. Named EMT-A (hon.) Ill. Dept. Pub. Health, 1983. Mem. Ill. State Bar Assn., Chgo. Bar Assn., Assn. Trial Lawyers Am., ABA. Club: Brookwood Country. Real property, State civil litigation, General corporate. Home: 408 Harmony Wheeling IL 60090 Office: Denkewalter & Assocs Ltd 790 Frontage Rd Northfield IL 60093

DENMAN, ALEXANDRA, lawyer; b. Oklahoma City, June 22, 1947; d. Dale and Norma Jean (Warmack) Denman; m. Benjamin J. Stein, Sept. 7, 1977. B.A., Vassar Coll., 1969; student Yale Coll., 1968-69; J.D., George Washington U., 1973. Bar: D.C. 1973, Calif. 1978. Assoc. Donovan Leisure Newton & Irvine, Washington, 1973-77, Overton, Lyman & Prince, Los Angeles, 1977-78; sr. atty. motion picture div. Paramount Pictures Corp., Los Angeles, 1982-85; v.p.-legal United Arts and Pictures, Inc., MGM/UA Entertainment Co., Beverly Hills, Calif., 1986—. Researcher books: Moneypower, 1981, Manhattan Gambit, 1983. Mem. ABA, Attys. for Animal Rights, Bar Assn. County Los Angeles. Republican. Presbyterian. Antitrust, Entertainment, Trademark and copyright. Office: MGM/UA Communications Co 450 N Roxbury Dr Beverly Hills CA 90210

DENMAN, JAMES BURTON, lawyer; b. Brownwood, Tex., Nov. 15, 1947; s. James Burton and Margaret Gwendolyn D.; m. Donna Van Tuyle, Feb. 18, 1978; children—Tuyle, Lindsay. A.A., Porterville Jr. Coll., 1968; B.S., Calif. State U.-Fresno, 1970; J.D., Samford U., 1973. Bar: Fla. 1974. Ptnr., assoc. Dolan, Denman & Gramling, P.A., Fort Lauderdale, 1975-78;

prin. James B. Denman & Assocs., P.A., Fort Lauderdale, 1978-80; ptnr. Bunnell, Denman & Woulfe, P.A., Fort Lauderdale, 1980— . Bd. dirs. Bethany Christian Sch., Fort Lauderdale, 1984. Mem. Assn. Trial Lawyers Am., Acad. Fla. Trial Lawyers. Democrat. Lutheran. Clubs: Lauderdale Yacht, Tower. Personal injury, State civil litigation, Aviation. Home: 901 Cordova Rd Fort Lauderdale FL 33316 Office: Bunnell Denman & Woulfe PA 1080 SE 3d Ave Fort Lauderdale FL 33316

DENNEEN, JOHN PAUL, lawyer; b. N.Y.C., Aug. 18, 1940; s. John Thomas and Pauline Jane (Ludlow) D.; m. Mary Veronica Murphy, July 3, 1965; children—John Edward, Thomas Michael, James Patrick, Robert Andrew, Daniel Joseph, Mary Elizabeth. B.S., Fordham U., 1963; J.D., Columbia U., 1966. Bar: N.Y. 1966. Assoc. Seward & Kissel, N.Y.C., 1966-75; sr. v.p., gen. counsel, sec. GK Techs., Inc., Greenwich, Conn., 1975-83; exec. v.p., gen. counsel, sec. Chromalloy Am. Corp., St. Louis, 1983—. Mem. ABA, Internat. Bar Assn., N.Y. State Bar Assn., N.Y.C. Bar Assn., Bar Assn. Met. St. Louis. General corporate, Securities, Contracts commercial. Office: Chromalloy Am Corp 120 S Central Ave Saint Louis MO 63105

DENNEMEYER, JOHN JAMES, lawyer; b. Los Angeles, Feb. 17, 1921; s. Jean and Mary (Gindt) D.; m. Margaret Juliette Adair, June 10, 1950; children: Paul Adair, Mary Catherine, James Eric. Baccalaureat, Athene Grand-Ducal, Luxembourg, 1941; student, U. Munich, 1941-42; JD, George Washington U., 1949. Bar: D.C., 1949. Patents translator U.S. Patent Office Dept. Commerce, Washington, 1949-50; fgn. patents searcher Gen. Electric Co., Washington, 1950-55; patent atty. N.Y.C., 1955-59; sole practice patent law Washington, 1959-62; patent atty. Office Dennemeyer, Luxembourg, 1962—, also bd. dirs.; bd. dirs. S.A.B., S.A., Luxembourg, Datatrust S.A., Luxembourg, Dennemeyer & Co., Luxembourg, Riccardi & Co., Milan, Italy. Served with U.S. Army, 1943-46. Mem. Assn. Internat. pour la Protection dela Propriete Industrielle, Fedn. Internat. des Conseils en Propriete Industrielle, Union des Conseils en Propriete Industrielle, Assn. Luxembourgeoise des Conseils en Propriete Industrielle, Am. Patent Law Assn., Delta Theta Phi. Roman Catholic. Clubs: Am. Luxembourg Soc., Am. Bus. Men's, Golf Grand-Ducal, Tastevin St. Cunibert, Spora Football. Patent, Trademark and copyright, Patent and trademark software development. Home: 5 Rue Jean l'Aveugle, Luxembourg Gr-D, Luxembourg Office: PO Box 1502, 55 Rue des Bruyeres, Luxembourg Gr-D Luxembourg

DENNIS, EDWARD S(PENCER) G(ALE), JR., lawyer; b. Salisbury, Md., Jan. 24, 1945; s. Edward Spencer and Virginia Monroe (Monroe) D.; m. Lois Juliette Young, Dec. 27, 1969; 1 son, Edward Brookfield. B.S., U.S. Merchant Marine Acad., 1967; LL.D., U. Pa., 1973. Bar: Pa. 1973. Law clk. Hon. A. Leon Higginbotham, Jr., U.S. Dist. Ct., Phila., 1973-75; asst. U.S. atty. U.S. Atty. Office, Phila., 1975-80; dep. chief.Criminal Div. U.S. Atty. Office, 1978-80; chief Narcotic and Dangerous Drug sect. U.S. Dept. Justice, Washington, 1980-83; U.S. Atty. Eastern Dist. Pa., Phila., 1983—. Mem. ABA, Nat. Bar Assn., Fed. Bar Assn., Phila. Bar Assn., Delaware County Bar Assn., Nat. Orgn. Black Law Enforcement Execs. Office: US Attys Office 601 Market St 3310 US Courthouse Philadelphia PA 19106

DENNIS, JAMES LEON, justice La. Supreme Court; b. Monroe, La., Jan. 9, 1936; s. Jenner Leon and Hope (Taylo) D.; m. Camille Smith; children: Stephen James, Gregory Leon, Mark Taylo, John Timothy. B.S. in Bus. Adminstrn, La. Tech. U., Ruston, 1959; J.D., La. State U., 1962; LL.M., U. Va., 1984. Bar: La. 1962. Assoc. firm Hudson, Potts & Bernstein, Monroe, 1962-65; ptnr. Hudson, Potts & Bernstein, 1965-72; judge 4th Dist. Ct. La. for Morehouse and Ouachita Parishes, 1972-74, La. 2d Circuit Ct. Appeals, 1974-75; asso. justice La. Supreme Ct., 1975—; coordinator La. Constnl. Revision Commn., 1970-72; del., chmn. judiciary com. La. Constnl. Conv., 1973; Mem. La. Ho. of Reps., 1968-72; mem. La. Commn. on the Bicentennial of U.S. Constitution. Served with AUS, 1955-57. Mem. Am., La. 4th Jud. bar assns. Methodist. Club: Rotary. Office: Supreme Ct La Supreme Ct Bldg 301 Loyola Ave New Orleans LA 70112

DENNIS, RALPH EMERSON, JR., lawyer; b. Marion, Ind., Dec. 19, 1925; s. Ralph Emerson Sr. and Martha Elnora (Bahr) D.; m. Virginia Lea Harter, June 19, 1949 (dec. Oct. 1981); children: Nancy J. Barefoot, Kathleen Ann Polk, Amel Joseph, Mary Elizabeth Saler, Ralph E. III; m. Barbara Grose, May 31, 1985. BS, Dartmouth Coll., 1946; JD, Ind. U., 1950. Bar: Ind. 1950, U.S. Supreme Ct. 1971. Sr. ptnr. Dennis, Cross, Raisor, Jordan & Marshall, P.C., Muncie, Ind., 1956-80, Dennis, Raisor, Wenger & Haynes, P.C., Muncie, 1980-85, Dennis & Wenger, P.C., Muncie, 1985-86, Dennis, Wenger & Orlosky, P.C., Muncie, 1986—; bd. dirs. Bahr Bros. Mfg. Inc., Marion; pres. Eastern Electric Supply Inc., Muncie; pres., chmn. bd. dirs., chief exec. officer Lift-A-Loft Corp., Muncie. City judge, Muncie, 1951-59, city atty., 1964-67; trustee Muncie Community Schs., 1960-63. Served with USN, 1944-46. Recipient Disting. Service award, Muncie Jaycees, 1959, Good Govt. award, Muncie Jaycees, 1959. Mem. ABA, Ind. Bar Assn. Republican. Lutheran. Club: Del. Country (Muncie). Lodges: Elks, Masons. General corporate, Estate planning, Probate. Home: 411 Wildwood Ln Muncie IN 47304 Office: Dennis Wenger & Orlosky PC 201 E Jackson Suite 300 Muncie IN 47305

DENNIS, WILLIAM ROBERT, lawyer; b. Columbus, Ohio, Oct. 22, 1955; s. Robert Vernon Dennis and Freida Irene (Reichley) Swackhamer; m. Tina Marie Frangowlakis, Mar. 22, 1980. BS in Secondary Edn., Ohio State U., 1977; JD, Cleve. Marshall Coll. Law, 1980. Bar: Ohio 1980, U.S. Dist. Ct. (no. and so. dists.) Ohio 1981. Legal intern dept. transp. Ohio Atty. Gen.'s Office, Cleve., 1978-80; jud. law clk. Ohio Ct. Appeals (4th dist.), Athens, Ohio, 1980-84; lectr. bus. law Ohio U., Athens, 1982-84; labor relations hearing officer State Employment Relations Bd., Columbus, 1984—. Mem. Ohio Stater's Inc., Columbus, 1976—; capt. Athens County United Appeal Dr., 1983; pres. Athens County Humane Soc., 1981-83, Cen. Ohio chpt. Nat. Hemophilia Found., 1984-86, bd. trustees, 1986—; appointed to adv. com. Ohio Dept. Health, 1987—. Named one of Outstanding Young Men of Am., U.S. Jaycees, 1983. Mem. ABA, Ohio State Bar Assn., Columbus Bar Assn., Am. Judicature Soc., Am. Lawyers Assn., Tri-State Regional Bus. Law Assn., Ohio State Life Alumni Assn., Cleve. Marshall Law Alumni Assn., Tau Epsilon Rho (vice chancellor Delta chpt. 1978-80). Democrat. Lutheran. Avocations: tennis, movies, music, softball. Labor, Health. Home: 920 Cummington Rd Columbus OH 43213 Office: State Employment Relations Bd 65 E State St 12th Fl Columbus OH 43215

DENNISTON, JOHN BAKER, lawyer; b. Cin., June 3, 1936; s. John B. Denniston and Edna (Gentile) Denniston Langlois; divorced; children—Derek C., Lavinia H., Miles S.; m. Carol L. McCollum Ellis. B.E. in Physics, Cornell U., 1958; LL.B., Harvard U., 1962; postgrad. Sydney U., Australia, 1962-63. Bar: U.S. Claims Ct., U.S. Ct. Appeals (D.C. cir.) 1963, U.S. Supreme Ct. 1964. Research engr. Rocketdyne div. N.Am. Aviation, 1958-59; research analyst Inst. for Drf. Analysis, 1960-61; Teaching asst. MIT, 1960-61; assoc. Covington & Burling, Washington, 1963-1971, ptnr., 1971—. Author: (with others) McGraw-Hill Construction Business Handbook. Mem. ABA, D.C. Bar Assn. (exec. council 1969-70, young lawyer of yr. 1971) Club: Metropolitan. Government contracts and claims, Immigration, naturalization, and customs, Public international. Home: 2800 Foxhall Rd NW Washington DC 20007 Office: Covington & Burling 1201 Pennsylvania Ave NW PO Box 7566 Washington DC 20044

DENNISTON, THOMAS ROBERT, lawyer, insurance consultant; b. N.Y.C., Sept. 19, 1953; s. Herbert A. and Helen (Ford) D.; m. Julia Therel Boody, Aug. 1, 1980; children: Graham, Bradford, Garrett. BS in Econs., SUNY, Oneonta, 1975; JD, NYU, 1979. Bar: N.J. 1980, U.S. Dist. Ct. N.J. 1980, U.S. Dist. Ct. (ea. and so. dists.) N.Y. 1981, U.S. Ct. Appeals (2d, 3d and 5th cirs.) 1983, U.S. Supreme Ct. 1984, U.S. Ct. Appeals (4th cir.) 1984, N.Y. 1985. Staff exec. Transport Mut. Services, Inc., N.Y.C., 1979-81; trial atty. Evans, Koelzer, Osborne & Kreizman, N.Y.C., 1981-85; gen. counsel Bradshaw & Assocs. Ltd., San Francisco, 1985—. Served with USNR, 1978-79. Mem. ABA, N.Y. Bar Assn., N.J. Bar Assn., Bar Assn. of Fifth Fed. Cir., Maritime Law Assn. of U.S., Average Adjusters Assn. of U.S. Club: Mchts. Exchange (San Francisco). Avocation: skiing. Admiralty, Insurance, Federal civil litigation. Office: Bradshaw & Assocs Ltd 1 Maritime Plaza Suite 620 San Francisco CA 94111

DENSBORN, DONALD KEITH, lawyer; b. Logansport, Ind., July 25, 1951; s. William Thomas Jr. and Betty Jo (Swearingen) D.; m. Kathryn Anne Mallette, May 18, 1974; children: Peter Thomas, Elissa Adrienne. BS in Bus. magna cum laude, Ind. U., 1973, JD magna cum laude, 1976. Bar: Ind. 1976, U.S. Dist. Ct. (so. dist.) Ind. 1976, U.S. Tax Ct. 1985. Assoc. Krieg, DeVault, Alexander & Capehart, Indpls., 1976-79, Johnson & Gross, Indpls., 1979-81; ptnr. Johnson, Gross, Densborn & Wright, Indpls., 1981—. Editor Real Estate Securities Jour., 1981-82. Assoc. mem. 500 Festival Assocs., Indpls., 1978—; mem. Butler Tarkington Neighborhood Assn., Indpls., 1976-85; fund raiser Marion County Assn. Retarded Citizens, Inpls., 1976—, Jr. Achievement, Indpls. Children's Mus., Meth. Hosp., United Way, Conner Prairie Mus., White Star Endowment. Mem. ABA (corp. banking, real property sects.), Ind. Bar Assn., Indpls. Bar Assn. (bus. law div. chmn. 1984, bus. law vice chmn. 1985, bus. law chmn. elect 1986), Sigma Nu Nat. Fraternity (div. comdr. 1985—), Sigma Nu Alumni Assn. of Ind. Univ. (pres. 1983-84, bd. dirs. 1977—). Republican. Methodist. Clubs: Indpls. Athletic, Econ. of Indpls. Avocations: handball, jogging, softball, tennis. Contracts commercial, Real property, Securities. Home: 7647 Washington Blvd Indianopolis IN 46240 Office: 151 N Delaware St Suite 1000 Indianapolis IN 46204

DENSEN-GERBER, JUDIANNE, psychiatrist, lawyer, educator; b. N.Y.C., Nov. 13, 1934; d. Gustave A. and Beatrice D.; m. Michael M. Baden, June 14, 1958; children: Trissa Austin, Judson Michael, Lindsey Robert, Sarah Densen. A.B. cum laude, Bryn Mawr Coll., 1956; JD, Columbia U., 1959; MD, NYU, 1963. Bar: N.Y. 1961. Rotating intern French Hosp., N.Y.C., 1963-64; resident psychiatry Bellevue Hosp., N.Y.C., 1964-65, Met. Hosp., N.Y.C., 1965-67; mem. core staff Addiction Services Agy., N.Y.C., 1966-67; founder Odyssey House (psychiat. residence for rehab. narcotics addicts), N.Y.C., Mich., Maine, N.H., Utah, La., Australia, N.Z., 1967, clin. dir., 1967-69, exec. dir., 1967-74, pres. bd., 1974-82; pres., founder, chief exec. officer Odyssey Inst. Am., 1974-82; pres. Odyssey Inst. Australia, 1977-86, Odyssey Inst. Internat., Inc., 1978—; attending physician Gracie Sq. Hosp., N.Y.C., 1982—, Park City Hosp., Bridgeport, Conn., 1985—, Bridgeport Hosp., 1985—, Northwest Gen. Hosp., Detroit, 1986—; assoc. vis. prof. law U. Utah Law Sch., 1973-75; adj. prof. law N.Y. Law Sch., 1973-76; chairperson plenary session drug abuse Am. Acad. Forensic Scis., 1972, sec. psychiatry sect., 1973, chmn. sect., 1974—; founder, 1973, since pres. Inst. Women's Wrongs; founder, since pres. Odyssey Inst. (health care for socially disadvantaged), 1974—; bd. dirs. Simpson St. Devel. Assn., An Extraordinary Event (One to One for Mental Retardation), Bridge House; mem. Nat. Adv. Commn. Criminal Justice Standards and Goals, 1971-74, Pres.'s Commn. on White House Fellows, 1972-76; mem. drug experience adv. com. HEW, 1973-76; v.p. psychiat. sect. Internat. Forensic Medicine Conf., Budapest, 1967; pres. N.Y. Council Alcoholism, 1978—; cons. to Mich. State Legislature to draft legislation on The Best Interests of the Child vs. the New Reproductive Techs., 1986; guest lectr. narcotics addiction NYU Sch. Medicine, also Sch. Law; cons. in field; dir. Daitch Shopwell, Inc. Author: (with Trissa Austin Baden) Drugs, Sex, Parents and You, 1972, We Mainline Dreams, The Odyssey House Story, 1973, Walk in My Shoes, 1976; co-author (with David Sandberg) The Role of Child Abuse in Delinquency and Juvenile Court Decision-Making, 1984, Chronic Acting-Out Students and Child Abuse: A Handbook for Intervention, 1986; contbr. articles to profl. jours.; editor: Jour. Corrective and Social Psychiatry, 1975. Mem. N.Y.C. Crime Control Commn., 1975-79, Gov.'s Task Force on Crime Control, Albany, N.Y., 1977-79, N.Y. State Crime Control Planning Bd., 1975-79; del. White House Conf. on Youth, 1971; bd. dirs. Nat. Coalition for Children's Justice, 1975—, Am. Soc. for Prevention of Cruelty to Children, 1979—, Mary E. Walker Found., 1978. Recipient Woman of Achievement award AAUW, 1970; Myrtle Wreath award Hadassah, 1970; B'nai B'rith Woman of Greatness award, 1971; Otty award for service to N.Y.C. Our Town Newspaper, 1977; named Dame of White Cross Australia, Dame of Malta, Ky. Col., N.Y. State Hon. Fire Chief. Fellow Am. Coll. Legal Medicine; mem. AMA, N.Y. State, N.Y. County Med. Socs., Soc. Med. Jurisprudence, Therapeutic Communities of Am. (founding mem., 1st v.p. 1975—), Am. Acad. Psychiatry and Law, Am. Psychiat. Assn., Women's Forum N.Y., Nat. Women's Forum, Conn. Med. Assn., Am. Orthopsychiat. Assn., ABA, N.Y. State Bar Assn., N.Y. County Women's Bar Assn., N.Y. Assn. Vol. Agys. Narcotics Addiction and Substance Abuse (dir. 1968—), Am. Psychiat. Assn., N.Y. Med. Assn. Republican. Unitarian. Club: Women's City (N.Y.C.). Family and matrimonial, Health, Legislative. Office: Odyssey Inst Internat 817 Fairfield Ave Bridgeport CT 06604

DENT, GEORGE E., lawyer; b. New Orleans, Aug. 9, 1950; s. William Wilkinson and Girdelle Elia (Smith) D.; m. Pamela Adams, May 5, 1977 (div. Dec. 1980); m. Terri Lynne Vaughan, Dec. 29, 1984; children: Elena L., E. Alex, Lindsey D. Whitfield, Ashley B. Whitfield. BS, U. So. Miss.; JD, U. Miss. Bar: Miss. 1980, U.S. Ct. Appeals (5th cir.) 1980. Assoc. Aultmon, Tyner, McNeece, Weathers & Ruffin, Hattiesburg, Miss., 1980-85, Soper & Russell, Tupelo, Miss., 1985-86; ptnr. Soper, Russell, Richardson &Dent, Tupelo, 1987—. Served to capt. U.S. Army, 1972-77. Mem. Miss. State Bar (chmn. character and fitness com.) Def. Research Inst., U. So. Miss. Alumni Assn. (pres. 1980—). Presbyterian. Club: Tupelo Exchange. Lodge: Lions. Avocations: jogging, swimming, nature. Federal civil litigation, State civil litigation, Insurance. Home: 731 N Madison Tupelo MS 38801

DENTON, ROGER MARIUS, lawyer; b. Galveston, Tex., Feb. 23, 1946; s. Dan N. and Frances Elizabeth (Hotopp) D.; m. Beverly Joyce Bauer. B.A., Loyola U., New Orleans, 1968, J.D., 1971. Bar: La. 1971, U.S. Dist. Ct. (ea. dist.) La. 1971, U.S. Ct. Appeals (5th cir.) 1971, U.S. Supreme Ct. 1976. Pres. Roger M. Denton, P.C., Metairie, La., 1971—. Vice-chmn. Jefferson Parish Charter Adv. Bd., 1980; chmn. East Jefferson chpt. ARC, 1980-81; pres. Civic Council East Jefferson, 1975-76; pres. Willowdale Civic Assn., 1973-74; bd. dirs. Lafreniere Park Found., 1982-87, sec., 1986-87; pres. Friends of Lafreniere Park, 1983-84; trustee United Way of Greater New Orleans, 1983—, vice chmn. bd. of trustees, 1986—; bd. dirs., mem. exec. com. S.E. La. chpt. ARC, 1983-85, bd. dirs., 1983—. Served to capt. USAR. Recipient award of merit ARC, 1969; Silver Beaver award Boy Scouts Am., 1976. Mem. ABA, La. Bar Assn. (ho. of dels. 1987—), Fed. Bar Assn., Jefferson Bar Assn., Assn. Trial Lawyers Am., La. Trial Lawyers Assn., New Orleans Acad. Trial Lawyers, New Orleans and River Region C. of C. (bd. dirs. 1981-83, chmn. East Jefferson Council 1982), Veterans Blvd. Bus. Assn. (pres. 1982). Republican. Roman Catholic. Club: Rotary (pres. 1978-79, dist. chmn. Internat. Service, 1985—, mem. dist. coordinating com. 1985—). Author La. Civil Practice Forms, 1985. Assoc. editor Loyola Law Rev., 1970-71; editor Jefferson Bar Assn. Record, 1979-80. Personal injury, Probate. Home: 2401 Elise Ave PO Box 73789 Metairie LA 70033 Office: 1900 Veterans Blvd Suite 104 Metairie LA 70005

DENVIR, JAMES PETER, III, lawyer; b. N.Y.C., Oct. 8, 1950; s. James P. and Catherine Jane (Scully) D.; m. Lee Rangeley Wallace, Nov. 24, 1979; children: Daniel, James. BA, Yale U., 1972; JD, U. Fla., 1975. Bar: Fla. 1975, D.C. 1979. Trial atty. U.S. Dept. Justice, Washington, 1975-82, chief atty. U.S. vs. AT&T trial staff, antitrust div., 1982-84; ptnr. Akin, Gump, Strauss, Hauer & Feld, Washington, 1984—. Club: Yale (Washington). Administrative and regulatory, Antitrust, Federal civil litigation. Office: Akin Gump Strauss Hauer & Feld 1333 New Hampshire Ave NW #400 Washington DC 20036

DENZEL, KEN JOHN, lawyer, corporate executive; b. Chgo., Jan. 21, 1940; s. John E. and Estelle K. D.; m. Mary Sue Plummer, Feb. 1, 1964; children—Michael B., Kyle J., Kristyn M., Karyn L., Mark R. B.S. in Econs. and Bus. Adminstrn., St. Ambrose Coll., 1962; J.D., Loyola U. of Chgo., 1967. Bar: Ill. 1968, U.S. Dist. Ct. (no. dist.) Ill. 1978, U.S. Ct. Appeals (7th cir.) 1978. Assoc. Yates, Haider, Hunt & Burke, Chgo., 1968-69, Philip H. Corboy & Assocs., Chgo., 1969; poverty lawyer Neighborhood Legal Services Program of Legal Aid Bur. (OEO), 1969-71; of counsel Burditt & Calkins, Chgo., 1971-78; ptnr. Ken J. Denzel & Assocs., Chgo., Des Plaines and Park Ridge, Ill., 1971—; rep. to U.S. Mil. Acad., West Point, N.Y., 1976-80; consul adviser, lectr. in sports, sports law; arbitrator Am. Arbitration Assn.; lectr. sports law Ill. Inst. Continuing Legal Edn., De Paul U. Sch. Law. Mem. adv. bd. Passionists Religious Community, 1981—; mem. U.S. Olympic Com., arbitrator 1984 Olympics; founder Internat. Center for Athletic and Ednl. Opportunities, 1967—; bd. mgrs. King Chgo. Boys Clubs, 1967-80; mem. parish sch. bd., 1973-74, mem. parish council, chmn. athletic bd., 1977-78; v.p. Orgn. of NW Communities, 1966-68; pres. Pulaski Civic Club, 1965-66; mem. O.L.S. Youth Council, 1968-75; coach Crane High Sch. Basketball Team, Chgo., 1969-72, Chgo. City Champs, 1972; coach Chgo. team in Nat. Neighborhood Invitational Basketball Tournament, 1972, Prairie State Games (Ill. Olympics), 1984—; founding mem., dir., atty. Cen. for Students Rights and Responsibilities U. Ill., Chgo., 1972; active numerous civic and community orgns. Recipient Loyola Law Sch. award for Outstanding Leadership and Scholastics Achievement, 1967; award for assistance to Chgo. Police Dept. Youth Program, 1970. Mem. Chgo. Bar Assn. (founding chmn. sports law com. 1981-84, mem. nominating com. 1983, judiciary com.), Ill. Bar Assn., ABA, Am. Judicature Soc., Ill. Trial Lawyers Assn., Am. Trial Lawyers Assn., Assn. of Evening Law Students (pres. 1965-67), Phi Alpha Delta (outstanding mem. and Nat. Justice award 1967). Roman Catholic. Contbr. articles to legal jours. Sports law, General practice, State civil litigation. Home: PO Box 141 Park Ridge IL 60068-0141 Office: 3 South Prospect Park Ridge IL 60068-4101

DEPEW, HARRY LUTHER, lawyer; b. Neodesha, Kans., Nov. 18, 1923; s. Clarence William and Dorothy J. (Bushaway) D.; m. Frances Allene Crisp, Mar. 27, 1951; children—Douglas D., Dennis D. B.S. in Bus., Kans. U., 1948, LL.B., 1951. Bar: Kan. 1951. County atty. County of Wilson (Kans.), 1955-58; ptnr. Depew Law Firm, Neodesha, Kans., 1952—. Served with U.S. Army, 1942-45, 51-52; Korea. Mem. ABA, C. of C., Kans. Bar Assn. (various coms.), S.E. Kans. Bar Assn. (past pres.), Wilson County Bar Assn. (past pres.). Republican. Clubs: Ducks Unltd.; Lions. Bankruptcy, General practice, Probate. Home: 1222 N 6th St Neodesha KS 66757 Office: 620 Main St Neodesha KS 66757

DERBER, ROBERT RAYMOND, lawyer, accountant; b. Lynwood, Calif., July 31, 1956; s. Robert Raymond and Mary Ann (Potts) D.; m. Patricia Ann Low, July, 26, 1980; children: Whitney Elizabeth, Bryden Lee. BA in Econs., U. Calif., Santa Cruz, 1978; MBA, U. Santa Clara, 1981, JD, 1982; LLM in Taxation, Golden Gate U., 1985. Bar: Calif. 1982, U.S. Dist. Ct. (no. dist.) Calif. 1986, U.S. Ct. Appeals (9th cir.) 1986. Supervising sr. accountant Arthur Young & Co., San Francisco, 1982-86; assoc. Atchison & Anderson, Santa Cruz, 1986—. Assoc. editor Santa Clara U. Law Rev., 1982. Mem. ABA, Am. Inst. CPA's, Santa Cruz Bar Assn., Profl. Software Programmers Assn. Democrat. Roman Catholic. Club: Toastmasters. Lodge: Rotary. Computer, Corporate taxation, Estate taxation. Office: Atchison & Anderson 333 Church St Santa Cruz CA 95060

DERDENGER, PATRICK, lawyer; b. Los Angeles, June 29, 1946; s. Charles Patrick and Drucilla Marguerite (Lange) D.; m. Jo Lynn Dickins, Aug. 24, 1968; children—Kristin Lynn, Bryan Patrick, Timothy Patrick. B.A., Loyola U., Los Angeles, 1968; M.B.A., U. So. Calif., 1971, J.D., 1974; LL.M. in Taxation, George Washington U., 1977. Bar: Calif. 1974, U.S. Ct. Claims 1975, Ariz. 1979, U.S. Ct. Appeals (9th cir.) 1979, U.S. Dist. Ct. Ariz. 1979, U.S. Tax Ct. 1979, U.S. Supreme Ct. 1979. Trial atty. honors program Dept. Justice, Washington, 1974-78; ptnr. Lewis and Roca, Phoenix, 1978—; adj. prof. taxation Golden Gate U., Phoenix, 1983—. Author: Arizona State and Local Taxation, Cases and Materials, 1983, Arizona Sales and Use Tax Guide, 1986; Served to capt. USAF, 1968-71. Recipient U.S. Law Week award Bur. Nat. Affairs, 1974. Mem. ABA (taxation sect., various coms.), Ariz. Bar Assn. (taxation sect., various coms., chmn. dept. revenue com.), Maricopa County Bar Assn., Nat. Assn. Bond Lawyers, Inst. Property Taxation, Phoenix Met. C. of C., Ariz. C. of C. (sales tax com.), Phi Delta Phi. State and local taxation, Corporate taxation, Personal income taxation. Home: 9501 N 49th Pl Paradise Valley AZ 85253 Office: Lewis and Roca 2200 1st Interstate Bank Plaza 100 W Washington St Phoenix AZ 85003

DEREN, DONALD DAVID, lawyer; b. Westfield, Mass., Oct. 2, 1949; s. Charles William and Margaret Bernice (Ryan) D.; m. Juanita Maria Marino, Apr. 10, 1982; children: Derek D., Jana L., Dustin M. B.B.A., Nichols Coll., 1971; J.D., Suffolk U., 1974. Bar: Mass. 1974, U.S. Dist. Ct. Mass. 1975, U.S. Ct. Appeals (1st cir.) 1980, U.S. Ct. Internat. Trade 1984. Pub. defender Mass. Defenders Commn., Worcester, 1975-79; assoc. Sullivan & Sullivan, Webster, Mass., 1980; assoc. Collins & Monopoli, Shrewsbury, Mass., 1980-83; sole practice, Dudley, Mass., 1983—; one of 3 attys. who successfully briefed and argued unconstitutionality of Mass. Death Penalty Statue before Supreme Judicial Ct., 1984. Recipient Atty. award Mass. Citizens Against the Death Penalty, 1985. Mem. ABA (criminal justice sect.), Nat. Assn. Criminal Def. Lawyers, Worcester County Bar Assn., Boston Bar Assn., Worcester County Bar Advs., Inc. (bd. dirs. 1986—), Calif. Pub. Defenders Assn. Criminal, Constitutional. Home: Fairfield Dr Dudley MA 01570

DERIN, GREG DAVID, lawyer; b. San Francisco, Sept. 30, 1954; s. Henry Maurice and Ruth (Rainglass) D.; m. Bonnie Audrey Smigel, Sept. 2, 1979; 1 child, Henry Matthew. AB, U. Calif., Berkeley, 1976, JD, 1979. Bar: Calif. 1979, U.S. Dist. Ct. (cen. and no. dist.) Calif. 1980, U.S. Ct. Appeals (9th cir.) 1980, U.S. Dist. Ct. (so. and ea. dist.) Calif. 1983, U.S. Supreme Ct. 1984, U.S. Ct. Appeals (Fed. cir.) 1985. Ptnr. Dern, Mason & Floum, Los Angeles, 1979—; Mem. adv. bd. Cal in the Capital, Berkeley, 1980—. Research and book rev. editor Calif. Law Rev., 1978-79. Charles Mills Gayley fellow U. Calif., 1976. Mem. ABA (com. trial practice 1984—), U. Calif. Alumni Assn. (bd. dirs. 1984-87, v.p.-at-large 1987—), Am. Polit. Items Collectors, Phi Beta Kappa. Club: West Los Angeles U. Calif. Alumni (bd. dirs. 1980—). Avocations: collecting polit. memorabilia, tennis. Federal civil litigation, State civil litigation, Trademark and copyright. Office: Dern Mason & Floum 2049 Century Park East Suite 2060 Los Angeles CA 90067

DERIVAN, HUBERT THOMAS, lawyer; b. Hamilton, Ohio, Mar. 14, 1940; s. Hubert Thomas and Cecilia Elizabeth (Pater) D.; m. Ann Elaine Anderson, July 6, 1963; m. 2d, Linda L. Morris, Aug. 7, 1975; children—Michael H., Marianne E., Lynn A. Stearns, Laura K. Student, U. Notre Dame, 1958-60, Xavier U., 1960; B.A. in Polit. Sci., U. Dayton, 1962; J.D., Ohio No. U., 1967. Bar: Ohio 1967, U.S. Dist. Ct. (so. dist.) Ohio, 1968, U.S. Supreme Ct., 1978. Ptnr., Crist, Kaup & Derivan, Middletown, Ohio, 1967-68; sole practice, 1968-85; ptnr. Derivan & Smith, Middletown, 1986—; part owner Vanlin Investments, Inc., Alcanzar Investments, Inc., Gt. Miami Canoe Trails, Inc.; owner Daladad Internat., Supplemental Income Systems, Freeman Internat., Diversified Enterprises. Mem. ABA, Ohio Bar Assn., Butler County Bar Assn., Middletown Bar Assn. (past pres.), Assn. Trial Lawyers Am., Ohio Acad. Trial Lawyers, Phi Alpha Delta. Club: K.C. General practice, Family and matrimonial, Personal injury. Home: 3009 Flemming Rd Middletown OH 45042 Office: 4000 Roosevelt Rd Middletown OH 45044

DEROIN, JAN ELIZABETH, lawyer; b. Beatrice, Nebr., Feb. 11, 1952; d. Glenn W. and Mary Jane (Fry) Plucknett; m. David DeRoin, Aug. 27, 1977; children—David A., Erik W. B.A. in Polit. Sci., U. Nebr., 1974; J.D., Creighton U., 1977. Bar: Nebr. 1977. Assoc. firm Mitchell & Demerath, Omaha, 1977-80; asst. trust officer First Nat. Bank Omaha, 1981-86; trust officer 1st Nat. Bank Omaha, 1987—. Mem. Am. Inst. Banking, ABA, Nebr. Bar Assn., Omaha Bar Assn., Omaha Estate Planning Council. Republican. Estate planning, Probate, Estate taxation. Office: First National Bank Omaha One First National Ctr Omaha NE 68102

DERONDE, JOHN ALLEN, JR., lawyer, author; b. Albany, N.Y., July 22, 1947; s. John Allen and Kathleen (Doran) DeR.; m. Marianne E. Karlsson, Mar. 19, 1983. B.A., U. Calif.-Davis, 1969; J.D., U. Pacific, 1972. Bar: Calif. 1974, U.S. Dist. Ct. (ea. and no. dists.) Calif. 1978, U.S. Supreme Ct. 1981, U.S. Tax Ct. 1984. Law clerk DeRonde & Brewer, Vacaville, Calif., 1972-73; dep. trial counsel State Dept. Motor Vehicles, Sacramento, 1973-74; ptnr. DeRonde & Geandrot, Fairfield, Calif., 1974-76, sole practice, Fairfield, 1976-78; ptnr. DeRonde & DeRonde, Fairfield and Pleasant Hill, Calif., 1978—; dir. Calif.-Hawaii Corp., 1979—, Pietro's Pizza Parlors, Inc., 1975—. Contbr. numerous articles to profl. jours. Active Vacaville, Fairfield and Concord, Calif. chambers of commerce. Recipient Highest Score award Jessup Internat. Moot Ct. Competition, Seattle, 1972. Mem. Calif. State Bar Assn. (legal econs. and family law sect.), ABA, Calif. Trial Lawyers Assn., Assn. Trial Lawyers Am., Am. Judicature Soc., Barristers Club No. Calif., No. Calif. Soc. Cert. Family Law Specialists, Calif. Assn. Realtors, Notaries Pub. Assn. Calif., Am. Overseas Employees Assn., Nat. Fedn. Ind. Bus.,

U.S. Justice Found., Pacific Legal Found., Bay Area Auto Dismantlers Assn., Nat. Restaurant Assn. Republican. Roman Catholic. Lodge: Lions Internat. Family and matrimonial, Real property, Personal injury. Home: 47 Portsmouth Circle Pleasant Hill CA 94523 Office: 627 Delaware St Fairfield CA 94533 also: 101 Gregory Ln Suite 30 Pleasant Hill CA 94523

DEROSE, JAMES DOMINIC, lawyer; b. Plainfield, N.J., Dec. 31, 1946; s. Anthony and Elizabeth DeLello DeR.; m. Elizabeth Agnes Clinch, June 5, 1982. B.A., Wagner Coll., 1969; J.D., Columbus Sch. Law, Cath. U. Am., 1978. Bar: N.J. 1978, U.S. Ct. Claims, U.S. Ct. Customs and Patent Appeals 1978, U.S. Supreme Ct. 1982, U.S. Ct. Appeals 1982; cert. civil trial atty., N.J. Dep. Washington rep. Volkswagen of Am., Inc., 1974-77, mgr. congl. matters, 1977-78, sr. atty. Office Gen. Counsel, 1978-79; assoc. gen. counsel, sec. Fiat Motors of N.Am., Inc., 1979-80; ptnr. Devlin Norton & DeRose, Westfield, N.J., 1980-84, Norton & DeRose, Westfield, 1984—; asst. sec. Alfa Romeo, Inc.; chmn. Mountainside Democratic Com., N.J. Mem. ABA, N.J. Bar Assn., Union County Bar Assn., Trial Attys. N.J., Automobile Importers Am. (lawyers com.), Def. Research Inst. (product liability com.). Served with Army N.G., 1968-74. Democrat. Roman Catholic. Club: Chadwick Beach and Yacht (trustee, sec. 1984-87), Lions. General corporate, State civil litigation, Personal injury. Home: 352 Ackerman Ave Mountainside NJ 07092 Office: 114 Elm St Westfield NJ 07090

DEROUSIE, CHARLES STUART, lawyer; b. Adrian, Mich., May 24, 1947; s. Stuart J. and Helia I. (Juntunen) DeR.; m. Patricia Jean Fetzer, May 31, 1969; children—Jennifer, Jason. B.A. magna cum laude, Oakland U., 1969; J.D. magna cum laude, U. Mich., 1973. Bar: Ohio, 1973, U.S. Dist. Ct. (so. dist.) Ohio 1974. Ptnr. Vorys, Sater, Seymour and Pease, Columbus, Ohio, 1973—. Trustee Ballet Met., Inc., Columbus, 1978—, pres., 1986—; trustee Gladden Community House, Columbus, 1975-81, pres., 1979-81. Mem. ABA, Columbus Bar Assn., Ohio Bar Assn., Order of Coif. Banking, Health, General corporate. Office: Vorys Sater Seymour and Pease PO Box 1008 52 E Gay St Columbus OH 43216

DERQUE, JOSEPH ALEXANDER, III, state agency administrator, lawyer; b. Whittier, Calif., Nov. 15, 1948; s. Joseph A. and Katherine (England) D.; m. Nancy L. Vaughn, Aug. 12, 1972; 1 child, Beau Charles. BA in History, Westminster Coll., 1970; JD, Washington U., St. Louis, 1973. Bar: Mo. 1973. Asst. pros. atty. St. Louis County, Clayton, Mo., 1974, Jefferson County, Hillsboro, Mo., 1974-75; sole practice Crystal City, Mo., 1975-77; asst. gen counsel Mo. Dept. Conservation, 1977-82; atty. div. legal services Mo. Dept. Social Services, 1982-85, exec. coordinator adminstrv. hearings unit, 1985—; Performing mem. Jefferson City Symphony Orchestra, Mid-Mo. Concert Band. Served with Mo. Army N.G., 1980—. Mem. Mo. Bar Assn., Am. Fedn. Musicians (bd. dirs.). Republican. Baptist. Lodges: Masons, Shriners. Avocations: French horn, ice hockey, softball, running, weight lifting. Administrative and regulatory, State civil litigation, Criminal. Home: 2814 Dwayne Dr Jefferson City MO 65101 Office: Mo Dept Social Services Legal Services Div PO Box 1527 Jefferson City MO 65102

DERRICK, GARY WAYNE, lawyer; b. Enid, Okla., Nov. 3, 1953; s. John Henry and Leota Elaine (Glenn) D.; m. Susan Adele Goodwin, Dec. 22, 1979 (div. June 1981); m. Francys Hollis Johnson, May 3, 1986; 1 child, Meghan. BA in History, English, Okla. State U., 1976; JD, U. Okla., 1979. Bar: Okla. 1979. Assoc. Andrews, Davis, Legg, Bixler, Milsten & Murrah, Oklahoma City, 1979-84, ptnr., 1985—; active Securities Law and Acctg. Group, Oklahoma City, 1979—; chmn. Bus. Corp. Act Commn., Okla., 1984—, chmn. Securities Liaison Com., Okla., 1985—; lectr. sem. Okla. Corp. Act, 1986. Mem. Okla. State U. Found., Stillwater, 1983—, U. Okla. Found., Norman, 1982—; conductors circle Okla. Symphony Orchestra, 1981—. Mem. ABA (taxation and corp. sect., banking and bus. law sect.), Okla. Bar Assn. (chmn. bus. assn. sect. 1985—), Okla. County Bar Assn. (bd. govs. young lawyers div. 1981-82). Republican. Episcopalian. Club: Oklahoma City Boat. Avocations: sailing, violin. Securities. Home: 500 NW 15th Oklahoma City OK 73103 Office: Andrews Davis Legg Bixler Milsten & Murrah 500 W Main Oklahoma City OK 73102

DERRICK, JACK HOLLEY, lawyer; b. Augusta, Ga., Jan. 17, 1947; s. Jasper Otto and Mildred Elizabeth (Holley) J.; Dagmar Irmgard Baartz, May 31, 1975; 1 child, John Christopher. BS in Indsl. Mgmt., Ga. Inst. Tech., 1969; JD, Wake Forest U., 1977. Bar: N.C. 1977, U.S. Dist. Ct. (ea. dist.) N.C. 1978, U.S. Supreme Ct. 1982. Assoc. Twiford, Trimpi & Thompson, Elizabeth City and Manteo, N.C., 1977-79; ptnr. Twiford, Trimpi, Thompson & Derrick, Elizabeth City and Manteo, 1979-83; gen. atty. Carolina Tel. & Tel. Co., Tarboro, N.C., 1983-85, sr. atty., 1985—. Chmn. Pasquotank County Chpt. Red Cross, Elizabeth City, 1979-81. Served to capt. U.S. Army, 1970-74. Mem. ABA, N.C. Bar Assn., Nash-Edgecombe County Bar Assn., Pasquotank County Bar Assn. (pres. 1979), N.C. Acad. of Trial Lawyers. Democrat. Episcopalian. Avocations: travel, water sports. General corporate, State civil litigation, Administrative and regulatory. Home: 1105 Vance Dr Tarboro NC 27886 Office: Carolina Tel and Tel Co 720 Western Blvd Tarboro NC 27886

DERRICK, WILLIAM ALFRED, JR., financier, lawyer; b. Washington, Oct. 15, 1943; s. William A. and Sara (M.) D.; m. Dianne Elizabeth Delmear, Aug. 26, 1967; children—William A. III, Christopher B., B. Alexander. A.B., John Carroll U., 1965; J.D., Howard U., 1968; LL.M., George Washington U., 1970. Bar: Ohio 1969, U.S. Tax Ct. 1970, U.S. Ct. Claims 1970, U.S. Ct. Appeals (D.C. cir.) 1970. Chief staff atty. Model Inner-City Community Orgn., Washington, 1969-70; staff atty. Office of Sec., HUD, Washington, 1968-69; assoc. atty. Squire, Sanders & Dempsey, Cleve., 1970-72; prin. James, Hill, Heggs, Derrick & Douglas, Cleve., 1972-75; mng. dir. Internat. Agts. & Cons. Inc., Cleve., 1983-86; mng. dir. W.A. Derrick Commodities Corp., 1985—; bd. dirs. Leisure Industries, Inc., Channel 19, Inc.; adj. prof. law Cleve. State U. Law Sch., 1973-76. Author: (with Allen) Real Estate Investment Trusts, The Bureau of National Affairs, Inc., 1973. Ford Found. student fellow, 1965-68, 69-70; speaker conf. Am. Mgmt. Assn., 1976. Mem. ABA (partnership com. tax sect. 1973-77), Ohio State Bar Assn., Phi Alpha Delta. Corporate taxation, Private international, General corporate.

DERSHOWITZ, ALAN MORTON, lawyer, educator; b. Bklyn., Sept. 1, 1938; s. Harry and Claire (Ringel) D.; married; children: Elon Marc, Jamin Seth. B.A. magna cum laude, Bklyn. Coll., 1959; LL.B. magna cum laude, Yale, 1962; M.A. (hon.), Harvard, 1967. Bar: D.C. 1963, Mass. 1968, U.S. Supreme Ct 1968. Law clk. to chief judge David L. Bazelon, U.S. Ct. Appeals, 1962-63; to justice Arthur J. Goldberg, U.S. Supreme Ct., 1963-64; mem. faculty Harvard, 1964—, prof. law, 1967—; Fellow (Center for Advanced Study of Behavioral Scis.), 1971-72; Cons. to dir. NIMH, 1967-69, NIMH (Pres.'s Commn. Civil Disorders), 1967, NIMH (Pres.'s Com. Causes Violence), 1968, NIMH (NAACP Legal Def. Fund), 1967-68, NIMH (Pres.'s Commn. Marijuana and Drug Abuse), 1972-73, NIMH (Council on Drug Abuse), 1972—, NIMH (Ford Found. Study on Law and Justice), 1973-76; rapporteur Twentieth Century Fund Study on Sentencing, 1975-76. Author: (with others) Psychoanalysis, Psychiatry and the Law, 1967, Criminal Law: Theory and Process, 1974, The Best Defense, 1982; Reversal of Fortune: Inside the vonBülow Case, 1986; also articles.; Editor-in-chief: Yale Law Jours, 1961-62. Mem. commn. on law and social action Am. Jewish Congress, 1978—; bd. dirs. ACLU, 1968-71, 72-75, Assembly Behavioral and Social Scis. at Nat. Acad. Scis., 1973-76; chmn. civil rights com. New Eng. region Anti-Defamation League, B'nai B'rith, 1980. Guggenheim fellow, 1978-79. Mem. Order of Coif, Phi Beta Kappa. Jewish. Legal education. Office: Harvard Law Sch Cambridge MA 02138

DERSHOWITZ, NATHAN ZEV, lawyer; b. Bklyn., May 5, 1942; s. Harry and Claire (Ringel) D.; m. Marilyn Barlach, Dec. 29, 1963; children—Adam, Rana. Grad. Bklyn. Coll., 1963; J.D., NYU, 1966. Bar: N.Y. 1966, U.S. Ct. Appeals (2d, 3d, 5th, 6th, 7th, 8th, 11th cirs.), U.S. Supreme Ct. Atty., Legal Aid Soc., N.Y.C, 1966-69; assoc. Stroock & Stroock & Lavan, N.Y.C., 1969-73, Greenbaum, Wolff & Ernst, N.Y.C., 1974-77; bd. dirs. Commn. Law and Social Action, Am. Jewish Congress, N.Y.C., 1977-83; sr. ptnr. Dershowitz & Eiger, N.Y.C., 1983—; gen. counsel Pearl, N.Y.C. and Washington, 1981—; spl. prof. Hofstra U. Law Sch., Hempstead, N.Y., 1979. Contbr. articles to profl. jours. Mem. ch. state com. ACLU, N.Y., 1980-84. Federal civil litigation, Criminal, Civil rights. Home: 2 Tudor City Pl New York NY 10017 Office: Dershowitz & Eiger 225 Broadway New York NY 10007

DERWIN, JORDAN, lawyer, consultant, actor; b. N.Y.C., Sept. 15, 1931; s. Harry and Sadie (Baruch) D.; m. Barbara Joan Concool, July 4, 1956 (div. 1970); children—Susan Lee and Moira Ellen; m. Joan Linda Wolfberg, May 6, 1973. B.S., NYU, 1953, J.D., 1959. Bar: N.Y. 1959, U.S. Dist. Ct. (so. and ea. dists.) N.Y. 1960, U.S. Ct. Appeals (2d. cir.) 1960, U.S. Supreme Ct. 1962. Arthur Garfield Hays research fellow NYU, 1958-59, research assoc. Duke U. Sch. of Law, Durham, N.C., 1959-60; assoc. Brennan, London, Buttenwieser, N.Y.C., 1960-64; sole practice Jordan Derwin, N.Y.C., 1964-70; gen. counsel N.Y.C. Off Track Betting Corp., 1970-74; assoc. gen. counsel Gen. Instrument Corp., N.Y.C., 1974-79, cons., 1980—. Author (with F. Hodge O'Neal), Expulsion or Oppression of Business Associates: Squeeze Outs in Small Business, 1960. Contbr. articles to prof. jours. Served to lt. j.g., USNR, 1953-56, Korea, Vietnam. Mem. Am. Soc. of Mag. Photographers, Screen Actors Guild (dir. nat. bd. 1982—, sec. N.Y. br. 1983—, nat. v.p. 1984—), AFTRA (dir. N.Y. local 1980-83, dir. nat. bd. 1982—), Actors Equity Assn., Phi Delta Phi. Labor, Legislative, General corporate. Home: 305 E 86 St New York NY 10028

DERZAW, RICHARD LAWRENCE, lawyer; b. N.Y.C., Mar. 6, 1954; s. Ronald Murray and Diana (Diamond) D. B.A. magna cum laude, Fairleigh-Dickinson U., 1976; J.D., Ohio No. U., 1979. Bar: Fla. 1979, U.S. Dist. Ct. (so. dist.) Fla. 1981, U.S. Ct. Appeals (5th cir.) 1981, U.S. Ct. Appeals (11th cir.) 1981, N.Y. 1982, U.S. Dist. Ct. (ea. dist.) N.Y. 1986, U.S. Tax Ct. 1986. Sole practice, Boca Raton, Fla., 1979-82, N.Y.C., 1982—. Mem. ABA, N.Y. State Bar Assn., Fla. Bar Assn., Am. Arbitration Assn., Assn. of Bar of City of N.Y., Phi Alpha Delta, Phi Zeta Kappa, Phi Omega Epsilon. Lodge: Lions of Boca Raton (treas. 1981-82). General corporate, Contracts commercial, Federal civil litigation. Home: 32 Pecan Valley Dr New City NY 10956

DESANTO, JAMES JOHN, lawyer; b. Chgo., Oct. 12, 1943; s. John Joseph and Erminia Asunda (Cassano) DeS.; m. Denise Clare Caneva, Feb. 3, 1968; children: Carrie Ann, James Thomas, John Joseph. BA, U. Ill., 1965; JD, DePaul U., 1969. Bar: Ill. 1969, U.S. Dist. Ct. (no. dist.) Ill. 1969, U.S. Ct. Appeals (7th cir.) 1972, U.S. Supreme Ct. 1974. Asst. state's atty. Waukegan, Ill., 1969-72; assoc. Finn, Geiger & Rafferty, Waukegan, 1972-74; ptnr. Rawles, Katz & DeSanto, Waukegan, 1975-80; sole practice Waukegan, 1980—; lectr. trial technique and practice Ill. Inst. for Continuing Legal Edn.; lectr. bus. law Coll. of Lake County, 1974-84. Fellow Ill. Bar Inst.; mem. Ill. Bar Assn., Lake County Bar Assn. (sec. 1979-80), Assn. Trial Lawyers Am., Lake County Trial Lawyers Assn. (sec. 1985—). Lodge: Rotary (sec. 1978). Avocations: raquetball, soccer, fishing. State civil litigation, Personal injury, Federal civil litigation. Home: 169 Blueberry Libertyville IL 60048 Office: 7 N County St Waukegan IL 60085

DESHAZO, GARY FORREST, lawyer; b. Bolivar, Tenn., Feb. 5, 1945; s. Warren and Verna (Scott) DeS; m. Carolyn Youngblood, July 11, 1969; children: Scott Forrest, Darcie Caroline, Elizabeth Annette. BA, Tex. Christian U., 1967, MA, 1970; JD, U. Tex., 1973. Bar: Tex. 1973, U.S. Dist. Ct. (we., ea., so. and no. dists.) Tex. 1973, U.S. Ct. Appeals (5th cir.) 1973, U.S. Supreme Ct. 1973. Exec. dir. criminal def. lawyers Tex. Bar Assn., Austin, 1975-77; sole practice Austin, 1976-86; ptnr. Herman, Spellings & DeShazo, Austin, 1986—; bd. dirs. Intercontinental Life Ins. Co., Elizabeth, N.J., Standard Life Ins. Co. Jackson, Miss. Mem. ABA, Tex. Bar Assn., Travis County Bar Assn. Baptist. State civil litigation, Federal civil litigation, General corporate. Home: 3705 Hillbrook Austin TX 78731 Office: Herman Spellings & DeShazo 600 Congress Ave 2560 1 American Ctr Austin TX 78701

DE SIMONE, DANIEL V., engineer, association executive; b. Chgo., May 4, 1932; s. James L. and Helen Catherine (Lattanzio) De S.; m. Virginia Carey, Aug. 13, 1955; children—Jane Ellen, James Michael, Daniel Carey. B.S. in Elec. Engring. with highest honors, U. Ill., 1956; J.D., NYU, 1960. Bar: N.Y. 1960, U.S. Supreme Ct. 1964, Va. 1981. Teaching asst. U. Ill., 1954-56; engr. Bell Telephone Labs., 1956-62; cons. to asst. sec. commerce for sci. and tech. Dept. Commerce, Washington, 1962-64; dir. Office Invention and Innovation, Nat. Bur. Standards, 1964-69; exec. dir. Study of Nat. Conversion to Metric System for U.S. Congress,, 1969-71; sci. policy asst. White House, Washington, 1971-73; exec. dir. Fed. Council for Sci. and Tech., Exec. Office of Pres., Washington, 1972-73; dep. dir. Congl. Office Tech. Assessment, Washington, 1973-80; pres. The Innovation Group, Inc., Arlington, Va., 1980-84; exec. dir. Am. Assn. Engring. Socs., Washington, 1984—; v.p. World Fedn. Engring. Socs., 1985—. Author: Technological Innovation—Its Environment and Management, 1967, Education for Innovation, 1968, A Metric America, 1971, To Preserve the Sense of Earth from Space, 1984. Served with USAF, 1948-52. Recipient Outstanding Achievement award IEEE, 1956, Gold Medal award for disting. achievement in fed. service, 1969, Career Service award Nat. Civil Service League, 1972; Ford Found. fellow, 1963. Environment, Legislative, Patent. Home: 2743 N Wakefield St Arlington VA 22207 Office: Am Assn Engring Socs 415 2d St NE Washington DC 20002

DESSONVILLE, LOREN EDWARD, lawyer; b. Watertown, S.D., Apr. 9, 1953; s. Norman Wendell and Margie Ann (Lebert) D.; m. Margaret Mary Reinmuth, Dec. 30, 1980 (div. Oct. 1983); m. Kathryn Ann Anderson, Aug. 10, 1985. BS, MIT, 1975; JD, U. Chgo., 1978. Bar: Nebr. 1978. Assoc. Kutak Rock & Campbell, Omaha, 1978-83, ptnr., 1983—. Mem. ABA, Nebr. Bar Assn., Omaha Bar Assn. Republican. Methodist. FERC practice, Securities, Public utilities. Office: Kutak Rock & Campbell 1650 Farnam St Omaha NE 68102

DESTEIN, BEVERLEE JEAN, government official; b. Beverly, Mass., Nov. 27, 1950; d. S. Robert and Doris L. (Bennett) D. Student Grove City Coll., 1969-71; B.A. summa cum laude, Gordon Coll., 1978; J.D., Vt. Law Sch., 1981. Bar: Pa. 1981, U.S. Dist. Ct. (we. dist.) Pa. 1982, U.S. Supreme Ct. 1986. TV talk show host WYTV-TV, Youngstown, Ohio, 1971-73; spl. events coordinator Strouss Dept. Stores, Youngstown, 1973-75; TV producer/dir. WPSX-TV, University Park, Pa., 1975-77; trial atty. Office of Allegheny Pub. Defender, 1981-82; TV legal contbr. WTAE-TV, Pitts., 1981-85; city magistrate City of Pitts., 1982-85; spl. asst. to dir. pub. affairs U.S. Dept. Justice, 1985-86; spl. asst. to asst. Atty. Gen., Criminal Div., dir. Ctr. for Obscenity and Child Pornography Prosecution, Washington, 1986—; lectr. in field. Creator, TV-Law Promotion, Law 4 You, 1984. Bd. advisors, bd. dirs. The Alcohol Recovery Ctr., Pitts., 1983-84. Mem. ABA, Pa. Bar Assn., Pa. Assn. Dist. Justices, Allegheny County Bar Assn. (pub. relations com.), AFTRA, Nat. Rifle Assn. Republican. Presbyterian. Criminal, Public Education legal. Office: Ctr for Obscenity and Child Pornography Prosecution US Dept Justice Room 2209 Washington DC 20530

DETEC, DAVID ALAN, lawyer; b. Youngstown, Ohio, Sept. 26, 1953; s. Philip J. Jr. and Mary (Abraham) D.; m. Maribeth Noga, Aug. 31, 1975; children: Rachel Ellen, Leah Alice, Hannah Beth. BA cum laude, Youngstown State U., 1976; JD, U. Akron, 1980. Bar: Ohio 1980, U.S. Dist. Ct. (no. dist.) Ohio 1980. Assoc. Letson, Griffith, Woodall & Lavelle, Warren, Ohio, 1980-85; assoc. Dragelevich & Carney, Warren, 1985, ptnr., 1986—. Articles editor U. Akron Law Rev., 1979-80. Mem. ABA (banking and corp. law sect., constrn. industry forum com.), Ohio Bar Assn., Trumbull County Bar Assn., Mahoning-Sheango Valley Estate Planning Commn., Mahoning County Bar Assn., Warren Area C. of C. (small bus. council 1984-85). General corporate, Contracts commercial, Banking. Home: 3252 Kirk Rd Youngstown OH 44511 Office: Dragelevich Carney & Detec 4087 Youngstown Rd SE Warren OH 44484

DETERMAN, SARA-ANN, lawyer; b. Palmerton, Pa., Aug. 17, 1938; d. Albert H. and Evelyn (Tucker) Heimbach; m. Dean W. Determan, July 28, 1957 (div. Nov. 1981); children: Dann, David. Student, Conn. Coll., 1956-57, Stanford U., 1958; AB, U. Del., 1960; LLB, George Washington U., 1967. Bar: U.S. Dist. Ct. D.C. 1968. Law clk. to sr. justice U.S. Ct. Appeals (D.C. cir.), Edgerton, 1967-68; assoc. Hogan & Hartson, Washington, 1968-75, ptnr., 1975—; trustee Lawyers Com. for Civil Rights Under Law, Washington, 1982—. Fellow Am. Bar Found.; mem. ABA (chmn. individual rights sect. 1985—, commr. legal problems elderly 1983—), ACLU (bd. dirs.), Mex. Am. Legal Def. and Ednl. Fend (bd. dirs. 1983—). Democrat. Unitarian. Estate taxation, Probate, Estate planning. Office: 815 Connecticut Ave NW Suite 500 Washington DC 20006

DETLING, GLENN EUGENE, judge lawyer; b. Ansonia, Ohio, Oct. 13, 1906; s. Elmer Frank and Edith Gertrude (Kershner) D.; m. Dorothy Eldise Weaver, Dec. 22, 1938; children—Robert Glenn, John Franklin. B.A., Ohio State U., 1927, M.A., 1933, J.D., 1940. Bar: Ohio 1942, U.S. Dist. Ct. (2d dist.) Ohio 1949, U.S. Tax Ct. 1956, U.S. Supreme Ct. 1960. Tchr., Springfield High Sch., Ohio, 1926-44; police ct. pros. atty. City of Springfield, 1944-45; prof. atty. County of Clark, Ohio, 1945-46, 58-61, judge Common Pleas Ct., 1961-73; instr. Wittenberg Coll., 1945-47; vis. judge Ohio Judiciary, Springfield, 1973—. Bd. dirs. Community Welfare Council, Springfield, 1953-55; chmn. United Appeals, 1953; pres. YMCA, 1958-59. Recipient Humanitarian award Humane Soc. Ohio, 1971, Disting. Service award Optimist Club, 1973. Mem. Ohio Assn. Juvenile Ct. (pres. 1971), Supreme Ct. Ohio, Springfield Bar and Library Assn. (pres. 1974), Ohio State Alumni Assn. (pres. 1969-70). Republican. Presbyterian. Club: University. Lodges: Kiwanis (Gov.'s award 1973), Masons, Elks. Probate, Personal injury, Criminal. Home and Office: 671 Westchester Park Springfield OH 45504

DETTINGER, WARREN WALTER, lawyer; b. Toledo, Feb. 13, 1954; s. Walter Henry and Elizabeth Mae (Zoll) D.; m. Patricia Marie Kasper, June 21, 1975; 1 child, John Robert. BS cum laude, U. Toledo, 1977, JD magna cum laude, 1980. Bar: Ohio 1980, U.S. Dist. Ct. (no. dist.) Ohio 1980, U.S. Ct. Appeals (6th cir.) 1980, U.S. Tax Ct. 1981. Law clk. to presiding judge U.S. Ct. Appeals (6th cir.), Grand Rapids, Mich., 1980-81; assoc. Fuller & Henry, Toledo, 1981-84; atty. Sheller-Globe Corp., Toledo, 1985—. Committeeman precinct Lucas County (Ohio) Dems., 1985—. Mem. Ohio Basr Assn., Toledo Bar Assn. (cert. commendation pro bono legal service program 1984), Phi Kappa Phi. Democrat. Roman Catholic. Club: Laurel Hill (Toledo). Avocations: tennis, travel, photography, golf. General corporate, Computer, Private international. Home: 2267 Heatherview Dr Maumee OH 43537 Office: Sheller-Globe Corp 1505 Jefferson Toledo OH 43624

DETTLOFF, RICHARD WARD, lawyer, chemical engineer; b. Detroit, May 10, 1930; s. Arthur Earl and Marian Jean (McCallum) D. BSChemE, Wayne State U., 1959; JD, Detroit Coll. Law, 1980. Bar: Mich. 1980, U.S. Dist. Ct. (ea. dist.) Mich. 1980. Staff engr. truck and bus div. Gen. Motors Corp., Pontiac, Mich., 1962-86; sole practice Farmington Hills, Mich., 1980—. Served to staff sgt. USAF, 1950-53. Republican. Lutheran. Avocation: travel. Real property, Probate. Home: 27785 Wellington Farmington Hills MI 48018

DETTMANN, MARC JOHN, health science facility adminstrator; b. Milw., Apr. 3, 1951; s. Karl Frederick and Beverly Jean (Rusdal) D.; m. Mary Elizabeth Gallagher, Oct. 6. 1979; children: Andrew Charles, Kathleen Mary, Bridget Kayle. BA, Luther Coll., 1972; MBA, U. Pa., 1976; JD, Harvard U., 1979. Bar: Minn. 1979. Acct. Peat, Marwick & Mitchell and Co., Mpls., 1972-74; assoc. Faegre & Benson, Mpls., 1979-81; sole practice Rochester, Minn., 1981-83; chief of ins. processing Mayo Clinic, Rochester, 1983—; bd. dirs. Affiliated Credit Services, Inc., Rochester. Mem. Minn. Bar Assn., Toastmasters, Beta Gamma Sigma. Republican. Lutheran. Avocation: model railroading. Health, Consumer commercial, Licensing. Home: 422-15th Ave SW Rochester MN 55902 Office: Mayo Clinic 200 1st St SW Rochester MN 55905

DETTMER, SCOTT CHARLES, lawyer; b. Long Beach, Calif., Sept. 16, 1957; s. Philip Bradshaw and Lucille Dettmer. BA, U. Calif., Santa Barbara, 1978; JD, U. So. Calif., 1982. Bar: Calif. 1982. Assoc. Cooley, Godward, Castro, Huddleson & Tatum, San Francisco, 1982—. Bd. dirs. Marin Conservation Corps, San Rafael, Calif., 1984—, North Market Child Devel. Ctr., San Francisco, 1985—. Mem. ABA, San Francisco Bar Assn., Lawyers Club San Francisco. General corporate, Securities, Computer. Office: Cooley Godward Castro et al One Maritime Plaza San Francisco CA 94111

DETTMERING, WILLIAM O'NEAL, JR., lawyer; b. Atlanta, Nov. 10, 1948; s. William O'Neal and Helen Ann (McElwaney) D.; m. Jerri Bradley, Dec. 16, 1967; children: Trey, David. Student, Davidson Coll., 1966-67; BS, Auburn U., 1970; JD, U. Ga., 1974. Bar: Ga. 1974, U.S. Dist. Ct. (no. dist.) Ga. 1974, U.S. Ct. Appeals (5th and 11th cirs.) 1974. Assoc. James R. Dollar Jr. P.A., Douglasville, Ga., 1974-75; ptnr. Dollar and Dettmering P.C., Douglasville, 1975-84, Howe, Sutton, McCreary & Dettmering P.C., Douglasville, 1984—. Mem. Ga. Bar Assn. (bd. govs. 1986—), Douglas County Bar Assn. (pres. 1981-82, law exploring com. younger lawyer sect. 1977), Ga. Trial Lawyers Assn., Kappa Delta Pi. Lodge: Rotary (bd. dirs. Douglas County 1982-84). Personal injury, State civil litigation, Banking. Home: 5441 S Lake Dr Douglasville GA 30135 Office: Howe Sutton McCreary & Dettmering PC 8486 Price Ave PO Box 1074 Douglasville GA 30133

DEUTSCH, DAVID, lawyer; b. Bklyn., Sept. 9, 1952; s. Morris and Frieda (Rosenblatt) D.; m. Deborah Auerbach, Aug. 21, 1977. BA, SUNY, Buffalo, 1973, JD, 1977; M Pub. Adminstrn., U. Wis., 1974. Bar: N.Y., D.C., U.S. Dist. Ct. D.C., U.S. Ct. Appeals (2d, 5th, 11th, D.C. and 7th cirs.). Law clk. to judge Buffalo, 1977; jud. clk. CAB, Washington, 1978-79; sr. trial atty. HUD, Washington, 1979-86; sr. assoc. Haley, Bader & Potts, Washington, 1986—; instr. continuing legal edn. programs Dept. Justice, 1982—, George Washington U., 1984—. Mem. U.S. Pub. Housing Desegregation Task Force, Washington, 1982-85. Mem. Assn. Trial Lawyers Am., ABA, N.Y. State Bar Assn., D.C. Bar Assn., Phi Beta Kappa. Avocation: karate. Federal civil litigation, Civil rights, Pension, profit-sharing, and employee benefits. Home: 6807 Breezewood Terr Rockville MD 20852 Office: Haley Bader & Potts 2000 M St NW Suite 600 Washington DC 20036

DEUTSCH, DENNIS STUART, lawyer; b. Perth Amboy, N.J., May 19, 1949; s. David and Esther (Berenfield) D.; m. Lempert, Oct. 20, 1979; 1 child, Dara Shana. B.A., U. Pitts., 1971, M.A., 1972; J.D., Dickinson Sch. Law, 1975. Bar: Pa. 1975, Fla. 1975, N.J. 1979, N.Y. 1981. U.S. Dist. Ct. (so. dist.) N.Y. 1980, U.S. Dist. Ct. N.J. 1975, U.S. Dist. Ct. (e. dist.) N.Y. 1980. Asst. dir. Fla. Legal Services, Tallahassee, 1975-78; adj. instr. bus. law Fla. State U., Tallahassee, 1976-78; sole practice, Englewood, N.J., 1979—. adj. assoc. prof. computer law Fordham U., N.Y.C. Author: Protect Yourself: The Guide to Understanding and Negotiating Contracts for Business Computers and Software, 1984. Contbr. articles to profl. jours. Mem. Bergen County Bar Assn., Computer Law Assn., Pa. Bar Assn., N.J. Bar Assn. Jewish. State civil litigation, Contracts commercial, Computer and high technology law. Home: 17 Grayson Pl Teaneck NJ 07666 Office: Gallo Geffner Farrell Fenster et al 265 Main St Hackensack NJ 07601

DEUTSCH, HARVEY ELLIOT, lawyer; b. Bklyn., Aug. 18, 1940; s. Harry Deutsch and Beulah (Deutsch) Koft; m. Paula Kantor, Nov. 26, 1964; children—Stacia Francine, Steven Harold, Karen Gail. B.A., So. Methodist U., 1962; LL.B., U. Tex., 1966. Bar: U.S. Dist. Ct. Colo. 1967, U.S. Ct. Appeals (10th cir.) 1967. Assoc., Holland & Hart, Denver, 1967-69; ptnr. Isaacson, Rosenbaum, Spiegleman & Friedman, Denver, 1970-82; v.p., gen. counsel Bill L. Walters Cos., Englewood, Colo., 1982—; lectr. in field. Contbr. chpt. to book. Dir., Anti-Defamation League of B'nai B'rith, Denver, 1976—, cochmn. civil rights com., 1980-84. Served with USNR, 1966. Mem. Tex. Bar Assn., Colo. Bar Assn. Real property, Environment. Home: 10291 E Powers Ave Englewood CO 80111 Office: Deutsch & Sheldon 7951 E Maplewood Suite 326 Englewood CO 80111

DEUTSCH, IRWIN FREDERICK, lawyer; b. N.Y.C., July 19, 1932; s. Melvin H. and Ethel (Steinberg) D.; m. Ingrid V.K. Rindfleisch, Nov. 23, 1968 (div. 1982). Student, U. Paris, 1951; AB, Amherst Coll., 1954; JD, Columbia U., 1957. Bar: N.Y. 1958, D.C. 1960, U.S. Supreme Ct. 1961. Asst. to U.S. Senator Herbert H. Lehman, Washington, 1954-55; atty. SEC, Washington, 1960-62; asst. counsel to comptroller of currency U.S. Treasury, Washington, 1962; ptnr. Upham, Meeker & Weithorn, N.Y.C., 1962-76; sole practice N.Y.C., 1976—; spl. dep. atty.gen. N.Y. State, 1959; lectr. Practicing Law Inst., N.Y.C. Contbr. articles to profl. jours. Mem. ABA, N.Y. State Bar Assn., Assn. Bar City of N.Y., D.C. Bar Assn., N.Y. County Lawyers Assn., Phi Beta Kappa, Delta Sigma Rho, Phi Delta Phi. General practice, Securities, General corporate. Home and Office: 117 E 57th St New York NY 10022

DEUTSCH, JAMES BERNARD, lawyer; b. St. Louis, Aug. 24, 1948; s. William Joseph and Margaret (Klevorn) D.; m. Deborah Marie Hallenberg, June 26, 1978; children: Michael, Gabriel. BA, Southeast Mo. State U., 1974; JD, U. Mo., 1978. Bar: Mo. 1978, U.S. Dist. Ct. (we. dist.) Mo. 1978. Assoc. Gt. Plains Legal Found., Kansas City, Mo., 1978-79; sole practice Kansas City, 1979-81; gen. counsel Mo. Dept. Revenue, Jefferson City, Mo., 1981-83; commr. Mo. Adminstrv. Hearing Commn., Jefferson City, 1983—. Served to lance cpl. USMC, 1968-70, Vietnam. Named one of Men of Yr. in Constrn. Industry, Engring. News, McGraw-Hill Pub., N.Y.C., 1985. Mem. ABA (jud. adminstrn. com.), Mo. Bar Assn. (council mem. taxation com. 1985—, adminstrn. law and jud. adminstrn. coms.), Mo. Inst. for Justice (bd. dirs. 1977—), VFW. Republican. Presbyterian. Administrative and regulatory, Judicial administration, State and local taxation. Office: Adminstrv Hearing Commn PO Box 1557 Jefferson City MO 65102

DEUTSCH, JAN C., legal educator; b. 1935. B.A., Yale U., 1955; Ph.D., Yale U, 1962; M.A., Cambridge U., Eng., 1963. Bar: D.C. 1963, Ohio 1965. Law clk. to Justice Stewart U.S. Supreme Ct., 1962-66; assoc. Jones Day Cockley & Reavis, Cleve., 1964-66; asst. prof. Yale U. Law Sch., New Haven, Conn., 1966-67; assoc. prof. Yale U. Law Sch., 1967-68, prof., 1968—; lectr. Case Western Res. U., 1965-66; cons. Pres' Commn. on Law Enforcement And Adminstrn. of Justice, 1966, Pres' Task Force on Telecommunications, 1968, Aetna Life and Casualty Co., 1979—. Author: (with Bianco) International Transactions: The Law of Corporations, 1976, Selling the People's Cadillac, 1976. Mem. Order of Coif. Legal education. Office: Yale Law Sch Drawer 401A Yale Sta New Haven CT 06520 *

DEVANEY, DENNIS MARTIN, lawyer, legal educator; b. Cheverly, Md., Feb. 25, 1946; s. Peter Paul and Alice Dorothy (Duffy) D.; m. Christine Marie Gallant, June 29, 1969; children: Jeanne Marie, Susan Theresa. BA in History, U. Md., 1968, MA in Govt. Politics, 1970; JD, Georgetown U., 1975. Bar: Md. 1976, D.C. 1976, Fla. 1977, U.S. Supreme Ct. 1980. Asst. gen. counsel U.S. Brewers Assn., Washington, 1975-77; counsel Food Mktg. Inst., Washington, 1977-79; jr. ptnr. Randall, Bangert & Thelen, Washington, 1979-81; assoc. Tighe, Curhan & Piliero, Washington, 1981-82; mem. U.S. Merit System Protection Bd., Washington, 1982—; instr. European div. U. Md., Bremerhaven, Fed. Republic of Germany, 1971-72; legis. asst. Md. Senate Jud. Commn., Annapolis, 1973-74; adj. prof. George Washington U., Washington, 1982—. Coach Columbia (Md.) Youth Baseball Assn., 1984—; campaign mgr., counsel Conroy for U.S. Senate, Bowie, Md., 1980. Served with USN, 1970-72, ETO. Mem. ABA, Md. Bar Assn., D.C. Bar Assn., Fla. Bar Assn., Fed. Bar Assn., Phi Alpha Theta, Pi Sigma Alpha, Delta Theta Phi, Omicron Delta Kappa. Democrat. Roman Catholic. Administrative and regulatory, Labor. Home: 7526 Yellow Bonnet Place Columbia MD 21046 Office: US Merit Systems Protection Bd 1120 Vermont Ave NW Washington DC 20419

DEVEAU, FRANCIS JOSEPH, lawyer; b. Ft. Wayne, Ind., Aug. 10, 1953; s. Edward Joseph Deveau and Helen R. (Krapf) Hurlbert; m. Linda Lee Heller, Aimee Marie, Katherine Elizabeth. BA, Ind. U., 1976, JD summa cum laude, 1980. Bar: Ind. 1980, U.S. Dist. Ct. (so. dist.) Ind. 1980. From assoc. to ptnr. Sommers & Barnard, Indpls., 1980—; legis. liaison DPMA Cen. Indpls., Indpls., 1985-86; bd. dirs. Ind. Entrepreneurs Alliance, AMD Inc., Ft. Wayne, Ind. Mem. ABA (natural resources sect.), Indpls. Bar Assn. (litigation sect.), Ind. Bar Assn. (litigation sect., natural resources sect.). Democrat. Roman Catholic. Avocations: tennis, golf, jogging, squash, family. Federal civil litigation, Environment, Computer. Office: Sommer & Barnard 54 Monument Circle Suite 900 Indianapolis IN 46204

DEVENDORF, ALFRED ERVIN, lawyer; b. Great Neck, N.Y., Mar. 12, 1935; s. George Epworth and Adelina (Spinetti) D.; m. Barbara Lancaster, Jan. 30, 1965; children: Diana Metcalf, George Epworth II. BA, Cornell U., 1956; JD, Bklyn. Law Sch., 1970. Bar: N.Y. 1973, U.S. Dist. Ct. (so. and ea. dists.) N.Y. 1975, U.S. Ct. Appeals (2d cir.) 1975, U.S. Supreme Ct. 1978. Coordinator sales promotions L.I. Lighting Co., Mineola, N.Y., 1966-68, pub. affairs rep., 1968-69; asst. dist. atty. Nassau County, Mineola, 1973-76, sr. dep. atty., counsel Commr. Health, 1976-80, exec. asst. to counsel Dept. Health, 1980—; bd. dirs., exec. com. Nassau Children's House Inc., Mineola. Pres. Locust Valley (N.Y.) Rep. Club, 1980. Served as 1st lt. U.S. Army, 1957-59. Mem. N.Y. State Pub. Health Assn. Roman Catholic. Lodges: Sons of Italy, Elks, KC. Avocations: paddle tennis, golf, tennis, softball, movies. Health, Environment, Criminal. Home: 40 Laurel Ln Locust Valley NY 11560 Office: Nassau County Health Dept 240 Old Country Rd Mineola NY 11501

DEVENS, PAUL, lawyer; b. Gary, Ind., June 8, 1931; s. Zenove and Anna (Brilla) Dewenetz; m. Setsuko Sugihara, Aug. 14, 1955; children: Paula, Vladimir, Mignon. BA in Econs. cum laude, Ind. U., 1954; LLB, Columbia U., 1957. Bar: N.Y. 1958, U.S. Dist. Ct. Hawaii 1960, Hawaii 1961, U.S. Ct. Appeals (9th cir.) 1962, U.S. Ct. Customs and Patent Appeals 1963, U.S. Supreme Ct. 1970. Lawyer N.Y.C., 1958-60; ptnr. Lewis, Saunders & Key, Honolulu, 1960-69; corp. counsel City and County of Honolulu, 1969-72, mng. dir., 1973-75; ptnr. Ikazaki, Devens, Lo, Youth & Nakano, Honolulu, 1975—; bd. dirs. Hotel Kaimana, Inc., Honolulu, Cen. Pacific Bank, Honolulu, CPB, Inc., Honolulu. Mem. Japan-Hawaii Econ. Council, 1975, Honolulu Charter Reorganization Com, 1979-80, Pacific and Asian Affairs Council, 1983, Wailupe Valley Elem. Sch. PTA, 1967, Niu Valley Intermediate Sch. PTA, 1970, Kalani High Sch. PTA, 1980; sec., v.p., trustee Japan-Am. Soc. of Hawaii, 1981. Served to sgt. U.S. Army, 1948-50. Mem. ABA, Hawaii State Bar Assn., Am. Trial Lawyers Assn., Columbia U. Alumni Assn. Democrat. Eastern Orthodox. Club: The Plaza(Honolulu). Federal civil litigation, State civil litigation, Real property. Address: Ikazaki Devens Lo Youth & Nakano 220 S King St Suite 1600 Honolulu HI 96813

DEVEREUX, ANTHONY QUENTIN, lawyer; b. Utica, N.Y., June 19, 1929; s. Nicholas Edward and Anne Madeline (Quinlan) D.; m. Monica Overton, June 14, 1974 (div. June 1979). B.A. with honors in History, Princeton, U., 1951; J.D., Harvard U., 1954. Bar: N.Y. 1957, S.C. 1974, U.S. Dist. Ct. S.C. 1978, U.S. Claims Ct. 1983, U.S. Ct. Appeals (4th cir.) 1980. Law assoc. Gifford, Woody, Carter Hayes, N.Y.C., 1957-71: asst. to pres. Oneita Knitting Mills, Andrews, S.C., 1961-69, N.Y.C., 1969-71, asst. sec., Andrews, 1972-84; dir. Garcon Investments, Inc., Andrews, 1980-84, Hebron Textiles, Inc., Cades, S.C., 1980-84, Mars Bluff Industries, Inc., Florence, S.C., 1981-84. Author: The Rice Princes, 1973; The Life and Times of Robert F.W. Allston, 1976. Pres., Georgetown County United Way (S.C.), 1978; chmn. Hagley Water, Sewer & Fire Authority, Pawleys Island, S.C., 1971-82. Democrat. Roman Catholic. Club: Grand Strand Tennis (Surfside Beach, S.C.). Administrative and regulatory, General corporate, Real property. Home: 4 Lancer Dr Hagley Estates Pawleys Island SC 29585 Office: PO Box 286 Hwy 17 Pawleys Island SC 29585 Office: 49 E 34th St New York NY 10016

DEVERS, PETER DIX, lawyer; b. N.Y.C., Mar. 13, 1938. BS, Holy Cross Coll., 1961; JD, NYU, 1964. Bar: N.Y. 1965, U.S. Dist Ct. (so. and ea. dists.) N.Y. 1965, U.S. Ct. Appeals (2d cir.) 1965. Assoc. Shearman & Sterling, N.Y.C., 1965-73; v.p., counsel Equitable Life Assurance Soc. U.S., N.Y.C., 1973—. Mem. Assn. Life Ins. Counsel, Am. Agrl. Law Assn., N.Y. State Bar Assn., Phi Delta Phi. Insurance, Investment, Real property. Office: Equitable Life Assurance Soc US 787 7th Ave New York NY 10019

DEVIENCE, ALEX, JR., lawyer, educator; b. Chgo., Nov. 18, 1940; s. Alex and Charlotte (Patelski) D. B.A., U. Md., 1964; J.D., Loyola U., Chgo., 1967. Bar: Ill. 1968, U.S. Dist. Ct. (no. dist.) Ill. 1968, U.S. Tax Ct. 1968, U.S. Ct. Appeals (7th cir.) 1970, Supreme Ct. 1971, U.S. Ct. Internat. Trade 1984, U.S. Ct. Appeals (9th and fed. cir.) 1984. Sole practice, Chgo., 1967-71; prof. bus. law DePaul U., Chgo., 1975—. Author: Legal and Social Obligations of Business Managers, 1986. Apptd. by Gov. to Small Bus. Adv. Council, 1985; mem. Fed. and State Legis. Implementation Task Force, 1985. Mem. Am. Bus. Law Profs., Chgo. Bar Assn. Federal civil litigation, General corporate, Insurance. Home: 630 Sylviawood St Park Ridge IL 60068 Office: 175 N Franklin St Chicago IL 60606

DEVINE, DONN, lawyer, city official; b. South Amboy, N.J., Mar. 30, 1929; s. Frank Edward and Emily Theresa (DeRevere) D. m. Elizabeth Cecilia Baldwin, Nov. 23, 1951; children—Edward (dec.), Mary Elizabeth, Martin Joseph. B.S., U. Del., 1949; J.D. with honors, Widener U., 1975. Bar: Del. 1975, U.S. Dist. Ct. Del. 1976. Devel. chemist Allied Chem. Corp., Claymont, Del., 1950-52; newspaper writer, editor corp. publs. Atlas Powder Co., Wilmington, Del., 1952-60; mgmt. cons., Wilmington, 1960-68; dir. renewal planning City of Wilmington, 1968-79, dep. dir. planning, 1979-80, dir. planning, 1981-85; cons., Wilmington City Council, 1985—; pvt. practice, 1985—; past dir. Small Bus. Devel. Corp., Wilmington Econ. Devel. Corp. Author: Delaware National Guard, A Historical Sketch, 1968, DeRevere Family of Peekskill, New York, 1982. Editor jour Del. Genealogical Soc., 1980-81; assoc. editor Del. Jour. Corp. Law, 1974-75. Treas., past v.p. Delmarva Ecumenical Agy.; v.p., sec., dir. Geriatric Services Del.; past officer, bd. dirs. Christina Cultural Arts Ctr., Cath. Interraccial Council, Del. chpt. ACLU, St. Mary's-St. Patrick's Parish council; mem. planning council United Way. Served to sgt. USAR, 1950-54, 2d lt., Del. N.G., 1954-84, ret. Decorated Meritorious Service medal. Mem. ABA, Am. Planning Assn., Am. Inst. Cert. Planners, Urban Land Inst., Am. Chem. Soc., Del. Soc. Sons Am. Revolution (past pres.), Del. Geneal. Soc., Ft. Delaware Soc. (recognition award), Phi Kappa Phi, Delta Theta Phi. Democrat. Clubs: Univ. and Whist (Wilmington); Chemists (N.Y.C.). Lodges: Ancient Order Hibernians. Real property, Local government, Environment. Home: 2004 Kentmere Pkwy Wilmington DE 19806

DEVINE, EUGENE PETER, lawyer; b. Albany, N.Y., Oct. 14, 1948; s. Eugene Peter and Phyllis Jean (Albanese) D.; m. Theresa Rose Jennings, Mar. 21, 1973; children—Kimberly, Tracy. J.D., Albany Law Sch., 1975. Bar: N.Y. 1975, U.S. Dist. Ct. (no. dist.) N.Y. 1975, U.S. Supreme Ct. 1980. Atty. N.Y. Pub. Defender, Albany County, 1976-85; ptnr. Cooper, Erving, and Savage, Albany, 1975-85 ; ptnr. Devine, Piedment and Rutnik ; chief atty. Albany County Dept. Social Services, 1985—. Bd. dirs. Ronald McDonald House, Albany, 1980—, founding mem.; committeeman Albany County Democratic Com., 1979—; treas. com. to elect Jim Tully N.Y. State Comptroller, N.Y.C., 1980. Club: Woolferts Roost Country. Lodge: Albany Sons of St. Patrick (pres. 1984). Criminal, Labor, General practice. Office: Devine Piedmont and Rutnik 744 Broadway Albany NY 12207

DEVINE, JAMES RICHARD, legal educator; b. Newark, Jan. 31, 1948; s. Richard Caryl and Lucy Mae (Babcock) D.; m. Sharon Ann Jungquist, May 25, 1971; children: Zachary James, Joshua Calvin, Noah Brooks. AB, Franklin & Marshall Coll., 1970; JD cum laude, Seton Hall U., 1975. Bar: N.J. 1975, Mo. 1983. Law sec. N.J. Superior Ct., Freehold, 1975-76; assoc. Madden & Holobinko, Middletown, N.J., 1976-80; assoc. prof. U. Mo., Columbia, 1980-84, prof. law, 1984-85, David Ross Hardy prof. law, 1986—; sec. dist. ethics and fee commn. N.J. Superior Ct., Monmouth County, 1976-80; chmn. com. on lawyer advt. Mo. Supreme Ct., Jefferson City, 1982-84. Author: Materials on Lawyer Trust Accounting, 1984, Cases/Materials on Professional Responsibility, 1985, Missouri Civil Pleading, 1986. Bd. dirs. Children's House of Columbia, 1984—, Mid-Mo. Legal Services. Mem. Mo. Bar Assn., N.J. Bar Assn., Am. Judicature Soc. Jurisprudence, State civil litigation, Legal education. Home: 1408 W Georgetown Loop Columbia MO 65203 Office: U Mo Sch of Law Tate Hall Columbia MO 65211

DEVINE, MICHAEL BUXTON, lawyer; b. Des Moines, Oct. 25, 1953; s. Cleatie Hiram, Jr., and Katherine Ann (Buxton) D. Student St. Peter's Coll., Oxford U., Eng., 1975; B.A. cum laude, St. Olaf Coll., 1976; M.P.A., Drake U., 1980, J.D., 1980; diploma in Advanced Internat. Legal Studies, U. Pacific extension Salzburg, Austria, 1986. Bar: Iowa 1980, U.S. Dist. Ct. (no. and so. dists.) Iowa 1980, U.S. Ct. Appeals (8th cir.) 1980, Nebr. 1985, Supreme Ct. 1985, Minn. 1986, D.C. 1986; Assoc. Bump & Haesemeyer, P.C., Des Moines, 1980-85; sole practice, Des Moines, 1985—; legal intern Herbert, Oppenheimer, Nathan & Vandyk, London, England, 1986. Scholar St. Olaf Coll., 1972-76; nat. alt. U.S. Presdl. Mgmt. Intern Program, 1980. Mem. ABA, Fed. Bar Assn. (chmn. state of Iowa SBA export assistance program 1983-85, treas. Iowa chpt. 1984-85, exec. com. 1985—), Iowa Bar Assn., Nebr. Bar Assn., Minn. Bar Assn., D.C. Bar Assn., Internat. Bar Assn., Polk County Bar Assn., Phi Alpha Theta, Pi Alpha Alpha, Phi Alpha Delta. Presbyterian. Private international. Home and Office: 2611 40th St Des Moines IA 50310

DEVINE, SHANE, federal judge; b. 1926. B.A., U. N.H., 1949; J.D., Boston Coll., 1952. Bar: N.H. 1952. Judge U.S. Dist. Ct. N.H., 1978—, now chief judge. Mem. ABA, N.H., Manchester bar assns. Office: US Dist Ct NH 55 Pleasant St Concord NH 03301 *

DEVINE, SHARON JEAN, lawyer; b. Milw., Feb. 27, 1948; d. George John Devine and Ethel May (Langworthy) Devine Chase; m. Curtiss Coughlin; children—Devin Curtiss, Katharine Langworthy. B.S. in Linguistics, Georgetown U., 1970; J.D., Boston U., 1975. Bar: Ohio, Colo. Staff atty. FTC, Cleve., 1975-79; asst. regional dir., Denver, 1979-82; atty. Mountain Bell, Denver, 1982-84, U.S. West Direct, 1984-85; assoc. gen. counsel U.S. West Direct, 1985—; dir. Denver Consortium, 1982-83, Ctr. for Applied Prevention, Boulder, Colo., 1982—. Contbr. article to law rev. Mem. Colo. Bar Assn., Denver Bar Assn., Colo. Women's Bar Assn. Club: Jr. League of Denver. Administrative and regulatory, Antitrust, Trademark and copyright. Home: 2360 Dartmouth Ave Boulder CO 80303 Office: US West Direct 2500 S Havana Aurora CO 80014

DE VIVO, EDWARD CHARLES, lawyer; b. Newark, Dec. 10, 1953; s. Louis Joseph and Marian (Pistilli) De V. B.A. cum laude, NYU, 1975, M.A., 1982; J.D., U. Notre Dame, 1978. Bar: N.Y. 1979, U.S. Dist. Ct. (so. dist.) N.Y., U.S. Dist. Ct. (ea. dist.) N.Y. Assoc. Bigham Englar Jones & Houston, N.Y.C., 1978-82, Condon & Forsyth, N.Y.C., 1982-85, Windels, Marx, Davies & Ives, N.Y.C., 1985—; cons. Contbr. articles to legal pubis. Mem. bd. spl. advisors Pres. Reagan's Phys. Fitness Commn., 1985—; active Big Bros. Program, United Way, 1985—. NYU scholar, 1971-75. Republican. Roman Catholic. Club: N.Y. Health and Racquet (N.Y.C.). Aviation, Federal civil litigation, Private international. Home: 14 Robert Ct Verona NJ 07044 Office: Windels Marx Davies & Ives 51 W 51st St New York NY 10020

DE VLAMING, DENIS MICHAEL, lawyer; b. Amityville, N.Y., July 12, 1947; s. William Maurice and Evelyn (Kirchmer) de V.; m. Voncele A. Zimmerman, Dec. 9, 1983; 1 child, Lacey Reid. BA, Ohio State U., 1969; JD, Stetson U., 1972. Asst. state atty. Office State Atty., Clearwater, 1972-75; adj. prof. U. So. Fla., Tampa, Fla., 1977-78; sole practice Clearwater, 1975—. Mem. ABA, Fla. Bar Assn. (criminal law sect.), Clearwater Bar Assn., Nat. Assn. Criminal Def. Attys Assn., Fla. Criminal Def. Attys. Assn., Acad. Fla. Trial Lawyers (criminal law sect.). Criminal. Home: 878 Island Way Clearwater FL 33515 Office: 1101 Turner St Clearwater FL 33516

DEVLIN, EUGENE JOSEPH, lawyer; b. Bklyn., Nov. 29, 1902; s. Mark and Susanne (Graham) D.; A.B., U. Detroit, 1924, LL.B., 1927, LL.M., J.D., 1931. Bar: Mich. 1927, U.S. Dist. Ct. (ea. dist.) Mich. 1928, U.S. Supreme Ct. 1971. Sole practice, Detroit, 1927-68, St. Clair Shores, Mich., 1968—. Served with U.S. Army, World War II. Mem. Mich. Bar Assn., ABA, Macomb County Bar Assn., St. Clair Shores Bar Assn., Cath. Lawyers Soc., Irish-Am. Bar Assn., Am. Legion (judge adv. 1968—), DAV, Mich. Legionnaires. Clubs: Magi (past pres.). Author numerous poems. Probate, Real property, Federal civil litigation. Address: 22328 Hanson Ct Saint Clair Shores MI 48080

DEVLIN, GREG MARTIN, lawyer; b. Spokane, Wash., Oct. 10, 1950; s. John Pershing and Evelyn Joyce (Martin) D.; m. Linda Jean Skredsvig, Dec. 1, 1978; 1 child, Julie Christine. BS in Polit. Sci., Wash. State U., 1973; JD, Gonzaga U., 1976. Bar: Wash. 1976, U.S. Dist. Ct. (ea. dist.) Wash. 1980. Dep. pros. atty. Stevens County, Colville, Wash., 1976-77, pros. atty., 1977-80; ptnr. Gordon, Hipperson, Shogan & Devlin, Spokane, 1980—. Mem. ABA, Spokane County Bar Assn., Wash. State Trial Lawyers Assn. Republican. Congregationalist. Lodge: Eagles. Avocations: golf, biking, running, skiing, boating. General practice, State civil litigation, Criminal. Office: Gordon Hipperson Shogan & Devlin W 24 Indiana Spokane WA 99205

DEVLIN, JOHN GERARD, lawyer; b. Phila., Apr. 26, 1955; s. John and Catherine (Flannery) D.; m. Maureen Borneman, June 17, 1978. BA, Temple U., 1977, JD, 1980; postgrad., U. Pa., 1980—. Bar: Pa. 1980, U.S. Supreme Ct. 1983. Assoc. Spencer, Sherr & Moses, P.C., Norristown, Pa., 1980-82, Deasey, Scanlan & Bender, Ltd., Phila., 1982-84; sole practice Phila., 1984—; cons. Sentry Ins. Co., Parsippany, N.J., 1983—, John Hancock Co., Boston, 1984—. Mem. ABA, Phi Beta Kappa, Pi Sigma Alpha. Republican. Club: vesper (Phila.). Insurance. Office: 2325 The Fidelity Bldg Philadelphia PA 19109

DEVLIN, PAUL ANTHONY, lawyer; b. Boston, Jan. 28, 1956; s. Francis Carroll and Ann Marie (Conroy) D. AB, Dartmouth Coll., 1977; JD, Boston U., 1982. Bar: Mass. 1982, U.S. Dist. Ct. Mass. 1982, U.S. Ct. Appeals (1st cir.) 1982. Assoc. Lecomte, Barber & Emanuelson, Boston, 1982-84, Haussermann, Davison & Shattuck, Boston, 1984—. Mem. ABA, Mass. Bar Assn. Federal civil litigation, State civil litigation, Insurance. Home: 247 Washington St #28 Winchester MA 01890 Office: Haussermann Davison & Shattuck One Boston Pl Boston MA 02108

DEVNEY, JOHN LEO, lawyer; b. Duluth, Minn., Sept. 21, 1938; s. John Leo and Madeline Genevieve (O'Brien) D.; m. Judith Lee, Apr. 11, 1970; children—John, Elizabeth, Joseph. A.B., Notre Dame U., 1960; LL.B., U. Minn., 1963. Bar: Minn. 1963, Alaska 1965, U.S. Dist. Ct. Minn. 1967, U.S. Ct. Appeals (8th cir.) 1974, U.S. Supreme Ct. 1982. Asst. dist. atty. Office Atty. Gen., State of Alaska, 1964-65; practice, Anchorage, 1965-67; spl. asst. atty. gen. State of Minn., 1967-70; assoc. Briggs and Morgan, P.A., St. Paul, 1970-71, mem., 1971—. Mem. ABA, Minn. State Bar Assn., Ramsey County Bar Assn. Republican. Roman Catholic. Club: St. Paul Athletic. Editorial bd. U. Minn. Law Rev., 1962-63. Federal civil litigation, State civil litigation. Office: 200 First Nat Bank Bldg Saint Paul MN 55101

DEVRIES, DONALD LAWSON, JR., lawyer; b. Phila., May 1, 1947; s. Donald Lawson and Jeanne (Coleman) DeV.; m. Nancy Shafer, Aug. 10, 1977; children: Donald Lawson III, Emily Shafer; stepdaughter: Alison Brady Beale. BA with honors, Dartmouth Coll., 1969; JD with honors, U. Md., 1973. Bar: Md. 1973, U.S. Dist. Ct. Md. 1973, U.S. Ct. Appeals (4th cir.) 1975. Assoc. Semmes, Bowen & Semmes, Balt., 1973-80, ptnr., chmn. med. malpractice dept., 1980—; mem. faculty Md. Inst. Continuing Profl. Edn. for Lawyers, 1984-87; gov.'s task force on Med. Malpractice Ins., 1985; master Am. Inns of Court, 1986—. Contbr. Md. Law Rev., 1973. Bd. trustees Roland Park Country Sch., 1987, Woodbourne Ctr., 1981—; vestryman St. David's Ch., 1982-85; bd. trustees, exec. com. S. Balt. Gen. Hosp., 1983—; mem. Canons and Other Bus. Coms. of Episcopal Diocese Md., 1984—; bd. dirs. Md. affiliate Am. Heart Assn., 1986—. Mem. Md. State Bar Assn. (spl. com. health claims arbitration 1983), ABA (ann. meeting speaker 1984, vice chmn. medicine and law com. torts and ins. practice sect. 1982—, forum com. health law), Internat. Assn. Ins. Counsel, Am. Bd. Trial Advs., Md. Assn. Def. Trial Counsel, Def. Research Inst. Republican. Club: Maryland (Balt.). Personal injury, Insurance, Health. Home: 401 Woodlawn Rd Baltimore MD 21210 Office: Semmes Bowen Semmes 10 Light St Baltimore MD 21202

DEVRIES, JAMES HOWARD, manufacturing exec., lawyer; b. Chgo., Mar. 17, 1932; s. James and Ruth (Heuman) DeV.; m. Eleanor Devries, Mar. 6, 1956; children: James, Sara, Adam, Peter, Mary. BS in Bus. Mgmt., U. Colo., 1954; JD with distinction, U. Mich., 1961. Bar: Ill. 1961. Assoc. Hopkins & Sutter, Chgo., 1961-62; ptnr. McBride & Baker, Chgo., 1963-82; v.p., sec., gen. counsel, chmn., chief exec. officer LaserVideo, Inc. subs. Quixote Quixote Corp., Chgo., 1982—, also bd. dirs. Pres. Library International Relations, Chgo., 1980-82; mem. Chgo. Crime Commn., 1982—. Served to lt. USN, 1954-58. Mem. Ill. Bar Assn., Chgo. Bar Assn., Am. Electronics Assn., Am. Soc. Corp. Secs., Internat. Am. Club: University (Chgo.). Administrative and regulatory, General corporate, Private international. Office: Quixote Corp One E Wacker Dr Chicago IL 60601

DEVRIES, SCOTT PHILIP, lawyer; b. N.Y.C., Sept. 7, 1954; s. Harold and Marilyn (Green) DeV.; m. Deborah Lynn Jordan, Oct. 14, 1984. BA, Coll. William and Mary, 1976; JD, Case Western Res. U., 1979. Bar: Calif. 1979, U.S. Dist. Ct. (no. dist.) Calif. 1979, U.S. Dist. Ct. (ea. and so. dists.) Calif. 1985. Assoc. Boornazian, Jensen & Garthe, Oakland, Calif., 1979-84; assoc. Lasky, Haas, Cohler & Munter, San Francisco, 1984-86, ptnr., 1986—. Mem. steering com. to elect P. Moscone to Mcpl. Ct., San Francisco, 1980, No. Calif. Lawyers for Cranston, San Francisco, 1986; campaign mgr. Jim Kennedy for City Council, Alameda, Calif., 1982. Named One of Outstanding Young Men Am., 1980. Mem. ABA, Calif. Bar Assn., Alameda County Bar Assn., San Francisco Bar Assn., Barristers' Club (co-chmn. local govt. affairs com. 1984—). Democrat. Avocations: tennis, skiing, golf. State civil litigation, Insurance, Environment. Home: 1352 Ballena Blvd #209 Alameda CA 94501 Office: Lasky Haas Cohler & Munter 505 Sansome St San Francisco CA 94111

DEW, THOMAS EDWARD, lawyer; b. Detroit, Feb. 13, 1947; s. Albert Nelson and Irene Theresa (Morris) D.; m. Gail Ruth Tuesink, June 27, 1970. B.A., U. Mich., 1969; J.D., Detroit Coll. Law, 1974. Bar: Mich. 1974, U.S. Dist. Ct. (ea. dist.) Mich. 1974, U.S. Tax Ct. 1980. Agt., IRS, Detroit, 1969-74; trust officer Ann Arbor Trust Co., Mich., 1974-75, asst. v.p., 1975-78; ptnr. Conner, Harbour, Dew, Ann Arbor, 1978-83, Harris, Lax, Guenzel & Dew, Ann Arbor, 1983—; lectr. Am. Coll., Bryn Mawr, Pa., 1979-82, Am. Inst. Paralegal Studies, Detroit, 1982. Mem. Ann Arbor Housing Commn., 1979-81, pres., 1981. Law scholor Sigma Nu Phi, 1974. Mem. ABA, State Bar Mich., Washtenaw Estate Planning Council (pres. 1979-80), Washtenaw County Bar Assn. Republican. Lutheran. Lodge: Lions. Estate taxation, Corporate taxation, General corporate. Office: Harris Lax Guenzel & Dew PC 320 City Ctr Bldg Ann Arbor MI 48104

DEWALD, JOHN EDWARD, lawyer; b. Phila., Sept. 2, 1946; s. John and Helen DeWald; 1 child, Meredith. BA magna cum laude, LaSalle U., 1969; JD, U. Pa., 1972. Bar: Pa. 1973, U.S. Dist. Ct. (ea. dist.) Pa. 1973, U.S. Supreme Ct. 1978, Tex. 1981, U.S. Ct. Appeals (3d cir.) 1981. Asst. counsel First Investment Annuity, Valley Forge, Pa., 1972-74, Acme Markets, Phila., 1974-79; chief atty. legal services Bell Helicopter div. Textron, Ft. Worth, 1979-81; gen. counsel IMM, Phila., 1982; sole practice Phila. and Westchester, Pa., 1983-84; asst. counsel Prudential Ins., Ft. Washington, Pa., 1984—; Co-author Restatement In the Courts, 1973. Candidate for dist. atty. Dems., Chester County, Pa., 1983, mem. exec. com., 1983—; treas. ballet com. Phila. Vol. Lawyers for the Arts, 1986. Mem. ABA (corp. antitrust com.), Pa. Bar Assn., World Affairs Council (mem. exec. com. Forum 3, 1983—). Insurance, General corporate, Federal civil litigation. Office: Prudential Ins PO Box 388 Fort Washington PA 19034

DEWEESE, KATHLEEN BATCHELDER, lawyer; b. Washington, Feb. 28, 1949; d. Edward Barron and Anastasia Catherine (McCloud) Batchelder; m. J. Taylor DeWeese, Oct. 18, 1975; children: James Taylor, Jill Maura. BA, St. Josephs U., Phila., 1974; JD, U. Pa., 1977. Bar: D.C. 1978, Pa. 1977, U.S. Ct. Appeals (4th cir.) 1986. Spl. asst. to gen. counsel Potomac Electric Power Co., Washington, 1977-80, assoc. counsel, 1981-83, asst. gen. counsel, 1983-86, assoc. gen. counsel, 1986; gen. counsel IAV div. PEPCO, Washington, 1983—, Energy Use Mgmt. Corp., Washington, 1984—. Contbr. articles to profl. jours. Mem. steering com. Washington Area Olympics Com., 1983; pres. Wilson Lane Civic Assn., Bethesda, Md., 1983. Recipient Goldman Found. award Goldman Found., 1974. Mem. ABA, Pa. Bar Assn., Women's Bar Assn. D.C., Women's Bar Assn. Found. (bd. dirs., sec. 1987—), Washington Met. Area Corp. Counsel Assn. Republican. Avocations: writing fiction, tennis. Contracts commercial, Environment. Home: 7409 Fairfax Rd Bethesda MD 20814 Office: Potomac Electric Power Co 1900 Pennsylvania Ave NW Washington DC 20068

DEWEY, ANNE ELIZABETH MARIE, lawyer; b. Balt., Mar. 16, 1951; d. George Daniel and Elizabeth Patricia (Mohan) D.; m. Peter Michael Barnett, Aug. 27, 1977; children: Brendan M., Andrew P. BA, Mich. State U., 1972; JD, U. Chgo., 1975; grad., Stonier Grad. Sch. Banking, East Brunswick, N.J., 1983. Bar: D.C. 1976. Atty. FTC, Washington, 1975-78; atty. enforcement div. Comptroller of Currency, Washington, 1978-81, atty. office legis. counsel, 1981-83; atty. dist. office Comptroller of Currency, Dallas, 1983-86; sr. atty. legal adv. services div. Comptroller of Currency, Washington, 1986; assoc. gen. counsel corp. and adminstrv. law Farm Credit Adminstrn., McLean, Va., 1986—. Tchr. St. Rita's Ch., Dallas, 1984-85. Mem. ABA, D.C. Bar Assn., Women in Housing and Fin. (bd. dirs. 1982-83). Roman Catholic. Banking, Administrative and regulatory. Home: 833 Fontaine St Alexandria VA 22302 Office: Farm Credit Adminstrn Office Gen Counsel 1501 Farm Credit Dr McLean VA 22102-5090

DEWITT, FRANKLIN ROOSEVELT, lawyer; b. Conway, S.C., May 25, 1936; s. Matthew A. and Rebecca (Hughes) DeW.; m. Willa Waylis Johnson, Aug. 20, 1960; children—Rosalyn Abravaya, Sharolyn Rene. B.S., S.C. State Coll., 1962; J.D., 1964; cert. urban affairs adminstrn. Ga. State U., 1974. Bar: S.C. 1964, D.C., 1966. Trial atty. CSC, Washington, 1965-67; sole practice law, Conway, S.C., 1967—; town atty. Town of Atlantic Beach (S.C.), 1966-79, 1984—. Mem. Conway City Council, 1968—; mem. Waccamaw Econ. Opportunity Council, 1968-81, treas. to 1981; mem. Waccamaw Mental Health Ctr. for Horry, Georgetown and Williamsburg Counties, 1970—; del. Nat. Democratic Party Conv., 1972, 76, 80; sec. Dem. Precinct Com. Served with USAF. Named Father of Yr., Cherry Hill Baptist Ch., 1972, Usher of Yr., 1978; recipient Disting. Service in Housing award Horry County. Mem. ABA, Nat. Bar Assn. (life), Horry County Bar Assn., S.C. Bar Assn., NAACP (life), Kappa Alpha Psi. State civil litigation, Criminal, Workers' compensation. Home: 1708 Hwy 378 Conway SC 29526 Office: 510 Hwy 378 Conway SC 29526

DEWITT, SHERRI KANDEL, lawyer. BA cum laude, SUNY, Binghamton, 1973, PhD in Polit. Sci., 1978; JD, Cornell U., 1982. Asst. prof. Sch. Mgmt. SUNY, Binghamton, 1978-79; assoc. Lowndes, Drosdick, Doster, Kantor & Reed, P.A., Orlando, Fla., 1982-85, Litchford & Christopher P.A., Orlando, 1985-86; sole practice Orlando, 1987—; cons. IBM, White Plains, N.Y., 1977-81; pre-law advisor SUNY, Binghamton, 1977-79; lectr. in field. Editor: Cornell Law Rev.; vis. editor Florida State Law Rev., 1981-82; contbr. articles to profl. jours. Mem. Greater Orlando Project 2000 Inc. (arts, culture and recreation task force); bd. dirs. Adam Walsh Found., Parent Resource Ctr. Mem. ABA (real property, probate, trial lawyers sects.), Fla. Bar Assn., Cen. Fla. Assn. Women Lawyers (treas. bar directory com., chmn. jud. reception com., bd. dirs.), Orange County Bar Assn. (real property and legal edn. coms., chmn. legal forum com.), Orlando C. of C., Cen. Fla. Cornell Univ. Alumni Assn. (chmn. membership com.), Cornell U. Alumni Assn. (bd. dirs.). Federal civil litigation, State civil litigation, General corporate. Office: 125 S Court Ave Orlando FL 32801

DEWOLFE, GEORGE FULTON, lawyer; b. Oak Park, Ill., Jan. 22, 1949; s. John Chauncey and Dorothy Sinclair (Fulton) DeW. A.B., Yale U., 1971; LL.B., U. Toronto, Ont., Can., 1974. Bar: Ill. 1975, U.S. Dist. Ct. (no. dist.) Ill. 1975, U.S. Dist. Ct. (ea dist.) Wis. 1976, U.S. Ct. Appeals (7th cir.) 1980, N.Y. 1983, U.S. Supreme Ct. 1985. Assoc. DeWolfe, Poynton & Stevens, Chgo., 1975-80, ptnr., 1980—; legal adviser Brit. Consulate Gen., Chgo., 1984—; gen. counsel Suburban Hosp., Hinsdale, Ill., 1984—; adj. prof. law DePaul U., 1985—; mem. adv. bd. Health Law Inst., DePaul U., 1986—. Assoc. editor U. Toronto Faculty of Law Rev., 1973-74, Hospital Law, 1986—. Bd. dirs., sec. St. Leonard's House of Episc. Diocese of Chgo., 1975-83; mem. Chgo. Area AIDS Task Force, 1987—. Mem. ABA, Ill. Bar Assn., Chgo. Bar Assn. (cert. appreciation 1983-84), Ill. Assn. Hosp. Attys., Nat. Health Lawyers Assn., Am. Soc. Law and Medicine, Am. Acad. Hosp. Attys. Club: University (Chgo.). Health, Probate, State civil litigation. Home: 880 N Lake Shore Dr Chicago IL 60611 Office: DeWolfe Poynton & Stevens 135 S LaSalle St Chicago IL 60603

DEWOLFE, JOHN CHAUNCEY, JR., lawyer; b. Chgo., June 9, 1913; s. John Chauncey and Mabel (Spafford) DeW.; m. Dorothy Fulton, May 9, 1942; children: John Chauncey, III, George F. B.S., U. Ill.; J.D., U. Wis., 1939. Bar: Wis. 1939, Ill. 1940. Ptnr. firm DeWolfe, Poynton & Stevens and predecessor firms, 1946—. Contbr. articles to profl. jours. Trustee Village of Riverside, Ill., 1963-70; Chmn. West Suburban Mass Transit Dist., 1974-76. Served from lt. to maj. AUS, 1942-45, 51-52; lt. col. USAR ret. Mem. Am., Ill., Wis. bar assns., Chgo. Bar Assn. (chmn. corp. law com. 1973-74), Bar Assn. 7th Fed. Circuit, Assn. Trial Lawyers Am., SAR, Sigma Phi Epsilon. Republican. Episcopalian. Club: University (Chgo.). Federal civil litigation, State civil litigation, General corporate. Home: 1448 N Lake Shore Dr Chicago IL 60610 Office: 135 S La Salle St Chicago IL 60603

DEWOSKIN, ALAN ELLIS, lawyer; b. St. Louis, Sept. 10, 1940; s. Samuel S. and Lillian (Sachs) DeW.; m. Iris Lynn Shapiro, Aug. 15, 1942; children—Joseph, Henry, Franklin. B.A., Washington U., St. Louis, 1962, J.D., 1965; grad. U.S. Army Command and Gen. Staff Coll., 1978; grad. U.S. Army War Coll., 1985. Bar: Mo. 1968, U.S. Dist. Ct. (ea. dist.) Mo. 1968, U.S. Ct. Appeals (8th cir.) 1969, U.S. Ct. Mil. Appeals 1976. Sole practice, St. Louis, 1968-82, prin. Alan E. DeWoskin, P.C., St. Louis, 1982—; mem. Ho. of Dels., 1986-87. Active Boy Scouts Am. Served to col. JAGC, USAR, 1965-66. Mem. ABA (chmn. gen. practice sect. 1985-86, mem. House of Dels. 1986-87), Assn. Trial Lawyers Am., Mo. Bar Assn., Bar Assn. Met. St. Louis, Assn. Mo. Trial Lawyers, St. Louis County Bar Assn. Club: Masons (past master, dir. 1972—). General practice, State civil litigation, Federal civil litigation. Home: 14030 Deltona Dr Chesterfield MO 63017 Office: 225 S Meramec Ave Suite 426 Saint Louis MO 63105

DEYOUNG, JONATHAN HARVEY, lawyer; b. Phila., Mar. 4, 1937; s. Daniel and Reba (Berman) DeY.; m. Janice Toll, Sept. 14, 1985; children: Dale, Jeffrey, Laurie, Gary. BS, Georgetown U., 1958; JD, Temple U., 1961. Bar: Pa. 1962, U.S. Dist. Ct. (ea. dist.) Pa. 1962, U.S. Supreme Ct. 1978. Assoc. Fox & Fox, Norristown, Pa., 1962-63; ptnr. Torak & DeYoung, King of Prussia, Pa., 1963-69; sole practice King of Prussia, 1969—. Area leader Dem. Party, 1969-71; pres. Ambucs, King of Prussia, 1970; chmn. March of Dimes, Montogomery County, Pa., 1970-72. Mem. ABA, Pa. Bar Assn., Montgomery County Bar Assn., Assn. Trial Lawyers Am. Republican. Jewish. Lodge: B'nai B'rith (local chmn. 1971-72). Contracts commercial, General corporate, Family and matrimonial. Office: 144 E DeKalb Pike King of Prussia PA 19406

DE YOUNG, VINCENT GERALD, lawyer; b. Paterson, N.J., Sept. 12, 1938; s. Henry and Jemima (Malefyt) De Jonge; m. Carol Esther Fleming, Jan. 19, 1963; children: Donna, Mary, Cindy, John, Rebecca, Shannon. Student, Calvin Coll., 1956-58; BS, Fairleigh Dickinson U., 1960; JD with honors, U. Tex., 1968; MBA, Memphis State U., 1986. Bar: N.Y. 1968, Ky. 1971, Tenn. 1985. Assoc. Simpson, Thacher & Bartlett, N.Y.C., 1968-70; atty., corp. sec. Ky. Fried Chicken Corp., Louisville, 1970-75; sole practice Louisville, 1975-80; sr. atty., asst. sec., assoc. gen. counsel Holiday Corp., Memphis, 1980—; lectr. contract law U. Louisville, 1975-80. Assoc. editor U. Tex. Law Rev., 1967-68. Served to 1st lt., USAF, 1960-65. Mem. ABA, Ky. Bar Assn., N.Y. State Bar Assn., Tenn. Bar Assn., Order of Coif, Phi Delta Phi. Presbyterian. Avocations: music, running. General corporate, Pension, profit-sharing, and employee benefits, Real property. Home: 7760 Foster Ridge Germantown TN 38138 Office: Holiday Corp 1023 Cherry Rd Memphis TN 38117

DIAMANT, AVIVA F., lawyer; b. N.Y.C., Mar. 13, 1949; d. Herman and Anni (Silbermann) D.; m. Steven Kaufman, May 31, 1976; 2 children. BS cum laude, CCNY, 1969; JD, Columbia U., 1972. Bar: N.Y. 1973, U.S. Ct. Appeals (2d cir.) 1975, U.S. Dist. Ct. (so. dist.) 1976. Assoc. Fried, Frank, Harris, Shriver & Jacobson, N.Y.C., 1972-79, ptnr., 1979—. James Kent scholar, 1972. Mem. Assn. of Bar of City of N.Y. (com. on corps.), Phi Beta Kappa. Jewish. Securities, General corporate. Office: Fried Frank Harris Shriver & Jacobson One New York Plaza New York NY 10004

DIAMANT, WILLIAM, lawyer, financial consultant; b. Johnstown, Pa., May 30, 1928; s. James and Anna (Papanicholau) D.; m. Bertha Polydoros, Nov. 27, 1951; children—Anna Woods, Elaine Sikorski, Christine Kipp, James. B.S., U. Pitts., 1952, J.D., 1955; grad. in trust adminstrn. Naval Justice Sch., 1956; postgrad. Northwestern U., 1967. Bar: Pa. 1955, Ill. 1958, U.S. Dist. Ct. (no. dist.) Ill. 1984. Title legal officer Chgo. Title & Trust Co., 1957-62; v.p., gen. counsel Unibanctrust Co., Chgo., 1962-78; v.p., trust dept. head, counsel 1st Nat. Bank of Elgin, Ill., 1978-81; sr. v.p., gen. counsel, sec. bd. dirs. Elmhurst Inst. Bank, Ill., 1981-83; sole practice, Hinsdale, Ill., 1983—; tchr. Am. Inst. Banking, Chgo., 1972—. Sec. Sch. Bd. Unit Dist. 401, Elmwood Park, Ill., 1972-78. Served with USMC, 1949; capt. Res. (ret.). Recipient Meritorious Service award Sch. Bd. Unit Dist. 401, 1978, Disting. Service award Am. Inst. Banking, 1982. Mem. Ill. Bar Assn., Pa. Bar Assn., Chgo. Bar Assn., DuPage County Bar Assn. Club: Ahepa (Chgo.) (pres. 1960-62). Lodge: Elks. Probate, Real property, General corporate. Office: 119 E Ogden Ave Hinsdale IL 60521

DIAMOND, ANN LANDY, lawyer, consultant; b. Pecs, Hungary, Dec. 29, 1912; came to U.S., 1929; d. Louis and Hella Ladanyi; m. Bernard L. Diamond, Feb. 10, 1946; children: Joan, Lynn, Larry, Lisa, Judy, Jan. BA, Case Western Res. U., 1935, JD, 1937. Bar: Ohio 1937, Calif. 1945. Atty. Labor Relations Bd., Washington, 1938-41; sr. atty. Office Price Adminsrtn. Rationing, Washington, 1941-43, War Labor Bd., San Francisco, 1943-46; sole practice San Rafael, Calif., 1954-76; sr. ptnr. Diamond, Bennington & Simborg, Corte Madera, Calif., 1979—; lectr. U. Calif., Davis, 1974-80. Contbr. articles to profl. jours. Fellow Am. Acad. Matrimonial Lawyers (No. Calif. chpt. past pres.); mem. ABA (family law sect.), State Bar Calif. (family law adv. com., 1979-84), Marin County Bar Assn. (past pres.). Family and matrimonial. Home: 59 Bridge Rd Ross CA 94957 Office: Diamond Bennington & Simborg 300 Tamal Plaza Suite 280 Corte Madera CA 94925

DIAMOND, GLORIA BEVERLY, lawyer; b. Chgo., Sept. 24, 1937; d. Max and Sally (Cohen) Steinberg; m. Marvin Diamond, June 11, 1960 (div. May 1971); 1 child, Judith Lynne. AA, Wright Jr. Coll., 1957; BA, Rutgers U., 1974, JD, 1977. Bar: N.J. 1977. Assoc. Pressler & Pressler, PineBrook, N.J., 1978; prosecutor Essex County, Newark, 1979-80; sole practice Princeton, N.J., 1980-82; assoc. Guarini & Guarini, Jersey City, 1984, Law Offices of Louis B. Youmans P.A., Trenton, 1985-86, Heilbrunn, Finkelstein, Heilbrunn, Alfonso & Goldstein, Old Bridge, N.J., 1986—. Mem. ABA, N.J. Bar Assn., Middlesex County Bar Assn., Phi Theta Kappa. Club: Appalachian Mountain (N.Y.C.). Family and matrimonial, Contracts commercial, Workers' compensation. Office: Golden Shore & Zahn 141 Main St South River NJ 08882

DIAMOND, GUSTAVE, fed. judge; b. Burgettstown, Pa., Jan. 29, 1928; s. George and Margaret (Solinsky) D.; m. Emma L. Scarton, Dec. 28, 1974; 1 dau., Margaret Ann; 1 stepdau., Joanne Yoney. A.B., Duke U., 1951; J.D., Duquesne U., 1956. Bar: Pa. bar 1958, U.S. Ct. Appeals bar 1962. Law clk. to judge U.S. Dist. Ct., Pitts., 1955-61; 1st asst. U.S. atty. Western Dist. Pa., 1961-62, U.S. atty., 1963-69; partner firm Cooper, Schwartz, Diamond & Reich, Pitts., 1969-75; formerly individual practice law Washington, Pa.; former solicitor washington County, Pa.; now judge U.S. Dist. Ct. Western Dist. Pa. Mem. Am. Bar Assn., Pa. Bar Assn., Allegheny County Bar Assn., Washington County Bar Assn., Fed. Bar Assn. Office: US Dist Ct 7th and Grant St Pittsburgh PA 15230

DIAMOND, JEFFREY BRIAN, lawyer; b. N.Y.C., Sept. 17, 1950; s. Norman and Sylvia (Kurinsky) D.; m. Evalynn Joyce Stern, Apr. 15, 1977. BA, Dickinson Coll., 1972; JD, Pepperdine U., 1976. Bar: N.Mex. 1976, U.S. Dist. Ct. N.Mex. 1980, U.S. Ct. Appeals (10th cir.) 1985. Ptnr. Shuler & Diamond, Carlsbad, N.Mex., 1976-77, Paine, Blenden & Diamond, Carlsbad, 1977—; atty. Eddy County, Carlsbad, 1983-84. Chmn. Eddy County Dems., Carlsbad, 1981-85; pres. Carlsbad Jewish Congregation, 1979-81, Carlsbad Mental Health Assn., 1985—, also founder, Carlsbad Area Counselling and Resource Ctr., 1977-83, also bd. dirs. Mem. ABA, N.Mex. Bar Assn., Eddy County Bar Assn., Assn. Trial Lawyers Am., N.Mex. Trial Lawyers Assn., Am. Judicature Soc. Lodges: Rotary, Elks. Personal injury, Pension, profit-sharing, and employee benefits, Family and matrimonial. Home: 1427 Verdel Carlsbad NM 88220 Office: Paine Blenden & Diamond 208 W Stevens St PO Box 1387 Carlsbad NM 88220

DIAMOND, JOSEF, lawyer; b. Los Angeles, Mar. 6, 1907; s. Michael and Ruby (Shifrin) D.; m. Violett Diamond, Apr. 2, 1933 (dec. 1979); children—Joel, Diane Foreman; m. 2d, Ann Dulien, Jan. 12, 1981 (dec. 1984); m. Muriel Bach, 1986. B.B.A., U. Wash., 1929, J.D., 1931. Bar: Wash. 1931, U.S. Dist. Ct. (we. dist.) Wash. 1932, U.S. Ct. Appeals (9th cir.) 1934, U.S. Supreme Ct. 1944. Assoc. Caldwell & Lycette, Seattle, 1931-35; ptnr. Caldwell, Lycette & Diamond, 1935-45; ptnr. Lycette, Diamond & Sylvester, 1945-80, Diamond & Sylvester, 1980-82, of counsel, 1982—; owner, pres. Diamond Parking Inc., Seattle, 1945-70, chmn. bd., 1970—; chmn. Budget Rent a Car of Wash.-Oreg.; dir. Old Nat. Bank, various businesses. Bd. dirs. Am. Heart Assn., 1960; chmn. Wash. Heart Assn., 1962. Served as col. JAG U.S. Army, World War II. Decorated Legion of Merit. Mem. Assn. Trial Lawyers Wash., Wash. Bar Assn., Seattle Bar Assn., The Beavers, Mil. Engrs. Soc. Jewish. Clubs: Wash. Athletic, Bellevue, Athletic, Harbor, Seattle Yacht, Rainier, Columbia Tower. General corporate, Real property, Construction.

DIAMOND, PHILIP ERNEST, lawyer; b. Los Angeles, Feb. 11, 1925; s. William and Elizabeth (Weizenhaus) D.; m. Dorae Seymour (dec.); children—William, Wendy, Nancy; m. 2d, Jenny White Carson. B.A., UCLA, 1949, M.A., 1950; J.D., U. Calif.-Berkeley, 1953. Bar: Calif. 1953, U.S. Dist. Ct. (no., ea. and cen. dists.) Calif. 1953, U.S. Ct. Appeals (9th cir.) 1953. Law clk. to presiding justice Calif. Dist. Ct. Appeals, 1953-54; assoc. Landels & Weigel, San Francisco, 1954-60; ptnr. Landels Weigel & Ripley, San Francisco, 1960-62; sr. ptnr. Landels, Ripley & Diamond, San Francisco, 1962—; bd. dirs. Pierre Deux West, Berkley Ballet Theatre. Pres. Contra Costa Sch. Bd. Assn., 1966-68. Served with USN, 1943-46. Mem. ABA, Calif. State Bar Assn., San Francisco Bar Assn., Phi Beta Kappa. Democrat. Clubs: Commonwealth, Merchants and Exchange. Contracts commercial, General corporate, Real property. Office: 450 Pacific Ave San Francisco CA 94133

DIAMOND, STANLEY JAY, lawyer; b. Los Angeles, Nov. 27, 1927; s. Philip Alfred and Florence (Fadem) D.; m. Lois Jane Broida, June 22, 1969; children: Caryn Elaine, Diana Beth. B.A., UCLA, 1949; J.D., U. So. Calif., 1952. Bar: Calif. 1953. Practiced law Los Angeles, 1953—; dep. Office of Calif. Atty. Gen., Los Angeles, 1953; ptnr. Diamond & Tilem, Los Angeles, 1957-60, Diamond, Tilem & Colden, Los Angeles, 1960-79, Diamond & Wilson, Los Angeles, 1979—; lectr. music and entertainment law UCLA; Mem. nat. panel arbitrators Am. Arbitration Assn. Bd. dirs. Los Angeles Suicide Prevention Center, 1971-76. Served with 349th Engr. Constrn. Bn. AUS, 1945-47. Mem. Am., Calif., Los Angeles County, Beverly Hills bar assns., Assn. Trial Lawyers Am., Calif., Los Angeles trial lawyers assns., Am. Judicature Soc., Lawyers Club Los Angeles, Calif. Copyright Conf., Nat. Acad. Rec. Arts and Scis., Zeta Beta Tau, Nu Beta Epsilon. Entertainment. Home: 608 N Linden Dr Beverly Hills CA 90210 Office: 12304 Santa Monica Blvd 3d Floor Los Angeles CA 90025

DIAZ, BENITO HUMBERTO, lawyer; b. Guines, Cuba, Dec. 6, 1950; came to U.S., 1962; s. Benito Marcos and Concepcion (Valdes) D.; m. Maria Adelaida Badenes, May 7, 1983; children: Ana Maria, Benito Ignacio. B.A., St. Peter's Coll., Jersey City, 1973; J.D., Duke U., 1976. Bar: Fla. 1976, U.S. Dist. Ct. (so. dist.) Fla. 1977, U.S. Dist. Ct. (mid. dist.) Fla. 1979, U.S. Ct. Appeals (5th cir.) 1977, U.S. Ct. Appeals (11th cir.) 1981. Assoc. Blackwell, Walker, Gray, Powers, Flick & Hoehl, Miami, Fla., 1976-82, Carroll & Halberg, Miami, 1982—. Vol. United Way of Dade County, Miami, 1982-83. Mem. Fla. Bar, ABA, Dade County Bar Assn., Cuban Am. Bar Assn. Roman Catholic. Federal civil litigation, State civil litigation, Personal injury. Office: Carroll & Halberg 2701 S Bayshore Dr Miami FL 33133

DIAZ, RAMON VALERO, judge; b. Manila, Oct. 13, 1918; came to Guam, 1951; s. Vicente and Bibiana (Valero) D.; m. Josefina Dela Concepcion, July 3, 1945; children: Carlos, Marilu, Mariles, Maribel, Marilen, Maryann, Anthony, Vincent, Ramon, Maricar. PhB, U. St. Tomas, Manila, 1940, LLB, 1941; grad. U.S. Army J.A.G. Sch., 1945; Diploma Jud. Skills, Am. Acad. Jud. Edn., 1984. Bar: Philippines 1941, Guam 1956, U.S. Ct. Appeals (9th cir.) 1966, High Ct. of Trust Territories 1977, No. Marianas 1985. Assoc. Diokno Law Office, Manila, 1943-44; sole practice, Guam, 1960-80; judge Superior Ct. of Guam, Agana, 1980—; mem. U.S. Selective Service Bd. Appeals, Guam, 1950-62. Permanent deacon Roman Catholic ch. Served with PhilippineArmy, j.g., 1941-45. Mem. Am. Judges Assn., Nat. Council Juvenile and Family Ct. Judges, VFW. Survivor Bataan Death March, 1942. State civil litigation, Family and matrimonial, Juvenile. Home: 41 San Antonio St Dededo GU 96912 Home: PO Box AR Agana GU 96910 Office: Superior Ct of Guam Route 4 O'Brien St Agana GU 96910

DIB, ALBERT, lawyer, author; b. Bklyn., Apr. 6, 1923; s. John A. and Anastasia (Hanania) D.; m. Mary Toerner, Apr. 20, 1964; children—Susan, John, Arthur, Robert, Albert. B.A., Bklyn. Coll., 1947; J.D., St. John's U., 1951. Bar: N.Y. 1952, N.J. 1967, U.S. Ct. Appeals (2d cir.) 1952, U.S. Ct. Appeals (3d cir.) 1983. Assoc. Buhler King and Buhler, N.Y.C., 1957—; participant continuing edn. seminars on engring., constrn. and high tech. law; spl. cons. Concast Inc., 1970—, Catalyst Mag., 1976—; adj. prof. Stevens Inst. Tech.; lectr. Sch. Constrn. Studies, Fairleigh Dickinson U.; lectr. continuing edn. N.J. Inst. Tech. Counsel ch.-related cable TV. Served to lt. (j.g.) USNR, 1942-46. Recipient Spl. award as charter chmn. Am. Inst. Chem. Engrs. Engring. and Constrn. Contracting Com., 1972. Mem. N.Y. County Lawyers Assn., Am. Inst. Chem. Engrs. (affiliate), Am. Arbitration Assn. (constrn. panelist 1977—). Roman Catholic. Author: Forms and Agreements for Architects, Engineers and Contractors, 3 vols., 1976, also 8 semi-ann. supplements. Construction, Environment, Contracts commercial. Office: 274 Madison Ave New York NY 10016

DIBBLE, CHARLES LEMMON, lawyer; b. Sumter, S.C., July 30, 1943; s. Wortham Wyatt and Kathryn (Lemmon) D.; m. Virginia Newell, Sept. 18, 1982. Student, U. Paris (Sorbonne); BA, Davidson Coll., 1968; JD, U. S.C., 1977. Bar: S.C. 1977, U.S. Dist. Ct. S.C. 1978, U.S. Ct. Appeals (4th cir.) 1981, U.S. Claims Ct., U.S. Supreme Ct. Assoc. Cooper, Bowen, Beard & Smoot, Camden, S.C., 1977-78; ptnr. Cooper, Bowen, Beard & Smoot, Camden and Columbia, 1978-84, Cooper, Beard & Dibble, Columbia, 1984—. Mem. ABA (sect. internat. law), Fed. Bar Assn., Inter-Am. Bar Assn., S.C. Bar (internat. comml. transactions subcom. 1984—), Richland County Bar Assn., Kershaw County Bar Assn., Union Internat. des Advocats. Democrat. Episcopalian. Private international. Home: 914 Gregg St Columbia SC 29201 Office: Cooper Beard & Dibble PO Drawer 1240 Columbia SC 29202

DIBLASI, JOHN PETER, lawyer; b. N.Y.C., Sept. 22, 1955; s. Vincent Anthony and Roslyn Dorothy (Pizzitola) DiB.; m. Juliane Marvel Shafernich, June 13, 1981; 1 child, Elizabeth Lyn. A.B., Syracuse U., 1977; J.D., St. Johns U., 1980. Bar: N.Y. 1981, U.S. Dist. Ct. (so. and ea. dist.) N.Y. 1981. Examining atty. N.Y.C. Dept. Investigation, 1980-82; assoc. Pizzitola and DiBlasi, Bklyn., 1982—; counsel N.Y.C. Taxi and Limousine Commn., 1982. Active Mt. Vernon Youth Bd., N.Y., 1983-84; atty., advisor N.Y. State Bar Assn. Mock Trial Tournament, N.Y.C., 1980-83. Recipient Cert. Appreciation, Econ. Devel. Council N.Y.C., 1980-81, 81-82, 82-83. Mem. ABA (com. on complex criminal litigation 1981-82), N.Y. State Bar Assn. (com. automobile liability 1983—). Federal civil litigation, State civil litigation, Personal injury. Office: Pizzitola & DiBlasi PC 188 Montague St Brooklyn NY 11201

DICARLO, DOMINICK L., federal judge; b. Bklyn., Mar. 11, 1928; m. Esther Hansen; children: Vincent, Carl, Robert, Barbara. B.A., St. John's Coll., 1950, LL.B., 1953; LL.M., NYU. Asst. U.S. atty. Eastern Dist. N.Y., 1959-62, chief organized crime and racketeering sect., 1959-62; spl. asst. to U.S. atty. 1962; counsel to minority leader N.Y. Council, 1962-64; sole practice 1954—; mem. N.Y. State assembly, 1964-81, dep. minority leader, 1975-78; asst. sec. state for internat. narcotics matters Dept. State, Washington, 1981-84; judge U.S. Ct. Internat. Trade, N.Y.C., 1984—; vice chmn. N.Y. State Legis. Commn. on Crime, 1969-70, Select Commn. on Correctional Insts. and Programs, 1972-73. Office: US Ct Internat Trade One Federal Plaza New York NY 10007 *

DICHTER, BARRY JOEL, lawyer; b. Brookline, Mass., Feb. 19, 1950; s. Irving Melvin and Arlene Dichter; m. Judith Rand, Oct. 22, 1972; 1 child, Rebecca Lynn. AB magna cum laude, Harvard U., 1972, JD cum laude, 1975. Bar: Mass. 1975, N.Y. 1976, U.S. Dist. Ct. (so. and ea. dists.) N.Y. 1976, D.C. 1980, U.S. Dist. Ct. D.C. 1980, U.S. Ct. Appeals (D.C. cir.) 1985. Assoc. Webster & Sheffield, N.Y.C., 1975-82; assoc. Cadwalader, Wickersham & Taft, N.Y.C., 1983-84, ptnr., 1984—. Vice chmn. Harvard Law Sch. Fund, Cambridge, Mass., 1984—. Mem. Assn. of Bar of City of N.Y. (bankruptcy com.). Bankruptcy. Office: Cadwalader Wickersham & Taft 100 Maiden Ln New York NY 10038

DICHTER, MARK S., lawyer; b. Phila., Jan. 22, 1943; s. Harry B. and Mollie (Silverstein) D.; m. Tobey Gordon, Aug. 17, 1969; children—Aliza, Melissa. B.S.E.E., Drexel U., 1966; J.D. magna cum laude, Villanova U., 1969. Bar: Pa. 1969, U.S. Ct. Appeals (3d cir.) 1969, U.S. Supreme Ct. 1979. Assoc. Morgan, Lewis & Bockius, Phila., 1969-76, ptnr., 1976—. Bd. dirs. Phila. Singers. Mem. ABA (labor and employment law sect. mgmt. co-chmn. equal opportunity com., litigation sect., employment law com.), Fed. Bar Assn. (equal employment com. vice-chmn.), Def. Research Inst. (vice chmn. employment law com.). Mem. Nat. Employment Law Inst. (adv. bd. 1984—). Co-author Employee Dismissal Law: Forms and Procedures, 1986; editor-in-chief ann. Supplement Employment Discrimination Law, 1984—; co. editor Employment-at-will 1985,86, State-by-State Survey, 1984-85. Labor. Home: 1017 Clinton St Philadelphia PA 19107 Office: 2000 One Logan Sq Philadelphia PA 19103

DICKERSON, THOMAS ARTHUR, lawyer; b. Lockport, N.Y., Mar. 3, 1944; s. William Thomas II and Esther Rose (Gray) D.; m. Patricia Lynn Reddy, May 6, 1978; children: William, Briana. BA, Colgate U., 1979; MBA, JD, Cornell U., 1973. Bar: N.Y. 1975, U.S. Dist. Ct. (so. dist.) N.Y. 1975, U.S. Dist. Ct. (ea. dist.) N.Y. 1976, U.S. Ct. Appeals (2d cir.) 1982, U.S. Supreme Ct. 1984. Sole practice N.Y.C., 1977—. Contbr. articles to profl. jours. Mem. ABA, N.Y. State Bar Assn. (chmn. class action com. 1985—), Assn. of Bar of City of N.Y. (consumer affairs com.), Assn. Trial Lawyers Am. Federal civil litigation, Trademark and copyright, State civil litigation. Home: 34 Moore Rd Bronxville NY 10708 Office: 9 E 40th St New York NY 10016

DICKERSON, THOMAS PASQUALI, investment banker, lawyer; b. Ft. Benning, Ga., Mar. 8, 1950; s. John Osburn and Ina (de Pasquali) D.; m. Claire Anne Moore, May 22, 1976; children: Caroline, Susannah. AB in Econs., Harvard U., 1971, JD, 1974, MBA, 1979. Bar: N.Y. 1975, U.S. Dist. Ct. (ea. and so. dists.) N.Y. 1975, U.S. Ct. Appeals (2d cir.) 1975. Assoc. Coudert Bros., N.Y.C., 1974-77; asst. v.p. W.R. Grace & Co., N.Y.C., 1979-80; v.p. investment banking div. Lehman Bros. Kuhn Loeb, N.Y.C., 1981-85; 1st v.p. E.F. Hutton & Co., N.Y.C., 1985—. Trustee U.S. Commn. for United World Coll. Schs., N.Y.C., 1969-74, chmn., 1974-80, vice chmn., 1980—; treas., bd. dirs. Alliance to Save Energy, Washington, 1982—. Roman Catholic. Club: Harvard (N.Y.C.). Home: 76 Overlook Pl Rye NY 10580 Office: EF Hutton & Co 31 W 52d St New York NY 10019

DICKERSON, WILLIAM ROY, lawyer; b. Uniontown, Ky., Feb. 15, 1928; s. Banjamin Franklin and Honor Mae (Staples) D. B.A. in Acctg., Calif. State U.; J.D., UCLA, 1948. Bar: Calif. 1959. Dep. atty., ex-officio city prosecutor City of Glendale, Calif., 1959-62; assoc. James Brewer, Los Angeles, 1962-68, LaFollette, Johnson, Schroeter & DeHaas, Los Angeles, 1968-73; sole practice, Los Angeles, 1973—; lectr. and speaker in field. Bd. dirs. LosFeliz Improvement Assn., Zoning Commn.; co-chmn. Streets and Hwys. Commn. Mem. ABA, Calif. Bar Assn., Los Angeles County Bar Assn., Soc. Calif. Accts., Assn. Trial Lawyers Am., Century City Bar Assn., Fed. Bar Assn., Nat. Soc. Pub. Accts., Assn. So. Calif. Def. Counsel, Am. Film Inst., Internat. Platform Assn. State civil litigation, Professional negligence. Home and Office: 813 N Doheny Dr Beverly Hills CA 90210

DICKERT, NEAL WORKMAN, lawyer; b. Newberry, S.C., July 28, 1946; s. Elbert Jackson and Mary Elizabeth (Layton) D.; m. Floride Cantey Clarkson, June 4, 1969; 1 child, Neal Workman. B.A., Wofford Coll., 1968; M.B.A., U. S.C., 1969, J.D., 1974. Bar: S.C. 1974, Ga. 1975, U.S. Dist. Ct. S.C. 1975, U.S. Dist. Ct. (so. dist. Ga.) 1975, U.S. Ct. Appeals (11th cir.) 1981. Assoc. Hull, Towill, Norman and Barrett, Augusta, Ga., 1974—. Chmn., Richmond County Bd. Elections, Augusta, 1980—; bd. dirs. Episcopal Day Sch., 1982. Served with AUS, 1969-71. Decorated Bronze Star medal. Mem. Ga. Bar Assn. (bd. govs. 1986—), Ga. Def. Lawyers Assn., Def. Research Inst., Nat. Assn. R.R. Trial Counsel, Augusta Bar Assn. (past chmn. Law Day, past mem. exec. bd.), Wofford Coll. Nat. Alumni Assn. (dir. 1981-84). Episcopalian (sr. warden 1984). Lodge: Rotary (bd. govs. Augusta 1986—). Federal civil litigation, State civil litigation, Personal injury. Office: Hull Towill Norman & Barrett PO Box 1564 Augusta GA 30913

DICKEY, HARRISON GASLIN, lawyer; b. Mpls., June 26, 1937; s. Charles Lonsdale and Elizabeth Eakin (Haumerson) D.; m. Linda Strickland (div. Oct. 1981); children—Susan Elizabeth, Jennifer Lynn; m. Foye Jean Turner, Sept. 7, 1982. B.A., U. So. Calif., 1959; J.D., U. Ariz., 1962. Bar: Ariz. 1963, U.S. Dist. Ct. Ariz. 1963, U.S. Ct. Claims 1974, U.S. Tax Ct.

1974. Asst. atty. City of Tucson, Ariz., 1963-65; assoc., then ptnr. Holesapple-Conner-Jones-Mcfall & Johnson, 1965-72; sole practice, Tucson, 1972—. Served to 1st lt. USNG, 1962-68. Fellow Ariz. Bar Found. (founder); mem. Am. Judicature Assn., Ariz. Bar Assn., Pima County Bar Assn., Am. Arbitration Assn. (panel), Assn. Builders and Contractors, Alpha Tau Omega, Phi Delta Phi. Republican. Construction, Federal civil litigation, Contracts commercial. Home: 5942 Camino del Conde Tucson AZ 85718 Office: 2223 E Speedway Blvd Tucson AZ 85719

DICKEY, JOHN HORACE, lawyer; b. Edmonton, Alta., Can., Sept. 4, 1914; s. Horace Arthur and Catherine (Macdonald) D.; m. Eleanor Joyce Carney, Apr. 18, 1959; children—Thomas, Michael, John Robert, Stephen, Gregory, Mary. B.A., St. Mary's U., 1936, LL.D., 1980; LL.B., Dalhousie U., 1940; L.H.D., Mt. St. Vincent U., 1981. Bar: N.S. 1940, Apptd. Queen's Counsel 1957. Practiced in Halifax, 1940—; ptnr. McInnes, Cooper & Robertson, 1947-85, of counsel, 1985—; chmn., dir. Atlantic Trust Co. of Can.; hon. chmn. Stora Forest Industries Ltd.; dir. Dover Mills, Ltd.; mem. C.D. Howe Research Inst.; bd. dirs. C.D. Howe Meml. Found.; Canadian rep. Econ. and Social Council of UN, 1950; mem. Canadian Del. to UN, 1950. Mem. Canadian Ho. of Commons rep. Constituency Halifax, 1947-57; parliamentary asst. to minister Def. Prodn. and minister Trade and Commerce, 1952-57; Chmn. bd. Mt. St. Vincent U., 1969-73. Served to maj. Canadian Army, 1942-47. Mem. Canadian Bar Assn. (past v.p.), N.S. Barristers Soc. (past pres.), Liberal Fedn. Can. (past v.p.). General practice, Federal civil litigation, Oil and gas leasing. Home: 1532 Larch St, Halifax, NS Canada B3H 5W8 Office: PO Box 730, 1673 Bedford Row, Halifax, NS Canada

DICKEY, SAM S., lawyer; b. Wichita Falls, Tex., 1921; s. Charles Wallis and Edoline (Stephens) D.; m. Betty Alice Dickey, June 18, 1949; children: Andrew Charles, Stuart Gilbert. AB, Drury Coll., 1943; JD, U. Mo., 1949. Bar: Mo. 1949, U.S. Dist. Ct. Mo. 1949. Sole practice Springfield, Mo., 1949—; bd. dirs. Citizens Bank of Rogersville, Mo. Served to lt. comdr. USNR, 1942-63. Presbyterian. Avocations: golf, swimming, boating. Banking, General corporate, Estate planning.

DICKHANER, RAYMOND HENRY, lawyer; b. St. Louis, Mar. 4, 1950; s. Richard Alvin and Betty Rose (Zeis) D.; m. Lisa A. Ostrem, Oct. 26, 1974. B.A. cum laude, Westminster Coll., 1971, J.D., Washington U., 1974, LL.M., 1978. Bar: Mo. 1974, U.S. Dist. Ct. (ea. dist.) Mo. 1978, U.S. Tax Ct. 1978. Law clk. Mo. Ct. Appeals, St. Louis, 1974-75; assoc. Wegmann, Gasaway, Stewart, Schneider, Dickhaner, Tesreau & Stoll, P.C., Hillsboro, Mo., 1975—; city atty. City of Kimmswick, Mo., 1980-87. bd. suprs. Glaize Creek Sewer Dist., 1983-87. Recipient Lon O. Hocker Meml. Trial Lawyer award Mo. Bar Found., 1983. Mem. Univ. Mo. Extension Council Mem., 1986. Personal injury, State civil litigation, Estate taxation. Office: Wegmann Law Firm PO Box 127 Hillsboro MO 63050

DICKIE, ROBERT BENJAMIN, lawyer, consultant, educator; b. Glendale, Calif., Sept. 10, 1941; s. John A. and Dorothy C. (Merkel) D.; m. Susan J. Williams, Jan. 28, 1967; children—Amy, John, Thomas. B.A., Yale U., 1963; J.D., U. Calif.-Berkeley, 1967. Bar: Calif. 1967, N.Y. 1970, Mass. 1971. Assoc., Shearman & Sterling, N.Y.C., 1969-71, firm Sullivan & Worcester, Boston, 1971-77; asst. prof. mgmt. policy, Boston U., 1977-83, tenured assoc. prof., 1983—; cons. AT&T, Basking Ridge, N.J., World Bank, Washington, Fortune 1000 Cos., various law firms. Contbr. numerous articles to The Nat. Law Jour., Strategic Mgmt. Jour., Columbia Jour. of World Bus., others. Deacon Congl. Ch. of Weston, Mass., 1984—. Mem. Boston Bar Assn., Calif. Bar Assn., N.Y. Bar Assn., Acad. Mgmt. (bus. policy and planning div., social issues in mgmt. div.), Yale Club of Boston. Securities, Antitrust, General corporate. Home: 751 Boston Post Rd Weston MA 02193 Office: Sch Mgmt Boston Univ 621 Commonwealth Ave Boston MA 02215

DICKIESON, DAVID H., lawyer; b. Dearborn, Mich., Nov. 20, 1955; s. Harold Leonard and Victoria Catherine (Dolich) D.; m. Lisa Claire Bohlander, Aug. 27, 1983. BA, Cornell U., 1977; JD, U. Mich., 1979. Bar: D.C. 1980, U.S. Dist. Ct. D.C. 1981. Assoc. Bracewell & Patterson, Washington, 1980-82, Van Ness, Feldman et al, Washington, 1982-84, Barrett, Smith et al, Washington, 1984; trial atty. U.S. Dept. of Justice, Washington, 1984—. Mem. vestry Christ Epis. Ch., Dearborn, 1972-73. Mem. ABA, D.C. Bar Assn. Federal civil litigation, Personal income taxation, Administrative and regulatory. Home: 4651 Q St NW Washington DC 20007 Office: US Dept of Justice Tax Div 555 Fourth St NW Washington DC 20001

DICKINSON, THOMAS MORE, lawyer; b. Pitts., Dec. 15, 1955; s. Albert William and Doris Winefred (Gould) D.; m. Kathleen Marie Madigan, Sept. 22, 1985; 1 child, Kathleen Frances. AB in Polit. Sci., Holy Cross Coll., 1977; JD, Suffolk U., 1980. Bar: R.I. 1980, Mass. 1980, U.S. Dist. Ct. R.I. 1981, U.S. Dist. Ct. Mass. 1982, U.S. Ct. Appeals (1st cir.) 1982, U.S. Supreme Ct. 1985. Law clerk to presiding justice R.I. Supreme Ct., Providence, 1980-81; assoc. Weinstein, Bernstein & Burwick, P.C., Worcester, Mass., 1981-83; spl. asst. atty. gen. R.I. Dept. Atty. Gen., Providence, 1983-85, chief appellate div., 1986—. Editor-in-chief Suffolk U. Law Rev., Boston, 1979-80. Mem. ABA, R.I. Bar Assn., Assn. Trial Lawyers Am. Appellate practice, Federal civil litigation, Criminal. Home: 115 Morton Ave Woonsocket RI 02895 Office: 72 Pine St Providence RI 02903

DICKINSON, TIMOTHY L., lawyer, educator; b. Ann Arbor, Mich., Apr. 9, 1954; s. Thomas L. and Lois Jean (Smith) D. AB, U. Mich., 1975, JD, 1979; LLM, Columbia U., 1980. Bar: D.C. 1981; lic. pilot. Assoc. Gibson, Dunn & Crutcher, Washington, 1979—; stagiaire Commn. European Coms., Brussels, 1980-81; adj. prof. Georgetown U., Washington, 1983—. Jervey fellow, 1979; James B. Angell scholar U. Mich., 1975. Mem. ABA (chmn. com. fgn. claims 1983—, chmn. 1986—, task force internat. antitrust conflicts). Presbyterian. Private international, Insurance, Contracts commercial. Office: Gibson Dunn & Crutcher 1050 Connecticut Ave NW Washington DC 20036

DICKS, JACK WILLIAM, lawyer; b. Tampa, Fla., Sept. 12, 1949; s. James R. and June (Simmons) D.; m. Linda Edmunds, Apr. 29, 1972; children: Jennifer, Lindsay. BSc, U. Fla., 1971; JD, George Mason U., 1980. Bar: Va. 1980, Fla. 1981. Sole practice Orlando, Fla., 1980—; instr. Nat. Assn. Relators, Chgo., 1982—, Real Estate Securities and Syndication Inst., Chgo., 1982—. Author: Real Estate Forms, 1985, Questions and Answers on Real Estate, 1980, Syndicating Real Estate, 1985; contbr. articles to publs. Mem. Nat. Assn. Realtors, Real Estate Securities and Syndication Inst., Nat. Assn. Securities Dealers, Fla. Mortgage Brokerage Assn., Sigma Chi (v.p. 1970-71). Republican. Presbyterian. Avocations: skiing, travel, boating. Securities, Real property. Office: Dicks & Palmer 520 Crown Oak Centre Dr Longwood FL 32750

DICKSON, BRENT E., state judge. Judge Ind. Supreme Ct., Indpls., 1986—. Office: Ind Supreme Ct State House Indianapolis IN 46204 *

DICKSON, PETER DEAN, lawyer; b. Cin., Apr. 23, 1950; s. Donald Paul and Georganna Mary (Dean) D.; m. Janet Elisabeth Zoubek, May 24, 1975; children: Johanna Ann, Sean Donald. AB, Princeton U., 1973; JD with high honors, George Washington U., 1978. Bar: D.C. 1978, N.J. 1979. Asst. to governor State of N.J., Trenton, 1974-75; law sec. to chief justice Supreme Ct. N.J., Trenton, 1978-79; assoc. Van Ness, Feldman, Sutcliffe & Curtis, Washington, 1979-85, ptnr., 1985—. Mem. ABA, Am. Trial Lawyers Assn., Order of the Coif. Democrat. Episcopalian. Administrative and regulatory, Federal civil litigation, Legislative. Office: Van Ness Feldman Sutcliffe & Curtis 1050 Thomas Jefferson St Washington DC 20007

DICKSON, ROBERT JAY, lawyer; b. Waukegan, Ill., Sept. 20, 1947; s. Robert Jay and Suzanne Elizabeth (Smith) D.; m. J. Alyson Younghusband, June 21, 1969; children: Peter M., Joshua H., Theodore F., Ian A. BA, Northwestern U., 1969; JD, U. Ill., Champaign, 1972. Bar: Alaska 1972, U.S. Dist. Ct. Alaska 1972, U.S. Ct. Appeals (9th cir.) 1972, U.S. Supreme Ct. 1973. Assoc. Atkinson, Conway & Gagnon, Anchorage, 1972—, ptnr., 1974—; mem. Forum Com. Constrn. Industry, 1978—. Author: Alaska Construction Law, 1980, 6th rev. edit., 1986. Bd. dirs. Alaskan Scottish Club, 1973—, Meier Lake Conf. Ctr., Wasilla, Alaska, 1979—, Homer (Alaska) Soc. Natural History, 1985—. Served with USAR, 1970-76. Mem. ABA, Alaska Bar Assn., Anchorage Bar Assn., Am. Hosp. Attys. Episcopalian. Clubs: Tower, Capt. Cook Athletic (Anchorage). Avocations: piano, boating. Federal civil litigation, State civil litigation, Construction. Office: Atkinson Conway & Gagnon 420 L St Anchorage AK 99501

DICKSON, THOMAS PAGE, lawyer; b. Arlington, Va., June 4, 1944; s. Raymond Page and Mary Elizabeth (Hildebrand) D. AB, Harvard U., 1966, JD, 1972. Bar: N.Y. 1973, U.S. Dist. Ct. (so. and ea. dists.) N.Y. 1975, U.S. Ct. Appeals (2d cir.) 1975. Assoc. Milbank, Tweed, Hadley & McCloy, N.Y.C., 1972-80, ptnr., 1981—. Banking, Private international, General corporate. Office: Milbank Tweed Hadley & McCloy, 2-1 Uchisaiwai-Cho 2 Chome, Tokyo 100, Japan Home: 4-1-12 Minami-Azabu Minato-Ku, Hiroo Towers Apt 2032, Tokyo 106, Japan

DIDRIKSEN, CALEB H., III, lawyer; b. Cleve., Nov. 3, 1955; s. Caleb. H. Jr. and Eleanore Ann (Hoepli) D.; m. Megan L. Conway, Oct. 9, 1982. BS in Engring., U. Ill., 1977; JD, Tulane U., 1982. Bar: La. 1982, U.S. Dist. Ct. (ea., mid. and we. dists.) La. 1982, U.S. Ct. Appeals (5th cir.) 1982, U.S. Supreme Ct. 1987. Assoc. McGlinchey, Stafford, New Orleans, 1982-84, Monroe & Lemann, New Orleans, 1984—. Mem. counsel of Ministries Rayne United Meth. Ch., New Orleans, 1981-84, adminstrv. bd., 1982—. Mem. ABA, La. Bar Assn., New Orleans Bar Assn., La. Trial Lawyers Assn., World Trade Assn., Tau Beta Pi, Gamma Epsilon. Republican. Club: Paul Morphy Chess. Avocations: sport airplane piloting, travel, handyman. Personal injury, State civil litigation, Real property. Home: 2103 Calhoun St New Orleans LA 70118 Office: Monroe & Lemann 201 St Charles Ave New Orleans LA 70170

DIDZEREKIS, PAUL PATRICK, lawyer; b. Chgo., Mar. 17, 1939; s. Louis Joseph and Estelle (Traczyk) D.; m. Heather Joy Izod, Aug. 8, 1969; children—Alexandria, Alexis. B.B.A., Loyola U., Chgo., 1963, J.D., 1964. Bar: Ill. 1964, U.S. Sup. Ct. 1971. Atty. govt. affairs law and tax depts. Sears, Roebuck & Co., 1960-65; mem. Ashcraft & Ashcraft, Chgo., 1965-72; sole practice, Chgo., 1972-74; pres., ptnr. Didzerekis & Douglas Ltd., Chgo., 1974-78, sole practice, Chgo. and Wheaton, Ill., 1978—; mem. paraprofl. advb. bd. Lewis U. Coll. Law, Glen Ellyn, Ill., 1975, adj. prof. legal ethics in action program 1976-77. Bd. dirs., gen. counsel The Eleanor Assn., 1970—, pres., 1983-84. Recipient David C. Hilliard award Chgo. Bar Assn. 1973-74. Fellow Am. Acad. Matrimonial Lawyers; mem. DuPage County Bar Assn. Contbr. articles to profl. jours. State civil litigation, Family and matrimonial, Probate. Home: 2 S 209 Stuarton Dr Wheaton IL 60187 Office: 610 W Roosevelt Rd Suite B-2 Wheaton IL 60187

DIEDRICH, PETER JOSEPH, lawyer; b. San Francisco, Nov. 8, 1955; s. William Lawler and Margaret (Benson) D.; m. Donna Marie Ferullo, Mar. 8, 1986. BA, U. Calif., San Diego, 1977; JD, Georgetown U., 1981. Bar: Calif. 1981, U.S. Dist. Ct. (cen. dist.) Calif. 1981, U.S. Ct. Appeals (9th cir.) 1986. Assoc. Weissburg & Aronson, Los Angeles, 1981-83, Lawler, Felix & Hall, Los Angeles, 1983, Pettit & Martin, Los Angeles, 1983—. Republican. Roman Catholic. Avocation: motor racing. Federal civil litigation, State civil litigation, Government contracts and claims. Office: Pettit & Martin 355 S Grand Ave Los Angeles CA 90071

DIEDRICH, WILLIAM LAWLER, lawyer; b. De Kalb, Ill., Nov. 17, 1923; s. William Leo and Marie Antoinette (Lawler) D.; m. Margaret Lucille Benson, Aug. 6, 1949; children: Peter, Louise, Anne. B.A., St. Benedict's Coll., 1949; LL.B., Georgetown U., 1951. Bar: D.C. 1952, Calif. 1954, U.S. Supreme Ct. 1956. Assoc. Pillsbury, Madison & Sutro, San Francisco, 1952-63, ptnr., 1963—; dir. San Francisco Com. Urban Affairs, 1972-74. Coauthor: How to Defend an Employment Discrimination Case, 1982. Pres. bd. dirs. Catholic Social Service, San Francisco, 1980, 81; bd. dirs. Cath. Charities, 1982, Benedictine Coll., 1972-80; bd. dirs. San Francisco Bay Area Council Girl Scouts U.S., 1985—. Served to sgt. U.S. Army, 1943-46, Burma, India. Recipient Kans. Monk award Benedictine Coll., Atchison, 1977, Cross of St. Benedict, 1987. Mem. State Bar Calif., Bar Assn. San Francisco (joint chmn. com. equal employment 1969-72, chmn. com. labor laws 1979-81), Bar Assn. D.C. Democrat. Roman Catholic. Club: Commonwealth (San Francisco). Labor. Home: 355 Santa Clara Ave San Francisco CA 94127 Office: Pillsbury Madison & Sutro 225 Bush St San Francisco CA 94104

DIEFFENBACH, CHARLES MAXWELL, emeritus law educator, lawyer; b. Westfield, N.Y., July 9, 1909; s. Arthur Warren and Mary Bertha (Meyer) D.; m. Gladys Ethel Gray, June 29, 1935; children—Gretchen Dieffenbach Gehlbach, Roxann Huschard. B.S. in Civil Engring., U. Ala., 1934; postgrad. Bus. Sch., Harvard U., 1934-35; M.A. in Econs., U. Cin., 1948; J.D., Ohio No. U., 1957. Bar: Ohio 1957. Meat packing exec. H.H. Meyer Packaging Co., Cin., 1935-55; from asst. prof. to prof. law Chase Coll. Law, Cin., 1957-65; prof. bus. adminstrn. N.Mex. State U., Las Cruces, 1965-68; prof. law Chase Coll. Law, No. Ky. U., Highland Heights, 1968-79, prof. law emeritus, 1980—; vis. prof. law Detroit Coll. Law, 1979-80. Served to maj. U.S. Army, 1942-46, ETO. Republican. Episcopalian. Club: University (Cin.). Probate, Contracts commercial, General corporate. Home: 710 Ivy Ave Cincinnati OH 45246 Office: No Ky U Chase Coll Law 508 Nunn Hall Highland Heights KY 41076

DIEHL, DEBORAH HILDA, lawyer; b. Troy, N.Y., Feb. 13, 1951; d. Warren S. and Norma K. (Apple) D.; m. Peter W. Hoffman, Feb. 29, 1980; 1 child, Alexandra Ellen. Student, U. de Rouen, France, 1971-72; BA, St. Lawrence U., 1973; JD, Syracuse U., 1976; postdoctoral, George Washington U., 1978-79. Bar: N.Y. 1977, D.C. 1981, Ohio 1982. Atty. U.S. Dept. Agriculture, Washington, 1976-81; assoc. Thompson, Hine & Flory, Columbus, Ohio, 1981-87, Semmes, Bowen & Semmes, Balt., 1987—. Vol. German Village Soc., Columbus, 1982—, WOSU-AM-FM-TV, Columbus, 1983—. Mem. ABA, Ohio Bar Assn., Columbus Bar Assn. Avocations: gardening, running. General corporate, Municipal bonds, Public utilities.

DIEHL, JOSEPH BURNETT, lawyer; b. Kankakee, Ill., Mar. 25, 1949; s. Howard Everett and Bessie Mae (Burnett) D.; m. Dorene Marion Keller, July 12,1969 (div. July 1979); 1 child, Jennifer Lin; m. Debbi Lynn Sousa, Jan. 1, 1983; children: Gene Allen, Brian Francis. BS, Northern Ill. U., 1971; JD, John Marshall Law Sch., 1979. Bar: Ill. 1979. Controller Heitman Mortgage Investors, Chgo., 1976-79, Bayswater Realty and Investment Trust, Chgo., 1979; pres. Diehl Assocs., Ltd., Chgo., 1979-82; partnership controller Montgomery Realty Investors, San Francisco, 1982; ptnr., chief fin. officer TCW Realty Advisors, Los Angeles, 1982—; cons. in field, 1985—. Mem. ABA, Ill. Bar Assn., Chgo. Bar Assn., Ill. Soc. CPA's, Am. Inst. CPA's, Nat. Council Real Estate Investment Fiduciaries (chmn. acctg. com. 1986—), U.S. Parachute Assn. Avocations: distance running, sky diving, Civil War history, computer sci. Real property, Pension, profit-sharing, and employee benefits. Office: TCW Realty Advisors 400 S Hope #600 Los Angeles CA 90071

DIEHL, KRISTIN KNOELL, lawyer; b. Pitts., July 17, 1953; d. William H. and E. Anne (Kirkland) K.; m. Kerry N. Diehl, Nov. 12, 1983. BBA, Bucknell U., 1975; JD, U. Pitts., 1980. Bar: Pa. 1980, U.S. Dist. Ct. (we. dist.) Pa. 1980; CPA, Pa. Staff acct. Price, Waterhouse and Co., Washington, 1975-77; assoc. Meyer, Unkovic & Scott, Pitts., 1980—. Republican. Presbyterian. General corporate, Securities, Probate. Home: 93 Country Club Dr Pittsburgh PA 15241 Office: Meyer Unkovic & Scott 1300 Oliver Bldg Pittsburgh PA 15222

DIEHM, JAMES WARREN, lawyer; b. Lancaster, Pa., Nov. 6, 1944; s. Warren G. and Verna M. (Hertzler) D.; m. Cathleen M. Hohmeier; 1 child, Elizabeth Ann. B.A., Pa. State U., 1966; J.D., Georgetown U., 1969. Bars: D.C. 1969, V.I. 1975. Asst. U.S. atty. Washington, 1970-74; asst. atty. gen. Atty. Gen.'s Office U.S. V.I., St. Croix, 1974-76; from assoc. to ptnr. Isherwood, Hunter & Diehm, St. Croix, 1976-83; U.S. atty. U.S. V.I., St. Croix, 1983—; bar examiner U.S. V.I. Bar, 1979-87; vis. assoc. prof. Del. U. Law Sch., 1987—. Mem. ABA. Republican. Lutheran. Home: PO Box 722 RD 1 Newmanstown PA 17073 Office: Widener U Del Law Sch PO Box 7474 Concord Pike Wilmington DE 19803 *

DIEKER, JAMES WILLIAM, lawyer; b. Quincy, Ill., Mar. 7, 1955; s. William and Norma J. (Sullivan) D. BS in Accountancy, U. Ill., 1977; JD, John Marshall Law Sch., 1980. Bar: Ill. 1981, U.S. Dist. Ct. (cen. dist.) Ill. 1981. Assoc. Harrington, Porter & Pope, Champaign, Ill., 1980-83; sole practice Champaign, 1983—. Mem. council St. Matthews Ch., Champaign, 1983—; bd. dirs. Arrowhead council Boy Scouts Am., Champaign, 1983—, The Crisis Nursery of Champaign County, 1983—. Recipient Award of Merit Boy Scouts Am., 1986. Mem. ABA, Ill. Bar Assn., Chgo. Bar Assn., Champaign County Bar Assn. Republican. Roman Catholic. Club: Exchange (Champaign) (pres. 1985-86, dist. dir. 1986—, Champaign Exchangite of Yr., 1986). Lodge: K.C. Avocations: hiking, backpacking. Oil and gas leasing, Real property, Probate. Office: 1806 Round Barn Rd Champaign IL 61821-0805

DIENST, GERALD A., lawyer; b. Newark, Mar. 14, 1939; s. Arthur E. and Doris Elma (Snyder) D.; m. Rose G. Tobia, Aug. 7, 1972; stepchildren—Glenn S. Graef, Thomas F. Graef. B.A., Lafayette Coll., 1961; J.D., Rutgers U., 1964. Bar: N.J. 1964, D.C. 1965, U.S. Dist. Ct. (dist.) N.J. 1965, U.S. Dist. Ct. (ea. and so. dists.) N.Y. 1978, N.Y. 1983. Real estate examiner N.J. Realty Title Ins., Newark, 1965-66; sole practice, Clark and Red Bank, N.J., 1966-79; mem. Freeman & Bass, Newark, 1980-81; mem. Alan J. Karcher, P.A., Sayreville, N.J., 1981-84; mem. Friedman and Blank, 1984—. Mem. ABA, N.J. Bar Assn., D.C. Bar Assn., Monmouth County Bar Assn., N.Y. County Lawyers Assn., Trial Lawyers Assn. Am., N.J., Trial Lawyers Assn. Presbyterian. Club: Lions (Red Bank, N.J.). State civil litigation, Personal injury, Real property. Home: 1 Anderson St Monmouth Beach NJ 07750 Office: 1 Broad St Freehold NJ 07728

DIETER, JAMES GEORGE, lawyer; b. Abilene, Kans., June 21, 1926; s. Frank Henry and Ina Ruth (Brown) D.; m. Barbara Ann Berger, July 18, 1950; children—Diane Elizabeth, Douglas Michael. B.S. in Chem. Engring., Kans. State U., 1949; J.D., George Washington U., 1953; M.B.A., Mo. U., 1960. Bar: D.C. 1953, Kans. 1953, Mo. 1954, U.S. Patent Office 1954, Tex. 1968, U.S. Supreme Ct. 1977, Calif. 1978. Corp. atty. Spencer Chem. Co., Kansas City, Mo., 1953-62; staff atty. Gulf Oil Corp., Kansas City, 1962-67, counsel, Houston, 1967-71; v.p. law, sec. Gen. Atomic Co., La Jolla, Calif., 1972-77; div. counsel Bechtel Inc., Houston, 1977-81; chief Counsel Bechtel Petroleum, Inc., Houston, 1981-85; prin. counsel, Bechtel, Inc., Houston, 1985—. Bd. dirs. Kans. State U. Research Found., 1958-62. Served to lt. USCG, 1951-53. Mem. Am. Intellectual Property Law Assn., ABA, Tex. Bar Assn., Houston Bar Assn., Calif. Bar Assn., D.C. Bar Assn., Am. Corp. Counsel Assn. (pres., dir. Houston chpt. 1984-85), Kans. State U. Found. (trustee 1982-85). Republican. Presbyterian. Clubs: Petroleum, University, Champions Golf (Houston). Antitrust, Construction, Patent. Office: Bechtel Inc PO Box 2166 Houston TX 77252-2166

DIETERLY, DOUGLAS KEVIN, lawyer; b. Kokomo, Ind., Jan. 23, 1955; s. Grover Eugene and Sophie (Rezo) D.; m. Debra Ann Healton, June 6, 1976; 1 child, Jennifer Elizabeth. BA summa cum laude, Ball State U., 1977; JD magna cum laude, Ind. U., 1980. Bar: Ind. 1980, U.S. Dist. Ct. (no. and so. dists.) Ind. 1980, U.S. Ct. Appeals (7th cir.) 1980. Assoc. Barnes & Thornburg, South Bend, Ind., 1980—; advisor Nat. Moot Ct. Team, Indpls., 1980; cons., judge Notre Dame U. Trial Advocacy Program, South Bend, 1980—. Contbg. author The Student Mag., Nashville. Dir. Bapt. Student Union, Notre Dame U., 1980—; rep. United Way, South Bend, 1980—; speaker, lectr. Pub. Sch. System Law Day, South Bend, 1980-84. Mem. ABA, Ind. Bar Assn., St. Joseph County Bar Assn. Republican. Southern Baptist. Avocations: hunting, fishing, tennis. Federal civil litigation, State civil litigation, Insurance. Home: 18025 Crowhill Dr Apt C South Bend IN 46637 Office: Barnes & Thornburg 600 1st Source Bank Ctr 100 N Michigan South Bend IN 46601

DIETRICH, DEAN RICHARD, lawyer; b. Milw., Sept. 22, 1952; s. Leon Martin and Enid Mary (Gamalski) D.; m. Cecelia Ann Frank, June 25, 1976; children; Sarah Elizabeth, Kathleen Ann. BS in Polit. Sci., Marquette U., 1974, JD, 1977. Bar: Wis., U.S. Dist. Ct. (ea. and we. dists.) Wis. Assoc. Kramer, Nelson, Kussmaul, Howley, Fennimore, Wis., 1977-79, Mulcahy & Wherry, S.C., Wausau, Wis., 1979—. Bd. dirs. March of Dimes, Wausau; mem. Greater Wausau Cath. Edn. Com., 1985—; council mem. St. Anne's Parish. Mem. ABA (labor and local govt. sect.), Wis. Bar Assn. (labor and local govt. sect., bd. dirs. young lawyers div. 1984—, mem. services com. 1985—), Marathon County Bar Assn. (sec., treas.), Wausau C. of C. (chmn. legislature action subcom. on civil rights reform). Lodge: Rotary. Avocations: golf, ice hockey. Labor, Local government, Workers' compensation. Home: 320 S 8th Ave Wausau WI 54401 Office: Mulcahy & Wherry SC 408 3d StPO Box 1004 Wausau WI 54402-1004

DIETZ, CHARLTON HENRY, lawyer; b. LeMars, Iowa, Jan. 8, 1931; s. Clifford Henry and Mildred Verna (Eggensperger) D.; m. Viola Ann Lange, Aug. 17, 1952; children: Susan (Mrs. Jay Kakuk), Robin (Mrs. Jack Mayfield), Craig. B.A., Macalester Coll., 1953; J.D., William Mitchell Coll. Law, 1957. Bar: Minn. 1957. Mem. public relations staff Minn. Mining and Mfg. Co., St. Paul, 1952-58; atty. Minn. Mining and Mfg. Co., 1958-70, asso. counsel, asst. sec., 1970-72, asst. gen. counsel, sec., 1972-75, gen. counsel, sec., 1975-76, gen. counsel, v.p. legal affairs, 1976—, also dir.; bd. dirs. Eastern Heights State Bank, chmn., 1981—; bd. dirs. State Bond and Mortgage Co.; instr. William Mitchell Coll. Law, 1960-74, trustee, 1974-86, pres., 1980-83. Bd. dirs. St. Paul Area YMCA, 1973-80, chmn., 1978-80; bd. dirs. Minn. Citizens Council on Crime and Justice, 1976—, pres., 1982-84; trustee United Theol. Sem., 1976-82; bd. dirs. St. Paul United Way, 1980—, Ramsey County Hist. Soc., 1979-86; mem. Conferees of Minn. Citizens Conf. on the Cts., 1981-82; trustee Macalester Coll., 1983—; bd. dirs. Indian Head council Boy Scouts Am., 1985—. Fellow Am. Bar Found.; mem. ABA, Fed. Bar Assn., Minn. Bar Assn., Ramsey County Bar Assn., Am. Soc. Corp. Secs., Assn. Gen. Counsel. Republican. Mem. United Ch. of Christ. Clubs: Mason (Shriner, Jester), St. Paul Athletic, North Oaks, Minn. General corporate. Home: 1 Birch Ln North Oaks MN 55110 Office: Minn Mining and Mfg Co 3M Center Saint Paul MN 55144

DIETZ, RICHARD JOSEPH, lawyer; b. Milw., July 6, 1944; s. Roy Joseph and Esther Catherine (Murphy) D.; m. Candace A. Wifvat, Dec. 27, 1967; children: Brian, Kristin, Margaret, Colleen. BA, Marquette U., 1967, JD, 1969. Bar: Wis. 1969, U.S. Dist. Ct. (ea. dist.) Wis. 1969. Asst. dist. atty. Brown County, Green Bay, Wis., 1969-71; ptnr. McKay & Dietz, Green Bay, Wis., 1971-76; dep. city atty. City of Green Bay, Wis., 1976-77, city atty., 1977-79; city atty. City of De Pere, Wis., 1979—; labor cons. City of Seymour, Wis., 1981—, Police and Fire Commn. City of Green Bay, 1982.; lectr. labor relations Mcpl. Attys. Inst., 1977, 84. Bd. dirs. Cerebral Palsy N.E. Wis., Green Bay, 1971; mem. exec. com. Brown County Rep. Party, 1972. Mem. Wis. Bar Assn., Brown County Bar Assn., Nat. Inst. Mcpl. Law Officers. Roman Catholic. Lodge: Ancient Order of Hibernians in Am. (local pres. 1982-83). Avocations: golf, hunting, fishing. Local government, Labor. Home: 800 E St Francis Rd De Pere WI 54115 Office: City of De Pere 335 S Broadway De Pere WI 54115

DIETZE, JOHN LESLIE, corporate lawyer; b. N.Y.C., July 29, 1942; s. William E. and Iris E. (Buckle) D.; m. Jestina J. Nyenkan, May 22, 1971; children: Anthony, Nicholas. BA, Hofstra U., 1964; JD, George Washington U., 1967. Bar: D.C. 1968, N.Y. 1970. Assoc. counsel USLIFE Corp., N.Y.C., 1983—; v.p., gen. counsel, sec. USLIFE Realty Corp. Fla. subs. USLIFE Corp., N.Y.C., 1984—. Mem. N.Y.C. Bar Assn. Real property. Home: 56 S Portland Ave Brooklyn NY 11217 Office: USLIFE Corp 125 Maiden Ln New York NY 10038

DIGENOVA, JOSEPH E., lawyer. U.S. atty. Washington, 1987—. Office: US Courthouse 34th and Constitution Ave NW Room 2800 Washington DC 20001 *

DIGGES, EDWARD S(IMMS), JR., Lawyer; b. Pitts., June 30, 1946; s. Edward S. and Maria Jane (McHugh) D.; m. Wendy L. Worob May 31, 1969; children: Courtney, Edward III, Ashley, John, Brittany. A.B., Princeton U., 1968; J.D., U. Md., 1971. Bar: Md. 1972, D.C. 1981, U.S. Supreme Ct. 1975. With staff of gov. State of Md., Annapolis, 1973; ptnr. Piper & Marbury, Washington and Balt., 1977-84; mng. ptnr. Digges, Wharton & Levin, Annapolis, 1984—; instr. Advanced Bus. Law, Johns Hopkins U., 1975-78; lectr. Civil Procedure, U. Balt. Law Sch., 1976-78; on govs. commn. to revise Md. code, 1978—. Mem. Alumni Council Mercersburg Acad., 1982—, chmn. 1987—. Bd. Advisors Indian Creek Sch.,

1982—, chmn. 1985—; pres. Beacon Hill Community Assn., 1978-86. Served U.S. Army R.O.T.C. 1970-71. Fellow Am. Bar Found., Md. Bar Found.; mem. ABA, Md. State Bar Assn. (bd. govs. 1981-82), D.C. Bar Assn., Bar Assn. Balt. City (treas. 1982-83), Anne Arundel County Bar Assn., Am. Law Inst., Am. Bd. Trial Adv. (pres. Md. chpt. 1984—), Internat. Assn. Def. Counsel, Fedn. Ins. and Corp. Counsel, Am. Judicature Soc., Md. Assn. Def. Trial Counsel (pres. 1978), Def. Research and Trial Lawyers Assn., Scribes. Democrat. Roman Catholic. Clubs: Center (Balt.), Merchant's (Balt.), Annapolis Yacht, So. Md. Soc. (bd. govs., pres.-elect 1987); Mid Ocean (Bermuda). Contbr. articles to profl. jours. Federal civil litigation, State civil litigation. Home: Hinchingham Chestertown MD 21620-0209 Office: 225 Duke of Gloucester St Annapolis MD 21401-6610

DIGNAN, THOMAS GREGORY, JR., lawyer; b. Worcester, Mass., May 23, 1940; s. Thomas Gregory and Hester Clare (Sharkey) D.; m. Mary Anne Connor, Sept. 16, 1978; children—Kellyanne E., Maryclare E. B.A., Yale U., 1961; J.D., U. Mich., 1964. Bar: Mass. 1964, U.S. Supreme Ct. 1968. Assoc. firm Ropes & Gray, Boston, 1964-74; ptnr. firm Ropes & Gray, 1974—; spl. asst. atty. gen. State of Mass., 1974-76; dir. Boston Edison Co. Asst. editor: Mich. Law Review, 1963-64; contbr. articles to profl. jours. Bd. dirs. Family Counseling and Guidance Centers, Inc., 1967-76, 78—, v.p., 1983—; Bd. dirs. Gov.'s Mgmt. Task Force, 1979-81; mem. fin. com. Town of Sudbury, 1982-85; moderator Town of Sudbury, 1985—; bd. advisers Environ. Law Ctr., Vt. Law Sch., 1981—; mem. lawyers com. Atomic Indsl. Forum; mem. com. vis. U. Mich. Law Sch. Mem. Am. Bar Assn., Mass. Bar Assn., Boston Bar Assn., Assn. Internationale du Droit Nucleaire, Am. Nuclear Soc., Am. Law Inst., Order of the Coif.; mem. Phi Delta Phi. Republican. Roman Catholic. Clubs: Downtown, Union. Federal civil litigation, Nuclear power, Environment. Home: 8 Saddle Ridge Rd Sudbury MA 01776 Office: 225 Franklin St Boston MA 02110

DI JOSEPH, STEVEN, lawyer; b. N.Y.C., June 5, 1948; s. Arnold Edward and Christine (Mariano) Di J.; m. Jill Di Joseph, Aug. 2, 1976; children: Robin Brett, Justin Steven. B.A., N.Y.U., 1970; J.D., Bklyn. Law Sch., 1973. Bar: N.Y. 1974, U.S. Dist. (so. and ea. dists.) N.Y. 1974, U.S. Ct. Appeals (2d and 5th cirs.) 1974, U.S. Supreme Ct. 1977. Asst. dist. atty. Kings County, N.Y., 1973-75; assoc. Siff & Newman, P.C., N.Y.C., 1975-81, ptnr., 1982-83; mng. atty., Morris J. Eisen, P.C., N.Y.C., 1983-84, Peter E. DeBlasio P.C., N.Y.C., 1984-86; sr. ptnr., DiJoseph & Gluck, N.Y.C., 1986—; lectr. on appellate practice; cons. in field. Mem. ABA, (com. rules criminal procedure and evidence 1977-79, vice chmn. com. appellate practice 1983—). N.Y. Bar Assn. (award 1981), N.Y. County Lawyers Assn., Nat. Dist. Attys. Assn., Lawyer to Lawyer Consultation Panel. Author: The Liberalization of Discovery Rules with Respect to Relevant Medical Records and Related Materials, 1981. Contbr. articles on law to profl. jours. State civil litigation, Personal injury, Insurance. Office: 233 Broadway New York NY 10279

DIKMAN, MICHAEL, lawyer; b. Jamaica, N.Y., Oct. 23, 1936; s. Leo and Dorothy (Meyerson) D.; m. Priscilla Sherman, Sept. 11, 1960 (div. Dec. 1984); children: David, Donna. AB, Dartmouth Coll., 1958; LLB, Cornell U., 1961. Bar: N.Y. 1961, U.S. Dist. Ct. (ea. and so. dists.) N.Y. 1964, U.S. Supreme Ct. 1965. Ptnr. Jamaica, 1962-69, Dikman Dikman & Botter, Jamaica, 1969—. Contbr. articles to profl. jours. Mem. Jamaica Lawyers Club (past pres. 1965-66), Brandeis Assn. (past pres. 1974-75), Fed. Lawyers Club (past pres. 1972-73), Queens County Bar Assn. (past pres. 1978-79), N.Y. State Bar Assn. (bd. dirs. family law sect.), Am. Acad. Matrimonial Lawyers. Democrat. Jewish. Lodge: Lions (past pres. 1967). Avocations: magic, handball, tennis, squash, bridge. Family and matrimonial. Home: 152-18 Union Turnpike Flushing NY 11367 Office: Dikman Dikman & Botter 161-10 Jamaica Ave Jamaica NY 11432

DIKTAS, CHRISTOS JAMES, lawyer; b. Hackensack, N.J., June 17, 1955; s. Christos James and Elpiniki (Angelou) D. Student U. Salonika (Greece), 1976, U. Copenhagen (Denmark), 1976; B.A., Montclair State Coll., 1977; J.D., Calif. Western Sch. Law, 1981. Bar: N.J. 1982, U.S. Dist. Ct. N.J. 1982. Law sec. Honorable James F. Madden, Superior Ct. Judge, Hackensack, N.J., 1981-82; sr. assoc. Klinger, Nicolette, Mavroudis & Honig, Hackensack, 1982-85; ptnr. Montecallo & Diktas, Hackensack, 1985-86, Biagiotti, Marino, Montecallo & Diktas, Hackensack, 1986—; asst. counsel Bergen County, 1986-87; atty. zoning bd. adjustment Borough Cliffside Park, N.J., 1986—. Editor lead articles Calif. Western Internat. Law Jour., 1980-81. Campaign dir. Kingman for Senate Com., Bergen County, N.J., 1983; mcpl. coordinator Kean for Gov. campaign, 1985; asst. treas. Arthur F. Jones for Congress, 9th Congl. Dist., 1986—. Mem. ABA, N.J. Bar Assn., Bergen County Bar Assn., Phi Alpa Delta (Campbell E. Beaumont chpt.) (parliamentarian 1978-81). Order of Am. Hellenic Edn. Progressive Assn. Republican. Greek Orthodox. Lodge: Sons of Pericles (5th dist. gov. 1976-77, supreme gov. 1977-78). Real property, Contracts commercial, General practice. Home: 243 Columbia Ave Cliffside Park NJ 07010 Office: Biagiotti Marino Montecallo & Diktas 294 Union St Hackensack NJ 07601

DILEONE, PETER, JR., lawyer; b. Providence, R.I., Feb. 29, 1908; s. Peter Sr. and Antonietta (Giugliano) Di L.; m. Alice Ruth Broeckel; children: Linda Di Leone Klein, Paulette Di Leone Novak. AB, Case Western Res. U., 1932, LLB, 1936. Bar: U.S. Dist. Ct. Cleve. 1943, U.S. Supreme Ct. 1960. Sole practice Cleve., 1943—. Pres. City Club Forum Found., 1977-85. Mem. Cleve. Bar Assn., Am. Arbitration Assn., Nat. Acad. of Arbitrators (bd. of govs. 1972-75). Democrat. Club: Cleve. City (pres. 1965-66). General practice, Labor. Home: 17100 Van Aken Blvd Shaker Heights OH 44120 Office: 819 National City Bank Bldg Cleveland OH 44114

DILG, JOSEPH CARL, lawyer; b. Dallas, Apr. 1, 1951; s. Millard John and Helen Mary (Gill) D.; m. Alexandra Gregg, Aug. 5, 1972; children: Helen Lane, Mary Saunders. BA, So. Meth. U., 1973; JD with highest honors, U. Tex., 1976. Bar: Tex. 1976. Assoc. Vinson & Elkins, Houston, 1976-83, ptnr., 1983—. Editor U. Tex. Law Rev., 1976. Named Outstanding Editor U. Tex. Law Rev., 1976. Mem. ABA, Tex. Bar Assn., Houston Bar Assn., Chancellors, Order of Coif. General corporate, Private international. Office: Vinson & Elkins 3300 First City Tower 1001 Fannin Houston TX 77002-6760

DILKS, PARK BANKERT, JR., lawyer; b. Phila., Mar. 25, 1928; s. Park Bankert and Gertrude Scott (Hilton) D. A.B., U. Pa., 1948, J.D., 1951. Bar: Pa. 1952, D.C. 1951, U.S. Supreme Ct. 1962. Asst. dist. atty. Phila., 1952; assoc. firm Souser & Schumacker, Phila., 1953-60; assoc. firm Morgan, Lewis & Bockius, Phila., 1961-63, ptnr., 1964—; chmn. bd. U.S. Investment Fund, 1973—; dir. Broadstone Group, Inc., N.Y.C. Served as 1st lt. USAR, 1952-58. Mem. ABA, Pa. Bar Assn., Phila. Bar Assn., D.C. Bar Assn., Fed. Bar Assn., Assn. Bar City N.Y., Phi Beta Kappa. Club: Union League. Private international, Banking. Home: 605 W Gravers Ln Philadelphia PA 19118 Office: 2000 One Logan Sq Philadelphia PA 19103

DILL, EVERETT CHARLES, lawyer; b. Deshler, Ohio, May 8, 1929; s. Charles and Anna Maria Katharina (Schilling) D.; m. Karol Ann Kirkpatrick, Feb. 18, 1967; children—Anne Marie, Alyson Ruth, Alyssa Ellen. B.Sc. in Bus. Adminstrn., Ohio State U., 1951, J.D., 1952; M.B.A., U. Toledo, 1962. Bar: Ohio 1952, Mich. 1980. With Marathon Oil Co., Findlay, Ohio, 1954-66; tax adviser Esso Inter-Am., Inc., Coral Gables, Fla., 1966-67; tax atty., mgr. Gerber Products Co., Fremont, Mich., 1968-77; tax counsel Upjohn Co., Kalamazoo, Mich., 1977—. Served with U.S. Army, 1952-54. Mem. Ohio State Bar Assn., Mich. Bar Assn., ABA, Tax Execs. Inst. (nat. bd. dirs. 1975-77). Republican. Methodist. Corporate taxation. Office: Upjohn Co 7000 Portage Rd Kalamazoo MI 49001

DILL, JOHN CHRISTOPHER, lawyer; b. Oklahoma City, Oct. 17, 1951; s. Francis E. and Helen (Payne) D.; m. Aloah Kay Kincaid, Aug. 25, 1979. B.A., Okla. State U., 1973; J.D., U. Okla., 1979. Bar: Okla., D.C. Legis. dir. to Congressman James Jones U.S. Ho. of Reps., Washington, 1977-81, counsel to chmn. Budget Com., 1981-85; dir. govt. relations Dickinstein-Shapiro & Morin, Washington, 1985—. Recipient award of excellence HUD, 1981. Democrat. Legislative. Office: Dickstein Shapiro & Morin 2101 L St NW Washington DC 20037

DILL, WILLIAM ALLEN, lawyer; b. Sharon, Pa., May 18, 1918; s. Harry Armitage and Mary Rose (McCann) D.; m. Marjorie Croft, Sept. 3, 1946; children—Mary Alyson, Laurie Ann, Thomas Allen. B.S., U. Pitts., 1940, J.D., 1948. Bar: Pa. 1949. Pilot, Pan Am. Airways, North and South Atlantic, N.Y.C., 1941-42, Central and South Am., Miami, 1942-43; spl. lectr. U. Pitts. Sch. Transp., 1946-48; assoc. Fruit & Francis, Sharon, 1949-68; ptnr. Fruit Dill, Goodwin & Scholl, Sharon, 1968—; asst. dist. atty., 1952-54; solicitor City of Sharon, 1958-68; spl. dep. atty. gen., 1966-71; lectr. Pa. Bar Inst., Def. Research Inst., Pa. Def. Inst., Am. Arbitration Assn. Rep. state committeeman, 1954-78. Served to capt. USNR, 1944-70, ret. Mem. Am. Jurisprudence Soc., Pa. Bar Assn., Mercer County Bar Assn. (pres. 1969). State civil litigation, Probate, Workers' compensation. Home: 219 Case Ave Sharon PA 16146 Office: 32 Shenango Ave Sharon PA 16146

DILLAHUNTY, WILBUR HARRIS, lawyer; b. Memphis, June 30, 1928; s. Joseph S. and Octavia M. (Jones) D.; 1 child, Sharon K. JD, U. Ark., 1954. Bar: Ark. 1954. City atty. West Memphis, Ark., 1958-68; U.S. atty. (ea. dist.) Little Rock, 1968-79; exec. asst. adminstr. SBA, Washington, 1979-80; ptnr. Dillahunty, Skelton et al, Little Rock, 1980—. Served to lt. U.S. Army, 1945-48, ETO. Mem. ABA, Pulaski Bar Assn. Federal civil litigation, State civil litigation. Home: 9710 Catskill Rd Little Rock AR 72207 Office: 10800 Financial Pkwy Suite 255 Little Rock AR 72211

DILLARD, GEORGE DOUGLAS, lawyer; b. N.Y.C., May 14, 1942; s. George Pershing and Mary Elizabeth (Elarbee) D.; m. Myra Gail Huggins, June 18, 1966; children: Karen Asheley, George Douglas Jr., Mary Ellen, Allison Rustin. BA, Furman U., 1964; JD, Mercer U., 1967. Bar: Ga. 1968, U.S. Dist. Ct. (no. dist.) Ga. 1968, U.S. Ct. Appeals (5th cir.) 1979, U.S. Ct. Appeals (11th cir.) 1981. Ptnr. Dillard & Shearer P.C., Atlanta, 1968-82, Dillard Greer Westmoreland & Wilson P.C., Atlanta, 1983—; lectr. to various real estate orgns., ednl. instns. and seminars of the bar, 1982—. Active Ga. Dems., 1970—, Leadership Ga., 1975. Mem. ABA, Ga. Bar Assn., Am. Judicature Soc., Ga. Trial Lawyers Assn., Decatur-DeKalb Bar Assn., Atlanta Lawyers Club, Old War Horse Lawyers Club, DeKalb County C. of C. (bd. dirs. 1984-86), Phi Delta Phi, Kappa Alpha Order. Methodist. Club: Druid Hills Golf (Atlanta) (bd. dirs. 1982-86). Avocations: golf, fishing, hunting. Local government, Real property, Land use and planning law. Home: 10 Hunt Valley Dr Lithonia GA 30058 Office: Dillard Greer Westmoreland & Wilson PC 3414 Peachtree Rd NE 800 Monarch Plaza Atlanta GA 30326

DILLARD, JOHN ROBERT, lawyer; b. Sylva, N.C., Mar. 14, 1955; s. George Washington and Ethel Thomasine (Freeman) D.; m. Cathy Ann Irvin, Aug. 10, 1974. BBA cum laude, Western Carolina U., 1977; JD, Samford U., 1980. Bar: N.C. 1980, U.S. Dist. Ct. (we. dist.) N.C. 1981. Sole practice Cashiers, N.C., 1980-81; ptnr. Alley, Killian, Kersten & Dillard, Waynesville, N.C., 1981-85; v.p., atty. Commonwealth Land Title Co., Asheville, N.C., 1985—; legal counsel Woodmen of World Ins., Waynesville, 1982—, bd. dirs.; sec. Beta-Zeta Ltd., Waynesville, 1982-84, bd. dirs.; cons. Nereus Inc., Greenville, Tenn., 1986—. Legal counsel, bd. dirs. Lambda Chi Alpha, Cullowhee, N.C., 1983-85; adv. Jr. Achievement, Clyde, N.C., 1984; campaign mgr. Thornburg for Atty. Gen., Hayward County, 1984. Recipient Unsung Brother award, Lambda Chi Alpha, 1974. Mem. Assn. Trial Lawyers Am., N.C. Acad. Trial Lawyers, N.C. Coll. Advocacy, Am. Land Title Assn., N.C. Real Property Assn., MAC Users Group. Democrat. Episcopalian. Club: Rotissery Baseball (Waynesville) (computer statistician 1986—). Lodges: Masons, Woodmen (trustee 1982—). Avocations: computer programming, travel. General corporate, Real property. Home: 404 Auburn Rd Waynesville NC 28786 Office: Commonwealth Land Title Co NW Plaza Suite 507 Asheville NC 28801

DILLARD, W. THOMAS, lawyer; b. Dothan, Ala., Nov. 28, 1941; s. William T. and Gladys (Harris) D.; m. Glenda Jeanne Howard, Aug. 29, 1964 (div. 1973); children—Kerry Jeanne, William Thomas; m. Susan Jean Jakuboski, Oct. 26, 1974. B.A., U. Tenn., 1962, J.D., 1964. Bar: Tenn. 1965. Asst. U.S. atty. Dept. Justice, Knoxville, Tenn., 1967-76; chief asst. U.S. atty. Dept. Justice, Knoxville, 1978-83, U.S. atty., 1981; U.S. atty. Dept. Justice, Tallahassee, 1983-86; ptnr. Ritchie, Fels, and Dillard, P.C., Knoxville, Tenn., 1987—; U.S. magistrate 1976-78; adj. prof. East Tenn. State U., Knoxville, 1979-80; instr. Knoxville Police Acad., 1979-82, Nat. Inst. Trial Advocacy, Chapel Hill, N.C., 1985-87. Deacon Presbyterian Ch., Knoxville, 1972-76, elder, 1978-82. Mem. ABA, Am. Judicature Soc., Knoxville Young Lawyers (pres. 1972-73). Avocations: golf; tennis; reading. Criminal, Government contracts and claims, Jurisprudence. Home: 4800 Santa Monica Rd Knoxville TN 37918 Office: Ritchie Fels & Dillard 1130 First American Ctr Knoxville TN 37902

DILLER, THEODORE CRAIG, lawyer; b. Pitts., Aug. 3, 1904; s. Theodore and Rebecca (Craig) D.; m. Barbara Cox, May 16, 1936; children: Anne Cox Diller Sterling, Rebecca Crossette Diller Howe, Deborah Howard Diller Triant. Ph.B., Kenyon Coll., 1925; LL.B., Harvard U., 1928. Bar: Pa. 1928, Ill. 1929. Practice law Chgo., 1929-85; partner Lord, Bissell & Brook, 1946-85; sec. Magnaflux Corp., 1940-59. Mem. Am., Ill., Chgo. bar assns., Law Club Chgo., Legal Club Chgo. Republican. Episcopalian. Clubs: University. (Chgo.), Mid-Am. (Chgo.). General corporate, Probate. Home: 416 Cumnor Rd Kenilworth IL 60043 Office: 115 S LaSalle St Chicago IL 60603

DILLEY, THOMAS ROBERT, lawyer; b. Grand Rapids, Mich., June 11, 1953; s. Robert W. and Frances (Berger) D.; m. Debra Cooper, June 12, 1983; 1 child, Sarah Elizabeth. BA, U. Mich., 1975; JD, U. Nebr., 1978. Bar: Mich. 1978, U.S. Dist. Ct. (we. dist.) Mich. 1978. Ptnr. Dilley & Dilley, Grand Rapids, 1978—. Mem. ABA, Mich. Bar Assn., Grand Rapids Bar Assn., Assn. Trial Lawyers Am., Mich. Trial Lawyers Assn. Personal injury, Workers' compensation, Family and matrimonial. Office: Dilley & Dilley 201 Monroe Ave NW Grand Rapids MI 49503

DILLIN, SAMUEL HUGH, U.S. judge; b. Petersburg, Ind., June 9, 1914; s. Samuel E. and Maude (Harrell) D.; m. Mary Eloise Humphreys, Nov. 24, 1940; 1 dau., Patricia Jane. A.B. in Govt, Ind. U., 1936, LL.B., 1938. Bar: Ind. bar 1938. Partner firm Dillin & Dillin, Petersburg, 1938-61; U.S. dist. judge So. Dist. Ind., 1961—; Sec. Pub. Service Commn. Ind., 1942; mem. Interstate Oil Compact Commn., 1949-52, 61. Mem. Ind. Ho. of Reps. from Pike and Knox County, 1937, 39, 41, 51, floor leader, 1951; mem. Ind. Senate from Pike and Gibson County, 1951, 61, floor leader, pres. pro tem, 1961, candidate for gov. Ind., 1956. Served to capt. AUS, 1943-46. Mem. Am. Bar Assn., Am. Judicature Soc., Delta Tau Delta, Phi Delta Phi. Democrat. Presbyn. Club: Indianapolis Athletic. Office: U S Dist Ct U S Courthouse 46 E Ohio St Room 255 Indianapolis IN 46204 *

DILLING, KIRKPATRICK WALLWICK, lawyer; b. Evanston, Ill., Apr. 11, 1920; s. Albert W. and Elizabeth (Kirkpatrick) D.; m. Betty Ellen Bronson, June 18, 1942 (div. July 1944); m. Elizabeth Ely Tilden, Dec. 11, 1948; children—Diana Jean, Eloise Tilden, Victoria Walgreen, Albert Kirkpatrick. Student, Cornell U., 1939-40; B.S. in Law, Northwestern U., 1942; postgrad., DePaul U., 1946-47, L'Ecole Vaubier, Montreux, Switzerland; Degre Normal, Sorbonne U., Paris. Bar: Ill. 1947, Wis., Ind., Mich., Md., La., Tex., Okla., U.S. Dist. Ct. (ea. dist.) Wis., U.S. Ct. Appeals (2d, 3d, 5th, 7th, 8th, 9th, 10th, 11th, D.C. cirs.), U.S. Supreme Ct. Mem. firm Dilling, Gronek and Armstrong, Chgo., 1948—; gen. counsel Nat. Health Fedn., Am. Massage and Therapy Assn., Cancer Control. Soc.; dir. Adelle Davis Found., Dillman Labs.; v.p. Midwest Medic-Aide, Inc.; spl. counsel Herbalife (U.K.) Ltd., Herbalife Australasia Pty., Ltd.; lectr. on pub. health law. Contbr. articles to profl. publs. Bd. dirs. Nat. Health Fedn., Adele Davis Found. Served to 1st lt. AUS, 1943-46. Mem. ABA, Ill. Bar Assn., Chgo. Bar Assn., Assn. Trial Lawyers Am., Cornell Soc. Engrs., Am. Legion, Air Force Assn., Pharm. Advt. Club, Navy League, Delta Upsilon. Republican. Episcopalian. Clubs: Lake Michigan Yachting Assn., Tower, Cornell U., Club Chgo. Health, Administrative and regulatory, Federal civil litigation. Home: 1120 Lee Rd Northbrook IL 60062 Winter Home: Casa Dorado Indian Wells CA 92260 Office: 150 N Wacker Dr Chicago IL 60601

DILLON, ANDREW JOSEPH, lawyer; b. Chgo., Apr. 1, 1947; s. John Hubert and Rose (Delpriore) D.; m. Maria Nett Devitt, Aug. 23, 1969; children: Melissa Marie, Justin Michael. BSEE, Purdue U., 1972; JD, John Marshall Law Sch., 1979. Bar: Tex. 1979, U.S. Dist. Ct. (no. dist.) Tex. 1979, U.S. Patent Office 1979, U.S. Ct. Appeals (fed. cir.) 1983. Enlisted USN, 1966, commd. ensign, 1972, advanced through grades to lt., ret., 1978; atty. patent dept. Tex. Instruments, Dallas, 1978-80; ptnr. Hubbard, Thurman, Turner & Tucker, Dallas, 1980-85; chief patent counsel Gearhart Industries Inc, Ft. Worth, 1985—. Contbr. articles to profl. jours. Mem. ABA, Tex. Bar Assn., Dallas Ft. Worth Patent Assn. (pres. 1984-85), Soc. Profl. Well Logging Analysts (assoc.), Am. Arbitration Assn. Republican. Roman Catholic. Patent, Trademark and copyright, Computer. Home: 6 Kevin Ct Mansfield TX 76063 Office: Gearhart Industries Inc PO Box 1936 Fort Worth TX 76101

DILLON, CHARLES EDWARD, lawyer, solicitor; b. Butler, Pa., Mar. 18, 1920; s. John Coady and Ann Marie (Dougherty) D.; m. Nina Elizabeth Turnblacer, June 16, 1948; children: Ann, Charles Jr., Robert, Patricia, Daniel, Elizabeth, Mary Jo. BA, U. Notre Dame, 1941; JD, U. Pa., 1951. Bar: Pa. 1951, U.S. Dist. Ct. (we. dist.) Pa. 1951. Asst., solicitor City of Butler, 1960-68; solicitor Butler (Pa.) Area Sch. Dist., 1955—, Butler County City Flood Control Authority, 1962—, Mars (Pa.) Area Sch. Dist., 1964-84, Butler County Controller, 1966—; v.p. Butler Meml. Hosp., 1960-72, bd. dirs. Campaign chmn. ARC, 1960; profl. chmn. United Fund, 1958-62. Served to 1st lt. U.S. Army, 1941-46. Decorated Bronze Star. Mem. ABA, Pa. Bar Assn., Butler County Bar Assn. (pres. 1968-69), VFW. Republican. Roman Catholic. Clubs: Butler Country. Lodges: Elks, K.C. Avocations: golf, bridge, swimming. General practice, Local government, Probate. Home: 610 E Pearl St Butler PA 16001 Office: Dillon McCandless & King 128 W Diamond St Butler PA 16001

DILLON, CLIFFORD BRIEN, lawyer; b. Amarillo, Tex., Oct. 25, 1921; s. Clifford Newton and Leone (Brien) D.; m. Audrey Catherine Johnson, Jan. 16, 1945; children: Audrey Catherine Dillon Peters, Robert Brien, Douglas Johnson. B.B.A., U. Tex., 1943, LL.B. with honors, 1947. Bar: Tex. 1947. Practiced in Houston, 1947—; ptnr. Baker & Botts, 1957—; mem. faculty Southwestern Legal Found., 1968—. Author articles in field. Bd. dirs. Antitrust Inst.; bd. dirs. U. Tex. Health Sci. Ctr., Houston; mem. antitrust adv. bd. Bur. Nat. Affairs, Past bd. dirs., Houston Vis. Nurses Assn., bd. visitors Mc Donald Obs. and Astronomy, 1986—. Served to lt. (j.g.) A.C. USNR and USCGR, 1943-45. Fellow ABA (chmn. sect. antitrust law 1975-76, bd. govs. 1985-87), State Bar Tex., Am. Judicature Soc.; mem. Houston Bar Assn., U.S. C. of C. (adv. council antitrust policy), Houston C. of C., Phi Kappa Psi, Phi Delta Phi. Presbyterian. Clubs: Houston Country (Houston), Petroleum (Houston); Riverhill Country, Old Baldy, Headliners. Antitrust. Office: Baker & Botts 3000 One Shell Plaza Houston TX 77002

DILLON, JAMES JOSEPH, lawyer; b. Rockville Ctr., N.Y., June 18, 1948; s. James Martin and Rosemary (Peter) D.; m. Martha Stone Wiske, Mar. 19, 1977; 1 child, Eleanor. BA, Fordham U., 1970, Oxford U., 1972; JD, Harvard U., 1975; MA, Oxford U., 1982. Bar: Mass. 1975, U.S. Dist. Ct. Mass. 1975, U.S. Ct. Appeals (1st cir.) 1976, U.S. Ct. Appeals (5th cir.) 1986. Assoc. Goodwin, Procter & Hoar, Boston, 1975-83, ptnr., 1983—. Mem. ABA, Mass. State Bar Assn., Boston Bar Assn. Democrat. Club: St. Botolph (Boston). Federal civil litigation, State civil litigation. Office: Goodwin Procter & Hoar Exchange Place Boston MA 02109

DILLON, JANET JORDAN, lawyer; b. Denver, Feb. 2, 1947; d. Ellis F. and Eileen R. (McElwain) Etheridge; m. Harry Dillon Sr., Sept. 17, 1983; 1 child, Janet Lynn. BA in Anthropology with honors, Columbia U., 1969; PhD, U. Conn., 1974; JD, U. Calif., 1981. Bar: U.S. Dist. Ct. (no. dist.) Calif. 1981, U.S. Ct. Appeals (9th cir.) 1982, U.S. Dist. Ct. (we. dist.) Wash. 1983, U.S. Ct. Claims 1985, U.S. Supreme Ct. 1986. Asst. prof. Colo. State U., Ft. Collins, 1974-78; field supr. Calif. State Coll./Warm Springs Dam Project, Rohnert Park, 1978; ind. contractor Calif. Indian Legal Services, Ukiah, Calif., 1978; assoc. Vlassis and Ott, Phoenix, 1982-83, DeMers and Thomson, Federal Way, Wash., 1983; sole practice Tacoma, 1983—. Dir. Mendocino County Family Violence Diversion Program, Ukiah, 1980. Grantee NIMH, Bethesda, Md., 1971; NSF fellow, Washington, 1971. Fellow Am. Anthropol. Assn.; mem. ABA, Am. Soc. Applied Anthropology, Wash. Women Lawyers Assn., Tacoma Women's Sailing Assn., Assn. for Polit. and Legal Anthropology (chmn. 1976-77), Soc. for Applied Anthropology (symposium organizer 1983), Tacoma-Pierce County C. of C., Phi Beta Kappa, Phi Kappa Phi. Club: Pacific West Sport and Racquet Ball (Federal Way). Avocations: sailboating, internat. travel, mountain sports. Indian law, Federal civil litigation, General practice. Office: 5505 20th St E Tacoma WA 98424

DILLON, WILBURN, JR., lawyer; b. Tulsa, Aug. 17, 1940; s. Wilburn Sr. and Clara E. (Ogan) D.; m. Evelyn J. Wiebe, Aug. 11, 1963; children: Mark D., Michael S. BA, Bethel Coll., 1962; JD, Washburn U., 1966. Bar: Kans. 1966, U.S. Dist. Ct. Kans. 1966, U.S. Ct. Appeals (10th cir.) 1972, U.S. Ct. Mil. Appeals 1981. Ptnr. Jones, Schroer, Rice & Dillon, Topeka, 1966-73, Tilton, Dillon & Beck, Topeka, 1973—; mem. workers compensation examiners State of Kans., Topeka, 1971-76. Served to lt. col. USAR, 1966—. Mem. ABA, Kans. Bar Assn., Topeka Bar Assn., Assn. Trial Lawyers Am., Kans. Trial Lawyers Assn. Democrat. Methodist. Personal injury, Civil rights, General practice. Office: Tilton Dillon & Beck 1324 Topeka Ave Topeka KS 66612

DILORETO, ANN MARIE, legal systems consultant; b. Detroit, July 4, 1953; d. Gilbert Remo and Nathalie Marie (Gouine) DiL. BGS, U. Mich., 1975; MLS, Simmons Coll., 1976. Law librarian Widett, Slater & Goldman, Boston, 1978-79, Herrick & Smith, Boston, 1983-84; cons. Legal Info. Mgmt., Menlo Park, Calif., 1984—. Mem. Am. Assn. Law Libraries (profl. standards com. 1984), Spl. Libraries Assn. (sec., treas. legis. reference sect. 1984-85, chair-elect of sect., 1986-87), Assn. Boston Law Libraries (chmn. profl. standards com. 1979-84, consulting com., nominating com.). Litigation Support, Computer, Librarianship. Home and Office: Legal Info Mgmt 444 University Dr Menlo Park CA 94025

DILTS, THOMAS HAROLD, lawyer; b. Somerville, N.J., July 3, 1947; s. Harold Richard and Rhoda Elizabeth (Hughes) D.; m. Susan Wright, July 19, 1969; children—Stephen Thomas, Brian Matthew, Amy Tupper. B.A., Gettysburg Coll., 1969, J.D., Georgetown U. Law Center, 1972. Bar: N.J., 1972. assoc., Carpenter, Bennett & Morrissey, Newark, 1972-75; sole practice, Somerville, N.J., 1976-79, 86—; ptnr. Dilts & Kemp, Somerville, 1979-80, Dilts, DeLancey & Kemp, Somerville, 1980-81, Dilts, DeLancey & Welch, Somerville, 1982—; borough atty., Somerville, 1976-79; mcpl. prosecutor Borough of Raritan, N.J., 1982, South Bound Brook, 1982-83; atty. Somerville Bd. Edn., 1982-87. Candidate, N.J. Gen. assembly, 1981; csl. Somerset County Democratic Com., 1977—; trustee Somerset County Hospice, 1980-82; adv. YMCA Model Youth Legislature, 1982. Mem. ABA, N.J. State Bar Assn. (chmn. election law reform com. 1977-79), Somerset County Bar Assn. Democrat. Mem. Reformed Ch. Am. (elder 1982-85, com. on judiciary Mid Atlantic Synod 1982—, exec. com. Gen. Synod 1985—). Club: Somerville-Raritan Exchange. General corporate, Local government, Real property. Home: 304 Altamont Pl Somerville NJ 08876 Office: 4 E Cliff St PO Box 842 Somerville NJ 08876

DIMARE, CHARLES JOSEPH, lawyer; b. Revere, Mass., Mar. 1, 1952; s. Salvatore Robert DiMare and Carmela C. (Faro) Sicuso; m. Joan A. Antonino, Aug. 1, 1982. AA, Massachusetts Bay Community Coll., 1972; BA magna cum laude, U. Mass., 1974; JD cum laude, Vermont Law Sch., South Royalton, 1977; M in Pub. Adminstrn., U. Mass., 1983. Bar: Mass. 1978, U.S. Dist. Ct. Mass. 1979, U.S. Ct. Appeals (1st cir.) 1979, U.S. Supreme Ct., 1984. Asst. supr. U.S. Dept. Navy, Naval Air Sta., Calif., 1977-78; staff atty. North Shore Legal Clinic, Lynn., Mass., 1978-79; sole practice Amherst, Mass., 1978—; staff atty. legal service office U. Mass., 1979-80, directing atty., 1980—, law instr. 1980—; trainer various civil rights and civil liability seminars. Bd. dirs. Western Mass. Health Planning Council, 1980-82, legal support to various civil rights activities and demonstrations, 1979—; admissions counselor Vermont Law Sch. 1984—; vol. Greater Boston Legal Services, Roxbury, 1979. Mem. Mass. Bar Assn., Hampshire County Bar Assn. (governing bd. legal services office 1980—), Mass. Acad. Trial Attys., Nat. Legal Aid Defender Assn., Nat. Lawyers Guild (founder Vermont and Pioneer Valley chpts.). Mem. Christian Ch. Civil rights, Federal civil litigation, Personal injury. Home: PO Box 832 Amherst MA 01004 Office: Legal Services Office 922 Campus Ctr Amherst MA 01003

DIMATTEO, PHILIP STEPHEN, lawyer; b. N.Y.C., Oct. 6, 1947; s. Philip P. and Josephine (Domino) DiM.; m. Mariann Colucci, July 27, 1969; 1 child, Donna. BBA magna cum laude, St. Francis Coll., Bklyn., 1969; JD, U. Notre Dame, 1973. Bar: Ariz. 1973, U.S. Dist. Ct. Ariz. 1973, U.S. Ct. Appeals (9th cir.) 1973, U.S. Tax Ct. 1975. Law clk. to presiding justice Ariz. Ct. Appeals, Phoenix, 1973-74; assoc. Julian F. Weltsch, Ltd., Phoenix, Ariz., 1974; ptnr. Murphy & Posner, Phoenix, 1974-79; sec., treas., ptnr. Bosco & DiMatteo P.C., Phoenix, 1979—. Co-author: Professional Practice Alternatives, 1978. Served with Army Nat. Guard, 1970-76. Mem. ABA, Ariz. Bar Assn., Maricopa County Bar Assn. Roman Catholic. Avocations: sports, reading. Pension, profit-sharing, and employee benefits, Probate, General corporate. Home: 5019 W Seldon Ln Glendale AZ 85302 Office: Bosco & DiMatteo PC 3101 N Central Ave Suite 400 Phoenix AZ 85012

DIMITRY, THEODORE GEORGE, lawyer; b. New Orleans, Jan. 15, 1937; s. Theodore Joseph and Ouida Marion (Seiler) D.; m. M. Elizabeth Warren; children—Mary Elizabeth, Theodore Warren. B.S., Tulane U., 1958, J.D., 1960. Bar: La. 1960, Tex. 1964. Assoc. firm Phelps, Dunbar, Marks, Claverie & Sims, New Orleans, 1965-69, ptnr., 1969-75; ptnr. firm Vinson & Elkins, Houston, 1975—; research fellow Southwestern Legal Found., Dallas, 1973—; speaker on maritime law, offshore contracting, resource devel. at profl. seminars, 1975—. Contbr. articles to profl. jours. Mem. permanent adv. bd. Tulane U. Admiralty Law Inst., 1985—. Served with USN, 1960-64. Mem. Maritime Law Assn. U.S., Southeastern Admiralty Law Inst., Am. Soc. Internat. Law, ABA. Admiralty, Private international, Insurance. Office: Vinson & Elkins First City Tower Houston TX 77002

DIMMERS, ALBERT WORTHINGTON, lawyer; b. Hillsdale, Mich., July 25, 1904; s. Albert Worthington and Cora Hannah (Bailey) D.; m. Kathleen McFarland, Aug. 13, 1932; children—Alan M., David A. Student Mich. State U., 1922-23; A.B., Hillsdale Coll., 1927; LL.B., U. Mich., 1931. Bar: Mich., 1931, U.S. Dist. Ct. (ea. and we. dists.) Mich., 1932. Practice law, Hillsdale County, Mich., 1931—; pros. atty. Hillsdale County, 1934-40; city atty., Hillsdale, 1947-49; mem. firm Dimmers & Boyd, Hillsdale, and predecessors, 1962—, sr. ptnr., 1950-82; dir. emeritus Hillsdale County Nat. Bank. Former mem. Hillsdale Community Schs. Bd. Edn.; mem. Mich. Ho. of Reps., 1944-48. Fellow Am. Coll. Trial Lawyers, Am. Coll. Probate Counsel; mem. ABA, Mich. Bar Assn. Republican. Presbyterian. Clubs: Hillsdale Rotary, Masons, KP. Personal injury, Probate, General practice. Home: 5000 S Broad St Hillsdale MI 49242 Office: 25 Budlong St Hillsdale MI 49242

DIMMICK, CAROLYN REABER, federal judge; b. Seattle, Oct. 24, 1929; d. Maurice C. and Margaret T. (Taylor) Reaber; m. Cyrus Allen Dimmick, Sept. 10, 1955; children: Taylor, Dana. B.A., U. Wash., 1951, J.D., 1963; LL.D., Gonzaga U., 1982. Bar: Wash. Asst. atty. gen. Wash., 1953-55; judge Dist. Ct., 1965-75, Superior Ct., 1976-80; justice Wash. Supreme Ct., 1981-85; judge U.S. Dist. Ct. (we. dist.) Wash., 1985—; pros. atty. King County, Wash., 1955-59, 60-62; sole practice law, 1959-60, 62-65. Recipient Matrix Table award, 1981, World Plan Execs. Council award, 1981, others. Mem. Am. Judges Assn. (gov.), Nat. Assn. Women Judges, World Assn. Judges, Am., Wash. bar assns., Am. Judicature Soc. Clubs: Wash. Athletic, Wingpoint Golf and Country, Harbor. Jurisprudence. Office: U.S. District Court 816 US Courthouse 1010 Fifth Ave Seattle WA 98104

DIMMITT, LAWRENCE ANDREW, lawyer; b. Kansas City, Kans., July 20, 1941; s. Herbert Andrew and Mary (Duncan) D.; m. Lois Kinney, Dec. 23, 1962; children: Cynthia Susan, Lawrence Michael. BA, Kans. State U., 1963, MA, 1967; JD, Washburn U., 1968. Bar: Kans. 1968, U.S. Dist. Ct. Kans. 1968, U.S. Ct. Appeals (10th cir.) 1969, Mo. 1973, N.Y. 1975, U.S. Supreme Ct. 1986. Atty. Southwestern Bell Telephone Co., Topeka, 1968-73; atty. Southwestern Bell Telephone Co., St. Louis, 1973-74, gen. atty. regulation, 1979; gen. atty. Kans. Southwestern Bell Telephone Co., Topeka, 1979—; atty. AT&T, N.Y.C., 1974-79. Bd. dirs. First United Meth. Ch., Topeka, 1979-84, mem. nominating com., 1985. Recipient commendation Legal Aid Soc. Topeka, 1986. Mem. ABA (pub. utility sect.), Kans. Bar Assn. (sec. adminstrv. law sect. 1982-83, 2d v.p. 1983-84, pres. 1985-86), Topeka Bar Assn., Am. Judicature Soc., Phi Alpha Delta. Republican. Club: Topeka Country. Lodge: Rotary. Administrative and regulatory, Public utilities, Federal civil litigation. Home: 3123 W 15th St Topeka KS 66604 Office: Southwestern Bell Telephone Co 220 E 6th Room 515 Topeka KS 66603

DIMON, JOHN E., lawyer; b. Roebling, N.J., May 14, 1916; s. George and Mary (Vrabel) D.; m. Virginia Lee Treece, Sept. 6, 1946; children: Patricia Frazier, Blake, David, Mark, Matthew. B, Villanova U., 1937; LLB, Temple U., 1940. Bar: N.J. 1946. Ptnr. Dimon, Haines and Bunting, 1952-73, Dimon & Eleuteri, 1973-79, Dimon Eleuteri & Gilangi, Mt. Holly, N.J., 1979; sole practice Roebling, 1979—; chmn. bd. dirs. Bank Mid N.J., Bordentown; bd. dirs. BMJ Fin., Bordentown; corp. counsel County Burlington, N.J. Chmn. Burlington County Reps., Mt. Holy, 1964-71, N.J. Rep. Orgn., Trenton, 1970-73, N.J. Reappointment Commn.; del. N.J. Constl. Conv., New Brunswick, 1966-67, Nat. Rep. Conv., 1964, 68, 72, 76, 80; mem. N.J. Racing Commn., Trenton, 1986—. Served to maj. U.S. Army, 1940-46. Republican. Byzantine Catholic. Elks. Avocation: writing. Banking, Estate planning, Real property.

DINAN, DONALD ROBERT, lawyer; b. Nashua, N.H., Aug. 28, 1949; s. Robert J. and Jeanette F. (Farland) D.; m. Amy Littlepage, June 24, 1978. B.S. in Econs., U. Pa., 1971; J.D., Georgetown U., 1974; LL.M., London Sch. Econs., 1975. Bar: Mass. 1976, D.C. 1977, U.S. Supreme Ct. 1979, U.S. Ct. Internat. Trade 1982, N.Y. 1986. Atty. advisor U.S. Internat. Trade Commn., Washington, 1976-81, chief patent br., 1981-82, chief unfair imports investigation div., 1981-82; ptnr. Adduci Dinan & Mastriani, Washington, 1982—; dir. Eastern Caribbean Investment Corp., Washington. Mem. Mayor's Internat. Adv. Council, Washington, 1984—, Juvenile Justice Adv. Group, Washington, 1983—; chmn. Adv. Neighbor Commn.-Capitol Hill, Washington Dem. State Com., 1986. Mem. Fed. Bar Assn., ABA, ITC Trial Lawyers Assn. , Am. Intelligent Property Law Assn. (chmn. internat. trade com.). Democrat. Roman Catholic. Private international, Federal civil litigation, Legislative. Home: 129 D St SE Washington DC 20003 Office: Adduci Dinan & Mastriani 1140 Connecticut Ave NW Washington DC 20036

DINARDO, JOSEPH, lawyer; b. Rochester, N.Y., Jan. 6, 1947; s. Carmen and Bertha Mascirelli DiN.; m. Stephanie Artis, July 22, 1978. B.A., SUNY, Buffalo, 1968, J.D., 1972. Bar: N.Y. 1973, U.S. Ct. Appeals (2d cir.) 1974, Pa., Ohio, Mich. assco. Collins, Collins & DiNardo, Buffalo, 1973-75, ptnr. 1974—. Mem. Trial Lawyers Am., N.Y. State Bar Assn., Erie County Bar Assn., Brotherhood Locomotive Engrs. (counsel), Transp. Workers Am. (counsel). Recipient Book award Bancroft-Whitney, 1969. Federal civil litigation, State civil litigation, Probate. Office: Collins Collins & Dinardo PC 415 Franklin St Buffalo NY 14202

DINEEN, JOHN K., lawyer; b. Gardiner, Maine, Jan. 21, 1928; s. James J. and Eleanor (Kelley) D.; m. Carolyn Foley Reardon (dec. 1982); children—Jane, Martha, Louisa, Jessica, John; m. Susan Lowell Wales, Aug. 15, 1986; children: Theodore, Ralph, Andrew. B.A., U. Maine, 1951; J.D., Boston U., 1954. Bar: Maine 1954, Mass. 1954. Ptnr. Weston, Patrick & Stevens, Boston, 1954-67; ptnr. firm Peabody & Arnold, Boston, 1967-70, Gaston Snow & Ely Bartlett, Boston, 1970—; dir., mem. exec. com. Coolidge Bank & Trust Co., Watertown, Mass., and Boston, 1983—; bd. dirs. Fiduciary Trust Co., Boston, Town & City Properties Boston, Inc., London, Codman Co., Inc., Boston; mng. dir. Dingle Am. Properties Ltd., Dingle, County, Kerry, Ireland, 1973—; pres., trustee Boston Local Devel. Corp., 1982—. Trustee Waring Sch., Beverley, Mass., 1981—, U.S.S. Constitution Mus., U. Hosp., Boston, 1980—; former trustee Winsor Sch. Emmanuel Coll., Boston, Hebron Acad., Maine; spl. asst. atty. gen. Commonwealth of Mass., Boston, 1965-67. Served with U.S. Army, 1946-48. Mem. Boston Bar Assn., Mass. Bar Assn., Marshall Street Hist. Soc. Republican. Roman Catholic. Clubs: Tavern, Union, Cary Street, Apollo. Real property. Home: 40 Pleasant St Nahant MA 01908 Office: Gaston Snow & Ely Bartlett One Federal St Boston MA 02110

DINERSTEIN, ROBERT DAVID, lawyer; b. N.Y.C., May 3, 1953; s. Irving and Helen (Risch) D.; m. Joan Patricia Fread, June 4, 1983; children: Michael Fread, Jonathan Fread. AB in History magna cum laude, Cornell U., 1974; JD, Yale U., 1977. Bar: N.Y. 1978, D.C. 1983, Md. 1984, U.S. Dist. Ct. D.C. 1984, U.S. Dist. Ct. Md. 1985. Trial atty. U.S. Dept. Justice, Washington, 1977-82; clin. lectr., supervising atty. Am. U., Washington, 1983-84, acting dir. criminal justice clinic, 1984-85, dep. dir. office of clin. programs, 1985—; bd. dirs. D.C. Law Students in Ct., Washington, 1983—. Recipient Spl. Commendation award U.S. Dept. Justice, 1979, 80, Meritorious Service award U.S. Dept. Justice, 1981, Outstanding Performance Ratings 1978-82. Mem. ABA, Md. Bar Assn.(exec. bd. dirs.), Assn. Am. Law Schs. (co-chmn. long range planning com., clin. legal edn. sect. 1987—, chmn. integration of clin. methodology, clin. legal edn. sect. 1985-86). Democrat. Jewish. Avocations: piano, sports, reading, politics. Legal education, Civil rights, Lawyer skills-interviewing, counseling and negotiation. Home: 5909 Cranston Rd Bethesda MD 20816 Office: Am U 4400 Massachusetts Ave NW Washington DC 20016

DINKINS, CAROL EGGERT, lawyer; b. Corpus Christi, Tex., Nov. 9, 1945; d. Edgar H., Jr. and Evelyn S. (Scheel) Eggert; m. O. Theodore Dinkins, Jr., July 2, 1966; children: Anne, Amy. B.S., U. Tex., 1968; J.D., U. Houston, 1971. Bar: Tex. 1971. Adj. asst. prof. law U. Houston Coll. Law, also prin. asso. Tex. Law Inst. Coastal and Marine Resources, U. Houston, 1971-73; assoc., then partner firm Vinson & Elkins, Houston, 1973-81, 83-84, 85—; asst. atty. gen. land and natural resources Dept. Justice, 1981-83, dep. atty. gen., 1984-85; chmn. Pres.'s Task Force on Legal Equity for Women, 1981-83; mem. Hawaiian Native Study Commn., 1981-83; dir. Nat. Consumer Coop. Banks Bd., 1981, ELI; bd. dirs., chmn. govt. and pub. affairs com. Nat. Ocean Industries Assn. Author articles in field. Chmn. Tex. Gov.'s Task Force Coast Mgmt., 1979, Tex. Gov.'s Flood Control Action Group, 1980-81; bd. dirs. Energy and Environ. Study Inst., Houston Mus. of Natural Sci., Tex. Nature Conservancy, U. Houston Law Ctr. Found. (bd. dirs. 1985—). Mem. ABA, State Bar Tex., Houston Bar Assn., Tex. Water Conservation Assn., Houston Law Rev. Assn. (dir. 1978—), Fed. Bar Assn. (bd. dirs. Houston chpt. 1986—). Republican. Lutheran. Environment. Office: Vinson & Elkins 3300 First City Tower Houston TX 77002

DINNING, WOODFORD WYNDHAM, JR., lawyer; b. Demopolis, Ala., Aug. 15, 1954; s. Woodford W. and Gladys (Brown) D.; m. Joan Holliman, Aug. 11, 1979. AS, U. Ala., 1976, JD, 1979. Bar: Ala. 1979, U.S. Dist. Ct. (so. dist.) Ala. 1980. Judge City of Demopolis, 1980—; ptnr. Lloyd, Dinning, Boggs & Dinning, Demopolis, 1979—; pres. and bd. dirs. Tenn-Tom Marinas, Inc., Demopolis, Tenn-Tom Motel, Demopolis. Chmn. Marengo County (Ala.) Cancer Assn., 1982-83, Marengo County United Way, 1983-84. Mem. U. Ala. Alumni Assn. (chmn. 1985-86). Avocations: water skiing, snow skiing. State civil litigation, Contracts commercial, Family and matrimonial. Office: Lloyd Dinning Boggs & Dinning PO Drawer Z Demopolis AL 36732

DINWIDDIE, BRUCE WAYLAND, lawyer; b. New Orleans, Aug. 24, 1943; s. George Summey and Augusta Rosser (Benners) D.; m. Judith Zatarain, May 7, 1966 (div. 1971); 1 child, Patrick; m. Kate Marie Crawford, Aug. 2, 1972; children—Kate, Bruce, Wayland. B.S., Centenary Coll. of La., 1965; J.D., Tulane U., 1968. Bar: La. 1968, U.S. Dist. Ct. (ea. dist.) La. 1968, U.S. Dist. Ct. (we. dist.) La. 1978, U.S. Dist. Ct. (mid. dist.) La. 1970, U.S. Ct. Appeals (5th cir.) 1969, U.S. Supreme Ct. 1975. Law clk. to dist. atty. Orleans Parish, 1967-68; assoc. Terriberry, Carroll, Yancey & Farrell, New Orleans, 1968-72; ptnr. Ungar, Dulitz, Jacobs & Manuel, New Orleans, 1972-76; sole practice, Metairie, La., 1977-80; ptnr. Dinwiddie & Brandao, Metairie, 1981—. Mem. ABA, La. State Bar Assn., Assn. Trial Lawyers Am., La. Trial Lawyers Assn., Tulane Maritime Law Soc. (adv. editor 1976—). Republican. Methodist. Admiralty, Juvenile, Personal injury. Office: Dinwiddie & Brandao 2313 N Hullen St Metairie LA 70001

DIOSEGY, ARLENE JAYNE, lawyer, consultant; b. Pitts., Sept. 13, 1949; d. William Cornelius and Rosemarie Arlene (Voivoda) D.; m. Charles Richard Mansfield, Apr. 11, 1981; 1 child, Corey Redling. B.A., Allegheny Coll., 1971; J.D., Temple U., 1974. Bar: Pa. 1974, U.S. Dist. Ct. (mid. dist.) Pa. 1974, U.S. Supreme Ct. 1980, Colo. 1981, U.S. Dist. Ct. (ea. dist.) Colo. 1981, N.C. 1982. Assoc. Smith & Roberts, Harrisburg, Pa., 1974-75; asst. atty. gen. Pa. Dept. of Edn., Harrisburg, 1975-77; chief counsel Gov.'s Council on Drug and Alcohol Abuse, Harrisburg, 1977-80; acting dir. legal affairs and risk mgmt. U. Colo. Health Scis. Ctr., Denver, 1980-81; asst. univ. counsel Duke U. Med. Ctr., Durham, N.C., 1981-85, adj. asst. prof. grad. dept. health adminstrn., 1983—; v.p. legal services Coastal Group Inc., Durham, 1985-87; assoc. Faison, Brown, Fletcher and Brough, Durham, 1987—; cons. Colo. Dept. Health, Denver, 1980-81. Bd. dirs. YWCA, Durham, 1984—; mem. fin. com. Epworth Ch., Durham, 1984—. Mem. Am. Acad. Hosp. Attys., ABA, Am. Coll. Legal Medicine (assoc.-in-law), Nat. Health Lawyers Assn., N.C. Bar Assn. (sec. health law com. 1983-84, vice chmn. 1984-85, chmn. 1985-86, chmn. 1985-86, 86-87, mental health law com.), N.C. Soc. Health Care Attys. (legis. com. 1983, program chmn. 1983, bd. dirs. 1985), Durham Bar Assn. Republican. Methodist. Health, General corporate, Insurance. Office: Faison Brown Fletcher and Brough PO Box 2800 Durham NC 27705

DIPIERO, ANDREW EDWARD, JR., lawyer; b. Phila., Nov. 26, 1952; s. Andrew E. and Edna M. (Gulla) DiP.; m. Janet Doris Eggert, Oct. 26, 1975; children: Andrew, Michael, Kristin. BA, LaSalle U., 1974; JD, Del Law Sch., 1981. Bar: Pa. 1981, N.J. 1981, U.S. Dist. Ct. (ea. dist.) Pa. 1981, U.S. Dist. Ct. N.J. 1981. Asst. city solicitor City of Phila., 1981-82; assoc. Rutter, Turner & Stein, Phila., 1982-86, ptnr., 1986—; bd. dirs. Quaint Oak Bldg. and Loan Assn., Feasterville, Pa. Mem. ABA, Pa. Bar Assn., Phila. Bar Assn. Democrat. Roman Catholic. Club: Justinian (Phila.). Lodge: Sons of Italy, Vince Lombardi. Personal injury, Insurance, State civil litigation. Home: 3879 Whitman Rd Huntingdon Valley PA 19006 Office: 872 Public Ledger Bldg Independence Sq Philadelphia PA 19106

DIPIETRO, ANDREW MICHAEL, JR., lawyer; b. Waterbury, Conn., Sept. 23, 1932; s. Andrew Michael and Phyllis Diana DiP.; m. Patricia Mazzaluppo, Dec. 31, 1960 (div. June 1979); children: David Justin, Michael Andrew, Mathew Jason; m. Kate Spitzer, Jan 11, 1980. BA, St. Lawrence U., 1954; JD, Cornell U., 1961. Bar: Conn. 1961, U.S. Dist. Ct. Conn. 1961, U.S. Ct. Appeals (2d cir.) 1969, U.S. Supreme Ct. 1971. Assoc. Evans & Evans, New Haven, 1961-62, Gerald W. Brownstein, New Haven, 1962-65; ptnr. Brownstein & DiPietro, New Haven, 1965-76, DiPietro, Kantovitz & Brownstein P.C., New Haven, 1976—. Sr. topical editor Conn. Bar Jour., 1981—; contbr. articles to profl. jours. Trustee Morris Weisman Edn. Found., Inc., 1980—, Orch. New England, New Haven, 1982—; trustee Eastern Dist. Ednl. Fund Corp., 1982-85, pres. 1985—. Served as 1st lt. U.S. Army, 1954-58. Fellow Comml. Law Found, Inc.; mem. ABA (bus. bankruptcy com. 1978—, legis. com. 1983—, chpt. 11 com. 1983—), New Haven County Bar Assn., Am. Arbitration Assn., Conn. Trial Lawyers Assn., Comml. Law League Am. (nat. chmn. bankruptcy com. 1981-84, exec. council bankruptcy and insolvency sect. 1981—, chmn. eastern dist. 1984-86, nat. bd. govs. 1986—), Am. Bankruptcy Inst., Phi Delta Phi. Clubs: Quinnipiac, Graduates (New Haven); Pine Orchard Yacht and Country (Branford, Conn.) (pres. 1986—). Lodge: Rotary (pres. New Haven club 1982-83). Bankruptcy, Chapter 11 commercial, Contracts commercial. Home: 2 Prospect Hill Stony Creek CT 06405 Office: DiPietro Kantrovitz & Brownstein PC 64 Grove St PO Box 1406 New Haven CT 06505

DIPIETRO, MELANIE, lawyer; b. Greensburg, Pa., Oct. 29, 1944; d. Joseph and Jessie (Detoro) DiP. BA cum laude, Seton Hill Coll., 1969; MA, Occidental Coll., 1971; JD, Duquesne U., 1975; cert., Harvard U., 1985; candidate J.C.L., U. St. Thomas, Rome, 1986. Joined Sisters of Charity of Seton Hill, Roman Cath. Ch., 1962. Bar: Pa. 1975, U.S. Dist. Ct. (we. dist.) Pa. 1975, U.S. Ct. Appeals (3d cir.) 1980, U.S. Supreme Ct. 1980. Tchr. Diocese of Pitts., 1965-69, assoc. gen. counsel, 1974-81; tchr. Elizabeth Seton Sch., Pitts., 1971-74; assoc. Mansmann, Cindrich & Titus, Pitts., 1981—; lectr. bus. law Seton Hill Coll., Greensburg, 1978-79; lectr. adminstrv. agy. law grad. sch. bus. Duquesne U., Pitts., 1979-80; lectr. developmentally disabled law U. Pitts., 1979-81; cons. Sisters of St. Mary Health Care System, St. Louis, 1986—. Author: (monograph) Congregational Sponsorship, 1985; contbr. articles to profl. jours. Vol. Elderly Law Project Neighborhood Legal Services, 1976-80. Coro Found. grantee, 1970-71; recipient West Pub. award, 1975; named one of Outstanding Young Women Am., 1975, 77. Mem. ABA, Allegheny County Bar Assn. (religious and charitable orgns. com., pub. service com., mental health com.), St. Thomas More Soc. Democrat. Health, General practice. Home: 5115 Second Ave Pittsburgh PA 15207 Office: Mansmann Cindrich & Titus Two Chatham Ctr 15th Floor Pittsburgh PA 15219

DIPRIMA, MICHAEL THOMAS, lawyer; b. Rochester, N.Y., Dec. 1, 1947; s. Joseph Thomas and Lillian (Versage) DiP.; m. Kathleen Mary Camuso, Aug. 9, 1969; children: Richard Joseph, Robert Lawrence. BA, John Carroll U., 1969; JD, Syracuse U., 1972. Bar: N.Y. 1973, U.S. Dist. Ct. (we. dist.) N.Y. 1975, U.S. Ct. Appeals (2d cir.) 1980. Assoc. Fritz, Christ, O'Brien & Farrell, Mineola, N.Y., 1972-73; trial atty. Monroe County Pub. defender, Rochester, 1974-77; ptnr. DiPrima & Noce, Rochester, 1977—. Mem. Criminal Def. League Inc., Rochester, 1980—, spokesman, 1985; bd. dirs. Pre-Trial Services Inc., Rochester, 1978—, pres. 1981. Mem. Monroe County Bar Assn. (trustee 1985—), Assn. Trial Lawyers Am. Roman Catholic. Avocation: sports. Criminal, Personal injury. Office: DiPrima & Noce 30 W Broad St Rochester NY 14614

DIRACLES, JAMES CONSTANTINE, lawyer; b. Mpls., Sept. 26, 1948. BA, Colo. Coll., 1970; JD, U. Minn., 1973. Bar: Minn. 1973, U.S. Dist. Ct. Minn. 1974, U.S. Ct. Appeals (8th cir.) 1974, U.S. Supreme Ct. 1983. Ptnr. Best & Flanagan, Mpls., 1973—. Securities, General corporate, Contracts commercial. Office: Best & Flanagan 3500 IDS Ctr Minneapolis MN 55402

DISABATINO, ARTHUR FRANK, judge; b. Wilmington, Del., Mar. 24, 1938; s. Ernest J. and Margurite E. (Giacoma) DiS.; m. Sheila Donovan, June 6, 1964; children: David, Steven, Timothy. AB, U. Notre Dame, 1959; LLB, Georgetown U., 1962. Bar: Del. 1962. Assoc. Killoran & VanBrunt, Wilmington, Del., 1962-71; solicitor Odessa, Delaware, Wilmington, 1966-71, Delaware City, 1968-71; pub. defender Wilmington, 1965-70; judge Ct. of Common Pleas, Wilmington, 1971—. Recipient Hope Chest award Nat. Multiple Sclerosis Soc., 1979; named Young Man of Yr., Del. Jaycees, 1972. Mem. ABA, Am. Judges Assn., Del. Bar Assn. Judicial administration. Office: 1000 King St Wilmington DE 19801

DISANDRO, EDMOND A., lawyer; b. Providence, Aug. 9, 1932; s. Nicandro and Adeline (Mascio) DiS.; 2 children. A.B. magna cum laude, Providence Coll., 1955; J.D., Boston U., 1960. Bar: R.I. 1960, U.S. Dist. Ct. R.I. 1961, U.S. Ct. Appeals (1st cir.) 1980. Assoc., Goldberg & Goldberg, 1960-61; sr. assoc. Kiernan, Connors, and Kenyon, 1961-64; mng. ptnr. Coia, Hirsh and DiSandro, 1964-66, DeSimone, Sammartino and DiSandro, 1966-70; sr. assoc. DiSandro, Assocs., 1970-80; mng. ptnr. DiSandro-Smith & Assocs., P.C., Inc., Providence, 1980—; lectr. in field. Exec. dir. Smithfield (R.I.) Indsl. Devel. Commn., 1969-70; chmn. Smithfield Democratic Town Com., 1970-71; bd. dirs. R.I. Legal Services, Inc., 1971-73. Mem. ABA, Assn. Trial Lawyers Am. (treas. R.I. chpt. 1968-69), R.I. Trial Lawyers Assn. (v.p. 1979-81), Am. Judicature Soc., New Eng. Bar Assn., R.I. Bar Assn. (ho. dels. 1979-83), Fed. Bar Assn. Federal civil litigation, State civil litigation, Personal injury. Home: 6 Birch Rd Greenville RI 02828 Office: DiSandro Smith & Assocs PC Inc 155 S Main St Providence RI 02903

DISCIULLO, ALAN MICHAEL, lawyer; b. Long Branch, N.J., Mar. 18, 1950; s. Peter Michael and Marion (Kaney) DiS.; m. Mary Jo Coppola, Oct. 13, 1979; 1 child, Megan Eileen. AB cum laude, Georgetown U., 1972, JD, 1977; MBA, NYU, 1986. Bar: N.J. 1977, U.S. Dist. Ct. N.J. 1977, D.C. 1980, N.Y. 1980. Law clk. to presiding justice U.S. Tax Ct., Washington, 1975-76; assoc. Shanley & Fisher, Newark, 1977-78; asst. v.p. Paine Webber Jackson, N.Y.C., 1978-83; v.p. Dean Witter Reynolds Inc., N.Y.C., 1983—; v.p., dir. Wall St. Realty, N.Y.C., 1981-83; bd. dirs., gen. counsel, sec. polit. action com. Dean Witter Real Estate Co., N.Y.C., 1986—, v.p. North Brunswick (N.J.) Tenants Assn., 1979-81; mem. task force Pres.'s Pvt. Sector Survey on Cost Control, Washington, 1982-83. Contbr. articles to prof. jours. Advisor planning rev. bd. West Windsor Twp. Site, 1987—. Mem. Young Lawyers of N.Y.C. (treas. 1982-83, chmn. 1983-85), ABA (v.p. securities law div., young lawyers div. 1985-86, comml. leasing subcom., Corp. Banking and Bus. Law Sect.), Pi Sigma Alpha. Democrat. Roman Catholic. Club: Princeton (N.J.) Athletic. Avocations: athletics, photography. Landlord-tenant, Contracts commercial, General corporate. Home: 24 Fieldston Rd Princeton NY 08540 Office: Dean Witter Reynolds Inc 5 World Trade Ctr New York NY 10048

DISENHAUS, HELEN ELIZABETH, lawyer; b. Washington, Nov. 2, 1948; d. Nathan and Henrietta (Weiss) Disenhaus; m. Brian Girard Driscoll, Sept. 11, 1977; children—Daniel Benjamin, David Michael. A.B., Mt. Holyoke Coll., 1970; M.A.T., Wesleyan U., Conn., 1972; J.D., Yale U., 1977. Bar: D.C. 1977. Tchr. English, Glastonbury (Conn.) High Sch., 1971-74; atty. law firm Dow, Lohnes & Albertson, Washington, 1977-87; sole practice, Washington, 1987—; pres. D.C. chpt. Am. Women in Radio and TV, 1982-83, bd. dirs., 1983-84, nat. v.p. govt. industry affairs, 1984-86, sec.-treas., 1986—; mem. exec. com. Yale Law Sch., 1983-84. Sarah Williston scholar, 1968. Mem. D.C. Bar Assn., Women's Bar Assn. D.C., Fed. Communications Bar Assn., ABA, Yale Law Sch. Assn. D.C. (pres. 1982-83), Phi Beta Kappa. Jewish. Club: Yale (N.Y.), Mt. Holyoke Club (Washington). Administrative and regulatory, Communications. Office: 1742 N St NW Suite 300 Washington DC 20036

DISHEROON, FRED RUSSELL, lawyer; b. Hot Springs, Ark., Nov. 21, 1931; s. Andrew Russell and Ruth Fayrene (Bearden) D.; m. Laurel Joan Picou, Apr. 1, 1961 (div. Dec. 1977); children—Terri Suzanne, John Frederick. A.B., Hendrix Coll., 1953; J.D., So. Meth. U., 1956; LL.M. in Environ. Law, George Washington U., 1976. Bar: Tex. 1956, U.S. Ct. Appeals (1st, 5th, 6th, 8th, 9th, 10th, and 11th cirs.), U.S. Supreme Ct. 1964, Va. 1974. Atty. Superior Ins. Co., Dallas, 1960-64; claims atty. Sentry Ins. Co., Dallas, 1964-67; litigation counsel Stigall, Maxfield & Collier, Dallas, 1967-69; sole practice, Dallas, 1969-70; asst. gen. counsel for litigation C.E., U.S. Army, Washington, 1970-75; spl. litigation counsel Dept. Justice, Washington, 1975—; instr. environ. law U. Ala.-Huntsville, 1979-82; lectr. law George Washington U., 1981-86. Editor Southwestern Law Jour., 1955-56. Served to col. JAGC, USAR. Recipient numerous outstanding performance awards U.S. Army, Dept. Justice, Sr. Exec. Service Meritorious award Dept. Justice, 1984. Mem. Sr. Execs. Assn., Res. Officers Assn. Lodge: Kiwanis. Environment, Administrative and regulatory, Federal civil litigation. Home: PO Box 6464 Arlington VA 22206 Office: US Dept Justice Land and Natural Resources div 1000 Pennsylvania Ave NW Room 7332 Washington DC 20530

DISSEN, JAMES HARDIMAN, lawyer, personnel director; b. Pitts., Jan. 26, 1942; s. William Paul and Kathryn Grace (Reilly) D.; m. Shirley Ann Stark, Dec. 17, 1976; children: Elizabeth Ann, William Stark, Anna Kathryn. BS, Wheeling Coll., 1963; MBA, Xavier U., 1966; JD, Duquesne U., 1972. Bar: Pa. 1972, U.S. Dist. Ct. (we. dist.) Pa. 1972, W.Va. 1973, U.S. Dist. Ct. (so. dist.) W.Va. 1973, U.S. Supreme Ct. 1976. Personnel mgr. Columbia Gas Transmission Corp., Uniontown, Pa., 1969-73; dir. labor relations Columbia Gas Transmission Corp., Charlestown, W.Va., 1973-84, dir. personnel and labor relations, 1984-87, dir. employee relations, 1987—; chmn. Great Lakes Personnel, 1982-83. Vol. Rep. Party, Charleston, 1980; v.p. Charleston Sch. Bd., 1982; coach baseball, soccer, basketball, Charleston, 1984. Served as spl. agent U.S. Army, 1963-66. Mem. ABA, Fed. Bar Assn., W.Va. Bar Assn. (counsellor lawyer info. service 1981—, chmn. 1982-83, com. on continuing legal edn.), Pa. Bar Assn., Assn. Trial Lawyers Am., Am. Arbitration Assn. Roman Catholic. Club: Charleston Tennis. Labor. Home: 1501 Brentwood Rd Charleston WV 25314 Office: Columbia Gas Transmission Corp 1700 MacCorkle Ave SE Charleston WV 25314

DISSEN, RICHARD WILLIAM, lawyer; b. Pitts., Mar. 28, 1953; s. Joseph Philip and Margaret Elizabeth (Kubic) D.; m. Debra Carole Springston, Oct. 6, 1984. BA in English with honors, Carnegie-Mellon U., 1975; JD, U. Pitts., 1978. Bar: Pa. 1978, U.S. Dist. Ct. (we. dist.) Pa. 1978. Intern arbitration Nat. Acad. Arbitrators, 1977-80; sole practice arbitration Pitts., 1980—; mem. expedited panel, coordinating com. steel cos. United Steelworkers Am., 1982—. Contbr. articles on arbitration to profl. jours., 1985.

Mem. ABA, Allegheny County Bar Assn., Am. Arbitration Assn., Fed. Mediation and Conciliation Service. General practice, Labor. Office: 1425 Porter Bldg 601 Grant St Pittsburgh PA 15219

DITKOWSKY, KENNETH K., lawyer; b. Chgo., July 12, 1936; s. Samuel J. and Lillian (Plavnik) D.; m. Judith Goodman, Aug. 9, 1959; children—Naomi, Deborah, R. Benjamin. B.S., U. Chgo.; J.D., Loyola U., Chgo. Bar: Ill. 1961, U.S. Dist. Ct. (no. dist.) Ill. 1962, U.S. Ct. Apls. (7th cir.) 1973, U.S. Tax Ct. 1973, U.S. Sup. Ct. 1975. Ptnr., Ditkowsky & Contorer, Chgo., 1961—. Mem. Ill. Bar Assn., Chgo. Bar Assn. Club: Kiwanis. General practice, Federal civil litigation, State civil litigation. Address: 6150 Forest Glen Chicago IL 60646

DITMARS, LYLE WILLIAM, lawyer; b. Council Bluffs, Iowa, Jan. 15, 1951; s. William Martin and Opal Virginia (Hansen) D; m. Judy Kaye (Whitehill), Mar. 25, 1972; children: Andrew Lee, Natalie Kaye. BS, U. Nebr., 1973; JD, Creighton U., 1977. Bar: Iowa 1977, U.S. Dist. Ct. (so. dist.) Iowa 1977. With Peters Law Firm, P.C., Council Bluffs, 1977—. Bd. dirs., officer Lee. R. Martin Therapy Ctr., Council Bluffs, 1977—. Mem. Iowa Bar Assn. (exec. comm. young lawyers sect. 1978-81), Southwest Iowa Bar Assn. (sec., treas. 1981—), Pottawattamie County Bar Assn., Iowa Def. Council Assn., Iowa Trial Lawyers Assn. Republican. Presbyterian. Club: Lakeshore Country (Council Bluffs) (sec. 1981, v.p. 1982, pres. 1983). Lodge: Rotary. State civil litigation, Workers' compensation, Personal injury. Office: Peters Law Firm PC 233 Pearl St Council Bluffs IA 51501

DITTENHOEFER, MARC MITCHELL, lawyer; b. N.Y.C., Aug. 27, 1951; s. Harold F. and Shirley D. (Rosenberg) D. BA in History and English, C.W. Post Ctr. L.I.U., 1973; JD, Hofstra U., 1976. Bar: N.Y. 1977, U.S. Dist. Ct. (so. and ea. dists.) N.Y. 1977, U.S. Supreme Ct. 1983. Atty. Manhattan and Bronx Suface Transit Operating Authority, Bklyn., 1977-80; asst. gen. counsel N.Y.C. Transit Authority, Bklyn., 1980-82; assoc. Schneider, Kleinick & Weitz P.C., N.Y.C., 1982-83; ptnr. Siegel & Dittenhoefer, Bklyn., 1983-85, Blank, Goolnick & Dittenhoefer, N.Y.C., 1985—; lectr. Mcpl. and Transit Tort Liability, 1986. Committeeman Nassau County (N.Y.) Dems., 1979-80. Mem. Bklyn. Bar Assn., N.Y. State Trial Lawyers Assn., Assn. Trial Lawyers Am., Assn. Trial Lawyers of City of N.Y., Kings County Defenders Assn., Pi Gamma Mu, Sigma Tau Delta. State civil litigation, Personal injury, General practice. Office: Blank Goolnick & Dittenhoefer 401 Broadway Suite 202 New York NY 10013

DITTER, JOHN WILLIAM, JR., judge; b. Phila., Oct. 19, 1921. B.A., Ursinus Coll., 1943, LL.D., 1970; LL.B., U. Pa., 1948. Bar: Pa. 1949. Clk. Ct. Common Pleas, Montgomery County, Pa., 1948-51; judge Ct. Common Pleas, 1964-70; asst. dist. atty. Montgomery County, 1951, 53-55, 1st asst. dist. atty., 1956-60; mem. firm Ditter and Jenkins and predecessor firm, Ambler, Pa., 1953-63; judge U.S. Dist. Ct. Ea. Dist. Pa., Phila., 1970—; lectr. Villanova U. Past pres. bd. trustees Calvary Methodist Ch.; charter pres. Ambler Jaycees, 1954-55; bd. dirs. Riverview Osteo. Hosp., Norristown, Pa., 1964-71; bd. consulters Villanova U. Sch. Law, 1977—. Served to capt. USNR, 1943-68. Mem. Am., Fed., Pa., Montgomery County bar assns., Hist. Soc. U.S. Dist. Ct. Eastern Dist. Pa. (incorporator, bd. dirs.). Office: US Dist Ct 6614 US Court House Philadelphia PA 19106

DITTMEIR, THOMAS E., lawyer. U.S. atty. ea. dist. State of Mo., St. Louis. Office: US Court & Custom House 1114 Market St Room 414 Saint Louis MO 63101 *

DITTRICH, RAYMOND JOSEPH, medical device company executive; b. Wichita, Kans., Feb. 17, 1932; s. Raymond Joseph and Helen Sue (Sheehan) D.; m. Paula Ann Makielski, Feb. 20, 1954; children: Lisa Ann, Claire Louise, David Thomas, Mark Alan. A.B. magna cum laude, U. Notre Dame, 1953; LL.B., U. Mich., 1958. Bar: Minn. bar 1958, Fla. bar 1973. Atty. Cargill, Inc., Mpls., 1958-71; v.p., gen. counsel, sec. Burger King Corp., Miami, Fla., 1971-74; v.p., gen. counsel Pillsbury Co., Mpls., 1974-80; sec. Pillsbury Co., 1977-80; v.p., gen. counsel Ga. Pacific Corp., 1980; v.p., sec., gen. counsel Medtronic, Inc., Mpls., 1980—. Mem. Charter Commn., Minnetonka, Minn., 1968-70; bd. dirs., pres. Mpls. Aquatenniel Assn., 1984. Served with USMCR, 1953-55; lt. col. Res. Mem. ABA, Fla. Bar Assn., Minn. Bar Assn. (v.p., dir. corporate counsel sect.), Food and Drug Law Inst. (trustee), Phi Alpha Delta. Republican. Roman Catholic. Clubs: Royal Palm Tennis (Miami); Wayzata Country, Minneapolis. Home: 4775 Bayswater Rd Shorewood MN 55330 Office: 7000 Central Ave NE Minneapolis MN 55432

DI TULLIO, DONNA MARIE, lawyer; b. Rochester, N.Y., Aug. 8, 1952; d. Louis Paul and Florence Madaline (Ciocchi) Di T. BA, Duquesne U., 1974; JD, Potomac Sch. Law, 1979. Bar: Ga. 1979, U.S. Supreme Ct. 1984, D.C. 1985. Atty. Washington region Fed. Labor Relations Authority, 1979-84; chief legal counsel Fed. Service Impasses Panel, Washington, 1984—. Democrat. Roman Catholic. Avocations: scuba diving, white water rafting. Labor, labor arbitration and mediation. Home: 1658A Euclid St NW Washington DC 20009 Office: Fed Service Impasses Panel 500 C St SW Rm 215 Washington DC 20424

DIXON, BONNIE LYNN, lawyer; b. Pitts., Aug. 21, 1955; d. Kenneth Harold and Margaret Louise Dixon. BA, U. Mich., 1978, JD, 1981. Bar: N.Y. 1982. Fgn. assoc. Nagashima & Ohno, Tokyo, 1981-84; assoc. Mudge, Rose, Guthrie, Alexander & Ferdon, N.Y.C., 1984—. Founder, sec. Internat. Friends Kabuki, Tokyo, 1982-84. Mem. ABA, Am. Assn. for Comperative Study of Law, Roppongi Bar Assn. (founder, pres. 1982-84), Japanese-Am. Soc. Legal Studies, N.Y. State Bar Assn., Phi Beta Kappa, Zeta Tau Alpha. Avocation: translater of Japanese kabuki and bunraku drama. Contracts commercial, General corporate, Private international. Office: Mudge Rose Guthrie Alexander & Ferdon 180 Maiden Ln New York NY 10038

DIXON, CARL FRANKLIN, lawyer; b. Mansfield, Ohio, Feb. 17, 1948; s. Carl Hughes and Elizabeth (Kauffman) D.; m. Barbara Wagner, Dec. 27, 1969; children—Clare Elizabeth, Jane Allison. B.A., Ill. Wesleyan U., 1970, B.S., 1970; M.A., Harvard U., 1974; JD, U. Chgo., 1974. Bar: Ill. 1975, U.S. Dist. Ct. (no. dist.) Ill. 1975, Ohio 1983. Assoc., Keck, Mahin & Cate, Chgo., 1974-78; ptnr. Dixon & Kois, Chgo., 1978-82; assoc. Porter, Wright, Morris & Arthur, Cleve., 1982-85, ptnr., 1986—. Recipient Adlai E. Stevenson award UN Assn., 1970; Edward R. Murror fellow, 1971. Mem. ABA, Greater Cleve. Bar Assn., Phi Kappa Phi. Republican. Episcopalian. Club: Union League (Chgo.); Clifton (Lakewood, Ohio). Real property, Banking. Home: 31011 Manchester Ln Bay Village OH 44140 Office: Porter Wright Morris & Arthur 1500 Huntington Bldg Cleveland OH 44115

DIXON, HARRY THOMAS, lawyer; b. Buffalo, N.Y., July 24, 1929; s. Harry T. and Florence M. (Luksch) D.; m. Elsie Ann Schlau, Dec. 29, 1951; children: Harry Thomas Jr., Michael B., Claudia M. Dixon Kuechle. BS, Canisius COll., 1952; JD, U. Buffalo, 1955. Bar: N.Y. 1955, U.S. Dist. Ct. (we. dist.) N.Y. 1955. Ptnr. Dixon, DeMarie & Schoenborn P.C., Buffalo, 1956—. Mem. N.Y. State Bar Assn., Erie County Bar Assn., Western N.Y. Trial Lawyers Assn., N.Y. State Trial Lawyers Assn., Assn. Trial Lawyers of Am., Am. Arbitration Assn. (arbitrator 1971—). Republican. Roman Catholic. Clubs: Island Yacht (Wilson, N.Y.) (fleet legal counsel 1976-81); Niagara on Lake Sailing (Ontario, Can.). Avocation: sailing. Federal civil litigation, State civil litigation, Insurance company defense. Office: Dixon DeMarie & Schoenborn PC 930 Convention Tower Buffalo NY 14202

DIXON, JAMES MIKEL, lawyer; b. Knoxville, Tenn., Dec. 12, 1947; s. James Martin and Marjorie Flora (Trotter) D.; m. M. Susan Merritt, Dec. 27, 1969; 1 child, Jason Mikel. BBA in Real Estate, U. Tenn., 1969, JD, 1974. Bar: Tenn. 1974, U.S. Dist. Ct. (ea. dist.) Tenn. 1974, U.S. Ct. Appeals (6th cir.) 1974. Sole practice Knoxville, 1974-75, 1985—; assoc. Ambrose, Wilson, Lockridge & Grimm, Knoxville, 1975-81; prosecutor Knox County Dist. Atty. Staff, Knoxville, 1981-85. Served with U.S. Army, 1970-72. Mem. ABA, Tenn. Bar Assn., Knoxville Bar Assn. Methodist. Criminal, Federal civil litigation, State civil litigation. Home: 7216 Ambassador Pl Knoxville TN 37918 Office: Ball & Dunn 701 S Gay St Knoxville TN 37902

DIXON, JOHN ALLEN, JR., chief justice La. Supreme Ct.; b. Orange, Tex., Apr. 8, 1920; s. John A. and Louella (Stark) D.; m. Imogene K. Shipley, Oct. 20, 1945; children: Stella (Mrs. Paul Shepard), Diana (Mrs. L.C. Morehead, Jr.), Jeannette (Mrs. Michael Downing). B.A., Centenary Coll., 1940; LL.B., Tulane U., 1947. Bar: La. 1947. Tchr., coach Tallulah High Sch., 1940-42; pvt. practice law Shreveport, La., 1947-57; asst. dist. atty. Shreveport, 1954-57; judge 1st Dist. Ct., 1957-68, La. Ct. Appeal, Shreveport, 1968-70; asso. justice La. Supreme Ct., 1971, now chief justice. Served with AUS, 1942-45. Democrat. Methodist. Club: Mason. Jurisprudence. Office: Supreme Court of Louisiana 301 Loyola Ave New Orleans LA 70112 *

DIXON, PAUL EDWARD, chemical company executive; b. Bklyn., Aug. 27, 1944; s. Paul Stewart and Bernice (Mathisen) D.; B.A., Villanova U., 1966; J.D., St. Johns U., 1972; m. Kathleen Constance Kayser, Sept. 23, 1967; children—Jennifer Pyne, Paul Kayser, Meredith Stewart. Admitted to N.Y. State bar, 1972, U.S. Supreme Ct., 1976; asso. mem. firm Rogers & Wells, N.Y.C., 1972-77; sec., asst. gen. counsel Volvo of Am. Corp., Rockleigh, N.J., 1977-79, v.p., gen. counsel, 1979-81; v.p., gen. counsel, sec. Reichhold Chems. Inc., 1981—; chmn. Teeches Ltd., Bermuda; dir. Reichhold Internat., dir. Eschem, Inc. Mem. Bedford Hist. Soc. (dir.), Am. Bar Assn., Assn. Bar City N.Y., N.Y. State Bar Assn., U.S. Supreme Ct. Hist. Soc., Am. Corp. Counsel Assn., Westchester-Fairfield Corp. Counsel. Club: Waccabuc Country. Reichhold General corporate. Office: Reichhold Chems Inc 525 N Broadway White Plains NY 10603

DIXON, PHILLIP RAY, lawyer; b. Wake Forest, N.C., Mar. 26, 1949; s. Milton R. Dixon and Lottie Belle (Tippett) Larson; m. Candace (Mamie) Cicerone, Nov. 26, 1977; children: Phillip Ray Jr., Joseph David. BSBA, East Carolina U., 1971; JD, U. N.C., 1974. Bar: N.C. 1974, U.S. Dist. Ct. (ea. dist.) N.C. 1976, U.S. Ct. Appeals (4th cir.) 1981, U.S. Supreme Ct. 1981. Law clk. N.C. Ct. Appeals, Raleigh, 1974-75; assoc. Gaylord & Singleton, Greenville, N.C., 1975-78; ptnr. Dixon, Duffus & Doub and predecessor firms, Greenville, 1978—; instr. police sci. paralegal program Pitt Community Coll., 1975-79, advisor 1982—; instr. sch. law Martin County Community Coll., 1981, bd. and individual legal liability, 1984; bd. dirs. Peoples Bank and Trust Co., Greenville, chmn. 1984-85. Atty. Pitt County Schs. and Bd. of Edn., 1978—; local and state hearing officer Greenville Utilities Commn., 1981—, N.C. Dept. Pub. Instrn.; Pitt County Area Mental Health Mental Retardation and Substance Abuse Bd., 1983—, chmn. 1984-86; chmn. bd. dirs. 1st Christian Ch. of Greenville, 1981, chmn. bd. dirs. 1984; bd. dirs. Pitt-Greenville Arts Council, Inc., 1979-81, Pitt County United Way, Inc., 1981, vice chmn., 1986; mem. Downtown Greenville Assn., 1980—, Greenville Mus. of Art, 1980—, treas. 1986-87, v.p., 1987—, trustee, 1986—. Named one of Outstanding Young Men of Am., 1974-83. Mem. ABA, N.C. Bar Assn. (sustaining mem., family law sect., criminal law sect., real estate sect., probate sect., practical tng. com., instr. and seminar speaker on topic appeals, practical skills course 1975-81), Pitts County Bar Assn. (sec. law library com. 1976-77, chmn. 1976-82), N.C. Acad. Trial Lawyers, N.C. Coll. of Adv., N.C. Sch. Bd. of Attys. (bd. dirs. 1982—, pres. 1984-85, v.p. 1983-84, chmn. ins. com. 1983-84), Nat. Sch. Bd. Attys. Assn., Greenville C. of C. (exec. vice chmn.). Democrat. Club: Greenville Sports (chartered, sec., treas. 1975-77, pres. 1979-80). Lodge: Rotary (chartered, bd. dirs. Greenville chpt. 1981-83, dist. sec. 1982, v.p. 1983, pres. 1986-87, Paul Harris Fellow 1982). Probate, Family and matrimonial, General practice. Home: 700 Daventry Dr Greenville NC 27858 Office: Dixon Duffus & Doub 201 W 1st St NCNB Bldg PO Drawer 1785 Greenville NC 27835

DIXON, RICHARD DEAN, lawyer, educator; b. Columbus, Ohio, Nov. 6, 1944; s. Dean A. and Katherine L. (Currier) D.; m. Kathleen A. Manfrass, June 17, 1967; children—Jennifer, Lindsay. B.S. in Elec. Engring., Ohio State U., 1967, M.S. in Elec. Engring., 1968; M.B.A., Fla. State U., 1972, J.D., 1974. Bar: Fla. 1975, U.S. Dist. Ct. (mid. dist.) Fla. 1975, U.S. Patent and Trademark Office, 1975, Colo. 1985, U.S. Dist. Ct. Colo. 1985. Telemetry systems engr. Pan Am. World Airways, Patrick AFB, Fla., 1968-72; sole practice, Melbourne and Orlando, Fla., 1975-80; sr. counsel Harris Corp., Melbourne, 1980-85; corp. counsel Ford Microelectronics, Inc., Colorado Springs, Colo., 1985—; adj. prof. bus. law U. Central Fla., Cocoa, 1977, Fla. Inst. Tech., Melbourne, 1980-84. Cooper Industries Engring. scholar Ohio State U., 1964-67. Mem. Licensing Execs. Soc., Am. Intellectual Property Law Assn., Am. Corp. Counsel Assn., ABA, Sigma Iota Epsilon, Eta Kappa Nu, Phi Eta Sigma. Contracts commercial, Government contracts and claims, Patent. Home: 225 Woodmoor Dr Monument CO 80132 Office: Ford Microelectronics Inc 10340 State Hwy 83 Colorado Springs CO 80908

DIXON, SCOTT WILLIAM, lawyer; b. Colorado Springs, Colo., Nov. 6, 1953; s. Donald Roger and Kitty (Badgley) D.; m. Patricia Rende; 1 child, Michael. BA, U. Ill., 1975; JD, John Marshall Sch. Law, 1978. Bar: Ill. 1978, U.S. Dist. Ct. (so. dist.) Ill. 1978, U.S. Dist. Ct. (ea. dist.) Mo. 1980, U.S. Ct. Appeals (8th cir.) 1980. Ptnr. Ripplinger, Dixon, Hoffman & Ver Steegh and predecessor firms Ripplinger, Dixon & Hoffman; Ripplinger & Dixon; Ripplinger, Ransom & Dixon, Belleville, Ill., 1978—; assoc. to the asst. corp. counsel City of East St. Louis, Ill., 1978-79. Fellow Ill. Bar Found.; mem. ABA, Ill. Bar Assn., Mo. Bar Assn., St. Clair County Bar Assn. (mem. pub. relations com. 1980-81), East St. Louis Bar Assn., Assn. Trial Lawyers Am., (mem. sole practitioners and small firms com., gen. practice sect., 1982-83), Nat. Assn. Criminal Def. Lawyers, Phi Delta Phi. Personal injury, General practice, Family and matrimonial. Office: Ripplinger Dixon Hoffman & Ver Steegh 120 S Central Suite 1400 Claytonlle MO 63105

DIXON, STEVEN BEDFORD, lawyer; b. San Bernardino, Calif., Dec. 25, 1945; s. Harold James Dixon and Jane Anna (Bedford) Kennedy; m. Lucy Pearson; children—Melanie Anne, Zachary David; stepchildren: Michael, Katherine. B.A., U. Hawaii-Hilo, 1975; J.D., Calif. Western Sch. Law, 1978; postgrad. Chaminade U. of Hawaii, Hawaii Tax Inst., 1978-82. Bar: Hawaii, U.S. Dist Ct. Hawaii, U.S. Tax Ct. Law clk. firm Linley, McDougal, Meloche & Murphy, El Cajon, Calif., 1976, D. Stephen Boner, San Diego, 1977, Tyson & Churchill, San Diego, 1977; law intern Legal Aid Soc. of Hawaii, 1978; law clk., investigator Stephen Christensen, Hawaii, 1978; gen. ptnr. Altman, Dicker & Dixon, tax attys., Hilo, 1978-79, Altman Dixon & Assocs., tax attys., Hilo, 1979-81; sole practice as tax atty., Hilo, 1981-82; gen. ptnr. Dixon & Okura, Hilo, 1982—; speaker, news columnist in field; writer; instr. bus. law U. Hawaii-Hilo, 1979-80, Vitousek Real Estate Sch. (cert.); bd. dirs. Elec. Co-operative Hawaii Inc. Columnist Money, Real Estate and You; radio show 50 Minutes with Steve Dixon. Past v.p. Hawaii Concert Soc.; counsel discharge Vets. Outreach, San Diego, 1976; bd. dirs. Big Island Substance Abuse Council, Elec. Coop. of Hawaii, Inc; active community services. Served to 1st lt. 1967-70, Vietnam. Decorated Bronze Star. U. Hawaii-Hilo scholar, 1973. Mem. Hawaii County Bar Assn. Lodge: Rotary. Probate, Real property, General corporate. Office: 155 Wailuku Dr Hilo HI 96720 also: Kailua Kona HI 96740

DIXON, WILLIAM CORNELIUS, lawyer; b. Dexter, N.Y., July 1, 1904; s. Frank and Celia (Potter) D.; m. Arvilla Pratt, Nov. 20, 1934; children—Anne Arvilla, Nancy Cornelia. A.B., U. Mich., 1926, J.D., 1928. Bar: Ohio 1928, Calif. 1948, Supreme Ct. U.S 1948. Asso. Holliday-Grossman-McAfee, Cleve., 1928-32; asst. dir. law Cleve., 1932-33, practiced law, 1933-38; justice Supreme Ct. Ohio, 1938; spl. asst. in anti-trust div. to atty. gen. U.S. Dept. Justice, 1944-54, chief asst. trial sect. anti-trust div., 1945, apptd. chief West Coast offices Anti-trust div., 1946, chief trial counsel for Govt. U.S. versus Standard Oil Co. Calif. et al, 1948, chief Los Angeles Office, 1948-54; pvt. law practice Los Angeles, 1954-59, 63—; asst. atty. gen. in charge state anti-trust enforcement Calif., 1959-63; legal adviser and mem. Joint War and State Depts., Zaibatsu Mission to Japan, 1946. Dir. relief for Ohio under Emergency Relief Act, 1938-39; moderator Los Angeles Assn. Congl. Chs., 1957; moderator Congl. Conf. So. Calif. and S.W., 1960; mem. constn. comm. United Ch. of Christ; mem. United Ch. Bd. for Homeland Ministries, 1962-65. Papers included in Truman Library, Library of Contemporary History, U. Wyo., Ohio State U. and UCLA libraries. Mem. Calif., Los Angeles bar assns., Delta Sigma Rho, Pi Kappa Alpha. Democrat. Antitrust, Jurisprudence. Home: 1188 Romney Dr Pasadena CA 91105 Office: Subway Terminal Bldg 417 S Hill St Los Angeles CA 90013

DJOKIC, WALTER HENRY, lawyer; b. Schwaforden, Germany, Sept. 12, 1947; came to U.S., 1951, naturalized, 1959; s. Radovan and Martha (Schulenburg) D.; divorced; 1 child, Joshua David. B.A., U. Ill., 1969; J.D., DePaul U., 1972. Bar: Ill. 1972, Ariz. 1980. Assoc., Washowski & Wachowski, Chgo., 1972-73; atty. Pretzel & Stouffer, Chartered, Chgo., 1973-79; ptnr., 1979-85, Wood, Lucksinger & Epstein, Chgo., 1985-86, Finley Kumble Wagner, Heine, Underberg, Manley, Myerson & Casey, Chgo., 1986—. Mem. Chgo. Bar Assn., Ill. State Bar Assn., State Bar of Ariz. Personal injury, Federal civil litigation, State civil litigation.

DOAN, KIRK HUGH, lawyer; b. Independence, Iowa, Jan. 30, 1953; s. Arthur Nelson and Kathlyn (Kingsley) D.; m. Laura Leah Brown, Sept. 24, 1982. BA, Iowa State U., 1975; JD, U. Iowa, 1978. Bar: Mo. 1978, U.S. Dist. Ct. (we. dist.) Mo. 1978. Assoc. Hillix, Brewer, Hoffhaus, Whittaker & Horner, Kansas City, Mo., 1978-83, ptnr., 1983—. Contbr. articles to profl. jours. Advisor Heart of Am. council Boy Scouts Am., 1982—. Mem. Mo. Bar Assn., Kansas City Met. Bar Assn., Lawyers Assn. Kansas City (pres. young lawyers sect. 1984-85), Order of Coif. Republican. Methodist. Club: Kansas City. Securities, Oil and gas leasing. Home: 6330 Hadley-Vernon Pl Merriam KS 66202 Office: Hillix Brewer Hoffhaus et al 911 Main St Suite 2700 Kansas City MO 64105

DOAN, XUYEN VAN, lawyer; b. Hadong, Vietnam, Apr. 1, 1949; came to U.S., 1975; Licence en droit, U. Saigon Law Sch., Vietnam, 1971; MBA, U. Ark., 1977; JD, U. Calif., Hastings, 1982. Bar: Saigon 1972, Calif. 1982. Sole practice Costa Mesa and San Jose, Calif., 1982-84; ptnr. Doan & Vu, San Jose, 1984—. Personal injury, Private international, Public international. Office: Doan & Vu Law Firm Doan & Vu Bldg 556 N First St Suite 100 San Jose CA 95112

DOBKIN, DONALD SIDNEY, lawyer; b. Toronto, Ont., Can., Nov. 20, 1952; s. Irving and Mary (Gore) D.; m. Sally A. McMahon, May 30, 1975; children: Kelly, Spencer. Student, U. Waterloo, Ont., Can., 1970-72, Wayne State U., 1974-75; LLB, U. Windsor, Ont., Can., 1975; LLM, Northwestern U., 1976. Bar: Ill. 1977, U.S. Dist. Ct. (no. dist.) Ill. 1977, U.S. Dist. Ct. (ea. dist.) Mich. 1979. Atty. Karon, Morrison, & Savikas, Chgo., 1976-77, AMA, Chgo., 1977-79; sr. ptnr., pres. Donald S. Dobkin P.C., Troy, Mich., 1979—. Contbr. articles to profl. jours. Mem. ABA, Am. Immigration Lawyers Assn., Can. Am. Bar Assn., Oakland County Bar Assn. Avocation: golf. Immigration, naturalization, and customs. Office: Donald S Dobkin PC 888 W Big Beaver Rd Troy MI 48084

DOBRANSKI, BERNARD, legal educator; b. Pitts., Sept. 3, 1939; s. Walter John and Helen Dolores (Rudnick) D.; m. Carroll Sue Wood, Aug. 31, 1963; children—Stephanie, Andrea, Christopher. B.B.A. in Finance, U. Notre Dame, 1961; J.D., U. Va., 1964. Bar: Va. 1964, U.S. Supreme Ct. 1968, U.S. Cir. Ct. (D.C. cir.) 1971. Legal advisor to bd. Nat. Labor Relations Bd., 1964-67; profl. staff mem. Pres.'s Adv. Commn. on Civil Disorders, 1967-68; adminstrv. asst. U.S. Ho. of Reps., 1968-71; gen. counsel Washington Met. Area Transit Commn., 1971-72; mem. faculty Creighton U. Sch. of Law, Omaha, 1972-77, U. Notre Dame, 1977-83; prof., dean U. Detroit Sch. of Law, 1983—; labor arbitrator Fed. Mediation and Conciliation Service. Contbr. articles to profl. jours. Mem. Am. Arbitration Assn., Am. Law Inst., ABA, Frank Murphy Honor Soc. Roman Catholic. Club; University (Detroit). Labor, Private international, Jurisprudence. Office: U Detroit Sch Law 651 E Jefferson Ave Detroit MI 48226

DOBRIN, MITZI S., corporate lawyer. Exec. v.p. legal and corp. affairs Steinberg Inc., Montreal, Que., Can. Office: Steinberg Inc, 1500 Atwater Alexis Nihon Plaza, Montreal, PQ Canada H3Z 1Y3 *

DOBRY, STANLEY THOMAS, lawyer, arbitrator; b. Hamtramck, Mich., May 29, 1948; s. Stanley Marcel and Mary (Lomaka) D.; m. Bette J. Nichols, May 21, 1971; children: Jason Thomas, Jeremy Scott. BA, U. Mich., 1970; JD cum laude, Detroit Coll. Law, 1974. Bar: Mich., U.S. Dist. Ct. (ea. and we. dists.) Mich., U.S. Ct. Appeals (6th cir.), U.S. Supreme Ct. Asst. supervising atty. Wayne County Neighborhood Legal Services, Detroit, 1974-76; staff atty. Mich. Jud. Tenure Comm., Detroit, 1976-81; sole practice Detroit, 1981—; labor arbitrator various orgns., 1978—. Bd. dirs. Lakeshore YMCA, St. Clair Shores, Mich., 1986. Arthur F. Lederle scholar, 1973-74; fellow Mich. Bar Found., 1985—. Mem. ABA, Mich. Bar Assn. (rep. assembly 1979-82), Ukrainian Am. Bar Assn. Mich. (pres. 1985-87, v.p. 1984-85), Nat. Acad. Arbitrators (legal affairs com.), Indsl. Relations Research Assn. Detroit (chmn. membership 1983-86), Soc. Profl. in Dipsute Resolution (state program dir. 1982-84), Am. Arbitration Assn. (panel arbitrators). Roman Catholic. Avocations: sailing, running, bicycling, skiing. Labor, Family and matrimonial. Home: 12008 Susan Ave Warren MI 48093 Office: 65 Cadillac Sq Suite 2201 Cadillac Tower Detroit MI 48226

DOBSON, ROBERT ALBERTUS, III, lawyer, accountant; b. Greenville, S.C., Nov. 27, 1938; s. Robert A. Jr. and Dorothy (Leonard) D.; m. Linda Josephine Bryant, Nov. 18, 1956; children: Robert, William, Michael, Daniel, Jonathan, Laura; m. Catherine Elizabeth Cornmesser, Sept. 17, 1983; 1 child, Andrew. BS in Acctg. summa cum laude, U. S.C., 1960, JD magna cum laude, 1962. Bar: S.C. 1962, U.S. Dist. Ct. S.C. 1962, U.S. Ct. Appeals (4th cir.) 1962. Pvt. practice pub. acctg. Greenville, 1962-64; ptnr. Dobson & Dobson, Greenville, 1964—; sr. ptnr., CPA, Dobson, Lewis & Saad, P.A., Greenville, 1985—. Contbr. articles on tax and acctg. to profl. jours. Mem. ABA, S.C. Bar Assn., Am. Inst. CPA's, Am. Assn. Attys. and CPA's, S.C. Assn. CPA's, S.C. Assn. Pub. Accts., Kappa Sigma (dist. grand master 1970—), Phi Beta Kappa. Episcopalian. Lodges: Sertoma Internat. (dist. treas.), Sertoma Sunrisers (pres. Greenville club). Corporate taxation, Estate taxation, Personal income taxation. Home: 1219 Shadow Way Greenville SC 29615 Office: 1306 S Church St Greenville SC 29605

DOCKRY, MICHAEL BRIAN, lawyer; b. Youngstown, Ohio, May 22, 1956; s. Donald Richard and Marjorie (Herschel) D.; m. Marie Denise Witt, June 18, 1982. BS, Youngstown U., 1978; JD, U. Akron, 1982. Bar: Ohio 1982, Fla. 1983, U.S. Dist. Ct. (no. dist.) Ohio 1983. Sole practice Youngstown, 1982—. Mem. Fla. Bar Assn., Ohio Bar Assn., Mahoning County Bar Assn., Assn. Trial Lawyers Am., Ohio Trial Lawyers Assn. Republican. Roman Catholic. Avocations: golf, tennis, fishing, sports, travel. Personal injury, General practice, Consumer commercial. Office: 5825 Mahoning Ave Youngstown OH 44515

DODD, LAWRENCE ROE, lawyer; b. Alexandria, La., Oct. 17, 1944; s. Sylvester Abner and Annie Ruth (Chandler) D.; m. Nancy Meager, Apr. 11, 1979 (div.); children: Bruce Wayne, Lawrence Scott, Chandler Lane. BA, La. State U., 1966, JD, 1972. Bar: La. 1973, U.S. Dist. Ct. (ea., mid. and we. dists.) La., U.S. Ct. Appeals (5th cir.), U.S. Supreme Ct. Ptnr. Kizer & Kizer, Baton Rouge, 1973-76, Dodd, Achee & Burt, Baton Rouge, 1976-80; sole practice Baton Rouge, 1980—; instr. law Inst. Continuing Legal Edn., 1971-72, Am. Inst. Banking, 1975-76. Editor: Recent Developments in the Law of Maritime Torts, 1972. Pres., bd. dirs. Villa Del Rey Citizens, Sevretary, Walden Citizens Assn., 1979-80. Republican. Lutheran. Clubs: City (Baton Rouge). State civil litigation, Consumer commercial, General corporate. Office: 7414 Perkins Rd Baton Rouge LA 70808

DODD, ROBERT WARREN, lawyer; b. Springfield, Ill., Jan. 20, 1938; s. Warren F. and Florence C. (Mueller) D.; m. Joyce M. Rowley, May 30, 1971; children: Cathy, Stephen, Joan, Jean, Brenda, James. AB, Pontofical Coll., 1964, DD, 1964; JD, U. Ill., 1974. Bar: Ill. 1974, U.S. Dist. Ct. (cen. dist.) Ill. 1974. Sole practice Champaign, Ill., 1975-81; ptnr. Zimmerly, Dodd, Ansel & Stout, P.C., Champaign, 1981-82; sr. ptnr. Dodd & Beyers, P.C., Champaign, 1982—; dep. mayor City of Champaign, 1981-83, mayor, 1983-87. Councilman City of Champaign, 1974-83. Fellow Ill. Bar Assn.; mem. Champaign County Bar Assn., Ill. Bar Assn., Assn. Trial Lawyers Am. Roman Catholic. Club: Am. Bus. (Champaign). Lodge: Rotary. Avocations: flying, computers. General corporate, Family and matrimonial, General practice. Home: 2120 Seaton Ct Champaign IL 61821 Office: Dodd & Beyers PC 303 S Mattis Ave 201 Marine American National Bank Champaign IL 61821-3045

DODD, ROGER JAMES, lawyer; b. Sewickley, Pa., Sept. 15, 1951; s. Carl Roger and Dorothy Maude (Barley) D.; m. Emily Elizabeth Lilly, June 9,

1974; children—Matthew A., Andrew J. B.A. in Econs., Bucknell U., 1973; J.D., U. Pitts., 1976. Ga. 1976, Fla. 1977, U.S. Ct. Appeals (5th cir.) 1976, U.S. Ct. Appeals (11th cir.) 1981, U.S. Dist. Ct. (mid. dist.) Ga. 1976, U.S. Dist. Ct. (no. dist.) Ga. 1983, U.S. Dist. Ct. Fla. 1983, U.S. Supreme Ct. 1981. Ptnr., Blackburn, Bright, Edwards, Dodd & Joseph, Valdosta, Ga., 1976-87; sole practice, Valdosta, 1987—; spl. asst. atty. gen. State of Ga., 1979-85; mem. faculty Nat. Coll. Criminal Def., 1986—, Ga. Inst. Trial Advocacy, 1986—; bd. dirs. Ga. Inst. Trial Advocacy, 1987; guest lectr. Mercer U. Sch. Law., Ga. State U. Sch. Law. Contbr. articles to profl. jours., newspapers. Bd. dirs. Lowndes Country Assn. Retarded Citizens, Valdosta, 1977, Valwood Sch., Valdosta, 1984-86. Named Outstanding Law Day Chmn., State Bar Ga., 1977. Mem. Ga. Assn. Criminal Def. Lawyers (v.p. 1982-83, bd. dirs. 1982—, Pres.'s award 1982, exec. v.p. 1984, pres. 1986), State Bar Ga. (mem. exec. com. family law sect.), Internat. Platform Assn., Ga. Trial Lawyers Assn. (contbr. articles), Assn. Trial Lawyers Am., Nat. Assn. Criminal Def. Lawyers, Valdosta Bar Assn. (sec.-treas. 1977-78), Ga. Assn. Sch. Bd. Attys., MENSA, Nat. Inst. Trial Advocacy (Advance Trial Advocacy Skills 1985). Libertarian. Presbyterian. Clubs: William Pitt (Pitts.), William Bucknell Assn. Lodge: Elks. Personal injury, Criminal, Family and matrimonial. Home: 1415 Williams St Valdosta GA 31601 Office: PO Box 1066 613 N Patterson St Valdosta GA 31601

DODD, WILLIAM HORACE, lawyer; b. Richmond, Va., Jan. 8, 1934; s. William Horace and Myrtle Ann (Clark) D.; m. Carol Santoki, Dec. 20, 1961; children—Michael William, Anna Laura, A.B., Coll. William and Mary, 1959; postgrad. U. Va. 1959-60; LL.B., George Washington U., 1962. Bar: Va. 1962, Hawaii 1963, U.S. Ct. Appeals (9th cir.) 1963. Ptnr. Fong, Miho, Choy & Robinson, Honolulu, 1962-69, Chun, Kerr & Dodd, Honolulu, 1970—. Bd. dirs., sec. Boys Club, Honolulu; mem., pres. Big Bros. Hawaii; bd. dirs. Big Bros. Am. Served with USAF, 1952-56. Mem. Am. Judicature Soc., Va. Bar Assn., Hawaii Bar Assn. (dir. 1983-86, pres. 1986), ABA, Assn. Trial Lawyers Am. Clubs: Honolulu, Wakiki Yacht, Pacific, Adventures (Honolulu). Federal civil litigation, Bankruptcy, Real property. Office: 14th Floor 700 Bishop St Honolulu HI 96813

DODDS, MICHAEL BRUCE, lawyer; b. Spokane, Wash., June 27, 1952; s. Bruce Alison and Janet Lorraine (Swanbeck) D.; m. Karen Lynn Sifford, Jan. 5, 1972; children: Jennifer Ann, Stephanie Marie, Alexander Michael. BA, Gonzaga U., 1974, JD, 1979. Bar: Wash. 1980, U.S. Dist. Ct. (ea. dist.) Wash. 1983. Dep. prosecutor Okanogan (Wash.) County, 1980-87, Clark (Wash.) County, 1987—. Served to 2d lt. U.S. Army, 1974-76. Mem. ABA, Wash. State Bar Assn., Wash. State Assn. of Coroners and Med. Examiners, Phi Alpha Delta. Democrat. Lodge: Eagles. Criminal. Home: 15102 NE 86th St Vancouver WA 98682 Office: Clark County Pros Atty PO Box 5000 Vancouver WA 98668

DODDS, ROBERT JAMES, JR., retired lawyer; b. Pitts., Mar. 5, 1916; s. Robert James and Agnes Julia (Raw) D.; m. Kathryn Moore Bechman, June 6, 1942 (dec. Sept. 1943); 1 child, Robert James III; m. Virginia T. Enright, Feb. 13, 1961; children: Dana, Anthony. Grad., Shady Side Acad., Pitts., 1933; A.B., Yale, 1937; LL.B., U. Pa., 1940. Bar: Pa. 1940. Since practiced Pitts.; former mem. firm Reed, Smith, Shaw & McClay; gen. counsel U.S. Dept. Commerce, 1959-61. Trustee Shady Side Acad. (emeritus), YMCA, Pitts.; trustee, past pres. bd. Children's Hosp. of Pitts.; former dir. Blue Cross Western Pa.; bd. dirs., sec. Pitts. Symphony Soc. Served from pvt. to maj., inf. AUS, 1941-45, ETO. Decorated Bronze Star medal. Mem. Am., Pa., Allegheny County bar assns. Presbyn. (trustee). Clubs: Duquesne (Pitts.); Pitts. Athletic Assn; Longue Vue Country (N.Y.C.), Rolling Rock (N.Y.C.), Yale (N.Y.C.); Wilderness Country (Naples, Fla.). Home: 1740 Beechwood Blvd Pittsburgh PA 15217 Office: Reed Smith Shaw & McClay 435 6th Ave Pittsburgh PA 15230

DODEGGE, THOMAS ROLAND, lawyer; b. Chgo., Aug. 31, 1942; s. Otto Nicholas and Charlotte Hilda (Burkhardt) D. B.A., Northwestern U., 1964; J.D., Ill. Inst. Tech., Chgo., 1974. Bar: Ill. 1974. Staff analyst Ill. Ho. Reps., Springfield, 1975-77; legal counsel Office of Ill. State Comptroller, Springfield, 1977-84, dep. comptroller, 1984—. Served to capt. USAF, 1966-70. Mem. Ill. Bar Assn. Democrat. Legislative, Government contracts and claims, Administrative and regulatory. Home: 256 Durkin Dr Apt D Springfield IL 62704 Office: Office of Comptroller 201 State House Springfield IL 62706

DODGE, CYNTHIA ELLEN, lawyer; b. Washington, June 11, 1953; d. Austin Phelps and Lucy Ann (Hapeman) D.; m. Edward James Woodhouse Jr., Nov. 29, 1980; 1 child, Victoria Hapeman. BA, Radcliffe Coll., 1975; JD, NYU, 1978. Bar: Mo. 1978, Va. 1981. Assoc. Watson, Ess, Marshall & Enges, Kansas City, Mo., 1978-79; atty. Pub. Defender's Office, Kansas City, 1979-80, Roanoke, Va., 1981-84; ptnr. Woodhouse and Dodge, Radford, Va., 1984—; legal advisor Women's Resource Ctr., Radford, 1984—. Trustee New River Valley Young Dems., Radford, 1985—; mem. Va. EEO Council, Richmond, Va., 1986—. Mem. ABA, Va. State Bar Assn., Mo. Bar Assn., Montgomery-Floyd-Radford Bar Assn., Va. Trial Lawyers Assn., Va. Women Attys. Assn., AAUW (legis. com. 1985—), Bus. & Profl. Women (pres. elect Radford chpt. 1986). Episcopalian. General practice, Family and matrimonial, Criminal. Home: 207 Fairway Dr Radford VA 24141 Office: 206 First St PO Box 2837 Radford VA 24143

DODGE, DAVID A., lawyer; b. Grand Rapids, Mich., Mar. 3, 1946; s. Richard C. and Lorraine G. Dodge; m. Carol Ruth Longstreet, Apr. 27, 1968; children: David II, Brian, Julia, Mark. BA, U. Mich., 1968; JD, Ind. U., 1970. Bar: Ind., U.S. Dist. Ct. (we. dist.) Mich., U.S. Ct. Appeals (6th cir.), U.S. Supreme Ct. Asst. atty. Kent Prosecutor Office, Grand Rapids, 1973-74; ptnr. Catchick & Dodge, Grand Rapids, 1974—. Served to capt. (judge advocate) USMC, 1970-73. Mem. Mich. Bar Assn. (chmn. prisons and corrections com. 1983-86), Grand Rapids Bar Assn. (trustee 1982-84). Roman Catholic. Clubs: Peninsular, Cascade Hills Country. Criminal. Office: 200 N Division Grand Rapids MI 49503

DODGE, RICHARD EDGAR, lawyer; b. Eureka, Calif., Mar. 21, 1941; s. Laurence Ashmore and Genevieve (Dever) D.; m. Jeanne Michele Pavlovic, Oct. 12, 1965; children: Michele, Lauren, Adam. BA, U. Colo., 1963; LLB, U. Calif., San Francisco, 1966. Bar: Calif. 1966. Assoc. Dunn, Hart & McDonald, San Francisco, 1966-67; ptnr. McNamara, Houston, Dodge, McClure & Ney, Walnut Creek, Calif., 1967—. Mem. Am. Bd. Trial Advs., Am. Bd. Profl. Liability Attys., Calif. Bar Assn., Contra Costa Bar Assn. (pres. 1977-78), Assn. Def. Counsel. Republican. Roman Catholic. Personal injury, Insurance. Home: 1120 Walker Ave Walnut Creek CA 94598 Office: McNamara Houston Dodge et al 1211 Newell Ave Walnut Creek CA 94596

DODSON, WILMER BYRD, lawyer; b. Lancaster County, Va., Nov. 18, 1925; s. Henry Thadeus and Virginia Ala (Wilmore) D.; m. Janie E. Callihan, July 21, 1949; children: Mark G., Robin L. Dodson Paper. AB, U. Md., 1951, JD, 1953. Bar: Md. 1953. Asst. gen. counsel Md. Casualty Co., Balt., 1954-72; counsel U.S. Fidelity and Guaranty Co., Balt., 1972-77, Calvert Fire Ins. Co., Balt., 1978—; gen. atty. Comml. Credit Co., Balt., 1978—; v.p., sec., gen. counsel Am. Life and Health Ins. Co., 1984—, also bd. dirs.; v.p., asst. sec., gen. counsel Gulf Ins. Co., Atlantic Ins. Co., and Select Ins. Co.; mem. legal adv. panel Ins. Services Office, N.Y.C., 1975—; bd. dirs. Gulf Ins. Co., Irving, Tex., Atlantic Ins. Co., Irving, Select Ins. Co., Irving. Mem. ABA, Md. Bar Assn., Internat. Assn. Ins. Counsel. Republican. Avocations: golf, fishing, woodworking. Insurance. Home: 4100 Loch Raven Blvd Baltimore MD 21218 Office: Comml Credit Co 300 St Paul Pl Baltimore MD 21202

DOEHRMAN, THOMAS C., lawyer; b. Ft. Wayne, Ind., Apr. 28, 1951; s. Ralph Charles and Virginia (Drury) D.; m. Judie Lynn Blonder, June 1, 1974; children: Jacob Tyler, Andrew Gregory and Sally Emma (twins). BA, Ind. U., 1973, JD cum laude, 1976. Bar: Ind. 1976, U.S. Dist. Ct. (so. dist.) Ind. 1976. Ptnr. Petri, Fuhs & Doehrman, Indpls., 1980-84; sole practice Indpls., 1976-80, 84—. Adv. bd. Head Injury Found. Ind., Inc., Indpls., 1982-84, bd. dirs., 1984—. Mem. ABA, Ind. Trial Lawyers Assn. State civil litigation, Personal injury. Office: 610 Victoria Centre 22 E Washington St Indianapolis IN 46204

DOERR, JOHN MAXWELL, lawyer; b. Pontiac, Mich., Oct. 3, 1939; s. Maxwell Hilberg and Jane (Park) D.; m. Eleanor Kilmon, Feb. 11, 1967; children—Jennifer Anne, Julie Kristin. B.A., Coll. Wooster, 1961; postgrad., Johns Hopkins U., 1962-64; J.D., U. Md., 1973. Bar: Md. 1973, Pa. 1974, U.S. Dist. Ct. (ea. dist.) Pa. 1974. Various positions Acme Markets, Inc., Balt., 1961-73, dir. real estate, Phila., 1973-80, asst. sec., 1973—, counsel, 1980—. Del., Delaware County Bus. Task Force, Bryn Mawr, Pa., 1976-77. Recipient Freidlander award Coll. Wooster, 1961. Mem. ABA, Phila. Bar Assn. Republican. Presbyterian. General corporate, Real property, Landlord-tenant. Office: Acme Markets Inc 124 N 15th St Philadelphia PA 19101

DOGGRELL, HENRY PATTON, lawyer; b. Memphis, July 3, 1948; s. Frank Ernest Doggrell Jr. and Martha (Patton) Ferris; m. Beverly Gay Rhoda, Jan. 22. 1983; children: Henry Patton Jr., Dana Scott. BS in Commerce, U. Va., 1970; JD, Vanderbilt U., 1976. Bar: U.S. Dist. Ct. (mid. dist.) Tenn. 1977, U.S. Ct. Appeals (6th cir.) 1977, U.S. Dist. Ct. (we. dist.) Tenn. 1978, U.S. Ct. Appeals (fed. cir.) 1985. Assoc. Boult, Cummings, Conners & Berry, Nashville, 1976-78; ptnr. Burch, Porter & Johnson, Memphis, 1978—. Chmn. ad hoc com. Citizens on Govtl. Consolidation, Memphis, 1978. Served to lt. (j.g.) USN, 1970-71. Democrat. Presbyterian. Avocations: backpacking, fishing, hiking, scuba diving, reading. Municipal bonds, Securities, Real property. Home: 799 West Dr Memphis TN 38112 Office: Burch Porter & Johnson 6060 Poplar Ave Suite 411 Memphis TN 38119

DOHANEY, JOSEPH GEORGE, JR., lawyer; b. State Coll., Pa., Apr. 17, 1934; s. Joseph George Dohaney and Anna Pauline (Fohringer) Hughes; m. Dewayne C. Jones, Jan. 19, 1953 (div.); m. Tena Ruth Taylor, Apr. 29, 1968; 1 child, Sean Kevin. AA, St. Petersburg (Fla.) Jr. Coll., 1958; JD, Stetson U., 1961. Bar: Fla. 1961, U.S. Dist. Ct. (so. dist.) Fla. 1962, U.S. Ct. Appeals (5th cir.) 1962, U.S. Dist. Ct. (mid. dist.) Fla. 1962, U.S. Supreme Ct. 1973, U.S. Ct. Appeals (11th cir.) 1981. Ptnr. Wolfe, Bonner, Hogan & Donahey, Clearwater, Fla., 1961-66, Mosley & Donahey, Clearwater, 1966-71, Donahey & Furnell, Clearwater, 1971-76; sole practice Clearwater, 1976-78; ptnr. Tanney, Forde, Donahey, Eno & Tanney P.A., Clearwater, 1978—; founding mem., treas. First Step, Inc., 1973—; chmn. prisoner outplacement com. PRIDE, Inc., 1986; mem. com. on standard jury instructions in criminal cases Fla. Supreme Ct., grievance com. U.S. Dist. Ct. (mid. dist.) Fla., com. establishment of criminal court complex Pinellas County; lectr. criminal justice program U. S. Fla., Tampa, profl. seminars on criminal law, criminal procedures, criminal evidence code, insanity rules and procedures, wiretap and electronic surveillance D&S Publs., dept. criminal law and police adminstrn. and dept. polit. sci. St. Petersburg Jr. Coll.; speaker criminal justice various elem., secondary schs. and civic orgns., Stetson U. Coll. Law. Author: Fla. Criminal Trial Tactics. Served with U.S. Army, 1953-56. Recipient cert. of appreciation Fla. Council on Crime & Delinquency, 1984, North Cen. Pinellas Scottish Rite Club, 1986. Fellow Am. Coll. Trial Lawyers; mem. Assn. Trial Lawyers Am., Assn. Fla. Trial Lawyers, Nat. Assn. Criminal Def. Lawyers (regional coordinator for speakers bur. 1984—), Pinellas County Def. Lawyers Assn. Republican. Lodge: Elks. Criminal. Office: Tanney Forde et al 13584 49th St N #A Clearwater FL 34622

DOHENY, DONALD ALOYSIUS, lawyer, business exec.; b. Milw., Apr. 20, 1924; s. John Anthony and Adelaide (Koller) D.; m. Catherine Elizabeth Lee, Oct. 25, 1952; children: Donald Aloysius, Celeste Hazel Doheny Kennedy, John Vincent, Ellen Adelaide, Edward Lawrence II, William Francis, Madonna Lee. Student U. Notre Dame, 1942-43; BME, Marquette U., 1947; JD, Harvard, 1949; postgrad., Washington U., St. Louis, 1950-56. Bar: Wis. 1949, Mo. 1949, U.S. Supreme Ct. 1970; registered prof. engr., Mo. Asst. to civil engr. Shipbuilding div. Froemming Bros., Inc., Milw., 1942-43; draftsman, designer The Heil Co., Milw., 1944-46; assoc. Igoe, Carroll & Keefe, St. Louis, 1949-51; asst. to v.p. and gen. mgr., chief prodn. engr., gen. adminstr., dir. adminstrn. Granco Steel Products subsidiary Granite City Steel, Granite City, Ill., 1951-57; asst. to pres. Vestal Labs., Inc., St. Louis, 1957-63; exec. v.p., dir. Moehlenpah Engring., Inc., Hydro-Air Engring., Inc., 1963-67; pres. dir. Foamtex Industries, Inc., St. Louis, 1967-75; exec. v.p., dir. Seasonal Industries, Inc., N.Y.C., 1973-75; sole practice, St. Louis, 1967-81; ptnr., Doheny & Doheny, Attys., St. Louis, 1981—, Doheny & Assocs. Mgmt. Counsel, St. Louis, 1967—; pres., dir. Mktg. & Sales Counsel, Inc., St. Louis, 1975—; pres., dir. Mid-USA Sales Co., St. Louis, 1976—; lectr. bus. orgn. and adminstrn. Washington U., 1950-74; lectr. Grad. Sch. Bus., St. Louis U., 1980—. Served with AUS, 1943-44; 1st lt. Res., 1948-52. Mem. ABA, Am. Judicature Soc., Am. Marketing Assn. (nat. membership chmn. 1959), Mo. Bar Assn., Wis. Bar Assn., Fed. Bar Assn., Bar Assn. St. Louis (gen. chmn. pub. relations 1955-56, vice chmn., sec.-treas. jr. sect. 1950, 51), Marquette Engring. Assn. (pres. 1946-47), Engring. Knights, Am. Legion, Tau Beta Pi, Pi Tau Sigma. Clubs: Notre Dame (pres. 1955, 56), Marquette (pres. 1961), Harvard (St. Louis); Stadium, Engineers, Mo. Athletic. General corporate, Contracts commercial, Probate. Office: Heritage Bldg 11960 Westline Indsl Dr Suite 320 Saint Louis MO 63146

DOHERTY, ASHLEY, lawyer; b. Columbia, Mo., Nov. 12, 1949; d. William Thomas and Dorothy Ashley (Huff) D.; m. Joseph Edwin Fortenberry, Nov. 23, 1972; 1 child, Dorothy Ashley. BA, Bryn Mawr Coll., 1971; JD, NYU, 1975. Bar: N.Y. 1976, D.C. 1980. Assoc. Milbank, Tweed, Hadley & McCloy, N.Y.C., 1976-79, Washington, 1980-86; assoc. Leva, Hawes, Symington, Martin & Oppenheimer, Washington, 1979; trial atty. environ. def. sect. land and natural resources div. U.S. Dept. Justice, Washington, 1986—; seminar lectr. Internat. Law Inst., Washington, 1985; seminar faculty mem. office legal edn. U.S. Dept. Justice, Washington, 1986. Mem. ABA, Assn. of Bar of City of N.Y., Women's Bar Assn. of D.C., Women's Legal Def. Fund, Washington Area Lawyers for Arts. Roman Catholic. Administrative and regulatory, Federal civil litigation. Home: 2022 Columbia Rd NW Washington DC 20009 Office: US Dept Justice 10th St and Constitution Ave NW Washington DC 20530

DOHERTY, JOHN L., lawyer; b. Pitts., Dec. 17, 1934; s. John A. and Carmella G. (Conte) D.; m. Diane J. Passetti, Aug. 10, 1963; children: John F., Kathleen A. BA, Duquesne U., 1960, JD, 1966. Bar: Pa. 1966. Law clk. to chief judge U.S. Dist. Ct. Western Dist. Pa., 1966-67; assoc. Livingston, Miller & Haywood, Pitts., 1967-75; city solicitor Pitts., 1969-70; law clk. to judge Allegheny County Ct. Common Pleas, Pitts., 1971-73; ptnr. Manifesto, Doherty & Donahoe, P.C., Pitts., 1975—. Served with U.S. Army, 1954-56. Fellow Am. Coll. Trial Lawyers, Acad. Trial Lawyers (past pres.); mem. Allegheny County Bar Assn., Pa. Trial Lawyers Assn. (chmn. criminal trial sect.), Assn. Trial Lawyers Am. Criminal, Personal injury.

DOHERTY, JOSEPH LEO, JR., lawyer; b. Medford, Mass., May 5, 1953; s. Joseph L. and Margaret Ann (Laffey) D.; m. Patricia Brady, Dec. 4, 1977; children: Joseph L. III, Jacqueline Brady. BA, Colby Coll., 1975; JD, Suffolk U., 1978. Bar: Mass. 1978, U.S. Dist. Ct. Mass. 1979. Law clk. to justices Mass. Superior Ct., Boston, 1978-79; assoc. Martin, Magnuson, McCarthy & Kenney, Boston, 1979-85, ptnr., 1985—. Mem. Mass. Bar Assn. (bench, bar and press coms., rules of court com., law practice com., civil litigation, legis. coms.). Federal civil litigation, State civil litigation, Personal injury. Home: 45 Mystic St Medford MA 02155 Office: Martin Magnuson McCarthy & Kenney 73 Tremont St Boston MA 02108

DOHERTY, MARY CUSHING, lawyer; b. Evanston, Ill., Apr. 22, 1953; d. F. John and Margaret Louise (Wolf) Cushing; m. James Francis Doherty, Aug. 20, 1977; children—John Francis, Margaret Rose. B.A., U. Del., 1975; J.D., Villanova U., 1978. Bar: Pa. 1978, N.J., 1978, U.S. Dist. Ct. (ea. dist.) Pa. 1978, U.S. Dist. Ct. N.J. 1978. Assoc. Abrahams and Loewenstein, Phila., 1979—; also lectr., course planner Pa. Bar Inst., Pa. Bar Assn., others. Contbr. articles to Pa. Law Jour., 1981. Mem. staff Pre-Cana Counselling, Roman Cath. Chs., 1981—; counselor UNITE of Jeanes Hosp., Phila., 1984, bd. dirs., 1985-86, v.p., 1986-87, chair bd. dirs., 1987—. Minerva Schultz Found. grantee, 1978. Fellow Am. Acad. Matrimonial Lawyers; mem. Phila. Bar Assn. (chmn. family law sect. 1985, del. bd. govs. 1986), ABA, N.J. Bar Assn., Hidden Meadow Community Assn., Bus. Women's Network. Roman Catholic. Family and matrimonial. Office: Abrahams & Loewenstein United Engineers Bldg 30 S 17th St 14th Floor Philadelphia PA 19103-4096

DOHERTY, ROBERT CHRISTOPHER, lawyer; b. Elizabeth, N.J., Sept. 3, 1943; s. Christopher Joseph and Marie Veronica (McLaughlin) D.; m. Sarajane Frances Doherty, June 12, 1965; children—Dennis Michael, Amy Elizabeth, Tracey Carolan. A.B., St. Peter's Coll., 1965; J.D., Seton Hall U., 1970. Bar: N.J. 1970, U.S. Ct. Appeals (3rd cir.) 1982, U.S. Supreme Ct. 1977. Asst. prosecutor Union County, Elizabeth, N.J., 1971-72; mem. Schumann, Hession, Kennelly & Dorment, Jersey City, 1972-73, Robert D. Younghans, Westfield, N.J., 1973-76; ptnr. Doherty & Kopnicki, Westfield, 1976—; county counsel Union County, Elizabeth, 1981—. Mem. ABA, N.J. Bar Assn., Union County Bar Assn., N.J. Assn. County Counsels. Republican. Roman Catholic. Club: Mindowaskin Swim. Local government, General practice, State civil litigation. Home: 771 Fairacres Ave Westfield NJ 07090 Office: Law Dept Union County Administration Bldg Elizabeth NJ 07207

DOHN, GEORGE THOMAS, lawyer; b. Chillicothe, Mo., Nov. 6, 1935; s. George Eckel and Lula Mae (Handley) D.; m. Nancy Lorraine Moore, Oct. 29, 61; children—Kari L., Katrina S., Derek S., Kristin K.; m. 2d, Rita Rae Gardner, June 2, 1972. A.A.S., Yakima Valley Coll., 1959; B.B.A., U. Wash., 1961, LL.B., 1963, J.D., 1968. Bar: Wash. 1963. Assoc. Tunstall & Hettinger, Yakima, Wash., 1963-65; ptnr. Tunstall, Hettinger Dohn, Yakima, 1966-72; prin. McArdle, Dohn, Talbott and Simpson, Inc. P.S., Yakima, 1973—, pres., 1982-83; city atty. Ellensburg, Wash., 1964-84, Union Gap, Wash., 1973-74, Goldendale, Wash., 1979—; bd. dirs. Mut. of Enumclaw (Wash.) and Enumclaw Life Ins. Cos.; instr. legal research techniques U. Wash., 1963; arbitrator Am. Arbitration Assn., 1973—. Bd. dirs., legal counsel Spring Acres Group Homes, Inc., 1969-76; bd. dirs. Planned Parenthood Assn., Yakima, 1965-75, Yakima County Young Republicans, 1963-65; mem. adv. bd., Wash. Criminal Justice Edn. and Tng. Ctr., 1973-74; mem. legal adv. bd., Wash. Found. Handicapped, 1975-76. Served with USAF, 1953-57. Mem. ABA, Wash. State Bar Assn., Yakima County Bar Assn., Wash. Assn. Mcpl. Attys. (pres. 1972-73), Nat. Inst. Mcpl. Law Officers, Wash. Govtl. Lawyers Assn., Wash. Assn. Def. Counsel, Am. Arbitration Assn. (arbitrator), Def. Research Inst., Phi Theta Kappa, Phi Delta Phi. Republican. Presbyterian (deacon). Clubs: Yakima Ski, Yakima Tennis, Washington Athletic. Insurance, Personal injury, Local government. Office: 201 E Lincoln Suite 5 Yakima WA 98901

DOKE, MARSHALL J., JR., lawyer; b. Wichita Falls, Tex., June 9, 1934; s. Marshall J. and Mary Jane (Johnson) D.; m. Betty Marie Orsini, June 2, 1956; children: Gregory J., Michael J., Laetitia Marie. BA magna cum laude, Hardin-Simmons U., 1956; LLB magna cum laude, So. Meth. U., 1959. Bar: Tex. 1959. Assoc. Thompson, Knight, Wright & Simmons, Dallas, 1959, 62-65; founding ptnr. Rain Harrell Emery Young & Doke, Dallas, 1965-87, Doke & Riley, Dallas, 1987—; gen. counsel Tex. Rep. Com., 1976-77; mem. adv. council U.S. Claims Ct., 1982—; chmn. internat. com. City of Dallas, 1984-87. Editor-in-chief: Southwestern Law Jour, 1958-59; editor: ABA Ann. Devels. in Govt. Contract Law, 1975-78 . Pres. Hope Cottage-Children's Bur. Inc., 1969-70; visitor Law Sch., So. Meth. U., 1966-69; mem. law com. So. Meth. U. Bd. Trustees, 1977—; bd. dirs. Dallas Theater Center, 1976—, chmn. exec. com., 1981-85, pres., 1983-85; chmn. bd. dirs., pres. World Trade Assn. Dallas-Ft. Worth, 1979-80; bd. dirs., sec. Theater Trustees Am., 1983—. Served to 1st lt., JAGC U.S. Army, 1959-62. Fellow Am. Bar Found., Tex. Bar Found.; mem. ABA (chmn. sect. pub. contract law 1969-70, ho. of dels. 1970-72, 74—, bd. govs. 1980-82), Tex. Bar Assn. (chmn. com. responsible citizenship 1971-73), Am. Bar Retirement Assn. (bd. dirs., trustee 1980—, pres. 1982-84), Nat. Conf. Lawyers and CPA's (co-chmn. 1983-85), Nat. Contract Mgmt. Assn. (nat. bd. advisors 1983—), U.S. Claims Ct. Bar Assn. (bd. govs. 1987—), Dallas C. of C. (chmn. com. consular corps 1972-79, chmn. internat. com. 1979-83), U.S. C. of C. (council on procurement policy 1983—), So. Meth. U. Law Alumni Assn. (pres. 1976-77). Contracts commercial, Government contracts and claims, Private international. Home: 6910 Dartbrook St Dallas TX 75240 Office: 4300 Republic Bank Tower Dallas TX 75201

DOKURNO, ANTHONY DAVID, lawyer; b. Gardner, Mass., Mar. 14, 1957; s. Anthony Chester and Damey Anteena (Aleson) D.; m. Andee J. Rappazzo. BA, Holy Cross Coll., 1979; JD, Vt. Law Sch., 1982. Bar: Mass. 1982, U.S. Ct. Mil. Appeals, 1986. Sole practice Fitchburg, Mass., 1982—. Served to lt. USNR, 1986—. Mem. ABA, Mass. Bar Assn., Phi Beta Kappa. Military, Criminal, Admiralty. Home: 62 Oriole St Gardner MA 01440

DOLAN, JAMES FRANCIS, lawyer; b. Orange, N.J., Jan. 5, 1930; s. Thomas and Edna (Monahan) D.; m. Rita Hughes, June 27, 1953; children: James E., Stephen T., Michael, Richard F. B.S., Seton Hall U., 1950; LL.B., Columbia U., 1953. Bar: D.C. 1953, N.Y. 1957. Assoc. atty. Davis Polk & Wardwell, N.Y.C., 1957-66, ptnr., 1966—; dir. Triangle Pubs., Inc., Radnor, Pa. Served to lt. USN, 1953-57. Mem. ABA, N.Y. State Bar Assn., Assn. Bar City N.Y. Clubs: Knickerbocker (N.Y.C.); Seminole Golf (North Palm Beach, Fla.). Estate planning, Probate, Estate taxation. Home: N Beach Rd Town of Juniter Island Hobe Sound FL 33455 Office: 1 Chase Manhattan Plaza New York NY 10005

DOLAN, JAMES VINCENT, lawyer; b. Washington, Nov. 11, 1938; s. John Vincent and Philomena Theresa (Vance) D.; m. Anne McSherry Reilly, June 18, 1960; children: Caroline McSherry, James Reilly. A.B., Georgetown U., 1960, LL.B., 1963. Bar: U.S. Dist. Ct. 1963, U.S. Ct. Appeals (D.C.) cir. 1964, U.S. Ct. Appeals (4th cir.) 1976. Law clk. U.S. Ct. Appeals D.C., 1963-64; assoc. Steptoe & Johnson, Washington, 1964-71, ptnr., 1971-82; mem. Steptoe & Johnson Chartered, Washington, 1982-83; v.p. law Union Pacific R.R., Omaha, 1983—. Co-author: Construction Contract Law, 1981; contbr. articles to legal jours.; editor-in-chief: Georgetown Law Jour., 1962-63. Mem. ABA, D.C. Bar Assn., Barristers. Republican. Roman Catholic. Clubs: Congressional Country (v.p. 1982, pres. 1983), Metropolitan; Omaha Country. General corporate, Public utilities, Federal civil litigation. Home: 9789 Frederick St Omaha NE 68124 Office: Union Pacific RR 1416 Dodge St Omaha NE 68179

DOLAN, PETER BROWN, lawyer; b. Bklyn., Mar. 25, 1939; s. Daniel Arthur and Eileen Margaret (Brown) D.; m. Jacqueline Elizabeth Gruning, Sept. 9, 1961; children—Kerry Anne, Peter Brown Jr. B.S., U.S. Naval Acad., 1960; J.D., U. So. Calif., 1967. Bar: Calif. 1967, U.S. Ct. Appeals (9th cir.) 1968, U.S. Dist. Ct. (no. and cen. dists.) Calif. 1967, U.S. Dist. Ct. (ea. dist.) Calif. 1972, U.S. Dist. Ct. (so. dist.) Calif. 1973, U.S. Claims Ct. 1982, U.S. Supreme Ct. 1986. Dep. county counsel Los Angeles County, 1967-69; assoc. Macdonald, Halsted & Laybourne, Los Angeles, 1969-71, ptnr., 1972-77; ptnr. Overton, Lyman & Prince, Los Angeles, 1977-81; pres. Peter Brown Dolan P.C., Los Angeles, 1981—. Active Pasadena (Calif.) Tournament of Roses Assn., 1973—; pres. West Pasadena Residents Assn., 1979-81. Served to lt. U.S. Navy, 1960-64, to comdr. USNR, 1964-86. Mem. ABA, Fed. Bar Assn., State Bar Calif., Los Angeles County Bar Assn., Phi Delta Phi. Democrat. Roman Catholic. Clubs: Bel-Air Bay (Pacific Palisades, Calif.); Univ., Stock Exchange, Chancery (Los Angeles). Federal civil litigation, State civil litigation, Insurance. Office: Overton Lyman & Prince 550 S Flower St 6th Floor Los Angeles CA 90071

DOLEAC, CHARLES BARTHOLOMEW, lawyer; b. New Orleans, La., Sept. 20, 1947; s. Cyril Bartholomew and Emma Elizabeth (St. Clair) D.; m. Denise Kilfoyle, Feb. 2, 1972; children: Keith Gabriel, Jessa Lee. BS cum laude, U. N.H., 1968; JD, NYU, 1971. Bar: Mass. 1972, N.H. 1972, Maine 1973. Law clk. to Justice Grimes N.H. Supreme Ct., Concord, 1972-73; assoc. Boynton, Waldron, Dill & Aeschliman, Portsmouth, N.H., 1973-76; ptnr. Boynton, Waldron, Doleac, Woodman & Scott, Portsmouth, 1977—; delegation mem. on tour of Chinese legal system Chinese Ministry of Justice, 1982; pres. bd. of trustees Strawbery Banke, Inc.; prop. Portsmouth Athenaeum. Mem. citizens adv. council Portsmouth Community Devel. Program, 1976-77; pres. bd. dirs. Seacoast United Way, 1976; chmn. Portsmouth Bd. of Bldg. Appeals, 1976-77; chmn. stewardship com. Soc. Preservation New Eng. Antiquities, 1980-84, trustee. Fellow NEH, Aspen Inst. Fellow N.H. Bar Found.; mem. Mass. Bar Assn., Maine Bar Assn., N.H. Bar Assn. (chairperson citizens rights com., delivery of legal services com., ethics com., coop. with the dept. of labor com., code of profl. responsibilities revision com.), Assn. Trial Lawyers Am., N.H. Trial Lawyers Assn., Maine Trial Lawyers Assn. Contracts commercial, Personal injury,

Workers' compensation. Home: Little Harbor Rd Portsmouth NH 03801 Office: Boynton Waldron Doleac et al 82 Court St Portsmouth NH 03801

DOLGORUKOV, D. EDWARD, lawyer; b. Washington, Oct. 28, 1944; s. Gregory S. and E. Florence (Swanson) D.; children: Kristin, Julie, Jason, Kevin. BS in Indsl. Engring., Wayne State U., 1968, JD, 1972. Bar: Mich. 1972, U.S. Dist. Ct. (ea. dist.) Mich. 1972, U.S. Ct. Appeals (Fed. cir.) 1982. Assoc. Law Offices of Gregory S. Dolgorukov, Detroit, 1968-72; ptnr. Law Offices of Dolgorukov & Dolgorukov, Detroit, 1972-86, Gifford & Dolgorukov, Birmingham, Mich., 1986—. Mem. Mich. Bar Assn., Oakland County Bar Assn., South Oakland Bar Assn., Mich. Patent Law Assn., Troy C. of C. Avocation: travel and related activities. Patent, Trademark and copyright.

D'OLIER, H(ENRY) MITCHELL, lawyer; b. Chgo., June 10, 1946; s. Henry and Helen Elizabeth (Mitchell) D'O.; m. Barbara Ann Miller, June 12, 1971; children: Jason Mitchell, Justin Frank, Jordan Henry. BA in English and Gen. Sci., U. Iowa, 1968, JD with distinction, 1972. Bar: Iowa 1972, Hawaii 1972. Assoc. tax Goodsil, Anderson, Quinn & Stifel, Honolulu, 1972-77; ptnr. tax health mgmt. com. Goodsill, Anderson, Quinn & Stifel, Honolulu, 1977—; bd. dirs. Reyn's Men's Wear Inc., Kamuela, Hawaii. Chmn., co-chmn. Friends Of Fred Hemmings, Honolulu, 1984, 86; chmn., vice chmn. profl. div. campaign Aloha United Way, 1982-84; clk., deacon Cen. Union Ch., 1983-85; bd. dirs. Boys' and Girls' Club Honolulu, 1977—, v.p., pres.-elect 1987—. Mem. ABA (tax and health law sects.), Nat. Health Lawyers Assn., Hawaii State Bar Assn. (tax sect.), Order of Coif, Omicron Delta Kappa. Republican. Club: Plaza (Honolulu). Lodge: Rotary. Avocations: jogging, youth baseball and soccer coaching. Corporate taxation, Health, State and local taxation. Home: 1704 Kumakani Loop Honolulu HI 96821 Office: Goodsil Anderson Quinn & Stifel 130 Merchant St Suite 1600 Honolulu HI 96813

DOLIN, LONNY H., lawyer; b. Youngstown, Ohio, Jan. 24, 1954; d. Lawrence Joseph and Sonya (Sacks) Heselov ; m. Raphael Dolin, June 19, 1976; children: Nathaniel, Brooke. AB, Georgetown U., 1976; JD, Cath. U., 1979. Bar: Vt. 1980, N.Y. State Bar 1984, U.S. Dist. Ct. (we. dist.) N.Y. 1984. Assoc. Downs, Rachlin & Martin, Burlington, Vt., 1979-81; sole practice Burlington, 1981-84; assoc. Harris, Beach, Wilcox, Rubin & Levey, Rochester, N.Y., 1984—; of counsel to U.S. Congressman Fred J. Eckert, N.Y., 1985—; bd. dirs. Monroe County Legal Services Corp. Mem. Pittsford Town and County Com., N.Y., 1983—, Town of Pittsford Bd. of Zoning Appeals, N.Y., 1984; chmn. Monroe County Comparable Worth Task Force, Rochester, 1985—, Fred J. Eckert Women's Adv. Council, Rochester, 1985—; del. The Jud. Dist. N.Y., Rochester, 1985; bd. dirs. Nat. Council Jewish Women. Recipient Corpus Juris Secundum award West Pub. co., 1979. Mem. ABA, Vt. Bar Assn., N.Y. Bar Assn., Monroe County Bar Assn., Greater Rochester Women's Bar Assn. (treas. 1986). Republican. Avocations: sailing, swimming. State civil litigation, Federal civil litigation, Personal injury. Home: 22 Fletcher Rd Pittsford NY 14534 Office: Harris Beach et al 130 E Main St Rochester NY 14604

DOLIN, MITCHELL F., lawyer; b. Augusta, Ga., Feb. 6, 1956; Martin H. and Harriet S. (Aronow) D. BA, Tufts U., 1978; JD, NYU, 1981. Bar: D.C. 1982, U.S. Ct. Appeals (D.C. cir.) 1983, U.S. Ct. Appeals (5th cir.) 1984. Clk. to presiding chief judge U.S. Ct. Appeals (5th cir.), 1981-82; assoc. Covington & Burling, Washington, 1982—. Democrat. Jewish. Club: Capitol Hill Squash (Washington). Federal civil litigation, Antitrust, Insurance. Home: 407-A Fourth St SE Washington DC 20003 Office: Covington & Burling PO Box 7566 Washington DC 20044

DOLINER, NATHANIEL LEE, lawyer; b. Daytona Beach, Fla., June 28, 1949; s. Joseph and Asia (Shaffer) D.; m. Debra Lynn Simon, June 5, 1983. B.A., George Washington U., 1970; J.D., Vanderbilt U., 1973; LL.M. in Taxation, U. Fla., 1977. Bar: Fla. 1973, U.S. Tax Ct. 1973, U.S. Dist. Ct. (mid. dist.) Fla. 1974. Assoc. Smalbein, Eubank, Johnson, Rosier & Bussey, P.A., Daytona Beach, Fla., 1973-76; vis. asst. prof. law U. Fla., Gainesville, 1977-78; assoc. Carlton, Fields, Ward, Emmanuel, Smith & Cutler, P.A., Tampa, Fla., 1978-82, ptnr., 1982—, chmn. tax, corp. and securities dept., 1984—, treas. 1985-86, bd. dirs., 1983-87. Bd. dirs. Big Bros./Big Sisters of Greater Tampa, Inc., 1980-82., dist. commnr. Gulf Ridge council Boy Scouts Am., 1983; bd. dirs. Tampa Bay Jazz Soc., Inc., 1985—, v.p.; 1985-87 bd. dirs. Child Abuse Council, Inc. 1986—, Am. Heart Assn. (bd. dirs. Hillsborough County chpt. 1987—), Mem. ABA (vice chmn. continuing legal education com. tax sect. 1986—, chmn. subcom. on sales and exchanges, partnership com. ABA Tax Sect. 1986—), Fla. Bar Assn. (mem. exec. com. tax sect. 1980-83); Greater Tampa C. of C. (chmn. Ambassadors Target Task Force of Com. of 100, 1984-85), Anti-Defamation League (regional bd. mem. 1986—, exec. com. 1987—), Tampa Jewish Fedn. (bd. dirs. 1986—). Clubs: Tampa Rotary (bd. dirs. 1986—), Carrollwood Village Golf and Tennis. General corporate, Corporate taxation, Estate planning. Home: 3207 Tarabrook Dr Tampa FL 33618 Office: Carlton Fields Ward et al 777 S Harbour Island Blvd 5th Floor Tampa FL 33602

DOLLIVER, JAMES MORGAN, state supreme court justice; b. Ft. Dodge, Iowa, Oct. 13, 1924; s. James Isaac and Margaret Elizabeth (Morgan) D.; m. Barbara Babcock, Dec. 18, 1948; children: Elizabeth, James, Peter, Keith, Jennifer, Nancy. BA in Polit. Sci. with high honors, Swarthmore Coll., 1949; LLB, U. Wash., 1952; D in Liberal Arts (hon.), U. Puget Sound, 1981. Bar: Wash. 1952. Clk. to presiding justice Wash. Supreme Ct., 1952-53; sole practice Port Angeles, Wash., 1953-54, Everett, Wash., 1961-64; adminstrv. asst. to Congressman Jack Westland, 1955-61, Gov. Daniel J. Evans, 1965-76; justice Supreme Ct. State of Wash., 1976—, chief justice, 1985-86; 2d v.p. conf. Chief Justices, 1985-86. Chmn. United Way Campaign Thurston County, 1975, pres., 1976, mem. exec. bd., 1977—; chmn. Wash. chpt. Nature Conservancy, 1981—; pres. exec. bd. Tumwater Area council Boy Scouts Am., 1972-73, Wash. chpt. The Nature Conservancy, 1981-83, mem. 1979—, Wash. State Capital Hist. Assn., 1976-80, 85—, also trustee, 1983-84 ; trustee Deaconess Children's Home, Everett, 1963-65, U. Puget Sound, 1970—, Wash. 4-H Found., 1977-84, also v.p., 1983—, Claremont (Calif.) Theol. Sem., assoc. mem., Community Mental Health Ctr., 1977-84; bd. mgrs. Swarthmore Coll., 1980-84; bd. dirs. Thurston Mason Community Health Ctr., 1977-84, Thurston Youth Services Soc., 1969-84, also pres., 1983, mem. exec. com., 1970-84, Safety Tng. and Research Assn. Wash., 1979—, Wash. Women's Employment and Edn., 1982-84; mem. jud. council United Meth. Ch., 1984—, gen. conf., 1970-72, 80—, gen. bd. ch. and society, 1976-84; adv. council Retired Senior Vol. program, 1979-83; mem. bd. visitors Cen. Wash. U. Coll. of Letters, Arts and Scis., 1983—. Served as ensign USCG, 1945-46. Recipient award Nat. Council Japanese Am. Citizens League, 1976; Silver Beaver award, 1971; Silver Antelope award, 1976. Mem. Am., Wash. bar assns., Am. Judges Assn., Am. Judicature Soc., Pub. Broadcast Found. (bd. dirs. 1982—), Am. Acad. Youth Exchange (adv. council 1983—). Clubs: Masons, Rotary. Jurisprudence. Office: Wash Supreme Ct Temple of Justice Olympia WA 98504

DOLOWITZ, DAVID SANDER, lawyer; b. Balt., Mar. 30, 1940; s. David A. and Frances M. (Fleisher) D.; m. Anne M. Dolowitz, June 13, 1964; children—Alexander, David Peter, Annetta. B.A., Yale U., 1963; J.D., U. Utah, 1966. Bar: Utah 1966, U.S. Dist. Ct. Utah 1966, U.S. Ct. Appeals (10th cir.) 1967, U.S. Supreme Ct. 1971. Law clk. to judge U.S. Dist. Ct. Utah, 1966-68; Reginald Heber Smith Community lawyer 1968-71; dir. Salt Lake County Bar Legal Services, Inc., Salt Lake City, 1970-75; shareholder Parsons, Behle & Latimer, Salt Lake City, 1975—; mem. Utah Juvenile Ct. Adv. Com., 1975-85. Mem. United Jewish Council, 1980—, pres., 1983-85; voting dist. chmn. Democratic party, 1968—; Fellow Am. Acad. Matrimonial Lawyers; mem. Utah State Bd. Family Services, 1980-83. Mem. Utah Bar Assn. (chmn. family law sect. 1985-86), 10th Cir. Jud. Conf., ACLU (legal panel 1981—), Phi Alpha Delta. Federal civil litigation, State civil litigation, Family and matrimonial. Office: Parsons Behle & Latimer PO Box 11898 185 S State St Salt Lake City UT 84147

DOLT, FREDERICK CORRANCE, lawyer; b. Louisville, Oct. 10, 1929; s. O. Frederick and Margaret A. (Corrance) D.; m. Lucy M. Voelker, Dec. 8, 1960; 1 child, Frederick C. Jr. JD, U. Louisville, 1952. Bar: Ky. 1952, La. 1982. Assoc. Morris & Garlove, Louisville, 1955-59; sole practice Louisville, 1959-70, 79—; ptnr. Leibson, Dolt & McCarthy, Louisville, 1970-73. Mem. Inner Circle Advocates, 1981. Served with U.S. Army, 1953-55. Mem. ABA, Ky. Bar Assn. (chmn. ins./negligibility sect. 1968-70, mem. Ho. of Dels., 1970-80), Assn. Trial Lawyers Am. (state del. 1965-70), Ky. Trial Lawyers Assn. (pres. 1970). Republican. Presbyterian. Avocation: golf. Federal civil litigation, State civil litigation. Home: 7216 Heatherly Sq Louisville KY 40222 Office: 310 Starks Bldg Louisville KY 40202

DOMANSKIS, ALEXANDER RIMAS, lawyer; b. Chgo., June 3, 1952; s. Van and Alina Alexandra (Tamasauskas) D.; m. Frances Laucka, May 6, 1978; children: Maria Laucka, John Joseph Laucka. A.B., U. Mich., 1973, J.D., 1977. Bar: Ill. 1977, U.S. Dist. Ct. (no. dist.) Ill. 1977, U.S. Ct. Appeals (7th cir.) 1978, U.S. Supreme Ct., 1985. Law clk. U.S. Dist. Ct. (no. dist.) Ill., Chgo., 1977-79; assoc. Ross & Hardies, Chgo., 1979-84, ptnr., 1985-87, of counsel, 1987—; assoc. gen. counsel and v.p. Intercounty Title Co. of Ill., 1987—. Editor U. Mich. Jour. Law Reform, 1976-77. Mem. ABA, Am. Judicature Soc., Ill. Bar Assn., Chgo. Bar Assn., Lithuanian Am. Council (bd. dirs. Chgo. 1981—), Lithuanian Roman Catholic Fedn. Am. (bd. dirs. Chgo. 1980—), Phi Alpha Delta. Democrat. Federal civil litigation, State civil litigation, Real property. Home: 4236 Hampton St Western Springs IL 60558 Office: Intercounty Title Co 120 W Madison Suite 200 Chicago IL 60602 Office: Intercounty Title 120 W Madison Suite 200 Chicago IL 60602

DOMBROFF, MARK ANDREW, lawyer; b. N.Y.C., Mar. 8, 1947; s. Benjamin and Eunice Jacqueline (Glassbury) D.; m. Janet Elizabeth Smukler, Jan. 4, 1973; 1 child, Jessica Leigh. BA, Am. U., 1967, JD, 1970. Bar: D.C. 1971, Md. 1971. Trial atty. FAA, Washington, 1970-71; trial atty. U.S. Dept. of Justice, Washington, 1971-80, from asst. dir. to dir. civil div., 1980-85, spl. atty., 1985-86; spl. counsel Hughes, Hubbard & Reed, Washington, 1985—. Author: Dombroff on Demonstrative Evidence, 1983, Trial Hearsay, 1983, Litigation Organization and Management, 1983, Trial Objections, 1984, Dombroff on Unfair Tactics, 1984, Dombroff on Direct and Cross Examination, 1985, Dynamic Closing Arguments, 1985, Key Trial Control Tactics, 1985, Federal Trial Evidence, 1985, Federal and State Negligence Litigation Manual, 1986, Dombroff on Discovery, 1986, Dombroff on Expert Witness, 1986; editor Personal Injury Defense Techniques, 1986. Served with USAR, 1968-74. Mem. ABA, Fed. Bar Assn. Nat. Transp. Safety Bd. Bar Assn., Def. Trial Lawyers Research Inst., Assn. Trial Lawyers Am. Jewish. Avocation: magic. Aviation, Personal injury, Products liability. Office: Hughes Hubbard & Reed 1201 Pennsylvania Ave NW Washington DC 20004

DOMBROW, ANTHONY ERIC, lawyer; b. N.Y.C., Apr. 6, 1945; s. Oscar and Nettie (Maslow) D.; m. Penny McClurg, July 21, 1978; children: Joshua Alan, Ashley Smith. B.A., U. Wis., 1966, J.D., 1969. Bar: Wis. 1969, Ill. 1973, U.S. Ct. Apls. (8th cir.) 1974, U.S. Ct. Apls. (7th cir.) 1975, U.S. Sup. Ct. 1976, U.S. Ct. Appeals (9th cir.) 1987. Atty., Nat. Labor Relations Bd., Chgo., 1969-72; ptnr. Laner, Muchin, Dombrow & Becker Ltd., Chgo., 1972—. Labor, Pension, profit-sharing, and employee benefits. Office: Laner Muchin Dombrow & Becker Ltd 350 Clark St Chicago IL 60610

DOMINA, DAVID ALAN, lawyer; b. Laurel, Nebr., Nov. 27, 1950; s. Marvin Everett and Jacqueline Mae (Hansen) D.; m. Judy Mae Hanson, June 5, 1970; children—Thurston A., Salesia. J.D. with distinction, U. Nebr., 1972. Bar: Nebr. 1973, Mo. 1973, U.S. Tax Ct. 1973, U.S. Ct. Appeals (8th cir.) 1973. Assoc., Shook, Hardy & Bacon, Kansas City, Mo., 1973-74; ptnr. Jewell, Gatz & Domina, Norfolk, Nebr., 1974-82, Domina & Gerrard, P.C., Norfolk, 1982—; gen. counsel Affiliated Foods Coop., Norfolk, 1982—; dir. Farmers State Bank, Carroll, Nebr. Mem. state central com. Nebr. Democratic party, 1976-78; commr. Nebr. Econ. Devel. Commn., 1986—; trustee Nebr. Bd. Edn. Lands and Funds, Lincoln, 1983—; spl. atty. gen. Nebr. Dept. Justice, Lincoln, 1983-84; counsel Nebr. Dept. Banking, Lincoln, 1983-84. Mem. ABA, Mo. Bar Assn., Nebr. Bar Assn. (vice chmn. young lawyers sect. 1982, chmn. corrections com. 1983), Assn. Trial Lawyers Am., U. Nebr. Coll. Law Alumni Assn. (bd. dirs.), Norfolk C. of C., Order of Coif, Order of Barristers. Lutheran. State civil litigation, Banking, Contracts commercial. Office: Domina & Gerrard PC 2425 Taylor Ave Norfolk NE 68701

DOMINICK, DAVID DEWITT, lawyer; b. Phila., Jan. 24, 1937; s. DeWitt and Elizabeth (Pullman) D.; m. Mary Helen Stein, Sept. 8, 1966; children: Buck, Andrew, DeWitt. B.A., Yale U., 1960; J.D., U. Colo., 1966. Bar: Colo. 1966, Wyo. 1966, U.S. Supreme Ct. 1973, D.C. 1974, U.S. Ct. Claims, 1975. Legis. asst. U.S. Senator Clifford P. Hansen, Wyo., 1966-69; commr. Fed. Water Quality Adminstrn., Dept. Interior, 1969-71; asst. adminstr. for hazardous materials control EPA, Washington, 1971-73; practice law Washington, 1974-75, Denver, 1975—. Contbr. articles to profl. jours. Chmn. Colo. Land Use Commn., 1986-87. Served to capt. USMCR, 1960-63. Mem. ABA, Colo., Wyo., D.C. bar assns., Wyo. Hist. Soc., Nature Conservancy, Denver Audubon Soc. (pres. 1984-86), Rocky Mountain Planned Parenthood (v.p. 1983-84). Clubs: Metropolitan (Washington); Denver Country, University (Denver). Environment, Local government, Water rights law. Home: 300 Humboldt St Denver CO 80218 Office: Cogswell & Wehrle 1700 Lincoln Suite 3500 Denver CO 80203

DOMINICK, PAUL ALLEN, lawyer; b. Orangeburg, S.C., Feb. 13, 1954; s. Allen Etheredge and Ruby Estelle (Pardue) D.; m. Sharon Norment, May 15, 1982. BA, U. S.C., 1976; JD, Washington & Lee U., 1979. Bar: S.C. 1979, U.S. Dist. Ct. S.C. 1980, U.S. Ct. Appeals (4th cir.) 1982. Assoc. Nexsen, Pruet, Jacobs & Pollard, Columbia, S.C., 1979-85, ptnr., 1985—. Treas. Met. Sertoma Club (v.p. 1986-87), Columbia, 1986; participant Leadership Columbia-Columbia C. of C., 1986. Mem. ABA, S.C. Bar Assn., S.C. Def. Trial Attys. Assn., Def. Research Inst., Richland County Bar Assn., Columbia Forum, Com. of 100, Phi Beta Kappa. Presbyterian. Club: Columbia 100 (pres. 1983-84). Federal civil litigation, State civil litigation, Securities. Home: 2804 Sheffield Rd Columbia SC 29204 Office: Nexsen Pruet Jacobs & Pollard PO Drawer 2426 Columbia SC 29202

DOMINIK, JACK EDWARD, lawyer; b. Chgo., July 9, 1924; s. Ewald Arthur and Gertrude Alene (Crotzer) D.; children—Paul, David, Georgia Lee, Elizabeth, Sarah, Clare. B.S. in Mech. Engring. with distinction, Purdue U., 1947; J.D., Northwestern U., 1950. Bar: Ill. bar 1950, U.S. Patent Office 1953, Wis. bar 1959, Fla. bar 1964. Founder, sr. partner firm Dominik, Knechtel, Godula & Demeur (patent, trademark, and copyright attys.), Chgo., 1962-78, Jack E. Dominik P.A., Miami, Tampa, Fla., 1974—; ptnr. Dominik, Stein, Saccocio, and Reese. Served to 1st lt., C.E. AUS, 1943-46, ETO. Mem. Am., Wis., Fla., Chgo. bar assns., Am., Chgo., Milw. patent law assns., Tau Beta Pi, Pi Tau Sigma, Tau Kappa Alpha. Clubs: Chgo. Yacht, Union League. Federal civil litigation, Patent, Trademark and copyright. Office: Dominik Stein Saccocio & Reese Suite 225 6175 NW 153rd St Miami FL 33014

DOMITROVICH, STEPHANIE, lawyer, educator; b. Rochester, Pa., Mar. 20, 1954; d. Stephen Jude and Helen (Pappavasillion) D.; m. Ronald James Susmarski, Sept. 1, 1979; childre: Adam James, Aaron Edward. BA, Carlow Coll., 1976; JD, Duquesne U., 1979. Bar: Pa., U.S. Dist. Ct. Pa., U.S. Ct. Appeals (3d cir.), U.S. Supreme Ct. Assoc. Susmarski Law Offices, Erie, Pa., 1980—; instr. Pa. State U., Eire, 1982—; asst. soliciter County of Erie, 1983—. Co-dir. legal explorers program Boy Scouts Am., 1980-84; counsel Childbirth Edn. Assn., 1986—; bd. dirs. YWCA, 1986—. Mem. ABA, Pa. Bar Assn., Erie County Bar Assn. Democrat. Roman Catholic. Home and Office: Susmarski Law Office 4036 W Lake Rd Erie PA 16505

DOMNITZ, MERRICK ROBERT, lawyer; b. Omaha, Apr. 8, 1948; s. Hyman and Adeline (Dubin) D.; m. Anita Carol Kane, July 15, 1973; children: Ari Benjamin, Noah David. BA, U. Wis., 1971; JD, Hamline U., 1977. Bar: Wis. 1977, U.S. Dist. Ct. (ea. dist.) Wis. 1977. Assoc. Samster, Aiken & Peckerman, Milw., 1977-82; ptnr. Samster, Aiken & Mawicke, S.C., Milw., 1982—; lectr. U. Wis., Milw., 1980—; instr. trial practice, U. Wis. Law Sch., Madison, 1986—; teaching asst. Marquette U., Milw., 1980-85. Mem. ABA, Wis. Bar Assn., Milw. County Bar Assn., Assn. Trial Lawyers Am., Wis. Trial Lawyers Assn. (bd. dirs. 1984—, dir. Coll. Trial Advocacy 1985—). Jewish. Avocations: music, lit., sports. State civil litigation, Insurance, Personal injury. Home: 1048 E Lexington Blvd Whitefish Bay WI 53217 Office: Samster Aiken & Mawicke SC 1509 N Prospect Ave Milwaukee WI 53202

DOMZALSKI, KENNETH STANLEY, lawyer; b. Phila., May 6, 1949; s. Stanley Z. and Helen (Papuga) D.; m. Mary Christine Brennan, June 19, 1971; children: Meredith, Kyle. BA in Polit. Sci., LaSalle Coll., 1971; JD, Rutgers U., 1974. Bar: N.J. 1975, U.S. Dist. Ct. N.J. 1975. Assoc. Hartman, Schlesinger, Schlosser & Faxon, Mt. Holly, N.J., 1974-81, Forkin & Eory, Cherry Hill, N.J., 1981-82, Toll, Forkin, Sullivan & Luthman, Cherry Hill, 1982-83; ptnr. Bookbinder, Guest & Domzalski, Burlington, N.J., 1983—. Mem. Medford Twp. Bd. Edn., 1986—, YMCA, 1984—, Maple Shade Dem. County Com., 1975-76, Cinnaminson Dem. County Com., 1976-78, vice chmn., 1977-78, Medford Dem. County Com., 1979—, vice chmn., 1984—, chmn., 1980-81, treas., 1979-80; campaign mgr. Carmel Fischer for Cinnaminson Twp. Com., 1977; baseball coach Cinnaminson Police Athletic League, Lenape Youth Athletic Assn.; mem. by-laws com. Sherwood Forest Homeowners Assn.; chmn. Heart Fund Cinnaminson Twp., 1977; bd. dirs. Mt. Laurel Regional Ballet Co., 1984—, pres., 1985, v.p., 1984-85. Recipient award Cinnaminson Dem. County Com., 1978. Mem. ABA (family law and young lawyers sects.), N.J. Bar Assn. (exec. com. family law sect., young lawyers sect.), Burlington Bar Assn. (sec. 1986—, treas. 1985-86, trustee 1982-85, various coms., Robert W. Criscuolo Meml. award 1980, Boss Yr. award 1986), Am. Acad. Matrimonial Lawyers, N.J. Fedn. Planning Ofcls., N.J. Inst. Mcpl. Attys., Rutgers Sch. Law Alumni Assn., LaSalle Coll. Alumni Assn., Burlington County and City C. of C., Sigma Beta Kappa, Alpha Epsilon. Roman Catholic. Lodge: KC. Avocations: sports, music. Family and matrimonial, Local government, Probate. Home: 12 Normandy Dr Medford NJ 08055 Office: Bookbinder Guest & Domzalski 235 High St PO Box 429 Burlington NJ 08016

DON, ARTHUR, lawyer; b. Chgo., Sept. 24, 1953; s. Richard and Arlene Rita (Rose) D.; m. Roselynn Lee Gilbert, Apr. 12, 1975; children: David Kenneth, Katherine Rebecca. BS with honors, Northwestern U., 1975, JD cum laude, 1978. Bar: Ill. 1978, U.S. Ct. Appeals (7th cir.) 1980, U.S. Dist. Ct. (no. dsit.) Ill. 1982, U.S. Ct. Appeals (8th cir.) 1985. Assoc. D'Ancona & Pflaum, Chgo., 1978-84, ptnr., 1985—; instr. legal writing Northwestern U., Evanston, Ill., 1977-78. Mem. editorial bd. Northwestern U. Law Rev., 1977-78. Bd. dirs. prison reform group John Howard Assn., Chgo., 1982-85, sec., 1985—; bd. dirs. jr. govs. Chgo. Symphony Orch., 1986—. Mem. ABA, Decalogue Soc. Lawyers, Chgo. Council Lawyers, Chgo. Bar Assn. Jewish. Securities, General corporate, Computer. Home: 1910 Greenwood Wilmette IL 60091 Office: D'Ancona & Pflaum 30 N LaSalle Chicago IL 60602

DONAHUE, CHARLES, JR., legal educator, author; b. N.Y.C., Oct. 4, 1941; s. Charles James and Rosemary (Spang) D.; m. Sheila Finn, Aug. 22, 1964; 1 child, Sarah. A.B., Harvard Coll., 1962; LL.B., Yale U., 1965. Bar: N.Y. 1966, Mich. 1969, U.S. Supreme Ct. 1971. Atty.-adv. Office Gen. Counsel of Air Force, Washington, 1965-67; asst. gen. counsel Pres.'s Commn. on Postal Orgn., Washington, 1967-68; asst. prof. law U. Mich., 1968-70, assoc. prof., 1970-73, prof., 1973-79; prof. law Harvard U., 1980—; acad. visitor law dept. London Sch. Econs. and Polit. Sci., 1972-73; vis. prof. law Vrije Universiteit Brussel, 1975, Columbia U., 1976, U. Calif. Boalt Hall, 1976, Harvard U., 1978-79. Author: (with others) Cases and Materials on Property: An Introduction to the Concept and the Institution, 1974, 2d edit, 1983, (with others) A Course in Basic Property, 1975, 2d edit., 1983, (with N. Adams) Select Cases from the Ecclesiastical Courts of the Province of Canterbury, c. 1200-1301, 1981; articles editor Yale Law Jour, 1963-65; bd. editors Am. Jour. Legal History, 1977-82. Served with USAF, 1965-68. Mem. Am. Law Inst., Am. Soc. Legal History (dir. 1977-79, v.p. 1981-85), Selden Soc. (v.p. 1985—), Société d'histoire du droit, Société pour l'histoire des droits de l'antiquité, Medieval Acad. Am. Roman Catholic. Legal education. Home: 584 Centre St Newton MA 02158 Office: Harvard Law Sch Cambridge MA 02138

DONAHUE, JOHN M(ICHAEL), lawyer; b. Phila., Apr. 20, 1952; s. Joseph Henry and Helen Catherine (Fitzpatrick) D. BA in English, LaSalle Coll., 1974; JD, John Marshall Law Sch., 1978. Bar: Pa. 1978, U.S. Dist. Ct. (ea. dist.) Pa. 1978. Atty. legal dept. Transam. Ins. Co., Phila., 1978-82; trial atty. Transamerica Ins. Co., Phila., 1982—; assoc. Law Offices of Thomas J. McNally, Phila., 1982—. Mem. ABA, Pa. Bar Assn., Phila. Bar Assn., Phila. Assn. Def. Counsel, Brehon Law Soc., John Marshall Law Sch. Alumni Assn. (rep. 1985—). Democrat. Roman Catholic. Avocations: photography, golf, cycling. State civil litigation, Personal injury, Insurance. Home: 6531 Montour St Philadelphia PA 19111 Office: Law Offices of Thomas J McNally 1515 Market St Suite 1500 Philadelphia PA 19102

DONAHUE, KATHLEEN ANN, lawyer; b. Yonkers, N.Y., May 7, 1947; d. James P. and Margaret E. (O'Brien) D. BA, Albertus Magnus Coll., 1969; JD, Suffolk U., 1978. Bar: Mass. 1979, U.S. Dist. Ct. Mass. 1979, U.S. Ct. Appeals (1st cir.) 1979. Law clk. to presiding justice U.S. Ct. Appeals (1st cir.), Boston and Concord, N.H., 1979-80; assoc. Oteri & Weinberg, Boston, 1980-81; sole practice Cohasset, Mass., 1981—; dir. evaluation and tng. Pilgrim Advs., Inc., Brockton, Mass., 1987—, also bd. dirs.; adv. various political candidates, 1968-70. Staff mem. Suffolk Law Rev. Pettingill Law Scholar Greenwich Rotary, 1976-78. Mem. ABA, Mass. Bar Assn., Plymouth County Bar Assn., Phi Delta Phi. Democrat. Club: Cohasset Dramatic. Avocations: community theater, gardening, labrador retrievers. Criminal. Home: 28 Whitcomb Rd Minot MA 02055 Office: Box 421 Cohasset MA 02025

DONAHUE, MICHAEL CHRISTOPHER, lawyer; b. Norwood, Mass., Apr. 20, 1946; s. Michael Christopher and Helen (Joyce) D.; m. Erna Joyce Carrigan, Apr. 20, 1968; children—Kirsten, Michael, Brendan, Brian. A.B., Boston Coll., 1968; J.D., Boston U., 1972. Bar: Mass. 1972. Assoc., Klainer & Kappel, Boston, 1972-73, Sheridan, Garrahan & Lander, Framingham, Mass., 1981—; asst. atty. gen. Mass. Atty. Gen., 1973-79; gen. counsel Mass. Dept. of Corrections, Boston, 1979-81; spl. asst. atty. gen. Mass., Boston, 1979—; lectr. grad. criminal justice program Anna Maria Coll., Paxton, Mass., 1981-86. Contbr. articles to law review jours. Served with USAR, 1968-72. Mem. ABA, Assn. Trial Lawyers Am., Mass. Bar Assn., Mass. Acad. Trial Attys. (author, editor), South Middlesex Bar Assn. Democrat. Roman Catholic. Civil rights, Federal civil litigation, State civil litigation. Home: 167 Depot St S Easton MA 02375 Office: Sheridan Garrahan & Lander 161 Worcester Rd The Meadows Framingham MA 01701

DONAHUE, RICHARD KING, lawyer; b. Lowell, Mass., July 20, 1927; s. Joseph P. and Dorothy F. (Riordan) D.; m. Nancy Lawson, Sept. 19, 1953; children—Gail M., Timothy J., Michael R., Nancy C., Richard K., Daniel J., Alicia A., Stephen J., Christopher P., Tara E., Philip A. A.B., Dartmouth Coll., 1948; J.D., Boston U., 1951. Bar: Mass. 1951. Practice, Lowell, Mass., 1951-60, 63—; ptnr. Donahue & Donahue, Attys., P.C.; asst. to Pres. Kennedy, Washington, 1960-63. Served with USNR. Recipient Herbert Harley award Am. Judicature Soc., 1981. Mem. Am. Bd. Trial Advs., ABA (gov., ho. of dels. 1972—), Am. Coll. Trial Lawyers, Mass. Bar Assn. (past pres., Gold medal 1979), New Eng. Bar Assn. (past pres.). Clubs: Union League (Boston); Vesper Country (Tyngsboro, Mass.); Fed. City (Washington); Yorick (Lowell). Federal civil litigation, State civil litigation, Criminal. Office: 21 George St Lowell MA 01852

DONAHUE, THOMAS E., JR., corporate lawyer. Exec. v.p. sec., gen. counsel Am. Med. Internat. Inc., Beverly Hills, Calif. Office: Am Med Internat Inc 414 N Camden Dr Beverly Hills CA 90210 *

DONAHUE, TIMOTHY PATRICK, lawyer; b. Phila., Sept. 7, 1955; s. Joseph Thomas and Margaret Teresa (Golden) D.; m. Diane Gilbert, June 26, 1982; 1 child, Timothy Patrick Jr. BA, U. Ala., 1977, JD, 1981. Bar: Ala. 1982. Assoc., then ptnr. Clark & Scott, P.A., Birmingham, Ala., 1982—. Mem. Ala. Bar Assn., Ala. Trial Lawyers Assn., Birmingham Bar Assn. (exec. com. young lawyers sect. 1986-87). Republican. Roman Catholic. Club: Vestavia (Ala.) Country. Insurance, State civil litigation, Workers' compensation. Home: 1013 S Ridge Dr Birmingham AL 35216 Office: Clark & Scott PA 14 Office Park Circle Box 7687A Birmingham AL 35223

DONALD, NORMAN HENDERSON, III, lawyer; b. Denver, Nov. 1, 1937; s. Norman Henderson Jr. and Angelene (Pell) D.; m. Alice Allen, Oct. 31, 1970 (div. Aug. 1980); children: Norman H. IV, Helen P.; m. Kathryn Akers, Sept. 26, 1981. AB, Princeton U., 1959; LLB, Harvard U., 1962.

Bar: N.Y. 1962. Assoc. Davis, Polk & Wardwell, N.Y.C., 1962-67; assoc. Skadden, Arps, Slate, Meagher & Flom, N.Y.C., 1967-68, ptnr., 1968—; sec. Henderson Estate Co., N.Y.C., 1968—, bd. dirs; bd. dirs. Bonsal, Seggerman & Co. Inc., Roslyn, N.Y. Mem. Assn. of Bar of City of N.Y., Practising Law Inst. (editor Reit Restructuring 1977—), St. Paul's Sch. Alumni Assn. (v.p., bd. dirs. 1984—). Republican. Episcopalian. Clubs: Union, Racquet (N.Y.C.). General corporate. Home: Overlook on Rockledge Rd Rye NY 10580 Office: Skadden Arps Slate Meagher & Flom 919 3rd Ave New York NY 10022

DONALDSON, CHARLES RUSSELL, state justice; b. Helena, Mont., Feb. 2, 1919; s. Charles Mortimer and Mabel (King) D.; children: Karen, Holly, Jean, Laurel, Sarah, Charles. Student, Willamette U., 1937-38; B.A., U. Idaho, 1941, LL.B., 1948; postgrad., George Washington Law Sch., 1943-44. Bar: Idaho 1948. Practice law Boise, 1948-64; dist. judge 1964-68; justice Idaho Supreme Ct., Boise, 1969—, chief justice, 1973, 79-80, 83-86; mem. Idaho Ho. of Reps., 1955-57; justice of peace, 1960-64. Mem. governing com. Idaho chpt. Arthritis and Rheumatism Found. Served with Signal Corps, AUS, World War II. Mem. Conf. Chief Justices (dep. chmn. 1980—). Methodist. Lodges: Kiwanis (past pres.), Masons, Shriners. Jurisprudence. Office: Supreme Ct Bldg Boise ID 83720

DONALDSON, DAVID HOWARD, JR., lawyer; b. Midland, Tex., Oct. 1, 1951; s. David Howard and Joan (Steinberger) D.; m. Susan Arleen Kepple, Aug. 13, 1971; children: Matthew, Shannon. BA summa cum laude, Tex. A&M U., 1973; JD with high honors, U. Tex., 1976. Bar: U.S. Dist. Ct. (we. dist.) Tex. 1978, U.S. Ct. Appeals (5th and 11th cirs.) 1981, U.S. Dist. Ct. (so. dist.) Tex. 1983, U.S. Dist Ct. (ea. dist.) Tex., U.S. Supreme Ct. 1984. Law clk. to presiding judge U.S. Ct. Appeals (5th cir.), New Orleans, 1976-77; assoc. Graves, Dougherty, Hearon & Moody, Austin, Tex., 1977-83, ptnr., 1983—. Pres.'s scholar Tex. A&M U., 1970. Named Tex. Friend of 1st Amendment, Soc. Profl. Journalists, 1986. Mem. ABA, Tex. Bar Assn., Tex. Young Lawyers Assn., Austin Young Lawyers Assn. Democrat. Libel, Federal civil litigation, State civil litigation. Home: 3218 Park Hills Dr Austin TX 78746 Office: Graves Dougherty Hearon & Moody 2300 InterFirst Tower Austin TX 78701

DONALDSON, DOROTHEA E., judge; b. New Rochelle, N.Y., Mar. 1, 1911; d. Harnett B. and Amelia J. (Roeck) Donaldson. B.A., Hunter Coll., 1931; M.A., Tchrs. Coll., Columbia U., 1932; J.D., St. John's U., 1935, LL.D. (hon.), 1977. Bar: N.Y. 1936, U.S. Supreme Ct. 1946. Tchr., New Rochelle Pub. Schs., 1932-43; assoc. J. Lester Albertson, New Rochelle, 1943-50; mem., referee, supervising referee N.Y. State Workmen's Compensation Bd., 1944-60; chmn. N.Y. State Unemployment Ins. Appeal Bd., 1960-63; judge N.Y. State Ct. Claims, 1963-77. Trustee St. John's U., Jamaica, N.Y.; mem. adv. bd. Pace U. Law Sch., White Plains, N.Y. Recipient Golden Eaglet award Girl Scouts U.S.A., 1929; Woman of Yr. award New Rochelle Bus. and Profl. Women's Club, 1949; Benjamin Potoker meml. brotherhood award N.Y. State Employees, 1961; Pres.'s medal St. John's U., 1971, Pietas medal, 1974, Medal of Honor, 1982; medallion Westchester Community Coll., 1975; named to Hall of Fame, Hunter Coll., 1972. Mem. ABA, New Rochelle Bar Assn., Westchester County Bar Assn., N.Y. State Bar Assn., Am. Arbitration Assn. (arbitrator), Bus. and Profl. Women's Club (Orlando, Fla.) Republican. Methodist. Condemnation, Personal injury, Workers' compensation. Home: 915 Euclid Ave Orlando FL 32806

DONAT, MARSHALL JAMES, lawyer; b. Bronx, N.Y., Oct. 29, 1955; s. Walter and Margaret (Kennedy) D.; m. Mary Jean Gardner, Oct. 17, 1981. BA, Columbia U., 1977; JD, Fordham U., 1980. Bar: N.Y. 1981, U.S. Dist. Ct. (so. and ea. dists.) N.Y. 1982. Assoc. Reynolds, Richards, LaVenture, Hadley & Davis, N.Y.C., 1980-82; atty. Pan Am Corp., N.Y.C., 1982-86; corp. counsel Savin Corp., Stamford, Conn., 1986—. Mem. ABA, Westchester Fairfield County Bar Assn. Home: 21 Holly Ln Rye Brook NY 10573 Office: Savin Corp 9 W Broad St Stamford CT 06904

DONAT, WALTER KENNEDY, lawyer; b. Bronx, N.Y., June 24, 1954; s. Walter Alexander and Margaret (Kennedy) D.; m. Rhonda Ellen Shapiro, Aug. 12, 1979; children: Amanda, Michael. BA magna cum laude, Fordham U., 1976, JD, 1979. Bar: N.Y. 1980, U.S. Dist. Ct. (so. and ea. dists.) N.Y. 1982. Atty. MONY Fin. Services, N.Y.C., 1979-81, asst. counsel, 1982, assoc. counsel, 1983, counsel, 1984-85, asst. gen. counsel, 1986—. Mem. Apt. Owners Adv. Council, White Plains, N.Y., 1983—. N.Y. Regents scholar NYU, 1972. Mem. ABA, N.Y. State Bar Assn., Westchester-Fairfield County Corp. Counsel Assn., Ins. Co. Lawyers Assn., Guild of Cath. Lawyers (sec. 1984—), Psi Sigma Alpha. Lodge: Kiwanis. Avocations: politics, tennis, theatre. Insurance, Pension, profit-sharing, and employee benefits, Real property. Office: MONY Fin Services 1740 Broadway New York NY 10019

DONATO, ARTHUR THOMAS, JR., lawyer; b. Bryn Mawr, Pa., Nov. 6, 1955; s. Arthur Thomas and Vincenza (Ricci) D.; m. June Gilson, May 7, 1983. BS in Econs., Villanova U., 1977; JD, Del. Law Sch., 1980; postgrad., Villanova U., 1987—. Bar: Pa. 1980, U.S. Dist. Ct. (ea. dist.) Pa. 1980, U.S. Ct. Appeals (3d cir.) 1984, U.S. Supreme Ct. 1984. Assoc. Prodoehl, James & Donato, Media, Pa., 1980-83; ptnr. Prodoehl, Malady & Donato, Media, 1983-84, Malady & Donato, Media, 1984—; vis. lectr. Villanova (Pa.) U., 1981—. active several polit. campaigns. Named one of Outstanding Young Men in Am., 1977. Mem. ABA (corp. and banking com.), Pa. Bar Assn. (criminal law, legal ethics and profl. responsibility, civil litigation coms.), Delaware County Bar Assn. (co-chmn. civil rights com. 1982-84, chmn. criminal rules com., budget and fin., criminal trial practices coms.), Assn. Trial Lawyers Am., Pa. Trial Lawyers Assn. (criminal law com.), Nat. Assn. Criminal Def. Lawyers, Del. County Assn. Criminal Def. Lawyers (founding pres.). Republican. Roman Catholic. Club: Lawyers (Delaware County)(pres. 1983). Criminal. Office: Malady & Donato 211-213 N Olive St Media PA 19063

DONEGAN, CHARLES EDWARD, lawyer, educator; b. Chgo., Apr. 10, 1933; s. Arthur C. and Odessa (Arnold) D.; m. Patty Lou Harris, June 15, 1963; 1 son, Carter Edward. B.S.C., Roosevelt U., 1954; M.S., Loyola U., 1959; J.D., Howard U., 1967; LL.M., Columbia, 1970. Bar: N.Y. 1968, D.C. 1968, Ill. 1979. Pub. sch. tchr. Chgo., 1956-59; with Office Internal Revenue, Chgo., 1959-62; labor economist U.S. Dept. Labor, Washington, 1962-65; legal intern U.S. Commn. Civil Rights, Washington, summer 1966; asst. counsel NAACP Legal Def. Fund, N.Y.C., 1967-69; lectr. law Baruch Coll., N.Y.C., 1969-70; asst. prof. law State U. N.Y. at Buffalo, 1970-73; assoc. prof. law Howard U., 1973-77; vis. assoc. prof. Ohio State U., Columbus, 1977-78; asst. regional counsel U.S. EPA, 1978-80; prof. law So. U., Baton Rouge, 1980—; sole practice law Chgo. and Washington, 1984—; arbitrator steel industry, 1972—, U.S. Postal Service, New Orleans; vis. prof. law La. State U., summer 1981; real estate broker. Author: Discrimination in Public Employment, 1975; Contbr. articles to profl. jours., to Dictionary Am. Negro Biography. Active Americans for Democratic Action. Named Most Outstanding Prof. So. U. Law Sch., 1982; Ford Found. scholar, 1965-67; Ford Found. fellow Columbia U., 1972-73; Nat. Endowment for Humanities postdoctoral fellow in Afro-Am. studies Yale, 1972-73. Mem. ABA (vice chmn. com. edn. and curriculum local govt. law sect. 1972—, mem. pub. edn. com. sect. local govt. 1974—, chmn. liaison com. AALS), Nat. Bar Assn., D.C. Bar Assn., Chgo. Bar Assn., Fed. Bar Assn., Cook County Bar Assn., Am. Arbitration Assn. (arbitrator), Nat. Conf. Black Lawyers (bd. organizers), Assn. Henri Capitant, Roosevelt, Loyola, Howard and Columbia alumni assns., Alpha Phi Alpha, Phi Alpha Kappa, Phi Alpha Delta. Legal education, Labor, Civil rights. Home: 4315 Argyle Terrace NW Washington DC 20011 Office: 601 Indiana Ave NW Suite 900 Washington DC 20004 also: 30 W Washington Suite 1300 Chicago IL 60602

DONELSON, LEWIS RANDOLPH, III, lawyer; b. Memphis, Oct. 9, 1917; s. Lewis Randolph and Katherine Campbell D.; m. Janice Ost, Feb. 3, 1945; children: Janice Donelson Howell, Lewis R. IV, Loring Donelson Daniel. BA in Polit. Sci. with distinction, Southwestern at Memphis, 1938; JD, Georgetown U., 1941. Bar: Tenn. 1940, D.C. 1941. Chief exec. officer, ptnr. Heiskell, Donelson, Bearman, Adams, Williams & Kirsch P.C., Memphis, Knoxville, Chattanooga and Nashville, Tenn., 1954—; commr. fin. State of Tenn., Nashville, 1979-81; bd. dirs. Choctaw Inc., NCRD Inc., Memphis. Contbr. articles to profl. jours. and mags. Charter mem. Memphis City Council, 1967-71; vice chmn. Leadership Memphis, 1977, Tenn. Higher Edn. Commn.; mem. exec. com. Tenn. Tech.; chmn. campaign for Sen. Howard Baker, 1978; bd. dirs. St. Jude's Children's Hosp., Memphis, Biomed. Research Zone. Recipient Outstanding City Council Member award Memphis City Council, 1971, Americansim award Shelby County Reps., 1977, Outstanding Citizen award Civitan Club, 1981. Mem. ABA, Tenn. Bar Assn., Memphis Bar Assn., Shelby County Bar Assn. Republican. Presbyterian. Club: Memphis Country, Belle Meade Country (Nashville). Lodge: Rotary (dir. 1959) (community service award 1985). Avocation: golf. Banking, General corporate, Estate planning. Home: 134 E Cherry Rd Memphis TN 38117 Office: Heiskell Donelson Bearman et al 1st Tennesee Bldg Suite 2000 Memphis TN 38103

DONIGER, ANTHONY M., lawyer; b. N.Y.C., Feb. 16, 1950; s. Lester L. and Rita (Roth) D.; m. Elizabeth A. Lunt, June 7, 1974; children: Kate, Emma. BA, Oxford U., Eng., 1973; JD, Harvard U., 1977. Bar: Mass. 1977, U.S. Dist. Ct. Mass. 1977, U.S. Ct. Appeals (1st cir.) 1977, U.S. Supreme Ct. 1981. Assoc. Sugarman, Rogers, Barshak & Cohen, Boston, 1977-1980, ptnr., 1980—. Mem. Supreme Jud. Ct. Adv. Com. on Handicapped, Boston, 1983—, adv. com. Mass. Civil Liberties Union, 1986—, gen. counsel, 1987—; bd. dirs. Nat. Consumer Law Ctr., Boston, 1982—. Mem. ABA, Mass. Bar Assn., Boston Bar Assn. (chmn. com. indigent criminal def. 1983-85). State civil litigation, Federal civil litigation, Civil rights. Office: Sugarman Rogers Barshak & Cohen PC 33 Union St Boston MA 02108

DONLAN, MARTIN ANDREW, JR., lawyer; b. Chgo., May 10, 1948; s. Martin Andrew and Margaret Catherine (Shugrue); m. Mary Helen Bliley; children: M. Andrew III, Daniel Paul, Joseph Patrick. Student, U. Innsbruck, Austria, 1968; BBA, U. Notre Dame, 1970; JD, U. Denver, 1974. Bar: Ill. 1974, Va. 1976, U.S. Dist. Ct. (ea. and we. dists.) Va., U.S. Supreme Ct. Asst. pub. defender Office of Pub. Defender, Chgo., 1974-76; asst. atty. gen. Office of Atty. Gen., Richmond, Va., 1976-80; assoc. Crews, Hancock & Dunn, Richmond, 1980-84, ptnr., 1984—. Bd. dirs. St. Francis Home, 1985-87. Mem. ABA, Ill. Bar Assn., Va. Bar Assn., Va. Trial Lawyers Assn., Va. Assn. Def. Attys., Richmond Bar Assn., Nat. Health Lawyers Assn., Def. Research Inst. Health, Federal civil litigation, Administrative and regulatory. Office: Crews Hancock & Dunn 700 E Main St Richmond VA 23219

DONLEVY, JOHN DEARDEN, lawyer; b. Chgo., May 29, 1933; s. Frank and Alice Genevieve (O'Connor) D.; m. Kristin Bach Minnick, Apr. 20, 1963 (div. Sept. 1985); 1 son, John Dearden. Student, Stanford U., 1950-52; B.S., Northwestern U., 1954; J.D., U. Chgo., 1957; postgrad., Northwestern U., 1958. Bar: Ill. 1957, U.S. Dist. Ct. (no. dist.) 1957, U.S. Ct. Appeals (7th cir.) 1969, U.S. Supreme Ct. 1972. Asst. state's atty. Cook County Criminal Div., Chgo., 1958-61; city prosecutor City of Evanston, Ill., 1961; assoc. Mayer, Brown & Platt, Chgo., 1962-73, ptnr., 1974—; participant Hinton Moot Ct. Competition U. Chgo., 1955-56, judge, 1972. Bd. dirs. English-Speaking Union, Chgo., 1964-65; active Republican Orgn., 1958-60. Recipient Disting. Legal award Am. Legion, Chgo., 1960; named spl. prosecutor-labor racketeering Cook County State's Atty., Chgo., 1959-61. Mem. ABA, Ill. State Bar Assn. (workers' compensation, criminal law sections), Chgo. Bar Assn. (def. of prisoners and criminal law coms.), Workers' Compensation Lawyers Assn. (Ill.). Republican. Roman Catholic. Club: Chgo. Athletic. Criminal, Workers' compensation, State civil litigation. Office: Mayer Brown & Platt 190 S LaSalle St Chicago IL 60604

DONLEY, JERRY ALAN, lawyer; b. Denver, Feb. 17, 1930; s. Richard O. and Mildred K. (Bailey) D.; m. Dorothy Jean Mayhew, Sept. 5, 1953; children—Charles Alan, Jack Edward, David William. B.A., Beloit Coll., 1951; LL.B., U. Mich., 1954. Bar: Colo. 1954, U.S. Dist. Ct. Colo. 1954, U.S. Supreme Ct. 1977. Atty. Legal Aid Soc., Colorado Springs, Colo., 1957; dep. dist. atty. 4th Jud. Dist., Colorado Springs, 1957-60; sole practice, Colorado Springs, 1960-64; ptnr. Rector, Kane & Donley, 1964-68, Rector, Kane, Donley & Wills, 1968-71, Kane, Donley & Wills, 1971-83, Kane & Donley, 1983—. Active 1st Presbyterian Ch. of Colorado Springs; bd. dirs. Boys Club Colorado Springs and Vicinity, Colorado Springs Charter Assn., Pikes Peak Roadrunners; mem. track and field com. Colo. Assn. of Athletic Congress; chmn. masters track and field com. Athletics Congress U.S.A., 1984-85. Served to cpl. U.S. Army, 1954-56. Mem. Colorado Springs Estate Planning Council (sec. 1979), Colorado Springs Jaycees (bd. dirs.), El Paso County Bar Assn. Lodge: Kiwanis. Insurance, Probate, General practice. Home: 1715 Alamo Ave Colorado Springs CO 80907

DONLEY, JOSEPH FRANCIS, lawyer; b. Bklyn., Oct. 8, 1952; s. George Anthony and Grace Ann (McFadden) D.; m. Christine Marie Simms, May 28, 1977; one child, Lauren Georgina. BA magna cum laude, Allegheny Coll., 1974; JD cum laude, NYU, 1977. Bar: N.Y. 1977, U.S. Dist. Ct. (so. and ea. dists.) N.Y. 1977, U.S. Ct. Appeals (2d cir.) 1984, U.S. Ct. Appeals (3d cir.) 1985. Assoc. Cravath, Swaine & Moore, N.Y.C., 1977-81; assoc. Shereff, Friedman, Hoffman & Goodman, N.Y.C., 1981-85, ptnr., 1985—. Mem. ABA, N.Y.C. Bar Assn. Democrat. Roman Catholic. Federal civil litigation, State civil litigation, Securities. Home: 78 Allendale Dr Rye NY 10580 Office: Shereff Friedman Hoffman & Goodman 919 3d Ave New York NY 10022

DONLON, WILLIAM JAMES, lawyer; b. Colorado Springs, Colo., Apr. 22, 1924; s. John Andrew and Kathleen M. Donlon; m. Josephine A. Janssen, July 19, 1946; children—William James, Gregory A., Michele, Dru Ann Lees. Student Colo. Coll., 1941-43; B.S., U. Denver, 1949, J.D., 1950. Bar: Colo. 1950, Ohio 1964, Ill. 1969, U.S. Dist. Ct. Colo. 1956 (no. dist.) Ill. 1974, U.S. Ct. Apls. (10th cir.) 1957, U.S. Ct. Apls. (5th cir.) 1970, U.S. Ct. Apls. (7th cir.) 1974, U.S. Ct. Apls. D.C. 1979, U.S. Supreme Ct. 1965. Dep. clk. U.S. Dist. Ct. Denver, 1949-50; solo practice, Denver, 1953-63; gen. counsel Brotherhood Ry., Airline and S.S. Clks., Freight Handlers, Express and Sta. Employees, Rosemont, Ill., 1963-78, Rockville, Md., 1963-86; instr. labor U. Ill., 1972-78. Served with USAAF, 1942-45. Decorated Air medal with 2 oak leaf clusters. Mem. ABA (council sect. labor and employment law 1977-86), Ill. Bar Assn., D.C. Bar Assn., Am. Legion, Phi Alpha Delta, Phi Delta Theta. Democrat. Roman Catholic. Labor.

DONLON, WILLIAM JAMES, JR., lawyer; b. Denver, Feb. 18, 1948; s. William J. and Jo (Sanssen) D. BA, Morehead State U., 1971; JD, St. Louis U., 1974. Asst. atty. gen. State of Colo., Denver, 1974-76; sole practice Denver, 1976—. Mem. Colo. Bar Assn., Adams Bar Assn., Assn. Trial Lawyers Am. Democrat. Roman Catholic. Family and matrimonial, Personal injury, Landlord-tenant. Home: 1177 York Denver CO 80206 Office: 8933 N Washington Thornton CO 80229

DONNELLA, MICHAEL ANDRE, lawyer; b. Great Lakes, Ill., Oct. 16, 1954; s. Joseph Anthony and Jacqueline (Reddick) D. BA in Mathematics, Wesleyan U., Middletown, Conn., 1976; JD, U.Chgo., 1979. Bar: Ga. 1979, U.S. Ct. Appeals (D.C. and 11th cirs.) 1980, N.J. 1987. Assoc. Troutman, Sanders et al, Atlanta, 1979-83; atty. AT&T So. Region, Atlanta, 1983-86, AT&T Communications Internat., Basking Ridge, N.J., 1986—; vis. prof. Nat. Urban Legaue Black Exec. Exchange Porgram, 1986, Huston-Tillotson Coll., Austin, Tex.; bd. dirs. Foxhead Devel. Corp., Atlanta. Interviewer Wesleyan Schs. Com., Middletown, 1976—; active Big Bros./Big Sisters, Atlanta, 1979—, public relations com., 1983—; counsel Ga. Legis. Black Caucus, Atlanta, 1982—. Named one of Outstanding Young Men of Am., Montgomery, Ala., 1985, 87. Mem. Ga. Assn. Black Elected Ofcls. Found. (counsel 1982—, service citation 1985), Gate City Bar Assn. (continuing legal edn. com. 1984-85), Wesleyan Alumni Club (treas. 1984-86). Roman Catholic. Avocations: jazz, sports. Private international, Public utilities, General corporate. Office: AT&T Room 3235 B3 295 N Maple Ave Basking Ridge NJ 07920

DONNELLY, FREDERICK JAMES, lawyer; b. Utica, N.Y., Apr. 4, 1953; s. Frederick J. and Shirley (Woodruff) D. BA, St. Lawrence U., 1974; JD, Vanderbilt U., 1977. Bar: N.Y. 1977, S.D. 1981, Colo. 1982. Judge adv. U.S. Army, Stuttgaart, Fed. Republic Germany, 1978-81; assoc. David Stanton Law Offices, Rapid City, S.D., 1981-82; assoc. Stutz, Dyer, Miller & Delap, Denver, 1982-85, ptnr., 1985-86; ptnr. Slavin & Donnelly, Denver, 1986. Rep. precinct capt., Denver, 1984-85; mem. 1st Congl. com. Rep. Party, Denver, 1986. Mem. Denver Bar Assn., Colo. Bar Assn. Roman Catholic. Federal civil litigation, State civil litigation, Construction. Home: 1640 S Emerson St Denver CO 80210 Office: Slavin & Donnelly 1133 Pennsylvania Denver CO 80203

DONNELLY, ROBERT TRUE, state supreme court justice; b. Lebanon, Mo., Aug. 31, 1924; s. Thomas John and Sybil Justine (True) D.; m. Wanda Sue Oates, Nov. 16, 1946; children: Thomas Page, Brian True. Student, Tulsa U., 1942-43, Ohio State U., 1943; J.D., U. Mo., 1949. Bar: Mo. 1949. Mem. firm Donnelly & Donnelly, Lebanon; city atty. Lebanon, 1954-55; asst. atty. gen. Mo., 1957-61; justice Supreme Ct. Mo., Jefferson City, 1965—; chief justice Supreme Ct. Mo., 1973-75, 81-83; bd. govs. Mo. Bar, 1957-63. Mem. Lebanon Bd. Edn., 1959-65; trustee Sch. Religion, Drury Coll., Springfield, Mo., 1958-66, Mo. Sch. Religion, Columbia, 1971-72. Served with inf. AUS, World War II. Decorated Purple Heart. Mem. Am., Mo. bar assns., Phi Delta Phi. Presbyterian. Club: Mason. Home: PO Box 6818 Jefferson City MO 65102 Office: Supreme Ct Bldg Jefferson City MO 65101

DONNEM, ROLAND WILLIAM, lawyer, business executive; b. Seattle, Nov. 8, 1929; s. William Roland and Mary Louise (Hughes) D.; m. Sarah Brandon Lund, Feb. 18, 1961; children: Elizabeth Prince, Sarah Madison. B.A., Yale U., 1952; J.D. magna cum laude, Harvard U., 1957. Bar: N.Y. 1958, U.S. Dist. Ct. (ea. and so. dists.) N.Y. 1959, U.S. Ct. Appeals (2d cir.) 1959, U.S. Ct. Claims 1960, U.S. Tax Ct. 1960, U.S. Supreme Ct. 1963, U.S. Ct. Appeals (3d cir.) 1969, D.C. 1970, U.S. Ct. Appeals (D.C. cir.) 1970, Ohio 1976, U.S. Dist. Ct. (no. dist.) Ohio 1980, U.S. Ct. Appeals (7th cir.) 1980, U.S. Ct. Appeals (6th cir.) 1984. With Davis Polk & Wardwell, N.Y.C., 1957-63, 64-69; law sec. appellate div. N.Y. Supreme Ct., N.Y.C., 1963-64; dir. policy planning antitrust div. Justice Dept., Washington, 1969-71; v.p., sec., gen. counsel Standard Brands Inc., N.Y.C., 1971-76; v.p. law Chessie System, Cleve., 1976-78; sr. v.p. law Chessie System, 1978-86; ptnr. Meta Ptnrs., real estate devel., 1984—; dir., v.p. registered security rep. Cidco Investment Services, Inc., Cleve., 1985—; chmn., chief exec. officer Med. Facilities Devel. & Mgmt., Inc. and Retirement Developers, Inc., Cleve., 1986—. Bd. dirs., fin. v.p. Presbyn. Home for Aged Women, N.Y.C., 1972-76; bd. dirs., treas. James Lenox House, Inc., 1972-76; trustee Food and Drug Law Inst., 1974-76; trustee, sec. Brick Presbyterian Ch., 1974-76. Served from ensign to lt. (j.g.) USNR, 1952-54. Mem. ABA, Fed. Bar Assn., N.Y. State Bar Assn., N.Y.C. Bar Assn., D.C. Bar Assn., Ohio Bar Assn., Greater Cleve. Bar Assn., Am. Law Inst., Nat. Panel Arbitrators, Am. Arbitration Assn., Def. Orientation Conf. Assn., Grocery Mfrs. Assn. (legal com. 1971-76), Corn Refiners Assn. (lawyers adv. com. 1971-76), Assn. Am. R.R.s (legal affairs com. 1976-85), Yale U. Alumni Assn. Cleve. (treas. 1982-84, del. 1984-87, trustee), Assn. Yale Alumni (bd. govs. 1987—), Phi Beta Kappa. Republican. Presbyterian. Clubs: Tuxedo (N.Y.); Union (N.Y.C.); Capitol Hill, University, Metropolitan, Chevy Chase (Washington); Racquet, Kirtland, Cleve. Wine and Food, Mid Day (Cleve.). Real property, Securities, General corporate. Home: 2945 Fontenay Rd Shaker Heights OH 44120 Office: Med Facilities Devel & Mgmt Inc 1250 Superior Ave The Park Mall Cleveland OH 44114

DONNICI, PETER JOSEPH, lawyer, law educator, consultant; b. Kansas City, Mo., Sept. 5, 1939; s. Albert H. and Jennie (Danubio) D.; m. Diane DuPlantier, July 27, 1985; children—JuliaAnn Donnici Clifford, Joseph A., Joann L. B.A., U. Mo.-Kansas City, 1959, J.D., 1962; LL.M., Yale U., 1963. Bar: Mo. 1963, U.S. Supreme Ct. 1966, Calif. 1969. Asst. prof. law U. San Francisco, 1963-65, assoc. prof., 1965-68, prof., 1968—; assoc. Law Offices Joseph L. Alioto, San Francisco, 1967-72; sole practice, San Francisco, 1974—; spl. asst. prosecutor Jackson County Prosecutor's Office, Mo., 1963; No. Calif. bd. dirs. Council on Legal Ednl. Opportunity, San Francisco, 1969-70; conciliator for housing discrimination cases HUD, San Francisco, 1976; cons. Calif. Consumer Affairs' Task Force on Electronic Funds Transfer, Sacramento, 1978-79; dir. DHL Corp.; spl. counsel and del. to internat. confs. Commonwealth of No. Mariana Islands, 1983-84; faculty adviser U. San Francisco Law Rev., 1966—. Editor-in-chief U. Mo.-Kansas City Law Rev., 1961-62. Contbr. articles to profl. jours., 1964—. Cons.-advisor to mayor of San Francisco, 1967-73; active Lawyers' Com. for Urban Affairs, San Francisco, 1965-68. Wilson scholar U. Mo.-Kansas City, 1956-62; Sterling fellow Law Sch., Yale U., 1962-63. Mem. Bench and Robe, Phi Delta Phi. Democrat. Roman Catholic. Antitrust, Federal civil litigation, Civil rights. Home: 190 Cresta Vista San Francisco CA 94127 Office: U San Francisco Sch Law 2130 Fulton San Francisco CA 94117

DONOHOE, JAMES D., lawyer; b. Rochester, N.Y., Aug. 10, 1943; s. James Vincent and Constance Traganza (Day) D.; divorced; children—J. Douglas, Jeffrey D., Cynthia. B.S., Cornell U., 1965; J.D., Catholic U. Am., 1969; M.B.A., Case Western Res. U., 1979. Bar: N.Y., 1970, Ohio, 1974. Assoc., Pennie & Edmonds, N.Y.C., 1967-73; house counsel, Republic Steel Corp., Cleve., 1973-84, LTV Corp., Dallas, 1984—. Mem. ABA, Am. Patent Law Assn., Cleve. Bar Assn., Cleve. Patent Law Assn., Ohio Bar Assn., N.Y. State Bar Assn., Cleve. Growth Assn., Cleve. YMCA. Administrative and regulatory, Environment, Patent. Home: 12500 Edgewater Dr Apt 902 Cleveland OH 44107 Office: PO Box 6778 Cleveland OH 44101

DONOHUE, JOHN PATRICK, lawyer; b. N.Y.C., Sept. 16, 1944; s. Joseph Francis and Catherine Elizabeth (Feeney) D.; m. Patricia Ann Holly, June 11, 1977; children—Eileen Mary, Anne Catherine. B.A., Providence Coll., 1966; J.D., Catholic U. Am., 1969. Bar: N.Y. 1973, U.S. Ct. Appeals (2d cir.) 1973, U.S. Ct. Appeals (fed. cir.) 1974, N.J. 1975, U.S. Dist. Ct. N.J. 1975, U.S. Dist. Ct. (so., ea. dists.) N.Y. 1975, U.S. Supreme Ct. 1978, D.C. 1981, Pa. 1986. Spl. agt. FBI, Washington, 1969-71; assoc. Donohue & Donohue, N.Y.C., 1971-74, ptnr., 1974—; adj. prof. law internat. bus. transactions Seton Hall U. Sch. Law, Newark, 1986—. Author book sect. Customs Fraud Section on Business Crimes, 1982. Mem. panel arbitrators N.Y. Better Bus. Bur., 1974-83; pres. New Providence N.J. Taxpayers Assn., 1981-84; mem. budget com. Summit-New Providence United Way, 1983-84. Named Man of Yr., Phila. Customs, Brokers and Forwarders Assn., 1984. Mem. ABA, Customs and Internat. Trade Bar Assn., Assn. Trial Lawyers Am., N.J. State Bar Assn. Republican. Roman Catholic. Private international, Immigration, naturalization, and customs, Federal civil litigation. Home: 40 Johnson Dr New Providence NJ 07974 Office: Donohue & Donohue 26 Broadway New York NY 10004

DONOHUE, MICHAEL J., judge; b. Holyoke, Mass.; s. David I. and Mary (Fitzgerald) D.; m. Adeline L. O'Neil (dec. Mar. 1986); children—Michael J., Adeline L., Owen B., Anne C., Quentin, Maria. Student N. Tex. U., 1943, Stanford U., 1944, U. Pa., 1944; B.A., U. Mass., 1947; LL.B., Boston U., 1950. Bar: Mass. 1950. Sole practice, Holyoke, Mass., 1950-63; presiding judge Holyoke Dist. Ct., 1963—; asst. city solicitor Holyoke, 1959-60; pub. adminstr. Hampden County (Mass.), 1959-64. Chmn. Internat. Conf. on Judges on Violence and Terrorism; past pres. Am. Judges Found.; mem. exec. bd. Am. Coalition Against Crime, pres., 1983; mem. bldg. authority U. Mass. Served with AUS, 1943-46. Recipient award of merit Am. Judges Assn.; Centennial award Boston U. Mem. Judges of Am. (pres. 1982), Am. Judges Assn. (past pres.), Mass. Judges Conf., U. Mass. Alumni Assn. (past pres.). Club: KC (past grand knight). Co-author: R, 1983. Mem. editorial bd. Criminal Justice Rev.; editor Judicial Hilites; editor Court Rev. Jurisprudence. Office: PO Box 865 Courthouse Holyoke MA 01041

DONOHUE, PETER SALK, lawyer; b. St. Cloud, Minn., July 14, 1948; s. Howard I. and Madelon Donohue; m. Janet Salk, June 3, 1976; children: Faye Salk Donohue, Alex Salk Donohue, Audrey Salk Donohue. BA, St. John's U., Collegeville, Minn., 1970; JD, Hamlin U., 1977. Bar: Minn. 1977. Legal asst. Law Office Howard I. Donohue, St. Cloud, 1970-75; mem. St. Cloud Area Legal Services, 1975-76; ptnr. Donohue & Rajkowski, St. Cloud, 1976-79, Donohue & Ristvedt, St. Cloud, 1984—; sole practice St. Cloud, 1979-84; bd. dirs. Midwest Health Program Services, St. Joseph, Minn. Mem., past chmn. Human Rights Commn., St. Cloud; bd. dirs. County Stearns Theatrical Co., 1978-86. Probate, Local government, General practice. Office: Donohue & Ristvedt 916 St Germain St Saint Cloud MN 56301

DONOHUE, RICHARD HARNEY, lawyer; b. Brighton, Mass., June 30, 1950; s. Timothy Harney and Dorothy (Keenan) D.; m. Helen Lynch, Mar. 3, 1976; children: Mark T., Ellen C., Megan E. BA, Dartmouth Coll., 1972; JD, Northwestern U., 1979. Bar: Ill. 1979, U.S. Dist. Ct. (no. dist) Ill.

1979, U.S. Ct. Appeals (7th cir.) 1981. Litigation atty. Baker & McKenzie, Chgo., 1979—. Served to lt. comdr. USN, 1972-76, with Res. 1976—. Mem. ABA, Chgo. Bar Assn., Ill. State Bar Assn., Pilots Bar Assn., Def. Research Inst. Club: Legal. State civil litigation, Personal injury, Federal civil litigation. Home: 925 Elmwood Ave Wilmette IL 60091 Office: Baker & McKenzie 130 E Randolph Dr Chicago IL 60601

DONOHUE, ROBERT JOHN, lawyer; b. Orange, N.J., Oct. 12, 1934; s. Walter Joseph and Helen Gray (Quinby) D.; m. Patricia McKenzie, Sept. 28, 1968; children: Christine, Colleen, Robert, Daniel, David, Michael, Mary. AB, Villanova U., 1957; JD, Georgetown U., 1960. Bar: Pa. 1961, U.S. Supreme Ct. 1969. Assoc. Reilly & Pierce, Upper Darby, Pa., 1961-64, Kardas & Donohue, Upper Darby, 1965-73, Cantwell & Donohue, Upper Darby, 1974-77; sr. ptnr. Donohue & McKee, Havertown, Pa., 1978—; bd. dirs. various mfg. cos. Bd. dirs. Community YM-YWCA, 1976-84, chmn. bd., 1980-84; bd. dirs. St. Vincent's Home for Children, 1975-81, Jay Lau Meml. Scholarship Fund, 1979—; govt. appeal agt. U.S. Selective Service System, 1968-72; bd. dirs. Southeastern Del. County chpt. ARC, 1980-82; vice chmn. Upper Darby Mayor's Blue Ribbon Panel for 69th St., 1976-77. Served with U.S. Army, 1960-61. Mem. ABA, Pa. Bar Assn., Delaware County Bar Assn., Am. Judicature Soc., Am. Arbitration Assn. (nat. panel arbitrators 1965—), Am. Legion, Phi Alpha Delta (life). Club: Undine Barge. Lodge: Lions (pres. 1966—). Writer children's short stories. General practice, Probate, General corporate. Home: 1217 Mason Ave Drexel Hill PA 19026 Office: Township Line and N Drexel Ave Havertown PA 19083

DONOVAN, JAMES, lawyer; b. Napoleon, Ohio, Mar. 13, 1927; s. James Jr. and Mary Elizabeth (Kerr) D.; m. Louise Zbylot, Feb. 11, 1956; children: James Jr., John, Mary Elizabeth. AB, U. Mich., 1950, LLB, 1953. Bar: Ohio 1953. Ptnr. Meekison & Donovan, Napoleon, 1953—. Served with USN, 1945-46. Mem. ABA, Ohio Bar Assn., Am. Legion. Democrat. Presbyterian. Lodge: Elks. General practice, State civil litigation. Home: 635 W Washington St Napoleon OH 43545 Office: Meekison & Donovan 609 N Perry St Napoleon OH 43545

DONOVAN, RICHARD EDWARD, lawyer; b. Cleve., Dec. 3, 1952; s. Richard A. and Eileen (Karthaus) D.; m. Ellen Brode, June 16, 1979; 1 child, Colin. BS, U. Notre Dame, 1974; JD, Rutgers U., 1977. Bar: N.Y. 1978, U.S. Dist. Ct. (ea. dist.) N.Y. 1978, N.J. 1985, U.S. Dist. Ct. N.J. 1985, U.S. Ct. Appeals (2d cir.) 1987. Assoc. Breed, Abbott & Morgan, N.Y.C., 1977-80; assoc. Kelley, Drye & Warren, N.Y.C., 1980-86, ptnr., 1987—. Mem. ABA, Assn. of Bar of City of N.Y., N.J. Bar Assn., Rutgers Alumni Assn., N.Y. State Bar Assn. (sec. com. on fed. cts.), Fed. Bar Council. Club: Racquets (Short Hills, N.J.). Antitrust, Federal civil litigation, State civil litigation. Home: 175 South St Morristown NJ 07960 Office: Kelley Drye & Warren 101 Park Ave New York NY 10178

DONOVAN, ROBERT BICKFORD, lawyer; b. Cambridge, Mass., Nov. 25, 1930; s. George R. and Jean (Bickford) D.; m. Annette Cahoon, Aug. 9, 1952; children: Robert Jr., William, Michael, Richard. BA, U. Maine, 1952; LLB, U. Harvard, 1955. Bar: N.H. 1955, Mass. 1955, U.S. Dist. Ct. N.H. 1955. Ptnr. Holland, Donovan, Beckett & Welch P.A., Exeter, N.H., 1955—. Republican. Estate planning, Probate, General practice. Home: 51 South Rd East Kingston NH 03827 Office: Holland Donovan Beckett & Welch 151 Water St PO Box 1090 Exeter NH 03833

DONOVAN, WILLIAM JEREMIAH, lawyer, lobbyist; b. Newport, R.I., Dec. 30, 1949; s. William Jeremiah and Agnes Patricia (Egan) D.; m. Donna Coghlan, Aug. 16, 1980; children: Meaghan Elizabeth, Gerard Michael, Timothy James. BA, Coll. of Holy Cross, Worcester, Mass., 1972; MA, Cath. U. Am., 1975, JD, 1978. Bar: D.C. 1979, U.S. Ct. Appeals (D.C. cir.) 1979, U.S. Dist. Ct. D.C., 1980, U.S. Supreme Ct. 1982. Mgr. govt. affairs Kellogg Co., Battle Creek, Mich., 1978-79; v.p. govt. affairs, fed. legis. council Nat. Assn. Fed. Credit Unions, Washington, 1979—. Bd. dirs. St. Ann's Arlington (Va.) Fed. Credit Union, 1985—. Mem. ABA, Fed. Bar Assn. (long-range planning com. 1985—), Nat. Dem. Club. Roman Catholic. Clubs: Capitol Hill, Capitol Group, Regency. Lodge: KC. Legislative, Banking, Administrative and regulatory. Home: 5110 N 10th St Arlington VA 22205 Office: Nat Assn Fed Credit Unions 1111 N 19th St Arlington VA 22209

DOOLIN, JOHN B., state supreme ct. justice; b. Alva, Okla., May 25, 1918; s. John B. and Leo M. (Museller) D.; m. Marilyn B. Bruck, Oct. 3, 1981; children from previous marriage: John William, Mary L. Doolin Trembley, Katherine, Carole and Colleen (twins), Martha. B.S. in Bus. Adminstrn, Okla. U., 1941, LL.B., 1947. Bar: Okla. 1942. Practiced in Alva, 1947-63, Lawton, 1963-73; justice Okla. Supreme Ct., 1973—, now vice chief justice; mem. Okla. Hwy. Commn., 1959-63. Trustee Comanche County (Okla.) Meml. Hosp., 1967-73, chmn., 1968-73. Served to capt. AUS, 1941-45. Mem. Phi Delta Phi. Office: Okla Supreme Ct Room 244 State Capitol Bldg Oklahoma City OK 73105 *

DORADO, MARIANNE GAERTNER, lawyer; b. Neptune, N.J., May 18, 1956; d. Wolfgang Wilhelm and Marianne L. (Weber) Gaertner; m. Richard Manuel Dorado, Oct. 1, 1982. BA, Yale U., 1978; JD, U. Mich., 1981. Bar: N.Y. 1982. Assoc. Shearman & Sterling, N.Y.C., 1981—; bd. dirs. W.W. Gaertner Research Inc., Norwalk, Conn. Contbr. articles to profl. jours. Extern office legal advisor U.S. Dept. State, Washington, 1980. Republican. Roman Catholic. Banking, General corporate, Securities. Office: Shearman & Sterling 53 Wall St New York NY 10005

DORAN, KENNETH JOHN, lawyer; b. Janesville, Wis., Feb. 10, 1950; s. Henry James and Alice Elizabeth (Fanning) D.; m. Dianne Marie Carlson, Feb. 28, 1987. BA, U. Wis., 1974, JD, 1977. Atty. The Legal Clinic, Madison, Wis., 1978-79, Doran Law Offices, Madison, 1980-84, Smoler & Albert, S.C., Madison, 1984—. Bd. dirs. Wis. Madison chpt. Civil Liberties Union, Wis., 1983-85. Mem. Am. Bar Assn., Dane County Bar Assn. Democrat. Bankruptcy, Consumer commercial. Home: 2101 Fox Ave Madison WI 53711 Office: Smoler & Albert 119 King Blvd Suite 520 Madison WI 53703

DORE, FRED HUDSON, state supreme ct. justice; b. Seattle, July 31, 1925; s. Fred Hudson and Ruby T. (Kelly) D.; B.S.F.S., Georgetown Fgn. Service Sch., 1946; J.D., Georgetown U., 1949; m. Mary S. Shuham, Nov. 26, 1956; children: Margaret, Fred Hudson, Teresa, Tim, Jane. Bar: Wash. 1949. Practiced in Seattle, 1949-77; mem. Wash. Ho. of Reps., 1953-59, Wash. State Senate, 1959-74; judge Wash. State Ct. Appeals, 1977-80; justice Wash. State Supreme Ct., Olympia, 1981—. Jurisprudence. Office: State Supreme Ct Temple Justice Olympia WA 98504 *

DOREN, ROBERT ALAN, lawyer; b. Buffalo, Mar. 11, 1949; m. Teri B. Shaffer, Aug. 27, 1978; children: Lee Michael, Lindsey Marisa. B.S., SUNY-Buffalo, 1972; J.D., U. Buffalo, 1975. Bar: N.Y. 1976, U.S. Dist. Ct. (we. dist.) N.Y. 1976, U.S. Ct. Appeals (2d cir.) 1978. Assoc. Brizdle & Hankin, P.C., Buffalo, 1975-76; ptnr. Flaherty, Cohen, Grande, Randazzo & Doren, Buffalo, 1976—. Labor. Home: 252 Ranch Trail Williamsville NY 14221 Office: Flaherty Cohen Grande Randazzo & Doren 135 Delaware Ave Suite 210 Buffalo NY 14202

DORF, MICHAEL CHARLES, lawyer, consultant; b. Chgo., Aug. 8, 1952; s. Frank Leonard and Margaret (Odes) D.; m. Maury Collins, Oct. 27, 1985. BA, U. Chgo., 1973; JD, Columbia U., 1976. Bar: Ill. 1976, D.C. 1978, U.S. Dist. Ct. (no. dist.) Il.. 1980. Law clk. to judge U.S. Dist. Ct. Ill. (no. dist.), Chgo., 1976-78; spl. counsel congressman Sidney R. Yates, Washington, 1978-84; sole practice Chgo., 1984—; cons. City of Chgo., 1984—. Contbr. articles to profl. jours. Mem. adv. bd. Friends of Downtown, Chgo., 1985—, Chgo. Artists Coalition, 1986—. Mem. ABA, Chgo. Bar Assn., Chgo. Council of Lawyers, Lawyers for the Creative Arts. Democrat. Jewish. Legislative, General practice, Cultural planning. Home and Office: 7535 N Washtenaw Chicago IL 60645

DORF, ROBERT CLAY, lawyer, broadcaster; b. N.Y.C., Apr. 4, 1943; s. Irving and Jeanne (Hayflick) D.; m. Wendy Rappaport, Nov. 27, 1968; children—Andrew R., Jessica L. B.A. in History, U. Fla., 1964; student Alliance Francise, Paris, 1967; J.D., Bklyn. Law Sch., 1972. Bar: N.Y. 1973, U.S. Dist. Ct. (ea. and so. dists.) N.Y. 1974, U.S. Ct. Appeals (2d cir.) 1980. Announcer Sta. WIVI, V.I., 1964-65; office clk. Reuters News Service, Paris, 1967; film editor sta. WMAL-TV, Washington, 1968; asst. dist. atty. Bronx Dist. Atty.'s Office, 1972-76; practice law, N.Y.C., 1976—; ptnr. law firm Dorf & Perlmutter, N.Y.C., 1984—; arbitrator U.S. Dist. Ct. (ea. dist.) N.Y.; hearing officer Environ. Control Bd., N.Y.C., 1976-77; arbitrator N.Y. County Civil Ct., N.Y.C., 1981—. Methadone counselor Beth Israel Hosp., 1969. Served with U.S. Army, 1965-67. Mem. Bklyn. Bar Assn., N.Y. State Trial Lawyers Assn. Democrat. Jewish. Criminal, Personal injury, Family and matrimonial. Home: 101 Clark St Brooklyn NY 11201 Office: 56 Pine St New York NY 10005

DORFMAN, JOHN CHARLES, lawyer; b. Wilkinsburg, Pa., Feb. 3, 1925; s. Leo O. Dorfman; m. Ruth B. Davison; children: Beverly (Dorfman) Lenci, Laura, Carolyn, Bradley. BEE, Yale U., 1945; JD, Cornell U., 1949. Bar: N.Y. 1949, Conn. 1950, Pa., U.S. Dist. Ct. (ea. dist.) Pa. 1957. Patent counsel Machlett Labs. Inc., Springdale, Conn., 1949-54; assoc. Pennie & Edmonds, N.Y.C., 1954-55; assoc. Howson & Howson, Phila., 1955-59, ptnr., 1960-73; ptnr. Dann, Dorfman, Herrell & Skillman, Phila., 1974—. Served to lt. (j.g.) USN, 1943-46, with reserves. Mem. ABA (chmn. sect. patent, trademark and copyright law 1984-85), Nat. Council Patent Law Assn. (chmn. 1978-79), Am. Intellectual Property Law Assn. (bd. dirs.), Phila. Patent Law Assn. (pres. 1974-76), Nat. Inventors Hall of Fame found. (pres. 1977-78), Tau Beta Pi. Republican. Presbyterian. Clubs: Union League (Phila.), St. Davids Golf (Wayne, Pa.). Avocations: skiing, golf, travel. Patent, Trademark and copyright, Unfair competition. Home: 215 Midland Ave Wayne PA 19087 Office: Dann Dorfman Herrell and Skillman 123 S Broad St Philadelphia PA 19109

DORIA, ANTHONY NOTARNICOLA, college dean; b. Savona, Italy, June 2, 1927; s. Vito Sante and Jolanda (Giampaolo) Notarnicola. M.B.A., Wharton Sch., U. Pa., 1953; LL.M. (equivalent), U. Paris, 1960; D.Jr., U. Rome, 1962. Prof. history, bus. and internat. law Community Coll. at Suffolk County, Selden, N.Y., 1960-65, L.I. U., Southampton, N.Y., 1964-65; founder, pres. Royalton Coll. Sch. Internat. Affairs, S. Royalton, Vt., 1965-72; dean Royalton Coll. Sch. Internat. Affairs (Royalton Coll. Law Study Center), 1974—; founder, dean Vt. Law Sch., 1972-74; cons. internat. law and orgns.; panelist Am. Arbitration Assn.; mem. Vt. Gov.'s Commn. on Student Affairs, 1972-75. Author: Italy and the Free World, 1945, The Conquest of the Congo, 1947, Influences in the Making of Foreign Policy in the United States of America, Great Britain, and France, 1953, Introduction to International Law, 1976. Candidate for U.S. Senate, 1986. Served with underground resistance movement World War II. Recipient Merit cert. UN; citation Boy Scouts Am., 1965. Mem. Am. Judicature Soc., Internat. Bar Assn., Internat. Law Assn., Am. Soc. Internat. Law, AAUP, Acad. Polit. Sci., Noble Assn. Chevaliers Pontificaux (life). Clubs: Elysee (Paris); Pen and Pencil. Legal education, Private international, Public international. Home: The Royalton Inn South Royalton VT 05068 Office: Royalton Coll Law Study Ctr South Royalton VT 05068

DORIT, J NILEY, lawyer; b. Coral Gables, Fla., Nov. 12, 1954; s. Edmond E. and Elaine (Singer) D. BA, Swarthmore Coll., 1976; JD with honors, U. Fla., 1979. Bar: Fla. 1979, Calif. 1980, U.S. Dist. Ct. (no. dist.) Calif. 1980, U.S. Ct. Appeals (5th cir.) 1980, U.S. Supreme Ct. 1980. Assoc. Furth, Fahrner, Bluemle & Mason, San Francisco, 1981-83, Bostwick & Tehin, San Francisco, 1983-87; sole practice San Francisco, 1987—. Vol. Spl. Olympics, San Francisco, 1985-86; aide Presdl. candidate Askew, San Francisco, 1984. Mem. Fla. Bar Assn., Calif. Bar Assn., San Francisco Bar Assn., Assn. Trial Lawyers Am., Calif. Trial Lawyers Assn., Order of Coif. Democrat. Jewish. Avocations: squash, wine collecting, tennis. Personal injury, Federal civil litigation, State civil litigation. Home: 3210 Washington St No 12 San Francisco CA 94115

DORNAN, DONALD C., JR., lawyer; b. Columbus, Miss., Oct. 26, 1952; s. Donald C. and Virginia (Shelley) D.; m. Jennieann Abel, Apr. 27, 1974; children: Gloria Diana, Donald Patrick. BA, Miss. State U., 1974; JD, U. Miss., 1976. Diplomate Nat. Coll. Trial Advocacy. Bar: Miss. 1977, U.S. Dist. Ct. (no. and so. dists.) Miss. 1977, U.S. Ct. Appeals (5th and 11th cirs.) 1981. Atty. Page, Mannino & Peresich, Biloxi, Miss., 1976-80; ptnr. Denton, Persons, Dornan & Bilbo, Biloxi, 1980-87; sole practice Biloxi, 1987—; asst. city prosecutor City of Biloxi, 1977-80, city judge pro tem, 1982—; bd. dirs. Gulf Law Inst., 1981—. Mem. ABA, Fed. Bar Assn., Miss. Bar Assn. (bd. dirs. young lawyers sect. 1985-86), Harrison County Bar Assn., Harrison County Young Lawyers (treas. 1980-81, v.p. 1981-82, pres. 1982-83), Miss. Trial Lawyers Assn., Assn. Trial Lawyers Am., Am. Judicature Soc., Southeastern Admiralty Law Inst., Phi Delta Phi. Methodist. Insurance, Federal civil litigation, Admiralty. Office: 218 Magnolia Mall Biloxi MS 39530

DORNBUSCH, ARTHUR A., II, lawyer; b. Peru, Ill., Nov. 8, 1943; s. Arthur A. Sr. and Genevieve C. (Knudtson) D.; children: Kimberly, Brendan, Courtney, Eric. BA, Yale U., 1966; LLB, U. Pa., 1969. Bar: N.Y. 1970, U.S. Ct. Appeals (2d cir.) 1971, U.S. Dist. Ct. (so. and ea. dists.) N.Y. 1971. Assoc. Dewey, Ballantine, Bushby, Palmer & Wood, N.Y.C., 1969-72; asst. gen. counsel Boise Cascade Corp., N.Y.C., 1972-75; asst. gen counsel Teleprompter Corp., N.Y.C., 1975-76; v.p., gen. counsel, sec. Engelhard Corp., Edison, N.J., 1976—. Mem. Pelham (N.Y.) Union Sch. Dist. Bd. Edn., 1979-82. Mem. ABA, Assn. of Bar of City of N.Y., Am. Corp. Counsel Assn., Am. Intellectual Property Law Assn., Am. Soc. Corp. Secs., Machinery and Allied Products Inst. (law council). Club: Pelham Country. Antitrust, Contracts commercial, General corporate. Home: 576 Manor Ln Pelham Manor NY 10803 Office: Engelhard Corp Menlo Park CN 40 33 Wood Ave S Edison NJ 08818

DORNETTE, W(ILLIAM) STUART, lawyer, educator; b. Washington, Mar. 2, 1951; s. William Henry Lueders and Frances Roberta (Hester) D.; m. Martha Louise Mehl, Nov. 19, 1983; 1 child, Marjorie Frances. A.B., Williams Coll., 1972; J.D., U. Va., 1975. Bar: Va. 1975, Ohio 1975, U.S. Dist. Ct. (so. dist.) Ohio, 1975, D.C. 1976, U.S. Ct. Appeals (6th cir.) 1977, U.S. Supreme Ct. 1980. Assoc. Taft, Stettinius & Hollister, Cin., 1975-83, ptnr., 1983—; instr. law U. Cin., 1980—; dir. Eaton Hose & Fitting Co., Cin. Co-author: Federal Judiciary Almanac, 1984-86. Mem. Hamilton County Republican Exec. Com., 1982—; bd. dirs. Zool. Soc. Cin., 1983—. Mem. ABA, Cin. Bar Assn., Fed. Bar Assn., Am. Trial Lawyers Assn., Am. Phys. Soc. Republican. Episcopalian. Clubs: Cin. Racquet, Cin. Athletic. Federal civil litigation, State civil litigation. Home: 329 Bishopsbridge Dr Cincinnati OH 45230 Office: Taft Stettinius & Hollister 1800 First Nat Bank Ctr Cincinnati OH 45202

DOROCKE, LAWRENCE FRANCIS, lawyer; b. Chgo., Oct. 4, 1946; s. Walter P. and Effie M. (Gillis) D.; m. Diane L. Roberts, June 22, 1968; children: Todd D., Rob L., Jill A. BS in Econs., Purdue U., 1968, MS in Indsl. Relations, 1970; JD magna cum laude, Ind. U., 1973. Bar: Ind. 1973, U.S. Dist. Ct. (so. dist.) Ind. 1973, Iowa 1974, U.S. Ct. Appeals (7th cir.). Asst. mgr. personnel Comml. Solvents Corp., Terre Haute, Ind., 1970-71; law clk. to chief justice U.S. Dist. Ct. (so. dist.) Iowa, Des Moines, 1973-75; ptnr. Dann, Pecar, Newman, Talesnick & Kleiman P.C., Indpls., 1975—. Mem. ABA, Ind. Bar Assn. Democrat. Roman Catholic. Avocations: running, skiing, bicycling. Real property, General corporate, Landlord-tenant. Home: 6230 Deerfield Dr Greenwood IN 46142 Office: Dann Pecar Newman Talesnick & Kleiman 1 American Sq Box 82008 Indianapolis IN 46282

DORR, ROBERT CHARLES, lawyer; b. Denver, Jan. 7, 1946; s. Owen and Rose Esther (Tudek) D.; m. Sandra Leah Gehlsen, Feb. 25, 1971; children—Bryan, Aric. B.S.E.E., Milw. Sch. Engring., 1968; M.S.E.E., Northwestern U., 1970; J.D., U. Denver, 1975. Bar: Colo. 1975, U.S. Dist. Ct. Colo. 1975, U.S. Patent Office 1975. Mem. tech. staff Bell Labs., Naperville, Ill., 1968-72, patent staff, Denver, 1975-76; ptnr. Burton & Dorr, Denver, 1976-86; sr. ptnr. Dorr, Carson, Sloan & Peterson, Denver, 1986—; ptnr. Internat. Practicum Inst., Denver, 1979—; owner The Lawyers Edge, Inc., 1985—; seminar speaker various profl. orgns. Contbr. articles to profl. jours. Active Citizens Com. for Retention of Judges, Denver, 1984. Milw. Sch. Engring. scholar, 1964-68; named Outstanding Young Man Am., 1976. Mem. Douglas-Elbert County Bar Assn. (pres. 1983—), IEEE, AAAS, ABA, Colo. Trial Lawyers Assn., Sigma XI. Republican. Roman Catholic. Patent, Trademark and copyright, Computer. Home: 519 Willowlake Dr PO Box 116 Franktown CO 80116 Office: Dorr Carson Sloan Peterson 3010 E 6th Ave Denver CO 80222

DORR, RODERICK AKIN, lawyer; b. Oklahoma City, Aug. 10, 1937. BS in Aero. Engring., U. Okla., 1961, JD, 1975. Bar: Okla. 1975, N.Mex. 1975, Calif. 1983, U.S. Dist. Ct. N.Mex. 1975, U.S. Ct. Appeals (10th cir.) 1977, U.S. Dist. Ct. (no., cen., ea. and so. dists.) Calif. 1983, U.S. Supreme Ct. 1983. Assoc. Civerolo, Hansen & Wolf, Albuquerque, 1975-77; asst. atty. gen. State of N.Mex., Santa Fe, 1977-78, asst. dist. atty. 1st jud. dist., 1981-83; ptnr. Terrazas & Dorr, P.A., Santa Fe, 1978-81; assoc. T.H. Lambert, P.A., San Diego, 1983, Pothier, Moore & Hinrichs, Santa Ana, Calif., 1983, Magana, Cathcart, McCarthy et al., Los Angeles, 1984—. Served to capt. USAF, 1961-67; served to lt. comdr. USNR, 1967-72. Personal injury, Federal civil litigation, State civil litigation. Office: Magana Cathcart McCarthy et al 1801 Ave of the Stars Los Angeles CA 90067

DORRIER, LINDSAY GORDON, JR., lawyer; b. Scottsville, Va., Aug. 27, 1943; s. Lindsay Gordon and Anne Shirley (Bruce) D.; m. Jane Ikenberry, Feb. 14, 1982; children: Margaret Anne, Lindsay Gordon III. BA, Trinity Coll., 1966; JD, U. Va., 1972; MBA, James Madison U., 1987. Bar: Va. 1972, U.S. Dist. Ct. (we. dist.) Va. 1972. Law clk. to presiding judge U.S. Dist. Ct. (we. dist.) Va., Roanoke, 1972-73; assoc. Paxson, Smith, Boyd, Gillian & Gouldman, Charlottesville, Va., 1973-76; sole practice Charlottesville, 1976-80; commonwealth atty. Albemarle County, Charlottesville, 1980—. Pres. Charlottesville Abemarle Mental Health Assn., 1974-75; bd. supvs. Albenarle County, 1976-80; Dem. candidate for Congress 7th Dist., Va., 1982. Served to maj. JAGC, USAR, 1966—. Mem. Va. Bar Assn., Charlottesville Albermarle Bar Assn., Va. Trial Lawyers Assn., Va. Assn. Commonwealth Attys. (bd. dirs. 1984—), Va. Assn. Local Exec. Constl. Officers (pres. 1986—), Albemarle Hist. Soc. (pres. 1976-78), Fraternal Order Police, Am. Legion. Methodist. Lodges: Rotary, Lions, Elks, Ruritans. Criminal.

DORSEN, NORMAN, lawyer, educator; b. N.Y.C., Sept. 4, 1930; s. Arthur and Tanya (Stone) D.; m. Harriette Koffler, Nov. 25, 1965; children: Jennifer, Caroline Gail, Anne. B.A., Columbia U., 1950; LL.B. magna cum laude, Harvard U., 1953; postgrad., London Sch. Econs., 1955-56; LL.D. (hon.), Ripon Coll., 1981. Bar: D.C. 1953, N.Y. 1954. Law clk. to judge U.S. Ct. Appeals, Boston, 1956-57; law clk. to Justice John Marshall Harlan U.S. Supreme Ct., Washington, 1957-58; assoc. firm Dewey, Ballantine, Bushby, Palmer & Wood, N.Y.C., 1958-60; mem. faculty NYU Sch. Law, 1961—, prof. law, 1961—, Stokes prof., 1981—, dir. Hays civil liberties program, 1961—; vis. prof. law London Sch. Econs., 1968, U. Calif., Berkeley, 1974-75, Harvard U., 1980, 83, 85; cons. U.S. Commn. on Violence, 1968-69, Random House, 1969-73, B.B.C., 1969-73, Native Am. Rights Fund, 1977—, U.S. Commn. on Social Security, 1979-80, Native Am. Rights Fund, 1978—; exec. dir. spl. com. on courtroom conduct Assn. Bar N.Y.C., 1970-73; chmn. Com. for Pub. Justice, 1972-74; vice chmn. HEW sec.'s rev. panel on new drug regulation, 1975-76, chmn., 1976-77; mem. N.Y.C. Commn. on Status of Women, 1978-80. Author: (with others) Political and Civil Rights in U.S., 3d edit, 1967, 4th edit., Vol. I, 1976, Vol. II, 1979, Frontiers of Civil Liberties, 1968, Discrimination and Civil Rights, 1969, (with L. Friedman) Disorder in the Court, 1973, (with S. Gillers) Regulation of Lawyers, 1985; editor: (with L. Friedman) The Rights of Americans, 1971, (with S. Gillers) None of Your Business, 1974, Our Endangered Rights, 1984, Our Evolving Constitution, 1987. Served to 1st Lt., JAGC U.S. Army, 1953-55. Recipient medal French Minister of Justice, 1983. Mem. ABA (chmn. com. free speech and press 1968-70), Am. Law Inst., ACLU (gen. counsel 1969-76, pres. 1976—, dir.), Soc. Am. Law Teachers (pres. 1973-75), Phi Beta Kappa. Civil rights, Legal education. Home: Central Park W New York NY 10023 Office: NYU Sch Law 40 Washington Sq S New York NY 10012

DORSEY, CHARLES HENRY, JR., lawyer; b. Balt., May 18, 1930; s. Charles Henry and Olga Cornelia (Nicholson) D.; m. Agnes Smith, Jan. 17, 1953; children: Kathleen, Andrea, Judith, Claire, Charles III, Leonard, Peter, Martin, Nicholas. Student, Epiphany Coll., Loyola Coll., Balt.; LLB, U. Md., 1961. Bar: Md. 1961, U.S. Dist. Ct. Md. 1961. Ptnr. Brown, Allen, Dorsey & Josey, Balt., 1966-69; dep. dir. Legal Aid Bur. Inc., Balt., 1969-74, exec. dir., 1974—; spl. city solicitor Balt, 1969; mem. adv. bd. Pub. Defender Balt. City, 1972—, Md. Bd. Law Examiners, Annapolis, Md., 1972—, chmn., 1981—, Fed. Jud. Selection Commn., 1985-86. Mem. Archdiocesan Bd. Edn., 1969-72, pres. 1972; trustee Western Md. Coll., Westminster, 1976-82, St. Joseph Hosp., Towson, Md., 1983—; chmn. Gov.'s Commn. Child Support Enforcement, Balt., 1984—. Served to 1st lt. USAF, 1951-56, Korea. Recipient Reginald Heber Smith award Nat. Legal Aid and Defender Soc., 1982, Denison Ray award Papal Order of Knights of St. Gregroy, 1972; named Man for All Seasons St. Thomas More Soc., 1974, Loyola U. Alumni Laureate, 1983. Mem. ABA (standing com. on legal aid and indigent def. 1986), Mo. Bar Assn. (bd. of govs. 1987—), Md. Bar Assn. (chmn. jud. appointments), Balt. Bar Assn. (sec. 1972-73, library com. 1979, v.p. 1984, pres. 1986), Atty. Grievance Commn. Republican. Roman Catholic. General practice, State civil litigation, Civil rights. Office: Legal Aid Bur Inc 714 E Pratt St Baltimore MD 21202-3105

DORSEY, CLARENCE W., legal educator; b. June 25, 1949; s. Anorine Dorsey; divorced; 1 child, Deodato. BA, Tex. Coll., 1971; MA, Fisk U., 1972; JD, Tex. So. U., 1975. Bar: Tex., U.S. Dist. Ct. (so. dist.) Tex., U.S. Ct. Appeals (5th and 11th cirs.). Legal asst. rev. bd. FCC, Washington, 1975-76; pres. All-Star Inc., Atlanta, 1976-79; chmn. criminal justice dept. Prairie View (Tex.) A&M U., 1980—; prof. law Southeastern U., Washington, 1975-76. Fellow Ford Found., Earl Warren Legal Found., Tex. So. U. Sch. Law. Mem. Psi Delta Psi, Phi Alpha Delta, Kappa Alpha Psi. Personal injury. Office: 4900 Fannin Suite 204 Houston TX 77004

DORSEY, PETER COLLINS, judge; b. New London, Conn., Mar. 24, 1931; s. Thomas F., Jr. and Helen Mary (Collins) D.; m. Cornelia McEwen, June 26, 1954; children: Karen G., Peter C., Jennifer S., Christopher M. B.A., Yale U., 1953; J.D., Harvard U., 1959. Ptnr. Flanagan, Dorsey & Flanagan, New Haven, 1963-74; U.S. atty. Dept. Justice, New Haven, 1974-77; ptnr. Flanagan, Dorsey & Mulvey, New Haven, 1977-83; judge U.S. Dist. Ct. Conn., Hartford, 1983—. Councilman Town of Hamden, Conn., 1961-69; town atty., 1973-74; commr. Bd. of Police, Hamden, 1977-81. Served to lt. comdr., USNR, 1953-56. Fellow Am. Coll. Trial Lawyers; mem. ABA, Conn. Bar Assn. (pres. 1977-78), New Haven County Bar Assn., Conn. Def. Lawyers Assn. (pres. 1982-83). Roman Catholic. Office: US Dist Ct 450 Main St Hartford CT 06103 *

DORSEY, ROBERT KNICKERBOCKER, lawyer; b. N.Y.C., Jan. 20, 1931; s. Leo Patrick and Ruth Ella (Knickerbocker) D.; m. Janet O'Brien, Sept., 1956 (div. Apr. 1962); children: Richard, Alexandra; m. Ruth Elizabeth Sabath, Feb. 17, 1963; children: Christopher (dec.), Brian, Sean. Student, Princeton U., 1949-53; JD, U. Va., 1958. Bar: Calif. 1959, U.S. Dist. Ct. (no. dist.) Calif. 1959, U.S. Ct. Appeals (9th cir.) 1959, N.Y. 1961, U.S. Dist. Ct. (ea. and so. dists.) N.Y. 1961, U.S. Ct. Appeals (2d cir.) 1961, Nev. 1962, U.S. Dist. Ct. Nev. 1964, U.S. Ct. Claims 1971, U.S. Supreme Ct. 1972, U.S. Tax Ct. 1974, U.S. Dist. Ct. (cen. dist.) Calif. 1979. Law clk. to presiding justice U.S. Ct. Appeals (9th cir.), San Francisco, 1958-59; assoc. Elwood Wilson Atty., Monterey, Calif., 1959-60, Dorsey & Burke, N.Y.C., 1960-61; research and bill drafter Nev. Statute Revision Commn., Carson City, Nev., 1962; dep. dist. atty. Clark County, Las Vegas, Nev., 1963; sole practice Las Vegas, 1963-78, 80—, Torrance, Calif., 1978-80. Panel mem. Nev. Local Govt. Employee Relations, Las Vegas, 1981—. Served with U.S. Army, 1953-55, Korea. Mem. ABA, N.Y. State Bar Assn., Calif. Bar Assn., Nev. Bar Assn., Assn. Trial Lawyes Am., Calif. Trial Lawyers Assn., Nev. Trial Lawyers Assn., Los Angeles Trial Lawyers Assn. Republican. Lodge: Elks. Avocations: photography, aviation. State civil litigation, Consumer commercial, Probate. Home: 2204 Plaza Del Puerto Las Vegas NV 89102 Office: 302 E Carson #807 Las Vegas NV 89101-5908

DORWART, CHARLES EDWARD, lawyer; b. Sidney, Nebr., Dec. 21, 1952; s. Clinton Bonaventure and Lucille Margurite (Keller) D.; m. Teresa Marie Jelinek, June 25, 1976. BS, Creighton U., 1975, JD, 1980. Bar: Nebr. 1981, U.S. Dist. Ct. Nebr. 1981. Sole practice Papillion, Nebr., 1981—; atty. Sarpy County Pub. Defender, 1986—; ptnr. Swensen's Ice Cream Parlor,

Omaha, 1982—; atty., v.p., bd. dirs. Affilated Portable X-Ray, Inc., Papillion, 1986—. Mem. Assn. Trial Lawyers Am., Papillion C. of C. Democrat. Roman Catholic. Lodge: Kiwanis. Avocations: golf, reading, skiing, basketball, hiking. General practice, Family and matrimonial, Juvenile. Office: 712 Tara Pl Papillion NE 68046

DOSLAND, CHESTER ALLEN, lawyer; b. Fargo, N.D., June 14, 1928; s. Chester Arthur and Edna Amanda (Baker) D.; m. Mary Lou Hunting; children: Thomas Allen, Catherine Ann, Beth Mary. BS in Law, U. Minn., 1953, LLB, 1953. Bar: Minn. 1953, U.S. Dist. Ct. Minn. 1954, U.S. Ct. Appeals (8th cir.) 1979, U.S. Supreme Ct. 1979. Law clk. to presiding justice Minn. Supreme Ct., St. Paul, 1953-54; from assoc. to ptnr. Gislason, Dosland, Hunter & Malecki, New Ulm, Minn., 1954—; Pres., mem. Minn. Bd. Law Examiners, St. Paul, 1963-78; chmn. bd. dirs. Citizens Bank, New Ulm. Pres. New Ulm Library Bd., 1970-76. Served with U.S. Army, 1945-48. Fellow Am. Coll. Trial Lawyers, Am. Bar Found.; mem. ABA, Am. Bd. of Trial Advs. (diplomate 1975), Minn. Bar Assn. (bd. govs. 1978-82). Republican. Club: Mpls. Athletic. Lodge: Rotary. Avocations: reading, walking, golf. State civil litigation, Federal civil litigation. Home: 36 Woodland Dr New Ulm MN 56073

DOSLAND, WILLIAM BUEHLER, lawyer; b. Chgo., Nov. 10, 1927; s. Goodwin Leroy and Beatrice Florence (Buehler) D.; m. Donna Mae Mathisen, Sept. 15, 1956; children: David William, Susan Elizabeth. B.A., Concordia Coll., 1949; J.D., U. Minn., 1954. Bar: Minn. 1954. Dir. firm Dosland, Dosland, Nordhougen, Lillihaug & Johnson P.A., Moorhead, Minn., 1968—; gen. counsel, corp. sec. Am. Crystal Sugar Co., 1973—, No. Grain Co., 1975—; gen. counsel Am. Bank and Trust Co., 1969—. Regent U. Minn., 1979-85; mem. Minn. State Senate, 1959-73. Served to capt. USNR, 1945-46, 51-53. Mem. Minn. State Bar Assn., Clay County Bar Assn. Republican. Lutheran. Clubs: Masons, Lions. General corporate, Probate, Real property. Home: 3122 Rivershore Dr Moorhead MN 56560 Office: Dosland Dosland Nordhougen et al 730 Center Ave PO Box 100 Moorhead MN 56560

DOSS, MARION KENNETH, lawyer; b. Wildwood, Fla., Sept. 25, 1939; s. Marion D. and Clide (Maxwell) D.; m. Addren Taylor, July 8, 1977; children—M. Kenneth Jr., Lisa Marie. B.S., Ga. Inst. Tech., 1961; LL.B., U. Ga., 1963. Bar: Ga. 1965, N.C. 1979, U.S. Dist. Ct. (no. dist.) Ga. 1977, U.S. Ct. Apls. (5th cir.) 1976, U.S. Sup. Ct. 1978. Ptnr., Northcutt, Edwards & Doss, Atlanta, 1963-71; v.p., gen. counsel Roy D. Warren, Atlanta, 1971-73; ptnr. Doss & Sturgeon, Atlanta, 1973-75; atty. Rollins, Inc., Atlanta, 1975-78; assoc. gen. counsel, asst. sec. Fieldcrest Mills, Inc., Eden, N.C., 1978-86; gen. counsel, sec., 1986—. Past pres., bd. dirs. Eden YMCA; past pres., bd. dirs. Rockingham County Arts Council. Mem. Assn. Trial Lawyers Am., Def. Research Inst., Ga. Assn. Plaintiffs Trial Attys., Corp. Counsel Assn. Greater Atlanta, Atlanta Bar Assn., N.C. Trial Lawyers Assn., ABA (corp. counsel com.), N.C. State Bar, Ga. Bar Assn., Rockingham County Bar Assn., Internat. Assn. of Ins. Counsel, Am. Textile Mfrs. Assn., N.C. C. of C. (past dir.). Democrat. Club: Meadow Greens Country. State civil litigation, General corporate, Workers' compensation. Office: Fieldcrest Mills Inc 326 E Stadium Dr Eden NC 27288

DOSSETT, JAMES KEARNEY, JR., lawyer; b. Laurel, Miss., Mar. 21, 1943; s. James Kearney and Ina (Fewell) D.; m. Linda Suzanne Massey, Aug. 26, 1967; children—Emily Caroline, Elizabeth Suzanne, Claire Lovard. B.A., Millsaps Coll., 1965; J.D., U. Miss., 1968; LL.M., NYU, 1969. Bar: Miss. 1968, U.S. Dist. Ct. (no. and so. dists.) Miss. 1968, U.S. Tax Ct. 1968. With Dossett, Magruder & Montgomery, Jackson, Miss., 1969-82, ptnr., 1974-82; ptnr. Dossett, Dossett and Goode, Jackson, 1982—. Mem. adv. bd. Salvation Army, Jackson, 1981-86; trustee Jackson Acad., 1979—. Mem. ABA, Miss. Bar Assn., Hinds County Bar Assn., Miss. Soc. C.P.A.s. Club: University (Jackson). Lodge: Kiwanis (bd. dirs., 1985-86, v.p. 1986—). Probate, Corporate taxation, Estate taxation. Address: PO Box 2449 Jackson MS 39205

DOSTAL, JOHN ANTHONY, lawyer; b. Ft. Benton, Mont., Sept. 24, 1949; s. Elmer and Mary Patricia (Carr) D.; m. Susan Rae Olsen, Aug. 28, 1976; children: Nathaniel J., Daniel M., Mark E. Bin Chem. Engring., U. Notre Dame, 1972; JD, U. Mont., 1975; LLM in Taxation, U. Pacific, 1984. Bar: Mont. 1975, U.S. Dist. Ct. Mont. 1975, U.S. Ct. Appeals (9th cir.) 1980. Ptnr. Hirst, Dostal & Withrow, Missoula, Mont., 1975-82; assoc. Patterson & Marsillo, Missoula, 1982-83, Anderson, Brown, Gerbase & Ceball, P.C., Billings, Mont., 1984—. Mem. Billings Hist. Preservation Soc., Yellowstone County Estate Planning Council; bd. dirs. Mont. Assn. for Refugee Services, Billings. Mem. ABA, Mont. Bar Assn. Avocations: reading, running, gardening. Probate, Estate taxation, Corporate taxation. Home: 2416 Dahlia Ln Billings MT 59102 Office: Anderson Brown Gerbase & Ceball PC 315 N 24th St Billings MT 59101

DOSTAL, MILAN MATHIAS, lawyer; b. Hutchinson, Minn., Feb. 7, 1929; s. Mathias William and Mary (Miska) D.; m. Dorothy Agnes Olsen, Mar. 18, 1951; children—Richard George, Cynthia Marie, Pamela Ann. Student Macalester Coll., 1947-49; B.B.A., U. Minn., 1952; J.D., 1957. Bar: Minn. 1957, U.S. Dist. Ct. Md. 1959, U.S. Tax Ct. 1959, U.S. Ct. Mil. Appeals 1959, U.S. Supreme Ct. 1962, Calif. 1965, U.S. Dist. Ct. (cen. dist.) Calif. 1965, U.S. Ct. Appeals (9th cir.). Trial atty. U.S. Dept. Justice, Washington, 1957-63; asst. U.S. atty., Los Angeles, 1964-65; sole practice, Orange, Calif., 1965—; judge pro tem; lectr., cert. specialist family law Calif. State Bd. Legal Cert. Councilman, mayor City of Newport Beach, Calif., 1970-78; founder Oralingua Sch. Hearing Impaired; chmn. Intergovernmental Coordinating Counsel Orange County (Calif.); commr. Orange County Airport Land Use Commn.; dir. various Orange County Sanitation Dists. Served in USAF, 1951-54. Mem. ABA, Calif. Bar Assn., Orange County Bar Assn., Phi Delta Phi, Delta Sigma Pi. Republican. Presbyterian. Club: Balboa Bay. Contbr. articles to law jours. General practice, State civil litigation. Office: Milan M Dostal Law Firm 505 City Pkwy W Orange CA 92668

DOSTART, PAUL JOSEPH, lawyer; b. Riceville, Iowa, Nov. 12, 1951; s. Leonard Atchison and Lois Marie (Marr) D.; m. Joyce Alene Sicking, Aug. 14, 1976; children: Zachariah Paul, Samuel Paul. BS, Iowa State U., 1973; JD, U. Houston, 1977; LLM in Taxation, NYU, 1978. Bar: Tex, 1977, Calif. 1978; CPA, Ill. From assoc. to ptnr. Gray, Cary, Ames & Paye, San Diego, 1978—; adj. prof. U. San Diego, 1986—; lectr. U. Calif., La Jolla, 1985—. Editor U. Houston Law Rev.; contbr. articles to profl. jours. Mem. World Affairs Council San Diego. Lasker scholar, NYU, Nat. Merit scholar, Iowa State Spl. Merit scholar; recipient Cert. of Merit U. Houston Student Bar Assn. Mem. ABA (sect. taxation 1978—, chmn. various subcoms. 1982—), Calif. Bar Assn. (tax sect.), San Diego County Bar Assn. (vice chmn. tax sect. 1986—, western pension conf.), U. Houston Tax Law Soc. (co-founder), Order of Barons (chancellor), Phi Delta Phi (Hutcheson Inn magister). Club: World Trade Assn. Corporate taxation, Pension, profit-sharing, and employee benefits, International trade and U.S. customs service. Home: 4382 Pavlov Ave San Diego CA 92122-3710 Office: Gray Cary Ames & Frye 401 B St Suite 1700 San Diego CA 92101-4219

DOTI, FRANK JOHN, legal educator, consultant income taxes; b. Chgo., May 24, 1943; s. Roy and Carmelina (Siracusa) D.; m. Margaret Ann Elliott, Dec. 21, 1973; children: Matthew, Emily. BS in Accountancy, U. Ill., Urbana, 1966; JD, Chgo.-Kent Coll. Law, Ill. Inst. Tech., 1969. Bar: Ill. 1969, U.S. Dist. Ct. (no. dist.) Ill. 1969, Calif. 1985, U.S. Tax Ct. 1987. Assoc. McDermott, Will & Emory, Chgo., 1969-74; tax dir. CF Industries, Inc., Long Grove, Ill., 1974-77; v.p., tax dir. Leo Burnett Co., Inc., Chgo., 1977-82; prof. law Western State Law Sch., Orange, Calif., 1982—. Contbr. Chgo.-Kent Law Rev., 1967, Taxes Mag., 1972, Western State U. Law Rev., 1984, 86, Los Angeles Lawyer, 1985. Bd. dirs. Ill. Inst. Tech.-Chgo. Kent Alumni Assn., 1979-83. Recipient 1st place award Moot Ct. Chgo.-Kent Law Sch., 1967; Corpus Juris award, 1969. Mem. Tax Execs. Inst., Calif. Bar Assn., Chgo. Bar Assn., ABA, Am. Bus. Law Assn. Corporate taxation, Personal income taxation, State and local taxation. Home: 7431 Mill Stream Circle Anaheim CA 92808 Office: Western State Law Sch Fullerton CA 92631

DOTY, JAMES ROBERT, lawyer; b. Houston, May 14, 1940; s. Robert Earl and Vivian (Weaver) D.; m. Joan Richardson, June 10, 1972; children: Katherine Brooks, Robert, Daniel. B.A., Rice U., 1972; A.B., Oxford U., Eng., 1963; LL.B., Yale U., 1969. Bar: Tex. 1969. Ptnr. Baker & Botts, Houston, 1977—. Sr. warden Christ Ch. Cathedral; trustee Endowments Bd., St. Luke's Epsic. Ch.; bd. dirs. DePelchin Children's Ctr. Rhodes scholar, 1962. Mem. Am. Law Inst., Houston Bar Assn., State Bar Tex., ABA, Houston Philos. Soc. General corporate, Real property. Office: 3000 One Shell Plaza Houston TX 77002

DOUB, WILLIAM OFFUTT, lawyer; b. Cumberland, Md., Sept. 3, 1931; s. Albert A. and Fannabelle (Offutt) D.; m. Mary Graham Boggs, Sept. 12, 1959; children: Joseph Peyton, Albert A., II. A.B., Washington and Jefferson Coll., 1953; LL.B., U. Md., 1956. Bar: Md. 1956, D.C. 1974. With law dept. B. & O. R.R., 1955-57; assoc. Bartlett Poe & Claggett, Balt., 1957-61; ptnr. Niles Barton & Wilmer, Balt., 1961-71; commr. AEC, 1971-74; ptnr. LeBoeuf, Lamb, Leiby & MacRae, Washington, 1974-77, Doub & Muntzing, Washington, 1977—; chmn. Minimum Wage Commn., Balt., 1964-66; peoples' counsel Md. Pub. Service Commn., 1967-68, chmn., 1968-71; vice chmn. Washington Met. Area Transit Commn., 1968-71; mem. President's Air Quality Adv. Bd., 1970-71; mem. exec. adv. com. FPC, 1969-71, Nat. Gas Survey, 1975-78; pres. Great Lakes Conf. Pub. Utility Commrs., 1971; mem. nat. adv. bd. Am. Nat. Standards Inst., 1975-80; mem. Md. Adv. Com. Retardation, 1969-71. Mem. Adminstrv. Conf. U.S., 1973-75; chmn. U.S. Energy Assn. Inc. World Energy Conf., 1978-80, U.S. del., 1974, 77, 80, 83, 86; vice chmn. World Energy Conf., 1986—; mem. adv. groups Nat. Acad. Public Adminstrn., NSF; presdl. appointee as rep. to So. States Energy Bd., 1983—; trustee Thomas Alva Edison Found., mem. exec. com., 1983—, v.p., 1985—; bd. govs. Middle East Inst., exec. com., 1985—. Clubs: Met., City Tavern (Washington); East India (London). Nuclear power, Public utilities, Legislative. Home: 6 Warde Ct Potomac MD 20854

DOUCHKESS, GEORGE, lawyer; b. N.Y.C., Apr. 19, 1911; s. Frank A. and Dorothy (Grunberg) D.; m. Sonia Sloshay; children—Donald, Barbara. B.B.A. in Acctg., CCNY, 1936; J.D., Bklyn. Law Sch., 1939. Bar: N.Y. 1940, U.S. dist. Ct. (ea. dist.) N.Y., U.S. Dist. Ct. (so. dist.) N.Y. 1951. Claim supr. Aetna Casualty & Surety Co., N.Y.C., 1940-44; head examiner Liberty Mut. Ins. Co., N.Y.C., 1944-47; compensation atty. Preferred Accident & Ins. Co., N.Y.C., 1947-51; U.S. supt. compensation claims div., compensation atty. Gen. Fire & Casualty Co., N.Y.C., 1951-65; compensation atty. Zurich Am. Ins. Co., N.Y.C., 1965—, Mem. Torch and Scroll. Republican. Administrative and regulatory, Workers' compensation. Home: 715 Park Ave New York NY 10021 Office: Zurich Am Ins Co 20 Exchange Pl New York NY 10038

DOUGHERTY, BRIAN JAMES, lawyer; b. Bristol, Pa., Apr. 23, 1955. BS summa cum laude, Bucknell U., 1977; JD cum laude, Harvard U., 1980. Bar: Pa. 1980. Assoc. Thorp, Reed & Armstrong, Pitts., 1980-85, Ballard, Spahr, Andrews & Ingersoll, Phila., 1985—. Mem. ABA, Pa. Bar Assn., Phila. Bar Assn. Pension, profit-sharing, and employee benefits, Labor. Office: Ballard Spahr Andrews & Ingersoll 30 S 17th St Philadelphia PA 19103

DOUGHERTY, F. JAY, lawyer; b. Valley Forge, Pa., Jan. 30, 1950; s. Raymond Edward and Dolly Mae (Taylor) D. BA magna cum laude, Yale U., 1971; JD, Columbia U., 1981. Bar: N.Y. 1982, Calif. 1984. Assoc. Paul, Weiss, Rifkind, Wharton & Garrison, N.Y.C., 1981-84, Mitchell, Silberberg & Knupp, Los Angeles, 1984-86; atty. MGM/United Artists Communications Co., Beverly Hills, Calif., 1986—; lectr. copyright and entertainment law U. So. Calif. Law Ctr., 1987—. Stone scholar, 1978-81. Mem. ABA, Los Angeles County Bar Assn. Avocations: music, sailing. Entertainment, Trademark and copyright. Home: 2101 Ocean Ave Santa Monica CA 90405 Office: United Artists Pictures 450 N Roxbury Dr Beverly Hills CA 90210

DOUGHERTY, JAMES DOUGLAS, lawyer; b. Baldwin, N.Y., Dec. 29, 1936; s. Thomas Francis and Jean May (Young) D.; m. Nancy Harrington Decker, Dec. 29, 1971. A.B., Dartmouth Coll., 1958; LL.B., Columbia U., 1963; A.M.P., Harvard Bus. Sch., 1983. Bar: N.Y. 1963. Assoc. firm Hughes Hubbard & Reed, N.Y.C., 1963-69, Shea & Gould, N.Y.C., 1969-71; assoc. gen. counsel Supermarkets Gen. Corp., Woodbridge, N.J., 1971-72; sec., gen. counsel Supermarkets Gen. Corp., 1972—, v.p., 1975-81, sr. v.p., 1981-83, exec. v.p., 1983—, also bd. dirs.; pres., dir. 132 E. 19th St., Inc., N.Y.C., 1964-78; lectr. Practising Law Inst., N.Y.C., 1970-74, Advanced Mgmt. Research, N.Y.C., 1974-78; bd. advs. Arkwright Boston Ins. Co., 1983—. Trustee, Nature Conservancy, 1982—. Served to lt. (j.g.) USNR, 1958-60. Mem. ABA, Assn. Bar City N.Y. (spl. com. on consumer affairs 1973-77, spl. com. electronic funds transfer 1976-79), Am. Soc. Corp. Secs. Clubs: Shelter Island Yacht, Metropolitan. General corporate. Home: 144 E 19th St New York NY 10003 also: Tuthills Hill Shelter Island NY 11964 Office: 200 Milik St Carteret NJ 07008

DOUGHERTY, JAMES THOMAS, industrial company executive, lawyer; b. Chgo., Aug. 31, 1935; s. Edward Warren and Edna Margaret (Macadory) D.; m. Rosemary Saballus, Nov. 21, 1959; children: Janet, Michael, Scott. BS, DePaul U., 1957, JD, 1960. Bar: Ill. 1960. Assoc. Arnstein, Gluck, Lehr & Milligan, Chgo., 1960-65; asst. gen. counsel Maremont Corp., Chgo., 1965-69, Rockwell Internat. Corp., Pitts., 1969-71; gen. counsel NVF Co., Yorklyn, Del., 1971-76, Sharon Steel Corp., 1971-76; v.p., gen. counsel, sec. Allegheny Internat., Inc., Pitts., 1976—. Bd. dirs. Sharon Indsl. Devel. Authority, 1972-76, Shenango Valley Charitable Capital Fund, 1972-75. Mem. Ill. Bar Assn., Chgo. Bar Assn. Antitrust, General corporate, Securities. Office: Allegheny Internat Inc Two Oliver Plaza Pittsburgh PA 15222

DOUGHERTY, JOHN CHRYSOSTOM, III, lawyer; b. Beeville, Tex., May 3, 1915; s. John Chrysostom and Mary V. (Henderson) D.; m. Mary Ireland Graves, Apr. 18, 1942 (dec. July 1977); children: Mary Ireland, John Chrysostom IV; m. Bea Ann Smith, June 1978 (div. 1981); m. Sarah B. Randle, 1981. BA, U. Tex., 1937; LLB, Harvard, 1940; diploma, Inter-Am. Acad. Internat. and Comparative Law, Havana, Cuba, 1948. Bar: Tex. 1940. Atty. Hewit & Dougherty, Beeville, 1940-41; ptnr. Graves & Dougherty, Austin, Tex., 1946-50, Graves, Dougherty & Greenhill, Austin, 1950-57, Graves, Dougherty & Gee, Austin, 1957-60, Graves, Dougherty, Gee & Hearon, Austin, 1961-66, Graves, Dougherty, Gee, Hearon, Moody & Garwood, Austin, 1966-73, Graves, Dougherty, Hearon, Moody & Garwood, Austin, 1973-79, Graves, Dougherty, Hearon & Moody, Austin, 1979—; spl. asst. atty. gen., 1949-50; Hon. French Consul, Austin, 1971-86; lectr. on tax, estate planning, probate code, community property problems; bd. dirs. InterFirst Bank Austin, N.A.; mem. Tex. Submerged Lands Adv. Com., 1963-72, Tex. Bus. and Commerce Code Adv. Com., 1964-66, Gov.'s Com. on Marine Resources, 1970-71, Gov.'s Planning Com. on Colorado River Basin Water Quality Mgmt. Study, 1972-73, Tex. Legis. Property Tax Com., 1973-75. Co-editor: Texas Appellate Practice, 1964, 2d edit., 1977; contbr. Bowe, Estate Planning and Taxation; Texas Lawyers Practice Guide, 1967, 71, How to Live and Die with Texas Probate, 1968, 3d edit., 1979, 4th edit., 1983, Texas Estate Administration, 1975, 78; mem. bd. editors: Appellate Procedure in Tex., 1964, 2d edit., 1982; contbr. articles to legal jours. Bd. dirs. Grenville Clark Fund at Dartmouth Coll., 1976—; past bd. dirs. Advanced Religious Study Found., Holy Cross Hosp., Sea Arama, Inc., Nat. Pollution Control Found.; trustee St. Stephen's Episcopal Sch., Austin, 1969-83, U. Tex. Law Sch. Found., 1974—. Served as capt. C.I.C. AUS, 1941-44, JAGC, 1944-46, now maj. Res. Decorated Medaille Française France, Medaille d'honneur en Argent des Affairs Etrangeres France. Fellow Am. Bar Found., Tex. Bar Found., Am. Coll. Probate Counsel, Am. Coll. Tax Counsel, Tex. State Bar Coll.; mem. Am. Arbitration Assn. (mem. nat. panel arbitrators 1958—), Inter-Am. Bar Assn., ABA (mem. ho. dels. 1982—), Travis County Bar Assn. (pres.-elect 1978, pres. 1979-80), State Bar Tex. (chmn. sect. taxation 1965-66, pres.-elect 1978, pres. 1979-80, chmn. State Bar Coll. Bd. 1983-84), Am. Judicature Soc. (bd. dirs. 1986—), Internat. Law Assn., Am. Fgn. Law Assn., Am. Law Inst., Am. Soc. Internat. Law (exec. council 1959-62), World Assn. Lawyers, Internat. Acad. Estate and Trust Law (exec. com. 1986—), Am. Assn. Internat. Council Jurists, Cum Laude Soc., Phi Beta Kappa, Phi Eta Sigma, Beta Theta Pi (bd. dirs. Tex. Beta Students Aid Fund 1947-85). Presbyterian. Lodge: Rotary. Estate planning, Probate, Estate taxation. Home: 6 Green Lanes Austin TX 78703 Office: 2300 InterFirst Tower Austin TX 78701 also: PO Box 98 Austin TX 78767

DOUGHERTY, MAUREEN PATRICIA, lawyer, consultant, accounting educator; b. Vineland, N.J., May 30, 1948; d. John Francis and Kathryn Evelyn (Mattioli) D.; m. Walter G. Scheuerman III, Aug. 21, 1971 (div. 1984); children—Kathleen Meghan, Christian Michael. BA in Psychology, Rosemont Coll., 1970; JD, Seton Hall U., 1979; LLM in Taxation, NYU, 1986. Bar: N.J. 1979, U.S. Dist. Ct. N.J. 1979. With Sudler Real Estate, Chgo., 1971-73; mgr. Arlen Realty, Chgo., 1973-75; assoc. Bloom & Levitt, Millburn, N.J., 1980-82, Gutkin Miller Shapiro & Selesner, Milburn, 1982-85, Water, McPherson, McNeill P.A., Secaucus, N.J., 1985—; asst. prof. acctg. Fairleigh Dickinson U., Madison, N.J., 1986—. Author: Testamentary Trusts, N.J. Trans. Guide, 1986. Mem. Jr. League Oranges and Short Hills, 1978-81. Mem. ABA, N.J. Bar Assn., Essex County Bar Assn. Roman Catholic. Estate taxation, Probate, Corporate taxation. Home: 9 Essex Dr Mendham NJ 07945 Office: Waters McPherson McNeill 400 Plaza Dr Secaucus NJ 07094

DOUGHERTY, THOMAS PAUL, JR., lawyer, oil company executive; b. N.Y.C., Mar. 30, 1948; s. Thomas Paul and Mary Eva (Hildenbrand) D.; m. Catherine Mary Gallo, Jan. 23, 1971; children: Germaine Ryan, Amanda Catherine, Margaret Eve. BA, St. Bonaventure U., 1969; JD, Coll. William & Mary, 1972, LLM in Taxation, 1973. Bar: N.Y. 1973, U.S. Tax Ct. 1975, U.S. Supreme Ct. 1976, U.S. Ct. Appeals (1st cir.) 1977. Trial atty., dist. counsel IRS, Boston, 1973-80; tax atty. Texaco Inc., White Plains, N.Y., 1980-85, sr. tax atty., 1985—. Served to 1st lt. U.S. Army, 1972-81. N.Y. State Regents scholar, 1965; Marshall Wythe Tax fellow Coll. William & Mary, 1972. Roman Catholic. Corporate taxation, Personal income taxation. Home: Trinity Pass Pound Ridge NY 10576 Office: Texaco Inc 2000 Westchester Ave White Plains NY 10650

DOUGHTY, H. REED, lawyer; b. Davenport, July 30, 1939; s. Reed B. and Alice L. (Walker) D.; m. Frances S. Weissman, Sept. 5, 1965; children: Mara, Alicia, David. BA, U. Iowa, 1961, JD, 1964. Assoc. Pollock, Ward, Klobasa and McGinnis, St. Louis, 1967-69; asst. state's atty. State of Ill., Rock Island, 1969-70; ptnr. Winstein, Kavensky, Wallace and Doughty, Rock Island, 1970—. Pres. Rock Island County Info. and Referral Service, 1971; chmn. bd. Franciscan Mental Health Ctr., Rock Island, 1965, Franciscan Med. Ctr., Rock Island, 1983; mem. Rock Island-Milan Sch. Bd., 1979-84. Served to capt. USAF, 1965-67. Mem. ABA, Ill. State Bar Assn., Iowa State Bar Assn., Assn. Trial Lawyers Am., Ill. Trial Lawyers Assn. Democrat. Methodist. Club: Lake Davenport Sailing (commodore 1986—). Lodge: Masons, Shriners. Avocations: sailing, skiing, reading. State civil litigation, Family and matrimonial, Criminal. Home: 48 Woodley Rd Rock Island IL 61201 Office: Winstein et al 244 18th St PO Box 428 Rock Island IL 61201

DOUGLAS, ANDY, state justice; b. Toledo, July 5, 1932; 4 children. J.D., U. Toledo, 1959. Bar: Ohio 1960, U.S. Dist. Ct. (no. dist.) Ohio 1960. Former ptnr. Winchester & Douglas; judge Ohio 6th Dist. Ct. Appeals, 1981-84; justice Ohio Supreme Ct., 1985—; former spl. counsel Atty. Gen. of Ohio. Served with U.S. Army, 1952-54. Recipient award Maumee Valley council Girl Scouts U.S., 1976, Outstanding Service award Toledo Police Command Officers Assn., 1980, Toledo Soc. for Autistic Children and Adults, 1983, Extra-Spl. Person award Central Catholic High Sch., 1981, Disting. Service award Toledo Police Patrolman's Assn., 1982, award Ohio Hispanic Inst. Opportunity, 1985; named to Woodward High Sch. Hall of Fame. Mem. Toledo Bar Assn., Lucas County Bar Assn., Ohio Bar Assn., Lagrange Bus. and Profl. Men's Assn., Toledo U. Alumni Assn., U. Toledo Law Alumni, St. John's High Sch. Dads' Club, Macomber High Sch. Boosters, Internat. Inst., Pi Sigma Alpha, Delta Theta Phi. Lodges: North Toledo Old Timers Assn., Old Newsboys Goodfellow Assn., 4th Ward Old Timers Assn. Office: Ohio Supreme Ct 30 E Broad St Columbus OH 43215

DOUGLAS, CHARLES GWYNNE, III, lawyer; b. Abington, Pa., Dec. 2, 1942; s. Charles Gwynne and Blanche Elizabeth (Graham) D.; children by previous marriage: Charles Gwynne IV, Thomas A. B.A., U. N.H., 1965; J.D., Boston U., 1968. Bar: N.H. 1968. Asso. firm McLane, Carleton, Graf, Greene & Brown, Manchester, N.H., 1968-70; partner firm Perkins, Douglas & Brock, Concord, N.H., 1970-74; legal counsel to gov. N.H. 1973-74; assoc. justice N.H. Superior Ct., 1974-76, N.H. Supreme Ct., 1977-85; mem. faculty Am. Acad. Jud. Edn.; chmn. ct. tech. com. Appellate Judges Conf., 1981-84; chmn. N.H. Constl. Bicentennial Commn. Contbr. articles to law jours. Alt. del. Republican Nat. Conv., 1972; chmn. N.H. Task Force on Child Abuse, 1977, N.H. Fair Trial-Free Press Com., 1979—. Served to lt. col. Army N.G., 1968—. Named Outstanding Young Man of Yr. N.H. Jaycees, 1977; recipient Pub. Service award N.H. Assn. Counties, 1979. Mem. N.H. Bar Assn., Inter-Am. Bar Assn. (chmn. judges' adv. com. to ethics com. 1979-84), Phi Beta Kappa. Republican. Episcopalian. Office: New Hampshire Supreme Court 8 Centre St Concord NH 03301 *

DOUGLAS, HUBERT GENE, II, lawyer; b. Charleston, W.Va., Oct. 21, 1947; s. Hubert Gene and Virginia (Barker) D.; m. Daneen M. Martin, Oct. 8, 1977; children: Robin Lynne, Kevin Elliotte, Brian Stanley, Allan Daniel. BA, Fla. Atlantic U., 1969; JD, Am. U., 1972. Bar: Fla. 1972, U.S. Dist. Ct. (so. dist.) Fla. 1973, U.S. Supreme Ct. 1976, U.S. Dist. Ct. (mid. dist.) Fla. 1985. Assoc. Spear & Deuschle, Ft. Lauderdale, Fla., 1973-75; v.p. legal, gen. counsel Hvide Shipping Inc., Ft. Lauderdale, 1975—. Chmn. Police Civil Service Bd., Wilton Manors, Fla., 1975-84; deacon Bethel Presbyn. Ch., Lauderhill, Fla., 1978-86, elder, 1986—. Mem. ABA, Broward County Bar Assn., Maritime Law Assn. U.S. (proctor in admiralty). Republican. Admiralty, Contracts commercial, General corporate. Office: Hvide Shipping Inc PO Box 13038 Fort Lauderdale FL 33316

DOUGLAS, JAMES MATTHEW, law educator; b. Onalaska, Tex., Feb. 11, 1944; s. Desso D. and Mary L. (Durden) D.; div.; children—DeLicia, Renee. B.A. in Math., Tex. So. U., 1966, J.D., 1970. J.S.M., Stanford U., 1971. Bar: Tex. 1970. Programmer analyst Singer Gen. Precision Co., Houston, 1966-70, 71-72; asst. prof. law Tex. So. U., Houston, 1971-72; asst. prof. Cleve. State U., Cleve.-Marshall Coll. Law, 1972-75; asst. prof., asst. dean student affairs, 1974-75; assoc. prof. law, assoc. dean Coll. of Law Syracuse (N.Y.) U., 1975-80; prof. law Northeastern U., Boston, 1980-81; dean, prof. law Tex. So. U., Houston, 1981—; mem. Law Sch. Admissions Council; cons. computer law and computer contracts; bd. dirs. Civil Ct. Legal Services, Gulf Coast Legal Found. Editorial bd. The Tex. Lawyer. Mem. ABA (affirmative action com.), Tex. Bar Assn., Houston Bar Assn., Hiscock Legal Soc. (dir.), Houston C. of C. (chmns. club). Contracts commercial, Legal education. Home: 5318 Calhoun Rd Houston TX 77021 Office: Tex U Thurgood Marshall Law Sch Bldg 3100 Cleburne Ave Houston TX 77021

DOUGLAS, JOHN WOOLMAN, lawyer; b. Phila., Aug. 15, 1921; s. Paul H. and Dorothy S. (Wolff) D.; m. Mary Evans St. John, July 14, 1945; children: Katherine D. Torrey, Peter R. AB, Princeton U., 1943; LLB, Yale U., 1948; DPhil, Oxford U., 1950. Bar: N.Y. 1948, D.C. 1953. Law clk. to justice Harold H. Burton U.S. Supreme Ct., 1951-52; asst. atty. gen. U.S. Dept. Justice, 1963-66; assoc. Covington & Burling, Washington, 1950-51, 52-63, 1966—; Chmn. Carnegie Endowment for Internat. Peace, 1978-86. Served to lt. (j.g.) USNR, 1943-46, MTO, PTO. Rhodes scholar, 1948-50. Fellow Am. Coll. Trial Lawyers; mem. ABA, D.C. Bar Assn. (pres. 1974-75), Practising Law Inst. (bd. trustees 1986—), Nat. Lawyers Com. for Civil Rights Under Law (co. chmn. 1969-71), Nat. Legal Aid Defender Assn. (pres. 1970-71), Yale Law Sch. Assn. (pres. 1975-77). Democrat. Presbyterian. Federal civil litigation. Home: 5700 Kirkside Dr Chevy Chase MD 20815 Office: Covington & Burling 1201 Pennsylvania Ave NW PO Box 7566 Washington DC 20044

DOUGLAS, KERRY DELISLE, lawyer; b. Bolivar, Mo., Nov. 13, 1946; s. Elvin S. and Florence (DeLisle) D.; m. Synda L. Kelsey; children: Thomas H., K. Patrick. AB, U. Mo., 1968, JD cum laude, 1970. Bar: Mo. 1970, U.S. Dist. Ct. (we. dist.) Mo. 1970, U.S. Ct. Appeals (8th cir.) 1985. Ptnr. Douglas & Douglas, Bolivar, 1972-79, Douglas, Douglas & Lynch, Bolivar, 1979—; chmn bd. dirs. Citizens Meml. Hosp., Bolivar, 1979—. chmn. Danforth for Senate, Bond for Gov., Ashcroft for Gov., Polk County. Mo.

Mem. Mo. Assn. Trial Attys. (bd. dirs. 1984-86), Bolivar Area C. of C. (past pres.). Republican. Southern Baptist. Lodge: Rotary. State civil litigation, Probate, Real property. Office: Douglas Douglas & Lynch PC PO Box 117 Bolivar MO 65613

DOUGLAS, WAYNE RODGER, lawyer; b. Manchester, Conn., Jan. 23, 1952; s. Wilfred George and Joan (Rodger) D.; m. Martica Faulkner Sawin, Sept. 8, 1984; 1 child, William. Student, Oxford (Eng.) U., 1972-73; BA in History, Bates Coll., 1974; JD, U. Maine, 1979. Bar: Maine 1979, U.S. Dist. Ct. Maine 1979. Law clk. to judges Supreme Judicial Ct. and Dist. Ct., Maine, 1979-82; assoc. Pierce, Atwood, Scribner, Allen, Smith and Lancaster, Portland, 1982—. Editor-in-Chief U. Maine Law Rev., 1978-79. Recipient Legal Scholarship award West Publ. Co., 1979. Mem. ABA, Maine State Bar Assn., Cumberland Bar Assn. Administrative and regulatory, Health, Insurance. Home: 11 Munjoy St Portland ME 04101 Office: Pierce Atwood Scribner Allen et al 1 Monument Sq Portland ME 04101

DOUGLAS-HAMILTON, MARGARET HAMBRECHT, lawyer; b. Bklyn., July 28, 1941; d. William Matthew and Kathleen (Sheehan) H.; m. Diarmaid H. Douglas-Hamilton, Oct. 14, 1967 (Nov. 1982). BA, Wellesley Coll., 1963; MA, Syracuse U., 1965; LLB, Boston U., 1967. Bar: Mass. 1967, U.S. Supreme Ct. 1979, N.Y. 1981. Assoc. Ely, Bartlett, Brown & Proctor, Boston, 1967-72, Bingham, Dana & Gould, Boston, 1972-80; ptnr. Sullivan & Worcester, Boston and N.Y.C., 1980-87; v.p., gen. counsel Schroders Inc., N.Y.C., 1987—. Contbr. articles to profl. jours. Mem. Gov.'s Commn. on Status of Women, Boston, 1970-73; bd. dirs. DIA Art Found., N.Y.C., 1985—, The Royal Oak Found., N.Y.C., 1986—. Mem. ABA, Assn. of Bar of City of N.Y., Boston Jr. C. of C. (named one of ten outstanding leaders 1972). Clubs: Chilton (Boston); Doubles (N.Y.C.). Avocations: poetry, wine, tennis. Banking, General corporate, Securities. Office: Sullivan & Worcester 767 3d Ave New York NY 10017

DOUGLASS, ORION LORENZO, lawyer, judge; b. Savannah, Ga., Feb. 22, 1947; s. Otha Lafayette Sr. and C. Veronica (Redd) D.; m. Shirley Ann Hill, June 29, 1952; children: Orion Jr., Omar Lorne. BA, Holy Cross Coll., 1968; JD, Washington U., St. Louis, 1971. Staff atty. Legal Aid Soc., St. Louis, 1972-74; asst. cir. atty. City of St. Louis, 1973-74; staff atty. Hill, Jones & Farrington, Atlanta, 1974-75; sole practice Brunswick, 1975—; judge Recorder's Ct., City of Brunswick, 1981—. Panel mem. Spl. Adv. Bd. for Handicapped, State of Ga., 1985—. Mem. Ga. Bar Assn., Mo. Bar Assn. Presbyterian. Avocations: golf, music. Home: 642 Johnson Rd Saint Simons Island GA 31522 Office: 1516 Goodyear Ave Brunswick GA 31521

DOUGLASS, ROBERT DUNCAN, lawyer; b. Bklyn., Aug. 18, 1941; s. George Wilbur Douglass and Gladys (Harding) Naffke; children: Benjamin R., Samuel H. BA, Lafayette Coll., 1963; JD, Harvard U., 1966. Bar: Pa. 1967, U.S. Dist. Ct. (we. dist.) Pa. 1984, U.S. Cir. Ct. (3d cir.) 1984. Assoc. Joseph N. Mack, Indiana, Pa., 1966-69; ptnr. Pierce & Douglass, Indiana, 1969-75; sole practice Indiana, 1975—; asst. prof. Ind. U., Pa., 1970-72, lectr. continuing edn. Ind. U., Pa., 1982-84. Mem. ABA, Pa. Bar Assn., Ind. County Bar Assn. (sec. 1975-86, v.p. 1986-87, pres. 1987—). Club: Rivers (Pitts.). State civil litigation, General corporate, General practice. Office: 917 Philadelphia St PO Box 326 Indiana PA 15701

DOUMAR, ROBERT G., U.S. district judge; b. 1930; m. Dorothy Ann Mundy; children—Robert G., Charles C. B.A., U. Va., 1951, LL.B., 1953. Assoc. firm Venable, Parsons, Kyle & Hylton, 1955-58; sr. ptnr. Doumar, Pincus, Knight & Harlan, 1958-81; U.S. dist. judge Eastern Va., Norfolk, 1981—. Judicial administration. Office: 183 US Courthouse 600 Granby St Norfolk VA 23510

DOWD, DAVID D., JR., federal judge; b. Cleve., Jan. 31, 1929; m. Joyce; children—Cindy, David, Doug, Mark. B.A., Coll. Wooster, 1951; J.D., U. Mich., 1954. Ptnr. Dowd & Dowd, Massillon, Ohio, 1954-55, ptnr., 1957-75; asst. pros. atty. Stark County, 1961-67, pros. atty., 1967-75; judge Ohio 5th Dist. Ct. Appeals, 1975-80, Ohio Supreme Ct., 1980-81; ptnr. Black, McCuskey, Souers & Arbaugh, Canton, Ohio, 1981-82; judge U.S. Dist. Ct. (no. dist.) Ohio, 1982—. Judicial administration. Office: U S Dist Ct 510 Fed Bldg & U S Courthouse 2 S Main St Akron OH 44308

DOWD, DENNIS OWEN, prosecutor, law educator; b. Orange, N.J., Oct. 2, 1947; s. David William and Congetta S. (Sansone) D.; m. Mary White, Nov. 26, 1971; children: David W. III, Molly W., Padraic T.J. BA, Rutgers U., 1971; JD, Seton Hall U., 1974. Bar: N.J. 1974, U.S. Dist. Ct. N.J. 1982, U.S. Ct. Customs 1982, N.Y. 1982. Assoc. Judge, Dowd & Geddis, West Orange, N.J., 1974-78; ptnr. Dowd & Dowd, West Orange, 1978-86; pres. Dennis O. Dowd, P.A., West Orange, 1986—. Councilman Township of West Orange, 1976-84; mem. Young Polit. Leaders, Washington, 1983—. Mem. ABA, N.J. Bar Assn., Essex County Bar Assn. Democrat. Roman Catholic. Club: Unico (Orange). Equine law, Real property, Administrative and regulatory. Office: 59 Main St West Orange NJ 07052

DOWD, PAMELA J. CUPLIN, lawyer; b. Ft. Sill, Okla., Sept. 23, 1954; d. Morton C. and Patricia J. (Agee) Cuplin; m. Timothy C. Dowd, Jan. 24, 1976; children: Kelley J., Megan C. BA in French, U. Okla., 1975; JD, U. Tulsa, 1979. Bar: Okla. 1980, U.S. Dist. Ct. (we. dist.) Okla. 1980. Staff atty. Legal Aid Western Okla., Oklahoma City, 1980-81; assoc. Carson, Rayburn, Hirsch & Mueller, Oklahoma City, 1981-84; sole practice Oklahoma City, 1984—; pres., counsel Kappa Delta House Corp. Bd., Norman, Okla, 1986. Chancellor St. Augustine Episcopal Ch., Oklahoma City, 1983—; co-chmn. precinct 251, Dems., The Village, Okla., 1986. Mem. ABA, Okla. County Bar Assn. (appreciation award 1983), Kappa Delta. Club: PEO (Oklahoma City) (corr. sec. 1986—). Oil and gas leasing, Probate, Real property. Home and Office: 2505 NW 121st Oklahoma City OK 73120

DOWD, STEVEN MILTON, lawyer; b. Tyler, Tex., Feb. 1, 1951; s. Loyd Robertus and Roy Frances (Dickard) D.; m. Pamela Gayle Blacklock, Apr. 6, 1974; children—Anna Lisa, Lydia Caroline. B.A., Austin Coll., 1973; J.D., Baylor U., 1975; LL.M., So. Meth. U., 1977. Bar: Tex. 1975, U.S. Dist. Ct. (so. dist.) Tex. 1983, U.S. Dist. Ct. (ea. dist.) Tex. 1985. Tax Atty. Exxon Corp., Houston, 1979-82, Tyler, Tex., 1984-86; assoc. Covington & Reese, Houston, 1982-84; asst. gen. counsel Temple-Eastex Inc., Diboll, Tex., 1986—. Bd. dirs. Noonday Holiness Camp, Hallsville, Tex. Mem. Houston Bar Assn., Houston Young Lawyers Assn. Baptist. State civil litigation, Banking, Real property. Home: 2 Glenview Ct Lufkin TX 75901 Office: Temple-Eastex Inc 303 S Temple Diboll TX 75941

DOWD, WILLIAM TIMOTHY, lawyer, energy association executive; b. Muskogee, Okla., May 3, 1927; s. Timothy J. and Nelle (McCune) D.; m. Charlotte H. Engelkamp, Dec. 1, 1951; children: Timothy C., Terence R., Nancy C., Kathryn H. Johnson; m. 2d, Maria Revelis, June 4, 1966; children: William J., Ellen M. AB, Xavier U., 1951; LLB, U. Tulsa, 1957. Bar: Okla. 1957, U.S. Supreme Ct. 1967. Assoc. Landrith & McGee, Tulsa, 1957-63; ptnr. Landrith, McGee & Dowd, Tulsa, 1963-65, McGee & Dowd, Tulsa, 1965-66; pub. defender Tulsa County, 1958; mem. Okla. Ho. of Reps., 1963-64; chief legal officer to Gov. of Okla., 1967-69; exec. dir. Interstate Oil Compact Commn., Oklahoma City, 1969—. Mem. Okla. Gov.'s Energy Adv. Council, 1975-79, Nat. Petroleum Council Com. on Enhanced Recovery, 1976-77, Fed. Power Commn. Natural Gas Survey, 1971-72, U.S. Nat. Com. World Energy Conf., 1972-75, Task Force on Underground Injection Control Programs, EPA, 1975—, Dept. of Interior Adv. Com. on Minerals Accountability, 1982-83, royalty mgmt. adv. com. U.S. Dept. Interior, 1986—; chmn. petroleum tech. adv. com. to People's Republic of China, 1984. Served with U.S. Army, 1945-47. Mem. ABA, Okla. Bar Assn., Fed. Energy Bar Assn., Assn. Petroleum Writers. Republican. Roman Catholic. Club: Oklahoma City Petroleum. FERC practice, Environment, Administrative and regulatory. Office: Interstate Oil Compact Commn PO Box 53127 Oklahoma City OK 73152

DOWDLE, PATRICK DENNIS, lawyer; b. Denver, Dec. 8, 1948; s. William Robert and Helen (Schraeder) D.; m. Eleanor Pryor, Mar. 8, 1975; children: Jeffery William, Andrew Peter. BA, Cornell Coll., Mt. Vernon, Iowa, 1971; JD, Boston U., 1975. Bar: Colo. 1975, U.S. Dist. Ct. Colo. 1975, U.S. Ct. Appeals (10th cir.) 1976, U.S. Supreme Ct. 1978. Acad. dir. in Japan Sch. Internat. Tng., Putney, Vt., 1974; assoc. Decker & Miller, Denver, 1975-77; ptnr. Miller, Makkai & Dowdle, Denver, 1977—; designated counsel criminal appeals Colo. Atty. Gens. Office, Denver, 1980-81; guardian ad litem Adams County Dist. Ct., Brighton, Colo., 1980-83; affiliated counsel ACLU, Denver, 1980—. Mem. ABA, Colo. Bar. Assn., Denver Bar Assn. (various coms.), Assn. Trial Lawyers Am., Sierra Club, Boston U. Sch. Alumni Assn. (regional rep. 1977—). Democrat. Clubs: Porsche of Am.(Rocky Mountain region 1983—). Avocations: scuba diving, photography, wine making, travel. Civil litigation, Real property, Bankruptcy. Home: 11825 W 30th Pl Lakewood CO 80215 Office: Miller Makkai & Dowdle 2325 W 72d Ave Denver CO 80221

DOWDY, ROBERT ALAN, lawyer; b. Rochester, N.Y., June 12, 1941; s. Andrew Hunter and Helen Marie (Brandes) D.; m. Lynne Bryant, June 18, 1966; children—Roger Alan, Douglas John. B.A., U. Calif.-Berkeley, J.D., 1966. Bar: D.C. 1967, Calif. 1968, Wash., 1974. Atty. Am. Airlines, N.Y.C., 1969-72; atty. Weyerhaeuser Co., Tacoma, 1972-75, legal counsel, 1975-78, sr. legal counsel, 1978-86, asst. gen. counsel, 1986—; dir. Green Arrow Motor Co., Tacoma; mem. Wash. Bd. Bar Examiners, 1982—; arbitrator King County Superior Ct., 1986—; vis. com. U. Wash. Sch. Law, U. Wash., Seattle, 1986—. Contbr. articles to profl. jours. Bd. dirs. N.W. Chamber Orch., Seattle, 1975-76; elder St. Elizabeth Episcopal Ch., Burien, Wash., 1976-78; trustee St. James Sch., Kent, Wash., 1982-84. Served to capt. U.S. Army, 1966-69. Decorated Army Commendation medal. Mem. Wash. Bar Assn. (exec. com. corp. sect. 1977-79, chmn. exec. com. law dept. 1977-79, mem. legal edn. sect. 1982-84). Republican. General corporate, Administrative and regulatory, Transportation. Home: 9329 SE Shoreland Dr Bellevue WA 98004 Office: Weyerhaeuser Co CH 2J28 Tacoma WA 98477

DOWELL, DOUGLAS MELVIN, lawyer; b. Louisville, Oct. 25, 1955; s. Clinton Melvin Dowell and Katherine L. Mueller; m. Angela A. Johnson, June 15, 1984. BA in Polit. Sci., DePauw U., 1977; JD, U. Louisville, 1980. Bar: Ky. 1980, U.S. Dist. Ct. (we. dist.) Ky. 1980, U.S. Dist. Ct. (ea. dist.) Ky. 1984, U.S. Tax Ct. 1984, U.S. Ct. Appeals (6th cir.) 1985. Atty. pub. defender's office Jefferson County, Louisville, 1981-84; assoc. Lynch, Sherman & Cox, Louisville, 1984-85; atty. Revenue Cabinet Commonwealth of Ky., Frankfort, 1985—. Mem. ABA, Ky. Govt. Bar Assn., Louisville Bar Assn. Democrat. State and local taxation, Administrative and regulatory, State civil litigation. Office: Revenue Cabinet PO Box 423 State Capitol Annex Frankfort KY 40602

DOWER, HARRY ALLEN, lawyer; b. Bethlehem, Pa., Nov. 29, 1918. AB, Lafayette Coll., 1940; JD, Yale U., 1948. Bar: Pa. 1949, U.S. Supreme Ct. 1974. Sole practice Allentown, Pa., 1949—; gen. counsel Alpo Pet Foods div. Allen Products Co., 1964-69; adj. prof. law Lehigh U., Bethlehem, 1969—. Author: (with Charles Vihon) Cases on Legal Problems of Business in Free Society, 1973. Legal counsel ACLU of Lehigh Valley, Pa., 1950—; trustee Allentown br. NAACP Scholarship Fund, 1965—; bd. dirs. Wiley House, Bethlehem, 1973-82. Mem. Pa. Bar Assn. Home: 1665 Lehigh Pkwy N Allentown PA 18103 Office: PO Box 950 Allentown PA 18105

DOWLING, MICHAEL ANTHONY, lawyer; b. Norwalk, Conn., Aug. 29, 1953; s. John Edward and Regina (Malkiewicz) D.; m. Susan Cappon, may 20, 1978; 1 child, Jeffrey Michael. BA cum laude, St. Michael's Coll., 1975; JD, Western New Eng. Coll., 1979. Bar: Conn. 1979, U.S. Dist. Ct. Conn. 1980, U.S. Tax Ct. 1980. Research assoc. Conn. Jud. Dept., Hartford, 1978; assoc. Santaniello, Posnik & Basile, Springfield, Mass., 1979-80, Willis & Holahan, Bridgeport, Conn., 1980-84, Marsh, Day & Calhoun, Bridgeport, 1984—. Mem. Conn. Bar Assn. (econs. com. office 1985—), Bridgeport Bar Assn., Danbury Bar Assn. Democrat. Roman Catholic. State civil litigation, Federal civil litigation, Real property. Home: 511 Riverside Dr Fairfield CT 06430 Office: Marsh Day Calhoun Bridgeport CT 06404

DOWLING, RODERICK ANTHONY, investment banker; b. N.Y.C., Dec. 29, 1940; s. John Joseph and Anne (Chisholm) D.; m. Lavinia Seibels, May 6, 1977; children: Lavinia Crosby, Roderick A.; children by previous marriage: Anne Chisholm, Katherine Burke. B.S., Fairfield U., 1962; J.D., Fordham U., 1965. Bar: N.Y. 1965, Ga. 1974. Assoc. Cahill, Gordon & Reindel, N.Y.C., 1965-72; v.p., gen. counsel U.S. Industries N.E. Corp., N.Y.C., 1972-73, Fugua Industries, Inc., Atlanta, 1973-81; mng. dir. Robinson Humphrey Inc., Atlanta, 1981—; bd. dirs. Forstmann & Co., Inc., L.S. Brown & Co., Nat. Consumer Prodn., Inc., Ocilla Industries, Inc. Mem. ABA, Bar Assn. City N.Y., Georgia, Atlanta bar assns., S.R. Clubs: University, Union, Capitol City, Lawyers. General corporate, Banking. Home: 380 Argonne Atlanta GA 30305

DOWLING, SARAH T., lawyer; b. Cleve., Nov. 7, 1941; d. Robert Herman and Wilma (Simon) Trenkamp; m. Joseph Leo Dowling Jr., July 28, 1962; children: Joseph III, Robert, Charles, Ruth. AB, Wellesley Coll., 1963; JD, Northeastern U., 1977; LLM, Boston U., 1982. Bar: R.I. 1977, U.S. Dist. Ct. R.I. 1977. Law clk. to presiding justice R.I. Bankrupcy Ct., 1975; assoc. Adler, Pollock & Sheehan, Providence, 1977-85, ptnr., 1985—. Mem. adv. bd. Trinity Sq. Repertory Co., Providence, 1984—. Mem. R.I. Bar Assn. (com. on taxation, com. on debtors and creditors rights). General corporate, Corporate taxation, Banking. Home: 109 Hazard Ave Providence RI 02906 Office: Adler Pollock & Sheehan 2300 Hospital Trust Tower Providence RI 02903

DOWLING, THOMAS PATRICK, lawyer; b. Yonkers, N.Y., Sept. 20, 1928; s. John T. and Mary E. (Rooney) D.; m. Rosemary A. McLoone, June 14, 1958; children: Rosemary, Thomas, James, Maureen, Kristina. BSEE, Poly. Inst. N.Y., 1958; LLB, St. John's U., 1957. Bar: N.Y. 1958, U.S. Patent Office 1958, U.S. Dist. Ct. (ea. and so. dists.) N.Y. 1959, U.S. Supreme Ct. 1960, U.S. Ct. Appeals (2d cir.) 1964, U.S. Ct. Appeals (9th cir.) 1970. Assoc. Morgan, Finnegan, Pine, Foley & Lee, N.Y.C., 1957-64, ptnr., 1964—; sr. ptnr., Morgan & Finnegan, N.Y.C., 1975—. Co-chmn. N.Y. State Gov.'s Health Adv. Council, 1975-80; vice chmn. Public Health Council State of N.Y., 1978—. Served with USN, 1946-48, 50-52. Mem. ABA, N.Y. State Bar Assn., Assn. Bar City N.Y., IEEE. Federal civil litigation, Trademark and copyright, Patent. Home: 129 Baldwin Ave Point Lookout NY 11569 Office: Morgan & Finnegan 345 Park Ave New York NY 10154

DOWLING, VICTOR JAMES, lawyer; b. N.Y.C., July 15, 1923; s. Victor Hurlin and Joan Agnes (Reardon) D.; m. Ruth E. Decker, Nov. 27, 1954 (dec. Mar. 1965); 1 son, Victor James; m. Mary G. Cole, Aug. 4, 1969. B.S., Harvard U., 1945; J.D., U. Conn., 1951. Bar: Conn. 1951. Sr. ptnr. Dowing & Dowling, Simsbury, Conn., 1952—; state trial referee Hartford/New Britain Jud. Dist. Conn., 1984—; corp. counsel Town of West Hartford, Conn., 1958-59. Town chmn. Republican Party, West Hartford, 1959-69. Mem. ABA, Conn. Bar Assn., Hartford County Bar Assn. Roman Catholic. Real property, Personal income taxation, General corporate. Home: 168 Westledge Rd West Simsbury CT 06092

DOWLING, VINCENT JOHN, lawyer; b. N.Y.C., Dec. 20, 1927; s. Victor Hurlin and Joan Agnes (Reardon) D.; m. Jane Cooney, Apr. 16, 1958; children—Vincent John, Jr., Douglas J., S. Colin, Joseph G. B.S., Lehigh U., 1949; J.D., U. Conn., 1957. Bar: Conn. 1957, U.S. Dist. Ct. Conn. 1958, U.S. Ct. Appeals (2d cir.) 1960, Mass. 1985, Fla. 1986, U.S. Ct. Claims 1986. Chief mfg. engr. Veeder-Root, Inc., Hartford, Conn., 1949-58; ptnr. Dowling & Dowling, Hartford, 1958-65; ptnr. Cooney, Scully & Dowling, Hartford, 1965—; lectr. constrn. law. Served to capt. U.S. Army, 1951-53. Mem. ASME, ABA, Conn. Bar Assn., Fed. Bar Assn., Diocesan Attys. Assn., Kappa Alpha Soc. Roman Catholic. Club: Golf (Hartford), Johns Island (Vero Beach, Fla.). Construction, Federal civil litigation. Address: 266 Pearl St Hartford CT 06103

DOWLING, WILLIAM FRANCIS, lawyer; b. Holyoke, Mass., July 24, 1941; s. William Francis and Rita (Morache) D.; m. Susan Torre, Oct. 13, 1973; children: Elizabeth Anne, Caroline T. BA, Columbia U., 1970; JD, Boston Coll., 1973. Bar: N.Y. 1974. Dep. chief asst. atty. gen. State of N.Y., N.Y.C., 1979-86; v.p., gen. counsel N.Y. Yankees, Bronx, 1986—. Mem. ABA, N.Y. State Bar Assn. (award 1979), N.Y. County Bar Assn. Criminal, Entertainment. Office: NY Yankees Yankee Stadium Bronx NY 10451

DOWNER, MICHAEL JOSEF, corporate legal counsel; b. Los Angeles, Feb. 25, 1955; s. Lowell Howard and Cora Marie (Masek) D.; m. Janet Lee Gewecke, Aug. 20, 1983. BA with honors, UCLA, 1977; JD, Southwestern U., 1981. Bar: Calif. 1982. Corp. legal counsel The Capital Group, Inc., Los Angeles, 1982-86, sr. counsel, 1986—. Mem. ABA, Calif. Bar Assn., Los Angeles County Bar Assn., Investment Co. Inst. (tax com.), Calif. Bankers Assn. (trust state govtl. affairs com.). Republican. Roman Catholic. Banking, General corporate, General taxation. Home: 3725 Mayfair Dr Pasadena CA 91107 Office: The Capital Group Inc 333 S Hope St 52d Floor Los Angeles CA 90071

DOWNES, ROBERT BRUCE, lawyer; b. Boston, Oct. 20, 1942; s. Arthur Bruce and Helen (Rita) Downes; m. Esther C. Weiss, Dec. 31, 1969 (div. July 1982); m. Melissa Ann Williams, Nov. 27, 1983; 1 stepchild, Amy Jo Coletta. BS, St. Vincent, Latrobe, Pa., 1965; JD, Boston Coll., 1968. Bar: Mass. 1969, Alaska 1971, U.S. Dist. Ct. Alaska 1971. Assoc. Elliot Goldman, Natick, Mass., 1969-70; asst. dist. atty. State of Alaska, Fairbanks, 1970-75; assoc. Jay Hodges, Fairbanks, 1975-76, ptnr., 1976-77; ptnr. Dick Cole, Fairbanks, 1977-80; sole practice Fairbanks, 1980-84; ptnr. Downes & McKelvie, Fairbanks, 1984—. Mem. Alaska Bar Assn., Tamara Valley Bar Assn., Assn. Trial Lawyers Am., Mens Hockey Assn. (pres. 1986—), Alaska Goldpanners (bd. dirs. 1978-86). Methodist. Lodge: Kiwanis (pres. 1975). Avocations: hockey, hunting, fishing. Criminal, State civil litigation, Family and matrimonial. Office: 1008 16th Ave Fairbanks AL 99701

DOWNEY, ARTHUR HAROLD, JR., lawyer; b. N.Y.C., Nov. 21, 1938; s. Arthur Harold Sr. and Charlotte (Bailey) D.; m. Gwen Vanden Berg, May 28, 1960; children: Anne Leigh, Neal Arthur, Drew Thomas. BA, Cen. Coll., Pella, Iowa, 1960; LLB, Cornell U., 1963. Bar: Colo. 1963, U.S. Dist. Ct. Colo. 1963, U.S. Ct. Appeals (10th cir.) 1963. From assoc. to ptnr. Weller, Friedrich, Hickisch, Hazlitt & Ward, Denver, 1963-82; ptnr., chief exec. officer Downey & Gulley P.C., Denver, 1982—. Contbr. articles to profl. jours. Vice moderator Presbytery Denver, 1972; past pres. Columbine Village Homeowners Assn., Trails End Homeowners Assn., Upper Village Homeowners Assn., Powderhorn Condominium Homeowners Assn., Breckenridge, Colo. Fellow Internat. Soc. Barristers; mem. ABA, Colo. Bar Assn., Denver Bar Assn., Def. Research Inst. (disting. service award), Nat. Inst. Trial Advocacy (teaching faculty, team leader 1973—), Colo. Def. Lawyers Assn. (pres. 1977-78), Am. Coll. Legal Medicine (assoc. in law). Republican. Mem. Reformed Ch. Am. Avocations: photography, woodworking, skiing. Federal civil litigation, State civil litigation, Insurance. Office: Downey & Gulley PC 950 S Cherry St #1210 Denver CO 80222

DOWNEY, JOSEPH W., lawyer; b. Ft. Meade, Md., July 22, 1945; s. William J. and Mary Elizabeth (Nobles) D. BA, St. Louis U., 1967, JD, 1972. Bar: Mo. 1973, U.S. Dist. Ct. (we. dist.) Mo. 1973, U.S. Supreme Ct. 1980. Research atty. Mo. Ct. Appeals, St. Louis, 1972-74; asst. pub. defender Pub. Defender Office, Clayton, Mo., 1974-81, pub. defender, 1981—; mem. Jail Population Mgmt. Bd., St. Louis, 1983—; bd. dirs. Mo. Coalition for Alternatives to Imprisonment, Jefferson, Mo., 1984—. Mem. Leadership St. Louis, 1985—. Served with U.S. Army, 1969-71. Avocations: travel, cooking, photography, music. Criminal. Home: 2626 Caroline St Saint Louis MO 63104 Office: Public Defender 1320 Market St Room 62 Saint Louis MO 63103

DOWNEY, RICHARD MORGAN, lawyer; b. S.I., N.Y., Nov. 13, 1946; s. William Sexton and Marion (Herbert) D.; m. Judith Yestrumskas, May 31, 1980. B.A., Fairfield U., 1968; J.D., Georgetown U., 1971. Bar: D.C. Regional dir. Common Cause, 1975-77; atty. Pub. Citizen, 1973-74; with Democratic Nat. Com., 1972, Ams. for Indian Opportunity, 1970-72; now dir. govt. affairs dept. Am. Speech-Lang.-Hearing Assn., Rockville, Md. Mem. Nat. Health Lawyers Assn.; Nat. Com. for Research (bd.dirs.). Democrat. Roman Catholic. Editor: Govt. Affairs Rev. Health, Legislative, Administrative and regulatory. Home: 4411 42d St NW Washington DC 20016

DOWNEY, WILLIAM GERALD, JR., lawyer; b. Bklyn., June 20, 1914; s. William Gerald and Mary Veronica (Ryder) D.; m. Ellen Wagle, Apr. 22, 1942 (dec. Nov. 1944); m. 2d Laufey Arnadottir, June 5, 1947; children—William Gerald III (dec.), Robert, Richard, Elizabeth, Mary, Catherine, William Gerald IV, Karen. B.S.S., CCNY, 1937; M.A., Cath. U. Am., 1938; J.D., Georgetown U., 1951; diploma Trinity Coll., Dublin, Ireland, 1976. Bar: D.C. 1951, Va. 1955, U.S. Ct. Mil. Appeals 1952, U.S. Supreme Ct. 1963. Fellow in internat. law Cath. U. Am., 1936-37, Georgetown U., 1937-40; commd. 2d lt. Inf., U.S. Army, 1936, advanced through grades to col. JAGC; served in various locations in U.S., Iceland, Eng., France, Germany, Formosa; ret., 1955; sr. ptnr. Downey & Lennhoff, Springfield, Va., 1955-85, of counsel Duvall, Blackburn, Hale & Downey, Fairfax, Va., 1985—; founder, v.p., past chmn. No. Va. Bank, Springfield; prof. law Soochow U., Taipei, Formosa, 1952-53. Decorated Army Commendation medal. Mem. D.C. Bar Assn., Va. Bar Assn., Fairfax County Bar Assn., Phi Alpha Delta. Roman Catholic. Clubs: Army-Navy (Washington); Army-Navy Country (Arlington, Va.). Contbr. articles to jours. Banking, Public international, Military. Office: Duvall Blackburn Hale & Downey 4031 University Dr Suite 202 Fairfax VA 22030

DOWNING, GEORGE, lawyer; b. Girard, Pa., Oct. 21, 1934; s. Jerome Francis and Anna M. (Strasswimmer) D.; m. Molly B. Downing, Dec. 30, 1966; children: Matthew, Gwynne. BA, Gannon Coll.; LLB, Case-Western Res. U. Bar: Ohio 1962, U.S. Dist. Ct. (no. dist.) Ohio 1962. Ptnr. Baker & Hostetler, Cleve., 1962—. V.p., exec. com. Cleve. Music Sch. Settlement, 1969—. Mem. ABA, Ohio Bar Assn., Cleve. Bar Assn., Copyright Soc., Cleve. Law Library Assn. (trustee, v.p. 1974—). Episcopalian. Clubs: Philos. (Cleve.) (pres. 1982-83), Cleve. Skating. Avocations: music, lit., theatre. Entertainment, Trademark and copyright, Libel. Office: Baker & Hostetler 3200 National City Ctr Cleveland OH 44114

DOWNING, JAMES CHRISTIE, lawyer; b. Los Angeles, Dec. 17, 1924; s. Dorman Perkins and Merle Grace (Christie) D.; m. Betty Griggs, Dec. 23, 1949; children—Colleen, James, Kimberly, Kelly, Kathleen. B.S., U. Calif., 1949; LL.B., U. Calif.-San Francisco, 1952. Bar: Calif. 1953, U.S. Dist. Ct. (no. dist.) Calif. 1953, U.S. Dist. Ct. (ea. dist.) Calif. 1975, U.S. Ct. Appeals (9th dir.) 1953. Assoc. Walkup, Downing, Shelby, Bastian, Melodia, Kelly & O'Reilly, and predecessors, San Francisco, 1954-59, ptnr., 1959-70, exec. v.p., 1970-84; ptnr. Downing & Downing, 1985—; lectr. Calif. Continuing Edn. of Bar Program. Served in AC, U.S. Army, 1943-45. Decorated Air medal with 5 oak leaf clusters. Fellow Am. Coll. Trial Lawyers; mem. ABA, State Bar Calif., Bar Assn. San Francisco (vice chmn. trial practice com. 1970), Calif. Trial Lawyers Assn., San Francisco Trial Lawyers Assn. (pres. 1972), Am. Bd. Trial Advs. (nat. exec. com. 1970-73, nat. sec. 1971, nat. chmn. membership 1972-73, 76-77, nat. pres. 1974, pres. San Francisco chpt. 1974, Calif. Trial Lawyer of Yr. 1978), Internat. Soc. Barristers, Internat. Acad. Trial Lawyers. Republican. Club: Bankers of San Francisco. litigation. Federal civil litigation, State civil litigation. Office: Downing & Downing 1460 Maria Ln Suite 200 Walnut Creek CA 94596

DOWNS, THOMAS EDWARD, IV, lawyer; b. South Amboy, N.J., Sept. 27, 1950; s. Thomas Edward III and Theresa Mary (Jaje) D.; m. Marie Popik, Oct. 6, 1979; 1 son, Thomas Edward, V. B.A., St. Peter's Coll., 1972; J.D., Seton Hall U., 1975. Bar: N.J. 1975, U.S. Dist. Ct. N.J. 1975, U.S. Dist. Cts. (so. and ea. dists.) N.Y. 1981. Law clk. to presiding judges Middlesex County, N.J., 1975; assoc. Irving Tabman, Old Bridge, N.J., 1975-76; ptnr. Tabman, Downs & McDonnell, Old Bridge, 1976-77, Tabman & Downs, Old Bridge, 1978-82; sole practice, Old Bridge, 1982—. Sec., South Amboy Shade Tree Com., 1974; co-chmn. South Amboy Blood Bank; pres. South Amboy Young Democratic Orgn. Mem. Assn. Trial Lawyers Am., N.J. State Trial Lawyers Assn., Middlesex County Trial Lawyers Assn., Middlesex County Bar Assn., N.J. State Bar Assn. Roman Catholic. Lodges: Lions (dist. zone chmn. 1984), Rotary (South Amboy). Real property, Local government, General practice. Home: 26 Carter Pl Sayreville PO Box Parlin NJ 08859 Office: 250 Route 516 Suite F PO Box 498 Old Bridge NJ 08857

DOWNSBROUGH, BRUCE OWEN, lawyer; b. Morristown, N.J., May 5, 1953; s. George Atha and Margaret Elizabeth (McDougall) D. BA, Union Coll., 1975; JD, U. Colo., 1978. Bar: Colo., U.S. Dist. Ct. Colo., U.S. Ct.

Appeals (10th cir.) 1978, U.S. Supreme Ct. 1982. Law clk. judge U.S. Dist. Ct. Colo., Denver, 1978-79; assoc. Williams, Trine, Greenstein & Griffith PC, Boulder, Colo., 1979-85, ptnr., 1985—. Class agt., mem. exec. com. Union Coll. Annual Fund, Schenectady, N.Y., 1975—. Recipient Alumni Recognition award U. Colo. Alumni Assn., 1985. Mem. Boulder County Bar Assn. (chmn. judiciary com. 1985—), Colo. Bar Assn., Colo. Trial Lawyer's Assn., ABA, Assn. Trial Lawyers Am. Personal injury, State civil litigation, Federal civil litigation. Home: 3355 Longwood Ave Boulder CO 80303 Office: Williams Trine Greenstein & Griffith PC 1435 Arapahoe Ave Boulder CO 80302-6390

DOYLE, AUSTIN JOSEPH, JR., lawyer; b. Atlanta, Aug. 2, 1941; s. Austin Joseph Sr. and Marguerite Clare (Sheridan) D.; m. Marian Frances Murphy, June 24, 1980; children: Kelly, Deborah. BBA, U. Notre Dame, 1963; JD, Am. U., 1973. Bar: D.C. 1974, U.S. Dist. Ct. D.C. 1974, U.S. Tax Ct. 1974, U.S. Ct. Appeals (D.C. cir.) 1986; CPA, D.C. CPA Williams & Connolly, Washington, 1967-73; sole practice Washington, 1973—. Served to 1st lt. U.S. Army, 1963-65. Mem. ABA, D.C. Bar Assn., Am. Assn. Atty. CPA's (bd. dirs. 1985—), D.C. Inst. CPA's. Republican. Roman Catholic. Corporate taxation, Federal civil litigation, White collar and tax fraud defense. Office: 1050 Connecticut Ave NW Suite 1200 Washington DC 20036

DOYLE, GERARD FRANCIS, lawyer; b. Needham, Mass., Oct. 25, 1942; s. John Patrick and Catherine Mary (Lawler) D.; BS in Indsl. Adminstrn., Yale U., 1966; JD, Georgetown U., 1972; m. Paula Marie Dervay, May 14, 1983; children: Laura Dervay, Meredith Lawler. Group head for operating submarine reactors and reactor tech. Div. Naval Reactors, AEC, Washington, 1970-72; atty. firm Morgan, Lewis & Bockius, Washington, 1972-76; legal counsel Am. Nuclear Energy Council, Washington, 1975-76; ptnr. Cotten, Day & Doyle, Washington, 1976—; legal counsel Assn. Fed. Data Peripheral Suppliers, Washington, 1979; dir. M Internat., Inc.; lectr. in field. Served with USN, 1966-71. Recipient Outstanding Young Man of Year award, 1976. Mem. ABA, D.C. Bar Assn., Fed. Bar Assn., Am. Arbitration Assn. (panel arbitrators), Nat. Contract Mgmt. Assn. Republican. Roman Catholic. Clubs: Washington Golf and Country. Government contracts and claims, Computer. Home: 6304 Stoneham Ln McLean VA 22101 Office: Cotten Day & Doyle 1899 L St NW Washington DC 20036

DOYLE, JOSEPH ANTHONY, lawyer; b. N.Y.C., June 13, 1920; s. Joseph A. and Jane (Donahue) D.; m. Eugenie A. Fleri, Aug. 19, 1944; children: Christopher, Stephen, Eugenie, Jane, Richard. B.S., Georgetown U., 1941; LL.B., Columbia U., 1947. Assoc. Shearman & Sterling, N.Y.C., 1947-57, ptnr., 1957-79, 81—; asst. sec. for manpower, res. affairs and logistics U.S. Navy, Washington, 1979-81; dir. The Fuji Bank & Trust Co., N.Y.C., Heller Internat. Corp., Chgo., Heller Fin. Inc., Chgo., OKI Am., Inc., Hackensack, N.J., U.S.O. Met., N.Y.C. Served to lt. USNR, 1941-45. Decorated Navy Cross; decorated D.F.C. with 3 gold stars, Air medal with 7 gold stars; recipient Disting. Pub. Service award Sec. of Navy, 1981. Mem. Assn. Bar City N.Y., N.Y. State Bar Assn., ABA. Democrat. Roman Catholic. Clubs: Broad St (N.Y.C.), Downtown Athletic (N.Y.C.); Metropolitan (Washington). Banking, General corporate. Home: 32 Washington Sq W New York NY 10011 Office: 53 Wall St New York NY 10005

DOYLE, JOYCE ANN, lawyer; b. Youngstown, Ohio, Aug. 13, 1937; d. Norbert Harry Doyle and Corinne (Johnson) McCoy. BA, Youngstown U., 1960; MSW, Cath. U., 1964; JD, Fordham U., 1972. Bar: N.Y. 1973. Assoc. Fogarty, McLaughlin & Semel, N.Y.C., 1973-76; asst. gen. counsel Belco Petroleum Corp., N.Y.C., 1976-85; commr. Fed. Mine Safety and Health Rev. Commn., Washington, 1985—. Mem. ABA, Women's Bar Assn. D.C., Fordham Law Sch. Alumni Assn. Judicial administration, Labor, Family and matrimonial. Home: 4701 Connecticut Ave NW #503 Washington DC 20008 Office: Fed Mine Safety & Health Rev Commn 1730 K St NW 6th Floor Washington DC 20006

DOYLE, MARTIN, lawyer; b. Elmira, N.Y., Mar. 29, 1954; m. Kathleen S., Oct. 3, 1982; 1 child, Riley Owen. AB, Dartmouth Coll., 1976; JD, Boston Coll., 1979. Bar: Ill. 1979, U.S. Dist. Ct. (no. dist.) Ill. 1979, Fla. 1984. Assoc. Lord, Bissell & Brook, Chgo., 1979-83, Shutts & Bowen, Miami, Fla., 1983-85, Sparber, Shevin et al, Miami, Fla., 1985—; chmn. seminars on doing bus. in Caribbean, 1984, 85. Securities, Private international, Contracts commercial. Office: Sparber Shevin et al 1 SE 3d Ave Suite 3000 Miami FL 33131

DOYLE, MICHAEL ANTHONY, lawyer; b. Atlanta, Nov. 4, 1937; s. James Alexander and Wilma (Summersgill) D.; m. Mary Fenton Ottley, June 29, 1963; children—John, David, Peter; m. 2d, Bernice H. Winter, Nov. 12, 1977. B.A., Yale U., 1959, LL.B., 1962. Bar: Ga. 1961, D.C. 1967, U.S. Dist. Ct. D.C. 1967, U.S. Dist. Ct. (no. dist.) Ga. 1962, U.S. Ct. Appeals (5th cir.) 1962, U.S. Ct. Appeals (11th cir.) 1982, U.S. Ct. Appeals (D.C. cir.) 1968, U.S. Supreme Ct. 1972, U.S. Ct. Appeals (4th cir.) 1985. Assoc. Alston, Miller & Gaines, Atlanta, 1962-67; ptnr. Alston & Bird, and predecessor, Atlanta, 1967—. Bd. dirs. Atlanta Legal Aid Soc., 1969-84, pres., 1975-76; bd. dirs. Ga. Legal Services Program. Served to lt. USNR, 1964-69. Mem. ABA, State Bar Ga., Atlanta Lawyers Club, Yale Law Sch. Assn. (v.p. 1982-85, mem. exec. com. 1978-85). Roman Catholic. Clubs: Piedmont Driving, Commerce, Yale of Ga. (pres. 1982-84), Yale of N.Y. Antitrust, Federal civil litigation, Private international. Office: Alston & Bird C&S Nat Bank Bldg Atlanta GA 30335

DOYLE, MORRIS MCKNIGHT, lawyer; b. Bishop, Cal., Jan. 4, 1909; s. Guy P. and Helen (McKnight) D.; m. Juliet H. Clapp, Sept. 15, 1934 (dec. 1985); children: Barbara Doyle Roupe, Thomas M.; m. Jean G. Kuhn, May 10, 1986. A.B., Stanford U., 1929; LL.B., Harvard U., 1932; L.H.D., Nat. Coll. Edn., 1965. Bar: Calif. 1932. Asso. McCutchen, Olney, Mannon & Greene, San Francisco, 1932-42; partner McCutchen, Thomas, Matthew, Griffiths & Greene, San Francisco, 1942-58, McCutchen, Doyle, Brown & Enersen, 1958—. Trustee Stanford U., 1959-79, pres. bd. trustees, 1962-65; trustee, chmn. James Irvine Found.; dir. Stanford Research Inst.; bd. overseers Hoover Instn. Fellow Am. Bar Found., Am. Coll. Trial Lawyers; mem. Am., Calif. San Francisco bar assns., Bar Assn. City N.Y., Am. Law Inst., Am. Judicature Soc. Clubs: Pacific Union, Bohemian, Commonwealth (San Francisco). Antitrust, Federal civil litigation, General corporate. Office: 3 Embarcadero Center San Francisco CA 94111

DOYLE, RICHARD HENRY, IV, lawyer; b. Elgin, Ill., Aug. 8, 1949; s. Richard Henry and Shirley Marian (Ohms) D.; m. Debbie Kay Cahalan, Aug. 2, 1975; children—John Richard, Kerry Jane. B.A., Drake U., 1971, J.D., 1976. Bar: Iowa 1976, U.S. Dist. Ct. (no. and so. dists.) Iowa 1977, U.S. Ct. Appeals (8th cir.) 1977, U.S. Supreme Ct. 1986. Asst. atty. gen. Iowa Dept. Justice, Des Moines, 1976-77; assoc. Lawyer, Lawyer & Jackson, Des Moines, 1977-79; assoc. Law Offices of Verne Lawyer & Assocs., Des Moines, 1979—. Contbr. articles to profl. jours. Served with U.S. Army, 1971-73. Fellow Iowa Acad. Trial Lawyers; mem. Assn. Trial Lawyers Am., Assn. Trial Lawyers Iowa, ABA (jud. adminstrn. and tort and ins. practice sects.), Am. Judicature Soc., Iowa Bar Assn., Polk County Bar Assn. (law library trustee 1986—), SAR (registrar Iowa 1983—), Phi Alpha Delta (chpt. pres. 1975), Republican. Presbyterian. Personal injury, State civil litigation. Home: 532 Waterbury Circle Des Moines IA 50312 Office: Law Offices Verne Lawyer & Assocs 427 Fleming Bldg Des Moines IA 50309

DOYLE, WILLIAM A., lawyer; b. Darby, Pa., Apr. 7, 1949; s. William J. and Yolanda T. (Casale) D.; m. Joan M. Menginie, Mar. 1, 1980; 1 child, Jennifer. BS in Math., St. Joseph's U., Phila., 1971; MA in Math., Villanova U., 1973; JD, Temple U., 1980. Bar: Pa. 1980. Systems programmer Burroughs Corp., Downington, Pa., 1973-81; contracts mgr. Burroughs Corp., Paoli, Pa., 1981-82; asst. gen. counsel Colonial Penn Group, Inc., Phila., 1982-86, Martin Marietta Corp., Princeton, N.J., 1986—. Contbg. author: Computer Law: Buying and Selling Computer Hardware and Software, 1983, Computer Law: Computer and Telecommunications Contracts, Licenses and Litigation, 1986; mem. editorial adv. bd. Computer User's Legal Reporter, 1985—. Mem. Computer Law Assn., ABA (sci. and tech. sect., computer law div.), Phila. Bar Assn. (computer law com.), Pa. Bar Assn., Delaware Valley (Pa.) Computer Law Group (co-founder). Avocations: golf, basketball, tennis. Computer, General corporate, Trademark and copyright. Office: Martin Marietta Data Systems 2000 Market St 28th Floor Philadelphia PA 19103

DOZIER, DANIEL PRESTON, lawyer; b. Detroit, May 30, 1944; s. Daniel P. and Phyllis Ann D.; 1 child, Daniel P. B.A., Wayne State U., 1968, J.D., 1971. Bar: Mich. 1971, D.C. 1979. Asst. gen. counsel UAW, Detroit, 1971-74; exec. asst. to mayor City of Detroit, 1974-76; dir. congl. liaison HEW, Washington, 1977-79; legal counsel Fed. Mediation and Conciliation Service, Washington, 1979—; mem. Adminstrv. Conf. of U.S. Mem. Soc. Profls. in Dispute Resolution, Indsl. Relations Research Assn. Democrat. Mem. Soc. of Friends. Labor, Legislative, Administrative and regulatory. Office: Fed Mediation and Conciliation Service 2100 K St NW Washington DC 20427

DOZIER, RUSH WATKINS, JR., lawyer, journalist; b. Madisonville, Ky., July 20, 1950; s. Rush Watkins and Patricia Joy (Sisk) D. AB, Harvard U., 1972; JD, Vanderbilt U., 1976. Bar: Ky. 1977. Reporter, editorial writer Lexington (Ky.) Herald-Leader, 1976-77, city editor, 1977-79; exec. asst., gen. counsel Gov. John Y. Brown Jr., Frankfort, Ky., 1979-83; vice chmn. Ky. Pub. Service Commn., Frankfort, 1983—; sec.-treas. Great Lakes Conf. Pub. Utilities Commrs., 1986—. Author numerous newspaper articles and editorials. Chmn. bd. Gov.'s Scholars Program, Frankfort, 1983—. Mem. ABA, Ky. Bar Assn., Nat. Assn. Regulatory Utility Commrs. (chmn. com. on fin. and tech. 1986—). Democrat. Episcopalian. Administrative and regulatory, Public utilities. Home: 3405 Tishoff Ct Lexington KY 40502 Office: Ky Pub Service Commn 730 Schenkel Ln Frankfort KY 40602

DRABKIN, MURRAY, lawyer; b. N.Y.C., Aug. 3, 1928; s. Max Drabkin and Minnie (Masin) Weiner; m. Mary Elizabeth Hooper, Nov. 27, 1971. AB, Hamilton Coll., 1950; LLB, Harvard U., 1953. Bar: D.C. 1953, U.S. Ct. Appeals (D.C. cir.) 1954, N.Y. 1966, U.S. Supreme Ct. 1972. Counsel com. on judiciary U.S. Ho. of Reps., Washington, 1957-66; spl. asst. to mayor City of N.Y., 1966-68; sole practice N.Y.C. and Washington, 1968-82; ptnr. Cadwalader, Wickersham & Taft, Washington, 1983—; dir. Conn. State Revenue Task Force, 1969-71; mem. adv. com. FRS, Washington, 1970-71, D.C. Tax Revision Com., 1976-77; lectr. law George Washington U., Washington, 1978-80; trustee in reorgn. Auto-Train Corp., 1980—. Contbr. articles to profl. jours. Served with USN, 1953-57, to lt. commdr. USNR. Mem. D.C. Bar, Assn. of Bar of City of N.Y., N.Y. Lawyers' Assn., Nat. Bankruptcy Conf. (exec. com., chmn. com. RR reorgn. 1984—), Phi Beta Kappa, Delta Sigma Rho. Clubs: Cosmos (Washington), Harvard (N.Y.C.). Bankruptcy, State and local taxation.

DRACHMAN, FRANK EMANUEL, JR., lawyer; b. Tucson, July 28, 1930; s. Frank Emanuel Sr. and Isabel (Baptist) D.; m. Joan Hiestand, Dec. 19, 1953; children: Brud, Deborah, Diane, Daren. BA, U. Ariz., Tucson, 1952, JD, 1957. Bar: Ariz. 1957. Assoc. Law Offices of L.V. Robertson, Tucson, 1957-59; ptnr. Robertson, Childers & Drachman, Tucson, 1959-66, Robertson, Childers, Everett, Burke & Drachman, Tucson, 1966, Robertson & Fickett, Tucson, 1967; counsel Univ. Mech., San Diego, 1967-75; gen. counsel Univ. Industries, San Diego, 1975—. Served as 1st lt. U.S. Army, 1952-54, Korea. Decorated Silver Star. Mem. ABA, Am. Arbitration Assn. (arbitrator), Ariz. Bar Assn., Assn. Trial Lawyers Am., Ariz. Trapshooting Assn. (pres. 1965), Tucson Trap and Skeet Club (pres. 1966), Miramar Gun Club. Democrat. Presbyterian. Construction, Labor, State civil litigation. Office: Univ Industries 3430 Camino del Rio N San Diego CA 92108

DRAGOO, DENISE ANN, lawyer; b. Colorado Springs, Colo., Mar. 28, 1952; d. Harold E. and Irma A. Dragoo; m. Craig W. Anderson, Nov. 25, 1977. BA with distinction in History, U. Colo., 1973; cert. planning U. Utah, 1976, JD, 1976; LLM in Environ./Land Use Law, Washington U., St. Louis, 1977. Bar: Utah 1978. Mem. staff Environ. Law Inst., Washington, 1977; spl. asst. atty. gen. for energy and natural resources, State of Utah, Salt Lake City, 1978-81; ptnr. Fabian and Clendenin, P.C., Salt Lake City, 1981—. Trustee, Salt Lake City Rape Crisis Ctr., 1975; mem. coal com. Western States Policy Office, 1980-81. Mem. Utah State Bar (chmn. oil and gas sect., natural resources com. 1981, environ. law com. 1978—, co-chmn. law related edn. and law day com., Natural Resources Lawyer of Yr. 1985, Disting. Service award 1986, 87), ABA (law day USA, Pub. Service award 1986, Rocky Mountain Mineral Law Assn., Utah Petroleum Assn., Utah Mining Assn. (pub. lands com.), Utah Bar and Gavel Soc. Contbr. articles on environ. law to profl. jours.; editorial bd. Jour. Contemporary Law, 1975-76. Environment, Mining and minerals. Home: 1826 Hubbard Ave Salt Lake City UT 84108 Office: Fabian & Clendenin 215 S State Suite 1220 Salt Lake City UT 84111

DRAKE, DAVID ALLEN, lawyer; b. Elkhart, Kans., Apr. 27, 1951; s. James Allen and Joy (Garrison) D.; m. Janet Lynn Giles, May 15, 1971; children: Justin David, Elisabeth Allyn. BA, U. Okla., 1973; JD, U. Tulsa, 1976. Bar: Okla. 1977, U.S. Dist. Ct. (we. dist.) Okla. 1981. Sole practice Perry, Okla., 1977-83; ptnr. Drake & Drake, Perry, 1983—; atty. City of Perry, 1979-81; asst. dist. atty. 8th jud. dist., Perry, 1981-82. Chmn. bd. dirs. United Way, Perry, 1977, pres. 1979. Mem. ABA, Okla. Bar Assn. (del. 1979, 85, lawyer referral com. 1984-85), Noble County Bar Assn. (pres. 1977-78, sec./treas. 1978-81), Phi Delta Phi. Republican. Avocations: astronomy, music. Banking, Oil and gas leasing, Probate. Home: 102 E Skyline Perry OK 73077 Office: Drake & Drake PC 319 7th St Perry OK 73077

DRAKE, E. THAYER, lawyer; b. Ridgewood, N.J., Jan. 19, 1923; s. Ervin T. and Elizabeth (Lum) D.; m. Jane Barbara Quist, July 20, 1946 (dec. July 1984); children: Anne B., Robert T. AB, Harvard U., 1944, LLB, 1949. Labor counsel CBS Inc., N.Y.C., 1952—. Mem. ABA (internat. labor law com.), N.Y. State Bar Assn., Assn. of Bar of City of N.Y. Republican. Clubs: Harvard (N.Y.C.); Harvard (Boston). Avocation: tennis. Labor. Office: CBS Inc Assoc Gen Counsel 51 W 52d St Room 687 New York NY 10019

DRAKEMAN, DONALD LEE, lawyer; b. Camden, N.J., Oct. 21, 1953; s. Fred J. and Jean (Faucett) D.; m. Lisa Natale Drakeman, Aug. 23, 1975; children: Cynthia, Amy. AB magna cum laude, Dartmouth Coll., 1975; JD, Columbia U., 1979; MA, Princeton U., 1984. Bar: N.J. 1979, U.S. Dist. Ct. N.J. 1979, N.Y. 1980, U.S. Supreme Ct. 1984. Assoc. Milbank, Tweed, Hadley & McCloy, N.Y.C., 1979-82; gen. counsel Essex Chem. Corp., Clifton, N.J., 1982—; adj. prof. polit. sci. Montclair (N.J.) State Coll., 1984. Co-editor Church and State in American History, 1986; contbr. articles to profl. jours. Chmn. Montclair Bd. Adjustment, 1984. Harlan Fiske Stone scholar, Columbia U., 1976-79. Mem. ABA, Assn. of Bar of City of N.Y., Nat. Council Chs. (religious liberty com.), Am. Corp. Counsel Assn., Am. Soc. Legal History, Am. Arbitration Assn. (arbitrator), Am. Acad. Religion. Republican. Episcopalian. General corporate, Constitutional-- church state. Home: 98 Magnolia Ln Princeton NJ 08540 Office: Essex Chem Corp 1401 Broad St Clifton NJ 07015

DRAKESMITH, FREDERICK WILLIAM, lawyer; b. Wiesbaden, W.Ger., Nov. 19, 1947 (parents Am. citizens); s. Charles Walter and Marion (Coleman) D.; m. Mary Margaret Tesno, Oct. 4, 1975; children—F. Matthew, Meredith Marie, Bradley Russell. B.A., U. Mo., 1970; J.D., St. Louis U., 1975. Bar: Mo. 1975, Calif. 1976, U.S. Dist. Ct. (no. dist.) Calif. 1976, U.S. Dist. Ct. (ea. dist.) Mo. 1976, U.S. Ct. Appeals (8th cir.) 1980. Assoc., Angell, Adams & Holmes, San Francisco, 1975-76, Cundiff, Turken & Londoff, St. Charles, No., 1976-79; ptnr. Cundiff, Turken, Londoff & Drakesmith, St. Charles, 1980-82; sole practice, St. Charles, 1983—; city atty., pros. atty. Village of Velda Village Hills, Mo., 1977-80; pros. atty. City of Lake Saint Louis, Mo., 1980—, St. Charles, 1984—; spl. pros. atty. Pros. Atty.'s Office, St. Charles County, 1978-79. Bd. dirs. Boone Ctr. Workshop, St. Charles, 1982—; chmn. campaign state rep., St. Charles, 1980. Mem. St. Charles County Bar Assn. (pres. 1982), ABA, Assn. Trial Lawyers Am., Mo. Trial Lawyers Assn., Bar Assn. Met. St. Louis. Democrat. Roman Catholic. Personal injury, State civil litigation, General corporate. Office: Law Office Frederick W Drakesmith 501 First Capitol Dr Suite 2 St Charles MO 63301

DRAN, ROBERT JOSEPH, lawyer; b. Abington, Pa., Apr. 12, 1947; s. Joseph A. and Claire B. (Kowalski) D.; m. Sandra Ann Hyatt, Aug. 16, 1969; children: Arjay, Stacy, Elizabeth. AB, Stanford U., 1969; JD, MBA, Harvard U., 1973. Bar: Calif. 1973, U.S. Dist. Ct. (cen. dist.) Calif. 1973. Assoc. Adams, Duque & Hazeltine, Los Angeles, 1973-75; assoc. gen. counsel Envirotech Corp., Menlo Park, Calif., 1975-79; mgr. legal dept. Cooper Labs. Inc., Palo Alto, Calif., 1979-82, assoc. gen. counsel, 1982-85, v.p., 1983-85; v.p., gen. counsel CooperVision Inc., Palo Alto, 1985—. Commr. Am. Youth Soccer Orgn., Redwood City, Calif., 1982-83; mgr., coach Little League Baseball, Redwood City and San Carlos, Calif., 1983—. Mem. Am. Corp. Counsel Assn., Peninsula Assn. Gen. Counsel. Republican. Roman Catholic. General corporate. Office: CooperVision Inc 3145 Porter Dr Palo Alto CA 94304

DRAPER, DANIEL CLAY, lawyer; b. Boston, June 7, 1920; s. John W. and Lulu H. (Clay) D.; m. Marjorie Walker, Dec. 22, 1950; children: John William, Elisabeth Orsini, Louise Antonia. BA, W.Va. U., 1940, MA, 1941; LLB, Harvard U., 1947. Assoc. Kelly, Drye & Warren, N.Y.C., 1947-55; ptnr. Cadwalader, Wickersham & Taft, N.Y.C., 1962—; bd. dirs. Union Devel., Montclair, N.J. Contbr. articles to profl. jours. Mgr. campaign Montclair's Community Com. Candidates, 1964; trustee Montclair Art Mus., 1966-71, Bloomfield Coll., Montclair, 1974-81, 87—. Served with USN, 1942-46. Decorated Bronze Star, European Service Ribbon (3 stars). Mem. N.Y. State Bar Assn. (chmn. banking com. 1981-85), Assn. of Bar of City of N.Y. (pres. young lawyers assn. 1984-86), N.Y. County Lawyers Assn. (pres. 1984-87, v.p. 1981-84, sec. 1978-81, chmn. banking com. 1968-78, housing and urban affairs and real property coms.), Am. Bar Council, Fed. Bar Council, St. George Soc. Episcopalian. Clubs: Harvard, N.Y.C. Downtown, THe Pilgrimds; Montclair Golf. Home: 124 Lloyd Rd Montclair NJ 07042 Office: Cadwalader, Wickersham & Taft 100 Maiden Ln New York NY 10038

DRAPER, MONETTE ELAINE, lawyer; b. Ft. Wayne, Ind., Feb. 22, 1952; d. Gordon Philip and Elinor Grace (Tussing) Putman; m. Thomas Wayne Draper, Oct. 28, 1972; 1 child, Michael Thomas. BA in English, Purdue U., 1974; JD, Ind. U., Indpls., 1980. Bar: Ind. 1980, U.S. Dist. Ct. (so. dist.) Ind. 1980, U.S. Ct. Claims 1984, U.S Tax Ct. 1985, U.S. Ct. Appeals (7th cir.) 1985. Legal editor R&R Newkirk, Indpls., 1980-81; sole practice Indpls., 1981-83, 83-84; ptnr. Pollen, Brazill, Impicciche & Bennet, Indpls., 1984-85; sole practice Whitestown, Ind., 1985—. Pro bono atty. St. Vincent's Stress Ctr. Hospice, 1982—; 1st v.p. Marion County Med. Soc. Aux., 1985—. Mem. ABA, Ind. Bar Assn., Indpls. Bar Assn. Club: Woodland Country (Carmel, Ind.). Estate taxation, Probate, Labor. Home and Office: Rural Rt #2 Box 188B Whitestown IN 46075

DRATLER, JAY, JR., lawyer, educator; b. Los Angeles, June 11, 1945; s. Jay Dratler and Berenice (Tolins) Eunson. AB in Physics, U. Calif., Berkeley, 1966; MS in Physics, U. Calif. San Diego, 1968, PhD in Physics, 1971; JD, Harvard U., 1978. Bar: Calif. 1978, U.S. Dist. Ct. (no. dist.) Calif. 1978, Hawaii 1987. Physicist Diax Corp., La Jolla, 1972-73; research scientist U. Calif., Berkeley, 1973-75; geophysicist U.S. Geol. Survey, Menlo Park, Calif., 1975; assoc. Morrison & Foerster, San Francisco, 1978-81, Fenwick, Davis & West, Palo Alto, Calif., 1981-86; assoc. prof. law U. Hawaii, Honolulu, 1986—; cons. York U., Downsview, Ont., Can., 1974, Geonomics, Inc., Berkeley, 1975, Fenwick, Davis & West, Palo Alto, Calif., 1986—. Articles editor Harvard U. Law Rev., 1976-78. Fellow NSF, 1966-70, NATO, 1971-72. Mem. AAAS, ABA (chmn. subcom. 1985—), Computer Law Assn., Sierra Club, Mensa, Phi Beta Kappa. Democrat. Jewish. Avocations: jogging, guitar, symphony, hiking, opera. Legal education, Trademark and copyright, Antitrust.

DRAUGHON, JOHN ALBERT, lawyer; b. Macon, Ga., Mar. 13, 1947; s. Elmo L. and Elizabeth (Glass) D.; m. Sally Hines, Aug. 31, 1968; children: Ashley, Jack. BBA, Emory U., 1969; JD, Mercer U., 1975; MBA, Ga. Coll., 1979. Bar" Ga. 1975, U.S. Dist. Ct. (mid. dist.) Ga. 1975, U.S. Ct. Appeals (5th cir.) 1975, U.S. Ct. Appeals (11th cir.) 1981. Assoc. Sell, Comer and Popper, Macon, 1975-78, ptnr., 1978-80; ptnr. Sell & Melton, Macon, 1980—; sec. Politex U.S. Inc., Macon, 1985—. Mem. Leadership Macon, 1982; pres. Macon Youth Found.; bd. dirs. Macon Health Ctr., 1980-85, Macon Bibb County Heart Assn., 1983-85; bd. dirs., spl. event chmn. Am. Cancer Soc., 1979. Served to 1st lt. USAF, 1969-72. Mem. ABA, Ga. Bar Assn., Macon Bar Assn. (ct. liaison 1986—), Assn. Trial Lawyers Am., Ga. Trial Lawyers Assn. Methodist. Clubs: Macon Civic, Idle Hour Country (Macon). Federal civil litigation, State civil litigation, General corporate. Home: 4768 Brae Burn Ln Macon GA 31210 Office: Sell & Melton 1414 Charter Med Bldg Macon GA 31297

DRAUGHON, SCOTT WILSON, lawyer, journalist, financial planner; b. Muskogee, Okla., June 17, 1952; s. Arthur Eugene and Helen Carrie (Vanhooser) D. AA, Tulsa Jr. Coll., 1972; BA, Okla. State U., 1974; JD, U. Tulsa, 1977; postgrad., Oxford U., Eng., 1978. Bar: Okla. 1979, U.S. Tax Ct. 1979, U.S. Dist. Ct. (no. dist.) Okla. 1980, U.S. Ct. Appeals (10th cir.) 1984, U.S. Supreme Ct. 1984. Sole practice Tulsa, 1979—; stockbroker Tenneco Fin. Services, Inc., 1983—; pvt. practice fin. planning Tulsa, 1984—; founder, exec. dir. The Fin. Hotline, Tulsa, 1984—; adj. faculty Tulsa Jr. Coll., 1986—. Fin. columnist The Tulsa Single Spirit, 1986. Bd. dirs. Arts and Humanities Council, Tulsa, 1982-83, Meals on Wheels, Tulsa, 1985, Internat. Council of Tulsa, 1987—; v.p. Family Action Ctr., Inc., Tulsa, 1984-85; adv. bd. Am. Indian Theatre Co., Tulsa, 1985, YWCA, Tulsa, 1985—, Okla. Tribal Assistance Program, 1985—; minority bus. enterprise com. Tulsa Human Rights Commn.; alumni community involvement com. Leadership Tulsa, Inc., 1985, mem. adv. com. Am. Indian Law Orgn., 1986—; candidate tribal counsel Cherokee Nation of Okla., 1987—; mem. adv. bd. Native Am. Communications and Career Devel., Inc. Mem. ABA, Nat. Assn. Accts., Okla. Bar Assn., Tulsa County Bar Assn., Phi Delta Phi, Leadership Tulsa IX. Republican. Methodist. Club: All-Am. Fitness (Tulsa). Lodges: Rotary, Masons, Shriners. Avocations: travel, golf, swimming, reading, acting. Labor, General corporate, Estate planning. Home: 9071 E 28th St Tulsa OK 74129 Office: PO Box 471280 Tulsa OK 74147-1280

DRAY, WILLIAM PERRY, lawyer; b. Cheyenne, Wyo., Sept. 20, 1940; s. George N. and Velda (Gamble) D.; m. Judy A. Gardner, Aug. 22, 1962; children—Todd, Lisa, Christopher. B.S., U. Wyo., 1962, J.D., 1964, LL.M., George Washington U., 1968. Bar: Wyo. 1965. law clk. Hirst, Applegate & Thomas, Cheyenne, Wyo., 1964-65, ptnr., 1968-75; sole practice, Cheyenne, 1975-76; ptnr. Dray, Madison & Thomson, P.C. (and predecessor firm), Cheyenne, Wyo., 1976—; dir. Unicover Corp., Unicover World Trade Corp., Unicover Internat. Sales Corp. Mem. Laramie County Republican Precinct Com., 1970-74. Mem. ABA, Wyo. State Bar Assn., Laramie County Bar Assn., Indsl. Devel. Assn., Am. Trial Lawyers Assn., Wyo. Trial Lawyers Assn., Def. Lawyers Assn. Wyo., Rocky Mountain Law Inst., Wyo. Estate Planning Council, Rocky Mountain Oil and Gas Assn., Am. Bankers Assn. Served with U.S. Army, 1965-68. Republican. Methodist. Clubs: Cheyenne Quarterback, Kiwanis. Estate taxation, Probate, General corporate. Office: Dray Madison & Thomson P C 204 E 22d St Cheyenne WY 82001

DRAZNIN, ANNE L., legal educator; b. Mpls., Mar. 25, 1945; s. Julius Nathan and Yaffa (Bernstein) D. BA, Earlham Coll., 1966; JD, U. Ill., Champaign, 1971. Bar: Ill., D.C., U.S. Dist. Ct. (no. dist.) Ill., U.S. Ct. Appeals (7th cir.), U.S. Supreme Ct. Trial atty. FTC, Chgo., 1972-76; sole practice Chgo., 1976-77; dir. legal services ABA, Chgo., 1977-81; regional dir. Am. Arbitration Assn., Chgo., 1981-82; prof. Sangamon State U., Springfield, Ill., 1982—; arbitrator, mediator, Chgo., 1982—; mem. arbitration panels Amer. Fed. State, County, Municipal Employees, Ill. Edn. Labor Relations Bd., Springfield, 1984-85, Ill. End. Labor Relations Bd., Springfield, 1984-85, Ind. Employment Labor Relations Bd., Fed. Mediation Conciliation Service. Mem. arbitration panel Cen. Ill. Dem. Women, Springfield, 1985. Fellow Chgo. Bar Found. (Maurice Weigle award for Service to Bar 1977); mem. ABA (labor law sect., chmn. subcom. alts. to litigation), Chgo. Bar Assn. (chmn. arbitration com. 1984-85), Indsl. Relations Research Assn. (pres. cen. ill. chpt. 1983-85, sec. 1985—), Soc. for Profls. in Dispute Resolution, Nat. Assn. of Concilliators, Mont. Arbitration Assn., Am. Arbitration Assn., Endispute, Inc., Cen. Ill. Women's Bar Assn. (treas. 1986-87). Arbitration and mediation, Labor, Legal education. Home: 1122 W Edwards Springfield IL 62704 Office: Sangamon State U Public Affairs Center 482 Springfield IL 62708

DREBSKY, DENNIS JAY, lawyer; b. N.Y.C., Sept. 28, 1946; s. Benjamin and Ronnie (Penso) D.; m. Norma Louise Linschitz, Aug. 16, 1970; children:

Richard Michael, Joshua William Evan. BBA magna cum laude, CCNY, 1967; JD, Cornell U., 1970. Bar: N.Y. 1971, U.S. Ct. Appeals (2d cir.) 1971, U.S. Dist. Ct. (so. dist.) N.Y. 1972, U.S. Ct. Appeals (5th cir.) 1980, U.S. Ct. Appeals (1st cir.) 1981, U.S. Ct. Appeals (10th cir.) 1984, U.S. Ct. Appeals (4th cir.) 1986. Assoc. Skadden, Arps, Slate, Meagher & Flom, N.Y.C., 1970-77, ptnr., 1978—; trustee Community Law Offices, N.Y.C., 1980—. Mem. Assn. of Bar of City of N.Y. (mem. com. on corp. reorgn. 1985—). Jewish. Avocations: reading, jogging, theater. General corporate, Corporate litigation, Bankruptcy. Home: 7 Glen Hill Ct Dix Hill NY 11746-4819 Office: Skadden Arps Slate Meagher & Flom 919 3d Ave New York NY 10022-9931

DRENGLER, WILLIAM ALLAN JOHN, lawyer; b. Shawano, Wis., Nov. 18, 1949; s. William J. and Vera J. (Simmonds) D.; m. Kathleen A. Hintz, June 18, 1983; 1 child, Ryan. BA, Am. U., 1972; JD, Marquette U., 1976. Bar: Wis. 1976, U.S. Dist. Ct. (ea. and we. dists.) Wis. 1976. Assoc. Herrling, Swain & Drengler, Appleton, Wis., 1976-78; dist. atty. Outagamie County, Appleton, 1979-81; corp. counsel Marathon County, Wausau, Wis., 1981—; vice chmn. Wis. Council on Criminal Justice, Madison, 1983—. Nat. delegation Dems., 1974-76; mem. adminstrv. com. Wis. Dems., Madison, 1977-81, 86—; chmn. local Selective Service Bd., Wausau, 1983—. Mem. ABA, Wis. Bar Assn. (bd. dirs. 1982-86, sec. 1986-87, pres.-elect 1987—). Democrat. Roman Catholic. Lodges: Kiwanis (lt. gov. 1985-86); Elks K.C. Avocations: baseball, softball, camping, fishing, gardening. Local government, General practice, Legislative. Office: Marathon County 500 Forest Wausau WI 54401

DRENNAN, D. JANE, lawyer; b. Champaign, Ill., Mar. 4, 1944; d. Walter E. and Marcella (Cavanaugh) Judson; m. William W. Sproul III; children: Judson W., James B. BA, Ind. U., 1965, JD, 1969; LLM, Georgetown U., 1975. Bar: Ind., D.C., U.S. Supreme Ct. Asst. to gen. counsel Fed. Power Commn., Washington, 1972-73; gen. counsel for policy Fed. Property Council, Washington, 1973-74; spl. asst. Fed. Power Commn., Washington, 1974-76; atty. FERC, Washington, 1976-79; ptnr. McDermott, Will & Emery, Washington, 1979-82, Pillsbury, Madison & Sutro, Washington, 1982—. Mem. FERC Transition Team, Pres. Elect Reagan, Wsahington, 1980-81, Presidential Pvt. Sector Task Force, Washington, 1982. Mem. ABA (chmn. adminstrv. law sect., natural resources law and pub. utility law sects.), Fed. Energy Bar Assn. (exec. council 1981-84). Club: Georgetown (Washington). FERC practice, Administrative and regulatory, Public utilities. Home: 9406 Brooke Dr Bethesda MD 20817 Office: Pillsbury Madison & Sutro 1667 K St NW Suite 1100 Washington DC 20006

DRENNAN, JOSEPH PETER, lawyer; b. Albany, N.Y., Apr. 15, 1956; s. Richard Peter and Ann Marie (Conlon) D. BA in Polit. Sci., U. Richmond, 1978; JD, Cath. U. of Am., Washington, 1981. Bar: D.C. 1981, U.S. Dist. Ct. D.C. 1983, U.S. Ct. Appeals (fed. cir.) 1983, Va. 1984, U.S. Ct. Appeals (D.C. cir.) 1984, U.S. Dist. Ct. (no. dist.) Va. 1987, U.S. Ct. Appeals (4th cir.) 1987. Sole practice Washington, 1981—. Mem. ABA, Assn. Trial Lawyers Am., Bar Assn. D.C. Republican. Roman Catholic. Personal injury, Federal civil litigation, Jurisprudence. Home: 1215 N Fort Myer Dr 704 Arlington VA 22209-3509 Office: 1420 16th St NW Washington DC 20036-2218

DRENTH, THOMAS LEE, lawyer; b. Charlevoix, Mich., Feb. 10, 1948; s. Henry John and Jennette Berndina (Ter Avest) D.; m. Carol Lee Wittenbach, Aug. 17, 1979; children: Todd William, Cori Lee. BA, Mich. State U., 1970; JD, U. Mich., 1973; MST, Grand Valley State Coll., 1982. Bar: Mich. 1973, U.S. Dist. Ct. (we. dist.) Mich. 1973, U.S. Ct. Appeals (6th cir.) 1973. Assoc. Clary, Nantz, Wood, Hoffius, Rankin & Cooper, Grand Rapids, Mich., 1973-79; mem. Clary, Nantz, Wood, Hoffius, Rankin & Cooper, Grand Rapids, 1979—. Deacon 1st Park Congl. Ch., Grand Rapids, 1983-86. Mem. Grand Rapids Jaycees (legal counsel 1977-78), Mich. State U. Alumni Club West Mich. (v.p. 1978-84). Republican. Mem. United Ch. Christ. Club: Les Amis Du Vin (Grand Rapids). Avocations: golf, reading. Labor. Home: 122 Forest Hill SE Grand Rapids MI 49506 Office: Clary Nantz Wood Hoffius et al 500 Calder Plaza Bldg Grand Rapids MI 49503

DRESCHER, ANN MARIE, lawyer; b. Scarsdale, N.Y., Feb. 19; d. Gustave O. and Mary Catherine (Sullivan) D. B.A., Coll. New Rochelle, 1960; J.D., Fordham U., 1963; LL.M., NYU, 1967. Bar: N.Y. 1964, Ga. 1981, N.J. 1982, U.S. Supreme Ct. 1971. Assoc. Edward F. Sweeney, N.Y.C., 1964-69; asst. to nat. exec. dir. and nat. bd. dirs. Girl Scouts U.S.A., N.Y.C., 1967-70; dir. youth div. Keep Am. Beautiful, N.Y.C., 1970-71; atty. AT&T, N.Y.C., 1971-79, gen. atty. so. region, Atlanta, 1979—. Mem. ABA, Ga. Bar Assn., N.J. Bar Assn., N.Y. State Bar Assn. Clubs: Ansley, Women's Commerce. General corporate, Federal civil litigation, Public utilities. Office: 1200 Peachtree St Room 4072 Atlanta GA 30309

DRESNER, BYRON, lawyer; b. N.Y.C., Nov. 13, 1927; s. Leo and Minnie (Plisner) D.; m. Irene Helen Dresner, Nov. 18, 1956; children—Lisa, Cheryl, Andrea. B.S.S., CCNY, 1949; LL.B., NYU, 1951. Bar: N.Y. 1952, U.S. Supreme Ct. 1961, U.S. Ct. Appeals (2d cir.), U.S. Dist. Ct. (no., so., ea. dists.) N.Y. Assoc. Alexander Rockmore, N.Y.C., 1952-57; ptnr. Kronish, Dresner & Henle, 1957-66, Dresner & Henle, N.Y.C., 1966—; spl. master N.Y. State Supreme Ct., 1977—. Chmn., Anti-Defamation League Young Adults, 1954-55; treas. Maspeth Jewish Ctr., 1959-71; pres., trustee Flushing Jewish Ctr., 1971—; exec. v.p. Queens Jewish Community Council, 1981-84, pres., 1984—; bd. dirs. YMHA-YWHA, Flushing, 1979—. Served with AUS, 1946-47. Mem. Bankruptcy Lawyers Bar Assn., N.Y. County Lawyers Assn., Brandeis Assn., Comml. Law League Am. Clubs: Camera, B'nai B'rith. Bankruptcy, General corporate, Real property. Home: 45-57 189th St Flushing NY 11358 Office: 419 Park Ave S #1206 New York NY 10016

DRESSER, RAYMOND H., JR., lawyer; b. Sturgis, Mich., Feb. 23, 1931; s. Raymond H. and Lola (Juckette) D.; m. Gretchen G. Meier, Aug. 7, 1954; children—John, Amy, Marcia. B.A. cum laude, Amherst Coll., 1953; J.D., U. Mich., 1956. Bar: Mich. 1956, U.S. Dist. Ct. (we. dist.) Mich. 1958, U.S. Ct. Appeals (6th cir.) 1958. Ptnr. Dresser & Dresser et al, Sturgis, 1956-85; sr. ptnr. Dresser Law Office P.C., Sturgis, 1986—; city atty. City of Sturgis, 1962—. Bd. dirs. Mich. Assn. Professions, 1981-85; bd. dirs. Glen Oaks Community Coll. Found., Jane A. Sturges Meml. Home Assn., Sturgis, Econ. Devel. Corp. Sturgis; elder Sturgis Presbyn. Ch. Fellow Am. Coll. Probate Counsel; mem. Am. Judicature Soc., ABA, State Bar Mich. (bd. dirs. 1980—, treas. 1985—). Republican. Clubs: Klinger Lake Country (pres. 1978) (Sturgis); Rotary (pres. 1960-61), KT, Elks, Masons, Shriners. Probate, General corporate, Corporate taxation. Office: 112 S Monroe St Sturgis MI 49091

DRESSLER, ROBERT A., lawyer; b. Fort Lauderdale, Fla., Aug. 20, 1945; s. R. Philip and Elisabeth (Anthony) D.; m. Patricia Kate Toth, Nov. 7, 1981; 1 child, James Philip. A.B. cum laude, Dartmouth Coll.; J.D. cum laude, Harvard U. Bar: Fla. 1974, Mass. 1973, D.C. 1980, U.S. Dist. Ct. (so. dist.) Fla., U.S. Dist. Ct. Mass., U.S. Ct. Appeals (1st cir.), U.S. Ct. Appeals (5th cir.), U.S. Supreme Ct. Assoc. Goodwin, Proctor & Hoar, Boston, 1973-75; ptnr. Dressler & Dressler, Ft. Lauderdale, 1975-82, English, McCaughan & O'Bryan, Ft. Lauderdale, 1982—; mayor City of Ft. Lauderdale, 1982-86. Vice chmn. Broward Tng. and Employment Adminstrn., Ft. Lauderdale, 1982-86; bd. dirs. Broward County League of Cities, 1985-86; nat. committeeman Fla. Fedn. Young Republicans, 1981-83. Served to capt. USMC, 1969-72. Mem. Greater Ft. Lauderdale County C. of C. (bd. dirs. 1982-86, 87—), ABA, Broward County Bar Assn. (mem. legis. com. 1983-85), Estate Planning Council Broward County, Fla. Bar, D.C. Bar, Vietnam Vets. Am., Phi Beta Kappa. Presbyterian. Clubs: Drummers; Tower (bd. govs. 1983-86). Lodge: Kiwanis. Avocations: jogging, scuba diving, hiking. Estate planning, Probate, Local government. Home: 1608 NE 6th St Fort Lauderdale FL 33304 Office: English McCaughan & O'Bryan PO Box 14098 Fort Lauderdale FL 33302

DREXLER, KENNETH, lawyer; b. San Francisco, Aug. 2, 1941; s. Fred and Martha Jane (Cunningham) D.; BA, Stanford U., 1963; JD, UCLA, 1969. Bar: Calif. 1970. Assoc., David S. Smith, Beverly Hills, Calif., 1970, McCutchen, Doyle, Brown and Enersen, San Francisco, 1970-77; assoc. Chickering & Gregory, San Francisco, 1977-80, ptnr., 1980-82; ptnr. Drexler & Leach, San Rafael, Calif., 1982—. Served with AUS, 1964-66. Mem. ABA, Calif. State Bar (resolutions com. conf. of dels. 1979-83, chmn. 1982-83, adminstrn. justice com. 1983—), Marin County Bar Assn. (bd. dirs. 1985—), Bar Assn. San Francisco (dir. 1980-81), San Francisco Barristers Club (pres. 1976, dir. 1975-76), Marin Conservation League (bd. dirs. 1985—). State civil litigation, Family and matrimonial, General practice. Office: 1330 Lincoln Ave Suite 300 San Rafael CA 94901

DREXLER, MARK ANDREW, lawyer; b. Rochester, N.Y., Mar. 14, 1953; s. Sheldon Francis and Rhea (Lipchitz) D. BA magna cum laude, SUNY, Buffalo, 1975; JD, Cornell U., 1979. Bar: N.Y. 1980, U.S. Dist. Ct. (we. dist.) N.Y. 1982. Assoc. Friedman & Greenfield, Rochester, 1979-83; ptnr. Brent & Drexler, Rochester, 1983—; bd. dirs. Farmworkers Legal Services N.Y. Inc., Rochester. atty. Vol. Lawyers for Arts, Rochester, 1980—; bd. dirs. N.Y. Civil Liberties Union. Mem. ABA, N.Y. State Bar Assn., Monroe County Bar Assn., Omicron Delta Epsilon. Real property, Consumer commercial, Family and matrimonial. Office: Brent & Drexler 30 W Broad St Suite 301 Rochester NY 14614

DREYER, HAROLD EMIL, lawyer, consultant; b. Wayne County, Nebr., Dec. 24, 1920; s. Paul Martin and Augusta (Splittgerber) D.; m. Irene Starkel, Feb. 19, 1943; children—Thomas, Douglas, James. B.S., U. Nebr., 1942; Ph.D., MIT, 1952; J.D., Suffolk U., 1964. Bar: Mass. 1964. Orgn. and methods examiner VA, St. Louis, 1946-48; personnel adminstr. MIT, Cambridge, 1951-73; personnel adminstr. C.S. Draper Lab., Inc., Cambridge, 1973-80, cons., 1980—; sole practice, Belmont, Mass., 1964—; faculty Suffolk U. Law Sch., Boston, 1965—. Mem. Belmont Personnel Bd., 1974-77; bd. dirs., chmn. personnel com. Mass. Easter Seal Soc., 1970—. Served with QMC, AUS, 1943-46. Mem. ABA, Mass. Bar Assn., Middlesex Bar Assn., Am. Mgmt. Assn., Am. Arbitration Assn., Phi Beta Kappa, Beta Gamma Sigma, Pi Mu Epsilon. Lutheran. Pension, profit-sharing, and employee benefits, Probate, Real property. Address: 437 Trapelo Rd Belmont MA 02178

DREYSPOOL, ANTHONY ALAN, lawyer; b. N.Y.C., Mar. 10, 1945; s. A. Anthony Dreyspool and Jeanne (Cohen) Bourg; m. Phyllis Cooper, Sept. 12, 1981. AB, U. Pa., 1967, JD, 1970. Bar: N.Y. 1971, U.S. Dist. Ct. (so. dist.) N.Y. 1980, U.S. Ct. Appeals (2d cir.) 1980. Assoc. Dewey, Ballantine, Bushby, Palmer & Wood, N.Y.C., 1970-74; sr. atty. J.C. Penney Co., N.Y.C., 1974-82; v.p., counsel Equitable Life Ins. Co., N.Y.C., 1982—. Phi Beta Kappa. Pension, profit-sharing, and employee benefits. Office: Equitable Life Ins Co 787 7th Ave New York NY 10019

DRIGGS, CHARLES MULFORD, lawyer; b. East Cleveland, Ohio, Jan. 26, 1924; s. Karl Holcomb and Lila Vandeveer (Wilson) D.; m. Jean Ellen Johnson, Nov. 16, 1974; children: Ruth, Rachel, Carrie, Karl H. Charles M. B.S., Yale U., 1947, J.D., 1950. Bar: Ohio 1951. Assoc. Squire, Sanders & Dempsey, Cleve., 1950-64, ptnr., 1964—. Pres. Bratenahl Sch. Bd., Ohio, 1958-62; pres. bd. trustees Unity Ch. of Christianity 1978—; mem. adv. council Cleve. Ctr. Theol. Edn., 1978—. Mem. ABA, Ohio Bar Assn., Bar Assn. Greater Cleve., Greater Cleve. Growth Assn., Cleve. Law Library Assn. (trustee 1977—), Ct. Nisi Prius, Citizens League Greater Cleve., Phi Delta Phi, Tau Beta Pi, Phi Gamma Delta. Probate, Estate taxation. Home: 350 Wilson Mills Rd Chardon OH 44024 Office: Squire Sanders & Dempsey 1800 Huntington Bldg Cleveland OH 44115

DRIKS, JORDAN JOSEPH, lawyer; b. N.Y.C., Oct. 7, 1931; s. Max and Rose (Friedland) D.; m. Ellen Clair Haber, Sept. 29, 1956; children—Alicia, Michele, Eric. B.S. in Chemistry, Bklyn. Coll., 1955; J.D., Bklyn. Law Sch., 1960. Bar: N.Y. 1960, U.S. Patent Office 1963, U.S. Ct. Customs and Patent Appeals 1964, U.S. Ct. Appeals (D.C. cir.) 1983. Patent atty. Colgate-Palmolive Co., N.Y.C., 1962-66, Borden, Inc., N.Y.C., 1966-68, M.W. Kellogg Co., N.Y.C., 1968-69; patent counsel Witco Chem. Co., N.Y.C., 1969-76; sr. atty. Rohm and Haas Co., Phila., 1977—; patent and trademark counsel Chem. Mfrs. Assn., Washington, 1982—; observer Bd. dirs. Fedn. Housing, 1986—. Commr. Ramapo Housing Authority, N.Y., 1974-76, chmn., 1976-77; pres. Viola Civic Assn., Monsey, N.Y., 1970; committeeman Rockland County Democratic Com., New City, N.Y., 1969-77. Recipient Resolution of Appreciation, Ramapo Town Council, 1977, Plaque of Appreciation, Ramapo Housing Authority, 1977. Mem. Licensing Exec. Soc., N.Y. Patent Law Assn. (vice-chmn. employment com. 1972-74). Democrat. Patent. Home: 284 Melrose Ave Merion PA 19066 Office: Rohm and Haas Co Independence Mall W Philadelphia PA 19105

DRINAN, ROBERT FREDERICK, lawyer, Congressman, educator, clergyman; b. Boston, Nov. 15, 1920; s. James Joseph and Ann Mary (Flanagan) D. A.B., Boston Coll., 1942, M.A., 1947; LL.B., Georgetown U., 1949, LL.M., 1950; Th.D., Gregorian U., Rome, 1954; study, Florence, Italy, 1954-55; LL.D., Worcester State Coll., 1970, L.I. U., 1970, R.I. Coll., 1971, St. Joseph's Coll., Phila., 1975, Syracuse U., 1977, Villanova U., 1977, Framingham (Mass.) State Coll., 1978, U. Santa Clara, 1980, Kenyon Coll., 1981, Lowell U., 1981, U. Bridgeport, 1981, Loyola U., Chgo., 1981, Gonzaga U., 1981, Curry Coll., 1982, De Paul U., 1984, U. San Diego, 1984, Mt. St. Mary Coll., 1985, Hebrew Coll., 1987. Bar: D.C. 1950, U.S. Supreme Ct. 1955, Mass. 1956. Entered S.J., 1942; ordained priest Roman Cath. Ch., 1953; asst. dean Boston Coll. Law Sch., 1955-56, dean, 1956-70; vis. prof. U. Tex. Law Sch., 1966-67; mem. 92d-96th congresses from 4th Dist. Mass.; mem. jud. com., govt. ops. com., house select com. on aging, chmn. subcom. on criminal justice; columnist Nat. Cath. Reporter, 1980; prof. Law Center, Georgetown U., Washington, 1981—; Chmn. adv. com. Mass. U.S. Commn. Civil Rights, 1962-70; mem. vis. com. Div. Sch., Harvard U., 1975-78; bd. dirs. Bread for the World; founder Nat. Interreligious Task Force on Soviet Jewry.; Mem. exec. com. Assn. Am. Law Schs. Author: Religion, the Courts and Public Policy, 1963, Democracy, Dissent and Disorder, 1969, Vietnam and Armageddon, 1970, Honor the Promise, America's Commitment to Israel, 1977, Beyond the Nuclear Freeze, 1983. Editor: The Right To Be Educated, 1968, God and Caesar on the Potomac, 1985, Cry of the Oppressed: The History and Hope of the Human Rights Revolution, 1987; editor-in-chief: Family Law Quar, 1967-70; contbr. editor: nat. Cath. weekly America, 1958-70. Contbr. articles to jours. of opinion. Fellow Am. Acad. Arts and Scis.; mem. ABA, Mass. Bar Assn. (v.p. 1961), Boston Bar Assn., Am. Law Inst., Ams. for Dem. Action (pres. 1981-84), NCCJ (nat. trustee), Common Cause (nat. governing bd. 1981-86). Office: Georgetown U Law Center 600 New Jersey Ave NW Washington DC 20001

DRISCOLL, KATHLEEN ELIZABETH, lawyer; b. Worcester, Mass., Dec. 29, 1920; d. Patrick and Delia (McInerney) D. AB, Boston U., 1942, JD, 1951. Bar: D.C. 1951. Atty. Liberty Mut. Ins. Co., Boston, 1951-56, from asst. counsel to assoc. counsel, 1956-84, counsel, 1984—. Served with USCG, 1944-46. Mem. ABA, Women Lawyers Mass. Workers' compensation. Office: Liberty Mut Ins Co 175 Berkeley St Boston MA 02117

DRISCOLL, MICHAEL HARDEE, county attorney; b. Houston, Mar. 24, 1946; s. Victor Amadale and Inez Mildred (Hardee) D. B.B.A., U. Houston, 1969, J.D., 1972. Bar: Tex. 1972. Precinct judge Harris County, Tex., 1969-73; justice of peace Harris County, Tex., 1973-78; judge City of Friendswood, Tex., 1978-80; hearing judge Tex. Edn. Agy., 1978-80; ptnr. Burge, Shults & Driscoll, Houston, 1978-80; elected county atty. Harris County, Houston, 1980—. Bd. dirs. Bay Area Drug Abuse Com., 1975-80, Riverside Gen. Hosp., 1977-80; mem. Salvation Army Boys' Club Adv. Council. Mem. State Bar Tex., Houston Bar Assn., Tex. Dist. and County Attys. Assn. (bd. dirs.), Houston C. of C. Democrat. Baptist. Lodges: Rotary, Scottish Rite, Shriners (Houston.). State civil litigation, Criminal. Office: County Atty's Office 1001 Preston Houston TX 77002

DRISCOLL, NEIL JOSEPH, III, lawyer; b. Chgo., Nov. 14, 1948; s. Neil Joseph and Regina Frances (Golden) D.; m. Linda Rae Fallon, June 30, 1973; children—Amelia Tara, Ethan Hancock. B.S., Portland State U., 1974; J.D., Lewis & Clark Law Sch., 1977. Bar: Oreg. 1978, U.S. Dist. Ct. Oreg. 1978, U.S. Tax Ct. 1982. Sole practice, Portland, Oreg., 1980—. Served with U.S. Army, 1971-72. Decorated Air medal, Purple Heart, U.S. Army Commendation medal, Armed Forces Honor medal (Vietnam). Mem. Oreg. Bar Assn., Multnomah Bar Assn. Republican. Club: Willamette Athletic (Portland). Home: 63 Aquinas Lake Oswego OR 97035 Office: 3405 SW Barbur Blvd Portland OR 97201

DRISCOLL, PATRICK THOMAS, JR., lawyer; b. Chgo., Oct. 30, 1942. B.S., Regis Coll., 1964; J.D., DePaul U., 1967. Bar: Ill. 1967, U.S. Dist. Ct. (no. dist.) Ill. 1967, U.S. Ct. Appeals (7th cir.) 1969, U.S. Supreme Ct. 1971. Asst. corp. counsel City of Chgo., 1968; asst. state's atty. Cook County (Ill.), 1968-74, chief appeals div., 1973-74, spl. asst. state's atty., 1976, 78, spl. state's atty., 1983; ptnr. Patrick T. Driscoll, Jr., P.C., Chgo., 1978—; mem. com. to study delay in criminal appeals Ill. Supreme Ct., 1984—, Inquiry Bd.; atty. registration and disciplinary com. Ill. Supreme Ct. Mem. ABA (appellate practice com. of litigation sect.), Ill. Bar Assn. (assembly 1979-85, chmn. unauthorized practice of law com. 1983-84; mem. Fellows Ill. Bar Found.), Chgo. Bar Assn. (criminal law com. 1969-82, evaluation of candidates 1978-83, tort litigation com. 1975-76, jud. evaluation com. 1984—), Ill. Trial Lawyers Assn. (criminal law com. 1982—), Assn. Trial Lawyers Am., Appellate Lawyers Assn. (dir. 1977-79), Am. Arbitration Assn. (panel). Contbr. articles to legal jours. State civil litigation, Criminal, Personal injury. Home: 1408 Elizabeth Ln Glenview IL 60025 Office: 77 W Washington St Suite 916 Chicago IL 60602

DRISCOLL, ROBERT GEORGE, lawyer; b. Newport, R.I., Sept. 1, 1949; s. George Albert and Eloise Mae (Phillips) D.; m. Gay Carpenter, July 29, 1978. AB, Brown U., 1971; JD, U. Maine, 1976. Bar: R.I. 1976. Sole practice Portsmouth and Middletown, R.I., 1976—; solicitor Town of Portsmouth, R.I., 1978-80. Mem. Portsmouth Town Council, R.I., 1982—, v.p., 1984—. Mem. ABA, R.I. Bar Assn. Republican. Episcopalian. Lodges: Lions, Masons. Real property, Family and matrimonial, Local government. Home: 116 Emmanuel Dr Portsmouth RI 02871 Office: 314 Oliphant Ln Middletown RI 02040

DRIVER, ALBERT WESTCOTT, JR., chain store executive; b. Bridgeport, Conn., Aug. 4, 1927; s. Albert W. and Bessie (Ferns) D.; m. Martha Lou Miller, Aug. 5, 1951; children: Martha, Sara. B.A., Yale, 1949; LL.B., U. Va., 1952. Bar: N.Y. 1952. Assoc. Cravath, Swaine & Moore, N.Y.C., 1952-60; asst. gen. counsel J.C. Penney Co., Inc., 1961-78, asst. sec., 1964-69, sec., 1969-74, 78—, v.p., 1974-81, gen. counsel, 1978—, sr. v.p., 1981—. Served with USNR, 1945. Fellow Am. Bar Found.; mem. ABA (corp., banking and bus. law sect., mem. com. on corp. law depts., chmn. 1977-79, com. on law and acctg., sect. planning rev. com., com. on corp. laws, com. on regulatory reform, com. on counsel responsibility and liability, litigation sect., com. on corp. counsel), N.Y. State Bar Assn. (exec. com. banking, corp. and bus. law sect., chmn. 1978-79, mem. bus. law com., chmn. 1977-78, task force on simplification), Assn. Bar City N.Y. (chmn. com. on corp. law depts. 1982-85), Nat. Retail Mchts. Assn. (mem. govt. and legal affairs com., chmn. 1977-79, mem. lawyers com., chmn. 1972-73). General corporate. Home: PO Box 268 Allamuchy NJ 07820 Office: JC Penney Co Inc 1301 Ave of the Americas New York NY 10019

DROST, MARIANNE, lawyer; b. Waterbury, Conn., Feb. 21, 1950; s. Albin Joseph and Henrietta Jean (Kremski) D. BA, Conn. Coll., 1972; JD, U. Conn., 1975. Bar: Conn. 1975. Assoc. Ritter, Tapper & Totten, Hartford, Conn., 1975-77; sr. atty. GTE Service Corp., Stamford, Conn., 1977-84, Chesebrough-Pond's Inc., Greenwich, Conn., 1984-85; corp. sec. GTE Corp., Stamford, 1985—. Tutor Literacy Vols., Stamford, 1985—. Mem. ABA, Am. Soc. Corp. Secs., Westchester-Fairfield County Corp. Counsel Assn. Democrat. Roman Catholic. Avocations: ballet, hiking, reading. General corporate, Securities. Office: GTE Corp 1 Stamford Forum Stamford CT 06904

DROWOTA, FRANK F., III, state supreme court justice; b. Williamsburg, Ky., July 7, 1938; (married); 2 children. B.A., Vanderbilt U., 1960, J.D., 1965. Practice law 1965-70; chancellor Tenn. Chancery Ct. Div. 7, 1970-74; judge Tenn. Ct. Appeals, Middle Tenn. Div., 1974-80; asso. justice Tenn. Supreme Ct., 1980—. Served with USN, 1960-62. State civil litigation, General practice, Criminal. Office: 311 Supreme Ct Bldg Nashville TN 37219

DROZDA, ROBERT LEE, lawyer; b. Omaha, June 19, 1954; s. Joseph Peter Sr. and Carroll Ann (McCreery) D.; m. Sue Ellen Wintz, June 12, 1982; children: Jennifer Lee, Phillip Richard. BSBA in Acctg., U. Nebr., Omaha, 1976; JD, Creighton U., 1980. Bar: Nebr. 1980, U.S. Dist. Ct. Nebr. 1980, U.S. Tax Ct. 1986. Mgr. tax dept. Peat, Marwick, Mitchell and Co., Omaha, 1980-84; mgr. tax planning Union Pacific R.R. Co., Omaha, 1984—; instr. U. Nebr., Omaha, 1981-83, 86. Sub chmn. Am. Cancer Soc., Omaha, 1981-83. Fellow Nebr. Soc. CPA's, ABA, Nebr. State Bar Assn., Am. Inst. CPA's. Republican. Roman Catholic. Clubs: Omaha Field, Omaha Raquetball. Avocations: softball, basketball, music, parenting. Corporate taxation, State and local taxation, Personal income taxation. Home: 4412 Woolworth Ave Omaha NE 68105 Office: Union Pacific RR Co 1416 Dodge St Norchem Room 301 Omaha NE 68179

DRUCKER, LEONARD MURRAY, lawyer; b. Hartford, Conn., Mar. 10, 1953; s. Jacob and Alice (Cahn) D.; m. Gail E. Wollman, June 14, 1981; children: Carol Ann, Rachel Jessie. BA, U. Conn., 1975; JD, U. Bridgeport, 1980. Bar: Conn. 1980, U.S. Dist. Ct. Conn. 1980, Mass. 1980, N.H. 1981. Sole practice Belmont, N.H., 1981—. Mem. Planning Bd., Belmont, 1982—, chmn., 1986—. Mem. ABA, N.H. Bar Assn. Democrat. Jewish. Avocations: radio, snow skiing, boating. General practice, Family and matrimonial, Juvenile. Office: 34 Main St PO Box 693 Belmont NH 03220

DRUKER, JAMES OWEN, lawyer; b. Cambridge, Mass., Apr. 9, 1942; s. Melvin and Charlotte (Zelermyer) D.; m. Joan Eleanora Smith, June 9, 1968; children—Scott Michael, Brian Daniel. A.B. in Polit. Sci., U. N.C., 1963; J.D., Boston Coll. Law, 1969. Bar: Mass. 1969, U.S. Ct. Appeals (1st cir.) 1969, U.S. Supreme Ct. 1973, U.S. Ct. Appeals (2d cir.) 1974, N.Y. 1974, Fla. 1979. Dep. asst. atty. gen. Dept. Atty. Gen. Mass., 1969-70; spl. atty. U.S. Dept. Justice, Washington, 1970-73; asst. U.S. atty., chief spl. prosecutions Eastern Dist. N.Y., Bklyn., 1974-75; asst. dist. atty. chief rackets, Nassau County, N.Y., Mineola, 1976-78; mng. ptnr. Kase & Druker, Garden City, N.Y., 1978—; lectr. in field. Recipient Meritorious Service award Justice Dept., 1974. Mem. ABA, Fla. Bar Assn., Mass. Bar Assn., N.Y. State Bar Assn., Nassau County Bar Assn. Personal income taxation, Criminal. Home: 140 West End Ave 11C New York NY 10023 Office: Kase & Druker 1325 Franklin Ave Suite 225 Garden City NY 11530

DRUMM, FRANCIS JOSEPH, JR., chief clerk of courts; b. Bronx, N.Y., Mar. 26, 1946; s. Francis Joseph Sr. and Mary (Tobin) D.; m. Susan M. Cormier, Oct. 18, 1986; children: Francis III, Bethany. AA, Greater Hartford Community Coll., 1974; BS, Cen. Conn. State U., 1977; JD, U. Conn., 1981. Bar: Conn. 1981. Enlisted USN, 1963, released from active duty, 1971; adminstrv. asst. Supreme Ct. Conn., Hartford, 1971-79, 1st asst. clk., 1979-83; chief clk. Supreme and Appellate Cts., Hartford, 1983—. Served with USNR, 1971—. Mem. ABA, Conn. Bar Assn., Nat Conf. Appelate Ct. Clks. Avocations: jogging, team sports. State civil litigation, Judicial administration. Office: Supreme Ct Conn 231 Capitol Ave Hartford CT 06106

DRUMMOND, DONALD FRANCIS, educational administrator; b. Kalamazoo, Sept. 24, 1917; s. Merle Vaughn and Phyllis (DeWindt) D.; m. Elizabeth Ruth Biddle, Aug. 30, 1944; 1 son, Robert Ward. A.B., Western Mich. U., 1938; A.M., U. Mich., 1939, Ph.D., 1949. Instr., asst. prof. history U. Mich., Ann Arbor, 1948-57; prof. history SUNY-Geneseo, 1957-58; head dept. history and social scis. Eastern Mich. U., Ypsilanti, 1958-65, dean Coll. Arts and Scis., 1965-77, 79—, interim v.p. for acad. affairs, 1977-79. Author: Passing of American Neutrality, 1937-41, 1955; co-author: Five Centuries in America, 1964. Served with U.S. Army, 1941-45. Mem. Phi Beta Kappa, Phi Kappa Phi. Republican. Club: Forum (pres. 1971-72). Federal civil litigation, State civil litigation. Home: 1813 Waltham Dr Ann Arbor MI 48103 Office: Eastern Mich U Ypsilanti MI 48197

DRUMMOND, DONALD FRANCIS, lawyer; b. Kansas City, Mo., Apr. 7, 1946; s. Donald Holland and Francis Elizabeth (Woodruff) D.; m. Page Wedlake, Dec. 28, 1973; children: Haley Page, Derek Edward. BA, Claremont Mens Coll.; LLB, U. Calif., San Francisco. Assoc. O'Gara & McGuire, San Francisco, 1971-78, ptnr., 1979-84; sole practice San Francisco, 1984-85; ptnr. Lukens, St. Peter & Cooper, San Francisco, 1986—. Mem. ABA, San Francisco Bar Assn., San Francisco Trial Lawyers

Assn. (bd. dirs. 1976-78). Avocations: tennis, fishing. Federal civil litigation, State civil litigation. Office: Lukens St Peter & Cooper 250 Alcoa Bldg San Francisco CA 94111

DRUMMOND, WINSLOW, lawyer; b. Phila., Jan. 29, 1933; s. Winslow Shaw and Dorothy (Moore) D.; m. Katherine Pace, June 18, 1983; children: Judith L., Kathryn W., Winslow Shaw II. AB, Coll. of Wooster, Ohio, 1954; LLB, Duke U., 1957. Bar: Ark. 1957, U.S. Dist. Ct. Ark. 1957, U.S. Ct. Appeals (8th cir.) 1958; diplomate Am. Bd. Trial Advocates. Since practiced in Little Rock; mem. firm Wright, Lindsey & Jennings, 1957-82, ptnr., 1962-82; ptnr. McMath Law Firm, 1982—; faculty Coll. of Advocacy, Hastings Coll. of Law, 1974-86, Nat. Inst. Trial Advocacy, 1979-86; chmn. com. on jury instrns. Ark. Supreme Ct., 1980—. Co-author: Arkansas Model Jury Instructions-Civil, 1965, 2d edit., 1974. Pres., bd. dirs. Urban League Greater Little Rock; bd. dirs. Little Rock Sch. Dist. Served with U.S. Army, 1957-58. Fellow Am. Coll. Trial Lawyers, Ark. Bar Found.; mem. ABA, Ark. Bar Assn. (past chmn. exec. com., ho. of dels.), Pulaski County Bar Assn., Assn. Trial Lawyers Am., Am. Judicature Soc., Ark. Trial Lawyers Assn. (pres. 1985-86), Order of Coif, Phi Alpha Theta. Democrat. Presbyn. Federal civil litigation, State civil litigation, Personal injury. Home: 13001 Crabapple Pl Little Rock AR 72209 Office: McMath Law Firm 711 W 3d St Little Rock AR 72201

DRUMMY, WILLIAM WALLACE, III, lawyer; b. Omaha, Nov. 12, 1948; s. William Wallace Jr. and Lillian Ann (Hubenthal) D.; m. Kathleen Therese Heffernan, July 3, 1971; children: Erin Marie, Rebecca Ann, Brian Robert. BS in Bus. Mgmt., Ind. U., 1970; JD, Creighton U., 1975. Bar: Nebr. 1975, Ind. 1977. Assoc. Kennedy, Holland, Delacy & Svoboda, Omaha, 1975-77; ptnr. Patrick, Wilkinson, Goeller & Modesitt, Terre Haute, 1977—. Served to capt. U.S. Army, 1970-71. Mem. ABA, Ind. Bar Assn., Am. Bd. Trial Advs. Roman Catholic. Federal civil litigation, State civil litigation, General corporate. Home: 763 Cambridge Ct Terre Haute IN 47802 Office: Patrick Wilkinson Goeller & Modesitt 333 Ohio St Terre Haute IN 47807

DRURY, RONALD EUGENE, judge; b. East Saint Louis, Ill., Apr. 15, 1947; s. Wilbert Warren and Eunice Melvina (Harvill) D.; m. Becky Sue Sheeler, Aug. 30, 1969 (div. Feb. 1986); children—Laura, Matthew, Jeremy. B.S., Ind. State U., 1969, M.S., 1971; J.D., Ind. U.-Indpls., 1975. Bar: Ind. 1975, U.S. Dist. Ct. (so. dist.) Ind. 1975. Ptnr. Adney & Drury, Lebanon, Ind., 1975-77; county ct. judge Boone County, Lebanon, 1977-79; circuit judge Ind. 20th Jud. Cir., Lebanon, 1979—; instr. Ind. Vocat.-Tech. Coll., Indpls., 1972-77. Pres., bd. dirs. Tri-County Mental Health Ctr., Indpls., 1979-83; county chmn. United Way, Lebanon, 1979; pub. relations officer Boone County Cancer Soc., Lebanon, 1978-82; chmn. Ind. Juvenile Justice Improvement Com., 1980—; bd. mgrs. Ind. Judge's Assn. 1987—. Mem. Ind. Bar Assn., Boone County Bar Assn. (pres. 1978-79), Pi Sigma Alpha. Democrat. Roman Catholic. Lodges: Kiwanis (sec. 1975-78), Elks, Masons, Shriners. Judicial administration, Juvenile. Home: 1005 Fordice Rd Lebanon IN 46052 Office: Boone Circuit Ct 1 Courthouse Sq Lebanon IN 46052

DRUTCHAS, GREGORY G., lawyer; b. Detroit, June 2, 1949; s. Gilbert Henry and Elaine Marie (Rutkowski) D.; m. Cheryl Aline June 9, 1973; children—Gillian Aline, Gregory Ryan. A.B., U. Mich., 1970; J.D., Duke U., 1973. Bar: Mich. 1973, U.S. Dist. Ct. (ea. dist.) Mich. 1974, U.S. Ct. Appeals (6th cir.) 1978, U.S. Supreme Ct. 1984. Assoc. Kitch & Suhrheinrich, P.C. (now Kitch, Saurbier, Drutchas, Wagner & Kenney, P.C.), Detroit, 1973-78, prin., 1978—; lectr., seminar presenter on med. profl. liability. Served to capt., USAFR, 1972-82. Mem. State Bar Mich., Detroit Bar Assn., Oakland County Bar Assn., Mich. Defense Trial Counsel, Mich. Soc. Hosp. Attys., Am. Acad. Hosp. Attys. Republican. Unitarian. Club: Detroit Golf. Author: (with others) Michigan Court of Appeals Practice: A Primer, 1981; contbr. articles to profl. publs. Health, Insurance, Federal civil litigation. Home: 1386 Lakeside St Birmingham MI 48009 Office: One Woodward Ave Detroit MI 48226

DRYDEN, ROBERT EUGENE, lawyer; b. Chanute, Kans., Aug. 20, 1927; s. Calvin William and Mary Alfreda (Foley) D.; m. Jetta Rae Burger, Dec. 19, 1953; children: Lynn Marie, Thomas Calvin. A.A., City Coll., San Francisco, 1947; B.S., U. San Francisco, 1951, J.D., 1954. Bar: Calif. 1955; diplomate: Am. Bd. Trial Advs. Assoc. Barfield, Barfield, Dryden & Ruane (and predecessor firm), San Francisco, 1954—; jr. partner Barfield, Barfield, Dryden & Ruane (and predecessor firm), 1960-65, gen. partner, 1965—; lectr. continuing edn. of the bar, 1971-77. Served with USMCR, 1945-46. Fellow Am. Coll. Trial Lawyers, Am. Bar Found; mem. ABA, San Francisco Bar Assn., State Bar Calif., Am. Judicature Soc., Assn. Def. Counsel (dir. 1968-71), Def. Research Inst., Internat. Assn. Ins. Counsel, Fedn. Ins. Counsel, Am. Arbitration Assn., U. San Francisco Law Soc. (mem. exec. com. 1970-72), U. San Francisco Alumni Assn. (bd. govs. 1977), Phi Alpha Delta. State civil litigation, Insurance, Personal injury. Home: 1320 Lasuen Dr Millbrae CA 94030 Office: Suite 3125 1 California St San Francisco CA 94111

DRYDEN, WILLIAM GEORGE, lawyer; b. Los Angeles, Jan. 24, 1953; s. Lowell Leroy and Oral (Robertson) D.; m. Debrha Jo Carnahan, June 15, 1985. BA, Stanford U., 1975; JD, Willamette U., 1978. Bar: Idaho 1979, U.S. Dist. Ct. Idaho 1979. Law clk. to presiding justice Idaho Supreme Ct., Boise, 1978-79, Fed. Dist. Ct., Boise, 1979-80; assoc. Elam, Burke & Boyd, Boise, 1978-85, ptnr., 1985—; Fundraiser YMCA, Boise, 1980—, ARC, Boise, 1980—. Mem. ABA, Boise Bar Assn., Idaho Trial Lawyers Assn., Assn. Trial Lawyers Am., Idaho Def. Counsel, Def. Research Inst. Democrat. Avocations: triathalons, snow skiing, water skiing, tennis, golf. Federal civil litigation, State civil litigation, Insurance. Office: Elam Burke & Boyd 710 W Idaho Box 1559 Boise ID 83701

DRYDEN, WOODSON E., lawyer; b. Anadarko, Okla., Dec. 21, 1924; s. Harry Ernest and Ruth Sally (Woodson) D.; divorced; children: Judith, Carol, Kim, Christine, Erich. BBA, Kans. U., 1948; LLB, Tex. U., 1951. Sole practice Beaumont, Tex., 1951—. Served to lt. (j.g.) USNR, 1942-46. Mem. Tex. Trial Lawyers Assn. (pres. 1972-73). Democrat. Episcopalian. Personal injury. Home: 6625 Windwood Beaumont TX 77701 Office: 915 Goodhue Bldg Beaumont TX 77701

DRYMALSKI, RAYMOND HIBNER, lawyer, banker; b. Chgo., June 1, 1936; s. Raymond P. and Alice H. (Hibner) D.; m. Sarah Fickes, Apr. 1, 1967; children—Robert, Paige. B.A., Georgetown U., 1958; J.D., U. Mich.-Ann Arbor, 1961. Bar: Ill. 1962. Lawyer, Chgo. Title & Trust Co., 1963-65; asst. sec., atty. No. Trust Co., Chgo., 1965-68; ptnr. Boodell, Sears, Giambalvo & Crowley, Chgo., 1968—; dir. Chicago Heights Nat. Bank, Chicago Heights Bancorp, Inc. Trustee Northwestern Meml. Hosp.; chmn., bd. dirs. Lincoln Park Zool. Soc. Mem. ABA, Chgo. Bar Assn. Roman Catholic. Club: Econ. (Chgo.). Contbr. articles to profl. jours. General corporate, Banking, Corporate taxation. Home: 443 Eugenie St Chicago IL 60614 Office: 69 W Washington St Room 500 Chicago IL 60602

DRYOVAGE, MARY MARGARET, lawyer; b. Dearborn, Mich., May 14, 1954; s. Henry John and Kathleen T. (Naughton) D.; m. Robert P. Carasik, Dec. 29, 1983. BA in History, U. Mich., 1975; JD, Wayne State U., 1978. Bar: Mich. 1979, U.S. Dist. Ct. (ea. dist.) Mich. 1979, U.S. Dist. Ct. (no. dist.) Calif. 1981, Calif. 1984, U.S. Ct. Appeals (9th cir.) 1985, U.S. Dist. Ct. (cen. and ea. dists.) Calif. 1986, U.S. Ct. Appeals (fed. cir.) 1987, U.S. Supreme Ct. 1987. Hearing officer Mich. Employee Relations Commn., Detroit, 1978-81; trial counsel Fed. Labor Relations Authority, San Francisco, 1981-82; sole practice San Francisco, 1984—; prof. Wayne State U., Detroit, 1980; instr. labor studies program San Francisco Community Coll., 1982—. Contbr. articles to profl. jours. Mem. ABA, Fed. Bar Assn., Assn. Trial Lawyers Am., Nat. Lawyers Guild, NOW, Coalition Labor Union Women. Civil rights, Federal civil litigation, Labor. Home: 4083 25th St San Francisco CA 94114 Office: 3929 24th St San Francisco CA 94114

DUB, LARRY, lawyer; b. Montreal, Quebec, Can., Feb. 24, 1954; s. Michael and Zahava (Schwimmer) D.; m. Karen Alster, Aug. 5, 1979; children: Ayelet, Alona, Yishai, Sharona. BA, Columbia U., 1975; BHL, Jewish Theol. Sem., 1975, MA, 1976; JD, Cardozo U., 1979. Bar: R.I. 1979, U.S. Dist. Ct. R.I. 1979, N.Y. 1980, U.S. Supreme Ct. 1982, U.S. Ct. Appeals (1st cir.) 1983, Israel 1985. Assoc. Pearlman & Vogel, Providence, 1979-84; atty. Ministry of Justice State of Israel, Jerusalem, 1984-85; of counsel Gordon & Levitt, Providence, 1985—. Author: R.I. Collection Law, 1982. Mem. R.I. Bar Assn., N.Y. Bar Assn., Israel Bar Assn., Assn. Trial Lawyers Am., R.I. Trial Lawyers Assn. Republican. Consumer commercial, State civil litigation, Real property. Home: 97 Emeline St Providence RI 02906 Office: 339 Angell St Providence RI 02906

DUBBS, THOMAS ALLAN, lawyer; b. Chgo., Nov. 30, 1947; s. Joseph Allan and Martha Elaine (Moore) D.; m. Elizabeth M.R. Dubbs, May 8, 1982; 1 child, Alexander Joseph. Grad., Culver Mil. Acad., 1965; BA, U. Wis., 1970; MA in Internat. Relations, Tufts U., 1971; JD, U. Wis., 1974. Bar: Wis. 1974, N.Y. 1976, U.S. Dist. Ct. (so. and ea. dists.) N.Y. 1976. Assoc. Chadbourne, Burke, Whiteside & Wolff, N.Y.C., 1974-84; ptnr. Hall, McNicol, Hamilton & Clark, N.Y.C., 1985—. Mem. ABA (litigation sect.), N.Y. State Bar Assn., Am. Soc. Internat. Law, Assn. of Bar of City of N.Y. Democrat. Clubs: Union, University (N.Y.C.). Federal civil litigation, State civil litigation, Public international. Home: 139 E 94th St Apt 3C New York NY 10128 Office: Hall McNicol Hamilton & Clark 220 E 42d St The News Bldg New York NY 10017

DUBÉ, LAWRENCE EDWARD, JR., lawyer; b. Chgo., Sept. 25, 1948; s. Lawrence Edward and Rosemary Nora (Cooney) D.; m. Paula Ann Googdal, Jan. 10, 1982; 1 child, Charles Bernard. BA in Polit. Sci. cum laude, Knox Coll., 1970; JD with distinction, U. Iowa, 1973. Bar: Ill. 1973, Md. 1982, Pa. 1982, D.C. 1983. Field atty. NLRB, Chgo., 1973-80, supr. atty., 1980-81; sole practice Balt., 1981-85; assoc. Grove, Jaskiewicz, Gilliam & Cobert, Washington, 1985-87; ptnr. Dubé & Googdal, Balt., 1987—. Author: Management on Trial-The Law of Wrongful Discharge, 1987; co-author: The Maryland Employer's Guide to Labor and Employment Law, 1984. Mem. ABA, Md. Bar Assn., D.C. Bar Assn., Balt. Bar Assn., Am. Soc. for Personnel Adminstrn. Labor, Pension, profit-sharing, and employee benefits, Federal civil litigation. Home: 622 W University Pkwy Baltimore MD 21210 Office: Dubé & Googdal 400 E Pratt St Suite 800 Baltimore MD 21202

DUBER, MICHAEL JOSEPH, lawyer; b. Columbus, Ohio, Mar. 3, 1947; s. Herbert Charles and Pauline Selma (Yaross) D.; m. Cindy A. Roller, Feb. 29, 1976; children—Herbert, Brandon, Craig. B.S. in Bus. Adminstrn., Ohio State U., 1970; J.D., U. Cin., 1973. Bar: Ohio 1973, U.S. Dist. Ct. (no. dist.) Ohio 1973. Assoc. F.J. Bentoff Co., L.P.A., Cleve., 1973-79; ptnr. Bentoff & Duber Co., L.P.A., Cleve., 1979—; instr. Ohio Paralegal Inst., Cleve., 1984. Bd. dirs. Wahoo Club (Cleve. Indians Baseball booster club), 1979—; Bd. dirs. Orange Community Athletic Assn.; mem. Holden Arboretum, Cleve., 1978—; mem. Sports Adv. Council, Orange, Ohio, 1984. Mem. Ohio Bar Assn., Cleve. Bar Assn., Cuyhoga County Bar Assn. (vice chmn. workers' compensation sect. 1984-86), Cleve. Law Library Assn., Ohio Acad. Trial Lawyers, Tau Epsilon Phi. Democrat. Jewish. Workers' compensation. Home: 3952 White Oak Trail Orange OH 44122 Office: Bentoff and Duber Co LPA 230 Leader Bldg Cleveland OH 44114

DUBERSTEIN, CONRAD B., judge; b. N.Y.C., Oct. 22, 1915; s. Alex N. and Esther (Drucks) D.; m. Anne Saggio, May 11, 1928; 1 dau., Elysa Rice. Student Bklyn. Coll., 1934-38; LL.B., St. John's U., 1942. Bar: N.Y. 1942, U.S. Dist. Ct. (ea. dist.) N.Y. 1945, U.S. Dist. Ct. (so. dist.) N.Y. 1949, U.S. Dist. Ct. (no. dist.) N.Y. 1963; Supreme Ct. , 1960, U.S. Ct. Appeals (2d cir.) 1966. Ptnr., Schwartz, Rudin & Duberstein, Bklyn., 1954-60, Schwartz & Duberstein, Bklyn., 1960-70; ptnr. Otterbourg, Steindler, Houston & Rosen, P.C., N.Y.C., 1970-80, sr. atty. insolvency dept.; bankruptcy judge U.S. Dist. Ct. (ea. dist.) N.Y., N.Y.C., 1981—, chief judge, 1984—. Pres., Levittown (N.Y.) Republican Club, 1960-61. Served with AUS, 1943-45; ETO. Decorated Purple Heart. Fellow Am. Bar Found.; mem. ABA, Fed. Bar Council, Comml. Law League, Nat. Conf. Bankruptcy Judges, N.Y. State Bar Assn., Bankruptcy Lawyers Bar Assn. N.Y., Assn. Bar City N.Y.; Bklyn. Bar Assn., Community Mayors of N.Y. State, Mil. Order of Purple Heart, DAV. Lodge: B'nai B'rith. Author: A Broad View of the New Bankruptcy Code, 1979; contbg. author: Bankruptcy Reform Act Manual, Bankruptcy Practice and Strategy. Bankruptcy. Home: 96 Schermerhorn St Brooklyn NY 11201 Office: US Ct House 75 Clinton St Room 313 Brooklyn NY 11201

DUBIN, JAMES MICHAEL, lawyer; b. N.Y.C., Aug. 20, 1946; s. Benjamin and Irene (Wasserman) D.; m. Susan Hope Schraub, Mar. 15, 1981; children—Alexander Philip, Elizabeth Joy. B.A., U. Pa., 1968; J.D., Columbia U., 1974. Bar: N.Y. 1975, D.C. 1984, U.S. Dist. Ct. (so. and ea. dist.) N.Y. 1975, U.S. Ct. Appeals (2d cir.) 1975. Assoc. Paul, Weiss, Rifkind, Wharton & Garrison, N.Y.C., 1974-82, ptnr. 1982—. Bd. editors Columbia Law Rev., 1973-74. Bd. dirs. YM-YWHA of Mid-Westchester, Scarsdale, N.Y., 1983-86, chmn. budget and fin. com., 1984-85; chmn. Cable Oversight Com., Harrison, N.Y., 1983-85; dir. Reiss Media Enterprises, Inc., 1985-86. Served with U.S. Army, 1969-71. Mem. ABA, Assn. Bar City N.Y., Phi Delta Phi. Club: Sunningdale Country (Scarsdale); Hemisphere (N.Y.C.). Securities, Banking, General corporate. Office: Paul Weiss Rifkind Wharton & Garrison 1285 Ave of Americas New York NY 10019

DUBIN, STEPHEN VICTOR, holding company executive lawyer; b. Bklyn., June 17, 1938; s. Herman E. and Rhoda (Fogel) D.; m. Paula L. Dubin, June 28, 1959; children—Jeffrey D., Michelle L. B.A., CUNY, 1961; J.D., Boston U., 1961. Bar: N.Y. 1961, Ill. 1975, Pa. 1984, U.S. Dist. Ct. (so. and ea. dists.) N.Y. 1966, U.S. Dist. Ct. (no. dist.) Ill. 1975, U.S. Cts. Apls. (2d cir.) 1966 (7th cir.) 1975, U.S. Supreme Ct. 1970. Assoc. Kronish, Lieb, Shainswit, Weiner & Hellman, N.Y.C., 1965-67; counsel corp. sec. Seligman & Latz, N.Y.C., 1967-72; gen. atty. Montgomery Ward & Co., Inc., N.Y.C., 1972-75, regional counsel and asst. sec., Chgo., 1975-78; gen. counsel and v.p., sec. CSS Industries Inc. (formerly known as City Stores Inc.), Phila., 1978—; v.p. Bankers Securities Corp., Phila., 1982—, Phila. Industries, Inc.; lectr. consumer law Am. Mgmt. Assn., 1974, 79, 81. Nassau County Democratic committeeman, 1967-75, mem. county jud. screening com., 1972-75, del. Nat. Dem. Issues Conv., 1974. Served to capt. JAGC AUS, 1961-65. Mem. ABA, N.Y. State Bar Assn., Pa. Bar Assn., Ill. Bar Assn., Chgo. Bar Assn., Phila. Bar Assn., Bar Assn. Nassau County, N.Y. County Lawyers Assn., Am. Soc. Corp. Secs. Jewish. Club: Masons. General corporate, Real property, State civil litigation. Office: CSS Industries Inc 1401 Walnut St Philadelphia PA 19102

DUBLIKAR, RALPH F(RANK), lawyer; b. Niles, Ohio, Aug. 31, 1949; s. Frank J. and Lucille M. (Guacci) D.; m. Nancy Ellen Fladung, Nov. 30, 1974; children: Justin, Randall, Ellen, Eric. BA in Polit. Sci., Xavier U., 1971; JD, U. Cin., 1974. Bar: Ohio 1974, U.S. Dist. Ct. (no. and so. dists.) Ohio 1976, U.S. Ct. Appeals (6th cir.) 1976. Law clk. to presiding justice U.S. Dist. Ct. (so. dist.) Ohio, Cin., 1974-76; ptnr. Day, Ketterer, Raley, Canton, Ohio, 1976-85, Baker, Meekison & Dublikar, Canton, 1986—. Served to capt. USAR. Mem. ABA, Ohio Bar Assn., Ohio Assn. Trial Lawyers Attys., Stark County Bar Assn. (exec. com. 1985—), Canton Jaycees (bd. dirs. 1978-79). Roman Catholic. State civil litigation, Insurance, Personal injury. Home: 3525 N Market St Canton OH 44714 Office: Baker Meekison & Dubikar 115 DeWalt NW Canton OH 44702

DUBOFF, LEONARD DAVID, legal educator; b. Bklyn., Oct. 3, 1941; s. Rubin Robert and Millicent Barbara (Pollach) DuB.; m. Mary Ann Crawford, June 4, 1967; children—Colleen Rose, Robert Courtney, Sabrina Ashley. J.D. summa cum laude, Bklyn. Law Sch., 1971. Bars: N.Y. 1974, U.S. Dist. Cts. (so. and ea. dists.) N.Y. 1974, U.S. Ct. Appeals (2d cir.) 1974, U.S. Customs Ct. 1975, U.S. Supreme Ct. 1977, Oreg. 1977. Teaching fellow Stanford (Calif.) U. Law Sch., 1971-72; mem. faculty Lewis & Clark Coll. Northwestern Sch. Law, Portland, Oreg., 1972—, prof. law, 1977—; instr. Hastings Coll. Law Coll. Civil Advocacy, San Francisco, summers 1978, 79. Founder, past pres. Oreg. Vol. Lawyers for Arts; mem. lawyers' com. ACLU, 1973-78, bd. dirs. Oreg., 1974-76; mem. Mayor's Adv. Com. Security and Privacy, 1974; bd. dirs. Portland Art Mus. Asian Art Council, 1976-77, Internat. Assn. Art Security, N.Y.C., 1976-80; Gov. Oreg. Com. Employment of Handicapped, 1978-81; cons., panelist spl. projects Nat. Endowment for Arts, 1978-79; mem. Mayor's Adv. Com. on Handicapped, 1979-81; mem. Wash. State Atty. Gen.'s Com. to Reorganize Maryhill Mus.; Oreg. Commn. for Blind; Oreg. Com. for Humanities, 1981-87. Recipient Bklyn. Law Sch. Stuart Hirschman Property, Jerome Prince Evidence, Donald W. Matheson Meml. awards, 1st scholarship prize; Hofstra U. Lighthouse scholar 1965-71; recipient Hauser award, 1967, Howard Brown Pickard award, 1967-69. Mem. Am. Soc. Internat. Law, Assn. Alumni and Attenders of Hague Acad. Internat. Law, Assn. Am. Law Schs. (chmn. sect. law and arts 1974-80, standing com. sect. activities 1975), ABA, N.Y. State Bar Assn., Oreg. Bar Assn., Delta Kappa Phi, Sigma Pi Sigma, Sigma Alpha. Spl. columnist on craft law, The Crafts Report; editor, contbr. materials to legal and art textbooks; author textbooks and articles for legal and art jours. Securities, General corporate, Art law. Office: Lewis & Clark Law Sch 10015 SW Terwilliger Portland OR 97219

DU BOFF, MICHAEL H(AROLD), lawyer; b. N.Y.C., June 27, 1945; s. Rubin Robert and Millicent Barbara (Pollack) Du B.; m. Diane Gail Gumenick, July 29, 1972; children—Jill Bonnie, Robert Evan. B.B.A., Pace U., 1967; J.D., Bklyn. Law Sch., 1970. Bar: N.Y. 1971, U.S. Dist. Ct. (so. and ea. dists.) N.Y. 1972, U.S. Supreme Ct. 1974, U.S. Tax Ct. 1973, U.S. Ct. Internat. Trade 1973. Sr. trial asst. dist. atty. Bronx County N.Y.C., 1970-73; ptnr. Gainsburg, Gottlieb, Levitan & Cole, N.Y.C., 1973-81; counsel firm Hahn & Hessen, N.Y.C., 1981-84; ptnr. Salon, Marrow & Dyckman, N.Y.C., 1985—; dir., cons. Harwell Group, Inc., N.Y.C., 1982—; v.p. Classic Antique & Restored Spls., Ltd., N.Y.C., 1980—. Contbr. article to Bklyn. Law Sch. Law Rev., 1969. Patron Children's Art Workshop, Mamaroneck, N.Y., 1979—; sponsor Children's Med. Ctr., Lake Success, N.Y., 1979—; mem. Westchester Council for Arts, N.Y., 1980—; assoc. chmn. fin. industries div. Nat. Asthma Ctr., Denver, 1981. Recipient award for disting. service Bronx Dist. Atty., 1973. Mem. Am. Arbitration Assn. (panel of arbitrators 1979—, guest speaker 1983), Assn. Bar City of N.Y. (com. uniform state laws 1972-81), Fed. Bar Council, ABA, N.Y. State Bar Assn., Alpha Phi Omega (v.p. N.Y.C. 1964-67). Consumer commercial, Contracts commercial, General corporate. Home: 7 McKenna Pl Mamaroneck NY 10543

DUBOFSKY, JEAN EBERHART, justice Colorado Supreme Court; b. 1942; B.A., Stanford U., 1964; LL.B., Harvard U., 1967; m. Frank N. Dubofsky; children: Joshua, Matthew. Admitted to Colo. bar, 1967; legis. asst. to U.S. Senator Walter F. Mondale, 1967-69; atty. Colo. Rural Legal Services, Boulder, 1969-72, Legal Aid Soc. Met. Denver, 1972-73; ptnr. Kelly, Dubofsky, Haglund & Garnsey, Denver, 1973-75; dep. atty. gen. Colo., 1975-77; counsel Kelly, Haglund, Garnsey & Kahn, 1977-79; justice Colo. Supreme Ct., Denver, 1979—. Jurisprudence. Office: 465 State Judicial Bldg 2 E 14th Ave Denver CO 80203 *

DUBOSE, CHARLES WILSON, lawyer; b. Sumter, S.C., Mar. 2, 1949; s. Frank Elsivan and Fannie Louise (Wilson) DuB.; m. Myra Ketus Cawthon, Nov. 21, 1981 (div. Feb. 1986). AB magna cum laude, Harvard U., 1971; JD, U. Va., 1974. Bar: Ga. 1974, U.S. Dist. Ct. (no. dist.) Ga. 1974, U.S. Ct. Appeals (5th cir.) 1976, U.S. Ct. Appeals (4th cir.) 1978, U.S. Supreme Ct. 1979, U.S. Ct. Appeals (11th cir.) 1981, U.S. Dist. Ct. (mid. dist.) Ga. 1982. Assoc. Kutak, Rock & Huie and predecessor firms, Atlanta, 1974-79; ptnr. Kutak, Rock & Huie, Atlanta, 1979-84; of counsel Griffin, Cochrane & Marshall P.C., Atlanta, 1985-86, ptnr., 1986—. Mem. ABA, State Bar Ga., Atlanta Bar Assn., Lawyers Club of Atlanta. Avocations: photography, piano, architecture, historic preservation. Construction, Federal civil litigation, General corporate. Home: 1217 Cumberland Rd Atlanta GA 30306 Office: Griffin Cochrane & Marshall 100 Peachtree St Suite 2800 Atlanta GA 30303

DUBOSE, CLARKE WARDLAW, lawyer; b. Winston-Salem, N.C., Apr. 5, 1954; s. Hugh Hammond and Katherine (McCants) DuB. BA, U. N.C., 1976; JD, U. S.C., 1980. Bar: S.C. 1980, U.S. Dist. Ct. S.C. 1982, U.S. Ct. Appeals (4th cir.) 1985. Law clk. to presiding justice S.C. Cir. Ct., 1980-82; assoc. Sinkler & Boyd, P.A., Columbia, S.C., 1982—. Episcopalian. Federal civil litigation, State civil litigation. Office: Sinkler & Boyd PA 1426 Main St Suite 1200 The Palmetto Ctr Columbia SC 29206

DUBOSE, GUY STEVEN, lawyer; b. Hollywood, Calif., June 12, 1954; s. Donald Thomas DuBose and Normalee Carol (Johnson) Farris. AB, U. So. Calif., 1976; JD, Whittier Coll., 1979; LLM, Cambridge U., Eng., 1981; cert., The Hague Acad. Internat. Law, The Netherlands, 1981. Bar: Calif. 1979, U.S. Dist. Ct. (cen. dist.) Calif. 1979. In house counsel Di-Line Corp., Orange, Calif., 1980-82; project contract adminstr. Rockwell Internat., Los Angeles, 1982-84; asst. v.p., corp. counsel So. Calif. Savs., Beverly Hills, Calif., 1984—. Mem. Los Angeles County Bar Assn., Beverly Hills Bar Assn., Am. Soc. Internat. Law, Middle Temple Inn Ct., Cambridge Soc., Phi Alpha Delta. Club: Los Angeles Adventurers. Avocation: world travel. General corporate, Contracts commercial, Real property. Home: 405 S Greenbriar Ln Brea CA 92621 Office: So Calif Savs 9100 Wilshire Blvd Beverly Hills CA 90212

DUBOW, ALAN MARTIN, lawyer; b. Kew Gardens, N.Y., Nov. 19, 1956; s. Arthur and Shirley Dubow; m. Marjorie H. Corn; 1 child, Sara Faye. BA in Philosophy, SUNY, 1977; JD, Bklyn. Law Sch., 1980. Bar: N.Y. 1980, U.S. Dist. Ct. (so. and ea. dists.) N.Y. 1980, U.S. Ct. Appeals 1983. Assoc. Epstein, Reiss & Goodman, N.Y.C., 1980-84, ptnr., 1985-86; ptnr. Robinowitz, Bianchi, Cohlan, White Plains, N.Y., 1986—. V.p. Sylvan Lake Homeowners Assn., Hopewell Junction, N.Y., 1979—; counsel Murray Hill Assn., N.Y.C., 1984—. Mem. ABA, N.Y. Trial Lawyers Assn., N.Y. County Lawyers Assn., Assn. of Bar of the City of N.Y. Avocations: tennis, sailing, jogging. State civil litigation, Real property, Probate. Home: 681 Long Hill Rd W Briarcliff Manor NY 10510 Office: 199 Main St White Plains NY 10601

DUBUC, CARROLL EDWARD, lawyer; b. Burlington, Vt., May 6, 1933; s. Jerome Joachim and Rose (Bessette) D.; m. Nart Jane Lowe, Aug. 31, 1963; children: Andrew, Steven, Matthew. BS in Acctg., Cornell U., 1955; LLB, Boston Coll., 1962; postgrad. NYU, 1966-67. Bar: N.Y. 1963, D.C. 1972, U.S. Supreme Ct. 1970, U.S. Ct. Claims 1975, U.S. Ct. Appeals (4th cir. 1977, U.S. Ct. Appeals (7th cir.) 1984, U.S. Ct. Appeals (5th and 9th cirs.) 1985. Assoc. Haight Gardner Poor & Havens, N.Y.C., 1962-70, partner, 1970-83, resident ptnr. D.C. office, 1975-83; sr. ptnr. Finley, Kumble, Wagner, Heine, Underberg, Manley, Myerson, Myerson & Casey, Washington, 1983—. Served as capt. AC, USN, 1955-59. Mem. ABA (past chmn. com. aviation law 1985-86, chmn. subcom. aviation ins.), N.Y. State Bar Assn. (past chmn. aviation law com.), D.C. Bar Assn., Fed. Bar Assn., Assn. Bar City N.Y. (aeros. com.), Maritime Law Assn. U.S., Nav. Aviation Commandery (vice comdr.), Internat. Assn. Ins. Counsel (aviation law com.), Fedn. Ins. Counsel (aviation law com.), Sigma Chi. Clubs: World Trade Center, Wings (N.Y.C.); University, Capitol Hill (Washington); Congressional Country (Potomac, Md.). Aviation, Antitrust, Federal civil litigation. Home: 2430 Inglewood Ct Falls Church VA 22043 Office: Finley Kumble et al 1120 Connecticut Ave NW Washington DC 20036

DUCANTO, JOSEPH NUNZIO, lawyer, educator; b. Utica, N.Y., Mar. 18, 1927; s. Joseph and Martha (Purchine) D'Acunto; m. Constance Alice Snow Davis, May 24, 1957; children—Anthony Davis, James Charner. B.A., Antioch Coll., 1952; J.D., U. Chgo., 1955. Bar: Ill. 1955, U.S. Tax Ct. 1960, U.S. Ct. Mil. Appeals 1960, U.S. Supreme Ct. 1960. Research asst. Law and Behavioral Sci. Research Project, U. Chgo., 1954-55; assoc. Cotton, Fruchtman & Watt, Chgo., 1955-62; ptnr. Bentley, Campbell, DuCanto & Silvestri, Chgo., 1962-80; prin. Schiller, DuCanto & Fleck, Ltd., Chgo., 1981—; vis. prof. family law Loyola U., Chgo., 1968—; arbitrator Am. Arbitration Assn.; frequent lectr. on family law, taxation, fin. planning and estate planning in connection with divorce. Served with USMCR, 1944-46; CBI, PTO. Nat. Honor Law scholar, 1952-55; Ford Found. fellow, 1954-55. Fellow Am. Acad. Matrimonial Lawyers (nat. pres. 1977-79, chmn.-dir. Inst. Matrimonial Law 1976-82), Am. Coll. Probate Counsel; mem. Chgo. Bar Assn. (chmn. matrimonial law com. 1973-74, bd. mgrs. 1976-78), ABA (vice chmn. taxation div. family law sect. 1983-84, mem.-at-large council family law 1983-86), Ill. State Bar Assn. (bd. govs. 1983—), Scribes. Democrat. Unitarian. Clubs: Chgo. Soc. Clubs, Cliff Dwellers, Arts of Chgo. (Chgo.). Author: Tax Aspects of Litigation, 1979; contbr. articles, essays on family law and fed. taxation, trusts and estates to profl. publs.; editor, pub. Tax, Fin. and Estate Planning Devels. in Connection With Divorce and Family Law, 1970-85; mem. editorial bd. Fair Share, 1981—, Equitable Distbn.

Reporter, 1981—, Matrimonial Lawyer strategist, 1982—. Family and matrimonial. Office: 200 N LaSalle 27th Floor Chicago IL 60601

DUCKENFIELD, THOMAS ADAMS, gas company executive, lawyer, consultant; b. Richmond, Va., July 30, 1935; s. John Samuel Sr. and Florence (Davis) D.; m. Evelyn Roberta Newman, May 11, 1963; children: Thomas A., David A., Pace A. BS in Math., Hampton U., 1957; JD, Georgetown U., 1970; MBA, So. Ill. U., 1977. Bar: D.C. 1972, U.S. Supreme Ct. 1984. Mathmetician and div. head Taylor Ship Research & Devel., Carderock, Md., 1960-69; systems analyst Wolf Research and Devel. Co., Riverdale, Md., 1969-70; mgmt. intern Nat'l Savings and Trust Co., Washington, 1970-72; asst. v.p. United Nat. Bank Washington, 1972-73; chief dep. register of wills D.C. Superior Ct., 1973-80; clk. D.C. Superior Ct., Washington, 1980-85; v.p. and gen. mgr. D.C. Natural Gas Co., Washington, 1985—. Bd. dirs., co-chmn. Neighborhood Legal Services Program, Washington, D.C. 1979; bd. dirs. Combined Health Appeal, Bethesda, Md., 1979, Council for Ct. Excellance, Washington, 1983. Served to 1st lt. U.S. Army, 1957-59. Mem. ABA, Nat. Bar Assn. (v.p. 1984—, service award 1984, 85), Washington Bar Assn. (pres. 1980-82, service award 1982), Bar Assn. D.C., Beta Kappa Chi, Alpha Kappa Mu, Am. Gas. Assn., Md.-D.C. Pub. Utilities Conf. Democrat. Baptist. Club: Lawyers (D.C.). Public utilities, General corporate, Probate. Home: 1415 Whittier St NW Washington DC 20012 Office: DC Natural Gas 1100 H St NW Washington DC 20080

DUCKER, BRUCE, lawyer; b. N.Y.C., Aug. 10, 1938; s. Allen and Lillian (Goldner) D.; m. Jaren Jones, Sept. 1, 1962; children: Foster, Penelope, John. AB, Dartmouth Coll., 1960; MA, Columbia U., 1963, LLB, 1964. Bar: Colo. 1964, U.S. Dist. Ct. Colo. 1964, U.S. Ct. Appeals (10th cir.) 1964. Gen. counsel Great Western United Corp., Denver, 1972-73; pres., chmn. bd. dirs. Great Western Cities Inc., Denver, 1974-75; pres. Ducker, Gurko & Roble P.C., Denver, 1979—. Author: Rule by Proxy, 1976, Failure at the Mission Trust, 1986; contbr. articles to profl. jours. Trustee Denver Symphony Assn., Kent Denver Country Day Sch. Mem. ABA, Colo. Bar Assn., Denver Bar Assn. General corporate. Office: Ducker Gurko & Roble PC 1560 Broadway Suite 1500 Denver CO 80202

DUCKETT, DOUGLAS EDWARD, lawyer, personnel director; b. Cin., June 8, 1957; s. Charles and Margaret Lillian (Iglehart) D. BA, Ohio State U., 1979, JD, 1982. Bar: Ohio 1982, U.S. Dist. Ct. (so. dist.) Ohio 1983. Assoc. Strauss, Troy & Ruehlmann Co., L.P.A., Cin., 1982-85; labor counsel, personnel dir. Butler County, Hamilton, Ohio, 1985—. V.p. Cin. NOW, 1984; vol. coordinator Gary Hart campaign-Hamilton County, Cin., 1984. Mem. ABA, Ohio Bar Assn., Cin. Bar Assn., Butler County Bar Assn., Cin. Astron. Soc., Phi Beta Kappa. Democrat. Avocations: amateur astronomy, shortwave radio. Labor, Civil rights, General practice. Home: 3542 Stettinius Ave Cincinnati OH 45208 Office: Butler County Commrs Butler County Adminstrv Ctr 130 High St Cincinnati OH 45011

DUCKETT, WARREN BIRD, JR., state's attorney; b. Annapolis, Md., Aug. 28, 1939; s. Warren B. Sr. and Mary Knight (Linthicum) D.; m. Judith Livingstone, Mar. 25, 1961; children—Pamela, Stephanie, Warren. A.B., U. Md., 1962, J.D., 1966. Bar: Md. 1967, U.S. Ct. Appeals (4th cir.) 1967, U.S. Supreme Ct. 1972. Asst. state's atty. Anne Arundel County, Annapolis, Md., 1967-69, state's atty., 1973—; ptnr. Turk, Manis & Duckett, Annapolis, 1968-75; prof. law and evidence Anne Arundel Community Coll.; mem. Anne Arundel County Council, Annapolis, 1970-73. Del. Democratic Nat. Conv., 1972; pres. Anne Arundel County YMCA, 1985-87. Named Outstanding Young Annapolitan, Jaycees, Annapolis, 1970; Prosecutor of Yr., Washington Bd. Trade, 1978; recipient Human Relations award Frontiers Internat., Annapolis, 1981, Exceptional Service award HHS, 1986. Mem. Nat. Dist. Attys. Assn. (dir. 1975-77, 82-86), Md. State's Attys. Assn. (dir. 1973—, pres. 1975-77, 82-86), Md. Bar Assn., Anne Arundel County Bar Assn. Episcopalian. Club: Touchdown (sec. 1985—) (Annapolis). Lodges: Lions (sec. Annapolis 1968-70), Rotary. Criminal, Local government, Legal education. Home: 206 Wardour Dr Annapolis MD 21401 Office: State Attys Office Anne Arundel County 101 South St Annapolis MD 21401

DUCKWORTH, MARVIN E., lawyer, educator; b. Des Moines, Aug. 16, 1942; s. Marvin E. and Maryann D.; m. Janice Ann Brady, Apr. 18, 1970; children—Matthew, Brian, Jennifer, Jeffrey. B.S. in Indsl. Engring., Iowa State U., 1964; J.D., Drake U., 1968. Bar: Iowa 1968, U.S. Dist. Ct. (no. and so. dists.) 1969 . Assoc., Davis, Huebner, Johnson & Burt, Des Moines, 1968-70; asst. prof. Drake U., 1970-71, lectr. law, 1971-85, assoc. dean clin. programs, 1979-80, adj. prof., 1986—; shareholder Hopkins & Huebner, Des Moines, 1971—; speaker in field. Coach Little and Sr. League, Des Moines; sr. warden St. Andrews Episcopal Ch., Des Moines. Mem. ABA (chmn. workers compensation and employers liability law, 1986-87), Iowa Bar Assn. (pres. young lawyers sect. 1977-78, Award Merit 1982), Am. Soc. Agrl. Engrs., Def. Research Inst., Fedn. Ins. Counsel, Iowa Assn. Workers Compensation Lawyers (treas. 1986—), Iowa Acad. Trial Lawyers (adv. com., chmn. legis. subcom.). Clubs: Hyperion Field, Variety (Des Moines). Workers' compensation, Personal injury, Insurance. Office: 1040 5th Ave Des Moines IA 50314

DUCKWORTH, R(OY) DEMAREST, III, lawyer; b. Bronxville, N.Y., Apr. 25, 1948; s. Roy Demarest Jr. and Janet (Cook) D.; m. Margaret Holmberg, Jan. 29, 1977; children: Heather, Gret, Roy IV, Drew. BA, Dartmouth Coll., 1970; JD, Suffolk U., 1976. Bar: N.Y. 1977. Assoc. Carter, Ledyard & Milburn, N.Y.C., 1976-86; ptnr. McKenzie, Meaders & Ives, N.Y.C., 1986—. Served with USN, 1970-73. Club: Apawamis (Rye, N.Y.) (trustee 1984—). Estate planning, Probate, Real property. Office: McKenzie Meaders & Ives 535 Fifth Ave New York NY 10017

DUDLEY, DENNIS MICHAEL, lawyer; b. Kalamazoo, Mich., Dec. 24, 1949; s. Arthur Kenneth and Marcia Louise (Rapaport) D.; m. Elizabeth Jane Mann, Apr. 7, 1971; children—Jennifer Elizabeth, Ruth Ellen. B.A., Western Mich. U., 1971; J.D., U. Cin., 1975. Bar: Mich. 1975, U.S. Dist. Ct. (ea. and we. dists.) Mich. 1975, U.S. Ct. Appeals (6th cir.) 1975, Minn. 1983. Assoc. Sablich, Ryan, Dudley & Rapaport, P.C., Lansing, Mich., 1975-79, Farhat, Story & Kraus, P.C., East Lansing, Mich., 1979—, also bd. dirs. Author med. malpractice casebooks, 1981, 84. Mem. Ingham County Dem. Exec. Bd., Lansing, 1983, chmn. 3d Congl. Dist.; candidate for sch. bd., Lansing, 1983. Mem. Mich. Trial Lawyers Assn. (lectr. 1980—, bd. dirs. 1981-87, co-chmn. med. malpractice com. 1982, chmn. legis. com. 1985-87). Jewish. Club: Civitan (Lansing). Personal injury, Workers' compensation, Environment. Home: 1900 Rockway Lansing MI 48910 Office: Farhat Story & Kraus PC 1111 Michigan Ave Suite 300 East Lansing MI 48823

DUDLEY, J. JEFFREY, lawyer; b. Cin., Sept. 19, 1948; s. Jack Duncan and Wilma Ruth (Nebel) D.; m. Hanan Gablan Zawideh, Aug. 12, 1972; children: Layla Zawideh, Carmel Zawideh, Suraya Zawideh. BS in Chem. Engring. magna cum laude, U. Mich., 1970; JD, Stanford U., 1974. Bar: Ohio 1974, Calif. 1978, Wash. 1978, U.S. Dist. Ct. (we. dist.) Wash. 1978, U.S. Ct. Appeals (9th cir.) 1979, U.S. Supreme Ct. 1980. Assoc. Steer, Strauss, White & Tobias, Cin., 1974-78; ptnr. Cartano Botzer Larson & Birkholz, Seattle, 1978—. Mem. ABA, Wash. State Bar Assn., Seattle-King County Bar Assn., Tau Beta Pi. Club: Olympic (pres. 1985) (Seattle). State civil litigation, Public utilities, Libel. Office: Cartano Botzer Larson & Birkholz One Union Sq 25th Floor Seattle WA 98101

DUDLEY, ROBERT HAMILTON, state supreme court justice; b. Jonesboro, Ark., Nov. 18, 1933; s. Denver Layton and Helen (Paslay) D.; m. Sarah Wentzel, Apr. 2, 1954; children: Debbie, Kathy, Cindy, Bob. Student, George Washington U., 1952-54; J.D., U. Ark., 1958. Bar: Ark. 1958, U.S. Supreme Ct. 1959. Dep. pros. atty. Randolph County, Ark., 1958; spl. mcpl. judge 1959; pros. atty. 16th Jud. Dist. Ark., 1965-70; chancery judge 3d Jud. Dist. Ark., 1971-80; justice Ark. Supreme Ct., Little Rock, 1981—. Dist. chmn. Boy Scouts Am., 1960; mem. Ark. State Crime Commn., 1970-80. Mem. Ark. Jud. Council (chmn. exec. com. 1978-79); Am. Bar Assn. Ark. Bar Assn., U. Ark. Alumni Assn. (dir. 1972-75). Democrat. Jurisprudence. Office: Supreme Court 3004 Painted Valley Little Rock AR 72212 *

DUDLEY, TIMOTHY OLIVER, lawyer; b. Vernon, Tex., Jan. 27, 1954; s. George Autrey and Mary Belle (Garrison) D.; m. Bobbie Jean Knowles, May 26, 1972; children: Timothy Oliver Jr., Matthew Christopher. BA, U. Ark., Little Rock, 1980, JD, 1982. Bar: Ark. 1982, U.S. Dist. Ct. (ea. and we. dists.) Ark. 1982, U.S. Ct. Appeals (8th cir.) 1985. Assoc. Friday, Eldredge & Clark, Little Rock, 1982-84; sole practice Little Rock, 1984-86; ptnr. Wilson, Engstrom, Corum & Dudley, Little Rock, 1986—. Served to sgt. U.S. Army, 1972-76. Mem. ABA, Assn. Trial Lawyers Am., Ark. Bar Assn., Pulaski County Bar Assn., Ark. Trial Lawyers Assn. Avocations: hunting, fishing. Personal injury, Criminal, Federal civil litigation. Home: 2704 Ozark Dr North Little Rock AR 72116 Office: PO Box 71 Little Rock AR 72203

DUENAS, CRISTOBAL CAMACHO, judge; b. Agana, Guam, Sept. 12, 1920; s. Jose Castro and Concepcion Martinez (Camacho) D.; m. Juanita Castro Calvo, May 8, 1954; children: Christopher, Therese, Vincent, Zerlina, Joanna, Richard, David. Student, Aquinas Coll., Grand Rapids, Mich., 1946-48; A.B., U. Mich., 1950, J.D., 1952. Bar: Guam 1952. Asst. atty. gen. Dept. of Law, Govt. of Guam, Agana, 1952-57; dir. dept. of Land Mgmt. Govt. Guam, Agana, 1957-60; judge Island Ct. of Guam, Agana, 1960-69, U.S. Dist. Ct. for Guam, Agana, 1969—; now chief judge U.S. Dist. Ct. for Guam. Mem. ABA, Guam Bar Assn. (v.p. 1966-67), Am. Judicature Soc. Club: K.C. Jurisprudence. Office: US District Court 6th Floor Pacific News Bldg 238 O'Hara St Agana GU 96910 *

DUENSER, RUTH EDWARDS, lawyer; b. Norfolk, Va., Aug. 22, 1954; d. Roy Woodrow and Ruth Harding (Miller) Edwards; m. Mark William Duesner, July 7, 1984. BA, Coll. William and Mary, 1976; JD, George Washington U., 1979. Bar: N.Y. 1980, Tex. 1982, U.S. Dist. Ct. (so. dist.) Tex. 1983, U.S. Ct. Appeals (5th cir.) 1983. Atty. Exxon Co. U.S.A., Pelham, N.Y. and Norwalk, Conn., 1979-81, Houston, 1981—. General corporate, Oil and gas leasing, Election law. Office: Exxon Co USA 800 Bell PO Box 2180 Houston TX 77252-2180

DUER, ANDREW ADGATE, lawyer; b. Balt., Aug. 27, 1917; s. A. Adgate Sr. and Ellen Gowen (Robinson) D.; m. Phyllis F.R. Bolton; children: Margaret, A. Adgate Jr., P. Bolton. BA, Princeton U., 1939; LLB, U. Va., 1942. Bar: Va. 1941, Md. 1946. Assoc. Niles, Barton & Wilmer, Balt., 1946-51, ptnr., 1951—. Served to maj. U.S. Army, 1942-46. Mem. ABA, Md. Bar Assn., Md. Bar Found., Balt. City Bar Assn., Am. Judicature Soc. Clubs: Md., Green Spring Valley Hunt (Balt. County). General corporate, Labor, Health. Office: Niles Barton & Wilmer 929 N Howard St Baltimore MD 21117

DUERBECK, HEIDI BARBARA, lawyer; b. Duisburg, Fed. Republic Germany, July 19, 1947; came to U.S., 1956; d. Kurt and Irmgard (Gottsche) D.; m. Jenik R. Radon, June 10, 1971; 1 child, Kaara. BA cum laude, UCLA, 1968, MA, 1969; student Gottingen U., Fed. Republic Germany, 1967-68; JD, Stanford U., 1972. Bar: Calif. 1973, N.Y. 1975, U.S. Dist. Ct. (so. dist.) N.Y. 1975. Atty. Sullivan & Cromwell, N.Y.C., 1972-77; ptnr. Walter, Conston & Schurtman, P.C., N.Y.C., 1980—. contbr. articles to German legal bus. jours.; Bd. dirs. Hugh O'Brien Youth Found., N.Y.C., 1984—; mem. N.Y. State Trade Mission, Europe, 1982, N.Y.C. Trade Mission, Europe, 1983; mem. Am. Council on Germany, N.Y.C., German Forum, N.Y.C. Soroptimist fellow, 1970. Mem. German-Am. Law Assn. (bd. dirs. 1982-86, pres. 1982—), ABA, Assn. of Bar of City of N.Y. Lutheran. General corporate, Private international, Securities. Home: 269 W 71st St New York NY 10023 Office: Walter Conston & Shurtman PC 90 Park Ave New York NY 10016

DUERK, WILLIAM ADAM, lawyer; b. Indpls., Nov. 12, 1942; s. William Adam Duerk; m. Judith Burhop, June 12, 1966 (div. 1980); children: W. Adam, Joshua M. AB, Ind. U., 1967; MBA, Pace U., 1968; JD, DePaul U., 1972. Bar: D.C. 1973, U.S. Ct. Claims 1976, U.S. Supreme Ct. 1976, U.S. Tax Ct. 1978. Adminstr. Ill. Drug Abuse Council, Chgo., 1968-71; spl. counsel Exec. Office of Pres., Washington, 1971-73; ptnr. Perito, Duerk & Pinco, Washington, 1973-85; counsel Finley, Kumble, Wagner, Heine, Underberg, Manley & Casey, Washington, 1985-86; ptnr. Ross & Duerk P.C., Washington, 1986—; adj. prof. Georgetown U., Washington, 1976-78. Mem. Endowment Bd., DePaul U., Chgo., 1981-82; bd. dirs. Abraxas Found., Pitts. Mem. ABA, Fed. Bar Assn, Nat. Old Timers Game (Washington). Real property, Government contracts and claims, Health. Office: Ross & Duerk PC 1700 K St NW Suite 1100 Washington DC 20006

DUESENBERG, RICHARD WILLIAM, lawyer; b. St. Louis, Dec. 10, 1930; s. John August) Hugo and Edna Marie (Warmann) D.; m. Phyllis Evelyn Buehner, Aug. 7, 1955; children: Karen, Daryl, Mark, David. B.A., Valparaiso U., 1951, J.D., 1953; LL.M., Yale U., 1956. Bar: Mo. 1953. Prof. law N.Y. U. Sch. Law, N.Y.C., 1956-62; dir. N.Y. U. Sch. Law (Law Center Publs.), 1960-62; sr. atty. Monsanto Co., St. Louis, 1963-70; asst. gen. counsel, asst. sec. Monsanto Co., 1975-77, sr. v.p., sec., gen. counsel, 1977—; dir. law Monsanto Textiles Co., St. Louis, 1971-75; corp. sec. Fisher Controls Co., Marshalltown, Iowa, 1969-71, Olympia Industries Inc., Spartanburg, S.C., 1974-75; vis. prof. law U. Mo., 1970-71; faculty Banking Sch. South, La. State U., 1967-83; mem. legal adv. com. Chem. Mfrs. Assn., Washington. Author: (with Lawrence P. King) Sales and Bulk Transfers Under the Uniform Commercial Code, 2 vols, 1966, rev., 1984, New York Law of Contracts, 3 vols, 1964, Missouri Forms and Practice Under the Uniform Commercial Code, 2 vols, 1966; Editor: Ann. Survey of Am. Law, N.Y. U., 1961-62; Mem. bd. contbg. editors and advisors: Corp. Law Rev, 1977-86; Contbr. articles to law revs., jours. Mem. adv. council Southwestern Legal Found., Dallas, 1977—, lawyers adv. council NAM, Washington, 1980, Adminstrv. Conf. of U.S., 1980-86, legal adv. com. N.Y. Stock Exchange, 1983—, corp. law dept. adv. council Practising Law Inst., 1982; bd. dirs. Bach Soc. St. Louis, 1965-86, pres. 1973-77, Valparaiso U., 1977—, chmn. bd. visitors Law Sch. 1966—, Luth. Charities Assn., 1984—, vice chmn. 1986—; bd. dirs. Luth Med. Ctr., St. Louis, 1973-82, vice chmn., 1975-80. Served with U.S. Army, 1953-55. Named Disting. Alumnus Valparaiso U., 1976. Mem. Am. Law Inst., Luth. Acad. Scholarship, Am. Arbitration Assn. (nat. panel arbitrators 1960, bd. dirs. 1987—), ABA (chmn. com. uniform comml. code 1976-79, council sect. corp., banking and bus. law 1979-83, sec. 1983-84, chmn. 1986-87), Mo. Bar Assn., St. Louis Bar Assn., Internat. Bar Assn., Assn. Gen. Counsel, Am. Soc. Corp. Secs. (securities com., bd. dirs. 1983—, chmn. 1987-88), Fellow of the ABA, Am. Judicature Soc., Order of Coif. Contracts commercial, General corporate, General practice. Home: One Indian Creek Lane Saint Louis MO 63131 Office: Monsanto Co 800 N Lindbergh Blvd Saint Louis MO 63167

DUESENBERG, ROBERT H., corporate lawyer; b. 1930. BA, Valparaiso (Ind.) U., 1951, JD, 1953; MA, Harvard U., 1956. Atty. Wabash R.R. Co., 1958-64, Norfolk & Western Ry. Co., 1964-65; v.p., gen. counsel Pet Inc., St. Louis, 1965-83; staff v.p., dep. gen. counsel Gen. Dynamics Corp., St. Louis, 1983-84, v.p., gen. counsel, 1984—. Office: Gen Dynamics Corp Pierre Laclede Ctr Saint Louis MO 63105 *

DUETSCH, JOHN EDWIN, lawyer; b. Newark, Sept. 25, 1915; s. John J. and Barbara A. (Nickl) D.; m. Gertrude A. Stewart, Aug. 31, 1940; children: John E., Karen A. Duetsch Gammond, Thomas F. LLB, Fordham U., 1941. Bar: N.Y. 1941. Clk. Ira Haupt & Co., N.Y.C., 1933-34; with Morris & McVeigh, N.Y.C., 1934—, ptnr., 1961-85, of counsel, 1985—. Mem. planning bd. Township of Livingston, N.J., 1955-56, mayor, councilman, 1957-64. Served with U.S. Army, 1945. Mem. ABA, N.Y. Bar Assn., Am. Arbitration Assn. (panel), Guild Cath. Lawyers, N.J. State Sr. Golf Assn. (v.p., bd. dirs.). Republican. Roman Catholic. Clubs: Spring Brook Country (hon. life, pres. 1970-77) (Morristown, N.J.); Country of Jacaranda West (Venice, Fla.). Lodges: KC, Kiwanis. Real property, Probate, Estate taxation. Home: 900 N Doral Ln Venice FL 34293 Office: Morris & McVeigh 767 3d Ave New York NY 10017

DUFENDACH, CARL WILLIAM, lawyer; b. Palo Alto, Calif., June 25, 1953; s. William Reid and Marilee Ann (Kroft) D.; m. (Mary) Karen Claybrook, June 12, 1976; children: Kyle W., Kevin R., Kelsey M. BA with honor, Wheaton Coll., 1975; JD with distinction, Duke U., 1979. Bar: Mich. 1979, U.S. Dist. Ct. (we. dist.) Mich. 1979. Assoc. Warner Norcross & Judd, Grand Rapids, Mich., 1979-86, ptnr., 1986—. Bd. Dirs. Maranatha Bible and Missionary Conf., Muskegon, Mich., 1985—; trustee Mich. Christian Home, Grand Rapids, 1984—. Mem. ABA, Mich. Bar Assn., Grand Rapids Bar Assn., Christian Legal Soc., Christian Businessmens Com., Grand Rapids C. of C. (small bus. council), Order of Coif. Western Mich. Estate Planning Council. Avocation: soccer. Probate, Estate taxation, Securities. Office: Warner Norcross & Judd 900 Old Kent Bldg Grand Rapids MI 49503

DUFF, DAVID POTTER, lawyer; b. Chgo., Apr. 4, 1947; s. Elmer Potter and Helen Cecelia (Bolger) D. A.B. in Polit. Sci., U. Ill., 1969; M.S. in Adminstrn. Justice, So. Ill U., 1972; J.D., Washington U., 1975. Bar: Ill. 1975. Prin., David Potter Duff and Assocs., Ltd., Oak Park, Ill., 1975—; prof. law DePaul U., Chgo., 1975-82; vis. asst. prof. Northwestern U., Chgo., 1976-77; vis. asst. prof. bus. law and adminstrn. of justice U. Ill., Chgo. 1975—; vis. asst. prof. Loyola U., Chgo., 1976-77. Mem. Am. Trial Lawyers Assn., Ill. Trial Lawyers Assn., ABA, Ill. State Bar Assn. State civil litigation, General practice, Airline litigation. Home: 7305 W Lake St Apt 308 River Forest IL 60305 Office: 840 S Oak Park Ave Oak Park IL 60304

DUFF, GERALD PATRICK, lawyer; b. Haverhill, Mass., Mar. 5, 1947; s. Henry Ira and Kathleen Frances (McCarthy) D.; m. Rena Patry, Aug. 22, 1970; children: Joseph P., Kathleen R., Christine M. BA, Merrimack Coll., 1968; JD, U. Notre Dame, 1971. Bar: Ohio 1971, Mass. 1972, U.S. Dist. Ct. (so. dist.) Ohio 1973, U.S. Ct. Appeals (6th cir.) 1980, U.S. Supreme Ct. 1984. Law clk. to presiding judge U.S. Dist. Ct., Columbus, Ohio, 1971-73; from assoc to ptnr. Kinder, Kinder and Hanlon, St. Clairsville, Ohio, 1973-84; ptnr. Hanlon, Duff & Palendis, St. Clairsville, 1984—. Mem. Ohio Bar Assn., Mass. Bar Assn., Belmont County Bar Assn. Club: Belmont Hills Country (St. Clairsville). Federal civil litigation, State civil litigation, Insurance. Home: 67230 S Almar Ln Saint Clairsville OH 43950 Office: Hanlon Duff & Palendis 46770 National Rd W Saint Clairsville OH 43950

DUFF, JAMES CLAIR, lawyer, arbitrator; b. Pitts., Feb. 14, 1947; s. Clair Vincent and Mary (McDonald) D.; m. Sue Ellen Duffy, Jan. 3, 1976; children: Shannon Kathleen, Devon Clair, Taryn Kaleen. BA, U. Pitts., 1969; JD, Duquesne U., 1974. Bar: Pa. 1974, U.S. Dist. Ct. (we. dist.) Pa. 1974, U.S. Supreme Ct. 1978. Labor arbitrator Pitts., 1974—. Mem. Nat. Acad. Arbitrators, Am. Arbitration Assn. Avocation: flying. Labor. Home: 207 Devonwood Dr Pittsburgh PA 15241 Office: 1700 N Highland Rd Suite 313 Pittsburgh PA 15241

DUFF, VAUGHN W., computer services company executive, lawyer; b. Norton, Va., June 24, 1947. B.S., U.S. Naval Acad., 1970. M.B.A., J.D., Rutgers U., 1977. Bar: N.Y. 1978, N.J. 1979. Assoc., Mudge Rose Guthrie Ferdon & Alexander, N.Y.C., 1977-80; v.p., sec., gen. counsel TTS, Inc., Parsippany, N.J., 1980—. Served to lt. USN, 1970-74. Dupont Scholar, 1965-66. Mem. ABA, Beta Gamma Sigma, Sigma Pi Sigma. General corporate, Securities. Office: 181 E Halsey Rd Parsippany NJ 07054

DUFFEY, WILLIAM SIMON, JR., lawyer; b. Phila., May 9, 1952; s. William Simon and Elinor (Daniluk) D.; m. Betsy Byars, Dec. 17, 1977; children: Charles, Scott. BA in English, honors, Drake U., 1973; JD cum laude, U. S.C., 1977. Bar: S.C. 1977, Ga. 1982, U.S. Dist. Ct. (no. and mid. dist.) Ga. 1982, U.S. Ct. Appeals (11th cir.) 1983. Atty. Nexson, Pruet, Jacobs & Pollard, Columbia, S.C., 1977-78, King & Spalding, Atlanta, 1982—. Pres. Pine Hills Civic Assn., Atlanta, 1984—; mem. Atlanta Task Force-Neighborhood Buyouts, 1986. Served to capt. JAGC, USAF, 1978-82. Mem. ABA (litigation sect.), Atlanta Bar Assn. (chmn. alternate dispute resolution com. 1984—). Republican. Methodist. Club: Lawyers. Avocations: flying, running. Federal civil litigation, State civil litigation. Home: 2990 W Roxboro Rd Atlanta GA 30324 Office: King & Spalding 2500 Trust Co Tower Atlanta GA 30303

DUFFY, EDMUND CHARLES, lawyer; b. N.Y.C., Jan. 16, 1942; s. Thomas and Helen (Fisher) D.; m. Terry D. Davis, Oct. 21, 1973; children: Elisabeth, Margot. AB in Eng., Boston Coll., 1963; LLB, Columbia U., 1966. Bar: N.Y. 1967. Assoc. Cravath, Swaine & Moore, N.Y.C., 1968-77; from assoc. to ptnr. Skadden, Arps, Slate, Meagher & Flom, N.Y.C., 1977—. Served to capt. U.S. Army, 1966-68, Vietnam. Mem. ABA, N.Y. State Bar Assn. General corporate, Private international, Securities. Home: 15 W 81st St New York NY 10024 Office: Skadden Arps Slate Meagher & Flom 919 3d Ave New York NY 10022

DUFFY, JAMES EARL, JR., lawyer; b. St. Paul, June 4, 1942; s. James Earl and Mary Elizabeth (Westbrook) D.; m. Jeanne Marie Ghiardi, June 7, 1969; children—Jennifer, Jessica. B.A., Coll. St. Thomas, 1965; J.D., Marquette U., 1968. Bar: Wis. 1968, Hawaii 1969. Assoc. Cobb & Gould, Honolulu, 1968-71, Chuck & Fujiyama, Honolulu, 1972-74; ptnr. Fujiyama, Duffy & Fujiyama, Honolulu, 1975—; mem. Am. Bd. Trial Advocates. Bd. dirs. Aloha United Way, 1984—; mem. med. ethical resources com. Kapiolani Children's Med. Ctr., 1984—. Mem. Hawaii Bar Found. (bd. dirs. 1984—), Hawaii Bar Assn. (pres. 1982), Hawaii Trial Lawyers Assn. (pres. 1981), Trial Lawyers Assn. Am. (bd. govs. 1982—), Hawaii Acad. Plaintiff's Attys. (pres. 1986), Am. Inns of Court IV. Roman Catholic. Personal injury, State civil litigation, Federal civil litigation. Home: 1567 Ulueo St Kailua HI 96734 Office: Fujiyama Duffy & Fujiyama 1001 Bishop St Honolulu HI 96813

DUFFY, JAMES HENRY, lawyer, author; b. Lowville, N.Y., Feb. 3, 1934; s. William Christopher and Phyllis Catherine (Rofinot) D.; m. Martha McDowell, May 25, 1968. A.B., Princeton U., 1956; LL.B., Harvard U., 1959. Bar: N.Y. 1960. Assoc. Cravath, Swaine & Moore, N.Y.C., 1959-67, ptnr., 1968—. Author: Domestic Affairs: American Programs and Priorities, 1979 (under pseudonym Haughton Murphy) Murder for Lunch, 1986, Murder Takes a Partner, 1987. Mem. Mayor's Commn. Cultural Affairs, 1981—; bd. dirs. Nat. Corp. Fund for Dance, Inc., 1981—. Mem. Council Fgn. Relations, ABA, N.Y. State Bar Assn., Assn. Bar City N.Y. Democrat. Roman Catholic. Clubs: Wall Street (N.Y.C.), Century Assn. (N.Y.C.). General corporate, Banking, Private international. Office: Cravath Swaine & Moore One Chase Manhattan Plaza New York NY 10005

DUFFY, JAMES P., III, lawyer; b. Jamaica Estates, N.Y., July 14, 1942; s. James P. and Bessie Isabel Duffy, Jr.; m. Elaine M. Higgins, Aug. 8, 1964; children—Jenifer E., James P. IV. B.S., Webb Inst. Naval Architecture and Marine Engring., 1964; LL.B., J.D., Fordham U., 1967; portgrad. N.Y.U. Grad. Sch. Law, 1968-69. Bar: N.Y. 1968, N.J. 1975, U.S. Ct. Appeals (2d cir.) 1968, U.S. Supreme Ct. 1973. Assoc. Poletti, Freidin Prashker, Feldman & Gartner, N.Y.C., 1968; minority counsel U.S. Senate Select Com. on Small Bus., Washington, 1969-70; assoc. Cravath, Swaine & Moore, N.Y.C., 1971; ptnr. Berg and Duffy, Lake Success, N.Y., 1972—; village atty. Inc. Village of East Williston (N.Y.). Bd. sponsors Mercy Hosp., Rockville Centre, N.Y., 1982—. Mem. ABA, N.Y. State Bar Assn., N.J. Bar Assn., Nassau County Bar Assn., Fordham U. Law Alumni Assn. (pres. Nassau-Suffolk chpt. 1975-76). Republican. Roman Catholic. General corporate, Corporate taxation, Private international. Home: 29 E Williston Ave East Williston NY 11596 Office: 3000 Marcus Ave Suite 1W7 Lake Success NY 11042

DUFFY, KEVIN THOMAS, federal judge; b. N.Y.C., Jan. 10, 1933; s. Patrick John and Mary (McGarrell) D.; m. Irene Krumeich, Nov. 9, 1957; children: Kevin Thomas, Irene Moira, Gavin Edward, Patrick Giles. A.B., Fordham Coll., 1954, J.D., 1958. Bar: N.Y. 1958. Clk. to chief circuit judge N.Y.C., 1955-58; asst. chief criminal div. U.S. Atty.'s Office, N.Y.C., 1958-61; asso. Whitman, Ransom & Coulson, N.Y.C., 1961-66; partner Gordon & Gordon, N.Y.C., 1966-69; regional adminstr. SEC, N.Y.C., 1969-72; judge U.S. Dist. Ct. So. Dist. N.Y., 1972—; adj. prof. securities law Bklyn. Law Sch., 1975-80; prof. trial advocacy NYU, 1982—. Recipient Achievement in Law award Fordham Coll. Alumni Assn., 1976. Mem. N.Y. State, Westchester County bar assns., Assn. Bar N.Y.C., Fed. Bar Council (trustee 1970-72), Fordham Law Sch. Alumni Assn. (trustee 1969—). Clubs: Adventurers (N.Y.C.), Merchants (N.Y.C.). Judicial administration. Office: US District Court US Courthouse Foley Sq New York NY 10007 *

DUFOUR, R(ICHARD) W(ILLIAM), JR., lawyer; b. Mpls., Apr. 11, 1940; s. Richard William and Maxine P. (Kerr) DuF.; m. Mary S. Spooner, Apr. 3, 1971; children—Nicole R., Richard W., III. B.A., U. Minn., 1964, J.D. cum laude, 1967. Bar: Minn. 1967, U.S. Dist. Ct. Minn. 1968. Assoc. Dorsey, Marquart, Windhorst, West & Halladay, 1967-70; sole practice, Mpls., 1970-72; ptnr. Dorfman, Rudquist & DuFour, Mpls., 1972-76; sole practice,

Mpls., 1976-81; ptnr. DuFour & Himlie P.A. and predecessor, Mpls., 1982—; instr. U. Minn., 1970-71, William Mitchell Coll. Law, 1970-71. Served with U.S. Army, 1960-61. Mem. ABA, Minn. State Bar Assn., Hennepin County Bar Assn., Order Coif. Club: Masons. Estate planning, Probate, General corporate. Office: 5200 Willson Rd Suite 210 Minneapolis MN 55424

DUGAN, MICHAEL THOMAS, II, judge; b. Indpls., May 26, 1944; s. Michael Thomas and Ella Joyce (Cox) D.; m. Kathleen W. Dugan, May 14, 1983; 1 son, James P. B.S., Murray State U., 1965; J.D., Ind. U., 1969, MBA, Ind. U., 1987. Bar: Ind. 1969, U.S. Dist. Ct. (so. dist.) Ind. 1969, U.S. Dist. Ct. (no. dist.) Ind. 1970, U.S. Ct. Apls. (7th cir.) 1970, U.S. Tax Ct. 1971. Broadcaster Sta. WNBS, Murray, Ky., 1964-65; bailiff Marion County (Ind.) Probate Ct., 1966-66; housing insp. Marion County Health and Hosp. Corp., 1967; tchr. Indpls. Pub. Schs., 1967-68; instr. English Ind. U.-Purdue U., Indpls., 1970-71; ptnr. Poore, Popcheff, Wurster & Dugan, Indpls., 1969-74; judge Marion County Superior Ct., 1975-86; presiding judge civil div., 1980, 84. Mem. nat. adv. council Eureka (Ill.) Coll.; bd. dirs. Julian Ctr.; v.p. Nat. Sports Festival, Indpls., 1982; bd. dirs. Circle Theater Assocs., Indpls. Humane Soc., Met. YMCA, Crossroads of Am. council Boy Scouts Am.; Democratic nominee Ind. Ho. of Reps., 1972; press sec. Ind. State Young Democrats, 1970; mem. Mayor's Task Force on Recreation, 1969-70. Mem. ABA (sect. corp., banking and bus. law, sect. internat. law), Indpls. Bar Assn., Bar Assn. 7th Fed. Cir., Indpls. Lawyers Assn. (Trial Judge of Yr.), Ind. Judges Assn., Am. Arbitration Assn., Am. Assn. Conciliation Cts., Am. Mgmt. Assn., Indpls. C. of C., Indpls. Legal Aid Soc., Ind. U. Sch. Law Alumni Assn. (pres. bd. dirs.), NAACP (life), Common Cause, So. Poverty Law Ctr., Sigma Chi. Methodist. Club: Indpls. Athletic. State civil litigation, General corporate, Public international. Home: 3144 Sandpiper Dr S Indianapolis IN 46268 Office: Marion Superior Ct 507 City County Bd W Indianapolis IN 46204

DUGAN, SEAN FRANCIS XAVIER, lawyer; b. Bklyn., June 21, 1951; s. Thomas Joseph and Maureen (Brett) D.; m. Martha S. Dones, 1981; 1 child, Vanessa. BA, SUNY, Oneonta, 1973; JD, Bklyn. Law Sch., 1977. Bar: N.Y. 1978, U.S. Dist. Ct. (so. and ea. dists.) N.Y. 1979. Assoc. Martin, Clearwater & Bell, N.Y.C., 1978-84, ptnr., 1985—. State civil litigation, Insurance, Personal injury. Home: 747 E 26th St Brooklyn NY 11210 Office: Martin Clearwater & Bell 220 E 42d St New York NY 10017

DUGAS, DAVID ROY, lawyer; b. New Iberia, La., July 4, 1953; s. Claude Anthony and Gladys Marie (Hippler) D.; m. Dolores Ann Broussard, Mar. 22, 1974; children: Brandy Nicole, Kelly Ann, Mary Katherine. JD, La. State U., 1978. Bar: La. 1978, U.S. Dist. Ct. (mid. dist.) La. 1978, U.S. Dist. Ct. (we. dist.) 1980, U.S. Ct. Appeals (5th cir.) 1981, U.S. Dist. Ct. (ea. dist.) 1984. Assoc. Sanders, Downing, Kean & Cazedessus, Baton Rouge, 1978-80; from assoc. to ptnr. Caffery, Oubre, Dugas & Campbell, New Iberia, 1980—. Editor La. State U. Law Rev., 1977. Chmn. Iberia Parish Reps., 1984, Dist. H delegation to Rep. State Convention, 1984. Mem. ABA, La. Bar Assn., Iberia Parish Bar Assn., La. Assn. Def. Counsel (bd. dirs. 1985—), Order of Coif, Phi Kappa Phi, Omicron Delta Kappa. Republican. Roman Catholic. Lodge: Kiwanis. Avocations: golf, sailing. Federal civil litigation, State civil litigation, Insurance. Home: 3918 Ave Bonne Terre New Iberia LA 70560 Office: Caffery Oubre Dugas & Campbell PO Box 789 New Iberia LA 70560

DUGGAN, THOMAS MICHAEL, lawyer; b. Bakersfield, Calif., Mar. 13, 1950; s. Hugh Quinn and Fern (Martin) D. BA, Calif. Poly. State U., 1973, MBA, 1974; JD, U. San Francisco, 1977. Bar: Calif. 1978. Assoc. DiGiorgio et al, Bakersfield, Calif., 1978-80; ptnr. Klein, Wegis & Duggan, Bakersfield, 1980—; bd. dirs. Kern County Cath. Services. Bd. dirs. Calif. Poly. State U. Alumni Assn., San Luis Obispo, 1980-84; mem. Calif. Poly. Pres's. Round Table, San Luis Obispo, 1985; v.p. Calif. Poly. State U. Athletic Fund Raising Orgn. Mem. ABA, Kern County Bar Assn. (bd. dirs. 1981-85, sec., treas. 1986—, v.p. 1987—), Calif. Trial Lawyers Assn., Assn. Trial Lawyers Am., Los Angeles Trial Lawyers Assn., Calif. State Bar Assn. (v. chmn. trust fund com. sect. 1986, mem. legal services trust fund com. 1985), Mustang Football Alumni Assn. (pres. 1984—). Democrat. Roman Catholic. Clubs: Petroleum (Bakersfield, Calif.), Commonwealth (San Francisco). Environment, State civil litigation, Personal injury. Office: Klein Wegis & Duggan 1111 Truxtun Ave Bakersfield CA 93301

DUGHI, LOUIS JOHN, JR., lawyer; b. Westfield, N.J., June 22, 1946; s. Louis John and Maybelle Helen (Albano) D.; m. Virginia Kiss, Aug. 9, 1974; stepchildren: Christopher Polek, David Polek; 1 child, Christina Blair. BA, Cornell U., 1969, JD, 1972. Bar: N.J. 1972, U.S. Dist. Ct. N.J. 1972. Assoc. Shanley & Fisher, Newark, 1972-79; ptnr. Dughi & Hewit, Cranford, N.J., 1979—; lectr. Inst. Continuing Legal Edn., Newark, 1973—. Trustee, Blair Acad., Blairstown, N.J., 1975—. Mem. ABA, N.J. State Bar Assn., Fed. Bar Assn., Am. Bd. Trial Advocates, Def. Research Inst. Episcopalian. Clubs: Echo Lake Country (Westfield), Bayhead Yacht, Beacon Hill (Summit). State civil litigation, Federal civil litigation. Home: 921 Kimball Ave Westfield NJ 07090

DUHE, JOHN M., JR., U.S. district judge; b. Iberia Parish, La., Apr. 7, 1933; s. J. Malcolm and Rita (Arnandez) D.; children—Kim Duhe Hollerman, Richard, Jeanne Duhe Sinitiero, Edward, M. Bofill. B.B.A., Tulane U., 1955, LL.B., 1957. Atty. firm Helm, Simon, Caffery & Duhe, New Iberia, La., 1957-78; state dist. judge, New Iberia, 1979-84; U.S. dist. judge Western La. dist., Lafayette, 1984—. Judicial administration. Office: Room 237 Federal Bldg Lafayette LA 70501

DUKE, CHARLES JEFFREY, lawyer, energy company executive; b. Olean, N.Y., May 31, 1949; s. Charles Leon and Betty (Jack) D.; m. Drenda Jean Wilcox, June 6, 1982; children: Elissa Nicole, Charles Adam. BA, Fla. State U., 1972, JD, 1976. Bar: Pa. 1976, Fla. 1976. Sole practice, Duke Center, Pa., 1977-79; ptnr. Pecora & Duke, Bradford, Pa., 1979-83, Garber, Pecora & Duke, Bradford, 1983-85, Pecora, Duke & Babcox, 1985—; chmn. FBD Duke Energy, Inc., 1986—; pres. Duke Energy, Inc., Bradford, 1983—; pub. defender McKean County, Pa., 1980-85; v.p. McKean Natural Gas Co., Bradford, 1984—, Messer Oil Co., Olean, N.Y., 1985—; v.p. Penn. Salt. Inc., Cambridge, Mass., 1986—; pres. the Guidance Ctr., Bradford, 1986—; solicitor City of Bradford, 1985—. V.p. Am. Cancer Soc., Bradford, 1984—; mem. McKean County Republican Com., 1984—; bd. dirs. Legal Services North Western Pa., Erie, 1980-82. Mem. Fla. Bar Assn., Pa. Bar Assn., N.Y. Bar Assn., Assn. Trial Lawyers Am. Avocations: cross-country skiing, sailing, cycling, water skiing. Personal injury, Oil and gas leasing, Insurance. Home: Box 337 Main St Duke Center PA 16729 Office: Pecora Duke & Babcock 222 W Washington St PO Box 548 Bradford PA 16701

DUKE, ROBERT DOMINICK, mineral company executive; b. Goshen, N.Y., Oct. 14, 1928; s. Robert DeWitt and Elma Christina (Dominick) D.; m. Jeannette Parham, Apr. 24, 1954; children: Katherine Campbell, Robert Dominick, Peter Benjamin DeWitt, Lois Christina. B.A., Va. Mil. Inst., 1947; LL.B., Yale U., 1950; M.B.A., U. Pa., 1952. Bar: N.Y. 1950. With Cravath, Swaine & Moore, N.Y.C., 1951-52, 54-64, Freeport-McMoRan Inc. and predecessors, N.Y.C., 1964-84; gen. counsel Freeport-McMoRan Inc. and predecessors, 1970-84, sr. v.p., 1973-84; sr. v.p., gen. counsel Pittston Co., Greenwich, Conn., 1984—; dir. Brink's Inc., Burlington Air Express Inc., Brink's Home Security, Inc. Served as 1st lt. JAGC, U.S. Army, 1952-54. Mem. Assn. Bar City N.Y., Am., N.Y. State bar assns. Presbyterian. Clubs: Yale (N.Y.C.), Sky (N.Y.C.); Wilton Riding, Silvermine Golf. General corporate, Securities, Contracts commercial. Home: 67 Ridgefield Rd Wilton CT 06897 Office: One Pickwick Plaza Greenwich CT 06830

DUKE, STEVEN BARRY, legal educator; b. Mesa, Ariz., July 31, 1934; s. Alton and Elaine (Altman) D.; m. Janet Truax, 1956; children: Glenn, Warren, Alison, Sally; m. Margaret Munson, 1984; 1 child, Jennifer. B.S., Ariz. State U., 1956; J.D., U. Ariz., 1959; LL.M., Yale U., 1961. Bar: Ariz. 1959. Law clk. to Supreme Ct. Justice Douglas, 1959; grad. fellow Yale Law Sch., 1960, mem. faculty, 1961—, prof. law, 1966—, Law of Sci. and Tech. prof., 1982—; vis. prof. U. Calif.-Berkeley, 1965, Hastings Coll. Law, 1981, Ariz. State U., 1986; Bd. dirs. New Haven Legal Assistance Assn., 1968-70; cons. Commn. to Revise Fed. Criminal Code; mem. Conn. Commn. on Medicolegal Investigations, 1976—. Contbr. profl. jours.; Editor-in-chief: Ariz. Law Rev. Mem. Woodbridge (Conn.) Bd. Edn., 1970-72; mem. Woodbridge Democratic Town Com., 1967-72. Mem. Nat. Assn. Criminal Def. Lawyers, Am. Trial Lawyers, Am. Civil Liberties Union, Phi Kappa Phi, Alpha Tau Omega. Criminal, Federal civil litigation. Home: 250 Grandview Ave Hamden CT 06514 Office: 401A Yale Station New Haven CT 06520

DUKEMINIER, JESSE, legal educator; b. West Point, Miss., Aug. 12, 1925; s. Jesse J. and Lucile (Weems) D. A.B., Harvard U., 1948; LL.B., Yale U., 1951. Bar: N.Y. 1952, Ky. 1957. Practice in N.Y.C., 1951-53; asst. prof. law U. Minn., 1954-55; prof. law U. Ky., 1955-63, UCLA, 1963—; vis. prof. U. Chgo., 1959, U. Miss., 1958; adv. Calif. Law Revision Commn. Author: Perpetuities Law in Action, 1962, Wills, Trusts, and Estates, 3d edit., 1984, Summary of the Law of Future Interests, 2d edit, 1979, Property, 1981, Summary of the Law of Property, 12th edit, 1985; also numerous articles. Served with inf. AUS, 1943-45. Mem. Am. Bar Assn., Phi Beta Kappa. Legal education, Probate, Real property. Home: 630 Burk Pl Beverly Hills CA 90210

DUKER, ANN, lawyer; b. Rockford, Ill., Nov. 3, 1950; d. Richard Peterson and Phyllis Ann (Nelson) Field; m. Gregory J. Duker, July 15, 1972; children: Joanna, Eric. BS in Urban Planning, U. Ill., 1972; JD, Loyola U., Chgo., 1979. Bar: Ill. 1979, Va. 1981. Staff planner Ill. Dept. Local Govt. Affairs, Chgo., 1972-73; planner Gov.'s Task Force on Flood Control, Chgo., 1973-75; coordinator flood ins. Ill. Dept. Transp., Chgo., 1975-76; assoc. McDermott, Will & Emery, Chgo., 1979—. Mem. ABA, Va. Bar Assn., Ill. Bar Assn., Chgo. Bar Assn. Club: Monroe (Chgo.). Real property. Home: 5445 Ranier Dr Lisle IL 60532 Office: McDermott Will & Emery 111 W Monroe St Chicago IL 60603

DUKES, JAMES OTIS, lawyer; b. Quitman, Miss., Aug. 4, 1946; s. James O. and Helen (Carlson) D.; m. Leslie Ann McIntyre, Jan. 24, 1970; children: Leslie Macon, William James. BS in Math., U. Miss., 1968, MS in Math., 1970, JD, 1975. Bar: Miss. 1975, U.S. Dist. Ct. (no. and so. dists. Miss.) 1975, U.S. Ct. Appeals (5th cir.) 1981. Law clk. to presiding justice U.S. Dist. Ct. (so. dist.) Miss., Biloxi, 1975-77; assoc. Bryant, Stennis & Colingo, Gulfport, Miss., 1977-79, ptnr., 1979—. Vestry, jr. warden, sr. warden St. Peters Episc. Ch., Gulport, 1976-83; mem. standing com. Episcopal Diocese Miss., Jackson. Served to 1st lt. U.S. Army, 1969-71. Fellow Miss. Bar Found.; mem. ABA, Fed. Bar Assn., Def. Research Inst., Southeastern Admirality Inst., Miss. Bar Assn. (bd. commrs. 1986—, unauthorized practice law com. 1982-85), Miss. Def. Lawyers Assn., Harrison County Bar Assn. (sec. 1979-80), Harrison County Jr. Bar Assn. (pres. 1981-82). Lodge: Rotary. Admiralty, Insurance, Personal injury. Home: 77 Bayou Circle Gulfport MS 39501 Office: Bryant Stennis & Colingo 2223 14th St PO Box 10 Gulfport MS 39502

DULANY, WILLIAM BEVARD, lawyer; b. Sykesville, Md., Sept. 4, 1927; s. William Washington and Helen Marie (Bevard) D.; m. Anna Winifred Spencer, Aug. 16, 1952; children: William Bryant, Thomas Patrick, Anne French. AB, Western Md. Coll., 1950; postgrad., U. Mich. Law Sch., 1950-51; JD, U. Md., 1953. Bar: Md. 1953, U.S. Dist. Ct. Md. 1954. Assoc. Baldwin, Jarman & Norris, Balt., 1953-59; sr. ptnr. Dulany, Parker & Scott, Westminster, Md., 1959—; mem. character com. Md. Ct. Appeals, Annapolis, 1974—; chmn. bd. dirs. Carroll County Bank and Trust, Westminster, 1987—; bd. dirs. Mut. Fire Ins. Carroll County, Westminster. Mem. Md. Ho. Dels., Annapolis, 1962-66, Md. Constl. Conv., Annapolis, 1967-68; mem. Md. Regional Planning Council, 1964-66; chmn. Md. Fair Campaign Practices Commn., 1975-78, Carroll County Community Coll. Adv. Com., 1976; trustee Western Md. Coll., Westminster, 1972—; bd. dirs. nat. office Am. Heart Assn., Dallas, 1982—, chmn., 1987, Episcopal Ministries Aging, Sykesville, 1982—, chmn., 1986—. Served with USN, 1945-48. Named one of Outstanding Young Men in Am. Westminster Jaycees, 1961, Outstanding Citizen award Westminster Rotary, 1985, Alumnus of Yr. Western Md. Coll., 1986. Fellow Am. Bar Found., Md. Bar Found. (pres. 1986—, bd. dirs.); mem. ABA, Md. Bar Assn. (v.p. 1970-71), Carroll County Bar Assn. (pres. 1966-67), Am. Judicature Soc., Phi Alpha Delta. Club: Timber Ridge Bassets (Upperco, Md.); Bachelor's Cotillon (Balt.). Avocations: travel, vol. work in non-profit orgns. General practice, Probate, Administrative and regulatory. Home: 1167 Old Taneytown Pike Westminster MD 21157 Office: Dulany Parker & Scott 127 E Main St PO Box 525 Westminster MD 21157

DULBERG, MICHAEL SETH, lawyer; b. N.Y.C., Nov. 25, 1954; s. Murray Harris and Clare (Beilenson) D.; m. Marcy Anne Morgen, Aug. 25, 1979; 1 child, Adam. BA, Columbia Coll., 1975; JD, Harvard U., 1978. Bar: N.Y. 1979, Ariz. 1984. Asst. dist. atty. N.Y. County, N.Y.C., 1978-84; assoc. Horne, Kaplan & Bistrow P.C., Phoenix, 1984-86, ptnr., 1987—; mem. state governing bd. Ariz. Common Cause, 1987—. Researcher Common Cause, Phoenix, 1985; dep. voter registrar elections dept. Maricopa County, Phoenix, 1986; precinct committeman Maricopa County Dems., Phoenix, 1984—. Mem. ABA, Ariz. Bar Assn., Maricopa County Bar Assn., N.Y. County Lawyers Assn. Jewish. Club: Phoenix City. Avocations: softball, basketball, politics. State civil litigation, Construction, Personal injury. Home: 6137 E Sandra Terr Scottsdale AZ 85254 Office: Horne Kaplan & Bistrow PC 201 N Central Ave Suite 2480 Phoenix AZ 85073

DULEBOHN, DIANA GAY, lawyer; b. Lima, Ohio, Feb. 2, 1950; s. Howard Beau and Doris Louise (Gay) Ridenour; m. William Joe Dulebohn, Oct. 17, 1969; children: Dustin Joe, Rustyn Billie, Justin Joe. BS cum laude, Ohio State U., 1977; JD, Ohio No. U., 1980. Bar: Ohio 1980, U.S. Dist. Ct. (no. dist.) Ohio 1982, U.S. Ct. Appeals (6th cir.) 1983. Sole practice Waynesfield, Ohio, 1980—; instr. bus. and real estate law Lima (Ohio) Tech. Coll., 1979-82; village soliciter Waynesfield, Ohio, 1984—; domestic relations investigator Auglaize County Ct. of Common Pleas, Wapakoneta, Ohio, 1984-86. Mem. ABA, Ohio Bar Assn. Democrat. Methodist. Consumer commercial, Family and matrimonial, General practice. Home and Office: 215 W Mulberry St Waynesfield OH 45896

DULIN, THOMAS N., lawyer; b. Albany, N.Y., May 26, 1949; s. Joseph Paul and Mary Carol (Keane) D.; m. Pamela Lee Kendall, May 14, 1983; 1 child, Chelsea K.; stepchildren: Danielle Y., Amanda L., Thomas M. BA, Siena Coll., 1972; JD, Western New England U., 1976. Bar: N.Y. 1977, U.S. Dist. Ct. (no. dist.) N.Y. 1977, U.S. Supreme Ct. 1984. Asst. dist. atty. Albany County, 1977-81; assoc. McCarthy & Evanick, Albany, 1981-83; staff atty. Albany County Pub. Defender's Office, 1983—; sole practice Albany, 1983—. Bd. dirs. Big Bros. and Sisters of Albany County, Inc., 1984—. Mem. ABA, N.Y. State Bar Assn. (lectr. criminal justice sect.), Albany County Bar Assn., Assn. Trial Lawyers Am., N.Y. State Trial Lawyers Assn., Albany Colonie C. of C. (crime prevention com.). Democrat. Avocations: skiing, golfing, swimming. Criminal, Personal injury. Home: 15 Criswood Dr Albany NY 12205 Office: 75 Columbia St Albany NY 12210

DULL, WILBUR ROBBINS, lawyer; b. Gallatin, Mo., Oct. 4, 1914; s. Albert Ross and Ola Mae (Vipond) D.; m. Doris Lister, June 5, 1938; children: James Allan, Mary Beth Brockman, William Lister. Student, Drake U., 1932-33; BA, U. Iowa, 1936, JD with distinction, 1938. Bar: Iowa 1938, U.S. Dist. Ct. (so. dist.) Iowa 1938, U.S. Ct. Appeals (8th cir.) 1965. Sole practice Ottumwa, Iowa, 1938-42; assoc. Gilmore, Moon & Bannister, Ottumwa, 1942-46; ptnr. Dull, Keith, Beaver & Orsborn, Ottumwa, 1946-86. Served with USN, 1943-46. Mem. ABA, Iowa Bar Assn. (chmn. jud. adminstrn. com. 1969-70, bd. govs. 1964-68), Wapello County Bar Assn. (pres. 1960), Ottumwa C. of C. Republican. Methodist. Lodges: Rotary (pres. Ottumwa 1962-63), Elks. Probate, Insurance, General corporate. Home: 1577 N Van Buren Ottumwa IA 52501 Office: Keith & Orsborn PO Box 218 Ottumwa IA 52501

DUMBAUGH, ROBERT FREDERICK, lawyer; b. Storm Lake, Iowa, June 22, 1939; s. Robert S. and Elma E. (Paul) D.; m. Janet Lyn Budack, Dec. 23, 1961; children—Daniel F., Thomas M., Sarah E. B.B.A., U. Iowa, 1961, J.D., 1964. Bar: Iowa 1964, Minn. 1986, U.S. Dist. Ct. (no. dist.) Iowa 1964, U.S. Supreme Ct. 1967, U.S. Dist. Ct. (so. dist.) Iowa 1968, U.S. Ct. Appeals (8th cir.) 1968, Minn. 1986. Sole practice, Cedar Rapids, Iowa, 1964-83; ptnr. Dumbaugh and Childers, P.C., Cedar Rapids, 1983—; lectr. in field. Contbg. author: The New Iowa Criminal Code, A Comparison, 1976. Mem. Mt. Vernon City Council, Iowa, 1982-83; mem. central com. Linn County Democratic Com., Cedar Rapids, 1971-83; precinct committeeman Mt. Vernon Dem. Com., 1971-83. Fellow Iowa Acad. Trial Lawyers; mem. Assn. Trial Lawyers Am., Iowa Bar Assn. (lectr. 1982), Linn County Bar Assn. Lodge: Rotary (pres. Mt. Vernon 1979-80). Bankruptcy. Home: 201 2d Ave N Mount Vernon IA 52314 Office: 9th Floor The Center Cedar Rapids IA 52401

DUMENY, MARCEL JACQUE, lawyer; b. Teaneck, N.J., Oct. 25, 1950; s. Marcel Lawrence and Mary Jane Elizabeth (White) D.; m. Kathryn Paulette Smith, Apr. 29, 1979; children: Marcel Ryan, Riva Collette. Student, Eastbourne Coll., Sussex, Eng., 1968-69; BS, U. Pa., 1972, JD, 1975. Bar: Ohio 1975, Tex. 1986. Of counsel Diamond Shamrock Chems. Co., Cleve., 1975-80, sr. counsel, 1980-83; gen. counsel Diamond Shamrock Chems. Co., Irving, Tex., 1983-85; v.p., gen. counsel Diamond Shamrock Chems. Co., Irving, 1985-86; sr. v.p. law and devel. Fairfield Communities, Inc., Little Rock, 1987—. Eastbourne Coll. scholar, 1968, English Speaking Union scholar, 1968. Mem. ABA. General corporate, Private international, Real property. Office: Fairfield Communities Inc 2800 Cantrell Rd Little Rock AR 72202

DUMIT, THOMAS A., corporate lawyer; b. 1942. BA, U. Notre Dame, 1964; JD, Northwestern U., 1967. Group counsel Am. Hosp. Supply Corp., Evanston, Ill., 1976-81, dep. gen. counsel, 1981-84, v.p., gen. counsel, 1984-85; v.p., gen. counsel Baxter Travenol Labs., Deerfield, Ill., 1985—. Office: Baxter Travenol Labs One Baxter Pkwy Deerfield IL 60015 *

DUMONT, JAMES ALLAN, lawyer; b. N.Y.C., May 14, 1953; s. Allan Eliot and Joan (Auerbach) D. BA, Harvard U., 1975; JD, Columbia U., 1978. Law clk. to presiding justice U.S. Dist. Ct. Vt., Rutland, 1978-79; pub. defender Chittenden County, Burlington, Vt., 1979-81; assoc. Sessions & Keiner, Middlebury, Vt., 1981-82, ptnr., 1982—; reporter Vt. Supreme Ct. Adv. Coms. on Civil Procedure, Criminal Procedure, Probate Procedure and Evidence, 1985—; adj. prof. Vermont Law Sch., 1985—. Environment, Criminal. Home: West Hill Rd RFD Bristol Lincoln VT 05443 Office: Sessions Keiner & Dumont 72 Ct St Middlebury CT 05753

DUNAWAY, WAYLAND FULLER, III, lawyer; b. Waverly, Va., Mar. 23, 1912; s. Wayland Fuller, Jr., and Mary Warren (May) D.; m. Marjorie Louise Weick, May 29, 1948; children: Carol Dunaway Irwin, Thomas Weick. AB, Pa. State U.; LLB, U. Pa. Bar: Pa. 1937, U.S. Dist. Ct. (we. dist.) Pa. 1937, U.S. Dist. Ct. (mid. dist.) Pa. 1946. Ptnr. Willard, Dunaway & Mazza, State College, Pa., 1945-67; ptnr. Dunaway, Weyandt, McCormick & Jones State Coll., 1967—; chmn. emeritus bd. Mellon Bank Cen., State Coll.; bd. dirs. United Fed. Savs. Bank; chmn. hearing com. disciplinary bd. Supreme Ct. Pa. Served to maj. U.S. Army, 1941-45. Decorated Bronze Star. Mem. ABA, Pa. Bar Assn., Centre County Bar Assn. Democrat. Baptist. Lodges: Rotary, Elks, Masons. General corporate, Probate, Real property. Address: 919 University Dr State College PA 16801

DUNBAR, BYRON HERBERT, lawyer, legal educator; b. Three Forks, Mont., June 8, 1927; s. Bryon B. and Georgette (Walsh) D.; m. Margaret Jo Lovelace, Dec. 23, 1948; children: Lynn Dunbar Ryerson, Michael, Patrick, Lisa. J.D., U. Mont., 1952. Bar: Mont. 1952. Spl. agt. FBI, 1952-79; pros. atty. Bozeman, Mont., 1979-80; legal cons. Mont. Law Enforcement Acad., 1980-81; U.S. atty. Billings, Mont., 1981—; chief legal instr. Mont. Law Enforcement Acad., 1966-79; legal instr. Mont. Supreme Ct., Helena, 1980—. Served to lt. U.S. Mcht. Marine, 1944-47. Mem. Mont. Bar Assn., Gallatin County Bar Assn., Yellowstone County Bar Assn. Lodges: Elks; Bozeman Rotary. Criminal, General practice. Home: 1400 Poly Dr Suite 2A Billings MT 59101 Office: U S Attorneys Office 310 N 26th St Billings MT 59103 *

DUNBAR, JAMES V., JR., lawyer, educator, real estate broker, broadcaster, business consultant; b. Union, S.C., June 4, 1937; s. James V. and Hatten (Crawford) D.; m. Nancy Mayer, Feb. 26, 1960; children—Nancy Phillips, Katherine Crawford. B.S. in Bus., U. S.C., 1959; J.D., U. Va., 1965. Bar: S.C. 1965, Va. 1965, Colo. 1965, U.S. Supreme Ct. 1980. Assoc. Holme, Roberts & Owen, Denver, 1965-68; v.p. Cosmos Broadcasting Corp., Columbia, S.C., 1969-74; mng. ptnr. Berry Dunbar & Woods, Columbia, 1974—; pres. Mid-Carolina Communications, Inc., 1978—, Selected Brokerage Realty, 1975—; grad. prof. U. S.C.; lectr. corp. structure and immigration, U.S. and abroad. Chmn. S.C. Lawyers for Reagan, 1980; pres. Columbia Philharm. Orch., 1981-82, Trinity Cathedral Men's Club, 1979-80, Mid-Carolina Council on Alcohol and Drug Abuse, 1974-78; gen. counsel S.C. Broadcasters Assn., So. Edn. Communications Assn. Served to lt. col. USMCR, 1959—. Named Young Man of Year, S.C. Jaycees, 1970. Mem. ABA, Colo. Bar Assn., S.C. Bar Assn., Va. Bar Assn., Fed. Communications Bar Assn., Am. Immigration Lawyers Assn., Kappa Alpha Order, Phi Alpha Delta. Episcopalian. Clubs: Forest Lake Country, Belle Isle, Summit, Kiwanis. Contbr. articles to profl. publs. Real property, Legal education, General corporate. Office: 1325 Laurel St Columbia SC 29201 Office: 2400 Cain Tower Peachtree Ctr Atlanta GA 30303

DUNCAN, CHARLES TIGNOR, lawyer; b. Washington, Oct. 31, 1924; s. Robert Todd and Nancy Gladys (Jackson) D.; m. Dorothy Adelena Thrasher, July 31, 1947 (dec. Dec. 1972); 1 child, Charles Todd. B.A., Dartmouth Coll., 1947; LLD (hon.), Harvard U., 1950, J.D., 1986, LLD (hon.), 1986. Bar: N.Y. 1951, D.C. 1953, Md. 1955, U.S. Supreme Ct. 1954; FAA licensed comml. pilot, instrument rating. Assoc. Rosenman, Goldmark, Colin & Kaye, N.Y.C., 1950-53; partner Reeves, Robinson & Duncan, Washington, 1953-60; prin. asst. U.S. atty. Washington, 1961-65; gen. counsel U.S. Equal Employment Opportunity Commn., Washington, 1965-66; corp. counsel D.C., 1966-70; acting dir. pub. safety 1969; partner Epstein, Friedman, Duncan & Medalie, Washington, 1970-74; dean, prof. law Sch. Law Howard U., 1974-78; partner Peabody, Lambert & Meyers, Washington, 1978-84, Reid & Priest, Washington, 1984—; dir. Eastman Kodak Co., Procter & Gamble, TRW, Inc. Trustee Northfield Mt. Hermon Sch., chmn., 1987—; trustee NAACP Legal Def. and Edn. Fund. Served with USNR, 1944-46. Recipient Distinguished Service award D.C. Bar, 1974. Fellow Am. Bar Found. (life); mem. ABA, Nat. Bar Assn., D.C. Bar Unified (Pub. Service award 1974, pres. 1973-74), Supreme Ct. Hist. Soc. (v.p., trustee), Phi Beta Kappa, Alpha Phi Alpha, Sigma Pi Phi, Delta Theta Phi. Democrat. Club: Burning Tree (Bethesda, Md.). Lodge: Masons (32 deg.). Active participant in preparation and presentation of sch. desegregation cases before U.S. Supreme Ct., 1953-55. General corporate, Local government. Home: 1812 Upshur St NW Washington DC 20011

DUNCAN, EDWARD ROGERS, JR., lawyr; b. Joliet, Ill., Oct. 23, 1945; s. Edward Rogers and Margaret Frances (Haynes) D.; m. Jane MacKenzie Runyon, Oct. 2, 1976; children: Robert, Kathryn, Lindsay, Ann. BA, Cornell U., 1967; JD, U. Ill., 1972. Bar: Ill. 1972, U.S. Dist. Ct. (no. dist.) Ill. 1972. Assoc. Baker & McKenzie, Chgo., 1972-75; assoc. O'Reilly & Cunningham, Wheaton, Ill., 1975-80, ptnr., 1980-85; O'Reilly, Cunningham, Duncan & Huck, Wheaton, 1985—. Served to capt. USAR, 1967-73, Vietnam. Decorated Bronze Star with first oakleaf cluster. Mem. ABA, Def. Research Inst., Ill. Bar Assn., Ill. Assn. Def. Trial Counsel, DuPage County Bar Assn. Republican. Presbyterian. Personal injury, Insurance, State civil litigation. Home: 188 Spring Ave Glen Ellyn IL 60137 Office: O'Reilly Cunningham Duncan and Huck 109 N Hale Wheaton IL 60189-0846

DUNCAN, ERNEST LOUIS, JR., lawyer; b. Roscoe, Tex.; s. Ernest Louis and Velma Fern (Carll) D.; m. Sheila Darlene Mc Dougal, May 29, 1965; children—Andrew Louis, Elizabeth Diane. Student, Tex. Tech. Coll., 1961-64; J.D. cum laude, Baylor U., 1967. Bar: Tex., 1967, Fla., 1972. Briefing atty. Sup. Ct. Tex., 1967-68; assoc. Smith, Hulsey, Schwalbe & Nichols, Jacksonville, Fla., 1972-77, Branscomb & Miller, Corpus Christi, 1978-81, Barnhart, Mallia, Cochran & Luther, Corpus Christi, 1982-86, Luther & Duncan, Corpus Christi, 1987—. Served as lt. JAGC, USNR, 1968-72. Mem. ABA, Nueces County Bar Assn., Phi Gamma Delta, Phi Alpha Delta. Methodist. Real property, State civil litigation. Home: 429 Haroldson St Corpus Christi TX 78412 Office: 805 MBank Ctr N Corpus Christi TX 78471

DUNCAN, JOHN ALEXANDER, lawyer; b. Seattle, May 5, 1937; s. John A. Sr. and Elizabeth M. Duncan. BA in Econs., U. Wash., 1960; JD, U.

Calif., San Francisco, 1963. Bar: Calif. 1964. Sole practice Santa Ana, Calif., 1968-76, Newport Beach, Calif., 1976—; lectr., cons., Calif. Continuing Edn. of Bar, 1986—. Fellow Am. Coll. Probate Counsel; mem. Newport Beach Estate Planning Council, Orange County Estate Planning Council (chmn. probate trust law sect. 1977). Probate, Estate taxation, General corporate. Home and Office: 610 Newport Beach Ctr Dr #1530 Newport Beach CA 92660

DUNCAN, JOHN MILTON, lawyer, real estate broker; b. Mt. Carmel, Ill., Jan. 5, 1926; s. Roscoe Carter and Edna Elizabeth (McRoberts) D.; m. Edith Ruth Pauley, July 2, 1946 (div.); children—William Leroy, James Lawrence, Mary Jane, Barbara Jean, Dona Kay; m. 3d, Joanne B. Wood, May 31, 1980. B.S. in Chemistry, N.Mex. Inst. Mining and Tech., 1950; M.S. in Chemistry, Purdue U., 1952; J.D., St. Louis U., 1968. Bar: Mo. 1968, Ill. 1968, Calif. 1970, Tex. 1973. Analytical chemist Shell Oil Co., Wood River, Ill., 1951, chemist in charge, 1953-55, sr. technologist, 1955-69; patent atty. Shell Devel. Co., San Francisco and Houston, 1969-74, lic. atty., 1974-77, sr. lic. atty., 1977-80, sr. patent atty., 1980-84, mgr. lic. coordinating, 1984—. Served with USN, 1943-46. Mem. ABA, State Bar Tex. (chmn. intellectual property law sect. 1986—), Houston Bar Assn. (vol. lawyers com.), Houston Patent Law Assn. (pres. 1982-83), Licensing Execs. Soc. Republican. Presbyterian. Clubs: Quail Valley Country (Missouri City, Tex.); Arabia Temple Shrine Golf (Houston); Masons, Shriners. Patent, Real property. Home: 3027 La Quinta Dr Missouri City TX 77459 Office: One Shell Plaza PO Box 2463 Suite 1156 Houston TX 77001

DUNCAN, NORA KATHRYN, lawyer; b. Chgo., Feb. 23, 1946; d. Robert Ferrie and Elise Grace (Walker) D. BA in Sociology, MacMurray Coll., 1968; JD, La. State U., 1973; LLM in Internat. and Comparative Law, George Washington U., 1979. Bar: La. 1973, U.S. Dist. Ct. (mid. dist.) La. 1974, U.S. Supreme Ct. 1978, D.C. 1979, U.S. Dist. Ct. (we. dist.) La. 1981, U.S. Ct. Appeals (5th and 11th cirs.) 1981. Staff atty. La. Dept. of Justice, Baton Rouge, 1973-76; contract counsel lands and natural resource La. Dept. of Justice, Washington, 1976-78; staff atty. La. Dept. of Justice, Shreveport, 1980; assoc. Cady & Thompson, Shreveport, 1981-82; ptnr. Cady, Thompson & Duncan, Shreveport, 1983; sole practice Shreveport, 1984-86, 87—; ptnr. Walker, Tooke, Perlman & Lyons, Shreveport, 1986; instr., dir. paralegal studies program Draughon Bus. Coll., 1987—. Mem. Caddo-Pine Island Oil and Hist. Soc., Oil City, La., 1984—; atty., speech writer Gahagan for U.S. Senate, Augusta, 1978; bd. dirs. Better Bus. Bur., Shreveport, 1985-86. Paul Harris fellow Rotary Found., 1981. Mem. ABA (natural resources sect., oil and gas com.), Shreveport Bar Assn., NOW (pres. 1975). Republican. Club: Toastmaster Internat. (area II gov. 1986—, pres. Eagle chpt. 1986—). Oil and gas leasing, General corporate, Probate. Office: PO Box 78452 Shreveport LA 71137

DUNCAN, ROBERT MICHAEL, lawyer; b. N.Y.C., May 23, 1931; s. John Collamer and Doris (Bullard) D.; m. Nancy Young, Mar. 23, 1958; children: Angus M., Diana G. BA, Yale U., 1953; LLB, Harvard U., 1958. Bar: D.C. 1958. Trial atty. tax div. U.S. Dept. Justice, Washington, 1958-62; assoc. Cleary, Gottlieb, Steen & Hamilton, Washington, 1962-68; ptnr. Cleary, Gorrlieb, Steen & Hamilton, Washington, 1968—. Served to 1st lt. U.S. Army, 1953-55. Corporate taxation, Personal income taxation. Office: Cleary Gottlieb Steen & Hamilton 1752 N St NW Washington DC 20036

DUNCAN, STEPHEN MACK, lawyer; b. Oklahoma City, Mar. 28, 1941; s. Marion Claude and Helen Colleen (Stone) D.; m. Luella S. Rinehart, Mar. 13, 1965; children: Kelly Lue, Paige Anne. BS, U.S. Naval Acad., 1963; AM in Govt., Dartmouth Coll., 1969; JD, U. Colo., 1971. Bar: Colo. 1972, U.S. Dist. Ct. Colo. 1972, U.S. Ct. Appeals (10th cir.) 1972, U.S. Ct. Mil. Appeals 1973, U.S. Supreme Ct. 1975. Asst. U.S. atty. U.S. Attys. Office, Denver, 1972-73; ptnr. Gorsuch, Kirgis, Campbell, Walker & Grover, Denver, 1973-79, Morrison & Foerster, Denver, 1979-82, Hopper, Kanouff, Smith, Peryam, Terry and Duncan, Denver, 1982—; mem. faculty U. Va. Trial Adv. Inst., Charlottesville, 1986, Nat. Inst. Trial Adv., Boulder, Colo., 1981. Contbr. articles to profl. jours. Nominee for atty. gen. Colo., 1978. Served as ensign USN, 1963-69; capt. USNR, 1969—. Fellow Internat. Soc. Barristers; mem. Colo. Bar Assn. (vice chmn. litigation council 1984—, bd. govs. 1979-81), Denver Bar Assn. (bd. of trustees 1984—), Colo. Trial Lawyers Assn. Republican. Presbyterian. Club: Colo. Mountain (Denver). Avocations: mountain climbing, cross-country skiing, sailing. Federal civil litigation, State civil litigation, Military. Home: 28110 Pine Dr Evergreen CO 80439 Office: Hopper Kanouff Smith Peryam Terry & Duncan 1610 Wynkoop St Suite 200 Denver CO 80202

DUNCOMBE, RAYNOR BAILEY, lawyer; b. Washington, July 17, 1942; s. Raynor Lockwood and Avis Ethel (Bailey) D.; m. Janice Assunta Rini, Apr. 12, 1969; children: Christina Luccioni, Raynor Luccioni. AB, Franklin & Marshall Coll., 1965; JD, Syracuse U., 1968. Bar: N.Y. 1972, U.S. Dist. Ct. (no. dist.) N.Y. 1972. Staff atty. State of N.Y., Albany, 1968-70; mgmt. trainee State Bank Albany, 1970-72; staff atty. Vibbard, Donaghy & Wright, Schoharie, N.Y., 1972-73, F. Walter Bliss, Esq., Schoharie, 1973-74; sole practice Schoharie, 1974—; exec. bd. dirs. Fulmont Mut. Ins. Co.; town atty. 8 towns in Schoharie County, 1975—; sch. atty. Middleburgh (N.Y.) Sch., 1981-85; county atty., Schoharie County, 1982—. Rep. committeeman Schoharie County, 1984—; dist. commr. Boy Scouts Am., Middleburgh, 1987. Mem. ABA, N.Y. Bar Assn., Schoharie County Bar Assn. (sec.-treas. 1975—). Methodist. Lodges: Rotary (past pres.), Masons, Lions. Avocations: camping, cross country skiing, collecting stamps. Local government, General practice, Real property. Home: Rural Rt 2 Box 320 Middleburgh NY 12122 Office: 319 Main St Schoharie NY 12157

DUNE, STEVE CHARLES, lawyer; b. Vithkuqi, Korca, Albania, June 15, 1931; s. Costa Pappas and Evanthia (Vangel) D.; m. Irene Duff Boudreau, Sept. 4, 1955; children: Michelle Dune Hopper, Christopher Michael. A.B., Clark U., 1953; J.D., NYU, 1956. Bar: N.Y. 1957. Law clk. U.S. Ct. Appeals 1st Cir., 1956-57; assoc. firm Cadwalader, Wickersham & Taft, N.Y.C., 1957-65, ptnr., 1965—. Trustee Clark U., Worcester, Mass., 1974-86, vice-chmn. bd. trustees, 1980-84, chmn. bd. trustees 1984-86, chmn. presdl. search com., 1983-84. Root-Tilden scholar, 1953-56. Mem. ABA, N.Y. State Bar Assn., Fed. Bar Council, N.Y. County Lawyers Assn., Assn. Bar City N.Y. (admiralty com. 1976-79), Maritime Law Assn. U.S. (marine fin. com. 1980—), Am. Soc. Internat. Law, Phi Beta Kappa. Club: India House. Admiralty, Contracts commercial, General corporate. Office: Cadwalader Wickersham & Taft 100 Maiden Ln New York NY 10038

DUNGAN, MALCOLM THON, lawyer; b. Butler County, Kans., Mar. 17, 1922; s. Quintin Randolph and Henrietta Mathilde (Blumer) D.; m. Nancy Murray Traverso, Feb. 7, 1950; children: Nicholas William Fitz-Randolph, Sally Murray. A.A., Bartlesville Jr. Coll., 1941; B.A., Stanford U., 1947, LL.B., 1948. Bar: Calif. 1949, U.S Supreme Ct. 1956. Assoc. Brobeck, Phleger & Harrison, San Francisco, 1949-58, ptnr., 1958—. Contbr. articles to legal jours. Served to 1st lt. USMCR, 1942-46, PTO. Decorated Air medal; decorated D.F.C. Fellow Am. Bar Found.; mem. Am Law Inst., ABA (fellow sect. of litigation). Republican. Episcopalian. Clubs: Bohemian (San Francisco), Presidio Golf (San Francisco). Antitrust, Federal civil litigation, Public utilities. Office: Brobeck Phleger Harrison One Market Plaza San Francisco CA 94105

DUNHAM, CORYDON BUSHNELL, broadcasting executive, lawyer; b. Yonkers, N.Y., Nov. 14, 1927; s. Corydon Busnhell and Marion (Howe) D.; m. Janet Burke, Oct. 29, 1966; children: Corydon B. III, Christopher B. B.A., Bowdoin Coll., 1948; LL.B., Harvard U., 1951. Bar: N.Y. Assoc. Cahill, Gordon, Reindel & Ohl, N.Y.C., 1951-65; asst. gen. atty. NBC Inc., N.Y.C., 1965-68, v.p., gen. counsel, 1971-76, exec. v.p., gen. counsel, 1976—. Served to 2d lt. Arty AUS, 1944-46, Japan. Mem. ABA, Fed. Communications Bar Assn., Am. Arbitration Assn. (dir.), Am. Corp. Counsel Assn. (dir.), Assn. Bar City N.Y. Episcopalian. Clubs: Harvard (N.Y.C.); Riverside Yacht (Conn.). Administrative and regulatory, Libel, Private international. Office: NBC Inc 30 Rockefeller Plaza New York NY 10020

DUNHAM, DAN STEVEN, lawyer; b. El Paso, Tex., June 27, 1952; s. Dan Smith and Helen Louise (Steinbaker) D.; m. Judith Mary Waltrich, Sept. 21, 1985; 1 child, Dan Scott. BA, U. S.D., 1974; JD, Columbia U., 1978. Bar: N.Y. 1979, U.S. Dist. Ct. (so. and ea. dists.) N.Y. 1979. Assoc. Gilbert, Segall & Young, N.Y.C., 1978-80, Hale, Russell & Gray, N.Y.C., 1980-85, Winthrop, Stimson, Putnam & Roberts, N.Y.C., 1985—. Editor in chief Columbia Human Rights Law Rev., 1978. Mem. Assn. of Bar of City of N.Y. (com. profl. and jud. ethics). Federal civil litigation, State civil litigation, Jurisprudence. Home: 23 E 10th St New York NY 10003 Office: Winthrop Stimson Putnam & Roberts 40 Wall St New York NY 10005

DUNHAM, DOUGLAS SPENCE, lawyer; b. Anchorage, Apr. 11, 1943; s. Alexander Spence and Thelma Gladys (Akridge) D.; m. Ellen Marie Bailey, Mar. 22, 1980; children: Dana Addison, Michael Jens. BA in Econs., Willamette U., 1965, JD cum laude, 1969; LLM, Harvard U., 1975. Bar: Wash. 1969, U.S. Dist. Ct. (we. dist.) Wash. 1970, U.S. Ct. Appeals (9th cir.) 1970, U.S. Supreme Ct. 1979. Dep. pros. atty. King County, Seattle, 1969-72, sr. dep. pros. atty., 1973; assoc. Skeel, McKelvy, Henke, Evenson & Betts, Seattle, 1973-78; ptnr. Crane, Stamper, Boese, Dunham & Drury, Seattle, 1978—. Contbg. editor Willamette U. Law Rev., 1969, Wash. Lawyer Practise Manual, 1972-83. Mem. Wash. State Bar Assn. (bd. examiners 1980-81, sec.-treas. trial sect. 1983-85, dist. counsel disciplinary bd. 1985—, chairperson 1986-87), Seattle-King County Bar Assn. (trustee young lawyers sect. 1977-80, treas. 1978-79). State civil litigation, Federal civil litigation, General practice. Home: 10770 Valmay NW Seattle WA 98104 Office: Crane Stamper Boese Dunham & Drury 5700 Columbia Ctr Seattle WA 98104-7094

DUNHAM, WOLCOTT BALESTIER, JR., lawyer; b. N.Y.C., Sept. 14, 1943; s. Wolcott Balestier and Isabel Caroline (Bosworth) D.; m. Joan Findlay, Jan. 26, 1974; children: Mary Findlay, James Wolcott. B.A. magna cum laude, Harvard U., 1965, LL.B. cum laude, 1968. Bar: N.Y. 1969. Vol. VISTA, 1968-69; assoc. Debevoise & Plimpton and predecessor Debevoise, Plimpton, Lyons & Gates, N.Y.C., 1969-76, ptnr., 1977—; exec. dir. N.Y. State Exec. Adv. Commn. on Ins. Industry Regulatory Reform, 1982. Contbr. articles to profl. jours. Treas., trustee Fund for Astrophys. Research, N.Y.C., 1970—, sec., 1970-84, pres., 1984—; bd. dirs. UN Assn. N.Y.C., 1973-79, vice chmn., 1975-79; bd. dirs. Neighborhood Coalition for Shelter, Inc., 1983—. Fellow Am. Coll. Investment Counsel; mem. ABA (chmn. com. on ins. sect. adminstrv. law 1979-83), Assn. Bar City N.Y. (com. on ins. 1981—, chmn. com. 1984—), Union Internationale des Avocats, Am. Soc. Internat. Law, Harvard Law Sch. Assn. N.Y.C. (dir. 1978-81). Episcopalian. General corporate, Securities, Insurance. Office: Debevoise & Plimpton 875 3d Ave New York NY 10022

DUNIPACE, IAN DOUGLAS, lawyer; b. Tucson, Dec. 18, 1939; s. William Smith and Esther Morvyth (McGeorge) D.; B.A. magna cum laude, U. Ariz., 1961; J.D. cum laude, 1966; m. Janet Mae Dailey, June 9, 1963; children: Kenneth Mark, Leslie Amanda. Reporter, critic Long Branch (N.J.) Daily Record, 1963; admitted to Ariz. bar, 1966, U.S. Supreme Ct. bar, 1972; assoc. firm Jennings, Strouss, Salmon & Trask, Phoenix, 1966-69, Jennings, Strouss & Salmon, 1969-70, ptnr., 1971—. Reporter, Phoenix Forward Edn. Com., 1969-70; bd. mgmt. Downtown Phoenix YMCA, 1973-80, chmn., 1977-78; bd. dirs. Phoenix Met. YMCA, 1976—, chmn., 1984-85; bd. mgmt. Paradise Valley YMCA, 1979-82, chmn., 1980-81; bd. mgmt. Scottsdale/Paradise Valley YMCA, 1983, mem. legal affairs com. Pacific Region YMCA, 1978-81; bd. dirs. Beaver Valley Improvement Assn., 1977-79, Pi Kappa Alpha Holding Corp., 1968-72; trustee Paradise Valley Unified Sch. Dist. Employee Benefit Trust, 1980—, chmn., 1987—; trustee First Meth. Found. of Phoenix, 1984—; mem. Greater Paradise Valley Community Council, 1985—. Served to capt. AUS, 1961-63. Mem. State Bar Ariz. (securities regulation sect. 1970—, sect. council 1983—, mem. sect. unauthorized practice of law 1972-84, chmn. 1975-83, mem. corp. law sect. 1981—, chmn., 1984-85), Am., Fed. (sec. Ariz. chpt. 1978-79, pres. 1980-81), Maricopa County bar assns., Ariz. Zool. Soc., U. Ariz. Law Coll. Assn. (bd. dirs. 1983—, pres. 1985-86), Heard Mus. Assn., Smithsonian Assn., U. Ariz. Alumni Assn. (bd. dirs. 1985-86), Phi Beta Kappa, Phi Kappa Phi, Phi Delta Phi, Phi Alpha Theta, Sigma Delta Pi, Phi Eta Sigma, Pi Kappa Alpha (nat. counsel 1968-72). Democrat. Methodist (mem. met. Phoenix commn. 1968-71, lay leader 1975-78, trustee 1979-81, pres. 1981; mem. Pacific S.W. ann. conf. 1969-79, lawyer commn. 1980-85, chancellor Desert S.W. ann. conf. 1985—). Clubs: Mansion, Renaissance. Lodges: Masons, Kiwanis (pres. Phoenix 1984-85, lt. gov. 1986-87). Comments editor Ariz. Law Rev., 1965-66. Securities, General corporate, Banking. Home: 3601 E Mountain View Phoenix AZ 85028 Office: Jennings Strouss & Salmon 2 N Central 1 Renaissance Square Phoenix AZ 85003

DUNLAP, CHARLES LEONARD, lawyer; b. Charleston, W.Va., Feb. 17, 1941; s. Fritz H. Dunlap and Edythe (Hamlet) McGrath; m. Eric Dwayne, Laura Denise. BSBA, U. Fla., 1964; JD, Mercer U., 1967; MBA, Rollins Coll., 1986. Bar: Fla. 1967, U.S. Tax Ct. 1967, U.S. Dist. Ct. (mid. dist.) Fla. 1970, U.S. Ct. Claims Ct. 1971, U.S. Ct. Appeals (5th cir.) 1971, U.S. Dist. Ct. (no. dist.) Fla. 1972, Ohio 1973. Gen. atty. chief counsel's office IRS, Washington, 1967-71; sole practice Jacksonville, Fla., 1971-73; asst. gen. counsel Nationwode Ins. Co., Columbus, Ohio, 1973-83, Tupperware Internat., Orlando, Fla., 1983—. Editorial bd. Mercer U. Law Rev., 1967; contbr. articles to profl. jours. Mem. IRS Commr./Tax Execs. Inst. (active various coms.), ABA (taxation sect. 1972—, gen. income tax problems com. 1972-73, annual reports co. 1973-74, ins. cos. com. 1974-83, internat. sect. 1983—), Fed. Bar Assn. (tax sect.), Ohio Bar Assn., Fla. Bar Assn. (tax sect. 1967—). Public international, Corporate taxation, General corporate. Office: Tupperware Internat PO Box 2353 Orlando FL 32802

DUNLAP, TAVNER BRANHAM, lawyer; b. Lexington, Ky., Oct. 19, 1953; s. Tavner and Anna (Miller) D.; m. Celia Muller, Aug. 18, 1979; 1 child, Sarah Jordan. Grad., Denison U.; JD, U. Dayton. Bar: Ohio, Ky. Ptnr. Dunlap & Dunlap, Lexington, 1981-86, Bunch & Brock, Lexington, 1986—; v.p. Sugar Hill Farm Inc., Versailles, Ky., 1986—. Scoutmaster Lexington Boy Scouts Am., 1982-85. Mem. Fed. Bar Assn., Ky. Bar Assn., Fayette Bar Assn. Republican. Avocation: scuba diving. Family and matrimonial, Personal income taxation. Office: Bunch & Brock 271 W Short St Suite 805 Lexington KY 40507

DUNLAVEY, DEAN CARL, lawyer; b. Waterloo, Iowa, Oct. 31, 1925; s. Ralph Earnest and Lou Emma (Caffall) D.; m. Dorian Brown, Sept. 8, 1948; children: Dudley Ralph, Dean Geoffrey, Dana Charles. B.S., Harvard U., 1949, LL.M., 1956; Ph.D., U. Calif., Berkeley, 1952, LL.B., 1955. Bar: Calif. 1956. Assoc. firm Gibson, Dunn & Crutcher, Los Angeles, 1956-61; partner Gibson, Dunn & Crutcher, 1962—. Served to capt. AUS, 1943-45. Mem. Calif. State Bar, Am. Coll. Trial Lawyers. Republican. Federal civil litigation, State civil litigation. Home: 3255 Parkhurst Rolling Hills CA 90274 Office: 333 S Grand Ave Los Angeles CA 90071

DUNN, CHRISTOPHER ALLAN, lawyer; b. Maracaibo, Venezuela, June 1, 1951; s. Alexander Leslie and Honor Sheila (Maingot) D.; m. Christine Louise Vaughn, May 23, 1975; children: Conor Alexander, Reed Christopher. BA, Brown U., 1972; JD, Georgetown U., 1975. Bar: U.S. Ct. Appeals (D.C. cir.) 1975, U.S. Ct. Claims 1980, U.S. Ct. Internat. Trade 1980, U.S. Ct. Appeals (fed. cir.) 1985. Law clk. to presiding justice U.S. Ct. Claims, Washington, 1975-77; assoc. Sutherland, Asbill & Brennan, Washington, 1977-79, Arter & Hadden, Washington, 1979-83; ptnr. Wald, Harkrader & Ross, Washington, 1983-85, Willkie, Farr & Gallagher, Washington, 1985—. Republican. Roman Catholic. Club: University (Washington). Private international, Public international. Home: 3753 Kanawha St NW Washington DC 20015 Office: Willkie Farr & Gallagher 818 Connecticut Ave NW Washington DC 20006

DUNN, GEORGE J., oil company executive, lawyer; b. Cleve., Apr. 29, 1935; married. B.S., Yale U., 1957; J.D., Harvard U., 1960. With McAfee, Hanning, Newcomer & Hazlett, 1960-67; with Squire, Sanders & Dempsey, 1967; with legal dept. Standard Oil Co. (Ohio Corp.), Cleve., 1968-74, v.p., gen. counsel, 1974—. General corporate. Office: The Standard Oil Co 1725 Midland Bldg Cleveland OH 44115 *

DUNN, HERBERT IRVIN, lawyer; b. Balt., July 19, 1946; s. Albert M. and Hilda F. (Winakur) D.; m. Marsha Edith Greenfield, Apr. 1, 1979; children—Marla Phyllis, Jonathan Howard. B.S. with high honors, U. Md., 1969, J.D., 1971. Bar: Md. 1971, D.C. 1971, U.S. Ct. Claims 1972, U.S. Tax Ct. 1972, U.S. Dist. Ct. D.C. 1971, U.S. Ct. Appeals (D.C. cir.) 1971, U.S. Supreme Ct. 1975. Atty.-adviser Office of Gen. Counsel U.S. Gen. Acctg. Office, Washington, 1971-83, sr. atty., 1983—. Served with USAR, 1968-74. Mem. Fed. Bar Assn. (exec. council Capitol Hill chpt. 1975-83, treas. Young Lawyers div. 1977-79, nat. council 1978-79), Md. Bar Assn., Omicron Delta Epsilon. Administrative and regulatory. Office: 441 G St NW Washington DC 20548

DUNN, JACKSON THOMAS, JR., lawyer, legal educator; b. Charlotte, N.C., Nov. 30, 1943; s. Jackson Thomas and Dorothy Holland (Schweiger) D.; m. Mary Louise Miller, Apr. 23, 1944; children—Jackson Thomas, Michael Lansing, Mary Katherine Holland. A.B., Belmont Abbey Coll., 1965; J.D., U. N.C., 1968. Bar: N.C. 1968, U.S. Dist. Ct. (mid. dist.) N.C. 1977, U.S. Dist. Ct. (we. dist.) N.C. 1974, U.S. Supreme Ct. 1982. Asst. prof. East Carolina U., Greenville, N.C., 1968-69, U. Ga., Athens, 1969-75; ptnr. Edwards & Dunn, Charlotte, N.C., 1975; counsel The Ervin Co., Charlotte, 1976; v.p., sr. counsel Northwestern Fin. Corp. and Northwestern Bank, North Wilkesboro, N.C., 1976-85; v.p., assoc. gen. counsel 1st Union Corp. and 1st Union Nat. Bank, 1985—; dir. M & J Group, Inc., Northwestern Leasing Corp., Northwestern Ins. Corp.; instr. N.C. Bankers Assn. Seminars. Bd. govs. U. N.C. Law Sch. Alumni Assn. Mem. ABA, N.C. Bar Assn. (fin. instns. com.), N.C. Bankers Assn. (chmn. N.C. Bank Counsel Com.). Democrat. Contbr. writings to legal publs. Banking, General corporate, Legislative. Office: 1st Union Corp LEG Charlotte NC 28288

DUNN, JAMES MELVIN, lawyer; b. Booneville, Ark., Apr. 30, 1948; s. Melvin Ralph and Jeanette (Atwood) D.; m. Suzanne Vinson, June 27, 1970; children: Amy Jackson, Julie Suzanne, James Matthew. BA, Hendrix Coll., 1970; JD, U. Ark., 1974. Bar: Ark. 1974, U.S. Dist. Ct. (ea. and we. dists.) Ark. 1974, U.S. Ct. Appeals (8th cir.) 1974, U.S. Supreme Ct. 1986. Ptnr. Warner & Smith, Ft. Smith, Ark., 1974—. Pres. Ft. Smith Regional Playground for All Children, 1981-86; Chmn. adminstrv. bd. Goddard Meth. Ch., Ft. Smith, 1985—; bd. dirs. Interfaith Community Ctr., Ft. Smith, 1986—. Recipient Distinguished Service award Ft. Smith Jaycees, 1982-83; named Individual Yr. Ark. Recreation and Parks Assn., 1983. Mem. ABA, Ark. Bar Assn., Sebastian County Bar Assn. (pres.1986-87). Democrat. Methodist. Club: Noon Civics (Ft. Smith). Lodge: Rotary (pres. Ft. Smith 1981-82, Paul Harris fellow 1983). Avocations: scuba diving, photography, swimming. Federal civil litigation, State civil litigation, General practice. Home: 5601 S Enid Fort Smith AR 72903 Office: Warner & Smith 214 N 6th Fort Smith AR 72902-1626

DUNN, JOHN BENJAMIN, lawyer; b. Washington, July 12, 1948; s. Read P. Jr. and Barbara (Butts) D.; m. Virginia Ann Hughes, July 3, 1983; 1 child, Lily Conti Hughes-Dunn. BA, Ohio Wesleyan U., Delaware, 1970; JD, George Washington U., 1973. Bar: D.C. 1973, Md. 1974, U.S. Ct. Appeals (D.C. cir.) 1974. Assoc. Schultz & Overby, Washington, 1973-76, Law Offices of Daniel E. Schultz, Washington, 1976-80; prin. Schultz & Dunn (now Schultz, Dunn & Murray), Washington, 1980-85; sole practice Takoma Park, Md., 1985—. Family and matrimonial, Probate, Workers' compensation. Office: 7030 Carroll Ave Suite 2 Takoma Park MD 20912

DUNN, MELVIN EDWARD, judge; b. Chgo., Oct. 31, 1933; s. Raymond E. and Josephine (Fitzgerald) D.; m. Judith Wilkinson, Oct. 28, 1972; children: Lori Dunn Mulley, Richard A. Vester Jr., Jonathan T. Vester, Geoffrey A. Vester, Andrea Lynn. JD, Chgo.-Kent Coll. Law, Ill. Inst. Tech., 1971. Bar: Ill. Assoc. Melvin E. Dunn, Ltd., Elburn, Ill., 1972-82; assoc. judge 16th Jud. Circuit, Kane County, Ill., 1982-86, cir. judge, 1986—. Served with USCG, 1952-56. Mem. Am. Acad. Matrimonial Lawyers (bd. mgrs. Ill. chpt.), ABA, Ill. Bar Assn. (chmn. family law sect. council), Kane County Bar Assn. Methodist. Club: Masons. Family and matrimonial. Office: Kane County Courthouse PO Box 354 Geneva IL 60134

DUNN, M(ORRIS) DOUGLAS, lawyer; b. Ionia, Mich., Nov. 1, 1944; s. Morris Frederick and Lola Adella (Gee) D.; m. Jill Lynn Fasbender, July 22, 1967; children—Brooks, Gillian, Joshua. B.S. in Mech. Engring., U. Mich., 1967; J.D., Vanderbilt U., 1970. Assoc. Winthrop Stimson, Putnam & Roberts, N.Y.C., 1970-78, ptnr. 1978-84; sr. v.p., mng. dir. Shearson Lehman Bros. Inc., N.Y.C., 1984-85; part. Milbank, Tweed. Hadley & McCloy, N.Y.C., 1985—. Contbr. articles to profl. jours. Bd. dirs. Madison Area YMCA, N.J., 1978-82. Mem. ABA (ann. reporter devels. in securities law, corp. financing com. 1986—, vice chmn. 1980-86, fed. regulation of securities com. 1981—), N.Y.C. Bar Assn. (chmn. nuclear tech. and law com. 1976-77), Internat. Bar Assn. (vice chmn. com. K 1986—), Chatham Fish and Game Protective Assn. Club: Down Town (N.Y.C.). Securities, Public utilities, Private international. Home: 72 Chandler Rd Chatham NJ 07928 Office: Milbank Tweed Hadley & McCloy 1 Chase Manhattan Plaza New York NY 10005

DUNN, PAUL JAMES, lawyer; b. Tiffin, Ohio, Sept. 23, 1939; s. James Marion and Elenora Rosina (Theis) D.; m. Carolyn Ann Bittner, Mar. 20, 1965; children: Cheryl Ann, Brian James. BA, Cath. U., 1962; JD, Ohio State U., 1964. Bar: Ohio 1965, Ariz. 1981. Sole practice Tiffin, 1965-84, Prescott, Ariz., 1982—. Law dir. City of Tiffin, 1972-73; mem. Prescott St. Commn., 1983—; bd. dirs. Tiffin C. of C., 1975-78; trustee Yavapai Regional Med. Ctr., Prescott, 1986. Named Boss of Yr., Seneca County, Ohio Legal Secs., 1983. Mem. ABA (taxation, real property, probate and trust sects.), Ariz. Bar Assn. (exec. com. probate and trust law sect. 1986—, editor newsletter 1986—, cert. 1987), Seneca County Bar Assn. (pres. 1975). Lodges: Kiwanis (pres. Tiffin 1981), Elks. Avocations: computers, motorcycling. Home: 2155 Nolte Dr Prescott AZ 86301 Office: 915 E Gurley St Prescott AZ 86301

DUNN, RICHARD CLEMENT, lawyer; b. Dallas, Sept. 20, 1956; s. Marvin Richard and Rosemary (Clement) D.; m. Terre Dea Finley, June 4, 1983. BA with highest honors, U. Tex., 1979, JD, 1982. Bar: Tex. 1982. 1st asst. dist. atty. Gregg County Dist. Atty.'s Office, Longview, Tex., 1982—; vis. instr. East Tex. Police Acad., Kilgore, 1982—. Mem. U. Tex. Ex-students Assn., Longview, 1982—; sponsor Longview Theatre Project, 1986—. Democrat. Presbyterian. Criminal, Government contracts and claims, Local government. Office: Gregg County Dist Attys Office PO Box 3403 Longview TX 75606

DUNN, RICHARD DEVERE, judge; b. Washingtonville, Ohio, July 4, 1916; s. Richard and Margaret (McBride) D.; m. Theda Sersen, Sept. 6, 1941. Student Wayne State U., 1946-47; LL.B., Detroit Coll. Law, 1950. Atty., Dearborn Twp., Mich., 1956-62; corp. counsel Town Dearborn Heights, Mich., 1962-63, mcpl. judge, 1963-69; judge 20th Dist. Ct. Mich., Dearborn Heights, 1969-75; judge 3d Jud. Circ. Mich., Wayne County, 1975—, chief judge, 1977-87; exec. chief judge Wayne Cir. Ct., 1981-87. Trustee, Detroit Coll. Law, 1961—; chmn. United Fund, 1983. Mem. Mediation Tribunal Assn. (founder, bd. dirs. 1979—), Mich. Assn. Trial Lawyers, Detroit Assn. Def. Counsel, Conf. Met. Cts. (pres. nat. 1984), Mich. Judges Assn., Am. Judicature Soc. Roman Catholic. Club: Washtenaw Country. Lodge: Elks. Judicial administration. Home: 27094 Havelock Dr Dearborn Heights MI 48127 Office: 1201 City County Bldg 2 Woodward Ave Detroit MI 48226

DUNN, SUSAN M., law librarian; b. Sioux City, Iowa, Oct. 16, 1956; d. Clifton H. and Carol M. (Heide) D. BFA, Doane Coll., 1978; MLS, Emporia State U., 1979. Librarian, census coordinator Sioux City (Iowa) and Interstate Met. Planning Commn., 1980-81; law librarian Woodbury County Bar Assn., Sioux City, 1981—. Vol. sta. KWIT FM 90 pub. radio, W. Iowa Community Coll., 1986—, YWCA, Sioux City, 1985. Mem. ALA, Iowa Library Assn. Republican. Baptist. Librarianship support staff. Home: 905 Jennings Sioux City IA 51105 Office: Woodbury County Bar Assn County Courthouse 6th Floor Sioux City IA 51101

DUNN, THOMAS TINSLEY, lawyer; b. Petersburg, Va., Aug. 27, 1901; s. George White and Emma (Tinsley) D.; m. Elizabeth Emogene Campbell, Dec. 31, 1927 (dec. 1983); children: Janet D. Tillery, Thomas Churchill; m. Mary Brooks Schwager, June 16, 1984. BS, U. Va., 1925, LLB, 1926. Bar: Va. 1925, Fla. 1926. Asst. trust officer First Nat. Bank, St. Petersburg, Fla., 1926-30; v.p., trust officer United Savs. Bank, Detroit, 1930-35; asst. v.p. Pub. Nat. Bank & Trust Co., N.Y.C., 1936-37; dir. trust and estate planning Citizens and So. Nat. Bank, Atlanta, 1938-41; v.p., trust officer First Nat. Bank, St. Petersburg, Fla., 1941-54; sole practice, 1954-72; of counsel Dunn & Dunn Attys., P.A., St. Petersburg, 1980—. Author: A Lawyer's Advice to

Retirees, 1981. Mem. ABA, Alpha Chi Rho, Phi Alpha Delta. Republican. Episcopalian. Clubs: St. Petersburg Yacht, Bath. Lodges: Masons, Shriners. Probate, Estate planning.

DUNN, WESLEY BRANKLEY, lawyer; b. Baskerville, Va., Oct. 9, 1951; s. Charles Richard III and Nancy Carolyn (Wells) D.; m. Lynda Reeves, Nos. 12, 1980; children: Elle, Anslyn. BA, Ga. State U., 1974; JD, Emory U., 1978. Bar: Ga. 1978, U.S. Dist. Ct. (no. dist.) Ga. 1978, U.S. Ct. Appeals (5th cir.0 1978, U.S. Supreme Ct. 1985. Assoc. Hansell & Post, Atlanta, 1978-81, Levine & D'Alessio, Atlanta, 1981-85; ptnr. Hancock, Dunn & Shuping, Riverdale, Ga., 1985—. State rep. Ga. Gen. Assembly, Atlanta, 1983—; pres. Henry County Heart Assn., McDonough, Ga., 1985. Mem. Ga. Bar Assn., Atlanta Bar Assn., Clayton Bar Assn., Henry County Bar Assn. Democrat. Presbyterian. Avocations: flying, tennis, golf. Legislative, Real property. Home: 840 McGarity Rd McDonough GA 30253 Office: Hancock Dunn & Shuping 7316 Hwy 85 Riverdale GA 30274

DUNN, WILLIAM DAVID, lawyer, writer; b. Tampa, Fla., July 2, 1933; s. Thomas Henry and Eleanor (Stephens) D. B.S. in Journalism, Fla. State U., 1953; J.D., U. Fla., 1958; postgrad. in French studies U. Paris, 1965-66, in art history Ecole du Louvre, Paris, 1966-67. Bar: N.Y. 1972, U.S. Dist. Ct. (so. and ea. dists.) N.Y. 1974. Night news editor Nippon Times, Tokyo, 1954-55; arts editor St. Petersburg Times, Fla., 1958-65; bur. chief MacNens News Agy., Paris, 1965-66; account exec. Foote, Cone & Belding, Paris, 1967-68; editorial dir. Advt. Trade Publs., N.Y.C., 1968-70; def. atty. Legal Aid Soc., N.Y.C., 1972—. Editor monthly mag. Art Direction, 1968-70, FotoTimes, 1970-71. Area coordinator Gt. Books Found., discussion groups, Fla., 1959-63; mem. coordinating council Great Decisions, fgn. policy discussion groups, St. Petersburg, Fla., 1961-64; bd. dirs. Fla. Arts Council, 1963-65, Performing Arts Alumni Theatre, N.Y.C., 1983—; mem. adv. bd. New Mus., N.Y.C., 1975—. Served with U.S. Army, 1953-55. Recipient Key to City, Mayor of St. Petersburg, 1965. Mem. N.Y. State Bar Assn., New York County Bar Assn., N.Y. State Defenders (bd. dirs. 1976—, amicus curiae com. 1983—), Gold Key, Alpha Tau Omega, Delta Sigma Pi. Democrat. Clubs: Union (Tokyo); American (Paris). Criminal, Entertainment. Home: 77 W 85th St Apt 2-C New York NY 10024 also: 2118 Marjory Ave Tampa FL 33606 Office: Legal Aid Society 80 Lafayette St New York NY 10013

DUNNAN, WEAVER WHITE, lawyer; b. Paxton, Ill., Sept. 23, 1923; s. J. Wallace and Mabel (White) D.; m. Diana Barrett Baldwin, Feb. 14, 1953; children—Bruce B., Douglas M., Donald S., Winifred B., John M. A.B., Harvard U., 1947, LL.B., 1949. Bar: D.C. 1951, U.S. Supreme Ct. 1954, U.S. Tax Ct. 1957, U.S. Ct. Appeals (D.C. cir.) 1960. Law clk. U.S. Ct. Appeals 2d cir., N.Y.C., 1949-50; law clk. to justice Felix Frankfurter, U.S. Supreme Ct., Washington, 1950-51; assoc., ptnr. firm Covington & Burling, Washington, 1960—. Bd. govs. St. Albans Sch., Washington, 1974-80; bd. dirs. Beauvoir Sch., Nat. Cathedral Sch., Washington, 1969-74. Served to sgt. U.S. Army, 1943-46; PTO. Decorated 2 Overseas Service bars, Am. Campaign medal, Asiatic Pacific Theater ribbon with 3 bronze battle stars, Phillippine Liberation ribbon with 2 bronze stars. Mem. ABA (chmn. com. tax reform, sect. corp., banking and bus. law, vice chmn. com. on profit policy, pub. contract sect.). Republican. Clubs: Metropolitan (Washington); Chevy Chase. General corporate, Government contracts and claims, Corporate taxation. Home: 5110 Cammack Dr Bethesda MD 20816 Office: Covington & Burling 1201 Pennsylvania Ave NW PO Box 7566 Washington DC 20044

DUNNE, FRANCIS HUGH, lawyer; b. Bklyn., Oct. 6, 1942; s. Frank H. and Virginia M. (Genovese) D.; m. Margaret A. DiTommaso, Aug. 1, 1964; children: Francis H. Jr., Karen, Stephen. BA, Villanova U., 1964; LLM, Fordham U., 1967; MBA, Mich. State U., 1975. Bar: N.Y. 1968, Mich. 1971, U.S. Dist. Ct. (ea. and so. dists.) N.Y. 1971. Assoc. Olwine, Connelly, Chase, O'Donnell & Weyher, N.Y.C., 1967-71; atty. legal dept. Gen. Motors Corp., Detroit, 1971-73, supervisory atty., 1973-75, atty. trade regulation, 1975-79, atty. in charge trade regulation, 1979-83, asst. gen. counsel legal dept., 1983—. Bd. consultors Villanova U. Sch. Law, 1986—. Recipient Young Alumnus award Villanova U., 1979, Alumni Medallion award, 1982. Mem. ABA, Mich. Bar Assn., U.S. C. of C. (council antitrust policy). Antitrust, Administrative and regulatory, Federal civil litigation. Office: Gen Motors Corp Legal Dept New Ctr 1 Bldg 3031 W Grand Blvd Detroit MI 48232

DUNNE, GERARD FRANCIS, lawyer; b. Huntington, N.Y., Aug. 23, 1947; s. Frank and Adele A. (Malerba) D.; m. Judith Ellen Gordon, Dec. 5, 1976; 1 child, Heather Chelsey. B in Engring., Manhattan Coll., 1969; JD, U. Balt., 1974. Bar: D.C. 1974, N.Y. 1974, U.S. Patent Office, U.S. Dist. Ct. (ea. and so. dists.) N.Y. 1976, U.S. Ct. Appeals (fed. cir.) 1982, U.S. Ct. Appeals (2d and 8th cirs.) 1985. Examiner patents U.S. Patent Office, Washington, 1969-74; assoc. Law Offices of Albert C. Johnston P.C., N.Y.C., 1974-76; assoc. Wyatt, Gerber, Shoup, Scobey & Badie, N.Y.C., 1976-82, ptnr., 1982—. Mem. ABA, IEEE, Assn. of Bar of City of N.Y., Fed. Bar Council. Federal civil litigation, Patent, Trademark and copyright. Home: 89-04 63d Ave New York NY 11374 Office: Wyatt Gerber Shoup Scobey & Badie 261 Madison Ave New York NY 10016

DUNNE, STEPHEN LEWIS, lawyer; b. Chester, Pa., Aug. 16, 1945; s. Lewis Stephen and Claudine (Rawlings) D.; m. Charlotte Robinson, Feb. 4, 1987; children: James Gregory, Jacob Aran, Heather Annette. B.A., La. State U., 1967; J.D., Tulane U., 1970. Bar: La. 1970, Oreg. 1974, U.S. Supreme Ct. 1977, Calif. 1983. Assoc., Deutsch, Kerrigan & Stiles, New Orleans, 1970-71; asst. U.S. atty., 1971-72; trial atty. antitrust div. U.S. Dept. Justice, 1972-74; chief counsel antitrust div. Dept. Justice, 1974-79; spl. counsel antitrust div. Dept. Justice, State of Calif., 1975; prof. antitrust law Willamette U., 1975-76; guest lectr. U. Oreg., 1978; faculty Hastings Coll. Law-U. Calif., 1983—; speaker Lewis & Clark Antitrust Seminar, 1978, Nat. Assn. Accts., 1978, multi-dist. litigation programs Nat. Assn. Attys. Gen., 1977; mem. faculty Practicing Law Inst., 1976; spl. asst. atty. gen. Oreg., 1979-81; spl. asst. atty. gen. Fla., 1979—; adviser, mem. faculty Nat. Jud. Coll., 1978-79. Mem. Phi Alpha Delta. Presbyterian. Antitrust, Federal civil litigation, State civil litigation. Home: PO Box 1228 Rancho Santa Fe CA 92067 Office: 4490 Fanuel St Suite 222 San Diego CA 92109

DUNNINGTON, WALTER GREY, JR., lawyer, food company executive; b. N.Y.C., Feb. 5, 1927; s. Walter Grey and Allen (Gray) D.; m. Jacqueline Cochran, Apr. 26, 1958; m. Patricia MacPhee, Sept. 21, 1972; children—Walter Grey III, India M. B.A., U. Va., 1948, LL.B., 1950. Bar: N.Y. 1952. Assoc. Rathbone, Perry, Kelley & Drye, N.Y.C., 1950-54; ptnr. Dunnington, Bartholow & Miller, N.Y.C., 1954-75, sr. ptnr., 1976-81; sr. v.p., gen. counsel Standard Brands Inc., N.Y.C., 1981, dir., 1964-81; exec. v.p., gen. counsel, dir. Nabisco Brands, Inc., East Hanover, N.J., 1981-87, sr. v.p., dep. gen. counsel RJR Nabisco, Inc., Atlanta, 1987—, also dir.; mem. legal steering com. Grocery Mfrs. Am., Inc., Washington. Bd. govs. N.Y. Hosp., N.Y.C.; trustee Algernon Sydney Sullivan Found., Morristown, N.J., Boys' Club N.Y., N.Y.C., Sprague Found., N.Y.C., Food and Drug Law Inst., Washington. Served with USNR, 1945. Mem. Assn. Bar City N.Y., N.Y. State Bar Assn., ABA. Episcopalian. Clubs: Brook; Racquet and Tennis (N.Y.C.); Nat. Golf Links Am.; Deepdale (L.I., N.Y.); Somerset Hills Country (Bernardsville, N.J.). General corporate. Office: RJR Nabisco Inc 9 W 57th St New York NY 10019

DUNSMORE, E. EDWARD, lawyer; b. New Castle, Ind., Feb. 26, 1947; s. Earl Edward Dunsmore and Joyce D. (Bolden) Dunsmore Estell; m. Judith L. Feigel, Sept. 8, 1972; children—Jessica Elizabeth, Sarah Michele. B.S., Ball State U., 1969; J.D., Ind. U.-Indpls., 1972. Bar: Ind. 1972, U.S. Dist. Ct. (so. dist.) Ind. 1972. Sole practice, Knightstown, Ind., 1972—; atty. Student Legal Services, Ball State U., Muncie, Ind., 1973-76; pub. defender Henry County Ct., New Castle, Ind., 1976, Henry Circuit Ct., New Castle, 1980-83; town atty. Town of Knightstown, 1980-84, 87, Town of Spiceland (Ind.), 1983—; atty. Rush County Area Planning Commn., Ind., 1983-86, Rush County Bd. Zoning Appeals, Rushville, 1983-86, Charles A. Beard Meml. Sch. Corp., Knightstown, 1984—; adj. prof. adminstrv. law Ind. U.-Purdue U., 1977; workshop participant Nat. Inst. Trial Advocacy, Indpls., 1981. Bd. dirs. Henry County Heart Assn., New Castle, 1981-83; mem. philanthropy adv. com. Ball State U. Found. State of Ind. scholar Ball State U., 1965-69; bail project fellow Ind. U. Law Sch., 1971-72. Mem. ABA, Ind. Bar Assn., Henry County Bar Assn., Nat. Assn. Criminal Def. Lawyers, Assn. Trial Lawyers Am., Ind. Trial Lawyers Assn., Blue Key, Pi Gamma Mu. Lodges: Masons, KP. General practice, State civil litigation. Office: 18 N Jefferson St PO Box 155 Knightstown IN 46148

DUPLANTIER, ADRIAN GUY, federal judge; b. New Orleans, Mar. 5, 1929; s. F. Robert and Amelie (Rivet) D.; m. Sally Thomas, July 15, 1951; children: Adrian G., David L., Thomas, Jeanne M., Louise M., John C. J.D. cum laude, Loyola U., New Orleans, 1949. Bar: La. bar 1950, U.S. Supreme Ct 1954. Practiced law New Orleans, 1950-74; judge Civil Dist. Ct. Parish of Orleans, 1974-78, U.S. Dist. Ct., New Orleans, 1978—; part-time prof. code of civil procedure Loyola U., 1951—, lectr. dental jurisprudence, 1960-67, lectr. English dept., 1948-50; mem. La. State Senate, 1960-74; 1st asst. dist. atty., New Orleans, 1954-56. Editorial bd.: Loyola Law Rev, 1947-48; editor-in-chief, 1948-49. Del. Democratic Nat. Conv., 1964; pres. Associated Cath. Charities New Orleans, Social Welfare Planning Council Greater New Orleans; mem. adv. bd. St. Mary's Dominican Coll., 1970-71, Ursuline Acad., 1968-73, Mt. Carmel Acad., 1965-69; chmn. pres.'s adv. council Jesuit High Sch., 1979—; active Assn. Retarded Children, Cystic Fibrosis Found. Recipient Meritorious award New Orleans Assn. Retarded Children, 1965; Gov.'s Cert. of Merit, 1970. Mem. Am. Bar Assn. (award 1960), La. Bar Assn., New Orleans Bar Assn., Order of Coif, Alpha Sigma Nu. Office: Chambers C-205 U S Courthouse 500 Camp St New Orleans LA 70130 *

DUPONT, RALPH PAUL, lawyer, educator; b. Fall River, Mass., May 21, 1929; s. Michael William and Gertrude (Murphy) D.; m. Barbara A. Irwin; children—Ellen O'Neill, Antonia Chafee, William Albert. A.B. cum laude with highest honors in Am. Civilization, Brown U., 1951; J.D. cum laude, Harvard U., 1956. Bar: Conn. 1956, U.S. Supreme Ct. 1967; diplomate Nat. Bd. Trial Advocacy. Assoc. Davies, Hardy & Schenck, N.Y.C., 1956-57; ptnr. Copp and Dupont, New London, Conn., 1957-60; mem. Suisman, Shapiro & Wool, New London, Conn., 1961-63; ptnr. Dupont & Dupont (and predecessor firms), New London, 1963—; chmn. bd. dirs. Dupont, Tobin, Levin, Carberry & O'Malley, New London, 1986—; instr. Am. history and bus. law Mitchell Coll., New London, 1955, 57-58; vis. prof., Northeastern U. Sch. Law, Boston, 1977-78; lectr. Am. legal history U. Conn. Sch. Law, 1980-86; mem. adv. bd. Conn. Bank & Trust Co., New London, 1984—; mem. Conn. Legal Services Adv. Council, 1980-82. Mem. bd. edn. New London, Conn., 1959-61; pres. Wamphassuc Point Assn.; Dem. candidate for Conn. Senate, 1960; bd. dirs. Conn. Bar Found., 1975-79; 1st v.p., trustee U.S. Atlantic Tuna Tournament. Served as lt. USNR, 1951-53. Named Outstanding Young Man of Yr., Conn. Jr. C. of C., 1960; recipient Disting. Service award Greater New London Jr. C. of C., 1960. Fellow Am. Coll. Probate Counsel; mem. ABA, Conn. Bar Assn., New London County Bar Assn., Assn. Trial Lawyers Am., Harvard Law Sch. Assn. Conn. (bd. govs.), Internat. Acad. Estate Planners, Newcomer Soc., Delta Sigma Rho, Kappa Sigma. Roman Catholic. Clubs: Faculty of Brown U. (Providence): Harvard (N.Y.C., Boston); Thames (New London). Personal injury, Probate, General practice. Home: RFD Route 1 Box 119 Wamphassuc Point Stonington CT 06378 Office: Dupont Tobin Levin et al 43 Broad St PO Box 58 New London CT 06320

DUPRE, JOHN LEACY, lawyer; b. Ogdensburg, N.Y., Oct. 8, 1956; s. Thomas Edward and Anna L. (Seymour) DuP.; m. Colleen Lyons, Oct. 11, 1980; children: Christopher James, Allison Leacy. BA, Williams Coll., 1978; JD, Fordham U., 1981. Bar: N.Y. 1982, N.H. 1987. Assoc. Hopgood, Calimafde, Kalil, Blaustein & Judlowe, N.Y.C., 1981-86, Hamilton, Brook, Smith & Reynolds, Lexington, Mass., 1986—. Mem. ABA, N.H. State Bar Assn., Boston Patent Law Assn. Federal civil litigation, Patent, Trademark and copyright.

DUPREE, CHARLES PATRICK, lawyer; b. Washington, June 9, 1949; s. Jack C. and Jeanne (Funderburg) D. B.A. in English, U. Tenn., 1971, J.D., 1974. Bar: Tenn. 1974, U.S. Dist. Ct. (ea. dist.) Tenn. 1975, U.S. Supreme Ct. 1978, U.S. Ct. Appeals (6th cir.) 1983. Ptnr. Curtis & Dupree, Chattanooga, 1974-76, Wassick & Dupree, Chattanooga, 1981-84, sole practice, Chattanooga, 1976-81, 84—; bd. dirs. S.E. Tenn. Legal Services, Chattanooga, 1974-83; counsel Chattanooga Area Urban League, 1980-83; v.p., mem. state com. Chattanooga area ACLU, 1977—; mem. Tenn. adv. com. U.S. Commn. on Civil Rights, Washington, 1978—. Mem. Chattanooga Mayor's Human Relations Com., 1979-84, pres., 1983-84; bd. dirs. Chattanooga Area Law Enforcement Com., 1980-87; charter mem. bd. dirs. Chattanooga Area Urban League, 1980-87. Mem. Assn. Trial Lawyers Am., ABA, Tenn. Bar Assn. (ho. of dels. 1978-79), Chattanooga Bar Assn. Jewish. Federal civil litigation, State civil litigation, Criminal. Office: 707 Georgia Ave 2d Floor Flatiron Bldg Chattanooga TN 37402

DURAND, PHILIP POYNTELL, lawyer; b. Madison, Wis., Dec. 24, 1933; s. Loyal and Dorothy (Lee) D.; m. Dianne Roberts, May 11, 1967; children—Peter Mac Dearmon, Dorothy Amanda; m. 2d, Judy Dunkin, Dec. 26, 1982. A.B., Yale U., 1955, J.D., U. Tenn., 1961. Bar: Tenn. 1970, U.S. Dist. Ct. (ea. dist.) Tenn. 1970, U.S. Ct. Appeals (6th cir.) 1972, U.S. Supreme Ct. 1972. Assoc. Roberts, Boradman, Suhr & Curry, Madison, Wis., 1961-63; with U.S. Peace Corps, African Regional Lawyers Project, Malawi, 1963-65, instr. Malawi Inst. Pub. Adminstrn.; with Sailer Project (Ford Found.), 1966-67; Internat. Legal Ctr. instr. in law Keynya Inst. Pub. Adminstrn., Nairobi, 1967-69; sole practice, Knoxville, Tenn., 1970-73; ptnr. Ambrose, Wilson, Grimm& Durand, Knoxville, 1973—. Served with USMC, 1955-59. Mem. Tenn. Assn. Criminal Def. Lawyers (pres. 1974-75), Tenn. Bar Assn. (ho. of dels., chmn. 1977-79), Author: Index of East African Cases Referred to, 1868-1968, 1968; Evidence for Magistrates, 1969; contbr. articles to legal jours. Civil rights, Federal civil litigation, Criminal. Office: 9th Floor Valley Fidelity Bank Bldg PO Box 2466 Knoxville TN 37901

DURANT, JAMES ROBERT, lawyer; b. Binghamton, N.Y., Dec. 31, 1946; s. Edward Joseph and Mary Elizabeth (Karnes) D.; m. Kristy Lou Ritterby, June 26, 1976; children: Jennifer Ryan, Cassie Lynn. BS summa cum laude, Western Mich. U., 1973; JD, Thomas M. Cooley Coll., 1976. Bar: Mich. 1976, U.S. Dist. Ct. (we. dist.) Mich. 1978. Sole practice Kalamazoo, Mich., 1976-82; ptnr. Lilly, Domeny, Durant, Byrne & Schanz P.C., Kalamazoo, 1982—; lectr. in field. Served with U.S. Army, 1967-69. Mem. Nat. Health Lawyers Assn., Mich. Health Lawyers Assn. (corp. law sect., real property law sect.). Republican. Roman Catholic. General corporate, Health, Real property. Office: Lilly Domeny Durant Byrne & Schanz 505 S Park St Kalamazoo MI 49007

DURANT, MARC, lawyer; b. N.Y.C., Jan. 17, 1947; s. Sidney Irwin and Estelle (Haas) D.; m. Karen Rose Baker, June 9, 1968 (div. July 1975); children: Lauren, Elyssa; m. Rita Mary Tatar, Dec. 31, 1979; 1 child, David. BS, Cornell U., 1968; JD, Harvard U., 1968-71. Bar: Pa. 1972, U.S. Dist. Ct. (ea. dist.) Pa. 1972, U.S. Supreme Ct. 1980, U.S. Ct. Appeals (3d cir.) 1981. Law clk. U.S. Dist. Ct., Wilmington, Del., 1971-72; assoc. Schnader, Harrison, Segal & Lewis, Phila., 1972-75; asst. U.S. Atty. U.S. Dept. Justice, Phila., 1975-77; dep. chief criminal div. U.S. Atty.'s Office, Phila., 1977-81; ptnr. Marc Durant and Assocs., Phila., 1981—. Mem. ABA, Fed. Bar Assn., Phila. Bar Assn. Federal civil litigation, Criminal. Office: Marc Durant & Assocs 400 Market St Philadelphia PA 19106

DURELL, JAY GLENN, lawyer; b. Memphis, June 8, 1956; s. Jack Lorren and Glenda Joy (Brigance) D.; m. Denise Diane McCandless, June 26, 1982; children: David Jayson, Daniel Glenn. Student, U. N.C., Charlotte, 1975-76; BA, Tex. Tech U., 1978, JD, 1981. Bar: Tex. 1982. PTNR. Hollmann, Lyon, Patterson & Durell, Inc., Odessa, Tex., 1981—; alt. mcpl. judge City of Odessa, 1984. Bd. dirs. Odessa Cablevision Adv. Bd., 1985—. Mem. ABA, Ector County Bar Assn., Young Lawyers Assn. Club: Tex. Tech Red Raider (Odessa) (chmn. 1985—). Avocations: golf, spectator sports. Real property, Probate, General corporate. Home: 6 Foote Ct Odessa TX 79762 Office: Hollmann Lyon Patterson & Durell Inc 1205 W University Odessa TX 79764

DURFEE, AMY LEE MCELHENY, lawyer; b. Denver, May 2, 1954; d. Richard Lee and Evelyn May (Gagos) McElheny; m. Steven Lee Durfee, Mar. 20, 1973; children: Casey Samuel, Benjamin Patrick, Lillian Elizabeth. BA with distinction, U. Colo., 1975; JD, U. Denver, 1979. Bar: Colo. 1980, U.S. Dist. Ct. Colo. 1980. Assoc. Carpenter & Klatskin P.C., Denver, 1980-82, Haligman & Lottner P.C., Denver, 1983—. Mem. ABA, Colo. Bar Assn., Denver Bar Assn. (chmn. community concerns com. 1984-86). Democrat. United Methodist. Avocations: gardening, photography, backpacking. Real property, Contracts commercial, Banking. Office: Haligman Zall & Lottner PC 7887 E Belleview #700 Englewood CO 80110

DURHAM, BARBARA, state justice; b. 1942. B.S.B.A., Georgetown U.; law degree, Stanford U. Bar: Wash. 1968. Formerly judge Wash. Superior Ct., King County; then judge Wash. Ct. Appeals; assoc. justice Wash. Supreme Ct., 1985—. Judicial administration. Office: Temple of Justice Olympia WA 98504 *

DURHAM, CHRISTINE MEADERS, justice Supreme Court Utah; b. Los Angeles, Aug. 3, 1945; d. William Anderson and Louise (Christensen) Meaders; m. George Homer Durham II, Dec. 29, 1966; children: Jennifer, Meghan, Troy, Melinda, Isaac. A.B., Wellesley Coll., 1967; J.D., Duke U., 1971. Bar: N.C. 1971, Utah 1974. Sole practice law Durham, N.C., 1971-73; instr. legal medicine Duke U., Durham, 1971-73; adj. prof. law Brigham Young U., Provo, Utah, 1973-78; ptnr. Johnson, Durham & Moxley, Salt Lake City, 1974-78; judge Utah Dist. Ct., 1978-82; justice Utah Sup. Ct., 1982—; faculty Nat. Jud. coll., Reno, 1983. Fellow Am. Bar Found.; mem. ABA (edn. com. appellate judges' conf.), Nat. Assn. Women Judges (pres. 1986—), ABA, Utah Bar Assn., Am. Law Inst., Am. Judicature Soc. (bd. dirs.). Mormon. Jurisprudence. Home: 1702 Yale Ave Salt Lake City UT 84108 Office: Utah Supreme Court 332 State Capital Salt Lake City UT 84114

DURHAM, HARRY BLAINE, III, lawyer; b. Denver, Sept. 16, 1946; s. Harry Blaine and Mary Frances (Oliver) D.; m. Lynda L. Durham, Aug. 4, 1973; children: Christopher B., Laurel A. BA cum laude, Colo. Coll., 1969; JD, U. Colo., 1973. Bar: Wyo. 1973, U.S. Tax Ct. 1974, U.S. Ct. Appeals (10th cir.) 1976. Assoc., Brown, Drew, Apostolos, Massey & Sullivan, Casper, Wyo., 1973-77, ptnr., 1977—. Permanent class pres. Class of 1969, Colo. Coll.; bd. dirs. Casper Symphony Assn., 1974—, v.p., 1979-82, pres., 1983—; bd. dirs., sec. Wyo. Amateur Hockey Assn., 1974-85, pres., 1985—; bd. dirs. Natrona County United Way, 1974-76, pres., 1975-76; pres. City of Casper Parks and Recreation Commn., 1985—. Mem. Wyo. Bar Assn., Natrona County Bar Assn., ABA, Phi Beta Kappa. Republican. Articles editor U. Colo. Law Rev., 1972-73. Oil and gas leasing, Real property, Probate. Home: 3101 Hawthorne Casper WY 82601 Office: 111 W 2d 500 Petroleum Bldg Casper WY 82601

DURHAM, JAMES GEOFFREY, law educator; b. Antioch, Calif., July 17, 1951; s. Gentry William and Nancy Virginia (Gilmore) D.; m. Joan Ellen Drake, Sept. 7, 1974; children: Christopher Drake, Matthew Gentry. AB, U. Calif., Berkeley, 1973; JD, U. Calif., Davis, 1976. Bar: Calif. 1976, U.S. Dist. Ct. (no. dist.) Calif. 1976. Asst. counsel Calif. Farm Bur. Fedn., Berkeley, 1976-77; assoc. Hawkins & Cooper, San Francisco, 1977-79; lectr. U. Calif. Sch. Law, Davis, 1979-80; prof. U. Dayton (Ohio) Sch. Law, 1980—; vis. prof. Vt. Law Sch., South Royalton, 1983. Contbr. articles to profl. jours. Bd. Trustees Legal Aid Soc. Dayton Inc., 1982-85, v.p. 1984, pres. 1985. Mem. Calif. Bar Assn. Democrat. Methodist. Legal education. Office: U Dayton Sch Law Dayton OH 45469

DURHAM, RICHARD MONROE, lawyer; b. Winston-Salem, N.C., July 7, 1954; s. George Washington and Martha Rebecca (Teague) D.; m. Tina Marie Tunks, Dec. 1, 1984. BA with honors, U. N.C., 1976, JD, 1979. Bar: N.C. 1982, U.S. Dist. Ct. (ea. and mid. dists.) N.C. 1982, U.S. Ct. Appeals (4th cir.) 1983, U.S. Supreme Ct. 1986. Legal asst. Robert A. Ades & Assocs., PC, Springfield, Va., 1980-82; assoc. H. Weldon Lloyd, Esq., Henderson, N.C., 1982-83, Jenkins, Lucas, Babb and Rabil, Winston-Salem, 1983-85, James J. Booker, PA, Winston-Salem, 1985-87; sole practice Winston-Salem, 1987—. Mem. ABA, Fed. Bar Assn. (pres. Piedmont chpt. 1985—), N.C. Bar Assn., N.C. Acad. of Trial Lawyers, N.C. Coll. of Advocacy, Phi Delta Phi (exchequer 1977-79). Democrat. Moravian. Club: Twin City (Winston-Salem). Lodge: Lions. Avocations: basketball, tennis, music. State civil litigation, Personal injury, Real property. Home: 2313 Walker Ave Winston-Salem NC 27103 Office: BB & T Bldg Suite 360 8 W 3d St Winston-Salem NC 27101

DURHAM, RONALD DALE, lawyer; b. Albuquerque, Jan. 25, 1953; s. Billie Jack and Annie Liberia (Ward) D.; m. Joy Lynn Miller, Sept. 4, 1976; children—Christopher Eric, DeAnna Marie. Student, U.S. Coast Guard Acad., 1971-73; B.A., Okla. Bapt. U., 1976; J.D., U. Tulsa, 1981. Bar: Okla. 1981, U.S. Dist. Ct. (ea., we., no. dist.) Okla. 1982, U.S. Ct. Appeals (10th cir.) 1982. Staff law librarian U. Tulsa, 1977-81; assoc. atty. Jones, Gungoll, Jackson, Collins & Dodd, Enid, Okla., 1981-83; atty., ptnr. Jones, McNaughton & Blakeley, Enid, 1983-85; sr. assoc. atty. Jones & Jennings, Enid, Okla., 1985-86; sr. assoc. atty. Steward & Calbert, Oklahoma City, 1986-87. Co-counsel Okla. State Rep. Com., 1985-86. Served with USCG, 1971-73. Mem. Okla. Bar Assn. (mineral, real property and bankruptcy sect.), ABA (mineral and banking law sect.), Mineral Lawyers Soc. of Okla. City. Author: (with others) The Surface Damages Act After Davis Oil Company vs. Cloud, 1987. Oil and gas leasing, Real property, Contracts commercial. Home: 2301 Regis Ct Norman OK 73071 Office: PO Box 19290 Oklahoma City OK 73144

DURIE, JACK FREDERICK, JR., lawyer; b. Lexington, Ky., Jan. 25, 1944. BS, U. Ky., 1966, JD, 1969. Bar: Ky. 1969, Fla. 1969, U.S. Ct. Mil. Appeals 1970, U.S. Dist. Ct. (so. dist.) Fla. 1974, U.S Supreme Ct. 1975, U.S. Dist. Ct. (mid. dist.) Fla. 1978. Sole practice Orlando, Fla., 1979—. Served to capt. JAGC, USAF, 1970-74. Mem. Ky. Bar Assn., Fla. Bar Assn. (chmn. aviation and space law com. 1978-79, vice chmn. 1980-81), Orange County Bar Assn., Dade County Bar Assn. (bd. dirs. 1976-78, pres. young lawyers sect. 1978-79), Am. Bar Assn., Assn. Trial Lawyers Am., Acad. Fla. Trial Lawyers, Lawyers-Pilots Bar Assn., Beta Alpha Psi, Phi Delta Phi. State civil litigation, Insurance, Personal injury. Office: 620 Day Bldg 605 E Robinson St Orlando FL 32801

DURN, RAYMOND JOSEPH, lawyer; b. Cleve., Nov. 28, 1925; s. Joseph Frank and Mary (Spenko) D.; m. Emmy Reboly, June 5, 1954; children: David, Sarah, Tamara. B.A., Harvard U., 1950, LL.B., 1953. Bar: Ohio 1953, U.S. Dist. Ct. Ohio 1954, U.S. Ct. Appeals 6th cir. 1974. Assoc. Jones, Day, Reavis & Pogue, Cleve., 1953-60, ptnr., 1960—. Trustee Cleve. Neighborhood Health Services, Inc., 1969—; trustee Chester Twp., Ohio, 1972-75; mem. Chester Twp. Bd. Zoning Appeals, 1969-72. Serves with USAAF, 1944-46. Mem. Ohio Bar Assn., Cleve. Bar Assn. Democrat. Unitarian. Club: City (Cleve.). Home: 13088 W Geauga Tr Chesterland OH 44026 Office: Jones Day Reavis & Pogue North Point 901 Lakeside Ave Cleveland OH 44114

DURNYA, LOUIS RICHARD, lawyer; b. Plainfield, N.J., July 24, 1950; s. Louis and Mary Ann (Pellegrino) D.; m. Elizabeth Trabue Shelton, July 16, 1977; children: Cameron, Sarah. B.B.A., Seton Hall U., 1972; J.D., U. Richmond, 1975. Bar: N.J. 1975, U.S. Dist. Ct. N.J. 1975, U.S. Supreme Ct. 1979, U.S. Ct. Claims 1981, Ct. Appeals (Fed. cir.) 84. Assoc. Orlando & McGimpsey, Esquires, New Brunswick, N.J., 1975-76; atty. Office of Chief Counsel Kennedy Space Center, Fla., 1979-82; assoc. chief counsel Marshall Space Flight Ctr., Ala., 1982—. Served to maj. JAGC, USAR, 1986—. Recipient Superior Achievement award NASA, 1982; named an Outstanding Young Man of Am., Jaycees, 1977. Mem. Fed. Bar Assn. (nat. del. North Ala. chpt.), Ky. Col. Assn., Delta Theta Phi (scholarship key 1973-74). Government contracts and claims. Home: 1005 Appalachee Dr Huntsville AL 35801 Office: Office of Chief Counsel Marshall Space Flight Ctr Huntsville AL 35812

DU ROCHER, JAMES HOWARD, lawyer; b. Racine, Wis., Aug. 4, 1945; s. Howard James and Frances Ann (Rasmussen) DuR.; m. Rosalyn Ann, Sept. 2, 1972; children—Jessica Lynn, James Howard, Emily Rosalyn. Student U.S. Mil. Acad., 1963-65, Ripon Coll., 1965-66; J.D., U. Wis., 1969. Bar: Wis. 1969. Assoc. Stewart, Peyton, Crawford & Josten, Racine, 1969-78; ptnr. Josten, DuRocher, Murphy & Pierce, S.C., Racine, 1978—. Bd. dirs. Racine Area United Way, 1973-79, v.p., 1977-79; chmn. Park Trails Dist. Boy Scouts Am., 1979-82; bd. dirs. Careers for Retarded Adults, Inc., 1978-82, pres., 1983; bd. dirs. A-Center of Racine, Inc., 1978-82, pres., 1985; deacon Atonement Lutheran Ch., Racine, 1978-81; mem. adv. bd. Children's Service Soc. Wis. Served as capt. JAGC, U.S. Army, 1969-73. Decorated Bronze

Star. Mem. State Bar Wis., ABA, Fed. Bar Assn. Club: Mason. General corporate, Probate, Labor. Home: 5531 Whirlaway Ln Racine WI 53402 Office: 927 Main St PO Box 1514 Racine WI 53401

DURONI, CHARLES EUGENE, lawyer, food company executive; b. McCune, Kans., Apr. 9, 1933; s. Charley S. and Dorothy M. D.; m. Charlene D. White, Feb. 18, 1978; children: Renee, Ashley, Michele, Lance. B.S., U. Kans., 1955; LL.B., U. Wis., 1962. Bar: Wis. 1962, Pa. 1979, U.S. Supreme Ct. 1979, U.S. Dist. Ct. (mid. dist.) Pa. 1980, U.S. Ct. Appeals (3d cir.) 1982. Staff atty. FTC, 1962-64; staff counsel Rockwell Internat. Co., Pitts., 1964-68; sr. atty. H.J. Heinz Co., Pitts., 1968-77; sr. assoc. counsel, asst. gen. counsel Hershey (Pa.) Foods Corp., 1977-79, v.p., gen. counsel, 1979—; bd. dirs. U.S. Trademark Assn., 1972-76. Served with USAF, 1955-59. Mem. ABA (com. corp. law depts., com. corp. cousel), Wis. Bar Assn., Pa. Bar Assn., Dauphin County Bar Assn., Mid-Atlantic Legal Found. (GMA steering com. of legal com.), Sigma Chi, Phi Delta Phi. Club: Met. (N.Y.C.). General corporate, General counsel. Office: 100 Mansion Rd E Hershey PA 17033

DURRETT, JAMES FRAZER, JR., lawyer; b. Atlanta, Mar. 23, 1931; s. James Frazer and Cora Frazer (Morton) D.; m. Lucretia McPherson, June 9, 1956; children: James Frazer III, William McPherson, Lucretia Heston, Thomas Ratcliffe. A.B., Emory U., 1952; postgrad., Princeton U., 1952-53; LL.B. cum laude, Harvard U., 1956. Bar: Ga. 1955. Ptnr. Alston & Bird (and predecessor firm), Atlanta, 1956—; adj. prof. Emory U. Law Sch., 1961-77. Trustee Student Aid Found., Howard Schs., Inc., Trinity Sch.; chmn., bd. govs. Ga. Assn. for Pastoral Care, 1978—. Fellow Am. Coll. Probate Counsel; mem. Am. Law Inst. (adv. estate and gift tax project, restatement, second, property), Am. Bar Assn., Ga. Bar Assn., Atlanta Bar Assn., Lawyers Club of Atlanta, Atlanta Tax Forum (dir., pres. 1985-86). Presbyterian. Clubs: Capital City; Harvard, Georgian (Atlanta). Estate planning, General corporate, Personal income taxation. Home: 3483 Ridgewood Rd NW Atlanta GA 30327 Office: Alston & Bird 1200 Citizens & So Nat Bank Bldg Atlanta GA 30335

DUSSAULT, WILLIAM L.E., lawyer; b. New Westminster, B.C., Can., May 9, 1947; Came to U.S., 1960; s. Eugene Leo and Louise (Hobbs) D.; m. Cheri Behrns, Jan. 25, 1979; 1 child, Amy Louise. BA, U. Wash., 1969, JD, 1972. Bar: Wash. 1972, U.S. Dist. Ct. (we. dist.) Wash. 1973, U.S. Supreme Ct. 1982. Ptnr., prin. Law Offices of William L.E. Dussault P.S., Seattle, 1972-84; sole practice Seattle, 1984—; adj. prof. U. Wash. Sch. Law, dept. spl. edn. Cen. Wash. U.; mem. faculty U. Wash. Sch. Nursing; guest lectr. U. Oreg., Seattle U.; former judge pro-tempore Seattle Mcpl. Ct.; cons. Guardian, Advocacy and Protective Services Program, Oreg., supt. of pub. instruction, devel. disabilities planning council, protection and advocacy agy., Assn. for Retarded Citizens, Devel. Diabilities Residential Service Assn., Coalition for Spl. Edn. State of Wash., Assn. Retarded Citizens, div. mental health State of Oreg., Devel. Disabilities Council State of Mont., Dept. Edn. States of N.D. and Kans., Protection Advocacy Agy. State of Tenn., Northwest Assn. Rehab. Industries. Mem. Editorial bd. The Assn. for the Severely Handicapped; author: drafted legislation concerning edn. rights of the handicapped; conbr. articles to profl. jours. Nat. bd. dirs., chmn. bylaws com. Soc. for Autistic Children and Adults; counsel The Assn. for the Severely Handicapped; bd. dirs., chmn. by-laws com., mem. exec. com. Accreditation Council for Services for the Mentally Retarded and Other Develmentally Disabled Persons; trustee Found. for the Handicapped; former mem. Wash. Spl. Edn. Commn., Wash. State Legis. Rev. Com. Spl. Edn., Gov.'s Com. on Employment of the Handicapped, Wash. State Human Rights Commn. Adv. Council for the Physically, Mentally and Sensory Handicapped; adv. bd. Sr. Rights Assistance Found. Wash.; exec. dir. Wash. State Develop. Disabilities Planning Commn.; vol. atty. Wash. Assn. for Persons with Disabilities; vol. Wash. State Spl. Olympics; bd. dirs. Wash. State Disabilities Polit. Action Com. Served to capt. USAR, 1967-75. Mem. ABA (family law com. on mental disability, cons. to guardianship/limited guardianship report 1981), Wash. Bar Assn. (civil rights com.), Seattle-King County Bar Assn. Civil rights, Probate, Disability and mental health law. Office: 219 E Galer Seattle WA 98102

DUTCHER, B(ENJAMIN) ANDREW, lawyer; b. Elmira, N.Y., Apr. 15, 1950; s. Benjamin A. and Jean M. (Erbelding) D.; m. Margaret A. Scott; May 1, 1980. BA, U. Rochester, 1972; JD, Boston U., 1975, LLM in Taxation, 1976. Bar: N.Y. 1976, Fla. 1978. Ptnr. Goodelle, Adams, Newman & Dutcher, Rochester, N.Y., 1976-80, Remington, Gifford, Williams & Colicchio, Rochester, 1981—. Chairperson Würzburg (Fed. Republic Germany)-Rochester Sister City Com., 1985—; trustee Asbury 1st United Meth. Ch., Rochester, 1984—. Mem. ABA, Monroe County Bar Assn. Avocations: music, reading, travel. Probate, Estate taxation, Personal income taxation. Home: 26 Elmdorf Ave Rochester NY 14619 Office: Remington Gifford et al 183 E Main St Suite 1400 Rochester NY 14604

DUTKA, ROBERT JOSEPH, lawyer; b. Three Rivers, Mich., Dec. 15, 1951; s. Joseph Frank and Stella Mary (Konieczka) D.; m. Charlene Virginia Wrogg, Sept. 11, 1982; children: Rosemary Lynn, Joseph Michael. AB, U. of Notre Dame, Notre Dame, Ind., 1974; JD, Loyola U., New Orleans, 1977. Bar: Mich. 1977. Solo practice Three Rivers, 1978—; instr. Glen Oaks Community Coll. Centerville, Mich., 1984; bd. dirs. Carter Assocs., Inc., Sturgis, Mich. Mem. ABA, Mich. State Bar Assn., St. Joseph County Bar Assn. (pres. 1983-84). Roman Catholic. Lodges: Kiwanis (pres. Three Rivers chpt. 1982-83), Elks (exalted ruler local club 1984-85). Avocations: reading, golf, bowling. Criminal, Probate, General practice. Home: 61884 Bay Shore Dr Sturgis MI 49091 Office: 205 Portage Ave PO Box 461 Three Rivers MI 49093

DUTTON, CLARENCE BENJAMIN, lawyer; b. Pitts., May 31, 1917; s. Clarence Benjamin and Lillian (King) D.; m. Marian Jane Stevens, June 21, 1941; children: Victoria Lynn, Barbara King. B.S. with distinction, Ind. U., 1938, LL.B. with high distinction, 1940, LL.D., 1970. Bar: Ind. 1940. Instr. bus. law Ind. U. Sch. Bus., 1940-41; atty. E.I. duPont de Nemours & Co., Inc., Wilmington, Del., 1941-43; asst. prof. law Ind. U. Sch. Law, 1946-47; pvt. practice Indpls., 1947—; dir. Sarkes Tarzian, Inc., The Hunt Corp., Central Supply Co., J L Realty, Inc.; mem. Ind. Jud. Study Commn., 1965-74; mem. regional adv. group Ind. U. Sch. Medicine, 1966-75; mem., sec. Ind. Civil Code Study Commn., 1967-73; mem. Ind. Commn. on Uniform State Laws, 1970—, chmn., 1980—. Author: (bus. law sect.) Chemical Business Handbook, 1954; contbr. articles to profl. jours. Bd. dirs. Found. Ind. U. Sch. Bus., Found. Econ. and Bus. Studies; bd. visitors Ind. U. Sch. Law, 1971—, chmn., 1974-75, bd. dirs., pres. Soc. for Advanced Study, Ind. U., 1984—. Served to comdr. USNR, 1943-45. Mem. ABA (ho. dels. 1960-62); Mem. (state del. 1967-72, chmn. gen. practice sect. 1971-72, gov. 1971-74), Ind. Bar Assn. (bd. mgrs. 1957-63, pres. 1961-62), Indpls. Bar Assn. (v.p. 1957), Ind. Soc. Chgo. Republican. Presbyn. Clubs: Lawyers (pres. 1959-60), Indianapolis Country (pres. 1955), Columbia, Woodstock (Indpls.); Wilderness Country (Naples, Fla.). Construction, General corporate, Probate. Home: 1402 W 52d St Indianapolis IN 46208 Office: 710 Century 36 S Pennsylvania St Indianapolis IN 46204

DUTTON, DIANA CHERYL, lawyer; b. Sherman, Tex., June 27, 1944; d. Roy G. and Monett (Smith) D.; m. Anthony R. Grindl, July 8, 1974; children: Christopher, Bellamy. BS, Georgetown U., 1967; JD, U. Tex., 1971. Bar: Tex. 1971. Regional counsel U.S. EPA, Dallas, 1975-79, dir. enforcement div., 1979-81; ptnr. Akin, Gump, Strauss, Hauer & Feld, Dallas, 1981—. Mem. ABA, Tex. Bar Assn. (chmn. environ. and natural resources law sect. 1985-86), Dallas Bar Assn. (chmn. environ. law sect. 1984). Episcopalian. Environment, General corporate. Office: Akin Gump Strauss Hauer & Feld 1700 Pacific Ave Dallas TX 75201

DUTTON, DOMINIC EDWARD, lawyer; b. New Orleans, Aug. 21, 1944; s. Lee M. and Fara C. (Cusimano) D. B.S., Lamar Coll. Tech., 1968; J.D., U. Houston, 1973. Bar: Tex. 1973, N.Mex. 1973, U.S. Dist. Ct. (we. dist.) Tex., U.S. Dist. Ct. N.Mex., U.S. Tax Ct., U.S. Ct. Appeals (10th cir.). Assoc. Bivins, Wienbrenner P.A., Las Cruces, N.Mex., 1973-76; ptnr. Dutton, Winchester, Las Cruces, 1976-81, Underwood & Dutton Ltd., Ruidoso, N.Mex., 1982-85, Underwood, Dutton & Griffin, Ltd., Ruidoso, 1985—; village atty. Ruidoso Downs, N.Mex., 1982-86, Carrizozo, N.Mex., 1983-85. Bd. dirs. Open Door Ctr., Inc., Las Cruces, 1976-80; del. Democratic State Conv., 1980, 84. Mem. Tex. State Bar Assn., Doña Ana County Bar Assn., Lincoln County Bar Assn. (sec.-treas. 1983-84, pres. 1985-87), N.Mex. State Bar Assn. (chmn. ethics 1976-77). Clubs: Cree Meadows Country (Rui, N.Mex.); Alto Lakes Country (Alto, N.Mex.). Lodge: Lions (past bd. dirs. Las Cruces club). Real property, Insurance, Family and matrimonial. Home: PO Box 1668 Ruidoso NM 88345 Office: Underwood Dutton & Griffin Ltd 229 Rio St Ruidoso NM 88345

DUTTON, HAROLD HILBERT, JR., lawyer; b. Washington, Sept. 18, 1944; s. Harold Hilbert and Dorothy (Mugler) D.; m. Julia Mason, Mar. 12, 1966; children: Katherine, Carolyn, Bryan. BA, George Mason U., 1969. Bar: Va. 1977, U.S. Ct. Customs and Patent Appeals 1977, U.S. Dist. Ct. (ea. dist.) Va. 1978, U.S. Ct. Appeals (4th cir.) 1978, U.S. Ct. Appeals (D.C. cir.) 1982. Patent agt. Shlesinger, Arkwright, Garvey & Dinsmore, Arlington, Va., 1970-77, ptnr., 1977-82; sole practice Alexandria and Triangle and Manassas, Va., 1982—. Chmn. Prince William Soil and Water Conservation Dist., Manassas, Va., 1980; chmn. Prince William County Planning Commn., 1981—; chmn. shoreline commn. Va. Assoc. Soil and Water Conservation Dist., Gloucester, 1982—; bd. dirs., legal counsel Prince William Crime Prevention Council, Woodbridge, Va., 1984—; mem. Woodbridge Art Guild, 1984—. Recipient merit award for conservation Goodyear Tire & Rubber Co., Akron, Ohio, 1984. Mem. ABA, Am. Patent Law Assn., Am. Intellectual Property Law Assn. Lutheran. Lodge: Lions. Patent, Trademark and copyright, Contracts commercial. Home: 3147 Lookout Point Triangle VA 22172 Office: 8711 Plantation Ln Suite 301 PO Box 3110 Manassas VA 22110

DUTTWEILER, LARRY L., lawyer; b. Bethpage, N.Y., Feb. 26, 1957; s. Ralph W. and Gloria June (Minch) D.; m. Marcia C. Henry, July 14, 1984. AB, Lafayette Coll., 1979; JD, Mercer U., 1982. Bar: Ga. 1982. Law clk. to presiding justice Dublin (Ga.) Jud. Cir. Ct., 1982-83; chief asst. dist. atty. Piedmont Jud. Cir., Winder, Ga., 1983-84; ptnr. Clark, McLaughlin & Duttweiler, Lawrenceville, Ga., 1984-86; sole practice Lawrenceville, 1986—. Mem. Gwinnett County Bar Assn. (v.p. criminal law sect. 1986—). Criminal, Family and matrimonial, Personal injury. Home: 1985 Pinella Dr Grayson GA 30221 Office: PO Box 747 Lawrenceville GA 30246

DUTY, TONY EDGAR, lawyer, judge, historian; b. Golinda Tex., May 14, 1928; s. Tony and Glennie Mae (Butler) D.; m. Kathleen Lou Lear, children - Valerie Ann, Barbara Diane, Dan Richard. Student, U. Colo., 1947-49; B.B.A., Baylor U., 1952, J.D., 1953, Bar: Tex. 1954, U.S. Dist. Ct. (we. dist.) Tex. 1970, U.S. Ct. Appeals (5th cir.) 1978, U.S. Ct. Appeals (llth cir.) 1981, U.S. Supreme Ct. 1982, U.S. Dist. Ct. (no. dist.) Tex. 1983. Sole practice Waco, Tex., 1954 - 56, 64 - ; lst asst. atty City of Waco, 1957 - 63; mcpl. judge City Woodway, Tex., 1963-80, City of Lacy-Lakeview, Tex., 1976-78, City of Waco, 1957 -86, City of Bellmead, Tex., 1964-86; prof. bus. law, corps. and real estate Baylor U. 1967-78; ptnr. Indian Creek Estates; dir. Shannon Devel. Co., Telco Systems Inc., Sun Valley Water and Devel. Co., Inc., Hewitt Devel. Co., Susans, Inc., Woodway Seed and Garden Co., Inc. Author: The Coronado Expedition, 1540-1542, 1970, James Wilkinson: 1757-1825, 1971, Champ D'Asile, 1972, The Home Front: McLennan County in the Civil War, 1974; contbr. articles to hist. jours. Mem. Waco Plan Commn., 1966-69, Waco-McLennan County Library Commn., 1968-72, chmn., 1971-72; mem. Waco Fire and Police Civil Service Commn., 1975-81, chmn., 1980-81; mem. Waco Am. Revolution Bicentennial Commn., 1974-76; chmn. Waco Heritage '76, 1974-76; mem. McLennan County Hist. Survey Commn., 1970 - ; chmn. Ft. House Mus., Waco, 1968-72; bd. dirs. Waco Heritage Soc., 1960 -. Served with USAF, 1946-49. Mem. State Bar Tex., Waco-McLennan County Bar Assn., Waco-McLennan County Def. Lawyers Assn.(v.p.), Delta Theta Phi. Democrat. Baptist. Lodges: Masons, K.P. Criminal, Probate, General practice. Home: 613 Camp Dr Waco TX 76710 Office: 2317 Austin Ave Waco TX 76701

DUVAL, ROBERT, steel fabrication and construction company executive; b. Bronx, N.Y., June 23, 1937; s. Jack Leon and Cornelia (Gerry) D.; m. Harriet Elin, June 4, 1960; children: Stacey R., Jennifer E. B.S., Cornell U., 1959; LL.B., St. Johns U., 1967. Bar: N.Y. 1968, Pa. 1976, U.S. Supreme Ct. 1971. Asso. firm Hart & Hume, N.Y.C., 1967-69, Kelley, Drye & Warren, N.Y.C., 1969-72, Gates & Laber, N.Y.C., 1972-75; mem. law dept. Westinghouse Electric Corp., Pitts., 1976-78; gen. counsel, sec. Pitts.-Des Moines Co., Pitts., 1978—; sec., gen. counsel PDM Internat. Ltd. Served with U.S. Army, 1961. Mem. Am. Bar Assn., N.Y. Bar Assn., Am. Arbitration Assn. (arbitrator). General corporate, Private international. Home: 1350 Old Meadow Rd Pittsburgh PA 15241 Office: Pittsburgh-Des Moines Co 3400 Grand Ave Neville Island Pittsburgh PA 15225

DUVALL, GARY ROSS, lawyer; b. Seattle, June 29, 1952; s. Donald Raymond Duvall and Shirley Joan Weeks; m. Gay Elizabeth Croteau, Aug. 16, 1975; children: Catherine, Mark, Luke. BA in Polit. Sci. magna cum laude, U. Wash., 1974, JD, 1977. Bar: Wash. 1977, U.S. Dist. Ct. (we. dist.) Wash. 1977. Assoc. Carney Stephenson, Seattle, 1977-78; sole practice Seattle, 1978-85; ptnr. Merkel, Caine, Jory, Donohue & Duvall, Seattle, 1985—. Contbr. articles to profl. jours. Mem. coordinating bd. Ravenna-Bryant Community Assn., Seattle, 1978. Mem. ABA (forum com. franchising antitrust div.), Wash. State Bar Assn. (franchise act rev. com.), Internat. Franchising Assn. (council franchise suppliers), Wash. State Soccer League, Phi Beta Kappa. Roman Catholic. Clubs: Wash. Athletic, Columbia Tower (Seattle). General corporate, Securities, Franchising. Office: Merkel Caine Jory Donohue & Duvall Columbia Ctr 64th Floor Seattle WA 98104

DUVALL, PAUL HAMILTON, lawyer; b. Chgo., Sept. 23, 1947; s. Anthony Charles and Betty Louise (Rathburn) D.; m. Nancy Louise Moon, May 31, 1969; 1 child, William. BA, Cornell Coll., 1969; JD, Northwestern U., 1972. Bar: Ill. 1972, Calif. 1976, U.S. Dist. Ct. (fed. dist.) Calif 1976, U.S. Supreme Ct. 1976. Law clk. to presiding justice U.S. Dist. Ct., San Diego, Calif., 1977; ptnr. Sullivan and Jones, San Diego, 1977-83, Hewitt, Sullivan & Marshall, San Diego, 1983-85, Sullivan, Duvall & Noya, San Diego, 1986—. Editor: Jour. Criminal Law and Criminology, 1970-72. Pres. San Diego Vol. Lawyers Program, 1985-86. Served to capt. USMC, 1972-76. Mem. ABA, Calif. Bar Assn., San Diego County Bar Assn. (chmn. ethics com. 1985-86). Democrat. Lutheran. Antitrust, Federal civil litigation, Criminal. Office: Sullivan Duvall & Noya 101 W Broadway Suite 1410 San Diego CA 92101

DUVALL, RICHARD OSGOOD, lawyer; b. Washington, Sept. 25, 1942; s. Charles F. and Edith (Osgood) D.; m. Donna Morris; children—Julianne T., Tyler D. B.A., U. Ill., 1964; LL.B., U. Va., 1967. Bar: Md. 1967, D.C. 1970, U.S. Dist. Ct. Md. 1975, U.S. Ct. Appeals (D.C. cir.) 1975, U.S. Claims Ct. 1979, Assoc. Pierson, Ball & Dowd, Washington, 1970-73, Dunnells, Duvall, Bennett & Porter, 1973—, mng. ptnr., 1980-84. Served to lt. JAGC, USNR, 1967-70. Mem. D.C. Bar Assn. (chmn. fed. practice com. adminstrv. law sect.), ABA, Md. Bar Assn., Fed. Bar Assn., Sigma Chi. Republican. Editor: Administrative Practice Manual, vol. I.; contbr. to profl. publs. Government contracts and claims, Administrative and regulatory, Federal civil litigation. Home: 5210 Worthington Dr Bethesda MD 20816 Office: Dunnells Duvall Bennett & Porter 1220 Nineteenth St NW Washington DC 20036

DUVIN, ROBERT PHILLIP, lawyer; b. Evansville, Ind., May 18, 1937; s. Louis and Henrietta (Hamburg) D.; m. Darlene Chmiel, Aug. 23, 1961; children: Scott A., Marc A., Louis A. B.A. with honors, Ind. U., 1958, J.D. with highest honors, 1961; LL.M. with highest honors, Columbia U., 1963. Bar: Ohio 1964. Since practiced in Cleve.; pres. Duvin, Flinker & Cahn (L.P.A.), 1972—; lectr. law schs.; labor adviser corps., cities and hosps. Contbr. to books and legal jours.; bd. editors: Ind. Law Jour., 1961, Columbia Law Rev., 1963. Served with AUS, 1961-62. Mem. Am., Fed., Ohio, Cleve. bar assns. Jewish. Club: Cleve. Racquet. Labor. Home: 2775 S Park Blvd Shaker Heights OH 44120 Office: Duvin Flinker & Cahn 1400 Transohio Savs Bank Bldg 2000 E 9th St Cleveland OH 44115

DUVIVIER, KATHARINE KEYES, lawyer; b. Alton, Ill., Jan. 1, 1953; d. Edward Keyes and Marjorie (Attebery) DuV.; m. James Wesley Perl, Mar. 30, 1985; 1 child, Alice Katharine Perl. BA in Geology and English cum laude, Williams Coll., 1975; JD, U. Denver, 1982. Bar: Colo. 1982, U.S. Dist. Ct. Colo. 1982, U.S. Ct. Appeals (10th cir.) 1982. Curator geology Hudson River Mus., Yonkers, N.Y., 1975; geologist French Am. Metals Corp., Lakewood, Colo., 1976-79; assoc. Sherman & Howard, Denver, 1982-84, Arnold & Porter, Denver, 1984—. Contbr. articles to profl. jours. Mem. Denver Botanic Garden, 1981—, Vols. Outdoor Colo., Denver, 1985—. Mem. ABA (vice chmn. subcom. 1985—), Colo. Bar Assn., Denver Bar Assn., Rocky Mountain Mineral Law Found., Colo. Mining Assn., Alliance Profl. Women (bd. dirs. 1985—), Phi Beta Kappa, Order of St. Ives, Williams Coll. Alumni Assn. (co-pres. Colo. chpt. 1984-86), Colo. Mountain Club. Avocations: geology, hiking, skiing, dancing, swimming. Real property, General corporate, Natural resources. Home: 510 Humboldt St Denver CO 80218 Office: Arnold & Porter 1700 Lincoln St Suite 4000 Denver CO 80203

DWECK, JACK S., lawyer; b. Bklyn., Aug. 15, 1938; s. Salim S. and Anna (Cohen) D.; m. Judith Amy Gitlin, Aug. 20, 1960; children: Alyssa, Stuart, H.P. Sean. BBA, City Coll. N.Y., 1958; JD, NYU, 1961. Bar: N.Y. 1961, U.S. Dist Ct. (so. dist.) N.Y. 1963, U.S. Dist. Ct. (ea. dist.) N.Y. 1964, Fla. 1973, U.S. Dist. Ct. (so. dist.) Fla., 1974. Assoc. Epstein, Burke & Shapiro, N.Y.C., 1961-62, Raymond Gitlin, N.Y.C., 1962-66, Jay Leo Rothschild, N.Y.C., 1966-67; ptnr. Dweck & Sladkus, N.Y.C., 1968-85, Feiden, Dweck & Sladkus, N.Y.C., 1985—; arbitrator Am. Arbitration Assn., 1969—, Civil Ct. N.Y., 1978—. Mem. ABA, N.Y. Bar Assn., Bar Assn. of City of N.Y., Fla. Bar Assn., Am. Judges Assn. Federal civil litigation, State civil litigation, Personal injury. Office: 295 Madison Ave New York NY 10017

DWORKIN, MICHAEL LEONARD, lawyer; b. Bridgeport Ct., Oct. 10, 1947; s. Samuel and Frances (Stein) Dworkin; m. Christina Lyn Hildreth, Sept. 25, 1977; children: Jennifer Hildreth, Amanda Hildreth. B.A. in Gov. with honors, Clark U., 1969; J.D. with honors, George Washington U., 1973. Bar: D.C. 1973, Calif. 1975, U.S. Ct. Appeals (9th cir.) 1982, U.S. Supreme Ct. 1978, U.S. Claims Ct. 1983. Atty. FAA, Washington, Los Angeles, 1973-77, United Airlines, San Francisco, 1977-81; sole practice, San Francisco, 1981—; instr. Embry Riddle Aeronautical U., San Francisco, 1980-81; dir. Poplar Ctr., San Mateo, Calif. Jonas Clark scholar Clark U., 1966-69. Mem. ABA, Lawyer Pilot's Bar Assn., Nat. Transp. Safety Bd. Bar Assn. (regional v.p. 1986-87, chmn. rules com. 1985-87), Aircraft Owners and Pilots Assn., Soaring Soc. Am., Internat. Soc. Air Safety Investigators (bd. dirs. San Francisco regional chpt.), State Bar Assn. Calif., D.C. Bar Assn. Jewish. Aviation, Contracts commercial, Insurance. Office: Law Offices of Michael L Dworkin 3 Embarcadero Ctr Suite 1620 San Francisco CA 94111

DWYER, GERALD PARKER, lawyer; b. New Haven, Feb. 16, 1936; s. Andrew Parker and Katherine (Dunn) D.; m. Mary Falsey, Dec. 26, 1961; children—Christopher, Meegan, Gerald, Timothy, David, Jared, Michael. B.A., U. Conn., 1958; LL.B., 1963, J.D., 1975. Bar: Conn. 1964, U.S. Dist. Ct. Conn. 1965, Mass. 1985. Assoc., Gormley & Gormley, New Haven, 1964-74; ptnr. Gormley & Dwyer, New Haven, 1974—; town counsel Town of Bethany, Conn., 1967—; arbitrator Am. Arbitration Assn., 1967—; spl. master state and fed. cts., Conn., 1967—. Mem. Bethany Zoning Bd. Appeals, 1965-66; chmn. Community Drug Task Force, Bethany, 1983—. Served to sgt. U.S. Army, 1958-60. Mem. Conn. Bar Assn., New Haven Bar Assn. Republican. Roman Catholic. Federal civil litigation, State civil litigation, Criminal. Office: Gormley & Dwyer 246 Church St New Haven CT 06506

DWYER, RALPH DANIEL, JR., lawyer; b. New Orleans, Apr. 23, 1924; s. Ralph Daniel Sr. and Carolyn (Nolting) D.; m. Gwendolyn Betpouey, Feb. 12, 1955; children: Ralph, Bridget Mary, Frederick Henry, Patrick Rees, John Betpouey, Timothy Paul, Kathleen Mary, Mary Megan, Pegeen Mary. BS in Econs., Loyola U., New Orleans, 1943; Japanese area and lang. program, U. Chgo., 1945; JD, Loyola U., New Orleans, 1950; grad., Army War Coll., 1976. Bar: La. 1950. Law clk. to presiding justice Civil Dist. Ct., Parish Orleans, 1950-51; legal research asst. New Orleans City Civil Service Commn., 1963—; sole practice New Orleans, 1951—. Mem. La. Civil Service League, 1968—, bd. govs., 1984—; past pres. Japanese Soc. New Orleans. Served to col. AUS, La. N.G., 1978. Awarded Order of Sacred Treasure, Japanese Govt., 1973, Order of Medallion of St. Louis, Archdiocese of New Orleans, 1982. Mem. ABA, La. State Bar Assn. (com. on law reform 1971-82, ho. of dels. 1975-77), New Orleans Bar Assn. (1st v.p. 1968-69), St. Thomas More Cath. Lawyers Assn. (pres. 1968-70). Democrat. Roman Catholic. Avocations: reading, family, fly-fishing. State civil litigation, Civil rights, Federal civil litigation. Office: 1622 Cadiz St New Orleans LA 70115

DWYER, ROBERT JEFFREY, lawyer; b. Elizabeth, N.J., Oct. 13, 1947; s. John Edward and Helen Patricia (Callahan) D.; m. Marice Eleanor White, Aug. 21, 1976; children: Angus White, Duncan White, Eleanor Grissom. BA magna cum laude, Amherst Coll., 1969; JD cum laude, Harvard U., 1972. Bar: N.Y. 1973, U.S. Dist. Ct. (so. and ea. dists.) N.Y. 1973, U.S. Ct. Appeals (2d cir.) 1973, U.S. Dist. Ct. (no. dist.) Calif. 1983. Assoc. Cravath, Swaine & Moore, N.Y.C., 1972-80; ptnr. Davis, Markel, Dwyer & Edwards, N.Y.C., 1980-86, Bryan, Cave, McPheeters & McRoberts, N.Y.C., 1986—. Mem. bd. govs. Misquamicut Club, Watch Hill, R.I., 1985—. Mem. ABA, Fed. Bar Council. Roman Catholic. Avocation: tennis. Federal civil litigation, State civil litigation, Computer. Office: Bryan Cave McPheeters & McRoberts 350 Park Ave New York NY 10022

DWYER, ROBERT VINCENT, JR., lawyer; b. Omaha, Sept. 8, 1940; s. Robert Vincent and Rosemary Frances (Daly) D.; m. Suzanne N. Dwyer, Aug. 3, 1963 (div. Jan. 1976); children: Coreen, Robert, Christopher, Eileen & Daniel; m. Marcia Grant, Mar. 7, 1980; 1 child, Robert Leo. BA, Creighton U., 1962, JD, 1964. Bar: Nebr. 1964. Assoc. Schmid, Ford et al, Omaha, 1964-67, McGrath, North et al, Omaha, 1967-78; ptnr. Dwyer & O'Leary, Omaha, 1978-83, Dwyer, Pohren, Wood, Heavey & Grimm, Omaha, 1983—; bd. dirs. Northern Bank, Omaha. Mem. ABA, Nebr. Bar Assn., Omaha Bar Assn. State civil litigation, Pension, profit-sharing, and employee benefits, General corporate. Office: Dwyer Phoren Wood Heavey & Grimm 300 Historic Library Plaza Omaha NE 68102

DWYER, STEPHEN IRWIN, lawyer; b. New Orleans, Jan. 15, 1949; s. Irwin J. and Catherine (LaRocca) D.; m. Nancy Peters, Aug. 8, 1970; children: Rachel, Jeremy, Jessica. AB, Coll. of Holy Cross, 1970; MA, U. New Orleans, 1972; JD, Loyola U., New Orleans, 1976. Bar: La. 1976, U.S. Dist. Ct. (ea. dist.) La. 1976, U.S. Ct. Appeals (5th cir.) 1976. Assoc. Shushn, Meyer et al, New Orleans, 1976-78, Gordon, Arata et al, New Orleans, 1978-83; atty., of counsel Camp, Carmouch et al, New Orleans, 1983-85; ptnr. Becknell, Dwyer, Bencomo & McDaniel, New Orleans, 1985—; bd. dirs. Plaza Properties, Inc., New Orleans. Editor Loyola U. Law Rev., 1975-76. Trustee New Orleans Home Mortgage Authority, 1985—. Mem. ABA (real estate fin. com.), La. Bar Assn., Am. Arbitration Assn. (arbitrator), Coll. of Holy Cross Alumni (pres. La. and Miss. 1980—), Loyola U. Alumni Assn. (pres. 1981). Democrat. Roman Catholic. Real property, Municipal bonds, Banking. Office: Becknell Dwyer Bencomo & McDaniel 639 Loyola Ave Suite 1600 New Orleans LA 70113

DWYER, SUSAN TATE, lawyer; b. Kansas City, Mo., June 21, 1953; s. Francis Xavier and Betty Lou (Crisp) D.; m. Jeffrey Arthur Lichtman, Aug. 26, 1978; 1 child, Brett William. Student, U.S. Internat. U., 1971-73; BA in English Lit., Colo. Coll., 1975; JD, U. Notre Dame, 1978. Bar: Fla. 1978, N.Y. 1979, U.S. Dist. Ct. (so. and ea. dists.) N.Y. 1980, U.S. Ct. Appeals (2d cir.) 1981. Assoc. Reid & Priest, N.Y.C., 1979-83, Herrick, Feinstein, N.Y.C., 1983—. Federal civil litigation, State civil litigation. Home: 251 W 89th St New York NY 10024 Office: Herrick Feinstein 2 Park Ave New York NY 10016

DWYER, WILLIAM EDWARD, lawyer; b. Hadley, Mass., Mar. 11, 1901; s. John and Ellen M. (Ryan) D.; m. Margaret Clifford, Apr. 25, 1953; 1 son, William E. A.B., Amherst Coll., 1924; J.D., Boston U., 1928. Bar: Mass. 1928. Assoc., Shaw, Hickey & Cook, Northampton, Mass., 1928-39; ptnr. Shaw, O'Brien & Dwyer, Northampton, 1936-38, Shaw & Dwyer, Northampton, 1938-42, Hemenway, Dwyer & Hemenway, Northampton, 1946-48; sr. ptnr. William E. Dwyer, Northampton, 1948-60, 74—, Dwyer & Cross, 1961-67, Dwyer & Collins, 1967-74. Trustee Hopkins Acad., Hadley, 1941—, pres., 1956—; bd. dirs. Cooley Dickinson Hosp., 1937—; mem. Hadley Sch. Com., 1928-41; chmn. Hampshire County chpt. ARC, 1948-55; pres. Hampshire County Pub. Health Assn., Inc., 1955-66; pres. Hist. Deerfield, Inc., 1974-81. Served to comdr. USNR, 1942-46. Recipient Disting. Alumnus award Williston Acad., 1969. Fellow Am. Coll. Probate Counsel;

mem. ABA, Hampshire County Bar Assn., Mass. Bar Assn., Nat. Assn. Coll. and Univ. Attys., Am Assn. Mus. Trustees, Roman Catholic. (Knight of Holy Sepulchre). Club: Colony (Springfield, Mass.). General practice, General corporate, Probate. Office: William E Dwyer Law Firm 39 Main St Northampton MA 01060

DYE, DAVID ALAN, lawyer, educator; b. Lexington, Mo., Sept. 11, 1950; s. Donald Alfred and Dorothy Sue D.; m. Julia Yolanda Zapata, June 21, 1979; 1 child, Soyal Chaski. B.A., U. Mo., 1972, J.D., 1976. Sole practice, Kansas City, Mo., 1976—; prof., coordinator Legal Asst. Program, Mo. Western State Coll., St. Joseph, 1977—; lawfirm cons. Co-founder, pres. Mid-Coast Radio Project, Inc., 1978-79, bd. dirs., 1978-80, chmn. adv. council, 1980—; legal cons. Greater Kansas City Epilepsy League, pres., 1982-84, mem. exec. com., 1984—, bd. dirs. 1978—; mem. ho. of dels. Epilepsy Found. Am., 1982-83. State of Mo. grantee, 1980, 82. Mem. ABA, Mo. Bar Assn. (vice chmn. legal asst. com.), Kansas City Met. Bar Assn., Am. Assn. for Paralegal Edn. (organizer, pres. 1987—, bd. dirs. 1983—, chair membership com. 1986), Nat. Assn. of Legal Assts. (assoc.). Editor: (with John Calvert) Systems for Legal Assistant: A Resource Manual of Selected Articles and Materials., 1980; author articles on paralegal edn. and profession; organizer, condr. nat. and regional seminars, confs., workshops on legal assts. programs. Legal education, General practice. Home: 6220 Harrison Kansas City MO 64110 Office: Mo Western State Coll St 4525 Downs Dr Saint Joseph MO 64507

DYE, DEWEY ALBERT, JR., lawyer; b. Bradenton, Fla., June 12, 1926; s. Dewey Albert and Lucy Ann (Edmondson) D.; m. Charlotte Healey, Feb. 1, 1948; children—Deborah Dye McKay, James Dewey, Stephen Richard. B.A., U. Fla., 1948, LL.B. with honors, 1949. Bar: Fla. 1949, U.S. Supreme Ct. 1959. Assoc. D.A. Dye, Bradenton, 1949-53; sr. ptnr. Dye, Scott, and Deitrich, P.A., Bradenton, 1954—; atty. Manatee County, 1954-56; gen. counsel West Coast Inland Navigation Dist. Fla., 1954-79; lectr. on environment and land use U. So. Fla., Sarasota, Contbr. articles to profl. jours. Mem. exec. bd. South Fla. Mus., Bishop Planetarium; trustee Eaton Found. Served as officer USNR, 1943-46, 51-53. Mem. ABA, Am. Coll. Probate Counsel, Manatee County Bar Assn. (pres. 1961), Fla. Bar Assn., Naval Res. Assn. (past pres. Manasota chpt.), Fla. Waterway Assn. (past pres.), Hernando DeSoto Hist. Soc. (past pres.), U. Fla. Alumni Assn. (pres. Sarasota-Bradenton chpt. 1950-51), Sigma Alpha Epsilon, Phi Delta Phi. Presbyterian. Clubs: Bradenton Yacht (past commodore), Bradenton Country. Environment, Real property, Administrative and regulatory. Office: Dye Scott and Deitrich PA 1111 3d Ave W Bradenton FL 33505

DYE, SHERMAN, lawyer; b. Portland, Oreg., Nov. 18, 1915; s. Trafton M. and Mary (Ward) D.; m. Jean Forsythe, Dec. 22, 1939; children—Peter S., Kathleen, Richard F., Alice, William T., Mary H. A.B., Oberlin Coll., 1937; LL.B., Case Western Res. U., 1940. Bar: Ohio bar 1940, U.S. Supreme Ct. bar 1972. Jr. atty. SEC, Washington, 1940-41; law clk. Tax Ct. U.S., Washington, 1941-42; assoc. mem. firm Baker, Hostetler & Patterson, Cleve., 1942-51; partner firm Baker & Hostetler, Cleve., 1952—. Trustee, chmn. First Bapt. Ch. Greater Cleve.; trustee, treas. Am. Cancer Soc., Cleve.; trustee PACE Assn. Served with USAF, 1945. Mem. Am. Bar Assn., Ohio Bar Assn., Cleve. Bar Assn. (trustee 1954-57), Soc. Benchers, Order of Coif, Phi Delta Phi. Republican. Baptist. Club: Union. General corporate, Corporate taxation, Personal income taxation. Home: 2300 Overlook Rd Cleveland Heights OH 44106 Office: 3200 National City Center Cleveland OH 44114

DYE, WILLIAM ELLSWORTH, lawyer; b. Detroit, Oct. 15, 1926; s. Edward Ellsworth and Elizabeth (Esther Bloom) D.; m. Joy Ann Kuehneman, Apr. 28, 1956 (div.); children—Constance, Elizabeth, William. B.A., U. Wis., 1948, LL.B., 1951. Bar: Wis., 1951. Assoc. John F. Thompson, Racine, Wis., 1951-75; ptnr. Heft, Dye, Paulson & Nichols, Racine, Wis., 1975—; instr. Law Sch., U. Wis., 1970-71; gov. State Bar Wis., 1972-78; Bd. Visitors U. Wis., 1982-85. Served as cpl. U.S. Army, 1946-47. Mem. ABA, Racine County Bar Assn. (pres. 1985-86), Am. Judicature Soc. Republican. Episcopalian. Clubs: Racine Country, U. Milw., Somerset of Racine. Banking, General corporate, Local government. Home: 5811 Cambridge Ct Racine WI 53406 Office: 827 Main St S Racine WI 53403

DYEKMAN, GREGORY CHRIS, lawyer; b. Ft. Collins, Colo., Aug. 2, 1955; s. Elmer Clifford and Patsy Joyce (Hill) D. BS with honors, U. Wyo., 1977, JD, 1980. Bar: Wyo. 1980, U.S. Dist. Ct. Wyo. 1980, U.S. Ct. Appeals (10th cir.) 1980, U.S. Tax Ct. 1981. Assoc. Dray, Madison & Thomson, Cheyene, Wyo., 1980-82, ptnr., 1983—. Editor-in-chief Land and Water Law Rev., 1978-79. Mem. dist. com. Boy Scouts Am., Cheyenne, 1980-83, dist. chmn., 1987—; bd. counsel Symphony and Choral Soc. of Cheyenne, 1983-85; pres. Cheyenne Family YMCA, 1984-85; pres., elder 1st Presbyn. Ch., Cheyenne, 1983-85, treas. 1986—. Named one of Outstanding Young Men Am., 1984-87. Mem. ABA, Laramie County Bar Assn. (sec., treas. 1985-86), Assn. Trial Lawyers Am., Wyo. Trial Lawyers Assn. (editor newsletter 1983—). Republican. Lodge: Kiwanis. Avocations: music composition, debate judging. Federal civil litigation, State civil litigation, Banking. Home: 6012 Osage Ave Cheyenne WY 82009

DYER, CHARLES ARNOLD, lawyer; b. Blairstown, Mo., Aug. 29, 1940; s. Arnold and Mary Charlotte (West) D.; children—Kristine, Erin, Kathleen, Kerry. B.J., U. Mo., 1962; J.D., U. Calif., 1970. Bar: Calif. 1971, U.S. Sup. Ct. 1976. Ptnr., Dyer & White, Menlo Park, Calif.; lectr. in field. Bd. dirs. Boys Club of San Mateo, Calif., 1971-83, pres., 1975; mem. exec. council Boys Clubs of the Bay Area, 1977-83; mem. Democratic Nat. Fin. Com., 1978. Served with USNR, 1963—. Mem. ABA, Calif. Bar Assn., San Mateo County Bar Assn., Assn. Trial Lawyers Am., Calif. Trial Lawyers Assn., San Mateo County Trial Lawyers Assn., Trial Lawyers Pub. Justice. Roman Catholic. State civil litigation, Federal civil litigation. Address: 800 Oak Grove Ave Menlo Park CA 94025

DYER, CHARLES HERBERT, lawyer; b. Haverhill, Mass., Oct. 21, 1949; s. Thomas William and Helen (Fisk) D.; m. Danna Lewis, July 1, 1972 (div. Oct. 1985); children: Daniel Spofford, David Charles. BA, Yale U., 1971; JD, U. Pa., 1974. Bar: Conn. 1974, U.S. Dist. Ct. Conn. 1975, U.S. Ct. Appeals (2d cir.) 1975, U.S. Tax Ct. 1975, U.S. Ct. Claims 1975, U.S. Dist. Ct. (so. and ea. dists.) N.Y. 1976; CLU. Assoc. Day, Berry & Howard, Hartford, Conn., 1974-77; assoc. counsel Conn. Mut. Life Ins. Co., Hartford, 1977—; treas. Conn. Mut. Life Polit. Action Com., Hartford, 1984; bd. dirs. Conn. Life and Health Ins. Guaranty Assn., Hartford. Mem. Fin. Adv. Bd., West Hartford, 1982-83, West Hartford Dem. Town Com., 1983. Named one of Outstanding Young Men Am., 1982. Fellow Life Mgmt. Inst.; mem. ABA, Conn. Bar Assn. Avocation: squash. Insurance. Home: 164B Brittany Farms Rd New Britain CT 06053 Office: Conn Mut Life Ins Co 140 Garden St Hartford CT 06154

DYER, GEORGE LEWIS, JR., lawyer; b. Detroit, Dec. 30, 1931; s. George Lewis and Florence Coote (Rock) D.; m. Dolores Lei Eaton, Nov. 8, 1957; children—Matthew E., Jennifer F.P., Mary F. B.A., Cornell U., 1955; LL.B. cum laude, Harvard U., 1961. Bar: Hawaii 1961. mem. Goodsill Anderson & Quinn, Assocs., Honolulu, 1961-66, ptnr., 1967-80; sole practice Honolulu, 1981-87; pres. George L. Dyer, Jr., Law Corp., Honolulu, 1981-87; lectr. U. Hawaii, Hawaii Inst. Continuing Legal Edn. Mem. rules com., del. Republican Nat. Conv., 1972, 76; 4th vice chmn. Rep. Party Hawaii, 1971-73; chmn. Rep. State Conv., 1972; chmn. Hawaii Lawyers Com. to Re-elect the Pres., 1972; chmn. rules com. Rep. Com. Hawaii, 1970-73, 83—; mem. State of Hawaii ofcl. observers primary and gen. elections, 1974, chmn., 1976, 78; mem. State of Hawaii Lt. Gov.'s election adv. com. 1974-76, chmn., 1976-78; mem. Hawaii Bicentennial Commn., 1986—; bd. dirs. Legal Aid Soc. Hawaii 1969-72, Friends of Hawaii Pub. TV, 1977-79, Arts Council Hawaii, 1980-83, Small Bus. Hawaii, 1983—. Served to lt. (j.g.) USNR, 1955-58. Mem. ABA, Hawaii Bar Assn. (dir. 1972). Club: Pacific. Editor, Hawaii Bar Jour., 1965-66. Consumer commercial, Contracts commercial, Banking. Home: 1001 Koohoo Pl Kailua HI 96734 Office: 220 S King St #1520 Honolulu HI 96813

DYER, JOHN GILBERT, lawyer; b. Richland, Wash., Sept. 2, 1945; s. Gilbert Benjamin and Marie Kathrine (Mousley) D. B.A., U. Mo.-Kansas City, 1968, J.D., 1974; cert. employee benefit specialist Wharton Sch., U. Pa., 1981. Bar: Mo. 1975, U.S. Dist. Ct. (we. dist.) Mo. 1975. Tax examiner IRS, Kansas City, 1967-68; ptnr. Hamilton and Dyer, Joplin, Mo., 1975-76; sole practice, Kansas City, 1976-77; chief counsel Elections and Govtl. Rev. Com., Mo. Ho. of Reps., Jefferson City, 1977; v.p., legal counsel UMB Mutual Fund Group; legal counsel Jones and Babson, Inc., Kansas City, 1977—, also v.p. various subs.; part-time instr. Rockhurst Coll., Kansas City, 1984—. Mem. Kansas City Pub. Improvements Adv. Com., 1984—; bd. dirs. Fairlane Homes Assn. Served with USN, 1968-72. Mem. ABA (Corp. Law and Fin., Family Law, Law, Sci. and Tech., Urban Law and Devel. sects.), Mo. Bar Assn., Internat. Soc. Cert. Employee Benefit Specialists. Republican. Episcopalian. General corporate, Pension, profit-sharing, and employee benefits, Real property. Home: L-36 Rt 1 Lake Lotawana MO 64063 Office: Jones & Babson Inc 2440 Pershing Rd Kansas City MO 64108

DYER, MATTHEW FINIS, lawyer; b. Pitts., June 12, 1945; s. Robert Clayton and Rosemary (Farr) D.; m. Nancy Pamela McBride, Aug. 25, 1976; 1 child, Jonathan McBride. B.S., U. Bridgeport, 1970; J.D., N.Y. Law Sch., 1975. Bar: N.Y. 1976, U.S. Dist. Ct. (so. and ea. dists.) N.Y. 1976, Maine 1978, U.S. Dist. Ct. Maine 1979. Dep. spl. prosecutor State of N.Y., N.Y.C., 1975-78; asst. atty. gen. State of Maine, Augusta, 1979-84; sole practice, Augusta, 1984—. Sec. zoning appeals bd. City of Augusta, 1984—; mem. Maine Criminal Law Adv. Commn., 1986—; bd. dirs. Vietnam Vets. Leadership Program, Portland, Maine, 1984. Served to sgt. U.S. Army, 1963-66, Vietnam. Recipient Am. Jurisprudence award Lawyers Coop. Pub. Co., 1973. Mem. ABA, Maine State Bar Assn., Maine Trial Lawyers Assn. Democrat. Lodge: Kiwanis. State civil litigation, Personal injury, Family and matrimonial. Home: 18 Duncan Rd Augusta ME 04330 Office: 132 State St Augusta ME 04330

DYER, MICHAEL JOSEPH, lawyer; b. Washington, Aug. 30, 1947; s. Edward Joseph and Helen Irene (O'Donnell) D.; m. Cheryl Ann Melof, Aug. 21, 1971; children: michael, Katharine. BA, Spring Hill Coll., 1969; MSW, U. Ala., 1972; JD, Loyola U., New Orleans, 1976. Bar: La. 1976, D.C. 1977, U.S. Dist. Ct. D.C. 1978, U.S. Ct. Appeals (D.C. cir.) 1980, U.S. Supreme Ct. 1980. Asst. prof. Norfolk (Va.) State U., 1976-78; govt. affairs Specialist Am. Assn. Dental Sch., Washington, 1978-81; counsel U.S. Senate Com. on Labor and Human Resources, Washington, 1981; staff dir., chief counsel Congressman, Mick Staton, Washington, 1982; sole practice Washington, 1983—; bd. dirs. Coalition for Health Funding, Washington, 1980-81. Mem. Norfolk State U. Faculty Senate., 1977-78, rev. commn. charter City of Laurel, 1986—; bd. dirs. Tidewater Legal Aid Assn., 1977. Contbr. articles to profl. jour. Mem. ABA, La. BAr Assn., Bar Assn. of D.C., Fed. Bar Assn., Nat. Health Lawyers Assn., Laurel Hist. Soc. Roman Catholic. Legislative, Health, Government contracts and claims. Home: 310 Fourth St Laurel MD 20707 Office: 888 17th St NW Suite 1050 Washington DC 20006

DYKSTRA, DANIEL D., lawyer; b. Patterson, N.J., Oct. 29, 1955; s. H. Allan and Evelyn M. (Brown) D.; m. Sharon R. Leensvaart, June 4, 1976; children: Josiah, Jesse, Jordan. BA, Dordt Coll., 1977; JD with distinction, U. Iowa, 1980. Bar: Iowa 1980, U.S. Dist. Ct. (no. dist.) Iowa 1980. Assoc. Gleysteen, Harper, Eidsmoe, Heidman & Redmond, Sioux City, Iowa, 1980-83; ptnr. Eidsmoe, Heidman, Redmond, Fredregill, Patterson & Schatz, Sioux City, 1983—; lectr. various orgns., 1980—. Mem. Siouxland Com. for Handicapped, Sioux City, 1980—; treas., bd. dirs. Council on Sexual Assault and Domestic Violence Inc., Sioux City, 1981-85. Mem. ABA (spl. com. problems of farmers and ranchers real property probate and trust div.), Iowa Bar Assn. (legal forms com.), Woodbury County Bar Assn. (probate com.), Estate Planning Council Greater Siouxland Inc., Dordt Coll. Alumni Assn. (coordinator 1985—). Mem. Reformed Ch. Am. Avocations: softball, gardening, travel. Real property, Contracts commercial, Probate. Home: 3372 Stone Park Blvd Sioux City IA 51104 Office: Eidsmoe Heidman Redmond et al 200 Home Fed Bldg PO Box 3086 Sioux City IA 51102

DYWAN, JEFFERY JOSEPH, lawyer; b. Hammond, Ind., Apr. 26, 1949; s. Joseph Michael and Florence Marie (Buda) D.; m. Jacque Ann Shulmistras, June 20, 1971; children: Dina, Abigail, Kathryn. BS in Indsl. Engring., Purdue U., 1971; JD, Valparaiso U., 1974. Bar: Ind. 1971, U.S. Dist. Ct. (no. and so. dists.) Ind. 1974, U.S. Ct. Appeals (7th cir.) 1975, Ill. 1984, U.S. Dist. Ct. (no. dist.) Ill. 1986. Assoc. Breclaw & Dywan, Griffith, Ind., 1974-78; sole practice Griffith, 1978-81; dep. prosecuting atty. Lake County, Crown Point, Ind., 1978-80, pub. defender, 1981-83; assoc. Chudom & Meyer, Schererville, Ind., 1981—; instr. Calumet Coll., Hammond, Ind., 1974-76, Ind. Vocat. and Tech. Coll., Gary, Ind., 1978-79. Mem. Ind. Bar Assn., Lake County Bar Assn., Dyer Jaycees. Democrat. Roman Catholic. Lodges: Elks, KC. Personal injury, Federal civil litigation, State civil litigation. Office: Chudom & Meyer 833 W Lincoln Hwy Schererville IN 46375

DZURAK, STEVEN J., lawyer; b. Brookfield, Wis., Jan. 27, 1955; s. Stephen J. and Irene D. (Hage) D. BS, Marquette U., 1977; MA, U. Chgo., 1978; JD, U. Wis., 1981. Bar: Wis. 1981, U.S. Dist. Ct. (we. dist.) Wis. 1981, U.S. Dist. Ct. (ea. dist.) Wis. 1983, U.S. Tax Ct. 1983, Minn. 1985. Tax acct. Arthur Young, Milw., 1981-83; assoc. Petrie, Stocking, Milw., 1983-85, O'Connor & Hannar, Mpls., 1985—. Editor: Wis. TAXNEWS, 1983—, Milw. Lawyer, 1984-86. Mem. ABA, Wis. Bar Assn., Am. Inst. CPA's, Minn. Soc. CPA's, Am. Swedish Inst. Lutheran. Club: Nordic Ski (Milw.) (bd. dirs. 1984-85). Lodge: Sons of Norway. Avocation: cross country skiing. General corporate, Pension, profit-sharing, and employee benefits, Corporate taxation. Office: O'Connor & Hannan 80 S 8th St Minneapolis MN 55402

DZURIK, JOHN GERARD, lawyer; b. Bridgeport, Conn., May 2, 1950; s. John Joseph and Mary Ann (Orlovski) D. Grad., Sch. Fgn. Service, Georgetown U., 1972; JD, Georgetown U., 1975. Bar: Conn. 1975, U.S. Dist. Ct. Conn. 1975. Assoc. Goldstein & Peck, P.C., Bridgeport, 1975-81; corp. counsel Gen. Electric. Credit Corp., Stamford, Conn., 1981-82; assoc. Gamm & Gamm, P.C., Hamden, Conn., 1982-83; of counsel Harlow, Knott & Adams, Stratford, Conn., 1983-85; ptnr. Chaplowe, Dzurik & Jaekle, Stratford, 1986—. Mem. ABA (state membership chmn. 1984—, dist. del. young lawyers div. 1981-83), Conn. Bar Assn. (ho. of dels. 1986—), Bridgeport Bar Assn., Georgetown U. Alumni Assn. (bd. dirs. 1981—), Delta Phi Epsilon. Real property, General corporate, Personal injury. Home: 350 Grovers Ave Unit 8B Bridgeport CT 06605 Office: Chaplowe Dzurik & Jaekle 2268 Main St Stratford CT 06497

EADES, RONALD WAYNE, law professor; b. Lexington, Ky., Sept. 6, 1948; s. Thomas William and Evelyn Louise (Smith) E.; m. Lillian Arpi Aivazian, July 2, 1971; children: Matthew Adrian, Emily Rachael. BA in English, Rhodes Coll., 1970; JD, Memphis State U., 1973; LLM, Harvard U., 1977. Bar: Tenn. 1974, Ky. 1984. Staff atty. Tenn. Valley Authority, Knoxville, Tenn., 1974-76; law prof. U. Louisville, 1977—. Author: Wrongful Death Actions - The Law in Kentucky 1981, supplement 1982, 85; Products Liability Actions - The Law in Kentucky 1981, supplement 1982, 85; Watson vs. Jones - The Walnut Street Presbyterian Church And the First Amendment (research funded by grant from the com. for academic excellence, U. of Louisville, summer 1979) 1982; Kentucky Damages Law 1985; Products Liability, Actions and Remedies, Callaghan 1985, Ky. Jurisprudence Evidence, 1987—; (with Laurence W. Knowles) Law For Asphalt Athletes 1983. Mem. ABA, Ky. Bar Assn., Assn. Trial Lawyers Am. Democrat. Presbyterian. Avocation: jogging. Legal education, Personal injury, Workers' compensation. Office: U Louisville Sch of Law Louisville KY 40292

EADIE, RICHARD DOUGLAS, lawyer; b. Seattle, Jan. 1, 1941; s. Richard Andrus and Myrtle B. (Bushey) E.; m. Colleen Sharon Dunn, June, 1968 (div. 1971); 1 child, Barbara Elaine; m. Claire Stephens Mapes, Aug. 4, 1973; children—Lorraine Mary, Russell Norman, Bryce Douglas, Meredith Claire. B.A., U. Wash., 1965, J.D., 1969. Bar: Wash. 1969, U.S. Dist. Ct. (we. dist.) Wash. 1971, U.S. Ct. Appeals (9th cir.) 1972, Calif. 1975, U.S. Dist. Ct. (so. dist.) Calif. 1976. Dep. pros. atty. Snohomish County, Everett, Wash., 1969-71; dep. pros. atty. King County, Seattle, 1971-74; presiding official Dept. HEW, San Diego, 1974-75; sole practice, Seattle, Edmonds, Wash., 1975—. Contbr. articles to profl. jours. Chancellor, St. Dunstan's Ch. of Highlands Parish, Seattle, 1981—, vestryman, 1981-84; del. Diocese of Olympia, Seattle, 1984-85; bd. dirs. Northwest Hosp. Found., 1986—. Mem. ABA, Assn. Trial Lawyers Am., Wash. State Bar Assn., Wash. Trial Lawyers Assn., Calif. Bar Assn., Seattle-King County Bar Assn., Snohomish County Bar Assn., San Diego County Bar Assn. Episcopalian. Club: Wash. Athletic (Seattle). State civil litigation, Administrative and regulatory, Labor. Home: 1455 NW 188th St Seattle WA 98177 Office: 115 3d Ave North Edmonds WA 98020

EADS, WAYNE BUCHANAN, lawyer; b. Roseboro, N.C., Apr. 15, 1950; s. Ora Wilbert and Ivaree (Cochran) E.; m. Frances Melinda King, Mar. 15, 1970; children—Christopher Wayne, Derrick Brandon. B.A., East Carolina U., 1970; J.D., U. N.C., 1974. Bar: Fla. 1975, N.C. 1979, U.S. Ct. Appeals (4th cir.) 1979, U.S. Supreme Ct. Sole practice law, Raleigh, N.C., 1978—, Miami, Fla., 1975—; cons. U.S. Dept. of State, Washington, 1978-82. Author: Federal Sanctions for Official Misconduct, 1973. Cons. Terry Sandford Presdl. Campaign, Durham, N.C. Mem. ABA, Nat. Acad. of Criminal Defense Lawyers, N.C. Acad. Trial Lawyers, Assn. Trial Lawyers Am. Democrat. Criminal, Banking, Private international. Office: 227 W Martin St Raleigh NC 27601

EAGAN, CHARLENE ANN, lawyer; b. Phila., Mar. 29, 1951; d. Paul F. and Helen (Pietruszak) Tholey; m. Paul A. Eagan, June 5, 1971 (div. Oct. 1981); m. Robert L. Gallagher, Feb. 28, 1986. BS in Pharmacy, Temple U., 1974, JD, 1980. Bar: Pa. 1980, N.J. 1980, U.S. Dist. Ct. (ea. dist.) Pa. 1980, U.S. Dist. Ct. N.J. 1980, U.S. Ct. Appeals (3d cir.) 1981, U.S. Supreme Ct. 1984. Pharm. chemist Rorer Group, Ft. Washington, Pa., 1974-76; pharmacist Suburban Gen. Hosp., Norristown, Pa., 1976-79; assoc. White & Williams, Phila., 1980-84, Wyeth Labs., Radnor, Pa., 1984—. vol. Women Against Abuse, Phila., 1985-86. Mem. Pa. Bar Assn. (medico-legal com. 1982—), Phila. Bar Assn. (medico-legal com. 1980—), Pharm. Mfrs. Assn. (product liability com. 1986—). Federal civil litigation, State civil litigation, Food and drug. Office: Wyeth Labs PO Box 8299 Philadelphia PA 19101

EAGAN, R(ODERICK) RUSSELL, lawyer; b. Chgo., June 3, 1919; s. Roderick and Marcella (Russell) E.; m. Shirley J. Nelson, Apr. 20, 1944; children—Wendy J., Russell Nelson, J. Roger, Elizabeth Ann Eagan Beaven. A.B., U. Mich., 1941; J.D., Northwestern U., 1947. Bar: Ill. 1947, D.C. 1947. Assoc., ptnr. Kirkland & Ellis, Washington, 1947-83; ptnr. Wiley & Rein, Washington, 1983—; dir. Gilmore Broadcasting Corp., Kalamazoo, Gilmore Enterprises Corp. Kalamazoo, Mich., Mem. bd. trustees Cedar Lane Unitarian Ch., Bethesda, Md., and Fund Dr. Ch., 1955, 61-64; pres. Elem. Sch. PTAs, Montgomery County, Md., 1955, 63. Served to maj. inf. USAF, 1942-46. Decorated Bronze Star. Mem. The D.C. Bar: Bar Assn. of D.C.; ABA (chmn. communication com. of administrv. law sect.) and Fed. Communications Bar Assn. (pres. 1978-79), Phi Delta Phi. Republican. Clubs: Metropolitan, International, Congressional Country. Administrative and regulatory, Estate planning. Home: 5724 Durbin Rd Bethesda MD 20817-6140 Office: Wiley Rein & Fielding 1776 K St NW Washington DC 20006

EAGAN, WILLIAM LEON, lawyer; b. Tampa, Fla., Feb. 10, 1928; s. John Robert and Margaret (Williams) E.; m. Marjorie Young, Mar. 6, 1949; children—Barbara Anne, Rebecca Elizabeth, Laurel Lea. Student U. Tampa, 1959, LL.B., U. Fla., 1961. Bar: Fla. 1961, U.S. Dist. Ct. (mid. dist.) Fla. 1959, U.S. Dist. Ct. (so. dist.) Fla. 1962, U.S. Ct. Appeals (5th cir.) 1972; bd. cert. civil trial lawyer, Fla. Assoc. Dexter, Conlee & Bissell, Sarasota, Fla., 1961-62; ptnr., v.p. Arnold, Matheny & Eagan, P.A., Orlando, 1962—; mem. Fla. Bar Ninth Circuit Grievance Com., 1982-84; mediator Family Law Mediation Program. Articles editor U. Fla. Law Rev., 1961. Chmn. bd. trustees First Baptist Ch. Winter Park, Fla., 1970-72, chmn. bd. deacons, 1967-69; active Indsl. Devel. Commn. Mid-Fla., Orlando, 1979-84. Served to seaman 2d class USN, 1945-46. Mem. ABA, Acad. Fla. Trial Lawyers, Am. Trial Lawyers Assn., Lawyers Title Guaranty Assn., Orange County Bar Assn. (exec. council), Order of Coif, Phi Alpha Delta, Phi Kappa Phi. Democrat. Baptist and Methodist. Clubs: University, Citrus (Orlando). Federal civil litigation, State civil litigation, Real property. Office: Arnold Matheny & Eagan PA 853 N Orange Ave Orlando FL 32802

EAGEN, FRANK P., judge, educator; b. Scranton, Pa., Sept. 26, 1949; s. Francis Peter and Helen (Gowden) E.; m. Eleanor Patricia Walters, June 19, 1982. ABA with honors, Lackawanna Jr. Coll., 1969; BA in Polit. Sci. with honors, U. New Haven, 1972; JD with honors, Western New Eng. U., 1976. Bar: Pa. 1976. Sole practice Scranton, 1976—; prof. law Lackawanna Jr. Coll., Scranton, 1976—; dist. judge Lackawanna County, Scranton, 1982—; solicitor Lackawanna County Funeral Dirs. Assn., Scranton, 1978—. Solicitor South Scranton Residents Assn., 1977—; chmn. Am. Cancer Soc., Scranton, 1979. Mem. Pa. Bar Assn., Lackawanna County Bar Assn., Pa. Trial Lawyers Assn. Democrat. Roman Catholic. Lodges: Lions (v.p. 1977-81), Elks, KC. Avocations: coin collecting, jogging, golf. Personal injury, Probate, Workers' compensation. Home: 312 Conroy Ave Scranton PA 18505 Office: O'Malley Eagen & O'Malley Chamber of Commerce Bldg #307 Scranton PA 18503

EAGLETON, EDWARD JOHN, lawyer; b. Tulsa, Jan. 22, 1931; s. William L. and Pauline (Dellinger) E.; m. Norma Lee, Oct. 6, 1956; children: Courtney Jean, Richard John. BA, Okla. U., 1954, JD, 1956. Bar: Okla. 1956, U.S. Dist. Ct. (ea., we. and no. dists.) Okla. 1956, U.S. Tax Ct. 1958, U.S. Supreme Ct. 1964. Acct. Peat Marwick Mitchell, Dallas, 1956-58; with IRS, Dallas and New Orleans, 1958-62; assoc. Houston & Klein, Tulsa, 1962-65, ptnr., 1974—; ptnr. Kothe & Eagleton, Tulsa, 1965-74. Served with U.S. Army, 1956. Republican. Unitarian. Corporate taxation, Federal civil litigation, State and local taxation. Home: 3210 E 65th Tulsa OK 74136 Office: Houston & Klein Inc PO Box 2967 Tulsa OK 74101

EAKELEY, DOUGLAS SCOTT, lawyer; b. Morristown, N.J., Mar. 2, 1946; m. Priscilla Van Tassel, June 2, 1973. BA, Yale U., 1968, JD, 1972; MA in Jurisprudence, Oxford U., Eng., 1970. Bar: N.Y. 1973, U.S. Ct. Appeals (2d cir.) 1974, N.J. 1978, U.S. Ct. Appeals (3d cir.) 1980, U.S. Supreme Ct. 1981. Law clk. to presiding justice U.S. Dist. Ct. (so. dist.) N.Y., N.Y.C., 1972-73; assoc. Debevoise, Plimpton, N.Y.C., 1973-80; ptnr. Riker, Danzig, Scherer, Hyland & Perretti, Newark and Morristown, N.J., 1980—; chmn. Legal Services N.J., North Brunswick, 1981—; pres. Legal Services Fedn. Essex County, Newark, 1981—. Chmn. bd. editors N.J. Law Jour., 1984—. Pres. N.J. Shakespeare Festival, Madison, 1982-86. Rhodes scholar Oxford U., 1968. Mem. ABA, N.J. Bar Assn., Essex County Bar Assn., Assn. of Bar of City of N.Y., Fed. Bar Assn. N.J. (v.p. 1983—), Phi Beta Kappa. Democrat. Federal civil litigation, Antitrust. Office: Riker Danzig Scherer Hyland & Perretti Hdqrs Plaza Morristown NJ 17960-1981

EAKIN, MARGARETTA MORGAN, lawyer; b. Ft. Smith, Ark., Aug. 27, 1941; d. Ariel Thomas and Oma (Thomas) Morgan; m. Harry D. Eakin, June 7, 1959; 1 dau., Margaretta E. B.A. with honors, U. Oreg., 1969, J.D., 1971. Bar: Oreg. 1971, U.S. Dist. Ct. Oreg. 1971, U.S. Ct. Appeals (9th cir.) 1977. Law clk. to chief justice Oreg. Supreme Ct., 1971-72; Reginald Heber Smith Law Reform fellow, 1972-73; house counsel Hyster Co., 1973-75; assoc. N. Robert Stoll, 1975-77; mem. firm Margaretta Eakin, P.C., Portland, Oreg., 1977—; tchr. bus. law Portland State U., 1979-80; speaker; mem. state bd. profl. responsibility Oreg. State Bar, 1979-82. Mem. ann. fund com. Oreg. Episc. Sch., 1981, chmn. subcom. country fair, 1981. Paul Patterson fellow. Mem. ABA, Assn. Trial Lawyers Am., Oreg. Trial Lawyers Assn., Oreg. Bar Assn., Multnomah County Bar Assn., 1000 Friends of Oreg. Land Use Attys. Democrat. Club: City (cooperating atty.). Federal civil litigation, State civil litigation, Contracts commercial. Office: 1220 Orbanco Bldg 1001 SW Fifth Ave Portland OR 97204

EALY, F. RONALD, lawyer; b. Effingham, Ill., Dec. 7, 1934; s. John Raymond and Florence (Bock) E.; m. Jude Louise Gerstenmeier, Aug. 23, 1958; children: Angela Donsbach, Scott, Rhonda. AS, Eastern Ill. U., 1954; JD, DePaul U., 1961. Bar: Ill. 1961, U.S. Dist. Ct. (no. dist.) Ill. 1962, U.S. Dist. Ct. (ea. dist.) Ill. 1966, U.S. Dist. Ct. (so. dist.) Ill. 1978, U.S. Supreme Ct. 1972. Spl. asst. atty. gen. State of Ill., Springfield, 1966-68, 80-83; sole practice Effingham, 1965—; field counsel Fed. Nat. Mortgage Assn., 1970—, Govt. Nat. Mortgage Assn., 1970—, Escrow Atty. Farmer's Home Administrn., 1970—; mem. Gov.'s Task Force on Children, Ill., 1982; prof. bus. law Lakeland Jr. Coll., Mattoon, Ill., 1976-81; conservator, guardian County of Effingham, 1979—. Contbr. articles to profl. jours. Pres. Effingham Community Unit 40 Sch. Bd., 1979; founder, chmn. Effingham County Operation Drug Alert Council, 1969; pres. Heart Shrine Club, 1971; mem. Atty.'s Title Guarantee Fund. Inc., 1977—; bd. dirs. United Fund, Effingham, 1975-78, Effingham County Mental Health Bd., 1972-75. Served with U.S. Army, 1955-57. Fellow Am. Acad. Matrimonial Lawyers (chmn.

membership com. 1986), Fellows Ill. Bar Found. (charter, life); mem. Ill. Bar Assn. (chmn. family law council 1981-82), Ill. Trial Lawyers Assn. (bd. dirs. 1979—, chmn. matrimonial law com. 1985—), Effingham County Bar Assn. (pres. 1976-77), Effingham C. of C. (v.p. 1973). Lodges: Kiwanis (pres. local chpt. 1970), Elks, Masons (32 degree). Avocation: scuba diving. Family and matrimonial. Home: PO Box 452 Effingham IL 62401 Office: 105 E Jefferson Ave PO Box 97 Effingham IL 62401

EARLE, VICTOR MONTAGNE, III, lawyer; b. N.Y.C., June 13, 1933; s. Victor Montagne and Marian Jeanette (Litonius) E.; m. Lois MacKennan, Dec. 28, 1955 (div. Jan. 1980); children: Jane Stewart, Susan Elizabeth, Anne McCallum; m. Karen Peterson Howard, Aug. 24, 1985. A.B., Williams Coll., 1954; LL.B., Columbia U., 1959. Bar: N.Y. 1960, U.S. Supreme Ct. 1963. Law clk. to Hon. Leonard P. Moore U.S. Ct. Appeals 2d Circuit, 1959-60; assoc. firm Cravath, Swaine & Moore, N.Y.C., 1960-68; gen. counsel Peat, Marwick, Mitchell & Co., N.Y.C., 1968-86, Peat, Marwick Internat., 1978-86; ptnr. Cahill, Gordon & Reindel, N.Y.C., 1986—; lectr. constl. and corp. law issues, U.S. and abroad. Contbr. articles to profl. jours. and popular mags. Served with U.S. Army, 1954-56. Mem. Am. Bar Assn., N.Y. State Bar Assn., Internat. Bar Assn., Assn. Bar City N.Y. (judiciary com.), Am. Law Inst., Lawyers Com. Civil Rights under Law (trustee), Legal Aid Soc. (dir.), Fund for Modern Cts. (dir.), Columbia Law Sch. Alumni Assn. (dir.). Administrative and regulatory, Federal civil litigation, State civil litigation. Office: Cahill Gordon & Reindel 80 Pine St New York NY 10005

EARLE, WILLIAM GEORGE, lawyer; b. Monroe, Mich., July 10, 1940; s. George Nelson and Ruth Elizabeth (Davies) E.; m. Cassandra Jane Mayer, Mar. 12, 1966; children—Dana, William, George. Student Yale U., 1958-59; A.B., U. Mich., 1963, LL.B., 1966. Bar: Fla. 1967, U.S. Ct. Appeals (2d cir.), U.S. Ct. Appeals (5th cir.) 1967, U.S. Dist. Ct. (so. dist.) Fla. 1967, U.S. Supreme Ct. 1972, U.S. Ct. Appeals (11th cir.) 1981; cert. civil trial lawyer, advocate. Law clk. to judge U.S. Ct. Appeals (5th cir.), 1966-67; trial atty. organized crime and racketeering sect. Dept. of Justice, 1967-69; ptnr. Kelly, Black, Black, Earle & Patchen, Miami, Fla., 1969-84; ptnr. Earle & Patchen, 1984—; bd. dirs. Fla. Bar Found., 1984—. Mem. emeritus nat. com. law sch. fund U. Mich., also mem. Pres.'s Club; chmn. eminent domain com. Fla. Bar, 1975-77. Mem. ABA, Fla. Bar Assn. (civil trial adv. nat. bd. trial advocacy 1984—, bd. dirs.), Dade County Bar Assn., Fed. Bar Assn. Episcopalian. Contbr. articles to profl. jours. Club: U. Mich. (Miami). Condemnation, Federal civil litigation, State civil litigation. Office: 1000 Brickell Ave Suite 660 Miami FL 33131

EARLEY, ANTHONY FRANCIS, JR., lawyer; b. Jamaica, N.Y., July 29, 1949; s. Anthony Francis and Jean Ann (Draffen) E.; m. Sarah Margaret Belanger, Oct. 14, 1972; children: Michael Patrick, Anthony Matthew, Daniel Cartwright, Matthew Sean. BS in Physics, U. Notre Dame, 1971, MS in Engring., 1979, JD, 1979. Bar: Va. 1980, N.Y. 1985, U.S. Ct. Appeals (5th cir.). Assoc. Hunton & Williams, Richmond, Va., 1979-85, ptnr., 1985; gen. counsel L.I. Lighting Co., Hicksville, N.Y., 1985—. Contbr. articles to profl. jours. Served to lt. USN, 1971-76. Mem. ABA, Va. Bar Assn., Assn. of Bar of City of N.Y. Roman Catholic. Club: Notre Dame (Richmond) (sec./treas. 1980-84, v.p. 1984). Avocations: tennis, skiing, furniture restoration. Nuclear power, Public utilities, Administrative and regulatory. Office: LI Lighting Co 175 E Old Country Rd Hicksville NY 11530

EARLS, MARGARET BERNARDINE HOLLEY, lawyer; b. N.Y.C., Aug. 2, 1951; d. Floyd Bernard and Margaret (Hardison) Holley; m. Phillip Martin Earls, Aug. 10, 1974; 1 child, Helen Marguerite. BA, Dillard U., 1973; JD, Boston Coll., 1977. Bar: Ga. 1981, U.S. Dist. Ct. Ga. 1981, U.S. Ct. Appeals 1981, Ga. 1981, U.S. Ct. Appeals (11th cir.) 1982. Instr. bus. law Ga. State U., Atlanta, 1980-83; sole practice Atlanta, 1981-83; spl. judiciary counsel State Ho. of Reps., Atlanta, 1982-83; asst. pub. def. Office of Def. of the Indigent, Atlanta, 1983-85; asst. dist. atty. Atlanta Jud. Cir., Fulton County, 1986—. Spl. asst. Neighborhood Justice Ctr. of Atlanta, Ga. 1978-83, mediator 1978—; mem. allocations panel United Way, Atlanta, 1981-83; arbitrator Better Bus. Bur., Atlanta, 1982—; study group facilitator Leadership Atlanta, 1986-87. Mem. Atlanta Bar Assn., Gate City Bar Assn., Ga. Assn. Black Women Attys., Am. Bus. Law Assn., Phi Alpha Delta. Criminal, Mediation and Arbitration. Office: Fulton County Court House Office Dist Atty 136 Pryor St 3d Floor Atlanta GA 30303

EARLY, BERT HYLTON, lawyer, legal search consultant; b. Kimball, W.Va., July 17, 1922; s. Robert Terry and Sue Keister (Hylton) E.; m. Elizabeth Henry, June 24, 1950; children—Bert Hylton, Robert Christian, Mark Randolph, Philip Henry, Peter St. Clair. Student, Marshall U., 1940-42; A.B., Duke U., 1946; J.D., Harvard U., 1949. Bar: W.Va. 1949, Ill. 1963, Fla. 1981. Assoc. Fitzpatrick, Marshall, Huddleston & Bolen, Huntington, W.Va., 1949-57; asst. counsel Island Creek Coal Co., Huntington, W.Va., 1957-60, assoc. gen. counsel, 1960-62; dep. exec. dir. ABA, Chgo., 1962-64, exec. dir., 1964-81; sr. v.p. Wells Internat., Chgo., 1981-83, pres., 1983-85; pres. Bert H. Early Assocs. Inc., Chgo., 1985—; Instr., Marshall U., 1950-53; cons. and lectr. in field. Bd. dirs. Morris Meml. Hosp. Crippled Children, 1954-60, Huntington Pub. Library, 1951-60, W.Va. Tax Inst., 1961-62, Huntington Galleries, 1961-62; mem. W.Va. Jud. Council, 1960-62, Huntington City Council, 1961-62; bd. dirs. Community Renewal Soc., Chgo., 1965-76, United Charities Chgo., 1972-80, Am. Bar Endowment, 1983—, Hinsdale Hosp. Found., 1987—; mem. vis. com. U. Chgo. Law Sch., 1975-78; trustee David and Elkins Coll., 1960-63. mem., Hinsdale Plan Commn., Ill., 1982-85. Served to 1st lt. AC, U.S. Army, 1943-45. Life Fellow Am. Bar Found., Ill. State Bar Found. (charter); mem. Am. Law Inst. (life), Internat. Bar Assn. (asst. sec. gen. 1967-82), ABA (Ho. of Dels. 1958-59, 84—, chmn. Young Lawyers div. 1957-58, Disting. Service award Young Lawyers div. 1983), Nat. Legal Aid and Defender Assn., Am. Jud. Soc. (bd. dirs. 1981-84), Fla. Bar, W.Va. State Bar, Chgo. Bar Assn. Presbyterian. Clubs: Harvard (N.Y.C.); Metropolitan (Washington); University, Economic (Chgo.); Hinsdale Golf (Ill.). legal search consultant. Office: Bert Early Assocs 111 W Washington St Suite 1421 Chicago IL 60602

EARLY, JOHN COLLINS, lawyer; b. N.Y.C., Jan. 24, 1919; s. Ernest Rhea and Elizabeth Jane (Collins) E.; m. Eleanor Livingston, Dec. 21, 1941; children—Elizabeth, Alison, Nancy. B.A. cum laude, Princeton U., 1940; J.D., Harvard U., 1947. Bar: N.Y. 1947, U.S. Tax Ct. 1948, U.S. Supreme Ct. 1951, U.S. Ct. Claims 1954, U.S. Ct. Mil. Appeals, 1956. Assoc. McCanliss & Early, N.Y.C., 1947-48, ptnr., 1950—; assoc. Conboy, Hewitt, O'Brien & Boardman, 1948-50. Past pres. United Campaign of Madison and Florham Park, N.J.; past v.p., trustee Kent Place Sch., Summit, N.J. Served to maj. U.S. Army, 1941-46; ETO. Decorated Bronze Star. Mem. Assn. Bar City N.Y., ABA, N.Y. State Bar Assn. Republican. Episcopalian. Clubs: Down Town Assn., Princeton, Church (N.Y.C.); Nassau, Charter (Princeton, N.J.). General practice, Estate planning, Probate. Home: Dellwood Park S Madison NJ 07940 Office: 90 Broad St New York NY 10004

EARNEST, JACK EDWARD, lawyer; b. Dallas, June 18, 1928; s. William Hubert and Uma Mae (Jolly) E.; m. Billie Jo Young, Aug. 1, 1953; children: Laura Ellen, Jack Edward. Student (Founders scholar), Vanderbilt U., 1944-46; B.B.A., So. Methodist U., 1948, LL.B., 1952; postgrad., Stanford U., summer 1967. Bar: N.Y. 1962, Tex. 1952, U.S. Supreme Ct. 1957. With Mobil Oil Corp., 1946-79; v.p. natural gas N. Am. Mobil Oil Corp., Houston, 1970-76; v.p. natural gas (worldwide) Mobil Oil Corp., N.Y.C., 1976-79; pres., chief operating officer Transcontinental Gas Pipe Line Corp., Houston, 1979-80; sr. v.p., gen. counsel Tex. Eastern Corp., Houston, 1981-83. Mem. Southeastern Gas Assn., So. Gas Assn. (dir.), Interstate Natural Gas Assn. Am. (dir.), Am. Bar Assn., Natural Gas Supply Assn. (chmn. 1979). Methodist. Clubs: Jesters, Wee Burn Country, Univ. of Houston, Ramada. Office: 4600 Post Oak Pl Houston TX 77027

EARNHART, MARK WARREN, lawyer, accountant; b. Sterling, Colo., May 19, 1955; s. Jack Warren and Bina Mae (Walker) E.; m. Cathy Kay Frinks, Sept. 6, 1980; children: Benjamin, Alison. BS in Acctg., U. Denver, 1977, JD, 1981. Colo. 1982, U.S. Dist. Ct. Colo. 1982, U.S. Tax Ct. 1985; CPA, Colo. Acct. Earnhart & Gorman CPA, Sterling, 1975-78, Earnhart & Assocs., Inc., Sterling, 1978—; sole practice Sterling, 1981—; prof. Northeastern Jr. Coll., Sterling, 1984—. Vice chmn., chmn. edn. adv. council Northeastern Jr. Coll., 1984—; legal counsel Sterling Centennial Com., 1984, Gary DeSoto Youth Ctr., Logan County, Colo., 1985; mem. legal council, bd. dirs. Friends Sterling Pub. Library, 1986—. Mem. ABA, Colo. Bar Assn., Nat. Assn. Estate Planning Councils, Colo. Soc. CPA's, Phi Delta Phi, Beta Alpha Psi. Republican. Mem. Foursquare Ch. Lodge: Elks. Probate, Corporate taxation, Personal income taxation. Home: 329 Elwood Sterling CO 80751 Office: 316 Poplar PO Box 1201 Sterling CO 80751

EASON, CARL EDWARD, JR., lawyer; b. Suffolk, Va., Apr. 3, 1954; s. Carl Edward Sr. and Katherine (Scott) E.; m. Katherine Wetterer, June 12, 1982; 1 child, Margaret Kelly. BA in Econs., Hampden-Sydney Coll., 1976; JD, Coll. of William & Mary, 1979. Bar: Va. 1979, U.S. Dist. Ct. (ea. dist.) Va. 1979. Ptnr. Pretlow, Eason & Pretlow, Suffolk, 1979—; treas., bd. dirs. Riddicks Folly, Inc., Suffolk, 1976. Chmn. City of Suffolk Commn. on Bicentennial of U.S. Constn. Mem. ABA, Va. Bar Assn. (dist. rep. 1985—), City of Suffolk Bar Assn. Democrat. Mem. Ch. of Christ. Club: Rumitan (Windsor, Va.) (bd. dirs. 1983-86). Avocation: skiing,. Bankruptcy, Real property, General practice. Home: 919 Virginia Ave Suffolk VA 23434 Office: Pretlow Eason & Pretlow 104 Western Ave Suffolk VA 23434

EASTERBROOK, FRANK HOOVER, judge; b. Buffalo, Sept. 3, 1948; s. George Edmund and Vimy (Hoover) E. B.A., Swarthmore Coll., 1970; J.D., U. Chgo., 1973. Bar: D.C. Law clk. to judge U.S.Ct. Appeals, Boston, 1973-74; asst. to solicitor gen. U.S. Dept. Justice, Washington, 1974-77, dep. solicitor gen. of U.S., 1978-79; asst. prof. law U. Chgo., 1979-81, prof. law, 1981-84, Lee & Brena Freeman prof., 1984-85; prin. employee Lexecon Inc., Chgo., 1980-85; judge U.S. Ct. Appeals (7th cir.), Chgo., 1985—; mem. adv. com. on tender offers SEC, Washington, 1983. Author: Antitrust, 1981; editor Jour of Law and Econs., Chgo., 1982—; contbr. articles to profl. jours. Recipient Prize for Disting. scholarship Emory U., Atlanta, 1981. Mem. Am. Law Inst., Phi Beta Kappa, Order of Coif. Antitrust, General corporate, Jurisprudence. Home: 1648 E 54th St Chicago IL 60615 Office: U S Ct of Appeals 219 S Dearborn St Chicago IL 60604

EASTERLING, CHARLES ARMO, lawyer; b. Hamilton, Tex., July 22, 1920; s. William Hamby and Jennie (Arilla) E.; m. Irene A. Easterling, Apr. 25, 1943; children—Charles David, Danny Karl, Jan Easterling Petty. B.B.A., Baylor U., 1951, LL.B., 1951, J.D. 1969. Bar: Tex. 1950, U.S. Supreme Ct. 1954. Sr. asst. city atty. City of Houston, 1952-64; sole practice, Houston, 1964-70; city atty. Pasadena (Tex.), 1970-82; sr. ptnr. Easterling and Easterling, Houston, 1982—; instr. So. Tex. Coll. Law, 1954-69. Served to lt. col. (ret.) USAFR. Mem. Houston-Harris County Bar Assn., Assn. Trial Lawyers Am., Phi Alpha Delta. Democrat. Methodist. Clubs: Masons (33d deg.; insp. gen. (hon.), Shriners. General practice, Probate, Workers' compensation.

EASTIN, KEITH E., lawyer; b. Lorain, Ohio, Jan. 16, 1940; s. Keith Ernest and Jane E. (Heimer) E. A.B., U. Cin., 1963, M.B.A., 1964; J.D., U. Chgo., 1967. Bar: Ill. 1967, Tex. 1974, Calif. 1975, U.S. Supreme Ct. 1975, D.C. 1983. Atty. Vedder, Price, Kaufman & Kammholz, Chgo., 1967-73; v.p., sec., gen. counsel Nat. Convenience Stores, Inc., Houston, 1973-79; partner Payne, Eastin & Widmer, Houston, 1977-83; dep. under sec. U.S. Dept. Interior, 1983-86; dep. asst. USN, 1986—; dir. Nat. Money Orders, Inc., Feast & Co., Inc., Kempco Petroleum Co., Bertman Drilling Co., Pacific Options, Inc., Del Rey Food Services, Inc., Stratford Feedyards, Inc. Bd. dirs. Theatre Under the Stars, Houston, Statue of Liberty-Ellis Island Found.; mem. exec. com. Harris County Republican Party, 1976-83. Mem. Am., Ill., Tex. bar assns., State Bar Calif., Beta Gamma Sigma, Phi Delta Phi, Beta Theta Pi. Clubs: University (Houston); Capitol Hill (Washington). General corporate, Environment, Administrative and regulatory.

EASTLAND, S. STACY, lawyer; b. Houston, Oct. 27, 1948; s. Seaborn and Anne (Stacy) E.; m. Tara Gardner, Mar. 24, 1972; children: Tara Doran, Seaborn Gardner. BS, Washington & Lee U, 1971; JD, U. Tex., 1974. Assoc. Baker & Botts, Houston, 1974-81, ptnr., 1982—; bd. dirs. Hoston Estate and Fin. Forum, Camp Mystic, Inc. Bd. dirs. Oscar Neuhaus Found., St. John Meml. Endowment Fund, Houston chpt. Ortin Soc. Fellow Am. Coll. Probate Counsel; mem. ABA (chmn. com. real property, probate and trust law sects.), Tex. State Bar Assn., Houston Bar Assn., Tex. Bd. Legal Specialization in Estate Planning and Probate Law. Episcopalian. Clubs: Houston Country, Tex. Allegro. Avocations: tennis, golf. Estate planning, Probate, Estate taxation. Home: 2525 Locke Ln Houston TX 77019 Office: Baker & Botts 3000 One Shell Plaza Houston TX 77002

EASTMAN, FOREST DAVID, lawyer; b. Iowa City, Mar. 30, 1950; s. Forest Emery and Wanda Mae (Lightner) E.; m. Susan Laurie Chenous, Jan. 4, 1975; children: Jeffrey David, Chad Ryan. BA, U. Wis., Plattville, 1975; JD, Washburn U., 1982. Bar: Iowa 1982, U.S. Dist. Ct. (no. dist.) Iowa 1982, U.S. Dist. Ct. (so. dist.) Iowa 1983. Assoc. Law Offices of Walter C. Schroeder, Mason City, Iowa, 1982—. Vol. Vol. Lawyers Project, Mason City, 1986—. Served with U.S. Army, 1968-72. Mem. ABA, Iowa Bar Assn., Cerro Gordo County Bar Assn. Republican. Lodge: Elks (inner guard, esquire 1986—, esteemed lecturing knight 1987). Avocations: racquetball, fishing, skiing, golf. State civil litigation, Personal injury, Health. Home: 622 S Maryland Mason City IA 50401 Office: Law Offices of Walter C Schroeder 119 2d St NW Mason City IA 50401

EASTWOOD, MYLES ERIC, lawyer; b. Springfield, Mass., Mar. 9, 1945; s. Eric and Allison Fairlee (Judd) E.; m. Linda Lee Revai, Dec. 29, 1975; 2 children. A.B. (Lovett Sch. scholar), U. N.C., 1967; J.D. (law scholar), Emory U., 1970; M.B.A., Ga. State U., 1982. Bar: Ga. 1970. Assoc. Lanier, Freeman, Elliott & Price, Atlanta, 1975-76; acting chief Edn. and Adminstrv. Law div. Office of Gen. Counsel Region IV, HEW, Atlanta, 1977-80; asst. U.S. atty. No. Dist. of Ga., Atlanta, 1980—. Served to lt. USN, 1971-75; to comdr. USNR, 1968-71, 75—. Recipient Outstanding Merit award Ga. State U., 1979. Mem. Ga. Internat. Trade Assn. (scholar 1979), ABA, Fed. Bar Assn. (pres. Atlanta chpt. 1984-85), Atlanta Bar Assn., Internat. Legal Soc. Tokyo, U.S. Naval Inst. Democrat. Episcopalian. Clubs: Kiwanis (Northside Atlanta chpt., chmn. com. 1977-78, 80-81, dir. 1982-84, treas. 1985-86, pres.-elect 1986—, co-chmn. Internat. Students Reception 1979-81); Lawyers. Contbr. articles to profl. publs. Federal civil litigation, Labor, Personal bankruptcy and injury. Office: 1800 US Courthouse 75 Spring St Atlanta GA 30335

EATMAN, ROBERT EMERSON, lawyer; b. Ft. Worth, Jan. 20, 1924; s. Phelan Williams and Annie (Bains) E.; m. Evelyn Marcom, July 2, 1950; children—Robert Emerson, John David. B.A., Centenary Coll., 1944; J.D., La. State U., 1949. Bar: La. 1949, U.S. Dist. Ct. (we. dist.) La. 1951, U.S. Ct. Appeals, (5th cir.) 1954, U.S. Dist. Ct. (ea. dist.) La. 1970. Gen. practice law, Shreveport, La., 1949—; sr. ptnr. Eatman & Hunter, Shreveport, 1970—; part-time lectr. oil and gas law Centenary Coll., 1979-83; asst. city atty. Shreveport, 1955-58. Served with USNR, 1944-46. Mem. La. Bar Assn., ABA, Am. Judicature Soc., Comml. Law League Am. (exec. council so. region 1978-83), Order of Coif, Phi Delta Phi. Democrat. Baptist. Club: Rotary (past pres.). Bankruptcy, Federal civil litigation, State civil litigation. Address: PO Box 4115 Shreveport LA 71134

EATON, BERRIEN CLARK, lawyer, author; b. Chgo., Feb. 12, 1919; s. Berrien Clark and Gladys (Hambleton) E.; m. Donna K. Prestwood; children: Theodore Hambleton, Ann Berrien. Student, Williams Coll., 1936-38; B.S., U. Va., 1940, LL.B., 1948, J.D., 1970. Bar: Mich. 1948, Ariz. 1969, Ga. 1971. Practiced in Detroit, 1948-69, Phoenix, 1969—; assoc. Miller, Canfield, Paddock & Stone, 1948-58, partner, 1958-69; mem. Leibsohn, Eaton, Gooding & Romley, P.C., 1971-79; partner Gray, Plant, Mooty, Mooty & Bennett, Phoenix, 1979-80; mem. firm Eaton, Lazarus, & Dodge Ltd., 1981—; instr. Wayne State U. Law Sch., 1954-69; prof. U. Ga. Law Sch., 1970-71; lectr. at law Ariz. State U. Coll. Law, 1970-71. Author: Professional Corporations and Associations, 6 vols., updated annually; co-author: tax newsletter Employee Benefits (Veba) Report, 1984-87; editorial bd. jour. Estate Planning; contbr. articles to profl. jours. Served to capt. F.A., AUS, 1941-46. Decorated Bronze Star; named hon. Ky. Col. Fellow Am. Coll. Probate Counsel, Am. Coll. Tax Counsel (regent); mem. ABA. (past com. chmn. tax sect.), Mich. Bar Assn. (past chmn. tax sect.), Detroit Bar Assn. (past chmn. tax sect.), Ariz. Bar Assn. (past chmn. tax sect.), Ga. Bar Assn., AAUP, Valley Estate Planning Council, Am. Law Inst. (program chmn.), Nat. Coll. Tax Practice (bd. trustees), Newcomen Soc. N.Am., Order of Coif, Kappa Alpha. Episcopalian. Clubs: Paradise Valley Country, Waweatonong. Home: 7239 N Mockingbird Ln Paradise Valley AZ 85253 Office: Eaton Lazarus & Dodge 3636 N Central 12th Floor Phoenix AZ 85012

EATON, DAVID FOSTER, lawyer; b. Kansas City, Kans., Sept. 6, 1955; s. Merrill Thomas and Louise (Foster) E.; m. Margaret Mary Dorsey, Oct. 13, 1979; children—Abigail, Ann-Louise, Eric James. B.S., Ind. U., 1977; J.D., Creighton U., 1980. Bar: Nebr. 1980, U.S. Dist. Ct. Nebr. 1980, U.S. Ct. Mil. Appeals 1981, U.S. Ct. Appeals (8th cir.) 1984. Assoc. Gallup & Schaefer, Omaha, 1984—; spl. asst. U.S. atty., 1983-84. Served to capt. USAF, 1980-84; capt. Res. Mem. Nebr. State Bar Assn., Omaha Bar Assn., Nat. Geog. Soc., Air Force Assn., Phi Alpha Delta. Republican. Criminal, Military, Environment. Home: 310 S 50th Ave Omaha NE 68132 Office: Gallup & Schaefer 1001 Farnam on Mall Omaha NE 68102

EATON, J(AMES) TIMOTHY, lawyer; b. Decatur, Ill., Sept. 2, 1951; s. Edward Loftus and Helen Christine (Carlson) E.; m. Jane Katzenberg, Dec. 10, 1983. BA, Miami U., Oxford, Ohio, 1973; JD, So. Ill. U., 1977; LLM, Washington U., 1979. Bar: Ill. 1977. Law clk. to presiding justice Ill. Supreme Ct., Decatur, Ill., 1977-79; ptnr. Baird, Latendresse, McCarthy & Rowden, Decatur, 1979-83, Hinshaw, Culbertson, Moelmann, Hoban & Fuller, Chgo., 1983-86, Coffield, Ungaretti, Harris & Slavin, Chgo., 1986—. Contbr. articles to profl. jours. Dept. legal counsel Ill. campaign Mondale for Pres., 1983-84; mem. St. Matthews Episc. Ch., Evanston. Fellow Ill. Bar Found.; mem. Ill. Bar Assn. (active various coms.), Lawyers Trust Fund Ill., Appellate Lawyers Assn. (bd. dirs. 1982-84), Miami U. Alumni Assn. (pres. elect 1986—). State civil litigation, Defense of pharmaceutical companies in products liability actions. Home: 723 Park Ave Wilmette IL 60091 Office: Coffield Ungaretti Harris & Slavin 3500 3 1st Nat Plaza Chicago IL 60602

EATON, JIMMY DON, lawyer; b. Evansville, Ind., Nov. 14, 1949; s. Lloyd Levi and Tellie B. (Martin) E.; m. Rosemary B. White, Aug. 29, 1972; children: Robert L., Patrick H. BA, U. Ark., 1972, JD, 1976. Bar: Ark. 1977, U.S. Dist. Ct. (ea. and we. dists.) Ark. 1977, U.S. Tax Ct. 1977, U.S. Ct. Appeals (8th cir.) 1978. Ptnr. Eaton & Benton, North Little Rock, 1980-82, Eaton & Embry, Little Rock, 1982—. Coach Burns Park Athletic Assn., North Little Rock, 1986—. Mem. ABA, Debtor-Creditor Bar Assn. Democrat. Avocations: bridge, baseball, coach. Bankruptcy, Consumer commercial. Office: Eaton & Embry 2416 Arch St Little Rock AR 72206

EATON, JOEL DOUGLAS, lawyer; b. Miami, Fla., Oct. 31, 1943; s. Joe Oscar and Patricia (MacVicar) E.; m. Mary Benson, June 24, 1967; children—Douglas, Darryl, David. B.A., Yale U., 1965; J.D., Harvard U., 1975. Bar: Fla. 1975, U.S. Dist. Ct. (so. dist.) Fla. 1976, U.S. Ct. Appeals (5th cir.) 1976, U.S. Supreme Ct. 1978, U.S. Ct. Appeals (11th cir.) 1981. Ptnr. Podhurst, Orseck, Parks, Josefsberg, Eaton, Meadow & Olin, P.A., Miami, 1975—. Served with USN, 1965-71. Decorated Air medal with Bronze Star and numeral 14, Navy Commendation medal with 2 gold stars, Cross of Gallantry (Vietnam). Mem. Acad. Fla. Trial Lawyers, ABA, Assn. Trial Lawyers Am., Dade County Bar Assn., Fla. Bar Assn. (appellate rules com. 1981—). Democrat. State civil litigation, Federal civil litigation, Personal injury. Office: Podhurst Orseck Parks et al City Nat Bank Bldg Suite 800 25 W Flagler St Miami FL 33130

EATON, LARRY RALPH, lawyer; b. Quincy, Ill., Aug. 18, 1944; s. Roscoe Ralph and Velma Marie (Beckett) E.; m. Janet Claire Rosen, Oct. 28, 1978. B.A., Western Ill. U., 1965; J.D., U. Mich., 1968. Bar: Ill. 1968, U.S. Dist. Ct. (no. dist.) Ill. 1976, U.S. Supreme Ct. 1978, U.S. Ct. Appeals (7th cir.) 1978, U.S. Ct. Appeals (D.C. cir.) 1984. U.S. Peace Corps vol. Instr. law U. Liberia Sch. Law, Monrovia, 1968-70; lawyer Forest Park Found., Peoria Heights, Ill., 1970-71; asst. atty. gen. State of Ill., Springfield, 1971-75; ptnr. Peterson, Ross, Schloerb & Seidel, Chgo., 1975—; instr. environ. law Quincy Coll., Ill., 1973-75; mem. Ill. Indsl. Pollution Control Financing Authority, 1979. Contbg. writer Chgo. Daily Law Bull., 1975-77; field editor Pollution Engring., 1976. Mem. Ill. Bar Found. (charter fellow), Ill. Bar Assn. (chmn. environ. control law sect. 1976-77, editor sect. newsletter 1972-77, mem. assembly 1980-86), ABA, Chgo. Bar Assn., Bar Assn. for 7th Jud. Cir., Law Club Chgo. Environment, Antitrust, Federal civil litigation. Office: Peterson Ross Schloerb Seidel 200 E Randolph Dr Suite 7300 Chicago IL 60601

EATON, WILLIAM LAWRENCE, lawyer; b. Boston, Mar. 12, 1946; s. Lawrence V. and Jeanne K. Eaton; m. Sally Ackerman, 1986. AB, Stanford U., 1969; JD, Boston Coll., 1972; LLM in Taxation, Boston U., 1980. Bar: Mass. 1972. Law clk. to presiding justice Mass. Superior Ct., Boston, 1972-73; trial atty. U.S. Dept. Justice, Washington, 1973-75; assoc. Parker, Coulter, Daley & White, Boston, 1975-77; ptnr. Snyder, Tepper & Comen, Boston, 1977-82, Woodman & Eaton P.C., Concord, Mass., 1982—. Assoc. editor Boston Coll. Indsl. and Comml. Law Rev., 1972. Mem. ABA, Mass. Bar Assn., Order of Coif. General corporate, Probate, Real property. Home: 7 Camden Pl Cambridge MA 02138 Office: Woodman & Eaton PC 801 Main St Concord MA 01742

EATON, WILLIAM MELLON, lawyer; b. N.Y.C., Oct. 5, 1924; s. Ernest Risley and Carolyn (Mellon) E.; m. Elizabeth Waring Witsell, Dec. 21, 1956; children: Carolyn Taylor, Alexander, Sarah, Lisa. B.S., Duke, 1945; J.D., Harvard, 1949. Bar: N.Y. 1949, U.S. Supreme Ct. 1961. Since practiced in N.Y.C.; asso. firm White & Case, 1949-60; mem. firm Hardy, Peal, Rawlings, Werner & Maxwell, 1960-65; sr. partner firm Eaton & Van Winkle, 1965-85, of counsel, 1986—; pres. BT Capital Corp., SBIC of Bankers Trust, N.Y. Corp., 1972-80, dir., 1972-83; pres. BT Capitol Corp., SBIC of Bankers Trust N.Y. Corp., 1972-80, bd. dirs. 1972-83. Trustee, executor pvt. estates; dir. various corps. and founds.; Trustee Skowhegan Sch. Painting and Sculpture, Hartford Family Fund, other charitable orgns.; asst. sec., ofcl. adviser U.S.-Japan Found., 1980-85; sec. Moroccan Am. Found., 1982-86; Ann. fellow Met. Mus. of Art and Pierpont Morgan Library. Served with USNR, 1943-46, PTO. Fellow N.Y. State Bar Found.; mem. ABA. (chmn. com. investment securities 1969-73, mem. 1973-83), Internat. Bar Assn., N.Y. State Bar Assn. (chmn. investment com. 1974-81), Assn. of Bar of City of N.Y., Soc. Colonial Wars (chancellor Gen. Soc. 1978—), St. Nicholas Soc. (gov. 1965-68). Episcopalian. Banking, General corporate, Private international. Office: Eaton & Van Winkle 600 3d Ave New York NY 10016

EBBEN, DAVID WILLIAM, lawyer; b. Oakland, Calif., Dec. 16, 1952; s. Donald Joseph and Dorothy May (Olson) E.; m. Lynn Agnes Essen, Aug. 7, 1977 (div. Mar. 1982); 1 child, Nicholas Donald. BS in Econs., U. Wis., 1975; JD, U. of Pacific, 1978. Bar: Wis. 1978. Assoc. Melby & Schiek, Rhinelander, Wis., 1978—. Mem. ABA, Wis. Bar Assn., Vilas-Oneida-Forest County Bar Assn. Roman Catholic. Lodge: Kiwanis. Avocations: fishing, hunting, camping, skiing. Home: 4360 Aberdeen Rd Rhinelander WI 54501 Office: Melby & Schiek SC PO Box 1047 Rhinelander WI 54501

EBERHARD, ROBERT VINCENT, lawyer; b. N.Y.C., Feb. 6, 1951; s. Daniel V. and Catherine Rita (Quinn) E.; B.A. in Econs., Fairfield U., 1973; J.D., Catholic U., 1976. Bar: Conn. 1976, U.S. Dist. Ct. Conn. 1980. Assoc. Daniel T. Eberhard, Danbury, Conn., 1976-77, DeFabritis & Eberhard, Danbury, 1977-81, Louis A. DeFabritis, Danbury, 1981-83; ptnr. Eberhard & Eberhard, Danbury, 1983—; atty. Fairfield County Campfire, Inc., 1978—. Mem. Danbury Bar Assn. (treas. 1981-86, v.p. 1986—). Roman Catholic. General practice, Real property, State civil litigation. Home: 28 Royal Rd Danbury CT 06811 Office: Eberhard & Eberhard 4 Moss Ave Danbury CT 06810

EBERHARDT, DANIEL HUGO, lawyer; b. Milw., Feb. 19, 1938; s. Erwin M. and Hazel M. (Daley) E.; m. Josephine E. Jeka, Sept. 10, 1960; children: Daniel Hugo Jr., Mark John. BS, Colo. State U., 1962; JD, Marquette U., 1968. Bar: Wis. 1968, U.S. Dist. Ct. (ea. dist.) Wis. 1968. Assoc. Morrissy, Morrissy, Sweet & Race, Elkhorn, Wis., 1968-70; ptnr. Sweet & Eberhardt, Elkhorn, 1970-76; sole practice Elkhorn, 1976—; commr. Walworth County Cir. Cts., 1975—. Served to 1st lt. U.S. Army, 1962-65, AUS. Mem. ABA, Wis. Bar Assn., Assn. Trial Lawyers Am., Walworth County Bar Assn. (sec., treas. 1983-85, v.p. 1985-86, pres. 1986—), VFW (comdr. 1980-81). Republican. Roman Catholic. Lodge: Rotary (pres. 1980-81). Family and matrimonial, Probate, Real property. Home: Rt 4 Box 463 Elkhorn WI 53121 Office: 18 S Broad St Elkhorn WI 53121

EBERHARDT, ROBERT SCHULER, JR., lawyer; b. Denver, Aug. 13, 1928; s. Robert Schuler and Kathryn Marie (Babington) E.; m. Lusetta Mary Bush, Aug. 6, 1955; children: Robert S. III, Gretchen Ann, Derek Bush, Krista Kathryn. BJ, U. Colo., 1952, JD, 1955; postgrad., Georgetown U. Law Sch., 1953-54. Bar: Colo. 1955, Denver 1955. Sole practice Littleton, Colo., 1955—. Rep. Colo. State Legis., Denver, 1960-65. Served with U.S. Army, 1947-48. Mem. Phi Delta Phi, Sigma Delta Chi. Personal injury, Probate, Legislative. Home: 5555 S King Crest Way-Bowmar Littleton CO 80123 Office: 8441 W Bowles Ave Suite 210 Littleton CO 80123

EBERHART, HARRY SIMON, lawyer; b. Allentown, Pa., May 21, 1934; s. Harry S.F. and Anna H. (Molchan) E.; m. Adele Gregg, Nov. 28, 1959; 1 child, Karen G. BS, Pa. State U., 1956; MA in Pub. Adminstrn., U. Pitts., 1964; JD, U. Bridgeport, 1980. Bar: Conn. 1980, Fla. 1981, Pa. 1981, U.S. Dist. Ct. Conn. 1981. Planning dir. City of Meriden, Conn., 1965-77, devel. cons., 1977-80; ptnr. Sargent & Eberhart, Meriden, 1980-84; sole practice, Meriden, 1985—; commr. small claims Conn. Superior Ct., 1982-85, magistrate, 1986—; judge moot ct. U. Bridgeport, Conn., 1980—; adj. prof. Post Coll., 1983—; lectr. in field. Contbr. articles to newspaper. Coordinator, City of Meriden-Expo '76, 1976; radio show host Sta. WWMW, Meriden, 1975-76. Served to lt. (j.g.) USN, 1956-58. Mem. Arts and Crafts Assn. (counsel 1982—), Internat. City Mgmt. Assn., Vol. Lawyers For Arts, ABA, Am. Trial Lawyers Assn., Delta Theta Phi (dist. chancellor). Democrat. Roman Catholic. Environment, Real property, Local government. Home: 100 Sandy Ln Meriden CT 06450

EBERLE, WILLIAM FREDERIC, lawyer; b. Lyndonville, N.Y., July 10, 1926; s. Arthur Mills and Doretta Fredericka (Rynders) E.; m. Barbara Lakin Wiese, Aug. 16, 1952; children—Elizabeth, John, James, Andrew. B.S., Cornell U., 1950; LL.B., St. John's U., 1956. Bar: N.Y. 1958, U.S. Supreme Ct. 1980, U.S. Ct. Claims 1980. Microbiologist, biochemist Gen. Foods Corp., Hoboken, N.J., 1950-52, patent law clk., 1952-55; assoc. Brumbaugh, Graves, Donohue & Raymond, N.Y.C., 1955-64, ptnr., 1964—. Mem. South Orangetown Sch. Bd., 1961-74; trustee Palisades Free Library, 1975-83, pres., 1978-79; trustee Hist. Soc. Rockland County, 1976—, pres., 1981-83. Mem. ABA, Am. Patent Law Assn., N.Y. State Bar Assn., Assn. Bar City N.Y., N.Y. Patent Law Assn. (pres. 1979-80). Patent, Trademark and copyright. Office: 30 Rockefeller Plaza New York NY 10112

EBERLY, RUSSELL ALBERT, lawyer, manufacturing company executive; b. Dover, Ohio, July 27, 1922; s. Herbert Lamoyne and Meta Charlotte (Bimeler) E.; B.S., Washington and Jefferson Coll., 1944; J.D., Akron U., 1950; m. Jean McWilliams Fisher, Jan. 19, 1946; children—Ann Eberly Calvert, James Allen. Bar: Ohio 1950, Pa. 1977. Patent atty. B.F. Goodrich Co., Akron, 1946-52; with PPG Industries, Inc., 1952—, asst. patent counsel, then corp. patent counsel, Pitts., 1970-77, corp. counsel, 1977-78, v.p. law, 1978-79, v.p., gen. counsel, 1979—; dir. PPG Industries Found. Mem. devel. council Washington and Jefferson Coll., 1979—, trustee, 1981—. Served with USNR, 1943-46. Mem. ABA, Am. Patent Law Assn., Assn. Gen. Counsel, Patent Law Assn. Pitts. Republican. Methodist. Clubs: Duquesne (Pitts.); South Hills Country. General corporate. Office: PPG Industries Inc 1 PPG Pl Pittsburgh PA 15272

EBERT, DARLENE MARIE, lawyer; b. Milw., Dec. 29, 1951; d. Frank James and Marie Antoinette (Ermenc) Leban; m. Lee Arthur Ebert, Dec. 30, 1972; children: Kristen Ann, Mark Alan. BA, U. Wis., 1973, MS, 1974, JD, 1977. Bar: Wis. 1977, Colo. 1977. Assoc. Lobato-Bleidt, Bleidt & Haight, Lakewood, Colo., 1978-79; asst. city atty. City of Denver, 1979—. Mem. ABA, Colo. Bar Assn., Denver Bar Assn., Wis. Bar Assn., Colo. Women's Bar Assn., Beta Sigma Phi (pres. 1981-82, v.p. 1986—). Democrat. Roman Catholic. Labor, Administrative and regulatory, State civil litigation. Home: 4015 S Niagara Way Denver CO 80237 Office: Denver City Atty 1445 Cleveland Pl Denver CO 80202

EBERT, LARRY PAUL, lawyer; b. Sandusky, Ohio, Apr. 10, 1952; s. James William and Joyce Ann (Schriempf) E.; m. Caren Odel Horn, Mar. 27, 1976; children: Lauren Elizabeth, Kathryn Elaine. BA, Case Western Res. U., 1974; JD, Ohio State U., 1977. Bar: Ohio 1978. Atty. Mead Corp., Dayton, Ohio, 1977-82; real estate mgr. Boise (Idaho) Cascade Corp., 1982—. Editor: Construction Contracts, 1985; contbr. articles to profl jours. Bd. dirs. Bus. for Idaho Found., Boise; mem. Boise Area Econ. Devel. Assn., 1986—. Mem. ABA, Indsl. Devel. Research Council Inc. (bd. dirs.), Boise Area C. of C. Club: The Court House (Boise). Real property, Construction. Home: 5270 Creswell Ave Boise ID 83704 Office: Boise Cascade Corp 1 Jefferson Sq Boise ID 83728

EBERT, REGAN DANIELLE, lawyer, educator; b. Chgo., June 13, 1954; d. Carl Henry and Florence (Sonerin) E.; m. Daniel Lee Balzano, July 13, 1981; 1 child, Daniel Carl. B.S., U. Ill., 1976, M.S., 1977; J.D., John Marshall Law Sch., Chgo., 1979. Bar: Ill. 1979, U.S. Dist. Ct. (no. dist.) Ill. 1979, U.S. Ct. Appeals (7th cir.) 1980, U.S. Dist. Ct. (no. dist.) Ill. Trial Bar 1983. Staff atty. City of Chgo., 1980; trial atty. Hartford Ins. Co., Chgo., 1980-84, Judge & Knight Ltd., Park Ridge, Ill., 1984, Carl H. Ebert & Assocs., Chgo., 1984—; prosecutor City of Park Ridge, 1984—; adj. faculty John Marshall Law Sch., 1980—. Legal advisor 41st Ward Democratic Orgn., Chgo., 1979—, precinct capt., 1977—. Grad. research asst. U. Ill., 1977; Ill. state scholar, 1972; mem. John Marshall Law Sch. Law Rev., 1977-79; recipient Order of John Marshall, 1979. Mem. ABA, Assn. Trial Lawyers Am., Ill. Bar Assn., Ill. Trial Lawyers Assn., Chgo. Bar Assn. Personal injury, State civil litigation, Criminal. Office: Carl H Ebert & Assocs 11 S La Salle Suite 2070 Chicago IL 60601

EBINER, ROBERT MAURICE, lawyer; b. Los Angeles, Sept. 2, 1927; s. Maurice and Virginia (Grand) E.; m. Paula H. Van Sluyters, June 16, 1951; children—John, Lawrence, Marie, Michael, Christopher, Joseph, Francis, Matthew, Therese, Kathleen, Eileen, Brian, Patricia, Elizabeth, Ann. J.D., Loyola U., Los Angeles, 1953. Bar: Calif. 1954, U.S. dist. ct. (cen. dist.) Calif. 1954. Solo practice, West Covina, Calif., 1954—; judge pro tem Los Angeles Superior Ct., 1964-66, arbitrator, 1979—; judge pro tem Citrus Mcpl. Ct., 1966-70; instr. law Alhambra Evening High Sch., 1955-58; mem. disciplinary hearing panel Calif. State Bar, 1968-75. Bd. dirs. West Covina United Fund, 1958-61, chmn. budget com. 1960-61; organizer Joint United Funds East San Gabriel Valley, 1961, bd. dirs. 1961-68; bd. dirs. San Gabriel Valley Cath. Social Services, 1969—, pres., 1969-72; bd. dirs. Region II Cath. Social Service, 1970—, pres. 1970-74; trustee Los Angeles Cath. Welfare Bur. (now Cath. Charities), 1978—; charter bd. dirs. East San Gabriel Valley Hot Line, 1969-74, sec., 1969-72; charter bd. dirs. N.E. Los Angeles County unit Am. Cancer Soc., 1973-78, chmn. by-laws com. 1973-78; bd. dirs. Queen of the Valley Hosp. Found., 1983—, West Covina Hist. Soc., 1982—; active Calif. State Democratic Central Com., 1963-68. Served with AUS, 1945-47. Recipient Los Angeles County Human Relations Commn. Disting. Service award, 1978; named West Covina Citizen of Yr., 1986. Mem. ABA, Calif. Bar Assn., Los Angeles County Bar Assn., Fed. Ct. So. Dist. Calif. Assn., Los Angeles Trial Lawyers Assn., Eastern Bar Assn. Los Angeles County (pres. Pomona Valley 1965-66), West Covina C. of C. (pres. 1960), Am. Arbitration Assn. Clubs: K.C., Bishop Amat High Sch. Booster (bd. dirs. 1973—, pres. 1978-80), Kiwanis (charter West Covina, pres. 1976-77, lt. gov. div. 35 1980-81, Kiwanian of Yr. 1978, 82, Disting. Lt. Gov. 1980-81, bd.dirs. Calif., Nev. and Hawaii Internat. Found. 1986—). State civil litigation, Personal injury, Probate. Office: 1502 W Covina Pkwy West Covina CA 91790

ECCARD, WALTER THOMAS, lawyer; b. Bklyn., May 19, 1946; s. Walter Stanley and Alice Lorenza (Thomas) E.; m. Joan Elizabeth Dufel, July 31, 1983; 1 child, David Thomas; 1 stepchild, Anne Linder. B.A., Capital U., 1968; M.A., U. Okla., 1973; J.D., Vanderbilt U., 1977. Bar: D.C. 1978, U.S. Dist. Ct. D.C. 1978. Assoc. LeBoeuf, Lamb, Leiby & MacRae, Washington, 1977-80; atty. adv. U.S. Dept. Treasury, Washington, 1980-85, dep. asst. gen. counsel banking and finance, 1985-86, ptnr. Brown & Wood, Washington, 1986—. Author: (textbook chpt.) Nurses, Nurse Practitioners, 1985. Served to capt. USAF, 1968-72. Recipient Performance award U.S. Dept. Energy, 1982, U.S. Dept. Treasury, 1984, 85, Meritorius Service award, 1986, Spl. Appreciation Adminstrn. award U.S. HHS, Washington, 1983. Mem. ABA, Order of Coif. Lutheran. Banking, Contracts commercial, Securities. Home: 9836 Dellcastle Rd Gaithersburg MD 20879 Office: Brown & Wood One Farragut Sq Washington DC 20006

ECHOHAWK, JOHN ERNEST, lawyer; b. Albuquerque, Aug. 11, 1945; s. Ernest V. and Emma Jane (Conrad) E.; m. Kathryn Suzanne Martin, Oct. 23, 1965; children: Christopher, Sarah. BA, U. N.M., 1967, JD, 1970. Bar: Colo. 1972, U.S. Dist. Ct. Colo. 1972, U.S. Appeals (8th cir.) 1976, U.S. Ct. Appeals (9th cir.) 1980. Research assoc. Calif. Indian Legal Services, Escondido, 1970, Native Am. Rights Fund, Berkeley Calif. and Boulder, Colo., 1970-72; dep. dir. Native Am. Rights Fund, Boulder, 1972-73, 1975-77, exec. dir., 1973-75, 1977—; mem. task force Am. Indian Policy Rev. Commn., U.S. Senate, Washington, 1976-77; bd. dirs. Am. Indian Lawyer Tng. Program, Oakland, Calif., 1975—, Nat. Com. Responsive Philanthropy, Washington, 1981—. Recipient Disting. Service award Ams. For Indian Opportunity, 1982, Pres. Indian Service award Nat. Congress Am. Indians, 1984. Mem. ABA, Am. Indian Bar Assn., Assn. Am. Indian Affairs (bd. dirs. 1980—). Democrat. Avocations: fishing, skiing. Indian law. Home: 2350 Panorama Boulder CO 80302 Office: Native Am Rights Fund 1506 Broadway Boulder CO 80302

ECHSNER, STEPHEN HERRE, lawyer; b. Columbus, Ind., Dec. 25, 1954; s. Herman Joseph and Virginia Blair (Lechleiter) E. BA, Marquette U., 1977; JD, St. Louis U., 1980. Bar: Fla. 1980, U.S. Dist. Ct. (no. dist.) Fla. 1980, U.S. Ct. Appeals (5th and 11th cirs.) 1980. Assoc. Levin, Warfield, Middlebrooks, Mabie, Thomas, Mayes & Mitchell P.A., Pensacola, Fla., 1980-85, ptnr., 1985—. Mem. ABA, Assn. Trial Lawyers Am., Acad. Fla. Trial Lawyers. Republican. Roman Catholic. Personal injury, Insurance. Office: Levin Warfield Middlebrooks Mabie et al PO Box 12308 Pensacola FL 32581

ECHT, GEORGE, lawyer; b. Grodek, Poland, Dec. 11, 1907; came to U.S., 1921; s. William and Leah (Wiletzky) E.; m. Helen Rosenberg, Sept. 18, 1938; children—David W., Rona F. Levi. A.A., Central YMCA Coll., 1930; LL.B., Chgo. Kent Coll. Law, 1934; J.D., Ill. Inst. Tech., 1972. Bar: Ill. 1934, U.S. Dist. Ct. (no. dist.) Ill. Counselor Service Corps Ret. Execs., SBA, San Diego, 1976—; mem. Inst. Continued Learning, U. Calif.-San Diego, 1976—. Mem. ABA, Ill. Bar Assn., San Diego County Bar Assn., Chgo. Bar Assn. (assoc.). Home: 400 Prospect St La Jolla CA 92037

ECKARDT, RICHARD WILLIAM, lawyer; b. St. Charles, Ill., Mar. 8, 1938; s. Frederick William and Mira Helen Louise (Vance) E.; B.A., Ohio State U., 1959; J.D., U. So. Calif., 1966. Bar: Calif. 1967, U.S. Dist. Ct. (no. and cent. dists.) Calif. 1967, U.S. Supreme Ct. 1972. Mem. legal staff Pacific Lighting Corp., Los Angeles, 1968-70; assoc. Mitchell and Mitchell, Los Angeles, 1970-71, Sprague and Clements, Los Angeles, 1971-73; sole practice, Los Angeles, 1973-81, 82-87; ptnr. Katsky, Ker, Eckardt & Hunt, Los Angeles, 1981-82, Eckardt & Ruonala, 1987—. judge pro tem Los Angeles Mcpl. Ct., 1978—; Mem. ABA, Fed. Bar Assn., Los Angeles Lawyers for Human Rights (sec. 1979-85, bd. of trustees 1979-85), Los Angeles County Bar Assn. (legal services for the poor com., del. to state bar conf. 1983—, exec. com. of delegation 1987—, bus. and corp. law sect., real property, taxation, probate and trust law sects., law office mgmt.), Assn. Bus. Trial Lawyers, Calif. Bar Assn., Am. Judicature Soc., Los Angeles World Affairs Council, Legion Lex., Phi Alpha Delta. Club: University (Los Angeles). Real property, General corporate, Banking. Home: 1155 Nithsdale Rd Pasadena CA 91105 Office: 530 W 6th St 5th Floor Los Angeles CA 90014

ECKELBERGER, JERRIE FRANCIS, lawyer; b. New Castle, Pa., Sept. 12, 1944; s. John Elton and Marian Elizabeth (Francis) E.; m. Judie Ann Ogstedal, July 22, 1978; children: David Francis, Kristen Elizabeth, John Irvin. BA, Northwestern U., 1966; JD, U. Colo., 1971. Bar: Colo. 1971, U.S. Dist. Ct. Colo. 1971. Dist. atty. Arapahoe County, Littleton, Colo., 1972-75; assoc. Meyers & Polidori, Denver, 1975-77; ptnr. Eckelberger & Feldman, Littleton, 1977—; bd. dirs. Roxborough Devel. Corp., Littleton, Roxborough Park Found., Littleton. Co-author: DUI Trial Manual, 1976. Chmn. task force Arapahoe County Juvenile Justice, Littleton, 1975. Mem. Colo. Bar Assn., Arapahoe County Bar Assn. Avocations: skiing, tennis, fishing. Real property, Personal injury, Civil litigation. Office: Eckelberger & Feldman One DTC Suite 690 5251 DTC Pkwy Englewood CO 80111

ECKELMAN, PAUL JOHN, lawyer; b. Denver, Nov. 2, 1950; s. Paul Frank and Mary Jane (Hakala) E.; children: Jennifer Marie, Paul Anthony, Justin Joseph, Jonathan Michael. BS, Marist Coll., 1974; JD, Vt. Law Sch., 1977. Bar: N.Y. 1978. Assoc. Mangold & Mahar, Poughkeepsie, N.Y., 1977-85; sole practice Poughkeepsie, 1985—. Mem. N.Y. State Bar Assn., Dutchess County Bar Assn. Republican. Roman Catholic. General practice, Family and matrimonial, Personal injury. Home: 22 Inwood Ave Poughkeepsie NY 12603 Office: 224 Mill St Poughkeepsie NY 12601

ECKER, JAMES MARSHALL, lawyer; b. Pitts., Nov. 4, 1929; s. I. Elmer and Belle Ruth (Berger) E.; m. Carole Dombro, Nov. 4, 1950; m. Barbara Van De Sande, Mar. 25, 1971; children—Michel Susan, Sharon Rose. B.A., Dickinson Coll., 1952, J.D., 1955. Bar: Pa. 1958, U.S. Dist. Ct. (we. dist.) Pa. 1958, U.S. Supreme Ct. 1960, Fla. 1979. Ptnr., Ecker, Ecker & Ecker, Pitts., 1957—; legal counsel Syria Shrine, Pitts., 1977—; counsel Pitts. Three Rivers Regatta, 1978—. Past pres. Variety Fund for Handicapped Children, Pitts.; past pres. Amen Corner; founder Ann. Police Luncheon for Pitts. Served with U.S. Army, 1955-57. Recipient St. Francis Hosp. award, 1974; Rosilia award, 1975; Variety Internat. award, 1977; I. Elmer Ecker Meml. award, 1975; citation Pres. U.S. Gerald Ford, 1976. Mem. ABA, Allegheny County Bar Assn. (judiciary com., bd. govs. family law and criminal bds.), Am. Acad. Matrimonial Lawyers (bd. govs. western Pa. br.), Am. Arbitration Assn., Turtle Creek C. of C. (pres.). Democrat. Jewish. Clubs: Variety (past chief barker), Dapper Dan, Pitts. Athletic Assn., Pitts. Press, Rivers, Shriners (Pitts.); Jockey (Fla.). Family and matrimonial, Criminal, General practice.

ECKERT, MICHAEL LOUIS, lawyer; b. Oshkosh, Wis., Jan. 14, 1950; s. Vincent Edward and Eileen Margaret (Lienum) E.; m. Mary Patricia Kroll, May 27, 1972; children—Brian W., Jeffrey V., Matthew J. B.A., U. Wis., 1972, J.D., 1975. Bar: Wis. 1975, U.S. Dist. Ct. (ea. and we. dists.) Wis. 1975, U.S. Ct. Appeals (7th cir.) 1976. Ptnr. Eckert Law Office, Rhinelander, Wis., 1975—; teaching atty. U. Wis. Law Sch., 1983, 86. Bd. dirs. Rhinelander Indsl. Devel. Corp., 1982—, Sacred Heart-St. Mary's Hosp., 1982—, Community Mental Health Services, 1986—, Sta. WXPR-FM Pub. Radio, 1986—, Older Am. Service Bur., 1986—, White Pines Community Broadcasting, 1987—. Recipient Wall Street Jour. Student Achievement award Dow-Jones, Inc., 1972. Mem. ABA, Oneida-Vilas-Forest County Bar Assn. (pres. 1982-83), Wis. Acad. Trial Lawyers, Def. Research Inst., Civil Trial Counsel Wis., Internat. Assn. Defense Counsel. Republican. Roman Catholic. Lodge: Kiwanis. Insurance, State civil litigation, Personal injury. Home: Kerry Ln Rhinelander WI 54501 Office: Eckert Law Office PO Box 1247 Rhinelander WI 54501

ECKERT, ROBERT LAIRD, judge; b. Garrison, N.D., Dec. 15, 1932; s. Joseph E. and Gertrude M. (Schlichting) E.; m. Dorothy Oddson, Sept. 21, 1963; children: Robert L. Jr., Ann Marie, Joseph Edward. BS in Commerce, U. N.D., 1954, JD, 1957. Bar: N.D. 1957, U.S. Dist. Ct. N.D. 1957. Assoc. Johnson, Milloy & Eckert, Wahpeton, N.D., 1957-75; dist. judge State of N.D., Wahpeton, 1975—; states atty. Richland County, Wahpeton, 1966-75; city atty. Wahpeton, 1965-75. Mem. Order of Coif. Methodist. Judicial administration. Home: 801 N 2d St Wahpeton ND 58075 Office: Richland County Courthouse PO Box 1109 Wahpeton ND 58075-1109

ECKERT, STEPHEN PAUL, lawyer; b. Ft. Wayne, Ind., Jan. 15, 1955; s. Aldhelm Joseph and Evangeline Betty (Hodson) E.; m. Diane Lynn Arend, Aug. 2, 1980; children: Jennifer Christine, Matthew Stephen, Katelin Diane. BA, Ind. U., Bloomington, 1978; JD, Ind. U., Indpls., 1981. Bar: Ind. 1981, U.S. Dist. Ct. (so. dist.) Ind. 1981, U.S. Ct. Mil. Appeals 1983. Researcher Civil Liberties Union, Indpls., 1979, Legal Services Orgn., Indpls., 1979-80; assoc. George Clyde Gray, P.C., Indpls., 1981-83; ptnr. Gray, Robinson, Eckert & Ryan, Indpls., 1984—. Mem. Ind. Bar Assn., Indpls. Bar Assn., Assn. Trial Lawyers Am., Ind. Trial Lawyers Assn. Roman Catholic. Personal injury, Insurance, Workers' compensation. Home: 329 Beechview Ln Indianapolis IN 46217 Office: Gray Robinson Eckert & Ryan 8122 S Meridian St Indianapolis IN 46217

ECKHARDT, WILLIAM RUDOLF, III, lawyer; b. Houston, Dec. 14, 1915; s. William Rudolf and Ura (Link) E.; m. Elra Hodges, Oct. 11, 1940; 1 son, Donald Kent. B.A., Rice Inst., 1937; LL.B., U. Tex., 1940. Bar: Tex. 1940. Asst. U.S. atty. Dept. Justice, So. Dist. Tex., 1940-44, 46-52; assoc. McGregor & Sewell, Houston, 1952-56, Vinson & Elkins, Houston, 1956—. Served to lt. (j.g.) USN, 1944-46. Fellow Am. Coll. Trial Lawyers; mem. ABA, Tex. Bar Assn., Maritime Law Assn., Tex. Def. Attys. Assn., Chancellors, Order of Coif, Phi Delta Phi, Chi Phi. Republican. Baptist. Clubs: Houst; Inns of Ct. (Houston). Admiralty, State civil litigation, Insurance. Home: 25 Robin Lake Ln Houston TX 77024 Office: Vinson & Elkins 3300 1st City Tower 10001 Fannin Houston TX 77002-6760

ECKHART, JAMES MILTON, lawyer; b. Miami, Fla., Mar. 13, 1944; s. Joseph W. and Elsie M. E. A.B., U. Miami (Fla.), 1965, J.D., 1968. Bar: Fla. 1968, D.C. 1979, U.S. Dist. Ct. (so. dist.) Fla. 1969, U.S. Ct. Appeals (11th cir.) 1981. Assoc., C.P. Lantz, Miami, 1968-70, Carey, Dwyer, Austin, Cole & Selwood, P.A., Miami, 1970-76; ptnr. Carey, Dwyer, Cole Selwood & Bernard, P.A., Miami, 1976-78, dir., 1978-81; dir., ptnr. Carey, Dwyer, Cole, Eckhart, Mason & Spring, P.A., Miami, 1981—; arbitrator, lectr. Am. Arbitration Assn.; guest lectr. U. Miami. Dade County Democratic committeeman, 1970-74. Served with U.S. Army, 1968-76. Mem. ABA, Fla. Bar Assn., D.C. Bar Assn., Dade County Bar Assn. (dir.), Am. Judicature Soc., Def. Research Inst., Fla. Def. Lawyers Assn., Delta Theta Phi, Phi Delta Theta. Roman Catholic. Clubs: Rod and Reel, Coral Reef Yacht (Miami). Personal injury, Insurance, State civil litigation. Office: 2180 SW 12th Ave Miami FL 33129

ECKHART, MORRIS LEE ROY, lawyer; b. Vinton, Iowa, Dec. 22, 1948; s. George L. and Nelda R. (Primmer) E.; m. Martha A. Milroy, Aug. 30, 1969; children: Peter J., Ann E. BA, U. No. Iowa, 1971; JD with honors, Drake U., 1973. Bar: Iowa 1974, U.S. Dist. Ct. (no. dist.) Iowa 1974. Asst. county atty. Benton County, Vinton, 1974; sole practice Milroy and Eckhart, Vinton, 1974—; pres., bd. dirs., Cedar Valley Abstract Co., Vinton, 1984—; sec., bd. dirs. Popcorn City, USA, Vinton, 1986—. V.p., bd. dirs. Vinton Unlimited, 1985—. Mem. ABA, Assn. Trial Lawyers Am., Iowa Bar Assn., Assn. Trial Lawyers Iowa, Benton County Bar Assn. Democrat. Presbyterian. Lodge: Kiwanis (pres. Vinton club 1980). Avocations: farming, conservation, boating. State civil litigation, Family and matrimonial, Personal injury. Home: 1608 G Ave Vinton IA 52349 Office: Milroy and Eckhart 218 W Fourth St Vinton IA 52349

ECKL, WILLIAM WRAY, lawyer; b. Florence, Ala., Dec. 2, 1936; s. Louis Arnold and Patricia Barclift (Dowd) E.; m. Mary Lynn McGough, June 29, 1963; children—Eric Dowd, Lynn Lacey. B.A., U. Notre Dame, 1959, LL.B., U. Va., 1962. Bar: Va. 1962, Ala. 1962, Ga. 1964. Law clk. Supreme Ct. of Ala., 1962; ptnr. Gambrell, Harlan, Russell & Moye, Atlanta, 1965-68, Swift, Currie, McGhee & Hiers, Atlanta, 1968-82, Drew, Eckl & Farnham, Atlanta, 1983—. Served to capt. JAGC, USAR, 1962-65. Mem. Def. Research Inst., State Bar of Ga. Roman Catholic. Clubs: Lawyers of Atlanta, Brookwood Hills. General practice, State civil litigation, Insurance. Home: 348 Camden Rd Atlanta GA 30309 Office: 1400 W Peachtree St PO Box 7600 Atlanta GA 30357

ECKLUND, JOHN EDWIN, lawyer, researcher; b. Jamestown, N.Y., Apr. 3, 1916; s. J. Edwin and Sagrid M. (Johnson) E.; m. Mary Theodora Sizer, Oct. 29, 1942 (dec. Dec. 1973); children—Hilda Ecklund Ollmann, Peter J., Elizabeth Ecklund Berger, John Edwin; m. Constance L. Cryer, Mar. 22, 1975. B.A., Yale U., 1938, LL.B., 1941, M.A. (hon.), 1966. Bar: Conn. 1941, U.S. Dist. Ct. Conn. 1946, U.S. Ct. Appeals (2d cir.) 1950. Assoc. Wiggin & Dana, New Haven, Conn., 1941, 46-51, ptnr., 1951-66; of counsel Yale U., New Haven, 1957-66, treas., 1966-78, researcher legal history, 1978—; bd. govs. Yale U. Press, 1966-78. Case editor Yale Law Jour., 1940-41. Contbr. articles to profl. jours. Bd. dirs. N.H. Symphony Orch., 1948-58, Yale New Haven Hosp., 1966-78; chmn. Woodridge Town Plan and Zoning Commn., 1954-64. Served to lt. (s.g.) USNR, 1941-46. Recipient Alpheus Henry Snow prize, Yale U., 1938. Mem. ABA, N.H. County Bar Assn., Order of Coif. Republican. Episcopalian. Clubs: Yale (N.Y.C.); Mory's Graduate (New Haven) (gov. 1970-76). Legal history, General practice, Jurisprudence. Home: 27 Cedar Rd Woodbridge CT 06525

ECKMAN, DAVID WALTER, lawyer; b. Ogden, Utah, Oct. 23, 1942; s. Walter and Ann-Marie Pauline (Nelson) E.; m. Laurie Alden Waters, Aug. 28, 1965; children: Christian Davidson, Catherine Marie. Student, Rice U., 1960-61; B.A. with honors, U. Tex., Austin, 1964, J.D. (Sam D. Hanna scholar), 1967. Bar: Tex. 1967, Calif. 1976, U.S. Dist. Ct. (so. dist.) Tex. 1983, U.S. Ct. Appeals (5th Cir.) 1983. With Exxon Co., U.S.A. div. Exxon Corp., 1967-78; mem. Prudhoe Bay Law Task Force Exxon Co., U.S.A. div. Exxon Corp., Houston and Los Angeles, 1974-75; counsel Pacific Region Exxon Co., U.S.A. div. Exxon Corp., Los Angeles, 1975-77; counsel hdqrs. Exxon Co., U.S.A. div. Exxon Corp., Houston, 1977-78; gen. counsel Natomas N.Am. Inc., Houston, 1978; v.p.-legal, corp. chief legal counsel Natomas N.Am. Inc., 1978-82; sole practice Houston, 1982—. Vestryman, dir. Christian edn. All Saints Episcopal Ch., Corpus Christi, 1968-70; leader adult study St. Mark's Episcopal Ch., Houston, 1971-74; v.p. St. Mark's Sch. PTO, 1981-82; lay reader St. John the Divine Episc. Ch., Houston, 1982—, leader adult study, 1983—; mem. St. Patrick's Sch. Bd., Thousand Oaks, Calif., 1976-77; pres. Houston Youth Soccer Assn., 1979-81, bd. dirs., 1979-83; pres. Neartown Soccer Club, 1980-83; v.p. Old Braeswood Civic Assn., 1982-83; bd. dirs. Friends of Pyramid House, Inc., 1985—. Recipient Am. Jurisprudence award in antitrust law U. Tex., 1967. Mem. ABA, Tex. State Bar, Calif. State Bar, Houston Bar Assn., Full Gospel Bus. Men's Fellowship Internat. (v.p. Downtown Houston chpt. 1985—), Lambda Chi Alpha, Phi Delta Phi. General practice, General corporate, Real property. Office: 6565 W Loop S Suite 240 Bellaire TX 77401

ECKOLS, THOMAS AUD, lawyer, assistant professor; b. Springfield, Ill., Oct. 3, 1950; s. Aud L. and Jean (Sutton) E.; m. Cynthia Marie Yontz, Aug. 19, 1973; children: Molly, Cally. BA, U. Iowa, 1972; JD, U. Ill., 1975. Bar: Ill. 1975, U.S. Dist. Ct. (cen. dist.) Ill. 1975. Assoc. Fleming, Messman & O'Connor, Bloomington, Ill., 1975-80; ptnr. Fleming, Messman, O'Connor & Eckols, Bloomington, Ill., 1980-81; sr. atty. State Farm Ins. Cos., Bloomington, Ill., 1981-85, asst. counsel, 1985—; asst. prof. legal studies Ill. State U., Normal, 1984—. Chmn. issues com. Sen. John Maitland, Ill., 1980—; program chmn. McLean County Lincoln Club, Bloomington, 1978-80; legis. aid Rep. John Hirschfeld, Champaign, Ill., 1972-75. Mem. ABA (commerce, banking and bus. subcom. 1985—, litigation sect. 1984—), Ill. Bar Assn., McLean County Bar Assn. (sec. 1977-78). Republican. Presbyterian. Avocations: swimming, running, golf. Insurance, Federal civil litigation, General corporate. Home: RR 13 Bloomington IL 61701 Office: State Farm Ins Cos Corp Law Dept One State Farm Plaza Bloomington IL 61710

ECKSTEIN, JOHN ALAN, lawyer; b. Iowa City, Aug. 11, 1948; s. John William and Imogene B. (O'Brien) E.; m. Ledy R. Garcia, June 10, 1972; children—Cody Brien, Maria Alejandra. Student Grinnell Coll., 1966-67; B.A., Iowa U., 1970; M.A., Johns Hopkins U., 1972; J.D., U. Va., 1975. Bar: Ind. 1975, U.S. Dist. Ct. (so. dist.) Ind. 1975, U.S. Tax Ct. 1975, Colo. 1981, U.S. Dist. Ct. Colo. 1981. Assoc. Ice, Miller, Donadio & Ryan, Indpls., 1975-81; assoc. Calkins, Kramer, Grimshaw & Harring, Denver, 1981-83, ptnr., 1983—; mng. bd. Va. Jour. Internat. Law, 1975. Contbr. articles to profl. jours. Colo. dir. Lawyers Who Care conf., Washington, 1981; rep. dist. 7 to 1981—3 Statehouse Conf. on Small Bus., Colo., 1983—; mem. fin. Colo. Dems., 1984—. Recipient Service award Indpls. Hispanic Community Ctr., 1981. Mem. Fed. Bar Assn. (bd. dirs. 1982—, pres. Colo. chpt. 1986—), Colo. Bar Assn., Denver Bar Assn., Ind. Bar Assn., Indpls. Bar Assn., Denver C. of C. Democrat. Roman Catholic. Clubs: Serra, City (Denver); Jewish Community Ctr. Securities, General corporate, Municipal bonds. Home: 1737 Glencoe St Denver CO 80220 Office: 1700 Lincoln St Suite 3800 Denver CO 80203

ECKSTEIN, STEVEN DOUGLAS, lawyer; b. Galion, Ohio, Oct. 19, 1946; s. Millard Mitchell and Kathryn Sarah (Heckler) E.; m. Trudy Lynne Dill, Sept. 3, 1977; children: Anastasia Lynne, Andrea Nicloe. BA in History and Polit. Sci., Ohio No. U., 1969, JD, 1972. Bar: Ohio 1972. Sole practice Galion, 1972-85; judge probate and juvenile divs. Common Pleas Ct., Bucyrus, Ohio, 1985—; acting judge County Ct., Galion, 1976-77, Mcpl. Ct., Bucyrus, 1977-84; referee, domestic relations Common Pleas Ct., Bucyrus,

1979-85, traffic, Mcpl. Ct., Bucyrus, 1980-84. Democrat. Mem. United Ch. Christ. Judicial administration, Juvenile, Probate. Home: 127 S Boston St Galion OH 44833 Office: Crawford County Courthouse 112 E Mansfield St Bucyrus OH 44820

ECONOMOU, STEWART CHARLES, lawyer; b. Worcester, Mass., Nov. 18, 1937; s. Constantine Spyridon and Ourania (Pliatsikas) E.; m. Lauretta Deimendes, Jan. 10, 1973; 1 child, Alexandra Celeste. BA, Dartmouth Coll., 1959; postgrad., McGill U., 1959-61; JD, Georgetown U., 1967. Bar: Va. Law clk. to presiding justice U.S. Dist. Ct. (ea. dist.) Va., Alexandria, 1967; assoc. Boothe, Prichard & Dudley, Alexandria, 1967-68; ptnr. Evans & Economou, Alexandria, 1969-77, Evans, Economou & Pickard, Alexandria, 1977-83; sole practice Alexandria, 1983—. Mem. jud. council U.S. Ct. Appeals (4th cir.). Served to lt. USN, 1963-66. Bar: ABA, Va. Bar Assn. (exec. com. young lawyers sect. 1972-73), Alexandria Bar Assn. (treas. 1970-72), Young Lawyers Assn. (pres. 1972, mem. 8th dist., grievance com. 1985—). Republican. Greek Orthodox. Federal civil litigation, State civil litigation, Criminal. Home: 214 Wilkes St Alexandria VA 22314 Office: 122 S Royal St Alexandria VA 22314

ECTON, DOUGLAS BRIAN, lawyer; b. Bozeman, Mont., Aug. 6, 1953; s. Zales Nelson and Patricia Jo (Jackson) E. BS, Mont. State U., 1976; JD, Gonzaga U., 1979. Bar: Wash. 1979, U.S. Dist. Ct. (ea. dist.) Wash. 1980, Idaho 1987, U.S. Dist. Ct. Idaho 1987. Sole practice Spokane, Wash., 1979-83; ptnr. Casey & Ecton, Spokane, 1983—. Mem. Wash. State Bar Assn., Spokane County Bar Assn., Wash. State Trial Lawyers Assn., Assn. Trial Lawyers Am., Idaho State Bar Assn. Personal injury, Federal civil litigation, State civil litigation. Office: W 1402 Broadway Spokane WA 99201

EDDINS, GERALD WAYNE, lawyer; b. Port Arthur, Tex., Oct. 20, 1950; s. Grady A. and Maggie (Bell) E.; m. Carol Sue Greiner, June 21, 1975; children: Christina, Elizabeth, Gerald Jr. BA, Tex. Tech U., 1974, JD, 1977. Bar: Tex. 1977, U.S. Dist. Ct. (ea. dist.) Tex. 1978, U.S. Ct. Appeals (5th cir.) 1979. Atty. Provost, Umphrey, Swearingen & Eddins, Port Arthur, 1977-80, ptnr., 1980—; bd. dirs. First Nat. Bank Mid-County, Port Neches, Tex. Mem. Tex. Trial Lawyers Assn., Assn. Trial Lawyers Am., Jefferson County Bar Assn. (bd. dirs.), Gulf Coast Conservation Assn. (bd. dirs. Beaumont chpt.). Democrat. Baptist. Avocations: hunting, fishing. Personal injury, Federal civil litigation, State civil litigation. Home: 2713 Ruth St Port Neches TX 77651 Office: Provost Umphrey Swearingen & Eddins PO Box 3837 Port Arthur TX 77643

EDEE, JAMES PHILIP, lawyer; b. Pawnee City, Nebr., Oct. 12, 1929; s. Allen Barnett and Helen (Reavy) E.; m. Sheila Grainger, Nov. 15, 1951; children: Alix Nardone, Eric Edee, Brooke Edee. BS in Law, U. Nebr., 1952, JD, 1954; MBA, Ga. State U., 1971; LLM in Taxation, Emory U., 1975. Bar: Nebr. 1954, U.S. Dist. Ct. Nebr. 1954, Ga. 1958, U.S. Dist. Ct. (no. dist.)Ga. 1973, U.S. Tax Ct. 1973, U.S. Supreme Ct. 1973. Trust rep. 1st Atlanta Bank, 1956-61; atty. estate tax IRS, Atlanta, 1961-73; sole practice Atlanta, 1973—. Served to capt. USAF, 1954-56. Mem. Lawyers Club Atlanta, Atlanta Estate Planning Council. Republican. Presbyterian. Club: Cherokee. Probate, Estate taxation. Home: 2639 Battle Overlook NW Atlanta GA 30327 Office: 305 Buckhead Ave NW Atlanta GA 30305

EDEL, MARTIN DAVID, lawyer; b. Bklyn., Mar. 11, 1952; s. Sidney and Rosalind (Panicz) E.; m. Pamela Kalish, Aug. 10, 1975; children: Charles, Eliza. BA, Columbia U., 1972; JD, Harvard U., 1975. Bar: N.Y. 1976, U.S. Dist. Ct. (so. dist.) N.Y. 1976, U.S. Dist. Ct. (ea. dist.) N.Y. 1978, U.S. Ct. Appeals (9th cir.) 1978, U.S. Ct. Appeals (2d cir.) 1984. Assoc. Cravath, Swaine & Moore, N.Y.C., 1975-81; ptnr. Miller & Wrubel P.C., N.Y.C., 1981—. Contbg. author: Public Control of Business, 1977. Mem. Assn. of Bar of City of N.Y. (trade regulation com. 1981-85). Clubs: Harvard (N.Y.C.); La Ronde (Westhampton Beach). Antitrust, Federal civil litigation, Securities. Office: Miller & Wrubel PC 30 Rockefeller Plaza 42d Floor New York NY 10112

EDELEN, FRANCIS HENNESSY, JR., lawyer; b. Lebanon, Ky., Feb. 26, 1944; s. Francis Hennessy Edelen Sr. and Martha Louise (Reed) Coldiron; m. Cheryl Ann Crawford, Aug. 1, 1970. BA, Centre Coll. Ky., 1966; postgrad., Victoria U., Manchester, Eng., 1967-68; MA, U. Ky., 1974, JD, 1977. Bar: Ky. 1978, U.S. Dist. Ct. (ea. dist.) Ky. 1979, U.S. Tax Ct. 1980, U.S. Supreme Ct. 1983, U.S. Ct. Appeals (6th cir.) 1985. Asst. corp. counsel City of Ashland, Ky., 1978-87; exec. dir. Ky. Mcpl. Law Ctr., Highland Heights, 1987—. Mem. ABA, Ky. Bar Assn., Ky. Mcpl. Atty.'s Assn. (pres. 1984-85), Ky. Mcpl. League (bd. dirs. 1984-85). Centre Coll. Alumni Club (bd. dirs. 1971-74). Democrat. Roman Catholic. Lodges: Lions (v.p. South Ashland club 1985-86, gov. dist. 43-T 1987-88, Internat. Extension award, Lexington, Ky. 1977), Rotary (found. fellow Eng. 1967-68), Elks, Masons. Avocations: gardening, photography, travel, philatelist, numismatist. Local government, Administrative and regulatory, Government contracts and claims. Home: 258 Farmington Dr Lakeside Park KY 41017 Office: No Ky U Mcpl Law Ctr Nunn Bldg Room 406 Highland Heights KY 41076

EDELMAN, DANIEL AMOS, lawyer; b. Chgo., Apr. 21, 1954; s. Szachna S. and Emily (Kerdeman) E.; m. Fran Karen Kravitz, July 15, 1984. BA with honors, U. Ill., 1973; JD with honors, U. Chgo., 1976. Bar: Ill. 1976, U.S. Dist. Ct. (no. dist.) Ill. 1976, U.S. Ct. Appeals (6th cir.) 1986. Assoc. Kirkland & Ellis, Chgo., 1976-81; assoc. Reuben & Proctor, Chgo., 1981-82, ptnr., 1982-85; ptnr. Torrado & Edelman, Chgo., 1985-87; sole practice Chgo., 1987—. Mem. Ill. Bar Assn., Chgo. Bar Assn. (antitrust and fed. procedure com.), ABA (antitrust, litigation sects.), Assn. Trial Lawyers Am., Order of Coif. Jewish. Antitrust, Federal civil litigation, State civil litigation. Home: 200 E Delaware Pl Chicago IL 60611 Office: 20 E Jackson Blvd Suite 800 Chicago IL 60604

EDELMAN, HYMAN, lawyer; b. St. Paul, Aug. 1, 1905; s. Morris and Molly (Goldberg) E.; m. Edith Linoff, Apr. 4, 1954; children by previous marriage—Peter B., Daniel B., Barbara L. Berman. B.A., U. Minn., 1926, J.D., 1928. Bar: Minn. 1928, U.S. Dist. Ct. Minn. 1936, U.S. Ct. Appeals (8th cir.) 1939, U.S. Supreme Ct. 1944. Ptnr. firm Maslon, Edelman, Borman & Brand, Mpls., 1956-84, of counsel, 1984—. Mem. editorial bd. Minn. Law Rev., 1926-27, recent case editor, 1927-28. Mem. Mayor's Council on Human Relations, Mpls., 1947-52, Mpls. Commn. on Human Relations, 1966-68. Fellow Am. Coll. Trial Lawyers, ABA; mem. Order of Coif. Democrat. Jewish. Clubs: Mpls., Oak Ridge Country (Mpls.). Contracts commercial, Family and matrimonial, Condemnation. Office: 1800 Midwest Plaza Minneapolis MN 55402

EDELMAN, PAUL STERLING, lawyer; b. Bklyn., Jan. 2, 1926; s. Joseph S. and Rose (Kaminsky) E.; m. Rosemary Jacobs, June 15, 1951; children—Peter, Jeffrey. A.B., Harvard U., 1946, J.D., 1950. Bar: N.Y. 1951, U.S. Dist. Ct. (so. dist.) N.Y. 1954, U.S. Dist. Ct. (ea. dist.) N.Y. 1954, U.S. Ct. Appeals (2d cir.) 1965, U.S. Supreme Ct. 1967. Ptnr. Kreindler & Kreindler, N.Y.C., 1953—. Served with U.S. Army, 1944-46. Mem. ABA (past chmn. admiralty com., toxic and hazardous substances litigation com.; mem. long range planning com., mem. TIPS council 1984), N.Y. State Bar Assn. (INCL award 1980, chmn. INCL sect. 1982-83), Am. Trial Lawyers Assn. (past chmn. admiralty coms.), Maritime Law Assn., World Peace Through Law Ctr. Democrat. Jewish. Clubs: Hudson Valley Tennis; Hastings on Hudson (past chmn., planning bd.). Author: Maritime Injury and Death, 1960; editor N.Y. State Bar Ins. Jour., 1973—; columnist N.Y. Law Jour. Admiralty, Personal injury, Private international. Home: 57 Buena Vista Dr Hastings-on-Hudson NY 10706 Office: 100 Park Ave New York NY 10017

EDELSON, GILBERT SEYMOUR, lawyer; b. N.Y.C., Sept. 15, 1928; s. Saul and Sarah (Sunshine) E.; m. Jane Barbara Levin, Sept. 6, 1953; children—Martha Jane, Paula Topal, Dorothy Rachel. BS, NYU, 1948; JD, Columbia U., 1955. Bar: N.Y. 1955, U.S. Ct. Appeals (2d cir.) 1959, U.S. Dist. Ct. (so. dist.) N.Y. 1959, U.S. Dist. Ct. (ea. dist.) N.Y. 1960. Assoc. Rosenman Goldmark Colin & Kaye, N.Y.C., 1955-63; ptnr. Rosenman & Colin, N.Y.C., 1963—; administrv. v.p., counsel Art Dealers Assn. Am., N.Y.C., 1985—. Bd. dirs. Coll. Art Assn. Am., N.Y.C., 1969—; sec., trustee Am. Fedn. Arts, N.Y.C., 1984—, Internat. Found. for Art Research, 1986—. Served with U.S. Army, 1950-52. Mem. ABA, N.Y. Bar Assn., Assn. of Bar of N.Y.C., Columbia Law Sch. Alumni Assn. (bd. dirs. 1981-84), Century Assn. Jewish. Avocation: art collector. Federal civil litigation, State civil litigation, Art law. Home: 580 West End Ave New York NY 10024 Office: Rosenman & Colin 575 Madison Ave New York NY 10022

EDELSON, HAROLD JESSE, lawyer; b. South Bend, Ind., July 16, 1921; s. William and Flora (Friedman) E.; m. Rita Beth Jacobs, Nov. 21, 1951; children: James I., William J. H. BSS, CCNY, 1942; MA, Columbia U., 1947, LLB, 1951. Bar: N.Y. 1951, U.S. Dist. Ct. (so. and ea. dists.) N.Y. 1953, U.S. Ct. Appeals (2d cir.) 1970, Del. 1971, U.S. Dist. Ct. Del. 1972, U.S. Supreme Ct. 1972. Fgn. service officer U.S. Embassy, Prague, Czechoslovakia, 1947-48; assoc. Casey, Lane & Mittendorf, N.Y.C., 1951-63; asst. to gen. counsel C.I.T. Fin. Corp., N.Y.C., 1963-70; sr. atty. Columbia Gas System Service Corp., N.Y.C., 1970; sr. atty. Columbia Gas System Service Corp., Wilmington, Del., 1970-73, counsel, 1973—. Served to cpl. U.S. Army, 1942-45, ETO. Mem. ABA, Del. State Bar Assn., Columbia Law Sch. Alumni Assn. Avocations: reading, professional activities, classical music, football, boxing. General corporate, Public utilities, Securities. Home: 35 Baynard Blvd Wilmington DE 19803 Office: Columbia Gas System Service Corp 20 Montchanin Rd Wilmington DE 19807

EDELSTEIN, DAVID NORTHON, federal judge; b. N.Y.C., Feb. 16, 1910; s. Benjamin and Dora (Mancher) E.; m. Florence Koch, Feb. 18, 1940; children—Jonathan H., Jeffrey M. B.S., M.A., LL.B., Fordham U. Bar: N.Y. State bar. Practiced in N.Y.C.; atty. claims div. U.S. Dept. Justice, 1944; asst. U.S. atty. So. Dist. N.Y., 1945-47, spl. asst. to atty. gen. in charge lands div., 1947-48, asst. atty. gen. in charge customs div., 1948-51; judge U.S. Dist. Ct. So. Dist. N.Y., 1951—, chief judge, 1971-80; former elected mem. Jud. Conf. U.S.; rep. Nat. Conf. Fed. Trial Judges, also mem. exec. and program coms., 1975-86; assisted Pres.'s Temporary Commn. on Employee Loyalty, chmn. preparation of report, 1946; mem. legis. com. Attys. Gen. Conf. on Crime, 1950; former mem. steering com. N.Y. Fed. Exec. Bd.; former mem. planning commn. Met. Conf. Chief Judges; founder student litigation tng. program So. Dist. N.Y.; mem. com. courtroom facilities Jud. Adminstrv. Div.; mem. White Plains Courthouse Com., 1983—, chmn. rules com., 1982—; mem. nat. adv. bd. Ctr. for the Study of the Presidency; planning and program com. Jud. Conf. (2d cir.), mem. Jud. Adminstrn. Div. Com. to coordinate revision of Code of Jud. Conduct, mem. com. on jury charge simplification; mem. Com. So. Dist. N.Y. Ct. History., Planning and Program com. of the Jud. Conf. 2d cir., Jud. Adminstrn. div. com. to Coordinate Revision of the Code of Jud. Conduct, com. on Jury Charge Simplification. Bd. advisors Health Edn. Found. Fellow Am. Bar Found.; mem. Fed. Bar Assn. (past pres. Empire chpt., past nat. del., past mem. jud. selection com., past alt. del. ho. of dels. for Fed. Bar Assn.), ABA (mem. spl. com. to survey legal needs 1971-77, past chmn., mem. speedy trial planning group, mem. subcom. on planning for Dist. Cts.), Fed. Judges Assn. (bd. dirs.), Maritime Lawyers Assn. (jud. mem.), Am. Trial Lawyers Assn. (hon.), Nat. Lawyers Club (hon.), Lawyers Assn. Textile Industry (1st hon. mem.), Pan Am. Med. Soc. (hon.), Chopin Found., Phi Delta Phi (hon.). Office: US Courthouse Foley Sq New York NY 10007

EDELSTEIN, STANLEY BARTON, lawyer; b. Pitts., Oct. 6, 1952; s. Joseph and Adeline (Herlick) E. BS in Econs., Carnegie Mellon U., 1974; JD with honors, George Washington U., 1977. Bar: Pa. 1977, U.S. Ct. Appeals (3rd cir.) 1978, U.S. Dist. Ct. (ea. dist.) Pa. 1978. Law clk. to judge U.S. Ct. Appeals (3d cir.), Pitts., 1977-78; assoc. Wolf, Block, Schorr & Solis-Cohen, Phila., 1978-81, Jacoby Donner & Jacoby, P.C., Phila., 1981—. Mem. ABA (forum com. constrn. industry), Pa. Bar Assn., Phila. Bar Assn. (state civil procedure com.). Democrat. Jewish. Avocations: sailing, composing music, photography. Construction, Federal civil litigation, Government contracts and claims. Home: 201 S 18th St 2309 Philadelphia PA 19103 Office: Jacoby Donner & Jacoby PC 123 S Broad St Philadelphia PA 19109

EDELSTEIN, STEVEN A(LLEN), lawyer; b. Newark, Nov. 18, 1943; s. Edwin M. and Frances R. (Rosenbloom) E.; m. Mary Lou Eisnor, June 4, 1973; children: Adam Craig, Jason Brett. B.A., Fairleigh Dickinson U., 1969. Bar: Fla. 1973, U.S. Dist. Ct. (so. dist.) Fla. 1974, U.S. Ct. Appeals (5th cir.) 1975, U.S. Ct. Appeals (11th cir.) 1981, U.S. Supreme Ct. 1977. Assoc. Hilery F. Silverman, Miami, Fla., 1973-74, Walton, Lantaff Schroeder & Carson, Miami, 1974-78, Storace, Hall & Hauser, Miami, 1978-79; asst. city atty. City of Miami Law Dept., 1979-83; assoc. Ress, Gomez, Rosenberg, Howland & Mintz, P.A., North Miami, Fla., 1983—. Co-editor: Handbook for Dade County Lawyers, 1979. Served with U.S. Army, 1965-66. Mem. Fla. Bar, ABA, Assn. Trial Lawyers Am., Am. Judicature Soc. Federal civil litigation, State civil litigation, Insurance. Home: 2720 Country Club Prado Coral Gables FL 33134 Office: Ress Gomez Rosenberg Howland & Mintz PA 1700 Sans Souci Blvd North Miami FL 33181

EDENFIELD, BERRY AVANT, judge; b. Bulloch County, Ga., Aug. 2, 1934; s. Perry and Vera E.; m. Vida Melvis Bryant, Aug. 3, 1963. B.B.A. U. Ga, 1956, LL.B., 1958. Bar: Ga. 1958. Partner firm Allen, Edenfield, Brown & Wright (and predecessors), Statesboro, Ga., 1958-78; judge U.S. Dist. Ct., So. Dist., Ga., 1978—. Mem. Ga. Senate, 1965-66. Office: Allen Edenfield Brown & Wright PO Box 9865 125 Bull St Rm 116 Savannah GA 31412

EDER, TODD BRANDON, lawyer; b. Englewood, N.J., Sept. 12, 1954; s. Harold Norman Eder and Jan (Schaffer) LeWinter; m. Lois Ann Friedman, July 31, 1983. B.A. in History magna cum laude, Boston U., 1977; J.D., U. Tulsa, 1980. Bar: N.J. 1980, U.S. Dist. Ct. N.J. 1980, N.Y. 1981, U.S. Dist. Ct. (so. dist.) N.Y. 1981, (ea. dist.) N.Y. 1981, U.S. Tax Ct. 1981, U.S. Ct. Claims 1981, U.S. Ct. Mil. Appeals 1981, U.S. Ct. Internat. Trade 1981, Fla. 1982, U.S. Ct. Appeals (3d cir.) 1982, (2d cir.) 1984, U.S. Supreme Ct. 1985. Congl. intern Robert F. Drinan, Washington, 1977; law librarian asst U. Tulsa Coll. Law Library, 1978-79; legal intern John B. Jarboe, Tulsa, 1979-80; law clk. Harold N. Eder, N.Y.C., 1980; asst. prosecutor Hudson County Prosecutor's Office, Jersey City, 1980-83; assoc. Morgan, Melhuish, Monaghan, Arvidson, Abrutyn & Lisowski, Livingston, N.J., 1984—. Mem. Phi Delta Phi. State civil litigation, Federal civil litigation, Personal injury. Office: Morgan Melhuish et al 651 W Mount Pleasant Ave Livingston NJ 07039

EDGAR, HAROLD S. H., legal educator; b. 1942. AB, Harvard U., 1964; LLB, Columbia U., 1967. Bar: N.Y. 1968. Law clk. to judge U.S. Ct. Appeals (D.C. Cir.); asst. prof. law Columbia U., N.Y.C.; now Julius Silver prof. law, sci. and tech., and dir. program in law, sci. and tech. Columbia U. Sch. Law, N.Y.C. Mem. Inst. Soc., Ethics and the Life Scis. Legal education. Office: Columbia U Law Sch 435 W 116th St New York NY 10027

EDGAR, R. ALLAN, federal judge; b. Munising, Mich., Oct. 6, 1940; s. Robert Richard and Jean Lillian (Hansen) E.; m. Frances Gail Martin, Mar. 31, 1968; children: Amy Elizabeth, Laura Anne. BA, Davidson Coll., 1962; LLB, Duke U., 1965. From assoc. to ptnr. Miller & Martin, Chattanooga, 1967-85; judge U.S. Dist. Ct. (ea. dist.) Tenn., Chattanooga, 1985—. Mem. Tenn. Ho. of Reps., Nashville, 1970-72, Tenn. Wildlife Resources Commn., Nashville, 1979-85. Served to capt. U.S. Army, 1966-67, Vietnam. Decorated Bronze Star, 1967. Mem. ABA, Fed. Bar Assn., Tenn. Bar Assn., Chattanooga Bar Assn. Epicopalian. Club: Civitan (Chattanooga) (pres. 1977-78). Office: US Dist Ct 317 Federal Bldg PO Box 1748 Chattanooga TN 37402 *

EDGELL, GEORGE PAUL, lawyer; b. Dallas, Mar. 9, 1937; s. George Paul and Sarah Elizabeth (McDonald) E.; B.S. in Aero. Engring., U. Ill., 1960; J.D., Georgetown U., 1967; M.B.A., Roosevelt U., 1983, BGS in Computer Sci., 1986; m. Karin Jane Williams; 1 son, Scott Rickard. Admitted to Va. bar, 1967, D.C. bar, 1968, Ill. bar, 1980; patent examiner U.S. Patent Office, Washington, 1963-65; ptnr. firm Schuyler, Birch, McKie & Beckett, Washington, 1969-80, assoc., 1965-69; group patent counsel Gould Inc., Rolling Meadows, Ill., 1980-86, asst. chief patent counsel, 1986—. Vol. tutor Hopkins Ho., 1968-69; officer St. Stephen's Dads' Club, 1975-77. Served with USMC, 1960-63. Mem. ABA, D.C., Ill., Va. bar assns., Am. Intellectual Property Law Assn., Licensing Execs. Soc. Republican. Presbyterian. Clubs: Army Navy Country, Meadow. Patent, Trademark and copyright, Antitrust. Home: 5403 Chateau Dr Rolling Meadows IL 60008 Office: Gould Inc Intellectual Property Law Dept 10 Gould Center Rolling Meadows IL 60008

EDGERTON, LYNNE TODD, lawyer; b. Nashville, Oct. 26, 1947; d. Kirkland Wiley and Adrienne (Hill) Todd; m. Bradford Wheatly Edgerton, Dec. 28, 1970; children: Bradford Wheatly Jr, Lauren Harrington. B.A., Vanderbilt U., 1969, J.D., 1972; LL.M., Yale, 1979. Bar: Tenn. 1972, Va. 1975, N.Y. 1980. Law clk. U.S. Ct. Appeals (4th cir.) Va., 1973-74; dir. Pub. Interest Law Ctr., Charlottesville, Va., 1974-78; assoc. Whitman & Ransom, N.Y.C., 1979-82; sr. project atty. Natural Resources Defense Council, Inc., N.Y.C., 1983—; bd. dirs. Adirondack Council, 1983—, Manitoga Nature Ctr., 1986—. Mem. Bar Assn. City N.Y. Environment, Oil and gas leasing, Federal civil litigation. Office: Natural Resources Defense Council 122 E 42d St New York NY 10168

EDLIN, SHIEL GRAHAM, lawyer; b. Cin., Sept. 26, 1954; s. Leonard I. and Rita (Harkavy) E.; m. Margo Weiller, Nov. 22, 1981; 1 child, Adrienne Bennah. BBA in Acctg., George Washington U., 1976; JD, Mercer U.w Sch., 1979. Bar: Ga. 1979, U.S. Dist. Ct. (no. dist.) Ga. Law clk. to presiding judge State Ct. Fulton County, Atlanta, 1979-80; assoc. Stern & Funk, P.C., Atlanta, 1981—. Editor Mercer Law Rev., 1978-79. Co-chmn. young leadership council Atlanta Jewish Fedn., 1985—, mem. leadership devel. com., 1985—. Mem. ABA, State Bar Ga. (authors ct., judicial study com., family law sect.), Atlanta Bar Assn. (family law sect.). Family and matrimonial. Office: Stern & Funk PC 225 W Wieuca Rd Atlanta GA 30342

EDLUND, CURTIS ERIC, lawyer; b. Chgo., July 4, 1945; s. Eric Gunner and Carrie A. (Feldhaus) E.; m. Lynnette Eleanor Fox, June 28, 1969; children—Brian, Jennifer. B.A., U. Ill., Chgo., 1972; J.D., Loyola U., Chgo., 1977. Bar: Ill. 1977, U.S. Dist. Ct. (no. dist.) Ill. 1977, U.S. Ct. Appeals (7th cir.) 1978, U.S. Supreme Ct. 1980. Sole practice, Park Ridge, Ill., 1977—; adviser Patent Moot Ct. teams Loyola U. Sch. Law, Chgo., 1977-82. Bd. dirs. Messiah Luth. Ch., Park Ridge, 1984; alderman City of Park Ridge, Ill., 1985—. Served with USN, 1963-67; Far East. Mem. Chgo. Bar Assn., Northwest Suburban Bar Assn., Ill. State Bar Assn., ABA, Assn. Trial Lawyers Am. Lodge: Kiwanis (pres. 1986-87) (Park Ridge). General practice, Federal civil litigation, State civil litigation. Office: 600 W Talcott Rd Park Ridge IL 60068

EDMISTON, CHARLES NATHAN, lawyer, educator; b. Shelbyville, Ill., Dec. 15, 1954; s. Robert Lee and Catherine Jean (Attebery) E.; m. Gretchen Elaine Bockhorst, May 21, 1977; children—Sarah, Benjamin. B.S. with honors, U. Ill., 1976; J.D. with honors, U. Iowa, 1979. Bar: Iowa 1980, Ill. 1980, U.S. Dist. Ct. (no. dist.) Iowa 1980, U.S. Dist.Ct. (so. dist.) Iowa 1980, U.S. Dist. Ct. (so. dist.) Ill. 1985. Assoc. Karr, Karr & Karr, P.C., Webster City, Iowa, 1980-82; asst. state's atty. Wayne county State's Atty.'s Office, Fairfield, Ill., 1982-84; sole practice, 1985—; pub. defender Wayne County, 1985—, Richland County, 1986—; bus. law Frontier Community Coll., Fairfield, Ill. Mem. ABA, Ill. State Bar Assn., Iowa Bar Assn., Wayne County Bar Assn. Republican. Methodist. Lodge: Lions (treas. local club 1983—). Criminal, Consumer commercial, Family and matrimonial. Home: 4 Windsor Ln Fairfield IL 62837 Office: 106 NE 2d St PO Box 651 Fairfield IL 62837

EDMISTON, ROBERT GRAY, lawyer; b. Louisville, July 25, 1954; s. George Harrell Sr. and Zan Mary (Gray) E.; m. Pamela Sue Blackwood, June 12, 1982; 1 child, Reed Gray. BA with high distinction, U. Ky., 1977, JD, 1981. Bar: Ky. 1981, Ohio 1982, U.S. Dist. Ct. (ea. dist.) Ky. 1982, U.S. Dist. Ct. (so. dist.) Ohio 1985. Assoc. Nippert & Nippert, Cin., 1981-83, Katz, Greenberger, Zied, Katz & Norton, Cin., 1983—. Mem. coordinating com. Hunger and Law Conf., U. Cin. Law Sch., 1983. Mem. ABA, Ky. Bar Assn., Cin. Bar Assn., Phi Beta Kappa. Presbyterian. Avocations: working out, golf, reading contemporary Am. fiction. Real property, Equine law, Probate. Home: 1269 Paddock Hills Ave Cincinnati OH 45229 Office: Katz Greenberger Zied Katz & Norton 105 E 4th St Suite 1400 Cincinnati OH 45202

EDMONDS, THOMAS LEON, lawyer, management consultant; b. Borger, Tex., May 10, 1932; s. Cline Azel and Flora (Love) E.; m. Virginia Marguerite Leon, June 20, 1960; 1 dau., Stephanie Lynn. B.S. in Chem. Engring., Tex. Tech. U., 1953, J.D., 1973. Bar: Tex. 1974, U.S. Tax Ct. 1975, U.S. Ct. Appeals (5th cir.) 1975, U.S. Dist. Ct. (no. dist.) Tex. 1976. Registered profl. engr., Tex. Engr. computers-exec. dept. Phillips Petroleum, Bartlesville, Okla., 1953-67; mktg. specialist Control Data, Dallas, 1967-68; exec. v.p. CUI, Austin, Tex., 1968-70; mgmt. cons. Mcauto, St. Louis, 1970-71; sr. ptnr. Edmonds Lagrone Smith, Borger, 1973—; mem. profl. staff Frank Phillips Coll.; bd. dirs., pres. council Tex. Tech. U. Found. Mem. Tex. Soc. Profl. Engrs. Club: Borger Country. Oil and gas leasing, Estate planning, Estate taxation. Home: 210 Broadmoor Borger TX 79007 Office: PO Box 985 Borger TX 79007

EDMONDSON, FRANK KELLEY, JR., lawyer; b. Newport, R.I., Aug. 27, 1936; s. Frank Kelley Sr. and Margaret (Russell) E.; m. Christiane Semirot, Mar. 5, 1959 (div. Sept. 1969); children: Mylene Anne, Yvonne Marie, Catherine May; m. Elaine Sueko Kaneshiro, Aug. 17, 1970. BBA, Ind. U., 1958; MBA, So. Ill. U., 1978; JD, U. Puget Sound, 1982. Bar: Wash. 1982, U.S. Dist. Ct. (we. dist.) Wash. 1983. Commd. 2d lt. USAF, 1959, advanced through grades to maj., 1969, ret., 1979; contracts specialist Wash. State Lottery, Olympia, 1982-85, asst. contracts adminstr., 1985—. Bd. dirs. Friends of Chambers Creek, Tacoma, 1981—; mem. pro bono panel Puget Sound Legal Assistance Found., Olympia, 1985-86. Mem. ABA, Wash. State Bar Assn., Tacoma/Pierce County Bar Assn., Govt. Lawyers Bar Assn. (sec. 1985-86, 1st v.p. 1986-87, pres 1987—), Beta Gamma Sigma. Club: College (Seattle). Administrative and regulatory, Contracts commercial, Government contracts and claims. Home: 7908 Sapphire Dr SW Tacoma WA 98498 Office: Washington State Lottery PO Box 9702 Olympia WA 98504

EDMONDSON, JOHN RICHARD, lawyer, pharmaceutical manufacturing company executive; b. N.Y.C., Mar. 1, 1927; s. Richard Emil and Josephine (Schroeter) E.; m. Rozanne Hume, Oct. 30, 1954; children: Lisa M., Kate H., Timothy H., Nicholas D., Julia N. A.B., Georgetown U., 1950; LL.B., Columbia U., 1953. Bar: N.Y. 1953. Asso. atty. Winthrop, Stimson, Putnam & Roberts, N.Y.C., 1953-59; with Bristol-Myers Co., N.Y.C., 1959—; asst. sec. Bristol-Myers Co., 1960-69, sec., 1969—, v.p., 1974-80, gen. counsel, 1977—, sr. v.p., 1980—. Served with AUS, 1945-47. Mem. Assn. Bar City N.Y. Clubs: University, The Board Room (N.Y.C.); Lake Waramaug Country (New Preston, Conn.); Hon. Co. Edinburgh Golfers (Gullane, Scotland). General corporate. Home: 60 E 96th St New York NY 10128 Office: Bristol-Myers Co 345 Park Ave New York NY 10154

EDMUNDS, FELIX ELMER, lawyer; b. Java, Va., Apr. 25, 1899; s. Doddridge Lee and Alice (Wood) E.; m. Frances Fitzpatrick, Oct. 5, 1935. Student, Mars Hill Coll., N.C. State U., U. Richmond, T.C. Williams Law Sch. Bar: Va. 1925, U.S. Dist. Ct. (we. dist.) Va. 1925. Ptnr. Edmunds, Willetts, Yount, Garber & Hicks, Waynesboro, Va.; commr. chancery Cir. Ct. Waynesboro; assoc. trial justice Augusta County, 1936-52. Mem. Ho. Dels., Va. Gen. Assembly, 1948-63; presidential elector 1949; pres. Waynesboro YMCA, 1968-70, bd. dirs., 1970—; trustee Jamestown Found., 1954-63, 1st Bapt. Ch., Waynesboro, deacon, Sunday sch. tchr.; bd. dirs. Fishburne-Hudgins Ednl. Found., pres., 1964-79. Mem. ABA, Va. Bar Assn. (v.p. 1966), Augusta County Bar Assn. (pres. 1964), Waynesboro C. of C. (past pres., sec.), Am. Legion (scoutmaster 1937-39). Democrat. Club: Farmington (Va.), Farmington Country; Waynesboro Country. Lodge: Rotary (past pres., sec., gov. 275th dist. 1950-51). Probate, Real property, General practice. Home: 848 Greenway Circle Waynesboro VA 22980 Office: Edmunds Willetts Yount et al 220 N Wayne Ave PO Box 1617 Waynesboro VA 22980

EDMUNDS, ROBERT H., JR., lawyer. U.S. atty. State of N.C., Asheville. Office: Post Office Box 132 Asheville NC 27402 *

EDSON, CHARLES LOUIS, lawyer, educator; b. St. Louis, Dec. 14, 1934; s. Harry G. and Mildred (Solomon) E.; m. Susan Kramer, Mar. 29, 1959; children—Richard, Nancy, Margaret. A.B., Harvard U., 1956, LL.B., 1959.

Bar: Mo. 1959, U.S. Supreme Ct. 1966, D.C. 1967. Assoc. Lewis, Rice, Tucker, Allen & Chubb, St. Louis, 1959-65; chief ops. officer Legal Services Program, OEO, Washington, 1966-67; gen. counsel Pres.'s Commn. on Postal Orgn., Washington, 1967-68; chief pub. housing sect. Officer of Gen. Counsel, HUD, Washington, 1968-70; ptnr. Lane and Edson, P.C., Washington, 1970—; adj. prof. law Georgetown U. Law Sch., Washington, 1970-76; HUD coordinator Pres. Carter's Transition Staff, 1976-77. Councilman, Town of Somerset (Md.), 1976-78. Served with USNR, 1953-61. Alt. White House fellow, 1965. Mem. ABA, D.C. Bar Assn., Harvard U. Law Sch. Assn. of D.C. (pres. 1972-73). Co-author: A Practical Guide to Low and Moderate Income Housing, 1972; A Leased Housing Primer, 1975; A Section 8 Deskbook, 1976; Guide to Federal Housing Programs, 1982; Secondary Mortgage Market Guide, 1985. Real property. Home: 5802 Surrey St Chevy Chase MD 20815 Office: 2300 M St NW Washington DC 20037

EDWARDS, ARTHUR MARTIN, III, lawyer; b. West Point, Miss., July 7, 1954; s. Arthur Martin Jr. and Lurlene (Tyer) E.; m. Cecile Champion, Aug. 14, 1976. BBA, U. Miss., 1976, JD, 1979; LLM in Taxation, NYU, 1980. Bar: Miss. 1979, U.S. Dist. Ct. (no. dist.) Miss. 1979, U.S. Dist. Ct. (so. dist.) Miss. 1980, U.S. Tax Ct. 1980, U.S. Ct. Appeals (5th cir.) 1980. Assoc. Magruder, Montgomery, Brocato & Hoseman, Jackson, Miss., 1980—, ptnr., 1986—. Mem. ABA. Methodist. Avocation: sports. Probate, Corporate taxation, State and local taxation. Home: PO Box 255 Jackson MS 39205 Office: Magruder Montgomery et al 1800 Deposit Guaranty Pl Jackson MS 39201

EDWARDS, BRUCE NEIL, lawyer; b. Des Moines, Iowa, Sept. 5, 1954; s. Alexander Eric and Francesanne (Chance) E.; m. Beatrix Millenkamp, June 7, 1980. BA, Colo. Coll., 1976; JD, U. Wash., 1979; LLM in Taxation, NYU, 1980. Bar: Wash. 1979, U.S. Ct. Claims 1981, U.S. Tax Ct. 1981, U.S. Ct. Appeals (9th and D.C. cirs.) 1981, U.S. Ct. Appeals (fed. cir.) 1982, U.S. Dist. Ct. (we. dist.) Wash. 1982, U.S. Supreme Ct. 1983. Law clk. assoc. judge U.S. Ct. Claims, Washington, 1980-82; assoc. Bassett, Morrison et al, Seattle, 1982-83; prin. Mackin, Sorensen Law Firm, Seattle, 1984—. Mem. ABA (real estate tax problem com., tax sect.), Wash. State Bar Assn. (fed. adminstrn. liaison com., tax sect.), Seattle Estate Planning Council. Republican. Methodist. Corporate taxation, Estate taxation, Personal income taxation. Home: 8112 W Mercer Way Mercer Island WA 98040 Office: Mackin Sorensen Law Firm 1301 Aetna Plaza 2201 6th Ave Seattle WA 98121

EDWARDS, CHARLES HENRY, III, lawyer, consultant; b. Jersey City, Jan. 14, 1952; s. Charles Henry and Elizabeth Genevieve (Shea) E.; m. Lee Newton Walker (div. Jan. 1986). BA, Duke U., 1973; JD, Georgetown U., 1977. Bar: D.C. 1978. Staff dir., gen. counsel com. on aging U.S. Ho. of Reps., Washington, 1978-82; gen. counsel Am. Assn. of Homes for the Aging, Washington, 1983-84; exec. dir. Nat. Com. for Future Health Policy, Washington, 1984—; dir. govt. affairs Nat. Council on Aging, Washington, 1982—. Author: Age Discrimination in Employment, 1983; editor: The History of the Senate Committee on Labor and Public Welfare, 1977. Mem. ABA. Health, Legislative, Labor. Office: Nat Com for Future Health Policy 2000 M St NW Suite 600 Washington DC 20003

EDWARDS, CLAUDE REYNOLDS, judge; b. Chester, S.C., Aug. 29, 1922; s. Claude R. and Mary (Walsh) E.; m. Sarah Chapman Walker, Sept. 27, 1948; children—Sarah, Claude R., James A. A.B., Wofford Coll., 1943; LL.B., Yale U., 1949. Bar: Fla. 1950. Asst. dir. Inst. Govt., Chapel Hill, N.C., 1949-50; legal cons. to gen. counsel Econ. Stablzn. Agy., Washington, 1950; pvt. practice, Deland, Fla., 1950-51, Orlando, Fla., 1951-68; judge 9th Jud. Circuit Ct., State of Fla., Orlando, 1968—, chief judge, 1973-74. City councilman, Orlando, 1955-58; chmn. Orlando Traffic Commn., 1955-58; mem. Orange County Republican Exec. Com., 1955-67; pres. Orange County Young Rep. Club, 1958; bd. dirs. Orlando Civil Service, 1960-67, chmn., 1967; trustee Orlando Public Library, 1958-70, pres., 1969-70; statutory trustee Legal Aid Soc. Orange County (Fla.), 1975-83; trustee Osceola County Children's Home, Kissimmee, Fla., 1979. Served with AUS, 1943-46; ETO. Recipient Spl. award for Outstanding Com. Chmn. Orlando area C. of C., 1977. Mem. Fla. Bar Assn., Orange County Bar Assn., Osceola County Bar Assn., Yale Alumni Assn. (past pres. Central Fla.), Blue Key, Phi Delta Phi, Sigma Alpha Epsilon (past pres. Central Fla. alumni), Pi Gamma Mu. Methodist. Club: Rotary (pres. 1983-84) (Orlando). Civil trial judge, General practice. Office: 9th Judicial Circuit Ct 479 Orange County Courthouse Orlando FL 32801

EDWARDS, DANIEL PAUL, lawyer; educator; b. Enid, Okla., Apr. 15, 1940; s. Daniel Paul and Joye Virginia (van Horn) E.; m. Virginia Lee, Mar. 27, 1976; 1 son, Austin Daniel. B.A., U. Okla., 1962; J.D., Harvard U., 1965. Bar: Colo. 1965. Ptnr., v.p. Cole, Helox, Tolley, Edwards & Keene, P.C., Colorado Springs, 1965-82; sole practice, Colorado Springs, 1983-85; of counsel Hughes & Dorsey, Denver, 1985—; lectr. law Colo. Coll., 1976-87. Pres. Springs Area Beautiful Assn., 1978. Mem. ABA, Colo. Bar Assn., Harvard Law Sch. Assn. Colo. (bd. govs. 1981-86, pres. 1986-87), Real Estate Securities and Syndication Inst., Phi Beta Kappa, Phi Delta Theta. Republican. Presbyterian. Clubs: El Paso, Broadmoor Golf, Cheyenne Mt., Garden of the Gods (Colorado Springs). Securities, Estate planning, Real property.

EDWARDS, DANIEL WALDEN, lawyer; b. Vancouver, Wash., Aug. 7, 1950; s. Chester W. Edwards and Marilyn E. Russell; m. Gwendolyn J. Marshall, June 29, 1974; children: Nathaniel, Matthew. BA in Psychology, Met. State Coll., Denver, 1973, BA in Philosophy, 1974; JD, U. Colo., 1976. Bar: Colo. 1977, U.S. Dist. Ct. Colo. 1977. Dep. pub. defender State of Colo., Denver, 1977-79, Littleton, 1979-81, Pueblo, 1981-86; head 10 atty. Brighton office Colo. State Pub. Defender, 1987—. Named Pub. Defender of Yr., Colo. State Pub. Defender's Office, 1985. Mem. ABA, Am. Trial Lawyers Assn., Colo. Bar Assn., Pueblo Bar Assn. Criminal. Home: 267 S Franklin Denver CO 80209 Office: Colo State Pub Defender 2627 Bridge St Brighton CO 80601

EDWARDS, HARRY LAFOY, lawyer; b. Greenville, S.C., July 29, 1936; s. George Belton and Mary Olive (Jones) E.; m. Suzanne Copeland, June 16, 1956; 1 dau., Margaret Peden. LL.B., U. S.C., 1963, J.D., 1970. Bar: S.C. 1963, U.S. dist. ct. S.C. 1975, U.S. Ct. Apls. (4th cir.) 1974. Assoc. Edwards and Edmunds, Greenville, 1963; v.p., sec., dir. Edwards Co., Inc., Greenville, 1963-65; atty. investment legal dept. Liberty Life Ins. Co., Greenville, 1965-67, asst. sec., asst. v.p., head investment legal dept., 1967-70; asst. sec. Liberty Corp., 1970-75; asst. v.p. Liberty Life Ins. Co., 1970-75; sec. Bent Tree Corp., CEL, Inc., 1970-75; sec., dir. Westchester Mall, Inc., 1970-75; asst. sect. Libco, Inc., Liberty Properties, Inc., 1970-75; sole practice, Greenville, 1975—. Com. mem. Hipp Fund Spl. Edn., Greenville County Sch. System; mem. Boyd C. Hipp II Scholarship Com. Wofford Coll., Spartanburg, S.C.; scholarship com. mem. Libety Scholars, U. S.C., 1984, 86; editor U.S.C. law rev., 1963 . Served with USAFR, 1957-63. Mem. ABA, S.C. Bar Assn., Greenville County Bar Assn., Phi Delta Phi. Baptist. Clubs: Greenville Lawyers, Poinsett (Greenville). General corporate, Estate planning, Real property. Home: 106 Ridgeland Dr Greenville SC 29601 Office: PO Box 10350 Federal Station Greenville SC 29603

EDWARDS, HARRY T., judge; b. N.Y.C., Nov. 3, 1940; children: Brent, Michelle. B.S., Cornell U., 1962; J.D., U. Mich., 1965. Assoc. firm Seyfarth, Shaw, Fairweather & Geraldson, Chgo., 1965-70; prof. law U. Mich., 1970-76, 77-80; vis. prof. law Harvard U., 1975-76, prof., 1976-77, part-time lectr. law, 1980—; now judge U.S. Ct. Appeals, Washington; vis. prof. Free U. Brussels, 1974; dir. AMTRAK, 1977-80, chmn. bd., 1979-80; disting. lectr. law Duke U., 1983—; lectr. law Georgetown Law Ctr., 1986—; lectr. Harvard Law Sch., 1981—. Mem. Adminstrv. Conf. of U.S., 1976-80. Co-author: Labor Relations Law in the Public Sector, 1975, 79, 85, Lawyer as a Negotiator, 1977, Collective Bargaining and Labor Arbitration, 1979, Higher Education and the Law, 1979. Mem. Nat. Acad. Arbitrators (dir. 1975-80, v.p. 1978-80), Am. Arbitration Assn. (dir. 1979-80), Am. Bar Assn. (sec. sect. labor law 1976-77), Am. Law Inst., Indsl. Relations Research Assn., Order of Coif. Office: US Courthouse 3d and Constitution NW Washington DC 20001

EDWARDS, HELEN JEX, lawyer; b. San Francisco, Nov. 17, 1938; d. Cooper Lee and Bettie Marian (Hayes) Jex; m. E. Daniel Edwards, Feb. 4, 1960 (div. 1972); children: Marian K., Steven Daniel. BS, U. Utah, 1976, U. Utah, 1978. Bar: Utah 1978, U.S. Ct. Appeals (9th cir.) 1985, D.C. 1987. Placement dir. U. Utah Law Sch., Salt Lake City, 1970-75; law clk. to presiding justice Utah Supreme Ct., Salt Lake City, 1976-78, atty., 1978-79; atty. Utah Power & Light, Salt Lake City, 1979—. Mem. ABA, Fed. Bar Assn., Utah State Bar Assn., Salt Lake County Bar Assn. General corporate, FERC practice, Public utilities. Home: 1057 Lake St Salt Lake City UT 84105 Office: Utah Power & Light Co PO Box 899 Salt Lake City UT 84110

EDWARDS, JAMES EDWIN, lawyer; b. Clarkesville, Ga., July 29, 1914; s. Gus Calloway and Mary Clara (McKinney) E.; m. Frances Lillian Stanley, Nov. 22, 1948; children—Robin Anne Edwards Ralston, James Christopher, Clare Wilkson. Student U. Tex. 1931-33; B.A., George Washington U., 1935, J.D. cum laude, 1946. Bar: Fla. 1938, D.C. 1981, Va 1987. Practice law, Cocoa, Fla., 1938-42; hearing and exam. officer USCG, 1943-45; div. asst. State Dept., Washington, 1945-50; practice law Ft. Lauderdale, Fla., 1951-55, 59-77; mem. firm Bell, Edwards, Coker, Carlon & Amsden, Ft. Lauderdale, 1956-59; sole practice, Coral Springs, Fla., 1977-81, 84-85; asst. city atty. Fort Lauderdale, 1961, 63-65; mem. firm. Edwards & Leary, Coral Springs, 1981-84; mem. panel Am. Arbitration Assn., 1984—. Commr., Coral Springs, 1970-76, mayor, 1972-74; mem. bd. suprs. Sunshine Water Mgmt. Dist., 1976-80; chmn. Ft. Lauderdale for Eisenhower, 1952; pres. Fla. Conservative Union, Broward County, 1976. Served to lt. USCGR, 1943-45, to lt. col. JAG, USAFR, 1950-68. Presbyterian. Club: English Speaking Union (Charlottesville, Va.). Lodge: Rotary. Author: Myths About Guns, 1978. General practice. Home and Office: PO Box 88 Keswick VA 22947-0088

EDWARDS, JAMES GARLAND, II, lawyer; b. Bluefield, W.Va., Jan. 13, 1951; s. B.C. and Mary Elizabeth (Shuff) E.; m. Beverly Anne White, Jan. 30, 1971; children: James Garland II, William Scott, Matthew Shuff. BS, BA, U. N.C., 1972; JD with distinction, Emory U., 1975. Bar: Ga. 1975. Assoc. Orr and Federal, Decatur, Ga., 1975-76; ptnr. Orr and Edwards, Decatur, 1976—. Mem. ABA, State Bar Ga., Decatur-DeKalb Bar Assn., Order of Coif, Beta Gamma Sigma. State civil litigation, General corporate, Real property. Home: 2891 Greenbush Pl Atlanta GA 30345 Office: Orr and Edwards 540 One W Court Sq Decatur GA 30030

EDWARDS, JOHN WESLEY, II, lawyer; b. Williamsport, Pa., Nov. 29, 1948; s. Robert Wesley Edwards and Jean Eleanor (Seitzer) Leprohon; m. Lee Ellen Berliner, May 22, 1971; children: Wesley David, Katherine Lee, Meredith Jean. BA, Colgate U., 1970; JD, Duke U., 1974. Bar: Ohio 1974, U.S. Dist. Ct. (no. dist.) Ohio 1974, U.S. Ct. Appeals (6th cir.) 1974. Assoc. Jones, Day, Reavis & Pogue, Cleve., 1974-82, ptnr., 1982—. Served to cpl. USMCR, 1970-76. Mem. Cleve. Bar Assn. (Fed. ct. com.), Order of Coif, Phi Beta Kappa. Republican. Presbyterian. Club: Mayfield Country (Lyndhurst, Ohio). Federal civil litigation, State civil litigation. Home: 3366 Lansmere Rd Shaker Heights OH 44122 Office: Jones Day Reavis & Pogue 1700 Huntington Bldg Cleveland OH 44115

EDWARDS, JOHN WHITE, lawyer; b. Columbus, Ohio; s. Harold Gardner and Virginia (Speidel) E.; m. Larrilyn Carr, Aug. 18, 1962 (div. Feb. 1986); children: Whitney Carr, Peter Frazier. AB, Amherst Coll., 1959; JD, U. Mich., 1962. Bar: Ohio 1962, U.S. Dist. Ct. (so. dist.) Ohio 1966, U.S. Ct. Appeals (6th cir.) 1967, U.S. Dist. Ct. (no. dist.) Ohio 1968, U.S. Ct. Appeals (7th cir.) 1968. Ptnr. Edwards & Edwards, Columbus, 1968-72, Lane, Alton & Horst, Columbus, 1972-79, Smith & Schanacke, Columbus, 1979—. Editor: A Country Law Study of the Philippines, 1964, An Administrative Law Handbook for Ohio Lawyers, 1984. Pres. Worthington Resource Ctr., Ohio, 1968, Ohio ALliance for the Environment, 1986—; trustee Columbus Jr. Theatre of the Arts, 1978, Les Cheneaux Islands Assn., 1985—. Served to lt. USNR, 1963-66. Mem. ABA, Ohio Bar Assn. (chmn. adminstrv. law com. 1984), Columbus Bar Assn. (chmn. legis. com. 1979-81), Nat. Coal Assn. (honored lawyer 1985). Clubs: Les Cheneaux Yacht (Cedarville, Mich.); Capital, Athletic (columbus). Avocations: sailing, flying, reading. Environment, Administrative and regulatory, Legislative. Office: Smith & Schancke 41 S High St Columbus OH 43215

EDWARDS, MARY FRANCES, lawyer, legal education administrator; b. Chgo., Sept. 4, 1950; d. Frank Byron and Marie (Koval) E. BA, U. Ill., 1971; JD, Northwestern U., 1975. Bar: Ill. 1975, U.S. Dist. Ct. (no. dist.) Ill. 1975, D.C. 1985. Asst. staff dir. ABA, Chgo., 1975-78, dir. nat. insts., 1978-79, project cons., 1979-80; mgr. ednl. materials Assn. Trial Lawyers Am., Washington, 1980-82, mgr. ednl. programs and devel., 1982-86, dep. dir. edn. dept., 1986—. Author: (with others) The Polygraph: A Discussion Guide, 1977; editor The Anatomy of a Personal Injury Lawsuit, 1981, Industrial and Toxic Torts, 1980, How to Recognize and Handle Recreation Liability Cases: Sports Torts, 1980, Settlement and Plea Bargaining, 1981; audio cassettes Philo on Tort Liability, 1981, Sturctured Settlements, 1981, The Psychology of a Trial, 1981. Bd. dirs. Ind. Voters of Ill., Chgo., 1971-72. Edmund J. James scholar, 1968-71. Mem. ABA, Internat. Bar Assn., Women's Bar Assn.of D.C., Assn. CLE Adminstrs. Legal association executive. Home: 3800 Jenifer NW Washington DC 20015 Office: Assn Trial Lawyers Am 1050 31st St NW Washington DC 20007

EDWARDS, ROBIN MORSE, lawyer; b. Glens Falls, N.Y., Dec. 9, 1947; d. Daniel and Harriet Lois (Welpen) Morse; m. Richard Charles Edwards, Aug. 30, 1970; children: Michael Alan, Jonathan Phillip. BA, Mt. Holyoke Coll., 1969; JD, U. Calif., Berkeley, 1972. Bar: Calif. 1972. Assoc. Donahue, Gallagher, Thomas & Woods, Oakland, Calif., 1972-77, ptnr., 1977—. Mem. ABA, Calif. Bar Assn., Alameda County Bar Assn. (bd. dirs. 1978-84, v.p. 1982, pres. 1983), Entrepreneurship Inst. East Bay (bd. dirs. 1985—). Jewish. Avocations: skiing, cooking. General corporate, Real property, Securities. Office: Donahue Gallagher Thomas & Woods 1900 Kaiser Ctr 300 Lakeside Dr Oakland CA 94612-3570

EDWARDS, VERN DOWNING, lawyer; b. Superior, Wis., May 23, 1916; s. Vern R. and Alice E. (Gallagher) E.; m. Lee H., Feb. 8, 1941; children—Nancy Edwards McNamara (dec.), Mark D., Catherine A., Linda E. Edwards Jenkins, Sara Edwards Kish. Ph.D., U. Wis., 1938, LL.B., 1939, LL.D., 1968. Bar: Wis. 1939. Atty., Wis. Dept. Revenue, Madison, 1940-45; mem. V. Downing Edwards & Assocs., Ltd., La Crosse, Wis., 1945—; chmn. bd. Coulee State Bank, La Crosse, 1962—; pub. adv. to Regional Commrs. Office, Chgo., 1968-69, to legis. counsel State of Wis., 1974-75. Served with USNR, 1940-45. Mem. ABA, Wis. Bar Assn., Milw. Bar Assn. Contbr. articles to legal jours. Corporate taxation, General corporate, Probate.

EDWARDS, W. CARY, JR., state attorney general; b. Paterson, N.J., July 20, 1944; s. William C. and Virginia (Duncan) E.; m. Lynn E. Cozzolino, 1970; children—Kari Lynn, Marcy Lynn. B.S., Seton Hall U., 1967, J.D., 1970. Bar: N.J. Mem. exec. staff R.H. Macy, 1964-67; instr., asst. dean students Seton Hall U., 1969-70; assoc. Villoresi & Flanagan, 1970-73; mcpl. atty., Boonton, N.J., 1970—; legis. asst. N.J. State Senate, 1972-73; sr. ptnr. Edwards & Gallo, Oakland, N.J., 1973-82; mcpl. atty., East Hanover, N.J., 1976-80, Franklin Lakes, N.J., 1979-82, Oakland, N.J., 1981-82; chief counsel, Gov. of N.J., 1982-86; atty. gen. State of N.J., 1986—. Author: The Student & Law, 1970. Borough councilman, fin. chmn., council pres., Oakland, N.J.; mem. N.J. State Assembly, 1977-82, asst. minority whip, 1979-81, asst. minority leader, 1981-82. Recipient Disting. Service award, N.J. Speech & Hearing Assn., 1981, Vol. in Parole, Top Ten Legislators award, 1981. Mem. Jr. C. of C. (assoc. legal counsel 1972-73), ABA, N.J. State Bar Assn., N.J. League Mcpl. Attys., Am. Judicature Soc. Roman Catholic. Address: 3 Morningstar Ln Oakland NJ 07436 *

EDWARDS, WILLIAM THOMAS, JR., lawyer; b. Eglin AFB, Fla., Feb. 8, 1956; s. William Thomas and Josephine (Fabian) E.; m. Karen Sue Foulk, July 1, 1978; children: Jennifer, Ali. BA, Fla. State U., 1977, JD, 1980. Bar: Fla. 1980, U.S. Dist. Ct. (mid. dist.) Fla. 1981, U.S. Ct. Claims 1981, U.S. Tax Ct. 1981, U.S. Ct. Appeals (11th cir.) 1983. Assoc. William T. Lassiter Jr., P.A., Jacksonville, Fla., 1980-82; sole practice Middleburg, Fla., 1982—. Pres. Middleburg Bus. Council, 1985, 87, v.p., 1984. Mem. ABA, Fla. Bar Assn., Jacksonville Bar Assn., Clay County Bar Assn., Clay County C. of C. (bd. dirs. 1985, 87). Republican. Roman Catholic. Lodge: KC. Avocation: tennis. Personal injury, General practice, Estate planning. Office: 2554 Blanding Blvd Suite B Middleburg FL 32068

EDWINN, EUGENE PAUL, lawyer; b. N.Y.C., July 16, 1927; s. Herman and Diana E.; m. Gloria Freeman, Aug. 2, 1953. PhB, U. Chgo., 1946; LLB, Bklyn. Law Sch., 1949; JD, Harvard U., 1951. Bar: N.Y. 1950, U.S. Dist. Ct. (so. and ea. dists.) N.Y. 1978. Assoc. Wasserman & Shagan, N.Y.C., 1950-60, ptnr., 1960-62; ptnr. Shagan, Edwinn & Golomb, N.Y.C., 1962-81; sole practice N.Y.C., 1981—; exec. sec. Paper Merchandising Assn. of N.Y., N.Y.C., 1972—; bd. dirs. numerous graphic arts cos. Mem. N.Y. County Dem. Com., N.Y.C., 1957-62. Served with U.S. Army, 1953-55, Korea. State civil litigation, Consumer commercial, General corporate. Home: 29 Cross Hwy Westport CT 06880 Office: 275 Madison Ave New York NY 10016

EFFRON, WAYNE DOUGLAS, lawyer, educator; b. Derby, Conn., Aug. 18, 1950; s. Harold S. and Rhea (Savelewitz) E.; m. Janet Marie Bepko, Mar. 16, 1986. BA summa cum laude, U. Conn., 1972, JD cum laude, 1977. Bar: Conn. 1977, U.S. Dist. Ct. Conn. 1977, U.S. Dist. Ct. (so. and ea. dists.) N.Y. 1980, U.S. Supreme Ct. 1980, N.Y. 1983. Assoc. Carter, Van Nostrand & Pacifico, Darien, Conn., 1977-79; prin. Kaye & Effron P.C., Greenwich, Conn., 1979—; adj. prof. Pace U. Sch. Law, White Plains, N.Y., 1983—. Co-author: Connecticut Practice Book Annotated, vol. II and III, 1979. Mem. ABA, Conn. Bar Assn., Assn. Trial Lawyers Am., Conn. Trial Lawyers Assn., Phi Beta Kappa. State civil litigation, Personal injury, Family and matrimonial. Office: Kaye & Effron PC 165 W Putnam Ave PO Box 499 Greenwich CT 06836

EFRON, MURIEL COHEN, law librarian; b. Phila., Nov. 15, 1925; d. Herman and Rose (Goldberg) Cohen; m. Martin Efron, Dec. 24, 1942; children: Nancy Efron Weisbein, Mark, Cynthia Efron Cieri, Neil. BA in Polit. Sci., U. Pa., 1969; MLS, Drexel U., 1970; MS in Mgmt., Fla. Internat. U., 1977; JD cum laude, U. Miami, 1981. Bar: Fla. 1981, U.S. Dist. Ct. (so. dist.) Fla. 1982, U.S. Ct. Appeals (11th cir.) 1982. Librarian Fla. Internat. U., Miami, 1971-84; law librarian Holland & Knight, Miami, 1984-85, Greenberg, Traurig, Askew et al, Miami, 1985—; instr. legal research paralegal program Fla. Internat. U., 1981—. Title II B Fellowship, Drexel U., 1969; Elder Scholar award Colonial Penn, U. Miami, 1983. Mem. ABA, Fla. Bar Assn., Am. Assn. Law Libraries, Fla. Assn. Women Lawyers, South Fla. Assn. Law Libraries (pres. 1985-86), Dade County Bar Assn., Am. Jewish Congress, LWV , U. Pa. Alumni Club (bd. mem. 1984—). Democrat. Jewish. Avocations: travel, reading. Librarianship, Legal education, Paralegal management and training.. Office: Greenberg Traurig et al 1401 Brickell Ave Miami FL 33131

EFRON, SAMUEL, lawyer; b. Lansford, Pa., May 6, 1915; s. Abraham and Rose (Kaduchin) E.; m. Hope Bachrach Newman, Apr. 5, 1941; children: Marc Fred, Eric Michael. B.A., Lehigh U., 1935; LL.B., Harvard U., 1938. Bar: Pa. 1938, D.C. 1949, N.Y. 1967. Atty. forms and regulations div., also registration div. SEC, 1939-40; Office Solicitor Dept. Labor, 1940-42; asst. chief real and personal property sect. Office Alien Property Custodian, 1942-43; chief debt claims sect., also asst. chief claims br. Office Alien Property, Dept. Justice, 1946-51; asst. gen. counsel internat. affairs Dept. Def., 1951-53, cons., 1953-54; partner firm Surrey, Karasik, Gould & Efron, Washington, 1954-61; exec. v.p. Parsons & Whittemore, Inc., N.Y.C., 1961-68; now partner Arent, Fox, Kintner, Plotkin & Kahn, Washington.; Mem. internat. relations vis. com. Lehigh U. Author: Creditors Claims Under the Trading with the Enemy Act, 1948, Foreign Taxes on United States Expenditures, 1954, Offshore Procurement and Industrial Mobilization, 1955, The Operation of Investment Incentive Laws with Emphasis on the U.S.A. and Mexico, 1977. Served to lt. USNR, 1943-46. Decorated Order of the Lion of Finland 1st class. Mem. Am., Fed., Inter-Am. bar assns., Am. Soc. Internat. Law, Assn. Bar City N.Y., Bar Assn. D.C., Phi Beta Kappa. Clubs: Army-Navy (Washington), Cosmos (Washington), Harvard, Internat. (Washington), Nat. Press (Washington), University (Washington), Fed. Bar (Washington); Harvard (N.Y.C.), Lehigh (N.Y.C.), Lotos (N.Y.C.). Private international, Public international, Contracts commercial. Home: 3537 Ordway St NW Washington DC 20016 Office: 1050 Connecticut Ave NW Washington DC 20036

EFROS, ELLEN ANN, lawyer; b. N.Y.C., Jan. 18, 1950; d. Edwin David and Judith (Breitman) E.; m. Fritz R. Kahn, June 26, 1983. BA, Case Western Res. U., 1971; MA, St. John's U., 1973; JD, Hofstra U., 1978. Bar: D.C. 1978, N.Y. 1979, U.S. Ct. Appeals (5th cir.) 1978, U.S. Ct. Appeals (D.C. and 2d, 7th cirs.) 1979, U.S. Dist. Ct. D.C. 1981, U.S. Ct. Claims 1986. Trial atty. ICC Gen. Counsel, Washington, 1978-79; assoc. Verner & Liipfert, Washington, 1979-81; ptnr. Vorys, Sater, Seymour & Pease, Washington, 1981—. Mem. ABA, Fed. Bar Assn., Internat. Trade Commn. Trial Lawyers Assn., D.C. Bar Assn., N.Y. Bar Assn. Federal civil litigation, Antitrust, Administrative and regulatory. Office: Vorys Sater Seymour & Pease 1828 L St NW Washington DC 20036

EGAN, KEVIN JAMES, lawyer; b. Chgo., June 24, 1950; s. Raymond Basil and Harriet Olene (Landbo) E.; m. Patricia Ann Kentner; children: Ryan, Daniel. BA, U. Ill., 1972; JD, Northwestern U., 1975. Bar: Ill. 1975, U.S. Dist. Ct. (no. dist.) Ill. 1975, U.S. Ct. Appeals (7th cir.) 1976, U.S. Ct. of Customs and Patent Appeals 1978. Law clk. to judge U.S. Dist. Ct. (no. dist.) Ill., Chgo., 1975-77; assoc. Pattishall, McAuliffe & Hofstetter, Chgo., 1977-78; asst. U.S. atty. City of Chgo., Chgo., 1978-82; assoc. Winston & Strawn, Chgo., 1982-84, ptnr., 1984—. article editor Jour. Criminal Law and Criminology, 1974-75. Mem. ABA, Chgo. Bar Assn. (mem. various coms.), Bar Assn. of 7th Cir. Roman Catholic. Club: Prestwick Country (Frankfort, Ill.). Avocation: hockey. Federal civil litigation, Health, State civil litigation. Home: 904 Huntsmoor Ln Frankfort IL 60423 Office: Winston & Strawn 1 First Nat Plaza Suite 5000 Chicago IL 60603

EGAN, ROBERT T., lawyer; b. Bklyn., Sept. 4, 1952; s. Thomas Edward and Gloria Elise (Rudolph) E.; m. Peggy Frances LaPointe, May 31, 1974; 1 child, Timothy. BA in Polit. Sci., U. Conn., 1974; JD, U. Pa., 1977. Bar: N.J., U.S. Dist. Ct. N.J. Assoc. Archer & Greiner, Haddonfield, N.J., 1977-84, ptnr., 1984—. Chmn. activities com. Kings Grant Open Space Assn., Evesham Twp., N.J., 1982-86. Mem. ABA, N.J. Bar Assn., Camden County Bar Assn. Club: Little Mill Country (Evesham Twp.). Avocations: softball, ice hockey, golf, boxing, furniture restoration and refinishing. Federal civil litigation, State civil litigation, Franchise litigation. Home: 4 Haddon Ct W Marlton NJ 08054 Office: Archer & Greiner 1 Centennial Sq Haddonfield NJ 08033

EGGEN, ERIC CARL, lawyer; b. Hemet, Calif., Apr. 16, 1946; s. Donald Tripp and Frances Allison (Dibelka) E.; m. Julie Harriet Stackhouse, Dec. 18, 1970; children—Jeffrey, Michael, Daniel. B.A. cum laude, Claremont Men's Coll., 1967; J.D., Emory U., 1974. Bar: Fla. 1975, U.S. Dist. Ct. (no. dist.) Fla. 1975. Assoc. Sherrill & Moore, Pensacola, Fla., 1975-76; sole practice, Pensacola, 1976-81; ptnr. Eggen, Bowden & Rasmussen, Pensacola, 1981-84, Eggen & Rasmussen, Pensacola, 1984—; atty. Fla. Dept. Health and Rehab. Services, Pensacola, 1977—. Mem. Escambia County Sch. Bd., Pensacola, 1984, vice chmn. 1985-86; mem. State of Fla. Computer Edn. Instrnl. Materials Council, 1986—; vice chmn. Escambia County Democratic Exec. Com., 1981-84; v.p. Escambia County Day Care Services, Inc., 1981-83. Served with USNR, 1969-72. Mem. ABA, Fla. Bar Assn. (continuing edn. com. 1986—), Escambia-Santa Rosa Bar Assn. (sec. 1977-78), Fla. Sch. Bds. Assn. (bd. dirs. 1985—) . Methodist. Club: Panhandle Tiger Bay (v.p. 1981-83) (Pensacola). Family and matrimonial, Bankruptcy, Consumer commercial. Home: 2437 Tronjo Terr Pensacola FL 32503

EGGERS, PAUL WALTER, lawyer; b. Seymour, Ind., Apr. 20, 1919; s. Ernest H. and Ottelia W. (Carre) E.; m. Frances Kramer, Dec. 29, 1946; 1 son, Steven Paul; m. Virginia McMillin, Feb. 23, 1974. B.A., Valparaiso U., 1941; J.D., U. Tex.-Austin, 1948. Bar: Tex. 1948. Sole practice, Wichita Falls, Tex., 1948-52; ptnr. Eggers, Sherrill & Pace, Wichita Falls, 1952-69; gen. counsel U.S. Treasury Dept., Washington, 1969-70; sole practice, Dallas, 1971-75; pres. Eggers & Wylie, P.C., Dallas, 1977-79, Eggers & Greene, P.C., Dallas, 1979—. Chmn. Wichita County Republican Club; mem. Pres.'s Task Force Narcotics and Dangerous Drugs, chmn. Tex. Gov.'s Task Force on Drug Abuse, 1987—; Republican candidate for gov. of Tex., 1968, 70; Treasury Dept. liaison with White House on Minority Affairs; trustee Episc. Ch. Bldg. Fund, 1972-84; sr. warden vestry St. Michael and All Angels Episc. Ch. of Dallas, 1983-85; dir. St. Michael and All Angels Found.; chancellor Episc. Diocese of Dallas, 1978—, pres. Corporation,

1983—. Served to maj. USAAF, World War II. Recipient Silver Anniversary All-Am. award Sports Illustrated, 1966, Layman of Yr. award Episc. Diocese of Dallas, 1968; Disting. Alumnus award Valparaiso U., 1978. Mem. ABA, Fed. Bar Assn., Am. Judicature Soc., Dallas Estate Planning Council, Tex. Bar Assn., Dallas Bar Assn. Republican. Clubs: Brook Hollow Golf (Dallas); Met., Capitol Hill (Washington). Office: Suite 3220 1999 Bryan St Dallas TX 75201

EGGERS, WILLIAM J., III, lawyer; b. Oakland, Calif., Feb. 18, 1939; s. William J. and Ida May (Jennings) E.; children by previous marriage—William J. IV, Loch Erich, Jason Hunter. A.A., Fresno State Coll., 1959; B.A., U. Calif.-Berkeley, 1962; J.D., U. Calif.-San Francisco, 1966. Bar: Hawaii 1967, U.S. Supreme Ct. 1968, U.S. Customs Ct. 1968, U.S. Ct. Appeals (9th cir.) 1969, U.S. Dist. Ct. 1967, U.S. Tax Ct. 1979. Adminstrv. asst. Dillingham Corp., 1966-67; dep. pros. atty. City and County Honolulu, 1967-69; sr. counsel Consumer Protection Office Gov., 1969-72; asst. U.S. atty. U.S. Dept. Justice dist. Hawaii, 1972-78; pres. William J. Eggers III, P.C., 1978—; spl. dep. atty. gen. State Hawaii, 1982-85 ; arbitrator judicial arbitration commn. Hawaii Ct. Appeals (1st cir.); cons. J.J. McMahon & Co., Andrew Donovan Party Ltd., T&L Hawaiian Wear, Inc., Holowave Hawaii, Inc.; Hawaii council Am. Indian Nations, 1977-79. Bd. dirs., pres. Outrigger Canoe Club, 1972-78, Aloha Tower Maritime Center, 1980-81; mem. Commn. Drug Abuse and Controlled Substances, 1983—. Dept. Interior scholar, 1964. Mem. ABA, Hawaii Bar Assn., Fed. Bar Assn. (pres. 1976), Assn. Trial Lawyers Am., Phi Gamma Delta. Club: Rotary. State civil litigation, General corporate, State and local taxation. Home: 1016 Kealaolu Ave Honolulu HI 96816 Office: 1164 Bishop St Suite 1502 Honolulu HI 96813

EGGLESTON, ROBERT DALE, lawyer; b. Hardtner, Kans., Nov. 5, 1949; s. J. Raymond and Josephine (Laws) E. BBA, U. Kans., 1972; JD, Washburn U., 1975; LLM, Georgetown U., 1980. Bar: Kans. 1975, Md. 1978. Tax atty. Chief Counsel Office IRS, Balt., 1975-80; mgr. taxes Sun Exploration & Prodns. Co., Dallas, 1980—. Served to capt. USAR, 1980-85. Corporate taxation. Home: 7510 Holly Hill #104 Dallas TX 75231 Office: Sun Exploration and Prodns PO Box 2880 Dallas TX 75221

EGGLESTON, THOMAS WARREN, lawyer, educator; b. Evansville, Ind., May 17, 1952; s. Warren Neil and Janice (Warren) E.; m. Katherine Ann Richardson, Oct. 5, 1985. AB, Dartmouth Coll., 1974; JD, U. Va., 1977. Bar: Ind. 1977, U.S. Dist. Ct. (so. and no. dists.) Ind. 1977, U.S. Ct. Appeals (7th cir.) 1979, U.S. Supreme Ct. 1982. Assoc. Ball & Eggleston, Lafayette, Ind., 1977-80, ptnr., 1980—; gen. counsel, v.p. corp. devel. 10th Pan Am. Games Orgn. Com., Indpls., 1986—; prof. Purdue U., W. Lafayette, Ind., 1980—; gen. counsel Warren Co., Lafayette, 1980-86. Rep. nominee State Senate, Lafayette, 1982. Mem. ABA, Ind. Bar Assn., Assn. Trial Lawyers Am., Ind. Trial Lawyers Assn., Phi Beta Kappa. Presbyterian. Lodge: Rotary. State civil litigation, Contracts commercial, Probate. Home: 601 W 91st St Indianapolis IN 46260 Office: Pax Indpls Inc 4475 Allisonville Rd Indianapolis IN 46287

EGINTON, WARREN WILLIAM, federal judge; b. Bklyn., Feb. 16, 1924. A.B., Princeton U., 1948; LL.B., Yale U., 1951. Bar: N.Y. 1952, Conn. 1954. Assoc. Donovan Leisure Newton & Irvine, N.Y.C., summer 1950, Davis Polk & Wardwell, N.Y.C., 1951-53; ptnr. Cummings & Lockwood, Stamford, Conn., 1954-79; judge U.S. Dist. Ct., Bridgeport, Conn., 1979—. Mem. Am. Judicature Soc., ABA, Am. Bar Found., Conn. Bar Assn., Fgn. Policy Assn. Office: US District Judge US Courthouse 915 Lafayette Blvd Bridgeport CT 06604

EGLER, FREDERICK NORTON, lawyer; b. Pitts., May 27, 1922; s. Frederick N. and Agnes (Norton) E.; m. Ruth Donnelly; 11 children. B.A., Duquesne U., 1943; J.D., U. Pitts., 1947. Bar: Pa. 1948. Mem. Egler, Anstandig, Garrett & Riley, Pitts., 1950—; mem. lawyers adv. com. U.S. Ct. Appeals (3d cir.), 1984—. Chmn. bd. dirs. Allegheny County San. Authority, Pitts., 1974-79. Fellow Am. Law Inst., Am. Coll. Trial Lawyers, Internat. Acad. Trial Lawyers; mem. Internat. Assn. Ins. Counsel, Acad. Trial Lawyers Allegheny County, ABA, Pa. Bar Assn., Allegheny County Bar Assn. Personal injury, Federal civil litigation, Workers' compensation. Office: Egler Anstandig Garrett & Riley 428 Forbes Ave 2100 Lawyers Bldg Pittsburgh PA 15219

EHINGER, JAMES OAKLEAF, lawyer; b. Los Angeles, Sept. 3, 1953; s. William Page and Jean Francis (Oakleaf) E.; m. Peggy Ellen Kuhlken, Dec. 20, 1975; children: Krista Anne, Jessica Lee. BA, UCLA, 1975, JD, 1981; MA in History, U. Calif., Berkeley, 1978. Bar: Calif. 1981, U.S. Dist. Ct. (cen. dist.) Calif. 1981, Ariz. 1984, U.S. Dist. Ct. Ariz. 1984. Assoc. Greenberg, Glusker, Fields, Claman & Machtinger, Los Angeles, 1981-83, Snell & Wilmer, Phoenix, 1984—. Mem. ABA, Calif. Bar Assn., Ariz. Bar Assn., Maricopa County Bar Assn., Order of Coif. Republican. Mem. Moravian Ch. Federal civil litigation, State civil litigation, Insurance. Office: Snell & Wilmer 3100 Valley Bank Ctr Phoenix AZ 85073

EHLERS, MICHAEL GENE, lawyer, transportation company executive; b. Waterloo, Iowa, Sept. 7, 1951; s. Gene Merle and Dorothy JoAnn (Vint) E.; m. Marlena Kay Hammonds, June 02, 1984. BA, U. No. Iowa, 1973; JD, U. Iowa, 1977. Bar: Iowa 1977. Ops. mgr. Gen. Leaseways, Inc., Davenport, Iowa, 1977-78; v.p., gen. counsel Gen. Leaseways, Inc., Davenport, 1978-84; exec. v.p., gen. counsel Gen. Car and Leasing System, Inc., Davenport, 1984—. Mem. ABA. Clubs: Davenport (Iowa), Crow Valley Golf (Davenport). General corporate, Antitrust. Home: 6401 Utica Ridge Rd # 12 Davenport IA 52807 Office: Gen Car and Truck Leasing System Inc 450 W 76th St Davenport IA 52806

EHMANN, ANTHONY VALENTINE, lawyer; b. Chgo., Sept. 5, 1935; s. Anthony E. and Frances (Verweil) E.; m. Alice A. Avina, Nov. 27, 1959; children—Ann, Thomas, Jerome, Gregory, Rose, Robert. B.S., Ariz. State U., 1957; J.D., U. Ariz., 1960. Bar: Ariz. 1960, U.S. Tax Ct. 1960, U.S. Sup. Ct. 1968. Spl. asst. atty. gen., 1961-68; mem. Ehmann, Waldman & Brody, P.C., Phoenix, 1969—. Republican dist. chmn. Ariz., 1964; pres., mem. exec. com. Theodore Roosevelt council Boy Scouts Am., Recipient Silver Beaver award Boy Scouts Am., 1982, Bronze Pelican award Cath. Com. on Scouting, 1981. C.P.A., Ariz. Mem. State Bar Ariz. (chmn. tax sect. 1968, 69), Central Ariz. Estate Planning Council (pres. 1968, 69). Republican. Roman Catholic. Clubs: Rotary (Phoenix); KC (grand knight 1964, 65) (Glendale, Ariz.). Pension, profit-sharing, and employee benefits, Estate planning, Corporate taxation. Office: 4722 N 24th St Suite 350 Phoenix AZ 85016

EHMLING, MILES ALLEN, lawyer; b. Circleville, Ohio, Sept. 3, 1955; s. Walter William and Elizabeth (Allen) E.; m. Rebecca Elizabeth Boyd, May 24, 1986. BA in Psychology, U. South, 1978; JD, U. Tenn., Knoxville, 1981. Bar: Tenn. 1981, U.S. Dist. Ct. (mid. dist.) Tenn. 1981. Assoc. McClellan & Powers P.C., Gallatin, Tenn., 1981-83; ptnr. McClellan, Powers & Ehmling P.C., Gallatin, 1983—. Bd. dirs. TRAC for Boys, Gallatin, 1985; v.p. Maples Homeowners Assn. sect. IV; sec. Sumner County Election Commn., 1987—. Named Outstanding Young Man of Am., 1986. Mem. ABA, Sumner County Bar Assn. (sec. 1984, treas. 1985, v.p. 1986, pres. 1987), Assn. Trial Lawyers Am., Tenn. Assn. Criminal Def. Lawyers, East Tenn. Alumni Assn., Beta Theta Pi. Episcopalian. Lodge: Rotary. Avocations: athletics, boating. Insurance, State civil litigation, Criminal. Home: 129 Cherry Hill Dr Unit 3C Hendersonville TN 37075 Office: McClellan Powers & Ehmling PC 116 Public Square Suite 101 Gallatin TN 37066

EHRENBERG, ROBERT JOHN, lawyer; b. St. Joseph, Mich., July 5, 1953; s. William Herman and Dorothy Lydia (Schadler) E.; m. Cynthia Joy Schipper, Sept. 12, 1981; 1 child, Elizabeth Mary. BS in Acctg. with distinction, Valparaiso U., 1975, JD, 1977. Bar: Mich. 1978, U.S. Dist. Ct. (we. dist.) Mich. 1980, U.S. Dist. Ct. (no. dist.) Ind. 1986. Law clk. Berrien County Cir. Ct., St. Joseph, 1978-79; assoc. Law Office of Elden W. Butzbaugh Jr., St. Joseph, 1979-82; ptnr. Butzbaugh & Ehrenberg, St. Joseph, 1982—. Bd. dirs. Lakeland Choral Soc., St. Joseph, 1981-86, pres., 1983-85, SW Mich. Symphony Orch., St. Joseph, 1984-86; mem. St. Joseph Planning Commn., 1985—. Mem. ABA, Mich. Bar Assn., Berrien County Bar Assn. (sec. 1985-86), Assn. Trial Lawyers Am., Mich. Trial Lawyers Assn., Berrien County Trial Lawyers Assn. (v.p. 1984—). Republican. Lutheran. Club: Berrien Hills Country (Benton Harbor, Mich.). Avocations: gardening, sports, music, theater. Office: Butzbaugh & Ehrenberg 316 Main St Saint Joseph MI 49085

EHRENHAFT, PETER DAVID, lawyer; b. Vienna, Austria, Aug. 16, 1933; came to U.S., 1940, naturalized, 1945; s. Bruno B. and Ann J. (Polacek) E.; m. Charlotte Kennedy, May 4, 1958; children: Elizabeth Ann, James Bruno, Daniel Parker. A.B. with honors, Columbia U., 1954; LL.B. and M.I.A. with honors, Schs. Law and Internat. Affairs, 1957. Bar: N.Y. 1958, D.C. 1961. Motions law clk. to U.S. Ct. Appeals, D.C. Circuit, 1957-58; sr. law clk. to Chief Justice U.S. Supreme Ct., 1961-62; assoc. firm Cox, Langford & Brown, Washington, 1962-66; partner Cox, Langford & Brown, 1966-68; ptnr. firm Fried, Frank, Harris, Shriver & Kampelman, Washington, 1968-77; dep. asst. sec., spl. counsel for tariff affairs Dept. Treasury, Washington, 1977-79; ptnr. firm Hughes, Hubbard & Reed, Washington, 1980-83, Bryan, Cave, McPheeters & McRoberts, Washington, 1984—; professorial lectr. in law George Washington U., 1965-72; mem. faculty Salzburg (Austria) Seminar in Am. Studies Law Session, 1973; lectr. in law U. Pa., 1980-85; mem. Fed. Jud. Center Study Group on Workload of Supreme Ct., 1971-74. Contbr. articles, revs., mainly on internat. trade, to law jours.; mem. adv. bd.: Jour. Law and Policy in Internat. Bus, 1967—, Patent, Trademark and Copyright Jour., 1970—; editorial bd.: Internat. Legal Materials, 1977-87. Pres. bd. trustees Nat. Child Research Center, Washington, 1976-77. Served with USAF, 1958-61, with Res., 1962—. Recipient Reginald Harmon award USAF, 1977, Meritorious Service medal, 1980; Exceptional Service medal Dept. Treasury, 1979. Mem. Am. Law Inst., ABA (council internat. law sect. 1983-86, co-chmn. internat. trade com. 1983-85), Am. Soc. Internat. Law, Washington Fgn. Law Soc. (bd. govs. 1982—, pres. 1986-87). Private international, Administrative and regulatory, General corporate. Home: 2932 Garfield Terr NW Washington DC 20008 Office: 1015 15th St NW Suite 1000 Washington DC 20005

EHRENWERTH, CHARLENE REIDBORD, lawyer, law educator; b. Pitts., Sept. 8, 1949; d. Julius Martin and Patricia B. (Postar) Reidbord; m. David H. Ehrenwerth, July 8, 1973; children—Justin Reid, Lindsey Royce. B.A., Barnard Coll. Columbia U., 1971; J.D., Duquesne U., 1974. Bar: Pa. 1974, U.S. Dist. Ct. (we. dist.) Pa. 1974, U.S. Ct. Appeals (3d cir.) 1977. Asst. dist. atty. Allegheny County, Pa., 1974-76; instr. Carlow Coll., 1977; asst. atty. gen. State of Pa., Pitts., 1976-79; asst. chief counsel Dept. Labor and Industry, Pitts., 1979-86, assoc. Nash and Co., P.C., 1986—; adj. prof. U. Pitts., 1982-85. Bd. dirs., vice-chmn. Mt. Lebanon Zoning Appeal Bd., Pitts., 1983; area rep. Barnard Coll Columbia U., 1972; social action chmn. Women's League of Conservative Judaism, 1982-83. Mem. Allegheny County Bar Assn. (mem. indigent divorce panel 1983-84, med. legal com. 1987—), ABA, Pa. Bar Assn., Assn. Trial Lawyers Am. Republican. Jewish. Clubs: 57 Club (asst. chmn.). Labor, Federal civil litigation, State civil litigation. Home;: 761 Pin Oak Rd Pittsburgh PA 15243

EHRENWERTH, DAVID HARRY, lawyer; b. Pitts., Apr. 22, 1947; s. Ben and Beatrice Lee (Schwartz) E.; m. Charlene Lee Reidbord, July 8, 1973; children: Justin Reid, Lindsey Royce. BA, U. Pitts., 1969; JD, Harvard U., 1972. Bar: Pa. 1972, U.S. Dist. Ct. (we. dist.) Pa. 1972, U.S. Ct. Appeals (3d cir.) 1976. Asst. atty. gen. Commonwealth of Pa., Pitts., 1972-74; assoc. Kirkpatrick & Lockhart, Pitts., 1974-79, ptnr., 1979—. Treas. Pitts. chpt. Am. Jewish Com., 1985—; mem. nat. adv. council FNMA, 1984-85; bd. dirs. Pa. Bd. Vocat. Rehab., Harrisburg, 1983—, Montefiore Hosp., Pitts., 1985—. Served as capt. USAR, 1969-77. Named Pittsburgher to Watch Pitts. Mag., 1980. Mem. Pa. Bar Assn. (chmn. real estate fin. com. 1985—), Allegheny County Bar Assn. (sec. real property sect. 1986), Harvard U. Law Alumni Assn. Western Pa. (pres. 1986—), Phi Beta Kappa. Republican. Jewish. Clubs: Harvard-Yale-Princeton (Pitts.), Concordia (Pitts.), Westmoreland Country (Export), Fifty-Seven (chmn. 1974—). Avocations: tennis, golf. Real property, Personal income taxation, Securities. Home: 761 Pin Oak Rd Pittsburgh PA 15243 Office: Kirkpatrick & Lockhart 1500 Oliver Bldg Pittsburgh PA 15222

EHRKE, WILLIAM WARREN, lawyer; b. Milw., June 6, 1956; s. Warren Dale and Elizabeth (Boswell) E. BS in Indsl. Engring., Northwestern U., 1978; JD, DePaul U., 1981. Bar: Wis. 1981, U.S. Dist. Ct. (ea. and we. dists.) Wis. 1981, Ill. 1982. Assoc. Prosser, Wiedabach & Quale S.C., Milw., 1981—; lectr. on career choices various schs., 1981—. Methodist. Avocations: triathalons, running, soccer, softball, swimming. State civil litigation, Insurance, Personal injury. Home: 1919 N Summit Milwaukee WI 53202 Office: Prosser Wiedabach & Quale SC 310 W Wisconsin Ave Suite 1000 Milwaukee WI 53203

EHRLE, WILLIAM LAWRENCE, lawyer, association executive; b. Colorado City, Tex., Dec. 11, 1932; s. Frank Lawrence and Mary Elma (Hinds) E.; m. Sandra Faye Luckey, Aug. 3, 1963; children—Sharon Elaine, William Lawrence, Rhonda Kay. B.A., McMurry Coll., 1953; J.D., U. Tex., 1961. Bar: Tex. 1961. Asst. gen. counsel Lone Star Gas Co., Dallas, 1961-67; pres. Coaches Life Ins. Co., El Paso, Tex., 1967-70; sole practice, Austin, Tex., 1970-78; pres., gen. counsel Tex. Manufactured Housing Assn., Austin, 1978—; dir. Nat. Manufactured Housing Fedn., Washington, 1978—; mem. adv. council Fed. Nat. Mortgage Assn., Dallas, 1983-84. Mem. Tex. Ho. of Reps., 1957-63. Served as 1st lt. USMC, 1953-56. Administrative and regulatory, Consumer commercial. Office: Tex Manufactured Housing Assn PO Box 14428 Austin TX 78761

EHRLICH, JEFF PASCHAL, lawyer; b. Wichita, Kans., Sept. 9, 1949; s. Norman H. and F. Ann (Paschal) E.; m. Mary L. Braddock, Dec. 27, 1969; children—Christopher Braddock, Jill Louise. B.A., Ft. Hays State U., 1971; J.D., So. Meth. U., 1974. Bar: Tex. 1974, U.S. Tax Ct. 1974, U.S. Dist. Ct. (central dist.) Ill. 1980. Atty., regional counsel, IRS, Denver, 1974-79, sr. atty., dist. counsel, 1979-80, dist. counsel, Springfield, Ill., 1980—. Recipient Performance award, Treasury Dept., 1982, 84, 85. Mem. Tex. Bar Assn., Sangamon County Bar Assn., Sigma Chi. Democrat. Methodist. Federal civil litigation, Personal income taxation, Corporate taxation. Home: 2417 Lindbergh Springfield IL 62704 Office: Dist Counsel IRS 320 W Washington Room 720 Springfield IL 62701

EHRLICH, JERROLD IVAN, lawyer; b. Bklyn., Jan. 21, 1934; s. Harvey B. and Belle R. (Crames) E.; m. Elaine J. Bergman, Dec. 26, 1954 (div. Jan. 1976); children: Mark S., Bruce D., Alan M., Philip L.; m. Vivian R. Fenster, June 27, 1976; children: Laurie B., Joshua B. AB, Oberlin Coll., 1955; LLB, Yale U., 1958. Bar: N.Y. 1958, U.S. Dist. Ct. (so. dist.) N.Y. 1961, U.S. Dist. Ct. (ea. dist.) N.Y. 1962, U.S. Supreme Ct. 1967, U.S. Ct. Appeals (2d cir.) 1968, N.J. 1969. Assoc. Law Office Harold Sylvan, N.Y.C., 1958-59, Burke & Groh, Jamaica, N.Y., 1959-66; asst. dist. atty. Queens County, N.Y., 1967; assoc. Law Office Harry Lipsig, N.Y.C., 1968-71; sole practice N.Y.C., 1971-73; asst. counsel Empire Blue Cross and Blue Shield, N.Y.C., 1973-82, assoc. gen. counsel, 1982—; bd. dirs., sec. Access Am. Inc., N.Y.C., 1985—. Sec. W. 91st St. Block Assn., N.Y.C., 1982—; bd. dirs., sec. Riverside Park Fund Inc., 1986—, Westside Yiddish Assn., 1986—. Mem. ABA, N.Y. State Bar Assn., Nat. Health Lawyers Assn, N.Y. County Lawyers Assn., Am. Soc. Law and Medicine. Democrat. Jewish. General corporate, Health, Insurance. Home: 186 Riverside Dr New York NY 10024 Office: Empire Blue Cross & Blue Shield 622 3d Ave New York NY 10017

EHRLICH, LESLIE SHARON, communications executive; b. Bklyn., July 30, 1952; d. Abraham and Evelyn (Kuznetz) E.; m. Lee Marc Kaswiner, Aug. 11, 1979; children: Adam Jason, Jessica Sarah. BA, New Coll. at Hofstra, 1973; paralegal cert., Adelphi U., 1974; MA, Montclair State U., 1977; JD, Pace U., 1981. Owner Paralegal Corp., Newark, 1975-77; supr. paralegal AT&T, N.Y.C., 1977-79, law clk., with sales dept., 1979-81; mgr. state regulatory N.Y. Telephone Co., N.Y.C., 1981-82; atty. Bell Communications Research, N.Y.C., 1983-84; mgr. contracts AT&T-IS, Morristown, N.J., 1984-86; mgr. contracts, adminstrn. and policies Timeplex, Woodcliff Lakes, N.J., 1986—; adj. prof. Am. Paralegal Inst., South Orange, N.J., 1982-83, Seton Hall, Newark, 1983-84. Chairperson Nat. Council Jewish Women, N.J., 1981-82, Edn./Programming, Suburban Jewish Ctr., Florham Park, N.J., 1984—; attendee Brookings Inst., Washington, 1986. Mem. ABA (vice chairperson young lawyers corp. council sect. 1984—, pub. utility com. 1986—, student liasion antitrust com. 1979-80, recipient Silver Key award 1979, Gold Key award 1980), N.Y. Bar Assn., N.J. Bar Assn. Democrat. Jewish. Avocations: tennis, horseback riding, water sports, arts, travel. Public utilities, Computer, Government contracts and claims. Home: 8 Pheasant Way Florham Park NJ 07932 Office: Timeplex Dept Contracts Adminstrn Policies Woodcliff Lakes NJ 07675

EHRLICH, RAYMOND, state judge; b. Swainsboro, Ga., Feb. 2, 1918; s. Ben and Esther Ehrlich; m. Miriam Bettman, Nov. 27, 1975; stepchildren—Jack Bettman, Gerald Bettman, Zelda Bettman, Carol Ann Bettman. B.S., U. Fla., 1939, J.D., 1942. Bar: Fla. 1942, U.S. Dist. Ct., U.S. Ct. Appeals (11th cir.), U.S. Supreme Ct. Ptnr. Mathews Osborne McNatt Ehrlich et al, Jacksonville, Fla., 1946-81; justice Supreme Ct. Fla., Tallahassee, 1981—. Served to comdr. USN, 1942-46. Mem. ABA, Fla. Bar Assn., Jacksonville Bar Assn., Am. Coll. Trial Lawyers, Internat. Acad. Trial Lawyers. Federal civil litigation, State civil litigation, Personal injury. Office: Supreme Ct Fla Tallahassee FL 32301

EHRLICH, THOMAS, university administrator, law educator; b. Cambridge, Mass., Mar. 4, 1934; s. William and Evelyn (Seltzer) E.; m. Ellen Rome, June 18, 1957; children—David, Elizabeth, Paul. AB, Harvard U., 1956, LLB, 1959; LLD (hon.), Villanova U., 1979, Notre Dame U., 1980, U. Pa., 1987. Bar: Wis. bar 1959. Law clk. Judge Learned Hand U.S. Ct. Appeals 2d Circuit, 1959-60; spl. asst. to legal adviser Dept. State, 1962-64; spl. asst. to under-sec. U.S. Dept. State, 1964-65; assoc. prof. law Stanford (Calif.) U., 1965-68, prof., 1968-75, also dean, 1971-75, Richard E. Lang dean and prof., 1973-75; pres. Legal Services Corp., Washington, 1976-79; dir. Internat. Devel. Coop. Agy., Washington, 1979-81; provost, prof. law U. Pa., Phila., 1981-87; pres., prof. law Ind. U., Bloomington and Indpls., 1987—. Author: (with Abram Chayes and Andreas F. Lowenfeld) The International Legal Process, 3 vols, 1968, (with Herbert L. Packer) New Directions in Legal Education, 1972, International Crises and the Role of Law, Cyprus, 1958-67, 1974; Editor: (with Geoffrey C. Hazard, Jr.) Going to Law School?, 1975. Legal education, Public international, Jurisprudence. Office: Ind Univ Office of President Bryan Hall Bloomington IN 47405

EHRMAN, JOSEPH S., lawyer; b. Milw., Mar. 28, 1931; s. Joseph S. and Pauline (Breslauer) E.; m. Hazel Hope Justus, June 16, 1962; children: Douglas Spencer, Robert Russell. B.S. in Econs. with highest distinction, U. Minn., 1953; J.D. cum laude, Harvard U., 1956, LL.M., 1957. Assoc. Sidley & Austin, Chgo., 1957-66, ptnr., 1966—; mem. inquiry bd. Atty. Registration and Disciplinary Commn., State of Ill., Chgo., 1973-78. Vice pres., dir. Chgo. Commons Assn., 1964-68; bd. dirs., bd. atty. Montessori Sch., Lake Forest, Ill., 1980-84; chmn. solictations com. Harvard Law Sch., Chgo. Fellow Am. Coll. Investment Counsel; mem. Legal Club Chgo. (past dir.), Law Club Chgo., ABA, Chgo. Bar Assn. Clubs: Union League; Mid-Day (Chgo.); Winter (Lake Forest). Home: 321 N Ahwahnee Rd Lake Forest IL 60045 Office: Sidley & Austin One 1st National Plaza Chicago IL 60603

EICHE, JAY S., lawyer; b. Topeka, Dec. 7, 1956; s. Carl E. and Harriet E. Eiche. BA in Bus., Mercer U., 1979, JD, 1982. Bar: Nebr. 1982, U.S. Ct. Mil. Appeals, U.S. Army Ct. Mil. Rev. Sole practice Altanta, 1982-83; atty. criminal appeals Office of Ind. Atty. Gen., Indpls., 1984-85; legal assistance claims atty. U.S. Army Adv. Gen. Corp., Aschaffenburg, Fed. Republic Germany, 1986—; instr. bus. law City Colls. of Chgo., Aschaffenburg, 1986. Served as capt. U.S. Army, 1985-86. Mem. ABA (family law div., mil. law div.), Am. Trial Lawyers Assn., Wilderness Soc. Republican. Military, Family and matrimonial, Government contracts and claims. Home: HHC 3d Brigade (SJA) APO New York NY 09162

EICHELBERGER, STEPHEN, lawyer; b. San Francisco, June 7, 1945; s. Sharon Stephen and Josephine Adelaide (Martinent) E.; m. Mary Ellen Town, Sept. 14, 1968; children: Ann Marie, John Thomas. BA, Lewis & Clark U., 1966; MAT, LaVerne Coll., 1972; JD, Willamette Coll. of Law, 1979. Bar: Oreg. 1979, U.S. Dist. Ct. Oreg. 1979. Ptnr. Churchill, Leonard, Brown & Donaldson, Salem, Oreg., 1979-83, Pound & Eichelberger, Salem, 1983—. Mem. Selective Service Local Bd. 10, Salem, 1981—. Served to capt. USMC, 1966-69, Vietnam. Mem. ABA, Oreg. Bar Assn., Marion County Bar Assn., Oreg. Trial Lawyers Assn., Def. Research Inst. Methodist. Lodge: Rotary. State civil litigation, Consumer commercial, Real property. Office: Pound & Eichelberger 805 Liberty St NE Salem OR 97301

EICHENBAUM, E. CHARLES, lawyer; b. Little Rock, Ark., May 30, 1907; s. E.H. and Sadie C. (Cohn) E.; m. Helen Lockwood; 1 child, Peggy Eichenbaum Jalenak. LLB, Washington U., St. Louis, 1928. Bar: Ark. 1928. Ptnr. Eichenbaum, Scott, Miller, Crockett, Liles & Heister, Little Rock. Fellow Am. Bar Found. (chmn. Ark. fellows 1973-83, vice chmn. com. quality lawyer's life, sect. gen. practice 1979-80, mem. adv. com. 1982-84), Ark. Bar Found. (mem. trust com. 1980—, Lawyer Citizens award 1978-79); mem. ABA (chmn. standing com. lawyer retirement benefits 1979-83, mem. sects. Taxation, Ins., Negligence and Compensation Law, Gen. Practice, mem. coms. corp. stockholder relationship 1975-84, implementing recommendations 1975-78, spl. com. retirement benefits 1976-78), Ark. Bar Assn. (chmn. com. taxation 1946-50, chmn. com. taxation, trusts and estate planning 1953-55, chmn. com. fed. legis. and procedures 1969—, chmn. sr. task force 1982—, Golden Gavel award 1982), Pulaski County Bar Assn., Am. Law Inst., Am. Judicature Soc., Am. Coll. Tax Counsel. General corporate, Estate taxation, Corporate taxation. Home: 12400 Hunters Glen Blvd #30 Little Rock AR 72211 Office: Eichenbaum Scott Miller Crockett et al Union Nat Bank Bldg Suite 1400 Little Rock AR 72201

EICHHORN, FREDERICK FOLTZ, JR., lawyer; b. Gary, Ind., Oct. 16, 1930; s. Frederick Foltz and Adele D. (DeLano) E.; m. Julia Abel, Aug. 27, 1955; children: Jill, Thomas, Timothy, Linda. B.S., Ind. U., 1952, J.D., 1957. Bar: Ind. 1957, U.S. Ct. Appeals (7th cir.) 1957, U.S. Dist. Ct. (no dist.) Ind. 1957, U.S. Supreme Ct. 1973. Assoc. Gavit, Eichhorn, Gary, 1957-62; ptnr. Eichhorn, Eichhorn & Link, and predecessor firm, 1963-76; sr. ptnr. Eichhorn, Eichhorn & Link and predecessor firm, 1977—. Bd. dirs. Gary Housing Authority, 1972-75, Planned Parenthood, Gary Police Civil Service Commn., 1975-82; bd. dirs., founder Miller Citizens Com., 1971; mem. Ind. Sesquicentennial Commn.; chmn. Lake County Community Devel. Com., 1984; bd. dirs. Northwest Ind. Symphony; Northwest Ind. Forum; chmn. World Affairs Council. Served with USAF, 1952-54. Fellow Am. Bar Found., Ind. Bar Found.; mem. Ind. Bar Assn. (inst. chmn. white collar crime 1979, treas. 1977-78, bd. mgrs. 1979-80, v.p. 1983-84, pres. 1985-86), Am. Gas. Assn. (state rate litigation com. 1982, regulation of gas supplies com., state regulatory matters com.), Midwest Gas Assn. (legal affairs sect. 1982), Ind. Soc. Chgo., Phi Delta Phi, Delta Tau Delta. Clubs: Columbia (Indpls.), University (Indpls.). General corporate, Public utilities, Securities. Office: Eichhorn Eichhorn & Link 200 Russell St PO Box 6328 Hammond IN 46325

EICHLER, BURTON LAWRENCE, lawyer; b. Newark, Mar. 1, 1933; s. Philip and Anna (Kessler) E.; children—Betsy, Peter, Thomas. B.S., Ohio State U., 1954; LL.B., Rutgers U.-Newark, 1957. Bar: N.J. 1958, N.Y. 1983, U.S. Dist. Ct. N.J. 1958, U.S. Ct. Appeals (3d cir.) 1981. Assoc., Zucker, Brach & Eichler and predecessor, Newark, 1958-59, ptnr., 1959-67; ptnr. Eichler, Rosenberg & Silver, Newark, 1967-69, Brach, Eichler, Rosenberg, Silver, Newark, 1969-72, Brach, Eichler, Rosenberg, Silver, Bernstein & Hammer P.A., East Orange, N.J., 1972-81, Brach, Eichler, Rosenberg, Silver, Bernstein, Hammer & Gladstone P.C., Roseland, N.J., 1981—; chmn. dist. fee arbitration com. for Essex County, Dist. V-C, N.J. Sup. Ct., 1983-86. Pres., chmn. bd. United Cerebral Palsy, East Oarnge, 1967-69; mem. South Orange/Maplewood Bd. Edn., 1979-83, v.p., 1981-83; bd. dirs. YM-YWHA Met. N.J., West Orange, 1970-74; former trustee Congregation B'nai Jeshurun, Short Hills, N.J. Recipient J. H. Cohn Outstanding Young Leadership award Jewish Community Fedn. Met. N.J., East Orange, 1961. Mem. Eseex County Bar Assn. (chmn. med.-legal affairs com. 1985-86), N.J. Bar Assn., ABA, Am. Health Lawyers Assn. Administrative and regulatory, Health, Real property. Office: Brach Eichler Rosenberg Silver Bernstein Hammer & Gladstone PC 101 Eisenhower Pkwy Roseland NJ 07068

EICHSTADT, CRAIG MARTIN, lawyer; b. Huron, S.D., Aug. 1, 1951; s. Martin Edward and Edith Marie (Scheibe) E.; m. Gail Lynn Carlson, June 1, 1975; children: Anne Elizabeth, Neil Craig, Carl Martin. BA, S.D. State U., 1973; postgrad., Ohio U., 1973-74; JD, U.S.D., 1978. Bar: S.D. 1978, U.S. Dist. Ct. S.D. 1979, U.S. Ct. Appeals (8th cir.) 1984, U.S. Supreme Ct. 1986.

Law clk. S.D. Supreme Ct., Pierre, 1978-79, U.S. Dist. Ct. S.D., Pierre, 1979-80; assoc. Bantz, Gosch & Cremer, Aberdeen, S.D., 1980-81; ptnr. Steele & Eichstadt, Plankinton, S.D., 1981-84; asst. atty. gen. State of S.D., Pierre, 1984—. Dem. chmn. Aurora County, Plankinton, 1983-84. W.W. French scholar U. S.D., 1977-78, Dean Marshall, Alice and Frances McCusick scholar U. S.D., 1976-77. Mem. ABA, S.D. Bar Assn. (com. criminal pattern jury instructions 1983—), Internat. Fish and Wildlife Assn. (legal com. 1984—), Phi Kappa Phi, Delta Phi Alpha. Lutheran. Avocations: furniture refinishing, coin collecting, reading. Administrative and regulatory, Federal civil litigation, State civil litigation. Home: 511 N Evans Pierre SD 57501 Office: Office Atty Gen State Capitol Bldg 500 E Capitol Ave Pierre SD 57501

EIDMAN, KRAFT WARNER, lawyer; b. Liberty Hill, Tex., Jan. 17, 1912; s. Kraft H. and Vera (Bates) E.; m. Julia Mary Bell, Aug. 31, 1940; children: Kraft Gregory, Dan Kelly, John Bates. Student, Rice U., 1929-30; A.B., U. Tex., 1935, LL.B., 1935. Bar: Tex. 1935. Since practiced in Housto; sr. partner Fulbright & Jaworski (and predecessors), 1947—; lectr. law sci. insts., medico-legal insts., state bar meetings.; v.p., dir. Def. Research Inst.; mem. centennial commn. U. Tex. Editor: Ins. Counsel Jour., 1961-63; contbr. articles to legal jours. Life trustee, pres. U. Tex. Law Sch. Found.; trustee, past chmn. U. Tex. Health Sci. Center Found. at Houston; mem. exec. com., chancellor's council U. Tex.; former trustee, mem. exec. com. Inst. Rehab. and Research; bd. dirs. Tex. Med. Ctr., Houston, Houston chpt. ARC; v.p., trustee M.D. Anderson Found. Served to lt. comdr. USNR, 1942-45. Named Disting. Alumnus, U. Tex., 1978. Fellow Am. Coll. Trial Lawyers (regent 1972-76, pres. elect 1976-77, pres. 1977-78), Am., Tex. bar founds.; mem. Anglo-Am. Exchange, Am. Counsel Assn., ABA (vice chmn. trial tactics coms.), Tex. Bar Assn. (chmn. tort and compensation law), Houston Bar Assn. (pres. 1960-61), Internat. Assn. Ins. Counsel (exec. com. 1957-60, 51-66, pres. 1964-65), Houston C. of C., U. Tex. Law Sch. Alumni Assn. (pres., Disting. Alumnus 1980), T Assn., Chancellors, Friar Soc. Democrat. Roman Catholic. Clubs: KC, Kiwanis (pres. S.W. Houston 1958), Houston, Colonneh, Houston Country, Briar (pres. 1952), Chaparral (Dallas); Lakeway Country (Austin), University (Austin), Capital (Austin), Tarry House (Austin). Home: 5559 Sugar Hill Houston TX 77056 Office: 41st Floor Gulf Tower 1301 McKinney St Houston TX 77010

EIDSMOE, ROBERT RUSSELL, lawyer; b. Sioux Falls, S.D., July 6, 1931; s. Russell M. and Beulah (Hoffert) E.; m. Leone M. Eidsmoe, June 6, 1958; children: Eric, Elizabeth. BA, Morningside Coll., 1952; JD, NYU, 1955. Bar: Iowa 1955, U.S. Dist. Ct. (no. dist.) Iowa 1958, U.S. Ct. Appeals (8th cir.) 1962, U.S. Supreme Ct. 1965, U.S. Ct. Appeals (10th cir.) 1966, U.S. Dist. Ct. (so. dist.) Iowa 1968. Ptnr. Eidsmoe, Heidman, Redmond, Fredregrill, Patterson and Schatz, Sioux City, Iowa, 1958—; pres. Tax Research Conf., Sioux City, 1978-85. Pres. Sioux City Symphony Orch. Assn., 1970, life bd. dirs., 1972—; chmn. bd. trustees 1st Congregational Ch., Sioux City, 1968. Mem. ABA, Iowa State Bar Assn. (pres. jr. sect. 1966-67), Woodbury County Bar Assn. (pres. 1986), Sierra Club (pres. Northwest Iowa sect. 1978-80). Congregationalist. Clubs: Sioux City Country (bd. dirs. 1971-74), Sioux Racquet. Banking, Federal civil litigation, State civil litigation. Home: 3649 Lindenwood Sioux City IA 51104 Office: Eidsmoe Heidman Redmond et al PO Box 3086 Sioux City IA 51102

EIKENBERRY, KENNETH OTTO, state attorney general; b. Wenatchee, Wash., June 29, 1932; s. Otto Kenneth and Florence Estelle E.; m. Beverly Jane Hall, Dec. 21, 1963. B.A. in Polit. Sci., Wash. State U., 1954; LL.B., U. Wash., 1959. Bar: Wash. 1959. Spl. agt. FBI, 1960-62; dep. pros. atty. King County (Wash.), Seattle, 1962-67; with firm Richey & Eikenberry, 1967-68, Clinton, Andersen, Fleck & Glein, Seattle, 1968-73; legal counsel King County Council, 1974-76; chmn. Wash. Republican party, 1977-80; atty. gen. State of Wash., 1981—; judge pro tem Seattle Mcpl. Ct., 1979-80; mem. Pres.'s Task Force on Victims of Crime, Pres.'s Child Safety Partnership, 1986—, state Criminal Justice Training Commn. 1980—, state Corrections Standards Bd. 1980—. Chmn., King County Rep. Conv., 1974, 78; mem. Wash. Ho. of Reps., 1970-74. Served with AUS, 1954-56. Named Legislator of Year, Young Americans for Freedom/Wash. Conservative Union, 1974, Rep. Man of Year, Young Men's Rep. Club King County, 1979. Mem. Wash. Bar Assn., Western Conf. Attys.-Gen. (chmn. 1983-84), Soc. Former Spl. Agts. FBI, Nat. Assn. Attys.-Gen. (chmn. energy com. 1983-84, sub-com. on RICO issues, 1984—), Internat. Footprint Assn., Delta Theta Phi, Alpha Tau Omega. Clubs: Kiwanis, Rainrunners. Office: Temple of Justice Office Atty Gen Olympia WA 98504

EILAND, GARY WAYNE, lawyer; b. Houston, Apr. 25, 1951; s. William N. and Louise A. (Foltin) E.; m. Sandra K. Streetman, Aug. 4, 1973; children; Trina L., Peter T. BBA, U. Tex., 1973, JD, 1977. Bar. Tex. 1976, U.S. Dist. Ct. (so. dist.) Tex. 1976, U.S. Ct. Claims 1977, U.S. Ct. Appeals (5th cir.) 1978, U.S. Ct. Appeals (11th cir.) 1981. Assoc. Wood, Lucksinger & Epstein, Houston, 1976-81, ptnr., 1981—; lectr. Aspen Health Care Industry seminars, Aspen Pubs., Inc., Rockville, Md., 1978—. Mem. Am. Acad. Hosp. Attys., Nat. Health Lawyers Assn. (editor Faculty Practice Forum 1984—), Nat. Assn. Coll. and Univ. Attys., Assn. Am. Med. Colls., Houston Young Lawyers Assn. Club: Houston Ctr. Home: 17215 Seven Pines Dr Klein TX 77379 Office: Wood Lucksinger & Epstein 1221 Lamar Suite 1400 Houston TX 77010

EILEN, HOWARD SCOTT, lawyer; b. N.Y.C., Mar. 28, 1954; m. Sharon R. Kornbluth, Oct. 21, 1956; 1 child, Michael. BA, MA, John Jay Coll., 1975; JD, St. John's U., 1979. Bar: N.Y. 1980, U.S. Tax Ct. 1980, U.S. Dist. Ct. (so. dist.) N.Y. 1980. Assoc. Bloom & Tese, N.Y.C., 1980-83; ptnr. Bloom & Eilen, N.Y.C., 1983-86; of counsel Spengler, Carlson, Gubar, Brodsky & Frischling, N.Y.C., 1986—; Arbitrator Nat. Assn. Securities Dealers, Inc., Nat. Futures Assn. Mem. N.Y. County Lawyers Assn. (com. on securities and exchanges 1983-86, chmn. subcom. on commodities regulation). Securities, Federal civil litigation, Commodities Regulation and Litigation. Home: 18 Fortune Ln Jericho NY 11753 Office: Spengler Carlson Gubar Brodsky & Frischling 280 Park Ave New York NY 10017

EILERS, JOHN WAGNER, JR., lawyer; b. Cin., Nov. 21, 1939; s. John Wagner and Mary (McEvilley) E.; m. Elizabeth Lamson, Aug. 16, 1969; children—Michael McE., Christopher R. B.A. in Econs., Marietta Coll., 1961; postgrad. Xavier Coll., 1961-62; J.D., Chase Coll. of Law, 1967. Bar: Ohio 1967, U.S. Dist. Ct. (so. dist.) Ohio 1968, U.S. Ct. Appeals (6th cir.) 1970, U.S. Supreme Ct. 1970, U.S. Tax Ct. 1980. Trust assoc. First Nat. Bank, Cin., 1962-65; tax law clk. Walker and Chatfield, Cin., 1965-68; asst. pros. atty. Hamilton County, Cin., 1968-69; assoc. Paxton and Seasongood, Cin., 1969-74; trust officer Fifth Third Bank, Cin., 1974-79; sole practice, Cin., 1979—; lectr. probate and tax law Ohio Legal Ctr. Inst. Treas. Com. to Re-elect Judge Painter, Hamilton County, Ohio, 1984; vice chmn., treas. Ohio State League of Young Republicans, 1969-70; chmn. Hamilton County Young Republicans, 1968; pres. Better Housing League, 1982-84. Mem. Internat. Assn. Fin. Planning (pres. 1983-84), Ohio State Bar Assn. (dist. rep. probate bd. govs. 1983—), Cin. Bar Assn. (vice chmn. probate com.), ABA (taxation and real property probate and trust law sects.), Friendly Sons St. Patrick, Cin. Assn., Cowan Lake Sailing Assn., Cin. Estate Planning Council (trustee 1986—), Cin. Assn., Mimosa Restoration, Inc. Republican. Roman Catholic. Avocation: sailing. General corporate, Estate planning, Probate. Home: 1131 Beverly Hill Dr Cincinnati OH 45226 Office: 511 Walnut St 2004 Dubois Tower Cincinnati OH 45202

EINCK, DEAN ROBERT, lawyer; b. Decorah, Iowa, Sept. 7, 1957; s. Robert J. and Dianna J. (Bushman) E.; m. Sharon A. Cunningham, Aug. 7, 1982. BA, U. No. Iowa, 1979; JD, U. Iowa, 1982. Bar: Iowa 1982, U.S. Dist. Ct. (no. dist.) Iowa 1982, U.S. Tax Ct.; CPA, Iowa. Assoc. Simmons, Perrine, Albright & Ellwood, Cedar Rapids, Iowa, 1982—. Mem. Linn County Rep. Cen. Com., Cedar Rapids, 1984; bd. dirs., treas. Cedar Rapids/ Marion Arts Council, 1985—. Named one of Outstanding Young Men Am., 1986. Mem. ABA, Iowa Bar Assn., Linn County Bar Assn., Cedar Rapids Tax Group, Cedar Rapids Area Estate Planning Council. Roman Catholic. Lodge: Rotary. General corporate, Pension, profit-sharing, and employee benefits, Probate. Home: 1817 Buckingham Dr NW Apt 10 Cedar Rapids IA 52405 Office: Simmons Perrine Albright & Ellwood 1200 MNB Bldg Cedar Rapids IA 52405

EINHORN, BRUCE JEFFREY, lawyer, historian; b. Orlando, Fla., Dec. 7, 1954; s. Arthur and Iris Joan (Maller) E.; m. Terri Jan Schneider, Mar. 9, 1980; children: Lee Michael, Matthew Mitchell. BA magna cum laude, Columbia U., 1975; JD, NYU, 1978. Bar: D.C. 1980, U.S. Dist. Ct. D.C. 1980, U.S. Ct. Appeals (D.C. cir.) 1980, U.S. Supreme Ct. 1983, U.S. Ct. Appeals (9th cir.) 1984, Pa. 1986. Law clk. to assoc. judge D.C. Ct. Appeals, Washington, 1978-79; sr. trial atty. office spl. investigations U.S. Dept. Justice, Washington, 1979—; annual judge law sch. Moot Ct. competition George Washington U., Washington, 1983—. Sr. fellow Am.-Israel Pub. Affairs Com., Washington, 1986. Recipient Recent Grad. award NYU Law Alumni Assn., 1986. Mem. ABA (internat. law sect.), Assn. of Holocaust Educators, Phi Beta Kappa. Democrat. Jewish. Club: Columbia U. (Washington). Avocations: reader of mystery and detective novels, collector of old movies, sports, civil war historian. Federal civil litigation, Public international, Immigration, naturalization, and customs. Home: 13275 Country Ridge Dr Germantown MD 20874 Office: US Dept Justice Office Spl Investigations 1400 New York Ave NW 11th Floor Washington DC 20530

EINHORN, EDGAR ROBERT, lawyer; b. Phila., Sept. 4, 1931; s. Benjamin and Minnie (Haber) E.; m. Barbara Orlinger, Mar. 31, 1957; children: David, Robert, Rebecca. BS in Econs., Wharton Sch. U. Pa., 1952; LLB, Harvard U., 1955. Bar: Pa. 1967. Asst. city solicitor Law Dept. City of Phila., 1962-77, dep. city solicitor, 1972-79; sole practice Phila., 1955—. Dem. committeeman, Phila., 1957-62. Mem. ABA, Phila. Bar Assn. Jewish. Federal civil litigation, State civil litigation, Personal injury. Home: 332 S 24th St Philadelphia PA 19103 Office: 42 S 15th St Philadelphia PA 19102

EINHORN, HAROLD, lawyer, writer; b. N.Y.C., Dec. 17, 1929; s. Abe and Pauline (Miller) E.; m. Jane Ellen, June 16, 1957; children—David, Edward. A.B., N.Y. U., 1951, M.A., 1957; J.D., Columbia U., 1960. Bar: N.Y., 1961. Pat. atty. Exxon Research & Engring. Co., Linden, N.J., 1960-65, sr. pat. atty., 1965-72, pat. csl., 1972-81; csl. Exxon Chem. Co., Florham Park, N.J., 1982—; lectr. Practicing Law Inst., Am. Mgmt. Assn., World Trade Inst. Bd. trustees Temple B'nai Israel, Elizabeth, N.J., 1980—, pres., 1985—. Served with CIC, U.S. Army, 1953-55. Mem. ABA (subcom. chmn. 1981, 1985, 86), N.Y. Patent Law Assn. (assoc. editor bull. 1968-76), Licensing Execs. Soc. (lectr.). Author: Patent Licensing Transactions, 2 vols., rev. ann., 1970—, Domestic and Foreign Technology, 1984; contbg. author: Domestic and International Licensing of Technology, 1980, Domestic and Foreign Technology Licensing, 1984; contbr. articles to profl. jours. Patent, Antitrust. Home: 382 Orenda Circle Westfield NJ 07090

EINHORN, JOSEPH HAROLD, lawyer; b. N.Y.C., May 1, 1906; s. Samuel and Ida Frimette (Jassem) E.; m. Rose Dorothy Weinberg, Jan. 2, 1933. B.A., Union Coll., 1928; J.D., Albany Law Sch., 1931. Bar: N.Y. 1932, U.S. Ct. Immigration Appeals 1948, U.S. Supreme Ct. 1965. Ptnr., Halter, Sullivan & Einhorn, Albany, N.Y., 1933-43; sole practice, Albany, 1943-81; of counsel Jeneroff, Brandow, Mancini & Roth, Albany, 1981—; referee incompetent accounts Albany County, 1935-45. Mem. Albany County Bd. Suprs., 1966-68, Albany County Democratic Com., 1935-70; chmn. Albany Area chpt. ARC, 1954-58; pres. Westland Hills Improvement Assn., 1940. Served with C.W.S., AUS, 1943, with USNG, 1940-43. Recipient Spier Law Sch. prize, Albany Law Sch., 1931, Covenant award B'nai B'rith, 1953, Anti-Defamation award, 1956, awards and certs. ARC, 1943-82. Mem. ABA, N.Y. State Bar Assn., Albany County Bar Assn., Am. Immigration Lawyers Assn., Estate Planning Council, Assn. Trial Lawyers Am., Am. Legion, DAV, Jewish War Vets., Nat. Chem. Warfare Assn. (nat. judge adv.), Zeta Beta Tau, Tau Epsilon Rho, Tau Kappa Alpha. Jewish. Clubs: Ft. Orange, Kiwanis (Albany), B'nai Brith, Elks, Travel Century, Union Coll. Alumni. Immigration, naturalization, and customs, Probate, Real property. Home: 152 Rosemont St Albany NY 12206 Office: 100 State St Suite 300 Albany NY 12207

EINHORN, LAWRENCE MARTIN, lawyer; b. N.Y.C., Jan. 15, 1943; m. Bonnie L. O'Niell, May 11, 1948; children: Aviva, Zen. BArch, Pratt Inst., N.Y.C., 1966; JD, Tulane U., 1982. Bar: La. 1982, U.S. Dist. Ct. (ea. dist.) La. 1982, U.S. Ct. Appeals (5th cir.) 1983, Calif. 1985, U.S. Dist. Ct. (no. dist.) Calif. 1985, U.S. Ct. Appeals (9th cir.) 1985. Assoc. Marvin I. Barish, New Orleans, 1982-83; sole practice New Orleans, 1983-85; assoc. Dorr, Cooper and Hays, San Francisco, 1985—. Mem. editorial bd. Tulane U. Law Rev. Mem. ABA, La. Bar Assn., Calif. Bar Assn, Nat. Trial Lawyers Assn., La. Trial Lawyers Assn., Calif. Trial Lawyers Assn., Order of Coif. Insurance, Personal injury, Admiralty. Office: Dorr Cooper & Hays 50 Francisco St Suite 210 San Francisco CA 94133

EINSTEIN, STEVEN HENRY, investment banker, lawyer, accountant; b. N.Y.C., Aug. 14, 1954; s. Ralph Gunther and Beatrice (Katz) E. B.S., Lehigh U., 1976; J.D., Seton Hall U., 1979; LL.M. in Taxation, NYU, 1985. Bar: N.J. 1979, U.S. Dist. Ct. N.J. 1979, U.S. Tax Ct. 1982, U.S. Ct. Appeals (3rd cir.) 1983, N.Y. 1985, U.S. Supreme Ct. 1985. Judicial law clk. to presiding justice Superior Ct., Hackensack, N.J., 1979-80; assoc. Wacks, Hirsch, Ramsey & Berman Esqs., Morristown, N.J., 1980-81; sr. tax mgr. Touche Ross, Newark, 1981-86; v.p., investment banking-corp. fin. div., mergers and acquistions dept. Paine Webber Capital Markets, N.Y.C., 1986—. Contbr. articles on tax and corp. fin./investment banking to legal publs. Mem. ABA, N.J. State Bar Assn., N.Y. State Bar Assn., Essex County Bar Assn. (taxation div.), Am. Inst. C.P.A.s, N.J. Soc. C.P.A.s, Beta Gamma Sigma, Phi Eta Sigma. Jewish. Corporate taxation, Estate taxation, Personal income taxation. Home: 6 Woodward Ln Basking Ridge NJ 07920 Office: Paine Webber Mergers and Acquisitions Dept 1285 Ave of Americas New York NY 10019

EISELE, GARNETT THOMAS, judge; b. Hot Springs, Ark., Nov. 3, 1923; s. Garnett Martin and Mary (Martin) E.; m. Kathryn Freygang, June 24, 1950; children: Wendell A., Garnett Martin II, Kathryn M., Jean E. Student, U. Fla., 1940-42, Ind. U., 1942-43; A.B., Washington U., 1947; LL.B., Harvard U., 1950, LL.M., 1951. Bar: Ark. Practiced in Hot Springs, 1951-52, Little Rock, 1953-69; asso. firm Wootten, Land and Matthews, 1951-52, Owens, McHaney, Lofton & McHaney, 1956-60; asst. U.S. atty. Little Rock, 1953-55; individual practice 1961-69; U.S. dist. judge Eastern Dist. Ark., 1970—, chief judge, 1975—; Legal adviser to gov. Ark., 1966-69. Del. Ark. 7th Constl. Conv., 1969-70; Trustee U. Ark., 1969-70. Served with AUS, 1943-46, ETO. Mem. Am., Ark., Pulaski County bar assns., Am. Judicature Soc., Am. Law Inst. Office: US Dist Ct PO Box 3684 Little Rock AR 72203 *

EISELE, R. JOSEPH, lawyer; b. Glendale, Calif., Mar. 19, 1943; s. William Joseph and Adele Emma (Schroeders) E.; m. Sandra Lynne Hamilton, June 27, 1980 (div. Apr. 1985); 1 child, Aiyana Nika. BA in Econs., UCLA, 1966, MS in Fin., 1969, postgrad., 1969-73; JD, U. Idaho, 1979. Bar: Idaho 1979, U.S. Dist. Ct. Idaho 1979, U.S. Tax Ct. 1979. Assoc. Hannon, Gabourie & Howard P.A., Coeur d'Alene, Idaho, 1979-81; prin., ptnr. Hannon, Gabourie, Howard & Eisele P.A., Coeur d'Alene, 1981-84, Hannon, Eisele & Lempesis P.A., Coeur d'Alene, 1984; sole practice Coeur d'Alene, 1984—. Bd. dirs. Kootenai County Emergency Med. Services, Coeur d'Alene, 1985—, Kootenai County Solid Waste Adv. Bd., 1985—. Mem. ABA, Idaho Bar Assn. Republican. Unitarian. Avocations: sailing, skiing, travel, soaring. General corporate, Real property, Bankruptcy. Home: PO Box 544 Coeur d'Alene ID 83814 Office: PO Box 968 Coeur d'Alene ID 83814

EISELT, ERICH RAYMOND, lawyer; b. Ancon, U.S. Canal Zone, Rep. of Panama, Sept. 25, 1953; s. Raymond Walter and Phyllis Jean (Clough) E. BA in Govt. and Fgn. Affairs, U. Va., 1976, JD, 1980. Bar: N.Y. 1981, U.S. Dist. Ct. (so. and ea. dists.) N.Y. 1982. Assoc. Anderson, Russell, Kill & Olick, N.Y.C., 1980-85; staff counsel Keene Corp., N.Y.C., 1985-86; gen. counsel VNU Amvest, Inc., Washington, 1986—. Bd. Editors Va. Jour. Internat. Law, 1979-80. Mem. ABA (bus., internat. law sects.). Contracts commercial, General corporate, Private international. Office: VNU Amvest Inc 3232 Ellicott St NW Washington DC 20008

EISEN, EDWIN ROY, lawyer; b. Bklyn., May 25, 1932; s. Edward and Cecile (Kurland) E.; m. Elaine Sollar, Feb. 15, 1963; 1 child, Marc. A.B., Colby Coll., 1954; LL.B., Cornell U., 1957. Bar: N.Y. 1958, U.S. Dist. Ct. (ea. and so. dists.) N.Y. 1963, U.S. Ct. Appeals (2d cir.) 1963. Ptnr., Tenzer, Greenblatt, Fallen & Kaplan, N.Y.C., 1973-74, Eisen & Fishman, N.Y.C., 1979-81; ptnr. Edwin Roy Eisen, P.C., 1974-78, 81—. Clubs: Brae Burn Country (exec. com.) (Purchase, N.Y.); City Athletic (bd. dirs) (N.Y.C.). Real property, Estate planning, Estate taxation.

EISENBERG, ANDREW LEWIS, lawyer; b. Brookline, Mass., Nov. 28, 1949; s. Eugene Robert and Shirley (Helman) E.; m. Sheryl Diane Fox, June 3, 1973; children: Benjamin Samuel, Lauren Beth. AB, Brown U., 1971; JD, Columbia U., 1974. Bar: Mass. 1974, U.S. Dist. Ct. Mass. 1975, U.S. Ct. Appeals (1st cir.) 1979, U.S. Supreme Ct. 1980. Assoc. Herrick & Smith, Boston, 1974-81, ptnr., 1982-84; ptnr. Goldstein & Manello, Boston, 1984—; dir. LEA Group, Inc., Boston, 1983—. Trustee Combined Jewish Philanthropies, Boston, 1983—; trustee Hebrew Coll., Brookline, 1983—, asst. treas., 1985-86, sec., 1986-87; chmn. Region I, UJA Young Leadership Cabinet, N.Y., 1984-85, co-chmn. Washington Conf., 1985-86, chmn. long-range planning com., 1986-87; bd. dirs. Jewish Community Relations Council, Boston, 1985—, Jewish Community Ctr., Newton, 1985—, v.p., 1986-87; bd. dirs. Am. Friends Hebrew U., 1985—; dir., sec. Jewish Vocat. Service, Boston, 1983-85, v.p., 1985—. Recipient Young Leadership award Combined Jewish Philanthropies, 1986. Mem. Mass. Bar Assn., Boston Bar Assn., ABA. Labor. Home: 185 Franklin St Newton MA 02158 Office: Goldstein & Manello 265 Franklin St Boston MA 02110

EISENBERG, BERTRAM WILLIAM, lawyer; b. Phoenix, Feb. 22, 1930; s. Louis and Mary Ethel (Fiddle) E.; m. Carlene Brown, Feb. 28, 1953; children: Stephen W., Lawrence D. AB, Syracuse U., 1948; LLB, Harvard U., 1951. Bar: N.Y. 1951, U.S. Dist. Ct. (so. dist.) N.Y. 1973. Assoc. Harrison and Coughlin, Binghamton, N.Y., 1954-60; ptnr. Appelbaum and Eisenberg, Liberty, N.Y., 1960—. Served as 1st lt. JAGC, 1951-54. Insurance, Real property. Office: Appelbaum and Eisenberg 6 N Main St Liberty NY 12754

EISENBERG, HARVEY ELLIS, lawyer; b. Bklyn., Sept. 7, 1949; s. Jack and Bobbie Lee (Starker) E. BBA with high honors, U. Md., 1971; JD cum laude, U. Balt., 1976. Bar: Md. 1977, U.S. Dist. Ct. Md. 1986. Personal aide Senator Paul S. Sarbanes, Washington, 1976; atty. Office of Chief Counsel, IRS, Washington, 1977-79; sr. trial atty. tax div., criminal sect. U.S. Dept. Justice, Washington, 1979-1986; asst. U.S. atty., coordinator Organized Crime Drug Enforcement Task Force Mid-Atlanic Region, U.S. Atty.'s Office, Balt., 1986—. Recipient John Marshall award U.S. Atty. Gen., 1984. Democrat. Criminal, Federal civil litigation. Office: Organized Crime Drug Enforcement Task Force Mid-Atlantic Regional Offices 101 W Lombard St Baltimore MD 21201-2692

EISENBERG, JONATHAN LEE, lawyer; b. Hornell, N.Y., Jan. 10, 1955; s. Louis and Marcia (Jesiek) E.; m. Jill Levenson, May 22, 1976; 1 child, Samuel David. BA summa cum laude, Macalester Coll., 1976; JD, Yale U., 1979. Bar: Minn. 1979, U.S. Dist. Ct. Minn. 1980, U.S. Ct. Appeals (8th cir.) 1980. Law clk. to assoc. justice Minn. Supreme Ct., St. Paul, 1979-80; assoc. Pepin, Dayton, Herman, Graham & Getts, Mpls., 1980-84, ptnr., 1985-86; litigation atty. Pillsbury Co., Mpls., 1986—. Mem. ABA, Fed. Bar Assn., Minn. State Bar Assn., Hennepin County Bar Assn., Macalester Coll. Alumni Assn. (bd. dirs. 1982-84). Federal civil litigation, State civil litigation. Office: Pillsbury Co Pillsbury Ctr Minneapolis MN 55402

EISENBERG, MELVIN A., legal educator; b. New York, Dec. 3, 1934; s. Max and Laura (Wallance) E.; m. Helen Garlitz, Feb. 5, 1956; children: Bonnie Jean, David Abram. A.B., S.C.L., Columbia U., 1956; LL.B., S.C.L., Harvard U., 1959. Bar: N.Y. 1960. Assoc. firm Kaye Scholer Fierman Hays & Handler, 1959-63, 64-66; asst. counsel Pres.'s Commn. on Assassination of Pres. Kennedy, 1964; asst. corp. counsel City of N.Y., 1966; acting prof. U. Calif.-Berkeley, 1966-69, prof. law, 1969-83, Koret prof. law, 1983—; vis. prof. Harvard U., 1969-70; counsel Mayor's Task Force on Reorgn. N.Y.C. Govt., 1966; mem. Mayor's Task Force on N.Y.C. Transp. Reorgn., 1966, Mayor's Task Force on Mcpl. Collective Bargaining; reporter Am. Law Inst., Principles of Corp. Governance: Analysis and Recommendations, 1980-84, chief reporter, 1984—; prov. in residence, Cologne U., 1984. Author: (with L. Fuller) Basic Contract Law, 1981, The Structure of the Corporation, 1977, (with W. Cary) Corporations—Cases and Materials, 1980, numerous articles. Pres. Queen's Child Guidance Ctr., 1963-66. Guggenheim fellow, 1971-72; Cooley lecturer U. Mich.; recipient Faye Diploma Harvard Law Sch. Mem. Phi Beta Kappa, Am. Law Inst.; Fellow Am. Acad. Arts and Scis. Legal education. Office: U Calif Sch Law 385 Boalt Hall Berkeley CA 94720 Home: 1197 Keeler Ave Berkeley CA 94708 *

EISENBERG, MEYER, lawyer; b. Bklyn., Dec. 15, 1931; s. Samuel and Bella (Fishman) E.; m. Carolyn Schoen, Dec. 25, 1954; children—Julie S., Ellen M. B.A., Bklyn. Coll., 1953; LL.B., Columbia U., 1958. Bar: N.Y. State bar 1960, D.C. bar 1970, U.S. Supreme Ct. bar 1963. Law clk. to Chief Justice William McAllister, Supreme Ct. Oreg., Salem, 1958-59; atty. SEC, Washington, 1959-70; counsel spl. study securities markets SEC, 1962-64, asst. gen. counsel, 1966-68, exec. asst. to chmn., 1968-69, assoc. gen. counsel, 1969-70; with firm Lawler, Kent & Eisenberg, Washington, 1970-79, Rosenman, Colin, Freund, Lewis & Cohen, Washington, 1980-87, Ballard, Spahr, Andrews & Ingersoll, Washington, 1987—; cons. in field; adj. prof. law George Washington U., 1972-75; vis. prof. law U. Calif. Boalt Hall Nat. Ctr. Fin. Services, Berkeley, 1985-86, bd. dirs.; exec. com. U. Calif. Securities Law Inst. Contbr. articles to profl. publs. Chmn. Nat. Law Commn.; mem. nat. exec. com. Anti-Defamation League, B'nai B'rith; pres. dist. 5 B'nai B'rith., 1981-82. Mem. ABA (chmn. com. on devels. in investment services 1981-86, chmn. com. on long range issues affecting bus. law practice, sect. corp. banking and bus. law 1986—), Fed. Bar Assn. (chmn. securities law com. 1984-85), Am. Law Inst. Securities, Financial services, General corporate. Office: Ballard Spahr Andrews & Ingersoll 555 13th St NW Suite 900E Washington DC 20004

EISENBERG, RONALD ALAN, lawyer; b. Hornell, N.Y., June 9, 1953; s. Louis and Marcia (Jesiek) E.; m. Gena M. Savolainen, July 10, 1976. BA, Macalester Coll., 1975; JD, NYU, 1981. Bar: Minn. 1981, U.S. Dist. Ct. Minn. 1981, N.Y. 1983, Fla. 1984. Assoc. Faegre & Benson, Mpls., 1981-82, Rubin Baum Levin Constant & Friedman, N.Y.C., 1983—. Root-Tilden scholar NYU, 1978-81. Mem. ABA, N.Y. State Bar Assn. (trust and estates sect., com. on estate planning 1985—), Assn. of Bar of City of N.Y., Phi Beta Kappa, Pi Sigma Alpha. Club: Macalester of N.Y. (dir. 1984—). Probate, Estate planning, Estate taxation. Office: Rubin Baum Levin Constant & Friedman 30 Rockefeller Plaza New York NY 10112

EISENBERG, STEPHEN PAUL, lawyer; b. Chgo., July 16, 1944; s. Morris and Esther (Greenberg) E.; m. Susan Irene Sair, July 4, 1968; children: Morris Robert, Jamie Sharon. BA, Wahington U., 1966; JD, DePaul U., 1969. Bar: Ill. 1969, U.S. Dist. Ct. (no. dist.) Ill. 1969, U.S. Supreme Ct. 1980. Assoc. Upton, Conklin & Leahy, Chgo., 1969-72; ptnr. Conklin, Leahy & Eisenberg, Chgo., 1972-79; mng. ptnr. Leahy & Eisenberg Ltd., Chgo., 1979—. Author: RICO: The Insurers Best Friend, 1985. Sec. Ill. Adv. Com. on Arson Prevention, Chgo., 1976-79, chmn. 1979-83, bd. dirs., 1983—; speaker, trainer Ins. and Law Enforcement, Ill., 1977—; patrolman Flossmoor (Ill.) Auxiliary Police, 1978—; mem. Ill. Arson award com., Springfield, 1983—, Gov.'s Arson Adv. Bd., 1983—. Mem. ABA, Ill. Bar Assn., Assn. Trial Lawyers Am., Ill. Trial Lawyers Assn., Internat. Assn. Arson Investigators. Jewish. Clubs: Union League (Chgo.), Idlewild Country (Flossmoor). Avocations: golf, white water river rafting, wine collecting. Insurance, State civil litigation, Federal civil litigation. Office: Leahy & Eisenberg Ltd 29 S LaSalle St Chicago IL 60603

EISENBERG, THEODORE, legal educator; b. Bklyn., Oct. 26, 1947; s. Abraham Louis and Esther (Waldman) E.; m. Lisa Wright, Nov. 27, 1971; children—Katherine Wright, Ann Marie. B.A., Swarthmore, Pa. Coll., 1969; J.D., U. Pa., 1972. Bar: Pa. 1972, N.Y. 1974, U.S. Ct. Appeals (2d cir.) 1974, Calif. 1977. Law clk. U.S. Ct. Appeals, D.C. Cir., 1972-73; law clk. to U.S. Supreme Ct. Justice Earl Warren, 1973; assoc. Debevoise & Plimpton, N.Y.C., 1974-77; prof. law UCLA Law Sch., 1977-81; prof. law Cornell U. Law Sch., Ithaca, N.Y., 1981—; vis. prof. law Harvard U. Law Sch., 1984-85; vis. prof. Law, Stanford U. Law Sch., 1987. Author: Civil Rights Legislation, 1981, 2d edit. 1987; Debtor-Creditor Law, 1984; contbr. articles to profl. jours. Am. Bar Found. grantee, NSF grantee. Mem. ABA, Assn. Bar

City N.Y. Bankruptcy, Civil rights, Consumer commercial. Office: Cornell U Law Sch Myron Taylor Hall Ithaca NY 14853

EISENBERG-MELLEN, VIVIANE, lawyer; b. Brussels, July 18, 1952; came to U.S., 1975; s. Samuel and Laura (Preiss) E.; m. Richard Mellen, Dec. 5, 1980; 1 child, Joshua. Lic. en Droit, U. Brussels, Belgium, 1975; LLM, Columbia U., 1976. Bar: N.Y. 1977. Assoc. Proskauer, Rose, Goetz & Mendelsohn, N.Y.C., 1976-80; v.p., chief counsel original programming Home Box Office, Inc., N.Y.C., 1980—. Mem. Assn. Bar of City of N.Y. Jewish. Entertainment, Trademark and copyright, General corporate. Office: Home Box Office Inc 1100 Ave of the Americas New York NY 10036

EISENBRAUN, ERIC CHARLES, lawyer; b. Quinn, S.D., Dec. 26, 1955; s. Emmanuel Edward and Glenda Mae (Cleveland) E.; m. Sharon Patricia Connolly, Jan. 29, 1977; children: Quinn, Alec, Erika. BS, Augustana Coll., 1978; JD, So. Meth. U., 1981. Bar: Tex. 1981, U.S. Dist. Ct. (no. dist.) tex. 1981, U.S. Ct. Appeals (5th cir.) 1985. Assoc. Coke & Coke, Dallas, 1981-84, Gibson, Dunn & Crutcher, Dallas, 1984—. Contbr. articles to profl. jours. East Dallas chmn. Assn. for Retarded Citizens,1982; vol. advisor East Dallas Legal Clinic, 1986. Named one of Outstanding Young Men Am. U.S. Jaycees, 1984. Mem. Tex. Bar Assn., Dallas Bar Assn., Assn. Trial Lawyers Am., Am. Bankruptcy Inst., Dallas Assn. Young Lawyers (chmn. social com. 1983, vice-chmn. continuing legal edn. com. 1982). Democrat. Avocations: reading, constrn./carpentry, animal husbandry, fishing, racquetball. Federal civil litigation, State civil litigation, Bankruptcy. Office: Gibson Dunn & Crutcher 1700 Pacific Ave Suite 4400 Dallas TX 75201

EISENMAN, GERARD PAUL, lawyer; b. Bridgeport, Conn., Oct. 6, 1949; s. Karl John and Mary (Carr) E. BA, Marist Coll., 1971; JD, U. Bridgeport, 1980. Bar: U.S. Dist. Ct. Conn. 1980, Conn. 1986. Assoc. Ganim & Ganim, Stratford, Conn., 1980-83; dep. asst. states atty. crim. justice div. State of Conn., Bridgeport, 1983—. Mem. law adv. com. U. Bridgeport Sch. Law. Served to sgt. USAF, 1972-76. Mem. ABA, Bridgeport Bar Assn., Nat. Dist. Attys. Assn., U. Bridgeport Law Alumni Assn. (pres. 1983—). Democrat. Roman Catholic. Lodge: Elks. Criminal. Office: States Attys Office 172 Goldenhill St Bridgeport CT 06604

EISENSTAT, ALBERT A., lawyer; b. N.Y.C., July 20, 1930; m. Constance Kend; children: Michael, Melissa. BS in Econs., U. Pa., 1952; JD, NYU, 1960. Bar: N.Y. 1961. Co-founder United Data Ctrs., N.Y.C., 1967-74; v.p., gen. counsel Tymeshare, Cupertino, Calif., 1974-79; sr. v.p., gen. counsel Bradford Nat. Corp., N.Y.C., 1979-81, sr. v.p., 1981—; v.p., gen. counsel Apple Computer, Inc., Cupertino, 1981-85, also bd. dirs.; bd. dirs. Adobe Systems, Palo Alto, Calif., Computer Task Group, Buffalo, Comml. Metals, Dallas. Served to lt. USAF, 1952-56, ETO. Antitrust, Computer, Construction. Office: Apple Computer Inc 20525 Mariana Ave Cupertino CA 95014

EISENSTAT, DAVID H., lawyer; b. Scranton, Pa., May 23, 1951. BA, MA, U. Pa., Phila., 1973; JD, Syracuse U., 1976. Bar: D.C. 1977. Ptnr. Akin, Gump, Strauss, Hauer & Feld, Washington. Office: Akin Gump Strauss Hauer & Feld 1333 New Hampshire Ave NW #400 Washington DC 20036 *

EISERT, EDWARD GAVER, lawyer; b. N.Y.C., May 26, 1948; s. Israel Jay and Bess (Gaver) E.; m. Cynthia G. Klieger, Aug. 26, 1973; children: Carolyn B., Stephen J. AB, Cornell U., 1969; JD, NYU, 1973. Bar: N.Y. 1974. Law clk. to chief judge U.S. Dist. Ct. (so. dist.) N.Y., N.Y.C., 1973-74; assoc. Simpson Thacher & Bartlett, N.Y.C., 1974-76; assoc. Schulte Roth & Zabel, N.Y.C., 1976-80, ptnr., 1981—. Note and comment editor NYU, 1972-73. Mem. ABA (com on fed. regulation of securities 1983—, subcom. on annual rev. fed. regulation of securities 1983—, subcom. on mcpl. and govtl. obligations 1984—), N.Y. State Bar Assn., Assn. of Bar of City of N.Y., Nat. Assn. Bond Lawyers (joint ABA/Nat. Assn. Bond Lawyers task force on roles of counsel in state and local govt. securities transactions 1984—). Club: University (N.Y.C.). Securities, Municipal bonds, General corporate. Home: 28 Secor Rd Scarsdale NY 10583 Office: Schulte Roth & Zabel 900 3d Ave New York NY 10022

EISNER, LAWRENCE BRAND, lawyer, real estate developer; b. New Haven, Sept. 27, 1951; s. Robert Raphael and Anita Stanton (Brand) E.; m. Karen Marie Menne, Nov. 11, 1979; children: Benjamin, Anna, Julia. B.A., Union Coll., 1973; J.D., Georgetown U., 1976. Bar: Conn. 1976, D.C. 1978, Mass. 1982. Atty., adviser Commodity Futures Trading Commn., Washington, 1977-79; treas. Continental Lumber Co., West Haven, Conn., 1979-85; pres. Eisner Devel. Group, Hamden, Conn., 1985—. Mem. Conn. Bar Assn., Phi Beta Kappa. Democrat. Jewish. Private international. Home: 88 Churchill Rd Hamden CT 06517 Office: Eisner Devel Group 2911 Dixwell Ave Hamden CT 06518

EISNER, THOMAS SULTAN, lawyer; b. Bklyn., Apr. 28, 1944; s. Lester Ludwig and Dorothy (Sultan) E.; m. Ellyn Dee Bachrach, Aug. 28, 1966; children: Lee Benjamin, Anna Sharon. BA in Fin., U. Ill., 1965, JD, 1968. Bar: Ill. 1969, U.S. Dist. Ct. (no. dist.) Ill. 1969, U.S. Ct. Appeals (7th cir.) 1973, U.S. Supreme Ct. 1974. Assoc. Aaron, Aaron, Schimberg & Hess, Chgo., 1968-71; sr. ptnr. Eisner, Miller, Frank & Melamed, Chgo., 1971-76, LeVine, Wittenberg, Eisner, Newman & Silverman, Harvey, Ill., 1976-82; pres. LeVine, Wittenberg, Eisner, Newman & Silverman, Homewood, Ill., 1982—, also bd. dirs. V.p. Congregation Beth Sholom, Park Forest, Ill., 1973-75, Anita Stone Jewish Community Ctr., Flossmoor, Ill., 1982-83; pres. Graymoor Landowners Assn., Olympia Fields, Ill, 1981. Served with USAR, 1968-74. Mem. ABA, Ill. Bar Assn., Chgo. Bar Assn., Am. Judicature Soc. Democrat. Club: Ravisloe Country (Homewood). General corporate, Real property. Home: 89 Graymoor Ln Olympia Fields IL 60461 Office: LeVine Wittenberg Eisner et al 930 W 175th St Homewood IL 60430

EISZNER, JAMES RICHARD, JR., lawyer; b. Chicago Heights, Ill., June 6, 1953; s. James R. Sr. and Joyce Carolyn (Holland) E.; m. Barbara Lynn Bonavita, Aug. 15, 1976; children: Nicole, James, Richard. AB, Princeton U., 1975; JD, NYU, 1978. Bar: N.Y. 1979, U.S. Dist. Ct. (so. and ea. dists.) N.Y. 1979, U.S. Supreme Ct. 1982, U.S. Ct. Appeals 1982. Assoc. Lord, Day & Lord, N.Y.C., 1978-86; ptnr. Coudert Brothers, N.Y.C., 1986—. Bd. dirs. Cooley's Anemia Found., N.Y.C. Mem. ABA. Republican. Presbyterian. Club: Princeton (N.Y.C.). Antitrust, Federal civil litigation, Criminal. Home: 903 Hillcrest Rd Ridgewood NJ 07450 Office: Coudert Brothers 200 Park Ave New York NY 10166

EITTREIM, RICHARD MACNUTT, lawyer; b. Neptune, N.J., Feb. 10, 1945; s. Wilbur Lawrence and Leta Blanch (MacNutt) E.; m. Margaret Anne Nolan, June 11, 1967; children—Theodore Scott, Elisabeth Marie, Samantha Leta. A.B., Yale U., 1967; J.D., U. Va., 1973. Bar: N.J. 1973, U.S. Dist. Ct. N.J. 1973, U.S. Ct. Appeals (3d cir.) 1984. Assoc., McCarter & English, Newark, N.J., 1973-80, ptnr., 1980—. Trustee, Children's Psychiat. Ctr., Eatontown, N.J., 1977—. Mem. ABA, N.J. State Bar Assn., Essex County Bar Assn., Phi Alpha Delta. Democrat. Presbyterian. Clubs: Sea Bright Lawn Tennis and Cricket (Rumson); Monmouth Boat (treas. 1983-86) (Red Bank, N.J.); Essex (Newark), Yale (pres. 1986—) (Monmouth, Ocean Counties). Federal civil litigation, Insurance, Libel. Home: Windmill Ln Rumson NJ 07760 Office: McCarter & English 550 Broad St Newark NJ 07102

EKERN, GEORGE PATRICK, lawyer; b. Mexico, Mo., June 12, 1931; s. Paul Chester and Sallie Mays (McCoy) E.; m. Anita Elizabeth Poynton, June 3, 1961; children—Stephen G., Nigel P., Adrienne E. A.B., U. Mo., 1953, J.D., 1958. Bar: Mo. 1958, N.Y. 1962. Assoc. Dewey, Ballantine, Bushby, Palmer & Wood, N.Y.C., 1960-68; asst. gen. atty. Cerro Corp., N.Y.C., 1968-71; asst. sec. Freeport Minerals Co., N.Y.C., 1971-75, assoc. gen. counsel, 1975-83; v.p. legal services Homequity Inc., Wilton, Conn., 1984; sec., gen. counsel Handy & Harman, N.Y.C., 1984-87, v.p., sec. and gen. counsel, 1987—. Mem. Darien Bd. Edn., Conn., 1978-81. Fulbright scholar, The Netherlands, 1955-56; fellow Rotary Internat., London, 1959-60. Mem. N.Y. State Bar Assn. (exec. com. corp. counsel sect. 1982—), Bar City N.Y., Am. Soc. Corp. Secs., Phi Beta Kappa. Republican. Presbyterian. Club: Mining (N.Y.). Avocations: sports; music. General corporate, Antitrust, Private international. Office: Handy & Harman 850 Third Ave New York NY 10022

EKLUND, CARL ANDREW, lawyer; b. Denver, Aug. 12, 1943; s. John M. and Zara (Zerbst) E.; m. Nancy Jane Griggs, Apr. 23, 1946; children—Kristin, Jessica, Peter. B.A., U. Colo., 1967, J.D., 1971. Bar: Colo. 1971, U.S. Dist. Ct. Colo. 1971, U.S. Ct. Appeals (9th cir.) 1975, U.S. Ct. Appeals (10th cir.) 1978, U.S. Supreme Ct. 1978. Dep. dist. atty. Denver Dist. Attys. Office, 1971-73; ptnr. DiManna, Eklund, Ciancio & Jackson, Denver, 1975-81, Smart, DeFurio, Eklund & McClure, Denver, 1982-84, Roath & Brega, P.C., Denver, 1984—; local rules com. Bankruptcy Ct. D.C., 1979-80; reporter Nat. Bankruptcy Conf., 1981-82; lectr. Continuing Legal Edn. Colo., Inc., Colo. Practice Inst., Colo. Bar Assn., Nat. Ctr. Continuing Legal Edn., Inc., Profl. Edn. Systems, Inc., Comml. Law Inst. Am., 1977—. Mem. ABA (bus. law and corp. banking sect., bus. bankruptcy com. subcom. on rules 1981—), Colo. Bar Assn. (bd. govs. 1980-82, corp. banking and bus. law sect. 1977—, ethics com. 1981-82), Denver Bar Assn. (trustee 1983-86), Law Club Denver. Democrat. Episcopalian. Club: Athletic (Denver). Bankruptcy. Office: One United Bank Center Suite 2222 1700 Lincoln St Denver CO 80203

EKLUND, ROBERT D., lawyer; b. Muskegon, Mich., Jan. 5, 1953; s. James D. and Kathryn (Albers) Eklund; m. Diane Sue Colby, May 9, 1981; children: Kathryn Ann, Colby Marie. BBA, U. Mich., 1976; JD, Wayne State U., 1979. Ptnr. O'Toole, Johnson, Knowlton, Muskegon, Mich., 1979—. Bd. dirs. Muskegon County unit Am. Cancer Soc., 1985—, West Mich. chpt. National SIDS Found., 1985—. Served with USAF, 1972-74. Mem. ABA, State Bar Mich., Muskegon County Bar Assn. General corporate, Estate planning, Probate. Office: O'Toole Johnson et al 175 W Apple Muskegon MI 49443

EKLUND-EASLEY, MOLLY SUE, lawyer; b. Benton Harbor, Mich., Aug. 17, 1953; d. Robert Gordon and Arlene Ann (Weinlander) Eklund; m. Herman Easley, Jr., July 18, 1981; 1 child, Rachel Nicole. B.A., Grand Valley State Coll., 1975; J.D. U. Detroit, 1979. Bar: Mich. 1979, U.S. Dist. Ct. (ea. dist.) Mich. 1979. Assoc. Stalburg, Fisher & Weberman, Detroit, 1979-87. Mem. ABA, Women Lawyer's Assn. Mich., Assn. Trial Lawyers Am., Mich. Trial Lawyers Assn., Mich. Bar Assn. Lutheran. Criminal, Family and matrimonial, General practice. Office: 2228 Inkster Rd at Michigan Ave Inkster MI 48141

EKSTRUM, B. WILLIAM, lawyer; b. Mpls., Jan. 1, 1948; s. Bertil William and Doris Elizabeth (Norton) E.; m. Margaret Jean Davidson, June 22, 1968; children : Karen Ann, Kristen Sara. BA, U. Minn., 1971; JD, William Mitchell Coll. Law, 1979. Bar: Minn. 1979, U.S. Dist. Ct. Minn., 1980. Sole practice Mpls., 1979-80; assoc. Smith, Juster et al, Fridley, Minn., 1980-85, mem., 1985—; counsel Blaine (Minn.) Community Scholarship Assn., 1981—; bd. dirs. Anoka County Econ. Devel. Partnership, Coon Rapids, Minn., 1985—. Served with U.S. Army, 1968-71. Mem. ABA, Minn. Bar Assn., Anoka County Bar Assn., Anoka County C. of C. (pres. 1983-84, bd. dirs. 1983—), Blaine Area C. of C. (pres. 1982). Methodist. Lodge: Rotary (local treas. 1984-85). Avocations: music, poetry, tennis, bridge. State civil litigation, General practice, Real property. Home: 9476 Tyler St NE Blaine MN 55434 Office: Smith Juster et al 6401 University Ave NE Fridley MN 55432

ELAM, JOHN WILLIAM, lawyer, academic administrator; b. Columbus, Ohio, Oct. 1, 1956; s. John Carlton and Virginia (Mayberry) E.; m. Shelley Lynn Nelson, May 21, 1981. BA in Polit. Sci., Earlham Coll., 1978; JD, U. Mich., 1981. Bar: Ohio 1982. Assoc. Vorys, Sater, Seymour & Pease, Columbus, Ohio, 1981-84; asst. dir. employment services Ohio State U., Columbus, 1984-86, assoc. to sec. of bd. trustees, 1985—, dir. employment services, 1986—; asst. atty. gen. State of Ohio, 1986—. Mem. ABA (fellow litigation sect., mem. labor and employment law sect., law student liason), Am. Immigration Lawyers Assn., Ohio State Bar Assn. Labor, Immigration, naturalization, and customs, Civil rights. Office: Ohio State U 2130 Neil Ave Columbus OH 43210

ELBERGER, RONALD EDWARD, lawyer; b. Newark, Mar. 13, 1945; s. Morris and Clara (Denes) E.; m. Rena Ann Brodey, Feb. 15, 1975; children: Seth, Rebecca. AA, George Washington U., 1964, BA, 1966; JD, Am. U., 1969. Bar: Md. 1969, D.C. 1970, Ind. 1971, U.S. Ct. Appeals (7th cir.) 1971, U.S. Supreme Ct. 1973. Atty. Balt. Legal Aid Bur., 1969-70; chief counsel Legal Services Orgn., Indpls., 1970-72; ptnr. Elberger & Stanton, Indpls., 1974-76, Bose, McKinney & Evans, Indpls., 1976—. Mem. Med. Licensing Bd. Ind., 1982—; pres. chmn. bd. dirs. Ind. Civil Liberties Union, Indpls., 1972-77, bd. dirs., 1984-86, ACLU, N.Y.C., 1972-77. Reginald Heber Smith fellow U. Pa., 1969-71. Mem. ABA, Ind. Bar Assn., Ind. Trial Lawyers Assn., Md. Bar Assn., D.C. Bar Assn., Indpls. Bar Assn. Democrat. Jewish. Avocations: fishing, music, gardening. Federal civil litigation, State civil litigation, Entertainment. Office: Bose McKinney & Evans 1100 First Ind Bldg Indianapolis IN 46204

ELBERT, CHARLES STEINER, lawyer; b. St. Louis, May 18, 1950; s. Harold I. and Carol B. (Steiner) E.; m. Karen Berry, Dec. 9, 1979; children: Matthew Berry, Lisa Beth. A.B., Washington U., St. Louis, 1972; J.D. cum laude, St. Louis U., 1976. Bar: Mo. 1976, Ill. 1977, U.S. Dist. Ct. (ea. and we. dists.) Mo. 1977, U.S. Ct. Appeals (8th cir.) 1977, U.S. Supreme Ct. 1985. Assoc. Kohn, Shands, Elbert, Gianoulakis & Giljum, St. Louis, 1976-81, ptnr., 1982—; spl. rep. 22d Jud. Bar Com., St. Louis, 1978. Contbr. articles to profl. jours. Trustee Clayton Gardens Neighborhood Assn., Mo., 1983-84, 85-86, pres., 1984-85; bd. dirs. St. Louis chpt. Am. Jewish Com., 1984—; mem. Nursery Found., St. Louis, 1986—, Mo. Coalition Against Censorship, 1986—. Mem. Mo. Bar Assn. (labor law com. 1977—), Ill. State Bar Assn., ABA (labor law sect. 1984—), Bar Assn. Met. St. Louis (labor law com. 1977—, grievance com. 1978—). Jewish. Labor, General corporate, Real property. Home: 8137 University Dr Saint Louis MO 63105 Office: Kohn Shands Elbert et al 411 N 7th St Saint Louis MO 63101

ELDRIDGE, DOUGLAS ALAN, lawyer; b. Boulder, Colo., Mar. 15, 1944; s. Douglas Hilton and Clara Effie (Young) E.; m. Benna June Germann, June 24, 1967; children: Heather Dana, Ethan Douglas, Hilary Beca. BA, Yale U., 1966; LLB, U. Pa., 1969; cert. Nat. Inst. Trial Advocacy, Boulder, 1973. Bar: N.Y. 1972, U.S. Dist. Ct. (no. dist.) N.Y. 1973, U.S. Supreme Ct. 1975. Legal asst. Hartford Neighborhood Legal Services, Conn., 1969-71; staff. atty. Onondaga Neighborhood Legal Services, Syracuse, N.Y., 1971-74, exec. dir., 1974-76; counsel N.Y. State Div. of Substance Abuse Services, Albany, 1976-79; dep. counsel N.Y. State Health Dept., Albany, 1979-80; asst. counsel N.Y. State Energy Office, Albany, 1980-86, asst. to commr., 1987—. Contbr. articles to legal jours. Chmn., N.Y. State Health and Welfare Coalition, 1975-76; pres. Coalition for Health and Welfare Syracuse and Onondaga County, N.Y., 1973-75; v.p. Consumer Credit Counseling Services, Albany, 1980-85; bd. dirs. Council of Community Services of United Way of Northeastern N.Y., Albany, 1980—, chmn. urban affairs com., 1982-86, v.p., 1983-85, pres., 1986—. Recipient Reginald Heber Smith Community Lawyer fellowship OEO, 1969-71. Mem. N.Y. State Bar Assn., Albany County Bar Assn., Onondaga County Bar Assn., Yale Alumni Schs. Com., Yale Alumni Assn. Northeastern N.Y. (bd. dirs. 1979—, del. 1985—), Assembly of Yale Alumni (rep. 1985—). Clubs: University. Administrative and regulatory, Nuclear power, Real property. Home: 9 Pinedale Ave Delmar NY 12054 Office: NY State Energy Office 2 Rockefeller Plaza Albany NY 12223

ELDRIDGE, JOHN COLE, judge; b. Balt., Nov. 3, 1933; s. Arthur Clement and Bertha Jean (Klitch) E.; m. Dayne S. Worsham, July 15, 1961; children—Kathryn Chandler, John Cole. B.A., Harvard U., 1955; LL.B., U. Md., 1959. Bar: Md. 1960, D.C. 1961. Law clk. to chief judge U.S. Ct. Appeals 4th Circuit, 1959-61; trial atty. appellate sect., civil div. Dept. Justice, 1961-67, asst. chief appellate sect., 1967-69; chief legis. officer, counsel Staff of Gov. of Md., 1969-74; judge Ct. Appeals Md., Annapolis, 1974—; Chmn. Md. Adv. Bd. Correction, 1969-70; dir. Annapolis Fine Arts Found., 1974-77. Mem. Anne Arundel County Bar Assn. Democrat. Methodist. Clubs: Nat. Lawyers, Annapolis Yacht. Office: Court of Appeals 361 Rowe Blvd Annapolis MD 21401

ELDRIDGE, RICHARD MARK, lawyer; b. Okmulgee, Okla., June 20, 1951; s. H.G. and Marcheta (Barnes) E.; m. Nellene Jane Mark, Aug. 20, 1971; children: Richard Mark Jr., Christopher Bryan, Ryan Matthew. BA, Okla. State U., 1973; JD, U. Tulsa, 1975. Bar: Okla. 1976, U.S. Dist. Ct. (no. dist.) Okla. 1976, U.S. Ct. Appeals (10th cir.) 1977. Ptnr. Jacobus, Green & Eldridge, Tulsa, 1976-78; spl. judge Dist. Ct., Tulsa, 1979-82; ptnr. Rhodes, Hieronymus, Jones, Tucker & Gable, Tulsa, 1982—; adj. prof. Oral Roberts U., Tulsa, 1985. Tchr. Couples for Christ, Asbury United Meth. Ch., Tulsa, 1979—; pres., sec. Christian Businessmen's Com., Tulsa, 1981—; chmn. Asbury Presch. Bd., Tulsa, 1985—. Recipient Cert. of Achievement, Am. Acad. Jud. Edn., 1979. Mem. Okla. Bar Assn., Tulsa County Bar Assn. Democrat. Avocation: basketball. State civil litigation, Federal civil litigation, Personal injury. Home: 2916 E 88th St Tulsa OK 74137 Office: Rhodes Hieronymus et al 2800 Fourth National Bldg Tulsa OK 74119

ELFMAN, ERIC MICHAEL, lawyer; b. Phila., Oct. 24, 1954; s. Isaac Selig and Mae (Kline) E.; m. Barbara Cecile Feldstein, Oct. 9, 1982; 1 child, Elizabeth. BS in Econs., U. Pa., 1975, MS in Acctg., 1976; JD, George Washington U., 1980. Bar: Calif. 1980, U.S. Tax Ct. 1981, Mass. 1986; CPA, Pa. Acct. Peat, Marwick, Mitchell and Co., Phila., 1976-78; assoc. Pettit & Martin, San Francisco, 1980-83; assoc. office of tax legis. counsel U.S. Dept. of Treas., Washington, 1983-85, Ropes & Gray, Boston, 1985—. Mem. ABA (taxation sect.), Mass. Bar Assn., Boston Bar Assn., Am. Inst. CPA's. Corporate taxation, Personal income taxation. Home: 49 Willis Rd Sudbury MA 01776 Office: Ropes & Gray 225 Franklin St Boston MA 02110

ELFVIN, JOHN THOMAS, judge; b. Montour Falls, N.Y., June 30, 1917; s. John Arthur and Lillian Ruth (Dorning) E.; m. Peggy Pierce, Oct. 1, 1949. B.E.E., Cornell U., 1942; J.D., Georgetown U., 1947. Bar: D.C. 1948, N.Y. 1949. Confidential clk. to U.S. Circuit Ct. Judge E. Barrett Prettyman, 1947-48; asst. U.S. atty. Western Dist. N.Y., Buffalo, 1955-58; U.S. atty. Western Dist. N.Y., 1972-75; with firm Cravath, Swaine & Moore, N.Y.C., 1948-51, Dudley, Stowe & Sawyer, Buffalo, 1951-55, Lansdowne, Horning Elfvin, Buffalo, 1958-69, 70-72; justice N.Y. Supreme Ct., 1969; judge U.S. Dist. Ct. for Western Dist. N.Y., Buffalo, 1975—; Mem. bd. suprs. Erie County, N.Y., 1962-65, mem. bd. ethics, 1971-74, chmn., 1971-72; mem., minority leader Buffalo Common Council Delaware Dist., 1966-69; trustee Buffalo Assn. Blind. Mem. Harvard Law Assn., Engring. Soc. Buffalo (pres. 1958-59), Tech. Socs. Niagara Frontier (pres. 1960-61), Phi Kappa Tau, Delta Sigma Chi. Republican. Clubs: Cornell (pres. 1957-58); City (Buffalo), Buffalo Country (Buffalo), Saturn (Buffalo). Office: 609 US Courthouse Buffalo NY 14202

ELIAS, JOHN SAMUEL, lawyer; b. Lawrence, Mass., May 2, 1951; s. Fred G. and Evon (Erban) E.; m. Cynthia Lee Eppley, Jan. 29, 1979; children: Daniel, Allison. A.B. summa cum laude, Dartmouth Coll., 1973; M.A., Oxford U., Eng., 1975; J.D., Harvard U., 1979; LL.M. in Taxation, NYU, 1982. Bar: Ill. 1979, Ohio 1980, U.S. Tax Ct. 1980, N.Y. 1981, Mass. 1982. Law clk. Ohio Supreme Ct., Columbus, 1979-81; assoc. Goodwin, Proctor & Hoar, Boston, 1982-84; ptnr. Sutkowski & Washkuhn Assocs., Peoria, Ill., 1984—; lectr. Ill. Inst. Continuing Legal Edn., Springfield, 1984. Contbr. articles to legal jours. Recruiter Dartmouth Coll., Peoria, 1984—. Dartmouth Coll. Reynolds Meml. scholar Oxford U., 1974. Mem. ABA, Ill. State Bar Assn., Peoria County Bar Assn., Phi Beta Kappa. Roman Catholic. Club: Peoria Country. Lodge: Rotary. Corporate taxation, General corporate, Securities. Home: 1017 Greenfield Dr Peoria IL 61614 Office: Sutkowski & Washkuhn Assocs 560 Jefferson Bank Bldg Peoria IL 61602

ELIAS, WILLIAM KEITH, lawyer; b. Atchison, Kans., Feb. 21, 1955; s. William Keith and Ruth Ann (Meier) E.; m. Amy S. Elias, Aug. 5, 1978; 1 child, Adrienne Michelle. BA, Okla. State U., 1977; JD, U. Tulsa, 1981. Bar: Okla. 1981, U.S. Dist. Ct. (we. dist.) Okla. 1981, U.S. Dist. Ct. (ea. dist.) Okla. 1985, U.S. Ct. Appeals (10th cir.) 1986. Assoc. Watson & McKenzie, Oklahoma City, 1981-86; mem. Watson & McKenzie, 1986—. Mem. ABA, Okla. Bar Assn., Okla. County Bar Assn. Democrat. Roman Catholic. Lodge: KC. Oil and gas leasing, Federal civil litigation, State civil litigation. Office: Watson & McKenzie 1900 Liberty Tower Oklahoma City OK 73112

ELICKER, GORDON LEONARD, lawyer; b. Cleve., May 27, 1940. BA in Math., U. Mich., 1962, JD, 1965; postdoctoral, U. Aix-Marseille, Aix-En Provence, France, 1965-66. Bar: Mich. 1967, N.Y. 1968, U.S. Dist. Ct. (so. dist.) N.Y. 1973. Stagiaire EEC, Brussels, 1966-67; assoc. Shearman & Sterling, N.Y.C., 1967-77, ptnr., 1977—; speaker in field. Contbr. articles to profl. jours. Mem. legal com. U.S.-U.S.S.R. Trade and Econ. Council, N.Y.C., 1978—; chmn. legis. com. N.Y. Dist. Export Council, N.Y.C., 1980-86; mem. Dem. Town Com., New Canaan, 1985-87; mem. bd. edn., New Canaan, Conn. Fulbright scholar, 1965. Mem. ABA (middle east and Soviet law coms.), Internat. Bar Assn., Assn. of Bar of City of N.Y. Democrat. Banking, Oil and gas leasing, Private international. Office: Shearman & Sterling 53 Wall St New York NY 10005

ELIKANN, PETER TODD, television reporter, lawyer; b. N.Y.C., May 6, 1953; s. Gerald Arthur and Leonore Rita (Reiser) E. BS in Journalism magna cum laude, Boston U., 1975; JD, Western New England Sch. Law, 1980. Bar: Mass. 1981, U.S. Dist. Ct. Mass. 1981, U.S. Ct. Appeals (1st cir.) 1982. Assoc. Nathan & Clayman, Bloomfield, Conn., 1980; asst. reporter jud. decisions Conn. Supreme Ct., Hartford, 1981-82; investigative legal reporter TV Channel Twelve, Norwalk, Conn., 1982-84; reporter news WRC-TV NBC, Washington, 1984—; instr. Western New England Coll., Springfield, Mass., 1981-82, Baypath Jr. Coll., Longmeadow, Mass., 1982. Author: The Boston Tenant's Guide to Housing, 1975. Mem. ABA, Mass. Bar Assn., Nat. Lawyers Guild. Jewish. Avocations: ballet, boxing, writing. Reporting television news. Home: 3020 Dent Pl NW Washington DC 20007 Office: WRC-TV NBC 4001 Nebraska Ave NW Washington DC 20016

ELION, GARY DOUGLAS, lawyer; b. N.Y.C., Mar. 3, 1947; s. Herbert A. and Sheila (Thall) E.; m. Sally Lloyd, June 30, 1968 (div. Oct. 1979); m. Kathy Dees, Nov. 20, 1979; 1 child, Leslie. BA, Williams Coll., 1969; MBA, Harvard U., 1974; JD, U. San Francisco, 1982. Bar: Calif., U.S. Dist. Ct. (no. dist.) Calif., U.S. Ct. Appeals (9th cir., 3d cir., 5th cir.). Assoc. dir. WNAC-TV, Boston, 1969-70; producer, dir. Westinghouse Broadcasting, Boston, 1970-74; exec. producer WJZ-TV, Balt., 1974-77; news dir. KPIX-TV, San Francisco, 1977-79; assoc. Alioto & Aliotoion, San Francisco, 1982-85, Bianco, Brandi & Jones, San Francisco, 1985-86; ptnr. Sturdevant & Elion, San Francisco, 1986—; cons. Program Devel., San Francisco, 1979-82; gen. counsel Inter Optical Telecommunications, Hyannis, Mass., 1985; dir. Inter Communications and Energy, 1985—. Recipient Emmy award 1979. Mem. Am. Trial Lawyers Assn., Calif. Bar Assn., San Francisco Bar Assn., Barristers Club. Federal civil litigation, State civil litigation, General corporate. Home: 594 48th Ave San Francisco CA 94121 Office: Sturdevant & Elion 120 Montgomery Suite 1800 San Francisco CA 94104

ELISBURG, DONALD EARL, lawyer; b. Chgo., Aug. 1, 1938; s. Herb and Evelyn (Feldman) E.; m. Nancy Meyers, June 26, 1966; children: Andrew, Michelle. BS, Ill. Inst. Tech., 1960; JD, U. Chgo., 1963. Bar: Ill. 1963, U.S. Supreme Ct. 1968, D.C. 1971. Trial atty. U.S. Dept. of Labor, Washington, 1963-70; asst. sec. of labor Washington, 1977-81; gen. counsel, staff dir. senate Labor and Human Resources Commn., Washington, 1970-77; ptnr. Connerton & Bernstern, Washington, 1981-86; adminstr. Occupational Health Legal Rights Found., Washington, 1986—. Bd. of trustees Nat. Capitol YMCA, Washington, 1983-86; vice chmn. Muscle, Inc., 1983—. Mem. ABA (chmn. labor standards com.), Fed. Bar Assn. (chmn. adminstrv. labor law com.), D.C. Bar Assn. (chmn. labor sect., workers compensation com.). Democrat. Jewish. Labor, Legislative, Workers' compensation. Office: 1211 Connecticut Ave NW #414 Washington DC 20036

ELKIN, PAUL STANLEY, lawyer; b. Lafayette, Ind., July 24, 1951; s. Jacob and Ruth (Paul) E.; m. Deane Ava Yaffe, Aug. 22, 1973; children: Matthew S., Stuart L. AB, Ind. U., 1973, JD, 1975. Bar: Ind. 1975. Law clk. to presiding justice Ind. Ct. Appeals, Indpls., 1975-76; ptnr. Dann, Pecar, Newman, Talesnick & Kleiman, Indpls., 1976—. Real property, General corporate. Home: 8949 Sourwood Ct Indianapolis IN 46260 Office: Dann Pecar Newman Talesnick & Kleiman 2300 AUL PO Box 82008 Indianapolis IN 46282

ELKINS, BETTYE SWALES, lawyer; b. San Antonio, Apr. 3, 1941; d. Franklin Easterby and Eddy Bernice (Henderson) Swales; m. Aubrey Christian Elkins, Jr., June 3, 1962; children: Duncan Christian, Ellen Vivian. B.J., U. Tex.-Austin, 1962; J.D., U. Mich., 1970. Bar: Mich. 1971, U.S. Supreme Ct. 1975. Assoc. firm Dykema, Gossett, Spencer, Goodnow & Trigg, Detroit, 1971-78; ptnr. firm Dykema, Gossett, Spencer, Goodnow & Trigg, Ann Arbor, 1978—; asst. prof. law U. Toledo, 1973-74; vis. lectr. U. Mich., 1978-80, 85-86; adj. asst. prof. Wayne State U., 1978-80. Bd. dirs. Met. Hosp., Detroit, Hospice of Washtenaw, Ann Arbor, Ann Arbor Art Assn., 1978-82; trustee Greenhills Sch., Ann Arbor, 1981—. Mem. ABA, Mich. Bar Assn., Am. Hosp. Attys. Acad., Mich. Soc. Hosp. Attys. Democrat. Presbyterian. Health, General corporate. Home: 3791 Waldenwood Dr Ann Arbor MI 48105 Office: 35th Floor 400 Renaissance Ctr Detroit MI 48243

ELL, DOUGLAS WILLIAM, lawyer; b. Manchester, Conn., Aug. 3, 1949; s. William Victor Ell and Joyce Elizabeth (Arnold) Hall; m. Sharon Denise Scott, May 23, 1981; children: Matthew, Christina. BA, M.I.T., 1971; MA, U. Md., 1974; JD, U. Conn., 1979. Bar: D.C. 1979. Assoc. Arnold & Porter, Washington, 1979-82; assoc. Groom & Nordberg, Washington, 1982-86, ptnr., 1986—. Pension, profit-sharing, and employee benefits, Legislative, Corporate taxation. Office: Groom & Nordberg 1775 Pennsylvania Ave NW Washington DC 20006

ELLEBRECHT, MARK GERARD, lawyer; b. St. Louis, July 13, 1954; married Alisse C. Camazine. BBA, St. Louis U., 1976, MBA, JD, 1980. Bar: Mo. 1980, U.S. Dist. Ct. (ea. and we. dists.) Mo. 1980. Assoc. Wolff & Frankel, St. Louis, 1980-83; atty. Mercantile Bank, St. Louis, 1983—. Mem. ABA (young lawyers div., corporations sect.), Bar Assn. Met. St. Louis (chmn.-elect young lawyers sect.). Banking, Contracts commercial, General corporate. Home: 150 Linden Saint Louis MO 63105 Office: Mercantile Bank 721 Locust Saint Louis MO 63101

ELLEFSON, JAMES C., lawyer; b. Boone, Iowa, Dec. 26, 1951; s. Theodore R. and Rebecca J. (Brown) E.; m. Brenda J. Fisher, Aug. 6, 1983. BA, Wartburg Coll., 1974; JD, Drake U., 1977. Bar: Iowa 1977, U.S. Dist. Ct. (no. and so. dists.) Iowa 1977, U.S. Ct. Appeals (8th and D.C. cirs.) 1977, U.S. Supreme Ct. 1983. Law clk. to judge Iowa Ct. Appeals, Des Moines, 1977-78, Iowa Supreme Ct., 1978-79; assoc. Lundy, Butler & Lundy, Eldora, Iowa, 1979-82, ptnr., 1982-85; assoc. Welp, Harrison, Brennecke & Moore, Marshalltown, Iowa, 1985-86, ptnr., 1987—; mem. nominating commn. Jud. Dist. 2B, 1984—. Mem. ABA, Iowa Bar Assn. (bd. govs. 1984—), Marshall County Bar Assn., Assn. Trial Lawyers Am., Assn. Trial Lawyers Iowa, Order of Coif, Order of Barristers. Republican. Lutheran. Avocation: flying. Federal civil litigation, State civil litigation, Personal injury. Home: 2325 S 5th Ave Marshalltown IA 50158 Office: Welp Harrison Brennecke & Moore 302 Masonic Temple Bldg Marshalltown IA 50158

ELLENBERG, MICHAEL ARON, lawyer; b. Flushing, N.Y., Dec. 30, 1951; s. Harold Louis and Lenora (Beck) E.; m. Karen Hutson, May 17, 1980; 1 child, Noah Eli Hutson. BA, SUNY, Albany, 1973; JD, NYU, 1976. Bar: N.Y. 1977, U.S. Dist. Ct. (so. and ea. dists.) N.Y. 1977, U.S. Ct. Appeals (2d cir.) 1981. Staff atty. office of chancellor Bd. Edn., Bklyn., 1976; law clk. to presiding justice N.Y. State Ct. Appellate Div., Bklyn., 1976-77; assoc. LeBoeuf, Lamb, Leiby & MacRae, N.Y.C., 1977-84, ptnr., 1985—. Mem. N.Y. State Bar Assn. Avocations: running, squash, basketball, chess. Insurance, Federal civil litigation, State civil litigation. Office: LeBoeuf Lamb Leiby & MacRae 520 Madison Ave New York NY 10022

ELLENBERGER, JACK STUART, law librarian; b. Lamar, Colo., Sept. 5, 1930; s. Emmert C. and Ruby F. (Overstreet) E. B.S., Georgetown U., 1957; M.L.S., Columbia U., 1959. Law librarian HEW, 1957; librarian Carter, Ledyard & Milburn, N.Y.C., 1957-60, Jones, Day, Reavis & Pogue (and predecessor firm), Cleve., 1960, Bar Assn. of D.C., Washington, 1961-63, Covington & Burling, Washington, 1963-78, Shearman & Sterling, N.Y.C., 1978—. Editor: (with Mahar) Legislative History of the Securities Act of 1933 and the Securities Exchange Act of 1934, 1973. Served with USAF, 1951-54. Mem. Am. Assn. Law Libraries (pres. 1976-77), Spl. Libraries Assn. Librarianship. Office: Shearman & Sterling 53 Wall St New York NY 10005

ELLENBOGEN HANDELSMAN, JOAN, lawyer, accountant; b. Pitts., June 30, 1954; d. Alex and Marjory (Blons) Ellenbogen; m. George B. Handelsman, July 30, 1982; 1 child, Michelle Josephine. BBA summa cum laude, Duquesne U., 1976, JD magna cum laude, 1981. Bar: Pa. 1981, U.S. Dist. Ct. (we. dist.) Pa. 1981, U.S. Tax Ct. 1982, U.S. Supreme Ct. 1985; CPA, Pa. ptnr., acct. Crawford & Ellenbogen, Pitts., 1972—; instr. U. Pitts., 1983. Named one of Outstanding Young Women Am., 1984. Mem. ABA, Am. Inst. CPA's, Pa. Bar Assn., Pa. Inst. CPA's (mem. various coms.), Allegheny County Bar Assn. (mem. various coms.), Estate Planning Council Pitts. Corporate taxation, Personal income taxation, Estate taxation. Office: 2300 Lawyers Bldg Pittsburgh PA 15219

ELLENPORT, ROBERT SAUL, lawyer; b. Irvington, N.J., July 25, 1949; s. Lawrence Reuben and Clara (Milstein) E.; m. Beverly Ida Libes, June 19, 1971; children: Aaron Scott, Rachel Carly. BA cum laude, Amherst Coll., 1971; JD cum laude, NYU, 1974. Bar: N.J. 1975, N.Y. 1975, U.S. Dist. Ct. N.J. 1975, U.S. Dist. Ct. (so. dist.) N.Y. 1975, U.S. Ct. Appeals (3d cir.) 1975, U.S. Dist. Ct. (ea. dist.) N.Y. 1976, U.S. Ct. Appeals (4th cir.) 1980, U.S. Supreme Ct. 1986. Law clk. to presiding judge U.S. Ct. Appeals (3d cir.), 1975; assoc. Kaye, Scholer, Fierman, N.Y.C., 1975-78, Graubard, Moskovitz, N.Y.C., 1978-80, Cole, Scholtz, Rochelle Park, N.J., 1980-82; ptnr. Ellenport & Holsinger, Roseland, N.J., 1982—; pres. Southeastern Casualty N.J., Inc., Livingston, 1985-86; bd. dirs. Harcourt Bindery Inc., Boston, Southeastern Ins. Group, Plantation, Fla. Fin. sec. Temple Beth O'R, Clark, N.J., 1985; counsel Clark Twp. Zoning Bd. Adjustment, 1985—; councilman Clark Twp., N.J., 1987—. Mem. ABA (equal employ oppurtunity com. 1983—), N.J. Bar Assn., N.Y. County Bar Assn., Assn. of Bar of City of N.Y., Order of Coif, NYU Law Alumni Assn. (bd. dirs. 1984—), NYU Law Rev. Alumni Assn. (bd. dirs. 1982-84). Democrat. Jewish. General corporate, Federal civil litigation, Labor. Office: Ellenport & Holsinger PA 75 Livingston Ave Roseland NJ 07068

ELLETT, JOHN SPEARS, II, taxation educator, accountant; b. Richmond, Va., Sept. 17, 1923; s. Henry Guerrant and Elizabeth Firmston (Maxwell) E.; m. Mary Ball Ruffin, Apr. 15, 1950; children—John, Mary Ball, Elizabeth, Martha, Henry. B.A., U. Va., 1948, J.D., 1957, M.A., 1961; Ph.D., U. N.C., 1969; C.P.A., Va., La.; bar: Va. 1957. Lab. instr. U. Va., Charlottesville, 1953-58; instr. Washington and Lee U., 1958-60; asst. prof. U. Fla., 1967-71; assoc. prof. U. New Orleans, 1971-76, prof. taxation, 1976—; trainee Va. Carolina Hardware Co., Richmond, 1948-51; acct. Equitable Life Assurance Soc., Richmond, 1951-52; staff acct. Musselman & Drysdale, Charlottesville, 1952-54; staff acct. R.M. Musselman, Charlottesville, 1957-58; mem. U. New Orleans Oil and Gas Acctg. Conf., 1973—; bd. dirs., publicity chmn., treas. U. New Orleans Estate Planning Seminar, 1975-78, lectr. continuing edn.; CPCU instr. New Orleans Ins. Inst., 1975-78. Served with AUS, 1943-46. Mem. Am. Inst. C.P.A.s, Am. Acctg. Assn., Am. Assn. Atty.-C.P.A.s, Va. Soc. C.P.A.s, La. Soc. C.P.A.s, Va. Bar Assn., New Orleans Estate Planning Council. Democrat. Episcopalian. Author books; contbr. articles to profl. jours. Corporate taxation, Personal income taxation, Estate taxation. Home: 430 Country Club Blvd Slidell LA 70458 Office: U of New Orleans Dept of Acctg New Orleans LA 70148

ELLICKSON, ROBERT CHESTER, legal educator; b. Washington, Aug. 4, 1941; s. John Chester and Katherine Heilprin (Pollak) E.; m. Ellen Zachariasen, Dec. 19, 1971; children—Jenny, Owen. A.B., Oberlin Coll., 1963; LL.B., Yale U., 1966. Bar: D.C. 1967, Calif. 1971. Atty. adviser Pres.'s Com. on Urban Housing, Washington, 1967-68; mgr. urban affairs Levitt & Sons Inc., Lake Success, N.Y., 1968-70; prof. law U. So. Calif., Los Angeles, 1970-81, Stanford U., Calif., 1981—. Legal education, Real property. Office: Stanford U Law Sch Stanford CA 94305

ELLICOTT, JOHN LEMOYNE, lawyer; b. Balt., May 26, 1929; s. Valcoulon LeMoyne and Mary Purnell (Gould) E.; m. Mary Lou Ulery, June 19, 1954; children: Valcoulon, Ann. AB summa cum laude, Princeton U., 1951; LLB cum laude, Harvard U., 1954. Bar: Md. 1954, D.C. 1957, U.S. Supreme Ct. 1959. Assoc. Covington & Burling, Washington, 1958-65, ptnr., 1965—. Pres. Fairfax County Fedn. Citizens Assn., Va., 1964; chmn. governing bd. Nat. Cathedral Sch., Washington, 1980-81; trustee Landon Sch., Bethesda, Md., 1972-76; bd. dirs. Protestant Episcopal Cathedral Found., Washington, 1984—. Mem. ABA, D.C. Bar Assn., Washington Inst. Fgn. Affairs. Democrat. Clubs: Metropolitan, 1925 F St (Washington); Chevy Chase (Md.). Private international, Administrative and regulatory, General corporate. Home: 3210 Macomb St NW Washington DC 20008 Office: Covington & Burling Box 7566 1201 Pennsylvania Ave NW Washington DC 20044

ELLINGER, STEVEN, lawyer; b. Amityville, N.Y., Nov. 1, 1952; s. Ernst and Claire (Kane) E.; m. Barbara Sue Jordan, Nov. 24, 1979. BA, Fairleigh Dickinson U., 1974; JD, South Tex. Coll. of Law, 1978. Bar: Tex. 1978, U.S. Dist. Ct. (so. dist.) Tex. 1979, U.S. Ct. Appeals (5th cir.) 1979, N.Y. 1985, U.S. Supreme Ct. 1985. Assoc. Stauffacher Assocs., Houston, 1978—; bd. dirs. Southwest Harris County Mcpl. Utility Dist. #1, Houston. Editorial bd. mem., contbr. Referee mag., Racine, Wis., 1983—. Mem. capital improvement com. Missouri City (Tex.) Citizens, 1984; bd. dirs. Fonmeadow Property Owners Assn., Houston, 1983-86. Mem. ABA (sports and entertainment industry forum com.), Tex. Bar Assn., Houston Bar Assn., Sports Lawyers Assn., Houston Amateur Basketball Assn. Inc. (bd. dirs. 1984—), Internat. Assn. Approved Basketball Officials Inc. (sec., chmn. constitution com. 1976—). Democrat. Jewish. Avocations: officiating collegiate and international basketball. Contracts commercial, Sports, General practice. Home: 12718 Arbor Ridge Houston TX 77071 Office: 3501 W Alabama Suite 201 Houston TX 77027

ELLINGSWORTH, PATRICK JAMES, lawyer; b. Mpls., Apr. 4, 1948; s. Leo Patrick and Debres A. (Bonner) E.; m. M. Kristine Newman, Sept. 22, 1973; children: Conrad, John, Patrick. BA, St. Johns U., 1970; MA, U. Minn., 1971; JD, U. Chgo., 1974. Bar: Ohio 1974, U.S. Dist. Ct. (no. dist.) Ohio 1974, U.S. Tax Ct. 1978, Minn. 1984. Ptnr. Hahn, Loeser, Freedheim, Dean & Wellman, Cleve., 1974-84; asst. tax counsel The Pillsbury Co., Mpls., 1984—. Trustee Citizens League of Greater Cleve., 1980-84. Mem. ABA (taxation sect., small bus. com., officer 1982—), Tax Execs. Inst. Corporate taxation, Pension, profit-sharing, and employee benefits, State and local taxation. Office: The Pillsbury Co Pillsbury Center Minneapolis MN 55402

ELLIOT, RALPH GREGORY, lawyer; b. Hartford, Conn., Oct. 20, 1936; s. K. Gregory and Zarou (Manoukian) E. BA, Yale U., 1958, LLB, 1961. Bar: Conn. 1961, U.S. Dist. Ct. Conn. 1963, U.S. Ct. Appeals (2d cir.) 1966, U.S. Supreme Ct. 1967. Law clk. to assoc. justice Conn. Supreme Ct., Hartford, 1961-62; assoc. Alcorn, Bakewell & Smith, Hartford, 1962-67, ptnr., 1967-83; ptnr. Tyler, Cooper & Alcorn, Hartford, 1983—; adj. prof. law U. Conn., Hartford, 1973—; sec. Superior Ct. Legal Internship, Conn., 1971—; chmn. Superior Ct. Legal Specialization Screening Com., Conn., 1981—, U.S. Dist. Ct. Panel Spl. Masters, Hartford, 1983—. Chmn. bd. editors Conn. Law Tribune, 1986—. Chmn. U.S. Constn. Bicentennial Commn. Conn. Fellow Am. Bar Found.; mem. ABA (ho. of dels. 1984—), Conn. Bar Assn. (officer 1971-79, bd. govs. 1983-87, pres. 1985-86), Am. Law Inst., Yale Law Sch. Assn. (v.p. 1985—), Phi Beta Kappa. Republican. Episcopalian. Clubs: Yale (pres. 1977-79, Nathan Hale award 1984), Hartford; Grad. (New Haven, Conn.). Federal civil litigation, State civil litigation, Libel. Office: Tyler Cooper & Alcorn City Place 35th Floor Hartford CT 06103-3488

ELLIOTT, A. IRENE, lawyer; b. N.Y.C., Dec. 9, 1944; d. James J. and Elizabeth (Temme) E. B.A. magna cum laude, Bklyn. Coll., 1974; J.D., Bklyn. Law Sch., 1978. Bar: N.Y. 1979, U.S. Dist. Ct. (so. and ea. dists.) N.Y. 1979, U.S. Tax Ct. 1980, U.S. Ct. Appeals (2d cir.) 1981, U.S. Supreme Ct. 1982. Assoc. Silver Feigen & Drucker, N.Y.C., 1979-80; hearing examiner Family Ct., Kings County, N.Y., 1984; sole practice, Bklyn., 1980—; (adminstrv. law judge N.Y.C. Dept. Transp., 1985—. Mem. Bklyn. Bar Assn. (trustee 1984—), Bklyn. Women's Bar Assn. (treas. 1983-84), Kings County Criminal Bar (sec. 1983-86, v.p. 1986—), N.Y. State Bar Assn., N.Y. State Defenders Assn., Phi Beta Kappa, Phi Delta Kappa. Democrat. Roman Catholic. Real property, Family and matrimonial, Criminal. Office: 50 Court St Brooklyn NY 11201

ELLIOTT, BRADY GIFFORD, lawyer, municipal judge; b. Harlingen, Tex., Nov. 26, 1943; s. Clyde Andres Elliott and Mildred (Parker) Bounds; m. Rhea Elizabeth Ricks, May 15, 1967; children—Adrian Winthrope, Jason Lawrence. B.B.A., McMurray Coll., 1970; J.D., S. Tex. Coll. Law, 1973. Bar: Tex. 1973, U.S. Dist. Ct. (so. dist.) Tex. 1974, U.S. Tax Ct. 1974, U.S. Ct. Appeals (5th cir.) 1974, U.S. Supreme Ct. 1979, U.S. Ct. Appeals (11th cir.) 1981. Asst. sec., asst. treas., asst. gen. counsel Gordon Jewelry Corp., Houston, 1970-79; sec., gen. counsel Oshman's Sporting Goods, Inc., Houston, 1979-82; sole practice, Sugar Land, Tex., 1982—; legal counsel Ft. Bend C. of C., Stafford, Tex., 1982—; mcpl. judge Missouri City, Tex., 1983—. Vice pres., bd. dirs. Ft. Bend chpt. Texans' War on Drugs, Sugar Land, 1981—; bd. dirs. Ft. Bend Boys Choir, 1984—. Mem. ABA, Houston Bar Assn. Republican. Baptist. Lodges: Masons; Rotary (treas. 1983—). General corporate, Contracts commercial, Real property. Office: Suite 360 Southwestern Bank Plaza 12603 SW Freeway Stafford TX 77477

ELLIOTT, CLIFTON LANGSDALE, lawyer; b. Kansas City, Mo., Oct. 26, 1938; s. John M. and Kate (Langsdale) E.; m. Bronwyn A. Reese, Mar. 30, 1963 (div.); children—Evan R., Kate L. B.A., Dartmouth Coll., 1960; J.D., Northwestern U., 1963. Bar: Mo. 1963, U.S. Dist. Ct. (we. dist.) Mo. 1963, U.S. Ct. Appeals (2d and 9th cirs.) 1980, U.S. Ct. Appeals (4th cir.) 1968, U.S. Ct. Appeals (8th cir.) 1965, U.S. Ct. Appeals (10th cir.) 1975, U.S. Ct. Appeals (D.C. cir.) 1973, U.S. Supreme Ct. 1979. Assoc., Spencer, Fane, Britt & Browne, Kansas City, Mo., 1963-79, Roan & Grossman, Kansas City, 1979-81; ptnr. Elliott & Kaiser, Kansas City, 1981—; instr. labor law U. Mo., 1966; mem. U.S. C. of C. Nat. Labor Relations Act Task Force, 1980—. Mem. ABA, Mo. Bar, Kansas City Bar Assn., Am. Soc. Hosp. Attys. (ad hoc com. labor relations 1975—). Contbr. articles to profl. jours. Labor. Office: 1550 City Center Sq 1100 Main St PO Box 26190 Kansas City MO 64196

ELLIOTT, DARRELL STANLEY, lawyer; b. Denver, May 11, 1953; s. Frank and Mattie (Wynn) E. BA, U. Denver, 1975, JD, 1978. Bar: Colo. 1980, U.S. Dist. Ct. Colo. 1980. Landman Anaconda, Denver, 1978-80; land acquisitions supr., counsel Gold Fields Mining, Lakewood, Colo., 1980-81; regional land mgr., counsel Union Oil Co. Calif., Los Angeles; Casper, Wyo.; Parachute, Colo., 1981-84; owner, prin. Darrell S. Elliott, P.C. Attys. at Law, Denver, 1984—. Mem. ABA, Colo. Bar Assn., Denver Bar Assn., Rocky Mountain Mineral Law Found., Assn. Trial Lawyers Am. Entertainment, Oil and gas leasing, General corporate. Office: 50 S Steele Suite 777 Denver CO 80209

ELLIOTT, EDWIN DONALD, JR., law educator; b. Chgo., Apr. 4, 1948; s. Edwin Donald and Mary Jane (Bope) E.; m. Geraldine Gennet (div. 1980); m. Mary Ellen Savage, Nov. 22, 1980; children: Eve Christina, Ian Donald. BA, Yale U., 1970, JD, 1974. Bar: D.C. 1975, U.S. Dist. Ct. D.C. 1975, U.S. Ct. Appeals (2d cir.) 1982. Law clk. to judge U.S. Dist. Ct. D.C., Washington, 1974-75, U.S. Ct. Appeals, Washington, 1975-76; assoc. Leva, Hawes et al, Washington, 1976-80; assoc. prof. law Yale U., New Haven, 1981-84, prof. law, 1984—; cons. Overseas Pvt. Investment Corp., Washington, 1983-85, Adminstrv. Conf. U.S., 1987—; spl. litigation counsel Gen. Electric Co., Fairfield, Conn., 1985—; faculty affiliate Inst. for Health Policy Analysis, Georgetown U., Washington. Contbr. articles on evolutionary theories of law, constl. law, environ. and toxic tort law to profl. jours. Mem. ABA (vice chmn. com. on separation of powers 1985—). Environment, Administrative and regulatory, Federal civil litigation. Home: 81 McKinley Ave New Haven CT 06515 Office: Yale Law Sch 401A Yale Station New Haven CT 06520

ELLIOTT, FRANK WALLACE, lawyer, foundation executive; b. Cotulla, Tex., June 25, 1930; s. Frank Wallace and Eunice Marie (Akin) E.; m. Winona Trent, July 3, 1954 (dec. 1981); 1 dau., Harriet Lindsey; m. Kay Elkins, Aug. 15, 1983. Student, N.Mex. Mil. Inst., 1947-49; B.A., U. Tex., 1951, LL.B., 1957. Bar: Tex. 1957. Asst. atty. gen. State of Tex., 1957; briefing atty. Supreme Ct. Tex., 1957-58; prof. U. Tex. Law Sch., 1958-77; dean, prof. law Tex. Tech U. Sch. Law, 1977-80; pres. Southwestern Legal Found., 1980-86; ptnr. Baker, Smith & Mills, Dallas, 1987—; parliamentarian Tex. Senate, 1969-73; dir. research Tex. Constl. Revision Commn., 1973. Author: Texas Judicial Process, 2d edit, 1977, Texas Trial and Appellate Practice, 2d edit, 1974, Cases on Evidence, 1980, West's Texas Forms, 20 vols, 1977—. Served with U.S. Army, 1951-53, 73-74. Decorated Purple Heart, Meritorious Service medal, Army Commendation medal. Mem. Am. Bar Assn., Judge Advs. Assn., Am. Judicature Soc., Am. Bar Found., Tex. Bar Found., Am. Law Inst., Southwestern Legal Found. (trustee). Federal civil litigation, State civil litigation, Private international. Home: 7710 Scotia Dr Dallas TX 75248 Office: 500 LTV Center 2001 Ross Ave Dallas TX 75201

ELLIOTT, HOMER LEE, lawyer; b. Madison, Ind., Aug. 3, 1938; s. William A. and Mabel E. (Talbot) E.; m. Judith A. Langley, Sept. 2, 1964; children—Homer, Charles, Jane. A.B., Ind. U., 1960; postgrad. Princeton U., 1960-61; J.D., Coll. William and Mary, 1969. Bar: Va. 1969, D.C. 1970, Pa. 1977, U.S. Supreme Ct. 1973, U.S. Tax Ct. 1971. Assoc., Steptoe & Johnson, Washington, 1969-77; ptnr. Drinker Biddle & Reath, Phila., 1977—. Served with U.S. Army, 1961-65. Mem. ABA, Pa. Bar Assn., D.C. Bar Assn., VA State Bar, Phi Beta Kappa. Club: Princeton (Phila). Contbr. articles to profl. jours. Pension, profit-sharing, and employee benefits, Corporate taxation, Personal income taxation. Home: 688 Thomas Jefferson Rd Wayne PA 19087 Office: 1100 Philadelphia National Bank Bldg Philadelphia PA 19107

ELLIOTT, IVAN A., lawyer; b. White County, Ill., Nov. 18, 1889; s. Benjamin Franklin and Nellie B. (Stroup) E.; m. Malen Stinson, Oct. 12, 1922; children—Ivan A., Norman J. Student, Ill. Wesleyan Acad., 1909-11, U. Ill., 1913; LL.B., Ill. Wesleyan U., 1916. Bar: Ill. 1917, U.S. Dist. Ct. (so. dist.) Ill. 1922, U.S. Ct. Appeals (7th cir.) 1930, U.S. Supreme Ct. 1953. Ptnr. Conger & Elliott, Carmi, Ill., 1919-49, 53-78, 78-86; dir. White County Abstract Co., White County Democratic Tribune; asst. atty. gen. State of Ill., 1932-40, atty. gen., 1949-53; city atty. City of Carmi, 1933-43; states atty. White County, Carmi, 1936-42; Home service sec. White County ARC, 1923-43; pres. grade sch. bd. Carmi Twp. 1933-43; Dem. state cen. committeeman 24th Congl. Dist., Ill., 1932-40. Served to lt. col., U.S. Army, 1917-1918, 1942-44, ETO. Mem. Ill. Bar Assn., ABA, White County Bar Assn., Chgo. Bar Assn., Carmi C. of C., White County Hist. Soc., Am. Legion (comdr. 1920-21, post service officer 1920-42), VFW, Sigma Phi Epsilon, Phi Alpha Delta. Presbyterian. Lodges: Kiwanis (pres. 1933), Elks. General practice, State civil litigation, Probate. Home: 206 S 3d St Carmi IL 62821 Office: Farm Bur Bldg Carmi IL 62821

ELLIOTT, IVAN A., JR., lawyer; b. Carmi, Ill., Oct. 31, 1923; s. Ivan A. and Malen (Stinson) E.; m. Lauralynn Parkerson, Sept. 17, 1950; children: Cynthia Ann, Rebecca Sue Griffin, Marjorie Kay. BA, U. Ill., 1948, LLD, 1950. Bar: Ill. 1950, U.S. Dist. Ct. (so. dist.) Ill. 1954, U.S. Ct. Appeals (7th cir.) 1959, U.S. Supreme Ct. 1967. Ptnr., pres. Conger & Elliott, P.C. and predecessor firm Conger & Elliott, Carmi, 1952—; bd. dirs. 1st Nat. Bank, Carmi, Tecumseh Internat. Corp., Carmi Area Indsl. Corp., Carmi Times Pub. Co., v.p. 1966-74, White County Abstract Co., pres. 1966—; asst. atty. gen. State of Ill., 1961-68; atty. City of Carmi, 1960-61. Contbr. articles to profl. jours. Mem. Ednl. Service Region Study Commn., 1979; gen. counsel Presbytery Southern Ill., 1965-71, 72-76, 79—, trustee, 1962-65, 72-76, 79—, pres. bd. trustees, 1972-76, 79—, State Us. Civil Service System, 1968—, chmn. 1969-78, 81—, Bd. Higher Edn., 1973-77; moderator Presbytery Southeastern Ill., 1982-83; trustee Southern Ill. U., 1967—, chmn. 1973-77, Police Pension Fund City of Carmi, 1957—, pres. 1957—; bd. dirs. Southern Ill. U. Found., 1968—, exec. com., 1970—, McKinely Found. at U. Ill., 1954-71. Served to lt. col. U.S. Army, 1942-46, 50-52, ETO. Recipient Kathryn G. Hansen award U.S. Civil Service System Ill., 1972. Fellow Am. Coll. Probate Counsel; mem. ABA, Ill. Bar Assn. (com. on publs. 1979—, chmn. 1986—, sec. exec. com. legal edn. 1955-57, subcom. merchantability of title real estate sect., various others), White County Bar Assn. (sec. 1960-64), Southeastern Ill. Bar Assn., Fedn. Local Bar Assn. Ill. (pres. so. div. 5th dist. 1965-66), Am. Judicature Soc., Ill. Inst. for Continuing Edn. (trustee 1956-58), VFW, Am. Legion (post judge adv. 1957—), Ill. Oil and Gas Assn., Wabash Valley Assn., Carmi C. of C. (pres. 1955-56, Outstanding Citizen of Yr. award 1981), Order of Coif, Phi Beta Kappa, Phi Kappa Phi, Phi Alpha Delta, Sigma Phi Epsilon. Democrat. Lodges: Kiwanis (pres. Carmi 1957, sec. 1953-56), Elks. Probate, Estate taxation, State civil litigation. Home: 806 W Kerney St Carmi IL 62821 Office: Conger & Elliott PC Farm Bur Bldg W Robinson St Carmi IL 62821

ELLIOTT, J. VICTOR, lawyer; b. Fredericksburg, Va., Apr. 6, 1954; s. David Nathaniel and Suzanne (Hill) E.; m. Linda Sue Melnick, July 17, 1977; children: Troy Steffen, Jon Trevor, Timothy Quinn. BA in Psychology, Columbia Union Coll., 1976; JD, Potomac Sch. Law, 1981. Bar: Ga. 1982, U.S. Dist. Ct. (no. dist.) Ga. 1982, Md. 1984. Surveyor Security Reporting Co., Ellicott City, Md., 1976-77; claims rep. United Ins. Service Inc., Washington, 1977-81; asst. mgr. claims Gencon Risk Mgmt. Service, Takoma Park, Md., 1981-83, mgr. hosp. liability claims, 1983-84, legal counsel, 1984-86; sr. legal counsel Risk Mgmt. Service Seventh-Day Adventists, Takoma Park, 1986—. Mem. ABA, Ga. Bar Assn., Md. Bar Assn., Fed. Bar Assn., Howard County Bar Assn., Assn. Trial Lawyers Am., Def. Research Inst., Nat. Notary Assn. Mem. Seventh-Day Adventists Ch. Insurance, Personal injury, General practice. Home: 6317 Dewey Dr Atholton Manor MD 21044-3910 Office: Risk Mgmt Service Seventh-Day Adventists 6930 Carroll Ave Takoma Park MD 20912-4494

ELLIOTT, JAMES ROBERT, Judge; b. Gainesville, Ga., Jan. 1, 1910; s. Thomas M. and Mamie Lucille (Glenn) E.; m. Brownie C. Buck, Aug. 3, 1949; children: Susan G., James Robert. Ph.B., Emory U., 1930, LL.B., 1934. Bar: Ga. 1934. Practiced law Columbus, Ga., 1934-62; judge U.S. Dist. Ct. for Middle Dist. Ga., Columbus, 1962—; Mem. Ga. Ho. of Reps., 1937-43, 47-49; Democratic nat. committeeman, 1948-56. Served as lt. USNR, 1943-46, PTO. Mem. Ga. Bar Assn., Lambda Chi Alpha, Phi Delta Phi, Omicron Delta Kappa. Lodge: Kiwanis. Home: 2612 Carson Dr Columbus GA 31906 Office: PO Box 2017 Columbus GA 31902 *

ELLIOTT, JAMES SEWELL, lawyer; b. Augusta, Ga., Dec. 30, 1922; s. Lester Franklin and Frances (Sewell) E.; m. Mary Jones Grace, June 25, 1947; children: James Sewell Jr., Lester Franklin III, Walter Grace, Randolph Squire, Robert Bruce. BS, The Citadel, 1943, U.S. Mil. Acad., 1946; JD, Mercer U., 1952. Bar: Ga. 1952, U.S. Dist. Ct. (mid. dist.) Ga. 1953, U.S. Ct. Appeals (11th cir.) 1953, U.S. Supreme Ct. 1959. Asst. U.S. atty. U.S. Dist. Ct. (mid. dist.) Ga., Macon, 1953-57; prin. Law Offices of J. Sewell Elliott, Macon, Ga., 1957—. Mem. Ga. Ho. of Reps. 107th dist., Atlanta, 1966; chmn. exec. com. Bibb County Reps., Macon, 1985. Served to maj. U.S. Army, 1946-50. Mem. ABA, Ga. Bar Assn., Macon Bar Assn. Episcopalian. Lodge: Kiwanis (pres. Macon). General practice, General corporate, State civil litigation. Office: 506 Fulton Fed Bldg Macon GA 31201

ELLIOTT, JOHN DEWEY, lawyer; b. Charleston, W.Va., July 14, 1948; s. John Franklin and Anne Marie (Petticrew) E. BJ, U. Mo., 1970; JD, U. S.C., 1977. Bar: S.C. 1977, U.S. Dist. Ct. S.C. 1978, U.S. Ct. Appeals (4th cir.) 1982. Children's atty. family ct. Richland County, Columbia, S.C., 1978-80; dir. Alston Wilkes Advocacy for Youth, Columbia, 1980-82; sole practice Columbia, 1982—; cons. Gov.'s Sentencing Guidelines Commn., Columbia, 1984. Pres. S.C. Coalition for Choice, Columbia, 1981-82; mem. exec. bd. S.C. chpt. ACLU, Columbia, 1981-83; pres. Council on Child Abuse, Columbia, 1984-85; adv. Joint Legis. Com. on Children, Columbia, 1979—. Mem. ABA (vice chmn. juvenile justice com. criminal justice sect. 1982-83, Pro Bono Publico award 1985), S.C. Bar Assn. (chmn. family law sect. 1984-85, chmn. com. on legal needs of children 1984—). Family and matrimonial, Juvenile, Personal injury. Office: 1136 Washington St Columbia SC 29201

ELLIOTT, JOHN MICHAEL, lawyer; b. Girardville, Pa., July 8, 1941; s. John T. and Clair C. E.; children: John P., Heather D., Kirwan B., Kyle M. A.B. in Econs. magna cum laude, St. Vincent Coll., 1963, LL.D. (hon.), 1985; LL.B. cum laude, Georgetown U., 1966. Bar: Pa. 1966, U.S. Dist. Ct. (ea. dist.) Pa. 1967, U.S. Ct. Appeals (3d cir.) 1967, U.S. Supreme Ct. 1968, U.S. Dist. Ct. (we. dist.) Pa. 1986. Sr. ptnr. Dilworth, Paxson, Kalish & Kauffman, Phila., 1968-86, Baskin, Flaherty, Elliott & Mannino, 1986—;

mem. Phila. Coal Rail Task Force, Rockefeller Commn., White House Coal Adv. Commn., 1980; bd. dirs. James A. Finnegan Fellowship Found., Irish Ednl. Devel. Found. Inc., chmn.; mem. Pa. Citizens Adv. Council Dept. Environ Resources, 1970-78, chmn. urban com.; mem. environ quality bd. Commonwealth of Pa., 1970-78; commr. Del. River Port Authority; rep. auditor gen. Robert P. Casen; mem. Phila. City Planning Commn., 1970-75, Del. Valley Citizens Council for Clean Air.; chmn. Disciplinary Bd. Supreme Ct. Pa., 1985-86, vice chmn., 1985, chmn. rules com., 1982. Contbr. articles to profl. jours. Williston research fellow, 1965. Mem. ABA (lectr. on trial practice), Pa. Bar Assn. (ho. of dels. 1983, task force on civil ct. rules), Pa. Bar. Inst. (course planner, faculty), Am. Law Inst. (ABA appellate practice program), Nat. Inst. Trial Advocacy (lectr.), Fed. Bar Assn., Phila Bar Assn. (environ. quality com.), Nat. Lawyers Com. for Civil Rights Under Law, Braehon Law Soc., NACCP (legal def. com.), Friendly Sons of St. Patrick, Pa. Hist. Soc., Chestnut Hill Community Assn., John Buchan Soc. Edinborough, Mil. History Soc. Ireland. State civil litigation, Antitrust, Constitutional law. Home: 6001 Cricket Rd Flourtown PA 19031 Office: Baskin Flaherty Elliott & Mannino 1800 Three Mellon Bank Ctr Philadelphia PA 19102

ELLIOTT, JOSEPH BRYAN, lawyer; b. Roanoke Rapids, N.C., Mar. 12, 1949; s. G.H. and Mamie Marie (Nash) E., Miriam Renee Adderholdt, Aug. 10, 1985. BA in History, U. N.C., 1971, JD, 1975. Bar: N.C. 1975, U.S. Dist. Ct. (we. dist.) N.C., 1977. Assoc. Samuel D. Smith, Hickory, N.C., 1976-79; sole practice Hickory, 1979—. Mem. ABA, N.C. Bar Assn. (bankruptcy and criminal law sect.), N.C. Acad. Trial Lawyers, N.C. Coll. Advocacy, Hickory Jaycees, Inc. (assoc.). Democrat. Roman Catholic. Avocations: jogging, reading history. Bankruptcy, Criminal, General practice. Office: PO Box 2710 620 4th St SW Hickory NC 28603

ELLIOTT, RICHARD HOWARD, lawyer; b. Astoria, N.Y., Apr. 30, 1933; s. Alexander and Elsie (Saphire) E.; m. Judith A. Kessler, Dec. 26, 1956; children—Marc Evan, Jonathan Hugh, Eve; m. 2d, Diane S. Schaefer, Nov. 18, 1978; children—Alexis, Sara Jane, Benjamin, David. B.S., Lehigh U., 1954; J.D. cum laude, U. Pa., 1962. Bar: U.S. Dist. Ct. (ea. dist.) Pa. 1962, Pa. Supreme Ct. 1962, U.S. Ct. Appeals (3d cir.) 1963, U.S. Dist. Ct. (mid. dist.) Pa. 1976. Assoc. Clark, Ladner, Fortenbaugh & Young, Phila., 1962-69; ptnr., 1970-75; ptnr. Cotlar, Aglow & Elliott, Doylestown, Pa., 1976—; bd. dirs. Bucks County Soc. Prevention Cruelty to Animals. Gen. counsel Pa. Soc. Prevention Cruelty to Animals. Mem. Pa. Nav. Commn., 1977-80. Served as lt. USN, 1954-59. Mem. ABA, Pa. Bar Assn., Phila. Bar Assn., Bucks County Bar Assn. Democrat. Federal civil litigation, General corporate, Probate. Home: 1205 Victoria Rd Warminster PA 18974 Office: Cotlar Aglow & Elliott 1795 S Easton Rd Doylestown PA 18901

ELLIOTT, SAM DAVIS, lawyer; b. Chattanooga, Tenn., July 31, 1956; s. Charles Eugene and Mary Ruth (Davis) E.; m. Karen Marie Honkanen, Mar. 2, 1985. BA, U. of the South, 1978; JD, U. Tenn., 1981. Bar: Tenn. 1981, U.S. Dist. Ct. (ea. dist.) Tenn. 1982, U.S. Ct. Appeals (6th cir.) 1985, U.S. Ct. Appeals (11th cir.) 1987. Law clk. to U.S. magistrate Tenn. State Ct., Chattanooga, 1981-82; assoc. Gearhiser, Peters & Horton, Chattanooga, 1982—. Mem. ABA, Tenn. Bar Assn., Chattanooga Bar Assn., Tenn. Trial Lawyers Assn. Methodist. Personal injury, General practice. Office: Gearhiser Peters & Horton 801 Chestnut Chattanooga TN 37402

ELLIOTT, STEPHEN K., lawyer; b. Southington, Conn., Dec. 22, 1910; s. Richard and Rosamond (Kenny) E.; m. Ruth Holcomb, June 24, 1939; children—Stephen K., Miriam E. Keefe, Rosemary E. DeLoach. Student Holy Cross Coll., 1927-30; AB, Trinity Coll., 1932; J.D., U. Conn., 1937. Bar: Conn., U.S. Dist. Ct. Conn., U.S. Supreme Ct. Judge Town Ct. of Southington, 1946-49; probate judge Dist. of Southington, 1949-66; ptnr. Elliott, Forgione & Stanek, Southington, 1966—. Trustee Bradley Meml. Hosp., Southington, 1948-85 ; naval aide to 3 Conn. govs. Served to lt. USN, 1943-46. Mem. ABA, Conn. Bar Assn., Internat. Soc. Barristers, Am. Coll. Probate Counsel. Democrat. Roman Catholic. Clubs: Waterbury Country, Southington Country, Elks. General corporate, Estate planning, Probate. Office: Elliott Forgione Stanek PO Box 578 Southington CT 06489

ELLIOTT, WILLIAM HOMER, JR., lawyer; b. Washington, Mar. 21, 1918; s. William Homer and Mildred Crawford (Stier) E.; m. Patricia Mary Seitz, June 28, 1950; children—Margaret Ann, W. Crawford. A.B., Wesleyan U., 1940; J.D., George Washington U., 1950. Bar: Pa. 1952, U.S. Sup. Ct. 1960. Chemist, Innis Spieden & Co., N.Y.C., 1940-42; pat. adv. Dept. Justice, Washington, 1946-50; assoc. Synnestvedt & Lechner, Phila., 1950-57, ptnr., 1957—, sr. ptnr., 1969—. Served to lt. comdr. USNR, 1942-46; PTO. Mem. ABA (council sect. at 1980-84, council sect. patents 1982-86), Phila. Bar Assn., Am. Pat. Law Assn., Phila. Pat. Law Assn. (pres. 1982), U.S. Trademark Assn., Patent and Trademark Inst. Can., Internat. Pat. and Trademark Assn. Clubs: Huntingdon Valley (Pa.) Country; Racquet (Phila.); Univ. (Washington). Antitrust, Patent, Trademark and copyright. Home: 801 Crosswicks Rd Jenkintown PA 19046 Office: 2600 One Reading Ctr 1101 Market St Philadelphia PA 19107

ELLIOTT, WILLIAM MCBURNEY, lawyer; b. Preeceville, Sask., Can., Aug. 8, 1922; s. William Stanley and Jean (McBurney) E.; m. Margaret Anderson Esson, May 30, 1946; children—Frances Jean McVea, William Stewart. LL.B., U. Sask., 1949. Bar: Sask. 1950. Assoc., MacPherson, Leslie & Tyerman, Regina, Sask., Can., 1949-62, ptnr., 1963—; apptd. queen's counsel, 1965; dir. Toronto-Dominion Bank, Ipoco, Inc.Potash Corp. Sask., Petro-Can. Producers Pipelines, Inc. Served with RCAF, 1942-46. Fellow Am. Coll. Trial Lawyers; mem. Internat. Bar Assn., Canadian Bar Assn. (past provincial pres.), Regina Bar Assn. (past pres.). Progressive Conservative. Clubs: Assiniboia, Wascana, Desert Island (Rancho Mirage, Calif.), Royal United Services Inst. Federal civil litigation, State civil litigation, General corporate. Office: MacPherson Leslie & Tyerman, 2161 Scarth St, Regina, SK Canada S4P 2V4

ELLIS, ALAN, lawyer; b. Phila., Nov. 17, 1943; s. Max and Mildred (Sladovsky) E.; m. Lianne Cordero Scherr, June 1, 1975; 1 dau., Amanda Ellis-Scherr. B.A., Pa. State U., 1964; J.D., Villanova U., 1967. Bar: Pa. 1968, U.S. Dist. Ct. (ea. dist.) Pa. 1968, U.S. Supreme Ct. 1978, U.S. Dist. Ct. (mid. dist.) Pa. 1979, U.S. Ct. Appeals (3d cir.) 1980, U.S. Ct. Appeals (11th cir.) 1982, U.S. Ct. Appeals (5th cir.) 1983, U.S. Ct. Appeals (2d cir.) 1986. Law clk. U.S. Dist. Ct. (ea. dist.) Pa., Phila., 1967-69; instr. in law Wharton Sch. Bus. and Fin., U.Pa., 1969-70; asst. prof. law Golden Gate U., 1970-71; ptnr. Ellis & Newman, P.C., Phila., 1971—; lectr. criminal def. seminars; mem. lawyers com. Amnesty Internat.; mem. Internat. Commn. Jurists. Named 1 of 82 People to Watch in '82, Phila. Mag., 1982. Mem. Internat. Bar Assn., Inter-Am. Bar Assn., ABA, Pa. Bar Assn., Phila. Bar Assn., Nat. Assn. Criminal Def. Lawyers (Presdl. commendation 1982, 84, Exec. Com. Award 1986, Robert C. Heeney Meml. award 1983, bd. dirs. 1981-85, sec. 1985, 3d v.p. 1986—), Young Lawyers Internat. Assn., Internat. Lawyers Alliance for Human Rights. Contbr. articles to profl. jours.; editor Villanova Law Rev., 1965-67; mem. ethics adv. bd. Pa. Law Jour., 1980—; editorial adv. bd. Drug Law Report, 1982—; mem. editorial adv. bd. Criminal Law Manual, Bur. Nat. Affairs, 1987—. Criminal, Private international, Public international. Home: 200 Locust St Apt 22-B Philadelphia PA 19106 Office: Ellis & Newman 9th and Chestnut Suite 400 Philadelphia PA 19107

ELLIS, BOBBY JAMES, lawyer; b. Gainesboro, Tenn., Oct. 14, 1941; s. Langford Charlie and Mamie (Bowman) E.; m. Ali June Zachary, Aug. 7, 1968; 1 child, Misty Dawn. BS, Tenn. Tech. U., 1965; JD, Nashville YMCA Law Sch., 1976. Bar: Tenn. 1976, U.S. Dist. Ct. (mid. dist.) 1980. Auditor State of Tenn., Nashville, 1965-66, auditor, legis. aid, 1969-76; sales rep. Columbia (Tenn.) Mill, 1966-67; sole practice Gainesboro, 1976—. Dem. chmn., Jackson County, Tenn., 1978—. Served with U.S. Army, 1967-69. Mem. ABA, Tenn. Bar Assn., Tenn. Trial Lawyers Assn., 7 County Bar Assn. (pres. 1984-86), Am. Legion (Gainseboro comdr. 1978-80). Lodges: Rotary (local pres. 1984-86), Tanneshill, Al Menah Temple (Ambassador 1984-85). Avocation: collecting Indian artifacts. Family and matrimonial, Criminal, Personal injury. Office: 111 S Union PO Box 192 Gainesboro TN 38562

ELLIS, COURTENAY, lawyer; b. Cottingham, Eng., Jan. 4, 1946. BA, Oxford U., Eng., 1967, MA, 1974; LLM, George Washington U., 1972. Bar: D.C. 1970. Ptnr. Akin, Gump, Strauss, Hauer & Feld, Washington. Office: Akin Gump Strauss Hauer et al 1333 New Hampshire Ave NW #400 Washington DC 20036 *

ELLIS, DAVID DALE, lawyer; b. Columbus, Ga., Dec. 22, 1952; s. Audie Stammattee and Eva Grace (Thomas) E. B.A. cum laude Mercer U., Macon, Ga., 1974; J.D., Drake U., 1976, M.P.A., 1977. Bar: Iowa 1977, Ga. 1978, U.S. Dist. Ct. (no. dist.) Ga. 1979, U.S. Ct. Appeals (11th cir.) 1979, U.S. Supreme Ct. 1983, Tex. 1986. Instr. Grad. Sch., Drake U., Des Moines, 1977; claims adjuster Farm Bur. Ins. Co., Des Moines, 1977; assoc. firm Cotton, White & Palmer, Atlanta, 1978-82; mng. atty. Hyatt Legal Services, Marietta and Smyrna, Ga., 1982-84, regional ptnr., Houston, 1984-86; sr. assoc. Hughes & Hilbert P.C., 1986-87, Jeffers & Ellis, P.C., Houston, 1987—. Career awareness chmn. Houston council Boy Scouts Am., 1984-85; instr. project bus., legal adviser Jr. Achievement, Houston, 1984-85. Mem. Iowa Bar Assn., Ga. Bar Assn., State Bar Tex., Am. Soc. Tng. and Devel., Atlanta Jaycees (chmn. Empty Stockings Fund 1982, v.p. individual devel. 1983-84; Officer of Yr. 1984), U.S. Jaycees (life, ambassador award 1985, named JCI senator), Houston Jaycees (exec. v.p. 1986—, chmn. govt. affairs 1984-85, pres. 1987—), Tex. Jaycees (legal counsel 1985—), ABA (bankruptcy com. 1985—). Lodge: Masons. General practice, Bankruptcy. Office: Jeffers & Ellis PC 3013 Fountainview #275 Houston TX 77057

ELLIS, DONALD LEE, lawyer; b. Dallas, Oct. 2, 1950; s. Truett T. and Rosemary (Tarrant) E.; m. Barbara Jo Moss, June 5, 1977; children—Angela Nicole, Laura Elizabeth, Natalie Dawn. B.S., U. Tulsa, 1973; J.D., Oklahoma City U., 1976. Bar: Tex. 1979, Okla. 1977, U.S. Dist. Ct. (ea. dist.) Tex. 1978, U.S. Dist. Ct. (we. dist.) Okla. 1978, U.S. Ct. Appeals (5th cir.) 1984, U.S. Supreme Ct., 1984, U.S. Ct. Appeals (11th cir.). Spl. agt. FBI, Washington, 1976-78; asst. dist. atty. Smith County, Tyler, Tex., 1979-80; mem. firm Barron & Ellis, Tyler, 1980-84, Woods, Ellis & Tyler, 1984-85, Ellis & Woods, Tyler, 1985-86; sole practice, Tyler, 1986—. Bd. dirs. Mental Health Assn., Tyler, 1983—. Mem. Tex. Bar Assn., Okla. Bar Assn., Smith County Bar Assn., Soc. Former Spl. Agts. FBI, Tex. Trial Lawyers Assn., FBI Agents Assn. Personal injury, Environment, Workers' compensation. Home: 3209 Lakepine Cir Tyler TX 75707 Office: PO Box 131221 Tyler TX 75713-1221

ELLIS, EDWARD PRIOLEAU, lawyer; b. Atlanta, May 31, 1929; s. Frampton E. and Eloise (Oliver) E.; m. Harriet L. Witham, Sept. 5, 1954; children: Harriet, Edward, Andrew. AB cum laude, U. Ga., 1951; LLB, Harvard U., 1956. Bar: Ga. 1956. Ptnr. Ellis, Moore & Simons, Atlanta, 1976—; pres. First Security and Exchange Co., Atlanta, 1965—. Pres. Peachtree Heights Civic Assn., Atlanta, 1985. Served to 1st lt. U.S. Army, 1952-54. Fellow Am. Coll. Probate Counsel; mem. Ga. Bar Assn. (chmn. taxation sect.), Phi Beta Kappa. Estate taxation, Probate, Personal income taxation. Home: 2804 Habersham Rd NW Atlanta GA 30305 Office: Ellis Moore & Simons 134 Peachtree St Suite 700 Atlanta GA 30303

ELLIS, EMORY NELSON, JR., lawyer; b. Washington, Nov. 13, 1929; s. Emory Nelson Sr. and Sadie (Morris) E.; m. Helen Jean Hargrove; children: Teresa M. Ellis Brown, Christopher A., Timothy J., Brian D., Emory Nelson III. BS, Georgetown U., 1952, LLB, 1958. Bar: D.C. 1958, U.S. Dist. Ct. D.C. 1958, U.S. Ct. Appeals (D.C. cir.) 1958, U.S. Supreme Ct. 1975. Assoc. Law Office of A.L. Wheeler, Washington, 1958-61; atty. CAB, Washington, 1961-70, exec. asst. to chmn., 1968-70; exec. sec. Adminstrn. Conf. of U.S., Washington, 1970-71; ptnr. Fulbright & Jaworski, Washington, 1971—; rep. steering com. U.S. internat. air transport policy CAB, 1968-69; mem. com. procedural reform CAB, 1973-74; bd. dirs. KHEMCO Energy Corp., Washington, 1983—. Served to lt. USNR, 1952-55. Mem. ABA (vice chmn. aviation com. pub. utility sect.), Fed. Bar Assn., Aero Club Washington, Internat. Aviation Club. Democrat. Roman Catholic. Administrative and regulatory, Transportation. Office: Fulbright & Jaworski 1150 Connecticut Ave NW Washington DC 20036

ELLIS, GEORGE DAWLIN, lawyer; b. Little Rock, June 26, 1946; s. Dawlin C. and Joan Marie (Savage) E.; m. Selena T. Duncan, Jan. 25, 1969; children: John Andrew, Mary Elizabeth. BA, Little Rock U., 1969; JD, U. Ark., 1972. Bar: Ark. 1972, U.S. Dist. Ct. (ea. dist.) Ark. 1972, U.S. Ct. Appeals (8th cir.) 1974, U.S. Supreme Ct. 1975. Atty. Ark. Ins. Dept., Little Rock, 1972; sole practice Little Rock, 1972-73; assoc. Spitzberg, Mitchell & Hays, Little Rock, 1973-74, Boswell Law Firm, Bryant, Ark., 1974-80; ptnr. Gibson & Ellis, Benton, Ark., 1980—. Mem. Ark. Govs. Mansion Commn., Little Rock, 1984—; chmn. Benton (Ark.) Planning Commn., 1982—; bd. dirs. Saline County Boys Club, Benton, 1980-83. Mem. ABA, Ark. Bar Assn. (chmn. young lawyers sect. 1974-75), Saline County Bar Assn. (pres. 1975-76), Assn. Trial Lawyers Am., Ark. Trial Lawyers Assn. Democrat. Episcopalian. Personal injury, Federal civil litigation, State civil litigation. Home: 1725 Cedarhurst Dr Benton AR 72015 Office: Gibson & Ellis 224 S Market St Benton AR 72015

ELLIS, HERBERT WAYNE, lawyer; b. Jacksonville, Fla., Jan. 20, 1948; s. Herbert White and Sophie Cecilia (Myrna) E.; m. Diane Joyce Bookman, Apr. 2, 1977; children: Austin Wayne, Gordon Blake. BA, U. Fla., 1970, JD, 1975. Bar: Fla. 1978, U.S. Dist. Ct. (mid. dist.) Fla. 1979. Asst. pub. defender 3d Jud. Cir. Fla., Lake City, 1978—. Deacon First Presbyn. Ch., Lake City, 1985—; bd. dirs. Columbia Assn. for Retarded Citizens, Lake City, 1981-86. Mem. ABA, Columbia County Bar Assn., 3d Cir. Bar Assn. Democrat. Club: Missions Trail Shooting (Lake City) (pres. 1983-85). Avocations: pistol competitions, photography. Criminal. Home: 17 Chapel Hill Blvd Lake City FL 32055 Office: Office of Pub Defender PO Drawer 1209 Guerdon Rd Lake City FL 32055

ELLIS, JAMES ALVIS, JR., lawyer; b. Lubbock, Tex., Mar. 19, 1943; s. James Alvis and Myrle Alice (Peden) E.; m. Sandra Gay Gillespie, June 18, 1966; children—Claire Elizabeth, James Alvis III. B.A., Tex. Tech U., 1965; J.D., U. Tex., 1968. Bar: Tex. 1968, U.S. Dist. Ct. (no., ea. and we. dists.) Tex. 1969, U.S. Ct. Appeals 1970, U.S. Supreme Ct. 1979—; cert. in civil trial law Tex. Bd. Legal Specialization. Law clk. to presiding judge U.S. Dist. Ct. (we. dist.) Tex., 1968-69; assoc. Carrington, Coleman Sloman & Blumenthal, Dallas, 1970-74, ptnr., 1975—. Pres. Dallas Jr. Bar Assn., 1972. Fellow Tex. Bar Found.; mem. ABA, State Bar Tex., Dallas Bar Assn. Methodist. Clubs: Cresent, Plaza Athletic, Chandlers Landing Yacht. Federal civil litigation, State civil litigation. Office: Carrington Coleman Sloman & Blumenthal 200 Cresent Ct Suite 1500 Dallas TX 75201

ELLIS, JAMES HENRY, lawyer, savings and loan executive; b. Hartford, Conn., May 6, 1933; s. Robert Isaac and Eve (Alperin) E.; m. Linda Abess, Feb. 22, 1959; children—James Arthur, Nancy Jean, Arthur Ungar. B.S., U. Conn., 1955; M.B.A., Harvard U., 1957; J.D., U. Miami, 1968. Bar: Fla. 1968, D.C. 1969, N.Y. 1975. Vice pres., sec. Fed. Fire & Casualty Co., Miami, Fla., 1959-68; atty. SEC, Washington, 1968-70; exec. v.p., sec., gen. counsel CNA Mgmt. Corp. and 5 related mut. funds, N.Y.C., 1970-79; pres., gen. counsel Mut. Fund Cons. Group, Scarsdale, N.Y., 1979—; founder, pres., bd. dirs. Sentry Savs. and Loan Assn., Stamford, Conn., 1983—. Bd. dirs., v.p. White Plains (N.Y.) Symphony Orch., 1975—. Served with USCGR, 1960-63. Mem. ABA. Democrat. Jewish. Club: Scarsdale Town, Landmark Athletic. Contbr. numerous articles to profl. jours. Securities, General corporate. Home: 36 Butler Rd Scarsdale NY 10583

ELLIS, JAMES REED, lawyer; b. Oakland, Calif., Aug. 5, 1921; s. Floyd E. and Hazel (Reed) E.; m. Mary Lou Earling, Nov. 18, 1944 (dec.); children: Robert Lee, Judith Ann (dec.), Lynn Earling, Steven Reed. B.S., Yale, 1942; J.D., U. Wash., 1948; LL.D., Lewis and Clark U., 1968, Seattle U., 1981. Bar: Wash. 1949, D.C. 1971. Partner firm Preston, Thorgrimson, Horowitz, Starin & Ellis, 1952-69; Preston, Thorgrimson, Starin, Ellis & Holman, Seattle, 1969-72, Preston, Thorgrimson, Ellis, Holman & Fletcher, 1972-79; sr. partner firm Preston, Thorgrimson, Ellis & Holman, 1979—; dep. pros. atty., King County, 1952; gen. counsel Municipality of Met. Seattle, 1958-79. Mem. Nat. Water Commn., 1970-73; mem. urban transp. adv. council U.S. Dept. Transp., 1970-71; mem. Wash. Planning Adv. Council, 1965-72; pres. Forward Thrust Inc., 1966-73; chmn. Mayors Com. on Rapid Transit, 1964-65; Trustee Ford Found., 1970-82, mem. exec. com., 1978-82; bd. regents U. Wash., 1965-77, pres., 1972-73; trustee Resources for the Future, 1983—; mem. council Nat. Municipal League, 1968-76, v.p., 1972-76; chmn. Save our Local Farmlands Com., 1978-79, King County Farmlands Adv. Com., 1980-82; pres. Friends of Freeway Park, 1976—; bd. dirs. Nat. Park and Recreation Assn., 1979-82; bd. dirs. Wash. State Conv. and Trade Ctr., 1982—, vice chmn., 1982-86, chmn., 1986—. Served to 1st lt. USAAF, 1943-46. Recipient Bellevue First Citizen award, 1968, Seattle First Citizen award, 1968, Nat. Conservation award Am. Motors, 1968, Distinguished Service award Wash. State Dept. Parks and Recreation, 1968, Distinguished Citizen award Nat. Municipal League, 1969, King County Distinguished Citizen award, 1970, La Guardia award Center N.Y.C. Affairs, 1975, Environ. Quality award EPA, 1977, Am. Inst. for Public Service award, 1974, U. Wash. Recognition award, 1981. Fellow Am. Bar Found.; Mem. ABA (ho. dels. 1978-82, past chmn. urban, state and local govt. law sect.), Wash. Bar Assn., Seattle Bar Assn., D.C. Bar Assn., Am. Judicature Soc., Acad. Public Adminstrn., Council on Fgn. Relations, Municipal League Seattle and King County (past pres.), Order of Hosp. of St. John of Jerusalem, AIA (hon.), Order of Coif (hon.), Phi Delta Phi, Phi Gamma Delta. Club: Rainier (Seattle). Local government, General practice. Home: 903 SE Shoreland Dr Bellevue WA 98004 Office: 5400 Columbia Ctr Seattle WA 98104

ELLIS, JOHN PATRICK, lawyer; b. Bronx, N.Y., Aug. 13, 1957; s. John Harold and Mary (Dowd) E.; m. Teresa Lynn Dundis, Aug. 1, 1981; children: Ryan, Caitlan. BA, U. Notre Dame, 1979; JD, Creighton U., 1982. Bar: Nebr. 1982. Ptnr. Spenceri, Kratina & Ellis, Omaha, 1982—. Mem. ABA, Nebr. Bar Assn., Omaha Bar Assn., Assn. Trial Lawyers Am., Nebr. Trial Lawyers Assn. Democrat. Roman Catholic. Avocations: sports, reading, traveling. Personal injury, Family and matrimonial, General practice. Home: 5037 Parker St Omaha NE 68104 Office: Spenceri Kretina & Ellis 300 Jackson Pl Omaha NE 68102

ELLIS, LEE T., lawyer; b. Phila., Apr. 15, 1945. BA, U. Tenn., 1967; JD, Georgetown U., 1970. Bar: D.C. 1970. Ptnr. Baker & Hostetler, Washington. Office: Baker & Hostetler 1050 Connecticut Ave NW #1100 Washington DC 20036 *

ELLIS, LESTER NEAL, JR., lawyer; b. Washington, Aug. 1, 1948; s. Lester Neal and Marie (Brooks) E.; m. Rhoda Goheen, June 14, 1970; children—Patrick Neal, Bret Hamilton, Ryan Renyer. B.S. U.S. Mil. Acad., 1970; J.D., U. Va., 1975. Bar: Va. 1975, U.S. Ct. Appeals (5th cir.) 1977, D.C. 1978, U.S. Ct. Appeals (4th and D.C. cirs.) 1979, U.S. Ct. Appeals (11th cir.) 1982. trial atty. litigation div. office JAG, Dept. Army, Washington, 1975-78; assoc. Hunton & Williams, Richmond, Va., 1978-84, ptnr., Raleigh, N.C., 1984—. Contbr. articles to profl. jours. Mem. Wake County Bd. Elections, 1986—. Served to maj. U.S. Army, 1970-78. Recipient Judge Paul W. Brosman award U.S. Ct. Mil. Appeals, 1975. Mem. ABA, Va. Bar Assn. (spl. issues com. 1982—), D.C. Bar Assn. (ct. rules com. 1981—, wake county bd. elections 1986—), Phi Kappa Phi. Republican. Episcopalian. Federal civil litigation. Home: 7204 Willmark Ct Raleigh NC 27612 Office: Hunton & Williams One Hanover Sq Raleigh NC 27602

ELLIS, MARK GREGORY, lawyer; b. Chgo., Apr. 11, 1953; s. Nicholas Peter and Nena A. (Kedo) E.; m. Margot Charles Meyerson. BS in Bus. Adminstrn., U. Denver, 1974, JD, 1978. Bar: Colo. 1979, U.S. Dist. Ct. Colo. 1979, U.S. Ct. Appeals (9th and 10th cirs.) 1984, D.C. 1985, U.S. Dist. Ct. D.C. 1985, U.S. Ct. Appeals (D.C. cir.) 1985. Atty. advisor office adminstrv. law judges Fed. Mine Safety and Health Rev. Commn., Denver, 1979-82; atty. advisor office gen. counsel Fed. Mine Safety and Health Rev. Commn., Washington, 1983-87; counsel Am. Mining Congress, Washington, 1987—. Mem. ABA, Fed. Bar Assn., D.C. Bar Assn., Colo. Bar Assn., Denver Bar Assn. Administrative and regulatory, Labor, Mining or natural resources. Office: Am Mining Congress 1920 N St NW Suite 300 Washington DC 20036

ELLIS, NEIL RICHARD, lawyer; b. Cleve., Apr. 13, 1955; s. Robert and Mary Ann (Yanover) E.; m. Bonnie Baugh; 1 child, Leah A. AB, Cornell U., 1976; JD, Yale U., 1980. Bar: D.C. 1981, U.S. Ct. Appeals (5th and 10th cirs.) 1982, U.S. Ct. Appeals (4th and D.C. cirs.) 1983, U.S. Ct. Appeals (Fed. cir.) 1986. Law clk. to presiding justice U.S. Ct. Appeals (6th cir.), Nashville, 1980-81; atty. antitrust div. U.S. Dept. Justice, Washington, 1981-83; gen. counsel U.S. Holocaust Meml. Council, Washington, 1983; assoc. Steptoe & Johnson, Washington, 1984—; pro bono U.S. Holocaust Meml. Council, 1984—. Mem. ABA, Phi Beta Kappa. Jewish. Avocations: creative writing, piano, orienteering. Antitrust, Private international, Administrative and regulatory.

ELLIS, RONNIE GENE, lawyer; b. Waynesville, Mo., Aug. 17, 1946; s. Leroy and Mabel Virginia (Tabor) E.; m. Carol Ann Connor, Feb. 2, 1972; children: Jean Ann, Marie Joelle. BS in Criminal Justice, U. Nebr., Omaha, 1974; JD, U. Nebr., Lincoln, 1978. Bar: Nebr. 1978, U.S. Dist. Ct. Nebr. 1978. Pianist, composer Ron Ellis Enterprises, Omaha, 1973—; sole practice Omaha, 1978—; pres. Omaha Musicians Assn., 1978—. Served to capt. (mil. intelligence) U.S. Army, 1966-73, Vietnam. Recipient service award Omaha Musicians Assn., 1981. Mem. ABA, Nebr. Bar Assn., Omaha Bar Assn. Democrat. Real property, General practice, Entertainment. Home: 3925 Terrace Dr Omaha NE 68134 Office: 3600 N 90th St NP Dodge Suite Omaha NE 68134

ELLIS, SHARON BARCLAY, lawyer; b. Pensacola, Fla., Dec. 19, 1956; d. Lee Roy and Nancy Carolyn (Chavis) Barclay; m. Charles Daniel Ellis, Aug. 22, 1981; children: Brian Daniel, Jordan Lee. BA, Carson Newman Coll., 1978; JD, U. Tenn., 1981. Bar: N.C. 1981, U.S. Dist. Ct. (mid. dist.) N.C. 1983, U.S. Dist. Ct. (we. dist.) N.C. 1987. Assoc. Coleman, Bernholz Law Firm, Hillsborough, N.C., 1981-83; sole practice Hendersonville, N.C., 1983-84; assoc. Prince, Youngblood & Massagee, Hendersonville, 1984—. Mem. ABA, N.C. Bar Assn., Henderson County Bar Assn., N.C. Acad. Trial Lawyers, Hendersonville C. of C. Democrat. Baptist. Family and matrimonial, General practice, Consumer commercial. Office: Prince Youngblood & Massagee 240 3d Ave W Hendersonville NC 28739

ELLIS, THOMAS TAYLOR, lawyer; b. Duncan, Okla., Sept. 18, 1950; s. Richard A. and Mary Evelyn (Hampton) E.; m. Sue Brunk Ellis, Jan. 8, 1972; children: Lauren Elizabeth, Jonathan Taylor. BA, U. Okla., 1971, JD, 1975. Bar: U.S. Dist. Ct. (we. dist.) Okla. 1975. Assoc. King & Roberts, Oklahoma City, 1975-77; ptnr. Sullivan, Steely & Ellis, Duncan, Okla., 1977-79, Sullivan, Ellis & Leonard, Duncan, Okla., 1979-81, Ellis, Leonard & Buckholts, Duncan, 1981—; temp. judge Okla. Ct. Appeals, 1981. Bd. dirs. Stephens County Youth Services, Duncan, Okla., 1982—, Stephens County United Way, Duncan, 1984—, Citizens Crime Commn., Duncan, 1985. Mem. Assn. Trial Lawyers Am., Okla. Trial Lawyers Assn., Stephen's County Bar Assn. (sec., treas., v.p., pres. 1978-82). Democrat. Club: Elks Golf and Country (Duncan). Avocations: golf, scuba diving, water sports. State civil litigation, Family and matrimonial, Personal injury. Home: 1014 Beech Duncan OK 73533 Office: Ellis Leonard & Buckholts 1032 Main Pl Suite 200 Duncan OK 73533

ELLISON, DAVID MCQUOWN, JR., laywer; b. Baton Rouge, Apr. 4, 1933. BA, La. State U., 1954, JD, 1956. Bar: La. 1956, U.S. Dist. Ct. (ea. dist.) La. 1956. From assoc. to ptnr. Taylor, Porter, Bonds, Fuller & Phillips, 1957-69; from ptnr. to sr. ptnr. Ellison & Smith, Baton Rouge, 1969—. Mem. ABA, Baton Rouge, La. Bar Assn., La. State Law Inst. (mem. continuing mineral law adv. com. 1969—), La. Assn. Def. Counsel, Phi Delta Phi. Probate, Oil and gas leasing, Workers' compensation. Office: Ellison & Smith 336 Louisiana Ave Baton Rouge LA 70802

ELLISON, JAMES OLIVER, judge; b. St. Louis, Jan. 11, 1929; s. Jack and Mary (Patton) E.; m. Joan Roberts Ellison, June 7, 1950; 1 son, Scott. Student, U. Mo., Columbia, 1946-48; B.A., U. Okla., 1951, LL.B., 1951. Bar: Okla. Individual practice Red Fork, Okla., 1953-55; partner Boone, Ellison & Smith, Davis & Minter, 1955-79; judge U.S. Dist. Ct. No. Dist. Okla., Tulsa, 1979—. Trustee Hillcrest Med. Center, Institution Programs, Inc.; elder Southminster Presbyterian Ch. Served to capt., inf. AUS, 1951-53. Mem. ABA, Okla. Bar Assn., Tulsa County Bar Assn., Alpha Tau Omega. Jurisprudence. Office: US Dist Ct Room 4-500 US Courthouse 333 W 4th St Tulsa OK 74103 *

ELLISON, W(ILLIE) JAMES, lawyer, educator; b. Rock Hill, S.C., Jan. 28, 1947; s. Leroy Sr. and Mattie (Watkins) E.; m. Star Davis, Feb. 12, 1977; children: Jonathan Daved, Clayton Davis. BA, Rutgers Coll., 1974; JD, U. Mich., 1977. Bar: Tenn. 1978, U.S. Dist. Ct. (we. dist.) Tenn. 1978, U.S. Ct. Appeals (6th. cir.) 1978, U.S. Supreme Ct. 1981. Asst. U.S. atty. Dept. Justice, Memphis, 1978-84; assoc. prof. law Samford U. Cumberland Sch. of Law, Birmingham, 1984—; mem. criminal procedure com. Supreme Ct. Ala., 1985—, adv. com. Ala. Dept of Corrections, 1985—. Speaker on U.S. Constn., Ala. Humanities Found., Birmingham, 1986. Served as sgt. USAF, 1965-69. Mem. ABA, Assn. Am. Law Schs. (exec. com. criminal justice sect. 1984—), Kappa Alpha Psi. Republican. Avocations: reading, research, writing. Legal education. Home: 5140 Crowley Dr Irondale AL 35210 Office: Samford U Cumberland Sch of Law 800 Lakeshore Dr Birmingham AL 35229

ELLMANN, DOUGLAS STANLEY, lawyer; b. Detroit, July 15, 1956; s. William Marshall and Sheila Estelle (Frenkel) E.; m. Claudia Joan Roberts, Feb. 16, 1985. AB, Occidental Coll., 1978; JD, U. Mich., 1982. Bar: Mich. 1982, U.S. Dist. Ct. (ea. dist.) Mich. 1982, U.S. Ct. Appeals (6th cir.) 1982. Assoc. Butzel, Keidan, Simon, Myers & Graham, Detroit, 1982-84; ptnr. Ellmann & Ellmann, Detroit, 1984—; spl. asst. atty. gen., 1986—. Founder, co-chmn. Amnesty Internat., Detroit, 1985—, Lawyer's Support Network; nat. com. U. Mich. Law Sch. Fund, 1986—. Mem. ABA, Mich. Bar Assn. (rep. Assembly 1983—, exec. counsel Young Lawyers sect. 1985—). General corporate, Contracts commercial, Bankruptcy. Home: 214 Koch Ann Arbor MI 48103 Office: Ellmann & Ellmann Penobscot Bldg Detroit MI 48226

ELLMANN, WILLIAM MARSHALL, lawyer; b. Highland Park, Mich., Mar. 23, 1921; s. James I. and Jeannette (Barsook) E.; m. Sheila Estelle Frenkel, Nov. 1, 1953; children: Douglas S., Carol E., Robert L. Student, Occidental Coll., 1939-40; AB, U. Mich., 1946; LLB, Wayne State U., 1951. Bar: Mich. 1951. Sole practice Detroit, 1951—; ptnr. Ellmann & Ellmann, 1970—; Spl. com. atty. gen. Mich. to study use state troops in emergencies, 1964-65; mem. exec. com. Inst. Continuing Legal Edn., 1964-68; mem. Mich. Employment Relations Commn., 1973—, chmn., 1983-86; commr. Mackinac Island State Park Commn., 1979-85, chmn., 1983-85. Served with USAAF, 1942-46. Fellow Am. Bar Found.; mem. Am. Arbitration Assn., Nat. Acad. Arbitrators, ABA (ho. of dels. 1969-72), Detroit Bar Assn. (vice chmn. pub. relations com. 1959), State Bar Mich. (commr. 1959-69, pres. 1966-67, co-chmn. com. on qualification jud. candidates 1970-78, mem. Detroit News secret witness panel 1983), Practicing Law Inst. (adv. council 1969-70, spl. asst. atty. gen. 1970—), Sigma Nu Phi. Labor, Civil litigation, Probate. Home: 28000 Weymouth Farmington MI 48018 Office: 1465 Penobscot Bldg Detroit MI 48226

ELLSWORTH, DAVID G., lawyer; b. Los Angeles, Jan. 20, 1941; s. Kennedy and Catherine C. (Carroll) E.; m. Gina Ellsworth; children—Brett, Erin. B.S., U. So. Calif., 1962, J.D., 1965. Bar: Calif. 1966, U.S. Ct. Appeals 1982. Law clk. to judge U.S. Dist. Ct. (cen. dist.) Calif. 1965-66; assoc. Meserve, Mumper & Hughes, Los Angeles, 1966-70, ptnr., 1970-80; ptnr. Memel, Jacobs & Ellsworth, Los Angeles, 1980—; ptnr. Finley, Kumble, Wagner, Heine, Underberg, Manley, Myerson & Casey, 1987—; head dept. real estate; guest lectr. on land devel. law U. So. Calif., spring 1980. Mem. bd. commrs. Housing Authority of County of Los Angeles (Calif.), 1977-78, chmn. bd. commrs., 1978-81; mem. Los Angeles County Beach Adv. Commn., 1981—; chmn. Los Angeles County Housing Commn., 1982-84, Los Angeles County Commn. Disposal of Hazardous Waste, 1984—. Mem. Am. Land Devel. Assn. (dir.; chmn. internat. council), Nat. Timesharing Council (dir.; chmn. com. on internat. affairs), Pacific Area Travel Assn. (devel. authority), Nat. Assn. Corp. Real Estate Execs. Clubs: The Wilshire Country (Los Angeles); The Vintage (Indian Wells, Calif.); Malibu (Calif.) Riding and Tennis; San Carlos (Guaymas, Sonora, Mexico) Country. Contbr. articles to profl. publs.; assoc. editor Land Devel. Law Reporter, Resort Timesharing Law Reporter. Real property. Home: 26104 Pacific Coast Hwy Malibu CA 90265 Office: 9100 Wilshire Blvd 6th Floor E Beverly Hills CA 90212

ELLSWORTH, GARY GEORGE, lawyer; b. Hartford, Conn., Apr. 18, 1948; s. Elbert Thelus and Anita (Skarin) E.; m. Meredith Scott Spencer, Jan. 6, 1984; 1 child, Spencer Thelus. B.A., Dartmouth Coll., 1970; J.D., George Mason Sch. Law, 1976. Bar: D.C. 1976. Sole practice Washington, 1976-77; counsel to Congressman Joe Skubitz U.S. Ho. of Reps., Washington, 1977, minority counsel Interior and Insular Affairs Com., 1977-81; dep. chief counsel Energy and Natural Resources Com. U.S. Senate, Washington, 1981-84, chief counsel, 1984-87, chief counsel to minority, 1987—. Served as lt. USN, 1970-73, Vietnam. Mem. ABA, D.C. Bar Assn. Republican. Methodist. Office: US Senate Energy and Natural Resources Com SD Senate Office Bldg Washington DC 20510

ELLSWORTH, MAURICE OWENS, lawyer; b. Globe, Ariz., Mar. 11, 1948; s. Maurice Chapman and Norma (Owens) E. BS, Ariz. State U., 1972, JD, 1975. Bar: Idaho 1975, U.S. Dist. Ct. Idaho 1975, U.S. Supreme Ct. 1984. Sole practice Hailey and Carey, Idaho, 1975-76, 79-80; pros. atty. Blaine County, Hailey, 1977-79; assoc. solicitor U.S. Dept. Interior, Washington, 1981-85; U.S. atty. Dist. of Idaho, Boise, 1985—. Republican. Mormon. Administrative and regulatory, Criminal, Environment. Home: PO Box 668 Boise ID 83701 Office: Office of US Atty 550 W Fort Box 037 Boise ID 83724

ELLWANGER, J. DAVID, lawyer; b. St. Louis, Feb. 11, 1937; s. Walter Henry and Jessie Lorraine (Hanger) E.; m. Barbara Ann Koehneke, Apr. 11, 1970; children—Carrie Louise, Jay David. Student, Valparaiso U., 1956; B.S., U. Ala., 1959, J.D., 1962. Asst. atty. gen. State of Ala., Montgomery, 1962-66; staff atty. Office of Econ. Opportunity Legal Services Program, Washington, 1967, Nat. Legal Aid and Defender Assn., Chgo., 1967-68; asst. dir. Pub. Services Activities div. ABA, Chgo., 1968-69, dir., 1969-73; dir. Commn. on Nat. Inst. Justice, Washington, 1973-74,, Office Relations with other Orgns., 1975; exec. dir. Los Angeles County Bar Assn., 1976-78, D.C. Bar, Washington, 1979-81; chief exec. officer State Bar of Calif., San Francisco, 1982-86. Democratic primary candidate for state senate, Selma, Ala., 1966; bd. dirs. English Synod of Assn. of Evangelical Luth. Chs., 1973-77; bd. dirs. Luth. Wheatridge Found., Chgo., 1974-83. Fellow Am. Bar Found.; mem. ABA (mem. commn. Nat. Inst. Justice 1976-81, chmn. individual rights and responsibilities sect. 1984-85, Commn. on Pub. Understanding About the Law 1982—), D.C. Bar, Ala. State Bar (award merit 1975), Nat. Assn. of Bar Execs. (exec. com. 1985), Nat. Legal Aid and Defender Assn., Am. Judicature Soc., House of Dels., 1985. Democrat. Avocation: photography. General practice, Bar executive. Home: 90 Cedro Way San Francisco CA 94127

ELLWANGER, THOMAS JOHN, lawyer; b. Summit, N.J., Feb. 26, 1949; s. James Warren and Lorean (Nicholson) E.; m. Mary Frances Comly, Dec. 28, 1970; children: James Hunter, Margaret Lorean. BA, Northwestern U., 1970; JD, U. Fla., 1974. Bar: Fla. 1975, U.S. Dist. Ct. (mid. dist.) Fla. 1976, U.S. Ct. Appeals (11th cir.) 1976, U.S. Dist. Ct. (so. dist.) Fla. 1977, U.S. Tax Ct. Assoc. Fowler, White, Gillen, Boggs, Villareal & Banker P.A., Tampa, Fla., 1975—; instr. law U. Fla., Gainesville, 1975. Editor: Gadsden County Times, 1970-72. Pres. Neighborhood Housing Services Hyde Park, Tampa, 1978. Mem. Fla. Bar Assn. (vice-chmn. div. state tax 1985-86), Hillsborough County Bar Assn. (chmn. com. probate liaison 1985-86). Democrat. Presbyterian. Club: Tampa. Avocations: music. lit., sports. Estate taxation, Probate, Personal income taxation. Office: Fowler White Gillen et al 501 E Kennedy Blvd Tampa FL 33602

ELLWOOD, SCOTT, lawyer; b. Boston, July 8, 1936; s. William Prescott and Doris (Cook) E.; m. Karen Lindquist; children: Victoria, W. Prescott II, Marjorie. Student, Williams Coll., 1954-56; AB, Eastern Mich. U., 1958; LLB, Harvard U., 1961. Bar: Iowa 1961, Ill. 1961, U.S. Dist. Ct. (no. dist.) Ill., 1961. Assoc. McBride & Baker, Chgo., 1961-67, ptnr., 1968-84; ptnr. McDermott, Will & Emery, Chgo., 1984—; pres. Miller Investment Co., 1973—, bd. dirs.; v.p. SMI Investment Corp., 1978—, bd. dirs., FRC Investment Corp., 1984—, bd. dirs. Pres., bd. dirs. 110 N Wacker Dr Found., 1974-84, Northfield Found., 1978-84, Leadership Found., 1979-84, Woodbine Found., 1980-84, The Cannon River Found., 1982-84, L.M. McBride Found., 1982-84, Bellarmine Found., 1982-84, Mark Morton Meml. Fund, 1982—. Mem. Iowa Bar Assn., Chgo. Bar Assn., Harvard Law Soc. Ill. (bd. dirs.). Republican. Episcopalian. Clubs: Monroe, Tower, Skokie Country (Glencoe, Ill.). Probate, Corporate taxation, Personal income taxation. Home: 2235 N Lakewood Apt E-N Chicago IL 60614 Office: McDermott Will & Emery 111 W Monroe St Chicago IL 60603

ELMAN, GERRY JAY, lawyer; b. Chgo., Oct. 7, 1942; s. Earl Samuel and Lucille Paulyne (Greenberger) E.; divorced; children—Jason Farrel, Floren Haley. B.S., U. Chgo., 1963; M.S. in Chemistry, Stanford U., 1964; J.D., Columbia U., 1967. Bar: N.Y. 1967, U.S. Patent Office 1967, Pa. 1969, U.S. Supreme Ct. 1973, U.S. Dist. Ct. (so. and ea. dists.) N.Y., 1971, U.S. Dist. Ct. (ea. dist.) Pa. 1973, U.S. Dist. Ct. (mid. dist.) Pa. 1974. Assoc. Hubbell, Cohen and Stiefel, N.Y.C., 1967-68; patent atty., enzymes and health products Rohm and Haas Co., Phila., 1968-72; dep. atty. gen. Pa. Dept. Justice, Harrisburg, Pa., 1972-76; trial atty. middle Atlantic office antitrust div. U.S. Justice Dept., Phila., 1976-82; sole practice, Phila., 1982-83; ptnr. Elman Assocs., Phila., 1984—; instr. short course in computer law Temple U., Phila., 1984. Contbg. author: Lawyers' Microcomputer Users Group Jour., 1985—; editor: Columbia Jour. Transnat. Law, 1966-67; mem. adv. bd. Jour. Computer Law Reporter, 1983—; mem. editorial bd. Jour. Trademark Reporter, 1968; founder, editor-in-chief legal newsletter Biotechnology Law Report, 1982—. Chmn. Three Steps Nursery Sch., Phila., 1977; arbitrator Phila. Ct. Common Pleas, 1971-72, 1983—. Mem. Am. Chem. Soc., Licensing Execs. Soc., Assn. Biotech. Cos., AAAS, ABA, Am. Arbitration Assn. (arbitrator computer disputes 1987), Am. Intellectual Property Law Assn., Phila. Bar Assn. (chmn. jurimetrics com. 1975-77), Phila. Patent Law Assn. (chmn. biotech. subcom. 1982-86, Computer Law Assn., Phila. Area Computer Soc. Lodge: B'nai B'rith (v.p. Society Hill 1977). General corporate, Patent, Administrative and regulatory. Home: Hopkinson House 1907 Philadelphia PA 19106 Office: Elman Assocs Bourse Bldg Suite 900 Philadelphia PA 19106

ELMAN, WILLIAM, lawyer; b. Evanston, Ill., Jan. 6, 1932; s. Mandel and Esther (Perkins) E.; B.A., Grinnell Coll., 1953; J.D., Harvard U., 1956. Bar: Ill. 1959, U.S. Dist. Ct. (no. dist.) Ill. 1960, U.S. Dist. Ct. (so. dist.) Ill. 1964, U.S. Dist. Ct. (we. dist.) Wis. 1965, U.S. Ct. Appeals (7th cir.) 1971, U.S. Supreme Ct. 1971, U.S. Dist. Ct. (ea. dist.) Wis. 1976, U.S. Dist. Ct. (no. dist.) Ill. 1982. Assoc., Levin, Upton & Glink, Chgo., 1959-60; assoc. firm Morton H. Meyer, Chgo., 1961-63; ptnr., pres. Elman and Ehardt, Ltd. and predecessor firm Elman and Ehardt, Harvard, Ill., 1963—; atty. City of Harvard, Ill., 1985—; mem. panel arbitrators Am. Arbitration Assn. Mem. Local Bd. 41 SSS. Served to specialist 3d class U.S. Army, 1956-58. Mem. ABA, Ill. Bar Assn. (hon. mention Annual Lincoln Award Legal Writing Contest, 1967), Chgo. Bar Assn. (civil practice com. 1971-73), McHenry County Bar Assn. (bd. govs. 1973-78), Ill. Trial Lawyers Assn., Am. Judicature Soc. Jewish. Clubs: Athletic, Rotary (pres. 1981-82), Moose (Harvard); Elks (Woodstock, Ill.). Contbr. articles to law jours. Personal injury, Workers' compensation, General practice. Office: 205 E Front St Harvard IL 60033

ELMORE, EDWARD WHITEHEAD, lawyer; b. Lawrenceville, Va., July 15, 1938; s. Thomas Milton and Mary Norfleet (Whitehead) E.; m. Gail Harmon, Aug. 10, 1968; children: Mary Jennifer, Edward Whitehead Jr. B.A., U. Va.-Charlottesville, 1959, J.D., 1962. Bar: Va. 1962. Assoc. firm Hunton & Williams, Richmond, Va., 1965-69; staff atty. Ethyl Corp., Richmond, 1969-78, asst. gen. counsel, 1978-79, gen. counsel, 1979-80, gen. counsel., sec., 1980-83, v.p., gen. counsel, sec., 1983—. Served to capt. AUS, 1962-65. Decorated Army Commendation medal. Mem. ABA, Va. Bar Assn., Internat. Bar Assn., Va. State Bar, Am. Corp. Counsel Assn., Bar Assn. Richmond, Am. Soc. Corp. Secs., Raven Soc., Phi Beta Kappa. General corporate. Home: 2901 W Brigstock Rd Midlothian VA 23113 Office: Ethyl Corp 330 S 4th St Richmond VA 23219

ELMORE, ELBERT FRANCIS, lawyer; b. Chgo., Feb. 3, 1932; s. Elbert Earl and Margaret (Roberts) E.; m. Gloria D. Elmore, Mar. 29, 1957; children: Cynthia E., Stephen E. LLD, DePaul U., 1957. Bar: Ill. Assoc. Williams & Leonard, Chgo., 1957-60; sr. ptnr. Elmore & DeMichael, Oak Forest, Ill., 1960—; bd. dirs. Ingalls Meml. Hosp., Harvey, Ill., Interstate Bank of Oak Forest, various bus. orgns. in Ill. Elected magistrate Bremen Twp., 1957-61; village atty. Villages of Midlothian and Olympia Fields, 1957-76. Served with U.S. Army, 1953-55. Mem. Chgo. Bar Assn., Ill. State Bar Assn., Ill. Trial Lawyers Assn. Republican. Clubs: Flossmoor (Ill.) Country; Mid-Am. (Chgo.). Banking, Probate, Real property. Office: Elmore & DeMichael 15507 S Cicero Ave Suite 200 Oak Forest IL 60452

ELMORE, MARVIN JEROME, lawyer; b. Eufala, Ala., May 9, 1948; s. Marvin C. and Lillian Elizabeth (Sutton) E.; m. Susan Margaret Hester, June 20, 1970; children: Scott McCollister, Bartow Jerome. BA with high honors, U. Va., 1970; JD, Emory U., 1976. Bar: Ga. 1976, Fla. 1976, U.S. Dist. Ct. (no. and mid. dists.) Ga. 1976, U.S. Dist. Ct. (so. dist.) Fla. 1976, U.S. Ct. Appeals (5th and 11th cirs.) 1976. Assoc. Fleming, O'Bryan & Fleming, Ft. Lauderdale, Fla., 1976-77, Trotter, Bondurant, Griffin, Miller & Hishon, Atlanta, 1977-81; ptnr. Trotter, Bondurant, Miller & Hishon, Atlanta, 1981-85, Bondurant, Mixson & Elmore, Atlanta, 1985—. Mem. editorial bd. Emory U. Law Rev. Served to lt. (j.g.) USN, 1970-73. Recipient Good Govt. award League of Women Voters, 1980. Mem. ABA, Fla. Bar Assn., Ga. Bar Assn. (chmn. mock trial com. 1979-80), Atlanta Bar Assn., Phi Delta Phi (magister 1975). Presbyterian. Clubs: Lawyers, Ashford (Atlanta). Federal civil litigation, State civil litigation. Home: 410 Breakwater Ridge Atlanta GA 30328 Office: Bondurant Mixson & Elmore Two Peachtree St NW 2200 First Atlanta Tower Atlanta GA 30383-4501

ELROD, EUGENE RICHARD, lawyer; b. Roanoke, Ala., May 14, 1949; s. James Woodrow and Selma Fromer (Steinbach) E. AB, Dartmouth Coll., 1971; JD, Emory U., 1974. Bar: Ga. 1974, D.C. 1976, U.S. Ct. Appeals (D.C. cir.) 1985, U.S. Ct. Appeals (5th cir.) 1987, U.S. Dist. Ct. D.C. 1987. Trial atty. Fed. Power Com., Washington, 1974-76; atty.-advisor Fed. Energy Adminstrn., Washington, 1977; assoc. Sidley & Austin, Washington, 1977-80, ptnr., 1981—; mem. adv. bd. The Keplinger Cos., Houston. Mem. selection com. for Woodruff scholars Emory U. Law Sch. Mem. ABA, D.C. Bar Assn., Ga. Bar Assn., Fed. Energy Bar Assn. (chmn. oil pipelne com. 1982-83, tax com. 1980-81, liaison with adminstrv. law judges 1986-87). Clubs: Dartmouth, Mt. Vernon Swimming and Tennis (Washington). Avocations: running, tennis, gardening, travel. FERC practice, Public utilities, Administrative and regulatory. Home: 4300 Hawthorne St NW Washington DC 20016 Office: Sidley & Austin 1722 Eye St NW Washington DC 20006

ELROD, LINDA DIANE HENRY, lawyer, educator; b. Topeka, Kans., Mar. 6, 1947; d. Lyndus Arthur Henry and Margorie Jane (Hammel) Allen; m. Mark Douglas Elrod, June 5, 1971; children: Carson Douglas, Bree Elizabeth. BA in English with honors, Washburn U., 1969, JD cum laude, 1971. Bar: Kans. 1972. Instr. U. S.D., Topeka, 1970-71; research atty. Kans. Jud. Council, Topeka, 1972-74; asst. prof. Washburn U., Topeka, 1974-78, assoc. prof., 1978-82, prof. law, 1982—; cons. Kans. Jud. Council, Topeka, 1974-76. Author: Kansas Family Law Handbook, 1983; contbr. articles to law jours. Pres. YWCA, Topeka, 1982-83; vice chmn. Kans. Commn. on Child Support, 1984—. Recipient Disting. Service award Washburn Law Sch. Assn., 1986. Mem. ABA (chmn. Schwab Meml. Grant Implementation 1984—), Topeka Bar Assn. (sec. 1981-85, v.p. 1985-86, pres. 1986-87), Kans. Bar Assn. (pres. family law sect. 1984-86, Disting. Service award 1985), Phi Kappa Phi, Phi Alpha Delta Alumni Assn. (justice 1976-77). Presbyterian. Avocations: bridge, reading, quilting. Family and matrimonial, Real property. Office: Washburn U Law Sch 17th and College Topeka KS 66210

ELROD, RICHARD BRYAN, lawyer; b. Denver, July 14, 1949; s. Walter Frank and Doris Beach (Kinnison) E.; m. Martha Jane Riddell, June 8, 1974; children: Jacob Jonathan, Kenin Casey. BS, U. No. Colo., 1971; JD, U. Denver, 1975. Bar: Colo., U.S. Dist. Ct. Colo., U.S. Tax Ct. U.S. Ct. Appeals (10th cir.). Assoc. Thomas & Esperti P.C., Denver, 1975-78; ptnr., founder Esperti, Elrod, Katz, Peterson, Schmit and Preeo, Denver, 1978-80, Esperti, Elrod and Wills, Denver, 1980-82, Schmidt, Elrod and Wills, Denver, 1982-85, Elrod, Katz, Preeo and Look P.C., Denver, 1985—; tchr. advanced CLU course on taxation, Denver, 1981. Contbr. articles to profl. jours., chpts. to books. Mem. Fellowship of Christian Fin. Advisors, Denver, 1984— (lectr.), exec. council St. Joseph's Hosp., Denver, 1985—; elder Cherry Hills Community Ch., Denver, 1984—. Mem. ABA (tax div. 1975—), Colo. Bar Assn., Denver Estate Planning Council (lectr. 1980—). Avocations: golf, fly fishing, reading, writing. Estate planning, General corporate, Pension, profit-sharing, and employee benefits. Office: Elrod Katz Preeo & Look PC 1120 Lincoln St Suite 1100 Denver CO 80203

ELSEN, SHELDON HOWARD, lawyer; b. Pitts., May 12, 1928; m. Gerri Sharfman, 1952; children: Susan Rachel, Jonathan Charles. A.B., Princeton U., 1950; A.M., Harvard U., 1952, J.D., 1958. Bar: N.Y. 1959, U.S. Supreme Ct. 1971. Mem. firm Orans, Elsen & Lupert, N.Y.C., 1965—; adj. prof. law Columbia Law Sch., 1969—; chief counsel N.Y. Moreland Act Commn., 1975-76; asst. U.S. atty. So. Dist. N.Y., 1960-64; cons. Pres's. Commn. Law Enforcement Adminstrn. Justice, 1967; mem. faculty Nat. Inst. Trial Advocacy, 1973. Contbr. articles to legal jours. Fellow Am. Coll. Trial Lawyer•. mem. Am. Law Inst., Assn. Bar City N.Y. (chmn. com. on fed. legislation 1969-72, mem. com. on judiciary 1972-75, chmn. com. on fed. courts 1983-86, chmn. nominating com. 1986—), Phi Beta Kappa. Federal civil litigation, State civil litigation, Criminal. Home: 50 Fenimore Rd Scarsdale NY 10583 Office: 1 Rockefeller Plaza New York NY 10020

ELSENER, G. DALE, lawyer; b. Frederick, Okla., Mar. 26, 1951; s. Gordon Lee and Anita Lois (Vaughan) E.; m. Janet Lynn Scism, June 21, 1980; children—Kelli Jan, Hayley Lynn, Garrett Dale. B.S., Okla. State U., 1973; J.D., Okla. U., 1976. Bar: Okla. 1976, U.S. Dist. Ct. (ea. and we. dists.) Okla. 1984. Assoc., Richard S. Roberts, Wewoka, Okla., 1976-78; ptnr. Roberts & Elsener, Wewoka, 1979-86; sole practice, 1986—; city atty. City of Wewoka, 1986—. Chmn. bd. trustees Seminole County Law Library, 1986; chmn. Seminole County Econ. Devel. Adv. Com., 1986; bd. dirs. Wewoka Campfire Council, Rural Water Dist. 3, Cromwell, Okla. Mem. Seminole County Bar Assn., Wewoka C. of C. (bd. dirs., pres.-elect 1987), ABA, Okla. Bar Assn. (mineral law sect.). Republican. Methodist. Oil and gas leasing, Real property, Probate. Office: Roberts & Elsener PO Box 839 Wewoka OK 74884

ELSMAN, JAMES LEONARD, JR., lawyer; b. Kalamazoo, Sept. 10, 1936; s. James Leonard and Dorothy Isabell (Pierce) E.; m. Janice Marie Wilczewski, Aug. 6, 1960; children—Stephanie, James Leonard III. B.A., U. Mich., 1958, J.D., 1962; postgrad., Harvard Div. Sch., 1958-59. Bar: Mich. bar 1963. Clk. Mich. Atty. Gen.'s Office, Lansing, 1961; atty. legal dept. Chrysler Corp., Detroit, 1962-64; founding partner Elsman, Young, O'Rourke, Bruno & Bunn, Birmingham, 1964—. Author: novel The Seekers, 1962; screenplay, 1976, 200 Candles for Whom?, 1973; Contbr. articles to profl. jours.; Composer, 1976, 1974. Mem. Regional Export Expansion Council, 1966-73, Mich. Partners for Alliance for Progress, 1969—; Candidate U.S. Senate, 1966, 76, U.S. Ho. of Reps., 1970. Rockefeller Brothers Found. fellow Harvard Div. Sch., 1969. Mem. Econ. Club Detroit, Council on Fgn. Relations, World Peace Through Law Center, Am. Soc. Internat. Law, ABA, Full Gospel Businessmen. Democrat. Mem. Christian Ch. Clubs: Rotarian, Bloomfield Open Hunt; Presidents (U. Mich.); Circumnavigators; Naples Bath and Tennis. State civil litigation, Private international, Personal injury. Home: 4811 Burnley Dr Bloomfield Hills MI 48013 Office: 635 Elm St Birmingham MI 48011

ELSON, JOHN S., law educator; b. 1943. BA, Harvard U., 1964, JD, 1967; MA, U. Chgo., 1968. Staff atty. Mandel Legal Aid Clinic U. Chgo., 1971-75; assoc. prof. Northwestern U., Evanston, Ill., 1976-79, prof., 1979—. Office: Northwestern U Law Sch 357 Chicago Ave Chicago IL 60611 *

ELTERMAN, WARREN BART, lawyer, legal educator; b. N.Y.C., July 23, 1945; s. Benjamin and Estelle E.; m. Lynne Haller, Dec. 25, 1968; children—Scott, Amy, Julie. B.S. in Econs., Wharton Sch. U. Pa., 1966; J.D. cum laude, Boston U., 1969. Bar: N.Y. 1969, U.S. Dist. Ct. (so., ea. dists.) N.Y., 1974, D.C. 1982. Assoc., Hale Russell & Gray, N.Y.C., 1969-78, ptnr., 1979-85; ptnr. Latham & Watkins, 1985—; panel arbitrators Am. Arbitration Assn.; adj. prof. law St. John's U. Law Sch., 1981—. Served in USAR, 1969-74. Mem. Bar Assn. City N.Y., ABA. Mem. Boston U. Law Rev. Club: Players (N.Y.C.). General corporate, Contracts commercial, Private international.

ELTZROTH, CARTER WEAVER, lawyer; b. Inpls., Mar. 7, 1952; s. Carter Weaver and Marjorie (Turk); m. Arline Wheat, Feb. 12, 1983; 1 child, Rebecca. Baccalaureate in Letters, Coll. Stanislas, Paris, 1971; BA, Columbia U., 1973; MA, U. Coll., Oxford, Eng., 1977; JD, Columbia U., 1980. Bar: N.Y. 1982, U.S. Ct. Appeals (7th cir.) 1982. Law clk. U.S. Ct. Appeals (7th cir.), Chgo., 1980-82; assoc. Shearman & Sterling, N.Y.C., 1982-86, Morgan, Lewis & Bockius, N.Y.C., 1986—. Mem. steering com. Whitney Mus., N.Y.C., 1985—. Oxford Soc. grantee, 1976. Mem. ABA (internat. sect.), Assn. Bar of City of N.Y., Am. Soc. Internat. Law, East/West Round Table, Hellenic Soc., French-Am. Found. General corporate, Securities, Private international. Home: 21 Highland Ave Darien CT 06820 Office: Morgan Lewis & Bockius 101 Park Ave New York NY 10178

ELTZROTH, CLYDE ALFRED, JR., lawyer; b. Savannah, Ga., Aug. 4, 1948; s. Clyde Alfred and Sarah Caroline (Platts) E.; m. Emily Jackson, June 26, 1976; children: Clay, Nyle, Mim. BA, The Citadel, Mil. Coll. S.C., 1970; JD, U. S.C., 1973. Assoc. Murdaugh, Eltzroth & Peters, Hampton, S.C., 1973-76; ptnr. Peters, Murdaugh, Parker, Eltzroth & Detrick P.A., Hampton, S.C., 1976—. Trustee Hampton Meth. Ch., S.C., 1984-86, grievance com., 1983-86, long-range planning com., 1985-86; mem. improvement com. Varnville Elem. Sch., S.C., 1985—, Hampton County Election Commn., 1987—. Mem. ABA, S.C. Bar Assn. (grievance com. 1983—, long range planning com. 1985—), Hampton County Bar Assn. (sec., treas. 1975-82), Assn. Trial Lawyers Am., S.C. Trial Lawyers Assn. Democrat. Methodist. Avocations: golf, hunting, fishing. Local government, Personal injury, Workers' compensation. Office: Peters Murdaugh et al 1st St E Box 457 Hampton SC 29924

ELWIN, JAMES WILLIAM, JR., university dean, lawyer; b. Everett, Wash., June 28, 1950; s. James William Elwin and Jeannette Georgette (Zichy-Litscheff) Sherman; m. Regina K. McCabe, Oct. 25, 1986. B.A., U. Denver, 1971, M.A., 1972; J.D., Northwestern U., 1975. Bar: Ill. 1975, U.S. Dist. Ct. (no. dist.) Ill. 1975, U.S. Ct. Appeals (7th cir.) 1977, U.S. Supreme Ct. 1980. Trial atty. antitrust div. U.S. Dept. Justice, Chgo., 1975-77; asst. dean Northwestern U. Sch. Law, Chgo., 1977-82, assoc. dean, 1982—, exec. dir. Corp. Counsel Ctr. Northwestern U., 1984—; planning dir. Corp. Counsel Inst., Chgo., 1983—; dir. Short Course for Pros. Attys., Chgo., 1981—, Short Course for Def. Lawyers in Criminal Cases, Chgo., 1979—. Bd. dirs. Legal Assistance Found. of Chgo., 1985—; vice chmn. Gov.'s Adv. Council on Criminal Justice Legislation, 1986—. Fellow German Academic Exchange Service, 1986. Mem. Chgo. Bar Assn. (bd. mgrs. 1983-85), Chgo. Bar Found. (bd. dirs. 1985—), Ill. Inst. Continuing Legal Edn. (chmn. 1987—), Assn. Am. Law Schs. (chmn. sect. Instl. Advancement 1985), Phi Beta Kappa, Pi Gamma Mu. Clubs: Legal, Univ. (Chgo.). Antitrust, Legal education. Office: Northwestern Univ Sch Law 357 E Chicago Ave Chicago IL 60611

ELY, ALBERT LOVE, JR., lawyer; b. Washington, June 27, 1911; s. Albert Love and Elizabeth Armstrong (Coe) E.; m. Jean Gallagher, Sept. 9, 1963; children—Albert Love III, Eugene S. II, Elizabeth Ely Palay, Jonathan D. M.E., Cornell U., 1933; LL.B., George Washington U., 1937. Bar: D.C. 1936, Ohio 1938, U.S. Patent Office, 1937, U.S. Supreme Ct. 1951. Law clk. U.S. Patent Office, 1933-37; jr. ptnr. Ely & Barrow, Cleve., 1938-42; ptnr. Ely, Frye & Hamilton, Cleve., 1942-55; sr. ptnr. Ely, Pearne & Gordon, Cleve., 1955-68, Ely, Golrick & Flynn, Cleve., 1968-73, Ely & Golrick, Cleve., 1973-77; of Counsel Bosworth, Sessions & McCoy, Cleve., 1978, John H. Mulholland, Cleve., 1979-81, Baldwin, Egan, Wallings & Fetzer, Cleve., 1981—; Consumer adv. bd. Cardinal Fed. Savings Bank, Ariz. Mem. Am. Judicature Soc., ABA, Cleve. Bar Assn., Am. Intellectual Property Law Assn., Cleve. Patent Law Assn. Republican. Episcopalian. Club: Cleve. Yachting. Contbr. to math. game dept. Sci. Am., 1977. Federal civil litigation, Patent, Trademark and copyright. Address: 18951 Inglewood Rd Rocky River OH 44116

ELY, BRUCE PETER, lawyer; b. Pitts., Aug. 6, 1955; s. Harold E. and Lorraine D. (Verstegen) E.; m. Karen Thompson, Aug. 13, 1977; 1 child, David Patrick. BS in Acctg., U. Ala., 1977, JD, 1980; LLM in Taxation,

NYU, 1981. Bar: Ala. 1980, U.S. Tax Ct. 1980, U.S. Dist. Ct. (no. dist.) Ala., U.S. Ct. Claims, U.S. Ct. Appeals (5th and 11th cirs.). Assoc. Hubbard, Waldrop & Tanner, Tuscaloosa, Ala., 1981-84, Johnstone, Adams, Howard, Bailey & Gordon, Mobile, Ala., 1984-85; ptnr. Tanner, Guin, Ely & Lary P.C., Tuscaloosa, 1985—; adj. prof. U. Ala. Sch. Law, Tuscaloosa, 1982-84; vice chmn. tax sect. Ala. State Bar, 1987—. Author: Tax-Free Reorganizations, 1985. Mem. Joint Com. to Revise Ala. Income Tax Laws, Birmingham, 1984—; vice chmn. tax com. Bus. Council of Ala., Birmingham, 1986—. Mem. ABA, Ala. Bar Assn. (energy law com.), Tuscaloosa Bar Assn., Christian Legal Soc., Eastern Mineral Law Found. (Ala. editor Case Update). Republican. Avocations: reading, sports. General corporate, Oil and gas leasing, Corporate taxation. Office: Tanner Guin Ely & Lary PC 2711 University Blvd Suite 100 Tuscaloosa AL 35401

ELY, CLAUSEN, JR., lawyer; b. Montgomery, Ala., Feb. 18, 1945. AB, Huntingdon Coll., 1967; JD, U. Ala., 1972. Ptnr. Covington & Burling, Washington. Office: Covington & Burling 1201 Pennsylvania Ave NW Box 7566 Washington DC 20044 *

ELY, HIRAM, III, lawyer; b. Lexington, Ky., May 14, 1951; s. Hiram and Buena E. (Wright) E.; m. Deborah A. Johnson, Oct. 22, 1977. B.A., Centre Coll. Ky., 1973; J.D., Washington and Lee U., 1976. Bar: Ky. 1976. U.S. Dist. Ct. (we. dist.) Va. 1976, U.S. Dist. Ct. (we. dist.) Va., U.S. Dist. Ct. (we. dist.) Ky., 1976. U.S. Dist. Ct. (ea. dist.) Ky. 1979, U.S. Supreme Ct. 1979, U.S. Ct. Appeals (6th cir.) 1979, U.S. Ct. Claims, 1979, U.S. Tax Ct. 1984. Clk. to presiding justice U.S. Dist. Ct. Va., Roanoke, 1976-77; assoc. Ewen, MacKenzie & Peden, P.S.C., Louisville, 1977-81; assoc. Greenebaum, Doll & McDonald, Louisville, 1981-84, ptnr., 1984—. Fund raising capt. Old Ky. Home council Boy Scouts Am., 1984; fund raiser profl. div. Metro United Way, Louisville, 1983-85; bd. dirs. Goodwill Industries, 1985—, Louisville C. of C., 1985—. Legal Research Assn. grantee, 1974; named among Top Ten Outstanding Kentuckians, Ky. Jaycees, 1969. Mem. Young Lawyers Club (v.p. 1982-83, pres. 1983-84), Louisville Bar Found. (chmn. continuing legal edn. sect. 1985—, bd. dirs. 1986—), Louisville Bar Assn. (subcom. chmn. 1983—, spl. subcom. SP mem. 1983-84, mem. litigation, internat. law, young lawyers, fed. practice sects.) Ky. Bar Assn., ABA (discovery com. litigation sect. 1981-84), Ky. Acad. Trial Atty's., Ky. Def. Counsel, Def. Research Inst., Sigma Chi. Club: Jefferson, Harmony Landing Country (Louisville). State civil litigation, Federal civil litigation. Office: Greenebaum Doll & McDonald 3300 First Nat Tower Louisville KY 40202

ELY, JAMES WALLACE, JR., legal educator; b. Rochester, N.Y., Jan. 20, 1938; s. James Wallace and Edythe (Farnham) E.; m. Ruth Buell MacCameron, Aug. 27, 1960; children—A. Elizabeth, Kimberly Farnham, Suzanne B., James W. A.B., Princeton U., 1959; LL.B., Harvard U., 1962; Ph.D., U. Va., 1971. Bar: N.Y. 1962, U.S. Dist. Ct. (we. dist.) N.Y. 1963. Assoc., Harris, Beach and Wilcox, Rochester, N.Y., 1962-67; instr. U. Va., 1970; instr. to asst. prof. Va. Commonwealth U., Richmond, 1970-73; asst. prof. law Vanderbilt U., Nashville, 1973-75, assoc. prof., 1975-78, prof., 1978—; vis. prof. law U. Leeds, Eng., 1981-82; Chapman disting. vis. prof., U. Tulsa, 1985. Author: The Crisis of Conservative Virginia: The Byrd Organization and the Politics of Massive Resistance, 1976. Co-author: (with Bruce and Bostick) Modern Property Law: Cases and Materials, 1984; (with Bodenhamer) Ambivalent Legacy: A Legal History of the South, 1984; asst. editor Am. Jour. Legal History, 1987—. Mem. Am. Soc. Legal History (treas. 1980-81, 82-83, 84-85), Orgn. Am. Historians, So. Hist. Assn. Legal history, Real property. Office: Vanderbilt U Sch Law 21st Ave S Nashville TN 37240

ELY, JOHN HART, lawyer, university dean; b. N.Y.C., Dec. 3, 1938; s. John H. and Martha Foster (Coyle) E.; children: John Duff, Robert Allan Duff. A.B. summa cum laude, Princeton U., 1960; LL.B. magna cum laude, Yale U., 1963; M.A. (hon.), 1971, Harvard U., 1973. Bar: D.C. 1965, Calif. 1967. Atty. Warren Commn., 1964; law clk. to Chief Justice Warren, 1964-65; Fulbright scholar London Sch. Econs., 1965-66; atty. Defenders, Inc., San Diego, 1966-68; asso. prof., then prof. law Yale U. Law Sch., 1968-73; mem. faculty Harvard U. Law Sch., 1973-1982, Ralph S. Tyler, Jr. prof. constl. law, 1981-1982; Richard E. Lang prof. law Stanford U. Law Sch., Calif., 1982—, dean, 1982—; gen. counsel U.S. Dept. Transp., 1975-76. Author: Democracy and Distrust, 1980. Served with USAR, 1963-69. Fellow Woodrow Wilson Internat. Center scholars (1978-79), Am. Acad. Arts and Scis. Legal education. Office: Stanford U Law Sch Stanford CA 94305

ELY, JOHN P., lawyer; b. Lubbock, Tex., Apr. 21, 1945; s. John O. and Laverne (Barton) E.; m. Julie McCall Sherman, Dec. 27, 1967. B.A., U. N.H., 1967; J.D., Boston U., 1976. Bar: Mass. 1977, U.S. Dist. Ct. Mass. 1977, U.S. Dist. Ct. Conn. 1980, U.S. Supreme Ct. 1980. Sole practice, Agawam, Mass., 1977-78; assoc. Laming, Smith, et al, Springfield, Mass., 1978-80; jr. ptnr. Auchter, Bozenhard & Socha, Springfield, 1980-83, ptnr., 1984-85; ptnr. Bozenhard, Socha, Ely & Kolber, Springfield, 1985—. Served to 1st lt. USMC, 1968-71. Mem. Marine Corps Assn., 3d Marine Div. Assn., ABA, Mass. Bar Assn., Hamdpen County Bar Assn., Mass. Conveyancers Assn. Club: Exchange (Springfield) (bd. dirs.). Real property, Probate, General practice. Office: Bozenhard Socha Ely & Kolber 1275 Elm St West Springfield MA 01089

ELY, NORTHCUTT, lawyer; b. Phoenix, Sept. 14, 1903; s. Sims and Elizabeth (Northcutt) E.; m. Marica McCann, Dec. 2, 1931; children—Michael and Craig (twins), Parry Haines. A.B., Stanford U., 1924, J.D., 1926. Bar: Calif. 1926, N.Y. 1927, D.C. 1930, U.S. Sup. Ct. 1930. Sole practice N.Y., 1926-29, Washington, Calif., 1933—; exec. asst. to Sec. Interior, Washington, 1929-33; chmn. tech. adv. com. Fed. Oil Cons. Bd., Washington, 1931-33; represented Sec. Interior in negotiation of Hoover Dam power and water contracts 1930-33; counsel to Gov. of Okla. in negotiating Interstate Oil Compact, 1934-35; co-executor of estate of ex-Pres. Herbert Hoover, 1964-68; spl. counsel colo. River Bd. of Calif., 1946-76 and various Calif. water and power agys.; spl. Asst. Atty. Gen. State of Calif., 1953-64 in Ariz. v. Calif.; counsel in 7 U.S. Supreme Ct cases involving rights in Colo., Columbia, Cowlitz, Niagara Rivers and fed. natural resource statutes; legal advisor to Ruler of Sharjah in boundary disputes with Iran, Umm al Qawain, and internat. arbitration of boundary with Dubai; counsel to Swaziland in internat. river dispute with Republic of South Africa and to Mekong Commn. (U.N.) in settling principles for devel. of Mekong Basin; counsel to govts. and cos. in determination of seabed boundaries in Gulf of Thailand, Mediterranean, East China, South China, Caribbean seas; represented U.S. Mining cos. in enactment of Deepsea Hard Minerals Act, & subsequent reciprocal internat. recognition of mining leases; gen. counsel Am. Pub. Power Assn., 1941-81; counsel Los Angeles, So. Calif. Edison Co. in renewal of Hoover Power contracts, 1980—; counsel to Govts. of Saudi Arabia, Turkey, Malagasy Republic, Ethiopia, Grenada, Thailand on mining and petroleum legis.; mem. U.S. del. to UN Conf. on application of Sci. and Tech. for Benefit Less Developed Areas, 1963, UN Conf. on mineral legislation, Manila, 1969, Bangkok, 1973; mem. bd. overseers Hoover Instn.; trustee Herbert Hoover Found., Hoover Birthplace Found. Author: Summary of Mining & Petroleum Laws of the World, Oil Conservation Through Interstate Agreement, The Hoover Dam Documents; co-author Law of International Drainage Basins, Economics of the Mineral Industries. Fellow Am. Bar Found.; mem. ABA (chmn. natural resource sect. 1973-74, ho. dels. 1974-80, regulatory reform com.), Calif. State Bar Assn., D.C. Bar Assn., Am. Law Inst. (life), Internat. Law Assn. (chmn. Am. br. com. on deep sea mineral resources 1970-79), Nat. Petroleum Council, Internat. Bar Assn., Sigma Nu, Phi Delta Phi, Sigma Delta Chi. Republican. Clubs: Bohemian (San Francisco); California (Los Angeles); Metropolitan, Chevy Chase, University (Washington); Fortnightly (Redlands); Redlands Country, Berkeley Tennis (Calif.). Natural resources, Public international. Home: 222 Escondido Dr Redlands CA 92373 Office: Law Offices Northcutt Ely 300 E State St Redlands CA 92373

EMANUEL, IRA MICHAEL, lawyer; b. Yonkers, N.Y., Oct. 10, 1956; s. Wilbert and Elaine (Lesikin) E. BA, U. Rochester, 1977; JD, Albany Law Sch., 1980. Bar: N.Y. 1981, U.S. Dist. Ct. (so. and ea dists.) N.Y. 1981, U.S. Ct. Appeals (2d cir.) 1984. Assoc. Lexow & Jenkins, P.C., Suffern, N.Y., 1981-84; sr. assoc. Lexow & Berbit, P.C., Suffern, 1984, Lexow, Berbit & Jason, Suffern, 1984-86; sole practice Suffern, 1987—; asst. village atty., Montebello, N.Y., 1986—; of counsel Lexow, Berbit & Jason, Suffern, 1987—. Dep. counsel Rockland County Legis., N.Y., 1987—; mem. Dem. Exec. Com., Rockland County, 1984—; committeeman N.Y. State Dem. Com., 1984—; chmn. Village Dem. Com., Suffern, 1986, Task Force on a More Harmonious Town, Ramapo, N.Y. 1986. Mem. N.Y. State Bar Assn., Rockland County Bar Assn. (chmn. continuing legal edn. com.). Condemnation, Local government, Real property. Office: 56 Park Ave PO Box 239 Suffern NY 10901

EMBRY, THOMAS ERIC, lawyer; b. Pell City, Ala., June 14, 1921; s. Frank Bernard and Isabella (Mungall) E.; m. Bedford Stall, Jan. 6, 1945 (dec. Sept. 1983); children—Corinne Embry, Vickers, Frances Alden Embry Burchfield. LL.B., U. Ala., 1947. Bar: Ala. 1947. Ptnr. Embry & Embry, Pell City, Ala., 1947-48; sole practice 1949-55; ptnr. Beddow, Embry & Beddow, Birmingham, Ala., 1956-74; justice Supreme Ct. Ala., Montgomery, 1975-85, ret., 1985; of counsel Emond & Vines, Birmingham, 1985—; adj. mem. faculty dept. criminal justice U. Ala., Birmingham, 1975-85. Served to capt. U.S. Army, 1943-46. Mem. Ala. Bar Assn., Birmingham Bar Assn., Assn. Trial Lawyers Am., Ala. Trial Lawyers Assn., Internat. Soc. Barristers. Democrat. Roman Catholic. Jurisprudence, Federal civil litigation, State civil litigation. Home: 3609 Springhill Rd Birmingham AL 35223 Office: Emond & Vines 1900 Daniel Bldg Birmingham AL 35233

EMERSON, ANDREW CRAIG, insurance company executive, lawyer; b. Fort Wayne, Ind., Feb. 11, 1929; s. Kenton Craig and Lucille Katherine (Godfrey) E.; m. Marilyn Annette Kling, June 17, 1951; children—Daniel, Mark, John, Michael. B.S., Purdue U., 1951; LL.B., Ind. U., 1953, M.B.A., 1958. Bar: Ind. 1953. Atty. Indpls. Life Ins. Co., 1958-66, counsel, 1966-68, gen. counsel, 1968-72, v.p. gen. counsel, 1972—. Vice pres. Meridian Kessler Assn., Indpls., 1973. Served to capt. USAF, 1953-56. Mem. Assn. Ind. Life Ins. Cos. (sec., treas. 1971—), Ind. Life and Health Ins. Guaranty Assn. (sec. 1981-86, chmn. 1986—), Ind. State Bar Assn. (chmn. com. 1972—), Indpls. Bar Assn., ABA, Indpls. Estate Plan Council, Am. Council Life Ins. (com.), Health Ins. Assn. Am. (com.). Democrat. Presbyterian. Clubs: Literary, Sertoma (Indpls.). Avocation: American history. Insurance. Home: 5671 Central St Indianapolis IN 46220 Office: Indpls Life Ins Co PO Box 1230 Indianapolis IN 46206

EMERSON, CARTER WHITNEY, lawyer; b. Oak Park, Ill., Mar. 18, 1947; s. Garner P. and Daisy M. (Carter) E.; m. Susan D. Emerson, June 28, 1969. BS in Fin., Miami U., Oxford, Ohio, 1969; JD magna cum laude, Northwestern U., 1972. Law clk. to judge U.S. Dist. Ct. (no. dist.) Ill., 1972-73; assoc. Kirkland & Ellis, Chgo., 1974-78, ptnr., 1978—. Mem. ABA (business corps. and banking sect.), Order of Coif. Club: Mid-Am. (Chgo.). Securities, Acquisitions, Venture capital. Office: Kirkland & Ellis 200 E Randolph Dr Chicago IL 60601

EMERSON, S. JONATHAN, lawyer; b. Pasadena, Calif., July 2, 1929; s. Sterling H. and Mary Foote (Randall) E.; m. Virginia B. Emerson, July 3, 1954; children: Margaret Ellen, Henry Rollins, Peter Randall. BA, U. Calif., Berkeley, 1955; JD, U. Mich., 1957. Bar: Pa. 1958. Assoc., ptnr. Montgomery, McCracken, Walker & Rhoads, Phila., 1958—; Mem. Continental Bank Trust Com., Phila., 1973—. Served to cpl. U.S. Army, 1950-52. Fellow Am. Coll. Probate Counsel. Republican. Club: Union League (Phila.). Avocations: tennis, gardening, travel. Probate, Estate taxation, General corporate. Home: 16 Oberlin Ave Swarthmore PA 19081 Office: Montgomery McCracken et al One Mennonite Church Rd Spring City PA 19475

EMERSON, WILLIAM HARRY, lawyer, oil company executive; b. Rochester, N.Y., Jan. 13, 1928; s. William Canfield and Alice Sarah (Adams) E.; m. Jane Anne Epple, Dec. 27, 1956; children: Elizabeth Anne, Carolyn Jane. B.A., Cornell U., 1951, LL.B., 1956. Bar: Ill. 1974. Atty. Amoco Corp., 1956—; sec., dir. Amoco Gas Co., 1979—. Pres., dir. Undercraft Montessori Sch., Tulsa, 1965-67, Tulsa Figure Skating Club, 1969; bd. dirs. v.p. Lake Forest Found. for Historic Preservation, Ill., 1983—. Served to 1st lt. AUS, 1945, 52. Federal civil litigation, State civil litigation, FERC practice. Home: 593 Greenvale Rd Lake Forest IL 60045 Office: 200 E Randolph Dr Chicago IL 60601

EMERTON, ROBERT WALTER, III, lawyer; b. Hanover, Pa., Feb. 4, 1950; s. James Leonard and Dorothy (Davenport) E.; m. Sharon Whitaker, June 9, 1973 (div. Mar. 1982); children—Chad, Ryan. B.A., U. Fla., 1972, J.D., 1975. Bar: Fla. 1975, U.S. Dist. Ct. (mid. dist.) Fla. 1976, U.S. Ct. Appeals (11th cir.) 1981, U.S. Supreme Ct. 1982. Asst. pub. defender State of Fla., Tampa, 1975-76; litigation counsel Jim Walter Corp., Tampa, 1976-79, sr. litigation counsel, 1979-82, asst. v.p., 1982-85, dir. Asbestos Claims Facility, Inc., 1985—; bd. dirs. Asbestos Claims Facility, Inc.; legal cons. Com. for Equitable Compensation, Washington, 1982—. Spl. award Ctr. for Pub. Resources, 1985. Mem. Hillsborough County Bar Assn. (corp. counsel subcom. 1977—). Republican. General corporate, Insurance, Personal injury. Home: 928 W Cimmeron Dr Tampa FL 33603 Office: Jim Walter Corp 1500 N Dale Mabry Hwy Tampa FL 33607

EMERY, HERSCHELL GENE, lawyer; b. Hobart, Okla., Oct. 19, 1923; s. W. Herschell and L. Norean (Lewis) E.; m. Charlotte Chrisney, Oct. 28, 1948; children—Kathy Emery Miller, Steve . A.B., U. Ill., 1945; LL.B., Harvard U., 1948. Bar: Ind. 1949, Tex. 1955, U.S. Tax Ct. 1956, U.S. Ct. Appeals (5th cir.) 1980, U.S. Ct. Claims, 1980. Assoc., Ross McCord Ice & Miller, Indpls., 1948-55; assoc., ptnr. Thompson Knight Wright & Simmons, Dallas, 1955-65; ptnr. Rain Harrell Emery Young & Doke, Dallas, 1965-87, ptnr. Lucke, Purwell, Rain & Harrell, 1987—; lectr. various tax and legal insts.; dir. various corps. Served with U.S. Army, 1943. Fellow Am. Coll. Probate Counsel; mem. ABA, Tex. Bar Assn., Dallas Bar Assn. Presbyterian. Clubs: Dallas Country, Northwood, Dallas Petroleum, Old Baldy. Corporate taxation, Probate, Estate taxation. Office: Suite 4200 Republic Bank Tower Dallas TX 75201

EMHARDT, CHARLES DAVID, lawyer; b. Indpls., Feb. 13, 1931; s. John William and Martha Jack (Macdougall) E.; m. Ann Devaney, Nov. 12, 1954; children—John D., Carol A., Frederick D., Martha A., Lucy E. B.S. in Engring. Mechanics, Purdue U., 1952, A.S. in Elec. Engring. Tech., 1966; LL.B., Harvard U., 1955. Bar: D.C. 1955, Ind. 1958, U.S. Patent Office 1955. Patent atty. Western Electric Co., Washington, Balt., 1955-57; assoc. Harold B. Hood, Indpls., 1957-59, Lockwood, Woodard, Smith & Weikart, Indpls., 1959-64; ptnr. Woodard, Emhardt, Naughton, Moriarty & McNett and previous firm Woodard, Weikart, Emhardt & Naughton, Indpls., 1964—. Republican precinct committeeman, 1965-70. Served with Army NG, 1955-66. Mem. ABA, Ind. State Bar Assn. (chmn. pat. sect. 1967-68), Indpls. Bar Assn. (bd. 1979-81, chmn. ethics com. 1982-83). Presbyterian. Clubs: Woodstock, Indpls. Athletic, Masons, Shriners. Federal civil litigation, Trademark and copyright, Patent. Home: 4801 Fauna Ln Indianapolis IN 46234 Office: Woodard Emhardt Naughton et al 2670 1 Indiana Sq Indianapolis IN 46204

EMLER, JAY SCOTT, lawyer; b. Denver, May 25, 1949; s. Joseph Fredrick and Lois Justine (Scott) E.; m. Lorraine Kristine Pearson, May 30, 1970. BA, Bethany Coll., 1971; JD, U. Denver, 1976; emergency med. technician degree, Hutchinson Community Coll., 1979. Bar: Colo. 1977, Kans. 1977. Sole practice Lindsborg, Kans., 1977—; judge Lindsborg (Kans.) Mcpl. Ct., 1978—; instr. Barton County (Kans.) Community Coll., 1979; bd. dirs. Falun (Kans.) State Bank, 1983—, sec., 1986—. adminstr. Lindsborg Vol. Ambulance Corps., 1979-85; chmn. Lindsborg chpt. McPherson County March of Dimes, 1979-86; mem. Kans Emergency Med. Services Council, 1985—, chmn., 1987—; bd. dirs. Lindsborg Community Hosp., 1981—, v.p., 1987—. Mem. ABA (family law sect.), Kans. Bar Assn., McPherson County Bar Assn. (chmn. law day com. 1978, sec. treas. 1985-86), Kans. Assn. Hosp. Attys., Kans. Mcpl. Judges Assn. (bd. dirs. 1981—, pres. 1985—, chmn. legisl. action com. 1983-85), Kans. Supreme Ct. Mcpl. Judges Adv. Com., Kans. Judicial Council (mcpl. ct. manual rev. com.), Kans. Assn. Emergency Med. Services Aminstrs. (sec. 1980-84). General practice. Office: 115 W Lincoln St PO Box 292 Linsborg KS 67456

EMMANUEL, MICHEL GEORGE, lawyer; b. Clearwater, Fla., May 16, 1918; s. George M. and Alexandra (Damianakes) E.; m. Betty Boring, Dec. 19, 1942; children: George Michel II, Martha Alexandra. B.S., U. Fla., 1940, LL.B., 1948; LL.M., NYU, 1949. Bar: Fla. 1948. Research fellow NYU, N.Y.C., 1948-49; partner Mabry, Reaves, Carlton, Fields & Ward, Tampa, 1951-63; mem. firm Carlton, Fields, Ward, Emmanuel, Smith & Cutler, 1963—; mem. adv. com., lectr. NYU Tax Inst.; lectr. Estate Planning Inst. U. Miami. Contbr. articles to profl. jours. and yachting mags. Bd. dirs., past pres. Hillsborough County Crime Commn.; chmn. Mayor's Com. on Juvenile Delinquency; bd. dirs. Anclote Found., U. of South Fla. Found., Univ. Community Found., U. Tampa, Saunders Found., Fla. Hist. Soc., Univ. Community Hosp., Fla. Yacht Club Council, United Fund, Tampa Improvement Found., Fales Com., U.S. Naval Acad. Served to comdr. USNR, World War II. Decorated D.F.C., Air medal with 2 stars, Purple Heart; recipient Gov.'s award for distinguished service to State of Fla. Fellow Am. Coll. Probate Counsel, Am. Coll. Tax Counsel; mem. Am., Hillsborough County, Tampa bar assns., D.C. Bar, Fla. Bar (past chmn. tax sect.), Am. Judicature Soc., Tampa C. of C. (past pres.), U.S. C. of C. (taxation com.), Ancient and Secret Order of Quiet Birdmen, Sigma Chi, Phi Delta Phi. Episcopalian. Clubs: Ye Mystic Krewe of Gasparilla (past king), University (past pres.), Tampa Executives , Tampa Yacht and Country, Tower (all Tampa); Gainesville (Fla.) Golf and Country; Cruising Club of Am. Lodge: Rotary (Tampa past pres.). Probate, Corporate taxation, Estate taxation. Home: 2806 Terrace Dr Tampa FL 33609 Home: Kritonos 9, Aegina Greece Office: One Harbour Pl Tampa FL 33602

EMMERT, STEVEN MICHAEL, lawyer; b. Zanesville, Ohio, July 6, 1957; s. Edward Francis and Doris Jean (Sigrist) E.; m. Margaret Teresa Brosnan, Aug. 8, 1981. BA with distinction, Ohio State U., 1979, JD, 1982. Bar: Ohio 1982, U.S. Dist. Ct. (so. dist.) Ohio 1984. Staff atty. Ohio Dept. Energy, Columbus, 1981-83, Ohio Bur. Workers' Compensation, Columbus, 1983; adminstrv. law judge energy Ohio Dept. Devel., Columbus, 1983-85; corp. atty. Online Computer Library Ctr., Dublin, Ohio, 1985—. Participant, supr. Vol/ Income Tax Assistance IRS, 1981-82. Named one of Outstanding Young Men Am. U.S. Jaycees, 1983-86. Mem. ABA, Ohio Bar Assn., Columbus Bar Assn. Democrat. Roman Catholic. Club: Ohio State U. Karate. Avocations: tennis, golf, karate. Computer, Trademark and copyright, Immigration, naturalization, and customs. Home: 1122A Weybridge Rd Columbus OH 43220 Office: Online Computer Library Ctr Inc 6565 Frantz Rd Dublin OH 43017

EMMETT, JAMES ROBERT, lawyer; b. Gary, Ind., Jan. 24, 1940; s. Robert Gerald and Jeannette Louise (Pinkerton) E.; m. Marian Carol Yanney, Jan. 28, 1967; children: Jennifer Kathleen, Robert Yanney. BCE, Purdue U., 1963; JD, Ind. U., 1966. Bar: Ind. 1967, U.S. Dist. Ct. (so. dist.) Ind. 1967. Engr. design GE Snyder & Assocs., Jackson, Mich., 1968-70; atty. real estate Amoco Oil Co., Chgo., 1970-72; rep. property tax Amoco Oil Corp., Chgo., 1972-74, atty. state tax, 1974—. Mem. Ind. Bar Assn., Inst. Property Taxation. Avocations: golf, tennis, guitar, reading. Corporate taxation, State and local taxation. Office: Amoco Corp 200 E Randolph Dr Chicago IL 60601

EMMETT, ROBERT ADDIS, III, lawyer; b. Washington, July 2, 1943; s. Robert Addis Jr. and Marjorie (Slater) E.; m. Anne Ellen Flanigan, Aug. 29, 1969; children: Jennifer, Laura, Robert, Andrew. BA, U. Mich., 1965; JD, Stanford U., 1968. Bar: Calif. 1969, D.C. 1976, U.S. Ct. Appeals (D.C. cir.) 1978, U.S. Supreme Ct. 1980, U.S. Ct. Appeals (8th cir.) 1981, U.S. Ct. Appeals (4th cir.) 1985, U.S. Ct. Appeals (3d and 6th cirs.) 1986. Vol. U.S. Peace Corps., Acarigua, Venezuela, 1969-70; atty. br. chief U.S. EPA, Washington, 1971-77; from assoc. to ptnr. Reed Smith Shaw & McClay, Washington, 1978—; bd. dirs. Detrex Corp., Southfield, Mich., 1984—. Mem. ABA, D.C. Bar Assn. Club: Edgemoor (Bethesda, Md.). Environment, Administrative and regulatory, Federal civil litigation. Home: 5408 Moorland Ln Bethesda MD 20814 Office: Reed Smith Shaw & McClay 1150 Connecticut Ave NW Suite 900 Washington DC 20036

EMMONS, ALISON LOBB, lawyer; b. Greensburg, Ky., Aug. 2, 1952; d. William Densil and Barbara Joy (Root) Lobb; m. William Charles Kline, Jan. 8, 1980 (div. July 1984); m. Dale C. Emmons, Jan. 11, 1986. BS, Campbellsville Coll., 1972; JD, U. Ky., 1977. Bar: Ky. 1977, U.S. Dist. Ct. (ea. dist.) Ky. 1978, U.S. Dist. Ct. (we. dist.) Ky. 1980, U.S. Ct. Appeals (6th cir.) 1982, U.S. Supreme Ct. 1982. Law clk. Ky. Office of Public Advocacy, Frankfort, 1976; ptnr. Walker, Emmons & Baird, P.S.C., Richmond, Ky., 1978—; asst. atty. Madison County, Ky., 1978; adj. prof. law U. Ky., Lexington, 1978-79. Bd. dirs. Appalachian Research & Def. Fund, Prestonsburg, Ky., 1980—; pres., bd. dirs. Madison County Estate Planning Council, 1982-83. Mem. Assn. Trial Lawyers Am., Am. Soc. Legal History, Ky. Acad. Trial Lawyers, Ky. Bar Assn., Madison County Bar Assn. (pres. 1982-83), Business and Profl. Women's Club (v.p. Richmond 1985-86, asst. dir. cen. region, 1985-86, Women of Yr. 1983), Younger Women's Club, (pres. Richmond 1983-84), Order of Coif. Democrat. Methodist. Probate, Public utilities, Personal injury. Office: Walker Emmons & Baird PSC 224 W Main St Richmond KY 40475

EMMONS, PETER RIBEIRO, lawyer; b. Salvador, Brazil, Mar. 29, 1955; s. Robert Mitchell and Aidil (Ribeiro) E.; m. Susan Joan Cohen, Nov. 3, 1984. BA, Bowdoin Coll., 1976; JD, Emory U., 1979. Bar: Ga. 1980, Fla. 1981, U.S. Dist. Ct. Staff atty. Ga. Legal Services Corp., Statesboro, Ga., 1980-81; corp. counsel Imperial Aviation, West Palm Beach, Fla., 1981-82; atty. White & Daum, Atlanta, 1982; sole practice Atlanta, 1982-84; v.p. Inperial Systems, Atlanta, 1984-86; ptnr. Whtie, Ravis, & Emmons, Atlanta, 1986—. Recipient Cert. of Achievement, NAACP, 1980. Mem. ABA (vice chmn. gen. practice com for systems in computer automation), Ga. Bar Assn., Fla. Bar Assn. Civil rights, Federal civil litigation, Family and matrimonial. Home: 3405 Old Plantation Rd Atlanta GA 30327 Office: White Ravis and Emmons 1126 Ponce de Leon Ave Atlanta GA 30306

EMRICH, EDMUND MICHAEL, lawyer; b. N.Y.C., Apr. 12, 1956; s. Edmund and Mary Ann (Picarella) E. BA, SUNY, Albany, 1978; JD, Hofstra U., 1981. Bar: N.Y. 1982, U.S. Dist. Ct. (so. and ea. dists.) N.Y. 1982, U.S. Ct. Appeals (2d cir.) 1987. Law clk. to presiding justice U.S. Bankruptcy Ct. (ea. dist.) N.Y., Westbury, 1982-83; assoc. Levin & Weintraub & Crames, N.Y.C., 1983—; mem. local rules com. U.S. Bankruptcy Ct. (ea. dist.) N.Y., 1985-86; mem. local rules drafting subcom. U.S. Bankruptcy Ct. (so. dist.) N.Y., 1985-86. Mem. Hofstra U. Law Rev., 1981-82. Mem. N.Y. State Bar Assn., N.Y. County Lawyers Assn. Roman Catholic. Avocations: golf, tennis. Bankruptcy. Home: 46 W 73d St New York NY 10023 Office: Levin & Weintraub & Crames 225 Broadway New York NY 10007

EMROCH, EMANUEL, lawyer; b. Richmond, Va., Apr. 13, 1908; s. Herman and Tobie (Weinstein) E.; m. Bertha Vitsky, June 10, 1931; children: Walter Herman, Brenda Sue, Linda Ann Leithner. BA, U. Richmond, 1928, LLB, 1931. Bar: Va. 1930, U.S. Dist. Ct. (ea. and we. dists.) Va. 1954, U.S. Ct. Appeals (4th cir.) 1956, U.S. Supreme Ct. 1960, U.S. Ct. Mil. Appeals 1985. Ptnr. Emroch & Williamson, Richmond, 1982—. Co-author: (with biennial supplements) Virginia Jury Instructions, 1964; contbr. numerous articles to law jours. Lecture series named in his honor T.C. Williams Sch. of Law, U. Richmond, 1985. Fellow Am. Coll. Trial Lawyers, Internat. Acad. Trial Lawyers (nat. bd. 1973-79), Am. Bd. Trial Advs. (pres. Va. chpt. 1985), Va. Trial Lawyers Assn. (pres. 1962), Richmond Bar Assn. (bd. dirs. 1960-63), Richmond Trial Lawyers Assn. (pres. 1959-60). Jewish. Club: Downtown. Lecture series established in name of Emanuel Emroch at U. Richmond T.C. Williams Sch. Law. Avocations: classical music, opera, reading. Federal civil litigation, State civil litigation, Personal injury. Home: One Roslyn Hills Dr Richmond VA 23229 Office: Emroch & Williamson 6800 Paragon Place Suite 233 Richmond VA 23230

ENBERG, HENRY WINFIELD, legal editor; b. Bethlehem, Pa., Oct. 4, 1940; s. Henry Winfield and Mildred Elizabeth (Jordan) E. B.S., U. Denver, 1962; LL.B., NYU, 1965. Bar: N.Y. 1967. Digester, Winthrop, Stimson, Putnam & Roberts, N.Y.C., 1965-69; sr. legal editor Practising Law Inst., N.Y.C., 1969—; bd. dirs. ZPPR Prodns., Inc. Contbr. articles. Republican. Episcopalian. Clubs: Wolfe Pack, Priory Scholars (N.Y.C.). Legal Writing. Home: 250 W 27th St New York NY 10001 Office: Practising Law Inst 810 7th Ave New York NY 10019

ENDEMAN, RONALD LEE, lawyer; b. Riverside, Calif., May 13, 1936; s. Walter Metsger and May Florence (Higdon) E.; m. Judith Lynn Sherman, May 27, 1959; children—Michael Scott, Melissa May. B.A., U. Calif.-River-

side, 1959; J.D., U. So. Calif., 1966. Bar: Calif. 1967, U.S. Dist. Ct. (so. dist.) Calif. 1967, U.S. Ct. Claims 1972, U.S. Ct. Appeals (9th cir.) 1973, U.S. Supreme Ct. 1972. Trial atty. Calif. Legal Div., San Diego, 1967-71; ptnr. Jackson, Turner, Endeman & Mulcare, Burlingame, Calif., 1971-73; ptnr. Jennings, Engstrand & Henrikson, San Diego, 1973—. Mem. ABA, Calif. Bar Assn., San Diego County Bar Assn., Assn. Trial Lawyers Am., Calif. Trial Lawyers Assn., San Diego County Trial Lawyers Assn., Am. Arbitration Assn., Internat. Right of Way Assn., Guild of Real Estate Appraisers (Man of Yr. 1971). Republican. Condemnation. Home: 10602 Noakes Rd La Mesa CA 92041 Office: 2255 Camino del Rio S San Diego CA 92108

ENDIEVERI, ANTHONY FRANK, lawyer; b. Syracuse, N.Y., May 21, 1939; s. Santo and Anne Rose (Zeolla) E.; m. Arlene Rita McDonald, May 20, 1967; children: Anne C., Steven A. BA, Syracuse U., 1961, JD, 1965. Bar: N.Y. 1967, U.S. Dist. Ct. (no. dist.) N.Y. 1967, U.S. Ct. Appeals (2d cir.) 1969, U.S. Supreme Ct. 1970. Assoc. Ronald Crowley, Atty., North Syracuse, N.Y., 1965-67, Love, Balducci & Scacciz, Syracuse, 1967; sole practice, Camillus, N.Y., 1968—; appellate counsel Hiscock Legal Aid, Syracuse, 1968-70; asst. corp. counsel, prosecutor City of Syracuse, 1970-74; participant Nat. Coll. Advocacy, 1981-83, 86; speaker seminar, 1987. Mem. ministry program Syracuse Diocese Pre-Deacon Study, 1980—. Served to maj. USMC, 1972—. Mem. ABA, N.Y. Bar Assn., Onondaga County Bar Assn., N.Y. Trial Lawyers Assn., Assn. Trial Lawyers Am. Democrat. Roman Catholic. Personal injury, Insurance, State civil litigation. Home: 205 Emann Dr Camillus NY 13031

ENDRELUNAS, RICHARD MICHAEL, lawyer; b. Hartford, Conn., Dec. 21, 1942; s. Robert J. and Helen K. (Karanda) E.; divorced; children: Mary Elisbeth, Kathleen, Robert. BA in History, St. Michael's Coll., Winooski, Vt., 1964; JD, U. Conn., 1969. Bar: Conn. 1969. Assoc. Ronald F. Storms, Windsor Locks, Conn., 1969-73; prosecutor State of Conn., Windsor, 1973-76; assoc. Bromson & Reiner, Windsor Locks, 1976—; mem. adv. com. to revise criminal rules State of Conn., 1976. Mem. Am. Trial Lawyers Assn. Roman Catholic. Avocations: hunting, fishing, skiing, growing bonsai. Criminal, Personal injury. Office: Bromson & Reiner 546 Halfway House Rd Windsor Locks CT 06096

ENERSEN, BURNHAM, lawyer; b. Lamberton, Minn., Nov. 17, 1905; s. Albert H. and Ethel (Rice) E.; m. Nina H. Wallace, July 21, 1935; children: Richard W., Elizabeth. A.B., Carleton Coll., 1927, L.H.D., 1974; LL.B., Harvard U., 1930. Bar: Calif. 1931. Assoc. McCutchen, Doyle, Brown & Enersen, San Francisco, 1930-43, ptnr., 1943-78, counsel, 1978—; dir. Pomfret Estates, Inc., Calif. Student Loan Fin. Corp.; Chmn. Gov.'s Com. Water Lawyers, 1957; mem. Calif. Jud. Council, 1960-64; vice chmn. Calif. Constn. Revision Commn., 1964-75; mem. com. to rev. Calif. Master Plan for Higher Edn., 1971-72. Mem. Calif. Citizens Commn. for Tort Reform, 1976-77; chmn. Assn. Calif. Tort Reform, 1979-83; mem. Calif. Postsecondary Edn. Com., 1974-78; bd. dirs. Criminal Justice Legal Found., 1982—, chmn., 1985-86; bd. dirs. Fine Arts Mus. Found., 1983—, pres., 1985—; pres. United Bay Area Crusade, 1962, United Crusades of Calif., 1969-71; trustee Mills Coll., 1972-82, chmn., 1976-80. Fellow Am. Bar Found.; mem. Am. Judicature Soc., ABA (ho. of dels. 1970-76), State Bar Calif. (pres. 1960), Bar Assn. San Francisco (pres. 1955), Bar Assn. City N.Y., Am. Law Inst., Calif. C. of C. (dir. 1962-78, pres. 1971), Calif. Hist. Soc. (dir. 1976-78, 83—). Clubs: Bohemian, Pacific-Union, Commercial (pres. 1966), Commonwealth Calif, San Francisco Golf, Cypress Point. General practice, Real property. Home: 40 Arguello Blvd San Francisco CA 94118 Office: 3 Embarcadero Center San Francisco CA 94111

ENFIELD, MYRON LEROY, lawyer; b. Anita, Iowa, Aug. 24, 1930; s. Lee Roy and Ella Christina (Quist) E.; m. Virginia Lee Jacobs, Feb. 3, 1957; children: Christy Lynn Enfield Todd, Steven Lee, Melanie Ann, Nancy Marie. BA, U. Iowa, 1957, JD, 1959. Bar: Oreg. 1960. Assoc. Rhoten, Rhoten and Speerstra, Salem, Oreg., 1960-69; sole practice Salem, 1969-79; ptnr. Enfield & McConville, Salem, 1969-82, Enfield, Guimond and Brown, Salem, 1982—. Chmn. Salam Sch. Adv. Com., 1969-72, Community Relations Adv. Com., 1973. Served as cpl. U.S. Army. Mem. ABA, Oreg. State Bar Assn., Marion County Bar Assn. Democrat. Mem. Covenant Ch. Club: Salem Swim and Tennis (chmn. 1975). State civil litigation, Family and matrimonial, Probate. Home: 568 Juntura Ct SE Salem OR 97302 Office: Enfield Guimond and Brown 117 Commercial NE Suite 214 Salem OR 97301-3498

ENGEL, ALBERT JOSEPH, judge; b. Lake City, Mich., Mar. 21, 1924; s. Albert Joseph and Bertha (Bielby) E.; m. Eloise Ruth Bull, Oct. 18, 1952; children: Albert Joseph, Katherine Ann, James Robert, Mary Elizabeth. Student, U. Md., 1941-42; A.B., U. Mich., 1948, LL.B., 1950. Bar: Mich. 1951. Ptnr. firm Engle & Engel, Muskegon, Mich., 1952-67; judge Mich. Circuit Ct., 1967-71; judge U.S. Dist. Ct. Western Dist. Mich., 1971-74; circuit judge U.S. Ct. Appeals, 6th Circuit, Grand Rapids, Mich., 1974—. Served with AUS, 1943-46, ETO. Fellow Am. Bar Found.; mem. Am., Fed., Cin., Grand Rapids bar assns., Am. Judicature Soc., Am. Legion, Phi Sigma Kappa, Phi Delta Phi. Episcopalian. Club: Grand Rapids Torch. Home: 7287 Denison Dr SE Grand Rapids MI 49506 Office: 640 Fed Bldg Grand Rapids MI 49503

ENGEL, DAVID CHAPIN, lawyer; b. N.Y.C., Oct. 6, 1931; s. Robert Albert and Mabel Gretchen (Eshbaugh) E.; m. Joan Talbot, June 6, 1954 (div. May 1972); children: Karen, Kathleen, Julie, Peter, Rebekah; m. Priscilla Gail Stevens, May 26, 1972; 1 adopted child, Terri, 1 child, Heidi. BA, St. Lawrence U., 1954; LLB, NYU, 1956. Bar: N.H. 1956, U.S. Dist. Ct. N.H. 1957, Mass. 1969, U.S. Dist. Ct. Mass. 1969, U.S. Ct. Appeals (1st cir.) 1969. Law clk. Atty. Gen. Office, Concord, N.H., 1956-58; ptnr. Shute, Engel & Morse, Exeter, N.H., 1958-84, Engel & Morse, Exeter, 1984—; arbitrator Am. Arbitration Assn., 1962—; chmn. Gov.'s Commn. on Child Support Enforcement, 1985—. del. Rep. Nat. Conv., 1964, Rep. State Conv., 1965, 67, 69, Nat. Conf. State Legis., Charleston, South Carolina, 1985; bd. dirs. Greenland (N.H.) Community Congl. Ch., 1975-78, deacon 1980-83; mem. Greenland Planning Bd., 1980—, Greenland Budget Com., 1986. Mem. N.H. Bar Assn. (legis. com. 1963-64). Federal civil litigation, State civil litigation, Personal injury. Home: 47 Park Ave Greenland NH 03840 Office: Engel & Morse PA 23 Portsmouth Ave Stratham NH 03885

ENGEL, DAVID WAYNE, judge advocate officer; b. Salisbury, Md., Nov. 29, 1956; s. Robert Peter Engel and Joan (King) Bradshaw; m. Laura Marie Tuck, June 25, 1983; children: Michael Andrew, Jennifer Lynn. AB, William & Mary Coll., 1978; JD, Washington & Lee U., 1981. Bar: Va. 1981, U.S. Dist. Ct. (ea. and we. dists.) Va. 1981, U.S. Ct. Mil. Appeals 1981, U.S. Ct. Appeals (4th cir.) 1981, U.S. Tax Ct. 1982, U.S. Ct. Appeals (5th cir.) 1985, Tex. 1985, U.S. Dist. Ct. (we. dist.) Tex. 1985. Claims atty. Ft. Leonard Wood, Ft. Wood, Mo., 1981-82, trial counsel, 1982-84; med. claims judge adv. William Beaumont Army Med. Ctr., El Paso, Tex., 1984—. Served to capt. U.S. Army (JAGC), 1981—. Mem. ABA, El Paso Bar Assn., Am. Polit. Sci. Assn. Military, Personal injury, Federal civil litigation. Home: 7145 Gran Vida El Paso TX 79912 Office: William Beaumont Army Med Ctr Attn: HSHM-MCJA El Paso TX 79920

ENGEL, EDWARD IGNATIUS, lawyer; b. Portland, Oreg., Feb. 18, 1926; s. Ignatius Loyola and Katherine Loretta (McDonald) E. m. Virginia Elizabeth Clay, June 7, 1952; children: Susan E. Muller, Mary V., Kathleen A., Janet M. BA, U. Portland, 1949; JD, Lewis & Clark Coll., 1954. Bar: Oreg. 1955, U.S. Supreme Ct. 1970. Ptnr. Goldsmith, Siegel, Engel & Littlefield, Portland, 1955—; cir. judge pro tem State Oreg., 1970; bd. dirs. Multnomah Law Library. Recipient Honor award Oreg. Jr. C. of C., 1961, Service Youth award YMCA, 1964. Mem. ABA, Oreg. Bar Assn., Oreg. Trial Lawyers Assn., Multnomah Bar Assn. (pres. 1972-78, Oustanding Service award 1970). Republican. Roman Catholic. Club: Multnomah Athletic. State civil litigation, Insurance, Probate. Home: 6209 SW Tower Way Portland OR 97221 Office: Goldsmith Siegal Engel 875 Boise Cascade Bldg Portland OR 97201

ENGEL, GEORGE LARRY, lawyer; b. Chgo., Apr. 19, 1947; s. George Albert and Jane Elizabeth (Hoyle) E.; m. Stephanie Fuller, May 29, 1971; children: Laura Elizabeth, Bryan Arthur. BA magna cum laude, Northwestern U., 1969, JD cum laude, 1972. Bar: Calif. 1972, U.S. Dist. Ct. (no., cen., ea. and so. dists.) Calif., U.S. Ct. Appeals (9th cir.). Assoc. Brobeck, Phleger & Harrison, San Francisco, 1972-79, ptnr., 1979—. Exec. editor Northwestern U. Law Rev., 1971-72; contbr. articles to profl. jours. Mem. ABA (subcom. chmn. comml. fin. services com. 1981—), Calif. Bar Assn. (uniform comml. code com.), Phi Beta Kappa, Order of Coif. Methodist. Avocations: writing, backpacking, scuba diving. Contracts commercial, Bankruptcy, Banking. Home: 31 Charles Hill Circle Orinda CA 94563 Office: Brobeck Phleger & Harrison 1 Market Plaza San Francisco CA 94105

ENGEL, R. JAY, lawyer; b. Sacramento, Aug. 28, 1937; s. Ralph Joseph and Mona Irene (Chubb) E.; m. Pamalee G. Hamilton, Oct. 27, 1973; children—Lisa, Curran, Scott, Brandon. B.A., U. of Calif.-Berkeley, 1959; LL.B., Hastings Coll. Law, 1962. Bar: Calif. 1962, U.S. Dist. Ct. (no. dist.) Calif. 1962, U.S. Ct. Appeals (9th cir.) 1962, U.S. Supreme Ct. 1967. Clerkship, Calif. Dist. Ct. of Appeal, San Francisco, 1962-63; atty. Walkup & Downing, San Francisco, 1963-67, Jarvis, Miller & Stender, San Francisco, 1967-70, R. Jay Engel, Inc., San Francisco, 1970—. Mem. Am. Bd. Profl. Liability Attys., Nat. Bd. Trial Advocacy, Assn. Trial Lawyers Am., Calif. Trial Lawyers Assn., ABA, Calif. State Bar. Democrat. Personal injury. Home: Berkeley CA 94701 Office: 22 2d St 6th Floor San Francisco CA 94105

ENGEL, RALPH MANUEL, lawyer; b. N.Y.C., May 13, 1944; s. Werner Herman and Ruth Fredericke (Friedlander) E.; m. Diane Linda Weinberg, Aug. 10, 1968; children—Eric M., Daniel C., Julie R. B.A. with highest honors in Econs., NYU, 1965, J.D., 1968. Bar: N.Y. 1968, U.S. Supreme Ct. 1972. Atty. firm Gilbert, Segall and Young, N.Y.C., 1968-71, Trubin Sillcocks Edelman & Knapp, N.Y.C., 1971-76; atty. firm Summit Rovins & Feldesman and predecessor firms, N.Y.C., 1976—, ptnr., 1978—. Contbr. articles to legal and other publs.; editor-in-chief The Commentator, NYU, 1968. Fellow Am. Coll. Probate Counsel; mem. Estate Planning Council Westchester County (bd. dirs. 1985—), N.Y. State Bar Assn., Assn. Bar City N.Y., Am. Arbitration Assn. (arbitrator). Probate, Estate planning, Estate taxation. Home and Office: 6 Rockwood Dr Larchmont NY 10538 Office: 445 Park Ave New York NY 10022

ENGEL, RICHARD LEE, lawyer, educator; b. Syracuse, N.Y., Sept. 19, 1936; s. S. Sanford and Eleanor M. (Gallop) E.; m. Karen K. Engel, Dec. 26, 1965; children—Todd Sanford, Gregg Matthew. B.A., Yale U., 1958, J.D., 1981. Bar: N.Y. 1961. Law asst. justices Appellate Div., N.Y. 4th Jud. Dist., 1961-63; law clk. judge N.Y. Supreme Ct., 1963-65; sr. ptnr. Nottingham, Engel, Gordon, Kerr & Watt, Syracuse, 1970—; adj. prof. law Syracuse U. Coll. of Law lectr. in field. Contbr. articles to profl. jours., seminars. Pres. Temple Soc. Concord, 1985—; trustee AFC Intercultual Internat. Scholarship, 1974-78; bd. dirs. Am. Field Service Internat. and Intercultural Programs, Inc., 1972-78. Mem. ABA, N.Y. State Bar Assn., Onondaga Bar Assn. (mem. trial lawyers com. 1978-80, chmn. med. legal liaison com 1976-77), N.Y. State Trial Attys. Assn., Upstate Trial Attys. Assn. (dir. 1968—; pres. 1973-74, chmn. bd. 1974-77), Def. Research Inst., Inc. Clubs: Cavalry Country, Yale (pres.). Federal civil litigation, State civil litigation, Personal injury. Home: Brockway Ln Fayetteville NY 13066 Office: One Lincoln Center 8th Floor Syracuse NY 13202

ENGEL, STEVEN IRA, lawyer; b. Bklyn., Oct. 8, 1946; s. Jack and Lillian (Kofsky) E.; m. Judith L. Cohen, Jan. 18, 1970; children—Jeffrey, Adam. A.A., U. Fla., 1966; B.B.A., U. Miami (Fla.), 1968, J.D., 1971. Bar: Fla. 1971, U.S. Ct. Appeals (D.C. cir.) 1979, U.S. Ct. Appeals (11th and 5th cirs.) 1972. Ptnr., Huysman, Engel & Gold, P.A., 1971-72; corp. counsel Sterling Capital Investments, 1973-74; v.p., gen. counsel Robins-Ladd Co., Wilmington, Del., 1974-76; ptnr. Liebman & Engel, P.A., Homestead, Fla., 1976-78; v.p., gen. counsel Devel. Corp. Am., Miami, 1978—. Mem. ABA, Broward County Bar Assn. General corporate, Real property. Address: 12829 SW 103d Pl Miami FL 33176

ENGEL, TALA, lawyer; b. N.Y.C., Aug. 29, 1933; d. Volodia Vladimir Boris and Risia (Modelevska) E.; m. James Colias, Nov. 22, 1981. AA, U. Fla., 1952; BA, U. Miami, 1954, JD, 1957; postgrad., Middlebury Coll., 1953; JD. Bar: Fla. 1957, U.S. Dist. Ct. (so. dist.) Ill. 1962, U.S. Dist. Ct. (no. dist.) Ill. 1965, U.S. Supreme Ct. 1982, D.C. 1982. Sole practice Miami, Fla. and Chgo., 1957-61, 66-86, Washington, 1987—; atty. Immigration and Naturalization Service, Chgo., 1961-62; parole agt. Ill. Youth Commn., Chgo., 1963-66. Editor The Editor, 1956. Bd. dirs. Cordi-Marian Settlement, Chgo., 1977—. Mem. ABA, Fla. Bar Assn., D.C. Bar Assn., Ill. Bar Assn. (gen. assembly 1984-86), Chgo. Bar Assn. (devel. of law com. 1985-87), Chgo. Bar Found., Am. Immigration Lawyers Assn., Platform Soc., MENSA, Alpha Lambda Delta. Avocations: travelling, theater, singing, writing plays, writing in code. Immigration, naturalization, and customs. Home: 4701 Willard Ave Chevy Chase MD 20815 Office: 1000 Connecticut Ave NW Suite 1200 Washington DC 20036 also: 69 W Washington Chicago IL 60602

ENGELHARDT, JOHN HUGO, lawyer; b. Houston, Feb. 3, 1946; s. Hugo Tristram and Beulah Lillie (Karbach) E.; m. Jasmin Inge Nestler, Nov. 12, 1976; children: Angelique D, Sabrina N. BA, U. Tex., 1968; JD, St. Mary's U., San Antonio, 1973. Bar: Tex. 1973. Tchr. history Pearsall High Sch., Tex., 1968-69; examining atty. Comml. Title Co., San Antonio, 1975-78, San Antonio Title Co., 1978-82; sole practice, New Braunfels, Tex., 1973-75, 1982—; adv. dir. M Bank Brenham, Tex., 1983—. Mem. ABA, Coll. State Bar Tex., Pi Gamma Mu. Republican. Roman Catholic. Real property, Probate. Office: HC 3 Box 1 New Braunfels TX 78132

ENGERRAND, KENNETH GABRIEL, lawyer, law educator; b. Atlanta, June 30, 1952; s. Gabriel H. and Doris A. (Dieskow) E.; m. Anne Walts, Mar. 16, 1985; 1 child, Caroline Elizabeth Turner. B.A., Fla. State U., 1973; J.D., U. Tex., 1976. Bar: Tex. 1976, U.S. Dist. Ct. (so. dist.) Tex. 1977. U.S. Ct. Appeals (5th cir.) 1978, U.S. Supreme Ct. 1980, U.S. Ct. Appeals (11th cir.) 1981, U.S. Dist. Ct. (ea. dist.) Tex. 1987. Assoc. Royston, Rayzor, Vickery & Williams, Houston, 1976-80, Brown, Sims & Ayre, Houston, 1980; v.p., gen. counsel Huthnance Offshore Corp., Houston, 1980-86; assoc. Brown, Sims, Wise & White, Houston, 1986— ; adj. prof. law S. Tex. Coll. Law, Houston, 1979—. Columnist The Reporter, 1984—; contbr. articles to profl. jours. Faculty advisor to spl. maritime edits. S. Tex. Law Jour., 1981—. Fund drive vol. Houston Grand Opera, 1985—, trustee, 1986—. Named Best Prof., S. Tex. Coll. Law, Houston, 1981-82, 83-84; recipient Outstanding Contrbn. to Community award, Houston Jaycees, 1983; Mem. ABA (vice chmn. admiralty and maritime law com., tort and ins. practice sect. 1986—), Maritime Law Assn., Order of Coif, Phi Beta Kappa, Phi Delta Phi. Republican. Methodist. Avocation: legal writing, cultivating roses. Admiralty, General corporate, Federal civil litigation. Home: 773 W Creekside Dr Houston TX 77024 Office: Brown Sims Wise & White 2000 Post Oak Blvd Suite 2300 Post Oak Central Houston TX 77056

ENGLAND, JOHN MELVIN, lawyer, clergyman; b. Atlanta, June 29, 1932; s. John Marcus and Frances Dorothy (Brown) E.; m. Jane Cantrell, Aug. 2, 1953; children—Kathryn Elizabeth, Janette Evelyn, John William, Kenneth Paul, James Andrew, Samuel Robert. Student Ga. State U., 1951-53; J.D., U. Ga., 1956; B.D. magna cum laude with honors in Theology, Columbia Theol. Sem., Decatur, Ga., 1964. Bar: Ga. 1959, U.S. Dist. Ct. (no. dist.) Ga. 1967, U.S. Ct. Mil. Appeals 1976, U.S. Ct. Appeals (5th cir.) 1967, U.S. Ct. Appeals (11th cir.) 1981, U.S. Supreme Ct. 1977; ordained to ministry Presbyterian Ch., 1964. Spl. agt. FBI, Washington, 1956-57, Indpls., 1957-59, Charlotte, N.C., 1959, Greenville, S.C., 1959-60; student supply pastor Bethel and Buford Presbyn. Chs., Atlanta, 1960-63; pastor Mullins (S.C.) Presbyn. Ch., 1964-67; asst. dist. atty. Fulton County (Ga.), 1967-75; sr. ptnr. England and Weller, Atlanta, 1975—; legal seminar lectr. and speaker throughout the country under auspices of Christian orgns.; spl. pros. for gov. Ga., 1976-79; spl. cons. on appellate reform Supreme Ct. Ga., 1979-80; state bar rep. to Superior Ct. Uniform Rules Com., 1984. Elder, tchr. Presbyn. Ch. USA; chmn., Christian Bus. Men's Coms. of U.S.A., Atlanta, 1971-73, chmn. internat. conv., Atlanta, 1979, bd. dirs., 1971-81. Mem. ABA, State Bar Ga., Atlanta Bar Assn., Lawyers Club Atlanta, Assn. Trial Lawyers Am., Ga. Trial Lawyers Assn.; Nat. Assn. Criminal Def. Lawyers, Ga. Assn. Criminal Def. Lawyers, North Fulton Bar Assn. Civil rights, General practice, Personal injury. Office: 250 Piedmont Ave NE Suite 1220 Atlanta GA 30308

ENGLAND, WILLIAM THOMAS, lawyer, energy company executive; b. Manchester, Conn., Mar. 28, 1934; s. George John and Helen (Dimlow) E.; B.A., U. Conn., 1958, LL.B. with high honors, 1963; postgrad. George Washington U. Grad. Sch. Law, 1964-65, Parker Sch. Internat. Law, Columbia U., 1982; m. Alice G. O'Rourke, Oct. 12, 1956; children—William Thomas, Jr., Kerry J., Nancy J., Kelly M. Admitted to Conn. bar, 1963, D.C. bar, 1980; reporter Hartford (Conn.) Times, 1961-62; atty. U.S. AEC, Washington, 1963-65; chief counsel Joint Com. on Atomic Energy, U.S. Congress, Washington, 1965-70; v.p. for corp. affairs, gen. counsel Exxon Nuclear Co., Bellevue, Wash., 1970-81; counsel Exxon Corp., N.Y.C., 1981-82; gen. counsel Exxon Enterprises, N.Y.C., 1982-86; sr. counsel Exxon Corp., 1986—. cons. U.S. Commn. Govt. Procurement, 1972; dir. Zilog, Inc., Campbell, Calif., 1983—. Served with U.S. Army, 1958-60. Recipient Author's award Fed. Bar Assn., 1967-68. Mem. Am. Bar Assn., Fed. Bar Assn. Contbr. articles to various legal periodicals. General corporate, Nuclear power, Labor. Home: 51 Greenlea Ln Weston CT 06883 Office: Exxon Corp 1251 Ave of Americas New York NY 10005

ENGLANDER, PAULA TYO, lawyer; b. Syracuse, N.Y., Dec. 25, 1951; d. Howard James and Pauline Harriet Henderson; m. Ronald Englander, Jan. 24, 1971; children: David, Lisa. BA, SUNY, 1978; JD, Syracuse U., 1981. Bar: Colo. 1982, U.S. Dist. Ct. Colo. 1983, U.S. Ct. Appeals (10th cir.) 1983. Law clerk Kintzele & Collins, Denver, 1981-82; sole practice Denver, 1982—; cons. Orthotic and Prosthetic Assn., 1980; bd. dirs. Orthopedic Techs., Inc., Syracuse, Aurora (Colo.) Orthopedics, Inc. Contbr. articles to profl. jours. Asst. founding mem., asst. coordinator Export Assistance Program, 1984—. Mem. (founding) Alliance of Profl. Women, Colo. Bar Assn. (gen. and small firm sect., mem. council), ABA (legal econs. section). Avocations: skiing, hiking, swimming. General corporate, State civil litigation, Federal civil litigation. Home: 2055 Ivanhoe St Denver CO 80207 Office: 1321 Delaware St Denver CO 80204

ENGLAR, JOHN DAVID, lawyer; b. Feb. 19, 1947; s. Jack Donald and Edith (Blackwell) E. B.A. magna cum laude, Duke U., 1969, J.D., 1972. Bar: N.Y. 1973. Assoc. Davis Polk and Wardwell, N.Y.C. and Paris, 1972-78; corp. atty. Burlington Industries, Inc., Greensboro, N.C., 1978—, v.p., gen. counsel, sec., 1984—. Chmn. bd. trustees Central N.C. chpt. Nat. Multiple Sclerosis Soc., 1984-86; mem. bd. visitors Wake Forest U. Sch. Law. Mem. ABA, N.C. Bar Assn., Am. Soc. Corp. Secs. Office: Burlington Industries Inc 3330 W Friendly Ave Greensboro NC 27410

ENGLE, DONALD EDWARD, retired railway executive, lawyer; b. St. Paul, Mar. 5, 1927; s. Merlin Edward and Edna May (Berger) E.; m. Nancy Ruth Frank, Mar. 18, 1950; children: David Edward, Daniel Thomas, Nancy Ann. B.A., Macalester Coll., St. Paul, 1948; J.D., U. Minn., 1952, B.S.L., 1950. Bar: Minn. 1952, Mo. 1972. Law clk., spl. atty. Atty. Gen.'s Office Minn., 1951-52; atty., asst. gen. solicitor, asst. gen. counsel G.N. Ry., St. Paul, 1953-70; asso. gen. counsel Burlington No., Inc., 1970-72; v.p., gen. counsel S.L.-S.F. Ry., St. Louis, 1972-79; v.p. law, sec. S.L.-S.F. Ry., 1979-80; v.p. corp. law Burlington No., Inc., St. Paul, 1980-81; v.p. corp. law Burlington No. Ry., St. Paul, 1981-83, sr. v.p. law and govt. affairs, sec., 1983-86, also dir.; ptnr. Oppenheimer, Wolff & Donnelly, 1986—; continuing edn. lectr. U. Minn. Bd. dirs. YMCA, St. Paul, 1981-84; bd. dirs. ARC, 1981-84. Served with USNR, 1945-46. Mem. Am., Mo., Minn., Ramsey County, St. Louis bar assns., Phi Delta Phi. Republican. Lutheran. Clubs: St. Paul Athletic, North Oaks Golf, Minnesota (St. Paul); Bellerive Country (St. Louis);. Administrative and regulatory, General corporate. Home: 9 West Bay Ln Saint Paul MN 55110 Office: 1700 1st Bank Bldg Saint Paul MN 55101

ENGLE, WILLIAM THOMAS, JR., lawyer; b. Galveston, Tex., Nov. 14, 1957; s. William Thomas Sr. and Dixie Faris (Moody) E.; m. Susan Byrnes Mann, Feb. 11, 1984; 1 child, Erin Patricia. BA, Tex. Christian U., 1980; JD, Baylor U., 1982. Bar: Tex. 1982, U.S. Dist. Ct. (no. dist.) 1983, U.S. Ct. Appeals (5th cir.) 1983. Assoc. Adams, Meier & Addison, Hurst, Tex., 1982-84; ptnr. Markey & Engle, Bedford, Tex., 1984, Markey, Ash & Engle, Bedford, 1984-86; sole practice Bedford, 1986—. Mem. Bldg. Commn., Bedford, 1983, Planning and Zoning Commn., Euless, 1985-86; alt. mem. Parks and Recreation Bd., Euless, Tex., 1984-85. Mem. Tex. Bar Assn., Northeast Tarrant County Bar Assn. Republican. Baptist. Avocations: softball, flag football, spectator sports. Real property, General corporate, General practice. Office: 803 Forest Ridge Suite 100 Bedford TX 76022

ENGLEBRECHT, BRUCE, lawyer; b. Passaic, N.J., Feb. 21, 1944; s. William G. and Mary (Bottari) E.; m. Yolande Lichon, Apr. 18, 1982. Student, Calif. State Poly. U., 1965-67; BS, Waseda U., Japan, 1968; JD, U. S.D., 1971. Bar: Calif. 1972, D.C. 1983, U.S. Dist. Ct. (so. dist.) Calif. 1972, U.S. Dist. Ct. (cen. dist.) Calif. 1974, U.S. Ct. Claims 1976, U.S. Tax Ct. 1972, U.S. Ct. Appeals (9th cir.) 1974, U.S. Ct. Appeals (D.C. cir.) 1983, U.S. Supreme Ct. Ptnr. Burton, Englebrecht, Harrison & Lerch, Newport Beach, 1972—. Served with U.S. Navy. Mem. Fed. Bar Assn. (Orange County chpt., officer). Republican. Episcopalian. Club: Balboa Bay (Newport Beach). Lodge: Kiwanis. Federal civil litigation, Bankruptcy, General corporate.

ENGLER, W. JOSEPH, JR., lawyer; b. Fountain Springs, Pa., May 7, 1940; s. W. Joseph and Mary Rita (King) E.; m. Leslie Carroll, Aug. 8, 1964; children: W. Joseph III, Mary Margaret, Thomas Carroll. AB, LaSalle Coll.; JD, Boston Coll. Bar: Pa., U.S. Dist. Ct. Pa., U.S. Ct. Appeals (3d cir.). Law clk. to presiding justice U.S. Dist. Ct., 1965-66; assoc. Duane, Morris & Heckscher, Phila., 1966-71; v.p., gen. counsel Rochester and Pitts. Coal Co., Indiana, Pa., 1971—. Bd. dirs. Indiana Area Sch. Dist., 1975—. Mem. ABA, Pa. Bar Assn., Nat. Coal Assn., Am. Mining Congress, Keystone Bituminous Coal Assn. (chmn. lawyers com.). Clubs: Oakmont Country (Pitts.); Indiana Country. Administrative and regulatory, General corporate, Environment. Office: Rochester and Pitts Coal Co 655 Church St Indiana PA 15701

ENGLERT, DENNIS M., lawyer; b. Schenectady, N.Y., May 10, 1938; s. Adolf Otto and Irene (Mego) E.; m. Judith Ann Scott, June 9, 1962; children: Dennis Jr., Michael, Jeffrey, Matthew, Darcy. BA, Rutgers U., 1961; LLB, Albany Law Sch., 1964. Bar: N.Y. Ptnr. Quinn, Englert & Reilly, Schenectady, 1966-69; pres. Englert, Reilly & McHugh, P.C., Schenectady, 1970-84; asst dist. atty. Schenectady County Dist. Atty's. Office, 1972-78; pres. Englert, Stillman & McHugh (formerly Englert & McHugh, P.C.), Schenectady, 1984—; pres. Schenectady Legal Aid, 1974—; bd. dirs. Northeast Legal Aid, Albany, N.Y.; justice Town of Glenville, Scotia, N.Y., 1985—. Mem. Burnt Hills PTA, Ballston Lake, N.Y.; mem. advising bd. Scotia-Glenville Bd. of Edn.; bd. dirs., former v.p. Schenectady Alcoholism Council, 1974—; bd. dirs. YMCA, Schenectady. Served to capt. U.S. Army, 1964-66. Mem. N.Y. State Bar Assn., N.Y. State Defenders Assn., N.Y. State Magistrates Assn., Deputy Sheriffs Assn. (Schenectady chpt.), Schenectady Bar Assn. (bd. dirs. 1981). Republican. Roman Catholic. State civil litigation, Personal injury, Criminal. Home: 66 Stephens Ln W Scotia NY 12302 Office: Englert & McHugh P.C. 144 Barrett St Schenectady NY 12305

ENGLING, ROBERT JOHN, lawyer; b. Elmhurst, Ill., May 9, 1945; s. Alfred John and Betty (Seger) E.; m. Suzanne Shoemaker, Oct. 2, 1971; children: Nancy, Erica. B.S., No. Ill. U., 1967, M.S.B.A., 1970; J.D., U. Iowa, 1974. Bar: Ill. 1974, U.S. Dist. Ct. (7th cir.) 1974. Instr. bus. St. Bonaventure U., Olean, N.Y., 1969-71, Augustana Coll., Rock Island, Ill., 1971-73; sr. v.p., sec., gen. counsel Kemper Fin. Services, Inc., Chgo., 1974—. Mgr. Glen Ellyn Speed Skating Club, Ill., 1984-85. Mem. ABA, Chgo. Bar Assn., Ill. Bar Assn., Investment Co. Inst. Club: Union League (Chgo.). Securities, General corporate, Insurance. Office: Kemper Fin Services Inc 120 S LaSalle St Chicago IL 60603

ENGLISH, CHARLES ROYAL, lawyer; b. Santa Monica, Calif., Apr. 9, 1938; s. Charles James and Antoinette Frieda (Schindler) E.; m. Marylyn Gray, Sept. 6, 1969; children—Mitchell Lloyd, Charles James, Julia Catherine. A.A., Santa Monica City Coll., 1958; B.S., UCLA, 1961, LL.B., 1965. Bar: Calif. 1966. Sole practice, Santa Monica, 1967; with Los Angeles County Pub. Defender's Office, 1967-78, sr. trial dep. until 1978; ptnr. Chaleff & English, and predecessor Lafaille, Chaleff & English, Santa Monica, 1978—; lectr. in field. Served with USAR, 1961-67. Mem. Santa

Monica Bar, State Bar Calif., ABA, Criminal Cts. Bar Assn., Bur. Automotive Repair, Los Angeles County Bar Assn. (trustee 1980-83), UCLA Law Alumni Assn. (pres. 1980). Criminal, Juvenile. Office: 1337 Ocean Ave Garden Suite Santa Monica CA 90401

ENGLISH, DALE LOWELL, lawyer; b. Madison, Wis., Nov. 12, 1956; s. Richard Dale and Grace Elaine (Piehler) E.; m. Patricia Kay Becker, Sept. 11, 1982; 1 child, Kristopher Scott. BA cum laude, Luther Coll., 1979; JD, Marquette U., 1982. Bar: Wis. Supreme Ct. 1982, U.S. Dist. Ct. (ea. and we. dist.) Wis. 1982, U.S. Ct. Appeals (7th cir.) 1986. Ptnr. Colwin, Fortune, Colwin, Pomeroy & English S.C., Fond du Lac, Wis., 1982—. Mem. Fond du Lac Planning Commn., 1986, adv. com. for Legal Sec. Assocs. Degree Program, Fond du Lac, 1986. Mem. Fond du Lac County Bar Assn., Wis. Bar Assn., ABA, Jaycees (legal counsel 1983—, state dir. 1983-84, bd. dirs. 1983-85), Omicron Delta Epsilon. Avocations: weightlifting, sports. Civil rights, General corporate. Home: 366 17th St Fond du Lac WI 54935 Office: Colwin Fortune Colwin Pomeroy & English 201 S Marr St Fond du Lac WI 54935

ENGLISH, GREGORY BRUCE, lawyer; b. Lynchburg, Va., Nov. 8, 1946; s. Edgar George and Mavis Clark (Daniel) E.; m. Elaine Coleman Patton, Sept. 18, 1971; 1 child, Erik Todd. B.A., Lynchburg Coll., 1969; J.D., U. Va., 1973; LL.M., George Washington U., 1979. Bar: Pa. 1973, U.S. Dist. Ct. (no. dist.) Ohio 1981, U.S. Ct. Mil. Appeals 1976, U.S. Ct. Appeals (6th cir.) 1981, U.S. Supreme Ct. 1977. Atty., Navy Gen. Counsel, 1977-78; sr. trial atty. U.S. Dept. Justice, narcotic and dangerous drug sect., criminal div., Washington, 1978—; staff judge advocate, maj. JAGC D.C. Army Nat. Guard, Washington, 1977—. Contbr. articles to profl. jours. Bd. dirs. ACLU, Lynchburg, Va., 1969; dir. Democratic Central Com., Lynchburg, 1969. Served to capt. JAGC, U.S. Army, 1973-77. Recipient Atty. Gen.'s Spl. Commendation award, 1981; Commr.'s Meritorious Service award IRS, 1982, Meritorious award Justice Dept., 1982, Outstanding Contbns. award Drug Enforcement Adminstrn., 1983, Meritorious Contbns. award, 1984; Carey Brewer Alumni award Lynchburg Coll., 1983. Mem. ABA (prosecution function subcom. 1978—). Republican. Unitarian. Clubs: U. Va. Student Aid Found. (Washington) (dir. 1977—), Lee Dist. Basketball Assn. (Alexandria, Va.) (commr. 1984—). Criminal. Office: US Dept Justice Criminal Div Narcotic and Dangerous Drug Sect PO Box 521 Washington DC 20044

ENGLISH, HARRY GORDON, lawyer; b. N.Y.C., June 10, 1921. BBA in Acctg. (N.Y. State Regents scholar), St. John's U., Bklyn., 1946; MBA, NYU, 1949; JD, N.Y. Law Sch., 1951, SJD, 1965; postgrad. (scholar) Wellesley Coll. Summer Inst. Social Progress, 1952. Bar: N.Y., U.S. Dist. Ct. N.Y., U.S. Tax Ct., U.S. Ct. Customs and Patent Appeals, U.S. Supreme Ct., U.S. Ct. Claims, U.S. Ct. Mil. Appeals; lic. real estate broker; registered tchr.; lic. ins. broker; lic. life ins. agent. Jr. underwriter Royal Ins. Co., N.Y.C., 1940-41; staff acct. Nat. Biscuit Co., N.Y.C., 1941-42; acct. Alex, Grant & Co., CPA's, 1942-46; dir. internal audit div. C.A.R.E., 1946-53; asst. v.p., controller H.L. Green Co., Inc., 1953-54; comptroller, asst. v.p. Weisglass Milk Corp., S.I., N.Y., 1954-55; ptnr. Restaine & English, Bklyn., 1955-56; ptnr. English, English & Hansen, pub. accts., tax cons., Bklyn., 1956—; sole practice, Bklyn., 1959—; pres. Bliss Realty Co., 1951—; acctg. taxation and bus. law tchr. Brown's Bus. Coll., 1951-53, chmn. acctg. dept., 1953-55; instr. acctg. Staten Island Community Coll., 1955-57; asst. prof. bus. fin. Connelly Coll., Long Island U., 1964-65, adj. assoc. prof., 1968-75, adj. asst. prof. Sch. Bus., 1965-68, adj. assoc. prof., 1969-75, mem. faculty Weekend Coll., 1975-76, adj. prof. law and taxation Grad. Sch. Bus., 1978-84, prof. law grad. div. Sch. Profl. Accountancy, 1984—; adj. prof. fin. Touro Coll. and Law Sch., 1984-86; lectr. Long Island U.; mem. adv. com. paralegal studies program, 1978—; instr. in charge real estate courses St. Francis Coll.; mem. Bklyn. Bd. Realtors, 1974—; master, referee civil ct. City of N.Y.; pres. Council Provincial Bar Assns., 1980-82. Contbr. articles to profl. jours. Chmn. bd. overseers Coll. of Bay Ridge, Long Island U., coordinator Bay Ridge extension, 1980—; mem. Bay Ridge Forum; mem. Bay Ridge Bicentennial Commn., 1974-77; bd. dirs. Ragamuffin, Inc., F.O.R.C.E., 1965-70, Soc. Old Brooklynites; pres. Bay Ridge Day Nursery, 1980; active Bay Ridge Hist. Soc.; bd. dirs. ARC; bd. mgrs. YMCA, 1976—; sec. Bay Ridge Devel. Corp., 1979—; pres. 3d Avenue Mchts. Assn., 1971-75; treas. Bay Ridge Community Council, 1970; mayor 3d Avenue South, Community Mayors State N.Y.; mem. adv. bd. Bay Ridge Salvation Army, Lutheran Med. Ctr.; mem. fin. adv. com. Guild for Exceptional Children, 1960—; bd. dirs. Bklyn. Businessmen's Coordinating Council; mem. Bay Ridge Estate Bd., 1950—. Recipient Cert. of Appreciation Boy Scouts of Am., Cert. of Appreciation Civil Ct. City of N.Y. Mem. ABA (com. on taxation, com. on real property, probate and trust law), N.Y. State Bar Assn. (com. on trusts and estates), Bay Ridge Lawyers Assn. (pres. 1965-66, mem. com. on estates and trusts, chmn. com. on 'Anatomy of an Estate', chmn. estate law and proceedings, appointed mem. fed. judiciary com. for Am. inns of Ct.), N.Y. State Trial Lawyers Assn. (com. on estates), Nat. Real Estate Bd., Bay Ridge Real Estate Bd., Inst. Internal Auditors, Nat. Soc. Pub. Accts., Am. Fin. Assn., N.Y. State Assn. Plaintive Trial Attys., Real Estate Assn., Nat. Assn. Tax Cons., Am. Trial Lawyers, Am. Assn. Univ. Profs., Am. Assn. Urban and Real Estate Devel. Clubs: Forest Knolls Boat (commodore), Men's of Bay Ridge (pres. 1968-69), Bay Ridge Lions (pres. 1980), Danish Athletic (counsel 1975—), Masons. Probate, Personal income taxation, Real property. Office: 7219 3d Ave Brooklyn NY 11209

ENGLISH, JERRY FITZGERALD, lawyer; b. Houston, Dec. 18, 1934; d. William Edward Michael and Viola Catherine (Christopherson) Fitzgerald; m. Alan Taylour English, July 23, 1955; children—Holly, Christopher, Anderson, Eric. B.A., Stanford U., 1956; J.D., Boston Coll., 1963; spl. student Harvard U., 1963. Bar: N.J., 1963, U.S. Dist. Ct. N.J. 1963. Clk., assoc., ptnr. Moser, Griffin, Kerby & Cooper, Summit, N.J., 1964-74; mem. N.J. Senate, 1971-72; asst. counsel to N.J. Senate, 1972-74; legis. counsel Gov. N.J., Trenton, 1974-79; commr. N.J. Dept. Environ. Protection, 1979-82; of counsel Kerby, Cooper, Schaul & Garvin, Summit, 1982-85, ptnr., 1986—; adj. prof. N.J. Inst. Tech., 1983—. Commr. Port Authority of N.Y. and N.J., 1979—; trustee N.J. Harvard Law Sch. Assn., 1973; mem. Gateway Nat. Recreation Area Adv. Commn., 1981; mem. exec. com. Democratic Nat. Com., 1978-84. Mem. ABA, N.J. Bar Assn., Summit Bar Assn. Unitarian. Club: Essex. Environment, Private international. Home: 4 Drum Hill Dr Summit NJ 07901

ENGLISH, MARK GREGORY, lawyer; b. Mpls., Oct. 14, 1951; s. Earl Mark and Georgia Corrine (Lastrange) E.; m. Renee Ann Thielen, Aug. 31, 1979; children—Janelle, Brandon. B.E.E. with high distinction, U. Minn., 1973, J.D. magna cum laude, 1976. Bar: Minn. 1976, Mo. 1981. Assoc. Arvesen, Donoho, Lundeen, Hoff, Svingen & English and predecessor Arvesen Donoho Lundeen, Hoff & Svingen, Fergus Falls, Minn., 1976-77, ptnr., 1978-80; atty. Kansas City Power & Light Co., Mo., 1981-82, staff atty., 1982-86, sr. atty., 1986—. Gen. counsel Minn. Jaycees, Mpls., 1978-79. Recipient Silver medal Royal Soc. Arts, London, 1973. Mem. Mo. Bar Assn., Mensa. Public utilities, Administrative and regulatory, General corporate. Home: 8504 Richards Rd Lenexa KS 66215 Office: Kansas City Power & Light Co 1330 Baltimore Kansas City MO 64105

ENGLISH, RICHARD D., government official; b. Beaumont, Tex., Jan. 11, 1948; s. Richard Wilfred and Clara Elizabeth (Dunshie) E. B.A., U. Tex., 1970, J.D., 1974. Bar: Tex. 1974, U.S. Dist. Ct. (so. dist.) Tex. 1975. Law clk. U.S. Dist. Ct. judge, Laredo, Tex., 1975-76; atty. Tenneco Inc., Houston, 1976-80; policy asst. Gov. of Tex., Austin, 1980-81; dep. asst. dir. ACTION, Washington, 1981-83; dep. asst. sec. Dept. State, Washington, 1983—. Assoc. Tex. Lyceum Assn., 1984; del. Republican Nat. Conv., Detroit, 1980. Mem. ABA, Fed. Bar Assn., State Bar Tex. Public international, Immigration, naturalization, and customs, General corporate.

ENGLISH, WILLIAM DESHAY, lawyer; b. Piedmont, Calif., Dec. 25, 1924; s. Munro and Mabel (Michener) English; m. Nancy Ames, Apr. 7, 1956; children—Catherine, Barbara, Susan, Stephen. A.B. in Econs., U. Calif.-Berkeley, 1948; J.D., U. Calif. Hastings Sch. Law, 1951. Bar: Calif. 1952, D.C. 1972. Trial atty, spl. asst. to atty. gen. U.S. Dept. Justice, Washington, 1953-55; sr. atty. AEC, Washington, 1955-62; legal advisor U.S. Mission to European Communities, Brussels, 1962-64; asst. gen. counsel internat. matters COMSAT, Washington, 1965-73, v.p., gen. counsel, dir., 1973-76; sr. v.p. legal and govtl. affairs Satellite Bus. Systems, McLean, Va., 1976-86; v.p., gen. counsel Satellite Transponder Leasing Corp. (IBM), McLean, 1986-87; bd. dirs. RealCom Communications Corp., McLean. Served with USAAF, 1943-45. Decorated air medal. Fellow Council on Econ. Regulation, 1985—; mem. Am. Corp. Counsel Assn. (bd. dirs. 1982-86), Competitive Telecommunications Assn. (bd. dirs. 1985-86, exec. com. 1985-86), ABA, Washington Met. Area Corp. Counsel Assn., D.C. Bar Assn., Fed. Communications Bar Assn., State Bar Calif., Fgn. Policy Discussion Group. Club: Metropolitan. Administrative and regulatory, Private international, Legislative. Home: 7420 Exeter Rd Bethesda MD 20814 Office: 8283 Greensboro Dr Suite 720 McLean VA 22102

ENGMAN, PATRICIA HANAHAN, lawyer; b. Hinesville, Ga., May 1, 1942; d. Ralph Bailey and Phyllis Harriet (Anderson) Hanahan; m. Lewis A. Engman, Dec. 2, 1978; children: Geoffrey Ponton, Jonathan Lewis, Richard Ransford. AB in Social Sci. with honors, Coker Coll., 1965; JD, U. Fla., 1969. Bar: Fla. 1969, D.C. 1972, U.S. Supreme Ct. 1975. Jud. research aide to Justice Dist. Ct. Appeals Fla., Vero Beach, 1969; campaign research coordinator, office mgr., asst. to campaign mgr. for State Senator, Lakeland, Fla., 1970; staff atty., asst. to U.S. Senator, Washington, 1971; congl. liaison officer Fed. Trade Commn., Washington, 1971-73; counselor legis. and adminstrv. affairs Bristol-Myers Co., Washington, 1974-84; sole practice McLean, Va., 1985-87; asst. exec. dir. The Bus. Roundtable, 1987—. Recipient Dist. Service award FTC, 1973. Mem. ABA, Fed. Bar Assn., Fla. Bar Assn., Nat. Assn. Women Lawyers, Phi Alpha Delta. Democrat. Episcopalian. Clubs: Kent Country (Grand Rapids, Mich.); George Town, Internat. (Washington), 116 Club. Legislative. Office: 1615 L St NW Suite 1350 Washington DC 20036

ENGSTRAND, PAUL DAVID, JR., lawyer; b. Hutchinson, Kans., Apr. 27, 1919; s. Paul David Sr. and Helena Sophia (Stromquist) E.; m. Parthena Pauline Grigsby, Aug. 30, 1941 (div. 1969); children: David Charles, Craig Steven; m. Iris Ann Higbie, June 20, 1970; 1 child, Kristin Clare. AB, Bethany Coll., 1940; postgrad., Baylor U., 1941-42; LLB, U. Calif., Berkeley, 1948. Bar: Calif. 1948. Ptnr. Jennings, Engstrand & Henrikson, La Mesa, Calif., 1949-66, Higgs, Jennings, Fletcher & Mack, San Diego, 1966-71, Jennings, Engstrand & Henrikson P.C., San Diego, 1971—. Served to 1st lt. USAF, 1942-45. Mem. ABA, Calif. Bar Assn., San Diego County Bar Assn. (bd. dirs. 1953-55, 66-68, v.p. 1955-68, found. pres. 1986-87), Am. Judicature Soc., San Diego C. of C. (bd. dirs. 1984—). Republican. Lutheran. Administrative and regulatory, Federal civil litigation, State civil litigation. Home: 6602 Norman Ln San Diego CA 92120 Office: Jennings Engstrand & Henrikson 2255 Camino del Rio S San Diego CA 92108

ENGSTROM, MARK WILLIAM, lawyer; b. Bridgeport, Conn., Mar. 15, 1955; s. Henry W. and Ingrid F. (Johnson) E.; m. Nina F. Tyrrell, Aug. 9, 1980; 1 child, Anna Fredrika. BA, Ithaca Coll., 1977; JD, Am. U., 1980. Bar: Ohio 1981, Conn. 1985, U.S. Dist. Ct. Conn. 1985. Atty. NLRB, Cin., 1980-84, Hartford, Conn., 1984—. Mem. ABA (labor law sect.). Congregationalist. Avocation: tennis. Administrative and regulatory, Labor. Home: 77 Overbrook Rd West Hartford CT 06107 Office: NLRB 1 Commercial Plaza 21st Floor Hartford CT 06103

ENGWALL, GREGORY BOND, lawyer; b. Sioux City, Iowa, May 23, 1950; s. Glen Leslie and Maxine Lillian (Bond) E.; m. Jeanne Ann Van Drasek, July 22, 1977; children: Thomas Gregory, Daniel Henry. BA, Gustavus Adolphus Coll., 1972; JD, U. Minn., 1975. Bar: Minn. 1975. Assoc. Larson Law Offices, Winthrop, Minn., 1975—. Mem. ABA, Minn. Bar Assn., Iota Delta Gamma, Guild of St. Angsgar. Republican. Roman Catholic. Probate, Real property, General practice. Home: Rt 1 Box 238 Brownton MN 55312 Office: Larson Law Office 110 E 2d St Winthrop MN 55396

ENIS, THOMAS JOSEPH, lawyer; b. Maryville, Mo., July 2, 1937; s. Herbert William and Loretta M. (Fitzmaurice) E.; m. Harolyn Gray Westhoff, July 24, 1971; children—Margaret Elizabeth, David Richard, John Anthony, Brian Edward. B.S., Rockhurst Coll., 1958; J.D., U. Mo.-Columbia, 1966. Bar: Mo. 1966, Okla. 1973. Law clk. U.S. dist. Ct. (we. dist.) Mo., 1966-67; prof. law U. Okla. Coll. Law, Norman, 1967-74, assoc. dean, 1970-74; atty. Southwestern Bell Telephone Co., Oklahoma City, 1974-79; ptnr. Bulla and Enis, Oklahoma City, 1979-81; sole practice, Oklahoma City, 1981—; lectr. Okla. Bar Rev. Bd. dirs. Okla. Symphony Orch., 1978—, legal counsel, 1981—; spl. counsel Okla. Ethics Commn., 1986—. Mem. ABA, Okla. Bar Assn., Mo. Bar Assn., Oklahoma County Bar Assn., Order of Coif, Phi Delta Phi. Democrat. Roman Catholic. Editor-in-chief Mo. Law Rev., 1965-66. Oil and gas leasing, Administrative and regulatory, Real property. Home: 3016 Stoneybrook Rd Oklahoma City OK 73120 Office: 2300 1st City Pl Oklahoma City OK 73102

ENNIS, RICHARD JACKSON, judge; b. Spokane, Sept. 24, 1921; s. William Walter and Clara (Donart) E.; m. Joy L. Davis, Feb. 27, 1945; children: Sherry, Brad. Pre-law student, U. Wash.; JD, Gonzaga U. Sole practice Wilbur, Wash., 1950-57; judge Lincoln County Superior Ct., Davenport, Wash., 1957-77; judge pro-tem Spokane, 1977—. Author: Ghost Havoc, 1980; contbr. articles on aviation to mags. Served to 1st lt. USAC, 1942-45. Mem. Am. Arbitration Assn. (arbitrator 1977—), Superior Ct. Judges Assn., Wash. State Bar Assn. Avocation: aviation, photography, piano. Home: S 5812 Custer Spokane WA 99203

ENNS, RODRICK JOHN, lawyer; b. Wichita, Kans., May 28, 1955; s. Harold John and Martha Jane (McElhinney) E.; m. Marcia Goldman, Aug. 11, 1979; 1 child, Samantha Marie. BA magna cum laude, U. Wash., 1976; JD cum laude, Harvard U., 1979. Bar: Colo. 1979, U.S. Dist. Ct. Colo. 1979, N.C. 1984, U.S. Dist. Ct. N.C. 1984. Assoc. Lohf & Barnhill P.C., Denver, 1979-83, Petree, Stockton & Robinson, Winston-Salem, N.C., 1983—. Mem. ABA (antitrust sect.), N.C. Bar Assn. (law day com. young lawyers com.), Forsyth County Bar Assn., Forsyth County Young Lawyers Assn. Antitrust, Federal civil litigation, State civil litigation. Office: Petree Stockton & Robinson 1001 W 4th St Winston-Salem NC 27101

ENO, LAWRENCE RAPHAEL, lawyer; b. N.Y.C., Jan. 19, 1914; s. Charles and Esther Hannah (Walfish) E.; m. Ruth Lillian Smolen, Apr. 19, 1939; children: Richard David, Robert Jonathan. AB with honors, Columbia U., 1933, LLB, 1935. Bar: N.Y. 1935, U.S. Dist. Ct. (so. dist.) N.Y. 1940, U.S. Ct. Appeals (2d. cir.) 1941, U.S. Dist. Ct. (ea. dist.) N.Y. 1958. Law clk. to justice N.Y. Supreme Ct., 1935-38; atty. office gen. counsel U.S. Treasury Dept., Washington, 1938-39; assoc. Wagner, Quillinan & Rifkind, N.Y.C., 1939-43, 46-48; sr. ptnr. and counsel Rosenman & Colin and predecessor firm Rosenman Colin Freund Lewis & Cohen, N.Y.C., 1955—. Served to capt. JAGD, U.S. Army, 1943-46. Mem. ABA, N.Y. State Bar Assn. (profl ethics com. 1970-73), Assn. of Bar of City of N.Y. (various coms.), N.Y. County Bar Assn., Judge Adv. Gens. Assn., Phi Beta Kappa. Jewish. Avocations: western Am. history 1800-1850, mid. east affairs. Federal civil litigation, State civil litigation, Jurisprudence. Home: 175 Riverside Dr New York NY 10024 Office: Rosenman & Colin 575 Madison Ave New York NY 10022

ENOCHS, ELIZABETH M., lawyer; b. Bklyn., Dec. 18, 1930; d. Alexa B. and Elizabeth V. (Hoey) Gunderson; m. Rodney L. Enochs, Feb. 11, 1961; children—Karen Elizabeth, Ross Alexander. Dr. Law, Fordham U., 1958. Bar: N.Y. 1959. Assoc. Nims, Martin, Halliday, Whitman & Williamson, N.Y.C., 1958-61; researcher, writer ct. decisions Am. Legal Publs. Inc., Irvington, N.Y., 1974-75, trademark mag., 1960-62; sole practice, Irvington, 1972—, Briarcliff, N.Y., 1982-86. Author legal publs. Mem. N.Y. State Bar Assn. Roman Catholic. Club: Ardsley Country (Ardsley-on-Hudson, N.Y.). Real property, Probate, Family and matrimonial. Home: 41 Carla Ln Irvington NY 10533 Office: 369 Ashford Ave Dobbs Ferry NY 10522

ENOS, PRISCILLA BETH, lawyer, consultant; b. Memphis, Jan. 9, 1952; d. James Galen and Arlena R. (Spurlock) E. BA, Memphis State U., 1978, JD, 1981. Bar: Tenn. 1981, U.S. Ct. Appeals (8th cir.) 1982. Law clk. to judge U.S. Ct. Appeals (8th cir.), Harrison, 1981-83; atty. Fed. Express Corp., Memphis, 1983-84; cons. Baker & Mckenzie, Bangkok, Thailand, 1985—. Mem. ABA, Internat. Bar Assn., Asia-Pacific Laweyrs Assn. Private international, Professional development. Home: 6906 Petworth Memphis TN 38119 Office: Baker & McKenzie, 18/8 Soi Asoke Sukhumvit, Bangkok Thailand

ENSENAT, DONALD BURNHAM, lawyer; b. New Orleans, Feb. 4, 1946; s. Alonzo G. and Genevieve (Burnham) E.; m. Taylor Harding, June 5, 1976; children: Farish, Will. BA, Yale U., 1968; JD, Tulane U., 1973. Bar: La. 1973, U.S. Dist. Ct. (ea. dist.) La. 1973, U.S. Ct. Appeals (5th cir.) 1974, U.S. Supreme Ct. 1975, U.S. Dist. Ct. (we. dist.) La. 1979, U.S. Ct. Appeals (11th cir.) 1982. Legis. asst. Congressman Hale Boggs, U.S. Ho. of Reps., Washington, 1969-70, legis asst. Congressman Lindy Boggs, 1973-74; personal aide Hon. George Bush Houston, Tex., 1970; asst. atty gen. State of La., New Orleans, 1974-80; dir. Carmouche, Gray, & Hoffman, A.P.L.C., New Orleans, 1982; mng. dir. Carmouche, Gray & Hoffman, A.P.L.C., New Orleans, 1985—; pres. Enzoil, Inc., New Orleans, 1981—. Bd. dirs. World Trade Ctr., New Orleans, 1985—; del. Dem. Conv., 1976, 78. Served with La. N.G., 1968-74. Mem. ABA, La. State Bar Assn., New Orleans Bar Assn., Am. Bd. Trial Advocates, Maritime Law Assn. U.S., Yale Alumni Assn. La. (bd. dirs., pres. 1976—), Assn. Yale Alumni (rep. 1986—). Democrat. Roman Catholic. Club: Yale (N.Y.C.),. Avocations: ranching, tennis, swimming, golf. Federal civil litigation, State civil litigation, Admiralty. Home: 1233 Harmony St New Orleans LA 70115-3422 Office: Carmouche Gray & Hoffman APLC 650 Poydras St New Orleans LA 70130-6121

ENSIGN, GREGORY MOORE, lawyer; b. Cleve., June 3, 1949; s. Gerald Edward and Patricia Mae (Komlos) E.; m. Nancy Beth Udelson, Jan. 9, 1977, divorced; children—Julie Ann, Jennifer Brooke. B.A., Ohio Wesleyan U., 1971; J.D., Capital U., 1975. Bar: Ohio 1975, U.S. Dist. Ct. (so. dist.) Ohio 1975, U.S. Dist. Ct. (no. dist.) Ohio 1978, U.S. Ct. Appeals (6th cir.) 1984. Mgr. legal sect. Dept. Mental Health and Mental Retardation, Columbus, Ohio, 1972-77, chief counsel, 1977-78; assoc. Weltman, Strachan and Green Co., L.P.A., Cleve., 1978-79; ptnr. Sindell, Sindell & Rubenstein, Cleve., 1979-86; v.p. adminstrn., gen. counsel, sec. Kirkwood Industries, Inc., Cleve., 1986—. Contbr. articles to profl. jours. Mem. Univ. Heights Communications and Devel. Commn., Ohio, 1981-84. Mem. Assn. Trial Lawyers of Am., Ohio State Bar Assn., Ohio Acad. Trial Lawyers, Cleve. Acad. Trial Attys. (bd. dirs. 1985-87), Greater Cleve. & Cuyahoga County Bar Assns., Nat. Orgn. Social Security Claimants Reps. Republican. Club: Shaker Heights (Ohio) Country. Lodge: Rotary. General corporate, Environment, Labor. Office: Kirkwood Industries Inc 4855 W 130th St Cleveland OH 44135

ENSLEIN, JERALD STEPHEN, lawyer; b. Kansas City, Mo., Aug. 9, 1954; s. Leonard and Barbara Lee (Planzer) E.; m. Terri Turner; 1 child, Alana. BA, Tulane U., 1976, JD, 1979. Bar: Mo. 1980, U.S. Dist. Ct. (we. dist.) Mo. 1980, U.S. Ct. Appeals (8th cir.) 1980, Ill. 1981. Assoc. Meise, Cope & Coen, Kansas City, 1980-82, Berman, DeLere, Kuchan & Chapman, Kansas City, 1982—. Mem. ABA, Mo. Bar Assn., Ill. Bar Assn., Kansas City Bar Assn., Lawyers Assn. of Kansas City. Democrat. Jewish. Bankruptcy. Home: 10934 W 100th Pl Overland Park KS 66214 Office: Berman DeLere Kuchan & Chapman 1006 Grand Suite 600 Kansas City MO 64106

ENSLEN, RICHARD ALAN, judge; b. Kalamazoo, May 28, 1931; s. Ehrman Thrasher and Pauline Mabel (Dragoo) E.; m. Pamela Gayle Chapman, Nov. 2, 1985; children—David, Susan, Sandra, Thomas, Janet, Joseph. Student, Kalamazoo Coll., 1949-51, Western Mich. U., 1955; LL.B., Wayne State U., 1958; LL.M., U. Va., 1986. Bar: Mich. bar 1958, Western Dist. Mich 1960, Ct. Appeals for 6th Circuit 1971, 4th Circuit 1975, U.S. Supreme Ct 1975. Mem. firm Stratton, Wise, Early & Starbuck, Kalamazoo, 1958-60, Bauckham & Enslen, Kalamazoo, 1960-64, Howard & Howard, Kalamazoo, 1970-76, Enslen & Schma, Kalamazoo, 1977-79; dir. Peace Corps. Costa Rica, 1965-67; judge Mich. Dist. Ct., 1968-70; U.S. dist. judge Kalamazoo, 1979—; mem. faculty Western Mich. U., 1961-62, Nazareth Coll., 1974-75, adj. prof. polit. sci. Western Mich. U., 1982—. Co-author: The Constitution Law Dictionary: Volume One, Individual Rights, 1985; Volume Two, Governmental Powers, 1987, Constitutional Law Deskbook, 1987. Served with USAF, 1951-54. Recipient Disting. Alumni award Wayne State Law Sch., 1980, Disting. Alumni award Western Mich. U., 1982; Outstanding Practical Achievement award Ctr. Pub. Resources, 1984; award for Excellence and Innovation in Alternative Dispute Resolution and Dispute Mgmt., Legal Program; Jewel Corp. scholar, 1956-57; Lampson McElhone scholar, 1957. Mem. ABA (spl. com. on dispute resolution 1983—), Am. Judicature Soc. (bd. dirs. 1983-85), Mich. Bar Assn. Jurisprudence. Office: U S Dist Ct 410 W Michigan Ave Kalamazoo MI 49005

ENTENMAN, JOHN ALFRED, lawyer; b. White Plains, N.Y., Apr. 14, 1948; s. Alfred Morris and Mae Muriel (Hamilton) E. B.A., U. Mich., 1970, J.D., Harvard U., 1973. Bar: Mich. 1973, U.S. Dist. Ct. (ea. dist.) Mich. 1973, U.S. Ct. Appeals (6th cir.) 1974, U.S. Supreme Ct. 1974. Assoc. Oykema, Gossett et al., Detroit, 1973-80, ptnr. 1980—; adj. prof. labor law U. Detroit Sch. Law, 1975-78. Mem. State Bar Assn. Mich., ABA, Indsl. Relations Research Assn., Theta Delta Chi (sr. exec. 1969-70). Club: Renaissance (Detroit). Labor. Home: 638 Westchester Grosse Pointe Park MI 48230 Office: Dykema Gossett Spencer Goodnow & Trigg 400 Renaissance Ctr 35th floor Detroit MI 48243

EOVALDI, THOMAS L., legal educator; b. 1940. B.S., U. Ill., 1962, LL.B., 1965. Bar: Ill. 1965. Assoc., Jenner & Block, Chgo., 1965-67; asst. prof. Northwestern U. Law Sch., Chgo., 1967-70, assoc. prof., 1970-73, prof., 1973—, asst. dean, 1974-76, assoc. dean, 1976-77. Author: (with Louis W. Stern) Legal Aspects of Marketing Strategy: Anti-Trust and Consumer Protection Issues, 1984; mem. U. Ill. Law Rev. Mem. Chgo. Council Lawyers (bd. govs.), Order of Coif. Legal education, Bankruptcy, Consumer protection.

EPHRAIM, DONALD MORLEY, lawyer; b. Chgo., Jan. 14, 1932; s. Jacob H. and Belle (Freundlich) E.; m. Sylvia Zupnik, Aug. 13, 1964 (div. 1981); children—David Marc, Eliot Scott, Eric Alan. B.S.C., DePaul U., 1952; postgrad., Northwestern U.; C.P.A., U. Ill., 1953; J.D., U. Chgo., 1955. Bar: Ill. 1955; C.P.A., Ill. Atty. Ross, McGowan & O'Keefe, Chgo., 1955; acct. Arthur Andersen & Co., Chgo., 1957-60; atty. Pennish, Steel & Rockler, Chgo., 1960-63, Schradzke, Gould & Ratner, Chgo., 1963-65; practice law Chgo., 1965—; pres., dir. Presdl. Properties, Ltd., 1970—, Donald M. Ephraim, Ltd., 1976—, Franklin Nat. Marine Corp., 1977; v.p., dir. Continental Marine Corp., 1976—, Kurtis Prodns., Ltd., 1977—; trustee various pension and profit sharing trusts. Served with AUS, 1956-57. Mem. ABA, Ill. Bar Assn., Chgo. Bar Assn., Am. Assn. Atty.-C.P.A.s, Am. Inst. C.P.A.s, Ill. Soc. C.P.A.s, Chgo. Estate Planning Council, Nat. Acad. TV Arts and Scis. (gov. Chgo. chpt., 2d v.p.), Art. Inst. Chgo. (Chgo. council fgn. relations), Phi Sigma Delta, Pi Gamma Mu. Entertainment, Estate planning, Personal income taxation. Office: 172 N Franklin St Chicago IL 60606

EPLEY, LEWIS EVERETT, JR., lawyer; b. Ft. Smith, Ark., Apr. 28, 1936; s. Lewis Everett and Evelyn (Wood) E.; m. Donna Louise Swopes, Feb. 24, 1962. B.S., J.D., U. Ark., 1961. Bar: Ark. 1961. Since practiced in Eureka Spring, city atty., 1969-71; dir. Bank of Eureka Springs.; del. Ark. Constl. Conv., 1969-70; appointed spl. assoc. justice Ark. Supreme Ct., 1984. Mem. Ark. Bldg. Services Council, 1975-80, chmn., 1976-78, mem. Carroll County Central Democratic Com., 1964-68; bd. dirs. Eureka Springs Ozark Folk Festival, 1964-69, NW Ark. Radiation Therapy Inst., 1984—; chmn. adv. bd. Eureka Springs Mcpl. Hosp., 1963-71; mem. Beaver Lake Adv. Com., 1982—. Mem. ABA, Ark. Bar Assn. (del. 1975-78), Carroll County Bar Assn. (past pres.), Eureka Springs C. of C. (dir., past pres.), Phi Alpha Delta, Kappa Kappa Psi. Baptist. General practice, Probate, Real property. Home: Pivot Rock Rd Eureka Springs AR 72632 Office: PO Box 470 104 Spring St Eureka Springs AR 72632

EPLEY, MARION JAY, oil company executive; b. Hattiesburg, Miss., June 17, 1907; s. Marion Jay and Eva (Quin) E.; m. Dorris Glenn Ervin, Feb. 12, 1934; children: Marion Jay III, Sara Perry (Mrs. Richard H. Davis). LL.B., Tulane U., 1930. Bar: La. 1930. Practiced in New Orleans, 1930-42, 45-47; gen. atty. Texaco, Inc., New Orleans, N.Y.C., 1948-58; v.p., asst. to chmn. bd. Texaco, Inc., N.Y.C., 1958-60; sr. v.p. Texaco, Inc., 1960-61, exec. v.p., 1961-64, pres., 1964-70, chmn. bd., 1970-71; also dir.; pres., dir. Dormar Ltd., 1986—. Served as lt. USNR, 1942-45. Decorated officer Ordre de la Couronne, Belgium. Mem. ABA, La. Bar Assn. Clubs: Boston (New Orleans); Everglades, Bath and Tennis, Seminole Golf (Palm Beach, Fla.); Governors (West Palm Beach, Fla.); Roaring Gap (N.C.); Royal Norwegian

Yacht (Norway). Private international. Address: 340 S Ocean Blvd Palm Beach FL 33480

EPLING, RICHARD LOUIS, lawyer; b. Waukegan, Ill., Aug. 16, 1951; s. Carrol Franklin and Mary Teresa (Fiscella) E.; m. Suzanne Braley, Aug. 4, 1973. BA in English and History magna cum laude, Duke U., 1973; JD, U. Mich., 1976. Bar: Ill. 1977, U.S. Dist. Ct. (no. dist.) Ill. 1977, U.S. Ct. Appeals (7th cir.) 1979, Ariz. 1981, U.S. Dist. Ct. Ariz. 1981, U.S. Ct. Appeals (9th cir.) 1982. Law clk. to presiding justice Mich. Supreme Ct., Southfield, 1976-77; assoc. Katten, Muchin, Zavis, Pearl & Galler, Chgo., 1977-81; ptnr. Brown & Bain, P.A., Phoenix, 1981—; assoc. conferee Nat. Bankruptcy Conf., Washington, 1985—. Contbr. articles to profl. jours. Mem. Am. Bankruptcy Inst., Phi Beta Kappa. Democrat. Club: Phoenix City. Avocations: jogging, gardening. Bankruptcy, Banking, Contracts commercial. Office: Brown & Bain PA 222 N Central Ave Phoenix AZ 85004

EPPERSON, JOEL RODMAN, lawyer; b. Miami, Fla., Aug. 29, 1945; s. John Rodman and Ann Louise (Barrs) E.; m. Gretchen Jean Meyer, Apr. 16, 1968; children—Joel Rodman, David Michael, Sandra Elizabeth. B.S., U. South Fla., 1967; J.D., South Tex. Coll., 1976. Bar: Fla. 1976, U.S. Dist. Ct. (mid. dist.) Fla. 1976, U.S. Ct. Appeals (5th cir.) 1976, U.S. Supreme Ct. 1979. Asst. states atty. State of Fla., Tampa, 1976-79; ptnr. Brant & Epperson, 1979-86, Assocs. & Bruce L. Scheiner, Ft. Myers, Fla., 1987—. Served to capt. USMC, 1968-72. Mem. ABA, Assn. Trial Lawyers Am., Fla. Criminal Def. Lawyers Assn., Fla. Trial Lawyers Assn., Hillsborough County Bar Assn. Democrat. Personal injury, Trial practice. Home: 1306 Anglers Ln Lutz FL 33549 Office: Assocs & Bruce L Scheiner PO Box 06049 Fort Myers FL 33906

EPPS, JAMES HAWS, III, lawyer; b. Johnson City, Tenn., Sept. 15, 1936; s. James Haws and Anne Lafayette (Sessoms) E.; m. Nancy Jane Mahoney, Oct. 9, 1976; children from previous marriage—James Haws IV, Sara Stuart. B.A., U.N.C., 1955-59; J.D., Vanderbilt U., 1962. Bar: Tenn. 1962, U.S. Ct. Appeals (6th cir.) 1971, U.S. Dist. Ct., ICC bar 1962, U.S. Supreme Ct. 1967. Assoc. Cox, Taylor, Epps, Miller & Weller, Johnson City, Tenn., 1962; assoc. Epps, Powell, Weller, Taylor & Miller, 1962-69, ptnr., 1969-72; ptnr. Epps, Powell, Weller & Epps, 1972-73, Epps, Powell, Epps & Lawrence, 1973-76, Powell & Epps, 1976-84; sole practice, 1984—; atty. City of Johnson City, 1967—, Johnson City Bd. Edn., 1967-86; spl. counsel State of Tenn., 1966-70; legal counsel Salvation Army. Past bd. dirs. Washington County Mental Health Assn., Tenn. Mental Health Assn., budget com. United Fund of Johnson City, 1964-68, East Tenn. and Western N.C. Transp. Co., East. Tenn. and Western N.C. R.R., Tennolina Corp., Appalachian Air Lines Inc., Appalachian Flying Service Inc., Farmers and Merchants Bank Limestone, Tenn.; legal counsel Salvation Army, Assault Crime Counsel Early Support Services Inc.; former legal adviser Appalachian Council Girl Scouts U.S.A.; mem. Tenn. Law Revision Commn., 1970-71; mem. adv. bd. Salvation Army, 1974—, Civil Def., 1967—; mem. exec. com. Washington County Democratic Party, 1962—. Mem. Fed. Bar Assn., ABA, Nat. Orgn. Legal Problems Edn., Nat. Sch. Bd. Attys. Assn., Nat. Assn. R.R. Trial Counsel, Nat. Inst. Mcpl. Law Officers, Nat. Legal Aid Defender Assn., Nat. Rifle Assn., Tenn. Bar Assn., Am. Judicature Soc., Washington County Bar Assn. (past pres.), Assn. Trial Lawyers Am., Tenn. Sch. Bd. Attys. Assn., Tenn. Trial Lawyers Assn., Tenn. Mcpl. Attys. Assn., Assn. ICC Practitioners (past com. profl. ethics and grievances), Motor Carrier Lawyers Assn., Am. Counsel Assn., Johnson City C. of C. (Disting. Service award 1968), Internat. Platform Assn., Lawyers Com. for Civil Rights Under Law, World Peace Through Law Ctr., Tenn. Lung Assn., Tenn. Correctional Assn., Tenn. Taxpayers Assn. (past bd. dirs.), Tennesseans for Better Transp., Supreme Ct. Hist. Soc., Def. Research Inst., Tipton Haynes Hist. Assn. (past dir.), Phi Delta Phi, Phi Delta Theta. Episcopalian. Clubs: Hurstleigh J.C. Country, Unaka Rd. and Gun, Highland Stable, LeConte (bd. dirs., pres. 1966-67 North Johnson City), Nat. Lawyers, Eastern Tenn. State U. Centry, Boys' Club (charter) (Johnson City). Lodges: Masons, Elks (legal counsel 1963-67). First bd. govs. Transp. Law Jour. General practice, Local government, Administrative and regulatory. Home: 705 Judith Dr Johnson City TN 37604 Office: 115 E Unaka Ave Johnson City TN 37601 Mailing: PO Drawer 2288 Johnson City TN 37605-2288

EPSTEIN, BARRY DAVID, lawyer; b. N.Y.C., Oct. 27, 1940; s. Emanuel and Edna (Goldman) E.; m. Elaine Soltz, June 7, 1964; children: Eric, Michael. AB, Clark U., 1962; JD, Rutgers U., 1965. Bar: N.J. 1965, U.S. Dist. Ct. N.J. 1965, U.S. Supreme Ct. 1971. Assoc. Asch & Asch, Elizabeth, N.J., 1966-68, Luebowitz, K & L, Englewood, N.J., 1968-69; sole practice Saddle Brook, N.J., 1969-86, Rochelle Park, N.J., 1986—. Arbitrator Am. Arbitration Assn., New Brunswick, N.J., 1974—. Mem. Bergen County Bar Assn. (sec. 1982-83, treas. 1983-84, 2d v.p. 1984-85, 1st v.p. 1985-86, pres. 1986—). Club: Wayne (N.J.) Racquet (bd. govs. 1984—). Avocations: tennis, running, reading. Personal injury, State civil litigation, Workers' compensation. Home: 10 Webster Ave Wayne NJ 07662 Office: 340 W Passaic St Rochelle Park NJ 07662

EPSTEIN, DAVID, lawyer, arbitrator; b. San Antonio, June 19, 1935; s. Jerome and Sara (Furman) E.; m. Ellen Robinson; children—Jeremy, Asher, Barak, Dina, Kira. A.B. cum laude, Harvard U., 1957, LL.B., 1960. Bar: Tex. 1960, D.C. 1962, U.S. Supreme Ct. 1967, Md. 1981, N.Y. 1982. Gen. atty. Nat. Capital Planning Commn., Washington, 1961-62; asst. U.S. Atty. for D.C., 1962-66; prin. David Epstein Group, P.C., Washington, 1983-86; ptnr. Thompson, Hine & Flory, Washington, 1986—; staff cons. Commn. Administrn. of Justice Jud. Council of D.C. Cirs., 1968-69; cons. study for new D.C. court facility, Westinghouse Pub. Systems Mgmt. Services, 1970-71; adj. prof. Georgetown U. Law Ctr., 1970-75; mem. disciplinary bd. D.C. Bar, 1972-76, treas., 1977-78. Mem. D.C. Bar, ABA. Contbr. articles to profl. jours. Federal civil litigation, Contracts commercial, Private international. Home: 7507 Wyndale Rd Chevy Chase MD 20815 Office: 1920 N St NW Suite 700 Washington DC 20036

EPSTEIN, EDNA SELAN, lawyer; b. Yugoslavia, July 26, d. Carl and Lotte (Eisner) Selan; came to U.S., 1944, naturalized, 1951; A.B. cum laude, Barnard Coll., 1960; M.A. (AAUW fellow), Johns Hopkins U., 1961; Ph.D., Harvard U., 1967; J.D. cum laude (Law Rev.), U. Chgo., 1973; m. Wolfgang Epstein, June 12, 1961; children—Matthew, Ezra, Tanya. Asst. prof. French, U. Ill., Chgo. Circle, 1967-70; Bar: Ill. 1973; with Cook County State's Atty., 1973-75; ptnr. Sidley & Austin, Chgo., 1976—; mem. faculty Nat. Inst. Trial Advocacy, 1979-86; vis. lectr. U. Chgo. Sch. Law, 1979-81; vis. lectr. NITA programs Hofstra U., Emory U., 1980-86. Bd. govs. Hyde Park-Kenwood Community Conf., 1974-77, Chgo. Fin. Exchange, 1985-86; bd. dirs. Friends of Parks, 1978-80 ; mem. Citizens Com. for Victim Assistance, 1976-78, Cook County State's Atty.'s Profl. Adv. Com., 1981-84 Mayor Byrne's Transition Task Force, 1979, Chgo. Econ. Club, Chgo. Execs. Club, Jefferson Found.; del. Dem. Nat. Conv., 1980, also mem. rules com.; mem. Ill. Humanities Council, 1982-86, treas., 1983-84 Mem. Internat. Bar Assn., ABA (chmn. trial evidence com. 1979-83, mem. litigation sect. council 1984—), Chgo. Bar Assn., Chgo. Council Lawyers (bd. govs. 1975-77), Phi Beta Kappa, Order of Coif. Author: Client Privilege; Conflicts of Interest; Sanctions; contbr. articles to learned jours. Federal civil litigation, State civil litigation. Office: Sidley & Austin 1 First Nat Plaza Suite 4800 Chicago IL 60603

EPSTEIN, GARY MARVIN, lawyer; b. Bklyn., Nov. 28, 1946; s. Arthur and Juliett (Winick) E.; m. Jeralyn Needel, June 29, 1969; children: Daniel, Deborah. B.S.E.E., Lehigh U., 1968; J.D., Harvard U., 1971. Engr. Gordon Engring. Co., Wakefield, Mass., 1967-70; assoc. Arent, Fox, Kinter, Plotkin & Kahn, Washington, 1971-79, ptnr., 1979-81; chief Common Carrier Bur. FCC, Washington, 1981-83; ptnr. Latham & Watkins, Washington, 1983—; pub. mem. Adminstrv. Conf. U.S., 1983-86; chmn. adv. com. FCC, 1983—. Mem. Adminstrv. Conf. U.S., 1984—; chmn. adv. com. reduced orbitral spacing FCC, 1985—. Mem. ABA, Fed. Bar Assn., D.C. Bar Assn., Eta Kappa Nu, Tau Beta Pi. Administrative and regulatory, Computer, Private international. Home: 5706 Ogden Rd Bethesda MD 20816 Office: Latham & Watkins 1333 New Hampshire Ave NW Suite 1200 Washington DC 20036

EPSTEIN, HYMAN DAVID, lawyer, lecturer; b. Bklyn., Jan. 2, 1910; s. Samuel and Jennie (Winning) E.; m. Bertha Goncharow, Oct. 21, 1934; children—Robert Joseph, Jonathan Edward. B.S. in Commerce, NYU, 1932, LL.M., 1949; LL.B., Bklyn. Law Sch., 1936, J.D., 1967, J.S.D., 1949. Bar: N.Y. 1937, U.S. Ct. Internat. Trade 1939, U.S. Tax Ct. 1939, U.S. dist. ct. (ea. and so. dists.) N.Y. 1954, U.S. Supreme Ct. 1972, U.S. Ct. Mil. Appeals 1978. Sole practice Staten Island, N.Y., 1937—; with tax adminstrn. Kuhn, Loeb & Co., N.Y.C., 1946-54; account exec. Schweickart & Co., N.Y.C., 1957-74; staff lectr. N.Y. Stock Exchange, N.Y.C., 1956-68; lectr. Community Coll., Staten Island, 1960, 62, New Sch., N.Y.C., 1968. Author article in legal publ. Chmn. workshop Assn. for Brain Injured Children, Wagner Coll., Staten Island, 1968; committeeman Democratic Party Richmond County, Staten Island, 1959-61; advisors Richmondtown Prep. Sch., 1966—; v.p. Staten Island Council Boy Scouts Am., 1957-68; pres. Temple Tifereth Israel, Staten Island, 1952-55. Served with USAAF, 1944-46. Recipient Silver Beaver award Boy Scouts Am., 1961, Shofar award, Nat. Jewish Com. on Scouting, 1963. Mem. ABA, Richmond County Bar Assn., Am. Legion. Lodges: B'nai B'rith, K.P., Masons. Probate, Real property, Personal income taxation. Home: 14 Grand Ave Staten Island NY 10301 Office: 14 Grand Ave Staten Island NY 10301

EPSTEIN, JOSEPH MARC, lawyer; b. Phila., Oct. 31, 1944; s. Arthur and Shirley (Rubenstone) E.; m. Susan Nancy Landerson, June 25, 1967; children—Daniel, Samara. B.A., SUNY-Buffalo, 1966; J.D., NYU, 1969. Bar: N.J. 1969, U.S. Dist. Ct. N.J. 1969, U.S. Ct. Appeals (3d cir.) 1971, U.S. Dist. Ct. Colo. 1973, U.S. Ct. Appeals (10th cir.) 1980, U.S. Supreme Ct. 1973. Assoc., Neville & Pendleton, Denville, N.J., 1970-71; asst. U.S. Atty., Newark, 1971-73; assoc. Kripke, Carrigan & Bragg, Denver, 1973-75; ptnr. Epstein & Gilbert, Denver, 1975-78; sole practice, Denver, 1978-80; ptnr. Kripke, Epstein & Lawrence P.C., Denver, 1980—; lectr. in field. Contbr. articles to profl. jours. Bd. dirs. Colo. Assn. Retarded Citizens, 1976-80, Theodore Herzl Day Sch., 1981-84. Recipient Leadership award Denver C. of C., 1978-79. Mem. ABA, Colo. Bar Assn., Denver Bar Assn., Assn. Trial Lawyers Am., Colo. Trial Lawyers Assn. (sec.), Am. Soc. Law and Medicine, Trial Lawyers for Public Justice. Republican. Jewish. Personal injury, Federal civil litigation, State civil litigation. Office: Kripke Epstein & Lawrence PC 4100 E Mississippi Suite 710 Denver CO 80222

EPSTEIN, JUDITH ANN, lawyer; b. Los Angeles, Dec. 23, 1942; d. Gerald Elliot and Harriet (Hirsch) Rubens; m. Joseph I. Epstein, Oct. 4, 1964; children: Mark Douglas, Laura Ann. AB, U. Calif., Berkeley, 1964; MA, U. San Francisco, 1974, JD, 1977. Bar: Calif. 1978, U.S. Dist. Ct. (no. dist.) Calif 1978, U.S. Supreme Ct. 1983, U.S. Ct. Appeals (9th cir.) 1984. With social services dept. Sutter County, Yuba City, Calif., 1964-66; bus. devel. assoc. Yuba County C. of C., Marysville, Calif., 1968-70; research clk. Calif. Supreme Ct., San Fransisco, 1977; ptnr. Crosby, Heafey, Roach & May, Oakland, Calif., 1978—; bd. dirs. Sierra Pacific Steel, Hayward, Calif. Bd. dirs., v.p. Oakland Ballet, 1980—. Recipient Pres.'s award Oakland Ballet. Mem. Calif. Women Lawyers Assn., Alameda Bar Assn. Club: Berkeley Tennis. Libel, General corporate, Antitrust. Office: Crosby Heafey Roach & May 1999 Harrison Oakland CA 94612

EPSTEIN, MELVIN, lawyer; b. Passaic, N.J., Jan. 4, 1938; s. Hyman and Lillian (Rozenblum) E.; m. Rachel Judith Stein, Dec. 20, 1964; children: Jonathan Andrew, Emily Sarah. AB, Harvard U., 1959, LLB, 1962. Bar: N.Y. 1963. Assoc. Stroock & Stroock & Lavan, N.Y.C., 1962-71, ptnr., 1972—. bd. dirs. Bklyn. Philharmonic Symphony Orch., 1974—, Jewish Assn. for Coll. Youth, N.Y.C., 1985—. Mem. N.Y. State Bar Assn., Assn. of Bar of City of N.Y. General corporate, Private international, Securities. Office: Stroock & Stroock & Lavan 7 Hanover Sq New York NY 10004

EPSTEIN, MICHAEL A., lawyer; b. N.Y.C., June 26, 1954; s. Herman and Lillian (King) E. BA, Lehigh U., 1975; JD, NYU, 1979. Ptnr. Weil, Gotshal & Manges, N.Y.C., 1979—. Author: Modern Intellectual Property, 1984; editor: Corporate Counsellors Deskbook, 1982, Trade Secrets, Restrictive Covenants and Other Safeguards, 1976; contbr. articles to profl. jours. Mem. ABA, N.Y. State Bar Assn. Antitrust, Computer, Trademark and copyright. Home: 3333 Henry Hudson Pkwy Riverdale NY 10463 Office: Weil Gotshal & Manges 767 Fifth Ave New York NY 10153

EPSTEIN, MILTON AARON, lawyer; b. Newark, Nov. 14, 1912; s. Julius and Anna (Gomber) E.; m. Violet Brown, Mar. 7, 1937; 1 child, Andrew M. BA, U. Pa., 1932; JD, Rutgers U., 1935. Bar: N.J. 1935. Sole practice Elizabeth, N.J., 1936-47; ptnr. Epstein & Epstein, Elizabeth, 1947-55, Epstein, Epstein & Brown, Elizabeth, 1955-81, Epstein, Epstein, Brown & Bosek, Springfield, N.J., 1981—; counsel N.J. Credit Union League, Hightstown, 1947—; chmn. attys. com. N.J. Svgs. League, Cranford, 1965—. Pres. Cong. B'nai Israel, Elizabeth, 1949-50. Recipient Dist. Service award N.J. Svgs. League, 1975; named Man of the Yr. N.J. Credit Union League, 1977. Mem. ABA, N.J. Bar Assn., Union County Bar Assn. Club: U. Pa., Metro (No. N.J.) (pres. 1964-65). Lodges: Shriner, Masons. Probate, Real property, Contracts commercial. Home: 600 Union Ave Elizabeth NJ 07208 Office: Epstein Epstein Brown & Bosek 505 Morris Ave Springfield NJ 07081

EPSTEIN, PHILIP EDWARD, lawyer; b. Balt., Aug. 3, 1942. B.A. with honors, U. Md., 1963, LL.B., 1965, J.D., 1969. Bar: Md. 1965. With estate tax div. IRS, Washington, 1965-66; assoc. Azrael & Gann, Balt., 1966-68; asst. states atty. Baltimore City, 1968-72; trial atty. U.S. Dept. Justice, Washington, 1973-76; dep. assoc. gen. counsel Presidential Clemency Bd., 1975-76; sole practice, Bowie, Md., 1976—. Mem. ABA, Md. Bar Assn., Prince George's County Bar Assn. Democrat. Jewish. General practice. Office: 14300 Gallant Fox Lane Suite 102 Bowie MD 20715

EPSTEIN, RICHARD A., legal eduator; b. 1943. A.B., Columbia U., 1964; B.A., Oxford U., 1966; LL.B., Yale U., 1968. Bar: Calif. 1969, Asst. prof. U. So. Calif. Sch. Law, Los Angeles, 1968-70, assoc. prof., 1970-73; vis. assoc. prof. U. Chgo. Law Sch., 1972-73, prof., 1973-82, James Parker Hall prof. law, 1982—. Mem. Yale Law Jour.; author: (with Gregory and Kalven) Cases and Materials in Torts, 4th edit., 1984, Takings: Private Property And the Power of Eminent Domain, 1985; editor Jour. Legal Studies, 1981—. Mem. Order of Coif. Legal education. Office: U Chgo Law Sch 1111 E 60th St Chicago IL 60637 *

EPSTEIN, ROBERT E., lawyer; b. Detroit, Dec. 21, 1941; s. Jack W. and Carrie (Lazarus) E.; m. Renee Newman, June 16, 1963; children: Michelle, Daniel. BA, Wayne State U., 1963; JD, U. Mich., 1966. Bar: Mich. 1967. From assoc. to ptnr. Sommers, Schwartz, Silver, P.C., Southfield, Mich., 1966-76; exec. v.p. Dearborn (Mich.) Refining Co., 1976-81, Herman Frankel Orgn., West Bloomfield, Mich., 1981-82; asst. gen. counsel Borman's, Inc., Detroit, 1983-84, gen. counsel, 1984—. Mem. Mich. Bar Assn., Am. Corp. Counsel Assn., Am. Soc. Corp. Secs., Order of Coif, Phi Beta Kappa. General corporate, Real property. Office: Borman's Inc PO Box 33446 Detroit MI 48232-5446

EPSTEIN, ROGER HARRIS, lawyer; b. Washington, May 8, 1945; s. Morris Herman and Dorothy (Mushinsky) E.; m. Barbara Joyce Kirk, July 31, 1983; 1 child, Marisa Kirk. BS, U. Md., 1967; JD, Goergetown U., 1972. Agt. IRS, Washington, 1967-70, tax law splist., 1970-72; assoc. Cades, Schutte, Fleming & Wright, Honolulu, 1972-78, ptnr., 1978—; bd. dirs. Theo H. Davies & Co., Ltd., Honolulu, 1985—; of counsel Kanung-Prok & Assoc. Internat. Attys., Bangkok, Thailand, 1985—. Editor Georgetown U. Jour., 1970-72. Pres., bd. dirs. The Maitreya Inst., Honolulu, 1983—; bd. dirs. The T'ai H'suan Found., Honolulu, 1983—; prin. Lily Suio Sch. Acupuncture, Honolulu, 1983. Mem. ABA, Hawaii Bar Assn. Avocations: Chi Kung, piano, skiing. Corporate taxation, Estate taxation, Personal income taxation. Home: 1531 Hoaaina St Honolulu HI 96821 Office: Cades Schutte et al 1000 Bishop St Honolulu HI 96813

EPSTEIN, STANLEY MURRAY, lawyer; b. Lowell, Mass., Jan. 10, 1918. A.B., Harvard U., 1939, LL.B., 1942. Bar: Mass. 1942, U.S. Supreme Ct. 1955. Law clk. to judge U.S. Dist. Ct. Mass., Boston, 1943-44; assoc. Mintz, Levin and Cohn, Boston, 1944-46; sole practice, Boston, 1946-65; ptnr. Epstein, Salloway & Kaplan, Boston, 1965-77, Epstein, King & Isselbacher, Boston, 1977—. Chmn. United Fund, Newton, Mass., 1964; chmn. fin. com. Mass. Bay Red Cross Chpts., 1971-75; mem. nat. conv. resolutions com. ARC, 1974, now mem. bd. govs., exec. com.; mem. adv. bd. Paralegal Inst., Bentley Coll., 1974—; trustee Social Law Library, Boston. Mem. ABA, Mass. Bar Assn., Boston Bar Assn., Assn. Trial Lawyers Am., Phi Beta Kappa. General practice. Home: 32 Fairview Rd Weston MA 02193 Office: 131 State St Boston MA 02109

ERBEN, RANDALL HARVEY, lawyer; b. San Antonio, Aug. 23, 1956; s. Harvey and Dona Lou (Orndorff) E. AB, Princeton U., 1978; JD, U. Tex., 1981. Bar: Tex. 1981, U.S. Ct. Appeals (5th cir.) 1982, U.S. Dist. Ct. (we. dist.) Tex. 1985, U.S. Tax Ct., 1986. Ptnr. Foster, Lewis, Langley, Gardner & Banack, Inc., San Antonio, 1981-87; asst. sec. state Tex., 1987—. Mem. Rep. Candidate Recruitment Com., San Antonio, 1985—, transp. com. Target 90/Future San Antonio, 1985—; del. Rep. State Convention, 1984—; chmn. Bexar County GOP Ballot Security Program, San Antonio, 1984—; spl. counsel Tex. Ballot Security Program, 1984, Spl. Congl. Election for Ballot Security, 1985; witness Tex. SEnate Subcom. on Civil Matters, Austin, Tex., 1984. Mem. Tex. Bar Assn. (minimum continuing legal edn. com.), San Antonio Bar Assn. (legis. com.), San Antonio Young Lawyers Assn. (sec., bd. dirs. 1981—), Nat. Inst. Mcpl. Law Officers, Tex. Mcpl. League, Rep. Men's Club of Bexar County (pres., sec. 1984-85), Christmas Cotillion Bachelor's Club, World Affairs Council, Young Art Patrons (bd. dirs. 1983—). Federal civil litigation, State civil litigation, Local government. Home: 201 Ellwood #120 San Antonio TX 78205 Office: State Capitol Room 127 Austin TX 78711

ERCKLENTZ, ENNO WILHELM, JR., lawyer; b. N.Y.C., Jan. 27, 1931; s. Enno Wilhelm and Hildegard (Schlubach) E.; m. Mai A. Vilms, Sept. 20, 1969; children—Cornelia, Stephanie. A.B., Columbia U., 1954; J.D., Harvard U., 1957. Bar: N.Y. 1958. Assoc. Curtis, Mallet-Prevost, Colt & Mosle, N.Y.C., 1957-60; sec., gen. csl. Channing Fin. Corp., N.Y.C., 1960-69; v.p., sec., gen. csl. Inverness Mgmt. Corp., N.Y.C., 1969-75; sole practice, N.Y.C., 1975-78; ptnr. Whitman & Ransom, N.Y.C., 1978-87, Greevan & Ercklentz, N.Y.C., 1987—. Mem. Assn. Bar City N.Y., ABA, N.Y. State Bar Assn., Am. Soc. Internat. Law, Am. Fgn. Law Assn. Republican. Roman Catholic. Clubs: Mid-Atlantic, Knickerbocker (N.Y.C.). Author: Modern German Corporation Law, 1979. General corporate, Private international, Securities. Office: Greeven & Ercklentz 30 Rockefeller Plaza Suite 3030 New York NY 10112

ERES, THOMAS W., lawyer. m. Jacquelyn Lee Bertagna; children: Kimberly, Kelly, Marty, Robbie. BA, U. Redlands, 1968; grad., calif. Mil. Acad., 1970; JD, U. Pacific, 1972. Bar: Calif., U.S. Dist. Ct. (ea. and cen. dists.) Calif., U.S. Ct. Claims, U.S. Tax Ct., U.S. Ct. Mil. Appeals, U.S. Ct. Appeals (9th cir.), U.S. Supreme Ct. Prin. Kronick, Moskovitz, Tiedemann & Girard, Sacramento, Calif., 1976—; mem. Gov.'s Task Force Pub. Broadcasting, Calif. Chmn. McGeorge Sch. Law Capital Fund Campaign; sec., treas. Sacramento Make-A-Wish Found.; arbitrator Sacramento Better Bus. Bur., Sacramento Superior Ct.; mem. adv. commn. Victims Rights, McGeorge Sch. Law; mem. Sacramento Met. C. of C.; bd. dirs. Calif. Attys. Fed. Credit Union. Named One of Outstanding Young Men Am., 1978. Fellow Am. Bar Found.; mem. ABA (editorial bd. human rights sect., mem. bus., litigation and taxation com.), Calif. Bar Assn. (bd. govs., chmn. spl. com. rev. jud. nominations evaluation commn.), Sacramento County Bar (past pres.), Am. Judicature Soc., N.G. Assn. U.S., McGeorge Sch. Law Alumni Assn., Phi Alpha Delta. Corporate taxation, Real property, General corporate. Office: Kronick Moskovitz Tiedemann & Girard Suite 1200 770 L St Sacramento CA 95814

ERICKSON, DAVID BELNAP, lawyer; b. Ogden, Utah, Oct. 13, 1951; s. Eldred H. and Lois (Belnap) E.; m. Julie Ann Hill, Apr. 19, 1974; children: Rachel, John, Michael, Jared, Emily, Steven, Katherine, Daniel. BA, Brigham Young U., 1975; MEd, Utah State U., 1979; JD, Gonzaga Sch. Law, 1982. Bar: Utah 1982, U.S. Dist. Ct. Utah 1982, U.S. Ct. Appeals (10th cir.) 1984, U.S. Ct. Appeals (9th cir.) 1987. English tchr. Bonneville High Sch., Ogden, 1976-79; law clk. U.S. Atty.'s Office, Spokane, Washington, 1980-81; law clk. to presiding justice U.S. Dist. Ct., Salt Lake City, 1982-83; assoc. Kirton, McConkie & Bushnell, Salt Lake City, 1983—. Coauthor Utah Appellate Practice Manual, 1986; Editor-in-Chief Gonzaga Law Review, 1981-82; assoc. editor Utah Barrister, 1986-87; contbr. articles to profl. jours. Mem. ABA, Fed. Bar Assn., Utah Bar Assn. (law jour. com.), Salt Lake City Bar Assn., Weber County Bar Assn., Phi Delta Phi. Mormon. Federal civil litigation, State civil litigation. Office: Kirton McConkie & Bushnell 330 S 300 E Salt Lake City UT 84111

ERICKSON, DAVID L., lawyer; b. Okmulgee, Okla., Mar. 21, 1939; s. Herbert R. and Jean (Russell) E.; m. Jeanne E. Jarvis, Jan. 22, 1965; children: Jennifer L., Russell D. BME, Western New England U., 1963; JD, U. Denver, 1966. Bar: U.S. Dist. Ct. Colo. 1966, U.S. Ct. Appeals (10th cir.) 1966, U.S. Supreme Ct. 1971. Legis. asst. U.S. Senator, Washington, 1966-67; sole practice Denver, 1968-79; ptnr. Erickson, Holmes, Nicholls, Kusic & Sussman, Denver, 1980-85; spl. counsel Kelly, Stansfield & O'Donnell, Denver, 1986; panel mem. Supreme Ct. Grievance Com. Author: Colorado Corporate Forms, 1984. Bd. dirs., officer Met. Denver Sewage Disposal Dist., 1976-84; pres., bd. dirs. Bellevue-Hale Neighborhood Assn., Denver, 1979—. Mem. ABA, Colo. Assn. Corp. Counsel, Supreme Ct. Bd. Law Examiners. Club: Denver Athletic. General corporate, Contracts commercial, Real property. Home: 1364 Ash Denver CO 80220 Office: Kelly Stansfield & O'Donnell 550-15th St Suite 900 Denver CO 80202

ERICKSON, GAIL, lawyer; b. Pasadena, Calif., Feb. 9, 1934; d. Alfred Louis and Helen Hield (Baker) E. BA, Stanford U., 1955; JD, Harvard U., 1958. Bar: N.Y. 1959. Atty. W. R. Grace and Co., N.Y.C., 1958—. Mem. ABA. Democrat. Club: Harvard. General corporate, Securities. Office: WR Grace and Co 1114 Ave of the Americas New York NY 10036

ERICKSON, GEORGE EVERETT, JR., lawyer; b. Ft. Scott, Kans., July 20, 1937; s. George Everett Sr. and Cora Kathleen (Hayden) E.; m. Carrol Ann Guthridge, Dec. 23, 1966; children: Ingrid Ann, Karin Ruth. BS, U.S. Naval Acad., 1959; JD, Washburn U., 1966. Bar: Kans. 1966, Okla. 1966, U.S. Dist. Ct. Kans. 1966, U.S. Ct. Appeals (10th cir.) 1967, U.S. Supreme Ct. 1972, D.C. 1985. Commd. ensign USN, 1959, advanced through grades to lt. comdr., resigned, 1963; atty. Amerada-Hess Corp., Tulsa, 1966-69; ptnr. Cosgrove, Webb & Oman, Topeka, 1969-73; sole practice Topeka, 1973-84; ptnr. Erickson & Hall, Topeka, 1984—; prof. Washburn U. Law Sch., Topeka, 1973-74; bd. dirs. The Am. Cos., Topeka, 1973—; atty. City of Auburn, Kans., 1976-82. Mem. Auburn-Washburn Rural Sch. Bd., Topeka, 1977-79. Mem. ABA, Fed. Bar Assn., D.C. Bar Assn., Kans. Bar Assn., Judge Advocates Assn, Nat. Lawyers Club. Republican. Clubs: Army, Navy (Washington); Shawnee Country (Topeka). General corporate, Federal civil litigation, State civil litigation. Home: 6000 Urish Rd Topeka KS 66604 Office: Erickson & Hall 3320 Harrison Topeka KS 66611

ERICKSON, PHILLIP ARTHUR, lawyer, food service equipment company executive; b. Duluth, Minn., June 27, 1941; s. Carl Edward and Velma Cecilia (Pera) E.; BA, U. Minn., 1967, JD, 1970; m. Marcia Diane Engman, July 22, 1967; children: Michael Phillip, Amy Diane. Bar: Minn. 1970, U.S. Supreme Ct. Gen. counsel and sec. N. Cen. Cos., Inc., St. Paul, 1970-73; gen. atty. JFP Enterprises, Duluth, 1973-74; corp. atty., The Cornelius Co., Anoka, Minn., 1974-80, sr. v.p. law and corp. sec., IMI Cornelius (Americas) Inc., 1986—. Pres. Homeward Bound, Inc., 1981-83, bd. dirs., 1977—; bd. dirs. Marc, 1978-80; mem. adv. com. to legal advocacy for persons with developmental disabilities. Served with USAF, 1959-63. Mem. ABA, Minn. State Bar Assn., Am. Corp. Counsel Assn. General corporate, Contracts commercial, Diverse practice. Home: 18905 9th Ave N Plymouth MN 55447 Office: Cornelius Co One Cornelius Pl Anoka MN 55303-1592

ERICKSON, RALPH ERNEST, lawyer; b. Jamestown, N.Y., Oct. 3, 1928; s. Lawrence Harold and Myrtle (Jespersen) E.; m. Janet Cass, June 6, 1953; children: Sandra Lynne, John Cass. B.S., Cornell U., 1952; J.D., Harvard U., 1955. Bar: Calif. 1956, U.S. Supreme Ct. 1968, D.C. 1973. Ptnr. Musick, Peeler & Garrett, Los Angeles, 1962-70, 74-75; asst. atty. gen. U.S. Dept. Justice, 1971-72, dep. atty. gen., 1972-73; ptnr. Erickson, Zerfas & Adams, Los Angeles, 1976-79, Jones, Day, Reavis & Pogue, Los Angeles, 1979—; spl rep. of U.S. for Am. Indian Movement Wounded Knee negotiations, 1973; mem. steering com. Am. Businessmen of Riyadh, Saudi Arabia, 1986—. Founding mem., trustee Victor Gruen Found. Environ Planning; chmn. legal adv. com. San Marino Sch. Dist., Calif., 1979-81; mem. Invest-

ment Commn., 1979—, Los Angeles Citizens Olympics Commn., Los Angeles World Affairs Council, 1984—. Fellow Huntington Library and Gallery, San Marino, Calif., 1984—. Mem. ABA (ho. of dels. 1972-73), Calif. State Bar, D.C. Bar. Republican. Episcopalian. Clubs: Calif. (Los Angeles); Met. (Washington); Springs (Rancho Mirage, Calif.); Annandale Golf (Pasadena, Calif.); Town Hall (Los Angeles) (life mem.). Administrative and regulatory, Private international, General corporate. Office: Reavis & Pogue 355 S Grand Ave Suite 3000 Los Angeles CA 90071

ERICKSON, ROBERT STANLEY, lawyer; b. Kemmerer, Wyo., Apr. 17, 1944; s. Stanley W. and Dorothy Marie (Johnson) E.; m. Alice Norman, Dec. 27, 1972; children—Robert Badger, Erin Elizabeth, Andrew Carl, Scott Stanley, Courtney Ellen, Brennan Marie. B.S. in Bus., U. Idaho, 1966; J.D., U. Utah, 1969; LL.M. in Taxation, George Washington U., 1973. Bar: U.S. Supreme Ct. 1973, U.S. Ct. Appeals (9th cir.) 1980, U.S. Dist. Ct. Idaho 1973, U.S. Tax Ct., 1969, Idaho 1973, Utah, 1969. Assoc. atty. Office of Chief Counsel, Dept. Treasury, Washington, 1969-73; assoc. Elam, Burke, Jeppesen, Evans & Boyd, Boise, Idaho, 1973-77; ptnr. Elam, Burke, Evans, Boyd & Koontz, Boise, 1977-81; spl. counsel Holme Roberts & Owen, Salt Lake City, 1981-83; ptnr. Hansen & Erickson, Boise, 1983-85; ptnr. Hawley Troxell Ennis & Hawley, Boise, 1985—. Mem. deferred gifts com. Primary Children's Hosp., Salt Lake City. Named Citizen of Yr., Boise Exchange Club, 1980. Mem. ABA, Idaho State Bar, State Bar Utah, Treasure Valley Estate Planning Council, Idaho State Tax Inst. (exec. com.). Mormon. Contbr. articles to profl. jours. Probate, Corporate taxation, Pension, profit-sharing, and employee benefits. Office: Suite 701 999 Main St Boise ID 83702

ERICKSON, ROY LYDEEN, agribusiness exec.; b. Kelliher, Minn., Apr. 20, 1923; s. Albert E. and Victoria (Lydeen) E.; m. Beverly E. Hurrle, July 12, 1957. B.B.A., U. Minn., 1948; J.D., Wm. Mitchell Coll. Law, 1961. Bar: Minn. bar 1961. With treas. dept. financial and computer areas Archer-Daniels-Midland Co., Decatur, Ill., 1948-60; atty., asst. sec. Archer-Daniels-Midland Co., 1961-68, sec., gen. counsel, 1969—, v.p., 1970—; practice law Mpls., 1961-69, Decatur, Ill., 1969—; Chmn. Planning and Zoning Com., Columbia Heights, Minn., 1962; spl. Municipal Ct. judge Columbia Heights, 1964-68. Served with USNR, 1940-45. Mem. Am., Minn., Hennepin County bar assns. General corporate. Home: 494 Shoreline Dr Decatur IL 62521 Office: 4666 Faries Pkwy Decatur IL 62525

ERICKSON, WILLIAM HURT, judge; b. Denver, May 11, 1924; s. Arthur Xavier and Virginia (Hurt) E.; m. Doris Rogers, Dec. 24, 1953; children: Barbara Ann, Virginia Lee, Stephen Arthur, William Taylor. Petroleum Engr., Colo. Sch. Mines., 1947; postgrad., U. Mich., 1949; LL.B., U. Va., 1950. Bar: Colo. 1951. Practiced law Denver; justice Colo. Supreme Ct., 1971—, chief justice, 1983-85; faculty NYU Appellate Judges Sch., 1972-85; mem. exec. com. Commn. on Accreditation of Law Enforcement Agys., 1980-83. Served with USAAF, 1943. Recipient award of merit Colo. Com. Continuing Legal Edn., 1968. Fellow Internat. Acad. Trial Lawyers (former sec.), Am. Coll. Trial Lawyers, Am. Bar Found. (chmn. 1985), Internat. Soc. Barristers (past pres.); mem. Am. Law Inst. (council), Practising Law Inst. (nat. adv. council, bd. govs. Colo. chpt.), Denver Bar Assn. (past pres., trustee), ABA (bd. govs. 1975-79, former chmn. com. on standards criminal justice, former chmn. council criminal law sect., former chmn. com. to implement standards criminal justice, mem. long-range planning com., action com. to reduce ct. costs and delay), Am. Bar Found. (chmn. 1985-86), Freedoms Found. at Valley Forge (nat. council trustees, 1986—), Order of Coif, Scribes (pres. 1978). Home: 10 Martin Ln Englewood CO 80110 Office: State Judicial Bldg 2 E 14th Ave Denver CO 80203

ERICKSTAD, RALPH JOHN, state supreme ct. justice; b. Starkweather, N.D., Aug. 15, 1922; s. John T. and Anna Louisa (Myklebust) E.; m. Lois Katherine Jacobson, July 30, 1949; children: John Albert, Mark Anders. Student, U. N.D., 1940-43; B.Sc. in Law, U. Minn., 1947, LL.B., 1949. Bar: N.D. bar 1949. Practiced in Devils Lake, 1949-62; State's atty. Ramsey County, 1953-57; mem. N.D. Senate from, Ramsey County, 1957-62; asst. majority floor leader N.D. Senate from, 1959, 61; asso. justice Supreme Ct. N.D., 1963-73, chief justice, 1973—; Treas. N.D. States Attys. Assn., 1955, v.p., 1956; mem. N.D. Legislative Research Com., 1957-59, N.D. Budget Bd., 1961-63, Gov. N.D. Spl. Com. Labor, 1960. Past mem. exec. com. Mo. Valley council Boy Scouts Am.; chmn. bd. trustees Mo. Valley Family YMCA, 1966-77. Served with USAAF, 1943-45, ETO. Recipient Silver Beaver award Boy Scouts Am., 1967; Sioux award U. N.D., 1973; 1st Disting. Service award Missouri Valley Family YMCA, 1978. Mem. Am., N.D., Burleigh County bar assns., Nat. Conf. Chief Justices (exec. council), Am. Judicature Soc., Am. Law Inst. Lutheran (del. 1st biennial conv., mem. nominating com.). Clubs: Am. Legion, VFW, Kiwanian. Judicial administration, Judicial administration. Office: Supreme Ct North Dakota State Capitol Bismarck ND 58505 *

ERICSON, BRUCE ALAN, lawyer; b. Buffalo, Feb. 28, 1952; s. Carl H. and Jean (Herman) E. AB, U. Pa., 1974; JD, Harvard U., 1977. Bar: Calif. 1977, U.S. Dist. Ct. (no. dist.) Calif. 1977, U.S. Ct. Appeals (9th cir.) 1981, U.S. Supreme Ct. 1982. Assoc. Pillsbury, Madison & Sutro, San Francisco, 1977-84, ptnr., 1985—; judge pro tem. San Francisco Mcpl. Ct., 1984—. Mem. ABA, San Francisco Bar Assn., Lawyers Club San Francisco, Phi Beta Kappa. Republican. Club: Olympic (San Francisco). Avocations: skiing, golf, squash. Antitrust, Federal civil litigation, State civil litigation. Office: Pillsbury Madison & Sutro 225 Bush St San Francisco CA 94104

ERICSON, JAMES DONALD, lawyer; b. Hawarden, Iowa, Oct. 12, 1935; s. Elmer H. and Martha (Sydness) E.; children: Linda Jean, James Robert. B.A. in History, State U. Iowa, 1958, J.D., 1962. Bar: Wis. 1965. Asso. firm Fitzgerald, Brown, Leahy, McGill & Strom, Omaha, 1962-65; with Northwestern Mut. Life Ins. Co., Milw., 1965—; asst. to pres. Northwestern Mut. Life Ins. Co., 1972-75, dir. policy benefits, 1975-76, v.p., gen. counsel, sec., 1976-80, sr. v.p., 1980; pres., dir. Grand Ave. Corp.; bd. dirs. Regis Group Inc., Mortgage Guaranty Ins. Corp., Baird Capital Devel. Fund., Inc., Baird Blue Chip Fund, Inc. Bd. dirs., treas. Performing Arts Center; v.p., dir. Florentine Opera Co.; treas., dir. Lynde and Harry Bradley Found., Inc.; bd. dirs. Blood Ctr. Southeastern Wis., Inc., Milw. County Research Park Commn., YMCA; bd. dirs., mem. adv. bd. U. Wis. Ctr. for Health Policy and Program Evaluation. Mem. Am., Wis. bar assns., Assn. Life Ins. Counsel, Phi Beta Kappa. Republican. Presbyterian. General corporate. Office: 720 E Wisconsin Ave Milwaukee WI 53202

ERICSON, ROGER DELWIN, forest products company executive; b. Moline, Ill, Dec. 21, 1934; s. Carl D. and Linnea E. (Challman) E.; m. Norma F. Brown, Aug. 1, 1957; children: Catherine Lynn, David. A.B., Stetson U., DeLand, Fla., 1958; J.D., Stetson U., 1958; M.B.A., U. Chgo., 1971. Bar: Fla. 1958, Ill. 1959, Ind. 1974. Atty. Brunswick Corp., Skokie, Ill., 1959-62; asst. sec., asst. gen. counsel Chemetron Corp., Chgo., 1962-73; asst. v.p. Inland Container Corp., Indpls., 1973-75, v.p., gen. counsel, sec., 1975-83; gen. counsel, sec. Temple-Inland, Inc., 1983—; v.p., sec., dir. Ga. Kraft Co.; pres., dir. Kraft Land Services, Inc.; vice chmn. bd., pres., dir. G.K. Investments, Inc.; bd. dirs. Inland Container Corp., Inland-Orange, Inc., Temple-Eastex Inc., Inland Real Estate Investments, Inc. Trustee Chgo. Homes for Children, 1971-74; mem. alumni council U. Chgo., 1972-76; mem. Palatine Twp. Youth Commn., 1969-72; sect. chmn. Chgo. Heart Assn., 1972, 73; alumni bd. dirs. Stetson U. Mem. ABA, Chgo. Bar Assn., Ill. State Bar Assn., Ind. Bar Assn., Fla. Bar Assn., Indpls. Bar Assn. (chmn. corp. counsel sect., mem. profl. responsibility com. 1982), Am. Soc. Corp. Secs., Am. Paper Inst. (past mem. govt. affairs com.), Indpls. C. of C. (mem. govt. affairs com.), Omicron Delta Kappa, Phi Delta Phi. Clubs: Plum Grove (Chgo.) (pres. 1969); Crown Colony Country (Lufkin, Tex.). General corporate, Antitrust, Administrative and regulatory. Office: Temple-Inland Inc Drawer N Diboll TX 75941

ERIM, AHMET MARTIN, lawyer; b. Adapazari, Turkey, Dec. 15, 1952; came to U.S., 1957; s. Seyfettin and Mecbure (Coroglu) E.; m. Rachel Lee McRorie, Jan. 3, 1980; 1 child, Kimberly Rena. BA, Pa. State U., 1973; JD, Am. U., Washington, 1977. Bar: Ill. 1978. Project mgr. Aspen Systems Corp., Rockville, Md., 1977-79; pres., chief exec. officer Am. Legal Systems, N.Y.C., 1979—. Contbr. articles to profl. jours. Mem. ABA, Am. Turkish Assn., Ill. Bar Assn. Computer, Federal civil litigation, General corporate. Home: 121 Victory Blvd New Rochelle NY 10804 Office: Am Legal Systems 475 Park Ave New York NY 10016

ERKENBRACK, STEPHEN K., lawyer; b. Washington, June 28, 1952; s. Phillip Frederick and Irene (Brady) E.; m. Lysa Marie Loew, Aug. 18, 1979; children: Kenneth, Elizabeth, Daniel. BA, Washington & Lee U., 1972-74; JD, U. Colo., 1975-78. Bar: Colo. 1975, U.S. Dist. Ct. Colo. 1978. Clk. Colo. Supreme Ct., Denver, 1979; dep. dist. atty. Mesa County Dist. Atty., Grand Junction, Colo., 1979-82; assoc., office mgr. Tipping & Beckner, Grand Junction, 1982-83; v.p. Beckner & Erkenbrack, Grand Junction, 1983-86. vice chmn. Attention to Youth, Grand Junction, 1979-84. Mem. ABA, Colo. Bar Assn., Mesa County Bar Assn., Assn. Trial Lawyers of Am., Colo. Trial Lawyers Assn. Republican. Avocations: music, history, philosophy, skiing, camping. State civil litigation, Criminal. Office: Beckner & Erckenbrack Valley Fed Bldg Suite 705 Grand Junction CO 81501

ERLEBACHER, ARLENE CERNIK, lawyer; b. Chgo., Oct. 3, 1946; d. Laddie J. and Gertrude V. (Kurdys) Cernik; m. Albert Erlebacher, June 14, 1968; stepchildren—Annette, Jacqueline. B.A., Northwestern U., 1967, J.D., 1973. Bar: Ill. 1974, U.S. Dist. Ct. (no. dist.) Ill. 1974, U.S. Ct. Appeals (7th cir.) 1974, Fed. Trial Bar, 1983, U.S. Supreme Ct. 1985. Assoc. Sidley & Austin, Chgo., 1974-80, ptnr., 1980—. Fellow Am. Bar Found.; mem. ABA, Ill. Bar Assn., Chgo. Bar Assn., Chgo. Council Lawyers, Order Coif. Federal civil litigation, State civil litigation, Personal injury. Office: Sidley & Austin One First Nat Plaza Chicago IL 60603

ERLICH, BARRY ARNOLD, lawyer; b. Bklyn., Nov. 19, 1947; s. Saul Michael and Sara R. (Steinman) E.; m. Merle Nona Rovel, June 13, 1971; children—Seth Michael, Rachel Beth, Joshua David. B.A., Calif. State U.-Los Angeles, 1968; J.D., U. Ill., 1971. Bar: Ill. 1971, U.S. Dist. Ct. (no. dist.) Ill. 1971, U.S. Ct. Appeals (7th cir.) 1975, U.S. Supreme Ct. 1975, Trial Bar 1982. Atty., Continental Ill. Nat. Bank, Chgo., 1971-72; assoc. Aaron, Aaron, Schimberg & Hess, Chgo., 1972-75; assoc. Solomon, Rosenfeld, Elliott, Stiefel & Engerman, Chgo., 1975-77, ptnr., 1978-80; ptnr., firm Engerman, Erlich, Jacobs & Berman, Ltd., Chgo., 1980—; mem. panel of arbitrators Am. Arbitration Assn. Mem. U. Ill. Law Forum, 1969-71, notes and comments editor, 1970-71. Mem. ABA, Ill. Bar Assn., DuPage County Bar Assn., Chgo. Bar Assn., Assn. Trial Lawyers Am. Contbr. writings to legal publs. State civil litigation, Federal civil litigation. Office: Suite 2300 55 W Monroe Chicago IL 60603

ERLICH, JACOB NATHAN, lawyer; b. Milford, Mass., Mar. 27, 1940; s. Jack and Sara (Londner) E.; m. Laura Yessin, Sept. 17, 1967; children—Adam and Shari. B.S. in Mech. Engring., Worcester Poly. Inst., 1962; J.D., Georgetown U., 1966. Bar: D.C. 1967, U.S. Ct. Appeals (D.C. cir.) 1967, Mass. 1972, U.S. Supreme Ct. 1972, U.S. Patent and Trademark Office, Canadian Patent Office. Patent examiner U.S. Patent Office, Washington, 1962-67; chief patent adviser U.S. Air Force, Waltham, Mass., 1967—. Bd. dirs. Citizens Scholar. Found., Bedford, Mass., 1979—, v.p., 1984-85, pres., 1985-86; mem. bd. Standards, Bedford, 1978—. Recipient Spl. Achievement award Dept. Air Force, 1969-72, 73-79, Superior Performance award Dept. Air Force, 1981-84, Sci. Achievement award, 1983; Disting. Service award Worcester Poly. Inst., 1982, 83. Mem. Boston Patent Law Assn. (sec. 1981, v.p. 1982, pres.-elect. 1983, pres. 1984, bd. govs. 1979, 81-85), ASME (pres. 1961-62). Club: Georgetown Patent Law (treas. 1965-66). Patent, Trademark and copyright, Government contracts and claims. Home: 19 Fox Run Rd Bedford MA 01730 Office: Dept Air Force 424 Trapelo Rd Waltham MA 02154

ERLICH, RICHARD HENRY, lawyer; b. Montreal, Que., Can., Aug. 9, 1949; came to U.S., 1959; s. Arthur and Felicia (Lefkovitch) E.; m. Suzy T. Savok, June 23, 1972; children: John, Sandy, Ian. BA, Antioch Coll., 1972; JD, Antioch Law Sch., Washington, 1981. Bar: Alaska 1981, U.S. Dist. Ct. Alaska 1982. Mgr. Puyallup Tribe, Tacoma, 1975-79; lawyer Alaska Legal Services, Kotzebue, Alaska, 1981-82; pres. Kikiktagruk Inupiat Corp., Kotzebue, Alaska, 1982-83; lawyer, prin. Law Office of Richard H. Erlich, Kotzebue, Alaska, 1983—. Mem. ABA, Alaska Bar Assn., Assn. Trial Lawyers, Nat. Assn. Criminal Def. Attys. Democrat. Jewish. Lodge: Lions (Service award 1985). General corporate, Criminal, General practice. Home: PO Box 565 Kotzebue AK 99752 Office: 333 Front St Suite 400 Kotzebue AK 99752

ERLICHSTER, JOE, lawyer; b. Warsaw, Poland, July 19, 1944; came to U.S., 1950; s. Leon and Lola (Kirshenbaum) E. Student, Princeton U., 1966, Calif. State U., Dominguez Hills, 1969, Yeshiva U., 1979, NYU, 1981. Bar: N.Y. 1980, U.S. Dist. Ct. (so. and ea. dists.) N.Y. 1980, U.S. Ct. Appeals (1st cir.) 1980, N.J. 1981. Sole practice N.Y.C., 1980—. Mem. governing council Am. Jewish Congress, N.Y.C., 1983-85. Mem. ABA, N.Y. State Bar Assn., Assn. of Bar of City of N.Y., Am. Soc. Inst. Law, Am. Physical Soc. Avocation: photography. Real property, Public international, Civil rights. Home: 275 W 96th St New York NY 10025 Office: 111 John St Penthouse New York NY 10038

ERLICK, EVERETT HOWARD, broadcasting company executive; b. Birmingham, Ala., Sept. 12, 1921; s. Julian H. and Bertha Lorraine (Engel) E.; m. Nancy Ruth Jacobs, July 11, 1953; children—James M., Lorre Bert. A.B., Vanderbilt U., 1942; LL.B., Yale, 1948. Bar: N.Y. 1948. Assoc. atty. Engel, Judge & Miller, N.Y. C., 1948-51; asst. gen. counsel Young & Rubicam, N.Y.C., 1951-55, v.p; asso. dir. media relations dept. 1955-58, v.p. radio-TV dept., 1959-61; v.p., gen. counsel Am. Broadcasting-Paramount Theatres, Inc. (now CCC/ABC Inc.), 1961-68, dir., 1962—, group v.p., gen. counsel, 1968-72, sr. v.p., gen. counsel, 1972—, exec. v.p., 1983-86, cons., 1986—; dir. AB-PT, Inc., WLS, Inc.; Mem. Pres.'s Bus. Adv. Com. on Desegregation, 1963, Pres.'s Nat. Citizens Com. for Community Relations, 1964, Nat. Com. for Immigration Reform, 1965. Mem. campaign Am. Cancer Soc., 1965—; nat. chmn. parents com. Duke U., 1974-76, pres.'s assoc., 1976—; trustee Everglades Protection Assn., 1980—. Mem. Phi Beta Kappa. Home: 22 Chester Dr Rye NY 10580 Office: 1330 Ave Americas New York NY 10019

ERMENTROUT, JOHN CURTIS, lawyer, state official; b. Potomac, Ill., Mar. 30, 1912; s. Arthur Clayton and Arie Genella (Kinney) E.; m. Alberta Ferabee Goodwine, May 8, 1937. B.S. in Commerce and Law, U. Ill., 1934, LL.B., J.D., 1936. Bar: Ill. 1936, U.S. Supreme Ct. 1945, U.S. Ct. Claims 1946, U.S. Dist. Ct. (cen. dist.) Ill. 1953, U.S. Tax Ct. 1958. Sole practice, Champaign, Ill., 1936—; sec. to justices Ill. Supreme Ct., 1951-63; spl. asst. atty. gen. Ill., 1968-82; dir. Prospect Foods, Inc., Champaign; grader Ill. State Bar Examination, Chgo., 1952-68. Author articles on genealogy. Campaign dir. Republican candidates in nat., state, jud., county and dist. elections, Ill., Champaign County, 1940-78. Served as maj. Gen. Staff Corps, War Dept., Pentagon, 1945-46. Recipient Army Commendation ribbon Hdqrs. Army Services Forces, Pentagon, Washington, 1945. Mem. Champaign County Bar Assn., Ill. Bar Assn. (sr. counsellor cert. 1986), ABA. Republican. Presbyterian. Clubs: Champaign Country, Champaign Athletic. Banking, General corporate, Estate planning. Home: 405 W University Ave Champaign IL 61820 Office: Bank of Ill Exec Ctr 115 N Neil St Suite 213 Champaign IL 61820

ERNST, CHARLES STEPHEN, lawyer; b. Mt. Vernon, N.Y., May 20, 1951; s. Charles and Dora (Dran) E.; m. Barbara Jean Crompton, Jan. 10, 1981; 1 child, Jessica Lynn. BA, U. Md., 1973; JD, Georgetown U., 1976. Bar: Del. 1976, U.S. Dist. Ct. Del. 1977. Assoc. Prickett, Ward, Burt & Sanders, Wilmington, Del., 1976-78; atty. Crum & Forster Corp., Morristown, N.J., 1979, asst. v.p., atty., 1979-82; v.p., atty. Crum & Forster Corp., Morristown, 1982—. Advisor Explorers, Wilmington, Del., 1978-79; mem. Rep. County Com., Hanover Twp., N.J., 1985-86. Mem. ABA (staff mem. The Tax Lawyer jour. 1974-75, sr. editor 1975-76), Del. Bar Assn., Assn. Corp. Counsel N.J., Phi Beta Kappa, Phi Kappa Phi, Phi Alpha Theta. Republican. Avocations: tennis, stamp collecting, golf, gardening, reading. General corporate, Real property, Computer. Office: Crum & Forster Corp 305 Madison Ave Morristown NJ 07960

ERRECART, JOYCE HIER, lawyer; b. Vergennes, Vt., July 1, 1950; d. Lloyd Maurice and Lillian Adela (Jay) Hier; m. Michael Terry Errecart, Mar. 30, 1971; children: Michael Jay, Jacqueline Marie. BA, Wellesley Coll., 1972; JD, Am. U., 1976; LLM in Taxation, Georgetown U., 1981. Bar: Md. 1976, U.S. Tax Ct. 1977, Vt. 1984, U.S. Dist. Ct. Vt. 1984. Law clk. to spl. trial judge U.S. Tax Ct., Washington, 1975-76; trial atty. dist. counsel IRS, Washington, 1976-83; assoc. Dinse, Erdmann & Clapp, Burlington, Vt., 1983-86; sole practice Burlington, 1986—; bd. dirs. Shelburne (Vt.) Newsletter, Inc. Bd. dirs. Vt. YWCA, 1986—; bd. trustees United Meth. Ch., Shelburne, Vt., 1987—; assoc. bd. dirs. Med. Ctr. Hosp. of Vt., Burlington, 1986—; mem. UVM Vt. Council, 1984—. Mem. ABA (tax sect.), Vt. Bar Assn. (tax sect.), Lake Champlain Region C. of C. Republican. Club: Wellesley (Vt.) (v.p. 1986—). Lodge: Zonta. Avocation: quilting. Corporate taxation, Personal income taxation, Estate taxation. Home: Fletcher Ln Shelburne VT 05482 Office: 444 S Union St Burlington VT 05401

ERSCHEN, GAIL LEE, lawyer; b. Kempton, Ill., July 12, 1944; s. Edmund N. and Bessie E. (Williams) E.; m. Pamela K. Farthing, Aug. 20, 1966; children: Jennifer, Paul. BS in Edn., Western Ill. U., 1966; JD, Loyola U., Chgo., 1969. Bar: Ill. 1969, U.S. Dist. Ct. (no. dist.) Ill. 1969. Assoc. Tyler, Peskind & Solomon, Aurora, Ill., 1969-76; sole practice, Aurora, 1976—. Bd. dirs. United Way of Aurora, exec. com., 1985—; chmn. bd. Family Support Ctr., Aurora, 1982-84; sch. bd. mem. Dist. 129 of West Aurora, 1985—. Mem. Ill. Bar Assn. (mem. assembly 1978-84), Kane County Bar Assn. (pres. 1979-80), Ill. Trial Lawyers Assn., Assn. Trial Lawyers Am., Comml. Law League. Methodist. Consumer commercial, Personal injury, General practice. Office: 8 E Galena Blvd Aurora IL 60506

ERTMAN, WILLIS MARION, lawyer; b. Boston, Aug. 27, 1927; s. Clarence S. and Thalia (Marion) E.; m. Carol J. Gardner, July 6, 1957; children—Deborah, Douglas, Elisabeth, Jeffrey. B.S. in Elec. Engring., Tufts U., 1951; LL.B., Harvard U., 1956. Bar: Mass. 1956, U.S. Dist. Ct. Mass. 1958, U.S. Patent Office 1957, U.S. Ct. Cust. and Pat. Appeals 1967, U.S. Ct. Appeals (Fed. cir.) 1982. Assoc., Fish & Richardson, Boston, 1956-70, ptnr., 1970—. Mem. mcpl. bds. Hingham (Mass.) Capital Outlay Com., 1960-70; mem. Hingham Planning Bd., 1966-71, Hingham Charter Commn., 1972-73, Hingham Sch. Com., 1974-83, Hingham Mcpl. Light Bd., 1984—. Served with USAAF, 1945-48. Mem. ABA, Mass. Bar Assn., Boston Patent Law Assn. (pres. 1976-77), Am. Patent Law Assn., IEEE. Club: Hingham Yacht. Patent.

ERVIN, HOWARD GUY, III, lawyer; b. Newark, Ohio, Oct. 18, 1947; s. Howard Guy Jr. and Janet H. Ervin; m. Elizabeth Harper, June 20, 1981; 1 child, Howard Guy IV. Student, Wabash Coll., 1965-67; BA, Harvard U., 1969; JD, U. Chgo., 1972. Bar: Calif. 1973, U.S. Dist. Ct. (no. dist.) Calif. 1973. Law clk. to presiding justice Calif. Supreme Ct., San Francisco, 1972-73; assoc. Cooley, Godward, Castro, Huddleson & Tatum, San Francisco, 1973-79, ptnr., 1979—. Contbg. editor U. Chgo. Law Rev., 1971-72. Mem. ABA, Calif. Bar Assn., San Francisco Bar Assn., Order of Coif. Clubs: Bohemian, Commonwealth (San Francisco). Contracts commercial, General corporate, General practice. Office: Cooley Godward Castro et al 1 Maritime Plaza San Francisco CA 94111

ERVIN, ROBERT MARVIN, lawyer; b. near Ocala, Fla., Jan. 19, 1917; s. Richard William and Carrie (Phillips) E.; m. Frances Anne Cushing, Dec. 25, 1941; children: Anne Cushing (Mrs. Henry Lamar Rowe), Robert Marvin. B.S. in Bus. Adminstrn, U. Fla., 1941, LL.B., 1947. Bar: Fla. 1947. Practice in Tallahassee, 1947—; partner firm Ervin, Varn, Jacobs, Odom & Kitchen (and predecessor firms), 1947—; U.S. referee in bankruptcy No. Dist. Fla., part time 1952-72. Mem. Fla. Constn. Revision Commn., 1966-68; Trustee U. Fla. Law Center Assn.; mem. bd. visitors Fla. State U. Coll. Law. Served with USMCR, 1941-45, PTO; col. Res.ret. Recipient Distinguished Service award for legal edn. John B. Stetson U., 1966; Distinguished Service award Armed Forces League, 1966. Fellow Fla. Bar Found., Am. Bar Found. (sec. 1987—), Nat. Coll. Criminal Def. Lawyers, Am. Coll. Trial Lawyers; mem. Fla. Bar (pres. 1965-66, Disting. Service award 1966), Am. Bar Retirement Assn. (pres. 1980-82), ABA (ho. of dels., bd. govs., chmn. sect. criminal justice 1975-76, mem. resource devel. council, audit com., vice-chmn. sr. lawyers div., chmn. spl. com. on fiscal policy 1984-85), Am. Coll. Trial Lawyers (regent 1983-84), Am. Law Inst., Am. Judicare Soc., Nat. Conf. Referees in Bankruptcy (pres. 1963-64), Res. Officers Assn., Marine Corps Res. Officers Assn., Fla. Blue Key, Phi Alpha Delta, Alpha Kappa Psi. Democrat. Baptist. Club: Elk. Federal civil litigation, State civil litigation, General practice. Home: 530 North Ride Tallahassee FL 32303 Office: Ervin Varn Jacobs Odom & Kitchen 305 S Gadsden St PO Box 1170 Tallahassee FL 32302

ERVIN, SAMUEL JAMES, III, federal judge; b. Morganton, N.C., Mar. 2, 1926; s. Sam E. B.S., Davidson Coll., 1948; LL.B., Harvard U., 1951. Bar: N.C. Pvt. practice law Morganton, 1952-57; mem. firm Patton, Ervin & Starnes and predecessors, Morganton, 1957-67; judge Superior Ct. 25th Jud. Dist. N.C., 1967-80; U.S. Ct. Appeals (4th cir.), Morganton, N.C., 1980—; solicitor Burke County (N.C.) criminal Ct., 1954-56. Pres. Davidson Coll. Nat. Alumni Assn., 1973-74; trustee Davidson Coll., 1982-86. Named Young Man of Yr. Morganton Jaycees, 1954. Mem. Borke County C. of C. (pres. 1962). Office: US Court Appeals PO Drawer 2146 Morganton NC 28655 *

ERVIN, SUSAN CHADWICK, lawyer; b. Aberdeen, Md., May 16, 1951; s. A.R. and Ellyn (Wiegert) E. BA, Mt. Holyoke Coll., 1973; JD, Rutgers U., 1976. Bar: N.Y. 1977, D.C. 1985. Assoc. Kronish, Lieb, Shainswit, Weiner & Hellman, N.Y.C., 1976-78, Kramer, Levin, Nessen, Kamin & Frankel, N.Y.C., 1978-83; asst. gen. counsel Commodity Futures Trading Commn., Washington, 1983-86, assoc. dir. div. of trading and markets, 1986—. Mem. ABA. Office: Commodity Futures Trading Commn 2033 K St NW Washington DC 20581

ERWIN, RICHARD C., federal judge; b. McDowell County, N.C., Aug. 23, 1923; s. John Adam and Flora (Cannon) E.; m. Demerice Whitley, Aug. 25, 1946; children—Richard Cannon, Jr., Aurelia Whitley. B.A., Johnson C. Smith U., 1947; LL.B., Howard U., 1951; LL.D., Pfeiffer Coll., 1980, Johnson C. Smith U., 1981. Bar: N.C., U.S. Supreme Ct. Practice law Winston-Salem, N.C., 1951-77; judge N.C. Ct. Appeals, 1978, U.S. Dist. Ct. Middle Dist., N.C., 1980—; rep. N.C. Gen. Assembly, chmn. hwy. safety com. Trustee Forsyth County Legal Aid Soc., Amos Cottage, Inc.; chmn. bd. trustees Bennett Coll.; bd. dirs. N.C. 4-H Devel. Fund, Inc.; bd. visitors Div. Sch., Duke U.; trustee Children's Home, Winston-Salem; mem. steering com. Winston-Salem Found.; bd. dirs. United Fund; bd. dirs., pres. Citizens Coalition Forsyth County and Anderson High Sch., PTA.; mem. N.C. Bd. Edn., 1971-77, N.C. State Library Bd. Trustees, 1968-69; mem., chmn. personnel com. Winston-Salem/Forsyth County Sch. Bd.; chmn. bd. trustees St. Paul United Methodist Ch. Mem. N.C. Bar Assn. (v.p. 1983-84), N.C. Assn. Black Lawyers, Forsyth County Bar Assn. (pres.), N.C. State Bar. Jurisprudence. Office: U S Dist Court PO Box 89 Greensboro NC 27402

ERWIN, SUE CARLANNE, lawyer; b. Rock Hill, S.C., Oct. 30, 1950; d. Arthur McMurray and Wilma (Maddox) E. BA, Queens Coll., 1972; JD, U. S.C., 1979. Bar: S.C. 1979, U.S. Dist. Ct. S.C. 1980, U.S. Ct. Appeals (4th cir.) 1982. Law clk. to presiding judge U.S. Dist. Ct. S.C., Columbia, 1979-81; assoc. Sinkler & Boyd, P.A. (and predecessor firm Boyd, Knowlton, Tate & Finlay, P.A.), Columbia, 1981—. White House intern, Washington, 1972; mem. exec. com. Columbia Action Council, 1984—; active Jr. League of Columbia. Mem. ABA, S.C. Bar Assn., Richland County Bar Assn., Columbia Young Lawyers (pres. 1985-86), Def. Trial Lawyers. Republican. Presbyterian. Labor, Federal civil litigation. Home: 724 Arbutus Rd Columbia SC 29205 Office: Sinkler & Boyd PA 1426 Main St Suite 1200 The Palmetto Ctr Columbia SC 29201

ESAKI, AMY ITSUMI, lawyer; b. Hilo, Hawaii, Apr. 3, 1955; d. James Umetaro and Chiyoko (Mori) Ishii; m. Clement Teruo Esaki, July 21, 1979; children—Ryan Akira, Stephen James Kiyoshi. B.B.A., U. Hawaii, 1977; J.D., U. Oreg., 1980. Bar: Hawaii 1980. Law clk. to county council, Lihue, Hawaii, 1980-81; 3d dep. county atty. County of Kauai, Lihue, 1981-84; pvt. practice law, 1984—. Mem. ABA, Hawaii Bar Assn., Kauai Bar Assn. (sec. 1983-84), Kapaa Businessman Assn., Anahola Japanese Community Assn., Beta Alpha Psi, Beta Gamma Sigma, Phi Kappa Phi, Phi Delta Kappa. Democrat. General practice. Home: 1981 Hulali Loop Kapaa HI 96746 Office: 4561 Mamane St Suite 100 Kapaa HI 96746

ESCARRAZ, ENRIQUE, III, lawyer; b. Evergreen Park, Ill., Aug. 30, 1944; s. Enrique Jr. and Mary Ellen (Bandy) E.; m. Ruth Ann Hess, Aug. 12, 1967; children: Erin Christine, Martina Mary. BA, U. Fla., 1966, JD, 1968. Bar: Fla. 1969, U.S. Dist. Ct. (so. and mid. dists.) Fla. 1969, U.S. Ct. Appeals (5th cir.) 1971, U.S. Ct. Appeals (11th cir.) 1981. VISTA atty. Community Legal Counsel, Chgo., 1968-69; mng. atty. Fla. Rural Legal Services, Ft. Myers, 1969-71; sole practice St. Petersburg, Fla., 1971-82, 1985-87; ptnr. Anderson & Escarraz, St. Petersburg, 1982-85; asst. gen. counsel U. South Fla., 1987—; part-time atty. Pub. Defender's Office Fla. 6th Cir., St. Petersburg, 1973-74; local counsel Lawyers Com. for Civil Rights Under Law, Washington, 1982. Coordinator James B. Sanderlin for Judge, Pinellas County, Fla., 1972-76; mem. ACLU Legal Panel, St. Petersburg, 1972—; cooperating atty. NAACP Legal Def. Edn. Funds, Inc., N.Y.C., 1973—; pres. Creative Care, Inc., Clearwater, Fla., 1974-80; mem. allocations com. United Way, Pinellas County, 1976, 1978-81; pres., treas. Community Youth Services, Inc., St. Petersburg, 1977-82; co-chmn. Blue Ribbon Com. Pinellas County Dem. Exec. Com., 1977-82; mem. Fla. HRS Dist. V Adv. Council, Pinellas County, 1982, St. Petersburg Relations Rev. Bd., 1982—; local counsel Lawyers Com. for Civil Rights Under Law, Washington, 1982—. Mem. ABA, Assn. Trial Lawyers Am., Acad. Fla. Trial Lawyers, Pinellas County Criminal Def. Lawyers (v.p. 1980-81), Pinellas County Trial Lawyers Assn., St. Petersburg Bar Assn. College and university law, Civil rights, State civil litigation. Home: 2320 14th St N Saint Petersburg FL 33704 Office: 4202 E Fowler Ave Adm 254 Tampa FL 33620 Office: PO Box 847 Saint Petersburg FL 33731

ESCHBACH, JESSE ERNEST, judge; b. Warsaw, Ind., Oct. 26, 1920; S. Jesse Ernest and Mary W. (Stout) E.; m. Sara Ann Walker, Mar. 15, 1947; children: Jesse Ernest III, Virginia. BS, Ind. U., 1943, JD with distinction, 1949, LLD (hon.), 1986. Bar: Ind. 1949. Ptnr. Graham, Rasor, Eschbach & Harris, Warsaw, 1949-62; city atty. Warsaw, 1952-53; dep. pros. atty. 54th Jud. Circuit Ct. Ind., 1952-1954; judge U.S. Dist. Ct. Ind., 1962-81; chief judge judge U.S. Dist. Ct. Ind., 1974-81; judge U.S. Ct. Appeals (7th cir.), Chgo., 1981-85, sr. judge, 1985—; Pres. Endicott Church Furniture, Inc., 1960-62; sec., gen. counsel Dalton Foundries, Inc., 1957-62. Editorial staff: Ind. Law Jour, 1947-49. Trustee Ind. U., 1965-70. Served with USNR, 1943-46. Hastings scholar, 1949; Recipient U.S. Law Week award, 1949. Mem. U.S. C. of C. (labor relations com. 1960-62), Warsaw C. of C. (pres. 1955-56), Nat. Assn. Furniture Mfrs. (dir. 1962), Ind. Mfrs. Assn. (dir. 1962), ABA, Ind. Bar Assn. (bd. mgrs. 1953-54, ho. dels. 1950-60), Fed. Bar Assn., Am. Judicature Soc., Order of Coif. Presbyn. Club: Rotarian (pres. Warsaw 1956-57). Home: 11709 N Lake Dr Boynton Beach FL 33436 Office: US Ct Appeals 7th cir 253 US Courthouse 701 Clematis St West Palm Beach FL 33401

ESHELMAN, DAVID RICHARD, lawyer; b. West Reading, Pa., Aug. 12, 1949; s. William Richard and Mary Prudence (Mackie) E.; m. Elizabeth Josephine Hayes, Aug. 24, 1974; children: Sarah Elizabeth, Suzanne Chandler. BA, Dickinson Coll., 1971, JD, 1974. Bar: Pa. 1974, U.S Dist. Ct. (ea. dist.) Pa. 1975, U.S. Dist. Ct. (cen. dist.) Pa. 1980, U.S. Ct. Appeals (3d cir.) 1980, U.S. Supreme Ct. 1980, U.S Tax Ct. 1981. Asst. pub. defender Berks County, Reading, Pa., 1975-78; assoc. Stevens & Lee, Reading, 1975-79, ptnr., 1980-83; sole practice Reading, 1983—. Mem. Mohnton Reps., Pa., 1980-84, Berks County Reps., Reading, 1980-84, exec. com., 1980-81; pres. Berks County Prison Soc., Inc., Reading, 1984—. YMCA Leaders fellow, 1977. Mem. ABA, Pa. Bar Assn., Pa. Trial Lawyers Assn., Nat. Assn. Criminal Def. Lawyers, Assn. Trial Lawyers Am., Berks County Bar Assn. (chmn. criminal law com. 1979, 82, 84). Methodist. Criminal, Family and matrimonial, State civil litigation. Office: 424 Walnut St Reading PA 19601

ESKIN, BARRY SANFORD, court investigator; b. Pitts., Mar. 6, 1943; s. Saul and Dorothy (Zaron) E.; m. M. Joyce Rosalind, Sept. 12, 1965; 1 child, David. AA, Los Angeles City Coll., 1963; BA, Calif. State U., Los Angeles, 1965; JD, Citrus Belt Law Sch., 1976. Bar: Calif. 1976. Social service worker San Bernardino (Calif.) Dept. Pub. Social Services, 1965-77; assoc. Law Office of Lawrence Novack, San Bernardino, 1978; ct. investigator San Bernardino Superior Ct., 1978, supervising investigator, 1978—; pro bono atty. Mex. Am. Commn., 1977-78. Mem. Am. Red Cross Service Ctr. Advising. Bd., San Bernardino, 1980-82; bd. dirs. Golden Valley Civ. Assn., San Bernardino, 1978-81, Congregation Emanuel, San Bernardino, 1984—. Mem. ABA, Calif. Assn. of Superior Ct. Investigators (pres. 1980-81, treas. 1984-85, bd. dirs.), Alpha Phi Omega. Democrat. Jewish. Avocations: reading, photography, baseball. Probate, Conservatorships, guardianships. Office: Conservatorship Ct Investigator 351 N Arrowhead Ave Room 200 San Bernardino CA 92415-0240

ESKIN, JEFFREY LAURENCE, lawyer; b. N.Y.C., May 10, 1952; s. Jordan Harlan Eskin and Charlette (Davies) Krane; m. Darla Lynn Gugel, Aug. 5, 1977; children: Jennifer, Jonathan, Emily. BA, Yale U., 1974; JD, Emory U., 1978. Bar: Nev. 1978, U.S. Dist. Ct. Nev. 1979, U.S. Ct. Appeals (9th cir.) 1980, U.S. Supreme Ct. 1982. Assoc. Vargas, Bartlett & Dixon, Las Vegas, Nev., 1978-79; dep. atty. gen. State of Nev., Las Vegas, 1979-81; sole practice Las Vegas, 1981—; spl. prosecutor State of Nev., Las Vegas, 1982-84. Mem. Employee Mgmt. Relations Bd., Las Vegas, 1983—, chmn., 1986-87; moderator Youth Forum; active VISTA 1974-75. Mem. ABA, Clark County Bar Assn., Assn. Trial Lawyers Am., Nev. Trial Lawyers Assn., Yale U. Alumni Assn. (assembly 1980-83). Democrat. Jewish. Home: 3110 Carnelian Ct Las Vegas NV 89121 Office: 101 Convention Ctr Dr Suite 1202 Las Vegas NV 89109

ESPINOSA, JOSE A., JR., lawyer; b. San Luis, Oriente, Cuba, Aug. 21, 1952; s. Jose A. Sr. and Besaida C. (Gonzales) E. BA, Northeastern U., Boston, 1975; JD, Boston Coll., 1978. Bar: Mass., U.S. Dist. Ct. Mass., U.S. Ct. Appeals (1st cir.). Staff atty. Roxbury (Mass.) Pub. Defenders, 1978-82; assoc. Law Offices of Richard Shalhoub, Boston, 1982-84; sr. ptnr. Espinosa and Assoc., Boston, 1984—. Bd. dirs. Jamaica Plain APac, Mass., 1978-79, Alianza Hispana, Roxbury, 1978-80. Mem. Mass. Bar Assn., Boston Bar Assn., Nat. Trial Lawyers Assn. Democrat. Roman Catholic. General practice, Criminal, Personal injury. Office: Espinosa and Assocs 15 Court Sq Boston MA 02108

ESPOSITO, JOHN VINCENT, lawyer; b. Logan, W.Va., Dec. 25, 1946; s. Vito T. and Mary Frances (Lamp) E. B.A. magna cum laude, W.Va. U., 1968, J.D., 1971. Bar: W.Va. 1971, S.C. 1980, U.S. dist. ct. (no. and so. dists.) W.Va., S.C. Legis. aide to Congressman Ken Hechler, 4th Dist. W.Va., 1971; counsel to Hans McCourt, Pres. W.Va. State Senate, 1972; instr. So. W.Va. Community Coll., 1972-74; sr. ptnr. Esposito & Esposito, Logan, W.Va. and Hilton Head Island, S.C., 1972—; arbitrator United Mine Workers Am.-Coal Operators Assn.; spl. judge Cir. Ct. Logan County (W.Va.); commr. in chancery Cir. Ct. Logan County; judge Mcpl. Ct. City of Chapmanville (W.Va.); spl. pros. atty., W. Va. Author: An Evil Heart Indeed, 1986. Founder Citizens Environ. Quality, 1983. Served to 2d lt. U.S. Army. U. Calif. Hastings Coll. Law Coll. Advocacy scholar. Mem. ABA, Assn. Trial Lawyers Am., Am. Judicature Soc., W.Va. State Bar, S.C. Bar, Internat. Platform Assn. Co-author: Laws for Young Mountaineers, 1973-74. Federal civil litigation, State civil litigation, Criminal. Office: One Saint Augustine PO Box 5705 Hilton Head Island SC 29938 also: 401 Stratton ST PO Box 1680 Logan WV 25601

ESPOSITO, ROBERT S., lawyer; b. Phila., Dec. 18, 1952; s. James J. and Emma M. (Jacobs) E.; m. Elaine P. Spada, June 1, 1974; children—Robert P., Laura E., David A. B.B.A., Temple U., 1974, J.D., 1977. Bar: Pa. 1977, U.S. Dist. Ct. (ea. dist.) Pa. 1977, U.S. Ct. Appeals (3d cir.) 1982, U.S. Tax Ct. 1982. Mem. McGill & McGreal, Phila., 1977-85; sole practice, Phila., 1979—; lectr. Temple U., 1979. Mem. Pa. 176th Legis. Adv. Com., 1979. Mem. ABA, Pa. Bar Assn., Phila. Bar Assn., Phi Alpha Delta, Beta Gamma Sigma. Republican. Roman Catholic. Real property, Probate, General practice. Office: 301 Noble Plaza Jenkintown PA 19046

ESSER, CARL ERIC, lawyer; b. Montclair, N.J., Feb. 12, 1942; s. Josef and Elly (Graber) E.; m. Barbara A. B. Stelzer, Oct. 12, 1968; children: Jennifer, Eric, Brian. A.B., Princeton U., 1964; J.D., U. Mich., 1967. Bar: Pa. 1967. Assoc. firm Reed Smith Shaw & McClay, Phila, 1967-72, ptnr., 1973—. Served with USMCR, 1965. Mem. ABA, Pa. Bar Assn., Phila. Bar Assn. Republican. Clubs: Racquet (Phila.); Penllyn (Pa.). General corporate, Health. Home: 10 Haddon Pl Fort Washington PA 19034 Office: 1600 Ave of the Arts Bldg Philadelphia PA 19107 Other Address: Film World Knight Publishing Co 8060 Melrose Ave Los Angeles CA 90046

ESSIG, WILLIAM JOHN, lawyer; b. South Bend, Ind., July 13, 1938; s. William Frederick and Grace Dorothea (Adelheit) (Hennig) E.; m. Agnes Constance Yodelis, July 13, 1968; children—William Victor, Peter Frederick. B.A., Yale U., 1959; J.D., U. Chgo., 1965. Bar: Ill. 1966, U.S. Dist. Ct. (so. dist.) Ill. 1966, U.S. Dist. Ct. (no dist.) Ill. 1981. CLU, chartered fin. cons. Atty., Lawyers Title Ins. Corp., 1965-67; title officer Pioneer Nat. Title Ins. Corp., Chgo., 1967-69; assoc. Ralph E. Brown, Chgo., 1969-71; asst. gen. counsel Benefit Trust Life Ins. Co., Chgo., 1971-85; sole practice, 1985-86; mem. Ill. State Scholarship Commn., 1986—. Served with USAR, 1961-62. Fellow Life Mgmt. Inst.; mem. ABA, Ill. State Bar Assn., Chgo. Bar Assn. Republican. Lutheran. Insurance. Home: 1601 10th St Wilmette IL 60091

ESSMYER, MICHAEL MARTIN, lawyer; b. Abilene, Tex., Dec. 6, 1949; s. Lytle Martin Essmyer and Roberta N. Essmyer Nicholson; m. Cynthia Rose Piccolo, Dec. 27, 1970; children: Deanna, Mike, Brent Austin. BS in Geology, Tex. A&M U., 1972; student Tex. Christian U., 1976; JD cum laude, South Tex. Coll. Law, 1980. Bar Tex. 1980, U.S. Ct. appeals (5th cir.) 1981, U.S. Dist. Ct. (no., so., ea. dists.) Tex. 1982. Briefing atty. Supreme Ct. Tex., Austin, 1980-81; ptnr. Haynes & Fullenweider, Houston, 1981—. Lead article editor south Tex. Law Jour., 1979. Democratic candidate for state rep., Bryan, Tex., 1972; del. Dem. Party, Houston, 1982, 84; precinct chmn. Harris County Democratic Exec. Com., Houston, 1983-86. Served to capt. USAF, 1972-78. Nat. Merit Scholar, 1968-72. Mem. ABA, Houston Bar Assn., Houston Young Lawyers Assn., Assn. Trial Lawyers Am., Tex. Criminal Def. Lawyers Assn., Harris County Criminal Lawyers Assn. (dir. 1986—). Roman Catholic. Club: Metropolitan Racquet (Houston). Criminal, Personal injury, Federal civil litigation. Home: 1122 Glourie Houston TX 77055 Office: Haynes & Fullenweider PLC 4300 Scotland Houston TX 77007-7328

ESTEP, SAMUEL D., lawyer, educator; b. Kans., Mar. 13, 1919; s. Alvernon D. and Mary E. (Paul) E.; A.B., Kans. State Tchrs. Coll., Emporia, 1940; J.D., U. Mich., 1946; m. Doris V.; children: Michael D., Julia L., David F. Admitted to Mich. bar, 1946; asso. firm Cook, Smith, Jacobs & Beake, Detroit, 1946-48; mem. faculty U. Mich. Law Sch., 1948—, prof. law, 1954—; cons. to govt., 1956—. Vice pres. Ann Arbor United Fund, 1957-58. Served with USNR, 1942-45. Mem. Am., Mich. bar assns., Order of Coif. Prin. author: Atoms and the Law, 1959; co-author: Atomic Energy Technology for Lawyers, 1956; State Regulation of Atomic Energy, 1956; also articles. Legal education. Office: U Mich Law Sch Ann Arbor MI 48109 *

ESTES, CARL L., II, lawyer; b. Fort Worth, Tex., Feb. 9, 1936; s. Joe E. and Carroll E.; m. Gay Gooch, Aug. 29, 1959; children: Adrienne Virginia, Margaret Ellen. B.S., U. Tex., 1957, LL.B., 1960. Bar: Tex. 1960. Law clk. U.S. Supreme Ct., 1960-61; assoc. firm Vinson & Elkins, Houston, 1961-69; ptnr. Vinson & Elkins, 1970—. Bd. dirs. Houston Grand Opera Assn. Fellow Am Bar Found., Tex. Bar Found.; mem. Am. Law Inst., Am. Coll. Probate Counsel, ABA, Internat. Bar Assn., Tex. Bar Assn., Internat. Fiscal Assn. (v.p.), Internat. Acad. Estate and Trust Law. Clubs: Houston, Ramada, Houston Country, Allegro; Marks (London). Corporate taxation, Personal income taxation, Private international. Home: 101 Broad Oaks Circle Houston TX 77056 Office: 3400 First City Tower Houston TX 77002

ESTES, HARPER, lawyer; b. Pecos, Tex., Dec. 16, 1956; s. Bobby Frank and Gayle (Harper) E.; m. Deidre Dement, Mar 19, 1976; 1 child, Andrew Kimble. BA, Tex. Tech U., 1977; JD, Baylor Sch. Law, 1979. Bar: Tex. 1980, U.S. Dist. Ct. (no. dist.) Tex. 1980, U.S. Dist. Ct. (we. dist.) Tex. 1981, U.S. Ct. Appeals (5th cir.) 1982, U.S. Supreme Ct. 1983. Ptnr. Lynch, Chappell, Allday & Alsup, Midland, Tex., 1980—; mem. admissions com. Dist. 16 State Bar Tex., 1982—. Mem. Tex. Tech U. Coll. Edn. Devel. Council, Lubbock, 1986—; vol. Big Bros., Midland, 1983—, bd. dirs. 1985—. Named Big Brother of Yr., Big Bros./Big Sisters of Midland, 1985; recipient Trimble Vol. Service award, Leadership Midland Alumni, 1986. Mem. ABA, Midland County Young Lawyers Assn. (sec., treas. 1986—), Midland County Bar Assn., Tex. Young Lawyers Assn., Phi Delta Phi. Presbyterian. Federal civil litigation, State civil litigation. Home: 3518 Humble Midland TX 79705 Office: Lynch Chappell Allday & Alsup The Summitt Bldg 300 N Marienfeld 7th Fl Midland TX 79701

ESTES, JERRY NELSON, lawyer; b. Sweetwater, Tenn., Sept. 19, 1951; s. William Edgar Jr. and Mary Helen (Wrinn) E.; m. Patricia Torbett, Mar. 16, 1974 (div. June 1976); m. Robin Ann Hall, May 2, 1981; 1 child, William Hall. BS, U. Tenn., 1973, JD, 1976. Bar: Tenn. 1976, U.S. Dist. Ct. (ea. dist.) Tenn. 1977. Sole practice Athens, Tenn., 1976-82; atty. gen. 10th jud. dist. State of Tenn., Athens, 1982—; atty. McMinn County Bd. Edn., Athens, 1978-82; mem. exec. com. Tenn. Dist. Attys. Gen. Conf., Nashville, 1983-84; co-chmn. com. Tenn. Child Sexual Abuse Task Force, Nashville, 1985—. Treas. McMinn County Reps., Athens, 1979-82, pres., 1977-78; mem. com. McMinn County Correctional Facility, 1985, advisory com. Victims-Assistance Program, Tenn., 1986, advisory bd. Bauchman Home, Cleve., Tenn., 1984—. Mem. ABA, Tenn. Bar Assn. (task force on alcohol and drug abuse), McMinn County Bar Assn. (pres. 1979-80). Methodist. Lodges: Rotary (pres. Athens 1981-82), Elks (presiding justice 1980-81). Avocations: hunting, fishing, swimming, reading. Criminal, Judicial administration. Home: 1604 Brentwood Dr Athens TN 37303 Office: Dist Attys Office 114 Washington Ave Athens TN 37303

ESTES, JOE EWING, judge; b. Commerce, Tex., Oct. 24, 1903; s. Joe Guinn and Della Marshall (Loy) E.; m. Carroll Virginia Cox, Dec. 1, 1931; children: Carl Lewis, Carroll. Student, E. Tex. State Tchrs. Coll., 1923-24; LL.B., U. Tex., 1927; LL.D., E. Tex. State U., 1974. Bar: Tex. 1927. Partner Crosby & Estes, Commerce, 1928-30, Phillips, Trammell, Estes, Edwards & Orn, Ft. Worth, 1930-45, Sanford, King, Estes & Cantwell, Dallas, 1946-52, Estes & Cantwell, 1952-55; U.S. dist. judge Dallas, 1955-60; chief judge U.S. Dist. Ct. No. Dist. Tex., Dallas, 1959-72; sr. judge U.S. Dist. Ct. No. Dist. Tex., 1972—; also judge Temp. Emergency Ct. Appeals U.S., 1972—; mem. adv. com. on rules evidence U.S. Supreme Ct. Contbr. articles to profl. jours.; also to: Handbook of Recommended Procedures for the Trial of Protracted Cases; co-author: Handbook for Newly Appointed U.S. District Judges; editorial bd.: Manual for Complex Litigation. Trustee, mem. exec. com. S.W. Legal Found.; Research fellow, mem. med.-legal com., chmn. Oil and Gas Inst. of S.W. Legal Found.; chmn. exec. com. bd. trustees St. Mark's Sch. of Tex., Dallas, 1951-55. Served as lt. comdr. USNR, 1942-45; mem. Res. Recipient Hatton W. Sumners award S.W. Legal Found., 1972, Citizen of Yr. award Kiwanis Club of Dallas, 1972. Fellow Am. Bar Found.; mem. Nat. Conf. Commrs. on Uniform State Laws, Am. Law Inst., Inter-Am., Fed., ABA (chmn. sect. jud. administrn. 1961-62, mem. ho. dels.), Dallas Bar Assn. (past v.p.), Fort Worth Bar Assn. (past dir.), State Bar Tex., Am. Judicature Soc., Jud. Conf. U.S. (chmn. com. on trial practice and technique, mem. exec. com. 1969-71, dist. judge rep.), Nat. Lawyers Club, Inst. Jud. Adminstrn., Philos. Soc. Tex., Newcomen Soc., Am. Legion, Chancellors, Phi Delta Phi, Kappa Sigma, Order of Coif. Methodist. Clubs: Masons (33 deg.), Shriners (hon. insp. gen., Jester). Jurisprudence. Home: 5846 Desco Dr Dallas TX 75225

ESTILL, JOHN STAPLES, JR., lawyer; b. Grapevine, Tex., Jan. 29, 1919; s. John Staples and Ada Beauchamp (Chambers) E.; m. Dorothy Finlayson, Nov. 27, 1940; children: John S. III, James C., Sally Finlayson Muhlbach. BS in Commerce, Tex. Christian U., 1940; JD, So. Meth. U., 1948. Bar: Tex. 1948, U.S. Dist. Ct. (no. dist.) Tex. 1950, Okla. 1966, D.C. 1975, U.S. Ct. Appeals (5th cir.) 1972. Sole practice Ft. Worth, 1948-53; counsel Sinclair Oil and Gas Co., Sinclair Pipe Line Co., Ft. Worth, Independence, Kans., and Tulsa, 1953-67; pres. Hall, Estill, Hardwick, Gable, Golden & Nelson, Tulsa, 1967—; sec. Williams Pipe Line Co., Tulsa, 1969—. Served to lt. USNR, 1942-46. Mem. ABA, Okla. Bar Found. (trustee 1984—), D.C. Bar Assn., Kans. Bar Assn., Tex. Bar Assn., Tulsa County Bar Assn., Tulsa Execs. Assn., Tulsa C. of C. Democrat. Methodist. Clubs: So. Hills Country (Tulsa), The Tulsa. Avocation: golf. General corporate, Oil and gas leasing, Public utilities. Home: 7221 S Atlanta Tulsa OK 74136 Office: Hall Estill et al 4100 Bank of Okla Tower One Williams Ctr Tulsa OK 74172

ESTIS, DENNIS ARNOLD, lawyer; b. Newark, May 4, 1947; s. Harold and Anne (Rosensweig) E.; m. Rebecca D. Perkins, May 30, 1982; 1 child, Sara Rebbeca. BA in Polit. Sci., Johns Hopkins U., 1969; JD, NYU, 1972. Bar: N.J. 1972, U.S. Dist. Ct. N.J. 1972, U.S. Ct. Appeals (3d cir.) 1982, N.Y. 1983, U.S. Supreme Ct. 1984. Law sec. appellate div. N.J. Judiciary, Newark, 1972-73; assoc. Greenbaum, Greenbaum, Rowe & Smith, Newark, 1973-79; ptnr. Greenbaum, Rowe, Smith, Ravin, Davis & Bergstein, Newark, 1979—; atty. Borough of Keansburg, N.J., 1983-84, Borough of Roselle Park, N.J., 1984-86. Councilman Roselle Park, 1976-81; chmn. Union County Dem. Com., N.J., 1980-81, Fanwood Dem. Com., N.J., 1986—. Mem. ABA, N.J. Bar Assn. (chmn. equity com. 1985-86), NYU Alumni Assn. (bd. dirs. 1984—, pres. N.J. chpt. 1983-85). Jewish. Avocation: sports. Construction, Local government, State civil litigation. Office: Greenbaum Rowe Smith Ravin et al Box 5600 Woodbridge NJ 07095

ESTLE, MARK DAVID, lawyer; b. Urbana, Ill., Nov. 20, 1955; s. Thomas Leo and Arlene Ruth (Poggermiller) E. BA, Tex. A&M U., 1978; JD, Baylor U., 1981. Bar: Tex. 1981, U.S. Dist. Ct. (so. and ea. dists.) Tex. 1983, U.S. Ct. Appeals (5th cir.) 1983. Assoc. Rowland & Keim, Houston, 1981-82, Mills, Shirley, McMiken & Eckel, Galveston, Tex., 1983—. Mem. ABA, Tex. Bar Assn., Galveston Bar Assn., Galveston Young Lawyers Club, Phi Alpha Delta. Avocations: tennis, raquetball. Banking, Contracts commercial, Real property. Home: 7019 Lasker #1321 Galveston TX 77551 Office: Mills Shirley McMiken & Eckel 700 Interfirst Bank Bldg Galveston TX 77550

ESTREICHER, SAMUEL, lawyer, educator; b. Bergen, Democratic Republic Germany, Sept. 29, 1948; came to U.S., 1951; s. David and Rose (Abramowicz) E.; m. Aleta Glaseroff, Aug. 10, 1969; 1 child, Michael. BA, Columbia U., 1970, JD, 1975; MS, Cornell U., 1974. Bar: N.Y. 1976, D.C. 1978, U.S. Dist. Ct. (so. and ea. dists.) N.Y., U.S. Ct. Appeals (2d cir.), U.S. Supreme Ct. Law clk. to presiding justice U.S. Ct. Appeals (D.C. cir.), 1975-76; assoc. Cohn, Glickstein, Lurie, Ostrin & Lubell, N.Y.C., 1976-77; law clk. to assoc. justice Lewis F. Powell Jr. U.S. Supreme Ct., Washington, 1977-78; prof. law NYU, 1978—; of counsel Cahill, Gordon & Reindel, N.Y.C., 1984—. Author: Redefining the Supreme Court, 1986; contbr. articles to profl. jours.; editor in chief Columbia U. Law Rev., 1974-75. Pulitzer Fund scholar, 1966-70; Herbert H. Lehman fellow, 1970-72. Mem. ABA (labor and employment law sect. 1978—), N.Y. State Bar Assn. (labor and employment law sect. 1980—), Assn. of Bar of City of N.Y. (chmn. lawbor and employment law com. 1984—). Labor, Administrative and regulatory, Federal civil litigation. Office: Cahill Gordon & Reindel 80 Pine St New York NY 10005

ESTRINE, ANDREW BRADLEY, lawyer; b. Washington, Feb. 10, 1953; s. Lewis and Dolores (Roskin) E.; m. Jan M. Markowitz. BA, U. Mich., 1975; JD, Syracuse U., 1979. Bar: Mass. 1979, U.S. Dist. Ct. Mass. 1979, U.S. Ct. Appeals (1st cir.) 1979. Assoc. Rich, May, Bilodeau & Flaherty, Boston, 1979-82; atty. New Eng. Electric System, Westborough, Mass., 1982-87, Rubin, Hay & Gould, Framingham, Mass., 1987—. Federal civil litigation, State civil litigation, General corporate. Office: Rubin Hay & Gould 205 Newbury St Framingham MA 01701

ETHERIDGE, DONALD MCGEE, JR., lawyer, educator; b. Raleigh, N.C., Mar. 5, 1952; s. Donald McGee Sr. and Betty Anne (Sawyer) E.; m. Dalby Chandler, Aug. 5, 1978; 1 child, Ashton Chandler. AB magna cum laude, Duke U., 1974, JD, 1977; LLM, Georgetown U., 1980; postdoctoral, U. N.C., 1986—. Bar: N.C. 1977, U.S. Dist. Ct. (we. dist.) N.C. 1980; CPA, N.C. Assoc. Akins, Harrel, Mann & Pike, Raleigh, 1977-78; atty. chief counsel IRS, Washington, 1978-80; assoc. Caudle, Underwood & Kinsey, Charlotte, N.C., 1980-84; assoc. univ. counsel, adj. law faculty Duke U., Durham, N.C., 1984—; adj. faculty mem. U. N.C. Sch. Law, Chapel Hill, 1986, Duke U., Durham, 1984—. Contbr. articles to profl. jours. Mem. ABA (vice chmn. subcom. on income taxation of trusts and estates probate and trust sect., tax sect.), N.C. Bar Assn. (vice chmn. tax sect. 1985—, lectr.), Am. Inst. CPA's, N.C. Assn. CPA's, Phi Kappa Psi. Democrat. Methodist. Lodge: Order of DeMolay (master councilor N.C. 1971-72), Masons (master), Shriners. Personal income taxation, Estate taxation, Corporate taxation. Home: 1724 Tisdale Durham NC 27707 Office: Duke U Durham NC 27706

ETHERINGTON, WILLIAM FISHER, lawyer; b. Hartford, Conn., Aug. 15, 1946; s. Sandford G. Jr. and Rhea (Robotham) E.; m. Martha Moon Beck, Aug. 28, 1971; children: Sandford G. III, Emily Hall McCue. AB, Princeton U., 1968; JD, Washington & Lee U., 1974. Bar: Va. 1974, U.S. Dist. Ct. (ea. dist.) Va. 1975, U.S. Ct. Appeals (4th cir.) 1975, U.S. Dist. Ct. Md. 1976, U.S. Supreme Ct. 1979. Assoc. Christian, Barton, Epps, Brent & Chappell, Richmond, Va., 1975-82, ptnr., 1982—. Sec., bd. dirs. Sr. Ctr. of Richmond, 1986—; bd. dirs. Va. Com. for Guard Res., Richmond, 1986—. Served to 1st lt. U.S. Army, 1968-71, Vietnam. Mem. Order of Coif. Episcopalian. Labor, Family and matrimonial. Home: 1312 Loch Lomond Ln Richmond VA 23220 Office: 1200 Mutual Bldg Richmond VA 23219

ETHRIDGE, LARRY CLAYTON, lawyer; b. Houston, Feb. 27, 1946; s. Robert Pike and Gladys J. (Grant) E.; m. Edith Kirkbride Gilbert, May 21, 1977; children: Elizabeth K., Grant H. BA, Duke U., 1968; JD cum laude, U. Louisville, 1975. Bar: Ky. 1975, D.C. 1977, U.S. Ct. Claims 1978, U.S. Dist. Ct. (we. dist.) Ky. 1981, U.S. Ct. Appeals (6th cir.) 1981. Intern Adv. Commn. on Intergovtl. Relations, Washington, 1975-76; asst. dir. model procurement code project ABA, Washington, 1976-80; assoc. Nold, Miller, Mosley, Clare, Hubbard & Townes, Louisville, 1980-83, ptnr., 1983—; cons. model procurement code project ABA, Washington, 1980-84. Mem. com. Am. Cancer Soc., Louisville, 1985—; elder Highland Presbyn. Ch., Louisville, 1984—; co-chmn. 34th Rep. Legis. Dist., Louisville, 1983-85. Served to lt. USNR, 1969-80, Vietnam. Mem. ABA (chmn. coordinating com. on a model procurement code 1985—), Ky. Bar Assn., Louisville Bar Assn. Republican. Presbyterian. Avocations: gardening, tennis, travel. State civil litigation, Contracts commercial, Construction. Home: 2402 Longest Ave Louisville KY 40204 Office: Nold Miller Mosley Clare Hubbard & Townes 730 W Main St #500 Louisville KY 40204

ETRINGER, WALTER JAMES, JR., lawyer; b. Bklyn., Dec. 23, 1947; s. Walter James Sr. and Alice Elizabeth (Balduf) E.; m. Barbara Joan Erickson, Apr. 5, 1969; children: Beth Lee, James Lee. BA with high honors, N.C. State U., 1972; JD, Wake Forest U., 1976. Bar: N.C. 1976, U.S. Dist. Ct. (mid. dist.) N.C. 1977. Assoc. Gardner, Gardner, Bell & Johnson, Mt. Airy, N.C., 1976-77; ptnr. Gardner, Gardner, Johnson, Etringer & Donnelly, Mt. Airy, 1978-83; gen. counsel No. Hosp. Dist. Surry County, Mt. Airy, 1983-85; sole practice Mt. Airy, 1985—; atty. City of Mt. Airy, 1977-83. Served to capt. U.S. Army, 1968-72, Vietnam. Mem. ABA, N.C. Bar Assn., Surry County Bar Assn., Am. Soc. Hosp. Attys., Phi Alpha Delta. Republican. Lodge: Rotary. State civil litigation, Health, Real property. Office: 134 Moore Ave Mount Airy NC 27030

ETTERS, RONALD MILTON, lawyer, government official; b. San Antonio, Nov. 6, 1948; s. Milton William and Ilse Charlotte (Ostler) E.; m. Anna Colleen Wesson, Feb. 12, 1977; children—William Lawrence, Elizabeth Charlotte, Margaret Lawrence, B.A., Am. U., 1971, J.D., 1975. Bar: Va. 1976, U.S. Ct. Appeals (D.C. cir.) 1977, U.S. Dist. Ct. (ea. dist.) Va. 1978, U.S. Ct. Appeals (4th and 9th cirs.) 1978, U.S. Supreme Ct. 1979, D.C. 1980, U.S. Ct. Appeals (1st and 2d cirs.) 1980, U.S. Ct. Appeals (7th cir.) 1981, U.S. Ct. Appeals (3rd, 11th and Fed. cirs.) 1982. Intern to gen. counsel Adminstrv. Office of U.S. Cts., Washington, 1970-71; fed. mgmt. intern IRS, Washington, 1971-72, labor relations officer, 1972-75; ptnr. Nusbaum & Etters, Burke, Va., 1976-80; hearing officer, chief hearing officer Nat. Mediation Bd., Washington, 1975-80, gen. counsel, 1980—; professorial lectr. Am. U., Washington, 1978-83; adj. prof. law Georgetown U., Washington, 1985—. Contbr. ABA reports. Mem. ABA, Christian Legal Soc. Republican. Methodist. Labor, Federal civil litigation. Home: 5315 Indian Rock Rd Centreville VA 22020 Office: Nat Mediation Bd 1425 K St NW Washington DC 20572

ETTINGER, ALBERT FRANKLIN, lawyer; b. Cin., Feb. 21, 1954; s. Morris Block and Mary Caroline (Eimer) E.; m. Susan Denise Lannin; 1 child, Franklin Karl. B in Gen. Studies, U. Mich., 1975, JD, 1979. Bar: Ill. 1979, U.S. Dist. Ct. (no. dist.) Ill. 1981, U.S. Ct. Appeals (5th cir.) 1981,

U.S. Dist. Ct. (cen. dist.) Ill. 1983, U.S. Ct. Appeals (9th cir.) 1983, U.S. Ct. Appeals (7th cir.) 1985. Assoc. Freeman, Freemen & Salzmen, Chgo., 1979—. Mem. Sierra Club (chmn. conservation Great Lakes chpt. 1983—). Democrat. Avocation: philosophy. Antitrust, Federal civil litigation, Environment. Home: 2724 N Central Park Chicago IL 60647 Office: Freeman Freeman & Salzman 401 N Michigan Ave Chicago IL 60611

ETTINGER, JOSEPH ALAN, lawyer, educator; b. N.Y.C., July 21, 1931; s. Max and Frances E.; B.A., Tulane U., 1954, J.D. with honors, 1956; m. Julie Ann Ettinger; children—Amy Beth, Ellen Jane. Admitted to La. bar, 1956, Ill. bar, 1959; asst. corp. counsel City of Chgo., 1959-62; practiced in Chgo., 1962-73, 76—; sr. partner firm Ettinger & Schoenfield, Chgo., 1980—; asso. prof. law Chgo.-Kent Coll., 1973-76; chmn. Village of Olympia Fields (Ill.) Zoning Bd. Appeals, 1969-76; chmn. panel on corrections Welfare Council Met. Chgo., 1969-76. Served to capt., Judge Adv. Gen. Corps, U.S. Army, 1956-59. Recipient Service award Village of Olympia Fields, 1976. Mem. Chgo. Bar Assn., Assn. Criminal Def. Lawyers (gov. 1970-72). Clubs: Ravisloe Country, Carlton Club, Contbr. articles to profl. publs. Criminal, Personal injury, Federal civil litigation. Office: 180 N La Salle St Chicago IL 60601

EUBANK, CHRISTINA, oil company executive; b. Temple, Tex., Jan. 17, 1944; d. G. R. and Catherine (Andrews) E. B.A., Baylor U., 1966, J.D., 1973. Bar: Tex. 1973. Atty., Champlin Petroleum Co., Ft. Worth, Tex., 1973-76, asst. gen. atty., 1976-78, staff atty., 1978-79, sr. staff atty., 1979-81, gen. atty., 1981-83, sr. gen. atty., 1983-84, asst. gen. counsel, 1984—. Contbg. author, mem. task force Presdl. Commn. War on Waste, 1984; contbr. Baylor Law Rev. Recipient Am. Jurisprudence award, 1973; Presdl. Letter of Commendation, 1982. Disting. Alumnae Hill Coll., 1987. Mem. ABA, Tex. Bar Assn., Am. Corp. Counsel Assn. Greek Orthodox. Clubs: Shady Oaks Country, Woman's, Petroleum. Administrative and regulatory, Labor. Home: 1239 Roaring Springs Rd Fort Worth TX 76114 Office: Champlin Petroleum Co 801 W Cherry St Fort Worth TX 76101

EUBANK, J. THOMAS, lawyer; b. Port Arthur, Tex., Mar. 17, 1930; s. J.T. and Ada (White) E.; m. Nancy Moore, Feb.10, 1956; children: John, Marshall, Stephen, Laura. B.A., Rice U., 1951; J.D., U. Tex., 1954. Bar: Tex. 1954, U.S. Supreme Ct. 1960. Assoc. Baker & Botts, Houston, 1954-66, ptnr., 1966—, sr. ptnr., 1979—. Mem. joint editorial bd. Uniform Probate code, 1972-86. Bd. govs. Rice U., 1985—. Mem. ABA (chmn. sect. real property, probate and trust law 1978-79), Am. Coll. Probate Counsel (pres. 1984-85, pres. Found. 1986—), State Bar Tex. (chmn. sect. real estate, probate and trust law 1972-73), Am. Bar Found., Tex. Bar Found., Houston Philos. Soc., Rice U. Alumni Assn. (pres. 1979-80), Am. Law Inst., Internat. Acad. Estate and Trust Law. Estate taxation, Personal income taxation, Probate. Home: 26 Liberty Bell Circle Houston TX 77024 Office: Baker & Botts One Shell Plaza Houston TX 77002

EUBANK, THOMAS FLEMING, lawyer; b. Riverside, Calif., May 13, 1952; s. Emmett F. and Gladys S. Eubank; m. Debra S. Eubank, Nov. 23, 1974; children: Thomas F. Jr., Nicholas C. BBA, Va. Tech. U., 1974; JD, U. Richmond, 1978. Bar: Va. 1979, U.S. Dist. Ct. 1979. Ptnr. Spinella, Owings & Shaia, Richmond, Va., 1978—; counsel St. Mary's Hosp., Richmond, 1985—. Mem. Va. Bar Assn., Henrico County Bar Assn. (bd. dirs. 1984—), Am. Acad. Hosp. Attys., Am. Soc. Law and Med. Attys., Va. Trial Lawyers Assn. Clubs: Raintree Racket (Richmond), Bull and Bear. Lodge: Lions (pres. Tuckahoe chpt. 1984-85). Avocations: boating, tennis, travel. Home: 1909 Windingridge Way Richmond VA 23233 Office: Spinella Owings & Shaia 8550 Mayland Dr Richmond VA 23229

EUBANKS, GARY FRANKLIN, lawyer; b. Marietta, Ga., Feb. 15, 1945; s. J. Robert and Hazel (Bentley) E.; m. Virginia Jones, July 31, 1971; children—Catherine F., James S. B.S. in Econs., U. Pa., 1967; J.D., U. Ga., 1971. Bar: Ga. 1972, U.S. dist. ct. (no. dist.) Ga. 1972; U.S. Ct. Appeals (11th cir.) 1982, U.S. Supreme Ct. 1982. Mem. law dept. So. Ry. Co., Washington, 1971-73; assoc. Custer, Smith & Eubanks, and predecessors, Marietta, Ga., 1973-74, ptnr., 1974-79; officer Smith, Eubanks & Smith, P.C., Marietta, 1980—. Chmn. long range planning com. First Baptist Ch. Marietta, 1976-78, chmn. bd. deacons, 1979-80, chmn. fin. com., 1982; bd. dirs. Cobb County Youth Mus. Mem. Cobb County Bar Assn., Alpha Kappa Psi. Club: Rotary. Editor in chief: Ga. Jour. Internat. and Comparative Law, 1970-71. Banking, Contracts commercial, General corporate. Home: 544 Bouldercrest Dr Marietta GA 30064 Office: 94 Church St Marietta GA 30060

EUBANKS, GARY LEROY, lawyer; b. North Little Rock, Ark., Nov. 22, 1933; s. Herman and Gertrude (Carmack) E. children—Gary L., Jr., Bobby Ray; m. Beverly Gayle Mauldin, Apr. 21, 1971 (div. 1983); 1 child, Shane Mauldin. J.D., U. Ark., 1960. Bar: Ark. 1970, U.S. Dist. Ct. Ark. 1970, U.S. Supreme Ct. 1970. Ptnr. Bailey, Jones, and Eubanks, Little Rock, 1960-63, Eubanks and Deane, Little Rock, 1963-65, Eubanks, Hood, and Files, Little Rock, 1965-69, Eubanks, Files and Hurley, Little Rock, 1969-76, Haskins Eubanks and Wilson, Little Rock, 1976-79, Gary Eubanks and Assocs., Little Rock, 1979—. Mem. Ark. Ho. of Reps., 1963-66; mem. Pulaski County (Ark.) Sch. Bd., 1967. Served with USN, 1952-54. Mem. ABA, Ark. State Bar Assn., Pulaski County Bar Assn., Ark. Trial Lawyers Assn., Assn. Trial Lawyers Am., Am. Bd. Trial Advocacy (civil trial advocate). Republican. Methodist. Personal injury. Home: #4 Wayside Dr North Little Rock AR 72116 Office: 708 W 2d St Little Rock AR 72201

EUBANKS, RONALD W., lawyer; b. Montgomery, Ala., Sept. 17, 1946; s. William Shell and Violet Lavern (Walker) E.; m. Tamara Ann Todd, July 3, 1985. Student, Auburn U., 1964-65; B.A., U. Ala., 1968; J.D., U. Utah, 1974. Bar: Utah 1974, Nebr., 1979, Minn. 1983, U.S. Ct. Appeals (10th cir.), 1977, U.S. Ct. Appeals (8th cir.), 1979, U.S. Supreme Ct., 1977, Wash. 1983, U.S. Ct. Appeals (9th cir.) 1985. Gen. mgr. Sta. WVMI and Sta. WQID, Biloxi Gulfport, Miss., 1968-71; with FCC, Washington, 1974-75; assoc. Hansen & Hansen, Salt Lake City, 1975-77; with law dept. Union Pacific R.R., Omaha, 1977-83; asst. gen. counsel Burlington No. R.R. Co., St. Paul, 1983-84, gen. counsel Western region, 1984-87, v.p. law and corp. affairs, Glacier Park Co., 1987—; dir. Camas Prairie R.R., Longview Switching Co. Bd. dirs., mem. exec. com., legal counsel Utah Boys Ranch, Salt Lake City, 1977-79; bd. dirs. Children and Youth Services, Salt Lake City, 1977-84, Nebr. affiliate Am. Diabetes Assn., 1982-83. Mem. ABA (sect. on litigation, coms. on publs. and trial techniques, sect. on tort and ins. practice, com. on r.r. law), Washington State Bar Assn., Utah Bar Assn. (com. on long range planning), Seattle-King County Bar Assn., Wash. Assn. Def. Counsel, Wash. R.R. Assn. (chmn. 1984—), Oreg. R.R. Assn. (bd. dirs.), Nat. Assn. R.R. Trial Counsel, Def. Research Inst. (chmn. com. on r.r. law 1984-86, mem. com. on practice and procedure), Jason's Soc., Phi Alpha Delta, Alpha Tau Omega. Republican. Presbyterian. Co-author: Practical Law in Utah, 1978; contbr. to profl. publs. General corporate, State civil litigation, Federal civil litigation. Home: 4163 Beach Dr Seattle WA 98116 Office: 1011 Western Ave Suite 700 Seattle WA 98104

EULE, JULIAN N., law educator; b. Kew Gardens, N.Y., Sept. 23, 1949; s. Leo Eule and Hanna (Gruenbaum) Minkin; m. Carole Lynn Rubin, Aug. 8, 1971; children: Lisa, Brian. BA, SUNY, Stony Brook, 1970; JD, Cornell U., 1973; LLM, Harvard U., 1977. Bar: N.Y. 1974, U.S. Ct. Appeals (2d cir.) 1974, U.S. Supreme Ct. 1977, U.S. Ct. Appeals (3d cir.) 1980, Pa. 1981, U.S. Ct. Appeals (9th and D.C. cirs.) 1984. Assoc. Shearman & Sterling, N.Y.C., 1973-74; spl. legal counsel Gov. of Conn., Hartford, 1974-75; law clk. U.S. Ct. Appeals (2d cir.), N.Y.C., 1974, 76-77; acting univ. counsel Temple U., Phila., 1982, asst. prof. law sch., 1977-80, assoc. law sch., 1980-82, prof. law sch., 1982-84; prof. law sch. UCLA, 1984—; vis. prof. Hebrew U., Jerusalem, 1977. Mem. gov.'s task force on off-shore oil State of Conn., 1974; hearing examiner EEOC, Washington, 1979-80, Pa. Bd. Med. and Edn. Licensure, 1980-82; cons. Calif. Com. Bar Examiners, San Francisco, 1985—. Mem. Order of Coif. Legal education, Constitutional law, Federal civil litigation. Office: UCLA Law Sch 405 Hilgard Ave Los Angeles CA 90024

EUSTICE, FRANCIS JOSEPH, lawyer; b. LaCrosse, Wis., Feb. 2, 1951; s. Frank R. and Cecelia T. (Babler) E.; m. Mary J. McCormick, July 28, 1971; children: Cristen L., Tara L. BS in Chemistry, Kansas Newman Coll., 1976; JD, U. Wis., 1980. Bar: Wis. 1980, U.S. Dist. Ct. (ea. and we. dists.) Wis. 1980, U.S. Tax Ct. 1981. Ptnr. Brill & Eustice, S.C., Sun Prairie, Wis., 1980—. Bd. dirs. Exchange Club Ctr. for Prevention of Child Abuse, Inc., Dane County, Wis., 1984—. Served to staff sgt. USAF, 1973-77. Mem. Wis. Bar Assn., Dane County Bar Assn., Assn. Trial Lawyers Am. Roman Catholic. Club: Sun Prairie Exchange (sec., pres., bd. dirs. 1980—). Avocations: camping, canoeing, cross-country skiing. Contracts commercial, Real property, Bankruptcy. Office: Brill & Eustice SC 1500 W Main St PO Box C Sun Prairie WI 53590

EUSTICE, JAMES SAMUEL, legal educator, lawyer; b. Chgo., June 9, 1932; s. Burt C. and Julia (Bohon) E.; m. LaVaun Schild, Jan. 29, 1956; children—Cynthia, James M. B.S., U. Ill., 1954, LL.B., 1956; LL.M. in Taxation, NYU, 1959. Assoc. White & Case, N.Y.C., 1958-60; prof. law NYU, N.Y.C., 1960—; counsel Kronish Lieb, N.Y.C., 1970—. Mem. N.Y. State Bar Assn., ABA, Order of Coif. Republican, Presbyterian. Club: University (N.Y.C.). Author: (with Bittker) Federal Income Taxation of Corporations and Shareholders, 1979; (with Kuntz) Federal Income Taxation of Subchapter S Corporations, 1985. Corporate taxation, Legal education. Office: 40 Washington Sq S 440 New York NY 10012

EUSTIS, ALBERT ANTHONY, lawyer, diversified industry corporate executive; b. Mahanoy City, Pa., Nov. 8, 1921; s. Anthony and Anna E.; m. Mary Hampton Stewart, Apr. 25, 1959; children: Thomas Stewart, David Anthony. B.S., Columbia U., 1948; LL.B., Harvard U., 1951. Bar: N.Y. 1952, U.S. Dist. Ct. (So. dist.) N.Y 1955. Atty. firm Kelley, Drye & Warren, N.Y.C., 1951-61; atty. W.R. Grace & Co., N.Y.C., 1961-66; asst. gen. counsel W.R. Grace & Co., 1966-76, v.p., gen. counsel, sec., 1976-78, sr. v.p., gen. counsel, sec., 1978-82, exec. v.p., gen. counsel, sec., 1982—; chmn. bd. trustees, spl. counsel Found. for President's Pvt. Sector Survey on Cost Control; adj. prof. law Fordham Law Sch. Served with AUS, 1942-46. Mem. ABA, Am. Arbitration Assn. (bd. dirs., comml. arbitration panel). Clubs: Harvard, Am. Yacht. General corporate. Home: 2 Northwest Way Bronxville NY 10708 Office: W R Grace & Co 1114 Ave of the Americas New York NY 10036-7794

EUSTIS, WARREN PENHALL, lawyer, educator; b. Fairmont, Minn., Nov. 30, 1927; s. Irving Nelson and Florence (Penhall) E.; m. Doris Anne Grieser, Mar. 1951 (div. Nov. 1968); children: Lillian, Paul; m. Nancy N. Anderson, Jan. 15, 1971; 1 child, Soren. B.A., Carleton Coll., 1950; J.D., U. Chgo., 1953; M.A., U. Ark., 1956. Bar: Minn. 1953. Practice law Rochester and Mpls., 1953—; prof. law U. Minn., 1974—; chmn. Granville, Ctrs., Inc.; counsel Upper Midwest Research and Devel. Council; dir. Twin Cities Health Project, 1972—; orgnl. cons. in health and ednl. delivery systems. Mem. Rochester Charter Commn., 1960-70, Minn. Higher Edn. Commn., 1965-67; pres. Rochester Council Chs., 1966; pres. emeritus Minn. Chem. Dependency Assn.; chmn. 1st Congl. Dist. Minn. Democratic-Farmer Labor Party, 1959-66; state fin. chmn. 1962-67; chmn. Granville Ctr., Inc. Served with Sci. and Profl. Corps, AUS, 1954-56. Mem. Minn. Trial Lawyers Assn. (gov.), Olmsted County Bar Assn. (past pres.), Delta Upsilon, Phi Alpha Theta. Federal civil litigation, Personal injury. Home: 58 Groveland Terr Minneapolis MN 55403 Office: 140 Shelard Plaza N Minneapolis MN 55426

EVAN, CHARLES, lawyer, educator; b. Domazlice, Czechoslovakia, Oct. 4, 1905; came to U.S., 1939, naturalized, 1947. JUDr, Charles U., Prague, Czechoslovakia, 1929; LL.B., Bklyn. Law Sch., 1943, J.D., 1967. Bar: N.Y. 1947. Advocate, Czechoslovakia, 1934-39; hon. vice consul of Spain, Czechoslovakia, 1936-39; with U.S. Office War Info., Dept. State, Washington, 1943-47; sole practice, N.Y.C., 1947—; adj. prof. law NYU Sch. Law, N.Y.C., 1950—; mem. faculty Benjamin N. Cardozo Sch. Law, N.Y.C., 1978-82; lectr. profl. orgns. Recipient Scroll of Honor, N.Y.U. Law Alumni Assn. 1976. Mem. ABA, Internat. Law Assn. (former com. chmn.), Am. Soc. Internat. Law, Am. Fgn. Law Assn. Club: N.Y.U. Contbr. articles on internat. trade law, comparative law and internat. monetary (currency) law to legal publs. Legal education, Private international, Public international. Office: 25 W 43d St Suite 1001 New York NY 10036

EVANGELISTA, DONATO A., computer and information processing systems manufacturing company executive, lawyer; b. Port Chester, N.Y., 1932. BS U. Rochester, 1954, LLB Cornell U., 1957. With IBM Corp., Armonk, N.Y., 1961—, atty., 1961-64, area counsel fed. systems div., Oswego, 1964-66, regional counsel data processing div., Washington, 1966-69, counsel data processing product group, 1969-75, corp. asst. gen. counsel, 1975-83, v.p. & deputy gen. counsel, 1983-85, v.p. & gen. counsel, 1986—. Office: IBM Corp Old Orchard Rd Armonk NY 10504

EVANOFF, MICHAEL BLAINE, lawyer; b. Flint, Mich., Mar. 13, 1946; s. Michael Welchner and Genevieve Ethel (Williamson) E.; m. Susan Kennedy, May 30, 1981. BA, Mich. State U., 1968; JD, U. Mich., 1971; LLM, U. London, 1982. Bar: N.Y. 1972, U.S. Dist. Ct. (so. dist.) N.Y. 1973, U.S. Ct. Appeals (2d cir.) 1974. Assoc. Breed, Abbott & Morgan, N.Y.C., 1971-73, Morgan, Lewis & Bockius and predecessor firm Wickes, Riddell, Bloomer, Jacobi & McGuire, N.Y.C., 1973-81; of counsel Youngstein & Gould, London, 1982-83, Wildman, Harrold, Allen & Dixon, London, 1983-84; v.p., gen. counsel Hyatt Internat. Corp., Chgo., 1984—; bd. dirs. James Electronics Inc., Chgo. Contbg. editor International Tax Report, 1982—; contbr. articles to profl. jours. Mem. ABA. Club: N.Y. Athletic (N.Y.C.); Chgo. Athletic. Private international, Corporate taxation. Home: 3000 N Sheridan Rd Chicago IL 60657 Office: Hyatt Internat Corp 200 W Madison St Chicago IL 60606

EVANS, BARRY LEONARD, lawyer; b. Mt. Vernon, N.Y. Oct. 24, 1938; s. Myer Herman and Helen Naomi (Uslan) E.; m. Elizabeth Hart Thompson, Mar. 25, 1967; children—Jonathan, Sarah, Samuel. B.Chem. Engring., Cornell U., 1960; J.D., NYU, 1965. Bar: N.Y. 1965. Chem. engr. Scientific Design Co., N.Y.C., 1960-64; patent atty. Halcon Internat., Inc., N.Y.C., 1964-66; assoc. McLean, Morton & Bousted, N.Y.C., 1966-68; ptnr. Curtis, Morris & Safford, P.C., 1968—. Mem. ABA, N.Y. Patent Trademark and Copyright Law Assn. (bd. govs. 1982—). Jewish. Patent, Trademark and copyright. Home: 134 W 78th St New York NY 10024 Office: Curtis Morris & Safford PC 530 Fifth Ave New York NY 10036

EVANS, BRUCE DWIGHT, lawyer; b. Mt. Hope, W.Va., May 27, 1934; s. M. Albert and Eleanor E. (Fowler) E.; m. Sallie Lee Hazen, Aug. 24, 1957 (div. Jan. 1974); children: Scott C., Leigh F., Randolph D.; m. Doris M. Stritzinger Webster, Sept. 2, 1978. A.B., Princeton U., 1956; LL.B., Harvard U., 1959. Bar: N.Y. 1960, Pa. 1970. Assoc. Debevoise, Plimpton, Lyons & Gates, N.Y.C., 1959-68; ptnr. Reed Smith Shaw & McClay, Pitts., 1969—. Trustee Ellis Sch., Pitts., 1972-78. Mem. ABA, Allegheny County Bar Assn., Phi Beta Kappa. Republican. Episcopalian. Clubs: Harvard-Yale-Princeton; Rivers (Pitts.). Office: Reed Smith et al 435 6th Ave Pittsburgh PA 15219

EVANS, CRAIG FLETCHER, lawyer; b. Dover, N.H., Sept. 2, 1948; s. George Newell and Eleanore (Dane) E.; m. Kathleen Marie McDermott, May 5, 1979. BA, U. N.H., 1970; JD, U. Maine, 1978. Bar: N.H. 1978, Maine 1978, U.S. Dist. Ct. N.H. 1978, U.S. Dist. Ct. Maine 1978, U.S. Ct. Appeals (1st cir.) 1978. Assoc. Michael, Jones & Wensley, Rochester, N.H., 1978-81; sole practice Durham, N.H., 1981—. Mem. selectmen Town of Madbury, N.H., 1984—. Served to capt. U.S. Army, 1970-75, Vietnam. Mem. ABA, N.H. Bar Assn., Maine Bar Assn., Assn. Trial Lawyers Am., Phi Kappa Theta. Republican. Episcopalian. Avocations: sports, softball, collecting history books. Personal injury, Real property, Criminal. Home: 3 Evans Rd Madbury Dover NH 03820 Office: PO Box 887 Durham NH 03824

EVANS, DANIEL FRALEY, JR., lawyer; b. Indpls., Apr. 19, 1949; s. Daniel Fraley and Julia (Sloan) E.; m. Marilyn Shultz, Aug. 11, 1973; children: Meredith, Benjamin, Suzannah, Theodore. BA, Ind. U., 1971, JD, 1976. Bar: Ind. 1976, U.S. Dist. Ct. (so. dist.) Ind. 1976, U.S. Ct. Appeals (7th cir.) 1983, U.S. Supreme Ct. 1983. Assoc. Sparrenberger, Duvall, Tabbert & Lalley, Indpls., 1976-77; ptnr. Duvall, Tabbert, Lalley & Newton, Indpls., 1977-81, Bayh, Tabbert & Capehart, Indpls., 1981-85, Baker & Daniels, Indpls., 1985—. Chmn. Ind. Bd. Correction, Indpls., 1976—, Quayle for Senate Com., 1980, 86; mem. Fed. Jud. Merit Selection Com., Indpls., 1981—, Adminstrv. Conf. U.S., 1983—, Indpls. Dist. Fed. Home Loan Bank Bd. Mem. Indpls. Bar Assn., Ind. Bar Assn., ABA. Republican. Methodist. Clubs: University, Woodstock, (Indpls.). Administrative and regulatory, Federal civil litigation, General corporate. Office: Baker & Daniels 810 Fletcher Trust Bldg Indianapolis IN 46204

EVANS, DAVID LEE, lawyer, accountant; b. Johnson City, N.Y., Sept. 11, 1953; s. Donald L. and Betty (Knight) E.; m. Deborah Tapping, Aug. 5, 1978; children: Elizabeth, Lee, Christopher. BBA, Hofstra U., 1975; JD, SUNY, Buffalo, 1978. Bar: N.Y. 1979, U.S. Tax Ct. 1981, U.S. Supreme Ct. 1986. Adminstrv. law judge N.Y. State Dept. Tax, Albany, 1978-79; ptnr. Urbach, Kahn & Werlin, P.C., Albany, 1980—. Author: (with others) New York Taxation, 1985. Mem. ABA, N.Y. State Bar Assn., Am. Inst. CPA's, N.Y. State Soc. CPA's. Corporate taxation, State and local taxation, Estate taxation. Office: Urbach Kahn & Werlin PC 66 State St Albany NY 12207

EVANS, DONALD CHARLES, JR., lawyer; b. New London, Conn., Nov. 1, 1938; s. Donald Charles and Henrietta Agnes (Perkins) E.; m. Magda Anna Wehr, Apr. 30, 1966; children—Donald Charles III, Sean Thomas. B.A., U. Miami, 1961; J.D., U. Fla., Gainesville, 1967; LL.M., N.Y.U., 1968. Bar: Fla. 1967, D.C. 1974, U.S. Tax Ct. 1974. Legis.-adminstrv. asst. Fla. State Senate, 1967; atty.-adviser legis. and regulations div. Office Chief Csl., IRS, 1968-71; legis. atty. U.S. Congress Joint Com. on Internal Revenue Taxation, Washington, 1971-74; mem. Williams & Jensen, P.C., Washington, 1974-83; mem. Evans & Assocs., Washington, 1983—. Served to 1st lt. AUS, 1963-65. Mem. ABA, Fla. Bar Assn. (gov. 1979-83), D.C. Bar Assn., U. Fla. Alumni Assn. (pres. D.C. chpt. 1974-75), Fla. State Soc. (dir. 1972-77). Corporate taxation, Personal income taxation, Legislative. Home: 9315 Winbourne Rd Burke VA 22015 Office: Evans & Assocs 655 15th St NW Suite 310 Washington DC 20005

EVANS, DOUGLAS HAYWARD, lawyer; b. Pawtucket, R.I., July 21, 1950; s. Jerrold Merton and Gladys Jean (Snelgrove) E.; m. Sarah Edwards Cogan, May 28, 1983. AB, Franklin & Marshall Coll., 1972; JD, Cornell U., 1975. Bar: N.J. 1975, U.S. Dist. Ct. N.J. 1975, N.Y. 1976. Assoc. Windels, Marx, Davies & Ives, N.Y.C., 1975-85, Sullivan & Cromwell, N.Y.C., 1985—; faculty NYU Inst. Fed. Taxation, N.Y.C., 1984; counsel, bd. dirs. St. David's Soc. State of N.Y., N.Y.C., 1984—. Co-author: Estate Accounting, 1980, Probate and Estate Administration, 1982, Administration of Estates, 1985; also articles. Mem. Ch. Club of N.Y. Mem. ABA, N.J. Bar Assn., N.Y. State Bar Assn. (estate litigation and adminstrn. of trusts and estates com.), Phi Beta Kappa, Phi Delta Phi, Phi Alpha Theta, Pi Gamma Mu. Episcopalian. Estate planning, Probate, Estate taxation. Home: 69 W 9th St Apt 7-K New York NY 10011 Office: Sullivan & Cromwell 250 Park Ave New York NY 10177

EVANS, GEORGE FREDERICK, JR., lawyer; b. Cleve., Feb. 23, 1952; s. George Frederick and Doris Ayn (Stickle) E.; m. Laraine Hoerter, May 16, 1981; children: Whitney, Reid, Ross. BA Ohio Wesleyan U., 1974; JD cum laude, Cleveland-Marshall Coll. Law, 1977. Bar: Ohio 1977, Tex. 1982, U.S. Dist. Ct. (no. dist.) Ohio 1977, U.S. Dist. Ct. (we. dist.) Tex. 1983. Assoc. Cronquist, Smith & Marshall, Cleve., 1977-79; with Johns-Manville Corp., 1979-82; assoc. Wiley & Garwood, San Antonio, 1982-84; ptnr. Groce, Locke & Hebdon, San Antonio, 1984—. assoc. prof. health sci. ctr. and med. sch. U. Tex. Author: (booklet series) Franklin County Legal Aid Assn., 1974; assoc. editor: Cleveland-Marshall Law Rev., 1975. Recipient "A" award Johns-Manville Corp., 1982. Mem. Def. Research Inst. (advocate), Tex. Assn. Def. Counsel, ABA, Tex. Bar Assn., Ohio State Bar Assn., Mensa. Republican. Roman Catholic. Personal injury, State civil litigation, Insurance. Home: 10414 Mount Hope San Antonio TX 78230 Office: Groce Locke & Hebdon 2000 Frost Bank Tower San Antonio TX 78205

EVANS, GEORGE MICHAEL, lawyer; b. Bogota, Colombia, Jan. 14, 1953; s. Jerry and Mary (Rychter) E.; m. Julia Marie Gillen, Feb. 16, 1980; children: Shannon Marie, George Michael Jr. BA in History, U. Md., 1973; JD, Nova U., 1977. Bar: Fla. 1977, U.S. Dist. Ct. (so. dist.) Fla. 1977, U.S. Tax Ct. 1977, U.S. Supreme Ct. 1980, U.S. Ct. Appeals (11th cir.) 1984, U.S. Dist. Ct. (mid. and no. dists.) Fla. 1986. Agt. departure service Eastern Air Lines, Washington, 1971-74; assoc. Koppen & Watkins, Miami, Fla., 1977—. Mem. ABA, Fla. Trial Lawyers Assn., Assn. Trial Lawyers Am., Nat. Coll. of Adv., Phi Alpha Delta. Avocations: sports, collecting baseball cards, music. Criminal, Personal injury, Federal civil litigation. Home: 930 NE 96th St Miami Shores FL 33138 Office: Koppen & Watkins 700 NE 90th St Miami FL 33138

EVANS, GEORGE WALTON, JR., lawyer; b. Wilkes-Barre, Pa., Aug. 18, 1954; s. George W. and Mildred Amelia (Kozmoski) E.; m. Susan Wood, Aug. 20, 1977; children: George W. III, Timothy P. BA, Williams Coll., 1976; JD and MBA, Columbia U., 1980. Bar: N.Y. 1981, U.S. Dist. Ct. (so. and ea. dists.) N.Y. 1982. Atty. Pfizer Inc., N.Y.C., 1980—. Contracts commercial, Legislative, General corporate. Home: 17 Irving Pl Pelham NY 10803 Office: Pfizer Inc 235 E 42d St New York NY 10017

EVANS, JACK D., lawyer; b. Marshfield, Mo., Jan. 20, 1944; s. Winston and Goldie (Williamson) E.; m. JoAnn Morse, May 13, 1978; children: Amy Rebecca, Jeffrey Derick. BA, U. Wash., 1966, JD, 1969. Ptnr. Evans & Kerr, Kennewick, Wash.; lectr. in field. Office: Evans & Kerr 3311 W Clearwater Ave Kennewick WA 99336

EVANS, JAMES A., lawyer; b. Hallettsville, Tex., May 10, 1940; s. Alton and Myrtle Alice (Koch) E.; m. Judy Lynne Gerdes, Sept. 9, 1962; children: James A., John C., Jeff G. BA, U. Tex., Austin, 1961, JD, 1963. Assoc. Allen & Allen, Hallettsville, 1963-66; asst. atty. gen. State of Tex., Austin, 1966-67; sole practice Victoria, Tex., 1967; atty. law dept. Shell Oil Co., Midland, N.Y.C. and Houston, Tex., 1967—; asst. gen. counsel Shell Oil Co., Houston, 1984—. Election judge Harris County, Houston, 1986—. Mem. Tex. Bar Assn. (mem. exec. council 1984—). Avocations: cattle ranching, horseback riding. Environment, Personal injury, Labor. Office: PO Box 2463 Houston TX 77090

EVANS, JOHN, sugar company executive; b. Jan. 13, 1932. A.B., U. Va., 1953; LL.B., George Washington U., 1958, LL.M., 1959. Bar: D.C. 1958, Colo. 1961, Calif. 1972. Sr. v.p., sec. Holly Sugar Corp., Colorado Springs, Colo., 1961-72, gen. counsel, 1981—, also bd. dirs.; bd. dirs. HSC Export Corp. div. Holly Sugar Corp., Colo. Springs. Member Order of Coif. Office: Holly Sugar Corp PO Box 1052 Colorado Springs CO 80901

EVANS, JOHN F., lawyer; b. Athens, May 8, 1941; s. Raymond Louis Evans and Augusta (Farnham) Larson; m. Margaret Alice McClendon, July 10, 1957; children: Deborah Jean, John Clayton, Timothy Courtney. BA, U. N.C., 1964, LLB, 1966. Bar: N.C. 1966, D.C. 1968, Fla. 1977, U.S. Dist. Ct. (so. dist.) Fla. 1979, U.S. Dist. Ct. (no. dist.) Fla. 1980, U.S. Ct. Appeals (5th cir.) 1980, U.S. Ct. Appeals (11th cir.) 1984. Law clk. U.S. Dist. Ct. (ea. dist.), Clinton, N.C., 1966-68; asst. U.S. atty. D.C., Washington, 1968-75; spl. atty. U.S. Dept. Justice Miami (Fla.) Strike Force, 1975-79; ptnr. Zuckerman, Spaeder, Taylor & Evans, Miami, 1979—. Mem. ABA, Fed. Bar Assn. Criminal, Federal civil litigation, State civil litigation. Office: Zuckerman Spaeder Taylor & Evans Gables Corp Plaza Suite 1100 2100 Ponce De Leon Blvd Coral Gables FL 33134

EVANS, JOHN KEDRICH, lawyer; b. Nanticoke, Pa., Oct. 31, 1953; s. John K. Sr. and Kathryn M. (Hibbard) E. BS in Econs., U. Pa., 1975; JD, U. Pitts., 1978. Bar: Pa., 1978, Va., 1980, D.C., 1982, Supreme Ct., 1983. Sr. counsel SEC, Washington, 1978-84; assoc. Epstein, Becker, Borsody & Green, Washington, 1984—. Securities, General corporate, Health. Home: 1718 P St NW #506 Washington DC 20036 Office: Epstein Becker Borsody & Green 1140 19th St NW Washington DC 20036

EVANS, JOHN THOMAS, lawyer; b. N.Y.C., Feb. 28, 1948; s. John Arthur and Dorothy (Reilly) E.; m. Marie Tolnay, June 2, 1979; children—Claire, Grace. B.A., U. Wis., 1970; J.D., Fordham U., 1973. Bar: N.Y. 1974, U.S. Dist. Ct. (so. and ea. dists.) N.Y., U.S. Tax Ct. Asst. dist. atty. N.Y. County, N.Y.C., 1973-79; assoc. Blumenthal & Lynne, N.Y.C., 1979-81; ptnr. Morris & Duffy, N.Y.C., 1982-85, Belair, Klein, Groman & Evans, N.Y.C., 1985—; cons. Vol. Lawyers for Arts, N.Y.C., 1979-84, Hofstra U. Law Sch. Moot Ct. Program, Uniondale, N.Y., 1982; cons., lectr. N.Y.C. Police Dept. Detectives Endowment Assn., 1981—. Recipient Highest award

Manhattan Detective Area, N.Y.C., 1979. Mem. N.Y. State Bar Assn., Assn. Bar City of N.Y., N.Y. Criminal Bar Assn. Club: N.Y. Athletic (N.Y.C.). Personal injury, Criminal, State civil litigation. Home: 362 W Broadway New York NY 10013 Office: Belair Klein Groman & Evans 61 Broadway New York NY 10006

EVANS, JOHN WILLIAM, lawyer; b. Brookhaven, Miss., July 26, 1955; s. James William and Chu Ke (Ko) E. BA, UCLA, 1978; JD, Southwestern U., 1981. Bar: Calif. 1981, U.S. Dist. Ct. (cen. dist.) Calif. 1981, U.S. Ct. Appeals (9th cir.) 1981. Assoc. Harlan, Huff & Marugg, Irvine, Calif., 1981-82, Erickson & Agan, Encino, Calif., 1983-85, Hill, Genson, Even, Crandall & Wade, Los Angeles, 1986, Liebman & Reiner, Los Angeles, 1986—. Mem. ABA, Los Angeles County Bar Assn., So. Calif. Assn. Def. Counsel, Phi Alpha Delta. Personal injury, Real property, State civil litigation. Home: 506 Dartmouth Dr Placentia CA 92670 Office: Liebman & Reiner 3255 Wilshire Blvd Los Angeles CA 90010

EVANS, LAWRENCE JACK, JR., lawyer; b. Oakland, Calif., Apr. 4, 1921; s. Lawrence Jack and Eva May (Dickinson) E.; m. Marjorie Hisken, Dec. 23, 1944; children—Daryl S. Kleweno, Richard L., Shirley J. Coursey, Donald B. Diplomate Near East Sch. Theology, Beirut, 1951; M.A., Am. U. Beirut, 1951; Ph.D., Brantridge Forest Sch., Sussex, Eng., 1968; J.D., Ariz. State U., 1971; grad. Nat. Jud. Coll., 1974. Bar: Ariz. 1971, U.S. Dist. Ct. Ariz. 1971, U.S. Ct. Claims 1972, U.S. Customs Ct., 1972, U.S. Tax Ct. 1972, U.S. Ct. Customs and Patent Appeals 1972, U.S. Ct. Appeals (9th cir.) 1972, U.S. Supreme Ct. 1975. Served as enlisted man U.S. Navy, 1938-41; enlisted man U.S. Army, 1942-44, commd. 2d lt., 1944, advanced through ranks to lt. col., 1962; chief, field ops. and tactics div., U.S. Army Spl. Forces, 1963, chief spl. techniques div., 1964, unconventional warfare monitor, 1964-65; assigned to Command and Gen. Staff Coll., 1960; ops. staff officer J-3 USEUCOM, 1965-68; mem. Airborne Command Post Study Group, Joint Chiefs of Staff, 1967; ret., 1968; sole practice law, cons. on Near and Middle Eastern affairs, Tempe, Ariz., 1971-72, 76—; v.p., dir. Trojan Investment & Devel. Co., Inc., 1972-75; active Ariz. Tax Conf., 1971-75; mem. adminstrv. law com., labor mgmt. relations com., unauthorized practice of law com. Ariz. State Bar. Author: Legal Aspects of Land Tenure in the Republic of Lebanon, 1951; (with Helen Miller Davis) International Constitutional Law, Electoral Laws and Treaties of the Near and Middle East, 1951. Contbr. articles to mags., chpts. to books. Chmn. legal and legis. com. Phoenix Mayor's Com. To Employ Handicapped, 1971-75; active Tempe Leadership Conf., 1971-75; chmn. Citizens Against Corruption in Govt.; mem. Princeton Council on Fgn. and Internat. Studies. Decorated Silver Star, Legion of Merit, Bronze Star, Purple Heart; named Outstanding Adminstrv. Law Judge for State Service for U.S., 1974; named to U.S. Army Ranger Hall of Fame, 1981. Mem. Ranger Bns. Assn. World War II (life), Tempe Rep. Mens Club (v.p., bd. dirs. 1971-72, U.S. Army Airborne Ranger Assn. (life), Mil. Order Purple Heart (life), Nat. Rifle Assn. (life), Phi Delta Phi, Delta Theta Phi. Episcopalian. Lodges: Masons, KT (past master, past thrice illustrious master, past comdr.). General corporate, General practice. Home: 539 E Erie Dr Tempe AZ 85282 Office: Tempe AZ 85282

EVANS, MARTIN FREDERIC, lawyer; b. Nashville, June 12, 1947; s. Robert Clements and Adelaide Hawkins (Roberts) E.; m. Margaret Carroll Kidder, Apr. 17, 1982. BA, U. Va., 1969; JD, Yale U., 1972. Bar: N.Y. 1973, U.S. Dist. Ct. (so. dist.) N.Y. 1973, U.S. Ct. Appeals (2d cir.) 1974, U.S. Ct. Appeals (D.C. cir.) 1981, U.S. Supreme Ct. 1981, D.C. 1982. Assoc. Debevoise & Plimpton, N.Y.C., 1972-80, ptnr., 1981—; researcher Nat. Commn. for Rev. of Antitrust Laws and Procedure, Washington, 1978. Mem. ABA (sect. for antitrust law), Assn. of Bar of City of N.Y., Phi Beta Kappa. Club: Yale (N.Y.C.). Antitrust, Federal civil litigation, State civil litigation. Office: Debevoise & Plimpton 875 3d Ave New York NY 10022

EVANS, ORINDA D., federal judge; b. Savannah, Ga., Apr. 23, 1943; d. Thomas and Virginia Elizabeth (Grieco) E.; m. Roberts O. Bennett, Apr. 12, 1975; children: Wells Cooper, Elizabeth Thomas. B.A., Duke U., 1965; J.D. with distinction, Emory U., 1968. Bar: Ga. 1968. Ptnr. Alston, Miller & Gaines, Atlanta, 1974-79; U.S. dist. judge No. Dist. Ga., Atlanta, 1979—; adj. prof. Emory U. Law Sch., 1974-77; counsel Atlanta Crime Commn., 1970-71. Mem. Atlanta Bar Assn. (dir. 1979). Democrat. Episcopalian. Jurisprudence. Home: 200 The Prado NE Atlanta GA 30309 Office: US District Court 1988 US Courthouse 75 Spring St SW Atlanta GA 30303

EVANS, PAUL VERNON, lawyer; b. Colorado Springs, Colo., June 19, 1926; s. Fred Harrison and Emma Hooper (Austin) E.; m. Frances Irene Pool, Sept. 7, 1947 (div. Jan. 1964); m. Patricia Gwyn Davis, July 27, 1964; children—Bruce, Paula, Mike, Mark, Paul. B.A. cum laude, Colo. Coll., 1953; J.D., Duke U., 1956. Bar: Colo. 1956, U.S. Dist. Ct. Colo. 1956, U.S. Supreme Ct. 1971, U.S. Ct. Appeals (10th cir.) 1974. Field mgr. Keystone Readers Service, Dallas, 1946-50; sole practice, Colorado Springs, 1956-60; ptnr. Goodbar, Evans & Goodbar, 1960-63; sr. ptnr. Evans & Briggs Attys., Colorado Springs, 1963—; city atty. City of Fountain, Colo., 1958-62, City of Woodland Park, Colo., 1962-78; atty. Rock Creek Mesa Water Dist., Colorado Springs, 1963—. Author instruction materials. Precinct com. man Republican Com., Colorado Springs, 1956-72. Served with USNR, 1944-46, PTO. Recipient Jr. C. of C. Outstanding Achievement award, 1957. Mem. Colo. Mining Assn., Am. Jud. Soc., ABA, Colo. Bar Assn. (com. chmn. 1966-67, 84), El Paso County Bar Assn. (com. chmn. 1956—), Assn. Trial Lawyers Am., Colo. and Local Trial Lawyers, Rocky Mountain Mineral Law Inst., Isaac Walton Contractors Assn. (sec. 1957-75), Tau Kappa Alpha (pres.), Phi Beta Kappa. Republican. Club: Optimist (pres. 1966-67). Mining and minerals, Family and matrimonial, Personal injury. Home: 3116 Wellshire Blvd Colorado Springs CO 80910 Office: Evans & Briggs 532 S Weber St Colorado Springs CO 80903

EVANS, RICHARD JOSEPH, lawyer; b. Buffalo, May 28, 1947; s. Morris amd Adeline (Kaufman) E.; m. Cheryl A. Covey, Jan. 6, 1982; children: Steven Noah, Leigh Allison. BA, SUNY, Buffalo, 1969, JD cum laude, 1972. Bar: N.Y. 1973, U.S. Dist. Ct. (we. dist) N.Y. 1973, U.S. Supreme Ct. 1978. Assoc. Harris, Carroll & Creary, Rochester, N.Y., 1972-74, Harris, Maloney & Horwitz, Rochester, 1974-75; ptnr. Harris, Maloney, Horwitz & Evans, Rochester, 1976-78, Harris, Maloney, Horwitz, Evans & Fox, Rochester, 1978—. Gen. counsel ALCU, Rochester, 1975-85. Mem. ABA, Assn. Trial Lawyers Am., N.Y. State Bar Assn., Monroe County Bar Assn (trustee 1985-87). Democrat. Jewish. Avocations: sailing, skiing. State civil litigation, Federal civil litigation, General practice. Office: Harris Maloney et al 700 1st Federal Plaza Rochester NY 14614

EVANS, ROBERT COLLIN, lawyer, consultant; b. Balt., June 2, 1954; s. Robert Garfield Collin and Estelle Theresa (Konieczny) Evans. BA, Columbia U., 1975; postgrad., Johns Hopkins U., 1975-76; JD, U. Md., 1980. Bar: La. 1980, Md. 1980, U.S. Dist. Ct. Md. 1980, U.S. Dist. Ct. (ea., mid. and we. dists.) La. 1980, U.S. Ct. Appeals (5th cir.) 1982, U.S. Ct. Internat. Trade 1982, U.S. Ct. Customs 1982, U.S. Patent Appeals 1982. Assoc. Phelps, Dunbar, Marks, Claverie & Sims, New Orleans, 1980-84; prin. Law Officesof Robert C. Evans, New Orleans, 1984—; gen. counsel Algiers Point Assn., New Orleans, 1982-83; cons. Law Processing Corp., New Orleans, 1984—. Columnist: The Proctor's Bench, 1985—. Mem. Rep. Exec. Counsel La., 1984—. Mem. ABA, La. Bar Assn., Maritime Law Assn. U.S. (com. 1982—), Computer Law Assn., New Orleans Assn. Def. Counsel. Presbyterian. Club: Paul Morphy Chess (bd. dirs. 1983-85). Avocations: computer implementation, computer programming, electronics, creative writing. Admiralty, Federal civil litigation, Computer. Office: 822 Perdido St New Orleans LA 70112

EVANS, ROBERT DAVID, legal association executive; b. Vergennes, Vt., Mar. 1, 1945; B.A., Yale U., 1966; J.D., U. Mich., 1969. Bar: Ill. 1969. Assoc., Sachnoff Schrager Jones & Weaver, Chgo., 1969-72; asst. dir. div. pub. service activities ABA, Chgo., 1972-73, asst. dir. govtl. relations office, Washington, 1973-78, assoc. dir. govtl. relations office, 1978-82, dir. govtl. affairs office, 1982—; asst. exec. dir., dir. Washington Office, 1986—. Mem. Washington Grove (Md.) Town Council, 1977-81, Washington Grove Town Planning Commn., 1977-81; mayor Washington Grove, 1981-83; vice chmn. Assns. div. Nat. Capital Area United Way, 1986-87, chmn., 1987—. Mem. ABA. Legal assn. exec.. Home: 317 Brown St Washington Grove MD 20880 Office: 1800 M St NW Washington DC 20036

EVANS, ROGER, lawyer; b. Syracuse, N.Y., Apr. 18, 1951; s. David Longfellow and Louise Maude (Crawford) E.; m. Claudia Thérèse Benack, Mar. 27, 1976; children: Jonathan Longfellow, Gillian Crawford. AB, Cornell U., 1974; postgrad., Columbia U., 1976-77; JD, Harvard U., 1977. Bar: Ohio 1977, U.S. Dist. Ct. (no. dist.) Ohio 1978, Tex. 1981, U.S. Dist. Ct. (no. dist.) Tex. 1981, U.S. Ct. Appeals (5th, 6th and 11th cirs.) 1981, U.S. Ct. Appeals (10th cir.) 1982. Assoc. Jones, Day, Reavis & Pogue, Cleve., 1977-81, Dallas, 1981-84; ptnr. Shank, Irwin & Conant, Dallas, 1984-86, Gardner, Carton & Douglas, Dallas, 1986—. Gen. counsel, bd. dirs. Freedom Ride Found., Dallas, 1985—; active Dallas Dem. Forum, 1986—. Mem. ABA, State Bar of Tex., Ohio State Bar Assn., Cornell U. Alumni Assn. (class pres. 1984—), Harvard Law Sch. Assn. of No. Ohio (sec. 1978-81). Democrat. Episcopalian. Club: Harvard (Dallas). Federal civil litigation, State civil litigation, Bankruptcy. Home: 11410 Strait Ln Dallas TX 75229 Office: Gardner Carton & Douglas 600 N Pearl Dallas TX 75201

EVANS, STANLEY ROBERT, lawyer; b. Youngstown, Ohio, July 12, 1955; s. Stanley Evan and Loretta Josephine (Capuano) E.; m. Barbara Jean Brunow, Nov. 16, 1985. AB, Coll. Holy Cross, 1978; JD, MBA, U. Toledo, 1982. Bar: Ohio 1982, U.S. Dist. Ct. (no. dist.) Ohio 1983, U.S. Dist. Ct. (so. dist.) Ohio 1986. Law clk. to presiding justice Ohio Ct. Appeals (6th dist.), Toledo, 1982-84; assoc. Elsass, Schmitt, Wallace & Co., L.P.A., Sidney, Ohio, 1984—. Editor U. Toledo Law Rev., 1981-82; contbr. articles to profl. jours. Mem. ABA, Ohio Bar Assn., Shelby County Bar Assn., Lucas County Bar Assn., Phi Alpha Delta. Roman Catholic. State civil litigation, Jurisprudence, General practice. Home: 213 Bon Air Dr Sidney OH 45365 Office: Elsass Schmitt Wallace & Co LPA 101 S Ohio Ave PO Box 499 Sidney OH 44511

EVANS, SUSAN ANN, lawyer; b. Washington, Aug. 31, 1954; d. Robert David and Clara Mae (Messick) E.; m. Robert Stevens Greenlief, Dec. 26, 1980 (Oct. 1983); m. Ralph Nicholas Boccarosse, May 27, 1986. BA, U. Va., 1976; JD, U. Richmond, 1979. Bar: Va. 1979, U.S. Ct. Appeals (4th cir.) 1979, D.C. 1982, U.S. Dist. Ct. D.C. 1982. Law clk. to presiding justice Va. Cir. Ct. (19th cir.), Fairfax, 1979-80; assoc. Siciliano, Ellis, Dyer & Boccarosse, Fairfax, 1980-85, ptnr., 1986—; atty. Va. Med. Malpractice Panel Rev., 1984—. Mem. Fairfax Bar Assn. (membership com.), No. Va. Def. Lawyers Assn. (treas. 1983-85, v.p. 1985—, pres. 1987—), Va. Assn. Def. Attys. Baptist. Personal injury, Workers' compensation, Insurance. Home: 11561 Southington Ln Reston VA 22070 Office: Sicilino Ellis Dyer & Boccarosse 10521 Judicial Dr #300 Fairfax VA 22030

EVANS, TERENCE THOMAS, judge; b. Milw., Mar. 25, 1940; s. Robert Hansen and Jeanett (Walters) E.; m. Joan Marie Witte, July 24, 1965; children: Kelly Elizabeth, Christine Marie, David Rourke. B.A., Marquette U., Milw., 1962; J.D., Marquette U., 1967. Bar: Wis. 1967. Law clk. to justice Wis. Supreme Ct., 1967-68; dist. atty. Milw. County, 1968-70; pvt. practice Milw., 1970-74; circuit judge State of Wis., 1974-80; judge U.S. Dist. Ct. Eastern Dist. Wis., Milw., 1980—. Mem. ABA, State Bar Wis., Milw. Bar Assn. Roman Catholic. Jurisprudence. Office: U S Dist Ct 371 U S Courthouse 517 E Wisconsin Ave Milwaukee WI 53202 *

EVANS, THOMAS MARTIN, lawyer; b. Athens, Ala., Nov. 20, 1914; s. Henry Bugg and Betty (Ross) E.; m. Virginia Richey, June 26, 1941 (dec.); children—Dorothy E., Thomas Martin. LL.B., Cumberland U., 1937. Bar: Tenn. 1937, U.S. Dist. Ct. (mid. dist.) Tenn. 1937. Sole practice, Nashville, 1937—. Served with USNR, 1942-46. Mem. Nashville Bar Assn., Tenn. Bar Assn., ABA. Methodist. Banking, Probate, General corporate. Office: 3d Nat Bank Bldg Nashville TN 37219

EVANS, THOMAS WILLIAM, lawyer; b. N.Y.C., Dec. 9, 1930; s. William J. and R. Helen (Stenvall) E.; m. Lois deBaun Logan, Dec. 22, 1956; children—Heather, Thomas Logan, Barbara Paige. B.A., Williams Coll., 1952; J.D., Columbia U., 1958. Bars: N.Y. 1958, U.S. Supreme Ct. 1961. Assoc. Simpson, Thacher & Bartlett, N.Y.C., 1958-64; asst. council to spl. state commn. of investigation, spl. dep. asst. N.Y. Atty. Gen., N.Y.C., 1964-65; assoc. Mudge Rose Guthrie Alexander & Ferdon, N.Y.C., 1965-66, ptnr., 1967—; mem. bd. visitors Columbia U. Law Sch., N.Y.C., 1973—; founder MENTOR, nat. law-related edn. program pub. sch. students, 1983. Author: The School in the Home, 1973; (with others) Nuclear Litigation, annually, 1979-84; patentee fly ash amalgam in pothold repair. Trustee, sec. N.Y. Alliance for Pub. Schs., N.Y.C., 1981—; mem. exec. com., chmn. edn. com. Presdl. Bd. Advisors on Pvt. Sector Initiatives, Washington, 1983—; trustee Tchrs. Coll., Columbia U., 1985—, Marine Corps Command and Staff Coll. Found., Inc. Served to capt. USMCR, 1950-54, Korea. Decorated Silver Star, Purple Heart (2). Mem. Fed. Bar Council (pres.-elect, trustee 1981—), ABA, N.Y. State Bar Assn., Assn. Bar N.Y.C. Republican. Episcopalian. Clubs: Century Assn., Down Town Assn., River (N.Y.C.); Met. (Washington). Federal civil litigation, State civil litigation. Home: 132 E 72d St New York NY 10021 Office: Mudge Rose Guthrie Alexander & Ferdon 180 Maiden Ln New York NY 10038

EVANS, WILLIAM ELLIS, lawyer; b. Starkville, Miss., June 8, 1952; s. Leslie Lee Evans and Beth (York) Fisher; m. Kathleen Thurmond, June 1, 1974 (div. Apr. 1979); m. Pamela Sue Marlin; 1 child, Blake Ellis. BA, So. Meth. U., 1974, LLM in Taxation, 1980; JD, U. Mo., 1977. Jr. ptnr. Bryan, Cave, McPheeters and McRoberts, St. Louis, 1977-79; assoc. Woolsey, Fisher, Whiteacre, McDonald and Ansley, Springfield, Mo., 1980-81; prin. Carnahan, Carnahan, Evans and Cantwell, P.C., Springfield, 1981—; lectr. various programs Ark. Fed. Tax Inst., Mo. Assn. Tax Practitioners. Mem. ABA (com. on civil and criminal tax penalties), Mo. Bar Assn. (taxation sect., chmn. continuing legal edn. com., taxation sect.), Greene County Bar Assn., Bar Assn. of Met. St. Louis, U.S. Tax Ct. Bar Assn., Acad. of Magical Arts, Internat. Brotherhood of Magicians. Avocations: magic, guitar, golf, fishing. Corporate taxation, Personal income taxation, State and local taxation. Office: Carnahan Carnahan Evans & Cantwell 1949 E Sunshine Suite 4-300 Springfield MO 65804

EVANS, WILLIAM JAMES, lawyer; b. Appleton, Wis., July 27, 1954; s. Robert Clifford and Beverly Kathryn (Wehrle) E.; m. Sonia del Carmen Hernández, June 24, 1978; children: Marisol del Carmen, Sara Lissette. BA, U. Wis., 1976; JD, Marquette U., 1980. Bar: Wis. 1980, U.S. Dist. Ct. (ea. and we. dists.) Wis. 1980. Sole practice Waukesha, Wis., 1980-85; atty. West Bend (Wis.) Mut. Ins., 1985—. Mem. ABA, Washington County Bar Assn., Waukesha County Bar Assn., Def. Research Inst., Civil Trial Counsel of Wis. Methodist. Lodge: Kiwanis. Insurance, Personal injury. Home: 217 S James St Waukesha WI 53186 Office: West Bend Mutual Ins 115 S Main St West Bend WI 53095

EVANS-HARRELL, VALERIE DIANNE, lawyer; b. Bronx, N.Y., Nov. 6, 1955; d. Royal Clarence and Clara Diana (Cross) Evans; m. Durand Harrell, Mar. 17, 1984. BA cum laude, CUNY, 1977; JD, George Washington U., 1980. Bar: Pa. 1981, U.S. Ct. Appeals (D.C. cir.) 1984. Atty., advisor employees compensation appeals bd. U.S. Dept. Labor, Washington, 1981—. Mem. Asbury United Meth. Ch. (spl. com. on nominations, chairperson com. on involvement, adminstrv. bd.). Named one of Outstanding Young Women Am., 1983. Mem. ABA, Fed. Bar Assn., Pa. Bar Assn., NAACP, Kappa Beta Pi, Alpha Kappa Alpha. Democrat. Avocations: choir singing, handball, music, movies. Labor, Workers' compensation. Home: 1806 Bryant St NE Washington DC 20018 Office: US Dept Labor Employees Compensation Appeals Bd 300 7th St SW Suite 300 Washington DC 20210

EVE, ROBERT MICHAEL, JR., lawyer; b. Charlotte, N.C., Apr. 26, 1953; s. Robert Michael and Carolyn Elizabeth (Roesel); m. Kimberly Denise Davenport, June 9, 1984. B.A. with honors, U. N.C.; J.D. cum laude Samford U. Bar: Ala. 1978, N.C. 1979, U.S. Dist. Ct. (mid. dist.) Ala. 1978, U.S. Dist. Ct. (we. dist.) N.C. 1979, U.S. Ct. Appeals (4th cir.) 1980. Dep. clk. Superior Ct., Mecklenburg County, N.C., 1972-73; dep. sheriff, 1974-75; law clk. to justice Supreme Ct. of Ala., Montgomery, 1978-79; assoc. Bailey, Sitton, Patterson and Bailey, P.A., Charlotte, N.C., 1979-84; ptnr. Justice, Parnell and Eve, P.A., Charlotte, 1984—; law clk. U.S. Dist. Ct. (no. dist.) Ala., 1978. Mem. Mecklenburg County Eagle Scout Rev. Bd., Boy Scouts Am.; mem. Mecklenburg County Young Republicans. Recipient Order of the Old Well, U. N.C., 1975. Mem. N.C. Bar Assn., N.C. Acad. Trial Lawyers. Lutheran. Club: Order of the Arrow. Editor-in-chief Cumberland Law Rev., 1977-78; contbr. articles on law to profl. jours. State civil litigation, Personal injury, Contracts commercial. Home: 2000 Brandon Circle Charlotte NC 28211 Office: BB&T Ctr 200 S Tryon St Suite 900 Charlotte NC 28202

EVELIUS, JOHN CHARLES, lawyer; b. Balt., May 21, 1926; s. Charles Carl and Gertrude (Brady) E.; m. Mary Agnes Kelly, Sept. 16, 1926; children—John Thomas, Joseph Charles, Mark Edward, Paul Francis, Mary Beth. A.B., Loyola Coll. Balt., 1949; J.D., U. Md., 1954. Bar: Md. 1954, U.S. Supreme Ct. 1973, U.S. Ct. Claims 1960, U.S. Dist. Ct. Md. 1958, Md. Ct. Appeals 1954. Mem. firm Gallagher, Evelius & Jones, Balt., 1962—, sr. ptnr., 1972—; grad. prof. Loyola Coll., Balt., 1981-82; dir. Light St. Savs. & Loan Assn. Trustee, Loyola Coll. Balt., Good Samaritan Hosp. of Md., Inc., Cath. High Sch. of Md. Served with USN, 1944-46. Mem. ABA, Am. Soc. Hosp. Attys., Assn. Trial Lawyers of Am., Nat. Assn. Coll. and Univ. Attys., Md. Bar Assn., Md. Trial Lawyers Assn., Balt. Bar Assn., U.S. Diocesan Attys. Assn. Democrat. Roman Catholic. Clubs: Barristers, K.C. Personal injury, Probate, Legal education. Address: 218 N Charles St Park Charles Baltimore MD 21201

EVERARD, GERALD WILFRED, lawyer, trust company executive; b. Green Bay, Wis., Sept. 25, 1952; s. Wilfred A. and Regina P. (Arendt) E.; m. Paula M. Devroy, Sept. 17, 1977. BA, St. Norbert Coll., 1974; JD, U. Wis., 1977. Bar: Wis. 1977. Assoc. Boaroman, Suhr, Curry & Field, Madison, Wis., 1977-81; trust officer 1st Wis. Nat. Bank, Madison, 1981—; law instr. U. Wis., Madison, 1985. Bd. dirs. Cen. YMCA, Madison, 1983—. Mem. Wis. Bar Assn., Dane County Bar Assn., ABA. Probate. Office: 1st Wis Nat Bank PO Box 7900 Madison WI 53707

EVERBACH, OTTO GEORGE, lawyer; b. New Albany, Ind., Aug. 27, 1938; s. Otto G. and Zelda Marie (Hilt) E.; m. Nancy Lee Stern, June 3, 1961; children: Tracy Ellen, Stephen George. B.S., U.S. Mil. Acad., 1960; LL.B., U. Va., 1966. Bar: Va. 1967, Ind. 1967, Calif. 1975, Mass. 1978. Counsel CIA, Langley, Va., 1966-67; corp. counsel Bristol-Meyers Co., Evansville, Ind., 1967-74, Alza Corp., Palo Alto, Calif., 1974-75; sec., gen. counsel Am. Optical Corp., Southbridge, Mass., 1976-81; assoc. gen. counsel Warner-Lambert Co., Morris Plains, N.J., 1981-83; v.p. Kimberly-Clark Corp., Neenah, Wis., 1984-86, sr. v.p., gen. counsel, 1986—. Served with U.S. Army, 1960-63. Mem. Am., Va., Ind., Calif. bar assns. Office: Kimberly-Clark Corp DFW Airport Station Box 619100 Dallas TX 75261-9100

EVERED, DONNA R., lawyer; b. Seattle, Apr. 24, 1955; d. J. Metz and Charlotte (Woosley) E. BBA, U. Wash., 1977, JD, 1982. Bar: Wash. 1982. Tax cons. Touche Ross & Co., Seattle, 1981-84, tax supr., 1984-86; tax supr. Benson & McLaughlin, Seattle, 1986—. Mem. Wash. State Bar Assn., Wash. Soc. CPA's, East King County Estate Planning Council, Am. Soc. Women Accts. (bd. dirs. 1985—). Personal income taxation, State and local taxation, Corporate taxation. Office: Benson & McLaughlin 401 2d Ave W Seattle WA 98119

EVERETT, C. CURTIS, lawyer; b. Omaha, Aug. 9, 1930; s. Charles Edgar and Rosalie (Cook) E.; m. Joan Rose Bader, Sept. 7, 1951; children: Jeffrey, Ellen, Amy, Jennifer. B.A. cum laude, Beloit Coll., 1952; J.D., U. Chgo., 1957. Bar: Ill. 1957. Since practiced in Chgo.; ptnr. Bell, Boyd, Lloyd, Haddad & Burns, 1965-81, successor firm Bell, Boyd & Lloyd, 1981—; v.p., sec., dir. H. Bader, Cons., Inc., Clearwater, Fla.; vis. com. U. Chgo. Law Sch., 1986—; lectr. Ill. Inst. Continuing Legal Edn. Editorial bd.: U. Chgo. Law Rev, 1956-57; contbr. articles to profl. jours. Chmn., So. suburban area Beloit Coll. Ford Found. challange program, 1964-65; pres. The Players, Flossmoor, 1970-71; bd. govs. Lake Shore Dr. Condominium Assn., 1986—. Served with AUS, 1952-54. Mem. ABA, Ill. Bar Assn., Chgo. Bar Assn., U. Chgo. Law Sch. Alumni Assn. (dir. 1973-76, pres. Chgo. chpt. 1979-80), Order of Coif, Sigma Chi, Phi Alpha Delta. Mem. Community Ch. (deacon). Clubs: Legal, Law, Monroe (bd. govs. 1976—), University (Chgo.). Lodge: Order Demolay (past master counselor Rock River chpt.). General corporate, Securities, Municipal bonds. Home: 1212 N Lake Shore Dr 26AS Chicago IL 60610 Office: 3 First Nat Plaza 70 W Madison St Chicago IL 60602

EVERETT, CARL BELL, lawyer; b. Plainfield, N.J., Mar. 23, 1947; s. Edward F. and Catherine (Bell) E.; m. Julie Elizabeth Lund, June 25, 1971; children: Andrew, Martha. BS Chem. Engring., MIT, 1969; JD, U. Houston, 1973. Bar: Tex. 1974, Del. 1974, U.S. Dist. Ct. Del. 1977, U.S. Ct. Appeals (6th cir.) 1977, U.S. Ct. Appeals (5th cir.) 1978, U.S. Ct. Appeals (1st cir.) 1979, U.S. Ct. Appeals (D.C. cir.) 1979. Sr. counsel E.I. du Pont de Nemours & Co. Inc., Wilmington, Del., 1974-86, Liebert, Short, FitzPatrick & Hirshland, Phila., 1986—. Environment. Home: 214 Elm Ave Swarthmore PA 19081 Office: Liebert Short FitzPatrick & Hirshland 1200 One Franklin Plaza Philadelphia PA 19103

EVERETT, ROBINSON OSCAR, judge, law educator; b. Durham, N.C., Mar. 18, 1928; s. Reuben Oscar and Kathrine McDiarmid (Robinson) E.; m. Linda Moore McGregor, Aug. 27, 1966; children: Robinson Oscar, James Douglas McGregor, Lewis Moore. A.B. magna cum laude, Harvard U., 1947, J.D. magna cum laude, 1950; LL.M., Duke U., 1959. Bar: N.C. 1950, D.C. 1954. Mem. faculty Law Sch., Duke U., Durham, N.C., 1950-51, 56—; commr. U.S. Ct. Mil. Appeals, Washington, 1953-55; chief judge U.S. Ct. Mil. Appeals, 1980—; practice law Durham, 1955-80; councilor N.C. State Bar Council, 1978-83; pres., dir. Triangle Telecasters, Durham, 1966-77. Author: Military Justice, 1956; assoc. editor Law and Contemporary Problems, 1950-51, 56-66; contbr. articles to legal jours. Chair, Durham Redevel. Commn., 1959-75. Served as 1st lt. USAF, 1951-53; to col. Res. (ret.). Mem. Am. Law Inst., Conf. Commrs. Uniform State Laws (life), Durham Bar Assn. (pres. 1976-77). Democrat. Presbyterian. Legal education. Office: US Ct Mil Appeals 450 E St NW Washington DC 20442 *

EVERETT, STEPHEN EDWARD, lawyer; b. Shreveport, La., Jan. 16, 1944; s. Rufus Webb and Myrtle (Morgan) E.; m. Patricia Hostetter, Jan. 19, 1965; children—Michael Stephen, Morgan Terez. B.A., La. Tech. U., 1965; J.D., Tulane U., 1967. Bar: La. 1967, U.S. Dist. Ct. (ea. dist.) La. 1968, U.S. Dist. Ct. (we. dist.) La. 1969, U.S. Ct. Appeals (5th cir.) 1976, U.S. Dist. Ct. (mid. dist.) La. 1982, U.S. Supreme Ct. 1983. Assoc. Montgomery, Barnett, Brown & Read, New Orleans, 1967-69, Gravel & Burnes, Alexandria, La., 1969-73; sole practice, Alexandria, 1973—. Mem. La. Trial Lawyers Assn., Assn. Trial Lawyers Am. Republican. Unitarian. Criminal, Civil rights, Federal civil litigation. Home: 8512 Fairway Dr Pineville LA 71360 Office: Stephen E Everett 827 Johnston St Alexandria LA 71301

EVERSBERG, HELEN M., lawyer. U.S. atty. we. dist. State of Tex., San Antonio. Office: John H Wood Jr Fed Bldg 655 E Durango Blvd San Antonio TX 78206 *

EVEY, MERLE KENTON, lawyer; b. Altoona, Pa., Oct. 9, 1930; s. Merle Houser and Dorothy Ellen (Miller) E.; m. Veronica Nuala Moran, Sept. 1, 1962; children: Eileen Veronica, Kathleen Marie. BA, Pa. State U., 1952; JD, Dickinson Sch. of Law, 1955. Bar: Pa. 1956, U.S. Dist. Ct. (we. dist.) Pa. 1959, U.S. Supreme Ct. 1959. Ptnr. Evey, Routch, Black, Dorezas, Magee & Andrews, Hollidaysburg, Pa., 1957—; bd. dirs. Hollidaysburg Trust Co., Penn Cen. Bancorp, Huntingdon, Pa. Solicitor County of Blair, Pa., 1978—, Blair County Hosp. Authority, Hollidaysburg, 1978—; bd. dirs., solicitor Home Nursing Affiliates, Altoona, Pa., 1978—. Served with U.S. Army, 1955-57. Mem. ABA, Blair County Bar Assn. (bd. govs. 1964-67, pres. 1982-83), Pa. Bar Assn. (ho. of dels. 1980-83, bd. govs. 1983-86). Republican. Methodist. Club: Spruce Creek (Pa.) Rod & Gun. Lodge: Masons. Avocation: golf. State civil litigation, General corporate, Probate. Home: PO Box 16 Elm St Sylvan Hills Hollidaysburg PA 16648 Office: Evay Routch Black et al 401 Allegheny St Hollidaysburg PA 16648

EWALT, HENRY WARD, lawyer; b. Pitts., July 3, 1940; s. Henry Ward and Jane Elizabeth (Stewart) E.; m. Mary Alice Jabsen, June 1, 1968; children: Andrew, Sarah. BA in Polit. Sci. cum laude, Allegheny Coll., 1962; MA in Polit. Sci., U. Mich., 1963, JD, 1966. Bar: U.S. Dist. Ct. Pa. 1966, Pa. 1967, U.S. Ct. Appeals (3d cir.) 1975, U.S. Supreme Ct. 1984. Field atty. NLRB, Pitts., 1966-71; ptnr. Reding, Blackstone, Rea & Stewart, Pitts., 1971-75; chief labor counsel Allegheny County, Pitts., 1971—; founder, pres. Brooks & Ewalt, Pitts., 1975-84; ptnr. Tucker Arensberg, P.C., Pitts.,

1984—. Author: Practical Planning-A How To Guide for Solos and Small Law Firms, 1985. Mem. Pitts. City Planning Commn., 1978-82; trustee Children's Home of Pitts., 1976-85; bd. dirs. Zoar Home, Pitts., 1984—; pres. Perry Hilltop Citizens Council, Pitts., 1970-76. Served to capt. U.S. Army, 1967-70, Vietnam. Decorated Bronze Star, Purple Heart. Mem. ABA (chmn. practice mgmt. div. econs. of law practice sect. 1986), Fed. Bar Assn. (past pres. Pitts. chpt.). Avocations: outdoor sports, gardening. Home: 4436 Mount Royal Blvd Allison Park PA 15101 Office: Tucker Arensberg PC 1200 Pittsburgh Nat Bldg Pittsburgh PA 15222

EWELL, A(USTIN) B(ERT), JR., lawyer; b. Elyria, Ohio, Sept. 10, 1941; s. Austin Bert and Mary Rebecca (Thompson) E.; m. Kristine Lynn Ballantyne, Feb. 14, 1976; children—Austin Bert III, Brice Ballantyne. B.A., Miami U., Oxford, Ohio, 1963; J.D., Hasting Coll. Law, U. Calif.-San Francisco, 1966. Bar: Calif. 1966, U.S. Dist. Ct. (ea. dist.) Calif. 1967, U.S. Supreme Ct. 1982, U.S. Ct. Appeals (9th cir.) 1967. Pres. A. B. Ewell, Jr., A. Profl. Corp., Fresno, 1984—; gen. counsel Kings River Water Assn., 1979—, Dudley Ridge Water Dist., 1980—, MidValley Water Dist., 1984—, Friant Water Users Authority, 1985—; pres. Western Water Recharge Corp., 1985—; chmn. San Joaquin River Flood Control Assn., 1984—; mem. task force on prosecution, cts. and law reform Calif. Council Criminal Justice, 1971-74; mem. Fresno Bulldog Found., Calif. State U. Mem. affiliated San Joaquin Valley Agrl. Water Com. 1979—; co-chmn. nat. adv. council SBA, 1981, 82, mem. 1981—; bd. dirs. Fresno East Community Ctr., 1971-73; mem. Fresno County Water Adv. Com., Fresno Community Council, 1972-73; chmn. various polit. campaigns and orgns., including Reagan/Bush, 1984, Deukmejian for Gov., 1986; mem. adv. com. St. Agnes Med. Ctr. Found., 1983—; trustee Fresno Met. Mus. Art, History and Sci. Mem. ABA (water resources com. of natural resources sect., real property probate and trust law sect.), Internat. Platform Assn., Phi Alpha Delta, Assn. Calif. Water Agys. (affiliate), U.S. Supreme Ct. Hist. Soc., Sigma Nu. Clubs: Downtown, Racquet (Fresno), Commonwealth (San Francisco), President's. Congregationalist. Real property, General corporate. Office: 83 E Shaw Ave Suite 203 Fresno CA 93710

EWIN, GORDON OVERTON, lawyer, farmer; b. New Orleans, June 1, 1923; s. James Perkins and Lucille Havard (Scott) E.; m. Katharine Elise Keller, Sept. 6, 1947; 1 dau., Katharine Adair. B.A., Tulane U., 1943, J.D., 1948; postgrad. Faculté de Droit, U. Paris, 1948-49. Bar: La. 1948, U.S. Dist. Ct. (ea. dist.) La. 1949, U.S. Ct. Appeals (5th cir.) 1949. Assoc. Milling, Saal, Saunders, Benson & Woodward, New Orleans, 1949-52; ptnr. Ewin & Robertson, New Orleans, 1952-55; staff atty. Humble Oil & Refining Co., New Orleans, 1955-59; ptnr. Chaffe, McCall, Phillips, Toler & Sarpy, New Orleans, 1959—; pres. Greenwood Planting Co., 1979—; dir. Farmers Bank & Trust of Cheneyville (La.). Bd. dirs. New Orleans Philharm. Orch., 1961; mem. Young Life Adv. Council, 1972; bd. dirs. Garden Dist. Assn., 1967-74, pres., 1973-74; bd. dirs. Friends of the Cabildo, 1976-82, pres., 1981-82. Served to lt. (j.g.) USNR, 1943-46; PTO. Mem. New Orleans Bar Assn. (treas.), La. Bar Assn., ABA. Republican. Episcopalian. (vestryman Trinity Ch. 1976-80). Clubs: La., Boston (New Orleans); Petroleum, Soc. Colonial Wars (past La. gov.). Oil and gas leasing, Probate, Real property. Home: 1220 Antonine St New Orleans LA 70115 Office: 210 Baronne St 1500 First NBC Bldg New Orleans LA 70112

EWING, KY PEPPER, JR., lawyer; b. Victoria, Tex., Jan. 7, 1935; s. Ky Pepper and Sallie (Dixon) E.; m. Almuth Rott, Apr. 6, 1963; children: Kenneth Patrick, Kevin Andrew, Kathryn Diana. B.A. cum laude, Baylor U., 1956; LL.B. cum laude, Harvard U., 1959. Bar: D.C. 1959, U.S. Supreme Ct 1963. Assoc. firm Covington & Burling, Washington, 1959-64; partner firm Prather, Seeger, Doolittle, Farmer & Ewing, Washington, 1964-77; dep. asst. atty. gen. antitrust div. Dept. Justice, Washington, 1978-80; partner firm Vinson & Elkins, Washington, 1980—; dir., sec. Washington Inst. Fgn. Affairs. Pres. Potomac Valley League, 1977, Carderock Springs Citizens Assn., 1975-78. Mem. ABA, D.C. Bar Assn., Fed. Bar Assn., Am. Soc. Internat. Law. Democrat. Episcopalian. Clubs: Metropolitan (Washington), 1925 F Street, City (Washington). Antitrust, Federal civil litigation, Environment. Home: 8317 Comanche Ct Bethesda MD 20817 Office: 1455 Pennsylvania Ave NW Washington DC 20004

EWING, LYNN MOORE, JR., lawyer; b. Nevada, Mo., Nov. 14, 1930; s. Lynn Moore and Margaret Ray (Blair) E.; m. Peggy Patton Adams, July 10, 1954; children: Margaret Grace, Melissa Lee, Lynn Moore. A.B., U. Mo., Columbia, 1952, J.D., 1954. Bar: Mo. 1954. Partner Ewing, Carter, McBeth, Smith, Gosnell, Vickers & Hoberock, Nevada, Mo.; trustee Mo. Law Sch. Found., 1974—, pres., 1981-85. Mem. Mo. Ho. of Reps., 1959-64; mem. Nevada City Council, 1967-73, mayor, 1979-70, 72-73; mem. Nevada Charter Commn., 1978-79, Mo. Land Reclamation Commn., 1971-75; bd. dirs. Nevada Hosp., 1974-83; bd. dirs., pres. Nev. Area Econ. Devel. Commn., 1985—; vestryman, sr. warden All Saints Episcopal Ch. Served to 1st lt. USAF, 1954-56. Recipient Legis. award St. Louis Globe-Democrat, 1960, 62; named Citizen of Year, Nevada Rotary Club, 1975. Mem. ABA, Fellows of Am. Bar Found. (life mem.), Am. Coll. Probate Counsel, Am. Coll. Mortgage Attys., Am. Judicature Soc., U.S. League Savs. Assn. (chmn. attys. com. 1977-79), Mo. Bar (adv. com. 1975-84, bd. govs. 1974-78), Mo. League Savs. Assns., Vernon County Bar Assn. Democrat. Episcopalian. Clubs: Nevada Rotary (pres. 1969-70), Nevada Country, Elks. Banking, General corporate, Insurance. Home: 146 Country Club Dr Nevada MO 64772 Office: 223 W Cherry St Nevada MO 64772

EWING, MARY ARNOLD, lawyer; b. Shreveport, La., Feb. 21, 1948; d. George and Christine (Cocek) Hengy; m. Robert Craig Ewing, Aug. 30, 1981; 1 child, Kyle Ross. BA, U. Colo., 1972; JD, U. Denver, 1975. Bar: Colo. 1975, U.S. Supreme Ct. 1979. Assoc. Johnson & Mahoney, Denver, 1975-80; ptnr. Branney, Hillyard, Ewing & Barnes, Englewood, Colo., 1980-85, Bucholtz, Bull & Ewing, Denver, 1985—; asst. prof. law U. Denver, 1977-78, part time prof. 1978—; mem. faculty Nat. Inst. Trial Advocacy, 1984-87; instr. nat. session 1984, 85, 87, Nat. Bd. Trial Advocacy, regional session, 1984, 85, 86, 87. Chmn. Denver County Task Force, 1976-77; treas. Cen. Com. 1st Congl. Dist., 1976-77; v.p. Young Rep. League Denver, 1975, pres. 1976; mem. govt. relations com. Jr. Symphony Guild, 1978—. Mem. ABA, Colo. Bar Assn. (ethics com.), Denver Bar Assn. (vice chmn. new lawyers assistance com. 1977), Colo. Women's Bar Assn., Internat. Platform Assn., Mountain States Combined Tng. Assn., Rocky Mountain Dressage Soc. (sec. High Plains chpt. 1979-80), Assn. Trial Lawyers Am., Colo. Trial Lawyers Assn. (bd. govs., chmn. interprofl. com. 1980, dir. 1981—), Am. Arbitration Assn., Am. Trakehner Assn., Rocky Mountain Trakehner Assn. (v.p. 1987), U. Denver Coll. Law Alumni Council, Kappa Beta Pi (pres. 1977-78). Club: Toastmasters; Arapahoe Hunt; Greenwood Athletic. Home: 816 W Quarry Rd Littleton CO 80124 Office: Bucholtz Bull & Ewing 1666 S University Blvd Denver CO 80210

EWING, ROBERT, lawyer; b. Little Rock, July 18, 1922; s. Esmond and Frances (Howell) E.; m. Elizabeth Smith, May 24, 1947; 1 child, Elizabeth Milbrey. B.A., Washington and Lee U., 1943; LL.B., Yale U., 1945. Bar: Conn. 1945. Assoc. Shipman & Goodwin, Hartford, Conn., 1945-50; partner Shipman & Goodwin, 1950—; asst. pros. atty. West Hartford, Conn., 1953-55; dir., asst. sec. H.W. Steane Co. Inc., Rocktide Inc.; dir., pres. Still Pasture Corp.; asst. sec. Linvar Marwin, Inc. Mem. U.S. Constitution Bicentennial Commn. of Conn.; incorporator Hartford Hosp., Mt. Sinai Hosp.; bd. dirs. Travelers Aid Soc. of Hartford, 1951-57, treas., 1954-57; bd. dirs. Family Service Soc., 1961-65; bd. dirs. Greater Hartford chpt. ARC, 1974—, chmn., 1977-79, also vice chmn. exec. and blood services coms.; bd. dirs. Conn. Pub. Expenditure Council, 1986—. Mem. ABA, Conn. Bar Assn. (chmn. fed. practice com. 1976-79, exec. com. corp. sect. 1981-85), Hartford County Bar Assn., Am. Law Inst., Conn. Hist. Soc. (trustee, v.p. 1982—, chmn. personnel com.), Newcomen Soc. N.Am. Congregationalist. (sr. deacon 1972-75). Clubs: Twentieth Century (pres. 1975-76), Hartford (counsel, ex officio bd. govs.), Mory's Assn, Dauntless, Rotary (pres. Hartford 1966-67). General corporate, Probate, Contracts commercial. Home: 28 Birch Rd West Hartford CT 06119 Office: 799 Main St Hartford CT 06103

EWING, WILLIAM HICKMAN, JR., U.S. attorney; b. Memphis, June 11, 1942; s. William Hickman and Addie Carolyn (Young) E.; m. Mary Clair Deyling, May 13, 1972; children: Jessica, Adam, Abigail. B.A., Vanderbilt U., 1964; J.D., Memphis State U., 1972. Bar: Tenn. 1972, U.S. Supreme Ct. 1978, U.S. Ct. Appeals, 6th cir. 1974. Asst. U.S. atty. Dept. Justice, Memphis, 1972-77; 1st asst. U.S. atty. Dept. Justice, 1977-81, U.S. atty., 1981—; mem. Nat. Econ. Crime Council. Served with USN, 1964-69, to capt. USNR. Mem. Memphis and Shelby County Bar Assn. (dir. young lawyers sect. 1974-75), ABA, Fed. Bar Assn. Criminal. Office: US Attys Office 1026 Fed Bldg 167 N Main St Memphis TN 38103

EXUM, JAMES GOODEN, JR., state chief justice; b. Snow Hill, N.C., Sept. 14, 1935; s. James Gooden and Mary Wall (Bost) E.; m. Judith McNeill Jamison, June 29, 1963; children—James Gooden, Steven Jamison, Mary March Williams. B.A., U. N.C. (1957), Chapel Hill; LL.B., N.Y. U., 1960. Bar: N.C. bar 1960. Law clk. to Justice Emery Denny, N.C. Supreme Ct., 1960-61; asso. firm Smith, Moore, Smith, Schell & Hunter, Greensboro, N.C., 1961-67; resident judge Superior Ct., 1967-74; assoc. justice N.C. Supreme Ct., Raleigh, 1975-86, chief justice, 1986—; mem. adj. faculty Law Sch. U. N.C. Rep. N.C. Gen. Assembly, 1967; vice chmn. central selection com. Morehead Scholarships. Served to capt. USAR, 1963-67. Recipient Disting. Service award Greensboro Jaycees, 1969, Psi Disting. Achievement and Service award Psi chpt. Sigma Nu, 1974. Mem. ABA (council criminal justice sect. 1981-85, chmn. ad hoc com. on death penalty costs), N.C. Bar Assn. (mem. com. on alternative dispute resolution 1985-87, appellate rules 1985-87), U. N.C. Alumni Assn. (pres.), U.S. Power Squadron. Democrat. Clubs: Raleigh Racquet, Capital City, Milburie Fishing, Watauga. Home: 2240 Wheeler Rd Raleigh NC 27607 Office: PO Box 1841 Raleigh NC 27602

EYERMAN, LINDA KATHLEEN, lawyer; b. Buffalo, Aug. 17, 1948; d. Constantine C. and Dorothy (Misner) Boyle; m. David L. Slader, Sept. 27, 1980; children: Jillian Eyerman, Anna Slader. Student, U. Leicester, Eng., 1968-69; BA, Elmira Coll., 1970; JD, U. Oreg., 1976. Bar: Oreg. 1976, U.S. Dist. Ct. Oreg. 1983. Staff atty. Met. Pub. Defender Service, Portland, Oreg., 1977-82; ptnr. Gaylord, Thomas & Eyerman, Portland, 1982—; chief atty. misdemeanor sect. Met. Pub. Defender Service, Portland, 1979-80, training dir., 1980-81. Mem. Oreg. Bar Assn., Assn. Trial Lawyers Am., Oreg. Trial Lawyers Assn. (lectr. 1985—), Oreg. Criminal Def. Lawyers Assn. (lectr. 1982-83), Oreg. Law Inst. (lectr. 1983-85). Democrat. Personal injury, Federal civil litigation, State civil litigation. Office: Gaylord Thomas & Eyerman 1400 SW Montgomery Portland OR 97201

EYNON, ERNEST ALFRED, II, lawyer; b. Cin., Jan. 2, 1944; s. Ernest E. and Joan (Babcock) E.; m. Angela Barrett; children: Teddy, May, Elizabeth, Barrett, Emily, Christina. BS, Williams Coll., 1966; JD, U. Cin., 1969. Bar: Ohio 1969, U.S. Dist. Ct. (so. dist.) Ohio 1970, U.S. Ct. Appeals (6th cir.) 1970, U.S. Supreme Ct. 1978. From assoc. to ptnr. Strauss & Troy, Cin., 1969—; bd. dirs. Am. Nursing Care Inc., Cin. Trustee Cin. Ballet Co., 1977-83, Cin. May Festival Assn., 1978—, Merchantile Library Assn., 1981—. Mem. ABA, Ohio Bar Assn., Cin. Bar Assn., Assn. Trial Lawyers Am. Republican. Episcopalian. Clubs: Cin. Country, Univ. (trustee 1983—). Federal civil litigation, State civil litigation, General corporate. Home: 2592 Perkins Ln Cincinnati OH 45208 Office: Strauss & Troy 201 E 5th St Cincinnati OH 45202

EZELL, KENNETH PETTEY, JR., lawyer; b. Murfreesboro, Tenn., June 9, 1949; s. Kenneth Pettey Sr. and Dorothy (Johnson) E.; m. Carol Anne Carter, Apr. 14, 1984. BA, U. South, 1971; MBA, Nat. U., 1976; JD, Vanderbilt U., 1979. Bar: Tenn. 1979. Assoc. Thompson & Crawford, Nashville, 1979-82, Bone & Woods, Nashville, 1982-83; ptnr. Bone, Langford & Armistead, Nashville, 1983—. Pres. Nashville br. Arthritis Found., 1986; bd. dirs. Legal Found. Inc., Nashville, 1985. Served to lt. USNR, 1972-76. Mem. ABA, Tenn. Bar Assn., Nashville Bar Assn., Nat. Assn. Bond Lawyers, Nashville Area Jr. C. of C. (legal counsel 1983). Republican. Presbyterian. Avocations: golf, basketball, softball. General corporate, Municipal bonds, Real property. Home: 711 Branch Creek Rd Nashville TN 37209 Office: Bone Langford & Armistead 2100 W End Ave Nashville TN 37203

EZELL, MICHAEL R., lawyer; b. Tyler, Tex., Jan. 11, 1944; s. Howard Lovelace and Elizabeth (Slawson) E.; m. Sharron Jarrett, Aug. 1, 1971; children: Stephen, Julie, Wendy. BS in Chemistry, Southwest Tex. State U., 1967; MA in Econs., St. Mary's U., San Antonio, 1970, JD, 1974. Bar: Tex. 1974, U.S. Dist. Ct. (so. dist.) Tex. 1975, U.S. Ct. Appeals (5th cir.) 1977, U.S. Supreme Ct. 1978. Ptnr. Koppel, Ezell, Jackson & Powers, Harlingen, Tex., 1974—. Pres. Arroyo Youth Soccer Club, Inc., Harlingen, Tex., 1982-84. Served to capt. USAF, 1968-77. Mem. ABA, Tex. Bar Assn., Cameron County Bar Assn. Lodge: Rotary. State civil litigation, Contracts commercial. Office: Koppel Ezell Jackson & Powers 312 E Van Buren Harlingen TX 78551

EZERSKY, WILLIAM MARTIN, lawyer; b. N.Y.C., Sept. 14, 1951; s. Abraham David and Ada Ezersky; m. Karen Gail Hecht, June 30, 1985. BA in Communications, Philosophy, Queens Coll., 1974; JD, Hofstra U., 1977. Bar: N.Y. 1979, U.S. Dist. Ct. (so. and ea. dists.) N.Y. 1979. Sole practice N.Y.C., 1979—. Mem. ABA. Bar Assn. City N.Y., N.Y. State Trial Lawyers Assn., N.Y. County Trial Lawyers Assn., Queens Bar Assn., Jewish Lawyers Guild. Democrat. Jewish. Lodge: Masons. Avocations: rowing, walking, sailing, tennis, swimming. Personal injury, Criminal, State civil litigation. Office: 3333 New Hyde Park Rd New Hyde Park NY 11042

EZRATTY, HARRY AARON, lawyer; b. N.Y.C., Aug. 25, 1933; s. Joseph Aaron and Mathilda (Samo) E.; m. Barbara Tasch; children—Laurie, Michelle. B.A., N.Y.U., 1955; grad. Bklyn. Law Sch., 1958. Bar: N.Y. 1958, P.R. 1970, D.C. 1971, Md. 1986. Ptnr. Rolnick, Tabak, Ezratty & Huttner, N.Y.C. and San Juan (P.R.), 1965-76; sole practice San Juan, 1976—. Head of Human Rights Com., San Juan, 1970-73; mem. Latin-Am. com. Anti-Defamation League. Mem. ABA, N.Y. State Bar Assn., Bronx Bar Assn., Assn. Trial Lawyers Am., Maritime Law Assn., Fed. Bar Assn., Md. Bar Assn., Authors' Guild Am. Author: How to Get Admitted to Other Jurisdictions, 1972, Seaman's Handbook of Rights, 1986; contbr. articles to legal jours. Admiralty, Federal civil litigation. Home: 664 McKinley 2 San Juan PR 00907 Office: 306 Ponce de Leon Suite 201 San Juan PR 00906

EZZELL, JAMES MICHAEL, lawyer; b. Borger, Tex., Nov. 15, 1950; s. Robert C. and Flora Katherine (Wallace) E.; m. Linda Christine Clark, Oct. 11, 1950; 1 child, Amy Elizabeth. BSEE, U. Houston; postgrad., Loyola U., New Orleans; JD, U. Houston. Bar: Tex. 1980, U.S. Dist. Ct. (we. dist.) Tex. 1980. Engr. Shell Oil Co., New Orleans and Houston, 1974-80; ptnr. Groce, Locke & Hubdon, San Antonio, 1980—. Mem. ABA, Tex. Bar Assn., Tex. Assn. Def. Counsel, Phi Kappa Phi, Phi Delta Phi, Tau Beta Pi. State civil litigation, Federal civil litigation, Personal injury. Office: Groce Locke & Hebdon 2000 First Bank Tower San Antonio TX 78205

EZZO, RALPH PATRICK, lawyer; b. Cleve., Aug. 4, 1934; s. Louis and Esther Marie (Fergus) E.; m. Carol Ann Jurenick, Aug. 18, 1956; children: Kimberly Ann, Carolyn Sue, Gina Marie. BSc, Ohio U., 1956; JD, U. Miami, 1959. Bar: Fla. 1959, Ohio 1980. Assoc. Sams, Anderson et al, Miami, Fla., 1959-62; ptnr. Highsmith & Ezzo, Miami, 1962-69; sole practice Miami, 1969-75, 83—, Cleve., 1980—; ptnr. Ezzo & Garel, Miami, 1975-83. Editor U. Miami Law Rev., 1957-59. Fellow Acad. Fla. Trial Lawyers; mem. Assn. Trial Lawyers Am., Cleve. Bar Assn., Dade County Bar Assn. Roman Catholic. Club: Lakewood Country (Westlake, Ohio). Personal injury. Home: 15600 SW 79th Ave Miami FL 33157 Office: 825 S Bayshore Dr Tower III Suite 1650 Miami FL 33131

FAALEVAO, AVIATA FANO, attorney general; b. Fagalele, Leone, Am. Samoa, Mar. 3, 1946; s. Faalevao Amitoelau Fano and Safua Akulu Pepe; m. Lia Sausau Faamausili, June 29, 1970; children: Aviata Jr., Sualua, Lora-Tufanua, Lia-Chalene, SauSau, Tafamoa. Student, Warren Wilson Coll.; BS, U. Tenn., 1969; JD, Valparaiso U., 1974. Bar: Pa. 1974, Am. Samoa 1975. Asst. atty. gen. Am. Samoa, 1975-78, dep. atty. gen., 1978-80, atty. gen., 1980—. V.p. PTA Pago Pago Sch., 1978—. Mem. Nat. Assn. Attys. Gen. Mem. Congregational Christian Ch. Am. Samoa. Criminal, General practice, Personal injury. Office: Office of Atty Gen, Pago Pago American Samoa

FABE, DANA ANDERSON, public defender; b. Cin., Mar. 29, 1951; d. George and Mary Lawrence (Van Antwerp) F.; m. Randall Gene Simpson, Jan. 1, 1983; 1 child, Amelia Fabe Simpson. B.A., Cornell U., 1973; J.D., Northeastern U., 1976. Bar: Alaska 1977, U.S. Supreme Ct. 1981. Law clk. to justice Alaska Supreme Ct., 1976-77; staff atty. pub. defenders State of Alaska, 1977-81; dir. Alaska Pub. Defender Agy., Anchorage, 1981—. Named Alumna of Yr., Northeastern Sch. Law, 1983. Mem. Alaska Bar Assn., Anchorage Assn. Women Attys. Criminal. Office: Pub Defender 900 W Fifth Ave Suite 200 Anchorage AK 99501

FABER, PETER LEWIS, lawyer; b. N.Y.C., Apr. 29, 1938; s. Alexander W. and Anne L. Faber; m. Joan Schuster, June 14, 1959; children: Michael, Julia, Thomas. AB, Swarthmore Coll., 1960; LLB, Harvard U., 1963. Bar: N.Y. 1964. Assoc. Wiser, Shaw, Freeman, Ickes & Williams, Rochester, N.Y., 1963-65; assoc. Parker, Chapin & Flattau, N.Y.C., 1965-66; ptnr. Harter, Secrest & Emery, Rochester, N.Y., 1966-82; ptnr. Winthrop, Stimson, Putnam & Roberts, N.Y.C., 1982-84, Kaye, Scholer, Fierman, Hays & Handler, N.Y.C., 1984—; mem. adv. com. Miami U. Inst. Estate Planning, N.Y. U. Ann. Inst. on Fed. Taxation. Chmn. Rochester Econ. Devel. Com., 1979-82; pres. Rochester Philharmonic Orch., Inc., 1980-82; bd. dirs. Met. Rochester Devel. Council, Harley Sch., 1978-81; mem. fin. com. Monroe County Democratic Party, 1979-82. Fellow Am. Bar Found., Am. Coll. Tax Counsel. Mem. ABA (chmn. com. corp. stockholder relationships tax sect. 1980-82, liaison to IRS for North Atlantic region, vice chmn. spl. com. on integration 1979-81, vice chmn. tax sect. 1986—), N.Y. State Bar Assn. (chmn. sect. taxation 1976-77, exec. com. sect. taxation 1969—), Monroe County Bar Assn., Am. Law Inst. (tax project adv. group), Rochester Area C. of C. (trustee 1980-82). Contbr. articles to profl. jours. Corporate taxation, State and local taxation. Home: 300 Central Park W New York NY 10024 Office: 425 Park Ave New York NY 10022

FABIAN, JOANNE FRANCES, lawyer; b. Bridgeton, N.J., Apr. 14, 1934; d. Joseph Anderson and Lucy (Garrison) Newkirk; 1 child, Gabrielle. BS, Ursinus Coll., 1955; MA, Seton Hall U., 1962; JD, U. Calif., San Francisco, 1974. Bar: Calif. 1974. Biochemist Merck & Co., Rahway, N.J., 1955-68; with administrv. dept. Merck Internat., Rahway, 1968-71; ptnr. McNeil, Silveira & Fabian, San Rafael, Calif., 1974—; bd. dirs., sec. New Horizons Savs., San Rafael, Filmvest, Inc., San Rafael. Bd. dirs., pres. Planned Parenthood of Marin/Sonoma, San Rafael, 1984—. Real property, Banking, General corporate. Office: McNeil Silveira & Fabian 55 Professional Ctr Pkwy San Rafael CA 94903

FACER, ERIC FOUTS, lawyer; b. Urbana, Ill., July 28, 1953; s. Clarence E. and Mary Jane (Fouts) F.; m. Vivian Margaret Crawford, Apr. 28, 1976; children: Ryan, Alisha, Danielle. BA, Brigham Young U., 1977; JD, Georgetown U., 1980, LLM in Taxation, 1983. Bar: D.C. 1980, U.S. Dist. Ct. D.C. 1981. Assoc. Cadwalader et al, Washington, 1980-83; tax counsel Satellite Bus. Systems, McLean, Va., 1983-86; assoc. Lewis, Mitchell & Moore, Vienna, Va., 1985-86, ptnr., 1987—. Sr. editor Georgetown U. Law and Policy Rev., 1979. Mem. ABA. Republican. Mormon. Avocations: flying, golf, tennis, piano. Corporate taxation, State and local taxation. Home: 11814 Pittson Rd Wheaton MD 20906 Office: Lewis Mitchell & Moore 8000 Towers Crescent Dr Suite 800 Vienna VA 22180

FACEY, JOHN ABBOTT, III, lawyer; b. Springfield, Mass., June 14, 1950; s. John Abbott and Mary Agnes (Murphy) F.; m. Patricia Marie Otto, Sept. 27, 1975; children: Justin Abbott, Christopher John. BA, Coll. of the Holy Cross, 1972; JD, Suffolk U., 1975. Bar: Mass. 1975, Vt. 1976, U.S. Dist. Ct. Vt. 1977. Assoc. Bishop & Crowley, Rutland, Vt., 1975-81; ptnr. Keyser, Crowley, Banse & Facey, Rutland, 1981—. Corporator Rutland Regional Med. Ctr.; bd. dirs. South Vt. chpt. March of Dimes. Mem. ABA, Mass. Bar Assn., Vt. Bar Assn., Rutland County Bar Assn., New Eng. Land Title Assn. Republican. Roman Catholic. Lodge: Rotary. Local government, Real property. Home: 82 Davis St Rutland VT 05701 Office: Keyser Crowley Banse et al 29 S Main St PO Box 975 Rutland VT 05701

FACHER, IRWIN LEE, lawyer; b. Newark, Sept. 13, 1939; s. Saul and Sylvia (Brody) F.; m. Marylou Portnoy, May 29, 1966; children: Scott Alan, Betsy Joan. AB, Dartmouth Coll., 1961; JD, Harvard U., 1964. Bar: N.J. 1964, U.S. Dist. Ct. N.J. 1964. Ptnr. Zucker, Facher & Zucker, West Orange, N.J., 1965—. Counsel South Orange Bd. Adjustment, N.J., 1984—. Mem. ABA (editor The Brief 1976-81, vice chmn. com. products gen. liability and consumer law 1976-81). Democrat. Jewish. Club: Dartmouth (Essex and Morris). Insurance, Personal injury, Real property. Home: 52 Collinwood Rd Maplewood NJ 07040 Office: Zucker Facher & Zucker 100 Executive Dr West Orange NJ 07052

FACTOR, MAX, III, lawyer, investment advisor; b. Los Angeles, Sept. 25, 1945; s. Sidney B. and Dorothy (Levinson) F.; m. Susan Barg, June 19, 1966; 1 child, Jennifer Lee. B.A. in Econs. magna cum laude, Harvard Coll., 1966; J.D., Yale U., 1969. Bar: Calif. 1970, U.S. Ct. Appeals (6th cir.) 1971, U.S. Dist. Ct. (cen. dist.) Calif. 1971. Law clk. U.S. Ct. Appeals (6th cir.), 1969-71; exec. dir. Calif. Law Ctr., Los Angeles, 1973-74; dir. Consumer Protection Sect., Los Angeles City Atty., 1974-77; pres. MF Capital Ltd., Beverly Hills, Calif., 1978-86; ptnr. Cooper, Epstein & Hurewitz, Beverly Hills, Calif., 1986—; expert witness numerous state and fed. bds., 1974-78; guest lectr. UCLA, U. So. Calif., Los Angeles County Bar Assn., Calif. Dept. Consumer Affairs, 1974-76; hearing examiner City of Los Angeles, 1975. Contbr. articles to profl. jours. Bd. dirs. Western Law Ctr. for the Handicapped, Los Angeles, 1977-79, Beverly Hills Unified Sch. Dist., 1979-83; pres. Beverly Hills Bd. Edn., 1983; bd. councilors U. So. Calif. Law Ctr., Los Angeles, 1983—. Recipient scholarship award Harvard Coll., 1965; Max Factor III Day proclaimed in his honor Beverly Hills City Council, 1979; recipient Disting. Service to Pub. Edn. award Beverly Hills Bd. Edn., 1979. Mem. Los Angeles County Bar Assn. (chmn. various coms. 1976-78), Beverly Hills C. of C. (pres.-elect 1986—), Beverly Hills Edn. Found. (pres. 1977-79). Democrat. Jewish. General corporate, Probate, Real property. Office: Cooper Epstein & Hurewitz 9465 Wilshire Blvd Suite 800 Beverly Hills CA 90212

FACUSSÉ, ALBERT SHUCRY, lawyer; b. Tegucigalpa, Honduras, Feb. 10, 1921; s. Nicholas and Maria (Barjum) F.; m. May Bandak, Dec. 22, 1946 (dec.); children—Vivian Neuwirth, Denise Lentz. J.D. cum laude, Loyola U., New Orleans, 1943. Bar: La. 1957. Sole practice, New Orleans, 1957—; pub. speaker. Mem. La. State Bar Assn., ABA, Internat. Platform Assn. Democrat. Roman Catholic. Comment editor Loyola U. Law Rev., 1943. General practice, Family and matrimonial, Personal injury. Home: 6731 Manchester St New Orleans LA 70126 Office: 234 Loyola Ave Suite 832 New Orleans LA 70112

FADAOL, ROBERT FREDERICK, lawyer; b. Opelousas, La., Oct. 3, 1939; s. Joseph Charles and Marie (Nassar) F.; m. Carolyn Ann Chapman, Jan. 1, 1970; children: Charles, Tracy, Robert. BS in Pharmacy, Auburn U., 1962; JD, Loyola U., New Orleans, 1970. Bar: La. 1971, U.S. Dist. Ct. (ea. and mid. dists.) La. 1971, U.S. Ct. Appeals (5h cir.) 1971, U.S. Dist. Ct. (we. dist.) La. 1975, U.S. Supreme Ct. 1976, U.S. Ct. Appeals (11th cir.) 1980. Sole practice New Orleans, 1971—; judge ad hoc Parish Ct., 1986. Served to 2nd lt. U.S. Army, 1962-67. Mem. ABA, La. Bar Assn., Assn. Trial Lawyers Am., La. Trial Lawyers Assn. Republican. Roman Catholic. General corporate, Insurance, Probate. Home: 348 Terry Pkwy Gretna LA 70056 Office: 1108 Stumpf Blvd Gretna LA 70054

FADEL, WILLIAM ISAAC, lawyer; b. Cleve., June 23, 1943; s. Fadel A. and Betty (Jacob) F.; m. Gail Joan Vanraalte, July 20, 1968; children: Matthew, Timothy, Michael, Rebecca. BA, Case Western Res. U., 1965, JD, 1969. Bar: Ohio 1969, U.S. Dist. Ct. (no. dist.) Ohio 1971, U.S. Ct. Appeals (6th cir.) 1982, U.S. Supreme Ct. 1985. Law clk. Cuyahoga County Ct. Common Pleas, Cleve., 1969-71; trial atty. Pub. Defenders Office, Cleve., 1971-72; house counsel Internat. Union Operating Engrs., Cleve., 1972-77; ptnr. Wuliger, Fadel & Beyer, Cleve., 1977—; Mem. AFL-CIO Lawyer Coordinating Com. Editor: Labor Lookout (newsletter), 1986. Legal counsel St. George Antiochian Orthodox Ch., Cleve., 1980—; legal counsel River's Bend Park Assn., Cleve., 1983-85. Mem. Ohio Bar Assn., Cuyahoga County Bar Assn. Democrat. Antiochian Orthodox Christian. Avocations: racquetball, golf. Labor, Federal civil litigation, General practice. Office: Wuliger Fadel & Beyer 1340 Sumner Ct Cleveland OH 44115

FAGAN, JOHN ERNEST, lawyer; b. Phila., June 30, 1949; s. George Vincent and Ernestine (Hudak) F. BA with highest honors, U. Notre Dame, 1971; JD, Northwestern U., 1974; LLM, NYU, 1986. Bar: Ill. 1974, Wis. 1977, N.Y. 1979. Assoc. McDermott Will & Emery, Chgo., 1974-76; internat. tax analyst Allis-Chalmers Corp., Milw., 1976-78; tax counsel Mobil Corp., N.Y.C., 1978—; bd. dirs. Overseas Products Inc., N.Y.C. Mem. ABA, Internat. Fiscal Assn., Can. Tax Found., Internat. Bar Assn., Am. Petroleum Inst. (com. mem.). Private international, Corporate taxation. Office: Mobil Corp 150 E 42d St New York NY 10017

FAGAN, PETER THOMAS, lawyer; b. Evanston, Ill., Nov. 20, 1948; s. Peter Thomas and Elisabeth (Bashe) F.; m. Virginia Ann Schurr, Apr. 8, 1982; children: Wendy Lynn, Carrie Jayne. BBA in Acctg., U. Notre Dame, 1970, JD, 1973; LLM with honors, George Wash. U., 1976. Bar: Ill. 1973, Ind. 1973, U.S. Ct. Mil. Appeals 1973, U.S. Ct. Appeals (7th cir.) 1979, U.S. Dist. Ct. (so. dist.) Ind. 1973, U.S. Dist. Ct. (no. dist.) Ill. 1978, U.S. Ct. Claims 1978. Assoc. Brydges, Riseborough, Morris, Franke & Miller, Waukegan, Ill., 1979-81; assoc. gen. counsel Magnavox, Ft. Wayne, Ind., 1981-85; chief counsel McDonnell Douglas Helicopter Co., Mesa, Ariz., 1985—. Served to capt. U.S. Army, 1973-79. Mem. ABA. Government contracts and claims, General corporate.

FAGAN, THOMAS JAMES, lawyer; b. Marquette, Mich., Feb. 6, 1915; s. William Thomas and Kathryn Mary (Reidy) F.; m. Elizabeth Ann Bowlen, July 17, 1944; children—W. Thomas, Ann, Mary, James, Paul, John, Michael. B.A., No. Mich. U., 1935; J.D., U. Mich., 1940. Bar: Mich. 1940. Trust officer Central Trust Co., Lansing, Mich., 1946-47; asst. atty. gen. State of Mich., Lansing, 1947-51; asst. sec., counsel Motor Wheel Co., Lansing, 1951-61; sole practice, Lansing, 1961—; U.S. commr., Lansing, 1962-65. Served to lt. A.C., USNR, 1941-45, PTO. Mem. Ingham County Bar Assn. Republican. Roman Catholic. Club: Walnut Hills Country (bd. dirs. 1962-70) (East Lansing, Mich.). Lodges: Elks, K.C. Probate, Public utilities, Personal injury. Home: 2593 Woodhill Okemos MI 48864 Office: 935 N Washington Ave Suite 201 Lansing MI 48906 also: PO Box 16027 Lansing MI 48901

FAGEN, LESLIE GORDON, lawyer; b. N.Y.C., Apr. 12, 1950; s. Herman and Estelle (Garber) F. BA, Yale U., 1971; JD, Columbia U., 1974. Bar: N.Y. 1975, U.S. Dist. Ct. (so. and ea. dists.) N.Y. 1975, U.S. Ct. Appeals (2d cir.) 1975, U.S. Supreme Ct. 1978, D.C. 1985. Law clk. to presiding judge U.S. Dist. Ct. (ea. dist.) N.Y., Bklyn., 1975; assoc. Milbank, Tweed, Hadley & McCloy, N.Y.C., 1975-76; from assoc. to ptnr. Paul, Weiss, Rifkind, Wharton & Garrison, N.Y.C., 1976—; adj. faculty CCNY, NYU. Mem. Assn. of Bar of City of N.Y. Federal civil litigation, State civil litigation. Office: Paul Weiss Rifkind Wharton & Garrison 1285 Ave of Americas New York NY 10019

FAGERBERG, ROGER RICHARD, lawyer; b. Chgo., Dec. 11, 1935; s. Richard Emil and Evelyn (Thor) F.; m. Virginia Fuller Vaughan, June 20, 1959; children: Steven Roger, Susan Vaughan, James Thor, Laura Craft. B.S. in Bus. Adminstrn., Washington U., St. Louis, 1958, J.D., 1961, postgrad., 1961-62. Bar: Mo. 1961. Grad. teaching asst. Washington U., St. Louis, 1961-62; assoc. firm Rassieur, Long & Yawitz, St. Louis, 1962-64; ptnr. Rassieur, Long, Yawitz & Schneider and predecessor firms, St. Louis, 1965—. Mem. exec. com. Citizens' Adv. Council Pkwy. Sch. Dist., 1974—, pres.-elect, 1976-77, pres., 1977-78; bd. dirs. Parkway Residents Orgn., 1969—, v.p., 1970-73, pres., 1973—; scoutmaster Boy Scouts Am., 1979-83; Presbyn. elder, 1976—, pres. three local congs. 1968-70, 77-78, 83-84. Mem. ABA, Mo. Bar Assn., St. Louis Bar Assn., Christian Bus. Men's Com. (bd. dirs. 1975-78, 87—), Full Gospel Bus. Men's Fellowship, Christian Bus. Men's. Com. (bd. dirs. 1975-78), Order of Coif, Omicron Delta Kappa, Beta Gamma Sigma, Pi Sigma Alpha, Phi Eta Sigma, Phi Delta Phi, Kappa Sigma. Republican. Lodges: Kiwanis (past bd. dirs.), Masons, Shriners. Home: 13812 Clayton Rd Town and Country MO 63011 Office: Rassieur Long Yawitz & Schneider 1150 Boatmen's Tower Saint Louis MO 63102

FAGG, GEORGE GARDNER, judge; b. Eldora, Iowa, Apr. 30, 1934; s. Ned and Arleene (Gardner) F.; m. Jane E. Wood, Aug. 19, 1956; children: Martha, Thomas, Ned, Susan, George, Sarah. B.S. in Bus. Adminstrn., Drake U., 1965, J.D., 1956. Bar: Iowa 1958. Ptnr. Cartwright, Druker, Ryden & Fagg, Marshalltown, Iowa, 1958-72; judge Iowa Dist. Ct., 1972-82, U.S. Ct. Appeals (8th cir.), 1982—; mem. faculty Nat. Jud. Coll., 1979. Mem. Am. Judicature Soc., ABA, Iowa Bar Assn., Order of Coif. Office: 301 US Courthouse E 1st and Walnut Sts Des Moines IA 50309

FAGGERT, DAVID YOUNG, lawyer; b. Richmond, Va., Sept. 29, 1947. BA, U. Va., 1969, JD, 1974. Bar: Va. 1974, U.S. Dist. Ct. (ea. dist.) Va. 1975, U.S. Ct. Appeals (4th cir.) 1975. Law clk. to presiding justice Va. Supreme Ct., Richmond, 1974-75; assoc. Kaufman, Oberndorfer & Spainhour, Norfolk, Va., 1975-77; ptnr. Scanelli & Shapiro, Norfolk, 1977—. Served to 1st lt. U.S. Army, 1969-71, Vietnam. Mem. ABA, Va. Bar Assn., Norfolk Bar Assn., Portsmouth Bar Assn., Phi Beta Kappa, Phi Eta Sigma. Real property, Banking, Contracts commercial. Home: 4740 Eastwind Rd Virginia Beach VA 23464 Office: Scanelli & Shapiro 1600 United Va Bank Bldg Norfolk VA 23510

FAGIN, GEORGE J., lawyer, author; b. N.Y.C., Mar. 6, 1908; s. Louis and Rose Fagin; m. Maxine Appleman, 1940; children: David H., Ronald. LLB, U. Okla., 1930. Bar: Okla. 1930, U.S. Supreme Ct. 1940. Asst. atty. gen. State of Okla., 1930-35; ptnr., mcpl. bond atty. J. Berry King & George J. Fagin, 1935-47; sr. ptnr. Fagin, Brown, Bush, Tinney, Kiser & Rogers, 1948-80; sole practice, author 1980—. Mem. Anti Defamation League, B'nai B'rith, 1950-55; pres. Emanuel Synagogue, 1960-61; bd. dirs. NCCJ, 1960-66. Mem. ABA (chmn. com. 1972-75), Oklahoma County Bar Assn. Democrat. Municipal bonds. Office: 1900 First National Ctr Oklahoma City OK 73102

FAHEY, JOSEPH EDMUND, lawyer; b. Syracuse, N.Y., June 30, 1949; s. James Joseph and Mary Gertrude (McGuire) F.; m. Katharine Olivia Hamler, Aug. 16, 1975; children: Meghan, Katharine. AA, Onondaga Community Coll., 1969; BS, U. Tenn., 1971; JD, Syracuse U., 1975. Bar: N.Y. 1976, U.S. Dist. Ct. (no. dist.) N.Y. 1977, U.S. Ct. Appeals (2d cir.) 1980, U.S. Supreme Ct. 1980. Staff atty. Hiscock Legal Aid Soc., Syracuse, 1975-79; sole practice Syracuse, 1979-80; ptnr. Wiles, Wiles & Fahey, Syracuse, 1980-83, Wiles, Fahey & Lynch, Syracuse, 1980—. Bd. dirs. Onondaga County Met. Water Bd., Syracuse, 1979—, Salt City Performing Arts Ctr., Syracuse, 1986—; del. 1972 Dem. Nat. Convention, Miami Beach, Fla.; vice chmn. Onondaga County Dem. County Com., Syracuse, 1984—; commr. City of Syracuse Bd. of Edn., 1986—. Mem. N.Y. State Bar Assn., Onondaga County Bar Assn. (chmn. criminal law com. 1976—, judiciary com. 1984—, bd. dirs. 1986—),N.Y. State Defenders Assn., Nat. Assn. Criminal Def. Lawyers (strike force com. 1985—). Democrat. Roman Catholic. Club: Syracuse Track. Avocations: long distance running, photography. Criminal, Federal civil litigation, State civil litigation. Home: 411 Robineau Rd Syracuse NY 13207 Office: Wiles Fahey & Lynch 1010 State Tower Bldg Syracuse NY 13202

FAHEY, ROBERT FRANCIS, lawyer; b. Peoria, Ill., Sept. 11, 1939; s. Edward J. and Catherine M. (Waterloo) F.; m. Anne M. Ferrell, Aug. 24, 1963; children—Bonnie, Rosemarie, Robert. B.S. in Fin., U. Ill., 1962; J.D., DePaul U., 1965. Bar: Ill. 1965, U.S. Dist. Ct. (cen. dist.) Ill. 1977, U.S. Supreme Ct. 1982. Atty. law dept. Chgo. Bd. Edn., 1967; atty. legal dept. Employers Ins. Wausau, Chgo., 1967-69; compensation atty. Caterpillar Tractor Co., Peoria, Ill., 1969—; instr. bus. law Harper Coll., Elk Grove Village, Ill., 1968-69. Served as capt. U.S. Army, 1965-67. Mem. ABA, Ill. Bar Assn., Peoria County Bar Assn., Ill. Workers' Compensation Lawyers Assn.; Am. Legion, Peoria Area Radio Club, Phi Delta Theta, Alpha Kappa Psi. Clubs: Peoria Boat (commodore 1977-78) Ill. Valley Yacht, K.C. Workers' compensation, Personal injury. Home: 903 W Kensington Dr Peoria IL 61614 Office: 100 NE Adams Peoria IL 61629

FAHNER, TYRONE CLARENCE, lawyer, former state attorney general; b. Detroit, Nov. 18, 1942; s. Warren George and Alma Fahner; B.A., U. Mich., 1965; J.D., Wayne State U., 1965; LL.M., Northwestern U., 1971; m. Anne Beauchamp, July 2, 1966; children—Margaret, Daniel, Molly. Admitted to Mich. bar, 1968, Ill. bar, 1969, Tex. bar 1984; mem. criminal def. litigation unit Northwestern U., 1969-71; asst. U.S. atty. for No. Dist. Ill., Chgo., 1971-75, dep. chief consumer fraud and civil rights, 1973-74, chief ofcl. corruption, 1974-75; mem. firm Freeman, Rothe, Freeman & Salzman, Chgo., 1975-77; dir. Ill. Dept. Law Enforcement, 1977-79; partner firm Mayer, Brown & Platt, Chgo., 1979-80, 83—; atty. gen. State of Ill., Springfield, 1980-83; instr. John Marshall Law Sch., 1973—. Ford Found. fellow, 1969-71. Mem. Am. Bar Assn., Ill. Bar Assn., Mich. Bar Assn., Chgo. Bar Assn., Tex. Bar Assn., Am. Judicature Soc., Nat. Assn. Attys. Gen. Republican. Lutheran. Antitrust, Federal civil litigation, Securities. Office: Mayer Brown & Platt 190 S LaSalle St Chicago IL 60603

FAIGIN, ARNOLD JEFFREY, lawyer, sports agent; b. Cleve., Aug. 11, 1947; s. Howard B. and Naomi F. BA, Ohio State U., 1970; JD, Case Western Res. U., 1973. Bar: Ohio 1973, U.S. Dist. Ct. (no. dist.) Ohio 1980. Aide to U.S. Senator Howard Metzenbaum, Cleve., 1973; asst. prosecutor Cuyahoga County Pros. Atty.'s Office, Cleve., 1974-78; sole practice, Cleve., 1978-80; pres. Lustig Pro Sports, Akron, Ohio, 1980-87, A.J. Faigin Co. LPA, Akron, 1980-87. Campaign mgr. Schecter for U.S. Congress, Cleve., 1979. Served to 1st lt. U.S. Army, 1973. Federal civil litigation, Criminal, Sports. Office: 24718 Hazelmate Rd Beechwood OH 44122

FAIGNANT, JOHN PAUL, lawyer, educator; b. Proctor, Vt., Mar. 24, 1953; s. Joseph Paul and Ann (DeBlasio) F.; m. Sandra Ellen Hoinski, Nov. 27, 1976; children: Janelle, Melissa. BA, U. New Haven, 1974; JD, George Mason U., 1978. Bar: Va. 1978, Vt. 1979, U.S. Dist. Ct. Vt. 1979, U.S. Ct. Appeals (4th cir.) 1979. Assoc. Griffin & Griffin, Rutland, Vt., 1978-79; ptnr. Miller, Norton & Cleary, Rutland, 1979—; adj. prof. Coll. St. Joseph, Rutland, 1982—. Supr. solid waste dist. Rutland County, 1986—. Mem. Va. Bar Assn., Vt. Bar Assn., Assn. Trial Lawyers Am. Roman Catholic. Avocation: antique trucks. Insurance, Personal injury, Environment. Home: 5 Shepard Ln Rutland VT 05701 Office: Miller Norton & Cleary 110 Merchants Row Rutland VT 05701

FAILE, WENDELL WAYNE, lawyer; b. Birmingham, Ala., May 8, 1939; s. Jason Alby and Dorothy Genieve (Crews) F.; m. Chestene Duncan, Feb. 9, 1959 (div. Feb. 1986); children: Stephen, John, Lawrence, Jason; m. Teresa Elizabeth Heller, July 4, 1986. AA, SUNY, Albany, 1973, BS, 1976; JD with honors, Western State U., Fullerton, Calif., 1978. Bar: Calif. 1979, U.S. Dist. Ct. (cen. dist.) Calif. 1979. Sole practice Long Beach, Calif., 1979—; ptnr. Hawk Devel., Long Beach, 1986—, Charwen Properties, Long Beach, 1984-86. Cen. committeeman Reps., Long Beach, 1982-84. Served with USAF, 1953-54. Fellow Am. Acad. Neurol. and Orthopedic Surgeons; mem. Long Beach Bar Assn., Assn. Trial Lawyers Am., Calif. Trial Lawyers Assn. Republican. Avocations: writing, history. Personal injury, Workers' compensation, Insurance. Office: 3629 Atlantic Ave Long Beach CA 90807

FAIN, JOEL MAURICE, lawyer; b. Miami Beach, Fla., Dec. 11, 1953; s. William Maurice and Carolyn Genievive (Baggett) F.; m. Moira Joan Slocum, June 15, 1974; children: Hannah Ruth, Dylan Michael, Rachel Joan. BA, Yale U., 1975; JD, U. Conn., 1978. Bar: Conn. 1978, U.S. Dist. Ct. Conn. 1978. Assoc. Kahan, Kerensky, Capossela, Levine & Breslau, Vernon, Conn., 1978-83, ptnr., 1984—; bd. dirs. Conn. Legal Services, Middletown, Conn. Chmn. Youth Adv. Bd., Tolland, Conn., 1983—. Mem. ABA, Conn. Bar Assn., Tolland County Bar Assn., Assn. Trial Lawyers Am., Conn. Trial Lawyers Assn. Democrat. Congregationalist. Lodge: Lions (sec. 1985—). Personal injury, State civil litigation, Federal civil litigation. Home: 76 Tolland Green Tolland CT 06084 Office: Kahan Kerensky Capossela Levine & Breslau 45 Hartford Turnpike Vernon CT 06066

FAIN, MIKE, judge; b. Miami, Fla., July 15, 1946; s. James Edward and Laura Bennett (Turner) F.; m. Catherine Amelia Smith, Mar. 29, 1969; children: Paul Augustus, James Marshall. BS in Polit. Sci., Yale U., 1968; JD, U. Pa., 1972. Bar: Ohio 1973, U.S. Dist. Ct. (so. dist.) Ohio 1973, U.S. Ct. Appeals (6th cir.) 1980. Assoc. Estabrook, Finn & McKee, Dayton, Ohio, 1973-77; ptnr. Bogin & Patterson, Dayton, 1977-87; judge Ohio Ct. Appeals (2d dist.), Dayton, 1987—; bd. commrs. character and fitness Ohio Supreme Ct., 1979-85 . Chmn. various coms. Dayton United Way, 1983-85 ; gen. counsel Montgomery County Democratic Com., Ohio, 1982-86 . Served with USNR, 1969-71. Recipient cert. of merit Epilepsy Found. Am., 1979. Mem. Dayton Bar Assn., Ohio State Bar Assn., ABA (jud. qualification and selection com. 1983—), Leadership Dayton Alumni Assn. (chmn. 1982). Methodist. Lodge: Kiwanis. Avocation: computer and non-computer simulations. Judicial administration, Jurisprudence, State civil litigation. Home: 110 Greenmount Blvd Dayton OH 45419 Office: Ohio Ct Appeals (2d dist) 41 N Perry St Dayton OH 45402

FAINSBERT, ANN RUBENSTEIN, lawyer; b. Los Angeles, June 13, 1944; d. Victor G. and Florence (Fox) Rubenstein); m. Henry Lewin, July 18, 1965 (div. Feb. 1986); children: Debra, Michelle; m. Stephen B. Fainsbert, Dec., 1986. BA, Mills Coll., 1964; JD, Glendale Coll. Law, 1978. Bar: Calif. 1979. Ptnr. Lewin & Lewin, Pasadena, Calif., 1979-85; sole practice Rolling Hills, Calif., 1985—. Panel mem. South Bay Jewish Ctr., Mediation, Torrance, Calif., 1985-86; bd. dirs. Palos Verdes Peninsula Symphony Assn., Rolling Hills, 1986—. Mem. South Bay Bar Assn., South Bay Women Lawyers, Los Angeles Women Lawyers, Palos Verdes Peninsula Horsemens Assn. (pres. 1983-86). Democrat. State civil litigation, Real property, Family and matrimonial. Home: 4736 Ferncreek Dr Rolling Hills Estates CA 90274 Office: 4030 Palos Verdes Dr N #108 Rolling Hills Estates CA 90274

FAINTER, JOHN WELLS, JR., lawyer; b. Pecos, Tex., Apr. 20, 1939; s. J. Wells and Ruth (Alexander) F.; m. Frances Barclay, June 7, 1969; 1 child, John Wells III. BA, U. Tex., 1962, LLB, 1963. Bar: Tex. 1963, U.S. Dist. Ct. (so., ea. and we. dists.) Tex. 1979, U.S. Supreme Ct. 1979, U.S. Ct. Appeals (10th cir.) 1980, U.S. Ct. Appeals (5th and 11th cirs.) 1981. Investigator state securities bd. State of Tex., Austin, 1963-64, asst. atty. gen., 1964-69; v.p. Underwood, Neuhaus and Co., Inc., Houston, 1969-79; 1st asst. atty. gen. State of Tex., Austin, 1979-83, sec. of state, 1983-84; ptnr., dir. Reynolds, Allen & Cook Inc., Austin, 1984-86; ptnr. McCall, Parkhurst & Horton, Austin, 1986—; bd. dirs. Allied Bank Austin, Guardian Svgs., Houston. Mem. adv. council coll. of bus. adminstrn. found. U. Tex., Austin, 1983—; chmn. ex-students pub. affairs assn. U. Tex., Austin, 1978—, Pub. Safety Commn., Austin, 1985—; bd. dirs. U. Tex. Law Sch. Assn., Austin, 1980—. Mem. U. Tex. Law Sch. Alumni Assn. (chmn. bd. of visitors 1982—), Order of Coif. Democrat. Episcopalian. Clubs: Headliners, Country Club of Austin, University, Metropolitan. Avocation: golf. Administrative and regulatory, Legislative, Municipal bonds.

FAIRBANK, ROBERT HAROLD, lawyer; b. Northampton, Mass., Mar. 4, 1948; s. William Martin and Jane (Davenport) F.; m. Karen Genkins, May 29, 1976; children: Sarah Julia, David King. A.B. in Polit. Sci., Stanford U., 1972; M.L.S., U. Calif.-Berkeley, 1973; J.D., NYU, 1977. Bar: Calif. 1977, U.S. Dist. Ct. (cen. and no. dists.) Calif. 1978. Ptnr., Gibson, Dunn & Crutcher, Los Angeles, 1985—. Author: Effective Pretrial and Trial Motions, 1983. Mem. editorial bd. NYU Law Rev., 1975-76. Mem. Assn. Bus. Trial Lawyers (bd. govs. 1984-85, treas. 1986-87, sec. 1987—), Los Angeles County Bar Assn. (fed. cts. com. 1983-85). Federal civil litigation, State civil litigation, Securities. Home: 609 S Burlingame Ave Los Angeles CA 90049 Office: Gibson Dunn & Crutcher 333 S Grand Ave Los Angeles CA 90071

FAIRBANKS, ROBERTA R(ONYA), lawyer; b. Los Angeles, July 21, 1945; d. Paul and Ethel R. (Brownstein) Stein; m. Aaron H. Fairbanks, Dec. 29, 1963; children: Joel Paul, Rachel Ilene. BA, Calif. State U., Los Angeles, 1975; JD, Southwestern U. Sch. Law, 1978. Bar: Calif. 1980, U.S. Dist. Ct. (cen. dist.) Calif. 1980, Wis. 1982. Assoc. Wilson, Elser, Edelman & Dicker, Los Angeles, 1980-81; atty. The Trane Co., La Crosse, Wis., 1981-83, sr. atty., 1983—. Mem. ABA, Calif. Bar Assn., Def. Research Inst. Avocation: gourmet cooking. Antitrust, General corporate, Labor. Home: 1220 King St La Crosse WI 54601 Office: The Trane Co Div of Am Standard Inc 3600 Pammel Creek Rd La Crosse WI 54601

FAIRCHILD, RAYMOND FRANCIS, lawyer; b. Springfield, Ill., June 29, 1946; s. Francis M. and Estelle G. Fairchild; m. Ann Louise Templeton, Dec. 28, 1968. BA, U. Ill., 1968; JD, Ind. U., 1971. Bar: Ind. 1971, U.S. Dist. Ct. (so. dist.) Ind. 1971. Sole practice Indpls., 1971—. Mem. Assn. Trial Lawyers Am., N.Y. State Trial Lawyers Assn., Ind. Trial Lawyers Assn. Club: Manor House, Skyline (Indpls.). Personal injury, State civil litigation, Federal civil litigation. Office: 246 N College Ave Indianapolis IN 46202

FAIRLAMB, MILLARD SCHUYLER, lawyer; b. Telluride, Colo., Nov. 2, 1942; s. Charles Nutter and Ethel Faye (Schuyler) F.; m. Melanie Springer, Aug. 16, 1969; children: Elizabeth, Laura Rose. BA, U. Denver, 1965, JD, 1968. Bar: Colo. 1968, U.S. Dist. Ct. Colo. 1968. Ptnr. Fairlamb & Fairlamb, Delta and Telluride, Colo., 1968—. Pres. Delta County Hist. Soc., 1970-83; elder Delta Presbyn. Ch., 1985—. Recipient cert. excellence in bills and notes Bancroft Whitney Pub. Co., 1968. Mem. Colo. Bar Assn., Delta County Bar Assn., 7th Jud. Dist. Bar Assn, Order St. Ives, Delta C. of C. (past bd. dirs.). Lodges: Rotary, Elks, Masons (master 1971-72). Avocations: hunting, bowling, hiking, skiing, horseback riding. Probate, Real property. Home: PO Box 289 Delta CO 81416 Office: Fairlamb & Fairlamb 540 Main Delta CO 81416

FAISON, WILLIAM FRANKLIN, II, elec. equipment mfg. corp. exec., lawyer; b. Jersey City, Apr. 7, 1933; s. John Butler and Mary Elizabeth (Murphy) F.; m. Susan Preston, June 20, 1959; children—John, Prudence, Dulcie. Student Princeton U., 1951-54; B.S., Columbia U., 1958; LL.B., U. Va., 1961. Bar: Va. 1961, N.Y. 1963, U.S. dist. ct. (so. dist.) N.Y. 1968, U.S. Ct. Apls. (2d cir.) 1966, U.S. Sup. Ct. 1967. Law clk. to judge U.S. Dist. Ct. N.J., 1961-63; assoc. Haight, Gardner, Poor & Havens, N.Y.C., 1963-68; atty. Commonwealth Oil Refining Co., Inc., N.Y.C., 1968-70; counsel, assoc. gen. counsel Gen. Electric Credit Corp., Stamford, Conn., 1970-78, counsel Gen. Electric Co., Fairfield, Conn., 1978-86; counsel Gen. Electric Co., Schenectady, N.Y., 1986—. Served with AUS, 1954-56. Mem. ABA, Va. State Bar, N.Y. State Bar Assn. Republican. Unitarian-Universalist. General corporate, Administrative and regulatory, Antitrust. Home: 1175 Stratford Rd Schenectady NY 12308 Office: Gen Electric Co 1 River Rd Schenectady NY 12345

FAISS, ROBERT DEAN, lawyer; b. Centralia, Ill., Sept. 19, 1934; s. Wilbur and Theresa Ella (Watts) F.; m. Barbara L. Roventini, Jan. 28, 1967; children—Michael Dean, Robert Mitchell, Philip Grant. B.A., Am. U., 1969, J.D., 1972. Bar: Nev. 1972, D.C. 1973, U.S. Dist. Ct. Nev. 1973, U.S. Supreme Ct. 1977, U.S. Ct. Appeals (9th cir.) 1978. City editor Las Vegas Sun, 1957-58; asst. exec. sec. Nev. Gaming Commn., Las Vegas, 1962; exec. asst. to gov. of Nev., 1963-67; asst. to Pres. Lyndon B. Johnson, 1968-69; ptnr. Lionel Sawyer & Collins, Las Vegas, 1973—; co-dir. ann. libel seminar Soc. Profl. Journalists. Recipient Bronze medal Dept. of Commerce, 1972. Mem. ABA (chmn. gaming law com. 1985-86), Nev. Bar Assn., Clark County Bar Assn., Internat. Assn. Gaming Attys. (charter trustee, pres. 1984-85), Sigma Delta Chi. Democrat. Author: (with others) Legalized Gaming in Nevada—Its History, Economics and Control, 1963; also articles. Administrative and regulatory, Legislative, Libel. Office: 1700 Valley Bank Plaza Las Vegas NV 89101

FALCON, RAYMOND JESUS, JR., lawyer; b. N.Y.C., Nov. 17, 1953; m. Debra Mary Bomeisl, June 4, 1977; children: Victoria Marie, Mark Daniel. BA, Columbia U., 1975; JD, Yale U., 1978. Bar: N.Y. 1979, U.S. Dist. Ct. (so. and ea. dist.) N.Y. 1979, U.S. Ct. Appeals (D.C. and 2d cirs.) 1983. Assoc. Webster and Sheffield, N.Y.C., 1978-82; ptnr. Falcon and Hom, N.Y.C., 1982-85; atty. Degussa Corp., Teterboro, N.J., 1985—; exec. v.p., bd. dirs., cons. IBG, Ltd., N.Y.C., 1984—; corp. counsel Village of Port Chester, N.Y., 1987—. Contbr. articles to profl. jours. Dem. candidate Town Justice, Town of Rye, N.Y., 1983; Dem. judicial del., Westchester, N.Y., 1984—. Mem. ABA, N.Y. State Bar Assn., Bar Assn. City of N.Y., Fed. Bar Council, Assn. Trial Lawyers Am. Clubs: Yale (N.Y.C.); Columbia Alumni of Westchester County (v.p., dir. 1983—). General corporate, Contracts commercial, Real property. Home: 1 Halstead Ave Port Chester NY 10573 Office: Degussa Corp Rt 46 at Hollister Rd Teterboro NJ 07608

FALCONE, RICHARD EDWARD, lawyer; b. N.Y.C., Apr. 27, 1945; s. John R. and Helen (Stucchio) F.; m. Karyn Louise Glassman, July 25, 1970; children: Jennifer, Mary. BA, NYU, 1965; JD, Fordham U., 1968. Bar: N.Y. 1969, Colo. 1972, U.S. Dist. Ct. Colo. 1972, U.S. Ct. Appeals (10th cir.) 1985. With Colo. Title, Colorado Springs, 1971-72; assoc. L.E. Addy, Colorado Springs, 1972-75; sole practice Colorado Springs, 1975-79, 1985—; ptnr. Falcone & Alexander, Colorado Springs, 1979-85. Mem. Colo. Bar Assn., El Paso County Bar Assn., Assn. Trial Lawyers Am., colo. Trial Lawyers Assn. Lutheran. Workers' compensation, Personal injury, Bankruptcy. Office: 740 Citadel Dr E Suite 205 Colorado Springs CO 80904

FALES, HALIBURTON, 2D, lawyer; b. N.Y.C., Aug. 7, 1919; s. DeCoursey and Dorothy Mildred (Mitchell) F.; m. Katharine Ladd, Dec. 27, 1941; children: Nancy, Haliburton, Priscilla, Lucy, William E. Ladd. Student, Harvard U., 1938-41; LL.B., Columbia U., 1947. Bar: N.Y. 1948, U.S. Supreme Ct. 1957, D.C. 1974. Assoc. firm White & Case, N.Y.C., 1947-58; ptnr. firm White & Case, 1959—; counsel Frick Collection; spl. master Appellate div. 1st dept. N.Y. State Supreme Ct. Contbr. articles to profl. jours. Trustee, pres. Pierpont Morgan Library; vice chmn. St. Barnabas Hosp.; trustee Victoria Found.; sr. warden St. Luke's Ch.; bd. dirs. Union Theol. Sem., Legal Aid Soc., Vols. for Legal Service, Inc. Served to lt. comdr. USNR, 1941-45. Fellow Am. Bar Found., N.Y. Bar Found. (dir.), Inst. Judicial Administration, Am. Coll. Trial Lawyers; mem. Albert Gallatin Assos., Am. Bar Assn., Am. Judicature Soc., Am. Law Inst. (life), Am. Soc. Internat. Law, Assn. Bar City N.Y. (life), Internat. Bar Assn. (patron), Internat. Law Assn., Internat. Legal Aid and Defender Assn., N.Y. County Lawyers Assn., N.Y. State Bar Assn. (pres. 1983-84). Home: Pottersville Rd Gladstone NJ 07934 Office: White & Case 1155 Ave of Americas New York NY 10036

FALEY, R(ICHARD) SCOTT, lawyer; b. Trenton, N.J., Aug. 18, 1947; s. Henry and Winifred (Goeke) F.; m. Josepha Ann Bartlett, Aug. 29, 1970; children: Scott Joseph, Zachary Lorin. J.D., Georgetown U., 1972; LL.M., George Washington U., 1975. Bar: D.C. 1973, U.S. Tax Ct. 1973, U.S. Dist. Ct. D.C. 1973. Assoc., ptnr. Danzansky, Dickey, Tydings, Quint & Gordon, Washington, 1972-78; prin. R. Scott Faley, P.C., Washington, 1978—; dir. Fed. Employees News Digest, Inc., Fairfax, Va., 1980—; dir., officer NCC Trout Unltd., 1985—. Inst. for Safety Analysis, Inc., Rockville, Md., 1980—. Contbr. articles to profl. jours. Mem. instl. rev. com. Sibley Meml. Hosp., Washington, 1980—. Served to capt. USAF, 1974. Mem. Fed. Bar Assn., ABA, Alpha Phi Omega, Phi Alpha Delta. Roman Catholic. Club: Univ. (Washington). Pension, profit-sharing, and employee benefits, Estate planning, Corporate taxation. Home: 25 Primrose St Chevy Chase MD 20815 Office: R Scott Faley PC 1706 New Hampshire Ave NW Washington DC 20009

FALGOUT, WOLLEN J., judge; b. Gheens, La., Nov. 2, 1927; s. Horace J. and Adail (Matherne) F.; m. Wanda Leslie, Oct. 26, 1952; children—Jane Ellen, Bill, Elizabeth, Lauren Ann, Kathleen, Robyn, James Leslie. B.A., La. State U., 1949, LL.B., 1951. Bar: La. Sole practice, Raceland, La., 1951-53, Thibodaux, 1953-76; city atty., Thibodaux, 1956-75; 1st asst. dist. atty. 17th Jud. Dist., 1964-67; judge La. Dist. Ct. 17th Jud. Dist., Thibodaux, 1976—. Mem. La. Ho. of Reps., 1960-64. Mem. La. State Bar Assn. Democrat. Clubs: Lions, Raceland Riding. Home: PO Box 126 Thibodaux LA 70302

FALK, GLENN PHILLIP, lawyer, educator; b. Providence, Apr. 13, 1946; s. Benjamin and Bella (Volpe) F.; m. Cheryl Faye Falk, July 24, 1969; children: Jodele, Kelly, Glenn Jr., Tiffany, Courtney, Tyler. AA, Miami-Dade Jr. Coll., 1966; BA, U. Miami, 1969, JD, 1973. Bar: Fla. 1973, U.S. Dist. Ct. (so. dist.) Fla., U.S. Ct. Claims, U.S. Ct. Appeals (5th and 11th cirs.). Police officer Coral Gables (Fla.) Police Dept., 1969-73; from assoc. to ptnr. Preddy, Kutner & Hardy, Miami, Fla., 1973-83; ptnr. Parenti & Falk P.A., Miami, 1983—; adj. prof. U. Miami, Coral Gables, 1981-86. Named one of Outstanding Young Men in Am. Coral Gables Jaycees, 1972. Mem. ABA, Fla. Bar Assn. (grievance com.), Dade County Bar Assn. (community relations com. young lawyers sect.), Dade County Def. Bar Assn., Assn. Trial Lawyers Am., Am. Arbitration Assn., Fla. Def. Lawyers Assn., Dade County Assn. Chiefs of Police (legal advisor), Phi Kappa Phi. Republican. Roman Catholic. Avocations: jogging, karate. State civil litigation, In-

surance, Personal injury. Office: Parenti & Falk PA 44 W Flagler St #1150 Miami FL 33130

FALK, ROBERT HARDY, trial lawyer; b. Houston, Dec. 27, 1948; s. Arnold Charles and Sara Holmes (Pierce) F.; m. Donna Kay Watts, Aug. 18, 1973; children: Dorian Danielle, Dillon Holmes. BS summa cum laude, U. Tex., 1971; BA cum laude, Austin Coll., 1972; JD, U. Tex., 1975. Bar: Tex. 1975, U.S. Dist. Ct. (so. dist. Tex.) 1975, U.S. Patent Office, U.S. Ct. Appeals (5th cir.) 1976, Ct. Customs and Patent Appeals 1976, U.S. Ct. Appeals (D.C. cir.) 1977, N.C. 1979, U.S. Dist. Ct. (we. dist. N.C.) 1982, U.S. Ct. Appeals (fed cir.) 1982, U.S. Ct. Appeals (5th cir.) 1983, U.S. Ct. Internat. Trade 1985. Process engr. Exxon Co., USA, Baytown, Tex., 1971-72; atty. Pravel, Wilson & Gambrell, Houston, 1975-77; patent and trademark counsel Organon Inc. div. Akzona, Inc., Asheville, N.C., 1977-84; ptnr. Hubbard, Thurman, Turner & Tucker, Dallas, 1984—; pres. Robert Hardy Falk, P.C. Pres. Haw Creek Vol. Fire Dept., Asheville, 1979-84; deacon Cen. Christian Ch., Dallas, 1985—. Fellow U. Tex., 1972. Mem. ABA, Am. Patent Law Assn., Am. Trial Lawyers Assn., Dallas Patent Law Assn., Carolina Patent Law Assn., Houston Bar Assn., Asheville Bar Assn. Republican. Club: University (Dallas). Avocation: golf. Patent, Trademark and copyright, Federal civil litigation. Home: 2116 Tiburon Carrollton TX 75006 Office: Hubbard Thurman Turner Tucker 2100 One Galleria Tower Dallas TX 75240

FALK, VICTOR S., III, lawyer; b. Madison, Wis., Mar. 20, 1945; s. Victor S. Jr. and Marjorie Jane (Shearer) F.; m. Linda R. Spooner, June 26, 1971; children: Christian V., Megan E. AB, Princeton U., 1971; JD, U. Wis., 1973; LLM in Taxation, U. Miami, Coral Gables, 1974. Bar: Fla. 1975, Wis. 1975, U.S. Dist. Ct. (we. dist.) Wis. 1975. Assoc. gen. counsel, asst. sec. Wometco Enterprises, Inc., Miami, Fla., 1975-84; v.p., sec., gen. counsel Wometco Cable TV, Inc., Miami, 1985—; sec., gen. counsel Wometco Broadcasting Co., Inc., Miami, 1985—. Served to specialist 5th class U.S. Army, 1967-68. Mem. ABA, Dade County Bar Assn., Dade Corp. Counsel Assn. (sec., bd. dirs. 1980-81). Republican. Clubs: Coral Oaks Tennis, Mont. Tennis (Miami, Fla.), Thiebeau Hunt (Wis.). General corporate, Entertainment, Corporate taxation. Home: 8951 SW 82d St Miami FL 33173 Office: Wometco Cable/Wometco Broadcasting 316 N Miami Ave Miami FL 33128

FALKIN, JEFFREY CURTIS, lawyer; b. N.Y.C., May 1, 1943; s. Leo Eli and Sylvia J. Falkin; m. Rochelle G. Tonkon; 1 dau., Lisa Mary. B.S., Cornell U., 1965; J.D., Syracuse U., 1968; LL.M., Georgetown U., 1971. Bar: N.Y. 1969. With NLRB, 1968-79, supervisory atty., Phila., 1976-79; labor counsel Ingersoll Rand Co., Woodcliff Lake, N.J., 1979—. Mem. ABA. Contbr. articles to profl. jours. Labor. Office: Ingersoll Rand Co Woodcliff Lake NJ 07675

FALKSON, SUSAN DORY, lawyer; b. N.Y.C., Mar. 20, 1948; d. Leo and Mildred (Novick) Rashkin; m. Joseph L. Falkson, May 22, 1971; 1 child, Adam L. BA, NYU, 1968; MS, U. Mich., 1969, JD, 1977. Bar: D.C. 1977, U.S. Dist. Ct. D.C. 1978, U.S. Ct. Appeals (D.C. cir.) 1979, U.S. Ct. Claims 1981. Systems analyst Ann Arbor (Mich.) Computer Corp., 1969-71, EPA, Washington, 1971-74; assoc. Shaw, Pittman, Potts & Trowbridge, Washington, 1977-81, Willkie, Farr & Gallagher, Washington, 1981-85; assoc. gen counsel Electronic Data Systems Corp., Bethesda, Md., 1985—. Mem. Computer Law Forum, Nat. Contracts Mgmt. Assn., Order of Coif, Phi Beta Kappa. Government contracts and claims, Computer. Home: 907B Seneca Rd Great Falls VA 22066 Office: Electronic Data Systems Corp 6430 Rockledge Dr Bethesda MD 20817

FALLMAN, JAMES MITCHELL, JR., lawyer; b. Kansas City, Mo., Oct. 24, 1944; s. James Mitchell Sr. and Ima L. (Allen) F.; children: James Mitchell III, Tamra, John, Jennifer. BA with honors, U. Nev., 1965; MA, U. Calif., Davis, 1967; JD, U. of Pacific, 1974; AA with honors, Am. River Coll., 1977. Bar: Nev. 1974, Calif. 1975, U.S. Ct. Appeals (9th cir.) 1975, U.S. Supreme Ct. 1977. Ptnr. Moe & Fallman, Sacramento, Calif., 1974-77; asst. dist. atty. Humboldt County, Nev., 1977; ptnr. Fallman & Janof, Sacramento, 1978—; instr. Humphreys Coll. Law, Stocton, Calif., 1975-77, 78-80, Nat. U., Sacramento, 1982-84; judge pro tem Sacramento Mcpl. Ct., 1981—, Small Claims Ct., Sacramento, 1981—. Mem. ABA, Nev. Bar Assn., Calif. Bar Assn., Sacramento Bar Assn. Lodge: Masons. State civil litigation, Criminal, Workers' compensation. Office: Fallman & Janof 2131 Capitol Ave SUite 205 Sacramento CA 95816

FALLON, JOHN FRANCIS, lawyer; b. White Plains, N.Y., Jan. 16, 1950; s. Walter Joseph and Marie (McKenna) F.; m. Jane Cook, June 22, 1974; children: Kerry Elizabeth, Eileen Noel, Katelyn Marie. BA, Fairfield U., 1971; JD, Fordham U., 1976. Bar: Conn. 1976, U.S. Dist. Ct. Conn. 1976. Assoc. Hershberg, Pettingill, Greenwich, Conn., 1976-78, Whitman & Ransom, Stamford, Conn., 1978-80; ptnr. Trager & Trager, P.C., Fairfield, Conn., 1981—; majority counsel judiciary com. Conn. Gen. Assembly, Hartford, 1979, Conn. State Senate, Hartford, 1980. Mem. Fairfield Bd. Edn., 1978-84, Fairfield Police Commn., 1985—. Served with USAR, 1971-77. Mem. ABA, Conn. Bar Assn., Assn. Trial Lawyers Am., Fairfield U. Alumni Assn. (v.p. 1984—). Democrat. Roman Catholic. Club: Fairfield Chamber (pres. 1986—). Avocation: jogging. State civil litigation, Condemnation, Real property. Office: Trager & Trager PC 1305 Post Rd Fairfield CT 06430

FALLON, JOHN JOSEPH, lawyer; b. New Rochelle, N.Y., Feb. 2, 1923; s. Francis X. and Beatrice (Hume) F.; m. Ethel Mary Schwartz, Dec. 27, 1948; children—Michael Brian, Kevin Christopher, Moira Anne, Mary Patricia, John Hume. A.B., U. Notre Dame, 1948; J.D., Cornell U., 1951. Bar: Mo., Kans. 1951. Assoc. Stinson, Mag, Thomson, McEvers and Fizzell, Kansas City, Mo., 1951-54; ptnr. Fallon Guffey and Jenkins and predecessors, Kansas City, Mo., 1955-69; counsel Popham, Conway, Sweeny, Fremont & Bundschu, Kansas City, Mo., 1970-78; ptnr. Fallon and Sappington and predecessors, Kansas City, Mo., 1979—; founding pres. Nat. Catholic Reporter Pub. Co., 1964-68. Co-chmn. Kansas City region NCCJ, 1966-68; pres. Mo. C. of C., 1967-69; trustee Avila Coll., 1982-86; mem. Jackson County Bond Adv. Com., 1967-72; co-chmn. Mo. Lawyer's Com. for Re-election Pres., 1972. Served with AUS. Decorated Bronze Star, Purple Heart. Health, Banking, General corporate. Home: 2029 W 96th St Leawood KS 66206 Office: Fallon & Sappington 9233 Ward Pkwy Suite 200 Kansas City MO 64114

FALLON, WILLIAM HUME, lawyer; b. Grand Rapids, Mich., Oct. 23, 1956; s. Francis Xavier and Rita Katherine (Kelly) F.; m. Mary Theresa Pintar, Aug. 4, 1979; children: Michael, Emily, Brian. BA, U. Notre Dame, 1977; MA, U. Wis., 1978; JD, U. Mich., 1981. Bar: Mich. 1981, U.S. Dist. Ct. (we. dist.) Mich. 1981, U.S. Ct. Appeals (6th cir.) 1981. Assoc. Miller, Johnson, Snell & Cummiskey, Grand Rapids, 1981—. Exec. bd. dirs. West Mich. Shores council Boy Scouts Am., Grand Rapids, 1982—. Mem. ABA (litigation, labor and employment sects.), State Bar of Mich. (labor relations sect.), Grand Rapids Bar Assn. Roman Catholic. Avocations: outdoor sports, gardening, woodworking. Labor, Federal civil litigation, Civil rights. Home: 526 Lakeside Dr NE Grand Rapids MI 49503 Office: Miller Johnson Snell & Cummiskey 800 Calder Plaza Bldg Grand Rapids MI 49503

FALLS, CRAIG THOMAS, lawyer; b. Dallas, Oct. 5, 1952; s. Carl Thomas and Agnes Frances (Clayton) F.; m. Karen Pitts, Dec. 23, 1978; children: Taylor Keegan, Adam Thomas. BS, Stephen F. Austin State U., 1976, MS, 1978; JD magna cum laude, St. Mary's U., San Antonio, 1982. Bar: Tex. 1982, U.S. Dist. Ct. (no. dist.) Tex. 1983. Jud. law clk. to assoc. justice State of Tex., San Antonio, 1982-83; assoc. Moore & Peterson, Dallas, 1983—. Mem. ABA, Tex. Bar Assn., Dallas Bar Assn., Dallas Young Lawyers Assn. Real property, Financial institutions. Office: Moore & Peterson 2800 First City Centre Dallas TX 75201

FALLS, RAYMOND LEONARD, JR, lawyer; b. Youngstown, Ohio, Feb. 24, 1929; s. Raymond Leonard and Vernita Belle (Bowden) F.; m. Alice Van Fleet, June 22, 1952; children: Janette Rae, Nancy Margaret, Raymond Taylor, Thomas Alan, Lawrence David. B.A., Coll. of Wooster, 1950; LL.B., Harvard U., 1953. Bar: N.Y. 1957, U.S. Supreme Ct. 1961. Law clk. to judge U.S. Ct. Appeals 2d Cir., 1955-56; assoc. Cahill, Gordon & Reindel, N.Y.C., 1956-63, ptnr., 1963—; assoc. adj. prof. NYU Law Sch., 1967-73. Mem. Mayor's Task Force on Reorgn. Govt., N.Y.C, 1965-66. Mem. Am. Coll. Trial Lawyers, ABA, Assn. Bar City N.Y. Federal civil litigation, State civil litigation, Antitrust. Office: Cahill Gordon & Reindel 80 Pine St New York NY 10005

FALSGRAF, WILLIAM WENDELL, lawyer; b. Cleve., Nov. 10, 1933; s. Wendell A. and Catherine J. F.; children: Carl Douglas, Jeffrey Price, Catherine Louise. A.B. cum laude, Amherst Coll., 1955; J.D., Case Western Res. U., 1958. Bar: Ohio 1958, U.S. Supreme Ct. 1972. Ptnr. Baker & Hostetler, Cleve., 1971—; chmn. vis. com. Case Western Res. U. Law Sch., 1973-76. Trustee Case Western Res., 1976—, chmn. bd. overseers, 1977-78; trustee Cleve. Health Mus. Recipient Disting. Service award; named Outstanding Young Man of Year Cleve. Jr. C. of C., 1962. Fellow Am. Coll. Probate Counsel, Am. Bar Found., Ohio Bar Found.; mem. ABA (chmn. young lawyers sect. 1966-67, mem. ho. of dels. 1967-68, 70—, bd. govs. 1971-75, pres. elect 1984-85, pres. 1985-86, bd. dirs., v.p., treas. Am. Bar Endowment 1974-84, chmn. standing com. on scope and correlation of work 1978-79), Ohio Bar Assn. (mem. council of dels. 1968-70), Cleve. Bar Assn. (trustee 1979-82), Amherst Alumni Assn. (pres. N.E. Ohio 1964). Clubs: Union, Canterbury Golf. Environment, General corporate, Probate. Home: 616 North St Chagrin Falls OH 44022 Office: 3200 National City Ctr Cleveland OH 44114

FALSTAD, DAVID BERGFELD, manufacturing company executive, lawyer; b. Eau Claire, Wis., May 15, 1936; s. Clarence Henry and Rose Marie (Bergfeld) F.; m. Carol Joanne Spurgeon, Sept. 2, 1962; children—Kristin, Ann, Becky. B.S., U. Wis.-Madison, 1958, J.D., 1963. Bar: Wis. 1963. Atty. Continental Ill. Bank, Chgo., 1964-65; atty. Grede Industries, Inc., Milw., 1965-69; atty. J.I. Case Co., Racine, Wis., 1969-73, asst. gen. counsel, 1973-81, assoc. gen. counsel, 1981-83, sr. v.p., gen. counsel, sec., 1983—. Bd. dirs. Downtown Racine Devel. Corp., Wis., 1983—, vice chmn., 1984, chmn., 1985—; chmn. Racine Lakefront Steering Com.; bd. dirs. St. Lukes Hosp., Racine, 1984-85, Jr. Achievement Racine, 1983-85. Served to 1st lt. U.S. Army, 1958-60. Mem. Am. Corp. Counsel Assn. (bd. dirs. Wis. chpt. 1985—), ABA, Wis. Bar Assn., Racine County Bar Assn., The Lawyers Council of the Constrn. Industry Mfrs. Assn. Milw. (chmn. exec. com. 1975, 83, vice chmn. 1982). General corporate. Home: 3815 Lighthouse Dr Racine WI 53042 Office: JI Case Co 700 State St Racine WI 53404

FALVEY, PATRICK JOSEPH, lawyer; b. Yonkers, N.Y., June 29, 1927; s. Patrick J. Falvey and Nora Falvey Rowley; m. Eileen Ryan, June 29, 1963; 1 son, Patrick James. Student Iona Coll., 1944-47; J.D. cum laude, St. John's U., Jamaica, N.Y., 1950. Bar: N.Y. 1951, U.S. Supreme Ct. 1972. Law asst. Port Authority of N.Y. and N.J., 1951, atty., 1951-65, chief condemnation and litigation, 1965-67, asst. gen. counsel, 1967-72, gen. counsel, 1972-79, gen. counsel, asst. exec. dir., 1979—. Served with USN, 1945-46. Recipient Howard S. Cullman disting. service medal Port Authority of N.Y. and N.J., 1982; Loftus award and Trustees' Honoree Iona Coll., 1982. Fellow Am. Bar Found.; mem. ABA (chmn. urban state and local govt. law sect. 1983-84, vice-chmn. model procurement code project), Am. Pub. Transit Assn. (legal affairs com.), Assn. Bar of City of N.Y., Airport Operators Council Internat. (legal com.), Fed. Bar Council (labor com.), N.Y. County Lawyers Assn., N.Y.C. C. of C. (transp. and state and local affairs sect., indsl. relations coms.), N.Y. State Bar Assn., Nat. Inst. Mcpl. Law Officers, Internat. Assn. Ports and Harbors (chmn. legal counsellors com.). Local government, General corporate, Real property. Office: Suite 67 E 1 World Trade Ctr New York NY 10048

FAMILO, EDWARD DOUGLAS, lawyer; b. Detroit, July 15, 1921; s. Joseph and Josephine (Ostrum) F.; m. Gloria Blessing, Apr. 8, 1943; children—Nancy Familo Hamilton, Timothy E. A.B., Adelbert Coll., Western Reserve U., 1943, LL.B., 1948; Bar: Ohio 1948, U.S. Dist. Ohio 1948. Assoc. Grossman, Schlesinger, & Carter, Cleve., 1948-53, ptnr., 1953-64; ptnr. Grossman, Familo, Cavitch, Kempf & Durkin, Cleve., 1964-69, Grossman, Stotter, Familo & Cavitch, Cleve., 1969-70, Stotter, Familo, Cavitch, Elden & Durkin, Cleve., 1970-77, Cavitch, Familo & Durkin, Cleve., 1978—, pres. Served to capt. USMC, 1942-50. Mem. Greater Cleve. Bar (exec. com. 1959-62), Ohio State Bar Assn. ABA. Methodist. Clubs: Westwood Country (Rocky River, Ohio), Cleve. Yachting (past commodore 1964), Mid-Day of Cleve. (pres. 1978-85—). Real property, General corporate, Contracts commercial.

FANNIN, DAVID CECIL, lawyer; b. Catlettsburg, Ky., Feb. 5, 1946; s. Cecil and Marie (Conley) F.; m. Lucille Ann Stewart, Jan. 1, 1985; children: Christopher, Brian, Catherine. BA, U. Ky., 1968, JD, 1973; MA, U. Ill., 1971. Bar: Ky., U.S. Dist. Ct. (ea. and we. dists.) Ky., U.S. Ct. Appeals (6th cir.). Assoc. Wyatt, Tarrant & Combs, Louisville, 1974-79, ptnr., 1979—. Bd. dirs. English Speaking Union, Louisville, 1976—, Louisville Redbirds Basaball Club Inc., 1982-86. Woodrow Wilson fellow, 1968. Mem. ABA, Ky. Bar Assn., Lousville Bar Assn. Democrat. Baptist. Club: Jefferson (Louisville). Avocations: music, running. Banking, Contracts commercial, Real property. Office: Wyatt Tarrant & Combs Citizens Plaza Louisville KY 40202

FANNING, BARRY HEDGES, lawyer; b. Olney, Tex., Dec. 5, 1950; s. Robert Allen and Carolyn (Parker) F.; m. Rebecca Sue Cobbs, May 24, 1975. B.B.A., Baylor U., 1972, LL.B., 1973. Bar: Tex. 1973, Fla. 1974, U.S. Dist. Ct. (no., ea. and we. dists.) Tex. 1974, U.S. Ct. Appeals (5th and 11th cirs.) 1974. Mem. firm Fanning, Harper & Martinson, Dallas, 1974—. Social v.p. Dallas Symphony Orch. Guild, 1975-77; mem. Dallas Metro Young Life Bd., 1977—, fund raising chmn., 1982-84, 86-87. Mem. ABA (vice-chmn. young lawyers com. 1980, pub. relations com. torts sect.), Baylor U. Student Found. (steering com. 1971-72), Baylor Alumni Assn. (dir. 1978-82), Tryon Coterie (pres. 1971), Phi Eta Sigma, Omicron Kappa Delta. Baptist. Clubs: Dervish (Dallas), Calyx (Dallas), Dallas Baylor (Dallas) (dir. 1976-84, pres. 1981-82), Christian Men's (Dallas). State civil litigation, Federal civil litigation, Insurance. Home: 4213 Greenbrier Dallas TX 75225 Office: Fanning Harper & Martinson 4303 N Central Expressway Dallas TX 75205

FANNON, STEPHEN THOMAS, lawyer; b. Wilkes-Barre, Pa., Dec. 9, 1954; s. James Richard and Elaine (McLean) F.; m. Victoria Joy Colonna, Aug. 24, 1985; 1 child, Patrick Stephen. BA cum laude, Glassboro State Coll., 1976; JD with honors, Drake U., 1980. Bar: N.J. 1980, U.S. Dist. Ct. N.J. 1980. Assoc. Capehart and Scatchard, P.A., Moorestown, N.J., 1980-86, ptnr., 1987—. Mem. ABA, N.J. Bar Assn., Camden County Bar Assn., Burlington County Bar Assn. (chmn. workers' compensation sect. 1985-86, 86-87, vice chmn. workers' compensation sect. 1984-85), Order of Coif. Republican. Roman Catholic. Lodge: Rotary. Workers' compensation. Home: 20 Lady Diana Circle Marlton NJ 08053 Office: Capehart and Scatchard PA 304 Harper Dr Moorestown NJ 08057

FANT, DOUGLAS VERNON, lawyer; b. Cleve., Apr. 3, 1952; s. Arthur Vernon and Helen Barbara (Becker) F. BA, Stanford U., 1974, JD, 1977. Bar: Ariz. 1977, Calif. 1977, D.C. 1980, U.S. Dist. Ct. Ariz. 1982, Tex. 1984. Atty. U.S. Dept. of the Interior, Washington, 1977-81, Union Oil Co. of Calif., Los Angeles, 1981-83; asst. counsel Union Oil Co. of Calif., Houston, 1983-86; sr. atty. Arco, Houston, 1986—; bd. dirs. Kramer's Diner and Club Inc., Corpus Christi, Tex. A.P. Sloan Found. Scholar, 1970-74; named one of Outstanding Young Men Am., 1986. Mem. Houston Jaycees, (bd. dirs. 1985, v.p. 1986—, Outstanding Dir. 1986, Leadership Achievement award 1986), Houston C. of C. (internal programs com.). Republican. Methodist. Avocations: onomastics, wine tasting, soccer. Oil and gas leasing, Private international, General corporate. Home: 704K Bering Dr Houston TX 77057 Office: Arco 15375 Memorial Dr Houston TX 77079

FANT, LESTER GLENN, judge; b. Holly Springs, Miss., Nov. 14, 1906; s. Lester Glenn and Cordelia (Leach) F.; m. Gladys Sage, Aug. 3, 1935; children—Nancy Fant Smith, Lester Glenn III, William H.S. A.B., Vanderbilt U., 1927; LL.B., Harvard U., 1930. Bar: Miss. 1930, U.S. Dist. Ct. (no. dist.) Miss. 1931, U.S. Ct. Appeals (5th cir.) 1952. Co-practice, Holly Springs, 1930-41; mem. firm Fant & Bush, Fant & Crutcher and predecessor firms, Holly Springs, 1946-80; judge Miss. Chancery Ct., 1980—; prof. law U. Miss., 1941-63; dir. Bank of Holly Springs. Served to lt. USNR, 1942-45. Mem. ABA, Am. Judicature Soc., Amincourt III. Methodist. Clubs: Rotary (Holly Springs); Summit (Memphis). Judicial administration, Jurisprudence, Family and matrimonial. Home: 330 E Salem Holly Springs MS 38635

FANWICK, ERNEST, lawyer, business executive; b. N.Y.C., Feb. 28, 1926; s. Jacob and Jeanette (Lossof) F.; m. Lee Nathan, Sept. 1, 1951; children: Lewis, Leslie, Eric. B.S. in Elec. Engring., Pa. State U., 1948; J.D., Columbia U., 1951. Bar: N.Y. 1952, U.S. Patent Office 1952, U.S. Ct. Appeals (2d cir.) 1952, U.S. Ct. Appeals (fed. cir.) 1982, U.S. Supreme Ct. 1958. Sr. patent atty. ITT Fed. Telephone Labs., Nutley, N.J., 1951-55; div. counsel Avion div. ACF, Paramus, N.J., 1955-57; patent counsel Burndy Corp., Norwalk, Conn., 1957-65, dir. legal dept., 1965-75, gen. counsel, 1975-82, v.p., gen. counsel, sec., 1982—; mem. faculty Practising Law Inst., N.Y.C., 1964—; lectr. Conf. Legal Execs., Pa., 1970, 72. Bd. dirs. Aid to Retarded, Stamford, Conn., pres., 1982; arbitrator Am. Arbitration Assn. Mem. ABA, Am. Patent Law Assn., Am. Soc. Corp. Secs., Conn. Patent Law Assn. (pres. 1966), N.Y. Patent Law Assn., Westchester-Fairfield Corp. Counsel Assn. Club: Masons. General corporate, Patent. Home: 1403 Newfield Ave Stamford CT 06905 Office: Burndy Corp Richards Ave Norwalk CT 06856

FARAGE, DONALD J., lawyer. A.B., U. Pa., 1930, LL.B. with 1st honors, 1933; LL.D. hon., Dickinson Sch. Law, 1966. Bar: Pa. 1933. Asst. to prof. Francis H. Bohlen, reporter for Restatement of Torts 1933-36; prof. law Dickinson Sch. Law, 1934-46, 50—, George Washington U. Law Sch., 1948-50; sr. ptnr. firm Farage & McBride; vis. prof. med. jurisprudence Jefferson Med. Coll., Phila., 1948-76. Author: Pennsylvania Annotations to Restatement of Restitution, 1940, Pennsylvania Annotations to Restatement Judgments, 1957; co-editor: Hazards of Medication, 1971, 2d edit., 1978. Fellow Law Sci. Acad.; fellow Internat. Soc. Barristers (dir. 1971-74), Am. Coll. Trial Lawyers, Internat. Acad. Law and Sci., Southwestern Legal Found., Internat. Acad. Trial Lawyers (pres. 1970-71); mem. ABA (council, chmn. com. on rules and procedure, sect. ins., negligence and compensation law 1971-73, mem. council sect. torts and ins. practice law 1977-81, chmn. class actions com. 1981-83, chmn. motions and resolutions com. 1983—), Pa. Bar Assn. (ho. of dels. 1966-73, 75-78, 82—), Phila. Bar Assn., Assn. Trial Lawyers Am. (v.p. Pa. 1956-58), Am. Law Inst., Scribes, Order of Coif. Clubs: Lawyers, Union League, Urban (Phila.). Office: 836 Suburban Sta Bldg 1617 John F Kennedy Blvd Philadelphia PA 19103

FARAH, BENJAMIN FREDERICK, lawyer; b. Cleve., Mar. 29, 1956; s. Benjamin Hallack and Janice Elizabeth (Gassan) F.; m. Ann Ruth Livingston, Sept. 8, 1984. BBA, George Washington U., 1978; JD, Case Western Res. U., 1981. Bar: Ohio 1981, U.S. Dist. Ct. (no. dist.) Ohio 1981, U.S. Tax Ct. 1981, U.S. Ct. Appeals (6th cir) 1983, U.S. Supreme Ct. 1984. Assoc. Steuer, Escovar & Berk, Cleve., 1981-85; sole practice Rocky River, Ohio, 1985—. Mem. ABA, Ohio Bar Assn., Cuyahoga County Bar Assn., Cleve. Bar Assn., Phi Alpha Delta. Republican. General corporate, Probate, General practice. Home: 2230 Olive Ave Lakewood OH 44107 Office: 1154 Linda St Suite 250 Rocky River OH 44116

FARBER, DANIEL ALAN, law educator; b. Chgo., July 16, 1950; s. Bernard Farber and Annette (Shugan) Holland; m. Dianne S. Farber, Mar. 25, 1972; children: Joseph, Sonia, Nora. BS, U. Ill., 1971, MD, 1972, JD, 1975. Bar: Ill. 1975, D.C. 1977, U.S. Ct. Appeals (7th cir.) 1976. Law clk. to presiding justice U.S. Ct. Appeals, Chgo., 1975-76, U.S. Supreme Ct., Washington, 1976-77; assoc. Sidley & Austin, Washington, 1977-78; asst. prof. U. Ill., Urbana, 1978-80; prof. U. Minn., Mpls., 1981—. Co-author: Environmental Law, 1981, 85. Mem. Am. Law Inst. Civil rights, Environment, Jurisprudence. Office: U Minn Law Ctr 229 19th Ave S Minneapolis MN 55455

FARBER, HOWARD, lawyer; b. N.Y.C., Dec. 7, 1931; s. Joseph and Mamie (Aronson) F.; m. June R. Polinger, Dec. 20, 1953; children: Shelly G., Carol R. BBA, CCNY, 1953; MS, Columbia U., 1957; JD, Temple U., 1972. Bar: Pa. 1972, Del. 1972, U.S. Dist. Ct. (ea. dist.) Pa. 1972, U.S. Ct. Appeals (3d cir.) 1975, U.S. Supreme Ct. 1975, N.Y. 1980. Ptnr. Farber & Halligan, P.C., Media, Pa., 1972-80; sole practice Media, 1980—; solicitor Twp. of Marple, Pa., 1975-78. Bd. dirs. Marple-Newton Sch. Dist., Newton Square, Pa., 1972-75. Served with U.S. Army, 1954-56. Recipient Disting. Service to Community award Marple Township Bd. Coms., 1978, Outstanding Service to Edn., Pa. Sch. Bds. Assn., 1976. Mem. ABA, Assn. Trial Lawyers Am., Pa. Bar Assn., Pa. Trial Lawyers Assn., Delaware County Bar Assn. Personal injury, Family and matrimonial, Probate. Office: 1 Veterans Sq Media PA 19063

FARESE, LAWRENCE ANTHONY, lawyer; b. Jersey City, Nov. 22, 1952; s. Gerald Albert and Ann (Tramontano) F.; m. Patti Lee Proctor; children: Laurie, Kevin, Michael. BBA, Fairleigh Dickinson U., 1974; JD, U. Miami, 1977. Bar: Conn. 1977, Fla. 1978, U.S. Dist. Ct. Conn. 1979, U.S. Dist. Ct. (so., mid. and no. dists.) Fla. 1981, U.S. Ct. Appeals (5th and 10th cirs.) 1981, U.S. Supreme Ct. 1986. Assoc. Cummings & Lockwood, Stanford, Conn. and Naples, Fla., 1977-85; ptnr. Cummings & Lockwood, Naples, Fla., 1985—. Trustee Youth Haven Inc., Naples, Fla., 1985—. Mem. ABA, Fla. Bar Assn. (exec. com. gen. practice sect. 1983-85), Fla. Acad. Trial Lawyers, Collier County Bar Assn. (pres. trial lawyers sect. 1987). Republican. Lodge: Rotary. Federal civil litigation, State civil litigation. Office: Cummings & Lockwood 3001 Tamiami Trail N Naples FL 33940

FARINO, SAL LOUIS, judge; b. Pitts., June 4, 1930; s. Louis and Mary (Iorfida) F.; m. Catherine Jean LeDonne, June 23, 1956; children—Maureen, Stephen. B.A., Duquesne U., 1953; LL.B., George Washington U., 1958. Bar: Pa. 1959. Sole practice, Allegheny County, Pa., 1959-74; solicitor City of Pitts., 1966-75, Sch. Dist. of Pitts., 1966-75; judge Ct. Common Pleas, Pitts., 1975—. Active United Fund, Miltiple Sclerosis, Home Exceptional Children, NAACP. Served as 1st lt. U.S. Army, 1953. Mem. Am. Judicature Soc., Pa. Bar Assn., Allegheny County Bar Assn. Roman Catholic. Clubs: Italian Sons and Daughters Am. (nat. pres.), Sons Columbus. Home: 122 High Park Pl Pittsburgh PA 15206 Office: 701 City-County Bldg Pittsburgh PA 15219

FARLEY, ANDREW NEWELL, lawyer; b. Brownsville, Pa., Oct. 31, 1934; s. Andrew Polycarp and Sarah Theresa (Landymore) F.; m. Marta Olha Pisetska, May 5, 1963; children—Andrew Daniel, Mark Landymore. A.B., Washington and Jefferson Coll., 1956; M.P.A., U. Pitts., 1961, J.D., 1961; diploma, U.S. Army Command and Gen. Staff Coll., 1972, Indsl. Coll. Armed Forces, 1967; grad., U.S. Army War Coll., 1976. Bar: Pa. 1962, U.S. Supreme Ct. 1965. Assoc. Reed Smith Shaw & McClay, Pitts., 1961-65; ptnr. Reed Smith Shaw & McClay, 1966—; lectr. in fed. jurisprudence and adminstrv. law U. Pitts; adminstrv. asst. Pa. Atty. Gen., 1959; counsel to Pa. Constl. Conv., 1968; mem. Pa. Atty. Gen.'s Task Force on Adminstrn., 1970. Assoc. editor Pitts. Legal Jour, 1963—; contbr. articles to law jours. Mem. Luth. Council Region III; chmn. Pitts. Area Consortium Ind. Schs.; bd. dirs. Ind. Schs. Chmn. Assn., Health Research and Services Found.; v.p., bd. dirs. World Affairs Council, Pitts.; sec., bd. dirs. Found. for Calif. U. Pa. Served with U.S. Army; brig. gen. Res. Decorated Meritorious Service medal, Army Commendation medal; recipient Gubernatorial citation Commonwealth of Pa., 1978, Omicron Delta Kappa award, 1960; Nat. Def. Transp. Assn. fellow, 1956. Mem. Pa. Bar Assn. (ho. of dels., chmn. sect. internat. law), Am. Law Inst., ABA (vice chmn. sect. adminstr. law com. on ombudsman), Assn. U.S. Army (pres. Ft. Pitt chpt.), Sr. Army Res. Comdrs. Assn. (exec. com.). Clubs: Pitts. Athletic Assn., Duquesne (Pitts.), Pa. State Grange. Lodge: Masons. Banking, General corporate. Office: James H Reed Bldg 435 6th Ave PO Box 2009 Pittsburgh PA 15230

FARLEY, BARBARA SUZANNE, lawyer; b. Salt Lake City, Dec. 13, 1949; d. Ross Edward Farley and Barbara Ann (Edwards) Farley Swanson; m. Arthur Hoffman Ferris, Apr. 9, 1982; 1 child, Barbara Whitney. BA with honors, Mills Coll., 1972; JD, U. Calif.-San Francisco, 1976. Bar: Calif. 1976. Extern law clk. to presiding justice Calif. Supreme Ct., San Francisco, 1975; assoc. Pillsbury, Madison & Sutro, San Francisco, 1976-78, Bronson, Bronson & McKinnon, San Francisco, 1978-80, Goldstein & Phillips, San Francisco, 1980-84; ptnr., head litigation, Rosen, Wachtell & Gilbert, San Francisco, 1984—; arbitrator U.S. Dist. Ct. (no. dist.) Calif., San Francisco, 1981—, Calif. Superior Ct., San Francisco, 1984—; judge pro tem San Francisco Mcpl. Ct., 1983—. Contbg. author Calif. Continuing Edn. of the Bar; mng. editor U. Calif.-San Francisco Constl. Law Quarterly, 1975-76;

civil litigation reporter. Active San Francisco Attys. for Better Govt., 1982—. Scholar Mills Coll., 1970-72, U. Calif., 1973-76. Mem. ABA, San Francisco Bar Assn., Am. Trial Lawyers Assn., San Francisco Trial Lawyers Assn. Federal civil litigation, State civil litigation, Probate. Office: Rosen Wachtell & Gilbert 345 California St Suite 2200 San Francisco CA 94104

FARLEY, JAN EDWIN, lawyer; b. Bartlesville, Okla., Dec. 4, 1948; s. Earl Franklin Farley and Martha Lynn Crisp; m. Sybil Anne Bova, Aug. 3, 1974; children—Elizabeth Anne, Christopher George. B.A. magna cum laude, Midwestern U., Wichita Falls, Tex., 1971; cert. Inst. Advanced Internat. Studies, U. Paris, 1973; J.D. with honors, U. Tex., 1975. Bar: Tex. 1975. Assoc. firm Baker & Botts, Houston, 1975-81; asst. sec., asst. gen. counsel Weatherford Internat. Inc., Houston, 1981-85 ; asst. gen. counsel ARA Services, Inc., Houston, 1986—; lectr. in internat. comml. trans. U. Houston Law Sch., 1976. Sec. Houston-Nice Sister City Assn., 1977-78. Rotary Found. fellow U. Paris, 1972-73. Mem. ABA, Tex. Bar Assn., Houston Bar Assn. (treas. internat. law sect. 1981, exec. council 1982-85, chmn.-elect 1985-86, chmn. 1986-87), Petroleum Equipment Suppliers Assn. (corp. counsel com., steering com. 1983-85), U. Tex. Internat. Law Jour. Alumni Assn. (pres. 1980-81). Presbyterian. Club: Houston Athletic. Contracts commercial, General corporate, Health. Home: 2927 Deer Creek Dr Sugarland TX 77478 Office: ARA Services Inc 15415 Katy Freeway Suite 800 Houston TX 77094

FARLEY, JOHN JOSEPH, III, lawyer; b. Hackensack, N.J., July 30, 1942; s. John Joseph and Patricia (Earle) F.; m. Kathleen Mary Wells, June 27, 1970; children: Maura, Brendan, Thomas. AB in Econs., Holy Cross Coll., 1964; MBA, Columbia, 1966; JD cum laude, Hofstra U., 1973. Bar: N.Y. 1974, D.C. 1975, U.S. Supreme Ct. 1977. Trial atty. torts sect. civil div. U.S. Dept. Justice, Washington, 1973-78, asst. dir. torts br. civil div., 1978-80, dir. torts br. civil div., 1980—; mem. faculty OPM Exec. Seminar Ctrs., Denver and Kings Point, N.Y., 1980—; lectr. Atty. Gen's. Advocacy Inst., Washington, 1976—, FBI Acad., Quantico, Va., 1978—. Editor-in-chief Hofstra Law Rev., 1971-73. Served to capt. U.S. Army, 1966-70, Vietnam. Decorated Bronze Star with V device and 3 oak leaf clusters, Purple Heart with oak leaf cluster; recipient Sr. Exec. Service Spl. Achievement award U.S. Dept. Justice, 1984, Civil Div. Spl award U.S. Dept. Justice, 1980; Samuel Bronfman fellow, 1964-65. Mem. ABA, Fed. Bar Assn., Sr. Exec. Assn. (bd. dirs.), DAV, Nat. Amputation Found. Roman Catholic. Avocations: skiing, tennis, bicycling, reading. Federal civil litigation, Personal injury. Home: 12400 Stretton Ln Bowie MD 20715 Office: US Dept Justice Torts Br Civil Div Washington DC 20530

FARLEY, WILLIAM PATRICK, lawyer; b. N.Y.C., Jan. 16, 1955; s. Herbert Francis and Frances Theresa (Moser) F.; m. June Mary Besek, May 30, 1981. BA, Harvard U., 1977; JD, NYU, 1981. Bar: N.Y. 1982, U.S. Dist. Ct. (so. and no. dists.) N.Y. 1982. Assoc. Paul, Weiss, Rifkind, Wharton & Garrison, N.Y.C., 1981-85; atty. McGraw Hill, Inc., N.Y.C., 1985-86, asst. gen. counsel, 1986—. Mem. ABA (patent, trademark and copyright law sect.), Assn. of Bar of City of N.Y. Federal civil litigation, Computer, Libel. Office: McGraw Hill Inc 1221 Ave of Americas 48th Floor New York NY 10020

FARMER, GUY, lawyer; b. Foster Falls, Va., Sept. 13, 1912; s. Harbert and Kate (Bell) F.; m. Helen Joura (dec.); children: Mary, Mark, Jane. B.A., W.Va. U., 1934, LL.B., 1936; Rhodes scholar, Oxford (Eng.) U., 1936-37. Bar: W.Va., D.C., U.S. Supreme Ct. Asso. gen. counsel NLRB, 1943-45, atty., 1945, chmn., 1953-55; assoc. Steptoe & Johnson, 1945-49, ptnr., 1949-60; sr. ptnr. Farmer, Wells, McGuinn, Flood & Sibal, 1960-83; of counsel Vedder, Price, Kaufman & Kamholtz, 1983-86; sole practice Washington, 1986—; lectr. labor law W.Va. U., 1948-49, Georgetown U., 1957-59; dir. Bartlett Tree Co., Stamford, Conn. Author articles labor topics. Mem. Am., D.C., W.Va. bar assns., Order of Coif, Phi Beta Kappa, Phi Alpha Delta. Club: Cosmos. Labor. Office: 1919 Pennsylvania Ave NW Washington DC 20006

FARMER, RYLAND LEE, lawyer; b. Hagerstown, Md., May 5, 1948; s. Samuel Ryland and Sarah Hodges (Dameron) F.; m. Elizabeth Layman Mundy, Sept. 4, 1976; children—Joshua P., Cameron L., Samuel M. B.A., Elon Coll., 1970; J.D., Wake Forest, 1973. Bar: N.C. 1973, D.C. 1974, U.S. Dist. Ct. (mid. dist.) N.C. 1974 (ea. dist.) 1975, U.S. Ct. Appeals (4th cir.) 1974, U.S. Tax Ct. 1976, U.S. Dist. Ct. (we. dist.) N.C. 1982, U.S. Ct. Mil. Appeals 1985, U.S. Supreme Ct. 1986. Assoc., Pemberton & Blackwell, Yanceyville, N.C., 1973; county atty. County of Caswell, Yanceyville, 1973—; ptnr. Blackwell & Farmer, 1974-82, Blackwell-Farmer & Watlington, 1982, Farmer & Watlington, Yanceyville, 1982—; mem. N.C. Criminal Code Commn., Raleigh, N.C., 1979-85, State Jud. Nominating Com., 1981-85. Bd. editors Law Jour., 1970-73. Town atty. Town of Yanceyville, 1982—; mem. N.C. Dem. Exec. Com., 1976-83, chmn. Caswell County, 1976-81. Recipient Silver Beaver, Boy Scouts Am., 1984. Mem. 17A Jud. Dist. Bar Assn. (pres. 1984-85), N.C. Acad. Trial Lawyers, ABA, N.C. Bar Assn., Caswell County Bar Assn., N.C. County Attys. Assn. (pres. 1986-87), Assn. Trial Lawyers Am. Methodist. Club: Ducks Unltd. General practice, State civil litigation, Criminal. Home: PO Drawer B Yanceyville NC 27379 Office: Farmer & Watlington 109 W Main St Yanceyville NC 27379

FARNELL, ALAN STUART, lawyer; b. Hartford, Conn., Mar. 14, 1948; s. Denis Frank and Katherine Dorothy (Dettenborn) F.; m. Roberta Ann Arquilla, May 21, 1983; children: Thomas Alan, Jeffrey Stuart. B.A. with honors, Trinity Coll., 1970; J.D., Georgetown U., 1973. Bar: D.C. 1973, N.Y. 1975, Ill. 1980, U.S. Dist. Ct. (no. dist.) Ill. 1980, U.S. Ct. Appeals (7th cir.) 1980. Assoc. Kaye, Scholer, Fierman, Hayes & Handler, N.Y.C., 1973-79; assoc. Isham, Lincoln & Beale, Chgo., 1979-83, ptnr., 1983—; gen. counsel 1550 N. State Pkwy. Condominium Assn., Chgo., 1984—; gen. counsel, bd. govs. Ginger Creek Community Assn., Oak Brook, Ill., 1984—. Editor Georgetown Law Jour., 1972-73. Mem. ABA. Club: Butterfield Country (Oak Brook). Federal civil litigation, General corporate, Securities. Home: 31 Baybrook Ln Oak Brook IL 60521 Office: Isham Lincoln & Beale Three First Nat Plaza Chicago IL 60602

FARNHAM, JAMES EDWARD, lawyer; b. Knoxville, Tenn., Feb. 28, 1942; s. Edward L. and Dorothy (Jones) F.; m. Carole Erksine, Aug. 29, 1964; children: Pamela, Katherine, Samuel, Sarah. BS, U. Tenn., 1963; LLB, Yale U., 1966. Bar: Va. 1967, U.S. Dist. Ct. (ea. dist.) Va. 1967, U.S. Ct. Appeals (4th cir.) 1968, D.C. 1980, U.S. Dist. Ct. D.C. 1982. Assoc. Hunton & Williams, Richmond, Va., 1966-73, ptnr., 1973—. Presbyterian. Club: Commonwealth (Richmond). Avocations: skiing, fishing, tennis. Federal civil litigation, State civil litigation, Insurance. Home: 6514 Westham Station Rd Richmond VA 23229 Office: Hunton & Williams 707 E Main St PO Box 1535 Richmond VA 23212

FARNSWORTH, EDWARD ALLAN, lawyer, educator; b. Providence, June 30, 1928; s. Harrison Edward and Gertrude (Romig) F.; m. Patricia Ann Nordstrom, May 30, 1952; children—Jeanne Scott, Karen Ladd, Edward Allan, Pamela Ann. B.S., U. Mich., 1948; M.A., Yale U., 1949; LL.B. (Ordronaux prize 1952), Columbia U., 1952. Bar: D.C 1952, N.Y. 1956. Mem. faculty Columbia U., 1954—, prof. law, 1959—, Alfred McCormack prof. law, 1970—; vis. prof. U. Instanbul, 1960, U. Dakar, 1964, U. Paris, 1974-75, Harvard Law Sch., 1970-71; mem. faculty Salzburg Seminar Am. Law, 1963, Columbia-Leyden-Amsterdam program Am. law, 1964, 69, 73, 85, San Diego Inst. on Internat. and Computer Law, Paris, 1982, China Ctr. for Am. Law Study, Beijing, 1986; dir. orientation program Am. law Assn. Am. Law Schs., 1965-68; U.S. rep. UN Commn. Internat. Trade Law, 1970—; reporter Restatement of Contracts 2d, 1971-80; cons. N.Y. State Law Revision Commn., 1956, 58, 59, 61; mem. coms. validity and agy. internat. sales contracts Internat. Inst. Unification Pvt. Law, Rome, 1966-72, mem. governing council, 1978—; spl. counsel city reorgn. N.Y.C. Council, 1966-68; U.S. del. Vienna Conf. on Internat. Sales Law, 1980, Bucharest and Geneva Conf. on Internat. Agy., 1979, 83. Author: An Introduction to the Legal System of the United States, 2d edit., 1983, (with J. Honnold) Cases and Materials on Commercial Law, 4th edit, 1985, (with W.F. Young) Cases and Materials on Contracts, 4th edit, 1985, Cases and Materials on Commercial Paper, 3d edit, 1984, Treatise on Contracts, 1982. Served to capt. USAAF, 1952-54. Mem. ABA, Am. Law Inst., Assn. Bar City N.Y. (chmn. com. fgn. and comparative law 1967-70, chmn. spl. com. on products liability 1979-82), Phi Beta Kappa, Phi Delta Phi. Unitarian. Contracts commercial, Private international. Home: 201 Lincoln St Englewood NJ 07631 Office: 435 W 116th St New York NY 10027

FARNSWORTH, T BROOKE, lawyer; b. Grand Rapids, Mich., Mar. 16, 1945; s. George Llelwyn and Gladys Fern (Kennedy) F.; m. Cherrill Kay Bowers, Aug. 24, 1968; children—Leslie Erin, T Brooke. B.S. in Bus., Ind. U., 1967; J.D., Ind. U.-Indpls., 1971. Bar: Tex. 1971, U.S. Dist. Ct. (so. dist.) Tex. 1972, U.S. Tax Ct. 1972, U.S. Ct. Appeals (5th cir.) 1977, U.S. Ct. Appeals D.C. Cir. 1977, U.S. Sup. Ct. 1978, U.S. Ct. Appeals (11th cir.) 1982. Adminstrv. asst. to treas. of State of Ind., Indpls., 1968-71; assoc. Butler, Binion, Rice, Cook & Knapp, Houston, 1971-74; counsel Damson Oil Corp., Houston, 1974-78; prin. Farnsworth & Assocs., Houston, 1987—; dir. Dorill Enterprises; pres., chmn. bd. TME, Inc; corp. sec. Lomax Oil & Gas Co. Mem. State Bar of Tex., Houston Bar Assn., ABA, Fed. Energy Bar Assn., Comml. Law League of Am. Republican. Mem. Christian Ch. (Disciples of Christ). Clubs: Petroleum of Houston, Champions Golf, Greenspoint (Houston). Contbr. articles on law to profl. jours. Contracts commercial, State civil litigation, Oil and gas leasing. Home: 5903 Bermuda Dunes Dr Houston TX 77069 Office: Farnsworth and Assocs 333 N Belt Suite 800 Houston TX 77060

FARNUM, HENRY MERRITT, lawyer, researcher, patent designer; b. Lewiston, Maine, June 19, 1919; s. Samuel Merritt and Florence Natalie (Hardy) F. A.B. magna cum laude, Bates Coll., 1939; J.D., Yale U., 1942. Bar: D.C. 1974, Maine 1974, N.Y. 1976, U.S. Patent Office 1976, U.S. Ct. Appeals (fed. cir.) 1986. Owner Farnum Industries, Inc., Auburn, Maine, 1942-49; patent designer, N.Y.C., 1952-55; automatic setup staff Kollsman Instrument Co., Elmhurst, N.Y., 1952-59; faculty services staff John Jay Coll. Criminal Justice, N.Y.C., 1972-78; sole practice, N.Y.C., 1966—; patent designer, N.Y.C., 1966—. Author: 725 Years of Magna Carta: 1215--1776--Today.; patentee Computer-Human responses for tests, Circumferential Stereo spectacular, universal constrn. elements for stage and film sets, multiple use direct mail graphics; inventor 3-D Spectacular and TV by Natural Vision. Originator, chmn. Bates Liberal Arts Expn., Lewiston, 1939; state chmn. Maine Young Republicans, 1947-48. Mem. Maine Bar Assn., D.C. Bar Assn., N.Y. Patent, Trademark and Copyright Law Assn. (fgn. law com.), ABA (patent sect., fgn. law com., automated search com.), Internat. Patent Club, Phi Beta Kappa, Delta Sigma Rho. Democrat. Dutch Reformed. Patent, Private international, Legal history. Home: Executive House 225 E 46th St New York NY 10017

FARON, ROBERT STEVEN, lawyer; b. N.Y.C., Jan. 10, 1947; s. Jack and Ceil Faron; m. Linda A. Baumann, May 18, 1975; children: Gregory Andrew, Douglas James. BS in Engring., Princeton U., 1968; JD, Columbia U., 1975. Bar: D.C. 1978, U.S. Ct. Appeals (D.C. cir.) 1978, U.S. Ct. Claims 1986. Systems engr. IBM Corp., Holmdel, N.J., 1968-69; atty. U.S. Dept. of Commerce, Washington, 1975-76; fgn. service officer U.S. Dept. of State, Washington, 1976-77; assoc. LeBoef, Lamb, Leiby & MacRae, Washington, 1977-82; of counsel Lane & Mittendorf, Washington, 1982-85; ptnr. Barnett & Alagia, Washington, 1986—. Served to capt. USAF, 1969-72. Mem. ABA (v.p. TIPS energy sect. 1984—), Assoc. Internat. de Droit des Assurances (U.S. pollution law working party). Environment, Insurance, Federal civil litigation. Office: Barnett & Alagia 1000 Thomas Jefferson St NW Washington DC 20007

FARR, CHARLES SIMS, lawyer; b. Hewlett, N.Y., June 29, 1920; s. John and Hazel Zealy (Sims) F.; m. Mary Randolph Rue, Dec. 21, 1946 (dec. Dec. 1980); children: Charles Sims, Virginia Farr Ramsey, Randolph Rue, John, II. Student, Princeton U., 1938-40; LLB, Columbia U., 1948. Bar: N.Y. 1949. Assoc. White & Case, N.Y.C., 1948-58, ptnr., 1959—; mem. bd. visitors Columbia U. Sch. Law. Contbr. articles to profl. publs. Chmn. Commonwealth Fund, N.Y.C.; trustee St. Luke's-Roosevelt Hosp. Center, Gen. Theol. Sem., 1968-77, N.Y. Zool. Soc.; mem. bd. fgn. parishes Protestant Episc. Ch., 1954-78, pres., 1977; chancellor to pres. bishop Protestant Episc. Ch. in U.S.A., 1977-85; mem. vestry St. James' Ch., N.Y.C., 1966-76, 77-82; sr. warden St. James' Ch., 1973-76, jr. warden, 1984-86; mem. council Rockefeller U.; sec. and bd. dirs. Am. Hosp. in Paris Found. Served to lt. comdr. USN, 1941-45, PTO. Decorated Sec. Navy Commendation Ribbon; recipient Alumni Assn. medal Columbia U., 1977. Fellow Am. Coll. Probate Counsel, Am. Bar Found.; mem. Am. Law Inst., ABA, N.Y. State Bar Assn. Republican. Clubs: Century, Links, Racquet and Tennis, River, Everglades, Pilgrims. Probate, Family and matrimonial. Home: 200 E 66th St New York NY 10021 Office: White & Case 1155 Avenue of Americas New York NY 10036

FARR, G(ARDNER) NEIL, lawyer; b. Los Angeles, Jan. 9, 1932; s. Gardner and Elsie M. (Schuster) F.; m. Lorna Jean, Oct. 26, 1957; children—Marshall Clay, Jennifer T., Thomas M. B.A., U. Calif.-Berkeley, 1957, J.D., 1960. Bar: Calif. 1961, U.S. Supreme Ct. 1977. Cert specialist family law Calif. Bd. Specialization, 1980. Dep. dist. atty. Solano County, 1961-66; recreation commr. City of Fairfield, 1964-66; dep. dist. atty. Kern County, 1966-69; ptnr. Young, Wooldridge, Paulden, Self, Farr & Hugie, now Farr & Griffin, Bakersfield, Calif., 1969—. Served with USNR, 1950-52. Mem. ABA, Calif. Bar Assn., Kern County Bar Assn. (pres. 1984), Calif. Trial Lawyers Assn., Los Angeles Trial Lawyers Assn. Family and matrimonial. Office: Young Wooldridge Paulden Self Farr & Griffin 4th Floor 1675 Chester Ave Bakersfield CA 93301

FARR, LINUS GILBERT, lawyer, writer, researcher; b. Bound Brook, N.J., Aug. 28, 1951; s. Asa Hursey and Norma Ardell (Gilbert) F.; m. Joyce G. Farr, Sept. 11, 1976 (div.). B.A. in Govt. and Sociology, Bates Coll., 1974; J.D., U. Miami, 1977. Bar: N.J., Pa. and Fla. 1977, D.C. 1978. Legal asst. Somerset County Prosecutors Office, Somerville, N.J., 1977-78, asst. prosecutor, 1978-82; sole practice, Somerville, 1982—; tchr. Am. Ednl. Inst., Somerset County Coll. Life gold membership N.J. P.B.A.; 1980. Mem. Assn. Trial Lawyers Am., Nat. Dist. Attys. Assn., N.J. Bar Assn., Fla. Bar Assn., Pa. Bar Assn., D.C. Bar Assn., ABA, Somerset County Bar Assn. Criminal, State civil litigation, Environment. Home and Office: PO Box 1098 Somerville NJ 08876

FARR, SIDNEY LAVELLE, lawyer; b. Haynesville, La., Jan. 20, 1923; s. Jesse Lavelle and Sybil Winifred (Yates) F.; m. Evalyn Louise Freeman, May 29, 1946; children: Nancy, Molly, Katy, William. Student, La. State U., 1939-43, 46, S.W. Tex. U., 1946, Vanderbilt U., 1946-48; LLB, So. Meth. U., 1949. Bar: Tex. 1949, U.S. Dist. Ct. (so. dist.) Tex. 1950, U.S. Ct. Appeals (5th cir.) 1952, U.S. Dist. Ct. (ea. dist.) Tex. 1960, U.S. Dist. Ct. (we. dist.) Tex. 1973, U.S. Tax Ct. 1973, U.S. Supreme Ct. 1973. Ptnr. Gray & Farr, Corpus Christi, Tex., 1949-50; staff atty. Nat. Assn. Broadcasters, Washington, 1950; asst. U.S. atty., chief of civil sect. So. Dist. Tex., Houston, 1955-57; ptnr. Barrow & Bland, Houston, 1958-72, Farr & Fillion, Houston, 1973-76; sole practice Houston, 1976—. Served to 1st Lt. U.S. Army, 1943-46, ETO. Democrat. Methodist. State civil litigation, Bankruptcy, Federal civil litigation. Home: 3743 Tangley Rd Houston TX 77005 Office: 711 Polk Suite 666 Houston TX 77002

FARR, THOMAS CAREY, lawyer; b. Des Moines, Sept. 11, 1952; s. Charles Edwin and Marilyn Marie (Herselius) F.; m. Deirdre Ilene Schechtman, May 25, 1975; children: Matthew, Kathleen, Rachel. BA, Grinnell Coll., 1974; JD, Drake U., 1981. Bar: Iowa 1981, U.S. Dist. Ct. (so. and no. dists.) Iowa 1981, U.S. Ct. Appeals (8th cir.) 1982, U.S. Supreme Ct. 1986. Assoc. Peddicord, Simpson & Sutphin, Des Moines, 1981-84; ptnr. Peddicord & Wharton, Des Moines, 1986; assoc. gen. counsel Preferred Risk Group, Des Moines, 1987—. Recipient Prentice-Hall Tax award, 1980. Mem. ABA, Fed. Bar Assn. (treas. 1982-83, 85-86), Iowa Bar Assn., Polk County Bar Assn., Order of Coif. Democrat. Federal civil litigation, State civil litigation, General corporate. Home: 608 46th St Des Moines IA 50312

FARRAR, ELIZABETH GRACE TURRELL, lawyer; b. Steubenville, Ohio, May 22, 1957; s. Ronald Sherman and Joanna Marguerite (Van Orden) T. BA, Smith Coll., 1979; JD, U. Va., 1982. Bar: Ohio 1982, U.S. Dist. Ct. (so. dist.)Ohio 1983. Assoc. Vorys, Sater, Seymour and Pease, Columbus, Ohio, 1982—. Dillard fellow U. Va. 1981-82. Mem. ABA (exec. comm. young lawyers div. 1986—), Ohio Bar Assn., Columbus Bar Assn. (admissions com. 1984—), U. Va. Alumni Club, Smith Coll. Alumnae Club. Republican. Presbyterian. Clubs: Capital (Columbus), Smith (Columbus) (candidate chmn. 1984—). Avocation: sports. Banking, General corporate, Securities. Home: 4820 F Pennfair St Columbus OH 43214 Office: Vorys Sater Seymour & Pease 52 E Gay St Columbus OH 43215

FARRAR, FRANK LEROY, lawyer, former governor of S.D.; b. Britton, S.D., Apr. 2, 1929; s. Virgil William and Venetia Soule (Taylor) F.; m. Patricia Jean Henley, June 5, 1953; children—Jeanne Marie, Sally Ann, Robert John, Mary Susan, Ann M. B.S., U. S.D., 1951, LL.B., 1953; LL.D., Huron Coll. Bar: S.D. 1953. Practiced law Britton, 1957-63; agt. IRS, 1955-57; judge Marshall County, S.D., 1958, state's atty., 1959-62; atty. gen. State of S.D., 1963-69, gov., 1969-70; chmn. Cardinal and Gold Ins. Co., Frank L. Farrar & Assocs., Performance Bankers, Inc., Capital, Fulda, Beresford, Wanbay, Sidney, Uptown, Versailles, Glenrock, Wolf Point Bancorps., Inc., NW Investment Inc., Carlton Agy., Inc., 1st Agy. Hasting, Cairo, First, Inc., Peoples Holding Co.; adv. bd. dirs. Citicorp, Correspondent Resources Inc. Past pres. Pheasant council Boy Scouts Am.; past chmn. S.D. March of Dimes; past fund raising chmn. S.D. Mental Health Assn.; bd. dirs. Rural Coalition Am.; chmn. Marshall County Republican Party, 1959; asst. sgt.-at-arms Rep. Nat. Conv., 1960. Served to capt. U.S. Army. Recipient Alumnus Achievement award U. S.D., 1981, named Alumnus of Yr. Sch. Bus., 1979. Mem. S.D. Bar Assn., Ind. Bar Assn., Wash. Bar Assn., S.D. States Attys. Assn. (asst. pres.), Nat. Dist. Attys. Assn., Alpha Tau Omega, Phi Delta Phi. Lodges: Masons, Shriners, Jesters, Lions, Elks, Odd Fellows, Sportsmen. Address: Britton SD 57430

FARRELL, CLIFFORD MICHAEL, lawyer; b. Gallup, N.Mex., Jan. 17, 1956; s. Francis and Carolyn Louise (Evans) F.; m. Ariane Pinkerton, Nov. 10, 1984. B.A., Moravian Coll., 1978; J.D., Capital U., 1982. Bar: Ohio 1982, Pa. 1983, U.S. Dist. Ct. (we. dist.) Pa. 1983, U.S. Ct. Appeals (3d cir.) 1983, U.S. Dist. Ct. (so. dist.) Ohio 1984, U.S. Ct. Appeals (6th cir.) 1984, U.S. Ct. Appeals (4th and 11th cirs.) 1985. Staff atty. HHS, Columbus, Ohio, 1982-83; mem. firm Robert N. Peirce, Jr., P.C., Pitts., 1983-84, Barkan & Neff Co. L.P.A., Columbus, 1984—. Mem. Ohio Mock Trial Program, N.W. Civic Assn. Mem. ABA, Assn. Trial Lawyers Am., Ohio Bar Assn., Ohio Acad. Trial Lawyers, Pa. Bar Assn., Allegheny County Bar Assn., Columbus Bar Assn. (common pleas ct. com., med. malpractice com.). Personal injury, State civil litigation, Administrative and regulatory. Home: 5280 Rockport St Columbus OH 43220 Office: Barkan & Neff Co LPA 50 W Broad St Suite 1515 Columbus OH 43215

FARRELL, GEORGE EDWIN, lawyer; b. Escalon, Calif., Dec. 10, 1916; s. John George and Ivy Myrtle (Rager) F.; m. Joan Abouchar, Apr. 10, 1966 (div. Aug. 1985); children: Taylor E., Katherine. AB, Stanford U., 1941; JD, DePaul U., 1959; grad., Naval Justice Sch., 1960. Bar: D.C. 1959, N.Y. 1965, U.S. Supreme Ct. 1969, U.S. Ct. Appeals (2d, 4th, 5th, and 11th cirs.), U.S. Dist. Ct. D.C., U.S. Dist. Ct. (ea. and so. dist.) N.Y. Commd. 2d lt. USMC, 1941, advanced through grades to lt. col., pilot, 1941-64, ret., 1964; assoc. Kreindler & Kreindler, N.Y.C., 1964-66, Speiser, Shumate et al, N.Y.C. and Washington, 1968-72; chief aviation litigation sect. U.S. Dept. Justice, Washington, 1972-75; ptnr. Healey, Farrell & Lear, Washington, 1975—; spl. asst. to atty. gen. U.S. Dept. Justice, Washington, 1975. Decorated Disting. Flying Cross, 1945, 50. Mem. ABA, Fed. Bar Assn., D.C. Bar Assn., Nat. Aviation Club. Republican. Roman Catholic. Avocation: golf. Personal injury, Administrative and regulatory, Insurance. Home: 5717 Bradley Blvd Bethesda MD 20814 Office: Farrell & Lear 1216 16th St NW Washington DC 20036

FARRELL, J. MICHAEL, lawyer; b. Darby, Pa., Mar. 22, 1953; s. James and Eleanor Marie (McLaughlin) F.; m. Margaret Mary Eichman, June 17, 1971 (div. May 1979); children—Kristin Maureen, Margaret Mary; m. Sharon Blakeny Marston, Mar. 27, 1982; children—James Michael, Brian Lance. B.A., U. S.C., 1975; J.D., Georgetown U., 1978. Bar: D.C. Ct. Appeals 1978, S.C. 1979, U.S. Dist. Ct. S.C. 1979, N.J. 1980, U.S. Dist. Ct. N.J. 1980, Pa. 1981, U.S. Dist. Ct. (ea. dist.) Pa. 1982, U.S. Supreme Ct. 1983, U.S. Ct. Appeals (3d and 4th cirs.) 1984, U.S. Ct. Appeals (6th cir.) 1985. Assoc. prof. U. S.C., Columbia, 1978-80; staff atty. Defender Assn. Phila., 1980-82; assoc. Brobyn & Forceno, Phila., 1982-85; ptnr. Sleet & Farrell, Phila. and Woodbury, N.J. 1985—; co-founder, dir. Legal Awareness Within, Va., 1977-78. Contbr. articles to legal publs. Served with U.S. Army, 1970-71. Named Tchr. of Yr., Coll. Criminal Justice, U. S.C., 1980. Mem. Phila. Bar Assn., Nat. Assn. Criminal Def. Lawyers, N.J. Bar Assn., S.C. Bar Assn., D.C. Bar Assn., Assn. Trial Lawyers Am. Democrat. Roman Catholic. Criminal, Personal injury, Entertainment. Home: 502 S 49th St Philadelphia PA 19143 Office: Sleet & Farrell 230 S Broad 8th Floor Philadelphia PA 19102 also: 231 S Broad St Woodbury NJ 08096

FARRELL, JOHN BRENDAN, lawyer; b. Gary, Ind., Jan. 26, 1946; s. Edward Lawrence and Margaret (Byrnes) F.; m. Sue Ann Schulte, June 8, 1974; children—Sean Edward, Brian Patrick, Joseph Brendan. B.A., Marquette U., 1968; J.D., Thomas F. Cooley Law Sch., Lansing, Mich., 1977. Bar: Mich. 1977, U.S. Dist. Ct. (we. dist.) Mich. 1977. Midwest div. claims supt. Foremost Ins. Co., Grand Rapids, 1974-77, claims atty., 1978-81, claims counsel, 1981-84, asst. v.p. claims, 1984—; assoc. Seth Barsky, Southfield, 1977-78. Sec., Kentwood Zoning Bd. Appeals, 1982—; mem. Kentwood Citizens Safety Commn., 1983—; adviser Jr. Achievement, Grand Rapids, 1980. Mem. Def. Research Inst., Mich. Def. Trial lawyers Assn., Assn. Trial Lawyers Am., ABA. Republican. Roman Catholic. Club: Charlevoix. Insurance, Personal injury, State civil litigation. Home: 5830 Pinetree SE Kentwood MI 49508 Office: Suite 103 Lucerne Bldg PO Box 2450 Grand Rapids MI 49501

FARRELL, PATRICK JOSEPH, JR., lawyer; b. Miami, Fla., Dec. 28, 1953; s. Patrick J. Sr. and Mary Edith (Odem) F.; m. Jann Johnson, June 30, 1979 (div. July 1985); 1 child, Rosemary J. BS in Acctg., Fin., Fla. State U., 1975; JD cum laude, Mercer U., 1978. Bar: Ga. 1978, Fla. 1979, U.S. Dist. Ct. (so., mid. and no. dists.) Fla. 1980, U.S. Dist. Ct. ((mid. and no. dists.) Ga. 1978, U.S. Ct. Appeals (5th cir.) 1978, U.S. Ct. Appeals (11th cir.) 1981. Assoc. Long, Weinberg, Ansley & Wheeler, Atlanta, 1978-80, Fuller & Johnson P.A., Tallahassee, Fla., 1980—. Mem. ABA, Ga. Bar Assn., Fla. Bar Assn., Atlanta Bar Assn., Atlanta Claims Assn., Tallahassee Bar Assn., Tallahassee Claims Assn., Ct. Practice Inst. (dipolomate), Def. Research Inst., Fla. Def. Lawyers Assn., Internat. Assn. Def. Counsel, Phi Delta Phi. Insurance, Personal injury, Products liability and professional malpractice. Office: Fuller & Johnson PA 111 N Calhoun St Tallahassee FL 32301

FARRELL, RICHARD JAMES, lawyer; b. Uniontown, Pa., Nov. 7, 1916; s. John and Nora Catherine (Moran) F.; m. Hope H. Hudson, Feb. 20, 1942; children—Patricia, Thomas, Richard, Jane. B.S., Wash. and Jefferson, 1938; J.D., U. Pa., 1941; LL.D. (hon.), Washburn U., 1970. Bar: Pa. 1942, N.Y. 1946, Ill. 1955, U.S. Dist. Ct. (no. dist.) Ill. 1956. Assoc., Cadwalader, Wickersham & Taft, N.Y.C., 1941-42; atty. Amoco Corp., Chgo., 1942-62, gen. counsel, 1962-72, v.p. law pub. affairs, 1972-78; of counsel Rooks, Pitts & Poust, Chgo., 1978—. Bd. dirs. Am. Petroleum Inst., Am. Enterprise Inst., 1966-81; chmn. Ravinia Festival Assn., 1978-81; trustee Seabury-Western Theol. Sem., 1978-84, Washington and Jefferson Coll., 1979—. Served to lt. USAAF, 1942-46. Mem. ABA. Clubs: Chgo., Mid-Day, Westmoreland Country (Chgo.); Tucson Country, Oro Valley Country (Tucson). General corporate, Private international. Office: Rooks Pitts & Poust Suite 1500 55 W Monroe Chicago IL 60603

FARRELL, THOMAS DINAN, lawyer; b. Chgo., Feb. 14, 1948; s. Francis George and Marian Elizabeth (Zadorozny) F.; m. Elizabeth Ann McElyea, Apr. 26, 1975; children: Brian, Timothy. AB in Politics, Princeton U., 1970; JD, U. Calif., Berkeley, 1973. Bar: N.J. 1974, Calif. 1977. Asst. counsel Nat. Gambling Commn., Washington, 1974-76; asst. U.S. atty. U.S. Dept. Justice, Los Angeles, 1976-78; assoc. Pitney, Hardin & Kipp, Morristown, N.J., 1978-80; v.p. Hilton Hotels Corp., Beverly Hills, Calif., 1980-82, Harrah's, Atlantic City, 1982-85; v.p., gen. counsel Trusthouse Forte, Inc., N.Y.C., 1985—. Commr. Alcoholic Beverage Study Commn., Trenton, N.J., 1983-85. Served to capt. USAR, 1972-80. Nat. Merit Scholar 1966. Mem. N.J. Bar Assn. (chmn. casino law com. 1984-85). Presbyterian. General corporate, Administrative and regulatory, Entertainment. Home: 9 W Shore Dr Pennington NJ 08534 Office: Trusthouse Forte Inc 645 Fifth Ave New York NY 10022

FARRELLY, FRANCIS J., lawyer; b. Hartford, Conn., Apr. 15, 1941; s. Francis J. and Elizabeth H. (Mulryan) F.; m. Delphine M. Johns, Apr. 19, 1969; children: Sean Patrick, Meeghan Kathleen. BS, Boston Coll., 1963; JD, U. Conn., 1966. Bar: Conn. 1966, U.S. Dist. Ct. Conn. 1966, U.S. Ct. Appeals (2d cir.) 1971, U.S. Supreme Ct. 1976, U.S. Tax Ct. 1982. Assoc. O'Connor & O'Connor, Hartford, Conn., 1966-74; ptnr. O'Connor, Farrelly & DiCorleto, Hartford, 1974-82, Farrelly & DiCorleto, Hartford, 1982-84, Farrelly, Tapper & Elkin, Hartford, 1984—; magistrate State of Conn. Jud. Dept., West Hartford, 1982—. Bd. mgrs. Wethersfield YMCA, Conn., 1981—, vice-chmn., 1984—. Served to lt. USNG, 1966-72. Mem. ABA, Conn. Bar Assn., Hartford County Bar Assn., Am. Judicature Soc., Acad. Continuing Profl. Devel. (charter), Am. Arbitration Assn. (arbitrator 1978—). Democrat. Roman Catholic. State civil litigation, Probate, Real property. Home: 24 Deer Ledge Ln Wethersfield CT 06109 Office: Farrelly Tapper & Elkin 780 Farmington Ave West Hartford CT 06119

FARRINGTON, RICHARD, lawyer; b. Springfield, Mo., Dec. 7, 1912; s. John Sebree and Blanche (McCann) F.; m. Edel Thompson, Apr. 16, 1938 (div. 1949); m. Dorothy M. Heying, Dec. 28, 1950. Student, Drury Coll., 1929-32; JD, U. Mo., 1935. Bar: Mo. 1934, U.S. Dist. Ct. (we. dist.) Mo. 1934, U.S. Ct. Appeals (8th cir.) 1948. Asst. pros. atty. Greene County, Springfield, 1941-43; asst. atty. gen. State of Mo., 1953-56, 58-60; ptnr. Farrington, Curtis, Knauer, Hart, Garrison & Powell, Springfield, 1946—; bd. dirs. Springfield Grocer Co., Acme Structural Inc., Springfield; trustee U.S. Bankruptcy Ct., 1965-85. Chmn. Dem. Cen. Com., Greene County, 1950-54, mem. Dem. State Com., 1954-58. Served to lt. (j.g.) USNR, 1942-45, PTO. Mem. ABA, Mo. Bar Assn., Greene County Bar Assn. (pres. 1964), Am. Judicature Soc. Club: Hickory Hills Country. Lodge: Elks (exalted ruler Springfield 1949-50). Home: 2255 Catalina Springfield MO 65804 Office: Farrington Curtis Knauer Hart Garrison & Powell 750 N Jefferson Springfield MO 65802

FARRIOR, J. REX, JR., lawyer; b. Tampa, Fla., June 5, 1927; s. J. Rex and Lera Spotswood (Finley) F.; m. Mary Lee Nunnally, May 30, 1958; children—J. Rex III, Preston Lee, Hugh Nunnally, Robert Pendleton. Student Auburn U., 1945-46; B.S. in Bus. Adminstrn., U. Fla., 1949, J.D., 1951. Bar: Fla. 1951. Assoc. Shackleford, Farrior, Stallings & Evans, P.A. and predecessors, Tampa, Fla., 1951-55, ptnr., 1955—, sr. ptnr.; permanent guest lectr. U. Fla., Coll. Engring.; mem. Fed. Jud. Nominating Comm., 1980—. Pres. Pres. Round Table of Tampa, 1965. Served with USNR, World War II. Named to Hall of Fame, U. Fla., 1951. Fellow Am. Coll. Probate Counsel, Fellows of ABA; mem. ABA (ho. of dels. 1976-81), Fla. Bar (pres. Fla. young lawyers sect. 1958, pres. 1975-76, Most Outstanding Local Bar Pres. 1977), Hillsborough County Bar Assn. (pres. 1966), Acad. Fla. Trial Lawyers, Am. Judicature Soc., Inter-Am. Bar Assn., Am. Counsel Assn. (pres. 1983-84), Assn. Trial Lawyers Am., Greater Tampa C. of C. (bd. govs.), Phi Delta Phi, Kappa Alpha Alumni Assn. (pres. 1957). Episcopalian. Clubs: Rotary, Sertoma (founder club 1952, pres. club 1964) Tampa), Masons, Shriners. General corporate, Probate, Estate planning. Office: PO Box 3324 Tampa FL 33601

FARRIS, FRANK MITCHELL, JR., lawyer; b. Nashville, Sept. 29, 1915; s. Frank M. and Mary (Lellyett) F.; m. Genevieve Baird, June 7, 1941; 1 dau., Genevieve B. B.A., Vanderbilt U., 1937; postgrad. N.Y. Law Sch., 1938-39. Bar: Tenn., 1939, U.S. Tax Ct., 1948, U.S. Supreme Ct., 1968. Conciliation commr. in bankruptcy U.S. Dist. Ct. Middle Dist. Tenn., 1940-42; ptnr. Farris, Warfield & Kanaday, and predecessors, Nashville, 1946—; gen. counsel, trustee George Peabody Coll. for Tchrs., 1968-79; counsel 3d Nat. Corp., Nashville, Cherokee Equity Corp., Nashville. Chmn. commrs. Watkins Inst., Nashville, 1953-76; trustee, exec. com. Vanderbilt U., 1979—; chmn. bd. Oak Hill Sch., Nashville, 1968-74, 80-81. Mem. ABA, Tenn. Bar Assn., Nashville Bar Assn. Banking, General corporate, Estate planning. Home: 940 Overton Lea Rd Nashville TN 37220 Office: Third Nat Fin Ctr 19th Floor Nashville TN 37219

FARRIS, JEROME, judge; b. Birmingham, Ala., Mar. 4, 1930; s. William J. and Elizabeth (White) F.; m. Jean Shy, June 27, 1957; children—Juli Elizabeth, Janelle Marie. B.S., Morehouse Coll., 1951, LL.D., 1978; M.S.W., Atlanta U., 1955; J.D., U. Wash., 1958. Bar: Wash. 1958. Mem. firm Weyer, Roderick, Schroeter and Sterne, Seattle, 1958-59; ptnr. Weyer, Schroeter, Sterne & Farris and successor firms, Seattle, 1959-61, Schroeter & Farris, Seattle, 1961-63, Schroeter, Farris, Bangs & Horowitz, Seattle, 1963-65, Farris, Bangs & Horowitz, Seattle, 1965-69; judge Wash. State Ct. of Appeals, Seattle, 1969-79, U.S. Ct. of Appeals for 9th circuit, Seattle, 1979—; lectr. U. Wash. Law Sch. and Sch. of Social Work, 1976—; mem. faculty Nat. Coll. State Judiciary, U. Nev., 1973; adv. bd. Nat. Ctr. for State Cts. Appellate Justice Project, 1978-81; founder First Union Nat. Bank, Seattle, 1965, dir., 1965-69. Del. White House Conf. on Children and Youth, 1970; mem. King County (Wash.) Youth Commn., 1969-70; vis. com. U. Wash. Sch. Social Work, 1977—; mem. King County Mental Health-Mental Retardation Bd., 1967-69; past bd. dirs. Seattle United Way; mem. Tyee Bd. Advisers, U. Wash., 1984—, bd. regents, 1985—; trustee U. Law Sch. Found., 1978-84. Served with Signal Corps, U.S. Army, 1952-53. Recipient Disting. Service award Seattle Jaycees, 1965, Clayton Frost award, 1966. Mem. ABA (exec. com. appellate judges conf. 1978-84, chmn. conf. 1982-83), Wash. Council on Crime and Delinquency (chmn. 1970-72), State-Fed. Jud. Council of State of Wash. (vice chmn. 1977-78, chmn. 1983-87), Order of Coif, U. Wash. Law Sch. Home: 1908 34th Ave S Seattle WA 98144 Office: 1030 US Courthouse Seattle WA 98104

FARRIS, ROBERT LEE, lawyer; b. Edson, Kans., Dec. 31, 1935; s. Alvin Eugene and Florence Dora (Tuttle) F.; m. Mary Ann Clark, Dec. 27, 1961; children: Kenneth E., Kathryn A., Patrick L. BSME, U. Kans., 1961, LLB, 1964. Bar: Kans. 1964, U.S. Dist. Ct. Kans. 1964, Mich. 1969, U.S. Ct. Appeals (Fed. cir.) 1982. Patent examiner U.S. Dept. Commerce, Washington, 1965-68; patent atty. Massey-Ferguson Ltd., Detroit, 1968-80, patent counsel, 1980—; mng. dir. Massey-Ferguson Services N.V., Curacao, Netherlands Antilles, 1980—. Served to lt. U.S. Army, 1959-60. Mem. ABA, Mich. Bar Assn., Assn. Corp. Patent Counsel, Mich. Patent Law Assn., Res. Officers Assn. Episcopalian. Patent, Trademark and copyright. Home: 4380 Squirrel St Bloomfield Hills MI 48013 Office: Massey-Ferguson Inc PO Box 322 Detroit MI 48232

FARRUG, EUGENE JOSEPH, lawyer; b. Detroit, May 22, 1928; s. Michael and Bridget Mary (Foley) F.; m. Dolores Marie Augustine, Apr. 14, 1951; children—Elizabeth Marie Streit, Eugene Joseph Jr., Matthew Augustine, Pamela Ann, Bridget Louise, Donna Michele. B.B.A., U. Mich., 1950, J.D., 1958. Bar: Ill. 1958, U.S. Dist. Ct. (no. dist.) Ill. 1958; U.S. Supreme Ct. 1980. With Lincoln-Mercury div. Ford Motor Co., Dearborn, Mich., 1950, Aircraft Engine div., Chgo., 1951; assoc. McKenna, Storer, Rowe, White & Farrug, Chgo., 1958-62, ptnr., 1962—. Mem. Citizens of Greater Chgo., 1970-80, pres., 1976-79. Served with USN, 1951-55. McGreggor Fund scholar, 1946; Mich. Bd. Realtors scholar, 1949. Mem. ABA, Ill. Bar Assn., Chgo. Bar Assn., DuPage County Bar Assn., Am. Judicature Soc., Cath. Lawyers Guild, Soc. Trial Lawyers, Trial Lawyers Club Chgo., Fedn. Ins. and Corp. Counsel, Phi Alpha Delta. Lodge: Kiwanis (pres. 1964). State civil litigation, Personal injury, Federal civil litigation. Address: 206 N Lincoln St Hinsdale IL 60521

FARUKI, CHARLES JOSEPH, lawyer; b. Bay Shore, N.Y., July 3, 1949; s. Mahmud Taji and Rita (Trownsell) F.; m. Nancy Louise Glock, June 5, 1971; children—Brian Andrew, Jason Allen, Charles Joseph. B.A. summa cum laude, U. Cin., 1971; J.D. cum laude, Ohio State U., 1973. Bar: Ohio 1974, U.S. Dist. Ct. (no. and so. dists.) Ohio 1975, U.S. Ct. Appeals (9th cir.) 1977, U.S. Tax Ct. 1977, U.S. Supreme Ct. 1977, U.S. Ct. Appeals (6th cir.) 1978, U.S. Dist. Ct. (no. dist.) Tex. 1979, U.S. Dist. Ct. (ea. dist.) Ky. 1982, U.S. Ct. Appeals (D.C. cir.) 1982, U.S. Ct. Customs and Patent Appeals 1982, U.S. Ct. Appeals (4th cir.) 1986. Assoc. Smith & Schnacke, Dayton, Ohio, 1974-78, ptnr., 1979—, also dir.; lectr. various continuing legal edn. programs. Contbr. articles in field. Served to capt. U.S. Army Res., 1971-79. Mem. ABA, Fed. Bar Assn. Ohio Bar Assn., Dayton Bar Assn. Avocation: numismatics. Antitrust, Securities, Federal civil litigation. Home: 238 Greenmount Blvd Oakwood OH 45419 Office: Smith & Schnacke PO Box 1817 2000 Courthouse Plaza NE Dayton OH 45401-1817

FARVER, HARRY CRAIG, lawyer; b. Bishopville, S.C., Feb. 14, 1954; s. Harry Edwin and Nancye (McGuigan) F.; m. Jenny Nichols, Jan. 10, 1981; 1 child, Matthew Craig. BS in Acctg. with high honors, Clemson U., 1976; JD cum laude, Wake Forest U., 1979. Bar: N.C. 1979, S.C. 1979, U.S. Dist. Ct. (mid. dist.) N.C. 1979. Assoc. Gwyn, Gwyn and Farver, Reidsville, N.C., 1979-81, ptnr., 1981—. Bd. dirs. Best Friends of Rockingham County/Big Bros., Inc., Eden, N.C., 1982-86; deacon 1st Presbyn. Ch., Reidsville, 1986—. Recipient Am. Jurisprudence award Bancroft-Whitney Co., 1980. Mem. ABA, N.C. Bar Assn., N.C. Acad. Trial Lawyers, S.C. State Bar Assn., Rockingham County Bar Assn., Reidsville Jaycees (bd. dirs., Presdl. award Honor 1985). Republican. Presbyterian. Lodge: Elks. Bankruptcy, Criminal, Family and matrimonial. Home: Rt 8 Box 476-A Reidsville NC 27320 Office: Gwyn Gwyn and Farver 108 S Main Reidsville NC 27320

FASHBAUGH, HOWARD DILTS, JR., lawyer; b. Monroe, Mich., Jan. 31, 1922; s. Howard Dilts and Ninetta Esther (Greening) F.; m. Joyce Dallas MacCurdy, Dec. 25, 1946; children—James Howard, Linda Carol, Patricia Lee. B.S.E., U. Mich., 1947, M.S.E. in Chem. Engring., 1948, M.B.A. with high distinction, 1960; J.D. cum laude, Wake Forest U., 1972; M.Law and Taxation, Coll. William and Mary, 1983. Bar: Va. 1973, Mich. 1975. Mgr. engring. and mfg. Dow Corning Corp., Midland, Mich., 1952-70; assoc. Williams, Worrell, Kelly & Greer, Norfolk, Va., 1972-76, ptnr., 1976-77; corp. counsel Va. Chems. Inc., Portsmouth, Va., 1977-83; ptnr. Williams, Worrell, Kelly & Greer, Norfolk, 1983-85, sole practice, Chesapeake, 1985—; gen. counsel CEP, Inc., 1985—; adj. prof. Sch. of Law CBN U., 1987—; adj. prof. law CBN U., 1987—. Elder Presbyterian Ch., 1966—; chmn. adv. bd. Salvation Army, Midland, Mich., 1967-69, mem. adv. bd., Portsmouth, 1975—. Served to lt. USNR, 1943-46, 50-52. Decorated Bronze Star medal. Mem. ABA, Va. Bar Assn., Norfolk-Portsmouth Bar Assn., Beta Gamma Sigma. Club: Kiwanis (pres. club 1977-78) (Portsmouth). General corporate, Contracts commercial, Corporate taxation. Home and Office: 3905 Stonebridge Ct Chesapeake VA 23321

FASMAN, ZACHARY DEAN, lawyer; b. Chgo., Oct. 27, 1948; s. Irving D. and Lillian V. (Vilatzer) F.; m. Sally Ann Metzger, Aug. 22, 1971; children: Jonathan, Benjamin, Rebecca. BA, Northwestern U., 1969; JD, U. Mich., 1972. Bar: Ill. 1972, D.C. 1977, Supreme Ct. 1977. From assoc. to ptnr. Seyfarth, Shaw et al, Chgo. and Washington, 1972-81; ptnr. Wald, Harkrader et al, Washington, 1981-83, Crowell & Moring, 1983—. Author: Equal Employment Audit Handbook, 1983. Mem. ABA (labor law sect., equal employment law com. individual rights sect.), Order of Coif. Republican. Jewish. Civil rights, Labor. Home: 11329 Marcliff Rd Rockville MD 20852 Office: Crowell & Moring 1001 Pennsylvania Ave Washington DC 20004

FASOLO, WILLIAM ALEXANDER, lawyer; b. N.Y.C., May 15, 1915; s. Angelo and Mary (Borgaro) F.; m. Geraldine Vivian Garoni, May 27, 1945; children: William Jeffrey, Jerilyn Fasolo Dexter. AB, Dartmouth Coll., 1938; LLB, Harvard U., 1941. Bar: N.Y. 1941, N.J. 1942. Assoc. Law Office Milton T. Lasher, Hackensack, N.J., 1945-70; ptnr. Fasolo, Krause & Dexter, Hackensack, 1970—; borough atty. New Milford, N.J., 1951-53, Demarest, N.J., 1953-75; judge Borough of Tenafly, N.J., 1953-72. Active numerous civic coms., Carefree, Ariz. and Tenafly. Served to 1st lt. USAF, 1942-45. Mem. ABA, N.J. Bar Assn., Bergen County Bar Assn., Lawyers Club Bergen County (past pres.), Am. Judicature Soc., Am. Arbitration Assn. Clubs: Knickerbocker Country (Tenafly), Republican (pres. 1951-52); Desert Forest Golf (Carefree). Avocations: golf, civic matters. Local government, Banking, Estate planning. Home: PO Box 1485 9542 Quail Trail Carefree AZ 85377 Office: Fasolo Krause & Dexter 90 Main St Hackensack NJ 07601

FAUCHER, JOHN DENNIS, lawyer; b. Vancouver, Wash., Oct. 29, 1936; s. Bernard A. and Florence M. (Kern) F.; m. Michael J. Beglan, Aug. 29, 1959; children—Robert A., Augustine D., John A. B.S. high honors, U. Idaho, 1960, LL.B. high honors, 1962. Bar: Idaho 1962, Pa. 1973, U.S. Dist. Ct. Idaho 1963, U.S. Ct. Appeals (9th cir.) 1966, U.S. Tax Ct. 1968, U.S. Dist. Ct. (ea. dist.) Pa. 1971, U.S. Supreme Ct. 1971, U.S. Ct. Appeals (3d cir.) 1981, U.S. Ct. Appeals (2d cir.). Asst. prof. law U. Idaho Coll. Law, 1962-63; pvt. practice, Boise, 1963-71; counsel for the trustees Penn Central Reorgn., 1971-72; ptnr. Saul, Ewing, Remick & Saul, Phila., 1973—. Served with USMC, 1954-56. Mem. ABA, Pa. Bar Assn., Idaho Bar Assn., Phila. Bar Assn. Federal civil litigation, State civil litigation, Bankruptcy. Home: 316 S Wayne Ave Wayne PA 19087 Office: Saul Ewing Remick & Saul Centre Sq W 38th Floor Philadelphia PA 19102

FAULK, MICHAEL ANTHONY, lawyer; b. Kingsport, Tenn., Sept. 10, 1953; s. Loy Glade and Rosella E. (Dykes) F.; m. Janet Lynn McLain, Aug. 31, 1974; children: Katherine Lea, Andrew McLain. BS, U. Tenn., 1975; M in Pub. Adminstrn., Memphis State U., 1978, JD, 1979. Bar: U.S. Dist. Ct. (we. dist.) Tenn. 1980, U.S. Dist. Ct. (ea. dist.) Tenn. 1985. Dep. clk. to presiding justice Shelby County Chancery Ct., Memphis, 1977-79; assoc. Weintraub & Dehart, Memphis, 1980-82; ptnr. Frazier & Faulk, Church Hill, Tenn., 1982-83; sole practice Church Hill, 1983—; commr. Tenn. Human Rights Commn., Nashville, 1985—; referee Hawkins County Juvenile Ct., Rogersville, Tenn., 1985—; bd. dirs. Legal Services Inc., Johnson City, Tenn. Bd. dirs. Upper East Tenn. Div. Am. Heart Assn., Blountville, 1984—. Named one of Outstanding Young Men in Am. U.S. Jaycees, 1977. Mem. ABA, Hawkins County Bar Assn. (v.p. 1985-86), Assn. Trial Lawyers Am., Ducks Unltd. (chmn. Holston River chpt. 1984-86). Republican. Baptist. Lodge: Moose. Avocation: outdoors. State civil litigation, Labor, General practice. Office: 107 E Main Blvd Church Hill TN 37642

FAULKNER, JAMES HARDIN, state justice; b. Louisville, Miss., Mar. 17, 1921; m. Eleanor Jane Wyatt; children: Kate Faulkner Hubbard, Christopher. Ed., San Diego State Coll.; J.D., U. Ala.; LL.M., U. Va.; postgrad., U. Calif., Boalt Hall; L.L.D. (hon.), Faulkner U., 1984; attended, N.Y. U. Sch. Law Seminar for Appellate Judges, Am. Acad. Jud. Edn., U. Colo. (Appellate Judges Seminars), La. State U. Sch. Law. Bar: Ala. bar 1949. Practiced law Birmingham, Ala., 1949-51, Birmingham and Montevallo, 1958-72; with Dept. Treasury, 1951-55; asso. justice Ala. Supreme Ct., Montgomery, 1972—; former city atty. City of Montevallo; former judge Recorder Ct.; trust officer Birmingham Trust Nat. Bank, 1955-58; instr. Am. Inst. Banking. Mem. Ala. State Bar, Birmingham Bar Assn., Shelby County Bar Assn. Club: Masons. Jurisprudence. Office: Supreme Court 445 Dexter Ave PO Box 218 Montgomery AL 36130

FAUNTLEROY, JOHN DOUGLASS, retired judge; b. Washington, Sept. 6, 1920; s. Frederick Douglass and Esther Mary (Webb) F.; m. Phyllis Elizabeth Gibbs, Sept. 21, 1946; children—Phylicia A., Jacqueline I. Fauntleroy Barber, John Douglass, Frederick G. LL.B, Robert H. Terrell Law Sch., Washington, 1941; B.S. in Govt., Am. U., Washington, 1953; postgrad., Georgetown U., Nat. Coll. State Judiciary, U. Nev. Bar: D.C. 1942, U.S. Dist. Ct. D.C., U.S. Ct. Appeals (D.C. cir.), U.S. Supreme Ct. Adjudicator, reviewer, sr. adjudicator, supr., instr. Office Dependency Benefits, Newark, 1942-46; pvt. practice law Washington, 1947-67; law mem. Bd. of Appeals and Rev., Washington, 1960-67; mem. Spl. Police Trial Bd., Washington, 1966-67; assoc. judge Juvenile Ct. of D.C., Washington, 1967-71, Superior Ct. of D.C., Washington, 1971-83; sr. judge Superior Ct. of D.C., 1983-85; ct. monitor, spl. asst. to mayor to insure D.C. compliance with ct. orders City of Washington, 1986—; mem. Jud. Conf. D.C. Circuit, 1960-67, 1981, 1982; mem. adv. bd. Law Students in Court, Washington, 1974—; mem. vol. faculty continuing legal edn. program Georgetown U. Law Sch., 1978-81; bd. dirs. Potomac Sch. Law, Washington, 1976-78, 1979-81. Mem. D.C. Democratic Central Com.; vice chmn. spl. com. on met. orgns. Inter-Fedn. Council of Greater Washington Met. Area, 1962-64; mem. panel on human relations Police Acad., Met. Police Dept., 1962-63; bd. dirs. Neighbors, Inc., 1962-65; mem. Citizens Adv. Com. to Supt. of Schs., 1966-68; pres. United Planning Orgn., 1971-72; bd. dirs. Info. Ctr. for Handicapped Children, 1971—, Capitol View Devel. Corp., 1967—, past mem. bd. dirs. D.C. Soc. for Crippled Children, 1971-78; mem. adv. bd. Crime Stoppers Club, Inc., Continental Soc.; substitute trustee Marion P. Shadd Scholarship Fund for Needy Female Grads. of McKinley Tech. High Sch., 1956—; consumer rep. Devel. Disabilities State Planning Council, 1979-84; trustee Tabor Presbyn. Ch. (name now Northeastern Presbyn. Ch.), 1942-57, pres. bd. trustees, 1947-56, ch. atty., 1947-66, elder, 1971-74 76-78; info. program officer U.S. Naval Acad., 1975—, D.C. coordinator, 1979—; mem. recruiting dist. adv. com., U.S. Navy, 1975—, ; mem. vis. com. Sch. Social Work, Howard U., 1976-85; mem. adv. bd. Georgetown U. Child Devel. Ctr., 1978—; mem. genetics adv. panel Georgetown Hosp., George Washington Hosp., Howard U. Hosp., Children's Hosp., 1980—. Served to comdr. USNR, 1973-81. Recipient George W. Norris Civil Rights award Anti-Defamation League, B'nai B'rith and Am. Vets. Com., 1965; plaque of appreciation for service D.C. Assn. for Retarded Citizens, Inc., 1977; Mayor of D.C. Proclamation Day in his honor, 1983; Meritorious Service award Am. Vets. Com., 1983; named Disting. Alumnus, Am. U., 1984; plaque for outstanding service Washington Recruiting Dist., U.S. Navy, 1984; numerous other honors and awards. Mem. Bar Assn. D.C. (cert. of appreciation 1983), D.C. Bar, Washington Bar Assn. (pres. 1962-64, plaque 1968), ABA (del. jud. adminstrv. div. 1969-83, chmn. standing com. lawyers in armed forces 1982-85), Nat. Bar Assn. (chmn. jud. com. 1979-81), Judge Advs. Assn. (nat. pres. 1984-85),VFW, Nat. Naval Officers Assn. (disting. mem.; pres. 1980-82). Democrat. Presbyterian. Avocations: traveling; fishing. Home: 1435 Kennedy St NW Washington DC 20011

FAURI, ERIC JOSEPH, lawyer; b. Lansing, Mich., Feb. 16, 1942; s. Fedele Fauri and Iris M. Petersen; m. Sherrill Lynn Nurenberg, July 15, 1969; children—Lauren, Nadia, Kirk. B.A., U. Del., 1963; J.D. with distinction, U. Mich., 1966. Bar: Mich. 1967, U.S. Dist. Ct. (ea. dist.) Mich. 1967, U.S. Dist. Ct. (we. dist.) Mich. 1972, U.S. Ct. Appeals (6th cir.) 1974. Assoc. Dykema, Gossett, Spencer, Goodnow & Trigg, Detroit, 1966-71, Parmenter, Forsythe, Rude et al, Muskegon, Mich., 1971-73; ptnr. Parmenter, Forsythe, Rude et al, Muskegon, 1973—. Served to capt. U.S. Army, 1967-68. Mem. ABA, State Bar Mich. Banking, Contracts commercial. Address: 500 Lumbermans Bank Bldg Muskegon MI 49443-0417

FAUST, LELAND HOWARD, lawyer; b. Los Angeles, Aug. 30, 1946; s. Joseph Milton and Jane Green (Moyse) F.; m. Susan Elaine Weitzman, June 29, 1969; children: Aaron, Jeremy. AB, U. Calif., Berkeley, 1968; JD, Harvard U., 1971. Bar: Calif. 1972, U.S. Dist. Ct. (no. dist.) Calif. 1972, U.S. Ct. Appeals (9th cir.) 1972. Assoc. Taylor, Winokur, Schoenberg, San Francisco, 1971-75; ptnr. Taylor & Faust, San Francisco, 1975—. Co-author: Personal Tax Planning, 1983. Fellow Am. Bar Found. Probate, Estate taxation, Personal income taxation. Home: 49 Heather Ave San Francisco CA 94118 Office: Taylor & Faust PC 1 Montgomery St #2820 San Francisco CA 94104

FAVERO, JAMES ANTHONY, lawyer; b. Pitts., Nov. 13, 1956; s. Bartholomew Joseph and Aleda Gloria (Gallino) F.; m. Antoinette Davila, June 5, 1982; 1 child, Anthony James. BA, W.Va. U., 1978; JD, Ohio No. U., 1981. Bar: Pa. 1982, U.S. Dist. Ct. (we. dist.) Pa. 1984. Assoc. McCue, Bertocchi & Heim, Kittanning, Pa., 1982-85; asst. dist. atty. Armstrong County, Kittanning, 1983—; sole practice Kittanning, 1985—. Councilman Leechburg Borough, Pa., 1984—; lector St. Catherine Cath. Ch., Leechburg, 1985—. Mem. ABA, Pa. Bar Assn., Assn. Trial Lawyers Am., Pa. Trial Lawyers Assn., Armstrong County Bar Assn. Republican. Lodges: Elks, William Marconi. Avocations: tennis, reading. General practice, Family and matrimonial, Probate. Home: 552 Pitt St Leechburg PA 15656 Office: 217 Market St Kittanning PA 16201

FAWCETT, CHARLES WINTON, lawyer; b. Long Beach, Calif., May 26, 1946; s. Phillip Nimmons and Beatrice Stricker (Winton) F.; m. Kathleen Gloria Mayes, Dec. 15, 1975; children: Reid Charles, Tracie Diane, Ryan Mayes, Marni Taylor. BA, U. Calif., Santa Barbara, 1968; JD, U. Calif., Berkeley, 1971. Bar: Idaho 1971, Wash. 1975, U.S. Tax Ct. 1982. Staff atty. Idaho Legal Aid Services, Lewiston, 1971-73, Caldwell, 1973-74; adminstrv. law judge State of Wash., Seattle, 1974-76; asst. atty. gen. State of Idaho, Boise, 1976-77; sr. ptnr. Skinner, Fawcett and Mauk, Boise, 1977—. Contbr. articles to law jour. Mem. Idaho Bar Assn., Boise Bar Assn., Nat. Assn. Bond Lawyers, Comml. Law League Am. Municipal bonds, Consumer commercial, General corporate. Office: Skinner Fawcett and Mauk PO Box 700 Boise ID 83701

FAWCETT, DWIGHT WINTER, lawyer; b. Springfield, Ohio, Sept. 24, 1927; s. Dwight Ansley and Hazel (Winter) F.; m. Anne N. Langfitt, Apr. 27, 1957; children—Dwight P., Jane F. Dearborn, Donald N. B.S., Ind. U., 1948; J.D., Harvard U., 1951. Bar: Ill. 1951, U.S. Supreme Ct. 1975. Assoc. Mayer, Brown & Platt, Chgo., 1951-61, ptnr., 1961—; dir. White Pigeon Paper Co., Pickard Inc. Bd. dirs., mem. legal aid bur. United Charities of Chgo. Served with USN, 1945-46. Republican. Episcopalian. Clubs: Law, Legal, U. Chgo., Economic (Chgo.); Indian Hill (Winnetka, Ill.); Lost Tree (North Palm Beach, Fla.). Administrative and regulatory, Banking, Contracts commercial. Home: 711 Locust St Winnetka IL 60093 Office: Mayer Brown & Platt 190 S LaSalle St Chicago IL 60603

FAWCETT, KIM ROBERT, lawyer; b. Windsor, Ont., Can., Apr. 14, 1949; s. John Robert and Margaret Jean (Clarridge) F. BA, U. Mich., 1971; JD, Wayne State U., 1975. Bar: Mich. 1975, U.S. Dist. Ct. (ea. dist.) Mich. 1975, U.S. Supreme Ct. 1985, U.S. Ct. Appeals (6th cir.) 1986. Research atty. Mich. Appellate Defender's Office, Detroit, 1976, asst. defender, 1976—, tng. dir., 1981—; adj. lectr. law U. Mich., Ann Arbor, 1980-81. Author, editor: Michigan Criminal Appeals: Practice and Procedure, 1985. Adminstrv. aide ACLU, Detroit, 1972. Mem. Mich. Bar Assn., Criminal Def. Attys. Mich. (edn. com. 1977—, bd. dirs. 1978—), Nat. Legal Aid and Def. Assn. (chmn. amicus com. 1985—). Democrat. Criminal, Legal history, Constitutional law. Office: State Appellate Defender Office 1200 6th Ave North Tower 3d Floor Detroit MI 48226

FAXON, THOMAS BAKER, lawyer; b. Des Moines, Oct. 15, 1924; s. Ralph Henry and Prue (Baker) F.; m. Virginia Webb, Sept. 8, 1949; children—Rebecca Webb, Thomas Baker Jr. B.A., Princeton U., 1949; LL.B., Harvard U., 1952. Bar: Colo. Asst. prof., asst. dir. Inst. Govt. U. N.C., Chapel Hill, 1952-53; assoc. firm Pershing, Bosworth, Dick and Dawson, Denver, 1953-57; ptnr. firm Dawson, Nagel, Sherman and Howard, Denver, 1957-84; of counsel firm Sherman and Howard, Denver, 1984—; trustee Colo. Legal Aid Found., Denver, 1984—. Bd. dirs. Urban League Colo., Denver, 1968; pres. bd. trustees 1st Unitarian Ch., Denver, 1969; mem. Denver Equality of Edn. Com., 1969. Mem. ABA (local govt. com.), Nat. Assn. Bond Lawyers, Rocky Mountain Princeton Club (v.p. 1967), Harvard Law Sch. Assn. Colo. (pres. 1968). Democrat. Club: Cactus (Denver). Municipal bonds. Home: 830 Race St Denver CO 80206 Office: Sherman & Howard 633 17th St Denver CO 80202

FAY, PETER THORP, judge; b. Rochester, N.Y., Jan. 18, 1929; s. Lester Thorp and Jane (Baumler) F.; m. Claudia Pat Zimmerman, Oct. 1, 1958; children: Michael Thorp, William, Darcy. B.A., Rollins Coll., 1951, LL.D., 1971; J.D., U. Fla., 1956; LL.D., Biscayne Coll., 1975. Bar: Fla. 1956, U.S. Supreme Ct. 1961. Partner firm Nichols, Gaither Green, Frates & Beckham, Miami, Fla., 1956-61, Frates, Fay, Floyd & Pearson (and predecessors), Miami, 1961-70; judge U.S. Dist. Ct. for So. Fla., Miami, 1970-76, U.S. Ct. Appeals (5th cir.), 1976-81, U.S. Ct. Appeals (11th cir.), 1981—; prof. Fla. Jr. Bar Practical Legal Inst., 1959-65; lectr. Fla. Bar Legal Inst., 1959—; faculty Fed. Jud. Center, Washington, 1974—; mem. Jud. Conf. Com. for Implementation Criminal Justice Act, 1974-82, Adv. Com. on Codes of Conduct, 1980—. Mem. Orange Bowl Com., 1974—; dist. collector United Fund, 1957-70; mem. adminstrv. bd. St. Thomas U., 1970—. Served with USAF, 1951-53. Mem. Law Sci. Acad., Fla. Acad. Trial Attys., Am., Fla., Dade County, John Marshall (past pres.) bar assns., Fla. Council of 100, U. Fla. Alumni Assn. (dir.), Miami C. of C., Medico Legal Inst., Order of Coif, Phi Delta Phi (past pres.), Omicron Delta Kappa (past pres.), Pi Gamma Mu (past pres.), Phi Kappa Phi, Phi Delta Theta (past sec.). Republican. Roman Catholic. Clubs: Wildcat Cliffs (N.C.); Snapper Creek Lakes (Miami), Coral Oaks (Miami). Home: 11000 Snapper Creek Rd Miami FL 33156 Office: US Court Appeal 300 NE 1st Ave Miami FL 33132

FAY, RAYMOND CHARLES, lawyer; b. Middletown, Ohio, Oct. 24, 1947; s. Robert Joseph and Eva Carolyn (Mail) Fay; m. Rochelle V. Rowlette, Dec. 1, 1984; 1 child, Meredith. Student, Xavier U.; AB magna cum laude, St. Louis U., 1969, student; JD, Georgetown U., 1973. Bar: D.C. 1974, U.S. Dist. Ct. D.C. 1975, U.S. Ct. Appeals (D.C. cir.) 1975, U.S. Ct. Appeals (2d, 7th, 9th and 10th cirs.) 1977, Ill. 1978, U.S. Dist. Ct. (no. dist.) Ill. 1978, U.S. Supreme Ct. 1978, U.S. Ct. Appeals (5th cir.) 1983, U.S. Ct. Appeals (11th cir.) 1984. Tchr. St. Louis Pub. Schs., 1969-70, Notre Dame Acad.,

Washington, 1970-72; atty. FUNDACOMUN, Caracas, Venezuela, 1973-74; assoc. Haley, Bader & Potts, Washington and Chgo., 1975-79, ptnr., 1980-87; ptnr. Bell, Boyd & Lloyd, Washington, 1987—. Trustee Notre Dame Acad., Washington, 1976-77. Mem. Phi Beta Kappa. Labor, Pension, profit-sharing, and employee benefits, Administrative and regulatory. Home: 3223 Rittenhouse St NW Washington DC 20015 Office: Bell Boyd & Lloyd 1615 L St NW Suite 1200 Washington DC 20036

FAY, THOMAS F., state judge. JD, Boston U., 1965. Judge R.I. Supreme Ct., Providence, 1978—. Office: Ct House 250 Benefit St Providence RI 02903 *

FAYE, STANLEY ETHAN, lawyer; b. N.Y.C., June 12, 1935; s. Benjamin and Beatrice F.; m. Marilyn E. Epstein, Nov. 26, 1966; children—Jodi, Robin. A.B. Duke U. 1957, J.D. 1960. Bar: N.Y. 1963, Tex. 1974. With H. Bravin and Assos., N.Y.C., 1961-66, Pell & Le Viness Esq., N.Y.C., 1966-70; with Dresser Industries, Inc., Dallas, 1970-73; v.p., sec., gen. counsel Datapoint Corp., San Antonio, 1973-78; v.p., gen. counsel La Quinta Motor Inns, Inc., San Antonio, 1978-83; ptnr. Russell & Vickers, San Antonio, 1984-86; v.p., gen. counsel Church's Fried Chicken, Inc., 1986—. Served with USMCR, 1960-61. Mem. ABA, Am. Soc. Corp. Secs. Securities, General corporate, Real property. Home: 9223 Bent Elm Creek San Antonio TX 78230 Office: Churchs Fried Chicken Inc 355 Spencer Ln San Antonio TX 78284

FAZIO, JOHN CESARE, publishing company executive, lawyer; b. Ridley Park, Pa., Oct. 30, 1938; s. Charles and Lucy Adina (Calandra) F.; divorced; children: Melanie, Jennifer, Cassandra; m. Ruth Morton, Mar. 18, 1972; children: Alison, Daniel. BA, Case Western Res. U., 1961, JD, 1965. Bar: Ohio 1965. V.p. Walter H. Drane Co., Cleve., 1967-73; pres., mng. editor Justinian Pub. Co., Cleve., 1973—. Author: (play) A Time for War, 1982. Mem. Ohio Bar Assn., Delta Sigma Rho. Democrat. Club: Cleve. Automobile. Avocations: reading, fishing, tennis. Legal publishing, General practice, Legislative. Home: 37200 Fox Run Solon OH 44139 Office: Justinian Pub Co 2940 Noble Rd Cleveland OH 44121

FAZIO, PETER VICTOR, JR., lawyer; b. Chgo., Jan. 22, 1940; s. Peter Victor and Marie Rose (LaMantia) F.; m. Patti Ann Campbell, Jan. 3, 1966; children—Patti-Marie, Catherine, Peter. A.B., Holy Cross Coll., Worcester, Mass., 1961; J.D., U. Mich., 1964. Bar: Ill. 1964, U.S. Dist. Ct. (no. dist.) Ill. 1965, U.S. Ct. Appeals (7th cir.) 1972, U.S. Ct. Appeals (D.C. cir.) 1981, U.S. Supreme Ct. 1977. Assoc. Schiff, Hardin & Waite, Chgo., 1964-70, ptnr., 1970-82, 84—; exec. v.p. Internat. Capital Equipment, Chgo., 1982-83, also dir., 1982-84, sec., 1982-87; dir. Planmetrics Inc., Chgo., 1984—, Chgo. Lawyers Commn. for Civil Rights Under Law, 1976-82, co-chmn., 1978-80, Seton Health Corp. Northern Ill., 1986—. Trustee Barat Coll., Lake Forest, Ill., 1977-82; mem. exec. adv. bd. St. Joseph's Hosp., Chgo., 1984—, chmn., 1986—. Mem. ABA, Ill. State Bar Assn., Chgo. Bar Assn., Am. Soc. Corp. Secs. Clubs: Saddle & Cycle (sec. 1983-86), Tavern, Metropolitan. (Chgo.). Public utilities, Contracts commercial, FERC practice. Office: Schiff Hardin & Waite 7200 Sears Tower Chicago IL 60606

FEAGLEY, MICHAEL ROWE, lawyer, educator; b. Exeter, N.H., Feb. 1, 1945; s. Walter Charles and Laura (Rowe) F. BA, Wesleyan U., 1967; JD, Harvard U., 1973. Bar: Mass. 1973, Ill. 1973, U.S. Dist. Ct. Mass., U.S. Dist. Ct. (no. dist.) Ill., U.S. Ct. Appeals (7th cir.) 1973, U.S. Ct. Appeals (10th cir.) 1986. Assoc. Mayer Brown & Platt, Chgo., 1973-79, ptnr., 1980—; instr. Nat. Inst. Trial Advocacy, Chgo., 1977—, John Marshall Law Sch., Chgo., 1980—. Served to 1st lt. U.S. Army, 1968-71, Vietnam. Mem. ABA, Chgo. Council of Lawyers. Club: Union League (Chgo.). Federal civil litigation, State civil litigation. Office: Mayer Brown & Platt 190 S LaSalle Chicago IL 60603

FEATHER, MARK RANDOLPH, lawyer; b. Troy, N.Y., Sept. 7, 1955; s. Arthur Philip and Wanda Agnus (Adamczyk) F.; m. Marilyn Schlapbach, Aug. 22, 1981; 1 child, Carl Edward. BS in Chem. Engring., U. Ky., 1977; JD, Stanford U., 1980. Bar: Ky. 1980. Ptnr. Brown, Todd & Heyburn, Louisville, 1980—. Vestry St. Matthews Episcopal Ch., Louisville, 1986—. Mem. ABA, Ky. Bar Assn., Louisville Bar Assn., Ky. Def. Counsel, Tau Beta Pi, Omega Chi Epsilon. Democrat. Club: Jefferson (Louisville). Environment, Federal civil litigation, Personal injury. Home: 2517 Valley Vista Rd Louisville KY 40205 Office: Brown Todd & Heyburn 1600 Citizens Plaza Louisville KY 40202

FEATHERLY, HENRY FREDERICK, lawyer; b. Stillwater, Okla., Aug. 10, 1930; s. Henry Ira and Lucy Anne (Borsch) F.; m. Dorcas Diane Rowley, July 19, 1952; children—Henry Frederick, Charles Alan. B.S., Okla. State U., Stillwater, 1952; LL.B., Okla. U., Norman, 1957. Bar: Okla. 1957, U.S. Dist. Ct. (we. and ea. dists.) Okla. 1957, U.S. Ct. Appeals (10th cir.) 1958. Assoc. Pierce, Mock & Duncan, Oklahoma City, 1957-63; ptnr. Chiles & Featherly, Oklahoma City, 1963-64; sole practice, Oklahoma City, 1964-66; ptnr. Lamun, Mock, Featherly, Baer & Timberlake, Oklahoma City, 1966-85; ptnr. Lamun, Mock, Featherly, Kuehling & Cunningham, Oklahoma City, 1986—. Mem. commrs. staff Dan Beard Dist. council Boy Scouts Am., 1966—, Last Frontier council; trustee Heritage Hall Sch., Oklahoma City, 1974-77. Mem. Am. Trial Lawyers Assn., Okla. Trial Lawyers Assn., Okla. Assn. Def. Counsel, Am. Judicature Soc. Republican. Methodist. Lodge: Lions (pres. 1970-71, 83-84). Workers' compensation, State civil litigation, Federal civil litigation. Home: 2433 NW 46th Oklahoma City OK 73112

FEATHERSTONE, BRUCE ALAN, lawyer; b. Detroit, Mar. 2, 1953; s. Ronald A. and Lois R. (Bosshart) F.; m. Sherry L. Winters, Sept. 22, 1979; children: Leigh Allison, Edward Alan. BA cum laude with distinction in Econs., Yale U., 1974; JD magna cum laude, U. Mich., 1977. Bar: Ill. 1977, U.S. Dist. Ct. (no. dist.) Ill. 1978, U.S. Ct. Appeals (5th cir.) 1980, U.S. Ct. Appeals (7th cir.) 1981, U.S. Dist. Ct. (ea. dist.) Wis. 1982, Colo. 1983, U.S. Dist. Ct. Colo. 1983, U.S. Dist. Ct. Mont. 1983, U.S. Ct. Appeals (10th cir.) 1983, U.S. Supreme Ct. 1984. Assoc. Kirkland & Ellis, Chgo., 1977-83, ptnr., 1983—; bd. dirs. Am. Inst. for Law Training Within Office, Phila. Articles editor U. Mich. Law Rev., 1976-77. Mem. ABA (litigation sect.), Colo. Bar Assn., Denver Bar Assn., Nat. Inst. Trial Advocacy (teacher 1982—), Order of Coif. Avocations: swimming, biking, running. Federal civil litigation, State civil litigation, Antitrust. Home: 7947 S Wabash Ct Englewood CO 80112 Office: Kirkland & Ellis 1999 Broadway Suite 4000 Denver CO 80202

FEAZELL, THOMAS LEE, lawyer, oil company executive; b. Mount Hope, W.Va., Feb. 25, 1937; s. Thomas Lee and Drema Lyal (Walker) F.; m. Virginia Scott, Feb. 3, 1961; children—Ann Lindsay, Thomas Lee, Robert Kent. Student, W.Va. U., 1954-56; B.B.A., Marshall U., 1959; LL.B., Washington and Lee U., 1962. Bar: W.Va. 1962, Ky. 1965. Atty. Ashland Oil, Inc., Ky., 1965-74, sr. atty., 1975-76, gen. atty., 1976-78, asst. gen. counsel, 1978-79, assoc. gen. counsel, 1979-80, v.p., 1980—, gen. counsel, 1981—, also dir. Bd. dirs. Marshall U. Found., Inc., Huntington, W.Va., 1984—. Mem. ABA, W.Va. Bar Assn., Ky. Bar Assn., Maritime Bar Assn., Assn. Trial Lawyers Am. Democrat. Presbyterian. Club: Bellefonte Country (bd. dirs.) (Ashland). General corporate, Contracts commercial, Banking. Office: Ashland Oil Inc PO Box 391 Ashland KY 41114

FECHTEL, EDWARD RAY, lawyer, educator; b. Pocatello, Idaho, Apr. 20, 1926; s. Edward Joseph and Frances Lucille (Myers) F.; m. Jewell Reagan, Apr. 7, 1950 (div.); children—Scot Gerald, Mark Edward, Kim; m. 2d Mary K. Milligan, Dec. 1983. B.A. in Bus., Idaho State U., 1949; J.D., U. Oreg., 1967; M.B.A. in Fin., 1968. Bar: Oreg. 1967, U.S. Dist. Ct. Oreg. 1967, U.S. Ct. Appeals (9th cir.) 1968. Sales rep. Genesco, 1950-59; gen. mdse. mgr. Fargo Wilson Wells Co., Pocatello, 1960-64; ptnr. Husband, Johnson & Fechtel, Eugene, Oreg., 1967-83, Ray Fechtel, P.C., 1984—; prof. bus. law U. Oreg.; lectr. Oreg. State Bar. Bd. dirs. Legal Aid Soc., Lane County, Oreg., Oreg. Citizens for Fair Land Planning. Served with USN, 1944-46. Mem. ABA, Oreg. State Bar Assn., Phi Alpha Delta. Republican. Federal civil litigation, State civil litigation, Antitrust. Home: 2858 Greentree Way Eugene OR 97405 Office: 975 Oak St Suite 990 Eugene OR 97401

FECHTEL, VINCENT J., parole commissioner; b. Leesburg, Fla., Aug. 10, 1936; s. Vincent John and Annie Jo (Hayman) F.; divorced; children: John, Katherine. BS in Bus. Adminstrn., U. Fla., 1959. Mem. Fla. Ho. of Reps., 1972-78, Fla. Senate, 1978-80; parole commr. U.S. Dept. Justice, Chevy Chase, Md., 1983—. Served with USNR and Fla. Nat. Guard. Mem. Alpha Tau Omega. Republican. Roman Catholic. Home: PO Box 1675 Leesburg FL 32748 Office: Dept Justice US Parole Commn 5550 Friendship Blvd Chey Chase MD 20815

FECTEAU, FRANCIS ROGER, lawyer; b. Worcester, Mass., July 8, 1947; s. Arthur F. and Rita F. (Jubinville) F.; m. Margaret M. Sharry, Mar. 26, 1972; children—Mary, Matthew, Daniel. B.A., Holy Cross Coll., 1969; J.D., Boston Coll., 1972. Bar: Mass. 1972, U.S. Dist. Ct. Mass. 1973, U.S. Ct. Appeals (1st cir.) 1973. Asst. dist. atty. Worcester County Dist. Atty.'s Office, Worcester, Mass., 1973-79; assoc. Lawrence H. Fisher, Worcester, Mass., 1979-82; assoc. law firm Healy & Rocheleau, Worcester, Mass., 1982-84, ptnr., 1984—; instr. Anna Maria Coll., 1976—. Mem. Worcester County Bar Assn. (exec. com. 1981-83), Mass. Bar Assn., Mass. Acad. Trial Lawyers, Am. Soc. Law and Medicine. Personal injury, Insurance, Criminal. Office: Healy and Rocheleau PC 484 Main St Suite 560 Worcester MA 01608

FEDER, ARTHUR A., lawyer; b. N.Y.C., Mar. 23, 1927; s. Leo and Bertha (Franklin) F.; m. Ruth Musicant, Sept. 4, 1949; children—Gwen Lisabeth, Leslie Margaret, Andrew Michael. B.A., Columbia Coll., 1949; LL.B., Columbia U., 1951. Bar: N.Y. 1951. Assoc. Fulton Walter & Halley, 1951-53; research asst. Am. Law Inst. Fed. Income, Estate and Gift Tax Project, 1953-54; assoc., partner Roberts & Holland, N.Y.C., 1954-66; partner Willkie, Farr & Gallagher, N.Y.C., 1966-69, Fried, Frank, Harris, Shriver & Jacobson, N.Y.C., 1970—; lectr. in law Columbia U., 1961-63; lectr. Am. Law Inst., N.Y. U. Inst. on Fed. Taxation, Practicing Law Inst., various profl. groups. Contbr. articles on fed. income tax to various publs. Served with USN, 1945-46. Mem. Am. Bar Assn. (sect. of taxation, chmn. com. on real property tax problems 1964-66, com. on legis. drafting 1968-84), Assn. of Bar of N.Y.C. (various coms.), N.Y. State Bar Assn. (sec. taxation sect. 1987—, chmn. various coms. 1982-86), Internat. Fiscal Assn. (council U.S.A. Br.), Am. Law Inst., Phi Beta Kappa. Democrat. Clubs: University, India House, Stockbridge Golf and Tennis. Corporate taxation, Estate taxation, Personal income taxation. Home: 25 W 81st St New York NY 10024 Office: 1 New York Plaza New York NY 10004

FEDER, BRUCE STANLEY, lawyer; b. N.Y.C., May 9, 1950; s. Morton and Ruth F. Student, Sch. for Internat. Tng. of Experiment in Internat. Living, 1971; BS, U. Ariz., 1972; JD, George Wash. U., 1976. Bar: Ariz. 1977, D.C. 1981, U.S. Dist. Ct. Ariz. 1977, U.S. Ct. Appeals (9th cir.) 1980. Sole practice Phoenix, 1977—. Mem. ACLU, Amnesty Internat., Natural Resources Defense Council, Nat. Assn. Criminal Defense Lawyers. Criminal, Personal injury, State civil litigation. Office: PO Box 25129 826 N 3rd Ave Phoenix AZ 85002

FEDER, GARY HAROLD, lawyer; b. Cin., Dec. 12, 1948; s. Max Henry and Marian Alice (Blumenthal) F.; m. Robin Melman; Aug. 19, 1973; children: Jessica, Amy. AB, Washington U., 1970, JD, 1974, LLM in Taxation, 1980. Bar: Mo. 1974, U.S. Dist. Ct. (we. and ea. dists.) Mo., U.S. Tax Ct., U.S. Ct. Appeals (8th cir.), U.S. Supreme Ct. Assoc. Teamfour, Inc., St. Louis, 1974-78; assoc. Shifrin & Treiman, St. Louis, 1978-84, ptnr., 1984—; sec. radio KWMU, st. Louis Mo., 1984—; treas. Sch. Dist. Clayton, Mo., 1986—. Co-author: The Abatement Alternatives, 1978; editor in chief urban law annual Washington U. Law Rev., 1974. Mem. ABA, Mo. Bar Assn., Met. St. Louis Bar Assn. (chmn. real sect. 1984-85). Real property, Federal civil litigation. Office: Shifrin & Treiman 8182 Maryland Saint Louis MO 63105

FEDER, HAROLD ABRAM, lawyer; b. Denver, Aug. 22, 1932; s. Harry A. and Surriee A. (Aarons) F.; m. Flora Sue Dunn, June 6, 1954; children: Harlan M., Sharon J., Janet B. B.A., U. Colo., 1954, LL.B., 1959, J.D., 1968. Bar: Colo. 1959, U.S. Dist. Ct. Colo. 1959, U.S. Ct. Appeals (10th cir.) 1969, U.S. Supreme Ct. 1971. Assoc. Feder, Morris, Denver, 1959-61; ptnr. Feder, Morris & Feder, Denver, 1961-71; ptnr. Feder, Morris & Tamblyn P.C., Denver, 1971—, pres., 1978—; spl. asst. atty. gen. Denver, 1960-71; adj. prof. law U. Denver, 1963; arbitrator Am. Arbitration Assn.; also lectr. U.S. and Can. Contbr. articles on condemnation trial technique and law practice mgmt. to profl. jours. Served with USNR, 1954-56. Mem. Fed. Bar Assn., ABA (litigation and local govt. sect., council econs. of law practice sect. 1980-86), Colo. Bar Assn. (bd. govs. 1972-74), Denver Bar Assn., Continental Divide Bar Assn., Assn. Trial Lawyers Am. (former state committeeman), Colo. Trial Lawyers Assn. (pres. 1971-72), Internat. Soc. Barristers, Am. Acad. Forensic Scis., Phi Delta Phi, Sigma Nu. Avocations: handball, skiing, tennis, lit., travel. Federal civil litigation, State civil litigation, Condemnation. Home: 460 S Marion Pkwy 1556 B Denver CO 80209 also: PO Box 238 Eagle CO 81631 Office: Feder Morris & Tamblyn PC 1441 18th St Suite 400 Denver CO 80202

FEDER, MIRIAM, lawyer; b. Dallas, May 27, 1955; s. Sylvan Irwin and Laura (Metzger) F.; m. Edward A. Finklea, Sept. 1, 1985. BA, U. Minn., 1977; JD, Lewis & Clark U., 1980. Bar: Calif. 1980, D.C. 1981, Oreg. 1982. Atty.-advisor Commodity Futures Trading Commn., Washington, 1981-82; assoc. Rankin, McMurray, & Var Rosky, Portland, Oreg., 1982-83; asst. atty. gen. Oreg. Atty. Gen.'s Office, Salem, 1983-84; staff atty. Tektronix Inc., Beaverton, Oreg., 1984—; mem. natural resources and environment exec. com. Oreg. Bar. Jewish Family and Child Service, Portland, 1986—. Democrat. Club: City (Portland). Environment, General corporate, Private international. Office: Tektronix Inc PO Box 500 Beaverton OR 97007

FEDER, ROBERT, lawyer; b. N.Y.C., Nov. 29, 1930; s. Benjamin and Bertha (Bloodstein) F.; m. Marjorie Feder, Dec. 3, 1950; children—Susan E., Judith D., Benjamin D., Jessica R., Abigail M. B.A. cum laude, CCNY, 1953; LL.B., Columbia U., 1953. Bar: N.Y. 1953, U.S. Tax Ct. 1956, U.S. Dist. Ct. (so. dist.) N.Y. 1973. Vice pres., gen. counsel Presdl. Realty Corp., White Plains, N.Y., 1953-71; ptnr. Cuddy & Feder, White Plains, 1971—; bd. dirs. Westchester County (N.Y.) Legal Aid Soc., 1972—, pres., 1974-78. Pres., White Plains Community Action Program, 1967-69; bd. dirs. White Plains Hosp. Med. Ctr., 1979—, also vice chmn., sec.; commr. White Plains Housing Authority, 1984—; adj. prof. Pace U. Law Sch., 1985—. Mem. ABA, N.Y. State Bar Assn., Westchester County Bar Assn., White Plains Bar Assn. Real property, Environment, General corporate. Home: 9 Oxford Rd White Plains NY 10605 Office: 90 Maple Ave White Plains NY 10601

FEDER, ROBERT DAVID, lawyer; b. Freeport, N.Y., Apr. 11, 1957; s. Jay Paul and Fredrica (Martel) F.; m. Madelyn Merrill Kleiner, Aug. 5, 1979. BA magna cum laude, Brown U., 1979; JD, U. Pa., 1982. Bar: Pa. 1982, U.S. Dist. Ct. (ea. dist.) Pa. 1983. Assoc. Abrahams & Loewenstein, Phila., 1982—. Mem. Lawyers Alliance for Nuclear Arms Control, Phila., 1985-86. Mem. ABA (family law sect.), Pa. Bar Assn. (family law sect.), Phila. Bar Assn. (family law sect., mem. exec. com. 1986—). Club: Brown of Phila.; Phila. Cheltenham Racquet (Elkins Park, Pa.). Family and matrimonial. Office: Abrahams & Loewenstein 30 S 17th St United Engrs Bldg 14th Floor Philadelphia PA 19103-4096

FEDER, SAUL E., lawyer; b. Bklyn., Oct. 8, 1943; s. Joseph Robert and Toby Feder; m. Marcia Carrie Weinblatt, Feb. 25, 1968; children: Howard Avram, Tamar Miriam, Michael Elon, David Ben-Zion Aaron. BS, NYU, 1965; JD, Bklyn. Law Sch., 1968. Bar: N.Y. 1969, U.S. Ct. Claims 1970, U.S. Customs Ct. 1972, U.S. Ct. Customs & Patent Appeals 1974, U.S. Ct. Appeals (2nd cir.) 1969, U.S. Supreme Ct. 1972. Mng. lawyer Queens Legal Services, Jamaica, N.Y., 1970-71; ptnr. Previte-Glasser-Feder & Farber, Jackson Heights, N.Y., 1972-73, Hein-Waters-Klein & Feder, Far Rockaway, N.Y., 1973-78, Regosin-Edwards-Stone & Feder, N.Y.C., 1979—; spl. investigator Bur. Election Frauds, Atty. Gen.'s Office, N.Y.C., 1976-77, spl. dep. atty. gen., 1969-70; arbitrator, consumer counsel small claims div. Civil Ct. City of N.Y., 1974—. Pres. Young Israel Briarwood, Queens, N.Y., 1978; chmn. polit. affairs com. Young Israel Staten Island, 1985—; rep. candidate State of N.Y. Assembly, Queens, 1976; chmn. Stat Pac Polit. Action Com., Young Israel Staten Island Pub. Affairs Com. Mem. N.Y. Bar Assn., Queens County Bar Assn. Nassau County Bar Assn., Am. Judges Assn., N.Y. Trial Lawyers Assn., Internat. Acad. Law & Sci., Am. Jud. Soc., Soc. Med. Jurisprudence, Am. Arbitration Assn. Republican. Contracts commercial, General practice, State civil litigation. Home: 259 Ardmore Ave Staten Island NY 10314 Office: Regosin Edwards Stone & Feder 225 Broadway New York NY 10007

FEDER, SCOTT JAY, lawyer; b. Paterson, N.J., Aug. 28, 1958; s. Richard Yale and Irma Rose (Robbins) F. BA, U. Fla., 1979, JD, MBA, 1982. Bar: Fla. 1982, U.S. Dist. Ct. (so. dist.) Fla. 1983, U.S. Ct. Appeals (11th cir.) 1985. Assoc. Floyd, Pearson, Richman, Greer, Weil, Zack & Brumbaugh, Miami, Fla., 1982—. Mem. Assn. Trial Lawyers Am., Fla. Bar Assn., Fla. Trial Lawyers Assn., S. Fla. JD/MBA Assn., Dade County Bar Assn. (bd. dirs. young lawyers sect. 1986—). Democrat. Jewish. Federal civil litigation, State civil litigation, Personal injury. Home: 6618 San Vicente Coral Gables FL 33146 Office: Floyd Pearson Richman et al One Biscayne Tower 25th Floor Miami FL 33131

FEDERICO, ANDREW JOHN, lawyer; b. Cleve., June 13, 1950; s. Sam and Angeline (Costa) F.; m. Hee Soo Hwang, Dec. 20, 1975; children: Regina Hoyoung, Peter Homin. BA, Ohio Wesleyan U., Delaware, 1972; JD, Capital U., 1978. Bar: Ohio 1978. Assoc., examiner Ohio Div. Securities, Columbus, 1978-80; assoc. Carlile Patchen Murphy & Allison, Columbus, 1980-83, ptnr., 1983—; sec. Lowe and Assocs. Inc., Columbus, 1983—. Served with U.S. Army, 1972-74. Mem. ABA, Ohio State Bar Assn., Columbus Bar Assn. Securities, Municipal bonds, General corporate. Office: Carlile Patchen Murphy & Allison 366 E Broad St Columbus OH 43215

FEDERLINE, ROBERT LOUIS, lawyer; b. Pitts., May 21, 1955; s. James J. and Alice V. (Hannon) F.; m. H. Victoria Dudley, June 3, 1979; 1 child, Megan Lynne. B.A., U. Pitts., 1977, J.D., 1980. Bar: Pa. 1980, U.S. Dist. Ct. (we. dist.) Pa. 1980. Assoc. firm Davis & Mazzotta, P.C., Pitts., 1980-81, Thomas J. Dempsey, Pitts., 1981—. Cantor, St. Iraneus Ch., Oakmont, Pa., 1982—. Recipient U.S. Law Week award U. Pitts. Sch. Law, 1980; Nat. Merit scholar, 1973-77; named one of Outstanding Young Men in Am., 1984. Mem. ABA (law student div. 1978-80, sect. econs. of practice of law, v.p. gen. practice sect. com. on professionalism 1985—, litigation sect. 1980—), Pa. Bar Assn. (sect. real property, probate and trust law, family law, ethics and profl. responsibility, litigation sect. 1984—), Allegheny County Bar Assn. (sect. young lawyers, speakers bur., young lawyers pub. service com., indigent div. panel), Assn. Trial Lawyers of Am., Pa. Trial Lawyers Assn., Phi Alpha Delta. Democrat. Roman Catholic. State civil litigation, Personal injury, General practice. Home: 1346 Della Dr Verona PA 15147 Office: Robert L Federline 820 Frick Bldg Pittsburgh PA 15219

FEDIRKO, ROBERT JOHN, lawyer; b. Elizabeth, N.J., May 8, 1949; s. John and Lorraine (Evans) F.; m. Judith Ellen Dervitz, July 4, 1976. BA, Tulane U., 1972; JD, U. San Fernando Valley, 1980. Bar: Calif. 1980, U.S. Dist. Ct. Calif. 1982. Assoc. Rand & Goodchild Inc., Sherman Oaks, Calif., 1980-85, Koszdin & Siegel, Van Nuys, Calif., 1985-86, Slipock & Feinberg, Van Nuys, 1986—; judge protem Workers Compensation Appeals Bd., Van Nuys, 1986. Mem. ABA, Calif. Bar Assn. (cert. specialization in workers compensation 1985), Los Angeles County Bar Assn., Applicants Atty.'s Assn., Def. Attys. Assn. Democrat. Avocations: traveling, stamp collecting. Workers' compensation, Social security. Office: Slipock & Feinberg 14553 Delano St Suite 207 Van Nuys CA 91411

FEDOTA, MARK CLARKE, lawyer; b. Chgo., Apr. 15, 1944; s. John and Dorothy (Strutzel) F.; m. Cherilyn Frances Radous, Aug. 12, 1967; children: Jennifer, Rebecca, Matthew Christopher. AB, Loyola U., 1966; JD, Georgetown U., 1969. Bar: Ill. 1969, U.S. Dist. Ct. (no. dist.) Ill. 1969. Assoc. Phillip H. Corboy & Assocs., Chgo., 1969-73; assoc. Wildman Harrold Allen & Dixon, Chgo., 1973-76, ptnr., 1977—. Mem. ABA (vice chmn. r.r. law), Assn. Trial Lawyers of Am., Nat. Assn. of R.R. Trial Counsel, Ill. Bar Assn., Ill. Trial Lawyers Assn., Chgo. Bar Assn., Def. Research and Trial Lawyers Assn., Ill. Assn. Def. Trial Counsel, Internat. Assn. Ins. Counsel. Personal injury, State civil litigation, Labor. Home: 211 N Elmwood Oak Park IL 60302 Office: Wildman Harrold Allen & Dixon One IBM Plaza Chicago IL 60611

FEEDORE, JEREMY RANDOLPH, lawyer; b. Bklyn., Apr. 23, 1951; s. Frederick W. and Leonore (Suchar) F.; m. Mary Marsh, Aug. 3, 1974; children: Sarah Elizabeth, Elliott Marshall. AB, Syracuse U., 1972; JD, U. Louisville, 1974. Bar. U.S. Ct. Mil. Appeals 1976, N.Y. 1984, U.S. Dist. Ct. (we. dist.) N.Y. 1984, U.S. Dist. Ct. (no. dist.) N.Y. 1987. Commd. 1st lt. USMC, 1975, advanced through grades to capt., 1977; judge adv. USMC, various locations, 1976-83; resigned from active duty USMC, 1983; assoc. Gallo & Iacovangelo, Rochester, N.Y., 1983-87, McClung, Peters & Simon and predecessor firm McClung, Peters, Simon & Arensberg, Albany, N.Y., 1987—. Mem. Monroe County Reps., Rochester, 1983—; vestry St. Luke's Episcopal Ch., Fairport, N.Y., 1986—. Mem. N.Y. State Bar Assn., Monroe County Bar Assn., N.Y. State Trial Lawyers Assn., Assn. Trial Lawyers Am. Criminal, Personal injury, Military. Office: McClung Peters Simon & Arensberg 41 State St Albany NY 12207

FEENEY, ANDREA CHARLTON, lawyer; b. San Francisco, June 8, 1955; d. Francis Joseph and Phyllis Dorothy (Mutch) Charlton; m. Thomas Joseph Feeney, Sept. 10, 1983; 1 child, Joseph Edward; B.A. English, Stanford U., 1977; J.D., U. Pacific, Mc George Sch. Law, 1980. Bar: Calif. 1980. Environ. policy analyst Nat. Commn. on Air Quality, Washington, 1980-81; Pacific Gas & Elec. Co., San Franciso, 1981, legis. rep., adminstr. legis. services, 1982, adminstr. state issues, 1983, adminstr. fed. issues, 1985—. Bd. dirs. Monterey Heights Homes Assn., 1985-86. Recipient writing and speech awards U. Pacific McGeorge Sch. Law, 1979; mem. Internat. Law Moot Ct. Honors Bd., 1979-80; recipient regional award Jessup Internat. Law Moot Ct., 1979. Mem. State Bar Calif. Democrat. Roman Catholic. Club: Spinsters of San Francisco (charity chmn. 1981-82, mem. adv. bd. 1982-83). Public utilities, Legislative, Administrative and regulatory. Office: Pacific Gas & Elec Co 77 Beale St San Francisco CA 94106

FEENEY, DAVID WESLEY, lawyer; b. Phila., Nov. 1, 1938; s. William James McKay and Mary Catherine (Watkins) Feeney; m. Elizabeth Butler Shamel, Aug. 15, 1959; children: Shawn, Shari, David, Darryl. BS, Cornell U., 1960, LLB with distinction, 1963. Bar: U.S. Tax Ct. 1966, U.S. Dist. Ct. (so. dist.) N.Y. 1976, U.S. Ct. Claims 1976, U.S. Ct. Appeals (2d cir.) 1976. Assoc. Cadwalader, Wickersham & Taft, N.Y.C., 1963-64, 66-71, ptnr., 1971—. Served to 1st lt. U.S. Army, 1964-66. Mem. N.Y. State Bar Assn. (tax sect.). Republican. Presbyterian. Clubs: Downtown Athletic, Cornell (N.Y.C.). Corporate taxation. Home: 1 Blackpoint Horseshoe Rumson NJ 07760 Office: Cadwalader Wickersham & Taft 100 Maiden Ln New York NY 10038

FEENEY, PATRICK JOSEPH, lawyer; b. Clarksburg, W.Va., Jan. 21, 1952; s. Patrick J. and Mary Virginia (Hardman) F. BA, U. Notre Dame, 1974; JD, U. Tex., 1977. Bar: Tex. 1977, U.S. Dist. Ct. (we. dist.) Tex. 1980, U.S. Dist. Ct. (so. dist.) Tex. 1981, U.S. Dist. Ct. (no. dist.) Tex. 1982, U.S. Ct. Appeals (5th cir.) 1983, U.S. Supreme Ct. 1983. Sole practice Austin, Tex., 1977-78, 84-85; ptnr. Feeney, O'Hanlon & Moore, Austin, 1979-83; asst. atty. gen. State of Tex., Austin, 1985—. Roman Catholic. Club: Notre Dame Austin (v.p. 1985—). State civil litigation, Personal injury, Contracts commercial. Office: Atty Gen's Office PO Box 12548 Austin TX 78711

FEERICK, JOHN DAVID, university dean, lawyer; b. N.Y.C., July 12, 1936; s. John D. and Mary J. F.; m. Emalie Platt, Aug. 25, 1962; children: Maureen, Margaret, Jean, Rosemary, John, William. B.S., Fordham U., 1958, LL.B., 1961. Bar: N.Y. 1961. Assoc. Skadden, Arps, Slate, Meagher & Flom, N.Y.C., 1961-68; partner Skadden, Arps, Slate, Meagher & Flom, 1968-82; dean Fordham U. Sch. Law, 1982—. Author: From Failing Hands: The Story of Presidential Succession, 1965, The 25th Amendment, 1976; co-author: The Vice Presidents of the United States, 1967, NLRB Representation Elections-Law, Practice and Procedure, 1980; also articles; editor-in-chief Fordham Law Rev., 1960-61; bd. editors Nat. Law Jour. Recipient Eugene J. Keefe award Fordham U. Law Sch., 1975, 85, spl. award Fordham U. Law Rev. Assn., 1977. Fellow Am. Bar Found.; mem. Am. Bar Assn. (chmn. spl. com. election law and voter participation 1976-79, spl. award 1966), N.Y. State Bar Assn. (chmn. com. fed. constn. 1979-83, exec. com.

1985-87), Assn. Bar City N.Y. (v.p. 1986-87), Am. Arbitration Assn., Fordham U. Law Sch. Alumni Assn. (dir. 1972—, medal of achievement 1980), Phi Beta Kappa.

FEESE, BRETT OWEN, lawyer; b. Danville, Pa., May 21, 1954; s. Henry Owens and Phyllis Mae Feese; m. Gwendolyn Bergesen, May 3, 1985. BA, Ind. U. of Pa., 1975; JD, Dickinson Sch. Law, 1979. Bar: Pa. 1979, U.S. Dist. Ct. (mid. dist.) Pa. 1980, U.S. Ct. Appeals (3d cir.) 1982. Ptnr. McNerney, Page, Vanderlin & Hall, Williamsport, Pa., 1980—; dist. atty. Lycoming County, Williamsport, 1984—. Mem. Lycoming County Rep. Com., 1982—; pres. Lycoming County Prison Bd., Williamsport, 1984—; West Br. Drug & Alcohol Abuse Commn., Williamsport, 1985; pastor search commn. New Covenant United Ch., Williamsport, 1985, pastorial relations com., 1985—, sec. ch. council, 1986—. Mem. ABA, Pa. Bar Assn., Assn. Trial Lawyers Am., Pa. Trial Lawyers Assn., Nat. Dist. Attys. Assn., Lycoming County Law Assn. (bench bar com. 1984—). Lodges: Eureka, Masons. Avocations: running, hiking, gardening. Federal civil litigation, State civil litigation, Criminal. Home: RD No 3 PO Box 499E Montoursville PA 17754 Office: McNerney Page Vanderlin & Hall 433 Market St Williamsport PA 17701

FEGAN, DAVID ALBERT, lawyer; b. Washington, July 13, 1918; s. David B. and Elizabeth (Jost) F.; m. Lorraine Coyle, Aug. 14, 1943; children: David, Stephen. Student, Harvard U., 1938; LLB, George Washington U., 1942. Bar: S.C. 1943, D.C. 1943, U.S. Supreme Ct. 1944, Md. 1945. Ptnr. Morris, Pearce, Gardner & Pratt, Washington, 1943-60; sole practice Washington, 1960—; Queen's counsel, U.K., 1969—; bd. dirs. Calvert Bank & Trust Co., Prince Frederick, Md.; bd. dirs., pres. Old Line Brick and Tile Co., Mar-Bar Devel. Corp.; bd. dirs., v.p. Capitol Clay Products Inc., St. Leonard's Devel. Corp. Served with USNR, 1942-43. Mem. ABA, D.C. Bar Assn. Club: Reciprocit. Avocation: golf. Federal civil litigation, General corporate, Private international. Home: 8709 Seven Locks Rd Bethesda MD 20817 Office: Suite 927 1511 K ST NW Washington DC 20005

FEGAN, DAVID COYLE, lawyer; b. Washington, July 9, 1944; s. David Albert and Lorraine Margaret (Coyle) F.; m. Joan Pooley, Apr. 10, 1976; children—Alison Marie, Paige Elizabeth. B.A., Washington Coll., Chestertown, Md., 1967; J.D., U. Md., 1970; LL.M., George Washington U., 1974. Bar: Md. 1970. Tax law specialist individual income tax br. IRS, Washington, 1970-75, sr. atty. Office of Chief Counsel, 1975—. Mem. Adv. Neighborhood Commn., 1979-81, Neighborhood Service award, 1982. Corporate taxation, Personal income taxation, Federal civil litigation. Home: 2307 Senseney Lane Falls Church VA 22043 Office: 1111 Constitution Ave NW Washington DC 20224

FEHELEY, LAWRENCE FRANCIS, lawyer; b. Phila., Oct. 9, 1946; s. Francis Edward and Dorothy May (Greenhalgh) F.; divorced; 1 child, Matthew Francis; m. Janet Kay Douglass, Apr. 6, 1979; children: Brendan Patrick, Lawren Kaitlin, Tyne Brielle. BA, Cornell U., 1969, JD with distinction, 1973. Bar: Ohio 1973, U.S. Dist. Ct. (so. dist.) Ohio 1974, U.S. Ct. Appeals (6th cir.) 1980. Assoc. Emens, Hurd, Kegler & Ritter, Columbus, Ohio, 1973-77, ptnr., 1977—, also bd. dirs., mng. dir., 1986; bd. dirs. Aleda Inc., Columbus. Mem. Franklin County Reps. Chmn's. Club., 1985—. Served with USAR, 1968-74. Mem. ABA, Ohio Bar Assn. (bd. govs. labor law sect.), Columbus Bar Assn. Republican. Episcopalian. Club: Shamrock (Columbus). Avocations: art, soccer. Labor, Administrative and regulatory. Office: Emens Hurd Kegler & Ritter 65 E State St Columbus OH 43215

FEIBLEMAN, GILBERT BRUCE, lawyer; b. Portland, Oreg., Jan. 29, 1951; s. Herbert Frank and Bernice (Kaplan) F.; m. Ellen L. Hobson, June 20, 1981; 1 child, Benjamin. BS, U. Oreg., 1972; JD, U. Pacific, 1976. Bar: Oreg. 1976, U.S. Dist. Ct. Oreg. 1976, U.S. Ct. Appeals (9th cir.). Assoc. Goodenough & Pierson, Salem, Oreg., 1976-78; mng. ptnr. Ramsay, Stein, Feibleman & Myers, Salem, 1978—; instr. bus. law Chemeketa Community Coll., Marion County, Oreg., 1977, trial law Willamette U.; arbitrator Oreg. State Bar, Salem, 1979—, Marion County Ct., Salem, 1985—; pro-tem judge Oreg. Dist. Cts., 1982—, Oreg. Cir. Cts., 1987—. Mem. Oreg. Trial Lawyers Assn., Am. Trial Lawyers Assn. Democrat. Avocations: skiing, gourmet cooking. Family and matrimonial, State civil litigation, Personal injury. Home: 552 Stagecoach Way SE Salem OR 97221 Office: Ramsay Stein Feibleman & Myers 960 Liberty St SE Suite 110 Salem OR 97302

FEIDLER, ROBERT ERNEST, lawyer; b. Grand Forks, N.D., Jan. 27, 1950; s. Robert August and Marie Louise (Mynster) F.; m. Patricia Ann Ward, June 3, 1978; children: Alex, William. BA, U. N.D., 1971, JD, 1974. Bar: N.D. 1974. Dep. counsel cts. sub-com. Com. on Judiciary, U.S. Senate, Washington, 1974-76, chief counsel cts. sub-com., 1976-80, chief minority counsel constn. subcom., 1981-86, chief counsel constn. subcom., 1986, chief counsel, staff dir. patent, trademark, copyright subcom., 1987; legis. and pub. affairs officer Adminstrv. Office of U.S. Cts., Washington, 1987—. mem. adminstrv. bd., trustee Mt. Olive United Meth. Ch., Arlington, Va., 1980-82, 84—. Served to maj. USAR, 1971—. Mem. Fed. Bar Assn. (pres. Capitol Hill chpt. 1982-83, Outstanding Younger Fed. Lawyer 1980), N.D. Bar Assn., Am. Bankruptcy Inst. (bd. dirs. exec. com. 1983—), Flat Tax Found. (pres. 1985—), Res. Officers Assn. (pres. local chpt. 1983-84, Outstanding Jr. Officer 1981-82). Club: Army-Navy (Arlington). Bankruptcy, Judicial administration, Antitrust. Home: 1411 N Glebe Rd Arlington VA 22207

FEIERSTEIN, MARK ERROL, lawyer; b. N.Y.C., May 22, 1948; s. Lester and Rose (Feingersh) F. BA, Miami U., Oxford, Ohio, 1970; MS in Bus., L.I. U., 1975; JD, N.Y. Law Sch., 1979. Bar: N.Y. 1979. Assoc. Olvaney, Eisner and Donnelly, N.Y.C., 1977-79, Oppenheim, Appel and Co., N.Y.C., 1981-82; law guardian Family Ct. of N.Y., Westchester, 1983—; atty. Article 18-B Panel, Westchester, 1984—; of counsel Thomas and Sykes, Yonkers, N.Y., 1985-86; adminstrv. law judge N.Y.C. Taxi and Limousine Commn., 1984—, N.Y.C. Parking Violations Bur., 1984—; arbitrator Civil Ct. of N.Y.C., 1985—. Mem. Bronx Citizens Com., N.Y., 1986. Mem. ABA, N.Y. State Bar Assn., Assn. Adminstrv. Law Judges, N.Y. Law Sch. Alumni Assn., Am. Arbitration Assn. Jewish. Avocations: tennis, golf, movies, theater, reading. Home: 5614 Netherland Ave 4C Riverdale NY 10471 Office: 27 Wendover Rd Yonkers NY 10705

FEIGER, LYNN DIAMOND, lawyer; b. San Francisco, Oct. 12, 1946; d. Bernard L. and Ann (Landy) Diamond; m. Alan David Feiger, June 26, 1966; 1 child, Joshua. Student, Brandeis U., 1964-66; BA, UCLA, 1968; JD, U. So. Calif., 1971; MS in Law and Soc., U. Denver, 1974. Bar: Calif. 1974, Colo. 1974, U.S. Dist. Ct. Colo. 1974, U.S. Ct. Appeals (10th cir.) 1979, U.S. Supreme Ct. 1979. Assoc. Donald S. Molen, Denver, 1974-76; sole practice Denver, 1976-77, 82-85; ptnr. Feiger & Lawson, Denver, 1977-82, Feiger & Hyman, Denver, 1985—; mem. initial com. on conduct U.S. Dist. Ct. Colo., 1979-82, mem. hearing bd. Colo. Supreme Ct. Grievance Com., 1983—. Contbr. articles to profl. jours. Fellow NSF. Fellow Am. Acad. Matrimonial Lawyers; mem. ABA (equal employment opportunity commn. liaison regional com.), Colo. Women's Bar Assn. (bd. dirs., chmn. profl. adv. com. 1984-85), Colo. Supreme Ct. Grievance Com. (hearing bd. mem. 1983—), Plaintiff Employment Litigation Assn. (pres. 1985—). Democrat. Jewish. Labor, Family and matrimonial, Personal injury. Home: 1742 Montane Dr E Golden CO 80401 Office: Feiger & Hyman 1860 Blake St #520 Denver CO 80202

FEIGIN, PHILIP ALAN, assistant commissioner; b. Manhattan, N.Y., Mar. 7, 1949; s. William Murray and Dora (Levenkron) F. BA, U. Wis., 1971; JD, Pepperdine U., 1977. Bar: Calif. 1977, Wis. 1978, U.S. Dist. Ct. (we. dist.) Wis. 1978, U.S. Dist. Ct. (ea. dist.) Wis. 1981, Colo. 1986. Assoc. Eisenberg, Giesen, Ewers & Hayes, Madison, Wis., 1977-79; chief atty. enforcement div. Wis. Commn. of Securities, Madison, 1979-82; asst. sec. commr. Colo. Div. of Securities, Denver, 1982—. Mem. ABA (state securities regulation subcom.), N.A. Securities Adminstrn. Assn. (chmn. commodities com. 1986—). Securities. Office: Colo Div of Securities 1560 Broadway Suite 1450 Denver CO 80202

FEIKENS, JOHN, judge; b. Clifton, N.J., Dec. 3, 1917; s. Sipke and Corine (Wisse) F.; m. Henriette Dorothy Schulthouse, Nov. 4, 1939; children: Jon, Susan Corine, Barbara Edith, Julie Anne, Robert H. A.B., Calvin Coll., Grand Rapids, Mich., 1939; J.D., U. Mich., 1941; LL.D., U. Detroit, 1979, Detroit Coll. Law, 1981. Bar: Mich. 1942. Gen. practice law Detroit; dist. judge Ea. Dist. Mich., Detroit, 1960-61, 70-79, chief judge, 1979-86, sr. judge, 1986—; past co-chmn. Mich. Civil Rights Commn.; past chmn. Rep. State Central Com.; past mem. Rep. Nat. Com. Past bd. trustees Calvin Coll. Fellow Am. Coll. Trial Lawyers; mem. ABA, Detroit Bar Assn. (dir. 1962, past pres.), State Bar Mich. (commr. 1965-71). Club: University of Michigan. Jurisprudence, Administrative and regulatory, Civil rights. Home: 1574 Brookfield Dr Ann Arbor MI 48103 Office: Fed Bldg 231 W Lafayette Blvd 7th Floor Detroit MI 48226

FEIMAN, RONALD MARK, lawyer; b. N.Y.C., Feb. 28, 1951; s. Richard and Patricia (Spalter) F.; m. Hilary J. Ronner, Jan. 7, 1954. BA, Yale U., 1972; JD, MBA, NYU, 1977. Bar: N.Y. 1978. Assoc. Gordon Hurwitz Butowsky Weitzen Shalov & Wein, N.Y.C., 1977-85, ptnr., 1985—. Mem. ABA, Assn. Bar of City of N.Y., Am. Inst. CPA's. Club: Yale (N.Y.C.). Securities, General corporate, Entertainment. Home: 401 E 80th St New York NY 10021 Office: Gordon Hurwitz Butowsky et al 101 Park Ave New York NY 10178

FEIN, ERIC DAVID, lawyer; b. Bklyn., Sept. 3, 1954; s. Norman and Harriett (Mehr) F.; m. Sharyn L. Hoffman, Dec. 15, 1984. BS, SUNY, Buffalo, 1975; JD, Capital U., 1978. Bar: N.Y. 1980. Atty. Am. Internat. Group, N.Y.C., 1978-79; assoc. Marsh & McLennan, N.Y.C., 1979-80, Kroll, Killarney, Pomerantz & Cameron, N.Y.C., 1980-81; sole practice N.Y.C., 1981—. Mem. N.Y. County Bar Assn. State civil litigation, Personal injury, General corporate. Office: 50 E 42d St New York NY 10017

FEIN, ROGER G., lawyer; b. St. Louis, Mar. 12, 1940; s. Albert and Fanny (Levinson) F.; m. Susanne M. Cohen, Dec. 18, 1965; children—David I., Lisa J. Student Washington U., St. Louis, 1959, NYU, 1960; B.S., UCLA, 1962; J.D., Northwestern U., 1965; M.B.A., Am. U., 1967. Bar: Ill. 1965, U.S. Dist. Ct. (no. dist.) Ill. 1968, U.S. Ct. Appeals (7th cir.) 1968, U.S. Supreme Ct. 1970. Atty. div. corp. fin. SEC, Washington, 1965-67; ptnr. Arvey, Hodes, Costello & Burman, Chgo., 1967—, mem. exec. com., 1977—; mem. Securities Adv. Com. to Sec. State Ill., 1973—, chmn., 1973-79, vice chmn., 1983—; spl. asst. atty. gen. State of Ill., 1974-83, 85—; mem. Appeal Bd., Ill. Law Enforcement Commn., 1980-83; mem. lawyer's adv. bd. So. Ill. Law Jour., 1980-83; mem. adv. bd. securities regulation and law report Bur. Nat. Affairs Inc., 1985—; lectr., author; bd. dirs. United Nat. Bank of Arlington Heights. Mem. Bd. Edn., Sch. Dist. No. 29, Northfield, Ill., 1977-83, pres., 1981-83; vice-chmn. Chgo. regional bd. Anti-Defamation League of B'nai B'rith, 1980—; chmn. lawyers' com. for ann. telethon Muscular Dystrophy Assn., 1983; past bd. dirs. Jewish Nat. Fund., Am. Friends Hebrew U., Northfield Community Fund. Recipient Sec. State Ill. Pub. Service award, 1976, Citation of Merit, WAIT Radio, 1976, Sunset Ridge Sch. Community Service award, 1984; City of Chgo. Citizen's award 1986. Fellow Am. Bar Found., Ill. Bar Found. (bd. dirs. 1978—, v.p. 1982-84, pres. 1984-86, chmn. Fellows 1983-84, Cert. of Appreciation 1985, 86), Chgo. Bar Found.; mem. Fed. Bar Assn., Am. Judicature Soc., Decalogue Soc. Lawyers, Attys. Title Guaranty Fund, ABA (state regulation of securities com. 1982—, Ill. liaison of com.), ho. of dels. 1981-85), Ill. Bar Assn. (bd. govs. 1976-80, del. assembly 1976—, sec. 1977-78, cert. of appreciation 1980, chmn. Bench and Bar com. 1982-83, sect. council 1983-84, chmn. bar elections supervision com. 1986-87), Chgo. Bar Assn. (mem. task force delivery legal services 1978-80, cert. of appreciation 1976, chmn. land trusts com. 1978-79, chmn. consumer credit com. 1977-78, chmn. state securities law subcom. 1977-79), Legal Club Chgo., Tau Epsilon Phi, Alpha Kappa Psi, Phi Delta Phi. Clubs: Standard, Legal (Chgo.). General corporate, Banking, Securities. Office: Arvey Hodes Costello & Burman 180 N LaSalle St Suite 3800 Chicago IL 60601

FEIN, RONALD LAWRENCE, lawyer; b. Detroit, Aug. 26, 1943; s. Lee Allen and Billie Doreen (Thomas) F.; m. Rosemary Heath, Sept. 2, 1966; children: Samantha, Mark. AB with honors, UCLA, 1966; JD with honors, U. San Diego, 1969. Bar: Calif. 1970, U.S. Dist. Ct. (cen. dist.) Calif. 1970. Assoc. Gibson, Dunn & Crutcher, Los Angeles, 1969-75; chmn. dep. commr. of corps. State of Calif., Los Angeles, 1975-78; ptnr., mem. adv. com., chmn. corp. fin./mergers and acquisitions sect. Jones, Day, Reavis & Pogue, Los Angeles, 1978-87; ptnr., mem. exec. com., chmn. gen. corp. and corp. securities group Wyman, Bautzer, Christensen, Kuchel & Silbert, Los Angeles, 1987—; bd. dirs. Executours, Inc., Los Angeles, Lottery Info., North Hollywood, Calif., Malibu Grand Prix, Woodland Hills, Calif.; adj. prof. law Loyola U., Los Angeles, 1978—; mem. Commr.'s Circle Adv. Com. to the Calif. Commr. of Corps., Fin. Lawyers Conf. Articles editor San Diego Law Rev., 1969; contbr. articles to profl. jours. Co-dir. protocol for boxing Los Angeles Olympic Organizing Com., 1984. Served to 1st lt. USAF, to 1966-69. Mem. ABA (corp., banking and bus. law sect., mem. ad hoc com. on merit regulation, mem. fed. regulation of securities com., mem. ad hoc com. on the Uniform Limited Offering Exemption, mem. ad hoc com. on Regulation D, mem. subcom. on Registration Statements—1933 Act, vice chmn. state regulation securities com., chmn. pvt. offering exemption and simplification of capital formation subcom.), Calif. Bar Assn. (exec. com. bus. law sect.), Los Angeles County Bar Assn. (bus. and corps. law sect.), Nat. Assn. of Securities Dealers, Inc. (mem. subcom. on indemnification, mem. arbitration panel). Club: Regency, Sand and Sea (Los Angeles). Avocations: athletics, reading, theater. Administrative and regulatory, Bankruptcy, General corporate. Home: 120 Homewood Rd Los Angeles CA 90049 Office: Wyman Bautzer Christensen Kuchel & Silbert 2049 Century Park E Los Angeles CA 90067

FEIN, SCOTT NORRIS, lawyer; b. N.Y.C., Oct. 22, 1949; s. Sidney and Charlotte (Blaustein) F.; m. Patricia Martinelli, Oct. 16, 1983. BA, Am. U., 1971; JD, Georgetown U., 1975; LLM, NYU, 1979. Bar: N.Y. 1976, U.S. Dist. Ct. (ea. dist.) N.Y. 1978, U.S. Dist. Ct. (no. dist.) N.Y. 1982, U.S. Dist. Ct. (so. dist.) N.Y. 1978, U.S. Dist. Ct. (we. dist.) N.Y. 1985. Asst. dist. atty. Nassau County, Mineola, N.Y., 1975-79; asst. counsel to Gov. Hugh Carey of N.Y., Albany, 1979-82, Gov. Mario Cuomo, 1982-83; ptnr. Whiteman Osterman & Hanna, Albany, 1983—; litigation counsel N.Y. State Civil Liberties Union, 1984—. Mem. Assn. Trial Lawyers Am., ABA, N.Y. State Bar Assn. (co-chmn. com. criminal environ. litigation), N.Y. State Defenders Assn. Federal civil litigation, Criminal, Environment. Home: 534 Huron Rd Delmar NY 12054 Office: Whiteman Osterman & Hanna 99 Washington Ave Albany NY 12210

FEIN, SHERMAN EDWARD, lawyer, psychologist; b. Springfield, Mass., June 17, 1928; s. Samuel L. and Mildred B. (Sherman) F.; m. Myra N. Becker, Nov. 13, 1955; children—Dina, Julia, Sara. B.A., Bowdoin Coll., 1949; J.D., Boston U., 1953; M.S., Springfield Coll., 1962; Ed.D., U. Mass., 1969; Sc.M.D., Sch. Medicine, Ross U., Portsmouth, Dominica, West Indies, 1983. Bar: Maine 1952, Mass. 1953, U.S. dist. Ct. Mass. 1957, U.S. Supreme Ct. 1965. Ptnr., Fein, Schulman, Pearson & Emond, Springfield, 1953—; pvt. practice psychology, Springfield, 1962—; hon. consul Republic of Costa Rica, 1963—. Author: Selected Cases on Shoplifting, 1975; Divorce Handbook, 1978. Served to sgt. USAF, 1950-52; to lt. col. CAP, 1953-77. Mem. Hampden County Bar Assn., Mass. Bar Assn., ABA, Assn. Trial Lawyers Am., Am. Psychology-Law Assn. Republican. Jewish. Lodges: Masons, Shriners. Personal injury, Workers' compensation, Health. Home: 224 Longmeadow St Longmeadow MA 01106 Office: Fein Schulman Pearson & Emond 52 Mulberry St Springfield MA 01105

FEINBERG, JACK, lawyer; b. Atlantic City, Mar. 24, 1949; s. Jules and Sara Rae (Schleimer) F.; m. Judy I. Levine, July 27, 1972; children—Jason B., Jamie L. B.A., Syracuse U., 1971; J.D., U. Akron, 1974. Bar: N.J. 1974, U.S. Dist. Ct. N.J. 1974, U.S. Supreme Ct. 1986. Ptnr. firm Goldenberg, Mackler & Feinberg, Atlantic City, 1974-81, Mairone, Biel, Zlotnick, Feinberg & Griffith, Atlantic City, 1982—; sole practice, Ventnor, N.J., 1981-82. Contbr. articles to profl. jours. County com. mem. Atlantic County Democrats, 1979. Named Boss of Yr., Atlantic County Legal Secs., 1980. Mem. ABA, Atlantic County Bar Assn., Assn. Trial Lawyers Am., N.J. Trial Lawyers Assn., Nat. Health Lawyers Assn., Greater Atlantic City Jaycees (legal counsel 1975-76, pres. 1976-77). Democrat. Jewish. Lodge: Rotary. Personal injury, State civil litigation, Real property. Office: Mairone Biel Zlotnick Feinberg & Griffith 3201 Atlantic Ave Atlantic City NJ 08401

FEINBERG, ROBERT JULIAN, judge; b. Plattsburgh, N.Y., Feb. 13, 1924; s. Benjamin Franklin and Leah (Mendelsohn) F.; m. Laurie Covert, Mar. 22, 1974. B.A., Yale U., 1945, J.D., 1947. Bar: N.Y. 1948. Assoc. Costello, Conney & Fearon, Syracuse, N.Y., 1947-50; mem. Feinberg, Jerry & Lewis, Plattsburgh, 1950-60; sole practice, Plattsburgh, 1961-67; mem. Jerry, Lewis, Feinberg & Lyon, Plattsburgh, 1967-70; judge Clinton County (N.Y.) Ct. and Family Ct., Plattsburgh, 1970—; asst. atty. gen. N.Y. State, 1948; mem. N.Y. State Assembly, 1957-64. Mem. N.Y. State Bar Assn., Clinton County Bar Assn., Am. Judicature Soc., County Judges Assn., Family Ct. Judges Assn. Republican. Jewish. Clubs: Rotary (past pres.), Elks, Masons (32 deg.), Shriners, Moose, B'nai B'rith. Mng. editor Yale Law Jour., 1946-47. Jurisprudence. Address: PO Box 827 Plattsburgh NY 12901

FEINBERG, SIDNEY S., lawyer; b. Bklyn., Aug. 30, 1910; s. Samuel and Minnie (Komaroff) F.; m. Elizabeth H. Hoffman, Sept. 4, 1931; children—Thomas, Sherry Ruth Feinberg Israel. Student, Carleton Coll., 1924-25; B.A., U. Minn., 1928, J.D., 1930. Bar: Minn. 1930, U.S. Dist. Ct. Minn. 1932, U.S. Ct. Apls. (8th cir.) 1947, U.S. Ct. Appeals (9th cir.) 1951. Atty., Davis & Michel, Mpls., 1926-35; sole practice, Worthington, Minn., 1935-43; enforcement atty. Office Price Adminstrn., Washington, 1943-47; sole practice, Mpls., 1947-48; assoc. Robins, Zelle, Larson & Kaplan and predecessor, Mpls., 1948-51, ptnr., 1951—. Chmn., Minn. State Civil Service Bd., 1968-72; trustee local Multiple Sclerosis chpt., 1963—; bd. dirs. Legal Rights Ctr., 1970—; mem. Minn. Pub. Employee Relations Bd., 1979-82. Mem. ABA (ho. of dels. 1968-69), Nat. Conf. Bar Presidents, Minn. State Bar Assn. (pres. 1967-68, sr. counselor 1980), Hennepin County Bar Assn. (pres. 1962-63), Fed. Bar Assn., Am. Judicature Soc. Republican. Jewish. Clubs: Mpls. Downtown Kiwanis (pres. 1984-85), B'nai B'rith, Masons, Shriners; Oak Ridge Country (Hopkins, Minn.). General practice. Office: Robins Zelle Larson & Kaplan 1800 Internat Centre 900 2d Ave S Minneapolis MN 55402

FEINBERG, THOMAS DAVIS, lawyer; b. St. Paul, Dec. 18, 1932; s. Sidney S. and Elizabeth (Hoffman) F.; m. Corrine Gottstein, Nov. 18, 1956; children: Jane Susan, Judith Ann Wert, Karen Beth. BA, U. Minn., 1952; JD, Harvard U., 1955. Bar: Minn. 1955, U.S. Dist. Ct. Minn. 1955. Ptnr. Robins, Davis & Lyons, Mpls., 1955-78, Leonard, Street & Deinard, Mpls., 1978—; sec. Lamaur Inc., Mpls., 1982—, XTAL Corp., Mpls., 1983—, bd. dirs., Thiele Enging. Co., Mpls., 1984—, bd. dirs.; bd. dirs. MF Bank and Co. Inc., Mpls. Pres. Mpls. Fedn. Jewish Service, 1975-78; bd. dirs. Nat. Council Jewish Fedns. and Welfare Funds, N.Y.C., 1976-80, Fund for Legal Aid Soc., 1986—; bd. visitors U. Minn. Law Sch., 1984—. Recipient Young Leadership award Mpls. Fedn. for Jewish Service, 1962. Mem. ABA, Minn. Bar Assn., Hennepin County Bar Assn., Minn. Orchestral Assn. (bd. dirs. 1986—). Club: Oakridge Country (Mpls.) (bd. dirs. 1975-76). Avocation: golf. Home: 1235 Yale Pl #609 Minneapolis MN 55403 Office: Leonard Street & Deinard 100 S 5th St #1500 Minneapolis MN 55402

FEINBERG, WILFRED, federal judge; b. N.Y.C., June 22, 1920; s. Jac and Eva (Wolin) F.; m. Shirley Marcus, June 23, 1946; children—Susan, Jack, Jessica. B.A., Columbia U., 1940, LL.B., 1946, LL.D. (hon.), 1985; LL.D. (hon.), Syracuse U., 1985. Bar: N.Y. 1947. Law clk. U.S. dist. judge 1947-49; assoc. Kaye, Scholer, Fierman & Hays, N.Y.C., 1949-53; mem. McGoldrick, Dannett, Horowitz & Golub, N.Y.C., 1953-61; dep. supt. N.Y. State Banking Dept., 1958; U.S. judge So. Dist. N.Y., 1961-66; U.S. judge Ct. Appeals 2d Circuit, 1966-80, chief judge, 1980—; Madison lectr. NYU Law Sch., 1983; Sonnett lectr. Fordham U. Law Sch., 1984. Editor-in-chief Columbia Law Rev, 1946. Served with AUS, 1942-45. Mem. ABA, Assn. Bar City N.Y., N.Y. County Lawyers Assn., Am. Judicature Soc., Am. Law Inst., Phi Beta Kappa. Jurisprudence. Office: US Cthouse Foley Sq New York NY 10007

FEINERMAN, JAMES VINCENT, law educator; b. Chgo., Oct. 30, 1950; s. Albert and Ann Marie (Donnelly) F. BA, Yale U., 1971, MA, 1974, PhD, 1979; JD, Harvard U., 1979. Bar: N.Y. 1981. Assoc. Davis Polk & Wardwell, N.Y.C., 1979-83; adminstrv. dir. East Asian legal studies Harvard U. Sch. Law, Cambridge, Mass., 1983-85; assoc. prof. Georgetown U. Sch. Law, Washington, 1985—. Editor jour. China Law Reporter, 1986—. Fulbright lectr. Peking U., 1982-83; Fulbright grantee Japan, 1986. Mem. ABA, Assn. Asian Studies. Roman Catholic. Avocations: jogging, rowing. Private international, Public international, General corporate. Office: Georgetown U Law Ctr 600 New Jersey Ave NW Washington DC 20001

FEINGOLD, VICTOR, lawyer; b. Bklyn., Feb. 19, 1912; s. Isadore and Rebecca (Wolkowiski) F.; m. Elizabeth Postman, Aug. 13, 1939; children—Jane Goldman, Lisa Cohen. B.A., CCNY, 1933; J.D., Fordham U., 1936; LL.M. in Labor Law, N.Y.U., 1955. Bar: N.Y. 1936, U.S. Dist. Ct. (so. dist.) N.Y. 1939, U.S. Supreme Ct. 1958, U.S. Ct. Appeals (2d cir.) 1960, U.S. Dist. Ct. (ea. dist.) N.Y. 1976. Sole practice, N.Y.C. and New Rochelle, N.Y., 1936—; lectr. Columbia U. Mem. ABA, N.Y. State Bar Assn., N.Y. County Lawyers Assn., Internat. Acad. Law and Sci. Bd. editors: Fordham Law Rev., 1935-36; contbr. articles to legal publs. Labor, Estate planning, Pension, profit-sharing, and employee benefits.

FEINOUR, JOHN STEPHEN, lawyer; b. Kingston, Pa., July 30, 1951; s. John Gouger and Ethel Cooke (Peterson) F.; m. Bernadette Barattini, Apr. 16 1977; children—J. Stephen, Kathleen M. B.A., Dickinson Coll., 1973; J.D., Temple U., 1976. Bar: Pa. 1976, U.S. Dist. Ct. (mid. dist.) Pa. 1979, U.S. Supreme Ct. 1983. Law clk. to presiding justice Dauphin County Ct. Common Pleas, Harrisburg, Pa., 1976-77; assoc. Nauman, Smith, Shissler & Hall, Harrisburg, 1977-82, ptnr., 1982—; arbitrator Dauphin County Ct. Common Pleas, 1982-84, chmn. arbitration bd., 1984—. Co-editor Dauphin County Young Lawyers Handbook. Bd. dirs. Camp Shikellimy br. Harrisburg Area YMCA, 1981-82, bd. dirs. Harrisburg Area, 1981-82, 85—, bd. mgrs. , 1979-84, asst. sec.; moderator, bd. deacons, ruling elder Paxton Presbyterian Ch., Pa., 1982-83. Mem. ABA, Assn. Trial Lawyers Am., Pa. Bar Assn. (litigation and workmen's compensation sects.), Dauphin County Bar Assn. (ct. relations, ct. rules and arbitration coms.), Kappa Sigma (alumnus advisor 1982). Republican. State civil litigation, Federal civil litigation, Insurance. Home: 333 Willow Ave Camp Hill PA 17011

FEINSTEIN, FRED IRA, lawyer; b. Chgo., Apr. 6, 1945; s. Bernard and Beatrice (Mines) F.; m. Judy Cutler, Aug. 25, 1968; children—Karen, Donald. B.S.C., DePaul U., 1967, J.D., 1970. Bar: Ill. 1970, U.S. Supreme Ct. 1977. Ptnr. McDermott, Will & Emery, Chgo., 1976—; lectr. in field. Pres., Skokie/Evanston (Ill.) Action Council, 1981-84; bd. dirs. Temple Judea Mizpah, Skokie, 1982-84, Deborah Goldfine Meml. Cancer Research, 1968—, YMCA of Chgo., 1985—. Mem. ABA, Ill. Bar Assn., Chgo. Bar Assn., Am. Coll. Real Estate Attys., Blue Key, Beta Gamma Sigma, Beta Alpha Psi, Pi Gamma Mu, Lambda Alpha. Club: Union League. Contbr. articles to profl. jours. Real property, Landlord-tenant, Contracts commercial. Office: McDermott Will & Emery 111 W Monroe St Chicago IL 60603

FEINSTEIN, LARRY BURTON, lawyer; b. Salt Lake City, Sept. 28, 1947; s. Herman N. and Muriel B. (Berenter) F.; m. Pamela Hooper, July 4, 1974; children: Joshua, Brian, Max. BA, U. Wash., 1970; JD, U. Utah, 1973. Bar: N.Y. 1973, Wash. 1975, U.S. Dist. Ct. (ea. and we. dists.) Wash 1975. Ptnr. Steiner & Feinstein, Seattle, 1975-78, Watson, Grosse & Feinstein, Seattle, 1978-82, Feinstein, McAulay & Bartlett, Seattle, 1982-85, Feinstein & Bull, Seattle, 1985—. Contbr. articles to profl. jours. Mem. Wash. Bar Assn. (officer debtor/creditor sect. 1980-82), Seattle-King County Bar Assn. (officer bankruptcy sect. 1981-83). Bankruptcy. Home: 2129 130th Pl SE Bellevue WA 98005 Office: Feinstein & Bull 910 5th Ave Seattle WA 98104

FEINSTEIN, PAUL LOUIS, lawyer; b. Chgo., Jan. 5, 1955; s. Sherman C. and Sara (Steinman) F.; m. Andrea Lee Albaum, June 26, 1983. BA, Tulane U., 1977; JD, Emory U., 1980. Bar: Ga. 1980, Ill. 1980, U.S. Dist. Ct. (no. dist.) Ill. 1980. Assoc. Jones, Baer & Davis, Chgo., 1980-81; sr. assoc. Marshall Auerbach and Assocs., Chgo., 1981-84, 86—; sr. ptnr. Chausow & Feinstein, Chgo., 1984-86. Chmn. programming Tulane U. Chgo. Alumni Council, 1984-86, pres., 1986—; bd. dirs. 3600 Lake Shore Dr. Condominium Assn., Chgo., 1986—. Mem. ABA, Ill. Bar Assn., Ga. Bar Assn., Chgo. Bar Assn. (lectr. battered women project), Pi Sigma Alpha, Phi Alpha Delta, Tau Epsilon Phi. Avocation: running. Family and matrimonial. Office: Marshall Auerbach & Assocs 180 N La Salle St Chicago IL 60601

FEINSTEIN, SHELDON, lawyer; b. Mar. 21, 1932; s. Moe and Sara Feinstein; married; children: Susan, Donna. BCE, City Coll. N.Y., 1954; LLB, Bklyn. Law Sch., 1961. Civil engr. City of N.Y., 1956-61; sole practice Queens, N.Y., 1961—. Mem. Queens County Bar Assn. Construction. Office: 136-55 37th Ave Flushing NY 11354

FEIRICH, JOHN COTTRILL, lawyer; b. Chgo., Jan. 2, 1933; s. John K. and Mary R. F.; m. Diane Suitt, June 29, 1985; children—John Charles, Elizabeth Suzanne, Lee Elizabeth. Student, Northwestern U., Evanston, Ill., 1950-53; J.D., U.Ill., Champaign, 1956. Bar: Ill. 1956. Mem. Feirich & Feirich, Carbondale, Ill., 1956-68; sole practice law Carbondale, 1968-72, John C. Feirich Assoc., Carbondale, 1972-77; sr. ptnr. Feirich, Schoen, Mager, Green & Assocs., Carbondale, 1977—. Author: Illinois Civil Practice Before Trial, 1985; co-author: Illinois Pattern Instructions, 2d edit., 1971; contbr. articles to profl. jours. Founder, 1st pres. Air Ill., Inc., Carbondale; bd. dirs. Carbondale YMCA, 1958-65, Carbondale United Fund, 1959-67; mem. Carbondale Community High Sch. Bd. Edn., 1969-74. Named to Scribes. Fellow Am. Coll. Trial Lawyers, Am. Bar Found.; mem. ABA (chmn. gen. practice sect. 1984-85, com. professionalism 1985—), Ill. State Bar Assn. (pres. 1982-83), Lawyer's Trust Fund Ill. (v.p.), Am. Judicature Soc. (bd. dirs.). Clubs: Yacht (Chgo.); Marathon Yacht (Fla.). Avocation: yachting. Federal civil litigation, General corporate, Real property. Office: Feirich Schoen Mager Green 2001 W Main St PO Box 2408 Carbondale IL 62901

FEITELSON, ROBERT JOEL, lawyer, accountant; b. Yonkers, N.Y., Jan. 6, 1935; s. Louis Leo and Miriam (Kaplan) F.; m. Doris Joan Markowitz, Apr. 19, 1956; children—Todd M., Glenn R. Student U. Vt., 1952-55; B.S., NYU, 1956, LL.B., 1962. Bar: N.Y. 1963; C.P.A. C.P.A. Elson & Steinman, Yonkers, 1956-73; ptnr., C.P.A. Elson, Steinman & Feitelson, Yonkers, 1973-75, Platt, Barth, Elson & Steinman, P.C., Yonkers, 1975—; sole practice law, Yonkers, 1963—. Mem. N.Y. State Bar Assn., Democrat. Jewish. Real property, Estate planning, Probate. Home: 6 Windsor Rd Hastings-on-Hudson NY 10706 Office: 984 N Broadway Yonkers NY 10701

FEKETE, GEORGE O., lawyer, pharmacist; b. Budapest, Hungary; came to U.S., 1949; s. Bela and Ilona (Meer) F.; divorced; children: Jacqueline Kim, Jeanette Lee. BS, Wayne State U., 1954; PharmD, U. So. Calif., 1960; JD, Pepperdine U., 1973. Bar: Calif. 1973, U.S. Dist. Ct. (so. dist.) Calif. 1973, U.S. Supreme Ct. 1980, U.S. Dist Ct. (no. dist.) Calif. 1986. Chief pharmacist Hylo Drug Co., Huntington Beach, Calif., 1960-73; pres. G.O. Fekete Law Corp., Anaheim, Calif., 1973-86; lead trial lawyer Melvin Belli Law Offices, San Francisco, 1986—. Served to maj. USAF, 1954-59. Mem. ABA, Assn. Trial Lawyers Am., Calif. Trial Lawyers Assn. (legis. com. 1976-78), Alameda County Bar Assn., Orange County Trial Lawyers Assn (bd. dirs. 1977). Personal injury, Insurance, State civil litigation.

FELCHER, PETER L., lawyer; b. Bklyn., 1939; s. Irving and Thelma (Hodes) F.; m. Nancy Kane, 1964; children: Andrew, Benjamin. AB, Princeton U., 1960; LLB, Yale U., 1963. Bar: N.Y. 1964, D.C. 1984. Assoc. Dewey, Ballantine, Bushby, Palmer & Wood, N.Y.C., 1964-68; ptnr. Paul, Weiss, Rifkind, Wharton & Garrison, N.Y.C., 1968—. Served with U.S. Army, 1963-69. Mem. ABA, N.Y. State Bar Assn., Assn. of Bar of City of N.Y. Democrat. Jewish. Entertainment, General corporate. Home: 54 Spring Ln Chappaqua NY 10514 Office: Paul Weiss Rifkind Wharton & Garrison 1285 Ave of the Americas New York NY 10019

FELD, ALAN DAVID, lawyer; b. Dallas, Nov. 13, 1936; s. Henry R. and Rose (Scissors) F.; m. Anne Sanger, June 1, 1957; children: Alan David, Elizabeth S., John L. B.A., So. Methodist U., 1957, LL.B., 1960. Bar: Tex. 1960. Since practiced in Dallas; partner Akin, Gump, Strauss, Hauer & Feld, 1966—; lectr. Southwestern U. Med. Sch.; mem. Tex. State Securities Bd.; dir. Knoll Internat. Inc., Clear Channel Communications, Inc., Sheller-Globe Corp., Color Tile Inc. Contbr. articles to legal jours. Trustee Brandeis U.; bd. dirs. Dallas Day Nursery Assn., Timberlawn Found., Dallas Symphony Orch. Mem. Am., Tex., D.C., Dallas bar assns., Salesmanship Club, Phi Delta Phi. Clubs: Dallas, Royal Oaks Country. Home: 4235 Bordeaux St Dallas TX 75205 Office: 4100 1st City Ctr Dallas TX 75201

FELD, ARTHUR MICHAEL, lawyer; b. York, Pa., June 1, 1942; s. Sidney and Rose E. (Stein) F.; m. Rosalind I. Sperling, July 3, 1966; children—Jennifer, Marjorie, Debra. B.S., Pa. State U., 1964; J.D., Dickinson Sch. Law, 1967. Bar: Pa. 1967, U.S. Dist. Ct. (ea. dist.) Pa. 1970, U.S. Dist. Ct. (mid. dist.) Pa. 1971. Clk. typist Pa. Liquor Control Bd., Harrisburg, 1964-65; legal asst. Pa. Dept. Health, Harrisburg, 1966-68; atty. Techner, Rubin & Shapiro, Phila., 1970, Shumaker, Williams & Placey, Harrisburg, Pa., 1970-71, Pa. Dept. Environ. Resources, Harrisburg, 1971-86; sole practice, Harrisburg, 1971-86, ptnr. Gross, Casper & Feld, 1987—. Bd. dirs. Chisuk Emuna Synagogue, Harrisburg, 1979-82. Served to capt. U.S. Army, 1968-70. Mem. Pa. Bar Assn. (pub. contracts law com. 1980—), Dauphin County Bar Assn. Democrat. Jewish. Administrative and regulatory, Consumer commercial, Government contracts and claims. Home: 1413 Regency Circle Harrisburg PA 17110 Office: Gross Casper & Feld 3003 N Front St Harrisburg PA 17110

FELDBERG, MICHAEL SVETKEY, lawyer; b. Boston, May 21, 1951; s. Sumner Lee Feldberg and Eunice (Svetkey) Cohen; m. Ruth Lazarus, Sept. 23, 1978; children: Rachel, Jesse. BA, Harvard U., 1973, JD, 1977. Bar: N.Y. 1978, U.S. Dist. Ct. (ea. and so. dists.) N.Y. 1978, U.S. Ct. Appeals (2d cir.) 1983. Assoc. Orans, Elsen, Polstein & Naftalis, N.Y.C., 1977-80; asst. U.S. atty. State of N.Y., N.Y.C., 1981-84; ptnr. Shea & Gould, N.Y.C., 1985—. Mem. Assn. of Bar of City of N.Y. (criminal law com.). Federal civil litigation, Criminal. Office: Shea & Gould 330 Madison Ave New York NY 10017

FELDCAMP, LARRY BERNARD, lawyer; b. Hannibal, Mo., Nov. 24, 1938; s. Bernard Ernest and Mildred Elizabeth (Lehenbauer) F.; m. Irma Elaine Dahse, Mar. 13, 1964; children: David Allen, Michael Neal. BS in Chem. Engring., U. Mo., 1961; JD, U. Tex., 1967. Bar: Tex. 1967, U.S. Dist. Ct. (so. dist.) Tex. 1968, U.S. Ct. Appeals (5th cir.) 1970, U.S. Supreme Ct. 1973. Chem. engr. Union Carbide Corp., Texas City, Tex., 1963-65; ptnr. Baker & Botts, Houston, 1967—; gen. counsel Tex. Chem. Council, Austin, 1981—. Chmn. Houston Area Oxidant Study Steering Com., 1976-80; pres. Woodlands Med. Ctr. Inc., Tex., 1978—; bd. dirs. Gulf Coast chpt. Air Pollution Control Assn., 1984—. Served to 1st lt. U.S. Army, 1961-63. Mem. ABA, Tex. Bar Assn. (bd. dirs., treas. environ. sect. 1983—), Am. Intellectual Property Assn., Houston Intellectual Property Assn., Houston C. of C. (chmn. environ. com. 1976-78), Order of Coif, Phi Delta Phi, Omicron Delta Kappa, Tau Beta Pi. Presbyterian. Environment, Patent. Office: Baker & Botts 910 Louisiana One Shell Plaza Houston TX 77002

FELDER, RAOUL LIONEL, lawyer; b. N.Y.C., May 13, 1934; s. Morris and Millie (Goldstein) F.; m. Myrna, May 26, 1963; children—Rachel, James. B.A., NYU, 1955, J.D., 1959; postgrad. U. Bern (Switzerland), 1955-56. Bar: N.Y., 1959, U.S. Dist. Ct. (so. and ea. dists.) N.Y., 1962, U.S. Ct. Appeals (2d cir.), 1962, U.S. Supreme Ct., 1970. Sole practice, N.Y.C., 1959-61, 1964—; asst. U.S. atty., N.Y.C., 1961-64; mem. faculty, Practicing Law Inst., 1979, Marymount Coll., 1982, 83, 84, 85, 86, 87, Ethical Culture Sch., 1981, 82. Fellow Internat. Acad. Matrimonial Lawyers; mem. Assn. Bar City N.Y. (spl. com. matrimonial law 1975-77), ABA (judge nat. finals client counseling competition), N.Y. State Bar Assn., N.Y. State Dist. Attys. Assn., N.Y. State Trial Lawyers Assn. (past chmn. matrimonial law 1974-75), Nat. Criminal Def. Lawyers Assn., N.Y. State Soc. Med. Jurisprudence, Am. Judicature Soc., Am. Acad. Matrimonial Lawyers, Am. Arbitration Assn., Nat. Council on Family Relations. Author: Divorce, The Way Things Are, Not the Way Things Should Be, 1971; Lawyers Practical Handbook to the New Divorce Law, 1981; contbr. articles on law to profl. jours. Family and matrimonial. Home: 985 Fifth Ave New York NY 10021 Office: 437 Madison Ave New York NY 10022

FELDMAN, ALAN M., lawyer; b. Phila., Sept. 6, 1951; s. Manny and Bernice F.; m. Maureen Pelta, June 6, 1975; children: Erica, Julia. BA, Temple U., 1973, JD, 1976. Bar: Pa. 1976, U.S. Ct. Appeals (3d cir.) 1982, U.S. Supreme Ct. 1982. Law clk. to presiding judge Ct. of Common Pleas, Phila., 1976-77; assoc. Raynes, McCarty, Binder, Ross & Mundy, Phila., 1977-87; ptnr. Feldman & Wohlgellernter, Phila., 1987—. Fellow Acad. of Advocacy, 1978. Mem. ABA, Pa. Bar Assn., Phila. Bar Assn. (chmn. young lawyers sect. 1986, bd. of govs., fee disputes coms.), Am. Trial Lawyers Assn., Pa. Trial Lawyers Assn. (bd. of govs., lawpac devel. com. eastern dist. seminers co-chmn., amicus curiae com., editorial bd. Barrister mag.), Phila. Trial Lawyers Assn. (bd. dirs., mem. Verdict staff newsletter). Democrat. Jewish. Avocations: running. Office: Feldman & Wohlgelernter 200 S Broad St Philadelphia PA 19102

FELDMAN, CLARICE ROCHELLE, lawyer; b. Milw., Dec. 2, 1941; d. Harry and Beatrice (Hiken) Wagan; m. Howard J. Feldman, July 11, 1965; 1 child, David Lewis. B.S., U. Wis., 1963, LL.B., 1965. Bar: Wis. 1965. Appellate atty. NLRB, Washington, 1965-69; co-counsel to Joseph A. Yablonski, Washington, 1969; atty. Washington research project Clark Coll., 1970-72; asso. gen. counsel United Mine Workers Am., Washington, 1972-74; partner Becker, Channell, Becker & Feldman, Washington, 1974-76, Becker & Feldman, 1976-77; gen. counsel Ams. for Energy Independence, Washington, 1978-80; atty. Office of Spl. Investigations, Dept. Justice, 1980-84; sole practice Washington, 1984—. Advisor Assn. Union Democracy. Mem. Wis., D.C. bar assns. Democrat. Jewish. Federal civil litigation, Family and matrimonial, Immigration, naturalization, and customs. Home: 4455 29th St NW Washington DC 20008 Office: 1050 Thomas Jefferson St NW Suite 609 Washington DC 20007

FELDMAN, EDWARD STEVEN, lawyer; b. N.Y.C., June 22, 1947; s. Samuel and Sophie (Goldner) F.; m. Lynne Maxine Edwards, Apr. 15, 1973; children: Stephanie Robyn, Seth Ira. BA, Syracuse U., 1969; JD, Fordham U., 1973. Bar: D.C. 1974, N.Y. 1975, N.J. 1976, U.S. Dist. Ct. (ea. and so. dists.) N.Y. 1976, U.S. Dist. Ct. N.J. 1976, U.S. Supreme Ct. 1986. Atty. N.Y. State Dept. of Law, N.Y.C., 1974-75; assoc. Herman L. Pedowitz, Garden City, N.J., 1975-77; asst. gen. counsel United Jersey Bank, Hackensack, N.J., 1977-78; assoc. Dreyer & Traub, N.Y.C., 1978-81; v.p. gen. counsel J.I. Sopher & Co., Inc., N.Y.C., 1981-83; sr. atty. Kaye, Scholer, Fierman, Hays & Handler, N.Y.C., 1983-85; ptnr. Snow, Becker, & Krauss P.C., N.Y.C., 1985—. Mem. ABA, N.Y. State Bar Assn., Bergen County Bar Assn. Avocation: theatre, music. Real property, Cooperatives and condominiums, Banking. Home: 329 Glenwood Ave Leonia NJ 07065 Office: Snow Becker Krauss PC 605 3d Ave New York NY 10158

FELDMAN, FRANKLIN, lawyer; b. N.Y.C., Nov. 12, 1927; s. Reuben and Anne (Schulman) F.; m. Naomi Goldstein, June 3, 1956; children: Sarah, Eve, Jacob. B.A., NYU, 1948; LL.B., Columbia U., 1951. Bar: N.Y. 1952. Mem. office Gen Counsel, U.S. Air Force, Dept. Def., Washington, 1951-53; atty. office gen. counsel to gov. State of N.Y., 1954; assoc. firm Stroock & Stroock & Lavan, N.Y.C., 1955-64, ptnr., 1965—; cons. Temp. N.Y. Commn. on Constl. Conv., 1967; lectr. in law Columbia Law Sch. Editor-in-chief: Columbia U. Law Rev., 1950-51; author: (with Stephen E. Weil) Art Works—Law, Policy and Practice, 1974, Art Law, 1986; contbr. articles to profl. jours. Yaddo Fellow, Saratoga Springs, 1983. Mem. ABA, N.Y. State Bar Assn., Assn. Bar City N.Y., N.Y. County Lawyers Assn., Internat. Found. for Art Research (pres. 1971-76). Home: 15 W 81st New York NY 10024 Office: Stroock & Stroock & Lavan 7 Hanover Sq New York NY 10004

FELDMAN, H. LARRY, lawyer; b. Tyler, Tex., Apr. 18, 1941; s. Henry and Bess (Booken) F.; m. Janice Kay Asner, June 26, 1960; children—Joseph, Katherine. B.A., U. Okla., 1963; J.D., So. Methodist U., 1966. Bar: Tex. 1966, U.S. Dist. Ct. (no. dist.) Tex. 1969, U.S. Sup. Ct. 1976. Adj. prof. law U. Dallas, 1967-68; mem. dept. tax Peat Marwick & Mitchell, 1968-69; atty. Marks, Time & Aranson, 1970; ptnr. Feldman, O'Donnell & Neil, Dallas, 1971; sole practice, Dallas, 1971—. Mem. Assn. Trial Lawyers Am., Tex. Trial Lawyers Assn., Phi Alpha Delta. Jewish. State civil litigation, Personal injury, Workers' compensation. Home: 6204 Shadycliff Dr Dallas TX 75240 Office: 8300 Douglas Law Suite 8th Floor Dallas TX 75225

FELDMAN, JAY N., telecommunications, film and TV production company executive, lawyer; b. N.Y.C., Nov. 11, 1936; s. Morris Kenneth and Della (Newman) F.; m. Nancy Tobias, Dec. 7, 1963; children—Nina Cheryl, Karen Elise. A.B. magna cum laude, Colgate U., 1958; J.D., Harvard U., 1961. Bar: N.Y. 1962, U.S. Dist. Ct. (so. and ea. dists.) N.Y. 1962. Assoc. Jacobs Persinger and Parker, 1961-68; sec., treas., gen. counsel Lynch Corp., 1968-69; counsel Allied Artists Industries, Inc., N.Y.C., 1970-80, sec., 1970-76, v.p., 1975-76, v.p. adminstrn., 1976-77, group v.p., 1977-80, dir., 1973-80; sec. Allied Artists Pictures Corp., 1973-74, dir., 1974-80; gen. corp. atty. NYNEX Corp., 1983—; sec. NYNEX Devel. Co., 1984—, NYNEX Internat. Co., 1985—, Data Group Corp., 1985—, NYNEX Info. Solutions Group Inc., 1987—; sec. NYNEX Info. Solutions Group, Inc., 1987—; sec., counsel, dir. PSP, Inc., 1970-76; sec., dir. D. Kaltman & Co., Inc., 1970-79, v.p., 1977-79; sec., dir. Vitabath, Inc., 1970-72, Apollo Motor Homes, Inc., 1970-80, v.p., 1977-80; sec., dir. Westwood Import Co., Inc., 1972-79, v.p., 1977-79; sec., dir. Paul-Marshall Products Inc., 1972-75, Adstat Co., 1972-74; v.p., sec., dir. Allied Artists Video Corp., 1978-80; v.p., dir. Palmland Fashions, Inc., 1971-78; resident counsel Lorimar Prodns., Inc., 1980-83; mem. com. on criminal cts. Legal Aid Soc., 1969-72; trustee Temple Beth Israel, Port Washington, N.Y., 1981-83, rec. sec., 1983-85, fin. sec., 1985-87. Mem. Am. Bar Assn., Westchester-Fairfield Corp. Counsel Assn., N.Y. State Bar Assn., Phi Beta Kappa. General corporate, Securities, Mergers and acquisitions. Home: 61 Roger Dr Port Washington NY 11050 Office: NYNEX Corp 1113 Westchester Ave White Plains NY 10604

FELDMAN, JEFFREY MARC, lawyer; b. Providence, Nov. 8, 1949; s. Samuel and Shirley (Halpern) F.; m. Marjorie Burrows, Aug. 15, 1971; children: Peter, James. BA, Northeastern U., Boston, 1972, JD, 1975. Bar: Alaska 1976, U.S. Dist. Ct. Alaska 1976, R.I. 1976, U.S. Dist. Ct. R.I. 1976, U.S. Ct. Appeals (9th cir.) 1976, U.S. Supreme Ct. 1980. Law clk. Alaska Supreme Ct., Anchorage, 1975-76; asst. pub. defender Alaska Pub. Defender Office, Anchorage, 1976-78; mem. Gilmore & Feldman, Anchorage, 1978—; mem. Supreme Ct. Com. on Pattern Jury Instrns., 1979-85, Alaska Com. Bar Examiners, 1981—; chmn. Supreme Ct. on Criminal Rules, 1985—; atty. rep. Jud. Conf. 9th Cir. Ct. Appeals, 1983—. Contbr. articles to profl. jours. Mem. ABA, Am. Judicature Soc., Assn. Trial Lawyers Am., Nat. Assn. Criminal Def. Lawyers, Alaska Acad. Trial Lawyers, R.I. Bar Assn., Alaska Bar Assn. (mem. bd. govs. 1986—), Anchorage Bar Assn. Federal civil litigation, State civil litigation, Criminal. Home: 1014 H St Anchorage AK 99501 Office: Gilmore & Feldman 310 K St Suite 308 Anchorage AK 99501

FELDMAN, JOEL HARVEY, lawyer; b. Bklyn., July 12, 1954; s. William Carl and Arline (Karu) F.; children: Maria Rene, Eric Richard. BA, Georgetown U., 1976; JD, Duke U., 1979. Bar: Fla. 1979, U.S. Dist. Ct. (so. dist.) Fla. 1980, U.S. Ct. Appeals (11th cir.) 1980, U.S. Supreme Ct. 1986. Assoc. Lavalle, Woochna, Rutherford & Brown, Boca Raton, Fla., 1979-81; ptnr. Weiss & Feldman, P.A., Boca Raton, 1981-83, Feldman & Mallinger, P.A., Boca Raton, 1983-84, Friedman, Leeds, Shorenstein, Feldman, Mallinger & Kaplan, P.A., Boca Raton, 1984—. Mem. Dems. of Boca Raton, 1986. Mem. ABA, Fla. Bar Assn. (summary procedures rules com., grievance com.), Palm Beach County Bar Assn., S. Palm Beach County Bar Assn. (chmn. law week 1980), Fla. Bar Summary Procedures Rules Com. Democrat. Jewish. Lodge: Kiwanis (bd. dirs. West Boca Raton club 1981—, youth services award, 1984). Avocations: tennis, golf, snorkeling. State civil litigation, General corporate, Real property. Office: Friedman Leeds et al 4400 N Federal Hwy # 401 Boca Raton FL 33431

FELDMAN, MARK B., lawyer, arbitrator; b. Rochester, N.Y., Oct. 3, 1935; s. Edward P. and Grace (Relin) F.; m. Marcia Smith, Nov. 23, 1963; children: Ilana, Rachel. A.B., Wesleyan U., 1957; LL.B., Harvard U., 1960. Bar: N.Y. 1961, D.C. 1974. Assoc. Kaye, Scholer, Fierman, Hays & Handler, N.Y.C., 1960-65; with Office Legal Adviser, Dept. State, 1965-81, dep. legal advisr, 1974-81, acting legal adviser, 1981; of counsel Donovan, Leisure, Newton & Irvine, Washington, 1981-84, ptnr., 1984—; adj. prof. law Georgetown U. Mem. Council Fgn. Relations, Am. Law Inst., Am. Soc. Internat. Law, Am. Arbitration Assn., U.S. Council Internat. Bus., ABA, Internat. Law Assn. Private international, Public international, Federal civil litigation. Address: 4010 48th St NW Washington DC 20016

FELDMAN, MARTIN L. C., federal judge; b. St. Louis, Jan. 28, 1934; s. Joseph and Zelma (Bosse) F.; m. Melanie Pulitzer, Nov. 26, 1958; children: Jennifer Pulitzer, Martin L.C. Jr. B.A., Tulane U., 1955, J.D., 1957. Bar: La., Mo. 1957. Law clk. to Hon. J.M. Wisdom, U.S. Ct. Appeals, 1958-59; assoc. Bronfin, Heller, Feldman & Steinberg, New Orleans, 1959-60; ptnr. Bronfin, Heller, Feldman & Steinberg, 1960-83; U.S. dist. judge New Orleans, 1983—; trustee, former chmn. Sta. WYES-TV; spl. counsel to Gov. of La., 1979-83. Contbr. articles to profl. jours. Former nat. sec. Anti-Defamation League; former pres. bd. mgrs. Touro Infirmary; bd. dirs. Public Broadcasting Service. Mem. ABA, La. Bar Assn. (chmn. law reform com. 1981-82), Mo. Bar Assn., Am. Law Inst., Order of Coif. Republican. Jewish. Antitrust, Federal civil litigation, General corporate. Home: 12 Rosa Park New Orleans LA 70115 Office: U S Dist Court 500 Camp St Room C-316 New Orleans LA 70130

FELDMAN, MICHAEL HARRIS, lawyer; b. Phila., Apr. 15, 1949; s. Morris Jack and Catherine (Goldblatt) F.; m. Joanne S. Feldman, June 18, 1972 (div. Oct. 1981); m. Anne C. Owen, Feb. 2, 1986. BA in Polit. Sci., Am. U., 1971; JD, George Washington U., 1974. Bar: D.C. 1975, U.S. Dist. Ct. D.C. 1979, Md. 1980, U.S. Dist. Ct. Md. 1980, U.S. Supreme Ct. 1980, U.S. Ct. Appeals (D.C. cir.) 1981. Atty. Adminstrv. Office of U.S. Cts., Washington, 1974-79; assoc. Law, Murphy & McKee, Washington, 1979-80; assoc. Ashcraft & Gerel, Washington, 1980-87, ptnr., 1987—. Treas. Pa. Fedn. Temple Youth, 1966-67. Recipient U.S. Ct. Spl. Act award, 1977; named one of Outstanding Young Men Am., 1985. MEM. D.C. Bar Assn., Md. Bar Assn., Assn. Trial Lawyers Am., D.C. Trial Lawyers Am. Jewish. Avocations: ice hockey, skiing, tennis. Personal injury, Insurance, Federal civil litigation. Home: 206 Indian Spring Dr Silver Spring MD 20901 Office: Ashcraft & Gerel 2000 L St NW Suite 700 Washington DC 20036

FELDMAN, MICHAEL SANFORD, lawyer; b. Highland Park, Mich., Dec. 10, 1948; s. Martin and Gertrude F. (Weberman) F.; m. Susan Sophie Charney, May 20, 1979; children: Matthew, Sarah. BA, U. Mich., 1971, MBA, 1972; JD, U. Detroit, 1976. Bar: U.S. Dist. Ct. (ea. dist.) Mich. 1977. Tax acct. Price Waterhouse, Detroit, 1973-75; sole practice Southfield, Mich., 1975—; adj. prof. Walsh Coll., Troy, 1975—, Wayne State U., 1985—. Mem. Mich. Bar Assn., Oakland County Bar Assn., Accts. Guild (pres. 1985—). Jewish. Lodge: B'nai B'rith Accts. (pres. 1985—). Avocations: spectator sports, golf, ice skating, bowling. Probate, Real property, Corporate taxation. Home: 18614 Webster Southfield MI 48076 Office: 3000 Town Ctr #2690 Southfield MI 48075

FELDMAN, RICHARD DAVID, lawyer; b. Providence, R.I., Apr. 15, 1951; s. George Berthold and Jeanne Marion (Diamond) F.; m. Elizabeth Brown, Mar. 16, 1985. BA, Clark U., 1973; JD, Rutgers U., 1976. Bar: Pa. 1976, U.S. Supreme Ct. 1980, D.C. 1985. Atty. U.S. Gen. Acctg. Office, Washington, 1976-81; sr. atty. procurement EPA, Washington, 1981—. Mem. ABA, Fed. Bar Assn. Government contracts and claims. Home: 955 26th St NW Apt 203 Washington DC 20037 Office: US EPA Office Gen Counsel 401 M St NW Washington DC 20460

FELDMAN, RICHARD JAY, lobbyist, political consultant; b. Bklyn., Feb. 12, 1952; s. Joseph Herbert Feldman and Selma Ruth Steinberger. BA, Boston U., 1974; JD, Vt. Law Sch., 1982. Bar: D.C. 1986, U.S. Dist. Ct. D.C. 1986, U.S. Ct. Appeals (D.C. cir.) 1987. Spl. asst. U.S. Dept. of Commerce, Washington, 1982—; former constable, aux. police officer City of Cambridge, Mass.; regional polit. dir. Nat. Rifle Assn. Inst. for Legis. Action, Washington. Named one of Outstanding Young Men in Am., 1983. Republican. Jewish. Legislative, Political consulting. Office: US Dept Commerce 5817 22d St N Arlington VA 22205

FELDMAN, ROGER DAVID, lawyer; b. N.Y.C., Apr. 7, 1943; s. Louis and Dora (Goldsmith) F.; m. Gail Steg, May 31, 1969; children: Rebecca, Seth. A.B., Brown U., 1962; LL.B., Yale U.; M.B.A., Harvard U. Bar: N.Y. 1966, D.C. 1977. Ops. research analyst Office Asst. Sec. Def., Washington, 1967-68; staff asst. Office of Pres. U. S., Washington, 1968-69; assoc. LeBoeuf Lamb Leiby & MacRae, 1969-75, ptnr., 1977-83; ptnr. Nixon Hargrave Devans & Doyle, Washington, 1983—; dep. asst. adminstr. Fed. Energy Adminstrn., Washington, 1975-77; dir. Pan Atlantic Group Inc., R.J. Rudden & Assocs. Inc., Oxford Energy, Inc., Cogeneration Inst. Assn. Energy Engrs. mem. bd. advisors Energy Bur. Inc.; vice chmn., dir. Privatization Council, 1983—. Mem. bd. editors Law Jour., Yale Law Sch., 1965; editor Cogeneration Letter; contbr. to profl. jours. Mem. ABA (chmn. energy law com. 1980-83, chmn. alt. energy sources com. 1981-85, spl. com. on energy law 1981-84, environ. values com. 1983—, spl. com. on privatization 1985—), Fed. Energy Bar Assn. (chmn. cogeneration com.), Internat. Cogeneration Soc. (bd. dirs. 1982-85), Phi Beta Kappa. Environment, General corporate, Energy. Office: Nixon Hargrave Devans & Doyle 1 Thomas Circle Suite 800 Washington DC 20005

FELDMAN, SAMUEL BOTWINIK, lawyer; b. Worcester, Mass., Nov. 23, 1954; s. Richard Noah and Reyna Mae (Botwinik) F. BA, Syracuse U., 1976; JD, U. Miami, 1979. Bar: Conn. 1979, U.S. Dist. Ct. Conn. 1979. Atty. Cohen & Silver, Hartford, Conn., 1979-81, Lublin, Wolfe, Kantor & Silver, East Hartford, Conn., 1981—. Mem. ABA, Assn. Trial Lawyers Am., Conn. Trial Lawyers Assn., Conn. Bar Assn., Hartford Bar Assn. Democrat. Jewish. Club: Tumblebrook Country (Bloomfield, Conn.). Avocation: sports. State civil litigation, Federal civil litigation, Contracts commercial. Office: Lublin Wolfe Kantor & Silver 546 Burnside Ave East Hartford CT 06108

FELDMAN, STANLEY GEORGE, judge; b. N.Y.C., Mar. 9, 1933; s. Meyer and Esther Betty (Golden) F.; m. Norma Arambula; 1 dau., Elizabeth L. Student, U. Calif., Los Angeles, 1950-51; LL.B., U. Ariz., 1956. Bar: Ariz. 1956. Practiced in Tucson, 1956—; partner firm Miller, Pitt & Feldman, 1968—; justice Ariz. Supreme Ct., 1982—; lectr. Coll. Law, U. Ariz., 1965-76, adj. prof., 1976—. Bd. dirs. Tucson Jewish Community Council. Mem. Am. Bd. Trial Advocates (past pres. So. Ariz. chpt.), ABA, Ariz. Bar Assn. (pres. 1974-75, bd. govts. 1967-76), Pima County Bar Assn. (past pres.), Am. Trial Lawyers Assn. (dir. chpt. 1967-76). Democrat. Jewish. Home: 3490 Via Guadalupe Tucson AZ 85716 Office: Supreme Ct State of Ariz State Capitol Bldg Phoenix AZ 85007 *

FELDMAN, STEPHEN E., lawyer; b. N.Y.C., Sept. 11, 1937; s. Manuel and Dorothy (Alpert) F. B.M.E., Rensselaer Poly. Inst., 1959; J.D., N.Y.U., 1962; postgrad. in electronics Union U. Bar: N.Y. 1963, D.C. 1962, U.S. Pat. & Trademark Office, 1965. Pat. examiner U.S. Pat. Office, 1962-64; pat. atty. Gen. Electric, Schenectady, 1964-65; sr. pat. atty. div. pat. council Litton Industries, Orange, N.J., 1965-71; sole practice, N.Y.C., 1971-76; ptnr. Feldman & Feldman, N.Y.C., 1976-83, Stephen & Feldman P.C., 1983—; lectr. in field. Mem. Suffolk Bar Assn., Assn. Bar City N.Y., Am. Patent Law Assn. Patent, Trademark and copyright. Office: 12 E 41st St New York NY 10017

FELDMAN, WARREN BRUCE, lawyer, consultant; b. N.Y.C., Oct. 29, 1948; s. Albert A. and Fae Ethel (Farber) F.; m. Eileen Rose Weisen, June 28, 1970; children—Jesse Ross, Eli Aaron. B.A., cum laude, SUNY-Buffalo, 1966, J.D., 1976. Bar: N.Y. 1977, U.S. Dist. Ct. N.Y. 1977. Assoc. Grove, Hogan & Hogan, Lockport, N.Y., 1976-80; ptnr. Feldman, Kramer & Fleisher and successor firm Feldman & Kramer, P.C., Hauppage, N.Y., 1980—; cons. Nationwide Legal Services, Inc., Hartsdale, N.Y., 1981—. Co-chmn. NCCJ, Lockport, 1979. Mem. Assn. Trial Lawyers Am., Am. Pre-Paid Inst., Nat. Resource Ctr. Consumer Legal Services, ABA, N.Y. State Bar Assn., Erie County Bar Assn. (trial excellence award 1976). Jewish. Personal injury, Prepaid Legal Services, Family and matrimonial. Office: Feldman & Kramer 350 Motor Pkwy Hauppauge NY 11788

FELDMANN, LOUIS GEORGE, lawyer; b. Wilkes-Barre, Pa., Sept. 10, 1909; s. John Thomas and Jessica Anne (Cole) F.; m. Anne Regina McKernan, June 3, 1931. BS in Econs., U. Pa., 1933; JD, Duquesne U., 1943. Bar: Pa. 1946, Pa. 1948, U.S. Dist. Ct. (mid. dist.) Pa. 1951, U.S. Ct. Appeals (3d cir.) 1954, U.S. Supreme Ct. 1954. Sole practice Hazelton, Pa., 1946—; dist. atty. Luzerne County, Wilkes-Barre, 1951-55; pres. Freeland (Pa.) Bldg. and Loan Assn. 1946-57; bd. dirs. Northeastern Bank Pa., Scranton; lectr. in field. Sec. Pa. State Civil Def. Council, 1951-57; vice

chmn., mem. Pa. Hwy. Commn., Harrisburg, 1962-68; mgr. Rep. senatorial campaign, Pa., 1972. Recipient commendation U.S. Info. Service, 1960, Disting. Service award Pa. Legislature, 1960, Gold Medal, Appalachian Regional Commn., 1986; knighted by Grand Cross Holy Sepulchare, 1965. Mem. ABA, Pa. Bar Assn., Luzerne County Bar Assn., Lower Luzerne County Bar Assn., Salvation Army. Roman Catholic. Lodges: KC, Kiwanis. Avocations: travelling, gardening. Industrial development, Administrative and regulatory, Insurance. Home: 9 W Diamond Ave Hazelton PA 18201 Office: 1009 Northeastern Bldg Hazleton PA 18201

FELDSTEIN, JAY HARRIS, lawyer; b. Elizabeth, Pa., June 23, 1937; s. Norman George and Gladys Shirley (Goldstein) F.; m. Judith Mae Stern, Sept. 8, 1963; children: Wendy Shawn, David Eric, Marc Howard. BA, Pa. State U., 1959; JD, Yale U., 1962. Bar: Fla. 1963, Pa. 1963, U.S. Dist. Ct. (we. dist.) Pa. 1963, U.S. Supreme Ct. 1967. Sole practice, Pitts., 1963-65; ptnr. Feldstein, Grinberg, Stein & McKee and predecessors, Pitts., 1965—. Chmn. Pa. Lottery Commn., Harrisburg, 1980-82; pres. Southview Apts. for Sr. Citizen Housing, Mt. Lebanon, 1980-84, State U. Nat. Alumni Assn., 1979-81; v.p. Am. Jewish Com., Pitts., 1984—. Served with USAF, 1963-69. Recipient Outstanding Young Man in Pitts. Area award Jr. C. of C., 1969. Mem. Pa. Trial Lawyers Assn. (bd. govs. 1984—), Allegheny County Acad. Trial Lawyers, Nat. Bd. Trial Advocacy (cert.). Democrat. Jewish. Club: Harvard, Yale, Princeton. Lodge: Masons (master 1972). Personal injury, State civil litigation. Home: 592 Sandrae Dr Mount Lebanon PA 15243 Office: Feldstein Grinberg Stein & McKee 428 Blvd of Allies Pittsburgh PA 15219

FELDWISCH, DAVID LEWIS, lawyer; b. Lima, Ohio, Jan. 24, 1952; s. Vernon Benjamin and Joann Elizabeth (Lammers) F.; m. Diane Lynn May, Sept. 25, 1982. BA, Ohio State U., 1974, JD, 1979. Bar: Ohio 1979. Atty. domestic prodn. Marathon Oil Co., Findlay, Ohio, 1979-82; atty. refining and mktg. Marathon Oil Co., Findlay, 1982-85; atty. internat. Marathon Oil Co., Houston, 1985—. Legal counsel, bd. dirs. Hancock County Mental Health Soc. Inc., Findlay, 1980-85. Mem. ABA, Tex. Bar Assn., Ohio Bar Assn., Order of Coif, Phi Beta Kappa. Democrat. Lutheran. General corporate, Oil and gas leasing, Private international. Home: 14803 Long Oak Dr Houston TX 77070 Office: Marathon Oil Co 5555 San Felipe Rd Houston TX 77056

FELFE, PETER FRANZ, lawyer; b. Dresden, Germany, Jan. 8, 1939; came to U.S., 1951; s. Frederick Christian Felfe and Ruth (Haberland) Hayden; m. Margareta K. Lindgren, July 19, 1971 (div. June 1976); m. Jenny Leueen Fishel, June 18, 1982; 1 child, Tess Claudia. B.S. in Chem. Engring., Yale U., 1960; J.D., Fordham U., 1964. Bar: N.Y. 1965, U.S. Patent and Trademark Office 1961, U.S. Dist. Ct. (so. and ea. dists.) N.Y., 1974, U.S. Ct. Appeals (2d cir.) 1975, U.S. Ct. Appeals (D.C.) 1983, U.S. Supreme Ct. 1985, U.S. Dist. Ct. (ea. dist.) Mich. 1985. Staff atty. Union Carbide, N.Y.C., 1964-69; assoc. Burgess & Dinklage, N.Y.C., 1969-77; sr. ptnr. Sprung, Felfe et al, N.Y.C., 1977-81; founding ptnr. Felfe & Lynch, N.Y.C., 1981—; lectr. in field; cons. German-Am. C. of C., N.Y.C., 1981—. Contbr. articles to profl. jours. Mem. ABA (patent, trademark and copyright law com.), Internat. Assn. Protection Indsl. Property, Am. Intellectual Property Law Assn. (com. on internat. and fgn. law), N.Y. Patent, Trademark and Copyright Law Assn., Bar Assn. City N.Y., Internat. Trade Commn. Trial Lawyers Assn., Fed. Cir. Ct. Bar Assn. (patent appeals from cts. com.), Yale Alumni Assn., Tau Beta Pi. Club: Yale (N.Y.C.). Patent, Trademark and copyright, Federal civil litigation. Office: Felfe & Lynch 805 Third Ave New York NY 10022

FELGER, THOMAS ROBERT, lawyer; b. Hartford city, Ind., Aug. 24, 1944; s. Victor Herman and Margaret Elizabeth (Schmidt) F.; m. Ruth Elaine Shrader, July 15, 1967; children: Michelle Leigh, Lisa Renee. BS, U.S. Naval Acad., 1966; JD, U. Tex., 1976. Bar: Tex. 1977, U.S. Patent Office 1978; registered profl. engr., 1976. Commd. ensign USN, 1966, advanced through grades to lt., resigned active duty, 1974; atty. patent div. Otis Engring. Corp., Dallas, 1977-84, asst. gen. counsel, 1984—; sec., bd. dirs. Employee's Credit Union, Carrolton, Tex., 1978-81. Served to capt. USNR, 1974—. Mem. ABA, Dallas Bar Assn. (arbitrator, fee dispute com.), Tex. Bar Assn., Am. Arbitration Assn. (comml. arbitrator 1977—), U.S. Naval Acad. Alumni Assn. Republican. Lutheran. Patent, General corporate, Trademark and copyright. Office: Otis Engring Corp PO Box 819052 Dallas TX 75381-9052

FELIX, ROBERT LOUIS, law educator; b. Detroit, Apr. 7, 1934; s. Camille Herbert and Rosalie (Le Floch) F.; m. Judith Joan Grossman, Aug. 25, 1962; children—Marie, Bridget, Robert, Conan. A.B., U. Cin., 1956, LL.B., 1959; M.A., U. B.C., 1962; postgrad. Oxford U. 1962-63; LL.M., Harvard U., 1967. Asst., assoc. prof. law Duquesne U., Pitts., 1963-67; assoc. prof. law U. S.C., 1967-72, prof., 1973—; chair James P. Mozingo III prof., 1984—; faculty assoc. Inst. Internat. Studies. Served with U.S. Army, 1960. Ford fellow Harvard Law Sch., 1966-67; Fulbright vis. lectr. U. Clermont-Ferrand, France, 1975-76; lectr. Program on Internat. Legal Coop., Free U., Brussels, Belgium, 1976. Mem. Assn. Am. Law Schs. (sect. on Conflict of Laws), S.C. Fulbright Alumni Assn. (pres.). Roman Catholic. Author: (with R. Leflar, L. McDougal) Cases and Materials on American Conflicts Law, 1982, American Conflicts of Law, 1986; (with others) New Directions in Legal Education, 1969, The Vanity Fair Gallery, 1979. Contbr. articles to profl. jours. Home: 6233 Macon Rd Columbia SC 29209 Office: Sch Law U of SC Columbia SC 29208

FELLER, DAVID E., legal educator; b. 1916. A.B., Harvard U., 1938, LL.B., 1941. Bar: Mass. 1941, D.C. 1942. Lectr. law and econs. U. Chgo., 1941-42; atty. U.S. Dept. Justice, Washington, 1946-48; law clk. U.S. Supreme Ct., 1948-49; assoc. gen. counsel CIO, Washington, 1949-53, United Steelworkers, Washington, 1949-60; gen. counsel ind. union dept. AFL-CIO, Washington, 1961-66, United Steelworkers, 1961-65; ptnr. Goldberg Feller & Bredhoff, Washington, 1955-60, Feller, Bredhoff & Anker, 1961-65, Feller & Anker, 1965-67; now John H. Boalt prof. U. Calif.-Berkeley Sch. Law. Editor Harvard Law Rev. Bd. dirs. NAACP Legal Def. and Edn. Fund, 1960—; pres. Council Univ. Calif. Faculty Assns., 1973—. Mem. Nat. Acad. Arbitrators (v.p. 1985-87), Fed. Mediation and Conciliation Service Roster of Arbitrators, ABA (sec. labor law sect. 1972-73), Phi Beta Kappa. Legal education, Labor, Federal civil litigation. Office: Univ of Calif Sch of Law 225 Boalt Hall Berkeley CA 94720

FELLER, LLOYD HARRIS, lawyer; b. New Brunswick, N.J., Aug. 27, 1942; s. Alexander and Freda (Kaminsky) F.; m. Susan Sydney Weinberg, Aug. 6, 1967; children—Jennifer, Andrew. B.S. in econs. Wharton Sch. U. Pa., 1964; LL.B., NYU, 1967. Bar: N.Y. 1967, D.C. 1980. Assoc., Rubin, Wachtel, Baum & Levin, 1967-70; trial atty. organized crime sect. div. enforcement SEC, Washington, 1970-72, legal asst. Commr. A. Sydney Herlong, Jr., 1972-73, Commr. A.A. Sommer, Jr., 1973-76; chief counsel Office of the Chief Acct., 1976-77, assoc. dir. div. market regulation Office of Market Structure and Trading Practices, 1977-79, of counsel, 1979-81; ptnr. Morgan, Lewis & Bockius, Washington, 1981—. Mem. ABA, D.C. Bar Assn. Securities, General corporate, Contracts commercial. Home: 419 S Lee St Alexandria VA 22314 Office: 1800 M St NW Suite 800N Washington DC 20036

FELLERS, JAMES DAVISON, lawyer; b. Oklahoma City, Apr. 17, 1913; s. Morgan S. and Olive R. (Kennedy) F.; m. Margaret Ellen Randerson, Mar. 11, 1939; children: Kay Lynn (Mrs. Fred. A. Grieder), Lou Ann (Mrs. James B. Street), James Davison. A.B., U. Okla., 1936, J.D., 1936; LL.D. (hon.), Suffolk U., 1974; LL.D. hon., William Mitchell Coll. Law, 1976; LL.D. (hon.), San Fernando Valley U., 1976; D.H.L. (hon.), Okla. Christian Coll., 1974. Bar: Okla. 1936. Since practiced in Oklahoma Cit; sr. mem. Fellers, Snider, Blankenship, Bailey & Tippens; mem. U.S. Com. Selection of Fed. Jud. Officers, 1977-79; Mem. bd. Nat. Legal Aid and Defender Assn., 1973-76; bd. dirs. Am. Bar Endowment, 1977—; mem. adv. bd. Internat. and Comparative Law Center. Trustee Southwestern Legal Found.; hon. consul Belgium, for Okla., 1972—. Served to lt. col. USAF, 8 campaigns, 1941-45, ETO, MTO. Decorated Bronze Star, Knight Order of Crown (Belgium); recipient Hatton W. Sumners award, 1975; Distinguished Service citation U. Okla., 1976; selected as outstanding young man Oklahoma City C. of C., 1948; named to Okla. Hall of Fame, 1982. Fellow Am. Coll. Trial Lawyers, Am. Bar Found., Okla. Bar Found., Nat. Jud. Coll. (dir. 1967-70); mem. Am. Bar Assn. (nat. chmn. jr. bar conf. 1946-47, gov. 1962-65, chmn. ho. of dels. 1966-68, pres. 1974-75), Barra Mexicana (hon. mem.), Can. Bar Assn. (hon. mem.), Internat. Bar Assn., Inter-Am. Bar Assn., Minn. Bar Assn. (hon. mem.), Okla. Bar Assn. (pres. 1964), W.Va. Bar Assn. (hon. mem.), Am. Judicature Soc., Am. Law Inst. (com. continuing legal edn. 1947-49), Inst. Jud. Adminstrn., Internat. Assn. Ins. Counsel (v.p. 1955-56), Nat. Conf. Bar Pres.'s, World Peace through Law Center, Fellows of Young Lawyers Am. Bar (hon. chmn. 1977-79), Oklahoma City C. of C. (dir. 1976), Phi Kappa Psi. Episcopalian. Clubs: Beacon, Petroleum. Federal civil litigation, State civil litigation, General practice. Home: 6208 Waterford Blvd #92 Oklahoma City OK 73102 Office: 2400 1st National Ctr Oklahoma City OK 73102

FELLERS, RHONDA GAY, lawyer; b. Gainesville, Tex., July 29, 1955; d. James Norman and Gaytha Ann (Sanders) F.; m. Bruce C. Hinton, Oct. 15, 1981 (div. Oct. 1985). BA, U. Tex., 1977, JD, 1980; LLM in Taxation, U. Denver, 1986. Bar: Tex. 1981, Colo. 1981, U.S. Dist. Ct. (no. dist.) Tex. 1982, U.S. Dist. Ct. Colo. 1985, U.S. Tax Ct. 1985, U.S. Ct. Appeals (5th cir.) 1986. Assoc. Walters & Assocs., Lubbock, Tex., 1981-83; gen. counsel Security Nat. Bank, Lubbock, 1983; assoc. Melvin Coffee & Assocs., P.C., Denver, 1984-85; sole practice Lubbock, 1983—. Mem. ABA, Tex. Bar Assn., Colo. Bar Assn., Lubbock County Women's Bar Assn., Lubbock County Bar Assn. Avocations: archaeology, tennis, photography, skiing, golf. Personal income taxation, State civil litigation, Federal civil litigation. Office: PO Box 16817 Lubbock TX 79490

FELLMETH, SCOTT EUGENE, lawyer; b. Canton, Ohio, Aug. 19, 1955; s. Eugene M. and M. Ruth (Sheriff) F.; m. Amy S. Paulik, Sept. 21, 1985. BA in Polit. Sci., Ohio U., 1977; JD, Ohio No. U., 1979. Bar: Ohio 1980, U.S. Dist. Ct. (no. dist.) Ohio 1983, U.S. Ct. Appeals (6th cir.) 1984. Ptnr. Kettler, Centrone & Fellmeth, Massillon, Ohio, 1980—; asst. prosecutor Massillon Mcpl. Ct., 1981-83, chief prosecutor, 1984—. Mem. ABA, Ohio Bar Assn., Stark County Bar Assn., Stark County Acad. Trial Lawyers. Lodge: Elks. Probate, Real property, Personal injury. Home: 808 Locust St Canal Fulton OH 44614 Office: Kettler Centrone & Fellmeth 921 Lincoln Way E Massillon OH 44646

FELLOWS, JERRY KENNETH, lawyer; b. Madison, Wis., Mar. 19, 1946; s. Forrest Garner and Virginia (Witte) F.; m. Patricia Lynn Graves, June 28, 1970; children: Jonathon, Aaron, Daniel. BA in Econs., U. Wis., 1968; JD, U. Minn., 1971. Bar: U.S. Dist. Ct. (no. dist.) Ill. 1971. Ptnr. McDermott, Will & Emery, Chgo., 1971—; speaker Bur. Nat. Affairs, Washington, 1985—. Contbr. articles to profl. jours. Pres. Project Home, Downers Grove, Ill., 1982, Downers Grove Track Club Inc., 1985—. Mem. Chgo. Bar Assn., Chgo. Assn. Commerce and Industry (chmn. employee benefits subcom. 1982—), U.S. C. of C. (employee benefits com. 1984—), U. Minn. Law Alumni Assn., Gamma Eta Gamma. Club: Chgo. Athletic Assn. Avocations: coaching track, basketball, baseball. Pension, profit-sharing, and employee benefits, Administrative and regulatory, Personal income taxation. Home: 4541 Middaugh Downers Grove IL 60515 Office: McDermott Will & Emery 111 W Monroe St Chicago IL 60603

FELLOWS, JOHN WHITE, lawyer; b. Walpole, Mass., June 20, 1909; s. Frank Marshall and Bessie Brackett (Frame) F.; m. Clara Louise Kelley, June 28, 1936; children—Barbara Louise Fellows Costas, Clara Joan Fellows Chapman, June Beth Fellows. A.B. cum laude, Harvard U., 1930, LL.B., 1935, J.D., 1969. Bar: Mass. 1935, U.S. Dist. Ct. Mass. 1936, U.S. Supreme Ct. 1969. Mem. firm Norman & Campbell, Worcester, Mass., 1935-41; ptnr. Baxter, Fellows, Pierce & Barnes, 1941-55; sr. ptnr. Fellows, Travers & Hoaglund, 1955-70, Fellows & Hoaglund, 1970—; town counsel Town of Boylston (Mass.), 1941-75, Town of Oxford (Mass.), 1936-39, Town of Hubbardston (Mass.), 1965-74. Served to 1st lt. USMC, 1944-45. Town playground named in his honor, Boylston, 1977. Mem. ABA, Mass. Bar Assn., Worcester County Bar Assn. Republican. Congregationalist. Club: Masons. Probate, Real property, Local government. Office: 339 Main St Worcester MA 01608

FELPER, DAVID MICHAEL, lawyer; b. Springfield, Mass., Dec. 17, 1954; s. Lawrence Allen and Edith Charlotte (Flesher) F.; m. Kimberlee White, May 19, 1979; children: Andrew Martin. BA in Polit. Sci., George Washington U., 1976; JD cum laude, Western New Eng. Coll., 1980. Bar: Mass. 1980, U.S. Dist. Ct. Mass. 1981. Assoc. Michelman & Feinstein, Springfield, 1980-82; asst. regional counsel Dept. Social Services, Commonwealth of Mass., Springfield, 1982-83; labor relations counsel Sprague Electric Co., Lexington, Mass., 1983—; lectr. various human resource orgns. throughout U.S., 1984—. Manuscript reviewer Personnel Administrator, Alexandria, Va., 1986—. Mem. ABA (labor law com.), Mass. Bar Assn. (labor law com.), New Eng. Labor Counsel. Avocations: golf, running, reading. Labor, Pension, profit-sharing, and employee benefits, Workers' compensation. Office: Sprague Electric Co 92 Hayden Ave Lexington MA 02173-7929

FELS, NICHOLAS WOLFF, lawyer; b. White Plains, N.Y., Mar. 19, 1943; s. Lawrence P. and Fredericka (Gaines) F.; m. Susan T. McEwan, Dec. 28, 1968; 1 child, Sarah. BA, Harvard U., 1964; MA, U. Calif., Berkeley, 1965; LLB, Harvard U., 1968. Bar: N.Y. 1968, Calif. 1970, U.S. Dist. Ct. (cen. dist.) Calif. 1970, D.C. 1971, U.S. Dist. Ct. D.C. 1971, U.S. Ct. Appeals (10th cir.) 1976, U.S. Ct. Appeals (D.C. cir.) 1977, U.S. Supreme Ct. 1978, U.S. Ct. Appeals (4th cir.) 1979, U.S. Ct. Appeals (8th cir.) 1981, U.S. Ct. Appeals (5th cir.) 1982. Law clk. to presiding justice U.S. Ct. Appeals, New Orleans, 1968-69; atty. OEO Legal Services, Los Angeles, 1969-70; assoc. Covington & Burling, Washington, 1970-76, ptnr., 1976—; mem. Nat. Com. on U.S.-China Relations, N.Y.C., 1982—. Contbr. articles to profl. jours. Mem. Harvard Schs. and Scholarships com., Washington, 1971—. Mem. ABA (adminstrv. law sect.), Fed. Communications Bar Assn., Fed. Energy Bar Assn. FERC practice, Communications. Home: 3534 Edmunds St NW Washington DC 20007 Office: Covington & Burling 1201 Pennsylvania Ave NW Washington DC 20044

FELSENTHAL, STEVEN ALTUS, lawyer; b. Chgo., May 21, 1949; s. Jerome and Eve (Altus) F.; m. Carol Judith Greenberg, June 14, 1970; children—Rebecca Elizabeth, Julia Alison. A.B., U. Ill., 1971; J.D., Harvard U., 1974. Bar: Ill. 1974, U.S. Dist. Ct. (no. dist.) Ill. 1974, U.S. Ct. Claims 1975, U.S. Tax Ct. 1975, U.S. Ct. Appeals (7th cir.) 1981. Assoc. Levenfeld & Kanter, Chgo., 1974-78, ptnr., 1978-80; sr. ptnr. Levenfeld, Eisenberg, Janger, Glassberg & Lippitz, Chgo., 1980-84, Sugar, Friedberg & Felsenthal, Chgo., 1984—; lectr. Kent Coll. Law, Ill. Inst. Tech., Chgo., 1978-80. Mem. ABA, Ill. State Bar Assn., Chgo. Bar Assn., Harvard Law Soc. Ill., Phi Beta Kappa. Clubs: Standard, Harvard (Chgo.). Corporate taxation, Estate planning, Real property. Office: Sugar Friedberg & Felsenthal 200 W Madison St Suite 3550 Chicago IL 60606

FELTER, EDWIN LESTER, JR., lawyer, agency administrator; b. Washington, Aug. 11, 1941; s. Edwin L. Felter and Bertha (Peters) Brekke; m. Yoko Yamauchi-Koito, Dec. 26, 1969. B.A., U. Tex., 1964; J.D., Cath. U. of Am., 1967. Bar: Colo. 1970, U.S. Dist. Ct. Colo. 1970, U.S. Ct. Appeals (10th cir.) 1971, U.S. Supreme Ct. 1973, U.S. Tax Ct. 1979, U.S. Ct. Claims 1979, U.S. Ct. Internat. Trade 1979. Dep. pub. defender State of Colo., Ft. Collins, 1971-75; asst. atty. gen. Office of the Atty. Gen., Denver, 1975-80; state adminstrv. law judge Colo. Div. of Adminstrv. Hearings, Denver, 1980-83, chief adminstrv. law judge, dir., 1983—; discipline prosecutor Supreme Ct. Grievance Com., 1975-78. Contbg. editor: International Franchising, 1970. Mem. Colo. State Mgmt. Cert. Steering com., 1983—; No. Colo. Criminal Justice Planning council, Ft. Collins, 1973-75; bd. dirs., vice chmn. The Point Community Crisis Ctr., Ft. Collins, 1971-73; mem. Denver County Democratic Party Steering Com., 1978-79; chmn. 12th legis. dist., 1978-79. Mem. Colo. Bar Assn., Arapahoe County Bar Assn., Nat. Assn. of Adminstrv. Law Judges (pres. Colo. chpt. 1982—). Workers' compensation, Administrative and regulatory. Office: Colo Div of Hearing Officers 1525 Sherman St #550 Denver CO 80203

FELTER, JOHN KENNETH, lawyer; b. Monmouth, N.J., May 9, 1950; s. Joseph Harold and Rosanne (Bautz) F. BA magna cum laude, MA in Econs., Boston Coll., 1972; JD cum laude, Harvard U., 1975. Bar: Mass. 1975, U.S. Dist. Ct. Mass. 1976, U.S. Ct. Appeals (1st cir.) 1977, U.S. Supreme Ct. 1982. Assoc. Goodwin, Procter & Hoar, Boston, 1975-83, ptnr., 1983—; spl. asst. atty. gen. Commonwealth of Mass., 1982-84; spl. counsel Town of Plymouth, Mass., 1983—, Town of Salisbury, Mass., 1983-85, Town of Edgartown, Mass., 1985—; active devel. com. Greater Boston Legal Services, 1982—, bd. dirs. 1980—; mem. faculty Mass. Continuing Legal Edn., Inc., Boston, 1984—, Am. Law Inst.-ABA Com. Continuing Edn., 1986—; instr. trial adv. program Harvard Law Sch., 1981—; judge moot ct. competition Harvard Law Sch., 1978—. Mem. adv. com. The Boston Plan for Excellence in Pub. Schs.; VIP panelist Easter Seals Telethon, Boston, 1978-79. Mem. ABA (litigation sect., gen. practice sect., personal rights litigation com.), Mass. Bar Assn., Boston Bar Assn. (bd. dirs. law firm resources project 1985—, coll. and univ. law com. 1986—), Am. Arbitration Assn. (comml. arbitrator 1985—), Greater Boston C. of C. (edn. com., health care com.). Federal civil litigation, State civil litigation, Civil rights. Office: Goodwin Procter & Hoar Exchange Place Boston MA 02109

FELTON, DALE WILEY, lawyer; b. Bartlesville, Okla., Sept. 19, 1944. BA, Okla. State U., 1967; JD, U. Houston, 1970. Bar: Tex. 1970, U.S. Dist. Ct. (so. dist.) Tex. 1971. Prin. Felton & Assocs., Houston, 1970—; instr. accident reconstrn. for attys. Tex. A&M U. Mem. Tex. Bar Assn., Houston Bar Assn., Ft. Bend Bar Assn. (bd. dirs. 1984-85), Assn. Trial Lawyers Am. (sustaining), Tex. Trial Lawyers Assn. (assoc. dir. 1975-80), Houston Trial Lawyers Assn. (pres. 1980-81), Ct. Practice Inst. (diplomate 1975). Lodge: Optimists (bd. dirs.). Personal injury, Workers' compensation. Home: 2710 Williams Grant Sugar Land TX 77479 Office: Felton and Assocs 10101 Southwest Freeway Suite 350 Houston TX 77074

FELTON, JULE WIMBERLY, JR., lawyer; b. Macon, Ga., July 22, 1932; s. Jule Wimberly and Mary Julia (Sasnett) F.; m. Kate Gillis, May 15, 1965; children—Jule Wimberly III, Mary Katherine, Laura Borden. Student, Emory U., Atlanta, 1949-50; A.B., U. Ga., Athens, 1954, LL.B, 1955. Bar: Ga. 1954. Assoc. Hansell & Post, Atlanta, 1955-70, mng. ptnr., 1970—. Mem. Ga. Gen. Assembly, Atlanta, 1969-72; mem. official bd. dirs. Northside United Meth. Ch., Atlanta, 1974-85 Served to 1st lt. JAGC, U.S. Army, 1955-56. Mem. State Bar Ga. (pres. 1985-86), Atlanta Bar Assn. (pres. 1973-74), ABA, Lawyers Club Atlanta, Nat. Conf. Bar Pres., Am. Judicature Soc., U. Ga. Law Sch. Assn. (pres. 1984-85), Old War Horse Lawyers Club, Inc. (pres. Atlanta 1983). Clubs: Commerce, Piedmont Driving, Capital City. Avocations: piano; golf; boating. Federal civil litigation, State civil litigation, Personal injury. Home: 2580 Woodward Way NW Atlanta GA 30305 Office: Hansell & Post 3300 First Atlanta Tower Atlanta GA 30383-3101

FENDERSON, FAUN LOUISE, lawyer, law librarian; b. Ft. Leonard Wood, Mo., June 2, 1952; d. John Richard and Joan Marie (Rose) F. m. Timothy Evan Joder, Jan. 1, 1972 (div. Oct. 1978). BA, Fla. Atlantic U., 1976; MLS, La. State U., Baton Rouge, 1977; JD, So. U., Baton Rouge, 1981. Bar: La. 1982, Nebr. 1985, U.S. Dist. Ct. (mid. dist.) La. 1983, U.S. Dist. Ct. (ea. dist.) La. 1984, U.S. Ct. Appeals (5th cir.) 1984. Law clk. to presiding justice La. Dist. Ct., Baton Rouge, 1981-82, New Orleans, 1982-83; assoc., law librarian Herman, Herman, Katz & Cotlar, New Orleans, 1984—. Mem. ABA, La. State Bar Assn., Nebr. State Bar Assn., La. Trial Lawyers Assn., New Orleans Assn. Legal Librarians. Democrat. Jewish. Avocations: gourmet cooking, gardening, swimming. Probate. Office: Herman Herman Katz & Cotlar 820 O'Keefe Ave New Orleans LA 70113

FENDLER, OSCAR, lawyer; b. Blytheville, Ark., Mar. 22, 1909; s. Alfred and Rae (Sattler) F.; m. Patricia Shane, Oct. 26, 1946; children—Tilden P. Wright III (stepson), Frances Shane. B.A., U. Ark., 1930; LL.B., Harvard, 1933. Bar: Ark. bar 1933. Practice in Blytheville, 1933-41, 46—; spl. justice Ark. Supreme Ct., 1965; Mem. Ark. Jud. Council, 1959- 60; pres. Conf. Local Bar Assn., 1958-60; pres. bd. dirs. Ark. Law Rev., 1961-67; mem. Ark. Bd. Pardons and Paroles, 1970-71. Mem. Miss. County Democratic Central Com., 1948—. Served with USNR, 1941-45. Fellow Am. Coll. Probate Counsel, Am. Bar Found.; mem. ABA (chmn. gen. practice sect. 1966-67, mem. council sect. gen. practice 1964—, ho. dels. 1968-80, mem. com. edn. about Communism 1966-70, com. legal aid and indigent defendants 1970-73, chmn. com. law lists 1973-76), Ark. Bar Assn. (chmn. exec. com. 1956-57, pres. 1962-63), Am. Judicature Soc. (dir. 1964-68), Scribes, Nat. Conf. Bar Presidents (exec. council 1963-65), Blytheville C. of C. (past v.p., dir.), Navy League, Am. Legion. Clubs: Blytheville Country, Blytheville Rotary (past pres.). Home: 1062 W Hearn St Blytheville AR 72315 Office: 104 N 6th St Blytheville AR 72315

FENICHEL, SAUL MICHAEL, lawyer; b. Lakewood, N.J., Nov. 10, 1952; s. Lester J. and Rachel (Tilis) F.; m. Isabel Strauss, May 23, 1982; children: Jessica, Matthew. BS in Econs., U. Pa., 1974; JD, Rutgers U., 1977. Bar: N.J. 1977, U.S. Dist. Ct. N.J. 1977. Tax ptnr. Coopers & Lybrand, Newark, 1977-80, 82—; tax atty. Coopers & Lybrand, Washington, 1980-82. Mem. ABA, Am. Inst. CPAs, N.J. Soc. CPAs. Corporate taxation, Personal income taxation, Real property. Office: Coopers & Lybrand 80 Park Plaza Newark NJ 07102

FENLON, THOMAS BOLGER, lawyer; b. Long Branch, N.J., Nov. 12, 1904; s. John T. and Elizabeth (Cole) F.; m. Juliet O. Ludford, June 30, 1930; children—Mary Ann (Mrs. William V. Knowles), Henry L., Thomas Bolger, Juliet (Mrs. Frederick L. Nagle, Jr.), Lois (Mrs. Michael W. Brinkman). A.B., Georgetown U., 1925; LL.B., Columbia, 1928. Bar: N.Y. bar 1928. Partner firm Emmet, Marvin & Martin, N.Y.C., 1942—; Village atty. North Pelham, N.Y., 1933-35; town supr., Pelham, 1942-43. Mem. Pelham Bd. Edn., 1945-58, pres., 1955-58; bd. dirs., mem. exec. com. United Fund of Westchester, 1969-72; bd. dirs. Traphagen Sch. Fashion; trustee St. Catharine's Ch., Pelham. Named Man of Year in Pelham, 1967. Mem. ABA, N.Y. State Bar Assn. (chmn. com. state legislation 1944-46), Assn. Bar City N.Y. (chmn. com. state legislation 1944-46). Clubs: Pelham Mens (pres. 1952-53); Down Town Assn. (N.Y.C.); Huguenot Yacht (New Rochelle, N.Y.). Home: 72 Clifford Ave Pelham NY 10803 Office: 48 Wall St New York NY 10005

FENN, BRUCE HUNTER, lawyer; b. Mt. Kisco, N.Y., Nov. 16, 1954; s. Rutherford Hunter and Jean (Voss) F. BA, U. Conn., 1976; JD cum laude, Thomas M. Cooley Law Sch., 1981. Bar: Mich. 1981, U.S. Dist. Ct. (ea. dist.) Mich. 1982, U.S. Dist. Ct. (we. dist.) Mich. 1983, U.S. Supreme Ct. 1985. Sole practice Lansing, Mich., 1981—; bd. dirs. Ingham County Felony Appointment Bar. Clinton County coordinator Friends of David A. Thayer for State Senate, 1986. Mem. ABA, Mich. Bar Assn., N.H. Bar Assn., Ingham County Bar Assn., Clinton County Bar Assn. Avocations: music, travel, language, golf, outdoors. Criminal, Family and matrimonial, Juvenile. Office: 121 E Allegan St Lansing MI 48933

FENN, GEORGE KARL, JR., lawyer; b. Chgo., Dec. 19, 1930; s. George K. Sr. and Vera (Wallace) F. AB, Harvard U., 1951, LLB, 1954. Bar: Ill. 1954, N.Y. 1955. Atty. Met. Life Ins. Co., N.Y.C., 1954-65, asst. gen. counsel, 1965-70, assoc. gen. counsel, 1970-75, v.p., investment counsel, 1976—; chmn. Children's Books U.S.A., Amenia, N.Y., 1985—; bd. dirs. MetLife Capital Corp., Bellevue, Wash., Stamford, Conn. Served to sgt. U.S. Army, 1955-57. Fellow Am. Coll. Investment Counsel (trustee 1982—, pres. 1984-85); mem. ABA. Club: Harvard (N.Y.C.). General corporate, Insurance, Securities. Home: Rural Rt 1 Box 299 Amenia NY 12501 Office: Met Life Ins Co 1 Madison Ave New York NY 10010

FENNELL, DENNIS EUGENE, lawyer; b. Caldwell, Idaho, May 7, 1949; s. Horace Christopher and Velda (Abbott) G.; m. Michele O'Neil, Feb. 28, 1981 (div. Jan. 1987); 1 child, Sean Gyshen. BA, U. Oreg., 1971; JD, Willamette U., 1974. Bar: Oreg. 1974, U.S. Dist. Ct. Oreg. 1985. Spl. agt. FBI, Seattle, 1975-78; dep. dist. atty. Clackamas County, Oregon City, Oreg., 1978-79; dep. dist. atty. Deschutes County, Bend, Oreg., 1979-83, chief dep. dist. atty., 1983-87. Criminal. Home: 12375 Mount Jefferson Terr Apt 9F Lake Oswego OR 97035 Office: Dist Attys Office 720 SW Washington St Suite 215 Portland OR 97205

FENNELL, WILLIAM ALFRED, lawyer; b. Upper Darby, Pa., Sept. 1, 1948; s. Joseph Peter and Mary Delores (Parenteau) F.; m. Hillary Antoinette Schmitt, Apr. 17, 1971; children: Philippa C., Piers A., Isabelle E., Edwina M., Louisa A. AB, Princeton U., 1970; JD, Am. U., 1976. Bar: Md. 1977, D.C. 1978. Computer specialist U.S. Dept. Transp., Washington, 1970-77; sr. research computer scientist Fed. Jud. Ctr., Washington, 1978, 80-82; assoc. Brown & Tighe, Chevy Chase, Md., 1979; asst. chief ct. systems

br. U.S. Cts. Adminstrv. Office, Washington, 1982-84; chief tech. br. Edgar Project SEC, Washington, 1985; assoc. Stewart & Stewart, Washington, 1985—; cons. U.S. Ct. Mil. Appeals, Washington, 1982; assoc. professorial lectr. Grad. Sch. of Arts and Scis. George Washington U., Washington, 1985. Contbr. articles to profl. jours. Vol. Princeton Schs. Com., Washington, 1980—; coach Montgomery Soccer, Inc., Chevy Chase, 1983—. Mem. ABA, Fed. Bar Assn. Republican. Roman Catholic. Avocation: soccer. Computer, Private international. Home: 7008 Hillcrest Pl Chevy Chase MD 20815 Office: Stewart & Stewart 1001 Connecticut Ave NW Washington DC 20036

FENNER, JOHN BENJAMIN, lawyer; b. Buffalo, June 2, 1918; s. Benjamin Charles and Bessie (Peck) F.; m. Dorothy Louise Harstad, Oct. 12, 1940; children: Barbara Fenner Sjostrom, Thomas William, David Michael. BBA, Oreg. State U., 1940; JD, Stanford U., 1951. Bar: Oreg. 1951, Calif. 1951. Assoc. Freed & Failing, Portland, Oreg., 1951-54; ptnr. Mix & Fenner, Corvallis, Oreg., 1954-58; sole practice Corvallis, 1958-70; ptnr. Fenner & Barnhisel and successors, Corvallis, 1970—; dist. atty. Benton County, Corvallis, 1957-61. Mem. bd. visitors Stanford U., 1969-71; chmn. Oreg. Jud. Fitness Commn., 1972-74; pres. Oreg. State U. Found., Corvallis, 1987—, trustee 1960—. Served to col. U.S. Inf., 1940-46, ETO. Decorated Croix de Guerre (France). Fellow Am. Bar Found.; mem. Calif. Bar Assn., Oreg. Bar Assn. (bd. govs. 1965-68), Oreg. State U. Alumni Assn. (pres. 1960-61), Phi Delta Phi. Republican. Presbyterian. Clubs: Arlington (Portland), Corvallis Country, Timberhill Racquet (Corvallis). Avocations: tennis, gardening, photography. Probate, General corporate, Charitable foundations. Office: Fenner Barnhisel Willis & Barlow 123 NW 7th St Corvallis OR 97330

FENNER, SUZAN ELLEN, lawyer; b. Grand Junction, Colo., Dec. 5, 1947; d. Harry J. and Louise (Bain) Shaw; m. Michael Lee Riddle, Apr. 24, 1969 (div. Feb. 1976); m. Peter R. Fenner, Nov. 24, 1978; children: Laura Elizabeth, Adam Kyle. BA, Tex. Tech U., 1969, JD, 1971. ar: Tex. 1972, U.S. Dist. Ct. (no. dist.) Tex. 1972. Assoc. Smith & Baker, Lubbock, Tex., 1971-72; law clk. to presiding justice U.S. Dist. Ct., Dallas, 1972, 1973; assoc. Gardere & Wynne, Dallas, 1973-78, ptnr., 1978—; bd. dirs. Tex. Lawyers Ins. Exchange. Bd. dirs. East Dallas Devel. Ctr., 1982—; pres. Dallas Bus. League, 1986. Mem. ABA, Tex. Bar Assn. (chmn. bar jour. com. 1982—), Dallas Bar Assn. Republican. Episcopalian. Club: 500 Inc. (Dallas). Avocation: sailing. Pension, profit-sharing, and employee benefits. Home: 600 Goodwin Dr Richardson TX 75081 Office: Gardere & Wynne 1500 Diamond Shamrock Tower Dallas TX 75201

FENSTER, FRED A., lawyer, educator; b. Hartford, Conn., Oct. 8, 1946; s. Albert J. and Eleanor S. (Meyers) F.; m. Andrea Reifman, Jan. 2, 1972; children—Amanda Susanne, Monica Danielle. B.A., U. So. Calif., 1968, J.D., 1971. Bar: Calif. 1972, U.S. Dist. Ct. (cen. and so. dists.) Calif. 1972. Assoc. Richards, Watson, Dreyfuss & Gershon, Los Angeles, 1971-76, ptnr., 1977—; adj. prof. U. So. Calif., Los Angeles, 1977—. Campaign organizer Democratic Party, Los Angeles. Recipient 4 Am. Jurisprudence awards U. So. Calif., 1968-71; Asso. Men's Student's Scroll of Honor, 1968; scholar Cambridge U., Eng., 1967. Mem. Los Angeles County Bar Assn., Calif. Bar Assn., ABA, Order of Coif, Phi Beta Kappa, Phi Kappa Phi, Phi Eta Sigma, Pi Sigma Alpha. State civil litigation. Office: Richards Watson Dreyfuss & Gershon 333 S Hope St 38th Floor Los Angeles CA 90071

FENSTER, HERBERT LAWRENCE, lawyer; b. N.Y.C., Mar. 29, 1935; s. Oscar Samuel and Bessie Estelle (Schafran) F.; m. Gail Frances Meier, Apr. 18, 1964; children—Christopher Lawrence, Jennifer Gail, Jonathan Adam. A.B., U. Pa., 1957, M.A., 1958; J.D., U. Va., 1961. Bar: Va. 1961, D.C. 1962, U.S. Supreme Ct. 1967. Assoc., Sellers, Conner & Cuneo, Washington, 1961-66, ptnr., 1967-78, sr. ptnr., 1978-80; sr. ptnr. McKenna, Conner & Cuneo, 1980—. Author treatise Anti Deficiency Act, ABA, 1979. Litigationcounsel Reagan-Bush Campaign Com., Washington, 1980-83, pres.'s pvt. sector survey Grace Commn., 1982—; bd. dirs. Nat. Chamber Litigation Ctr., Washington, 1983—; bd. dirs. Keewaydin Found., Middlebury Vermont, 1982—, also trustee. Fellow Assn. Trial Lawyers Am.; mem. ABA, Fed. Bar Assn., D.C. Bar Assn. Republican. Episcopalian. Clubs: Metropolitan, University. Government contracts and claims, Product liability, Environment. Home: 5213 Albermarle St Westmoreland Hills MD 20816 Office: McKenna Conner & Cuneo 1575 Eye St NW Washington DC 20005

FENSTER, MARVIN, lawyer, department store executive; b. Bklyn., Jan. 19, 1918; s. Isaac and Anna (Greenman) F.; m. Louise Rapoport, Nov. 13, 1953; children—Julie, Mark. A.B., Cornell U., 1938; LL.B., Columbia U., 1941. Bar: N.Y. 1942. Assoc. Lauterstein, Spiller, Bergerman & Dannett, N.Y.C., 1941-42, 46-48; atty., asst. gen. atty. R.H. Macy & Co., Inc., N.Y.C., 1948-60, sr. v.p., gen. counsel, sec., 1960-84, sr. v.p. spel. counsel, sec., 1984—; sr. v.p., sec. Macy Acquiring Corp., N.Y.C., 1986—; pres. Macy's Bank, 1981—; dir., v.p., sec. Macy Credit Corp., N.Y.C., 1961-86, dir., pres., 1986—; dir., sec. Garden State Plaza Corp., Paramus, N.J., 1960—. Served to 1st lt. U.S. Army, 1943-46. Mem. Assn. of Bar, City of New York (corp. law depts. post-admission legal edn. council jud. adminstrn. 1983). Jewish. Clubs: Harmonie, Beach Point, Phi Epsilon Pi. General corporate, Landlord-tenant, Real property. Office: R H Macy & Co Inc 151 W 34th St New York NY 10001

FENSTER, ROBERT DAVID, lawyer; b. N.Y.C., Sept. 25, 1946; s. Alfred Howard and Esther (Eisenberg) F.; m. Janet Lynne Shanes, July 27, 1969; children: Lori Beth, Eric Steven. BA, Queens Coll., 1968; JD, Bklyn. Law Sch., 1973. Bar: N.Y. 1974, U.S. Dist. Ct. (so. and ea. dists.) N.Y. 1974, U.S. Supreme Ct. 1977. Investigator, prosecutor N.Y. Stock Exchange, N.Y.C., 1972-73; assoc. various law firms, Rockland County, N.Y., 1973-80; sole practice New City, N.Y., 1980—; bd. dirs. Brit. Pub. Corp., various other corps. Advisor Youth Ct. Town of Clarkstown, New City, N.Y., 1982; bd. dirs. Legal Aid Soc., Rockland County, 1974-78. Mem. ABA, N.Y. State Bar Assn., Rockland County Bar Assn., Am. Arbitration Assn. (arbitrator). General corporate, Oil and gas leasing, Real property. Office: 337 N Main St New City NY 10956

FENSTERSTOCK, BLAIR COURTNEY, lawyer; b. N.Y.C., Aug. 20, 1950; s. Nathaniel and Gertrude (Isaacson) F.; m. Joyce Narins, Sept. 16, 1979; children—Michael Bayard, Evan Steele. A.B. summa cum laude, Bowdoin Coll., 1972; J.D., Columbia U., 1975. Bar: N.Y. 1976, U.S. Dist. Ct. (so. ea. and no. dists.) N.Y., U.S. Ct. Appeals (2d cir.), Ind., U.S. Customs Ct., U.S. Ct. Internat. Trade, U.S. Supreme Ct. Assoc. firm Simpson, Thacher & Bartlett, N.Y.C., 1975-79, firm Dewey, Ballantine, Bushby, Palmer & Wood, N.Y.C., 1979-83; v.p., asst. gen. counsel, asst. sec. Reliance Group Holdings, Inc., N.Y.C., 1983—. Harlan Fiske Stone scholar Columbia U., 1975. Mem. Assn. Bar City N.Y., N.Y. State Bar Assn., ABA, Council N.Y. Law Assocs. (bd. dirs. 1979-82), Lawyers Com. for Internat. Human Rights (bd. dirs. 1979-80), Am. Arbitration Assn. (panel of arbitrators), Internat. Peace Acad. (sec. 1977-79), Phi Beta Kappa. Republican. Jewish. Clubs: University (N.Y.C.); Aspetuck Valley Country (Weston, Conn.). Federal civil litigation, State civil litigation, Securities. Home: 120 E 75th St New York NY 10021 Office: Reliance Group Holdings Inc 55 E 52d St New York NY 10055

FENTON, ELLIOTT CLAYTON, lawyer; b. Oklahoma City, Nov. 26, 1914; s. Edgar R. and Mary (Gaddo) F.; m. LeNoir Massey, July 6, 1939; children: Elliott, Ann Wallis. BA, U. Okla., 1935, LLB, 1937. Bar: Okla. 1937, U.S. Dist. Ct. (no., ea. and we. dists.) Okla., U.S. Ct. Appeals (10th cir.), U.S. Supreme Ct., U.S. Ct. Mil. Appeals. Atty. Looney & Fenton, Oklahoma City, 1937-38; atty., claims rep. Nat. Mut. Casualty Co., Tulsa, 1938-40, Hartford Ins. Group, Oklahoma City, 1940-47; atty. Fenton & Fenton, Oklahoma City, 1947—. Chmn. bd. trustees United Meth. Found., Oklahoma City, 1973-83; chancellor United Meth. Found., Oklahoma City, 1983—. Served to comdr. USNR, 1942-45, PTO. Fellow Am. Bar Found; mem. Am. Bd. Trial Advs., Def. Research Inst. (state chmn. 1978-83), Okla. Assn. Def. Counsel (pres. 1972), Okla. County Bar Assn. (bd. dirs.). Democrat. United Methodist. Lodge: Optimists (Oklahoma City). Avocations: golf. Federal civil litigation, State civil litigation, Personal injury. Home: 1213 Westchester Oklahoma City OK 73114 Office: Fenton Fenton Smith et al 1 Leadership Sq Suite 800 Oklahoma City OK 73102

FENTON, HOWARD NATHAN, III, legal educator; b. Toledo, May 6, 1950; s. Howard Nathan, Jr. and Maxine Claire (LaFountaine) F.; m. Kathleen Kay Scimeca, Dec. 29, 1971; children—William Carl, Margaret Claire, Andrew Scimeca, Julie Marie, Christopher Howard. BS with honors, U. Tex., 1971, JD with honors, 1975. Bar: Tex. 1975, D.C. 1976, U.S. Dist. Ct. D.C. 1976, U.S. Ct. Appeals (D.C. cir.) 1976. Assoc. Williams & Jensen, P.C., Washington, 1975-77; ptnr. Swift & Swift, P.C., Washington, 1978; supervisory compliance officer Office Antiboycott Compliance, Internat. Trade Adminstrn., U.S. Dept. Commerce, Washington, 1979-80, dir. compliance policy, 1981-84; assoc. prof. Miss. Coll. Sch. Law, Jackson, 1984—; fellow Nat. Ctr. for Export/Import Studies, Georgetown U., Washington, 1983-86; mem. adj. faculty Cath. U. Law Sch., Washington, spring 1984. Cons. editor Boycott Law Bull., 1984-85. Mem. ABA. Democrat. Legal education, Administrative and regulatory, Private international. Office: Miss Coll Sch of Law 151 E Griffith St Jackson MS 39201

FENTON, JOHN HENRY, judge; b. Boston, Aug. 11, 1927; s. Francis Patrick and Christine Wilhelmina (Tucker) F.; m. Gloria Anne Adams, May 2, 1959; children: John, Michael, Francis, Anne. B.S.S., Georgetown U., 1948, LL.B., 1952. Bar: Md. 1952. Atty. advisor NLRB, Washington, 1952-56, trial and supervisory trial atty., Atlanta, 1956-63, asst. gen. counsel, Washington, 1963-72; assoc. chief adminstrv. law judge Dept. Labor, Washington, 1972-79; chief adminstrv. law judge Fed. Labor Relations Authority, Washington, 1979—. Democrat. Roman Catholic. Labor, Workers' compensation, Administrative and regulatory. Office: Adminstrv Law Judges 500 C St SW Washington DC 20424 •

FENTON, MARC IRA, lawyer; b. Chgo., July 8, 1953; s. Donald Raymond and Esther Alice (Cohen) F.; m. Ellen Desnet, June 15, 1980; children—Alison, Aaron. B.A., Loyola U., 1975; J.D., No. Ill. U., 1981. Bar: Ill. 1981, U.S. Dist. Ct. (no. dist.) Ill. 1981, U.S. Ct. Appeals (7th cir.) 1982. Asst. pub. defender Cook County, Ill., 1981-82; staff atty. Office of U.S. Trustee, U.S. Dept. Justice, Chgo., 1982-84; assoc. Fagel, Haber & Maragos, Chgo., 1984—. Mem. ABA, Ill. Bar Assn., Am. Bankrupcy Inst., Comml. Law League, Chgo. Bar Assn. (bankruptcy subcom.). Jewish. Bankruptcy, General corporate. Home: 313 Redwing Dr Deerfield IL 60015 Office: Fagel Haber & Maragos 140 S Dearborn Suite 1400 Chicago IL 60603

FENTON, THOMAS CONNER, lawyer; b. Cin., Feb. 9, 1954; s. William Conner and Virginia (Rawnsley) F.; m. Karen Lois Haswell, Oct. 20, 1979; children: Margaret Lois, Rebecca Conner. BA, Centre Coll., 1976; JD, Ohio State U., 1979. Bar: Ky. 1979, U.S. Dist. Ct. (we. dist.) Ky. 1979, U.S. Ct. Appeals (D.C. cir.) 1981, U.S. Dist. Ct. (ea. dist.) Ky. 1985, U.S. Ct. Appeals (6th cir.) 1986. Assoc. Greenebaum, Young, Treita & Maggiolo, Louisville, 1979-85; ptnr. Greenebaum, Young, Treitz & Maggiolo, Louisville, 1985—. Bd. dirs. Sr. House, Inc., Louisville, 1983—, sec., 1984-86, v.p., 1986—. Mem. ABA (labor and employment law sect.), Ky. Bar Assn. (chmn. labor relations law sect. 1981-83), Louisville Bar Assn. Episcopalian. Labor, General corporate, General practice. Home: 4615 Fox Run Rd Louisville KY 40207 Office: Greenebaum Young Treitz & Maggiolo 2700 First National Tower Louisville KY 40202-3101

FENWICK, LYNDA BECK, lawyer; b. Great Bend, Kans., Oct. 24, 1944; d. Ralph George and Margaret Pauline (Hawk) Beck; m. Larry Dean Fenwick, Dec. 23, 1962. BS with distinction, Fort Hays State U., 1966; JD, Baylor U., 1975. Bar: U.S. Dist. Ct. (we. dist.) Tex. 1980, U.S. Dist. Ct. (no. dist.) Tex. 1986. Atty. VA, Waco, Tex., 1975-79; assoc. Pakis, Cherry, Beard & Giotes, Waco, 1979-81; sole practice Dallas, 1981-85; assoc. Taylor & Mizell P.C., Dallas, 1985—; adj. faculty law Baylor U., Waco, 1979-81; grader exams Supreme Ct. of Tex., 1981-85. Assoc. editor Baylor U. Law Rev., 1974-75. Docent Dallas Mus. Art., 1982-85. Mem. ABA, Tex. Bar Assn., Dallas County Bar Assn., Phi Delta Phi, Southwest Watercolor Soc., Pastel Soc. of the Southwest. State civil litigation, Federal civil litigation, Real property. Office: Taylor & Mizell PC 500 N Akard St Suite 3000 Dallas TX 75201

FENZA, WILLIAM JOSEPH, JR., financial co. exec.; b. Ridley Park, Pa., May 21, 1929; s. William Joseph and Leona (Lane) F.; m. Myra Ann Wolf, Dec. 14, 1968; children—David, Christine, Jennifer, Richard. A.B., Johns Hopkins U., 1951; LL.B., U. Pa., 1956. Bar: Pa. bar. Law clk. firm Joseph E. Pappano, Chester, Pa., 1956-57; claims office mgr. State Farm Ins. Co., Dover, Del., 1957-59; partner firm Bernstein, Corcoran, Mueller & Fenza, Upper Darby, Pa., 1960-62; with Chrysler First Inc. (formerly Finance Am. Corp.), Allentown, Pa., 1962—; sr. v.p., gen. counsel. Chrysler First Inc. (formerly Finance Am. Corp.). Served with AUS, 1951-53. Mem. Am., Pa., Lehigh County bar assns. General corporate. Home: 2830 Old S Pike Ave Allentown PA 18103 Office: 1105 Hamilton St Allentown PA 18101

FEOLA, EUGENE DAVID, lawyer, food products executive; b. N.Y.C., Oct. 29, 1948; s. Valentine and Rachel (Chernack) F.; m. Theresa Catherine Rendini, June 20, 1971; children: Craig Scott, Michael Todd. BA, CCNY, 1971; JD, U. Miami, 1974. Bar: Fla. 1974, U.S. Dist. Ct. (so. dist.) Fla. 1976, U.S. Ct. Appeals (5th cir.) 1976, U.S. Supreme Ct. 1978. Corp. counsel real estate Burger King Corp., Miami, Fla., 1974-77, sr. corp. counsel real estate, 1977-82, group counsel, 1982-84, v.p., asst. gen. counsel, 1984—. Mem. ABA, Fla. Bar Assn., Am. Corp. Counsel Assn. Contracts commercial, Real property, Landlord-tenant. Office: Burger King Corp 7360 N Kendall Dr PO Box 520783 - GMF Miami FL 33152

FERCHLAND, WILLIAM THOMAS, lawyer, lecturer; b. Chgo., Jan. 15, 1945; s. William H. and Veronica (August) F.; m. Candace Nilsson, Sept. 8, 1973; children: William, Kyle, Kathleen. BS in Fin., U. Ill., 1970; JD, John Marshall Law Sch., Chgo., 1975. Bar: Calif. 1975, U.S. Dist. Ct. Calif. 1975; cert. specialist in workers compensation law. Assoc. Richens L. Wootton, Santa Rosa, Calif., 1975-79; prin. Ferchland Law Office, Santa Rosa, 1979—; judge pro tem Workers Compensation Appeals Bd. Bd. dirs. Sonoma County Legal Services Found., Sonoma County Legal Aid. Served with U.S. Army, 1967-69. Mem. Calif. Applicant Atty. Assn., ABA, Calif. Bar Assn., Am. Trial Lawyers Assn., Nat. Orgn. Social Security Claimants Reps., Redwood Empire Trial Lawyers Assn., VFW. Republican. Roman Catholic. Workers' compensation, Pension, profit-sharing, and employee benefits. Office: 716 College Ave Santa Rosa CA 95404

FERENCIK, ROBERT ELMER, JR., lawyer; b. Fort Belvoir, Va., July 25, 1947; s. Robert Elmer Sr. and Elizabeth (Bartlett) F.; m. Kathleen Dayton Smith, Sept. 5, 1970 (div. Aug. 1980); 1 child, Douglas Alan: m. Patrice Tedsko, June 15, 1982; 1 child, Robert Joseph. EdB, U. Miami, 1970; Med, Wichita State U., 1975; JD cum laude, U. Miami, 1978. Bar: Fla. 1978, U.S. Ct. Mil. Appeals 1979, U.S. Dist. Ct. (so. dist.) Fla. 1980, U.S. Ct. Appeals (11th cir.) 1985, U.S. Supreme Ct. 1985. Commd. 2d lt. USAF, 1970, advanced through grades to maj., 1985; asst. staff judge area def. counsel USAF, Whiteman AFB, Mo., 1978-80; cir. trial counsel USAF, Ramstein AB, Fed. Republic Germany, 1980-81, Ramstein AFB, Fed. Republic Germany, 1980-81; chief cir. trail counsel USAF, Rheinmain AFB, Fed. Republic Germany, 1981-83; assoc. apppelate govt. counsel USAF, Washington, 1983-85; ret. USAF, 1985; assoc. Leiby and Elder, Miami, Fla., 1985—. Mem. Fed. Bar Assn., Fla. Bar Assn., Assn. Trial Lawyers Am. Republican. Episcopalian. Avocations: sports, boating. Construction, Government contracts and claims, State civil litigation. Office: Leiby and Elder 17131 NE 6th Ave Miami FL 33162

FERENCZ, ROBERT ARNOLD, lawyer; b. Chgo., Sept. 10, 1946; s. Albert and Frances (Reiss) F.; m. Marla J. Miller, May 20, 1973; children: Joseph, Ira. BS in Acctg., U. Ill., 1968; JD magna cum laude, U. Mich., 1973. Bar: Ill. 1973. From assoc. to ptnr. Sidley & Austin, Chgo., 1973—. Mem. ABA, Ill. Bar Assn., Chgo. Bar Assn. Corporate taxation, Pension, profit-sharing, and employee benefits. Office: Sidley & Austin One 1st Nat Plaza Chicago IL 60603

FERGUS, WILLIAM LEE, lawyer; b. Memphis, Sept. 23, 1948; s. William Dane and Pearle White (Cartwright) F.; m. Marla Jo Henson, Nov. 25, 1978; 1 child, Jensie Elizabeth. BA, Westminster Coll., 1970; JD, U. Ark., 1975. Bar: Ark. 1975, U.S. Dist. Ct. (ea. dist.) Ark. 1980, U.S. Tax Ct. 1980, U.S. Ct. Appeals (8th cir.) 1980, U.S. Supreme Ct. 1980. Dir. criminal investigation, 2d. jud. dist. State of Ark., Osceola, 1975-78; sole practice Osceola, 1975—. Mem. Gideons Internat., Osceola, 1978—; deacon Sunday Sch. Calvary Bapt., Osceola, 1980—; chmn. South Miss. County Red Cross, Osceola, 1980—. Served to capt. USAR, 1973—. Mem. ABA, Ark. Bar Assn., Osceola Bar Assn., Assn. Trial Lawyers Am., Christian Legal Soc., Phi Alpha Delta. Lodge: Masons (numerous offices), KT (grand capt. gen. 1986). Personal injury, Real property, Probate. Home: 605 W Union Osceola AR 72370 Office: 101 N Walnut PO Box 985 Osceola AR 72370

FERGUSON, APRIL ROSE W., lawyer, editor; b. Detroit, Mar. 28, 1943; d. Arthur and Hilda (Pavek) Wyss; m. Joseph J. Ferguson (dec.); 1 child, Alyce Theresa. BA, Wayne State U., 1973; JD, Cath. U. Am., 1976. Bar: Fla. 1978, Tenn. 1979, U.S. Ct. Appeals (5th, 6th and 11th cirs.). Assoc. dir. Washington for Citizens Commn. of Inquiry, 1975-76; sole practice, Memphis; asst. pub. defender, Memphis. Bd. dirs. Peace and Justice Ctr.; mem. citizens rev. bd. Selective Service, 1984—. Mem. ACLU (past dir.), NOW (pres. Memphis chpt.), Tenn. Assn. Criminal Def. Lawyers (bd. dirs.). Editor: Code Name Zorro; The Strongest Poison. Criminal, Civil rights, Jurisprudence. Address: 1258 Forrest Ave Memphis TN 38104

FERGUSON, CHARLES ALAN, lawyer; b. Fulton, Mo., Jan. 7, 1940; s. Charles Milton and Hazel A. (Jackson) F.; m. Sandra Minter, Dec. 21, 1963; children: Stacy Christine, Scot Alan. BA, So. Meth. U., 1962, JD, 1965. Bar: Tex. 1965, U.S. Dist. Ct. (we. dist.) Tex. 1967, U.S. Supreme Ct. 1976; CLU. Assoc. McGown, McClanahan & Hamner, San Antonio, 1965-69; atty. Govt. Personnel Mut. Life Ins. Co., San Antonio, 1969—, assoc. gen. counsel, asst. sec., 1970-79, v.p., gen. counsel and sec., 1979—, also bd. dirs.; pres., bd. dirs. G.P.M. Fed. Credit Union, San Antonio, 1971-80; sec., bd. dirs. Greenwood Life Ins. Co., San Antonio, 1970-76; Mem. adv. com. on replacement, Tex. State Bd. Ins., 1981-82; mem. legis. com. Tex. Life Ins. Assn.; com. chmn. Aero. Med. Div. and Wilford Hall USAF Hosp., San Antonio, 1972-73, Joint Jr. Officers Council, San Antonio, 1974, Brooks AFB, 1980-81. Pres., bd. dirs. Scenic Oaks Property Owners Assn., 1986—. Fellow Life Mgmt. Inst.; mem. ABA, San Antonio Bar Assn., San Antonio Jr. Bar Assn. (v.p. 1973), State Bar Tex. (Coll.), Fiesta Men (v.p. 1974-76), Assn. Life Ins. Counsel, San Antonio C. of C., Phi Gamma Delta, Phi Alpha Delta. Clubs: Turtle Creek Country (bd. govs.), Diez y Seis Handball (sec.-treas. 1975). Insurance, General corporate. Home: 8601 Barn Swallow Dr San Antonio TX 78255 Office: 800 NW Loop 410 San Antonio TX 78216

FERGUSON, ELIZABETH NORTON, lawyer; b. Cleve., Mar. 25, 1933; d. James Nicolas and Ruth Elizabeth (Cannell) Wychgel; m. Henry Wacks Norton, July 16, 1954 (div. 1971); children: James, Henry, Peter, Fred; m. James Cory Ferguson, Dec. 14, 1985. BA in Math., Wellesley Coll., 1954; JD cum laude, U. Minn., 1974. Bar: Minn. 1974. Assoc. Gray, Plant, Mooty, Mooty & Bennett, P.A., Mpls., 1974-79, ptnr., 1980—. Trustee YWCA, Mpls., 1979-84, co-chmn. deferred giving com., 1980-81, chmn. bylaws com., bd. dirs. 1976-77, lectr.; treas. Minn. Women's Campaign Fund, 1985, guarantor, 1982-83, budget and fin. com., bd. dirs. 1984—; trustee Ripley Meml. Found., 1980-84; treas. Jones-Harrison Home, 1967, bd. dirs. 1962-69, 2d v.p., chmn. fin., 1968-69; mem. senator David Durenberger's Women's Network, 1983—. Durant scholar. Mem. ABA (family law sect. mediation task force 1983-84), Minn. Bar Assn. (family law sect., human rights com. mem., lectr., task force on uniform marital property act 1984-85), Hennepin County Bar Assn. (pres.-elect 1986-87, pres. 1987-88treas. 1985-86, sec. 1984-85, chmn. task force pub. edn. 1985, chmn. family law sect. 1980-81, exec. com. family law sect. 1979—, lectr.), Lawyer's Bd. Profl. Responsibility (task force study com. proposals 1985), Minn. Inst. Legal Edn. (lectr.), Minn. Women's Lawyers Inc. (co-chmn. appointments com. 1980-81, exec. com.), U. Minn. Law Sch. Alumni Assn. (bd. dirs. 1975-81, exec. com. alumnae 1981-83), Horizon 100 (steering com.), Phi Beta Kappa. Clubs: Minneapolis, Mpls. Wellesley; Woodhill; Minikahda. Family and matrimonial, Probate. Home: 3200 W Calhoun Pkwy Apt #302 Minneapolis MN 55416 Office: Gray Plant Mooty Mooty & Bennett 33 S 6th St 3400 City Ctr Minneapolis MN 55402

FERGUSON, GERALD PAUL, lawyer; b. Teaneck, N.J., Oct. 17, 1951; s. James Richard and Ilene Veronica (Meyer) F.; m. Nancy Ivers, Aug. 20, 1977; 1 child, James Ralph. BA, Fairleigh Dickinson U., 1974; JD, Capital U., 1979. Bar: Ohio 1979, U.S. Dist. Ct. (so. dist.) Ohio 1980, U.S. Ct. Appeals (6th cir.) 1986. Ptnr. Vorys, Sater, Seymour and Pease, Columbus, 1979—. Mem. ABA (trial evidence subcom. 1985-86), Ohio State Bar Assn. (unauthorized practice law com. 1985-86), Columbus Bar Assn. (chmn. juror subcom. 1979-86). Republican. Roman Catholic. Avocation: fishing. Federal civil litigation, State civil litigation, Construction. Office: Vorys Sater Seymour & Pease 52 E Gay St Columbus OH 43215

FERGUSON, HAROLD LAVERNE, JR., lawyer; b. Cleveland, Miss., Dec. 3, 1938; s. Harold Laverne and Allene Thompson (Burford) F.; m. Jamie Frances Flemming, Nov. 20, 1965; children: Harold Laverne III, Samuel Christopher, Julie Allene. BA in Pub. Adminstrn., U. Miss., 1960; JD, Samford U., 1973. Bar: Ala. 1973. Ptnr. Spain, Gillon, Riley, Tate & Etheredge, Birmingham, Ala., 1973-80, Dominick, Fletcher, Yeilding, Wood & Lloyd P.A., Birmingham, 1980—; bd. dirs. S.P. Food Services Inc., Birmingham. Served with Miss. and Tenn. N.G., 1955-63. Mem. ABA, Ala. Bar Assn., Tenn. Bar Assn., Birmingham Bar Assn., Ala. Def. Lawyers Assn., Def. Research Inst., Birmingham Ole Miss. Alumni Club (pres. 1985-86). Republican. Baptist. Lodge: Rotary. Insurance, Personal injury, Workers' compensation. Home: 440 Hillwood Dr Birmingham AL 35209

FERGUSON, MARVIN ELWOOD, retired state court judge; b. Los Angeles, Dec. 10, 1926; s. Elwood Lynn and Marjorie (Greeley) F.; m. Shirley Eileen Abbot, 1947 (div. 1963); children—Thomas Marvin, Daniel Lynn; m. Julie Mary Alonde, Sept. 25, 1965; stepchildren—Larry B. Briscoe, Shellie Julie Briscoe. Student Pepperdine Coll., 1947; LL.B., U. Calif.-San Francisco, 1952. Bar: Calif. 1953. Ct. clk. County of Kern, Bakersfield, Calif., 1952-53, asst. dist. atty., 1953-63, mcpl. ct. judge, 1963-66; judge Calif. Superior Ct., Bakersfield, 1966-86. prin. Bus. Jud. Arbitration and Settlement Services, Bakersfield, 1986—. Served with U.S. Army, 1945-46. State civil litigation, Criminal, Juvenile.

FERGUSON, MILTON CARR, JR., lawyer; b. Washington, Feb. 10, 1931; s. Milton Carr and Gladys (Emery) F.; m. Marian Evelyn Nelson, Aug. 21, 1954; children: Laura, Sharon, Marcia, Sandra. B.A., Cornell U., 1952; LL.B., 1954; LL.M., N.Y. U., 1960. Bar: N.Y. State 1954. Trial atty. tax div. Dept. Justice, Washington, 1954-60; asst. atty. gen. Dept. Justice, 1977-81; asst. prof. law U. Iowa, 1960-62; asso. prof. N.Y. U., 1962-65, prof., 1965-77; vis. prof. law Stanford (Calif.) U., 1972-73; of counsel Wachtell, Lipton, Rosen & Katz, N.Y.C., 1969-76; partner firm Davis Polk & Wardwell, N.Y.C., 1981—; spl. cons. to Treasury Dept., Commonwealth P.R., 1974. Author: (with others) Federal Income Taxation Legislation in Perspective, 1965, Federal Income Taxation of Estates and Beneficiaries, 1970. Mem. Am., N.Y. State bar assns., Soc. Illustrators. Corporate taxation, Estate taxation. Home: 32 Washington Sq W New York NY 10011 Office: Davis Polk & Wardwell One Chase Manhattan Plaza New York NY 10005

FERGUSON, SANFORD BARNETT, lawyer; b. Boston, Feb. 3, 1947; s. Albert Barnett and Louise (Enequist) F.; m. Louise King, Oct. 13, 1978; children: Andrew, Robert. BA, Dartmouth Coll., 1970; MA, Oxford U., Eng., 1972; JD, Yale U., 1975. Bar: Pa. 1975, U.S. Dist. Ct. (we. dist.) Pa., U.S. Tax Ct., U.S. Ct. Appeals (3d cir.). Ptnr. Kirkpatrick & Lockhart, Pitts., 1981—. Presbyterian. Computer, General corporate, Real property. Office: Kirkpatrick & Lockhart 1500 Oliver Bldg Pittsburgh PA 15222

FERGUSON, STANLEY LEWIS, lawyer; b. Evanston, Ill., Aug. 2, 1952; s. Richard G. and Alberta Ann (Crebo) F.; m. Mary M. Pyle, Aug. 16, 1980; children: Kate, Brooke. BA, Northwestern U., 1975; JD cum laude, Boston U., 1978. Bar: Ill. 1978, U.S. Dist. Ct. (no. dist.) Ill. 1978, U.S. Ct. Appeals (6th and 7th cirs.). Assoc. Kirkland & Ellis, Chgo., 1978-85, ptnr., 1985-87; asst. gen. counsel USG Corp., Chgo., 1987—. Mem. ABA (faculty, joint program antitrust issues in health care industry 1986), Ill. Bar Assn., Legal Club Chgo. Club: Univ. (Chgo.). Federal civil litigation, State civil litigation. Home: 317 Glendale Ave Winnetka IL 60093 Office: USG Corp 101 S Wacker Dr Chicago IL 60606

FERGUSON, STEPHEN LUTHER, lawyer; b. Indpls., Jan. 3, 1941; s. Luther and Arline F.; m. Jean Byrd (div.); children: Elizabeth, Matthew, Amy. AB, Wabash Coll., 1963; JD with distinction, Ind. U., 1966. Ptnr. Ferguson, Ferguson & Lloyd, Bloomington, Ind., 1966—; pres. CFC, Inc., Bloomington, Ind., 1976—. Mem. Ind. Ho. of Reps., 1967-75; mem. Ind. Criminal Law Study Com., Indpls., 1979—; mem. Commn. for Bloomington (Ind.) Downtown Inc., 1984—; bd. dirs. YMCA, Hoosier Trails council Boy Scouts Am. Mem. ABA, Am. Judicature Soc., Assn. Trial Lawyers Am., Ind. Bar Assn., Monroe County Bar Assn. (pres.). Republican. Avocations: basketball, coaching basketball. General practice, General corporate, Public utilities. Office: Ferguson Ferguson & Lloyd 403 E Sixth St Bloomington IN 47401

FERGUSON, THEODORE JAMES, lawyer; b. San Antonio, Dec. 19, 1954; s. James Homer and Ellen (Ball) F.; m. Lee Ann Merry, June 26, 1982. AB, Wabash Coll., Crawfordsville, Ind., 1977; JD, Ind. U., 1980. Bar: Ind. 1980, U.S. Dist. Ct. (so. dist.) Ind. 1980, U.S. Tax Ct. 1983. Ptnr. Ferguson, Ferguson & Lloyd, Bloomington, Ind., 1980—; sec. and bd. dirs. Pub. Investment Corp., WFD, Inc. Bd. dirs. Hoosier Trails Council Boy Scouts Am., 1983—. Mem. ABA, Ind. State Bar Assn., Monroe County Bar Assn., Def. Lawyers Assn. Real property, Probate, General corporate. Office: Ferguson Ferguson & Lloyd 403 E 6th St Bloomington IN 47401-3698

FERGUSON, TRACY HEIMAN, lawyer, educational administrator; b. Syracuse, N.Y., Sept. 2, 1910; s. George Joshua and Fannie (Heiman) F.; m. Babbette R. Oberdorfer, Dec. 22, 1938; children: Babbette Tracy, Earl Mark. A.B., Syracuse U., 1931; LL.B., Harvard, 1934. Bar: N.Y. 1934, U.S. Supreme Ct 1944, other U.S. cts 1934. Practice in Syracuse, 1934—; ptnr. Bond, Schoeneck & King, 1947—; mem. faculty Coll. Law Syracuse U., 1946-48, sr. fellow Employment Studies Inst., Sch. Mgmt., 1982—; adj. prof. labor law U. Miami, 1977-78, Nova U., 1978, 79; adj. prof. Maxwell Sch. Citizenship, Syracuse U., 1981-83. Contbr. articles to legal jours. Industry mem. N.Y.-N.J. Regional Wage Stblzn. Bd., 1951-52; v.p. Citizens Found. Syracuse, 1949-50; nat. vice chmn. jr. div. Am. Jewish Joint Distbn., 1937; chmn. Syracuse Jewish Welfare Fedn., 1950-51, 62, pres., 1951; chmn. Onondaga County chpt. March of Dimes, 1956; mem. labor mgmt. adv. panel N.Y. State Mediation Bd., 1969-78; mem. nat. adv. com. NYU Inst. Labor Relations, 1968-83; Pres. Republican Citizens Com. Onondaga County, 1962-63; Regent LeMoyne Coll., Syracuse, 1967-72; bd. dirs., sec. Community-Gen. Hosp. Greater Syracuse, 1967-74, hon. dir., 1976—; former bd. dirs. Midtown Hosp., Syracuse, United Community Chest and Council; trustee Onondaga County Community Coll., 1961-66, Cazenovia Coll., 1965-66, Syracuse Pub. Library, 1965-69, Union of Am. Hebrew Congregations, 1969-83; bd. dirs. N.Am. Bd., World Union for Progressive Judaism, 1981-83. Served as officer USNR, 1943-46. Recipient Letterman of Distinction award Syracuse U., 1976, Alumni award Syracuse U., 1983. Fellow Am. Bar Found., N.Y. State Bar Assn. (chmn. labor law com. 1964-66); mem. ABA (chmn. labor relations law sect. 1963-64, mem. council 1957-66, hon. mem. council 1973—, sect. del. 1965-66), Fed. Bar Assn. (pres. N.Y. upstate chpt. 1973-74, mem. nat. council), Onondaga County Bar Assn., Am. Arbitration Assn. (mem. exec. com. 1977-79, former chmn. N.Y. State adv. council), Indsl. Relations Research Assn. Central N.Y. (co-pres. 1979-80). Jewish (trustee temple, pres. 1966-71). Clubs: Century, University (Syracuse); Nat. Lawyers (Washington). Labor, Antitrust. Home: 15 Pebble Hill Rd S Syracuse (Dewitt) NY 13214 also: 3039 Deer Creek Lake Shore Dr Deerfield Beach FL 33442 Office: 1 Lincoln Center Syracuse NY 13202

FERGUSON, WARREN JOHN, federal judge; b. Eureka, Nev., Oct. 31, 1920; s. Ralph and Marian (Damele) F.; m. E. Laura Keyes, June 5, 1948; children: Faye F., Warren John, Teresa M., Peter J. B.A., U. Nev., 1942; LL.B., U. So. Calif., 1949; LL.D. (hon.), Western State U., San Fernando Valley Coll. Law. Bar: Calif. 1950. Mem. firm Ferguson & Judge, Fullerton, Calif., 1950-59; city atty. for cities of Buena Park, Placentia, La Puente, Baldwin Park, Santa Fe Springs, Walnut and Rosemead, Calif., 1953-59; mcpl. ct. judge Anaheim, Calif., 1959-60; judge Superior Ct., Santa Ana, Calif., 1961-66, Juvenile Ct., 1963-64, Appellate Dept., 1965-66; U.S. dist. judge Los Angeles, 1966-79; judge U.S. Circuit Ct. 9th Circuit, Los Angeles, 1979-86, sr. judge, 1986—; faculty Fed. Jud. Ctr., Practising Law Inst., U. Iowa Coll. Law, N.Y. Law Jour.; sr. judge U.S. Cir. Ct. (9th cir.), Santa Ana, Calif., 1986—; assoc. prof. psychiatry (law) Sch. Medicine, U. So. Calif.; assoc. prof. Loyola Law Sch. Served with AUS, 1942-46. Decorated Bronze Star. Mem. Phi Kappa Phi, Theta Chi. Democrat. Roman Catholic. Jurisprudence. Office: 34 Civic Ctr Plaza Santa Ana CA 92701

FERGUSON, WHITWORTH, III, lawyer, trust company executive; b. Buffalo, Aug. 16, 1954; s. Whitworth Jr. and Elizabeth (Rice) F.; m. Mary Barstow, May 30, 1981. BA in Econs., St. Lawrence U., Canton, N.Y., 1976; MBA in Fin., U. Pa., 1978; JD, Cornell U., 1981. Bar: Ill. 1981, N.Y. 1983. Assoc. McDermott, Will & Emery, Chgo., 1981-82, Damon & Morey, Buffalo, 1982-84; officer fin. planning Key Trust Co., Buffalo, 1984—. Bd. dirs. Senecare Corp., 1983—, YMCA Greater Buffalo, 1985—; ho. of dels. United Way, Buffalo and Erie County, 1984—. Mem. ABA, Internat. Assn. Fin. Planners. Presbyterian. Business law. Office: Key Trust Co 284 Main St Buffalo NY 14202

FERINGA, SCOTT DOUGLAS, lawyer; b. Paterson, N.J., July 9, 1953; s. Philip John and Margaret Martina (Van Der Wiele) F.; m. Karen Ann Kronberger, Aug. 2, 1980; 1 child, Lauren Ashley. BA, Calvin Coll., 1975; JD, U. Detroit, 1978. Bar: Mich. 1978, U.S. Dist. Ct. (ea. dist.) Mich. 1978. Assoc. Kitch, Suhrheinrich, Detroit, 1978-80; assoc. Sullivan, Ward & Bone, Detroit, 1980-86, ptnr., 1986—, also bd. dirs. Recipient Am. Jurisprudence award (evidence) Lawyers Coop. Pub. Co., Detroit, 1977. Fellow Am. Acad. Hosp. Attys.; mem. ABA, Mich. Bar Assn., Mich. Soc. Hosp. Attys., Detroit Bar Assn., Oakland County Bar Assn., Ski Def. Attys. Assn. (bd. dirs., sec.). Club: Grosse Pointe (Mich.) Yacht. Avocations: sailing, skiing, tennis. State civil litigation, Federal civil litigation, Personal injury. Office: Sullivan Ward et al 220 W Congress 5th floor Detroit MI 48226

FERMAN, IRVING, lawyer, educator; b. N.Y.C., July 4, 1919; s. Joseph and Sadie (Stein) F.; m. Bertha Paglin, June 12, 1946; children—James Paglin, Susan Paglin. B.S., N.Y.U., 1941; J.D., Harvard, 1948. Bar: La. 1948, D.C. 1974. Partner Provensal, Faris & Ferman, New Orleans, 1948-52; dir. Am. Civil Liberties Union, Washington, 1952-59, Am. Civil Liberties Clearing House, 1952-54; exec. vice chmn. Pres.'s Com. Govt. Contracts, 1959-60; v.p. Internat. Latex Corp., 1960-66; pres. Piedmont Theaters Corp., 1966-69; adj. asso. prof. mgmt. N.Y.U. Grad. Sch. Bus., 1964-68; adj. prof. law Howard U., 1968-69, prof. law, 1969-86, prof. emeritus, 1986—; dir. Project for Legal Policy, 1976—; vis. prof. law Am. U., 1971-72; mem. Am. Com. Cultural Freedom, 1954—; mem. Com. of Arts and Scis. for Eisenhower, 1956; mem. citizens adv. com. U.S. Commn. on Govt. Security, 1957; chmn. Police Complaint Review Bd., 1965-73; mem. Dept. HEW Reviewing Authority, 1969-79; chmn. Interdisco Ltd., London, 1986—; bd. dirs. Control Fluidics, Inc., Greenwich, Conn. Contbr. to books and revs. Mem. bd. dirs. New Orleans Acad. Art, 1948-51. Served from cadet to 1st lt. USAAF, 1942-46. Mem. Am., La., D.C., New Orleans bar assns. Jewish. Clubs: Capitol Hill (Washington), International (Washington); Army-Navy Country (Arlington, Va.); Harvard (N.Y.C.), Caterpillar (N.Y.C.). Legal education, General corporate, Jurisprudence. Home: 3818 Huntington St NW Washington DC 20015 Other: Route 1 Sullivan Harbor ME 04689 Office: 2935 Upton St NW Washington DC 20015

FERMOILE, DOUGLAS KEITH, lawyer; b. Niagara Falls, N.Y., Apr. 20, 1956; s. Robert Joseph Fermoile and Joan (Wojcik) Hanchette; m. Christy Lynn Hamar, May 22, 1985. BA in English Lit., U. Nev., 1978; JD, Willamette U., 1981. Bar: Nev. 1981, U.S. Dist. Ct. Nev. 1981, U.S. Supreme Ct. 1986. Assoc. Fahrenkopf, Mortimer, Sourwine, Mousel & Sloane, Reno, 1981-83; sole practice Reno, 1983—; adj. prof. criminal justice U. Nev., Reno, 1983—. Author and editor: Judicial Function Outline, 1978, Significant State Appellate Decisions Outline, 1978, Judicial Function Outline for Administrative Law Judges, 1978. Trustee Sierra Nev. Ednl. Found. Inc., Reno, 1983—. Mem. ABA, Nev. Bar Assn., Washoe County Bar Assn., Assn. Trial Lawyers Am., Nev. Trial Lawyers Assn., Barristers Club (pres. 1983-84). Republican. Roman Catholic. Home: 1440 Westfield Ave Reno NV 89509 Office: 522 Lander St Reno NV 89509

FERN, FREDERICK HAROLD, lawyer, pharmacist; b. Newark, Feb. 27, 1954; s. William Herman and Selma (Schwartz) F.; m. Marilyn Ann Edelman, May 29, 1977; 1 child, Stuart Brett. Student, Boston U., 1972-74; BS in Pharmacy cum laude, Northeastern U., Boston, 1977; JD cum laude, St. Louis U., 1980. Bar: N.Y. 1981, N.J. 1981, U.S. Dist. Ct. N.J. 1981, U.S. Dist. Ct. (so. and ea. dists.) N.Y. 1982. Registered pharmacist in charge Frontenac Drugs, Ladue, Mo., 1977-78, Medicare Pharmacy, St. Louis, 1978-79; ptnr. Lester, Schwab, Katz & Dwyer, N.Y.C., 1980—; lectr. pharmacy Rutgers U. Contbr. articles to profl. jours. Mem. exec. bd. Congl. B'nai Jacob and David. Fellow Am. Soc. Pharmacy Law (James Hartley Beal award 1985); mem. ABA, N.Y. State Bar Assn., N.J. Bar Assn., Union County Pharmacist Assn. (v.p., bd. dirs. 1983—), Am. Pharm. Assn. (del. 1981, 84, 85, 86, 87), N.J. Pharm. Assn. (organizational affairs com.), Def. Research Inst. Democrat. Jewish. State civil litigation, Personal injury, Federal civil litigation. Office: Lester Schwab Katz & Dwyer 120 Broadway New York NY 10271

FERNANDEZ, JOSE WALFREDO, lawyer; b. Cienfuegos, Cuba, Sept. 19, 1955; came to U.S., 1967; s. Jose Rigoberto and Flora (Gomez) F.; m. Andrea Gabor, June 22, 1985. BA, Dartmouth Coll., 1977; JD, Columbia U., 1980. Bar: N.Y. 1981, N.J. 1981, U.S. Dist. Ct. (so. dist.) N.Y. 1981, U.S. Dist. Ct. N.J. 1981. Assoc. Curtis, Mallet, Prevost, Cott & Mosle, N.Y.C., 1981-84, Baker & McKenzie, N.Y.C., 1984—; adj. prof. N.Y. Law Sch., 1984—. Contbr. articles to profl. jours. Mem. ABA (com. Inter-Am. law 1985—, Cen. Am. task force 1985—, presdl. commn. Latin Am. 1986—), N.Y.C. Bar Assn. (com. fgn. and comparative law), U.S.-Spain C. of C., Am. Fgn. Law Assn., Am. Arbitration Assn. (arbitrator 1984—). Avocations: sports, non-fiction writing, travel. Private international, Contracts commercial, Banking. Home: 241 W 108th St New York NY 10025 Office: Baker & McKenzie 805 3rd Ave New York NY 10022

FERNANDEZ, LILLIAN, lawyer; b. N.Y.C., Feb. 11, 1954; d. Victor Manuel and Nilsa (Vazquez) F. BA, CCNY, 1976; JD, U. Pa., 1979. Bar: Pa. 1979, D.C. 1981. Atty. advisor EEOC, Washington, 1979-82; exec. dir. Minority Civic Assn., Inc., N.Y.C., 1982-83, Congl. Hispanic Caucus, Washington, 1983-84; staff dir. subcom. on postal operations U.S. Ho. of Reps., Washington, 1984-85, staff dir., chief counsel subcom. on census and population, 1985-87; dir. trade policy Pfizer Inc., N.Y.C., 1987—. Mem. adv. bd. N.J. Dept. Higher Edn., Trenton, 1983—; bd. dirs. Washington Correctional Found., 1983—. Mem. Hispanic Bar Assn. (D.C. chpt.), ABA, Fed. Bar Assn., D.C. Bar Assn. (adv. com. Observance of Bicentennial of U.S. Constitution, adv. com. multi-door dispute resolution program). Democrat. Civil rights, Labor, Private international. Home: 519 N Armistead St Alexandria VA 22312 Office: Pfizer Inc 235 E 42d St New York NY 10017

FERNANDEZ, WILLIAM WARREN, lawyer; b. Washington, Aug. 31, 1943; s. Gumersindo Alonso and Kathryn Naomi (Nycum) F.; m. Kathryn-Patricia Letford, Jan. 11, 1969; children—William Warren, James Robert, Rosemarie Patricia. A.A., U. Fla., 1964, B.A., 1967, J.D., 1969. Bar: Fla. 1969, U.S. Dist. Ct. (mid. dist.) Fla. 1970, U.S. Ct. Claims 1973, U.S. Tax Ct. 1973, U.S. Ct. Appeals (5th cir.) 1972, U.S. Ct. Appeals (11th cir.) 1981, U.S. Supreme Ct. 1972. Staff atty. Law, Inc. of Hillsborough County (Fla.), 1969-70; assoc. Pope & Burton, P.A., Tampa, Fla., 1970-71; ptnr. Fernandez & Scarito, Orlando, Fla., 1971-79; sole practice, Orlando, 1979—; mem. Fla. Bar Study and Standardization of Disciplinary Enforcement Com., 1972-73; chmn. Altamonte Springs Code Enforcement Bd., 1982—. Mem. Altamonte Springs (Fla.) Charter Revision Commn., 1974, 79, 85; mem. citizens adv. com., sec. Seminole County Expressway Authority, 1984—; bd. dirs. Muscular Dystrophy Assn. Am., 1972-77, pres., 1975-76; bd. dirs. Seminole County Mental Health Ctr., Inc., 1979-84, pres., 1982-83; bd. dirs. Council of 100 of Seminole County (Fla.), 1975—, pres., 1978-80, sec., 1980—; bd. dirs. T.H.E. Wayfarer Inc. (Transp. for Handicapped and Elderly), Orlando, 1976-79, treas., 1977-79; bd. dirs. Easter Seals Soc. Orange, Seminole and Osceola, 1978-79. Served with U.S. Army, 1968-69. Recipient various civic awards, including certs. of appreciation from Muscular Dystrophy Assn., Easter Seals, YMCA, T.H.E. Wayfarer, Inc., Seminole County Mental Health Ctr. Service award City Altamonte Springs, 1974, 83. Mem. Orange County Bar Assn., ABA, Assn. Trial Lawyers Am., Orange County Legal Aid Soc., Aircraft Owners and Pilots Assn., Acad. Fla. Trial Lawyers, Central Fla. Gen. Aviation Assn. Democrat. Roman Catholic. State civil litigation, General practice, Personal injury. Office: 1309 E Robinson St Orlando FL 32801

FERNBACH, ROBERT DENNIS, lawyer; b. Cheektowaga, N.Y., May 27, 1917; s. Louis P. and Katherine (Kinsella) F.; m. Beth M. Hager, July 18, 1947; children—Robert Dennis, John P. Grad. cum laude, U. Notre Dame, 1938; LL.B. with distinction, Cornell U., 1941. Bar: N.Y. 1941. With Moot & Sprague, Buffalo, 1941—; now ptnr. Moot & Sprague; dir. Monroe Abstract & Title Corp.; lectr. U. Buffalo Sch. Bus. Adminstrn., 1947-50, Law Sch., 1950-54. Bd. dirs., mem. exec. com., now pres. Greater Buffalo Devel. Found.; chmn. legal div. United Way of Buffalo.; chmn. bd. dirs. Downtown Buffalo Mgmt. Corp.; bd. dirs. Western N.Y. Tech. Devel. Center, Devel. Downtown Inc.; mem. exec. com. Erie County Indsl. Devel. Agy.; bd. dirs. Buffalo Waterfront Devel. Corp.; mem. Main-Genesee Urban Design Task Group. Served with USAAF, 1942-45. Decorated Bronze Star medal. Mem. Am., N.Y. State, Erie County bar assns., Trial Lawyers Assn., Ry. Trial Counsel Assn. Republican. Roman Catholic. General corporate, General practice, Public service and not for profit organizations. Home: 117 Hyledge Dr Eggertsville NY 14226 Office: 2300 Main Place Tower Buffalo NY 14202

FERNSLER, JOHN PAUL, lawyer; b. Lebanon, Pa., Dec. 24, 1940; s. K. Paul and Elizabeth Mary (Snyder) F.; m. Christine Joan Chester, July 31, 1965; children: Euan, Scott. A.B., Dickinson Coll., 1962; J.D., U. Mich., 1965. Bar: Pa. 1965. Assoc. Balmer, Mogel, Speidel & Roland, Reading, Pa., 1965-66; dep. atty. gen. Commonweatlh of Pa., Harrisburg, 1968-70; area counsel HUD, Pitts., 1970-81; ptnr. Reed Smith Shaw & McClay, Pitts., 1981—. Contbr. articles to profl. jours. Mem. Mt. Lebanon Zoning Hearing Bd., 1979—, sec., 1979-82; chmn., 1983—; bd. dirs., counsel Council for Luth. Campus Ministry in Greater Pitts., 1979-82. Served to capt. U.S. Army, 1966-67. Decorated Commendation medal. Mem. ABA, Pa. Bar Assn., Allegheny County Bar Assn. (council real property sect., vice chmn.), Am. Judicature Soc., Am. Coll. Real Estate Lawyers (elected). Republican. Lutheran. Real property, Local government, Banking. Home: 852 N Meadowcroft Ave Pittsburgh PA 15216 Office: Reed Smith Shaw & McClay James H Reed Bldg 435 6th Ave Pittsburgh PA 15129

FERRARA, ANTHONY JOSEPH, lawyer; b. New Brunswick, N.J., Jan. 11, 1940; s. Anthony Joseph and Josephine Filomena (Barbano) F.; m. Virginia Lee Cushman, Apr. 1, 1976; children—Amy Katrin, Justin Michael. B.A., Temple U., 1962; M.A., Johns Hopkins, U., 1967, Ph.D., 1971; J.D., U. N.Mex., 1977. Bar: N.Mex. 1979, U.S. Dist. Ct. N.Mex. 1979, U.S. Ct. Claims 1979, U.S. Ct. Appeals (10th cir.) 1981, U.S. Supreme Ct. 1982, U.S. Ct. Appeals (fed. cir.) 1983. From asst. prof. to prof. U. Ill.-Chgo., 1970-74; sole practice law, Albuquerque, 1979—, adminstrv. law judge 2d Jud. Dist. N.Mex., Albuquerque, 1984—, spl. asst. atty. gen. State of N.Mex., Albuquerque, 1985—; lectr. U. N.Mex., 1977—. Author: Studia Pohl Series Maior I, 1974; also articles. Recipient Marcus Buell award Boston U., 1963; Daniel Coit Gilman fellow, 1968; Ford Found. grantee, 1969. Fellow Am. Acad. Polit. and Social Sci.; mem. State Bar N.Mex. (fee arbitration com. 1981—, CLE com. 1983-84), Am. Oriental Soc., Nat. Assn. Criminal Def. Attys., Assn. Trial Lawyers Assn., N.Mex. Trial Lawyers Assn., Alpha Chi Rho. State civil litigation, Criminal, Family and matrimonial. Office: 601 Tijeras NW Albuquerque NM 87102

FERRARIO, RAYMOND WILLIAM, lawyer; b. Portsmouth, N.H., Oct. 5, 1956; s. James J. and Eva R. (Grunow) F.; m. Barbara J. O'Hara, Aug. 20, 1983. BA, Pa. State U., 1978; JD, Temple U., 1981. Bar: Pa. 1981, U.S. Dist. Ct. (mid. dist.) Pa. 1981, U.S. Ct. Appeals (3d cir.) 1982. V.p. Mattes, Mattes & Mattes P.C., Scranton, Pa., 1981—; solicitor Covington (Pa.) Twp. Bd. of Suprs., 1982—. Mem. adminstrv. bd. dirs. Elm Park Meth. Ch., Scranton, 1984—; pres. Lackawanna Arts Council, Scranton, 1984—. Mem. ABA, Pa. Bar Assn., Lackawanna County Bar Assn., Pa. Trial Lawyers Assn., Comml. Law League of Am. Democrat. Methodist. Lodge: Kiwanis (sec. 1985—). Personal injury, General practice, Federal civil litigation. Office: Mattes Mattes & Mattes PC Wyoming and Spruce 900 Bank Towers Bldg Scranton PA 18503

FERREIRA, BEATRIZ VALADEZ, lawyer; b. Scottsbluff, Nebr., June 16, 1947; d. Genovevo Valadez and Priscilla (Jimenez) Cansino; 1 child, Miguel. B in Sociology, N.Mex. State U., 1970; M in Edn., U. So. Calif., 1974; JD, U. N.Mex., 1980. Bar: N.Mex. 1982, U.S. Dist. Ct. N.Mex. 1982, U.S. Ct. Appeals (10th cir.) 1982, U.S. Dist. Ct. (we. dist.) Tex. 1986. Edn. specialist U.S. Dept. of Def., Darmstadt, Fed. Republic of Germany, 1972-76; acting coordinator Farmworker Legal Rights, Las Cruces, N.Mex., 1979; atty., advisor U.S. Dept. of Transp., Washington, 1980-81; ptnr. Saenz, Gonzales & Ferreira, Las Cruces, 1982-85; sole practice Las Cruces, 1985—. Mem. voter task force Sec. of State, Santa Fe, 1983; bd. dirs. Gov.'s Environ. Adv. Bd., Santa Fe, 1983-84, Planned Parenthood, Las Cruces, 1985, United Way, Las Cruces, 1985, Internat. Good Neighbor Council, Las Cruces, 1985—, Internat. Border Resources, Las Cruces, 1986—. Named one of Outstanding Young Women in Am., 1980. Mem. Internat. Bar Assn., Assn. Trial Lawyers Am., N.Mex. Trial Lawyers Assn. (liaison com.), Am. Com. Assn., Asia Pacific Lawyers Assn. Lodge: Internat. Seroptimists (historian 1986—). Avocations: foreign languages, outdoors, international travel and study. Immigration, naturalization, and customs, Private international, Personal injury. Home: PO Box 374 Fairacres NM 88033 Office: 1100 S Main Pueblo Plaza Suite 22 Las Cruces NM 88005

FERRELL, MILTON MORGAN, JR., lawyer; b. Coral Gables, Fla., Nov. 6, 1951; s. Milton M. Ferrell and Annie (Blanche) Bradley; m. Lori R. Sanders, May 22, 1982; children: Milton Morgan III, Whiteny Connolly. BA, Mercer U., 1973, JD, 1975. Bar: Fla. 1975. Asst. state's atty. State's Atty.'s Office, Miami, 1975-77; ptnr. Ferrell & Ferrell, Miami, 1977-84; sole practice Miami, 1985-87; ptnr. Ferrell & Williams, P.A., Miami, 1987—. Bd. dirs. Mus. Sci. and Space Transit Planetarium, 1977; mem. Ambassadors of Mercy, Mercy Hosp. Found., Inc., 1986—; trustee, mem. legal com., Com. Chairperson U. Miami Project, 1986—. Fellow Nat. Assn. Criminal Def. Lawyers, Am. Bd. Criminal Lawyers (bd. of govs. 1981-82, sec. 1983-84, v.p. 1984-86, pres. 1987—); mem. ABA (grantee 1975), Dade County Bar Assn. (bd. dirs. 1977-80). Clubs: The Bath, The Palm Bay, Downtown Athletic (Miami). Federal civil litigation, State civil litigation, Criminal. Home: 610 Sabal Palm Rd Bay Point Miami FL 33137 Office: Ferrell & Williams PA 100 Chopin Plaza Suite 1920 Miami FL 33131

FERRELL, WAYNE EDWARD, JR., lawyer; b. Pascagoula, Miss., Jan. 26, 1946; s. Wayne E. and Bessie (Ryals) F.; m. Susan Jane Nicholson, Mar. 28, 1970; children—Taylor N., Matthew G. B.A. in Bus. Adminstrn. & Econs., Millsaps Coll., 1969; J.D., Miss. Coll. Sch. Law, 1975; LL.M. in Aviation and Space Law, McGill U., 1981. Bar: Miss. 1976, U.S. Dist. Cts. (so. and no. dists.) Miss. 1976, U.S. Ct. Appeals (5th and 11th cirs.) 1978, U.S. Supreme Ct. 1985; lic. instrument-rated comml. pilot. Assoc. Satterfield, Allred & Colbert, Jackson, Miss., 1976-78; assoc., ptnr. Cothren, Pittman & Ferrell, Jackson, 1978-81; sole practice, Jackson, 1981-83; ptnr. Ferrell & Hubbard, Jackson, 1983—. Served to maj. Air N.G., 1970—. Named Alumnus of Yr., Miss. Coll. Sch. Law, 1983. Fellow ABA (young lawyers assn.); mem. Miss. Young Lawyers Assn. (sec. 1980-81), Miss. Bar Assn. (ethics com., 1985-87, character and fitness com., 1982—), Miss. Coll. Sch. of Law Alumni Assn. (pres. 1979-80), Phi Alpha Delta (charter mem. Virgil A. Griffin chpt.). Methodist. Aviation, Personal injury, Admiralty. Home: 5326 Red Fox Rd Jackson MS 39211 Office: Ferrell & Hubbard Bldg 405 Tombigbee St PO Box 1080 Jackson MS 39215-1080

FERREN, JOHN MAXWELL, appellate judge; b. Kansas City, Mo., July 21, 1937; s. Jack Maxwell and Elizabeth Anne (Hansen) F.; m. Ann Elizabeth Speidel, Sept. 4, 1961; children—Andrew John, Peter Maxwell. A.B. magna cum laude, Harvard U., 1959, LL.B., 1962. Bar: Ill. 1962, Mass. 1967, D.C. 1970. Asso. Kirkland, Ellis, Hodson, Chaffetz & Masters, Chgo., 1962-66; dir. Neighborhood Law Office Program, Harvard U. Law Sch., 1966-68; teaching fellow, dir. Neighborhood Law Office Program, Harvard Law Sch. (Legal Services Program), 1968-69, lectr. law, dir., 1969-70; partner Hogan & Hartson, Washington, 1970-77; asso. judge D.C. Ct. Appeals, 1977—, mem. disciplinary bd., 1972-76; mem. exec. com., bd. dirs. Council on Legal Edn. for Profl. Responsibility, 1970-82; exec. com. Washington Lawyers Com. for Civil Rights Under Law, 1970-77. Contbr. articles to profl. jours. Treas., bd. dirs. Firman Neighborhood House, Chgo., 1964-66; legis. subcom. on consumer credit Chgo. Commn. on Human Relations Com. on New Residents, 1964-66; originator, chmn. Neighborhood Legal Advice Clinics, Ch. Fedn. Greater Chgo., 1964-66; bd. dirs. Peoples Devel. Corp., Washington, 1970-74; exec. com. of legal adv. com. Nat. Com. Against Discrimination in Housing, 1974-77; steering com. Nat. Prison Project of ACLU Found., 1975-77; bd. dirs. George A. Wiley Meml. Fund, 1974-84, Nat. Resource Center for Consumers of Legal Services, 1973-77. Fellow Am. Bar Found.; mem. ABA (Commn. on Nat. Inst. Justice 1972-80, mem. Consortium on Legal Services and Public 1972-73, 76-79, chmn. 1979-82, chmn. spl. com. on public interest practice 1976-78), Am. Law Inst., Nat. Legal Aid and Defender Assn., Phi Beta Kappa. Presbyterian. Office: DC Court Appeals 500 Indiana Ave NW Washington DC 20001

FERRERI, VITO RICHARD, lawyer; b. Phila., Feb. 17, 1949; s. Vito and Lucrecia (Poleo) F.; m. Sheila Diane Palmer, June 24, 1972; 1 child, Michelle Lee. B.A., U. Pitts., 1970; J.D., Rutgers U., 1973; postgrad. Nat. Coll. Advocacy, 1976. Bar: N.J. 1973, U.S. Dist. Ct. N.J. 1973, U.S. Supreme Ct. 1977, U.S. Ct. Appeals (3d cir.) 1978. Ptnr., Moss, Thatcher, Moss, McNeill & Ferreri, Runnemede, N.J., 1972-86, Ferreri & Manos, 1986—; arbitrator Am. Arbitration Assn., Somerset, N.J., 1980—, adv. bd., 1984—. Advocate KC, Turnersville, N.J., 1975-86; pres. Wedgewood Civic Assn., Turnersville, 1975-77. Named Boss of Yr., Camden County Legal Secs. N.J., 1980. Mem. Camden County Bar Assn., Gloucester County Bar Assn., Assn. Trial Lawyers Am. Republican. Roman Catholic. General practice, State civil litigation, Criminal. Office: Ferreri & Manos PC 1000 White Horse Rd Suite 402 Voorhees NJ 08043

FERRI, KAREN LYNN, lawyer, retail food company executive; b. McKeesport, Pa., Aug. 15, 1956; d. Edward James and Carole Elizabeth (Petterson) Ferri. B.A., Duquesne U., 1977, J.D., 1981. Bar: Pa. 1981, U.S. Dist. Ct. (we. dist.) Pa. 1981., U.S. Supreme Ct. 1986. Law clk. Weiler & Dolfi, Pitts., 1980-81, assoc., 1981-84; assoc. Stokes, Lurie & Cole, Pitts., 1984—; weekend mgr. Ferri Land Co., Inc., Murraysville, Pa., 1977—; atty. Ferri Enterprises, 1981—. Recipient Sr. Leaders award Duquesne U., 1977, Am. Jurisprudence award Joint Pubs. Total Client-Service Library Pitts., 1978-79. Mem. Allegheny County Bar Assn. (vol. indigent divorce program, high sch. edn. program, family law sect.), Pa. Bar Assn. (family law sect.), Westmoreland County Bar Assn., ABA. Republican. Roman Catholic. Clubs: AMAA Investment, Young Republicans, Variety (Pitts.) Family and matrimonial, General practice, Probate. Home: Chatham Tower Unit 3C Chatham Ctr Pittsburgh PA 15219 Office: Stokes Lurie & Cole 2100 Law and Fin Bldg Pittsburgh PA 15219

FERRIER, JON TODD, lawyer; b. Grand Rapids, Mich., May 9, 1951; s. Elmer Earl Ferrier and Jeanne Marie (Smolenski) Mikita; m. Dinah P. Wells, Mar. 15, 1974 (div. Feb. 1976); m. Kayne Lyn Kulpa, Feb. 4, 1978; 1 child, Valerie Katherine. BA, St. John's Coll., Annapolis, Md., 1973; JD, Wayne State U., 1978. Bar: Mich. 1979, U.S. Dist. Ct. (we. dist.) Mich. 1979, U.S. Ct. Appeals (6th cir.) 1982. Atty. Legal Aid Office Mich., Grand Rapids, 1979-81; referee 17th Cir. Ct., Kent County, Mich., 1981—. Mem. Referees Assn. Mich. (pres. 1985—), Friends of Ct. Assn. of Mich. (hon.), Grand Rapids Bar Assn. (dir. legal explorers program 1982-83). Family and matrimonial, Bankruptcy, Personal income taxation. Office: 50 Monroe NW Suite 260 Grand Rapids MI 49503

FERRIS, EVELYN SCOTT, lawyer; b. Detroit, d. Ross Ansel and Irene Mabel (Bowser) Nafus; m. Roy Shorey Ferris, May 21, 1969 (div. Sept. 1982); children—Judith Ilene, Roy Sidney, Lorene Marjorie. J.D., Willamette U., 1961. Bar: Oreg. 1962, Fed. Dist. Ct. 1962. Law clk. Oreg. Tax Ct., Salem, 1961-62; dep. dist. atty. Marion County, Salem, 1962-65; judge Mcpl. Ct., Stayton, Oreg., 1965-76; ptnr. Brand, Lee, Ferris & Embick, Salem, 1965-82; chmn. Oreg. Workers' Compensation Bd., Salem, 1982—. Bd. dirs. Friends of Deepwood, Salem, 1979-82, Salem City Club, 1972-75; bd. dirs. Marion County Civil Service Commn., 1970-75; com. mem. Polk County Hist. Commn., Dallas, Oreg., 1976-79; mem. Oreg. legis. com. Bus. Climate,

1967-69, Govs. Task Force on Liability, 1986. Recipient Outstanding Hist. Restoration of Comml. Property award Marion County Hist. Soc., 1982. Mem. Oreg. Mcpl. Judges Assn. (pres. 1967-69), ABA, Altrusa, Internat., Mary Leonard Law Soc., Phi Delta Delta. Republican. Episcopalian. Club: Capitol (Salem) (pres. 1977-79). Home: 747 Church St SE Salem OR 97301 Office: Oreg Workers' Compensation Bd 480 Church St SE Salem OR 97310

FERRIS, WILLIAM MICHAEL, lawyer; b. Jackson, Mich., May 1, 1948; s. Franklyn C. and Betty J. (Dickerson) F.; m. Cynthia L. Muffitt, June 26, 1970 (div.); 1 child, Christina M.; m. Kathleen S. Santacroce, Mar. 21, 1987. BS with distinction, U.S. Naval Acad., 1970; JD summa cum laude, U. Balt., 1978, postdoctoral, 1982. Bar: Md. 1978, U.S. Dist. Ct. Md. 1978, U.S. Ct. Appeals (4th cir.) 1978, U.S. Supreme Ct. 1983, U.S. Tax Ct. 1986. Commd. ensign USN, 1970, advanced through grades to lt., 1974, resigned active duty, 1977; staff atty. Md. Legis., Annapolis, 1977-78, 80-81; assoc. Semmes, Bowen & Semmes, Balt., 1978-80; ptnr. Ferris & Robin, Annapolis, 1981-83, Krause & Ferris, Annapolis, 1983—. Author: Maryland Style Manual for Statutory Law, 1985; articles editor Md. Annotated Code, 1981-84. Elder Woods Meml. Presbyn. Ch., Severna Park, Md., 1980—; sec. PTA Belvedere Elem. Sch., Arnold, Md., 1984-86; treas. Bay Hills Swim Team, Arnold, 1985-86—; chmn. Com. to Rev. Anne Arundel County Code, Annapolis, 1985-86; temporary zoning hearing officer, Anne Arundel County, Annapolis, 1984—; pres. elect Md. Bd. Dental Examiners, Balt., 1986. Served to comdr. USNR, 1984—. Mem. ABA, Md. Bar Assn., Maritime Law Assn., Anne Arundel County Bar Assn. Republican. Avocations: golfing, running, bowling, tennis. General practice, Family and matrimonial, Admiralty. Home: 606 Bay Green Dr Arnold MD 21012 Office: Krause & Ferris 91 Cathedral St Annapolis MD 21401

FERRITER, MAURICE JOSEPH, lawyer; b. Holyoke, Mass., Aug. 14, 1930; s. John J. and Aldea (Brouilette) F.; m. Margaret M. Hennigan, June 19, 1954; children—Maurice J., John J., Mary M., Joseph P. A.A., Holyoke Jr. Coll., 1952, B.A., U. Mass., 1979; J.D., Western New Eng. Law Sch., Springfield, Mass., 1957. Bar: Mass. 1957, U.S. Dist. Ct. Mass. 1960, U.S. Supreme Ct. 1967, U.S. Ct. Appeals (1st cir.) 1980. Pres., treas. Begley, Ferriter, LaVelle & Welsh, P.C., Holyoke, Mass., 1957—; chmn. bd. dirs. Ferriter, Scobbo, Sikora, Caruso & Rodophele, P.C., Boston; gen. counsel Mass. Mcpl. Wholesale Electric Co. Pres. Holyoke Heritage Park R.R.; dir. ARC. Served with U.S. Army, 1948-51. Recipient Outstanding Servant of Pub. award Springfield TV Sta. WWLP Channel 22, 1976; Spl. Service award Mcpl. Electric Assn. Mass. 1981; award of merit Bur. Exceptional Children, 1979. Mem. ABA, Mass. Bar Assn., Hampden County Bar Assn., Holyoke Bar Assn., Assn. Trial Lawyers Am., Mass. Acad. Trial Lawyers, Am. Judicature Soc., Holyoke C. of C. (past pres., appreciation award 1975). General corporate, Administrative and regulatory. Home: 31 Longfellow Rd Holyoke MA 01040 Office: Ferriter Scobbo Sikora et al 1 Milk St Boston MA 02109 Office: Begley Ferriter Lavelle & Welch 1 Court Plaza Holyoke MA 01040

FERRUCCIO, SAMUEL JOSEPH, JR., lawyer; b. Canton, Ohio, Oct. 14, 1952; s. Samuel Joseph and Joan Ruth (Onesto) F.; m. Nancy Leigh Eichenlaub, Nov. 19, 1983; children: Nikki, Noelle. BA in Psychology, Bowling Green State U., 1974; JD, Ohio No. U., 1979. Bar: Ohio 1979, U.S. Dist. Ct. (no. dist.) Ohio, 1980, U.S. Ct. Appeals (6th cir.) 1981. Sole practice Canton, 1980—; spl. counsel State of Ohio, Canton, 1984—. Exec. editor Ohio No. Law Rev., 1978. Mem. Save the Palace Theatre, Canton, 1984—. Named one of Outstanding Young Men in Am., 1983. Mem. Am. Trial Lawyers Assn., Ohio State Bar Assn., Stark County Bar Assn., Stark County Trial Lawyers Assn., Canton C. of C., Sigma Chi (v.p. 1973-74). Democrat. Roman Catholic. Personal injury, State civil litigation, Criminal. Office: Nat City Bank Bldg Suite 403 Canton OH 44702

FERRY, JOSEPH DEAN, lawyer; b. St. Louis, May 20, 1954; s. Dean Doering and Willie Hall (Young) Ferry. Student, U. Mo., St. Louis, 1972-74; BS in Physics magna cum laude, U. Mo., Rolla, 1976; JD, U. Mo., Columbia, 1979. Bar: Mo. 1979, U.S. Dist. Ct. (ea. dist.) Mo. 1979, U.S. Dist. Ct. (we. dist.) Mo. 1982, U.S. Ct. Appeals (8th cir.) 1985. Law clk. to presiding justice Mo. Ct. Appeals, Kansas City, 1979-80; sole practice Kansas City, 1980-81; asst. county counsel St. Louis County, 1981—. Violinist St. Louis Philharm. Orch., 1971—, bd. dirs., 1982—, chmn. patron drive, 1983—, sec. 1986—; mem. Landolfi String Quartet, St. Louis. Mem. Am. Fedn. Musicians. Republican. Mem. Ch. of Christ. Local government, Government contracts and claims, Administrative and regulatory. Home: 2666 Park Ave Saint Louis MO 63104 Office: Office St Louis County Counselor 41 S Central Clayton MO 63105

FERSKO, RAYMOND STUART, lawyer; b. Newark, Dec. 6, 1947; s. Seymoure Arnold and Hannah Judith (Geffner) F.; m. Francine Iris Poses, Aug. 23, 1970; children—Stacey Michelle, Madeline Poses. B.A., Am. U., 1969; J.D., 1972. Bar: N.Y. 1973, U.S. Ct. Appeals (D.C. cir.) 1973, U.S. Dist. Ct. (so., ea. and we. dists.) N.Y. 1975, U.S. Ct. Appeals (2d cir.) 1975, U.S. Supreme Ct. 1982. Trial atty. CAB, Washington, 1972-75; assoc. Demov Morris Levin & Shein, N.Y.C., 1975-76; assoc. Walsh & Levine, N.Y.C., 1976-80, ptnr., 1980-82; ptnr. Shapiro Shiff Beilly Rosenberg and Fox, N.Y.C., 1982-84, Goldschmidt Fredericks & Oshatz, N.Y.C., 1984, Tanner Gilbert Propp & Sterner, N.Y.C., 1984—; cons. World Aviation Services, Ltd., London, 1982—, Internat. Joint Ventures, Ltd., London, 1983—; sec. Tradewinds Express Inc., N.Y.C., 1982—; pres. Cornwell Corp., N.Y.C., 1986—. Treas., Paine Heights Orgn., New Rochelle, N.Y., 1978—. Mem. Assn. Bar City N.Y. (mem. com. on state legis. 1976-78), N.Y. County Bar Assn., ABA (mem. anti-trust sect. civil practice and procedure com. 1973—, mem. adminstrv. law sect. aviation com. 1973-77), N.Y. State Bar Assn., Internat. Bar Assn., Argentine U.S. C. of C., Spain U.S. C. of C., Phi Alpha Delta. Jewish. Clubs: Harmonie (N.Y.C.); Mamaroneck Yacht and Tennis (N.Y.). Aviation, Federal civil litigation, Private international. Home: 61 Bayeau Rd New Rochelle NY 10804 Office: Tanner Gilbert Propp & Sterner 99 Park Ave New York NY 10016

FETZNER, MICHAEL ALAN, lawyer; b. Erie, Pa., Dec. 24, 1947; s. Leonard Lawrence and Winifred Ann (Tarr) F.; m. Cassandra Jean Fidorra, Oct. 12, 1979; children: Stephen Michael, Daniel John, Laura Mary. BS, Gannon U., 1969; JD, Dickinson Sch. of Law, 1972. Bar: Pa. 1972, U.S. Dist. Ct. (we. dist.) Pa. 1973, U.S. Supreme Ct. 1976. Assoc. Magenau & Gornall, Erie, 1972-76; ptnr. Knox, Graham, McLaughlin, Gornall & Sennett, Erie, 1976—; asst. dist. atty. Erie County Dist. Attys. Office, 1975-76; spl. prosecutor Pa. Atty. Gen.'s Office, 1980, 86. Mem. exec. bd. Luth. Home for the Aged, Erie, 1978—, Erie Glenwood Park YMCA, 1978—, Erie Met. YMCA, 1982—. Mem. ABA (author, editor, actor film Mock Trial-Armed Robbery, 1976, Honorable Mention award 1977), Pa. Bar Assn. (workers compensation com. 1981—, civil litigation com. 1980—), Erie County Bar Assn. (mem. exec. bd. 1981-85, chmn. L.A.V.A. com. 1982-83, treas. 1984-85, chmn. long range planning com. 1985-86). Democrat. Roman Catholic. Clubs: Erie Maennerchor, Erie, Lawrence Park Golf. Avocations: softball, golf, boating. State civil litigation, Real property, Workers' compensation. Home: 4681 Harbor View Dr Erie PA 16508 Office: Knox Graham McLaughlin et al 120 W 10th St Erie PA 16501

FEUERSTEIN, DONALD MARTIN, lawyer; b. Chgo., May 30, 1937; s. Morris Martin and Pauline Jean (Zagel) F.; m. Dorothy Rosalind Sokolsky, June 3, 1962 (dec. Mar. 1978); children: Eliza Carol, Anthony David. B.A. magna cum laude, Yale U., 1959; J.D. magna cum laude, Harvard U., 1962. Bar: N.Y. 1962. Asso. firm Cleary, Gottlieb, Steen & Hamilton, N.Y.C., 1962-63; law clk. to U.S. dist. judge N.Y.C., 1963-65; asso. firm Saxe, Bacon & Bolan, N.Y.C., 1965; asst. gen. counsel, chief counsel instl. investor study SEC, Washington, 1966-71; partner, counsel Salomon Bros., N.Y.C., 1971-81; mng. dir., sec. Salomon Bros. Inc., 1981—; mem. adv. council U. Pa. Center for Study of Fin. Instns., 1973—. Mem. editorial adv. bd.: Securities Regulation Law Jour, 1973—; bd. editors: Nat. Law Jour, 1978—. Bd. dirs. 1st All Children's Theatre, 1976-85, chmn., 1976-82; mem. adv. bd. Solomon R. Guggenheim Mus., N.Y.C., 1984—; bd. dirs. Arts and Bus. Council, 1980-85, v.p., 1985—; bd. dirs. Legal Aid Soc., N.Y.C., 1985—; trustee, v.p., mem. exec. com. Dalton Sch., 1983—. Served with U.S. Army, 1962-63. Mem. Am., N.Y. State bar assns., Assn. Bar City N.Y., Phi Beta Kappa, Pi Sigma Alpha. Club: Harvard. Home: 11 E 77th St New York NY 10021 Office: 1 New York Plaza New York NY 10004

FEUERSTEIN, HOWARD M., lawyer; b. Memphis, Sept. 16, 1939; s. Leon and Lillian (Kappel) F.; m. Tamra Lynn Saperstein, May 19, 1968; children: Laurie, Daniel. BA, Vanderbilt U., 1961, JD, 1963. Bar: Tenn. 1963, Oreg. 1965. Law clk. to presiding justice U.S. Ct. Appeals (5th cir.), Montgomery, Ala., 1963-64; teaching fellow Stanford U., 1964-65; assoc. Davies, Biggs et al (now Stoel, Rives, Boley, Fraser & Wyse), Portland, Oreg., 1965-71; ptnr. Stoel, Rives, Boley, Fraser & Wyse, Portland, 1971—; mem. Oreg. Gov.'s Task Force on Land Devel. Law, 1974; bd. realtors Condominium Study Com., Oreg., 1975-76. Editor-in-chief Vanderbilt Law Rev., 1962-63. Trustee Congregation Beth Israel, Portland, 1977-83; bd. dirs. Jewish Family & Child Service, Portland, 1975-81. Recipient Founder's medal Vanderbilt Law Sch., 1963. Mem. ABA, Oreg. State Bar, Multnomah County Bar Assn. (pres. real property com. 1976), Am. Resort & Residential Devel. Assn. (assoc.), Community Assn. Inst. (bd. dirs. Oreg. chpt. 1980-86), Am. Coll. Real Estate Lawyers. Real property. Office: Stoel Rives Boley et al 900 SW Fifth Ave Suite 2300 Portland OR 97204

FEVURLY, KEITH ROBERT, lawyer; b. Leavenworth, Kans., Oct. 30, 1951; s. James R. Fevurly and Anne (McDade) Kaiser; m. Peggy L. Vosburg, Aug. 4, 1978; children: Rebecca Dawn, Grant Robert. BA in Polit. Sci., U. Kans., 1973; JD, Washburn U. of Topeka Sch. Law, 1976; postgrad., U. Mo. Sch. Law, 1984. Bar: Kans. 1977, Colo. 1986; cert. fin. planner. Sole practice Leavenworth, 1977; atty. estate and gift tax IRS, Wichita and Salina, Kans., Austin, Tex., 1977-83; atty., acad. assoc. Coll. for Fin. Planning, Denver, 1984—; adj. faculty in retirement planning and estate planning Coll. Fin. Planning; instr. bus. law Highland (Kans.) Jr. Coll. Contbg. author tng. modules, articles on tax mgmt., estate planning. Mem. ABA, Kans. Bar Assn., Colo. Bar Assn., Internat. Assn. for Fin. Planning (Rocky Mountain chpt.), Delta Theta Phi, Pi Sigma Alpha. Republican. Presbyterian. Club: Toastmasters Internat. (pres. Salina chpt. 1981-82). Avocations: softball, racquetball. Estate planning, Probate, Estate taxation. Home: 18774 E Quinn Place Aurora CO 80015 Office: Coll for Fin Planning 9725 E Hampden Ave Denver CO 80231

FEWELL, TERRY GLENN, moving company executive, lawyer; b. Greenwood, Ind., Jan. 11, 1940; s. Wilbur Glenn and Martha Jean (Petrakos) F.; m. Johanna Theresa Planker, July 15, 1962; children—John Bradley, Jason Glenn, Jeffrey Joseph, Johanna Theresa, II. A.B., Wabash (Ind.) Coll., 1962; J.D., Ind. U., 1965. Bar: Ind. bar 1965, Ill. bar 1979. Atty., then gen. atty. N. Am. Van Lines, Inc., Ft. Wayne, Ind., 1965-76; v.p., gen. counsel Allied Van Lines, Inc., Broadview, Ill., 1976—; sec. Allied Ins. Bermuda, Ltd., Vanguard Ins. Agy., Inc. Mem. Ill. Bar Assn., Ind. Bar Assn., Transp. Lawyers Assn., Am. Corp. Counsel Assn. (pres. 1987-88, bd. dirs. Chgo.). Republican. Lutheran. Administrative and regulatory, Trademark and copyright, General corporate. Home: Route 2 Box 380 West County Line Rd Barrington IL 60010 Office: Allied Van Lines Inc 25th Ave and Roosevelt Rd Broadview IL 60153

FIALA, DAVID MARCUS, lawyer; b. Cleve., Aug. 1, 1946; s. Frank J. and Anna Mae (Phillips) F.; m. Maryanne E. McGowan, Jan. 4, 1969 (div. Mar. 1986); 1 child, D. Michael; m. Lyn McDonald Jones, May 31, 1986. B.B.A., U. Cin., 1969; J.D., Chase Coll., No. Ky. State U., 1974. Bar: Ohio 1974, U.S. Dist. Ct. (so. dist.) Ohio 1974, U.S. Tax Ct. 1974. Assoc., Walker, Chatfield & Doan, Cin., 1974-78, ptnr., 1979—; lectr. Southwestern Ohio Tax Inst., 1978-79; bd. dirs. Elkhorn Collieries, Cin. Trustee, sec. Sta. WCET-TV, Cin., 1983—, auction chmn., 1979; trustee Jr. Achievement Greater Cin., 1979—, Mental Health Services West, 1974-83, Contemporary Dance theatre, 1974-80. Mem. ABA, Ohio State Bar Assn., Cin. Bar Assn., Les Chefs de Cuisine Assn. (trustee Cin. chpt. 1985—). Personal income taxation, Probate, General corporate. Home: 3718 Mt Carmel Rd Cincinnati OH 45244 Office: Walker Chatfield & Doan 1900 Carew Tower Cincinnati OH 45202

FIALKOFF, JAY R., lawyer; b. N.Y.C., Apr. 3, 1951; m. Iris Fialkoff. JD, Bklyn. Law Sch., 1976. Bar: N.Y. 1977, U.S. Dist. Ct. (so. and ea. dist.) N.Y. 1977, U.S. Ct. Appeals (2d cir.) 1979. Assoc. Stroock & Stroock & Lavan, N.Y.C., 1976-84, ptnr., 1985—. Mem. ABA, Assn. of Bar of City of N.Y. Federal civil litigation, State civil litigation. Office: Stroock & Stroock & Lavan 7 Hanover Square New York NY 10004

FICK, NATHANIEL CROW, JR., lawyer; b. Columbus, Ohio, Oct. 9, 1947; s. Nathaniel Crow and Margaret (Smith) F.; m. Jane Ella Stimola, July 13, 1974; children—Nathaniel Charles, Maureen Poydras, Stephanie Noelle. B.A., U. Md., 1972; J.D., U. Balt., 1974. Bar: Md. 1975, U.S. Dist. Ct. Md. 1975. Sole practice trial atty., Towson, Md. lectr. practice skills and personal injury representation U. Balt. Law Sch., 1981-85. Served with U.S. Army, 1970-72. Recipient Am. Spirit Honor medal U.S. Govt., 1971. Fellow Roscoe Pound-Am. Trial Lawyers Found. (life); mem. ABA (trial evidence com. litigation sect.), Assn. Trial Lawyers Am. (state del. 1987—), Am. Soc. Law and Medicine, Trial Lawyers for Pub. Justice (founder), Md. Trial Lawyers Assn. (bd. govs.), Balt. County Bar Assn. (judiciary com., chmn. bench and bar com. 1986-87), Md. Bar Assn. (atty. grievance commn. 1982—, consumer advocacy com.). State civil litigation, Personal injury, Product liability. Home: Timonium MD 21093 Office: 1426 E Joppa Rd Towson MD 21204

FIDDLER, ROBERT WILLIAM, lawyer; b. Cleve., June 25, 1927; s. Solomon R. and Fannie (Yannes) F.; m. Vera M. Margolin, Oct. 3, 1950; children—Noah, Ann. B.M.E., CCNY, 1947; LL.B., George Washington U., 1952; postgrad. Columbia U. Bar: N.Y. 1953. Mech. engr. N.Y.C. Bd. Transp., 1947-48; examiner U.S. Patent Office, 1948-51; ptnr. Fiddler & Levine, N.Y.C., 1973—. Contbr. articles to profl. jours. Patent, Trademark and copyright, Federal civil litigation. Home: 21 Linford Rd Great Neck NY 11021 Office: 7814 Empire State Bldg NY 10118

FIDNICK, LINDA SUSAN, lawyer; b. Newark, Oct. 27, 1953; d. Paul and Mary Ellen (Smith) F. AB, Smith Coll., 1975; JD, U. Conn., 1979. Bar: Mass. 1979, U.S. Dist. Ct. Mass. 1979. Ptnr. Burres, Fidnick & Sheppard, Amherst, Mass., 1979—; faculty U. Mass. Continuing Legal Edn., Amherst, 1984—; adj. prof. law Western. New Eng. Coll., Springfield, Mass., 1985-86. Bd. dirs. Mass. div. Am. Cancer Soc., 1986—, mem. speakers bur., 1983-86, faculty Mass. div., 1986—; pres. Hampshire County unit Am. Cancer Soc., 1984-86, faculty, 1986; chmn. human rights com. Pioneer Sr. Services, Amherst, 1983—. Recipient Award Am. Cancer Soc., 1986. Mem. ABA, Mass. Bar Assn. (chmn. Implementation of lawyers trust accounts com. Hamphire County, speaker's bur., Outstanding Community Service award), Hampshire County Bar Assn. (exec. com. 1985-86), Assn. Trial Lawyers Am. Democrat. Club: Amherst (founder). Family and matrimonial, Real property, General practice. Office: Burres & Fidnick 19 Pray St Amherst MA 01002

FIEBACH, H. ROBERT, lawyer; b. Paterson, N.J., June 7, 1939; s. Michael M. and Silvia Irene (Nadler) F.; m. Elizabeth D. Carlton, Mar. 17, 1984; 1 child, Michael; children by previous marriage: Jonathan, Rachel. B.S., U. Pa., 1961, LL.B. cum laude, 1964. Bar: Pa. 1965, U.S. Supreme Ct. 1971. Law clk. to Chief Judge U.S. Ct. Appeals for 3d Cir., 1964-65; assoc. Wolf, Block, Schorr and Solis-Cohen, Phila., 1965-71, ptnr., 1971-79, sr. ptnr., 1979—; permanent mem. U.S. Jud. Conf. for 3d cir., 1967—; arbitrator Phila. Common Pleas Ct., U.S. Dist. Ct. (ea. dist.) Pa., Am. Arbitration Assn., 1966—. Research editor U. Pa. Law Rev., 1964-65; contbr. articles to legal jours. Mem. Phila. adv. bd. Anti-Defamation League of B'nai B'rith; mem. Greater Phila. Regional Commn. on Law and Social Action, Am. Jewish Congress; bd. dirs. Greater Phila. chpt. ACLU, past chmn. criminal justice and police practices com.; past bd. dirs. Pa. chpt. ACLU; bd. dirs. Welsh Valley Civic Assn., past pres.; past bd. dirs., treas. A Better Chance in Lower Merion; founder, mem. bd. dirs. Penn Valley Jr. Sports Assn.; mem. legal com. Main Line Reform Temple, Phila. Mem. ABA (litigation sect. 3d cir. discovery com.), Pa. Bar Assn. (ho. of dels. 1983—, vice chmn. jud. selection com., past chmn. jud. retention election com. 1980-83, chmn. spl. com. on profl. liability, past chmn. polit. action com. for merit retention of judges 1980-83), Phila. Bar Assn. (bd. govs., past chmn. fed. cts. com., past. vice chmn. arbitration com., past mem. spl. com. to study appellate cts., past chmn. spl. com. on ins. 1983—, mem. civil jud. precedures com., speaker various panels), Pa. Bar Inst. (bd. dirs.), Defender Assn. Phila. (bd. dirs.), Am. Judicature Soc., Assn. Trial Lawyers Am., Phila. Trial Lawyers Assn. (past chmn. bus. litigation com.), Defender Assn. Phila. (bd. dirs.), Order of Coif (past dir. U. Pa. chpt.). Federal civil litigation, State civil litigation. Home: Independence Pl Philadelphia PA 19106 Office: 12th Floor Packard Bldg Philadelphia PA 19102

FIELD, ARTHUR NORMAN, lawyer; b. N.Y.C., Sept. 28, 1935; s. Harry and Rose (Lemberg) F.; m. Doris Helen Rabbiner, Sept. 1, 1957; children: Michael, Karen. B.B.A., CCNY, 1955; LL.B., Harvard U., 1958. Assoc. firm Shearman & Sterling, N.Y.C., 1959-68, ptnr., 1968—; dir. North Central Oil Corp., Houston, Sunset Realty Corp., Punta Groda, Fla.; chmn. bd. Western Maine Radio Inc., Rumford, Maine, 1981—. Bd. dirs. Wave Hill Inc., N.Y.C., 1968-80; bd. dirs. Washington Sq. Legal Services, 1979—; chmn., dir. Community Action for Legal Services, 1972-77; trustee Brookdale Found., 1983—. Fellow Am. Bar Found., N.Y. Bar Found.; mem. N.Y. County Lawyers Assn. (dir., v.p.), N.Y. State Bar Assn. (mem. ho. of dels. 1978-85), ABA, Assn. Bar City of N.Y. Club: Metropolitan.

FIELD, CHARLES G., regulatory counsel; b. N.Y.C., Oct. 13, 1940; s. Leonard G. and Beatrice (Koppe) F.; m. Cynthia Ann Rosenburg, June, 1963; children: Alexandra M., Aaron G. BA, Cornell U., 1962; M in Urban Planning, NYU, 1967; PhD, Harvard U., 1971; JD, Georgetown U., 1978. Bar: D.C. 1978. Research mgr. HUD, Washington, 1971-74, office dir., 1975-78, spl. asst., 1983-84; assoc. Troy, Malin & Pottinger, Washington, 1979; staff atty. EPA, Washington, 1980-82; staff v.p., regulatory counsel Nat. Assn. Home Builders, Washington, 1984—. Co-author: Building Code Burden, 1975. Pres. Woodley Park Hist. Soc., 1986. Served to 1st lt. U.S. Army, 1963-65. Louise D. Lasker Found. fellow, 1967-69; Joint Ctr. for Urban Studies fellow, 1969; recipient Hieneman award, NYU, 1966. Mem. ABA, D.C. Bar Assn., Am. Tort Reform Assn. (vice-chmn. 1986). Republican. Jewish. Club: Harvard (Washington) (bd. dirs. 1986-89). Avocations: tennis, skiing. Real property, Administrative and regulatory, Construction. Home: 2638 Woodley Pl NW Washington DC 20008 Office: Nat Assn Home Builders 15th and M St NW Washington DC 20005

FIELD, HAROLD GREGORY, lawyer; b. Chgo., Fb. 27, 1923; s. Harold Gregory and Catherine (Crowley) F.; m. Marilyn Daw, June 21, 1947 (div. July 1977); children—Lnda, Karen, Jennifer, Gregory; m. Nancy L. Kesecker, Sept. 30, 1977. BS, Ariz. State U., 1948; LLB, Chgo. Kent Coll. Law, 1952. Bar: Ill. 1953. Sole practice, Wheaton, Ill., 1965—. Mem. Dist. 41 Bd. Edn., Glen Ellyn, Ill., 1960-65, chmn., 1965. Served with U.S. Army, 1942-45, ETO. Decorated Bronze Star. Fellow Am. Bar Found., Ill. Bar Found.; mem. Ill. Bar Assn. (bd. govs. 1983—), DuPage County Bar Assn. (pres. 1977-78, Man of Yr. 1982), ABA, Assn. Trial Lawyers Am., Ill. Trial Lawyers Assn., Am. Acad. Matrimonial Lawyers (chpt. pres.-elect 1983—, nat. bd. dirs. 1981—, pres. 1985-86). Republican. Club: Naperville Country (pres. 1975-76) (Ill.). Avocations: golf, skiing, tennis, running. Family and matrimonial. Home: 979 Creekside Circle Naperville IL 60540 Office: 107 E Front St Wheaton IL 60187

FIELD, MARTHA AMANDA, law educator, lawyer; b. Boston, Aug. 20, 1943; d. Donald T. and Adelaide (Anderson) F.; children: Maria Adelaide, Gabriel Hartry, Lucas Anthony. B.A., Harvard U., 1965; J.D., U. Chgo., 1968. Bar: D.C. 1969. Law clk. to justice Abe Fortas, U.S. Supreme Ct., 1968-69; from asst. prof. to prof. law U. Pa., 1969-78; prof. law Harvard U., 1978—. Contbr. numerous articles to law revs. Family and matrimonial, Civil rights, Federal civil litigation. Office: Harvard U Law Sch Langdell Hall 255 Cambridge MA 02138 *

FIELD, RICHARD CLARK, lawyer; b. Palo Alto, Calif., July 13, 1940; s. John and Sally (Miller) F.; m. Barbara Faith Butler, May 22, 1967 (dec. Apr. 1984); 1 child, Amanda Katherine; m. Eva Sara Halbreich, Dec. 1, 1985. BA, U. Calif., Riverside, 1962; JD, Harvard U., 1965. Bar: Calif. 1966, U.S. Supreme Ct., 1971, U.S. Ct. Appeals (9th cir.) 1979. Assoc. Thompson & Colegate, Riverside, 1965-69; ptnr. Adams, Duque & Hazeltine, Los Angeles, 1970—, mem. mgmt. com., 1981-84, chmn. litigation dept., 1985—. Contbr. articles to law jours. Counsel ARC, Los Angeles, 1984—, also bd. dirs. Mem. ABA (litigation, torts and ins. practice sects., bus. torts com., products, gen. liability and consumer law com.), Los Angeles County Bar Assn. (trial lawyers sect., fair jud. practices com.), Assn. Bus. Trial Lawyers (bd. govs. 1978-82), Am. Arbitration Assn. (comml. arbitration panel), So. Calif. Def. Counsel, Conf. Ins. Counsel. Republican. Episcopalian. Federal civil litigation, State civil litigation, Insurance. Office: Adams Duque & Hazeltine 523 W 6th St Los Angeles CA 90014

FIELD, ROBERT EDWARD, lawyer; b. Chgo., Aug. 21, 1945; s. Robert Edward and Florence Elizabeth (Aiken) F.; m. Jenny Lee Hill, Aug. 5, 1967; children—Jennifer Kay, Kimberly Anne, Amanda Brooke. B.A., Ill. Wesleyan U., 1967; M.A., Northwestern U., 1969, J.D., 1973. Bar: Ill. 1973, U.S. Dist. Ct. (no. dist.) Ill. 1974, U.S. Supreme Ct. 1979. Exec. dir. Winnetka Youth Orgn., Ill., 1969-73; assoc. firm Seyfarth, Shaw, Fairweather & Geraldson, Chgo., 1973-79, ptnr., 1979—; bd. dirs. Gt. Lakes Fin. Resources, Blue Island, Ill.; chmn. bd. dirs. 1st Nat. Bank of Blue Island, Winchester Mfg. Co., Wood Dale, Ill., Comml. Resources Corp., Naperville, Ill.; dir., sec. Ellis Corp., Chgo.; chmn. bd. dirs. Community Bank of Homewood-Flossmoor, Homewood, Ill. Pres. bd. dirs. Family Service and Mental Health Ctr. S. Cook County, Chgo. Heights, 1979—, treas., 1981-82, pres. 1986—; trustee Village of Olympia Fields, Ill., 1981—. Mem. Ill. Bar Assn., ABA. Republican. Methodist. Club: Calumet Country (Homewood). Banking, Contracts commercial, Real property. Home: 3424 Parthenon Way Olympia Fields IL 60461 Office: Seyfarth Shaw Fairweather & Geraldson 55 E Monroe St Chicago IL 60603

FIELD, SAMUEL SUMMERS, III, lawyer; b. Balt., Dec. 30, 1931; s. Samuel Summers and Margaret Rose (Sutton) F.; m. Joann Vilma Chester, Nov. 3, 1962; children: Samuel Summers IV, Catherine Margaret. AA, U. Balt., 1957, JD, 1959. Bar: Md. 1959. Sr. claims investigator Balt. Dept. Law, 1956-61, asst. soliciter, 1962-63; sole practice Balt., 1963—; auditor Balt. Cir. Ct., 1983—. Served with U.S. Army, 1953-55. Mem. ABA, Md. Bar Assn., Balt. Bar Assn. Democrat. Methodist. Consumer commercial, Probate, State civil litigation. Home: 10 Gittings Ave Baltimore MD 21212 Office: 9 W Hamilton St Baltimore MD 21201

FIELDS, HENRY MICHAEL, lawyer; b. N.Y.C., Feb. 11, 1946; s. Jack and Sylvia (Eggert) F.; m. Barbara Ann Schinman, June 20, 1971; children: Alexandra Wynne, Matthew Wyatt. BA magna cum laude, Harvard U., 1968; JD, Yale U., 1972. Bar: N.Y. 1973, N.J. 1974, Calif. 1981. Law clk. to presiding judge U.S. Dist. Ct. N.J. and U.S. Ct. Appeals (3d cir.), Newark, 1972-73; assoc. Cleary, Gottlieb, Steen & Hamilton, N.Y.C. and Paris, 1973-80; from assoc. to ptnr. Morrison & Foerster, Los Angeles, 1981—; lectr. on banking law topics various orgs.; bd. dirs. Stockton Wire Products, Burbank, Calif. Mng. editor Yale U. Law Rev., 1971-72; contbr. articles to profl. jours. Tower fellow Harvard U., 1968. Mem. ABA, Internat. Bar Assn., Calif. Bar Assn. (chmn. fin. insts. com. bus. law sect. 1985-86), Los Angeles County Bar Assn., Union Internationale des Avocats, French-Am. C. of C., Phi Beta Kappa. Club: Harvard-Radcliffe So. Calif, University (Los Angeles). Avocations: tennis, softball, photography. Banking, Private international, Securities. Home: 2121 Balsam Ave Los Angeles CA 90025 Office: Morrison & Foerster 333 S Grand Ave Los Angeles CA 90071

FIELDS, HOWARD M., lawyer, accountant; b. Highland Park, Ill., June 7, 1956; s. Milton and Sophy (Trachtenberg) F.; m. Pennie Dee Grusin, May 20, 1979; children: Lauren, Caryn. BS in Fin., U. Ill., 1977; JD, Wash. U., 1980. Bar: Ill. 1980, U.S. Dist. Ct. (no. dist.) Ill. 1980. Supr. sr. tax acct. Peat Marwick, Chgo., 1980-83; tax mgr. Deloitte, Haskins & Sells, Chgo., 1983-85, Allstate Ins. Co., Northbrook, Ill., 1985—. Contbr. articles to profl. jours. Mem. ABA, Am. Inst. CPAs, Ill. CPA Soc., Chgo. Bar Assn. Corporate taxation, Personal income taxation, Personal Financial Planning. Home: 1144 Devonshire Rd Buffalo Grove IL 60089 Office: Allstate Ins Co Allstate Plaza N B-6 Northbrook IL 60062

FIELDS, JAMES RALPH, lawyer, lobbyist, consultant; b. Los Angeles, Mar. 14, 1943; s. Paul Raymond Fields and Della Louise (Brabb) Klebe; m. Barbara Smith Knudson, May 18, 1985. BS in Bus. Adminstrn., U. Idaho, 1965, JD, 1973. Bar: Idaho 1973, U.S. Dist. Ct. Idaho 1973. Staff counsel U.S. Sen. James McClure, Washington, 1973-76; gen. counsel Idaho Assn.

Commerce and Industry, Boise, 1976-83, v.p., gen. counsel, 1983-87; cons. Knudson-Fields Human Devel. Cons., Boise, 1985—. Organizer, pres. Idaho Liability Reform Coalition; mem. Gov.'s Adv. Com. on Workers' Compensation, Idaho, 1978—; pres. Idaho Liability Reform Coalition, 1986. Served to 1st lt. U.S. Army, 1968-71, Vietnam. Mem. ABA, Idaho Bar Assn., Am. Soc. Personnel Adminstrn., Human Resources Assn. Treasure Valley (bd. dirs. 1986). Republican. Baptist. Lodge: Kiwanis (pres. Boise chpt. 1985-86). Avocations: travel, outdoor activities, sports. Legislative, General corporate, International-Private Arbitration. Home: 1183 Wild Phlox Way Boise ID 83709

FIELDS, ROBERT MEDDIN, lawyer; b. Savannah, Ga., Sept. 9, 1953; s. Maurice and Phyllis (Meddin) Fields; m. Robyn Elleen, Apr. 12, 1981; 1 child, Michael Benjamin. BA, Duke U., 1975; JD, Cornell U., 1978; LLM, Georgetown U., 1982. Bar: Ga. 1979, N.J. 1980, Conn. 1983, D.C. 1986. Tax law specialist IRS, Washington, 1979-82; assoc. Reid & Riege, P.C., Washington, 1982-84, Winthrop, Stimson, Putnam & Roberts, N.Y.C., 1984—. Mem. ABA (employee benefits com.). Pension, profit-sharing, and employee benefits. Office: Winthrop Stimson et al 40 Wall St New York NY 10005

FIER, ELIHU, lawyer; b. N.Y.C., Mar. 25, 1931; s. Charles H. and Helen N. (Nadel) F.; m. Jane Lee Saltser, Jan. 10, 1956 (dec. Jan. 1964); children—Jennifer, Michael; m. Dorothy Elaine Broman, Sept. 25, 1977; children—Paige, Carlyn. B.A., Dartmouth Coll., 1952; LL.B., Harvard U., 1958. Bar; N.Y. 1959, U.S. Dist. Ct. (so. and ea. dists.) N.Y. 1960 U.S. Tax Ct. 1961, U.S. Ct. Appeals (2d cir.) 1961. Ptnr. Weil, Gotshal & Manges, N.Y.C., 1969-80; ptnr. Morgan, Lewis & Bockius, N.Y.C., 1980-83; ptnr. Finley, Kumble, Wagner, Heine, Underberg, Manley & Casey, Beverly Hills, Calif., 1983—, N.Y.C., 1983—; adj. assoc. prof. NYU, N.Y.C., 1969-76; lectr. N.Y. Law Jour., Law and Bus., Practicing Law Inst. Served to lt. (j.g.) USNR, 1952-60. Mem. ABA (com. creditors' rights in real estate financing 1983—), Assn. Bar City N.Y., N.Y. Bar Assn. Home: 623 N Bedford Beverly Hills CA 90210 Office: Finley Kumble Wagner Heine Underberg Manley & Casey 9100 Wilshire Blvd Beverly Hills CA 90212 also: 425 Park Ave New York NY 10022

FIERST, BRUCE PHILIP, lawyer; b. Chgo., Jan. 26, 1951; s. Robert Jay and Esther Toby (Kaplan) F. BA with honors, Tulane U., 1973; JD, U. Denver, 1975. Bar: Colo. 1976, U.S. Dist. Ct. Colo. 1976. Assoc. Epstein, Lozow & Preblud, P.C., Denver, 1976-79; pres. Bruce P. Fierst, P.C., Denver, 1979—. Co-author manual Handling the DUI case, 1981. Big Brother, Big Bros. of Colo., Denver, 1975-81. Mem. ABA, Colo. Bar Assn., Denver Bar Assn., Am. Trial Lawyers Assn., Colo. Trial Lawyers Assn. (lectr., mem. coms. on driving under the influence, bd. dirs. 1986—). Democrat. Jewish. Avocations: sports. Criminal, Personal injury. Home: 5431 S Dayton Ct Greenwood Village CO 80111 Office: 1120 Lincoln St 1007 Denver CO 80203

FIERSTEIN, RONALD KARL, lawyer; b. Bklyn., Dec. 4, 1950; s. Irving and Jacqueline H. (Gilbert) F.; m. Dorothea E. Regal; children: Bradley, Matthew. BS, SUNY, Stony Brook, 1971; JD, Bklyn. Law Sch., 1978. Bar: N.Y. 1979, U.S. Dist. Ct. (so. and ea. dists.) N.Y. 1979. Assoc. Fish & Neave, N.Y.C., 1978-83; sole practice N.Y.C., 1983—. Entertainment, Trademark and copyright. Office: 1500 Broadway Suite 2805 New York NY 10036

FIFER, SAMUEL, lawyer; b. Chgo., May 5, 1950; s. Joseph and Zipporah (Berkowicz) F.; m. Barabra Lee Brown, Apr. 8, 1980; children: Jessica, Max. BS, Northwestern U., 1971; JD cum laude, DePaul U., 1974. Bar: Ill. 1974, U.S. Dist. Ct. (no. dist.) Ill. 1974, U.S. Ct. Appeals (7th cir.) 1976, U.S. Supreme Ct. 1977. Intern U.S. Dept. Justice, Pitts., 1973; assoc. Kirkland & Ellis, Chgo., 1974-78; assoc. Reuben & Proctor, Chgo., 1978-80, ptnr., 1980-86; ptnr. Isham, Lincoln & Beale, Chgo., 1986—. Mem. ABA, U.S. Trademark Assn., Ill. Bar Assn., Chgo. Bar Assn. Lutheran. Clubs: Chgo. Athletic, Chgo. Literary. Entertainment, Libel, Trademark and copyright. Home: 1733 N Cleveland Ave Chicago IL 60614 Office: Isham Lincoln & Beale 19 S LaSalle Chicago IL 60603

FIFLIS, TED J., lawyer, educator; b. Chgo., Feb. 20, 1933; s. James P. and Christine (Karakitsos) F.; m. Vasilike Pantelakos, July 3, 1955; children: Christina Eason, Antonia Fowler, Andreanna Lawson. B.S., Northwestern U., 1954; LL.B., Harvard U., 1957. Bar: Ill. 1957, Colo. 1975. Individual practice law Chgo., 1957-65; mem. faculty U. Colo. Law Sch., Boulder, 1965—; prof. U. Colo. Law Sch., 1968—; vis. prof. N.Y. U., 1968, U. Calif., Davis, 1973, U. Chgo., 1976, U. Va., 1979, Duke U., 1980, Georgetown U., 1982, Am. U., 1983; cons. Rice U. Author: (with Homer Kripke, Paul Foster) Accounting for Business Lawyers, 1970, 3d edit., 1984; Editor-in-chief: Corp. Law Review, 1977—; Contbr. articles to profl. jours. Mem. Am. Assn. Law Schs. (past chmn. bus. law sect.), Colo. Bar Assn. (council mem. sect. of corp., banking and bus. law 1974-75), Am. Law Inst., ABA. Greek Orthodox. Securities, Contracts commercial. Home: 1636 Columbine Boulder CO 80302 Office: Univ of Colo Law Sch Boulder CO 80309

FIGA, PHILLIP SAM, lawyer; b. Chgo., July 27, 1951; s. Leon and Sarah (Mandelkorn) F.; m. Candace Cole, Aug. 19, 1973; children—Benjamin Todd, Elizabeth Dawn. B.A., Northwestern U., 1973; J.D., Cornell U., 1976. Bar: Colo. 1976, U.S. Dist. Ct. Colo. 1976, U.S. Ct. Appeals (10th cir.) 1980, U.S. Supreme Ct. 1980. Assoc. Sherman & Howard, Denver, 1976-80; ptnr. Burns & Figa, P.C., Denver, 1980—; lectr. U. Denver Law Sch., 1984—; bd. dirs. Colo. Lawyers Com., Denver, 1984—; mem. adv. com. on group legal services and advt. Colo. Supreme Ct. 1982—. Contbr. articles to legal jours.; articles editor Cornell Internat. Law Rev., 1975-76. Bd. dirs. B'nai B'rith Anti-Defamation League, Denver, 1984. Evans scholar, 1969. Mem. Colo. Bar Assn. (chmn. ethics com. 1984—, bd. of govs. 1986—), ABA, Denver Bar Assn., Am. Judicature Soc., Phi Beta Kappa, Phi Eta Sigma. Democrat. Jewish. Antitrust, Federal civil litigation, State civil litigation. Home: 9928 E Ida Ave Englewood CO 80111 Office: 3773 Cherry Creek N Dr Ptarmigan Pl Denver CO 80209

FIGARI, ERNEST EMIL, JR., lawyer, educator; b. Navasota, Tex., Feb. 18, 1939; s. Ernest Emil and Louise (Campbell) F.; m. Cynthia Wright, Dec. 3, 1981; 1 child, Alexandra Caroline. BS, Tex. A&M U., 1961; LLB, U. Tex.-Austin, 1964; LLM, So. Meth. U., 1970. Bar: Tex. 1964, U.S. Ct. Appeals (5th cir.) 1965, U.S. Dist. Ct. (no. dist.) Tex. 1964, U.S. Supreme Ct. 1967. Law clerk to judge U.S. Dist. Ct. (no. dist.) Tex., Dallas, 1964-65; assoc. Coke & Coke, Dallas, 1965-70, ptnr., 1970-75; ptnr. Johnson & Swanson, Dallas, 1975-86, Figari & Davenport, Dallas, 1986—; adj. prof. law So. Meth. U., Dallas, 1982-84. Contbr. articles to legal jours. Fellow Tex. Bar Found.; mem. State Bar Tex., ABA. Democrat. Roman Catholic. Federal civil litigation, State civil litigation, Legal education. Office: Figari & Davenport 4800 Inter First Plaza 901 Main St Dallas TX 75202

FIGG, ROBERT MCCORMICK, JR., lawyer; b. Radford, Va., Oct. 22, 1901; s. Robert McCormick and Helen Josephine (Cecil) F.; m. Sallie Alexander Tobias, May 10, 1927; children: Robert McCormick, Emily Figg Dalla Mura, Jefferson Tobias. A.B., Coll. of Charleston, 1920, Litt.D., 1970; law student, Columbia U., 1920-22; LL.D., U. S.C., 1959. Bar: S.C. 1922. Practiced in Charleston, 1922-59; gen. counsel S.C. State Ports Authority, 1942-72; circuit solicitor 9th Jud. Circuit of S.C., 1935-47; spl. circuit judge 1957, 75, 76; dean Law Sch., U. S.C., 1959-70; sr. counsel Robinson, McFadden, Moore, Pope, Williams, Taylor & Brailsford, Columbia, 1970—; dir. Home Fed. Savs. & Loan Assn., Charleston. Co-author: Civil Trial Manual (joint com. Am. Coll. Trial Lawyers-Am. Law Inst.-Am. Bar Assn.), 1974. Mem. S.C. Reorgn. Commn., 1948—, chmn., 1951-55, 71-75; elector Hall Fame for Gt. Americans, 1976; mem. S.C. Ho. of Reps., 1933-35; first pres., now hon. life chmn. Coll. of Charleston Found.; trustee Saul Alexander Found., Columbia Mus. Art. Recipient DuRant award for disting. pub. service S.C. Bar Found., 1982; Founders medal Coll. of Charleston, 1986. Fellow Am. Coll. Trial Lawyers; mem. Am. Soc. Internat. Law, Am. Acad. Polit. Sci., Am. Law Inst. (life), Am. Judicature Soc., Inst. Jud. Adminstrn., World Assn. Lawyers, Inter-Am. Bar Assn., Charleston County Bar Assn. (pres. 1953), ABA (ho. of dels. 1971-72, com. fair trial-free press 1965-69, com. spl. study legal edn. 1974—), S.C. Bar Assn., S.C. State Bar (pres. 1971), Order Coif, Blue Key (hon.), Phi Beta Kappa (hon.), Phi Delta Phi (hon.). Clubs: Forum, Forest Lake, Palmetto U. S.C. Faculty. Lodge: Masons (33 degree, grand master S.C. 1972-74). General practice, Federal civil litigation, Libel. Home: 1522 Deans Ln Columbia SC 29205 Office: Jefferson Bldg Columbia SC 29201

FIGNAR, EUGENE MICHAEL, lawyer, mortgage executive; b. Hazleton, Pa., Aug. 12, 1946; s. Basil W. and Helen (Hannock) F.; m. R. Casey, June 15, 1968. BBA, King's Coll., Wilkes-Barre, Pa., 1963; JD, Duquesne U., 1967. Bar: Pa. 1972, U.S. Dist. Ct. (we. dist.) Pa. 1972. Counsel Westinghouse Electric Corp., Pitts., 1972-80; asst. gen. counsel Champion Internat. Corp., Stamford, Conn., 1980-81; v.p., gen. counsel, sec. Merrill Lynch Realty, Stamford, Conn., 1981-82; v.p., gen. counsel, sec. Merrill Lynch Mortgage, Stamford, Conn., 1982-85, v.p. quality, product devel., 1985—, also bd. dirs. Bus. adv. council King's Coll., Wilkes-Barre, 1985—; allocations com. Greenwich (Conn.) United Way, 1985-86. Served to sgt. U.S. Army, 1969-71. Mem. ABA, Allegheny County Bar Assn., Mortgage Bankers Assn. Democrat. Catholic. Club: West End Yacht (Greenwich) (commodore 1986—). Avocations: sailing, bicycling, model railroading, gardening. Banking, Contracts commercial, Real property. Home: 21 West End Ave Old Greenwich CT 06870 Office: Merrill Lynch Mortgage Corp 10 Stamford Forum Stamford CT 06904

FIGUEORA, NICHOLAS, judge; b. N.Y.C., Oct. 1, 1933; s. Nicanor and Isabel (Gonzalez) F.; m. Carmen Gonzalez, Sept. 22, 1968 (div. Mar. 1976). BBA, CUNY, 1956; LLB, Bklyn. Law Sch., 1964. Bar: N.Y. 1964, U.S. Dist. Ct. (so. dist.) N.Y. 1973, U.S. Ct. Appeals (2d cir.) 1973, U.S. Dist. Ct. (ea. dist.) N.Y. 1975. Asst. dist. atty. Borough of Bronx, N.Y., 1966-69; assoc. counsel Knapp Commn., N.Y.C., 1970-71; asst. U.S. atty. U.S. Justice Dept. (so. dist.), N.Y.C., 1972-75; dep. police commr. City of N.Y., 1977-80; criminal ct. justice State of N.Y., Bronx, 1980-85; justice supreme ct. State of N.Y., N.Y.C., 1986—; dep. pub. adminstr. Surrogate Ct., Bronx, 1969-70; bd. dirs. Legal Services Corp., Bronx. Mem. Mayor's Com. on Judiciary, N.Y.C., 1976-77; trustee Bd. of Higher Edn., N.Y.C., 1976-77. Served to 1st lt. U.S. Army, 1956-58, Korea. Mem. P.R. Bar Assn. (pres. 1980), Hispanic Soc. N.Y.C. Police Dept. Democrat. Roman Catholic. Avocations: literature, racquetball. Criminal, Administrative and regulatory, General practice. Home: 50 King St Apt 1B New York NY 10014 Office: NY Supreme Ct 851 Grand Concourse Bronx NY 10451

FIGUEROA, LUIS ANTONIO, lawyer; b. Zapata, Tex., Oct. 17, 1953; s. Arturo M. and Rebeca (Adam) F. BA, Tex. A & I, 1976; JD, Tex. So. U., 1979. Bar: Tex. 1979, U.S. Dist. Ct. (so. dist.) Tex. 1979, U.S. Ct. Appeals (5th cir.) 1979. Sole practice Laredo, Tex., 1979-81; ptnr. Figueroa, Rubio & Czar, Laredo, 1981—; juvenile referee Zapata County, 1982-86; atty. Tex-Mex. R.R. Credit Union, Laredo, 1983-86; alt. juvenile referee Webb County, Laredo, 1984-86; cons. Falcon Nat. Bank, Laredo, 1986—. Nat. legal advisor, dist. dir. Lulac, Laredo and Corpus Christi, Tex., 1982-84; chmn. Zapata County Dems., 1986—; v.p. Laredo Legal Aid Soc., 1984. Named one of Outstanding Young Men of Am. Jaycees, 1983. Mem. Tex. Bar Assn., Laredo Bar Assn. (treas. young lawyers div. 1982-83), Zapata County Fair Assn. Democrat. Roman Catholic. Criminal, Real property, Family and matrimonial. Office: Figueroa Rubio & Czar 1319 Convent Laredo TX 78043

FIGULI, DAVID JOHN, lawyer, educational consultant; b. Cleve., Aug. 23, 1949; s. Joseph John and Dorothy Ellen (Schurdell) F.; m. Sandra Lee Colavecchio, Feb. 14, 1970; children—Keri Lee, Joshua David. B.A. in Math., Cleve. State U., 1972, J.D., 1975. Bar: Ohio 1975, S.D. 1977, Nebr. 1976, Mont. 1980, Colo. 1984, U.S. Dist. Ct. (no. dist.) Ohio 1981, U.S. Dist. Ct. S.D. 1977, U.S. Dist. Ct. Mont. 1981. Legal counsel Bethesda Found., Omaha, 1975-76; gen. counsel S.D. Bd. Regents, Pierre, 1977-80, labor relations cons., 1980-81; chief legal counsel Mont. Bd. Regents, Helena, 1980-81; ptnr. Wickens, Herzer, and Panza Co., L.P.A., Lorain, Ohio, 1981—; asst. to pres. for legal affairs, 1983—, sec. bd. trustees U. No. Colo., Greeley, 1983-86; gen. counsel, exec. sec. Regis Coll., Denver, 1986—; seminar speaker, commentator. Mem. editorial bd. Cleve. State U. Law Rev., 1974-75. Contbr. chpts. to scholarly texts. Mem. med. services plan bd. U. S.D., 1979-80. Recipient Exegesis award Cuyahoga County Bar Assn., 1975. Mem. Mont. State Bar Assn., Nebr. State Bar Assn., Colo. Bar Assn., Lorain County Law Library Assn., Ohio Assn. of Civil Trial Attys., Nat. Assn. Coll. and Univ. Attys., Ohio Bar Assn. (sch. law com. 1983—), State Bar S.D. (law sch. com. 1980). Administrative and regulatory, Federal civil litigation. Office: Wickens Herzer & Panza PC Lake Plaza Bldg Suite 201 3545 W 12th St Greeley CO 80634

FILDES, RICHARD JAMES, lawyer; b. N.Y.C., Nov. 9, 1952; s. Edgar E. and Lucille (Sanna) F.; m. Deborah D. Davenport, June 21, 1979; children: Matthew, Melissa. BS in Psychology and Econs. magna cum laude, Duke U., 1973; JD cum laude, U. Fla., 1977. Bar: Fla. 1977. Ptnr. Lowndes, Drosdick, Doster, Kantor & Reed, Orlando, Fla., 1977—, also bd. dirs.; bd. dirs. Fla. Citrus Sports Assn., Inc. Democrat. Roman Catholic. Clubs: University (Orlando), Bay Hill. Avocations: golf, tennis, fishing, reading. Real property, Contracts commercial, General corporate. Office: Lowndes Drosdick Doster et al 215 N Eola Dr Orlando FL 32802

FILES, GORDON LOUIS, lawyer, judge; b. Ft. Dodge, Iowa, Mar. 5, 1912; s. James Ray and Anna (Louis) F.; m. Kathryn Thrift, Nov. 24, 1942; children—Kathryn Allen, James Gordon. A.B. in Polit. Sci. with honors, UCLA, 1934; LL.B., Yale U., 1937. Bar: Calif., U.S. Supreme Ct. Law clk. U.S. Ct. Appeals (8th cir.), 1937-38; enforcement atty. Office Price Adminstrn., 1942; ptnr. Freston & Files, Los Angeles, 1938-59; judge Los Angeles Superior Ct., 1959-62; assoc. justice 2d dist., div. 4 Calif. Ct. Appeals, 1962-64, presiding justice, 1964-82, adminstrv. presiding justice, 1970-82; now arbitrator, referee and mediator; mem. Jud. Council Calif., 1964-71, 73-77; mem. governing com. Ctr. for Jud. Edn. and Research, 1981-82; mem. bd. govs. State Bar Calif., 1957-59. Bd. editors Yale Law Jour., 1935-37. Served to lt. USN, 1942-45. Fellow Am. Bar Found.; mem. ABA, Am. Judicature Soc., Inst. Jud. Adminstrn., Los Angeles County Bar Assn. (trustee 1952-56), Calif. Judges Assn. (exec. com. 1971-72), Am. Legion, Order of Coif, Phi Beta Kappa, Phi Delta Phi. Democrat. Clubs: Chancery (pres. 1972-73) (Los Angeles); Valley Hunt (Pasadena). Judicial administration, Jurisprudence. Home: 154 S Arroyo Blvd Pasadena CA 91105

FILIPPINE, EDWARD L., fed. judge; b. 1930. A.B., St. Louis U., 1951, J.D., 1957. Bar: Mo. 1957. Sole practice law St. Louis, 1957-77; spl. asst. atty. gen. State of Mo., 1963-64; judge U.S. Dist. Ct., Eastern Dist. Mo., St. Louis, 1977—. Served with USAF, 1951-53. Mem. ABA, Mo. Bar Assn., Bar Assn. Met. St. Louis, St. Louis County Bar Assn. Jurisprudence. Office: U S Dist Ct 1114 Market St Saint Louis MO 63101 *

FILLER, RONALD HOWARD, lawyer; b. St. Louis, Apr. 11, 1948; s. Leon Isaac and Jeanette Frances (Sanofsky) F.; m. Wendy L. Fink, June 28, 1970; children—Stephen Paul, Lindsay Ann. B.S., U. Ill.-Urbana, 1970; J.D., George Washington U., 1973; LL.M. in Taxation, Georgetown U., 1976. Bar: D.C. 1973, Ill. 1976. Atty., SEC, Washington, 1973-76; assoc. Abramson & Fox, Chgo., 1976-77; assoc. counsel Conti Commodity Service, Chgo., 1977-78, dir. mgmt. accts., 1978-80; mng. ptnr. Filler Zaner & Assocs., Chgo., 1980-85; ptnr. Vedder, Price, Kaufman & Kammholz, Chgo., 1985—; dir. Commodities Law Inst., IIT/Chgo. Kent Law Sch., 1978—, adj. prof. law, 1977—, bd. overseers, 1982—; lectr. Commodities Ednl. Inst., 1977—. Contbr. articles to jours., futures mags. Mem. Nat. Futures Assn. (bd. dirs. 1984-87), Am. Arbitration Assn. (arbitrator), Mid Am. Commodity Exchange (bd. dirs. 1984-86), ABA (chmn. sub futures comm. merchants 1986—), Chgo. Bar Assn. (chmn. commodities law com. 1981-82), Nat. Assocs. Futures Traders Assn., Futures Industry Assn. (exec. com. Chgo. div. 1986—), Law and Comp. div. of Futures Industry Assn. (exec. com. 1985—), D.C. Bar Assn., Ill. State Bar Assn. Democrat. Jewish. Commodities, Securities, Federal civil litigation. Home: 125 Lockerbie Ln Wilmette IL 60091 Office: Vedder Price Kaufman & Kammholz 115 S LaSalle St #3000 Chicago IL 60603

FILLION, THOMAS JOHN, lawyer; b. Detroit, Apr. 21, 1953; s. George Joseph and Patricia Vera (Roy) F. B in Gen. Studies with distinction, U. Mich., 1975, JD, 1980. Bar: Mich. 1981, U.S. Dist. Ct. (ea. dist.) Mich. 1981. Sole practice Dearborn Heights, Mich., 1981—. Mem. ABA. State civil litigation, Criminal. Home and Office: 25251 Hopkins Detroit MI 48125

FILLNER, RUSSELL KENNETH, lawyer; b. Forsyth, Mont., Apr. 18, 1926; s. George William and Jane (Dowson) F.; m. D. Jane Jackson, Aug. 28, 1949; children—Clifford Allen, William Edward, Myrna Jane, Russell Kendall, John Charles. LL.B., U. Mont., 1952, J.D., 1967. Bar: Mont. 1952. City atty. City of Forsyth, 1952-66; county atty. Rosebud County (Mont.), 1952-66; sole practice, Billings, Mont., 1967-86; dist. ct. judge 13 Jud. Dist. Mont., 1986— ; pub. defender Yellowstone County, Mont.; lectr. Mont. State Law Enforcement Acad.; mem. Mont. Criminal Law Commn.; mem. fee arbitration com., judiciary com. State Bar Mont. Pres., Yellowstone County Democratic Club, 1969-70; mem. City Council, Billings, 1971-74, pres., 1973-74. Served to cpl. U.S. Army, 1944-46. Mem. ABA, Mont. Bar Assn., State Bar Mont. (judiciary com., fee arbitration com.), Yellowstone County Bar Assn., Yellowstone County Claimants Attys. Assn. (trustee 1981-84), Am. Trial Lawyers Assn. Presbyterian. Clubs: Hilands Golf, Lions, Masons. Judicial administration.

FILLON, RICHARD, lawyer; b. Boston, Mar. 21, 1951; s. Charles William and Rita (Baino) F. AB, Bridgewater State Coll., 1969-73; JD, Southwestern U., Los Angeles, 1981; postdoctoral, Harvard U., 1984—. Bar: Mass. 1982, U.S. Dist. Ct. Mass. 1982, U.S. Ct. Appeals (1st cir.) 1982. Sole practice Boston, 1982-83, Hingham, Mass., 1984—; owner, mgr. Joy Marie Realty, Hingham, 1984—. Mem. Mass. Bar Assn. State civil litigation, Civil rights, Criminal. Office: 190 Lincoln St Hingham MA 02043

FILORAMO, JOHN ROBERT, lawyer; b. N.Y.C., Mar. 3, 1951; s. Anthony and Arlene (Heldoorn) F.; m. Kathy Lou Speyer, Oct. 13, 1973; children: James Anthony, Joseph Donald. BS, Eastern Mich. U., 1973; JD, Detroit Coll. Law, 1979. Bar: Mich., U.S. Dist. Ct. (we. dist.) Mich. Asst. pros. atty. Delta County, Escanaba, Mich., 1980-81; ptnr. Davis, Olsen, Filoramo, Plackowski, Jarvi P.C., Escanaba, 1981—. Fellow ABA, Mich. Bar Assn., Delta County Bar Assn. (v.p. 1984-86, pres. 1986—), Mich. Trial Lawyers Assn. Democrat. Roman Catholic. Lodge: Kiwanis (K-club advisor Escanaba chpt. 1982-86). Avocations: hunting, fishing. State civil litigation, Criminal, Family and matrimonial. Home: 1625 S 16th St Escanaba MI 49829 Office: Davis Olsen Filoramo et al 504 Ludington Escanaba MI 49829

FINBERG, ALAN ROBERT, lawyer, communications company executive; b. Bklyn., July 2, 1927; s. Chester F. and Anne B. (Gorfinkle) F.; m. Barbara J. Denning, June 21, 1953. B.A., Yale U., 1950; J.D., Harvard U., 1953. Bar: N.Y. 1954, D.C. 1974, U.S. Supreme Ct. 1974. Assoc. firm Cravath, Swaine & Moore, N.Y.C., 1953-61; partner firm Stein, Kripke & Rosen, N.Y.C., 1961-64; asst. gen. counsel Gen. Dynamics Corp., N.Y.C., 1964-71; v.p., sec., gen. counsel Washington Post Co., Washington and N.Y.C., 1971—; dir. Newsweek, Inc., Daily Herald Co. Trustee Bard Coll.; sec., bd. dirs. Hudson Valley Festival of the Arts, Inc., The Copper Horse, Inc. Served with USNR, 1945-46. Mem. Am. Bar Assn., Assn. Bar City N.Y., Helsinki Watch (mem. exec. com.), Am. Arbitration Assn. (arbitration panel), Am. Soc. Corporate Secs., Phi Beta Kappa. Democrat. Clubs: Board Room (N.Y.C.), Coffee House (N.Y.C.). General corporate, Libel, Securities. Home: 165 E 72d St New York NY 10021 Office: Washington Post Co 444 Madsion Ave New York NY 10022

FINCH, DAVID SAMUEL, lawyer; b. Chgo., Dec. 19, 1950; s. Herman Manuel and Frances (Gutlow) F.; m. Ruth Deborah Lion, Oct. 30, 1982. BS, Cornell U., 1973; JD, U. Ill., 1977. Bar: Ill. 1977, U.S. Dist. Ct. (no. dist.) Ill. 1977, U.S. Ct. Appeals (7th cir.) 1979, U.S. Ct. Appeals (5th cir.) 1983, Calif. 1986, U.S. Dist. Ct. (cen. dist.) Calif. 1987. Assoc. Gottlieb and Schwartz, Chgo., 1977-82; atty. Quaker Oats Co., Chgo., 1982-83; assoc. Friedman & Koven, Chgo., 1983-85, ptnr., 1985-86; ptnr. Folger & Levin, Los Angeles, 1986—. Mem. ABA, Chgo. Bar Assn. Club: The Standard, Chgo. Labor, Federal civil litigation, State civil litigation. Office: Folger & Levin 1900 Ave of the Stars Los Angeles CA 90067

FINCH, EDWARD RIDLEY, JR., lawyer, diplomat, author; b. Westhampton Beach, N.Y., Aug. 31, 1919. A.B. with thesis honors, Princeton U., 1941; J.D., NYU, 1947; LL.D. (hon.), Mo. Valley Coll., 1963; D.Sc. (hon.), Cumberland Coll., 1985. Bar: N.Y. 1948, U.S. Supreme Ct. 1953, D.C. 1978, Fla. 1980. Ptnr. Finch & Schaeffer, N.Y.C., 1950-85, Le Boeuf, Lamb, Leiby at MacRae, 1986—; commr. City of N.Y., 1955-58; gen. counsel St. Giles Found.; U.S. del. 4th UN Congress, Geneva, 1970, 5th UN Congress, Japan, 1975; U.S. spl. ambassador to Panama, 1972; legal advisor U.S. Del. Unispace, Vienna, 1982; lectr. in field. Author: Hands In Your Pockets, Astro Business-A Guide to Commerce and Law of Outer Space. Contbr. articles to legal jours. Mem. faculty adv. com. dept. politics Princeton U.; pres. N.Y. Inst. for Edn. of Blind, 1969-71; treas. Jessie Ridley Found., N.Y.C.; pres. Crippled Children's Friendly Aid Assn. Inc., Finch Trusts, Adams Meml. Fund Inc.; trustee St. Andrew's Dune Ch. Decorated Legion of Merit with oak leaf cluster, Order of Brit. Empire Eng., Legion of Honor France; Knight Order of St. John. Mem. ABA (ho. of dels. 1971-72, chmn. com. aerospace law of sect. internat. law 1973-79), Fed. Bar Assn., Inter-Am. Bar Assn., Internat. Bar Assn., Judge Advs. Assn. U.S. (past pres.), Am. Law Inst., Am. Judicature Soc., AIAA, Internat. Astronautical Acad. (Hall of Fame 1985), Am. Arbitration Assn. (panelist), N.Y. State Bar Assn. Clubs: University, Union League, Union, Princeton, L.I., Bathing of Southampton. Estate planning, Probate, Public international. Home: 860 Park Ave New York NY 10021 Office: LeBoeuf Lamb Leiby & MacRae 520 Madison Ave New York NY 10022

FINCH, FRANK HERSCHEL, JR., lawyer; b. Mpls., Mar. 13, 1933; s. Frank H. and Louise A. (Henry) F.; m. Margaret Lee Samuel, June 13, 1953; children: Frank H. III, Lani D.L. BA, Harvard U., 1953; LLB, Harvard U. Law Sch., 1959. Bar: Conn. 1959, U.S. Supreme Ct. 1967. Assoc. Howd & Lavieri, Winsted, Conn., 1959-61; ptnr. Howd, Lavieri & Finch, Winsted, 1961—; pros. atty. Conn. Cir. Ct., 1961-78; mem. adv. bd. Conn. Bank and Trust Co., 1976—; bd. dirs. Northwest Conn. Health Corp., 1986—. Chmn., bd. dirs. Winsted Meml. Hosp., 1975-77; chmn. personnel com. Town of Barkhamsted, Conn., 1984—. Served to lt. USNR, 1953-59. Mem. ABA, Conn. Bar Assn. (bd. govs. 1985—), Litchfield County Bar Assn. (pres. 1974-76, grievance com. 1982-86, state trial referee 1984—), Am. Arbitration Assn. (arbitrator 1975—), Nat. Assn. Dist. Attys., Northwest Conn. C. of C. (chmn., bd. dirs. 1980-81). Club: University (exec. com. 1985—). Lodge: Rotary (pres. Winsted club 1967-68). General corporate, Real property, General practice. Office: Howd Lavieri & Finch 682 Main St Winsted CT 06098

FINCH, FREDERICK EARL, lawyer; b. Ross, Calif., Oct. 16, 1943; s. Glenn E. and Luella (Johnson) F.; m. Teresa Elizabeth Soland, June 10, 1972; children: Jason, Vin, Frederick, Elliot. BA, U. Minn., 1967; JD, William Mitchell Coll. Law, 1973. Bar: Minn. 1973, U.S. Dist. Ct. Minn. 1973, U.S. Ct. Appeals (8th cir.) 1974, U.S. Supreme Ct. 1982. Assoc. Fredrikson & Byron, Mpls., 1972-79, ptnr., 1979—. Editor: The Hennepin Lawyer, 1976—; contbr. articles to profl. jours. Mem. ABA, Minn. Bar Assn. (ho. dels. 1979—), Hennepin County Bar Assn. (sec. 1985-86, treas. 1986-87, pres. elect 1987—, bd. dirs. Legal Advice Clinics Ltd. 1974—), Hennepin County Bar Found. (bd. dirs. 1985—). Mem. Democratic Farm Labor Party. Mem. United Ch. Christ. Labor, Federal civil litigation, State civil litigation. Home: 5100 Highland Rd Minnetonka MN 55345 Office: Frederikson & Byron 900 2d Ave S Minneapolis MN 55402

FINCH, JOHN MARSHALL, lawyer; b. Caripito, Monagas, Venezuela, Mar. 14, 1944; came to U.S., 1956; m. Heide Elmene Perner, Dec. 31, 1968 (div. Apr. 1982); m. Dorothea Potter Teipel, Dec. 11, 1982; 1 child, Marshall Potter. AB, Georgetown U., 1966; JD, U. Mich., 1971. Bar: D.C. 1973. Assoc. Mayer, Brown & Platt, Washington, 1971-73; dep. gen. counsel Nat. Assn. Mfrs., Washington, 1973-78; ptnr. Arthur Young & Co., Washington, 1978-86. Vol. Peace Corps, San Jose, Costa Rica, 1966-68; mem. Peace Corps. Nat. Adv. Com., 1986. Mem. ABA, Fed. Bar Assn., D.C. Bar Assn. Democrat. Roman Catholic. Clubs: University. Avocations: reading, gardening. Private international, Legislative, Securities. Home: 1505 Oakview Dr McLean VA 22101 Office: 1255 23d St NW Suite 850 Washington DC 20037

FINCH, MICHAEL PAUL, lawyer; b. Galveston, Tex., Jan. 4, 1946; s. Albert Lynn and Ila Belle (Robertson) F.; m. Rebecca Jean Minnear, Dec. 27, 1969; children: Michael Paul, Rachelle Jean. BEE cum laude, Rice U.,

1969, MEE, 1969; JD magna cum laude, U. Houston, 1972. Bar: Tex. 1973. Petroleum engr. Exxon Corp., Houston, 1969-72; assoc. Vinson & Elkins, Houston, 1972-79, ptnr., 1980—. V.p. PTO Holy Spirit Episc. Sch., Houston, 1985—. Mem. ABA, Tex. Bar Assn., Houston Bar Assn. Republican. Methodist. Clubs: Houston Ctr., Century (Houston). Rice U. (founder). Avocations: electronics, video photography, snow skiing, snorkeling, gardening. Securities, General corporate. Home: 12531 Overcup Dr Houston TX 77024 Office: Vinson & Elkins First City Tower Suite 3636 Houston TX 77002

FINCH, NATHAN C., lawyer; b. Los Angeles, Aug. 14, 1909; s. Nathan Swain and Jeannette Cochrane F.; m. Janet Snedden, Feb. 21, 1935; children—Douglas S., James C., Barbara Finch Lawson. A.B., Stanford U., 1931, LL.B., 1934. Bar: Calif. 1934. Assoc. Howe & Finch, Palo Alto, Calif.; ptnr. Finch, Montgomery & Wright, Palo Alto, 1961-79, of counsel, 1979—. Bd. dirs. David and Lucille Packard Found., Monterey Bay Aquarium Found., Watkins-Johnson Co. Mem. Palo Alto Bd. Edn., 1951-61. Recipient Gold Spike award Stanford U., 1980. Mem. ABA, Calif. Bar Assn., Santa Clara County Bar Assn. Republican. Club: Palo Alto. Estate planning, Probate, General practice. Office: 350 Cambridge Ave Suite 178 Palo Alto CA 94306

FINCH, RONALD CORYDON, lawyer; b. Anna, Ill, Apr. 27, 1934; s. Eleazer Corydon and Beulah Mae (Adams) F.; m. Mickey Martin; children: Jennifer, Andrew. B.A., So. Ill. U., 1956; J.D., U. Chgo., 1959. Bar: Ill. 1959, U.S. Dist. Ct. (so. dist.) Ill. 1961, U.S. Ct. Appeals (7th cir.) 1985, U.S. Supreme Ct. 1985. Assoc. Dallstream, Schiff, Hardin, Waite & Dorschel, Chgo., 1959-60; sole practice, Anna, Ill., 1960-87; ptnr., finch & Karraker, P.C., Anna, 1987—. Bd. dirs. Union County Counselling Service, 1979-83, Friends of Morris Library, 1972-73. Mem. Ill. Bar Assn., Ill. Trial Lawyers Assn. Episcopalian. State civil litigation, Banking, General practice. Office: Finch & Karraker PC 402 E Vienna St Anna IL 62906

FINCK, KEVIN WILLIAM, lawyer; b. Whittier, Calif., Dec. 14, 1954; s. William Albert and Ester (Gutbub) F. BA, U. Calif., Santa Barbara, 1977; JD, U. Calif., San Francisco, 1980. Bar: Calif. 1980. Assoc. Law Offices of E.O.C. Ord, San Francisco, 1980-85; ptnr. Ord & Finck, San Francisco, 1985—. Author: California Corporation Start Up Package and Minute Book, 1982, 4th rev. edit. 1987. Republican Methodist. Avocations: hiking, golf, skiing, softball. General corporate, Private international, Securities. Office: Ord & Finck 1 Maritime Plaza #1313 San Francisco CA 94111

FINE, A(RTHUR) KENNETH, lawyer; b. N.Y.C., June 29, 1937; s. Aaron Harry and Rose (Levin) F.; m. Ellen Marie Jensen, July 11, 1964; children—Craig Jensen, Ricki-Barie, Desiree-Ellen. A.B., Hunter coll., 1959; J.D., Columbia U., 1963; C.L.U. cert. Coll. Ins., 1973; diploma Command and Gen. Staff Coll., 1978. Bar: N.Y. 1974. Joined U.S. Army N.G., 1955, advanced through grades to maj., 1973, ret., 1980; cons. U.S. Life Ins. Co., N.Y.C., 1970-74, atty., 1975-78, asst. gen. counsel, 1978; asst. counsel US-LIFE Corp., N.Y.C., 1978-79, assoc. counsel, 1979—. Mem. ABA, N.Y. State Bar Assn. (spl. com. on mil. and veterans affairs), N.Y. County Lawyers Assn. (chmn. com. on corp. law depts. 1981-84), Nat. Guard Assn. U.S., Militia Assn. N.Y. (chmn. vet. officers com. 1981—), Am. Legion (7th regt. post). Republican. Lutheran. Consumer commercial, General corporate, Insurance. Home: 3 Tallman St Staten Island NY 10312 Office: USLIFE Corp 125 Maiden Ln New York NY 10038

FINE, ELEANOR ROSE, lawyer; b. N.Y.C., Dec. 13, 1927; d. Herman and Frances (Morris) Jampole; m. David M. Fine, Dec. 12, 1945 (dec. Oct. 1985); children: Jeannette Morina Clark, Polagaya Deborah Allsop, Seth Aaron. BS in Nursing, U. Wash., 1948, MA, 1970; JD, U. Puget Sound, 1978. Bar: Wash. 1979, U.S. Dist. Ct. (we. dist.) Wash. 1979. Pub. health nurse Seattle-King County, 1948-50; nurse Swedish Hosp., Seattle, 1951-57; nurse emergency room Group Health Hosp., Seattle, 1957-62; nurse hosp. imp. program Fircrest Sch. for Retarded, Seattle, 1962-64; nursing cons., support and legal affairs unit State of Wash., Olympia, 1966-79; sole practice Tacoma, 1980—; legal cons. to editor Nursing Life Mag., Springfield, Ill., 1981—; lectr. health law various univs., western Wash., 1981—. Contbg. editor: Nurses Reference Library, 1984. Bd. dirs. Altrusa, Tacoma, 1982-85, Tacoma Urban League, 1983—; commr. Tacoma Housing Authority, 1983—. U. Wash. fellow, 1951. Mem. ABA, Wash. State Bar Assn., Pierce County Bar Assn. (fitness com.), Smithsonian Inst., Zoo Soc., Sigma Eplison, Phi Delta Phi. Avocation: violin. Health, General practice, Personal injury. Office: 609 Tacoma Ave S Tacoma WA 98402

FINE, LOUIS BERNARD, lawyer; b. Norfolk, Va., Oct. 3, 1904; s. Morris and Mamie (Heller) F.; m. Minnie Snyder, Nov. 12, 1929; children: Morris Heller, Andrew S. LLB, Georgetown U., 1925, LLD (hon.), 1968. Bar: Va. 1924, U.S. Dist. Ct. (ea. and we. dists.) Va. 1944, U.S. Ct. Appeals (4th cir.) 1944, U.S. Supreme Ct. 1944. Sole practice Norfolk; ptnr. Fine, Fine, Legum & Fine, Virginia Beach. Pres. Jewish Family Service of Norfolk, 1950-53; gen. chmn. United Jewish Appeals, 1951. Mem. ABA (com. on pension, welfare and related plans, labor relations law sect. 1974-75), Va. Bar Assn. (com. on domestic relations 1975-76, com. on matrimonial law 1977-78), Norfolk-Portsmouth Bar Assn. (com. on jud. fitness for candidates 1977-78), Va. Trial Lawyers Assn. (bd. govs. 1960, parliamentarian 1960, pres. 1966), The Assn. of Trial Lawyers of Am. (parliamentarian 1954-64); pres. Georgetown U. Alumni Assn. 1966-68; life mem. bd. regents Georgetown U.; bd. visitors Old Dominion U. 1980—. Clubs: Civitans, Townpoint, Harbor, Caviler (Tidewater, Va.). Office: Fine Fine Legum & Fine PC PO Box 61546 Virginia Beach VA 23462

FINE, MICHAEL WILLIAM, lawyer; b. N.Y.C., Jan. 21, 1957; s. Robert George Fine and Marna (Spiegel) Hovine; m. Aneta Ioannidis, Sept. 23, 1984. BA in Polit. Sci., SUNY, Binghamton, 1977; JD, Cleve. State U., 1980. Bar: Ohio 1981, U.S. Dist. Ct. (no. dist.) Ohio 1981. Staff atty. Legal Aid Soc. Lorain County (Ohio), Elyria, 1980-82; staff atty. Hyatt Legal Services, North Olmsted, Ohio, 1982-85, mng. atty., 1985—; comml. arbitrator Am. Arbitration Assn., N.Y., Ohio, 1985—. Mem. ABA, Ohio Bar Assn., Ohio Acad. Trial Lawyers, Tau Epsilon Rho. Democrat. Avocations: body building, photography, tennis. Bankruptcy, Family and matrimonial, Real property. Home: 2840 Northglen Dr Westlake OH 44145 Office: Hyatt Legal Services 4615 Great Northern Blvd North Olmsted OH 44070

FINE, PHIL DAVID, lawyer; b. Brookline, Mass., Aug. 20, 1925; s. Joseph H. and Ann M. (Rosenblum) F.; m. Norma Loew, Dec. 28, 1952; children—Susan Ellen, Lauri Joan Friedman, Debra Jane. Student Northeastern U., Boston, 1942-43. 46-47, Norwich U., 1943—; LL.B., Boston U., 1950; LL.D. (hon.), St. Michael's Coll., 1972. Bar: Mass. 1950, U.S. Dist. Ct. Mass. 1952, U.S. Ct. Appeals (1st cir.) 1952, U.S. Dist. Ct. (D.C. cir.) 1961, U.S. Tax Ct. 1962, U.S. Supreme Ct. 1961. Assoc. Parker Coulter, Daley & White, Boston, 1950-55, ptnr., 1955-57; ptnr. Peabody, Koufman & Brewer, Boston, 1957-59, Fine & Ambrogne, Boston, 1959—. White, Fine & Verville, Washington, 1967—; dep. adminstr. SBA, Washington, 1961-63; cons. Dept. Commerce, Washington, 1964-67; chmn. bd. Commonwealth Nat. Corp., 1969-82, Stadium Realty Trust, 1970-80; Commonwealth Bank & Trust Co., Boston, 1964-82; bd. govs. Mass Gen. Hosp., 1983—; hon. trustee Joslin Diabetes Center, 1983—; trustee Boston U., 1973-78; hon. consul Republic of Costa Rica to Boston; past pub. mem. bd. govs. Boston Stock Exchange. Vice chmn. Housing Authority, Newton, Mass., 1961-63; trustee Pub. Library, Newton, 1964-70; co-chmn. Democratic Congl. Campaign Com., Washington, 1975. Mem. ABA, Mass. Bar Assn. (chmn. corp. law com. 1979-81), Boston Bar Assn. (chmn. banking law com. 1981-83). Democrat. Jewish. Lodge: Mason. Corporate finance, Real property, Federal civil litigation. Home: 3 Charles River Sq Boston MA 02114 Office: Fine & Ambrogne Exchange Pl Boston MA 02109 also: White Fine & Verville 1156 15th St NW Washington DC 20005 Address: PO Box 5 Hartford CT 05047

FINE, RICHARD ISAAC, lawyer; b. Milw., Jan. 22, 1940; s. Jack and Frieda F.; m. Maryellen Olman, Nov. 25, 1982; 1 child, Victoria Elizabeth. B.S., U. Wis., 1961; J.D., U. Chgo., 1964; Ph.D. in Internat. Law, U. London, 1967; cert., Hague (Netherlands) Acad. Internat. Law, 1965, 66; cert. comparative law, Internat. U. Comparative Sci., Luxembourg, 1966; diplome superiere, Faculte Internat. pour l'Ensignment du Droit Compare, Strasbourg, France, 1967. Bar: Ill. 1964, D.C. 1972, Calif. 1973. Trial atty. fgn. commerce sect. antitrust div. Dept. Justice, 1968-72; chief antitrust div. U.S., Los Angeles City Atty.'s Office, also spl. counsel gov. efficiency com., 1973-74; prof. internat., comparative and EEC antitrust law U. Syracuse (N.Y.) Law Sch. (overseas program), summers 1970-72; individual practice Richard I. Fine and Assocs., Los Angeles, 1974; mem. antitrust adv. bd. Bur. Nat. Affairs, 1981—. Contbr. articles to legal publs. Mem. ABA (chmn. subcom. internat. antitrust and trade regulations, internat. law sect. 1972-77, co-chmn. com. internat. econ. orgn. 1977-79), Am. Soc. Internat. Law (co-chmn. com. corp. membership 1978-83, mem. exec. council 1984-87), Am. Fgn. Law Assn., Internat. Law Assn., Brit. Inst. Internat. and Comparative Law, World Peace Through Law Center, State Bar Calif. (chmn. antitrust and trade regulation law sect. 1981-84, exec. com. 1981—), Retinitis Pigmentosa Internat. (bd. dirs. 1985—), Los Angeles County Bar Assn. (chmn. antitrust sect. 1977-78), Ill. Bar Assn., Am. Friends London Sch. Econs. (bd. dirs. 1984—, co-chmn. So. Calif. chpt. 1984—), Phi Delta Phi. Antitrust, Federal civil litigation, State civil litigation. Address: Suite 250 10100 Santa Monica Blvd Los Angeles CA 90067

FINE, ROBERT PAUL, lawyer; b. Buffalo, June 10, 1943; s. Leonard and Sylvia (Wagner) Finkelstein; m. Eileen Joyce Levitsky, Nov. 26, 1967; children—Lisa Robin, Julie Beth. B.A., SUNY-Buffalo, 1965, J.D., 1968. Bar: N.Y. 1968, U.S. dist. ct. (we. dist.) N.Y. 1969, U.S. Tax Ct. 1973, Fla. 1985. Intern, U.S. Dept. Justice, Washington, 1967; law asst. app. div. 4th jud. dept. N.Y. sup. ct., Rochester, 1968-69, chief law asst., 1969-70; assoc. Williams, Stevens, McCarville & Frizzell, P.C., Buffalo, 1970-74, ptnr., 1974-77; co-founder, sr. ptnr. Hurwitz & Fine, P.C., Buffalo, 1977—; participant, panelist Fed. Tax Inst. Western N.Y., 1976-85, chmn. inst., 1978-81; instr. pension planning course Am. Coll. C.L.U.s, 1979-82; instr. SUNY, Buffalo Sch. Mgmt., 1982-83. Bd. dirs. QRS Arts Found., Inc., 1981-82, Jewish Family Service Erie County, 1976-82; bd. dirs. United Jewish Fedn., 1979-84, treas., 1982-84, v.p., 1986—; trustee Theodore Roosevelt Inaugural Site Found., 1980-83; chmn. exec. bd. Western N.Y. Israel Bonds Orgn., 1980-82; mem. dean search com. SUNY, Buffalo, 1986—. Mem. ABA, N.Y. State Bar Assn., Erie County Bar Assn. (chmn. tax com. 1978-81, chmn. corp. law com. 1981-84, bd. dirs. 1985—), Fin. Planning Counselors Western N.Y. (v.p.), Estate Analysts Western N.Y., Nat. Health Lawyers Assn., SUNY Sch. Law Alumni Assn. (pres. 1976-77). Democrat. Clubs: Mid-Day of Buffalo; Westwood Country (Williamsville, N.Y.). General corporate, Pension, profit-sharing, and employee benefits, Probate.

FINE, THOMAS FLEMING, lawyer; b. Beverly, Mass., Nov. 30, 1949; s. Jacob Harold and Katherine (Fleming) F.; m. Patricia Anne Maffeo, May 22, 1983. BA, Duke U., 1971; JD, Boston U., 1974. Bar: Tenn. 1975. U.S. Dist. Ct. (ea. dist.) Tenn. 1975, U.S. Ct. Appeals (5th and 6th cirs.) 1976, U.S. Ct. Appeals (11th cir.) 1981. Law clk. to presiding justice U.S. Dist. Ct. (no. dist.) Ala., Birmingham, 1974-75; staff atty. TVA, Knoxville, Tenn., 1975-86, sr. litigation atty., 1986—. Mem. ABA, Am. Corp. Counsel Assn. (chpt. pres. 1986—). Federal civil litigation, Labor. Office: TVA 400 W Summit Hill Dr Knoxville TN 37901

FINE, TIMOTHY HERBERT, lawyer; b. Washington, Oct. 11, 1937; s. Nathan and Emily Newhall (Brown) F.; m. Mary Ellen Fox, June 16, 1960; children: Margaret Carol, Susan Emily, Rachel Winslow. B.E.E., U. Va., 1959; M.S. in E.E., U. So. Calif., 1962; LL.B., U. Calif.-Berkeley, 1965. Bar: Calif. 1966, U.S. Dist. Ct. (no., ea. and cen. dists.) Calif. 1966, U.S. Ct. Appeals (9th cir.) 1966, U.S. Supreme Ct. 1971. Law clk. to Hon. William T. Sweigert, U.S. Dist. Judge, San Francisco, 1965-67; assoc. G. Joseph Bertain, Jr., San Francisco, 1967-77; prin. Law Offices of Timothy H. Fine, San Francisco, 1977—; del. White House Conf. Small Bus., 1980, chmn. No. Calif. delegation, 1986; del. Calif. State Confs. Small Bus., 1980, 82, 84, 86, 1st v.p., 1984-86; chmn. San Francisco Bay Area Small Bus. Caucus, 1984, Small Bus. Legal Def. Com., 1982—; author, lectr., cons., trial atty. on antitrust, franchise and small bus. legal matters.; mem. nat. adv. council U.S. Senate Small Bus. Com., 1983—; mem. adv. bd. Calif. Senate Select Com. Small Bus., 1983—; mem. Calif. Bd. Registration Profl. Engrs., 1982-86. Bd. dirs. Boalt Hall Law Sch. Alumni Assn., 1983-86; nat. advisor drafting com. Uniform Franchise and Bus. Oppurtunites Act, 1985—. Served to lt. USAF, 1959-62. Mem. ABA (mem. governing bd., forum com. on franchising 1977-84, chmn. 1983 forum on franchising, mem. gov. bd. standing com. on specialization 1986—, nat. advisor drafting com. on Uniform Franchise and Bus. Opportunities Act 1985—), Fed. Bar Assn., State Bar of Calif., The Bar Assn. San Francisco, Lawyers Club of San Francisco. Antitrust, Franchising, Federal civil litigation. Home: 747 San Diego Rd Berkeley CA 94707 Office: 49 Geary St Suite 450 San Francisco CA 94108

FINEBERG, DAVID L(EMAN), lawyer; b. Hartford, Conn., Nov. 21, 1931; s. Morris W. and Ida (Leman) F.; m. Barbara E. Gold, Sept. 5, 1955; children—Marcia E., Diane E., Laura E. B.A., Colgate U., 1953; LL.B., Columbia U., 1956. Bar: Conn. 1956, Fla. 1976. With Schatz & Schatz, Hartford, 1956-76; mem. firm Albrecht & Richman, Hartford, 1976-77; ptnr., Moller, Horton & Fineberg, P.C., Hartford, 1978—. Mem. town council Town of Bloomfield, Conn., 1965-67, chmn. charter revision com. 1969-70; v.p., legal counsel Conn. Opera Assn., Hartford, 1972-83. Harlan Fiske Stone scholar 1956. Mem. ABA, Conn. Bar Assn., Fla. Bar Assn., Hartford County Bar Assn. Banking, Bankruptcy, Contracts commercial. Home: 49 Hurdle Fence Dr Avon CT 06001 Office: 90 Gillett St Hartford CT 06105

FINEMAN, S. DAVID, lawyer; b. Phila., Oct. 23, 1945. B.A., Am. U., 1967; J.D. with honors, George Washington U., 1970. Bar: Pa. 1971, U.S. Dist. Ct. (ea. dist.) Pa. Trial atty. Defender Assn., Phila., 1971-72; law clk. Superior Ct. Commonwealth Pa., 1972-73; mng. ptnr. Hunt & Fineman, Phila., 1981—. Instr. bus. law Temple U., 1974-83. Bd. dirs. Help Inc., Phila., 1976-81. Mem. Phila. Bar Assn., Pa. Bar Assn., Pa. State Trial Lawyers Assn., Def. Research Inst. General practice, Legal education. Home: 8233 Seminole St Philadelphia PA 19118 Office: 1608 Walnut St 19th Floor Philadelphia PA 19103

FINERTY, MARGARET JOAN, lawyer; b. Chgo., June 6, 1953; d. Martin James and Elaine Beatrice (Wolniewicz) F.; m. Neil Victor Getnick, May 21, 1978. BA, U. Chgo., 1975; JD, Cornell U., 1978. Bar: N.Y. 1979. Asst. dist. atty. N.Y. County, N.Y.C., 1978—; dep. bur. chief trial bur., sr. trial counsel, 1985—. Mem. N.Y. County Lawyers Assn. (criminal law com.). Criminal. Office: NY County Dist Atty 1 Hogan Place New York NY 10013

FINESILVER, SHERMAN GLENN, judge; b. Denver, Oct. 1, 1927; s. Harry M. and Rebecca M. (Balaban) F.; m. Annette Warren, July 23, 1954; children: Jay Mark, Steven Brad, Susan Lynn. B.A., U. Colo., 1949; LL.B., U. Denver, 1952; certificate, Northwestern U. Traffic Inst., 1956; LL.D. (hon.), Gallaudet Coll., Washington, 1970. Bar: Colo. bar 1952, also U.S. Supreme Ct 1952, U.S. Ct. of Appeals 1952, 10th Circuit, U.S. Dist. Ct., Colo 1952. Legal asst. Denver City Atty.'s Office, 1949-52; asst. Denver city atty. 1952-55; judge Denver County Ct., 1955-62; judge Denver Dist. Ct., 2d Jud. Dist., 1962-71, presiding judge domestic relations div., 1963, 67, 68; judge U.S. Dist. Ct., Denver, 1971—; Faculty Denver Opportunity Sch., 1949-54, U. Denver Coll. Law and Arts and Sci. Sch., 1955—; Faculty Westminster Law Sch., 1955-61, Nat. Coll. Judiciary, Reno, 1967—, Atty. Gen.'s Advocacy Inst., Washington, 1974—, seminars for new fed. judges, 1974—; cons. HEW, 1958-62. Author: Model Law for Interpreters in Court Proceedings, 1968, Protect Your Life-Wise Words for Women, 1969, Timely Tips When Disaster Strikes-No Second Chance, 1970; Contbr.: chpt. to Epilepsy Rehabilitation, 1974; Editor: chpt. to Proceedings Nat. Symposium on the Deaf, Driving and Employability, 1964; Contbg. editor: chpt. to Lawyers Coop. Pub. Co, Rochester, N.Y., 1958-60, Teaching Driver and Traffic Safety Education, 1965; Contbr. articles to profl. jours. Founder Denver Driver Improvement Sch., 1959, dir., 1959-71; chmn. Denver Citizenship Day, 1967; organizer Denver Youth Council, 1968; dir. leadership conf. Neighborhood Youth Corps, 1969; mem. Pres.'s Task Force on Hwy. Safety, 1969-71; mem. advisory com. Nat. Hwy. Traffic Safety Adminstrn., Dept. Transp., 1969-72; mem. task force White House Conf. on Aging, 1972; chmn. Gov.'s Adv. Com. on Hwy. Safety, 1960-71; commr. Gov.'s Commn. on Aging, 1967-71; mem. nat. youth commn. B'nai B'rith, 1970-74; Pres. Jewish Family and Childrens Service of Colo., 1962-64; bd. dirs. Nat. Council Orgns. Serving Deaf, Washington, 1968-71; trustee Am. Med. Center, Denver, 1960-72. Decorated Knight Comdr. Ct. of Honor K.C., Rocky Mountain Consistory, 1967; recipient numerous awards including citation Nat. Safety Council, 1958, Paul Gray Hoffman award Automotive Safety Found., 1960, spl. award N.Am. Judges Assn., merit award Colo. Assn. Deaf and Nat. Soc. Deaf, 1966, Service to Mankind award Denver Sertoma Club, 1969, Freedoms Found. award, 1969, medallion for outstanding service by a non-handicapped person to physically disabled Nat. Paraplegia Found., 1972, certificate of commendation Sec. Transp., 1974, numerous others. Mem. ABA (nat. chmn. Am. citizenship com. 1968, award of merit Law Day 1968), Colo. Bar Assn. (chmn. Law Day 1964, chmn. Am. citizenship com. 1963), Denver Bar Assn. (chmn. Law Day 1964), Am. Judicature Soc., Hebrew Ednl. Alliance, Allied Jewish Community Council, Phi Sigma Delta (trustee 1960-66); mem. B'nai B'rith. Clubs: Mason (Shriner), Am. Amateur Radio. Jurisprudence. Office: US Dist Ct Room C-236 US Courthouse 1929 Stout St Denver CO 80294 *

FINESTEIN, RUSSELL MARK, lawyer; b. Bklyn., Jan. 10, 1956; s. Norman and Claire M. (Bogitsh) F.; m. Eve F. Ozimek, Aug. 20, 1978; children: Sara, Daniel. BS in Commerce with distinction, U. Va., 1978; JD cum laude, U. Mich., 1981. Bar: N.J. 1981, U.S. Dist. Ct. N.J. 1981, Fla. 1984. Assoc. McCarter & English, Newark, 1981-85; ptnr. Nochimson, Schablik, Kessler & Finestein, Livingston, N.J., 1985—; bd. dirs. WP Inc., Media, Pa. Coach soccer Woodbridge (N.J.) Little League, 1982; v.p., bd. dirs. Aspen Manor Condominium Assn., Woodbridge, 1982-83. Echols scholar U. Va., 1975. Mem. ABA, N.J. Bar Assn., Essex County Bar Assn., Beta Gamma Sigma. Republican. Jewish. Avocations: tennis, skiing. Real property, Contracts commercial, Banking. Home: 973 Cherokee Ct Westfield NJ 07090 Office: Nochimson Schablik Kessler & Finestein 293 Eisenhower Pkwy Livingston NJ 07039

FINGER, JOHN HOLDEN, lawyer; b. Oakland, Calif., June 29, 1913; s. Clyde P. and Jennie (Miller) F.; m. Dorothy C. Riley, Dec. 30, 1950; children: Catherine, John Jr., David, Carol. A.B., U. Calif., 1933. Bar: Calif. 1937. Pvt. practice of law San Francisco, 1937-42; chief mil. commn. sect. Far East Hdqrs. War Dept., Tokyo, 1946-47; mem. firm Hoberg Finger Brown Cox & Molligan, San Francisco, 1947—; adv. bd. Central Savs. & Loan Assn.; Trustee Pacific Sch. Religion, bd. chmn., 1969-78; bd. dirs. Calif. Maritime Acad., San Francisco Legal Aid Soc., 1955-70; bd. visitors Judge Adv. Gen. Sch., Charlottesville, Va., 1964-76, Stanford U. Law Sch., 1969-71. Pres. Laymen's Fellowship, No. Calif. Conf. Congl. Chs., 1951-53, moderator, 1954-55. Served to maj. JAGC AUS, 1942-46; col. Res. ret.; comdg. officer 5th Judge Adv. Gen. Detachment, 1962-64; U.S. Army Judiciary, 1967-68. Decorated Legion of Merit. Fellow Am. Bar Found., Am. Coll. Trial Lawyers; mem. Am. Judicature Soc., Am. Bar Assn. (ho. of dels. 1970-78, council jud. adminstrn. div. 1972-77, standing com. assn. communications), Bar Assn. San Francisco (dir. 1960-62, recipient John A. Sutro award for legal excellence 1980), Judge Adv. Assn. (dir. 1957—, pres. 1964-65), Lawyers Club San Francisco (pres. 1953, dir. 1950—), State Bar Calif. (bd. govs. 1965-68, pres. 1967-68), Sierra Club (exec. com. legal def. fund), Phi Alpha Delta, Sigma Phi Epsilon, Alpha Kappa Phi. State civil litigation, Personal injury. Home: 12675 Skyline Blvd Oakland CA 94619 Office: Hoberg Finger et al 703 Market St San Francisco CA 94103

FINGERMAN, ALBERT ROSS, lawyer; b. Cin., Sept. 29, 1920; s. Louis and Freda (Skyletsky) F.; m. Shirley Eskind, June 2, 1946; children—Naomi Osher, David, Joel, Jeremy. LL.B., U. Cin., 1948. Bar: Ohio 1948, U.S. Supreme Ct. 1955. Assoc. Schmidt, Effron, Josselson & Weber, Cin., 1970-83; ptnr. Fingerman, Guckenberger & Assocs., Cin., 1983—; chmn. bd. trustees Ohio Legal Services Fund, Inc.; guest instr. U. Cin. Law Sch., Chase Coll. Law, No. Ky. State Coll. Chmn. Woodward High Sch. Alumnal Endowment Fund. Served with USAAF, 1941-45. Decorated Air medal. Mem. ABA (past mem. bar pres. sect.), Ohio Bar Assn. (past com. chmn.), Cin. Bar Assn. (past pres.), Lawyers Club Cin. Mem. B'nai B'rith (past pres. Cin.). General practice, Criminal, Family and matrimonial. Office: 524 Walnut St Suite 700 Cincinnati OH 45202

FINGERMAN, MICHAEL ELLIOTT, lawyer; b. Phila., July 11, 1952; s. David and Isabele (Lipoff) F.; m. Wendy Segal, June 19, 1976. BA, Emory U., 1974; JD, Villanova U., 1977. Bar: Pa. 1977. Assoc. Astor, Weiss and Newman, Phila., 1977-79, Pepper, Hamilton and Sheetz, Phila., 1979-82, Hamberg and Rubin, Lansdale, Pa., 1982-84; ptnr. Shainberg & Fingerman, Phila., 1984—; lectr. Temple U., Phila., 1986, Pa. Bar Inst., Phila., 1984-86. Contbr. articles to profl. jours. atty. Support Ctr. for Child Advs., Phila., 1979-82. Fellow Am. Acad. Matrimonial Lawyers; mem. ABA (Family Law sect. 1977—), Pa. Bar Assn. (lectr. 1982-86), Phila. Bar Assn. (chmn. Family Law sect. 1983). Family and matrimonial. Office: Shainberg & Fingerman 1500 Walnut St Suite 300 Philadelphia PA 19102

FINK, JANET ROSE, lawyer, consultant; b. N.Y.C., May 10, 1950; d. Karl K. and Sona (Holman) F. AB, Bryn Mawr Coll., 1971; JD, Georgetown U., 1974. Bar: N.Y. 1975, U.S. Dist. Ct. (so. and ea. dists.) N.Y. 1977, U.S. Ct. Appeals (2d cir.) 1978, U.S. Supreme Ct. 1980. Fellow Met. Applied Research Ctr., N.Y.C., 1970-71; research intern Urban Inst., Washington, 1972-73, Russel Sage Found., N.Y.C., 1974-75; atty. family ct. and spl. litigation units Legal Aid Soc., N.Y.C., 1974-79, dir. spl. litigation unit, 1979-84, asst. atty. in charge juvenile rights div., 1984—; bd. dirs. N.Y. Coalition for Juvenile Justice and Youth Services, N.Y.C., Nat. Ctr. for Youth Law; cons. juvenile justice Harvard U., 1984-86; mem. adv. com. appellate div. Family Ct., 1984—; lectr. various agys. Contbr. articles to profl. jours. mem. task force Citizens Com. for Children, N.Y.C., 1984—. Mem. ABA (editorial bd. Criminal Justice Jour., vice chmn. juvenile justice subcommitte 1986—), Assn. Bar of City of N.Y. (family ct. com. 1979-82, legal asst. com. 1982-85, children and law com. 1985—, family ct. coms. 1985—), NLADA (steering com. juvenile justice sect. 1978—). Juvenile, Civil rights, Legislative. Office: Juvenile Rights Div Legal Aid Soc 15 Park Row 21 Floor New York NY 10038

FINK, JOSEPH LESLIE, III, law educator; b. Altoona, Pa., May 27, 1947; s. J. Leslie Jr. and Drucie Mardell (Stover) F.; m. Maureen Mae Malaney, Aug. 12, 1972; children: Joseph Leslie IV, Jonathan Morgan. BS in Pharmacy, Phila. Coll. Pharmacy and Sci., 1970; JD, Georgetown U., 1973. Bar: Pa. 1973, U.S. Dist. Ct. (ea. dist.) Pa. 1973, U.S. Ct. Appeals (3d cir.) 1973, U.S. Supreme Ct. 1977. From asst. prof. to prof. Phila. Coll. Pharmacy and Sci., 1973-81; exec. dir. Del. Pharm. Soc., Wilmington, 1976-78; asst. dean, prof. pharm. law U. Ky., Lexington, 1981—. Author: Manager's Guide to Third Party Programs, 1983; editor: Pharmacy Law Digest, 1981—; contbr. numerous articles to research and profl. jours. Named to Nat. Fink Hall of Fame, Finks Internat., 1980; recipient Great Tchr. award U. Ky. Alumni Assn., 1984; Am. Council on Edn. fellow, 1985-86. Fellow Am. Soc. for Pharmacy Law (Pres. award 1984); mem. ABA, Am. Pharm. Assn., Am. Assn. Colls. Pharmacy, Ky. Bar Assn. Republican. Presbyterian. Avocations: gardening, household projects. Health, Pharmacy law, Food and drug. Home and Office: 2009 Ermine Ct Lexington KY 40513-1008

FINK, MONROE, lawyer; b. Bklyn., June 4, 1925; s. William Samuel and Regina (Flusser) F.; m. Lauretta Lubin, Nov. 25, 1948; children—Karl, Sarah, Susan, Regina; m. 2d, Patricia Hunt, May 29, 1965; 1 son, Jonathan. A.B., U. Mich., 1945; J.D., U. Mich., 1947; LL.M., NYU, 1978. Bar: N.Y. 1948. Assoc. Hawkins, Delafield & Wood, N.Y.C., 1947-52; with Weldon Mfg. Corp., 1952-54; assoc. Wood, Wilklow & Ritter, Hempstead, N.Y., 1955, John L. Molloy, Westbury, N.Y., 1956-58; sole practice, Glen Cove, N.Y., 1958—; atty. of record N.Y. State Tax Commn. for Nassau County, 1959-74; ofcl. referee 2d dept. Appellate Div., 1974-78; counsel Glen Cove Housing Authority, 1957-76; dist. clk. North Shore Sch. Dist., 1977—. Bd. zoning appeals, Town of Oyster Bay, 1982—; bd. dirs. L.I. Philharm., 1960-67, L.I. Symphony, 1973-79, N.Y. Virtuosi, 1984. Mem. Nassau County Bar Assn., N.Y. Bar Assn. Republican. Jewish. Clubs: Bklyn., Beaver Dam Winter Sports, Hempstead Harbour. Lodge: Kiwanis. Probate, Estate taxation, State and local taxation.

FINK, NORMAN STILES, lawyer, educational adminstrator; b. Easton, Pa., Aug. 13, 1926; s. Herman and Yetta (Hyman) F.; m. Helen Mullen, Sept. 1, 1956; children—Hayden Michael, Patricia Carol. A.B., Dartmouth Coll., 1947; J.D., Harvard U., 1950. Bar: N.Y. 1951, U.S. Dist. Ct. (ea. and so. dists.) N.Y. 1954, U.S. Supreme Ct. 1964. Mem. legal staff Remington Rand, Inc., N.Y.C., Washington, 1949-54; ptnr. Lans & Fink, N.Y.C., 1954-68; counsel devel. program U. Pa., Phila., 1969-80; v.p. devel. and univ.

relations Brandeis U., Waltham, Mass., 1980-81; dep. v.p. devel. and alumni relations, assoc. gen. counsel devel. Columbia U., N.Y.C., 1981—. Served with U.S. Army, 1945-46. Recipient Alice Beeman award for excellence in devel. Writing Council Advancement and Support of Edn.; Lilly Endowment grantee, 1979-80. Mem. ABA (mem. com. on exempt orgns. sect. taxation), Council Advancement and Support Edn., Nat. Assn. Coll. and Univ. Attys. (com. on taxation), Am. Arbitration Assn. (panelist), Am. Council Edn. (com. on taxation), Nat. Assn. Ind. Colls. and Univs. (com. on taxation), N.Y. County Lawyers Assn., Assn. Bar City N.Y., Harvard Law Sch. Assn., Nat. Soc. Fund Raising Execs. Democrat. Jewish. Clubs: Nat. Lawyers (Washington); University (N.Y.C.). Editor: Deferred Giving Handbook, 1977; author: (with Howard C. Metzler) The Costs and Benefits of Deferred Giving, 1982. Legal education, Estate planning, Personal income taxation. Home: Valeria #64 Furnace Dock Rd Peekskill NY 10566 Office: Columbia U Central Mail Room PO Box 400 New York NY 10027

FINK, ROBERT STANLEY, lawyer; b. Los Angeles, Aug. 7, 1947; s. Irving I. and Ruth (Alexander) F.; m. Linda Teresa Romero, Aug. 23, 1975; children—James A., David A. A.A., Los Angeles Valley Coll., 1968; B.A., Calif. State U.-Northridge, 1970; J.D., Whittier Coll., 1974. Bar: Calif. 1975, U.S. Dist. Ct. (cen. dist.) Calif. 1980. Assoc., Erwin Sobel Law Offices, Los Angeles, 1975-78, Richard Dunsay, Los Angeles, 1978-81; sole practice Los Angeles, 1981—. Bd. dirs. Ctr. Improvement Child Care, Los Angeles, 1984—. Mem. Los Angeles Trial Lawyers Assn. (bd. govs. 1984-85), Calif. Trial Lawyers Assn. Federal civil litigation, Insurance, Personal injury. Office: 6404 Wilshire Blvd Suite 1001 Los Angeles CA 90048

FINK, ROBERT STEVEN, lawyer; writer; b. Bklyn., Dec. 7, 1943; s. Samuel Miles and Helen Leah (Bogen) F.; m. Abby Deutsch, Mar. 20, 1980; children—Juliet Leah, Robin Rachel. Diploma, U. Vienna, 1962; B.A., Bklyn. Coll., 1965; J.D., N.Y. U., 1968, LL.M., 1973. Bar: N.Y. 1969, U.S. Dist. Ct. (so. dist.) N.Y. 1970, U.S. Dist. Ct. (ea. dist.) N.Y. 1970, U.S. Dist. Ct. (we. dist.) N.Y. 1975, U.S. Dist. Ct. (no. dist.) N.Y. 1985, U.S. Tax Ct. 1970, U.S. Ct. Apls. (2d cir.) 1970, U.S. Sup. Ct. 1972, U.S. Ct. Claims 1984. Assoc. Kostelanetz & Ritholz, N.Y.C., 1968-75, ptnr. Kostelanetz, Ritholz, Tigue & Fink, 1975—; lectr. in field; expert witness IRS; mem. adv. com. tax div. Dept. Justice; adj. prof. law NYU. Mem. ABA (chmn. com. civil and criminal tax penalties 1983-85, chmn. task force for revision of tax penalties 1982), N.Y. State Bar Assn. (chmn. com. criminal and civil tax penalties 1982-85, chmn. compliance and unreported income 1985-87 , chmn. commodities and fin. futures 1987—), Fed. Bar Assn., N.Y. County Lawyers Assn., Assn. Bar City N.Y., Am. Arbitration Assn. (arbitrator 1973—). Author: Tax Fraud: Audits, Investigations, Prosecutions, 2 vols., 1980, 2d rev. edition, 1986; Co-author: How to Defend Yourself Against the IRS, 1985, You Can Protect Yourself form the IRS, 1987; contbr. numerous articles in field to profl. jours. Litigation, Taxation, White collar criminal defense. Office: 80 Pine St New York NY 10005

FINK, ROSALIND SUE, lawyer, university administrator; b. Cleve., May 24, 1946; d. Sanford and Bess (Tiktin) F.; m. Robert Cannel Herz, Feb. 4, 1979; 1 child, Zachary Robert. A.B., Barnard Coll., 1968; J.D., Yale U., 1972. Bar: N.Y. 1973, U.S. Dist. Ct. (so. dist.) N.Y., 1973, U.S. Ct. Appeals (2d cir.) 1975, U.S. Supreme Ct., 1977. Assoc. Proskauer Rose Goetz & Mendelsohn, N.Y.C., 1972-74, Dretzin & Kauff, P.C., N.Y.C., 1974-75; asst. atty. gen. N.Y. State Dept. Law, N.Y.C., 1975-80; dir. Office Equal Opportunity and Affirmative Action, Columbia U., N.Y.C., 1980—. Exec. bd. Barnard Coll. Women's Ctr., N.Y.C., 1980-84; chair subcom. Handicapped Accessability of Local Adv. Com. for 150th Annual Meeting AAAS, Washington, 1983-84; staff Am. Council Edn. Task Force on Affirmative Action, Washington, 1981-83. Mem. N.Y. County Lawyers' Assn. (bd. dirs. 1982—, spl. bd. com. programs and pub. issues 1985—, com. women's rights 1973—, chair 1981-84, house com. 1983—, word processing com. 1982-84), Assn. Bar City of N.Y. (civil rights com. 1980-83, edn. com. 1985—), Nat. Assn. Coll. and Univ. Attys. (vice chmn. affirmative action and nondiscrimination section 1983-84, chmn. 1984—, program com. 1985-86). Democrat. Jewish. Civil rights, Federal civil litigation, Labor. Office: Columbia U 305 Low Meml Library 116th St & Broadway New York NY 10027

FINK, SALLY CLAIRE, lawyer; b. Detroit, Mar. 16, 1942; d. Harry and Lillian (Roth) F.; m. Stephen G. Josephson, May 1, 1977. BA, U. Mich., 1964; JD, Wayne State U., 1974. Bar: Mich. 1974, U.S. Dist. Ct. (ea. dist.) Mich. 1974. Asst. pub. defender Washtenaw County, Ann Arbor, Mich., 1974-77; ptnr. Josephson & Fink, Ann Arbor, 1977—; hearing panelist Mich. Atty. Discipline Bd., 1987—; speaker Nat. Conf. on Women and the Law, Washington, 1983. Bd. dirs. Domestic Violence Project, Ann Arbor, 1979-86. Recipient Susan B. Anthony NOW award, 1979. Mem. Mich. Bar Assn., Washtenaw County Bar Assn., Assn. Trial Lawyers Am. (v.p. Washtenaw County chpt. 1984-85), Mich. Women Lawyers Assn. (regional dir. 1980-81), Am. Arbitration Assn., Nat. Lawyers Guild. Democrat. Jewish. General practice, Family and matrimonial, Civil rights. Office: Josephson & Fink 201 E Liberty St Ann Arbor MI 48104

FINK, SCOTT ALAN, lawyer; b. Aurora, Ill., Sept. 18, 1953; s. Harold Lawrence and Lois (Franch) F.; m. Kathy Ellen Klein, May 14, 1978; 1 child, Lindsay Klein. AB, Stanford U., 1974; JD, U. Mich., 1978. Bar: Calif. 1978, U.S. Dist. Ct. (no. dist.) Calif. 1978, U.S. Ct. Appeals 9th cir.) 1981, U.S. Supreme Ct. 1985. Assoc. Heller, Ehrman, White & McAuliffe, San Francisco, 1978-84, ptnr., 1984—. Securities, Federal civil litigation, Accountant liability. Office: Heller Ehrman White & McAuliff 333 Bush St San Francisco CA 94104

FINKE, ROBERT FORGE, lawyer; b. Chgo., Mar. 11, 1941; s. Robert Frank and Helen Theodora (Forge) F. A.B., U. Mich., 1963; J.D., Harvard U., 1966. Bar: Ill. 1966, U.S. Dist. Ct. (no. dist.) Ill. 1966, U.S. Ct. Appeals (4th and 6th cirs.) 1982, U.S. Ct. Appeals (7th cir.) 1966, U.S. Ct. Appeals (9th cir.) 1980, U.S. Supreme Ct. 1970. Law clk., 1966-67; assoc. firm Mayer, Brown & Platt, Chgo., 1967-71, ptnr., 1972—. Bd. dirs. Lyric Opera Guild; assoc. Rush Presbyterian St. Luke's Med. Ctr. Mem. ABA (sects. litigation, antitrust, legal edn. and admissions to the bar, vice chmn. 1974-75, corp., banking and bus. law sect.), Law Club Chgo., Legal Club Chgo. Clubs: University, Economic (Chgo.). Antitrust, Federal civil litigation, General corporate. Address: 190 S LaSalle St Chicago IL 60603

FINKEL, GERALD MICHAEL, lawyer; b. N.Y.C., July 29, 1941; s. Abraham B. and Elizabeth B. (Michaels) F.; m. Beverly Lynne Jaffee, Aug. 26, 1962; children: Bruce Daniel, Judith Michelle. B.A., NYU, 1962; J.D., U. S.C., 1970. Bar: S.C. 1970, U.S. Dist. Ct. S.C. 1970, U.S. Ct. Appeals (4th cir.) 1973, U.S. Supreme Ct. 1973, D.C. 1973. Prin. Finkel, Georgaklis, Goldberg, Sheftman and Korn, P.A., Columbia, S.C., 1970—; adj. prof. trial advocacy U. S.C.; mem. faculty fed. trial practice AM. Law Inst., ABA; lectr. S.C. Bar, S.C. Trial Lawyers Assn., Richland County Bar and Profl. Insts.; spl. judge Richland County Family Ct., 1974-78, Ct. Gen. Sessions 5th Jud. Cir., 1976. Author: (with Ralph C. McCullough II) A Guide to South Carolina Torts, 1st edit., 1981, 2d edit., 1986. Hearing officer S.C. Dept. Health and Environ. Control, 1979-82; mem. S.C. Appellate Def. Commn., 1982-83, Gov.'s Sentencing Guidelines Commn., 1982-83. Served to capt. U.S. Army, 1962-67. Recipient Outstanding Alumni cert. Phi Alpha Delta, 1972. Mem. ABA, S.C. Bar Assn. (bd. of govs. 1985—), Richland County Bar Assn., Am. Judicature Soc., Assn. Trial Lawyers Am., Am. Law Inst., S.C. Trial Lawyers Assn. (pres. 1982-83), Phi Alpha Delta (dist. justice 1976-78). Democrat. Jewish. Federal civil litigation, General corporate, Contracts commercial. Office: Finkel Georgaklis et al PO Box 1799 Columbia SC 29202

FINKELSTEIN, ALLEN LEWIS, lawyer; b. N.Y.C., Mar. 19, 1943; s. David and Ella (Miller) F.; m. Judith Elaine Stutman, June 20, 1964 (div. Mar. 1980); children: Jill, Jennifer; m. Shelley Gail Barone, June 15, 1980; 1 child, Amanda. BS, NYU, 1964; JD, Bklyn. Law Sch., 1967; MBA, Long Island U., 1969. Bar: N.Y. 1968, U.S. Dist. Ct. (ea. and so. dists.) N.Y. 1973, U.S. Ct. Appeals (2d cir.) 1973, U.S. Supreme Ct. 1976, U.S. Tax Ct. 1979. Sr. ptnr. Finkelstein, Bruckman, Wohl, Most & Rothman and predecessor firms, N.Y.C., 1986—; assoc. prof. Long Island U., N.Y.C., 1969-73, adj. prof. 1973-74; bd. dirs. Amotrophic Lateral Sclerosis Assn., Myser Found. Fund. Mem. dem. adv. com. N.Y. State Senate, N.Y.C., 1985-86. Mem. ABA (family law sect.), N.Y. State Bar Assn., Assn. of Bar of City of N.Y., Queens County Bar Assn. Jewish. Lodge: Masons. Real property, General corporate, Family and matrimonial. Home: 425 E 63rd St New York NY 10021 Office: Finkelstein Bruckman Wohl et al 801 2d Ave New York NY 10017

FINKELSTEIN, ANITA JO, lawyer; b. Cleve., Jan. 2, 1957; d. Denis and Helen (Graber) Fabian; m. Ben Finkelstein, Mar. 20, 1983. BA in Econs. and Bus. Adminstrn., Wittenberg U., 1979; JD, Yale U., 1982. Bar: D.C. 1982; CPA, Ill. Assoc. Shaw, Pittman, Potts & Trowbridge, Washington, 1982—. General corporate, Securities. Home: 4434 Garrison St NW Washington DC 20016 Office: Shaw Pittman Potts & Trowbridge 2300 N St NW Washington DC 20037

FINKELSTEIN, BERNARD, lawyer; b. N.Y.C., Jan. 21, 1930; s. Irving and Sadie (Katz) F.; m. Adele S. Levine, June 29, 1952; children: Sharon Ann, Marcia Lyn. B.A., NYU, 1951; LL.B., Yale U., 1954. Bar: N.Y. 1954, D.C. 1970. Assoc. Paul, Weiss, Rifkind, Wharton & Garrison, N.Y.C., 1956-64, ptnr., 1965—; mem. wills and trusts adv. com. Practicing Law Inst. Trustee Altman Found., N.Y.C., 1985—. Fellow Am. Coll. Probate Counsel; mem. ABA (chmn. com. on pre-death planning, probate and trust div. of sect. on real property, probate and trust law 1985—), N.Y. State Bar Assn. (chmn. gift and tax com.- tax sect. 1978-80), Assn. of Bar of City of N.Y. (trusts, estate and surrogate's ct. com. 1986—), N.Y. Bar Found., Yale Law Sch. Assn. (exec. com. 1983-86), Phi Beta Kappa, Phi Alpha Delta, Order of Coif. Club: Elmwood Country (White Plains, N.Y.). General corporate, Estate planning, Probate. Home: 1 Tory Ln Scarsdale NY 10583 Office: Paul Weiss Rifkind Wharton & Garrison 1285 Ave of Americas New York NY 10019

FINKELSTEIN, IRA ALLEN, lawyer; b. N.Y.C., Oct. 7, 1946; s. Louis and Lillian (Reiser) F.; m. Madelyn Kay Hoffman, May 30, 1982; 1 dau., Sarah Rebekah. B.A., CCNY, 1967; J.D., Harvard U., 1972. Bar: N.Y. 1974, U.S. Supreme Ct. 1978, U.S. Ct. Appeals (2d cir.) 1976, U.S. Dist. Ct. (ea. dist.) N.Y., 1975, U.S. Dist. Ct. (so. dist.) N.Y. 1976. Assoc. firm Cahill, Gordon & Reindel, N.Y.C., 1972-81; assoc. firm Tenzer, Greenblatt, Fallon & Kaplan, N.Y.C., 1981-83, ptnr., 1983—. Mem. Harvard Law Rev. 1970-72. Mem. ABA, Fed. Bar Council, N.Y. State Bar Assn., Assn. Bar City N.Y., Democrat. Federal civil litigation, State civil litigation, Antitrust. Office: Tenzer Greenblatt Fallon & Kaplan 405 Lexington Ave New York NY 10174

FINKELSTEIN, JOSEPH JUDAH, lawyer; b. Melbourne, Australia, Feb. 15, 1952; came to U.S., 1952; s. Leo and Sylvia (Zubovsky) F.; m. Wendy Ehrenreich, Sept. 22, 1974; children: Tami, Jason, Lisa, Michael. BA cum laude, Wayne State U., 1971; JD, Detroit U., 1974. Bar: Mich. 1975, Fla. 1975, U.S. Dist. Ct. (so. dist.) Mich. 1975, U.S. Supreme Ct. 1978, U.S. Ct. Appeals (5th cir.) 1978. Ptnr. Pelzner, Schwedock, Finkelstein & Klausner, Miami, Fla., 1974—. Bd. dirs. Greater Miami Hebrew Acad., Miami Beach, Fla., 1975—, Beth-El Hebrew Acad. Cong. Toras Emes Acad., 1984—. Mem. ABA, Fla. Bar Assn., Mich. Bar Assn., Dade County Bar Assn., Assn. Trial Lawyers Am., Phi Beta Kappa. Personal injury, Family and matrimonial, Workers' compensation. Home: 2835 Fairgreen Dr Miami Beach FL 33140 Office: Pelzner Schwedock Finkelstein & Klausner PA 28 W Flagler St #800 Miami FL 33130 also: 1922 Tyler St Hollywood FL 33020

FINKELSTEIN, JOSEPH SIMON, lawyer; b. Vineland, N.J., Feb. 28, 1952; s. Absalom and Goldie (Cukier) F.; m. Sara M. Green, May 30, 1976; children: Adam, Julia. BA, Rutgers U., 1973; JD, U. Pa., 1976. Bar: Pa. 1976, N.J. 1976, U.S. Supreme Ct. 1982. Assoc. Wolf, Block, Schorr and Solis-Cohen, Phila., 1976-85, ptnr., 1985—. Mem. exec. bd. young leadership council bd. Fedn. of Jewish Agys., Phila., 1986—. Mem. ABA, Pa. Bar Assn., N.J. Bar Assn., Phila. Bar Assn. Club: Golden Slipper (Phila.). Real property, Contracts commercial. Home: 716 Oxford Rd Bala Cynwyd PA 19004 Office: Wolf Block Schorr and Solis-Cohen Packard Bldg 12th Floor Philadelphia PA 19102

FINKELSTEIN, SAUL HAYM, lawyer; b. Queens, N.Y., Feb. 2, 1958; s. Bernard A. and Carolyn (Greenberg) F.; m. Anne M. Friedman, July 3, 1984. BA, Yeshiva U., 1978, JD magna cum laude, 1981. Bar: N.Y. 1982. Assoc. Breed, Abbott & Morgan, N.Y.C., 1981-84, Paul, Weiss, Rifkind, Wharton & Garrison, N.Y.C., 1984—. Articles editor Cardozo Law Rev., 1980-81. V.p., treas. 140 W 74th St Corp., N.Y.C., 1985—. Mem. ABA. Democrat. Jewish. Avocation: jogging. General corporate, Securities, Contracts commercial. Office: Paul Weiss Rifkind Wharton & Garrison 1285 Ave on the Americas New York NY 10019

FINKELSTEIN, WILLIAM BERNDT, lawyer; b. Austin, Tex., June 19, 1949; s. Willard Casper and Doris Jean (Frennesson) F.; m. Jeri Helen Goldberg, Feb. 6, 1972; children: Robin, Lisa, Shana. BA, U. Tex., 1971; JD cum laude, Baylor U., 1974. Bar: Tex. 1974, U.S. Dist. Ct. (no. dist.) Tex. 1975, U.S. Ct. Appeals (5th and 11th cirs.) 1975, U.S. Supreme Ct. 1978. Law clk. to assoc. justice Supreme Ct. Tex., Austin, 1974-75; from assoc. to ptnr. Hughes & Luce, Dallas, 1975—; lectr. in field. Vol. Jewish Fedn. Greater Dallas, 1982—; bd. dirs. Jewish Nat. Fund, Dallas, 1984—, Shaaray Zedek Hosp., Dallas Region, 1985. Mem. ABA, Tex. Assn Bank Counsel, State Bar Tex., Dallas Bar Assn. (courthouse com. 1982, judiciary com. 1987). Lodges: Masons, Shriners. Banking, Bankruptcy, State civil litigation. Home: 7425 Kenshire Dallas TX 75230 Office: Hughes & Luce 1000 Dallas Bldg Dallas TX 75201

FINLAYSON, DAWN BRUNER, lawyer; b. Dallas, June 2, 1952; d. Fred and Joy (Groves) Bruner; m. Daniel Wallace Finlayson Jr., Oct. 1, 1981. BA, U. Tex., 1974; JD, St. Mary's U., 1978. Bar: Tex. 1978, U.S. Dist Ct. (no. dist.) Tex. 1979, U.S. Dist. Ct. (we. and so. dists.) Tex. 1980, U.S. Ct. Appeals (5th cir.) 1980. Assoc. Bruner & Matlock, Dallas, 1978-80; asst. atty. gen. Austin, Tex., 1980-82; law clk. to presiding chief judge U.S. Dist. Ct. (we. dist.) Tex., San Antonio, Tex., 1982-83; assoc. Manitzas, Harris & Padgett, San Antonio, 1983-85, Matthews & Branscomb, San Antonio, 1985—. Democrat. Methodist. Labor, Federal civil litigation, Civil rights. Home: 226 W Fair Oaks San Antonio TX 78209 Office: Matthews & Branscomb 800 One Alamo Ctr San Antonio TX 78205

FINLEY, JOHN CYRUS, III, lawyer, municipal judge; b. Texarkana, Ark., Jan. 10, 1949; s. John Cyrus and LaVerne (Kenneweg) F.; B.A. magna cum laude, Ouachita Bapt. U., 1971; J.D., U. Ark., 1974. Bar: Ark. 1974, U.S. Dist. Ct. (we. dist.) Ark. 1974, U.S. Supreme Ct. 1980. Ptnr. firm Finley and Finley, Attys.-at-Law, Ashdown, Ark., 1974—; judge Ashdown and Little River County Mcpl. Ct., 1983—. Mem. ABA, Ark. Bar Assn., S.W. Ark. Bar Assn. (past pres.), Am. Judges Assn., Little River County Hist. Soc. (v.p. 1983). Democrat. Baptist. Club: Rotary. General practice, Probate, Real property. Home: Hwy 32 W Ashdown AR 71822 Office: Finley and Finley 20 E Main St Ashdown AR 71822

FINLEY, JOHN CYRUS, JR., lawyer; b. Ashdown, Ark., Sept. 7, 1912; s. John Cyrus Sr. and Edna Lynah (Evans) F.; m. LaVerne Kenneweg, Aug. 15, 1942; 1 child, John C. III. BA, Coll. of Ozarks, 1935; JD, U. Ark., Fayetteville, 1938. Bar: Ark. 1941, U.S. Dist. Ct. (we. dist.) Ark. 1941, U.S. Supreme Ct. 1943. Sole practice Ashdown, 1938-74; ptnr. Finley & Finley, Ashdown, 1974—; dep. pros. atty. Little River County, Ark., 1938-40; mem. Ark. Ho. of Reps., 1947-50. Served as agt. Counter Intelligence Corps, U.S. Army, 1942-45, ETO. Mem. Ark. Bar Assn., Southwest Ark. Bar Assn., Am. Legion. Baptist. Lodge: Masons. Avocations: golf, playing the violin. Probate, Real property, General practice. Home: Hwy 32 West Ashdown AR 71822 Office: Finley & Finley 20 E Main St Ashdown AR 71822

FINLEY, JOHN JORDAN, lawyer; b. Arlington, Va., Sept. 8, 1946; s. William Thompson and Mary Catherine (Jordan) F.; m. Mary Cary Ambler, Sept. 29, 1973; children—John Thompson Ambler, Jaquelin Cary. A.B., Harvard Coll., 1968; J.D., U. Va., 1971. Bar: N.Y. 1972. Assoc. Reid & Priest, N.Y.C., 1971-73, Wender, Murase & White, N.Y.C., 1973-74, 75-77, ptnr., 1977-82; cons. in U.S. law Lane and Ptnrs., London, 1974-75; ptnr. Boulanger, Finley & Hicks, N.Y.C., 1982-84, Drinker Biddle & Reath, N.Y.C., 1984—; dir. Hanover Ptnrs. Ltd., N.Y.C. Mem. ABA, Internat. Bar Assn., N.Y. State Bar Assn., Assn. Bar City of N.Y., Brit. Am. C. of C. (coms.). Episcopalian. Clubs: Union, Sleepy Hollow Country, Harvard. General corporate. Home: 282 Evandale Rd Scarsdale NY 10583 Office: Drinker Biddle & Reath 405 Park Ave New York NY 10022

FINLEY, LUCINDA MARGARET, educator; b. Washington, Mar. 2, 1956; d. Joseph E. and Joanne (Otte) F. BA, Barnard Coll., 1977; JD, Columbia U., 1980. Bar: D.C. 1980, U.S. Dist. Ct. D.C., U.S. Ct. Appeals (D.C. cir.), U.S. Ct. Appeals (2d cir.). Law clk. to presiding judge U.S. Ct. Appeals 3d cir., Phila., 1980-81; assoc. Shea & Gardner, Washington, 1981-83; prof. law Yale U., New Haven, 1983—; bd. dirs. Conn. Women's Edn. and Legal Fund, Initiative for Pub. Interest Law at Yale, Inc. Contbr. articles to profl. jours. Grantee Rockefeller Found., 1986—. Mem. ABA, Soc. Am. Law Tchrs. Labor, Personal injury. Office: Yale U Law Sch 127 Wall St New Haven CT 06520

FINMAN, TERRY JEANETTE, lawyer, financial planner; b. San Francisco, June 17, 1954; d. Theodore and Susan Florence (Heifetz) F.; m. James Dorian Ballotti, June 20, 1981; 1 child, James Benjamin. BS, U. Wis., 1977, JD, 1982. Bar: Ill. 1982, Wis. 1982. Homebound tchr. River Valley Sch. Dist., Spring Green, Wis., 1978-79; assoc. Schiller, Du Canto & Fleck, Chgo., 1982-84; fin. planner Waddell & Reed Inc., Countryside, Ill., 1985—; instr. N. Cen. Coll., Naperville, Ill., 1985. Mem. ABA, Ill. Bar Assn., Wis. Bar Assn., Chgo. Bar Assn. Office: Waddell & Reed Inc 6406 Joliet Rd Countryside IL 60525

FINN, CHESTER EVANS, lawyer; b. Dayton, Ohio, July 13, 1918; s. Samuel Lawrence and Lillian Rose (Evans) F.; m. Phyllis Muriel Kessel, Apr. 29, 1942; children: Chester E. Jr., Natalie K., Samuel J. BA, Yale U., 1940; LLB, Harvard U., 1946. Bar: Ohio 1947, U.S. Dist. Ct. (so. dist.) Ohio 1949, U.S. Ct. Claims 1949, U.S. Ct. Appeals (6th cir.) 1966, U.S. Supreme Ct. 1975, U.S. Ct. Internat. Trade 1984. Assoc. Estabrook, Finn & McKee, Dayton, 1947-53, ptnr., 1953-83; ptnr. Porter, Wright, Morris & Arthur, Dayton, 1983—. Pres. Dayton United Way, 1969; trustee various civic groups. Served to lt. USNR, 1942-45, PTO. Mem. ABA, Ohio Bar Assn., Dayton Bar Assn. (pres. 1969). Clubs: Moraine Country (Dayton); Moss Creek Golf (Hilton Head, S.C.). Avocations: golfing, traveling. Banking, Labor, Libel. Home: 514 Valewood Ln Dayton OH 45405 Office: Porter Wright Morris & Arthur 2100 First Nat Bank Bldg Dayton OH 45402

FINN, HAROLD BOLTON, III, lawyer; b. Bronxville, N.Y., Nov. 7, 1938; s. Harold Bolton and Anita Genevieve (Blackburne) F.; m. Catherine Cecelia Young, Sept. 11, 1965; children: Denyse, Alison, Douglas, Katherine. B.A., Yale Coll, 1960; LL.B. magna cum laude, Columbia U., 1966. Bar: N.Y. State 1967, D.C. 1968, Conn. 1974. Law clk. to Assoc. Justice Stanley F. Reed and Chief Justice Earl Warren, U.S. Supreme Ct., 1966-67; assoc. Covington & Burling, Washington, 1967-69, Cravath, Swaine & Moore, N.Y.C., 1969-73, Cummings & Lockwood, Stamford, Conn., 1973-74; ptnr. Cummings & Lockwood, 1975-87, Finn Dixon & Herling, Stamford, 1987—. Mem. adv. com. Conn. Banking Commr.; mem. Atty. Gen.'s Blue Ribbon Commn., Conn. Served with USN, 1960-63. Mem. Am. Bar Assn. (banking law com. and fed. regulation of securities com. sect. corps.), Conn. Bar Assn. (exec. com. sect. corps., exec. com. banking law sect.), Am. Law Inst. Club: Field of Greenwich (Conn.). Banking, General corporate. Office: Finn Dixon & Herling One Landmark Sq Suite 600 Stamford CT 06901

FINN, JERRY MARTIN, lawyer; b. Newark, Dec. 10, 1932; s. Harry and Meriam (Dichne) F.; m. Terri Lowen, June 13, 1954; children: David, Lawrence, Brian. BA, Emerson Coll., 1954; JD, Boston U., 1956. Bar: Mass. 1956, U.S. Dist. Ct. Mass. 1956, N.J. 1959, U.S. Dist. Ct. N.J. 1959, U.S. Supreme Ct. 1965. Assoc. Greenstone & Greenstone, Newark, 1959-62; ptnr. Goldberger & Finn, West Orange, N.J., 1962—. Mem. ABA, Assn. Trial Lawyers Am. (pres. N.J. br., chmn. nat. legis. 1964). Democrat. Jewish. Avocations: profl. and coll. soccer referee, breeder and exhibitor of doberman pinschers. Workers' compensation, Personal injury, Labor. Office: Goldberger & Finn 81 Northfield Ave West Orange NJ 07052

FINN, JOHN JOSEPH, lawyer; b. Boston, Jan. 6, 1952; s. Francis Raymond and Catherine B. (Connors) F. BA, Boston U., 1974; MA, U. Chgo., 1976; JD, Boston U., 1980. Bar: Mass. 1980, N.Y. 1981, U.S. Dist. Ct. Mass. 1982. Asst. atty. Kings County Dist. Atty's Office, Bklyn., 1980-81; sole practice Boston, 1981-84; assoc. Gallagher & Gallagher, P.C., Boston, 1984—. Mem. ABA, Mass. Bar Assn., Am. Trial Lawyers Assn. Federal civil litigation, Insurance, Personal injury. Home: 80 Sanborn Ave West Roxbury MA 02132 Office: Gallagher & Gallagher PC 1 Constitution Plaza Boston MA 02129

FINN, MARVIN RUVEN, lawyer; b. Boston, Sept. 9, 1938; s. Max and Edith N. (Goldstein) F.; m. Norma R. Cadiff, July 4, 1965; children—Jonathan, Andrew. B.S. cum laude, Babson Coll., 1959; J.D., Boston Coll., 1962. Bar: Mass. 1962, U.S. Dist. Ct. Mass. 1964, U.S. Ct. Appeals (1st cir.) 1980. Assoc. Fox, Orlov & Cowin, Boston, 1962-63; atty. Mass. Crime Commn., Boston, 1963-65; spl. asst. atty. gen. Mass., Boston, 1965-69; ptnr. Spencer & Stone, Boston, 1969-82; chief trial dept. Fulman & Fulman, Malden, Mass., 1982—; cons. civil litigation; rep. extradition proc. U.S. State Dept., Israel, 1968; speaker WBZ Radio, 1966. Coach, Youth Basketball Team, North Shore Jewish Community Ctr., 1976-81; mem. sch. com. Temple Beth El Sch., Swampscott, Mass., 1980. Mem. ABA, Mass. Bar Assn. (civil litigation com.), Boston Bar Assn., Assn. Trial Lawyers Am., Mass. Acad. Trial Lawyers, Am. Judicature Soc., Boston Coll. Alumni Assn., Babson Coll. Alumni Assn. Jewish. Lodges: K.P., Masons. Personal injury, State civil litigation, Workers' compensation. Office: Fulman & Fulman 7 Dartmouth St Malden MA 02148

FINNEGAN, EDWARD JAMES, lawyer; b. Yonkers, N.Y., Mar. 27, 1948; s. Edward Bernard and Ann Marie (Conway) F.; m. Elizabeth Whiting, Sept. 18, 1976; children: James, Thomas. AB in Econs., Coll. Holy Cross, 1969; JD, U. Va., 1976. Bar: Va. 1976, U.S. Dist. Ct. (ea. dist.) Va. 1977, U.S. Ct. Appeals (D.C. cir.) 1979, U.S. Ct. Appeals (4th cir.) 1980, U.S. Ct. Appeals (5th cir.) 1981, U.S. Supreme Ct. 1984. Asst. county atty. Fairfax (Va.) County, 1976-80; atty. Loudoun County, Leesburg, Va., 1980—. Served to lt. (j.g.) USN, 1969-73. Mem. ABA, Fairfax County Bar Assn., Loudoun County Bar Assn. (chmn. bench-bar com.), Local Govt. Attys. Va. (bd. dirs., pres. 1986—), Nat. Inst. Mcpl. Law Officers. Roman Catholic. Federal civil litigation, State civil litigation, Local government. Home: 241 Edwards Ferry Rd NE Leesburg VA 22075 Office: Office County Atty 18 N King St Leesburg VA 22075

FINNEGAN, GEORGE BERNARD, JR., lawyer; b. Nevada City, Calif., June 13, 1903; s. George B. and Margaret (Gillespie) F.; m. Elisabeth B. Morgan, Oct. 23, 1926; children—Marcus B., George Bernard III, Dana G.; m. Dorothy J. Conte, Dec. 9, 1978. B.S., U.S. Mil. Acad., 1924; postgrad., George Washington Law Sch., 1926-27; J.D., Fordham U., 1929. Bar: N.Y. 1930. Asst. examiner U.S. Patent Office, 1926-27; since practiced in N.Y.C.; sr. ptnr. Morgan, Finnegan, Pine, Foley & Lee, 1939—. Served with U.S. Army, 1924-26; from maj. to col. AUS, 1942-46. Decorated Legion of Merit; recipient Nat. Patent prize, 1978. Mem. ABA, Am. Judicature Soc., Am., N.Y., N.J. patent law assns., Am. Coll. Trial Lawyers, Assn. Grads. U.S. Mil. Acad., West Point Soc. N.Y., West Point Alumni Found. (bd. dirs.), Newcomen Soc. Clubs: Anglers, Marco Polo (N.Y.C.); Bohemian (San Francisco). Co-inventor, licensor Aetna Drivo-Trainer. Patent, Trademark and copyright, Federal civil litigation. Office: Morgan Finnegan Pine Foley & Lee 345 Park Ave New York NY 10154

FINNEGAN, THOMAS JOSEPH, lawyer; b. Chgo., Aug. 18, 1900; s. Thomas Harrison and Marie (Flanagan) F.; J.D., Chgo. Kent Coll. of Law, 1923; m. Hildreth Millslagel, July 1, 1933 (dec. Mar. 1977). Admitted to Ill. bar, 1923, and since practiced in Chicago; mem. firm Fithian, Spengler & Finnegan, 1935-51; mem. firm Korshak, Oppenheim & Finnegan, 1951-86. Mem. ABA, Fed., Ill., Chgo. bar assns., Chgo. Law Inst., Phi Alpha Delta. Personal injury, Probate, Labor. Home: 5630 Sheridan Rd Chicago IL 60660 Office: 29 S LaSalle St Chicago IL 60603

FINNELL, ROBERT KIRTLEY, lawyer; b. Covington, Ky., May 30, 1949; s. Robert Kirtley and Mildred (Manning) F.; m. Sherry Kay Plyler, Sept. 17, 1977; 1 child, Kirtley Andrew. BA, U. Ky., 1971; JD, Samford U., 1975.

Bar: Ga. 1975, U.S. Supreme Ct. 1982. Assoc. Jackson B. Harris, Rome, Ga., 1975-77; ptnr. Patton & Finnell, Rome, 1977-81; chief of staff U.S. senator Mattingly, Washington, 1981-82; ptnr. Sawhill & Finnell, Rome, 1982-85; sole practice Rome, 1985—. Mem. Assn. Trial Lawyers Am., Ga. Trial Lawyers Assn. Republican. Presbyterian. Club: Rome 7001 (bd. dirs.). Avocation: golf. Personal injury, Workers' compensation, Federal civil litigation. Office: PO Box 63 Rome GA 30161

FINNEY, JOSEPH CLAUDE JEANS, lawyer, investment adviser, psychologist, psychiatrist; b. Urbana, Ill., Mar. 18, 1927; s. Claude Lee and Margaret Ellen (Boillin) F.; m. Mary Littlefield, Jan. 21, 1955; children: Carol, Michael, John, Ellen. B.A., Vanderbilt U., 1946; postgrad., U. Notre Dame, 1947; M.D., Harvard U., 1949; postgrad., U. Calif. at Berkeley, 1950-51, 52-53; Ph.D., Stanford U., 1959; LL.B., LaSalle U., 1972; postgrad. in law, U. Ky., 1972-75. Bar: Calif. 1972, U.S. Ct. Appeals (9th cir.) 1973, U.S. Dist. Ct. (no. dist.) Calif. 1974, U.S. Ct. Appeals (D.C. cir.) 1974, U.S. Ct. Appeals (fed. cir.) 1974. U.S. Ct. Mil. Appeals 1978, U.S. Supreme Ct. 1978; ordained priest, 1969; registered investment adviser SEC.; CPA. Med. intern Johns Hopkins Hosp., Balt., 1949-50; resident physician U.S. VA Hosp., Palo Alto, Calif., 1953-56; dir. Champaign County Mental Health Center, 1956-60; chief research Hawaii State Mental Health System, 1960-63; assoc. prof. psychiatry U. Ky., 1963-67, prof. ednl. psychology, 1967-77; dir. psychology curriculum Liberal Cath. Inst. Studies, Ojai, Calif., 1977-80; dir. continuing edn. Am. Inst. Higher Studies, 1977—; pres. Finney Inst. for Study Human Behavior, 1977—; dir. research in psychiatry Loyola U. of Chgo., 1980-83; chief psychiatry and psychology U.S. Army Hosp., Fort Ord, Calif., 1983-87; cons. U.S. Dept. Justice, 1967-79, U.S. Social Security Adminstrn., 1967-80; nat. chaplain mems.-at-large Liberal Cath. Ch. in U.S., 1979-87, sec., treas. Nat. Chpt. Priests, 1987—; del. Internat. Liberal Cath. Synod, 1976, 81; pres. Computer Assisted Profl. Services, 1986—; mem. adv. bd. Am. Coll. Forensic Psychiatry, 1987—. Author: Culture Change, Mental Health and Poverty, 1969; editorial bd.: Jour. Marriage and Family Counseling, 1974-80, Family Law Quar, 1977-78, Jour. Psychol. Anthropology, 1976-83. Del. Libertarian Party Nat. Conv., 1977, 79; sec. Ky. Libertarian Party, 1979-80; nominee Electoral Coll., 1980. Served to lt. (j.g.) USPHS, 1951-53, col. U.S. Army, 1983-87. Recipient research grants NIMH, 1966-68, research grants U.S. Social and Rehab. Services, 1967-70. Fellow Am. Psychiat. Assn., Am. Coll. Forensic Psychiatry (adv. bd. 1987—), Am. Psychol. Assn., Am. Coll. Legal Medicine, Am. Anthrop. Assn.; mem. ABA (vice chmn. law and psychiatry liaison com. 1973-76, 80-81, chmn. 1976-80), Linguistic Soc. Am., Assn. Research in Nervous and Mental Disease, Soc. Crosscultural Research, Soc. Sci. Study Religion, Religious Research Assn., Polynesian Soc., Soc. Sci. Study of Sex, Am. Assn. Sex Educators, Counselors and Therapists (dir. 1981-83), VFW, Mensa, Phi Beta Kappa. Liberal Catholic. Club: Kiwanis. Inventor, developer computer systems for interpretation psychol. tests and for econometric forecasting. Health, Computer, Trademark and copyright. Home: 2109 Ridgetop St Tallahassee FL 32303 Office: PO Box 6849 Salinas CA 93912

FINSON, LOWELL WAYNE, lawyer; b. Cleve., June 23, 1949; s. Norman Elliot and Maxine Muriel (Gerber) F.; m. Beth Allyson Bernstein, Mar. 20, 1977; 1 child, Lee Warren. BBA, Miami U., Oxford, Ohio, 1971; JD, Cleve. State U., 1974. Assoc. Rollins & Mosesson, Cleve., 1974-76, Berger & Kirschenbaum, Cleve., 1976-78, Sindell & Sindell, Cleve., 1978-80; ptnr. Finson & Shapiro, Cleve., 1980-86, Van Baalen Law Offices, Phoenix, 1987—; auctioneer, dir. Finson & Co. Inc., Cleve., 1971—. Mem. Ohio State Bar Assn., Ariz. Bar Assn., Cuyahoga County Bar Assn., Cleve. Bar Assn., Assn. Trial Lawyers Am. State civil litigation, Personal injury, Contracts commercial. Home: 2257 E Mercier Dr Phoenix AZ 85016 Office: Van Baalen Law Offices 111 W Monroe Phoenix AZ 85001

FINTON, TIMOTHY CHRISTOPHER, lawyer; b. Washington, Feb. 5, 1952; s. James Robert and Iris Clinton (Hammer) F.; m. Tonya Cecile Thomas, June 3, 1983. AB, Ohio U., 1974; MA, Oxford U., Eng., 1976; JD, Am. U., 1979. Bar: D.C. 1980, U.S. Dist. Ct. D.C. 1980, U.S. Ct. Internat. Trade 1980, U.S. Ct. Appeals (D.C. cir.) 1980, U.S. Supreme Ct. 1983. Trade policy advisor Internat. Trade Adminstrn. U.S. Dept. of Commerce, Washington, 1979-85; policy advisor Bur. of Internat. Communications and Information U.S. Dept. of State, Washington, 1985—. Author: A Competitive Assessment of the U.S. Fiber Optics Industry, 1984. Mem. ABA (internat. communications com.), Fed. Bar Assn. (editorial bd. 1981-83, Dist. Service award 1982), Phi Alpha Delta. Republican. Episcopalian. Clubs: Oxford and Cambridge University (London), Army Navy Country, The City Tavern (Washington). Private international, international communications. Home: 1112 Noyes Dr Silver Spring MD 20910 Office: Bur Internat Communications and Info US Dept State Room 6317 Washington DC 20520

FINZEN, BRUCE ARTHUR, lawyer; b. Mpls., Mar. 11, 1947; s. Floyd Arthur Finzen and Lorraine Jeannette (Offerdahl) Krans; m. Julianna Margaret Ryan, July 12, 1975; children: Margaret, Sara, Stephanie. BA, U. Minn., 1970; JD, U. Kans., 1973. Bar: Minn. 1973, U.S. Dist. Ct. Minn. 1973, U.S. Ct. Appeals (8th cir.) 1973, U.S. Ct. Appeals (7th cir.) 1983, U.S. Ct. Appeals (2nd cir.) 1986. Law clk. to presiding justice Minn. Supreme Ct., St. Paul, 1973-74; assoc. Robins, Zelle, Larson & Kaplan, Mpls., 1974-79, ptnr., 1979—. Bd. dirs. Union Gospel Mission, St. Paul, 1983—; sec. bd. dirs. Boys & Girls Clubs St. Paul, 1984—. Mem. ABA, Minn. Bar Assn., Assn. Trial Lawyers Am., Minn. Trial Lawyers Assn. Presbyterian. Avocations: hunting, fishing. Federal civil litigation, State civil litigation, Personal injury. Office: Robins Zelle Larson & Kaplan 1800 International Ctr 900 Second Ave S Minneapolis MN 55402

FIORAMONTI, FRANK ROBERT, lawyer; b. Washington, May 20, 1943; s. Frank Joseph and Virginia Grace (Hayes) F. B.S., U. Pa., 1965; LL.B., Columbia U., 1968, LL.M., NYU, 1970. Bar: N.Y. 1969, U.S. Dist. Ct. (so. dist.) N.Y. 1981. VISTA vol., N.Y.C., 1968-70; asst. corp. counsel City N.Y., 1970-71; legis. counsel N.Y.C. Councilman Carter Burden, 1971-75; Eastern regional coordinator Nat. Orgn. Reform Marijuana Laws, N.Y.C., 1975-79; asst. atty. gen. in charge legis. bur. N.Y. State Dept. Law, N.Y.C. and Albany, 1979—; adj. prof. law N.Y. Law Sch., N.Y.C., 1977—. Bd. dirs. Jobs for Youth, Inc., N.Y.C., 1976—, Nat. Orgn. Reform Marijuana Laws, 1972-81. Mem. ABA (chmn. com. alcoholism and drug law reform, sect. individual rights and responsibilities 1975-81). Contbg. editor Juris Doctor mag., 1971-79. Legislative. Office: 120 Broadway Suite 25-82 New York NY 10271

FIORENTINO, CARMINE, lawyer; b. Bklyn., Sept. 11, 1932; s. Pasquale and Lucy (Coppola) F. LL.B., Blackstone Sch. Law, Chgo., 1954, John Marshall Law Sch., Atlanta, 1957. Bar: Ga, D.C., U.S. Supreme Ct., U.S. Dist. Ct. D.C., U.S. Ct. Appeals (2d cir.), U.S. Dist. Ct. (no. dist.) Ga., U.S. Ct. Appeals (5th cir.), U.S. Ct. Claims. Mem. N.Y. State Workmen's Compensation Bd., N.Y. State Dept. Labor, 1950-53; ct. reporter, hearing stenographer N.Y. State Com. State Counsel and Attys., 1953; public relations sec. Indsl. Home for Blind, Bklyn., 1953-55; legal stenographer, researcher, law clk., Atlanta, 1955, 57-59; sec. import-export firm, Atlanta, 1956; sole practice, Atlanta, 1959-63, 73—; atty., advisor, trial atty. HUD, Atlanta and Washington, also legal counsel Peachtree Fed. Credit Union, 1963-74; acting dir. Elmira (N.Y.) Disaster Field Office, HUD, 1973. Mem. Smithsonian Instn., Republican Nat. Com., Rep. Presdl. Task Force, Nat. Hist. Soc.; Life Dynamics fellow; mem. Atlanta Hist. Soc., Atlanta Bot. Gardens, Am. Mus. Natural History, Mus. Heritage Soc. Mem. ABA, Fed. Bar Assn., Atlanta Bar Assn., Decatur-DeKalb Bar Assn., Am. Judicature Soc., Old War Horse Lawyers Club, Assn. Trial Lawyers Am., AAAS, Internat. Platform Soc., Nat. Audubon Soc. Presbyterian. Clubs: Toastmasters, Gaslight, Sierra. Writer non-fiction and poetry; composer songs and hymns. General corporate, General practice, Personal injury. Home and Office: 4764 Wieuca Rd NE Atlanta GA 30342

FIORITO, EDWARD GERALD, patent lawyer; b. Irvington, N.J., Oct. 20, 1936; s. Edward and Emma (DePascale) F.; m. Charlotte H. Longo; children—Jeanne C., Kathryn M., Thomas E., Lynn M., Patricia A. B.S.E.E., Rutgers U., 1958; J.D., Georgetown U., 1963. Bar: U.S. Patent and Trademark Office 1960, Va. 1963, N.Y. 1964, Mich. 1970, Ohio 1975, Tex. 1984. Patent staff atty. IBM, Armonk, N.Y., 1958-69; v.p. patent and comml. relations Energy Conversion Devices, Troy, Mich., 1969-71; mng. patent prosecution Burroughs Corp., Detroit, 1971-75; gen. patent counsel B.F. Goodrich Corp., Akron, Ohio, 1975-83; dir. patents and licensing Dresser Industries, Inc., Dallas, 1983—; dir. LIM Holding, S.A., Luxembourg, 1978-82. Bd. dirs. Akron's House Extending Aid on Drugs, 1976. Mem. ABA (sci. and tech. sect. chmn. 1984-85, program chmn. Nat. Inst. on Law, Sci. and Tech. in Health Risk Regulation 1979, 81, patent, trademark and copyright sect. council 1985—), Tex. Bar Assn. (council intellectual property law sect.), Assn. Corp. Patent Counsel (exec. com. 1982-84), IEEE, Tau Beta Pi. Roman Catholic. Avocations: musician; running. Office: Dresser Industries Inc 1600 Pacific Ave Dallas TX 75201

FIRESTONE, CHARLES MORTON, lawyer, educator; b. St. Louis, Oct. 16, 1944; s. Victor and Betty (Solomon) F.; m. Pattie Winston Porter, Apr. 19, 1975; children—Laurel, Asa. B.A., Amherst Coll., 1966; J.D., Duke U., 1969. Bar: D.C. 1969, U.S. Ct. Appeals (D.C. cir.) 1970, U.S. Ct. Appeals (5th cir.) 1972, U.S. Ct. Appeals (9th cir.) 1973, U.S. Ct. Appeals (2d cir.) 1975, U.S. Ct. Appeals (3d cir.) 1976, U.S. Ct. Appeals 8th cir.) 1977, U.S. Supreme Ct. 1977, Calif. 1983. Litigation atty. FCC, Washington, 1969-73; dir. litigation Citizens Communications Ctr., Washington, 1973-77; adj. prof. law, dir. communications law program, UCLA, 1977-86; vis. lectr. UCLA Sch. Law, 1986-87; counsel firm Mitchell, Silberberg & Knupp, Los Angeles, 1983—; faculty adviser Fed. Communications Law Jour., Los Angeles, 1977-86; cons. FTC, Washington, Pub. Agenda Found., N.Y.C., 1978; counsel statewide television debates LWV, Los Angeles, 1978—; pres. Bd. Telecommunications Commrs., City of Los Angeles, 1984-86. Editor case materials, symposia resource manuals on communications; contbr. articles to profl. jours. Bd. dirs. Corp. for Disabilities and Telecommunications, Los Angeles, 1980-82, KCRW Found., Santa Monica, Calif., 1982—; adv. com. campaign Mondale for Pres., Los Angeles, 1984. Recipient Am. Jurisprudence award, 1968, 69; Cert. Commendation award Mayor Los Angeles, 1986; Resolution Commendation award City Council Los Angeles, 1986; Recognition award NOW, Nat. Black Media Coalition, Nat. Latino Media Coalition, Nat. Citizens Com. for Broadcasting, Washington, 1977; Luther Ely Smith scholar and Andrew Laurie scholar Amherst Coll., 1965-66. Mem. ABA (chmn. broadcast and spectrum use com., sect. sci. and tech. 1981-83, chmn. electronic campaigning com. 1984-86), Fed. Communications Bar Assn., Soc. Satellite Profls. (sec. bd. dirs. So. Calif. chpt. 1984—). Democrat. Jewish. Communications/Telecommunications, Administrative and regulatory, Public utilities. Office: Mitchell Silberberg & Knupp 11377 W Olympic Blvd Los Angeles CA 90064

FIRTH, PETER ALAN, lawyer; b. Rockville Center, N.Y., Jan. 7, 1943; s. Richard V. and Patricia (Gilmour) F.; m. Carol A. Smith, Aug. 21, 1965; children: Andrew, Marysusan, Patrick, James, William. AB in Econs., Georgetown U., 1964; LLB, Albany Law Sch., 1967. Bar: N.Y. 1967, U.S. Dist. Ct. (no. dist.) N.Y. 1967, U.S. Tax Ct. 1971, U.S. Ct. Appeals (2d cir.) 1985. Assoc. LaPann & Reardon, Glens Falls, N.Y., 1967-71; ptnr. LaPann, Reardon, FitzGerald & Firth, Glens Falls, 1971-86, LaPann, Reardon, Morris, Fitzgerald & Firth P.C., Glens Falls, 1986—; asst. dist. atty. Warren County, Lake George, N.Y., 1972-74. Assoc. editor Albany Law Rev., 1966-67. Mem. ABA, N.Y. State Bar Assn., Warren County Bar Assn. (sec. 1969-72, treas. 1985—), Assn. Trial Lawyers Am., N.Y. State Trial Lawyers Assn., Am. Arbitration Assn. (arbitrator 1977—). Republican. Roman Catholic. Lodge: Lions. State civil litigation, Insurance, Personal injury. Home: 6 Meadow Dr Glens Falls NY 12801 Office: LaPann Reardon Morris et al 1 Broad St Plaza Glens Falls NY 12801

FISCH, EDITH L., lawyer; b. N.Y.C., Mar. 3, 1923; d. Hyman and Clara L. Fisch; m. Steven Ludwig Werner, Dec. 14, 1963 (dec.). B.A., Bklyn. Coll., 1945; LL.B., Columbia U., 1948, LL.M., 1949, J.Sc.D., 1950. Bar: N.Y. 1948, U.S. Supreme Ct. 1957. Grad. asst. Columbia U. Law Sch., N.Y.C., 1948, fellow in law, 1949-50; assoc. firm Conrad & Smith, N.Y.C., 1951-57; sole practice, N.Y.C., 1957-62, 65—; asst. prof. law N.Y. Law Sch., 1963-65; counsel firm Brodsky, Lenett & Altman, N.Y.C., 1973-75; pres. Lond Publs., 1958—; ednl. dir. Found. for Continuing Legal Edn., 1964—; editor N.Y.C. Charter and Adminstrv. Code, 1965—; presenter lectures, seminars and courses for profl. groups. Author: The Cy Pres Doctrine in the U.S., 1950; (with others) State Laws on the Employment of Women, 1953; Lawyers in Industry, 1956; Fisch on New York Evidence, 1959, 2d edit. 1977; (with others) Charities and Charitable Foundations, 1974; contbr. numerous articles to legal publs. County committeewoman 7th Dist. N.Y. Dem. party, 1949-52; bd. dirs., treas. nat. women's com. Brandeis U., 1964-68. Mem. N.Y. Women's Bar Assn. (pres. 1970-71, bd. dirs. 1971-73, adv. council 1974—), Nat. Assn. Women Lawyers, Assn. Bar City N.Y., Bklyn. Coll. Lawyers Group (rec. sec. 1961-63, bd. govs. 1963-65), Am. Arbitration Assn. (nat. panelist), Acad. Polit. Sci., AAUW, Alumni Assn. Columbia U., Bklyn. Coll. Alumni Assn. Probate, State civil litigation. Home: 250 W 94th St New York NY 10025 Office: Call Hollow Rd Pomona NY 10970

FISCH, JOSEPH, lawyer; b. N.Y.C., Apr. 7, 1939; s. Israel Ben Zion and Esther Leah (Spielvogel) F.; m. Norma Potter, Aug. 7, 1960; children: Adam Jeffrey, Jennifer Anne, Rachel Lynne. BA, Tufts U., 1960; JD, NYU, 1963, LLM in Taxation, 1969. Bar: N.J. 1964, U.S. Dist. Ct. (3d dist.) 1964, U.S. Tax Ct. 1966, U.S. Supreme Ct. 1969, U.S. Ct. Appeals (3d cir.) 1971. Law sec. to judge N.J. Supreme Ct., Jersey City, 1963-64; assoc. Hannock, Wiseman, Stern and Besser, Newark, 1964-65, Blume and Kalb, Newark, 1965-66; sole practice Kendall Park, N.J., 1966—; asst. prof. Rutgers U., New Brunswick, N.J., 1971-81; arbitrator Am. Arbitration Assn., 1969—, N.J. Superior Ct., Somerville, 1985—; atty. Franklin Twp. Rent Leveling Bd., Somerset, 1980—. Contbr. articles to law jours. Pres. Franklin Housing and Neighborhood Devel. Corp., Somerset, 1975-78, Temple Beth El Men's Club, Somerset, 1971-72, trustee, 1970. Mem. ABA, N.J. Bar Assn., Somerset County Bar Assn., Assn. Trial Lawyers Am., N.J. Trial Lawyers Assn. Republican. Jewish. Lodge: Rotary. State civil litigation, Real property, General practice. Office: Congl Office Complex 3084 Route 27 Suite 7 Kendall Park NJ 08824

FISCHBACH, DONALD RICHARD, lawyer; b. Ventura, Calif., Sept. 26, 1947; s. Richard A. and Ruth (Blevins) F.; children: Amy, Sara. BS in Bus. adminstrn. with honors, Calif. State Poly. Coll., 1979; JD, U. Calif., San Francisco, 1972. Bar: Calif. 1972. Assoc. Baker, Manock & Jensen, Fresno, Calif., 1972-75, ptnr., 1976—; adj. asst. prof. San Joaquin Coo. Law., Fresno, 1980-82; commr. jud. State Bar Calif., 1983; lectr. in field. Vol. atty. Fresno County Legal Services, 1973-79; chmn. fund raising United Way, 1979, Am. Cancer Soc., 1980-81, bd, dirs, 1980-82, Fresno Met. Mus., 1982, Rally for Ratcliffe, 1983, Valley Childrens Hosp., 1986; bd. dirs. Fresno County Legal Services, 1976-79. Mem. ABA (del. young lawyers div. 1977-79), Calif. Bar Assn. (del. 1975-81, 84, treas. young lawyers assn. 1978, 1st v.p. 1979, bd. dirs. 1976-79), Fresno County Bar Assn. (pres. 1985, v.p. 1984, bd. dirs. 1975, 78-81, 1983—), Assn. Trial Lawyers Am., Calif. Trial Lawyers Assn., Fresno County Young Lawyers Assn. (pres. 1975, bd. dirs. 1975-79), No. Calif. Def. Counsel Assn., So. Calif. Def. Council Assn., Fresno Trial Lawyers Assn. (bd. dirs., officer 1978-82), Am. Soc. Law and Medicine, Def. Research Inst. State civil litigation, Personal injury, Insurance. Home: 6578 N Safford Fresno CA 93711 Office: Baker Manock & Jensen 5260 N Palm Suite 421 Fresno CA 93704

FISCHEL, SHELLEY DUCKSTEIN, lawyer; b. N.Y.C., Dec. 30, 1950; d. Saul and Dorothy (Rebitch) Duckstein; m. Robert E. Fischel, July 27, 1980; 1 child, Joseph Jacob. BA, Wellesley Coll., 1972; JD, Columbia U., 1977. Bar: N.Y. 1978, U.S. Dist. Ct. (so. dist.) N.Y. 1978. Assoc. Sullivan & Cromwell, N.Y.C., 1977-79; v.p., chief counsel labor and litigation Home Box Office Inc., N.Y.C., 1979-84, v.p. human resources, 1984-86, sr. v.p. human resources, 1986—. Founder, chmn. Jewish Advs. for the West Side, N.Y.C., 1978-80. Harlan Fiske Stone scholar, 1974-77. Democrat. Labor, Entertainment, Antitrust. Office: Home Box Office Inc 1100 Ave of Americas New York NY 10036

FISCHER, DALE SUSAN, lawyer; b. East Orange, N.J., Oct. 17, 1951; d. Edward L. and Audrey (Tenner) F. BA magna cum laude, U. So. Fla., 1977; JD, Harvard U., 1980; student Dickinson Coll., 1969-70. Bar: Calif. 1980. Ptnr. law firm Kindel & Anderson, Los Angeles, 1980—; lawyer in classroom Constl. Rights Found., 1981—. Mem. ABA, Los Angeles County Bar Assn., Beverly Hills Bar Assn. Federal civil litigation, State civil litigation, Family and matrimonial. Home: 3695 Hampton Rd Pasadena CA 91107 Office: Kindel and Anderson 555 S Flower Los Angeles CA 90071

FISCHER, DAVID JON, lawyer; b. Danville, Ill., July 27, 1952; s. Oscar Ralph and Sarah Pauline (Pomerantz) F. BA, U. Miami, 1974, JD, 1977. Bar: Fla. 1977, Iowa 1978, U.S. Dist. Ct. (so. dist.) Iowa 1978, U.S. Ct. Appeals (8th cir.) 1978, D.C. 1979, U.S. Ct. Appeals (D.C. cir.) 1979, U.S. Dist. Ct. D.C. 1980, U.S. Ct. Appeals (11th cir.) 1984. Atty. Iowa Dept. Social Services, Des Moines, 1978; assoc. Parrish & Del Gallo P.C., Des Moines, 1978-79, Donald M. Murtha & Assocs., Washington, 1979-80; assoc. editor Lawyers Coop. Pub. Co., Washington, 1980-82; sole practice Washington, 1982-83, Des Moines, 1983-84, Atlanta, 1984—; prof. law John Marshall Law Sch., Atlanta, 1986—. Author: The Aeronaut's Law Handbook, 1986; contbg. editor Balloon Life mag., 1986—; tech. editor various manuals; contbr. articles to profl. jours. Mem. ABA (sect. com. 1980-82), Fed. Bar Assn., Iowa Bar Assn., Fla. Bar Assn., D.C. Bar Assn., Polk County Bar Assn., Pros. Attys. Council Ga. (tech. editor Computer Crime jour.), Balloon Fedn. Am. (chmn. com. 1986—), Carolinas Balloon Assn., Ga. Balloon Assn. (chmn. com. 1985—), Chesapeake Balloon Assn. Jewish. Avocations: hot air balloon pilot, writing, competetive sports. General practice, Aviation, Legal education. Office: PO Box 2166 Roswell GA 30077-2166

FISCHER, ERIC ROBERT, lawyer, banker, law educator; b. N.Y.C., Aug. 22, 1945; s. Maurice and Pauline (Pilcer) F.; m. Anita Ellen Cohen, July 31, 1977; children—Joshua, Lauren. B.A., U. Pa., 1967; M.B.A., J.D., Stanford U., 1971; LL.M. in Taxation, Boston U., 1982. Bar: N.Y. 1975, Mass. 1977. Assoc. Fried, Frank, Harris, Shriver & Jacobson, N.Y.C., 1971-76; v.p., asst. gen. counsel, asst. sec. bd. dirs. 1st Nat. Bank of Boston, 1976-86, sr. v.p., gen. counsel UST Corp., 1986—; lectr. law Boston U. Law Sch., 1984—. Mem. Bank Capital Markets Assn. (chmn. banking law subcom. 1984—), UN Assn. Boston (treas. 1978—). Jewish. Banking, General corporate, Securities. Home: 205 Waban Ave Newton MA 02168 Office: UST Corp 40 Court St Boston MA 02108

FISCHER, JAY DAVID, lawyer; b. N.Y.C., Aug. 13, 1931; s. Sol and Ruth (Teitelbaum) F.; m. Laurel Simon, Feb. 3, 1957; children: Tamar, Toby, Judith, Jessica. BA, CCNY, 1952; LLB, Columbia U., 1955. Bar: N.Y. 1955, U.S. Ct. Mil. Appeals 1958, U.S. Supreme Ct. 1959, U.S. Dist. Ct. (so. and ea. dists.) N.Y. 1960, N.J. 1970, U.S. Dist. Ct. N.J. 1970, U.S. Tax Ct. 1979, U.S. Ct. Appeals (2d and 3d cirs.). Assoc. Corcoran, Kostelanetz, N.Y.C., 1959-61; ptnr. Mermelstein, Burns & Lesser, N.Y.C., 1961-69, Marcus, Rosen, Breslow, Levy & Fischer, Totowa, N.J., 1970-73, Fischer, Kagan, Ascione & Zaretsky, Clifton, N.J., 1973—. Chmn. Bronx (N.Y.) Com. Dem. Voters, 1965-69; vice chmn. N.Y. Com. Dem. Voters, N.Y.C., 1966-69. Served to capt. JAGC, U.S. Army, 1957-59. Named one of Outstanding Young Men in Am. Jaycees. Mem. N.J. Bar Assn., Assn. of Bar of City of N.Y., Passaic County Bar Assn., Phi Beta Kappa. State civil litigation, General corporate, General practice. Office: Fischer Kagan Ascione & Zaretsky 1373 Broad St Clifton NJ 07013 also: 10 E 40th St New York NY 10016

FISCHER, JOHN FREDERICK, lawyer; b. Stillwater, Okla., Sept. 23, 1948; s. John Frederick and Jo Ruth (King) F.; m. Pamela Lynne Correia, May 13, 1972; children: Jennifer Leigh, Andrea Lynne. BA, U. Okla., 1971, MA in English, 1972, JD, 1975. Bar: Okla. 1976, U.S. Dist. Ct. (we., no. and ea. dists.) Okla. 1976, U.S. Ct. Appeals (10th cir.) 1977, U.S. Supreme Ct. 1979. Asst. atty. gen. State of Okla., Oklahoma City, 1976-80; assoc. Andrews, Davis, Oklahoma City, 1980-84, ptnr., 1984—; judge temporary ct. appeals, Oklahoma City, 1984. Contbr. articles to profl. jours. Mem. Mesta Park Assn., Oklahoma City, 1976—, Speaker's Bur., Oklahoma City, 1986; awards chmn. Reunion Com., Oklahoma City, 1986; assoc. Okla. Mus. Art, Oklahoma City, 1986. Recipient Liberty Research award Liberty Nat. Bank, 1975. Mem. ABA (antitrust and litigation coms.), Okla. Bar Assn. (pub. info. com.), Okla. County Bar Assn. Democrat. Mem. Unitarian Ch. Club: Okla. Ctr. Athletics (Oklahoma City). Avocations: running, sailing, reading, skiing, swimming. Antitrust, Federal civil litigation, Real property. Office: Andrews Davis 500 W Main Oklahoma City OK 73102

FISCHER, MARK ALAN, lawyer, law educator; b. Evanston, Ill., Sept. 28, 1950; s. Lee Earle and Zelda (Dlugo) F. BA magna cum laude, Emerson Coll., 1975; JD, Boston Coll., 1980. Bar: Mass. 1980, U.S. Dist. Ct. Mass. 1980. Sole practice Cambridge, Mass., 1980-83; mem. Cohen & Burg, Boston, 1983-86; of counsel Wolf, Greenfield & Sacks, Boston, 1986—; lectr. copyright and trademark law Boston Coll. Law Sch.; lectr. entertainment law New Eng. Sch. Law. Contbr. articles to profl. jours. Mem. ABA, Mass. Bar Assn., Boston Patent Law Assn. (chmn. copyright law com.), Copyright Soc. U.S.A. Entertainment, Copyright and trademark, Computer. Office: Wolf, Greenfield & Sacks 201 Devonshire St Boston MA 02110

FISCHER, MICHAEL DAVIN, lawyer; b. Louisville, Sept. 2, 1948; s. Arch G. and Dorothy (Davin) F.; m. Deborah M. Walther, Aug. 3, 1973; children: Anna, Davin. AB, Georgetown U., 1970; JD, Harvard U., 1973. Bar: D.C. 1973, Wis. 1985. Mem. Foley & Lardner, Milw., 1973—. Mem. ABA, Fed. Bar Assn., D.C. Bar Assn., Wis. Bar Assn. Antitrust, Federal civil litigation. Home: 1441 E Goodrich Ct Milwaukee WI 53217 Office: Foley & Lardner 777 E Wisconsin Ave Milwaukee WI 53202

FISCHER, RICHARD LAWRENCE, lawyer; b. Pitts., Oct. 22, 1936; s. Francis William and Catherine Ellen (Haggerty) F.; m. Virginia Mae Fullerton, Aug. 19, 1961; children—Richard F., Lynn A., Laura A., Greg L. A.B. in Econs., U. Pitts., 1958, J.D. in Law, 1961; LL.M. in Internat. Law, Georgetown U., 1965. Bar: Pa. 1963, D.C. 1963. Spl. agt. FBI, Washington, 1961-65; atty. Aluminum Co. Am., Pitts., 1965-69, gen. atty., 1969-72, internat. counsel, 1973-74, asst. gen. counsel, 1975-82, gen. mgr. Brazilian project, 1980-82, v.p., dep. gen. counsel, 1982-83, v.p., gen. counsel, 1984, sr. v.p., gen. counsel, 1984-85, sr. v.p. corp. affairs, gen. counsel, 1985-86, sr. v.p. devel. corp affairs, gen. counsel, 1986—. bd. dirs. Alcoa Found., Pitts., 1984—, St. Francis Health System, Pitts., 1985—; bd. visitors U. Pitts. Sch. Law, 1984—. Mem. ABA, Pa. Bar Assn., Assn. Gen. Counsel, Pitts. Gen. Counsel Group, Internat. and Comparative Law Ctr. of Southwestern Legal Found. (adv. bd. 1983—), Am. Corp. Counsel Assn. (bd. dirs.), Am. Judicature Soc., World Assn. Lawyers, Allegheny County Bar Assn., U. Pitts. Sch. Law Alumni Assn. (bd. govs. 1984—). Clubs: Duquesne, Oakmont Country. General corporate. Office: Aluminum Co Am Alcoa Bldg Pittsburgh PA 15219

FISCHER, RICHARD SAMUEL, lawyer; b. Buffalo, July 31, 1937; s. Richard D. and Isabel B. (Van Dorn) F.; m. Malinda Berry, June 3, 1960; children: Richard B., Van D. A.B., Harvard U., 1959, J.D., 1963. Bar: N.Y. 1963. Law clk N.Y. Ct. Appeals, Albany, 1963-65; assoc. Nixon, Hargrave, Devans & Doyle, Rochester, N.Y., 1965-71, ptnr., 1972—. Sec., trustee Highland Hosp.; past pres. Harley Sch. Mem. ABA, N.Y. State Bar Assn. (chmn. com. ins. programs and retirement plans), Monroe County Bar Assn., NYU Inst. Fed. Taxation (adv. com.). Club: Genessee Valley, Country Club of Rochester (Rochester, N.Y.). Pension, profit-sharing, and employee benefits, Personal income taxation, Health. Office: 2200 Lincoln Tower Rochester NY 14603

FISCHER, THOMAS COVELL, legal educator, consultant, writer, lawyer; b. Cin., May 2, 1938; s. Vilas Uber and Elizabeth Mary (Holland) F.; m. Katherine Brenda Andrew, Sept. 29, 1972; A.B., U. Cin., 1960; postgrad. U. Wash., 1960-62, Loyola U., Chgo., 1964-66; J.D., Georgetown U., 1966. Asst. dir. U. Ill.-Chgo., 1964-66; asst. dean Georgetown U. Law Ctr., 1966-72; cons. Antioch Sch. Law, 1972-73; asst. exec. dir. Am. Bar Found., Chgo., 1974-76; assoc. dean, prof. law U. Dayton, 1976-78; dean, prof. New Eng. Sch. Law, 1978-81, prof. 1981—; cons. ednl. instns. Project dir. Commn. on Legal Edn. and Practice and the Economy of New Eng. Recipient Elaine R. Maham award U. Cin., 1960; Pi Kappa Alpha Meml. scholar, 1960-62. Mem. Delta Theta Phi, Pi Delta Epsilon, Phi Alpha Theta. Roman Catholic. Author: Due Process in the Student/Institutional Relationship, 1970; (with Duscha) The Campus Press: Freedom and Responsibility, 1973; (with Zenhle) Introduction to Law and Legal Reasoning, 1977. Administrative and regulatory, Civil rights, Legal education. Office: New Eng Sch Law 154 Stuart St Boston MA 02116

FISE, THOMAS FRANCIS, lawyer; b. Wheeling, W.Va., July 13, 1950; s. Francis Clarence and Marcella Marie (Megale) F.; m. Mary Ellen Rextor, Dec. 27, 1975; 1 child, Peter. BA with high honors, George Washington U.,

1972, MA with high honors, 1975, LLM in Taxation with high honors, 1983; JD with high honors, U. Md., 1977. Bar: Md. 1978. Dir. adminstrv. services Am. Dental Trade Assn., Washington, 1975-78; dir. adminstrn. Nat. Park. Found., Washington, 1978-84; gen. counsel Nat. Spa and Pool Inc., Alexandria, Va., 1984—; spl. counsel Am. Dental Trade Assn., Washington, 1978—. Editor: Complete Guide to America's National Parks, 1979. Trustee scholarships George Washington U., Washington, 1968-72. Mem. ABA, Am. Soc. Assn. Execs. Democrat. Roman Catholic. Administrative and regulatory, Personal income taxation, Personal injury. Home: 3016 Q St NW Washington DC 20007

FISH, A. JOE, judge; b. Los Angeles, Nov. 12, 1942; s. John Allen and Mary Magdalene (Martin) F.; m. Betty Fish, Jan. 23, 1971; 1 child, Abigail. B.A., Yale U., 1965, LL.B., 1968. Bar: Tex. Assoc. firm McKenzie & Baer, Dallas, 1968-80; judge Tex. Dist. Ct., 1980-81; assoc. judge Tex. Appeals Ct., 1981-83; judge U.S. Dist Ct. (no. dist.) Tex., Dallas, 1983—. Mem. ABA, State Bar Assn. Tex., Dallas Bar Assn. Office: Room 15-A-3 US Courthouse 1100 Commerce St Dallas TX 75242 *

FISH, JOHN MANCIL, JR., lawyer; b. Tulsa, Mar. 13, 1937; s. John Mancil and Alice Jean (Shearer) F.; m. Gayle Marie Bruner, Aug. 29, 1959; children: Cara Jean, Carla Jo. BS MechE, U. Okla., 1960, LLB, 1963. Bar: Okla. 1963, U.S. Dist. Ct. (we. dist.) Okla. 1971, U.S. Patent and Trademark Office 1971. Tech. staff adminstr. Sperry Univac, Bristol, Tenn., 1967-70; patent atty., assoc. Dunlap, Laney, Hessin & Dougherty, Oklahoma City, 1970-73; patent atty., ptnr. Laney, Dougherty, Hessin & Fish, Oklahoma City, 1973-77; patent atty. Phillips Petroleum Co., Bartlesville, Okla., 1977—. Mem. Bartlesville Symphony Orch., 1977—; pres. Bartlesville Symphony Orch. Assn. Inc., 1979-80. Served to capt. U.S. Army, 1963-67. Mem. Okla. Bar Assn. (pres. patent, trademark & copyright sect. 1976-77), Washington County Bar Assn., Am. Intellectual Property Law Assn., Phi Alpha Delta. Lodge: Elks. Avocations: fishing, running, music. Patent, Trademark and copyright, Licensing and Technology Transfer. Home: 4620 Rolling Meadows Rd Bartlesville OK 74006 Office: Phillips Petroleum Co 259 PLB Bartlesville OK 74004

FISH, PAUL MATHEW, lawyer; b. N.Y.C., Sept. 27, 1947; s. Louis and Shirley (Aaronowitz) F.; m. Patrice Ellen Schooley, Nov. 27, 1976. B.A., Drake U., 1969; J.D., Harvard U., 1972. Bar: N. Mex. 1972, U.S. Dist. Ct. N.Mex. 1972, U.S. Ct. Appeals (10th cir.) 1972. Mem. Modrall, Sperling, Roehl, Harris & Sisk, P.A., Albuquerque, 1972—; chmn. Chpt. 11 Local Rules Com., Albuquerque, 1981, bankruptcy law sect. N.Mex. State Bar, Albuquerque, 1983. Mem. ABA, N.Mex. Bar Assn., Albuquerque Bar Assn. Federal civil litigation, Bankruptcy, Construction. Home: Box 7 Tunnel Springs Rd Placitas NM 87043 Office: PO Box 2168 500 4th St NW Albuquerque NM 87103

FISH, PETER GRAHAM, law educator; b. 1937. AB, Princeton (N.J.) U., 1960, AM, 1965; PhD, John Hopkins U., 1968. Vis. instr. Oberlin (Ohio) Coll., 1965-66; instr. polit. sci. Princeton (N.J.) U., 1966-68, lectr. polit. sci., 1968-69; asst. prof. Duke U., Durham, N.C., 1969-71, assoc. prof. polit. sci., 1971-80, prof., 1980—. Office: Duke U Law Sch Durham NC 27706 *

FISHBEIN, PETER MELVIN, lawyer; b. N.Y.C., June 20, 1934; s. Arthur L. and Lotta (Chary) F.; m. Bette Klinghoffer, June 16, 1957; children: Stephen, Bruce, Gregory. B.A. magna cum laude, Dartmouth Coll., 1955; J.D., Harvard U., 1958. Bar: N.Y. 1959, U.S. Supreme Ct. 1973. Note editor Harvard Law Rev., Cambridge, Mass., 1956-58; law clk. to Justice William J. Brennan, Jr. U.S. Supreme Ct., Washington, 1958-59; dep. sec.gen. Internat. Peace Corps., Washington, 1962-64; ptnr. Kaye, Scholer, Fierman Hays & Handler, N.Y.C., 1967—, mng. ptnr., 1984—; chief counsel N.Y. State Constl. Conv., Albany, 1967; mem. Presdl. Commn. to Nominate Candidates for Fed. Ct. of Appeals, N.Y.C., 1980. Contbr. articles to profl. jours. Trustee Goddard Coll., 1967-75; mem. N.Y. State Gov.'s Bd. Pub. Disclosure, Albany, 1975-77; trustee Fedn. Jewish Philanthropies, N.Y.C., 1975-81; compaign mgr. Justice Arthur J. Goldberg's Campaign for gov., 1970. Fellow Am. Coll. Trial Lawyers; mem. N.Y.C. Bar Assn., ABA, Phi Beta Kappa. Club: Beach Point (bd. govs. 1981-86). Home: 101 Woodlands Rd Harrison NY 10528 Office: Kaye Scholer Fierman Hays & Handler 425 Park Ave New York NY 10022

FISHBERG, GERARD, lawyer; b. Bronx, N.Y., May 23, 1946; s. Alfred and Sarah (Goldberg) F.; m. Eileen Taubman, Dec. 23, 1972; children: David, Dana. BA, Hofstra U., 1968; JD, St. John's U., Bklyn., 1971. Bar: N.Y. 1972, U.S. Dist. Ct. (ea. and so. dists.) N.Y. 1973, U.S. Ct. Appeals (2d cir.) 1975, U.S. Supreme Ct. 1976. Assoc. Cullen & Dykman, Garden City, N.Y., 1972-79, ptnr., 1980—. Assoc. editor St. John's U. Law Rev., 1970-71. Mem. legis. com. N.Y. Conf. of Mayors and Mcpl. Officials, Albany, 1976—. Served to capt. USAR, 1968-77. St. Thomas Moore scholar St. John's U. Sch. Law, 1969-71. Mem. N.Y. State Bar Assn. (exec. com. 1978—, sec. 1985-87, 2d vice chmn. 1987—, mcpl. law sect., labor law sect.), Nassau County Bar Assn. (chmn. mcpl. law com. 1981-83, 1985—, labor law com.), Garden City C. of C. Jewish. Lodge: Rotary. Labor, Local government. Home: 1 Bucknell Dr Plainview NY 11803 Office: Cullen & Dykman 1010 Franklin Ave Garden City NY 11530

FISHER, ANN BAILEN, lawyer; b. N.Y.C., Oct. 15, 1951; s. Eliot and Elise (Thompson) Bailen; m. John C. Fisher, Apr. 6, 1980. BA magna cum laude, Radcliffe Coll., 1973; JD, Harvard U., 1976. Bar: N.Y. 1977. Assoc. Sullivan & Cromwell, N.Y.C., 1976-80, 82-84, ptnr., 1984—; assoc. Sullivan & Cromwell, Paris, 1980-82. Mem. ABA, N.Y. State Bar Assn. Episcopalian. Clubs: Cosmopolitan, Harvard (N.Y.C.). Securities, General corporate. Office: Sullivan & Cromwell 125 Broad St New York NY 10004

FISHER, BARRY ALAN, lawyer; b. Los Angeles, May 15, 1943; s. Harry Benjamin and Fay Doris (Sternfeld) F.; m. Susan E. Landman, June 16, 1968; children—J. Benjamin, Jonathan J., Robert A. A.B., UCLA, 1965, J.D., 1968. Bar: Alaska 1969, R.I. 1969, Calif. 1971, U.S. Supreme Ct. 1972. Law clk. to chief justice Alaska, 1968-69; Reginald Heber Smith fellow U. Pa., 1969-71; staff counsel Sierra Club Legal Def. Fund, San Francisco, 1972-74; mem. Fleishman, Brown, Weston & Rhode, Beverly Hills, Calif., 1974-76; sr. ptnr. Fisher & Moest, Los Angeles, 1976—; v.p. Human Rights Advs.; justice of peace, R.I., 1971; co-founder, gen. counsel U.S. Romani Council; mem. com. on persons with spl. needs, Calif. State Bar; speaker profl. confs. Mem. adv. bd. Constitutions Research Centre; bd. dirs. Pacifica Found.; mem. bd. Sta. KPFK-FM. Mem. ABA (religious freedom subcommn.), World Assn. Lawyers, Judges (chmn., World Peace thru Law Ctr., religion and law commn.). Contbg. author Government Intervention in Religious Affairs, 1982; mem. adv. bd. Religious Freedom Reporter. Constitutional, Environment, Federal civil litigation. Office: Fleishman Fisher & Moest 2049 Century Park E Suite 3160 Los Angeles CA 90067

FISHER, BART STEVEN, lawyer, lecturer; b. St. Louis, Feb. 16, 1943; s. Irvin and Orene (Moskow) F.; m. Margaret Cottony, Mar. 1, 1969; 1 child, Ross Alan. A.B., Washington U., 1963, M.A., Johns Hopkins Sch. Advanced Internat. Studies, 1967, Ph.D., 1970; J.D., Harvard Law Sch., 1972. Bar: D.C. 1972. Assoc. Patton, Boggs & Blow, Washington, 1972-78, ptnr., 1978—; adj. prof. internat. relations Georgetown Sch. Fgn. Service, Washington, 1974-82; professorial lectr. internat. relations Johns Hopkins Sch. Advanced Internat. Studies, Washington, 1983—. Author: The International Coffee Agreement, 1972; (with John H. Barton) International Trade and Investment: Regulating International Business, 1986. Editor: Regulating the Multinational Enterprise, 1983; Barter in the World Economy, 1985. Treas., adv. com. chmn. Aplastic Anemia Found. Am. Inc., Balt., 1983—; program com. Georgetown Leadership Seminar, Washington, 1981—. Recipient Dean's Cert. Appreciation Georgetown U. Sch. Fgn. Service, Washington, 1984. Mem. ABA, Am. Soc. Internat. Law (rapporteur, panel trade policy and insts. 1974-77), Wash. Fgn. Law Soc. Jewish. Clubs: Georgetown, Reston Racquet (Va.), Great Falls Swim and Tennis (Va.). International trade, Public international, Administrative and regulatory. Home: 723 Walker Rd Great Falls VA 22066 Office: Patton Boggs & Blow 2550 M St NW Washington DC 20037

FISHER, BERTRAM DORE, lawyer; b. N.Y.C., July 10, 1928; s. Samuel and Dorothy (Eisman) F.; m. Barbara Marks, Aug. 23, 1959; children—Beth Carlyle Cutler, Priscilla Brooke. Student Johns Hopkins U.; B.A., U. Miami, Fla., 1949; LL.B., Bklyn Law Sch., 1951; postgrad. NYU Grad Sch. Law. Bar: N.Y., D.C. Sr. ptnr. Queller, Fisher, Bower & Wisotsky, N.Y.C.; mem. Supreme Ct. Com., 1985—, Med. Malpractice Jud. Panel, Supreme Ct., N.Y. County; lectr. N.Y. Acad. Trial Lawyers; frequent lectr. to profession on trial techniques, evidence, cross-examination. Served with U.S. Army, 1951-53, Korea. Decorated Bronze Star. Recipient Man of Year award NCFJE, 1984. Mem. ABA, N.Y. State Trial Lawyers Assn. (bd. dirs., mem. jud. screening com. 1978-85), N.Y. State Bar Assn. (mem. ethics com. 1979-80, toxic waste com., negligence com. 1984—), Assn. of Bar of City of N.Y., D.C. Bar Assn., N.Y. County Lawyers Assn. (com. on Supreme Ct. 1978-83, forum com. 1984-85), Assn. Trial Lawyers City N.Y., N.Y. Criminal and Civil Bar Assn., Bklyn. and Manhattan Trial Counsel Assn., Bklyn. Bar Assn. (mem. ethics com. 1978-80), Met. Women's Bar Assn., Jewish Lawyers Guild (pres. 1984—), Assn. Trial Lawyers Am. (Roscoe Pound Found., M Club), Joint Bar Assn. (jud. screening com. 1983—), Internat. Assn. Jewish Lawyers and Jurists (bd. dirs. Merit award 1986), Bklyn. Law Sch. Alumni Assn., Am. Coll. Legal Medicine (assoc. in law), Network of Bar Leaders (com. of 24 bar assns. 1983—). Clubs: Downtown Athletic (N.Y.C.), Iota Theta; Dunes Racquet (Ammagamset, N.Y.); Port Washington Tennis Acad. (N.Y.); North Shore H.C. (Manhasset, N.Y.). Personal injury. Office: Queller Fisher Bower & Wisotsky 110 Wall St New York NY 10005

FISHER, CATHERINE AMBROSIANO, lawyer; b. Bklyn., Aug. 5, 1946; d. Taddeo and Gilda (Caressa) Ambrosiano; B.A., Marygrove Coll., 1968; M.A. (fellow), U. Detroit, 1970; J.D., Detroit Coll. Law, 1977; m. Eugene J. Fisher, Dec. 31, 1970. Admitted to Mich. bar, 1977, D.C. bar, 1978; atty. ICC Office Hearings, Washington, 1977-80; atty. div. corp. regulation SEC, Washington, 1980-84, dep. asst. dir. Office Pub. Utility Regulation, Div. Investment Mgmt., 1984—. Sec., bd. dirs. Chs.' Center for Theology and Public Policy, Washington, 1981-87; mem. nat. adv. com. Secretariat for Catholic-Jewish Relations, Nat. Conf. Cath. Bishops. Mem. ABA (pub. utility law sect.). Roman Catholic. Co-author Family article series Nat. Cath. News, 1979-80. Public utilities, Securities, Administrative and regulatory. Home: 11296 Spyglass Cove Ln Reston VA 22091

FISHER, CHERYL SMITH, lawyer; b. Corning, N.Y., Sept. 4, 1951; d. Norman Albert and Betty (Manzella) Smith; 1 child, Daniel Terence. BA, SUNY-Oswego, 1973; JD, SUNY-Buffalo, 1976. Bar: N.Y. 1977, U.S. Dist. Ct. (we. dist.) N.Y. 1977, U.S. Ct. Appeals (2d cir.) 1980. Assoc. Runfola, Birzon & Renda, Buffalo, 1976-77, Kavinoky Cook et al, Buffalo, 1977-79; asst. U.S. atty. Western Dist. N.Y., Buffalo, 1979-84; assoc. Cohen Swados Wright Hanifin Bradford & Brett, Buffalo, 1984-86; assoc. Magavern & Magavern, Buffalo, 1986—; spl. asst. U.S. atty. Dept. Justice, Buffalo, 1984. Pres. Cathedral Park Counseling Sevice, Inc., Buffalo, 1979-83; bd. dirs. Child and Family Service Erie County, Buffalo, 1984—; mem. vestry St. Paul's Cathedral, Buffalo, 1979-82, 84-87. Recipient Trial Practice award Trial Lawyers Assn. Erie County, 1976. Mem. Erie County Bar Assn., N.Y. State Women's Bar Assn., Women Lawyers Assn., Alpha Psi Omega. Democrat. Episcopalian. Federal civil litigation, State civil litigation. Home: 441 Crescent Ave Buffalo NY 14214 Office: Law Offices 20 Cathedral Park Buffalo NY 14202

FISHER, CLARKSON SHERMAN, judge; b. Long Branch, N.J., July 8, 1921; s. Albert Emmanuel and Katherine Morris (Sherman) F.; m. Mae Shannon Hoffmann, Dec. 26, 1949; children—Albert James, Clarkson Sherman, Scott Laurus, Daniel Russell. LL.B. cum laude, U. Notre Dame, 1950. Bar: N.J. bar 1951. Law clk., atty. Jacob Steinbach, Jr. (Atty. at Law), Long Branch, 1950, 51; atty. Edward F. Juska (Lawyer), Long Branch, 1951-58; partner Juska & Fisher (Counsellors at Law), Long Branch, 1958-64; Monmouth County (N.J.) Ct. judge 1964-66; judge N.J. Superior Ct., 1966-70; judge U.S. Dist. Ct., Dist. of N.J., 1970-79, chief judge, 1979—. Trustee Central Jersey Bank & Trust Co.; Atty. Long Branch Planning Bd., Partrolmen's Benevolent Assn., Long Branch, Monmouth County, and Bayshore (N.J.); Mem. West Long Branch Fire Co. 2, 1955—, West Long Branch Bd. Adjustment, 1958; mem. Borough Council, West Long Branch, 1959-64; N.J. State assemblyman from Monmouth County, 1964; Trustee Monmouth Coll., West Long Branch, 1971-76. Served to staff sgt. Signal Corps, also Inf. AUS, 1942-45. Mem. ABA., N.J. Bar Assn., Monmouth County Bar Assn. (trustee 1962-64), Am. Legion, Holy Name Soc. (pres. chpt. 1960), VFW. Home: 11 Pinewood Ave West Long Branch NJ 07764 Office: Fed Bldg and US Courthouse Bldg Trenton NJ 08608

FISHER, CLYDE OLIN, JR., lawyer; b. Middletown, Conn., Nov. 5, 1927; s. Clyde Olin and Agnes Hawthorne (Johnston) F.; m. Alice Marshall Daltry, Apr. 11, 1953; children—Timothy, Andrew. B.A., Wesleyan U., 1949; J.D., Yale U., 1954, M.S. in Conservation, 1956. Bar: Conn. 1954. Cons. on water law Conservation Found., N.Y.C., Conn. Water Resources Commn., Hartford, 1955-56; zoning dir. City of New Haven, 1956-60; zoning adminstr. City of San Francisco, 1960-66; dir. land use policies and controls project P.R. Planning Bd., San Juan, 1966-69; div. chief Conn. Dept. Community Affairs, Hartford, 1969-71; environ. planning dir. N.E. Utilities, Hartford, 1971-77, environ. counsel, 1978-81; sole practice, Hartford, 1982—. Mem. citizen adv. bd. New Eng. River Basins Commn., 1970-71, chmn., 1973-74; counsel on planning and zoning legis. Conn. Gen. Assembly, 1977-78; vice chmn. Conn. Sr. Exec. Service Bd., 1979-83; bd. dirs. Conn. Forest and Park Assn., 1980—; trustee Unitarian Soc., Hartford, 1980-85. Served with USNR, 1945-46. Mem. Conn. Bar Assn. (exec. com. environ. sect.), Am. Planning Assn., Am. Inst. Cert. Planners (chmn. nat. nominating com. 1970-72). Author various publs. on water law, land planning and zoning, and environ. planning of electric utility facilities. Environment, Land use and planning. Home and Office: 15 Sunfield Ln West Hartford CT 06107

FISHER, EDWARD JOSEPH, lawyer; b. Ft. Leavenworth, Kans., Apr. 23, 1943. BA, So. Ill. U., 1967; JD, John Marshall Law Sch., Chgo., 1971. Bar: Ill. 1971, U.S. Dist. Ct. (so. dist.) Ill. 1972. atty. City of Chester, Ill., 1967—; pub. defender Randolph County, Chester, 1972-73; spl. asst. atty. gen. State of Ill., 1983—. Served with USMC, 1961-64. Mem. Ill. Trial Lawyers Assn. (workers compensation com.), Chester C. of C. (rural dir.). General practice, Local government, Workers' compensation. Office: Nehrt Sachtleben Fisher Smith & Kerkhover 1300 1/2 Swanwick St Chester IL 62233

FISHER, EDWARD WALTER, lawyer; b. Jackson, Mich., Oct. 12, 1953; s. William Paul and Grace (Monroe) F.; m. D'lyn Star Kulpa, Jan. 31, 1976. BA in Social Sci., Mich. State U., 1975; JD, U. Detroit, 1979; LLM, Wayne State U., 1986. Bar: Mich. 1980, U.S. Dist. Ct. (ea. dist.) Mich. 1982, U.S. Ct. Appeals (6th cir.) 1986. Legal asst. Blue Cross & Blue Shield of Mich., Detroit, 1977-80, asst. gen. counsel, 1980—. Mem. ABA, Detroit Bar Assn., Mensa. Methodist. Club: Econ. of Detroit. Lodge: Masons. Avocation: youth advisor to DeMolay. State civil litigation, General corporate, Insurance. Office: Blue Cross Blue Shield of Mich 600 Lafayette E Suite 2115 Detroit MI 48226

FISHER, EVERETT, lawyer; b. Greenwich, Conn., May 23, 1920; s. Henry Johnson and Alice Gifford (Agnew) F.; m. Catherine Gray Marshall, Aug. 21, 1943; children: Catherine (Mrs. Eliot Field), Emily Trenholm Griswold. Grad., Phillips Acad., 1937; B.A., Yale U., 1941, LL.B., 1948. Bar: Conn. 1948, N.Y. 1949. Assoc. Littlefield, Miller & Cleaves, N.Y.C., 1948-51; ptnr. Pullman, Comley, Marshall & Parker, Greenwich, 1951-58, Parker, Badger & Fisher, 1958-72, Badger, Fisher, Cohen & Barnett, 1972—; Dir., sec., mem. exec. com. Times Mirror Mags., Inc.; trust bd. dirs. Union Trust Co. Past chmn. Bd. Estimate and Taxation, Greenwich.; Bd. dirs., v.p. Greenwich Boys' Club; trustee Internat. Coll., Beirut, Lebanon. Mem. Internat., Am. bar assns., State Bar of Conn., Am. Coll. Probate Counsel, Phi Delta Phi. Republican. Clubs: Pine Valley Golf (Clementon, N.J.); Royal and Ancient Golf (St. Andrews, Scotland); Round Hill (Greenwich) (dir., past pres), Field (Greenwich); Yale (N.Y.C.); Royal St. George's Golf (Sandwich, Eng.); Honourable Company of Edinburgh Golfers (Muirfield, Scotland); U.S. Seniors Golf Assn. (sec., gov.). Probate, Estate taxation, Estate planning. Home: 53 Pecksland Rd Greenwich CT 06831 Office: 49 W Putnam Ave Greenwich CT 06830

FISHER, FREDRICK LEE, lawyer; b. Charleston, W.Va., Nov. 12, 1952; s. Ahaz and Lois Mildred (O'Dell) F.; m. Roberta Lee Lane, Sept. 16, 1972; children: Jamie Elizabeth, John Fredrick. BA in Econs., Ohio State U., 1973; JD, Harvard U., 1976. Bar: Ohio 1976, U.S. Dist. Ct. (no. dist.) Ohio 1976, U.S. Claims Ct. 1978, U.S. Tax Ct. 1978. Assoc. Squire, Sanders & Dempsey, Cleve., 1976-80, Columbus, Ohio, 1981-85; ptnr. Squire, Sanders & Dempsey, Columbus, 1985-87, Schottenstein, Zox & Dunn, Columbus, 1987—; sec. DirectCare Inc., Columbus, 1986—, bd. dirs. Trustee Players Theatre of Columbus Found., 1982—; sec., treas., trustee The Bill and Edith Walter Found., Columbus, 1982—; v.p., trustee Meadow Park Ch., Columbus, 1985—. Mem. ABA (corps. com. tax sect. 1982—), Ohio Bar Assn., Columbus Bar Assn. (organizing com. Columbus tax conf. 1981-84), Phi Beta Kappa. Republican. Club: University (Columbus). Avocations: golf, basketball, softball, reading, gardening. General corporate, Health, Probate. Home: 6711 Elmers Ct Worthington OH 43085 Office: Schottenstein Zox & Dunn 41 S High St Columbus OH 43215

FISHER, HAROLD LEONARD, lawyer, banker; b. N.Y.C., Dec. 10, 1910; s. Jacob and Pauline (Sherman) F.; m. Betty Kahn, July 24, 1934; children—H. Leonard, Alice Fisher Rubin, Stephanie Fisher Cooper, Andrew S., Kenneth K. LL.B. cum laude, St. John's U., 1932. Bar: N.Y. 1935, U.S. Dist. Ct. (ea. dist.) N.Y. 1937, U.S. Dist. Ct. (so. dist.) N.Y. 1938, U.S. Ct. Appeals (2d cir.) 1946. Sole practice, Bklyn., 1935-76; ptnr. Fisher & Fisher, Bklyn., 1976—; chmn. bd. Dime Savs. Bank of Williamsburgh, 1976-85; Bd. dirs. HIP of Greater N.Y., Nat. Housing Conf.; chmn. bd. Met. Transit Authority, 1977-79, dir., 1968-79; mem. presdl. del. at Mt. Sinai Transfer; chmn. urban transp. del. to People's Republic of China, 1979; bd. dirs. Bklyn. Acad. Music, Borough Hall Restoration Fund; mem. Nat. Citizens Coalition for the Windfall Profits Tax; treas. Democratic County Com. Kings County, N.Y. Recipient B'nai B'rith Youth Service Am. Traditions award, 1981; Gonen Soc. Man of Year award, 1978; L.I. Rail Road Club Transp. Man of Year award, 1977; named March of Dimes Transit Man of Year, 1978. Mem. Bklyn. Bar Assn. (pres. 1977-78, Ann. award for outstanding achievement in law and pub. service 1983), Fed. Bar Council, ABA, N.Y. State Bar Assn., Bklyn. Criminal Bar Assn., N.Y. State Trial Lawyers Assn. Jewish. Clubs: Bklyn., B'nai B'rith, The Towers. General practice, General corporate, Real property. Office: 189 Montague St Brooklyn NY 11201

FISHER, JEFFREY B., lawyer; b. Balt., Dec. 2, 1949; s. Irving H. and Esther Ida (Sandler) F.; children: Aaron Benjamin, Ethan Israel. BS, U. Md., 1971, JD, 1974. Ptnr. Fisher & Walcek, Marlow Heights, Md., 1974—. Bd. dirs. Shaare Tikvah Congregation, Temple Hills, Md., 1985—. Mem. ABA, Md. Bar Assn., Prince George's County Bar Assn. (bd. dirs. 1982-83), Atty. Greivance Commn. (inquiry panel 1981—, rev. bd. 1986—). Democrat. Avocations: skiing, folk music, computing. Probate, Family and matrimonial, General corporate. Office: Fisher & Walcek 4465 Old Branch Ave Marlow Heights MD 20748

FISHER, JOHN EDWIN, insurance company executive; b. Portsmouth, Ohio, Oct. 26, 1929; s. Charles Hall and Bess (Swearingin) F.; m. Eloise Lyon, Apr. 25, 1949. Student, U. Colo., 1947-48, Ohio U., 1948-49, Franklin U., Columbus, Ohio, 1950-51. With Nationwide Mut. Ins. Co., Columbus, 1951—, v.p., office gen. chmn., 1970-72, pres., gen. mgr., dir., 1972-81, gen. chmn., chief exec. officer, 1981—, also dir.; gen. chmn., chief exec. officer, dir. Nationwide Gen. Ins. Co., Nationwide Mut. Fire Ins. Co., Nationwide Property & Casualty Ins. Co., Nationwide Life Ins. Co., Nationwide Variable Life Ins. Co.; dir. Neckura Versicherungs A.G., Oberursel, Germany, 1976—; gen. chmn., dir. Employers Ins. of Wausau, 1985—, Farmland Ins. Cos., 1985—; trustee Ohio Cener Co. Chmn. bd. Nationwide Found., 1981—; pres. bd. trustees Children's Hosp., 1984-87. Mem. Chartered Property and Casualty Underwriters Assn., Chartered Life Underwriters Soc., Assn. Ohio Life Ins. Cos. (past pres.), Ohio Ins. Inst. (pres. 1975-77), Nat. Assn. Ind. Insurers, Am. Risk and Ins. Assn., Griffith Ins. Found. (chmn. 1981), Property-Casualty Ins. Council (chmn. 1981-82), Property and Liability Underwriters, Ins. Inst. Am., Am. Inst. Property-Liability Insurers (chmn. 1985—), Am. Inst. Property and Liability Underwriters, Ins. Inst. Am., Internat. Coop. Ins. Fedn. (chmn. 1984—), Columbus C. of C. (chmn. 1981-82). Federal civil litigation, State civil litigation, Insurance. Office: Nationwide Mutual Ins Co One Nationwide Plaza Columbus OH 43216

FISHER, J(OHN) ROBERT, lawyer; b. Duncan, Okla., Dec. 26, 1946; s. John Earl and Ena (Salas) F.; m. Jane Lee Kleier, Jan. 20, 1968; children—Jennifer, Katherine, Andrew, Rebecca. B.A., U. Okla., 1968, J.D., 1973. Bar: Tex. 1974, U.S. Dist. Ct. (so. dist.) Tex. 1974, U.S. Dist. Ct. (no. dist.) Tex. 1975, U.S. Ct. Appeals (5th cir.) 1977, U.S. Supreme Ct. 1979. Atty. Conoco, Inc., Houston, 1973-75; assoc. Matthews, Matthews, Sechrist & Madrid, Dallas, 1975-76; assoc., ptnr. real estate sect. Winstead, McGuire, Sechrest & Minick, Dallas, 1976—, mem. mgmt. com., 1985-87. Bd. dirs. The Chance Ctr., Dallas, 1985; fund raiser Am. Heart Assn., Dallas, 1984. Served to capt. U.S. Army, 1968-71. Decorated Bronze Star. Mem. ABA, Tex. Bar Assn., Dallas Bar Assn., Order of Coif. Republican. Episcopalian. Real property, Landlord-tenant, Banking. Home: 2921 University Blvd Dallas TX 75205 Office: Winstead McGuire Sechrest & Minick 400 Allied Bank Tower Dallas TX 75202

FISHER, JOSEPH FREILER, lawyer; b. Highland Park, Ill., Dec. 25, 1955; s. Milton Leonard and Jean (Freiler) F. BA, Lake Forest Coll., 1978; JD, Northwestern U., 1981. Bar: Ill. 1982, U.S. Dist. Ct. (no. dist.) Ill. 1982, U.S. Ct. Appeals (7th cir.) 1982, U.S. Tax Ct. 1985; lic. real estate broker, Ill. 1986. Assoc. Frankel, McKay & Orlikoff, Chgo., 1981-82, Altheimer & Gray, Chgo., 1983-85; sole practice Chgo., 1985—. Young Profls. chmn. Stevenson for Gov., Chgo., 1985-86. Mem. ABA, Ill. Bar Assn., Chgo. Bar Assn., Chgo. Council Lawyers. Democrat. Jewish. Club: Cliffdwellers (Chgo.). Consumer commercial, Bankruptcy.

FISHER, KENNETH KNIGHT, lawyer; b. Bklyn., Feb. 22, 1953; s. Harold Leonard and Betty (Kahn) F.; m. Kirsten Moller Jensen, Sept. 18, 1977; children: Jacob Neil, Penelope Anne. BA, U. Pacific, 1973; JD, Syracuse U., 1976. Bar: N.Y. 1977, U.S. Dist. Ct. (ea. dist.) N.Y. 1979, U.S. Dist. Ct. (so. dist.) N.Y. 1980, U.S. Supreme Ct. 1980, U.S. Ct. Appeals (2d cir.) 1985. Asst. counsel N.Y. State Energy Research & Devel. Authority, N.Y.C., 1976-78; ptnr. Fisher & Fisher, Bklyn., 1978—. Treas. Com. for Golden Future, Bklyn., 1982—; mem. com. Bklyn. Friends Sch., 1977-84; trustee Interfaith Hosp., Bklyn., 1986—. Mem. N.Y. State Bar Assn. (ho. dels. 1979-85, various coms.), Am. Arbitration Assn. (arbitrator 1987—), Assn. of Bar of City of N.Y. (various coms.), Am. Scandinavian Soc. (v.p., bd. dirs. 1984-86). Democrat. Club: Brooklyn. General practice, Real property, Health. Office: Fisher & Fisher 189 Montague St Brooklyn NY 11201

FISHER, MICHAEL BRUCE, lawyer, corporate executive; b. Montgomery, Ala., Jan. 2, 1945; s. Philip and Rita (Joss) F.; m. Noreen Rene Zidel, June 25, 1967; children—Anne Elizabeth, Alex Nicholas. B.A., U. Minn., 1967; J.D., U. Calif.-Berkeley, 1970. Bar: N.Y. 1971, Minn. 1972, U.S. Dist. Ct. Minn. 1972. Assoc. Rosenman, Colin, et al, N.Y.C., 1970-71, Mullin, Swirnoff & Weinberg, P.A., Mpls., 1972-73; staff atty. Fingerhut Corp., Mpls., 1974, assoc. gen. counsel, 1975-80, gen. counsel, 1980-83, v.p., gen. counsel, sec., 1983—; dir. Mchts. Research Council, Chgo., 1976-80. Exec. com., dir. Big Sisters Mpls., Inc., 1976-83, Big Bros./Big Sisters Mpls., Inc., 1984—; v.p., bd. dirs. Herzl Camp Assn., Inc., Mpls., 1975—; vol. Minn. Pub. TV, St. Paul, 1980—. Mem. Minn. Bar Assn., ABA, Am. Corp. Counsel Assn. Minn., Minn. Retail Mchts. Assn. (trustee 1983—), Direct Mktg. Assn. (govt. affairs com. 1980—), 3d Class Mail Assn. (sec., bd. dirs. 1981-86, exec. vice chmn. 1987—), Parcel Shippers Assn. (v.p., bd. dirs. 1980-86, pres. 1987—). Jewish. Club: Calhoun Beach (Mpls.). General corporate, Legislative, Contracts commercial. Office: 4400 Baker Rd Minnetonka MN 55343

FISHER, MILTON LEONARD, lawyer; b. Pitts., Jan. 17, 1922; s. Jacob Morris and Sara (Weiner) F.; m. Jean Freiler, Apr. 30, 1950; children: Susan Yellen, Janet Sara, Joseph Freiler. A.B., Oberlin Coll., 1943; J.D., Northwestern U., 1949. Bar: Ill. 1949, Ohio 1949. Assoc. Suekoff & Frost, Chgo., 1949-50; assoc. Mayer, Brown & Platt, Chgo., 1950-60, ptnr., 1960—. Mem. ednl. region service commn. Ill. State Bd. Edn., 1979; chmn. Highland Park Civil Service Commn., Ill., 1959-68; bd. dirs. Better Govt. Assn.; mem. Spl. Commn. on Jud. Discipline; bd. dirs. Chgo. Bar Found. Mem. ABA, Ill. Bar Assn., Chgo. Bar Assn., Chgo. Council Lawyers, Law Club.

Clubs: Lake Shore Country (Glencoe, Ill.); Cliff Dwellers (Chgo.). Home: 349 Woodland Rd Highland Park IL 60035 Office: Mayer Brown & Platt 190 S LaSalle St Chicago IL 60603

FISHER, MYRON R., lawyer; b. Chgo., Aug. 13, 1935. B.A., Calif. State U., Long Beach, 1964; J.D., Southwestern U., 1969. Bar: Calif. 1970, U.S. Dist. Ct. (cen. dist.) Calif. 1970, U.S. Supreme Ct. 1974. Dep. pub. defender San Bernardino County (Calif.), 1970-71; assoc. Anderson, Adams & Bacon, Rosemead, Calif., 1971-74; sole practice, San Clemente, Calif., 1974—; judge pro tem South Orange County Mcpl. Ct., 1978—. Served with U.S. Army, 1955-57. Mem. State Bar Calif., South Orange County Bar Assn. (dir. 1978-83), Orange County Bar Assn., Los Angeles Trial Lawyers Assn., Orange County Trial Lawyers Assn., Calif. Trial Lawyers Assn., Assn. Trial Lawyers Am. Criminal, Insurance, Personal injury. Office: Fisher Profl Bldg 630 S El Camino Real San Clemente CA 92672

FISHER, NED LAWRENCE, lawyer; b. Waukegan, Ill., Dec. 28, 1947; s. Henry Dayton and Florence Charlotte (Cook) F.; m. Mary Jen Gavigan, May 19, 1979; stepchildren: Richard James Kennedy, Nora Maureen Kennedy; 1 child, Bradley Lawrence. BA, Cornell U., 1970; JD, U. Mich., 1973. Bar: Ill. 1978. Assoc. Hall, Holmberg, Roach, Johnston, Fisher & Lessmon, Waukegan, 1973-80, ptnr., 1981—; spl. asst. atty. gen. Ill. Dept. Transp. and Conservation, Waukegan, 1975-84; commr. Attys. Registration and Disciplinary Commn. Chmn. com. to re-elect congressman Robert McClory, 1976, 80; pres. Waukegan Young Reps., 1976-78, Jacob Blumberg Meml. Blood Bank, Waukegan, 1980-83, Lake County Reps. Fedn., Ill., 1983—. Served to capt. U.S. Army, 1974. Recipient Distinguished Service award Jaycees, 1979. Mem. Ill. Bar Assn. (council sec. 1982-83, v.p. 1983-84, pres. young lawyers div.), Lake County Bar Assn. (treas. 1980-82, chmn. found. 1984—, 2d v.p. 1986—). Republican. Jewish. Lodges: Moose, B'nai B'rith. Real property, Banking. Home: 2430 N Poplar St Waukegan IL 60087 Office: Hall Holmberg Roach et al 25 N County St Waukegan IL 60085

FISHER, PATRICIA SWEENEY, lawyer; b. Chgo., Sept. 11, 1954; d. Michael C. and Mary J. (Moore) Sweeney; m. Edward Vogler Fisher, Sept. 23, 1982. BA, Northwestern U., 1975; JD, Northwestern U., Chgo., 1978. Bar: Ill. 1978. Assoc. Isham, Lincoln & Beale, Chgo., 1978-81; atty. Amoco Corp., Chgo., 1981—; corp. sec. Amoco Credit Corp. Securities, General corporate. Home: 26060 W Cuba Rd Barrington IL 60010 Office: Amoco Corp 200 E Randolph Dr Suite 2106 Chicago IL 60601

FISHER, PETER FRANCIS, lawyer; b. Washington, Aug. 14, 1955; s. Charles M. and Eleanor A. (Akers) F. BA in History with honors, U. Md., 1977; JD, U. Ala., 1980. Bar: Ariz. 1980, U.S. Dist. Ct. Ariz. 1980, U.S. Ct. Appeals (9th cir.) 1982, U.S. Supreme Ct. 1986. Assoc. Laird & Schmidt, P.C., Phoenix, 1980-84; sole practice Scottsdale, Ariz., 1984-86; ptnr. Schmitt & Assocs. P.C., Phoenix, 1986—; adj. faculty Ottawa U., Phoenix, 1985—. Hugo Black scholar U. Ala., 1977; named one of Outstanding Young Men Am., 1981, 82. Mem. Assn. Trial Lawyers Am., Ariz. Trial Lawyers Assn., Phoenix Trial Lawyers Assn. (bd. dirs. 1984—). Republican. Avocations: weight tng., golf. State civil litigation, General corporate, Personal injury. Home: 8225 E Thomas Rd Scottsdale AZ 85251 Office: Schmitt & Assocs PC 4725 N 19th Ave Phoenix AZ 85015

FISHER, PHILIP WAYNE, lawyer; b. Cameron, Tex., June 22, 1937; s. George Noel and Mary Jane (Diver) F.; m. Patsy Mullinax, July 25, 1958; children: Terri, Bryan. BBA, Baylor U., 1959, LLB, 1961. Bar: Tex. 1961. Assoc. Fulbrigst & Jaworski, Houston, 1961-66; founding ptnr. Fisher, Gallagher, Perrin & Lewis, Houston, 1966—. Contbr. articles to law jours. Guest artists sponsor Houston Symphony Soc., 1986; patron Soc. for Performing Arts, Houston, 1985—; bd. dirs. Houston Symphony Soc. Fellow Tex. Bar Assn.; mem. State Bar Assn. of Tex. (pres. 1981-82), Tex. Trial Lawyers Assn. (pres. 1974-75), Internat. Acad. Trial Lawyers (bd. dirs. 1985—), Houston Trial Lawyers Assn. (pres. 1971-72), Am. Bd. Trial Advs., Inner Circle Advs., Am. Coll. Trial Lawyers, Baylor Alumni Assn. (bd. dirs.). Democrat. Baptist. Avocations: Tex. history, keyboard jazz. Personal injury. Office: Fisher Gallagher Perrin & Lewis Allied Bank Plaza 1000 70th floor Houston TX 77002

FISHER, RANDALL EUGENE, lawyer, educator; b. Wichita, Kans., June 3, 1949; s. George Allen Fisher and LaVonna (Brooks) Jackson; m. Arlena L. Eveleigh, May 20, 1970 (div. 1976); 1 child, Scott N.; m. Kathy R. Vetter, July 21, 1978 (div. 1985). BA, Wesleyan U., Salina, Kans., 1971; JD, Washburn U., 1976. Bar: Kans. 1976, U.S. Dist. Ct. Kans. 1976, U.S. Ct. Appeals (10th cir.) 1981, U.S. Supreme Ct. 1981. Ptnr. McDonald, Tinker, Skaer, Quinn & Herrington PA, Wichita, 1974-81, also bd. dirs.; law clk. to assoc. justice Kans. Supreme Ct., Topeka, 1976-78; assoc. Barta & Barta, Salina, 1978-80; staff atty. Legal Aid of Wichita, 1980-81; adj. prof. Wichita State U., 1982—; trustee, vice chmn. Wichita Legal Aid, 1983—;faculty mem. Nat. Inst. Trial Advocacy, 1985—. Author: (with others) Settling Personal Injury Cases in Kansas, 1986, KBA KS Worker's Compensation Practice Manual, 1985-87, Kansas Uninsured and Underinsured Motorist Issues, 1987; ann. supplements. Advisor Law Explorer Post, Wichita, 1985-86. Recipient Dist. Advocacy Internat. Trial Lawyers Assn., 1975. Mem. ABA, Kans. Bar Assn., Wichita Bar Assn., Assn. Trial Lawyers Am., Kans. Trial Lawyers Assn. (bd. editors 1978-80), Kans. Assn. Def. Counsel, Internat. Trial Lawyers Assn., Order of Barristers. Democrat. Methodist. Avocations: photography, writing, computers. Workers' compensation, Personal injury, Federal civil litigation. Office: McDonald Tinker Skaer et al 300 W Douglas Wichita KS 67202

FISHER, ROBERTA LANE, lawyer; b. Cleve., Apr. 11, 1952; s. James Edward and Betty Jayne (Bucy) Lane; m. Fredrick Lee Fisher, Sept. 16, 1972; children: Jamie Elizabeth, John Fredrick. BA in Linguistics with distinction summa cum laude, Ohio State U., 1973; JD, Harvard U., 1976. Bar: Ohio 1976. Assoc. Squire, Sanders & Dempsey, Cleve. and Columbus, Ohio, 1976-85; ptnr. Squire, Sanders & Dempsey, Columbus, 1985—. Mem. ABA, Ohio Bar Assn., Columbus Bar Assn., Nat. Assn. Bond Lawyers, Bond Atty.'s Workshop (steering com.). Avocations: gardening, woodworking. Municipal bonds. Home: 6711 Elmers Ct Worthington OH 43085 Office: Squire Sanders & Dempsey 155 E Broad St Columbus OH 43215

FISHER, ROGER DUMMER, lawyer, educator, negotiation expert; b. Winnetka, Ill., May 28, 1922; s. Walter Taylor and Katharine (Dummer) F.; m. Caroline Speer, Sept. 18, 1948; children: Elliott Speer, Peter Ryerson. A.B., Harvard U., 1943, LL.B. magna cum laude, 1948. Bar: Mass. 1948, D.C. 1950. Asst. to gen. counsel, then asst. to dep. U.S. spl. rep. ECA, Paris, 1948-49; with firm Covington & Burling, Washington, 1950-56; asst. to solicitor gen. U.S., 1956-58; lectr. law Harvard Law Sch., 1958-60, prof. law, 1960-76, Samuel Williston prof. law, 1976—; sr. cons., dir. Conflict Mgmt. Inc.; dir. Harvard Negotiation Project, 1980—; vis. prof. internat. relations dept. London Sch. Econs., 1965-66; cons. pub. affairs editor WGBH-TV, Cambridge, 1969; tech. adv. Found. for Internat. Conciliation, Geneva. Originator, 1st exec. editor: series on pub. TV The Advocates, 1969-70; moderator, 1970-71; co-originator, exec. editor: series on pub. TV Arabs and Israelis, 1975; Author: International Conflict for Beginners, 1969, Dear Israelis, Dear Arabs, 1972, International Mediation: A Working Guide, 1978, International Crisis and the Role of Law: Points of Choice, 1978, Improving Compliance with International Law, 1981; Co-author: Getting to Yes: Negotiating Agreement Without Giving In, 1981; co-author, editor: International Conflict and Behavioral Science-The Craigville Papers, 1964; lectr. contbr. articles on internat. relations, negotiation, internat. law and TV. Mem. Mass. Gov.'s Commn. on Citizen Participation, 1973-74; Bd. dirs. Council for Livable World, Overseas Devel. Council, Pub. Interest Communications Services; trustee Hudson Inst. Served to 1st lt. USAAF, 1942-46. Recipient Sziland Peace award, 1981. Guggenheim fellow, 1965-66. Fellow Am. Acad. Arts and Scis.; mem. Am. Soc. Internat. Law (exec. council 1961-64, 66-69, v.p. 1982-84), ABA, Mass. Bar Assn., Commn. to Study Orgn. of Peace, Council Fgn. Relations. Clubs: Metropolitan (Washington); Harvard (N.Y.C.). Public international, Negotiation and Conflict Resolution. Office: Harvard U Law Sch Cambridge MA 02138

FISHER, STANLEY MORTON, lawyer; b. Dover, Ohio, Feb. 15, 1928; s. Jacob M and Sara (Weiner) F.; m. Lee I., Barbara Ann, Richard S., Suzanne Debra. BA, Oberlin Coll., 1950; JD, U. Mich., 1953. Bar: Ohio 1953, Mich. 1953, Fla. 1974, U.S. Ct. Appeals (3d, 6th and 7th cirs.), U.S. Supreme Ct. Law clk. to chief justice U.S. Ct. Appeals (6th cir.), Cin., 1953-54; assoc. Ulmer, Berne & Laronge, Cleve., 1954-56; ptnr. Fuerst, FIsher, Levy & Goulden, Cleve., 1956-74, Guren, Merritt & Sogg, Cleve., 1974-84; of counsel Arter & Hadden, Cleve., 1984—; adj. prof. Cleve. Marshall Law Sch., 1981-83; mem. State Bd. Uniform Laws, 1983—; bd. dirs. Welcome Radio, Inc., Cleve., Cook United, Inc., Cleve. Trustee United Cerebral Palsy, Cuyahoga County, 1980-86. Served to tech. sgt. U.S. Army, PTO. Mem. Fed. Bar Assn. (pres. 1985-86), Nat. Panel Arbitrators. Clubs: Commerce (Cleve.), Cleve. Racquet Club (Pepper Pike). Avocation: tennis. Antitrust, General corporate, Federal civil litigation. Office: Arter & Hadden 1100 Huntington Bldg Cleveland OH 44115

FISHER, THOMAS GEORGE, lawyer, media company executive; b. Debrecen, Hungary, Oct. 2, 1931; came to U.S., 1951; s. Eugene J. and Viola Elizabeth (Rittersporn) F.; m. Rita Knisley, Feb. 14, 1960; children: Thomas G., Katherine Elizabeth. B.S., Am. U., 1957, J.D., 1959; student, Harvard U., 1956. Bar: D.C. 1959, Iowa 1977; registered real estate broker, Iowa. Atty and legal asst. FCC, Washington, 1959-61, 65-66; pvt. law practice Washington, 1961-65, 66-69; asst. counsel Meredith Corp., N.Y.C., 1969-72; assoc. gen. counsel Meredith Corp., Des Moines, 1972-76, gen. counsel, 1976-80, v.p. gen. counsel, 1980—. Contbr. articles to profl. jours. Bd. dirs. Des Moines Met. Opera Co., Indianola, 1979—; bd. dirs. Civic Music Assn., Des Moines, 1982—; chmn. legis. com. Greater Des Moines C. of C., 1976-77; bd. dirs. Des Moines Housing Counsel, Inc.; bd. dirs. Legal Aid Soc. Polk County, 1986—. Served with U.S. Army, 1952-54. Mem. Iowa State Bar Assn. (chmn. corp. counsel subcom. 1979-82), ABA, Fed. Communications Bar Assn., Polk County Bar Assn., Am. Corporate Counsel Assn., Com. Fgn. Relations (Des Moines chpt.), Am. Advt. Fedn. (legal affairs com.). Clubs: Wakonda Country; Embassy (Des Moines). General corporate. Office: Meredith Corp 1716 Locust St Des Moines IA 50336

FISHER, THOMAS GRAHAM, judge; b. Flint, Mich., May 15, 1940; s. John Corwin and Bonnie Decou (Graham) F.; m. Barbara Molnar, June 2, 1963; children—Anne Corwin, Thomas Molnar. A.B., Earlham Coll., 1962; J.D., Ind. U., 1965. Bar: Ind. 1965, U.S. Sup. Ct. 1969. Assoc., John R. Nesbitt, Remington and Rensselaer, Ind., 1965-68; ptnr. Nesbitt & Fisher, Remington and Rensselaer, 1968-73, Nesbitt, Fisher & Daugherty, Rensselaer, Remington, 1973-78, Nesbitt, Fisher, Daugherty & Nesbitt, 1978-82, Nesbitt, Fisher & Nesbitt, 1982-83, Fisher & Nesbitt, 1983-86, judge, Ind. Tax Ct., Indpls., 1986—; pros. atty. Jasper County, Ind., 1967-86; lectr. bus. law St. Joseph's Coll., Rensselaer, 1970-86 . Mem. Ind. Bar Assn., Jasper County Bar Assn. Republican. Presbyterian. Lodge: Rotary. State and local taxation. Home: 227 Brown St Remington IN 47977 Office: Ind Tax Ct Merchants Plaza 115 W Washington St 1188 S Tower Chamber 23 Indianapolis IN 46204

FISHMAN, CHARLES LOUIS, lawyer; b. Providence, Oct. 10, 1942; s. Harold and Tessie Fishman; m. Margaret Morgan; children: Jessica, Morgan. BA, U. R.I., 1964; LLB, Howard U., 1967; LLM, Harvard U., 1968. Bar: D.C. 1967, U.S. Supreme Ct. 1967, U.S. Ct. Appeals (D.C. cir.) 1969, U.S. Ct. Appeals (1st cir.) 1971, U.S. Dist. Ct. D.C. 1972. Prof. law Howard U., Washington, 1968-70, U. Vt., Burlington, 1970-71; cons. Washington, 1971-74, sole practice, 1974—; bd. dirs. Sumitomo Trust and Banking Co. Ltd. Mem. ABA, D.C. Bar Assn. Nuclear power, FERC practice, Private international. Office: 1717 K St NW #502 Washington DC 20036

FISHMAN, EDWARD MARC, lawyer; b. Cambridge, Mass., Apr. 28, 1946; s. Eli Manuel and Marian (Goldberg) F.; m. Barbara Ellen Stern, June 29, 1969 (div. Sept. 1982); m. Tracy Ann Lind, July 13, 1985. AB, Bowdoin Coll., 1968; JD, Columbia U., 1972. Bar: Tex. 1972. Assoc. Akin, Gump, Strauss, Hauer & Feld, Dallas, 1972-73, Luce, Hennessy, Smith & Castle, Dallas, 1973-76; corp. counsel Centex Corp., Dallas, 1976-78; from assoc. to ptnr. Brice & Barron, Dallas, 1978-82; v.p. Baker, Smith & Mills, Dallas, 1982-86; pres. Kuhn, Fishman, Jones & Walsh, Dallas, 1986—, also bd. dirs. Bd. dirs. Space Found. Roundtable, Dallas, 1985—; officer local pub. TV sta., Dallas, 1976—. Mem. ABA, Tex. Bar Assn., Dallas Bar Assn. Avocations: reading, bicycling, swimming, running, skiing. Real property, General corporate, Landlord-tenant. Home: 6721 Southpoint Dallas TX 75248 Office: Kuhn Fishman Jones & Walsh RPR Tower 700 Pearl Plaza of the Americas Suite 2000 Dallas TX 75201

FISHMAN, FELIX ARTHUR, lawyer; b. N.Y.C., May 23, 1904; s. Joseph L. and Annie (Kaplan) F.; m. Sylvia Marshak, Aug. 2, 1929; children: Joseph L., Daniel B., Andrew M. AB, City Coll. of N.Y., 1925; LLB, Columbia U., 1927. Bar: N.Y. 1928. From assoc. to ptnr. Moses & Singer, N.Y.C., 1927—. Mem. N.Y. State Bar Assn. Democrat. Jewish. Probate. Home: Kirby Ln Rye NY 10580 Office: Moses & Singer 1271 Ave of Americas New York NY 10020

FISHMAN, FRED NORMAN, lawyer; b. N.Y.C., Aug. 21, 1925; s. Arthur Elihu and Frederica (Greenspan) F.; m. Claire S. Powsner, Sept. 19, 1948; children: Robert J., Nancy K. S.B. summa cum laude, Harvard U., 1946, LL.B. magna cum laude, 1948; postgrad., Yale U., 1945-46. Bar: N.Y. State 1950, U.S. Supreme Ct. 1954. Law clk. to Chief Judge Calvert Magruder, U.S. Ct. Appeals, 1st Circuit, Boston, 1948-49; to Asso. Justice Felix Frankfurter, Supreme Ct. U.S., 1949-50; asso. firm Dewey, Ballantine, Bushby, Palmer & Wood (and predecessors), N.Y.C., 1950-57; with Freeport Minerals Co., N.Y.C., 1957-61; asst. sec. Freeport Minerals Co., 1958-59, asst. v.p., 1959-61; partner firm Kaye, Scholer, Fierman, Hays & Handler, N.Y.C., 1962—; chmn. exec. com. Kaye, Scholer, Fierman, Hays & Handler, 1981-83. Editor, officer: Harvard Law Rev. Chmn. Harvard Law Sch. Fund, 1977-79; mem. Harvard Bd. Overseers' Com. to Visit Harvard Law Sch., 1975-81; chmn. Com. for Harvard Law Sch. Class of 1948 Twenty-Fifth Anniversary Gift; mem. Harvard U. Bd. Overseers' Com. to Visit Grad. Sch. Edn., 1971-77, Harvard Coll. Class of 1946 Permanent Class Com.; trustee Public Edn. Assn., N.Y.C., 1956-73, chmn. bd., 1970-71; dir. Harvard Alumni Assn., 1981-83; trustee Hosp. for Joint Diseases and Med. Center, N.Y.C., 1971-73; trustee Lawyers' Com. for Civil Rights under Law, 1979—, bd. dirs., 1983—, co-chmn., 1983-85. Mem. Assn. Bar City N.Y. (chmn. com. fed. legis. 1963-66, exec. com. 1966-70, chmn. com. on corp. law 1980-82), ABA, N.Y. State Bar Assn., New York County Lawyers Assn., Am. Law Inst. (adviser corp. governance project 1980—), Harvard Law Sch. Assn. (pres. 1986—, 1st v.p. 1984-86, council 1978-82, exec. com. 1980-82, trustee N.Y.C. chpt. 1966-69, v.p. N.Y.C. chpt. 1974-75), Phi Beta Kappa. Club: Harvard of N.Y.C. General corporate. Home: 650 Park Ave New York NY 10021 Office: 425 Park Ave New York NY 10022

FISHMAN, JAMES BART, lawyer; b. Mt. Vernon, N.Y., June 26, 1954; s. Ernest Martin and Adele (Goldstein) F.; m. Carol Merle, June 18, 1977; 1 child, Sarah Rose. AB, Bard Coll., 1976; JD, N.Y. Law Sch., 1979. Bar: N.Y. 1980, U.S. Dist. Ct. (so. dist.) N.Y. 1980, U.S. Dist. Ct. (ea. dist.) N.Y. 1987. Asst. atty. gen. State of N.Y., N.Y.C., 1979-84; staff atty. The Legal Aid Soc., N.Y.C., 1984—, sr. staff atty., 1985—; arbitrator N.Y. County Small Claims Ct., N.Y.C., 1985. Mem. Kings County Dem. com., 1984. Mem. Nat. Lawyers Guild (bd. dirs.). Jewish. Consumer commercial, Landlord-tenant, General practice. Office: The Legal Aid Soc 11 Park Place New York NY 10007

FISHMAN, LEWIS WARREN, lawyer, educator; b. Bklyn., Dec. 19, 1951; s. Sidney N. and Bess (Lefkowitz) F.; m. Juno M. Van Winkle, Aug. 27, 1978 (dec.); 1 child, Rachael; m. Nancy Massey, July 27, 1986. B.A. in Political Sci., Syracuse U., 1972; M.P.A., Maxwell-Syracuse U., 1973; J.D., U. Miami, 1976. Bar: Fla. Supreme Ct. 1976, U.S. Dist. Ct. (so. dist.) Fla. 1977, D.C., 1978, U.S. Ct. Appeals (5th and 11th cirs.) 1981. Assoc. Simons & Fishman P.A. (and predecessor firm), Miami, 1976-80, ptnr., 1980-81; assoc. law firm Wood, Lucksinger & Epstein, Miami, 1981-82; pres. Lewis W. Fishman P.A., Miami, 1982—; adj. prof. law Fla. Internat. U., 1981, 83, 84. Mem. Fla. Assn. Hosp. Attys. (bd. dirs.), Nat. Health Lawyers Assn. (lectr. 1983), Fla. Hosp. Assn. (lectr., sec. 1986), Fla. Med. Records Assn. (lectr. 1982, 83, 84), Am. Acad. Hosp. Attys., Nat. Health Lawyers Assn., Cath. Health Assn., Fla. Bar Assn. (mem. health law com.). Democrat. Jewish. Health, General corporate, Insurance. Home: 14140 SW 104 Ave Miami FL 33176 Office: 9400 S Dadeland Blvd #420 Miami FL 33156

FISHMAN, MITCHELL STEVEN, lawyer; b. N.Y.C., July 27, 1948; s. Abraham and Sylvia (Sher) F.; m. Alison Rivard, Sept. 7, 1980; children: Danielle, Matthew. BA cum laude, Harvard U., 1970, JD cum laude, 1973. Bar: N.Y. 1974, D.C. 1984. Assoc. Breed, Abbott & Morgan, N.Y.C., 1973-74; dir. communications to U.S. Congressman Richard Vander Veen, Washington, 1974; assoc. Paul, Weiss, Rifkind, Wharton & Garrison, N.Y.C., 1975-80, ptnr., 1980—; exec. dir. Temporary State Commn. on Banking, Ins. and Fin. Services, N.Y., 1983-84. Mem. ABA, N.Y. State Bar Assn., Assn. of Bar of City of N.Y. (sec. com. on corp. law 1976-79). Democrat. Securities, General corporate, Banking. Home: 617 The Parkway Mamaroneck NY 10543 Office: Paul Weiss Rifkind Wharton & Garrison 1285 Ave of Americas New York NY 10019

FISHMAN, ROBERT MICHAEL, lawyer; b. Bloomington, Ill., Dec. 28, 1953; s. Hank and Lucy (Moscovitch) F.; m. Victoria M. Swan, Aug. 12, 1979; 1 child, Eric B. BA, U. Ill., 1972-76; JD, George Washington U., 1979. Bar: Ill. 1979, U.S. Dist. Ct. (no. dist.) Ill. 1979. Atty. Office of Ill. Atty. Gen., Chgo., 1979-80; ptnr. Levit and Mason Ltd., Chgo., 1980—. Mem. ABA (bus. bankruptcy sect.), Chgo. Bar Assn., Am. Bankruptcy Inst. (chmn. programs and seminars com.), Comml. Law League. Bankruptcy, Banking, Contracts commercial. Office: Levit & Mason Ltd 135 S LaSalle Suite 1525 Chicago IL 60603

FISKE, ROBERT BISHOP, JR., lawyer; b. N.Y.C., Dec. 28, 1930; s. Robert Bishop and Lenore (Seymour) F.; m. Janet Tinsley, Aug. 21, 1954; children: Linda Goucher, Robert Bishop, Susan Seymour. B.A., Yale U., 1952; J.D., U. Mich., 1955. Bar: Mich. 1955, N.Y. 1956, U.S. Supreme Ct. 1961. Assoc. Davis, Polk, Wardwell, Sunderland & Kiendl, 1955-57; asst. U.S. atty. So. Dist. N.Y., 1957-61; assoc. Davis, Polk & Wardwell, 1961-64, ptnr., 1964-76, 80—; U.S. atty. So. Dist. N.Y., N.Y.C., 1976-80. Mem. Darien Police Commn., Conn. Fellow Am. Coll. Trial Lawyers (regents); mem. ABA (chmn. standing com. on fed. judiciary), Bar Assn. City N.Y., Fed. Bar Council (pres. 1982-84), N.Y. State Bar Assn. Republican. Congregationalist. Club: Noroton Yacht. Federal civil litigation, State civil litigation, Criminal. Home: 19 Juniper Rd Darien CT 06820 Office: 1 Chase Manhattan Plaza New York NY 10005

FISS, OWEN M., legal educator; b. 1938. B.A., Dartmouth Coll., 1959; B.Phil., Oxford U., 1961; LL.B., Harvard U., 1964. Bar: N.Y. 1965. Law clk. to Judge Thurgood Marshall, U.S. Ct. Appeals 2d Cir., 1964-65, to Justice Brennan, U.S. Supreme Ct., 1965; spl. asst. to asst. atty. gen., civil rights div. U.S. Dept. Justice, Washington, 1966-67, acting dir. Office of Planning Coordination, 1968; prof. U. Chgo. Law Sch., 1968-74; prof. Yale U. Law Sch., New Haven, 1974-84, Alexander M. Bickel prof. pub. law, 1984—; vis. prof. Stanford U., 1973. Mem. Harvard Law Rev.; author: Injunctions, 1972; The Civil Rights Injunction, 1978; (with R.M. Cover) The Structure of Procedure, 1979; (with D. Rendleman) Injunctions, 2d edit., 1984; editorial bd. Philosophy and Pub. Affairs. Mem. Soc. Ethical and Legal Philosophy. Legal education. Office: Yale Law Sch Drawer 401A Yale Sta New Haven CT 06520

FITCH, HOWARD MERCER, lawyer, labor arbitrator; b. Jeffersonville, Ind., Dec. 23, 1909; s. J. Howard and Kate Orvis (Girdler) F.; m. Jane Rogers McCaw, Dec. 25, 1930 (dec. 1983); children: Catherine Mercer Druitt, Jane Rogers Butterworth; m. Nancy Dolt Langley, Apr. 28, 1984. B.M.E., U. Ky., 1930, M.S., 1936, M.E., 1939; J.D. magna cum laude, U. Louisville, 1942. Bar: Ky. 1942, Ill. 1954, U.S. Patent Office 1943; registered profl. engr., Ky. Engr. Western Electric Co., Kearney, N.J., 1930-32; joined Am. Air Filter Co. Inc., 1936, served as sales engr., prodn. mgr., mgr. legal and patent dept., asst. to exec. v.p., 1936-53, mgr. Herman Nelson div., 1953, v.p., 1954-72, dir. ops., 1958-63; practice law Louisville, 1942—; ptnr. Hunt & Fitch, 1945-58. Patentee in field. Mem. nat. com. Atlantic Union Com.; mem. Louisville Labor-Mgmt. Com.; bd. dirs. Louisville Urban League, Louisville Better Bus. Bur., Consumers Adv. Council. Mem. ASME, ASHRAE, Am. Arbitration Assn. (panel arbitrators), Nat. Acad. Arbitrators, ABA, Ky. Bar Assn., Louisville Bar Assn., Hon. Order Ky. Cols., Louisville C. of C., Assoc. Industries Quad Cities (past pres.), Am. Soc. Personnel Adminstrn., Louisville Personnel Assn., SAR. Episcopalian. Clubs: Filson, Pendennis, Arts (past pres.), Ky. Soc. Natural History, Louisville Photog. Soc. Labor, Patent. Home and Office: 1704 Spruce Ln Louisville KY 40207

FITCH, RAYMOND WILLIAM, lawyer, musician; b. Mpls., Apr. 10, 1931; s. Ray W. and Eleanor (Fleetham) F.; m. Antoinette C. Suwalsky, May 31, 1958; children—Albert, Robert, Michael, Anne. B.S.L., U. Minn., 1953, LL.B., 1955. Bar: Minn. 1955. Assoc. Tyrrell, Jardine, St. Paul, 1957-65, Robb & Van Eps, Mpls., 1965-68; ptnr. Fitch & Johnson, Mpls., 1968—; advisor Minn. Legislature, 1970—; tchr. legal affairs Mpls. pub. schs., 1975—; tchr., advisor, musician Basilica St. Mary, Mpls., 1968—; owner, operator Arabian horse farm, Shakopee, Minn. Served to lst lt. U.S. Army, 1955-57. Mem. Minn. Bar Assn., Hennepin County Bar Assn., Am. Arbitration Assn. (arbitrator 1980—), Delta Tau Delta. Roman Catholic. Lodge: Knight of Holy Sepulchre. Workers' compensation, Insurance, Personal injury. Office: Fitch & Johnson 15 N 16th St Minneapolis MN 55403

FITT, BENJAMIN JONES, lawyer; b. Detroit, Sept. 23, 1952; s. Alfred Bradley and Patricia (Hewitt) F.; m. Lawton Wehle, Mar. 29, 1975 (div. Dec. 1985); m. Nina Buckler Eckhoff, Mar. 22, 1986. BA, Yale U., 1975; postgrad., Columbia U., 1980; JD, U. Va., 1980. Bar: N.Y. 1981, U.S. Dist. (ea. and so. dists.) N.Y. 1981, U.S. Tax Ct. 1985, U.S. Dist. Ct. (no. and we. dists.) N.Y. 1986. Assoc. Milbank, Tweed, Hadley & McCloy, N.Y.C., 1980-82, Slade & Pellman, N.Y.C., 1982-85; asst. atty. gen. N.Y. State Dept. Law, Albany, 1986. Harlan Fiske Stone scholar, 1980. Mem. ABA, Albany county Bar Assn. Federal civil litigation, State civil litigation, Administrative and regulatory. Office: The Capitol Dept of Law Albany NY 12224

FITTERER, RICHARD CLARENCE, lawyer; b. Ellensburg, Wash., Jan. 22, 1946; s. L. George and Margaret H. (Lewis) F.; m. Janice M. Ivey, Feb. 14, 1968; children: Christian C., Zane I., Aaron G. BCS, Seattle U., 1968; JD, U. Puget Sound, 1976. Assoc. Patrick R. Acres, Moses Lake, Wash., 1977; sole practice Moses Lake, 1977-79, 83—; ptnr. Milne, Lemargie & Fitterer, Ephrata, Wash., 1979—. Bd. dirs. Columbia Basin Rodeo Assn. Moses Lake Roundup, 1984—, United Way, Moses Lake, 1978-81, Moses Lake C. of C., 1979-83. Mem. ABA, Wash. State Bar Assn., Grant County Bar Assn., Assn. Trial Lawyers Am., Wash. State Trial Lawyers Assn. Republican. Roman Catholic. Club: Moses Lake Golf and Country. Lodges: Elks (bd. dirs. 1984), Moose, Rotary. Avocations: skiing, boating, golfing. Consumer commercial, Construction, Personal injury. Home: 322 N Crestview Moses Lake WA 98837 Office: PO Box 1118 Moses Lake WA 98837

FITTON, GARVIN, lawyer; b. Harrison, Ark., Oct. 5, 1918; s. David Edwards and Lulu Vance (Garvin) F.; m. Martha Ann Hamilton, Sept. 21, 1941; children—John Dennis, Thomas Garvin, Ann Fitton Kelly. LL.B., U. Ark., 1941, J.D., 1969. Bar: Ark. 1941, U.S. Dist. Ct. (ea. and we. dists.) Ark. 1949, U.S. Supreme Ct. 1982. Sole practice, Harrison, 1946—; mem. Ark. Bd. Law Examiners, 1971-73. Mem. bd., officer Harrison Sch. Dist. Served to col. U.S. Army, 1940-46, ETO. Mem. Boone County Bar Assn. (pres. 1959), Ark. Bar Assn. (bd. govs. 1981-83), ABA. Democrat. Methodist. Lodges: Rotary (pres. 1970-71), Mason. Probate, Real property, General corporate. Home: 921 W Nicleson Harrison AR 72601 Office: PO Box 249 224 W Stevenson Harrison AR 72601

FITZGERALD, EDWARD BROWNE, lawyer; b. New Haven, Oct. 30, 1934; s. Edward George Benedict and Katherine Cecilia (Browne) FitzG.; m. Susan Fisher Browne, Jan. 18, 1963; children—Karen S., Edward B., A.B., Cornell U., 1956; LL.B., U. Conn., 1959. Bar: Conn. 1959, U.S. Dist. Ct. Conn. 1965. Assoc. Kinney & Reynolds, New Haven, 1959-61; pros. atty. State of Conn., New Haven, 1961-69; ptnr. Maretz & Korn, New Haven, 1964-66, Maretz, FitzGerald & Maretz, New Haven, 1966-71, McNerney, FitzGerald & Tiernan, P.C., New Haven, 1971—. Bd. dirs. Quinnipiak Valley Health Dist., 1979-86; trustee Hamden Hall Country Day Sch., 1978—. Mem. ABA, Conn. Bar Assn., New Haven County Bar Assn. Roman Catholic. Clubs: New Haven Country (Hamden, Conn.); Quinnipiac. Contbr. articles to profl. jours. Personal injury, State civil litigation, General corporate. Home: 236 Santa Fe Ave Hamden CT 06517 Office: 59 Elm St New Haven CT 06507

FITZGERALD, JAMES MARTIN, judge; b. Portland, Oreg., Oct. 7, 1920; s. Thomas and Florence (Linderman) F.; m. Karin Rose Benton, Jan. 19, 1950; children: Dennis James, Denise Lyn, Debra Jo, Kevin Thomas. BA, Willamette U., 1950, LLB, 1951; postgrad., U. Wash., 1952. Bar: Alaska 1953. Asst. U.S. atty. Ketchikan and Anchorage, Alaska, 1952-56; city atty. City of Anchorage, 1956-59; legal counsel to Gov. Alaska, Anchorage, 1959; commr. pub. safety State of Alaska, 1959; judge Alaska Superior Ct., 3d Jud. Dist., 1959-69, presiding judge, 1969-72; assoc. justice Alaska Supreme Ct., Anchorage, 1972-75; judge U.S. Dist. Ct. for Alaska, Anchorage, 1975—. Mem. advisory bd. Salvation Army, Anchorage, 1962—, chmn., 1965-66; mem. Anchorage Parks and Recreation Bd., 1965-77, chmn., 1966. Served with AUS, 1940-41; Served with USMCR, 1942-46. Jurisprudence. Office: US District Court US Courthouse 701 C St Anchorage AK 99513 *

FITZGERALD, JOHN EDWARD, III, lawyer; b. Cambridge, Mass., Jan. 12, 1945; s. John Edward Jr. and Kathleen (Sullivan) FitzG.; m. Nancy Balik; children: Katie, Patrick, Jana. BCE, U.S. Mil. Acad., West Point, N.Y., 1969; JD, M in Pub. Policy Analysis, U. Pa., 1975. Bar: Pa. 1975, N.Y. 1978, Calif. 1983. Commd. 2d lt. U.S. Army, 1969, advanced through grades to capt., 1971, resigned, 1972; assoc. Saul Ewing, Remick & Saul, Phila., 1975-77, Shearman & Sterling, N.Y.C., 1977-78; atty., dir. govt. relations Pepsico, Inc., Purchase, N.Y., 1978-82; sr. v.p., dept. head Security Pacific Nat. Bank, Los Angeles, 1982-83; ptnr. Schlesinger, FitzGerald & Johnson, Palm Springs, Calif., 1983-87, John E. FitzGerald and Assocs., Palm Springs, 1987—; prof. law U. Pa., Temple U., and Pace U.; judge pro tem Desert Jud. Dist., Palm Springs, Nat. Council Freedom Found., Valley Forge, Pa.; mem. Pvt. Industry Council. Bd. dirs. Wilde Woode Sch. for Gifted Children, Palm Springs, U. So. Calif. of Pub. Adminstrn.; chmn. bd. Palm Springs Sister Cities Com., 1986. Served to capt. U.S. Army, 1969-72. Named Outstanding Tchr. The Wharton Sch. U. Pa., 1977. Mem. ABA (1st place award in legal essay contest 1973), Calif. Bar Assn. (exec. com., law practice mgmt. sect.), Desert Bar Assn., Am. Trial Lawyers Assn., Calif. Trial Lawyers Assn, Am. Arbitration Assn. (arbitrator). Republican. Roman Catholic. Clubs: O'Donnell Golf (Palm Springs); Jonathan (Los Angeles); Racquet of Phila. Business law, State civil litigation, Real property. Home: 555 Via Lola Palm Springs CA 92262

FITZGERALD, JOHN ELMER, lawyer; b. Somerville, Mass., Apr. 6, 1932; s. John E. and Annie (Shaw), F.; m. Carol E. Mathisen, June 12, 1954 (div. Sept. 1985); children—John H., Mark D., Timothy, Cara Beth, Elyce; m. Laura J. Fitzgerald, Aug. 29, 1986. A.A., Boston U., 1952, B.A., 1954, LL.B., 1960; postgrad. U. Colo., 1970-71, Northwestern U., 1973. Bar: Mass. 1961, U.S. Dist. Ct. Mass. 1965, S.D. 1973, U.S. Dist. Ct. S.D. 1973, U.S. Ct. Appeals (1st and 8th cirs.) 1964, U.S. Ct. Claims 1977, U.S. Supreme Ct. 1977. Sole practice, Boston, 1960-68; regional atty. SBA, Denver, 1969-72; pub. defender Pennington County (S.D.), 1972-73; ptnr. Nelson & Harding, Rapid City, S.D., 1974—; adj. prof. criminal justice dept. U. S.D., 1977—, adj. prof. Grad. Sch., West River Ctr., 1980-82. Mem. Rapid City Sch. Bd., 1977-78; mem. Rapid City Police Dept. Rev. Bd., 1971, legal adviser, 1974-76. Served with U.S. Army, 1954-57. Mem. ABA, Nat. Coll. Criminal Def., Assn. Trial Lawyers Am., Assn. Criminal Def. Lawyers, Mass. Bar Assn., S.D. Bar, Mass. Trial Lawyers Assn., S.D. Trial Lawyers Assn. Mem. Evangelical Free Ch. Am. Club: Lions (Rapid City, S.D.). Criminal, General practice, Personal injury.

FITZGERALD, JOHN WARNER, legal educator; b. Grand Ledge, Mich., Nov. 14, 1924; s. Frank Dwight and Queena Maud (Warner) F.; m. Lorabeth Moore, June 6, 1953; children: Frank Moore, Eric Stiles, Adam Warner. B.S., Mich. State U., 1947; J.D., U. Mich., 1954. Bar: Mich. 1954. Practiced in Grand Ledge 1955-64; chief judge pro tem Mich. Ct. Appeals, 1965-73; justice Mich. Supreme Ct., 1974-83, dep. chief justice, 1975-82, chief justice, 1982; prof. law Thomas M. Cooley Law Sch., Lansing, Mich., 1982—; mem. Mich. Senate from 15th Dist., 1958-64. Served with AUS, 1943-44. Mem. ABA, State Bar Mich. (bd. commrs. 1985—), Am. Judicature Soc. Legal education, Real property, Judicial administration. Office: Thomas M. Cooley Law Sch PO Box 13038 Lansing MI 48901

FITZGERALD, STEPHEN PATRICK, lawyer; b. Detroit, Feb. 6, 1954; s. William John and Jean Marie (Fitzgerald) F.; m. Mary Alice Franco, Apr. 11, 1981. BGS magna cum laude, U. Mich., 1976, JD cum laude, 1978. Bar: Calif. 1979, U.S. Dist. Ct. (cen. and so. dists.) Calif. 1979. Assoc. Averil D. Vallier Law Office, Los Angeles, 1980-83, Regal & Levy, Los Angeles, 1983-85; sole practice Santa Monica, Calif., 1983—. Mem. Santa Monica Dem. Club, 1984—. Mem. ABA, Assn. Trial Lawyers Am., Los Angeles County Bar Assn., Los Angeles Trial Lawyers Assn., Santa Monica Bar Assn. State civil litigation, Insurance, General practice. Home: 2449 29th St Santa Monica CA 90405 Office: 309 Santa Monica Blvd Suite 209 Santa Monica CA 90401

FITZGERALD, TAMI LYNN, lawyer; b. Wichita Falls, Tex., Dec. 6, 1957; d. Gary Wynn and Betty Jo (Stewart) Tibbits; m. Craig Quentin Fitzgerald, Jan. 6, 1979. BS, Okla. State U., 1979; JD, U. Okla., 1982. Bar: Okla. 1982, U.S. Dist. Ct. (we. dist.) Okla., U.S. Ct. Appeals (10th cir.). Assoc. Watson & McKenzie, Oklahoma City, 1982-85, ptnr., 1985—. Mem. Norman (Okla.) Jr. League, 1985-86; vol. Norman Sch. for Handicapped, 1986—. Mem. ABA, Okla. County Bar Assn. (young lawyers' div., bd. govs. 1985-86), Christian Legal Soc., Phi Alpha Delta. Republican. Baptist. Bankruptcy, Consumer commercial, Oil and gas leasing. Office: Watson & McKenzie 1900 Liberty Tower Oklahoma City OK 73102

FITZGERALD, THOMAS RAYMOND, lawyer; b. Yonkers, N.Y., Mar. 9, 1946; s. Thomas Raymond and Lucy (Howley) F.; m. Jeanne Marie Harder, May 27, 1973; children: Kelly Ann, Thomas Joseph. BSEE, Manhattan Coll., 1967; JD, Fordham U., 1972. Bar: N.Y. 1973, U.S. Patent Office 1974, U.S. Ct. Appeals (2d and D.C. cirs.), U.S. Dist Ct. (ea. and so. dists.) N.Y. Assoc. Fitzpatrick, Cella, Harper & Scinto, N.Y.C., 1972-74; patent atty. Gen. Electric Co., Fairfield, Conn., 1974-76, Pitney Bowes Inc., Stamford, Conn., 1976-78; group patent counsel Gen. Signal Corp., Stamford, 1978—. Served to lt. USNR, 1969-71. Mem. Westchester-Fairfield Corp. Counsel Assn. (patent, trademark and copyright com. 1986—). Roman Catholic. Patent, Trademark and copyright, Federal civil litigation. Home: 2757 Boston Post Rd Darien CT 06820 Office: Gen Signal Corp High Ridge Park Stamford CT 06904

FITZGERALD, WILLIAM BRENDAN, JR., lawyer; b. Waterbury, Conn., May 4, 1936; s. William Brendan Sr. and Margaret (Cunning) F.; m. Teresa Vannini, Oct. 12, 1963 (div. Oct. 1980); children: W. Brendan III, Nicholas S., Francesca V. BA cum laude, Yale U., 1958; JD, Harvard U., 1961; cert. in higher European Studies, Coll. Europe, Bruges, Belgium, 1962. Bar: Conn. 1961, Calif. 1985. Ptnr. Fitzgerald & Fitzgerald, Waterbury, Conn., 1961-72, Carmody & Torrance, Waterbury, 1972-85, Haight, Dickson, Brown & Bonesteel, Santa Monica, Calif., 1985—. Rotary fellow, 1961. Fellow Am. Coll. Trial Lawyers, Roscoe Pound Found; mem. ABA (litigation, torts and ins. sects.), Calif. Bar Assn., Conn. Bar Assn. (acad. continuing profl. devel. 1982, judiciary com. 1982-85, jud. liason com. 1985), Def. Research inst., Assn. So. Calif. Def. Counsel, Am. Arbitrations Assn. (panelist), Conn. Trial Lawyers Assn. (pres. 1985). Democrat. Club: Yale (N.Y.C.). Federal civil litigation, State civil litigation. Office: Haight Dickson Brown & Bonesteel 201 Santa Monica Blvd Santa Monica CA 90406

FITZGIBBON, DANIEL HARVEY, lawyer; b. Columbus, Ind., July 7, 1942; s. Joseph Bales and Margaret Lenore (Harvey) FitzG.; m. Joan Helen Meltzer, Aug. 12, 1973; children: Katherine Lenore, Thomas Bernard. BS in Engring., U.S. Mil. Acad., 1964; JD cum laude, Harvard U., 1972. Bar: Ind. 1972, U.S. Dist. Ct. (so. dist.) Ind. 1972, U.S. Tax Ct. 1977. Commd. 2d lt. U.S. Army, 1964, advanced through grades to capt., 1967; served with inf. U.S. Army, West Berlin, Vietnam; resigned U.S. Army, 1969; assoc. Barnes & Thornburg, Indpls., 1972-79, ptnr., 1979—; adminstr. tax and estate depts., 1981—, Barnes and Thornburg, mgmt. com., 1983—, compensation com., 1984-87, exec. com. 1987—; chmn. legal personnel com., 1983-85, exec. com. 1987—; mgmt. com. Barnes and Thornburg Bldg. Co., 1981-84; speaker various insts. Served to capt. U.S. Army, 1964-69, Vietnam. Mem. ABA (tax, corp. bus. and bank law sects.), Ind. State Bar Assn. (chmn. scholarship com. of tax sect. 1983—), Indpls. Bar Assn. (chmn. tax sect. 1982-83, council 1982—). Clubs: Indpls. Athletic, Woodstock. Corporate taxation, General corporate. Home: 5833 Eastview Ct Indianapolis IN 46250 Office: Barnes & Thornburg 11 S Meridian St Indianapolis IN 46204

FITZGIBBON, SCOTT THOMAS, law educator; b. Louisville, Apr. 11, 1945; s. William Charles and Miriam Ruth (James) F.; m. Kwan Kew Lai, May 26, 1979; children: Timothy James Lai, Cara Lai. BA, Antioch Coll., 1967; JD, Harvard U., 1970; BCL, Oxford U., Eng., 1972. Bar: Mass. 1972. Law clk. U.S. Ct. Appeals (4th cir.), Balt., 1970-71; assoc. Ropes & Gray, Boston, 1972-78; prof. law Boston Coll. Law Sch., Newton Centre, Mass., 1978—. Editor Harvard U. Law Rev., 1968-70, articles officer 1969-70. Mem. Mass. Bar Assn. (com. profl. ethics 1980-85), Alliance for Nuclear Arms Control (founding), Cath. Commn. Cultural and Intellectual Affairs. Democrat. Roman Catholic. Jurisprudence, General corporate, Securities. Home: 104 School St Belmont MA 02178 Office: Boston Coll Law Sch 885 Centre St Newton Centre MA 02159

FITZGIBBONS, ANN, lawyer; b. Estherville, Iowa, Sept. 5, 1951; d. Francis and Evelyn Louise (Murray) F. BA, U. Iowa, 1973; JD, Drake U., 1977. Bar: Iowa 1978, U.S. Dist. Ct. Iowa 1979. Asst. atty. gen. State of Iowa, Des Moines, 1977-79; assoc. Scalise, Scism, Sandre & Uhl, Des Moines, 1979-83; ptnr. Scalise, Scism, Sandie & Uhl, Des Moines, 1983—; mem. adv. com. rules of criminal procedure Iowa Supreme Ct., 1986—. Dist. rep. Des Moines Reps., 1980, Iowa Reps., Cedar Rapids, 1980; mem. Des Moines Jr. League, 1986—. Mem. Iowa Bar Assn. (various coms. young lawyers sect.), Polk County Bar Assn., Polk County Women Attys. Assn. Republican. Roman Catholic. State civil litigation, Family and matrimonial, Criminal. Office: Scalise Scism Sandre & Uhl 2910 Grand Ave Des Moines IA 50312

FITZGIBBONS, JOHN MURRAY, lawyer; b. Estherville, Iowa, Aug. 17, 1950. BA, St. Norbert Coll., DePere, Wis., 1972; JD, U. Iowa, 1975. Bar: Iowa 1975, U.S. Ct. Appeals (8th cir.) 1976, U.S. Ct. Appeals (5th cir.) 1978, U.S. Supreme Ct. 1979, D.C.1983, U.S. Ct. Appeals (11th and D.C. cirs.) 1983, Fla. 1986. Asst. county atty. Polk County, Des Moines, 1975-76; asst. U.S. atty.so. dist. Iowa U.S. Atty.'s Office, Des Moines, 1976-78, chief criminal div. and 1st. asst. U.S. atty., 1977-78, spl. asst. U.S. atty., 1978; spl. asst. U.S. atty. ea. dist. Ky. U.S. Atty.'s Office, Lexington, 1983; asst. U.S. atty. mid. dist. Fla. U.S. Atty.'s Office, Tampa, 1983-87, dep. chief criminal div. mid. dist. Fla., 1985-86; spl. counsel U.S. Ho. Reps., Washington, 1978-80; trial atty. pub. integrity sect. criminal div. U.S. Dept. Justice, Washington, 1980-83. Roman Catholic. Criminal. Home: 2413 Bayshore Blvd Suite 1601 Tampa FL 33629 Office: Law Offices of John M Fitzgibbons 600 N Florida Ave Suite 1550 Tampa FL 33602

FITZHUGH, DAVID MICHAEL, lawyer; b. San Francisco, Nov. 24, 1946; s. William DeHart and Betty Jean (Jeffries) F.; m. Jenny Lu Conner, Dec. 22, 1967; children—Ross DeHart, Cameron Hyatt, Michael Jeffries. Student Carleton Coll., 1964-67; B.A., Coll. William and Mary, 1972; J.D., U. Va., 1975. Bar: D.C. 1975, U.S. Dist. Ct. D.C. 1979, U.S. Ct. Claims 1980, U.S. Ct. Appeals (fed. cir.) 1982, U.S. Supreme Ct. 1982. Assoc. McKenna, Conner & Cuneo, Washington, 1975-80, ptnr., 1980—. Mem. editorial bd. Nat. Contract Mgmt. Assn. Jour., 1975—. Contbr. articles to legal publs. Referee Alexandria Soccer Assn., Alexandria, Va., 1984. Served to capt. USMC, 1967-71, Vietnam. Mem. ABA (litigation sect., discovery com. pub. contracts sect.) Club: Army-Navy Country. Federal civil litigation, Government contracts and claims. Home: 3606 Cameron Mills Rd Alexandria VA 22305 Office: McKenna Conner & Cuneo 1575 Eye St NW Suite 800 Washington DC 20005

FITZHUGH, J. MICHAEL, lawyer; b. 1947. BS, JD, U. Ark. U.S. atty. we. dist. State of Ark., Ft. Smith. Office: PO Box 1524 Fort Smith AR 72901 *

FITZHUGH, JOHN HARDY, lawyer; b. Greenwich, Conn., June 1, 1948; s. William Wyvill and Florence (Hardy) F.; m. Georgianna Brush, June 17, 1973; children: Nicholas, Eliza. BA, Dartmouth Coll., 1970; JD, Bklyn. Law Sch., 1977. Bar: N.Y. 1978, Vt. 1980, U.S. Dist. Ct. Vt. 1981. Reporter AP, N.Y.C., 1972-75, N.Y. Law Jour., N.Y.C., 1975-77; editor in chief Nat. Law Jour., N.Y.C., 1977-80; hearing examiner Vt. Dept. Labor and Industry, Montpelier, Vt., 1980-81; assoc. Sheehey, Brue & Gray, Burlington, Vt., 1981-84; ptnr. Sheehey, Brue & Gray, Burlington, 1984—. Editor mag. Vt. Bar Digest, 1982; contbr. articles to profl. jours. Treas. Vt. Mozart Festival, Burlington, 1985—; trustee Bklyn. Law Sch., 1979-80. Mem. ABA, Vt. Bar Assn., Chittenden County Bar Assn. Republican. Episcopalian. Avocations: music, fishing, tennis, canoeing. General practice, State civil litigation, Real property. Home: 39 Liberty St Montpelier VT 05602 Office: Sheehey Brue & Gray 119 S Winooski Ave Burlington VT 05402

FITZPATRICK, BARRY LANE, lawyer; b. Athens, Ga., July 1, 1950; s. Alton Lord and Virginia Roberta (Ginn) F.; m. Norma Ellen Finch, Mar. 18, 1973; children: Sara, Sallie. BA in English, U. Ga., 1973, JD, 1976. Bar: Ga. 1976, U.S. Dist. Ct. (mid. dist.) Ga. 1978, U.S. Ct. Appeals (11th cir.) 1981, U.S. Supreme Ct. 1981, U.S. Dist. Ct. (no. dist.) Ga. 1984. Assoc. Graham & Graham, Danielsville, Ga., 1976-80; sole practice Danielsville, 1980—. Mem. Assn. Trial Lawyers Am., Ga. Trial Lawyers Assn., Ga. Assn. Criminal Def. Lawyers, Nat. Sch. Bd. Assn., Council of Sch. Attys. Baptist. Club: Ga. Coliseum (Athens) (bd. dirs. 1978-86). General practice, State civil litigation, Local government. Home: Danielsville/Colbert Rd Danielsville GA 30633 Office: Courthouse Sq Danielsville GA 30633

FITZPATRICK, DUROSS, lawyer; b. Macon, Ga., Oct. 19, 1934; s. Mark W. and Jane L. (Duross) F.; m. Beverly O'Connor, Mar. 17, 1963; children—Mark O'Connor, Devon Hart. B.S. in Forestry, U. Ga., 1961, LL.B., 1966. Bar: Ga. 1965. Assoc. Elliott & Davis, Macon, 1966-67; sole practice, Cochran, Ga., 1967-83; ptnr. Fitzpatrick & Mullis, Cochran, 1983-86; judge U.S. Dist. Ct. (mid. dist.) Ga., Macon, 1986—. bd. govs. State Bar Ga., 1976-83, mem. exec. com., 1979-84, pres., 1984-85. Legal counsel Republican del. Gen. Assembly Ga., 1969. Served with USMC, 1954-57. Fellow Ga. Bar Found., ABA; mem. Oconee Bar Assn. (pres. 1970), Am. Judicature Soc., Am. Law Inst. Republican. Episcopalian. Clubs: Rotary (pres.) (Cochran); Lawyers (Atlanta). State civil litigation, Family and matrimonial, General practice. Home: Route 1 Box 167 Jeffersonville GA 31044 Office: US Dist Ct PO Box 1014 Macon GA 31202

FITZPATRICK, FRANCIS JAMES, lawyer; b. N.Y.C., Apr. 29, 1916; s. Francis James and Susan Clemens (Tompkins) FitzP.; m. Ethel Marie Peters, Mar. 2, 1956. A.B., Duke U., 1938; postgrad. Harvard U. Grad. Sch. Bus. Adminstrn., 1939-40; J.D., Cornell U., 1947. Bar: Iowa 1951, N.J. 1954. Exec. trainee U.S. Fidelity & Guaranty Co., N.Y., 1940-41; counsellor, Western Electric Co., Kearny, N.J., 1942-45; practice, Orange, N.J., 1954—. Served with M.C., U.S. Army, 1941-42. Mem. ABA, N.J. State Bar Assn., Essex County Bar Assn., Am. Judicature Soc., Cornell Law Student Assn. (sec.-treas.), Cornell U. Law Assn., Duke U. Met. Alumni Assn., Delta Theta Phi (pres.), Am. Legion (former judge adv. Orange), Sigma Alpha Epsilon. Democrat. General practice, Personal injury, Probate. Home: 5 Ledgewood Ct Warren NJ 07060 Office: 308 Main St Orange NJ 07050

FITZPATRICK, HAROLD FRANCIS, lawyer; b. Jersey City, Oct. 16, 1947; s. Harold G. and Anne Marie Fitzpatrick; m. Joanne M. Merry, Sept. 22, 1973; children: Elizabeth, Kevin, Matthew. AB, Boston Coll., 1969; MBA, NYU, 1971; JD, Harvard U., 1974. Bar: N.J. 1974, U.S. Dist. Ct. N.J. 1974, U.S. Ct. Internat. Trade, 1986. Securities analyst Chase Manhattan Bank, N.Y.C., 1970-71, Brown Bros., Harriman & Co., N.Y.C., 1971; staff asst. U.S. Senate, Washington, 1972; law clk. to assoc. justice N.J. Supreme Ct., Trenton, 1974-75; assoc. Cleary, Gottlieb, Steen & Hamilton, N.Y.C., 1975-78; mng. ptnr. Fitzpatrick & Israels, Bayonne, N.J., 1978—; gen. counsel Housing Authority City of Bayonne, 1976—, Dry Color Mfrs. Assn., Alexandria, Va., 1978—, N.J. Assn. Housing & Redevel. Authorities, Bayonne, 1979—, Housing Authority Town of Secaucus, N.J., 1980—, Rahway Geriatrics Ctr. Inc., N.J., 1981—, Housing Authority City of Englewood, N.J., 1985—, Housing Authority City of Rahway, N.J., 1986—, Edgewater Mcpl. Utilities Authority, 1986—. Mem. ABA, N.J. Ban Assn., Hudson County Bar Assn. (trustee 1984-87, officer 1987—), Nat. Assn. Bond Lawyers, Nat. Health Lawyers Assn., Am Soc. Assn. Execs. (legal sect.), Beta Gamma Sigma. General corporate, Environment, Municipal bonds. Office: Fitzpatrick & Israels 90 W 40th St Bayonne NJ 07002

FITZPATRICK, JOHN MICHAEL, lawyer, military officer; b. Portsmouth, Va., May 29, 1952; s. John Patrick and Margaret Helen (Fiocca) F.; m. Judith Patricia Waltz, July 24, 1976; children: Michael, Ryan, James. BSME, U.S. Mil. Acad., 1974; JD, U. Notre Dame, 1981; postdoctoral, The Army JAG Sch., 1986. Bar: Ind. 1981. Commd. 2d lt. U.S. Army, 1974, advanced through grades to maj., 1986; prosecutor U.S. Army, Ft. Carson, 1981-82, chief prosecutor, 1982-83; chief prosecutor 8th U.S. Army, Seoul, Republic of Korea, 1983-85; atty. civil litigation torts br., Pentagon U.S. Army, Washington, 1986—. Mem. ABA. Roman Catholic. Avocations: concert piano, U.S. history. Federal civil litigation, Personal injury. Home: 10230 Antietam Ln Fairfax VA 22030-2102 Office: HQDA (DAJA-LTT) Washington DC 20310-2210

FITZPATRICK, JOSEPH MARK, patent lawyer; b. Jersey City, May 27, 1925; s. Joseph Francis Stephen and Meave (Wilson) F.; M.E., Stevens Inst. Tech., 1945; J.D., Georgetown U., 1951; m. Elizabeth Anne Keane, June 18, 1949; children—Elizabeth A., Susan E., Christopher M., Stephen R. Examiner, U.S. Patent Office, 1946-50; admitted to Va. bar, 1950, N.Y. bar, 1954; trial atty., anti-trust div. Dept. Justice, 1951-53; mem. firm Ward, McElhannon, Brooks & Fitzpatrick, N.Y.C., 1954-70, Fitzpatrick, Cella, Harper & Scinto, N.Y.C., 1970—. Served with USNR, 1943-46. Fellow Am. Coll. Trial Lawyers; mem. N.Y., Va. bar assns., Assn. Bar City N.Y., Am., N.Y. patent law assns. Clubs: City Midday; Manasquan River Yacht, Fox Meadow Tennis. Patent, Trademark and copyright, Federal civil litigation. Home: 17 Oak Ln Scarsdale NY 10583 Office: 277 Park Ave New York NY 10017

FITZPATRICK, LAWRENCE SCOTT, lawyer; b. Rochester, Minn., Jan. 18, 1950; s. Thomas Bernard and Beatrice L. (Devaney) F. Student U. Wis., 1968-69, U. Ariz., 1969-70; B.A., U. Mass., 1977; J.D., U. Pa., 1981. Bar: Mass. 1981. Prodn. supr., analyst Energy Resources Inc., Cambridge, Mass., 1974-77; assoc. Choate, Hall & Stewart, Boston, 1981-83; asst. atty. gen. antitrust div. State of Mass., Boston, 1984—. Author: The Antinomian Controversy, 1981. Antitrust, Estate planning, State civil litigation. Home: 5-5 Concord Greene Concord MA 07142 Office: Office of Atty Gen Antitrust Div 1 Ashburton Place Boston MA 02108

FITZPATRICK, PETER BRYAN, lawyer; b. New Orleans, June 30, 1945; s. William H. and Frances (Westfeldt) F.; m. Anne L. Wallace, Aug. 24, 1968; children—Bryan W.W., Lydia W.C. B.A., Princeton U., 1968; M.A., Stanford U., 1969; J.D., U. Va., 1973; postgrad. St. Antony's Coll. Oxford Univ., 1976. Bar: Va. 1974, N.Y. 1977, D.C. 1978. Assoc. Winthrop, Stimson, Putnam & Roberts, N.Y.C., 1976-80; asst. counsel Newsweek Inc., N.Y.C., 1980-83; counsel Hunton & Williams, Norfolk, Va., 1983—. Contbr. articles to profl. jours. Trustee St. Antony's Coll. Trust, Pembroke Coll. Found., Oxford; bd. advisors Va. Ctr. World Trade, Norfolk, 1984; pres. World Affairs Council Greater Hampton Rds., Norfolk, 1986; communications com. campaign U. Va. Mem. ABA, D.C. Bar Assn., Va. Bar Assn., Assn. Bar City N.Y. (com. human rights). Avocations: tennis, hiking, squash, reading, history. Office: Hunton & Williams 101 St Paul's Blvd Norfolk VA 23510

FITZPATRICK, SANDRA MARLENE, lawyer; b. East St. Louis, Ill., Jan. 21, 1940; d. Clottis F. and Louise (Campbell) Gray; m. Lorenzo Fitzpatrick, May 5, 1961; children—Andre Renard, Eric D'Wayne. B.A., U. Tex., 1973, J.D., 1976. Bar: Tex. 1977, U.S. Dist. Ct. (we. dist.) Tex. 1980, U.S. Ct. Appeals (5th and 11th cirs.) 1981, U.S. Supreme Ct. 1982. Appeals referee Tex. Employment Commn., Austin, 1976-78; hearings examiner Tex. Water Commn., Austin, 1978-83; sole practice, Austin, 1983—; mcpl. ct. relief judge City of Austin, 1980-82; trustee Travis County Lawyer Referral Service; bd. dirs. Austin Ctr. Battered Women; pro bono Austin Lawyers Care, 1982—. Bd. dirs. Austin Ctr. for Battered Women; bd. of trustees Travis County Lawyer Referral Service. Mem. Black Austin Dems., Nat. Polit. Congress Black Women (parliamentarian cen. Tex. chpt.), Tex. Coalition Black Dems., Lawyers (rec. sec.), Tex. State Bar (environ. sect.), Nat. Womens Polit. Caucus, Austin Womens POlit. Caucus, Travis County Women Lawyers, Travis County Bar Assn., NAACP (appreciation award 1980). Democrat. Baptist. General practice, Family, Probate. Home: 7516 Downridge Dr Austin TX 78731 Office: 314 Highland Mall Blvd Suite 407 Austin TX 78752

FITZPATRICK, THOMAS BERNARD, federal agency judge; b. N.Y.C., Nov. 19, 1924; s. Patrick and Mary (Mulligan) F.; m. Margaret Catherine McDonald, Sept. 15, 1951; children: Maureen, Colleen, Ilene, Kathleen, Thomas, Eileen. BBA, CCNY, 1946; JD, NYU, 1949. Atty.-advisor FCC, Washington, 1950-55, trial atty., 1955-61, asst. chief, hearing div., broadcast bur., 1961-63, chief hearing div., broadcast bus., 1963-73, adminstrv. law judge, 1974-79, asst. chief judge, 1979-84, chief judge, 1984—. Mem. Fed. Adminstrv. Law Judges Conf. Avocations: church related activities. Home: 4711 Surry Pl Alexandria VA 22304 Office: FCC Adminstrv Law Judges 2000 L St NW Washington DC 20554

FITZSIMMONS, RICHARD M., lawyer; b. New Haven, Apr. 4, 1924; s. Irving F. and Nina G. (Moore) FitzS.; m. Estelle M. Naughton, Nov. 27, 1954; children: Estelle J., Anne H. B.A., Hamilton Coll., 1947; J.D., Yale U., 1950. Bar: N.Y. 1950, U.S. Supreme Ct. 1954, Wis. 1958, Ill. 1964, Ky. 1966. Assoc. Winthrop, Stimson, Putnam & Roberts, N.Y.C., 1950-51, Satterlee, Warfield & Stephens, N.Y.C., 1951-54; counsel Gen. Electric Co., various locations, 1954-70; counsel Hotpoint div. Gen. Electric Co., various locations, Chgo., 1963-66; appliance and TV group Gen. Electric Co., various locations, Louisville, 1966-70; gen. counsel, sr. v.p., sec. Allis-Chalmers Corp., Milw., 1970-85; mem. firm Cook & Franke S.C., 1986—; dir. Marine Trust (N.A.); mem. adv. bd. Internat. and Comparative Law Center, Southwestern Legal Found., Dallas, 1970—; mem. panel neutrals Asbestos Claims Facility. Editor Yale Law Jour., 1948-50; contbr. articles to profl. jours. Trustee Hamilton Coll., 1975-79. Served to capt. USAAF, 1943-46. Mem. Am., Wis., N.Y.C., Chgo., Ky. bar assns., Am. Arbitration Assn. (panel arbitrators), Corbey Ct., Yale Law Sch. Assn. (exec. com. 1978), Delta Kappa Epsilon, Phi Delta Phi. Clubs: Milwaukee Country, University of Milwaukee; Shenorock (Rye, N.Y.); Yale (N.Y.C.). General corporate, Labor. Home: 4720 N Lake Dr Milwaukee WI 53211 Office: 660 E Mason St Milwaukee WI 53202

FITZSIMON, JEAN KATHLEEN, lawyer; b. Evanston, Ill., Jan. 23, 1951; d. Robert Theodore and Kathleen Theresa (Daley) FitzSimon. B.A., St. John's Coll., Annapolis, Md., 1973; J.D., U. Notre Dame, 1976. Bar: Ill. 1976, D.C. 1982, U.S. Ct. Appeals (D.C. cir.) 1983, U.S. Dist. Ct. D.C. 1984. Staff atty. U.S. Dept. Justice, Washington, 1976-80, unit chief, 1980-81, dep. dir., 1981-82, asst. U.S. trustee, Chgo., 1982-83, sr. atty.-advisor, Washington, 1983—; dir. Am. Bankruptcy Inst. Mem. ABA, Dist. Bar Assn., St. John's Coll. Alumni Assn. (v.p. 1982—). Bankruptcy, Administrative and regulatory, Legislative. Office: Office of Legal Policy US Dept Justice Washington DC 20530

FIX, BRIAN DAVID, lawyer; b. Rochester, N.Y., May 31, 1944; s. Meyer and Elizabeth (Goldsmith) F. AB cum laude, Columbia U., 1965, LLB, 1968. Bar: N.Y. 1968, D.C. 1969. Ptnr. Surrey & Morse, Beirut, Lebanon, 1975, Washington, 1976-78, Paris, 1974-75, 78-81, N.Y.C., 1981-85; ptnr. Jones, Day, Reavis & Pogue, N.Y.C., 1986—. Mem. ABA, Internat. Bar Assn. Clubs: 29 (N.Y.C.); Circle de l'Union Interallieé (Paris). Avocations: tennis, skiing. Office: Jones Day Reavis & Pogue 599 Lexington Ave New York NY 10022

FIX, MEYER, lawyer; b. Manchester, Eng., July 29, 1906; came to U.S., 1910, naturalized, 1917; s. Morris and Leah (Katz) F.; m. Elizabeth Goldsmith, July 27, 1937; children: Terry E., Brian D. AB, U. Rochester, 1928; JD, Harvard U., 1931. Bar: N.Y. 1932, U.S. Supreme Ct. 1950. Assoc. John Van Voorhis' Sons, Rochester, N.Y., 1936-43; ptnr. Fix & MacCameron, Rochester, 1943-55, Meyer, Fix, Rochester, 1955-61, Fix & Spindelman, Rochester, 1961-74, Fix, Spindelman, Turk & Himelein, Rochester, 1974-77; sr. ptnr. Fix, Spindelman, Turk, Himelein & Schwartz, Rochester, 1977-83, Fix, Spindelman, Turk, Himelein & Shukoff, Rochester,

1983—; lectr. Cornell Law Sch., 1958-68. Contbr. articles to Scribes. Mem. ABA, N.Y. State Bar Assn., Monroe County Bar Assn., Am. Law Inst., Internat. Assn. Ins. Counsel, Fedn. Ins. Counsel, Assn. Ins. Attys., N.Y. State Trial Lawyers Assn. Club: Irondequoit Country. Lodges: Masons, Shriners. Insurance, General practice. Home: 2501 East Ave Rochester NY 14610 Office: 500 Crossroads Bldg 2 State St Rochester NY 14614

FLACK, CHARLES HAYNES, lawyer; b. Macomb, Ill., June 15, 1927; s. Charles Earl and Mary Helen (Gesler) F.; m. Barbara Joan Hull, Sept. 14, 1952; 1 dau., Teresa Flack Hillyer. Student Western Ill. U., 1946; B.S., Northwestern U., 1951, J.D., 1954. Bar: Ill. 1954. Ptnr., Flack & Kerman, Macomb, 1954-59, Flack & Flack, 1959-62, Flack & Dye, 1963-72, Flack & Kwacala, 1975-79, Flack, Kwacala & Murphy, 1979-85, Flack, Kwacala, Murphy & Ashenhurst, 1986—; spl. asst. Ill. Atty. Gen., 1983—; dir. Union Nat. Bank of Macomb. Bd. dirs. Western Ill. U. Found. Served with USNR, 1945-46. Fellow Am. Coll. Probate Csl. Mem. ABA, Ill. Bar Assn., McDonough County Bar Assn. Democrat. Presbyterian. Clubs: Macomb Country, Masons, Elks. Probate, Real property, Estate taxation. Home: 401 S Pearl St Macomb IL 61455 Office: 32 1/2 West Side Sq Macomb IL 61455

FLADUNG, RICHARD DENIS, patent lawyer; b. Kansas City, Mo., Aug. 1, 1953; s. Jerome Francis and Rosemary (Voeste) F.; m. Leslie Lynn Cox, June 1, 1985. BSCE, U. Kans., 1976, postgrad., 1977; JD, Washburn U., 1980. Bar: Kans. 1980, U.S. Dist. Ct. Kans. 1980, Ind. 1981, U.S. Dist. Ct. (so. dist.) Ind. 1981, U.S. Patent Office 1982, Mo. 1983, Tex. 1984, U.S. Dist. Ct. (we. dist.) Mo. 1983, U.S. Dist. Ct. (so. dist.) Tex. 1984, U.S. Ct. Appeals (fed. cir.) 1984, U.S. Ct. Appeals (5th cir.) 1987. Engr. Black and Veatch Cons. Engrs., Kansas City, 1975-80; corp. counsel CTB Inc., Milford, Ind., 1980-82; patent atty. Linde Thompson et al., Kansas City, 1982-83, Dodge, Bush & Moseley and predecessor firm, Houston, 1983-87, Pravel, Gambrell, Hewitt Kimball & Krieger, Houston, 1987—. Contbr. articles on patent applications to profl. jours. Legal aide to speaker of Kans. Ho. of Reps., Topeka, 1980, mem. Johnson County Rep. Com., 1980. Named One of Outstanding Young Men of Am., 1985. Mem. ABA, ASCE, Am. Intellectual Property Law Assn., Tex. Young Lawyers Assn., Mo. Bar Assn., Ind. Bar Assn., Houston Young Lawyers Assn. (pres. elect 1986-87, pres. 1987—, Outstanding Com. Chmn. award 1985-86), Houston Bar Assn., Kansas City Bar Assn., Houston Intellectual Property Law Assn. Pi Alpha Kappa (treas. 1974-75). Roman Catholic. Club: Kansas City. Avocations: tennis, sailing, jogging, raquetball. Patent, Trademark and copyright, Federal civil litigation. Office: Pravel Gambrell Hewitt et al 1177 W Loop S Suite 1010 Houston TX 77027

FLAGG, RONALD SIMON, lawyer; b. Milw., Dec. 3, 1953; s. Arnold and Marian (Levy) F.; m. Patricia Sharin, June 20, 1982; 1 child, Laura Sharon. AB, U. Chgo., 1975; JD, Harvard U., 1978. Bar: U.S. Dist. Ct. (ea. dist.) Wis. 1978, U.S. Ct. Appeals (7th cir.) 1979, D.C. 1980, U.S. Dist. Ct. D.C. 1980, U.S. Ct. Appeals (D.C. cir.) 1980, U.S. Ct. Appeals (3d cir.) 1984, U.S. Supreme Ct. 1986. Law clk. to presiding judge U.S. Dist. Ct. (ea. dist.) Wis., Milw., 1978-80; atty., adv. office of intelligence policy and rev. U.S. Dept. Justice, Washington, 1980-82; assoc. Sidley & Austin, Washington, 1982-85, ptnr., 1986—. Mem. ABA, D.C. Bar Assn. Democrat. Jewish. Administrative and regulatory, Federal civil litigation, Antitrust. Home: 4537 Grant Rd NW Washington DC 20016 Office: Sidley & Austin 1722 I St NW Washington DC 20006

FLAHERTY, DAVID THOMAS, JR., lawyer; b. Boston, June 17, 1953; S. David Thomas Sr. and Nancy Ann (Hamill) F.; m. Margaret Lynn Hoyle, Oct. 2, 1986. BS in Math., German, U. N.C., 1974, JD, 1978. Bar: Mass. 1979, N.C. 1979, U.S. Dist. Ct. (we. dist.) N.C. 1979, U.S. Dist. Ct. (mid. dist.) N.C. 1981, U.S. Ct. Appeals (4th cir.) 1981, U.S. Tax Ct. 1982. Assoc. Wilson & Palmer, Lenoir, N.C., 1979-80, Ted West P.A., Lenoir, 1980-82; ptnr. Robbins, Flaherty & Lackey, Lenoir, 1982-85, Robbins & Flaherty, Lenoir, 1985—. Mem. exec. com. Caldwell County Reps., Lenoir, 1985—. Mem. N.C. Bar Assn., Assn. Trial Lawyer Am., N.C. Acad. Trial Lawyers, Catawba Valley Estate Planning Council, Reps. Men's Club, Young Reps., Blue Key. Methodist. Avocations: water and snow skiing, motorcycling. General practice, Criminal, State civil litigation. Home: 228 Pennton Ave SW Lenoir NC 28645 Office: Robbins & Flaherty 204 Main St NW Lenoir NC 28645

FLAHERTY, JOHN P., supreme court justice; b. Pitts., Nov. 19, 1931; s. John Paul and Mary G. (McLaughlin) F. B.A. in Philosophy, Duquesne U., Pitts., 1953; J.D., U. Pitts., 1958. Bar: Pa. 1958. Pvt. practice Pitts., 1958-73; mem. faculty Carnegie-Mellon U., 1958-73; judge Ct. Common Pleas Allegheny County, 1973-79, pres. judge civil div., 1978-79; justice Supreme Ct. Pa., 1979—; USIA speaker in Far East, 1985-86. Served as officer AUS, 1953-55. Named Man of Year in Law and Govt. Greater Pitts. Jaycees, 1978. Mem. Pa. Acad. Sci. (Disting. Alumnus 1977, chmn. hon. exec. bd. 1979—), Pa. Soc., Mil. History Soc. Ireland, Irish Soc. Pitts., Friendly Sons St. Patrick, Irish-Am. Cultural Inst., Gaelic Arts Soc., Knights Equity, Ancient Order Hibernians, Am. Legion. Jurisprudence. Home: 901 William Penn Ct Pittsburgh PA 15221 Office: 6 Gateway Center Pittsburgh PA 15222

FLAHERTY, THOMAS VINCENT, lawyer; b. Wheeling, W.Va., Dec. 8, 1949; s. Leo Joseph and Irma Hazel (Cole) F.; m. Paula L. Wheatley, Jan. 1, 1972; children: Ian Cole, Colin O'Donnell. BS, W.Va. U., 1971, JD, 1974. Bar: W.Va. 1974, U.S. Dist. Ct. (so. dist.) W.Va. 1974, U.S. Ct. Appeals (4th and 6th cirs.) 1978, U.S. Dist. Ct. (no. dist.) W.Va. 1979. Assoc. Kay, Casto & Chaney, Charleston, W.Va., 1974-77, ptnr., 1977—; spl. asst. W.Va. Atty. Gen.'s Office, Charleston, 1976; bd. dirs. Ronal McDonald Ho., Charleston. Fin. agt., campaign mgr. various W.Va. Trial and Ct. and Supreme Ct. judges, 1976—; pres. St. Anthonys Sch. Bd., Charleston, 1983-85. Mem. ABA, W.Va. Bar Assn. (bd. of govs. 1981—), Kanawha County Bar Assn. (pres. 1983-84), Def. Trial Counsel W.Va. (officer, bd. of govs. 1981—). Democrat. Roman Catholic. Avocations: running, carpentry. Federal civil litigation, State civil litigation, Personal injury. Home: PO Box 2031 Charleston WV 25327 Office: Kay Casto & Chaney 1600 Charleston Nat Plaza Charleston WV 25301

FLAMM, LEONARD N(ATHAN), lawyer; b. Newark, May 23, 1943; s. Sydney Lewis and Lillian (Schreiber) F. Cert., London Sch. Econs., 1964; BA, Dartmouth Coll., 1965; JD, Harvard U., 1968. Bar: N.J. 1968, N.Y. 1970, U.S. Ct. Appeals (2d cir.) 1970, Fla. 1976, U.S. Dist. Ct. (so. and ea. dists.) N.Y. 1976, U.S. Ct. Appeals (7th cir.) 1986. Assoc. Marshall, Bratter, Greene, Allison & Tucker, N.Y.C., 1968-70, Donovan, Leisure, Newton & Irvine, N.Y.C., 1970-72, Glass, Greenberg & Irwin, N.Y.C., 1972-75; ptnr. Hockert & Flamm, N.Y.C., 1975—; bd. dirs. Falchi Enterprises Inc., N.Y.C. Named one of Best Lawyers in U.S., Town & Country Mag., 1985. Mem. Assn. of Bar of City of N.Y. (legal referral panel 1975—), Plaintiff Employment Lawyers Assn. (exec. com. N.Y.C.). Federal civil litigation, Labor, Civil rights. Home: 8 Ridgecrest W Scarsdale NY 10583 Office: Hockert & Flamm 880 3d Ave Suite 1300 New York NY 10022

FLAMM, MARTIN BENJAMIN, lawyer; b. N.Y.C., July 30, 1943; s. Herbert Herman and Rose Hilda (Yudson) F. AB, Columbia U., 1964; MD, Med. Coll. of Va., 1968; JD, Loyola U., New Orleans, 1984. Bar: La. 1984; Diplomate Am. Bd. Radiology, Am. Bd. Nuclear Medicine. Pvt. practice specializing in radiology New Orleans, 1971—, sole practice, 1984—. Fellow Am. Coll. Legal Medicine (diplomate); mem. Radiol. Soc. N.Am., Am. Soc. Law and Medicine. Club: Bards of Bohemia (New Orleans). Health, Legal education.

FLAMMER, GEORGE HERBERT, lawyer, educator; b. Rahway, N.J., Aug. 21, 1947; s. Herbert Stanley and Verna Anna (Zuckschwerdt) F. BS, Rider Coll., 1969; JD, Detroit Coll. Law, 1974. Bar: N.J. 1975, U.S. Supreme Ct. 1980. Law clk. to presiding justice Atlantic County Ct., Atlantic City, 1975-76; assoc. Valore, McAllister, DeBrier, Aron & Westmoreland, Northfield, N.J., 1976-77, Lashman & Kupperman, Atlantic City, 1977-78; atty., dir. Atlantic County Sr. Citizens Legal Service, Atlantic City, 1978-81; sole practice Atlantic City and Ocean City, N.J., 1981—; adj. prof. law Stockton State Coll., 1977-80, Atlantic Community Coll., Mays Landing, N.J., 1976—. Served with U.S. Army, 1970-72. Mem. ABA, Assn. Trial Lawyers Am., N.J. Bar Assn., Atlantic County Bar Assn., Delta Theta Phi. Republican. Avocations: golf, tennis. State civil litigation, General practice, Legal education. Home: 57 DeFeo Ln Somers Point NJ 08244 Office: 1421 Atlantic Ave Atlantic City NJ 08401

FLANAGAN, DEBORAH MARY, lawyer; b. Hackensack, N.J., Sept. 17, 1956; d. Joseph Francis and Mary Agnes (Fitzsimmons) F.; m. Glen H. Koch, Aug. 27, 1983. BA summa cum laude, Fordham U., 1978, JD, 1981. Bar: N.Y. 1982. Tax atty. McGraw-Hill Inc., N.Y.C., 1981—; sec., v.p. Internat. Archtl. Found. Inc., N.Y.C., 1982—; v.p. MHFSCO, Ltd. subs. McGraw-Hill, Inc., N.Y.C., 1984—. Mem. ABA, N.Y. State Bar Assn., Assn. of Bar of City of N.Y., N.Y. County Lawyers Assn., Fordham U. Law Alumni Assn. Corporate taxation, Personal income taxation, State and local taxation. Home: 114 Harrison Ave Hasbrouck Heights NJ 07604 Office: McGraw-Hill Inc 1221 Ave of Americas New York NY 10020

FLANAGAN, JAMES HENRY, JR., lawyer; b. San Francisco, Sept. 11, 1934; s. James Henry Sr. and Mary Patricia (Gleason) F.; m. Charlotte Anne Nevins, June 11, 1960; children: Nancy, Christopher, Christina, Alexis, Victoria, Grace. AB in Polit. Sci., Stanford U., 1956, JD, 1961. Bar: Calif. 1962, U.S. Dist. Ct. (no. dist.) Calif. 1962, U.S. Ct. Appeals (9th cir.) 1962, U.S. Dist. Ct. (so. dist.) Calif. 1964, U.S. Dist. Ct. (ea. dist.) 1967, Oreg. 1984. Assoc. Creede, Dawson & McElrath, Fresno, Calif., 1962-64; ptnr. Pettitt, Blumberg & Sherr and successor firms, Fresno, 1964-75; sole practice Clovis, Calif., 1975—; instr. Humprey's Coll. Law, Fresno, 1964-69, bus. Calif. State U., Fresno, 1986—; judge pro tem Fresno County Superior Ct., 1974-77; gen. counsel Kings River Water Assn., 1976-79. Author: California Water District Laws, 1962. Mem. Fresno County Rep. Cen. Com., 1964-66, exec. com. parish council St. Helen's, 1982-85, chmn. 1985; pres. Fresno Opera Assn., 1965-69, parish council St. John's Cathedral, 1974-82; pres. bd. dirs. 3d Floor, Cen. Calif.; bd. dirs. Fresno Facts Found., 1969-70, Fresno Dance Reperatory Assn., St. Anthony's Retreat Ctr., Three Rivers, Calif. Served to 1st lt. USMC, 1958-61. Recipient President award Fresno Jaycees, 1964. Mem. Calif. Bar Assn., Oreg. Bar Assn., Fresno County Bar Assn. (various coms.), Assn. Trial Lawyers Am., Calif. Trial Lawyers Assn. (pres. Fresno chpt. 1975, 83), Oreg. Trial Lawyers Assn., Fresno Trial Lawyers Assn., Stanford Alumni Assn. (life, service award), Fresno Region Stanford Club (pres. 1979-80), Celtic Cultural Soc. Cen. Calif. (pres. 1977-78), Fresno County and City C. of C. (chmn. natural resources com. 1977-78), Clovis Dist. C. of C. (bd. dirs. 1977—, award of merit 1982), Clovis-Big Dry Creek Hist. Soc. (past vice chmn.), Phi Alpha Delta. Republican. Roman Catholic. Club: Fresno Serra (pres. 1980-81, v.p. 1986—). Lodge: Rotary. Avocations: writing, music, gardening, sailing, fishing. Family and matrimonial, Personal injury, Probate. Home: 1770 Robinwood Clovis CA 93612 Office: PO Box 1048 Clovis CA 93613

FLANAGAN, JOSEPH PATRICK, JR., lawyer; b. Wilkes-Barre, Pa., Sept. 18, 1924; s. Joseph P. and Grace B. F.; m. Mary Elizabeth Mayock, Aug. 5, 1950; children: Maureen Elizabeth, Joseph P. III. B.S., U.S. Naval Acad., 1947; J.D., U. Pa., 1952. Bar: Pa. 1953, U.S. Dist. Ct. (ea. dist.) Pa. 1953, U.S. Ct. Appeals (3d cir.) 1953. Assoc. Saul, Ewing, Remick & Saul, Phila., 1952-56; ptnr. Ballard, Spahn, Andrews & Ingersoll, Phila., 1956—; chmn. pub. fin. dept. Ballard, Spahn, Andrews & Ingersoll, 1961—. Editor: Practicing Law Inst., Health Facilities Financing, 1976; co-author: "In Search of Capital-A Trustee's Guide to Hospital Financing"; editor-in-chief: U. Pa. Law Rev., 1951-52; contbr. articles to profl. jours. Bd. dirs. Phila. Com. of 70, 1952-56; trustee Wyoming Sem., Kingston, Pa. Served to lt. (j.g.) USN, 1946-49. Fellow Am. Bar Found.; mem. Phila. Bar Assn. (past founding chmn. tax exempt fin. com., past chmn. profl. edn. com., client's security fund com., fee disputes com., sec. corp. bus. banking com., treas. corp. banking and bus. com.), Pa. Bar Assn., ABA (chmn. urban state and local govt. sect.), Pa. Bar Inst. (pres. 1983, chmn. curriculum and course planning com. 1976-83), Am. Law Inst. Republican. Roman Catholic. Clubs: Philadelphia, Racquet, Phila. Cricket (Phila.); Army Navy Country of Va; Princeton (N.Y.C.). Public finance, Health. Home: 401 E Mill Rd Flourtown PA 19031 Office: 30 S 17th St 20th Floor Philadelphia PA 19103

FLANAGAN, NORMAN PATRICK, lawyer; b. Pitts., Feb. 3, 1953; s. Norman Patrick and Janice (Smith) F.; m. Caroline E.E. Reverdin, Aug. 2, 1975; children: Erin Elizabeth, Sean Patrick. BS in Edn., Duquesne U., 1975; JD, Calif. Western U., 1978. Bar: Pa., Nev., U.S. Dist. Ct. Nev., U.S. Ct. Appeals (9th cir.), U.S. Supreme Ct. Dep. pub. defender Washoe County Pub. Defender's Office, Reno, 1979-81; asst. pub. defender Pub. Defender's Office, Reno, 1982—. Mem. Nev. State Bar Assn. (continuing legal edn. sect.), Legal Def. Fund (capital litigation sect.). Republican. Roman Catholic. Avocations: tennis, cross-country skiing. Criminal. Office: Pub Defenders Office 300 Booth St Reno NV 89509

FLANAGIN, NEIL, lawyer; b. Chgo., Dec. 2, 1930; s. Norris Cornelius and Virginia (Riddell) F.; m. Mary Mead, Nov. 19, 1960; children: John Mead, Margot, Nancy, Jill. B.A., Yale U., 1953; J.D., U. Mich., 1956. Bar: Ill. 1956. Assoc. Leibman, Williams, Bennett, Baird & Minow, Chgo., 1960-66, ptnr., 1966-72; ptnr. Sidley & Austin, Chgo., 1972—. Bd. dirs. Dr. Scholl Found., Chgo., 1973—. Served to 1st lt. AUS, 1956-59. Fellow Am. Coll. Investment Counsel; mem. Internat. Bar Assn., ABA, Chgo. Bar Assn. Clubs: University; Law (Chgo.); Indian Hill (Winnetka). General corporate, Securities. Home: 1010 Mt Pleasant Winnetka IL 60093 Office: Sidley & Austin One First Nat Plaza Chicago IL 60603

FLANARY, DONALD HERBERT, JR., lawyer; b. Texarkana, Ark., July 27, 1949; s. Donald Herbert and Tenney-Margaret (Webb) F.; m. Janet Gail Lymnan, June 3, 1971; children—Donald Herbert III, Shannon Gail. B.S. with honors, East Tex. State U., 1971; J.D., U. Houston, 1974. Bar: Tex. 1974, U.S. Dist. Ct. (no. dist.) Tex. 1975, U.S. Dist. Ct. (ea. dist.) Tex. 1976, U.S. Dist. Ct. (so. dist.) Tex. 1982, U.S. Tax Ct. 1982, U.S. Ct. Appeals (5th cir.) 1976, U.S. Ct. Appeals (11th cir.) 1984, U.S. Supreme Ct. 1983. Law clk. Ct. Appeals (7th cir.), Amarillo, Tex., 1974-75; asst. dist. atty. Dallas County, Tex., 1975-76; ptnr. Henderson Bryant & Wolfe, Sherman, Tex., 1976—; lectr. for bar assns. on tort law, 1981-84. Bd. dirs. Texoma Valley council Boy Scouts Am., Cancer Soc., Sherman. Named one of Outstanding Young Men Am., U.S. Jaycees, 1981; Eagle Scout, Boy Scouts Am., 1963. Fellow Tex. Bar Found.; mem. Tex. Assn. Def. Counsel (bd. dirs. 1981-84), Grayson County Bar Assn. (pres. 1983-84), Internat. Assn. Ins. Counsel (bd. cert. personal jury trial law), Bd. Legal Specialization (civil trial law), Nat. Bd. Trial Adv. Democrat. Roman Catholic. Lodges: Masons, Shriners. Federal civil litigation, State civil litigation, Insurance. Home: 2803 Mimosa Sherman TX 75090 Office: Henderson Bryant & Wolfe PO Box 239 Sherman TX 75090

FLANDERS, GILBERT LEE, lawyer; b. San Diego, Sept. 18, 1935; s. James L. and Josephine (Medrano) F.; m. Amy, Dec. 2, 1961; children—Therese, Sean, Patrick. Student U. San Diego, 1954-57; J.D., Southwestern Sch. Law, Los Angeles, 1964. Bar: Calif., 1965, U.S. dist. ct. (cent. dist.) Calif. 1965. Assoc., H. H. Hiestand, Los Angeles, 1965-66, English & MacDowell, Lynwood, Calif., 1966-68; sole practice Downey, Calif., 1968—; csl. Mexican-Am. Polit. Assn., 1965-68; mem. Los Angeles Dist. Atty. Adv. Council, 1967-70; bd. dirs. Legal Services S.E. Dist. Los Angeles 1970—; mem. Calif. Atty. Gen. Adv. Council, 1970-77; gen. csl. United Nat. Italian Charitable Orgns., 1978—. Bd. dirs. Downey YMCA, 1979—; found. bd. mem. Downey Community Hosp., 1980—. Served with U.S. Army, 1958-60. Mem. Themis Legal Soc. (founding), Calif. Trial Lawyers Assn., ABA, Am. Trial Lawyers Assn., S.E. Bar Assn., Los Angeles County Bar Assn. Republican. Roman Catholic. Federal civil litigation, Federal civil litigation, Personal injury. Office: 11510 S Downey Ave Downey CA 90241

FLANDERS, HOWARD BARRETT, JR., lawyer; b. San Francisco, Apr. 21, 1935; s. Howard Barrett Sr. and Emma Marion (Stewart) F.; m. Jean Hammond Curtis, June 21, 1958; children: Julia Hammond, Keith Howard. AB, Harvard U., 1956; LLB, Columbia U., 1963. Bar: N.Y. 1963, N.J. 1972. Assoc. Carter, Ledyard & Milburn, N.Y.C., 1963-71; from atty. corp. law dept. to staff v.p., assoc. gen. counsel Allied-Signal Inc., Morris Twp., N.J., 1971—. Served to lt. (j.g.) USNR, 1956-60. Mem. ABA, Assn. of Bar of City of N.Y., N.J. Bar Assn. General corporate, Securities, Real property. Home: 198 Central Ave Madison NJ 07940 Office: Allied-Signal Inc Columbia Rd & Park Ave Morris Township NJ 07960

FLANDERS, LAURENCE BURDETTE, JR., lawyer; b. Longmont, Colo., Feb. 7, 1917; s. Laurence Burdette and Harriet (Secor) F.; m. Eleanor Carlson, June 6, 1941; children—Laurel Flanders Umile, John C., Lynette Flanders Moyer, Paul L. B.S. with honors, U. Colo., 1938; J.D., 1940. Bar: Colo. 1940, U.S. Dist. Ct. Colo. 1965. Dep. dist. atty. Boulder County, Colo., 1948-52; ptnr. Flanders, Wood, Sonnesyn & Steinkamp, Longmont, Colo., 1946—; dir. First Nat. Bank Longmont; pres., trustee Flanders Found., Inc. Bd. trustees Colo. Bar Found.; mem. Longmont Charter Conv., 1961; mem. Longmont Water Bd., 1952-85; chmn. Longmont Long Range Planning Commn., 1971-72. Served with USNR, 1942-45. Fellow Am. Coll. Probate Counsel, Am. Bar Found.; mem. Colo. Bar Assn. (bd. of govs. 1963-67, v.p. bd. govs. 1967-68, chmn. probate and trust law sect. 1965-66), Boulder County Bar Assn., Am. Judicature Soc., Delta Sigma Pi, Order of Coif. Republican. Mem. United Ch. of Christ. Clubs: Rotary Internat., Boulder Country, Masons. Probate, Estate taxation. Home: 917 3d Ave Longmont CO 80501 Office: FNB Bldg #1 401 Main ST Longmont CO 80501

FLANNAGAN, FRANCIS WILLS, lawyer; b. Clintwood, Va., Apr. 30, 1919; s. John William and Frances Deal (Pruner) F.; m. Florine Bibee, Dec. 18, 1943; 1 child, Flo Tallman. BA, King Coll., 1940; postgrad., Am. U., 1941; JD, Washington & Lee U., 1947. Bar: Va. 1947. Ptnr. Flannagan & Flannagan, Bristol, Va., 1947-66; sr. ptnr. Woodward, Miles & Flannagan, P.C., Bristol, 1966—. Served with USAF, 1942-45. Mem. ABA, Va. Bar Assn., Internat. Assn. Ins. Counsel, Am. Coll. Trial Lawyers, Def. Research Inst. Presbyterian. Insurance, State civil litigation, Labor. Home: 102 Flannagan Dr Bristol VA 24201 Office: Woodward Miles & Flannagan PC 510 Cumberland Suite 200 Bristol VA 24203-0789

FLANNERY, DAVID MICHAEL, lawyer; b. Logan, W.Va., Nov. 20, 1946; s. Clyde H. and Helen (Leedy) F.; m. Janice S. Howell, Aug. 14, 1971; children: Michael Scott, Charles Henderson. BEE, W.Va. U., 1969, JD, 1972. Bar: W.Va., 1972. Assoc. James, Wise, Robinson & Magnuson, Charleston, W.Va., 1972-75; ptnr. Love, Wise, Robinson & Woodroe, Charleston, 1976-83, Robinson & McElwee, Charleston, 1983—. Served to capt. U.S. Army, 1969-77. Mem. ABA (natural resources sect.), W.Va. Bar Assn., Kanawha County Bar Assn. Democrat. Methodist. Environment, Administrative and regulatory. Office: Robinson & McElwee PO Box 1791 Charleston WV 25326

FLANNERY, HARRY AUDLEY, lawyer; b. New Castle, Pa., June 11, 1947; s. Wilbur Eugene and Ruth (Donaldson) F.; m. Maureen Louise Flaherty, June 28, 1969; children: Preston Wilbur, Courtney Lilyan. BA, Wesleyan U., 1969; JD, Ohio No. U., 1972; LLM in Taxation, Boston U., 1973. Bar: Pa. 1972, U.S. Tax Ct. 1973, U.S. Dist. Ct. (we. dist.) Pa. 1975, U.S. Supreme Ct. 1976, U.S. Ct. Appeals 1984. Trust legal officer Pitts. Nat. Bank, 1973-76; atty. Pa. Power Co., New Castle, 1977—, sec. fed. and state polit. coms., 1983—. Assoc. editor Pitts. Legal Jour., 1979; contbr. articles to profl. jours. Mem. Highland United Presbyn. Ch., New Castle. Mem. ABA (labor and employment law sect. com. on labor arbitration and law of collective bargaining agreements, tax sect. com. excise and employment taxes, subcom. payroll tax issues), Pa. Bar Assn. (com. workmen's compensation), Allegheny County Bar Assn., Pitts. Legal Jour. Com., Lawrence County Bar Assn., Allegheny Tax Soc., Pa. Soc., Assn. Trial Lawyers Am., Phi Alpha Delta (life). Republican. Clubs: Duquesne, Lawrence, New Castle Country. Lodge: Lions (bd. dirs. 1982—, tailtwister 1983-84, 3d v.p. 1984-85, 2d 1985—, 1st 1986—). Avocations: writing, tennis, boating. Workers' compensation, Corporate taxation, Labor. Home: 116 Valhalla Dr New Castle PA 16105 Office: Pa Power Co One E Washington St New Castle PA 16103

FLANNERY, JAMES LLOYD, lawyer; b. N.Y.C., Jan. 29, 1949; s. Lloyd F. and Mary K. (Stewart) F.; m. Kathryn P. Thoms, Aug. 29, 1970. BA, Miami U., Oxford, Ohio, 1971; M in Urban and Regional Planning, Va. Tech., 1974. Bar: Pa. 1982, U.S. Dist. Ct. (we. dist.) Pa. 1982, U.S. Dist. Ct. (ea. dist.) Pa. 1984, U.S. Ct. Appeals (3d cir.) 1984, Ind. 1986m U.S. Dist. Ct. (so. dist.) Ind. 1986m U.S. Ct. Appeals (7th cir.) 1986. Planner regional planning commn. Merrimack Valley, Haverhill, Mass., 1974-77; sr. planner Fargo-Morehead (Minn.) Council of Govts., 1977-79; law clk. to presiding justice U.S. Ct. Appeals (3d cir.), Pitts., 1982-84; assoc. Schnader, Harrison, Segal & Lewis, Phila., 1984-86, Barnes & Thornburg, Indpls., 1986—. Editor-in-chief U. Pitts. Law Rev., 1981-82. Real property, Federal civil litigation, State civil litigation. Office: Barnes & Thornburg 1313 Merchants Bank Bldg Indianapolis IN 46204

FLANNERY, J(OHN) HAROLD, judge, lawyer; b. West Pittston, Pa., Apr. 2, 1933; s. J. Harold and Anne (Allan) F.; m. Barbara Marie Nash, Nov. 25, 1967. B.A. in History, Wilkes Coll., 1955; LL.B., U. Pa., 1958. Bar: U.S. Ct. Appeals (D.C. cir.) 1959, U.S. Ct. Appeals (1st, 4th, 5th, 6th, 7th, 10th cirs.), Mass. 1976, U.S. Supreme Ct. 1971. Trial atty. U.S. Dept. Justice, Washington, 1958-70; dep. dir. Law and Edn. Ctr., Cambrige, Mass., 1970-74; bd. dirs. Lawyers Com. for Civil Rights, Washington, 1974-75, trustee, 1975—; ptnr. Foley, Hoag & Eliot, Boston, 1975-84; assoc. justice Superior Ct. of Mass., 1984—, First v.p. Mass. Civil Liberties Union, 1983-84; mem. Town Fin. Com. Town of Weston, Mass., 1981-85. Jud. fellow Am. Coll. Trial Lawyers. Democrat. Roman Catholic. Judicial administration. Office: New Court House Penberton Sq Boston MA 02108

FLANNERY, JOHN PHILIP, II, lawyer; b. N.Y.C., May 15, 1946; s. John Philip and Agnes Geraldine (Applegate) F.; m. Bettina Gregory, Nov. 14, 1981. B.S. in Physics, Fordham Coll., 1967; B.S. in Engring., Columbia U., 1969, J.D., 1972; student Art Student League, 1972-73. Bar: N.Y. 1973, U.S. Dist. Ct. (so. dist.) N.Y. 1973, U.S. Ct. Appeals (2d cir.) 1973. Mem. staff Ford Found. Project to Restructure Columbia U., 1968; news rep. nat. press relations IBM, 1970; law clk. Adminstrv. Conf. U.S., 1971; law clk. U.S. Ct. Appeals 2d cir., 1972-74; asst. U.S. atty. Narcotics and Ofcl. Corruption units So. Dist. N.Y., 1974-79; sr. assoc. Poletti Freidin Prashker Feldman & Gartner, N.Y.C., 1979-82; spl. counsel U.S. Senate Judiciary Com., 1982; spl. counsel U.S. Senate Labor Com., 1982-83; Dem. candidate for U.S. Congress from Va. 10th Dist., 1983-84; sole practice in civil and criminal litigation, 1984—; spl. counsel Sen. Howard Metzenbaum, 1985-87; asst. dist. atty., Bronx, N.Y., 1986-87; lectr. in field. Committeeman Dem. Party N.Y. County, 1979-80; mem. legis. commn. Citizen's Union, 1971-72; mem. Arlington Transp. Commn., 1983-85; chmn. bus. council Va. Gov.'s War on Drugs Task Force, 1983-84; committeeman Dem. Party Arlington County, 1983-84; coordinator N.Y. State Lawyers Com. for Senator Edward M. Kennedy, 1979-80; dir. Citizens for Senator M. Kennedy, 1980; pres. Franklin Soc., 1979-80. Recipient U.S. Justice Dept. award for Outstanding Contbns. in the Field of Drug Law Enforcement 1977; U.S. Atty. Gen.'s Spl. Commendation for Outstanding Service, 1979. Mem. ABA, Bar Assn. City N.Y., N.Y. County Lawyers Assn., Arlington County Bar Assn., Loudon County Bar Assn., Acad. Polit. Sci. Democrat. Author: Commercial Information Brokers, 1973; Habeas Corpus Bores Hole in Prisoners' Civil Rights Action, 1975; Pro Se Litigation, 1975; Prison Corruption: A Mockery of Justice, 1980. Federal civil litigation, Criminal, Civil rights. Home: Shamrock Farm Rt 2 Box 144A Leesburg VA 22075

FLASTER, RICHARD JOEL, lawyer; b. N.Y.C., Jan. 7, 1943; s. Charles and Sylvia (Moss) F.; m. Esther S. Stomel, Aug. 10, 1945; children—Kiva Moss, Eben Scott. B.S. in Econs., U. Pa., 1963; J.D., Harvard U., 1966. Bar: N.Y. 1967, U.S. Tax Ct. 1971, N.J. 1972, D.C. 1972. Law clk. to judge U.S. Dist. Ct. (ea. dist.) N.Y., 1966-68; Reginald Heber Smith fellow U. Pa., 1968-69; assoc. Stroock, Stroock & Lavan, N.Y.C., 1969-72; v.p. Liebman & Flaster, P.C., Cherry Hill, N.J., 1972-86; pres. Flaster, Greenberg, Mann & Wallerstein, P.C., Marlton, N.J., 1986—; frequent lectr. on various tax subjects ABA, N.J. Inst. Continuing Legal Edn. Mem. Camden County Bar Assn., N.J. State Bar Assn., N.Y. State Bar Assn., ABA, Beta Gamma Sigma, Beta Alpha Psi, Pi Gamma Mu. Author: Basic Federal Tax Aspects of Real Estate Transactions, 1976; Tax Aspects of Separation and Divorce, 1982; tax editor N.J. Family Lawyer. Corporate taxation, Estate taxation, Personal income taxation. Office: Flaster Greenberg Mann & Wallenstein PC Five Greentree Ctr Suite 200 Rt 73 & Lincoln DrW Marlton NJ 08053

FLATE, RONALD ALLEN, lawyer, real estate broker; b. Cleve., Nov. 26, 1937; s. Arthur J. and Hilda R. (Rosenberg) F.; m. Greta Gail Scheiner, Dec. 19, 1965; children—David Scott, Samantha Leigh, Lisa Ann, Robert Steven. B.S., U. Wis., 1960; J.D., Calif. Western Sch. Law, 1966. Bar: Calif.

1967, U.S. Dist. Ct. (cen.) Calif., 1967, U.S. Supreme Ct. 1974. Atty.-agt. IRS, Los Angeles, 1966-68; supervisory atty. SBA, Los Angeles, 1971-72; sr. ptnr. Ronald A. Flate, Los Angeles, 1968-71, 72—; judge pro tem Los Angeles Mcpl. Ct., 1977—; owner Ron Realty; lectr. bus. and real estate groups. Mem. ABA, Calif. Bar Assn., Los Angeles Bar Assn. (mem. coms. tax, real estate, probate, bus. corp.), Nat. Assn. Realtors, Los Angeles Bd. Realtors (author monthly real estate article for apt. owner and builder mag.), Phi Delta Phi. Contbr. articles to legal and bus. jours. General corporate, State civil litigation, Real property. Office: 4929 Wilshire Blvd #700 Los Angeles CA 90010

FLATLEY, DANIEL KEVIN, lawyer; b. Milw., Aug. 5, 1953; s. James Michael and Suzanne Nell (Futch) F. AB magna cum laude, U. Notre Dame, 1975; JD, Georgetown U., 1978; MBA, U. Pa., 1982. Bar: Fla. 1978, U.S. Dist. Ct. (no. and mid. dists.) Fla., 1979, U.S. Ct. Appeals (5th and 11th cirs.) 1979. Law clk. to presiding justice U.S. Dist. Ct. Fla., Tallahassee, 1978-80; assoc. Johnson, Blakely, et al, Clearwater, Fla., 1982-85; mng. dir. Madsen & Co., Inc., Los Angeles, 1985-86, Donaldson, Lufkin & Jenrette Inc., N.Y.C., 1986—. Conv. del. Dem. Exec. Com., Clearwater, Fla., 1982-85; mem Leadership Pinellas County, Clearwater, 1983—; bd. dirs. Clearwater Progress, 1984-85; treas., bd. dirs. Manger 2, Los Angeles, 1985-86. Strong Found. fellow, Washington, 1977-78, 80-82. Democrat. Roman Catholic. Banking, Securities. Home: 45 E 25th St #8A New York NY 10010 Office: Donaldson Lufkin & Jenrette Inc 140 Broadway 48th Floor New York NY 10005

FLATLEY, ROBERT RAHR, lawyer; b. Green Bay, Wis., June 28, 1929; s. D. Francis and Eleanor (Rahr) F.; m. Jeanne Rae Buerschinger, May 15, 1964; children: Mary Jean, John Robert. BS, U. Wis., 1951, JD, 1954. Bar: Wis. 1954, U.S. Dist. Ct. (ea. dist.) Wis. 1960. Dist. atty. Brown County, Green Bay, 1964-67, corp. counsel, 1967-76; ptnr. Will & Flatley, Green Bay, 1974—; pres. Heritage Hill Corp., Green Bay, 1976-79. Pres. Brown County Hist. Soc., Green Bay, 1963-67. Served to sgt. U.S. Army, 1954-56. Mem. Wis. Bar Assn., Brown County Bar Assn., Assn. Trial Lawyers Am. Lodge: Kiwanis (pres. Green Bay 1975). General practice, Probate, Criminal. Home: 253 Little Rd Green Bay WI 54301 Office: Will & Flatley 220 N Madison St Green Bay WI 54301

FLATTERY, PAUL CHARLES, lawyer; b. Jamaica, N.Y., Apr. 15, 1935; s. Henry and Alice V. (Heverin) F.; m. Dorothy Ellen Fenelon, Aug. 1, 1959; children: Paul C. Jr., Kevin M., William H., Patrick J., Steven R. BEE, U. Notre Dame, 1957; JD, Georgetown U., 1964. Bar: U.S. Patent Office 1964, N.Y. 1965, Ill. 1976, U.S. Dist. Ct. (ea. and so. dists.) N.Y. 1973, U.S. Ct. Appeals (Fed. cir.) 1978, U.S. Dist. Ct. (no. dist.) Ill. 1982. From assoc. to ptnr. Fish & Neave, N.Y.C., 1964-75; assoc. gen. counsel Baxter Travenol Labs., Deerfield, Ill., 1975—. Served to capt. USMC, 1957-60. Mem. ABA, Am. Intellectual Property Law Assn., Patent Law Assn. Chgo. (bd. mgrs. 1981-82, 2d v.p. 1985, pres. elect 1986, pres. 1987-88). Roman Catholic. Club: Chgo. Curling (v.p. 1987-88). Patent, Trademark and copyright. Home: 917 Oxford Rd Deerfield IL 60015 Office: Baxter Travenol Labs One Baxter Pkwy Deerfield IL 60015

FLATTERY, THOMAS LONG, manufacturing company executive, lawyer; b. Detroit, Nov. 14, 1922; s. Thomas J. and Rosemary (Long) F.; m. Gloria M. Hughes, June 10, 1947 (dec.); children: Constance Marie, Carol Dianne Lee, Michael Patrick, Thomas Hughes, Dennis Jerome, Betsy Ann Bagnall; m. Barbara J. Balfour, Oct. 4, 1986. B.S., U.S. Mil. Acad., 1947; J.D., UCLA, 1955; LL.M., U. So. Calif., 1965. Bar: Calif. 1955, U.S. Patent Office 1957, U.S. Customs Ct. 1968, U.S. Supreme Ct. 1974, Conn. 1983, N.Y. 1984. With Motor Products Corp., Detroit, 1950, Equitable Life Assurance Soc. Am., 1951, Bohn Aluminum & Brass Co., 1952; mem. legal staff, asst. contract adminstr. Radioplane Co., Van Nuys, Calif., 1955-57; successively corp. counsel, gen. counsel, asst. sec. McCulloch Corp., Los Angeles, 1957-64; sec., corp. counsel Technicolor, Inc., Hollywood, Calif., 1964-70; successively corp. counsel, asst. sec., v.p., sec. and gen. counsel Amcord, Inc., Newport Beach, Calif., 1970-72; v.p., sec., gen. counsel Schick Inc., Los Angeles, 1972-75; counsel, asst. sec. C.F. Braun & Co., Alhambra, Calif., 1975-76; sr. v.p., sec., gen. counsel Automation Industries, Inc. (now PCC Tech. Industries Inc. a unit of Penn Cen. Corp.), Greenwich, Conn., 1976-86; v.p., gen. counsel G&H Tech. Inc. (a unit of Penn Cen. Telecommunications Co.), Santa Monica, Calif., 1986—. Contbr. articles to various legal jours. Served to 1st lt. AUS, 1942-50. Mem. ABA, State Bar Calif. (co-chmn. corp. law dept. com. 1978-79, lectr. continuing edn. program), Los Angeles County Bar Assn. (chmn. corp. law dept. com. 1966-67), Century City Bar Assn. (chmn. corp. law dept. com. 1979-80), Conn. Bar Assn., Am. Soc. Corp. Secs. (Los Angeles regional group pres. 1973-74), Patent Law Assn. Los Angeles, Fgn. Law Assn. Los Angeles, Licensing Exec. Soc. U.S., Westchester-Fairfield Corp. Counsel Assn., West Point Alumni Assn., Army Athletic Assn., Friendly Sons St. Patrick, Phi Alpha Delta. Roman Catholic. Clubs: Los Angeles Athletic, Jonathan (Los Angeles); Darien Country (Conn.). General corporate, Patent, Trademark and copyright. Home: 439 Via de la Paz Pacific Palisades CA 90272 Office: 1541 Ocean Ave Suite 200 Santa Monica CA 90401

FLAUM, JOEL MARTIN, judge; b. Hudson, N.Y., Nov. 26, 1936; s. Louis and Sally (Berger) F.; m. Thea Kharasch, July 3, 1960; children: Jonathan, Alison. B.A., Union Coll., Schenectady, 1958; J.D., Northwestern U., 1963, LL.M., 1964. Bar: Ill. 1963. Asst. state's atty. Cook County, Ill., 1965-69; 1st asst. atty. gen. Ill., 1969-72; 1st asst. U.S. atty. No. Dist. Ill., Chgo., 1972-75; judge U.S. Dist. Ct. No. Dist. Ill., Chgo., 1975-83, U.S. Ct. Appeals 7th Cir., 1983—; lectr. Northwestern U. Sch. Law, 1967-69, 84—; mem. Ill. Law Enforcement Commn., 1970-72; cons. U.S. Dept. Justice, Law Enforcement Assistance Adminstrn. Mem.: Northwestern U. Law Rev., 1962-63; contbr. articles to legal jours. Mem. adv. bd. Loyola U. Sch. Law, 1978—; mem. vis. com. U. Chgo. Law Sch., 1983-86, Northwestern U. Sch. Law, 1984—; trustee Congregation Anshe Emet, Chgo., 1978—. Served to lt. JAGC, USNR. Ford Found. fellow, 1963-64; Am. Bar Found. fellow, 1984. Mem. Fed. Bar Assn., ABA, Bar Assn. 7th Circuit, Ill. Bar Assn., Chgo. Bar Assn., Legal Club Chgo., Maritime Law Assn., Law Club Chgo., Judge Advs. Assn., Am. Judicature Soc. Jewish. Jurisprudence. Office: U S Ct of Appeals 219 S Dearborn St Room 2602 Chicago IL 60604

FLAX, SAMUEL ALLAN, lawyer; b. Washington, May 24, 1956; s. Louis and Mary (Burke) F. B in Indsl. Engrng., Ga. Inst. Tech., 1978; JD, Washington and Lee U., 1981. Bar: Ga. 1981, U.S. Dist. Ct. (no. dist.) Ga. 1981, D.C. 1982, U.S. Ct. Appeals (4th cir.) 1982. Law clk. to presiding judge U.S. Ct. Appeals (4th cir.), Abingdon, Va., 1981-82; assoc. Morgan, Lewis & Bockius, Washington, 1982-85, Arnold & Porter, Washington, 1985—. Mem. ABA. Democrat. General corporate, Bankruptcy. Home: 4914 41st St NW Washington DC 20016 Office: Arnold & Porter 1200 New Hampshire Ave NW Washington DC 20036

FLAX-DAVIDSON, RON HUNTER, lawyer, bank executive; b. Passiac, N.J., Jan. 27, 1953; s. Sol M. and Penny (Goldfinger) Davidson; m. Cheryl S. Flax, Aug. 175, 1975; children: Skylar Anne, Devorah Gillian. BS, New Coll., 1974; JD, Stetson U., 1978; EdM, Harvard U., 1982. Bar: Fla. 1978. Exec. dir. Colo. Pub. Interest Research Group, Denver, 1974-75; v.p. Chase Manhatten Bank, Miami, Fla., 1978—; v.p. western hemisphere Chase Manhatten Bank, 1984—; s.v.p. Drexel Burnham Lambert Caribe Internat., Inc., 1986—. Campaign mgr. Duprey for State Rep., N. Conway, N.H., 1971. Mem. ABA (internat. sect.). Private international, Banking. Home: 2204 General Patton Ocean Park PR 00915 Office: Drexel PR Bco de Ponce 12th Floor Hato Rey PR 00915

FLECHNER, STEPHEN E., lawyer; b. N.Y.C., Oct. 2, 1942; m. Jane B. Berylson, Sept. 24, 1978; 1 dau., Laura Ellen. B.A. cum laude, NYU, 1964; J.D., Yale U., 1967. Bar: N.Y. 1968. Assoc., Shea, Gould, Climenko & Casey, N.Y.C., 1967-69, Danziger, Bangser & Klipstein, N.Y.C., 1969-71; asst. gen. counsel Supermarkets Gen. Corp., Woodbridge, N.J., 1971-73; gen. counsel Pueblo Internat., N.Y.C., 1973-77; asst. gen. counsel Azcon Corp., N.Y.C., 1978; v.p., gen. counsel, sec. Gold Fields Mining Corp., N.Y.C. and Denver, 1979—. Mem. ABA, Rocky Mountain Mineral Law Found., Phi Beta Kappa. Clubs: Yale, Mining (N.Y.C.). General corporate.

FLEDDERMANN, STEPHEN ROY, lawyer; b. St. Louis, Apr. 30, 1956; s. Roy O. and Louise (Harris) F.; m. Victoria Lynn Bartnett, May 4, 1985. AA, St. Louis Community Coll., 1976; BA, U. Mo., 1978, JD, 1981. Bar: Mo. 1981, U.S. Dist. Ct. (ea. dist.) Mo. 1983. Assoc. Cundiff, Turken & Londoff, St. Charles, Mo., 1981-85; ptnr. Cundiff, Turken & Londoff, St. Charles, 1986—. Mem. St. Louis Met. Bar Assn., St. Charles Bar Assn., Order of Barristers. Republican. Avocations: tennis, SCUBA. State civil litigation, Personal injury, Family and matrimonial. Home: 12270 Prince Towne Creve Coeur MO 63141 Office: Cundiff Turken & Londoff 320 N 5th St Saint Charles MO 63301

FLEECE, STEVEN MICHAEL, judge; b. Louisville, Apr. 13, 1950; s. John Burton and Bonnie Jean (Shepherd) F.; m. Pamela Haas Simpson, Sept. 6, 1975; children: Jennifer Robyn, Jamie Heather. BA, Ind. U., 1972; JD, U. Louisville, 1982. Bar: Ind. 1982, U.S. Dist. Ct. (so. dist.) Ind. 1982. Assoc. Fifer, Vogt & Lanum, Jeffersonville, Ind., 1982; dep. prosecutor Clark County Prosecutors Office, Jeffersonville, Ind., 1982-84; judge Clark County Ct., Jeffersonville, Ind., 1985—. Mem. vestry St. Pauls Episcopal Ch., Jeffersonville, 1986—, allocation com. United Way, Jeffersonville, 1986—; program coordinator Leadership Clark County, Jeffersonville, 1986. Mem. ABA, Ind. Bar Assn., Ind. Judges Assn., Phi Beta Phi, Omicron Delta Kappa, English Speaking Union. Democrat. Clubs: Filson (Louisville). Lodges: Lions (Charlestown, Ind., sec. 1982-83); SAR (Southern Ind.). General practice, Judicial administration, Jurisprudence. Home: Rt 2 PO Box 389 Charlestown IN 47111 Office: Clark County Courthouse 501 E Ct Ave City County Bldg Jeffersonville IN 47130

FLEGLE, JIM L., lawyer; b. Paducah, Ky., Dec. 3, 1951; s. J. L. and Alice M. (Goodman) F.; m. Melissa D'Ann Suhr, July 24, 1980; children: Lauren Tyler, Brittanie Len, James Brendan. BA, U. Ky., 1974; JD, U. Va., 1977. Bar: Tex. 1977, U.S. Dist. Ct. (so. dist.) Tex. 1977, U.S. Ct. Appeals (5th and 11th cirs.) 1981, U.S. Dist. Ct. (no. dist.) Tex. 1984. Assoc. Bracewell & Patterson, Houston, 1977-83, ptnr., 1983—. Vol. Houston Pro Bono program; mem. Vol. Lawyers and Accts. for Arts, Houston, 1982-85, St. Paul's Chamber Music Soc.; pres., bd. dirs. Cimarron Wind Quintet, Houston, 1983—. Mem. ABA, Tex. Bar Assn., Houston Bar Assn., Houston Young Lawyers Assn. (chmn. com. 1984-85), Phi Beta Kappa, Omicron Delta Kappa, Sigma Nu. Democrat. Methodist. Federal civil litigation, State civil litigation. Home: 2015 Dryden Houston TX 77030 Office: Bracewell & Patterson 2900 S Tower Pennzoil Pl Houston TX 77002

FLEISCHAKER, JACK, lawyer; b. Joplin, Mo., Mar. 3, 1912; s. Isadore and Johanna (Ehrlich) F.; m. Elaine Barlow, Apr. 23, 1939; children: James, Jacelaine Fleischaker Horn, William Johanna. Grad., U. Mo., 1936; JD, Washington U., St. Louis, 1937. Bar: Mo. 1937, U.S. Dist. Ct. (we. dist.) Mo. 1937. Assoc. Thompson & Roberts, Joplin, 1938-57; ptnr. Roberts & Fleischaker, Joplin, 1957—; asst. atty. gen. State of Mo., 1955-58. Chmn. Jasper County Dem. Com., 1956-62; chmn. Congl. Dem. Com., 1960-62; mem. Mo. Dem. Com., 1960-62, Joplin Bd. Edn., 1951-56, pres. 1955-56, Joplin Airport Bd. 1956-79, 81—, chmn. 1960-79, 82; mem. adv. com. YWCA, Joplin; bd. dirs. Freeman Hosp. 1951-84; active Little Theatre, Community Concert Bd. Served to lt. col. U.S. Army, 1941-46. Recipient Appreciation award Freeman Hosp., 1975, Airport Bd. 1979. Mem. ABA, Mo. Bar Assn., Assn. Trial Lawyers Am., Mo. Assn. Trial Lawyers, Joplin C. of C., Mo. Pilots Assn., S.W. Mo. Pilots Assn., Am. Legion, VFW. Jewish. Club: Twin Hills Country. Lodges: Elks, Masons. Real property, General practice, Probate. Home: 2539 E 11th St Joplin MO 64301 Office: Roberts Fleischaker & Scott PO Box 996 Joplin MO 64802

FLEISCHER, ARTHUR, JR., lawyer; b. Hartford, Conn., Jan. 27, 1933; s. Arthur and Clare Lillian (Katzenstein) F.; m. Susan Abby Levin, July 6, 1958; children: Elizabeth, Katherine. B.A., Yale U., 1953, LL.B., 1958. Bar: N.Y. State 1959. Assoc. firm Strasser, Spiegelberg, Fried & Frank, N.Y.C., 1958-61; legal asst. SEC, Washington, 1961-62; exec. asst. to chmn. SEC, 1962-64; assoc. Fried, Frank, Harris, Shriver & Jacobson, N.Y.C., 1964-67; partner Fried, Frank, Harris, Shriver & Jacobson, 1967—; Vis. lectr. law Columbia U. Law Sch., N.Y.C., 1972-73; adviser to advisory com. Fed. Securities Code Project, Am. Law Inst., 1970-78; adviser to com. to consider new issue proposals Nat. Assn. Securities Dealers, 1973-75, mem. com. corporate financing, 1976-80; chmn. Ann. Inst. on Securities Regulation, Practising Law Inst., 1969-81; mem. indsl. issuers adv. com. SEC, 1972-73, mem. adv. com. corporate disclosure, 1976-77; bd. govs. Am. Stock Exchange, 1977-83. Author: Tender Offers: Defenses, Responses and Planning, 1978; Co-editor: Annual Institute on Securities Regulation, 1970-81; contbr. to publs. in field. Mem. adv. council Center for Study of Fin. Instns., U. Pa. Law Sch., 1969—. Served with AUS, 1953-55. Recipient disting. community service award Brandeis U., 1983, Judge Learned Hand human relations award Am. Jewish Com., 1983. Mem. ABA (mem. com. on fed. regulation of securities regulation 1969—), Assn. Bar City N.Y. (mem. spl. com. on lawyers role in securities transactions 1973-77, chmn. com. securities regulation 1972-74). Club: Century Country (N.Y.C.). Securities. Home: 1050 Park Ave New York NY 10028 Office: 1 New York Plaza New York NY 10004

FLEISCHER, JAMES SIDNEY, lawyer; b. Youngstown, Ohio, Nov. 14, 1951; s. Oscar and Sylvia (Solomon) F.; m. Sarah Elizabeth Perry, Apr. 27, 1980; children: Jeffrey, Sydney Elizabeth. BA, Dartmouth Coll., 1973; JD, Duke U., 1976. Bar: Colo. 1976, Ohio 1978, D.C. 1979. Assoc. Nadler & Nadler, Youngstown, 1977-79; atty. Fed. Home Loan Bank Bd., Washington, 1979-81; assoc. Hamel & Park, Washington, 1981-83; assoc. Silver, Freedman & Taff, Washington, 1983-85, ptnr., 1985—. Banking, Securities. Home: 5419 Moorland Ln Bethesda MD 20814 Office: Silver Freedman & Taff 1735 Eye St NW Washington DC 20006

FLEISCHER, SARAH PERRY, lawyer; b. Redfield, S.D., June 1, 1951; d. Edmond Joseph and Mary Elizabeth (Sanders) Perry; m. James S. Fleischer, Apr. 28, 1980; children: Jeffrey, Sydney Elizabeth. BA, Cornell Coll., Mt. Vernon, Iowa, 1972; JD, Duke U., 1976. Bar: D.C. 1976, U.S. Supreme Ct. 1981. Assoc. Zuckert et al, Washington, 1976-81; atty. Air Line Pilots Assn., Washington, 1981—. Mem. ABA, D.C. Bar Assn., Women's Bar Assn., Assn. Part-Time Profls. Club: Edgemoor (Bethesda, Md.). Labor, Federal civil litigation, Administrative and regulatory. Home: 5419 Moorland Ln Bethesda MD 20814 Office: Air Line Pilots Assn 1625 Massachusetts Ave NW Washington DC 20036

FLEISCHLI, FRANZ K., III, lawyer; b. Springfield, Ill., Apr. 29, 1943; s. Franz K. and Dorothy Jane (Johnston) F.; m. Margaret Mary O'Beirne, Aug. 6, 1966; children: Franz, Jacob. BS, Purdue U., 1965; MBA, Washington U., St. Louis, 1973; JD, Washington U., 1973. Bar: Ill., U.S. Dist. Ct. Ill., U.S. Ct. Appeals, U.S. Tax Ct. Sole practice Springfield, 1974—; dir. Washington U. Sch. Law Exec. Com. Served with U.S. Army, 1965-71. Mem. Ill. Bar Assn., Sangamon County Bar Assn., Assn. Trial Lawyers Am., Ill. Trial Lawyers Assn. Roman Catholic. Personal injury, Bankruptcy, General practice. Home: 2005 Willamore Springfield IL 62704 Office: 833 S 4th St Springfield IL 62705

FLEISCHLI, JACK A., lawyer; b. Long Beach, Calif., Oct. 5, 1949; s. Jack Edward and Jeanette (Lorraine) F.; m. Kathy Graham, June 28, 1978 (div. Nov. 1984). BA, U. Calif., Santa Barbara, 1971; JD cum laude, Pepperdine U., 1975. Bar: Calif., U.S. Dist. Ct. (cen. dist) Calif., U.S. Ct. Appeals (9th cir.). Dep. pub. defender Orange County Office of Pub. Defender, Santa Ana, Calif., 1974-80; sole practice Long Beach, 1980—. Mem. Assn. Trial Lawyers Am., Los Angeles County Bar Assn., Long Beach Bar Assn., Screen Actors Guild, AFTRA. Avocations: acting, songwriting, playing guitar, swimming, snow skiing. Family and matrimonial, Construction, State civil litigation. Office: 5030 E 2d St Suite 200 Long Beach CA 90803

FLEISCHMAN, EDWARD A., federal government official; b. Cambridge, Mass., June 25, 1932. AB, Harvard U., 1953; LLB, Columbia U., 1959. Assoc. Beekman & Bogue, Boston, 1959-67; ptnr. Gaston, Snow, Beekman & Bogue, Boston, 1968-85; commr. SEC, Washington, 1986—; adj. prof. law NYU, 1976-85. Office: SEC Office of the Chmn 450 5th St NW Washington DC 20549 *

FLEISCHMAN, EDWARD HIRSH, lawyer, government official; b. Cambridge, Mass., June 25, 1932. B.A., Harvard U.; LL.B., Columbia U., 1959. Bar: N.Y. 1959, U.S. Supreme Ct. 1980. Assoc. Beekman & Bogue, N.Y.C., 1959-67; partner Beekman & Bogue, 1968-81; ptnr. Gaston Snow Beekman & Bogue, 1981-86; commr. SEC, Washington, 1986—; adj. prof. NYU Law Sch. Contbr. articles to legal jours. Mem. Am. Law Inst., Am. Coll. Investment Counsel, ABA (chmn. ad hoc subcom. rule 144 1970-72, broker-dealer matters 1973-78, model simplified indenture 1980-83, chmn. adminstrv. law com. securities, commodities and exchanges 1981-84). Securities, General corporate, Administrative and regulatory. Office: SEC 450 5th St NW Washington DC 20549

FLEISCHMANN, PAMELA, lawyer; b. Balt., Jan. 3, 1947; d. Albert Joseph and Janie Ruth (Crowe) F. BA, U. Miami, 1968, JD, 1981. Bar: Fla. 1981, U.S. Ct. Appeals (5th, 11th and D.C. cirs.) 1981. Supr. Claims Kemper Ins. Group, Miami, Fla., 1974-78; assoc. Kaplan, Sicking, et al, Miami, 1981-83; sole practice Miami, 1983—. Mem. ABA, Fla. Bar Assn. Workers' compensation. Office: 7600 Red Rd Suite 202 South Miami FL 33143

FLEISSNER, PHILLIP ANTON, lawyer; b. Chattanooga, Tenn., Sept. 19, 1945; s. Raymond Anton and Hazel Orene (Powell) F.; m. Janet Virginia Harwell, Dec. 21, 1968; 1 child, Lisa Harwell. BA, Yale U., 1967; JD, U. Tenn. 1971. Bar: Tenn. 1971, U.S. Dist. Ct. (ea. dist.) Tenn. 1971, U.S. Ct. Appeals (6th cir.) 1972. Assoc. Chambliss, Bahner, Crutchfield, Gaston & Irvine, Chattanooga, 1971-75, ptnr., 1975-79; ptnr. Fleissner, Cooper & Marcus, 1979—. Author: (with others) Tennessee Automobile Liability Insurance, 1985. Served to capt. USMC, 1968-74. Mem. ABA, Tenn. Bar Assn., Chattanooga Bar Assn., Fedn. of Ins. and Corp. Counsel, Tenn. Def. Lawyers Assn., Def. Research Inst. Republican. Episcopalian. Club: Yale of Ga. Insurance, Workers' compensation, Labor. Office: Fleissner Cooper & Marcus 555 River St Suite 200 Chattanooga TN 37405

FLEMING, GEORGE MATTHEWS, lawyer; b. Houston, Mar. 26, 1946; s. George McMillian and Mary Kathryn (Matthews) F.; m. Francine Mikulik, May 27, 1972; children: Matthew Joseph, Kathryn Nicole. B.B.A., U. Tex., Austin, 1968, J.D., 1971. Bar: Tex. 1971, U.S. Dist. Ct. (so., no., we. and ea. dists.) Tex. 1976, U.S. Dist. D.C. 1973, U.S. Ct. Appeals (5th cir.) 1976, U.S. Ct. Appeals (7th cir.) 1979, U.S. Ct. Appeals (11th cir.) 1982, U.S. Ct. Appeals (D.C. cir.) 1974, U.S. Supreme Ct. 1974. Trial atty. torts sect. U.S. Dept. Justice, Washington, 1972-76; ptnr. Byrd, Davis & Eisenberg, Austin, 1976-82, Fleming, Betts & Cooke, Houston, 1982-86; prin. Law Offices of George M. Fleming, P.C., Houston, 1986—; lectr. South Tex. Coll. Law, Houston, Embry-Riddle Aero. U., Orlando, Fla., So. Meth. U. Air Law Symposium; lectr. aviation accident law litigation N.Y. Law Jour. Seminar, N.Y.C. Served to lt. U.S. Army, 1972. Mem. D.C. Bar Assn., ABA (ins. and compensation law com., chmn. mil. aviation com.), Houston Bar Assn., Assn. Trial Lawyers Am., Tex. Trial Lawyers Assn., Fed. Bar Assn., Lawyer Pilots Bar Assn., Internat. Soc. Air Safety Investigators. Democrat. Roman Catholic. Contbr. articles to legal jours. Federal civil litigation, State civil litigation, Personal injury. Home: 3922 Holder Forest Dr Houston TX 77088 Office: 1330 Post Oak Blvd Suite 3030 Houston TX 77056

FLEMING, J. CLIFTON, JR., legal educator; b. 1942. B.S., Brigham Young U., 1964; J.D. with honors, George Washington U., 1967. Bar: Wash. 1967, Utah 1979. Assoc., Bogle & Gates, Seattle, 1967-73; assoc. prof. U. Puget Sound Sch. Law, 1973-74; assoc. prof. Brigham Young U. Law Sch., Provo, Utah, 1974-76, prof., 1976—, assoc. dean acad. affairs, 1986—; Fulbright-Hayes vis. prof. Faculty of Law, U. Nairobi (Kenya), 1977-78; prof.-in-residence Office of IRS Chief Counsel, Washington, 1985-86. Notes editor George Washington Law Rev.; author: Estate and Gift Tax, 1976; Tax Aspects of Buying and Selling Corporate Businesses, 1984. Mem. ABA (mem. corp. stockholder relations com. of tax sect.). Order of Coif, Pi Sigma Alpha. Legal education. Office: Brigham Young U Law Sch Provo UT 84602 *

FLEMING, JOHN C., lawyer; b. Mar. 18, 1942. BA, St. John's U., Jamaica, N.Y., 1963; JD cum laude, Harvard U., 1966. Bar: N.Y. 1967, U.S. Supreme Ct. 1970, N.J. 1982. Assoc. Willkie, Farr & Gallagher, N.Y.C., 1969-74, Rosenman, Colin, Freund, Lewis & Cohen, N.Y.C., 1974-76; mem. faculty sch. law Rutgers U., Camden, N.J., 1976-81; sr. atty. Am. Homes Products Corp., N.Y.C., 1981—. Mem. editorial bd. Harvard U. Law Rev., 1964-66. Mem. ABA, N.Y. State Bar Assn. Antitrust, General corporate, Federal civil litigation. Office: Am Home Products Corp Law Dept 685 3d Ave New York NY 10017

FLEMING, JOHN GUNTHER, legal educator; b. Berlin, July 6, 1919; came to U.S., 1960; m. Valerie Joyce Beall, Apr. 16, 1946; children—Anthony, Barbara, Colin, Stephen. BA, Oxford U., Eng., 1939, MA, 1941, PhD, 1948, DCL, 1959, LLD, 1985. Bar: Eng. 1947. Lectr. in law King's Coll., London, 1946-48; prof., dean faculty law Australian Nat. U., 1949-60; prof. law U. Calif.-Berkeley, 1957-58, 60—, Shannon Cecil Turner prof. law, 1974—; Goodhart prof. Cambridge U., 1987-88. Author: Law of Torts, 7th edit, 1987, Introduction to the Law of Torts, 1967, 2d edit., 1986; editor-in-chief: Am. Jour. Comparative Law, 1971-87. Served with Royal Armoured Corps, Brit. Army, 1941-45. Hon. fellow Brasenose Coll., Oxford U.; mem. Am. Law Inst., Internat. Acad. Comparative Law, Internat. Assn. Legal Sci. (pres. 1980-82). Comparative, Trademark and copyright, Torts. Home: 401 Western Dr Point Richmond CA 94801

FLEMING, JOSEPH Z., lawyer; b. Miami, Fla., Jan. 30, 1941; s. Richard Marion and Lenore C. F.; m. Betty Corcoran, Feb. 12, 1947; 1 dau., Katherine Anne. B.A. in Engish, U. Fla., 1958; spl. courses U. Chgo., 1959, Hague Acad. of Internat. Law, 1966; J.D., U. Va., 1965; LL.M. in Labor Law, NYU, 1966. Bar: Fla. 1965, D.C. 1981. Assoc., Paul & Thomson, Miami, 1966-72, ptnr., 1972-74; ptnr. Fleming & Neuman, 1974-81, Fleming & Huck, Miami, 1981-86; sole practice, Miami, 1986-87; Fleming and Klink, 1987—; lectr. profl. programs, seminars. Trustee, Met. Dade County Ctr. for Fine Arts, 1982-86; mem. Biscayne Bay Environ. Task Force Subcom., 1982-83, well field protection adv. com. Dade County Task Force, 1984—; mem. Noguchi-Bayfront Park Task Force, Miami, 1983—; pres., bd. dirs. Fla. Rural Legal Services, 1967-78, Pres.'s Water Policy Implementation Workshops, Dept. of Interior Water Task Force, 1979; bd. dirs. Miami chpt. Am. Jewish Com. Recipient conservation award Fla. Audubon Soc., 1981, Tropical Audubon Soc., 1979, award Dade County Mental Health Assn., 1974, award Miami Design Preservation League, 1982, 83, award Progressive Architecture, 1982. Mem. ABA (continuing profl. edn. com. 1985—), Am. Soc. Internat. Law, Internat. Bar Assn., Inter-Am. Bar Assn., Fla. Bar Assn. (past chmn. environ. and land use law sect., labor law and employment discrimination law sect.). Clubs: Aviation Execs., City, Bath. Author: Airline Labor Law, 1981, 87; editor, contbg. author: Environmental Regulation and Litigation in Florida, 1980, 82; contbg. author: Environmental Pollution and Individual Rights, 1978; Reporter's Handbook, 1979—. Labor, Environment, Administrative and regulatory. Home: 34 La Gorce Circle Miami Beach FL 33141 Office: 25 SE 2d Ave 620 Ingraham Bldg Miami FL 33131

FLEMING, JULIAN DENVER, JR., lawyer; b. Rome, Ga., Jan. 12, 1934; s. Julian D. and MargaretMadison (Mangham) F.; m. Sidney Howell, June 28, 1960; 1 dau., Julie Adrianne. Student, U. Pa., 1951-53; B. Chem. Engring., Ga. Inst. Tech., 1955, Ph.D, 1959; J.D., Emory U., 1967. Bar: Ga. 1966, D.C. 1967; registered profl. engr., Ga., Calif. Research engr., prof. chem. engring. Ga. Inst. Tech., 1955-67; ptnr. Sutherland, Asbill & Brennan, Atlanta, 1967—. Contbr. articles to profl. jours.; patentee in field. Bd. dirs. Mental Health Assn. Ga., 1970-80; bd. dirs. Mental Health Assn. Met. Atlanta, 1970-80, pres., 1974-75; mem. council legal advisers Rep. Nat. Com., 1981-85. Fellow Am. Inst. Chemists, Am. Coll. Trial Lawyers; mem. ABA (council sect. sci. and tech. 1980-82, vice chmn. 1982-84, chmn.-elect 1984-85, chmn. 1985-86), Am. Inst. Chem. Engrs. Federal civil litigation, State civil litigation, Nuclear power. Home: 2238 Hill Park Ct Decatur GA 30033 Office: 3100 First Atlanta Tower Atlanta GA 30383

FLEMING, MACK GERALD, lawyer; b. Hartwell, Ga., May 3, 1932; s. Mack Judson and Dessie Leola (Vickery) F.; m. Elizabeth McClellan, Mar. 30, 1963; children: Katharine Lee, John McClellan. B.S., Clemson (S.C.) U., 1956; J.D., Am. U., Washington, 1966. Asst. dir. prodn. control Woodside Mills, Simpsonville, S.C., 1959-60; adminstrv. asst. to mem. congress 1960-64; dir. Congressional Liaison Office, VA, Washington, 1965-68; spl. asst. to adminstr. Congressional Liaison Office, VA, 1968-69; adminstrv. asst.,

counsel to mem. congress 1969-70; pvt. practice law Washington, 1970-74; chief counsel Com. on Vets. Affairs, U.S. Ho. of Reps., 1974-80, staff dir. and chief counsel, 1980—. Served to 1st lt. U.S. Army, 1956-58. Mem. D.C., S.C. bar assns. Democrat. Methodist. Legislative, Administrative and regulatory, Military. Home: 805 E Capitol St SE Washington DC 20003 Office: 335 Cannon House Office Bldg Washington DC 20003

FLEMING, MILO JOSEPH, lawyer; b. Roscoe, Ill., Jan. 4, 1911; s. John E. and Elizabeth (Shafer) F.; m. Dorothea H. Kunze, Aug. 15, 1942 (dec. 1944); m. Lucy Anna Russell, June 30, 1948; stepchildren: Michael Russell, Jo Ann Russell (Mrs. Clemens); 1 child, Elizabeth Fleming Weber. AB, U. of Ill., 1933, LLB, 1936. Bar: Ill. 1936, U.S. Dist. Ct. (cen. dist.) Ill. 1936, 53, U.S. Tax Ct. 1936, 84, U.S. Ct. Appeals (7th cir.) 1936, 85, U.S. Supreme Ct. 1986. Sole practice law, 1936-42, 58-59; ptnr. Pallissard and Fleming, Watseka, Ill., 1942-46, Pallissard, Fleming & Oram, 1946-58, Fleming & McGrew, 1960-77, Fleming, McGrew and Boyer, 1977, Fleming & Boyer, 1977-79, Fleming, Boyer & Strough, 1980-82, Fleming & Strough, 1982—; master in chancery, Iroquois County, Ill., 1943-44; asst. atty. gen. Ill. for Iroquois County, 1964-69; city atty., Watseka, 1949-57, 61—, Gilman, Ill., 1966-69; village atty. Milford, Ill., 1942-70, Wellington, 1962-72, Woodland, 1958-79, Danforth, 1961-78, Crescent City, Martinton, Sheldon, 1946-79, Onarga, Cissna Park, 1977-82, Beaverville, Papineau; atty. Lake Iroquois Lot Owners Assn. and Cen. San. Dist.; asst. atty. gen. Iroquois County, 1964-69; pres. Iroquois County Devel. Corp., 1961-68; bd. dirs. Belmont Water Co., 1963-81, pres., 1976-81. Chmn. Iroquois County Universities Bond Issues Campaign, 1960; mem. State Employees Group Ins. Adv. Commn., Ill., 1975-78; trustee Welles Sch. Fund, Watseka, 1978—; candidate state rep., Apr. 1940; life mem. U. Ill. Pres.'s Council, 1979—. Recipient Merit award for indsl. relations Watseka Area C. of C., 1983. Mem. ABA (vice chmn. com. ordnances and adminstrv. regulations 1968-69, 73-75, chmn. 1969-72, 75-78, mem. council local govt. sect. 1976-79, mem. council sect. urban, state and local govt. law 1979-80)), Ill. Bar Assn., Iroquois County Bar Assn. (pres. 1966-67), Internat. Platform Assn., Smithsonian Instn., Phi Eta Sigma, Sigma Delta Kappa. Democrat. Methodist. Lodges: Masons (32 deg.), Shriners, Odd Fellows (mem. jud. and appeals com. Ill. 1960-62, grand warden Ill. 1962, dep. grand master 1963, grand master 1964-65; grand rep. 1966; trustee Old Folks Home, Mattoon, Ill., 1966-71, sec. bd. 1966-68, vice chmn. bd. 1970—, atty. 1966—; 2d v.p. No. Assn. Odd Fellows and Rebekahs Ill. 1981, 1st v.p., 1982, pres. 1983; Meritorious Service jewel, Grand Encampment of Ill. 1980, elected Grand Sr. Warden Grand Encampment of Ill. 1984, Grand Patriarch Grand Encampment of Ill. 1986). Prepared Municipal Code for City of Watseka, 1953, 80, Milford, 1957, Martinton, 1960, Crescent City, 1960, 66, Woodland, 1961, Cissna Park, 1961, Papineau, 1978. Local government, Probate, General practice. Home: 120 W Jefferson Ave Watseka IL 60970 Office: Fleming & Strough Odd Fellows Bldg PO Box 297 216 E Walnut St Watseka IL 60970

FLEMING, PETER EMMET, JR., lawyer; b. Atlantic Highlands, N.J., Aug. 18, 1929; s. Peter Emmet and Anna (Sullivan) F.; m. Jane Breed, June 2, 1956; children—Peter Emmet III, James M., William B., David W., Jane H. A.B., Princeton U., 1951; LL.B., Yale U., 1958. Bar: N.Y. 1959, U.S. Dist. Ct. (so. and ea. dists.) N.Y. 1960, U.S. Ct. Appeals (2d cir.) 1963, U.S. Ct. Appeals (4th cir.) 1979, U.S. Supreme Ct. 1985. Assoc. Davis, Polk & Wardwell, N.Y.C., 1958-61; asst. U.S. atty. U.S. dist. Ct. (so. dist.) N.Y., N.Y.C., 1961-70; mem. Curtis, Mallet-Prevost Colt & Mosle, N.Y.C., 1970—. Federal civil litigation, State civil litigation, Criminal. Home: 122 Old Church Rd Greenwich CT 06830 Office: Curtis Mallet-Prevost Colt & Mosle 101 Park Ave New York NY 10178

FLEMING, ROBERT LAURENCE, lawyer; b. Grand Island, Nebr., Dec. 7, 1955; s. Bruce Austin and Patricia Ann (Cross) F.; m. Julie Ann Again, May 19, 1978; children: Jennifer Clare, Laura Ann. BA, U. Mo., 1978, JD, 1982. Bar: Mo. 1982, U.S. Dist. Ct. (we. dist.) Mo. 1982. Asst. counsel Mo. Tax Commn., Jefferson City, 1982-84; asst. pros. atty. Boone County, Columbia, Mo., 1984-86; assoc. Knight, Ford, Wright, Atwill, Parshell & Baker, Columbia, 1986—; instr. property appraisal Internat. Assn. Assessing Officers, Jefferson City and elsewhere, 1982-84. Editor Iowa Bar Assn. Young Lawyers Real Estate Practice Manual, 1980. Mem. Mo. Bar. Assn., Boone County Bar Assn., Phi Alph Delta. Democrat. Methodist. Lodge: Optimists (sec.-treas. 1984—). Avocations: skiing, hunting, car repair, softball, basketball. Criminal, Personal injury, State and local taxation. Home: 1314 St Christopher Columbia MO 65203

FLEMING, RUSSELL, JR., lawyer and utility company executive; b. New Brunswick, N.J., Aug. 20, 1938; s. Russell and Margaret Olga (Kebly) F.; m. Cheryl Hall; children: Eileen, Russell III. A.B., Rutgers U., 1960; J.D., Columbia U., 1963. Bar: N.J. 1964. Partner firm Sailer and Fleming, Elizabeth, N.J., 1970-73; v.p., gen. counsel Elizabethtown Gas Co., 1973-80, exec. v.p., gen. counsel, 1980-85, chief operating officer, 1985; pres., gen. counsel services div. NUI Corp., Bridgewater, N.J., 1985—; gen. atty. Elizabethtown Water Co., 1973-80; v.p., gen. counsel NUI Corp., 1975-85; exec. com. Associated Gas Distbrs., 1979-85; counsel boroughs of, Milltown and Middlesex, 1969, 73. Pres. Milltown Bd. Edn., 1968-69; sec. Middlesex County Charter Study Commn., 1973. Served to capt. USAR, 1963-65. Mem. ABA, N.J. Bar Assn. (chmn. public utility law sect. 1975). Roman Catholic. General corporate, Public utilities, Administrative and regulatory. Office: 1011 Route 22 PO Box 6060 Bridgewater NJ 08807

FLEMING, VICTOR ANSON, lawyer; b. Jackson, Miss., Dec. 26, 1951; s. Elijah Anson and Norfleet Leo (Cranford) F.; m. Susan Theresa Burnside, Dec. 28, 1973; children: Elizabeth Anson, Edward Davidson. BA, Davidson Coll., 1974; JD, U. Ark., Little Rock, 1978. Bar: Ark. 1978, U.S. Dist. Ct. (ea. and we. dists.) Ark. 1978, U.S. Ct. Appeals (8th cir.) 1979, U.S. Supreme Ct. 1982. Asst. atty. City Atty.'s Office, North Little Rock, Ark., 1976-78; ptnr. Hoover, Jacobs & Storey, Little Rock, 1978-86, Catlett, Stubblefield, Bonds & Fleming, Little Rock, 1986—. Columnist Ark. Lawyers Mag., 1984—. Sunday Sch. tchr. 2d Presbyn. Ch., Little Rock, 1980—; deacon, 1984-86; bd. dirs. Ark. Ednl. TV Found., Conway, Ark., 1984—; pres. bd. dirs. Friends of Ark. Ednl. TV, Conway, Ark., 1985-86; commr. Ark. Ednl. TV Commn. Served as cadet (ROTC) U.S. Army, 1970-74. Recipient 2d Place Gov.'s award Ark. Writers Conf.,1985, 1st Place Nonfiction award Burlington Writers Festival, 1976, 3d Place Pop Category award Ark. Songwriters Assn.,1981. Fellow Ark. Bar Found.; mem. ABA, Ark. Bar Assn., Assn. Trial Lawyers Am., Ark. Trial Lawyers Assn., Pulaski County Bar Assn. Democrat. Presbyterian. Club: Polit. Animals (Little Rock). Federal civil litigation, State civil litigation, Jurisprudence. Office: Catlett Stubblefield Bonds & Fleming 1800 Tower Bldg Little Rock AR 72201

FLEPS, JOHN JOSEPH, lawyer; b. Lewes, Del., Feb. 1, 1954; s. Carl John and Josephyne (Waples) F.; m. Petronella Mesdag, July 17, 1982; children: John R., Caroline L., Peter J. BA, Northwestern U., 1976; JD with honors, George Washington U., 1979. Bar: Ill. 1979, U.S. Dist. Ct. (no. dist.) Ill. 1979, U.S. Ct. Appeals (10th cir.) 1982, U.S. Ct. Appeals (5th cir.) 1983, U.S. Ct. Appeals (7th cir.) 1984, U.S. Supreme Ct. 1984. Atty. Santa Fe Industries, Inc., Chgo., 1979-83, asst. gen. atty., 1984-85; asst. gen. atty. Santa Fe Southern Pacific Corp., Chgo., 1985—, gen. atty., 1987—. Served to 1st lt. JAGC, USAR, 1986—. Mem. ABA, Ill. Bar Assn., Conf. R.R. and Airline Labor Lawyers, Assn. Am. R.R.s (subcom. safety rulemaking proceedings 1985—). Republican. Clubs: Northwestern U. Rugby Football (Evanston, Ill.) (coach 1986—); Chgo. Lions Rugby Football. Avocations: rugby football, military history, zoology, model making. Labor, Administrative and regulatory, Federal civil litigation. Office: Santa Fe Southern Pacific Corp 224 S Michigan Ave Chicago IL 60604

FLESSLAND, DENNIS MICHAEL, lawyer; b. Pontiac, Mich., Feb. 6, 1954; s. Christian and Irma (Blomquist) F.; m. Janet Saunders, Aug. 19, 1977; 1 child, Natalie. BA with high honors, Mich. State U., 1976; JD, U. Ill., 1979. Bar: Mich. 1979, U.S. Dist. Ct. (ea. dist.) Mich. 1981, U.S. Supreme Ct. 1985. Sole practice Bloomfield Hills, Mich., 1979-84; ptnr. Snavely, Lightbody & Flessland, Bloomfield Hills, 1984-87, Wierzbicki & Flessland P.C., Huntington Woods, Mich., 1987—. Vol. atty. Common Ground, Birmingham, Mich., 1983-85; active Rep. Com. of Oakland County, Pontiac, 1982—. Mem. ABA (litigation sect.), Mich. Bar Assn., Oakland County Bar Assn., Commercial Law League, Oakland County C. of C. (legis. affairs com.). Lutheran. Consumer commercial, General corporate, General practice. Home: 10815 Kingston Huntington Woods MI 48070 Office: Wierzbicki & Flessland PC 26789 Woodward Suite 104 Huntington Woods MI 48070

FLETCHER, ANTHONY L., lawyer; b. Washington, Dec. 12, 1935; s. Robert J. and Lyndell (Pickett) F.; m. Juliana Schump, Sept. 3, 1960 (div. 1977); children—Leigh Anne, Kristin Marie, Julie Bowen; m. Zelda L. Fletcher, Mar. 30, 1986. B.A., Princeton U., 1957; J.D., Harvard U., 1962. Bar: N.Y. 1963, U.S. Ct. Appeals (2d cir.) 1966, U.S. Ct. Appeals (7th cir.) 1966, U.S. Supreme Ct. 1966, U.S. Ct. Appeals (3d cir.) 1969, U.S. Ct. Appeals (fed. cir.) 1972, U.S. Ct. Appeals (5th cir.) 1973, U.S. Ct. Appeals (1st cir.) 1981, U.S. Ct. Appeals 9th cir. 1983. Assoc. Simpson Thacher & Bartlett, N.Y.C., 1962-71, Conboy, Hewitt, O'Brien & Boardman, N.Y.C., 1971-74, ptnr., 1974-86, ptnr. Hunton & Williams, N.Y.C., 1986—. Editor-in-chief Trademark Reporter, 1982-84. Contbr. articles to profl. jours. Served with inf. U.S. Army, 1957-59. Mem. Bar City of N.Y., U.S. Trademark Assn. (bd. dirs. N.Y.C. 1983-85). Episcopalian. Club: Princeton. Trademark and copyright, Federal civil litigation, State civil litigation. Office: Hunton & Williams 100 Park Ave New York NY 10017

FLETCHER, HON. BETTY B., judge; b. Tacoma, Mar. 29, 1923. B.A., Stanford U., 1943; LL.B., U. Wash., 1956. Bar: Wash. 1956. Former mem. firm Preston, Thorgrimson, Ellis, Holman & Fletcher, Seattle, 1956-1979; judge U.S. Circuit Ct. for 9th Circuit, Seattle., 1979—. Mem. ABA, Wash. Bar Assn., Order of Coif, Phi Beta Kappa. Jurisprudence. Office: US Court of Appeals 1010 5th Ave Seattle WA 98104 *

FLETCHER, DAVID JAMES, lawyer; b. Yukon, Fla., May 1, 1946; s. James Spencer and Jean (Paton) F.; m. Marcia Lee Bishop, June 7, 1969; children—Emily, William. A.B., Tufts U. magna cum laude, 1968; J.D. with honors, U. Maine, 1971. Bar: Maine 1971. Ptnr. Brown, Tibbetts & Fletcher, Calais, Maine, 1971-74; sole practice, Calais, 1975-81; ptnr. Fletcher & Foster, Calais, 1982—. Mem. ABA, Maine Bar Assn. (pres. 1984, bd. dirs. 1984—), Maine Bar Found. (pres. 1987—), Washington County Bar Assn. (pres. 1976). Democrat. Episcopalian. General practice, Probate, Real property. Office: Fletcher & Foster 138 Main St Calais ME 04619

FLETCHER, JOHN RICHARD, lawyer; b. Chatham, N.Y., Sept. 24, 1950; s. Francis Edward and Helma Ann (Jensen) F. BA, Coll. of William and Mary, 1968-72, JD, 1975. Bar: Va. 1975, U.S. Dist. Ct. (ea. dist.) Va. 1975, U.S. Ct. Appeals (4th cir.) 1975. Assoc. Ellenson, Fox & Wittan, Newport News, Va., 1975; asst. atty. Commonwealth Atty.'s Office, Hampton, Va., 1976-78; assoc. Richard J. Tavss, P.C., Norfolk, Va., 1978-79; ptnr. Tavss, Fletcher & Earley P.C., Norfolk, 1980—. Served to 1st lt. U.S. Army, 1975-76. Mem. ABA, Va. Bar Assn. (mem. exec. com. young lawyers sect. 1986—, chmn. criminal law and corrections com. 1984, 85, ad hoc com. on indigent defendants), Omicron Delta Kappa, Lambda Chi Alpha (pres. Epsilon Alpha chpt. 1971-72). Democrat. Roman Catholic. Avocations: golf, tennis. Personal injury, Criminal, State civil litigation. Home: 206 55th St Virginia Beach VA 23451 Office: Tavss Fletcher & Earley PC 2 Commercial Place Norfolk VA 23510

FLETCHER, PAUL GERALD, lawyer; b. Boston, Mar. 20, 1945; s. Samuel and Rosamond Rebecca (Gold) F.; m. Susan Mary Beckerman, Aug. 11, 1968; children: Lynne, Michael, Allison. BAE, U. Fla., 1967; JD, U. Miami, 1970. Bar: Fla. 1970, U.S. Dist. Ct. (so. dist.) Fla. 1970, U.S. Ct. Mil. Appeals 1971, U.S. Supreme Ct. 1973, U.S. Ct. Appeals (11th cir.) 1982. Judge adv. USAF, 1970-74; ptnr. Peskoe, Fletcher & Cahan, Homestead, Fla., 1974-77, Fletcher & Langer, Homestead, 1977-84; sole practice Homestead, 1984—; instr. No. Mich. U., Marquette, 1970-72; mem. adv. bd. Amerifirst Fla. Trust Co., 1987—. Co-chmn. ARC, 1976-78. Recipient Service award ARC, 1977, Leadership award Jewish Fedn., 1980. Mem. Fla. Bar Assn., Homestead Bar Assn. (pres. 1980-81), Assn. Trial Lawyers Am., Am. Arbitration Assn. (arbitrator), Homestead C. of C., Tau Epsilon Phi. Lodges: Kiwanis (v.p. 1983, pres. 1980), B'nai B'rith (adv. bd. 1974—, v.p. 1979-80). Avocations: tennis, racquetball, photography, World War II history, baseball cards. Family and matrimonial, Real property, State civil litigation. Office: 850 Homestead Blvd Suite 201 Homestead FL 33030

FLETCHER, RILEY EUGENE, lawyer; b. Eddy, Tex., Nov. 29, 1912; s. Riley Jordan and Lelih Etta (Gill) F.; m. Hattie Inez Blackwell, June 11, 1954. B.A., Baylor U., 1950, LL.B., 1950. Bar: Tex. 1950, U.S. Dist. Ct. (no. dist.) Tex. 1958, U.S. Ct. Appeals (5th cir.) 1959, U.S. Ct. Mil. Appeals 1965, U.S. Ct. Appeals (11th cir.) 1981, U.S. Supreme Ct. 1965. Asst. county atty. Navarro County, Corsicana, Tex., 1951-52, county atty., 1952-54; sole practice, Corsicana, 1955-56; asst. atty gen. Atty. Gen. dept., Austin, Tex., 1956-62, chief Law Enforcement div., 1958-61, chief Tax div., 1961-62; asst. gen. counsel Tex. Mcpl. League, Austin, 1962-63, gen. counsel, 1963-78, special counsel, 1978—. Served to capt. U.S. Army, 1942-46, New Guinea, Philippines; lt. col. AUS ret. Recipient Disting. Service award Tex. Mcpl. Courts Assn. 1980, Appreciation award Tex. City Atty.'s Assn. 1982, Assn. Mayors, Councilmen & Commrs. Tex. 1984, City Bowie, Tex. 1984. Mem. ABA, State Bar Tex., Travis County Bar Assn., Judge Advocates Assn. Baptist. Local government. Home: PO Box 1762 Austin TX 78767 also: 7201 Creekside Dr Austin TX 78752 Office: Tex Mcpl League 1020 Southwest Tower Austin TX 78701

FLETCHER, ROBERT WESLEY, lawyer, patent management company executive; b. Balt., July 27, 1940; s. Wesley Howard and Dawn Rose (Bell) F.; m. Elizabeth Ann Birks, Sept. 11, 1965; children—Robin, Deborah, Mary, Bonnie, Timothy. B.S. in Chem. Engring., U. Wis., 1963, J.D., 1967; postgrad. U. Mo., 1964-65; M.B.A., U. Louisville, 1976. Bar: Wis. 1967, Ill. 1968, U.S. Dist. Ct. (no. dist.) Ill. 1968, U.S. Patent Office 1970, Ky. 1972. Patent atty. Standard Oil (Ind.), Chgo., 1967-71, Am. Air Filter Co., Louisville, Ky., 1971-73; div. patent counsel Gen. Electric Co., Louisville, 1973-76; pres. Hilliard Lyons Patent Mgmt., Inc., Louisville, 1976— exec. dir. Coaltech Ltd. (Australia); chmn. bd. CT Research, Inc.; mng. dir. HLPM Netherlands B.V. Patented low temperature primary cells, plastic stackable cup. Mem. Dane County Bail Bond Release Project, Madison, Wis., 1965-67; pres. Camelot Improvement Assn., Louisville, 1971-74. Recipient Hon. Sci. award Bausch & Lomb, Baraboo, Wis., 1958. Mem. Bar Assn. Wis., Bar Assn. Ill., Bar Assn. Louisville, ABA. Patent. Home: 3009 Lightheart Rd Louisville KY 40222 Office: Hilliart Lyons Patent Mgmt Inc 545 S 3d St Louisville KY 40222

FLETCHER, R(UFUS) BURTON, JR., lawyer, educator; b. Fla., Dec. 25, 1950; s. Rufus Burton Sr. and Emma Callie (Hunter) F. BS, U. West Fla., 1975, MBA, 1976; JD, Western State U., 1980. Bar: Ga. 1980, Calif. 1981. Prof. El Camino Coll., Torrance, Calif., 1980—; ptnr. Fletcher and Assocs., Torrance, 1982—; dir. Honors Most Ct., 1979-80. Editorial bd. Western State U. Law Rev., 1979-80. Served to cpl. to USMC, 1970-73. Named one of Outstanding Young Men Am., 1973. Mem. ABA, Calif. Bar Assn., Ga. Bar Assn., Los Angeles County Bar Assn., South Bay Bar Assn., Calif. Trial Lawyers Assn., Los Angeles Trial Lawyers Assn. Republican. Personal injury, Family and matrimonial, Criminal. Home: 17009 Ainsworth Ave Torrance CA 90504 Office: Fletcher and Assocs 18436 Hawthorne Blvd Suite 101 Torrance CA 90504

FLICK, JOHN EDMOND, newspaper publishing company executive; b. Franklin, Pa., Mar. 14, 1922; s. Edmond Leroy and Mary M. (Weaver) F.; m. Lois Anna Lange, Apr. 20, 1946; children: Gregory Allan, Scott Edmond, Lynn Ellen, Ann Elizabeth. Student, Northwestern U., 1941-44, U. Pa., 1945; LL.B., Northwestern U., 1948. Bar: Ill. 1948, Calif. 1971, fed. cts 1971, U.S. Supreme Ct 1974. Commd. 1st lt. Judge Adv. Gen. Corps U.S. Army, 1950, advanced through grades to lt. col. Res., 1968; ret. 1972; faculty U.S. Mil. Acad., 1954-57, Judge Adv. Gen. Sch., U. Va., 1960-61; counsel Litton Industries, 1963-67; sr. v.p., sec., gen. counsel, dir. Bangor Punta Corp., 1967-69; sr. v.p., gen. counsel Times Mirror Co., Los Angeles, 1970-87, cons., 1987—; dir. Tejon Ranch Co., Piper Aircraft Co., 1969. Mem., past chmn. Los Angeles adv. bd. Salvation Army; mem. adv. bd. Nat. Salvation Army; past mem. vis. com. Northwestern U. Law Sch. Recipient Am. Bar Assn. Acad. award, 1961. Mem. Am., Los Angeles County bar assns., state bars Calif., Ill., Am. Soc. Corp. Secs. Club: Wigmore (Northwestern U. Law Sch.) (life mem.). Administrative and regulatory, Antitrust, General corporate. Office: Times Mirror Sq Los Angeles CA 90053

FLICK, SHEILA ANN, lawyer; b. New Orleans, Oct. 31, 1951; d. James Gerard and Ethel Edna (Schneider) Nolan; m. Dana Dominick Flick, June 9, 1973; 1 child, Shana. BA in English and Spl. Edn. summa cum laude, St. Mary's Dominican Coll., New Orleans, 1973; JD in Civil Law with honors, Loyola U., New Orleans, 1982. Bar: La. 1982, U.S. Ct. Appeals (5th cir.) 1983. Tchr. english Mt. Carmel Acad., New Orleans, 1973-76; tchr. spl. edn. Jefferson Parish Sch. Bd., Metairie, La., 1976-77; law clk. to justice La. Supreme Ct., New Orleans, 1982-83; staff atty. La. Supreme Ct. Cen., New Orleans, 1983-84; atty. La. Ct. Appeals (4th cir.), New Orleans, 1984—. Named one of Outstanding Young Women in Am., 1981. Mem. ABA, La. Bar Assn., Assn. Women Attys., Phi Alpha Delta, Delta Epsilon Sigma. Democrat. Roman Catholic. Avocations: creative writing, reading, swimming. Jurisprudence, State civil litigation, Criminal. Home: 1109 Houma Blvd Metairie LA 70001 Office: La Ct Appeals 4th Cir 421 Loyola Ave New Orleans LA 70112

FLICKINGER, DWIGHT CHARLES, lawyer; b. Logan, Utah, Sept. 4, 1939; s. Dwight Wright and Violet (Goodsell) F.; m. Lorna May Flickinger, June 18, 1964; children: Wendy, Rodney, Mark, Troy, Craig. BA, U. Utah, 1964, JD, 1967. Ptnr. Blake, Colter, Flickinger, Daudet & Shields P.C., 1968-79; sole practice 1979—. Pres. Phoenix Symphony Council, 1983. Mem. Utah Bar Assn., Ariz. Bar Assn., Maricopa County Bar Assn., Assn. Trial Lawyers Am., Ariz. Trial Lawyers Assn. (bd. dirs.), Phoenix Trial Lawyers Assn. (pres.), Am. Arbitration Assn., So. for Preservation and Encouragement of Barbershop Quartet Singing in Am. (pres.). LSD. Club: Phoenicians (pres.). Office: 2001 N 3d St 2d Floor Phoenix AZ 85004

FLINK, RICHARD ALLEN, lawyer, manufacturing company executive; b. N.Y.C., Mar. 1, 1935; s. Jack and Claire (Goldberg) F.; children: Andrea L., Gary R. B.A., Brandeis U., 1955; J.D., NYU, 1959, LL.M., 1962. Bar: N.Y. 1959, N.J. 1969. Sole practice N.Y.C., 1960-65; gen. atty. Becton Dickinson & Co., Rutherford, N.J., 1966-70; with C.R. Bard, Inc., Murray Hill, N.J., 1970—, gen. counsel, 1971—, v.p., 1973—, sec., 1984—; adj. asst. prof. indsl. adminstrn. Columbia Coll. Pharm. Scis., 1966-75; co-adj. instr. Rutgers U. Coll. Pharmacy, 1976—. Mem. Internat., Fed., Am., N.Y., N.J., Bergen County bar assns., Assn. Fed. Bar N.J., Assn. Advancement of Med. Instrumentation (dir.). Office: CR Bard Inc 731 Central Ave Murray Hill NJ 07974

FLINN, THOMAS D., lawyer; b. Jersey City, July 1, 1956; s. John D. and Elizabeth L. (Collins) F.; m. Debora E. Schnell, Sept. 18, 1982; 1 child, Patrick. BA, Fordham U., 1978; JD, Seton Hall U., 1981. Bar: N.J. 1981, U.S. Dist. Ct. N.J. 1981, N.Y. 1982, U.S. Supreme Ct. 1986. Law clk. to presiding justice Bergan County (N.J.) Dist. Ct., 1981-82; trial atty. Farabaugh & Friedland, West Orange, N.J., 1982-85; assoc. DeGonge, Garrity & Fitzpatrick, Bloomfield, N.J., 1985—. Com. chmn. Lake Hopatcong (N.J.) Regional Planning Bd., 1983—. Named one of Outstanding Young Men Am., 1985. Mem. ABA, N.J. Bar Assn., Bergen County Bar Assn., N.J. Def. Assn., Lake Hopatcong Star Class Yacht Racing Assn. (fleet capt.). Roman Catholic. Avocations: yacht racing, swimming, music. Personal injury, Insurance, Legal malpractice defense. Home: 6 C Lakeview Ave Leonia NJ 07605 Office: DeGonge Garrity & Fitzpatrick 430 Broad St Bloomfield NJ 07003

FLINT, DANIEL WALDO BOONE, lawyer; b. Phila., Nov. 24, 1926; s. Ralph Woodberry and Laura Chapin (Schontz) F.; m. Joan Graebe, Dec. 14, 1957; children: Daniel Waldo Boone, Adam P., Charlton G. B.A., U. Pa., 1950; J.D., Temple U., 1956. Bar: Pa. 1957. Practiced law Phila., 1960—, King of Prussia, Pa., 1972—; farmer Perkiomenville, Pa., 1966—; sec., gen. counsel Nat. Liberty Life Ins. Co., 1967-72. Dir. Montgomery County (Pa.) Conservation Dist., 1972-76; pres. gen. Gen. Soc. SR, 1974-76, pres. emeritus, 1976; pres. emeritus King of Prussia Hist. Soc., 1968—; bd. dirs., legal counsel Freedom Forge Found., 1969-76, Daniel Boone Nat. Found., 1986—; pres., legal counsel Soc. Preservation Am. Indian Culture, 1968-76; former pres., legal counsel, Scudder Assn., Inc.; former gen. counsel Keystone Christian Edn. Assn.; founder, v.p., counsel Valley Forge Tours, 1968-78; mem. sch. bd. Upper Bucks Christian Sch., 1975-78. Served with USNR, 1945-46. Recipient Washington Gold medal Freedoms Found., at Valley Forge, 1973, Scudder of Yr. award, 1985; named Man of Year award Patriotic Order Sons of Am., 1970; Ky. Col. Mem. ABA, Pa. Bar Assn., Phila. Bar Assn., Montgomery Bar Assn., Descs. Signers of Declaration Independence, Mil. Order Loyal Legion U.S., Soc. War 1812, Am. Arbitration Assn., Valley Forge Hist. Soc., Valley Forge Interpretive Assn. (bd. dirs. 1986—), Goschenhoppen Historians, Am. Vets. Assn. (pres. 1977—), Am. Legion. Baptist. Club: Union League (Phila.). Lodge: Rotary. Probate, Personal injury, State civil litigation. Home: Flintlock Farm Perkiomenville PA 18074 Office: 570 W DeKalb Pike King of Prussia PA 19406

FLOOD, KEVIN PATRICK, lawyer; b. Bklyn., Apr. 1, 1939; s. Arthur Eugene and Margaret Wilhelmina (Hepp) F. BBA, St. John's U., N.Y.C., 1963, JD, 1967. Bar: N.Y. 1968, U.S. Dist. Ct. (so. and ea. dists.) N.Y. 1970, U.S. Ct. Internat. Trade 1971, Fla. 1978, U.S. Ct. Mil. Appeals 1984. Ptnr. Pfister & Flood, Bklyn., 1968-78; sole practice Bklyn., 1978-81, 84—; ptnr. Alvey & Flood, Bklyn., 1981-82, Flood & Sawaya, Bklyn., 1982-84; mem. faculty L.I. U., N.Y., 1980-84; mem., judge Congl. Com. on Art 14CD, 14th congl. dist., 1983. Mem. adv. bd. Salvation Army, Bklyn., 1982—; mem. Kings County Rep. Com., Bklyn., 1970-76; v.p. Friendly Sons of St. Patrick, Bklyn., 1985—; legis. aid to state assemblyman, Bklyn., 1968-76. Served to capt. JAGC, USNR, 1960—. Mem. ABA (standing com. on legal assistance for mil. personnel, editor LAMP quarterly newsletter, probate and real property sects.), N.Y. State Bar Assn. (probate and real property sects., mil. affairs com.), Fla. Bar Assn., Bklyn. Bar Assn., Bay Ridge Lawyers Assn. (pres. 1983-84), Richmond County Bar Assn., N.Y. State Trial Lawyers Assn., Judge Adv. Assn., Navy Marine Lawyers Assn., Naval Res. Assn., Bay Ridge Hist. Soc., Mensa. Roman Catholic. Clubs: 12:30 (pres. 1980), Mcpl. (Bklyn.). Lodge: Lions. Avocations: sailing, skiing. Probate, Real property, Estate taxation. Home: 8314 10th Ave Brooklyn NY 11228

FLOOD, VINCENT PATRICK, lawyer; b. Chgo., Oct. 9, 1946; s. Vincent Patrick and Virginia Eileen (Reilly) F.; m. Suzanne M. Severt, Aug. 21, 1982; 1 child, Abigail E. BS, John Carroll U., 1968; JD, Ill. Inst. Tech., 1975. Bar: Ill. 1975; CPA 1977. Atty. Ill Pollution Control Bd., Chgo., 1974-78; atty., asst. sec. Masonite Corp., Chgo., 1978—; cons. econs. Chgo., 1977-78. Editor: Chgo. Kent Law Rev., 1972-75. Pres. Uptown Ctr., Chgo., 1984—; trustee Hull House Assn., Chgo., 1985—. Served to 1st lt. U.S. Army, 1969-71, Korea. Mem. ABA, Chgo. Bar Assn. (co-chmn. young lawyers/environment com. 1976-77). Democrat. Roman Catholic. Environment, Takeover defense, General corporate. Home: 741 Forest Evanston IL 60202 Office: Masonite Corp 1 S Wacker Chicago IL 60606

FLORENCE, DOROTHY M., lawyer; b. Danville, Va., Sept. 9, 1942; s. Irene I. (Towler) F.; 1 child, Michael Paul Wright. BA, U. San Diego, 1973; JD, U. Calif., Davis, 1976. Bar: Minn. 1979, U.S. Dist. Ct. Minn. 1979, U.S. Supreme Ct. 1983, U.S. Tax Ct. 1984. Ptnr. D.M. Florence and Assocs., Edina, Minn., 1979-82; div. atty. Minn. Dept. Revenue, St. Paul, 1982-84; corp. counsel 1st Bank System, Inc., Mpls., 1984—; pro bono atty. Legal Advice, Mpls., 1979—; faculty continuing legal edn. program Minn. State Bar, advance legal studies State of N.Y.; vice chmn. CETA Service (PIC), Mpls., 1980-82; bd. dirs. Legal Rights Ctr., Hennepin Parks. Contbr. articles to profl. jours. Vol. Minn. Vikings Charity, Mpls., 1983—; mem. U.S. Senator Boschwitz senate page selection com., St. Paul, 1984—; contbr. U.S. Senator Rudy Boschwitz 1990 Club and Wash. Club, 1984—. Recipient Woman of Distinction award San Diego Bus. Women, 1972, First Vol. award First Banks Community, 1986. Mem. ABA (litigation, banking and corp. sects.), Minn. Bar Assn. (bd. govs. 1986—, litigation, corp. law, banking and corp. counsels assn. sect.), Hennepin County Bar Assn. (community relations sect. 1979-84, speakers referral panel 1979—, chairperson 2d annual bar benefit 1981-82, bd. govs. 1983-84, 86—, chairperson social events 1981-82, programs com. 1983—, vice chmn. 1985-86, chmn. 1985-86, co-vice chmn. 1986—), Minn. Trial Lawyers Assn. (comml. law com.), Minn. Def. Lawyers, Fed. Bar Assn., Twin West C. of C. (recipient Woman of Achievement award 1985). Republican. Avocations: container gardening, weightlifting, chess, reading. Banking, State civil litigation, General corporate. Office: First Bank System Inc 200 S Sixth St Minneapolis MN 55402

FLORENCE, HENRY JOHN, lawyer; b. Rockville Centre, N.Y., Dec. 11, 1934; s. Henry Dulap and Mary (Hanley) F.; m. A. Jean Butler, June 13, 1959; 1 child, Henry John Jr. BS in Econs., Villanova U., 1956; JD, Fordham U., 1961. Bar: N.Y. 1962, Ariz. 1963, U.S. Dist. Ct. Ariz. 1967, U.S. Ct. Appeals (9th cir.) 1970, U.S. Supreme Ct. 1970. Advisor legal aid Navajo Indian Tribe, Window Rock, Ariz., 1962-63; asst. atty. Maricopa County, Phoenix, 1964-65, chief civil dep., 1965-67; ptnr. Stewart & Florence Ltd., Phoenix, 1967-73; sole practice Phoenix, 1973—. Pres. Ariz. Family, Phoenix, 1972-78. Served to lt. (j.g.) USN, 1956-58. Mem. Ariz. Bar Assn. (atty.), Nat. Assn. Criminal Def. Lawyers, Assn. Trial Lawyers Am., Calif. Attys. for Criminal Justice, Ariz. Attys. for Criminal Justice. Democrat. Roman Catholic. Avocation: philatelist. Criminal. Office: 13 W Jefferson St Phoenix AZ 85003

FLORENCE, KENNETH JAMES, lawyer; b. Hanford, Calif., July 31, 1943; s. Ivy Owen and Louella (Dobson) F.; m. Verena Magdalena Demuth, Dec. 10, 1967. B.A., Whittier Coll., 1965; J.D., Hastings Coll. Law, U. Calif.-San Francisco, 1974. Bar: Calif. 1974, U.S. Dist. Ct. (cen. dist.) Calif. 1974, U.S. Dist. Ct. (ea. and so. dists.) Calif., 1976, U.S. Dist. Ct. (no. dist.) Calif. 1980, U.S. Ct. Appeals (9th cir.) 1975, U.S. Supreme Ct. 1984. Dist. mgr. Pacific T&T, Calif., 1969-71; assoc. Parker, Milliken, et al, Los Angeles, 1974-78; ptnr. Dern, Mason, et al, 1978-84, Swerdlow & Florence, A Law Corp., Beverly Hills, 1984—; pres. Westside Legal Services, Inc., Santa Monica, Calif., 1982-83. Served to lt. USNR, 1966-69, Vietnam. Col. J.G. Boswell scholar, 1961. Mem. ABA (co-chmn. state labor law com. 1982-83). Democrat. Labor. Home: 1124 21st St #2 Santa Monica CA 90403 Office: Swerdlow & Florence 9401 Wilshire Blvd Suite 828 Beverly Hills CA 90212

FLOWE, BENJAMIN HUGH, JR., lawyer; b. Durham, N.C., Feb. 8, 1956; s. Benjamin H. and Dorothy Amelia (Bell) F.; m. Sharon Eileen Delaney, July 14, 1979 (div.); m. Carol Connor, Apr. 21, 1984. AB in Sociology, Psychology, Duke U., 1978; JD, U. N.C., 1981. Bar: U.S. Ct. Appeals (D.C. cir.) 1981. Assoc. Arent, Fox et al, Washington, 1981-84, Bowman, Conner & Touhey P.C., Washington, 1984—. Contbr. articles to profl. jours. Mem. ABA, Am. Soc. Internat. Law, Order of the Coif. Democrat. Presbyterian. Avocations: skiing, writing, golf, tennis. Private international, Admiralty, Commercial financing. Home: 8120 Paisley Pl Potomac MD 20854 Office: Bowman Conner Touhey and Petrillo 2828 Pennsylvania Ave NW Washington DC 20007

FLOWER, DAVID JEFFREY, lawyer; b. Homestead, Pa., Dec. 1, 1951; s. Albert H. and Mary L. (Liggitt) F.; m. Sandra L. Novison, Aug. 23, 1975; children: Matthew, Jeffrey. BA, Westminster Coll., 1973; JD, U. Pitts., 1976. Bar: Pa. 1976, U.S. Dist. Ct. (we. dist) Pa. 1976. Assoc. Kimmel, Rascona, Yelovich & Bowman, Somerset, Pa., 1976-80; mental health officer Somerset County Ct., 1977-80; 1st asst. dist. atty. Somerset County, 1980—; ptnr. Yelovich & Flower, Somerset, 1984—. Editor Somerset Legal Jour., 1977-79. Chmn. Citizens for Yelovich, Somerset, 1975-79, 83-85; chmn. Com. to Retain Judge Shaulis, 1984. Mem. Am. Trial Lawyers Assn., Pa. Trial Lawyers Assn., Pa. Bar Assn., Somerset County Bar Assn. Democrat. Lutheran. Lodge: Kiwanis (local pres. 1980-81), Masons. Avocations: fishing, racquetball, flying. Criminal, General practice, Personal injury. Home: 269 W Sanner St Somerset PA 15501 Office: Yelovich & Flower 166 E Union St Somerset PA 15501

FLOWER, EDWARD, b. N.Y.C., Aug. 19, 1929; s. Isidor and Rose (Braunstein) F.; m. Marilyn Tonkelowitz, Nov. 5, 1955; children—Stephanie, Andrew. B.S.S., CCNY, 1950; M.A., Columbia U., 1952; LL.B., Bklyn. Law Sch., 1955. Bar: N.Y. 1956, U.S. Supreme Ct. 1959, U.S. Dist. Ct. (ea. and so. dists.) N.Y. 1969, U.S. Tax Ct. 1975. Assoc. Wagner, Quillan & Tennant, N.Y.C., 1956-57, Schwartz & Lockman, Massapequa, N.Y., 1957-59; asst. county atty. Suffolk County, 1960-64; spl. counsel Town of Huntington, 1964-66; ptnr. Koffler & Flower, Islip, N.Y., 1960-63, Koffler, Flower & Plotka, Islip, 1963-69, Flower & Plotka, Bay Shore, N.Y., 1969—; counsel West Islip Library Assn., 1956-57. Mem. Union Free Sch. Dist. Bd. Edn., West Islip, 1959-62; mem. Suffolk County Democratic Com., 1956-80; vice chmn. labor law com. Suffolk County Dem. Com.; vice chmn. Islip Town Dem. Com., 1959-62; del Jud. Nominating Conv., 1960, 62, 64. Mem. ABA, N.Y. State Bar Assn., Comml. Law League, Suffolk County Bar Assn. (trustee, chmn. com. condemnation and tax certiorari, chmn. com. real property, chmn. com. environ. law). State civil litigation, Condemnation, Real property. Office: 120 4th Ave Bay Shore NY 11706

FLOWERS, FRANCIS ASBURY, III, lawyer; b. Dothan, Ala., July 10, 1955; s. Francis Asbury Jr. and Janet (Herndon) F. BS, U. Ala., 1976, JD, 1979. Bar: Ala. 1979, U.S. Dist. Ct. (no. and mid. dists.) Ala. 1980, U.S. Ct. Appeals (11th cir.) 1981, U.S. Supreme Ct. 1983. Law clk. to presiding justice U.S. Dist. Ct. (no. dist.) Ala., Birmingham, 1979-80; assoc. Farmer, Farmer, Price & Espy, Dothan, Ala., 1980; from assoc. to ptnr. Burr & Forman, Birmingham, 1981—. Assoc. editor Jour. of Legal Profession, 1978-79. Hugo L. Black scholar U. Ala. Law Sch., 1978. Mem. ABA, Ala. Bar Assn., Birmingham Bar Assn., Order of Coif, Beta Gamma Sigma. Avocations: reading, legal history. Civil rights, Federal civil litigation, Appellate practice. Home: 3865 Overton Manor Ln Birmingham AL 35243 Office: Burr & Forman 3000 Southtrust Tower Birmingham AL 35203

FLOWERS, KENT GORDON, JR., lawyer; b. Aurora, N.C., Apr. 29, 1955; s. Kent Gordon Sr. and Shirley Temple (Deal); m. Debra Ann Henries, Aug. 21, 1981; 1 child, Kent Gordon III. BA in Social Sci., U. N.C., Wilmington, 1976, BA in Secondary Edn., 1977; postgrad., Emmanuel Coll., 1977-78; JD, U. Ark., Little Rock, 1981. Bar: N.C. 1982, U.S. Dist. Ct. (ea. dist.) N.C. 1986. Staff atty. Craven County, New Bern, N.C., 1982—. Cons. Craven County Foster Parents, New Bern, 1982—; com. chairperson Craven County Council for Children, New Bern, 1982-86. Mem. ABA, N.C. Bar Assn., Assn. Trial Lawyers of Am., N.C. Coll. of Advocacy, N.C. Assn. Social Service Attys. (sec. 1984-85). Republican. Avocations: collecting antiques, home restoration. Juvenile, Administrative and regulatory, Government contracts and claims. Home: 519 Broad St New Bern NC 28560 Office: PO Box 310 New Bern NC 28560

FLOWERS, MICHAEL EDWARD, lawyer; b. Columbus, Ohio, Nov. 20, 1953; s. Robert William and Cynthia Mai (McClennon) F. BS, Bucknell U., 1976; JD, Ohio State U., 1979. Bar: Ohio 1979, U.S. Dist. Ct. (so. dist.) Ohio 1979, U.S. Supreme Ct. 1984. Ptnr. Porter, Wright, Morris & Arthur, Columbus, 1979—. Trustee United Cerebral Palsy of Columbus and Franklin County, 1982—, Ch. of Christ, Columbus, 1979—, Willow Brook Christian Home, 1987—. Mem. ABA (corp., banking and bus. law sect. 1979—), Nat. Bar Assn., Ohio State Bar Assn., Columbus Bar Assn. (securities law com. 1984—), Robert B. Elliott Law Club (recording sec. 1980-82). Avocations: tennis, bicycling. General corporate, Oil and gas leasing, Securities. Home: 1300 Fahlander Dr N Columbus OH 43229 Office: Porter Wright Morris & Arthur 41 S High St Columbus OH 43215

FLOWERS, WILLIAM ELLWOOD, lawyer; b. N.Y.C., Apr. 9, 1942; s. Roy M. and Esther E. (Fischle) F.; m. Mary Kathryn Torrey, June 19, 1965; children—Michael T., Matthew C. A.B., Dartmouth Coll., 1964; LL.B., Vanderbilt U., 1967; LL.M. in Taxation, NYU, 1975. Bar: N.Y. 1969. Assoc., Shearman & Sterling, N.Y.C., 1967-76, ptnr., 1976—. Served to capt. U.S. Army, 1968-70. Decorated Bronze Star medal. Mem. ABA, N.Y. State Bar Assn., Assn. Bar City N.Y. Democrat. Presbyterian. Corporate taxation, Private international. Office: 53 Wall St New York NY 10005

FLOWERS, WILLIAM HAROLD, JR., lawyer; b. Chgo., Mar. 22, 1946; s. William Harold and Ruth Lolita (Cave) F.; m. Pamela Mays, Sept. 13, 1980. B.A., U. Colo., 1967, J.D., 1971. Bar: Colo. 1973, U.S. Dist. Ct. Colo. 1973, U.S. Ct. Appeals (10th cir.) 1978, U.S. Supreme Ct. 1985. Clk. Legal Aid Soc., Albuquerque, 1970; atty. Pikes Peak Legal Services, Colorado Springs, Colo., 1973; ptnr. Tate, Tate & Flowers, Denver, 1973-76; dep. dist. atty. Office Adams County Dist. Atty., Brighton, Colo., 1977-78; ptnr. Taussig & Flowers, Boulder, Colo., 1978-81; sole practice, Boulder, 1981—; mem. Boulder County Community Corrections Bd., 1985—. Mem. Boulder Bd. Zoning Adjustment, 1973-78, chmn., 1977-78; mem. Boulder Growth Task Force, 1980-82; mem. exec. bd. Longs Peak council Boy Scouts Am., 1983—; bd. dirs. Sta. KGNU, Boulder County Broadcasting, 1981-84. Mem. Nat. Bar Assn. (regional dir. 1983-86, bd. govs. 1983—), Colo. Criminal Def. Bar (bd. dirs. 1982-83), Boulder County Bar Assn. (criminal law com. 1979—, civil litigation com. 1978—), Colo. Trial Lawyers Assn., Assn. Trial Lawyers Am., Sam Cary Bar Assn. (pres. 1987). Democrat. Methodist. Personal injury, Criminal, Family and matrimonial. Office: 230 Peachtree St NW 10th Fl Atlanta GA 30303

FLOYD, SHELBY ANNE, lawyer; b. N.Y.C., Feb. 3, 1945; d. Darwin and Mary (Fredericks) F.; 1 child, Nicolas Paul. BS, Columbia U., 1973, JD, 1975. Bar: Calif. 1975, Hawaii 1976, U.S. Ct. Appeals (9th cir.) 1976. Atty. Legal Aid Soc. Hawaii, Honolulu, 1976-78; dir. Paul Johnson & Alston, Honolulu, 1978—; visiting fellow Ctr. for Law in Pub. Interest, Los Angeles, 1975. Mem. ABA, Hawaii Bar Assn., Hawaii Women Lawyers Assn. (outstanding woman lawyer 1984), Assn. Trial Lawyers Am. Federal civil litigation, Construction, Real property. Office: Paul Johnson & Alston 1001 Bishop St Suite 1300 Honolulu HI 96813

FLUHARTY, JESSE ERNEST, lawyer, former judge; b. San Antonio, Tex., July 25, 1916; s. Jesse Ernest and Gwendolyn (Elder) F.; m. Ernestine Gertrude Corlies, Oct. 25, 1945; 1 son, Stephen Robert. Student Calif. State U.-San Diego, 1935-36, Art Ctr. Sch. Design Los Angeles, 1938-39; J.D. with distinction, U. Pacific, 1951; grad. Nat. Jud. Coll. Adminstrv. Law 1982. Bar: Calif. 1952, U.S. Dist. Ct. (no. dist.) Calif. 1952, U.S. Ct. appeals (9th cir.) 1952, U.S. Dist. Ct. (cen. dist.) Calif. 1979, U.S. Supreme Ct. 1983. Sole practice, Sacramento, 1952-60; referee in charge Indsl. Accident Commn., Stockton, Calif., 1960-67; presiding referee so. Calif. Workers Compensation Appeals Bd., Los Angeles, 1967-71, workers compensation Judge, Los Angeles, 1971-79; presiding judge, Los Angeles, 1979-81, Long Beach, 1981-83; of counsel Law Office of Stephen Fluharty, Glendale, Calif., 1984—. Pres. Family Service Agy., Sacramento, 1958, 59, Community Council Stockton and San Joaquin County, 1965, Service Club Council Los Angeles, 1973-74, Glendale Hills Coordinating Council, 1976-78, Chevy Chase Estates Assn., 1971-77; chmn. San Joaquin County Recreation and Park Commn., 1963-67. Served with U.S. Army, 1943-45. Decorated Bronze Star, Philippine Liberation medal; recipient Meritorious citation Calif. Recreation Soc., 1967. Mem. Calif. State Bar, Los Angeles County Bar Assn., Glendale Bar Assn., Am. Judicature Soc., Lawyers Club Los Angeles (pres. 1980, Judge of Yr. 1982). Republican. Congregationalist. Clubs: Chevy Chase Country, Verdugo. Lodges: Lions (pres. Los Angeles 1971-72), Masons. Administrative and regulatory, Workers' compensation, General practice. Home: 3330 Emerald Isle Dr Glendale CA 91206 Office: 501 N Central Ave Suite B Glendale CA 91203

FLUKE, RANDALL LYNN, lawyer; b. Houston, Aug. 19, 1959; s. Albert Eugene and Valrie Yvonne (Smith) F.; m. Emily Louise Cauhape, Apr. 27, 1985. AA in Econs., San Jacinto Coll., 1979; BA in Econs., U. Tex., 1981; JD, Tex. Tech U., 1984; postgrad., Odessa (Tex.) Coll., 1987. Bar: Tex. 1985, U.S. Dist. Ct. (no. dist.) Tex. 1985. Assoc. Huffaker, Green & Huffaker Attys., Tahoka, Tex., 1984-86; asst. dist. atty. Lubbock (Tex.) County Criminal Dist. Atty., 1986-87; asst. dist. atty., appellate chief Midland (Tex.) County Dist. Atty., 1987—. Precinct chmn. Lubbock County Reps., Lubbock, 1982-83; bd. dirs. Gammill & Murphey Music Ministries, Lubbock, 1986—, treas., 1987—. Named one of Outstanding Young Men of Am., 1987-88. Mem. ABA (real estate, probate and trust divs.), Midland County Young Lawyers Assn., Lubbock County Young Lawyers Assn. (community liasison 1986-87), Tex. Dist. and County Attys. Assn. Baptist. Lodge: Rotary. Avocations: racquetball, hunting, tennis, fishing, writing. Criminal prosecution, Probate, Real property. Home: 2900 Emerson Midland TX 79705 Office: Office Midland County Dist Atty 4th Floor Midland County Ct Midland TX 79701

FLUKER, BRENDA ANN, lawyer; b. Demopolis, Ala., Mar. 3, 1952; d. Clinton and Pandora E. (Essex) F.; 1 child, Brandy Fluker Oakley. BS, Ala. A&M U., 1972; JD, Tulane U., 1978. Bar: Mass. 1979, U.S. Supreme Ct. 1984. Underwriter Liberty Mut. Ins. Co., Boston, 1972-74, filing analyst, 1974-75, assoc. counsel, 1979—; of counsel Rosa Parks Day Care Ctr., Roxbury, Mass., 1979—. Active Urban League Eastern Mass., Boston, 1984-85. Mem. ABA, Nat. Bar Assn. (regional dir. bd. govs. 1981-82, 1986—), Mass. Bar Assn. (corp. council com. 1980), Mass. Black Lawyers Assn. (sec. 1981-83, exec. com. 1981-83, 85-86, counsel), Mass. Black Women Attys. Assn. (exec. com. 1980-82). Democrat. Baptist. Insurance, Administrative and regulatory, General corporate. Office: Liberty Mut Ins Co 175 Berkeley St Boston MA 02117

FLYNN, DAVID KEVIN, lawyer; b. Troy, N.Y., Feb. 8, 1954; s. James Henry and Emma Rose (Petzler) F.; m. Janet Mary Boselovic, June 5, 1982. BA, U. Rochester, 1976; JD, Yale U., 1979. Bar: D.C. 1979, U.S. Dist. Ct. D.C. 1980, U.S. Ct. Appeals (D.C. cir.) 1980, N.Y. 1984, U.S. Dist. Ct. (so. and ea. dists.) N.Y. 1984, U.S. Ct. Appeals (5th and 6th cirs.) 1985, U.S. Supreme Ct. 1985, U.S. Ct. Appeals (11th cir.) 1986, U.S. Ct. Appeals (2d cir.) 1987. Assoc. Covington & Burling, Washington, 1979-83, Milbank, Tweed, Hadley & McCoy, N.Y.C., 1983-84; apellate counsel U.S. Dept. of Justice, Washington, 1984-86, spl. asst. to asst. atty. gen. civil rights div., 1986, chief appellate sect. civil rights div., 1986—. Mem. ABA, D.C. Bar Assn., Federalist Soc. Republican. Roman Catholic. Federal civil litigation, Civil rights. Home: 6808 N 31st St Arlington VA 22213 Office: US Dept of Justice 10th St and Pennsylvania Ave NW Washington DC 20530

FLYNN, JOHN ALLEN, lawyer; b. Riverside, Ill., Jan. 12, 1945; s. William and Marian Rae (Gustafson) F.; m. Kathey Walker, June 18, 1966; children—Judson John, Erin Courtney. A.B., Stanford U., 1966; J.D., U. Calif.-San Francisco, 1969. Bar: Calif. 1970, U.S. Dist. Ct. (no. dist.) Calif. 1970, U.S. Dist. Ct. (ea. dist.) Calif. 1970, U.S. Ct. Appeals (9th cir.) 1970, U.S. Supreme Ct. 1975. Assoc. Graham & James, San Francisco, 1969-75, ptnr., 1976—; speaker Practicing Law Inst., Los Angeles, 1980, San Francisco, 1982, Lloyds of London Press, San Francisco, 1984. Mem. ABA, Maritime Law Assn. (mem. com. on practice and procedure 1983—), San Francisco Bar Assn. (chmn. admiralty com. 1978—). Roman Catholic. Club: San Francisco Press. Admiralty, Private international. Office: Graham & James 1 Maritime Plaza San Francisco CA 94111

FLYNN, MICHAEL, lawyer; b. Bklyn., Sept. 20, 1952; s. James Thomas and Catherine Marie (Fratello) F.; m. Janet Marie DiPaolo, Jan. 11, 1975; children—Michael Sean, Ashley Brooke, Thomas James. B.A., Bklyn. Coll., 1970; J.D., N.Y. Law Sch., 1978. Bar: N.Y. 1979, U.S. Dist. Ct. (so. ea. we., no. dists.) N.Y. 1979, U.S. Ct. Appeals (2d cir.) 1979, U.S. Supreme Ct. 1985. Assoc. firm Elkind & Lampson, N.Y.C., 1979-83; sr. ptnr. firm Elkind, Flynn & Maurer, P.C., N.Y.C., 1983—; cons. counsel United Transp. Union, Cleve., Brotherhood R.R. Signalmen, Cleve.; judge (arbitration) Civil Ct., N.Y.C., 1980—; cons. atty. Oceanside civil counsel (N.Y.), 1984. Judge N.Y. Law Sch., N.Y.C., 1978. Recipient Am. Jurisprudence award, 1976; Goodrich award Western New Eng. Sch. Law, Springfield, Mass., 1977. Mem. N.Y. State Bar Assn., Civil Justice Found. (founding sponsor 1987), N.Y. State Trial Lawyers Assn., Assn. Trial Lawyers Am. Federal civil litigation, State civil litigation, Personal injury. Office: Elkind Flynn & Maurer PC 122 E 42d St New York NY 10168

FLYNN, RICHARD JAMES, lawyer; b. Omaha, Dec. 6, 1928; s. Richard T. and Eileen (Murphy) F.; m. Kay House Ebert, June 28, 1975; children: Richard McDonnell, William Thomas, Kathryn Eileen Merritt, James Daniel. Student, Cornell U., 1944-46; B.S., Nothwestern U., 1950; J.D., Northwestern U., 1953. Bar: D.C. 1953, Ill. 1954. Law clk. to Chief Justices Vinson and Warren, 1953-54; assoc. Sidley, Austin, Burgess & Smith, Chgo., 1954-63; ptnr. Sidley, Austin, Burgess & Smith, Washington, 1963-66, Sidley & Austin, 1967—. Contbr. articles to profl. jours. Mem. exec. com. Washington Lawyers Com. for Civil Rights Under Law. Served with USN, 1946-48. Fellow Am. Coll. Trial Lawyers, mem. ABA, Fed. Bar Assn., Fed. Energy Bar Assn., Assn. Transp. Practitioners, Nat. Lawyer Club, Chgo. Bar Assn., D.C. Bar Assn., Order of Coif, Phi Beta Kappa, Phi Delta Phi, Sigma Chi. Republican. Presbyterian. Clubs: Economic of Chgo, Legal, Kenwood Golf and Country; Metropolitan (Washington). Administrative and regulatory, Antitrust, Federal civil litigation. Home: 2342 S Queen St Arlington VA 22202 Office: 1722 Eye St NW Washington DC 20006

FLYNN, RORY CHRISTOPHER, lawyer; b. Bklyn., Dec. 31, 1956; s. John Joseph and Marianne Finola (Brady) F. BBA, CCNY, 1978; JD, Benjamin Cardozo Sch. Law, 1981. Bar: N.Y. 1982, Tex. 1982, U.S. Dist. Ct. (so. dist.) Tex. 1982, U.S. Dist. Ct. (so. and ea. dists.) N.Y. 1982, U.S. Ct. Appeals (5th cir.) 1982, U.S. Supreme Ct. 1985, D.C. 1986. Law clk. U.S. Ct. Appeals (5th cir.), Brownsville, Tex., 1981-82; asst. dist. atty. State of Tex., Houston, 1982-85; assoc. Law Offices of William Pannill, P.C., Houston, 1985—. Mem. ABA. Avocations: fencing, bicycling. Federal civil litigation, Oil and gas leasing, Criminal. Office: William Pannill PC 2 Houston Ctr Suite 1600 909 Fannin St Houston TX 77010-1007

FLYNN, THOMAS EDWARD, naval officer, lawyer; b. N.Y.C., Dec. 4, 1934; s. Thomas Edward and Sara Irene (Nolan) F.; m. Mary Ann Ward, Apr. 12, 1958; children—Mary Ann, Peter Ward, Christopher Jonathan. B.S. in Edn. with honors, Fordham U., 1956; LL.B., Georgetown U., 1963. Bar: D.C. 1965, U.S. Supreme Ct. 1968. Commd. officer U.S. Navy, advanced through grades to rear adm.; def. counsel, claims officer 12 Naval Dist., U.S. Navy, San Francisco, 1965-67; staff judge advocate Comdr. Fleet Air, U.S. Navy, Alameda, Calif., 1967-70; legis. atty. Office Legis. Affairs, U.S. Navy, Washington, 1970-73, spl. asst. for legal affairs Office Asst. Sec. Manpower and Res. Affairs,, 1973-76, spl. counsel sec. of Navy, 1976-77; dep. asst. Office JAG, U.S. Navy, Alexandria, Va., 1977-82, dept. judge adv. gen. Office JAG,, 1982-84, judge adv. gen. Office JAG,, 1984—. Decorated Legion of Merit, Meritorious Service medal, Navy achievement medal, Nat. Def. Service medal. Mem. Fed. Bar Assn., Judge Advocates Assn. (bd. dirs. 1982—). Military. Office: Judge Advocate Gen Navy 200 Stovall St Alexandria VA 22332

FLYNN, THOMAS JOSEPH, hospital management company executive; b. Pitts., Dec. 28, 1936; m. Elizabeth A. Gessner, May 28, 1960; children: Sean Patrick, Kelly Lynn Flynn. B.S., Mt. St. Mary's Coll., Emmitsburg, Md., 1958; LL.B., Duquesne U., Pitts., 1964. Bar: Pa. 1964, Ky. 1976. Atty. Westinghouse Electric Corp., Pitts., 1964-74; exec. v.p., gen. counsel Humana Inc., Louisville, 1974—. Mem. Am. Bar Assn., Am. Hosp. Assn., Ky. Bar Assn., Allegheny County Bar Assn. Roman Catholic. Clubs: Pendennis, Valhalla, Hunting Creek Country. Address: Humana Inc 500 W Main St Louisville KY 40201 *

FLYNN, WILLIAM BERNARD, lawyer; b. N.Y.C., May 31, 1949; s. Bernard Thomas and Mary Clare (Nolen) F.; m. Kathleen Theresa Costello, Sept. 1, 1974; children: Tara, Erin, Kerry. BA, St. John's U., N.Y.C., 1971, JD, 1974. Bar: N.Y. 1975, U.S. Dist. Ct. (ea. and so.) dists. N.Y. 1977, U.S. Ct. Appeals (2d cir.) 1984, U.S. Supreme Ct. 1985. Assoc. Goetz & Fitzpatrick, P.C., N.Y.C., 1974-80, ptnr., 1980-85; ptnr. Goetz, Fitzpatrick & Flynn, P.C., N.Y.C., 1985—. Served to 2d lt. N.Y. Army N.G., 1969-74. Mem. ABA (forum com. on constrn. industry), N.Y. State Bar Assn., Nassau County Bar Assn., Am. Arbitration Assn. (panel of arbitrators), Order of Barristers, Associated Builders and Contractors Inc. Avocations: tennis, volleyball. Construction, Government contracts and claims, State civil litigation. Office: Goetz Fitzpatrick & Flynn PC One Penn Plaza New York NY 10119

FLYNN, WILLIAM FREDERICK, lawyer; b. Washington, Nov. 15, 1952; s. L. Martin and Martha Jean (Rennie) F.; m. Deborah Ann Norton, Apr. 20, 1985. AB, U. Mich., 1975, JD, 1978. Bar: Wis. 1978. Assoc. Reinhart, Boerner, Van Deuren, Norris & Rieselbach S.C., Milw., 1978-85, ptnr., 1986—. Mem. ABA, Wis. Bar Assn., Milw. Bar Assn. Banking, Consumer commercial, Municipal bonds. Home: 4936 N Newhall Ave Whitefish Bay WI 53217 Office: Reinhart Boerner et al 111 E Wisconsin Ave Milwaukee WI 53202

FLYNN PETERSON, KATHLEEN A., lawyer; b. St. Paul, July 7, 1954; d. Richard Edward and Margaret (Flaig) Flynn; m. Steven R. Peterson; children: Christopher, Colin. BA in Nursing, Coll. St. Catherine, 1976; JD cum laude, William Mitchell Coll. Law, 1981. Bar: Minn. 1981, U.S. Ct. Appeals (8th cir.) 1981. Assoc. Robins, Zelle, Larson & Kaplan, St. Paul, 1981—; lectr. health law issues various med. orgns., 1979—; adj. prof. William Mitchell Coll. Law, St. Paul, 1984—; bd. dirs. Home Health Plus. Mem. ABA, Am. Soc. Health Lawyers, Am. Assn. Nurse Attys. (pres. Minn. chpt.), Minn. Bar Assn., Minn. Trial Lawyers Assn., Great Plains Orgn. Perinatal Health Care (bd. dirs.). Democrat. Health, Personal injury. Office: Robins Zelle Larson & Kaplan 345 Saint Peter St Saint Paul MN 55102

FLYNT, JOHN JAMES, JR., lawyer, former congressman; b. Griffin, Ga., Nov. 8, 1914; s. John James and Susan Winn (Banks) F.; m. Patricia Irby Bradley, Feb. 7, 1942; children: Susan, John James III, Crisp. A.B., U. Ga., 1936; postgrad., Emory U., 1937-38; LL.B., George Washington U., 1940; grad., Nat. War Coll., Command and Gen. Staff Sch., Air Corps Advanced Flying Sch., Brooks Field, Tex. Bar: Ga. 1938. Asst. U.S. atty. No. Dist. Ga., 1939-41, 45-46; mem. Ga. Ho. of Reps., 1947-48; solicitor gen. Griffin Jud. Circuit, 1949-54; mem. 83d-88th Congresses, 4th Ga. Dist., and 89th-95th Congresses from 6th Ga. Dist.; partner firm Smalley Cogburn & Flynt (P.C.), Griffin, 1979—; vice chmn., bd. dirs. Bank of Spalding County. Chmn. bd. trustees N. Ga. Meth. Children's Home; trustee La Grange Coll., Ga., Woodward Acad. Served in U.S. Army, 1936-37, 41-45, ETO; col. Ret. Decorated Bronze Star medal. Fellow Ga. Bar Found. (charter); Mem. ABA, Ga. Bar Assn. (pres.), Am. Legion, V.F.W., Phi Delta Phi, Sigma Alpha Epsilon. Democrat. Methodist (trustee, chmn. bd. stewards). Lodges: Masons; Kiwanis; Shriners. Administrative and regulatory, Public international, Private international. Office: 115 N 6th St Griffin GA 30224

FOARDE, MARY PATRICIA, lawyer; b. Evanston, Ill., July 13, 1954; d. John Joseph Jr. and Evelyn LaVon (Craver) F.; m. David William Deming, June 25, 1978; children: Kerry Jean Deming, Caitlin Elizabeth Deming. BA magna cum laude, Creighton U., 1975; JD cum laude, U. Minn., 1980. Bar: Minn. 1980, U.S. Dist. Ct. Minn. 1980. Assoc. Maslon Edelman Borman & Brand, Mpls., 1980-85, ptnr., 1985—. Mem. Am. Acad. Hosp. Attys., Nat. Health Lawyers Assn. General corporate, Health, Real property. Home: 1440 Fairlawn Way Golden Valley MN 55416 Office: Maslon Edelman Borman & Brand 1800 Midwest Plaza Minneapolis MN 55402

FOCHT, THEODORE HAROLD, lawyer, educator; b. Reading, Pa., Aug. 20, 1934; s. Harold Edwin and Ruth Naomi (Boyer) F.; m. Joyce Gundy, Aug. 11, 1956; children—David Scott, Eric Steven. A.B. in Philosophy, Franklin and Marshall Coll., 1956; J.D., Coll. of William and Mary, 1959. Bar: Va. 1959. Teaching assoc. Columbia U. Sch. Law, N.Y.C., 1959-60; atty. Office of Gen. Counsel SEC, Washington, 1960-61, legal asst. to Commr., Washington, 1961-63; mem. faculty U. Conn. Sch. Law, Hartford, 1963-71 (leave of absence, 1969-71); spl. counsel on securities legislation Interstate and Fgn. Commerce Com., U.S. Ho. of Reps., Washington, 1969-71; gen. counsel Securities Investor Protection Corp., Washington, 1971—, pres., 1984—; adj. prof. law American U. Sch. Law, Washington, 1979-84. Mem. Va. State Bar, ABA, Phi Beta Kappa. General corporate, Bankruptcy, Securities. Home: 7015 Petunia St Springfield VA 22152 Office: 900 17th St NW Suite 800 Washington DC 20006

FOERSTER, DAVID WENDEL, lawyer; b. Jacksonville, Fla., July 22, 1923; s. Robert Oscar and Ada Ewing (Wendel) F.; children—David, Margaret Foerster Bratton, Michael, Amy, Caroline; m. 2d, Margaret Vason, June 20, 1974. B.S. Washington and Lee U. 1947, J.D. 1951. Bar: Fla. 1951. Sole practice Jacksonville, Fla., 1951—; spl. asst. to Gov. of Fla., 1961; mem. Gov.'s Task Force on Eminent Domain, 1981. Co-founder, vice chmn. bd. trustees Jacksonville Episcopal High Sch., 1967-75. Served to lt. USN, 1943-45. Mem. ABA, Jacksonville Bar Assn. Democrat. Episcopalian. Clubs: Fla. Yacht, River, Rotary (Jacksonville). Contbr. articles to profl. jours. Condemnation. Home: 3577 Richmond St Jacksonville FL 32205 Office: 1550 Florida Bank Tower Jacksonville FL 32202

FOGARTY, EDWARD MICHAEL, lawyer; b. Woonsocket, R.I., Feb. 25, 1948; s. Raymond Henry and Mary (Hogan) F.; m. Gail Higgins, Jan. 8, 1977. B.A., Providence Coll., 1969; J.D., Georgetown U., 1972. Bar: R.I. 1972, D.C. 1973, U.S. Supreme Ct. 1977. Law clk. U.S. Dist. Ct. R.I., Providence, 1972-73; assoc. Wilkinson, Cragun & Barker, Washington, 1973-79, ptnr., 1979-82; ptnr. Baenen, Timme, De Reitzes & Middleton, Washington, 1982-83; counsel Spriggs, Bode & Hollingsworth, Washington, 1983—; legal counsel to speaker R.I. Ho. of Reps., Providence, 1987—. Mem. R.I. Bar Assn., D.C. Bar Assn., ABA, Am. Arbitration Assn. (nat. panel of arbitrators 1985—). Democrat. Roman Catholic. Club: University

(Washington). Federal civil litigation, Administrative and regulatory, General corporate. Home: 488 Lloyd Ave Providence RI 02906 Office: Rm 302 State House Providence RI 02903

FOGARTY, ROBERT JEROME, lawyer; b. Paterson, N.J., Jan. 5, 1952; s. Robert John and Mary Lou (Westfall) F.; m. Laura J. Pedone, Aug. 20, 1977; children: Robert, Caitlin. BA, U. Cin., 1974, JD, 1977. Bar: Ohio, Fla., U.S. Dist. Ct. (we. and so. dists.) Ohio, U.S. Ct. Appeals (6th cir.). Assoc. Dayton, Power & Light, Dayton, Ohio, 1977-79; asst. U.S. atty. So. dist. Ohio, 1979-82; ptnr. Parks, Eisele, Baxter & Wilsman, Cleve., 1982-86, Hahn, Loeser & Parks, Cleve., 1986—. Mem. Ohio State Bar Assn., Fla. Bar Assn., Cleve. Bar Assn., Assn. Trial Lawyers Am., Ohio Acad. Trial Lawyers. Democrat. Roman Catholic. Office: Hahn Loeser & Parks 800 Nat City E 6th Bldg Cleveland OH 44114

FOGEL, RICHARD, lawyer; b. Bklyn., Feb. 9, 1932; s. Sam and Anna (Markow) F.; m. Sheila Feldman, Dec. 21, 1957; children—Bruce, Lori Ellen. B.A., York Coll., CUNY, 1971; J.D., N.Y. Law Sch., 1974. Bar: N.J. 1976, U.S. Dist. Ct. N.J. 1976, N.Y. 1981, U.S. Tax Ct. 1977. Tax law specialist IRS, Newark, 1975-77; sr. pension cons., atty. N.Y. Life, N.Y.C., 1977-81; sole practice, Franklin, N.J., 1981-85, Wayne, N.J., 1985—; lectr. Inst. for Continuing Legal Edn., Newark, 1977—; mem. adj. faculty Upsala Coll., East Orange, N.J., 1978—. Recipient Certs. of Appreciation, IRS, Newark, 1977, Inst. Continuing Legal Edn., Newark, 1981-82, 84, Cert. in Recognition of Accomplishments, Coop. Extension Cook Coll., Rutgers U., 1982, Disting. Grad. award York Coll., 1984. Mem. N.J. State Bar Assn. (tax sect.). Jewish. Lodge: Masons. Pension, profit-sharing, and employee benefits, Estate planning, Real property. Home: RD 1 Box 28 Sussex NJ 07461 Office: 1044 Route 23 PO Box 186 Wayne NJ 07470

FOGELGAREN, ERIC ISRAEL, lawyer; b. Heidelberg, Fed. Republic Germany, Apr. 13, 1947; came to U.S., 1952; s. Samuel and Dina (Einstein) F.; m. Susan Eileen Pollock, Jan. 4, 1969; children: Lisa Renee, David Joshua. BA, SUNY, Albany, 1968; JD, Bklyn Law Sch., 1973. Bar: N.Y. 1974, U.S. Dist. Ct. (so. and ea. dists.) N.Y. 1975. Ptnr. Isaacson, Robustelli, Fox, Fine, Greco & Fogelgaren P.C., N.Y.C., 1971—. Mem. N.Y. County Bar Assn. (bd. dirs. 1975—). Workers' compensation, Pension, profit-sharing, and employee benefits, Personal injury. Home: 2 Gate Ct Dix Hills NY 11746 Office: Isaacson Robustelli et al 277 Broadway New York NY 10007

FOGELMAN, MARTIN, lawyer, law educator; b. N.Y.C., Mar. 16, 1928; s. Herman and Fanny (Abramowitz) F.; m. Suzanne Stern, Dec. 21, 1952; children: Henry Jonathan, Jeffrey Scott, Martin, Jr., Douglas Edmund. AB cum laude, Syracuse U., 1948, JD magna cum laude, 1950. Confidential law clk. N.Y. Ct. Appeals, Albany, 1950-54; assoc. Saxe, Bacon, O'Shea & Bryan, N.Y.C., 1955-58; adj. prof. Fordham Law Sch., N.Y.C., 1956-58, prof. law, 1958-62, Arthur A. McGivney prof. law, 1982—, pres. univ. senate, 1980-83, v.p. athletic bd., 1980-84, bd. dirs. Univ. Press, 1978—, chmn. 1986—; arbitrator Nat. Assn. Security Dealers, 1981—, Chgo. Bd. Trade, 1986—. Co-author: Cases and Materials on Mortgages, 1963; author: West's Forms and Text, New York Business Corporation Law, 1965, 2d edit., 1984; West's Forms and Text, New York Not-For-Profit Corporation Law, 1972. Mem. ABA, N.Y. State Bar Assn., Assn. Trial Lawyers Am., N.Y. State Trial Lawyers Assn., Assn. Am. Law Schs. (ho. of dels. 1969—), Phi Delta Phi. General corporate, Securities, Insurance. Home: 21 Brookside Dr Huntington NY 11743 Office: Fordham U Sch Law 140 W 62d St New York NY 10023

FOGELNEST, ROBERT CRAIG, lawyer; b. Phila., Aug. 29, 1946; s. Phillip Harold and Charlotte (Wolkov) F.; m. M.J. Wolf, Jan. 21, 1972 (div. 1980); 1 child, B. Jacob. B.A., Temple U., 1973; J.D., Rutgers U., 1976. Bar: Pa. 1976, U.S. Dist. Ct. (ea. dist.) Pa. 1976, U.S. Tax Ct. 1984. Asst. dist. atty. Phila., 1976-79; prin. firm Ellis, Fogelnest & Newman, P.C., Phila., 1979-85; sole practice, 1985—. Editorial adviser Inside Drug Law, 1984—. Co-author: Coming Home, 1984; Pennsylvania Drunk Driving Law, 2 vols. Mem. Nat. Assn. Criminal Def. Lawyers (bd. dirs.), Assn. Trial Lawyers Am., Pa. Trial Lawyers Assn., Pa. Bar Assn., Phila. Bar Assn., Internat. Legal Def. Counsel (founding mem. Phila. 1980). Democrat. Criminal, Private international. Home: 177 Prince St 5th Floor New York NY 10012 Office: 111 S 15th St 24th Floor Philadelphia PA 19103

FOGG, BLAINE VILES, lawyer; b. Boston, Mar. 29, 1940; s. Sanford L. and Dorothy (Viles) F.; m. Diane Abitbol, June 22, 1964; children: William, Matthew, Katherine. AB, Williams Coll., 1962; JD, Harvard U., 1965. Bar: N.Y. 1966. Assoc. Skadden, Arps, Slate, Meagher & Flom, N.Y.C., 1966-71, ptnr., 1971—. General corporate, Securities. Office: Skadden Arps Slate Meagher & Flom 919 Third Ave New York NY 10022

FOGLEMAN, JOHN NELSON, lawyer; b. Memphis, Jan. 2, 1956; s. Julian Barton and Margaret (Henderson) F.; m. Nancy Darlene Norris, Aug. 14, 1976; children: John Nelson Jr., Adam Barrett. BS in Edn., Ark. State U., 1978; JD, U. Ark., 1981. Bar: Ark. 1981, U.S. Dist. Ct. (ea. dist.) Ark. 1981. Assoc. Hale, Fogleman & Rogers, West Memphis, Ark., 1981-85, ptnr., 1985—; city atty. City of Marion, 1982—, dep. pros. atty. 2d jud. dist. Crittenden County, Marion, Ark., 1983—. Mem. sch. bd. Marion Sch. Dist., 1985—; pres. Marion C. of C., 1982-83. Mem. ABA, Ark. Bar Assn., Assn. Trial Lawyers Am., Ark. Trial Lawyers Assn. Methodist. Avocations: jogging, reading, gardening. General practice, Personal injury, Criminal. Home: 388 L P Mann Marion AR 72364 Office: Hale Fogleman & Rogers 108 Dover Rd West Memphis AR 72301

FOGNANI, JOHN DENNIS, lawyer; b. Pueblo, Colo., Dec. 7, 1950; s. Victor and Anne Marie (Biggi) F.; m. Nancy Lee Schnackenberg, Aug. 18, 1973; children: John Michael, Andrew Victor. BA in Polit. Sci. with distinction, U. Colo., 1973; JD cum laude, Northwestern U., 1977. Bar: Colo. 1977, U.S. Dist. Ct. Colo. 1977, U.S. Ct. Appeals (10th cir.) Colo. 1977, U.S. Ct. Appeals (D.C. cir.) 1979. Investigator Office of Dist. Atty. of Pueblo, 1973-74; assoc. Holland and Hart, Denver, 1977-83, ptnr., 1983—. Co-author: American Law of Mining, 2d edit., 1985; exec. editor Northwestern U. Law Rev. Mem. ABA (natural resources sect.), Colo. Bar Assn., Denver Bar Assn., Rocky Mountain Oil and Gas Assn., Am. Mining Congress, Colo. Mining Assn. Club: Denver Coal. Administrative and regulatory, Environment, Real property. Office: Holland and Hart 555 17th St Suite 2900 Denver CO 80202

FOHN, GERALD ANTHONY, lawyer; b. Uvalde, Tex., Dec. 25, 1945; s. Wilfred Joseph and Sara Erma (Rothe) F.; m. Dolores Ann Fuchs, June 8, 1974; children—Douglas, Stephen, Matthew. B.A., U. Tex.-Austin, 1968, J.D., 1973. Bar: Tex. 1973. Asst. dist. atty. 51st and 119th/Jud. Dist., San Angelo, Tex., 1973-75; dist. atty. 51st Jud. Dist. Tex., San Angelo, 1975—; mem. adv. com. Prosecutor Council Tex. Mem. Tex. Dist. and County Attys. Assn. (bd. dirs. 1983-85), State Bar Tex., Tom Green County Bar Assn. Democrat. Roman Catholic. Club: Kiwanis (bd. dirs. 1982). Criminal, Family and matrimonial, Juvenile. Home: 3349 Tanglewood Dr San Angelo TX 76904 Office: 51st Jud Dist Atty Tom Green County Courthouse San Angelo TX 76903

FOLEY, DANIEL ROBERT, lawyer; b. San Francisco, Mar. 15, 1947; s. Robert Daniel and Doris Marie (Glazer) F.; m. Carlyn Leiko Tani, Dec. 29, 1984; 1 child, Jason Tani. BA, U. San Francisco, 1969, JD, 1974. Bar: Calif. 1974, Trust Territory of the Pacific Islands 1974, Federated State of Micronesia 1982, Yap 1983, U.S. Dist. Ct. Hawaii 1984, U.S. Ct. Appeals (9th cir.) 1984, U.S. Supreme Ct. 1984. Assoc. Carrow, Jones, Apphen & Forest, Novato, Calif., 1974-75; legis. cousel Palau Nat. Congress, Koror, 1982, Yap (Federated State of Micronesia) Legislature, 1979-83; of counsel Aluli & Trask, Honolulu, 1983-84; staff atty. ACLU of Hawaii, Honolulu, 1984—; pro bono lawyer Micronisian indigents, 1975-83; cons. Micronesian govts., 1975—. Author: drafted constitutions of Truk, 1978, Yap, 1982, Kosrae, 1983 (Federated State of Micronesia). Mem. Calif. Bar Assn., Hawaii Bar Assn. Democrat. Buddhist. Avocations: jogging, swimming. Civil rights, Legislative, Constitutional law. Office: ACLU of Hawaii 33 S King St #412 Honolulu HI 96813

FOLEY, JOSEPH LLEWELLYN, lawyer; b. Phila., Oct. 22, 1937; s. Joseph A. and Edna M. (Llewellyn) F. B.S., Pa. State U., 1960; J.D., Temple U., 1968. Bar: Pa. 1968, U.S. Dist. Ct. Pa. 1968, U.S. Ct. Appeals 1968, U.S. Sup. Ct. 1974. With firm Detweiler, Hughes & Kokonos, Phila., 1968-72, Durban and Moore, Morrisville, Pa., 1972-73; sole practice, Glenside, Pa., 1973—; public defender Montgomery County (Pa.), 1972-77 solicitor to domestic relations office Montgomery County, 1980—. Served as 1st lt. U.S. Army, 1960-62. Mem. Montgomery Bar Assn., Montgomery Estate Planning Commn. Republican. Roman Catholic. Club: Abington Lions. General practice, Family and matrimonial, Probate. Office: 614 N Easton Rd Glenside PA 19038

FOLEY, MARGARET SWEENEY, lawyer; b. Lexington, Ky., Oct. 20, 1954; d. Woodrow Wilson and Magaret Kimbrough (Sweeney) F. BA, Transylvania U., 1976; JD, U. Ky., 1981. Bar: Ky. 1981, U.S. Dist. Ct. (ea. dist.) Ky. 1982. Law clk. to presiding justice U.S. Dist. Ct. (ea. dist.) Ky., Pikeville, 1981-82; assoc. Pratt. Weinberg, Perkins & Campbell, Hindman, Ky., 1982; ptnr. Morgan & Foley, Danville, Ky., 1983—. Mem. Danville Area Spouse Abuse Com., 1984—; bd. dirs. Boyle County Jr. Achievement, 1985—. Mem. ABA, Ky. Bar Assn., Ky. Acad. Trial Attys., Boyle County Bar Assn. General practice, Environment, Real property. Office: Morgan & Foley 316 W Main St Danville KY 40422

FOLEY, MARTIN JAMES, lawyer; b. Nebr., Nov. 7, 1946; s. James Gleason and Mary Elizabeth (O'Brien) F.; m. Linda Sivyer; children—James Gleason II, Daniel Patrick, Ryan Edward. Cert Completion, Cambridge U., 1967; B.A. in Philosophy, U. So. Calif. 1968, M.B.A., 1975, J.D., 1974. Bar: Calif. 1975, U.S. Dist. Ct. (cen. dist.) Calif. 1975, U.S. Dist. Ct. (ea., so. and no. dists.) Calif. 1980, U.S. Ct. Appeals (9th cir.) 1980. Acct., Ford Motor Co., San Jose, Calif., 1968, cost analyst, 1970-71; assoc. Adams, Duque & Hazeltine, 1975-80; sr. ptnr. Bryan, Cave, McPheeters & McRoberts, Los Angeles, 1980—. Mem. bd. govs. Gen. Alumni Assn., U. So. Calif., 1982-84. Served to lt. (j.g.) USNR, 1968-70. Mem. ABA (numerous coms.), Calif. Bar Assn. (conf. of del. 1979—), Los Angeles County Bar Assn. Republican. Roman Catholic. Clubs: Jonathan (Los Angeles); Annandale Golf (Pasadena, Calif.). Contbr. articles to profl. jours.; lectr. groups and profl. confs. High technology, Lenders liability, Private international. Office: 333 S Grand Ave Suite 3100 Los Angeles CA 90071

FOLEY, PATRICK JOSEPH, lawyer; b. N.Y.C., Oct. 2, 1930; s. John and Anne (Sheehan) F.; m. Ann Tubman; children: Maura, John. BA, Iona Coll., 1957; JD, N.Y. Law Sch., 1961. Bar: N.Y., U.S. Dist. Ct. (so., no., ea. and we. dists.) N.Y., U.S. Tax Ct., U.S. Ct. Customs, U.S. Ct. Claims, U.S. Ct. Appelas (2d cir.), U.S. Supreme Ct. Asst. underwriter Atlantic Mutual, N.Y.C., 1958-60; acct. exec. Hagedorn and Co., N.Y.C., 1960-62; v.p., assoc. gen. counsel Am. Internat. Group, Inc., N.Y.C., 1963—. Recipient Outstanding Young Ins. Man award, 1965. Mem. ABA (corp. banking and bus. law com.), N.Y. State Bar Assn. (ins. law sect.), Westchester County Bar Assn., N.Y. State Trial Lawyers Assn., Am. Judges Assn., Soc. Friendly Sons of St. Patrick, Ins. Fedn. of N.Y. (pres.), Phi Delta Phi. Republican. Roman Catholic. Lodge: Knights of Malta. Administrative and regulatory, Insurance, Legislative. Office: Am Internat Group 70 Pine St New York NY 10270

FOLEY, STEPHEN BERNARD, lawyer; b. Detroit, Sept. 8, 1950; s. William Stephen and Barbara Gregor (Winter) F.; m. Ruth Ann Burney, May 20, 1972; children: Shanna, Lauren. BS, Eastern Mich. U., 1972; JD, Detroit Coll. Law, 1976. Bar: Mich. 1977, U.S. Dist. Ct. (ea. dist.) Mich., U.S. Ct. Appeals (6th cir.) 1979. Asst. prosecutor Wayne County Prosecutors Office, Detroit, 1977-79, Redford Twp., Mich., 1979-84; ct. officer Wayne County Juvenile Ct., Detroit, 1976-77; assoc. Law Offices of Alan R. Miller P.C., Birmingham, Mich., 1984—; real estate Salesman Coaches Realty, Detroit, 1970—. Past pres., bd. dir. Brookside Village Homes Assn., Canton, Mich., 1980—. Mem. Am. Trial Lawyers Assn., Mich. Trial Lawyers Assn., Mich. Bar Assn., Canton Jaycees (past dir., Springboard of Yr. 1979-80). Democrat. Roman Catholic. Avocations: boating, skiing, reading. Personal injury, State civil litigation, Workers' compensation. Home: 39784 Fox Valley Dr Canton MI 48188 Office: Alan R Miller PC 300 E Maple Suite 200 Birmingham MI 48011

FOLGATE, HOMER EMMETT, JR., lawyer; b. Rockford, Ill., Nov. 10, 1920; s. Homer Emmett and Hazel J. (Grissinger) F.; m. Letty Rae Huber, Apr. 28, 1944; children—Randall Lind, Jill, John Ernest. J.D., U. Ill., 1948. Bar: Ill. bar 1948. Asst. states atty. Winnebago County, Ill, 1948-55; partner firm Reno, Zahm, Folgate, Lindberg & Powell, Rockford, 1955—. Chmn. Winnebago County Republican Central Com., 1955-64. Served with AUS, 1943-46. Decorated Purple Heart, Silver Star. Club: Mason (Shriner). Probate, Local government, General practice. Home: 5177 Norwich Dr Rockford IL 61107 Office: Camelot Tower Rockford IL 61108

FOLGER, OSCAR DAVID, lawyer; b. Stuttgart, Fed. Republic Germany, Apr. 11, 1947; came to U.S., 1948; s. Henry and Margaret (Schwartz) F.; m. Rita Carol Strenger, June 13, 1968; children: Jennifer, Jeffrey, Kenneth. BS, Columbia U., 1968, JD, 1971. Bar: N.Y. 1972. From assoc. to ptnr. Kramer, Levin, Nessen, Kamin & Frankel, N.Y.C., 1971-79; ptnr. Moses & Singer, N.Y.C., 1979-85; sole practice N.Y.C., 1986—. Mem. ABA (com. fed. regulation securities). General corporate, Securities. Office: One Rockefeller Plaza New York NY 10020

FOLK, THOMAS ROBERT, lawyer; b. Milford, N.J., Jan. 9, 1950; s. Conrad Frank and Isabella Ramsey (Sickels) F.; m. JoAnn Elizabeth Lo Pinto, June 21, 1975; children: Elizabeth Frances, Karina Marie. BS, U.S. Mil. Acad., 1972; JD, U. Va., 1978. Bar: Va. 1978, U.S. Ct. Mil. Appeals 1978, U.S. Ct. Appeals (4th cir.) 1978, U.S. Supreme Ct. 1983, U.S. Ct. Claims 1985, U.S. Ct. Appeals (9th and fed. cirs.) 1985, D.C. 1986., U.S. Dist. Ct. D.C. 1987. Commd. 2d lt. U.S. Army, 1972, advanced to maj., 1983, res., 1986; asst. to gen. counsel U.S. Army, Washington, 1980-82, atty. litigation, 1983-86; assoc. Hazel, Beckhorn & Hanes, Fairfax, Va., 1986—. Contbr. articles to profl. jours. Mem. Com. Armed Services and Vets. Affairs, 1985—. Mem. ABA, Va. bar Assn., West Point Soc. D.C. Federal civil litigation, State civil litigation, Military. Home: 4409 Pickett Rd Fairfax VA 22032 Office: Hazel Beckhorn & Haines 4084 University Dr PO Box 547 Fairfax VA 22030

FOLKS, ROBERT LOGUE, lawyer; b. Amityville, N.Y., Aug. 6, 1947; s. T. John Jr. and Bernice (O'Keefe) F.; m. Rosemary Elizabeth Ruggiero, June 28, 1975; children: Kelly, Shannon, Jennifer. BA, U. Notre Dame, 1969; LLD, St. John's U., Jamaica, N.Y., 1972. Bar: Fla. 1973, N.Y. 1973, U.S. Dist. Ct. (so. dist.) N.Y. 1980, U.S. Ct. Mil. Appeals 1980, U.S. Ct. Appeals (2d cir.) 1980, U.S. Supreme Ct. 1980. Asst. dist. atty. Suffolk County Dist. Atty.'s Office, Riverhead, N.Y., 1972-84; asst. county atty. Suffolk County Atty.'s Office, Hauppauge, N.Y., 1984; asst. atty. so. dist. U.S. Atty.'s Office, N.Y.C., 1984-87; ptnr. Rivkin, Radler, Dunne & Bayh, Uniondale, N.Y., 1987—; v.p. Edn. Assistance Corp., Port. Washington, N.Y., 1984—; pres. Suffolk County Acad. of Law, Ronkontoma, N.Y., 1985-87. 1st v.p. Community Mediation Bd., Coram, N.Y., 1983—, Police Athletic League, Yaphank, N.Y., 1985—. Recipient Recognition award Suffolk County Acad. of Law, 1981-85. Fellow N.Y. State Bar Found. (recognition award 1983); mem. N.Y. State Bar Assn. (chmn., county cts. com. recognition award 1982-85), Criminal Bar Assn. (bd. dirs. 1980-81, sec. 1981-82), Suffolk County Bar Assn. (bd. dirs. 1985-87, recognition award 1985), Suffold County Acad. of law (pres. 1985-87). Republican. Roman Catholic. Clubs: N.Y. Athletic (N.Y.C.); Southward Ho Country (Brentwood, N.Y.); Sayville (N.Y.) Yacht. Criminal. Home: 150 Kilburn Rd Garden City NY 11530

FOLLICK, EDWIN DUANE, chiropractic physician, legal educator, educational administrator; b. Glendale, Calif., Feb. 4, 1935; s. Edwin Fulfford and Esther Agnes (Catherwood) F. BA Calif. State U., Los Angeles, 1956, MA, 1961; MA Pepperdine U., 1957, MPA, 1977; PhD, D in Theology St. Andrews Theol. Coll., Sem. of the Free Protestant Episcopal Ch., London, 1958; MS in Literary Sci., U. So. Calif., 1963, MEd, 1964, AdvMEd, 1969; Calif. Coll. Law, 1965; LLB Blackstone Law Sch., 1966, JD, 1967; DC Cleve. Chiropractic Coll., Los Angeles, 1972; PhD, Academia Theatina, Pescara, 1978. Tchr., library adminstr. Los Angeles City Schs., 1957-68; law librarian Glendale U. Coll. Law, 1968-69; coll. librarian Cleveland Chiropractic Coll., Los Angeles, 1969-74, dir. edn. and admissions, 1974-84, prof. jurisprudence, 1975—, dean student affairs, 1976—, chaplain, 1985— ; assoc. prof. Newport U., 1982—; extern prof. St. Andrews Theol. Coll., London, 1961; dir. West Valley Chiropractic Health Ctr., 1972—. Contbr. articles to profl. jours. Served as chaplain's asst. U.S. Army, 1958-60. Decorated Cavaliere Internat. Order legion of Honor of Immacolata (Italy); knight of Malta, Sovereign Order of St. John of Jerusalem; chevalier Ordre Militaire et Hospitalier de St. Lazare de Jerusalem, numerous others. Mem. ALA, NEA, Am. Assn. Sch. Librarians, Los Angeles Sch. Library Assn., Calif. Media and Library Educators Assn., Assn. Coll and Research Librarians, Am. Assn. Law Librarians, Am. Chiropractic Assn., Internat. Chiropractors Assn., Nat. Geog. Soc., Internat. Platform Assn., Phi Delta Kappa, Sigma Chi Psi, Delta Tau Alpha. Democrat. Episcopalian. Administrative and regulatory. Home: 6435 Jumilla Ave Woodland Hills CA 91367 Office: 590 N Vermont Ave Los Angeles CA 90004 also: 7022 Owensmouth Ave Canoga Park CA 91303

FOLLOWS, JILL MARILYN, lawyer, consultant; b. Syracuse, N.Y., July 21, 1952; d. Alan Greaves and Elva Jean Follows; m. Frederick Niles Dorfman, April 23, 1983; children: Audrey Rachel, Robert Benjamin. BS in Nursing, SUNY, Albany, 1974; MS in Nursing, Syracuse U., 1976; JD, Villanova U., 1982. Bar: Pa. 1982. Sch. nurse, tchr. Westhill High Sch., Syracuse, N.Y., 1974-75; nursing instr. Syracuse U., 1977, Presbyt. U. Pa., Phila., 1977, Hahnemann Coll., Phila., 1978-79; assoc. Anapol, Schwartz, Weiss & Schwartz, Phila., 1982-85; sole practice Ardmore, Pa., 1985—; cons. T.S.O. Fin. Corp., Horsham, Pa., 1985—, Widener U. Sch. Nursing, 1986—; adj. faculty mem. Del. County Community Coll., Media, Pa., 1985. Campaign com. mem. Dems. for Anderson, Del. County, 1985. Mem. Pa. Bar Assn., Pa. Trial Lawyers Assn., Am. Assn. Nurse Attys. (corr. sec. 1985-86, bd. dirs. 1984—, treas. 1987), Sigma Theta Tau. Democrat. Episcopalian. Represented appellants in landmark case Amadio vs. Levin et al. before Pa. Supreme Ct., resulting in the state's recognition of the right of an estate to receive compensation for the death of a stillborn whose death was occasioned by malpractice, 1985. Avocations: golf, sailing. Personal injury, State civil litigation, Legal education. Home and Office: 2945 Mapleshade Rd Ardmore PA 19003

FOLMAR, OLIVER WILEY, lawyer; b. Troy, Ala., Aug. 9, 1913; s. Marshall Bibb and Lois (Wiley) F.; m. Portia Witherspoon Phillips, Apr. 17, 1943; children—Judith Wiley Folmar Songy, Clare Therita, Michelle Lois Mary. Student St. John's Coll., 1931-32; J.D., U. Miami, 1938, U. Ala., 1974. Bar: Fla. 1938, Tenn. 1982, U.S. Supreme Ct. 1954. Sole practice, Sarasota, Fla., 1938-41, Miami and Plantation Key, Fla., 1946-78, Mountain City, Tenn., 1978—. Served as officer paratroop-inf. U.S. Army, 1941-45. Mem. ABA, Tenn. Bar Assn., Fla. Bar, Am. Legion, Phi Delta Phi. Republican. Roman Catholic. Private international, Personal injury, Admiralty. Home: Portia's Parthenon Rainbow Rd Mountain City TN 37683 Office: PO Box 12 Mountain City TN 37683

FOLSE, PARKER C(AMILE), III, lawyer; b. Austin, Tex., July 8, 1954; s. Parker C. Folse Jr. and Marlee (Baker) Joseph; m. Carol Ann Marko, Mar. 30, 1985; 1 child, Alexis Brighton. BA magna cum laude, Harvard U., 1977; JD with high honors, U. Tex., 1980. Bar: Tex. 1980, U.S. Ct. Appeals (9th cir.) 1981, U.S. Dist. Ct. Ariz. 1983, U.S. Dist. Ct. (so. dist.) Tex. 1984, U.S. Dist. Ct. (no. dist.) Tex. 1985, U.S. Ct. Appeals (5th cir.) 1985. Law clk. to presiding judge U.S. Ct. Appeals (9th cir.), San Francisco, 1980-81; law clk. to justice William H. Rehnquist U.S. Supreme Ct., Washington, 1981-82; assoc. Martori, Meyer, Hendricks & Victor, Phoenix, 1982-84; assoc. Susman, Godfrey & McGowan, Houston, 1984-85, ptnr., 1985—. Editor in chief Tex. Law Rev., 1980. Mem. ABA, Tex. Bar Assn., Houston Bar Assn., Order of Coif. Antitrust, Federal civil litigation, State civil litigation. Office: Susman Godfrey & McGowan 2400 Allied Bank Plaza Houston TX 77002

FOLSOM, VICTOR CLARENCE, lawyer; b. Dallas, Dec. 31, 1909; s. Clarence S.T. and Mildred (Johnson) F.; m. Maude A. Ward, Dec. 23, 1933 (div.); children—Georgia, Dale John, Glen Victor, Alan Lynn; m. 2d, Victoria Vancza, 1948. Student U. Tex., 1929-33; LL.B., Pacific Coast U., 1935. Bar: Calif. 1935, N.Y. 1942, Mass. 1960. Ptnr., Mayhew & Folsom, Los Angeles, 1935-40; fgn. dept. Reid & Priest, N.Y.C., 1940-42; fgn. legal cons. U.S. Alien Property Custodian, 1942-44; fgn. counsel Sterling Drug Inc., N.Y.C., 1944-59; v.p. Sterling Products Internat., Inc., 1956-59; gen. counsel, mem. mgmt. com. United Fruit Co., Boston, 1960-61, v.p., gen. counsel, 1961-70, dir., 1962-70, legal adviser, 1970-74; counsel Escobar, Garcia, Ortiz, Antolinos & Inman, Mexico City, 1974-78; chmn. adv. bd. internat. and comparative law center Southwestern Legal Found., Dallas, 1968-70, also mem. faculty. Mem. World Trade Adv. Commn. Dept. Commerce; legal adviser U.S. Missions to various Latin Am. countries; mem. adv. bd. World Tax Series Harvard Law Sch.; chmn. adv. com. internat. legal studies program U. Tex. Sch. Law. Recipient gold medal Inter-Am. Bar Assn., 1967; William Roy Vallance award Inter-Am. Bar Found., 1977; Carl H. Fulda award Tex. Internat. Law Jour., 1981. Mem. ABA (ho. dels.), Inter-Am. Bar Assn. (pres. 1972-73, mem. exec. com.; U.S. council rep.), Fed. Bar Assn., Calif. Bar Assn., N.Y. State Bar Assn., Mass. Bar Assn., Boston Bar Assn., Assn. Gen. Counsel, Am. Fgn. Law Assn. (council), Am. Soc. Internat. Law, Acad. Polit. Sci., Pan-Am. Soc., Internat. C. of C., Proprietary Assn., Nat. Fgn. Trade Council (dir.), Controllers Inst. Am. (internat. operations com. N.Y.C. Control), Internat. Bar Assn., Am. Judicature Soc., Council on Fgn. Relations, Nat. Lawyers Club, Bolivarian Soc. U.S. Republican. Methodist. Clubs: Country of Green Valley (Ariz.); Univ. (Boston); Charles River Country. Contbr. articles in field to profl. jours. Private international, General corporate, Legal education. Home: 112 W Esperanza Blvd Green Valley AZ 85614

FOLTZ, RICHARD NELSON, III, lawyer; b. Balt., Jan. 14, 1953; s. Richard Nelson Jr. and Betty Rose (Dunn) F.; m. Deborah Marian Imbach, Oct. 23, 1982. BS in Acctg., Towson State U., 1974; JD, U. Balt., 1976, MS in Taxation, 1981; MBA, Loyola Coll., Balt., 1985. Bar: Md. 1977, U.S. Dist. Ct. Md. 1977, U.S. Ct. Appeals (4th cir.) 1977, U.S. Tax Ct. 1978, U.S. Ct. Claims 1979, U.S. Supreme Ct. 1980. Assoc. Hessey & Hessey, Balt., 1975-83; sole practice Balt., 1983—; pres. Am. Utilities Subs., Cherry Hill, N.J., 1984—; treas. Halethorpe Meth. Ch., Balt., 1972-73, bd. trustees, 1980-83. General practice, General corporate, Public utilities. Home and Office: 5504 Edmonson Ave Baltimore MD 21229

FONDREN, LOUIS, lawyer; b. Colony Town., Miss., May 16, 1932; s. Elmer Louis and Mary Lou (Hull) F.;m. Bobbie J. Fondren, June 29, 1963; stepchildren: Danny, Nancy, Charles, Suzanne, Michael. Student, Yale U., 1950-52; LLB, U. Miss., 1955. Bar: Miss. 1955, U.S. Dist. Ct. (so. dist.) Miss. 1963, U.S. Ct. Appeals (5th cir.) 1966. Claim rep. State Farm Auto Ins. Co., Greenwood, Miss., 1957-58; sole practice Jackson and Pascagoula, Miss., 1958—; pub. defender, justice judge, Pascagoula. Author: Mississippi Criminal Trial Practice, 1980, Mississippi Criminal Trial Practice Forms, 1982, Mississippi Civil Trial Practice Forms, 1983. Atty. City of Moss Point, Miss.; mayor City of Moss Point; state legislator Miss. House of Reps., Jackson. Served with U.S. Army, 1955-57. Mem. Am. Trial Lawyers Assn., Jackson County Bar Assn. Democrat. Baptist. Avocations: jogging, reading, writing. State civil litigation, Federal civil litigation, Personal injury. Home: 1205 Beach Blvd Pascagoula MS 39567 Office: 520 Live Oak Ave Pascagoula MS 39567

FONES, WILLIAM HARDIN DAVIS, state supreme court justice; b. Friendship, Tenn., Oct. 6, 1917; s. Roy Revelle and Kitty (Davis) J.; m. Rebecca Logan Barr, July 26, 1946; children: Jere, William Hardin Davis. Student, Memphis State U., 1934-37; J.D., U. Tenn., 1940. Bar: Tenn. 1942. Practiced in Memphis, 1945-71; judge div. 3 15th Jud. Circuit Ct. Tenn., Shelby County, Memphis, 1971-73; assoc. justice Supreme Ct., Tenn., 1973-74, 76—; chief justice Supreme Ct., 1974-76, 82-84; mem. exec. council Conf. Chief Justices, 1976-79. Active local Boy Scouts Am., ARC, Shelby United Neighbors fund drives. Served with USAAF, 1942-45. Decorated Air medal with 3 oak leaf clusters. Office: Supreme Ct Tenn 311 Supreme Bldg Nashville TN 37219 *

FONG, HAROLD MICHAEL, federal judge; b. Honolulu, Apr. 28, 1938; m. Judith Tom, 1966; children—Harold Michael, Terrence Matthew. A.B. cum laude, U. So. Calif., 1960; J.D., U. Mich., 1964. Bar: Hawaii 1965. Dep. pros. atty. City and County of Honolulu, 1965-68; assoc. Mizuha and Kim, Honolulu, 1968-69; asst. U.S. atty. dist. Hawaii, 1969-73; U.S. atty.

1973-78; ptnr. Fong and Miho, Honolulu, 1978-82; judge U.S. Dist. Ct., Dist. of Hawaii, 1982-84, chief judge, 1984—. Office: PO Box 50128 Honolulu HI 96850

FONG, VALERIE (WAI HIN), lawyer; b. Honolulu; d. Arthur Sun Kong and Victoria Kam Yuk (Chun) F.; m. Glenn Kum Lun Chang, May 31, 1986. BA, U. Oreg., 1979; JD, U. Calif., Davis, 1982. Bar: Calif. 1982, Hawaii 1983, U.S. Ct. Appeals (9th cir.) 1983. Assoc. Shim, Tam, Kirimitsu, Kitamura & Chang and predecessor firm Shim, Tam, Kirimitsu & Naito, Honolulu, 1982—. Personal injury. Office: Shim Tam Kirimitsu & Naito 333 Queen St Suite 900 Honolulu HI 96813

FONS, JOHN JOSEPH, lawyer; b. Milw., July 26, 1957; s. Eugene John and Jeanne Ellen (Coughlin) F.; m. Debra Lynn Mantei, Apr. 30, 1983. BBA, U. Wis., Milw., 1979; JD, Marquette U., 1982. Bar: Wis. 1982, U.S. Dist. Ct. (ea. and we. dists.) Wis. 1982, Nev. 1983. Assoc. David Goldwater Ltd., Las Vegas, Nev., 1982-83; field atty. ITT Fin. Corp., Milw., 1983-84; atty. Bear Automotive Service Equipment Co., Milw., 1984-87, assoc. gen. counsel, 1987—. Mem. ABA, Wis. Bar Assn., Nev. Bar Assn. Roman Catholic. Avocations: tennis, aerobics, golf, skiing, cycling. General corporate, Contracts commercial, Consumer commercial. Office: Bear Automotive Service Equipment Co 2855 James Dr New Berlin WI 53151

FONTANA, VINCENT ROBERT, lawyer; b. Bklyn., Mar. 1, 1939; s. Joseph E. and Sadie (Guastella) F.; m. Joanne F. D'Antonio, Aug. 5, 1967; children: Joseph John, Anne Louise. BS in Acctng., Holy Cross Coll., 1960; JD, Fordham U., 1964. Bar: N.Y. 1965, U.S. Ct. Appeals (2d cir.) 1967, U.S. Supreme Ct. 1974, U.S. Dist. Ct. (ea. so. and we. dists.) N.Y. 1981, U.S. Ct. Appeals (11th cir.) 1985, U.S. Ct. Appeals (9th cir.) 1987.. Assoc. Wilkie, Farr & Gallagher, N.Y.C., 1965-66; assoc. Mendes & Mount, N.Y.C., 1966-75, ptnr., 1975-77; assoc. Wilson, Elser, Edelman & Dicker, N.Y.C., 1977-78, ptnr., 1979—. Contbr. articles to profl. jours. Pres., Bklyn. Assn. Brain Injured Children, 1974-77; pres. N.Y. Assn. Learning Disabled, 1977-79. Recipient Am. Jurisprudence award Fordham Law Review, 1962-64. Mem. ABA, N.Y. State Bar Assn., Nat. Inst. Mcpl. Law. Republican. Roman Catholic. Civil rights, Insurance, Personal injury. Office: 420 Lexington Ave New York NY 10170

FOOTE, CALEB, legal educator, writer; b. Cambridge, Mass., Mar. 26, 1917; s. Henry Wilder and Eleanor (Cope) F.; m. Hope Stephens, Nov. 17, 1942; children: Robert, Heather, Andrew, Ethan, David. AB, Harvard U., 1939; MA, Columbia U., 1941; LLB, U. Pa., 1953. Bar: Pa. 1956, U.S. Supreme Ct. 1961. Instr. U. Pa., 1953-54; assoc. prof. U. Nebr. Law Sch., 1954-56, prof., 1956-65; Elizabeth Josselyn Boalt prof. law U. Calif.-Berkeley, 1965—; Walter E. Meter vis. Research prof. Harvard U. Law Sch., 1960-61. Co-author: (with R.J. Levt and F.E.A. Sander) Cases and Materials on Family Law, 1966, 3d edit., 1985, (with H. Mayer) The Culture of the University: Governance and Education, 1968, (with R.J. Levy) Criminal Law: Cases and Materials, 1981; editor: Studies on Bail, 1966. Legal education. Office: U Calif Law Sch 225 Boalt Hall Berkeley CA 94708 Office: PO Box 517 Port Reyes Station CA 94956 *

FOOTE, EDWARD THADDEUS, II, university president, lawyer; b. Milw., Dec. 15, 1937; s. William Hamilton and Julia Stevenson (Hardin) F.; m. Roberta Waugh Fulbright, Apr. 18, 1964; children: Julia, William, Thaddeus. B.A., Yale U., 1959; LL.B., Georgetown U., 1966; LL.D. (hon.), Washington U., St. Louis, 1981; hon. degree, Tokai U., Tokyo, 1984. Bar: Mo. 1966. Reporter, Washington Star, 1963-64, Washington Daily News, 1964-65; exec. asst. to chmn. Pa. Ave. Commn., Washington, 1965-66; assoc. Bryan, Cave, McPheeters & McRoberts, St. Louis, 1966-70; vice chancellor, gen. counsel, sec. to bd. trustees Washington U., St. Louis, 1970-73; dean Sch. Law Washington U., 1973-80, spl. adv. to chancellor and bd. trustees, 1980-81; pres. U. Miami, Coral Gables, Fla., 1981—; mem. task force on mandatory continuing legal edn. Mo. Bar, 1975-76, mem. peer performance subcom. of profl. responsibility com., 1977-78; chmn. citizens com. for sch. desegregation, St. Louis, 1980; chmn. desegregation monitoring and adv. com., St. Louis, 1980-81. Author: An Educational Plan for Voluntary Cooperation Desegregation of School in the St. Louis Met. area, 1981. Mem. Council on Fgn. Relations, St. Louis, 1966-69; bd. dirs. Expt. in Internat. Living, St. Louis, 1966-69, Jr. Kindergarten, St. Louis, 1966-70, Legal Services Ea. Mo., 1973-78, St. Louis City and County Legal Aid Soc., 1973-78; founding pres. bd. New City Sch., St. Louis, 1967-73; mem. gov.'s task force on reorganization State of Mo., 1973-74, steering com., chmn. goverance com. Mo. Gov.'s Conf. on Edn., UN Assn. (Greater St. Louis chpt.), 1977-79, adv. council Seminar on Edn. and Cts., Danforth Found, 1978-81, Conf. on Edn., St. Louis, 1978-81, adv. com. Naval War Coll., 1979-82, edn. com. Fla. Council 100, So. Fla. Coordinating Council, Miami Com. on Fgn. Relations, Metro-Miami Action Plan, exec. com. Miami Citizens Against Crime; trustee St. Louis Art Mux., 1979-80. Served with USMCR, 1959-62. Recipient Order of Sun (Peru). Mem. ABA, Greater Miami C. of C. (bd. govs.), Order of Coif. Democrat. Office: Univ of Miami Office of Pres PO Box 248006 Coral Gables FL 33124

FORBES, ARTHUR LEE, III, lawyer; b. Houston, Sept. 3, 1928; s. Arthur Lee Jr. and Corinne (Mayfield) F.; m. Nita R. Harrison, Mar. 25, 1957; children—Tricia, Kim, Arthur Lee. B.S.C.E., U. Tex.-Austin, 1952; J.D., S. Tex. Coll. Law, 1959. Bar: Tex. 1959, U.S. Ct. Appeals (5th cir.) 1960, U.S. Supreme Ct. 1967. Ptnr. firm Lee & Forbes, Houston, 1960-73, Shapiro, Forbes & Cox, Houston, 1974—. Served to lt. USMC, 1952-54. Mem. ABA, Tex. Bar Assn., Houston Bar Assn., Assn. Trial Lawyers Am., Houston Trial Lawyers Assn., Sigma Chi, Phi Delta Phi, Unitarian. Club: Houston Racquet. State civil litigation, Condemnation, General practice. Home: 5 Leisure Ln Houston TX 77024 Office: Shapiro Forbes & Cox 2919 Allen Pkwy Suite 1122 Houston TX 77019

FORBES, MORTON GERALD, lawyer; b. Atlanta, July 12, 1938; s. Arthur Mark and Mary Dean (Power) F.; m. Eunice Lee Haynsworth, Jan. 25, 1963; children: John, Ashley, Sarah. AB, Wofford Coll., 1962; LLB, U. Ga., 1965. Bar: Ga. 1965, U.S. Dist. Ct. (mid. dist.) Ga. 1965, U.S. Dist. Ct. (so. dist.) Ga. 1968, U.S. Ct. Appeals (5th cir.) 1974, U.S. Ct. Appeals (4th cir.) 1972, U.S. Ct. Appeals (11th cir.) 1981. Assoc. Pierce, Ranitz, Lee, Berry & Mahoney, 1967-70; ptnr. Pierce, Ranitz, Berry, Mahoney & Forbes, 1970-76, Pierce, Ranitz, Mahoney, Forbes & Coolidge, 1976-81; ptnr., sec. Ranitz, Mahoney, Forbes & Coolidge, P.C., 1981—; gen. counsel Ga. Fen. Young Rep. Clubs, 1971-72; guest lectr. dept. dental hygiene Armstrong State Coll., 1970-72. Mem. Savannah Port Authority, 1973—, chmn., 1979-81; mem. Chatham County Devel. Authority, 1973-80; mem. nat. com. Nat. Fedn. Young Reps., 1973; mem. econ. adv. council Coastal Area Planning and Devel. Authority, 1980—; bd. dirs. Savannah Symphony Soc., 1971-75; Ga. del. to Japan/Southeast Trade Mission, Kyoto, Japan, 1983, S.E. U.S.A./Japan Assn. meeting, Birmingham, Ala., 1984. Served with USN, 1965-67. Recipient Outstanding Service award Savannah Port Authority, 1981. Mem. ABA, State Bar Ga., Am. Judicature Soc., Nat. Assn. Bond Counsel, Ga. Def. Lawyers Assn. (bd. dirs.), Savannah Bar Assn., Libel Def. Resource Center, Def. Research Inst., Savannah Econ. Devel. Action Counsel (founding), Savannah Area Wofford Coll. Alumni Club (past pres.), S.R. Republican. Methodist. Clubs: Chatham, Savannah Yacht, Chatham Tennis. Libel, Insurance, Federal civil litigation. Office: PO Box 786 Savannah GA 31402

FORBES, THOMAS ALLEN, lawyer; b. Georgetown, Tex., Apr. 1, 1949; s. Charles Alexander and Mary (Cook) F.; m. Frances Potter Lochridge, Sept. 25, 1982. BA, Southwestern U., 1971; JD, Baylor U., 1975. Bar: Tex. 1975, U.S. Dist. Ct. (we. dist.) 1984, U.S. Ct. Appeals (5th cir.) 1984, U.S. Supreme Ct. 1984. Atty. State Bar of Tex., 1975-77; sole practice Austin, 1977-79; ptnr. Stone & Forbes, Austin, 1979-86; counsel Groce, Locke & Hebdon, Austin and San Antonio, 1986—. Trustee Southwestern U., 1983—; bd. dirs. Austin YMCA, 1983-85, AustinChoral Union. Fellow Tex. Bar Found.; mem. ABA (officer young lawyers div. 1980-83, ho. of dels. 1983-85, standing com. on law and electoral process, Inter-Am. affairs commn.), Am. Judicature Soc. (bd. dirs. 1983-85), Nat. Assn. Bond Lawyers, Tex. Young Lawyers Assn. (bd. dirs 1984-85), Inter Am. Bar Assn., Austin Council on Fgn. Affairs, Inc., Phi Delta Phi. Presbyterian. Avocations: golf, running. Administrative and regulatory, Legislative, Public finance. Home: 2103 Hartford Rd Austin TX 78703 Office: Groce Locke & Hebdon 823 Congress suite 1400 Austin TX 78701

FORBUS, SHARON ANN, lawyer, military officer; b. Indpls., Mar. 19, 1952; d. Herschel Moris and Lottie (Rogenski) Johnson; m. Jackie Earl Forbus, Mar. 27, 1976; 1 child, Scott Eric. BS in Criminal Justice, Ind. U., 1974; JD, Tulane U., 1981. Bar: Ind. 1981, U.S. Dist. Ct. (so. dist.) Ga. 1982, U.S. Ct. Mil. Appeals 1982, Army Ct. Mil. Rev. 1982. Tech. spl. agt. USAF, Washington, 1975-76; chief maintenance USAF, Shaw AFB, 1976-78; asst. staff judge advocate U.S. Army, Ft. Stewart, Ga., 1981-85; asst. dist. counsel U.S. Army C.E., Mobile, Ala., 1985—. Served to capt. U.S. Army, 1981—. Decorated U.S. Army commendation medal with one oak leaf cluster, 1985. Mem. Mensa (gifted children's coordinator Mobile br.). Avocation: computers. Military, Government contracts and claims. Home: PO Box 2341 Mobile AL 36602 Office: US Army Corps Engrs Office of Counsel PO Box 2288 Mobile AL 36628

FORCUM, RICHARD EUGENE, lawyer; b. Whitefish, Mont., June 22, 1939; s. Paul Eugene and Lillian (Jones) F.; m. Susan Meyer, Nov. 26, 1968; 1 son, Geoffrey E. B.S., Willamette U., 1962, J.D., 1964. Bar: Oreg., 1964. Assoc. Ralf Erlandson, Milwaukie, Oreg., 1965; title officer Pioneer Nat. Title Ins., Portland, Oreg., 1965-68; assoc. John T. Chinnock, Madras, Oreg., 1968-69; dist. atty. Jefferson County, Oreg., 1969-73; ptnr. Williver and Forcum, Bend, Oreg., 1973-77; ptnr. Forcum, West, Parker, Bend, 1977-82, Forcum, Parker & Speck, Bend, 1982-85, Forcum & Speck, Band, 1986—; instr. Central Oreg. Community Coll.; mem. com. unauthorized practice of law Oreg. State Bar, 1982-85, State Oreg. Indigent Def. Bd., 1985—. Bd. dirs. Deschutes County Fair Assn., 1983—. Mem. Oreg. Bar Assn., Oreg. Criminal Def. Lawyers Assn. Democrat. Clubs: Elks, Eagles. Criminal, Family and matrimonial, Real property. Office: 1101 NW Bond St Bend OR 97701

FORD, ASHLEY LLOYD, consumer products company executive, lawyer; b. Cin., Mar. 10, 1939; s. Starr MacLeod and Mary Lloyd (Mills) F.; m. Barbara Hill, Apr. 23, 1965; children—Christopher Ashley, Elizabeth Hill. A.B., Princeton U., 1960; J.D., Yale U., 1963. Bar: Ohio 1963. Assoc., Densmore & Shohl, Cin., 1965-69; counsel Procter & Gamble Co., Cin., 1969-71, div. counsel, 1971—, sec., 1979—. Shareholder, Cin. Mus. Assn., Cin. Hist. Soc. Served as lt. USNR, 1966-79. Mem. ABA, Ohio Bar Assn., Cin. Bar Assn., Am. Soc. Secs., Order of Coif, Phi Beta Kappa. Episcopalian. Clubs: Cin. Country, University (Cin.). Antitrust, General corporate. Office: Procter & Gamble Co 1 Procter & Gamble Plaza Cincinnati OH 45202

FORD, DAVID R(UCKER), lawyer; b. Richmond, Va., May 22, 1955; s. C. Rucker and Jane Broadus (Trevvett) F.; m. Elizabeth Ann Rauld, Aug. 11, 1979. BA, Rollins Coll., 1976; JD, U. Va., 1979. Bar: D.C. 1979, U.S. Dist. Ct. D.C. 1980, U.S. Ct. Appeals (D.C. cir.) 1980, U.S. Supreme Ct. 1985. Assoc. Winston & Strawn, Washington, 1979-81; assoc. Casson, Calligaro & Mutryn, Washington, 1981-85, ptnr., 1986-87; ptnr. Simons & Ford, Washington, 1987—. Health, General corporate, Real property. Office: Simons & Ford 1133 21st St NW Washington DC 20036

FORD, JOHN R., lawyer; b. Jersey City, June 12, 1950; s. Harold C. Ford and Margaret R. White; m. Dorothy Ann Kelly; children: Ashley, Colin. BA in History, Yale U., 1972; JD, Fordham U., 1975. Bar: N.J., U.S. Dist. Ct. N.J., U.S. Ct. Appeals (3d cir.). Asst. prosecutor Monmouth County Prosecutors Office, Freehold, N.J., 1975-77; assoc. McCarter & English, Newark, 1977; ptnr. Rudnick, Waldman, Ford, Addonizio, Pappa & Tonneman PC, Red Bank, N.J., 1977—; lectr. Inst. Continuing Legal Edn.; adj. prof. law, trial advocacy Fordham U., 1986—; legal contbr. The CBS Morning Program, 1986—. TV commentator on legal matters WCBS-TV Channel 2, 1983—. Pres. Mary Carmody Found., Red Bank, 1983—. Mem. Assn. Trial Lawyers Am., Trial Lawyers N.J., N.J. Criminal Def. Lawyers Assn., Yale U. Alumni Assn. (athletic steering com.). State civil litigation, Criminal. Office: Rudnick Waldman Ford Addonizio & Tonneman PC 656 Shrewsbury Ave PO Box 578 Red Bank NJ 07701

FORD, LEE ELLEN, scientist, educator, lawyer; b. Auburn, Ind., June 16, 1917; d. Arthur W. and Geneva (Muhn) Ford; B.A., Wittenberg Coll., 1947; M.S., U. Minn., 1949; Ph.D., Iowa State Coll., 1952; J.D., U. Notre Dame, 1972. CPA auditing, 1934-44; assoc. prof. biology Gustavus Adolphus Coll., 1950-51, Anderson (Ind.) Coll., 1952-55; vis. prof. biology U. Alta. (Can.), Calgary, 1955-56; asso. prof. biology Pacific Luth. U., Parkland, Wash., 1956-62; prof. biology and cytogenetics Miss. State Coll. for Women, 1962-64; chief cytogeneticist Pacific N.W. Research Found., Seattle, 1964-65; dir. Canine Genetics Cons. Service, Parkland, 1963-69. Sponsor Companion Collies for the Adult, Jr. Blind, 1955-65; dir. Genetics Research Lab., Butler, Ind., 1955-75, cons. cytogenetics, 1969-75; legis. cons., 1970-79; dir. chromosome lab. Inst. Basic Research in Mental Retardation, S.I., 1968-69; exec. dir. Legis. Bur. U. Notre Dame Law Sch., also editor New Dimensions in Legislation, 1969-72; editor Butler Record Herald, 1972-76; bd. dirs. Ind. Interreligious Com. on Human Equality, 1976-80; exec. asst. to Gov. Otis R. Bowen, Ind., 1973-75; dir. Ind. Commn. on Status Women, 1973-74; bd. dirs. Ind. Council Chs.; editor Ford Assos. pubs., 1972-86; mem. Pres.'s Adv. Council on Drug Abuse, 1976-77. Admitted to Ind. bar, 1972. Adult counselor Girl Scouts U.S.A., 1934-40; bd. dirs. Ind. Task Force Women's Health, 1976-80; mem. exec. bd., bd. dirs. Ind.-Ky. Synod Lutheran Ch., 1972-78; bd. dirs., mem. council St. Marks Lutheran Ch., Butler, 1970-76; mem. social services personnel bd.; mem. DeKalb County (Ind.) Sheriff's Merit Bd., 1983-87; founder, dir., pres. Ind. Caucus for Animal Legislation and Leadership, 1984-87. Mem. or ex-mem. AAUW, AAAS, Genetics Soc. Am., Am. Human Genetics Soc., Am. Genetic Assn., Am. Inst. Biol. Scis., Am. Soc. Zoologists, La., Miss., Ind., Iowa acads. sci., Bot. Soc. Am., Ecol. Soc. Am., Am. (dir.), Ind. (dir.), DeKalb County (dir.) bar assns., Humane Soc. U.S. (dir. 1970-88), DeKalb County Humane Soc. (founder, dir. 1970-86), Ind. Fedn. Humane Socs. (dir. 1970-84), Nat. Assn. Women Lawyers (dir.), Bus. and Profl. Women's Club, Nat. Assn. Republican Women (dir.), Women's Equity Action League (dir.), Assn. So. Biologists, Phi Kappa Phi. Club: Altrusa. Editor: Breeder's Jour., 1958-63; numerous vols. on dog genetics and breeding, guide dogs for the blind. Contbr. over 2000 sci. and popular publs. on cytogenetics, dog breeding and legal topics; contbr. Am. Kennel Club Gazette, 1970-81, also others. Researcher in field. Family and matrimonial, General practice, Civil rights. Home and Office: 824 E 7th St Auburn IN 46706

FORD, MICHAEL RAYE, lawyer; b. Blackwell, Okla., Sept. 1, 1945; s. Oscar Raye and Lucille Belton (Ray) F.; m. Carol Annette, June 17, 1972; children—Seth Michael, Jared Raye. Student Northwestern U., 1963-64; B.A., U. Okla., 1967, J.D., 1970; postgrad. (scholar) U. Wis., Madison, 1967, Georgetown U. Law Ctr., 1971-72; LL.M., George Washington U., 1974. Bar: Okla. 1970, U.S. Dist. Ct. (no. dist.) Okla. 1974, U.S. Dist. Ct. (we. dist.) Okla. 1978, U.S. Ct. Appeals (10th cir.) 1975, U.S. Supreme Ct. 1974. Mem. legal dept. Cities Service Oil Co., Tulsa, 1970; asso. Gable, Gotwals, Rubin, Fox, Johnson & Baker, Tulsa, 1974-77; ptnr. Baker, Baker, Wilson, Selph & Ford, Oklahoma City, 1977-79, McKnight, Gasaway, Beck, Seals & Ford, Enid, Okla., 1979-84; sole practice, 1984; ptnr. Ford & Brown, Enid, 1984-86; ptnr. Fellers, Snider, Blankenship, Bailey & Tippens, P.C., Oklahoma City, 1987—. Trustee Cen. Christian Ch., Enid, 1982-84, deacon, 1981-85, 85— , bd. dirs., 1981—, vice chmn., 1984—; mem. pres.'s adv. council on giving Phillips U., 1981-85 ; v.p. Enid Estate Planning Council, 1982-83, pres., 1983-84. Served to capt. JAG Corps, U.S. Army, 1971-74. Mem. ABA (com. sect. taxation 1978), Okla. Bar Assn. (v.p. taxation sect. 1982-83, chmn. 1983-84, program chmn. continuing legal edn. seminar 1982), Banking and Bus. Law and Constrn. Law Forum (sec. 1980), Greater Enid C. of C. (bd. dirs; 1983-85), Order of Coif, Phi Delta Phi, Pi Kappa Alpha. Democrat. Lodge: Kiwanis (com. chmn. Enid club 1980-81, dir. 1982-86, 2d v.p. 1982-83, 1st v.p. 1983-84, pres. 1984-85, lt. gov. 1986-87). Contbr. articles to profl. jours.; articles editors, book rev. editor U. Okla. Law Rev. 1969-70. Corporate taxation, Banking, Contracts commercial. Home: 2109 Woodhill Rd Edmond OK 73034 Office: 2400 First National Ctr Oklahoma City OK 73102

FORD, MORGAN, judge; b. nr. Wheatland, N.D., Sept. 8, 1911; s. Morgan J. and Mary (Langer) F.; m. Margaret Duffy, July 30, 1955; children: William, Patrick and Michael (twins), Mary Ellen. B.A., U. North Dakota, 1935; LL.B., Georgetown U., 1938. Tchr. Dist. 102, Everest Twp., Cass Co., N.D., 1933-34; state mgr. Royal Union Fund, Des Moines, 1938-39; in gen. law practice Fargo, N.D., 1939-49; pres. Surety Mut. Health & Accident Ins. Co., Fargo, 1939-49; v.p. 1st State Bank of Casselton, N.D., 1941-49; judge U.S. Customs Ct., N.Y.C., 1949—. City atty., Casselton, 1942-48, mem. adv. bd. for registrants in selective service, 1942. Address: US Ct of Internat Trade 1 Federal Plaza New York NY 10007 *

FORD, RICHARD EDMOND, lawyer; b. Ronceverte, W.Va., May 3, 1927; s. Grady Williams and Hazel Loraine (Fry) F.; m. Sally Frances Alexander, June 14, 1952; children: Richard Edmond, Sally Anne, Melinda J. Student, U. N.C., 1950; B.S. in Bus. Adminstrn., W.Va. U., 1951, LL.B., 1954. Bar: W.Va. 1954. Assoc. Holt & Haynes, Lewisburg, W.Va., 1954-55; ptnr. Haynes & Ford, Lewisburg, 1955-74; firm Haynes, Ford & Rowe, Lewisburg, 1975—; pres. W.Va. State Bar, 1978-79; dir. Greenbrier Cable Corp. Mem. W.Va. Legislature, 1961-64; bd. dirs. W.Va. U. Found., Daywood Found. (v.p. 1986—), Faculty Merit Found. W.Va., W.Va. Legal Services Plan, 1973-79; trustee Greenbrier Coll. for Women, 1960-73; mem. exec. bd. Buckskin council Boy Scouts Am.; mem. adv. bd. Greenbrier Community Coll. Center; mem. vis. com. Coll. Law, W.Va. U., 1972-74. Served as ensign U.S. Maritime Service, 1945-47. Recipient Outstanding Alumnus award W.Va. U. Coll. Law, 1980. Fellow Am. Bar Found., Am. Judicature Soc.; mem. ABA (ho. of dels. 1977-80), W.Va. Bar Assn. (v.p. 1965-66, 75-76), Greenbrier County Bar Assn. (pres. 1964-66, 81-82), W.Va. Law Sch. Assn. (pres. 1966-67), Nat. Conf. Commrs. Uniform State Laws, Am. Coll. Real Estate Lawyers, W.Va. U. Alumni Assn. (pres. 1971), Phi Beta Kappa, Sigma Chi, Phi Delta Phi, Order of Vandalia. Democrat. Methodist. Clubs: Masons, KT, Shriners, Lewisburg Elks. Real property, Probate, State civil litigation. Home: Buckingham Acres Lewisburg WV 24901 Office: 203 W Randolph St Lewisburg WV 24901

FORD, SEABURY HURD, lawyer; b. Burton, Ohio, Sept. 26, 1902; s. Carl Boughton and Elizabeth McKee (Hurd) F.; m. Helen Paar, Dec. 1940 (dec. Feb. 1976). A.B., Western Res. U., 1923, J.D., 1925. Bar: Ohio 1925, U.S. Supreme Ct. 1965. Pros. atty. Portage County (Ohio), 1945-53; mem. Portage County Bd. Elections, 1972-76; law dir. City of Aurora (Ohio), 1966-76; ptnr. Ford, Simon & Norris, Ravenna, Ohio; dir. Bank One of Ravenna. Mem. Ravenna C. of C.; bd. dirs. Aurora C. of C. Served with U.S. Army. Fellow Ohio Bar Assn.; mem. ABA, Cleve. Bar Assn., Akron Bar Assn., Portage County Bar Assn. Republican. Clubs: Pine Lake Trout, Aurora Country, Masons, Elks, Kiwanis. Personal injury, Probate, Real property. Home: 12 W Garfield Rd Aurora OH 44202 Office: 200 W Main St Ravenna OH 44266

FORDE, KEVIN MICHAEL, lawyer; b. Chgo., Sept. 5, 1938; s. John Patrick and Agnes M. (Considine) F.; m. Janice M. Reilly, June 28, 1968; children: Michael Kevin, Maura Francis. BBA, Marquette U., 1960; JD, Loyola U., Chgo., 1963. Bar: Ill. 1963, U.S. Ct. Appeals (7th cir.) 1966, U.S. Ct. Appeals (D.C. and fed. cir.) 1980, U.S. Supreme Ct. 1970. Counsel, pres. county Cook County, Chgo., 1964-66; law clk. to chief judge U.S. Dist. Ct. (no. dist.) Ill., Chgo., 1966-70; sole practice Chgo., 1970—; mem. faculty John Marshall Law Sch., Chgo., 1968-70. Cons. editor Class Action Handbook, 1979; contbr. articles to profl. jours. Chmn. compensation rev. bd. State of Ill., 1984—. Served to capt. USAR, 1966-69. Recipient Disting. Service award Ill. Judges Assn., 1982, Judges of Cook County, Chgo., 1982. Fellow Internat. Acad. Trial Lawyers, Am. Coll. Trial Lawyers; mem. Chgo. Bar Assn. (pres. 1981-82), Union League. Roman Catholic. Federal civil litigation, State civil litigation. Office: 111 W Washington Chicago IL 60602

FORDHAM, BENJAMIN CLEVELAND, lawyer; b. Statesboro, Ga., Jan. 30, 1953; s. Benjamin E. and Effie Helen (Cleveland) F.; children: Benjamin Richard, Christoper Russell. BA, Duke U., 1975; JD, Vanderbilt U., 1978. Bar: Ga. 1978, Tenn. 1979, U.S. Dist. Ct. (no. dist.) Ga. 1979, U.S. Dist. Ct. (mid. dist.) Tenn. 1979, U.S. Dist. Ct. (we. and ea. dists.) Tenn. 1982. Assoc. Swift, Currie, McGhee & Heirs, Atlanta, 1978-79; from assoc. to ptnr. Tune, Entrekin & White, Nashville, 1979—. Mem. rules subcom. Tenn. Reps., 1980, Mid. Tenn. Muscular Distrophy Telethon, 1982, Tenn. Med. Malpractice Rev. Bd., 1982-85, adv. com. mid. dist. Tenn. Duke U. Alumni Com., 1983-87; capt. group Clinic Bowl, 1984-85; asst. coach Pee Wee League baseball, 1984-86; bd. dirs. Tenn. Foster Grandparents Inc., 1984-85; co-head coach high sch. mock trial Tenn. Young Lawyers Conf., 1985-86. Patrick Wilson merit scholar Vanderbilt U., 1975-78. Mem. ABA, Tenn. Bar Assn. (legis. com. 1984, 85, polit. action com. study subcom. 1984-86), Nashville Bar Assn., Nashville Jr. C. of C. (group capt. bowl 1984, 85, legal adv. 1985-87, Clinic Bowl Bronze award 1982, Silver award 1983, 84, Gold award 1985, 86, Top 10 Percent award 1985, 86, Spotlight award 1986). Baptist. Avocation: sports. State civil litigation, Personal injury, Construction. Home: 239 Summit Ridge Dr Nashville TN 37215 Office: Tune Entrekin & White 2100 First American Ctr Nashville TN 37238

FOREMAN, DALE MELVIN, lawyer; b. Los Angeles, May 10, 1948; s. C. Melvin and Sylvia (Ahnlund) F.; m. Gail Burgener, June 24, 1972; children: Mari Elizabeth, Ann Marie, James Sterling. AB cum laude, Harvard U., 1970, JD, 1975. Bar: Wash. 1976, U.S. Dist. Ct. (we. dist.) Wash. 1977, U.S. Ct. Claims 1977, U.S. Dist. Ct. (ea. dist.) Wash. 1981, U.S. Ct. Appeals (9th cir.) 1981. Ptnr. Jeffers, Danielson & Foreman, Wenatchee, Wash., 1975-81, Jardine, Foreman & Appel, Wenatchee, 1981—; Mem. Spl. Adv. Commn. on Pub. Opinion, U.S. Dept. of State, 1970-72, Canon Mine Adv. Commn., 1984—. Author: Whiplash and The Jaw Joint, 1985, (novel) Panama'm Tombé, 1986. Chmn. Chelan County Rep. Cen. Com., Wenatchee, 1977-79, 82-84; bd. dirs. Am. and Fgn. Christian Union, N.Y.C., 1985—. Presbyterian. Lodge: Rotary. Avocation: quarterhorses. State civil litigation, Insurance, Antitrust. Home: 323 Chatham Hill Rd Wenatchee WA 98801 Office: Jardine Foreman & Appel 701 N Chelan Wenatchee WA 98801

FOREMAN, JAMES LOUIS, judge; b. Metropolis, Ill., May 12, 1927; s. James C. and Anna Elizabeth (Henne) F.; m. Mabel Inez Dunn, June 16, 1948; children—Beth Foreman Banks, Rhonda Foreman Riepe, Nanette. B.S., U. Ill., 1950, J.D., 1952. Bar: Ill. bar. Individual practice law Metropolis, Ill.; partner firm Chase and Foreman, Metropolis, until 1972; Ill. state's atty. Massac County; asst. atty. gen. State of Ill.; chief judge So. Dist. of Ill. East St. Louis, 1972—. Pres. Bd. of Edn., Metropolis. Served with USNR, 1945-46. Mem. Am. Bar Assn., Ill. State Bar Assn., Metropolis C. of C. (past pres.). Republican. Home: PO Box 866 Metropolis IL 62960 Office: PO Box 186 East St Louis IL 62202

FORER, LOIS G., judge; b. Chgo., Mar. 22, 1914; d. Harry Goldstein and Lorraine (Beilman) Goldstein Forer; m. Morris Forer, June 30, 1940; children—Stuart, John, Hope Abigail Forer Ross. A.B. with honors, Northwestern U., 1935, J.D., 1938. Bar: Ill. 1938, Pa. 1945, U.S. Dist. Ct. (ea. dist.) Pa. 1945, U.S. Ct. Appeals (3d cir.) 1945, U.S. Supreme Ct. 1942. Legal staff REA, Washington, 1938-40; law clk. to presiding judge U.S. Ct. Appeals (3d cir.) 1941-46; legal staff, Office of Price Stabilization, Phila., 1948; dep. atty. gen. Commonwealth of Pa., Harrisburg, 1955-63; atty.-in-charge Office for Juveniles, Community Legal Services, Phila., 1966-68; sole practice, Phila., 1946-71; judge Ct. of Common Pleas, Phila., 1971—; Cons. Kerner Commn. Author: No one Will Listen: How Our Legal System Brutalizes the Youthful Poor, 1970; The Death of the Law, 1975, Criminals and Victims: A Trial Judge Reflects on Crime and Punishment, 1980, paperback edit., 1984, Money and Justice: Who Owns the Courts, 1984, paperback edit., 1985; also articles. Editor-in-chief Jour. Nat. Assn. of Women Lawyers, 1966-67. Nat. bd. dirs. ACLU, 1960-80; mem. Lawyers Com. on Civil Rights under Law; mem. Lehman Com. on Immigration and Naturalization, Pa. Gov.'s Com. on Children and Youth; mem. drafting com. Interstate Compact on Del. River. Mem. Nat. Law Sci. Council, ABA (Ross Essay award 1950). Democrat. Jewish. Office: Ct of Common Pleas 1004 One E Pa Sq Philadelphia PA 19107

FORGER, ALEXANDER DARROW, lawyer; b. N.Y.C., Feb. 19, 1923. B.A. with honors, Princeton U., 1945; J.D., Yale U., 1950. Assoc. Milbank, Tweed, Hadley & McCloy, N.Y.C., 1950-57, ptnr., 1958—. Trustee Rockefeller U.; chmn. bd., trustee N.Y. Law Sch.; chmn. bd. Legal Aid Soc.; officer, mem. exec. com., bd. dirs. Whitney M. Young Jr. Meml. Found., Inc.; bd. dirs. Leonhardt Found., Inc., Gerard B. Lambert Meml. Found., Inc. Fellow Am. Bar Found., N.Y. Bar Found. (v.p., bd. dirs.), Am. Coll. Probate Counsel; mem. ABA (ho. of dels., council individual rights and responsibilities, N.Y. State del.), N.Y. State Bar Assn. (ho. of dels.), Nat. Conf. Bar Founds. (trustee), Assn. Bar City N.Y., N.Y. County Lawyers' Assn., Westchester County Bar Assn., Lawyers' Com. for Civil Rights Under

Law. Office: Milbank Tweed Hadley & McCloy 1 Chase Manhattan Plaza New York NY 10005

FORKIN, THOMAS S., lawyer; b. Berkeley Twp., N.J., Dec. 20, 1937; s. Thomas Francis and Sally Marie (Johnston) F.; m. E. Syvonne Keffer, June 27, 1964; children—Keith A., Tracey S. B.A. in English, Villanova U., 1959, LL.B., 1962. Bar: N.J. 1963, U.S. Dist. Ct. N.J. 1963, U.S. Supreme Ct. 1966, U.S. Ct. Appeals (3d cir.) 1970. Assoc. Brown, Connery, Kulp, Wille, Purnell & Greene, Camden, N.J., 1962-70, ptnr., 1970-72; ptnr. Forkin & McShane, P.A., Cherry Hill, N.J., 1972—; instr. Villanova U. Sch. Law, 1969-73, Burlington County Coll., 1974-75; spl. dep. atty. gen. Rate Counsel, 1970-71; lectr. in field. Co-author: Tax Strategies in Divorce, 1987; contbr. articles to legal publs. Mem. bd. consultors Villanova U. Law Sch., 1979—. Fellow Am. Acad. Matrimonial Lawyers (v.p. 1973-77, bd. govs. 1977-80), Internat. Acad. Matrimonial Lawyers; mem. N.J. Acad. Matrimonial Lawyers, Assn. Trial Lawyers Am., Burlington County Bar Assn. (chmn. family law sect. 1976, 80-82), Camden County Bar Assn. (chmn. family law sect. 1975, mem. law for layman adult edn. com. 1980—), N.J. Bar Assn. (sec. 1975, chmn. family law sect. 1977, exec. com. 1987-88), ABA. Republican. Roman Catholic. Clubs: Union League (Phila.); Metropolitan (Chgo.); Tavistock Country (Haddonfield, N.J.). Family and matrimonial, Personal income taxation, Estate planning. Office: Forkin & McShane PA 750 N Kings Hwy Cherry Hill NJ 08034

FORMAN, JONATHAN BARRY, law educator; b. Cleve.; m. Lani Lee Malysa, Nov. 18, 1984. BA in Psychology, Northwestern U., 1973; MA in Psychology, U. Iowa, 1975; JD, U. Mich., 1978; MA in Econs., George Washington U., 1983. Clk. U.S. Ct. Claims, Washington, 1978-79; trial atty. Tax Div. U.S. Dept. Justice (tax Div.), Washington, 1979-83; tax counsel U.S. senator Daniel Moynihan, Washington, 1983-84; editorial staff Tax Notes, Arlington, Va., 1985; assoc. prof. law U. Okla., Norman, 1985—; adj. prof. Antioch Sch. of Law, Washington, 1981-85. Author: The Administrations 1985 Tax Proposals, 1985. Mem. ABA (taxation sect.), D.C. Bar Assn. Democrat. Jewish. Avocations: camping, birdwatching, photography. Corporate taxation, Personal income taxation, State and local taxation. Office: U Okla Coll of Law 300 Timberdell Norman OK 73019

FORMAN, ROBERT STEVEN, lawyer; b. Oceanside, N.Y., Feb. 18, 1953; s. Joseph and Selma (Kissiloff) F.; m. Deborah Jean Spencer, July 11, 1976; children: Michael, Amanda. Student, Nassau Community Coll., 1971-74; BBA, Hofstra U., 1976; JD, U. Puget Sound, 1979. Bar: Wash. 1980, Fla. 1981. Title examiner Pioneer Nat. Title, Everett, Wash., 1979; staff atty. Safeco Ins. Co., Seattle, 1979-80; assoc. Law Office of James B. Chaplin, Ft. Lauderdale, Fla., 1980-82; sole practice Ft. Lauderdale, 1982—. Mem. Downtown Council, Ft. Lauderdale, 1986—. Recipient Corpus Juris Secundum award West Pub. Co., 1977. Mem. ABA, Broward County Bar Assn., Atty.'s Title Ins. Fund. Jewish. Avocations: boating, golf. General corporate, Real property, Contracts commercial. Office: 800 E Broward Blvd #608 Fort Lauderdale FL 33301

FORMAN, THOMAS M., corporate lawyer; b. 1945. BS, U. Mich., 1967, JD, 1973. Asst. gen. counsel Firestone Tire and Rubber Co., Akron, Ohio, 1981, asst. sec., 1981-83, assoc. gen. counsel, 1983-85, v.p. gen. counsel, 1985—. Office: Firestone Tire & Rubber Co 1200 Firestone Pkwy Akron OH 44317 *

FORNEY, SUSAN JANE, lawyer; b. York, Pa., Jan. 2, 1954; d. Charles Binkley and Miriam Irene (Meyer) F.; m. Michael Lynn Harvey, Oct. 22, 1983; 1 child, John Martin. BA, Pa. State U., 1975; JD, Cornell U., 1978. Bar: Pa. 1978, U.S. Dist. Ct. (mid. and ea. dists.) Pa., U.S. Ct. Appeals (3d cir.), U.S. Supreme Ct. Dep. atty. gen. Pa. Dept. Justice, Harrisburg, 1978-81; dep. atty. gen. Office Atty. Gen., Harrisburg, 1981-85, sr. dep. atty. gen., employment litigation coordinator, 1985—. Mem. Community Devel. Action Com., Harrisburg, 1983—; pres. Uptown Coalition, Harrisburg, 1984—. Mem. ABA, Pa. Bar Assn., Harrisburg Women Lawyers Assn. (sec. 1983-84), Phi Kappa Phi (fellow). Federal civil litigation, State civil litigation, Civil rights. Office: Office Atty Gen Strawberry Sq 15th Floor Harrisburg PA 17120

FORREST, HERBERT EMERSON, lawyer; b. N.Y.C., Sept. 20, 1923; s. Jacob K. and Rose (Fried) F.; m. Marilyn Lefsky, Jan. 12, 1952; children: Glenn Clifford, Andrew Matthew. B.A. with distinction, George Washington U., 1948; J.D. with highest honors, 1952; student, CCNY, 1941, Ohio U., 1943-44. Bar: Va. 1952, D.C. 1952, U.S. Supreme Ct. 1956, Md. 1959. Plate printer Bur. Engraving and Printing, Washington, 1946-52; law clk. to chief judge Bolitha J. Laws U.S. Dist. Ct., Washington, 1952-55; practice in Washington, 1952—; mem. firm Welch & Morgan, 1955-65; mem. firm Steptoe & Johnson, 1965-85, of counsel, 1986-87; trial atty. Fed. Programs Br. Civil div. U.S. Dept. Justice, Washington, 1987—; chmn. adv. bd. D.C. Criminal Justice Act, 1971-74; sec. com. admissions and grievances U.S. Ct. Appeals, D.C., 1973-79; mem. Title-1 audit hearing bd. U.S. Office Edn. HEW, 1976-79; mem. edn. appeals bd. U.S. Dept. Edn., 1979-82; mem. Lawyer's Support Com. for Visitors Service Center, 1975-87. Contbr. articles to legal jours.; advisory bd.: Duke Law Jour, 1969-75. Pres. Whittier Woods PTA, 1970-71. Served with U.S. Army, 1943-46. Recipient Walsh award in Irish history, 1952, Goddard award in commerce, 1952. Fellow Am. Bar Found.; mem. George Washington Law Assn., Am. Judicature Soc., ABA (council 1972-75, 1981-84, budget officer 1985—, vice chmn. task force on sect. devel. 1987—, chmn. com. on agy. rule making 1968-81, chmn. membership com. 1984-85, editor ann. reports 1973—, adminstrv. law sect., mem. communications com. public utilities law sect., vice chmn. industry regulation com. 1985-86, chmn. communications subcom. 1983-85 antitrust law sect., internat. law sect., sect. sci. and tech. communications forum), Va. State Bar Assn., Fed. Bar Assn. (chmn. jud. rev. com. 1981-85, vice chmn. adminstrv. law sect. 1985-87), Fed. Communications Bar Assn. (v.p. 1981-82, pres. 1982-83, chmn. telecommunications com. 1983—), D.C. Bar Assn. (past sec., exec. com.), NAM, Nat. Assn. Bar Pres., Washington Council Lawyers, Legal Aid and Pub. Defender Assn., Am. Arbitration Assn. (comml. panel 1976-87), D.C. Unified Bar (bd. govs. 1976-79, chmn. com. on employment discrimination complaint service 1973-79, chmn. task force on services to public 1974-78, chmn. com. on appointment counsel in criminal cases 1978—, co-chmn. com. on participation govt. employees in pro bono activities 1977-79), Broadcast Pioneers, Order of Coif, Phi Beta Kappa, Pi Gamma Mu., Artus, Phi Eta Sigma, Phi Delta Phi. Democrat. Lodge: B'nai Brith. Administrative and regulatory, Communications. Home: 8706 Bellwood Rd Bethesda MD 20817 Office: US Dept Justice 10th & Pennsylvania Ave NW Room 3342 Main Bldg Washington DC 20530

FORREST, ROBERT EDWIN, lawyer; b. Washington, July 31, 1949; s. Henry Smith and Jane (Witt) F.; m. Deirdre Loretto McGahey, Sept. 23, 1978; children: Matthew Henry, John Robert. BA, Northwestern U., 1971; JD, Georgetown U., 1974. Bar: D.C. 1975, U.S. Ct. Appeals (D.C. cir.) 1976, U.S. Dist. Ct. D.C. 1976, U.S. Supreme Ct. 1980, U.S. Dist. Ct. (ea. and we. dists.) Mich. 1981, Md. 1984. Law clk. to presiding justice U.S. Dist. Ct. D.C, Washington, 1974-75; tax div. trial atty. U.S. Dept. Justice, Washington, 1975-81; prin. ptnr. Raymond & Dillon, P.C., Detroit, 1981—. Mem. Fed. Bar Assn. (exec. bd. 1984—, sec. 1986—). Methodist. Personal income taxation, Federal civil litigation, Criminal. Home: 4861 Malibu Dr Bloomfield Hills MI 48013 Office: Raymond & Dillon PC 400 Renaissance Ctr Suite 2370 Detroit MI 48243

FORRESTAL, MICHAEL VINCENT, lawyer; b. N.Y.C., Nov. 26, 1927; s. James Vincent and Josephine (Ogden) F. Student, Princeton U., 1949; LL.B., Harvard U., 1953. Bar: N.Y. 1954. Since practiced in N.Y.C; partner Shearman & Sterling, 1960—; spl. asst. to Averell Harriman (dir. Marshall Plan), 1948-50; sr. mem. White House Nat. Security Staff, 1962-65; sec. tripartite Naval Commn., Berlin, 1946; asst. U.S. naval attache, Moscow, USSR, 1946-47. Chmn. Met. Opera Guild, 1965-70; bd. dirs., treas. Met. Opera Assn., 1967—, Nat. Opera Inst., 1971-80; exec. sec. adv. com. Kennedy Inst. Politics, Harvard U., 1967-82; trustee Inst. Advanced Study, Princeton, N.J., 1970—; trustee Phillips Exeter Acad., 1979—, pres. bd. trustees, 1981—. Mem. ABA, Assn. Bar City N.Y., Am. Arbitration Assn. (dir. 1980-83), Council Fgn. Relations. Episcopalian. Clubs: Racquet and Tennis (N.Y.C.), Links (N.Y.C.); Metropolitan (Washington); Travellers (Paris, France). Home: 25 Central Park West New York NY 10023 Office: 153 E 53d St New York NY 10022

FORRESTER, J. OWEN, judge; b. 1939. B.S., Ga. Inst. Tech., 1961; LL.B., Emory U., 1966. Bar: Ga. Staff atty. Ga. gubernatorial candidate, 1966-67; assoc. firm Fisher & Phillips, Atlanta, 1967-69; magistrate U.S. Dist. Ct. (no. dist.) Ga., Atlanta, 1976-81, judge, 1981—. Judicial administration. Office: US District Court 2367 US Courthouse 75 Spring St Atlanta GA 30303 *

FORRESTER, STEPHEN CARY, lawyer; b. San Antonio, Nov. 8, 1954; s. Cleveland Edward and Jane Evelyn (Pitman) F.; m. Erika Gertrude Zuehlke, July 17, 1982. BA, U. Ark., 1977; JD, Harvard U., 1980. Bar: Ariz. 1980, U.S. Dist. Ct. Ariz. 1980. Assoc. Fennemore, Craig, von Ammon, Udall & Powers, Phoenix, 1980-85; ptnr. Kalish & Forrester, P.C., Phoenix, 1985—. Mem. ABA, Ariz. Bar Assn. (bankruptcy sect., creditor/debtor's rights com.), Maricopa County Bar Assn., Am. Bankruptcy Inst. State civil litigation, Bankruptcy. Office: Kalish & Forrester PC 9002 N Central Ave Phoenix AZ 85020

FORSMAN, ALPHEUS EDWIN, lawyer; b. Montgomery, Ala., May 12, 1941; m. Greta Friedman, July 5, 1964; children: Ellen E., Jennifer Ann. BA, George Washington U., 1963, JD, 1967. Bar: Va. 1968, D.C. 1969, U.S. Supreme Ct. 1973, Mo. 1979. Trademark examiner U.S. Patent Office, Washington, 1967-69; staff atty. Marriott Corp., Washington, 1969-72; assoc. Roylance, Abrams, Berdo and Kaul, Washington, 1972-75, ptnr., 1975-78; trademark atty. Ralston Purina Co., St. Louis, 1978-81, trademark counsel, 1981—. Mem. ABA, Bar. Assn. Met. St. Louis, Inst. Trade Mark Agts. Trademark and copyright. Home: 417 Glan Tai Dr Manchester MO 63011 Office: Ralston Purina Co Checkerboard Sq Saint Louis MO 63164

FORSTADT, JOSEPH LAWRENCE, lawyer; b. Bklyn., Feb. 21, 1940; B.A., CCNY, 1961; LL.B., NYU, 1964. Bar: N.Y. 1965, U.S. Supreme Ct. 1968. Dep. commr. N.Y.C. Dept. Licenses, 1967-68, acting commr., 1968-69; acting commr. N.Y.C. Dept. Consumer Affairs, 1969; asst. adminstr. Econ. Devel. Adminstrn., 1969; assoc. Stroock & Stroock & Lavan, N.Y.C., 1969-75, ptnr., 1976—; lectr. in trial practice N.Y. County Lawyers Assn.; mem. N.Y.C. Rent Guidelines Bd., 1984—. Judge Jacob Markowitz scholar NYU, N.Y.C., 1964. Mem. Fed. Bar Council, Am. Judicature Soc. Federal civil litigation, State civil litigation. Office: Stroock & Stroock & Lavan 7 Hanover Sq New York NY 10004

FORSTER, JAMES FRANCIS, lawyer; b. N.Y.C., Apr. 26, 1956; s. James Joseph and Kathleen Ann (McCullaugh) F. BA in Polit. Sci. and Spanish, Bradley U., 1978; JD, Hofstra U., 1981. Bar: N.Y. 1982, U.S. Dist. Ct. (so. and ea. dists.) N.Y. 1982, N.J. 1986, U.S. Dist. Ct. N.J. 1986. Law clk. to presiding justice Long Beach (N.Y.) City Ct., 1979-80; assoc. Max E. Greenberg, Cantor & Reiss, N.Y.C., 1981-83, Ostrower & Gart P.C., Lake Success, N.Y., 1983-85, Postner & Rubin, N.Y.C., 1986—; vis. asst. prof. constrn. mgmt. program Sch. Architecture of Pratt Inst., Bklyn., 1987—. Columnist Consulting Engineer mag., 1980-85; assoc. editor Hofstra U. Law Rev., 1981-82. Mem. ABA, N.Y. Bar Assn., N.Y. County Lawyers Assn., N.J. Bar Assn. Roman Catholic. Government contracts and claims, Construction, State civil litigation. Office: Postner & Rubin 17 Battery Pl New York NY 10004

FORSYTH, JOHN EMERY, lawyer; b. Chgo., Nov. 26, 1954; s. John Smith and Geraldine (Mihalek) F.; m. Mary Lynn Gilliam, Jan. 11, 1975; 1 child, Bonnie Lynn. Student, Regis Coll., 1972-74; BSBA, Creighton U., 1976; JD, U. Okla., 1978. Bar: Okla. 1978, U.S. Dist. Ct. (we. dist.) Okla. 1982, U.S. Dist. Ct. (no. dist.) Okla. 1984, U.S. Dist. Ct. (ea. dist.) Okla. 1985. Sole practice Cushing, Okla., 1978—; asst. dist. atty. Payne County, Cushing, 1979-81; ptnr. Forsyth & Ahrberg, P.A., Cushing, 1981-82; gen. counsel TU Internat., Inc., Cushing, 1982-83. Editor U. Okla. Law Rev., 1977-78. Commr. Cushing Planning Commn., 1979-84, chmn. 1982-84; commr. Cushing City Commn., 1984—, chmn., 1985—; chmn. Cushing Hosp. Authority, 1985—. Recipient Outstanding Dedication to Law Enforcement award Cushing Police Dept., 1981; named one of Outstanding Young Men of Am., 1984-85. Mem. ABA, Okla. Bar Assn., Payne County Bar Assn., Cushing C. of C., Cushing Jaycees (treas. 1979-80; Jaycee of Month, 1980, one of three Outstanding Young Oklahomans 1985, Disting. Service award 1985). Roman Catholic. Lodge: Lions. General practice, Oil and gas leasing, Contracts commercial. Office: 317 W Broadway PO Box 7 Cushing OK 74023-0007

FORT, D. STEPHEN, lawyer; b. Waco, Tex., Jan. 31, 1955; s. David Lynson Fort and Ruth (Hutcherson) Baker. BS in Petroleum Engring., Tex. A&M U., 1977; JD, So. Meth. U., 1980. Bar: Tex. 1980, U.S. Dist. Ct. (no. dist.) Tex. 1981. Assoc. John L. Roach, Inc., Dallas, 1980-84; sole practice Dallas, 1984—. Mem. ABA (oil, gas, mineral law sects.), Soc. Petroleum Engrs., Dallas Bar Assn. Republican. Avocations: sports, hunting. Oil and gas leasing, Probate. Office: 880 Two Energy Sq Dallas TX 75206

FORT, JEFFREY EDWARD, lawyer; b. Honolulu, Apr. 9, 1952; s. William Edward and Shirley (Christ) F.; Elizabeth Jane Yetzer, Nov. 23, 1974; children: Jason, Julie. BS, U.S. Naval Acad., 1974; JD, Ohio State U., 1982. Bar: Ohio 1982. Commd. ensign USN, 1974, advanced through grades to lt., 1978, res., 1979; atty. Marathon Oil Co., Robinson, Ill., 1982-84, Findlay, Ohio, 1984—. Served with USNR, 1979—. Mem. ABA, Ohio Bar Assn. Republican. Avocations: running, weight lifting, tennis. Environment, Oil and gas leasing, General corporate. Home: 842 Beech Ave Findlay OH 45840 Office: Marathon Oil Co 539 S Main Findlay OH 45840

FORT, LYMAN RANKIN, lawyer; b. Stronghurst, Ill., June 8, 1922; s. Elbridge C. and Bess P. (Allison) F.; m. Mildred Lucille Gibb, June 1, 1946; children—Jeff, Jane Ann, Tim. Student Bradley U., 1940-43; J.D., Northwestern U., 1949. Bar: Ill. 1949, U.S. Dist. Ct. (no., so. and cen. dists.) Ill. 1955, U.S. Ct. Appeals (8th cir.) 1972, U.S. Tax Ct. 1977. Ptnr., Charles E. and Lyman R. Fort, 1949-69; sole practice, Stronghurst, 1969-82; sr. ptnr. Fort, Fort & Hennenfent, Stronghurst, 1982—. Served with AUS, 1943-46; ETO. Mem. ABA, Ill. Bar Assn., Assn. Trial Lawyers Ill., Am. Legion, VFW. Republican. Presbyterian. Estate planning, Probate, Personal income taxation. Address: Fort Fort & Hennenfent Stronghurst IL 61480

FORTADO, MICHAEL GEORGE, lawyer, diversified energy, engineering and construction company executive; b. Wichita Falls, Tex., Oct. 29, 1943; s. Antonio and Flossie Juanita (Bowers) F.; m. Avis Ann Smith, Mar. 12, 1964; children: Michael Scott, Angela Avis, Shannon Michelle. B.B.A., Midwestern U., Wichita Falls, 1965; LL.B., U. Tex., Austin, 1968. Bar: Tex. 1968. Asso. atty. firm McClure & Sharpe, Houston, 1968-69; atty. ENSERCH Corp. (and predecessor), Dallas, 1969-71; corp. sec., asst. gen. counsel ENSERCH Corp. (and predecessor), 1971—. Mem. Am. Soc. Corp. Secs. (dir. 1980-83), ABA, State Bar Tex., Dallas Bar Assn., Kappa Alpha Order, Delta Sigma Pi, Phi Alpha Delta. Mem. Christian Ch. (Disciples of Christ). Club: DAC Country. Securities, General corporate. Office: 300 S St Paul St Dallas TX 75201

FORTE, WESLEY ELBERT, insurance company executive; b. Worcester, Mass., Dec. 1, 1933; s. Elbert W. and Ethel M. (Lyons) F.; m. Margaret Ellen Layman, July 29, 1961; children—Laura Jean, Scott Montgomery. B.B.A., Clark U., 1956; J.D., N.Y. U., 1959, LL.M., 1965. Bar: Pa. 1960, Ohio 1972, U.S. Supreme Ct 1972, Tex. 1974, D.C. 1975, N.Y. 1980. Atty. Dechert, Price & Rhoads, Phila., 1959-62; atty. corporate law dept. Standard Brands, Inc., N.Y.C., 1962-66; atty., foods div. counsel Borden, Inc., N.Y.C., 1966-71; sr. counsel domestic ops. Borden, Inc., 1971-72; sr. v.p. legal affairs Campbell-Taggart, Inc., Dallas, 1972-73; exec. v.p., gen. counsel, dir. Campbell-Taggart, Inc., 1973-79; sr. v.p. law USLIFE Corp., N.Y.C., 1979-85; exec. v.p., gen. counsel USLIFE Corp., 1985—. Contbr. articles to profl. jours. General corporate, Administrative and regulatory, Antitrust. Home: 8 Paddington Circle Bronxville NY 10708 Office: USLIFE Corp 125 Maiden Ln New York NY 10038

FORTENBERRY, JOSEPH EDWIN, lawyer; b. Washington, Sept. 2, 1944; s. Charles Nolan and Mae (Edwards) F.; m. Dorothy Ashley Doherty, Nov. 24, 1972; 1 dau., Dorothy Ashley. A.B., Harvard Coll., 1966; LL.B., Yale U., 1969. Bar: Ala., 1969, U.S. Dist. Ct. (mid. dist.) Ala. 1969, U.S. Supreme Ct. 1972, N.Y. 1973, U.S. Dist. Ct. (so. dist.) N.Y. 1974, U.S. Ct. Appeals (2d cir.) 1974, D.C. 1982, U.S. Dist. Ct. D.C. 1986. Law clk. to judge U.S. Ct. Appeals (5th cir.), Montgomery, Ala., 1969-70; assoc. Rushton, Stakely, Johnston & Garrett, Montgomery, 1970-71, Donovan Leisure Newton & Irvine, N.Y.C., 1971-79; atty. antitrust div. U.S. Dept. Justice, Washington, 1979—, co-chmn. antitrust com. D.C. Bar, 1986-87. Recipient spl. achievement award U.S. Dept. Justice, 1980, 82. Mem. ABA, Fed. Bar Assn., Am. Econ. Assn., Selden Soc. Democrat. Episcopalian. Contbr. articles to profl. publs. Antitrust, Legal history, Federal civil litigation. Office: Room 8231 555 4th St Washington DC 20001

FORTGANG, CHAIM JACOB, lawyer; b. Benzheim, Frankfort, Fed. Republic Germany, July 6, 1947; came to U.S., 1947; s. Pinkas and Paula (Zoberman) F.; m. Fay Rosalyn Roiter, Nov. 16, 1969; children: Leyla, Shabtai, Chami, Gitti. BA summa cum laude, Bklyn. Coll., 1968; LLM, NYU, 1971. From assoc. to ptnr. Wachtell, Lipton. Rosen & Katz, N.Y.C., 1971—; adj. assoc. prof. N.Y.U. Sch. Law, 1984—. bd. dirs. Ethnic Millions Pol. Action Com., N.Y.C.; bd. dirs., v.p. Shulamith Sch. for Girls, Bklyn., Nat. Jewish Commn. Law and Public Affairs, N.Y.C. Mem. ABA, N.Y. State Bar Assn., Assn. of Bar of City of N.Y., Nat. Bankruptcy Conf., Order of Coif, Phi Beta Kappa. Jewish. Avocations: reading, sports. Bankruptcy. Office: Wachtell Lipton Rosen & Katz 299 Park Ave 35th Floor New York NY 10171

FORTIER, ALBERT MARK, JR., lawyer; b. Cambridge, Mass., July 22, 1936; s. Albert M. and Marie R. (Tagney) F.; m. Bente Mortensen, Nov. 10, 1964; children—John, Mark. A.B., U. Chgo., 1955; LL.B., Harvard U., 1958. Bar: Mass. 1958. Assoc. Richard S. Bowers, Boston, 1958-65; ptnr. Bowers, Fortier & Lakin, Boston, 1966-76, Rackemann, Sawyer & Brewster, Boston, 1976—. Served with USAR, 1958-64. Mem. ABA, Mass. Bar Assn., Boston Bar Assn., Am. Coll. Probate Counsel. Republican. Methodist. Clubs: Union (Boston); Brae Burn Country. Probate, General corporate. Home: 90 Craftsland Rd Chestnut Hill MA 02167 Office: One Financial Ctr Boston MA 02111

FORTIER, ROBERT FREDERIC, lawyer; b. Chgo., Sept. 5, 1949; m. Mardelle LaDonna Eide, July 27, 1974. BA with honors, U. Ill., 1971, JD, 1974. Bar: Ill. 1975, U.S. Dist. Ct. (no. dist.) Ill. 1975. Atty. Liberty Mut. Ins. Co., Chgo., 1975-76; assoc. Tews, Abbey & Theisen, Chgo., 1976-77; assoc. gen. counsel Alliance of Am. Insurer, Chgo., 1977-83; sole practice Lisle, Ill., 1983—; cons. govt. affairs Fortier Mangerial Systems Inc., Lisle, 1984—. Contbr. articles to Chgo. Sun-Times and Chgo. Tribune, 1983—. Served with USAR, 1971-76. Mem. Chgo. Bar Assn. Democrat. Roman Catholic. Avocations: history, nature. Legislative, General corporate, Insurance. Home and Office: Fortier Managerial Systems Inc 5515 E Lake Dr Suite A Lisle IL 60532

FORTIER, SAMUEL JOHN, lawyer; b. Spokane, Wash., Mar. 30, 1952; s. Charles Henry and Mary (Petersen) F.; m. Dagmar Christine Mikko, Sept. 15, 1983; 1 child, Nova Marie. BA cum laude, Boston U., 1974; JD magna cum laude, Gonzaga U., 1982. Bar: Alaska 1982, U.S. Dist. Ct. Alaska 1983. Acting exec. dir. Bristol Bay Native Assn., Dillingham, Alaska, 1974-76; fin. analyst Alaska Fedn. of Natives, Anchorage, Alaska, 1976-78; loan analyst State of Alaska, Anchorage, 1978-79; law clk. consumer ptotection div., atty. gen.'s office State of Wash., Spokane, 1980-82; assoc. Cummings & Rough P.C., Anchorage, 1982-84; ptnr. Fortier & Mikko, Anchorage, 1984—; adj. prof. U. Alaska, Anchorage, 1982-85; speaker workshop Small Bus. Adminstrn., Anchorage, 1982-85. Mem. ABA, Alaska Bar Assn. (native law sect.), Anchorage Bar Assn. Democrat. Avocations: reading, writing, camping, skiing. General corporate, Alaska native law, Federal civil litigation. Home: 8650 Pioneer Dr Anchorage AK 99504 Office: Fortier & Mikko 600 W Internat Airport Rd Suite 201 Anchorage AK 99518

FORTINO, ALFRED J., lawyer; b. Pontiac, Mich., Nov. 16, 1914; s. Michele and Giovannina F.; m. Mary Alice Damon, Feb. 15, 1941; children—Charles, Richard, Thomas. A.B., Alma Coll., 1937; M.A., U. Mich., 1938, J.D., 1940. Bar: Mich. 1940. Sr. ptnr. Fortino, Plaxton & Moskal and predecessors, Alma, Mich., 1940—. Trustee Central Mich. U., Mt. Pleasant, 1967-85; mem. Mich. State Bd. Canvassers, 1963-67. Served with U.S. Army, 1943-46. Decorated Bronze Star. Mem. ABA, Mich. Bar Assn. Republican. Presbyterian. Club: Pine River Country. State civil litigation, General corporate, Estate planning. Home: 313 E Saginaw St St Louis MI 48880 Office: 175 Warwick Dr Alma MI 48801

FORTMAN, MARVIN, legal educator, consultant; b. Bklyn., Oct. 20, 1930; s. Herman and Bess (Smith) F.; m. Sorale Esther Elpern, Aug. 3, 1958; children: Brian E., Anita J., Deborah J. BS in Acctg., U. Ariz., 1957, JD, 1960; LLM, NYU, 1961. Bar: Ariz. 1960, N.Y. 1961, U.S. Tax Ct. 1962, U.S. Ct. Appeals 1962, U.S. Supreme Ct. 1962. Assoc. Aranow, Brodsky, Bolinger, Einhorn & Dann, N.Y.C., 1961-63, O'Connor, Cavanaugh, Anderson, Westover & Beshears, Phoenix, Ariz., 1963-65; prof. bus. law, bus. and pub. adminstrn. U. Ariz., Tucson, 1965—; legal cons. various corps., 1963—. Author: Legal Aspects of Doing Business in Arizona, 1970; contbr. articles to profl. jours. Mem. legal com. Ariz. Council on Econ. Edn., Tucson, 1975—, Sabbar Shrine Temple, Tucson, 1978—, chmn. wills and gifts, 1981-84. Served to pvt. 1st class U.S. Army, 1951-53, ETO. Kenneson fellow NYU, 1960-61. Mem. N.Y. State Bar Assn., Ariz. Bar Assn. (tax sect.), Phi Kappa Phi, Beta Gamma Sigma (sec., treas. 1972—), Beta Alpha Psi, Alpha Kappa Psi. Legal education, Probate. Home: 5844 E 15th St Tucson AZ 85711 Office: U Ariz Coll of Bus and Pub Adminstrn Tucson AZ 85721

FORTUNE, PHILIP LEE, lawyer; b. High Point, N.C., Nov. 11, 1945; s. Porter Lee and Elizabeth (Cummings) F.; m. Janet Ellis, June 10, 1967; children: Molly Lynne, Philip Lee Jr. BA, U. N.C., 1967; JD, U. Toledo, 1970. Bar: Ga. 1971, U.S. Dist. Ct. (no. dist.) Ga. 1971. Ptnr. Smith, Currie & Hancock, Atlanta, 1971—; speaker in field. Construction, Environment. Office: Smith Currie & Hancock 233 Peachtree St NE 2600 Peachtree Ctr Harris Tower Atlanta GA 30043-6601

FOSCARINIS, MARIA, lawyer; b. N.Y.C.; d. Nicolas and Rosa F. BA, Barnard Coll., 1977; MA, Columbia U., 1978, JD, 1981. Bar: N.Y. 1982, U.S. Dist. Ct. (so. and ea. dists.) N.Y. 1983, D.C. 1986. Law clk. to judge U.S. Ct. Appeals (2d cir.), N.Y.C., 1981-82; assoc. Sullivan & Cromwell, N.Y.C., 1982-85; counsel Nat. Coalition for Homeless, Washington, 1985—. Notes editor Columbia U. Law Rev., 1980-81. Harlan Fiske Stone scholar, 1978-79; John Dewey fellow. Mem. ABA, N.Y. County Lawyers Assn., D.C. Bar Assn., Lawyers Alliance for Nuclear Arms Control. Civil rights, Federal civil litigation, Poverty law. Home: 1444 Rhode Island Ave Washington DC 20005 Office: Nat Coalition for Homeless 1620 I St NW Washington DC 20006

FOSHEIM, JON, lawyer, retired judge; b. Howard, S.D., Jan. 25, 1923; s. Oscar and Margaret F.; m. Mary Lou Olson, Dec. 28, 1948; children: Patsy, Jon, Douglas, Peggy, Todd. JD, U. S.D., 1946. Bar: S.D. 1946. Sole practice Huron, S.D., 1946-59; state's atty. Beadle County, S.D., 1950-55; dep. state's atty. Beadle County, 1955-57; judge S.D. Circuit Ct. for 9th Circuit, 1959-79, presiding judge, 1974-79; justice S.D. Supreme Ct., Pierre, 1979-82, chief justice, 1982-86; ptnr. Wehde, Fosheim & Haberstick, Huron, 1986—; mem. S.D. Constl. Revision Commn.; instr. bus. law N.W. Coll.; instr. criminal justice Huron Coll. Served with U.S. Army, World War II. Mem. Izaak Walton League, Am. Legion. Democrat. Roman Catholic. Constitutional, Real property, State and local taxation. Office: Wehde Fosheim & Haberstick 351 Wisconsin SW Huron SD 57350

FOSMIRE, MICHAEL SEAN, lawyer; b. Detroit, Aug. 17, 1954; s. George Woodward and Joan Grace (Solak) F.; m. Barbara Lynn Grant, Feb. 2, 1985. BA, Mich. State U., 1976; JD, Am. U., 1980. Bar: Mich. 1980, U.S. Dist. Ct. (ea. dist.) Mich. 1980, U.S. Ct. Appeals (6th cir.) 1982, U.S. Dist. Ct. (we. dist.) Mich. 1985, Wis. 1986. Atty. Kitch, Saurbier, Drutchas, Wagner & Kenney, P.C., Detroit, 1980-85; ptnr. Lynch, Andrews & Fosmire, P.C., Negaunee, Mich., 1985—; bd. dirs. Negaunee St. Paul Endowment Fund, Inc. Mem. ABA, Am. Soc. Law and Medicine, Mich. Def. Trial Counsel. Personal injury, State civil litigation, Federal civil litigation. Home: PO Box 108 Negaunee MI 49866 Office: Lynch Andrews & Fosmire PC 200 Marquette St Negaunee MI 49866

FOSSUM, DONNA L., government counsel; b. Cedar Rapids, Iowa, Feb. 5, 1949; d. Donald E. and Esther O. (Sondreal) F. BA, U. N.Mex., 1971; MA, SUNY, Buffalo, 1974, JD, 1975, PhD, 1981. Bar: N.Y. 1976, Ill. 1978., D.C. 1978. Research atty. Am. Bar Found., Chgo., 1975-80; counsel Com. on Govt. Ops., U.S. Ho. of Reps., Washington, 1981—; adv. com. legal advocacy fund AAUW, Washington, 1981—. Contbr. articles to profl. jours. Mem. Alexandria (Va.) Dem. Com., 1985—; chmn. Holmes Run com., Alexandria, 1985—. Mem. ABA (del. Nat. Conf. Lawyers & Collection Agys., 1983—), U. N.Mex. Alumni Assn. (pres. D.C. chpt. 1984—), Women's Bar Assn. of D.C. Fedn. (bd. dirs.), Phi Beta Kappa, Phi Kappa Phi. Avocations: painting, weaving, sewing, writing. Legislative.

FOSSUM, LEE LEIF, lawyer; b. Farmington, Minn., Oct. 27, 1934; s. Leif A. and Mabel (Sandmann) F.; m. Carol Johnson, Dec. 22, 1956; children: Kristin, Karin, John. BA, St. Olaf Coll., 1956; JD, William Mitchell Coll. Law, 1967. Bar: Minn. 1968, U.S. Dist. Ct. Minn. 1972. Tchr. high sch. english Clara City (Minn.) Pub. Schs., 1958-59; mgr. Johnson Road Constrn. Co., Montivideo, Minn., 1958-66; ptnr. Lampe, Fossum & Crow, Northfield, Minn., 1968—. Pres. Southern Minn. Legal Services, St. Paul, 1984-86, bd. dirs. 1977-86; pres. Northfield Hist. Soc. 1978-79, bd. dirs. 1976-86; chmn. com. Bicentennial, Northfield, 1975-76. Served to lt. (j.g.) USNR, 1956-58. Mem. Assn. Trial Lawyers Am., Minn. Trial Lawyers Assn., Minn. Bar Assn., Rice County Bar Assn. (sec., treas. 1972-73), 5th Dist. Bar Assn. (pres. 1985-86). Lutheran. Lodge: Rotary (pres. 1985-86). Avocations: skiing, folk singing, archeology. State civil litigation, Probate, Real property. Office: Lampe Fossum & Crow 105 E 5th St Northfield MN 55057

FOSTER, ARTHUR KEY, JR., lawyer; b. Birmingham, Ala., Nov. 22, 1933; s. Arthur Key and Vonceil (Oden) F.; m. Jean Lyles Foster, Jan. 7, 1967; children—Arthur Key III, Brooke Oden. B.S.E., Princeton U., 1955; LL.B., U. Va., 1960. Bar: Ala. 1960. Ptnr. Balch & Bingham, Birmingham, 1965—. Trustee Episcopal Found. Jefferson County, 1965—; bd. dirs. Met. YMCA, 1969—, Downtown Club, 1977—, Highlands Day Sch. Served to lt., USN, 1955-60. Mem. Estate Planning Council of Birmingham, Nat. Assn. Bond Lawyers, Newcomen Soc. of U.S. Republican. Club: Kiwanis (bd. dirs.). Estate planning, Probate, Municipal bonds. Address: PO Box 306 Birmingham AL 35201

FOSTER, BEN FRANK, JR., lawyer; b. Houston, May 28, 1941; s. Ben Frank and Maydelle (Vaughan) F.; m. Raye Boyer; children: Ben F. III, David Peyton, Katharine Raye. BBA, Tex. A&I U., 1964; JD, Baylor U., 1966. Atty. NLRB, Ft. Worth, 1966-68; asst. dean St. Mary's Law Sch., San Antonio, 1974-76; pres. Foster, Bettac & Heller, P.C., San Antonio, 1978—; bd. dirs. Vaughan & Sons, San Antonio. Alderman City of Alamo Heights, 1985—; bd. dirs. San Antonio Symphony, 1972—. Mem. ABA, Tex. Bar Assn., Fed. Bar Assn., Am. Judicature Soc. Clubs: Conopus, Governor's, German, Town (bd. dirs. 1976), Order of the Alamo. Labor, Government contracts and claims, Civil rights. Home: 901 Cambridge Oval San Antonio TX 78209 Office: 4040 Broadway San Antonio TX 78209

FOSTER, CHARLES ALLEN, lawyer; b. Monroe, La., Aug. 26, 1941; s. Charles Shearer and Bessie Lea (Long) F.; children—Meg, Stephanie. B.A. summa cum laude, Princeton U., 1963; postgrad., B.A. in Jurisprudence with 1st class honors, Oxford (Eng.) U., 1965, M.A. in Jurisprudence, 1971; J.D. magna cum laude, Harvard U., 1967. Assoc., McLendon, Brim, Brooks, Pierce & Daniels, Greensboro, N.C., 1967-72, ptnr., 1972-73; sec., dir., gen. counsel Spanco Industries, Inc., Greensboro and Sanford, N.C. and Conestee, S.C., 1973-75 ; ptnr. Turner, Enochs, Foster, Sparrow & Burnley, Greensboro, 1975-81, Foster, Conner & Robson, 1983—; sr. lectr. law Duke U., 1981—; arbitrator Am. Arbitration Assn., mem. nat. panels of labor, constrn. and internat. comml. arbitrators; mem. Nat. Acad. Arbitrators; pub. mem. N.C. Tax Rev. Bd., 1957-79; permanent panel arbitrators N.C. Mcpl. Power Agy., Duke Power Co.; U.S. rep. Internat. Energy Agy. Dispute Resolution Centre, Paris, 1983—; permanent panel arbitrator Union Carbide Corp. and Atomic Trades and Labor Council; hearing officer Guilford Tech. Inst., Greensboro, others. Co-founder, sec., bd. dirs. Greensboro Day Sch.; dir. Greensboro Opera Co.; atty. for and dir. YWCA, 1969; alumni council; exec. com. Princeton U. Alumni Assn.; exec. com. Harvard Law Sch. Assn. N.C., 1970; group chmn. United Fund Dr., 1969-70; precinct chmn. Guilford County Rep. Exec. Com., 1974-76, chmn. fin. com., 1975-76; Rep. candidate for atty.-gen. N.C., 1984. Mem. ABA, N.C. Bar Assn. (council sect. labor and employment law), Greensboro Bar Assn., 18th Jud. Dist. Bar Assn., N.C. State Bar, Phi Beta Kappa, Cap and Gown. Author: Construction and Design Law, 1984; Construction and Design Law Digest, 1984; Law and Practice of Commercial Arbitration in North Carolina, 1984; contbr. articles to profl. jours. Legal education, Federal civil litigation, Labor. Address: PO Drawer 20004 Greensboro NC 27420

FOSTER, CHARLES CRAWFORD, lawyer, educator; b. Galveston, Tex., Aug. 1, 1941; s. Louie Brown and Helen (Hall) F.; m. Marta Brito Foster, Sept. 7, 1967 (div. Apr. 1986); children: John, Ruth. AA, Del Mar Jr. Coll., 1961; BA, U. Tex., 1963, JD, 1967. Assoc. Reid & Priest, N.Y.C., 1967-69, Butler & Binion, Houston, 1969-73; ptnr. Tindall & Foster, Houston, 1973—; adj. prof. immigration law U. Houston, 1985—. Contbr. articles to profl. jours. Chmn. immigration reform Gov.'s Task Force, Tex., 1984-87. Rotary Internat. fellow U. Concepción, Chile, 1964. Mem. ABA (chmn. immigration com. 1982—), Am. Immigration Lawyers Assn. (pres. 1981-82, outstanding service award 1985), Tex. Bar Assn. (chmn. com. law relating to immigration and nationality 1984-86), Tex. Bd. Legal Specialization (chmn. immigration adv. commn. 1979—), Tex. Young Lawyers Assn. (chmn. bd. dirs. 1976-77), Houston Bar Assn. Democrat. Methodist. Lodge: Rotary. Avocations: mountain climbing, photography, travel. Immigration, naturalization, and customs. Home: 5000 Montrose #8D Houston TX 77006 Office: Tindall & Foster 2801 Tex Commerce Tower 600 Travis Houston TX 77002

FOSTER, DAVID LEE, lawyer; b. Des Moines, Dec. 13, 1933; s. Carl Dewitt and Dorothy Jo (Bell) F.; m. Marilyn Lee Bokemeier, Aug. 12, 1957 (div. June 1978); children—Gwendolyn Dawn, Cynthia Lee, David Lee Jr.; m. Kathleen Carol Walsh, Mar. 24, 1979; 1 child, John Wickersham Foster. Student, Simpson Coll., 1951-52; B.A., U. Iowa, 1954, J.D., 1957. Bar: N.Y. 1958, Ohio 1964, Iowa 1957, U.S. Supreme Ct. 1975. Assoc. Cravath, Swaine & Moore, N.Y.C., 1957-63; from assoc. to ptnr. Jones, Day, Cockley & Reavis, Cleve., 1963-72; ptnr. Willkie, Farr & Gallagher, N.Y.C., 1972—; lectr. So. Meth. U., 1979-84, N.E. Antitrust Conf., Boston, 1984, U. Pitts., 1984, Practicing Law Inst., N.Y.C., 1984-85. Contbr. chpt. to book, articles to legal jours. Served with USNR, 1952-60. Fellow Am. Coll. Trial Lawyers, Internat. Acad. Trial Lawyers; mem. Am. Counsel Assn. (bd. dirs. 1984—), Order of Coif, Phi Beta Kappa. Club: Wash. Athletic. Avocations: flying; fishing. Antitrust, Patent, Federal civil litigation. Office: Willkie Farr & Gallagher 153 E 53d St New York NY 10022

FOSTER, DAVID SCOTT, lawyer; b. White Plains, N.Y., July 13, 1938; s. William James and Ruth Elizabeth (Seltzer) F.; m. Eleanore Stalker, Dec. 21, 1959; children—David Scott, Robert McEachron. B.A., Amherst Coll., 1960; LL.B., Harvard U., 1963. Bar: N.Y. 1963, D.C. 1977, Calif. 1978. Jud. law clk. U.S. Dist. Ct. So. Dist. N.Y., 1963-64; assoc. Debevoise & Plimpton, N.Y.C., 1964-72; internat. tax counsel U.S. Treasury Dept., Washington, 1972-77; ptnr. Brobeck, Phleger & Harrison, San Francisco, 1978—. Bd. dirs. Mus. Soc., San Francisco. Mem. ABA (chmn. com. U.S. taxation of foreigners and tax treaties/tax sect.), Internat. Fiscal Assn., San Francisco Bar Assn., N.Y. State Bar Assn. Presbyterian. Club: St. Francis Yacht (San Francisco). Corporate taxation, Personal income taxation. Office: Brobeck Phleger & Harrison Spear St Tower One Market Plaza San Francisco CA 94105

FOSTER, GEORGE WILLIAM, JR., lawyer, educator; b. Boston, Nov. 23, 1919; s. George William and Marguerite (Werner) F.; m. Jeanette Raymond, May 26, 1950; children—Susan, Bill, Fred. Student, Antioch Coll., 1937-40; B.S. in Chemistry, Stanford U., 1947; LL.B., Georgetown U., 1951; LL.M., Yale U., 1952. Bar: Wis. bar 1972. Exec. asst. to U.S. Senator, 1949-50; spl. asst. to Sec. of State Dean Acheson, 1951; asst. prof. law U. Wis., Madison, 1952-56; asso. prof. U. Wis., 1956-59, prof., 1959—, asso. dean, 1969-72; reporter Wis. Long-Arm Process Statute, 1955-59; cons. sch. desegregation guidelines HEW, 1965; legal advisor Ministry of Justice, Kabul, Afghanistan, 1976. Served to lt. (j.g.) USN, 1942-46. Mem. Am. Bar Assn., Am. Ornithologists Union, State Bar Wis., Dane County Bar Assn., Am. Law Inst. Democrat. Legal education. Home: 5616 Lake Mendota Dr Madison WI 53705 Office: U Wis 501 Law Bldg Madison WI 53706

FOSTER, JOHN WITHERSPOON, lawyer; b. Columbia, S.C., Nov. 6, 1948; s. Charlie Cantzon and Isabel (Witherspoon) F.; m. Vesta Anne Haselden, Nov. 5, 1977; children: Vesta Murray, Isabel Witherspoon. BA, Davidson Coll., 1970; BA, MA, Oxford U., Eng., 1972; JD cum laude, Harvard U., 1976. Bar: N.Y. 1976, S.C. 1977. Analyst econ. Govt. Research Group, Washington, 1972-73; assoc. Sullivan & Cromwell, N.Y.C., 1976-79; from assoc. to ptnr. Boyd, Knowlton, Tate & Finlay, Columbia, 1979-83; ptnr. McNair, Glenn, Konduros, Corley, Singletary, Porter & Dibble, Columbia, 1983—; bd. dirs., mem. exec. com. Foster-Dixiana Sand Inc., Columbia, 1979—; chmn. S.C. Tax Bd. Rev., Columbia, 1981—. Served to 1st lt. U.S. Army, 1972-73. Mem. ABA, Nat. Assn. Bond Lawyers. Securities, Municipal bonds, Banking. Home: 2721 Wheat St Columbia SC 29205 Office: McNair Glenn Konduros et al NCNB Tower 18th Floor PO Box 11390 Columbia SC 29211

FOSTER, JUDITH CHRISTINE, lawyer; b. Columbus, Ohio, Nov. 25, 1952; d. Paul Marvel and Jean Harper (Uhland) F.; m. Sabah Amin Wali, Dec. 28, 1973; children: Samed Michel, Sabah, Russeen Paul Sabah. BS in Natural Sci. and BA in Linguistics, Pa. State U., 1973; JD, Coll. William & Mary, 1979. Bar: Va. 1979, U.S. Ct. Appeals (4th cir.) 1979, U.S. Supreme Ct. 1984. Sole practice Fairfax, Va., 1980—; of counsel U.S. Justice Found., Escondido, Calif., 1982—; judge Internat. Moot Ct. Competition Assn. of Student Internat. Law Soc., 1984, 86. Del. Va. Reps., Fairfax, 1981, 85. Mem. ABA, Am. Immigration Lawyers Assn. (Legis. com. 1985—, D.C. chpt. 1980—), Washington Foreign Law Soc., Fairfax County Bar Assn. (continuing leagal edn. com. 1980—). Republican. Lutheran. Immigration, naturalization, and customs, Private international. Office: 4021 University Dr Fairfax VA 22030

FOSTER, LLOYD BENNETT, lawyer, musician; b. Wellman, Iowa, May 6, 1911; s. George Elliott and Lulu Nettie (Bennett) F.; m. Rowene Stevens, Sept. 1, 1940. BA cum laude in Commerce and Fin., Coe Coll., 1937; MS in Econs., Iowa State U., 1939; JD, De Paul U., 1952. Bar: Ill. 1952, U.S. Supreme Ct. 1980. Instr. Shenandoah Coll., Va., 1939-41; acct. McGladrey, Hansen, Dunn and Co., Cedar Rapids, Iowa, 1941-42; agt. Office of Dist. Dir., IRS, Chgo., 1946-52, pension plan reviewer, 1952-53, tech. advisor Appellate div., 1953-60; atty. Office of Chief Counsel, Washington, 1961-67; dep. asst. chief counsel Bur. of Pub. Debt, Chgo., 1967-71, atty., Washington, 1967; atty., income tax hearing officer, supr. regulations legis. rulings sect., litigation counsel, adminstrv. law judge Ill. Dept. Revenue, Chgo., 1971—. Mem., Chgo. Met. Symphony Orch., 1969—, Deerfield Park Dist. Community Band, 1968—. Served to comdr. USN, 1942-46. Mem. Fed. Bar Assn., Ill. Bar Assn., Chgo. Fedn. Musicians, D.C. Fedn. Musicians, Naval Res. Assn., Retired Officers Assn. Corporate taxation, Personal income taxation, State and local taxation. Office: Ill Dept of Revenue Ill Ctr 100 W Randolph St Chicago IL 60601

FOSTER, PHILIP CAREY, lawyer, county government official; b. Salisbury, Md., Jan. 5, 1947; s. Philip Kyle and Betty (Carey) F. BA, Coll. of Wooster, 1969; JD, Vanderbilt U., 1972. Bar: D.C. 1973, Md. 1973. Atty., advisor U.S. Dept. of Interior, Washington, 1972-73; assoc. Henry, Hairston & Price, Easton, Md., 1973-75; sole practice Easton, 1975—; adj. instr. Chesapeake Coll., Wayne Mills, Md., 1973-75; asst. state's atty. Talbot County, Easton, 1975-77, dep. state's atty., 1977-86; state's atty. for Talbot County, 1986—. Chmn. Bd. of Zoning Appeals, Easton, 1978-81, Talbot County Dem. Cen. Com., Easton, 1974-78, 82-86; pres., coach, referee Talbot County Youth Soccer League. Served to capt. U.S. Army. Mem. ABA, D.C. Bar Assn., Md. Bar Assn., Talbot County Bar Assn. (pres. 1987). Democrat. Episcopalian. Lodges: Rotary, Elks. State civil litigation, General practice. Office: Federal St Stewart Bldg Suite 220 Easton MD 21601

FOSTER, RANDOLPH COURTNEY, lawyer; b. Boise, Idaho, Oct. 3, 1952; s. Lucius Fisher and Margaret Anne (McLaren) F.; m. Debra Lynne Schulstad, 1976; children: Cameron, Andrew. BA, U. Puget Sound, 1974; JD, Georgetown U., 1978. Bar: U.S. Ct. Appeals (9th cir.) 1986. Legis. asst. to Senator Frank Church U.S. Senate, Washington, 1974-78; ptnr. Stoel, Rives, Boley, Fraser & Wyse, Portland, Oreg., 1978—. Editor: Civil Litigation Manual, 1982, rev. edit., 1986. Bd. dirs. The New Rose Theater, Portland, 1984—. Recipient Charles T. Battin award U. Puget Sound, 1974. Mem. ABA, Wash. State Bar Assn., Oreg. Bar Assn., U. Puget Sound Alumni Assn. (bd. dirs. 1980—). Federal civil litigation, State civil litigation, Trademark and copyright. Office: Stoel Rives Boley Fraser & Wyse 900 SW 5th Ave Portland OR 97204

FOSTER, SCOTT RAYMOND, lawyer; b. Greenville, Tex., Jan. 11, 1932; s. Paul Raymond and Mary Lee (Scott) F.; m. Marjorie Ann Barry, Feb. 11, 1956; children: Lisa Lee, Adrea Adkinson. BS, U.S. Naval Acad., 1954; JD, Boston Coll., 1961. Bar: Mass. 1961, U.S. Patent Office 1962. Commd. ensign USN, 1950, advanced through grades to lt., 1958, resigned, 1958; patent atty. U.S. AEC, Washington, 1961-63, USM Corp., Boston, 1963-69; div. patent counsel The Gillette Co., Boston, 1969-81, asst. patent counsel, 1981, patent counsel, 1982—; bd. dirs. Medico Devels., Inc., Lancaster, Mass.; lectr. law corp. patent seminars, 1981, Internat. Bus. Ctr. New England, 1984, Franklin Pierce Law Sch., 1985, 2d Nat. Innovation Workshop, 1986. Contbr. articles to profl. jours. Mem. Town of Milton (Mass.) Meeting, 1966-71, warrant com., 1970. Mem. Assn. Corp. Patent Counsels, Boston Patent Law Assn. (lectr. 1963-85, gov. 1983), Social Law Library (trustee 1982-86), Milton Jaycees (pres. 1967), Mayflower Soc. (capt. Boston chpt. 1970-71, bd. trustees 1970-78), SAR (bd. govs. Boston chpt. 1966-69). Patent. Home: Born Free Farm Tubwreck Dr Dover MA 02030 Office: The Gillette Co Prudential Tower Bldg Boston MA 02199

FOSTER, TAD STEVENSON, lawyer; b. Boulder, Colo., Sept. 30, 1944; s. Frank W. and Doris W. F.; m. Melissa C. Smith, June 20, 1976; 1 child, Piper. B.A., U. Colo., 1966, J.D., 1969. Bar: Colo. 1970, Calif., 1973, U.S. Dist. Ct. Colo., U.S. Ct. Appeals (10th cir.), U.S. Supreme Ct., 1984. Asst. atty. City of Colorado Springs, 1974—; mem. Colo. Water Quality Control Commn., 1981—. Served with JAGC, USMC, 1969-74. Mem. ABA, Colo. Bar Assn. (chmn. environmental law sect. 1983), El Paso County Bar Assn., Air Pollution Control Assn., Colo. Water Congress, Nat. Water Resources Assn. Republican. Christian Scientist. Administrative and regulatory, Environment, Local government. Home: 1229 E High Point Ln Colorado Springs CO 80904 Office: PO Box 1575 Colorado Springs CO 80901

FOSTER, THOMAS GLEN, JR., judge; b. Greensboro, N.C., May 20, 1946; s. Thomas Glen and Mary Opal (Holloway) F.; m. Carolyn Sue Holder, May 17, 1975; children—Thomas Glen, Jeffrey Michael, Sarah Elizabeth. B.A., U. Va., 1968; J.D., U. Louisville, 1974. Bar: N.C. 1974, U.S. Dist. Ct. (mid. dist.) N.C. 1975, U.S. Supreme Ct. 1980. Dep. county atty. Guilford County, Greensboro, 1975-80; judge N.C. 18th Jud. Dist. Ct., Greensboro, 1980-86, chief dist. ct. judge, 1984-86. Bd. dirs. United Services for Older Adults, Greensboro, 1980-81, Youth Adv. Council, Greensboro, 1981-82, Commn. on Alcoholism, Greensboro, 1982-83. Served to capt. U.S. Army, 1968-72, Vietnam. Mem. N.C. State Bar, Greensboro Bar. Democrat. Baptist. Club: Civitan (Greensboro). Home: 4908 Batten Rd Greensboro NC 27406 Office: Guilford County Courthouse 201 S Elm St Greensboro NC 27402

FOUGEROUSSE, PHILIP, lawyer; b. Indpls., Apr. 22, 1945; s. Bernard J. and Mary I. (Kearney) F.; m. Linda L. Hamilton, Aug. 22, 1980. B.S., Ind. U., 1967, M.B.A., 1971, J.D., 1974. Bar: Ind. 1974, Ala. 1981, Fla. 1982. Computer programmer Economy Fin. Corp., Indpls., 1967-70; resident atty. Railroadmen's Fed. Savs. & Loan, Indpls., 1974-79; title ops. mgr. TICOR Title Ins. Co., Indpls., 1979-80, state counsel, Birmingham, Ala., 1980-82; pres. Fair Builders, Inc., Indian Harbour Beach, Fla., 1982-84; sole practice, Satellite Beach, Fla., 1984—. Instr. Inst. Savs. and Loan, Indpls., 1977-79, Ind. Central U., Indls., 1979; lectr. U. Ala., Samford U. Mem. Fla. Bar (real property and probate sect.), Brevard County Bar Assn. (continuing legal edn. program com. 1983—). Club: Exchange (bd. dirs., child abuse prevention com. 1986—). Lodge: Lions (community activity chmn. 1977-80) (Indpls.). Real property, State civil litigation, General practice. Home: 290 Paradise Blvd Unit 31 Indialantic FL 32903 Office: 411 Palm Springs Blvd Indian Harbour Beach FL 32937

FOULKE, EDWIN GERHART, JR., lawyer; b. Perkasie, Pa., Oct. 30, 1952; s. Edwin G. and Mary Clare (Keller) F. BA, N.C. State U., 1974; JD, Loyola U., New Orleans, 1978. Bar: S.C. 1979, U.S. Dist. Ct. S.C. 1979, U.S. Ct. Appeals (4th cir.) 1979, Ga. 1986, U.S. Ct. Appeals (11th cir.) 1986. Assoc. Thomson, Mann & Hudson, Greenville, S.C., 1978-82, Rainey, Britton, Gibbes & Clarkson, Greenville, 1982-85, Constangy, Brooks & Smith, Atlanta, 1985—; instr. St. Mary's Dominican Coll., New Orleans, 1977-78. Field rep. Reagan/Bush Campaign, Columbia, S.C. 1980, S.C. state coordinator, 1984; sec., treas. Employment Labor Law Sect., Columbia, 1981-82. Mem. ABA, S.C. Bar Assn., Ga. Bar Assn., Greenville County Bar Assn. (chmn. pub. relations Com. 1984-85). Roman Catholic. Avocations: swimming, tennis, skiing. Labor, Federal civil litigation, Administrative and regulatory. Home: 2577 Ridgewood Terr NW Atlanta GA 30318 Office: Constangy Brooks & Smith 230 Peachtree St NW Suite 2400 Atlanta GA 30303

FOUNTAIN, KENNETH PAUL, lawyer, oil company executive; b. Timpson, Tex., Oct. 21, 1934; s. Joe Graham and Hazel VanDora (Magness) F.; m. Sylvia Elaine Worthington, Dec. 20, 1957; children—Paula, Kenneth, Douglas, David. Student So. Meth. U., 1953-54; B.S. in Mech. Engring., La. Poly. U., 1957; J.D., S. Tex. Coll. Law, 1966. Bar: Tex. Mech. engr. Interstate Oil Pipe Line Co., Shreveport, La., 1957-61, Humble Pipe Line Co., Houston, 1961-66; atty. Humble Oil & Refining Co., Southwest Enco region, Dallas, 1966-68; mgr. contracts and law Trans Alaska Pipeline System, Houston, 1968-70; coordinator legis. and polit. affairs Exxon Co. U.S.A., Houston, 1970-73; mgr. pub. affairs Western div., Los Angeles, 1973-74, trial counsel, law dept., Houston, 1974-81; gen. counsel, dir. Exxon Pipeline Co., Houston, 1981-86; sr. staff counsel Exxon Co. USA, Houston, 1986—; trustee South Tex. Coll. Law; bd. dirs. Southwestern Legal Found. Served as capt. USAFR, 1958-61. Mem. ABA, Houston Bar Assn. Republican. Baptist. Clubs: Kingwood Country, Inns of Ct. Federal civil litigation, Oil and gas leasing. Office: Exxon Co USA 800 Bell Ave Houston TX 77002

FOUNTAIN, RICHARD MAURICE, lawyer; b. Pensacola, Fla., Aug. 4, 1948; s. Cleaveland L. and Rhonda (Hall) F.; m. Elna Francis McDowell, May 3, 1967 (div. Oct. 1979); children: Leslie Marie, Richard M. Jr.; m. Teresa Joyce Stratton, Aug. 7, 1982; 1 child, Claire Stratton. BA in Acctg., U. West Fla., 1970; JD, U. Miss., 1981; LLM in Taxation, U. Fla., 1982. Bar: Miss. 1981, U.S. Dist. Ct. (so. and no. dists.) Miss. 1981, U.S. Tax Ct. 1981, U.S. Ct. Appeals (5th cir.) 1985. Assoc. Dossett, McGruder & Montgomery, Jackson, Miss., 1981, Dosset, Dossett & Goode, Jackson, 1982-84; ptnr. Crockett, Neeld & Starling, Jackson, 198-86; sole practice Jackson, 1986—. Editor newsletter Easter Seals. Vice chmn. Mayor's Task Force on Pub. Housing., Pensacola, 1977; chmn. transp. adv. bd. Pensacola-Escambia, 1978; bd. dirs. Easter Seal Soc., Pensacola, 1978; exec. com., bd. dirs. ARC, Jackson, 1986—. Named Outstanding Vol. of Yr., Action '76 com., 1976. Mem. ABA, Hinds County Bar Assn., Jackson Tax Forum, Estate Planning Council Miss., Phi Delta Phi, Delta Sigma Pi. Republican. Episcopalian. Clubs: University, Capital City Petroleum (Jackson); Executive (Pensacola). Lodges: Masons, Sertoma (pres. Jackson 1986—, mem. of yr. 1977). Corporate taxation, Estate planning, Estate taxation. Home: 5040 Romany Dr Jackson MS 39211 Office: Crockett Neeld & Starling 610 Trustmark Nat Bank Jackson MS 39201

FOURNIER, ARTHUR EDMOND, JR., lawyer; b. Hartford, Conn., Mar. 25, 1935; s. Arthur Edmond and Alice Marie (Joly) F.; m. Elizabeth Ann Coope, Aug. 31, 1957; children—Jennifer M., Michael E., Kathleen A., Amy E., Andrew J., Peter A., Sarah R. B.Engring., Yale U., 1957; J.D., George Washington U., 1965. Bar: U.S. Patent Office 1965, Conn. 1966. Patent examiner U.S. Patent and Trademark Office, Washington, 1961-65; dept. patent atty. Gen. Electric Co., Bridgeport, Conn., 1965-73; assoc. Law Offices Peter L. Costas, Hartford, 1973-75; project exec. Conn. Product Devel. Corp., Hartford, 1975-78; sr. patent atty. Combustion Engring., Inc., Windsor, Conn., 1978—. Chmn. Canton Bd. Appeals, Conn., 1977, Canton Charter Commn., 1984; mem. Canton Bd. Edn., 1983; chmn. Canton Democratic Town Com., 1973. Served to capt. USMC, 1957-60. Mem. Conn. Patent Law Assn. Roman Catholic. Club: Yale (Hartford). Patent. Home: 16 Country Ln Collinsville CT 06022 Office: Combustion Engring Inc 1000 Prospect Hill Rd Windsor CT 06095

FOUST, C. WILLIAM, lawyer; b. Bethlehem, Pa., May 27, 1952; s. Alan Shivers and Helen Elizabeth (Aigler) F.; m. Melissa A. Cherney, July 31, 1982. BA, U. Wis., 1974, JD, 1978. Bar: Wis. Bar, U.S. Dist. Ct. (we. dist.) Wis. 1978. Asst. dist. atty. Dane County Dist. Atty.'s Office, Madison, 1979-82; asst. pub. defender State Pub. Defender's Office, Milw., 1982-83; assoc. Smoler & Albert SC, Madison, 1983—. Mem. ABA, Dane County Bar Assn. (criminal law sect.; bd. dirs. 1985—, chmn. 1985—), State Bar of Wis., Nat. Assn. Criminal Def. Attys., Dane County Criminal Def. Lawyers Assn. Criminal. Home: Rt 2 Box 70 Brooklyn WI 53521 Office: Smoler & Albert 119 Martin Luther King Jr Blvd Madison WI 53703

FOUTS, LOUIS MILNER, III, lawyer, real estate investor; b. Dallas, Mar. 3, 1944; s. Fredric Clark and Dorothy Jean (Frey) F.; m. Sondra Sue Tally, Jan. 25, 1969 (div. 1977); children—Molly Anne, Paul Louis. B.B.A., So. Meth. U., 1966; J.D., U. Tex., 1970. Bar: Tex., 1969. Assoc., Ramey, Brelsford, Flock, Devereux & Hutchins, Tyler, Tex., 1969-72; gen. counsel Southwestern Dynamics, Inc., Dallas, 1972-74; ptnr. Benners & Fouts, Dallas, 1974-83; sole practice, Dallas, 1983—; lectr. Dallas Bd. Realtors seminars; mem. Bar Candidate Admissions Bd.; dir. Child Welfare Bd.; co-chmn. Law Day Com. Mem. 500, Inc., Young Republicans, Fourth Session Club; bd. dirs. vestry Christ Episcopal Ch. Mem. Dallas Bar Assn., Phi Delta Theta, Phi Alpha Delta. Real property, Family and matrimonial, General practice. Home: 9125 Drumcliffe Dallas TX 75231 Office: 2522 McKinney Ave Suite 102 Dallas TX 75201

FOWLE, FRANK FULLER, lawyer; b. Chgo., May 28, 1908; s. Frank Fuller and Alice Edna (Cowper) F.; m. Elisabeth Sloan Ballard, June 27, 1938 (dec.); children—Elisabeth Sloan, Susan Rankin, Margaret Duryee, Frank Fuller III, William Cowper II. A.B., Williams Coll., 1929; J.D., Harvard U., 1932; M.A., Columbia U., 1946. Bar: Ill. 1932, D.C. 1970, U.S. Dist. Ct. (no. dist.) Ill. 1937, US. Ct. Appeals (7th cir.) 1952, U.S. Supreme Ct. 1954. Assoc. McKinney, Lynde & Grear, Chgo., 1932-34; mem. legal div. Nat. Recovery Adminstrn., Washington, 1935-36; mem. legal div. Pub. Works Adminstrn., Washington, 1936-37; assoc. Mayer, Meyer, Austrian, & Platt, Chgo., 1937-40; mem. Pope, Ballard, Shepard & Fowle, and precessors, Chgo., 1940-82, of counsel, 1983—; dir. Harris Winnetka Bank, Winnetka, Ill. Pres., dir. Winnetka Community Chest, 1958-61; pres. Combined Bds. Winnetka PTA, 1952-53; bd. dirs. Nat. Soc. Prevention Blindness, 1957-66; pres., trustee Ill. Soc. Prevention Blindness, 1956-79; pres. Rheumatic Fever Research, Northwestern U., 1955-58; v.p., trustee Library Internat. Relations, Chgo., 1948-53; governing mem. Glenwood Sch. for Boys, Chgo., 1949-64; mem. Cook County Rent Adv. Bd., 1952-53; 1st chmn. Ill. Community Coll. Bd., 1965-71; mem., 1971-77; mem. Ill. Bd. Higher Edn., 1965-71; mem. Chgo. Hist. Soc., Chgo. Zool. Soc., Chg. Art Inst., Chgo. Mus. Natural History, Chgo. Council Fgn. Relations; mem. vestry Christ Ch., Winnetka. Served to lt. comdr. USNR, 1942-45. Mem. Chgo. Bar Assn. (bd. mgrs. 1964-66), Ill. Bar Assn., ABA, 7th Cir. Bar Assn., Am. Law Inst., Am. Judicature Soc., Legal Club Chgo., Law Club Chgo., Harvard Law Sch. Soc. Ill. (pres. 1969), Chi Psi. Democrat. Club: Univ. Chgo. (sec. dir. 1954-57), Indian Hill Country (Winnetka). Federal civil litigation, State civil litigation. Office: 69 W Washington St Chicago IL 60602

FOWLER, DON WALL, lawyer; b. Clarksville, Tenn., Apr. 19, 1944; s. Slayden Grimes and Dorothy Lavenia (Wall) F.; m. Ruthann Arneson, July 20, 1942 (div.); 1 child, Scott Slayden; m. Deborah Dewar, Sept. 15, 1984 (dec. Feb. 1986). B.A., Emory U., 1966; J.D., U. Chgo., 1969. Bar: Ill. 1969, U.S. Dist. Ct. (no. dist.) Ill. 1969, U.S. Ct. Appeals (7th cir.) 1980. Assoc. Lord Bissell & Brook, Chgo., 1969-77, ptnr., 1977—. Mem. Chgo. Bar Assn., Ill. Bar Assn., ABA, Ill. Assn. Def. Trial Counsel, Def. Research Inst. Unitarian. Club: Union League. State civil litigation, Federal civil litigation, Insurance. Office: Lord Bissell & Brook 115 S LaSalle St Chicago IL 60603

FOWLER, DONALD RAYMOND, lawyer, educator; b. Raton, N.Mex., June 2, 1926; s. Homer F. and Grace B. (Honeyfield) F.; m. Anna M. Averyt, Feb. 6, 1960; children—Mark D., Kelly A. B.A., U. N.Mex., 1950; J.D., 1951; M.A., Claremont Grad. Sch., 1979, Ph.D., 1983. Bar: N.Mex. 1951, Calif. 1964, U.S. Supreme Ct. 1980. Atty. AEC, Los Alamos and Albuquerque, 1951-61, chief counsel Nev. Ops., 1962-63; pvt. practice, Albuquerque, 1961-62; asst., then dep. staff counsel Calif. Inst. Tech., Pasadena, 1963-72, staff counsel, 1972-75, gen. counsel, 1975—; lectr. exec. mgmt. program Claremont Grad. Sch., Calif., 1981-84. Contbr. articles to profl. publs. Served with USAAF, 1944-46. Recipient NASA Pub. Service award, 1981. Mem. ABA, Calif. State Bar Assn., N.Mex. State Bar Assn., Fed. Bar Assn., Los Angeles County Bar Assn., Nat. Assn. Coll. and Univ. Attys. (exec. bd. 1979-82, 84—, chmn. publs. com. 1982-84, pres.-elect 1987—). Government contracts and claims, General corporate. Office: Suite 305 Calif Inst Tech 4800 Oak Grove Dr Bldg 180 Pasadena CA 91109

FOWLER, FLORA DAUN, lawyer; b. Washington, Aug. 11, 1923; d. Herman Hartwell and Flora Elizabeth (Adams) Sanford; m. Kenneth Leo Fowler, Aug. 22, 1941; children: Kenneth Jr., Michael, Kathleen, Daun, Jonathan, Colin, Kevin, James, Shawn, Maureen, Wendelyn, Liam, Tobias, Melanie. Student, Wilson Tchrs. Coll., 1940-41; BA, U. Md., 1973; JD, U. Balt., 1976. Bar: Fla. 1977, U.S. Dist. Ct. (mid. dist.) Fla. 1979, U.S. Ct. Appeals (5th and 11th cirs.) 1981. Staff atty. Cen. Fla. Legal Services Inc., Daytona Beach, 1978-80, mng. atty., 1980-81; sole practice Daytona Beach, 1981—; pro bono work Lawyers' Referral, Daytona Beach. Past editor Seabrook Acres Citizens' League Newsletter; columnist Bowie Express & Community Times; contbr. poems to New Voices in American Poetry, 1974. V.p. Seabrook (Md.) Acres Citizens League, 1970; past v.p. Prince Georges County Civic Fedn., Md.; past unit chmn. League of Women Voters, Prince Georges County; past pres., v.p., publicity chmn. Lanham-Bowie Dem. Club, Seabrook. Recipient Evening Star Trophy award Prince Georges County Civic Fedn., 1969. Mem. ABA, Fla. Bar Assn., Volusia County Bar Assn., Am. Judicature Soc., Vol. Lawyers' Project. Democrat. Roman Catholic. Avocations: swimming, creative writing, collecting salt and pepper shakers, church activities, Cursillo. General practice, State civil litigation, Family and matrimonial.

FOWLER, GEORGE J., III, lawyer; b. Havana, Cuba, Oct. 12, 1950; s. George J. Fowler and Graciela (Estevez) Cosculluela; m. Cristina Jenkins, Dec. 19, 1971; children: George J., Cristina Maria. BS, La. State U., 1972; JD, Tulane U., 1975. Bar: Ind. 1975, U.S. Dist. Ct. (ea. dist.) La. 1975, U.S. Dist. Ct. (we. dist.) La. 1976, U.S. Ct. Appeals (5th cir.) 1981. Assoc. Phelps, Dunbar, Marks, Claverie & Sims, New Orleans, 1975-80, ptnr., 1980—, mng. ptnr. Latin Am. dept., 1986—; pro bono atty. Juvenile Ct., New Orleans, 1986—. Author: (transl.) Panamanian Maritime Code, 1984. Mem. ABA, Fed. Bar Assn., La. Bar Assn., New Orleans Bar Assn., New Orleans Assn. Defense Counsel, Southeastern Admiralty Law Inst., World Trade Ctr. New Orleans. Republican. Roman Catholic. Avocations: fishing, swimming, chess. Admiralty, Private international. Office: Phelps Dunbar Marks Claverie & Sims 400 Poydras St 30th Floor New Orleans LA 70130

FOWLER, JOHN BALLARD, lawyer; b. Berea, Ky., Oct. 4, 1949; s. John Thomas and Imogene (Ballard) F.; m. Jennifer Jan Johnson, July 10, 1976. B.A., Berea Coll., 1971; J.D., U. Ky., 1974. Bar: Ky. 1974, Tenn. 1977, U.S. Dist. Ct. (ea. dist.) Ky. 1974, U.S. Dist. Ct. (ea. dist.) Tenn. 1977, U.S. Supreme Ct. 1980. Atty. Dept. of Transp., Lexington, Ky., 1974-76; assoc. Ambrose, Wilson & Grimm, Knoxville, Tenn., 1976-80, ptnr., 1980—; instr. banking law State Tech. Inst., Knoxville, 1982; mem. Tenn. Lawyers Profl. Liability Ins. Com., 1984—. Recipient Alumni Leadership and Service award U. Ky. Alumni Assn., 1982. Mem. Ky. Bar Assn., Tenn. Bar Assn., Knoxville Bar Assn., ABA. Clubs: City, LeConte, Ft. Loudoun Yacht. Banking, Real property, General corporate. Home: 1825 Nantasket Rd Knoxville TN 37922 Office: Ambrose Wilson & Grimm 9th Floor VFB Bldg Knoxville TN 37901

FOWLER, SANDRA T., judge; b. Tampa, Fla.; d. Hobson R. and Lillian Ann (Dye) T.;. BA, U. South Fla., 1975; JD, Mercer U., 1978. Asst. pub. defender Office of Pub. Defender, Key West, Fla., 1978-81; sole practice Key West, 1981-87; judge County Ct., Key West, 1987—. Pres. bd. dirs. Monroe County Fine Arts Council, Key West, 1984—, Monroe Assn. Retarded Citizens, Key West, 1983—; bd. dirs. Handicapped Job Replacement Council, Key West, 1985—, Key West Cultural Commn., 1986—, Teach Young Minds Early, Inc., Key West, 1985—. Recipient Pres.'s Pro Bono award Fla. Bar Assn., 1986. Mem. ABA, Monroe County Bar Assn., League of Women Voters. Democrat. Baptist. Lodge: Zonta (Key West, Fla.). Criminal, Family and matrimonial, General practice. Home: 1210 Pine St Key West FL 33040 Office: County Ct 310 Fleming St Key West FL 33040

FOWLER, WILLIAM CRAIG, lawyer; b. Sandusky, Ohio, Nov. 26, 1952; s. R. James and Eleanor A. (Appell) F.; m. Christy Parker Seip, Sept. 24, 1977. BBA in Fin. with high honors, U. Notre Dame, 1975; JD, Northwestern U., 1978. Bar: Ill. 1978, U.S. Dist. Ct. (no. dist.) Ill. 1979. Assoc. Schuyler, Roche & Zwirner (formerly known as Hubachek, Kelly, Rauch & Kirby), Chgo., 1979-84; ptnr. Schuyler, Roche & Zwirner, Chgo., 1984—. Mem. ABA, Ill. Bar Assn., Chgo. Bar Assn., Newcomen Soc. of U.S., Beta Gamma Sigma. Episcopalian. Club: Notre Dame, Union League (Chgo.). General corporate, Private international, Real property. Home: 458 Linden St Winnetka IL 60093 Office: Schuyler Roche & Zwirner 3100 Prudential Plaza Chicago IL 60601

FOX, BYRON NEAL, lawyer; b. St. Louis, May 15, 1948; s. Meyer and Thelma (Werber) F.; m. Cynthia Penner, Aug. 25, 1984. B.S., Tulane U., 1966; M.B.A., Boston U., 1973; J.D., Kans. U., 1970. Bar: Mo. Pres. Byron Neal Fox, P.C., Kansas City, Mo., 1980—; of counsel Goodman, Terry, Stein & Quintano, P.C., Las Vegas. Bd. govs. Am. Royal Assn., Kansas City, 1979—. Served to 1st lt. U.S. Army, 1973. Mem. ABA, Mo. Bar Assn., Kansas City Bar Assn. Criminal, General corporate, State civil litigation. Office: 600 Broadway 560 Rivergate Bus Ctr Kansas City MO 64105 also: Goodman Terry Stein & Quintano PC 20 S 4th St Las Vegas NV 89101

FOX, FRANCIS ANTHONY, lawyer; b. Providence, Oct. 10, 1954; s. Frank Alstrup and Jane Mary (Raia) F.; m. Elizabeth Winter Greer, Oct. 2, 1982; 1 child, Justin Alstrop. BA, Bates Coll., 1976; JD, Washington and Lee U., 1980. Bar: R.I. 1981, Mass. 1981, U.S. Dist. Ct. R.I. 1981. Assoc. Hinckley & Allen, Providence, 1981-84; ptnr. Saunders, Dumas & Fleury, East Greenwich, R.I., 1984-86, Carroll, Kelly & Murphy, Providence, 1986—; counsel to house minority leader R.I. Ho. of Reps., Providence, 1985, 86. Mem. planning bd. Town of East Greenwich, 1984-85; mem. exec. com. Bates Coll., Lewiston, Maine, 1985—. Served with USMC, 1975-76; with USNR. Mem. ABA, R.I. Bar Assn., Mass. Bar Assn., U.S. Naval Inst. Avocations: Triathlon, reading, travel. State civil litigation, Consumer commercial, Personal injury. Home: 10 Midlands Dr East Greenwich RI 02818 Office: Carroll Kelly & Murphy 155 S Main St Providence RI 02903

FOX, FRANCIS HANEY, lawyer; b. Attleboro, Mass., May 28, 1933; s. Francis Joseph and Mary Frances (Brady) F.; m. Cynthia Ann Blundell, Dec. 27, 1959; children: Cynthia, Martin, Matthew, Kalan. BS in Econs., Coll. Holy Cross, 1955; LLB, Harvard U., 1963. Bar: Mass. 1963, U.S. Ct. Appeals (1st cir.) 1963, U.S. Supreme Ct. 1977. Assoc. Bingham, Dana & Gould, Boston, 1963-70, ptnr., 1970—. Served to capt. USNR, 1955-78. Fellow Am. Coll. Trial Lawyers. Federal civil litigation, State civil litigation, Libel. Home: 77 Cottage St Sharon MA 02067 Office: Bingham Dana & Gould 100 Federal St Boston MA 02110

FOX, GARY DEVENOW, lawyer; b. Detroit, Sept. 8, 1951; s. Edward J. Fox. BA in Polit. Sci. and Drama, Drury Coll., 1973; JD, U. Fla., 1976. Bar: Fla. 1976, U.S. Dist. Ct. (so. and mid. dists.) Fla. 1977, U.S. Ct. Appeals (5th and 11th cirs.) 1977, U.S. Supreme Ct. 1981. From assoc. to ptnr. Frates, Floyd, Pearson, Stewart, Richman & Greer, Miami, Fla., 1976-84; ptnr. Stewart, Tilghman, Fox & Bianchi, P.A., Miami, 1984—. Exec. editor U. Fla. Law Rev.; contbg. editor Court Handbook for Dade County Lawyers, 2d edition, 1979. Mem. ABA, Fla. Bar Assn. (cert. civil trial advocacy 1983, civil procedure rules com., lectr. young lawyers sect.), Dade County Bar Assn., Assn. Trial Lawyers Am. (sustaining, lectr.), Acad. Fla. Trial Lawyers (lectr.), Dade County Trial Lawyers Assn. (bd. dirs. 1986—). Clubs: Bankers, Grove Isle (Miami). Avocations: tennis, skiing. Personal injury, Federal civil litigation, State civil litigation. Office: Stewart Tilghman Fox & Bianchi PA 44 W Flagler St Suite 1900 Miami FL 33130

FOX, HAMILTON PHILLIPS, III, lawyer; b. Salisbury, Md., Sept. 18, 1945; s. Hamilton Phillips and Evelyn Louise (Jefferson) F.; m. Mary Shannon Lafans, Aug. 31, 1968 (dissolved); children: Gretchen Robinson, Hamilton Duke, Caleb Savage; m. Barbara Daniels Robinson, Dec. 13, 1986. BA with honors, U. Va., 1967; LLB, Yale U., 1970. Bar: Maine 1971, D.C. 1972, U.S. Dist. Ct. Md., U.S. Ct. Appeals (1st, 9th and D.C. cirs.), U.S. Supreme Ct. Law clk. to judge U.S. Ct. Appeals (1st cir.), Portland, Maine, 1970-71; law clk. to Hon. Stanley Reed and Lewis F. Powell Jr. U.S. Supreme Ct., Washington, 1971-72; asst. U.S. atty. U.S. Atty.'s Office, Washington, 1972-73, 74-77; asst. spl. prosecuter Watergate Prosecution Force, Washington, 1973-74; dep. chief organized crime sect. U.S. Dept. Justice, Washington, 1977-80; sole practice Washington, 1980-84; ptnr. Dewey, Ballantine, Bushby, Palmer & Wood, Washington, 1984—; lectr. law U. Va., Charlottesville, 1980-82; assoc. dep. counsel com. on standards of official conduct U.S. Ho. of Reps., 1983-84. Criminal, Federal civil litigation, State civil litigation. Home: 729 Massachusetts Ave NE Washington DC 20002 Office: Dewey Ballantine Bushby Palmer & Wood 1775 Pennsylvania Ave NW Washington DC 20006

FOX, JACQUELINE R., lawyer; b. Cleve., Sept. 4, 1949; d. Stanley and Lucille (McCollom) F. BA, Ohio U., 1970; MLS, Case Western Res., 1972; JD, Cleve. Marshall Coll. of Law, 1978. Bar: Ohio 1978, Tex. 1982. Law librarian U. San Francisco, 1978-79, U. Va., Charlottesville, 1979-81; staff atty. Mead Data Cen., Houston, 1981; landman Union Oil Co. Calif., Houston, 1982-84; assoc. McPherson & McPherson, Houston, 1984-85, Schechter, Eisenman & Solar, Houston, 1985—. Mem. steering com. Young Leadership, Houston, 1984-86, Women's Polit. Awareness Com., Houston, 1985—, Jewish Fedn. Community Relations Com., Houston, 1985—; co-chmn. AIPAC Metro Com., Houston, 1985-86. Named one of Outstanding Young Women of Am., 1985. Mem. ABA, Tex. Bar Assn., Assn. Trial Lawyers Am., Assn. Women Attys. Club: Hadassan, Forum (Houston), A.J.C. Avocations: swimming, travel. Personal injury, Workers' compensation. Office: Schechter Eisenman & Solar 525 Webster Houston TX 77002

FOX, JAMES CARROLL, judge; b. Atchison, Kans., Nov. 6, 1928; s. Jared Copeland and Ethel (Carroll) F.; m. Katharine deRosset Rhett, Dec. 30, 1950; children—James Carroll, Jr., Jane Fox Brown, Ruth Fox Jordan. B.S. in Bus. Adminstrn., U. N.C., 1950, LL.B. with honors, 1957. Law. clk. U.S. Dist. Ct. (ea. dist.) N.C., Wilmington, 1957-58; assoc. Carter & Murchison, Wilmington, N.C., 1958-59; ptnr. Murchison, Fox & Newton, Wilmington, N.C., 1960-82; judge U.S. Dist. Ct. (ea. dist.) N.C., Wilmington, 1982—; lectr. in field. Contbr. articles to profl. jours. Vestryman, St. James Episcopal Ch., 1973-75, 79-82. Mem. New Hanover County Bar Assn. (pres. 1967-68), Fifth Jud. Dist. Bar Assn. (sec. 1960-62), N.C. Bar Assn., ABA, N.C. Acad. Trial Lawyers Assn. Home: 124 Edge Hill Wilmington NC 28403 Office: Alton Lennon Fed Bldg and US Courthouse PO Box 2143 Wilmington NC 28402 *

FOX, JAMES ROBERT, law librarian, educator; b. Dayton, Ohio, June 30, 1950; s. Forest Maxwell and Edna Virginia (Swatz) F.; m. Patricia Schoeler, July 1, 1978; 1 child, Henry Maxwell. BA, Otterbein Coll., 1972; JD, Ohio State U., 1974; MS, Drexel U., 1978; diploma, McGill U., Montreal, Que., Can., 1983. Bar: Pa. 1976. Media specialist Ohio State U., Columbus, 1973-75; law librarian Dickinson Sch. Law, Carlisle, Pa., 1976—; vis. law librarian McGill U., 1982-83; mem. adv. bd. Law Library Microform, Honolulu, 1982-85. Reviewer, cons. Law Books in Rev., Dobbs Ferry, N.Y. 1979-83. Mem. Am. Assn. Law Libraries, Am. Assn. Law Schs. Republican. Methodist. Librarianship, Public international, Air and space law. Home: 219 W Yellow Breeches Rd Carlisle PA 17013 Office: Dickinson Sch Law 150 S College St Carlisle PA 17103

FOX, JOHN CHARLES, lawyer; b. Pensacola, Fla., Apr. 14, 1948; s. Lawrence Charles and Althea (Ruth) F.; m. Cheryl Perkins, June 21, 1975; children: Eric Charles, John Alexander. BS in Mgmt. Advt., U. Fla., 1970; JD, Birmingham (Ala.) Sch. of Law, 1974. Bar: Ala. 1974, U.S. Ct. Appeals (10th cir.) 1974; Securities Exchange Commn. Series 7 license. Clerk Balch, Bingham & Baker, Birmingham, 1971-74; sr. atty. Public Defenders Office, Birmingham, 1974-86; acct. mgr., legal advisor The Acacia Group, Birmingham, 1986—, also employee benefits coordinator and registered investment advisor. Council mem. Boy Scouts Am., Birmingham, 1984-86; pres. PTA, youth soccer coach Our Lady of the Valley School, Birmingham, 1985-86. Serves with USCGR. Fellow USCG Reserve Officers Assn. (life); mem. Ala. Def. Lawyers Assn., Alpha Delta Sigma (v.p.), Delta Sigma Pi (v.p.). Democrat. Roman Catholic. Pension, profit-sharing, and employee benefits, Personal income taxation, Estate planning. Home: 1541 Cape Cod Circle Alabaster AL 35007 Office: 3000 Riverchase Galleria Suite 400 Birmingham AL 35244

FOX, MARY ELLEN, lawyer; b. Upper Sandusky, Ohio, Aug. 8, 1956; d. Paul Eugene and Anna Marie (Walton) F. BA in Acctg. and Polit. Sci., Ohio No. U., 1978, JD, 1981. Bar: Ohio 1981, U.S. Dist. Ct. (no. dist.) Ohio 1982. Assoc. Stansbery, Schoenberger and Scheck, Upper Sandusky, 1981-85; ptnr. Stansbery, Schoenberger, Scheck & Fox, Upper Sandusky, 1985—; bd. dirs. Community 1st Bank, N.A., Forest, Ohio; solicitor Village of Nev., Ohio, 1982—; librarian Wyandot County Law Library, Upper Sandusky, 1983—. Bd. dirs. Wyandot County Council on Alcoholism, Upper Sandusky, 1983-86. Mem. ABA, Ohio Bar Assn., Wyandot County Bar Assn. (sec., treas. 1982, v.p. 1983, pres. 1984), Alpha Xi Delta (bldg. corp. bd. 1978—, pledge advisor 1979, province sec. 1981-85, province pres. 1986—, chpt. dir. 1986—). Republican. Methodist. Avocations: tennis, walking, sewing, music, swimming. General practice, Family and matrimonial, Banking. Home: 14370 SH 37 Rural Rt 2 Forest OH 45843 Office: Stansbery Schoenberger Scheck & Fox 106 E Wyandot Ave Upper Sandusky OH 45843

FOX, MICHAEL DAVID, lawyer; b. N.Y.C., Aug. 14, 1940; s. Sol and Faye R. (Goor) F.; m. Geraldine Hill, Ag. 16, 1964; children—Thaddeus Hill, Amanda Curry. B.S., Carnegie Mellon U., 1962, M.S. in Indsl. Adminstrn., 1963; J.D., U. Pitts., 1969. Bar: Pa. 1970. Corp. market planning staff, field and div. sales engr. positions Westinghouse Electric Corp., Pitts., Detroit and Youngwood, Pa., 1963-66, staff atty., Pitts., 1969-72, antitrust litigation counsel, 1973-74; assoc. Berkman Ruslander Pohl Lieber & Engel, Pitts., 1974-77, ptnr. 1978—; adj. lectr. Grad. Sch. Bus., U. Pitts. Sec., bd. dirs. Jr. Achievement Southwest Pa.; mem. nat. alumni adv. counsel Grad. Sch. Indsl. Adminstrn., Carnegie Mellon U., 1983—, chmn. elect. Andrew Carnegie Soc. Mem. ABA, Pa. Bar Assn., Allegheny County Bar Assn. (chmn. antitrust and class action com. 1977-78, vice chmn. intellectual property sect., 1987), Order of Coif. Club: Pitts. Athletic Assn. Antitrust, Computer, Contracts commercial. Home: 10 Dunmoyle Pl Pittsburgh PA 15217 Office: One Oxford Center 40th Floor Pittsburgh PA 15219

FOX, PATRICK JOSEPH, lawyer; b. Atlanta, May 30, 1950; s. Joseph M. and Betty J. (Garvey) F.; m. Martha Ann Adams, June 12, 1976; children: Meredith Ashley, Patrick Joseph Jr. AB, U. Ga., 1972, JD, 1975. Bar: U.S. Dist. Ct. (no. dist.) Ga. 1976, U.S. Ct. Appeals (11th cir.) 1981, U.S. Supreme Ct. 1979. Assoc. Thomas K. McWhorter, Jonesboro, Ga., 1975-78, Glaze McNally & Glaze, Jonesboro, 1978-80; ptnr. Glaze & McNally P.C., Jonesboro, 1980-86, McNally, Fox, Mahler & Cameron, P.C., Fayetteville, Ga., 1986—. Mem. Ga. Trial Lawyers Assn. (v.p. 1986), Assn. Trial Lawyers Am., State Bar Assn. Ga., Clayton Bar Assn., Fayette County Bar Assn., Lawyers Club Atlanta, Atlanta Bar Assn. Personal injury, Workers' compensation, Family and matrimonial. Home: 125 Partridge Pt Fayetteville GA 30214 Office: McNally Fox Mahler & Cameron PC 100 Habersham Dr Fayetteville GA 30214

FOX, REEDER RODMAN, lawyer; b. Easton, Pa., Oct. 18, 1934; s. Louis Rodman and Mary Catherine (Cannon) F.; m. Marion Laffey, May 12, 1962; children—Rodman R., Drew D., Vanessa S. B.A., Yale U., 1956; LL.B., Harvard U., 1959. Bar: Pa. 1960, U.S. Dist. Ct. (ea. dist.) Pa. 1960, U.S. Ct. Appeals (3d cir.) 1960. Assoc., Duane, Morris & Heckscher, Phila., 1960-65, ptnr., 1965—. Served with Pa. N.G., 1959-60. Mem. ABA, Pa. Bar Assn., Phila. Bar Assn. Republican. Roman Catholic. Federal civil litigation, Antitrust, State civil litigation. Office: Duane Morris & Heckscher 1 Franklin Plaza Philadelphia PA 19102

FOX, RICHARD PAUL, lawyer; b. N.Y.C.; m. Joan Thompson, Mar. 23, 1962; children—Joseph, Paul, Jonathan, Jeffrey. B.A., UCLA, 1966; J.D., Loyola U., Los Angeles, 1969; M.A. in Ethics, Pepperdine U., 1981. Bar: Calif. 1970, U.S. Supreme Ct., 1974, U.S. Ct. Claims 1973, U.S. Ct. Mil. Appeals 1973, U.S. Ct. Appeals (5th cir.) 1979, U.S. Ct. Appeals (6th cir.) 1980, U.S. Ct. Appeals (7th cir.) 1977, U.S. Ct. Appeals (9th cir.) 1971, U.S. Ct. Appeals (10th cir.) 1977, U.S. Ct. Appeals (D.C. cir.) 1983. Ptnr. firm Richard P. Fox & Max Gest, P.C., Los Angeles, 1970—. Mem. staff Loyola U. Law Rev., 1968-69. Contbr. articles to profl. jours. Served to maj. U.S. Army, 1951-63. Mem. Nat. Lawyers Guild, Christian Legal Soc. Lutheran. Military, Veterans, Federal employees. Office: Richard P Fox & Max Gest PC 9911 W Pico Blvd Suite 1030 Los Angeles CA 90035

FOX, SHAYLE PHILLIP, lawyer; b. Chgo., July 20, 1934; s. Charles Fox and Beatrice Chazin; m. Deanna Fingersh, May 30, 1959; children: Sara, Leslie, Anthony. BS with high honors, U. Ill., 1954; JD, DePaul U., 1957. Bar: Ill. 1957. Ptnr. Fox & Grove, Chgo., 1965-76, pres., 1977—. Fund raiser Jewish United Fund, Chgo., 1960—; bd. dirs. Schwab Rehab. Hosp., Chgo., 1981-84; v.p., bd. dirs. Jewish Community Ctrs. Chgo., 1975—. Served with USAFR, 1958-63. Mem. ABA, Am. Judicature Soc., Ill. Soc. CPA's, Chgo. Assn. Commerce and Industry, Ill. C. of C. Jewish. Clubs: Standard (Chgo.); Birchwood (Highland Park, Ill.). General corporate, Labor, Federal civil litigation. Home: 1 Rockgate Ln Glencoe IL 60022 Office: Fox & Grove 233 S Wacker Dr Suite 7818 Chicago IL 60606

FOX, TERRY ROY, lawyer; b. Sioux City, Iowa, Dec. 22, 1954; s. Mel R. and Marilyn M. (Miller) F.; m. Patricia Ann Quinlan, July 3, 1985. BSBA, U. S.D., 1977, JD, 1980. Bar: S.D. 1980, Iowa 1981. Atty. I Iowa Power and Light Co., Des Moines, 1981-83, atty. II, 1983-85, sr. atty., 1985—; chmn. mgmt. adv. council Iowa Resources Inc., Des Moines, 1987. Mem. ABA, S.D. Bar Assn., Iowa Bar Assn., Polk County Bar Assn., Corp. Counsel Assn., Phi Delta Phi. Avocations: tennis, golf, pvt. pilot. Administrative and regulatory, General corporate, Public utilities. Office: Iowa Power and Light Co 666 Grand Ave PO Box 657 Des Moines IA 50303

FOXHOVEN, JERRY RAY, lawyer; b. Yankton, S.D., July 24, 1952; s. Elmer William and Ida Elizabeth (Lubbers) F.; m. Julie Ann Greco, Apr. 6, 1985; 1 child, Anthony Michael. B.S., Morningside Coll., 1974; J.D., Drake U., 1977. Bar: Iowa 1977, U.S. Dist. Ct. (so. and no. dists.) Iowa 1977, U.S. Ct. Appeals (8th cir.) 1977, U.S. Supreme Ct. 1981, Nebr. 1985, U.S. Dist. Ct. Nebr. 1985, Wis. 1986. Assoc. Critelli & Pille, Des Moines, 1977-79; ptnr. Critelli & Foxhoven, Des Moines, 1979-82, Foxhoven & McCann, Des Moines, 1982—; instr. criminal justice dept. Des Moines Area Community Coll., Ankeny, Iowa, 1978-81, Am. Inst. Banking, 1982—. Mem. steering com. Culver for U.S. Senate, Des Moines, 1980; mem. parish council Sacred Heart Roman Cath. Ch., West Des Moines, 1982. Democrat. Lodge: Masons (jr. warden 1982-84). Personal injury, State civil litigation, Federal civil litigation. Home: 903 45th St Des Moines IA 50312 Office: Foxhoven & McCann 1100 Midland Fin Bldg Des Moines IA 50309

FRAICHE, DONNA DIMARTINO, lawyer; b. New Orleans, Dec. 8, 1951; d. Anthony and Rose Mary (Batchelona) DiM.; m. John F. Fraiche, Dec. 27, 1974; 1 child, Geoffrey Michael. Student St. Mary's Dominican Coll., New Orleans, 1969. La. State U. and A. & M. Coll., 1972; JD, Loyola U., 1975. Bar: La. 1975, U.S. Dist. Ct. (ea., we., mid. dists.) La. 1975, U.S. Dist. Ct. (no. dist.) W.Va. 1984, U.S. Dist. Ct. D.C. 1984, U.S. Ct. Claims 1979, U.S. Tax Ct. 1977, U.S. Ct. Appeals (D.C. cir.) 1977, U.S. Ct. Appeals (3d, 4th, 5th, 10th and 11th cirs.) 1975, U.S. Supreme Ct. 1979. Assoc. litigation sect. Martzell & Montero, New Orleans, 1975-76, McCollister, McCleary, Fazio & Holliday, Baton Rouge, 1976-78; pres., chmn. bd. Donna D. Fraiche, A Profl. Law Corp., New Orleans, 1978-82; of counsel Epstein, Becker, Borsody & Green, P.C., N.Y.C., Washington, Ft. Worth, San Francisco, Los Angeles, 1984—; equity ptnr., head health sect. Broadhurst, Brook, Mangham & Hardy, New Orleans, Lafayette, La., Baton Rouge, Washington, Houston, 1984—. Author: (with others) An Analysis of the Revised Medical Staff Standards of the Joint Commission on Accreditation of Hospitals, 1984; contbr. articles to profl. jours. Bd. dirs. Louise S. Davis Devel. Sch., 1983—; mem. pres. adv. council Our Lady of Holy Cross Coll., New Orleans, 1979—; mem. La. State Arts Council, pres., exec. com.; bd. dirs. Young Audiences, New Orleans chpt., 1982-84, adv. bd., 1984—; mem. women's com. New Orleans Symphony, 1981—; mem. jr. women's com. New Orleans Symphony, 1981—, bd. dirs., 1981-84, adv. bd., 1984—. Mem. LWV, Nat. Health Lawyers Assn. (bd. dirs. 1982, exec. com. sec. 1985, treas., v.p., mem. com. career opportunities, program chmn. med. staff legal issues 1985), Am. Hosp. Assn. (task force on revision JCAH standards for med. staff credentialing 1983—, antitrust considerations 1983—, mem. faculty med. staff credentialing: fundamentals and new dimensions div. med. affairs 1984), Am. Coll. Legal Medicine (assoc. law 1979—), Am. Soc. Law and Medicine, Am. Soc. Hosp. Attys., Am. Acad. Hosp. Attys., ABA (forum com. health law 1980— , chmn. New Orleans health law forum 1982—, health ins. law com. 1979—), Am. Trial Lawyers Assn. (admiralty law sect. 1975-80), Fed. Bar Assn., D.C. Bar Assn, Nat. Assn. Real Estate Investment Trusts (assoc.), Nat. Assn. Women Lawyers, La. Soc. Hosp. Attys. (chmn. by-laws com.), La. State Bar Assn. (mem. antitrust sect.), Phi Kappa Phi, Phi Alpha Delta. Democrat. Roman Catholic. Administrative and regulatory, Antitrust, Health. Home: 3924 St Charles Ave New Orleans LA 70115 Office: Broadhurst Brook Mangham & Hardy 400 Poydras St Suite 2500 New Orleans LA 70130

FRAIDIN, STEPHEN, lawyer; b. Boston, July 29, 1939; s. Morris and Freda (Rozeff) F.; m. Susan Greene, July 4, 1963; children—Matthew, Sam, Sarah. A.B., Tufts U., 1961; J.D., Yale U., 1964. Bar: N.Y. Ptnr. Fried, Frank, Harris, Shriver & Jacobson, N.Y.C., 1964—; bd. dirs. Sybron Corp.; lectr. Practising Law Inst. Contbr. numerous articles to profl. jours. Mem. Assn. Bar City N.Y., ABA. Office: Fried Frank Harris Shriver Jacobson One New York Plaza New York NY 10004

FRAME, NANCY DAVIS, lawyer; b. Brookings, S.D., Dec. 13, 1944; d. Wilmer L. and Adele N. (Swensen) D.; m. J. Davidson Frame, Mar. 28, 1970; 1 child, Katherine Adele. BS, S.D. State U., 1966; MA, Georgetown U., 1968, JD, 1976. Bar: D.C. 1976. Atty., advisor AID, Washington, 1976-81, asst. gen. counsel, 1981-86; dep. dir., legal advisor Trade and Devel. program, Internat. Devel. Cooperation Agy., Washington, 1986—. Recipient Superior Honor award AID, 1984; Fulbright fellow , 1966, NDEA fellow, 1967. Mem. ABA, Fed. Bar Assn. Public international, Government contracts and claims. Home: 5819 Magic Mountain Dr Rockville MD 20852 Office: Dept State Trade and Devel Program SA16 Washington DC 20523

FRANCIS, JEROME LESLIE, lawyer; b. Seattle, May 25, 1941; s. Leslie J. and Phyllis G. (Pike) F.; m. Jen H. Hough, Nov. 2, 1968; children—David S., Catherine E. B.A. in Bus. Adminstrn., U. Wash., 1963; J.D., San Francisco Law Sch., 1968. Bar: Mass. 1970. Sole practice, Sudbury, Mass., 1970-74; atty. legal dept. Texaco Inc., Cherry Hill, N.J., 1974-84, Denver, 1984—. Mem. ABA, Mass. Bar Assn. Republican. Episcopalian. Real property, General corporate, Environment.

FRANCISCOVICH, GEORGE, lawyer; b. N.Y.C., July 23, 1954; s. George Gregory and Lynda Joan (Wolter) F. BS, Syracuse U., 1976; JD, Union U., Albany, N.Y., 1979; postgrad. in trade regulation, NYU, 1987. Bar: N.Y. 1980. Govt. affairs adminstr. Westinghouse Broadcasting and Cable Co., N.Y.C., 1980-83; adminstr. sports sales NBC, N.Y.C., 1984—. Mem. ABA, Fed. Communications Bar Assn. (N.Y. coordinating com. 1980—). Avocation: running. Entertainment, Contracts commercial, Administrative and regulatory. Office: NBC 30 Rockefeller Plaza Room 4841A New York NY 10112

FRANCK, MICHAEL, lawyer, association executive; b. Berlin, Oct. 6, 1932; came to U.S., 1941, naturalized, 1950; s. Wolf and Marga (Oppenheimer) F.; m. Carol E. Eichert, May 29, 1965; children: Michele, Lauren, Rebecca, Jennifer. B.A., Columbia U., 1954, J.D., 1958. Bar: N.Y. 1958, Mich. 1970. Trial counsel Liberty Mut. Ins. Co., Bklyn., 1958-60; chief litigator com. on

grievances Assn. Bar City N.Y., 1960-70; cons. spl. com. on disciplinary procedures, bd. governance Pa. Supreme Ct., 1969-72; spl. counsel Phila. Ct. Common Pleas, 1970-73; exec. dir. State Bar Mich., Lansing, 1970—; mem. Commn. on Uniform State Laws, 1975—, Mich. Malpractice Arbitration Adv. Com., 1975—; mem. coordinating council on lawyer competence Conf. Chief Justices, 1981—. Contbr. articles to bar jours. Served with U.S. Army, 1954-56. Mem. ABA (com. on nat. coordination disciplinary enforcement 1970-73, reporter spl. com. on evaluation of disciplinary enforcement 1968-70, chmn. sect. bar activities 1975-76, mem. long-range planning council 1979-81, mem. council sect. on individual rights and responsibilities 1982—, mem. com. on ethics and profl. responsibility 1982-83, chmn. com. to implement model rules of profl. conduct 1983—, del. 1976-78, 82—, mem. ALI-ABA adv. com. on model peer rev. 1978-79, liaison to Commn. on Evaluation Profl. Standards 1977-83, chmn. com. profl. discipline 1979-82, mem. task force on lawyer advt. 1977), State Bar Mich., Ingham County Bar Assn. Home: 1211 N College Rd Mason MI 48854 Office: 306 Townsend St Lansing MI 48933

FRANCK, THOMAS MARTIN, legal educator; b. Berlin, July 14, 1931; naturalized, 1977; s. Hugo and Ilse (Rosenthal) F. B.A., U. B.C., 1952, LL.B., 1953; LL.M., Harvard U., 1954, S.J.D., 1956. Asst. prof. law U. Nebr., 1956-57; mem. faculty NYU, 1957—, prof. law, 1960—, dir. Center Internat. Studies, 1965—; acting dir. internat. law Carnegie Endowment Internat. Peace, 1973-75, dir., 1975-79; vis. prof. Stanford U., 1963, U. East Africa, 1964, 65, York U. Osgoode Hall Law Sch., 1972-73, 74-76; dir. research UN Inst. Tng. and Research, 1980-82; cons. U.S. AID Dept. State, 1970-72, 85; constl. adviser govts., Tanganyika, 1963, Zanzibar, 1963, 64, Mauritius, 1965; mem. Sierra Leone Govt. Commn. Legal Edn., 1964, Nat. Liberal Adv. Council Can., 1952-53. Author: Race and Nationalism, 1960, The United Nations in the Congo, 1963, East African Unity Through Law, 1965, Comparative Constitutional Process, 1968, The Structure of Impartiality, 1968, Why Federations Fail, 1968, A Free Trade Association, 1968, World Politics, 1971, Secrecy and Foreign Policy, 1973, Resignation in Protest, 1975, Control of Sea Resources by Semi-Autonomous States, 1978, Foreign Policy by Congress, 1979, U.S. Foreign Relations Law, Vols. I-III, 1980-81; editor: The Tethered Presidency, 1981, Human Rights in Third World Perspective, 1982, U.S. Foreign Relations Law, Vols. IV-V, 1984, Nation Against Nation: What Happened to the UN Dream and What the U.S. Can Do About It, 1985, Judging the World Court, 1986; editor-in-chief Am. Jour. Internat. Law. Served to lt. Can. Army, 1953. Guggenheim fellow, 1973-74, 82-83. Mem. Can. Council Internat. Law, African Law Assn., Assn. Am. Law Schs., Am. Soc. Internat. Law (exec. council), Internat. Law Assn. (v.p. U.S. br.), Council Fgn. Relations. Club: Century Assn. (N.Y.C.). Home: 15 Charlton St New York NY 10014

FRANCOEUR, ROBERT ALFRED, lawyer, educator; b. Fall River, Mass., Feb. 3, 1923; s. Edmond Joseph and Leonia (Giasson) F. BA, U. Montreal, Can., 1944; MA, Boston Coll., 1950; PhD, U. Notre Dame, 1958; JD, U. Akron, 1980. Various teaching positions 1941-58; dean LaMennais Coll., Alfred, Maine, 1958; dean Walsh Coll., Canton, Ohio, 1960, pres., 1970, prof., 1980; sole practice Canton, 1980—; legal asst. Avanti Corp., Canton, 1985—. Mem. ABA, Ohio Bar Assn., Stark County Bar Assn. Roman Catholic. Estate planning, General corporate. Home: 2020 Easton St NW Canton OH 44720

FRANCOIS, WILLIAM ARMAND, lawyer; b. Chgo., May 31, 1942; s. George Albert and Evelyn Marie (Smith) F.; m. Barbara Ann Sala, Aug. 21, 1965; children—Nicole Suzanne, Robert William. B.A., DePaul U., 1964, J.D., 1967. Bar: Ill. bar 1967. Practiced in Lyons, Ill., 1967-68; atty. Nat. Can Corp., Chgo., 1970—; sec. Nat. Can Corp., 1974—, v.p., 1978—. Served to capt. AUS, 1968-70. Mem. Am., Ill., Chgo. bar assns., Am. Soc. Corporate Secs. General corporate, Securities. Home: 326 Earls Ct Deerfield IL 60015 Office: 8101 W Higgins Rd Chicago IL 60631

FRANCOMB, LONNIE COLEMAN, lawyer; b. Savanna, Ill., Dec. 13, 1953; s. Lyle Avery and Rita Alma (Baumgartner) F. BA, Western Ill. U., 1975; JD, So. Ill. U., 1978. Bar: Ill. 1978. Assoc. Victor V. Sprengelmeyer, East Dubuque, Ill., 1978, ptnr., 1979; sole practice East Dubuque, 1980—; pub. defender Jo Daviess County, Galena, Ill., 1980—. Contbg. editor So. Ill. U. Law Jour. 1977-78. Fireman Elizabeth (Ill.) Vol. Fire Dept., 1980—, sec., 1981—; Rep. candidate for Ill. Ho. of Reps. 69th dist., 1984; dist. gov. Young Reps. Ill. 16th Cong. dist., 1985—; pres. Ulysses S. Grant Young Reps. Jo Daviess County, 1984—. Mem. ABA, Ill Bar Assn., Jo Daviess County Bar Assn., No. Ill. Pub. Defenders Assn., Galena/Jo Daviess Hist. Soc. Roman Catholic. Lodge: Elks. Avocations: racing automobiles, reading. State civil litigation, Criminal, Juvenile. Home: 302 N Ash St Elizabeth IL 61028 Office: 295 Sinsinawa East Dubuque IL 61025

FRANK, BERNARD, lawyer; b. Wilkes-Barre, Pa., June 11, 1913; s. Abraham and Fanny F.; m. Muriel I. Levy, June 19, 1938; children: Roberta R. Frank Penn, Allan R. Ph.B., Muhlenberg Coll., Allentown, Pa., 1935; J.D., U. Pa., 1938; postgrad., N.Y. U., 1940-42. Bar: Pa. bar 1939. Since practiced in Allentown; asst. U.S. atty. Eastern Dist. Pa., 1950-51; asst. city solicitor Allentown, 1956-60. Author articles on ombudsmen in profl. jours. Vice chmn. B'nai B'rith Nat. Commn. Adult Jewish Edn., 1959-61, chmn., 1961-63. Served with F.A. AUS, 1943-46. Decorated comdr. Order of North Star Sweden; recipient Disting. Service award Internat. Ombudsman Inst., 1980. Mem. Internat. Bar Assn. (chmn. com. ombudsman 1973-80), ABA (chmn. com. ombudsman 1970-76), Fed. Bar Assn. (chmn. com. ombudsman 1971-74), Pa. Bar Assn., Lehigh Bar Assn., Inter-Am. Bar Assn., World Assn. Lawyers, U.S. Assn. Ombudsmen (hon.), Internat. Ombudsman Inst. (dir. 1978—, pres. 1984—), Jewish Publ. Soc. Am. (dir. 1982—, v.p. 1986—), 94th Inf. Div. (pres. 1953-54). General corporate, Estate planning. Home: 745 N 30th St Allentown PA 18104 Office: 931 Hamilton Mall Allentown PA 18105

FRANK, BERNARD ALAN, lawyer; b. Rochester, N.Y., Nov. 12, 1931; s. Mark Louis and Ella Mildred) F.; m. Barbara L. Wilan, June 14, 1952; children—Jeffrey, Glenn, Lauren. B.S.L., Northwestern U., 1953, J.D., 1955. Bar: N.Y. 1955, Ill. 1955, U.S. Dist. Ct. (we. dist.) N.Y. Ptnr., Frank, Garrity & Tiernan, Rochester; ptnr. Weidman Williams Jordan Angeloff & Frank, Rochester, 1979-83, Goldstein, Goldman, Kessler & Underberg, Rochester, 1983—; dir. Monroe Abstract & Title Co., Voit Corp. Mem. N.Y. Bar Assn., Monroe County Bar Assn., U.S. Tennis Assn. Real property, General corporate, Probate. Address: 25 San Rafael Dr Rochester NY 14618

FRANK, FREDERICK NEWMAN, lawyer; b. Pitts., Jan. 10, 1947; s. Abraham C. and Nancy (Newman) F. B.A., U. Pitts., 1967, J.D., 1970. Bar: Pa. 1970, U.S. Dist. Ct. (we. dist.) Pa. 1970, U.S. Ct. Appeals (3d cir.) 1972. Law clk. Pa. Ct. of Common Pleas, Pitts., 1970-71; asst. atty. gen. Pa. Dept. of Justice, 1971-73; ptnr. Raphael-Sheinberg & Barmen, 1973-79, Baskin, Flaherty, Elliott & Mannino, P.C., Pitts., 1979—; solicitor Allegheny County Treas., 1974—. Contbr. articles to law revs. Chmn. Urban Affairs Found., Pitts., 1976-79; treas. Allegheny County Democratic Com., 1980—; bd. dirs. United Jewish Fedn. Recipient Stark Young Leadership award 1976, Levinson Human Relations award, 1984 (both United Jewish Fedn.). Mem. Pa. Bar Assn. (council family law sect. 1985—, editor newsletter, 1975-77), Allegheny County Bar Assn. (treas. family law sect. 1985—, vice chmn. council young lawyers div. 1978-79). Democrat. Jewish. Clubs: Concordia, Pitts. Athletic Assn. Family and matrimonial, State civil litigation, Federal civil litigation. Office: One Mellon Bank Ctr 29th Floor Pittsburgh PA 15219

FRANK, GEORGE ANDREW, lawyer; b. Budapest, Hungary, Apr. 6, 1938; came to U.S., 1957; s. Alex and Ilona (Weiss) F.; m. Carole Shames, Feb. 14, 1979; children: Cheryl, Charles. BS, Colo. State U., 1960; PhD in Organic Chemistry, MIT, 1965; JD, Temple U., 1977. Bar: Pa. 1977, U.S. Dist. Ct. (ea. dist.) Pa. 1977, D.C. 1980, U.S. Ct. Appeals (fed. cir.) 1982, U.S. Supreme Ct. 1984. Sr. chemist Rohm & Haas Co., Phila., 1965-69; lab. head Borden Chem., Phila., 1969-73; sr. scientist Thiokol Corp., Trenton, N.J., 1973-74; counsel Du Pont Corp., Wilmington, Del., 1974-85, sr. counsel, 1986—. Contbr. articles to profl. jours; patentee in field. Recipient Merck award Merck & Co., 1960; Sun Oil Co. grantee, 1964; fellow NIH. Mem. ABA, Phila. Patent Lawyer's Assn. (com. chmn. 1983—), Am. Intellectual Property Law Assn. (task force chmn. 1986). Republican. Avocations: tennis, squash. Patent. Home: 229 Gypsy Ln Wynnewood PA 19096 Office: Du Pont Corp 1007 Market St Wilmington DE 19898

FRANK, HARRY BENNETT, lawyer; b. N.Y.C., Mar. 6, 1905. LLB, NYU, 1926; LLD (hon.), St. John's U., 1978. Bar: N.Y. 1928. Sole practice N.Y.C., 1928-52; chief counsel Office Price Stabilization, N.Y.C., 1952; judge N.Y.C. Ct., 1954-63, N.Y.C. Civil Ct., 1963-65, N.Y. County Supreme Ct., 1965-75; appellate term 1973-75, ret., 1975; counsel Max E. Greenberg, Trayman, Cantor et al, N.Y.C., 1975-78; assoc. F. Lee Bailey and Aaron J. Broder, 1979--81; of counsel Weingrad & Weingrad, N.Y.C., 1981—; lectr. in field. Contbr. articles to profl. jours. Active Am. Jewish Congress, Young Men's Philanthropic League. Recipient awards, including Learned Hand award Joint Citizens Com. Advancement Cts., 1964, cert. of honor NYULaw Sch., 1969, Alumnae Meritorious Service award NYU, 1973, award Trial Bar, 1975. Mem. N.Y. County Lawyers Assn., Assn. Bar of City of N.Y., NYU Law Alumni Assn. (pres. 1969-70, medal of honor 1975). Home: 300 E 74th St New York NY 10021 Office: 350 Fifth Ave New York NY 10001

FRANK, HARVEY, lawyer, author; b. N.Y.C., Aug. 24, 1930; s. Leon and Hannah (Lehr) F.; m. Judith Ellen Lewis, Nov. 29, 1959; 1 child, David L. A.B., NYU, 1951, LL.M., 1961; J.D., Harvard U., 1954. Bar: N.Y. 1954, Va. 1977, Md. 1981, Ohio 1982. Ptnr. Hays Feuer Porter & Spanier, N.Y.C., 1963-69, Burns, Summit, Rovins & Feldesman, N.Y.C., 1970-74; prof. law Coll. William and Mary, Williamsburg, Va., 1974-80; adj. prof. Johns Hopkins U., Balt., 1981; ptnr. Benesch Friedlander, Coplan & Aronoff, Cleve., 1982—. Author: The ERC Closely Held Corporation Guide, 1981, 2d edit., 1984; contbr. articles to legal jours. Mem. ABA, Ohio Bar Assn. General corporate, Securities. Home: 18128 W Clifton Rd Lakewood OH 44107 Office: Benesch Friedlander Coplan & Aronoff 1100 Citizens Bldg Cleveland OH 44114

FRANK, JAMES STUART, lawyer; b. Milw., Aug. 22, 1945; s. Jerome M. and Sylvia (Segall) F.; m. Marjorie Slavick, July 16, 1967; children: Adam Robert, Benjamin Steven. B.S. in Econs., U. Wis., 1967, M.A. Indsl. Relations, 1971, J.D., 1971. Bar: Wis. 1971, D.C. 1971, N.Y. 1974. With NLRB, Washington, 1971-74, Simpson, Thacher & Bartlett, N.Y.C., 1974-83; mem. firm Vedder, Price, Kaufman, Kammholz & Day, N.Y.C., 1983—. Served with USAR, 1968-74. Mem. ABA (labor law and EEO com.), N.Y. State Bar Assn. (labor law com.; practice and procedure before NLRB com.), Fed. Bar Council, Assn. Trial Lawyers Am., D.C. Bar Assn., Wis. Bar Assn. Labor, Civil rights, Federal civil litigation.

FRANK, JULIE ANN, lawyer; b. Omaha, Aug. 5, 1953; d. Morton Stanley Frank and Elaine Edith (Meyerson) Potts; m. Howard Nathan Kaplan, Oct. 26, 1985. BA in Psychology, U. Tex., 1975; JD, Creighton U., 1979. Bar: Nebr. 1979, Tex. 1980. Clk. to presiding justice Nebr. Supreme Ct., Lincoln, 1979-80; assoc. Qualley, Larson & Jones, Omaha, 1980-81; sole practice Omaha, 1981-83; pntr. Pollak & Frank, Omaha, 1983—; instr. Met. Community Coll., Omaha, 1982-84, Buena Vista Coll., Omaha, 1982-84, U. Nebr., 1983. Bd. dirs. Nebr. Civil Liberties Union, 1981-85; adminstrv. coordinator Douglas County Dems., 1982; del. Douglas County Conv., 1984; mem. cen. com. Nebr. Dem. Party, 1984—; mem. Nat. Council Jewish Women, Omaha; del. Douglas County Conv., 1984, 86. Mem. ABA (family law sect.), Assn. Trial Lawyers Am., Omaha Bar Assn. Avocations: aerobics, tennis. Bankruptcy, Juvenile, Social security disability. Home: 960 S 119th Ct Omaha NE 68154 Office: Pollak & Frank 1823 Harney St #203 Omaha NE 68102

FRANK, KATHERINE MARIE, lawyer; b. Dubuque, Iowa, Oct. 23, 1952; d. Lester W. amd Marjorie K. (Fine) Amenda; m. Andrew H. Frank, Aug. 12, 1972; children: Amanda E., Matthew L. BS with honors, U. Wis., Platteville, 1973; JD, U. Wis., Madison, 1976. Bar: Wis. 1976, U.S. Dist Ct. (we. dist.) Wis. 1976. Ptnr. Frank & Frank, Janesville, Wis., 1976—; guest lectr. U. Wis. Madison, 1983, 85. Mem. Wis. Bar Assn., Rock County Bar Assn. (exec. com., v.p.). Family and matrimonial. Office: 1404 Creston Park Dr Janesville WI 53545

FRANK, LLOYD, lawyer, chemical company executive; b. N.Y.C., Aug. 9, 1925; s. Herman and Selma (Lowenstein) F.; m. Beatrice Silverstein, Dec. 26, 1954; children: Margaret Lois, Frederick. B.A., Oberlin Coll., 1947; J.D., Cornell U., 1950. Bar: N.Y. 1950, U.S. Supreme Ct. 1973. Practice law N.Y.C., 1950—; sr. ptnr. Parker Chapin Flattau & Klimpl; sec. Grow Group, Inc., N.Y.C., 1964—; bd. dirs. Madison Industries, Inc., N.Y.C., Metro-Tel Corp., Syosset, N.Y., Ketcham & McDougall, Inc., Roseland, N.J., Perrigo Co., Allegan, Mich., Public Art Fund, Inc., N.Y.C., Wilfred Am. Edn1. Corp., N.Y.C., Park Electrochem. Corp., Lake Success, N.Y.; lectr. Am. Mgmt. Assn., 1967-77, Probe Internat., Inc., 1975-77, Corporate Seminars, Inc., 1968-71. Mem. Assn. Bar City N.Y., N.Y. County Lawyers Assn. (mem. com. on corps., com. on SEC), ABA (com. affiliated and related corps. taxation sect.). Clubs: Chemists, Oberlin of N.Y. General corporate, Public international, Securities. Home: 25 Central Park W New York NY 10023 Office: 1211 Ave Of Americas New York NY 10036

FRANK, MARK KENNITH, III, lawyer; b. Havana, Cuba, Oct. 4, 1941 (parents Am. citizens); s. Mark Kennith and Dallas J. (Wilson) F.; m. Katherine S. White; children—Courtney R., Jessica C., Rachel K., Matthew C. B.S. in Fgn. Service, Georgetown U., 1964; J.D., George Washington U., 1967. Bar: D.C. 1968, Alaska 1970. Trial atty. merger div. FTC, Washington, 1968-70; asst. atty. gen. State of Alaska, Juneau, 1970-72; staff counsel ITT, Mass. and N.Y., 1972-75; sr. assoc. counsel, asst. sec. Champion Internat. Corp., N.Y.C. and Stamford, Conn., 1975—. Mem. ABA (past council natural resources sect., past chmn. forest resources com.). Clubs: Metropolitan (Washington); Greenwich (Conn.) Country. General corporate, Antitrust, Real property. Office: Champion Internat One Champion Plaza Stamford CT 06921

FRANK, MARK STEPHEN, lawyer; b. Pitts., July 24, 1949; s. Bernard H. and Yetta (Haught) F.; m. Lynne Marcovsky, Sept. 20, 1982; children: Rebecca Lynne, Alexander Geoffrey. AB, Kenyon Coll., 1971; JD, U. Pitts., 1974. Bar: Pa. 1974, U.S. Dist. Ct. (we. dist.) Pa. 1974, U.S. Ct. Appeals (3d cir.) 1975. Ptnr. Aderson, Frank & Steiner, Pitts., 1976—. V.p. Graymore Road Assn., 1984—; pres. bd. trustees Shadylane Presch., Pitts., 1986—. Mem. Am. Trial Lawyers Assn., Pa. Trial Lawyers Assn. State civil litigation, Federal civil litigation, Personal injury. Home: 7532 Graymore Rd Pittsburgh PA 15221 Office: Aderson Frank & Steiner 2320 Grant Bldg Pittsburgh PA 15219

FRANK, VINCENT ANTONIO, biomedical company executive, lawyer; b. Rochester, N.Y., Sept. 27, 1952; s. Vincent Pasquale and Angela (Palma) F.; m. Jill Kathryn Linehan, Oct. 22, 1977; children: Kathryn Maura, Patrick Vincenzo. BA, U. Rochester, 1974; JD, Northwestern U., 1977. Bar: Pa. 1977, N.Y. 1979, Ill. 1980, Calif. 1982, U.S. Dist. Ct. (we. dist.) Pa. 1977, U.S. Dist. Ct. (we. dist.) N.Y. 1979, U.S. Dist. Ct. (no. dist.) Ill. 1980, U.S. Dist. Ct. (so. dist.) Calif. 1982. Atty. U.S. Steel Corp., Pitts., 1977-78; assoc. Harter, Secrest & Emery, Rochester, N.Y., 1978-79; ptnr. Johnson & Colmar, Chgo., 1979-81; v.p. Molecular Biosytems, Inc., San Diego, 1981-83, exec. v.p., 1983-85, pres., 1985—; v.p. pub. relations Assn. Corp. Growth, San Diego, 1983—. Pres. bd. dirs. Beach Area Commn. Health Ctr., San Diego, 1983—. Mem. ABA, Calif. Bar Assn., San Diego Bar Assn. Republican. Roman Catholic. General corporate, Securities, Health. Home: 10967 Riesling Dr San Diego CA 92131 Office: Molecular Biosystems Inc 10030 Barnes Canyon Rd San Diego CA 92126

FRANK, WILLIAM HARRIS, editor; b. Cambridge, Mass., Jan. 23, 1948; s. Victor Samuel and Miriam (Goldberg) F.; m. Janet Laura Mirengoff, Aug. 20, 1972; children: Alexander Stephen, Elizabeth Julia. AB, Ripon Coll., 1970; JD, George Washington U., 1973. Bar: D.C. 1973. Legal editor Bur. Nat. Affairs, Washington, 1973-81, sr. legal editor, 1981-86, mng. editor, 1986—; instr. U. Md., College Park, 1976-80. Mng. editor: Toxics Law Reporter, 1986—. Served to capt. USAR, 1970-76. Mem. ABA. Avocations: chess, classical music, golf. Environment, Insurance, Personal injury. Office: Bur Nat Affairs Toxics Law Reporter 1231 25th St NW Washington DC 20037

FRANKEL, JAMES BURTON, lawyer; b. Chgo., Feb. 25, 1924; s. Louis and Thelma (Cohn) F.; m. Louise Untermyer, Jan. 22, 1956; children—Nina, Sara, Simon. Student U. Chgo., 1940-42; B.S., U.S. Naval Acad., 1945; LL.B., Yale U., 1952. Bar: Calif. 1953. Mem. Steinhart, Goldberg, Feigenbaum & Ladar, San Francisco, 1954-72; of counsel Cooper, White & Cooper, San Francisco, 1972—; sr. fellow, lectr. in law Yale U., 1971-72; lectr. Stanford U. Law Sch., 1973-75; vis. prof. U. Calif. Law Sch., 1975-76. Pres. Council Civic Unity of San Francisco Bay Area, 1964-66; chmn. San Francisco Citizens Charter Revision Com., 1968-70; mem. San Francisco Pub. Schs. Commn., 1975-76; trustee Natural Resources Def. Council, 1972-77, 79—, staff atty., 1977-79; chmn. San Francisco Citizens Energy Policy Adv. Com., 1981-82. Mem. ABA, Calif. Bar Assn., San Francisco Bar Assn. Democrat. General corporate, Probate, Real property. Office: 101 California St 16 Floor San Francisco CA 94111

FRANKEL, ROGER L., lawyer; b. Washington, Apr. 6, 1946; s. Louis Max and Sara Betty (Seltzer) F.; m. Betty Ann Frank, Oct. 15, 1978; children—Jason, Jessica, Jamie. B.A., Brandeis U., 1968; J.D. with honors, George Washington U., 1971. Bar: D.C. 1971, Md., 1972. Ptnr., Lerch Early Roseman & Frankel, Bethesda, Md. Mem. ABA, Md. Bar Assn., Montgomery County Bar Assn. (chmn. bankruptcy sect. 1980-82). Jewish. Club: Woodmont Country (Rockville, Md.) (bd. govs. 1985—). Bankruptcy. Home: 7321 Heatherhill Ct Bethesda MD 20817 Office: Lerch Early Roseman & Frankel 7101 Wisconsin Ave Suite 1300 Bethesda MD 20814

FRANKEL, SANDOR, lawyer, author; b. N.Y.C., Nov. 16, 1943; s. David and Bessie (Edelson) F. B.A., N.Y. U., 1964; LL.B., Harvard U., 1967. Bar: N.Y. 1967, D.C. 1968, U.S. Supreme Ct. 1976. Staff mem. White House Task Force on Crime, 1967; counsel Nat. Commn. Reform Fed. Criminal Laws, 1968; asst. U.S. atty. for D.C. 1968-71; practice law N.Y.C., 1971—; lectr. N.Y. U. Inst. on Fed. Taxation, 1976, 77. Author: Beyond a Reasonable Doubt, 1972 (Edgar Allan Poe award), The Aleph Solution, 1978; How to Defend Yourself Against the IRS, 1985. Contbr. articles to legal publs. Mem. Phi Beta Kappa. Criminal, Federal civil litigation, State civil litigation. Office: 225 Broadway New York NY 10007

FRANKENHEIM, SAMUEL, lawyer; b. N.Y.C., Dec. 20, 1932; s. Samuel and Mary Emma (Ward) F.; m. Nina Barbara Mennerich, Sept. 2, 1960; children—Robert Mennerich, John Frederick. B.A., Cornell U., 1954, LL.B., 1959. Bar: N.Y. 1959, Mass. 1976. Law clk. N.Y. Ct. Appeals, 1959-61; assoc. Shearman & Sterling, attys., N.Y.C., 1961-68; ptnr. Shearman & Sterling, attys., 1968-69; sr. v.p., dir. Damon Corp., Needham Heights, Mass., 1969-78; sr. v.p., gen. counsel mem. Office of Chmn. Gen. Cinema Corp., Chestnut Hill, Mass., 1979—; dir. Carter Hawley Hale Stores, Inc., Los Angeles. Trustee Newton-Wellesley Hosp., Newton, Mass., 1973-85, pres., 1980-82; bd. govs. Newell Health Corp., 1983—; overseer Wang Ctr. for Performing Arts, Boston, 1985—. Served to 1st lt. USAF, 1955-57. Mem. Assn. Bar City N.Y., Am., N.Y. State, Boston bar assns., Am. Corp. Counsel Assn., Am. Soc. Corp. Secs. Club: Broad St. (N.Y.C.). General corporate. Home: 115 Shornecliffe Rd Newton MA 02158 Office: 27 Boylston St Chestnut Hill MA 02167

FRANKFURT, MORTON ALLEN, lawyer; b. N.Y.C., Jan. 22, 1937; s. Stanley and Mary (Preisner) F.; m. Elaine P. Miller, June 26, 1965. B.S., NYU, 1958; LL.B., St. John's U., 1961. Bar: N.Y. 1962, Fla. 1980. Assoc. firm Margolin & Schekter, N.Y.C., 1962-68; legal counsel, v.p., dir. Bohack Corp., N.Y.C., 1968-77; pvt. practice law, N.Y.C., 1977—. Contbr. articles to profl. jours. Mem. N.Y. Bar Assn., Fla. Bar Assn., Alpha Epsilon Pi. Lodge: Masons. Real property, General corporate, Contracts commercial. Office: 10 Columbus Circle New York NY 10019

FRANKLIN, BLAKE TIMOTHY, lawyer; b. San Mateo, Calif., Sept. 28, 1942; s. Harvey James and Marie Agnes (Leane) F. A.B., Dartmouth Coll., 1963; J.D., Harvard U., 1966. Bar: Calif. 1966, D.C. 1969, U.S. Supreme Ct. 1970, N.Y. 1976. AID contractor Peace Corps; vis. prof. comml. law U. Costa Rica, San Jose, 1966-68; assoc. Coudert Bros., Washington, 1969-74, ptnr., N.Y.C., 1975-83; ptnr. Gibson Dunn & Crutcher, N.Y.C., 1983—; v.p., dir. South Am. Placers, Inc. Mem. ABA, Inter-Am. Bar Assn., Am. Soc. Internat. Law. Private international, Banking, General corporate. Office: Gibson Dunn & Crutcher 200 Park Ave New York NY 10166

FRANKLIN, BRUCE WALTER, lawyer; b. Ellendale, N.D., Feb. 26, 1936; s. Wallace Henry and Frances (Webb) F.; m. Kristy Ann Jones, Feb. 7, 1944; children—Kevin, Monica, Taylor. Student, U. Mich., 1954-56; grad. Eastern Mich. U., 1957; LL.B., Detroit Coll. Law, 1962. Bar: Mich. 1963. Sole practice, Troy, Mich., from 1962; now mng. ptnr. Franklin, Bigler, Berry & Johnston, P.C., Troy. Past chmn. Mich. Young Republicans. Served with U.S. Army. State civil litigation, Personal injury. Office: 14th Floor 900 Tower Dr Troy MI 48098

FRANKLIN, FREDERICK RUSSELL, legal association executive; b. Berlin, Germany, Mar. 20, 1929; s. Ernest James and Frances (Price) F.; A.B., Ind. U., 1951, J.D. with high distinction, 1956; m. Barbara Ann Donovan, Jan. 26, 1952; children—Katherine Elizabeth, Frederick Russell. Bar: Ind. 1956. Trial atty. criminal div. and ct. of claims sect., civil div. U.S. Dept. Justice, Washington, 1956-60; gen. counsel Ind. State Bar Assn., Indpls., 1960-67; dir. continuing legal edn. for Ind., adj. prof. law Ind. U., Indpls., 1965-68; staff dir. profl. standards Am. Bar Assn., Chgo., 1968-70; exec. v.p. Nat. Attys. Title Assurance Fund, Inc., Indpls., 1970-72; staff dir. legal edn. and admissions to the bar Am. Bar Assn., Chgo., 1972—. Trustee, Olympia Fields (Ill.) United Methodist Ch., 1980-84; treas. bd. dirs. Olympia Fields Pub. Library, 1984—; mem. Olympia Fields Police Bd., 1983—. Served to capt. USAF, 1951-53. Mem. Am., Ind., Ill. bar assns., Fed. Bar Assn. (officer, found. bd. dirs. 1974—, historian 1979—, nat. council 1965—, nat. v.p. 1967-69, chpt. pres. 1965-66, chmn. admission to practice and recert. com. 1980-82, bd. dirs. Chgo. chpt. 1984—), Nat. Orgn. Bar Counsel (pres. 1967), Order of Coif, Phi Delta Phi. Kiwanian, Elk. Legal association executive. Home: 3617 Parthenon Way Olympia Fields IL 60461 Office: 750 N Lake Shore Dr Chicago IL 60611

FRANKLIN, JUSTIN DUKE, JR., lawyer, author, publisher; b. Gadsden, Ala., Mar. 23, 1944; s. Justin D. and Gladys J. (Moore) F.; B.A., Auburn U., 1965; J.D., Samford U., 1968. Bar: Ala. 1968, Sole practice, Birmingham, Ala., 1968-69; legal editor Matthew Bender Co., N.Y.C., 1969-70; legal editor, mng. editor Clark Boardman Co. Ltd., N.Y.C., 1971-80, editor-in-chief, dir., 1980—, sec., 1983—. Mem. ABA, Nat. Lawyers Guild, Am. Soc. Corp. Secs. Co-author: Searches and Seizures, Arrests and Confessions, 1979; Guidebook to the Freedom of Information and Privacy Acts, 2d edit. 1986. Communications. Office: Clark Boardman Co Ltd 435 Hudson St New York NY 10014

FRANKLIN, LEONARD, lawyer; b. N.Y.C., Nov. 22, 1914; s. Louis and Sara F.; m. Hannah Myra Franklin, Nov. 1, 1940; 1 son, Alan M. B.A., N.Y. U., 1934, LL.B., 1937. Bar: N.Y., 1938. Sole practice, 1938-65; ptnr. Franklin, Weinrib, Rudell, Vassallo, P.C., and predecessors, N.Y.C., 1965—. Served to capt., USAAF, 1942-46. Mem. ABA, N.Y. State Bar Assn., N.Y. County Lawyers Assn. Entertainment. Office: 950 3d Ave New York NY 10022

FRANKLIN, LUCILLE ESPEY, lawyer; b. Washington, Pa., July 3, 1951; d. Harold George and Ruth Clarinda (Brown) E.; m. Paul Andrew Stephens Jr., Aug. 16, 1973 (div. July 1982); 1 child, Ruth Espey Stephens; m. Keith Barry Franklin, Jan. 3, 1987. BA, Washington & Jefferson Coll., 1973; MA, Wake Forest U., 1975; JD, Emory U., 1981. Bar: Ga. 1981, U.S. Dist. Ct. (no. dist.) Ga. 1982, Fla. 1984, U.S. Dist. (so. dist.) Fla. 1986. Assoc. P.M. Francoeur Jr., P.A., Naples, Fla., 1985; ptnr. Siesky, Lehman & Espey, P.A., Naples, 1985—. V.p. Naples Park Neighborhood Watch, Inc., 1985-86, treas. 1986—; mem. Naples Park PTO, 1985—, LWV; asst. coordinator local #177 Foster Parents Plan, Naples, 1985—; pres. Parents Without Partners, 1985. Served to capt. JAGC, U.S. Army, 1982-85. Mem. ABA (family and trial sects.), Fla. Bar Assn. (family sect.), Assn. Trial Lawyers Am., Collier County Bar Assn. (law day com.). Republican. Mem. United Ch. Christ. Lodge: Zonta. Avocations: running, chess, home restoration. State civil

litigation, Local government, Family and matrimonial. Office: Siesky Lehman & Espey PA 791 10th St S Naples FL 33963

FRANKLIN, MARC A., legal educator; b. 1932. AB, Cornell U., 1953, LLB, 1956. Bar: N.Y. 1956. Sole practice, N.Y.C., 1956-57; law clk. to judge U.S. Ct. Appeals 2d Cir., 1957-58, to Justice Earl Warren, U.S. Supreme Ct., 1958-59; asst. prof. Columbia U. Law Sch., 1959-61, assoc. prof., 1961-62; assoc. prof. Stanford (Calif.) U. Law Sch., 1962-64, prof., 1964—, now Frederick I. Richman prof. law; fellow Ctr. Advanced Study in Behavioral Scis., 1968-69; Fulbright research scholar Victoria U., Wellington, N.Z., 1973; vis. prof. U. Calif.-Berkeley, 1974, 77; Marshall Madison vis. prof., lectr. U. San Francisco Sch. Law, 1983. Editor-in-chief Cornell Law Quar.; author: Cases on Tort Law and Alternatives, 4th edit., 1987; Cases and Materials on Mass Media Law, 3d edit., 1987; The First Amendment and the Fourth Estate, 3d edit., 1985, The First Amendment and the Fifth Estate, 1986. Mem. Order of Coif. Legal education. Office: Stanford U Law Sch Stanford CA 94305

FRANKLIN, RANDY WAYNE, lawyer; b. Chgo., Mar. 28, 1945; s. Sidney Aaron and Hilda (Goldstein) Franklin Skora; m. Danette Penny Siegel, Dec. 21, 1974; children—Jennifer Rose, Jason Adam, Seth Peter. BS., Bradley U., 1967; J.D., Massey U., 1971. Bar: Ga. 1972, Ill. 1973. Tchr. high sch., Chgo. Bd. Edn., 1968-70; asst. pub. defender Cook County, Chgo., 1973-79; assoc. McLennon, Nelson, Gabriele & Nudo, Park Ridge, Ill., 1979-81; ptnr. Gabriele & Franklin, Park Ridge, 1981—. Bd. dirs. Young Men's Jewish Council, Chgo., 1974-76, Main Family and Mental Health Ctr., Little Mexico Convent Holy Spirit, Mt. Prospect, Ill., 1980—; advisor Northeastern Ill. U. Sch. of Bus. Mem. ABA, Ill. Bar Assn., Ga. Bar Assn., No. Suburban Bar Assn. (bd. of mgrs.), Nat. Assn. Criminal Def. Lawyers, Assn. Trial Lawyers Am. General practice, Family and matrimonial, State civil litigation. Home: 330 Landis Ln Deerfield IL 60015 Office: Gabriele & Franklin 1550 N Northwest Hwy Suite 308 Park Ridge IL 60068 also: 180 N Michigan Ave Suite 1605 Chicago IL 60601

FRANKLIN, RICHARD MARK, lawyer; b. Chgo., Dec. 13, 1947; s. Henry W. and Gertrude (Gross) F.; m. Marguerite June Wesle, Sept. 2, 1973; children: Justin Wesley, Elizabeth Cecilia. BA, U. Wis., 1970; postgrad., U. Freiburg, Fed. Republic Germany, 1968-69; JD, Columbia U., 1973. Bar: Ill. 1973, U.S. Dist. Ct. (no. dist.) Ill. 1973, U.S. Ct. Appeals (7th cir.) 1973. Assoc. Baker & McKenzie, Chgo., 1973-79, Frankfurt, Fed. Republic Germany, 1979-80; ptnr. Baker & McKenzie, Chgo., 1980—. Mem. ABA, Ill. Bar Assn., Chgo. Bar Assn. (com. on profl. responsibility). Mem. United Ch. Christ. Avocations: music, lit., theatre, outdoor activities. Federal civil litigation, State civil litigation, Private international. Home: 1179 Asbury Ave Winnetka IL 60093 Office: Baker & McKenzie Suite 2800 Prudential Plaza Chicago IL 60601

FRANKLIN, ROBERT V., judge; b. Toledo, Jan. 6, 1926; s. Robert V. Sr. and Josephine (Beard) F.; m. Kathryn Jane Harris, Aug. 3, 1952; children: Jeffery, Gary. BA, Morehouse Coll., 1947; JD, U. Toledo, 1950; LLD (hon.), Morehouse Coll., 1980. Pros. atty. City of Toledo, 1953-58, 2d asst. law dir., 1959-60; judge Toledo Mcpl. Ct., 1960-68, Lucas County Common Pleas Ct., Toledo, 1969-86; ret. 1986. Bd. trustees St. Luke's Hosp., Toledo, 1964-76, Morehouse Coll., Atlanta, 1980—, U. Toledo Alumni Found.; chmn. bd. trustees The Boule Found., nat. pres.; pres. Ohio Conf. NAACP Brs., 1958-59, Scholarship Fund, Inc., Toledo, 1980—; mem. Housing Dirs. of Greater Toledo. Served to sgt. U.S. Army, 1950-52, Korea. Mem. ABA, Ohio State Bar Assn., Toledo Bar Assn., Am. Judicature Soc., Ohio Common Pleas Judges Assn. (pres. 1982), Toledo C. of C. (named one of Outstanding Young Men of Am. 1960), U. Toledo Alumni Assn. (recipient Gold T award 1982), Toledo Automobile Club (pres.), Sigma Pi Phi. Democrat. Baptist. Home: 5018 Chatham Valley Dr Toledo OH 43615 Office: 1405 Toledo Trust Bldg Toledo OH 43602

FRANKLIN, WILLIAM JAY, lawyer; b. Logansport, Ind., Mar. 1, 1945; s. Frederick Arthur and Ferne (Friskney) F.; m. Cynthia Ann Boerger, July 26, 1969 (div. Oct. 1979). B.S. with highest distinction in Mech. Engring., Purdue U., 1968, M.S. in Computer Sci., 1970; J.D. Georgetown U., 1977. Bar: D.C. 1977, U.S. Dist. Ct. D.C. 1978, U.S. Ct. Appeals (D.C. cir.) 1977, U.S. Supreme Ct. 1981. Computer specialist antitrust div. U.S. Dept. Justice, Washington, 1976-77; assoc. Lowenstein, Newman Reis & Axelrad, Washington, 1977-80, Becker, Gurman, Lukas, Meyers & O'Brien, Washington, 1980-82; prin. Mahn, Franklin & Goldenberg, P.C., Washington, 1982-85; ptnr. Bell, Boyd & Lloyd, 1985—; guest lectr. Brookings Instn., Washington, 1982. Author monthly column: Legal Briefs, 1984—. Mem. ABA, Fed. Communications Bar Assn., Tau Beta Pi. Administrative and regulatory, Computer, Communications. Home: 1530 O St NW Washington DC 20005

FRANKOVITCH, CARL NICHOLAS, lawyer; b. Steubenville, Ohio, Aug. 26, 1947; s. Carl A. and Rose (Lalich) F.; m. Leslie W. Wild, Aug. 9, 1969; children: Marden, Nick, Allyn. BA, Coll. William & Mary, 1969; JD, U. W.Va., 1972. Bar: W.Va. 1972, Pa. 1985, U.S. Dist. Ct. (no. and so. dists.) W.Va., U.S. Ct. Appeals (4th cir.). Ptnr. Frankovitch & Antakd, Weirton, W.Va., 1972-85, Volk, Frankovitch, Anetakis, Recht, Robertson & Hellerstedt, Weirton, 1985—; bd. dirs. First Nat. Bank Weirton. Mem. ABA, Def. Research Inst., Am. Hosp. Assn., Am. Assn. Hosp. Counsel, Order of Coif. Labor, State civil litigation, Health. Office: Volk Frankovitch Anetakis Recht Robertson & Hellerstedt 334 Penco Rd Weirton WV 26062

FRANKS, HERBERT HOOVER, lawyer; b. Joliet, Ill., Jan. 25, 1934; s. Carol and Lottie (Dermer) F.; m. Eileen Pepper, June 22, 1957; children—David, Jack, Eli. B.S., Roosevelt U., 1954. Bar: Ill. 1961, U.S. Dist. Ct. (no. dist.) Ill. 1961, U.S. Supreme Ct. 1967. Ptnr. Franks & Filler, 1985—; chmn. Wonder Lake State Bank, Ill., 1979—; chmn. First Nat. Bank, Marengo, Ill., 1976-81, mem. exec. com., 1976—. Bus. editor Am. U. Law Rev. 1959, 60. State pres. Young Democrats of Ill., 1970-72; trustee Hebrew Theol. Coll., Skokie, Ill., 1974—; trustee, sec. Forest Inst. Profl. Psychology, Des Plaines, Ill., 1979—; chmn. Forest Hosp., Des Plaines, 1980—. Served with U.S. Army, 1956-58. Fellow Ill. State Bar; mem. Ill. Trial Lawyers (mng. bd. 1975-85, treas. 1985—), Sigma Nu Phi (pres. 1980-82). Lodges: Masons, Shriners. Workers' compensation, Banking, Health. Home: 19324 E Grant Hwy Marengo IL 60152 Office: Franks & Filler 19333 E Grant Hwy Marengo IL 60152

FRANKS, HERSCHEL PICKENS, judge; b. Savannah, Tenn., May 28, 1930; s. Herschel R. and Vada (Pickens) F.; m. Joan Loope, June 2, 1935; 1 dau., Ramona. Student U. Tenn.-Martin, U. Md.; J.D., U. Tenn.-Knoxville; grad. Nat. Jud. Coll. of U. Nev. Bar: Tenn. 1959, U.S. Supreme Ct. 1968. Claims atty. U.S. Fidelity & Guaranty Co., Knoxville, 1958; ptnr. Harris, Moon, Meacham & Franks, Chattanooga, 1959-70; chancellor 3d Chancery div. of Hamilton County, 1970-78; judge Tenn. Ct. Appeals, Chattanooga, 1978—; spl. justice Tenn. Supreme Ct., 1979, 86, 87; presiding judge Hamilton County Trial Cts., 1977-78. Served with USNG, 1949-50, USAF, 1950-54. Mem. Tenn. Bar Assn. (award of merit 1968-69), Chattanooga Bar Assn. (pres. 1968-69, Founds. of Freedom award 1986), ABA (award of merit), Am. Judicature Soc., Inst. Jud. Adminstrn., Phi Alpha Delta. Mem. United Ch. of Christ. Clubs: Optimist (pres. 1965-66), Community Service award 1971), Mountain City, LeConte, City Farmers, Torch. Address: 540 McCallie Ave Chattanooga TN 37402

FRANT, RONALD MAYER, lawyer; b. Detroit, Apr. 22, 1952; s. Murray Lee Frant and Ethel Janet Moss; m. Barbara Sue Kreiger, Nov. 19, 1984. BA, U. Calif., San Diego, 1974; JD, U. San Diego, 1977. Bar: Calif. 1977, U.S. Dist Ct. (so. dist.) Calif. 1977, U.S. Ct. Appeals (9th cir.) 1981, U.S. Supreme Ct. 1986. Assoc. Goldberg & Link, San Diego, 1977-81, Law Office Charles L. Goldberg, San Diego, 1981-83; ptnr. Goldberg & Frant, San Diego, 1983—; Judge pro tem El Cajon Mcpl. Ct., San Diego, 1985—, San Diego Mcpl. Ct., 1985—; lectr. San Diego State U., 1986. Mem. ABA, Assn. Trial Lawyers Am., Calif. Attys. for Criminal Justice, Foothills Bar Assn., San Diego County Bar Assn., Calif. Bar Assn., Criminal Lawyers Club of San Diego. Democrat. Jewish. Avocations: golf, travel. Criminal. Office: Goldberg & Frant 303 W A St San Diego CA 92101

FRANTZ, THOMAS RICHARD, lawyer; b. Waynesboro, Pa., Sept. 10, 1947; s. John Richard and Janet (Donnelly) F.; 1 son, Thomas Richard; m. Dianne Boffa, June 22, 1985; 1 dau., Lindsay Amore. B.A., Coll. William and Mary, 1970, J.D., 1973, LL.M., 1981. Bar: Va., U.S. Dist. Ct. (ea. dist.) Va. 1974, U.S. Ct. Appeals (4th cir.) 1974, U.S. Supreme Ct. 1978. Supr. tax dept. Peat, Marwick, Mitchell & Co., 1973-74; officer, dir. Clark & Stant P.C., Virginia Beach, Va., 1974—; adj. prof. law Coll. William and Mary, 1981-82, trustee tax conf. 1984—; planning com. Old Dominion U. Tax Conf., 1977-81, chmn., 1981. Trustee William and Mary Athletic Ednl. Found., 1985—, Old Dominion U. Ednl. Found., 1980—; trustee, mem. exec. com. Va. Mus. Marine Sci., 1980—; bd. dirs. Sovran Bank, 1984—; chmn. participants com. Va. Republican Conv., 1981; chmn. Virginia Beach Marathon, 1977, Va. Beach United Way Capital Funds Dr., 1986; bd. trustees Cape Henry Collegiate Sch., 1986— . Served to capt. USAR, 1972-79. Mem. Va. Soc. C.P.A.s, Am. Inst. C.P.A.s, Am. Assn. Attys.-C.P.A.s, Va. Bar Assn., Norfolk-Portsmouth Bar Assn. (exec. com. 1983-85), Va. State Bar (bd. govs. trusts and estates sect.), Virginia Beach Bar Assn. Lutheran. Club: Princess Anne Country. Contbr. articles profl. jours. Corporate taxation, Estate taxation, Personal income taxation. Address: 900 One Columbus Center Virginia Beach VA 23462

FRANTZE, DAVID W., lawyer; b. Kansas City, Mo., Jan. 28, 1955; s. James W. and Margaret M. (Pursley) F.; m. Geri L. Sexton, July 28, 1979; children: Kevin, Lisa. BA, Avila Coll., 1976; JD, U. Mo., Kansas City, 1981. Assoc. Stinson, Mag & Fizzell, Kansas City, 1981—. Bd. dirs. Kansas City Spirit, Inc., 1986, 87—. Mem. ABA, Mo. Bar Assn., Kansas City Met. Bar Assn., Lawyers Assn. Kansas City, Kansas City C. of C. (metro affairs com.). Roman Catholic. Real property, Landlord-tenant, Condemnation. Home: 407 E 105th Terr Kansas City MO 64131 Office: Stinson Mag & Fizzell 920 Main Suite 1900 Kansas City MO 64105

FRANZ, PAUL ALLEN, lawyer; b. Cin., June 16, 1951; s. Aloysius Leo and Eunice (Williams) F.; m. Shari Melissa Loo, Sept. 13, 1980; 1 child, Christopher Steven. BA, U. Cin., 1973; JD, UCLA, 1980. Bar: Calif. 1981, U.S. Ct. Appeals (6th cir.) 1981, Ohio 1982, U.S. Ct. Appeals (10th cir.) 1982, U.S. Ct. Appeals (11th cir.) 1985. Law clk. to judge U.S. Ct. Appeals (6th cir.), Cin., 1980-82; counsel Procter & Gamble, Cin., 1982—. Antitrust, General corporate. Office: Procter & Gamble 1 P&G Plaza Cincinnati OH 45202

FRANZ, WILLIAM MANSUR, lawyer; b. Dayton, Ohio, Dec. 3, 1930; s. Robert and Muriel (Bisbee) F.; m. Jane Speers, May 26, 1962; children: David, Julie, Elizabeth, Susan. BA in Russian Studies, Syracuse U., 1953; LLB, Chgo.-Kent Coll. Law, 1959. Bar: Ill. 1959, U.S. Dist. Ct. (no. dist.) Ill. 1959. Assoc. Righeimer & Righeimer, Chgo., 1959, Corcoran & Corcoran, Evanston, Ill., 1959-61; ptnr. Franz & Franz, Crystal Lake, Ill., 1961-73, Franz, Naughton & Leahy, Crystal Lake, 1974—. Served to 1st lt. USAF, 1951-53. Mem. Ill. Bar Assn., McHenry County Bar Assn. Republican. Club: Crystal Lake Country. Lodge: Lions. Construction, Real property, General practice. Home: 623 Leonard Pkwy Crystal Lake IL 60014 Office: Franz Naughton & Leahy 453 Coventry Green Crystal Lake IL 60014

FRANZÉN, STEPHEN EDWARDS, lawyer; b. Bloomington, Ind., July 17, 1953; s. Charles Kugler and Nancy Morris (Edwards) F.; m. Therese Lee Glisson, May 8, 1982; 1 child, Sarah. BA, Duke U., 1975; JD, U. Ga., 1979. Bar: Ga. 1979. Assoc. Kunes & Kunes, Tifton, Ga., 1979-80, Jones & Van Gerpen, Atlanta, 1980-81; asst. dist. atty. Gwinnett County, Lawrenceville, Ga., 1981-85, chief asst. dist. atty., 1985—. Mem. outreach com. Christ Ch., Norcross, Ga., 1985—. Mem. ABA, Ga. Bar Assn., Gwinnett County Bar Assn. (sec., treas. 1983-84). Episcopalian. Avocations: tennis, basketball, sailing, camping, reading history. Criminal. Office: Gwinnett County Dist Atty Office 142 Pike St Lawrenceville GA 30246

FRANZKE, RICHARD ALBERT, lawyer; b. Lewistown, Mont., Mar. 7, 1935; s. Arthur A. and Senta (Clark) F.; divorced; children: Mark, Jean, Robert. BA in Polit. Sci., Willamette U., 1958, JD with honors, 1960. Bar: Oreg. 1960, U.S. Dist. Ct. Oreg., 1960, U.S. Supreme Ct., 1961. Ptnr. Stoel, Rives, Boley, Fraser & Wyse, Portland, 1960—; bd. dirs., chmn. various coms. Assn. Gen. Contractors Am., Portland, 1972-79; mem. com. on legis. affairs Assn. Builders & Contractors, Portland, 1983—. Author: A Study of the Construct by Contract Issue, 1979. Mem. Gov.'s Task Force on Reform of Worker's Compensation, Salem, Oreg., 1980-81; atty. gen.'s com. on Pub. Contracting. Recipient SIR award Assn. Gen. Contractors, 1979, Outstanidng Oral Argument award U.S. Moot Ct., 1959. Mem. ABA, Oreg. Bar (law sch. liaison, com. on practice and procedure specialization), Multnomah County Bar Assn. Republican. Avocations: antique autos, antique furniture, boating, water skiing. Construction. Home: 14980 SW 133d Tigaro OR 97224 Office: Stoel Rives et al 900 SW 5th Ave Portland OR 97204

FRANZOI, JOSEPH FRANK, IV, lawyer; b. Neenah, Wis., May 31, 1955; s. Joseph F. and LaVerne L. (Reichow) F.; m. Patricia Ann Selingo, Aug. 2, 1980; 1 child, Joseph F. V, Forest A. BSBA summa cum laude, Georgetown U., 1976; JD, U. Chgo., 1979. Bar: Wis. 1979, Fla. 1980. Pres. Franzoi and Franzoi SC, Menasha, Wis., 1980—; bd. dirs. StratSeis, Inc., Denver, Corway (Ark.) Machine, Inc., Anchor Fish and Seafood, Appleton, Wis., Vehicle Search, Inc., Appleton. Recipient Wall St. Jour. award, 1976, Dean's award, Georgetown U., 1976. Mem. ABA (taxation sect.), Wis. Bar Assn., Fla. Bar Assn., Winnebago, Calumet & Waupaca Counties Bar Assn. Republican. Roman Catholic. Clubs: Milw. Athletic; Butte des Mortes Country (Appleton). Avocations: jogging, road rallying, hi-fi. Corporate taxation, Estate taxation, General corporate. Home: 819 Emily St Menasha WI 54952 Office: 514 Racine St Menasha WI 54952

FRASCH, DAVID EDWARD, lawyer; b. Columbus, Ohio, Mar. 28, 1947; s. William E. and Edith P. (Koch) F.; m. Evalyn W. Wiley, Aug. 30, 1969; children: Matthew M., Christopher D. BA, Lawrence U., 1969; JD, U. Mich., 1972; LLM, U. London, 1973. Bar: Ohio 1972, U.S. Dist. Ct. (so. dist.) Ohio 1972, Wis. 1974, U.S. Dist. Ct. (we. dist.) Wis. 1974, Minn. 1985, U.S. Dist. Ct. (ea. dist.) Minn. 1985. Assoc. Lane, Alton & Horst, Columbus, 1973-74; ptnr. Wiley, Rasmus, Colbert, Frasch, Norseng & Cray, Chippewa Falls, Wis., 1974-85; corp. sec., tech. counsel Cray Research Inc., Chippewa Falls, 1986—; bd. dirs. 1st Nat. Bank, Chippewa Falls. Chmn. Capital Devel. Com. Chippewa Valley Family YMCA; trustee Cen. Luth. Ch., Chippewa Falls. Mem. ABA, Wis. Bar Assn., Minn. Bar Assn. (computer law sect.), Chippewa County Bar Assn. (pres. 1975), Am. Soc. Corp. Secs., Lawrence U. Alumni Assn. (bd. dirs. 1983—). Avocations: traveling, sports. General corporate, Computer. Office: Cray Research Inc 900 Lowater Rd Chippewa Falls WI 54729

FRASER, BRUCE WILLIAM, lawyer; b. Glen Cove, N.Y., Sept. 4, 1957; s. Albert and Ernestine Beverly (Parillo) F. AB, Columbia U., 1978; JD, Harvard U., 1981. Bar: Calif. 1981, U.S. Dist. Ct. (cen. dist.) Calif. 1981. Assoc. Jones, Day, Reavis & Pogue, Los Angeles, 1981-85, Kadison, Pfaelzer, Woodard, Quinn & Rossi, Los Angeles, 1985—. Real property. Home: 11668 Kiowa Ave #205 Los Angeles CA 90049 Office: Kadison Pfaelzer Woodard Quinn & Rossi 707 Wilshire Blvd 39th Floor Los Angeles CA 90017

FRASER, D. LARRY, federal agency administrator, lawyer; b. Deadwood, S.D., June 3, 1940; s. David C. and June (Schloredt) F.; m. Glenna Roth, June 18, 1964; children: David, Eric. BS, No. Ariz. State U., 1976; JD, U. Kans., 1979, M in Pub. Adminstrn., 1980; cert. aviation safety, U. So. Calif., 1985. Bar: Kans. 1980, U.S. Dist. Ct. Kans. 1980. Pilot Air Am., Uourn, Thailand, 1968-73; owner Pioneer Planning, Prescott, Ariz., 1974-76; mgr. aviation program U.S. Forest Service, Atlanta, 1980-83; aviation safety mgr. U.S. Customs Service, Washington, 1983—. Served to capt., USMC, 1962-67. Mem. Prescott Jaycees (pres. 1975). Avocations: aviation. Administrative and regulatory, Criminal, Aviation. Office: US Customs Service 1301 Constitution Ave NW Washington DC 20229

FRASER, DONALD ROSS, lawyer; b. Toledo, May 21, 1927; s. Malcolm Wicks and Elizabeth (Ross) F.; m. Caroline Ann Pilliod, Aug. 16, 1951; children—Donald Ross Jr., Marguerite Ann. B.S. in Physics, U. Toledo 1952; J.D., George Washington U., 1954. Bar: D.C. 1957, Ohio 1963. Ptnr. Marshall & Melhorn and predecessor firms, Toledo, 1954—; adj. prof. patent law U. Toledo Coll. Law, 1979—; asst. solicitor of patents U.S. Dept. Interior, 1975-76; mem. Ohio Gen. Assembly, 1968-72. Served to sgt. U.S. Army Corps of Engrs., 1944-46. Mem. ABA; Ohio Bar Assn., Lucas County Bar Assn., Toledo Bar Assn., U.S. Trademark Assn.; Am. Intellectual Property Law Assn. Republican. Presbyterian. Clubs: Toledo; Belmont Country (Perrysburg, Ohio), University, Kenwood Golf and Country (Washington). Patent, Trademark and copyright. Home: 203 W Front St Perryburg OH 43551 Office: Marshall & Melhorn 4 SeaGate Suite 800 Toledo OH 43604

FRASER, EVERETT MACKAY, lawyer; b. Mpls., July 20, 1921; s. Everett and Barbara Lois (MacKay) F.; m. Elizabeth Barbara Graves, Mar. 9, 1966; children—Alexander Martin, Margaret Lois. B.A. in Math. and Physics, U. Minn., 1943; LL.B., J.D., Columbia U., 1948. Bar: Minn. 1949, Mass. 1968. Patent atty. ITT, 1948-50; patent adviser Signal Corps, U.S. Army, Ft. Monmouth, N.J., 1950-51, legal counsel Harlan Bradt Assocs., N.Y.C., 1952-53; patent atty. Burroughs Corp., N.Y.C., 1954-56, mgr. N.Y. patent operation, 1956-59; chief patent counsel LFE Corp., Clinton, Mass., 1959-61, gen. counsel, 1961—, sec., 1962—, v.p., 1970—. Mem. Town Meeting, Town of Arlington (Mass.), 1977—, mem. fin. com., 1981—. Served to lt. USNR, 1943-46; ATO, PTO. Mem. ABA, Mass. Bar Assn., Boston Bar Assn., Am. Patent Law Assn., Boston Patent Law Assn., Am. Soc. Corp. Secs. Democrat. Unitarian-Universalist. General corporate, Patent, Construction. Office: LFE Corp 55 Green St Clinton MA 01510

FRASER, ROBERT BURCHMORE, lawyer; b. Newton, Mass., Aug. 13, 1928; s. Alfred Alexander and Helen Louise (Comiskey) F.; A.B., Harvard U., 1949, LL.B., 1952, LL.M., 1955; m. Mary-Ann Jackson, Sept. 7, 1963; children: Melanie, Jennifer Amy, Matthew John. Admitted to Mass. bar; asso. atty. Goodwin, Procter & Hoar, Boston, 1955-63, partner, 1964—, chmn. exec. com., 1984—; dir. New Eng. Mchts. Leasing Corp., 1974-83. Mem. Mass. Gov.'s Jud. Nominating Commn., 1979-82; mem. adv. com. Mass. Commr. Revenue, 1979-82; chmn. adv. com. Mass. Housing Fin. Agy., 1979-83; mem. Mass. Fin. Adv. Bd., 1982-87; mem. bd. dirs. Greater Boston YMCA, 1981-87; trustee New Eng. Conservatory Music, 1982—, Boston Plan for Excellence in Pub. Schs., 1987—. Served with AUS, 1952-54. Mem. ABA, Mass. Bar Assn., Boston Bar Assn., Harvard Musical Assn. Club: Harvard (Boston). Contbr. articles to profl. jours. Home: 90 Allandale St Jamaica Plain MA 02130 Office: Goodwin Procter & Hoar Exchange Place Boston MA 02109

FRASIER, RALPH KENNEDY, banker, lawyer; b. Winston-Salem, N.C., Sept. 16, 1938; s. LeRoy Benjamin and Kathryn O. (Kennedy) F.; m. Jeannine Quick, Aug. 1981; children: Karen D. Frasier-Money, Gail S. Frasier Griffin, Ralph Kennedy Jr., Keith L. B.S., N.C. Central U., Durham, 1962, J.D., 1965. Bar: N.C. 1965, Ohio 1976. With Wachovia Bank and Trust Co., N.A., Winston-Salem, 1965-70; v.p., counsel Wachovia Bank and Trust Co., N.A., 1969-70; asst. counsel, v.p. parent co. Wachovia Corp., 1970-75; v.p., gen. counsel Huntington Nat. Bank, Columbus, Ohio, 1975—; sr. v.p. Huntington Nat. Bank, 1976-83, sec., 1981—, exec. v.p., 1983—, cashier, 1983—; v.p., gen. counsel Huntington Bancshares Inc., 1976—, sec., 1981—; sec., dir. Huntington Mortgage Co., Huntington State Bank, Huntington Leasing Co., Huntington Bancshares Fin. Corp., Huntington Investment Mgmt. Co., Scioto Life Ins. Co., Huntington Co., 1976—; v.p., asst. sec. Huntington Bank N.E. Ohio, 1982-84. Bd. dirs. Family Services Winston-Salem, 1966-74, sec., 1966-71, 74, v.p., 1974; chmn. Winston-Salem Transit Authority, 1974-75; bd. dirs. Research for Advancement of Personalities, 1968-71, Winston-Salem Citizens for Fair Housing, 1970-74, N.C. United Community Services, 1970-74; treas. Forsyth County (N.C.) Citizens Com. Adequate Justice Bldg., 1968; trustee Appalachian State U., Boone, N.C., 1973-83, trustee endowment fund, 1973—; trustee, vice chmn. Employment and Edn. Commn. Franklin County, 1981-85; mem. Winston-Salem. Forsyth County Sch. Bd. Adv. Council, 1973-74, Atty. Gen. Ohio Task Force Minorities in Bus., 1977-78; bd. dirs. Inroads Columbus, Inc., 1986—, Greater Columbus Arts Council, 1986—. Served with AUS, 1958-60. Mem. ABA, Nat. Bar Assn., Ohio Bar Assn., Columbus Bar Assn., Columbus Urgan League. Banking, Consumer commercial, General corporate. Address: 41 S High St PO Box 1558 Columbus OH 43260

FRASSINETI, JORDAN JOSEPH, lawyer; b. Florence, Italy, Mar. 30, 1929; came to U.S., 1946; s. Guido Gaetano Frassineti and Helen Elizabeth (Gill) Gordon-Mann; m. Elizabeth Hoyt Studdert, Oct. 26, 1957; children: Jordan Jr., Margaret Bragaw, William Studdert. AB, U. N.C., 1955, JD, 1957. Bar: N.C. 1957, U.S. Supreme Ct. 1976. Sr. ptnr. Frassineti & Glover, Greensboro, N.C., 1957—. Mem. Greensboro Airport Authority, 1970; chmn. Guilford County Reps., 1960-62. Served to capt. U.S. Army, 1951-53. Mem. ABA, N.C. Bar Assn., Greensboro Bar Assn., 18th Jud. Dist. Bar Assn. (pres. 1971-72), Nat. Assn. Bar Pres. Republican. Episcopalian. Bankruptcy, Consumer commercial, Private international. Office: Frassineti & Glover Box 1799 Greensboro NC 27402

FRAUENSHUH, RONALD RAY, SR., lawyer; b. St. Paul, July 7, 1936; s. Raymond Roy and Orple Elizabeth (Gagnon) F.; m. Phyllis Marie King, July 2, 1955; children—Ronald Ray, Sharon Rae Frauenshuh Hage, Colleen Marie. B.A., Macalester Coll., 1960; J.D., William-Mitchell Coll. Law, 1964. Bar: Minn. 1964, U.S. Dist. Ct. Minn. 1964, U.S. Supreme Ct. 1964, U.S. Ct. Appeals (8th cir.) 1968. Ptnr. Weis & Frauenshuh Law Firm, Paynesville, Minn., 1964-72; sole practice, Paynesville, 1972-74; ptnr. Frauenshuh & Fahlberg Law Firm, Paynesville, 1974-84, Frauenshuh, Fahlberg & Spooner Law Firm, Paynesville, 1984—; city atty. City of Paynesville, 1970—, City of Eden Valley, Minn., 1975—. Served with U.S. Army, 1955-58. Recipient Disting. Service award Paynesville Jaycees, 1970, Bronze Key award Minn. Jaycees, 1970. Mem. Stearns/Benton/Sherburne Bar Assn. (pres. 1979-80), Minn. State Bar Assn., ABA, Assn. Trial Lawyers Am., Minn. Trial Lawyers Assn., Paynesville C. of C. Republican. Lutheran. Lodge: Lions (pres. Paynesville club 1968—, dist. gov. 1981-82, chmn. multiple dist. council of govs. 1982-83, 100% Pres. award 1978, 100% Gov. award 1982, Internat. Pres. award 1985, bd. dirs. U. Minn. Eye Bank 1983—). Federal civil litigation, State civil litigation, Local government. Home: 803 Washburne Ave Paynesville MN 56362

FRAUMANN, WILLARD GEORGE, lawyer; b. San Francisco, July 21, 1948; m. Anne C. Derleth, Dec. 18, 1971; children: Ellen, Robert, Sarah. AB, U. Mich., 1970; JD, Harvard U., 1973. Bar: Ill., U.S. Dist. Ct. (no. dist.) Ill. Ptnr. Kirkland & Ellis, Chgo., 1977—. Served to lt. USNR, 1973-77. General corporate, Securities. Office: Kirkland & Ellis 200 E Randolph Dr Chicago IL 60601 Home: 1450 Wincanton Deerfield IL 60015

FRAZELLE, MICHAEL JEROME, lawyer; b. New Bern, N.C., Feb. 8, 1953; s. Gerald Cox Frazelle and Virginia I. (Brooks) Helber; m. Deborah Lynn Goldman, June 2, 1974. BA, U. Ariz., 1975; JD, Southwestern U., 1978. Bar: Ariz. 1979, Calif. 1980, U.S. Dist. Ct. Ariz. 1982, U.S. Ct. Claims 1985. Assoc. Kinkle, Rodiger & Spriggs, Los Angeles, 1980-82; gen. counsel Hartford Ins. Group, Phoenix, 1982-84; sr. assoc. Ridenour, Swenson, Cleere & Evans, Phoenix, 1985—; seminar lectr. State Farm Ins. Co., Phoenix, 1986, Hartford Ins. Group, Phoenix, 1984. Mem. editorial bd. Southwestern U. Law Rev., 1976. Mem. ABA (torts and ins. practice and bus. corps. and banking coms.). Republican. Methodist. Lodge: Kiwanis (bd. dirs. Phoenix 1985, organizer annual charity octoberfest 1982—). Avocations: golf, swimming. State civil litigation, General corporate, Insurance. Office: Ridenour Swenson Cleere & Evans 2350 Valley Bank Ctr Phoenix AZ 85073

FRAZIER, HENRY BOWEN, III, government official, lawyer; b. Bluefield, W.Va., Aug. 9, 1934; s. Henry Bowen and Margaret Beale (West) F.; m. Joan McIntosh, Dec. 30, 1959. B.A. with honors, U. Va., 1956; J.D. with honors, George Washington U., 1967; LL.M. in Labor Law, Georgetown U., 1969, M.L.T., 1985. Bar: Va. 1967, D.C. 1980. Personnel adminstr. Army Dept. Washington, 1959-63, spl. projects officer, 1963-67; dep. for civilian personnel policy and civil rights Office Sec. Army, 1967-70; chief program div. Fed. Labor Relations Council, Exec. Office Pres., 1970-71, dep. exec. dir., 1971-72, exec. dir., 1973-78; mem. Fed. Labor Relations Authority, Washington, 1979—, acting chmn., 1984-85; chmn. Employee Relations Commn., U.S. Fgn. Service, 1979-81; acting chmn. Fgn. Service Labor Relations Bd., 1984-85. Served with USAF, 1961-62. Recipient W.H. Kushnick award Sec. Army, 1968, Exceptional Civilian Service award, 1970, spl. commendation award Dir. OMB, 1978. Mem. ABA, Soc. Fed. Labor Relations Profs., Soc. Profs. in Dispute Resolution, Jefferson Soc., Indsl. Rela-

tions Research Assn., SAR, U. Va. Alumni Assn. (nat. v.p. 1984-85, nat. pres. 1985-86, bd. mgrs. 1980-87), Raven Soc., Order of Coif, Phi Beta Kappa, Omicron Delta Kappa, Phi Kappa Psi. Labor, Personal income taxation, Corporate taxation. Office: Fed Labor Relations Authority 500 C St SW Washington DC 20424

FRAZIER, LAWRENCE ALAN, lawyer; b. Hastings, Nebr., Dec. 29, 1936; s. Harold Ivan and Lila Rose (Eichler) F.; m. Anabeth Hormel, June 25, 1961; children: Stephanie, Andrea, Julia. AA, McCook (Nebr.) Coll., 1957; BS, U. Nebr., 1959, LLB, 1961. Bar: Nebr. 1961, U.S. Dist. Ct. Nebr. 1961, U.S. Ct. Mil. Appeals 1963. Ptnr. Russell, Colfer & Frazier, McCook, Nebr., 1964-69; atty. Farmers Mut. Ins. Co. Nebr., Lincoln, 1969—,zxsst. gen. counsel, 1969, v.p., 1974-79, gen. counsel, 1979-85, exec. v.p., sec., sr. counsel, 1985-86, pres., sec., 1986—. Active Lincoln United Way, 1971; bd. dirs. Lincoln Family Services Assn., 1975-83, pres., 1979; trustee, deacon First Plymouth Congregational Ch.; bd. dirs. Nebr. Soc. Prevention of Blindness, 1976-80. Served to maj. USAFR. Mem. ABA, Nebr. Bar Assn. (ins. com. 1980—), Lincoln Bar Assn., Nebr. Assn. Def. Counsel, Assn. Trial Lawyers Am., Nebr. Assn. Mut. Ins. Cos. (chmn. legis. com., pres. 1986), Nebr. Ins. Arbitration Com. (arbitrator), Soc. CPCU's, Am. Mgmt. Assn., Nebr. Ins. Info. Service (pres. 1980—). Club: Nebr. Lodge: Elks, Rotary. Republican. Contbr. articles to profl. jours. Insurance, Legislative, General corporate. Home: 2431 Marilynn Ave Lincoln NE 68502 Office: Farmers Mut Ins Co of Nebr 1220 Lincoln Mall PO Box 81529 Lincoln NE 68501

FRAZIER, STEVEN CARL, lawyer; b. Kingsport, Tenn., Jan. 8, 1954; s. Carl Dexter and Jean (Winegar) F.; m. Darline Nancy Anderson, Aug. 11, 1984; children: John Carl, Jacob Steven. BS, U. Tenn., 1976, JD, 1979. Bar: Tenn. 1980. Sole practice Church Hill, Tenn., 1980-82; ptnr. Frazier & Faulk, Church Hill, 1982-83; appeals referee dept. employment sec. State of Tenn., Kingsport, 1983; sole practice Church Hill, Tenn., 1983—; intern Senator Bill Brock, 1975; atty. City of Mount Carmel, Tenn, 1986—; chmn. Foster Care Rev. Bd., Rogersville, Tenn., 1981-85. Parlimentarian Hawkins County Young Reps., Rogersville, 1986. Mem. ABA, Tenn. Bar Assn., Tenn. Trial Lawyers Assn., Hawkins County Bar Assn., Kingsport Bar Assn., Church Hill Jaycees (pres. 1984—). Baptist. Club: Tenn. Capital. Lodge: Kiwanis (pres. 1983-84). Real property, Probate, General practice. Home: Rt 6 Rural Rt Box 630 Church Hill TN 37642 Office: PO Box 1208 Church Hill TN 37642

FRAZIER, THOMAS LOUIS, lawyer, law enforcement consultant; b. Biloxi, Miss., Mar. 24, 1948; s. Tom A. and Janet (Medeiros) F. AA, Monterey Peninsula Coll., 1973, JD, 1981; BA, Golden Gate U., 1976, MA in Pub. Adminstrn., 1978. Bar: Calif. 1981, U.S. Dist. Ct. (no. dist.) Calif., U.S. Ct. Mil. Appeals, U.S. Ct. Appeals (9th cir.). Sgt. Carmel (Calif.) Police Dept., 1970-78; cons. State of Calif., 1976—; sole practice Marina, Calif., 1981—; tchr. adminstrn. of justice Monterey (Calif.) Peninsula Coll., 1977—. Served with USMC, 1966-70, Vietnam. Republican. Lodges: Elks, Rotary. Military, Criminal, General practice. Home: 3146 Crescent Ave Marina CA 93933 Office: PO Box 639 Marina CA 93933

FRAZZA, GEORGE S., lawyer, business executive; b. Paterson, N.J., Jan. 21, 1934; s. Paul T. and Myrtle Mary (Van Riper) F.; m. Marie Pollara, Sept. 17, 1955; children: Caren, Janine, Leslie, Lauren. A.B., Marietta Coll., 1955; LL.B., Columbia U., 1958. Bar: N.Y. 1959. Atty. Rogers & Wells, N.Y.C., 1958-66, Johnson & Johnson, New Brunswick, N.J., 1966; assoc. gen. counsel Johnson & Johnson, 1973, corp. sec., 1975; gen. counsel 1978—. Bd. dirs. N.J. Ballet, Morristown, 1983—. Mem. Assn. Gen. Counsel (sec., treas.), ABA, N.Y. State Bar Assn., Assn. of Bar of City of N.Y. Club: Roxitious. General corporate. Home: Oak Knoll Rd Mendham NJ 07945 Office: One Johnson and Johnson Plaza New Brunswick NJ 08933

FREAD, JOAN P., lawyer; b. Tacoma, Dec. 19, 1950; s. Paul D. and Anne L. Fread; m. Robert D. Diverstein, June 4, 1983; 1 child, Michael Fread. BA, Seattle U., 1972; MA, Western Wash. State U., 1974; JD, Yale U., 1977. Bar: D.C. 1977. Assoc. Mayer, Brown & Platt, Washington, 1977-83, ptnr., 1983—. Mem. ABA, Women's Bar Assn. of D.C. Democrat. Roman Catholic. General corporate, Real property, Administrative and regulatory. Office: Mayer Brown & Platt 2000 Pennsylvania Ave NW Washington DC 20006

FRECCIA, VINCENT JOHN, III, lawyer; b. Stamford, Conn., Nov. 23, 1955; s. Vincent J. Jr. and Dolores A. (DeLuca) F. BS, Providence Coll., 1977; JD, Bridgeport U., 1980. Bar: Conn. 1980, U.S. Ct. Appeals (2d cir.). Sole practice Stamford, Conn., 1980. Mem. ABA, Conn. Bar Assn., Conn. Trial Lawyers Assn., Stamford/Darien Bar Assn. Republican. General practice, Bankruptcy, Real property. Home: 1200 Sumner St Stamford CT 06905 Office: 1318 Bedford St Stamford CT 06905

FRECON, ALAIN JEAN-CHRISTIAN, lawyer; b. Casablanca, Morocco, Jan. 27, 1946; came to U.S. 1974; s. Laurent Jean Benoit and Maria (Boroni) F.; m. Leslie Ann Myers, Aug. 4, 1978; 1 child, Laurent Jean Benoit. Diploma, Centre Notarial de Formation et D'information Professionnelle and Faculté de Droit-Paris II, 1969; Lic. en Droit, Faculté de Droit-Paris II, 1974; LLM in Internat. Bus., Stanford U., 1976; JD, William Mitchell Coll. Law, 1982. Assoc. Ader, Rochelois & Roy, Paris, 1969-74; of counsel Jones, Bell, Simpson, & Abbott, Los Angeles, 1976-81; assoc. Dorsey and Whitney, Mpls., 1981-85; ptnr., chmn. internat. bus. practice Popham, Haik, Schnobrich, Kaufman & Dotyand Popham, Haik, Schnobrich & Kaufman, 1985—; bd. dirs. Julian Jill, USA, Inc., Beverly Hills, Calif.; seminar promoter and guest speaker on internat. bus. Author: (handbooks) Negotiation of International Contracts,1984, Legal Issue of Doing Business in India, 1985, Practical Issues of Doing Business in the United States, 1986, Legal Issues of Doing Business in France, 1986. Reader Nat. Assn. Blind, Paris, 1973; internat. press relations com. Valery Giscard D'Estaing campaign, Paris, 1974; vol. Stanford, Calif. Legal Aid Soc., 1975; chmn. Minn. French Festival, Mpls., 1985-86; appointed to bd. dirs. Minn. Export Fin. Authority by Gov. Perpich, 1987—. Mem. Internat. Bar Assn., Fed. Bar Assn., ABA, Minn. Bar Assn., Hennepin Bar Assn., Am. Arbitration Assn. (internal. bus. sect.), Mpls. French Am. C. of C. (bd. dirs. 1984-86, v.p. 1986). Mem. French UDF/RPR party. Roman Catholic. Club: Mpls. Athletic. Lodge: Rotary. Avocations: marathon runner, hunting, fishing, sculpture. Private international, Contracts commercial, General corporate. Home: 3430 List Place Minneapolis MN 55416 Office: Popham Haik Schnobrich & Kaufman 3300 Piper Jaffray Tower Minneapolis MN 55402

FREDA, FRANK ANTHONY, lawyer; b. Bklyn., Apr. 12, 1952; s. Charles Adrian and Marianna (DeConstanza) F.; m. Maria Elvira Sarmiento, Aug. 30, 1975; children: Marianna, Cristina, Humberto. BA in Polit. Sci., Hofstra U., 1974; JD, St. John's U., Jamaica, N.Y., 1977. Bar: N.Y. 1978. Legal asst. Cushman & Wakefield Inc., N.Y.C., 1977-78, asst. counsel, asst. sec., 1978-79, assoc. counsel, asst. sec., 1979-80, assoc. counsel, asst. v.p., 1980-85, assoc. counsel, v.p., 1985-86, sr. counsel, v.p., mgr. law office, 1986—. Mem. N.Y. State Bar Assn., Assn. Bar of City of N.Y. Roman Catholic. Avocations: softball, football, golf. Real property, General corporate. Home: 33-29 156th St Flushing NY 11354 Office: Cushman & Wakefield Inc 1166 Ave of Americas New York NY 10036

FREDERICI, C. CARLETON, lawyer; b. Sioux City, Iowa, Jan. 17, 1938; s. Cecil Carleton and Lois Alida (Selzer) F.; m. Virginia A. Gregori, Oct. 14, 1961 (div.); m. Susan A. Low, Oct. 1, 1983; children—Gloria M., Carleton J., Charles W. Student Iowa State U., 1956; B.A., U. Iowa, 1960, J.D. with high distinction, 1965. Bar: Iowa 1965, N.Y. 1966, U.S. Dist. Ct. (no. dist.) Iowa 1968, U.S. Dist. Ct. (so. dist.) Iowa 1969, U.S. Supreme Ct. 1970, U.S. Ct. Appeals (8th cir.) 1970, U.S. Ct. Appeals (3d cir.) 1973. Assoc. firm Willkie, Farr & Gallagher, N.Y.C., 1965-68, firm Shull, Marshall & Marks, Sioux City, Iowa, 1968-69; assoc. firm Davis, Hockenberg, Wine, Brown, Koehn & Shors, Des Moines, 1969-71, jr. ptnr., 1971-73, sr. ptnr., 1973—; speaker Supreme Ct. Day, Law Sch. Drake U., 1973. Vestryman St. Luke's Ch., bd. dirs. 1976-78, 1982-85; mem. Polk County Rep. Cen. Com., 1969-71. Served to 1st lt. U.S. Army, 1961-62. Mem. ABA (chmn. 8th cir. commn. on class actions and derivative suits), Iowa Bar Assn. (chmn. prison reform com., adv. mem. fed. practice commn.), Polk County Bar Assn. (bench and bar com.), Assn. Bar City N.Y., Assn. Trial Lawyers Iowa, Am. Judicature Soc., Order of Coif. Episcopalian. Club: Wakonda (Des Moines). Contbr. articles to legal publs. Class actions, Federal civil litigation, State civil litigation. Office: Suite 2300 Financial Center Des Moines IA 50309

FREDERICK, JOEL DENNIS, judge; b. Salt Lake City, July 12, 1940; s. Jesse Allen and Echo Parker (Pollock) F.; m. Jonnee Lynn Perri, Dec. 28, 1974; children—Lisa Ann, Gia Ann, Jesse Allen II. Student Tulsa U., 1958-59, U. Ark., 1959-60; B.S. in Psychology, U. Utah, 1964, J.D., 1966. Bar: Utah, 1966, U.S. Dist. Ct. Utah 1966, U.S. Ct. Appeals (10th cir.) 1971, U.S. Supreme Ct. 1973, U.S. Ct. Appeals (9th cir.) 1977. Dep. dist. atty. Dist. Atty.'s Office, Salt Lake City, 1968-71; officer, dir. Kipp and Christian, P.C., Salt Lake City, 1966-82; judge 3d Dist. Ct., Salt Lake City, 1982—; mem. adv. com. Utah Ins. Law Revision Commn., 1980-81, nat. claims counsel adv. bd. Comml. Union Assurance Co., Boston, 1979-81; vice chmn. Utah Commn. Adminstrn. Justice in Dist. Cts., 1986—; recodification com. task force Utah State Div. Corrections, 1984-85. Pres., v.p. Cosgriff Home and Sch. Assn.-St. Ambrose Parish, Salt Lake City, 1982-85; legal counsel Children's Ctr., Salt Lake City, 1968; mem. trial advocacy program U. Utah Coll. Law, 1983-84. Nat. Office Mgmt. Assn. scholar, 1958-59; U. Utah scholar, 1980—. Mem. Am. Bd. Trial Advocates, ABA, Utah State Bar Assn. (examinations com. 1978-84, cts. and judges com. 1984-86, judiciary com. 1985—), Utah Jud. Council, Sutherland Inn of Ct. (master of bench 1986—), Salt Lake County Bar Assn. (mem. exec. com. 1980-83), U. Utah Coll. Law Alumni Assn. (charter), Phi Alpha Delta (treas. 1968). Office: Courts Bldg 240 E 400 S Salt Lake City UT 84111

FREDERICK, ROBERT GEORGE, lawyer; b. Evanston, Ill., Feb. 11, 1948; s. George D. and Lee (Miller) F.; m. Pamela Kaye Kline, June 13, 1970 (div. Sept. 1977); m. Ellen Marie Due, Oct. 25, 1980; children: Robert, Christina. BS, No. Ill. U., 1969; JD, U. Ill., 1972. Bar: Ill. 1972, U.S. Dist. Ct. (cen. dist.) Ill. 1974, U.S. Ct. Appeals (7th cir.) 1975, U.S. Supreme Ct. 1978. Asst. states atty. Champaign County, Urbana, Ill., 1972-75; pub. defender Champaign County, Urbana, 1975-79; commr. State Ill. Claims Ct., Springfield, 1984—; ptnr. Johnson, Frank & Frederick, Urbana, 1975—. Mem. ABA, Ill. State Bar Assn., Ill. Trial Lawyers Assn., Champaign County Bar Assn., Order of Coif. Republican. Methodist. Criminal, General practice, Family and matrimonial. Home: 915 W William Champaign IL 61821 Office: Johnson Frank Frederick & Walsh 129 W Main Urbana IL 61801

FREDERICK, SAMUEL ADAMS, lawyer; b. N.Y.C., Mar. 17, 1946; s. Robert George and Mary Elizabeth (Adams) F.; m. Elizabeth Lothrop Moore, June 18, 1977; children: Alyssa Adams, Julia Moore, Charles Payson. BA, Yale U., 1968; JD, U. Pa., 1974. Bar: N.Y. 1975, U.S. Dist. Ct. (so. and ea. dists.) N.Y. 1975, U.S. Ct. Appeals (2d cir.) 1975, Mass. 1983. Assoc. Wickes, Riddell, Bloomer, Jacobi & McGuire, N.Y.C., 1974-77, Milbank, Tweed, Hadley & McCloy, N.Y.C., 1977-78, Brown & Wood, N.Y.C., 1978-81; counsel Eastern Gas and Fuel Assocs., Boston, 1982—; sec. Eastern Associated Real Estate Corp., Boston, 1984—, Eastern Energy Systems Corp., Boston, 1984—; v.p., bd. dirs. U.S. Mut. Liability Ins. Co., Boston, 1984—. Author: Papering Procedures Manual for the Superior Court Division of the U.S. Attorney's Office for the District of Columbia, 1970. Served to lt. (j.g.) USNR, 1968-70. Mem. Internat. Bar Assn., ABA, N.Y. Bar Assn., Mass. Bar Assn., Boston Bar Assn., Assocs. Club (pres., bd. dirs. 1985-86). Avocations: reading, travel, tennis, squash, skiing. Contracts commercial, General corporate, Securities. Home: 35 Locust Ave Lexington MA 02173 Office: Eastern Gas and Fuel Assocs One Beacon St Boston MA 02108

FREDERICKS, DALE E., lawyer; b. Springfield, Ill.. BS with honors, Bradley U., 1965; JD, U. Ill., 1968. Ptnr. mgmt. com. Sedgwick, Detert, Moran & Arnold, San Francisco, Los Angeles, N.Y.C. and London. Served to capt. USMCR, 1968-72. Mem. ABA (antitrust law and litigation sects.), Calif. Bar Assn., San Francisco Bar Assn. Republican. Club: World Trade (San Francisco). Avocations: golf, tennis. Antitrust, Securities, Federal civil litigation. Office: Sedgwick Detert Moran & Arnold One Embarcadero Ctr San Francisco CA 94111

FREDERICKS, WESLEY CHARLES, JR., businessman, lawyer; b. N.Y.C., Mar. 31, 1948; s. Wesley Charles and Dionysia W. (Bitsanis) F.; m. Jeanne Maria Judson, May 19, 1973; children—Carolyn Anne, Wesley C. III. B.A., Johns Hopkins U., 1970; J.D., Columbia U., 1973. Bar: N.Y. 1974, Conn. 1976, U.S. Supreme Ct. 1979. Assoc. Shearman & Sterling, N.Y.C., 1973-76, 76-83, Cummings & Lockwood, Stamford, Conn., 1976; dir. Automobile Importers Am., Inc., Washington, 1983—, British Performance Car Imports, Inc., Norwood, N.J., 1982-86, Carbodies N. Am., Dover, Del., 1983-84; chmn. bd. Lotus Performance Cars, L.P., Norwood, 1983-86, chief exec. officer, 1986—. Honors judge Columbia U. Law Sch. Stone Moot Ct. Honors Program, 1980—; mem. Johns Hopkins U. Alumni Schs. Com.; trustee Wilton Hist. Soc., 1986—. Served with USMC, 1968-69.. Mem. Blue Key Soc., Sigma Chi Epsilon. Republican. Congregationalist. Clubs: India House (N.Y.C.); Steering Wheel (London), Sandonana (N.Y.). Antitrust, General corporate, Private international. Home: 190 Hurlbutt St Wilton CT 06897 Office: Lotus Performance Cars LP 530 Walnut St Norwood NJ 07648

FREDERICKSON, JOHN DREW, lawyer; b. Passaic, N.J., Oct. 28, 1956; s. C.M. and Margaret E. (Zechmeister). BS magna cum laude, Seton Hall U., 1978, JD, 1981. Bar: N.J. 1985, D.C. 1985, U.S. Dist. Ct. N.J. 1985, U.S. Supreme Ct. 1985. Assoc. Demetrakis, Sinisi & Carmel, Fort Lee, N.J., 1980—. Assoc. editor Seton Hall U. Law Rev., 1980-81. Mem. ABA, NSPE, N.J. Bar Assn., Bergen County Bar Assn., Essex County Bar Assn., Assn. Trial Lawyers Am., N.J. Trial Lawyers Assn., Internat. Soc. Law, Pi Sigma Alpha, Phi Alpha Theta. Republican. Roman Catholic. Avocations: golf, collecting coins, collecting stamps, tennis. Home: 37 Glendale St Nutley NJ 07110 Office: Oliver McCartney & Holmes Inc 8400 River Rd PO Box 59 Edgewater NJ 07020

FREEBERG, EDWARD RONALD, lawyer; b. Omaha, Nov. 26, 1943; s. Edward Frederic and Janice Ellen (Miller) F.; m. Norena Marie Anderson, Aug. 23, 1969; children: Edward Miller, Gregory Trent. BS, U. Nebr., 1970; JD, Creighton U., 1973. Bar: Nebr. 1973, Mich. 1977, U.S. Dist. Ct. Nebr. 1973, U.S. Ct. Appeals (8th cir.) 1974, U.S. Dist. Ct. (we. dist.) Mich. 1980, U.S. Dist. Ct. (ea. dist.) Mich. 1984, U.S. Ct. Appeals (6th cir.) 1985. Labor counsel Midwest Employers Council, Omaha, 1973-76; corp. labor relations atty. Whirlpool Corp., Benton Harbor, Mich., 1976-80; ptnr. Gemrich Moser, Dombrowski, Bowser and Fette, Kalamazoo, 1980—. Contbr. chpts. to legal publs. Mem. ABA (equal employment opportunity law com. 1977—), Internat. Found. Employee Benefit Plans. Republican. Lutheran. Labor, Pension, profit-sharing, and employee benefits. Home: 7689 N 14th St Kalamazoo MI 49007 Office: Gemrich Moser Dombrowski et al 222 S Westnedge Ave Kalamazoo MI 49007

FREEBORN, MICHAEL D., lawyer; b. Mpls., June 30, 1946; s. Andrew W. and Verena M. (Keller) F.; m. Nancie L. Siebel, Oct. 19, 1947; children—Christopher A., Nathan M., Joel C., Paul K. B.S., U.S. Air Force Acad., 1968; M.B.A., U. Chgo., 1975; J.D., Ind. U., 1972. Bar: Ill. 1972, Ind. 1972, Wis. 1983. Assoc., ptnr. Rooks, Pitts & Poust, Chgo., 1972-83; ptnr. Freeborn & Peters, Chgo., 1983—. Gen. editor: O.S.H.A. Law, 1981. Assoc. editor Ind. Law Rev., 1970-71. Contbr. articles to profl. jours. Chmn. citizens adv. council Ill. Coastal Zone Mgmt. Program, Chgo., 1979. Served as capt. USAF, 1968-72. Recipient Founders Day award Ind. U. Law Sch., 1972. Fellow Am. Coll. Environ. Lawyers; mem. Ill. Bar Assn., Ind. Bar Assn., Wis. Bar Assn. Republican. Lutheran. Clubs: Union League, Legal (Chgo.). Antitrust, Environment, Labor. Home: 122 S Kaspar Ave Arlington Heights IL 60005 Office: 11 S LaSalle St Suite 1500 Chicago IL 60603

FREEBURGER, THOMAS OLIVER, lawyer; b. Balt., Jan. 18, 1948; s. Oliver Adolphus and Hannah Marie (Heiss) F.; m. Sandra Lee Dubay, Jan. 19, 1980; children: Angela Christine, Jennifer Leanne. BA, U. Va., 1970; JD, U. Pacific, 1978. Bar: Calif. 1978, U.S. Dist. Ct. (ea. dist.) Calif. 1980, U.S. Dist. Ct. (so. dist.) Calif. 1983, U.S. Dist. Ct. (no. dist.) Calif. 1984. Assoc. Law Office of Clyde O. West, Sacramento, Calif., 1978-82; sole practice Sacramento, 1982—; instr. The Learning Exchange, Sacramento, 1984—. Served to lt. USN, 1970-75. Mem. ABA (real property/probate sect., law office econs. sect.), Calif. Bar Assn. (landlord-tenant subsect., real property sect.), Sacramento County Bar Assn. (pres. real estate sect. 1985, comml. law and probate sects.), Comml. Law League Am., Coalition Concerned Legal Profls. (bd. dirs. 1982—). Democrat. Club: Tahoe Park Soccer (Sacramento)(head coach, head referee). Avocations: soccer coaching and refereeing, backpacking. Real property, Consumer commercial, Probate. Home: 10 Fiesta Ct Sacramento CA 95817 Office: 716 10th St Suite 300 Sacramento CA 95814

FREED, GARY STUART, lawyer; b. Oceanside, N.Y., Aug. 28, 1956; s. Melvin and Babette (Schiff) F.; m. Helen Dillon, May 27, 1984. BA, Drew U., 1978; JD, Emory U., 1981. Bar: Ga. 1981, N.Y. 1982, U.S. Dist. Ct. (no. dist.) Ga. 1983, U.S. Ct. Appeals (11th cir.) 1985. Assoc. Montfort, Healy, McGuire & Salley, Mineola, N.Y., 1981-82, Labovitz, Rosenberg & Campbell, Atlanta, 1982-85; sole practice Atlanta, 1985-86; ptnr. Freed & Freed, Atlanta, 1986—. Mem. Va.-Highland Civic. Assn., Atlanta, 1983—, Am. Jewish Com., Atlanta, 1984—. Mem. ACLU. Democrat. State civil litigation, Federal civil litigation, Family and matrimonial. Office: Freed & Freed 4200 Northside Pkwy NW 6 N Parkway Sq Atlanta GA 30327

FREED, KENNETH ALAN, lawyer; b. Buffalo, Apr. 28, 1957; s. Sherwood E. and Renee (Liebesman) F.; m. Janese Swanson, July 29, 1986; 1 child, Jacqueline Kelly. BA in Econs. magna cum laude, Boston U., 1979; JD, U. Chgo., 1982. Bar: Calif. 1982, U.S. Dist. Ct. (no. dist.) Calif., 1982. Assoc. Feldman, Waldman & Kline, San Francisco, 1982—. Mem. ABA, Calif. Bar Assn. General corporate, Contracts commercial, Real property. Home: 752 Clipper St San Francisco CA 94114 Office: Feldman Waldman & Kline 235 Montgomery St #2700 San Francisco CA 94104

FREED, MAYER GOODMAN, law educator, lawyer; b. Phila., Oct. 26, 1945; s. Abraham H. and Fannie (Rothenberg) F.; m. Paulette Kleinhaus, Aug. 23, 1970; children: Daniel, Joshua. A.B. cum laude, Columbia Coll., 1967, J.D., 1970. Bar: N.Y. 1971, Ill. 1975, U.S. Dist. Ct. (so. and ea. dists.) N.Y. 1972, U.S. Ct. Appeals (2d cir.) 1972, U.S. Supreme Ct. 1974. Assoc. Proskauer Rose Goetz & Mendelsohn, N.Y.C., 1970-71; staff atty. Nat. Employment Law Project, N.Y.C. 1971-73, sr. staff atty., 1973-74; asst. prof. law Northwestern U., 1974-77, assoc. prof., 1977-79, prof., 1979—. Bd. dirs. Legal Assistance Found. Chgo., 1980-82. Stone scholar, 1968-69. Mem. ABA. Contbr. articles to legal publs.; bd. editors Columbia Law Rev., 1969-70. Labor, Federal civil litigation, Civil rights. Office: Northwestern U Sch Law 357 East Chicago Ave Chicago IL 60611 *

FREED, MICHAEL LEONARD, lawyer; b. San Diego, Dec. 5, 1942; s. Leonard T. and Violet Louise (French) F.; m. Pamela McDiramid Prentice, Aug. 23, 1971; children: Christopher, Candice, Bryan. BS, San Jose State U., 1966; JD, Hastings Coll., 1974. Bar: Hawaii 1974, U.S. Dist. Ct. Hawaii 1974, U.S. Ct. Appeals (9th cir.) 1981. Assoc. Rush, Moore, Craven, Kim & Stricklin, Honolulu, 1974-80, ptnr., 1980—. Served to lt. USNR, 1966-71, Vietnam. Mem. Order of Coif. Roman Catholic. Avocation: big game fishing. State civil litigation, Construction, Labor. Office: Rush Moore Craven Kim & Stricklin 745 Fort St 20th Floor Honolulu HI 96813

FREED, ROBERT LESLIE, lawyer; b. Phila., June 25, 1946; s. Bertram Monroe and Rose Claire (Artzis) F.; m. Janice Meryl Benenson, May 26, 1974; children: David, Daniel, Shelley. BS in Acctg., Va. Commonwealth U., 1969; JD, Marshall Wythe Sch. Law, 1972. Bar: Va. 1972, U.S. Tax Ct. 1973, U.S. Dist. Ct. (ea. dist.) Va. 1974, U.S. Ct. Appeals (4th cir.) 1974. Assoc. Harris, Tuck, Freasier & Johnson, Richmond, Va., 1973-76; ptnr. Norman & Freed, Richmond, 1976-78, Coates, Comess & Freed, Richmond, 1978-79; prin. Robert L. Freed, P.C., Richmond, 1979—; lectr. Am. Coll. CLU's, Bryn Mawr, Pa., 1978—; adj. prof. acctg. Va. Commonwealth U., 1973-76, law U. Richmond, 1979—. Mem. legal com. Richmond Jewish Community Found., 1984—. Recipient Tax Medallion Seidman & Seidman, 1972. Mem. ABA, Va. Bar Assn., Richmond Bar Assn., Va. Soc. CPA's, Estate Planning Council of Richmond, U. Richmond Estate Planning Council (adv. council 1986—). Jewish. Avocations: sailing, racquetball, youth soccer coaching. General corporate, Corporate taxation, Real property. Home: 2 Raven Rock Ct Richmond VA 23229 Office: 8100 ThreeChopt Rd Suite 102 Richmond VA 23229

FREEDMAN, BARBARA WIDMAN, lawyer; b. Phila., Sept. 1, 1947; d. Robert and Lillian (Kartoz) W.; m. Allan Perry Freedman, Dec. 22, 1968; children: Avraham T., Reena Z., Noam M. BA cum laude, Temple U., 1969, JD cum laude, 1977. Bar: Pa. 1977, D.C. 1980, U.S. Dist. Ct. (ea. dist.) Pa. 1980. Law clk. U.S Dist. Ct. (ea. dist.) Pa., 1977-78; assoc. Dechert Price & Rhoads, Phila., 1978-82; assoc. Rawle & Henderson, Phila., 1983-85, ptnr., 1985-86; ptnr. Saul, Ewing, Remick & Saul, Phila., 1987—; adj. prof. Temple U. Law Sch., Phila., 1981—; lectr. U. Pa. Tax Confs., 1986—; lectr. Temple Tax Planning Forum, 1984—, mem. planning com., 1985-86. Contbg. editor Temple Law Quarterly, 1975-76; contbr. articles to profl. jours. Recipient Hornbook award West Publishing Co., 1975, 76, 77; BarenKopf scholar, 1976-77. Mem. ABA (tax sect., real estate tax problems com.), Phila. Bar Assn. (exec. council sect. on taxation 1985—, vice chmn. fed. tax com. 1987—, lectr.), Phila. Tax Supper Group (treas. 1985-86, pres. 1986-87), Phila. Citywide Pension Lawyers Group. Club: Racquet (Phila). Partnership taxation, Corporate taxation, Pension, profit-sharing, and employee benefits. Office: Saul Ewing Remick & Saul 3800 Centre Sq W 1500 Market St Philadelphia PA 19102

FREEDMAN, CARL IRA, lawyer; b. Phila., June 30, 1950; s. Edward and Frances (Metter) F.; m. Beverly Ehrich, May 22, 1977; children: Jesse Matthew Ehrich Freedman, Adam Joshua Ehrich Freedman. AB, Haverford Coll., 1972; MA, The Fletcher Sch. of Law and Diplomacy, 1974; JD, Villanova U., 1977. Bar: Pa. 1977, U.S. Dist. Ct. (ea. dist.) Pa. 1977, R.I. 1979. Law clk. to presiding justice Pa. Superior Ct., Phila., 1977-78; atty. R.I. Legal Services, Providence, 1979-82; assoc. Licht & Semonoff, Providence, 1982-86, ptnr., 1986—; pres. The Work Place Inc., Providence, 1986-87. Spl. counsel R.I. Pub. Utilities Commn., Providence, 1982—; v.p. Brown-RISD Hillel Found., Providence, 1986—. Mem. ABA, R.I. Bar Assn., Pawtucket Bar Assn., Phi Beta Kappa. Democrat. Jewish. Real property, General corporate, Contracts commercial. Home: 17 Lowden St Pawtucket RI 02860 Office: Licht & Semonoff One Park Row Providence RI 02903

FREEDMAN, FRANK HARLAN, judge; b. Springfield, Mass., Dec. 15, 1924; s. Alvin Samuel and Ida Hilda (Rosenberg) F.; m. Eleanor Labinger, July 26, 1953; children: Joan Robin Freedman Goodman, Wendy Beth Greedman Mackler, Barry Alan. LL.B., Boston U., 1949, LL.M., 1950; Ph.D. (hon.), Western New Eng. Coll., Springfield, 1970. Practiced law 1950-68, mayor City of Springfield, 1968-72; judge U.S. Dist. Ct. Mass., Springfield, 1972-86, chief judge, 1986—. Chmn. fund raising drs. Muscular Dystrophy, Leukemia Soc.; mem. Susan Auchter Kidney Fund Raising Com.; mem. Springfield City Council, 1960-67, pres., 1962; del. Republican Nat. Conv., 1964, 68; mem. Springfield Rep. Com., 1959-72. Served with USNR, 1943-46. Greenaway Drive Elem. Sch. rededicated as Frank H. Freedman Sch., 1974; recipient Silver Shingle award for disting. service Boston U., 1984. Mem. Hampden County (Mass.) Bar Assn., Lewis Marshall Club on Jurisprudence (pres.). Jewish. Office: US Courthouse 1550 Main St Springfield MA 01103

FREEDMAN, HOWARD JOEL, lawyer; b. Cleve., Jan. 30, 1945; s. Samuel Brooks and Marian (Kirschner) F.; m. Terry Jay Greene, Dec. 22, 1966; children—Randall Greene, Jonathan Jay; m. 2d, Rita Bialosky, June 20, 1981. B.A., Tulane U., 1967; J.D., Case-Western Res. U., 1970. Bar: Ohio 1970. Assoc. Benesch, Friedlander, Coplan & Aronoff and predecessors, Cleve., 1970-75; founding ptnr. Friedman, Freedman & Kurland, and predecessors, Cleve., 1975-85, Goodman, Weiss & Freedman, Cleve., 1986—. Mem. ABA, Ohio Bar Assn., Bar Assn. Greater Cleve. Club: Cleve. Racquet (Pepper Pike, Ohio). General corporate, Real property, Securities. Home: 2951 Montgomery Rd Shaker Heights OH 44122 Office: 100 Erieview Plaza 27th Floor Cleveland OH 44114

FREEDMAN, KENNETH DAVID, lawyer; b. N.Y.C., Dec. 25, 1947; s. Samuel and Ethel Roberta (Myers) F.; m. Maxine Lantin, July 25, 1976; children—Jill Rose-Sophia, Robert Lantin. B.S., Ariz. State U., 1970; M.Ed., U. Ariz., 1973; J.D., Calif. Western Sch. Law, San Diego, 1979. Bar: Ariz. 1980, D.C. 1985, U.S. Dist. Ct. Ariz. 1980, U.S. Ct. Internat. Trade, 1980,

U.S. Ct. Mil. Appeals 1980, U.S. Ct. Appeals (9th cir.) 1980, U.S. Tax Ct. 1981, U.S. Supreme Ct. 1983, D.C. 1985. Grad. asst. U. Ariz., Tucson, 1972-73; adminstr. So. Colo. State Coll., Pueblo, 1973-74; adult probation officer Maricopa County Superior Ct., Phoenix, 1974-76, judge pro tem, 1986—, law clk. to chief presiding justices Maricopa County Superior Ct., 1979-80; assoc. Hocker, Yarbrough & Gilcrease, Tempe, Ariz., 1980-81; sole practice, Phoenix, 1981—; commr. pro tempore Juvenile div. Maricopa County Superior Ct., 1980—, instr. Park Coll., Williams AFB, 1976, Phoenix Coll., 1981—, U. Phoenix, 1985—; mem. disciplinary panel Ariz. State Bar, def. rep. exec. counsel criminal justice sect., mem. coms. legal edn., criminal and continuing legal edn. Served to 1st lt. U.S. Army, 1970-72. Mem. Nat. Assn. Criminal Def. Lawyers, Am. Arbitration Assn. (arbitration panel, 1986—), Ariz. State Univ. Greater Phoenix Alumni Assn. (bd. dirs.), Maricopa County Bar Assn. (chmn. com. on continuing legal edn. 1983-84, speakers bur.), Phi Alpha Delta. Republican. Jewish. Criminal, Family and matrimonial, General practice. Office: 11 W Jefferson St #16 Phoenix AZ 85003

FREEDMAN, MONROE HENRY, lawyer, educator; b. Mount Vernon, N.Y., Apr. 10, 1928; s. Chauncey and Dorothea (Kornblum) F.; m. Audrey Willock, Sept. 24, 1950; children: Alice Freedman Korngold, Sarah Freedman Izquierdo, Caleb, Judah. AB cum laude, Harvard U., 1951, LLB, 1954, LLM, 1956. Bar: Mass. 1954, Pa. 1957, D.C. 1960, U.S. Ct. Appeals (D.C. cir.) 1960, U.S. Supreme Ct. 1960, U.S. Ct. Appeals (2d cir.) 1968, N.Y. 1978, U.S. Ct. Appeals (9th cir.) 1982, U.S. Ct. Appeals (11th cir.) 1986. Assoc. Wolf, Block, Schorr & Solis-Cohen, Phila., 1956-58; ptnr. Freedman & Temple, Washington, 1969-73; dir. Stern Community Law Firm, Washington, 1970-71; prof. law George Washington U., 1958-73; dean Hofstra Law Sch., Hempstead, N.Y., 1973-77, prof. law, 1973—; faculty asst. Harvard U. Law Sch., 1954-56, instr. trial advocacy, 1978—; bd. dirs. U.S. Holocaust Meml. Council, 1980-82, gen. counsel, 1982-83, sr. adviser to chmn., 1982-87; cons. U.S. Commn. on Civil Rights, 1960-64, Neighborhood Legal Services Program, 1970; legis. cons. to Senator John L. McClellan, 1959; spl. com. on courtroom conduct N.Y.C. Bar Assn., 1972; bd. dirs. Criminal Trial Inst., 1965-66; expert witness on legal ethics state and fed. ct. proceedings U.S. Senate and House Coms., U.S. Dept. Justice; reporter Am. Lawyer's Code of Conduct, 1979-81; lectr. numerous profl. confs. Author: Contracts, 1973, Lawyers' Ethics in an Adversary System, 1975 (ABA gaval award cert. of merit 1976), Teacher's Manual Contracts, 1978, American Lawyer's Code of Conduct, 1981; vice chmn. editorial bd. ABA Human Rights; reviewing editor Georgetown Jour. Legal Ethics, 1986—; contbr. articles to profl. jours. Recipient Martin Luther King Jr. Humanitarian award, 1987. Mem. ACLU (nat. bd. dirs. 1970-80, nat. adv. council 1980—), Soc. Am. Law Tchrs. (gov. bd. 1974-79, exec. com. 1976-79, chmn. com. on profl. responsibility 1974-79, 87—), ABA (ethical considerations com. criminal justice sect.), D.C. Bar Assn. (chmn. legal ethics com. 1974-76, award of merit 1980, spl. com. on model rules profl. conduct 1983-86), Fed. Bar Assn. (chmn. com. on profl. disciplinary standards and procedures 1970-71), Am. Law Inst., Am. Jewish Congress (nat. governing council 1984—), Am. Arbitration Assn. (arbitrator, nat. panel arbitrators 1964—, arbitration panel U.S. Dist. Ct. (ea. dist.) N.Y. 1986—, cert. service 1986), Nat. Network on Right to Counsel (exec. bd., exec. com. 1986—, Cert. Service award 1986), N.Y. Lawyers Against Death Penalty, Assn. of Bar of City of N.Y. (com. on profl. responsibility 1987—), Internat. Assn. Jewish Lawyers and Jurists (chmn. acad. adv. com. Project Casaz 1987—), Nat. Prison Project (steering com. 1970—). Democrat. Jewish. Federal civil litigation, Criminal, Jurisprudence. Office: Law Bldg 1000 Fulton Ave Hempstead NY 11550

FREEDMAN, WALTER, lawyer; b. St. Louis, Oct. 30, 1914; s. Sam and Sophie (Gordon) F.; m. Maxine Weil, June 23, 1940; children—Jay W., Sandra Freedman Sabel. A.B., Washington U., 1937, J.D., 1937; LL.M., Harvard, 1938. Bar: Mo. bar, Ill. bar, D.C. bar. Atty. SEC, Washington, 1938-40, U.S. Dept. Interior, Washington, 1940-42; chief counsel Office Export Control, Foreign Econ. Adminstrn., 1942-44, dir., 1944-45; partner Freedman, Levy, Kroll & Simonds (and predecessor firm), Washington, 1946—; Fairchild fellow Harvard U. Law Sch., 1937-38. Editor-in-chief: Washington U. Law Quarterly, 1936-37; Contbr. articles to profl. jours. Decorated chevalier de l'Ordre de la Couronne (Belgium). Mem. Washington Bd. Trade, Am. Law Inst., Am., Fed., D.C. bar assns., Phi Beta Kappa, Omicron Delta Kappa; Phi Sigma Alpha. Jewish (trustee temple). Clubs: Internat, Woodmont Country (bd. mgrs.). Administrative and regulatory, General corporate, Probate. Home: 4545 W St NW Washington DC 20007 Office: 1050 Connecticut Ave NW Washington DC 20036

FREEDMAN, WARREN, lawyer, consultant in products liability, toxic torts and hazardous waste disposal; b. Scranton, Pa., May 2, 1921; s. Samuel N. and Sarah S. (Spitz) F.; m. Esther Rosenbluth, May 3, 1944; children—Debbie Freedman Stiebel, Douglas, Miriam. A.B., Rutgers U., 1943; J.D., Columbia U., 1949. Bar: N.Y. State 1949, U.S. Dist. Ct. (ea. dist.) N.Y. 1954, U.S. Ct. Appeals (2d cir.) 1954, U.S. Supreme Ct. 1955. Counsel, asst. sec. Bristol-Myers Co., N.Y.C., 1953-80; prof. law Rutgers U., New Brunswick, N.J., 1950-53; prof. sociology and the law New Sch. for Social Research, N.Y.C., 1959-66; hearing examiner, arbitrator; cons. in products liability; Am. counsel Israel Med. Assn. and Merephdi Med. Fedn. Served to capt. JAGC, U.S. Army, 1944-46; PTO. Mem. ABA, Internat. Assn. Jewish Lawyers and Jurists, World Peace Through Law Ctr., Anti-Defamation League of B'nai B'rith (hon. life). Author books on sociology, law and travel; contbr. articles to profl. jours. Product liability, Insurance, Transnational and international law. Home: 81 Stratford Rd New Rochelle NY 10804

FREEHLING, PAUL EDWARD, lawyer; b. Chgo., June 10, 1938; s. Norman and Edna (Wilhartz) F.; m. Susan Seder, June 27, 1961; children—Daniel, Joel. A.B., Harvard U., 1959, LL.B., 1962. Bar: U.S. Supreme Ct. 1974, Ill. 1962, U.S. Dist. Ct. (no. dist.) Ill. 1962, U.S. Ct. Appeals (7th cir.) 1973, U.S. Ct. Appeals (6th cir.) 1980; U.S. Ct. Appeals (D.C. cir.) 1983. Law clk. to judge U.S. Dist. Ct. No. Dist. Ill., Chgo., 1962-64; assoc. Pope, Ballard, Shepard & Fowle, Chgo., 1964-70, ptnr., 1970-82, dir., mem., 1982—. Mem. ABA, Am. Law Inst., Fed. Bar Assn., Ill. Bar Assn., Am. Judicature Soc., Chgo. Bar Assn., 7th Cir. Bar Assn., Chgo. Council Lawyers. Jewish. Clubs: Northmoor Country (Highland Park, Ill.); Standard (Chgo.). Federal civil litigation, State civil litigation. Office: Pope Ballard Shepard & Fowle 69 W Washington St Room 3200 Chicago IL 60602

FREELAND, CHARLES, lawyer, accountant; b. Balt., July 18, 1940; s. Benjamin and Beatrice (Polakoff) F.; m. Beverly Klaff, July 15, 1965; children—Stephen Jason, Jennifer Jill, Gwen Nicole, Kimberly Suzanne. B.S., U. Md., 1962, LL.B., 1965; diploma U.S. Naval Justice Sch., 1966. Bar: Md. 1965, U.S. Dist. Ct. Md. 1965, U.S. Tax Ct. 1966, U.S. Ct. Mil. Apls. 1966, U.S. Ct. Claims 1968, U.S. Supreme Ct. 1969, U.S. Ct. Appeals (4th cir.) 1974. Fin. v.p. Collins Electronics Mfg. Co.; dir. fin. planning Cellu-Craft, Inc., Stevensville, Md., 1963-65; controller Braun-Crystal Mfg. Co., Inc., Middle Village, N.Y., 1969-70, BCN Design Products, Inc., Bayshore, N.Y., 1969-70; asst. city solicitor City of Balt., 1972-82; sole practitioner, C.P.A., Balt., 1971-81; ptnr. Kaplan, Freeland & Schwartz, Balt., 1982-86; sole practice 1986—. Served to lt. USNR, 1965-68. Mem. Am. Judicature Soc., Am. Assn. Attys.-C.P.A.s, ABA, Md. Bar Assn., Am. Assn. C.P.A.s, Md. Assn. C.P.A.s, Am. Arbitration Assn. (nat. panel 1970—). Democrat. Jewish. Club: Woodholme Country. Corporate taxation, General corporate, Personal income taxation. Home: PO Box 422 4 Timothys Green Ct Brooklandville MD 21022 Office: 1300 York Rd Suite 180 Lutherville MD 21093

FREELAND, T. PAUL, lawyer; b. Princeton, Ind., Sept. 26, 1916; s. Leander Theodore and Leona B. (Tryon) F.; m. Caroline Van Dyke Ransom, July 7, 1941; 1 child, Caroline Carr (Mrs. Torrance C. Raymond). A.B., DePauw U., 1937; LL.B., Columbia U., 1940. Bar: N.Y., D.C., Mass. Assoc. firms Cravath, de Gersdorff, Swaine & Wood, N.Y.C., summer 1939, Dunnington, Bartholow & Miller, 1940-42; atty. office chief counsel IRS, 1945-48; partner firms Wenchel, Schulman & Manning, Washington, 1948-62, Sharp & Bogan, Washington, 1962-65, Bogan & Freeland, Washington, 1965-83, Sutherland, Asbill & Brennan, Washington, 1983—; lectr. various tax insts. Trustee Embry-Riddle Aero. U., 1972-82. Served as lt. USCGR, 1942-45, ETO. Fellow Am. Bar Found.; mem. Am., Inter-Am., Fed., D.C. bar assns., Internat. Fiscal Assn., U.S. C. of C. (task force on internat. tax policy), Phi Delta Phi. Clubs: Met. (D.C.), Chevy Chase (Md.). Corporate taxation. Home: 5525 Pembroke Rd Bethesda MD 20817 Office: 1275 Pennsylvania Ave NW Washington DC 20004

FREEMAN, ANTOINETTE ROSEFELDT, lawyer; b. Atlantic City, Oct. 7, 1937; d. Bernard Paul and Fannie (Levin) Rosefeldt; m. Alan Richard Freeman, June 22, 1958 (div. Apr. 1979); children—Barry David, Robin Lisa. B.A., Rutgers U., 1972; J.D., Ind. U., 1975; LL.M., Temple U., 1979. Bar: Pa. 1975, U.S. Dist. Ct. (ea. dist.) Pa. 1976, U.S. Ct. Appeals (3d cir.) 1982. Substitute tchr. Washington Twp. Sch. Dist., Indpls., 1972; dep. prosecutor intern Marion County Prosecutor, Indpls., 1974-75; asst. dist. atty. City of Phila., 1975-76; mgr. EEO, Wyeth Labs., Radnor, Pa., 1976-80, SmithKline & French Labs., Phila., 1980-82; atty. SmithKline Beckman Corp., Phila., 1982—; arbitrator Am. Arbitration Assn., 1976—. Counsel Regional Interests Developing Efficient Transp., 1983—; adv. bd. Family Service Phila., 1980-81, Greater Phila. C. of C., 1983; pres. Croskey Ct. Condominium Assn., 1983—; bd. dirs. Logan Sq. Neighborhood Assn., 1983—, pres., 1985—; v.p., sec. Friends of Logan Sq. Found.; chairperson Ctr. City Coalition for Quality of Life; atty. Vol. Lawyers fot the Arts, Phila., 1985—. Mem. ABA, Pa. Bar Assn., Phila. Bar Assn., Merit Employers Council (1st v.p. 1978-79), Phila. Women's Network, Phila. Lawyers Club, Phila. Vol. Lawyers for Arts. Democrat. Jewish. Administrative and regulatory, Government contracts and claims, Labor. Office: Smith Kline Beckman Corp One Franklin Plaza Philadelphia PA 19101

FREEMAN, BETH LABSON, lawyer; b. Washington, Nov. 21, 1953; d. Arnold and Dorothy (Deskin) Labson; m. William S. Freeman, Aug. 19, 1979; children: Laura, Scott. AB, U. Calif., Berkeley, 1976; JD, Harvard U., 1979. Bar: D.C. 1979, U.S. Dist. Ct. D.C. 1980, U.S. Ct. Appeals (9th and D.C. cirs.) 1980, Calif. 1981, U.S. Dist. Ct. (no. and ea. dists.) Calif. 1981. Assoc. Fried, Frank, Harris, Shriver & Jacboson, Washington, 1979-81, Lasky, Haas et al, San Francisco, 1981-83; dep. dist. atty. San Mateo County, Redwood City, Calif., 1983—. Pres., bd. dirs. Jr. Statemen Found., Menlo Park, Calif., 1981—; del. Dem. Nat. Conv., 1972; Dem. nominee Calif. Assembly, San Mateo, 1972. Mem. ABA, LWV. State civil litigation, Local government, Juvenile. Home: 484 Fairfax Ave San Mateo CA 94402 Office: Dist Attys Office 401 Marshall St Redwood City CA 94063

FREEMAN, DAVID JOHN, lawyer; b. N.Y.C., Aug. 9, 1948; s. John L. and Josephine F. (Wilding) F.; m. Ellen Gogolick, Dec. 29, 1974; children—Matthew, Julie. B.A., Harvard U., 1970, J.D., 1975. Bar: Mass. 1975, D.C. 1977, U.S. Ct. Appeals (D.C. cir.) 1979, U.S. Dist. Ct. D.C. 1981, N.Y. 1982, U.S. Dist. Ct. (so., ea. dists.) N.Y. 1982, U.S. Ct. Appeals (2d cir.) 1982. Spl. asst. to U.S. senator Frank E. Moss, 1970-72; trial atty. FTC, Washington, 1975-77; assoc. firm Ginsburg, Feldman & Bress, Washington, 1977-81; assoc. firm Holtzmann, Wise & Shepard, N.Y.C., 1981-84, ptnr., 1984—. Mem. ABA (antitrust sect., litigation sect.), Assn. Bar City N.Y. (environ. law com.), Harvard Law Sch. Assn. Federal civil litigation, Antitrust, Environment. Office: Holtzmann Wise & Shepard 745 Fifth Ave New York NY 10151

FREEMAN, DEBORAH LYNN, lawyer; b. Santa Monica, Calif., Jan. 12, 1955; d. T.L. Gordon and Patricia I. (von Walden) F. BA in History with distinction, Stanford U., 1976; JD with honors, U. Denver, 1982. Bar: Colo. 1982. With Saunders, Snyder, Ross & Dickson P.C., Denver, 1982—. Mem. ABA, Colo. Bar Assn. (mem. adv. council environ. law sect. 1987—), Denver Bar Assn. (sec. young lawyers div. 1985—). Environment, Real property. Office: Saunders Snyder Ross & Dickson PC 303 E 17th Ave Suite 600 Denver CO 80203

FREEMAN, FLORENCE ELEANOR, lawyer; b. Cambridge, Mass., Feb. 25, 1921; s. Elbern and Olive Blanche (Rice) F.; A.B., Wellesley Coll., 1942; J.D., U. Pa., 1945. Bar: Del. 1947, U.S. Dist. Ct. Del. 1948, U.S. Ct. Appeals (3d cir.) 1950, Mass. 1954, U.S. Dist. Ct. Mass. 1960. Assoc., Lynch & Hermann, Wilmington, Del., 1946-53; sole practice, Weston, Mass., 1954-69; ptnr. Freeman & Conceison, Weston, 1970-83, Freeman & White, Weston, 1984—; town counsel Town of Weston, 1968-86, spl. counsel, 1986—. Author: (play) Portrait of a Prince, 1965. Pres. Weston LWV, 1960-62, Weston Drama Workshop, 1963-71; mem. bd. selectmen Town of Weston, 1964-68; sec., trustee So. New Eng. Conf. United Meth. Ch., Boston, 1971-74, chancellor, 1976-86 ; bd. visitors Boston U. Sch. Theology, 1978-86 ; mem. council fin. and adminstrn. United Meth. Ch., Chgo., 1980—, alt. jud. council, 1980—, chmn. legal responsibilities com. 1984—. Mem. ABA, Am. Judicature Soc., Mass. Bar Assn. Republican. Club: Footlight (Boston) (pres. 1962-64); Wellesley Coll. Local government, Probate, Legal education. Office: Freeman & White 483 Boston Post Rd Weston MA 02193

FREEMAN, GEORGE CLEMON, JR., lawyer; b. Birmingham, Ala., Jan. 3, 1929; s. George Clemon and Annie Laura (Gill) F.; m. Anne Colston Hobson, Dec. 6, 1958; children: Anne Colston, George Clemon III, Joseph Reid Anderson. B.A., Vanderbilt U., 1950; LL.B., Yale U., 1956. Bar: Ala. 1956, Va. 1958, D.C. 1974. Law clk. Justice Hugo L. Black, U.S. Supreme Ct., 1956; practiced in Richmond, Va., 1957—; mem. firm Hunton & Williams, 1957—, partner, 1963—. Contbr. articles to profl. jours. Pres. Va. chpt. Nature Conservancy, 1962-63; mem. sect. 301 Superfund Act Study Group Congl. Adv. Com., 1981-82; mem. Falls of James Com., 1973—; chmn. Richmond City Democratic Com., 1969-71; chmn. adv. council Energy Policy Studies Ctr., U. Va., 1981—; chmn. legal adv. com. to Va. Commn. on Transp. in the 21st Century, 1986—; sec., bd. dirs. Richmond Symphony, 1960-63. Served to lt. (j.g.) USNR, 1951-54. Fellow Am. Bar Found.; mem. ABA (chmn. ad hoc on Fed. Criminal Code corp., banking and bus. law sect. 1979-81, chmn. program com. 1981-82, mem. coordinating group on regulatory reform 1981-85 , del. to ho. of dels. 1983-87, nominating com. 1984-87, sec. corp. banking and bus. law sect. 1987—), Richmond Bar Assn., Va. Bar Assn., Am. Law Inst. (council 1980—, advisor to council on project on compensation and liability for product and process injuries, 1986—), Am. Judicature Soc., Phi Beta Kappa, Phi Delta Phi, Omicron Delta Kappa, Alpha Tau Omega. Episcopalian. Clubs: Country of Virginia (Richmond); Knickerbocker (N.Y.C.); Metropolitan (Washington). Administrative and regulatory, Environment, Nuclear power. Home: 10 Paxton Rd Richmond VA 23226 Office: 707 E Main St Richmond VA 23212

FREEMAN, JAMES ATTICUS, III, lawyer; b. Gadsden, Ala., Jan. 27, 1947; s. James Atticus and Dorothy Mae (Watson) F.; m. Judith Gail Davis, June 19, 1970; children: Gwendolyn Gail, James Atticus IV, Laura Marie. BS, Vanderbilt U., 1969, JD, 1972. Bar: Tenn. 1972. Broadcaster, newsman Gen. Electric Broadcasting, Nashville, 1965-72; atty. The Murray Ohio Mfg. Co., Nashville, 1972-73, legal officer, 1973-81; asst. v.p., legal officer The Murray Ohio Mfg. Co., Brentwood, Tenn., 1981-86, asst. v.p., legal officer, dir. risk mgmt., 1986—; lectr. corp. law, bd. advisors Southeastern Inst. Paralegal Edn., Nashville, 1981—; guest lectr. U. Wis. Sch. Engring., Madison, 1983—; adj. faculty Am. Soc. of Metals, Cleve., 1984—. Mem. ABA, Tenn. Bar Assn., Nashville Bar Assn. (chmn. membership com. 1984, program chmn. corp. sect. 1985-86), Am. Soc. Metals, Outdoor Power Equipment Inst. (chmn. corp. counsel com. 1976-84), Bicycle Mfrs. Assn. (chmn. legal affairs com. 1978-81), Vanderbilt Alumni Assn., Phi Alpha Delta. Episcopal. Club: Bluegrass Yacht & Country (Hendersonville, Tenn.). Personal injury, Insurance, General corporate. Office: The Murray Ohio Mfg Co 219 Franklin Rd Brentwood TN 37027

FREEMAN, MARTIN HENRY, lawyer; b. Balt., Mar. 25, 1940; s. Aaron and Sophia Louise (Flocks) F.; m. Roslynn Mogel, June 16, 1963; children—Mark Allan, Jon Stuart, Thomas Randolph. B.A. in Applied Sci., Lehigh U., 1961, B.S. in Mech. Engring., 1961; J.D. with honors, George Washington U., 1965. Bar: Md. 1965, U.S. Ct. Appeals (4th cir.) 1966, U.S. Supreme Ct. 1969, U.S. Dist. Ct. Md. 1970, D.C. 1977, U.S. Dist. Ct. D.C. 1977, U.S. Ct. Appeals (D.C. cir.) 1977. Assoc. Sasscer, Clagett, Powers & Channing, Upper Marlboro, Md., 1965-70; ptnr. Sasscer, Clagett, Channing & Bucher, Upper Marlboro, 1970-71; assoc. Bulman, Goldstein, Feld & Dunie, Bethesda, Md. and Washington, 1971-73; sr. ptnr. Bulman, Dunie, Freeman, Burke & Feld, Bethesda and Washington, 1974-82; sole practice, Bethesda and Washington, 1983-86; sr. ptnr. Freeman & Richardson, 1986—; lectr. in field; people's counsel Pub. Service Commn. Md., Balt., 1971-73; mem. legis. task force utility rates and practices, Annapolis, Md., 1976-77; lobbyist Md. Gen. Assembly, Annapolis, 1983—. City councilman City of Bowie, Md., 1969-71, mayor pro tem, 1971; bd. dirs. Pub. Safety and Policy Commn., Met. Washington Council of Govts., 1969-71, Nat. Capital Region Transp. Planning Bd., Washington, 1970-71; bd. dirs., chmn. legis. and social action com. Jewish Social Service Agy. Met. Washington, Rockville, Md., 1969-70; mem. Health and Welfare Council Met. Washington, 1970; v.p. Temple Solel Congregation, Bowie, 1973; active Bowie Boys and Girls Club, PTA, Bowie Jaycees. Mem. ABA, Prince George's County Bar Assn., Montgomery County Bar Assn., D.C. Bar Assn., Md. State Bar Assn. (jud. adminstrn. council 1973-75, 84—), Am. Bd. Trial Advocates (diplomate, charter mem. Md. chpt. 1983—, nat. bd. dirs.), Am. Judicature Soc., Assn. Trial Lawyers Am., Md. Trial Lawyers Assn. (treas., bd. of govs.), Md. Tort Litigation Study Group (charter mem. 1977), J. Dudley Digges Inn of Ct. (chmn. organizing com., master of bench, 1st counselor), Am. Inns of Ct found. (chmn. fin. com., del.), Bethesda-Chevy Chase C. of C. (bd. dirs. 1977-81, pres. 1979-80, chmn. bd. 1979-81), Montgomery County C. of C. (bd. dirs. 1979-81), Md. C. of C. Democrat. Jewish. Personal injury, Public utilities, Federal civil litigation. also: 1053 Conundrum Rd Aspen CO 81612 Office: 4550 Montgomery Ave Suite 760-N Bethesda MD 20814

FREEMAN, MILTON VICTOR, lawyer; b. N.Y.C., Nov. 16, 1911; s. Samuel and Celia (Gelfand) F.; m. Phyllis Young, Dec. 19, 1937; children: Nancy Lois (Mrs. Gans), Daniel Martin, Andrew Samuel, Amy Martha (Mrs. Malone). A.B., Coll. City N.Y., 1931; LL.B., Columbia U., 1934. Bar: N.Y. 1934, D.C. 1946, U.S. Supreme Ct. 1943. With gen. counsel's office SEC, 1934-42, asst. solicitor, 1942-46; staff securities div. FTC, 1934; with firm Arnold & Porter and predecessor firms, Washington, 1946—; adj. prof. Yale U., 1947, Georgetown U. Law Sch., 1952; vis. scholar various univs., 1978-79; mem. adv. bd. Bur. Nat. Affairs, Securities Regulation and Law Report, Washington, Nat. Law Jour., N.Y., Internat. Fin. Law Rev., London. Contbr. articles to profl. jours.; bd. editors Columbia Law Rev., 1933-34. Mem. exec. com. U. Calif., San Diego; bd. visitors U. San Diego Law Sch. Mem. ABA (chmn. subcom. on SEC practice and enforcement 1972-83, exec. com. fed. regulation of securities com. 1983—, ad hoc com. on corp. governance project), Fed. bar Assn., D.C. Bar Assn., Internat. Law Inst. (hon. chmn. 1977—, trustee 1955—), Securities Regulation Inst. (exec. com.). Club: International (Washington). General corporate, Securities, Administrative and regulatory. Home: 3405 Woolsey Dr Chevy Chase MD 20815 Office: 1200 New Hampshire Ave NW Washington DC 20036

FREEMAN, PHILIP DAYNE, lawyer; b. Oklahoma City, Nov. 29, 1947. BA, Pa. State U., 1970; JD, Duquesne U., 1975. Bar: Pa. 1975, U.S. Dist. Ct. (we. dist.) 1975, U.S. Ct. Appeals (4th cir.) 1978, Tex. 1983. Atty. U.S. Steel Corp., Pitts., 1975-83; sr. counsel domestic ops. Datapoint Corp., San Antonio, 1983-85; v.p., gen. counsel, sec. Intelogic Trace, Inc., San Antonio, 1985—. Assoc. editor Duquesne Law Rev., Pitts., 1974-75. General corporate, Contracts commercial, Antitrust. Office: Intelogic Trace Inc 8415 Datapoint Dr San Antonio TX 78229

FREEMAN, RICHARD C., judge; b. Atlanta, Dec. 14, 1926. A.B., Emory U., 1950, LL.B., 1952. Bar: Ga. bar 1953. Since practiced in Atlanta; mem. firm Haas, Holland & Blackshear, 1955-58; partner Haas, Holland, Freeman, Levison & Gibert, 1958-71; judge U.S. Dist. Ct., 1971—; Alderman City of Atlanta, 1962-71; pres. Atlanta Humane Soc., 1981. Mem. Ga., Atlanta bar assns., Lawyers Club Atlanta, Chi Phi, Phi Delta Phi. Office: US Dist Ct 2121 US Courthouse 75 Spring St SW Atlanta GA 30303 *

FREEMAN, RICHARD LYONS, lawyer; b. Chgo., Oct. 29, 1932; s. Reuben L. and Bernice (Green) F.; m. Mary Leopold, May 2, 1959; children—Thomas R., Richard Lyons. A.B. cum laude, Harvard U., 1954; LL.B., Yale U., 1957. Bar: Ill. 1958. Assoc., Friedman, Zoline & Rosenfield, Chgo., 1958-60; investment analyst Robert J. Levy & Co., Chgo., 1960-62; assoc. Schwartz & Freeman, Chgo., 1962-68, ptnr., 1968—. Bd. dirs. Chgo. Hearing Soc., pres., 1972-74. Served with Air N.G., 1957-63. Fellow Am. Coll. Probate Counsel; mem. Chgo. Estate Planning Council, Chgo. Bar Assn., Ill. Bar Assn., ABA. Jewish. Clubs: Standard (Chgo.); Lake Shore Country (Glencoe, Ill.). Probate, Pension, profit-sharing, and employee benefits, Real property. Office: Suite 3400 401 N Michigan Ave Chicago IL 60611

FREEMAN, ROBERT JOHN, lawyer, state agency director; b. Newton, Mass., June 5, 1947; s. Bernard Sherman and Marian (Weiner) F.; m. Felice Wallach, Sept. 4, 1972; children: Melissa, Brandon, Elliot. BS, Georgetown U., 1969; postgrad., U. Dijon, France, 1967; JD, NYU, 1973. Bar: N.Y. 1974. Assoc. Ungerman, Harris & Ackerman, Albany, N.Y., 1973-74; atty. N.Y. State Dept of Social Services, Albany, N.Y., 1974; counsel N.Y. State Com. Pub. Access, Albany, N.Y., 1974-76; exec. dir. N.Y. State Com. on Open Govt., Albany, N.Y., 1976—; mem. editorial adv. bd. access reports Washington Monitor, 1983—; lectr. Nat. Jud. Coll., Reno, 1986. Contbr. articles to law jours. Recipient Friend of the Free Press award N.Y. Soc. Newspaper Editors, 1982, Pres.'s award Syracuse (N.Y.) Press Club, 1986. Mem. ABA, N.Y. State Bar Assn. Administrative and regulatory, Government information and privacy. Office: NY State Com on Open Govt 162 Washington Ave Albany NY 12231

FREEMAN, STEPHAN JOHN, lawyer; b. Boston, Feb. 17, 1956; s. Michael Sherwood and Corinne (Hirschfeld) F.; m. Bonnie Leigh Earley. BA, Emory Coll., 1978; JD, U. Fla., 1981. Bar: Fla. 1981, U.S. Dist. Ct. (mid. dist.) Fla. 1982, U.S. Ct. Appeals (11th cir.) 1982. Assoc. Lewis & Freeman, St. Petersburg, Fla., 1981-84, Mattson, McGrady & Todd P.A., St. Petersburg, 1984—. Bd. dirs. Suncoast Children's Dream Fund, St. Petersburg, 1985—. MMem. St. Petersburg Bar Assn., Nat. Assn. Remodeling Industry (bd. dirs. 1983—), Sunshine City Jaycees. Republican. Jewish. Lodge: Rotary. Avocations: swimming, reading. State civil litigation, General practice, Insurance. Office: Mattson McGrady & Todd PA 6500 1st Ave N Saint Petersburg FL 33710

FREERKSEN, GREGORY NATHAN, lawyer; b. Washington, Iowa, June 4, 1951; s. Floyd and Betty Jo (Frederick) F.; m. Patricia A. Menges, Mar. 21, 1981; children: Suzanna Lynn, Andrea Elizabeth. B.S., No. Ill. U., 1973; J.D., DePaul U., 1976. Bar: Ill. 1976, U.S. Dist. Ct. (no. dist.) Ill. 1976, U.S. Supreme Ct. 1980, U.S. Ct. Appeals (D.C. cir.) 1983. Law clk. Ill. Appellate Ct., Waukegan, Ill., 1976-78; assoc. Law Offices of A.E. Botti, Wheaton, Ill., 1978-79; assoc. DeJong, Poltrock & Giampietro, Chgo., 1979-86; mem. Poltrock & Giampietro, 1986—. Author: (annotated bibliography) Children in the Legal Literature, 1976; Non-Salary Provisions in Negotiated Teacher Agreements, 1975. Editor Ill. law issue DePaul U. Law Rev., 1975-76. Dem. candidate for State Senate, 1986; committeeman 26th precinct Downers Grove Twp. Mem. ABA, Ill. State Bar Assn., Chgo. Bar Assn., Appellate Lawyers Assn., DuPage Bar Assn. Democrat. Labor, Personal injury, Civil rights. Home: 5224 Fairmount Ave Downers Grove IL 60515 Office: DeJong Poltrock & Giampietro 221 N LaSalle St Chicago IL 60601

FREI, MICHAEL CLARK, lawyer; b. Salt Lake City, Apr. 4, 1946; s. Clark and Nina (Nisson) F.; m. Jacque Sloan, June 11, 1969; children: Christopher, Daniel, Jaime, Kelly, Tracie. JD, U. Utah, 1971. Bar: Calif. 1972, Utah 1979. Assoc. Duryea, Carpenter & Barnes, Newport Beach, Calif., 1972-76; asst. gen. counsel Albertson's Inc., Boise, Idaho, 1976-78; ptnr. Snow, Christensen & Martineau, Salt Lake City, 1978-81; v.p., gen. counsel Price Devel., Salt Lake City, 1981—. Mem. ABA, Calif. Bar Assn., Utah Bar Assn. Real property, General corporate, Landlord-tenant. Office: Price Devel Co 35 Century Park Way Salt Lake City UT 84115

FREILICH, DIANE M., lawyer; b. Detroit, Mar. 2, 1943; d. Norman and Nettie (Karpel) F. JD, Detroit Coll. Law, 1972. Bar: Mich., U.S. Dist. Ct. (ea. dist.) Mich., U.S. Supreme Ct. Assoc. Zeff & Zeff, Detroit, 1972-82; sole practice Farmington Hills, Mich., 1982—; bd. dirs. Detroit Coll. Law, 1984—. Mem. Mich. Bar Assn. (family law sect.), Oakland County Bar Assn. (family law sect., sec. 1974-75), Detroit Bar Assn. Personal injury, Family and matrimonial, Medical malpractice. Office: 30833 Northwestern Hwy Suite 214 Farmington Hills MI 48018

FREIS, JAMES HENRY, lawyer; b. New Brunswick, N.J., June 11, 1944; s. Peter Charles and Agnes (Clarkson) F.; m. Maria Felicia Peters, Aug. 10, 1968; children—Jean Marie, James Henry, Jr., Kathleen Marie. A.B. cum laude, St. Peter's Coll., 1966; J.D., Villanova U., 1969. Bar: N.J. 1969, N.Y. 1983. Law clk. to judge appellate div. Superior Ct. N.J., Newark, 1969-70;

ptnr. Shanley & Fisher, P.C., Morristown and Somerville, N.J., 1972—; mem. exec. com. banking law sect. N.J. State Bar Assn.; mem. adv. com. pension commn. Newark Archdiocese Roman Cath. Ch. Served to capt. U.S. Army, 1970-72. Mem. ABA, Nat. Assn. Bond Lawyers, Mortgage Bankers Assn. Club: Exchange (Metuchen). Municipal Bonds, Contracts commercial, Banking. Office: 131 Madison Ave Morristown NJ 07960

FREISER, LAWRENCE M., lawyer; b. Bklyn., Mar. 3, 1942; m. Frances A., June 7, 1970; children—Jeffrey A., Dana M., B.A., N.Y.U., 1963; LL.B., Bklyn. Law Sch., 1966. Bar: N.Y. 1966, Calif. 1972, U.S. Dist. Ct. (so. and ea. dists.) N.Y. 1968, U.S. Tax Ct. 1969, U.S. Customs Ct. and Patent Appeals 1969, U.S. Ct. Appeals (2d cir.) 1969, U.S. Ct. Claims 1970, U.S. Supreme Ct. 1970, U.S. Dist. Ct. (no. dist.) Calif. 1973, U.S. Ct. Appeals (9th cir.) 1973, U.S. Dist. Ct. (cen. dist.) Calif. 1976, U.S. Ct. Internat. Trade 1980. Assoc. Kaufman, Taylor, Kimmel & Miller, N.Y.C., 1967-68, Ruben Schwartz, N.Y.C., 1968; sole practice, N.Y.C., 1968-72, Pleasant Hill, Calif., 1973, N.Y.C., 1973-74, Los Angeles, 1974-75, 1977-79; atty. Hughes Aircraft Corp., San Mateo, Calif., 1972-73; assoc. Alvin B. Green, Los Angeles, 1975-77; adj. prof. Northrop U. Sch. Law, 1978-79; atty. Calif. Continuing Edn. of the Bar, State Bar of Calif./U. Calif. Extension, Berkeley, 1979—; tchr. math. bd. edn. N.Y.C., 1966-67. Cert. community coll. law instr., Calif. Mem. State Bar of Calif., ABA, N.Y. County Lawyers Assn. Editor, contbg. author several sects. Vol. 1, Calif. Civil Procedure During Trial, 1982; co-atty./editor Calif. Workers' Compensation Practice, 3d edit., 1985, chpts. 11, 21 Calif. Civil Appellate Practice, 2d. edit., 1985; supr. atty.-editor Calif. Civil Procedure, Vol. 2, 1984; mem. staff Bklyn. Law Rev., 1964-66. State civil litigation, Federal civil litigation, Jurisprudence. Home: 2877 Walnut Blvd Walnut Creek CA 94596 Office: 2300 Shattuck Ave Berkeley CA 94704

FRELING, RICHARD ALAN, lawyer; b. N.Y.C., June 21, 1932; s. Jack C. and Natalie F.; children—Darryl, Robert, Dana. B.B.A, U. Tex., 1954, LL.B. with honors, 1956. Bar: Tex. 1956, U.S. Dist. Ct. (no. dist.) Tex. 1959, U.S. Ct. Appeals (5th cir.) 1961, U.S. Supreme Ct. 1962. Ptnr. firm Johnson & Swanson, Dallas, 1983—; bd. dirs., research fellow Southwestern Legal Found. Editor-in-chief: (1955-56) Tex. Law Rev; contbr. articles to legal jours. Trustee St. Marks Sch. of Tex., 1971-78; sec., mem. exec. com., 1975-78; trustee Greenhill Sch., 1972—, sec., mem. exec. com. 1976-78; bd. govs., mem. exec. com. Southwest Outward Bound Sch., 1972-81, chmn., 1981—; trustee Retina Found. of S.W., 1975—, Southwestern Legal Found., 1983—, Pine Manor Coll., Chestnut Hill, Mass., 1982-85; bd. dirs. Colo. Outward Bound Sch., 1982—, Friends of Dallas Pub. Library, 1982—, Dallas Symphony, 1984—, Isthmus Inst., 1983—, Aperture Found., 1984—, Tex. Nature Conservancy, 1986—. Fellow Am. Coll. Tax Counsel, Tex. Bar Found.; mem. Am. Law Inst. (cons. fed. income tax project 1976—), ABA (council Taxation sect. 1982-85), Tex. Bar Assn., Dallas Bar Assn., Tex. Law Rev. Assn. (bd. dirs. 1973—). Corporate taxation, General corporate, Private international. Office: Johnson & Swanson 900 Jackson St Dallas TX 75202

FREMONT, ERNEST HOAR, JR., lawyer; b. Glenwood, Minn., Nov. 19, 1925; s. Ernest Hoar and Olga (Ostlund) F.; m. Johanne M. Ravenholt; children: Paula Marie, Alicia Ann. B.A., U. Minn., 1950; J.D., U. Mo. at Kansas City, 1956. Bar: Mo. bar 1956. Dir. firm Popham, Conway, Sweeny Fremont & Bundschu (P.C.), Kansas City, 1956—; Chmn. Mo. Adv. Com. Free Press-Fair Trial, 1968-70; chmn. Supreme Ct. (Mo.) Com. on Profl. Ethics and Responsibility, 1969-71; vice chmn. DRI Automobile Compensation Com. Chmn. law found. U. Mo. at Kansas City, 1973-74, trustee, 1962-68; active Vols. for Council on Pub. Higher Edn. for Mo.; trustee Kansas City U. Conservatory Music. Served with USNR, 1944-46; served to 1st lt. AUS, 1951-53. Recipient Alumni Achievement award U. Mo. at Kansas City, 1965, Ann. Law Day award, 1972. Hon. fellow Harry S. Truman Library Inst.; mem. steering com. Truman Statue project.; Fellow Internat. Soc. Barristers; mem. ABA (mem. standing com. pub. relations 1965-71, chmn. 1965-68, vice chmn. trial techniques com. of ins. sect. 1973-77, Mo. del. Ho. Dels. 1974-87, Ho. Dels. hearing com. 1974-80, chmn. 1978-79, spl. com. on automobile legislation 1977-80, gov. 1979-82, chmn. standing com. on mil. law 1981—), Mo. Bar Assn. (bd. govs. 1964-73, mem. control council 1963-70, chmn. pub. info. com. 1962-64, pres. 1971-72, chmn. coordinating com. state bar pres. 1972-73, chmn. task force on mandatory continuing legal edn. 1975-77), Kansas City Bar Assn., Internat. Bar Assn., Powell Inn (exchequer) (1952-53), Nat. Planning Assn. (mem. nat. council 1970-74), Fedn. Ins. Counsel, U. Mo. at Kansas City Alumni Assn. (dir. 1972-79, pres. 1978-79), Phi Delta Phi (Disting. Alumnus of Year 1970). Congregationalist (trustee 1966-68, chmn. 1967-68, moderator 1982-83). Club: Kansas City. Home: 6647 State Line Rd Kansas City MO 64113 Office: Commerce Bank Bldg Kansas City MO 64106

FRENCH, BRUCE HARTUNG, economist, lawyer; b. Canton, Ohio, May 2, 1915; s. Garnett Bruce and Marie (Hartung) F.; m. Jeanne Adrienne Aeberhard, June 27, 1942 (div. 1969); m. Dorothy Fleming Gorman, Nov. 29, 1969 (div. 1985); children: Robert Adrain, David Adrain. A.B., Haverford Coll., 1937; A.M., U. Pa., 1940, Ph.D., 1946; postgrad., Princeton U., 1941-42; LL.B., Rutgers U., 1945. Bar: N.J. 1948. Asst. in govt. Haverford Coll., 1937-39; instr. politics Princeton U., 1941-42, 46-47; asst. prof. econs. U. Coll., Rutgers U., 1947-53, assoc. prof. econs., 1953-83, emeritus, 1983—, chmn. dept. econs., 1951-75; practice in Princeto; mem. firm French & Cook, Princeton, N.J., 1950-59; pvt. practice law 1959-80, 82—; mem. firm French & Stockton, Princeton, 1981-82; chmn. bd. Am. Investors Services, Inc., Great Barrington, Mass., 1978-83; mem. Am. Investors Services, Inc., 1983—; pres. Estate Owners, Inc., Frenchlands Inc.; counsel, also exec. dir. Housing Authority Borough Princeton, 1949-58, Hightstown, 1958-75. Author: Banking and Insurance in New Jersey-A History, 1965, How to Avoid Financial Tangles, 1981. Pres. Princeton Community Chest, 1950; mem. N.J. Tercentenary Adv. Com., 1960; mem. corp. Haverford Coll.; pres. bd. trustees Princeton Meeting of Friends at Stony Brook, 1976-81; chmn. bd. trustees Am. Inst. for Econ. Research, Great Barrington, 1976—. Served to lt. comdr. USNR, 1942-46; as liaison officer with fgn. govts., officer-in-charge USN Internat. Aid Office N.Y.C. Recipient letter commendation USN. Mem. N.J., Princeton, Mercer County bar assns., Princeton Hist. Soc. (past pres.), Huguenot Soc., Am. Econs. Assn., Soc. War of 1812, St. Nicholas Soc., Soc. Colonial Wars, First Families of Ohio, S.R. (past pres. N.J.), Phi Beta Kappa (del. to Bicentennial meeting 1976). Republican. Mem. Soc. of Friends. Clubs: Nassau (Princeton) (past pres.), Pretty Brook Tennis (Princeton); Union (N.Y.C.); Princeton (N.Y.C.); Athenaeum (Phila.); Pot and Kettle (Maine), Bar Harbor (Maine); Founders (Haverford Coll.). Probate, Estate taxation, Real property. Home: 19 Winfield Rd Princeton NJ 08540 Office: 601 Ewing St Princeton NJ 08540

FRENCH, COLIN VAL, lawyer, estate planner; b. Phila., July 20, 1957; s. Calvin Valdean and Ella LaVon (Crum) F.; m. Amanda Mitchell, June 16, 1984. BS magna cum laude, Graceland Coll., 1979; JD, Drake U., 1982; LLM in Tax, So. Meth. U., 1983. Bar: Iowa 1982, Tex. 1983. Atty. Nat. Office Boy Scouts Am., Des Moines, 1984-86, So. Meth. U., Dallas, 1986—; cons. Am. Coll. Fin., Sunnyvale, Calif., 1984—; prof. U. Calif. system, 1985—; mem. Legal Ethics and Sports Law Coms., Dallas, 1985—. Editor newspaper The Gavel, 1981-82, newsletter Finance Update, 1985-86. Mem. ABA, State Bar Iowa, State Bar Tex., Dallas Bar Assn. Republican. Mem. Reorganized Ch. of Jesus Christ of Latter Day Saints. Avocations: music writing and performance, golf, tennis. Estate planning, Probate, Estate taxation. Home: 6215 Meadow Rd Dallas TX 75230 Office: So Meth U Box 4115 Dallas TX 75275

FRENCH, E. LAVON, lawyer; b. Centralia, Wash., Nov. 6, 1930; d. Carl Freeman and Melva Lavon (Ward) Crum; m. Calvin Valdean French, Aug. 30, 1950; children: Colin Val, Kelsey Ward. AA, Graceland Coll., 1950; BA, Drake U., 1969, MA, 1970, JD, 1975. Bar: Iowa 1975, D.C. 1980. Asst. county atty. Polk County, Des Moines, 1975-80; counsel small bus. com. U.S. Ho. of Reps., Washington, 1980—. Mem. ABA, Fed. Bar Assn. (council mem. Capital Hill chpt. 1985—). Democrat. Reorganized Ch. of Jesus Christ of Latter-day Saints. Club: PEO. Avocations: music, art. Legislative, Government contracts and claims. Home: 2711 35th Pl NW Washington DC 20007 Office: House Small Bus Com 2361 Rayburn Bldg Washington DC 20515

FRENCH, JOHN, III, lawyer; b. Boston, July 12, 1932; s. John and Rhoda (Walker) F.; m. Leslie Ten Eyck, Jan. 11, 1957 (div. 1961) children: John B., Lawrence C.; m. Ann Hubbell, Jan. 9, 1965; children: Daniel J., Susanna H. BA, Dartmouth Coll., 1955; JD, Harvard U., 1958. Bar: N.Y. 1959. Assoc. Milbank, Tweed, Hadley & McCloy, N.Y.C., 1961-68, Satterlee & Stephens, N.Y.C., 1968-73; asst. gen. counsel Continental Group, Inc., Stamford, Conn., 1973-81; v.p., gen. counsel, sec. Peabody Internat. Corp., Stamford, Conn., 1981-82; ptnr. Appleton, Rice & Perrin, N.Y.C., 1982-84, Beveridge and Diamond, N.Y.C., 1985—; lectr. Practising Law Inst., 1979-83, Am. Law Inst., 1978; dir. Sheba Foods, Inc., Resorts Mgmt., Inc., UAA Films, Inc., Los Angeles, Hart Environ. Mgmt. Corp., N.Y.C. Contbr. articles to profl. jours. Trustee Hudson River Found., 1982—, YM-YWCA Camping Services of Greater N.Y., Inc., 1983—; bd. dirs. Third St. Music Sch. Settlement House, Inc., Internat. House, Inc., N.Y.C., Young Concert Artists, Inc., 1980—; mem. Westchester County Planning Bd., 1974-85; mem. N.Y. State Environ. Bd., 1976—. Served to capt. JAGC, USAF, 1958-61. Mem. ABA, N.Y. State Bar Assn. (lectr.), Assn. Bar City N.Y. (lectr.), Environ. Law Inst., Am. Soc. Corp. Secs. Republican. Clubs: River, Harvard (N.Y.C.); Knickerbocker and Bedford (N.Y.) Golf and Tennis. General corporate, Antitrust, Environment. Home: 420 E 54th St New York NY 10022 Office: Beveridge & Diamond 101 Park Ave Suite 1202 New York NY 10178

FRENCH, JOHN DWYER, lawyer; b. Berkeley, Calif., June 26, 1933; s. Horton Irving and Gertrude Margery (Ritzen) F.; m. Annette Richard, 1955; m. Berna Jo Mahling, 1986. B.A. summa cum laude, U. Minn., 1955; B.A. postgrad, Oxford U., Eng., 1955-56; LL.B. magna cum laude, Harvard U., 1960. Bar: D.C. bar 1960, Minn. bar 1963. Law clk. Justice Felix Frankfurter, U.S. Supreme Ct., 1960-61; legal asst. to commr. FTC, 1961-62; asso. firm Ropes, & Gray, Boston, 1962-63, Faegre & Benson, Mpls., 1963-66; partner Faegre & Benson, 1967-75, mng. partner, 1975—; adj. faculty mem. Law Sch. U. Minn., 1965-70; mem. exec. com. Lawyers Com. for Civil Rights under Law, 1978—; co-chmn. U.S. Dist. Judge Nominating Commn., 1979; Vice chmn. adv. com., mem. dir. search com., chmn. devel. office search com. Hubert Humphrey Inst., 1979-80. Contbr. numerous articles and revs. to legal jours. Chmn. or co-chmn. Minn. State Democratic Farm Labor Party Conv., 1970, 72, 74, 78, 80, 82, 84, 86, chmn. Mondale Vol. Com., 1972, treas., 1974; assoc. chmn. Minn. Dem.-Farmer-Labor Party, 1985-86; mem. Dem. Nat. Com., 1985-86; del. Democratic Nat. Conv., 1976, 78, 80, 84; trustee Twin Cities Public TV, Inc., 1980—, mem. overseers com. to visit Harvard U. Law Sch., 1970-75, 77-82. Served with U.S. Army, 1955-56. Rotary Found. fellow, 1955-56. Mem. ABA (mem. editorial bd. jour. 1976-79), Minn. Bar Assn., Hennepin County Bar Assn., Jud. Council Minn., Lawyers Alliance for Nuclear Arms Control (nat. bd. dirs. 1982-84), U. Minn. Alumni Assn. (mem. exec. com. 1985—), Phi Beta Kappa. Episcopalian. Antitrust, Administrative and regulatory, Federal civil litigation. Office: 2300 Multifoods Tower Minneapolis MN 55402

FRENCH, THOMAS MCGUINNESS, lawyer; b. Muskegon, Mich., Nov. 15, 1934; s. Thomas Hart and Isabel (Mongeau) F.; m. Cecilie L. Franke, May 26, 1964; children: Danielle G. French-Hollander, Thomas H. BA, U. Mich., 1957; JD, U. Wis., 1961. Bar: Wis. 1961, Vt. 1966, U.S. Dist. Ct. Vt. 1966, Mass. 1986. Assoc. Fitts & Olson, Brattleboro, Vt., 1966-67; sole practice Brattleboro, 1967-77, 85—; ptnr. French & Zwicker, Brattleboro, 1977-85. Sect. chmn. Project 2000, Brattleboro, 1981, 86; bd. dirs. Housing Devel. Credit Corp., Brattleboro, 1985—. Served to capt. JAGC, USAF, 1961-65. Mem. ABA, Vt. Bar Assn., Windham County Bar Assn. (treas. 1966-69), Brattleboro Area C. of C. (bd. dirs. 1976-82, 85—), Phi Delta Phi. Democrat. Unitarian. Federal civil litigation, State civil litigation, Public international. Home: South St Box 492 Brattleboro VT 05301 Office: 231 Western Ave Box 492 Brattleboro VT 05301

FRETWELL, NORMAN ELLIOTT, lawyer; b. Joplin, Mo., Apr. 13, 1944; s. Delmar Elliott and Louise (Roehling) F.; m. Nancy Houx, Mar. 12, 1977 (div. Oct. 1984); 1 child, Jami. BS, U.S. Mil. Acad., 1966; JD, U. Mich., 1973. Bar: Mo. 1973. Commd. 2d lt. U.S. Army, 1966, advanced through to capt., resigned, 1970; from assoc. to ptnr. Watson, Ess, Marshall & Enggas, Kansas City, Mo., 1973—. Republican. Banking, Contracts commercial, General corporate. Home: 300 Avila Circle Kansas City MO 64114 Office: Watson Ess Marshall & Enggas 1010 Grand Kansas City MO 64106

FREUND, FRED A., lawyer; b. N.Y.C., June 18, 1928; s. Sidney J. and Cora (Strasser) F.; m. Rosalie Sampo, Nov. 18, 1975 (div. Apr. 1983); m. Patricia A. Gardner, Mar. 13, 1957 (div. Jan. 1967); children: Gregory G., K. Bailey. A.B., Columbia U., 1948, J.D., 1949. Bar: N.Y. 1949, U.S. Supreme Ct. 1968. Law clk. to chief judge U.S. Dist. Ct. So. Dist. N.Y., N.Y.C., 1949-51; assoc. Kaye, Scholer, Fierman, Hays & Handler, N.Y.C., 1953-58, ptnr., 1959. Served to 1st lt. USAF, 1951-53. Mem. ABA, Assn. Bar City N.Y., Phi Beta Kappa. Antitrust, Federal civil litigation, Employment discrimination. Home: 1085 Park Ave New York NY 10128 Office: Kaye Scholer et al 425 Park Ave New York NY 10022

FREUND, JAMES COLEMAN, lawyer; b. N.Y.C., July 26, 1934; s. Sylvan and Marcella (Coleman) F.; m. Barbara Fox, 1985; children by previous marriage—Erik Hellstrom, Thomas Hagstrom. B.A. magna cum laude, Princeton U., 1956; J.D. cum laude, Harvard U., 1962. Bar: N.Y. 1962. Since practice N.Y.C.; partner firm Skadden, Arps, Slate, Meagher & Flom, 1968—; spl. cons. SEC, 1980-81; lectr. law U. Pa. Law Sch., 1982; adj. prof. Fordham U. Sch. Law, 1986—. Author: Anatomy of a Merger: Strategies and Techniques for Negotiating Corporate Acquisitions, 1975, Lawyering—a Realistic Approach to Legal Practice, 1979; Legal-ease: Fresh Insights into Lawyering, 1984; also articles.; co-editor: Disclosure Requirement of Public Corporations and Insiders, 1967. Trustee Princeton U., 1981-84, Horace Mann Sch., N.Y.C., 1980-86; bd. dirs. The Beresford, 1978-80; pres. class of 1956 Princeton U., 1976-81 . Served to lt. (j.g.) USNR, 1956-59. Mem. Bar Assn. City N.Y. General corporate, Securities, Mergers and acquisitions. Home: 55 W 73rd St Apt 1 New York NY 10023 Office: 919 3d Ave New York NY 10022

FREY, A. JOHN, JR., lawyer; b. Little Falls, Minn., Dec. 2, 1944; s. Arnold John and Mae A. (Monk) F.; m. Cheryl Ann McCoy, June 11, 1966; children—Deborah Lynn, Robert Christopher, Laura Kathleen. B.A. in Polit. Sci., U. Iowa, 1967, J.D. with distinction, 1969. Bar: Iowa 1969, U.S. Dist. Ct. (no. and so. dists.) Iowa 1973. Spl. agt. FBI, Washington, 1969-73; assoc. Jurgemeyer & Eddy, Clinton, Iowa, 1973-74; ptnr. Jurgemeyer & Frey, Clinton, 1974-75, Jurgemeyer, Frey & Haufe, Clinton, 1975—; speaker Bridge-the-Gap Seminar, Des Moines, 1977; mem. faculty Clinton Community Coll., 1979-80. Bd. dirs. Eagle Point Nature Soc., Clinton, 1974-75, Clinton County Legal Aid, Inc., 1978-80, Clinton Y's Mens Club, 1978, Arch, Inc., Clinton, 1984, Clinton YMCA, 1984, Gateway United Way, Clinton, 1981-84; pres. Seton Sch. Bd. Edn., Clinton, 1982-84; councilman City of Clinton, 1984—. Recipient letters of commendation FBI, 1970-73. Mem. Clinton County Bar Assn. (pres. 1977-78), Iowa State Bar Assn., Assn. Trial Lawyers Am., Clinton C. of C. (pres. elect) Republican. Roman Catholic. Lodge: K.C. (adv. 1979—). General practice, Real property, Personal injury. Home: 723 N 4th St Clinton IA 52732 Office: Jurgemeyer Frey & Haufe 601 S 3d St Clinton IA 52732

FREY, ERIC ALAN, lawyer; b. Terre Haute, Ind., Sept. 3, 1942; s. Harry E. and Dorothy G. (Castle) F.; m. Susan C., Sept. 7, 1963 (div. Apr. 1985); children: Jennifer, Eric II, Sarah, Jonathan; m. Ann L. Sackrider, June 15, 1985. AB, Ind. U., 1964, JD, 1967. Bar: Ind. 1967, U.S. Ct. Appeals (7th cir.) 1973, U.S. Supreme Ct. 1978. Law clk. to presiding justice U.S. Dist. Ct., Ft. Wayne, Ind., 1967-68; assoc. Rosenfeld & Wolfe, Terre Haute, 1968-70; ptnr. Rosenfeld, Wolfe & Frey, Terre Haute, 1970-79, Wolfe, Frey, Hunt & Olah, Terre Haute, 1979-86, Frey, Hunt, Hassler & Lorenz, Terre Haute, 1986—. Mem. dem. precinct com. Vigo County, 1972-84; del. Ind. State Dem. Conv., Indpls., 1972—. Mem. Ind. Bar Assn. (counsel 1974-78), 7th Cir. Bar Assn., Ind. Trial Lawyers Assn., Terre Haute Bar Assn. (pres. 1974-75). Baptist. Clubs: Harry Truman, Terre Haute Country. Avocations: running, tennis, bicycling. General practice, State civil litigation, Federal civil litigation. Home: 307 Terre Vista Dr Terre Haute IN 47803 Office: Frey Hunt Hassler & Lorenz 100 Cherry St PO Box 1527 Terre Haute IN 47808

FREY, KELLY LEIBERT, lawyer; b. Nashville, Mar. 13, 1951; s. William B. and Louise M. (Gleaves) F.; m. Faye M. Stewart, June 2, 1973; children: Margaret Ashley Anderson, Kelly Leibert II. BA, Vanderbilt U., 1973, MS, 1979; JD, U. Tenn., 1982. Bar: Tenn. 1982. Programmer 1st Am. Bank, Nashville, 1973-74; corp. planner Fed. Express, Memphis, 1977-79; assoc. Harwell Barr Martin and Stegalll, Nashville, 1982-86; sole practice Nashville, 1986—; bd. dirs. Display Telecom, Dallas and Nashville, Mfg., Inc., Nashville; instr. bus. law, Nashville State Tech. Sch., 1985—; instr. corps., Southeastern Paralegal Inst., Nashville, 1986—. Contbr. articles to profl. jours. Mem. ABA (publs. com. computer div. 1984—, Digital Equipment Corp. user group of computer div. 1983-84, editorial bd. legal econs. prodn. media bd. 1984—). Real property, Contracts commercial, Computer. Home: 725 Tahlena Madison TN 37115 Office: One Church St Suite 301 Nashville TN 37201

FREY, MONROE LYNN, III, lawyer; b. Atlanta, June 28, 1956; s. Monroe Lynn Jr. and Barbara Jean (Kimbrell) F.; m. Julie Karen Slaughter, Aug. 16, 1975. BA in Religion, Emory U., 1977; JD cum laude, U. Ga., 1980. Bar: Ga. 1980, U.S. Dist. Ct. (so. dist.) Ga. 1981, U.S. Ct. Appeals (5th and 11th cirs.) 1981. Law clk. to presiding judge Brunswick, Ga., 1980-81; assoc. Bennett, Gilbert, Gilbert, Whittle, Harrell & Gayner, Brunswick, 1981-85, ptnr., 1986—. Recipient Cert. of Merit State of Ga., 1971; named one of Outstanding Young Men Am. 1987. Mem. ABA, Ga. Bar Assn., Brunswick Bar Assn. (v.p. 1986, pres. 1987), Def. Research Inst., Ga. Def. Lawyers Assn. Methodist. Avocations: fishing, golf, antiques, sailing. Federal civil litigation, Personal injury, Workers' compensation. Home: 1108 Union St Brunswick GA 31520 Office: Bennett Gilbert Gilbert Whittle Harrell & Gayner PO Box 190 777 Gloucester St Brunswick GA 31521

FREY, PHILIP SIGMUND, lawyer; b. Los Angeles, July 31, 1941; s. Victor Leslie and Virginia Alice (Smith) F.; m. Mary Catherine Rowland, Jan. 4, 1969; children—Philip Gregory and Grant Victor (twins). B.A. with honors, Calif. State U.-Long Beach, 1964; postgrad. U. So. Calif.; J.D., Stanford U., 1968. Bar: Hawaii 1969, U.S. dist. ct. Hawaii 1969, U.S. Customs Ct. 1972, U.S. Ct. Appeals (9th cir.) 1970, U.S. Supreme Ct. 1981. Assoc. Padgett, Greeley & Marumoto, Honolulu, 1968-70; ptnr. Ames-Frey Co., Los Angeles, 1968-73, Cowan & Frey, Honolulu, 1970—. Active various community drs. Fellow Roscoe Pound-Assn. Trial Lawyers Am. Found. (life); mem. Hawaii Bar Assn. (chmn. med.-legal com. 1972-75), Assn. Trial Lawyers Am. (state committeeman from Hawaii 1972-75), ABA, Am. Judicature Soc., Tex. Trial Lawyers Assn., Supreme Ct. Hist. Soc., Phi Kappa Phi. Republican. Episcopalian. Club: Waikiki Yacht (judge adv). Personal injury, Admiralty, State civil litigation. Office: 1600 Grosvenor Ctr 733 Bishop St Honolulu HI 96813

FREYER, DANA HARTMAN, lawyer; b. Pitts., Apr. 17, 1944; m. Bruce M. Freyer, Dec. 21, 1969. Student, L' Institut De Hautes Etudes Internationales, Geneva, 1963-64; BA, Conn. Coll., 1965; postgrad., Columbia U., 1968, JD, 1971. Bar: N.Y. 1972, Ill. 1974, U.S. Dist. Ct. (no. dist.) Ill. 1974, U.S. Ct. Appeals (7th cir.) 1976, U.S. Supreme Ct. 1977, U.S. Dist. Ct. (so. dist.) N.Y. 1978, U.S. Dist. Ct. (ea. dist.) N.Y. 1981, U.S. Ct. Appeals (2d cir.) 1982. Staff atty. Legal Aid Soc. Westchester County, Mt. Vernon, N.Y., 1971-72; assoc. Friedman & Koven, Chgo., 1973-77, Skadden, Arps, Slate, Meagher & Flom, N.Y.C., 1977—; pres. Westchester Legal Services, Inc., White Plains, N.Y., 1985—, bd. dirs. Mem. ABA, Bar Assn. of City of N.Y., Westchester County Women's Bar Assn., Westchester County Bar Assn. Federal civil litigation, State civil litigation. Office: Skadden Arps Slate Meagher & Flom 919 Third Ave New York NY 10022

FREYTAG, SHARON NELSON, lawyer; b. Larned, Kans., May 11, 1943; d. John Seldon and Ruth Marie (Herbel) Nelson; m. Thomas Lee Freytag, June 18, 1966; children: Kurt David, Hillary Lee. BS with highest distinction, U. Kans., Lawrence, 1965; MA, U. Mich., 1966; JD cum laude, So. Meth. U., 1981. Bar: Tex. 1981, U.S. Dist. Ct. (no. dist.) Tex. 1981, U.S. Ct. Appeals (5th cir.) 1982. Tchr. English, Gaithersburg (Md.) High Sch., 1966-70; instr. English, Eastfield Coll., 1974-78; law clk. U.S. Dist. Ct. for No. Dist. Tex., 1981-82, U.S. Ct. Appeals for 5th Circuit, 1982; assoc. in litigation Haynes and Boone, Dallas, 1983—, vis. prof. law Southern Meth. U., 1985-86. Editor-in-chief Southwestern Law Jour., 1980-81; contbr. articles to law jours. Mem. ABA, Tex. Bar Assn., Dallas Bar Assn., Dallas Mus. Fine Arts, Dallas Shakespeare Soc., Order of Coif, Barristers, Phi Delta Phi, Phi Beta Kappa. Lutheran. Federal civil litigation, State civil litigation. Office: Haynes & Boone 3100 Inter First Plaza Dallas TX 75202

FREYVOGEL, WILLIAM THOMAS, lawyer; b. Washington, July 1, 1951; s. William Robert and Catherine (Jenkins) F.; m. Pamela Joy Benjamin, Apr. 26, 1980. A.B., Georgetown U., 1972, J.D., 1975. Bar: Va. 1975, U.S. Dist. Ct. (ea. dist.) Va. 1975, U.S. Ct. Appeals (4th cir.) 1975, D.C. 1983, U.S. Dist. Ct. (D.C.) 1984. Ptnr. Adams, Porter & Radigan, Arlington, Va., 1975—. Mem. ABA, Va. State Bar, D.C. Bar, Assn. Trial Lawyers Am., Va. Trial Lawyers Assn., Phi Beta Kappa, Pi Sigma Alpha. Roman Catholic. Federal civil litigation, State civil litigation, Real property. Home: 890 Linganore Dr McLean VA 22102 Office: Adams Porter & Radigan 1415 N Court House Rd Arlington VA 22216

FRIAR, MARTHA JANE, lawyer; b. Milw., Apr. 22, 1952; d. John Henry and Jule Frances (Horschak) F.; m. Jeffrey Bruce Wilkins, July 21, 1984. AB, Boston Coll., 1974; JD, U. Conn., 1978. Bar: Conn. 1978, U.S. Dist. Ct. Conn. 1978, Mass. 1981, U.S. Dist. Ct. Mass. 1981, N.Y. 1985. Jud. law clk. Conn. State Ct., New Haven, 1978-79; assoc. Blume, Elbaum & Adams, Hartford, Conn., 1979-82; atty. Union Carbide Corp., Danbury, Conn., 1982—. Mem. ABA, Conn. Bar Assn., Mass. Bar Assn., N.Y. State Bar Assn., Westchester-Fairfield Corp. Counsel Assn., Inc. Democrat. Roman Catholic. Personal injury, State civil litigation, Federal civil litigation. Home: 14 Taunton Lake Rd Newtown CT 06470 Office: Union Carbide Corp Old Ridgebury Rd Danbury CT 06817

FRIBANCE, CAROLINE ELEANOR, insurance company executive, lawyer; b. Newport News, Va., June 1, 1945; d. Austin Edward and Annette Augusta F. BA, William Smith Coll., 1967; postgrad. in sociology, U. Rochester, 1968-71; JD, U. Wis., 1974. Bar: Wis. Project dir., atty. Wis. Dept. Industry, Labor and Human Relations, Madison, 1974-75, Ctr. for Pub. Representation, Madison, 1975-77; staff atty. Legal Action of Wis., Madison, 1977-79; assoc. counsel Sentry Ins. Group, Stevens Point, Wis., 1979-84, v.p., corp. sec., 1984—; bd. dirs., sec. many Sentry cos. Author: (with others) Workers with a Handicapping Condition and the Law, 1977. Bd. dirs., chmn. Project Equality of Wis., Milw., 1979-83; mem. Portage County Commn. on Women, 1983-84; trustee U. Wis.-Stevens Point Found., 1985—; charter mem., pres. Acad. of Letters and Sci., U. Wis., Stevens Point, 1984—. Mem. ABA, Wis. State Bar Assn., Portage County Bar Assn., Legal Assn. For Women. Lodge: Zonta. Avocations: gardening, hiking, reading. Labor, General corporate, Civil rights. Home: 1972 Church St Stevens Point WI 54481 Office: Sentry Ins 1800 N Point Dr Stevens Point WI 54481

FRICK, ROBERT HATHAWAY, lawyer; b. Cleve., June 28, 1924; s. Claude Oates and Urshal May (Hathaway) F.; m. Lenore R. Maurin, Aug. 16, 1947; children—Elaine D., Barbara A. Frick Bundick, Catherine L. Frick Cayer. B.B.A., U. Mich., 1948, J.D., 1950; postgrad. Harvard Bus. Sch., 1965. Bar: Mich. 1951, Ill. 1951, Ohio 1952, N.Y. 1962, U.S. Supreme Ct. 1981. Atty., Amoco Corp. (formerly Standard Oil Co. Ind.), Chgo., 1950, 52-60, Paris, 1960-62, N.Y.C., 1962-68, Chgo., 1968-71, assoc. gen. counsel, Chgo., 1972—; sole practice, Cleve., 1951-52. Served with USAAF, 1943-46. Mem. ABA, Am. Soc. Internat. Law, Ill. Bar Assn., Chgo. Bar Assn., Order of Coif, Sigma Phi Epsilon. Republican. Clubs: Westmoreland Country, Exces., Mid Am., Internat. (Washington). General corporate, Administrative and regulatory, Oil and gas leasing. Home: 330 Cumnor Rd Kenilworth IL 60043 Office: Amoco Corp 200 E Randolph Dr Chicago IL 60601

FRICKE, RICHARD JOHN, lawyer; b. Ithaca, N.Y., Apr. 17, 1945; s. Richard I. and Jeanne L. (Hines) F.; m. Carol A. Borelli, June 17, 1967; children—Laura, Richard, Amanda. B.A., Cornell U., 1967, J.D., 1970. Bar: Conn. 1970. Assoc., Gregory & Adams, Wilton, Conn., 1970-73; ptnr. Crehan & Fricke, Ridgefield, Conn., 1973—; dir. Village Bank & Trust Co.; town atty. Town of Ridgefield, 1973-81. Bd. dirs. Ridgefield Community Ctr., Ridgefield Montessori, Ridgefield Community Kindergarten; founder,

pres. Ridgefield Lacrosse League; mem. Conn. Bar Commn. on Women, 1976. Mem. ABA, Conn. Bar Assn., Danbury Bar Assn. Democrat. Roman Catholic. Co-patentee low reactive pressure foam. Family and matrimonial, Real property, General practice. Home: 94 Main St Ridgefield CT 06877 Office: 181 Main St Ridgefield CT 06877

FRIDAY, HERSCHEL HUGAR, lawyer; b. Lockesburg, Ark., Feb. 10, 1922; s. Herschel Hugar and Rosa Lee (Scarborough) F.; m. Nancy Elizabeth Hammett, Feb. 26, 1943; children—Gregory David, Steven Herschel, Pamela Friday Freeman (dec.). Student Little Rock Jr. Coll. (now U. Ark.-Little Rock), 1939-41, LL.D. (hon.), 1981; student air force program U. Minn., 1943; J.D., U. Ark., 1947. Bar: Ark. Law clk. to judge U.S. Dist. Ct. we. dist. Ark., 1947-52; assoc. Friday, Eldredge & Clark, and predecessors, Little Rock, 1952, sr. ptnr., 1974—; lectr. in law U. Ark.-Fayetteville, 1951-52; mem. Ark. Bd. Law Examiners, 1960-66; trustee Southwestern Legal Found., 1977—; sec. bd. dirs. Oaklawn Jockey Club, Inc., 1973—; dir. First Comml. Corp. in Little Rock, Gt. Lakes Chem. Corp., Southwestern Bell Corp. Trustee Ark. Children's Hosp., Little Rock, 1955—, pres. 1965-66, chmn. steering com., 1979-80; bd. dirs. Pulaski County (Ark.) chpt. ARC, 1977-81, Greater Little Rock C. of C. 1979—. Named Man of Yr. in Ark., Ark. Democrat, 1971; named Disting. Alumnus and recipient Shield of Trojan award U. Ark.-Little Rock Alumni Assn., 1976; recipient Harrison Tweed award Assn. Continuing Legal Edn. Adminstrs., 1979; named Citizen of Yr., Ark. chpt. March of Dimes, 1981; recipient Builders award U. Ark.-Little Rock, 1983. Fellow Am. Bar Found.; mem. Pulaski County Bar Assn., Ark. Bar Assn. (exec. com. 1954-68, chmn. exec. com. 1963-64, pres. 1976-77, chmn. law sch. com.; Outstanding Lawyer award 1971), ABA (ho. of dels. 1954-68, 71—, gov. 1968-71, 85—, chmn. cons. panel on advanced jud. and legal edn. 1978-81, chmn. task force on lawyer competence 1981-83, com. on continuing profl. edn. 1972-77, 83—), Am. Judicature Soc., Am. Law Inst., Am. Bar Endowment, Am. Coll. Trial Lawyers, Am. Law Inst. (bd. dirs.). Baptist. Club: Pleasant Valley Country (pres. 1964-65), Little Rock, Country of Little Rock. Banking, General corporate, Public utilities. Office: Friday Eldredge & Clark 2000 1st Commercial Bldg Little Rock AR 72201

FRIDKIN, JEFFREY DAVID, lawyer; b. Kansas City, Kans., Dec. 16, 1953; s. Harold Lozar and Lucille Ann (Smith) F.; m. Lucy June Wilson, June 8, 1974; children: Dustin Jacob, Elysia Dawn. BA, U. Mo., 1977, JD, 1980. Bar: Mo. 1980, U.S. Dist. Ct. (we. dist.) Mo. 1980, U.S. Ct. Appeals (8th cir.) 1980, Fla. 1985, U.S. Dist. Ct. (so. and mid. dists.) Fla. 1986. From assoc. to ptnr. Linde, Thompson, Fairchild, Langworthy, Kohn & Van Dyke, Kansas City, 1979-85; assoc. Mershon, Sawyer, Johnston, Dunwody & Cole, Naples, Fla., 1985—. Mem. Centurions, Kansas City, 1984-85. Mem. Collier County Econ. Devel. Counsel. Democrat. Federal civil litigation, State civil litigation. Home: 75 4th St N Naples FL 33940

FRIED, ALEXANDER, lawyer; b. N.Y.C., Aug. 29, 1956; s. Karl and Pearl (Goldner) F. BA in Econs., UCLA, 1977; JD, Harvard U., 1980. Bar: Calif. 1980, U.S. Dist. Ct. (cen. dist.) Calif. 1981, U.S. Dist. Ct. Calif. (ea. dist.) Calif. 1983, U.S. Tax Ct. 1983, U.S. Ct. Claims 1984. Assoc. Law Offices of Douglas P. Grim, Los Angeles, 1980-82, Sanger, Grayson, Givner & Booke, Encino, Calif., 1983—. Mem. ABA (gift tax com. 1982—), Calif. Bar Assn., Los Angeles County Bar Assn., Phi Beta Kappa. Democrat. Jewish. Avocations: sports, travel, hist. studies. General corporate, Estate planning, Probate. Office: Sanger Grayson Givner & Booke 16633 Ventura Blvd Suite 600 Encino CA 91436

FRIED, CHARLES, lawyer, U.S. solicitor general, educator; b. Prague, Czechoslovakia, Apr. 15, 1935; came to U.S., 1941, naturalized, 1948; s. Anthony and Marta (Wintersteinova) F.; m. Anne Sumerscale, June 13, 1959; children: Gregory, Antonia. A.B., Princeton U., 1956; B.A. Juris, Oxford (Eng.) U., 1958, M.A., 1961; LL.B., Columbia U., 1960. Bar: D.C., Mass. Law clk. to assoc. justice John M. Harlan, U.S. Supreme Ct., 1960; mem. faculty Harvard Law Sch., 1961-85, prof. law, 1965-85, Carter prof. gen. jurisprudence, 1981-85; dep. solicitor gen., counselor to solicitor gen. Dept. Justice, Washington, 1985; solicitor gen. Dept. Justice, 1985—; assoc. reporter model code prearraignment procedure Am. Law Inst., 1965—; spl. cons. Treasury Dept., 1961-62; cons. White House Office Policy Devel., 1982, Dept. Transp., 1981-82, Dept. Justice, 1983. Author: An Anatomy of Values, 1970, Medical Experimentation: Personal Integrity and Social Policy, 1974, Right and Wrong, 1978, Contract as Promise: A Theory of Contractual Obligation, 1981; contbr. legal and philos. jours. Mem. Lawyers for Ford, 1976, Reagan Task Force on Regulatory Reform, 1980. Guggenheim fellow, 1971-72. Mem. Am. Law Inst., Nat. Acad. Scis., Inst. Medicine, Am. Soc. Polit. and Legal Philosophy, Phi Beta Kappa. Republican. Constitution, Labor, Contracts commercial. Office: Solicitor General US Justice Dept 10th & Constitution Ave Washington DC 20530

FRIED, DONALD DAVID, lawyer; b. N.Y.C., Feb. 28, 1936; s. Fred and Sylvia (Falk) F.; m. Joan Hilbert, Sept. 15, 1963; children: Neil, Derek. BA, CCNY, 1956; JD, Harvard U., 1959. Bar: N.Y. 1959. Ptnr. Hunton & Williams and predecessor firm Conboy, Hewitt, O'Brien & Boardman, N.Y.C., 1960—. General corporate, Probate, Real property. Home: 37 W 12th St New York NY 10011 Office: Hunton & Williams 100 Park Ave New York NY 10017

FRIED, JOSEPH, lawyer; b. Borsha, Rumania, Mar. 27, 1948; came to U.S., 1975.; s. Solomon and Malka-Dina (Katz) F.; m. Rachel-Agnes Rosenthal, Mar. 8, 1971; children: Udi, Shevi, Avi, Shlomo. LLB, Hebrew U., 1971; MA, JD, U. Denver, 1978. Bar: Israel 1973, N.Y. 1981, Colo. 1982, U.S. Dist. Ct. Colo. 1982. Clk., legal researcher Weller, Friedrich, Hickish & Hazlitt, Denver, 1976-77, Hall & Evans, Denver, 1977-78; assoc. George S. Carter, Denver, 1978-80; sole practice Denver, 1981—. Served to capt. USAF, 1970-75. Mem. ABA, Israel Bar Assn., N.Y. State Bar Assn., Colo. Bar Assn. Avocations: travel, hiking, opera. General practice, Landlord-tenant, Real property. Home: 220 S Forest St Denver CO 80222 Office: 1670 Broadway #3335 Denver CO 80222

FRIED, L. RICHARD, JR., lawyer; b. N.Y.C., Apr. 3, 1941; s. L. Richard and Jane (Kent) Wick F.; m. Marsha Ann Scibella, July 30, 1966; 1 child, Paula Suzanne. B.S., U. Ariz., 1963, J.D., 1966. Bar: Ariz. 1966, Hawaii 1968, U.S. Dist. Ct. No. Mariana Islands 1978, U.S. Ct. Claims 1978, U.S. Ct. Internat. Trade 1977, U.S. Tax Ct. 1977, U.S. Ct. Appeals (9th cir.) 1969, U.S. Supreme Ct. 1977. Assoc. Case, Kay & Lynch, Honolulu, 1967-72; ptnr. Cronin, Fried, Sekiya, Kekina & Fairbanks, Honolulu, 1974—. Mem. ABA, Assn. Trial Lawyers Am. (nat. committeeman 1980-82), Am. Bd. Trial Advocates (v.p. 1986—), Hawaii Trial Lawyers Assn. (pres. 1981-82, 84—), Hawaii State Bar Assn., Hawaii Acad. Plaintiffs' Attys. (bd. dirs. 1984—), Episcopalian. Club: Exchange of Honolulu. Federal civil litigation, State civil litigation, Personal injury. Office: Cronin Fried Sekiya Kekina & Fairbanks 841 Bishop St Suite 1900 Honolulu HI 96813

FRIED, SAMUEL, lawyer; b. Bklyn., Aug. 16, 1951; s. Zoltan and Helen (Katina) F.; m. Avrama Panush, Dec. 27, 1981; children—Eva M., Orly Z., Jacob J., Molly R. A.B., Washington U., St. Louis, 1971; J.D., Boston U., 1974, LL.M., 1977. Bar: Mass. 1974, Ill. 1982. Assoc. Warner & Stackpole, Boston, 1974-77; staff atty. The Bendix Corp., Southfield, Mich., 1977-79, sr. atty., 1979-80, asst. treas., 1980-81; v.p., corp. counsel Clevite Industries, Inc., Glenview, Ill., 1981-83, v.p., sec., gen. counsel, 1983-87, v.p., sec., gen. counsel Exide Corp., Troy, Mich., 1987—. Editor: Psychosurgery, 1974. Mem. ABA, Phi Beta Kappa. General corporate, Securities, Corporate taxation.

FRIEDBERG, ALAN CHARLES, lawyer; b. Ft. Leavenworth, Kans., Dec. 22, 1945; s. Arnold Millard and Gisela Claire (Newkirk) F.; m. Jean Anderson, June 23, 1973; children—John, Michael. B.A. with honors, U. Va., 1967; J.D., Yale U., 1970. Bar: Va. 1970, Colo. 1973. Law clk. U.S. Ct. Appeals (10th cir.), Denver, 1974-75; dir. Pendleton & Sabian, P.C., Denver, 1975—. mem. faculty Nat. Inst. for Trial Adv., 1984, 85, 86; lectr. Continuing Legal Edn. of Colo., 1986—. Mem. ch. council Mt. Calvary Lutheran Ch., Boulder, Colo., 1980-82. Served as capt. JAG, U.S. Army, 1970-74. Decorated Bronze Star, Army Commendation medal, Vietnamese Cross of Gallantry, Vietnam Service medal. Mem. Denver Bar Assn. (vol. atty. pro bono program, Outstanding Young Lawyer of Yr. award 1981, past mem. interprofl., jud. selection and benefits com. jud. survey task force, pub. interest law com., exec. counsel young lawyers sect., chmn. 1979-80; chmn. legal service com. 1982-84), Colo. Bar Assn., ABA (mem. availability of legal services com.), Colo. Trial Lawyers Assn., Assn. Trial Lawyers Am., Nat. Inst. Trial Advocacy (mem. faculty, nat. sessions 1984-85, regional sessions 1984-86), Denver Law Club. Democrat. Club: Denver, Meadows (pres. 1986-87). Federal civil litigation, State civil litigation, Personal injury. Home: 275 Pawnee Dr Boulder CO 80303 Office: 303 E 17th Ave Suite 1000 Denver CO 80203

FRIEDBERG, HARRY JACOB, lawyer; b. N.Y.C., Nov. 27, 1937. BA, Wittenberg Coll., 1959; LLB, N.Y. Law Sch., 1962. Bar: N.Y. 1962, U.S. Dist. Ct. (so. and ea. dists.) N.Y. 1963, U.S. Supreme Ct. 1967, U.S. Ct. Appeals (2d cir.) 1971, U.S. Ct. Appeals (D.C. cir.) 1979, U.S. Dist. Ct. D.C. 1979. Sole practice N.Y.C., 1977—. Mem. Assn. of Bar of City of N.Y., N.Y. State Bar Assn., Phi Mu Delta. Federal civil litigation, State civil litigation, Family and matrimonial. Office: 551 Fifth Ave New York NY 10176

FRIEDEN, JAMES ANTHONY, lawyer; b. Los Angeles, Jan. 15, 1948; s. Earl and Esther (Handelman) F.; m. Deborah Elliott, Apr. 10, 1971; children: Jordan Nicholas, Piers Alexander. BA, Brandeis U., 1971; JD, Boston Coll., 1975. Bar: Mass. 1975, Calif. 1976, U.S. Dist. Ct. Mass. 1977. Sole practice Boston, 1975—. Co-author: Massachusetts Standardized Civil Practice Forms, 1986. Mem. Mass. Bar Assn., Boston Bar Assn. State civil litigation, Federal civil litigation, Personal injury. Office: 15 Court Sq Boston MA 02108

FRIEDEN, ROBERT M., lawyer; b. Norfolk, Va., Apr. 21, 1955; s. Joseph Lee and Jane (Heller) F. BA, U. Pa., 1977; JD, U. Va., 1980. Bar: Va. 1981, D.C. 1981, U.S. Ct. Appeals (4th cir.) 1981. Atty. FCC, Washington, 1980-82; assoc. Pepper, Hamilton & Scheetz, Washington, 1982-83, Dow, Lohnes & Albertson, Washington, 1983-85, Hogan & Hartson, Washington, 1985-86; program mgr. internat. satellite policies Nat. Telecommunications and Info. Adminstrn. Dept. Commerce, Washington, 1986—. Contbr. editor Telematics, 1985—. Mem. Fed. Communications Bar Assn., Am. Teleport Assn. (counsel 1985-86). Avocations: gemstone prospecting, shortwave radio, hiking. Administrative and regulatory, Public international, Computer. Home: 5996 9th Rd N Arlington VA 22205 Office: Nat Telecommunications Info Adminstrn Dept Commerce Room 4090 14th and Constitutional NW Washington DC 20230

FRIEDENTHAL, JACK H., educator; b. Denver, Sept. 22, 1931; married; 3 children. A.B., Stanford U., 1953; LL.B., Harvard U., 1958. Bar: Calif. 1959. Sole practice 1959—; from asst. prof. to assoc. prof. Stanford U., 1958-64, prof., 1964—, George E. Osborne prof. law, 1980—, now assoc. dean; cons. Law Revision Commn., 1964. Contbr. articles to profl. jours. Office: Stanford Univ Law Sch Stanford CA 94305 *

FRIEDERICHS, NORMAN PAUL, lawyer; b. Ft. Dodge, Iowa, Sept. 13, 1936; s. Norman Paul and Dorothy Mae (Vinsant) F.; m. Marjorie Darlene Farrand, Aug. 23, 1959; children—Laurie Lynne, Norman Paul, Stacie Lynne. A.A., Ft. Dodge Community Coll., 1956; B.A., Wartburg Coll., 1959, J.D., U. Iowa, 1966. Bar: Iowa 1966, Mich. 1968, Minn. 1974, U.S. Ct. Appeals (7th, 8th and fed. cirs.) 1978. Tchr. chemistry Janesville Sch. Dist., Iowa, 1960-63; mem. Woodhams, Blanchaud & Flynn, Kalamazoo, 1966-68; atty. PPG Industries, Pitts., 1968-69, Gen. Mills, Inc., Mpls., 1969-76; mem. Merchant, Gould, Smith, Edell, Welter & Schmidt, Mpls., 1976—. Editor: (booklet) Report of Economic Survey, 1983. Mem. Minn. Rep. Cen. Com.; chmn. St. Louis Park Sch. Dist., Minn., 1973; mem. Suburban Hennepin Vocat.-Tech. Bd., 1980-84, chmn. 1982-84. Mem. Eden Prairie C. of C. (bd. dirs.), Am. Patent Law Assn. (com. chmn. 1980-84), Minn. Patent Law Assn.(chmn. small bus. com.), ABA. Baptist. Clubs: Optimist (pres. 1971-72, lt. gov. 1976-77). Lodge: Masons. Patent, Trademark and copyright, Federal civil litigation. Home: 6421 Kurtz Ln Eden Prairie MN 55344 Office: Merchant Gould Smith Edell Welter & Schmidt PA 1600 Midwest Plaza Bldg Minneapolis MN 55402

FRIEDLAND, PAUL DANIEL, lawyer; b. Newark, Aug. 15, 1954; s. Abner Michel and Adele (Gottlieb) F.; m. Isabelle Heywang, Aug. 1, 1984. BA cum laude, Yale U., 1976; postgrad., Am. Sch. Classical Studies, Athens, Greece, 1976-77; JD, Columbia U., 1980. Bar: N.Y. 1981, N.J. 1981, U.S. Dist. Ct. (so. and ea. dists.) N.Y. 1981, U.S. Dist. Ct. N.J. 1981. Law clk. to judge U.S. Dist. Ct., N.Y.C., 1980-82; assoc. Coudert Bros., N.Y.C., 1982-84, 87—, Coudert Frères, Paris, 1984-87. Editor Columbia Law Rev., 1979-80. James Kent scholar, 1980, Harlan Fiske Stone scholar, 1979. Mem. ABA, Internat. Bar Assn., Am. Arbitration Assn. Private international, Federal civil litigation, State civil litigation. Office: Coudert Bros 200 Park Ave New York NY 10166

FRIEDLANDER, JEROME PEYSER, II, lawyer; b. Washington, Feb. 7, 1944; s. Mark Peyser and Helen (Finkel) F.; m. Irene Bluethenthal, Apr. 23, 1972; children—Jennifer R., Tyler Weil. B.S., Georgetown U., 1965; L.L.B., U. Va., 1968. Bar: Va. 1968, U.S. Dist. Ct. (ea. dist.) Va. 1968, D.C. 1968, U.S. Dist. Ct. D.C. 1968, U.S. Ct. Appeals (4th and D.C. cirs.) 1978, U.S. Supreme Ct. 1978. Ptnr. Friedlander, Friedlander & Brooks, P.C., Arlington, Va., 1972—; dir. Artech Corp., Fairfax, Va., 1976—, substitute judge Arlington (Va.) Gen. Dist. Ct. Served to capt. U.S. Army, 1969-71. Mem. ABA, Assn. Trial Lawyers Am., Internat. Bar Assn., Inter-Am. Bar Assn., Va. Trial Lawyers Assn., Fed. Bar Assn (treas. No. Va. chpt.). Personal injury, Contracts commercial, General practice. Office: Friedlander Friedlander & Brooks 2018 Clarendon Blvd Arlington VA 22201

FRIEDLANDER, SUSAN OLIVER, lawyer; b. Los Angeles, Sept. 2, 1934; s. John Pleasant and Virginia (Greelis) Oliver-Hill; m. Richard Worth, Dec. 15, 1956 (div. Jan. 1974); children: John, Sharon; m. Harry Peyser Friedlander, Sept. 4, 1978. BA, U. Calif., Santa Barbara, 1956; JD, Ariz. State U., 1975. Bar: Ariz. 1975, U.S. Dist. Ct. (Ariz.) 1979, U.S. Supreme Ct. 1980. Educator Various Sch. Bds., Calif., Guam, Ariz., 1956-72; law clk. to presiding justice Ariz. Supreme Ct., Phoenix, 1975-76; asst. city prosecutor City of Phoenix, 1976-79; ptnr. Friedlander & Friedlander P.C., Scottsdale, Ariz., 1979-82; sole practice Phoenix, 1982—; juvenile ct. referee Superior Ct. of Maricopa County, Phoenix, 1980-82. Mem. scholarship bd. U. So. Calif., 1980-84. Mem. ABA, Ariz. Bar Assn., Maricopa County Bar Assn., Ariz. Women Lawyers Assn., Kappa Alpha Theta (patron chmn. 1985-86). Club: Valley of Sun Alumni. Family and matrimonial, Probate, Personal injury. Home: 8106 Via del Desierto Scottsdale AZ 85258 Office: 4203 E Indian Sch #160 Phoenix AZ 85018

FRIEDLER, SYDNEY, lawyer; b. Jamaica, N.Y., Jan. 8, 1941; s. Benjamin and Evelyn (Feldman) F.; m. Dale Steckler, Feb. 20, 1965; children—Hillary, Lori. B.A., Hofstra U., 1962; LL.B., Bklyn. Law Sch., 1964. Bar: N.Y. 1964, Fla. 1978. Owner, Sheehy & Friedler, attys. at law, Hempstead, N.Y., 1970—. Served to col. JAGC, U.S. Army, 1964-70, now Res. Republican. Jewish. Clubs: Hofstra U., Woodcrest, Jockey of Fla. Consumer commercial, Criminal. Office: One Fulton Ave Hempstead NY 11550

FRIEDMAN, BARRY ALLEN, lawyer; b. Mobile, Ala., June 21, 1950; s. Louis and Grace Katherine (Ladezensky) F.; m. Eleanor Ann Capeloto, Dec. 26, 1971; children—Joshua Daniel, Scott David. B.S., U. Ala., 1972, J.D., 1975. Bar: Ala. 1975, U.S. Dist. Ct. (so. dist.) Ala. 1975, U.S. Ct. Appeals (11th cir.) 1981, U.S. Supreme Ct. 1979. Staff atty. Mobile County Legal Aid Soc., 1975-76, dir., 1976-78; ptnr. Copeland & Friedman, Mobile, 1978-79, Hall & Friedman, Mobile, 1979-83; sole practice, Mobile, 1983—. Trustee, U.S. panel trustees So. Dist. Ala.; bd. dirs. Dauphin St. Synagogue, Mobile, 1982—, v.p. 1985—. Served with USAFR, 1970-76. Mem. ABA, Ala. State Bar, Mobile County Bar Assn., Nat. Trial Lawyers Assn., Comml. Law League. Bankruptcy, Consumer commercial, Family and matrimonial. Home: 1621 Norwich Ct Mobile AL 36609 Office: 150 Government St La Clede Bldg Suite 3004 Mobile AL 36602

FRIEDMAN, BART, lawyer; b. N.Y.C., Dec. 5, 1944; s. Philip and Florence (Beckerman) F.; m. Wendy Alpern Stein, Jan. 11, 1986. AB, L.I. U., 1966; JD, Harvard U., 1969. Bar: N.Y. 1970, Mass. 1972. Research fellow Harvard U. Bus. Sch., Cambridge, Mass., 1969-70; assoc. Cahill, Gordon & Reindel, N.Y.C., 1970-72, ptnr., 1980—; assoc. Bingham, Dana & Gould, Boston, 1972-74; spl. counsel SEC, Washington, 1974-75, asst. dir., 1975-77; lectr. internat. tax program Harvard U. Law Sch., 1971, 85. Bd. dirs. Paul Taylor Dance Co., 1986—. Mem. Assn. Bar City N.Y., Explorers Club. Club: Down Town Assn. Securities, General corporate. Home: 1172 Park Ave Apt 5B New York NY 10128 Office: Cahill Gordon & Reindel 80 Pine St New York NY 10005

FRIEDMAN, BERNARD ALVIN, district court judge; b. Detroit, Sept. 23, 1943; s. David and Rae (Garber) F.; m. Rozanne Golston, Aug. 16, 1970; children: Matthew, Megan. Student, Detroit Inst. Tech., 1962-65; JD, Detroit Coll. Law, 1968. Bar: Mich. 1968, Fla. 1968, U.S. Dist. Ct. (ea. dist.) Mich. 1968, U.S. Ct. Mil. Appeals 1972. Asst. prosecutor Wayne County, Detroit, 1968-71; ptnr. Harrison & Friedman, Southfield, Mich., 1971-78, Lippitt, Harrison, Friedman & Whitefield, Southfield, 1978-82; judge Mich. Dist. Ct. 48th dist., Bloomfield Hills, 1982—. Bd. dirs. Easter Seals Soc., Oakland County, Mich., 1985—. Served to lt. U.S. Army, 1967-74. Recipient Disting. Service award Oakland County Bar Assn., 1986. Avocation: running. Home: 4432 Exmoor Circle Bloomfield Hills MI 48013 Office: 48th Dist Ct 2709 Telegraph Rd Bloomfield Hills MI 48013

FRIEDMAN, BRUCE A., lawyer; b. Los Angeles, June 6, 1935; s. Samuel L. and Irene L. (Oreck) F.; children—David, Julie, Stephen. B.A., UCLA, 1957; J.D., U. Calif.-Berkeley, 1960. Bar: Calif. 1961, U.S. Superior Ct. 1976. Research atty. Calif. Ct. Apl. 4th App. Dist., 1960-61; sole practice, Los Angeles, 1961—; instr. Southwestern U., Los Angeles, 1965; arbitrator Los Angeles Superior Ct., 1980—. Mem. Assn. Trial Lawyers Am., Calif. Trial Lawyers Assn., Los Angeles Trial Lawyers Assn., ABA, Los Angeles County Bar Assn. Personal injury. Office: 2029 Century Park E Suite 2610 Los Angeles CA 90067

FRIEDMAN, DANIEL MORTIMER, judge, lawyer; b. N.Y.C., Feb. 8, 1916; s. Henry Michael F. and Julia (Freedman) Fiedman; m. Elizabeth Ellis, Oct. 18, 1975. A.B., Columbia U., 1937, LL.B., 1940. Bar: N.Y. 1941. Practice law N.Y.C., 1940-42; with SEC, Washington, 1942-51, Justice Dept., Wahsington, 1951-78; asst. to solicitor gen. Justice Dept., Washington, 1959-62, 2d asst. to solicitor gen., 1962-68, 1st dep. solicitor gen., 1968-78; judge Ct. Claims and U.S. Ct. Appeals, Washington, 1978—. Served with AUS, 1942-46. Recipient Exceptional Service award Atty. Gen., 1969. Federal civil litigation. Office: US Ct Appeals 717 Madison Pl NW Washington DC 20439

FRIEDMAN, DAVID ALAN, lawyer, educator; b. Flushing, N.Y., July 7, 1952; s. Arnold S. and Bette Marion (Harris) F.; m. B. Elise Medinger, Apr. 19, 1986. Student, Clarkson Coll. of Tech., 1969-1970; BA, SUNY, Buffalo, 1973; JD, Boston U., 1977. Bar: Ga. 1977, U.S. Dist. Ct. (mid. and no. dists.) Ga. 1977, U.S. Ct. Appeals (5th cir.) 1978, U.S. Dist. Ct. (we. and ea. dists.) Ky. 1980, U.S. Ct. Appeals (6th cir.) 1980, U.S. Supreme Ct. 1982, Ky. 1983. Atty. Ga. Legal Services Program, Macon, 1977-80; mng. atty. Legal Aid Soc. Inc., Shelbyville, Ky., 1980-82; dir. litigation Legal Aid Soc. Inc., Louisville, 1983—; sole practice Atlanta, 1982-83; adj. faculty U. Louisville Sch. Law, 1983—. Bd. dirs., gen. counsel ACLU, 1984—. Mem. ABA, Fed. Bar Assn., Ga. Bar Assn., Ky. Bar Assn., Louisville Bar Assn. Democrat. Avocations: baseball, gourmet cooking, bicycling, backpacking, arts. Civil rights, Federal civil litigation. Office: Legal Aid Soc Inc 425 W Muhammad Ali Blvd Louisville KY 40202

FRIEDMAN, HARVEY, lawyer; b. N.Y.C., Aug. 26, 1938; s. Arthur L. and Ada (Zwerling) F.; m. Marsha Goetz, Sept. 8, 1962; children—David M., Cheryl J. B.B.A., Pace U., 1959; J.D., NYU, 1962, LL.M., 1963. Bar: N.Y. 1963, U.S. Tax Ct. 1964, U.S. Supreme Ct. 1980. Assoc., Herzfeld & Rubin, N.Y.C., 1963-65, Simpson, Thacher & Bartlett, N.Y.C., 1965-71; tax counsel Amstar Corp., N.Y.C., 1971-82, gen. tax atty., 1982—. Vice pres., treas. Oceanside (N.Y.) Little Leagues, 1976—. Mem. ABA, Assn. Bar City N.Y., Tax Execs. Inst., NYU Law Rev. Alumni Assn., Phi Alpha Delta. Corporate taxation, Pension, profit-sharing, and employee benefits, Personal income taxation. Office: Amstar Corp 1251 Ave of Americas New York NY 10020

FRIEDMAN, HERBERT JEROME, lawyer; b. Lincoln, Nebr., Aug. 24, 1936; s. Abe and Helen S. (Garson) F.; m. Brenda Geffen, June 11, 1961; children: Elizabeth, Charles, Daniel. LLB, U. Nebr., 1960. Bar: Nebr. 1960, U.S. Supreme Ct. 1982. Sole practice Lincoln, Nebr., 1962—. Democrat. Personal injury. Office: 633 S 9th #300 Lincoln NE 68501

FRIEDMAN, JEROME, pharmacist; b. Columbus, Ohio, Oct. 10, 1943; s. Max Jack and Marjorie Lois (Grundstein) F.; m. Cheryl Ilene Lando, June 30, 1968; 1 child, Julie Beth. B.A. in Zoology, Ohio State U., 1965; B.S. in Pharmacy, 1969. Pharmacist, Ohio State U. Hosp., Columbus, 1969-72, Eastmoor Pharmacy, 1972-73; pharmacist, Westland Med. Pharmacy, Columbus, 1973—, pres., owner, 1979—. Trustee, Nat. Kidney Found Central Ohio, Columbus, 1981-84; bd. govs. Internat. B'nai B'rith Bowling Assn., 1982—, v.p., 1985—. Fellow Am. Coll. Apothecaries; mem. Nat. Assn. Retail Druggists, Ohio State Pharm. Assn., Central Ohio Acad. Pharmacy. Lodge: B'nai B'rith (pres. 1982-83). Avocations: Bowling, tennis, gardening, reading. State civil litigation, Personal injury, Juvenile. Home: 345 S Cassingham Rd Columbus OH 43209 Office: Westland Med Pharmacy 455 Industrial Mile Rd Columbus OH 43228

FRIEDMAN, JERRELL DON, lawyer; b. Pell City, Ala., June 6, 1945; s. William W. and Clemmie Deloris (Henderson) F. BS, Troy State U., 1967; JD, Stetson U., 1973. Bar: Fla. 1973, U.S. Dist. Ct. Fla. 1974, U.S. Tax Ct. 1973, U.S. Customs and Patent Appeals 1973, U.S. Ct. Appeals (6th, 10th, 11th and D.C. cirs.) 1973. Law clk. to sr. judge U.S. Ct. Appeals (10th cir.), Denver, 1973-74; ptnr. O'Brien & Friedman, St. Petersburg, Fla., 1974-78; assoc. Pope & Henniger, St. Petersburg, 1978-80, Duncan & Duncan, Tavares, Fla., 1980-83; ptnr. Friedman & Friedman, P.A., Longwood, Fla., 1983—; city prosecutor Madeira Beach, Fla., 1977; instr. Fla. Inst. Tech., St. Petersburg, 1977. Served to lt. USN, 1967-69, Vietnam. Mem. ABA, Fla. Bar Assn. (probate law com. 1982—, probate rules com. 1983—), Seminole County Bar Assn. Democrat. Baptist. Probate, State civil litigation, General practice. Home: 926 Sherrington Rd Orlando FL 32804 Office: 165 W Jessup Ave Longwood FL 32750

FRIEDMAN, JOEL WILLIAM, law educator; b. N.Y.C., Mar. 16, 1951; s. Max Aaron and Muriel (Yudien) F. B.S., Cornell U., 1972; J.D., Yale U., 1975. Bar: Calif. 1975, U.S. Dist. Ct. (cen. dist.) Calif. 1975. Asst. prof. Tulane U., New Orleans, 1976-79, assoc. prof., 1979-82, prof. law, 1982—; vis. prof. law U. Tel Aviv, Israel, 1983, U. Tex. Law Sch., 1985-86; cons. La. Ho. of Reps., Baton Rouge, 1982—; bd. dirs. Legal Aid Bur., New Orleans, 1982—. Editor: Cases and Materials on Law of Employment Discrimination, 1983, 2d edit., 1987; contbr. articles to law revs. Named C.J. Morrow Prof. of Law Tulane U., 1985-86. Mem. New Orleans Community Relations Com., 1984. Mem. Soviet Jewry Legal Advocacy Ctr., Nat. Cont. Soviet Jewry. Civil rights, Labor. Home: 274 Audubon St New Orleans LA 70118 Office: Tulane U Law Sch New Orleans LA 70118

FRIEDMAN, JOHN MAXWELL, JR., lawyer; b. N.Y.C., Oct. 31, 1944; s. John M. and Jane (Blum) F.; m. Laurie Suzanne Nevin, July 8, 1973 (div. 1987); children: David Nevin, Michael Nevin. AB, Princeton U., 1966; MA, U. Sussex, Brighton, Eng., 1970; JD, U. Chgo., 1970. Bar: N.Y. 1971, U.S. Ct. Appeals (2d cir.) 1971, U.S. Dist. Ct. (so. and ea. dist.) N.Y. 1972, U.S. Supreme Ct. 1974. Assoc. Dewey, Ballantine, Bushby, Palmer & Wood, N.Y.C., 1970-78, ptnr., 1978—. Federal civil litigation, State civil litigation, Securities. Office: Dewey Ballantine Bushby Palmer & Wood 140 Broadway New York NY 10005

FRIEDMAN, JON GEORGE, lawyer; b. N.Y.C., Sept. 2, 1951; s. George Alexander and Viola Elizabeth (Elson) F. BBA, Adelphi U., 1972; MBA, Golden Gate U., 1972; MPA, NYU, 1974; JD, Hofstra U., 1977; MA, NYU, 1978. Bar: N.Y. 1978, U.S. Dist. Ct. (ea. dist.) N.Y. 1978, U.S. Dist. Ct. (so. dist.) N.Y. 1978, U.S. Supreme Ct. 1984, U.S. Dist. Ct. P.R. 1982. V.p., gen. counsel Allou Distbrs., Inc., Brentwood, N.Y., 1978-82; bus. cons. internat. trade, fin. Long Island, N.Y., 1982—; v.p., bus. editor Caribbean Bus., San Juan, P.R., 1983-84; sole practice Long Island, P.R., 1984—. Contbr. articles to profl. jours. Mem. ABA, N.Y. State Bar Assn., Assn. of

Bar of City of N.Y. Avocations: flying airplanes, parachuting, water skiing, reading, traveling. Federal civil litigation, Criminal, Private international. Home and Office: 82-46 268th St Floral Park NY 11004

FRIEDMAN, JOSEPH, lawyer; b. Pitts., Aug. 30, 1947; s. Irving and Yvette (Walters) F. Student, U. Cologne, Germany; BA, Pa. State U., 1968; JD, U. Pitts., 1972. Bar: Pa. 1972, U.S. Dist. Ct. (we. dist.) Pa. 1972, U.S. Dist. Ct. (mid. dist.) Pa. 1975, U.S. Ct. Appeals (3d cir.) 1976, U.S. Supreme Ct. 1976. Assoc. Springer & Perry, Pitts., 1972-77, ptnr., 1977-85; ptnr. Springer, Bush & Perry P.C., Pitts., 1985—. Bd. dirs. Hebrew Inst. Pitts., 1983—. Mem. ABA, Pa. Bar Assn., Allegheny County Bar Assn., Nat. Health Lawyers Assn., Nat. Assn. Bond Lawyers, Order of the Coif, Phi Alpha Delta. Federal civil litigation, State civil litigation, Health. Office: Springer Bush & Perry PC 2300-301 5th Ave Pittsburgh PA 15222

FRIEDMAN, LAWRENCE ANDREW, lawyer; b. N.Y.C., Aug. 28, 1951; s. Philmore H. and Patricia L. Friedman; m. Barbara Jean Rye; 1 child, Mark Randall. BA, SUNY, Binghamton, 1973; JD, NYU, 1976, LLM, 1982. Bar: N.Y. 1977, D.C. 1979, N.J. 1982, U.S. Tax Ct. 1983. Atty. U.S. Dept. Transp., Washington, 1977-81; assoc. Ozzard, Rizzolo, Klein, Mauro & Savo, Somerville, N.J., 1983—. Staff writer NYU Jour. Internat. Law and Politics, 1974-75, Note and Comment editor, bd. dirs. 1975-76; contbr. articles to profl. jours. Recipient Prize Environ. Law Legal Essay Contest, Assn. Trial Lawyers Am. Mem. ABA (various sects.), N.J. Bar Assn., Phi Beta Kappa. Corporate taxation, General corporate, Banking.

FRIEDMAN, LESTER JAMES, lawyer; b. Los Angeles, Apr. 10, 1951; s. Saul Abraham and Bella (Friedman) F.; m. Simone Frenk, Aug. 3, 1975; children: Joshua, Allana, Adam. BA, UCLA, 1973; JD, Southwestern U., 1976. Bar: Calif. 1977, U.S. Dist. Ct. (cen. dist.) Calif. 1977, U.S. Ct. Appeals (9th cir.) 1977. Sole practice Los Angeles, 1977—; judge protem Los Angeles Mcpl. Ct., Los Angeles Superior Ct. and Workers' Compensation Appeal Bd., 1982—. Mem. Am. Arbitration Assn. (Los Angeles arbitrator), Los Angeles County Bar Assn., Beverly Hills Bar Assn. Democrat. Jewish. State civil litigation, Workers' compensation, Personal injury. Home: 352 S Swall Dr Beverly Hills CA 90211 Office: 1776 N Highland Ave Los Angeles CA 90028

FRIEDMAN, LEWIS RICHARD, municipal judge; b. N.Y.C., May 24, 1941; s. Harold and Sylvia (Nirenberg) F.; m. Myra Weinroth, Jan. 25, 1964 (div. Dec. 1981); 1 child: Karen; m. Bernice Forman, June 13, 1982. BA, NYU, 1963, JD, 1966. Bar: N.Y. 1966, U.S. Dist. Ct. (ea. and so. dists.) N.Y. 1968, U.S. Dist. Ct. (no. dist.) N.Y. 1969, U.S. Ct. Internat. Trade 1969, U.S. Tax Ct. 1969, U.S. Ct. Appeals (2d cir.) 1968, U.S. Ct. Appeals (10th cir.) 1982, U.S. Supreme Ct. 1970. Asst. dist. atty. New York County, N.Y.C., 1966-74; ptnr. Litman, Friedman, Kaufman & Asche, N.Y.C., 1974-82; spl. asst. atty. gen. State of N.Y., N.Y.C., 1975-76; sole practice N.Y.C., 1982, 84; judge N.Y.C. Civil Ct., 1983, 1987—, judge housing, 1985-86. Bd. of editors NYU Law Rev., 1964-66. Mem. Am. Judicature Soc., Am. Law Inst., N.Y. State Bar Assn., N.Y. County Bar Assn., Assn. of Bar of City of N.Y., Bklyn. Bar Assn., Puerto Rican Bar Assn., N.Y. State Trial Lawyers Assn., N.Y. Assn. for New Ams. (bd. dirs. 1986—), Am. Ort Fedn. (bd. dirs., exec. com. 1982—), HIAS (bd. dirs., exec. com., assoc. treas., chmn. Latin Am. ops. com. 1981—). Home: 75 E End Ave New York NY 10028 Office: NYC Civil Ct 111 Centre St New York NY 10013

FRIEDMAN, MICHAEL PHILLIP, lawyer; b. N.Y.C., May 26, 1951; s. Jack and Babette (Schapiro) F.; m. Helene Gerstel, Aug. 30, 1981; children—Felice Eva Gerstel, Jaclin Maude Gerstel. Student Alvescot Coll., Oxfordshire, Eng., 1970; B.A., CUNY, 1973; J.D., New Eng. Sch. Law, 1976; postgrad. Harvard U., 1981. Bar: Mass. 1977, U.S. Dist. Ct. Mass. 1977. Law clk. to chief civil div. U.S. Atty.'s Office, Boston, 1975-76; of counsel Denner & Singer, Cambridge, Mass., 1977-81; prin. Sorett, Friedman & Bielitz, Cambridge, 1981-83; of counsel Brickley, Sears & Sorett, Boston, 1983-86 ; staff atty. Cambridgeport Problem Ctr., Mass., 1976-77; dir. Thermographic Diagnostics, Inc., Cambridge. Pres. Trustee's-Beaconsfield Condominium Trust, Brookline, Mass., 1983-86. Mem. Trial Lawyers Assn. Am., Mass. Bar Assn., Mass. Assn. Trial Attys., Boston Bar Assn., Middlesex County Bar Assn. (clin. counselor 1976-82). Named Face to Watch by Boston Mag., 1985. General practice, State civil litigation, Personal injury. Home: 27 Lyon Rd Chestnut Hill MA 02167 Office: Brickley Sears & Sorett 75 Federal St Boston MA 02110

FRIEDMAN, MORTON LEE, lawyer; b. Aberdeen, S.D., Aug. 4, 1932; s. Philip and Rebecca (Feinstein) F.; m. Marcine Lichter, Dec. 20, 1955; children—Mark, Philip, Jeffrey. Student, U. Mich., 1950-53; A.B., Stanford U., 1954, LL.B., 1956. Bar: Calif. bar 1956. Mem. firm Kimble, Thomas, Snell, Jamison & Russell, Fresno, 1957, Busick & Busick, Sacramento, 1957-59; sr. partner firm Friedman, Collard, Poswall & Virga, Sacramento, 1959—; lectr. various law schs. and seminars; mem. Calif. Bd. Continuing Edn. Pres. Mosaic Law Congregation, 1977-80; v.p. Sacramento Jewish Fedn., 1980-82; chmn. Sacramento campaign United Jewish Appeal, 1981; nat. v.p. Am. Israel Pub. Affairs Com. Served to 1st lt. USAF, 1956. Fulbright candidate Stanford Law Sch., 1956. Fellow Am. Coll. Trial Lawyers; mem. ABA, Calif. Bar Assn., Sacramento County Bar Assn. (pres. 1976), Am. Trial Lawyers Assn., Calif. Trial Lawyers Assn. (v.p. 1973-75), Capitol City Lawyers Club (past pres.), Am. Bd. Trial Advocates (adv., pres. 1977), West Sacramento C. of C. (dir.), Order of Coif. Democrat. Club: Kiwanis. Personal injury. Home: 1620 McClaren Dr Carmichael CA 95608 Office: Friedman Collard Poswall & Virga 7750 College Town Dr Suite 300 Sacramento CA 95826

FRIEDMAN, PAUL LAWRENCE, lawyer; b. Buffalo, Feb. 20, 1944; s. Cecil Alfred and Charlotte (Wagner) F.; m. Elizabeth Ann Friedman, May 25, 1975. B.A., Cornell U., 1965; J.D. cum laude, SUNY-Buffalo, 1968. Bar: N.Y. 1968, D.C. 1969, U.S. Supreme Ct. 1974. Law clk. to judge U.S. Dist. Ct. D.C., 1968-69, U.S. Ct. Appeals (D.C. cir.), 1969-70; asst. U.S. atty. D.C. 1970-74, asst. to solicitor gen. of U.S., 1974-76; assoc. White & Case, Washington, 1976-79, ptnr., 1979—; assoc. ind. counsel Iran-Contra Investigation, 1987—; adj. prof. Georgetown U., 1973-75; mem. adv. com. procedures U.S. Ct. Appeals (D.C. cir.), 1982—, mem. grievance com., 1980-87, vice chmn., 1981-83, chmn., 1983-85; mem. faculty Nat. Inst. Trial Advocacy. Contbr. articles to profl. jours. Bd. dirs. Stuart Stiller Meml. Found. Fellow Am. Coll. Trial Lawyers; mem. Am. Law Inst., ABA (standing com. continuing edn. of bar 1982—, ho. of dels. 1985—), D.C. Bar (gov. 1978-81, 85—, pres.-elect 1985-86, pres. 1986-87), Asst. U.S. Attys. Assn. of D.C. (pres. 1976-77). Jewish. Club: Fed. City (Washington). Federal civil litigation, Criminal, Administrative and regulatory. Home: 3042 P St NW Washington DC 20007 Office: 1747 Pennsylvania Ave NW Suite 500 Washington DC 20006

FRIEDMAN, RICHARD LLOYD, lawyer; b. Bklyn., Feb. 17, 1943; s. H. Martin and Naomi (Ortman) F.; m. Carole Anne Greenhause, Aug. 28, 1966; children: Melissa Joy, Jonathan Scott. BA, Rutgers U., 1964; JD, U. Calif.-Berkeley, 1967; LL.M., NYU, 1972. Bar: N.Y. 1968, U.S. Dist. Ct. (so. and ea. dists.) N.Y. 1968, U.S. Ct. Appeals (2d cir.) 1968, U.S. Supreme Ct. 1971, N.J. 1972, U.S. Dist. Ct. N.J. 1972, U.S. Ct. Appeals (3d cir.) 1982, U.S. Ct. Appeals (11th cir.) 1986. Asst. dist. atty. office N.Y. County Dist., Atty., N.Y.C., 1967-71; ct. planner Appellate Div., N.Y.C., 1971-72; exec. dir. Dist. Atty.'s Assn., N.Y.C., 1972-74, Office of Prosecutorial Services, N.Y.C., 1974-75; asst. U.S. atty. Newark, 1975-82; ptnr. Giordano, Halleran & Ciesla, Middletown, N.J., 1982—; lectr., advisor Inst. for Continuing Legal Edn., Newark, 1982—; lectr. Nat. Inst. Trial Advocacy; mem. Supreme Ct. Criminal Practice Com., Trenton, 1983-86, Mayor's Anti-Rape Task Force, N.Y.C., 1973-75; adj. assoc. prof. John Jay Coll. Criminal Justice, N.Y.C., 1973-74. Editor Dist. Atty. Newsletter, 1972-75, Criminal Law Sect. Newsletter, 1978-81. Recipient Dir.'s award Dept. Justice, 1982, Spl. Commendation award, 1983, Spl. Achievement awards, 1980, 1978. Mem. N.J. Bar Assn. (chmn. criminal law sect. 1983-84), Monmouth County Bar Assn., Union County Bar Assn., N.Y. State Bar Assn. (sec. criminal justice sect. 1974-75), Nat. Dist. Attys. Assn., Assn. Trial Lawyers Am., Nat. Assn. Criminal Def. Lawyers, N.J. Assn. Criminal Def. Lawyers. Criminal, Federal civil litigation, State civil litigation. Office: Giordano Halleran & Ciesla PC 270 State Hwy #35 Middletown NJ 07748

FRIEDMAN, ROBERT LAURENCE, lawyer; b. Mt. Vernon, N.Y., Mar. 19, 1943; s. Alvin S. and Frances (Feinsod) F.; m. Barbara Lander, Dec. 25, 1964; children: Lisa, Andrew. AB, Columbia Coll., 1964; JD, U. Pa., 1967. Bar: N.Y. 1968. Assoc. Simpson, Thacher & Bartlett, N.Y.C., 1967-74, ptnr., 1974—. Mem. ABA, Assn. of Bar of City of N.Y. General corporate, Securities. Office: Simpson Thacher & Bartlett One Battery Park Plaza New York NY 10004

FRIEDMAN, ROBERT MARTIN, lawyer; b. Newark, Sept. 12, 1941; s. Irving and Charlotte (Droll) F.; m. Leslie Janet Oppenheim, May 11, 1980; children—Nicole, Phoebe, Noah, Samantha. B.A., Bowdoin Coll., 1963; J.D., Rutgers U., 1966. Bar: N.J. 1966, U.S. Dist. Ct. N.J. 1966. Asst. dep. pub. defender, 1970-72; assoc. Slavitt, Fish & Cowen, Newark, 1969-70; staff atty. Foster Wheeler Energy Corp., Livingston, N.J., 1972-84, gen. counsel, 1984-86; asst. gen. counsel Foster Wheeler Corp., Livingston, 1986—. Served to capt. U.S. Army, 1967-69. General corporate, Contracts commercial. Office: Foster Wheeler Corp 110 S Orange Ave Livingston NJ 07039

FRIEDMAN, ROBERT MICHAEL, lawyer; b. Memphis, June 19, 1950; s. Harold Samuel and Margaret (Siegel) F.; m. Elaine Freda Burson, Dec. 21, 1975; children: Daniel Justin, Jonathan Aaron. B.S., U. Tenn., 1973, J.D., 1975; postgrad., Exeter U., Eng., 1974, Nat. Coll. Trial Advocacy, 1985. Bar: Tenn. 1976, U.S. Dist. Ct. (we. dist.) Tenn. 1977, U.S Dist Ct. (no. dist.) Miss. 1979, U.S. Ct. Appeals (5th cir.) 1979, U.S. Supreme Ct. 1983, U.S. Dist. Ct. (so. dist.) Tex. 1986, U.S. Ct. Appeals (6th cir.) 1986. Assoc., Cassell & Fink, Memphis, 1976-78; pres., sr. ptnr. Friedman & Sissman, P.C., Memphis, 1978—; legal counsel, dir. Tenn. Interpreting Service for Deaf, Memphis, 1981—, Mid-South Hospitality Mgmt. Ctr., Inc., Memphis, 1984—; legal counsel Moss Hotel Co., Inc., 1986—; legal counsel, pres. Biloxi Hotel Co., Inc., 1986—. Mem. staff, contbr. Tenn. Law Rev., 1974-75, recipient cert., 1975. Bd. dirs. Project 1st Offenders, Shelby County, Tenn., 1976-78; bd. dirs., legal counsel Memphis Community Ctr. for Deaf & Hearing Impaired, 1980-81; bd. dirs. Eagle Scout Day, Chickasaw council Boy Scouts Am., 1978—. Served with USCG, 1971-72. Recipient Outstanding Service award and Key Alpha Phi Omega, 1972, Am. Jurisprudence award Lawyers Co-op. Pubg. Co. and Bancroft-Whitney Co., 1973-74, Chancellor's Honor award George C. Taylor Sch. Law, U. Tenn., 1975; A.S. Graves Meml. scholar, 1974-75. Mem. ABA, Assn. Trial Lawyers Am., Bar Assn. Tenn., Tenn. Trial Lawyers Assn., Nat. Assn. Criminal Def. Lawyers, Nat. Criminal Justice Assn. (charter 1984—). Alpha Phi Omega, Delta Theta Phi. Democrat. Jewish. Criminal, Personal injury, General corporate. Home: 3303 Spencer Dr Memphis TN 38115 Office: Friedman & Sissman P C Suite 3010 100 N Main St Memphis TN 38103

FRIEDMAN, RONALD MICHAEL, judge; b. Miami, June 11, 1942; s. Milton A. and Sylvia S. (Stern) F.; m. Janyce L. Friedman, May 23, 1981. B.S. in Bus. Adminstrn., U. N.C., 1964; J.D., U. Miami, 1967; LL.M. in Taxation, N.Y.U., 1968. Bar: Fla. 1967, Calif. 1969. Assoc. Wyman, Bautzer, Rothman & Kuchel, Los Angeles, 1968-71, Lederer & Jacobs, Beverly Hills, Calif., 1971-73; ptnr. Sankary & Friedman, Los Angeles, 1973-76, Freidin, Silber & Friedman, Miami, 1976-77; sole practice, Coral Gables, Fla., 1977-85; cir. ct. judge State of Fla., Miami, 1985—; instr. Northrop U. Law Sch., 1975-76. Bd. dirs. South Fla. Epilepsy Found. Mem. Los Angeles County Bar Assn. (past chmn. income tax coms.), Beverly Hills Bar Assn., Greater Miami Jewish Fedn. (bd. dirs), Dade County Bar Assn. Democrat. Jewish. Clubs: B'nai B'rith (outstanding man of year Koach chpt. 1981, past pres., past pres. South Dade council). Author: How to Prove a Profit Motive in Horse Breeding 1976. General corporate, Probate, Personal income taxation. Office: 301 C Met Justice Bldg 1351 NW 12th St Miami FL 33125

FRIEDMAN, ROSELYN L., lawyer; b. Cleve., Dec. 9, 1942; s. Charles and Lillian Edith (Zalzneck) F. BS, U. Pitts., 1964; MA, Case Western Res. U., 1967; JD cum laude, Loyola U., Chgo., 1977. Bar: Ill. 1977, U.S. Dist. Ct. (no. dist.) Ill. 1977. Adminstrv. asst. Case Western Res. U. Reading Clinic, Cleve., 1966-67; cons. Chute Jr. High Sch., Evanston, Ill., 1967-69; editor Scott, Foresman & Co., Glenview, Ill., 1969-70, Sci. Research Assocs., Inc., Chgo., 1970-77; mem. legal dept. No. Trust Co. Chgo., 1977-79; assoc. Rudnick & Wolfe, Chgo., 1979-84, ptnr., 1984—. Mem. profl. adv. com. Chgo. Jewish Fedn. Mem. Chgo. Bar Assn. (probate practice com., cert. appreciation continuing legal edn. program 1984, chmn. div. III trust law com. 1986-87), ABA, Ill. State Bar Assn., Chgo. Estate Planning Council. Probate, Estate taxation, Estate planning. Office: Rudnick & Wolfe 30 N LaSalle St Suite 2900 Chicago IL 60602

FRIEDMAN, STANLEY JOSEPH, lawyer; b. N.Y.C., Feb. 26, 1928; s. Samuel J. and Gertrude (Rabinoff) F.; m. Shari O. Friedman, Mar. 17, 1957; children—Jessica, Alexandra, Sophia. A.B. magna cum laude, Harvard U., 1948; LL.B., Yale U., 1951. Bar: N.Y., 1951, U.S. dist. ct. (so. dist.) N.Y., 1961, U.S. dist. ct. (ea. dist.) N.Y., 1961, U.S. Ct. Appeals (2d cir.) 1961, U.S. Supreme Ct., 1961. Assoc., Berlack, Israels & Liberman, 1953-59, ptnr., 1960-71; ptnr. Shereff, Friedman, Hoffman & Goodman, N.Y.C., 1971—. Served with Signal Corps, AUS, 1951-53. Recipient Helen Choate Bell prize Harvard U., 1948. Mem. ABA, Assn. Bar City N.Y., Phi Beta Kappa. Democrat. Jewish. Club: Harvard (N.Y.C.). Bd. editors Yale Law Jour., 1950-51; contbg. editor and author chpts. in books. Securities, General corporate. Home: 4710 Grosvenor Ave Riverdale NY 10471 Office: Shereff Friedman Hoffman & Goodman 919 3d Ave New York NY 10022

FRIEDMAN, VICTOR STANLEY, lawyer; b. N.Y.C., May 9, 1933; s. Harry and Rose (Cohen) F.; m. Sara Ann Riesner, June 21, 1958 (div.); children—Eric H., Diana B., Michael C.; m. Victoria Schonfeld, Mar. 7, 1984; 1 child, Jared D. A.B., Harvard U., 1954; LL.B., Yale U., 1957. Bar: N.Y. 1958, U.S. Dist. Ct. (so. dist.) N.Y. 1964, U.S. Ct. Appeals (2d cir.) 1966, U.S. Ct. Appeals (4th cir.) 1981, U.S. Ct. Appeals (3d cir.) 1972, U.S. Ct. Appeals (8th cir.) 1970, U.S. Dist. Ct. (ea. dist.) N.Y. 1966, U.S. Supreme Ct. 1974. Asst. to dep. atty. gen. Dept. Justice, Washington, 1958-60; assoc. firm Fried, Frank, Harris, Shriver & Jacobson, N.Y.C., 1960-66, ptnr., 1967—. Served with USAR, 1958-59. Mem. ABA, Bar Assn. City N.Y., Am. Coll. Trial Lawyers, Fed. Bar Council. Antitrust, Federal civil litigation, Private international. Office: Fried Frank Harris Shriver & Jacobson 1 New York Plaza New York NY 10004

FRIEDMAN, WALLACE, lawyer; b. Bklyn., June 16, 1931; s. Max Paul and Belle (Rosen) F.; m. Beverly Nathalie Feinman, Dec. 7, 1952; children—Richard Bruce, Stephen Jay. A.A. in Bus., Los Angeles City Coll., 1951; B.A. in Sci. and Journalism, Calif. State U.-Los Angeles, 1957; J.D., U. San Fernando Valley, 1966. Bar: Calif. 1968, U.S. Dist. Ct. (cen. dist.) Calif. 1968, U.S. Supreme Ct. 1971. Engr., Aerospace, Los Angeles, 1955-68; sole practice, Los Angeles, 1968—; assoc. corp. counsel Marquardt, Los Angeles, 1967-68; counsel to chmn. bd. DayLin Inc., Los Angeles, 1971. Served to 1st lt. USAF, 1951-55. Mem. ABA, Los Angeles County Bar Assn., San Fernando Valley Bar Assn. Democrat. Jewish. Personal injury, State civil litigation, General corporate. Office: 16255 Ventura Blvd Suite 1001 Encino CA 91436

FRIEDMANN, JONATHON DAVID, lawyer; b. Phila., May 22, 1957; s. Jacob Bernard Friedman and Frances May (Payes) Neiman; m. Michele Ucci, Sept. 9, 1984. BA, Lafayette Coll., 1979; JD cum laude, Suffolk U., 1982. Bar: Mass. 1982, U.S. Dist. Ct. Mass. 1983, U.S. Ct. Appeals (1st cir.) 1983, U.S. Claims Ct. 1984, U.S. Supreme Ct. 1986. Assoc. Gargill, Sassoon & Rudolph, Boston, 1982—; legal specialist Mass. State Racing Commn., 1980-81; staff atty. Mass. Soc. of Prevention of Cruelty to Children, Boston, 1980-81, Exec. Office Consumer Affairs, Boston, 1981-82. Mem. Big Bros. Am., Phila., 1980—. Mem. Union League Phila. (Good Citizenship award 1975). Republican. Jewish. Avocations: skiing, horseback riding, photography. State civil litigation, Federal civil litigation, Contracts commercial. Home: 465 Washington St Unit 1 Brookline MA 02146 Office: Gargill Sassoon & Rudolph 92 State St Boston MA 02109

FRIEDRICH, BRUCE ROBERT, lawyer; b. Phila., Mar. 10, 1951; s. William Robert and Frances Elizabeth (Wagner) F.; m. Liora Lassinger, May 21, 1972; children: Joshua Evan, Todd Michael. AA, Monmouth Coll., 1971, BA, 1973; JD, Bklyn. Law Sch., 1977. Bar: Calif. 1977, U.S. Dist. Ct. (cen. dist.) Calif. 1979, N.Y. 1987. V.p., gen. counsel Physicians and Surgeons Underwriters Corp., Los Angeles, 1977-81; asst. sec. Physicians and Surgeons Ins. Exchange of Calif., Los Angeles, 1981, sec., 1978-81; assoc. Tyre, Kamin, Katz & Granof, Los Angeles, 1981-82, O'Brien & Hallisey, Santa Monica, Calif., 1982-84; v.p., gen. counsel The Doctors Mgmt. Co., Santa Monica, 1984-86; assoc. Pegalis & Wachsman, P.C., Great Neck, N.Y., 1986—. Recipient Elvin R. Simmill Meml. award Monmouth Coll., 1973. Mem. ABA, Los Angeles County Bar Assn., Conf. Ins. Counsel. Avocations: surfing, guitar. Personal injury, Insurance, Civil rights.

FRIEDRICH, CRAIG WILLIAM, lawyer; b. Oshkosh, Wis., Oct. 25, 1946; s. William Harold and Lorraine June (Pugh) F. AB, U. Wis., Madison, 1968; JD cum laude, Harvard U., 1972. Bar: N.Y. 1973, U.S. Tax Ct. 1973, U.S. Dist. Ct. (so., ea. dists.) N.Y. 1979, U.S. Ct. Internat. Trade 1980, Maine 1986. Atty., advisor Office Tax Legis. Counsel, U.S. Treasury Dept., Washington, 1974-76; assoc. Weil, Gotshal and Manges, N.Y.C., 1972-74, 1976-77, Debevoise and Plimpton, N.Y.C., 1977-81; assoc. prof. N.Y. Law Sch., N.Y.C., 1981-83; counsel Schoeman, Marsh, Updike and Welt, N.Y.C., 1982-83, ptnr., 1983-86; ptnr. Bernstein, Shur, Sawyer & Nelson, Portland, Maine, 1986—; cons. Bank Tax Inst., 1981-83; subject specialist Council Non Collegiate Continuing Edn., 1982. Mem. bd. contbg. editors, advisors Jour. Corp. Taxation, 1980—, author column, 1980—. Contbr. articles to profl. jours. Mem. ABA, N.Y. State Bar Assn., Maine Bar Assn., Am. Soc. Internat. Law, N.Y.C. Bar Assn., Phi Beta Kappa, Phi Kappa Phi, Phi Eta Sigma. Republican. Congregationalist. Clubs: Harvard (N.Y.C.); Cumberland (Portland). Home: 4 Hackmatack Dr Scarborough ME 04074 Office: Bernstein Shur Sawyer & Nelson 1 Monument Sq PO Box 9729 Portland ME 04109-5529

FRIEDRICHS, DAVID O., legal educator; b. White Plains, N.Y., Oct. 31, 1944; s. Kurt O. and Nellie (Bruell) F.; m. Jean L. Richards, Aug. 7, 1971 (div. Oct. 1974); m. Jeanne A. Windle, June 5, 1976; children: Jessica Pauline, Bryan Patrick. AB, NYU, 1966, MA, 1970, ABD. Lectr., asst. prof. CUNY, Staten Island, 1969-77; from asst. to assoc. prof. U. Scranton, Pa., 1977—. Contbr. articles to profl. jours. Bd. dirs. Friends of the Library, Scranton, 1979-84, Pa. Citizens for Better Libraries, Harrisburg, Pa., 1983-85. Faculty research grantee CUNY, U. Scranton, 1984. Mem. Assn. for Humanist Socioly (v.p. 1983), Acad. Criminal Justice Scis. (com. chmn. 1982-86), Soc. for the Study of Social Problems, Am. Legal Studies Assn. (editor Legal Studies Forum 1985—), Pi Gamma Mu (Frank Brown Scholarship medal 1984). Legal education, Jurisprudence. Office: U Scranton Dept Sociology & Criminal Justice Scranton PA 18510

FRIEL, KAREN EILEEN, lawyer; b. Phila., Aug. 24, 1957; d. George William John and Eleanor A. (Check) Kayati; m. Brian Paul Friel, June 21, 1980. BA, St. Joseph's U., Phila., 1979; JD, Temple U., 1982. Assoc. Banks & Banks, Phila., 1982-84, Eckell, Sparks, Levy, Auerbach & Monte, Media, Pa., 1984-85; sole practice Upper Darby, Pa., 1985—; pub. defender Del. County, Media, 1985-87; atty. Del. County Dist. Atty.s Office, 1987—. Adult advisor high sch. CYO, Upper Darby, 1984—; mem. Upper Darby Rep. Com, 1985—; mem. exec. com. Delaware County Women's Conf., Media, 1985—; sec., mem. exec. com. Del. County Lawyers for Life, 1985—; pres. Voice for the Unborn, Drexel Hill, Pa., 1985—. Mem. Del. County Bar Assn. (various coms. 1985—). Roman Catholic. Avocations: tennis, softball, racquetball. General practice, Criminal. Home: 228 Maypole Rd Upper Darby PA 19082 Office: Del County Dist Attys Office Media Courthouse Media PA 19063

FRIEND, DAVID LEE, lawyer; b. Houston, May 23, 1951; s. Leonard Nathan and Sharlee Baruch (Freedman) F.; m. Deborah S. Grubb, July 17, 1982; children: Nathan Douglas, Matthew Joseph. BA with honors, U. Tex., 1973, JD, 1976. Bar: Tex. 1976, Wash. 1977, U.S. Dist. Ct. (we. dist.) Wash. Law clk. to justice Seattle, 1976, 1976-77; assoc. Garvey, Schubert, et al, Seattle and Washington, 1977-82; ptnr. Weinrich, Gilmore et al, Seattle, 1982-85, Franco, Asia, Bensussen & Coe, Seattle, 1985—. Pres. U.S. Assn. Blind Athletes, Seattle region, 1979; organizer North End Jewish Community Ctr., Seattle, 1984—. Mem. ABA, Wash. State Bar Assn., Tex. Bar Assn., Assn. Trial Lawyers Am., Wash. State Trial Lawyers Assn., Seattle C. of C. (chmn. internat. trade com. 1984—). Club: Tower (chmn. under 45 com.) (Seattle). Private international. Office: Franco Asia Bensussen & Coe Tower Bldg 7th and Olive Seattle WA 98101

FRIEND, EDWARD MALCOLM, III, lawyer; b. Birmingham, Ala., Oct. 12, 1946; s. Edward M. Jr. and Hermione Frances (Curjel) F. BA in History, U. Ala., 1968, JD, 1971. Ptnr. Sirote, Permutt, McDermott, Slepian, Friend, Friedman, Held & Apolinsky P.C., Birmingham; mem. Family Ct. Jefferson County, 1981-84, Legal Services Corp. Ala.; treas. Birmingham Legal Aid. Soc., 1982-84; bd. dirs. Colonial BancGroup, Montgomery, Ala., Colonial Bank Ala., Birmingham, chmn. Mem. Birmingham Area chpt. Am. Red Cross, 1972—, exec. and fin. com. 1978—, vice chmn. adv. council Southeastern Area, 1979, vice chmn. 1983—, Nat. Conf. Christians and Jews, 1976—, exec. com., state vice chmn., 1979, nat. bd., 1981—, Pres.' Council, U. Ala., Birmingham, 1980—, adv. com. capital campaign, 1985—, Birmingham Jewish Fedn., 1984—, vice chmn. community relations council, 1982-85, trustee, 1985—, United Way Cen. Ala., 1984—, co-chmn. gen. campaign, 1978, exec. com., 1985—, Operation New Birmingham, 1984—, exec. com. community relations com., 1981-84, v.p., 1986—, Childrens Hosp. Ala., 1986—; exec. com. Ala. Symphony Assn., 1980-82, bd. dirs., 1982-85, Birmingham Festival Arts, 1978—, pres. 1984-85, chmn. 1985—; pres. Big Bros./Big Sisters Greater Birmingham, 1980, chmn., 1981-83; trustee St. Vincent's Hosp., 1982-86, v.p., 1984-86, Ala. Sch. Fine Arts Found., 1985—; chmn. bd. dirs. Thirteenth Place, 1974-79. Recipient Vol. of Yr. award Birmingham chpt. Am. Red Cross, 1973, Am. Nat. Red. Cross Disting. Service award Southeastern Area Adv. Council, 1974, Brotherhood award Nat. Conf. Christinas and Jews, 1987; named Lawyer of Yr., Birmingham Legal Secretarial Assn., 1976, one of Outstanding Young Men, Ala. Jaycees, 1978, Outstanding Alumnus, U. Ala. Sch. Law, 1984. Mem. Birmingham Mortgage Bankers Assn. (exec. com. 1981-83), So. Inst. Health Law (vice chmn. 1985—), Young Lawyers Assn. (sec./treas.), Farrah Law Soc. (vice chmn. 1980-82, chmn. 1982-84), Greater Birmingham Area C. of C. (v.p., gen. counsel). Office: Sirote Permutt McDermott et al 2222 Arlington Ave S Birmingham AL 35205

FRIEND, HENRY CHARLES, lawyer; b. Milw., Mar. 30, 1909; s. Charles and Caroline (Blumberg) F. AB, Harvard U., 1931, LLB, 1934. Bar: Wis. 1934, U.S. Supreme Ct. Assoc. Homeowners Loan Corp., Chgo., 1934-36; sole practice Milw., 1936-42, 43—; atty. Office Price Adminstrn., Washington, 1942-43. Contbr. legal and hist. articles to profl. jours. Abraham Lincoln fellow. Mem. ABA, Wis. Bar Assn., Milw. County Bar Assn., Am. Counsel Assn., Comml. Law League Am. Club: Milw. Rowing (pres. 1957-82). Avocation: rowing. Contracts commercial, Probate, Real property. Home: 1981 N Prospect Ave Milwaukee WI 53202 Office: 238 W Wisconsin Ave Milwaukee WI 53203

FRIEND, ISRAEL, lawyer; b. Passaic, N.J., Apr. 9, 1903; s. Noah and Frieda (Wasserstrum) F.; m. Bess Steckler, May 29, 1928; children: Herbert S., William M., Richard J., Gerald G. LLB, N.J. Law Sch., 1924. Bar: N.J. 1924, U.S. Dist. Ct. N.J. 1924, U.S. Supreme Ct. 1957. Ptnr. Friend & Friend, Clifton; mayor City of Clifton, N.J., 1972-74; sole practice Clifton. Sec. zoning bd., Clifton, 1928-32; mem. city council, Clifton, 1969-78. Mem. Passaic County Bar Assn. Democrat. Jewish. Lodge: Masons. Family and matrimonial, Probate. Office: 1000 Clifton Ave Clifton NJ 07013

FRIEND, JOSEPH ERNEST, lawyer; b. New Orleans, Oct. 5, 1931; s. Julius Weis and Elise (Weil) F.; m. Joan Anderson, June 30, 1956; children: Christopher, Anne, Duff, Courtney. BA, Yale U., 1953; JD, Tulane U., 1960. Bar: La. 1960. Assoc. Milling, Benson, Woodward, Hillyer & Pierson, New Orleans, 1960-62; ptnr. Friend, Wilson & Draper and predecessor firms, New Orleans, 1962—. Pres. New Orleans Speech and Hearing Ctr., 1968, Kingsley Ho., New Orleans, 1972; v.p. Touro Infirmary, New Orleans, 1986—. Served to lt. (j.g.) USNR, 1953-56. Mem. ABA, La. Bar Assn., New Orleans Bar Assn. (bd. dirs. 1969-71), Comml. Law League of Am. (pres.1982-83), Order of Coif. Democrat. Jewish. Avocation: sailing. Bankruptcy, Contracts commercial, Federal civil litigation. Home: 1666 Soniat St New Orleans LA 70115 Office: Friend Wilson & Draper 1335 First NBC Bldg New Orleans LA 70112

FRIEND, RICHARD E., lawyer; b. N.Y.C., Mar. 29, 1950; m. Lynne Isaacs Friend, Aug. 1972; 1 child, Robert Adam. BS in Econs. cum laude, U. Pa.,

1972; JD cum laude, NYU, 1975. Bar: N.J. 1975, N.Y. 1976, Fla. 1982. Assoc. Kronish, Lieb, Shainswit, Weiner & Hillman, N.Y.C., 1975-77; assoc. Weil, Gotshal & Manges, N.Y.C. and Miami, Fla., 1977-83, ptnr., 1983-85; ptnr. Shea & Gould, N.Y.C. and Miami, Fla., 1985—. Mem. Dade County strategic plan Task Force on Econ. Devel., 1984-85; bd. dirs. Friends of Art at the Lowe, 1986—. Mem. ABA, Fla. Bar Assn., N.Y. State Bar Assn., Greater Miami C. of C. (co-chmn. govtl. task force 1985-86, actice various coms.), Wharton Sch. Club of South Fla. (pres. 1985—, v.p. adminstrn. 1983-85), U. Pa. Dade Alumni Club (bd. dirs. 1985—). Club: City (Miami). Real property, General corporate, Contracts commercial. Home: 55 Arvida Pkwy Coral Gables FL 33156 Office: Shea & Gould 801 Brickell Ave Miami FL 33131

FRIERSON, SARAH STEWART, lawyer; b. Mobile, Ala., Feb. 8, 1949; d. John Calvin and Sarah Pace (Johnson) Stewart; m. Richard Scott Frierson, July 28, 1973; 1 child, John. BS in Commerce, U. Ala., 1969, JD, 1972, LLM in Taxation, 1979. Bar: Ala. 1972. Trust officer Birmingham (Ala.) Trust Nat. Bank, 1972-80; assoc. Collins, Galloway & Smith, Mobile, Ala., 1980-86; sole practice Mobile, 1986—. Episcopalian. Probate, Bankruptcy, Family and matrimonial. Home: 3920 Radnor Ave Mobile AL 36608 Office: 3280 Dauphin St Bldg B Suite 134 Mobile AL 36606

FRIES, JAY ROBERT, lawyer; b. Phila., July 30, 1954; s. George Bruce and Myrtle (Keck) F.; m. Annette Rooney, June 4, 1983. BA, Washington & Lee U., 1976; JD, Coll. William and Mary, 1979. Bar: Va. 1979, Ohio 1979, U.S. Dist. Ct. (so. dist.) Ohio 1979, Md. 1982, U.S. Dist. Ct. Md. 1983, U.S. Dist. Ct. Va 1984. Assoc. Taft, Stettinius & Hollister, Cin., 1979-82, Law Offices of John G. Kruchko, Balt., 1982-86; ptnr. Kruchko & Fries, Balt., 1986—. Bd. dirs. Cystic Fibrosis Found., Balt., 1986—. Mem. ABA (labor com. young lawyers sect., exec. council), Balt. County Bar Assn. (exec. council), Md. Bar Assn., Md. C. of C. (human relations com.), Balt. County C. of C. (small bus. council). Labor. Office: Kruchko & Fries 28 W Allegheny Ave Suite 606 Baltimore MD 21204

FRIES GARDNER, LISA, lawyer; b. N.Y.C., June 29, 1956; d. Leslie R. and Marie D. (Corsano) Fries; m. Kevin R. Gardner, Sept. 22, 1984. BA, Lynchburg Coll., 1978; JD, Seton Hall U., 1981. Bar: N.J. 1981, U.S. Dist. Ct. N.J. 1981. Atty. Foster Wheeler Corp., Livingston, N.J., 1981—. Author: Landlord and Tenant-Application of Implied Warranty of Habitability Expanded to Encompass Tenant Security, 1981. Recipient Tribute to Women and Industry award, 1987. Roman Catholic. General corporate, Contracts commercial, Securities. Office: Foster Wheeler Corp 110 S Orange Ave Livingston NJ 07039

FRIEZE, H(AROLD) DELBERT, lawyer; b. Tulsa, Feb. 15, 1943; s. Harold William and Violet Izenna (Schnelle) F.; m. Connie Dixon, Dec. 28, 1966; 1 child, Todd William. BBA, U. Okla., 1966; JD, U. Tulsa, 1975. Bar: Okla. 1975, U.S. Dist. Ct. (no. dist.) Okla. 1975, U.S. Dist. Ct. (ea. dist.) Okla. 1976. Ptnr. Petrik, Frieze & Moore, Broken Arrow, Okla., 1975—; bd. dirs. 1st Nat. Bank & Trust Co., Broken Arrow. Bd. mem. Broken Arrow Bd. Adjustment, 1976-78; asst. city atty. City Broken Arrow, 1978-81; charter mem., bd. dirs. Broken Arrow Citizens Crime Commn., 1983—. Served to major USAF, 1966-79. Mem. Tulsa County Bar Assn. Republican. Methodist. Lodge: Rotary (past pres. Broken Arrow club, Paul Harris fellow 1983). State civil litigation, Contracts commercial, Real property. Office: Petrik Frieze & Moore 121 E College Broken Arrow OK 74012

FRIGERIO, CHARLES STRAITH, lawyer; b. Detroit, Mar. 8, 1957; s. Louie John and LaVern (Straith) F.; m. Annette Angela Russo, Oct. 18, 1985. BA, St. Mary's U., 1979, JD, 1982. Bar: Tex. 1982. Pros. atty. City Attys. Office, San Antonio, 1982-84, trial atty., 1984—. Mem. Dem. Nat. Com., San Antonio, 1976; asst. mgr. local campaigns, San Antonio, 1976-84. Mem. ABA, Tex. Bar Assn., Fed. Bar Assn., San Antonio Bar Assn., Assn. Trial Lawyers Am., Cath. Lawyers Assn., Delta Epsilom Sigma. Democrat. Roman Catholic. State civil litigation, Personal injury, Workers' compensation. Home: 123 Brackenridge #106 San Antonio TX 78209 Office: City Attys Office 200 Main Plaza Suite 101 San Antonio TX 78205-2798

FRISBY, THOMAS NEWTON, lawyer; b. Tyler, Tex., Sept. 3, 1932; s. A.J. and Thelma Gene (Karr) F.; m. Barbee Machado, Mar. 6, 1973. B.A., La. State U., 1952, LL.B., 1954. Bar: La. 1954, Tex. 1983. Faculty law U.S. Air Force Acad., Colorado Springs, Colo., 1960-63; lectr. U. Denver Sch. Law, 1972-75, Fed. Publs., Washington, 1973-75; sole practice, Tyler, 1975—; lectr. seminars on constrn., contract law U. Houston, Assoc. Gen. Contractors, Tex. A&M U. Author: Cases and Materials on Government Contracting, 1962, Personal Estate Planning, 1963, Risk Management for Construction Contractors, 1973. Served to capt. JAG, USAF, 1958-63. Mem. ABA, La. Bar Assn., Tex. Bar Assn., Assn. Trial Lawyers Am., Nat. Acad. Sci. (productivity council). Construction, Administrative and regulatory, Federal civil litigation. Home: 1522 N Bois D'Arc Tyler TX 75702 Office: Riviere-Frisby Bldg 1604 N Bois D'Arc Tyler TX 75702

FRISCH, ROBERT EMILE, lawyer; b. Chgo., Aug. 18, 1925; s. Emile Leopold and Lillian Laverne (Ward) F.; m. Dolly Hemphill, Jan. 26, 1952; children: Katharine Frisch Malin, Robert P., Peter O. A.B., Harvard U., 1946, LL.B., 1950. Bar: N.Y. 1950, U.S. Supreme Ct. 1959, U.S. Tax Ct. 1954, U.S. Claims Ct. 1954, U.S. Ct. Appeals (2d cir.) 1954, U.S. Ct. Appeals (3d cir.) 1972, U.S. Ct. Appeals (7th and 9th cirs.) 1983. Teaching fellow Harvard Law Sch., Cambridge, Mass., 1950-51; asst. counsel U.S. Senate Crime Com., N.Y.C., 1951; assoc. firm Rogers & Wells, N.Y.C., 1951-57, ptnr., 1957—. Mem. ABA, N.Y. Bar Assn., Assn. Bar City N.Y. Republican. Episcopalian. Clubs: Sky, Am Yacht. Corporate taxation, Personal income taxation, State and local taxation. Office: 200 Park Ave New York NY 10166

FRISCH, SIDNEY, JR., lawyer, real estate developer; b. Evanston, Ill., Oct. 25, 1940; s. Sidney and Helen (Hunter) F. B.S. in Fin., U. Ill., 1962, J.D., 1965. Bar: Ill. 1966, U.S. Dist. Ct. (no. dist.) Ill. 1966, U.S. Ct. Appeals (7th cir.) 1968; Colo. 1977, U.S. Dist. Ct. (mid. dist.) Ga. 1974. Ptnr. Frisch & Frisch, Chartered, Chgo., 1966—; gen. counsel Weber-Stephen Products Co., Palatine, Ill., 1966—; gen. ptnr. The 312 Randolph Partnership, Chgo., 1981—; lectr. seminars in field; mem. sec. of state's adv. com. to revise Ill. Bus. Corp. Act, 1984. Author: Illinois Mechanic's Liens, 1972; Attorney's Guide to Negotiation, 1979. Asst. editor Ill. Law Forum, U. Ill. Coll. Law, 1964, 65; mem. editorial com. Illinois Business Act Annotated, 1978. Assoc. bd. mem. U. Chgo. Cancer Research Found., 1982, v.p. 1984. Served to lt. USNR, 1962-69. Recipient cert. of appreciation Ill. Inst. for Continuing Legal Edn., 1983. Mem. ABA, Ill. Bar Assn., Chgo. Bar Assn. (chmn. corp. law com. 1983-84, cert. of appreciation 1978, 83), Order of Coif. Club: Deans (U. Ill. Coll. Law). General corporate, Real property. Office: Frisch & Frisch Chartered 312 W Randolph St Chicago IL 60606

FRISCH, SIDNEY, lawyer; b. Chgo., May 4, 1899; s. Morris and Pauline (Unger) F.; m. Helen Carroll Hunter, Sept. 1, 1934; 1 son: Sidney. Ph.B., U. Chgo., 1920, J.D., 1922. Bar: Ill. 1922. Ptnr. Frisch & Frisch, Chgo., 1922—, sr. mem.; pres., dir. Rogers Park Apts., Inc., Chgo., 1934—. Bd. dirs. Highland Park (Ill.) Playground and Recreation Bd., 1954-58, Presbyterian Home, Evanston, Ill., 1965-69. Served with U.S. Army, 1918-20. Mem. Chgo. Bar Assn. (50 year mem., chmn. corp. law com. 1958-68), Ill. State Bar Assn. (chmn. real estate law sect. 1955-57, 50 year mem.), ABA (chmn. com. current lit. on real property law 1953-54). Republican. Presbyterian. General corporate, Probate, Real property. Home: 256 Ivy Ln Highland Park IL 60035 Office: 312 W Randolph St Suite 200 Chicago IL 60606

FRITH, DOUGLAS KYLE, lawyer; b. Henry County, Va., Sept. 2, 1931; s. Jacob and Sally Ada (Nunn) F.; m. Ella Margaret Tuck, Sept. 10, 1960; children—Margaret Frith Ringers, Susan Elaine. A.B., Roanoke Coll., 1952; J.D., Washington and Lee U., 1957. Bar: Va. 1957. Sole practice, 1957-58; assoc. Taylor & Young, Martinsville, Va., 1957-58; ptnr. Young, Kiser & Frith, 1960-71, Frith, Gardner & Gardner, 1973-78; pres. Douglas K. Frith & Assocs., P.C., Martinsville, 1979—; adv. bd. Sovran Bank, Frith Equipment Corp., others; dir. Frith Constrn. Co., Inc., Frith Equipment Corp.; substitute judge 21st Gen. Dist. Ct., 21st Juvenile and Domestic Relations Dist. Ct., 1969-80. Chmn., March of Dimes, 1960, Brotherhood Week, 1960; capt. profl. div. United Fund, 1971. Served with U.S. Army, 1952-54. Mem. Va. Bar Assn., Martinsville-Henry Count Bar Assn. (pres. 1970-71), Va. Trial Lawyers Assn. (dist. v.p. 1970-71, del. at large 1971-77). Republican. Baptist. Club: Kiwanis. Personal injury, Estate planning, Real property. Address: 58 W Church St Martinsville VA 24112

FRITTON, KARL ANDREW, lawyer; b. Olean, N.Y., Mar. 29, 1955; s. William John and Margaret (O'Brian) F.; m. Christine Evelyn Councill, June 9, 1984; children: Katherine Evelyn, Jessica Claire. BS in Econs., SUNY, Albany, 1977; JD, Rutgers U., 1980. Bar: Pa. 1981, N.Y. 1981, U.S. Supreme Ct. 1985. Assoc. Bond, Schoeneck & King, Syracuse, N.Y., 1980-81, Obermayer, Rebmann, Maxwell & Hippel, Phila., 1981-84; assoc. Sprecher, Felix, Visco, Hutchinson & Young, Phila., 1984-86, ptnr., 1987—. Contbr. articles to profl. jours. Active Phila. Vol. Lawyers For Arts, 1981—, Big Brs. Phila., 1981—. Mem ABA (labor law sect.). Democrat. Roman Catholic. Club: Racquet (Phila.). Labor. Home: 341 S 26th St Philadelphia PA 19103 Office: Sprecher Felix et al 123 S Broad St Philadelphia PA 19109

FRITZ, COLLIN MARTIN, lawyer; b. Des Moines, June 8, 1947; s. Collin Wilburn and Jeanne (Wills) F.; m. Susyn Miller; 1 child, Courtney. BA, U. Iowa, 1969, JD, 1973. Bar: Iowa 1974, Hawaii, 1977, U.S. Dist. Ct. Hawaii 1976, U.S. Ct. Appeals (9th cir.) 1980. Ptnr. Trecker Rosenberg & Fritz, Kailua, Hawaii, 1976-79, Trecker & Fritz, Kailua, 1979-80, McKenzie, Trecker & Fritz, Honolulu, 1980—. Bd. dirs. ARC, Honolulu, 1979-82, ACLU, Honolulu, 1977-83. Fellow Hawaii Acad. Plaintiffs Attys.; mem. Am. Trial Lawyers Assn., Hawaii Bar Assn. Club: Honolulu. Personal injury. Home: 829 Onaha St Honolulu HI 96816 Office: McKenzie Trecker and Fritz 820 Mililani St Suite 710 Honolulu HI 96813

FRITZ, TOBIAS BODWELL, lawyer; b. Kansas City, Mo., Apr. 15, 1953; s. William E. and Sarah J. (Bodwell) F.; m. Nancy J. Jones, Aug. 1, 1981; children: Samuel Lee, Joseph William. BA, Duke U., 1975; JD, U. Mo., Kansas City, 1980. Bar: Mo. 1980, U.S. Dist. Ct. (we. dist.) Mo. 1980. Staff regional solicitor U.S. Dept. Labor, Kansas City, 1980—. Avocation: outdoors. Administrative and regulatory, Federal civil litigation, Labor. Home: Box 2584 Kansas City MO 64142 Office: US Dept Labor Regional Solicitor 911 Walnut Room 2106 Kansas City MO 64106

FRITZ COHN, LORELI, lawyer; b. Bryan, Ohio, May 14, 1955; d. Ward Gerald and Shirley Elaine (Hilbert) Fritz; m. Steven Philip Cohn, Aug. 24, 1980; 1 child, Benjamin Russell. AB magna cum laude, Heidelberg Coll., 1977; JD cum laude, U. Pa., 1980. Bar: Ill. 1980, U.S. Dist. Ct. (no. dist.) Ill. 1980, U.S. Ct. Appeals (7th cir.) 1981. Assoc. Hedlund, Hunter & Lynch, Chgo., 1980-82; gen. atty. Centel Corp., Chgo., 1982—. Mem. ABA (antitrust law sect.), Chgo. Bar Assn. (antitrust com.). Democrat. Methodist. Club: Literary Soc. Avocations: reading, gardening, inning. Antitrust, Entertainment. Home: 505 Sheridan Rd 3E Evanston IL 60202 Office: Centel Corp 8725 Higgins Rd Chicago IL 60631

FRITZE, JAMES RONALD, lawyer; b. Chgo., July 23, 1947; s. William P. and Margaret Louise (Aspan) F.; m. Sheila Kay Fritze, June 17, 1972; children—Elizabeth Ann, Julia Louise. B.A., U. Wis., Whitewater, 1969; J.D., U. Ill., 1972. Bar admittee: Ill., 1973, Colo., 1982, U.S. Dist. Ct. (cen. dist.) Ill., 1978, U.S. Dist. Ct. Colo., 1982. Asst. state's atty. Iroquois County, Ill., 1972-74, asst. public defender, 1975, state's atty., 1976-80; sole practice, Watseka, Ill., 1974-76, 81-82; asst. county atty. Eagle County, Eagle, Colo., 1982-86, atty. Eagle County, 1986—; counsel Eagle County Airport Commn., 1982—. Pres., Iroquois County Young Republicans, 1974-76; dep. dist. gov. Ill. Young Reps., 1975; Rep. precinct committeeman, 1974; chmn. Echo Ranch Group Home for Neglected Children, 1984-85; pres. ch. council Mt. of Holy Cross Luth. Ch., Vail, Colo., chmn., 1985—; chmn. Indian Trails dist. Boy Scouts Am., 1977-78. Mem. ABA, Ill. Bar Assn., Iroquois County Bar Assn. (pres. 1979-82), Nat. Dist. Attys. Assn., Colo. County Attys. Assn. Lutheran. Clubs: Eagle Valley Lions (1st v.p. 1985, pres. 1986—). Local government, General practice, Criminal. Home: 101 Shorthorn Dr PO Box 985 Eagle CO 81631 Office: 550 Broadway PO Box 850 Eagle CO 81631

FRITZLER, RANDAL BRANDT, judge; b. Hollywood, Calif., Dec. 14, 1943; s. George Paul and Laurine A. (Brandt) F.; m. Barbara Jean Walters, June 21, 9171; children: Elizabeth, Jon, David, Mark. BS, U. Nebr., 1966; JD, U. Puget Sound, 1974. Bar: Wash. 1975, U.S. Dist. Ct. (we. dist.) Wash. 1976. Ptnr. Fritzler & Hall, Vancouver, Wash., 1976-78, Weber & Baumgartner, Vancouver, 1978, Eling, Fritzler & Lewis, Vancouver, 1980-85; dir. arbitration Arbitration Service of Southwest Wash., Vancouver, 1984-87; sole practice Vancouver, 1985-87; presiding judge Clark County Dist. Ct., Vancouver, 1987—; chmn. bd. dirs. Weinberg, Gilbert & Steibel, Vancouver; ct. commr., traffic magistrate Clark County Dist. Ct., 1979-80, 1986—. Author: Arbitration Handbook, 1985. Bd. dirs. Wash. Lawyer Referral Service, Seattle, 1984-86. Mem. ABA, Am. Judicature Soc., Wash. State Trial Lawyers. Democrat. State civil litigation, Real property, Arbitration and alternative dispute resolution methods. Home: 19106 NE 164th St Brush Prairie WA 98606 Office: Clark County Dist Ct PO Box 5000 Vancouver WA 98660

FROHNMAYER, DAVID BRADEN, state attorney general; b. Medford, Oreg., July 9, 1940; s. Otto J. and Marabel (Fisher) B.; m. Lynn Diane Johnson, Dec. 30, 1970; children: Kirsten, Mark, Kathryn, Jonathan, Amy. A.B. magna cum laude, Harvard U., 1962; B.A., Oxford (Eng.) U., 1964, M.A. (Rhodes scholar), 1971; J.D., U. Calif., Berkeley, 1967. Bar: Calif. 1967, Oreg. 1971. Assoc. firm Pillsbury, Madison & Sutro, San Francisco, 1967-69; asst. to sec. Dept. HEW, 1969-70; prof. U. Oreg. Law Sch., 1971-81, spl. asst. to pres., 1971-79; atty. gen. State of Oreg., 1981—; mem. Oreg. Ho. of Reps., 1975-81; chmn. Conf. Western Attys. Gen., 1985-86; pres.-elect Nat. Assn. Attys. Gen., 1986—. Recipient awards Weaver Constl. Law Essay competition Am. Bar Found., 1972, 74. Mem. ABA, (Ross essay winner 1980), Oreg. Bar Assn., Calif. Bar Assn., Assn. Attys. Gen. (v.p. 1985-86, pres. elect 1986—), Round Table Eugene, Order of Coif, Phi Beta Kappa. Republican. Presbyterian. Administrative and regulatory, State civil litigation, State government. Home: 2875 Baker St. Eugene OR 97403 Office: Office of Atty Gen 100 State Office Bldg Salem OR 97310

FROMBERG, MALCOLM HUBERT, lawyer, mayor; b. N.Y.C., Feb. 23, 1935; m. Arlene Kaplan; children: Risa Anne, Alyse Renee. BBA, Northwestern U., 1956; JD, U. Mich., 1959. Bar: Fla. 1960, Ill. 1960, Mich. 1960, U.S. Dist. Ct. (so. dist.) Fla. 1960, U.S. Ct. Appeals (5th cir.) 1960, U.S. Supreme Ct. 1971, U.S. Ct. Appeals (11th cir.) 1986. Legal research asst. to presiding justice U.S. Ct. Appeals (3d cir.), Miami Beach, 1962-63; sr. ptnr. Fromberg, Fromberg, Gross, Shore, Lewis & Rogel P.A., Miami, Hallandale, Coral Gables, Fla., 1967—; mayor City of Miami Beach, 1983-85; commr. City of Miami Beach, 1981-83. Adv. council Barry U.; sec. Temple Emanu-El, Miami Beach. Recipient Dist. Service award Latin Builders Assn., Dist. Service award Temple Emanu-El, Outstanding Pub. Leader award Greater Miami C. of C., 1985. Mem. ABA, Fla. Bar Assn. (continuing legal edn. com. 1966-73, vice chmn. 1970-71, rep. 1966-72, chmn. grievance com. 1970-71), Dade County Bar Assn. (chmn. 1971-72, vice chmn. 1972-73), Assn. Trial Lawyers Am., Acad. Fla. Trial Lawyers; Greater Miami Jewish Fedn. (co-chmn. family league, bd. dirs., bd. dirs. adv. com., exec. com., vice-chmn. non-local allocations com.). Lodges: Rotary, B'nai B'rith (sr. internat. v.p., mem. adminstrv. com., bd. govs., personnel com., v.p., chmn. fund raising com., chmn. legacy devel. and deferred giving program, fin. mgmt. com., past pres. Dist. 5, nat. commr. Anti-Defamation League, recipient Label A. Katz award), Elks (recipient Dist. Service award). Family and matrimonial, Personal injury, Federal civil litigation. Office: 420 S Dixie Hwy 3d Floor Coral Gables FL 33146

FROMHERCZ, STEPHEN P., lawyer; b. Cleveland Heights, Ohio, May 17, 1956; s. Steve E. and Dorothy R. (Szasz) F. BSBA in Acctg., Xavier U., 1978; MBA in Fin., JD, Loyola U., Chgo., 1982. Bar: Ohio 1982. Tax atty. Ernst & Whinney, Cleve., 1982-84, Progressive Corp., Cleve., 1982—. Active Citizens League, Cleve., 1984—. Mem. ABA. Address: 6724 Metro Park Dr Mayfield Village OH 44143

FROMHOLZ, HALEY JAMES, lawyer; b. Greenwich, Conn., Nov. 1, 1938; s. Adolph Stanley and Terese V. (Haley) F.; m. Anita Alden Bridgman, Aug. 6, 1965; children—Ann Haley, Julia Marie. Student, Dartmouth Coll., 1956-60; A.B., NYU, 1964; LL.B., Duke U., 1967. Bar: Calif. 1967, U.S. Dist. Ct. (no. dist.) Calif. 1967, U.S. Ct. Appeals (9th cir.) 1967, U.S. Dist. Ct. (cen. dist.) Calif. 1980. Assoc. Morrison & Foerster, San Francisco, 1967-73; ptnr. Morrison & Foerster, 1973-80; mgn. ptnr., litigation ptnr. Morrison & Foerster, Los Angeles, 1980—. Contbr. writings to legal jours. Trustee San Francisco County Law Library, 1980. Fellow Am. Bar Found.; mem. ABA (chmn. sect. sci. and tech. 1976-77), State Bar Calif. (chmn. com. computers and law 1972-74, chmn. com. county law libraries 1975-76), Bar Assn. San Francisco (chmn. clients relations com. 1975), Practicing Law Inst. (lectr. 1975, 76, 82), Nat. Inst. on Computers in Litigation. Republican. Club: Jonathan (Los Angeles). Computer, Federal civil litigation, State civil litigation. Home: 1325 Circle Dr San Marino CA 91108 Office: Morrison & Foerster 333 S Grand Ave 38th Floor Los Angeles CA 90071

FROMMER, WILLIAM S., lawyer; b. Bklyn., Sept. 27, 1942; s. Herbert S. and Molly B. (Stegman) F.; m. Karen Beagle, July 31, 1966; 1 dau., Hillary. B.E.E., Cornell U., 1965; J.D., Am. U., 1969. Bar: N.Y. 1970, U.S. Patent Office, 1970, U.S. Ct. Customs and Patent Appeals 1975, U.S. Ct. Appeals (fed. cir.) 82, U.S. Supreme Ct. 1985. Assoc. Marn & Jangarathis, N.Y.C., 1969-73, Curtis, Morris & Safford, P.C., N.Y.C., 1973-76, ptnr., 1976—. Mem. N.Y. Patent Law Assn., ABA, N.Y. State Bar Assn., Internat. Patent and Trade Assn., Internat. Bar Assn. Mem. staff, contbr. Am. U. Law Rev., 1967-69. Patent, Trademark and copyright. Office: 530 Fifth Ave New York NY 10036

FROST, CHARLES ESTES, JR., lawyer; b. Houston, Aug. 17, 1950; s. Charles Estes and Lucille Fourmey (DeGravelles) F. BS, U.S. Mil. Acad., 1972; MBA, Armstrong State Coll., 1979; JD, U. Tex., 1981. Bar: Tex. 1982, U.S. Dist. Ct. (no. and so. dists.) Tex. Commd. 2d lt. U.S. Army, 1972, advanced through grades to capt., 1979; resigned from active duty 1979; assoc. Strasburger & Price, Dallas, 1982-84, Chamberlain, Hrdlicka et al, Houston, 1985—. Note editor: Tex. Law Rev., U. Tex. Law Sch.1981-82. Served to maj. USAR, 1979—. Mem. ABA, Houston Bar Assn. Republican. Episcopalian. Avocations: running, church. Federal civil litigation, State civil litigation. Office: Chamberlain Hrdlicka et al 1400 Citicorp Ctr 1200 Smith St Houston TX 77002

FROST, GREGORY LYNN, judge; b. Newark, Ohio, Apr. 17, 1949; s. William Kenneth and Mildred Ellen (Swick) F.; m. Kathleen Schaller, May 27, 1972; children—Wesley Adam, Nicholas Brian, Andrew Gregory. B.A., Wittenberg U., 1971; J.D., Ohio No. U., 1974. Bar: Ohio 1974, U.S. Supreme Ct. 1979. Asst. Licking County prosecutor, Newark, Ohio, 1974-78; ptnr. Schaller, Frost & Hostetter, Newark, 1974-82; commn. clk. Heath' Civil Service Commn., Ohio, 1979-82; judge Licking County Mcpl. Ct., Newark, 1983—. Pres. exec. com. Licking County council Boy Scouts Am., 1985, mem. exec. com., 1980—, troop com. chmn., 1975—; bd. dirs. Licking Alcoholism Prevention Program, 1983—; county chmn. Licking County Heart Fund, 1981; mem. at large bd. dirs. Nat. Council Alcoholism, 1984-85; v.p. Symposiarchs Nat. Orgn., 1984-85; merit examiner for citizenship in community, nation, world and law Boy Scouts Am., 1976—; mem. Licking County Republican Exec. Com., 1975-82, ex-officio mem., 1983—; mem. Licking County Alcoholism Prevention Program, 1984—. Recipient Superior Jud. Conduct award Ohio Supreme Ct., 1983, 84, 85, Outstanding Young Man of Yr. award Jaycees, 1983, Service to Mankind award Moundbuilder's Sertoma Club, 1983, Disting. Service award Jaycee's, 1983, Wildlife award Ohio Dept. Natural Resources, 1984, Outstanding Service award Licking County Shrine Club, 1983-84, Cert. of Appreciation, Northwest Licking Kiwanis Club, 1983, Outstanding Community Service award Licking Alcoholism Prevention Program, 1984, Cert. of Appreciation, Buckeye Lake Fire Dept., 1984. Mem. Am. Judicature Soc., ABA, Ohio Jud. Conf., Ohio Mcpl. Judges Assn., Ohio State Bar Assn., Licking County Bar Assn., Newark Area C. of C., Ohio State Assn. Twp. Trustees and Clks. (hon.), Phi Mu Delta. Republican. Clubs: Teheran Grotto, Newark Rebounders, Newark Manennerchor, Big Red Touchdown, Symposiarchs, Ducks Unltd., Licking County Old Timers Athletic Assn. Lodges: Masons, Shriners, Elks, Moose, Rotary. Avocations: golf; fishing; swimming. Home: 229 Queens Dr N Newark OH 43055 Office: Licking County Mcpl Ct 40 W Main St Newark OH 43055

FROST, JEROME KENNETH, lawyer; b. Troy, N.Y., July 4, 1939; s. Carl Kenneth and Madeline May (Michel) F.; m. Carol Ann Brown, May 16, 1967; children—Arthur, Carl, Anya, Jonah, Jerome. B.A., Siena Coll., 1962; J.D., Boston Coll., 1965. Bar: N.Y. 1965, U.S. Dist. Ct. (no. dist.) N.Y. 1965, U.S. Ct. Appeals (2d cir.) 1982. Assoc. Wagar, Taylor, Howd & Brearton, Troy, 1965-66; ptnr. Lee, LeForestier & Frost, Troy, 1967-75; sole practice, Troy, 1976—; asst. corp. counsel City of Troy, 1970-73. Editor Boston Coll. Law Rev., 1965. Player, agt. Lansingburgh Little League, 1982—. Presdl. scholar Boston Coll., 1965. Mem. Rensselaer County Bar Assn., Order of Coif, Alpha Sigma Nu, Delta Epsilon Sigma, Alpha Kappa Alpha, Alpha Mu Gamma. Roman Catholic. Personal injury, Family and matrimonial, Criminal. Home: 20 Deepkill Ln Troy NY 12182 Office: 68 2d St Troy NY 12180

FROST, NORMAN COOPER, telephone company executive; b. Nashville, Feb. 6, 1923; s. Norman and Anna Martha (Cooper) F.; m. Katherine McDonald Shapard, Nov. 25, 1948; children: Kathy, Norman Cooper. B.A., Vanderbilt U., 1943, J.D., 1948. Bar: Tenn. 1946, Ga. 1954, N.Y. State bar 1964, D.C. bar 1965. Practiced in Nashville, 1948-50; trust officer Nashville Trust Co., 1952-53; atty. So. Bell Telephone Co., Atlanta, 1953-61; gen. atty. So. Bell Telephone Co., 1961-62; atty. Am. Tel. & Tel. Corp., N.Y.C., 1962-66; asst. gen. atty. Am. Tel. & Tel. Corp., 1966-67; v.p., gen. counsel South Central Bell, Birmingham, Ala., 1968-83; exec. v.p., gen. counsel Bell South Corp., Atlanta, 1983—. Served with USMCR, 1943-46, 50-52. Mem. Am., Ga., Tenn., N.Y., D.C. bar assns., Order of Coif. Methodist. Home: 9955 Huntcliff Trace Atlanta GA 30338 Office: 4515 Southern Bell Ctr Atlanta GA 30375

FROST, SMITH GIBBONS, lawyer; b. Snowflake, Ariz., Feb. 26, 1942; s. Austin and Rizpah Jayne (Gibbons) F.; m. Martha L. Litster, Dec. 18, 1969; children—Jennifer, Nathan, Paul, Allen, Joel, Stephen, Laurie Jayne. B.A., Brigham Young U., 1967; J.D., Ariz. State U., 1970. Bar: Ariz. 1970, U.S. Dist. Ct. Ariz. 1970. Assoc. Axline & Johnson, Holbrook, Ariz., 1970-72; sole practice, Show Low, Ariz., 1972-73; sr. ptnr. Frost & Porter, Show Low, 1973; city atty., Holbrook, Ariz., 1974-82; U.S. magistrate part time, 1972-75. Chmn. Community Bicentennial Com., 1976; mem. exec. bd. Grand Canyon council Boy Scouts Am., 1978—; founder Northland Pioneer Coll. Found. Mem. Assn. Trial Lawyers Am., Ariz. Trial Lawyers Assn., Navajo-Apache Bar Assn. (v.p. 1975-77), Show Low C. of C. (past pres.). Mormon. Lodge: Rotary. Columnist White Mountain Ind. newspaper, 1980-86, The Falcon, 1986—. Personal injury, General practice, Probate. Home: Box 2855 Low AZ 85901 Office: 1020 E Deuce of Clubs Show Low AZ 85901

FRUCCO, JOHN PETER, lawyer; b. New Rochelle, N.Y., Feb. 21, 1942; s. John J. and Mary M. (Inello) F.; children—John D., Karen Lynn, Jennifer Ann. B.A., U. Dayton, 1963; LL.D., N.Y. Law Sch., 1967. Bar: N.Y. 1967, U.S. Supreme Ct. 1971, U.S. Dist. Ct. (so. dist.) N.Y. 1972, U.S. Tax Ct. 1980, U.S. Ct. Mil. Appeals 1968. Asst. dist. atty. Western County, White Plains, N.Y., 1972-74; confidential law sec. Supreme Ct. Justice, White Plains, 1974-79; atty. Russo, Lombardi & Frucco, White Plains, 1979-81; sole practice, White Plains, 1981-85, ptnr. Bender, Bodnar & Frucco, White Plains, 1985—. Town justice Town of Yorktown (N.Y.), 1984—. Vice pres. Am. Com. on Italian Migration, Westchester County, 1975—; publicity chmn. Boystown of Italy, Westchester County 1981—. Served to capt. U.S. Army, 1968-72. Mem. Yorktown Bar Assn. (pres. 1979), Westchester Bar Assn., N.Y. State Bar Assn. Republican. Roman Catholic. Lodge: Elks (Yorktown). State civil litigation, Family and matrimonial, Personal injury. Office: 2 William St White Plains NY 10601

FRUG, GERALD E., legal educator; b. 1939. A.B., U. Calif.-Berkeley, 1960; J.D., Harvard U., 1963. Bar: Calif. 1964, N.Y. 1969. Frank Knox fellow London Sch. Econs., 1963-64; law clk. to chief justice Supreme Ct. Calif., 1964-65; assoc. Heller, Ehrman, White & McAuliffe, San Francisco, 1965-66;

spl. asst. to chmn. EEOC, 1966-69; assoc. Cravath, Swaine & Moore, N.Y.C., 1969-70; gen. counsel Health Services Adminstrn., N.Y.C., 1970-72, 1st dep. adminstr., 1972-73, adminstr., 1973-74; assoc. prof. U. Pa. Law Sch., Phila., 1974-78, prof., 1978-81; prof. Harvard U. Law Sch., 1981—. Mem. Phi Beta Kappa. Legal education. Office: Harvard U Dept of Law Cambridge MA 02138

FRUMENTO, AEGIS JOSEPH, lawyer; b. Sydney, New South Wales, Australia, Aug. 4, 1954; came to U.S., 1956; s. Salvador and Teresa (Rinaldi) F.; m. Jane Daggett Vagnoni, Aug. 11, 1979. AB cum laude, Harvard U., 1976; JD, NYU, 1979. Bar: N.Y. 1980, U.S. Dist. Ct. (so. and ea. dists.) N.Y. 1980, U.S. Ct. Appeals (3d cir.) 1984, U.S. Tax Ct. 1985, U.S. Ct. Appeals (2d cir.) 1985, U.S. Supreme Ct. 1986. Assoc. Schulte, Roth & Zabel, N.Y.C., 1979-86. Editor NYU Rev. Law and Social Change, 1978-79. Mem. ABA, N.Y. State Bar Assn., Assn. of Bar of City of N.Y. Roman Catholic. Avocations: computer programming, reading, writing, running, skiing. Federal civil litigation, State civil litigation, Securities. Home: 315 E 77th St #3J New York NY 10021 Office: 880 3d Ave New York NY 10022

FRUTKIN, HARVEY LEE, lawyer; b. San Antonio, Apr. 22, 1945; s. Arthur Marvin and Fay (Feren) F.; m. Maxine Doris Rosenberg, June 22, 1969; children—Jonathan, Elliott, Rachel. A.B. cum laude, Ohio U., 1967; J.D. magna cum laude, U. Mich., 1971. Bar: Ohio 1972. Assoc. Cavitch, Familo & Durkin, Cleve., 1972-74, ptnr., 1975—; lectr. law Case Western Res. U. Law Sch., Cleve., 1977-81. Author: Tax Planning for Executive Compensation, 1983. Co-editor: Current Legal Forms, 1976—. Mem. Greater Cleve. Bar Assn. (participant Tax Inst. 1974—). Jewish. Club: Mid-Day (Cleve.). Pension, profit-sharing, and employee benefits, Corporate taxation, General corporate. Home: 32300 Chestnut Ln Pepper Pike OH 44124 Office: Cavitch Familo & Durkin East Ohio Bldg 14th Floor Cleveland OH 44114

FRY, DONALD CURTIS, lawyer; b. Killeen, Tex., June 23, 1955; s. Lloyd Curtis and Kathleen (Gordy) F.; m. Bonnie F. Kreamer, Apr. 19, 1984. BS in Polit. Sci., Frostburg State Coll., 1977; JD, U. Balt., 1979. Bar: Md. 1980, U.S. Dist. Ct. Md. 1980, U.S. Bankruptcy Ct. 1981, U.S. Ct. Appeals (4th cir.) 1984. Assoc. Lentz, Hooper, Jacobs & Blevins, Bel Air, Md., 1980-81; ptnr. Miller, Fry & Protokowicz, Bel Air, 1981—; spl. asst. atty. gen. State Hwy. Adminstrn., 1987—. Citizen mem. Bd. Estimates for Harford County, Md., 1978-82; mem. Dem. Cen. Com., Harford County, Md., 1980-82, 86—; mgr. campaign Donald P. Hutchinson for U.S. Senate, Balt., 1986. Named one of Outstanding Young Men Am., 1979, 85. Mem. ABA, Md. Bar Assn. (local bar liason com. 1984), Harford County Bar Assn. (chmn. social activities 1984—), Bel Air Jaycees (pres. 1984, v.p. 1983). Methodist. Avocations: golf, politics. State civil litigation, General corporate, General practice. Home: 805 Chesney Ln Bel Air MD 21014 Office: Miller Fry & Protokowicz 5 S Hickory Ave Bel Air MD 21014

FRY, MORTON HARRISON, II, communications company executive, lawyer; b. N.Y.C., May 15, 1946; s. George Thomas Clark and Louise Magdalen (Cronin) F.; m. Patricia Laylin Coffin, May 29, 1971. A.B., Princeton U., 1968; J.D., Yale U., 1971. Bar: N.Y. 1973, U.S. Ct. Mil. Appeals 1973, U.S. Dist. Ct. (so. dist.) N.Y. 1975, U.S. Dist. Ct. (ea. dist.) N.Y. 1975, U.S. Ct. Appeals (2d cir.) 1975. Assoc. Cravath, Swaine & Moore, N.Y.C., 1971-72, 75-79; dep. gen. counsel Columbia Pictures Industries, Inc., N.Y.C., 1979-81; v.p., gen. counsel Warner Home Video Inc., N.Y.C., 1982-83; exec. v.p., gen. counsel Warner Electronic Home Services, N.Y.C., 1983-84; acquisitions and divestitures counsel Warner Communications Inc., N.Y.C., 1984-85, pres., chief exec. officer, bd. dirs. The Congress Video Group, Inc., 1986-87, ; mem. governing bd. Council N.Y. Law Assocs., 1976-78, presiding officer, 1977-78; counsel Hosp. Audiences Inc., N.Y.C., 1979-82; Served to capt. USMC, 1972-75. AIA grantee, 1970-71. Mem. ABA, Assn. Bar City N.Y., Liberal Democrat. Congregationalist. Clubs: University (N.Y.C.); Point O'Woods (N.Y.); Campus (Princeton). General corporate, Entertainment, Communications. Home: 719 Greenwich St New York NY 10014

FRY, STEPHEN, lawyer; b. Portsmouth, Va., Dec. 31, 1948. BS in Journalism, U. Fla., 1975, JD, 1977. Bar: Fla. 1978. Asst. county atty. Martin County, Stuart, Fla., 1978-80, county atty., 1980-82; ptnr. Boose, Ciklin, Martens & Fry, Stuart, 1982-86, Fry & Olenick, P.A., Stuart, 1986—. Mem. econ. council Martin County, Inc. Served with U.S. Army, 1969-72. Mem. Fla. Bar Assn., Martin County Bar Assn. Administrative and regulatory, Real property. Office: Fry & Olenick PA 900 E Ocean Blvd Suite 120 Stuart FL 33494

FRYBURGER, LAWRENCE BRUCE, lawyer; b. Cin., Apr. 7, 1933. BA, U. Cin., 1956; LLB with honors, U. Tex., 1958. Bar: Tex. 1959, U.S. Dist. Ct. (we. dist.) Tex. 1961, U.S. Ct. Appeals (5th cir.) 1962, U.S. Supreme Ct. 1963, U.S. Dist. Ct. (so. dist.) Tex. 1972, U.S. Dist. Ct. (no. dist.) Tex. 1981, U.S. Ct. Appeals (11th cir.) 1981. Sole practice San Antonio, Tex., 1959—; spl. prof. labor relations law San Antonio Coll., 1968—. Contbr. articles to law jours.; mem. editorial bd. Tex. Lawyers Practice Guide, 1964. Mem. San Antonio Bd. Adjustment, 1969-72; program chmn. EEO compliance and EEOC case processing procedures Small Bus. Council,1981—; chmn. lawyer's div. United Fund, San Antonio and Bexar County, 1967-68. Sutphin scholar U. Cin., 1956. Mem. ABA, Tex. Bar Assn. (program chmn. current devels. in labor law inst. 1978, mem. counsel labor law sect. 1978-80), Tex. Young Lawyer's Inst. (originator), San Antonio Bar Assn. (chmn. lawyer reference plan 1970-73), Tex. Young Lawyers Assn. (bd. dirs. 1964-66), San Antonio Young Lawyer's Assn. (pres. 1963-64, Outstanding Young Lawyer award 1967), Phi Delta Phi, Sigma Chi. Labor, Civil rights, Health. Office: 1441 Frost Bank Tower San Antonio TX 78205

FRYD, ROBERT, lawyer; b. Bklyn., Nov. 20, 1952; s. Benjamin and Ida (Rapaport) F.; married; 1 child, Brian Benjamin. BA, CUNY, Flushing, 1974; JD, U. Chgo., 1977. Bar: N.Y. 1978, U.S. Dist. Ct. (so. and ea. dists.) N.Y. 1978, U.S. Ct. Appeals (2d cir.) 1986. Assoc. Cahill, Gordon & Reindel, N.Y.C., 1977-81; assoc. Warshaw, Burstein, Cohen, Schlesinger & Kuh, N.Y.C., 1981-84, ptnr., 1985—. Mem. ABA, Assn. Bar of City of N.Y. Federal civil litigation, State civil litigation. Office: Warshaw Burstein Cohen et al 555 Fifth Ave New York NY 10017

FRYE, HELEN JACKSON, U.S. dist. judge; b. Klamath Falls, Oreg., Dec. 10, 1930; d. Earl and Elizabeth (Kirkpatrick) Jackson; m. Perry Holloman, July 10, 1980; children—Eric, Karen, Heidi. B.A. in English; B.A. with honors, U. Oreg., 1953, M.A., 1960, J.D., 1966. Bar: Oreg. bar 1966. Public sch. tchr. Oreg., 1956-63; pvt. practice Eugene, 1966-71; circuit ct. judge State of Oreg., 1971-80; U.S. dist judge Dist. Oreg. Portland, 1980—. Judicial administration. Office: US District Courthouse 706 US Courthouse 620 SW Main St Portland OR 97205

FRYE, HENRY E., state supreme court justice; b. Ellerbe, N.C., Aug. 1, 1932; s. Walter A. and Pearl Alma (Motley) F.; m. Edith Shirley Taylor, Aug. 25, 1956; children: Henry Eric, Harlan Elbert. B.S. in Biol. Scis., A & T U., N.C., 1953; J.D. with honors, U. N.C., 1959. Bar: N.C. 1959. Asst. U.S. atty. (middle dist.), N.C., 1963-65; prof. law N.C. Central U., Durham, 1965-67; practice law Greensboro, N.C., 1967-83; rep. N.C. Gen. Assembly, 1969-80, N.C. Senate, 1980-82; assoc. justice N.C. Supreme Ct., Raleigh, 1983—; organizer, pres. Greensboro Nat. Bank, 1971-80; dir. N.C. Mut. Life Ins. Co., 1972-82. Deacon tchr. youth Sunday Sch. Providence Baptist Ch. Served to capt. USAF, 1953-55. Fellow AAAS; mem. ABA, N.C. Bar Assn., Greensboro Bar Assn., Nat. Bar Assn., Kappa Alpha Psi. Judicial administration. Office: North Carolina Supreme Ct Justice Bldg PO Box 1841 Raleigh NC 27602

FRYE, JOHN H., III, judge; b. Birmingham, Ala., Aug. 10, 1936; s. John H. Jr. and Helen Lewis (Johnston) F.; m. Helen Susan Durkin, Sept. 30, 1967 (dec. Feb. 1977); m. Lucille Ann Bowie, Apr. 21, 1979. BA, Davidson Coll., 1958; LLB, Vanderbilt U., 1965. Bar: Tenn. 1965, D.C. 1966, U.S. Dist. Ct. D.C. 1966, U.S. Ct. Appeals (D.C. cir.) 1966. Assoc. Barnes, Richardson & Colburn, Washington, 1965-69; ptnr. Frye & Keeffe, Washington, 1969-73; counsel atomic safety and licensing bd. panel AEC, Washington, 1973-75; counsel atomic safety and licensing bd. panel U.S. Nuclear Regulatory Commn., Washington, 1975-81, adminstrv. judge, 1981—; adj. faculty Am. U. Coll. Law, Washington, 1979-85. Bd. dirs. 4200 Cathedral Ave. Condominium Assn., Washington, 1978. Served to 1st lt. AUS, 1958-61. Mem. ABA, Fed. Bar Assn. (chmn. internat. law council 1973-78, disting. service award 1973-78, nat. council 1973-78, chmn. adminstrv. law com. 1983-85), D.C. Bar Assn., Tenn. Bar Assn. Republican. Episcopalian. Club: West River Sailing (Galesville, Md.). Administrative and regulatory, Nuclear power, Environment. Home: 5002 Baltimore Ave Bethesda MD 20816 Office: US Nuclear Regulatory Commn Washington DC 20555

FRYER, HUGH NEVIN, lawyer; b. Phila., June 11, 1938; s. William Hugh and Myrtle S. Fryer; m. Geraldine Rose Caruse, Nov. 8, 1964; children: Jacqueline C., Robert H., John A., James N. AB, Brown U., 1960; LLB, U. Pa., 1963. Bar: N.Y. 1966, U.S. Ct. Appeals (2d cir.) 1968, U.S. Supreme Ct. 1969, U.S. Ct. Appeals (D.C. cir.) 1982, D.C. 1983. Assoc. Dewey, Ballantine, Bushby, Palmer & Wood, N.Y.C., 1963-71; ptnr. Dewey, Ballantine, Bushby, Palmer & Wood, N.Y.C. and Washington, 1971—. Served with USAR, 1963-69. Mem. ABA, Internat. Bar Assn., N.Y. State Bar Assn., Assn. of Bar of City of N.Y., Am. Judicature Soc., N.Y. Law Inst. Democrat. Episcopalian. Clubs: Yacht, N.Y. Yacht, Nat. Dem., Down Town, Knickerbocker. Federal civil litigation, Antitrust, State civil litigation. Home: 7200 Glenbrook Rd Bethesda MD 20814 Office: Dewey Ballantine Bushby Palmer & Wood 1775 Pennsylvania Ave NW Washington DC 20006

FRYMAN, VIRGIL THOMAS, JR., lawyer; b. Maysville, Ky., Apr. 9, 1940; s. Virgil Thomas and Elizabeth Louis (Marshall) F. A.B. cum laude, Harvard U., 1962, LL.B., 1966. Bar: N.Y. 1967, U.S. Ct. Appeals (2d cir.) 1967, U.S. Dist. Ct. (so. and ea. dists.) N.Y. 1968, U.S. Supreme Ct. 1970. Assoc. Cravath, Swaine & Moore, N.Y.C., 1966-73; asst. U.S. atty. U.S. Dist. Ct. (so. dist) N.Y., N.Y.C., 1973-78; assoc. gen. counsel Price Waterhouse, N.Y.C., 1978-86; staff counsel U.S. Ho. of Reps. select com. to investigate covert arms transactions with Iran, 1987—. Mem. ABA, Assn. Bar City of N.Y. Democrat. Episcopalian. Clubs: Harvard, West Side Tennis (N.Y.C.), Idle Hour Country (Lexington, Ky.). Contbr. to Proving Federal Crimes, 6th edit., 1976. Federal civil litigation, State civil litigation, Criminal. Home: 115 Rumsey Ct SE Washington DC 20003 Office: The Capitol H-419 Washington DC 20515

FUERSTENBERG, JAMES P., lawyer; b. Chgo., Dec. 12, 1954; s. Samuel and Eileen (Stone) F. BS in Mktg., Acctg., U. Ill., Chgo., 1977; JD, DePaul U., 1980. Bar: Ill. 1980, U.S. Dist. Ct. (no. dist.) Ill. 1980, U.S. Ct. Claims 1985. Assoc. Law Office of B.B. Hirsch, Chgo., 1980, Law Offices of B. O. Adolph & Bruggeman, Chgo., 1981-83, Howard, Pomper and Assocs., Chgo., 1983; atty., advisor Gen. Services Adminstrn. Office of Regional Counsel, Chgo., 1983—. Mem. ABA, Ill. Bar Assn., Porsche Club of Am., Gen. Techs. (Chgo.) (mktg. advisor 1977—). Government contracts and claims, General corporate, Labor. Home: 624 Elder Ln Winnetka IL 60093 Office: Gen Services Adminstrn Office of Regional Counsel 230 S Dearborn St Chicago IL 60604

FUHRER, ARTHUR K., lawyer, theatrical agency executive; b. N.Y.C., Oct. 19, 1926; s. Isadore and Toby (Schorr) Fuhrer; m. Lenore R. Lewis; children—Laura A., Robert A., David A. LL.B., Bklyn. Law Sch., 1949; postgrad. NYU, 1951, 52. Bar: N.Y. 1950, U.S. Dist Ct. (so. dist.) N.Y. 1951, U.S. Supreme Ct. 1977. Assoc. firm Sargoy and Stein, N.Y.C., 1951-52, firm Andrew D. Weinberger, N.Y.C., 1952-54; lawyer William Morris Agy., Inc., N.Y.C., 1954-75, v.p., 1975—; co-chmn. Television and Motion Picture Seminar Practicing Law Inst., 1973. Contbr.: Lindey on Entertainment and the Law. Entertainment. Office: William Morris Agy Inc 1350 Ave of Americas New York NY 10019

FUHRER, LEONARD, lawyer; b. Texarkana, Ark., Mar. 3, 1929; s. Jack H. and Belle (Friedman) F.; m. Eileen Patricia Miller, Dec. 24, 1955; children—Sara, Emily, Anne, Helen. B.A., Tulane U., 1950, LL.B., 1952. Bar: La., 1952, U.S. Ct. Mil. Apls., 1953, U.S. Supreme Ct., 1970. Ptnr., Gravel, Sheffield & Fuhrer, 1955-63, Neblett & Fuhrer, 1963-79; sr. ptnr. Fuhrer, Flournoy, Hunter & Morton, Alexandria, La., 1979—; mem. com. profl. responsibility La. Sup. Ct., 1971-81; lectr. legal seminars. Served to 1st lt. JAGC, AUS, 1952-55. Mem. La. Bar Assn., Alexandria Bar Assn. (pres. 1974), La. Trial Lawyers Assn. (pres. 1973), Am. Trial Lawyers Assn. Republican. Admiralty, Personal injury, Workers' compensation. Home: 2802 Elliott St Alexandria LA 71301 Office: 900 Foisy Ave Alexandria LA 71301

FUJIMOTO, WESLEY MINORU, lawyer; b. Papaaloa, Hawaii, Jan. 13, 1954; s. Frank Shigeo and Shizue (Inomoto) F.; m. Jennifer Vieira, Aug. 22, 1977. BA, U. Mich., 1976; JD, Georgetown U., 1979. Bar: D.C. 1979, Hawaii 1982. Atty. advisor, office of adminstrn. law judges Dept. Labor, Washington and San Francisco, 1979-81; ptnr. Torkildson, Katz, Jossem, Fonseca & Moore, Honolulu, 1981—. Bd. dirs. Arthritis Found., Honolulu, 1986—. Workers' compensation, Labor. Office: Torkildson Katz Jossem Fonseca & Moore 700 Bishop St Amfac Bldg Honolulu HI 96813

FUJIYAMA, RODNEY MICHIO, lawyer; b. Honolulu, Aug. 1, 1945; s. Wallace Sachio Fujiyama and Jean (Osumi) Shin; m. Vicki Ann Yamaguchi, Dec. 28, 1968; children—Christopher, Laurie, Sandra, Jonathan, Shannon. Student Oberlin Coll., 1963-64; B.A. with high honors, U. Hawaii, 1967; J.D., U. Calif.-San Francisco, 1970. Bar: Hawaii 1970, U.S. Dist. Ct. Hawaii 1970, U.S. Ct. Appeals (9th cir.) 1971. Assoc., Chuck & Fujiyama, Honolulu, 1970-74; assoc. Law Offices of Wallace S. Fujiyama, Honolulu, 1974; ptnr. Fujiyama, Duffy, Fujiyama, Honolulu, 1975-78, Fujiyama, Duffy, Fujiyama & Koshiba, Honolulu, 1979, Fujiyama, Duffy & Fujiyama, Honolulu, 1979—; per diem judge Dist. Ct. of 1st Cir., State of Hawaii, Honolulu, 1979-85. Mem. ABA, Hawaii State Bar Assn., Assn. Trial Lawyers Am., Phi Beta Kappa. General corporate, Administrative and regulatory, Real property. Office: Fujiyama Duffy & Fujiyama 1001 Bishop St 2650 Pacific Tower Honolulu HI 96813

FUJIYAMA, WALLACE SACHIO, lawyer; b. Honolulu, Aug. 8, 1925; s. George Susumu and Cornelia (Matsumoto) F.; m. Mildred Hatsue Morita, Jan. 24, 1959; children—Rodney Michio, Susan Misao, Keith Susumu. B.A., U. Hawaii, 1950; J.D., U. Cin., 1953. Bar: Hawaii 1954. Dep. atty. gen. State of Hawaii, Honolulu, 1954-56, examiner employment relations bd., 1956-59; ptnr. Chuck & Fujiyama, 1959-74; pres. Fujiyama, Duffy & Fujiyama, Honolulu, 1974—; dir. 1st Hawaiian Bank; chmn. adv. bd. Duty Free Shoppers Ltd., 1982—, lectr. William S. Richard Sch. Law, Honolulu, 1981—. Mem. Hawaii Statehood Commn., Honolulu, 1957-59; regent U. Hawaii, 1974-82; bd. dirs. Honolulu Symphony, 1983—, Hawaii Imin Centennial Corp., 1983—; mem. Palama Settlement Exec. Campaign Com., 1981—, Stadium Authority, 1982—. Served to pvt. U.S. Army, 1944-46. Mem. Hawaii Bar Assn. (bd. bar examiners 1962-82, pres. 1973, jud. appointments com. 1975), ABA mem. ho. of dels. 1973, active com. mem.), Hawaii Trial Lawyers Assn. (pres. 1971-79), Assn. Trial Lawyers Am., Calif. Trial Lawyers Assn., Fedn. Ins. Counsel, Def. Research Inst., Am. Judicature Soc., Trial Attys. Am., Am. Bd. Trial Advocates (pres. Hawaii chpt. 1980—), Am. Inn of Ct. (bencher 1982—), Hastings Ctr. Trial and Appellate Advocacy (bd. dirs. 1977—), Order of Coif, Phi Alpha Delta. Clubs: Honolulu Internat. Country (dir., gen. counsel), Waialae Country, Plaza (bd. dirs. 1985—). Federal civil litigation, State civil litigation, Banking. Home: 1803 Laukahi St Honolulu HI 96821 Office: Fujiyama Duffy & Fujiyama 1001 Bishop St 2650 Pacific Tower Honolulu HI 96813

FUKUMOTO, LESLIE SATSUKI, lawyer; b. Los Angeles, Mar. 10, 1955; s. Robert Fukumoto and Florence Teruko Kodama Kuroda. BA, U. Hawaii, 1977; JD, William S. Richard Sch. Law, 1980. Bar: Hawaii 1980, U.S. Dist. Ct. Hawaii 1980, U.S. Ct. Appeals (9th cir.) 1981. Dep. pub. defender State of Hawaii, Honolulu, 1980-81; assoc. Pyun, Kim & Okimoto, Honolulu, 1981-83; ptnr. Pyun, Okimoto & Fukumoto, Honolulu, 1983-84; sole practice Honolulu, 1984—; bd. dirs. Alexander Bros., Ltd., Honolulu. Assoc. editor U. Hawaii Law Rev., 1979-80. Mem. Assn. Trial Lawyers Am. Club: Honolulu. Personal injury, State civil litigation, Federal civil litigation. Office: 1001 Bishop St Pacific Tower 976 Honolulu HI 96813

FULLAM, JOHN P., federal judge; b. Gardenville, Pa., Dec. 10, 1921; s. Thomas L. and Mary Nolan F.; m. Alice Hilliar Freiheit, Apr. 15, 1950; children—Nancy, Sally, Thomas, Jeffrey. B.S., Villanova U., 1942; J.D., Harvard U., 1948. Atty. Bristol, Pa., 1948-60; judge Pa. Ct. Common Pleas, 7th Jud. Dist., 1960-66; judge U.S. Dist. Ct. (ea. dist.) Pa., Phila., 1966—, chief judge, 1986—. Democratic candidate for U.S. Congress, 1954, 56. Mem. Am. Judicature Soc., Pa. Bar Assn. Judicial administration. Office: 15614 US Courthouse 601 Market St Independence Mall W Philadelphia PA 19106

FULLEM, L. ROBERT, lawyer; b. Jersey City, Aug. 29, 1929; s. Laurence V. and Ethel A. Fullem; m. Elsbeth A. MacCulley, Feb. 6, 1954; children: John Christopher, Leslie Ann, Robert M., Terrance D. BA, Colgate U., 1951; LLB, Harvard U., 1954. Ptnr. Dewey, Ballantine, Bushby, Palmer & Wood, N.Y.C., 1958—; bd. dirs. Tesoro Petroleum Corp., San Antonio, Tex. Served to 1st lt. JAGC, U.S. Army, 1955-58. General corporate, Securities. Home: 236 Upper Mountain Ave Upper Montclair NJ 07043 Office: Dewey Ballantine Bushby Palmer & Wood 140 Broadway New York NY 10005

FULLER, ATHERTON, lawyer; b. Milton, Mass., June 8, 1916; s. Walter Atherton and Marjorie (Frank) F.; m. Elizabeth Louise Gillam, Aug. 9, 1941; children: Caroline Hutchinson, Cynthia Libby, Nancy Cameron, Walter A., David G. AB, Dartmouth Coll., 1938; LLB, Harvard U., 1941. Bar: Mass. 1941, Maine 1949, U.S. Dist. Ct. Mass., U.S. Dist. Ct. Maine. Assoc. Nutter, McCennen & Fish, Boston, 1941-49; sole practice Ellsworth, Maine, 1949-61; judge of probate Hancock County, Ellsworth, 1954-57; ptnr. Hale and Hamlin, Ellsworth, 1961-85, of counsel, 1985—; mem. Maine Probate Commn., 1976-80. Pres. Ellsworth C. of C., 1959; bd. dirs. Down East Family YMCA, Ellsworth, 1957—, Peninsula Retirement Group, Blue Hill, Maine, 1986—; mem. adv. com. Acadia Nat. Park, 1987—. Fellow Am. Coll. Probate Counsel; mem. ABA, Maine Bar Assn. (title standards com. 1967—, continuing legal edn. com. 1985—), Hancock County Bar Assn. (pres. 1962-67). Republican. Mem. Church of Christ. Lodge: Rotary. Avocations: canoeing, gardening. General corporate, Probate, Real property. Home: 1 Hillside Dr Ellsworth ME 04605 Office: Hale & Hamlin PO Box 729 Ellsworth ME 04605

FULLER, DAVID OTIS, JR., lawyer; b. Grand Rapids, Mich., May 28, 1939; s. David Otis and Virginia Chapin (Emery) F.; m. Isabelle Patrice Gigout, July 5, 1968; children: Thomas Andrew, Christian Scott, Pierre Emery, Margaret Isabelle. A.B., Wheaton Coll., 1961; J.D., Harvard U., 1964; postgrad. George Washington U., 1963, U. Paris, 1966. Bar: Mich 1964, N.Y. 1967, U.S. Sup. Ct. 1968. Law clk. U.S. Ho. of Reps. Judiciary Com., 1963; assoc. Amberg, Law & Fallon, Grand Rapids, 1964-65; asst. dist. atty. N.Y. County, 1966-72, law sec. to justice, 1972-73; corp. atty. Pan Am. World Airways, Inc., 1973-74; dep. gen. counsel Reader's Digest Assn., Inc., 1974-84; sole practice, N.Y.C., 1984-87; ptnr. Baker, Nelson & Williams, N.Y.C., 1987—; justice Tuckahoe Village, N.Y., 1986—; lectr. Am. Bar Assn., Practicing Law Inst., Bronx Community Coll. Bd. dirs. Family Consultation Service, Eastchester, N.Y., 1984—. Mem. ABA, Internat. Bar Assn., N.Y. State Bar Assn. (chmn. privacy com. 1982-84), Assn. Bar City N.Y. (comml. law com. 1984—), Am. Arbitration Assn. (arbitrator 1983—). Republican. Episcopalian. Clubs: Harvard (N.Y.C.), Shenorock Shore (Rye). Avocations: French, trout fishing, tennis, squash, ancient coins. Editor, Harvard Jour. on Legislation, 1962-64; contbr. articles to profl. jours. General corporate, Private international, Libel. Office: Baker Nelson & Williams 800 Third Ave New York NY 10022

FULLER, DIANA CLARE, lawyer; b. Omaha, Jan. 26, 1953; d. William Thomas and Dorothy Louise (Gallen) F. B.A., U. Nebr.-Omaha, 1974; J.D., Creighton U., 1977. Bar: Nebr. 1977, U.S. Dist. Ct. Nebr. Law clk. Nebr. 4th Jud. Dist., Omaha, 1978-79; atty. United Omaha, subs. Mut. Omaha, 1979-83; assoc. corp. counsel Mut. of Omaha, 1983-85; asst. v.p. Actuarial United of Omaha subs. Mut. of Omaha, 1985—. Explorers leader Boy Scouts Am., 1978-84; mem. membership com. bd. dirs. Campfire, Inc., Omaha, 1982-83; trustee Central Presbyterian Ch., Omaha, 1984—; mem. Leadership Omaha Program, 1986; bd. dirs. Omaha Folk Arts Alliance, 1981-83. Recipient award Boy Scouts Am., 1984, Merit award Boy Scouts Am., 1986; named one of 10 Outstanding Young Omahans, 1985. Mem. Omaha Fin. Planners (pres. 1982-83), Omaha Bar Assn. (pub. service com. 1983—), Nebr. Bar Assn. Democrat. Insurance, Legislative. Office: Mut Omaha Law Div Mutual of Omaha Plaza Omaha NE 68175

FULLER, DIANA L., lawyer; b. Morgantown, W.Va., Nov. 16, 1952; d. William Fleming and Amelia Marie (Lattanzi) F.; m. Robert Deeb Batey, July 21, 1979. B.S., W.Va. U., 1972, J.D., 1977. Bar: W.Va. 1977, U.S. Dist. Ct. (so. dist.) W.Va. 1977, Fla. 1978, U.S. Dist. Ct. (no., mid. and so. dists.) Fla., U.S. Ct. Appeals (5th and 11th cirs.). Law clk., ct. crier to chief judge U.S. Dist. Ct. (mid. dist.) Fla., Tampa, 1977-79, arbitrator arbitration program; ptnr. Fowler, White, Gillen, Boggs, Villareal & Banker, P.A., Tampa, 1983-85; ptnr. Smith & Fuller, P.A., Tampa, 1985—; lectr. in area of constrn. law. Contbr. articles to profl. jours. Mem. ABA (del. gen. assembly young lawyers div. 1984), Am. Judicature Soc., Fed. Bar Assn., Hillsborough County Bar Assn., W.Va. Trial Lawyers Assn., Greater Tampa C. of C., Phi Alpha Delta. Federal civil litigation, Construction. Home: 2418 W Palm Dr Tampa FL 33629 Office: 201 E Kennedy Blvd Suite 201 Tampa FL 33602

FULLER, MAURICE DELANO, JR., lawyer; b. San Francisco, Sept. 5, 1930; s. Maurice DeLano and Marie Elizabeth (Haub) F.; m. Martha Foster Hewett, June 13, 1953; children: Gwendolyn Hewitt, Katherine Hewitt, Daniel DeLano. AB with great distinction, Stanford U., 1953, JD, 1955. Bar: Calif. 1956, U.S. Dist. Ct. (no. dist.) Calif. 1956, U.S. Ct. Appeals (9th cir.) 1956, U.S. Supreme Ct. 1971. Assoc. Pillsbury, Madison & Sutro, San Francisco, 1956-63, ptnr., 1964—. Editor-in-chief Stanford Law Rev., 1954-55. Bd. visitors Stanford U. Law Sch., 1978-83, exec. com., 1979-83, chmn. 1981-82; mem. governing bd. Menlo Park (Calif.) City Sch. Dist., 1979-83; trustee Jr. Statesman Found., 1960-65. Served with USNR, 1950-51. Mem. ABA, Calif. Bar Assn., San Francisco Bar Assn., Santa Clara County Bar Assn., Order of Coif, Phi Beta Kappa. Republican. Club: Bohemian (sec., bd. dirs. 1979-82) (San Francisco). Contracts commercial, General corporate, Real property. Office: Pillsbury Madison & Sutro 225 Bush St San Francisco CA 94104 also: 333 W Santa Clara St San Jose CA 95113

FULLER, ROBERT FERREY, lawyer; b. St. Paul, Aug. 11, 1929; s. Robert Garfield and Gwendolen (Ferrey) F.; m. Marcelle McIntosh, June 6, 1953 (div. 1984); children—Julie, Gordon McIntosh; m. Sheila Nolan Mensing, May 25, 1985; stepchildren—Andrew Mensing, Allison Mensing. A.B. magna cum laude, Harvard, 1950, J.D., 1953. Bar: N.Y. bar 1956. Practiced in N.Y.C. with firm Patterson, Belknap & Webb, 1955-66; sec., gen. counsel Reuben H. Donnelley Corp., 1966-68; mng. dir. R.H. Donnelley Internat. Ltd., London, Eng., 1970-73; asst. sec., internat. counsel Am. Can Co., Greenwich, Conn., 1973-86; asst. sec., asst. gen. counsel Am. Can Co. (name changed to Am. Can Packaging Inc. 1986), 1986—; underwriting mem. LLoyd's , 1977—. Mem. Representative Town Meeting, Greenwich, 1986—. Served to lt. (j.g.) USCGR, 1953-55; lt. comdr. Res. ret. Mem. Am., Internat. bar assns., Assn. Bar City N.Y., Westchester-Fairfield Corp. Counsel Assn. Republican. Presbyn. Clubs: Harvard (N.Y.C.); Camp Fire (Chappaqua, N.Y.); Greenwich Country. Private international, Patent, General corporate. Office: American Can Packaging Inc American Ln 3C9 Greenwich CT 06836-2600

FULLER, ROBERT L(EANDER), lawyer; b. N.Y.C., Sept. 8, 1943; s. Robert (Leander) and Elsie (Virginia) F.; m. Barbara Braverman, Dec. 5, 1973. BS cum laude, SUNY, Stony Brook, 1971; MBA, Columbia U., 1972; JD, Cath. U., Washington, 1977; M. Laws in Taxation, Georgetown U., 1981. Bar: Md. 1977, D.C. 1978. Acct. Ernst & Whinney, N.Y.C., 1972-74; controller Warner-Jenkinson East Inc., N.Y.C., 1974-75, Atomic Indsl. Forum, Inc., N.Y.C., Washington, 1975-76; tax analyst So. Rwy. Co., Washington, 1976-78; asst. tax counsel CACI, Inc., Arlington, Va., 1978-84; tax counsel, mgr. VSE Corp., Alexandria, Va., 1984-87, dir. taxes Newmont Mining Corp., N.Y.C., 1987—. Served with USN, 1961-67. CPA, N.Y., D.C. Mem. ABA (tax sect.), Tax Execs. Inst. (chpt. dir. and officer 1983—), Am. Inst. CPA's, Mayflower Descs., SAR, Sigma Pi Sigma. Corporate taxation, Pension, profit-sharing, and employee benefits, State and local taxation. Home: 238 Christopher St Upper Mountain NJ 07043 Office: Newmont Mining Corp 200 Park Ave New York NY 10166

FULLER, S. WAYNE, lawyer; b. Cullman, Ala., June 7, 1950; s. Silas and Lois Nadine (Waldrep) F.; m. Joan Davidson, Aug. 3, 1974; children—Michael, Katie, Courtney. B.S. in Commerce and Bus., U. Ala., 1972; J.D., Samford U., 1975. Bar: Ala. 1975, U.S. Dist. Ct. Ala. 1976. Sole practice, Cullman, 1975—. Sec., treas., v.p., pres. Young Democrats, Cullman, 1975-79. Mem. Ala. Criminal Def. Lawyers, ABA, Cullman County Bar Assn., Ala. Bar Assn., Assn. Trial Lawyers Am. (sustaining), Ala. Trial Lawyers Assn. (bd. govs. 1980-83). Democrat. Lodge: Masons (32d degree). State civil litigation, Personal injury, General practice. Office: 413 1st Ave SW Cullman AL 35055

FULLER, SAMUEL ASHBY, lawyer; b. Indpls., Sept. 2, 1924; s. John L.H. and Mary (Ashby) F.; m. Betty Winn Hamilton, June 10, 1948; children—Mary Cheryl Fuller Hargrove, Karen E. Fuller Wolfe, Deborah R. B.S. in Gen. Engring, U. Cin., 1946, LL.B., 1947. Bar: Ohio 1948, Ind. 1951, Fla. 1984. Cleve. claims rep. Mfrs. and Mchts. Indemnity Co., 1947-48; claims supr. Indemnity Ins. Co. N.Am., 1948-50; with firm Stewart, Irwin, Gilliom, Fuller & Meyer (formerly Murray, Mannon, Fairchild & Stewart), Indpls., 1950-85, Lewis, Kappes, Fuller & Eads, 1985—; Pres., dir. Irsugo Consol. Mines, Ltd., 1953-80; dir. Ind. Pub. Health Found., Inc., 1972-84; staff instr. Purdue U. Life Ins. and Mktg. Inst., 1954-61; instr. Am. Coll. Life Underwriters, Indpls., 1964-74; mem. Ind. State Bd. Law Examiners, treas. 1985—. Bd. dirs. Southwest Social Centre, Inc., 1965-70; pres., dir. Westminster Village North, Inc. Fellow Am. Coll. Probate Counsel, Indpls. Bar Found.; mem. ABA, Ind. State Bar Assn. (bd. of mgrs. 1986—), 7th Circuit Bar Assn., Indpls. Bar Assn. (treas. 1961-62), Estate Planning Council Indpls. (pres. 1966), Mil. Order Loyal Legion U.S. (recorder 1970-76, comdr. 1977), Ind. Pioneer Soc., Central Ind. Bridge Assn., Inc. (pres. 1969), Brookshire Homeowners Assn. (pres. 1973), English Speaking Union (treas. Indpls. br. 1974-79), Beta Theta Pi, Phi Delta Phi. Republican. Mem. Disciples of Christ. Clubs: Mason. (Indpls.), Lawyers (Indpls.), Harbour Trees. Federal civil litigation, State civil litigation, Probate. Home: 8543 Quail Hollow Rd Indianapolis IN 46260 Office: One Am Sq Indianapolis IN 46282

FULLER, WILLIAM SIDNEY, lawyer; b. Auburn, Ala., Aug. 9, 1931; s. William Melton and Ernestine (Tolbert) F.; m. Joyce Jeffrey, Nov. 5, 1953; children: Jeffrey Melton, Barbara Rush. A.B., Auburn U., 1953; LL.B., U. Ala., 1956. Bar: Ala. 1956. Student asst. to dean U. Ala. Law Sch., 1952-53; law clk. to U.S. dist. judge, Montgomery, Ala., 1956-57; practice law Andalusla, 1957—; city atty. City of Andalusia; dir., sec. Covington County Bank; lectr. Southeastern Trial Inst.; mem. grievance com. Ala. State Bar, 1968-71, mem. bd. commrs., 1979-81; mem. law and contemporary affairs adv. council Auburn U. Author: Personal Injury Treatises. Mem. ABA, Ala., Covington County bar assns., Am. Trial Lawyers Assn., Am. Bd. Trial Advocates, Ala. Plaintiff Lawyers Assn., Ala. Trial Lawyers Assn. (pres. 1968), Phi Delta Phi, Kappa Alpha, Alpha Phi Omega. Presbyterian (elder, trustee, past chmn. bd. deacons Sunday sch. tchr.). Club: Andalusia (dir., pres. 1972). Federal civil litigation, State civil litigation, Personal injury. Home: 100 South Ridge Rd Andalusia AL 36420 Office: 28 S Court Sq Andalusia AL 36420

FULSHER, ALLAN ARTHUR, lawyer; b. Portland, Oreg., July 5, 1952; s. Rémy Walter and Barbara Lee (French) F.; m. Karen Louise Schmid, Dec. 28, 1974; children: Brian Rémy, Louise Katherine, Elizabeth Alane. BA in Biology, U. Oreg., 1974, BA in Econs., 1976; JD, U. of Pacific, 1979. Bar: Oreg. 1979, Calif. 1980, U.S. Dist. Ct. Oreg. 1980, U.S. Dist. Ct. (ea. dist.) Calif. 1981, U.S. Ct. Appeals (9th cir.) 1982, U.S. Dist. Ct. (no. dist.) Calif. 1985, U.S. Dist. Ct. (so. dist.) Calif. 1986. Assoc. Law Offices of Jacques B. Nichols P.C., Portland, 1979-82, Ragen, Roberts, O'Scannlain, Robertson & Neill, Portland, 1982-83; shareholder Bauer, Hermann, Fountain & Rhoades P.C., Portland, 1983—, v.p., 1984—; v.p., bd. dirs. Contemporary Motorsports, Ltd., 1986—. Editorial bd. mem. Oreg. Bus. and Corp. Law Digest, 1979—. Mem. commn.'s task force on securities and law reform Oreg. Corp., Portland, 1985. Mem. ABA (com. on fed. securities law regulation bus. and banking law sect. 1983—, com. on fed. securities litigation, litigation sect. 1985—), Oreg. Bar Assn., (exec. com. sect. on securities regulation 1984-85), Multnomah Bar Assn. Republican. Roman Catholic. Club: Multnomah Athletic (Portland). Avocations: basketball, automobile restoration, coaching youth and adult sports. Securities, General corporate, Banking. Home: 16399 SE Sager Rd Portland OR 97236-5509 Office: Bauer Hermann Fountain & Rhoades PC 1100 Commonwealth Bldg 421 SW 6th Ave Portland OR 97204

FULTON, ROBERT EDWARD, state agency administrator; b. St. Louis, Sept. 8, 1931; s. Hadley James and Gleta (Miinch) F.; m. Norma Maxine Heitman, May 10, 1952; children: Robin Edward, Colin Scott Cole, Kenton Wade. A.B., B.S. in Edn., Southeast Mo. State U., 1956; J.D., Am. U., 1960; M.S. in Bus. Adminstrn, George Washington U., 1965. Tchr. elem. schs. Patton, Mo., 1948-52; mgmt. analyst U.S. Navy Dept., Washington, 1956-59, AEC, Germantown, Md., 1959-66; nuclear cooperation specialist AEC, 1966-67, U.S. State Dept., 1967-68; community action adminstr. U.S. OEO, Chgo., 1968-70; regional dir. U.S. OEO, Boston, 1970-73, HEW, Boston, 1973-76; adminstr. Social and Rehab. Service, HEW, Washington, 1976-77; minority counsel U.S. Senate Budget Com., Washington, 1977-81, chief counsel, 1981-83; dir. Okla Dept. Human Services, Oklahoma City, 1983—. Mem. Bd. Social Services County of Montgomery, Md., 1978-81; chmn. nat. council of State Human Services Adminstrn., 1987—. Served with U.S. Army, 1952-54. Recipient Meritorious award for Achievement in Public Adminstrn. William A. Jump Meml. Found., 1967; Sec.'s Spl. citation HEW, 1977. Mem. ABA (bd. dirs. 1987—), Am. Public Welfare Assn. Republican. Public administration.. Office: Sequoyah Office Bldg State Capitol Compl PO Box 25352 Oklahoma City OK 73125

FULTON, ROBERT WRIGHT, lawyer; b. Mpls., Nov. 19, 1948; s. John Adams and Lois Marion (Cooper) F. BS, U. Minn., 1969; JD, U. Mich., 1981. Orderly Luth. Deaconness Hosp., Mpls., 1969-72; tchr. math. St. Peter's Sch., North St. Paul, 1972-74; pension actuary William M. Mercer, Mpls., 1974-78; assoc. Faegre & Benson, Mpls., 1981—. Mem. ABA, Minn. Bar Assn. Banking. Home: 2550 3d Ave S Minneapolis MN 55404 Office: Faegre & Benson 2300 Multifoods Tower Minneapolis MN 55402

FUNDERBURK, KENNETH LEROY, lawyer, banker; b. Phenix City, Ala., Sept. 13, 1936; s. Lemuel Leroy and Ruth (Duke) F.; m. Judy Barbee, Oct. 5, 1958; children—Rebecca, Kimberly, Eric. B.A., Howard Coll. (now Samford U.), 1957; LL.B., U. Ala., 1965. Bar: Ala. 1965, U.S. Dist. Ct. Ala. 1965, U.S. Ct. Appeals (5th cir.) 1965, U.S. Ct. Appeals (11th cir.) 1982, U.S. Supreme Ct. 1983. Ptnr. Phillips and Funderburk, Phenix City, 1965—. Chmn., Russell County Republican Party, Ala., 1973—. Recipient Appreciation award Russell County Bd. Realtors, 1977, 81; Ambassador award Alcazar Temple, 1982. Mem. Assn. Trial Lawyers Am., ABA, Ala. Criminal Def. Lawyers, Am. Coll. Mortgage Attys., Ala. Bar (bar commr. 1977-80), Russell County Bar Assn. (pres. 1977-80). Baptist. Lodge: Rotary. Contracts commercial, Personal injury, Real property. Home: 2000 38th Ct Phenix City AL 36877 Office: PO Box 1025 1313 Broad St Phenix City AL 36868

FUNDERBURK, RAYMOND, lawyer; b. Phila., Mar. 2, 1944; s. Walter and Inez (Prince) F. AA, Olive-Harvey Coll., 1972; BA, U. Ill., 1974; MPA, Roosevelt U., 1975; JD, U. Ill., 1978. Bar: Ill. 1979, U.S. Dist. Ct. (no. dist.) Ill. 1979, U.S. Ct. Appeals (7th and fed. cirs.) 1983, U.S. Supreme Ct. 1983. Staff atty. Cook County Legal Assistance, Harvey, Ill., 1978-80; mng. atty. Cook County Legal Assistance, Harvey, 1980-82; assoc. O. Kenneth Thomas Ltd., Harvey, 1982-83, Jones, Ware & Grenard, Chgo., 1983—; chmn., bd. dirs. Cook County Legal Assistance, Oak Park, Ill., 1985—; active legal adv. bd. Thornton Community Coll., South Holland, Ill., 1982—, Aunt Martha's Service, Park Forest, Ill., 1981-83. Commr. Zoning Bd. of Appeals, Park Forest, 1981—, Housing Bd. of Appeals, Park Forest, 1981—, Equal Employment Opportunity Bd., Park Forest, 1981—, Housing Rev. Bd., Park Forest, 1981—; bd. dirs. Park Forest Pub. Library, 1982. Served with U.S. Army, 1965-67. Recipient Cert. of Appreciation Thornton Community Coll., 1985, Cert. of Appreciation Wendell Phillips High Sch., 1985, Cert. of Appreciation South Suburban YMCA, 1986. Mem. ABA, Chgo. Bar Assn., Cook County Bar Assn., Chgo. Council of Lawyers, Phi Alpha Delta. Democrat. Avocations: running, chess, tennis. Probate, Real property, State civil litigation. Home: 2922 Western Ave Park Forest IL 60466 Office: Jones Ware & Grenard 180 N LaSalle St Suite 800 Chicago IL 60601

FUNK, DAVID ALBERT, law educator; b. Wooster, Ohio, Apr. 22, 1927; s. Daniel Coyle and Elizabeth Mary (Reese) F.; children—Beverly Joan, Susan Elizabeth, John Ross, Carolyn Louise; m. Sandra Nadine Henselmeier, Oct. 2, 1976. Student, U. Mo., 1945-46; student, Harvard Coll., 1946; B.A. in Econs., Coll. of Wooster, 1949; M.A., Ohio State U., 1968; J.D., Case Western Res. U., 1951, LL.M., 1972; LL.M., Columbia U., 1973. Bar: Ohio 1951, U.S. Dist. Ct. (no. dist.) Ohio 1962, U.S. Tax Ct. 1963, U.S. Ct. Appeals (6th cir.) 1970, U.S. Supreme Ct. 1971. Ptnr. Funk, Funk & Eberhart, Wooster, Ohio, 1951-72; assoc. prof. law Ind. U. Sch. Law, Indpls., 1973-76, prof., 1976—; vis. lectr. Coll. of Wooster, 1962-63; dir. Juridical Sci. Inst., Indpls., 1982—. Author: Oriental Jurisprudence, 1974; Group Dynamic Law, 1982; (with others) Rechtsgeschichte und Rechtssoziologie, 1985; contbr. articles to profl. jours. Chmn. bd. trustees Wayne County Law Library Assn., 1956-71; mem. Permanent Jud. Commn., Synod of Ohio, United Presbyn. Ch. in the U.S., 1968. Served to seaman 1st class USNR, 1945-46. Harlan Fiske Stone fellow Columbia U., 1973; recipient Am. Jurisprudence award in Comparative Law, Case Western Res. U., 1970. Mem. Assn. Am. Law Schs. (sec. comparative law sect. 1977-79, chmn. law and religion sect. 1977-81, sec., treas. law and soc. sci. sect. 1983-86), Japanese-Am. Soc. Legal Studies, Law and Soc. Assn., Am. Soc. Legal History. Pi Sigma Alpha. Republican. Legal history, Private international, Jurisprudence. Office: 735 W New York St Indianapolis IN 46202

FUNK, JONATHAN A., lawyer; b. New Brunswick, N.J., Aug. 4, 1957; s, Julius Jacob and Pearl (Wiseman) F. BA summa cum laude, Rutgers U., 1979; JD cum laude, Harvard U., 1982. Bar: Calif. 1982. Assoc. McCutchen, Doyle, Brown & Enersen, San Francisco, 1982—. class rep. Harvard U. Law Sch. Fund, San Francisco, 1982-86. Mem. ABA, Calif. Bar Assn., San Francisco Barristers, Bay Area Lawyers for Individual Freedom, Phi Beta Kappa. Democrat. Avocation: music. Real property. Home: 345 Church St Unit 1C San Francisco CA 94114 Office: McCuthen Doyle Brown & Enersen Three Embarcadero Ctr San Francisco CA 94111

FUNK, WILLIAM F., lawyer, law educator; b. Boston, Nov. 29, 1945; s. Ward L. and Mary Roberts (Fergusson) F.; m. Renate Dieckmann, June 5, 1971; children—Andrew Christopher, Jonas Peter, Rebecca Matthea. B.A., Harvard U., 1967; J.D., Columbia U., 1973. Bar: N.Y. 1974, D.C. 1979, U.S. Supreme Ct. 1983. Law clk. to Judge James Oakes, U.S. Ct. Appeals for 2d circuit, Brattleboro, Vt., 1973-74; atty. advisor Office Legal Counsel, Dept. Justice, Washington, 1974-77; prin. staff Intelligence Com., U.S. House Reps., Washington, 1977-78; asst. gen. counsel U.S. Dept. Energy, Washington, 1978-83; assoc. prof. law Lewis and Clark Coll. Law Sch., Portland, Oreg., 1983-86, prof., 1986—; cons. U.S. Dept. Energy, Washington, 1983-84, U.S. Adminstr. Conf., Washington, 1985-86. Served to 1st lt. U.S. Army, 1967-70. Mem. ABA (chmn. fed. register reports and paperwork com., adminstrv. law sect.). Legal education, Administrative and regulatory, Environment. Home: 10315 SW Terwilliger Pl Portland OR 97219 Office: Lewis and Clark Law Sch 10015 SW Terwilliger Blvd Portland OR 97219

FUNKHOUSER, DAVID EDWARD, lawyer; b. Ft. Madison, Iowa, Nov. 11, 1941; s. Floyd Franklin and Nellie Mae (Short) F.; m. Michaela Irene Lannon, June 28, 1969; children: Stacy Skye, Shelby Kathleen, David Edward III. BBA, U. Iowa, 1964, JD, 1967. Bar: Iowa 1967, U.S. Dist. Ct. (no. and cen. dists.) Iowa 1968, U.S. Supreme Ct. 1979. Clk. Iowa Supreme Ct., Des Moines, 1967-68; ptnr. Brown, Kinsey & Funkhouser, Mason City, Iowa, 1968—; CLE commr. Iowa Supreme Ct., Des Moines, 1979-83. Commr. Civil Service Commn., Mason City, Iowa, 1972-86; pres., bd. trustees Mason City Pub. Library, 1974-86. Fellow Iowa Acad. Trial Lawyers (bd. dirs. 1984-86, v.p. 1987—). Mem. Iowa State Bar Assn. (bd. govs. 1984-86, v.p. 1986, pres.-elect 1987). Democrat. Roman Catholic. Avocations: hunting, skiing, conservation. Home: 231 Lakeview Dr Mason City IA 50401 Office: Brown Kinsey & Funkhouser 214 N Adams Mason City IA 50401

FURBER, PHILIP CRAIG, lawyer; b. Grand Rapids, Mich., Sept. 21, 1943; s. Robert W. and Elinor J. (Hutchinson) F.; m. Valentina Baranyk, Feb. 21, 1982; children: Michele L., Bradley C. BS, Ind. U., 1967; JD, Cleve. State U., 1975. Bar: Ohio 1975, U.S. Tax Ct. 1976, U.S. Ct. Appeals (6th cir.) 1978, U.S. Ct. Claims 1979; CPA, Ohio. Staff acct. Arthur Andersen & Co., Chgo., 1967-68; adminstrn. asst. trust dept. Soc. Nat. Bank, Cleve., 1968-69; staff acct. John Dobson & Co., South Bend, Ind., 1969-72; prin. atty. McCarthy, Lebit, Crystal & Haiman Co., LPA, Cleve., 1975-86; sole practice Cleve., 1986—; asst. to spl. master Cleve. Sch. Desegregation U.S. Dist. Ct., 1976-80, bd. dirs. Murray Becker Industries, Inc., Twinsburg, Ohio, bd. dirs. Dreco, Inc. North Ridgeville, Ohio. Bd. dirs. Lakewood Luth. Sch., Cleve. Luth. High Sch., Fairview Park, Ohio, 1979-81. Mem. ABA, Ohio Soc. CPA's, Cleve. Bar Assn. General corporate, State and local taxation, Estate planning. Home: 5956 Woodside Dr Highland Heights OH 44143 Office: McCarthy Lebit et al 1300 Ohio Savs Plaza Cleveland OH 44115

FUREY, SHERMAN FRANCIS, JR., lawyer; b. Pocatello, Idaho, June 1, 1919; s. Sherman Francis and Julia Bartlett (Falls) F.; m. Jo Ann Horton, Feb. 18, 1951; children—Jan Furey Kirkpatrick, Stephen Horton (dec.), Sherman Francis III, Terrill Kay Furey Rust. B.A., U. Idaho, 1946, J.D., 1947. Bar: Idaho 1947, U.S. Dist. Ct. Idaho 1947, U.S. Ct. Appeals (9th cir.) 1955. Asst. atty. gen. State of Idaho, 1947-48; asst. U.S. atty. Dist. of Idaho, Boise, 1948-49, U.S. atty., 1953-57, 69-70; ptnr. Doane & Furey, Boise, 1949-51; sole practice, Salmon, Idaho, 1951-53, 57-69, 70-81; sr. ptnr. Furey & Furey, Salmon, 1981—. Mayor, City of Salmon 1959-61; chmn. Citizen's Com. on Legis. Compensation 1976-83. Served to capt. USAAF 1941-45. Decorated D.F.C., Air medal with 3 oak leaf clusters. Mem. Idaho Bar Assn. Republican. Episcopalian. Clubs: Masons, Elks (Salmon). General practice, State civil litigation, Probate. Office: 116 N Center St Salmon ID 83467

FURGANG, PHILIP, lawyer; b. N.Y.C., Apr. 18, 1937; s. William and Sadie (Ball) F.; m. Carol Toby Rubin, Aug. 25, 1962. B.A., Bklyn. Coll., CUNY, 1961; B.E.E., Poly. Inst. Bklyn., 1960; J.D., NYU, 1965. Bar: N.Y., 1966, U.S. Patent and Trademark Office, 1967, U.S. Supreme Ct., 1976, U.S. Ct. Appeals (fed. cir.) 1976, U.S. Internat. Trade Commn., 1976, U.S. Dist. Ct., (so. dist.) N.Y., 1967, U.S. Dist. Ct. (ea. dist.) N.Y., 1967, U.S. Ct. Appeals (5th cir.) 1971. Engring. staff RCA, 1961-64, mem. pat. staff, 1964-66; pat. atty. Curtiss Wright Corp., Woodbridge, N.J., 1966-67, Litton Industries, E. Orange, N.J., 1967-71; sole practice law, N.Y.C. and Spring Valley, N.Y., 1972—. Councilman Village of Suffern, 1973-75; county committeeman Dem. Party, 1969-80; mem. Rockland County Assn., 1975—; mem. transp. adv. com. Legis. Rockland County, 1978-81. Mem. ABA, Am. Patent Law Assn., U.S. Trademark Assn. (mem. long range forum com.), N.Y. Bar Assn., N.Y. Patent, Trademark and Copyright Law Assn. (bd. dirs.), Westchester County Bar Assn., Rockland County Bar Assn. (chmn. econs. of law com., chmn. legal referral com.). Patent, Federal civil litigation, State civil litigation. Office: 205 Lexington Ave New York NY 10016 also: 49 S Main St Spring Valley NY 10977

FURGESON, WILLIAM ROYAL, lawyer; b. Lubbock, Tex., Dec. 9, 1941; s. W. Royal and Mary Alyene (Hardwick) F.; m. Marion McElroy, Aug. 15, 1964 (div.); m. Juli Ann Bernat, July 29, 1973; children—Kelly Lynn, Houston, Joshua, Seth, Jill. B.A. in English, Tex. Tech Coll., 1964; J.D. with honors, U. Tex., 1967. Bar: Tex. 1969, U.S. Dist. Ct. (we. dist.) Tex. 1971, U.S. Ct. Appeals (5th cir.) 1974, U.S. Supreme Ct. 1976. Law clk. to presiding justice U.S. Dist. Ct. for No. Dist. Tex., 1969-70; ptnr. Kemp, Smith, Duncan & Hammond, El Paso, Tex., 1970—. Gen. campaign chmn. El Paso United Way, 1979, 1st v.p., 1980, pres., 1981; mem. Jewish Fedn., El Paso, 1980-86; trustee Baylor U. Coll. Dentistry, 1982-86; chmn. YWCA Capital Devel. Campaign, 1986-87. Served to capt. U.S. Army, 1967-69. Decorated Bronze Star; recipient Service award Social Workers of El Paso, 1982, Faculty award U. Tex. Law Sch., 1983. Mem. El Paso Bar Assn. (pres. 1982-83, Outstanding Young Lawyer award 1972), Am. Law Inst., U. Tex. Law Sch. Assn. (pres. 1978), U. Tex. Law Rev. Assn. (pres. 1982-83), El Paso Legal Assistance Soc. (bd. dirs. 1972-78), NCCJ (chmn. El Paso region 1980), ABA, Fed. Bar Assn. (pres. West Tex. chpt. 1987), Am. Law Inst., Tex. Bar Assn. (sec., treas. anti-trust and trade regulation sect. 1985-86), Tex. Bar Found. Democrat. Jewish. Antitrust, Federal civil litigation, State civil litigation. Home: 3927 Hillcrest El Paso TX 79999 Office: PO Drawer 2800 20th Floor State Nat Plaza El Paso TX 79999

FURMAN, MARK STEVEN, lawyer; b. Boston, Aug. 29, 1951; s. Joseph Marvin and Ann (Rapoport) F.; m. Amy Jean Stanger, Nov. 4, 1978; children: Matthew Stinger, Alexandra Sarah. BA, U. Mass., 1973; JD, Boston Coll., 1977. Bar: Mass. 1977, N.H. 1979, U.S. Dist. Ct. Mass. 1980, U.S. Ct. Appeals (1st cir.) 1980. Atty. N.H. Legal Assistance, 1977-80; assoc. Singer, Stoneman, Kunian & Kurland, Boston, 1980-84, ptnr., 1984—. Mem. ABA, Mass. Bar Assn., N.H. Bar Assn., Assn. Trial Lawyers Am., Mass. Acad. Trial Lawyers, Phi Beta Kappa, Phi Kappa Phi, Pi Sigma Alpha. Avocations: sports, reading. State civil litigation, Federal civil litigation, Personal injury. Office: Singer Stoneman Kunian & Kurland 100 Charles River Plaza Boston MA 02114

FURMAN, MICHAEL JOSEPH, lawyer; b. Chgo., Jan. 18, 1953; s. Joseph Edmund Furman and Ileane (Joyce) Jenness; m. Helen Colt Levey, Nov. 24, 1974; children: Mary Catherine, Michael Douglas. BS cum laude, La. Tech U., 1975; JD cum laude, Tulane U., 1979. Bar: La. 1979, U.S. Dist. Ct. (ea. and mid. dist.) La. 1979, U.S. Ct. Appeals (5th cir.) 1979, U.S. Dist. Ct. (we dist.) La. 1981, U.S. Ct. Appeals (11th cir.) 1981, U.S. Supreme Ct. 1982. Assoc. Lemle, Kellener, Konmeyer, Dennery, Huley, Moss & Frilot, New Orleans, 1979-86; ptnr. Lemle, Kelleher, Kohlmeyer, Dennery, Hunley, Moss & Frilot, New Orleans, 1986—; adj. asst. prof. Tulane U., New Orleans, 1984—. Served to capt. USAFR, 1975—. Mem. ABA, La. Bar Assn., New Orleans Bar Assn., Assn. Trial Lawyers Am., La. Trial Lawyers Assn., La. Assn. Def. Counsel, Def. Research Inst. Republican. Personal injury, Product liability defense, Insurance. Home: 6332 Cartwright Dr New Orleans LA 70122 Office: Lemle Kelleher Kohlmeyer et al 601 Poydras St 21st Floor Pan Am Life Ctr New Orleans LA 70130

FURNISH, DALE BECK, lawyer, educator; b. Iowa City, Iowa, Feb. 11, 1940; s. William Madison and Eula Bernice (Beck) F.; m. Roberta Rae Mahnke, Aug. 23, 1963 (div. Oct. 1975); 1 child, Katherine Elizabeth; m. Hannah Rose Arterian, May 27, 1978; children—William, Susannah, Diana. B.A., Grinnell Coll., 1962; J.D., U. Iowa, 1965; LL.M., U. Mich., 1970. Bar: Iowa, 1965, U.S. Ct. Appeals (8th cir.) 1966, Ariz. 1973, U.S. Dist. Ct. Ariz. 1976. Law clk. U.S. Ct. Appeals (8th cir.), Sioux City, Iowa, 1965-66; asst. prof. law U. Iowa, Iowa City, 1966-68; vis. prof. law Ford Found. Internat. Legal Ctr., Santiago, Chile, 1969-70; prof. law Ariz. State U., Tempe, 1970—; vis. prof. law U. Nacional Autonoma de Mexico, Mexico City, 1974-75; Fulbright prof. Pontificia U. Católica del Peru, 1984; lectr. USIA, Latin Am., 1972—. Author: Usury and the Monetary Control Act of 1980, 1981. Bd. editors Am. Jour. Comparative Law, 1972—, Revista Peruana del Derecho Internat., 1979—. Mem. Fgn. Relations Com., Phoenix, 1979—, mem. exec. bd. 1986—; mem. Gov.'s Ariz.-Mex. Commn., 1981—. Mem. Am. Assn. Law Schs. (chmn. creditor debtor sect. 1978, chmn. comparative law sect. 1979), ABA, Ariz. Bar Assn., Iowa Bar Assn., Interam. Bar Assn., Order of Coif. Democrat. Presbyterian. Bankruptcy, Contracts commercial, Private international. Office: Ariz State U Coll Law Tempe AZ 85287

FURR, O(LIN) FAYRELL, JR., lawyer; b. Clinton, S.C., Jan. 19, 1943; s. Olin Fayrell and Helen Ella (Osborn) F.; m. Ann Longwell, June 10, 1967 (div.); m. Karole Jensen, Apr. 1, 1983; children: Sara Shannon, Karolan Marie, Paul Andrew. B.S., U. S.C., 1965, J.D., 1968. Bars: S.C. 1968, U.S. Dist. Ct. S.C., 1968, U.S. Ct. Appeals (4th cir.) 1972, (5th cir.) 1977, U.S. Supreme Ct. 1977. Mem. Law Offices of Kermit S. King, Columbia, S.C., 1973-77; ptnr. King & Furr, Columbia, 1977-79; sole practice law, Columbia, 1980—; lectr. various univs. Pres. bd. dirs. Contact Help, 1975-76; bd. dirs. Appelate Pub. Defender Orgn., 1980. Served to capt. U.S. Army, 1968-73. Decorated Bronze Star. Mem. S.C. Trial Lawyers Assn. (pres. 1979-80; most valuable mem. 1974), S.C. Bar Assn., Am. Trial Lawyers Assn. (cert. trial adv.), Richland County Bar Assn., Horry County Bar Assn. Democrat. Baptist. Editor, S.C. Trial Lawyers Bull., 1974-77; contbr. articles to profl. jours. Personal injury, Federal civil litigation, State civil litigation. Office: 1534 Blanding St Columbia SC 29201 Office: PO Box 2909 Myrtle Beach SC 29577

FURRER, DAVID EUGENE, lawyer; b. Altoona, Pa., Sept. 12, 1950; s. Eugene Edward and Madeline Josephine (Strobel) F.; m. Hope Hughes, Sept. 22, 1973; children: Paul David, Andrew Edward. BA in Polit. Sci. and Russian, Pa. State U., 1972; JD, U. Balt., 1978. Bar: Md. 1978, U.S. Dist. Ct. Md. 1980. Ptnr. Steen, Seigel, Tully & Furrer, Balt., 1978—. bd. dirs, zoning chmn. Rodgers Forge Community Assn., Balt., 1979-81. Mem. ABA, Md. Bar Assn. (ins., negligence and compensation com.), Md. Trial Lawyers Assn. (bd. dirs. 1984—), Atty. Grievance Commn., Phi Beta Kappa. Republican. Roman Catholic. Avocations: coaching youth soccer and basketball. General practice, Federal civil litigation, Insurance. Home: 5700 Downing Pl Baltimore MD 21212 Office: Steen Seigel Tully & Furrer 712 Park Ave Baltimore MD 21201

FURSMAN, NANCY JOHANNA, lawyer; b. Iola, Kans., Jan. 28, 1952; d. John Anton Jr. and Florence L. (Hiser) F. AA, Allen County Jr. Coll., 1972; BS, Kansas State Tchrs. Coll., 1974; JD, Washburn U., 1978. Bar: Kans. 1978, U.S. Dist. Ct. Kans. 1978. Instr. Shawnee Heights, Topeka, 1974-75; legal advisor Kansas State Indsl. Reformatory, Hutchinson, 1979-80; asst. gen. counsel Fed. Intermediate Credit Bank, Wichita, Kans., 1980-85; section chief FDIC, Wichita, 1984—; adj. prof. Wichita U., 1981—. Mem. ABA, Kans. Bar Assn., Wichita Bar Assn., Corp. Counsel Soc. Consumer commercial, Banking, General corporate. Home: 2323 N Woodlawn Wichita KS 67220 Office: FDIC 2024 N Woodlawn PO Box 8192 Wichita KS 67218

FURST, STEPHEN W., lawyer; b. Bellefonte, Pa., Apr. 28, 1948; s. Austin O. and Margaret W. (Watkins) F.; m. Keveney Robinson, Apr. 28, 1979; children: Kathryn R., Taylor W. BS, U. Va., 1971; JD, Dickinson Sch. Law, 1975. Bar: Pa. 1975. Ptnr. Furst & Furst, Bellefonte, 1975—. Mem. ABA, Pa. Bar Assn., Centre County Bar Assn. General practice. Home: 177 E Curtin St Bellefonte PA 16823 Office: Furst & Furst 111 E High St Bellefonte PA 16823

FURUYA, LAURIE E., lawyer; b. Puunene, Hawaii, July 27, 1955; d. Jitsuo and Shizue (Katahara) Matsubara. BA, U. Hawaii, 1977, JD, 1980. Bar: Hawaii 1980, U.S. Dist. Ct. Hawaii 1980. Dep. atty. gen. State of Hawaii, 1980-83; assoc. Dudley G. Akama, Honolulu, 1983—; mem. Bd. Naturopathy, State of Hawaii, 1986—. Bd. dirs. Wailuna Town Assn., Pearl City, Hawaii, 1985-86, Hawaii Lupus Found., Honolulu, 1985—. Mem. ABA, Hawaii Bar Assn. (dir. young lawyers sect. 1984), Hawaii Women Lawyers Assn. (bd. dirs. 1984, sec. 1985, v.p. 1986, pres. 1987—). Democrat. Avocations: volleyball, skiing, cross-stitching. Workers' compensation. Office: Dudley G. Akama 1000 Bishop St Suite 806 Honolulu HI 96813

FUSCO, ANDREW G., lawyer; b. Punxsitawney, Pa., Jan. 11, 1948; s. Albert G. and Virginia N. (Whitesell) F.; children—Matthew, Geoffrey, David. B.S. in Bus. Adminstrn. and Fin., W.Va. U., 1970, J.D., 1973. Bar: W.Va. 1973, U.S. Supreme Ct. 1977, U.S. Ct. Appeals (4th cir.) 1974, U.S. Ct. Appeals (4th cir.) 1985. Sole practice, Morgantown, W.Va., 1973-85; ptnr. Fusco & Newbraugh, Morgantown, 1985—; pros. atty. Monongalia County, W.Va., 1977-81; instr. Coll. bus. and Econ., W.Va. U., 1975-76; dir. Pitts. Environ. Systems Inc., 1983—. Bd. dirs. W.Va. Career Colls., 1971-76; mem. profl. adv. bd. Childbirth and Parent Edn. Assn., Rape and Domestic Violence Info. Ctr.; mem. W.Va. Sec. State's Tribunal on Election Reform, 1977-81; chmn. Monongalia County Drug Edn. Task Force, 1978-80. Mem. ABA, Monongalia County Bar Assn., W.Va. Bar, Am. Trial Lawyers Assn., W.Va. Trial Lawyers Assn., Baker St. Irregulars of N.Y., W.Va. Dist. Attys. Assn., Nat. Dist. Attys. Assn., Am. Judicature Soc., Sons of Italy, W.Va. Law Sch. Assn., Monongalia Arts Center (pres.-elect, treas., trustee). Recipient Am. Jurisprudence award Bancroft-Whitney Publ. Co. 1971; named Outstanding Young Man of 1979, Morgantown, 1979. Editor, contbg. author: Twenty Feet From Glory (John R. Goodwin), 1970; Business Law (John R. Goodwin) 1972; Beyond Baker Street (Michael Harrison) 1976. Democrat. Roman Catholic. General corporate, Federal civil litigation, Antitrust. Home: 20 Harewood Morgantown WV 26505 Office: 220 Pleasant St Morgantown WV 26505

FUSCO, ARTHUR GEIGER, lawyer; b. Key West, Fla., Oct. 26, 1947; s. Arthur Anthony and Lucia Gertrude (Geiger) F.; m. Carol Jean Bower, Aug. 17, 1969 (div. Oct. 1978); 1 child, Mary Bennett; m. Barbara June Snyder, Apr. 2, 1983. AB in Govt., Wofford Coll., 1969; JD, U. S.C., 1975. Bar: S.C. 1975, U.S. Dist. Ct. S.C. 1977, U.S. Ct. Appeals (4th cir.) 1982. Sole practice Columbia, S.C., 1975-79; from staff atty. to gen. counsel S.C. Pub. Service Commn., Columbia, 1979—; Moot ct. judge U. S.C. Sch. of Law, Columbia, 1976-79; faculty participant ann. conference of Motor Carrier Lawyers Assn., S.C., 1982, S.C. Electric Coop. Assn., S.C., 1986; supr. law sch. clinic adminstrv. law program U. S.C., Columbia, 1984-85. Mem. Riverbanks Zool. Soc., 1975—, Columbia Area Mental Health Adv. Bd., 1981-82, County Dem. Exec. Com., 1980, state del., 1980, ward pres. 1979; vol. United Way, 1976-79, patron Columbia Town Theater, 1975-83, 85—; commr., coach Dentsville Youth Athletic Program, 1983-86. Served to 1st lt. U.S. Army, 1970-71. Mem. ABA, S.C. Bar Assn. (editorial bds. various publs., rep. young lawyers 2d congl. dist., faculty participant continuing legal edn. seminar), Richland County Bar Assn., Phi Delta Phi. Methodist. Lodge: Rotary (bd. dirs. Spring Valley club 1986, sec. 1987). Avocations: chess, paleontology. Administrative and regulatory, Public utilities. Home: 204 Stonegate Dr Columbia SC 29223 Office: SC Pub Service Commn PO Drawer 11649 Columbia SC 29211

FUSCO, CLAUDE EUGENE, JR., tax consultant, lawyer; b. Bronx, N.Y., Nov. 10, 1946; s. Claude Eugene and Betty (Simeone) F.; m. Kathryn Anne Blanton, Oct. 5, 1974; children: Dana, Claude III. BS, St. Francis Coll., Loretto, Pa., 1968; JD, Fordham U., 1971. Bar: N.Y. 1971. Staff Arthur Young, N.Y.C., 1971-76; mgr. Arthur Young, Brussels, 1976-79; ptnr. Arthur Young, N.Y.C. and internat., 1979-85; ptnr., dir. of tax Arthur Young, Newark, 1985—. Mem. ABA (internat. tax com.), N.Y. State Bar Assn. (internat. tax com.), Am. Soc. CPA's, N.Y. State Soc. CPA's (internat. tax com.), Kensico C. of C. (v.p.). Corporate taxation, Personal income taxation. Office: Arthur Young 99 Wood Ave S Metro Park Iselin NJ 08830

FUSELIER, LOUIS ALFRED, lawyer; b. New Orleans, Mar. 26, 1932; s. Robert Howe and Monica (Hanemann) F.; m. Eveline Gasquet Fenner, Dec. 27, 1956; children: Louis Alfred, Henri de la Claire, Elizabeth Fenner. B.S., La. State U., 1953; LL.B., Tulane U., 1959. Bar: La. 1959, Miss. 1964, U.S. Supreme Ct. 1965. Trial atty. NLRB, New Orleans, 1959-62; pres. firm Fuselier, Ott, McKee & Walker, P.A., and predecessors, Jackson, Miss. Served as pilot and squadron comdr. USAF, 1953-56. Mem. ABA (practice and procedure com. of labor law sect.), La. Bar Assn. (past chmn. labor law sect.), New Orleans Bar Assn., Miss. Bar Assn., Hinds County Bar Assn., Fed. Bar Assn., Miss. Bar Found., Miss. Def. Lawyers, Am. Law Inst., Am. Hosp. Attys. Assn., Miss. Wildlife Fedn. (pres. 1975-77), Newcomen Soc., Am. Judicature Soc., Am. Soc. Personnel Adminstrs. (accredited personnel diplomate), Jackson C. of C. Clubs: Boston (New Orleans), Country, Capital City Petroleum, University (Jackson). Lodge: Rotary. Labor, Civil rights, Defense. Home: 3804 Old Canton Rd Jackson MS 39216 Office: 2100 Deposit Guaranty Plaza Jackson MS 39201

FUSON, DOUGLAS FINLEY, lawyer; b. Ann Arbor, Mich., Jan. 19, 1944; s. William M. and Helen L. Fuson; m. Bernadette M. Nottling, May 9, 1980; children: Adrienne M., Erica L.; stepchildren: Bruce J. Paluch, Philip S. Paluch. BA, Oberlin Coll., 1965; JD, U. Chgo., 1968. Bar: Ill. 1968, U.S. Dist. Ct. (no. dist.) Ill. 1968, U.S. Ct. Appeals (7th cir.) 1968, U.S. Supreme Ct. 1974, U.S. Ct. Appeals (4th cir.) 1982. Assoc. Sidley & Austin, Chgo., 1968-74, ptnr., 1974—. Bd. dirs. Legal Found. Chgo., 1979—. Mem. ABA, Ill. Bar Assn., Chgo. Bar Assn., Chgo. Council Lawyers, Phi Beta Kappa. Club: Beaver Creek (Colo.). Federal civil litigation, State civil litigation, Antitrust. Office: Sidley & Austin 1 First Nat Plaza Chicago IL 60603

FUSON, HAROLD WESLEY, JR., lawyer; b. Galesburg, Ill., Jan. 8, 1945; s. Harold Wesley and Virginia May (Moon) F.; m. Pamela Lee Crist, Dec. 30, 1966; children—John Harold, Anne Crist. B.A., Grinnell Coll., 1967; M.S., Columbia U., 1968; J.D., Cleve. State U., 1976. Bar: Ohio 1976, Ill. 1976, Calif. 1979, U.S. Ct. Appeals (9th cir.) 1980, U.S. Supreme Ct., 1986. Instr. journalism Tex. So. U., Houston, 1968-70; copy editor, asst. news editor Houston Post, 1969-70; asst. prof. journalism Cuyahoga Community Coll., 1970-76, U. Ill., Urbana, 1976-79; staff counsel Times Mirror Co., Los Angeles, 1979-83; v.p., gen. counsel The Copley Press, Inc., La Jolla, Calif., 1983—; mem. task force ABA, Chgo., 1983—, legal affairs com. Am. Newspaper Pubs. Assn., Reston, Va., 1984—. Libel.

FUSTE, JOSE ANTONIO, federal judge; b. 1943. BBA, U. P.R., San Juan, 1965, LLB, 1968. Ptnr. Jimenez & Fuste, Hato Rey, P.R., 1968-85; judge U.S. Dist. Ct. P.R., San Juan, 1985—; prof. U. P.R., 1972—. Office: PO & Courthouse Bldg PO Box 3671 San Juan PR 00904 *

FUTRELL, JOHN WILLIAM, institute executive, lawyer; b. Alexandria, La., July 6, 1935; s. J.W. and Sarah Ruth (Hitesman) F.; m. Iva Macdonald, Aug. 13, 1966; children: Sarah, Daniel. B.A., Tulane U., 1957; postgrad., Free U. Berlin, 1958; LL.B., Columbia U., 1965. Bar: La. 1966. Atty. Lemle & Kelleher, New Orleans, 1966-71; prof. law U. Ala., 1971-74, U. Ga., 1974-80; pres. Environ. Law Inst., Washington, 1980—; lectr. Dept. State in Japan and India, 1978; Woodrow Wilson fellow Smithsonian Instn., Washington, 1979-80. Pres. Sierra Club, San Francisco, 1977-78, nat. bd. dirs., 1971-81; del. UN Conf. on Water, 1977, White House Conf. Inflation, 1974. Served as officer USMC, 1957-62. Fulbright scholar, 1958. Mem. ABA, Am. Law Inst., AAAS, Phi Beta Kappa, Order of Coif. Club: Cosmos. Environment, General corporate, Administrative and regulatory. Office: Environmental Law Inst 1616 P St NW Washington DC 20036

FUTTERER, EDWARD PHILIP, lawyer; b. Cleve., July 17, 1953; s. Stephan and Erna (Oswald) F.; m. Jane Leah Chizmar, Aug. 4, 1979. BBA, Cleve. State U., 1975, JD with honors, 1978. Bar: Ohio 1978, U.S. Dist. Ct. (no. dist.) Ohio 1979, U.S. Tax Ct. 1983; CPA, Ohio. Tax acct. Ernst & Whinney, Cleve., 1978-80, sr. tax acct., 1980-81; tax atty. Reliance Electric Co., Cleve., 1981-83, sr. tax atty., 1983-84; sr. tax atty. Exxon Co. USA Inc., Houston, 1984—. Mem. ABA (tax sect.), Ohio State Bar Assn., Ohio Soc. CPA's. Avocations: fishing, trap and skeet shooting, wood-carving. Corporate taxation, Personal income taxation, State and local taxation. Home: 2227 Riverlawn Dr Kingwood TX 77339 Office: Exxon Co USA Inc 800 Bell Houston TX 77001

FUTTERMAN, RONALD L., lawyer; b. Chgo., Mar. 5, 1943; s. Sol and Edythe (Greenberg) F.; m. Pamela Ann Hayes, June 5, 1966; children—Elizabeth, Samantha. B.B.A., U. Wis.-Madison, 1964; J.D., Northwestern U., 1967. Bar: Ill. 1967, U.S. Dist. Ct. (no. dist.) Ill. 1967, U.S. Ct. Appeals (7th cir.) 1975, U.S. Ct. Appeals (D.C. cir.) 1977, U.S. Supreme Ct. 1984. Atty. anti-trust div. U.S. Dept. Justice, Chgo., 1967-73; assoc. Pressman & Hartunian, Chgo., 1973-78, ptnr., 1978-82; ptnr. Hartunian, Futterman & Howard, Chartered, Chgo., 1982—. Mem. Ill. Sch. Dist. #113 Polit. Caucus, Deerfield, 1976-78, chmn. publicity, 1977-78; pres. South Park Elementary Sch. PTO, Deerfield, 1980-81. Mem. ABA, Ill. Bar Assn., Chgo. Bar Assn., Chgo. Council Lawyers (v.p. 1983-84, bd. govs. 1984—). Anti-trust, Civil rights, Federal civil litigation. Office: Hartunian Futterman & Howard Chartered 55 E Monroe St Chicago IL 60603

FUTTERMAN, STANLEY NORMAN, lawyer; b. N.Y.C., Aug. 18, 1940; s. Louis and Mildred (Friedman) F.; Linda Roth, Aug. 26, 1962; children: David, Daniel, Matthew. AB, Columbia U., 1961; LLB, Harvard U., 1964, MPA, 1969. Bar: N.Y. 1966, U.S. Dist. Ct. (so. and ea. dists.) N.Y. 1976, U.S. Ct. Apls. (2d cir.) 1977, U.S. Sup. Ct. 1977, U.S. Ct. Apls. (5th cir.) 1978. Law clk. to chief judge U.S. Ct. Appeals (1st cir.), Boston, 1964-65; spl. asst. to legal adviser U.S. Dept. State, Washington, 1965-67; asst. legal adviser for spl. polit. affairs, 1967-68, asst. legal adviser for East Asian and Pacific affairs, 1969-71; assoc. prof. law NYU, 1971-75; assoc. Poletti Freidin Prashker Feldman & Gartner, N.Y.C., 1976-78, ptnr., 1978-85; ptnr. Epstein Becker Borsody & Green, 1985—; vis. prof. law U. Wis., Madison, 1975. Chmn. spl. com. on campaign financing ACLU, mem. com. on free speech and assn., 1972-84; treas. Larchmont (N.Y.) Dem. Com., 1974-77; trustee Beth Emeth Synagogue, Larchmont, N.Y. Mem. ABA, N.Y. State Bar Assn., Assn. of Bar of City of N.Y., Fed. Bar Council, Supreme Ct. Hist. Soc. Club: Harvard (N.Y.C.). Contbg. author: None of Your Business, 1974, The Constitution and the Conduct of Foreign Policy, 1976; contbr. articles to law revs. Labor, Private international, Federal civil litigation. Office: Epstein Becker Borsody & Green 250 Park Ave New York NY 10177

FUZESI, STEPHEN, JR., lawyer, banker; b. Budapest, Hungary, Aug. 3, 1948; came to U.S., naturalized, 1962; s. Stephen, Sr. and Marta (Jancso) F; m. Nancy J. Steinhardt, Apr. 5, 1975; children—Stephen Joseph, Timothy Roger. A.B., Princeton U., 1970; J.D., U. Pa., 1974. Bar: N.Y. Atty. Davis, Polk & Wardwell, N.Y.C., 1974-82; ptnr./of counsel Reid & Riege, PC, Hartford, Conn., 1982-83; 1st. sr. v.p., gen. counsel and sec. Am. Savings Bank, FSB, N.Y.C., 1984—. Contbr. articles to jours., newspapers. Term mem. Council Fgn. Relations, N.Y., 1976-81; mem. Am. Council on Germany, 1977-80. Recipient Keedy Law Rev. award U. Pa. Law Sch., 1974. Mem. N.Y.C. Bar Assn. Clubs: Princeton of N.Y., Burning Tree Country (Greenwich, Conn.). Office: Am Savings Bank FSB 380 Madison Ave New York NY 10017

FYLSTRA, RAYMOND ALAN, lawyer; b. Grand Rapids, Mich., Oct. 12, 1947; s. Daniel H. and Winifred (Rameau) F.; m. Charlotte Buis, Aug. 17, 1968; children: Helen Rameau, Margaret Pell, Henry Buis. BA, Hope Coll., 1969; JD, Northwestern U., 1972. Bar: Ill. 1972, U.S. Dist. Ct. (no. dist.) Ill. 1973, U.S. Dist. Ct. (ea. dist.) Wis. 1974, U.S. Ct. Appeals (7th cir.) 1974, U.S. Supreme Ct. 1978, U.S. Dist. Ct. (ea. dist.) Mich. 1982. Assoc. Chapman & Cutler, Chgo., 1972-77, participant, 1977-82, ptnr., 1982—. Served to capt. USAR, 1973-80. Mem. Chgo. Bar Assn. Republican. Club: Union League (Chgo.). Federal civil litigation, State civil litigation, Construction. Home: 309 E 59th St Hinsdale IL 60521 Office: Chapman & Cutler 111 W Monroe St Chicago IL 60603

GAAR, NORMAN EDWARD, lawyer, former state senator; b. Kansas City, Mo., Sept. 29, 1929; s. William Edward and Lola Eugene (McKain) G.; student Baker U., 1947-49; A.B., U. Mich., 1955, J.D., 1956; children—Anne, James, William, John; m. Marilyn A. Wiegraffe, Apr. 12, 1986. Bar: Mo. 1957, Kans. 1962, U.S. Supreme Ct. 1969. Assoc. Stinson, Mag, Thomson, McEvers & Fizzell, Kansas City, 1956-59; ptnr. Stinson, Mag & Fizzell, Kansas City, 1959-79; mng. ptnr. Gaar & Bell, Kansas City and St. Louis, Mo., Overland Park and Wichita, Kans., 1979—; mem. Kans. Senate, 1965-84, majority leader, 1976-80; mem. faculty N.Y. Practising Law Inst., 1969-74; adv. dir. Panel Pubs., Inc., N.Y.C. Mcpl. judge City of Westwood, Kans., 1959-63, mayor, 1963-65. Served with U.S. Navy, 1949-53. Decorated Air medal (2); named State of Kans. Disting. Citizen, 1962. Mem. Am. Bar Assn., Am. Judicature Assn., Nat. Conf. State Legislatures, Am. Radio Relay League, Antique Airplane Assn., Exptl. Aircraft Assn. Republican. Episcopalian. Clubs: Woodside Racquet, Brookridge Country. Securities, Local government, Municipal bonds. Office: Gaar & Bell 8717 W 110th Suite 640 Overland Park KS 66210

GABALDON, THERESA A., law educator; b. Williams, Ariz., Sept. 4, 1954; d. Antonio A. and Jacqueline J. (Sykes) G. BS, U. Ariz., 1975; JD, Harvard U., 1978. Bar: Ariz. 1978. Assoc. Snell & Wilmer, Phoenix, 1978-84, ptnr., 1984—; assoc. prof. U. Ariz., Tucson, 1984—. Mem. Jr. League Phoenix, 1983—. Securities, General corporate. Office: Univ Arizona Coll of Law Mountain & Speedway Tucson AZ 85721

GABAY, DONALD DAVID, lawyer; b. Bklyn., Apr. 25, 1935; s. Harry I. and Rachel (Cohen) G.; m. Vicky R. Geula, Apr. 6, 1968; children—Rachel, Daniel, Sari. B.B.A., CCNY, 1956; LL.B., Bklyn. Law Sch., 1961. Bar: N.Y. 1962. Pvt. practice law, N.Y.C., 1962-75; chief counsel N.Y. State Assembly Com. on Ins., Albany, 1975-78; 1st dep. supt. N.Y. State Ins. Dept., N.Y.C., 1978-84; ptnr. Stroock & Stroock & Lavan, N.Y.C., 1984—; lectr. Coll. Ins., New Sch. for Social Research. Bd. dirs. NCCJ, Jerusalem Inst. Tech., N.Y.C., Israel Bonds, N.Y.C. Served with U.S. Army, 1956-58. Named Ins. Man of Yr., Ind. Ins. Brokers Assn., 1973; Pub. Service award Bklyn. Ins. Brokers Assn., 1977; ann. achievement award Council Ins. Brokers, 1981; Outstanding Achievement award, CCNY Alumni Assn., 1981, Pub. Service award Ind. Ins. Agts. Assn., 1984; Torch of Liberty award ins. div. Anti-Defamation League, 1984. Club: Broome and Allen Boys. Lodge: Abravanel. Insurance. Office: Stroock & Stroock & Lavan 7 Hanover Sq New York NY 10004

GABBARD, (JAMES) DOUGLAS, II, judge; b. Lindsay, Okla., Mar. 27, 1952; s. James Douglas and Mona Dean (Dodd) G.; m. Connie Sue Mace, Dec. 30, 1977 (div. Feb. 1979); m. Robyn Marie Kohlhaas, June 18, 1981; children: Resa Marie, David Ryan, James Douglas III, Michael Drew. BS, Okla. U., 1974, JD, 1977. Bar: Okla. 1978. Ptnr. Stubblefeild & Gabbard, Atoka, Okla., 1978; sole practice Atoka, 1979; asst. dist. atty. State of Okla., Atoka, 1979-82; 1st asst. dist. atty. State of Okla., Atoka, Durant and Coalgate, 1982-85; dist. judge 26th jud. dist. State of Okla., Atoka and Coalgate, 1985—; mcpl. judge City of Atoka, 1978-79; atty. Town of Wapanucka, Okla., 1979-80; officer advisor Counties of Atoka, Coal and Bryan, 1982-85. Mem. Bryan County/Durant Arbitration Com., 1984; negotiator Bryan Meml. Hosp. Bd., Durant, 1984-85. Mem. Okla. Bar Assn. (state law and edn. com. young lawyers div. 1986—), Nat. Dist. Attys. Assn. Democrat. Methodist. Lodges: Jaycees, Lions, Elks. Avocations: drawing, painting, tennis, bicycling, reading. Jurisprudence, Judicial administration, General practice. Home: Box 69 Atoka OK 74525 Office: County Ct House Atoka OK 74525

GABBAY, ALAN, lawyer; b. Oceanside, N.Y., Apr. 23, 1953; s. Maurice and Violet (Shashou) G. BA, Yale U., 1975; JD, Harvard U., 1978. Bar: N.Y. 1979, Ill. 1984. Assoc. Webster & Sheffield, N.Y.C., 1978-83, Sidley & Austin, Chgo., 1983—. Editor in chief, founder Harvard Environ. Law Rev., 1976-77. Mem. ABA, Ill. State Bar Assn., Chgo. Bar Assn. Avocation: bicycle riding. Contracts commercial, General corporate. Home: 30 E Elm St Apt 7A Chicago IL 60611 Office: Sidley & Austin One First Nat Plaza Chicago IL 60603

GABE, CARYL JACOBS, lawyer; b. N.Y.C., July 12, 1949; d. Herman and Ethel (Spector) Jacobs; m. Allen Sherwin Gabe, May 25, 1980. BA cum laude, Bklyn. Coll., 1972; JD with honors, John Marshall Law Sch., 1976. Bar: Ill. 1976, U.S. Dist. Ct. (no. dist.) Ill. 1976. Spl. asst. atty. gen. Ill. Atty. Gen.'s Office, Chgo., 1976-77; sole practice Chgo., 1977-79, 80-83; assoc. Kaufman & Litwin, Ltd., Chgo., 1979-80; ptnr. Gabe, Gabe & Assocs., Chgo., 1983—. Art juror Old Town Art Fair, Chgo. Mem. ABA, NOW, Women in Mgmt., Ill. Bar Assn., Chgo. Bar Assn. (matrimonial com.), Woodfield Bar Assn. Democrat. Jewish. Avocations: painting, sculpture, cellist, racquetball, softball. Family and matrimonial, Paternity. Office: Gabe Gabe & Assocs 180 N LaSalle Chicago IL 60601 Office: 1821 Walden Office Square Schaumburg IL 60194

GABEL, GEORGE DESAUSSURE, JR., lawyer; b. Jacksonville, Fla., Feb. 14, 1940; s. George DeSaussure and Juanita (Brittain) G.; m. Judith Kay Adams, July 21, 1962; children—Laura Elizabeth, Meredith Rion. A.B., Davidson Coll., 1961; J.D., U. Fla., 1964. Bar: Fla. 1964, D.C. 1972. Mem. firm Toole, Taylor, Moseley, Gabel & Milton, Jacksonville, 1966-74, Wahl and Gabel, Jacksonville, 1974—; mem. Fla. Jud. Nominating Commn., 4th Circuit, 1982-86. Pres. Willing Hands, Inc., 1971-72; chmn. N.E. Fla. March of Dimes, 1974-75; mem. budget com. United Way, 1972-74, chmn. rev. com., 1976; bd. dirs. Central and South brs. YMCA, 1973-79, Camp Immokalee, 1982-86; elder Riverside Presbyterian Ch., 1970-77, 80-86, clk. session, 1975-76, 85-86; pres. Riverside Presbyn. Day Sch., 1977-79; chmn. Nat. Eagle Scout Assn., 1974-75; bd. dirs., v.p. adminstrn, chmn. long range planning com. N. Fla. Boy Scouts Am., 1974—, Silver Beaver award, 1978; mem. Jacksonville Council on Citizen Involvement, 1976-79; trustee Davidson Coll., 1984—. Served to capt. U.S. Army, 1964-66. Fellow Am. Coll. Trial Lawyers, Am. Bar Found.; mem. ABA (chmn. admiralty and maritime law com. 1980-81, chmn. elect defamation torts com. 1977-78, tort and ins. practice sect. 1980-81), World Assn. Lawyers (founding mem.), Am. Counsel Assn. (bd. dirs. 1980-82), Assn. Trial Lawyers Am., Am. Judicature Soc., Maritime Law Assn. U.S., Fla. Bar (chmn. grievance com. 1973-75, chmn. admiralty law com. 1978-79), Acad. Fla. Trial Lawyers, Southeastern Admiralty Law Inst. (bd. govs. 1973-75), Duval County Legal Aid Assn. (bd. dirs. 1971-74, 81-84), Am. Inn of Ct. (master of bench). Democrat. Club: Rotary of Jacksonville (bd. mem. 1982-84, treas. 1985-86, pres. 1987—). Admiralty, Federal civil litigation, State civil litigation. Home: 1850 Shadowlawn St Jacksonville FL 32205 Office: Wahl and Gabel PA Suite 920 Barnett Bank Bldg Jacksonville FL 32202

GABERT, NORI LAUREN, lawyer; b. Houston, Aug. 15, 1953; d. Lenard Morris and Dahlia (Edelstein) G. BA, U. Houston, 1975, JD, 1979. Bar: Tex. 1980, U.S. Dist. Ct. (so. and ea. dists.) Tex. 1980. Staff atty. securities bd. State of Tex., Houston, 1980-81; assoc. gen. counsel, compliance rev. officer Am. Capital Asset Mmgt. Inc., Houston, 1981—; mem. pension and tax com., options and futures com. Investment Co. Inst., Washington, 1985—. Mem. ABA, Houston Bar Assn., Houston Young Lawyers Assn. Avocations: aerobics, needlework, reading. Securities. Office: Am Capital Asset Mgmt Inc 2800 Post Oak Blvd Houston TX 77056

GABLEHOUSE, TIMOTHY REUBEN, corporate attorney; b. Boulder, Colo., May 13, 1951; s. Reuben H. and Genevieve M. (Willburn) G.; m. Barbara Lynn Dorough, June 23, 1973; children: Brian, Kristin, Andrew. BA, U. Colo., 1973; JD, U. Denver, 1975, MBA, 1981. Bar: Colo. 1976, U.S. Dist. Ct. Colo. 1983. Assoc. Geddes, MacDougal & McHugh, Colorado Springs, Colo., 1976-77; regulatory analyst Adolph Coors Co., Golden, Colo., 1977-78, new products devel. mgr., 1978-79, regulatory affairs analyst, 1979-84, mng. atty., 1984—. Commr. City of Arvada (Colo.) Commn. for Prevention of Sexual Assault, 1982-85; arbitrator Better Bus. Bur., Denver, 1984—. Mem. ABA, Colo. Hazardous Waste Mgmt. Soc. (pres. 1985-86, bd. dirs. 1986—), Environ. Law Inst., Am. Corp. Counsel Assn. Avocations: fly fishing, mountain climbing. Environment, Administrative and regulatory, Biotechnology. Office: Adolph Coors Co BC 540 Golden CO 80401

GABOVITCH, STEVEN ALAN, lawyer, accountant; b. Newton, Mass., Feb. 7, 1953; s. William and Annette (Richman) G.; m. Rhonda Merle Kitover, Aug. 6, 1978; 1 child, Daniel J. BS in Acctg., Boston Coll., 1975, JD, 1978, LLM in Taxation, 1982. Bar: Mass. 1978, R.I. 1979, U.S. Dist. Ct. R.I. 1979, U.S. Tax Ct. 1980, U.S. Ct. Appeals (1st cir.) 1980, U.S. Dist. Ct. Mass. 1981, U.S. Ct. Appeals (fed. cir.) 1982, U.S. Supreme Ct. 1983. Tax specialist Peat, Marwick, Mitchell & Co., Providence, 1978-80; sole practice Boston, 1982-85; ptnr. William Gabovitch & Co., Boston, 1985—; instr. Brown Learning Community, Providence, 1985—. Mem. ABA, Am. Assn. Attys. and CPA's, Mass. Bar Assn., R.I. Bar Assn., Boston Bar Assn., Beta Gamma Sigma. Estate taxation, Corporate taxation, Personal income taxation. Office: 148 State St Suite 500 Boston MA 02109

GABOVITCH, WILLIAM, lawyer, accountant; b. Boston, June 18, 1922; s. Ezra and Lena Ruth (Elkins) G.; m. Annette Richman, Sept. 19, 1925; children—Steven A., Ellis. B.S. in Bus. Adminstrn., Boston U., 1943; J.D., Boston Coll., 1949; LL.M. in Taxation NYU, 1950. Bar: Mass. 1949, U.S. Dist. Ct. Mass., U.S. Dist. Ct. R.I., U.S. Ct. Appeals (1st cir.), U.S. Tax Ct., U.S. Ct. Claims, U.S. Ct. Appeals (fed. cir.), U.S. Supreme Ct.; C.P.A., Mass. Sr. ptnr. William Gabovitch & Co., C.P.A.s, Boston, 1962—; lectr. in legal acctg. and taxation Boston Coll. Law Sch., 1959-70; examiner and trustee in bankruptcy. Campaign treas. Congressman Robert F. Drinan, 1970-84. Served to lt. (s.g.) USNR, 1943-46; Tokyo. Mem. Am. Inst. C.P.A.s, Mass. Soc. C.P.A.s, ABA, Mass. Bar Assn., Boston Bar Assn., Mensa. Clubs: New Century (Boston); Masons. Corporate taxation, Bankruptcy. Home: 33 Old Nugent Farm Rd Gloucester MA 01930 Office: 148 State St Boston MA 02109

GABRIEL, EBERHARD JOHN, financial company executive, lawyer; b. Bucharest, Rumania, Mar. 22, 1942; came to U.S., 1952, naturalized, 1955; s. William and Margaret (Eberhart) Krzyzewski; m. Janice Josephine Jedrzejewski, Aug. 21, 1965; children—John, Stephanie, Christopher. B.A. in English, St. Joseph's Coll. of Ind., 1963; J.D., Georgetown U. Law, 1966. Bar: Md. 1966, U.S. Supreme Ct. 1972. Staff atty. Fgn. Claims Settlement Commn., Washington, 1966-68; corp. atty. Govt. Employees Ins. Co./GEICO, Washington, 1968-70; sr. v.p., gen. counsel Govt. Employees Fin. Corp. and subs., Denver, 1970-87, exec. v.p., corp. counsel Nat. Personal Fin. Corp./Am. Indsl. Banks, 1987—; fellow St. Joseph's Coll., 1978—; dir., sec., treas. Indsl. Bank Savs. Guaranty Corp. Colo., 1973-83, pres., 1983—; lectr., Am. Fin. Services Assn., Nat. Installment Banking Sch., 1974-81, 85; mem. Law Forum, 1974—, mem. law com., 1978—, dist. chmn. congl. action com., 1979-82, speaker 1980 Thrift Seminar. Bd. dirs. Lakewood (Colo.) C. of C., 1974-78, 79-80, 82-86, chmn. civic affairs council, 1975-76, chmn. govtl. action council, 1976-77, chmn. legis. action council, 1980-81, chmn. and mem. exec. com., 1984-85; mem. Jefferson County DA Adult Diversion Council, 1985—; mem. bus. adv. com. Jefferson Found., 1985—; mem. adv. council Colo. Office Regulatory Reform, Colo. Dept. Regulatory Agys., 1984—; trustee Lakewood Polit. Action Com., 1978—, chmn. 1986—; sr. v.p. fund raising Lakewood on Parade, 1980, chmn. bd. govs., 1982; vice chmn. fin. div. United Way Metro Denver, 1982. Mem. ABA, Md. Bar Assn., Indsl. Bankers Assn. Colo. (chmn. legis. com. 1980-84, chmn. polit. action com. 1981—, v.p. 1983-85, pres. 1985-86), Phi Alpha Delta, Democrat. Roman Catholic. Club: Pinehurst Country (Denver). General corporate, Banking, Consumer commercial. Home: 7546 S Wadsworth Ct Littleton CO 80123 Office: Nat Personal Fin Corp 15435 E Iliff Ave Aurora CO 80013

GACHET, THOMAS MCINNIS, lawyer; b. Arlington, Va., Nov. 30, 1943; s. Thomas Morton and Edna Lou (McInnis) G.; m. Patricia Veronica Arnold, May 21, 1976; children—Carolyn Leigh, Catherine Eleanor. B.A., Eckerd Coll., 1966; J.D., Harvard U., 1970; M.A., Vanderbilt U., 1971; LL.M. in Taxation, Georgetown U., 1976. Tax advisor Gulf Oil Co., London, 1971-73, supr. planning and research, Pitts., 1974; tax counsel CACI, Arlington, Va., 1974-75; sr. tax atty. Allied Chem. Co., London, 1976-78; internat. tax atty. Amerada Hess, Woodbridge, N.J., 1978-79; sr. counsel-tax Harris Corp., Melbourne, Fla., 1979—. Corporate taxation. Home: 1407 S Riverside Dr Indialantic FL 32903 Office: Harris Corp 1025 W Nasa Blvd Melbourne FL 32919

GAD, ROBERT K., III, lawyer; b. N.Y.C., Aug. 21, 1946; s. Robert K. Jr. and Alma Rose (Kelley) G.; m. Karen Anne Buerig, Nov. 30, 1968. AB, Brown U., 1968; JD summa cum laude, Boston U., 1972. Bar: Mass. 1972, U.S. Dist. Ct. Mass. 1973, U.S. Ct. Appeals (1st cir.) 1975, U.S. Supreme Ct. 1976, U.S. Ct. Appeals (2d cir.) 1978, U.S. Ct. Appeals (D.C. cir.) 1979, U.S. Tax Ct. 1980, U.S. Ct. Appeals (11th cir.) 1984. Assoc. Ropes and Gray, Boston, 1972-80, ptnr., 1980—. Mem. ABA, Mass. Bar Assn., Boston Bar Assn. Club: Downtown (Boston). Avocation: sailing. Federal civil litigation, State civil litigation, Nuclear power plant licensing. Home: 27 Fayette St Arlington MA 02174 Office: Ropes and Gray 225 Franklin St Boston MA 02110

GADBOIS, RICHARD A., JR., judge; b. Omaha, June 18, 1932; s. Richard Alphonse Gadbois and Margaret Ann (Donahue) Bartlett; m. Jeanne E. Roach, Dec. 15, 1956; children: Richard, Gregory, Guy, Geoffrey, Thomas. A.B., St. John's Coll., Camarillo, Calif., 1955; J.D., Loyola U., Los Angeles, 1958; postgrad. in law, U. So. Calif., 1958-60. Bar: Calif. 1959, U.S. Dist. Ct. (cen. dist.) Calif. 1959, U.S. Supreme Ct. 1966. Ptnr. Musick, Peeler & Garrett, Los Angeles, 1962-68; v.p. Denny's Inc., La Mirada, Calif., 1968-71; judge Mcpl. Ct., Los Angeles, 1971-72, Superior Ct., Los Angeles, 1972-82, U.S. Dist. Ct. (cen. dist.) Calif., Los Angeles, 1982—. Decorated knight Order of Holy Sepulchre (Pope John Paul II). Mem. ABA, Los Angeles County Bar Assn. (trustee 1966-67), State Bar Calif. (profl. ethics com. 1965-70). Republican. Roman Catholic. Home: 2155 El Molino Ave San Marino CA 91108 Office: US Dist Ct 176 US Courthouse 312 N Spring St Los Angeles CA 90012 *

GADDIS, LARRY ROY, lawyer; b. Pratt, Kans., Nov. 8, 1941; s. Wade G. and Lorena (Pierce) G.; m. Barbara Ann Law, June 14, 1972; children—Jeffrey Wade, Aaron Paul. BA., U. Colo., Boulder, 1963, J.D., 1969. Bar: Colo. 1969, U.S. Dist. Ct. Colo. 1969, U.S. Ct. Appeals (10th cir.), 1969. Staff atty. Pikes Peak Legal Services, Colorado Springs, Colo., 1969-71, dir., 1971-73; ptnr. Cross, Gaddis, Kin & Quicksall, P.C., Colorado Springs, 1973—; vis. prof. U. Colo.-Colorado Springs, 1971-74. Bd. dirs. Colorado Springs Sch., 1973—. Mem. El Paso County Bar Assn., Colo. Bar Assn. (exec. council 1978), ABA, Phi Kappa Alpha. Democrat. Episcopalian. Probate, General corporate, Real property. Office: 118 S Wahsatch St Colorado Springs CO 80903

GADDIS, STEPHEN MICHAEL, judge; b. Seattle, Mar. 15, 1946; s. Donald Earl and Mary Louise (DeBurgh) G.; m. Jeanne Jennison, Apr. 1, 1980; children—Clark, Carrie, Carolyn, Craig, Cynthia. B.A., U. Wash.,

1967, J.D., 1970. Bar: Wash. 1970, U.S. Dist. Ct. (we. dist.) Wash. 1970, U.S. Ct. Appeals (9th cir.) 1970, U.S. Ct. Mil. Appeals 1972, U.S. Supreme Ct. 1974. Assoc. firm Hilyer & Levinski, Seattle, 1968-73, firm Jonson & Jonson, Seattle, 1973-75; sole practice, Seattle, 1975-78; ptnr. firm Gaddis & Fox, Seattle, 1978-80; family court commr. King County Superior Ct., Seattle, 1980-83, court commr., 1983-86, judge, 1986—; founder Northwest Mediation Service, Seattle, pres, 1977-80; founder Childrens Legal Services, Seattle, pres., 1978-80; adj. prof. law U. Puget Sound, Seattle, 1983—; presenter, panelist numerous profl. assn. seminars, television programs on family law matters. Author numerous articles, pamphlets. Precinct committeeman, Seattle, 1968-70, 72-74; bd. dirs. Jane Addams Co-op Sch., Seattle, 1975-77; trustee Puget Sound Big Sisters 1985-87; vol. Family Ct. CASA program, 1983. Served to capt. U.S. Army, 1971. Recipient founding grant for Family Ct. CASA Program 1983; recipient Merit award Puget Sound Assn. for Edn. Young Children, Seattle, 1981. Mem. Wash. State Bar Assn. (trustee family law sect. 1984-87, pres. elect 1986—, chairperson 1986-87), Seattle-King County Bar Assn. (trustee 1977-80), Assn. Family and Conciliation Cts. (trustee 1982—), Superior Ct. Judges Assn. Family and matrimonial, State civil litigation, Jurisprudence. Office: King County Superior Ct 516 3d Ave Seattle WA 98104

GADDY, RODNEY EDWIN, lawyer; b. Bklyn., N.Y., Aug. 16, 1955; s. Joseph Lee and Avis Evelyn (James) G. BA in Polit. Sci., Wheeling Coll., 1977; JD, Georgetown U., 1980. Bar: Fla. 1980, U.S. Dist. Ct. (mid. dist.) Fla. 1981. Staff atty. Cen. Fla. Legal Services, Palatka, 1980-81; asst. pub. defender Jacksonville, Fla., 1981-83; field counsel Fla. Dept. Law Enforcement, Tampa, 1983-84; dep. gen. counsel Fla. Dept. Law Enforcement, Tallahassee, 1984—. Mem. Big Bros./Big Sisters, Jacksonville, 1981. Mem. Fla. Assn. Police Attys., Jacksonville Jaycees. Democrat. Baptist. Criminal, Administrative and regulatory, State civil litigation. Home: 2917 C Woodrich Dr Tallahassee FL 32301 Office: Fla Dept Law Enforcement 401 W Carolina St Tallahassee FL 32301

GADE, THOMAS ANDREW, lawyer; b. Amsterdam, N.Y., Mar. 3, 1932; s. Thomas Nelson and Olive Marjorie (Bornt) G.; m. L. Susan Sand, Aug. 5, 1972; children: Pamela Jean, Thomas Edward, Sandy Ann. BCE, Union Coll., 1961; JD, Western State U., 1970. Bar: Calif. 1972, U.S. Supreme Ct. 1977. Engr., planner Calif. Dept. Transportation, San Diego, 1961-71; sole practice San Diego, 1971-75; councilman City of San Diego, 1975-79; ptnr. Gade & Gade, San Diego, 1979—. Contbg. editor Dicta, 1974. Bd. dirs. San Diego Stadium Authority, 1979-83. Served with USN, 1951-55. Mem. ABA, Calif. Bar Assn., San Diego Bar Assn., Am. Soc. Civil Engrs., Engrs. Club San Diego. Lodges: Masons, Spreckels. Construction, General corporate, Real property. Office: Gade & Gade 110 W C St #1705 San Diego CA 92101

GADHIA, LALIT HARILAL, lawyer; b. Bombay, Maharashtra, India, Aug. 25, 1938; came to U.S., 1960; s. Harilal Premji and Santokben H. (Tanna) G.; m. Anu M. Jhaveri, Sept. 6, 1961 (div. Mar. 1971); 1 child, Anita L. BA with honors, Bombay U., 1960; MA, U. Md., College Park, 1964; JD, U. Md., Balt., 1978. Bar: Md. 1980, U.S. Dist. Ct. Md. 1980, U.S. Ct. Appeals (4th cir.) 1984. Instr. Morgan State U., Balt., 1962-67; chief of planning Community Action Agy. City of Balt., 1968-69; assoc. exec. dir. CAA City of Balt., 1969-74; economist State of Md., Annapolis, 1975-77; atty. Legal Aid Bur., Balt., 1978-81; sole practice Balt., 1982—. Candidate Md. State Assembly, Balt., 1974. Mem. ABA, Md. Bar Assn., Balt. City Bar Assn., Am. Immigration Lawyers Assn. Democrat. Hindu. Avocations: chess, reading, swimming. Immigration, naturalization, and customs, Contracts commercial, Federal civil litigation. Office: 355 N Calvert St Baltimore MD 21202

GADRIX, EDWARD WALLACE, JR., lawyer; b. Atlanta, Oct. 29, 1939; s. Edward Wallace and Madeline June (Rowe) G.; m. Mary Wade, May 29, 1952; children: Edward Markham, Christopher Guy, Martha Allison. Student, Young Harris Coll., 1959-60; BBA, Ga. State U., 1960-65; JD, John Marshall U., 1969-72. Bar: Ga., U.S. Dist. Ct. (no., mid. and so. dists.) Ga. Asst. v.p. 1st Nat. Bank Atlanta, 1960-70; gen. mgr. Kaiser-Aetna, Atlanta, 1970-72; ptnr. Gadrix & Assocs., Atlanta, 1972—; bd. dirs. H.H. Barvus Co., Santa Barbara, Calif.; pres. Family Law Alliance Inc., Atlanta, 1984—, pres. Sandy Springs Bar Assn., 1984; instr. real estate DeKalb Coll., Atlanta, 1976-79. Contbr. articles on landlord tenant law to profl. jours. Rep. nominee for 5th Congl. Dist., Atlanta, 1976; Rep. chmn. Fulton County, Atlanta, 1977. Served with USCG, 1959-65. Mem. Atlanta C. of C. (hon. life) (pres. 1970). Episcopalian. Lodge: Rotary. Avocations: karate, snow skiing, boating. Federal civil litigation, Real property, Insurance. Home: 110 Bonnie Ln Atlanta GA 30328 Office: 367 Hammond Dr Atlanta GA 30328

GAERTNER, GARY J., lawyer; b. Pitts., Oct. 20, 1954; s. Robert L. Sr. and Marie (Zelik) G.; m. Christine M. Cipriani, May 22, 1982. BA cum laude, U. Pitts., 1975, JD, 1979, MBA, 1980. Bar: Pa. 1979, U.S. Dist. Ct. (we. dist.) Pa. 1979. Dep. atty. gen. Pa. Office of Atty. Gen. in Pitts., 1980-82; dir. Pitts. Regional Office Bur. Consumer Protection, 1981-82; estate adminstr. U.S. Bankruptcy Ct. (we. dist.) Pa., Pitts., 1982-83; assoc. Berkman, Ruslander, Pohl, Lieber & Engel, Pitts., 1983-86; sole practice Pitts., 1986—; sec. editorial com. drafting local rules of bankruptcy practice. Mem. ABA, Pa. Bar Assn., Allegheny County Bar Assn., Comml. Law League Am. Bankruptcy, Contracts commercial, General practice. Home: 103 Spruce Valley Dr Pittsburgh PA 15229 Office: 436 7th Ave 2917 Koppers Bldg Pittsburgh PA 15219

GAERTNER, GARY M., judge; b. St. Louis; m. Maureen; children—Gary M., Lisa, Mark. Student in polit. sci. St. Louis U., J.D., Sch. Law; grad. Nat. Jud. Coll., U. Nev., Mo. Trial Judges Coll., Am. Acad. Jud. Edn., U. N.H., Sch. Law U. Va., Stanford U. Law Sch., Harvard U. Sch. Law; attended Oxford (Eng.) U. Bar: Mo., Ill., U.S. dist. ct., U.S. Ct. Appeals, U.S. Supreme Ct. After pvt. practice law, served as asst. city counselor City of St. Louis, until 1964, assoc. city counsel, 1964-67, city counselor, 1967-69; former judge 22d Jud. Cir. Mo., 1969-85, including presiding judge criminal divs., juvenile judge, asst. presiding judge and presiding judge and chief adminstrv. officer 22d Jud. Cir. Mo.; judge U.S. Ct. Appeals (ea. dist.) Mo., 1985; past pres. Mo. Council Juvenile Ct. Judges; former chmn., former chmn. juvenile subcom. Mo. Council Criminal Justice, region 5; former mem. St. Louis Commn. on Crime and Law Enforcement. Bd. dirs. Boys Town Mo.; v.p. Khoury Internat. Leagues, Policeman and Fireman's Fund of St. Louis; former dist. chmn., now dist. vice-chmn. Tomahawk dist. Boy Scouts Am.; past mem. exec. bd. St. Louis Area council Boy Scouts Am. Served with USCG. Recipient awards, including Judiciary award St. Louis Grand Jury Assn., Man of Yr. award George Khoury Internat. Assn., Spl. Act. award U.S. Assn. Fed. Investigators; named an Outstanding Young St. Louisian, St. Louis Jaycees; recipient diploma Jud. Skills Am. Acad. Jud. Edn. Mem. ABA, Mo. Bar Assn., Mo. Assn. Trial Attys., Bar Assn. Met. St. Louis, Lawyers Assn. Met. St. Louis, Am. Judicature Soc., Phi Delta Phi. Jurisprudence. Office: Civil Cts Bldg Saint Louis MO 63101

GAETANOS, CHRIST, lawyer; b. Wiesbaden, Essen, Fed. Republic of West Germany, Nov. 27, 1953; came to U.S., 1957; s. George and Argerolla (Lemonis) G.; m. Dianne R. Civello, June 28, 1980; children: George Nicholas, Benjamin Nelson. BA in Polit. Sci., SUNY, Buffalo, 1975, JD, 1979. Bar: N.Y. 1980, W.Va. 1980, U.S. Tax Ct. 1980, U.S. Ct. Appeals (4th cir.) 1980, U.S. Dist. Ct. (we. dist.) N.Y. 1980, U.S. Dist. Ct. (so. dist.) W.Va. 1980. Law clk. to presiding justice U.S. Dist. Ct. (so. dist.), W.Va.; assoc. Duke, Holzman, Yaeger & Radlin, Buffalo, 1981-83, Offermann, Fallon, Mahoney & Cassano, Buffalo, 1983-86; gen. counsel Bella Vista Mgmt., Inc. and Associated Cos., Lancaster, N.Y., 1986—; adj. prof. Marshall U., Huntington, W.Va.; bd. dirs. Ascar, Inc., Kenmore, N.Y., Buffalo Birth Ctr. Treas. com. Arcara for dist. atty., Buffalo, 1985—. Mem. ABA, N.Y. State Bar Assn., Am. Arbitration Assn. Republican. Greek Orthodox. Corporate taxation, General corporate, Real property. Office: Bella Vista Mgmt Inc 6495 Transit Rd Lancaster NY 14069

GAFFNEY, MARK WILLIAM, lawyer; b. Spokane, Wash., July 3, 1951; s. William Joseph and Anne Veronica (McGovern) G. B.A., U. Notre Dame, 1973, J.D., George Washington U., 1976. Bar: Wash. 1976, N.Y. 1982, D.C. 1984, Conn. 1984. Law clk. antitrust div. U.S. Dept. Justice, Washington, 1974-76, trial atty., N.Y.C., 1976-81; assoc. Solin & Breindel, P.C., N.Y.C., 1982-83; ptnr. Chapman, Moran & Gaffney, Stamford, Conn., 1984-85; of counsel Kaplan Kilsheimer & Foley, N.Y.C., 1985—. Recipient Spl. Achievement award U.S. Dept. Justice, 1978, 1979. Mem. ABA, Assn. Bar City N.Y., Conn. Bar Assn. Republican. Roman Catholic. Club: N.Y. Athletic. Antitrust, Federal civil litigation, State civil litigation. Home: 1395 Roosevelt Ave Pelham Manor NY 10803 Office: Kaplan Kilsheimer & Foley 122 E 42d St New York NY 10168

GAFFNEY, TERRENCE JOHN, lawyer; b. Fond du Lac, Wis., June 25, 1949; s. John Francis and Helen Catherine (Reilly) G.; m. Jane Ellen Salter, June 17, 1972; children: Michael Terrence John, Brendan Patrick Mackin. BA, St. Norbert Coll., 1971; JD, Tulane U., 1974. Bar: Wis. 1974, U.S. Dist. Ct. (ea. dist.) Wis. 1975, U.S. Ct. Appeals (7th cir.) 1978, Ill. 1985, U.S. Dist. Ct. (no. dist.) Ill. 1985. Assoc. Burke & Schoetz, Milw., 1975-79, Davis & Kuelthau, S.C., Milw., 1980-84, Seki & Jarvis, Chgo., 1984-87, Bell, Boyd and Lloyd (merger with Seki and Jarvis), Chgo., 1987—. Del. Wis. Dem. Conv., Appleton, 1984; v.p. St. Michael's Hosp. Friars, Milw., 1983-84, Cedarburg (Wis.) Jaycees, 1976-77. Served with U.S. Army, 1974-75. Mem. ABA, Wis. Bar Assn. (bd. dirs. bankruptcy sect. 1983-86), Chgo. Bar Assn., Bar Assn. 7th Fed. Cir., Assn. Trial Lawyers Am. Roman Catholic. Club: Chalet Racquet (Western Springs, Ill.). Avocations: oil painting, writing poetry, golf, tennis, skiing. Private international, Bankruptcy, State civil litigation. Home: 5332 Johnson Ave Western Springs IL 60558 Office: Bell Boyd & Lloyd 3 1st National Plaza Chicago IL 60602

GAFFORD, GEORGE NELSON, lawyer; b. Cleve., Mar. 25, 1916; s. George Armand and Rose (Freed) G.; m. Toni Williams, June 21, 1945 (dec. Apr. 1979); m. Martha Austin, May 17, 1980. AB, Yale U., 1936; JD, Case Western Res. U., 1939. Bar: Ohio 1939, U.S. Dist. Ct. (no. dist.) Ohio 1939, U.S. Supreme Ct. 1950. Atty. SEC, Washington, 1939-41; sole practice Cleve., 1946-69; prof. law Calif. Western Sch. Law, San Diego, 1969—; asst. atty. gen. Ohio, 1948-50; bd. dirs. Cockrell Production, Abilene, Tex., Jacena Corp., San Diego. Trustee La Jolla Playhouse, Calif., 1986—, San Diego Pops Orch., 1986—, Calif. Western Sch. Law, 1986—. Served as lt. USNR, 1942-65, PTO, Korea. Mem. ABA, San Diego Bar Assn., Assn. Trial Lawyers Am., San Diego Trial Lawyers Assn., Cleve. Skating Club. Democrat. Presbyterian. Club: La Jolla Beach and Tennis. General corporate, State civil litigation, Legal education. Home: 5270 Chelsea St La Jolla CA 92037

GAGE, JOHN BAILEY, II, lawyer; b. Lawrence, Kans., Oct. 27, 1951; s. John Cutter and Eleanor Jane (Pack) G. BA, U. Kans., 1974, JD, 1979. Bar: Mo. 1979, U.S. Dist. Ct. (we. dist.) Mo., U.S. Ct. Appeals (8th cir.) 1980, Kans. 1985, U.S. Dist. Ct. Kans. 1986. Claims adjuster Liberty Mut. Ins. Co., Des Moines, 1974-76; assoc. Gage & Tucker, Kansas City, Mo., 1979-85; ptnr. Gage & Hutton, Kansas City, Kans., 1985—. Mem. men's adv. com. Belles of Am. Royal Citizens Assn., Kansas City, Mo., 1986—, chief exec. officer, chmn. bd. dirs. young supporters chpt., 1986—, bd. dirs., 1986—. Mem. Kans. Bar Assn., Mo. Bar Assn., Lawyer's Assn., Wyandotte County Bar Assn., Johnson County Bar Assn., Kans. Head Injury Assn. Republican. Episcopalian. Home: 5066 Mission Rd Shawnee Mission KS 66205 Office: Gage & Hutton 212 Brotherhood Bldg Kansas City KS 66101

GAGEN, JOSEPH CHARLES, lawyer; b. Mpls., Oct. 2, 1951; s. Charles Anthony and Virginia (Elder) G.; m. Joanne Prescott Hopkins, Mar. 8, 1986. BA, U. Tex., 1974, JD, 1982. Bar: Tex. 1982, U.S. Dist. Ct. (so. dist.) Tex. 1983, U.S. Ct. Appeals (5th cir.) 1983, U.S. Supreme Ct. 1985. Legis. aide Tex. state rep. Ben Reyes, Austin, 1975; urban planner City of Houston, 1975-76; assoc. Reynolds, Allen & Cook, Houston, 1982-85; chmn. indsl. accident bd. State of Tex., Austin, 1985—. Exec. dir. Tex. Dems., Austin, 1978, 80, 82. Mem. ABA, Tex. Bar Assn., Houston Bar Assn. (legal edn. com. 1985-86), Phi Beta Kappa, Phi Eta Sigma. Roman Catholic. Home: 1816 Travis Heights Blvd Austin TX 78704 Office: Tex Indusl Accident Bd 200 E Riverside Dr Austin TX 78704

GAGLIARDI, PAUL, lawyer; b. Kenosha, Wis., Jan. 4, 1952; s. Frank and Carolyn (Stella) G.; m. Kathryn McCormick, June 15, 1974; children: Genevieve, Frank, Paul. BA, Boston Coll., 1974; JD, Marquette U., 1979. Bar: Wis., U.S. Dist. Ct. (ea. and we. dists.) Wis., U.S. Ct. Appeals (7th cir.). CPA Ernst & Winnie, Milw., 1974-76, Gordon J. Meier Co., Racine, Wis., 1974-76; ptnr. Madrigrano, Gagliardi, Zievers & Aiello, S.C., Kenosha; bd. dirs. Neighborhood Housing Services Inc. Pres. Kenosha Vis. Nurses Assn. Mem. Italian Businessmens' Assn. (bd. dir. 1984-86), ATAW. Personal injury, Workers' compensation, State civil litigation. Home: 3701 104 St Kenosha WI 53142 Office: Madrigrano Gagliardi et al 1108 56th St Kenosha WI 53140

GAGLIARDO, JOSEPH M(ICHAEL), lawyer; b. Chgo., Nov. 21, 1952; s. Joseph Anthony and Marie Vivian (Aiello) G.; m. Jennifer Ann Vozella, June 7, 1980; 1 child, Joseph Michael Jr. BS in Commerce, DePaul U., 1974; JD, John Marshall Law Sch., 1977. Bar: Ill. 1977, U.S. Dist. Ct. (no. dist.) Ill. 1977. Asst. corp. counsel law dept. City of Chgo., 1978-82, sr. atty. supr., 1982-83, chief asst. corp. counsel, 1983-85, dep. corp. counsel, 1985-86, first dep. corp. counsel, 1986—. Editor: (annual report) Personnel and Labor Relations 1984-1985, 1985. Mem. ABA, Ill. State Bar Assn., Chgo. Bar Assn., Justinian Soc. Lawyers, Assembly Ill. State Bar Assn., Delta Mu Delta, Delta Epsilon Sigma. Civil rights, Labor, Local government. Office: Office of Corp Counsel Room 511 City Hall Chicago IL 60602

GAGLIUSO, RICHARD CARON, lawyer; b. Rumford, Maine, Dec. 13, 1953; s. Richard Joseph and Marion Estelle (Caron) G.; m. Maria Concetta Dimauro, June 14, 1975; children: Laura Marie, Linda Christine. AB, Harvard U., 1976; JD, Boston U., 1979. Bar: N.H. 1979, U.S. Dist Ct. N.H. 1979, U.S. Ct. Appeals (1st cir.) 1985, U.S. Supreme Ct. 1986. Assoc. Hamblett & Kerrigan P.A., Nashua, N.H., 1979-84, ptnr., 1984—, also bd. dirs.; mem. N.H. Jud. Council, 1986—. Bd. dirs. Big Bros./Big Sisters of Greater Nashua, N.H., 1981-86. Mem. ABA, N.H. Bar Assn., Nashua Bar Assn., No. New Eng. Def. Counsel Assn. Roman Catholic. Avocations: music, tennis, running. State civil litigation, Insurance, Consumer commercial. Home: 29 Watersedge Dr Nashua NH 03063 Office: Hamblett & Kerrigan PA One Indian Head Plaza Nashua NH 03061

GAGNE, JAMES L., lawyer; b. Sanford, Maine, Jan. 26, 1954; s. Ronald Omer and Doris (Boudreau) G.; m. Debra Ann Etheridge, May 1, 1983. BA, U. Maine, 1976, JD, 1979; MBA, Keller Grad. Sch. Mgmt., Chgo., 1984. Bar: Mass. 1980, Ill. 1981. Asst. mgr. Village of Ogunquit, Maine, 1976; asst. to U.S. atty. Dept. Justice, Portland, Maine, 1979-80; editorial dept. mgr. Callaghan and Co., Wilmette, Ill., 1981—. Mem. ABA. Democrat. Club: N. Shore Running. Avocation: marathon running. Computer, Local government, Securities. Home: 42 Lincolnshire Dr Lincolnshire IL 60015

GAGNON, STEWART WALTER, lawyer; b. Beaumont, Tex., Jan. 29, 1949; s. Stewart Paul and Helen Anne (Payne) G.; m. Lynn Bass, July 29, 1972; children—Ashley Lynn, Jason Stewart. Student, Trinity U., 1967-69; B.A., U. Houston, 1971; J.D., S. Tex. Coll. Law, 1974. Bar: Tex. 19—, U.S. Dist. Ct. (so. dist.) Tex. 1975, U.S. Ct. Apls. (5th cir.) 1975, U.S. Supreme Ct. 1976. Assoc. firm Fulbright & Jaworski, Houston, 1974-83, participating assoc., 1983—; mem. Supreme Ct. Commn. on Child Support Guidelines; master/referee Harris County Dist. Cts., Houston, 1977—. Asst. scoutmaster Boy Scouts Am., Troop 642, Houston, 19—; mem. State Dem. Exec. Com., Tex., 1984—; mem. Houston Found. Bd. Pub. Trust, 1982—; lectr. Spring Branch Ind. Sch. Dist., 1976—. Recipient Award of Merit, Boy Scouts Am., 1982, Silver Beaver award, 1983. Fellow Am. Acad. Matrimonial Lawyers; mem. Houston Bar Assn., Tex. Bar Assn. (dist. 4 com. on admissions), Gulf Coast Family Law Specialists Assn. (dir., pres. 1986—), Tex. Acad. Family Law Lawyers (treas.). Presbyterian. Family and matrimonial. Home: 2303 Lexford Ln Houston TX 77080 Office: Fulbright & Jaworski 1301 McKinney Houston TX 77010

GAINES, EDWIN METCALF, JR., lawyer; b. Richmond, Va., Jan. 11, 1954; s. Edwin Metcalf Sr. and Anne-Roswell (Johns) G.; m. Tani D. Bahti, Dec. 21, 1974; children: Eric Michael, Justin Thomas, Todd Andrew. BS in Anthropology, U. Ariz., 1976, JD, 1981. Bar: Ariz. 1981, U.S. Dist. Ct. Ariz. 1981. Assoc. Chandler, Tullar, Udall & Redhair, Tucson, 1981-86, ptnr., 1986—. Editor U. Ariz. Law Rev., 1980-81. Mem. ABA (profl. liability litigation sect.), Ariz. Bar Assn., Pima County Bar Assn., Assn. Trial Lawyers Am. Avocations: skiing, scuba diving, racquetball, travel. State civil litigation, Insurance, Personal injury. Home: 5650 W Gerhart Tucson AZ 85745 Office: Chandler Tullar Udall & Redhair 33 N Stone Ave Suite 1700 Tucson AZ 85701

GAINES, IRVING DAVID, lawyer; b. Milw., Oct. 14, 1923; s. Harry and Anna (Finkelman) Ginsburg; m. Ruth Rudolph, May 22, 1947, (dec. Apr. 5, 1979); children—Jeffrey S., Howard R., Mindy S. Gaines Pearce; m. 2d, Lois Shier, Nov. 25, 1979. B.A., U. Wis., Madison, 1943, J.D., 1947; student U. Pa., Phila., 1943-44; Bar: Wis., 1947, Fla., 1971, U.S. Dist. Ct. (ea. dist.) Wis. 1947, U.S. Dist. Ct. (we. dist.) Wis. 1970, U.S. Dist. Ct. (so. dist.) Fla. 1972, U.S. Dist. Ct. (mid. dist.) Fla. 1976, U.S. Ct. Appeals (7th cir.) 1954, U.S. Ct. Appeals (11th cir.) 1981, U.S. Supreme Ct. 1954. Sole practice, Milw., 1947-72; ptnr. Gaines & Saichek, S.C. (and predecessor firm), Milw., 1972-78; sr. ptnr. Irving D. Gaines, S.C., Milw., 1979—. Served with AUS, 1943-46. Mem. Fla. Bar (bd. editors jour. 1973-84), Milw. Bar Assn. (past mem. exec. com., cts. com., econs. law com., past chmn. unauthorized practice of law com., past chmn. negligence sect., lectr. programs, seminars), State Bar Wis. (bd. govs. 1982-85, communications com. 1981-85), Broward County Bar Assn., ABA (various coms.), 7th Fed. Cir. Bar Assn., Inter-Am. Bar Assn., Mem. Acad. Fla. Trial Lawyers, Wis. Acad. Trial Lawyers (pres. 1958-59, 70-71), Assn. Trial Lawyers Am. (state committeeman 1981-83), Am. Judicature Soc., Am. Soc. Law and Medicine, Am. Coll. Legal Medicine. Cert. civil litigation specialist Nat. Bd. Trial Advocacy. Personal injury, Real property, Civil litigation. Home: 7821 N Mohawk Rd Milwaukee WI 53217 Office: 735 N Water St Suite 726 Milwaukee WI 53202

GAINES, PETER MATHEW, lawyer; b. N.Y.C., Mar. 5, 1951; s. Dan M. and Ellen M. Gaines; m. Jane Lausch, July 14, 1972; children: Matthew P., Eliizabeth C. BA, U. Wis., 1972, JD, 1975. Bar: Ill. 1975. Assoc. Mayer, Brown & Platt, Chgo., 1975-81, ptnr., 1982—. Note and comment editor U. Wis. Law Rev., 1975. Mem. ABA. Club: University (Chgo.). Banking, Contracts commercial. Office: Mayer Brown & Platt 190 S LaSalle St Chicago IL 60603

GAINES, ROBERT PENDLETON, lawyer; b. Daytona Beach, Fla., Apr. 6, 1927; s. Marion Toulmin and Marion (Howie) G.; m. Doris Bolton, July 8, 1961; children: Jennifer, Amante, Edmund. BA, U. Fla., 1950, LLB, 1956. Bar: Fla. 1956, U.S. Dist. Ct. (no. dist.) Fla. 1956, U.S. Ct. Appeals (5th cir.) 1958, U.S. Ct. Appeals (11th cir.) 1982. From assoc. to ptnr. Beggs & Lane and predecessor firms, Pensacola, Fla., 1956—. Mem. Fla. Commn. on Local Govt., Tallahassee, 1973-74. Served to lt. U.S. Army, 1945-47, 1950-53, Korea. Mem. ABA, Fla. Def. Lawyers Assn. (pres. 1974-75), Internat. Assoc. Def. Counsel, Maritime Law Assn. U.S., Southeastern Admirality Inst., Pensacola C. of C. (pres. 1969), Pensacola Jaycees (pres. 1961), Order of Coif, Phi Beta Kappa. Democrat. Episcopalian. Club: Scenic Hills Country (Pensacola) (v.p. 1986—). Lodge: Rotary (bd. dirs.). Avocations: fishing, golf. Federal civil litigation, State civil litigation, Admiralty. Home: 8839 Burning Tree Rd Pensacola FL 32514 Office: Beggs & Lane PO Box 12950 Pensacola FL 32576-2950

GAINES, SANFORD ERVIN, legal professor; b. N.Y.C., Sept. 23, 1945; s. Ervin James and Martha Twila (Zirbel) G.; m. Cassandra Labes, Oct. 25, 1969; children: Seth Daniel, Ingrid Anna-Theresa. AB, Harvard U., 1967, MA, JD, 1974. Bar: Mass. 1975, U.S. Ct. Appeals (5th cir.) 1986. Project dir. Environ. Law Inst., Washington, 1975-76; atty., sect. chief U.S. EPA, Boston, 1976-78; asst. environ. counsel Environ. Research Tech., Inc., Concord, Mass., 1978-80; asst. gen. counsel Chem. Mfrs. Assn., Washington, 1981-86; assoc. prof. law, dir. environ. liability law program U. Houston, 1986—. Contbr. articles to profl. jours. Bd. dirs. Holt-Elwell Meml. Found., East Hebron, N.H., 1985—. Mem. ABA, AAAS, Environ. Law Inst. (assoc.). Environment, Legal education. Office: U Houston Law Ctr University Park Houston TX 77004

GAINES, TYLER BELT, lawyer; b. Omaha, Oct. 21, 1924; s. Francis S. and Dorothy Tyler (Belt) G.; m. Elizabeth Bush Caldwell, Feb. 24, 1951; children—Katherine C., Elizabeth D., David T., Sarah R., Mary C.; m. Agneta Margareta Anderhagen, Nov. 27, 1977; stepchildren—Anna C., Anders C. Student Yale U., 1942-43, U. Omaha, 1946—; LL.B., Nebr. U., 1949. Bar: Nebr. 1949, U.S. Supreme Ct. 1964, U.S. Ct. Appeals (8th cir.) 1953, U.S. Dist. Ct. Nebr. 1949, U.S. Tax Ct. 1970. Ptnr., Gaines, Otis, Mullen & Carta and predecessors, Omaha, 1960—. Mem. Brownell Talbot Sch. Bd., 1964-75, pres., 1968-72; bd. dirs. Gilbert and Martha Hitchcock Found., 1970—. Served with USNR, 1943-45. Mem. ABA, Am. Coll. Probate Counsel, Nebr. Bar Assn., Omaha Bar Assn. (pres. 1982-83). Republican. Episcopalian. Clubs: Omaha Country, Omaha. Probate, Corporate taxation. Office: Gaines Otis Mullen & Carta 10050 Regency Circle Omaha NE 68114

GAINES, WEAVER HENDERSON, JR., lawyer; b. Ft. Meade, S.D., Aug. 31, 1943; s. Weaver Henderson and Bertha Louise (Harris) G. AB in Philosophy, Dartmouth Coll., 1965; LLB, U. Va., 1968. Bar: N.Y. 1969, Pa. 1979, U.S. Dist. Ct. (so. dist.) N.Y. 1973, U.S. Dist. Ct. (ea. dist.) N.Y. 1975, U.S. Ct. Appeals (2d cir.) 1975. Assoc. Dewey, Ballantine, Bushby, Palmer & Wood, N.Y.C., 1970-79; sr. staff counsel INA Corp., N.Y.C., 1979; asst. gen. counsel, sec. Thyssen-Bornemisza Inc., N.Y.C., 1979-82, v.p. strategic projects, 1982-85; v.p., dep. gen. counsel MONY Fin. Services, N.Y.C., 1985-86, sr. v.p., gen. counsel, 1985—; bd. dirs. Hyperion Inc. Participation chmn. Dartmouth Alumni Fund, 1980—; chmn. 59 W. 12th St. Tenents Assn., 1985—; bd. dirs. N.Y. Lawyers for Nixon, 1972. Served to capt. U.S. Army, 1968-70, Vietnam. Decorated Bronze Star. Mem. ABA, Assn. of Bar of City of N.Y., Fed. Bar Council. Republican. Episcopalian. Club: Hemisphere (N.Y.C.). Antitrust, General corporate, Insurance. Office: MONY Fin Services 1740 Broadway New York NY 10019

GAISER, RICHARD EDWARD, lawyer; b. N.Y.C., June 13, 1943; s. Charles H. and Winifred E. Gaiser; m. Ruth Ann Cavill, June 24, 1967; children: Kristin, Karin. BA cum laude, C.W. Post Coll., 1967; MA, Cen. Mich. U., 1982; JD, Woodrow Wilson Law Sch., 1980. Bar: Ga. 1981, U.S. Dist. Ct. (no. dist.) Ga. 1981, U.S. Ct. Appeals (11th cir.) 1981. Sole practice Lilburn, Ga., 1981—; contract adminstr. USAFR, Robins AFB, GA., 1983—. Served to maj. USAF, 1967-72, Vietnam. Decorated D.F.C., 1972. Mem. Air Force Assn. Club: Atlanta Navy Flying Club. Avocations: reading, jogging. General practice, Government contracts and claims. Home and Office: 2177 Lunceford Ln Lilburn GA 30247

GALAMAGA, ROBERT JOHN, lawyer; b. Bluefield, W.Va., Apr. 24, 1948; s. Peter and Margaret Mary (Bond) G.; m. Mary Frances Finnegan, Dec. 13, 1969; children: Kristen, Craig. BA, Fordham U., 1970; JD, U. Miami, 1973. Bar: Fla. 1974, U.S. Dist. Ct. (so. dist.) Fla. 1982. Assoc. Dixon, Dixon, Lane, Mitchell & Harris, Miami, Fla., 1975-78; sole practice Miami, 1978—. Mem. ABA, Dade County Bar Assn. (med. profl. liason com., cir. ct. gen. jurisdiction div.), Fla. Bar Assn. (legal ethics com. young lawyers sect., unauthorized practice law com., computer law com., legal forms com.), Acad. Fla. Trial Lawyers, Assn. Trial Lawyers Am., N.Y. State Trial Lawyers Assn., Maritime Law Assn. Democrat. Roman Catholic. Avocations: hunting, fishing, reading. Personal injury, State civil litigation, Federal civil litigation. Office: 7600 Red Rd Suite 214 South Miami FL 33143

GALANE, MORTON ROBERT, lawyer; b. N.Y.C., Mar. 15, 1926; s. Harry J. and Sylvia (Schenkelbach) G.; m. Rosalind Feldman, Dec. 22, 1957; children: Suzanne Galane Duvall, Jonathan A. B.E.E., CCNY, 1946; LL.B., George Washington U., 1950. Bar: D.C. 1950, Nev. 1955, Calif. 1975. Patent examiner U.S. Patent Office, Washington, 1948-50; spl. partner firm Roberts & McInnis, Washington, 1950-54; practice as Morton R. Galane, P.C., Las Vegas, Nev., 1955—; spl. counsel to Gov. Nev., 1967-70. Contbr. articles to profl. jours. Chmn. Gov.'s Com. on Future of Nev., 1979-80. Fellow Am. Coll. Trial Lawyers; mem. Am. Law Inst., IEEE, Am. Bar Assn. (council litigation sect. 1977-83), State Bar Nev., State Bar Calif., D.C. Bar. Federal civil litigation, Libel. Home: 2019 Bannies Ln Las Vegas NV 89102 Office: 302 E Carson Suite 1100 Las Vegas NV 89101

GALANIS, JOHN WILLIAM, insurance executive; b. Milw., May 9, 1937; s. William and Angeline (Koroniou) G.; m. Patricia Caro, Nov. 29, 1969; children: Lia, William, Charles, John. B.B.A. cum laude, U. Wis., 1959; J.D., U. Mich., 1963; postgrad. (Ford Found. grantee), London Sch. Econs., 1964. Bar: Wis. 1965; C.P.A., Wis. Assoc. firm Whyte & Hirschboeck S.C., Milw., 1964-68; sr. v.p., gen. counsel, sec. MGIC Investment Corp. and Mortgage Guaranty Ins. Corp., Milw., 1968—. Assoc. editor: Mich. Law Rev, 1962-63. Chmn. Milw. Found.; trustee Milw. Ballet; bd. dirs. Milw. Council on Alcoholism; v.p. and trustee Milw. Boys' and Girls' Club. Served to capt. Military Police U.S. Army, 1959-60. Mem. ABA, Wis. Bar Assn., Milw. Bar Assn., Internat. Assn. Ins. Counsel, Am. Hellenic Ednl. Progressive Assn., Am. Coll. Mortgage Attys., Order of Coif. Greek Orthodox. Clubs: Milw. Athletic, Western Racquet. General corporate. Home: 1200 Woodlawn Circle Elm Grove WI 53122 Office: MGIC Plaza Milwaukee WI 53201

GALANT, HERBERT LEWIS, lawyer; b. N.Y.C., Oct. 16, 1928; s. Charles A. and Bertha (Rosenberg) G.; m. Fern Judith Laikin, Feb. 10, 1957; children: Peter B., John M., Amy E. BA cum laude, U. Wis., 1949; LLB magna cum laude, Harvard U., 1952; LLM, NYU, 1960. Bar: N.Y. 1955, U.S. Dist. Ct. (so. dist.) N.Y. 1956, U.S. Ct. Appeals (2d cir.) 1959. Assoc. Fried, Frank et al, N.Y.C., 1955-61, ptnr., 1962—. Editor: Harvard Law Rev., 1950-52. Mem. Tenafly Twp. Bd. Ethics, (N.J.), 1978—. Served to 1st lt. USAF, 1952-54. MEM. ABA; mem. Assn. Bar City N.Y. Democrat. Jewish. Club: Harvard (N.Y.C.). General corporate, Finance. Home: 150 Tekening Dr Tenafly NJ 07670 Office: Fried Frank et al One New York Plaza New York NY 10004

GALANTER, ROBERT ALLEN, lawyer; b. Newark, Jan. 18, 1945; s. Irving S. and Beatrice (Sternberg) G.; m. Mary Jane McClurg, Aug. 14, 1971; children: Gregory, Beth. BA, Pa. State U., 1966; JD, Duquesne U., 1969. Bar: Pa. 1969, U.S. Dist. Ct. (we. dist.) Pa. 1969, U.S. Ct. Appeals (3d cir.) 1987. Ptnr. Phillips & Galanter, P.C., Pitts., 1971—. Mem. ABA, Pa. Bar Assn., Allegheny County Bar Assn., Comml. Law League Am., Nat. Ski Patrol. Clubs: Rivers (Pitts.); Williams Country (Weirton, W.Va.). Avocations: golf, running, skiing, coaching Little League baseball. Contracts commercial, Real property, Federal civil litigation. Office: Phillips & Galanter PC 428 Forbes Ave Pittsburgh PA 15219

GALASKA, MICHAEL FRANCIS, lawyer; b. Omaha, Apr. 25, 1950; s. Stanley Francis and Betty Ann (Garvey) G. BA, Creighton U., 1972; JD, 1975. Bar: Nebr. 1975, U.S. Dist. Ct. Nebr. 1975, Okla. 1982. Sole practice, Omaha, 1975-82, Geary, Okla., 1982—. Del. Nebr. White House Conf. on Handicapped Individuals, Lincoln, 1976; treas. Omaha chpt. Nat. Paraplegia Found., 1977; trustee Geary Library Bd., 1986—. Mem. ABA, Nebr. Bar Assn., Okla. Bar Assn., Okla. Trial Lawyers Assn., Blaine County Bar Assn., Canadian County Bar Assn., Geary C. of C. (2d v.p. 1986, 1st v.p. 1987). Republican. Roman Catholic. Lodge: Elks. General practice, Family and matrimonial, Probate. Home and Office: 205 S Galena Route 1 Box 113-C Geary OK 73040

GALATZ, HENRY FRANCIS, lawyer; b. N.Y.C., Feb. 5, 1947; s. Julius D. and Dorothy (Kirschen) G.; m. Colleen Prager, Aug. 19, 1973; children: Benjamin Chase, Brandon Kyle. BA, U. Ariz., 1970, MEd, MA with honors, 1973; JD, U. the Pacific, 1979. Bar: Ill. 1981, U.S. Dist. Ct. (no. dist.) Ill. 1981, U.S. Ct. Appeals (7th cir.) 1981, U.S. Dist. Ct. (ea. dist.) Mich. 1982, U.S. Ct. Appeals (6th cir.) 1982, U.S. Dist. Ct. (ea. dist.) Mo. 1985, U.S. Supreme Ct. 1985, U.S. Dist. Ct. Mont. 1986. Cons. labor relations Phoenix Closures, Chgo., 1974-75, Galatz Elec. Corp., Las Vegas, Nev., 1975-80; labor counsel W.W. Grainger, Inc., Skokie, Ill., 1980—; sole practice Olympia Fields, Ill., 1981—; hearing officer Ill. State Bd. Edn., Chgo., 1982—; atty. Chgo. Legal Services Found. (cert. merit 1983), 1983—; mem. com. Employment Law Inst. Northwestern U., Evanston, Ill. Coach Homewood-Flossmoor (Ill.) Soccer Club, 1985—, Intercollegiate Varsity Athletics, Lacrosse. Recipient Judge Mason Rothwell Award, 1979, Cert. of Merit Chgo. Legal Services Found., 1983. Mem. ABA, Ill. Bar Assn., Chgo. Bar Assn., Am. Arbitrators Assn. (arbitrator), Am. Judicature Soc., Assn. Am. Trial Lawyers, Ill. Trial Lawyers Assn., Phi Delta Phi, Alpha Epsilon Pi. Democrat. Jewish. Labor, Federal civil litigation, Public education law. Home: PO Box 288 Olympia Fields IL 60461 Office: W W Grainger Inc 5500 W Howard St Skokie IL 60077

GALBUT, MARTIN RICHARD, lawyer; b. Miami Beach, Fla., June 27, 1946; s. Paul A. and Ethel (Kolnick) G.; m. Cynthia Ann Slaughter, June 4, 1972; children: Keith Richard, Lindsay Anne. BS in Speech, Northwestern U., 1968, JD cum laude, 1971. Bar: Ariz. 1972, U.S. Dist. Ct. Ariz. 1972. Assoc. Brown, Vlassis & Bain P.A., Phoenix, 1971-75; ptnr. McLoone, Theobald & Galbut, Phoenix, 1975-86; sole practice Scottsdale, Ariz., 1986—; of counsel Furth, Fahrner, Bluemle & Mason, 1986—; adv. dir. Liberty Bank. Contbr. articles to profl. jours. Chmn. Ariz. State Air Pollution Control Hearing Bd., 1984—; mem. Govs. Task Force on Urban Air Quality, 1986; bd. dirs. Men's Art Council Phoenix Art Mus.; bd. dirs. founder Ariz. Asthma Found. Clarion de Witt Hardy scholar, Kosmerl scholar. Mem. ABA, Ariz. State Bar Assn. (lectr. securities law, securities law com. and sect.), Maricopa County Bar Assn., Am. Arbitration Assn. (arbitrator), Nat. Assn. Securities Dealers (arbitrator). Democrat. Jewish. Avocations: antique and fine art collecting, travelling to Asia, tennis. Federal civil litigation, State civil litigation, Antitrust. Office: 7373 N Scottsdale Rd Suite B-252 Scottsdale AZ 85253

GALE, CONNIE R(UTH), lawyer; b. Cleve., July 15, 1946; m. Curtis S. Gale, Dec. 20, 1967. Student, Miami U., Oxford, Ohio, 1964-66; BA with distinction, U. Mich., 1967, JD, 1971; MBA, Mich. State U., 1981. Bar: mich. 1971. Law clk. to presiding justice Mich. Supreme Ct., Lansing, 1971-72; asst. atty. gen. State of Mich., Lansing, 1973; corp. counsel Chrysler Corp., Highland Park, Mich., 1973-81; assoc. gen. counsel Fed.-Mogul Corp., Southfield, Mich., 1981-86; assoc. gen. counsel and asst. sec. Allnet Communication Services, Inc., Birmingham, Mich., 1987—. Chmn. Religious Edn. Com., Farmington, Mich. Mem. ABA, Mich. Bar Assn. (chmn. in-house counsel com. 1984—, council member corp. fin. bus. law sect. 1985—, alternate dispute resolution com. 1986—), Phi Kappa Phi. Contracts commercial, General corporate, Securities. Office: Allnet Communication Services 30300 Telegraph Rd Suite 350 Birmingham MI 48010

GALE, PETER L., lawyer; b. Chgo., Feb. 11, 1936; s. Eureka Ward and Gladys Dorothy (Field) G.; m. Sheila Kavanagh, Dec. 29, 1976; 1 stepchild: Jennifer; children: Alexander, Amanda. BA, Wilkes Coll., 1958; postgrad, Cornell U., 1958-62, LLB, 1965. Bar: Pa. 1965, U.S. Dist. Ct. (ea. dist.) Pa., U.S. Dist. Ct. (ea. dist.) N.Y. 1966, N.Y. 1979, U.S. Dist. Ct. (ea. dist.) N.Y. 1984. Assoc. Thomas Erskine, Phila., 1965-68; ptnr. Rosenthal & Gale, Phila., 1968-78; assoc. David Freedman, N.Y.C., 1978-80, Bruce G. Clark & Assocs., N.Y.C., 1980—. Personal injury, Labor, Civil service. Home: 363 Greenwich St New York NY 10013 Office: Bruce G Clark Assocs 233 Broadway New York NY 10279

GALE, RANDALL GLENN, lawyer; b. Nanticoke, Pa., Apr. 20, 1952; s. Joseph John and Mary Elizabeth (Glenn) G.; m. Pamela Louise Pethick, Aug. 10, 1974; children: Randall Glenn Jr., Christopher Scott. BA summa cum laude, Wilkes Coll., 1974; JD, Dickinson Sch. of Law, 1977. Bar: Pa. 1977, U.S. Dist. Ct. (mid. dist.) Pa. 1977, U.S. Ct. Appeals (3d cir.) 1977. Law clk. to judge U.S. Dist. Ct., Harrisburg, Pa., 1977-79; dep. atty. gen. Pa. Dept. of Justice, Harrisburg, 1979-81; sr. dep. atty. gen. Pa. Office Atty. Gen., Harrisburg, 1982-85; assoc. Thomas & Thomas, Harrisburg, 1985—. Mem. tort liabilities subcom. Pa. Transp. Adv. Com., Harrisburg, 1984-85. Mem. Pa. Bar Assn., Dauphin County Bar Assn., Assn. Trial Lawyers Am., Cen. Pa. Claims Assn., Luzerne County Law Library, Pa. Def. Inst. Republican. Presbyterian. Club: Country Club Hills Assn. (Camp Hill, Pa.). Avocations: gardening, golf. Insurance, Personal injury, Workers' compensation. Home: 2916 Rathton Rd Camp Hill PA 17011 Office: Thomas & Thomas 212 Locust St PO Box 999 Harrisburg PA 17108

GALEA, JOHN HENRY, lawyer; b. Albany, N.Y., Jan. 18, 1924; s. John Fortune and Virginia (Sterling) G.; m. Helen Flynn Conway, Aug. 14, 1948; children: Michelle Galea Jeter, Mark C., Mary Ellen, Monica, Madeleine. AB cum laude, Holy Cross Coll., 1947; LLB, Harvard U., 1951. Bar: Ohio 1952, Ky. 1953, Va. 1959. Assoc. Grossman Schlesinger & Carter, Cleve., 1951-53; with Reynolds Metals Co., Richmond, Va., 1953—, asst. gen. counsel, 1964-72, gen. atty., 1972-76, v.p., gen. counsel, 1976-85, sr. v.p., gen. counsel, 1985—, also dir. subs.; bd. dirs. Eskimo Pie Corp. Bd. dirs. Reynolds Metals Co. Found. Served in USAAF, 1943-45, ETO. Decorated D.F.C., Air medal with three oak leaf clusters. Mem. ABA, Aluminum Assn. (legal audit com.), Am. Corp. Counsel Assn., Assn. Gen. Counsel, Va. Bar Assn., Ky. Bar Assn., Richmond Bar Assn., NAM (legal adv. com.). Republican. Roman Catholic. Clubs: Internat. (Washington); Harvard of Va. General corporate. Office: 6601 W Broad St Richmond VA 23261

GALEF, STEVEN ALLEN, lawyer; b. N.Y.C., Mar. 10, 1940; s. Gabriel and Mildred (Rome) G.; m. Sandra Risk, Mar. 30, 1963; children—Gregory T., Gwendolyn. B.A. cum laude, Washington and Lee U., 1962; J.D., U. Va. 1965. Bar: N.Y. 1966. Assoc. Galef & Jacobs, N.Y.C., 1965-72, ptnr., 1972—, chmn. exec. com., 1984—; counsel Vittoria & Parker, N.Y.C., 1982—. Legislator Westchester County (N.Y.), 1975-79; vice chmn. ARC, 1974-76; founder Westchester Mcpl. Law Forum; bd. dirs. United Way of Westchester, 1979-83, chmn. allocations, 1979-81; bd. dirs. Westchester Council for Arts, 1976-79, 82-87 ; mem. N.Y. Hosp. Adv. Bd., 1981-85; v.p. Westchester Health Fund, 1984—; pres. Westchester Community Service Council 1981-84; bd. dirs. Westchester County Assn., 1980—. Served with USNG, 1966-72. Recipient Disting. Service award Ossining (N.Y.) Area Jaycees; Humanitarian of Yr. award B'nai B'rith of No. Westchester, 1977, Westchester County Disting. Service award, 1984. Mem. ABA (internat. and adminstrv. law sects.), N.Y. State Bar Assn. (internat. law com.), Westchester County Bar Assn., Assn. Bar of City of N.Y. (chmn. immigration and naturalization law com. 1975-77, admiralty law com. 1982-85). Club: Rotary of N.Y. (bd. dirs. 1975-78). Private international, General corporate, General practice. Home: 44 Orchard Dr Ossining NY 10562 Office: 275 Madison AVe New York NY 10016 also: 709 Westchester Ave White Plains NY 10604

GALELLA, JOSEPH PETER, lawyer; b. N.Y.C., Oct. 19, 1956; s. Joseph Anthony and Stella Agnes (McKee) G.; m. Elaine Fowler, Aug. 15, 1981. BA, Franklin & Marshall Coll., 1978; JD, U. Miami, 1981. Bar: Fla. 1981, N.Y. 1982, U.S. Dist. Ct. (so. dist.) Fla. 1982, U.S. Ct. Appeals (11th cir.) 1982. Assoc. Karsch & Meyer, N.Y.C., 1981-82; sole practice Peekskill, N.Y., 1983—; title atty. Kenneth Pregno Agy., Ltd., Peekskill, 1984—. Rep. Franklin & Marshall Coll. Alumni Admissions Program, 1979—; dir. Peekskill Field Library, 1985—. Mem. N.Y. Bar Assn., Fla. Bar Assn., Westchester County Bar Assn., Peekskill Bar Assn. Democrat. Roman Catholic. Avocations: swimming, racquetball, tennis, reading. Real property, Probate. Home: 434 Simpson Pl Peekskill NY 10566

GALER, BENJAMIN ANDERSON, lawyer, financial executive; b. Mt. Pleasant, Iowa, May 3, 1915; s. Paul B. and Ruth (Anderson) G.; m. Dorothy I. Mathews, Sept. 4, 1939; children—Dorothea Galer Higgins, Ernest L. Student Iowa Wesleyan Coll., Mt. Pleasant, 1931-33; B.A., U. Iowa, 1935, J.D. magna cum laude, 1937. Bar: Iowa 1937, U.S. Dist. Ct. (so. dist.) Iowa 1937, U.S. Supreme Ct. 1972. Ptnr., Galer & Galer, and predecessors, 1937—; county atty., 1942-46; counsel Capitol Savs. and Loan Assn., Mt. Pleasant, 1945-84 , also dir.; v.p. Peoples State Bank, Winfield, Iowa, 1960-72, also dir.; dir. United Service Corp., Mt. Pleasant, 1971-84. Chmn., Henry County (Iowa) Republican Com., 1949-58, dist. chmn. State Central Com., 1958-66, del. Nat. Conv., 1960; mem. Henry County Mental Health Commn., 1958-75. Mem. ABA, Iowa Bar Assn. (gov. 1964-68), Henry County Bar Assn., Order of Coif, Phi Alpha Delta, Beta Theta Pi, Pi Kappa Delta. Methodist. Clubs: Kiwanis (pres. 1940), Masons. Co-editor Iowa Law Rev., 1936-37. Estate planning, Real property, Personal income taxation. Home: 707 Alter Dr Mount Pleasant IA 52641 Office: 211 W Monroe St Mount Pleasant IA 52641

GALES, ROBERT ROBINSON, lawyer, consultant; b. N.Y.C., Feb. 15, 1941; s. Arthur S. and Gertrude L. (Robinson) G.; m. Karen A. Terry, Nov. 25, 1986; children: Laurie Ann, Thomas Michael, Brian Timothy, Victoria Marie. BA in History and Geography, Ohio Wesleyan U., 1962; JD, Syracuse U., 1965; LLM, George Washington U., 1966; postgrad. U. Philippines, 1969, Indsl. Coll. Armed Forces, 1971. Bar: N.Y. 1966, U.S. Dist. Ct. (so. and ea. dists.) N.Y. 1967, U.S. Dist. Ct. (we. dist.) Wash. 1967, U.S. Ct. Mil. Appeals 1967, U.S. Ct. Claims 1967, U.S. Ct. Appeals (9th cir.) 1968, D.C. 1973, U.S. Dist. Ct. (ea. dist.) Va. 1973, U.S. Ct. Appeals (4th cir.) 1973, U.S. Ct. Appeals (2d cir.) 1975, U.S. Customs Ct. 1977, U.S. Ct. Customs and Patent Appeals 1978, Ill. 1978, U.S. Ct. Internat. Trade, 1980, U.S. Ct. Appeals (Fed. cir.) 1982, U.S. Ct. Appeals (7th cir.) 1983, U.S. Dist. Ct. (no. dist.) Ill. 1983, U.S. Dist. Ct. (so. dist.) Ill. 1984. Travel cons. ESSO Touring Service, N.Y.C., 1960; dep. dir. internat. law 13th Air Force, Philippines, 1969-71; asst. legal advisor U.S. del. Renegotiation of Philippines-U.S. Status of Forces Agreement, 1969-71; chief civil law Tactical Air Command, USAF, Hampton, Va., 1971-72, chief adminstrv. law, 1972-73; assoc. Herzfeld & Rubin, P.C., N.Y.C., 1973-77; task force coordinator Volkswagen of Am., Inc., Englewood Cliffs, N.J., 1977; sr. atty. Velsicol Chem. Corp., sec. subsidiaries, 1977-80; asst. atty. gen. Consumer Protection div. Office of Ill. Atty. Gen., Bensenville and Joliet, 1981-83; chief Utility and Acquisition Law, 375th Air Base Group, Scott AFB, Dept. Air Force, Belleville, Ill., 1984-87; dept. counsel Def. Legal Services Agy., Directorate for Indsl. Security Clearance Rev., Arlington, Va., 1987—; vis. lectr. Manhattan Coll., 1973-77, N.J. Inst. Tech., 1975-77, Ill. Inst. Tech., 1978-84, So. Ill. Univ., Carbondale, 1984-86. Mem. Wash. State Soccer Commn., 1967-68; chmn. exploring com. Far East council Philippine dist. Boy Scouts Am., 1969-71; dist. judge adv. VFW, 1972-73; pres., chmn. exec. com. Briarcliff Citizens for Responsive Govt., 1973-74; bd. dirs. Ossining (N.Y.) Area Jaycees, 1973-74, sec., 1974-75; pres. Ossining Hist. Soc., 1974-76; Republican dist. leader Town of Ossining, 1974-78; dir. Soc. Prevention of Cruelty to Animals of Westchester, 1974-77; dir. Briarcliff-Ossining-Scarborough br. ARC, 1975-76; mem. Westchester County Rep. Com., 1975-78; commr. Wayne Twp. (Ill.) Soccer, 1979-83; Rep. precinct committeeman Wayne Twp., 1979-82; adv. bd. Elgin (Ill.) High Sch., 1979-83; trustee Wayne Twp., 1979-85. Served with USAF, 1966-73, Vietnam. Decorated Bronze Star, Meritorious Service medal with 1 oak leaf cluster, Air Force Commendation medal with 3 oak leaf clusters, Air Force Achievement medal (U.S.); various medals Republic of Vietnam, Outstanding Contribution award USAF, 1986. Mem. Internat. Bar Assn., Twp. Ofcls. Ill. (bd. dirs. 1984-85), Vietnam Vets. Bar Assn. (air force judge adv.), Am. Mosquito Control Assn., Ill. Mosquito Control Assn., Arnold Air Soc., Delta Phi Epsilon, Phi Alpha Delta. Republican. Club: Internat. Trade (Chgo.). Contbr. articles to profl. jours. Avocation: sports. Private international, Administrative and regulatory, Government contracts and claims. Home: 6411 Battle Rock Dr Clifton VA 22024 Office: Def Legal Services Agy Directorate Indsl Security Clearance Rev PO Box 3656 Arlington VA 22203

GALIARDO, JOHN WILLIAM, lawyer, diversified health care company executive; b. Elizabeth, N.J., Dec. 28, 1933; s. Joseph A. and Genevieve A. (Luxich) G.; m. Joan A. DeTurk, Aug. 26, 1961; children: Richard C., Christopher D., Elizabeth A. B.S., U. Md., 1956; LL.B., Columbia U., 1962. Bar: N.Y. 1962. Assoc. Dewey, Ballantine, Bushby, Palmer & Wood, N.Y.C., 1962-71; asst. gen. counsel E.R. Squibb & Sons, Inc., Princeton, N.J., 1971-77; v.p., gen. counsel Becton Dickinson and Co., Franklin Lakes, N.J., 1977—. Treas. Charter Commn. Scotch Plains, N.J., 1970-71; mem. Joint Consol. Com. Princeton, 1973-76; mem. legal adv. council Mid-Atlantic Legal Found.; trustee Ind. Coll. Fund of N.J. Served with AUS, 1956-58. Mem. Am. Bar Assn., N.Y. State Bar Assn., Assn. Bar City N.Y. General corporate. Home: 56 Crooked Tree Ln Princeton NJ 08540 Office: Becton Dickinson and Co One Becton Dr Franklin Lakes NJ 07417

GALIE, LAWRENCE PIUS, lawyer; b. Conshohocken, Pa., Jan. 4, 1952; s. Peter John and Mary Agusta (Schraeder) G. BA, Pa. State U., 1974; JD, U. Pitts., 1977. Bar: Pa. 1977, U.S. Dist. Ct. (we. dist.) Pa. 1977, U.S. Ct. Appeals (3d cir.) 1978. Assoc. McClure & Watkins, P.C., Pitts., 1977-80; atty. Duquesne Light Co., Pitts., 1980-81, asst. treas., 1981—; adj. prof. Point Park Coll., Pitts., 1980—; v.p. Whale's Tale, Pitts., 1986—, bd. dirs. Editor U. Pitts. Law Rev., 1977. Treas. Consumer Credit Counseling of Western Pa., Pitts., 1986—, bd. dirs. 1985-86. Club: Rivers (Pitts.). Avocations: travel, sports, public speaking. Public utilities, Bankruptcy, General corporate. Office: Duquesne Light Co 301 Grant St Pittsburgh PA 15279

GALIP, RONALD GEORGE, lawyer; b. Youngtown, Ohio, Feb. 28, 1934; s. George A. and Agnes A. (Ellis) G.; m. Eileen E. Bott, 1955; children: Rochelle D., Kathleen A. Galip Mootz. BA, Youngstown (Ohio) State U., 1955; JD, Ohio State U., 1957. Gen. counsel Cafaro Co., Youngstown, 1957-78; ptnr. Galip & Manos, Youngstown, 1978-83; sole practice Youngstown, 1983—; pres. Youngstown Title Agy., 1986; counsel, bd. dirs. Youngstown Devel. Co., 1986. Bd. dirs. Ohio Heart Inst.; trustee Easter Seal Soc., Youngstown. Mem. ABA, Ohio Bar Assn., Mahoning County Bar Assn., Internat. Council Shopping Ctrs., Am. Arbitration Assn. Roman Catholic. Avocations: golf, tennis, travel. Shopping centers, Real property, Landlord-tenant. Home: 3445 Logan Way Youngstown OH 44505 Office: 422 City Center One Youngstown OH 44503

GALLAGHER, DENNIS VINCENT, lawyer; b. Cleve., Aug. 28, 1952; s. Vincent Francis and Dolores Hariet (Hastings) G.; m. Deborah Scott, Aug. 12, 1978; children: Matthew, Luke. Bar: Calif. 1978, Nev. 1979, U.S. Dist. Ct. Nev. 1979, U.S. Dist. Ct. (no., so. and ea. dists.) Calif. 1980, U.S. Ct. Appeals (9th cir.) 1980. Dep. Legis. Counsel Bureau, Carson City, Nev., 1978-79; assoc. Law Offices of Daniel Walsh, Carson City, 1979-81; dep. atty. gen. Carson City, 1981-83; chief investigation div. Nev. State Gaming Control Bd., Carson City, 1983-84; assoc. gen. counsel Harrahs Hotels and Casinos, Reno, 1984—. Loaned exec. United Way No. Nev., Reno, 1985—; mem. No. Nev. Mental Health Adv. Commn., Reno, 1984-86. Named one of Outstanding Young Men Am., 1984. Mem. ABA (gen. practice sect., gaming law com., corp. counsel subcom.), Calif. Bar Assn., Nev. Bar Assn. (gaming sect.), Washoe County Bar Assn., Internat. Assn. Gaming Attys., Am. Corp. Counsel Assn. General corporate, Administrative and regulatory, Gaming. Office: Harrahs Hotels and Casinos 300 E 2d St Reno NV 89520

GALLAGHER, HENRY EDMOND, JR., lawyer; b. Wilmington, Del., Aug. 2, 1949; s. Henry E. and Matilda (Hondros) G.; m. Geri Lotierzo, July 9, 1977; children: Kristin E., Henry E. III. AB, Villanova U., 1971, JD, 1975. Bar: Del. 1975, U.S. Dist. Ct. Del., U.S. Ct. Appeals (3rd cir., 4th cir.), U.S. Ct. Claims, CAFC. Law clk. Superior Ct. of Del., Wilmington, 1975-76; assoc. Connolly, Bove & Lodge, Wilmington, 1976-82; ptnr. Connolly, Bove, Lodge & Hutz, Wilmington, 1982—; mem. bd. profl. responsibility, 1986—. Bd. dirs. United Cerebral Palsy of Delaware, Inc., 1979-86; chmn. Protection and Advocacy System of Del., Wilmington, 1978-82. Mem. ABA, Del. Bar Assn. (council corp. law sect. 1986—). Democrat. Roman Catholic. General corporate, Contracts commercial, Federal civil litigation. Office: Connolly Bove Lodge Hutz PO Box 2207 Wilmington DE 19899

GALLAGHER, JOHN M., JR., lawyer; b. Ocala, Fla., Jan. 20, 1957; s. John M. Sr. and Rosemary (Flahive) G. Grad., St. Leo Coll., 1976; JD, Loyola U., New Orleans, 1980. Bar: Fla. 1980, La. 1981. Assoc. Cooper & Hingle, New Orleans, 1981-84; ptnr. Wootan, Hennen, Pelayo & Gallagher, New Orleans, 1984-85; sole practice New Orleans, 1985—. Mem. Assn. Trial Lawyers Am., La. Trial Lawyers Assn., New Orleans Bar Assn. Republican. General corporate, Insurance, Personal injury. Office: 1811 Coliseum St New Orleans LA 70130

GALLAGHER, JOHN PAUL, lawyer; b. Phila., Dec. 13, 1947; s. Paul Francis and Kathryn Mary (Gallagher) G.; m. Frances Maureen Madden, Feb. 8, 1975; children: Matthew, Jean Marie, Stephen. BS, LaSalle U., 1969; JD, Temple U., 1973. Bar: Pa. 1974, U.S. Tax Ct. 1985. Auditor Arthur Andersen and Co., Phila., 1973-74; assoc. Schubert, Bellwoar, Mallon & Walheim, Phila., 1974-83, ptnr., 1983—, also chmn. real estate dept., 1985—; trustee retirement plan Schubert, Bellwoar, Mallon & Walheim, Phila., 1985—; bd. dirs. Sacred Heart Manor, Phila. Tchr. St. Luke CCD Program, Glenside, Pa., 1981—; mem. Sacred Heart Manor Aux., Phila., 1984. Served with U.S. Army, 1969-72. Recipient Bishop Neumann award Archdiocese of Phila., 1986. Mem. ABA, Pa. Bar Assn., Phila. Bar Assn. (unauthorized practice com.), St. Thomas More Soc. Democrat, Republican. Roman Catholic. CLub: Lawyers (Phila.). Avocations: basketball, reading. Pension, profit-sharing, and employee benefits, Probate, Personal income taxation. Home: 235 Sylvania Ave Glenside PA 19038 Office: Schubert Bellwoar Mallon & Walheim 1330 Two Penn Ctr Plaza Philadelphia PA 19102

GALLAGHER, MICHAEL GERALD, lawyer; b. Phila., Nov. 24, 1952; s. Gerald Joseph and Lucille Virginia (Kiess) G.; m. Joanne Wolfe, Aug. 16, 1975. BA, U. Del., 1975; JD, U. Baltimore, 1980; LLM, George Washington U., 1986. Bar: Md. 1980, U.S. Dist. Ct. Md. 1981, U.S. Ct. Mil. Appeals 1981, U.S. Appeals (fed. cir.) 1985, U.S. Ct. Appeals (D.C. cir.) 1986. Sr. atty. chief counsel IRS, Washington, 1984—. Served to capt. JAGC, U.S. Army, 1981-84. Mem. ABA, Assn. Trial lawyers Am., Res. Officers Assn. Democrat. Lutheran. Avocations: tennis, running. Labor, Federal civil litigation, Military.

GALLAGHER, MICHAEL STEPHEN, lawyer, priest; b. Easton, Pa., Dec. 9, 1948; s. James Stephen and Rosemary (Smith) G. BA, Spring Hill Coll., 1973; MA, U. Toronto, 1974; JD, Georgetown U., 1979; M in Divinity, Weston Sch. Theology, 1984; MST, Jesuit Sch. Theology, 1985. Bar: La. 1979, U.S. Dist. Ct. (ea. dist.) La., U.S. Ct. Appeals (5th and 11th cirs.) 1979, Mass., U.S. Dist. Ct. Mass. 1981, U.S. Supreme Ct. 1982. Instr. Spring Hill Coll., Mobile, Ala., 1974-76; supr. atty. Loyola Law Clinic, New Orleans, 1979-81, 85-86; atty Mass. Defenders, Boston, 1982-83; co-ordinator Gillis Long Poverty Law Ctr. Loyola U., New Orleans, 1986—; bd. dirs. New Orleans Legal Assistance Corp., 1985—. Mem. ABA, La. State Bar Assn., Audubon Soc. Democrat. Roman Catholic. Avocations: camping, fishing. Criminal, Family and matrimonial, Jurisprudence. Office: Gillis W Long Poverty Law Ctr 7214 St Charles Ave New Orleans LA 70118

GALLAGHER, SHAWN THOMAS, lawyer; b. Huron, S.D., Apr. 22, 1954; s. John Edward and Catherine (Thernes) G.; m. Mary Patricia Ruhlman, July 17, 1976; children: Kathleen, Jacquelyn. BA, Mt. Marty Coll., 1976; JD, U. Notre Dame, 1981. Bar: Neb. 1981, U.S. Dist. Ct. Neb. 1981, U.S. Army Ct. Milit. Rev. 1981. Commd. capt. U.S. Army, 1981; atty. JAGC U.S. Army, Ft. Knox, Ky., Washington and Honduras, 1981—. Mem. ABA, Nebr. Bar Assn. Democrat. Roman Catholic. Avocations: woodworking, chess. Government contracts and claims, Administrative and regulatory. Home: 7021 Bedrock Rd Alexandria VA 22306 Office: HQDA (DAJA-LTF) Washington DC 20310-2210

GALLAGHER, THOMAS ALLEN, lawyer; b. Cleve., Sept. 15, 1942; s. Thomas Joseph and Florence Allen G.; m. Leontina Kelly, July 29, 1966. B.E.E., Tulane U., 1965; J.D., George Washington U., 1968. Bar: Md. 1968, Calif. 1970. Patent staff atty. Communications Satellite Corp., Washington, 1968-69; assoc. Limbach, Limbach & Sutton, San Francisco, 1969-72, ptnr., 1972-82; ptnr. Majestic, Gallagher, Parsons & Siebert, San Francisco, 1982—. Mem. San Francisco Bar Assn., San Francisco Patent Law Assn., ABA, Am. Patent Law Assn., Licensing Exec. Soc., AIPPI, Audio Engring. Soc., Soc. Motion Picture and TV Engrs., IEEE. Club: Commonwealth of Calif. Patent. Office: 101 California St 39th Floor San Francisco CA 94111

GALLAGHER, THOMAS JORDAN, JR., lawyer; b. DeKalb, Ill., Sept. 10, 1947; s. Thomas Jordan Sr. and Rosella Jane (Conlin) G.; m. Deborah Lynn Steckhan, Aug. 16, 1975 (dec. Feb. 1980); 1 child, Sarah Jane. BA, U. Wis., 1969; JD, Ill. Inst. Tech., 1972. Bar: Ill. 1972, U.S. Dist. Ct. (no. dist.) Ill. 1972, U.S. Ct. Appeals (7th cir.) 1978, U.S. Supreme Ct. 1978. Instr. Northern Ill. U., DeKalb, 1972-73; from asst. state's atty. to state's atty. DeKalb County, Sycamore, Ill., 1973-84; ptnr. Gallagher, Fuenty & Klein, DeKalb, 1984—; lectr. various legal and civic groups. Mem. ABA, Ill. Bar Assn. (criminal justice council), DeKalb County Bar Assn., Ill. Trial Lawyers Assn. Lodge: Elks, K.C. Criminal, State civil litigation, Federal civil litigation. Home: 904 W State Sycamore IL 60178 Office: Gallagher Fuenty & Klein Suite 300 Hillcrest Centre 444 E Hillcrest Dr DeKalb IL 60115

GALLAGHER, WALTER EDWARD, lawyer; b. New Haven, Feb. 11, 1910; s. Lawrence James and Margaret Agnes (Donlon) G.; m. Nancy Lee Cooley, June 28, 1963; children—Janet (Mrs. Charles S. Linning, Jr.), Linda D. B.A., Georgetown U., 1931, LL.B., 1934, LL.M., 1935. Bar: D.C. bar 1934. Spl. asst. to U.S. Atty. Gen., U.S. Dept. Justice, Washington, 1934-39;

practiced in Washington, 1939—; partner firm Gallagher, Boland, Meiburger & Brosnan, 1945—. Author: (with F. Vinson Roach) Legislative History of Natural Gas Act, 1938-68, 2 vols., 1968, Legislative History of the Department of Energy Organization Act, 6 vols., 1978; contbg. author: (with F. Vinson Roach) Legislative History of the National Energy Acts, 6 vols., 1978, Regulation of the Gas Industry; Rate of Return Chpt. of American Gas Assn. Publ. Served as lt. (j.g.) USNR, 1944-45. Mem. Am. Bar Assn., Phi Alpha Delta. Roman Catholic. Clubs: Congressional Country (Bethesda, Md.) (pres. 1965-67), Burning Tree (Bethesda, Md.). Legislative, FERC practice, Legal history. Office: Gallagher Boland Meiburger & Brosnan 821 15th St NW Washington DC 20005

GALLANT, KENNETH STUART, lawyer, educator; b. Washington, June 21, 1951; s. Arthur and Martha (Forman) G. AB cum laude, Harvard U., 1973; JD cum laude, U. Pa., 1977. Bar: Pa. 1977, D.C. 1980, U.S. Dist. Ct. (ea. dist.) Pa. 1980, U.S. Ct. Appeals (3d cir.) 1980, U.S. Supreme Ct. 1984, Idaho 1986, U.S. Dist. Ct. Idaho 1986, U.S. Ct. Appeals (9th cir.) 1986. Law clk. to justice Pa. Supreme Ct., Erie, 1977-78; law clk. to judge U.S. Dist. Ct. (ea. dist.) Pa., Phila., 1978-79; asst. dist. atty. Phila. Dist. Atty.'s Office, 1979-84; vis. assoc. prof. law U. Okla., Norman, 1984-86; assoc. prof. law U. Idaho, Moscow, 1986—. Vol. Big Bros./Big Sisters, Phila., 1980-84; mem. steering com. Cleve. County Dems., Okla., 1985-86; mem. Latah County (Idaho) Dem. Com. Mem. ABA. Jewish. Criminal, Legal education, Legal history. Office: U Idaho Law Sch Moscow ID 83843

GALLANT, WADE MILLER, JR., lawyer; b. Raleigh, N.C., Jan. 12, 1930; s. Wade Miller and Sallie Wesley (Jones) G.; m. Sandra Kirkham, Sept. 15, 1979. BA summa cum laude, Wake Forest U., 1952, JD cum laude, 1955. Bar: N.C. 1955. Since practiced in Winston-Salem, N.C.; ptnr. Womble, Carlyle, Sandridge & Rice, 1963—; bd. dirs. EuroCaribe Bank & Trust Co. Ltd., Brenner Cos., Inc., Piece Goods Shops Corp., Trinity Am. Corp.; lectr. continuing edn. N.C. Bar Found., 1966—. Contbr. articles to legal publs. Pres. Forsyth County Legal Aid Soc., 1963-67; assoc. Family and Child Service Agy., Winston-Salem, 1962-65, Winston-Salem Symphony Assn., 1965-66, Forsyth Mental Health Assn., 1972-73, N.C. Mental Health Assn., 1974-75; dir.-at-large Nat. Mental Health Assn., 1978-84, v.p., 1981-82; bd. dirs., exec. com. Blumenthal Jewish Home for the Aged Inc. Fellow Am. Bar Found. (life); mem. Internat. Bar Assn., N.C. Bar Assn., Forsyth County Bar Assn., Am. Counsel Assn. (hon.), Am. Law Inst., Phi Beta Kappa, Omicron Delta Kappa, Phi Delta Phi. Democrat. Episcopalian. Clubs: Old Town, Twin City, Piedmont (Winston-Salem). Banking, General corporate, Securities. Home: 2534 Warwick Rd Winston-Salem NC 27104 Office: Womble Carlyle Sandridge & Rice 2400 Wachovia Bldg Winston-Salem NC 27101

GALLANTZ, GEORGE GERALD, lawyer; b. N.Y.C., Apr. 23, 1913; s. Samuel and Gussie (Safir) G.; m. Lillian Kolko, Nov. 12, 1939; children—Michael, Judith Coven. B.S., CCNY, 1932; LL.B. cum laude, Bklyn. Law Sch., 1935. Bar: N.Y. 1935. Atty. N.Y.C. Corp. Counsel's Office, 1939-42; clk. to judge N.Y. State Ct. Appeals, 1943-45; asso. firm Simpson Thacher & Bartlett, N.Y.C., 1946-56; partner firm Colton, Gallantz & Fernbach, N.Y.C., 1958-63; Proskauer Rose Goetz & Mendelsohn, 1963—. Trustee Bklyn. Law Sch., 1983—, Henry St. Settlement, 1985—. Mem. Am. Bar Assn., Assn. Bar City N.Y. (chmn. exec. com. 1974-75). Antitrust, Federal civil litigation, Trademark and copyright. Home: 37 W 12th St New York NY 10011 Office: 300 Park Ave New York NY 10022

GALLASPY, JOHN NORMAN, lawyer; b. Pelican, La., Nov. 8, 1932; s. Francis Norman and Hazel (Weeks) G.; m. Dixie Nell Yates, June 14, 1958; children: John Whithurst, Gardner Weeks, Leland Redding. BA, La. State U., 1952, JD, 1958. Asst. dist. atty. 22nd Jud. Dist., Bogalusa, La., 1969-77; atty. City of Bogalusa, 1978-84; ptnr. Gallaspy & Paduda, Bogalusa. Contbg. author: Pelican, Our Home, 1985. Pres. Bogalusa Community Affairs Com., Bogalusa, 1965. Served to 1st lt. U.S. Army, 1952-54, Korea. Mem. ABA, La. Bar Assn., Washington Parish Bar Assn. (pres. 1971), Bogalusa Jaycees (Disting. Service award 1965), Am. Legion. Democrat. Methodist. Avocation: horticulture. Probate, Real property, Condemnation. Home: 1737 Gaylord Dr Bogalusa LA 70427

GALLAVAN, MICHAEL LEE, lawyer; b. Richmond, Calif., Jan. 27, 1947; s. William Michael and Mary Elaine (Eichenberg) G.; m. Judith Lee Baldwin, Sept. 18, 1971; children—Sean William, Erin Louise, Megan Sarah. B.A., U. Notre Dame, 1969; J.D., Am. U., Washington, 1976. Bar: Md. 1976, D.C. 1977, U.S. Dist. Ct. Md. 1979, U.S. Dist. Ct. D.C. 1979, U.S. Ct. Appeals (4th cir.) 1980, U.S. Ct. Appeals (D.C. cir.) 1980, U.S. Supreme Ct. 1980. Asst. state's atty. Prince George's County State's Atty.'s Office, Upper Marlboro, Md., 1977-81; assoc. Goldman, Walker, Greenfeig & Metro, Rockville, Md., 1981-83; sole practice, Upper Marlboro, 1983—. Co-author: Bicycling Laws in U.S., 1974; Pedestrian Laws in U.S., 1974. Pres., Citizens Assn. of Marlton, Upper Marlboro, 1979-80, bd. dirs., 1978-79; bd. dirs. Brandywine Country Homeowners Assn., Upper Marlboro, 1979-84. Mem. Md. Bar Assn., D.C. Bar Assn., Prince George's County Bar Assn., Assn. Trial Lawyers Am., Md. Trial Lawyers Assn., Nat. Assn. Criminal Def. Lawyers, Md. Criminal Def. Attys. Assn. Democrat. Roman Catholic. Criminal, Personal injury, General practice. Home: 9606 Tam O Shanter Dr Upper Marlboro MD 20772 Office: 14749 Main St Suite 6 PO Box 82 Upper Marlboro MD 20772

GALLEGOS, LARRY DUAYNE, lawyer; b. Cheverly, Md., Mar. 23, 1951; s. Belarmino R. and Helen (Schlotthauer); m. Mary Louise, May 11, 1973 (div. Aug. 21, 1985); 1 child, Will Adam. BS summa cum laude, U. Puget Sound, 1978; JD, Harvard U., 1981. Bar: Colo. 1981, U.S. Dist. Ct. Colo. 1981. Assoc. Pendleton & Sabian, Denver, 1981-83, O'Conner & Hannan, Denver, 1983-86; ptnr. O'Connor & Hannan, Denver, 1986—. Served with U.S. Army, 1972-74. Mem. ABA (real property, probate and trust law sect.), Colo. Bar Assn., Colo. Trial Lawyers Assn., Denver Bar Assn., U.S. Tennis Assn. Avocation: tennis. Real property, Securities, Federal civil litigation. Office: O'Connor & Hannan 1700 Lincoln St #4700 Denver CO 80203

GALLEN, JAMES M., lawyer; b. East St. Louis, Ill., Jan. 29, 1952; s. James V. and Catherine Ellen (English) G.; m. JoAnn Bundschuh, July 26, 1980; 1 child, James W. BS in Commerce magna cum laude, St. Louis U., 1973, JD, 1976. Bar: Mo. 1976, U.S. Dist. Ct. (ea. dist.) Mo. 1976, Ill. 1977. Assoc. Evans & Dixon, St. Louis, 1976-83, ptnr., 1984—. Mem. adv. bd. SSM Rehab. Inst., St. Louis, 1986—. Mem. ABA (com. on workers' compensation and employers' liability law), Mo. Bar Assn., Ill. State Bar Assn., Met. St. Louis Bar Assn. Republican. Roman Catholic. Club: Mo. Athletic (St. Louis). Workers' compensation. Office: Evans & Dixon 314 N Broadway Ste 1600 Saint Louis MO 63102

GALLES, DUANE LEROY CHARLES MEALMAN, lawyer; b. Adrian, Minn., June 22, 1948; s. Lester D. and Nettie E. (Mealman) G. A.B., George Washington U., 1970; M.A., U. Minn., 1973; J.D., William Mitchell Coll., St. Paul, 1977; J.C.B., St. Paul U., Ont., Can., 1982. Bar: Minn. 1977, U.S. Supreme Ct. 1981. Compliance adminstr. Minn. Dept. Commerce, St. Paul, 1981—; of counsel Livingston-Griggs Preservation Assn., St. Paul, 1982—. Contbr. articles to profl. jours. Decorated officer Order of St. Lazarus of Jerusalem; fellow U. Toronto, 1972, Massey Coll., 1973; F.B. Olson scholar, 1976. Mem. ABA, Am. Soc. Internat. Law, Canon Law Soc. Am., Can. Canon Law Soc., Union Internat. des Avocats, Minn. SAR (pres. 1982-83), Soc. Colonial Wars (chancellor 1982—), Sons and Daus. of Pilgrims (gov. Minn. br. 1985-87, editor gen. 1986—), Order of Descendants of Colonial Govs. (corresponding sec. gen. 1987—), Order of Founders and Patriots (states atty. Wis. soc. 1987—), Phi Alpha Delta. Democrat. Roman Catholic. Home: 2546 Cedar Ave Minneapolis MN 55404 Office: Minn Dept Commerce 500 Metro Sq Saint Paul MN 55101

GALLET, JEFFRY HERSHEL, judge; b. N.Y.C., Nov. 18, 1942; s. Simon and Evelyn M. (Myers) G.; m. Jill M. Marks, Mar. 9, 1968; m. Gail A. Wasserman, Jan. 17, 1982. A.B., Wilkes Coll., 1964; J.D., Bklyn. Law Sch., 1967. Bar: N.Y. 1967, U.S. Dist. Ct. (ea. and so. dists.) N.Y. 1973, U.S. Ct. Claims 1973, U.S. Tax Ct. 1973, U.S. Supreme Ct. 1970, U.S. Ct. Appeals (2d cir.) 1973. Judge Civil Ct. City N.Y., 1980; ptnr. Gallet & Dreyer, N.Y.C., 1978-82; judge Family Ct. N.Y., 1982—; adj. asst. prof. law Bklyn. Coll., 1978-79, lectr., 1973-74; adj. lectr. Hunter Coll., 1975, Rockland Community Coll., 1974; instr. New Sch. Social Research, 1983-84. Mem. N.Y. State Temp. Commn. on Rental Housing, 1978-80; nat. v.p. Am. Jewish Congress, 1982-84, pres. N.Y. Met. council, 1981-83; bd. dirs. Service Program for Older People, 1981-84. Named Outstanding Alumnus Wilkes Coll., 1982. Mem. ABA, N.Y. State Bar Assn. (chmn. subcom. warranty of habitability), Assn. Bar City N.Y., Fed. Bar Council, Author: (with Joel Glass, Martin Minkowitz) Rent Stabilization and Control Laws of New York, 1971; Landlord Tenant Law and Summary Proceedings, 1985; contbg. author: Condominium and Cooperative Conversions, 1980; Warren's Weed N.Y. Real Property, 1984, Disputed Paternity Proceedings, 1984; contbr. numerous articles to profl. jours. Family and matrimonial, Juvenile, Criminal. Office: Family Ct 60 Lafayette St New York NY 10013

GALLIAN, RUSSELL JOSEPH, lawyer; b. San Mateo, Calif., Apr. 24, 1948; s. Phillip Hugh and Betty Jane (Boulton) G.; m. Marian Barbara Howard, Sept. 17, 1969; children: Lisa, Cherie, Joseph, Russell, Yvette, Jason, Ryan. BS, U. San Francisco, 1969, JD with highest honors, 1974. Bar: Calif. 1974, Utah 1975; CPA, Calif. Ptnr. Gallian & Westfall, St. George, Utah. Chmn. Tooele City Planning Commn., Utah, 1977; atty. City of Tooele, 1978-79, Town of Ivins, 1982—. Mem. ABA, Utah State Bar Assn., Tooele County Bar Assn. (pres. 1978), So. Utah Bar Assn. (pres. 1986—). Republican. Mormon. Real property, Banking, Local government. Home: 625 S Valleyview Dr Saint George UT 84770 Office: Gallian & Westfall 1 S Main St Saint George UT 84770

GALLIGAN, MATTHEW G., lawyer; b. New Haven, Sept. 1, 1923; s. Matthew J. and Mary J. (Gordon) G.; m. Anne Elizabeth Reynolds, Apr. 10, 1950. BS, Fordham U., 1947; JD, Georgetown U., 1950. Bar: Conn. 1951. Sole practice Wallingford, Conn., 1952—; asst. pros. atty. Town of Wallingford, 1953-55, atty., 1956-57, 1960-69; counsel joint senate ho. judiciary com. Conn. Gen. Assembly, 1971; mem. adv. bd. Am. Nat. Bank, 1979. Corporator Meriden-Wallingford (Conn.) Hosp., 1975. Mem. Conn. Bar Assn., New Haven County Bar Assn., Southington Bar Assn., Meriden-Wallingford Bar Assn. Roman Catholic. Lodge: Elks, Rotary. General practice, Probate, Real property. Office: 152 N Main St Wallingford CT 06492

GALLIHER, KEITH EDWIN, JR., lawyer; b. Fond du Lac, Wis., July 29, 1947; s. Keith Edwin and Dolores Mae (Hazen) G.; m. Linda Lee Dessauer, May 18, 1985; children: Patrick, Christy Lyn. B.S, U. Nev. at Las Vegas, 1970; J.D., Ariz. State U., 1974. Bar: Nev. 1974, U.S. Dist. Ct. Nev. 1974, U.S. Ct. Appeals (9th cir.) 1976. Assoc. Lionel, Sawyer & Collins., Las Vegas, 1974-75; atty. Clark County Pub. Defender, Las Vegas, 1975-76; sr. ptnr. Mills, Galliher, Lurens, Gibson, Schwartzer & Shinehouse, Las Vegas, 1976-80, Galliher & Tratos, Las Vegas, 1980-83; pres., sr. ptnr. Keith E. Galliher, Jr., Chartered, Las Vegas, 1983—; instr. hotel law U. Nev.-Las Vegas, 1980; alt. mcpl. judge City Las Vegas, 1983—. Author: Supplement to Comparison Analysis of ABA Criminal Justice Standards to Nevada Law, 1976. State del. Democratic Party, 1976; bd. govs. March of Dimes, Las Vegas, 1978. Mem. Nat. Assn. Trial Lawyers, Nev. Trial Lawyers Assn., ABA, Nev. Bar Assn., Clark County Bar Assn., State Bar Nev. (mem. fee dispute com. 1983), Comml. Law League Am., Real Estate Securities and Syndication Inst., Nat. Coll. Criminal Def. Lawyers and Pub. Defenders. Lutheran. State civil litigation, Personal injury, Criminal. Home: 6855 Stone Dr Las Vegas NV 89110 Office: 1850 E Sahara Ave Suite 100 Las Vegas NV 89104

GALLOP, DONALD PHILIP, lawyer; b. St. Louis, Aug. 28, 1932; s. Philip and Frieda (Olian) Gallop; m. Sue Ellen Steiner, Aug. 9, 1959; children—John S., Elizabeth I., Thomas J. and Emily J. A.B., U. Mo., 1954; J.D., Washington U., 1959. Bar: Mo. 1959, D.C. 1977. Mem. Gallop & Gallop, St. Louis, 1959-68, Shifrin, Treiman, Schermer & Gallop, St. Louis, 1968-73, Susman, Stern, Agatstein, Heifetz & Gallop, St. Louis, 1973-76; ptnr. Gallop, Johnson & Neuman, St. Louis, 1976—; dir. Landmark Bancshares Corp., Falcon Products, Inc., others. Mem., chmn. Mo. Housing Devel. Commn., 1977-80. Served to 1st lt. U.S. Army, 1954-56. Mem. Bar Assn. St. Louis, Bar Assn. D.C., Order of Coif. Democrat. Jewish. Clubs: St. Louis, Westwood Country. General corporate, Banking, Legislative. Home: 12 Glenview Rd Ladue MO 63124 Office: 7733 Forsyth Blvd Suite 1800 Clayton MO 63105

GALLOWAY, HUNTER HENDERSON, III, lawyer, small business owner; b. Abingdon, Va., Nov. 16, 1945; s. Hunter Henderson Jr. and Katherine Cosby (Hines) G.; m. Linda Sharlene Alley, June 20, 1971 (div. Feb. 1975); m. Deborah Lynn Brannon, Dec. 18, 1977; children: Andrew Michael, Hunter Henderson IV, Patrick B., Thomas J. BBA, U. N.C., 1968, JD, 1972. Bar: N.C. 1972, U.S. Dist. Ct. (mid. dist.) 1974, U.S. Tax Ct. 1976, U.S. Ct. Appeals (4th cir.) 1979, U.S. Supreme Ct. 1983. Assoc. Hoyle, Hoyle & Boone, Greensboro, 1972-78; sole practice Greensboro, 1978—; tchr. U. N.C., Greensboro, 1974-82; dealer Galloway Buick Co., Greensboro, 1978—. Served with N.C. N.G., 1968-74. Recipient Wall Street Jour. award, U. N.C., 1968. Mem. ABA, N.C. Bar Assn., Greensboro Bar Assn., N.C. Acad. Trial Lawyers. Democrat. Presbyterian. Club: Greensboro Country. Lodge: Rotary. Avocations: trap shooting, hunting, camping. Real property, Consumer commercial. Home: 1815 Nottingham Rd Greensboro NC 27408 Office: Galloway Buick Co 401 N Murrow Blvd Greensboro NC 27401

GALLUP, J. WILLIAM, lawyer; b. Three Hills, Alta., Can., Mar. 3, 1939; came to U.S., 1948; s. Ralph Wyman and Mary E. (Atwood) G.; m. Paula Sharon Fortune, Dec. 28, 1963; children—Pamela, John, Bridget, Sean. B.S., U. Nebr.-Omaha, 1957, M.S., 1961; J.D., Creighton U., 1964. Bar: Nebr. Sup. Ct. 1964, U.S. Dist. Ct. Nebr. 1964, U.S. Ct. Apls. 1965, U.S. Ct. Clms. 1966, U.S. Tax Ct. 1966, U.S. Sup. Ct. 1966. Dep. atty. County Cheyenne, Nebr., 1964; asst. prosecutor city of Omaha, 1965-67; dep. atty. County of Douglas, 1967-69; asst. U.S. dist. atty. Dist. Nebr., 1969-71; sole practice, Omaha, Nebr., 1971—; now ptnr. Gallup & Schaefer, Omaha; lectr. forensic medicine Creighton U. Med. Sch. Served with U.S. Navy, 1952-57, U.S. Army, 1957-59. Fellow Am. Bd. Criminal Lawyers (gov. 1975-82, pres. 1982-83). Criminal. Home: 158 Ginger Cove Rd Valley NE 68064 Office: Gallup & Schaefer 1001 Farnam on the Mall Omaha NE 68102

GALTON, STEPHEN HAROLD, lawyer; b. Tulare, Calif., Dec. 23, 1937; s. Harold Parker and Marie Rose (Tuck) G.; m. Grace Marilyn Shaw, Aug. 15, 1964; children—Mark, Bradley, Jeremy, Elisabeth. B.S., U. So. Calif., 1966, J.D., 1969. Bar: Calif. 1970, U.S. Ct. Appeals (9th cir.) 1973, U.S. Dist. Ct. (no. dist.) Calif. 1973, U.S. Dist. Ct. (cen. dist.) Calif. 1970, U.S. Dist. Ct. (ea. and so. dists.) Calif. 1973. Assoc. Martin & Flandrick, San Marino, Calif., 1970-71, ptnr., 1971-72; assoc. Booth, Mitchel, Strange & Smith, Los Angeles, 1973-77, ptnr., 1978-85; ptnr. Galton & Helm, Los Angeles, 1986—. Mem. ABA (litigation, tort, insurance sects.), Calif. State Bar Assn. (del. 1974-81), Wilshire Bar Assn. (pres. 1986-87), Los Angeles County Bar Assn. (bd. of trustees 1987—). Republican. Presbyterian. Contbr. articles to profl. jours. Insurance, Federal civil litigation, State civil litigation. Office: Galton & Helm 5900 Wilshire Blvd Suite 1800 Los Angeles CA 90036

GALVIN, CHARLES O'NEILL, legal educator; b. Wilmington, N.C., Sept. 29, 1919; s. George Patrick and Marie (O'Neill) G.; m. Margaret Edna Gillespie, June 29, 1946; children: Katherine Marie, George Patrick, Paul Edward, Charles O'Neill, Elizabeth Genevieve. B.S., So. Meth. U., 1940; M.B.A., Northwestern U., 1941, J.D., 1947; S.J.D., Harvard U., 1961. Bar: Ill. 1947, Tex. 1948; C.P.A., Tex. Practice law Dallas, 1947-52; asso. prof. So. Meth. U., Dallas, 1952-55; prof. So. Meth. U., 1955-83, dean Sch. Law, 1963-78; Centennial prof. law Vanderbilt U., Nashville, 1983—; Thayer teaching fellow Harvard U., 1956-57; vis. prof. U. Mich., 1957, Duke U., 1979-80, Pepperdine U., 1979-80. Served to lt. comdr. USNR, 1942-46. Mem. Am., Tex., Dallas bar assns., Am. Law Inst., Am., Tex. bar founds., Am. Judicature Soc., Tex. Soc. C.P.A.s, Am. Inst. C.P.A.s, Order of Coif, Phi Delta Theta, Beta Gamma Sigma. Estate taxation, Estate planning. Home: 6384 Chickering Circle Nashville TN 37215

GALVIN, MADELINE SHEILA, lawyer; b. N.Y.C., Jan. 31, 1948; d. Rod Sheil and Madeline (Twiss) G. BA cum laude with highest honors, Russell Sage Coll., 1970; JD, Albany Law Sch., 1973. Bar: N.Y. 1974, U.S. Dist. Ct. (no. dist.) N.Y. 1974, U.S. Supreme Ct. 1978; cert. parliamentarian, lic. real estate broker. Atty. N.Y. State Dept. Law, Albany, 1973-74; sr. atty. Dormitory Authority State of N.Y., Elsmere, 1974-78; sole practice, Delmar, N.Y., 1974—. Bd. dirs., mem. endowment com., mem. exec. bd. YMCA, Albany, 1980-86; bd. dirs. Mercy House, 1980-83, v.p., 1981-82; mem. fin. com. Ronald McDonald House, 1981-83; mem. Bethlehem Zoning Bd. Appeals; Rep. committeeman 15th dist. Town of Bethlehem. Kellas scholar, 1967-70. Mem. AAUW (recognition cert. Albany br., pres. 1983-84), Nat. Assn. Parliamentarians, ABA, N.Y. State Bar Assn. (numerous coms.), Albany County Bar Assn., N.Y. State Trial Lawyers Assn., Albany Claims Assn., Women's Bar Assn., Albany Law Sch. Alumni Assn., N.Y. Geneal. and Biog. Soc., Strafford Hist. Soc., Russell Sage Coll. Alumni Assn. (pres. 1983—), Albany Inst. History and Art, DAR (regent 1980-82, bd. dirs.), Bethlehem C. of C., Capital Dist. Trial Lawyers Assn., Bus. and Profl. Women Assn., Athenian Honor Soc., Phi Alpha Theta. Roman Catholic. Clubs: NYU; Zonta (Albany), Union U. Outing. General practice, Probate, Real property. Office: 217 Delaware Ave Delmar NY 12054

GALVIN, ROBERT J., lawyer; b. New Haven, Conn., Dec. 10, 1938; s. Herman I. and Freda (Helfand) G.; m. Susan I. Goldstein, Oct. 15, 1960 (div.); children—David B., Peter J. A.B., Union Coll., Schenectady, N.Y., 1961; J.D., Suffolk U., Boston, 1967. Bar: Mass. 1967, U.S. Dist. Ct. Mass. 1967. Sole practice, Boston, 1967-78; ptnr. firm Lippman & Galvin, Boston, 1978-84; of counsel Gage & Tucker, Boston, 1984-86; ptnr. firm Davis, Malm & D'Agustine, Boston, 1986—; lectr. Boston Ctr. Adult Edn., 1972—, Northeastern U., Boston, 1977-78. Real estate columnist Boston Ledger, 1981. Contbr. numerous articles to profl. jours. Bd. dirs., v.p. Rental Housing Assn. div. Greater Boston Real Estate Bd., 1974, Boston Ctr. Adult Edn., 1982—, chmn. fin. com., 1985— . Mem. Mass. Bar Assn. (council mem. property law sect. 1977-80, chmn. condominium com. 1979—), Mass. Continuing Legal Edn. (real estate curriculum adv. com. 1983—), Am. Arbitration Assn. (comml. arbitration panel), Mass. Conveyancers Assn., Thoreau Soc. (life, chmn. devel. com. 1985—). Real property. Home: 33 Pond Ave Brookline MA 02146 Office: Davis Malm & D'Agustine One Boston Pl Boston MA 02108

GAMBARO, ERNEST UMBERTO, lawyer, consultant; b. Niagara Falls, N.Y., July 6, 1938; s. Ralph and Teresa (Nigro) G.; m. Winifred Sonya Gambaro, June 3, 1961. B.A. in Aero. Engring. with honors, Purdue U., 1960, M.S. with honors, 1961; Fulbright scholar, Rome U., 1961-62; J.D. with honors, Loyola U., Los Angeles, 1975. Bar: Calif. 1975, U.S. Tax Ct. 1976, U.S. Supreme Ct. 1979, U.S. Ct. Appeals (9th cir.). With Aerospace Corp., El Segundo, Calif., 1962-80, counsel, 1975-80; asst. gen. counsel, asst. sec. Computer Scis. Corp., El Segundo, 1980—; cons. bus. fin. and mgmt., 1968—. Recipient U.S. Air Force Commendation for contbns. to U.S. manned space program, 1969; Purdue U. Pres.'s scholar, 1959-60. Mem. ABA (internat., taxation sects.), Los Angeles Bar Assn. (exec. com. 1976—, founder chmn. sect. law and tech. 1976-78, chmn. bar reorgn. com. 1981-82), Am. Arbitration Assn. Los Angeles Ctr. Internat. Comml. Arbitration (founder, bd. dirs.), Internat. Law Inst. (faculty), St. Thomas More Law Soc., Phi Alpha Delta, Omicron Delta Kappa (past pres.), Tau Beta Pi, Sigma Gamma Tau (past pres.), Phi Eta Sigma. Republican. Newspaper columnist Europe Alfresco; contbr. articles to profl. publs. General corporate, Private international, General practice. Home: 4221 Rousseau Ln Palos Verdes CA 90274 Office: 2100 E Grand Ave El Segundo CA 90245

GAMBESCIA, JOSEPH M(ARIO), JR., court administrator; b. Phila., June 13, 1945; s. Joseph and Mary Gambescia; m. Constance Conway, June 1969 (div. Mar. 1974); m. Barbara Jadick, Nov. 1980; children: Kerry, Joseph III, Maxwell. Adminstr. Phila. Ct. of Common Pleas, 1971—. Mem. Pa. Assn. of Probation, Parole and Corrections (treas.). Avocation: triathlon. Judicial administration, Jurisprudence, Criminal. Home: 926 Coopertown Rd Bryn Mawr PA 19010 Office: Phila Ct Common Pleas 121 N Broad St Philadelphia PA 19107

GAMBLE, E. JAMES, lawyer, accountant; b. Duluth, Minn., June 1, 1929; s. Edward James and Modesta Caroline (Reichert) G.; m. Lois Kennedy, Apr. 3, 1954; children—John M., Martha M., Paul F. A.B., U. Mich., 1950, J.D., 1953. Bar: Mich., D.C.; C.P.A., Mich. Tax acct. Ernst & Ernst, Detroit, 1957-59; assoc. Dykema, Gossett, Spencer, Goodnow & Trigg, Detroit, 1959-67, ptnr., 1967—; adj. prof. law Wayne State U., Detroit, 1972-79; adj. lectr. law U. Mich., Ann Arbor, 1979-81; counsel Mich. State Bd. Accountancy, Lansing, 1973-77; dir. Vermilion Bay Land Co., Lafayette, La., Ernst Concrete & Supply Co., Warren, Mich. Author: (handbook) The Revised Principal and Income Act, 1966; contbr. articles to profl. jours. Trustee Rehab. Inst., Inc., Detroit, 1961-84, chmn. bd., 1974-77; bd. dirs., sec. Jr. Achievement Southeastern Mich., 1973—; trustee Walsh Coll. Accountancy and Bus. Adminstrn., Troy, Mich., 1975—, Alma Coll., Mich., 1981—. Served to lt. USN, 1953-57. Recipient Bronze Leadership award Jr. Achievement, Inc., 1985. Fellow Am. Coll. Tax Counsel, Am. Coll. Probate Counsel, Am. Bar Found., Mich. State Bar Found.; mem. Fin. and Estate Planning Council Detroit (bd. dirs. 1969-76, pres. 1975), ABA (spl. com. on profl. relations with Am. Inst. C.P.A.s 1968-70), Mich. Bar Assn. (various coms.), Detroit Bar Assn. (chmn. taxation com. 1968-74), Detroit Bar Assn. Found. (trustee, treas. 1973-79). Presbyterian. Clubs: Detroit Athletic; Birmingham Athletic, Leland Country (Mich.). Estate planning, Estate taxation, Probate.

GAMBOL, ROBERT ALAN, lawyer; b. Cleve., July 26, 1947; s. Frank Clarence and Anna Delores (Janitor) G.; m. Suzanne Louise McCollum, Nov. 22, 1975; children: Melissa, Katrina, Frank, Anthony. AB, Boston Coll., 1969; JD, Duke U., 1973. Bar: Ohio 1973, U.S. Dist. Ct. (no. dist.) Ohio 1974, U.S. Supreme Ct. 1975. Counsel CIC Lake County, Madison, Ohio, 1974—, Lake County 503 Corp., Madison, 1983—; instr. Am. Inst. Paralegal Studies, 1982—. Trustee Birthright Lake County, Ohio, 1979; evaluator Mentor High Sch., 1985. Mem. Ohio State Bar Assn., Lake County Bar Assn. Democrat. Roman Catholic. Family and matrimonial, Municipal bonds, State civil litigation. Home: 1813 Sandgate Rd Madison OH 44057

GAMBONI, CIRO ANTHONY, lawyer; b. Bklyn., Aug. 16, 1940; m. Gail Pollack, Aug. 1, 1965; children: Dina, Lee. BBA, CCNY, 1963; LLB, NYU, 1965; LLM, Georgetown U., 1969. Bar: N.Y., U.S. Dist. Ct. (so. dist.) N.Y. Ptnr. Cahill, Gordon & Reindel, N.Y.C. Chmn. Circle Repertory Co., N.Y.C. Served to capt. JAGC, U.S. Amry, 1966-69. Mem. N.Y. State Bar Assn. (tax. sect.), Order of Coif, Beta Gamma Sigma, Beta Alpha Psi. Clubs: Downtown Assn., City Midday, Lotos (N.Y.C.). Avocation: theater. Corporate taxation. Home: 1 Fifth Ave New York NY 10003 also: 11 Jefferson Ave Short Hills NJ 07078 Office: Cahill Gordon & Reindel 80 Pine St New York NY 10005

GAMBRO, MICHAEL S., lawyer; b. N.Y.C., July 15, 1954; s. A. John and Rose A. (Grandinetti) G.; m. Joan L. Thurneyssen, Aug. 8, 1980; children: Dana E., Merrill R. BS summa cum laude, Tufts U., 1976; JD, Columbia U., 1980. Bar: N.Y. 1981, U.S. Dist. Ct. (so. dist.) N.Y. 1981, U.S. Dist. Ct. N.J. 1981, N.J. 1983. Ptnr. Cadwalader, Wickersham & Taft, N.Y.C., 1980—. Harlan Fisk Stone scholar, 1978-79, 1979-80. Mem. ABA, Phi Beta Kappa, Psi Chi. General corporate, Securities. Office: Cadwalader Wickersham & Taft 100 Maiden Ln New York NY 10038

GAMM, GORDON JULIUS, lawyer; b. Shreveport, La., July 14, 1939; s. Sylvian Willer Gamm and Leona (Gordon) Windes. BA, Drake U., 1963; JD, Tulane U., 1970. Ptnr. Hill & Gamm, Kansas City, Mo., 1977-79; sole practice Kansas City, 1979-83, Levine P.C. & Gamm, Kansas City, 1983—. Founder Bragg's Symposium, 1980—. Mem. Mo. Bar Assn., Kans. City Bar Assn., Assn. Trial Lawyers Am. (diploma), Nat. Inst. Trial Advocacy (cert.), Am. Humanist's Assn. (exec. com. 1980-86), ACLU (bd. dirs.). Democrat. Mem. Unitarian Ch. Federal civil litigation, State civil litigation, Consumer employee fraud litigation. Office: Levine PC & Gamm 106 W 14th St #2302 Kansas City MO 64105

GANDARA, DANIEL, lawyer; b. Los Angeles, July 7, 1948; s. Henry and Cecilia (Contreras) G.; m. Juleann Cottini, Aug. 26, 1972; children: Mario, Enrico. BA, UCLA, 1970; JD, Harvard U., 1974. Bar: Calif. 1974, Wash. 1978. Asst. city atty. City of Los Angeles, 1974-77; staff atty. FTC, Seattle, 1977-79; ptnr. Lane, Powell, Moss & Miller, Seattle, 1979-87; atty. Graham & Dunn, Seattle, 1987—. Mem. Wash. State Bar Assn., Seattle-King County

Bar Assn., Hispanic Nat. Bar Assn., Wash. Assn. of Def. Counsel, Wash. State Hispanic C. of C. (bd. dirs. 1986). Democrat. Roman Catholic. Club: Seattle. State civil litigation, Federal civil litigation, Antitrust. Home: 2010 E Lynn Seattle WA 98112 Office: Graham & Dunn 3400 Rainier Bank Tower Seattle WA 98101

GANDY, DEAN MURRAY, lawyer; b. Dallas, Mar. 5, 1927; s. Howard C. and Florine (Seay) G.; m. Virginia Brannan, Mar. 17, 1950; m. Beverly Ann Herrin, Dec. 29, 1972. BBA, So. Meth. U., 1948, LLB, 1950. Bar: Tex. 1950, U.S. Dist. Ct. (no., so., ea., we. dists.) Tex. Sole practice, Sherman, Tex., 1950-53; oil co. exec., exec. v.p. Magna Oil Corp., Dallas, 1953-66; ptnr. Rochelle, Gandy & King, Dallas, 1966-70; bankruptcy judge, Dallas, 1970-83; ptnr. Akin, Gump, Strauss, Hauer & Feld, Dallas, 1983—. Mem. Nat. Conf. Bankruptcy Judges (past pres.), Nat. Bankruptcy Conf. Bankruptcy, Oil and gas leasing. Home: 3310 Fairmount Dallas TX 75201 Office: 4100 First City Ctr 1700 Pacific Ave Dallas TX 75201-4618

GANDY, FRANCIS I., JR., lawyer; b. San Antonio, Jan. 20, 1937; s. Francis I. and Crystal A. (Robertson) G.; m. Nancy Bluntzer, June 27, 1959; 1 dau., Jennifer Lynn. B.A., Baylor U., 1961, LL.B., 1963. Bar: Tex. 1963, U.S. Dist. Ct. (so. dist.) Tex. 1965, U.S. Ct. Appeals (5th cir.) 1968; cert. civil trial law and personal injury trial law Tex. Bd. Legal Specialization. Sole practice, Corpus Christi, Tex., 1963—; mem. admissions com. State Bar of Tex., 1970—, vice chmn. admission com., Dist. 11, 1982—. Bd. dirs. Coastal Bend Youth City, 1968—, pres., 1981; bd. dirs. Driscoll Children's Hosp., 1981-83; trustee Corpus Christi Mus., 1970-72; bd. dirs. Am. Cancer Soc., 1965-70; mem. Nueces County Grievance Com., 1977-78, chmn., 1978. Mem. ABA, Assn. Trial Lawyers Am., Tex. Trial Lawyers Assn. (dir. 1968-72). Democrat. Episcopalian. Clubs: Corpus Christi Yacht (dir. 1975-79), Kiwanis. State civil litigation, Condemnation, Personal injury. Home: 225 Jackson Pl Corpus Christi TX 78411 Office: PO Box 1316 Corpus Christi TX 78475

GANDY, H. CONWAY, lawyer, state ofcl.; b. Washington, Nov. 3, 1934; s. Hoke and Anne B. (Conway) G.; m. Carol Anderson, Aug. 29, 1965; children—Jennifer, Constance, Margaret. B.A., Colo. State U., 1962; J.D., U. Denver, 1968. Bar: Colo. 1969, U.S. dist. ct. Colo. 1969. Sole practice, Ft. Collins, Colo., 1969-81; dep. chief adminstrv. law judge div. Adminstrv. Hearings, State of Colo., Denver, 1981—. Democratic candidate for Colo. Senate, 1974, dist. atty., 1976. Served with USN, 1954-58. Mem. Colo. Bar Assn., Larimer County Bar Assn., Nat. Assn. Adminstrv. Law Judges (pres. Colo. chot. 1985-86). Methodist. Club: Front Range Sertoma (Centurion award 1973, Tribune award 1975, Senator award 1977, 79, sec. Honor Club 1977-78, pres. 1978-79). Administrative and regulatory, Workers' compensation. Home: 724 Winchester Dr Fort Collins CO 80526 Office: 1525 Sherman St #550 Denver CO 80203

GANDY, KIM ALLISON, lawyer; b. Bossier City, La., Jan. 25, 1954; d. Alfred K. and Roma Rae (Young) G. B.S., La. Tech. U., 1973; J.D., Loyola U., 1978. Bar: La. 1978, U.S. Dist. Ct. (ea. and we. dists.) La. 1980, U.S. Supreme Ct. 1981, U.S. Ct. Appeals (5th cir.) 1982. Mgr., South Central Bell Telephone Co., New Orleans, 1973-77; asst. dist. atty. Orleans Parish, New Orleans, 1978-79; sole practice, New Orleans, 1979—; guest lectr. in field. Treas. ERA United Coalition La., 1977-78; chmn. New Orleans delegation La. Dem. Conv., 1980, 82, vice chmn., 1984; dir. Women's Lobby Network, 1980-85; co-founder Greater New Orleans Assn. Dem. Women, 1984. Recipient Law Alumni award Loyola U., 1976; Milton Sheen award, 1978; named New Orleans Outstanding Young Career Woman New Orleans Bus. and Profl. Women, 1980, New Orleans 100 Women in Forefront, 1986. mem. ABA, La. Bar Assn., La. Trial Lawyers Assn., Assn. Women Attys. (legis. chair 1982-84), La. Assn. Women Attys., NOW (nat. dir. 1982—; Woman of Yr.). State civil litigation, Family and matrimonial, Legislative. Home: 5509 Coliseum St New Orleans LA 70115 Office: 1826 St Claude Ave Suite 100 New Orleans LA 70116

GANG, IRVING LLOYD, lawyer; b. Passaic, N.J., Oct. 13, 1922; s. Solomon and Janet (Rosenberg) G.; m. Ruth Leon Jacoby, Mar. 28, 1950; children—Stephen R., Laura J., Meredith A. B.A., Amherst Coll., 1943; J.D., Yale U., 1949. Bar: N.J. 1949, U.S. Dist. Ct. N.J. 1949. Assoc. Hannoch & Lasser, Newark, N.J., 1949-51; sole practice, Passaic, 1951-55; ptnr. Gardner & Williams, Passaic, 1956-58; sole practice, Passaic and Montclair, N.J., 1958-83; ptnr. Gang and Smith, Montclair, 1983—; spl. counsel to Town of Montclair, 1976-81; mem. Passaic County Ethics Com., 1966-68, 74-76, chmn., 1969; mem. dist. fee arbitration com. N.J. Supreme Ct., 1982-84, chmn. Dist. V-C, 1983-84, mem. com. on code of profl. responsibility, 1969-70, mem. com. on enforcement ethical standards, 1970-72. Trustee Passaic County Legal Aid Soc., 1963-80, pres., 1964-68; pres. Aheka council Boy Scouts Am., 1960-64, mem. exec. bd., 1953-78; bd. dirs. Planning Assn. North Jersey, pres., 1957-60, chmn. bd., 1960-63; bd. dirs. Appalachian Highlands Assn., 1969-72; bd. dirs. Passaic chpt. ARC, 1969-74; bd. dirs. N.J. Fedn. Planning Ofcls., 1968-71, mem. adv. council, 1971-75; trustee United Community Service North Essex, 1964-73, N.J. Conservation Found., 1986—; bd. dirs. Home Health Services Passaic County, 1971-72; bd. dirs. Shelter Island Assn., 1970-86 , pres., 1970; mem. Montclair Planning Bd., 1959-68, chmn., 1962-68; mem. Com. on 2d Regional Plan, 1966-68; mem. N.J. Commn. To Study Reclamation of Meadowlands, 1963-66; chmn. Essex County Joint Council Mcpl. Planning Bds., 1965-67; past mem. bd. trustees United Fund of Clinton, Garfield, Passaic and Wallington, Essex County chpt. Am. Jewish Com., Family and Children's Services Montclair and Glen Ridge; past mem. bd. dirs. Passaic-Clifton YM-YWHA; trustee Orpheus Chamber Singers, 1979-84. Served with USAAF, 1943-46; 1st lt. Res. ret. Recipient Community Service award B'nai B'rith, Passaic, 1965; Silver Beaver award Aheka council Boy Scouts Am., 1959; Planning Pioneer award Planning Assn. North Jersey, 1978. Mem. ABA, Passaic County Bar Assn. (pres. 1973-74), Essex County Bar Assn., N.J. Bar Assn. (gen. council 1970—), Am. Judicature Soc., Montclair and West Essex Bar Assn., Yale Law Sch. Alumni Assn. N.J. (trustee 1966-74). Clubs: Rotary (pres. 1971-72); Loantaka Skeet; Shelter Island (N.Y.) Yacht (trustee); Amwell Valley Conservancy (pres.). General corporate, Probate, Real property. Office: 80 Park St Montclair NJ 07042

GANGLE, SANDRA SMITH, lawyer; b. Brockton, Mass., Jan. 11, 1943; d. Milton and Irene M. (Powers) S.; m. Eugene M. Gangle, Dec. 21, 1968; children—Melanie Jean, Jonathan Rocco. B.A., Coll. New Rochelle, 1964; M.A., U. Oreg.; J.D., Willamette U., 1980. Bar: Oreg. 1980. Instr. French, Oreg. State U., Corvallis, 1968-71, Willamette U., Salem, Oreg., 1971-74; instr. ESL, Chemeketa Community Coll., Salem, 1975-79; labor arbitrator Salem, 1980—; mem. Oreg., Idaho, Wash., Mont. Arbitration Panels; sole practice Salem, 1980-86; ptnr. Depenbrock, Gangle & Naucler, 1986—; clin. prof. Portland State U., 1981-84; cons. State Oreg., 1981. Contbr. articles to profl. jours. Land-use chmn. Faye Wright Neighborhood Assn., Salem, 1983-84; mem. Civil Service Commn., Marion County Fire Dist., Salem, 1983—; mem. U.S. Postal Service Expedited Arbitration Panel, 1984—; mem. Salem Neighbor-to-Neighbor Panel; mem. panel Fed. Mediation and Conciliation Service, 1986—. NDEA fellow, 1967. Mem. Am. Arbitration Assn. (arbitrator), Soc. Profls. in Dispute Resolution ABA, Oreg. Trial Lawyers Assn., Marion County Bar Assn., Oreg. Assn. Adminstrv. Law Judges. Arbitration, Personal injury, Probate. Office: Depenbrock Gangle & Naucler 831 Lancaster Dr NE Suite 209 Salem OR 97301

GANIS, STEPHEN LANE, lawyer; b. N.Y.C., Sept. 24, 1951; s. Milton and Beverly Ganis; m. Claudia S. Harris, Nov. 2, 1974; children: Bret Jason, April Michelle. BS in Journalism, Syracuse U., 1973; JD, Bklyn. Law Sch., 1981. Bar: N.Y. 1982, U.S. Dist. Ct. (so. and ea. dists.) N.Y. 1982. Editor Bklyn. Graphic, 1974-76; pub., editor The Bklyn. Times, 1976-78; assoc. Whitman & Ransom, N.Y.C., 1981-84, Robinson, Silverman, Pearce, Aronsohn & Berman, N.Y.C., 1984—. Mem. Vol. Lawyers for Arts, N.Y.C., 1982—. Mem. ABA, N.Y. State Bar Assn. (spl. com. media law 1986—). General corporate, Contracts commercial, Securities. Office: Robinson Silverman Pearce Aronsohn & Berman 230 Park Ave New York NY 10169

GANLY, DAVID MILTON, lawyer; b. Ridgewood, N.J., Nov. 15, 1937; s. Milton L. and Ruth A. (Tichenor) G.; m. Lorraine Bullock, Mar. 11, 1967; children: Samantha E., Winston B., Maxwell D. BA, Yale U., 1959; JD, N.C. Cen. U., 1980. Bar: N.C. 1980, U.S. Dist. Ct. (we. dist.) N.C. 1980, U.S. Ct. Appeals (4th cir.) 1981. Ptnr. Gudger, Reynolds, Ganly & Stewart, Asheville, N.C., 1981-84, Reynolds, Ganly & Stewart, Asheville, N.C., 1984-85, Ganly & Matney, Asheville, N.C., 1985—. Mem. Small Bus. Task Force, Asheville, 1985-86; gen. counsel Western Carolina Entrepreneurial Council, Asheville, 1985-86. Served to capt. USAR, 1959-63, Vietnam. Mem. Nat. Orgn. Social Security Claimants Reps. Republican. Presbyterian. Clubs: Asheville, Downtown City (Asheville, N.C.). Avocation: hiking. Pension, profit-sharing, and employee benefits, General corporate. Home: 23 Braddock Way Asheville NC 28803 Office: Ganly & Matney 1 Oak Plaza Asheville NC 28801

GANN, PAMELA BROOKS, legal educator; b. 1948. B.A., U. N.C., 1970; J.D., Duke U., 1973. Bar: Ga. 1973, N.C. 1974. Assoc. King & Spalding, Atlanta, 1973; assoc. Robinson, Bradshaw & Hinson, P.A., Charlotte, N.C., 1974-75; asst. prof. Duke U. Sch. Law, Durham, N.C., 1975-78, assoc. prof., 1978-80, prof., 1980—; vis. asst. prof. U. Mich. Law Sch., 1977; vis. assoc. prof. U. Va., 1980. Author: (with D. Kahn) Corporate Taxation and Taxation of Partnerships and Partners, 1979; article editor Duke Law Jour. Mem. Am. Law Inst., Order of Coif, Phi Beta Kappa. Legal education, Corporate taxation, Private international. Office: Duke U Law Sch Durham NC 27706

GANNAM, MICHAEL JOSEPH, lawyer; b. Savannah, Ga., Nov. 10, 1922; s. Karam George and Annie (Abraham) G.; m. Marion Collins DeFrank, June 11, 1949; children—James, Ann, Elizabeth, Joseph. B.A., U. Ga., 1949, J.D., 1948; M.A., U. N.C., 1950. Bar: Ga. 1948. Assoc. Bouhan, Lawrence, Williams & Levy, Savannah, 1950-59; ptnr. Findley, Shea, Friedman, Gannam, Head & Buchsbaum, Savannah, 1959-70; sole practice, Savannah, 1970-81; sr. ptnr. Gannam and Gnann, Savannah, 1981—; instr. bus. law, polit. sci. and history Armstrong State Coll., evenings 1951-62. Bd. dirs. Historic Savannah Found.; bd. dirs., legal counsel Telfair Acad. Arts and Scis.; past pres. Legal Aid Soc. Savannah; mem. Savannah-Chatham Bd. Zoning Appeals, 1961-63, Savannah Arts Com., 1982-85. Served with USAAF 1942-46, PTO. Mem. ABA, State Bar Ga. (gov. 1969—), Savannah Bar Assn. (pres. 1973-74), Assn. ICC Practitioners, Armstrong State Coll. Alumni Assn. (dir., past pres.), Am. Legion. Democrat. Roman Catholic. Club: Savannah Golf. Author: The Problems in the Caribbean and The Caribbean Commission, 1950. General practice, State civil litigation, Probate. Home: 235 E Gordon St Savannah GA 31401 Office: 130 W Bay St Savannah GA 31401

GANNASCOLI, RUDOLPH LANCE, lawyer; b. Bklyn., Sept. 26, 1950; s. Joseph and Vivian (Cottone) G.; m. Barbara JoAnn McKenna, June 10, 1984; 1 child, Vivian. BA, St. John's U., 1974; JD, Potomac Sch. of Law, 1980. Bar: Ga. 1981, Md. 1982. Wage hour investigator Washington Dept. Labor, 1979-83; sole practice Washington, 1984—. Pres. N.Y. Young Dems., 1972-76; bd. dirs. Potomac Sch. of Law, Washington. Mem. Fed. Bar Assn., Ga. Bar Assn., Md. Bar Assn., Am. Immigration Lawyers Assn., Lido Civic Assn. Roman Catholic. Avocation: golf. Immigration, naturalization, and customs, Personal income taxation, Labor. Home: 1856 Mintwood Pl NW Washington DC 20009 Office: 1801 Columbia Rd NW #105 Washington DC 20009

GANNON, CHRISTOPHER RICHARD, lawyer; b. Manchester, Conn., Sept. 16, 1955; s. Richard Edward and Barbara Lee (Selden) G.; m. Jan Allyn Johnston, Aug. 22, 1981. BA, Tufts U., 1978; JD, Boston U., 1981. Bar: Mass. 1981, U.S. Dist. Ct. Mass. 1982. Assoc. Burns & Levinson, Boston, 1981-84; corp. atty. Cabot Corp., Boston, 1984—. Antitrust, General corporate, Private international. Office: Cabot Corp 950 Winter St Waltham MA 02254-9073

GANSON, NORRIS LLOYD, lawyer; b. Buffalo, Jan. 8, 1929; s. Philip S. and Dora M. (Moskowitz) G.; m. Beverly Eckstein Tonkin, Jan. 1, 1950 (div. Apr. 1969); m. Marilyn M. Calhoun, Oct. 29, 1971; children: Steven C., Marjorie S. Ganson Mendelsohn. LLB, U. Cin., 1958. Bar: Ohio 1959, U.S. Dist. Ct. (so. dist.) Ohio 1960, U.S. Ct. Appeals (6th cir.) 1960, U.S. Dist. Ct. (ea. dist.) Ky. 1965, U.S. Supreme Ct. 1966, Ariz. 1970, U.S. Ct. Appeals (9th cir.) 1983. Sole practice Cin., 1959-70, Tucson, 1970—. State civil litigation, Personal injury, Probate. Home: 5021 N Calle Bujia Tucson AZ 85718 Office: 5671 N Oracle Rd Suite 1001 Tucson AZ 85704

GANT, HORACE ZED, lawyer; b. Van Buren, Ark., Apr. 1, 1914; s. George Washington and Ida Elizabeth (Stephenson) G.; m. Edith Imogene Farabough, Oct. 10, 1937; children—Alice Margaret, Linda Beth, Zed George, Paul David. LL.B., U. Ark., 1936, J.D., 1969. Bar: Ark. 1936, U.S. Dist. Ct. (we. dist.) Ark. 1937, U.S. Supreme Ct. 1943. Asst. pros. atty., Van Buren, 1936-41; sole practice, Van Buren, 1941-43; atty. War Relocation Authority, Washington, 1943, U.S. Dept. Interior, Washington, 1947; field atty. VA, Little Rock, 1947-73; chancery judge Ark. 15th Jud. Dist., Van Buren, 1973-75; ptnr. Gant & Gant, Van Buren, 1975—. Bd. dirs. Harbor House and Gateway House, Ft. Smith, Ark., 1974-84; chmn. Western Ark. Adv. Council, Ft. Smith, 1976-81; pres. Mental Health Assn., Ft. Smith, 1978; trustee Boggan Edn. Scholarship Trust Fund, chmn., 1979—; deacon 1st Baptist Ch., Van Buren. Served to lt. comdr. USN, 1943-46. Mem. Ark. Bar Assn. Democrat. Lodge: Masons (master 1942-43). Probate, Family and matrimonial, General practice. Home: 403 S 7th St Van Buren AR 72956 Office: Gant & Gant Attys at Law 200 S 7th St PO Box 416 Van Buren AR 72956

GANT, JOSEPH ERWIN, chemist, former state senator; b. Altamahaw, N.C., Feb. 4, 1912; s. Joseph Erwin and Mary (Banner) G.; B.S., U. N.C., 1934; m. Opal Martin, Feb. 11, 1938 (dec. June 1982); children—Joseph Erwin III, Mary Martin; m. Margaret Minter Doss, Dec. 28, 1985. With U.S. Potash Co., Carlsbad, N.Mex., 1934-56, U.S. Borax & Chem. Co., Carlsbad, 1956-67; chmn. N.Mex. Bd. Eddy Commrs., 1967-68; mem. N.Mex. Senate, 1969-84, mem. judiciary com., 1969-72, rules com., 1973-84, chmn. conservation com., 1973-84, chmn. majority caucus, 1973-84, also vice chmn. legis. univ. study com., 1971-75, mem. local govt. com., 1974-75, chmn. legis. higher edn. admissions standards com., 1976-77, legis. energy com., 1976-77, mem. legis. council, 1978-84, chmn. joint interim radioactive waste consultation com., 1979-84, vice chmn. com. on coms.; dir. Glen Raven Mills, Inc. (N.C.). Pub. mem. N.Mex. State Investment Council, 1959-60; v.p. N.M. Assn. Counties, 1969; dir. Southeastern N.Mex. Econ. Devel. Dist.; mem. Southwestern Regional Energy Council, 1975-84; mem. nat. resources task force intergovtl. com. Nat. Conf. State Legislatures, 1973-77; mem. state-fed. relations energy com., 1977-84; mem. Roswell Dist. Land Use Com., Bur. Land Mgmt., 1978-82, N.Mex. Water Resources Adv. Com., 1982-84; chmn., Eddy County Democratic Com., 1948-60; mem. N.Mex. Dem. Exec. Com., 1953-54. Mem. Am. Chem. Soc., Alpha Tau Omega. Episcopalian. Elk. Criminal, Family and matrimonial. Home: 602 Riverside Dr PO Box 909 Carlsbad NM 88220 Office: 111 W Menmod PO Drawer DD Carlsbad NM 88220

GANT, JOSEPH ERWIN, III, lawyer; b. Carlsbad, N.Mex., Mar. 17, 1940; s. Joseph Erwin Jr. and Opal (Martin) G.; m. Beverly Marrs, Dec. 20, 1975; children: Joseph Erwin IV, Carla Hollen, Mark Hensley. BA in Econs., U. N.Mex., 1965, JD, 1968. Bar: N.Mex. 1970, U.S. Dist. Ct. N.Mex. 1970. Assoc. Glasscock, Denny & McKim, 1972-73, Howden & Turden, Albuquerque, 1973; asst. dist. atty. 13th Jud. Dist., Grants, N.Mex., 1973-74; sole practice Carlsbad, 1974—; banker Carlsbad Nat. Bank; owner farm, Burlington, N.C. Mem. ABA, N.Mex. Bar Assn., Assn. Trial Lawyers Am., N.Mex. Trial Lawyers Assn., Christian Legal Soc., U. N.Mex. Alumni Assn. Episcopalian. Lodges: Lions, Elks, Masons (worshipful master), Shriners (local bd. dirs.). Avocation: tennis. Criminal, Family and matrimonial, State civil litigation. Home: 602 W Riverside Dr Carlsbad NM 88220 Office: 211 W Mermod PO Drawer DD Carlsbad NM 88220

GANT, WILLIAM MILTON, justice; b. Owensboro, Ky., Nov. 25, 1919; s. Archibald Stuart and Mattie Ellis (Sloane) G.; m. Mary Ellen Price, Dec. 27, 1952; children: Stuart Price, Walter Sloane. A.B., Transylvania U., 1940; LL.B., U. Ky., 1947. Bar: Ky. 1947, fed. cts. 1947, U.S. Supreme Ct. 1966. Commonwealth atty. 6th Jud. Dist., Owensboro, 1962-76; judge Ky. Ct. Appeals, Frankfort, 1976-83; justice Supreme Ct. Ky., Frankfort, 1983—. Curator Transylvania U., Lexington, Ky., 1968—. Served to 1st lt. USAAF, 1942-45. Recipient Disting. Service award Ky. Med. Assn., 1972; recipient Disting. Service award Ky. Council on Crime and Delinquency, 1973. Mem. ABA, Am. Judicature Soc., Ky. Bar Assn., U. Ky. Alumni Assn. (nat. pres. 1958-59, 64-65 Disting. Service award). Democrat. Mem. Christian Ch. Home: 1643 Sherwood Dr Owensboro KY 42301 Office: Supreme Ct Ky State Capitol Frankfort KY 40601 also: 100 St Ann Bldg Owensboro KY 42301 *

GANTT, CHARLES DAVID, lawyer; b. Winston-Salem, N.C., Oct. 2, 1956; s. Charles Heman and Augusta (Pharr) G.; m. Charise Lowery; children: Brett Daniel, Carrie Michelle. BA in Econs., U. N.C., 1978; JD, Campbell Sch. Law, 1981. Bar: N.C. 1981, U.S. Dist. Ct. (we. dist.) N.C. 1981, U.S. Dist. Ct. (middle dist.) N.C. 1984, U.S. Ct. Appeals (4th cir.) 1984, U.S. Supreme Ct. 1985. Assoc. Marvin P. Pope Jr. PA, Asheville, N.C., 1981-82; sole practice Asheville, N.C., 1982—. Pres. Santa Pal, Asheville, 1982. Mem. Young Lawyer's Buncombe County (v.p. 1983, treas. 1985), Toastmasters (charter pres. 1981), Jaycees (bd. dirs.). Democrat. Methodist. Lodges: Optimists (Asheville) (pres. 1986). State civil litigation, Family and matrimonial, Personal injury. Office: PO Box 7353 Asheville NC 28807

GANZ, CHARLES DAVID, lawyer; b. N.Y.C., Oct. 1, 1946; s. Harold Leonard and Mimi (Platzker) G.; m. Carol Susan Fisher, June 5, 1969; children: Jonathan, Adam, Melissa. AB, Franklin and Marshall Coll., 1968; JD, Duke U., 1972; LLM in Taxation, NYU, 1976. Bar: N.Y. 1973, U.S. Ct. Appeals (2d cir.) 1973, Ga. 1976, U.S. Dist. Ct. (so. and ea. dists.) N.Y. 1973, U.S. Ct. Appeals (11th cir) 1979, U.S. Dist. Ct. (no. dist.) Ga. 1979. Assoc. Cahill Gordon & Reindel, N.Y.C., 1972-76; assoc. Gambrell & Russell, Atlanta, 1976-77, ptnr., 1978-81; ptnr. Wildman, Harrold, Allen, Dixon & Branch, Atlanta, 1982—; bd. dirs. Videostar Connections Inc., Staging Connections, Inc. Trustee Atlanta Ballet, 1980-82. Served to staff sgt. U.S. Army, 1968-74. Mem. ABA, Ga. Bar Assn., Atlanta Bar Assn., Atlanta Tax Forum; trustee Ga. Tax Conf. (trustee, pres. 1985—). Jewish. General corporate, Securities, Corporate taxation. Office: Wildman Harrold et al 1360 Peachtree St Atlanta GA 30309-3209

GANZ, DAVID L., lawyer; b. N.Y.C., July 28, 1951; s. Daniel M. and Beverlee (Kaufman) G.; m. Barbara Bondanza, Nov. 3, 1974 (div. 1978); m. Sharon Ruth Lamnin, Oct. 30, 1981; children—Scott Harry, Elyse Toby. B.S. in Fgn. Service, Georgetown U., 1973; J.D., St. John's U., 1976. Bar: N.Y. 1977, D.C. 1980, N.J. 1985. Assoc. firm Regan, Dorsey & DeRiso, Flushing, N.Y., 1977-79; ptnr. firm Durst & Ganz, P.C., N.Y.C., 1979-80; mng. ptnr. firm Ganz, Hollinger & Towe P.C., N.Y.C., 1981—; cons. FAO, Money Office, Rome, 1975—; cons. to sub-com. on historic preservation and coinage House Banking Com., 94th and 95th Congresses; bd. dirs. Industry Council Tangible Assets, Washington, 1983—. Author: A Legal and Legislative History of 31 USC Sec 324d-324i, 1976; The World of Coins and Coin Collecting, 1980, 2d edit., 1985. Corr., Numis. News Weekly, 1969-73, asst. editor, 1973-74, spl. corr., 1974-75; contbg. editor, columnist COINage Mag., 1974—; columnist Coin World, 1974—, COINS Mag., 1973-83. Contbr. articles to legal publs. Mem. U.S. Assay Commn., 1974; bd. dirs. Georgetown Library Assocs., Washington, 1982—; mem. N.Y. County Draft Bd., 1984, Bergen County, N.J., 1985—. Mem. Nat. Assn. Coin and Precious Metals Dealers (assoc. mem., gen. counsel 1981-85), Flushing Lawyers Club (pres. 1982-83), N.Y. State Bar Assn. (mem. civil practice com., chmn. sub-com. 1978-84), Am. Soc. Internat. Law, Am. Numis. Assn. (legis. counsel 1978-81, 83—, elected bd. govs. 1985—). Democrat Jewish. Legislative, Private international, Contracts commercial. Office: Ganz Hollinger & Towe 1394 3rd Ave New York NY 10021-0404

GANZI, VICTOR FREDERICK, lawyer; b. N.Y.C., Feb. 14, 1947; s. Walter John and Gertrude (Meyer) G.; m. Patricia Frances Martin, July 10, 1971; children: Danielle Martin, Victoria Louise. BS, Fordham U., 1968; JD, Harvard U., 1971; LLM in Taxation, NYU, 1981. Bar: N.Y. 1973, U.S. Dist. Ct. (so. and ea. dists.) N.Y. 1975, U.S. Ct. Appeals (2d cir.) 1975, U.S. Tax Ct. 1975; CPA, Colo. Tax acct. Touche Ross & Co., Denver, 1971-73; from assoc. to mng. ptnr. Rogers & Wells, N.Y.C., 1973—; speaker various insts.; bd. dirs. Palm Mgmt. Corp., N.Y.C. Mem. ABA, Am. Inst. CPA's, Colo. Soc. CPA's. Club: Sky (N.Y.C.). Corporate taxation, Real property, Municipal bonds. Home: 303 Captain's Way West Bay Shore NY 11706 Office: Rogers & Wells Pan Am Bldg 200 Park Ave New York NY 10166

GARABEDIAN, CHARLES BAGDASAR, lawyer, educator; b. Everett, Mass., Mar. 19, 1917; s. Bagdasar and Elmas (Keljikian) G.; m. Nancy Carole Kocha, Apr. 25, 1976; 1 child, Mark Charles. BA, Tufts U., 1939; JD, Boston U., 1943. Bar: Mass. 1943, U.S. Dist. Ct. Mass. 1944, U.S. Supreme Ct. 1963, U.S. Ct. Appeals (1st cir.) 1969, U.S. Ct. Mil. Appeals 1970. Atty. New England Regional Enforcement Office of Price Stabilization, Boston, 1950-51; asst. prof. law Suffolk U., Boston, 1956-65, assoc. prof., 1965-69, prof., 1969—; examiner police promotional exams civil service comm. Commonwealth of Mass., Boston, 1965-72. Mem. ABA, Mass. Bar Assn., Boston Bar Assn., Assn. Trial Lawyers Am. Avocations: photography, tennis, football, basketball, baseball. State civil litigation, Legal education, General practice. Home: 9 Ginn Rd Winchester MA 01890 Office: Suffolk U Law Sch 41 Temple St Boston MA 02114

GARAY, ERICA BLYTHE, lawyer; b. Bklyn., Mar. 8, 1953; d. Harold and Gladys M. (Messing) G.; m. Gary Stuart Schachter, Dec. 22, 1973 (widowed Aug. 1980); m. Michael Bruce Siehs, June 10, 1984. BA, SUNY, Binghamton, 1973; JD, St. John's U., Jamaica, N.Y., 1978. Bar: N.Y. 1979, U.S. Dist. Ct. (ea. and so. dists.) N.Y. 1979. Asst. corp. counsel N.Y.C. Law Dept., 1978-82; assoc. Willkie, Farr & Gallagher, N.Y.C., 1982-83, Rivkin, Radler, Dunne & Bayh, Uniondale, N.Y., 1983-85; ptnr. Rivkin, Radler, Dunne & Bayh, Los Angeles, 1986—. Editor St. John's U. Law Rev., 1978. Mem. ABA. Federal civil litigation, Environment, Contracts commercial. Office: Rivkin Radler Dunne & Bayh 2049 Century Park Los Angeles CA 90067

GARBARINI, CHAS. J., lawyer, trade association consultant; b. N.Y.C., July 5, 1911; s. Victor Emanuele and Maria (Balzarini) G.; m. Lillian Michelina Penna, Jan. 23, 1937; children—Charles J., Rita Garbarini Nugent, Stephen A. B.A., Fordham Coll., 1933; J.D., St. John U., N.Y.C., 1936; trade assn. mgmt. cert. Eastern U. at Yale U., 1952. Bar: N.Y. 1941, U.S. Dist. Ct. (so. dist.) N.Y. 1947, U.S. Dist. Ct. (ea. dist.) N.Y. 1951. Ptnr. Garbarini & Kroll, N.Y.C., 1944-60, Garbarini, Scher & De Cicco, N.Y.C., 1961—; cons. trade assns. Penn Affiliates, Inc., New Rochelle, N.Y., 1960-80; cons.-constrn. Garco Constrn. Corp., N.Y.C., 1940-54. Mem. ABA, Assn. Bar City N.Y., N.Y. County Lawyers Assn., Columbian Lawyers Assn. (pres. 1967). Roman Catholic. Lodge: K.C. (grand knight 1974). Personal injury, Insurance. Home: 956 Edgewood Ave Pelham Manor NY 10803 Office: Garbarini Scher & DeCicco PC 1114 Ave of Americas New York NY 10036

GARBER, MARC RICKY, lawyer; b. Phila., Sept. 23, 1955; s. Irving Edward and Audrey (Aidenbaum) G.; m. Terry Lynn Ginsburg, June 25, 1978; children: Edward Alexander, Joshua Ryan. Student, Pa. State U., 1973-75; BA magna cum laude, Temple U., 1977; JD, Duquesne U., 1981. Bar: Pa. 1981, U.S. Dist. Ct. (ea. dist.) Pa., 1982, Mass. 1983, U.S. Dist. Ct. Mass. 1983, Okla. 1985, U.S. Tax Ct. 1985, U.S. Ct. Appeals (1st cir.) 1983. Assoc. Pelino & Lentz, P.C., Phila., 1981-82, Burns & Levinson, Boston, 1982-83, Hall, Estill, Hardwick, Gable et al, Tulsa, 1984-86, Pepper, Hamilton & Scheetz, Phila., 1986—. Mem. ABA (employee benefits com., tax sect.), Southwest Pension Conf., Tulsa Employee Benefits Group. Republican. Jewish. Avocations: reading, gardening, cooking. Pension, profit-sharing, and employee benefits, Health. Home: 6817 Kindred St Philadelphia PA 19149 Office: Pepper Hamilton & Scheetz 123 S Broad St Fidelity Bldg 20th Floor Philadelphia PA 19102

GARBER, PHILIP CHARLES, lawyer; b. Boston, Nov. 16, 1934; s. Rubin E. and Sarah Rose (Schick) G. B.A. cum laude, Harvard U., 1956, J.D., 1961. Bar: Mass. 1961, U.S. Ct. Appeals (1st cir.) 1977. Ptnr. Garber & Garber, Boston, 1961—; title examiner Land Ct., Mass., 1966. Translator: The Political Constitution of Chile, 1980. Pres. West End House Boys Club Alumni Assn., Allston, Mass., 1982-83; hon. consul, Chile, 1982. Mem. Comml. Law League. Club: Harvard (Boston); Caleuche (Valparaiso). Consumer commercial, Contracts commercial. Office: Garber & Garber Esquires PC 79 Milk St Suite 600 Boston MA 02109

GARBER, ROBERT EDWARD, lawyer, banker; b. N.Y.C., Jan. 4, 1949; s. Edward Robert and Estelle (Rosenberg) G.; m. Mary Ellen Roche, Jan. 17,

1981; 1 child, Edward Thomas. A.B., Princeton U., 1970; J.D., Columbia U., 1973. Bar: N.Y. 1974. Law clk. U.S. Dist. Ct. (so. dist.), N.Y.C., 1973-75; assoc. Debevoise, Plimpton, Lyons & Gates, N.Y.C., 1976-79; assoc. counsel, v.p. Irving Trust, N.Y.C., 1979-82, sr. v.p., 1982—. Served to capt. USAR, 1970-78. Mem. N.Y. Bar Assn., Am. Soc. Internat. Law. Banking, General corporate. Home: 2 Bacon Ct Bronxville NY 10708 Office: Irving Trust Co 1 Wall St New York NY 10015

GARBIS, GARY EDWARD, lawyer; b. Jersey City, Oct. 25, 1943; s. Benjamin and Lillian (Goldstein) G.; m. Michelle Renee Holtzman, June 20, 1970; 1 child, Shawn. BA, U. Tampa, 1966; JD, U. Miami, 1969. Bar: Fla. 1969, U.S. Ct. Mil. Appeals 1971, U.S. Supreme Ct. 1973, U.S. Dist. Ct. (so. dist.) Fla. 1973, U.S. Ct. Appeals (11th cir.) 1982. Assoc. Virgin, Whittle & Slatko, Miami, Fla., 1973-79; ptnr. Virgin, Whittle & Garbis, Miami, 1979-83; sole practice Miami, 1983—. Served to capt. JAGC, U.S. Army 1969-72. Mem. ABA, Fla. Bar Assn., Am. Acad. Trial Lawyers, Fla. Acad. Trial Lawyers, Jewish War Vets. (pres. post 778 1978.). Lodge: Lions (pres. Kendall club 1978). Avocations: tennis, theater. Federal civil litigation, State civil litigation. Home: 7300 SW 142d Ave Miami FL 33103 Office: 701 SW 27th Ave Suite 1000 Miami FL 33135

GARCIA, ADOLFO RAMON, lawyer; b. Havana, Cuba, Nov. 5, 1948; came to U.S., 1961; s. Adolfo Damiam and Luz I. (Garcia) G.; m. Elizabeth Ensor, July 17, 1971; children: Andrew, Laurence. AB magna cum laude, Harvard U., 1971; JD, Georgetown U., 1974. Bar: N.Y. 1975, Mass. 1981. Assoc. Cahill, Gordon & Reindel, N.Y.C., 1974-79, Choate, Hall & Stewart, Boston, 1979-82; sr. ptnr. McDermott, Will & Emery, Boston, 1982—. Sec., co-chmn. leagl affairs com., bd. dirs. Internat. Bus. Ctr. New England Inc., Boston, 1983—; past chmn. and pres., bd. dirs. Boston Ctr. for Internat. Visitors, 1981-86; mem. Mass. Internat. Trade Council, Boston, 1984—. Mem. Internat. Bar Assn., Boston Bar Assn. (co-chmn. pvt. internat. law sect. 1982-86), InterAm. Bar Assn. Republican. Clubs: Union (Boston); Essex County, Manchester (Mass.) Yacht. General corporate, Securities, Private international. Home: West Hollow Beverly Farms MA 01915 Office: McDermott Will & Emery 1 Post Office Sq Boston MA 02109

GARCIA, EVA, lawyer; b. McAllen, Tex., Dec. 12, 1950; d. Ruben Garcia and Soledad (Balderas) G.; m. John Greene, Dec. 26, 1970 (div. Apr. 1985); children: Teresa, Christina, Aaron. BA, U. Nev., 1973; JD, U. San Diego, 1981. Bar: Nev. 1981, U.S. Dist. Ct. Nev. 1981, U.S. Ct. Appeals (9th cir.) 1983. Social worker Nev. State Welfare Agy., Las Vegas, 1973; interpreter 8th jud. dist. Nev. Dist. Ct., Las Vegas, 1975-78; mem. commrs. adv. bd. Nat. Assn. Housing and Redevel. Officials, Washington, 1985; official atty. Mexican Consulate, San Bernadino, Calif., 1983—. Commr. Clark County Housing Authority, Las Vegas, 1984—; bd. dirs. Nev. State Pub. Works Bd., Carson City, 1984—, Las Vegas Adv. Bd., 1984-86, United Way Southern Nev., 1986. Recipient Profl. award Nev. Econ. Devel. Co., Las Vegas, 1984-86, Named Outstanding Young Women Am., 1980. Mem. Assn. Trial Lawyers Am., Latin Am. Bar Assn. (pres. 1983-85), Latin C. of C. (v.p. 1984—, Bus. award, 1983), Nev. Bar Assn., Nev. Trial Lawyers Assn., Nev. Assn. Latin Ams. (v.p. 1981-84), Southern Nev. Assn. Women Attys. (bd. dirs. 1982-83), Clark County Bar Assn. Club:s Lulac (Las Vegas). Avocation: scuba diving. General practice, Immigration, naturalization, and customs, Personal injury. Home: 3659 Cherokee Las Vegas NV 89121 Office: Garcia & Garcia Law Offices 501 S 7th St Las Vegas NV 89101

GARCIA, HIPOLITO FRANK, federal judge; b. San Antonio, Dec. 4, 1925; s. Hipolito and Francisca G. LL.B., St. Mary's U., San Antonio, 1951. Bar: Tex. bar 1952. With Dist. Atty's Office, San Antonio, 1952; judge County Ct. at Law, 1964-74, Tex. Dist. Ct. Dist. 144, 1975-79, U.S. Dist. Ct. Western Dist., San Antonio, 1980—. Recipient cert. of Merit Am. Legion. Mem. San Antonio Bar Assn., Am. Bar Assn., Delta Theta Phi. Democrat. Office: US Courthouse US Dist Ct 655 E Durango St Suite 165 San Antonio TX 78206 *

GARCIA, HUMBERTO SIGIFREDO, lawyer; b. Harlingen, Tex., June 7, 1944; s. Porfirio and Margarita (Herrera) G.; m. Lana Cheryl Caswell, Aug. 9, 1975. BA, Lamar U., 1974; JD, U. Tex., 1977. Bar: Tex. 1978, U.S. Dist. Ct. (ea. dist.) Tex. 1978, U.S. Dist. Ct. (so. dist.) Tex. 1979, U.S. Ct. Appeals (5th cir.) 1979, U.S. Supreme Ct. 1982. Ptnr. Mehaffy, Garcia & Bradford, Beaumont, Tex., 1977-83; asst. U.S. atty. east dist. State of Tex., Sherman, 1983—; instr. Lamar U., Beaumont, 1980-83; bd. dirs. Western State Bank, Denton, Tex. Served to capt. USMC, 1968-71. Mem. ABA, Fed. Bar Assn., Tex. Bar Assn, Kappa Sigma. Democrat. Presbyterian. Avocations: long distance running, fishing, photography, cars. Criminal, Condemnation, Federal civil litigation. Home: 2010 Meadows Ln Sherman TX 75090 Office: US Attys Office 101 E Pecan Sherman TX 75090

GARCIA, JOSEPH ANTONIO, lawyer, legislative consultant; b. Highland Park, Mich., Oct. 14, 1947; s. Joseph and Zena (Fesik) G.; m. Mary Christine Fredericks, June 19, 1970; children: Joseph Jr., Mark, Anthony, Jennifer. BA in Econs., Wayne State U., 1969; JD with distinction, Thomas M. Cooley Coll., 1978. Bar: Mich. 1979, U.S. Dist. Ct. (ea. dist.) Mich. 1980. Tchr., coach Pontiac (Mich.) Cath. High Sch., 1969-73; assoc. pub. affairs Mich. Cath. Conf., Lansing, 1973-78; legis. counsel Mich. Food Dealers Assn., Lansing, 1978-70; legis. cons. Karoub Assn., Lansing, 1980—; gen. counsel Mich. Racing Assn., Lansing, 1980—; gen. counsel Northville (Mich.) Driving Club, 1984—. Mem. ABA, Mich. Bar Assn. Roman Catholic. Lodge: KC. Administrative and regulatory, General practice, Legislative. Office: Karoub Assocs 200 N Capitol Suite 500 Lansing MI 48933

GARCIA, LAWRENCE L., lawyer, real estate investor; b. Kalamazoo, Oct. 28, 1946; s. Fidencio R. and Doris Marie (McDaniels) G.; m. Linda Casey, Sept. 10, 1966; children: William Frederick, Casey Marie. Student, U. Tex., 1964-65, U. Md., 1968; BA, U. Houston, 1971, JD, 1979. Bar: Tex. 1980, U.S. Dist. Ct. (we. dist.) Tex. 1983. Asst. personnel mgr. FMC Corp., Houston, 1974-76; employment mgr. TRW Inc., Houston, 1975-78; equal employment mgr. Tenneco, Inc., Houston, 1978-80; sole practice San Antonio, 1980-82; ptnr. Ehrlich & Garcia, San Antonio, 1982-84; prin. Lawrence L. Garcia & Assocs., San Antonio, 1984—; bd. dirs. KFI Services, Inc., San Antonio, 1985—; owner Lawrence L. Garcia Properties, San Antonio, 1984—; com. chmn. San Antonio Criminal Def. Lawyers, 1984-85. Chmn. bd. dirs. Wildlife Rescue and Rehab., Inc., San Antonio, 1985—; bd. dirs. Woman's Law Ctr., 1982-84; lic. coach Northeast Youth Soccer Assn., 1980-84. Served with U.S. Army, 1966-69. Named Sole Proprieter of Yr., Bexar County Legal Aid., 1985. Mem. ABA (semi- finalist moot ct. competition, 1977, finalist, 1978), Tex. Trial Lawyers Assn., San Antonio Trial Lawyers Assn., Tex. Criminal Def. Lawyer, Mex. Am. Bar Assn. (sec. 1982-84), Nat. Order Barristers. Democrat. Mem. Christian Ch. Criminal, Family and matrimonial, Personal injury. Office: 257 E Hildebrand San Antonio TX 78212

GARCIA, LUIS CESAREO, lawyer; b. Hato Rey, P.R., Apr. 19, 1949; came to U.S., 1965; s. Elena and John B. Amos (foster parents); s. Evelina Maura; m. Kathy Jo Mims, Dec. 4, 1970; children—Joseph Amos, Evelyn Kathleen. Student Columbus Coll., 1967-70; J.D., John Marshall Law U., Atlanta, 1973; postgrad. Harvard U., 1978, 84. Bar: Ga. 1974, U.S. Dist. Ct. (mid. dist.) Ga. 1974, U.S. Ct. Appeals (11th cir.) 1983, U.S. Supreme Ct. 1977. Assoc. Keil, Riley & Fort, Columbus, Ga., 1974-75; sole practice, Columbus, 1975-76; sr. ptnr. Garcia & Hirsch, P.C., Columbus, 1976-79; regional mgr. Am. Family Life Assurance Co., Columbus, 1979-82, exec. v.p., chief counsel, 1982—; sr. v.p. counsel internat. ops., 1986—; legal counsel LMI, Inc., 1979-82; mem. legis. com. Am. Prepaid Legal Inst., Chgo., 1983-85. Bd. dirs. Better Bus. Bur. of W. Ga.-E. Ala., 1984—; mem. bd. adv. council CETA, 1979-83; adv. bd. Ga. Pub. TV, 1979-82. Mem. Fed. Bar Assn., ABA, Ga. Bar Assn., Columbus Lawyers Club, Younger Lawyers Club, Sigma Delta Kappa. Episcopalian. Clubs: Toastmasters, Country of Columbus. General corporate, Insurance, Legal insurance and services. Office: Am Family Life Assurance Co 1932 Wynnton Rd Columbus GA 31999

GARCIA, MARIA ELIAS, lawyer; b. N.Y.C.; d. Mario Camargo and Carmen (Céspedes) Garcia; m. Peter V. O'Shea Jr.; children: Carmen Mary O'Shea, Kieran Robert O'Shea. BA, Barnard Coll., 1969; JD, Columbia U., 1974. Bar: N.Y. 1975. Area counsel IBM Corp., Kingston, N.Y., 1980-82; sr. atty. IBM Corp., White Plains, N.Y., 1982-83; regional counsel IBM Corp., Dallas, 1983-85; sr. atty. IBM Corp., Armonk, N.Y., 1985-86; staff counsel IBM Corp., Armonk, 1986—. Mem. Wetlands Control Commn. Town of Bedford, N.Y., 1986—; v.p. Suzuki Strings Dallas Parents Org., 1984-85; bd. dirs. No. Dutches Hosp., 1981-82. Mem. ABA, N.Y. State Bar Assn. Republican. Roman Catholic. Avocations: music, reading, cross country skiing. Labor, Computer, Antitrust. Home: Virginia Ave PO Box 702 Bedford NY 10506 Office: IBM Corp 3B 20 Old Orchard Rd Armonk NY 10506

GARCIA, PATRICIA A., lawyer; b. New Orleans, Feb. 18, 1956; d. Martin F. and Shirley (Polders) G. BA in History, U. New Orleans, 1976; JD, Loyola U., New Orleans, 1980. Bar: La. 1980, U.S. Tax Ct. 1982, U.S. Dist. Ct. (ea. dist.) La. 1984, U.S. Dist. Ct. (mid. dist.) La. 1986. Staff atty. office of chief counsel IRS, Washington, 1980-82; law clk. U.S. Ea. Dist. Ct. of La., New Orleans, 1983-86; assoc. Law Office of Eric A. Holden, New Orleans, 1986—. Mem. ABA (La. dist. gov. 1979-80, project dir. model project for effective delivery of law-related edn. to low income families 1985—, chmn. delivery of legal services com. young lawyers div. 1987—, recipient Gold Key award 1980), La. Bar Assn. (chmn. law week 1986, mem. young lawyers sect. 1986—, Achievement award 1985, 86, 87), New Orleans Bar Assn. (vice-chmn. young lawyers sect. 1984—, chmn.-elect 1986—, vice chmn. increasing membership com. 1986—, mem. profl. ehtics, pub. relations coms. 1984—, grantee to direct project for ABA 1985). Democrat. Roman Catholic. Federal civil litigation, State civil litigation, Consumer commercial. Home: 6850 Wuerpel St New Orleans LA 70124 Office: Law Office of Eric A Holden 101 W Robert E Lee Blvd #400 New Orleans LA 70124

GARCIA, RUDOLPH, lawyer; b. Phila., June 22, 1951; s. Rudolph Sr. and Assunta Rita (Marrara) G.; m. Randi Ellen Pastor, Aug. 3, 1980; 1 child, Jonathan P. BA magna cum laude, Temple U., 1974, JD cum laude, 1977. Bar: Pa. 1977, U.S. Dist. Ct. (ea. dist.) Pa. 1977, U.S. Ct. Appeals (3d cir.) 1982, U.S. Supreme Ct. 1982. Assoc. Wright, Thistle & Gibbons, Phila., 1977-78; assoc. Saul, Ewing, Remick & Saul, Phila., 1978-84, ptnr., 1984—. Fellow Acad. of Adv.; mem. ABA, Pa. Bar Assn., Phila. Bar Assn., Nat. Assn. R.R.Trial Counsel, Phila. Assn. Def. Counsel, Justinian Soc., Phi Beta Kappa. Avocations: photography, golf. Federal civil litigation, State civil litigation, Insurance. Home: 235 Lloyd Ln Wynnewood PA 19151 Office: Saul Ewing Remick & Saul 3800 Centre Sq W Philadelphia PA 19102

GARCIA, SYLVIA R., judge; b. San Diego, Sept. 6, 1950; d. Luis and Antonia (Rodriguez) G. BS, Tex. Womens U., 1972; JD, Tex. So. U., 1978. Bar: Tex. 1978, U.S. Dist. (so. dist.) Tex. 1979, U.S. Ct. Appeals (5th cir.) 1981. Law clk. City of Houston, 1978; atty. Gulf Coast Legal Found., Houston, 1978-81; vice-chmn. Appraisal Rev. Bd. City of Houston, 1982-83; gen. mgr., counsel ASI Universal Corp., Houston, 1981-84; ptnr. Hubacker and Garcia, Houston, 1984-85; sole practice Houston, 1985; hearings examiner EEOC, Houston, 1985-86; mcpl. ct. judge City of Houston, 1986—. Mem. ABA, State Bar Tex. (legal services to indigent com. 1979-81, legislation pub. interest com., 1980-81, women in law sect., council, 1981-82), Houston Bar Assn. (judicare com. 1985), Mex. Am. Bar Assn., Hispanic Women Lawyers Assn. (past pres.). Judicial administration. Home: 4103 Yupon Houston TX 77006

GARCIA, TERRY DONATO, lawyer; b. Jacksonville, Fla., Mar. 27, 1953; s. Joseph Donato and Marcelle (Cook) G.; m. Mary Talley, Mar. 27, 1982; 1 child, Alex Donato. BA in Internat. Relations, Am. U., 1975; JD, George Washington U., 1980. Bar: D.C. 1980, Calif. 1982. Dir. research UN Assn., Washington, 1972-74; dir. legislation World Federalists, Washington, 1974-76; lobbyist New Directions, Washington, 1976-78; legis. cons. Internat. Devel. Coop. Agy., Washington, 1979-80; assoc. Manatt, Phelps, Rotherberg & Tunney, Washington and Los Angeles, 1980-83; ptnr. Fried, King & Holmes, Los Angeles, 1983—. Author: Federal Regulation of Banking, 1980. Asst. counsel Brown for Gov., Los Angeles, 1982; asst. gen. counsel Mondal Com., Los Angeles, 1984; gen. counsel Ams. with Hart, Los Angeles, 1983-84, Calif. Dems. for New Leadership, Los Angeles, 1985—, Calif. Dem. Party, 1987—; counsel So. Calif. Freeze Voter, Los Angeles, 1984—. Mem. ABA, Calif. Bar Assn., D.C. Bar Assn., Los Angeles Bar Assn.,. Episcopalian. Avocation: amateur radio. Banking, General corporate, Securities. Office: Fried King & Holmes 1901 Ave of Stars Suite 760 Los Angeles CA 90067

GARCIA-PEDROSA, JOSE RAMON, lawyer; b. Havana, Cuba, May 2, 1946; came to U.S., 1960; s. Jose Ramon and Zoraida Garcia Pedrosa; m. Marjorie Baron; 1 child, Daniel. BA in Econs., Harvard U., 1968, JD, 1971. Bar: Fla. 1971. From assoc. to ptnr. Smathers & Thompson, Miami, Fla., 1971-82; atty. City of Miami, 1982-84; ptnr. Finley, Kumble, Wagner, Heine, Underberg, Manley & Casey, Miami, 1984—. Mem. visiting com. U. Miami, 1982—, U. Miami Citizens Bd., 1983—; fund raiser Harvard U. Fund, Harvard Law Sch., Bapt. Hosp. and Endowment Fund; trustee Metrozoo, Miami, 1984—; bd. dirs. Facts. About Cuban Exiles, 1982. Mem. ABA (law sch. accredation com. 1982—, council on legal edn. 1983—), Fla. Assn. for Women Lawyers, Cuban Am. Bar Assn. (founder). State civil litigation, Local government. Home: 3916 Granda Blvd Coral Gables FL 33134 Office: Finley Kumble Wagner Heine et al 777 Brickell Ave Flagship Ctr Suite 1000 Miami FL 33131

GARD, SPENCER AGASSIZ, lawyer, former judge; b. Iola, Kans., June 24, 1898; s. Samuel Arnold and Louisa (Irel) G.; m. Marjorie P. Garlinghouse, Sept. 27, 1924; 1 dau., Amy Lou (Mrs. Jack Brazil). LL.B., U. Kans., 1922, JD, 1968. Bar: Mo. bar 1922, Kans. bar 1942. Practiced in Kansas City, 1922-42, Iola, 1942-50; judge 37th Kans. Jud. Dist., Iola, 1950-69; county atty. Allen County, Kans., 1943-47; faculty Nat. Coll. State Trial Judges U. Colo., 1964. Author: Jones on Evidence, 6th edit, 1972, Illinois Evidence Manual and Kansas Code of Civil Procedure Annotated, 2d edit, 1979, Florida Evidence Manual, 2d edit, 1979, Missouri Evidence Law, 2 vols., 1985; Contbr. profl. jours. Vice pres. Kansas City Area council Boy Scouts Am., 1941; mem. Nat. Conf. Commrs. on Uniform State Laws, 1947-62; chmn. spl. com. which drafted Kans. Code Civil Procedure, 1963; Mem. Kan. Ho. of Reps., 1947, Kans. Senate, 1949; nominated for Kans. Supreme Ct., 1964, spl. commr., 1972-76. Recipient Disting. Alumnus citation U. Kans. Sch. Law, 1968, Disting. Service in Adminstrn. of Justice award Kans. Judges Assn., 1974; Disting. Service award Kans. Bar Assn., 1975; Justinian award Johnson County Bar Assn., 1978; Order of Smiling Bull award Jefferson County Bar Assn., 1986. Fellow Am. Bar Found.; mem. Am. Bar. Assn., Order of Coif, Scribes. Methodist. State civil litigation, Criminal, Consultant on evidence. Home and office: 9007 Salem Dr Apt 4 Lenexa KS 66215

GARDINER, LESTER RAYMOND, JR., lawyer; b. Salt Lake City, Aug. 20, 1931; s. Lester Raymond and Sarah Lucille (Kener) G.; m. Janet Ruth Thatcher, Apr. 11, 1955; children—Allison Gardiner Bigelow, Annette Gardiner Weed, John Alfred, Leslie Gardiner Crandall, Robert Thatcher, Lisa, James Raymond, Elizabeth, David William, Sarah Janet. B.S. with honors, U. Utah, 1954; J.D., U. Mich., 1959. Bar: Utah 1959, U.S. Dist. Ct. Utah 1959, U.S. Ct. Apls. (10th cir.) 1960. Law clk., U.S. Dist. Ct., 1959; assoc. then ptnr. Van Cott, Bagley, Cornwall & McCarthy, Salt Lake City, 1960-67; ptnr. ptnr. Gardiner & Johnson, Salt Lake City, 1967-72; ptnr. Christensen, Gardiner, Jensen & Evans, 1972-78; ptnr. Fox, Edwards, Gardiner & Brown, Salt Lake City, 1978-87, ptnr. Chapman & Cutler, 1987—; reporter, mem. Utah Sup. Ct. Com. on Adoption of Uniform Rules of Evidence, 1970-73, mem. com. on revision of criminal code, 1975-78; master of the bench Am. Inn of Ct. I, 1980—; mem. com. bar examiners Utah State Bar, 1973; instr. bus. law U. Utah, 1965-66; adj. prof. law Brigham Young U., 1984-85. Mem. Republican State Central Com. Utah, 1967-72, mem. exec. com. Utah Rep. Party, 1975-78, chmn. state convs., 1980, 81; mem. Salt Lake City Bd. Edn., 1971-72; mem. bd. dirs. Salt Lake City Pub. Library, 1974-75. Served to 1st. USAF, 1954-56. Mem. ABA, Utah State Bar Assn., Salt Lake County Bar Assn. (mem. exec. com. 1967-68). Mormon. Clubs: Ft. Douglas Hidden Valley Country, Sons of Utah Pioneers, Bonneville Knife & Fork (Salt Lake City). Lodge: Rotary. Antitrust, Federal civil litigation, General corporate. Office: 57 W 2 S Salt Lake City UT 84111

GARDINER, RICHARD ERNEST, lawyer; b. Bryn Mawr, Pa., Sept. 16, 1951; s. Frank John and Philippa (Tunis) G. BSEE, Union Coll., 1973; JD, George Mason U., 1978. Bar: Va. 1979, U.S. Supreme Ct. 1982. Staff atty. Nat. Rifle Assn., Washington, 1979-82, asst. gen. counsel, 1982—. Bd. dirs. ACLU of Va., Richmond, 1981—. Mem. ABA, Va. Trial Lawyers Assn., Fairfax Bar Assn. Libertarian. Avocations: squash, flying. Federal civil litigation, Legislative, Criminal. Home: 7404 Estaban Pl Springfield VA 22151 Office: Nat Rifle Assn 1600 Rhode Island Ave NW Washington DC 20036

GARDINER, STUART KORSON, lawyer, educational administrator; b. Phila., Oct. 13, 1948; s. Eli W. and Ruth Sylvia (Korson) G.; divorced. BA, Yale U., 1970; JD, U. Calif., Berkeley, 1973. Bar: Calif. 1975, U.S. Dist. Ct. (no. dist.) Calif. 1975, U.S. Ct. Appeals (9th cir.) 1985. Sr. budget analyst office of chancellor U. Calif., Berkeley, 1973-75, asst. dean, lectr. sch. law, 1975-82; atty. Pacific Gas & Electric Co., San Francisco, 1983—. Commr. commn. Police Rev., Berkeley, 1977-79, Planning commn., Berkeley, 1987—; chmn. commn. fair campaign practices, Berkeley, 1981-85, commr., 1986—. Mem. Calif. Bar Assn., Fed. Energy Bar Assn. Contracts commercial, FERC practice, Public utilities. Office: Pacific Gas & Electric Co Law Dept 77 Beale St San Francisco CA 94106

GARDINER, THOMAS G., lawyer; b. Harvey, Ill., Apr. 5, 1957; s. Lloyd Gene and Dona L. Gardiner; m. Margaret Lass, Sept. 17, 1982; 1 child, Katherine Julia. BS, U. Ill., Urbana, 1978; JD, Northwestern U., Chgo., 1981. Assoc. Sidley & Austin, Chgo., 1981; jud. clk. to presiding justice U.S. Dist. Ct., Chgo., 1982; asst. state's atty. State's Atty.'s Office, Chgo., 1983—. Contbr. articles to profl. jours. Chmn. Jud. Licensing Com., Glenwood, Ill., 1985; trustee Prairie State Coll., Chgo. Heights, Ill., 1981—, Village of Glenwood, Ill., 1985—. Edmund J. James scholar, 1978. Mem. Ill. Bar Assn., Chgo. Bar Assn., South Suburban Mayors and Mgrs., Ill. Community Coll. of Trustees, Assn. Community Coll. Trustees. Home: 122 W Main St Glenwood IL 60425

GARDNER, ALAN JOEL, lawyer; b. Los Angeles, July 18, 1945; s. Leonard and Charlotte M. (Cohen) G.; m. Trudi York, Mar. 19, 1947. B.A. cum laude, UCLA, 1967; J.D., U. Calif.-Berkeley, 1970. Bar: Oreg. 1970, U.S. Ct. Appeals (9th cir.) 1970, U.S. Dist. Ct. Oreg. 1971, Wash. 1971, U.S. Ct. Appeals (4th cir.) 1975, U.S. Ct. Appeals (D.C. cir.) 1975, D.C. 1976, U.S. Supreme Ct. 1976, U.S. Dist. Ct. (we. dist.) Wash. 1979. Law clk. U.S. Ct. Appeals (9th cir.), Seattle, 1970-71; assoc. McColloch, Dezendorf, Spears & Lubersky, Portland, Oreg., 1971-72; corp. atty. Pacific N.W. Bell Telephone Co., 1972-75, 77-78, Oreg. area, Portland, 1978-81, hdqrs., Seattle, 1981-83, Wash.-Idaho-Oreg. area, Seattle, 1983-84, legal head mktg., 1986—; head civil litigation, 1984-86, legal head mktg. services, 1986—; corp. atty. AT&T, N.Y.C., 1975-77; judge pro tempore Bellevue Dist. Ct.; instr. Nat. Inst. Trial Advocacy, 1979—. Active United Way, 1979—; bd. dirs. Wash. State Film Council, 1986—, v.p., 1987—; bd. dirs. Pacific Northwest Studio, 1986—. Mem. ABA (litigation com., trial advocacy sub-com.), Oreg. State Bar Assn., Wash. State Bar Assn., D.C. Bar Assn., Seattle-King County Bar Assn., FCC Bar Assn., Phi Beta Kappa. Clubs: Bellevue Athletic (Wash.) Seattle Skeet and Trap (past bd. dirs., treas., v.p.). Federal and state regulatory, Antitrust. Address: 3206 Bell Plaza Seattle WA 98191

GARDNER, ARNOLD BURTON, lawyer; b. N.Y.C., Jan. 3, 1930; s. Harry P. and Ruth G. (Gutfreund) G.; m. Sue Shaffer, Aug. 24, 1952; children—Jonathan H., Diane R. B.A. summa cum laude, U. Buffalo, 1950; LL.B., Harvard U., 1953. Bar: N.Y. State bar 1954. Assoc. firm Kavinoky & Cook (and predecessor), Buffalo, 1953-58, ptnr., 1958—; sr. ptnr. Kavinoky & Cook (and predecessor), 1977—; bd. dirs. Emmis Broadcasting Corp., Indpls. Mem. Buffalo Bd. Edn., 1969-74, pres., 1971-72; mem. nat. bd. govs. Am. Jewish Com., 1972—, nat. v.p., 1986—; chmn. N.Y. State Edn. Dept. Task Force on Tchr. Edn. and Certification, 1975-77; trustee SUNY, 1980—; bd. govs. Hebrew Union Coll., Jewish Inst. Religion, Cin., 1981—. Served with U.S. Army, 1954-56. Recipient Community Service award NCCJ, 1974. Mem. Erie County Bar Assn., N.Y. State Bar Assn., ABA, Am. Law Inst. Club: Buffalo. General corporate, Corporate taxation. Home: 89 Middlesex Rd Buffalo NY 14216 Office: 120 Delaware Ave Buffalo NY 14202

GARDNER, BRUCE ELWYN, lawyer; b. N.Y.C., Jan. 28, 1953; s. Parker and Mary P. (Pinkston) G. BA, UCLA, 1975; JD, Syracuse U., 1978; LLM in Taxation, Georgetown U., 1987. Bar: Ill. 1981, U.S. Dist. Ct. (no. dist.) Ill. 1981, U.S. Ct. Appeals (5th cir.) 1981, U.S. Dist. Ct. (so. dist.) Tex. 1982, U.S. Ct. Appeals (7th cir.) 1982, U.S. Ct. Appeals (9th cir.) 1983, U.S. Claims Ct. 1983, U.S. Ct. Mil. Appeals 1983, U.S. Supreme Ct. 1985. Estate tax atty. IRS, Chgo., 1979-80; appeals officer Ill. Dept. Revenue, Chgo., 1980-81, hearing officer, 1981-82; agt. IRS, Houston, 1982-84; tax law specialist IRS, Washington, 1984-86; appeals officer IRS, Houston, 1986—. Named One of Outstanding Young Men Am., U.S. Jaycees, 1983, 84, 85, 86; recipient Spl. Achievement award IRS, 1986. Mem. ABA. Avocations: tennis, racquetball, music, travel. Corporate taxation, Estate taxation, Personal income taxation. Home: 738 Corvette Ct Houston TX 77060 Office: IRS 10850 Richmond Ave Houston TX 77060 also: PO Box 770983 Houston TX 77215

GARDNER, DALE RAY, lawyer; b. Broken Arrow, Okla., May 8, 1946; s. Edward Dale and Dahlia Faye (McKeen) G.; m. Phyllis Ann Weinschrott, Dec. 27, 1969. BA in History, So. Ill. U., 1968; MA in History, St. Mary's U., San Antonio, 1975; JD, Tulsa U., 1979. Bar: Okla. 1979, U.S. Dist. Ct. (no. dist.) Okla. 1981, U.S. Dist. Ct. Colo. 1986, U.S. Ct. Appeals (10th cir.) 1986. Sole practice Sapulpa, Okla., 1979-80; asst. dist. atty. child support enforcement unit 24th Dist. Okla., Sapulpa, 1980-86; sole practice Aurora, Colo., 1986—. Mem. Child Support Enforcement, Sapulpa, 1985—; trustee United Way, Sapulpa, 1985, Domestic Violence Counsel, Sapulpa, 1985; chmn. bd. trustees 1st Prebyn. Ch., Sapulpa, 1985. Served to capt. U.S. Army, 1969-75, Vietnam. Mem. ABA, Okla. Bar Assn., Creek County Bar Assn., Nat. Dist. Atty. Assn., Okla. Dist. Atty. Assn., Colo. Bar Assn., Aurora Bar Assn. Democrat. Lodge: Sertoma (pres. Sapulpa 1985—, Sertoman of yr. award 1985). Avocations: fishing, post card collecting. Administrative and regulatory, Family and matrimonial, Child support enforcement. Home: 3333 E Florida Ave #1 Denver CO 80210 Office: 10333 E Colfax Ave Aurora CO 80010

GARDNER, JERRY LOUIS, JR., lawyer; b. New Orleans, Oct. 25, 1932; s. Jerome Louis and Marguerite F. (Marcour) G.; m. Gayle June Gardner, Dec. 27, 1958; children—Ylon M., Kevin M. B.A., Tulane U., 1954, J.D., 1960. Bar: La. 1960, U.S. Dist. Ct. (mid., ea., and we. dists.) La. 1960, U.S. Ct. Apls. (5th cir.) 1960, U.S. Ct. Apls. (D.C. cir.) 1974, U.S. Ct. Apls. (11th cir.) 1981, U.S. Supreme Ct. 1973. Atty. NLRB, 1960-67; ptnr. Baker, Boudreaux, Lamy, Gardner & Foley, New Orleans, 1967-84; ptnr. Gardner, Robein, Healey, 1984—; lectr. Tulane U., Loyola U., La. State U.; co-chmn. continuing legal edn. com. La. State Bar, past chmn. labor law sect. Served to capt. USAF, 1954-57. Mem. ABA (council labor and employment law sect.), Fed. Bar Assn., La. Bar Assn., New Orleans Bar Assn. Roman Catholic. Club: New Orleans Athletic. Labor, Workers' compensation. Office: Gardner Robein & Henley 2540 Severn Ave Suite 400 Metairie LA 70002

GARDNER, MARK S., lawyer; b. Fredericksburg, Va., June 28, 1953; s. Harold L. and Vera E. (Harvey) G.; m. Joan Elizabeth Mastin, Aug. 24, 1974; children: Matthew Adam, Jonathan Aaron. BA, Davidson Coll., 1975; JD, U. Richmond, 1978. Bar: Va. 1978, U.S. Dist. Ct. (ea. dist.) Va. 1978, U.S. Supreme Ct. 1982. Law clk. to presiding justice Va. Supreme Ct., Richmond, 1978-79; ptnr. Gardner & Maupin, Spotsylvania, Va., 1979—; commonwealth atty. Spotsylvania County, 1980—. Editor-in-chief U. Richmond Law Rev., 1977-78. Mem. ABA, Va. Bar Assn., Va. Trial Lawyers Assn., Va. Assn. Commonwealth Attys., Jaycees (v.p. 1985). Democrat. Baptist. State civil litigation, Criminal, General practice. Office: Gardner & Maupin PO Box 129 Spotsylvania VA 22553

GARDNER, PAUL HENDRICKS, lawyer; b. Kansas City, Mo., Jan. 7, 1954; s. Paul Hendricks and Elizabeth Jane (McCandless) G. B Gen. Studies, U. Kans., 1976; JD, U. Mo., 1979. Bar: Mo. 1979, U.S. Dist. Ct. (we. dist.) Mo. 1985. Research atty. Mo. Ct. Appeals, Kansas City, 1980-81, law clk. to presiding judge, 1981-83; asst. gen counsel Mo. Pub. Service Commn., Jefferson City, 1983—. Contbr. (book) Antitrust Law Developments, articles to law rev. Mem. ABA, Mo. Bar Assn. Avocations: running,

weightlifting, softball, fishing. Public utilities, Administrative and regulatory, Antitrust. Home: 1226 B Carter Jefferson City MO 65101 Office: Mo Pub Service Commn 301 W High PO Box 360 Jefferson City MO 65102

GARDNER, RAY DEAN, JR., lawyer; b. Huntington Park, Calif., July 9, 1954; s. Ray Dean Gardner Sr. and Wanda Lou (Banks) Goldman; m. Elizabeth Louise Davis, Dec. 28, 1976; 1 child, John Davis. BA, Humboldt State U., 1977; JD, U. Calif., San Francisco, 1981. Bar: Alaska 1981, U.S. Dist. Ct. Alaska 1981, U.S. Ct. Appeals (9th cir.) 1981, U.S. Supreme Ct. 1985. Assoc. Hartig, Rhodes, Norman, Mahoney & Edwards, Anchorage, 1981-85, ptnr., 1985—. Bd. dirs. Resource Devel. Council for Alaska Inc., Anchorage, 1985—, Alaska Mineral and Energy Resource Edn. Fund, 1987—. Alfred C. Piltz scholar Humboldt State U., 1975; Calif. State fellow, 1978-81. Mem. ABA, Alaska Bar Assn. (exec. com. natural resources sect. 1984—, chmn. bus. law sect. 1985-86, corp. code revision subcom. 1985—), Alaska Assn. Petroleum Landmen, Alaska Miners Assn. (state oversight com. 1985-86), Anchorage C. of C. (chmn. state legis. com. 1986-87). Republican. Presbyterian. Oil and gas leasing, General corporate. Home: 507 Big Diomede Eagle River AK 99577 Office: Hartig Rhodes Norman Mahoney & Edwards PC 717 K St Anchorage AK 99501

GARDNER, RICHARD NEWTON, lawyer, educator; b. N.Y.C., July 9, 1927; s. Samuel I. and Ethel (Elias) G.; m. Danielle Luzzatto, June 10, 1956; children: Nina Jessica, Anthony Laurence. A.B. magna cum laude, Harvard U., 1948; J.D., Yale U., 1951; Ph.D. (Rhodes scholar), 1951-53, Ph.D. Oxford (Eng.) U, 1954. Bar: N.Y. 1952. Corr. UP, 1946-47, AP, 1948; teaching fellow internat. legal studies Harvard Law Sch., 1953-54; with Coudert Bros., N.Y.C., 1954-57; assoc. prof. law Columbia U., 1957-60, prof., 1960-61, 65-66, Henry L. Moses prof. law and internat. orgn., 1967-77, 81—; of counsel Coudert Bros., 1981—; U.S. ambassador to Italy, 1977-81; dep. asst. sec. state internat. orgns. Dept. State, 1961-65; vis. prof. U. Istanbul, 1958, U. Rome, 1967-68; dep. U.S. rep. UN Com. on Peaceful Uses of Outer Space, 1962-65; U.S. alt. del. 19th UN Gen. Assembly; sr. adviser U.S. del. to 20th and 21st UN Gen. Assemblies; rapporteur UN Com. Experts on Econ. Restructuring, 1975; mem. Pres.'s Commn. on Internat. Trade and Investment Policy, 1970-71, U.S. Adv. Com. on Law of Sea, 1971-76; cons. to sec.-gen. UN Conf. on Human Environment, 1972. Author: Sterling-Dollar Diplomacy, 1956, New Directions in U.S. Foreign Economic Policy, 1959, In Pursuit of World Order, 1964, Blueprint for Peace, 1966, (with Max F. Millikan) The Global Partnership: International Agencies and Economic Development, 1968; note editor: Yale Law Jour, 1950-51. Bd. dirs. Freedom House. Served with AUS, 1945-46. Harvard Club scholar N.Y.C., 1944; recipient Detur prize for distinguished scholarship Harvard U., 1948, Arthur S. Flemming award, 1963. Mem. Am., N.Y. State bar assns., UN Assn. (dir.), Fgn. Policy Assn. (dir.), Assn. Bar City N.Y., Council Fgn. Relations, Am. Econ. Assn., Am. Acad. Arts and Scis., Phi Beta Kappa, Order of Coif. Clubs: Century Assn. (N.Y.C.); Met. (Washington). Public international, International Trade. Home: 1150 Fifth Ave New York NY 10128

GARDNER, ROMAINE LUVERNE, lawyer; b. Wallingford, Iowa, Aug. 19, 1933; s. Lloyd Gilbert and Olivia Agnes (Berge) G.; m. Jane Elder Andrews, June 16, 1956; children: Sibyl Kimerley, Nicholas Berge. BA cum laude, St. Olaf Coll., 1955; M in Divinity, Luth. Theol. Sem., 1958; PhD, Columbia U., 1966; JD cum laude, Bklyn. Law Sch., 1979. Bar: N.Y. 1980. Prof. Wagner Coll., Staten Island, N.Y., 1963-79, dept. chmn., 1971-75; assoc. Cadwalader, Wickersham & Taft, N.Y.C., 1979-82, 83—; dean Gustavus Adolphus Coll., St. Peter, Minn., 1982-83. Del. N.Y. 16th Congl. dist. Dem. Nat. Com., 1968. Jurisprudence, Securities, Commodities. Home: 31 Howard Ave Staten Island NY 10301 Office: Cadwalader Wickersham & Taft 100 Maiden Ln New York NY 10038

GARDNER, RUSSELL MENESE, lawyer; b. High Point, N.C., July 14, 1920; s. Joseph Hayes and Clara Emma-Lee (Flynn) G.; m. Joyce Thresher, Mar. 7, 1946; children—Winthrop G., Page Stansbury, June Thresher. A.B., Duke U., 1942, J.D., 1948. Bar: Fla. 1948, U.S. Ct. Appeals (5th cir.) 1949, U.S. Tax Ct. 1949. Mem. McCune, Hiaasen, Crum Ferris & Gardner and predecessor firms, Ft. Lauderdale, Fla., 1948-50, mem., 1950—; bd. govs. Nova Ctr. for Study of Law. Trustee Mus. of Art, Inc., Ft. Lauderdale, pres., 1964-67; bd. dirs., pres. Stranahan House, Inc., 1980-84, Ft. Laud Hist. Soc., 1975-85, Emeritus, 1985—; pres. Ft. Lauderdale Hist. Soc., 1975—; mem. estate planning council, Duke U. Sch. Law; bd. dirs., vice chmn. Broward Performing Arts Found., Inc., 1985—. Served to lt. USNR, 1943-49. Fellow Am. Coll. Probate counsel; mem. Am. Judicature Soc., ABA (real property, probate, trust sect.), Fla. Bar Assn. (probate, guardianship rules com.), Broward County Bar Assn. (estate planning council). Democrat. Presbyterian. Clubs: Coral Ridge Country, Lauderdale Yacht, Tower (Ft. Lauderdale). Probate, Real property, Estate taxation. Office: McCune Hiaasen Crum Ferris Gardner PO Box 14636 Fort Lauderdale FL 33302

GARDNER, WILLIAM COURTLEIGH, judge; b. Springfield, Ohio, Oct. 19, 1917; s. Glenn Gardner and Myrtle (Lewis) Artis; m. Ora Dowling, Sept. 2, 1943; 1 child, Glenn C. AB, Howard U., 1948; JD, Harvard U., 1951. Bar: D.C. 1951, U.S. Ct. Appeals (D.C. cir.) 1953, U.S. Supreme Ct. 1957, U.S. Ct. Appeals (6th cir.) 1962. Ptnr. Houston & Gardner and predecessor firms, Washington, 1951-80; presiding judge civil div. Superior Ct. of D.C., Washington, 1985—. Commr. Nat. Conf. of Commrs. on Uniform State Laws, 1969—, sec. 1982-85. Served as sgt. U.S. Army, 1942-46. Recipient cert. appreciation, D.C. Govt. Mem. ABA (jud. adminstrn. div.), Bar Assn. D.C. (hon., jud. appointment com., bd. dirs. 1971-72, lawyer of year award 1979), Assn. Trial Lawyers Am. (hon. jud. status), Am. Coll. of Trial Lawyers, The Counsellors, Harvard Law Sch. Assn. Baptist. Clubs: DePriest 15, Nat. Lawyers (hon.) (D.C.). Judicial administration. Office: Superior Ct DC 500 Indiana Ave NW Washington DC 20001

GARFINKEL, BARRY HERBERT, lawyer; b. Bklyn., June 19, 1928; s. Abraham and Shirley (Siegel) G.; m. Gloria Lorenz, Feb. 16, 1969; children—David, James, Paul. B.S.S., CCNY, 1950; LL.B., Yale U., 1955. Bar: N.Y. State 1955, U.S. Supreme Ct. 1959. Law clk. Judge Edward Weinfeld, U.S. Dist. Ct., N.Y.C., 1955-56; assoc. firm Skadden, Arps, Slate, Meagher & Flom, N.Y.C., 1956—; ptnr. Skadden, Arps, Slate, Meagher & Flom, 1961—; trustee Practising Law Inst., Law Center Found. of N.Y. U. Sch. Law, Legal Aid Soc.; chmn. program com. 2d. Circuit Jud. Conf. Mng. editor: Yale Law Jour. Bd. dirs. Jewish Mus.; trustee N.Y. Community Trust. Served to lt. USCG, 1953-55. Fellow Am. Coll. Trial Lawyers, Am. Bar Found.; mem. Am. Arbitration Assn., Nat. Choral Council (pres.), Assn. Bar of City of N.Y. (exec. com., judiciary com., past chmn. fed. cts. com.), Am. Bar Assn., N.Y. State Bar Assn., Am. Law Inst. Club: Yale (N.Y.C.). Federal civil litigation, State civil litigation, Securities. Home: 211 Central Park W New York NY 10024 Office: 919 3d Ave New York NY 10022

GARFINKEL, MARVIN, lawyer, real estate developer; b. Phila., Mar. 23, 1929; s. Simon L. and Theresa (Brier) G.; m. Marian Schwartz, Apr. 6, 1963; 1 son, Simson Leon. B.A., Pomona Coll., 1951; LL.B. magna cum laude, U. Pa., 1954; LL.M. in Taxation, NYU, 1962. Bar: Pa. 1955, N.Y. 1984. Law clk. to Curtis Bok, Gerald F. Flood and Louis E. Levinthal, Phila., 1954-55, W.H. Kirkpatrick, Phila., 1957-58; dep. atty. gen. Pa. 1955-57; sr. partner Garfinkel and Volpicelli; faculty, program chmn. Am. Bar Assn.-Am. Law Inst. on Profl. Edn., Com., 1971—; lectr. post admission program Law Sch., Temple U.; cons. real estate. Editorial bd.: Practical Lawyer; contbr. articles to legal jours. Mem. Internat. Bar Assn. (real estate com.), ABA (real estate sect., chmn. comml. leasing com.), Fed. Bar Assn., N.Y. State Bas Assn., N.Y.C. Bar Assn., Phila. Bar Assn., Pa. Bar Assn., Am. Law Inst., Commercial Law League of Am., Scribes, Am. Soc. Internat. Law, Am. Coll. Real Estate Lawyers, Internat. Law Assn., Order of Coif. Club: Locust (Phila.). General corporate, Real property, Franchising. Home: 426 Pine St Philadelphia PA 19106 Office: Phenox of London House 308 Walnut St Philadelphia PA 19106

GARFUNKEL, ALAN J., lawyer; b. Savannah, Ga., Oct. 26, 1947; s. Sylvan Adler Garfunkel and Eve D. (Darmstadter) Goldmann; m. Peggy D. Lasson, Nov. 26, 1972; children—S. Jonathan, Michael J. A.B., NYU, 1968, LL.M. in Taxation, 1975; J.D., Columbia U., 1972. Bar: N.Y. 1972, U.S. Dist. Ct. (so. and ea. dists.) N.Y. 1974, U.S. Ct. Appeals (2d cir.) 1975, U.S. Tax Ct. 1975. Sr. trial atty. Office of Chief Counsel, IRS, N.Y.C., 1972-77; assoc. firm Proskauer Rose Geotz & Mendelsohn, N.Y.C., 1977-80; ptnr. Garfunkel, Bllomfield & Driggin and predecessor firm Garfunkel & Driggin, N.Y.C., 1980—. Served with USAR, 1969-74. Mem. N.Y. State Bar Assn. (tax sect.), New York County Lawyers Assn., Omicron Delta Epsilon. Personal income taxation, Corporate taxation, State and local taxation. Home: 7 Hillview Dr Scarsdale NY 10583 Office: Garfunkel Bloomfield & Driggin 477 Madison Ave New York NY 10022

GARFUNKEL, STEVEN BROOKS, lawyer; b. N.Y.C., Oct. 25, 1948; s. Milton and Doris (Brooks) G.; m. Marilyn Licht, May 20, 1983; children: Meredith, Allison. BBA, Lehigh U., 1969; JD, Case Western Res. U., 1972. Bar: Ohio 1972, U.S. Dist. Ct. (no. dist.) Ohio 1973, Fla. 1975, U.S. Ct. Appeals (6th cir.) 1981. Asst. law dir. City of Cleve., 1972-79; asst. gen. soliciter Chessie System R.R., Cleve., 1979-86; sr. corp. atty. Progressive Corp., Beachwood, Ohio, 1986—. Mem. ABA, Ohio Bar Asn., Fla. Bar Assn., Nat. R.R. Trial Counsel, Order of Coif. Avocations: bridge, golf. General corporate, Insurance. Home: 3329 Stockholm Rd Shaker Heights OH 44120 Office: Progressive Corp 3401 Enterprise Pkwy Beachwood OH 44101

GARGIULO, ANDREA WEINER, lawyer; b. Hartford, Conn., Apr. 26, 1946; d. Charles M. and Irma S. (Rubin) Weiner; m. Richard A. Gargiulo, Nov. 26, 1975; 1 child, John K. BA, Smith Coll., 1968; JD cum laude, Suffolk U., 1972. Bar: Mass. 1972, U.S. Dist. Ct. Mass. 1975, U.S. Ct. Appeals (11th cir.) 1981, U.S. Supreme Ct. 1983. Asst. dist. atty. Middlesex County, Mass., 1972-75; chmn. Boston Fin. Commn., 1975-77; ptnr. Gargiulo & McMenimen, Boston, 1976—; master U.S. Dist. Ct. Mass., Boston, 1976-83; lectr. Northeastern U. Coll. Criminal Justice, Boston, 1978, 80. Chmn. Boston Licensing Bd., 1977—; commr. Mass. Ethics Commn., 1985—; co-chmn. John Glenn presdl. campaign, Mass., 1983-84; bd. overseers Children's Hosp., Boston, 1983—. Mem. Mass. Bar Assn., Boston Bar Assn. (council 1982-85), Assn. Trial Lawyers Am. Democrat. Clubs: Bay, Beacon Hill Garden (treas. 1984—). Avocation: sailing. Administrative and regulatory, General practice, Local government. Home: 13 W Cedar St Boston MA 02108 Office: Gargiulo & McMenimen One Court St Boston MA 02108

GARHART, JOHN PAUL, lawyer; b. Warren, Ohio, Sept. 30, 1946; s. Florence Irene G.; m. Nada Sue Kaplan, Oct. 30, 1968 (div.); children: Nate, Eden. BA, Youngstown (Ohio) State U., 1970; JD, Rutgers U., 1974. Bar: Pa. 1974, U.S. Ct. Appeals (3rd cir.) 1978, U.S. Supremem Ct. 1980. Asst. dist. atty. Mercer County, Pa., 1974-76; asst. U.S. atty. U.S. Dept. Justice, Pitts., 1976-81; pvt. practice Erie, Pa., 1981—; asst. county solicitor Erie County, 1981—. Served to lt. U.S. Army, 1968-74. Mem. ABA, Am. Trial Lawyers Assn., Pa. Bar Assn., Erie County Bar Assn. Clubs: Erie, Town. Avocations: sailing, reading. Criminal, Personal injury. Office: 400 French St Suite 120 Lafayette Pl Erie PA 16507

GARIBALDI, MARIE LOUISE, state supreme court justice; b. Jersey City, Nov. 26, 1934; d. Louis J. and Marie (Servente) G. B.A., Conn. Coll., 1956; LL.B., Columbia U., 1959; LL.M. in Tax. Law, NYU, 1963; LL.D., Drew U., 1983, St. Peter's Coll., Jersey City, 1983. Atty. Office of Regional Counsel, IRS, N.Y.C., 1960-66; assoc. McCarter & English, Newark, 1966-69; ptnr. Riker, Danzig, Scherer & Hyland, Newark, 1969-82; assoc. justice N.J. Supreme Court, Newark, 1982—. Contbr. articles to profl. jours. Trustee St. Peter's Coll.; co-chmn. Thomas Kean's campaign for Gov. of N.J., 1981, mem. transition team, 1981; mem. Gov. Byrne's Commn. on Dept. of Commerce, 1981. Recipient Disting. Alumni award NYU Law Alumni of N.J., 1982; recipient Disting. Alumni award Columbia U., 1982. Fellow Am. Bar Found.; mem. N.J. Bar Assn. (pres. 1982), Columbia U. Sch. Law Alumni Assn. (bd. dirs.). Judicial administration. Home: 34 Kingswood Rd Weehawken NJ 07087

GARIEPY, STEPHEN HENRY, lawyer; b. Salamanca, N.Y., Dec. 12, 1952; s. Henry Francis and Marjorie (Ramsdell) G.; m. Susan Lynn Mongell, Sept. 7, 1974; children—Lauren Elizabeth, Elizabeth Ellen, Alison Grace. BA magna cum laude, Case Western Res. U., 1974; JD cum laude, Ohio State U., 1977. Bar: Ohio 1977. Law clk. U.S. Dist. Ct., Columbus, Ohio, 1976-77; assoc. Cavitch, Familo & Durkin Co., L.P.A., Cleve., 1977-84, ptnr., 1985—. Co-author: Tax Planning for Executive Compensation, 1983; editor: Ohio Transaction Guide, 1978—, (Rabkin and Johnson) Current Legal Forms with Tax Analysis, 1978—, Ohio Taxation, 1986; contbr. articles to profl. jours. Recipient award of Merit Ohio Legal Center Inst. Mem. bd. Western Res. Sch., Chardon, Ohio, 1982—. Mem. Greater Cleve. Bar Assn., Ohio Bar Assn. Lodge: Kiwanis. Estate planning, Probate, Estate taxation. Home: 158 Hawthorne Dr Chagrin Falls OH 44022 Office: Cavitch Familo & Durkin Co LPA 1401 E Ohio Bldg Cleveland OH 44114

GARLAND, JAMES BOYCE, lawyer; b. Gastonia, N.C., June 16, 1920; s. Peter Woods and Kathleen (Boyce) G.; m. Elizabeth Matthews, Nov. 9, 1951; children—Elizabeth Garland Sarn, Woods Garland Potts, James Boyce Jr., Rebecca Middleton. B.S., U. N.C., Chapel Hill, 1941, LL.B., 1946. Bar: N.C. 1946. Ptnr. Garland & Garland, Gastonia, 1946-59, Garland & Eck, Gastonia, 1961-62, Garland & Alala, Gastonia, 1962—, also chmn. bd. dirs.; me . N.C. Ho. of Reps., 1949-51. Chmn. bd. trustees Lees McRae Coll.; trustee Gaston Coll., Lineberger Cancer Research Ctr.; bd. visitors U. N.C., Chapel Hill; mem. N.C. Local Govt. Commn., 1970-75, Gastonia City Council, 1985—; pres. Schiele Mus. Natural History and Planetarium, 1984-85. Served to capt. N.C. N.G., 1942-45. Decorated Bronze Star. Fellow Am. Bar Found; mem. Am. Bar Assn., N.C. Bar Assn. (chmn. edn. law com., v.p. 1984-85), Gaston County Bar Assn. (pres.), N.C. State Bar, Gaston County C. of C. (pres. 1980-81), N.C. Jaycees (v.p. 1954-55, Disting. Service award 1955), Phi Delta Phi. Democrat. Presbyterian. Clubs: Gaston Country, Rotary (dist. gov. 1966-67) (Gastonia). Estate planning, Real property, Legal education. Home: 2515 Pinewood Rd Gastonia NC 28054 Office: 192 South St Gastonia NC 28052

GARLAND, JOHN LOUIS, SR., lawyer, data processing executive; b. Seattle, Sept 18, 1928; s. Homer Alanson and Anne Margaret (Jurich) G.; m. Paula Mary Joy, Feb. 19, 1955; children: Anne, John Louis Jr., Thomas. AB, St. Edward's Sem., Kenmore, Wash., 1950; MLS, Cath. U. Am., 1953; JD, Georgetown U., 1960. Bar: N.Y. 1972. Mgr. project LITE, IBM, Bethesda, Md., 1963-65, mgr. advanced systems tech., Armonk, N.Y., 1965-72, mgr. info. systems mktg., White Plains, N.Y., 1972-79, mgr. info. mgmt., Franklin Lakes, N.J., 1979-82, mgr. bus. info. systems devel., Atlanta, 1982—; instr. bus. law Fairleigh Dickinson U., Rutherford, N.J., 1980-84; instr. Am. Mgmt. Assns., N.Y.C., 1980-83. Author: How to Develop Business Information Systems for End Users, 1986; contbr. articles to profl. publs., also book chpt. Served to lt. USCG, 1953-60. Mem. ABA. Democrat. Roman Catholic. Legal education, Librarianship, Computer. Home: 10240 Carleigh Ln Roswell GA 30076 Office: IBM PO Box 2150 Atlanta GA 30056

GARLAND, MERRICK BRIAN, lawyer; b. Chgo., Nov. 13, 1952; s. Cyril and Shirley Garland. AB summa cum laude, Harvard U., 1974, JD magna cum laude, 1977. Bar: D.C. 1979, U.S. Dist. Ct. D.C. 1980, U.S. Ct. Appeals (D.C. and 9th cirs.) 1980, U.S. Ct. Appeals (4th cir.) 1983, U.S. Supreme Ct. 1983. Law clk. to judge U.S. Ct. Appeals (2d cir.), N.Y.C., 1977-78; law clk. to justice U.S. Supreme Ct., Washington, 1978-79; from assoc. to ptnr. Arnold & Porter, Washington, 1981—; spl. asst. to U.S. atty. gen. U.S. Dept. Justice, Washington, 1979-81. Com. mem. Harvard U. Law Sch. Fund, Washington, 1983. Mem. ABA, Phi Beta Kappa. Federal civil litigation, Administrative and regulatory, Criminal. Office: Arnold & Porter 1200 New Hampshire Ave NW Washington DC 20036

GARLEY, BARRY ERNEST, lawyer; b. Chgo., May 22, 1945; s. Raymond J. Garley and Betty Jane (Corey) Bible; m. Deborah Ann Towers, Sept. 19, 1970; children: Kristin Elizabeth, Allison Brooke. JD, John Marshall Law Sch., 1975. Bar: Ill. 1975, U.S. Dist. Ct. (no. dist.) Ill. 1975, U.S. Ct. Appeals (7th cir.) 1976, U.S. Supreme Ct. 1977, U.S. Dist. Ct. (ea. dist.) Mich. 1984. Title officer Lawyers Title Ins. Co., Chgo., 1972-74; mem. real estate dept. Chgo. & Northwestern R.R., 1974-75; sole practice Oak Brook, Ill., 1975-82; ptnr. Conklin & Adler, Ltd., Chgo., 1982-85, Lapin, Hoff, Spangler & Greenberg, Chgo., 1985—. Precinct committeeman DuPage County Reps., 1978-80. Served with USAF, 1966-70, Vietnam. Mem. ABA, Ill. Bar Assn., Chgo. Bar Assn., Lawyer Pilots Bar Assn. Lodge: Rotary. Federal civil litigation, Insurance, Aviation. Home: 355 E Berkshire Ave Lombard IL 60148 Office: Lapin Hoff Spangler & Greenberg 115 S LaSalle St Suite 2780 Chicago IL 60603

GARLEY, R. SCOTT, lawyer; b. South Amboy, N.J., Apr. 12, 1956; s. Richard Edward Garley and Carol Marjorie (Fitzgerald) Novak; m. Janet Louise Mauger, Sept. 15, 1984; 1 child, Taylor Gregory. AB in English cum laude, Colgate U., 1978; JD, Fordham U., 1981. Bar: N.Y. 1982, U.S. Dist. Ct. (so. and ea. dists.) N.Y. 1982. Assoc. Haight, Gardner, Poor & Havens, N.Y.C., 1981-84, Seward & Kissel, N.Y.C., 1984—. Editor Fordham Internat. Law Jour., 1980-81, sponsor, 1983—. Coach Rumson (N.J.) Pop Warner, 1976-83. Mem. ABA, Vol. Lawyers for Arts. Roman Catholic. Club: Colgate U. Club of N.Y. Federal civil litigation, State civil litigation, General practice. Office: Seward & Kissel Wall Street Plaza New York NY 10005

GARLICK, MICHAEL, lawyer, franchise consultant; b. N.Y.C., Oct. 20, 1944; s. Nathan S. and Gertrude (Finkel) G.; m. Judith Ann Schaufeld, May 12, 1977; children—Nathan S., Max Aaron. B.A., Lehigh U., 1966; J.D., NYU, 1969. Bar: N.Y. 1970, Fla. 1971, Calif. 1973, D.C. 1974, U.S. Dist. Ct. (so. dist.) Fla. Gen. counsel Internat. House of Pancakes Fla., Miami, 1970-74, cons., 1983—; sr. ptnr. Garlick, Cohn, Darrow & Hollander, Miami, 1974-79; gen. counsel Internat. Adv. Group, Inc., Miami, 1980—; dir. Tao Inst., Inc.; chmn. bd. Attys. Profl. Assn., Inc., Miami, 1981-83. Author: The Karate Decision, 1984. Editor Lawletter, 1981-83. Mem. Floridians United for Safe Energy, Miami. Served with U.S. Army, 1969. Mem. Forum Com. on Franchising, ABA, Dade County Bar Assn. North Miami Beach Karate (pres. 1970-80), Tai Chi Chaun Assn. (pres. 1983—), Phi Beta Kappa, Beta Alpha Psi. Antitrust, General corporate, Real property. Office: 1110 Brickell Ave Suite 430 Miami FL 33131

GARLITZ, THOMAS DRAKE, lawyer; b. Cumberland, Md., May 5, 1953; s. Vincent LeRoy and Nancy Brandes (Holland) G. AB, U. N.C., 1975, JD with honors, 1978. Bar: N.C. 1978, U.S. Dist. Ct. (we. dist.) N.C. 1981, U.S. Dist. Ct. (ea. dist.) N.C. 1983, U.S. Dist. Ct. (mid. dist.) 1984. Law clk. to judge U.S. Ct Appeals (4th cir.), Durham, N.C., 1978-79; assoc. Cansler & Lockhart P.A., Charlotte, N.C., 1979-84, ptnr., 1984—. Research editor U. N.C. Law Rev., 1977-78. Mem. ABA, N.C. Bar Assn., Nat. Assn. R.R. Trial Counsel, 26th Jud. Dist. Bar Assn., Phi Beta Kappa. Democrat. Roman Catholic. Federal civil litigation, State civil litigation, Insurance. Home: 1519-101 Eastcrest Dr Charlotte NC 28205 Office: Cansler & Lockhart PA 200 S Tryon St Charlotte NC 28202

GARMAN, JOHN WILLIAM, lawyer; b. Hazeltown, Pa., Feb. 7, 1946; s. John Wilson and Mary Louise (Bonevich) G.; m. Eugenia Barbara Tukaj, Sept. 5, 1981; 1 child, Marta Cornelia. AA, Monmouth Coll., West Long Branch, N.J., 1971, BA, 1973; JD, U. LaVerne, 1978. Bar: Calif. 1980, U.S. Dist. Ct. (cen. dist.) Calif. 1983. Sole practice Calif., 1982-83; assoc. Marken, Parsons & Andersen, Los Angeles, 1983-85, Law Office of Paul Orszag, North Hollywood, Calif., 1985—. Served to sgt. USAF, 1964-68. Mem. ABA, Los Angeles County Bar Assn., Calif. Bar Assn., Assn. Trial Lawyers Am., Am. Legion, DAV. Republican. Roman Catholic. Avocations: skiing, golf. State civil litigation, Insurance, Personal injury. Office: Law Office of Paul Orszag 10999 Riverside Dr #300 North Hollywood CA 91602

GARMON, OLLIE LORANCE, III, state official; b. Memphis, Sept. 16, 1942; s. Ollie Lorance and Lillian Atherton (Tubb) G.; m. Patricia Ann Hill, July 21, 1963; children—Ollie Lorance IV, Todd Howard. Student U. Miss., 1960-61, J.D., 1970; B.S. in Agr., Miss. State U., 1966, Postgrad. in agrl. econs., 1966; grad. gen. jurisdiction session Nat. Jud. Coll., Reno, 1979; grad. summer coll. Nat. Coll. Juvenile Justice, Reno, 1980; also continuing legal edn. at U. Miss. Law Ctr. Bar: Miss. 1970, U.S. Dist. Ct. (no. dist.) Miss. 1970, U.S. Supreme Ct. 1977. Realtor, appraiser, assoc. Hal Fiser Agy., Clarksdale, Miss., 1968; assoc. Maynard, FitzGerald, Maynard and Bradley, Clarksdale, 1970-72; asst. city pros. atty. City of Clarksdale, 1971; sole practice, Clarksdale, 1972; ptnr. Garmon and Sadler, Clarksdale, 1973; county pros. atty. Coahoma County (Miss.), 1972-75; city atty. City of Clarksdale, 1977-78; ptnr. Garmon, Wood and Twiford, P.A., Clarksdale, 1977-78; judge Coahoma County Ct., Clarksdale, 1979-82; commr. Miss. Workers Compensation Commn., 1982-87; instr. in real estate principles and practice Coahoma Jr. Coll., 1980-82; tchr. various seminars, confs.; lectr. Miss. Prosecutors Assn.; mem. Miss. Standards and Goals Com. on Juvenile Justice, 1982-83; mem. Gov. Miss. Commn. on Children and Youth Task Force on Foster Care, Adoption and Permanency Planning, 1982-83; chmn. Miss. Juvenile Justice Adv. Com., 1981-83; mem. Miss. Criminal Justice Planning Commn., 1980-83; mem. county judges bench-book com. mem. continuing edn. com. Miss. Jud. Coll. Moderator Riverside Baptist Assn., Coahoma-Tunica Counties; interim pastor LuRand First Baptist Ch., 1981-82, Clarksdale. Mem. Hinds County Bar Assn., Miss. State Bar Assn., ABA, Conf. Miss. County Ct. Judges, Miss. Council Youth Ct. Judges (chmn.), Conf. Miss. Judges, Nat. Council Juvenile and Family Ct. Judges, Internat. Assn. Indsl. Accident Bds. and Commns., So. Assn. Workmen's Compensation Adminstrs., Phi Alpha Delta. Workers' compensation. Office: 1428 Lakeland Dr PO Box 5300 Jackson MS 39216

GARNER, JAMES PARENT, lawyer; b. Madison, Wis., Jan. 22, 1923; s. Harrison Levi and Mary (Parent) G.; m. Georgia Ann Trebilcock, Oct. 12, 1946; children: Gail G., Ann G., Thomas W., Mary F. B.A., U. Wis., 1947; LL.B., Harvard U., 1949. Bar: Wis. 1949, Ohio 1950. Assoc. firm Baker & Hostetler & Patterson, Cleve., 1949-58; ptnr. Baker & Hostetler, Cleve., 1959—. Served to capt. inf. U.S. Army, 1943-46. Mem. ABA, Ohio Bar Assn., Greater Cleve. Bar Assn. (trustee 1969-71), Selden Soc. Republican. Clubs: Union; Harvard (N.Y.C.); Sports. Sports. Home: 31000 Shaker Blvd Pepper Pike OH 44124 Office: 3200 National City Ctr Cleveland OH 44114

GARNER, ROBERT EDWARD LEE, lawyer; b. Bowling Green, Ky., Sept. 26, 1946; s. Alto Luther and Katie Mae (Sanders) G.; m. Suzanne Marie Searles, Aug. 22, 1981; 1 child, Jessica Marie. B.A., U. Ala.-Tuscaloosa, 1968; J.D., Harvard U., 1971. Bar: Ga. 1971, Ala. 1982, U.S. Dist. Ct. (no. dist.) Ga. 1974, U.S. Ct. Appeals (5th cir.) 1974, U.S. Ct. Appeals (11th cir.) 1981. Assoc., Gambrell, Russell & Forbes, Atlanta, 1972-76, ptnr., 1976-80; ptnr. Haskell, Slaughter & Young and predecessor firms, Birmingham, Ala., 1981—; sec., gen. counsel, dir. Builders Transport, Inc. Charter mem. Meadow Brook Bapt. Ch.; mem. Shelby County Rep. Com. Served to 1st lt. JAGC, USAF, 1971-72. Mem. ABA, Ga. Bar Assn., Ala. State Bar, Birmingham Bar Assn., U. Ala. Alumni Assn., Harvard U. Alumni Assn., Phi Alpha Theta, Pi Sigma Alpha. Republican. Clubs: Relay House, Cahaba Valley Lions (charter). Banking, General corporate, Securities. Home: 5204 Meadow Brook Rd Birmingham AL 35243 Office: Haskell Slaughter & Young 1st Nat Southern Natural Bldg Suite 800 Birmingham AL 35203

GARNETT, MARION WINSTON, circuit court judge; b. Jeffersonville, Ind., Feb. 18, 1919; s. Jerry M. and Mary (Winston) G.; m. Juanita Oretta Nogest, Apr. 29, 1944; children—Marion Francis, Galda Irma. Ph.B., U. Chgo., 1947, J.D., 1950. Bar: Ill. 1950, U.S. Dist. Ct. (no. dist.) Ill. 1954, U.S. Ct. Apls. (7th cir.) 1968, U.S. Supreme Ct. 1965. Ptnr. Wilson & Garnett, Chgo., 1950-53, Hunter, Wilson & Garnett, Chgo., 1954-64, Rogers, Strayhorn, Harth, Wilson & Garnett, Chgo., 1965-70, Rogers, Garnett, Harth, Vital & Stroger, Chgo., 1971-74; judge Circuit Ct. Cook County, Chgo., 1974—; supervising judge pretrial sect., spl. asst. atty. gen. Ill. Atty. Gen.'s Office, Chgo., 1966-68; guardian ad litem, Circuit Ct. Cook County, 1966-69; faculty Labor Law Seminars, 1969-70. Served with USN, 1942-45. Recipient Cert. of Merit, Mayor and City Council of Los Angeles, 1975, New Orleans, 1974; Resolution of Honor, State Legis. Mich., 1983. Mem. Nat. Bar Assn. (life mem., judicial council, exec. bd.), Ill. Judicial Council (chmn. 1984-85), Omega Psi Phi (life mem., former Basileus 1973-76). Democrat. Baptist. Lodge: Masons. Civil rights, Judicial administration. Office: Room 2301 Daley Center Chicago IL 60602

GAROD, HARVEY JAY, lawyer; b. Bklyn., Jan. 5, 1948; s. Mac Garod and Estelle (Schultz) White; m. Marla Lynn Teitler, Dec. 19, 1982. BA, U. N.H., 1972; JD, U. Fla., 1975. Bar: Fla. 1975, U.S. Dist. Ct. (mid. dist.) Fla. 1976, U.S. Dist. Ct. (so. dist.) Fla 1978, N.H. 1984, U.S. Dist Ct. N.H. 1984, U.S. Ct. Appeals (1st cir.) 1985. Assoc. T.G. LaGrone, Orlando, Fla., 1975-76, Fisher & Matthews, Altamonte Springs, Fla., 1976-77, Reasbeck & Fegars, Hollywood, Fla., 1977-79, Day, Grantham & Hess, Lakeworth, Fla.,

1979-82, Shutts & Bowen, Lakeworth, 1982-84, James J. Kalled, Ossipee, N.H., 1984—. Contbr. articles to Fla. Bar Jour. Served to sgt. USAF, 1966-70. Mem. ABA, Assn. Trial Lawyers Am., Phi Beta Kappa, Phi Kappa Phi, Pi Gamma Mu, Order of the Coif. Republican. Jewish. Lodges: Shriners. Avocations: karate. Personal injury, Criminal, State civil litigation. Home: Rural Rt 1 Box 186 Center Ossipee NH 03814 Office: Law Office of James J Kalled Box 132 Ossipee NH 03864

GAROFALO, JOHN RICHARD, lawyer; b. Chgo., Apr. 27, 1940; s. Mauro James and Lorraine Grace (Stevens) G.; m. Gloria Jean Prochazka, Feb. 18, 1966; children—Christine, John Thomas. B.B.A., U. Notre Dame, 1962; J.D., John Marshall Law Sch., Chgo., 1966. Bar: Ill. 1967. Trust adminstr. Am. National Bank, Chgo., 1965-68; assoc. Garbutt & Jacobson, Chgo., 1968-76, Kiesler & Berman, Chgo., 1976—; atty. Oak Park Twp., Ill., 1969—. Precinct committeeman Oak Park Republican Orgn., 1968—, mem. exec. com., 1976-83. Served with USMC, 1963-68. Mem. Ill. Bar Assn., Chgo. Bar Assn., Soc. Trial Lawyers, Ill. Def. Lawyers. Roman Catholic. Personal injury, Insurance, Local government. Home: 1001 N Belleforte St Oak Park IL 60302 Office: Kiesler & Berman 188 W Randolph St Chicago IL 60601

GARRETT, DAVID ISAIAH, JR., lawyer; b. Monroe, La., June 11, 1923; s. David Isaiah and Lessie Henrietta (Madison) G.; m. Dorothea Girault, June 12, 1948; children—Nancy Garrett Holder, David Isaiah III. Student La. State U., 1940-42, J.D., 1948. Bar: La. 1948. Assoc., Madison, Madison, Files and Shell, Monroe, 1948-50; sole practice, Monroe, 1950-56, 58-62; ptnr. Garrett and Bounds, Monroe, 1956-58, Madison, Garrett, Brandon, Hamaker, Wilson & Tugwell, P.C. Monroe, 1962—, sr. ptnr., Monroe and Bastrop, La., 1975—. Past pres. Twin Cities YMCA, Ouachita Valley council Boy Scouts Am.; chmn. adv. bd. Salvation Army. Served to 1st lt. AUS, 1942-46; to capt., 1951-52. Decorated Bronze Star with oak leaf cluster, Purple Heart. Mem. ABA, 4th Dist. Bar Assn., La. Bar Assn., La. Assn. Def. Counsel, Monroe C. of C. (dir.). Methodist. Club: Bayou DeSiard Country (past pres.). General corporate, Labor, Oil and gas leasing. Office: PO Box 2425 Monroe LA 71201

GARRETT, DUEJEAN C., corporate lawyer. BA, U. Tex., 1965; JD, Ind. U., 1967. With Pub. Service Co. of Ind. Inc., Plainfield, 1967-79, counsel, 1979-82, sr. counsel, 1982-83, v.p. gen. counsel, 1983—. Office: Pub Service Co of Ind Inc 1000 E Main St Plainfield IN 46168 *

GARRETT, HENRY LAWRENCE, III, lawyer, government official; b. Washington, June 24, 1939; s. Henry Lawrence II and Gladys Beatrice (Locknane) G.; m. Marilyn Kay Bender, Mar. 6, 1965; children: Juliana Kay, Henry Lawrence IV. BS, U. West Fla., 1969; JD cum laude, U. San Diego, 1972. Bar: U.S. Dist. Ct. (so. dist.) Calif. 1972, U.S. Ct. Mil. Appeals 1974, U.S. Supreme Ct. 1981. Enlisted USN, 1961, commd. ensign, 1964, advanced through grades to comdr. JAGC, 1979, ret., 1981; asst. counsel White House, Washington, 1981; exec. asst. to pres. U.S. Synfuels Corp., Washington, 1981-82; assoc. counsel to Pres. of the U.S. White House, Washington, 1983-86; gen. counsel Dept. of Def., Washington, 1986—. Decorated Air medal. Mem. Calif. Bar Assn., D.C. Bar Assn., Ret. Officers Assn., Phi Alpha Delta. Republican. Episcopalian. Clubs: Army-Navy (Washington), Army-Navy Country (Arlington). Avocations: reading; golf. Government contracts and claims, Public international, Legislative. Home: 3202 Cinch Ring Ct Oakton VA 22124 Office: The Dept of Def Pentagon Room 3E980 Washington DC 20301

GARRETT, STACY F., III, lawyer; b. Richmond, Va., Nov. 11, 1944; s. Stacy F., Jr., and Hazel (Hall) G.; m. Linda Gregg, Jan. 27, 1973; children—Sara Rebecca, Rachel Courtney. A.B., Coll. William and Mary, 1966; J.D., Marshall-Wythe Sch. Law, 1969; grad., FBI Nat. Law Inst., 1984. Bar: Va. 1969, U.S. Ct. Mil. Appeals 1969, U.S. Supreme Ct. 1973, U.S. Dist. Ct. (ea. dist.) Va. 1973, U.S. Ct. Appeals (4th cir.) 1974. Asst. atty. gen. State of Va., Richmond, 1973-75, asst. Commonwealth's atty., Commonwealth's Atty.'s Office, Richmond, 1975-76, dep. Commonwealth's atty. Commonwealth's Atty.'s office, Richmond, 1977—. Pres., Settlers Landing Community Assn., 1981-84. Served as capt. JAGC, U.S. Army, 1969-73. Decorated Bronze Star with oak leaf cluster. Mem. Nat. Dist. Atty's. Assn., Am. Judicature Soc., Va. Assn. Commonwealth Attys., Izaak Walton League Am., Nat. Rifle Assn. Republican. Presbyterian. Club: Izaak Walton Pistol (v.p. 1983-85, treas. 1985—. Criminal, Civil rights. Home: 1808 Sealing Wax Way Richmond VA 23235 Office: Commonwealth's Atty's Office John Marshall Cts Bldg 800 E Marshall St Richmond VA 23219

GARRETT, THEODORE LOUIS, lawyer; b. New Britain, Conn., Sept. 4, 1943; s. Louis and Sylvia (Greenberg) G.; m. Bonnie Garrett, Nov. 27, 1968; children—Brandon, Natalie. B.A., Yale U., 1965; J.D., Columbia U., 1968. Bar: N.Y. 1968, U.S. Supreme Ct. 1973, D.C. 1981. Law clk. to Judge J. Joseph Smith U.S. Ct. Appeals for 2d Circuit, 1968-69; spl. asst. to asst. atty. gen. William H. Rehnquist Dept. Justice, Washington, 1969-70; law clk. to Chief Justice Warren E. Burger U.S. Supreme Ct., 1970-71; assoc. Covington & Burling, Washington, 1971-76, ptnr., 1976—. Contbr. articles to profl. jours. Mem. ABA, D.C. Bar Assn. Environment, Administrative and regulatory, Federal civil litigation. Home: 6604 Broxburn Dr Bethesda MD 20817 Office: Covington & Burling 1201 Pennsylvania Ave NW Washington DC 20044

GARRIGLE, WILLIAM ALOYSIUS, lawyer; b. Camden, N.J. Aug. 6, 1941; s. John Michael and Catherine Agnes (Ebeling) G.; m. Jeannette R. Regan, Aug. 15, 1965 (div.); children—Maeve Regan, Emily Way; m. Rosalind Chadwick, Feb. 17, 1984; 1 child, Susan Chadwick. B.S., LaSalle Coll., 1963; LL.B., Boston Coll., 1966. Bar: N.J. 1966, U.S. Dist. Ct. N.J. 1966, U.S. Ct. Appeals (3d cir.) 1973, U.S. Supreme Ct. 1973; cert. civil trial atty. Assoc. Taylor, Bischoff, Neutze & Williams, Camden 1966-67; assoc. Moss & Powell Camden 1967-70; ptnr. Garrigle & Chierici and predecessors Cherry Hill, N.J. 1970—. Served with USAR, 1959-67. Mem. ABA, N.J. State Bar Assn., Burlington County Bar Assn., Camden County Bar Assn., Internat. Assn. Ins. Csl., Def. Research Inst., Fedn. of Ins. and Corp. Counsel, Trial Attys. N.J., Phila. Art Alliance. Clubs: Moorestown (N.J.) Field; Atlantic City Country (Northfield, N.J.); Downtown (Phila.). Federal civil litigation, State civil litigation, Insurance. Home: 223 E Main St Moorestown NJ 08057 Office: 2 W Evesham Ave Cherry Hill NJ 08003

GARRIGUES, GAYLE LYNNE, lawyer; b. Anchorage, Aug. 7, 1955; s. James Martin and Julia Ann (Harris) G. B.A. in Polit.Sci., U. Alaska, 1977; J.D., U. Idaho, 1980. Bar: Alaska 1981, U.S. Dist. Ct. Alaska 1982. Atty. Alaska Legal Services Corp., Kotzebue, 1980-82; assoc. Settles, Kalamarides & Assocs., P.C., Anchorage, 1982; sole practice, Kotzebue, 1982-84; asst. dist. atty. Dept. of Law 2d Jud. Dist., Kotzebue, 1984—; instr. criminal justice Chuckchi Community Coll., 1985-86. Bd. dirs. Kotzebue Womens Crisis Project, 1982-84; del. Alaska State Dem. Conv., 1974, 84; leader Girl Scouts U.S., 1981-83, 86. Mem. ABA, Assn. Trial Lawyers Am., Alaska Bar Assn., Anchorage Women Lawyers, Phi Alpha Delta. Criminal, Juvenile, Indian law.

GARRISON, PITSER HARDEMAN, lawyer, mayor; b. Lufkin, Tex., Mar. 7, 1912; s. Homer and Mattie (Milam) G.; m. Berneice Jones, Dec. 3, 1936. Student Lon Morris Jr. Coll., 1929-30, student Stephen F. Austin State U., 1930-32; LL.B., U. Tex., 1935. Bar: Tex. 1935; U.S. Dist. Ct. (ea. dist.) Tex. 1936, U.S. Dist. Ct. (so. dist.) Tex. 1938, U.S. Ct. Appeals (5th cir.) 1939. Ptnr. Garrison, Renfrow, Zeleskey, Cornelius & Rogers, Lufkin, 1935-52, sr. ptnr., 1952-68; chmn., gen. counsel Lufkin Nat. Bank, 1968-81; sole practice, Lufkin, 1981—; dir. First City Nat. Bank, Lufkin, First State Bank, Wells, Tex. Mayor City of Lufkin, 1970—; bd. dirs., past pres. Angelina and Neches River Authority, Lufkin; past pres. Deep East Tex. Council of Govts., Jasper; bd. dirs., past chmn. Angelina County Tax Appraisal Dist., Lufkin, bd. dirs. Meml. Hosp., Lufkin, 1975—. Served to maj. U.S. Army, 1942-46. Recipient Disting. Alumnus award Lon Morris Jr. Coll., 1974; Disting. Alumnus award Stephen F. Austin State U., 1976; named East Texan of the Month, East Tex. C. of C., 1966, East Texan of the Yr., 1981, East Texan of Yr., Deep East Tex. Council of Govts., 1980. Fellow Am. Coll. Trial Lawyers, Tex. Bar Found. (charter); mem. Angelina County Bar Assn. (past pres.), Tex. Bar Assn., ABA, Phi Delta Phi. Democrat. Methodist. Lodges: Rotary (pres.), Masons, Shriners. General practice, Federal civil litigation, State civil litigation. Home: 5 Trailwood Ct Lufkin TX 75901 Office: PO Box 789 203 S First St Lufkin TX 75901

GARRISON, RAY HARLAN, lawyer; b. Allen County, Ky., Aug. 6, 1922; s. Emmett Washington and Ollie Irene (Keen) G.; m. Eunice Anne Bolz, Oct. 7, 1961. B.A., Western Ky. U., 1942; M.A., U. Ky., 1944; postgrad., Northwestern U., 1945-46; J.D., U. Chgo., 1949. Bar: Ky. 1951, Ill. 1962, U.S. Ct. Appeals 1962, U.S. Tax Ct. 1962, U.S. Ct. Internat. Trade 1968, U.S. Supreme Ct. 1980. Tax acct. Ky. Dept. Revenue, Frankfort, 1943, supr. escheats, 1944-45, fiscal analyst, 1945; research asst. Bur. Bus. Research, U. Ky., Lexington, 1943-44; research assoc. Fedn. Tax Adminstrs., Chgo., 1946-52; spl. atty. U.S. Dept. Treasury, St. Louis, 1952-57; spl. asst. U.S. Dept. Treasury, 1957-59, asst. regional counsel, 1959-61; sr. counsel Internat. Harvester Co., Chgo., 1982-86; gen. tax atty. Navistar Internat. Corp., Chgo., 1986—; lectr. Loyola U., Chgo., 1949-51. Contbr. articles to various publs. Mem. Ill. Racing Bd., 1975—; mem. adv. bd. Ill. Thoroughbred Breeders Fund, 1976-80. Mem. NAM (taxation com. 1969—), Ill. Mfrs. Assn. (taxation com. 1969—), Motor Vehicle Mfrs. Assn. (taxation com. 1963—), ABA, Ill. Bar Assn., Ky. Bar Assn., Chgo. Bar Assn., Nat. Assn. State Racing Commrs., Chgo. Tax Club, South Suburban Geneal. and Hist. Soc. (bd. dirs. 1973-77), Ky. Hist. Soc., Mecklenburg Hist. Assn., Beta Gamma Sigma. Club: Filson. Corporate taxation, Administrative and regulatory, State and local taxation. Home: 2625F Hawthorne Ln Flossmoor IL 60422 Office: 401 N Michigan Ave Chicago IL 60611

GARRISON, STUART HUGH, lawyer; b. Buffalo, Apr. 13, 1945; s. Lloyd Roscoe and Lois Emiline (Schwab) G. BA, SUNY, Buffalo, 1968; JD, Woodland U., 1976; MS in Taxation, Northrup U., 1982. Bar: Calif. 1976, U.S. Dist. Ct. (cen. dist.) 1977. Claims adjuster Auto Club So. Calif., Los Angeles, 1972-76, LFC Ins., Beverly Hills, Calif., 1976; ptnr., trial atty. Shields, Anderson & Garrison, Los Angeles, 1977-82; ptnr., mng. atty. Shields, Garrison & Misity, Los Angeles, 1982-86, ptnr., trial specialist, 1986—. Mem. Town Hall, Los Angeles, 1982—. Served to 1st lt. U.S. Army, 1968-71, Vietnam, USNG, 1977—. Mem. Calif. State Bar Assn., Los Angeles County Bar Assn., Assn. So. Calif. Def. Attys., N.G. Assn. U.S. and Calif. Democrat. Club: Westwood Ski (Calif.). Avocations: water and snow skiing, photography, reading, camping. Insurance, Personal injury, State civil litigation. Home: 7601 Goddard Ave Los Angeles CA 90045 Office: Shields Garrison & Misity 4201 Wilshire Blvd Suite 200 Los Angeles CA 90010

GARRITY, THOMAS ANTHONY, JR., retired judge, lawyer; b. New Orleans, Aug. 17, 1925; s. Thomas A. and Viola (Roser) G.; m. Betty Jean Greenlee, May 1, 1953; 1 child, Thomas A. III. Geophys. Engr., Colo. Sch. Mines, 1952; J.D., N.Mex., 1964. Bar: N.Mex. 1964, U.S. Dist. Ct. N.Mex. 1964, U.S. Ct. Appeals (10th cir.) 1964, U.S. Supreme Ct. 1970, Tex. 1977. Atty. adviser Dept. Interior, Albuqueque, 1964-73; solicitor Amarillo, Tex., 1973-80; adminstrv. law judge Office Hearings and Appeals, chief adminstrv. law judge, 1981-87; sole practice, Waveland, Miss., 1987—. Author: Water Law Atlas; contbr. articles to profl. jours. Served as cpl. AUS, 1943-46. Mem. Fed. Bar Assn. (pres. 1967-68). Administrative and regulatory, Pension, profit-sharing, and employee benefits, Natural resources. Home: PO Box 439 220 S Beach Blvd Waveland MS 39576

GARRITY, W. ARTHUR, JR., judge; b. Worcester, Mass., June 20, 1920; s. W. Arthur and Mary B. (Kennedy) G.; m. Barbara A. Mullins, May 24, 1952; children: W. Arthur III, Charles, Anne, Jean. A.B., Holy Cross Coll., 1941; LL.B., Harvard U., 1946. Bar: Mass. 1956. Asst. U.S. atty. for Mass., 1948-50; U.S. atty. for Mass. 1961-66; judge U.S. Dist. Ct. Mass., 1966—. Jurisprudence. Office: John W McCormack PO & Courthouse US Dist Court Room 1104 Boston MA 02109

GARRO, ALEJANDRO MIGUEL, lawyer, legal educator; b. La Plata, Buenos Aires, Argentine, Apr. 8, 1950; came to U.S., 1977; s. Juan Manuel and Rina Margarita (Sureda) G.; m. Bonnie Gail McCullock, Aug. 24, 1971 (dec. Feb. 1973); m. Luisa Liliana Costa, Jan. 28, 1977; 1 child, Julia Liliana. JD, Nat. U. La Plata, Argentina, 1975; M in Civil Laws, La. State U., 1979. Bar: Buenos Aires 1975, N.Y. 1982, Madrid 1983. Staff atty. La. State Law Inst., Baton Rouge, 1979-80; asst. prof. law La. State U., Baton Rouge, 1980-81; lectr. in law Columbia U., N.Y.C., 1981-83, 85—; research assoc. Inst. Comparative Law, Lausanne, Switzerland, 1983-85. Contbr. articles to profl. jours. Mem. ABA, N.Y. State Bar Assn., Inter Am. Bar Assn., Argentine Assn. Comparative Law, Fedn. Argentina de Colegio de Abogados. Private international, Contracts commercial, Legal education. Home: 400 W 119th St Apt 15-O New York NY 10027 Office: Columbia U Sch of Law 435 W 116th St New York NY 10027

GARRY, JOHN THOMAS, II, lawyer; b. Albany, N.Y., Dec. 12, 1923; s. Joseph T. II and Jean Theresa (Cramond) G.; m. Mary Regina Hoffman; children: John, Michael, Regina, Maureen, Suzanne, Patricia. Student, Cornell U., 1942-43; BA, St. Bernadine of Siena Coll., 1949; LLB, JD, Union U., 1952. Bar: N.Y. 1952, U.S. Supreme Ct. 1952. Asst. corp. counsel City of Albany, 1953-55, asst. dist. atty., 1955-58, dist. atty., 1958-68; sr. ptnr. Garry, Cahill & Edmunds and Garry, Cahill, Edmunds & Calderone, Albany, 1968—. Exec. chmn. Dem. Cen. Com., Albany, Albany Big Bros./Big Sisters Am., 1971. Served with USAAF, 1943. Decorated Air medal. Mem. ABA, N.Y. State Bar Assn., Albany County Bar Assn., Am. Judicature Soc., Internat. Narcotic Enforcement Officers Assn., N.Y. State Dist. Attys. Assn. (v.p. 1967), St. Bernadine of Siena Coll. Alumni Assn. (pres. 1964), Am. Legion, VFW. Club: Wolfert's Roost Country. Lodges: K.C. (past grand knight), Elks. General practice, Criminal, Personal injury. Home: 10 Grey Ledge Dr Albany NY 12205

GARTH, LEONARD I., judge; b. Bklyn., Apr. 7, 1921; s. Frank A. and Anne F. (Jacobs) Goldstein; m. Sarah Miriam Kaufman, Sept. 6, 1942; 1 dau., Tobie Gail Garth Meisel. B.A., Columbia U., 1942; postgrad., Nat. Inst. Pub. Affairs, 1942-43; LL.B., Harvard U., 1952. Bar: N.J. bar 1952. Mem. firm Cole, Berman & Garth (and predecessors), Paterson, N.J., 1952-70; judge U.S. Dist. Ct. for Dist. N.J., Newark, 1970-73; U.S. Circuit judge Ct. Appeals for 3d Circuit, 1973—; lectr. Inst. Continuing Legal Edn.; lectr., coadj. mem. faculty Rutgers U. Law Sch., 1978—, Seton Hall Law Sch., 1980—; mem. N.J. Bd. Bar Examiners, 1964-68; mem. com. on revision gen. and admiralty rules Fed. Dist. Ct. NJ.; mem. commn. on jud. ethics Jud. Conf. U.S.; mem. adv. com. on law and society maj., Ramapo Coll, Mahwah, N.J. Adv. bd. Law and Soc. Major of Ramapo Coll.; trustee U.S. Dist. Ct. N.J. Hist. Soc. Served as 1st lt. AUS, 1943-46. Mem. ABA (N.J. fellows), Fed. Bar Assn., N.J. Bar Assn., Passaic County (N.J.) Bar Assn. (pres. 1967-68), Harvard Law Sch. Assn. (nat. v.p. 1963-64), Am. Law Inst. Jurisprudence, Legal education. Home: 17 Greenview Way Upper Montclair NJ 07043 Office: US PO and Courthouse Newark NJ 07101 Office: 20316 US Courthouse Philadelphia PA 19106

GARTH, THOMAS FEARN, lawyer; b. Huntsville, Ala., Nov. 10, 1948; s. Winston Fearn and Emily Hails (Thornton) G.; m. Susan Felder Price, June 12, 1971; children: Susan Price, Elizabeth H., Katherine D., Thomas Fearn Jr. BA, U. Va., 1970; JD, Samford U., 1974; LLM in Taxation, NYU, 1975. Bar: Ala. 1974. Ptnr. Lyons, Pipes & Cook, Mobile, Ala., 1975—. Served to lt. (j.g.) USN, 1970-71. Mem. ABA, Ala. Bar Assn., Mobile Bar Assn., Mobile Estate Planning Council (mem. exec. com.), Ala. Bd. of Bar Examiners. Episcopalian. Corporate taxation, Estate taxation, Personal income taxation. Home: 62 Fearnway Mobile AL 36604 Office: Lyons Pipes & Cook 2 N Royal Mobile AL 36602

GARTNER, RICHARD ANTHONY, lawyer; b. St. Louis, Nov. 16, 1954; s. Anthony John and Louise Dolores (Nickels) G.; m. Christine Marie Starke, Dec. 28, 1979; children: Nicholas Richard, Daniel Todd. BA in Polit. Sci., U. Mo., 1976, postgrad. in polit. sci., 1976-77; JD, St. Louis U., 1980. Bar: Sept. 1980, U.S. Dist. Ct. (ea. dist.) Mo. 1982, U.S. Ct. Appeals (8th cir.) 1982, U.S. Supreme Ct. 1984. Asst. gen. counsel Mass. Indemnity and Life Ins. Co., St. Louis, 1980-82; assoc. J.V. Hoskins & Assocs., St. Louis, 1982-83; sole practice St. Louis, 1983-86; ptnr. Brackman, Copeland, Oetting, Copeland, Schmidt & Stock, St. Louis, 1986-87, Copeland, Gartner, Thompson & Jeep, St. Louis, 1987—. Mem. Met. St. Louis Bar Assn., St. Louis County Bar Assn., St. Charles County Bar Assn., Am. Trial Lawyers Assn., Tau Kappa Epsilon Frat. Alumni Assn. Roman Catholic. Avocations: softball, skiing. Personal injury, Workers' compensation, General practice. Home: 2924 N Kristopher Bend Saint Charles MO 63303 Office: 231 S Bemiston Suite 520 Clayton MO 63105

GARTS, JAMES RUFUS, JR., lawyer; b. Meadville, Pa., Mar. 22, 1949; s. James Rufus and Priscilla Jane (Greer) G.; m. Susan Damian Hord, June 3, 1971; children—Katherine Elizabeth, James Rufus III, Emily Alice. B.A., Tulane U., 1971; J.D., 1974. Bar: Tenn. 1974, U.S. Dist. Ct. (we. dist.) Tenn. 1983, U.S. Ct. Appeals (6th cir.) 1984. Assoc., Chandler, Manire, Harris and Shelton, Memphis, 1974-76; asst. dist. atty. gen. State of Tenn., Memphis, 1976-79; ptnr. Harris, Shelton, Dunlap and Cobb, Memphis, 1979—; spl. judge Shelby County, 1984. Mem. ABA, Tenn. Bar Assn., Memphis and Shelby County Bar Assn., Phi Beta Kappa. Republican. Roman Catholic. Federal civil litigation, State civil litigation, Criminal. Home: 1200 Homewood Dr Memphis TN 38128 Office: Harris Shelton Dunlap & Cobb 1 Commerce Sq Suite 130 Memphis TN 38103

GARTZMAN, JEFFREY SCOTT, lawyer; b. Waterbury, Conn., May 4, 1957; s. Paul Jay and Helen Ann (Kronick) G. BSBA in Acctg., Bucknell U., 1979; JD, Emory U., 1982, postdoctoral, 1985—. Bar: Ga. 1982, U.S. Dist. Ct. (no. dist.) Ga. 1984, U.S. Tax Ct. 1984, U.S. Ct. Appeals (11th cir.) 1984; CPA, Ga. Tax cons. Touche Ross & Co., Atlanta, 1982-84; assoc. Law Office of D. Robert Autrey, P.C., Marietta, Ga., 1984-86, Stokes, Shapiro, Fussell, Fox & Wedge, Atlanta, 1986—. Mem. ABA, Ga. Bar Assn., Atlanta Bar Assn., Ga. Soc. CPAs. Republican. Jewish. Personal income taxation, General corporate, Corporate taxation. Office: Stokes Shapiro Fussell & Genberg 2300 1st Atlanta Tower Atlanta GA 30383

GARVEY, JOHN COTTON, lawyer; b. Washington, Apr. 9, 1953; s. George Aloysius and Cynthia Mary (Cotton) G.; m. Cheryl Colleen Sole, Aug. 6, 1977; 1 child, Ryan Elizabeth. BS in Engring., Duke U., 1975; JD, George Washington U., 1979. Bar: D.C. 1979, U.S. Dist. Ct. D.C. 1979, U.S. Ct. Appeals (Fed. cir.) 1979. From assoc. to ptnr. Staas & Halsey, Washington, 1979—. Mem. ABA, Am. Intellectual Property Law Assn., Computer Law Assn. Avocations: swimming, gardening. Patent, Trademark and copyright, Computer. Home: 4717 N 37th St Arlington VA 22207 Office: Staas & Halsey 1825 K St NW Washington DC 20006

GARVEY, KEVIN LEE, judge. m. Janet Elaine Bauer; children: Kimberly, Jennifer, Kristina. BA, U. Louisville, 1975, JD, 1979. Bar: U.S. Dist. Ct. (we. dist.) Ky. 1979. Trust officer United Ky. Bank, 1979-81; judge Jefferson Dist. Ct., Louisville, 1981—; guest lectr. law U. Louisville, 1985—. Mem. ad hoc Jud. Com. to Enlighten Young People, 1984—, bd. aldermen Task Force on Social Service Cut-backs, 1982; appointed safety dir., City of Plantation, 1979, city alderman, 1980; lector Holy Trinity Cath. Ch.; adminstrn. com. Mother of Good Council Cath. Ch., 1983. Mem. ABA, Ky. Bar Assn., Louisville Bar Assn. (bd. dirs., 1986, treas. young lawyers sect, 1984, chmn. 1986), Ky. Dist. Judges Assn. (bd. dirs. 1985—), Ky. Acad. of Trial Attys., Ky. Acad. of Justice, Am. Judicature Soc., Estate Planning Forum, Louisville Estate Planning Council, Louisville Assn. of Life Underwriters, Phi Kappa Tau, Phi Alph Delta. Club: Holy Spirit Cath. Ch. Men's (treas. 1972). Jurisprudence. Office: Hall of Justice Louisville KY 40202

GARVEY, MARGARET S., lawyer; b. Chgo., Jan. 10, 1947; d. Robert and Mercedes (Wampole) Schneider. BS, Loyola U., Chgo., 1971; JD, Northwestern U., Chgo., 1978. Bar: Ill. 1978, U.S. Dist. Ct. (no. dist.) Ill. 1978, U.S. Ct. Appeals (7th cir.) 1981. Research assoc. Am. Hosp. Assn., Chgo., 1973-75; assoc. Rooks, Pitts & Poust, Chgo., 1978-83; assoc. Freeborn & Peters, Chgo., 1984-86, ptnr., 1986—; author, lectr. Ill. Inst. Continuing Legal Edn., Chgo., 1981. Author: OSHA, 1981, 2nd edit., 1986. Mem. ABA, Chgo. Bar Assn. Federal civil litigation, State civil litigation, Labor. Office: Freeborn & Peters 11 S LaSalle Chicago IL 60603

GARVEY, MARY ANNE, lawyer; b. Cleve., Apr. 4, 1955; d. John Joseph and Anna May (Simonetti) G. BA, John Carroll U., 1977; JD, Case Western Res. U., 1980. Bar: Ohio 1980, U.S. Dist. Ct. (no. dist.) Ohio 1982. Trial atty. U.S. Dept. of Labor, Cleve., 1981—. Mem. Marinello Endowment Fund Com., Cleve., 1985—; vol. Playhouse Sq. Assn., Cleve., 1981—; class agt. Case Western Res. Law Sch., Cleve., 1983—; sec. Vol. Lawyers for the Arts, 1982—; v.p. North Coast Ballet Theatre, Cleve., 1985—. Mem. ABA, Cleve. Bar Assn. Administrative and regulatory, Federal civil litigation, Labor. Office: US Dept of Labor 1240 E 9th St Cleveland OH 44199

GARWOOD, WILLIAM LOCKHART, lawyer, federal judge; b. Houston, Oct. 29, 1931; s. Wilmer St. John and Ellen Burdine (Clayton) G.; m. Merle Castlyn Haffler, Aug. 12, 1955; children: William Lockhart, Mary Elliott. B.A., Princeton U., 1952; LL.B. with honors, U. Tex., 1955. Bar: Tex. 1955, U.S. Supreme Ct. 1959. Law clk. to presiding justice U.S. Ct. Appeals (5th cir.), 1955-56; judge U.S. Ct. Appeals (5th cir.), Austin, 1981—; mem. Graves, Dougherty, Hearon, Moody & Garwood (and predecessor firms), Austin, Tex., 1959-79, 81; assoc. justice Supreme Ct. Tex., Austin, 1979-80; dir. Anderson, Clayton & Co., 1976-79, 81, exec. com., 1977-79, 81. Pres. Child and Family Service of Austin, 1970-71, St. Andrew's Episcopal Sch., Austin, 1972; bd. dirs. Community Council Austin and Travis County, 1968-72, Human Opportunities Corp. Austin and Travis County, 1966-70, Mental Health and Mental Retardation Ctr. Austin and Travis County, 1966-69, United Fund Austin and Travis County, 1971-73; mem. adv. bd. Salvation Army, Austin, 1972—. Served with U.S. Army, 1956-59. Fellow Am. Bar Found., Tex. Bar Found. (life); mem. Am. Law Inst., ABA, Am. Judicature Soc., Order of Coif, Chancellors, Phi Delta Phi. Episcopalian. Office: Court of Appeals 111 US Courthouse 200 W 8th St Austin TX 78701

GARY, RICHARD DAVID, lawyer; b. Richmond, Va., Apr. 25, 1949; s. Morton Nathan and Blanche (Rudy) G.; m. Linda Levene, Aug. 6, 1972; children: Brent Ryan, Lauren Renee. AB in Econs., U. N.C., 1971; JD, U. Va., 1974. Bar: Va. 1974. From assoc. to ptnr. Hunton & Williams, Richmond, 1974—; guest lectr. law Coll. William and Mary, Williamsburg, 1983—. Mem. adv. bd. March of Dimes, Richmond, 1985—; v.p. Beth Sholom Home Cen. Va., Richmond, 1986—. Recipient Distinguished Service award Beth Shalom Hom Cen. Va., 1984. Mem. ABA, Va. State Bar (chmn. law sect. 1982-83), Va. Bar Assn., Richmond Bar Assn., Fed. Energy Bar Assn. Avocation: sports. Public utilities, Administrative and regulatory, FERC practice. Home: 1518 Helmsdale Dr Richmond VA 23233 Office: Hunton & Williams 707 E Main St PO Bos 1535 Richmond VA 23212

GARY, ROBERT DALE, lawyer; b. Lorain, Ohio, June 4, 1941; s. David Bear and Ruth Ida (Levine) G.; m. Karen Miriam Schiller, Aug. 14, 1962; children—Wendy, Tracy. B.A., Western Res. U., 1963, J.D., 1966; LL.M., NYU, 1967. Bar: Ohio 1966, U.S. Supreme Ct. 1969, U.S. Tax Ct. 1969. Dep. chief for Ohio organized crime strike force U.S. Dept. Justice, Cleve., 1967-71; dir. Organized Crime Prevention Council, Columbus, Ohio, 1972-73; spl. asst. Gov. Ohio, Columbus, 1973-75; asst. prosecutor Lorain County, Ohio, 1975-80; sole practice, Lorain, Ohio, 1975—; instr. Western Res. U., Cleve., 1978, Lorain County Community Coll., Elyria, Ohio, 1979; lectr. Law Enforcement Officers Tng. Program, Ohio, 1979. Mem. 7 County Supermarket Settlement Com., Lorain, 1982-83; trustee Agudath Bnai Israel Synagogue, Lorain, 1984; chmn. Lorain County Blue Ribbon Com., Elyria, 1983-84. Recipient Spl. Achievement award U.S. Dept. Justice, 1971, Lorain County Commrs., 1982, 84. Mem. Lorain County Bar Assn., Ohio State Bar Assn. Democrat. Jewish. Avocations: Art appreciation, bicycling, skiing, golf. Antitrust, Labor, Personal injury. Home: 3716 Woodstock Lorain OH 44053 Office: 446 Broadway Lorain OH 44052

GARY, STUART HUNTER, lawyer; b. Richmond, Va., Nov. 22, 1946; s. Morton Nathan and Blanche (Rudy) G.; m. Donna Rothman, Aug. 19, 1967; children—Kenneth Asher, Robin Leigh. B.A. in Econ., U. Va., 1968; J.D., Wash. Coll. Law Sch. Am. U., 1972. Bar: Va. 1972, D.C. 1973, U.S. Dist. Ct. (ea. dist.) Va. 1975, D.C. 1974, U.S. Tax Ct. 1976, U.S. Ct. Appeals (4th cir.) 1975, (D.C. Cir.) 1974, U.S. Supreme Ct. 1976. Law clerk D.C. Ct. Appeals, Washington, 1972-73; atty. antitrust div. Fed. Trade Commn., Washington, 1973-74; ptnr. Swift & Gary, Washington, 1974-75, Falcone & Gary, Fairfax, Va., 1975-81; prin. Stuart H. Gary & Assocs., McLean, Va., 1981-85; exec. v.p., Huntmar Assocs., Ltd., 1986—; bd. cons. Riggs Nat. Bank Va. Editorial bd. Am. U. Law Rev., Washington, 1971-72. Chmn., No. Va. Heart Fund Drive, 1976; bd. dirs. No. Va. Jewish Community Ctr., Fairfax, Va., 1983—. Mem. ABA, Va. Bar Assn., D.C. Bar Assn., Fairfax

County Bar Assn., Am. Arbitration Assn. (panel of arbitrators). Contracts commercial, General corporate, Real property. Home: 1704 Burlwood Ct Vienna VA 22180 Office: Huntmar Assocs Ltd 1100 Towers Crescent Dr Suite 600 Vienna VA 22180

GARY, SUSAN NANNETTE, lawyer; b. Zanesville, Ohio, June 29, 1955; d. Holland Merrick and Betty Jane (Roose) G.; m. Alexander Bailey Murphy, Aug. 15, 1981. BA cum laude, Yale U., 1977; JD, Columbia U., 1981. Bar: Ill. 1981. Assoc. Mayer, Brown & Platt, Chgo., 1981-85, 86—, DeBandt, Van Hecke & Lagae, Brussels, 1985-86. Author: A Lawyers Guide to Private Foundations, 1985. Mem. ABA, Chgo. Bar Assn. Charitable and not for profit organizations, Estate planning, Probate. Home: 5419 S Dorchester Chicago IL 60615 Office: Mayer Brown & Platt 190 S LaSalle St Chicago IL 60603

GARZA, GRACIANO JAIME, judge; b. McAllen, Tex., Mar. 12, 1948; s. Graciano L. and Juanita (Elizondo) G. B.A., Tex. A&I U., 1970; J.D., U. Tex.-Austin, 1973. Ptnr. firm Morin & Garza, Edinburg, Tex., 1974-78; sole practice, Edinburg, 1978-80; judge Hidalgo County Ct. at Law, 1981—. Bd. dirs. Assn. Retarded Children, 1980; bd. dirs. Image Youth Services, Inc., 1977, chmn. bd. dirs., 1980—; chief grievance officer Hidalgo Health Dept., Edinburg, 1984—. Mem. Hidalgo County Bar Assn. (mem. com. to preserve history of bar also com. on Tex. Young Lawyers Assn., 1983—). Democrat. Roman Catholic. Criminal, Family and matrimonial, General practice.

GARZA, REYNALDO G., judge; b. Brownsville, Tex., July 7, 1915; s. Ygnacio and Zoila (Guerra) G.; m. Bertha Champion, June 9, 1943; children: Reynaldo G., David C., Ygnacio Daniel, Bertha Victoria, Monica Bernadette. B.A., LL.B., U. Tex.; LL.D. (hon.), U. St. Edwards, Austin, Tex., 1965. Bar: Tex. 1939. Pvt. practice 1939-42, 46-50; partner firm Sharpe, Cunningham & Garza, 1950-60, Cunningham, Garza & Yznaga, 1960-61; U.S. dist. judge Dist. Tex., Brownsville, from 1961; U.S. dist. chief judge Dist. Tex., 1974-79; judge U.S. Ct. Appeals (5th cir.), 1979—. Treas. Cameron County Child Welfare Bd., 1950-52; mem. Tex. Good Neighbor Commn., 1957-61; Commr. City Brownsville, 1947-49; Trustee Brownsville Ind. Sch. Dist., 1941-42. Served with USAAF, 1942-45. Recipient Pro Ecclesia et Pontifice medal Pope Pius XII, 1952; decorated knight Order St. Gregory the Great e Pius XII, 1954. Mem. Am., Cameron County bar assns., State Bar Tex. Office: Court of Appeals PO Box 1129 Brownsville TX 78520

GARZA, RUDY A., lawyer; b. San Antonio, Aug. 30, 1952; s. Rudy A. and Maria (Villareal) G.; m. Connie Jo Dupuy, May 23, 1980; children: Thomas, Christine, Cassandra. BS with high honors, U. Tex., 1974, JD, 1977. Bar: Tex. 1977, U.S. Dist. Ct. (we. dist.) Tex., U.S. Ct. Appeals (5th cir.). Ptnr. Tinsman and Houser, San Antonio, 1977—; mem. grievance com. State Bar Dist. 10, San Antonio, 1985—; sec. grievance com. I.O.A., 1986—. Mem. Dem. exec. com. Bexar County, Tex., 1984-86. Fellow Tex. Bar Found.; mem. State Bar Tex., San Antonio Bar Assn. (bd. dirs. 1986—), Tex. Bar Assn., Tex. Trial Lawyers Assn., San Antonio Young Lawyers Assn. (pres. 1985-86, sec. 1983-84, bd. dirs. 1982-83). Roman Catholic. Avocations: golf, tennis, softball, chess. Federal civil litigation, State civil litigation, Personal injury.

GASCH, MANNING, lawyer; b. Washington, June 25, 1943; s. Manning and Hilda Gregg (Lynn) G. BS, Cornell U., 1966; JD, U. Va., 1972. Bar: Va. 1972, U.S. Ct. Appeals (4th cir.) 1972. Assoc. Hunton & Williams, Richmond, Va., 1972-79; ptnr. Hunton & Williams, Richmond, 1979—. Chmn. Va. chpt. Nature Conservatory, 1981. Served as spl. agt. M.I., U.S. Army, 1966-69. Republican. Episcopalian. Club: Commonwealth Club (Richmond). Avocations: hunting, fishing, farming. Environment. Home: Rt 1 Box 1400 Hanover VA 23069 Office: Hunton & Williams 707 E Main St Richmond VA 23219

GASIORKIEWICZ, EUGENE ANTHONY, lawyer; b. Milw., Jan. 7, 1950; s. Eugene Constantine and Loretta Ann (Kasprzak) G.; m. Jana Jamieson, Jan. 12, 1980; children: Suzanne A., Alexei E. AB, Regis Coll., 1971; JD, U. Miss., 1974. Bar: Wis. 1974, U.S. Supreme Ct. 1986. Law clk. to presiding justice Miss. Supreme Ct., Jackson, 1974-75; assoc. Schoone, McManus & Hanson S.C., Racine, Wis., 1975-79; ptnr. Hanson & Gasiorkiewicz S.C., Racine, Wis., 1979—; lectr. labor law U. Wis., Racine, 1975-76, worker's comp., State Bar Wis., 1984-86, med. malpractice, Wis. Acad. Trial Lawyers, 1986. Mcpl. judge Village of Wind Point, Wis., 1983-85; moot ct. instr., The Prairie Sch., Racine, 1986-87. Mem. Assn. Trial Lawyers Am., Am. Arbitration Assn., Wis. Acad. Trial Lawyers, Nat. Bd. Trial Advocacy (cert. civil trial advocate), State Bar Wis. Roman Catholic. Avocation: tennis. Personal injury, Federal civil litigation, Workers' compensation. Home: 101 Westminster Sq Racine WI 53402 Office: Hanson Gasiorkiewicz & Becker SC 212 Fifth St Racine WI 53403

GASKIN, LILLIAN BERNICE, lawyer; b. Harrisburg, Pa., July 21, 1946; d. Lillian Bernice Gaskin; m. Frederick S. Lipton, Oct. 17, 1976; children: Alissa K., Eric J. BA in Psychology, Dickinson Coll., 1968, JD, 1972. Bar: U.S. Supreme Ct. 1972, U.S. Ct. Appeals (D.C. cir.) 1977. Dep. atty. gen. Pa. Dept. Justice, Harrisburg, 1972-76; atty. govtl. affairs office ABA, Washington, 1977-78, staff dir. govtl. affairs office, 1978-83, legis. coordinator, 1983—. Contbr. articles to profl. jours. Mem. ABA, Pa. Bar Assn., D.C. Bar Assn. Democrat. Roman Catholic. Legislative. Office: ABA 1800 M St NW Washington DC 20036

GASS, DAVID, lawyer; b. Appleton, Wis., May 21, 1956; s. Orville Eugene and Lois Helen (Bellin) G.; m. Cheryl Ann Schloss, Feb. 22, 1986. BA, U. Wis., 1978, JD, 1981. Bar: Wis. 1981, U.S. Dist. Ct. (ea. and we. dists.) Wis 1981. Assoc. Rohde, Neuses & Dales, Sheboygan, Wis., 1981-85, ptnr., 1986—. Mem. Sheboygan County Dem. Com., Wis., 1982—, pub. relations dir., 1984—, mem City of Sheboygan Planning Commn., 1985—, Vis. Nurse's Assn., Sheboygan, 1984—, pres. 1986—; past v.p., bd. dirs. Big Bros./Big Sisters of Sheboygan County; mem. City of Sheboygan Park and Forestry Commn., 1985—; sec. Calvary Evang. Luth. Ch., Sheboygan, pres. 1984—. Mem. ABA, Wis. State Bar Assn., Sheboygan County Bar Assn., Jaycee's (pres. Sheboygan club 1984-85; named Outstanding pres. in Wis. 1985), Phi Beta Kappa. Democrat. Lutheran. Lodge: Optimists, Elks. Avocations: woodworking, reading, sports. Bankruptcy, Consumer commercial, General practice. Office: Rohde Neuses & Dales 607 Plaza 8 Suite 400 Sheboygan WI 53081

GASS, JAMES RIC, lawyer, legal educator; b. Green Bay, Wis., Mar. 13, 1943; s. F.E. and Wanda (Dobry) G.; m. Roxanne M. Loomis, June 19, 1965; children—Jenna, Jolie, Rebecca. B.S., U. Wis.-Stevens Point, 1965; J.D. cum laude, Marquette U., 1970. Bar: Wis. 1970, U.S. Dist. Ct. (ea. and we. dists.) Wis. 1970, U.S. Ct. Appeals (7th cir.) 1972, U.S. Supreme Ct. 1975. Law clk. Kivett & Kasdorf, Milw., 1967-70, assoc., 1970-73; ptnr. Kasdorf, Lewis & Swietlik, S.C., Milw., 1973—; adj. assoc. prof. law Marquette U.; lectr. legal and edn. seminars; faculty mem., torts program dir. advanced tng. seminars, continuing legal edn. State Bar Wis. Arbitrator Am. Arbitration Assn. Thomas More scholar, 1967-70. Mem. ABA, Wis. Bar Assn., Milw. Bar Assn., Bar Assn. 7th Cir., Ins. Trial Counsel Wis., Def. Research Inst. (state chmn. Wis.), Fedn. Ins. Corp. Counsel, Internat. Assn. Def. Counsel., Wis. Health Care (bd. govs.). Personal injury, State civil litigation, Legal education. Office: 1551 S 108th St Milwaukee WI 53214

GASSER, EMMETT CLARK, lawyer; b. Pocatello, Idaho, Mar. 2, 1929; s. Emmett William and Mae (Clarke) G.; m. Sallee G. Cox, Aug. 24, 1951; children: Kathryn, Janet, John. BA, St. Mary's Coll., 1951; LLB, George Washington U., 1956. Bar: D.C. 1957, Idaho 1957, U.S. Dist. Ct. Idaho 1957, U.S. Tax Ct. 1967, U.S. Supreme Ct. 1970, U.S. Ct. Appeals (9th cir.) 1983. Ptnr. Terrell & Gassee, Pocatello, 1957-62, Green, Service, Gasser & Kerl, Pocatello, 1962—; examiner Idaho State Bar, 1967-76. Mem. ABA, Idaho Bar Assn. (continuing legal edn. com. 1981-84), Idaho Bar Found. (bd. dirs. 1981-83), Assn. Trial Lawyers Am., Am. Judicature Soc., Def. Research Inst. Democrat. Roman Catholic. Lodge: Elks. Avocations: downhill and nordic skiing, tennis, golf, backpacking. Environment, Personal injury, Insurance. Home: 56 Cedar Hills Dr Pocatello ID 83201 Office: Green Service Gasser & Kerl PO Box 4883 C-1 Center Pl Pocatello ID 83201

GASSLER, FRANK HENRY, lawyer; b. N.Y.C., Apr. 21, 1951; s. Frank and Frieda (Grupe) G.; m. Pamela Kay Tedder, June 16, 1984; 1 child, Loren Nicole. BA, Villanova U., 1973; JD, Columbia U., 1976. Bar: Fla. 1976, U.S. Dist. Ct. (mid. dist.) Fla. 1976, U.S. Ct. Appeals (5th and 11th cirs.) 1983, U.S. Supreme Ct. 1983. Shareholder Fowler, White, Gillen, boggs, Villareal and Banker, Tampa, Fla., 1976—. Mem. Fla. Bar Assn., Hillsborough County Bar Assn., Def. Research Inst. Roman Catholic. Personal injury, Federal civil litigation, State civil litigation. Home: 4907 W Bay Way Dr Tampa FL 33629 Office: Fowler White Gillen Boggs Villareal Banker 501 E Kennedy Blvd Tampa FL 33602

GAST, RICHARD SHAEFFER, lawyer; b. Pueblo, Colo., Aug. 1, 1956; s. Robert Shaeffer and Ann (Day) G.; m. Beverly Paterson, Aug. 22, 1981; children: Charles Edward, Robert Shaeffer. BA, Stanford U., 1978; JD, U. Colo., 1981. Bar: Colo. 1981, U.S. Dist. Ct. Colo. 1981. Assoc. March, Myatt, Korb, Carroll & Brandes, Ft. Collins, Colo., 1981-85, ptnr., 1985—. Contbg. editor U. Colo. Law Rev., 1980-81. Organizer local fundraising Am. Cancer Soc., Ft. Collins, 1985-86; mem. Larimer County Land Use Plan Citizens' Rev. Com., Ft. Collins, 1986. Mem. ABA (corps., bus. and banking law sect.), Colo. Bar Assn., Larimer County Bar Assn. (chmn. legal aid program 1986, chmn.-elect young lawyers sect. 1986-87,chmn. 1987—). Democrat. Episcopalian. Lodge: Elks. Avocations: skiing, running, soccer, backpacking, bicycling. Banking, Probate, Real property. Home: 1736 Yucca Ct Fort Collins CO 80525 Office: March Myatt Korb Carroll & Brandes 110 E Oak Fort Collins CO 80524

GASTFREUND, IRVING, lawyer; b. Landsberg, Ger., Nov. 27, 1947; s. Morris and Sally G.; m. Diane Lynn Cohen, June 14, 1970; children—Sarah Heather, Michael. B.A., Brown U., 1969; J.D., Boston U., 1973. Bar: D.C. 1973, U.S. Dist. Ct. D.C. 1974, U.S. Ct. Appeals (D.C. cir.) 1974, U.S. Supreme Ct. 1977. Atty., adviser FCC, Washington, 1973-76; assoc. Fly, Shuebruk, Gaguine, Boros, Schulkind & Braun, Washington, 1976-81, ptnr. 1981-85; of counsel Kumble, Wagner, Heine, Underberg, Manley, Myerson & Casey, 1985—. Served with USAR, 1969-75. Recipient William Gaston prize for excellence in oratory Brown U., 1969. Mem. ABA (broadcast and spectrum use com. communications law div., vice chmn. 1982-83, chmn. 1983—), Fed. Bar Assn., Fed. Communications Bar Assn. Jewish. Communications, Administrative and regulatory, Trademark and copyright. Office: Finley Kumble Wagner Heine et al 1120 Connecticut Ave NW Washington DC 20036

GASTL, EUGENE FRANCIS, lawyer; b. Shawnee, Kans., Apr. 28, 1932; s. Bert J. and Bessie C. (Bell) G.; m. Deanna J. Cordon, June 7, 1959 (div. May 1978); children: Philip E., Catherine L., David B., Brenda M.; m. Arline Blackwood, June 15, 1979. BA, U. Kans., 1954, BL, 1956, JD, 1968. Bar: Kans. 1956, U.S. Dist. Ct. Kans. 1956. Sole practice Shawnee, 1959—. State rep. Kans. Legislature, Topeka, 1961-65, 71-79, senator, 1965-69. Served to specialist grade 3 U.S. Army, 1956-58. Mem. ABA, Kans. Bar Assn., Johnson County Bar Assn., Assn. Trial Lawyers Am., Shawnee C. of C. (v.p. 1965-67). Democrat. Methodist. Lodge: Optimist (bd. dirs. 1961-63). Avocation: reading. Probate, Family and matrimonial, Workers' compensation. Home: 5420 Bluejacket Shawnee KS 66203 Office: 5811 Nieman Rd Shawnee KS 66203

GATES, JAMES EDWARD, lawyer; b. Los Angeles, Nov. 18, 1954; s. Edward Dwight and June Elizabeth (Rowell) G. BA summa cum laude, Ursinus Coll., 1977; JD, Georgetown U., 1981, MS in Fgn. Service, 1985. Bar: D.C. 1981, Va. 1982, U.S. Ct. Appeals (4th and D.C. cirs.) 1982, N.C. 1985, U.S. Supreme Ct. 1985. Assoc. Smiley, Olson, Gilman & Pangia, Washington, 1981-83; law clk. to presiding justice U.S. Dist. Ct. (mid. dist.), Durham, N.C., 1983-85; assoc. Maupin, Taylor, Ellis & Adams, Raleigh, N.C., 1986. Mem. Arlington Va. Young Reps., 1979-83, Arlington Va. Rep. County Com., 1979-83. Mem. ABA, N.C. Bar Assn. Federal civil litigation, State civil litigation, Personal injury. Home: 6081-B Shadetree Ln Raleigh NC 27612 Office: Maupin Taylor Ellis & Adams PO Drawer 19764 Raleigh NC 27619

GATES, KENNETH W., lawyer; b. Spokane, Wash., Feb. 28, 1948; s. Charles Lee and Bertha Mae (Shannon) G.; m. Kim Gates, July 20, 1977; 1 child, Shannon Marie. AB, Whitman Coll., 1970; JD, Gonzaga U., 1977; LLM, U. Fla., 1978. Ptnr. Huppin, Ewing, Anderson, Spokane, 1978-85; sole practice Spokane, 1985—. Mem. ABA, Wash. State Bar Assn. Club: Neuro Comp (Spokane). Lodge: Lions. General corporate, Probate, Corporate taxation. Office: 628 S Maple Spokane WA 99204

GATES, SIGNE SANDRA, lawyer; b. Washington, Dec. 19, 1949; d. Russell and Signe Eva (Nelson) G.; m. Peter Benjamin Knock, Sept. 12, 1987. BA in English summa cum laude, Susquehanna U., 1971; JD, U. Mich., 1980. Bar: Conn. 1981, U.S. Dist. Ct. Conn. 1982. Mgmt. trainee Sears, Roebuck and Co., Alexandria, Va., 1971; mgmt. cons. Macro Systems, Inc., Silver Spring, Md., 1971-73; v.p. Program Resources, Inc., Rockville, Md., 1973-78; assoc. Cummings and Lockwood, Stamford, Conn., 1980-83; corp. atty. Tetley Inc., Shelton, Conn., 1983-85, Gen. Signal Corp., Stamford, 1985—; bd. dirs., sec. Tri-State Employment Law Forum, N.Y.C., 1984—. bd. dirs. Norwalk (Conn.) YMCA, Inc., 1985—. Mem. ABA, Conn. Bar Assn., Westchester-Fairfield Corp. Counsel Assn. Democrat. Lutheran. Contracts commercial, General corporate, Mergers and acquisitions. Office: Gen Signal Corp High Ridge Park Stamford CT 06904

GATES, STEPHEN FRYE, lawyer; b. Clearwater, Fla., May 20, 1946; s. Orris Alison and Olga Betty (Frye) G.; m. Laura Daignault, June 10, 1972. B.A. in Econs., Yale U., 1968; J.D., Harvard U., 1972, M.B.A., 1972. Bar: Fla. 1973, Mass. 1973, Ill. 1977, Colo. 1986. Assoc. Choate Hall & Stewart, Boston, 1973-77; atty. Amoco Corp., Chgo., 1977-82, gen. atty., 1982-86; regional atty. Amoco Production Co., Denver, 1987—; dir. XMR Inc, Santa Clara, Calif. Knox fellow, 1972-73. Mem. ABA, Chgo. Bar Assn. Clubs: Univ. (Chgo.); Yale (N.Y.C.); Petroleum (Denver). Securities, General corporate, Oil and gas leasing. Office: Amoco Production Co 1670 Broadway Denver CO 80202

GATEWOOD, DIANE RIDLEY, lawyer; b. St. Louis, June 20, 1951; s. Benjamin James and Vera Delores (Dickerson) R.; m. Lamerol Alexander, Sept. 1, 1979. AB, Washington U., 1973; JD, Northwestern U., 1976. Bar: Ill. 1982, U.S. Dist. Ct. (no. dist.) Ill. 1982, U.S. Ct. Appeals (7th cir.) 1982. Instr. YMCA Community Coll., Chgo., 1976-77; legal asst. Wilson, Smith & McCullin, St. Louis, 1977-78; securities analyst A.G. Edwards, St. Louis, 1978—; bd. dirs. KMT Vision Inc., St. Louis, 1986—. Treas. Equity Community Found., St. Louis, 1985-86. Recipient Award of Merit City of East St. Louis, 1981, Cert. Appreciation U.S. Govt. Fed. Exec. Bd., 1982; named one of Outstanding Young Women Am., 1985. Mem. ABA, Ill. Bar Assn., Mound City Bar Assn., Nat. Assn. Securities Profls. Avocations: egyptology, African history, fine art, langs., swimming. Securities. Office: AG Edwards Inc One N Jefferson Saint Louis MO 63103

GATHRIGHT, HOWARD T., lawyer; b. Phila., May 3, 1935; s. Howard W. and Rose (McGurk) G.; m. Natalie Acquaviva, June 22, 1963; children: Donna Marie, Gary Thomas. BA, U. Pa., 1957; JD, Temple U., 1963. Bar: Pa. 1964, U.S. Dist. Ct. Pa. 1964, U.S. Supreme Ct. 1968. Ptnr. Pratt, Gathright & Brett, Doylestown, Pa., 1964—; bd. dirs. BEan, Mason & Eyer, Doylestown. Pres. Am. Lung Assn., Doylestown, 1970-72, bd. dirs. 1970—. Served with U.S. Army, 1958-62. Mem. Bucks County Bar Assn. (pres. 1986—), Assn. Trial Lawyers Am., Pa. Trial Lawyers Assn., Bucks County Estate Planning Commn. (pres. 1972), Cen. Bucks C. of C. (pres. 1972, Man of Yr. 1975). Republican. Roman Catholic. Avocations: sports, tennis. State civil litigation, Estate planning, Real property. Office: Pratt Gathright & Brett 68 E Court St Doylestown PA 18901

GAUGHAN, JOHN ANTHONY, lawyer; b. Washington, Mar. 29, 1947; s. John Vincent and Marguerite (Portland) G.; m. Janelle Williams, Apr. 28, 1984. BS, U.S. Coast Guard Acad., 1970; JD, U. Md., 1977. Bar: D.C. 1978, U.S. Dist. Ct. D.C. 1978. Atty. Fed. Maritime Commn., Washington, 1980-81; officer congl. relations U.S. Dept. Transp., Washington, 1981-84, dir. external affairs U.S. maritime adminstrn., 1984-85, dep. asst. sec., 1985, adminstr. U.S. maritime adminstrn., 1985—. Served to lt. comdr. USCG, 1970-79. Mem. ABA, D.C. Bar Assn., Maritime Law Assn., Am. Legion (vice comdr. 1984—). Republican. Roman Catholic. Avocations: tennis, biking, reading. Administrative and regulatory, Public international, Admiralty. Home: 5301 Roosevelt St Bethesda MD 20814 Office: Maritime Adminstrn 400 7th St SW Washington DC 20590

GAUNT, WILLIAM L., corporate lawyer; b. 1945. BA, Washington (Pa.) and Jefferson Coll., 1968; JD, Case Western Res. U., 1971. Law clk. to presiding justice Phila. Ct. of Common Pleas, 1972-73; assoc. Truscott & Erisman, 1973-77, White & Williams, 1977-78; sr. v.p., gen. counsel Cen. Pa. Nat. Bank, 1978-82; sec., gen. counsel Meridian Bancorp Inc., Reading, Pa., 1978—. Served to 1st lt. USAR, 1968-74. Office: Meridian Bancorp Inc 35 N 6th St Reading PA 19601 *

GAUNTLETT, DAVID ALLAN, lawyer; b. Long Beach, Calif., May 16, 1954; s. Allan Leonard Gauntlett and Nelly (Brown) Mayne. BA in history magna cum laude, U. Calif., Irvine, 1976; JD, U. Calif., Berkeley, 1979. Bar: Calif. 1980, U.S. Dist. Ct. (cen. dist.) Calif. 1983, U.S. Dist. Ct. (ea., no. and so. dists.) Calif. 1986. Assoc. Paul, Hastings, Janofsky & Walker, Los Angeles, 1979-81, Vitti, Miles & Robinson, Newport Beach, Calif., 1981-83, Burkley, Moore, Greenberg & Lyman, Torrance, Calif., 1983-86, Callahan & Assocs., Irvine, Calif., 1986—. Production mgr. U. Calif. Law Rev., 1978-79. Calif. state scholar. Mem. ABA, Los Angeles County Bar Assn., Orange County Bar Assn., Assn. Bus. Trial Lawyers. Democrat. Episcopalian. Avocations: bicycling, art collection, cooking, sailing, tennis. Federal civil litigation, State civil litigation, Contracts commercial. Office: Callahan & Assocs 18400 Von Karman Suite 950 Irvine CA 92715

GAUTHIER, WENDELL HAYNES, lawyer; b. Iota, La., Apr. 14, 1943; s. Cylvert Joseph and Florence (Breaux) G.; m. Anne Barrios, Aug. 28, 1965; children—Cherie Anne, Michelle Anne, Celeste Anne. B.A., U. Southwestern La., 1966; J.D., Loyola U., New Orleans, 1970. Bar: U.S. Dist. Ct. (ea. dist.) La. 1971, U.S. Ct. Appeals (5th cir.) 1977, U.S. Supreme Ct. 1977. Assoc., John B. Hattier and Louis Heyd, Jr., New Orleans, 1970-71; sole practice, 1971-74; ptnr. Gauthier, Murphy, Sherman, McCabe & Chehardy and predecessors, 1974—; pres., sr. ptnr. Gauthier & Murphy P.L.C.; lectr. Loyola U., New Orleans. Served with USMCR, 1961-62. Mem. Jefferson Bar Assn., La. Bar Assn., ABA, Am. Trial Lawyers Assn., La. Trial Lawyers Assn. Democrat. Roman Catholic. Club: Lions. Federal civil litigation, State civil litigation, Personal injury. Home: 10025 Hyde Pl River Ridge LA 70123 Office: Gauthier Murphy et al 3500 N Hullen St Metairie LA 70002

GAVILANES, DIEGO P., lawyer; b. Guayaquil, Ecuador, Apr. 4, 1950; came to U.S., 1967; s. Hugo and Angela (Granja) G.; m. Peggy Ann McNeil, Aug. 19, 1972; children: Gabriel, Tony & Julian. BA, U. Wash., 1973, JD, 1976. Bar: Wash. 1979, U.S. Dist. Ct. (we. dist.) Wash. 1979, U.S. Ct. Appeals (9th cir.) 1980. Dep. prosecutor State of Wash., Everett, 1978-80; assoc. Ferguson, Maynard, Miller, Gavilanes & Wolff, Everett, 1980-84; sole practice Everett, 1984—; pres., legal counsel The Travel Connection, Ic., Everett, 1977—. Mem. Joint Task Force Salvadoran and Guatemalan Refugees, Seattle, 1984—, Snohomish County Leagl Clinic, 1982—. Mem. ABA, Am. Immigration Lawyers Assn., InterAm. Bar Assn., Wash. State Bar Assn. (exec. bd. internat. law sect. 1984—), Wash. State Trial Lawyers Assn. Lodge: Kiwanis Internat. Avocations: racquet ball, hiking, travel. Immigration, naturalization, and customs, Personal injury, Family and matrimonial. Office: 3325 Wetmore Ave Everett WA 98201

GAVIN, CONNIE KAY, lawyer; b. Monmouth, Ill., Sept. 18, 1957; d. Robert George and Imogene P. (Eversmeyer) G.; m. Robert Donald Rothacker, May 26, 1984. BA, Marquette U., 1979; JD, U. Mich., 1982. Bar: Wis. 1982, U.S. Dist. Ct. (ea. and we. dists.) Wis. 1982. Assoc. Quarles & Brady, Milw., 1982—. Advisor Law Explorers, Milw., 1982-84; active Future Milw., 1985-86; bd. dirs. Vol. Ctr. Greater Milw., 1985—; mem. Holy Family Ch. Mem. ABA, Milw. Bar Assn. (young lawyers div.), Wis. Bar Assn., Milw. Met. Assn. Profl. Mortgage Women, Phi Beta Kappa, Alpha Sigma Nu. Real property. Home: 1551 E Blackthorne Pl Whitefish Bay WI 53211 Office: Quarles & Brady 411 E Wisconsin Ave Milwaukee WI 53202

GAVIN, JOHN NEAL, lawyer; b. Chgo., Aug. 31, 1946; s. John Anthony and Mary Anne (O'Donnell) G.; m. Louise A. Sunderland, June 16, 1979; 1 child, Anne. AB, Coll. of Holy Cross, Worcester, Mass., 1968; JD, Harvard U., 1975. Bar: Ill. 1975. Law clk. to presiding judge U.S. Ct. Appeals (9th cir.), San Francisco, 1975-76; atty. office of legal counsel U.S. Dept. Justice, Washington, 1976-79; ptnr. Hopkins & Sutter, Chgo., 1981—. Served to lt. USNR, 1968-71. Mem. ABA, Chgo. Bar Assn. Administrative and regulatory, General corporate, Insurance. Home: 415 Aldine #7C Chicago IL 60657 Office: Hopkins & Sutter Three First National Plaza Chicago IL 60602

GAVIN, LOUIS BROOKS, lawyer; b. N.Y.C., July 15, 1907; s. Harry and Jennie (Krafchick) G.; m. Elizabeth S. Neivert, Oct. 15, 1936; children—Marlene Gavin Snedaker, Meritt B., Donald G. Grad. NYU, 1926, postgrad., 1959; J.D. with honors, Rutgers U., 1928. Bar: N.J. 1929, U.S. Dist. Ct. N.J., 1929, U.S. Tax Ct. 1948, U.S. Ct. Claims 1972, U.S. Supreme Ct. 1937. Sr. ptnr. Gavin, Sakinski & Gavin, Newark, 1966-70, Gavin & Gavin, Cranford, 1971—; lectr. on taxes. Chmn. ethics com., Point Pleasant Borough and Point Pleasant Beach (N.J.), 1974-77; co-counsel Zoning Bd. Adjustment Point Pleasant Borough, 1979, counsel Bd. Health, 1980; dist. leader. county com. Borough Point Pleasant, 1983—. Mem. ABA (chmn. subcom. taxes and divorce of gen. practice sect. 1975—), N.J. Bar Assn., Union Lawyers Club, N.Y. Soc. Accts. (pres. 1967-69), King's Bench (pres. 1929). Episcopalian. Club: Bay Head Shores P.O.A. Lodge: Rotary. Contbr. articles to legal and popular publs. Probate, Estate taxation, Real property. Office: 198 North Ave E Cranford NJ 07016

GAVIN, WILLIAM PATRICK, lawyer; b. East St. Louis, Ill., Nov. 17, 1955; s. Neil Patrick and Ruth Ann (Curry) G.; m. Kathleen Ann Sonnenberg, Apr. 20, 1985. AB, St. Louis U., 1977, JD, 1980. Bar: Ill., Mo., U.S. Dist. Ct. (cen. and so. dists.) Ill., U.S. Dist. Ct. (ea. dist.) Mo. Assoc. Gundlach, Lee Eggmann, Boyle & Roessler, Belleville, Ill., 1980-85, ptnr., 1986—. Bd. dirs. YMCA Southwest Ill., Belleville, 1985—. Recipient Service to Youth award YMCA Southwest Ill., 1976. Mem. ABA, Ill. Bar Assn., Mo. Bar Assn., Nat. Assn. RR Trial Counsel, Ill. Defense Counsel. Club: St. Clair Country (Belleville). Federal civil litigation, State civil litigation, Oil and gas leasing. Office: Gundlach Lee Eggman Boyle & Roessler 5000 W Main St Belleville IL 62222

GAWALT, GERARD W(ILFRED), historian, writer; b. Boston, Feb. 10, 1943; s. John R. and Regina M. (Chaloux) G.; m. Jane F. Cavanaugh, Aug. 6, 1966; children—Susan, Ann, Ellen. B.A., Northeastern U., 1965; M.A., Clark U., 1968, Ph.D., 1969. Reporter Milford Daily News, Mass., 1961-63; reporter Worcester Telegram, Mass., 1963-65; instr. Assumption Coll., 1967-68, Clark U., 1968-69; hist. specialist Library of Congress, Washington, 1969—, specialist in legal history, 1969—; adj. prof. George Mason U., 1972, Catholic U. Am., 1981; guest lectr. George Washington U., Smithsonian Instn. Author: Manuscript Sources in the Library of Congress for Research on the American Revolution, 1975; The Promise of Power: The Emergence of the Massachusetts Legal Profession 1760-1840, 1979 (Choice Outstanding Acad. Book of 1980). Author papers in legal history. Editor: Journal of Gideon Olmsted; Adventures of a Revolutionary War Sea Captain, 1978; John Paul Jones' Memoir of the American Revolution, 1979; The New High Priests: Lawyers in Modern Industrial America, 1984. Assoc. editor Letters of Dels. to Congress, 1774-1789, 15 vols., 1976—. Alumni scholar, 1960-61; NDEA fellow, 1965-68; Am. Council Learned Socs. fellow, 1979-80. Mem. Am. Soc. Legal History, Orgn. Am. Historians, Inst. Early Am. History, Library of Congress Profl. Guild (treas. 1977-78, pres. 1978-79). Democrat. Roman Catholic. Legal education, Legal history, Legislative. Home: 6808 Quebec Ct Springfield VA 22152

GAY, CARL LLOYD, lawyer; b. Seattle, Nov. 11, 1950; s. James and Elizabeth Anne (Rogers) G.; m. Robin Ann Winston, Aug. 23, 1975; children: Patrick, Joel, Alexander, Samuel, Nora. Student, U. of Puget Sound, 1969-70; BS in Forestry cum laude, Wash. State U., 1974; JD, Willamette U., 1979. Bar: Wash. 1979, U.S. Dist. Ct. (we. dist.) Wash. 1979. Assoc. Taylor & Taylor, Port Angeles, Wash., 1979-82; prin. Taylor, Taylor & Gay, Port

Angeles, 1982-85, Greenaway & Gay, Port Angeles, 1985—; pro tem judge Clallam County, Port Angeles, 1981—; superior ct. commr.; juvenile ct. judge, 1985—; guest lectr. Peninsula Coll., Port Angeles, 1983; instr. Guardian ad Litem program, Port Angeles, 1985—. Bd. dirs. Community Concert Assn., Port Angeles, pres. 1982-85; bd. dirs. Salvation Army Adv. Bd., Port Angeles, 1982—, Port Angeles C. of C., 1983-85; bd. dirs., pres. Friends of the Library polit. action com., Port Angeles, 1985—. Mem. ABA (real property, probate and trust and gen. practice sects.), Wash. Bar Assn. (real property, probate and trust sects.), Nat. Council Juvenile and Family Ct. Judges, Superior Ct. Judges Assn. (com. mem.). Methodist. Lodge: Kiwanis (local bd. dirs. 1982-84, pres. 1986—, Kiwanian of the Yr. 1983-84). Avocations: backpacking, cross country skiing, raquetball, sailing. Probate, Real property, Contracts commercial. Home: 3220 McDougal Ave Port Angeles WA 98362 Office: Greenaway & Gay 122 W 1st St Suite 201 Port Angeles WA 98362

GAY, JOE THOMAS, lawyer, consultant; b. Ripley, Miss., Oct. 18, 1947; s. Ross C. and Betty J. (Filgo) G.; m. Brenda Daniel, Aug. 12, 1967; children: Jennifer Jo, Daniel Christian. BBA, U. Miss., 1969; JD, Memphis State U., 1972. Bar: Miss. 1972, U.S. Dist. Ct. (no. and so. dists.) Miss. 1972, U.S. Supreme Ct. 1972. Sole practice Ripley, 1973—; atty. Town of Falkner, Miss., 1972—, Town of Blue Mountain, Miss., 1980—, Town of Walnut, Miss., 1982—; prosecutor Tippah County, Ripley, 1980—, City of Ripley, 1984—; v.p., legal counsel Gay Truck Lines, Falkner, 1980—; bd. dirs. Regular Common Carriers Conf. Served to maj. Miss. N.G., U.S. Army, 1969—. Mem. ABA, Miss. Bar Assn., Tippah County Bar Assn. (pres. 1985), Miss. Prosecutors Assn., Civitan Club. Democrat. Baptist. Lodge: Rotary. Avocations: soccer, softball. Criminal, Local government, General practice. Home: Hwy 15 N Rt 4 Box 150A Ripley MS 38663 Office: 104 S Main St 2d Floor Ripley MS 38663

GAY, MICHAEL HUBERT, lawyer; b. Honolulu, May 11, 1944; s. Hubert Henry and Betty Jane (Plaister) G.; m. Gloria Mildred Knox, Mar. 15, 1975. BS, UCLA, 1967; JD, Hastings Coll. Law, 1974; LLM, NYU, 1975. Bar: Calif. 1974, U.S. Supreme Ct. 1979. V.p., gen. counsel Dyna Industries Inc., Carlsbad, Calif., 1977-85; corp. counsel Fujitsu Systems of Am. Inc., San Diego, 1985—; bd. dirs. Interactive Inc., San Diego; adj. prof. bus. law San Diego State U., 1979-81. Mem. San Diego County Pub. Welfare Adv. Com., 1967-77; arbitrator San Diego Mcpl. & Superior Ct., 1980-85. Served to capt. U.S. Army, 1967-71, Vietnam. Mem. ABA, Am. Soc. Corp. Counsel, State Bar Calif., San Diego County Bar Assn. General corporate, Contracts commercial, Computer. Home: 722 Devon Ct San Diego CA 92109 Office: Fujitsu Systems of Am Inc 12670 High Bluff Dr San Diego CA 92130

GAY, SANDRA BATES, lawyer; b. Atlanta, Nov. 4, 1947; d. Charles W. and Barbara Adelle (Roberts) Bates: m. H. Paul Gay; children: Erin Elisabeth, Jeffrey Alan. BA, Emory U., 1969; JD, U. Wash., 1972. Bar: Wash. 1972, U.S. Dist. Ct. (we. dist.) Wash. 1973. Assoc. Carney, Stephenson, et al, Seattle, 1972-75, ptnr., 1976—; assoc. prof. City U., Seattle, 1980-82. Editor: U. Wash. Law Rev., 1970. Mem. ABA, Wash. Bar Assn., Seattle-King County Bar Assn. Republican. Presbyterian. General corporate, Probate, Securities. Office: Carney Stephenson et al 701 5th Ave Suite 2300 Seattle WA 98104

GAYER, KATHERINE L., lawyer; b. Kearney, Nebr.. BA, Kearney State Coll., 1972; JD cum laude, St. Louis U., 1979. Separations analyst Continental Telcom, St. Louis, 1972-76; law clk. to presiding justice Mo. Ct. Appeals, St. Louis, 1979-80; asst. county counselor St. Louis County, Clayton, Mo., 1980-85; assoc. counsel Continental Baking Co., St. Louis, 1985—. Mem. ABA, St. Louis Met. Bar Assn. General corporate. Office: Continental Baking Co 5CBC Checkerboard Sq Saint Louis MO 63164

GAYLE, GIBSON, JR., lawyer; b. Waco, Tex., Oct. 15, 1926; s. Gibson and Elsie (Little) G.; m. Martha Jane Wood, May 29, 1948; children: Sally Ann, Alice, Gibson III, Jane, Philip. A.B., LL.B., Baylor U., 1950. Bar: Tex. 1950. Since practiced in Houston; sr. partner, chmn. exec. com. Fulbright & Jaworski.; Instr. U. Houston Law Sch., 1951-55; dir. M Corp., M Bank, Houston, Daniel Industries Inc. Bd. editors: Am. Bar Assn. Jour, 1967-72. Trustee Kelsey-Seybold Found., M.D. Anderson Found., bd. govs. Harris County Center for Retarded 1956-76; Tex. Med. Center Inc., Leon Jaworski Found.; bd. dirs., pres. Am. Bar Endowment, 1956-76; chmn. bd. trustees Baylor Coll. Medicine. Served to 2d lt. F.A. AUS, 1945-47. Fellow Am. Bar Found. (dir. 1978-79), Tex. Bar Found. (chmn. 1968-69); mem. ABA (chmn. jr. bar conf. 1959-60, ho. of dels. 1960-62, 63—, sec. 1963-67), Houston Bar Assn., State Bar Tex. (dir. 1966-69, pres. 1976-77), Houston C. of C. (dir.). General practice, Federal civil litigation, State civil litigation. Home: 11727 Broken Bough Circle Houston TX 77024 Office: 1301 McKinney 51st Floor Houston TX 77010

GAYLORD, BRUCE MICHAEL, lawyer; b. Kearny, N.J., Mar. 31, 1948; s. George Makepeace and Doris (Bullock) G.; m. Gail Irene Kelly, Aug. 23, 1980; 1 child, Jesse Winsor. AB, Hamilton Coll., 1970; JD, N.Y. Law Sch., 1974; MBA, NYU, 1985. Bar: N.Y. 1976, U.S. Dist. Ct. (so. and ea. dists.) N.Y. 1976. Atty. Mfr. Hanover Trust Co., N.Y.C., 1974-76, asst. counsel, 1976-78, assoc. counsel, 1978-81, v.p., counsel, 1981-84, v.p., sr. counsel, 1984—; corp. sec., bd. dirs. Mfg.'s Hanover Data Services Corp. Mem. ABA, (sect. corp. bus. banking law, telecommunications com.), N.Y. State Bar Assn. Episcopalian. Avocations: travel, geography, hiking, communications. Computer, Telecommunications, Banking. Home: 12 Canterbury Close Westport CT 06880 Office: Mfrs Hanover Trust Co 270 Park Ave New York NY 10017

GAYLORD, HARRY EUGENE, lawyer; b. Syracuse, N.Y., Apr. 29, 1914; s. Earl Frank and Ellen Elnora (Patterson) G.; m. Faustene Blanche Town, Aug. 9, 1939; children: Harry Jr., Frank, John. JD, Stetson U., 1936. Bar: Fla. 1936. Ptnr. Gaylord, Gaylord, Stone & Evans, Eustis, Fla., 1936—. Mayor, mcpl. judge City of Eustis, 1937-41. Served to lt. USNR, 1942-46. Named Distinguished Alumnus Stetson U. Fellow Acad. Fla. Probate and Trust Litigants; mem. Fla. Bar Assn. (lectr., various coms.), Lake-Sumter Bar Assn. (pres. 1960-61), Nat. Council Presbyn. Men. (vice-pres. 1939-40). Democrat. Probate, Estate planning. Home: PO Box 1317 Eustis FL 32727-1317 Office: Gaylord Gaylord Stone & Evans 804 N Bay St Eustis FL 32737-2047

GAYMAN, BENJAMIN FRANKLIN, lawyer; b. Carlisle, Pa., Jan. 18, 1947; s. Joseph Franklin and Mary E. (Fields) G.; m. Carol Ann Steinen, Nov. 26, 1971; children: Rebecca, Megan, Katie, Anna. BA, Dickinson Coll., 1968; JD, Georgetown U., 1974; LLM in Taxation, Boston U., 1979. Bar: N.H. 1975, U.S. Dist. Ct. N.H. 1975, U.S. Tax Ct. 1984. From assoc. to ptnr. Wiggin & Nourie, Manchester, N.H., 1975—. Editor: Am. Criminal Law Rev., 1973-74. Trustee Manchester Girls and Boys Club, 1976—, Crotched Mountain Found., Greenfield, N.H., 1985—. Served to 1st lt. U.S. Army, 1968-71, Vietnam. Mem. ABA, N.H. Bar Assn. General corporate, Contracts commercial, Real property. Home: 300 Steinmetz Dr Manchester NH 03104 Office: Wiggin & Nourie PO Box 808 Manchester NH 03105

GAYNES, BRUCE HARVEY, lawyer; b. Newark, May 10, 1952; s. Abe and Yolanda Elaine (Diamond) G.; m. Shelley Anne Steele, Jan. 1, 1980. BA, Tulane U., 1973; JD, Emory U., 1977. Bar: Ga. 1977, N.J. 1978, U.S. Tax Ct. 1984; CPA, Ga. Acct. KMG Main Hurdman, Atlanta, 1977-80; sole practice Atlanta, 1980-82; ptnr. Land, Kitchens & Gaynes, Atlanta, 1982-85, Kitchens, Kelley, Gaynes, Huprich & Shmerling, Atlanta, 1985—; instr. Investment Tng. Inst., Atlanta, 1981-84. Active ops. com. Zoo Atlanta, 1985—, nat. young leadership cabinet United Jewish Appeal, N.Y.C., 1986—; trustee Atlanta Jewish Fedn., 1986—. Mem. Atlanta Bar Assn., Ga. Soc. CPA's (chmn. pub. service and info. com. 1983-84), Jaycees (pres. Atlanta chpt. 1984-85). Lodge: B'nai B'rith (pres. Ga. state assn. 1985—). Probate, Personal income taxation, General corporate. Home: 1068 Byrnwyck Rd Atlanta GA 30319 Office: Kitchens Kelley Gaynes et al 11 Piedmont Ctr Suite 900 Atlanta GA 30305

GEAREN, JOHN J., lawyer; b. Wareham, Mass., Sept. 1, 1943. BA, U. Notre Dame, 1965; MA, Oxford U., 1967; JD, Yale U., 1970. Bar: Ill. 1972. Ptnr. Mayer, Brown & Platt, Chgo., 1970—. Democrat. Roman Catholic. Home: 636 Linden Ave Oak Park IL 60302 Office: Mayer Brown & Platt 190 S LaSalle St Chicago IL 60603

GEARHISER, CHARLES JOSEF, lawyer; b. Dyersburg, Tenn., Aug. 14, 1938; s. Charles Josef Gearhiser and Mary Josephine (Plant) Wickham; m. Joy Edwards; children: Charles J. III, Laura, Christy. BS, Austin Peay State U., 1960; LLB, U. Tenn., 1961. Bar: Tenn. Assoc. Strang, Fletcher, Carriger & Walker, Chattanooga, 1961-63; law clk. to presiding justice U.S. Dist. Ct. (ea. dist.) Tenn., Chattanooga, 1963-64; asst. U.S. atty. Dept. Justice, Chattanooga, 1964-66; ptnr. Stophel, Caldwell & Heggie, Chattanooga, 1966-74, Gearhiser, Peters & Horton, Chattanooga, 1974—; U.S. commnr., 1966-73; U.S. magistrate U.S. Dist. Ct. (ea. dist.) Tenn., 1973-78, Chattanooga. Chmn. bd. dirs. S.E. Tenn. Legal Services, Chattanooga, 1978-81. Fellow Am. Coll. Trial Lawyers, Tenn. Bar Found.; mem. ABA, Tenn. Bar Assn., Chattanooga Bar Assn. (sec., treas 1972-73, pres. 1973-74), Assn. Trial Lawyers Am., Tenn. Trial Lawyers Assn., Chattanooga Trial Lawyers Assn., Nat. Inst. Trial Advocacy (civil trial adv. 1981), Am. Bd. Trial Advs. (charter mem. Tenn. chpt.), Order of Coif. Democrat. Methodist. Federal civil litigation, State civil litigation. Home: 12 North Crest Chattanooga TN 37404 Office: Gearhiser Peters & Horton 801 Chestnut St Chattanooga TN 37402

GEARY, JAMES H., lawyer; b. Midland, Mich., Nov. 8, 1946; s. James Edward and Ruth Alice (Cary) G.; m. Judith Ellery McHugh, Aug. 22, 1967; children: Patricia Jean, Christopher James. BA, U. Mich., 1968, JD, 1972. Bar: U.S. Dist. Ct. (we. dist.) Mich. 1972, U.S. Dist. Ct. (ea. dist.) Mich. 1974, U.S. Ct. Appeals (6th cir.) 1973, U.S. Ct. Appeals (5th cir.) 1978, U.S. Ct. Appeals (11th cir.) 1981, U.S. Supreme Ct. 1981. Law clk. to judge U.S. Ct. of Appeals 6th Cir., Mich., 1972-73; assoc. Howard & Howard, Kalamazoo, Mich., 1973-80; ptnr. Little & Geary, Kalamazoo, 1980-83, Howard & Howard, Kalamazoo, 1983—; chmn. Ad-Hoc Sub-Com. on Examinations, Grand Rapids, Mich., 1980-82; faculty Western Mich. Univ. Trial Advocacy Inst., 1982; guest lectr. Western Mich. Univ.; lectr. and commentator Inst. of Continuing Legal Edn., 1980—. Chmn. selective service Western Dist. of Mich. Appeal Bd., Grand Rapids, 1985. Served with U.S. Army, 1969-71. Mem. ABA, Kalamazoo County Trial Lawyers Assn. (pres. 1984-85), State Bar of Mich. (co-chmn. U.S. cts. com. 1985-86); bd. dirs. Kalamazoo County Bar Assn.; bd. dirs. Western Mich. Fed. Bar Assn., Kalamazoo Optimist Hockey Assn. Avocations: hockey, soccer officiating. State civil litigation, Federal civil litigation, Labor. Office: 400 Kalamazoo Bldg 107 W Mich Ave Kalamazoo MI 49007

GEBO, STEPHEN WALLACE, lawyer; b. Watertown, N.Y., Apr. 2, 1951; s. Wallace Anthony and Yolanda (Leana) G.; m. Kathleen Lenair Hunt, Aug. 7, 1976; children: Allison, Carolynn, Sarah. AB, Hamilton Coll., 1973; JD, Cornell U., 1976. Bar: N.Y. 1977, U.S. Dist. Ct. (no. dist.) N.Y. 1978, U.S. Ct. Appeals (2d cir.) 1980. Assoc. Proskauer, Rose, Goetz & Mendelson, N.Y.C., 1976-77, Pearis, Resseguie, Kline & Barber, Binghamton, N.Y., 1977-78; assoc. Conboy, McKay, Bachman & Kendall, Watertown, 1978-81, ptnr., 1981—. Assoc. editor Cornell U. Law Rev., 1974-75, editor, 1975-76. Bd. dirs. March of Dimes, Watertown, 1979-82, Jefferson County Women's Ctr., Watertown, 1980—. Mem. ABA, N.Y. State Bar Assn., Jefferson County Bar Assn., Phi Beta Kappa. Republican. Roman Catholic. Club: Ives Hill Country (Watertown). Avocation: golf. Insurance, Personal injury, Workers' compensation. Home: 155 Paddock St Watertown NY 13601 Office: Conboy McKay Bachman & Kendall 407 Sherman St Watertown NY 13601

GEBOW, THOMAS EUGENE, lawyer; b. Denver, Nov. 30, 1947; s. Charles Orville and Audrey Janet (Kropp) G.; m. Gail Bunting Mitchel, Aug. 23, 1969. BA, U. Pa., 1969; JD, U. Dnever, 1974. Bar: Colo. 1974, D.C. 1974. Assoc. Holland & Hart, Denver, 1974-80, ptnr., 1980-82; prin. Holt & Gebow, Denver, 1983—. Served with U.S. Army, 1970-72. Mem. ABA, Colo. Bar Assn., Denver Bar Assn., Order St. Ives. Democrat. Lutheran. Avocations: computer programming, bicycling, skiing. Contracts commercial, Computer, Architect and engineering malpractice. Office: Holt & Gebow 1576 Sherman St Denver CO 80203

GECK, DONNA DUNKELBERGER, lawyer; b. Durham, N.C., Oct. 1, 1949; d. Donald Edward and Daphene (Bowles) Dunkelberger; m. Timothy R. Geck, July 29, 1972. BA, Marquette U., 1971; JD with distinction, U. N.D., 1976. Bar: N.D. 1976, Minn. 1976, U.S. Dist. Ct. Minn. 1977, U.S. Ct. Appeals (8th cir.) 1977, U.S. Supreme Ct. 1980, U.S. Dist. Ct. N.D. 1981. Pub. defender Ramsey County, St. Paul, 1976-77; ptnr. Austin & Roth, P.A., Mpls., 1977-82, McDonough, Geck & Cronan, P.A., Mpls., 1982-85, Arthur, Chapman, Michaelson & McDonough, P.A., Mpls., 1985—. Mem. ABA, N.D. Bar Assn., Minn. Bar Assn., Minn. Def. Lawyers Assn., Minn. Women Lawyers Assn., Order of Coif. Insurance, Personal injury, State civil litigation. Office: Arthur Chapman Michaelson & McDonough PA 1219 Marquette Minneapolis MN 55403

GEE, DELBERT CALVIN, lawyer; b. Oakland, Calif., July 29, 1955; s. Stanley Hung and Amy (Sung) G.; m. Doris Louise Wong, Jan. 29, 1983. BA in Polit. Sci., U. Calif., Davis, 1977; JD, U. Santa Clara, 1979. Bar: Calif. 1980, U.S. Dist. Ct. (no. dist.) Calif. 1982, U.S. Ct. Appeals (9th cir.) 1982, U.S. Dist. Ct. (ea. dist.) Calif. 1985. Dep. dist. atty. County of Ventura, Calif., 1980-82; assoc. Hassard, Bonnington, Roges & Huber, San Francisco, 1982—. Mem. ABA, Calif. Bar Assn., San Francisco Bar Assn., Alameda County Bar Assn., Chinese Am. Citizens Alliance, Asian Am. Bar Assn., Wa Sung Service Club, Oakland Chinatown C. of C., Chinese Am. Polit. Assn. Democrat. Avocations: sports, music, politics. Insurance, Personal injury, State civil litigation.

GEE, THOMAS GIBBS, fed. judge; b. Jacksonville, Fla., Dec. 9, 1925; s. James Gilliam and Cecile (Gibbs) G.; m. Deborah Ann Bagg, June 15, 1986; children by previous marriage—Jennifer Gee Updegraf, John Christopher, Mary Cecile, Thomas Gibbs. Student, The Citadel, 1942-43; B.S., U.S. Mil. Acad., 1946; LL.B., U. Tex., 1953. Bar: Tex. bar 1953. Assoc. firm Baker & Botts, Houston, 1953-54, Graves, Dougherty, Gee, Hearon, Moody & Garwood (and predecessors), Austin, Tex., 1954; partner Graves, Dougherty, Gee, Hearon, Moody & Garwood (and predecessors), 1955-73; judge U.S. Ct. Appeals, 5th Circuit, Austin, 1973—. Contbr. articles to profl. jours., publs.; editor-in-chief: Tex. Law Rev, 1952-53. Served with USAAF, 1946-47; Served with USAF, 1947-50. Mem. Am. Law Inst., Am. Bar Assn., Am. Judicature Soc., Tex. Bar Found., Order of Coif. Home: 2708-A West Ln Houston TX 77027 Office: US Courthouse 515 Rusk Room 11009 Houston TX 77002

GEER, JOHN FARR, diversified company executive; b. N.Y.C., Oct. 15, 1930; s. William Montague and Edith Jaffray (Farr) G.; m. Carolyn Boston, June 25, 1954; children: Jennifer, Evelyn, John Farr. B.A., Princeton U., 1952; LL.B., Columbia U., 1957. Bar: N.Y. State 1957. Asso. firm Sullivan & Cromwell, N.Y.C., 1957-65, Whitman & Ransom (and predecessor firms), N.Y.C., 1965-67; partner Whitman & Ransom (and predecessor firms), 1967-73; v.p., gen. counsel, sec. Am. Standard Inc., N.Y.C., 1973—. Trustee Protestant Episcopal Soc. for Promoting Religion and Learning in State N.Y., 1960-82, treas., 1968-82; trustee Gen. Theol. Sem., 1980—; mem. Corp. for Relief Widows and Children of P.E. Clergymen in State N.Y., 1960—, treas., 1967—. Served to 1st lt. F.A. AUS, 1952-54, Korea. Mem. Phi Delta Phi. Episcopalian. Club: Princeton (N.Y.C.). Home: 151 Central Park W New York NY 10023 Office: 40 W 40th St New York NY 10018 *

GEER, THOMAS LEE, lawyer; b. Johnstown, Pa., Sept. 26, 1951; s. Frank Densmore, III, and Lillian Louise (Vivoda) G. BA cum laude, Boston U., 1973; JD, U. Pitts., 1976; MLT., Georgetown U., 1978. Bar: Pa. 1978, U.S. dist. (ea. dist.) Mich. 1978, U.S. Tax Ct. 1978, Ohio 1982. Clk. NW Pa. Legal Services, Sharon, 1975; assoc. Silverstein & Mullins, Washington, 1976-78, Dykema, Gossett, Spencer, Goodnow & Trigg, Detroit, 1978-80, Keywell & Rosenfeld, Troy, Mich., 1980-81; ptnr. Carson, Vieweg, Geer & Smereck, Bloomfield Hills, Mich., 1981-82, Schwartz, Kelm, Warren & Rubenstein, Columbus, Ohio, 1982—; adj. prof. Walsh Coll., Troy, Mich., 1981, Franklin U., Columbus, 1983-86, Capital U., Columbus, 1986—. Author: 274-2nd T.M. Casualty Losses, 1979; 298-2nd T.M. Private Foundation-Definition & Classification, 1982; 337-2nd T.M. Exempt Organizations, 1984; columnist The Tax Times, 1986—; also articles. Mem. ABA (chmn. continuing legal edn. subcom. tax acctg. problems com. 1981-82), Ohio State Bar Assn., Columbus Bar Assn. (chmn. task force on provision of legal services to nonprofit entities 1982-84). Pension, profit-sharing, and employee benefits, Corporate taxation, Labor. Home: 1062 S Cassingham Rd Columbus OH 43209 Office: Schwartz Kelm Warren & Rubenstein 41 S High St Columbus OH 43215

GEESEMAN, ROBERT GEORGE, lawyer; b. Shreveport, La., Oct. 23, 1944; s. George Robert and Cora (Hamilton) Glasgow; m. Rosemary Monahan, Aug. 19, 1967; 1 child, Regan Glasgow. B.A., Yale U., 1966; J.D., U. Mich., 1969. Bar: Pa. 1969, U.S. Dist. Ct. (we. dist.) Pa. 1969, U.S. Supreme Ct., 1973, U.S. Tax Ct. 1979. Assoc. Blaxter, O'Neill, Houston & Nash, Pitts., 1969-75; ptnr. Lynch, Lynch, Carr & Kabala, Pitts., 1975-81, Lynch, Kabala & Geeseman, Pitts., 1981, Kabala & Geeseman, Pitts., 1981—; lectr. on tax law and employee benefits; legal adv. bd. Small Bus. Council Am. Mem. ABA (mem. profl. service corps. com. sect. on taxation, chmn. profl. corp. com. sect. econs.; bd. editors Withdrawal Retirement and Disputes, What You and Your Firm Should Know), Pa. Bar Assn., Allegheny County Bar Assn., Am. Soc. Law and Medicine, Am. Judicature Soc., Estate Planning Council, Pitts. Inst. Legal Medicine, Phi Delta Phi. Clubs: Rosslyn Farms Country, Rivers, Harvard-Yale-Princeton (Pitts.); Mory's (New Haven, Conn.); John's Island Country (Vero Beach, Fla.). Pension, profit-sharing, and employee benefits, Corporate taxation, Personal income taxation. Office: Suite 700 316 4th Ave Pittsburgh PA 15222

GEFFEN, ARTHUR HAROLD, lawyer, pharmacist; b. Savannah, Ga., Apr. 18, 1945; s. Joseph and Pearl Lillian (Vogel) G.; m. Joan Leslie Solomon, Aug. 3, 1969; 1 dau., Wendi Shawn. Student Emory U., 1962-64; B.S., U. Ga., 1966, B.S.Ph., 1969; J.D., U. Houston, 1973. Bar: Tex. 1973, U.S. Ct. Appeals (5th cir.) 1974, U.S. Dist. Ct. (so. dist.) Tex. 1974, U.S. Supreme Ct. 1977, U.S. Tax Ct. 1979. Asst. mgr. Reed Drugs, Atlanta, 1969-71; assoc. firm Hirsch, Westheimer & Block, Houston, 1974-75; sole practice, Dallas, 1975-79; pres. Arthur H. Geffen, P.C. formerly known as Geffen & Jacobson, P.C., Dallas, 1979—. Served with USAR, 1970-75. Fellow Internat. Soc. Barristers; mem. ABA, Tex. Bar Assn., Dallas Bar Assn. Clubs: Brookhaven Country, Landmark, Park Cen. Athletic (Dallas). Contbg. editor Houston Law Rev., 1972-73. Estate planning, Corporate taxation, Personal income taxation. Office: 12750 Merit Dr Suite 801 Dallas TX 75251

GEHRES, JAMES, lawyer; b. Akron, Ohio, July 19, 1932; s. Edwin Jacob and Cleora Mary (Yoakam) G.; m. Eleanor Agnew Mount, July 23, 1960. B.S. in Acctg., U. Utah, 1954; M.B.A., U. Calif.-Berkeley, 1959; J.D., U. Denver, 1970, LL.M. in Taxation, 1977. Bar: Colo. 1970, U.S. Dist. Ct. Colo. 1970, U.S. Tax Ct. 1970, U.S. Supreme Ct. 1973, U.S. Ct. Appeals (10th cir.) 1978. Atty. IRS, Denver, 1965-80, atty. chief counsel's office, 1980—. Served with USAF, 1955-58, capt. Res. ret. Mem. ABA, Colo. Bar Assn., Am. Inst. C.P.A.s, Colo. Soc. C.P.A.s, Am. Assn. Atty.-C.P.A.s, Am. Judicature Soc., Am. Acctg. Assn., Order St. Ives, Beta Gamma Sigma, Beta Alpha Psi. Democrat. Contbr. articles to profl. jours. Corporate taxation, Personal income taxation, Estate taxation. Address: 935 Pennsylvania St Denver CO 80203

GEHRIG, MICHAEL FORD, lawyer; b. Cin., Jan. 25, 1947; s. John Richard and Mary Bonita (Ford) G.; m. Barbara Jane Rigg, June 16, 1973; children—Michael Ford, Caroline Christina. B.A., Ohio State U., 1970; J.D., Chase Coll. Law, Cin., 1974. Bar: Ohio 1974, U.S. Dist. Ct. (so. dist.) Ohio 1974, U.S. Dist. Ct. (ea. dist.) Ky. 1983, U.S. Supreme Ct., 1985. Assoc. Beall, Hermanies & Bortz, Cin., 1974-76; mem. firm Gehrig & Gehrig, Cin., 1976-79, Gehrig, Parker & Baldwin, Cin., 1979—; lectr. various legal seminars. Contbr. articles to jours., chpts. to books. Recipient book awards Chase Coll. Law, 1971, 73, 74. Mem. ABA, Ohio State Bar Assn., Cin. Bar Assn., Assn. Trial Lawyers Am. (sustaining), Ohio Acad. Trial Lawyers (sustaining), Cin. Hist. Soc., English Speaking Union, Mercedes Benz Club, Phi Gamma Delta. Republican. Episcopalian. Club: Cin. Athletic. Personal injury. Home: 3121 Portsmouth Cincinnati OH 45208 Office: Gehrig Parker & Baldwin 1140 Bartlett Bldg 36 E 4th St Cincinnati OH 45202

GEHRING, RONALD KENT, lawyer; b. Ft. Wayne, Ind., Feb. 5, 1941; s. Ronald G. and Beverly M. (Failor) G.; m. Teresa L. Eyer, June 18, 1966; children—Gregory D., Douglas K., Suzanne C. A.B., Ind. U., 1963, J.D., 1967. Bar: Ind. 1967, U.S. Dist. Ct. (no. dist.) Ind. 1967, U.S. Dist. Ct. (so. dist.) Ind. 1967, U.S. Ct. Appeals (7th cir.) 1975. Assoc., Peters, McHie, Enslen & Hand, Hammond, Ind., 1967-70; ptnr. Tourkow, Danehy, Crell, Hood & Gehring, Ft. Wayne, 1971-79, Grossman, Boeglin & Gehring and predecessor, Ft. Wayne, 1980-84; sole practice, 1984—; panelist Ind. Collection Law Seminar, 1982-83. Dir. Concordia Cemetery Assn., 1982-83, Luth. Assn. Broadcasting, Inc. Mem. Assn. Trial Lawyers Am., Ind. Trial Lawyers, Comml. Law League, Am. Judicature Soc., ABA, Ind. Bar Assn., Allen County Bar Assn. (dir.), Phi Delta Phi. Consumer commercial, Probate, Real property. Home: 5027 Wapiti Ct Fort Wayne IN 46802 Office: 1600 Lincoln Bank Tower Fort Wayne IN 46802

GEHRINGER, JOHN G., lawyer; b. Milw., Apr. 24, 1953; s. John J. and Lorayne M. (McKee) G.; m. Cheryl L. Nisenbaum; 1 child, Shannon M. BA cum laude, Marquette U., 1975, JD, 1978. Bar: Wis. 1978, U.S. Dist. Ct. (ea. and we. dists.) Wis., U.S. Ct. Appeals (7th cir.) 1978. Assoc. atty. Frisch Dudek & Slattery, Milw., 1978-83; ptnr. Frisch Dudek & Shattery, Milw., 1984—. Mem. ABA, Milw. Bar Assn. (legis. com.), Milw. Young Lawyers Assn., Wis. Realtors Assn. (speaker 1987), Waukesha Bar Assn., Wis. Bar Assn., Brookfield C. of C. (bd. dirs.), Phi Delta Phi (magistrate 1977-78). Republican. Roman Catholic. Lodge: Rotary. Avocations: golf, hunting, fishing. Banking, State civil litigation, Real property. Office: Frisch Dudek & Slattery Ltd 825 N Jefferson Milwaukee WI 53202

GEHRINGER, MICHAEL EDWARD, library administrator, lawyer; b. Darby, Pa., Nov. 5, 1950; s. Charles Matthew and Dorothea Veronica (Wood) G.; m. Suzanne Cormier, Dec. 18, 1971 (div. Oct. 1981); children: Alison, Katherine. BA cum laude, Duquesne U., 1972; MLS, Cath. U., 1974, JD, 1979. Bar: Va. 1979. Catalog and reference librarian Cath. U. Law Library, Washington, 1974-76; reference specialist Library of Congress, Washington, 1976-78; asst. librarian U.S. Supreme Ct., Washington, 1978-81; cons. FDR Online, Inc., Washington, 1981-83; mgmt. services librarian Joint Bank Fund Library, Washington, 1983-85, acting dir., 1985-86, dir., 1986—; adj. prof. U. Md. Sch. Library and Info. Systems, College Park, Md., 1983-85. Compiler column Questions and Answers Law Library Jour., 1977-81. Mem. ABA, D.C. Law Librarians Soc. (pres. 1986-87), Am. Assn. Law Librarians, Spl. Libraries Assn. Librarianship. Home: 8524 Lakinhurst Ln Springfield VA 22152 Office: Joint World Bank Internat Monetary Fund Library 700 19th St NW Washington DC 20431

GEHRINGER, SUSANNE ELKINS, law librarian; b. Phila., Feb. 21, 1941; d. Harry S. and Reba (Braun) Elkins; m. Peter Mathius Hahn, Sept. 15, 1962 (div. 1978); children: Karen Anne, Paul F., Roger J.; m. Michael Edward Gehringer, Apr. 3, 1982; children: Alison, Kate. BA, U. Pa., 1962; MLS, Villanova U., 1975. Librarian reference and circulation Villanova (Pa.) U., 1973-76; head librarian Schnader, Harrison, Segal & Lewis, Phila., 1976-82, Hamel & Park, Washington, 1985—; librarian, archivist office legal counsel U.S. Senate, Washington, 1982-85. Mem. Am. Assn. Law Libraries (chmn. com. 1984—, grantee 1984), D.C. Law Library Assn. (chmn. com. 1985—), D.C. Pvt. Law Librarians (pres. 1986—). Librarianship. Home: 8325 Wickham Rd Springfield VA 22152 Office: Hamel & Park 888 16th St NW Washington DC 20006

GEIGER, ALEXANDER, lawyer; b. Kosice, Czechoslovakia, May 21, 1950; came to U.S., 1965; s. Emil and Alice (Schwinger) G.; m. Helene R. Hurwitz, May 28, 1972; children: Theodore, Aviva. AB, Princeton U., 1972; JD, Cornell U., 1975. Bar: N.Y. 1976, U.S. Dist. Ct. (we. dist.) N.Y. 1976, U.S. Supreme Ct. 1980, U.S. Ct. Appeals (2d cir.) 1985, U.S. Tax Ct. 1986. Assoc. Nixon, Hargrave, Devans & Doyle, Rochester, N.Y., 1975-82; sr. ptnr. Geiger & Rothenberg, Rochester, 1982-86, Geiger, Rothenberg & Feldman, Rochester, 1986—; adj. asst. prof. St. John Fisher Coll., Rochester, 1977-78. Mem. ABA, N.Y. State Bar Assn., Monroe County Bar Assn., Assn. Trial Lawyers Am. Jewish. Federal civil litigation, State civil litigation, Personal injury. Home: 194 Edgemoor Rd Rochester NY 14618 Office: Geiger Rothenberg & Feldman 45 Exchange St Rochester NY 14614

GEIGER, DAVID R., lawyer. BS, Dickinson Coll., 1977; JD, Harvard U., 1980. Bar: Mass. 1980, U.S. Dist. Ct. Mass. 1981, U.S. Ct. Appeals (1st cir.) 1984. Law clk. to judge U.S. Dist. Ct. Mass., Boston, 1980-81; assoc. Foley, Hoag & Eliot, Boston, 1981—. Bd. dirs. Germaine Lawrence Sch., Arlington, Mass., 1981—. Mem. ABA, Mass. Bar Assn., Boston Bar Assn., Phi Beta Kappa, Omicron Delta Kappa. Federal civil litigation, State civil litigation. Office: Foley Hoag & Eliot One Post Office Square Boston MA 02109

GEIGER, JAMES NORMAN, lawyer; b. Mansfield, Ohio, Apr. 5, 1932; s. Ernest R. and Margaret L. (Bauman) G.; m. Paula Hunt, May 11, 1957; children—Nancy G., John W. Student Wabash Coll., Crawfordsville, Ind., 1950-51; B.A., Ohio Wesleyan U., 1954; J.D., Emory U., 1962. Bar: Ga. 1961, U.S. Dist. Ct. (mid. dist.) Ga. 1966, U.S. Ct. Appeals (5th and 11th cirs.) 1980, U.S. Dist. Ct. (so. dist.) Ga. 1983. Assoc., Henderson, Kaley, Geiger and Thurmond, Marietta, Ga., 1962-64; ptnr. Geiger and Pierce and predecessors, Perry, Ga., 1964—, sr. ptnr., 1971—. Trustee Westfield (Ga.) Schs., 1970-74; mem. civilian adv. bd. Warner Robins AFB, 1976; chmn. council ministries Perry United Meth. Ch., 1970-71, mem. adminstrv. bd., 1968—. Served to capt. USAF, 1954-57. Mem. ABA, Ga. Bar Assn., Houston County Bar Assn., Perry C. of C. (pres. 1976), Phi Delta Phi, Pi Sigma Alpha. Methodist. Clubs: Perry Kiwanis (pres. 1968, Man of Yr. 1968), Perry Council (pres. 1967). General practice, Contracts commercial, Real property. Home: 821 Forrest Hill Rd Perry GA 31069 Office: PO Drawer T Perry GA 31069

GEIGER, RICHARD STUART, lawyer; b. Dallas, Feb. 21, 1936; s. Gilbert A. and Letitia (Wells) G.; m. Phyllis Scott McGee, June 4, 1954; children—R. Scott, Angela G., Margaret L., P. Claire, Amy S. LL.B., So. Meth. U., 1962. Bar: Tex. 1962, U.S. Ct. Appeals (5th cir.) 1969, U.S. Supreme Ct. 1968. Sole practice, Dallas, 1962-75; ptnr. Thompson, Coe, Cousins & Irons, Dallas, 1975—. Co-editor Tex. Ins. Law Reporter. Mem. Tex. Ho. of Reps., 1972-76. Mem. Internat. Assn. Def. Counsel, Assn. Internat. de Droit des Assurances. Democrat. Episcopalian. Clubs: Austin, Chaparral, Crescent (Dallas). Administrative and regulatory, Insurance, Legislative. Office: Thompson Coe Cousins & Irons 200 Crescent Ct 11th Floor Dallas TX 75201-1840

GEIGER, WILLIAM DAVID, lawyer; b. Cleve., Apr. 5, 1950; s. William Theodore and Eleanor Virginia (Rodgers) G.; m. Constance Ann Esola, Aug. 16, 1975; children: Timothy Russel, Christina Leigh. BA, Pa. State U., 1972; JD, U. Pitts., 1979. Bar: Pa. 1979, U.S. Dist. Ct. (we. dist.) Pa. 1979, U.S. Supreme Ct. 1985. Ptnr., trial atty. Gragsby, Gaca & Davies, P.C., Pitts., 1979—. Mem. ABA, Pa. Bar Assn., Allegheny County Bar Assn. Democrat. Presbyterian. Avocations: skiing, sailing, golf, furniture making. Federal civil litigation, State civil litigation, Insurance. Office: Gragsby Gaca & Davies PC One Gateway Ctr 10th Floor Pittsburgh PA 15222

GEIGER, WILLIAM HAROLD, lawyer; b. Milw., June 1, 1947; s. Herb A. and Sydella F. (Gebhardt) G.; m. Margaret E. Boyer, Jan. 19, 1973; children: Budd W., Timothy W., Scott W. Student, Marquette U., 1965-68, Washington U., St. Louis, 1968-69; BA cum laude, Loyola U., New Orleans, 1972; JD, U. Wis., 1975. Bar: Wis. 1975, U.S. Dist. Ct. (we. dist.) Wis. 1975, Iowa 1976, U.S. Dist. Ct. (no. dist.) Iowa 1976, Fla. 1979. Assoc. Klauer, Stapleton, Ernst & Sprengelmeyer, Dubuque, Iowa, 1975-76; asst. gen. counsel Reliable Life and Casualty Ins. Co., Madison, Wis., 1976-78; v.p., gen. counsel Fla. Gen. Life Ins Co., Miami, Fla., 1978-80; sr. v.p., gen. counsel, sec. Home Life Fin. Assurance Corp. and Orange State Life and Health Ins Co., Largo, Fla., 1980—. Mem. adv. com. Fla. Ho. of Reps., Tallahassee, 1980-81. Mem. ABA, Fla. Bar Assn., Clearwater Bar Assn., Am. Council Life Ins. (corresponding officer 1982—), Health Ins. Assn. Am. (corresponding officer 1982—), Life Office Mgmt. Assn. (fellow Life Mgmt. Inst. 1987), Soc. Fin. Examiners (assoc.). Democrat. Methodist. Lodge: Elks (trustee, presiding justice Largo 1985—). Avocation: music. Insurance, Administrative and regulatory, General corporate. Office: Home Life Assurance Corp 2400 W Bay Dr Largo FL 33540

GEIL, JOHN CLINTON, lawyer; b. San Antonio, Oct. 27, 1951; s. William Clinton and Frances E. (Coverdale) G. B.A., Occidental Coll., 1972; J.D., Lewis and Clark Coll., 1976. Bar: Oreg. 1976, U.S. Dist. Ct. Oreg. 1977, U.S. Ct. Appeals (9th cir.) 1977, U.S. Supreme Ct. 1981. Sole practice, Portland, Oreg., 1976-78; ptnr. Rieke, Geil & Savage, P.C., and predecessor Portland, 1978—. Mem. Multnomah County Corrections Classifications System Adv. Commn., Oreg., 1982. Named to Outstanding Young Men Am., U.S. Jaycees, 1979, 81. Mem. Oreg. Young Attys. Assn. (pres. 1983-84), ABA (bd. dirs. law student div. 1975-76, exec. council young lawyers div. 1981-82, dir. young lawyers div. 1984-85, assembly clk. young lawyers div. 1986-87), Multnomah Bar Assn. (chmn. corrections com. 1981-83, chmn. legis. com. 1984-86, Recognition award 1983), Cornelius Honor Soc. State civil litigation, Federal civil litigation, Criminal. Office: Rieke Geil & Savage PC 820 SW 2d St Suite 200 Portland OR 97204

GEIL, KARL JAMES, lawyer; b. Rochester, N.Y., May 31, 1957; s. Gordon H. and Alma H. (Huehn) G. BA, Hamilton Coll., 1979; JD, U. Denver, 1982. Bar: Colo. 1982, U.S. Dist. Ct. Colo. 1982, U.S. Ct. Appeals (10th cir.) 1982. Assoc. Vranesic, Gordon & Visciano, Denver, 1982-84, Leonard M. Chesler, Denver, 1984—. Mem. ABA, Colo. Bar Assn., Denver Bar Assn. Democrat. Lutheran. Criminal, Family and matrimonial, State civil litigation. Office: Leonard M Chesler 1343 Delaware St Denver CO 80204

GEIS, JEROME ARTHUR, lawyer, legal educator; b. Shakopee, Minn., May 28, 1946; s. Arthur Adam and Emma Mary (Boegemann) G.; m. Beth Marie Bruger, Aug. 11. 1979; children: Jennifer, Jason, Joan. BA in History, Govt. magna cum laude, St. John's U., Collegeville, Minn., 1968; JD cum laude, U. Notre Dame, 1973; LLM in Taxation, NYU, 1975. Bar: Minn. 1973, U.S. Dist. Ct. Minn. 1973, U.S. Tax Ct. 1973, U.S. Ct. Appeals (8th cir.) 1973. Law clk. to presiding justice Minn. Supreme Ct., St. Paul, 1973-74; assoc. Dudley & Smith, St. Paul, 1975-76; assoc. Briggs & Morgan P.A., St. Paul, 1976-83, chief tax dept., 1983—; prof. tax law William Mitchell Coll. of Law, St. Paul, 1976—. Columnist: Minn. Law Jour., 1986. Bd. dirs. Western Townhouse Assn., West St. Paul, 1979, St. Matthews Cath. Ch., West St. Paul, 1981. Served to specialist 4th class U.S. Army, 1969-71. Mem. ABA, Minn. Bar Assn. (bd. dirs. tax council sect. 1984—), Ramsey County Bar Assn., Hennepin County Bar Assn., Minn. Inst. Legal Edn. (bd. dirs. 1984—), Cath. Aid Assn., Minn. Assn. Commerce and Industry, Minn. Taxpayers Assn. Clubs: Minn., St. Paul Athletic (St. Paul). Lodge: K.C. Corporate taxation, Personal income taxation, State and local taxation. Home: 1116 Dodd Rd Mendota Heights MN 55118 Office: Briggs & Morgan PA 2200 First National Bank Bldg Saint Paul MN 55101

GEISEL, HENRY JULES, lawyer; b. Cin., Oct. 3, 1947; s. Albert and Else Geisel; m. Ellyn Anne Levy, Sept. 1, 1975; children: Noah L., Gideon L. BS in Econs., U. Pa., 1969; JD, U. Cin., 1972. Bar: Colo. 1972, U.S. Dist. Ct. Colo. 1972. Dep. dist. atty. 20th Jud. Dist., Boulder, Colo., 1973-74, 10th Jud. Dist., Pueblo, Colo., 1974-76; assoc. John R. Naylor, Pueblo, 1976-82, Naylor & Geisel P.C., Pueblo, 1982—. Pres. Temple Emanuel, Pueblo, 1981-82, 85-86; bd. dirs. Pueblo Youth Services Bur., 1978—, Parkview Hosp. Found., Pueblo, 1986—. Mem. ABA, Colo. Bar Assn., Pueblo County Bar Assn., Colo. Trial Lawyers Assn. Clubs: Thirty, Pueblo Country. Avocations: tennis, skiing, scuba diving, travel. Consumer commercial, Family and matrimonial, State civil litigation. Office: Naylor & Geisel PC 201 W 8th St #760 PO Box 1421 Pueblo CO 81003

GEISLER, THOMAS MILTON, JR., lawyer; b. Orange, N.J., Jan. 16, 1943; s. Thomas M. Sr. and Helen (Thomas) G.; m. Sarah Farrell, Aug. 6, 1977; children: Sarah Claire, Ann Cathleen. AB, Harvard U., 1965, JD, 1968. Bar: N.J. 1968, U.S. Dist. Ct. N.J. 1968, U.S. Supreme Ct. 1972, N.Y. 1974, U.S. Dist. Ct. (so. and ea. dists.) N.Y. 1974, U.S. Ct. Appeals (2d cir.) 1975. Assoc. Shearman & Sterling, N.Y.C., 1973-80, ptnr., 1980—. Served as lt. JAGC, USNR, 1969-72. Mem. ABA (newsletter subcom. trial practice com. litigation sect. 1985—), Assn. of Bar of City of N.Y. Presbyterian. Club: Harvard (N.Y.C.). Federal civil litigation, State civil litigation. Home: 500 E 85th St #4A New York NY 10028 Office: Shearman & Sterling 53 Wall St New York NY 10005

GEITZ, MICHAEL M(EYER), investment company executive, lawyer; b. Pitman, N.J., Feb. 4, 1952; s. William Daniel and Laura (Rainey) G.; m. Elizabeth Bradley Rankin, June 8, 1974; 1 child, Charlotte. BA, Vanderbilt U., 1975; MBA, U. S.C., 1976, JD, 1979. Atty. William Sword & Co., Inc., Princeton, N.J., 1979-81, mng. dir., 1981-84; v.p. Merrill Lynch, Pierce Fenner & Smith, N.Y.C., 1984—; bd. dirs. Am. Reliance Ins. Co., Lawrenceville, N.J. Mem. ABA, S.C. Bar Assn. Republican. Episcopalian. Club: Bedens Brook (Skillman, N.J.). General corporate, Banking, Insurance. Office: Merrill Lynch Capital Markets Merrill Lunch World Hdqrs World Financial Ctr North Tower 29th Fl New York NY 10281-1201

GEKAS, CONSTANTINE JOHN, lawyer; b. Chgo., Mar. 1, 1946; s. John Constantine and Olga (Massias) G.; m. Markie Carlson Gekas, June 12, 1970; children—John C., Alexandra L. B.A. in Polit. Sci., U. Chgo., 1967; J.D., U. Ill., 1970. Bar: Ill. 1971, D.C. 1973, Va. 1973, U.S. Supreme Ct. 1974. Assoc. Chadwell, Keck, Kayser & Ruggles, Chgo., 1971-72; atty. criminal div. Dept. Justice, Washington, 1973; counsel Impeachment Inquiry, Com. on Judiciary, U.S. Ho. of Reps., Washington, 1974, assoc. counsel Com. on Judiciary subcom. on crime, 1974-76; asst. U.S. atty. D.C., 1976-80; regional counsel, central region div. enforcement Commodity Futures Trading Commn., Chgo., 1980-84; sole practice, Chgo., 1984-85; ptnr. Harvitt & Gekas, Ltd., 1985— . Served with USAR, 1969-75. Mem. ABA, Chgo. Bar Assn. Federal civil litigation, Criminal, Legislative. Home: 1111 Cherry St Winnetka IL 60093 Office: 135 S LaSalle St Suite 1235 Chicago IL 60603

GELATT, TIMOTHY ARTHUR, lawyer, educator; b. N.Y.C., Aug. 12, 1955; s. Roland Bernard and Esther Rachel (Frishkoff) G. BA, U. Pa., 1977; JD, Harvard U., 1981. Bar: D.C. 1981. Assoc. Baker & McKenzie, Hong Kong, Beijing, 1981-84, Paul, Weiss, Rifkind, Wharton & Garrison, N.Y.C., 1984—; lectr. law Harvard U., Cambridge, Mass., 1986—, U. Paris, 1986—. Author: Corporate and Individual Taxation in the People's Republic of China, 1986; contbr. articles on law of the People's Republic of China to profl. jours. Mem. Phi Beta Kappa. Club: Harvard (N.Y.C.). Private international, General corporate, Banking. Office: Paul Weiss Rifkind Wharton & Garrison 1285 Ave of the Americas New York NY 10019

GELB, JUDITH ANNE, lawyer; b. N.Y.C., Apr. 5, 1935; d. Joseph and Sarah (Stein) G.; m. Howard S. Vogel, June 30, 1962; 1 child, Michael S. B.A., Bklyn. Coll., 1955; J.D., Columbia U., 1958. Bar: N.Y. 1959, U.S. Dist. Ct. (so. dist. and ea. dist.) N.Y. 1960, U.S. Ct. Appeals (2d cir.) 1960, U.S. Ct. Mil. Appeals 1962. Asst. to editor N.Y. Law Jour., N.Y.C., 1958-59; confidential asst. to U.S. atty. ea. dist. N.Y., Bklyn., 1959-61; assoc. Whitman & Ransom, N.Y.C., 1961-70, ptnr., 1971—. Mem. ABA (individual rights sect.), Fed. Bar Counsel, N.Y. State Bar Assn. (trusts and estates com.), N.Y. State Dist. Attys. Assn., Assn. Bar City N.Y. Clubs: Princeton, Assn. Ex-mem. Squadron A. Estate planning, Probate, Estate taxation. Home: 169 E 69th St New York NY 10021 Office: Whitman & Ransom 200 Park Ave New York NY 10166

GELB, RICHARD MARK, lawyer; b. N.Y.C., June 12, 1947; s. Harold Seymour and Sylvia Mildred (Miller) G.; m. Gail Kleven, July 29, 1973; 1 child, Daniel Kleven. B.A., NYU, 1969; J.D., Boston Coll., 1973. Bar: Mass. 1973, N.Y. 1975, D.C. 1975, U.S. Dist. Ct. (so. and ea. dists.) N.Y. 1975, U.S. Ct. Appeals (2d cir.) 1975, U.S. Dist. Ct. Conn. 1977, U.S. Ct. Appeals (1st cir.) 1978, U.S. Dist. Ct. Mass. 1978, U.S. Supreme Ct. 1980. Assoc. Proskauer, Rose, Goetz & Mendelsohn, N.Y.C., 1975-77; ptnr. Gelb Heidlage & Reece, P.C., Boston, 1983—. Contbr. articles to profl. publs. Trustee North Shore Children's Hosp., Salem, Mass., 1979-84; chmn., bd. dirs. North Shore Human Services, 1984-85. Mem. Boston Bar Assn. (fee disputes com. 1983), Essex County Bar Assn., Mass. Bar Assn. (assoc. editor Mass. Law Rev. 1981), ABA, Assn. Trial Lawyers Am., Mass. Acad. Trial Attys., Pi Sigma Alpha. Democrat. Jewish. Federal civil litigation, State civil litigation, Personal injury. Home: 60 Pine Hill Rd Swampscott MA 01907 Office: Gelb Heidlage & Reece PC 1 Liberty Sq Boston MA 02109

GELBER, DON JEFFREY, lawyer; b. Los Angeles, Mar. 10, 1940; s. Oscar and Betty Sheila (Chernitsky) G.; m. Jessica Jeasun Song, May 15, 1967; children—Victoria, Jonathan, Rebecca, Robert. Student UCLA, 1957-58, Reed Coll., 1958-59; A.B., Stanford U., 1961, J.D., 1963. Bar: Calif. 1964, Hawaii 1964, U.S. Dist. Ct. (cen. and no. dists. Calif.) 1964, U.S. Dist. Ct. Hawaii 1964, U.S. Ct. Appeals (9th cir.) 1964. Assoc. Greenstein, Yamane & Cowan, Honolulu, 1964-67; reporter Penal Law Revision Project, Hawaii Jud. Counsel, Honolulu, 1967-69; assoc. H. William Burgess, Honolulu, 1969-72; ptnr. Burgess & Gelber, Honolulu, 1972-73; prin. Law Offices of Don Jeffrey Gelber, Honolulu, 1974-78; prin., pres. Gelber & Wagner, Honolulu, 1978-83; prin., pres. Gelber & Gelber, Honolulu, 1984—; legal counsel Hawaii State Senate Judiciary Com., 1965; adminstrv. asst. to majority floor leader Hawaii Senate, 1966, legal csl. Edn. Com., 1967, 68; majority counsel Hawaii Ho. of Reps., 1974. Contbr. articles to legal publs. Mem. State Bar Calif., ABA (sect. corp., banking, bus. law), Am. Bankruptcy Inst., Hawaii Bar Assn. (sect. corps. and securities), Am. Bankruptcy Inst., Hawaii Estate Planning Council. Clubs: Pacific, Plaza. (Honolulu). Bankruptcy, Federal civil litigation, Real property. Office: Gelber & Gelber 745 Fort St Suite 1400 Honolulu HI 96813

GELBER, LINDA CECILE, lawyer, bank executive; b. Hackensack, N.J., Oct. 30, 1950; d. Melvin W. and Beverly E. (Gilman) Gelber. B.A., Ind. U., 1972, M.B.A., 1974, J.D., 1978; cert. fin. services counselor, Am. Bankers Assn. National Grad. Trust Sch., 1983. Bar: Ind. 1978, U.S. Dist. Ct. (so. dist.) Ind. 1978, U.S. Supreme Ct. 1983. Program analyst Indiana Legis. Services Agy., Indpls., 1978-80; v.p., trust officer First National Bank, Kokomo, Ind., 1980-85, asst. v.p. Mchts. Nat. Bank, Indianapolis, 1985—; part time instr. Indiana U., Kokomo, 1981-82, Ball State U., Muncie, Ind., 1979-80. Bd. dirs. United Way, Kokomo, 1983-85, div. chmn. fund raising campaign, 1983. Mem. ABA, Am. Inst. Banking (v.p. 1983-85), Estate Planning Council Indpls., Howard County (Ind.) Bar Assn. (sec.-treas. 1981), Indiana State Bar Assn., Indpls. Bar Assn., Cen. Ind. Corp. Fiduciaries Assn. Club: Altrusa (Kokomo). Probate. Office: Merchants Nat Bank & Trust Co 1 Merchant Plaza Indianapolis IN 46255

GELBERG, FREDERICK, lawyer; b. N.Y.C., Sept. 21, 1919; s. Henry Bernard and Sophie (Schenk) G.; m. Terie Isaacs, June 30, 1948; children—Barbara Gelberg Angerman, Steven J., Jonathan D. B.B.S., CCNY, 1939; J.D., Columbia U., 1947; postgrad. U. Paris, 1945-46. Bar: N.Y. 1947, U.S. Dist. Ct. (so. dist.) N.Y. 1949, U.S. Ct. Appeals (2d cir.) 1950. Law clk. to judge U.S. Dist. Ct., 1947-48; assoc. Chadbourne, Wallace, Park & Whiteside, N.Y.C., 1948-51; atty. Am. Law Inst. Fed. Income Tax Project, 1951-52; ptnr. Silverson & Gelberg, N.Y.C., 1952-66, Kaye, Scholer, Fierman, Hays & Handler, N.Y.C., 1966-79, Gelberg & Abrams, N.Y.C., 1979—; lectr. on taxation. Served in U.S. Army, 1943-46. Mem. ABA, N.Y. State Bar Assn., Assn. Bar City N.Y., N.Y. County Bar Assn. Jewish. Club: Old Westbury Golf and Country. Corporate taxation, Estate planning, Estate taxation. Office: Gelberg & Abrams 711 3d Ave New York NY 10017

GELDON, FRED WOLMAN, lawyer; b. N.Y.C., July 18, 1946; s. Earl R. and Ruth Judith (Abrahams) G.; m. Anne Wolman, June 2, 1974; children: Todd Wolman, Elise Wolman. AB magna cum laude, Princeton U., 1968; MA in Physics, U. Calif., Berkeley, 1970; JD magna cum laude, Harvard U., 1973. Bar: Calif. 1973, D.C. 1974, U.S. Dist. Ct. D.C. 1974, U.S. Ct. Appeals (D.C. cir.) 1974, U.S. Supreme Ct. 1978, U.S. Ct. Claims 1981, Md. 1984, U.S. Ct. Appeals (4th cir.) 1984. Law clk. U.S. Dist. Ct. D.C., Washington, 1973-74; from assoc. to ptnr. Leva, Hawes, Symington, Martin, Oppenheimer, Washington, 1974-83; asst. dir. torts br. civil div. U.S. Dept. Justice, Washington, 1983-85; ptnr. Janis, Schuelke & Wechsler, Washington, 1985-87; sole practice Rockville, Md., 1987—. Contbr. articles to profl. jours. Pres. Potomac Springs Civic Assn., Rockville Md., 1983-84. Mem. ABA, Fed. cir. Bar Assn. (vice chmn. govt. contracts appeals com. 1986), Sigma Xi, Phi Beta Kappa. Democrat. Jewish. Avocations: tennis, softball, music, computer programming, stamp collecting. Government contracts and claims, Federal civil litigation, Administrative and regulatory. Home and Office: 5 Golden Crest Ct Rockville MD 20854

GELFAND, MICHAEL JOSEPH, lawyer; b. Chgo., July 14, 1957; s. Lionel John and Shirley (Weinstein) G.; m. Mary C. Arpe. BS, Northwestern U., 1979; JD, U. Fla., 1982. Bar: Fla. 1982, U.S. Dist. Ct. (so. dist.) Fla. 1982, U.S. Ct. Appeals (11th cir.) 1982, U.S. Dist. Ct. (middle dist.) Fla. 1985, U.S. Ct. Appeals (11th cir.) 1983. Assoc. Abramson, Sacant et. al., Miami, Fla., 1982-83; ptnr. Abramson, Ansel, Gelfand, Miami, Fla., 1983; assoc. Becker, Poliakoff, Ft. Land, Fla., 1984-85, West Palm Beach, Fla., 1985—. Mem. Boca Raton builders bd. of Adjustment and Appeals, 1983. Lodge: Kiwanis. Real property, Computer, State civil litigation. Office: 450 Australian Ave S Suite 720 West Palm Beach FL 33401

GELFMAN, MARY HUGHES BOYCE, lawyer; b. Boston, Apr. 3, 1935; d. Joseph Canon and Emily M. (Hughes) Boyce; m. Nelson A. Gelfman, Sept. 6, 1958; children: Celia, Kay, David. BA, Swarthmore Coll., 1957; MA, Columbia U., 1959; JD, U. Conn., 1978. Bar: Conn. 1979, U.S. Dist. Ct. Conn. 1986. Tchr. New Haven High Sch., 1958-60; cons. Conn. State Dept. Edn., Hartford, 1979-84; sole practice Ridgefield, Conn., 1984—; cons. Northeast Regional Resource Ctr., Burlington, Vt. 1984-86. Mem. Ridgefield Bd. Edn., 1969-80, Conn. State Adv. Council Spl. Edn., 1972-77; bd. dirs. Community Kindergarten, Ridgefield, 1965-77. Mem. ABA, Conn. Bar Assn., LWV, AAUW, Am. Arbitration Assn. (arbitrator). Democrat. Administrative and regulatory, Civil rights, Labor. Home and Office: 374 N Salem Rd Ridgefield CT 06877

GELHAUS, ROBERT JOSEPH, lawyer, publisher; b. Missoula, Mont., Oct. 17, 1941; s. Francis Joseph and Bonnie Una (Mundhenk) G. A.B. magna cum laude, Harvard Coll., 1963; LL.B., Stanford U., 1968. Bar: Calif. 1970, U.S. Dist. Ct., U.S. Ct. Appeals 1970. Assoc. firm Howard, Prim, Rice, Nemerovski, Canady & Pollak, San Francisco, 1970-74; sole practice, San Francisco, 1974—; editor in chief Harcourt Brace Jovanovich Legal & Profl. Publs., Inc., 1974-78; gen. ptnr. Flolex Publs., 1973—; pres. Horizon Publs. San Francisco, Inc., 1976—; instr. econs. U. Wash., 1964-65; instr. law Stanford Law Sch., 1968-69; cons. FCC, 1968-69; asst. Calif. Law Revision Commn., 1967-68. Mem. San Francisco Bar Assn., Calif. Bar Assn., ABA, Omicron Delta Epsilon, Order Coif. Club: Harvard of San Francisco. Author: (with James C. Oldham) Summary of Labor Law, 9th edit., 1972. Antitrust, Federal civil litigation, Labor. Home: 1756 Broadway San Francisco CA 94109

GELL, CARL LEDDIN, lawyer; b. San Diego, June 29, 1943; s. Charles F. and Edna (Leddin) G.; m. Jane Jensen, Apr. 20, 1979; children: Brittain, Charles, Christy, Anne. BA, North Tex. State U., 1967; JD, Am. U., 1973. Bar: D.C. 1974, U.S. Supreme Ct. 1977, U.S. Dist. Ct. D.C. 1980, U.S. Ct. Appeals (D.C. cir.) 1980. Trust officer Am. Security Bank, Washington, 1970-74, v.p., gen. counsel, 1974-80; ptnr. Cooter & Gell, Washington, 1980—; adj. prof. law Georgetown U., Washington, 1976-78; instr. Am. Inst. Banking, 1979-83. Chmn. bd. dirs. St. Albans Day Care Ctr., Washington, 1978—; bd. dirs., gen. counsel Nat. Capital Area Council Boy Scouts Am., Washington, 1980—; bd. dirs. Loughran Found., Washington, 1980—. Served to sgt. U.S. Army, 1967-69. Mem. ABA, Fed. Bar Assn., D.C. Bar Assn. Republican. C:ub: Army/Navy (Washington). Banking, General corporate, Bankruptcy. Home: 10001 New London Dr Potomac MD 20854 Office: Cooter & Gell 1333 H St NW Suite 600 Washington DC 20005

GELLER, DIANE JOYCE, lawyer; b. Glen Cove, N.Y., Aug. 6, 1953; d. Isadore and Rose (Herskovitz) Goldstein; m. Joseph H. Geller, July 4, 1973. BA, C.W. Post Coll., 1975; JD, Hofstra U., 1978. Bar: N.Y. 1978, U.S. Dist. Ct. (ea. and so. dists.) N.Y. 1978. V.p. adminstrn. Counsel Synergy Group, Farmingdale, N.Y., 1978-83; gen. counsel, assoc. risk mgr. LRF Risk Mgmt., Great Neck, N.Y., 1984-85; gen. cousel Alpha Surg. Enterprises, Inc., White Plains, N.Y., 1985-86, Am. Med. Ins. Co., Hicksville, N.Y., 1986—; bd. advisors lawyers assistance program Adelphi U. Bd. Advisors, Garden city, N.Y.. Mem. ABA, Nassau County Bar Assn. General corporate, Insurance. Home: 32 Broadfield Pl Glen Cove NY 11542 Office: Am Med Ins Co 35 Broadway Hicksville NY 11801

GELLER, STEVEN ANTHONY, lawyer; b. N.Y.C., Nov. 4, 1958; s. Marvin and Joan Beverly (Winikoff) G. BA, Fla. State U., 1979, JD, 1982. Assoc. Law Office of Joseph S. Geller, Hallandale, Fla., 1982-83; ptnr. Law Offices of Geller & Geller, Hallandale, 1983-86, Law Offices of Geller & Waterman, Hallandale, 1986—. Parliamentarian Fla. Dems., 1983—; nat. v.p. Young Dems. of Am., 1980-82, state pres., 1981-82; chmn. code rev. commn. City of Hallandale, 1985—. Named one of Outstanding Young Men in Am. U.S. Jaycees, 1980. Mem. Assn. Trial Lawyers Am., Broward County Trial Lawyers Assn., Acad. Fla. Trial Lawyers, Broward Forum, South Broward Jewish Fedn. (bd. dirs. attys. and accts. div.), Greater Hollywood Jaycees (pres. 1984-86). Lodges: B'nai B'rith (pres. 1986—), K.P. Personal injury, State civil litigation, Probate. Office: Geller Geller & Waterman 1920 E Hallandale Beach Blvd Suite 600 Hallandale FL 33009

GELLHORN, ERNEST ALBERT EUGENE, lawyer; b. Oak Park, Ill., Mar. 30, 1935; s. Ernst and Hilde Betty (Obermeier) G.; m. Jaquelin Ann Silker, Feb. 1, 1958; children: Thomas Ernest, Ann Lois. B.A. cum laude, U. Minn., 1956, LL.B. magna cum laude, 1962. Bar: Ohio bar 1962, Va. bar 1975, Ariz. bar 1976. With firm Jones, Day, Reavis & Pogue, Cleve. and Washington, 1962-66, 86—; prof. law Duke U. Law Sch., 1966-70, U. Va. Law Sch., 1970-75; dean Coll. Law, Ariz. State U., Tempe, 1975-78, Law Sch., U. Wash., Seattle, 1978-79; T. Munford Boyd prof. U. Va. Law Sch., Charlottesville, 1979-82; dean, Galen J. Roush prof. Case Western Res. U. Sch. Law, Cleve., 1982-86; mng. ptnr. Jones, Day, Reavis & Pogue, Washington, 1986—; sr. counsel Commn. CIA Activities Within U.S., 1975; cons. in field. Author: Antitrust Law and Economics, 3d edit, 1986; co-author: Administrative Law and Process, 2d edit, 1981, The Administrative Process, 3d edit, 1986. Served to lt. USNR, 1956-59. Mem. ABA, Ariz. Bar Assn., Va. Bar Assn., Ohio Bar Assn., D.C. Bar Assn., Phi Beta Kappa, Order of Coif. Administrative and regulatory, Antitrust, Legislative. Home: 1827 23d St NW Washington DC 20008 Office: Jones Day Reavis & Pogue 655 15th St NW Washington DC 20005

GELMAN, JON LEONARD, lawyer; b. Paterson, N.J., Mar. 14, 1946; s. Carl and Gussie (Weiss) G.; m. Nancy R. Sugarman, Oct. 2, 1971; children: Michael A., Jason L. BA, Rutgers U., 1967; JD, John Marshall Law Sch., 1971. Bar: N.J. 1971, U.S. Dist. Ct. N.J. 1971, U.S. Tax Ct. 1973, U.S. Ct. Appeals (D.C. cir.) 1973, U.S. Supreme Ct. 1974, U.S. Ct. Appeals (3d cir.) 1980, N.Y. 1985. Ptnr. Gelman and Gelman, Paterson, 1971-79; sole practice Wayne, N.J., 1979—. Contbg. columnist N.J. Law Jour.; contbr. articles to profl. jours. Trustee United Assn. for Handicapped Citizens, Inc., Paterson, 1981, Inner City Com. for Action, Paterson, Parents for Academically and Artistically Talented Students, Inc., Paterson, 1982. Mem. Assn. Trial Lawyers, Nat. Orgn. Social Security Claimants Rep., Asbestos Litigation Group, N.Y. Acad. Scis., Trial Attys. N.J., D.C. Bar Assn., N.J. Bar Assn. (workers'compensation sect., prepaid legal com., aviation law com.), Passaic County Bar Assn. (workers' compensation sect.), Morris County Bar Assn. Workers' compensation, Personal injury, Environment. Office: PO Box 2008 450 Hamburg Turnpike Wayne NJ 07474

GELSO, CHARLES PATRIC, lawyer; b. Pittston, Pa., Feb. 7, 1948; s. Samuel J. and Florence (Nardone) G.; m. Maryanne Compo, July 12, 1975. BA in English Lit., Boston Coll., 1969; JD, Boston U., 1972. Bar: Pa., U.S. Dist. Ct. (mid. dist.) Pa., U.S. Ct. Appeals (2d, 3d and 5th cirs.), U.S. Supreme Ct. Sole practice Wilkes-Barre, Pa., 1972—; solicitor Exeter (Pa.) borough, 1975—, Edwardsville (Pa.) borough, 1978—. Solicitor Luzerne County Dems. Mem. ABA, Pa. Bar Assn., Am. Trial Lawyers Assn., Luzerne County Bar Assn. (exec. com. 1985—), Pa. Assn. County Controllers (soliciter 1985-86), Luzerne County Controllers Assn. (soliciter). Criminal, Local government, Federal civil litigation. Office: 120 S Franklin St Wilkes Barre PA 18701

GELTZER, ROBERT LAWRENCE, department store executive, lawyer; b. Bronx, N.Y., Jan. 27, 1945; s. Edward and Grace Theresa (DeFeo) G.; m. Elise Anne Lewis, Nov. 11, 1972; 1 child, Joshua Alexander. BA in Biochemistry and Polit. Sci., Queens Coll., N.Y.C., 1965; JD, George Washington U., 1968. Bar: N.Y. 1969, U.S. Dist. Ct. (so. and ea. dists.) N.Y. 1974, U.S. Ct. Appeals (2d cir.) 1974, U.S. Supreme Ct. 1976. Sole practice N.Y.C., 1968-71; assoc. atty. legal and govtl. affairs Allied Stores Corp., N.Y.C., 1971-74; sr. atty. J.C. Penney Co., N.Y.C., 1974-84, northeastern regional counsel, 1984—; dir. credit specialist program Adelphi U., 1976-78; adj. prof. Pace Coll.; speaker state bar assns., Colo., Ill., Miss., N.J., Okla.,

Pa., W.Va. Author articles on fed. and state consumer credit legislation, regulation, litigation and compliance, and class action litigation. Pro bono gen. counsel Nat. Kidney Found. Fellow Am. Bar Found., N.Y. Bar Found.; mem. ABA (ho. of dels. 1980-86, , chair-elect sci. and tech. sect., 1986-87, vice chmn. corp. counsel coms. of various sects., mem. exec. com., lawyers' conf. jud. adminstrn. div., numerous other offices various sects.), N.Y. State Bar Assn. (mem. Action Unit 5 pertaining to regulatory reform 1980-83, ho. of dels. 1981—, chmn. corp. counsel sect. 1981-83, chmn. pub. relations com. 1983-86, chmn. membership com 1982-85, law simplification task force 1985—), Assn. Bar N.Y.C. (profl. jud. ethics com. 1982-83, sci. and law com. 1985—, children and the law com.), New York County Lawyers Assn. (bd. dirs. 1982—, 75th Anniversary steering com. 1982-84, mem. fed. legislation, state legislation, trade regulation, and alcoholism in the profl. coms.), Am. Law Inst., Am. Judicature Soc. (life mem., bd. dirs. 1979-82), Am. Soc. for Polit. and Legal Philosophy, Am. Soc. for Legal History, Nat. Assn. Women Lawyers (co-first male mem.), Am. Jewish Com., George Washington U. Law Sch. Alumni Assn., Phi Epsilon Phi, Phi Delta Phi. Lodge: KP (past chancellor comdr.). Consumer commercial, Legislative. Office: JC Penney Co Inc Legal Dept 1301 Ave of the Americas New York NY 10019

GEMIGNANI, MICHAEL CAESAR, computer scientist, lawyer, clergyman, university dean; b. Balt., Feb. 23, 1938; s. Hugo J. and Dorothy G.; m. Carol A. Federico, June 30, 1962 (dec.); children: Stephen, Susan; m. Nilda B. Keller, May 18, 1985. B.A., U. Rochester, 1962; M.S., U. Notre Dame, 1964, Ph.D., 1965; J.D., Ind. U., 1980. Bar: Ind. 1980, U.S. Dist. Ct. Ind. 1980, Maine 1987, U.S. Dist Ct. Maine 1987. Asst. prof. math. SUNY, Buffalo, 1965-68; asso. prof. Smith Coll., 1968-72; prof., chmn. dept. math. scis. Ind. U.-Purdue U. at Indpls., 1972-81; dean Coll. Scis. and Humanities, Ball State U., Muncie, Ind., 1981-86; dean Coll. Arts and Scis. U. Maine, Orono, 1986—; ordained to ministry Episcopal Ch., 1973; vicar St. Francis Episcopal Ch., Zionsville, Ind., 1974-79; pres. Met. Indpls. Campus Ministry, 1975-76, bd. dirs., 1974-81; mem. adv. bd. Ind. Office Campus Ministry, 1973-86, pres., 1983-85. Author: books including Elementary Topology, 1967, 2d rev. edit., 1972, Introductory Real Analysis, 1970, Law and the Computer, 1981, Computer Law, 1985; composer. Mem. Am. Math. Soc. (chmn. N.E. sect. 1970-71, chmn. Ind. sect. 1975-76), AAAS, ABA, Scribes, Sigma Xi, Kappa Sigma. Research, publs. in math. Computer. Home: 7 Colburn Dr 1 Orono ME 04473 Office: U Maine Stevens Hall 100 Orono ME 04469

GENAUER, MARTIN JAY, lawyer; b. Seattle, Aug. 2, 1949; s. Jack and Ruth (Rosen) G.; m. Leslie Jeanne marcus, Jan. 10, 1982; children: Gabriel, Deena, Stefanie. BS in Econs., U. Pa., 1971, JD, 1974. Bar: Ohio 1974, Fla. 1978. Assoc. Jones Day Reavis Pogue, Cleve., 1974-78, Greenberg, Traurig, Askew, Hoffman, Lipoff, Rosen and Quentel, Miami, Fla., 1978-80; assoc. Paul, Landy, Beiley and Harper, P.A., Miami, 1984, ptnr., 1984—. Mem. ABA, Dade County Bar Assn., Fla. Bar Assn. General corporate, Real property, Municipal bonds. Office: Paul Landy Beiley and Harper PA 200 SE First St Miami FL 33131

GENEVA, LOUIS BRION, lawyer, educator, consultant; b. Wilmington, Del., Feb. 2, 1947; s. Maurice L. and Constance J. (Welsh) G.; m. M. Jayne Hurst, May 31, 1969; children: Scott, Tyler, Keith, Shayne. BA, Miami U., Oxford, Ohio, 1969; JD, Suffolk U., 1973; LLM, NYU, 1974. Bar: Ohio 1973, Conn. 1976. Assoc. Bergman, Horowitz & Reynolds, P.C., New Haven, 1976-78; vis. assoc. prof. law Cleve. State U., 1978-80; assoc. prof. Cleve. Marshall Coll. Law, 1980—; sole practice Cleveland Heights, Ohio, 1978—; lectr. NYU Law Sch., N.Y.C., 1974-76. Mem. ABA (estate and gift tax sect. com. 1978—). Estate planning, Pension, profit-sharing, and employee benefits, Corporate taxation. Office: Cleve Marshall Coll Law 1801 Euclid Cleveland OH 44115

GENOVA, JOSEPH STEVEN, lawyer; b. Red Bank, N.J., Nov. 12, 1952; s. M. Leonard and Margaret (Coons) G.; m. Janet Scott, May 18, 1974 (div. Dec. 1980) ; m. Diane Melisano Genova, Jan. 15, 1983; 1 child, Anthony Robert. BA, Dartmouth Coll., 1974; JD, Yale U., 1977. Bar: N.Y. 1978, U.S. Dist. Ct. (so. and ea. dists.) N.Y. 1978. Assoc. Milbank, Tweed, Hadley & McCloy, N.Y.C., 1977-85, ptnr., 1986—; mem., sec. Community Law Offices Council, N.Y.C., 1980-86; exec. com. Lawyers for Legal Aid, N.Y.C., 1985—; ct. appointed arbitrator U.S. Dist. Ct. (ea. dist.) N.Y., 1986—. Mem. ABA, Assn. of Bar of City of N.Y. (com. on housing and urban devel. 1982-85), N.Y. State Bar Assn. (com. on legal aid 1980—, chmn. subcom. on Pro Bono tng. 1985-86, chmn. 1986—), Fed. Bar Council, Am. Judicature Soc. Roman Catholic. Club: Montauk (Bklyn.). Avocations: fishing, skiing. Federal civil litigation, State civil litigation, Bankruptcy. Office: Milbank Tweed Hadley & McCloy 1 Chase Manhattan Plaza New York NY 10005

GENOVESE, THOMAS L., corporation executive, lawyer; b. 1936; married. B.A., U. Va., 1957; J.D., Fordham U., 1960. Atty., FAA, 1961-66, NBC, 1966; counsel purchasing and subcontracts depts. Grumman Corp., Bethpage, N.Y., 1966-69, counsel staff gen. counsel, 1969-70, gen. counsel, sec. Grumman Data Systems Corp., 1970-73, dep. gen. counsel, 1973-79, gen. counsel, 1979-81, v.p., gen. counsel, 1981—; dir. Paumanock Ins. Co., Ltd.; sec. Grumman Credit Corp., Call Data Systems Devel., Inc. General corporate. Office: Grumman Corp 1111 Stewart Ave Bethpage NY 11714

GENRICH, WILLARD ADOLPH, lawyer, educational administrator; b. Buffalo, Feb. 19, 1915; s. John E. and Emma P. (Luescher) G.; m. Eleanor M. Merrill, Mar. 15, 1941; children—Willa Genrich Long, Ellen Genrich Rusling, Willard A., Jeffrey M. LL.B., U. Buffalo, 1938; L.H.D., Medaille Coll., 1973, SUNY, 1986, Hofstra U.; LL.D., Canisius Coll., 1975, L.I.U., 1979, Hobart Coll., 1981, Fordham U., 1984; Litt.D., N.Y. Inst. Tech., 1979; Dr. Comml. Sci., Niagara U., 1980; Dr. Civil Law, Mercy Coll., 1981; D.Chiropractic Sci., N.Y. Chiropractic Coll., 1983; . Bar: N.Y. 1939. Spl. agt. FBI, 1942-46; sole practice, Amherst, N.Y., 1946—; pres. Genrich Builders, Inc., Buffalo, 1966—; owner, operator 3 hotels; dir. real estate corps. Bd. dirs. N.Y. State Higher Edn. Assistance Corp., 1962-73; bd. Regents, 1973—, vice chancellor bd. regents, 1977-79, chancellor, 1980-85; del N.Y. State Constl. Conv., 1967; past trustee N.E. br. YMCA; ruling elder, trustee First Presbyn. Ch. Recipient Pres.'s award Daemen Coll., 1975; Disting. Citizen's award DeVeaux Sch., 1975; Disting. Alumni award U. Buffalo Law Sch., 1978; Disting. Alumni award Alumni Assn. SUNY-Buffalo, 1980; Disting. Citizen's Achievement award Canisius Coll. Bd. Regents, 1980; Citation of Appreciation, Commn. of Ind. Colls. and Univs. and Western N.Y. Consortium of Higher Edn., 1978; Pres.' award Hilbert Coll., 1983; John Jay award Commn. Ind. Colls. and Univs., 1984; Service award Daemen Coll., 1984, Bernard E. Hughes Recognition award N.Y. State Assn. Health, Phys. Edn. Recreation and Dance, 1986; Disting. Service award N.Y. State 4201 Schs. Assn., 1986. Mem. ABA, N.Y. State Bar Assn., Erie County Bar Assn., Am. Judicature Soc. Club: Rotary (Amhert). Real property, Landlord-tenant, General corporate. Home: 66 Getzville Snyder NY 14226 Office: 4287 Main St Snyder NY 14226

GENS, RICHARD HOWARD, lawyer, consultant; b. Lynn, Mass., Jan. 29, 1929; s. Aaron Leonard and Doris L. (Damsky) G.; m. Helen Diane Pransky, June 10, 1952; children—William, Sara Lee, Julie Ann, James, Cory, Noah. B.A., Ohio State, 1949; J.D. cum laude, Boston U., 1952. Bar: Mass. 1952, U.S. Dist. Ct. Mass. 1953, U.S. Ct. Claims 1953, U.S. Ct. Appeals (1st cir.) 1954, U.S. Ct. Appeals (5th cir.) 1975, U.S. Ct. Appeals (7th cir.) 1980, U.S. Supreme Ct. 1956. Atty., Isadore H.Y. Muchnick, Boston, 1952-54; mem. firm Sheff & Gens, Boston, 1954-58, Richard H. Gens, Boston, 1958-73, Leppo & Gens, Boston, 1973-77, Gens & Gens, Sherborn, Mass., 1978—; dir. Voice, Inc., Bellingham; asst. atty. gen. Commonwealth of Mass., 1958-61. Bd. dirs. of pub. charities Commonwealth of Mass., 1959-61. Republican. Jewish. State civil litigation, Criminal, Health. Home & Office: 54 Whitney St Sherborn MA 01770

GENTILE, JOSEPH F., lawyer, educator; b. San Pedro, Calif., Jan. 15, 1934; s. Ernest B. and Icy Otie (Martin) G.; m. Kathleen McMahon, Aug. 11, 1976; children—Kim Yvonne, Kevin James, Kelly Michele, Kristien Elyse, Kerri Nicole. B.A. cum laude, San Jose State U., 1955; J.D., U. San Fernando Valley, 1966; certificate in Indsl. Relations, U. Calif., Los Angeles, 1959; Teaching credential, Calif. Community Coll., 1972; M.Pub. Adminstrn., U. So. Calif., 1976. Bar: U.S. Supreme Ct. 1972. Mem. indsl. relations staff Kaiser Steel Corp., Fontana Works, 1957-62; labor relations counsel Calif. Trucking Assn., Burlingame, Calif., 1964-68; acting dir. indsl. relations, labor relations counsel McDonnell Douglas Corp., Santa Monica, Calif., 1968-70; sr. partner Nelson, Kirshman, Goldstein, Gentile & Rexon, Los Angeles, 1970-76; individual practice 1976—; Evening instr. bus. econs., indsl. relations U. Calif., 1969—; evening instr. personnel and indsl. relations San Bernardino Valley Coll., 1969-72; evening instr. transp. Mt. San Antonio Coll., 1972-74; lectr. labor law Loyola U., 1973-74; lectr. Grad. Sch. Pub. Adminstrn., U. So. Calif., 1975-80; adj. prof. law Pepperdine U., 1979—; chmn. Employee Relations Commn., Los Angeles County, 1979—; mem. arbitration panel Fed. Mediation and Conciliation Service, Calif. Conciliation Service. Contbr. articles to profl. jours. Served with AUS, 1955-57. Mem. ABA, Calif. Bar Assn., Los Angeles County Bar Assn. (former chairperson exec. com. labor law sect.), Am. Arbitration Assn. (chmn. regional adv. council, arbitration panel, nat. bd. dirs. 1985—), Phi Sigma Alpha, Phi Alpha Delta. Labor, Arbitration, Administrative and regulatory. Office: PO Box 491117 Los Angeles CA 90049-9117

GENTILE, MICHAEL ANTHONY, lawyer; b. Springfield, Mass., June 1, 1956; s. Edward Cyril and Margaret Mary (Cassidy) G. BA, U. Mass., 1978; JD, Western New England Coll., 1981. Bar: Mass. 1981, U.S. Dist. Ct. Mass. 1982. Assoc. Law Office Louis H. Cohen, Springfield, 1982-83; asst. reporter jud. decisions State of Conn., Hartford, 1983—; instr. bus. law Asnuntuck Community Coll., Enfield, Conn., 1985. Mem. ABA, Mass. Bar Assn., Hampden County Bar Assn. Democrat. Roman Catholic. Office of the Reporter of Judicial Decisions. Home: 148 Elm St East Longmeadow MA 01028 Office: Office Reporter Jud Decisions 231 Capitol Ave Hartford CT 06106

GENTRY, ELVIN LEROY, lawyer; b. Granite City, Ill., Sept. 12, 1937; s. Elvin Oliver and Verna Mae (Rider) G.; m. Patricia Lynn Bass, Aug. 14, 1965 (div. Jan. 1976); children—Alan Burton, William Seth; m. Sandra Jean Swan, Sept. 24, 1977. B.A., Ill. Wesleyan U., 1960, Specialist in Spanish, 1965; M.A., Western Res. U., 1962; J.D., U. Colo., 1969. Bar: Colo. 1970, U.S. Dist. Ct. Colo. 1970, Ill. 1970, U.S. Supreme Ct. 1979, U.S. Ct. Appeals (10th cir.) 1983. Instr. Spanish, Colo. Coll., Colorado Springs, 1965-67; dep. dist. atty., Colorado Springs, 1970-71, chief dep. dist. atty., 1971-72, asst. dist. atty., 1972-74; ptnr. Gresham, Stifler, Gentry, Colorado Springs, 1974-82; sole practice Elvin L. Gentry, P.C., Colorado Springs, 1982—; chief spl. prosecutor 11th Jud. Dist., Canon City, Colo., 1973; spl. prosecutor 10th Jud. Dist., Pueblo, 1977-79; part-time instr. Pikes Peak Community Coll., Colorado Springs, 1972-78. Author: A Century of Men, 1966. Contbr. articles to profl. jours. Precinct leader El Paso County, Republican Orgn., 1972; del. State Rep. Conv., Denver, 1972, Rep. County Assembly, El Paso County, 1974, 82. NDEA fellow, 1960-63; Fulbright fellow Universidad Nacional Autonoma de Mex., 1964; recipient Service award Colo. Dist. Attys. Assn., 1974; selected as eponym of Elvin L. Gentry award for criminal justice professionalism Chi Sigma Pi chpt. Lambda Alpha Epsilon, 1986. Mem. Colo. Bar Assn., El Paso County Bar Assn., Assn. Trial Lawyers Am., Colo. Trial Lawyers Assn., Colo. Criminal Def. Bar Assn. (chartered), Nat. Assn. Criminal Def. Lawyers. Republican. Presbyterian. State civil litigation, Criminal, General practice. Home: 3127 Westcliff Dr E Colorado Springs CO 80906 Office: Elvin L Gentry PC 105 E Vermijo Suite 600 Colorado Springs CO 80903

GENTRY, GAVIN MILLER, lawyer; b. N.Y.C., Oct. 5, 1930; s. Curtis Gavin and Grace (Wattenbarger) G.; m. Mary Jane Coleman, Sept. 28, 1963; children—Janie Coleman, Grace Eleanor. B.S., U. Tenn., 1954, J.D., 1954. Bar: Tenn. 1954, U.S. Dist. Ct. (we. dist.) Tenn. 1956, U.S. Supreme Ct. 1978. Trial counsel U.S. Army, 1954-56; with Armstrong, Allen, Prewitt, Gentry, Johnston & Holmes, Memphis, 1956—, sr. ptnr., 1976—; mem. redrafting com. Tenn. Corp. Law; guest lectr. Memphis State U., U. Tenn. Ctr. Health Scis.; dir. corps. Mem. Pres.'s council Southwestern Coll., 1970—; bd. dirs. Girl Scouts U.S.A., 1973-75; pres. Memphis Tennis Assn., 1960-66, Tenn. Tennis Assn., 1960-61; treas. Tenn. br. Maureen Connelly Brinker Tennis Found., 1972-79; pres. Les Passees Rehab. Ctr., 1977, Lausanne Sch., 1975-78; elder Idlewild Presbyn. Ch. Served to 1st lt. AUS, 1954-56. Recipient Faculty prize U. Tenn., 1953, 1st prize will writing U. Tenn., 1954; numerous awards and prizes for tennis, 1947—. Mem. Memphis and Shelby County Bar Assn., Tenn. Bar Assn., ABA, Am. Soc. Hosp. Attys., Tenn. Hosp. Assn., Nat. Health Lawyers Assn., Am. Soc. Law and Medicine. Club: Univ. (Memphis). Health, General corporate, State civil litigation. Office: One Commerce Sq Suite 1900 Memphis TN 38103

GENTRY, HUBERT, JR., lawyer; b. Sonora, Tex., Oct. 3, 1931; s. Hubert and Julia (Killin) G.; m. Patsy Lynn Bullington, Dec. 27, 1953; children: Julia Ruth, Chester Lindsey, Beth Marie, Hubert Michael, Patsy Jean. B.A., Tex. Tech. U., 1952; J.D., So. Meth. U., 1955. Bar: Tex. 1955. Mem. firm Fulbright & Jaworski, Houston, 1955-72; partner Fulbright & Jaworski, 1967-72; exec. v.p., then chief operating officer, pres. Southwest Bancshares, Inc., Houston, 1973-76; vice chmn. Southwest Bancshares, Inc., 1976-77; partner firm Tita, Phillips, Jensen & Gentry, Houston, 1977-78; sr. v.p., gen. counsel Entex, Inc., Houston, 1978—; mem. faculty Southwestern Grad. Sch. Banking So. Meth. U., 1972; chmn. consumer credit law sect. State Bar Tex., 1969-70, chmn. banking laws com. of corp., banking and bus. law sect., 1970-71, mem. counsel, pub. utility law sect., 1980-83, sec. pub. utility law sect., 1983-84, vice chmn. pub. utility law sect., 1984-85, chmn., pub. utility law sect., 1985-86. Mem. ABA, Tex. Bar Assn., Houston Bar Assn., So. Meth. U. Alumni Law Assn. (pres. 1963-64), Tex. Assn. Bank Holding Co. (v.p. 1976, dir. 1976-77), Am. Gas Assn., Southern Gas Assn., Tex. Gas Assn. Methodist. Clubs: River Oaks Country, Coronado. Office: Entex Inc 1600 Smith St Houston TX 77002

GENZ, MARY KEOHAN, lawyer; b. Weymouth, Mass., Nov. 17, 1954; d. Francis and Margaret (Quinn) Keohan; m. Alan H. Ganz, Sept. 7, 1980. BA magna cum laude, Emmanuel Coll., 1976; JD, Suffolk U., 1979. Bar: Mass. 1979, U.S. Dist. Ct. Mass. 1979, N.H. 1981, U.S. Dist. Ct. N.H. 1981. Sole practice Seabrook, N.H., 1981—. Bd. dirs. My Greatest Dream Inc., Seabrook, 1985—. Mem. Mass. Bar Assn., N.H. Bar Assn., Rockingham County Bar Assn., Seacoast Community Women, Seabrook Bus. and Profl. Assn. (pres. 1986—), Phi Delta Phi, Kappa Gamma Pi. Roman Catholic. General practice. Office: 549 Lafayette Rd Seabrook NH 03874

GENZLINGER, DOROTHEA, lawyer; b. Yonkers, N.Y., Oct. 9, 1900; d. Jacob and Katharine (Loetzerich) G. LL.B., NYU, 1926. Bar: N.Y. 1926. Assoc. Wallin, Beckwith & Edie, Yonkers, 1926-48; sole practice, Yonkers, 1948—. Charter mem., past pres. Bus. and Profl. Women, Yonkers, 1931; past pres. Yonkers LWV; sec., dir. Jr. Hostesses, USO, Yonkers, 1942-45. Mem. ABA, N.Y. State Bar Assn., Am. Judicature Soc., Women's Bar Assn. of Westchester County (pres. 1960). Republican. Mem. Reformed Ch. Club: Soroptimist (charter pres.). Probate. Office: 20 S Broadway Yonkers NY 10701

GEOGAN, FRANCIS JOSEPH, II, lawyer; b. Quincy, Mass., July 30, 1954; s. Robert Joseph and Mary Reardon (Donaher) G.; m. Amy Aldrich, Aug. 16, 1980; 1 child, Robert Aldrich. AB, Coll. Holy Cross, 1976; JD, New England Sch. Law, 1980. Bar: Mass. 1980, U.S. Dist. Ct. Mass. 1981. Ptnr. Geogan & Geogan P.C., Rockland, Mass., 1980—; counsel Rockland Savings Bank, 1980—, Rockland Trust Co., 1980—; approved atty. Chgo. Title Ins. Co., Boston, 1980—, Lawyers Title Ins. Co., Boston, 1980—; agent Ticor Title Ins. Co., Boston, 1985—. Trustee Rockland Meml. Librarym 1978-80' counsel Town of Rockland, 1982-85. Mem. ABA, Mass. Bar Assn., Boston Bar Assn., Plymouth County Bar Assn., Mass. Conveyancers Assn. Avocations: running, bicycling, weightlifing. Contracts commercial, Probate, Real property. Office: Geogan & Geogan PC 379 Union St Rockland MA 02370-0313

GEOGHEGAN, PATRICIA, lawyer; b. Bayonne, N.J., Sept. 9, 1947; d. Frank and Rita (Mihok) G. BA, Mich. State U., 1969; MA, Yale U., 1972, JD, 1974; LLM, NYU, 1982. Bar: N.Y. 1975. Assoc. Cravath, Swaine & Moore, N.Y.C., 1974-82, ptnr., 1982—. Mem. ABA, N.Y. State Bar Assn., Assn. of Bar of City of N.Y. Corporate taxation. Office: Cravath Swaine & Moore One Chase Manhattan Plaza New York NY 10005

GEORGALLIS, JOANN, lawyer; b. Sacramento, Aug. 6, 1956; d. Pericles and Katherine Mary (Thompson) G. AB in Rhetoric, U. Calif., Davis, 1978; JD, U. Santa Clara, 1981. Bar: Calif. 1981, U.S. Dist. Ct. (cen. dist.) Calif. 1982, U.S. Dist. Ct. (ea. dist.) Calif. 1983. Assoc. Surr and Hellyer, San Bernardino, Calif., 1981-83, Porter, Scott, Weiberg & Delehart, Sacramento, 1983—. Active Jr. League of Sacramento, 1984—; mem. U. Calif. Davis Pub. Affairs Com., 1985—. Recipient Am. Jurisprudence award for torts, 1979. Mem. Calif. Bar Assn., Sacramento County Bar Assn., Hellenic Law Soc., No. Calif. Assn. Def. Counsel, Am. Hellenic Profl. Soc. Republican. Greek Orthodox. Avocations: floral design, tennis, skiing, jogging, church choir. State civil litigation, Personal injury, Real property. Office: Porter Scott Weiberg Delehant 350 University Ave Suite 200 Sacramento CA 95864

GEORGE, ALEXANDER ANDREW, lawyer; b. Missoula, Mont., Apr. 26, 1938; s. Andrew Miltiadin and Eleni (Efstathiou) G.; m. Penelope Mitchell, Sept. 29, 1968; children—Andrew A., Stephen A. BBA honors, U. Mont., 1960, JD, 1962; postgrad. John Marshall U., 1964-66. Bar: Mont. 1962, U.S. Ct. Mil. Apls. 1964, U.S. Tax Ct. 1970. Sole practice, Missoula, 1966—; mem. adv. com. U. Mont. Tax Inst., 1973-76; lectr. in field. Pres., Missoula Civic Symphony, 1973; nat. dir. Assn. Urban and Community Symphony Orch., 1974. Served to capt JAG U.S. Army, 1962-66. Recipient Jaycee Disting. Service award, 1973. Mem. State Bar Mont. (pres. 1981), Western Mont. Bar Assn. (pres. 1971), Mont. Law Found. (treas. 1986—), Mont. Soc. C.P.A., Phi Delta Phi, Alpha Kappa Psi, Sigma Nu (alumni trustee 1966-71). Greek Orthodox (pres. 1978). Lodges: Rotary (pres. 1972, state chmn. found. 1977, membership com. chmn. 1978), Ahepa (pres. 1967, state gov. 1968). Probate, Corporate taxation, Real property. Home: 4 Greenbrier Ct Missoula MT 59802 Office: 127 E Front St Suite 201 Missoula MT 59802

GEORGE, BARRY BRIAN, lawyer; b. Flint, Mich., Apr. 21, 1945; s. Clark And Charlotte George; m. L. Joanne George, Aug. 18, 1973; children: Jennifer, Brian. BS in Aeronautical Engring., Purdue U., 1967; JD, U. Mich., 1970. Bar: Mich. 1971, U.S. Supreme Ct. 1977. Sole practice Midland, Mich., 1970—. Served to capt. with USAR, 1970-72, Vietnam. Avocations: music, home improvement, karate, soccer. Real property, Contracts commercial, Probate. Office: 414 Townsend Midland MI 48640

GEORGE, CAROLYN BURKE, lawyer; b. Mt. Vernon, N.Y., Dec. 12, 1953; d. Edmund Martin and Phyllis Frances (Curran) Burke; m. Andrew James George, Nov. 28, 1981; children: Daniel Joseph, Lauren Amanda. BA cum laude, Le Moyne Coll., 1975; JD, Syracuse U., 1978. Bar: N.Y. 1979, U.S. Dist. Ct. (no. dist.) N.Y. 1979, U.S. Ct. Appeals (2d cir.) 1983. Staff atty. N.Y. Commn. on Child Welfare, Syracuse and Albany, N.Y., 1978-79; assoc. Pentak, Brown & Tobin, Albany, 1979—. Arbitrator arbitration program Albany County Supreme Ct., 1982—, arbitration program Rensselaer County Supreme Ct., Troy, N.Y., 1983—. Mem. N.Y. State Bar Assn., Albany County Bar Assn. (young lawyers com. 1983-84), Capital Dist. Trial Lawyers Assn., Am. Arbitration Assn. (arbitrator). Democrat. Roman Catholic. Avocations: running, jazzercise, aerobics, gardening, sewing. Personal injury, Real property, State civil litigation. Home: 60 Euclid Ave Albany NY 12203 Office: Pentak Brown & Tobin 111 Pine St Albany NY 12207

GEORGE, DONALD ELIAS, lawyer; b. Akron, Ohio, July 8, 1950; s. George John and Thelma Beatrice (Goforth) G.; m. Christine Kaderle Cirignano, May 1, 1982; children: Michelle, Michael. B.A., U. Akron, 1972, J.D., 1975. Bar: Ohio 1975, U.S. Dist. Ct (no. dist.) Ohio 1975, U.S. Supreme Ct. 1979, U.S. Ct. Appeals (6th cir.) 1985. Sole practice, Akron, 1975—; bankruptcy trustee, U.S. Bankruptcy Ct., Akron, 1975-78; arbitrator Am. Arbitration Assn., Cleve., 1976-79. Author: Israeli Occupation: International Law and Political Realities, 1979. Mem. Akron Regional Devel. Bd., 1984—, guest speaker Sta. WHLO, Steve Fullerton Show, Akron, 1979-80; mem. adv. coms. for judicial candidates, 1979, 86; choir dir. St. George Orthodox Ch., 1969-75. Mem. ABA, Ohio State Bar Assn., Akron Bar Assn., Summit County Humane Soc., Akron Law Library Assn., Democrat. Avocation: piano playing. Bankruptcy, Labor, Personal injury. Office: 572 W Market St Suite 11 Akron OH 44303

GEORGE, DOUG, lawyer; b. East St. Louis, Ill., Apr. 27, 1949; s. Boyd Franklin and Norene Marie (Pennell) G.; m. Pamela Ann Abshier, Feb. 16, 1975. BA, So. Ill. U., 1971; JD, Ariz. State U., 1978. Bar: Colo. 1978, U.S. Dist. Ct. Colo. 1978. Staff atty. Colo. Rural Legal Services, Alamosa, 1978-80, mng. atty., 1981—. Mem. Colo. Bar Assn., San Luis Valley Bar Assn. Avocations: sports, fitness. State civil litigation, Administrative and regulatory, Family and matrimonial. Office: Colo Rural Legal Services 431 3d St Alamosa CO 81101

GEORGE, FREDRIC JOEL, lawyer; b. Huntington, W.Va., July 31, 1949; s. Fred and Salwa Jean (Mickel) G. AB, Marshall U., 1971; JD, U. N.C., 1974. Bar: N.C. 1974, W.Va. 1975, U.S. Dist. Ct. (no. and so. dists.) W.Va., U.S. Ct. Appeals (4th and D.C. cirs.). Staff atty, Atty Gens. Office State of W.Va., Charleston, 1975-77, 1st dep. atty., Atty. Gens. Office, 1977-83; atty. Columbia Gas Transmission Corp., Charleston, 1983—. Mem. ABA, W.Va. Bar Assn., Kanawha County Bar Assn. (pres. 1982-83). FERC practice, Government contracts and claims, Local government.

GEORGE, JOHN MARTIN, JR., lawyer; b. Normal, Ill., Dec. 17, 1947; s. John and Ada George; m. Judy Ann Watts; 1 child, Sarah. AB with high honors, U. Ill., 1970, AM, 1971; PhD, Columbia U., 1976; JD cum laude, Harvard U., 1982. Bar: Mass. 1982, U.S. Dist. Ct. Mass. 1983, Ill. 1984, U.S. Dist. Ct. (no. dist.) Ill. 1984. Assoc. Hill & Barlow, Boston, 1982-84, Sidley & Austin, Chgo., 1984—. Editor Harvard U. Law Rev., 1980-82. Mem. ABA, Ill. Bar Assn., Chgo. Bar Assn., Phi Beta Kappa. Democrat. Federal civil litigation, Securities, Accountants liability. Office: Sidley & Austin One 1st Nat Plaza Chicago IL 60603

GEORGE, JOYCE JACKSON, judge; b. Akron, Ohio, May 4, 1936; d. Ray and Verna (Popadich) Jackson; children: Michael Eliot, Michelle Renè. BA, U. Akron, 1962, JD, 1966; postgrad. Nat. Jud. Coll., Reno, 1976, NYU Sch. Law, 1983; LLM, U. Va., 1986. Bar: Ohio 1966, U.S. Dist. Ct. (no. dist.) Ohio 1966, U.S. Ct. Appeals (6th cir.) 1968, U.S. Supreme Ct. 1968. Tchr. Akron Bd. Edn., 1962-66; asst. dir. law City of Akron, 1966-69, pub. utilities advisor, 1969-70, asst. dir. law, 1970-73; sole practice, Akron, 1973-76; referee Akron Mcpl. Ct., 1975, judge, 1976-83; judge 9th Dist. Ct. Appeals, Akron, 1983—; tchr., lectr. Ohio Jud. Coll., Nat. Jud. Coll. Author: Judicial Opinion Writing Handbook, 1981, 2d edit, 1986; contbr. articles to profl. publs. Recipient Outstanding Woman of Yr. award Akron Bus. and Profl. Women's Club, 1982; Alumni Honor award U. Akron, 1983; named Woman of Yr. in politics and govt. Summit County, Ohio, 1983. Mem. Akron Bar Assn. (lawyers assistance com.), Ohio Bar Assn., Ohio Jud. Conf. and Ohio Jud. Coll. (chair revision project Resource Manual for Judges), Ohio Legal Ctr. Inst., ABA (victims com., criminal justice div.). Judicial administration, Legal education, Jurisprudence. Office: 9th Dist Ct Appeals 161 S High St Akron OH 44308

GEORGE, MAUREEN ROSE, lawyer; b. Atlantic City, NJ, Apr. 11, 1951; d. Fred Christopher and Rose (Kelly) G.; m. Dennis Vaughan, Dec. 29, 1978; 1 child, Kathleen Rose. BA in Polit. Sci., Loyola U., Chgo., 1973; JD, U. Ariz., 1976. Bar: Ariz. 1976, Ill. 1977, U.S. Dist. Ct. Ariz. 1977. Asst. city atty. City of Yuma, Ariz., 1977, dep. atty., 1977-78, city atty., 1978-86; assoc. Bill Stephens & Assocs. P.C., Phoenix, 1986—. Bd. dirs. Casa De Yuma, Inc., 1978-86; bd. edn. St. Francis Parish, Yuma, 1984-86. Mem. Nat. Inst. Mcpl. Law Officers, Ariz. City Atty. Assn. Democrat. Roman Catholic. Avocations: aerobics, reading, backpacking. Local government, Real property, Legislative. Home: 1869 E Tulane Dr Tempe AZ 85283 Office: Bill Stephens & Assocs PC 1112 E Washington Phoenix AZ 85034

GEORGES, PETER JOHN, lawyer; b. Wilmington, Del., Sept. 8, 1940; s. John Peter and Olga Demetrius (Kazitoris) G.; m. Joan Markessini, Jan. 29, 1981. BS in Chemistry, U. Del., 1962; JD, John Marshall Law Sch., 1970; LLM in Patent and Trade Regulations, George Washington U., 1973. Bar: Ill. 1970, U.S. Ct. Appeals (fed. cir.) 1972, D.C. 1973, Del. 1978. Chemist engring. labs Bell & Howell Co., Chgo., 1966; patent agt., atty. UOP Inc., Chgo., 1968-71; Washington counsel UOP Inc., Arlington, Va., 1972-77; ptnr. Kile, Gholz, Bernstein & Georges, Arlington, 1977-78; from assoc. to ptnr. Law Office Sidney W. Russell, Arlington, 1978-83; mng. officer Russell, Georges, & Breneman and predecessor firm Russell, Georges, Breneman,

Hellwege & Yee, Arlington, 1983—; patent coordinator Armour & Co., Chgo., 1967. Served to 1st lt. USMC, 1963-65, Vietnam. Mem. ABA, Ill. Bar Assn., D.C. Bar Assn., Del. Bar Assn., Fed. Cir. Bar Assn., Am. Intellectual Property Law Assn. Trademark and copyright, Patent, Federal civil litigation. Home: 2331 9th St S Arlington VA 22202 Office: Russell Georges Breneman et al 745 S 23d St Suite 304 Arlington VA 22202

GEORGES, RICHARD MARTIN, lawyer, educator; b. St. Louis, Nov. 17, 1947; s. Martin Mahlon Georges and Josephine (Cipolla) Rice. A.B. cum laude, Loyola U., New Orleans, 1969; J.D. cum laude, Stetson Coll. Law, 1972. Bar: 1972, U.S. Dist. Ct. (mid. dist.) Fla. 1973, U.S. Ct. Appeals (11th cir.) 1981, U.S. Supreme Ct. 1982. Ptnr., Kieffer & Georges, St. Petersburg, Fla., 1973-80, Kieffer, Georges & Rahter, St. Petersburg, 1980-85; sole practice St. Petersburg, 1985—; adj. prof. Fla. Inst. Tech., Melbourne, 1977-86, Stetson Coll. Law, 1985—; adj. prof. Eckerd Coll., St. Petersburg, 1986—. Contbg. author: Florida Law of Trusts, 1983. Arbitrator, United Steelworkers Union, Continental Can Co., 1975—; hearing examiner City of St. Petersburg, 1982—; mem. citizen's adv. com. Pinellas County Met. Planning Orgn., 1986—; exec. committeeman Pinellas County Republican Party, Clearwater, Fla., 1981-82. Served to 1st lt. U.S. Army, 1972. Recipient Rafael Steinhardt award Stetson Coll. Law, 1972, Clint Green award, 1972. Mem. ABA, Fla. Bar, St. Petersburg Bar Assn. (chmn. legal check-up course), Pinellas County Trial Lawyers Assn., Fla. Camera Club Council (pres. 1985), Phi Alpha Delta. Roman Catholic. Clubs: Feather Sound Country, Suncoast Camera (v.p. 1982-84; pres. elect 1984) (Clearwater). General corporate, Insurance, Real property. Office: 3656 First Ave N Saint Petersburg FL 33713

GEORGIADES, PETER NICHOLAS, lawyer, educator; b. Pitts., Nov. 17, 1951; s. Alexander Martin and Maria Georgiades. BA, Carnegie-Mellon U., 1974; JD, George Washington U., 1977. Bar: Pa. 1977, U.S. Dist. Ct. (we. dist.) Pa. 1977, U.S. Ct. Appeals (3d cir.) 1977, D.C. 1978, U.S. Dist. Ct. D.C. 1978, U.S. Dist. Ct. Appeals (D.C. cir.) 1978, U.S. Supreme Ct. 1981. Assoc. gen. counsel Action on Smoking and Health, Washington, 1977-78, gen. counsel, 1978-80; sole practice Pitts. and Washington, 1980-81; assoc. Samuel J. Reich & Assocs., Pitts., 1981-83; ptnr. Rothman, Gordon, Foreman & Groudine, Pitts. and Washington, 1983—; instr. law George Washington U., 1978-80; instr. law Carnegie-Mellon U., 1985—; gen. counsel Karpathian Ednl. Trust, Pitts., 1980—. Mem. ABA (chmn. subcom. on cult-related litigation 1984—), Pa. Bar Assn., D.C. Bar Assn., Phi Kappa Phi. Avocations: guitar, motorcycling, building. Civil litigation with cultic groups and orgns., Federal civil litigation, Personal injury. Office: Rothman Gordon Foreman & Groudine 300 Grant Bldg Pittsburgh PA 15219

GERAGHTY, THOMAS F., legal educator; b. 1944. A.B., Harvard U., 1966; J.D., Northwestern U., 1970. Bar: Ill. 1970. Staff atty. Northwestern U. Legal Clinic, Chgo., 1970-73, co-dir., 1973-75, dir., 1976—, assoc. prof. Sch. Law, 1976-79, prof., 1979—, asst. dean, 1977-81, assoc. dean, 1981—; teaching team leader Midwest regional session Nat. Inst. Trial Advocacy, also Midwest regional dir. Bd. dirs. Legal Assistance Found. Chgo., Chgo.-Cook County Criminal Def. Consortium, Chgo. Council of Lawyers. Legal education. Office: Northwestern U Law Sch 357 E Chicago Ave Chicago IL 60611 *

GERARD, STEPHEN STANLEY, lawyer; b. N.Y.C., June 2, 1936; m. Nancy Mercer Keith, Apr. 25, 1969; children: Robert, Lillian, Stephen. BS, NYU, 1958, JD, 1963; cert. in employee relations law, Inst. for Applied Mgmt. and Law, Newport Beach, Calif., 1983. Bar: N.Y. 1964, U.S. Dist. Ct. (so. and ea. dists.) N.Y. 1967, U.S. Ct. Appeals (2d cir.) 1968. Commd. 2d lt. U.S. Army, 1954, advanced through grades to capt. M.I. Corps, 1966, ret., 1974; assoc. Haight, Gardner, Poor & Havens, N.Y.C., 1965-72; counsel Am. Hoechst Corp., Somerville, N.J., 1972-77, asst. sec., sr. counsel, 1977-87, assoc. gen. counsel, 1987—. Patron N.J. Youth Symphony, 1986. Mem. ABA, Am. Corp. Counsel Assn., Am. Counsel Internat. Personnel, N.J. World Trade Council, N.J. Assn. Corp. Counsel, N.Y. Zool. Soc., Smithsonian Inst. Nat. Assocs., Morris Mus. Astron. Soc. Labor, Pension, profit-sharing, and employee benefits, General corporate. Office: Am Hoechst Corp Rt 202-206 N Somerville NJ 08876

GERB, BERNARD, lawyer; b. Gloversville, N.Y., Aug. 20, 1925; s. Joseph and Theresa G.; m. Alice Kirman, Nov. 24, 1957; children—Andrew, Jane, B.E.E., Cornell U., 1950; J.D., Rutgers U., 1955. Bar: N.Y. 1955. Ptnr., Ostrolenk Faber, Gerb, & Soffen, N.Y.C., 1955-86; dir. T. K. Communications, Inc., Metuchin, N.J., Wm. Steinen Mfg. Co., Parsippany, N.J. Mercer County Democratic Committeeman, Princeton, N.J., 1983-86. Served with U.S. Army, 1944-46. Mem. N.Y. Patent Law Assn., N.J. Patent Law Assn., Am. Patent Law Assn., N.Y. State Bar Assn., ABA. Clubs: Princeton Democratic. Patent, Trademark and copyright. Home: 127 Meadowbrook Dr Princeton NJ 08540

GERBER, ALBERT B., lawyer; b. Phila., July 10, 1913; s. Jacob and Jennie (Suffrin) G.; m. Rhona C. Posner, Nov. 22, 1939; children—Jack J., Gail, Lynne. B.S. in Edn., U. Pa., 1934, J.D., 1937, LL.M., 1941; M.A. in Govt., George Washington U., Washington, 1940. Bar: Pa. 1938. Chief opinion unit Dept. Agr., Washington, 1938-42; ptnr. Gerber & Gafand, Phila., 1946-72; adminstrv. dir. 1st Amendment Lawyers Assn., Phila., 1970—; pres. Assn. for Research, Inc., Phila., 1972-84; of counsel Galfand, Berger, et al., Phila., 1984—; cons. United Nat. Ins. Co., Phila., 1972—. Author: Bashful Billionaire, 1967, The Lawyer, 1972, Book of Sex Lists, 1981, Miracles on Park Avenue, 1985; also numerous articles; editor Tax Sense, 1980-83, Internat. Intelligence, 1981-84. Democratic committeeman, Phila., 1950-60, Montgomery County, Pa., 1979-81. Served to sgt. inf. U.S. Army, 1942-45, PTO. Recipient Best Novel award Pa. Assn. Writers, 1980. Mem. ABA, Phila. Bar Assn., Order of Coif. Jewish. Avocations: handball; tennis; volleyball. Office: 1737 Chestnut St Philadelphia PA 19103

GERBER, EDWARD F., lawyer, educator; b. Houston, Oct. 10, 1932; s. Edward F. and Lucille (Beaver) G.; m. Eileen Healy, Sept. 1, 1956; children—Gretchen, Eric, Nils. B.S., Syracuse U., 1957, LL.B., 1960, J.D., 1968. Bar: N.Y. 1960, U.S. Dist. Ct. (no. dist.) N.Y. 1960. Sole practice, Syracuse, N.Y., 1960-64; first asst. dist. atty. Onondaga County, Syracuse, N.Y., 1964-67; spl. prosecutor Onondaga County, 1976; sole practice, Syracuse, 1977—; lectr. Coll. of Law Syracuse U., 1968—; counsel Onondaga County Sheriff, Syracuse Police Benevolent Assn; faculty Criminal Law Services Syracuse U. Trial Practice Sessions. Bd. dirs. Onondaga County Young Republican Club, 1964-66. Served with USN, 1951-54. Fellow Am. Coll. Trial Lawyers; mem. N.Y. State Bar Assn. (lectr.), Upstate Trial Lawyers Assn. (pres. 1978-79), Onondaga County Bar Assn. (dir. 1969-71), Onondaga Bar Found. (pres. 1983), Assn. Trial Lawyers Am. Criminal, Federal civil litigation, State civil litigation. Home: 202 Scottholm Blvd Syracuse NY 13224 Office: 631 University Bldg Syracuse NY 13202

GERBER, JACK, lawyer; b. Uniontown, Pa., July 2, 1940; s. Benjamin and Sara Libby (Schwartzstein) G.; m. Marsha Eve Leff, Apr. 20, 1968 (May 1977). BA in Liberal Arts, U. Tampa, 1962; MA, Auburn U., 1964; ArtsD, Carnegie Mellon U., 1969; JD, Duquesne U., 1975; postgrad., U. Lund, Sweden, 1978—. Bar: Pa. 1975, U.S. Dist. Ct. (we. dist.) Pa. 1975, U.S. Patent Office 1979, N.J. 1982, U.S. Dist. Ct. N.J. 1982. Editor printing trades publs. Graphic Arts Found., Pitts., 1966-68; editor proposals mktg. publs. Rust Engring., Pitts., 1968-71; editor govt. research and devel. proposals mktg. documents Westinghouse Research and Devel., Pitts., 1972-78; adminstr. engring. and constrn. contracts and div. atty. Gen. Electric Environ. Scis., N.Y.C., 1979-81; sole practice Elizabeth, N.J., 1981—. Chmn. Elizabeth Juvenile Conf. Com., 1986—; atty. Vol. Lawyers Project, Essex County, N.J., Union County, N.J.; vis. supr. Family Part Superior Ct. N.J., Union County. Recipient Woodrow Wilson Found. Hon. Mention, 1962. Mem. Essex County Bar Assn., Union County Bar Assn., Assn. Criminal Trial Def. Lawyers N.J., Trial Attys. N.J., N.J. State Bar Assn., Internat. Narcotics Enforcement Officers Assn., Pi Delta Epsilon (pres. 1961-62), Sigma Tau Delta (pres. 1961-62). Club: Triton Rowing and Boat (Newark) (v.p. fin.). Avocations: sculling and crew, cycling. General practice, Trademark and copyright, Construction.

GERBER, JOEL, federal judge; b. Chgo., July 16, 1940; s. Peter H. and Marcia L. (Weber) G.; m. Judith R. Smilgoff, Aug. 18, 1963; children—Jay Lawrence, Jeffrey Mark, Jon Victor. B.S.B.A., Roosevelt U., Chgo., 1962; J.D., DePaul U., Chgo., 1965; LL.M., Boston U., 1968. Bar: Ill. 1965, Ga. 1974, Tenn. 1978. Trial atty. IRS, Boston, 1965-72; staff asst. to regional counsel IRS, Atlanta, 1972-76; dist. counsel IRS, Nashville, 1976-80; dep. chief counsel IRS, Washington, 1980-83, acting chief counsel, 1983-84; judge U.S. Tax Ct., Washington, 1984—; gen. counsel ATF Credit Union, Boston, 1968-70; lectr. Vanderbilt U. Sch. Law, Nashville, 1976-80, U. Miami Sch. Law, 1986—; lectr. U. Miami Grad. Law Sch., 1986-87. Recipient awards U.S. Treasury Dept., 1979, 81, 82. Mem. ABA. Corporate taxation, Estate taxation, Personal income taxation. Office: US Tax Ct 400 2d St NW Washington DC 20217

GERBER, ROBERT EVAN, lawyer; b. N.Y.C., Feb. 12, 1947; s. Milton M. and Miriam (Simon) G. B.S. with high honors, Rutgers U., 1967; J.D. magna cum laude, Columbia U., 1970. Bar: N.Y. 1971, U.S. Dist. Ct. (so. and ea. dists.) N.Y. 1972, U.S. Ct. Appeals (2d cir.) 1973, U.S. Ct. Appeals (9th cir.) 1974, U.S. Ct. Appeals (10th cir.) 1975, U.S. Ct. Appeals (11th cir.) 1983, U.S. Supreme Ct. 1983. Assoc. Fried, Frank, Harris, Shriver & Jacobson, N.Y.C., 1970-71, 72-78, ptnr., 1978—. Served to 1st lt. USAF, 1971-72. James Kent scholar, 1970; Harlan Fiske Stone scholar, 1969. Mem. Assn. Bar City N.Y. (sec. spl. com. on energy 1974-79), ABA, Fed. Bar Council, Tau Beta Pi. Federal civil litigation, State civil litigation. Home: 13 Colt Rd Summit NJ 07901 Office: Fried Frank et al 1 NY Plaza New York NY 10004

GERBERDING, MILES CARSTON, lawyer; b. Decatur, Ind., Oct. 25, 1930; s. Arnold H. and Luella E. (Lapp) G.; m. Ruth H. Hostrup, Aug. 20, 1955; children—Karla M., Greta E. Gerberding Kachmann, Kent E., Brian K. J.D., Ind. U., 1956. Bar: Ind. 1956, Mich. 1984. Ptnr., Nieter & Smith, Ft. Wayne, Ind., 1956-58, Barrett, Barrett & McNagny, Ft. Wayne, 1958-85, Barnes & Thornburg, Ft. Wayne, 1986—; lectr., writer Ind. Continuing Legal Ednl. Forum. Pres., Lutheran Assn. Elem. Edn., 1968-69; mem. Ind. Supreme Ct. Commn. on Mandatory Continuing Legal Edn.; bd. dirs. Big Bros., Ft. Wayne, Jr. Achievement, Ft. Wayne, Ft. Wayne Fine Arts Found.; pres. Concordia Ednl. Found., 1970; chmn. bd. visitors Ind. U. Sch. Law, Bloomington, 1984-85. Served with USMC, 1950-52. Decorated UN medal; recipient Christus Magister award, Lutheran Edn. Assn., 1971. Fellow Am. Bar Found., Am. Coll. Probate Counsel, Am. Coll. Tax Counsel; mem. ABA (rep. Nat. Conf. Lawyers and CPA's 1980-86, nominating com., ho. dels. credentials com., Ind. del. 1985—), Ind. Bar Assn. (pres. 1979-80; del. ABA 1981-85), Allen County Bar Assn. (dir.), Am. Judicature Soc., Ind. Continuing Legal Edn. Forum (pres. 1978-79), Ind. Bar Found. (dir.), Nat. Conf. Bar Pres. (exec. council 1983-86). Republican. Lutheran. Clubs: Ft. Wayne Country, Summit (Ft. Wayne); Columbia (Indpls.). Contbr. articles to profl. jours. Probate, General corporate, Corporate taxation. Home: 3908 Spanish Trail Fort Wayne IN 46815 Office: One Summit Sq Fort Wayne IN 46802

GERDE, CARLYLE NOYES (CY), lawyer; b. Long Beach, Calif., Oct. 22, 1946; m. Priscilla A. Murphy, July 4, 1976. BA in Am. Studies, Purdue U., 1967; JD, Ind. U., 1970. Bar: Ind. 1971, U.S. Supreme Ct. 1976, U.S. Tax Ct. 1980. Ptnr. Hanna & Gerde, Lafayette, Ind., 1972-86; registered lobbyist Ind. Twp. Assn., 1975—; spl. counsel Nat. Assn. Towns and Twps., Washington, 1976—; adj. prof. indsl. engring. Purdue U., 1972; participant White House Conf. Rural Policy, 1978, White House Conf. on Block Grants, 1980, White House Conf. on Liability Ins., 1986; mem. Ind. Gen. Assembly Study Commn. Bd. of govs. Tippecanoe County Hist. Assn., Lafayette, 1976—, Ams. for Nuclear Energy, Washington, 1986; pres. Battle Ground (Ind.) Hist. Corp., 1986; del. State of Ind. GOP Conventions. Mem. Assn. Trial Lawyers Am., Ind. State Bar Assn., Tippecanoe County Bar Assn., Nat. Assn. Town and Twp. Attys. (co-founder, v.p. 1985—). Clubs: Lafayette Country, Skyline, Columbia (Indpls.). Local government, Estate planning, State civil litigation. Office: Hanna & Gerde PO Box 1098 Lafayette IN 47902

GERDES, DAVID ALAN, lawyer; b. Aberdeen, S.D., Aug. 10, 1942; s. Cyril Frederick and Lorraine Mary (Boyle) G.; m. Karen Ann Hassinger, Aug. 3, 1968; children—Amy Renee, James David. B.S., No. State Coll., Aberdeen, 1965; J.D. cum laude, U. S.D., 1968. Bar: S.D. 1968, U.S. Dist. Ct. S.D., 1968, U.S. Ct. Appeals (8th cir.) 1973, U.S. Supreme Ct. 1973. Assoc., Martens, Goldsmith, May, Porter & Adam, Pierre, S.D., 1968-73; ptnr. successor firm May, Adam, Gerdes & Thompson, Pierre, 1973—; chmn. disciplinary bd. S.D. Bar, 1980-81, mem. fed. practice com. U.S. Dist. Ct., S.D., 1986—; bd. dirs. U.S.D. Law Sch. Found., 1973-84, pres., 1979-84. Mng. editor U. S.D. Law Rev., 1967-68. Chmn. Hughes County Republican Central Com., 1979-81; del. Rep. State Conv., 1980, 82, 84, 86; state cen. committeeman, 1985—. Served to lt. Signal Corps, AUS, 1965-68. Mem. ABA, Internat. Assn. Def. Counsel, Assn. Ins. Attys., Am. Judicature Soc., Am. Bd. Trial Advocates, Pierre Area C. of C. (pres. 1980-81), Lawyer-Pilots Bar Assn., Def. Research Inst., Am. Soc. Med. Assn. Counsel. Republican. Methodist. Clubs: Pierre Kiwanis, Pierre Elks. Author: Physician's Guide to South Dakota Law, 1982. Insurance, Federal civil litigation, Health. Office: 503 S Pierre St PO Box 160 Pierre SD 57501

GERDY, HARRY, lawyer; b. Chgo., Nov. 19, 1935; s. Abraham and Frances (Koerner) G. B.S. in Commerce, Roosevelt U., 1957; J.D., DePaul U., 1966. Bar: Ill. 1966, U.S. Dist. Ct. (no. dist.) Ill. 1967. Spl. agt. Criminal Investigation div. IRS, Chgo., 1961-67; atty. Law Offices of Merwin Auslander, Chgo., 1967-69; chief counsel Ill. Dept. Gen. Services, Chgo., 1969-73; pvt. practice law, Chgo., 1973-75; regional counsel U.S. Gen. Services Adminstrn., Chgo., 1975—. Mem. bus. adv. council Jones Comml. High Sch., Chgo., 1976-79; adv. council Nat. Assn. State Purchasing Ofcls., Washington, 1974. Mem. ABA, Ill. Bar Assn., Fed. Bar Assn. (dir. 1976-79), Chgo. Bar Assn. Government contracts and claims, Real property, Labor. Home: 2318 N Lakewood Ave Chicago IL 60614 Office: Regional Counsel GSA 230 S Dearborn St Chicago IL 60604

GERE, ELIZABETH SARAH, lawyer; b. Rochester, N.Y., Sept. 14, 1947; d. David Becker and Elizabeth (White) G.; m. Glenn V. Whitaker, Jan. 24, 1970. BA, Denison U., 1969; postgrad., Syracuse U., 1970; JD, George Washington U., 1972. Bar: Md. 1973, D.C. 1973, Ohio 1980. Atty. U.S. Dept. Justice, Washington, 1975-80; asst. U.S. atty. U.S. Dept. Justice, Cin., 1980-86; sr. trial counsel civil div. U.S. Dept. Justice, Washington, 1986—. Contbg. author Proving Federal Crimes, 1982. Sec. Cin. Council on Epilepsy, 1984-85. Home: 2737 Devonshire Pl NW Washington DC 20008 Office: US Dept Justice Fed Programs Branch Civil Div Washington DC 20530

GEREK, WILLIAM MICHAEL, lawyer; b. Bay Shore, N.Y., Mar. 2, 1950. AB, Dartmouth Coll., 1972; JD, U. Mich., 1975; LLM in Taxation, DePaul U., 1982. Bar: Minn. 1975, Ill. 1976. Assoc. Nisen, Elliott & Meier, Chgo., 1975-79, Greenberger & Kaufmann, Chgo., 1979-82; ptnr. Greenberger & Kaufman, Chgo., 1982-86, Katten, Muchin, Zavis, Pearl, Greenberger & Galler, Chgo., 1986—. Served to lt. USNR, 1974-76. Mem. ABA, Chgo. Bar Assn., Phi Beta Kappa. Avocations: theatre, athletics. Pension, profit-sharing, and employee benefits, Probate, Estate planning. Office: Katten Muchin Zavis et al 525 W Monroe St Suite 1600 Chicago IL 60606

GERGEL, RICHARD MARK, lawyer; b. Columbia, S.C., Aug. 14, 1954; s. Melvin and Meri (Friedman) G.; m. Belinda Bundy Friedman, May 19, 1979; children: Robert Richard, Joseph Friedman. Student, Oxford U., 1974; BA summa cum laude, Duke U., 1975, JD, 1979. Bar: S.C. 1979, U.S. Dist. Ct. S.C. 1979, U.S. Ct. Appeals (4th cir.) 1979. Assoc. Medlock & Davis, Columbia, 1979-80; ptnr. Medlock, Davis & Gergel, Columbia, 1981-82, Medlock & Gergel, Columbia, 1982-84, Gergel & Burnette, Columbia, 1984—; adj. prof. Columbia Coll., 1981. Mem. Bd. dirs. Tree of Life Synagogue, Columbia, 1985—. Mem. S.C. Bar Assn., S.C. Trial Lawyers Assn., Nat. Assn. of Tchr. Attys.. Democrat. Jewish. Personal injury, Federal civil litigation, Labor. Home: 719 Springlake Rd Columbia SC 29201 Office: Gergel Burnette & Nickles 1711 Pickens St Columbia SC 29201

GERHARDT, RICHARD LEE, lawyer; b. Circleville, Ohio, Nov. 25, 1941; s. George Edward and Dorothy A. (Riegel) G.; m. Marie A. Baldwin, June 28, 1964; children—Kara, Richard Lee, II. B.A., Ohio No. U., 1963; J.D., Georgetown U., 1966. Bar: Ohio 1966, U.S. Dist. (so. dist.) Ohio 1969. Mayor, Circleville, 1968-72; pros. atty. Pickaway County, Circleville, 1972-76; sole practice law, Circleville, 1976—; spl. counsel Office Atty. Gen., State of Ohio, 1972—. Asst. contbg. editor: Ohio Prosecutor's Handbook, 1975. Mem. staff Sen. John Glenn Campaign, 1970-74, 80, 86, Pres. Carter Campaign, 1978, 80, v.p. Mondale Campaign, 1980; precinct committeeman Democratic Party, 1968-72, 80, 83, 84; campaign chmn. United Way Pickaway County, 1981. Recipient Am. Jurisprudence award Georgetown U. Law Ctr., 1968. Mem. Ohio Bar Assn., Pickaway County Bar Assn. Lodges: Masons, Shriners. General practice. Home: 527 Willow Ln Circleville OH 43113 Office: 143 W Franklin St Circleville OH 43113

GERHART, EUGENE CLIFTON, lawyer; b. Bklyn., Apr. 7, 1912; s. Herman Eugene and Mary Elizabeth (Hamilton) G.; m. Mary Richardson Schreiber, Mar. 30, 1939; children: Catherine Gerhart Landon, Virginia Gerhart Mason. A.B., Princeton U., 1934; LL.B., Harvard U., 1937. Bar: N.J. 1938, N.Y. 1945. Practiced in Newark, 1938-43, Binghamton, N.Y., 1946—; sr. partner firm Coughlin & Gerhart, Binghamton; sec. to Judge Manley O. Hudson, Secretariat League of Nations, Geneva, 1934; lectr. bus. law U. Newark, 1942-43, Triple Cities Coll., 1946-48, Harpur Coll., Endicott, N.Y., 1953-55; lectr. indsl. and labor relations Cornell U., Ithaca, N.Y., 1946; dir., gen. counsel Columbian Mut. Life Ins. Co., 1949-83, acting pres., 1969-70, chmn. bd., 1970-82; dir. McIntosh Lab., Inc., Stickley Corp.; mem. nat. panel Am. Arbitration Assn., N.Y. State Mediation Bd. Arbitration Panel.; Mem. council SUNY, Cortland, 1967-77, chmn., 1971-77; mem. Select Task Force on Ct. Reorgn. N.Y. State Senate; mem. jud. nominating com. 3d Jud. Dept., State of N.Y.; mem. N.Y. Unified Ct. System Judicial Records Disposition and Archives Devel. Com. Author: American Liberty and Natural Law, America's Advocate: Robert H. Jackson, Robert H. Jackson: Lawyer's Judge, Quote It! Memorable Legal Quotations, Arthur T. Vanderbilt: The Compleat Counsellor; editor: The Lawyer's Treasury; spl. contbg. author: Law Office Econs. and Mgmt, 1962—; mem. editorial bd.: Quarterly Report of Conf. on Personal Fin. Law, 1965—; contbr. articles to legal, other publs. Chmn. Harpur forum SUNY, Binghamton, 1983-84. Served as lt. USNR, 1943-46. Fellow Am. Bar Found., Am. Coll. Probate Counsel; mem. Assn. Bar City N.Y., N.Y. State Bar Assn., Am. Law Inst., ABA (editor Jour. 1946-67, Ross Essay award 1946), N.Y. State Bar Assn. (editor in chief jour. 1961—), Broome County Bar Assn. (pres. 1961-62), Selden Soc., Internat. Assn. Ins. Counsel, Assn. Life Ins. Counsel, Am. Judicature Soc., Broome County Princeton Alumni Assn., Harvard Law Sch. Assn. Upstate N.Y. (pres. 1955-57), Scribes (pres., dir. 1966-67), St. Andrew's Soc. Republican. Clubs: Rotary (pres. 1969-70), Cosmos, Oteyokwa Lake (pres. 1971-73), Nassau, Harvard of N.Y., Princeton of N.Y. General corporate, Estate planning, Insurance. Home: 34 West End Ave Binghamton NY 13905 Office: One Marine Midland Plaza Binghamton NY 13901

GERHART, PETER MILTON, legal educator; b. Milw., July 4, 1945; s. Howard Leon and Ann (Baker) G.; m. Virginia Ann Herold, Feb. 9, 1969 (div. Oct. 1980); 1 child, Matthew; m. Ann Tarbutton, Apr. 9, 1983; 1 child, Mary Elizabeth. BA, Northwestern U., 1967; JD, Columbia U., 1971. Bar: N.Y. 1971, U.S. Dist. Ct. (so. dist.) N.Y. 1973. Assoc. Weil, Gotshal & Manges, N.Y.C., 1971-75; prof. law Ohio State U., Columbus, 1975—, assoc. dean, 1983-86; dean Case Western Res. U., Cleve., 1986—; cons. Pres.'s Commn. Antitrust, Washington, 1978-79, Adminstrv. Conf., Washington, 1976-77. Contbr. articles to profl. jours. Mem. ABA (cons. com. to study FTC 1969). Democrat. Presbyterian. Avocations: piano, jogging. Antitrust, Trademark and copyright, Legal education. Home: 16713 Fernway Rd Shaker Heights OH 44120 Office: Case Western Res U Sch Law 11075 East Blvd Cleveland OH 44106

GERJUOY, EDWARD, physicist, lawyer; b. Bklyn., May 19, 1918; s. Abraham and Clara (Hirsch) G.; m. Clark Jacqueline Reid, Aug. 26, 1940; children: Neil, David Leif. B.S. cum laude, CCNY, 1937; M.A., U. Calif., Berkeley, 1940, Ph.D., 1942; J.D. magna cum laude, U. Pitts., 1977. Bar: Calif. 1977, Pa. 1978. Asso. dir. sonar analysis group Div. War Research, Columbia, 1942-46; mem. faculty U. So. Calif., Los Angeles, 1946-51; vis. asso. prof. N.Y. U., 1951-52; mem. faculty U. Pitts., 1952-58, 64-82, prof. physics, 1964-82, prof. emeritus, 1982—; mem. Pa. Environ. Hearing Bd., 1982-86, cons. hearing examiner, 1987—; mem. research staff Gen. Atomic div. Gen. Dynamics Corp., San Diego, 1958-62; dir. plasma and space applied physics RCA Labs., Princeton, N.J., 1962-64; cons. Westinghouse Research Labs., 1952-58; mem. adv. com. health physics div. Oak Ridge Nat. Labs., 1967-71, chmn. com., 1971-74; asso. firm Tucker Arensberg Very & Ferguson, Pitts., 1978-80; vis. fellow Joint Inst. Lab. Physics, U. Colo., Boulder, 1970; cons. EPA, 1977-81; hearing examiner Pa. Environ. Hearing Bd., 1980-81; vis. scholar Stanford Math. Dept., 1987. Author: (with A. Yaspan) Reverberation, in series The Physics of Sound in the Sea, 1968; Editor: Physics Text Series, 1960-62, Jour. Comments on Atomic and Molecular Physics, 1971-74, Jurimetrics Jour. of Law Sci. and Tech, 1980—; Contbr. chpts. and numerous articles to tech. and legal lit. Bd. dirs. Pitts. ACLU, 1975-80. Fellow Am. Phys. Soc. (mem. panel on public affairs 1976-79, chmn. 1981), AAAS, Inst. Physics, Phys. Soc. (Eng.); mem. Am. Bar Assn. (chmn. phys. scis. com., sect. sci. and tech. 1976-77, mem. council sect. sci. and tech. 1977-80, 84-86), AAUP, Nat. Conf. Lawyers and Scientists, Phi Beta Kappa, Sigma Xi, Order Coif. Environment, Administrative and regulatory, Nuclear power. Home: 400 Richland Ln Pittsburgh PA 15208 Office: U Pitts 100 Allen Hall Pittsburgh PA 15260

GERLACH, FRANKLIN THEODORE, lawyer; b. Portsmouth, Ohio, Apr. 11, 1935; s. Albert T. and Nora Alice (Hayes), G.; m. Cynthia Ann Koehler, Aug. 1, 1958; children—Valarie, Philipp. B.B.A., U. Cin., 1958; M.P.A., Syracuse U., 1959; J.D., U. Cin., 1961. Bar: Ohio 1961, U.S. Dist. Ct. (so. dist.) Ohio 1969, U.S. Supreme Ct. 1971. Dir. Purchasing, Planning and Renewal, City of Portsmouth, 1961-62; city mgr., 1962-66; asst. dir. Ohio U., Portsmouth, 1966-68; sole practice, Portsmouth, 1968—; solicitor Village New Boston, Ohio, 1968-70; trustee Ohio Acad. Trial Lawyers, Columbus, Ohio, 1984-85. Recipient Outstanding Young Man of Ohio award (1 of 5) Portsmouth Jaycees, 1968, Ohio Jaycees, 1969. Mem. Portsmouth Bar and Law Library Assn. (pres. 1986), Ohio Acad. Trial Lawyers. Democrat. Lodges: Rotary. Avocation: antiques. Personal injury, Family and matrimonial, Workers' compensation. Home: 1221 20th St Portsmouth OH 45662 Office: 1030 Kinneys Ln Portsmouth OH 45662

GERLACH, G. DONALD, lawyer; b. Toledo, July 13, 1933; s. Werner George and Marian (Peiter) G.; m. Betty Lou Smith, Dec. 19, 1959 (dec.); children: Lisa A., Gregory D., Jeffrey S.; m. Diane Bonfigli, July 30, 1983; stepchildren: Kevin, Michael Chase. B.A., Princeton U., 1955; LL.B., Harvard U., 1960. Bar: Pa. 1961. Assoc. firm Reed Smith Shaw & McClay, Pitts., 1960-66; ptnr. Reed Smith Shaw & McClay, 1967—, mng. ptnr., 1983—. Trustee Shadyside Hosp., 1983—; v.p. United Way of Allegheny County, 1985—. Served to capt. U.S. Army, 1955-60. Fellow Am. Coll. Probate Counsel; mem. ABA (real property, probate and trust sect.), Pa. Bar Assn. (chmn. real property, probate and trust sect. 1977-78). Republican. Episcopalian. Clubs: Duquesne (bd. dirs. 1986—), Harvard, Yale, Princeton; Fox Chapel Golf (Pitts.), Teutonia Mannerchor; Dunkirk Yacht (N.Y.C.), Nassau Club (Princeton, N.J.). Office: Reed Smith Shaw & McClay James H Reed Bldg 435 6th Ave PO Box 2409 Pittsburgh PA 19530

GERLIN, WILLIAM LANCE, lawyer; b. Columbus, Ohio, Jan. 25, 1945; s. Jack Alfred and Jane Graham (Boyle) G.; m. Pamela Jean Gates, Sept. 21, 1974; children—William Sean, Matthew Graham. B.S., U. Fla., 1968, J.D., 1973. Bar: Fla. 1973, U.S. Supreme Ct. 1978, U.S. Dist. Ct. (so. dist.) Fla. 1974, U.S. Tax Ct. 1977, U.S. Ct. Appeals (5th and 11th cirs.). Sr. ptnr., dir. Stinson, Lyons & Schuette, Miami, Fla., 1973—; lectr. Acad. Fla. Trial Lawyers, Munich, Germany, Kitzbuehl, Germany, 1982. Served to capt. U.S. Army, 1968-70. Mem. ABA, Dade County Bar Assn. Republican. Presbyterian. Clubs: University (Miami); Riviera Country (Coral Gables, Fla.); Ocean Reef (North Key Largo); Snowmass (Colo.). State civil litigation, Federal civil litigation, Bankruptcy. Home: 6490 SW 100th St Miami FL 33156 Office: Stinson Lyons & Schuette 1401 Brickell Ave Miami FL 33131

GERLITS, FRANCIS JOSEPH, lawyer; b. Chgo., Mar. 29, 1931; s. John T. and May (Cameron) G.; m. Suzanne Long, June 20, 1953; children: Kathleen, Karen, Mary Cameron, Francis Jr. Ph.B., U. Notre Dame, 1953; J.D., U. Chgo., 1958. Bar: Ill. 1958. Ptnr. Kirkland & Ellis, Chgo., 1964—; gen. counsel Internat. Harvester Co. (now Navistar Internat. Corp.), Chgo.,

1983—. Mem. ABA, Order of Coif. Clubs: Tavern (Chgo.), Chicago (Chgo.). Office: Kirkland & Ellis 200 E Randolph Dr Chicago IL 60601

GERLT, WAYNE CHRISTOPHER, lawyer, consultant; b. Hartford, Conn., Mar. 7, 1948; s. Warren Russell and Marie Theresa (Yacconiello) G.; m. Elaine Della Bernarda, Feb. 27, 1970; children—Tabetha Elaine, Tiffany Elaine, Christopher Wayne. B.A., U. Conn., 1970; J.D., Capital U., 1975. Bar: Ohio 1975, Conn. 1976, U.S. Dist. Ct. Conn. 1976, U.S. Supreme Ct. 1979. Asst. chief legal services Ohio Dept. Health, Columbus, 1972-75; assoc. Gitlitz, Ronai & Berchem, Milford, Conn., 1975-76; sr. ptnr. Gerlt & Smith, South Windsor, Conn., 1983-84; sole practice, South Windsor, 1976-83, 84—; adj. prof. law Quinnipiac Coll., Hamden, Conn., 1975-76; town atty. Town of South Windsor, 1981-83. Sec. Pub. Health Council, Columbus, 1974-76; coach Sr. League, 1977-78, Girl's Softball, 1980-82, boy's basketball league, 1986—; mem. South Windsor Democratic Town Com., 1976—. Mem. ABA, Conn. Bar Assn., Conn. Assn. Mcpl. Attys. (bd. dirs., treas. 1981-84), Order of Curia. Roman Catholic. General practice, Real property, Family and matrimonial. Home: 970 Foster St South Windsor CT 06074 Office: 435 Buckland Rd PO Box 559 South Windsor CT 06074

GERMAN, EDWARD CECIL, lawyer; b. Phila., Dec. 28, 1922; s. Samuel Edward and Reba (Trimble) G.; m. Jane H., Sept. 2, 1950; 1 child, Jeffrey Neal. JD, Temple U., 1950. Bar: Pa. 1951. assoc. LaBrum & Doak, Phila., 1953-80; ptnr. German, Gallagher & Murtagh, Phila., 1980—; cons., lectr. to law schools including Harvard U., U. Pa., Syracuse U., others; bd. dirs., mem. products liability, def. research coms. Def. Research Inst., Def. Research Regional Library Inst.; instr. Practicing Law Inst. Contbr. chpts. to books, articles to profl. jours. Dist. dir. United Fund campaign, 1960; solicitor-counsel Civic Assns. Delaware County, 1955-60; sec. Haven Beach Assn., 1962-63, v.p., 1963-64; trustee Pop Warner's Little Scholars, 1968—; sec., treas. Henryville Conservation Club. Served with USAAF, 1942-46, with USAF, 1950-51. Mem. ABA (chmn. trial techniques com. 1969, mem. profl. and officers and dirs. liability law com. ins. sect. 1974—, pvt. antitrust litigation com. litigation sect. 1974—, subcom. miscellaneous malpractice re accts., bankers, etc. 1976—), Pa. Bar Assn (com. unauthorized practice 1976—), Phila. Bar Assn. (mem. Pa. rules of civil procedure com. 1963-71, unauthorized practice law com. 1965—, common pleas ct. com. 1964-71, com. antitrust laws corp. sect., mem. Federal bench-bar conf.), Am. Law Firm Assn. (chmn. bd. 1985—), Fedn. Ins. Counsel (bd. govs. 1960-62, v.p. 1962-63, sec.-treas. 1963-65, exec. v.p. 1965-66, pres. 1966-67, chmn. bd. 1967-68), Maritime Law Assn., U.S. Am. Legion, 40 and 8, Internat. Assn. Ins. Counsel (def. research com., profl. liability and malpractice com.), Internat. Assn. Humble Humbugs, Pa. C. of C., Phila. Def. Counsel Assn., Scribes, Phi Delta Phi. Lodges: Masons, Shriners. Clubs: Union League, Down Town, Maxwell Meml. Football (Phila.); Beach Haven (N.J.) Yach; Little Egg Harbor Yacht; Seaview Country (Absecon, N.J.); Little Mill Country; Belleplain Farms Shooting Preserve; India House. Federal civil litigation, State civil litigation, Securities. Home: 129 The Mews Haddonfield NJ 08033 Office: Suite 3100 1818 Market St Philadelphia PA 19103

GERMANN, DOUGLAS DEAN, SR., lawyer, accountant; b. South Bend, Ind., Oct. 23, 1946; s. Harold F. and LaVerne (Kepschull) G.; m. Linda Jo Schlundt, Dec. 21, 1968; children: Douglas Jr., Michael J. BSBA, Valparaiso U., 1969, JD, 1973. Bar: Ind. 1973, U.S. Dist. Ct. (no. and so. dists.) Ind. 1973, Mich. 1974, U.S. Tax Ct. 1974, U.S. Dist. Ct. (we. dist.) Mich. 1976. Tax atty. Clark Equipment Co., Buchanan, Mich., 1973-75; sole practice Manistique, Mich., 1975-77, Mishawaka, Ind., 1980—; assoc. Bingham, Loughlin, Means & Mick, Mishawaka, 1977-80; pres. St. Joseph County Estate Planning Council, South Bend, 1980-81. Bd. dirs. St. Peter Luth. Ch., Inc., Mishawaka, 1979—, pres. 1980-85. Mem. ABA, Mich. Bar Assn., Ind. Bar Assn., St. Joseph County Bar Assn., Am. Inst. CPA's, Ind. CPA Soc. Club: Toastmasters (South Bend). Avocation: fishing. Probate, General corporate, Personal income taxation. Office: 415 Lincoln Way W Mishawaka IN 46544

GERMANN, J. GARY, lawyer; b. Ventura, Calif., Dec. 13, 1946; s. Otto A. and Frances W. (Crawford) G.; m. Virginia Ann Vermeulen, May 10, 1975; 1 child, Vanessa Charlene. B.A. magna cum laude, Calif. State U.-Fresno, 1968; J.D., U. San Francisco, 1973. Bar: Calif. 1973, U.S. Dist. Ct. (no. dist.) Calif. 1973, U.S. Ct. Appeals (9th cir.) 1977, U.S. Dist. Ct. (cen. dist.) Calif. 1978, U.S. Dist Ct. (so. dist.) Calif. 1984. Assoc., Barfield, Barfield, Dryden & Ruane, San Francisco, 1974-76, Hunt, Liljestrom & Wentworth, Santa Ana, Calif., 1976-78; sole practice, Newport Beach, Calif., 1978-82; ptnr. Germann & Welputt, Irvine, Calif., 1982—. Chmn. Woodbridge Homeowners Assn. Legal and Fin. Com., Irvine, 1977. Mem. Calif. Young Lawyers Assn. (bd. dirs. 1978-81), Orange County Young Lawyers Assn. (bd. dirs. 1979-81), Orange County Bar Assn., Profl. Ski Instrs. Am., Calif Trial Lawyers Assn., Pi Gamma Mu. Republican. Roman Catholic. State civil litigation, Personal injury, Consumer commercial. Office: Germann & Welputt 19762 Mac Arthur Blvd Suite 200 Irvine CA 92715

GERNERT, RICHARD CHARLES, lawyer; b. Passaic, NJ, May 9, 1943; s. George Anton and Alice (Hughes) G. BS in Econ. and Mktg., St. Peter's Coll., Jersey City, 1970; JD, St. John's U., 1973. Bar: N.J. 1973, U.S. Dist. Ct. N.J. 1973, U.S. Supreme Ct. 1979. Mcpl. prosecutor Borough of Hasbrouck Heights (N.J.), 1978—; sole practice Hackensack, N.J., 1984—; cons. various law firms, 1984—. Served to sgt. U.S. Army, 1963-66, Vietnam. Mem. ABA, N.J. Bar Assn., Bergen County Bar Assn. Lodge: Lions (pres. Hasbrouck Heights. club 1977). Personal injury, Insurance, Criminal. Office: 200 Main St Hackensack NJ 07601

GERRARD, MICHAEL BURR, lawyer; b. N.Y.C., Aug. 14, 1951; s. Nathan L. and Louise (Burr) G.; m. Barbara E. Seuling, Aug. 29, 1976; children: David, William. BA, Columbia U., 1972; JD, NYU, 1978. Bar: N.Y. 1979, U.S. Dist. Ct. (so. and ea. dists.) N.Y. 1979. Assoc. Berle, Kass and Case, N.Y.C., 1978-81, 84-85, ptnr., 1985—. Columnist on environ. law N.Y. Law Jour., 1986—. Mem. bd. advisors Council on Mcpl. Performance, N.Y.C., 1979—; bd. dirs N.Y. State Environ. Planning Lobby, Albany, 1978—; spl. counsel to chmn. Met. Transp. Authority, N.Y.C., 1983; dep. dir. Mayor's Transit Office, N.Y.C., 1982; analyst Mayor's Council on Environment, N.Y.C., 1973-75. Root-Tilden scholar NYU, 1975-78; Rockefeller fellow, 1978. Mem. Assn. of Bar of City of N.Y. (chmn. transp. com. 1985—), N.Y. State Bar Assn. (co-chmn. transp. com. 1985—). Environment, Federal civil litigation, Local government. Office: Berle Kass and Case 45 Rockefeller Plaza New York NY 10111

GERRISH, JEFFREY C., lawyer; b. Washington, Aug. 24, 1951; s. Donald Hughes and Doris (Crane) G.; m. Carolyn Ann Campbell, June 3, 1972; children: Bryan Christopher, Elisabeth Anne. BA with highest honors, U. Md., 1972; JD, George Washington U., 1976. Bar: Md. 1976, U.S. Dist. Ct. Md. 1976, Tenn. 1983, U.S. Dsit. Ct. (we. dist.) Tenn. 1984. Sr. atty. dirs. liability FDIC, Washington, 1980-82; regional counsel FDIC, Memphis, 1982-83; ptnr. Borod & Huggins, Memphis, 1983—. Contbr. articles to profl. jours. Mem. ABA. Banking, Administrative and regulatory, Insurance. Home: 2137 Shallow Ford Cove Germantown TN 38138 Office: Borod & Huggins 80 Monroe Ave 7th Floor Memphis TN 38103

GERRY, JOHN FRANCIS, federal judge; b. Camden, N.J., Nov. 17, 1925; s. Francis P.; m. Jean June 21, 1952; children: Patricia, Kathleen, Ellen. A.B., Princeton U., 1950; LL.B., Harvard U., 1953. Solicitor Twp. of Mt. Laurel, N.J., 1971-72; judge Camden County Ct., 1972-73, N.J. Superior Ct., 1973-75, U.S. Dist. Ct. N.J., 1975—. Mem. ABA, N.J. Bar Assn. Judicial administration. Office: US District Court 401 Market St Camden NJ 08101 *

GERSHBERG, RICHARD LOUIS, lawyer; b. Balt., Oct. 3, 1954; s. Maurice Ray and Joan (Weinberg) G.; m. Elaine Kishter, Nov. 24, 1979; children: Jordan Benjamin, Jaime Lauren. AB, Washington U., St. Louis, 1976; JD, U. Balt., 1979. Bar; Md. 1980, U.S. Dist. Ct. Md. 1981, U.S. Ct. Appeals (4th cir.) 1981. Law clk. to presiding justice Md. Ct. Spl. Appeals, Balt., 1979; assoc. Gordon & Heneson, Balt., 1980-85; ptnr. Gershberg, Honeyman & Pearl, Balt., 1985—. Pres., bd. dirs. Queen Anne Village Assn., Owings Mills, Md., 1984-85, Rehab. Opportunities, Inc., Landover, Md., 1984—. Democrat. Jewish. Avocations: sailing, tennis, carpentry, children. General corporate, Real property, Banking. Home: 9314 Fitzharding Ln Owings Mills MD 21117 Office: Gershberg Honeyman & Pearl 110 Saint Paul St Baltimore MD 21202-1748

GERSON, JEROME HOWARD, lawyer; b. Chgo., Sept. 9, 1928; s. Bernard Jay and Minnie (Cooper) G.; children—Daniel, Bradley, Mitchell. Student U. Ill., 1946-48; J.D., Chgo. Kent Coll. Law, 1951. Bar: Ill. 1951, U.S. Dist. Ct. (no. dist.) Ill. 1952. Assoc. Teller, Levit & Silvertrust, Chgo., 1952-56, Joseph W. Bernstein, 1957-60, Philip Goodman, 1961-63; ptnr. Yacker & Gerson, Chgo., 1963-76; sr. ptnr. Rudnick & Wolfe, Chgo., 1976—. Contbr. articles to profl. publs. Fellow Honor Council, Chgo. Kent Coll. Law. Mem. Chgo. Bar Assn., Ill. State Bar Assn., ABA. Club: Lake Shore Country (Glencoe, Ill.). Real property. Office: Rudnick & Wolfe 30 N LaSalle St Chicago IL 60602

GERSON, RALPH JOSEPH, lawyer; b. Detroit, Nov. 30, 1949; s. Byron Hayden and Dorothy Mary (Davidson) G.; m. Erica Ann Ward, May 20, 1979. BA, Yale U., 1971; MSc, London Sch. Econs., 1972; JD, U. Mich., 1975. Bar: Mich. 1975, D.C. 1976, U.S. Dist. Ct. D.C. 1976, U.S. Ct. Appeals (D.C. cir.) 1976. Counsel Dem. Nat. Com., Washington, 1975-77; spl. asst. U.S. Spl. Trade Rep., Washington, 1978-79; counselor Pres. Spl. Middle East Negotiator, Washington, 1979-80; ptnr. Akin, Gump, Strauss, Hauer & Feld, Washington, 1981-83, 85—; dir. Mich. Dept. Commerce, Lansing, 1983-85; bd. dirs. Guardian Industries Corp., Northville, Mich. Bd. dirs. Mich. High Tech. Task Force Force, Detroit, 1985—. Mem. ABA, Mich. Bar Assn., D.C. Bar Assn. Clubs: Royal Automobile (London); Yale (N.Y.C.); Franklin (Mich.) Hills Country; Detroit. Private international, Legislative, General corporate. Home: 1719 Hoban Rd NW Washington DC 20007 Office: Akin Gump Strauss Hauer & Feld 1333 New Hampshire Ave NW #400 Washington DC 20036

GERSTEIN, JOE WILLIE, lawyer; b. Atlanta, July 29, 1927; s. Arthur and Tena (Hartman) G.; m. Doris Renate Florsheim, May 20, 1956; children: Ellen Claire Gerstein Crooke, Kim Carol Gerstein Wainer. AB, Duke U., 1949, JD, 1952. Bar: Ga. 1953, U.S. Tax Ct., U.S. Ct. Appeals (fed. cir.) 1965, U.S. Supreme Ct. 1967. Sr. ptnr. Gerstein, Carter & Chestnut and predecessor firm Gerstein & Carter, Atlanta and Doraville, Ga., 1957-76; sole practice Doraville, 1976—; former city atty, Doraville; lectr. on taxes, wills, trust and estates at various civic, profl. and ch. orgns.; bd. dirs. Atlanta Estate Planning Council. Contbg. editor Duke U. Law Rev. Past dir. Social Service Fedn. Atlanta. Served with USN, 1944-47. Mem. ABA, Ga. Bar Assn., Atlanta Bar Assn., Decatur-DeKalb Bar Assn., Met. Atlanta Council Rotary Club Pres. (past chmn.), Comml. Law League Am. (past nat. recording sec.), Atlanta Tax Forum, Big Canoe Men's Golf Assn. (golf com.), Zeta Beta Tau (v.p. AU chpt.), Phi Delta Phi. Jewish. Club: Standard (Atlanta) (legal and golf coms.). Lodges: Rotary (North DeKalb past pres.), Masons (past offices), B'nai B'rith (Gate City past v.p.). Corporate taxation, Probate, Pension, profit-sharing, and employee benefits. Home: 6909 B Roswell Rd Atlanta GA 30328 Office: 6485 Peachtree Ind Blvd Doraville GA 30360

GERSTEN, SANDRA JOAN PESSIN, lawyer; b. Hartford, Conn., June 21, 1936; d. Israel George and Gussie (Marcus) Pessin; m. Aaron L. Gersten, Mar. 29, 1957; children—Peter Samuel, Karen Sue. Student U. Geneva, 1955-56; B.A., Vassar Coll., 1957; LL.B., U. Conn., 1960. Bar: Conn. 1960. Sole practice, West Hartford, Conn., 1960—. Pres., Greater Hartford Chpt. Orgn. for Rehab. Through Tng., 1968; trustee U. Conn. Law Sch. Found. Mem. ABA, Conn. Bar Assn., Hartford County Bar Assn., U. Conn. Law Sch. Alumni Assn. (pres. 1981-82). West Hartford C. of C. (sec. 1981-82). Jewish. Club: Cliffside Country (Simsbury, Conn.). Family and matrimonial, Real property, Probate. Home: 25 Pioneer Dr West Hartford CT 06117 Office: 41 N Main St Hartford CT 06107

GERSTENHABER, MURRAY, educator, lawyer; b. Bklyn., May 6, 1927; s. Joseph and Pauline (Rosenzweig) G.; m. Ruth P. Zager, June 3, 1956; children: Jeremy J., David E., Rachel R. BS, Yale U., 1948; PhD, U. Chgo., 1951; JD, U. Pa., 1973. Bar: Pa. 1973. Prof. math U. Pa., Phila., 1953—, lectr. law, 1970—; cons. statis. issues law, 1974—. Contbr. numerous articles to profl. jours. Served with U.S. Army, 1945-47. Grantee NSF, 1955—. Fellow AAAS (council); mem. ABA, Am. Math. Soc. (council), Assn. Mems. Inst. Advanced Study (treas. 1974—, acting pres. 1985—). Jewish. Avocation: jogging. Legal education, Personal income taxation, Statistical questions in law. Home: 237 Hamilton Rd Merion Station PA 19066-1102 Office: U Pa Dept Math Philadelphia PA 19104-6395

GERSTMAN, GEORGE HENRY, lawyer; b. N.Y.C., July 25, 1939; s. Mortimer and Adelaide (Koteen) G.; m. Rozanne Millman, Dec. 24, 1960; children: Heidi Ann, Gary Daniel. BSEE, U. Ill., 1960; JD with honors, George Washington U., 1963. Bar: Ill. 1964, U.S. Dist. Ct. (no. dist.) Ill. 1964, U.S. Patent Office 1964, U.S. Supreme Ct. 1971, U.S. Ct. Appeals (7th cir.) 1971, U.S. Ct. Appeals (2d cir.) 1980, U.S. Ct. Appeals (Fed. cir.) 1982. Patent examiner U.S. Patent Office, Washington, 1960-63; assoc. Dressler, Goldsmith et al, Chgo., 1963-70; ptnr. Lettvin & Gerstman Ltd., Chgo., 1970-75, Pigott & Gerstman Ltd., Chgo., 1976—. Asst. editor George Washington Law Rev., 1962-63. Govt. appeal agt. Selective Service System, Evanston, Ill., 1967-73; mem. Northbrook (Ill.) Bd. Zoning Appeals, 1971—. Mem. ABA, Chgo. Bar Assn., Assn. Trial Lawyers Am., Am. Intellectual Property Law Assn., Patent Law Assn. Chgo., Internat. Trade Commn. Trial Lawyers Assn., Order of Coif. Clubs: Standard (Chgo.), Monroe. Avocations: tennis, art. Patent, Trademark and copyright, Federal civil litigation. Home: 4041 Picardy Dr Northbrook IL 60062 Office: Pigott & Gerstman Ltd 2 N LaSalle St Chicago IL 60602

GERTLER, MEYER H., lawyer; b. New Orleans, Oct. 28, 1945; s. David and Sadie (Redman) G.; m. Marcia Raye Goldstein, Aug. 23, 1967; children—Louis, Danielle, Joshua. B.A., Tulane U., 1967, J.D. 1969. Bar: La. 1970, U.S. Dist. Ct. (ea. and mid. dists.) 1970, U.S. Ct. Appeals (5th cir.) 1970, U.S. Supreme Ct. 1970. Ptnr. Uddo & Gertler, New Orleans, 1970-76, Gertler & Gertler, New Orleans, 1977-86, Gertler, Gertler & Vincent, New Orleans, 1986—; mem. Asbestos Litigation Group. Mem. La. Trial Lawyers Assn., Am. Trial Lawyers Assn., ABA, Sup. Ct. Hist. Soc., Am. Judicature Soc. Democrat. Jewish. Clubs: B'nai B'rith, Masons. Product liability, Federal civil litigation, State civil litigation. Home: 174 Country Club Dr New Orleans LA 70124 Office: 127-129 Carondelet New Orleans LA 70130

GERTNER, MICHAEL HARVEY, lawyer; b. Columbus, Ohio, Aug. 26, 1941; s. Abraham and Edythe Gertner. B.A. cum laude, Ohio State U., 1963, J.D., 1966. Bar: D.C. 1971, Ohio 1966, U.S. Dist. Ct. (D.C. dist.) 1971, U.S. Supreme Ct. 1971, U.S. Claims Ct. 1973, U.S. Tax Ct. 1973, U.S. Ct. Appeals (D.C. cir.) 1974, U.S. Dist. Ct. (so. dist.) Ohio 1979, U.S. Ct. Appeals (6th cir. and fed. cir.) 1983. Law clk. Ohio Supreme Ct., Columbus, 1966-68; legis. asst. to Sen. Wm. B. Saxbe, Washington, 1969-74; atty. advisor Office Atty. Gen., U.S. Dept. Justice, Washington, 1974; asst. U.S. atty, Washington, 1974-76; assoc. Vorys, Sater, Seymour & Pease, Columbus, 1977-79; ptnr. Gertner & Gertner, Columbus, 1979—. Mem. ABA, Ohio Bar Assn., Columbus Bar Assn., Fed. Bar Assn., Franklin County Trial Lawyers Assn., Phi Beta Kappa, Phi Eta Sigma, Eta Sigma Phi, Pi Sigma Alpha, Ohio Acad. Trial Lawyers, Assn. Trial Lawyers Am. Republican. Jewish. State civil litigation, Family and matrimonial, General practice. Home: 2753 Plymouth Ave Columbus OH 43209 Office: Gertner & Gertner 88 E Broad St Columbus OH 43215

GERTZ, THEODORE GERSON, lawyer; b. Chgo.; s. Elmer and Ceretta (Samuels) G.; m. Suzanne C. Feldman, Sept. 18, 1936; children—Craig M., Candace C., Scott W. B.A., U. Chgo., 1958; J.D., Northwestern U., 1962. Bar: Ill. 1962, U.S. Dist. Ct. (no. dist.) Ill. 1962. Assoc. Marks, Marks and Kaplan, Chgo., 1962-65; ptnr. Lowitz, Vihon, Stone, Kipnis and Gertz, Chgo., 1965-71; ptnr., dir., treas. Pretzel and Stouffer, P.C., Trustee and gen. counsel Hull House Assocs.; bd. dirs. Pub. Interest Law Internship, Lawyers for Creative Arts. Served with U.S. Army, 1962-68. Mem. Chgo. Bar Assn., Ill. Bar Assn., Chgo. Estate Planning Council. Jewish. Clubs: Monroe, Metropolitan, River. Co-author: A Guide to Estate Planning, 1983; Illinois Advanced Estate Planning, 1984. Estate planning, Pension, profit-sharing, and employee benefits. Office: 15 Wacker Dr Suite 2500 Chicago IL 60606

GESCHEIDT, RICHARD ANTHONY, lawyer, educator; b. S.I., N.Y., Feb. 24, 1948; s. Anthony Louis and Alice Mildred (Greendale) G.; m. Constance Heil, May 20, 1972. B.A., Hiram Coll., 1970; J.D., U. Louisville, 1972; LL.M., NYU, 1973. Bar: Fla. 1972, Ky. 1973, U.S. Dist. Ct. (we. dist.) Ky. 1973, U.S. Ct. Appeals (6th cir.) 1973, U.S. Tax Ct. 1973, U.S. Ct. Claims 1973, U.S. Dist. Ct. (so. dist.) Fla. 1975, U.S. Ct. Appeals (5th cir.) 1979, U.S. Supreme Ct. 1981, U.S. Ct. Appeals (11th and fed. cirs.) 1982, U.S. Ct. Mil. Appeals 1982, U.S. Ct. Internat. Trade 1982. Assoc. Goldberg, Steuterman & Nicholas, Louisville, 1973-75, Carlisle & Tworoger, Ft. Lauderdale, Fla., 1975-76; ptnr. Papa & Gescheidt, Boca Raton, Fla., 1976-85, Gescheidt & Foreman, 1985—; asst. prof. taxation Fla. Atlantic U., Boca Raton, 1976-85; gen. counsel code enforcement bd. City of Boca Raton. Mem. ABA, Palm Beach County Bar Assn., Lawyer-Pilot Bar Assn., Delta Theta Phi. Republican. Mem. Moravian Ch. Clubs: NYU (N.Y.C.), Deercreek Country (Deerfield Beach, Fla.), Masons. Contbr. articles on taxation to Penny Stock News. Estate taxation, Real property, General corporate. Office: Gescheidt & Foreman 400 S Dixie Hwy The Arbor Suite 320 Boca Raton FL 33432

GESELL, GERHARD ALDEN, judge; b. Los Angeles, June 16, 1910; s. Arnold Lucius and Beatrice (Chandler) G.; m. Marion Holliday Pike, Sept. 19, 1936; children—Peter Gerhard, Patricia Pike. A.B., Yale, 1932, LL.B., 1935. Bar: Conn. 1935, D.C. 1941. With SEC, Washington, 1935-40; tech. adviser to chmn. SEC, 1940-41; acted for Commn. as spl. counsel Temporary Nat. Econ. Com., study legal res. life ins. cos.; mem. Covington & Burling, Washington, 1941-67; judge U.S. Dist. Ct. D.C., 1968—; designated mem. Temporary Emergency Ct. Appeal, 1983; chief asst. counsel Joint Congl. Com. on Investigation Pearl Harbor Attack, 1945-46; Chmn. Pres.'s Com. on Equal Opportunity in the Armed Forces, 1962-64; chmn. com. on adminstrn. of justice D.C. Jud. Council, 1965-67; jud. mem. D.C. Commn. on Jud. Disabilities and Tenure, 1976-81. Co-author: Study of Legal Reserve Life Insurance Cos, 1940, Families and Their Life Insurance, 1940. Mem. Am. Bar Assn., Am. Law Inst., Am. Coll. Trial Lawyers, Phi Delta Phi, Zeta Psi. Clubs: Lawyers (Washington), Met. (Washington); Casino (North Haven, Maine). Jurisprudence. Home: 3304 N St Washington DC 20007 Office: US Courthouse Washington DC 20001

GESKE, ALVIN JAY, lawyer; b. Whitefish, Mont., Apr. 17, 1942; s. Alvin Emil and Ada Jay (Best) G.; m. Cheryl S. Glaze, Aug. 10, 1968; children—David, Daniel. B.A. in Econs. with highest honors So. Meth. U., 1964; J.D. with honors, U. Chgo., 1967; LL.M. in Taxation, with highest honors, George Washington U., 1974. Bar: Tex. 1967, D.C. 1972, U.S. Tax Ct. 1982, U.S. Ct. Appeals (4th cir.), 1984. Atty., Jackson, Walker, Winstead, Cantwell & Miller, Dallas, 1967-68; atty., then asst. br. chief legislation and regulation div. Office Chief Counsel, IRS, Washington, 1970-74; atty. Childs, Fortenbach, Beck & Guyton, Houston, 1974-75; legislation atty. Joint Com. on Taxation, U.S. Congress, Washington, 1975-78, asst. legislation counsel 1978-81; atty. Davis & McLeod, Washington, 1981-83; atty. Richard P. Sills, P.C., Washington, 1983-85, Stein, Sills & Brodsky P.C., Washington, 1985—. Served with U.S. Army, 1968-70. Mem. ABA (chmn. com. on agr. sect. taxation), Order of Coif, Phi Beta Kappa, Phi Delta Phi. Contbr. articles to profl. jours. Personal income taxation, Legislative. Office: 1106 16th St NW 6th Floor Washington DC 20003

GESSLING, JAMES PLACE, lawyer; b. Niagara Falls, N.Y., Feb. 7, 1954; s. Kurt Richard and Janice May (Pieta) G. Student, U. Nottingham, Eng., 1974-75; AB, Columbia U., 1976; JD, U. Denver, 1979. Bar: Colo. 1980, U.S. Dist. Ct. Colo. 1980, U.S. Ct. Appeals (10th cir.) 1980, U.S. Supreme Ct. 1986. Assoc. Wiegand & Assocs. P.C., Englewood, Colo., 1980-81; ptnr. Gessling & Minton, Englewood, 1981—. Mem. ABA, Assn. Trial Lawyers Am., Colo. Trial Lawyers Am., Colo. Bar Assn., Denver Bar Assn., Arapahoe County Bar Assn., Sports Car Club Am., Porsche Club Am. Avocation: car racing. Personal injury, Real property, Securities. Office: Gessling & Minton Southfield Park Tower 2 5th Floor 12835 Arapahoe Rd Englewood CO 80112-3940

GETLAN, NORMAN, lawyer; b. N.Y.C., June 21, 1927; s. Abraham David and Mildred (Rosenweig) G.; m. Phyllis Jane Kolbrener, Nov. 7, 1954; children: Robert Adam, Nancy Susan. B.BA in Acctg., CCNY, 1950; JD, NYU, 1952, LLM in Taxation, 1954. Bar: N.Y. 1952, U.S. Dist. Ct. (so. and ea. dists.) N.Y. 1953, U.S. Ct. Appeals (2d cir.) 1975, U.S. Supreme Ct. 1966. Assoc., Murray Rosen, N.Y.C., 1952-68; ptnr. Smith, Panish & Getlan, N.Y.C., 1968-75, Schoen, Getlan and Dun, N.Y.C., 1975—; lectr. Queens County Women's Bar Assn., 1978. Served with USMC, 1945-46. Mem. Am. Trial Lawyers Assn., N.Y. State Trial Lawyers Assn., N.Y. County Lawyers Assn. Federal civil litigation, State civil litigation, General corporate. Home: 198 Hickory Grove Dr Larchmont NY 10538 Office: Schoen Getlan and Dun 299 Broadway New York NY 10007

GETMAN, JULIUS GERSON, legal educator, lawyer; b. 1931. J.D., Harvard U., 1958, LL.M., 1963. Bar: D.C. 1959, Ind. 1970. Atty. NLRB, Washington, 1959-61; from asst. prof. to prof. law Ind. U., Bloomington, 1963-75; prof. Stanford U., Calif., 1975-77; William K. Townsend prof. law Yale U., New Haven, 1977-86; Earl E. Sheffield regent chair in law U. Tex., Austin, 1986—; cons. legal edn. Ford Found.; vis. prof. Benares Hindu U., 1967-68, Indian Law Inst., 1967-68; chief negotiator Conn. State Police, 1978—; spl. inst. for labor and mgmt. groups, arbitrator, 1963—; mem. editorial com. and exec. com. Labor Law Group; gen. conusel AAUP, 1980-82; regents chair Earl E. Sheffield U. Tex., Austin, 1986. Author: (with Steve Goldberg and Jeanne B. Herman) Union Representation Elections: Law and Reality, 1976, Labor Relations: Law, Practice and Policy, 1978; editor: (with John Blackbourn) Employment Discrimination Casebook, 1979. Mem. Nat. Acad. Arbitrators, Am. Assn. Univ. Profs. (pres. 1986—). Legal education. Office: U Tex Sch of Law 727 E 26th St Austin TX 78705

GETMAN, WILLARD ETHERIDGE, lawyer; b. Cin., Jan. 31, 1949; s. Frank Newton and Dorothy Dill (Etheridge) G. B.A., U. N.C., 1971; J.D., Stetson U., 1974. Bar: Fla. 1974, U.S. Dist. Ct. (so. dist.) Fla. 1975, N.Y. 1985. Assoc., Law Offices John M. Callaway, Lake Worth, Fla., 1974-75; sole practice, West Palm Beach, Fla., 1976-80, Boynton Beach, Fla., 1980—. Mem. ABA, N.Y. State Bar Assn., Assn. Trial Lawyers Am., Fla. Bar (trust law com. 1975-76, summary rules com. 1980-84, probate and guardianship rules com. 1981-82), Palm Beach County Bar Assn. (ethics com. 1977-78), South Palm Beach County Bar Assn., Delta Theta Phi. Republican. Presbyterian. Club: Delray Dunes Golf and Country (Boynton Beach). Lodges: Trailside Lions, Elks, Moose, Masons, Shriners. General practice. Home: 17 Holly Villas Delray Dunes Boynton Beach Fl 33436 Office: 112 S Federal Hwy Suite 4 Boynton Beach FL 33435 Office: Getman & Getman 38 Morgan St PO Box 477 Ilion NY 13357-0477

GETNICK, NEIL VICTOR, lawyer; b. Bklyn., Oct. 28, 1953; s. Irving Murray and Zita (Ellman) G.; m. Margaret Joan Finerty, May 21, 1978. BA in Govt. magna cum laude, Cornell U., 1975, JD, 1978. Bar: N.Y. 1979, U.S. Dist. Ct. (so. and ea. dists.) N.Y. 1983. Asst. dist. atty. trial div. N.Y. County, N.Y.C., 1978-81, asst. dist. atty. frauds bur., 1981-82; ptnr. Getnick & Getnick, Mineola, N.Y., 1983—; counsel Abberley, Kooiman, Marcellino & Clay, N.Y.C., 1983—; mem. criminal justice act panel U.S. Dist. Ct. (so. dist.) N.Y., N.Y.C., 1984—; bd. dirs., pres. Cast Iron Corp., N.Y.C., 1986-87. Recipient Pub. Citizenship award N.Y. Pub. Interest Research Group, 1977. Mem. ABA (litigation and criminal justice sects., fed. procedure com.), N.Y. State Bar Assn. (litigation and criminal law sects.), Assn. of Bar of City of N.Y., N.Y. County Lawyers Assn. General practice, Federal civil litigation, Criminal. Office: 521 Fifth Ave Suite 2200 New York NY 10175-0050

GETTNER, ALAN FREDERICK, lawyer; b. N.Y.C., Dec. 25, 1941; s. Victor Salomon and Henriette Seldner (Herrmann) G.; m. Monah Lawrence, Jan. 19, 1969. BA, Yale U., 1963; MA, U. Chgo., 1964; PhD, Columbia U., 1971, JD, 1979. Bar: N.Y. 1980. Assoc. Debevoise & Plimpton, N.Y.C. and Paris, 1979-84; assoc. Holtzmann, Wise & Shepard, N.Y.C., 1984-85, ptnr., 1986—. Mem. ABA, Assn. Bar of City of N.Y., Council on Ethics and Internat. Affairs. Private international, General corporate, Securities. Office: Holtzmann Wise & Shepard 745 Fifth Ave New York NY 10151

GETTO, ERNEST J., lawyer; b. Dubois, Pa., May 24, 1944; s. Ernest F. and Olga (Gagliardi) G.; m. Judith Payne, Aug. 19, 1967; children: Matthew

Payne, Christopher Ernest. BA, Cornell U., 1966; JD, Vanderbilt U., 1969. Assoc. Simpson, Thatcher & Bartlett, N.Y.C., 1969-73; froam assoc. to ptnr. Kadison, Pfaelzer, Woodard, Quinn & Rossi, Los Angeles, 1973-80; ptnr. Latham & Watkins, Los Angeles, 1980—; lectr. on product liability evidence and jud. disqualification. Contbr. articles to profl. jours. Bd. dirs. Calif. Pediatric Ctr., Los Angeles, 1977—. Mem. ABA, Calif. Bar Assn., Los Angeles Bar Assn., N.Y. State Bar Assn. Republican. Roman Catholic. Club: Jonathan, Wilshire Country (Los Angeles). Federal civil litigation, State civil litigation, Antitrust. Home: 109 S Rossmore Los Angeles CA 90004 Office: Latham & Watkins 555 S Flower St Los Angeles CA 90071

GETZENDANNER, SUSAN, U.S. dist. ct. judge; b. Chgo., July 24, 1939; d. William B. and Carole S. (Muehling) O'Meara; children—Alexandra, Paul. B.B.A., Loyola U., 1966, J.D., 1966. Bar: Ill. bar 1966. Law clk. to presiding justice U.S. Dist. Ct., 1966-68; assoc. Mayer, Brown & Platt, Chgo., 1968-74; ptnr. Mayer, Brown & Platt, 1974-80; judge U.S. Dist. Ct., Chgo., 1980—. Recipient medal of excellence Loyola U. Law Alumni Assn., 1981. Mem. Chgo. Council Lawyers. Jurisprudence. Office: US Dist Ct 219 S Dearborn St Chicago IL 60604

GEVERS, MARCIA BONITA, lawyer, lecturer, consultant; b. Mpls., Oct. 11, 1946; d. Sam and Bessie (Gottlieb) Fleisher; m. Michael A. Gevers, Sept. 13, 1970; children—Sarah Nichole, David Seth. B.A. Nat. Coll. Edn., 1968; M.A., N.E. Ill. U., 1973; J.D., DePaul U., 1980. Bar: Ill. 1980. Tchr., Chgo. Bd. Edn., Harris Sch., North Suburban Spl. Edn. Dist., Highland Park, Ill., 1968-73; legis. asst., campaign mgr. Ill. State Rep., Dolton, 1974-79; sole practice, Park Forest, Dolton, Ill., 1980-83; cons. LWV, Chgo., 1978; ptnr. Getty and Gevers, Dolton, 1983—. Producer, host cable TV show The Law and You, 1982-83. Bd. dirs. Park Forest Zoning Bd. Appeals, Fair Housing Rev. Bd., Housing Bd. Appeals, Equal Employment Opportunity Rev. Bd., 1975—; pres., bd. dirs. South Suburban Community Hebrew Day Sch., Olympia Fields, Ill., 1982-86; bd. dirs. Congregation Beth Sholom Ch., Park Forest, 1980-82; pres. Ill. Women Polit. Caucus; mem. steering com. Nat. Women's Polit. Caucus, Washington; pres., founder Metro South Women's Polit. Caucus, Chgo. suburbs; alt. del. Dem. Nat. Conv., N.Y.C., 1980. Mem. ABA, Ill. State Bar Assn., South Suburban Bar Assn. (unauthorized practices com.), Chgo. Bar Assn., Am. Arbitration Assn. (arbitrator), Decalogue Soc. Lawyers, LWV. Lodges: Hadassah, B'nai B'rith Women. Federal civil litigation, General practice, Real property. Office: Getty and Gevers 15000 Dorchester Ave PO Box 603 Dolton IL 60419

GEVURTZ, FRANKLIN ANDREW, legal educator; b. Portland, Oreg., Nov. 26, 1951; s. Marvin Merle and Manya Elizabeth Gevurtz; m. Carmen Caroline Bigard, May 31, 1981; 1 child, Sara Katherine. BS in Physics magna cum laude, UCLA, 1974; JD, U. Calif., Berkeley, 1977. Bar: Calif. 1977, U.S. Dist. Ct. (cen. dist.) Calif. 1978, U.S. Dist. Ct. (so. and ea. dists.) Calif. 1980, U.S. Dist. Ct. (no. dist.) Calif. 1981. Assoc. O'Melveny & Myers, Los Angeles, 1977-82; asst. prof. McGeorge Sch. Law, Sacramento, Calif., 1982-85, assoc. prof., 1985—. Editor: Survey of the International Sale of Goods, 1986. Mem. ABA, Order of Coif, Phi Beta Kappa. Democrat. Jewish. General corporate, Legal education. Office: McGeorge Sch Law 3200 5th Ave Sacramento CA 95817

GEWACKE, JOHN CLIFFORD, lawyer; b. Ohiowa, Nebr., Oct. 30, 1907; s. William George Gewacke and Elizabeth Wernimont; m. Dorothy Jeanette Knight, Aug. 16, 1942; children: Joan Sargent, Virginia Stockwell, Marilyn. B, Nebr. Wesleyn U., 1928; JD, Nebr. U., 1932. Ptnr. Gewacke & Bixby, Geneva, Nebr., 1932—; atty. Fillmore County, 1935-75. Served with U.S. Army, 1941-45, ETO. Mem. ABA, Nebr. Bar Assn. Lodges: Rotary (pres. Geneva), Masons (master). Probate, Federal civil litigation, Corporate taxation. Home: 620 N 12th St Geneva NE 68361

GEWIRTZ, ELLIOT, lawyer; b. N.Y.C., Apr. 8, 1947; m. Barbara Gewirtz; children: Lisa D., Eric S. BA summa cum laude, Colgate U., 1969; JD cum laude, Harvard U., 1972; M in Pub. Adminstrn., Princeton U., 1973. Ptnr. Milbank, Tweed, Hadley & McCloy, N.Y.C., 1973—. Banking, Private international, Public international. Home: 52 Greenacres Ave Scarsdale NY 10583 Office: Milbank Tweed Hadley & McCloy 1 Chase Manhattan Plaza 45F New York NY 10005

GEWIRTZ, PAUL D., lawyer, legal educator; b. May 12, 1947. s. Herman and Matilda (Miller) G.; m. Zoë Baird, June 8, 1986. A.B. summa cum laude, Columbia U., 1967; J.D., Yale U., 1970. Bar: D.C. 1973, U.S. Supreme Ct. 1976. Law clk. to judge U.S. Dist. Ct. So. Dist. N.Y., 1970-71, to Justice Thurgood Marshall, U.S. Supreme Ct., Washington, 1971-72; assoc. Wilmer, Cutler & Pickering, Washington, 1972-73; atty. Ctr. Law and Social Policy, Washington, 1973-76; assoc. prof., then prof. Yale Law Sch., New Haven, 1976—. Contbr. numerous articles to profl. jours. Legal education, Federal civil litigation. Office: Yale Law Sch Box 401A Yale Sta New Haven CT 06520

GEYER, DOUGLAS WARREN, judge; b. Springfield, Ohio, Nov. 19, 1942; s. Warren William and Doris Irene (Rust) G.; m. Sharon Ann Ondrejka, June 24, 1978; children: Matthew, Molly. BS, Ohio Northern U., 1965; JD, Ohio No. Coll. Law, 1968. Bar: Ohio 1968, U.S. Dist. Ct. Ohio 1969, U.S. Supreme Ct. 1973. Ptnr. Jewett, West & Geyer, Springfield, Ohio, 1968-70; Juergens, Juergens & Geyer, 1970-75; asst. atty. gen. Ohio, 1969-75; judge, Springfield Mcpl. Ct., Ohio, 1975—, presiding judge, 1982—. Co-author: Insanity and Psycopathy, 1967. Recipient Outstanding and Excellent Jud. Service awards Supreme Ct. of Ohio, 1975-86, Stephen Curtis award, 1967. Mem. Am. Judges Assn., Ohio State Bar Assn., Ohio Jud. Coll., Ohio Mcpl. Judges Assn., Springfield-Clark County Bar Assn. Democrat. Lutheran. Home: 2025 Cheviot Hills Dr Springfield OH 45505 Office: Springfield Mcpl Ct Springfield OH 45501

GHANDHI, MADONNA STAHL, lawyer, judge; b. Robinson, Ill., Sept. 26, 1928; d. Lawrence Joy and Inez Lucille (Kennedy) Stahl; children—Khushro, Rustom, Behram. B.S., U. Ill., 1950; J.D., Albany Law Sch., 1973. Bar: N.Y. 1974, U.S. Dist. Ct. (no. dist.) N.Y. 1974, U.S. Ct. Apls. (2nd cir.) 1975, U.S. Supreme Ct. 1978. Atty. trainee N.Y. State Dept. Commerce, Albany, 1973-74; atty. Legal Aid Soc., Albany, 1974-76; ptnr. Powers, Ghandhi and Somers and predecessor firm, Albany, 1976— ; judge Albany City Ct., part-time, 1984—; mem. com. on character and fitness N.Y. State Supreme Ct. A.D. 3d Dept., Albany, 1980-86. Lobbyist Com. for Progressive Legislation, Schenectady, 1968-70. Mem. N.Y. State Bar Assn., Albany County Bar Assn., Women's Bar Assn. State N.Y. (Capital dist. pres. 1983-84). Democrat. Unitarian. Club: Altrusa. General practice, Family and matrimonial, Real property. Office: Powers & Ghandhi 230 Delaware Ave Delmar NY 12054

GHERLEIN, GERALD LEE, diversified manufacturing company executive, lawyer; b. Warren, Ohio, Feb. 16, 1938; s. Jacob A. and Ruth (Matthews) G.; m. Joycelyn Hardin, June 18, 1960; children: David, Christy. Student, Ohio Wesleyan U., 1956-58; B.S. in Bus. Adminstrn, Ohio State U., 1960; J.D., U. Mich., 1963. Bar: Ohio 1963. Assoc. Taft Stettinius & Holister, Cin., 1963-66; corp. atty. Eaton Corp., Cleve., 1966-68; European legal counsel Eaton Corp., Zug, Switzerland, 1968-71; asst. sec., asso. counsel Eaton Corp., Cleve., 1971-76; v.p., gen. counsel Eaton Corp., 1976—. Trustee Citizen's League Greater Cleve., 1971-81, v.p., 1977-79, pres., 1979-81; trustee Cleve. Ballet, 1983—, vice chmn., 1985-87. Mem. ABA, Greater Cleve. Bar Assn. (vice chmn. 1985—, trustee), Ohio Bar Assn., Am. Soc. Corp. Secs. (pres. Ohio regional group 1977). Clubs: Union, Mayfield Country. General corporate. Home: 3679 Greenwood Dr Pepper Pike OH 44124 Office: Eaton Center Cleveland OH 44114

GHERLEIN, JOHN HARLAN, lawyer; b. Warren, Ohio, June 26, 1926; s. Jacob Alphonse and Ruth Ann (Matthews) G.; m. Rachel Ann Mills, Oct. 13, 1951; children—Ann Gherlein Vaughn, John M., Thomas M. B.A., Ohio Wesleyan U., 1948; LL.B., Case Western Res. U., 1951. Bar: Ohio 1951. Ptnr., mem. exec. com. Thompson, Hine and Flory, Cleve., 1951—. Former mem. bd. overseers Case Western Res. U., Cleve., now mem. vis. com. Sch. Law, trustee Alcoholism Services Cleve., pres., 1984-85; former trustee, pres. Citizens League Greater Cleve.; sec., trustee Martha Holden Jennings Found.; trustee, mem. fin. and devel. coms. St. Luke's Hosp. Assn.; trustee, sec. Vocat. Guidance Services; former trustee Fedn. for Community Planning, chmn. commn. on health concerns, 1983-84, mem. com. on health care for indigent, 1984-85. Served with USN, 1944-46. Fellow Am. Bar Found.; mem. ABA, Ohio Bar Assn., Cleve. Bar Assn. (trustee 1977-85, pres. 1983-84), Cuyahoga County Bar Assn., Soc. Benchers. Republican. Methodist. Clubs: Union, Pepper Pike, Mayfield Country (Cleve.). Avocations: golf, tennis. Banking, Real property, Contracts commercial. Home: 32975 Creekside Dr Pepper Pike OH 44124 Office: Thompson Hine and Flory 1100 Nat City Bank Bldg Cleveland OH 44114

GIACOMO, PAUL JOSEPH, JR., lawyer; b. Greenwich, Conn., Oct. 1, 1953; s. Paul Joseph Sr. and Mildred Rita (Santamauro) G. BA, Coll. William and Mary, 1975; JD, U. Notre Dame, 1978. Bar: N.Y. 1979, U.S. Dist. Ct. (so. and ea. dists.) N.Y. 1979, U.S. Ct. Appeals (2d cir.) 1984. Law clk. to judge U.S. Dist. Ct. (so. dist.) N.Y., N.Y.C., 1978-79; assoc. Bleakley, Platt, Schmidt & Fritz, White Plains, N.Y., 1979-82; ptnr. Gersten, Savage, Kaplowitz & Zukerman, N.Y.C., 1982—. Mem. ABA (litigation sect.), Fed. Bar Council, N.Y. State Bar Assn. (com. on fed. cts. 1979—), Assn. of Bar of City of N.Y.. Republican. Roman Catholic. Avocations: duplicate bridge, running. Federal civil litigation, Securities, State civil litigation. Home: 215 W 95th St New York NY 10025 Office: Gersten Savage Kaplowitz & Zukerman 575 Lexington Ave New York NY 10022

GIAMPIETRO, WAYNE BRUCE, lawyer; b. Chgo., Jan. 20, 1942; s. Joseph Anthony and Jeannette Marie (Zeller) G.; B.A., Purdue U., 1963; J.D., Northwestern U., 1966; m. Mary E. Fordeck, June 15, 1963; children—Joseph, Anthony, Marcus. Bar: Ill. 1966. Since practiced in Chgo.; assoc. Elmer Gertz, 1966-73; mem. firm Gertz & Giampietro, 1974-75; sole practice, 1975-76; ptnr. Poltrock & Giampietro, 1976—. Cons. atty. Looking Glass div. Traveler's Aid Soc. Pres. Chgo. 47th Ward Young Republicans, 1968. Bd. dirs. Ravenswood Conservation Commn. Mem. ABA, Ill. Bar Assn. (chmn. sect. on Individual Rights and Responsibilities, 1986-87, 2d pl. Lincoln award 1975), Chgo. Bar Assn., Assn. Trial Lawyers Am., Ill. Trial Lawyers Assn., First Amendment Lawyers Assn. (sec. 1982, treas. 1983, pres. 1986), Order of Coif, Phi Alpha Delta. Lutheran. Contbr. articles to profl. jours. Civil rights, Federal civil litigation, State civil litigation. Home: 23 Windsor Dr Lincolnshire IL 60015 Office: 221 N LaSalle St Chicago IL 60601

GIANNELLI, PAUL CLARK, law educator; b. N.Y.C., May 21, 1945; s. William John and Marjorie (Clark) g.; m. Susan Egan, Aug. 8, 1970; children: Michael, Adam. BA, Providence Coll., 1967; JD, U. Va., 1970, LLM, 1975; MS, George Washington U., 1973. Bar: Va. 1970, U.S. Supreme Ct. 1973. Prof. law Case Western Res. U., Cleve., 1975—; mem. rules adv. com. Ohio Supreme Ct., Columbus, 1985—. Author: Ohio Evidence Manual, 1982, Ohio Juvenile Law, 1985, Scientific Evidence, 1986; articles editor U. Va. Law Rev., 1969. Mem. Shaker Heights (Ohio) Charter Rev. Commn., 1985—. Served to capt. JAGC, U.S. Army, 1970-75. Criminal, Legal education, Juvenile. Home: 3129 Chadbourne Rd Shaker Heights OH 44120 Office: Case Western Res U Law Sch 11075 East Blvd Cleveland OH 44106

GIANNINI, MATTHEW C., lawyer, educator; b. Youngstown, Ohio, July 12, 1950; s. Matthew and Graziella (Nistri) G. BS, Youngstown State U., 1973, postgrad., 1973-75; JD, U. Dayton, 1978. Bar: Ohio 1978, U.S. Dist. Ct. (no. dist.) Ohio 1978, U.S. Supreme Ct. 1982. Assoc. D'Apolito, Infante, Huberman and Gentile,, Youngstown, 1978-84; ptnr. D'Apoloito, Infante and Giannini, A, Youngstown, 1984—; asst. prof. forensic psychiatry Northeastern Ohio U. Coll. Medicine, 1981-84, assoc. prof. forensic psychiatry, 1984—; agt. Safeco Title Ins. Co., 1978—; sr. cons. forensic medicine Fair Oaks Psychiatry Hosp., Summit, N.J., 1979—; instr. Paralegal Inst. Ohio, 1980—; instr. comml. law Youngstown State U., 1980—. Author: (with A.J. Giannini and A.E. Slaby) Physicians Guide to Overdose and Detoxification, 1984; contbr. numerous articles to profl. jours., chpts. to books. Mem. ABA, Am. Inst. Biol. Scis., Ohio Bar Assn. Republican. Roman Catholic. Avocations: tennis, golf. General corporate, Family and matrimonial, Personal injury. Home: 7377 Elmland Dr Poland OH 44514 Office: D'Apolito Infante & Giannini Attys at Law 120 Boardman St Youngstown OH 44503

GIANNOTTI, DAVID ALLEN, lawyer; b. Rome, N.Y., May 27, 1947; s. Dominick and Florence Mary (Wilkinson) G.; m. Kathy Ann Hanna, June 5, 1982. B.A. in Polit. Sci., Ithaca Coll., 1969; J.D., Emory U., 1971. Bar: Ga. 1972, Tenn. 1972, N.Y. 1976, Calif. 1981. Assoc., Stophel, Caldwell & Heggie, Chattanooga, 1972-75; assoc. gen. counsel Hooker Chems. & Plastics Corp., Niagara Falls, N.Y., 1975-78; counsel environ. affairs Occidental Chem. Corp., Houston, 1978-81; corp. counsel environ. health and safety Occidental Petroleum Corp., Los Angeles, 1981-84; ptnr. McKenna, Conner & Cuneo, Los Angeles, 1984—; lectr. in field. Contbr. in field. Mem. ABA, Am. Petroleum Inst., Chem. Mfrs. Assn., State Bar Calif. (com. on the environment). Republican. Environment. Home: 4251 Parva Ave Los Angeles CA 90027 Office: McKenna Conner & Cuneo 3435 Wilshire Blvd Los Angeles CA 90010

GIANOTTI, ERNEST F., lawyer; b. Price, Utah, Nov. 28, 1925; s. Ernest F. and Elizabeth (Crockett) G.; m. Alice Chambers, Oct. 31, 1960 (div. Apr. 1976); m. Rebecca Steinlicht, May 16, 1982; children: Stefani Knoeller, Christine, Lisa. JD, U. of Pacific, 1955. Bar: Mont. 1960, U.S. Dist. Ct. Mont. 1961, High Ct. Am. Samoa 1971, U.S. Ct. Appeals (9th cir.) 1972, High Ct. Trust Ter. 1977, U.S. Supreme Ct. 1977, Commonwealth, No. Marianas 1978, High Ct. Marshall Islands 1983, U.S. Dist. Ct. No. Marianas 1983, Hawaii 1985, U.S. Dist. Ct. Hawaii 1985. Sole practice Great Falls, Mont., 1960-77; assoc. judge High Ct., Trust Territory, Pacific Islands, 1977-85; sole practice Kona, Hawaii, 1985—; del. S. Pacific Judge's Conf., Australia, Saipan, 1982-84. Eastern chmn. State of Mont. Carter for Pres., 1976. Served with USN, 1943-46. Mem. AM. Trial Lawyers Assn., Mont. Bar Assn., Hawaii Bar Assn., VFW. Democrat. Clubs: Marshall Island Yacht, Kona Billiken (bd. dirs. 1986). Lodges: Shriners, Elks. Avocations: skiing, sailing, scuba diving. Criminal, Private international, Judicial administration.

GIBB, WILLIAM STEWART, lawyer; b. Des Moines, Nov. 6, 1939; m. Jane Gibb; children—Carol, John. B.S.B.A., Iowa State U., 1962; J.D. with honors, Drake U., 1968. Bar: Iowa 1968. Assoc., Betty, Neuman, McMahon, Hellstrom & Bittner, Davenport, Iowa, 1968; assoc. firm Johnson, Burnquist & Erb, Fort Dodge, Iowa, 1968-70; ptnr., Johnson, Erb, Latham, Gibb & Carlson, P.C., Fort Dodge, 1971—, pres. 1979—. Editor-in-chief Drake Law Rev., 1967-68. Bd. trustees First Congl. Ch., 1970-76; dir. Fort Dodge Sch. Bd., 1973-79, pres., 1978-79. Served to lt. USN, 1962-65 Fellow Iowa Acad. Trial Lawyers (bd. of govs. 1986—), Am. Coll. Trial Lawyers; mem. Assn. Trial Lawyers Iowa, (bd. govs. 1978—, pres. 1982-83; Outstanding Mem. of Yr. 1978), Assn. Trial Lawyers Am. (state committeeman 1982—), Webster County Bar Assn., Iowa State Bar Assn., ABA, Fort Dodge C. of C. (dir. 1970-76, chmn. indsl. devel. com.), Omicron Delta Kappa. Club: Fort Dodge Country (dir. 1973-76, pres. 1976). Lodge: Rotary. Federal civil litigation, State civil litigation, Construction. Office: Johnson Erb Latham Gibb & Carlson PC 600 Boston Centre Fort Dodge IA 50501

GIBBES, WILLIAM HOLMAN, lawyer; b. Hartsville, S.C., Feb. 25, 1930; s. Ernest Lawrence and Nancy (Watson) G.; m. Frances Hagood, May 1, 1954; children: Richard H., William H. Jr., Lynn. BS, U. S.C., 1952, LLB, 1953. Bar: S.C. 1953, U.S. Ct. Mil. Appeals 1954, U.S. Dist. Ct. S.C. 1956, U.S. Supreme Ct. 1959, U.S. Ct. Appeals (4th cir.) 1965. Asst. atty. gen. Columbia, S.C., 1957-62; ptnr. Berry & Gibbes, Columbia, 1962-68, Berry, Lightsey, Gibbes & Bowers, Columbia, 1968-72; sole practice Columbia, 1972-84; ptnr., sr. mem. Gibbes & Gibbes, Columbia, 1985—. Chmn. bd. dirs. U. S.C. YMCA. Served with JAGC, USAR, 1953-83; brig. gen., 1980—. Recipient Legion of Merit, U.S. Army, 1983. Mem. ABA (mil. laws com. 1984—, meml. com.), Judge Advs. Assn. (pres. 1982-83), Richland County Bar Assn., S.C. Credit Ins. Assn. (gen. counsel 1963—). Episcopalian. Clubs: The Summit, Forest Lake Country (Columbia). General practice, Federal civil litigation, State civil litigation. Home: 287 Windward Point Rd Lake Murray Columbia SC 29210 Office: 1518 Washington St Columbia SC 29201

GIBBONS, JOHN JOSEPH, judge; b. Newark, Dec. 8, 1924; s. Daniel Lehane and Julia (Murray) G.; m. Mary Jeanne Boyle, Apr. 19, 1952; children—Daniel J., Mary E., Nora F., Richard G., Deirdre E., Maude A., David C. B.S., Holy Cross Coll., 1947, LL.D., 1970; LL.B. cum laude, Harvard U., 1950; LLD, Seton Hall U., Suffolk U. Bar: N.J. bar 1950. Partner law firm Crummy, Gibbons & O'Neill, Newark, 1953-70; circuit judge U.S. Ct. of Appeals, 3d Circuit, 1970—; adj. prof. law Seton Hall U., Rutgers U., Suffolk U.; Mem. N.J. Bd. Bar Examiners, Trenton, 1959-64, chmn., 1963-64; mem. Gov.'s Select Commn. on Civil Disorders, N.J. Council Against Crime; mem. vis. com. law sch. U. Chgo. Author articles in field. Trustee Practising Law Inst., 1973—; trustee Holy Cross Coll., 1970—. Served to lt. (j.g.) USNR, 1943-46. Fellow Am. Bar Found.; mem. ABA (ho. of dels. 1968), N.J. Bar Assn. (pres. 1967-68), Essex County Bar Assn. (trustee 1961-64), Holy Cross Coll. Gen. Alumni Assn. (trustee, v.p. 1967-70). Home: 9 Winding Way Short Hills NJ 07078 Office: US Courthouse Newark NJ 07102

GIBBONS, JULIA SMITH, judge; b. Pulaski, Tenn., Dec. 23, 1950; d. John Floyd and Julia Jackson (Abernathy) Smith; m. William Lockhart Gibbons, Aug. 11, 1973; children: Rebecca Carey, William Lockhart Jr. B.A., Vanderbilt U., 1972; J.D., U. Va., 1975. Bar: Tenn. 1975. Law clk. to judge U.S. Ct. Appeals, 1975-76; assoc. Farris, Hancock, Gilman, Branan, Lanier & Hellen, Memphis, 1976-79; legal advisor Gov. Lamar Alexander, Nashville, 1979-81; judge 15th Jud. Cir., Memphis, 1981-83, U.S. Dist. Ct. (we. dist.) Tenn., Memphis, 1983—. Fellow Am. Bar Found.; mem. ABA, Tenn. Bar Assn., Memphis and Shelby County Bar Assn., Nat. Assn. Women Judges, Am. Judicature Soc., Phi Beta Kappa, Order of Coif. Presbyterian. Office: US Dist Ct 1157 Fed Bldg 167 N Main St Memphis TN 38103

GIBBONS, ROBERT JOHN, lawyer; b. Bklyn., Dec. 3, 1944; s. David Thomas and Virginia Marie (Saal) G.; m. Judith Ann Borst, Nov. 23, 1968; children: Robert, Sharon, Suzanne. BA, St. John's U., Jamaica, N.Y., 1966; JD, Fordham U., 1969. Bar: N.Y. 1970. Assoc. Mudge, Rose, Guthrie, Alexander & Ferdon, N.Y.C., 1969-76; ptnr. Wood, Dawson et al, N.Y.C., 1976-77, Debevoise & Plimpton, N.Y.C., 1977—. Trustee New Canaan County Sch., Conn., 1984—; bd. dirs New Canaan Baseball Inc., 1982—. Mem. ABA, N.Y. State Bar Assn., Assn. of Bar of City of N.Y. Clubs: Lake, Winter, New Canaan Field. Municipal bonds, Public utilities, Securities. Home: 221 Michigan Rd New Canaan CT 06840 Office: Debevoise & Plimpton 875 3d Ave New York NY 10022

GIBBONS, WILLIAM JOHN, lawyer; b. Chgo., Jan. 22, 1947; s. Edward and Lottie (Gasiorek) G.; m. Marcia Guthridge, Dec. 31, 1976; children: Maximilian Clay, Bartholomew David, Ariel Katherine. BA, Northwestern U., 1968, JD, 1972. Bar: Ill. 1972, U.S. Dist. Ct. (no. dist.) Ill. 1972, U.S. Ct. Appeals (9th cir.) 1980, U.S. Supreme Ct. 1982, U.S. Ct. Appeals (7th cir.) 1984. Assoc. Kirkland and Ellis, Chgo., 1972-76; ptnr. Hedlund, Hunter and Lynch, Chgo., 1976-82, Latham and Watkins, Chgo., 1982—; bd. dirs. Fin. Fed. Savings Bank. Participating atty. ACLU, Chgo., 1982—. Served with USAR, 1968-74. Mem. ABA, Chgo. Bar Assn., Chgo. Council of Lawyers, Seventh Cir. Bar Assn. Club: Met., River (Chgo.). Trademark and copyright, Federal civil litigation, State civil litigation. Home: 4900 S Kimbark Chicago IL 60615 Office: Latham and Watkins Sears Tower Suite 6900 Chicago IL 60606

GIBBS, JEFFREY NEIL, lawyer; b. Newark, Nov. 27, 1953; s. Stanley and Bernice (Siegel) G.; m. Jody Diane Katz, Dec. 4, 1983. BA summa cum laude, Princeton U., 1975; JD cum laude, NYU, 1978. Bar: N.J. 1978, U.S. Dist. Ct. N.J. 1978, U.S. Ct. Appeals (3d cir.) 1979, N.Y. 1981, U.S. Dist. Ct. (D.C. cir.) 1983, D.C. 1984. Law clk. to judge U.S. Dist. Ct. N.J., Newark, 1978-80; enforcement atty. office of gen. counsel FDA, Rockville, Md., 1980-83; spl. asst. civil div. U.S. Attys. Office, Washington, 1983-84; assoc. Hogan & Hartson, Washington, 1984-86; ptnr. Mackler, Cooper & Gibbs, Washington, 1986—. Contbr. articles to profl. jours. Mem. ABA, Fed. Bar Assn., Order of Coif. Avocations: travel, photography. Administrative and regulatory, Environment, Health. Home: 3809 N Military Rd Arlington VA 22007 Office: Mackler Cooper & Gibbs 1220 L St NW Washington DC 20005

GIBBS, LIPPMAN MARTIN, lawyer; b. N.Y.C., Feb. 27, 1938; s. Harold nd Shirley (Marks) G.; m. Dona Lynn Fagg, May 3, 1968; 1 son, Bradford, A.B., Brown U., 1959; J.D., Columbia U., 1962. Bar: N.Y. 1963, D.C. 1982. Atty., Port of N.Y. Authority, N.Y.C., 1963-64; assoc. Weiner, Neuberger & Sive, N.Y.C., 1964-65, Spear & Hill, N.Y.C., 1966-69, Finley, Kumble, Wagner, Heine & Underberg, N.Y.C., 1969-72; ptnr. Finley, Kumble, Wagner, Heine & Underberg, 1972—; arbitrator Am. Arbitration Assn., 1967—. Regional dir. United Fund Dr. Rye, 1979. Served with USAR, 1962-63. Mem. ABA, Assn. Bar City of N.Y., N.Y. State Bar Assn. Unitarian. Clubs: N.Y. Yacht, Univ., Fishers Island Yacht, Hay Harbor. General corporate, Contracts commercial. Home: 8 Woodland Dr Rye NY 10580 Office: 425 Park Ave New York NY 10022

GIBBS, NANCY PATRICIA, lawyer; b. Vancouver, B.C., Can., Dec. 22, 1946; d. Richard Brandreth and Ann Dorothy (Marriott) G.; m. Frank Weber Hughes, Aug. 28, 1971 (div.); 1 dau., Adrianne Elizabeth Hughes. B.A. in Chemistry, U. Wash., 1968, J.D., 1971. Bar: Wash. 1971, U.S. Dist. Ct. (we. dist.) Wash. 1971, U.S. Ct. Appeals (9th cir.) 1972, U.S. Supreme Ct. 1980. Assoc. Davis, Wright, Todd, Riese & Jones, Seattle, 1971-76, ptnr., 1977—. commr. on salaries of state elected officials Washington State Commn., 1987—. Trustee, Seattle Aquarium Soc., 1982-83, 2d v.p., 1983-84; trustee Northwest Chamber Orchestra, 1985-88, mem. exec. com. 1986-87; mem. adv. bd. Sr. Rights Assistance Project, 1978-80, Evergreen Legal Services Corp., 1980-81. Named Newsmaker of Future, Seattle C. of C./Time Mag., 1978; Cathedral fellow Cathedral Assocs., 1983-84. Mem. Seattle-King County Bar Assn. (treas. 1977-79, trustee 1979-82, 2d v.p. 1983-84, 1st v.p. 1984-85, pres. 1985-86), Seattle King County Bar Found. (trustee 1979-82, pres. 1981-82), U. Wash. Law Sch. Alumni Assn. (trustee 1978-82, treas. 1982-83, v.p. 1983-84, pres. 1984-85), Assn. Immigration and Nationality Lawyers, Fed. Bar Assn., ABA (mem. Nat. Met. Bar Leaders Caucus 1985—, mem. exec. com. 1986—), Wash. Bar Assn. (chmn. law related edn. com. 1980-82, disciplinary proceeding hearing officer, 1981—), Phi Alpha Delta. Episcopalian. Club: Wash. Athletic (Seattle). Bd. dirs. The Public Defender, 1987—; contbr. articles to profl. jours. Private international, Banking. Office: Century Sq Suite 2600 Seattle WA 98101-1688

GIBBS, RICHARD FREDERIC, lawyer, physician; b. Chelsea, Mass., June 11, 1931; s. Arthur I. and Shirley K. Gibbs; children by previous marriage—Robin Ann, Michele Lynn. A.B., Brandeis U., 1953; M.A., U. Mass., 1955; M.D., N.Y. Med. Coll., 1959; J.D., Suffolk U., 1970, LL.D., 1978. Bar: Mass. 1971, U.S. Dist. Ct. Mass. 1982, U.S. Supreme Ct. 1982. Intern Beverly Hosp., 1959-60; resident in anesthesia Mass. Gen. Hosp., Boston, 1960-62; atty. R.F. Gibbs Medicolegal Assocs., Boston, 1971—; asst. prof. anaesthesia Harvard Med. Sch., Boston, and Boston Hosp. Women, 1974-80; sr. anesthesiologist Brigham and Women's Hosp., Boston, 1978—. Mem. Mass. Med. Soc. (chmn. profl. liability com., chmn. jud. com.), Am. Bd. Legal Medicine (trustee 1980—), Mass. Bar Assn. (chmn. liaison com.), ABA (bd. govs. health law forum) Am. Coll. Legal Medicine (bd. govs. 1970-79, pres. 1979), Am. Soc. Law and Medicine (bd. dirs. 1971-82), Am. Soc. Anesthesiologists (chmn. profl. liability com. 1975-79, 82-84). Personal injury, Insurance, Health. Office: Harvard Med Sch Dept Anesthesiology 75 Francis St Boston MA 02115 also: RF Gibbs Medicolegal Assocs 241 Perkins St Suite J-401 Cabot Estate Boston MA 02130

GIBBS, STEPHEN MARK, lawyer; b. Ft. Bragg, N.C., June 15, 1955; s. Marvin Hugh and Helen Ruth (Scroggs) G.; m. Lynn Cecilia Hart, May 31, 1986; 1 child, Jeston Alexander. BA magna cum laude, Oglethorpe U., 1977; JD, Emory U., 1981. Bar: Ga. 1981, U.S. Dist. Ct. (no. dist.) Ga. 1982, U.S. Ct. Appeals (11th cir.) 1982. Assoc. Lowe, Barham, Eubanks & Lowe, Atlanta, 1981-83, Claude R. Ross, P.C., Atlanta, 1983-84, Zachary & Segraves, P.A., Decatur, Ga., 1984—. Mem. Ga. Bar Assn., Atlanta Bar Assn., Decatur-DeKalb Bar Assn. Democrat. Methodist. General practice, Bankruptcy, State civil litigation. Office: Zachary & Segraves PA 1000 Commerce Dr Atlanta GA 30030

GIBERSON, FRANCIS EUGENE, lawyer; b. Milw., Jan. 15, 1947; s. Walker Eugene and Helen (Crenshaw) G.; m. Judith Brooks, Aug. 21, 1976; children: Matthew, John, David. AB, Occidental Coll., 1973; JD, Boston Coll., 1976. Bar: Minn. 1976, U.S. Dist. Ct. Minn. 1976, U.S. Ct. Appeals

(8th cir.) 1976. Assoc. Larkin, Hoffman, Daly & Lindgren, Mpls., 1976-80, Kronish, Lieb, Sheinswit, Weiner, Boyle, Vogeler & Haimes, N.Y.C., 1980-82; dep. commr. Minn. Dept. Human Services, St. Paul, 1983-87; assoc. Larkin, Hoffman, Daly & Lindgren, Mpls., 1987—. Co-author: The Land Use Controversy in Massachusetts, 1975; editor Boston Coll. Indsl. and Comml. Law Rev., 1975-76. Co-chmn. mpls. mcpl. fin. com., 1978-79; mem. Life at Any Price Task Force, Mpls., 1984-85; treas. Westminster Bd. Deacons., Mpls., 1985—. Served with USN, 1965-69. Recipient resolution Minn. State Senate, 1983, cert. commendation Gov. and Commr. Human Services, 1985. Mem. Nat. Health Lawyers Assn. Mem. Democratic Farm Labor Party. Presbyterian. Health, General corporate, Securities. Home: 6932 W 83d St Bloomington MN 55438 Office: 2000 Piper Jaffray Tower 222 S 9th St Minneapolis MN 55402

GIBSON, BENJAMIN F., judge; b. Safford, Ala., July 13, 1931; s. Eddie and Pearl Ethel (Richardson) G.; m. Lucille Nelson, June 23, 1951; children: Charlotte, Linda, Gerald, Gail, Carol, Laura. B.S., Wayne State U., 1955; J.D. with distinction, Detroit Coll. Law, 1960. Bar: Mich. 1960. Acct. City of Detroit, 1955-56, Detroit Edison Co., 1956-61; asst. atty. gen. Mich., 1961-63; asst. pros. atty. Ingham County, Mich., 1963-64; pvt. practice law Lansing, Mich., from 1964; judge U.S. Dist. Ct. Western Dist. Mich., Grand Rapids., 1979—. Hearing officer, East Lansing; bd. dirs. Lansing Jr. Achievement, Greater Lansing Legal Aid Bur. Mem. Am. Trial Lawyers Assn., Am. Bar Assn., Ingham County Bar Assn., State Bar Mich. (grievance bd. hearing panel 1971), Sigma Pi Phi. Club: Rotary. Jurisprudence. Office: U S Dist Ct 616 Fed Bldg 110 Michigan St NW Grand Rapids MI 49503 *

GIBSON, CARROLL ALLEN, JR., lawyer; b. Greenville, S.C., May 1, 1957; s. Carroll Allen and Jeanne Preston (Beckwith) G.; m. Wendy Teresa Kaminski, Aug. 14, 1982; 1 child, Walker Allen. BA with high distinction, U. Va., 1979, JD, 1982. Bar: S.C. 1982, U.S. Dist. Ct. S.C. 1982, U.S. Ct. Appeals (4th cir.) 1984. Assoc. Buist, Moore, Smythe & McGee, Charleston, S.C., 1982—. Bd. dirs. Charles Webb Easter Seal Ctr., Charleston, 1984—. Mem. ABA (state chmn. membership com. young lawyers div. 1985—, asst. editor Affiliate Assistance 1986—), S.C. Bar Assn. (treas. young lawyers div. 1986—). Republican. Episcopalian. Federal civil litigation, State civil litigation, Insurance. Home: 1042 Plantation Ln Mount Pleasant SC 29464 Office: Buist Moore Smythe & McGee 5 Exchange St PO Box 999 Charleston SC 29402

GIBSON, DANIEL PETER, lawyer; b. Arlington, Mass., Apr. 6, 1957; s. G.W. and Mary (Butler) G.; m. Lynn Marie Sorensen, July 26, 1980; children: Daniel John, Brendan Paul. BS, Salem State U., 1979; JD, Villanova U., 1982. Bar: Mass. 1982, U.S. Dist. Ct. Mass. 1982, U.S. Ct. Appeals (1st cir.) 1982. Assoc. Morrison, Mahoney & Miller, Boston, 1982—. Mem. ABA, Boston Bar Assn. Federal civil litigation, State civil litigation. Home: 200 Stage Rd Hampstead NH 03841 Office: Morrison Mahony & Miller 250 Summer St Boston MA 02210

GIBSON, ERNEST WILLARD, III, state supreme court justice; b. Brattleboro, Vt., Sept. 23, 1927; s. Ernest William and Dorothy Pearl (Switzer) G.; m. Charlotte Elaine Hungerford, Sept. 10, 1960; children—Margaret, Mary, John. B.A., Yale U., 1951; LL.B., Harvard U., 1956. Bar: Vt. State's atty. Windham County, Vt., 1957-61; mem. Vt. Ho. of Reps., 1961-63, chmn. judiciary com., 1963; chmn. Vt. Pub. Service Bd., 1963-72; judge Vt. Superior Ct., Montpelier, 1972-83; justice Vt. Supreme Ct., 1983—. Chancellor Episcopal Diocese Vt., 1977—, trustee, 1973—. Served to 1st lt., arty. U.S. Army, 1945-46, 51-53, Korea. Mem. Vt. Bar Assn. Avocations: tennis. Home: 11 Baldwin St Montpelier VT 05602 Office: Vt Supreme Ct 111 State St Montpelier VT 05602

GIBSON, FLOYD ROBERT, judge; b. Prescott, Ariz., Mar. 3, 1910; s. Van Robert and Katheryn Ida G.; m. Gertrude Lee Walker, Apr. 23, 1935; children: Charles R., John M., Catherine L. Gibson Jobst. A.B., U. Mo., 1931, LL.B., 1933. Bar: Mo. 1932. Practiced law Independence, 1933-37, Kansas City, 1937-61; mem. firm Johnson, Lucas, Bush & Gibson (and predecessor), 1954-61; county counselor Jackson County, 1943-44; judge U.S. Dist. Ct. (we. dist.) Mo., 1961-65, chief judge, until 1965; judge U.S. Ct. Appeals (8th cir.), Kansas City, Mo., 1965—, chief judge, 1974-80; former chmn. bd. Mfrs. & Mechanics Bank, Kansas City, Mo., Blue Valley Fed. Savs. & Loan Assn.; mem. Nat. Conf. Commrs. Uniform State Laws, 1957—, Jud. Conf. U.S., 1974-80; chmn. Chief Judges Conf., 1977-78; bd. mgrs. Council State Govts., 1960-61; pres. Nat. Legis. Conf., 1960-61. Mem. Mo. Gen. Assembly from 7th Dist., 1940-46; mem. Mo. Senate, 1946-61, majority floor leader, 1952-56, pres. pro tem, 1956-60; del. Nat. Democratic Conv., 1956, 60; Mem. Mo. N.G. Named 2d most valuable mem. Mo. Legislature Globe Democrat, 1958, most valuable, 1960; recipient Faculty-Alumni award U. Mo., 1968; citation of merit Mo. Law Sch. Alumni, 1975; Spurgeon Smithson award Mo. Bar Found., 1978. Fellow ABA (adv. bd. editors Jour., chmn. jud. adminstrn. div. 1979-80, chmn. conf. sect. 1980-81, chmn. appellate judges conf. 1973-74, mem. ho. of dels.); mem. Fed. Bar Assn., Mo. Bar, Kansas City Bar Assn. (Ann. Achievement award 1980), Lawyers Assn. Kansas City (past v.p., Charles Evans Whittaker award 1985), Mo. Law Sch. Found. (life), Mo. Acad. Squires, Order of Coif, Phi Delta Phi, Phi Kappa Psi (Man of Yr. 1974). Clubs: University (Kansas City, Mo.), Carriage (Kansas City, Mo.), Mercury (Kansas City, Mo.). Jurisprudence. Home: 2102 3 San Francisco Tower 2510 Grand Kansas City MO 64108 Office: US Ct of Appeals 837 US Courthouse 811 Grand Ave Kansas City MO 64106

GIBSON, HUGH, federal judge; b. Cameron, Tex., Nov. 8, 1918; s. Hugh and Rene Louise (Blankenship) G.; m. Evalyn Grace Dunlop, Sept. 18, 1954. B.A., Rice U., 1940; LL.B., Baylor U., 1948. Bar: Tex. 1948. Asst. dist. atty. State of Tex., Galveston, 1949-52, probate judge, 1954-68, state dist. judge, 1968-79; judge U.S. Dist. Ct., Galveston, 1979—. Served with U.S. Army, 1941-45, PTO. Democrat. Judicial administration. Home: 2928 Ave P Galveston TX 77550 Office: US Dist Court 611 Post Office Bldg Galveston TX 77550 *

GIBSON, JAMES THOMAS, JR., consultant, antique dealer, lawyer; b. Bessemer, Mich., Nov. 22, 1921; s. James Thomas and Bernice Muriel (Roberts) G.; Ph.B., U. Chgo., 1948, J.D., 1952. Bar: Ill. 1952. Assoc. Gould & Ratner, Chgo., 1953-60; atty., asst. treas., treas., then v.p. Internat. Minerals & Chems., Northbrook, Ill., 1960-79, cons., 1979—; assoc. dean. U. Chgo. Law Sch., 1981-83; sec., gen. counsel, dir. JMG Fin. Group, Oakbrook Terrace, Ill.; dir. Coromandel Fertilisers, Secunderabad, India. Author case note U. Chgo. Law Rev., 1951. Pres. Library of Internat. Relations, Chgo., 1976-77; bd. dirs. Internat. Visitors Ctr.; bd. dirs., pres. Racine Art Assn. Served with U.S. Army, 1943-46, PTO. Mem. Chgo. Bar Assn., Racine Art Assn. (bd. dirs., v.p., chmn. exec. com. 1979—). Episcopalian. Clubs: Tavern, Economic (membership com. 1978) (Chgo.). Estate taxation, Probate, General corporate. Home: 2400 N Lakeview Apt 2102 Chicago IL 60614 Office: JMG Financial Group 1 Oakbrook Terr Oakbrook Terrace IL 60181

GIBSON, JOHN ROBERT, judge; b. Springfield, Mo., Dec. 20, 1925; s. Harry B. and Edna (Kerr) G.; m. Mary Elizabeth Vaughn, Sept. 20, 1952 (dec. Aug. 1985); children: Jeanne, John Robert; m. Diane Allen Larrison, Oct. 1, 1986; stepchildren: Holly, Catherine. AB, U. Mo., 1949, JD, 1952. Bar: Mo. 1952. Assoc. Morrison, Hecker, Curtis, Kuder & Parrish, Kansas City, Mo., 1952-58, ptnr., 1958-81; judge U.S. Dist. Ct. (we. dist.) Mo., 1981-82, U.S. Ct. Appeals (8th cir.), Kansas City, 1982—; mem. Mo. Press-Bar Commn., 1979-81. Vice chmn. Jackson County Charter Transition Com., 1971-72; mem. Jackson County Charter Commn., 1970; v.p. Police Commrs. Bd., Kansas City, 1973-77. Served with AUS, 1944-46. Fellow Am. Bar Found.; mem. ABA, Mo. State Bar (gov. 1972-79, pres. 1977-78; Pres.'s award 1974, Smithson award 1984), Kansas City Bar Assn. (pres. 1970-71), Lawyers Assn. of Kansas City (Charles Evan Whittaker award 1980), Phi Beta Kappa, Omicron Delta Kappa. Presbyterian. Home: 801 W 57th St Kansas City MO 64113 Office: US Ct of Appeals 851 US Courthouse 811 Grand Ave Kansas City MO 64106

GIBSON, JOSEPH LEE, lawyer, lecturer; b. Lufkin, Tex., Mar. 12, 1940; s. Mitchell Osler Gibson and W. Christine (Bennett) Gibson Abrams; m. Bethanna Bunn, May 27, 1983; 1 child, Mark Corbett. B.A., Baylor U., 1962; LL.B., Harvard U., 1965. Bar: Tex. 1965, D.C. 1967. Legis. counsel Maritime Adminstrn., Washington, 1965-66; counsel govt. activities subcom. U.S. Ho. of Reps., Washington, 1966-68; assoc. Kirkland & Ellis, and predecessor, Washington, 1968-69; ptnr. Gibson, Branham & Farmer, Washington, 1969-73; counsel Montgomery Ward & Co., Washington, 1974-78; gen. counsel Credit Union Nat. Assn., Washington, 1978-79; counsel Diplomat Nat. Bank, Washington, 1979-80, also dir.; asst. solicitor Econ. Regulatory Adminstrn., Dept. Energy, Washington, 1980—; lectr. on equal employment in broadcasting, 1971-77, on consumer credit, privacy, electronic fund transfers, 1975—; atty. for mem. Nat. Commn. on Electronic Fund Transfers, Washington, 1976-78. Mem. various campaign and conv. staffs Democratic Party, Young Democrats, Tex. and Washington, 1965-80. Recipient Disting. Service award Maritime Adminstrn., 1966, Disting. Service award Dept. Energy, 1983. Methodist. FERC practice, Banking, Real property. Home: 2148 Florida Ave NW Washington DC 20008 also: 702 N 2d St Lufkin TX 75901 Office: Dept Energy Econ Regulatory Adminstrn 1000 Independence Ave NW Washington DC 20585

GIBSON, LOUISE, lawyer; b. Flushing, N.Y., Apr. 15, 1947; s. Rubin H. and Beatrice T. (Chorna) G. BA, U. Mich., 1969; JD, Northeastern U., 1974. Bar: Ariz. 1975, U.S. Dist. Ct. Ariz. 1975, N.Mex. 1978, U.S. Dist. Ct. N.Mex., U.S. Ct. Appeals (10th cir.), U.S. Supreme Ct. Atty. DNAúPeople Legal Services, Tuba City, Ariz., 1975-77; law clk. State of N.Mex., Santa Fe, 1977-78; assoc. Butt, Thorton & Baehr, Albuquerque, 1978—. Bd. mem. YWCA, Albuquerque, 1983—. Mem. ABA, Ariz. Bar Assn., N.Mex. Bar Assn., N.Mex. Trial Lawyers Assn., N.Mex. Def. Lawyers Assn., Albuquerque Bar Assn. Democrat. Jewish. Avocations: snorkeling, travel. Federal civil litigation, State civil litigation, Personal injury. Office: Butt Thorton & Baehr PC PO Box 3170 Albuquerque NM 87190

GIBSON, MICHAEL FIELDING, lawyer; b. Gallipolis, Ohio, Oct. 8, 1948; s. Robert Fielding Gibson and Maria Louise (Holzer) Brink. BA, Coll. William and Mary, 1970; JD, U. Richmond, 1973. Bar: Va. 1973, W.Va. 1973, U.S. Dist. Ct. (no. and so. dists.) W.Va. 1973, U.S. Dist. Ct. (we. dist.) Va. 1975, U.S. Dist. Ct. (so. dist.) Ohio 1985, U.S. Dist. Ct. (mid. dist.) N.C. 1977, U.S. Ct. Appeals (4th cir.) 1978, U.S. Ct. Appeals (6th cir.) 1985. Ptnr. Sanders, Austin & Gibson, Princeton, W.Va., 1973-76, Johnston, Holroyd & Gibson, Princeton, 1976—; bd. dirs. First Nat. Bank Keystone, W.Va.; pres. Mercer County (W.Va.) Pub. Defender Corp. Named one of Outstanding Young Men of Am., U.S. Jaycees, 1976. Mem. W.Va. Trial Lawyers Assn. (gov.), W.Va. Bar Assn., Va. Bar Assn., Am. Trial Lawyers Assn., E. African Wildlife Soc. Democrat. Episcopalian. Personal injury, Workers' compensation, Criminal. Home: 1408 Lebanon St Bluefield WV 24701 Office: Johnson Holroyd & Gibson 1438 Main St Princeton WV 24740

GIBSON, MICHAEL MORGAN, lawyer; b. Enid, Okla., Apr. 1, 1950; s. Arrell Morgan and Dorothy Faye (Dietz) G.; 1 child, Alecia Beth; m. Janice Gaye Jones, June 5, 1987. BA with spl. distinction, U. Okla., 1972, JD, 1975. Bar: Okla. 1975, Tex. 1982. Atty. U.S. EPA, Dallas, 1975-82; assoc. Richards, Harris & Medlock, Dallas, 1982-83; trial atty. tax div. U.S. Dept. Justice, Dallas, 1983-87; assoc. Holtzman & Urquhart, Houston, 1987—. Co-author: Corporate Environmental Risk, 1983. Mem. Tex. Bar Assn. (author, speaker videotape on solid waste regulation, 1983), Fed. Bar Assn. (pres. Dallas chpt. 1983-84). Democrat. Methodist. Avocations: running, scuba diving. Federal civil litigation, Personal income taxation, Environment. Office: Holtzman & Urquhart 900 Two Houston Ctr 909 Fannin St Houston TX 77010

GIBSON, RANKIN MACDOUGAL, lawyer; b. Unionville, Mo., Oct. 9, 1916; s. Alexander R. and Murle L. (Fletcher) G.; m. Eloise M. Corns, Sept. 13, 1941; children: Phillip, Barbara. Student, N.E. Mo. State Tchrs. Coll., 1934-36; LL.B., U. Mo., 1939; B.S. in Law, St. Paul Coll. Law, 1948; LL.M., George Washington U., 1950. Bar: Mo. 1939, Ohio 1954, Supreme Ct. U.S 1951. Gen. practice law Unionville, 1939-40; atty. T.H. Mastin & Co., St. Louis, 1940-42, VA, Des Moines, St. Paul, Washington, 1945-51; enforcement and litigation atty. Nat. Wage Stblzn. Bd., 1951; asso. prof. law U. Toledo Coll. Law, 1951-56; mem. firm DiSalle, Green, Haddad & Lynch, Toledo, 1956-59; asst. to gov., Ohio, 1959-61; dir. Ohio Dept. Commerce, 1961-62; mem. Pub. Utilities Commn., Ohio, 1962-63; judge Supreme Ct., Ohio, 1963-65; now partner firm Lucas, Prendergast, Albright, Gibson & Newman, Columbus, Ohio; tchr. adminstrv. law Franklin Sch. Law, 1960; tchr. labor law Franklin Law Sch., Capitol U., 1967—; Mem. Nat. Enforcement Commn. Econ. Stblzn. Agy., 1952-53; chmn. labor law round table council Assn. Am. Law Schs., 1952-53; labor arbitrator panels Am. Arbitration Assn., Fed. Mediation and Conciliation Service, Toledo Labor-Mgmt. Citizens Com., 1952-53; rep. Ohio on interstate Coop. Com.; chmn. Gov. Ohio Com. Pub. Information, 1959-61; mem. Ohio Water Pollution Bd., Civil War Centennial Commn.; mem. Ohio Housing Bd.; Ohio rep. on Interstate Oil Compact Commn. and Nat. Rivers and Harbors Congress, 1961-62. Contbr. articles to profl. jours. Dem. nominee for rep. Mo. Gen. Assembly, 1940. Served to 2d lt. AUS, 1942-45. Mem. Fed. Bar Assn. (pres. Columbus chpt. 1967-68), Ohio Bar Assn., Columbus Bar Assn. (pres.), Indsl. Relations Research Assn. (pres. central Ohio chpt. 1966-68), Nat. Acad. Arbitrators (chmn. region 9 1975—), Am. Judicature Soc., Soc. Profls. in Dispute Resolution. Labor, Administrative and regulatory, General practice. Home: 7355 Feder Rd Galloway OH 43119 Office: 471 E Broad St Columbus OH 43215

GIBSON, REGINALD WALKER, federal judge; b. Lynchburg, Va., July 31, 1927; s. McCoy and Julia Ann (Butler) G.; 1 child, Reginald S. B.S., Va. Union U., 1952; postgrad., Wharton Grad. Sch. Bus. Adminstrn., U. Pa., 1952-53; LL.B., Howard U., 1956. Bar: D.C. 1957, Ill. 1972. Agt. IRS, Washington, 1957-61; trial atty. tax div. U.S. Dept. Justice, Washington, 1961-71; sr. tax atty. Internat. Harvester Co., Chgo., 1971-76, gen. tax atty., 1976-82; judge U.S. Claims Ct., Washington, 1982—. Mem. bus. adbv. council Chgo. Urban League, 1974-82. Served with AUS, 1946-47. Recipient cert. award U.S. Dept. Justice Atty. Gen., 1969; recipient spl. commendation U.S. Dept. Justice Atty. Gen., 1970. Mem. ABA, D.C. Bar Assn., Chgo. Bar Assn., Fed. Bar Assn., Nat. Bar Assn. Republican. Baptist. Club: Nat. Lawyers (Washington). General practice, Corporate taxation. Home: 6305 Chaucerview Circle Alexandria VA 22304 Office: US Claims Ct 717 Madison Pl NW Washington DC 20005

GIBSON, THOMAS HARRIS, III, lawyer, accountant; b. San Diego, May 5, 1947; s. T.H. and Dorothy (Wiggins) G.; m. Gretchen Schnieders, Aug. 4, 1973; children: Graham Alexander, Emily Elizabeth. B.A., UCLA, 1970; J.D., U. Calif.-Hastings, 1975. Bar: Calif. 1975. Tax mgr. Price Waterhouse, San Francisco, 1978-82; sr. internat. tax mgr., N.Y.C., 1982-83, San Francisco, 1984-85, internat. tax ptnr., 1985—; instr. U. Sherbrooke, Que., PQ, Can., 1983-87. Author (with others): The Art of Deduction, 1980. Bd. dirs. Bay Area Lawyers for Arts, San Francisco, 1981-82. Mem. ABA, Calif. State Bar Assn., Calif. Soc. C.P.A.'s, Am. Inst. C.P.A.'s. Clubs: Piping Rock Club, Racquet and Tennis (N.Y.C.). Private international, Corporate taxation. Office: Price Waterhouse 555 California St San Francisco CA 94104

GIBSON, THOMAS MARTIN, lawyer; b. Rahway, N.J., Nov. 1, 1935; s. William John and Louise (Schmitzer) G.; m. Judith A. Gibson, Aug. 19, 1960; children—Loretto, Kathleen, Timothy, Christopher. B.E.S. in Engring., Johns Hopkins U., 1957; LL.B., NYU Sch. Law, 1966. Bar: N.Y. 1967. Ptnr., Morgan, Finnegan, Pine, Foley & Lee, N.Y.C., 1974-81, Hedman, Gibson, Costigan & Hoare, N.Y.C., 1981—; lectr. Del. Law Sch., Wilmington, 1970-72. Mem. St. Gabriels Holy Name Soc., Marlboro, N.J., 1976—, pres. 1978-80. Fellow N.Y. Bar Assn., N.Y. Patent Law Assn.; mem. Johns Hopkins U. Alumni Assn. (pres. Central N.J. 1983-84). Patent, Trademark and copyright, Copyright. Home: 1 Northwood Place Colts Neck NJ 07702 Office: Hedman Gibson Costigan & Hoare PC 1185 Ave of the Americas New York NY 10036

GIBSON, VIRGINIA LEE, lawyer; b. Independence, Mo., Mar. 5, 1946. BA, U. Calif., Berkeley, 1972; JD, U. Calif., San Francisco, 1977. Bar: Calif. 1981. Assoc. Pillsbury, Madison & Sutro, San Francisco, 1980-83; ptnr. Chickering & Gregory, San Francisco, 1983-85, Baker & McKenzie, San Francisco, 1985—. Mem. ABA (employee benefits subcom. tax sect.), Calif. Bar Assn. (exec. com. tax sect. 1985—), Western Pension Conf. (chmn. program com. 1986—), Internat. Found. Employee Benefit Plans. Pension, profit-sharing, and employee benefits, Fiduciary services and institutional funds. Office: Baker & McKenzie 580 California St San Francisco CA 94104

GIDCUMB, LANCE EDWARD, lawyer; b. Harrisburg, Ill., Oct. 5, 1950; s. Charles F. and Barbara A. (Bigelow) G.; m. Candice Harper, Jan. 29, 1972; children—Kelly, Shaun. B.S. in Edn., Ill. State U., 1972; J.D., Baylor U., 1975. Bar: Tex. 1975, U.S. Mil. Appeals 1975, Alaska 1978, U.S. Ct. Appeals (9th cir.) 1979, U.S. Supreme Ct. 1979. Assoc. Groh, Eggers, Anchorage, 1979-81, ptnr., 1981—; guest lectr. Anchorage Sch. Dist., 1983-84. Negotiator, gen. counsel Kenai Natives Assn., Inc., Alaska, 1983—; lobbyist Tesoro Alaska Petroleum Corp., Alaska Land Title Assn., 1983—. Served to capt. JAGC, USAF, 1975-79. Mem. ABA (mil. law com. 1975-79, litigation, tort and ins. practice sects.), Assn. Trial Lawyers Am., Nat. Assn. R.R. Trial Counsel, Tex. Bar Assn., Alaska Bar Assn., Anchorage Bar Assn. Lodge: Masons. Real property, Personal injury, General corporate. Home: 2530 Brittany Dr Anchorage AK 99504 Office: Groh Eggers & Price 550 W 7th St Suite 1250 Anchorage AK 99501

GIDEL, DAVID DALE, lawyer; b. Ft. Dodge, Iowa, Apr. 17, 1948; s. Dale Raymond and Harriet Olivia (Schlachter) G.; m. Mary Eleanor Reideler, June 13, 1970; children: Michael, Robert. BBA, U. Iowa, 1970; JD, Creighton U., 1976. Assoc. Matthews & Cannon, Omaha, 1976-78; ptnr. Monaghan, Tiedeman, Lynch & Gidel, Omaha, 1978-83, Gray, Gray & Gidel, Rockwell City, Iowa, 1983—; asst. atty. Calhoun County, Rockwell City, 1984-85, atty., 1985—. Mem. adv. bd. Rockwell City Recreation, 1984—. Served with USN, 1970-73. Mem. ABA, Iowa Bar Assn. (lawyers profl. ins. com.), Nebr. Bar Assn., Calhoun County Bar Assn. (sec., treas. 1986—), Rockwell City C. of C. Republican. Roman Catholic. Club: Twin Lakes (Iowa) Golf and Country (bd. dirs. 1985—). Lodge: Rotary (bd. dirs. 1985—). Avocations: flying, golf, racquetball, officiating sports. General practice, Probate, State civil litigation. Home: 259 Morton Dr Rockwell City IA 50579 Office: Gray Gray & Gidel 423 Court St Rockwell City IA 50579

GIDEON, KENNETH WAYNE, lawyer; b. Lubbock, Tex., July 25, 1946; s. Melton Jean and Mary B. (Lanham) G.; m. Carol Almack, June 2, 1968; children—Christopher Lynn, Kevin Almack, Timothy Charles, Emily Susan. B.A., Harvard U., 1968; J.D., Yale U., 1971. Bar: Tex. 1971, U.S. Tax Ct. 1971, U.S. Ct. Claims 1972, U.S. Supreme Ct. 1981, D.C. 1984. Ptnr., assoc. Fulbright & Jaworski, Houston, 1971-81, Washington, 1983-86; chief counsel IRS, Washington, 1981-83; ptnr. Fried, Frank, Harris, Shriver & Jacobson, Washington, 1986—. Mem. Spring Valley City Council, Tex., 1978-79. Served to capt. U.S. Army, 1971-72. Mem. ABA (chmn. govt. relations com. tax sect. 1984-86). Corporate taxation, Personal income taxation. Office: Fried Frank Harris Shriver & Jacobson 1001 Pennsylvania Ave NW Washington DC 20004

GIEPERT, MELVIN JOHN, lawyer; b. New Orleans, Feb. 18, 1929; s. William Albert and Catherine (Rennenberg) G.; m. Sarah Catherine Dimitri, July 28, 1956; children—Elmore, Gary, Catherine. B.A., Southeastern U., 1956; J.D., Tulane U., 1959. Bar: La. 1959. Security clk. FBI, Washington, 1948-53; ptnr. Arnold & Giepert, New Orleans, 1959—; arbitrator Am. Arbitration Assn., N.Y.C., 1969—. Disaster chmn. ARC, New Orleans, 1982—. Served as sgt. U.S. Army, 1951-53, Korea. Fellow Nat. Bd. Trial Advocacy; mem. La. Trial Lawyers Assn. (bd. 1972-74), Acad. New Orleans Trial Lawyers Assn. (pres. 1969-70). Club: Sunshine (New Orleans). State civil litigation, Personal injury, Probate. Home: 319 Olivier St New Orleans LA 70114 Office: 500 Verret St New Orleans LA 70114

GIERBOLINI-ORTIZ, GILBERTO, federal judge; b. 1926. B.A., U. P.R., 1951, LL.B., 1961. Asst. U.S. atty. Commonwealth P.R., 1961-66; judge Superior Ct. Bayamon, P.R., 1966-67; asst. atty. gen. for litigation P.R., 1969-72; sole practice 1973-80; judge U.S. Dist. Ct. P.R., San Juan, 1980—. Judicial administration. Office: US District Court Post Office and Courthouse Bldg PO Box 3671 San Juan PR 00904 *

GIERHART, DOUGLAS MARK, lawyer; b. Shawnee, Okla., Mar. 29, 1956; s. Lew Dale and Carla Jeanne (Spangler) G.; m. Linda Susan Lanier, May 16, 1981; 1 child, Joshua Douglas. BA, Okla. U., 1978; JD, Okla. City U., 1981. Bar: Okla. 1982, U.S. Dist. Ct. (we. dist.) Okla. 1982. Asst. dist. atty. Child Support Enforcement Agy., Shawnee, 1981-83; sole practice Shawnee, 1984—. Candidate Dem. State Ho. of Reps., 1986. Mem. ABA, Okla. Bar Assn., Pottawatomie County Bar Assn., Assn. Trial Lawyers Am., Okla. Trial Lawyers Assn., Jaycees. Baptist. Lodge: Lions. Avocations: snow skiing, camping. Probate, Consumer commercial, General practice. Home: 1915 Chandler Cir Shawnee OK 74801 Office: 228 N Broadway Shawnee OK 74801

GIERKE, HERMAN FREDRICK, III, state supreme court justice; b. Williston, N.D., Mar. 13, 1943; s. Herman Fredrick, Jr. and Mary (Kelly) G.; m. Judith Lynn Olson, June 12, 1965; children—Todd H.F., Scott H.F., Craig H.F., Michelle Lynn. B.A., U. N.D., 1964, J.D., 1966; attended, JAG Sch., U. Va., 1967, 69. Bar: N.D. 1966, U.S. Dist. Ct. N.D., U.S. Supreme Ct. Practice law Watford City, N.D., 1971-83; state's atty. McKenzie County, 1974-82; city atty. City of Watford, 1974-83; justice N.D. Supreme Ct., Bismarck, 1983—. Served as capt. JAGC, U.S. Army, 1967-71. Recipient Outstanding Service award Gov. of N.D., 1984. Fellow Am. Coll. Probate Counsel; mem. N.D. Trial Lawyers Assn. (bd. govs. 1977-83), N.D. State Attys. Assn. (pres. 1979-80), N.D. Council Sch. Attys. (charter), NW Jud. Dist. Bar Assn. (pres. 1977-79), State Bar Assn. N.D. (pres. 1982-83), Am. Judicature Soc., Assn. Trial Lawyers Am., Nat. Dist. Attys. Assn., Aircraft Owners and Pilots Assn., Am. Legion (N.D. comdr. 1984, judge adv. state assn., nat. vice comdr. 1985—), ABA, Blue Key, Phi Delta Phi. Lutheran. Lodge: Elks. Avocations: racquetball; golf; tennis; raising horses. Office: ND State Supreme Ct Judicial Wing 1st Floor State Capitol Bismarck ND 58505

GIESE, HEINER, lawyer, real estate investor; b. Passau, Germany, Apr. 16, 1944; came to U.S., 1950, naturalized, 1957; s. Heinz Emil and Wilma Maria (Dunner) G.; m. Barbara Ann Kent, June 28, 1969; children—Anna, Peter. B.S. in Internat. Affairs, Georgetown U., 1966; J.D., U. Wis.-Madison, 1969. Bar: Wis. 1969, U.S. Dist. Ct. (ea. and we. dists.) Wis. 1969, U.S. Ct. Appeals (7th cir.) 1974, U.S. Supreme Ct. 1974. Law clk. U.S. Dist. Ct., Madison, 1969-70; assoc. Cannon, McLaughlin, Herbon & Staudenmeier, Milw., 1969-74; ptnr. Levin & Giese, Milw., 1974-85, Giese & Weden Law Offices, Milw., 1985—. Bd. dirs. German Fest Milw., 1981-84, legal counsel, 1981-84; bd. dirs. Grafton Dells, 1981—, v.p., 1981—; bd. dirs. German Lang. and Sch. Soc., 1976—; mem. adv. council Milw. World Festival, 1981-84; legal counsel United Festivals of Milw., Inc., 1984—; mem. Income Property Owners Assn., 1980—; bd. dirs. Goethe House, Milw.; Wis. gov.'s rep. Presdl. Commn. for German-Am. Tricentennial, 1983. Recipient Outstanding Young Lawyer award, 1979. Mem. ABA (Young Lawyers Div. Affiliate Outreach Team 1979-80, regional vice chmn. membership com. 1979-81), Wis. Bar Assn., Milw. Bar Assn. (chmn. lawyer referral service 1980-83), Milw. Young Lawyers Assn. (pres. 1978-79), Milw. Bar Found. (bd. dirs. 1979—). Democrat. Lutheran. General practice, Real property. Home: 2022 N 72d St Wauwatosa WI 53213 Office: 1216 N Prospect Ave Milwaukee WI 53202

GIESEKE, CORINNE JOYCE, lawyer; b. Barrington, Ill., May 28, 1954; s. Walter Henry and Carole Mae (Olney) G.; m. Paul Robert Wood, Jan. 14, 1978; children: Ashley, Brandon. BS, U. Ill., 1976; JD, Loyola U., Chgo., 1979. Bar: Ill. 1979, U.S. Dist. Ct. (no. dist.) Ill. 1979, U.S. Ct. Appeals (7th cir.) 1981. Gen. counsel Ill. Commr. Banks, Chgo., 1979-82; assoc. Hopkins & Sutter, Chgo., 1983-86; sole practice Chgo., 1986—. Mem. ABA (banking com.), Ill. Bar Assn., Chgo. Bar Assn. (sec. 1985-86, vice chmn. 1986-87), Jr. League Chgo., Phi Beta Kappa, Phi Kappa Phi, Alpha Lambda Delta. Banking, Consumer commercial, Legislative. Home and Office: 1448 N Lake Shore Dr Chicago IL 60610

GIEVERS, KAREN A., lawyer; b. Culver City, Calif., Apr. 27, 1949; d. Ernest Conrad and Josephine Theresa (Passolt) Prevost; m. Joseph R. Gievers, Nov. 16, 1968; children—Daniel Steven, Donna Ann. A.A., Miami Dade Community Coll., 1974; B.A., Fla. Internat. U., 1975; J.D. cum laude, U. Miami, 1978. Bar: Fla. 1978, U.S. Dist. Ct. (so. dist.) Fla. 1978, U.S.

Dist. Ct. (mid. and no. dist.) Fla. 1979, U.S. Ct. Appeals (5th cir.) 1979, U.S. Ct. Claims 1980, U.S. Ct. Appeals (11th cir.) 1981, U.S. Suprem Ct. 1982. Assoc. Sams, Anderson, Gerstein & Ward, P.A., Miami, Fla., 1978; assoc. Anderson, Moss, Russo & Gievers, P.A., Miami, 1979-83, ptnr. 1983—. Bd. editors So. Dist. Digest, 1981-85. Lectr. FACT, Miami, 1984. Mem. Fla. Bar Assn. (editor trial lawyers sect. 1984, vice-chmn. evidence com. 1985-86), ABA, Acad. Fla. Trial Lawyers (chmn. pub. com. 1984—, bd. dirs. 1985—, recipient Pres.'s award 1986), Am. Trial Lawyers Assn., Dade County Bar Assn. (bd. dirs. 1981-84, 85—), Dade County Trial Lawyers Assn. (sec. 1984, treas. 1985, pres. 1987), Fed. Bar Assn., Fla. Assn. Women Lawyers, Zool. Soc. Fla., Fla. Consumer Fedn. (bd. dirs. 1985—). Democrat. Club: City (Miami). Personal injury, Federal civil litigation, State civil litigation. Office: Anderson Moss Russo Gievers & Cohen PA 100 N Biscayne Blvd Suite 2300 Miami FL 33132

GIFFIN, GORDON D., lawyer; b. Springfield, Mass., Dec. 29, 1949; s. Earl K. and Sarah-Gwen (Davies) G.; m. Patti Alfred, July 31, 1976; 1 child, Kelley V. BA, Duke U., 1971; JD, Emory U., 1974. Bar: Ga. 1974, D.C. 1978. Assoc. McCurdy, Candler & Harris, Decatur, Ga., 1974; legis. dir. Sen. Sam Nunn, Washington, 1975-79; ptnr. Hansell & Post, Atlanta, 1979-86, Long, Aldridge & Norman, Atlanta, 1986—; adj. prof. Emory U. Sch. Law, Atlanta, 1986—. Mem. Leadership Ga., 1978, Atlanta Chamber Govt. Com., 1985—; treas. Sen. Nunn Campaign Com., 1979—. Clubs: Atlanta Lawyers, Gridiron Society. Administrative and regulatory, General corporate, Election law. Home: 172 N Mill Rd Atlanta GA 30328 Office: Long Aldridge & Norman 134 Peachtree St Suite 1900 Atlanta GA 30043

GIFFORD, DONALD ARTHUR, lawyer; b. Derry, N.H., Nov. 21, 1945; s. George Donald and Bertha Margaret (Gibbs) G.; m. Sandra Louise Robaldo, July 25, 1964; children—Adriana, Roy, Stacy. B.A., U. S. Fla., 1967; J.D. with high honors, Fla. State U., 1970. Bar: Fla. 1970, U.S. Dist. Ct. (mid. dist.) Fla. 1970, U.S. Dist. Ct. (no. dist.) Fla. 1981, U.S. Dist. Ct. (so. dist.) Fla. 1982, U.S. Ct. Appeals (5th cir.) 1975, U.S. Ct. Appeals (11th cir.) 1981, U.S. Supreme Ct. 1980. Assoc. Raymond, Wilson, Karl, Conway & Barr, Daytona Beach, Fla., 1972; law clk. U.S. dist. ct. (mid. dist.) Fla., Tampa, 1972-73; with Shackleford, Farrior, Stallings & Evans, P.A., Tampa, 1973—. Mem. ABA, Fed. Bar Assn., Fla. Bar, Hillsborough County Bar Assn. (dir. 1981—, pres. elect 1987—), U. S. Fla. Nat. Alumni Assn. (pres. 1976, dir. 1970—), Fla. State U. Coll. Law Alumni Assn. (dir. 1982—, pres. 1987—), Hall of Fame Bowl Assn. (mem team selection com. 1986—). Clubs: Tower (dir. 1982-85), Tiger Bay (Tampa). Lodge: Kiwanis. Antitrust, Federal civil litigation. Office: PO Box 3324 Tampa FL 33601

GIFFORD, ERNEST IRVING, lawyer, educator; b. Flint, Mich., Dec. 4, 1933; s. Gale L and Bergetta (Rice) G.; m. Marianne Janet Herod, Aug. 14, 1954; children: Kim, Kris, Kori. AA, Flint Community Coll., 1954; BA, Mich. State U., 1956; JD, Wayne State U., 1960. Bar: Mich, 1961, U.S. Supreme Ct., 1971, U.S. Patent and Trade Office, 1962, U.S. Ct. Appeals (6th cir.) 1964, U.S. Ct. Appeals (D.C. cir.) 1980. Ptnr. Hauke, Gifford et al, Lathrup Village, Mich., 1961-74, Gifford, Groh, Van Ophem, Sheridan, Sprinkle & Dolgorukov, Birmingham, Mich., 1975—; assoc. prof. Oakland U. paralegal program. Mem. ABA, State Bar Mich. (assembly rep. 1985—, chmn. patent-trademark-copyright sect. 1974), Mich. Patent Law Assn., Am. Intellectual Property Law Assn. Democrat. Lutheran. Patent, Trademark and copyright, Federal civil litigation. Home: 5210 Kings Gate Way Bloomfield Hills MI 48013 Office: Gifford Groh et al 280 N Woodward Birmingham MI 48011

GIFFORD, GEOFFREY L., lawyer; b. Kirksville, Mo., Nov. 26, 1946; s. Robert M. and Elnora Frances (Overstreet) G.; m. Jerrilyn A. Randall; children—Andrew, Katie. B.A., U. Mo., 1968; J.D., U. Mich., 1971. Bar: Mo. 1971, Mich. 1972, U.S. Dist. Ct. (we. dist.) Mo. 1973, Ill. 1977, U.S. Dist. Ct. (no. dist.) Ill. 1978. Assoc. firm Forsythe, Campbell, Vandenberg & Clevenger, Ann Arbor, Mich., 1972; ptnr. firm Gifford & Gifford, Green City, Mo., 1973-77; of counsel Gifford & Richardson, Green City; adj. prof. law Ill. Inst. Tech.-Chgo. Kent Coll. Law, 1977-78; prin. firm Asher, Pavalon, Gittler & Greenfield, Chgo., 1978—. speaker IICLE Automobile Products Liability Seminar, Chgo., 1986—. Fellow The Roscoe Pound Am. Trial Lawyers Found. (patron); mem. Ill. Trial Lawyers Assn. (assoc. editor 1980-82, editor 1982-86, bd. mgrs. 1982—, chmn. products liability com. 1984-86, chmn. seminar planning com. 1984-86, chmn. med. malpractice com., 1985-87), Assn. Trial Lawyers Am. (lectr. U. Wis., vice chmn. reorganization com.), Tenn. Trial Lawyers Assn. (guest lectr. 1986), W.Va. Trial Lawyers Assn. (guest lectr. 1986), Ill. Inst. Continuing Legal Edn. (author and lectr.), Soc. Trial Lawyers, Ill. Bar Assn., Trial Lawyers Club Chgo., Phi Beta Kappa, Phi Alpha Delta. Democrat. Personal injury, State civil litigation, Federal civil litigation. Home: 834 W George St Chicago IL 60657 Office: Asher Pavalon Gittler & Greenfield Ltd 2 N LaSalle St Chicago IL 60602

GIFFORD, WAYNE DANIEL, lawyer; b. Lebanon, Mo., Sept. 30, 1955; s. Elmer Lawrence and Velma Ruth (Sayers) G.; m. Linda Carol Butler, Jan. 1, 1979. B.S., Sch. of the Ozarks, 1975; J.D., U. Mo.-Columbia, 1977. Bar: Mo. 1978, U.S. dist. ct. (we. dist.) Mo. Pros. atty. Pulaski County (Mo.), 1979-80; atty. for Juvenile Officer of 25th Cir., 1981—; sole practice, Waynesville, Mo., 1978—; instr. Columbia Coll., Leonard Wood Campus. Democratic committeeman Union Twp. (Mo.), 1982-84 . Mem. Mo. Bar Assn., Pulaski County Bar Assn., ABA, Assn. Trial Lawyers Am. Baptist. Club: Kiwanis (Waynesville). General practice, Personal injury, Family and matrimonial. Address: 409 City Rt E Waynesville MO 65583

GIFFORD, WILLIAM DAVID, lawyer; b. Atlanta, Mar. 24, 1951; s. William and Charlotte (Reynolds) G.; m. Molly Marie Motes, July 10, 1976; children: Christopher Kelley, John David. BA in History, Mercer U., 1974, JD, 1981. Bar: Ga. 1981, U.S. Dist. Ct. (mid. dist.) Ga. 1982. Sole practice Macon, Ga., 1981-84; ptnr. Cook & Shaffer, Macon, 1984—. Coach Vinr-Ingle Little League, Macon, 1986; mem. Macon Assn. Retarded Citizens, 1986, past bd. dirs. Mem. Macon Bar Assn., Macon Assn. Criminal Def. Lawyers (treas. 1982-83, pres. elect 1986—). Democrat. Methodist. Lodges: Elks, Sertoma (chmn. freedom week 1986). Avocations: fishing, reading, sailing, golf. Criminal, Bankruptcy, Personal injury. Home: 181 Audubon Pl Macon GA 31210 Office: Cook & Shaffer 520 Liberty Fed Tower Macon GA 31201

GIGNILLIAT, WILLIAM ROBERT, III, lawyer; b. Sebring, Fla., Mar. 22, 1943; s. William Robert and Ann Josephine (Harris) G.; m. Rosemary Rebecca Bersch, May 29, 1971 (div. July 1979); 1 dau., Meigan Rebecca; m. Laura Crowell Lieberman Mar. 20, 1984; 1 child, William Robert, IV. B.A., U. South, 1965; J.D., Emory U., 1968. Bar: Ga. 1968, U.S. Dist. Ct. (no. dist.) Ga. 1970, U.S. Ct. Apls. (5th cir.) 1970, U.S. Supreme Ct. 1972, U.S. Ct. Apls. (11th cir.) 1982. Atty., Emory Neighborhood Law Office, Atlanta, 1967-71; ptnr. Mantegna, Gignilliat & Wiggins, Atlanta, 1974-75, Gignilliat, Manchel, Johnson & Wiggins, 1977-83; sole practice, Atlanta, 1983—. Pres., chmn. bd. Words of Art, Inc., Atlanta, 1982—. Author: Contracts for Artists, 1983, Handbook on the Georgia Print Law, 1986. Bd. sponsors Center for Puppetry Arts, Atlanta, 1979—. Served with AUS, 1968-70. Mem. Ga. Vol. Lawyers for the Arts, ABA, Ga. Criminal Def. Lawyers Assn. Democrat. Trademark and copyright, Criminal, Entertainment. Office: 918 Ponce de Leon Ave Atlanta GA 30306

GIGNOUX, EDWARD THAXTER, federal judge; b. Portland, Maine, June 28, 1916; s. Frederick Evelyn and Katherine (Denison) G.; m. Hildegarde Schuyler Thaxter, June 30, 1938; children: Marie Andrée (Mrs. James F. Grisé), Edward Thaxter. A.B. cum laude, Harvard U., 1937, LL.B. magna cum laude, 1940; LL.D. (hon.), Bowdoin Coll., 1962, U. Maine, 1966, Colby Coll., 1974, Nasson Coll., 1974, Bates Coll., 1977, Husson Coll., 1983, St. Joseph's Coll., 1984. Bar: D.C. bar 1941, Maine bar 1946. Asso. Slee, O'Brian, Hellings & Ulsh, Buffalo, 1940-41, Covington, Burling, Rublee, Acheson & Shorb, Washington, 1941-42; partner Verrill, Dana, Walker, Philbrick & Whitehouse, Portland, 1946-57; U.S. dist. judge Portland, 1957—; judge U.S. Temp. Emergency Ct. Appeals, 1980—; former corporator Maine Savs. Bank; former mem. adv. com. bankruptcy rules U.S. Supreme Ct.; former mem. council and vis. com. Harvard Law Sch.; also chmn. vis. com.; past mem. adv. panel internat. law U.S. State Dept.; faculty Salzburg Seminar for Am. Studies, 1972; asst. corp. counsel, City of Portland, 1947-48, mem. city council, 1949-55, chmn., 1952. Editor: Harvard Law Rev, 1939-40. Pres., bd. dirs. Greater Portland Community Chest, 1955-56, United Fund, 1956-57; former corporator, trustee Maine Med. Center; former trustee Maine Eye and Ear Infirmary, Portland Symphony Orch.; former bd. overseers Harvard Coll. Served as maj. AUS, 1942-46. Decorated Bronze Star, Legion of Merit. Mem. ABA (spl. com. on jud. conduct), Maine Bar Assn., Cumberland County Bar Assn., Inst. Jud. Adminstrn.; former mem. Jud. Conf. U.S. (chmn. standing com. on rules of practice and procedure 1980—, former mem. jud. ethics com.); mem. Am. Judicature Soc. (past dir.), Am. Law Inst. (council, 2d v.p.). Episcopalian. Clubs: Harvard (pres. Maine 1957); Harvard (N.Y.C.); Portland Country. Home: 25 Starboard Ln Cumberland Foreside ME 04110 Office: US Dist Ct 156 Federal St Portland ME 04112

GIKAS, RICK CHRISTOPHER, lawyer; b. Gary, Ind., May 17, 1957; s. Philip George and Lulu (Zervos) G. BA, Ind. U., 1979; JD, Valparaiso U., 1982. Bar: Ind. 1982, U.S. Dist. Ct. (no. and so. dists.) Ind. 1982, U.S. Ct. Appeals (7th cir.) 1984. Sole practice Valparaiso, Ind., 1982-84, Merrillville, Ind., 1984—; cons. Project Justice and Equality, Gary, 1982—. Published decisions include: Atty. for Defendant, Grimes vs. Smith, 1985, Atty. for Plaintiff, Wykoff vs. Resig, 1985, Atty. for Plaintiff, McChristion vs. Duckworth, 1985. Mem. ABA, Ind. Bar Assn., Am. Judicature Soc., Assn. Trial Lawyers Am., Jack Lynn Meml. Jaycees (pres. 1985). Avocations: rare books, antiques. Federal civil litigation, Civil rights, Labor. Office: 7895 Broadway Suite N Merrillville IN 46410

GILBERG, DAVID JAY, lawyer; b. Phila., Apr. 2, 1956; s. Edwin M. and Elaine (Greenbaum) G.; m. Judith Cohn, Oct. 24, 1982; 1 child, Anne Rachel. BA, MA in History, U. Pa., 1978; JD, Harvard U., 1981. Bar: D.C. 1981, U.S. Dist. Ct. D.C., U.S. Ct. Appeals (D.C. cir.). Assoc. Rogers & Wells, Washington and N.Y., 1981—; Author: Law Review article, 1983, 84, 85. Mem. ABA, D.C. Bar Assn. Democrat. Jewish. Banking, Securities, Commodities. Home: 6012 Walton Rd Bethesda MD 20817 Office: Rogers & Wells 1737 H St NW Washington DC 20006

GILBERG, HOWARD LARRY, lawyer; b. Chgo., Nov. 26, 1955; s. Barry Paul and Judith (Frank) G.; m. Catherine Caudle, Sept. 24, 1983. BA with honors, U. Va., 1977; JD cum laude, Ind. U., 1981. Bar: Ill. 1981, U.S. Dist. Ct. (no. dist.) Ill. 1982, Tex. 1985, U.S. Dist. Ct. (no. dist.) tex. 1986. Assoc. Nisen, Elliott & Meier, Chgo., 1981-85, Thompson & Knight, Dallas, 1985—. Mem. ABA (natural resources sect.), Dallas Bar Assn. (environ. law sect., exec. council 1986), Tex. Bar Assn., Ill. State Bar Assn. (environ. law com. 1981—), Cook County (Ill.) Bar Assn. (young lawyer's energy and environ. law sect., environ. law com. 1981—), Phi Delta Phi, Delta Sigma Phi. Avocations: sports, outdoor activities. Environment, Federal civil litigation, Administrative and regulatory. Office: Thompson & Knight 3300 First City Ctr Dallas TX 75201

GILBERT, BRUCE RITS, lawyer; b. Milw., Apr. 8, 1954; s. Eugene George and Inez Laurel (Rits) G.; m. Andrea L. Fenton, Aug. 13, 1981; children: Molly Rits, Emily Rits. BBA, U. Wis., 1976; JD, Antioch Sch. Law, 1981. Bar: D.C. 1981, U.S. Dist. Ct. D.C. 1982, U.S. Ct. Appeals (D.C. cir.) 1982, Pa. 1985. Assoc. Weissburg and Aronson, Washington, 1981-84, Case & Cohen, Washington, 1984-85; health law counsel, asst. sec., editor Counsellor newsletter Universal Health Law Services, Inc., King of Prussia, Pa., 1985—. Mem. ABA, Nat. Assn. Health Lawyers. Jewish. Health, General corporate, Labor. Office: Universal Health Services Inc 367 Gulph Rd King of Prussia PA 19406

GILBERT, DANIEL THOMAS, lawyer, educator; b. Rockford, Ill., Dec. 25, 1954; s. Thomas D. and Dorothy M. (Humpal) G.; m. Jan E. Parker, June 17, 1978; children: Katie, Emily. BS, Rockford Coll., 1976; JD, John Marshall Sch. Law, Chgo., 1980. Bar: Ill. 1980, U.S. Dist. Ct. (no. dist.) Ill. 1981, Wis. 1985. Sole practice Rockford, Ill., 1980—; frequent lectr. in Ill. and Wis.; adj. faculty Rock Valley Community Coll., Rockford, 1985—; instr. Cardinal Stritch Coll., Beloit, Wis., 1985—, Rockford Coll., 1982—. Contbr. articles to profl. jours. Bd. dirs. Responsible Peer Program, Inc., 1983—, Big Brothers/Big Sisters of No. Ill., Rockford, 1985—. Mem. ABA, Ill. State Bar Assn. (com. on profl. responsibility 1984—), Wis. Bar Assn., Winnebago County (Ill.) Bar Assn. (com. for mentally disabled, chair com. on fee disputes 1981-83), Ill. Trial Lawyers Assn., Am. Arbitration Assn. Civil rights, Federal civil litigation, State civil litigation. Home: 216 Welty Ave Rockford IL 61107 Office: 1600 N Main St PO Box 6374 Rockford IL 61125

GILBERT, HOWARD N(ORMAN), lawyer; b. Chgo., Aug. 19, 1928; s. Norman Aaron and Fanny (Cohn) G.; m. Jacqueline Glasser, Feb. 16, 1957; children—Norman Abraham, Harlan Wayne, Joel Kenneth, Sharon. Ph.B., U. Chgo., 1947; JD, Yale U., 1951. Bar: Ill. 1951, U.S. Dist. Ct. (no. dist.) Ill. 1955, U.S. Ct. Appeals (7th cir.) 1956. Assoc. firm Rusnak, Deutsch & Gilbert, Chgo., 1962-79; ptnr. Aaron, Schimberg, Hess, Rusnak, Deutsch & Gilbert, Chgo., 1980-84, sr. ptnr. Holleb & Coff, 1984—, now sr. ptnr.; dir. Reflector-Hardware Corp., Albany Bank & Trust Co. N.Am., Sharon Broadcasting Co. Bd. dirs. Jewish Fedn. Met. Chgo., 1977-83; pres. Mt. Sinai Hosp. Med. Ctr., Chgo., 1968-69; trustee Chgo. Hosp. Council, 1979-84; mem. Bd. Jewish Edn. Served to lt. (j.g.) USN, 1951-55. Mem. ABA, Ill. Bar Assn., Chgo. Bar Assn., Chgo. Council Lawyers, Ill. Soc. Health Lawyers. Democrat. Jewish. Club: Standard. Real property, Health, General corporate. Office: Holleb & Coff 55 E Monroe Suite 4100 Chicago IL 60603

GILBERT, JOHN JORDAN, lawyer; b. Americus, Ga., Nov. 18, 1907; s. Osceola Pinckney and Talulah Zuleme (Jordan) G.; m. Dorothy Adams, Apr. 2, 1932; children—Emily, Randall. LL.B., Mercer U., 1929. Bar, Brunswick-Glynn County, 1929; with Gilbert, Whittle, Harrell, Scarlett, & Skelton, and predecessor firms, Brunswick, Ga., 1929—; dir. Sea Island Co. (Ga.); dir. Brunswick Pupl and Paper Co., 1955-78, Am. Nat. Bank Brunswick, 1955-78, chmn. bd., 1972-78.Rep., Ga. Ho. of Reps., 1942-46; mem. Brunswick Port Authority, 1946-51, chmn., 1948-51; mem. pres.'s adv. council Med. Coll. Ga., 1978—; trustee Brunswick Coll. Found., 1968-84; mem. Glynn-Brunswick Meml. Hosp. Authority, 1970-82, chmn., 1979-82. Recipient Alfred W. Jones award Brunswick C. of C., 1981. Fellow Am. Bar Found.; mem. Ga. Bar Assn., ABA, Brunswick-Glynn County Bar Assn., Alpha Tau Omega, Delta Theta Phi. Baptist. Lodge: Rotary (pres.). Banking, General corporate, Real property. Home: 2502 Frederica Rd Saint Simons Island GA 31522 Office: Gilbert Whittle et al 1st Fed Plaza 777 Gloucester St Brunswick GA 31521

GILBERT, OSCAR LAWRENCE, lawyer; b. Norfolk, Va., May 6, 1945; s. Harry L. and Felice (Nelson) G.; m. Janet Twiddy, July 3, 1966; children: David, Shana. BBA, Old Dominion U., 1972; JD, Coll. William & Mary, 1975. Bar: Va. 1975, U.S. Dist. Ct. Va. 1975. Assoc. Cooper & Cooper, Norfolk, 1975-76; ptnr. Rabinowitz, Rafal, Swartz & Gilbert, Norfolk, 1976—. State civil litigation, Federal civil litigation, Personal injury. Office: Rabinowitz Rafal Swartz & Gilbert 229 W Bute St Suite 750 Norfolk VA 23510

GILBERT, PAUL NELSON, lawyer; b. Plainfield, N.J., Feb. 8, 1950; s. Paul Nelson and LaVerne (Biddulph) G.; m. Pamela Joan DeMarco, June 10, 1972; children—Carrie Anne, Peter Marc. B.A., Rutgers Coll., 1972, J.D. cum laude, 1975. Bar: N.J. 1975, U.S. Dist. Ct. N.J. 1975, U.S. Dist. Ct. (so. dist.) N.Y. 1984, U.S. Dist. Ct. (ea. dist.) N.Y. 1984. Assoc., Goldberg, Simon & Selikoff, Cherry Hill, N.J., 1976; gen. atty. U.S. Immigration & Naturalization Service, Newark, 1977-82; sr. ptnr. Parlapiano & Gilbert, Newark, 1982-85; sole practice, Newark, 1985—. Legal counsel, bd. dirs. Ironbound Ednl. & Cultural Center, Newark, 1982-85 ; mem. exec. bd. Glacier Hills Assn., Parsippany, N.J., 1983-86. Mem. Am. Immmigration Lawyers Assn., N.J. State Bar Assn. Democrat. Roman Catholic. Immigration, naturalization, and customs. Home: 605 Lynne Dr Morris Plains NJ 07950 Office: 142 Walnut St Newark NJ 07105

GILBERT, RICHARD ALLEN, lawyer; b. Pitts., Dec. 13, 1948; s. Donald T., Sr. and Sara Margaret (Fife) G.; m. Patricia Ann Ramsdale, Jan. 21, 1972; 1 child, Stephanie Ann. B.A., Miami U., Oxford, Ohio, 1970; J.D., U. Cin., 1973. Bar: Ohio 1973, Fla. 1974, U.S. Dist. Ct. (mid. dist.) Fla. 1975, U.S. Ct. Appeals (5th and 11th cirs.) 1975. Assoc. Fowler, White, Gillen, Boggs, Villareal & Banker, PA, Tampa, Fla., 1974-78; ptnr. de la Parte, Gilbert & Gramovot, Tampa, 1979—. Editorial bd. U. Cin. Law Rev., 1972. Co-chmn. United Way Tampa, 1984. Mem. Assn. Trial Lawyers Am., Fla. Bar Assn., Ohio Bar Assn., ABA, Hillsborough County Bar Assn. Republican. Presbyterian. Federal civil litigation, State civil litigation, General practice. Home: 3202 Chapin Ave Tampa FL 33611 Office: de la Parte Gilbert & Gramovot 705 E Kennedy Blvd Tampa FL 33602

GILBERT, RICHARD LEE, lawyer; b. Phila., Feb. 16, 1948; s. Simon A. and Ruth (Kaufman) G.; m. Louise Burda, Sept. 27, 1969. BA, U. Calif., Santa Barbara, 1969; JD, U. Calif., Davis, 1972. Bar: Calif., U.S. Dist. Ct. (ea. dist.) CAlif., U.S. Supreme Ct. Dep. dist. atty. Yolo County, Calif., 1972-76; assoc. Blease, Vanderlaan & Rothschild, Sacramento, 1976-79; dist. atty. County of Yolo, Calif., 1979-83; judge Placer County Superior Ct., Auburn, Calif., 1983—; judge pro tem Calif. Supreme Ct., 1984, Calif. Ct. Appeals, Sacramento, 1985; instr. U. Calif., Davis, 1970-78, Los Rios Community Coll., Sacramento, 1970-76. mem. ABA (jud. adminstrn. sect.), Calif. Judges Assn., U. Calif. Sch. Law Almni Assn. (v.p. 1980-84, bd. dirs.), U. Claif. Alumni Assn. Democrat. Avocations: sailing, horseback riding, cross country skiing, cooking. Juvenile, General practice, Judicial administration. Office: Placer County Superior Ct 11546 B Ave Dept 4 Auburn CA 95603

GILBERT, ROBERT BRUCE, lawyer, tax consultant, accountant; b. Boyne City, Mich., June 16, 1918; s. Wilbur Gladstone and Flora (Haire) G.; m. Barbara Elizabeth Wurth, Dec. 14, 1945; children: Richard Bruce, Herbert David, Jacqueline Ann, Mark Thomas. BA in Law, Mont. State U., 1941, LLB, 1942. Bar: Mont. 1942. Sole practice Dillon, Mont., 1946; contract officer VA, Ft. Harrison, Mont., 1946-53; assoc. Schmidt, Lynch, Schmidt, Ft. Benton, Mont., 1953-54; ptnr. Schmidt, Gilbert, Jungers, Ft. Benton, 1955-84, of counsel, 1984—. Bd. dirs. Community Improvement Assn., Ft. Benton, 1957—; v.p. Benton Med. Ctr., Ft. Benton, 1981—. Served to capt. U.S. Army, 1942-46. Mem. ABA, Mont. State Bar Assn. (v.p.), Am. Judicature Soc., Sigma Chi (life). Republican. Episcopalian. Lodge: Kiwanis (pres. Ft. Benton club 1969-70). Avocations: travel, boating. General practice, Probate, Personal income taxation. Home: 605 River Rd Fort Benton MT 59442 Office: Schmidt Gilbert Jungers 1216 Front St Fort Benton MT 59442

GILBERT, ROBERT WOLFE, lawyer; b. N.Y.C., Nov. 12, 1920; s. L. Wolfe and Katherine L. (Oestreicher) Wolfe; m. Beatrice R. Frutman, Dec. 25, 1946; children—Frank Richard, Jack Alfred. B.A., UCLA 1941; J.D., U. Calif., Berkeley, 1943. Bar: Calif. 1944, U.S. Ct. Apls. (9th cir.) 1944, U.S. Ct. Apls. (D.C. cir.) 1976, U.S. Sup. Ct. 1959. Pres. Gilbert & Sackman, P.C. and predecessors, Los Angeles, 1944—; judge pro tem Los Angeles Mcpl. Ct., Beverly Hills Mcpl. Ct. Commr. City of Los Angeles Housing Authority 1953-63; bd. dirs. Calif. Housing Council 1955-63. Mem. Internat. Bar Assn., Interam. Bar Assn. (co-chmn. labor law and social security com.), ABA (co-chmn. internat. labor law com.), Fed. Bar Assn., Beverly Hills Bar Assn., Los Angeles Bar Assn. (chmn. labor law sect.), Am. Judicature Soc., Order of Coif, Pi Sigma Alpha. Club: Nat. Lawyers. Contbr. articles to profl. jours. Labor, Pension, profit-sharing, and employee benefits, Private international. Home: 7981 Hollywood Blvd Hollywood CA 90046 Office: 6100 Wilshire Blvd Suite 700 Los Angeles CA 90048-5107

GILBERT, RONALD BART, lawyer; b. Washington, Jan. 21, 1944; s. George and Betty (Janofsky) G.; m. Nancy Marie Railsback, Apr. 19, 1973. AB, U. Miami, 1965, JD, 1968. Bar: Fla. 1968, U.S. Dist. Ct. (so. dist.) Fla. 1968, U.S. Ct. Appeals (5th cir.) 1969, U.S. Ct. Appeals (11th cir.) 1982. Assoc. Strauss & McCormack, Miami, Fla., 1968-73, Ronald J. Strauss, Miami, 1973-75; sole practice South Miami, 1975-77, 80-83; ptnr. Gilbert & Schumacher, Coral Gables, Fla., 1977-80; sole practice Miami, 1984—. Mem. ABA, Fla. Bar Assn., Assn. Trial Lawyers Am., Fla. Trial Lawyers Assn. Avocations: photography, cooking, travel, computers. Personal injury, Family and matrimonial. Office: 9100 S Dadeland Blvd Suite 410 Miami FL 33156

GILBERT, RONALD RHEA, lawyer, organization executive; b. Sandusky, Ohio, Dec. 29, 1942; s. Corvin and Mildred (Millikin) G.; m. Marilynn Davis, Aug. 26, 1966; children: Elizabeth, Lynne, Lisa. B.A., Wittenberg U., 1964; J.D., U. Mich., 1967, postgrad., 1967-68; postgrad., Wayne State U., 1973-74. Bar: Mich. Assoc. prosecutor Wayne County, Mich., 1969; assoc. Rouse, Selby, Dickinson, Shaw & Pike, Detroit, 1969-72; ptnr. Charfoos, Christensen, Gilbert & Archer, P.C., Detroit, 1972-84; founder, chmn. Aquatic Injury Safety Group, 1982—, speaker seminars, 1982-83; instr. Madonna Coll., Detroit, 1977-81; mem. faculty Inst. Continuing Legal Edn., 1977—; speaker symposium on social security law Detroit Coll. Law, 1984. Co-author: Social Security Disability Claims, 1983. Contbr. articles to legal jours. Patron Detroit Art Inst.; mem. Pres.'s Club U. Mich.; mem. data collection subcom. of Nat. Swimming Safety com. for Consumer Products Safety Commn.; bd. dirs. Nat. Spinal Cord Assn. Mem. Assn. Trail Lawyers Am., Mich. Trial Lawyers Assn., System Safety Soc., ABA, Mich Bar Assn., Detroit Bar Assn., Am. Judicature Soc., Nat. Spinal Cord Injury Assn., Nat. Closed Head Injury Assn., Nat. Spinal Cord Assn. (bd. dirs.). Clubs: Detroit Country, Renaissance, Detroit Athletic, U. Mich. Personal injury, State civil litigation, Insurance. Home: 290 McKinley St Grosse Pointe Farms MI 48236

GILBERT, STEVEN JOHN, lawyer; b. Freeport, Tex., Sept. 5, 1947; s. William Drew and Josephine (Inamoratti) G.; m. Phyllis Nan Innerarity, May 23, 1970; children: Steven Drew, Emily Clain, Nancy Catherine, Lauren Nicole. BA, Stephen F. Austin State U., 1969; JD, U. Houston, 1975. Bar: Tex. 1974, U.S. Dist. Ct. (so. and ea. dists.) Tex. 1977, U.S. Ct. Appeals (5th cir.) 1977. Asst. dist. atty. Ft. Bend County, Richmond, Tex., 1975; ptnr. Van Slyke & Gilbert, Richmond, 1976—. Mem. S.W. Football Officials, Houston. Mem. Tex. Bar Assn. (admissions com.), Ft. Bend Bar Assn. (bd. dirs. 1986), Ft. Bend Criminal Bar Assn. (pres. 1986). Democrat. Baptist. Lodge: Lions. Criminal, Personal injury, Family and matrimonial. Home: 3622 FM 359 Richmond TX 77469 Office: Van Slyke & Gilbert 500 Morton St Richmond TX 77469

GILBERTSON, JOEL WARREN, lawyer; b. Valley City, N.D., Nov. 9, 1949; s. Roy W. and Gwen D. (Haugen) G.; m. Jan Erikson, June 11, 1972; children: David, Lisa. BA, Concordia Coll., Moorhead, Minn., 1972; JD, U. N.D., 1975. Bar: N.D. 1976, U.S. Dist. Ct. N.D. 1976, U.S. Ct. Appeals (8th cir.) 1976. Assoc. Binek & Gilbertson, Bowman, N.D., 1976; atty. N.D. Supreme Ct., Bismarck, 1976-78; exec. dir. N.D. Bar Assn., Bismarck, 1978-81; ptnr. Pearce & Durick, Bismarck, 1981—. Served with N.D. Air N.G., 1972-78. Mem. N.D. Bar Assn. (chmn. legis. com. 1978—), N.D. Bar Found. (vice chmn. 1982-84, chmn., bd. dirs. 1986—). Republican. Lutheran. Lodges: Rotary (chmn. com.), Elks. Avocations: piano, softball. Federal civil litigation, Personal injury, Insurance. Home: 1025 Crescent Ln Bismarck ND 58501 Office: Pearce & Durick 314 E Thayer Bismarck ND 58501

GILBRETH, PETER NELSON, lawyer; b. Lowell, Mass., July 21, 1948; s. John Moller and Dorothy Frances (Girvan) G.; m. Patricia Anne Thuring, June 26, 1971; children: Jeffrey, Amy. BA, Lafayette Coll., 1970; JD, St. John's U., Jamaica, N.Y., 1973. Bar: N.J. 1974, U.S. Dist. Ct. N.J. 1974, U.S. Ct. Appeals (3d cir.) 1975, U.S. Supreme Ct. 1983, N.Y. 1984. Dep. N.J. Atty. Gen., Trenton, 1974-75; asst. prosecutor Essex County, N.J., 1976-79, Morris County, N.J., 1979-82; assoc. Stephen S. Weinstein P.A., Morristown, N.J., 1982—. Mem. N.J. State Bar Assn., Morris County Bar Assn., N.J. Assn. Criminal Def. Attys., Trial Attys. of State of N.J. Democrat. Avocations: raquetball, sailing. Criminal, Personal injury, Insurance. Office: Stephen S Weinstein PA 20 Park Pl Morristown NJ 07960

GILCHRIST, DENNIS CLINTON, lawyer; b. Long Beach, Calif., May 12, 1946; m. Jan McLane; 1 child, Meghan. BA in Econs., San Jose State U., 1971; JD cum laude, Washington & Lee U., 1974; LLM in Taxation, NYU, 1976. Bar: N.Y. 1975, U.S. Dist. Ct. (so. and ea. dists.) N.Y. 1975, U.S. Tax Ct. 1975, U.S. Ct. Appeals (2d cir.) 1975, S.C. 1976, U.S. Dist. Ct. S.C. 1976, U.S. Ct. Appeals (4th cir.) 1977. Assoc. Patterson, Belknap & Webb, N.Y.C., 1974-76; ptnr. Leatherwood, Walker, Todd and Mann, Greenville, S.C., 1976-82, Brown and Hagins P.A., Greenville, 1982—. Del. White House Conf. on Small Bus., Washington, 1986. Mem. ABA, N.Y. State Bar Assn., S.C. Bar Assn., Greenville County Bar Assn., Greenville Estate Plan-

ning Council, Phi Delta Phi. Republican. Episcopalian. Corporate taxation, Probate, Pension, profit-sharing, and employee benefits. Office: Brown and Hagins PA PO Box 2464 Greenville SC 29602

GILDEA, EDWARD JOSEPH, lawyer; b. Boston, Sept. 8, 1951; s. William Aloysius and Catherine Florence (Nickerson) G.; m. Susan Maynard, Aug. 25, 1974; children: Edward, Caitlin, Anne. AB, Coll. of Holy Cross, 1973; JD, Suffolk U., 1977. Bar: Mass., 1977, D.C., 1980. Asst. gen. counsel Nat. Assn. Govt. Employees, Washington, 1977-79, gen. counsel, 1979-81; asst. gen. counsel Grolier Inc., Danbury, Conn., 1981-84, asst. sec., corp. counsel, 1984-85, sec., corp. counsel, 1985-86, v.p., corp. counsel, sec., 1986—. Mem. Bd. Fin., City of Bethel, Conn., 1986. Mem. Am. Soc. Corp. Secs., Am. Corp. Counsel Assn., Conn. Bar Assn., Mass. Bar Assn., D.C. Bar Assn., Direct Selling Assn., Direct Mktg. Assn. Democrat. Roman Catholic. Avocation: tennis. General corporate, Securities. Office: Grolier Inc Sherman Turnpike Danbury CT 06816

GILDEN, RICHARD HENRY, lawyer; b. Waterbury, Conn., May 28, 1946; s. Samuel and Adele (Lipshez) G.; m. Lorraine Ellen Bitner, Aug. 23, 1970; children: Sarah, Andrew. AB, Lafayette Coll., 1968; JD, Cornell U., 1971. Bar: N.Y., U.S. Dist. Ct. (no. dist.) N.Y. 1972. Assoc. Rosenman, Colin, Freund, Lewis & Cohen, N.Y.C., 1971-80, ptnr., 1980-86; ptnr. Gelberg & Abrams, N.Y.C., 1986—. Bd. dirs. Cotswold Assn., 1983—. Mem. ABA, Assn. of Bar of City of N.Y. General corporate, Securities. Office: Gelberg & Abrams 711 3d Ave New York NY 10017

GILDENHORN, JOSEPH BERNARD, lawyer; b. Washington, Sept. 17, 1929; s. Oscar and Celia (Koval) G.; m. Alma Lee Gross, June 28, 1953; children: Carol Ann, Michael Saul. B.S., U. Md., 1951; LL.B., Yale U., 1954. Bar: D.C. 1954, Md. 1954. Counsel Office Gen. Counsel, SEC, 1956-58; individual practice Washington, 1958—; ptnr. Brown, Gildenhorn & Jacobs, 1958—; guest lectr. George Washington U., D.C. Bar Assn.; pres. JBG Properties, Inc., JBG Assocs., Inc.; vice chmn., dir. Sovran/D.C. Nat. Bank; bd. dirs. Sovran Fin. Corp. Chmn. State of Israel Bonds, Washington, 1974, Nat. Jewish Coalition, Republican Com., 1984—; past pres., bd. dirs. Hebrew Home Greater Washington, 1975-77; bd. dirs. Washington Jewish Community Found.; v.p., bd. dirs. United Jewish Appeal Fedn. Greater Washington. Served with AUS, 1954-56. Recipient David Ben Gurion award State of Israel, 1977, Hyman Goldman Humanitarian award, 1984, B'nai B'rith Humanitarian award, 1985, Ourisman Community Service award, 1987. Mem. Apt. and Office Bldg. Assn. Washington. Club: Woodmont Country. Lodge: Masons. Home: 7000 Loch Lomond Dr Bethesda MD 20034 Office: 1250 Connecticut Ave NW Suite 500 Washington DC 20036

GILES, HOMER WAYNE, lawyer; b. Noble, Ohio, Nov. 9, 1919; s. Edwin Jay and Nola Blanche (Tillison) G.; m. Zola Ione Parke, Sept. 8, 1948; children: Jay, Janice, Keith, Tim, Gregory. A.B., Adelbert Coll., 1940; LL.B., Western Res. Law Sch., 1943, LL.M., 1959. Bar: Ohio bar 1943. Mem. firm Davis & Young, Cleve., 1942-43, William I. Moon, Port Clinton, Ohio, 1946-48; pres. Strabley Baking Co., Cleve., 1948-53; v.p. French Baking Co., Cleve., 1953-55; law clk. 8th Dist Ct. Appeals, Cleve., 1955-58; ptnr. Kuth & Giles, Cleve., 1958-68, Walter, Haverfield, Buescher & Chockley, Cleve., 1968—; pres. Clinton Franklin Realty Co., Cleve., 1958—, Concepts Devel., Inc., 1980—; sec. Holiday Designs, Inc., Sebring, Ohio, 1964—; trustee Teamster Local 52 Health and Welfare Fund, 1950-53; mem. Bakers Negotiating Exec. Com., 1951-53. Contbr. articles to profl. publs.; editor: Banks Baldwin Ohio Legal Forms, 1962. Troop com. chmn. Skyline council Boy Scouts Am., 1961-63; adviser Am. Security Council; trustee Hiram House Camp, Florence Crittenton Home, 1965; chmn. bd. trustees Am. Econ. Found., N.Y.C., 1973-80, chmn. exec. com., 1973-80. Served with AUS, 1943-46, ETO. Mem. Am. Bar Assn., World Law Assn. (founding), Am. Arbitration Assn. (nat. panel), Com. on Econ. Reform and Edn. (life), Inst. Money and Inflation, Speakers Bur. Cleve. Sch. Levy, Citizens League, Pacific Inst., Phila. Soc., Aircraft Owners and Pilots Assn., Cleve. Hist. Soc., Mus. Modern Art, Mercantile Library, Delta Tau Delta, Delta Theta Phi. Unitarian. Clubs: Cleve. Skating, Harvard Bus. General corporate, Contracts commercial, Corporate taxation. Home: 2588 S Green Rd University Heights OH 44122 Office: Walter Haverfield et al 1215 Terminal Tower Cleveland OH 44113

GILES, JAMES T., federal judge. B.A., Amherst Coll., 1964; LL.B., Yale U., 1967. Mem. Nat. Labor Relations Bd., Phila., 1967-68; assoc. Pepper, Hamilton & Scheetz, 1968-79; judge U.S. Dist. Ct. (ea. dist.) Pa., Phila., 1979—. Mem. Fed. Bar Assn., Phila. Bar Assn. Judicial administration. Office: US Dist Ct 8613 US Courthouse Independence Mall W 601 Market St Philadelphia PA 19106 *

GILES, ROBERT EDWARD, JR., lawyer; b. Bremerton, Wash., Dec. 17, 1949; s. Robert Edward Sr. and Alice Louise (Morton) G.; m. Barbara Susan Miller, Aug. 21, 1971; children: Steven, William, Thomas, James. BA in Fin., U. Washington, 1971, JD, 1974. Bar: Wash. 1974, U.S. Tax Ct. 1974. Assoc. Perkins Coie, Seattle, 1974-80, ptnr., 1980-83, fin. ptnr., 1983-86, adminstrv. ptnr., 1986—. Bd. dirs. Jr. Achievement, Seattle, 1984—; bd. dirs., sec. Wash. Council for Econ. Edn., 1981—. Served to capt. U.S. Army, 1974. Mem. ABA, Wash. State Bar Assn. Avocations: hiking, climbing. General corporate, Corporate taxation, Personal income taxation. Home: 5208 NE 187th St Seattle WA 98155 Office: Perkins Coie 1900 Washington Bldg Seattle WA 98101

GILES, WILLIAM JEFFERSON, III, lawyer; b. Manila, Philippines, Apr. 10, 1936; came to U.S., 1938; s. William Jefferson and Gardner (Anderson) G.; m. Nancy Gifford Seff, May 9, 1957; children—William Jefferson IV, Gregory Gifford. B.S., U. Calif.-Berkeley, 1957; postgrad. Golden Gate Coll., 1958-59, Stanford U., 1960; J.D., U. S.D., 1961. Bar: Iowa, 1961, Nebr. 1982, U.S. Dist. Ct. Iowa, 1961, U.S. Ct. Appeals (8th cir.) 1971, U.S. Supreme Ct. 1971. Sole practice, Sioux City, Iowa, 1962—; of counsel Whicher & Whicher, Sioux City, 1968-75, Whicher & Hart, Sioux City, 1975-77; lectr. in field. Bd. dirs. Sioux City Mus. and Hist. Soc., 1976-79, Sioux City Community Theatre, 1974-76. Served to capt. USAR, 1957-68. Recipient Gold Seal award, Phi Beta Kappa, 1953. Mem. Iowa Bar Assn., Nebr. Bar Assn., ABA, Assn. Trial Lawyers Am., Assn. Trial Lawyers of Iowa, Nebr. Assn. Trial Attys. Republican. Clubs: Sioux City Country, Phi Delta Phi, Phi Phi. Contbr. articles to profl. jours. Bankruptcy, Family and matrimonial, Personal injury. Home: 3827 Country Club Blvd Sioux City IA 51104 Office: 722 Frances Bldg Sioux City IA 51101 also: 1107 W 2d St Crofton NE 68730

GILES, WILLIAM JEFFERSON, IV, lawyer; b. Columbus, Ga., Feb. 2, 1958; s. William Jefferson III and Nancy Gifford (Seff) G.; m. Barbara Joan Ryan, Apr. 9, 1983; 1 child, Katherine Elizabeth. BA, Carleton Coll., 1979; JD, Whittier Coll., 1982. Bar: Iowa 1982, Nebr. 1982, U.S. Dist. Ct. (no. dist.) Iowa 1982, U.S. Dist. Ct. Nebr. 1982. Assoc. Giles' Law Office, Sioux City, Iowa, 1982—. Fundraiser Boy Scouts Am., Sioux City, 1986—. Mem. ABA, Iowa Bar Assn. (juvenile law com. 1985—), Nebr. Bar Assn., Woodbury County Bar Assn. (civil rights com. 1983—), Assn. Trial Lawyer Am., Sioux City Young Lawyers Club, Whittier Coll. Sch. Law Student Bar Assn. (Outstanding Mem. award 1980-81). Club: Sioux City Country. Avocations: baseball, basketball, football, film, drama. Criminal, Family and matrimonial, Personal injury. Home: 3126 Pierce St Sioux City IA 51104 Office: Giles Law Office 722 Frances Bldg Sioux City IA 51101

GILFORD, STEVEN ROSS, lawyer; b. Chgo., Dec. 2, 1952; s. Ronald M. and Adele (Miller) G.; m. Anne Christine Johnson, Jan. 2, 1974; children—Sarah Julia, Zachary Michael, Eliza Rebecca. B.A., Dartmouth Coll., 1974; J.D., Duke U., 1978, M. Public Policy Scis., 1978. Bar: Ill. 1978, U.S. Dist. Ct. (no. dist.) Ill. 1978, U.S. Ct. Appeals (7th cir.) 1981, U.S. Ct. Appeals (D.C. cir.) 1984. Assoc., Isham, Lincoln & Beale, Chgo., 1978-85, ptnr. 1985—. Adminstrv. law editor Duke Law Jour., 1976-77. Bd. dirs. Evanston YMCA, 1982—, sec., 1985, vice chmn. 1986—; ; participating atty. ACLU, 1983—. Mem. Ill. Bar Assn. Federal civil litigation, Insurance, Libel. Home: 2728 Harrison St Evanston IL 60201 Office: Isham Lincoln & Beale 3 1st Nat Plaza Chicago IL 60601

GILHOOLY, EDWARD FOSTER, lawyer; b. Orange, N.J., July 2, 1946; s. Edward Henry and Vivian Ethel (Henze) G.; m. Susan Jacobs, Dec. 26, 1970; children—Ann Hull, Brian Thomas, Jonathan Edward. B.A. in Econs., Yale U., 1968; J.D., So. Meth. U., 1975. Bar: Pa. 1975, U.S. Dist. Ct. (ea. dist.) Pa. 1976, U.S. Ct. Appeals (3d cir.) 1976, D.C. 1982. Atty., Gulf Oil Corp., Phila., 1975-82; assoc. gen. counsel Johnson Matthey Investments, Inc., Malvern, Pa., 1982—. Served to capt. U.S. Army, 1968-72. Recipient Internat. Law prize So. Meth. U. Sch. Law, 1975. Mem. ABA, Am. Corp. Counsel Assn., Maritime Law Assn. U.S. General corporate, Insurance, Private international. Home: RD 2 Dowlin Forge Rd Downingtown PA 19335 Office: 4 Malin Rd Malvern PA 19355

GILHOUSEN, BRENT JAMES, lawyer; b. Anacortes, Wash., Sept. 24, 1946; s. Darrell James and Jean Sarah (Sabatine) G.; m. Sandra Mae King, Aug. 13, 1983; 1 child, Lindsay Elizabeth. B.A., Wash. State U., 1968; J.D., U. Oreg., 1973. Bar: Wash. 1973, U.S. Dist. Ct. (we. dist.) Wash. 1973, U.S. Ct. Appeals (9th cir.) 1976, Mo. 1980, U.S. Supreme Ct. 1980. Atty., EPA, Seattle, 1973-80; atty. Monsanto Co., St. Louis, 1980-83, asst. environ. counsel, 1983-85, environ. counsel, 1986—. Environment, Federal civil litigation, Administrative and regulatory. Office: Monsanto Co 800 N Lindbergh Blvd Saint Louis MO 63167

GILKES, ARTHUR GWYER, lawyer; b. Bronxville, N.Y., Feb. 6, 1915; s. Arthur Burton and Frances (Gwyer) G.; m. Ann Fullan, Feb. 26, 1942; children—Arthur Gwyer, Ann Colwell Gilkes Liu, Judith Porter Gilkes Benson, Jane Scott Gilkes Strausgütl. A.B., Princeton U., 1939; LL.B., NYU, 1947. Chemist, Standard Oil Devel. Co., Bayway, N.J., 1939-40; asst. advt. mgr. Mathieson Alkali Works, Inc., N.Y.C., 1940-42; assoc. Pennie, Edmonds, Morton & Barrows, N.Y.C., 1945-49; ptnr. Adams, Forward & McLean, N.Y.C., 1949-54; gen. mgr. patents and lic. dept., gen. patent atty. Standard Oil Co. (Ind.), Chgo., 1954-80; of counsel Leydig, Voit & Mayer, Ltd., Chgo., 1980—; pres., dir. Mid-Century Corp., 1967-74. Served with USN, 1942-45. Mem. ABA, Am. Intellectual Property Law Assn., Chgo. Patent Law Assn., Association Internationale pour la Protection de la Proprié té Industrielle, Assn. Bar. City N.Y., Internat. Patent and Trademark Assn., Licensing Execs. Soc., Am. Judicature Soc., Assn. Corp. Patent Counsel, Clubs: Mid-America, University, Racquet (Chgo.); Glen View (Ill.); Princeton (N.Y.C.); Nassau (Princeton); Northeast Harbor Golf, Tennis and Fleet (Maine); Country of Fla. Patent, Trademark and copyright. Office: One IBM Plaza Suite 4600 Chicago IL 60611

GILL, ANNE WHALEN, lawyer; b. Greenwich, Conn., Oct. 28, 1948; d. John James and Mary Jane (Stallcup) Whalen; m. David Masser Gill, May 27, 1972. BS, Dickinson College, 1969; postgrad., CUNY, 1969-71; JD, N.Y. Law Sch., 1979. Bar: N.Y. 1980, U.S. Dist. Ct. (so. dist.) N.Y. 1981, Colo. 1985. Sole practice N.Y.C., 1979-80; atty., editor N.Y. and Nat. Law Jour., N.Y.C., 1980-84; atty. Manville, Denver, 1984-85; sr. editor Shepard's McGraw Hill, Colorado Springs, Colo., 1985-86; law editor Wiley Law Publs., Colorado Springs, Colo., 1986—. Editor: N.Y. Law Jour. Digest (ann.) 1981-84. Sec. Bloomingdale Rep. Club, N.J., 1983; founder Jarre Canyon Protective Assn., Sedalia, Colo., 1985—; chmn. zoning planning com. Home Owner Assn., 1987. Mem. El Paso County Bar Assn. General practice, Legal publishing. Home: 1170 Madge Gulch Box 442 Sedalia CO 80135 Office: Wiley Law Publs 711 N Tejon St PO Box 1777 Colorado Springs CO 80901

GILL, E. ANN, lawyer; b. Elyria, Ohio, Aug. 31, 1951; d. Richard Henry and Laura (Beeler) G.; m. Robert William Hampel, Aug. 4, 1973; children: Lena, Richard. AB, Barnard Coll., 1972; JD, Columbia U., 1976. Bar: N.Y. 1977, U.S. Supreme Ct. 1982. Assoc. Mudge, Rose, Guthrie & Alexander, N.Y.C., 1976-77; assoc. Dewey, Ballantine, Bushby, Palmer & Wood, N.Y.C., 1977-84, ptnr., 1984—. Mem. ABA, N.Y. State Bar Assn., Nat. Assn. Bond Lawyers. Municipal bonds, General corporate. Home: 222 Central Park S New York NY 10019 Office: Dewey Ballantine Bushby et al 140 Broadway New York NY 10005

GILL, JOHN WELCH, JR., U.S. attorney; b. Monterey, Tenn., Mar. 17, 1942; s. John Welch and Billie Gene (Mackey) G.; m. Kathleen Gay Broughan, Apr. 15, 1983; 1 son, Andrew Welch. B.A., Vanderbilt U., 1964; J.D., Vanderbilt, 1967. Bar: Tenn. 1967. Spl. agt. FBI, New Haven and N.Y.C., 1967-70; asst. dist. atty. Knox County Dist. Atty.'s Office, Knoxville, Tenn., 1970-81; atty. Harwell & Nichols, Knoxville, 1981; U.S. atty. Eastern Dist. Tenn. U.S. Atty.'s Office, Dept. Justice, Knoxville, 1981—; mem. adv. com. U.S. Atty. Gen., Washington, 1985-86, vice chmn., 1985-86; mem. State of Tenn. Law Revision Commn., Nashville, 1973-76. Bd. dirs. Knoxville Ballet Co., 1983-86, Girls Club of Knoxville, 1986—, Leadership Knoxville, Class of 1986; v.p. bd. dirs. Knoxville Jr. Achievement, 1981-82. Mem. ABA, Tenn. Bar Assn., Knoxville Bar Assn. (pres. young lawyer sect. 1975-76, bd. dirs. 1974-76). Republican. Baptist. Club: Knoxville Civitan (pres. 1982-83). Criminal, Federal civil litigation, State civil litigation. Office: US Attys Office PO Box 872 Knoxville TN 37901

GILL, KEITH HUBERT, lawyer; b. Pocatello, Idaho, May 31, 1929; s. Hubert Samuel and Myrtle Frances (Olsen) G.; m. Glenna Jean Lowery, June 16, 1956; children—Suzanne Marie, Gina Michelle. B.A., Idaho State U., 1952; M.B.A., UCLA, 1962; J.D., U. So. Calif., 1968. Bar: Calif. 1969, U.S. Dist. Ct. (cen. dist.) Calif. 1969, U.S. Ct. Appeals (9th cir.) 1972, U.S. Supreme Ct. 1973, U.S. Tax Ct. 1974. Assoc. Kadison, Pfaelzer, Woodard, Quinn & Rossi, Los Angeles, 1968-73, ptnr., 1973-80; of counsel Mitchell, Silberberg & Knupp, Los Angeles, 1980-81; prin. Rodi, Pollock, Pettker, Galbraith & Phillips, Los Angeles, 1981-85; sole practice, Woodland Hills, Calif., 1985—; lectr. UCLA Law Sch. Clin. Program; dir. Sunland Ford, Inc. Judge pro tem Los Angeles Mcpl. Ct., 1977—; chmn. ballot measures Town Hall Calif., Los Angeles; mem. World Affairs Council Los Angeles County Art Mus. Bd. dirs. Las Virgenes Ednl. Fund, Calabasas Park Homeowners Assn. Mem. Calif. Bar Assn., Los Angeles County Assn., ABA, Calif. Conf. Dels., Phi Alpha Delta. Republican. Mormon. General corporate, Probate, Personal income taxation. Office: 5850 Canoga Ave Suite 400 Woodland Hills CA 91367

GILL, MARGARET GASKINS, lawyer; b. St. Louis, Mar. 2, 1940; d. Richard Williams and Margaret (Cambage) Gaskins; m. Stephen Paschall Gill, Dec. 21, 1961; children: Elizabeth, Richard. BA, Wellesley Coll., 1962; JD, U. Calif., Berkeley, 1965. Bar: Calif. 1966. Assoc. Pillsbury, Madison & Sutro, San Francisco, 1966-73, ptnr., 1973—; referee Calif. State Bar Ct., 1979-82. Mem. steering com. Trinity Episcopal Ch., Menlo Park, Calif., 1980-82, com. to revise constitution, Diocese Calif., 1981-82; trustee St. Luke's Hosp. Found., San Francisco, 1983—. Mem. ABA (spl. com. on corps.), Calif. Bar Assn. (corp. com. 1982-85, exec. com. 1985—, bus. law sect.), San Francisco Bar Assn. Republican. Episcopalian. Securities. Office: Pillsbury Madison & Sutro 235 Montgomery St San Francisco CA 94104

GILL, RULAND J., JR., lawyer; b. Roosevelt, Utah, Aug. 18, 1945; s. Ruland Jay and LeNore (Merkley) G.; m. Karen Morris Westergard, Sept. 27, 1974; children—Mary Elizabeth, Erin Lindsey, Jennifer Elise, David Paul. B.S. in Acctg., U. Utah, 1970, J.D., 1973. Bar: Utah 1973, U.S. Dist. Ct. Utah 1973, U.S. Ct. Appeals (10th cir.) 1976. Staff atty. Mountain Fuel Supply Co., Salt Lake City, 1973-79, Wexpro Co., Salt Lake City, 1979-82; staff atty. Celsius Energy Co., Salt Lake City, 1982-84; mng. atty., 1984—; trustee Rocky Mountain Mineral Law Found., 1982—. Author: Intergovernmental Restraints on Oil and Gas Development, 1981. Mem. editorial bd. Law of Federal Oil and Gas Leases, 2 vols., 1982—. Bd. dirs. Utah State Fair Found., 1983—; mem. Utah Gov's. Blue Ribbon Task Force on Oil and Gas Regulation, 1986—. Served to maj. JAGC, USAR, 1963—. Mem. Rocky Mountain Oil and Gas Assn. (vice chmn. legal com. 1982-85), Utah State Bar (chmn. energy and natural resources sect. 1983-84), Utah State Rifle and Pistol Assn. (bd. dirs. 1978—, mem. nat. champion service rifle team 1983, 84), Sigma Nu. Republican. Mormon. Oil and gas leasing, General corporate, Military. Home: 532 Heritage Dr Bountiful UT 84010 Office: Celsius Energy Co 79 S State St Salt Lake City UT 84111

GILLAM, MAX LEE, lawyer; b. Cleve., Apr. 28, 1926; s. Max Lee and Louise (Sellers) G.; m. Carol McCully; children: Marcheta, Wade, Lynn, Anne, Mary, Re, Eric, Alex, Kate. B.S., U.S. Naval Acad., 1949; LL.B., Harvard U., 1956. Bar: Calif. 1957. With Latham, & Watkins, Los Angeles, 1956—; now sr. partner Latham, & Watkins. Served with USN, 1944-45; USAF, 1949-53. Mem. ABA, Assn. Bus. Trial Lawyers, Am. Coll. Trial Lawyers, Los Angeles Bar, Calif. Bar.

GILLEN, JAMES ROBERT, insurance company executive; b. N.Y.C., Nov. 14, 1937; s. James Matthew and Katharine Isabel (Fritz) G.; m. Rita Marie Wahleithner, June 15, 1963; children: Jennifer Elaine, Nancy Louise, Paula Anne. A.B. magna cum laude, Harvard U., 1959, LL.B. cum laude, 1965. Bar: N.Y. 1966, N.J. 1975. Assoc. firm White & Case, N.Y.C., 1965-72; v.p., assoc. gen. counsel Prudential Ins. Co. Am., Newark, 1972-77, sr. v.p., assoc. gen. counsel, 1977-80, sr. v.p. pub. affairs, 1980-84, sr. v.p., gen. counsel, 1984—; mem. legal adv. com. New York Stock Exchange, 1986—. Trustee United Way Essex and West Hudson Counties, 1981—, pres., 1986—; mem. Mendham Twp. (N.J.) Bd. Edn., 1981-82; trustee Mendham Twp. Library, 1979-82. Served to lt. (j.g.) USN, 1959-62. Mem. ABA, N.J. Bar Assn., Assn. Life Ins. Counsel. Club: Essex (Newark). Home: 12 Hamilton Dr Morristown NJ 07960 Office: Prudential Ins Co Am Prudential Plaza-3 Plaza Newark NJ 07101

GILLEN, STEPHEN EARL, lawyer; b. Gallipolis, Ohio, July 24, 1953; S. John Crawford and Faye Elizabeth (O'Dell) G.; m. Ann Margaret Humphrey, May 14, 1983; 1 child, Sarah Christine. BSBA, Miami U., Oxford, Ohio, 1975; JD, No. Ky. U., 1980. Bar: Ohio 1980, U.S. Dist. Ct. (so. dist.) Ohio 1980. Atty., exec. editor, v.p. South-Western Pub. Co., Cin., 1976—; instr. Xavier U., Cin., 1986—. Editor: 8 textbooks in bus. and labor law; coauthor: A Canoeing and Kayaking Guide to the Streams of Ohio, 1983; Contbr. articles to profl. jours. Mem. ABA, Ohio Bar Assn., Cin. Bar Assn., Am. Bus. Law Assn. Republican. General corporate, General practice. Home: 3718 Woodland Ave Cincinnati OH 45227 Office: South-Western Pub Co 5101 Madison Rd Cincinnati OH 45227

GILLEN, WILLIAM ALBERT, lawyer; b. Sanford, Fla., May 26, 1914; s. William D. and Marie Carolyn (Holt) G.; m. Lillian Stevens Thornton, Aug. 19, 1939 (dec. May 1981); children: William Albert, Susan Marie Gillen Casper. Student, U. Tampa, 1932-33, LL.D., 1983; J.D., U. Fla., 1936. Bar: Fla. 1936, U.S. Dist. Ct. (mid. and so. dists.) Fla. 1937, U.S. Supreme Ct. 1950, U.S. Ct. Appeals (5th and 11th cirs.) 1981. Since practiced in Tampa; mem. Fowler, White, Gillen, Boggs, Villareal and Banker, P.A., 1946—, chmn. bd., pres., 1970-86; mem. Hillsborough County Home Rule Charter Com., 1969-70, 13th Circuit Jud. Nominating Com., 1972-76, Fla. Supreme Ct. Jud. Nominating Commn., 1979-83; bd. dirs. Freedom Savs. and Loan Assn., Tampa, chmn. bd. dirs., 1978-84. Asso. editor: Am. Maritime Cases, 1948—. Bd. dirs. U. South Fla. Found., 1965-68, pres., 1967-68; pres. Gulf Ridge council Boy Scouts Am., 1959; bd. dirs. United Fund Tampa, 1956-64, Greater Tampa Citizens Safety Council, 1966-69. Served to maj., inf. AUS, 1942-46. Fellow Am. Coll. Trial Lawyers, Am. Bar Found., Fla. Bar Found.; mem. Bar Assn. Tampa and Hillsborough County (pres. 1953), Fla. Bar (gov. 1951-57), Fedn. Ins. Counsel (pres. 1960-61, chmn. bd. dirs. 1961-62), Internat. Assn. Def. Counsel, Def. Research Inst. (v.p. 1961-62), Maritime Law Assn. U.S., Am. Bar Assn. (co-chmn. conf. lawyers, ins. cos. and adjusters 1975-78), Com. of 100, Tampa C. of C. (pres. 1968-69), Am. Legion, Gasparilla Krewe (capt. 1968-70, King LVII 1970-71), Phi Delta Phi, Sigma Alpha Epsilon. Democrat. Episcopalian. Clubs: Rotary (pres. 1959-60), Tampa Yacht and Country (dir. 1962-64), Tower, University (dir. 1976-79, pres. 1978-79), Merrymakers, Palma Ceia Golf and Country (Tampa). Lodge: Masons. General corporate, General practice, Insurance. Home: 3109 Sunset Dr Tampa FL 33629 Office: Fowler White Gillen Boggs et al 501 E Kennedy Blvd Suite 1700 Tampa FL 33602

GILLENWATER, MICHAEL ALLEN, lawyer; b. Jeffersonville, Ind., May 23, 1958; s. James H. Sr. and Marilyn A. (Enteman) G. BA, Ind. U., 1981; JD, U. Louisville, 1985. Bar: Ind. 1985, U.S. Dist. Ct (so. and no. dists.) Ind. 1985. Dep. prosecutor Clark County Ind., Jeffersonville, 1985—. Precinct committeman Clark County Dems., 1983—; bd. dirs. Clark County Council for the Arts, Jeffersonville, 1985—; mem. Clark County Child Protection Team, 1986—. Mem. ABA, Ind. Correctional Assn., Ind. Bar Assn., Assn. Trial Lawyers Am., Ind. Trial Lawyers Assn., Nat. Rifle Assn., Tau Kappa Epsilon. Mormon. Avocations: camping, 5 string banjo, sports. Criminal, Juvenile. Home: 10 Redbud Rd Jeffersonville IN 47130 Office: Clark County Prosecutors Office City County Bldg Jeffersonville IN 47130

GILLES, HERBERT JEFFREY, lawyer; b. Bay City, Mich., Dec. 1, 1955; s. William Barry and Lillian Blanche (Lane) G.; m. Suzanne DeMaret (Hicks) G., Sept. 1, 1985. Student, Oakland U., Rochester, Mich., 1973-74; BA with honors, Mich. State U., 1977; JD cum laude, Detroit Coll. Law, 1981. Bar: Mich. 1981, U.S. Dist. Ct. (no. dist.) Tex. 1981, U.S. Dist. Ct. (ea. dist.) Mich. 1981, Tex. 1982. Assoc. Law Office of D.J. Silman, Dallas, 1981-82, Winikates & Curtis, Dallas, 1982-83, Glast & Miller, Dallas, 1983-85, Palmer & Palmer, P.C. and Palmer, Palmer & Coffee, P.C., Dallas, 1985—. Mem. ABA (corp., banking and bus. law sect., bus. bankruptcy com., executory contracts and leases subcom.), Am. Bankruptcy Inst., Dallas Bar Assn., Mich. State Alumni Assn. (com. mem. 1985—). Republican. Jewish. Club: 500. Bankruptcy. Office: Palmer & Palmer PC 1510 One Main Pl Dallas TX 75250

GILLESPIE, ALEXANDER JOSEPH, JR., lawyer; b. N.Y.C., Sept. 2, 1923; s. Alexander Joseph and Catharine (Allen) G.; m. Elizabeth Margaret Roth, Dec. 4, 1944; children: Robert Daniel, James Edward, William Gerard, Patricia Elise, Anne Marie. A.B. magna cum laude, Dartmouth Coll., 1943; J.D., Fordham U., 1957. Credit mgr. cosmetic div. Vick Chem. Co., 1946-50; dist. sales mgr. Avco Mfg. Co., 1950-54; assoc. atty. Breed Abbot & Morgan, 1957-60; asst. gen. counsel ASARCO Inc. (formerly Am. Smelting & Refining Co.), N.Y.C., 1960-68; sec. ASARCO Inc. (formerly Am. Smelting & Refining Co.), 1968-69, sec., gen. counsel, 1969-86, v.p., 1972-77, sr. v.p., sec., gen. counsel, 1977-84, gen. counsel, 1984-86, vice chmn., dir., 1986—; dir. So. Peru Copper Corp., Mex. Desarollo Indsl. Minera, S.A., ASARCO Found.; arbitrator Nat. Assn. Security Dealers, Am. Arbitration Assn.; mem. adv. bd. Parker Sch. Internat. Law Columbia U. Mem. adv. bd. Southwest Legal Found., Parker Sch. Internat. Law of Columbia U.; bd. dirs. Silver Hill Found. Served to lt. (j.g.) USNR, 1943-46, PTO. Mem. ABA, N.Y. State Bar Assn., Assn. Bar City N.Y., Conn. Bar Assn., N.Y. County Lawyers Assn., Americas Soc., Assn. Gen. Counsel, N.Y. Chamber Commerce and Industry, Peruvian Am. Assn., Phi Beta Kappa, Delta Upsilon, Gamma Eta Gamma. Episcopalian. Clubs: Wall St. (gov. 1984—), Dartmouth Coll., World Trade (N.Y.C.); Stanwich (Greenwich, Conn.). Antitrust, General corporate, Private international. Home: 30 Will Merry Ln Greenwich CT 06831 Office: 180 Maiden Ln New York NY 10038

GILLESPIE, DAVID ARTHUR, lawyer. s. Walter M. and Mary L. (Long) G.; m. Camille O'Hara, Nov. 6, 1982. BA, Wesleyan U., Middletown, Conn., 1974; AM, U. Chgo., 1978; JD, Georgetown U., 1981. Bar: Ill. 1981, N.Y. 1985. Assoc. Isham, Lincoln & Beave, Chgo., 1981-83, Barrett, Smith, Schapiro, Simon & Armstrong, N.Y.C., 1983-84. Trustee Nat. Brit. Am. Ednl. Found., N.Y.C. Mem. ABA, N.Y. State Bar Assn., Assn. of Bar of City of N.Y. Corporate taxation, Banking, General corporate. Home: 39 Remsen St New York NY 11201 Office: Barrett Smith et al 26 Broadway New York NY 10004

GILLESPIE, GEORGE JOSEPH, III, lawyer; b. N.Y.C., May 18, 1930; s. George Joseph Jr. and Dorothy Elizabeth (McKenna) G.; m. Eileen Tracy Dealy, July 27, 1955; children—Gail Gillespie Garcia, John D., Myles D., Eileen T. A.B. magna cum laude, Georgetown U., 1952; LL.B. magna cum laude, Harvard U., 1955. Bar: N.Y. State bar 1957. Frederick Sheldon travelling fellow Harvard U., 1955-56; asso. firm Cravath, Swaine & Moore, N.Y.C., 1956-62; partner firm Cravath, Swaine & Moore, 1963—; bd. dir. Washington Post Co., Fireman's Fund Corp. Trustee, treas. John M. Olin Found., Pinkerton Found., ARW Found.; sec. Mus. of Broadcasting; trustee Rye Country Day Sch., 1969-75, Practising Law Inst., 1968-78, NYU Med. Ctr.; v.p., bd. dirs. Madison Sq. Boys Club; bd. dirs., dep. chmn. Nat. Multiple Sclerosis Soc. Mem. Assn. Bar City N.Y., Am., N.Y. State bar assns. Republican. Roman Catholic. Clubs: Winged Foot Golf, Prouts Neck Country, Am. Yacht, Sailfish Point Golf. Office: Cravath Swaine & Moore 1 Chase Manhattan Plaza New York NY 10005

GILLESPIE, JAMES DAVIS, lawyer; b. Elkin, N.C., Apr. 30, 1955; s. John Banner and Jerry Sue (Swaim) G.; m. Tommie Lee Johnson, Aug. 13,

1977; 1 child, John Foster. BA, U. N.C., 1977; JD, Samford U., 1980. Bar: N.C. 1980, U.S. Dist. Ct. (mid. dist.) 1982, U.S. Ct. Appeals (4th cir.) 1983, U.S. Dist. Ct. (we. dist.) N.C. 1984. Ptnr. Neaves & Gillespie, Elkin, 1980—. Bb. editors: Cumberland Law Rev., 1978-80. Commr. Town of Jonesville, N.C., 1983-85, mayor, 1985—. Mem. ABA, Assn. Trial Lawyers Am., N.C. Bar Assn., N.C. Trial Lawyers Assn., Surry and Yadkin Counties Bar Assn., Elkin Jaycees (bd. dirs. 1981-83, v.p. 1983-84), N.C. Acad. Trial Lawyers. Democrat. Baptist. Avocations: tennis, basketball, reading. State civil litigation, Criminal, Personal injury. Home: 310 W Wagoner St Jonesville NC 28642 Office: Neaves & Gillespie 112 A Church St Elkin NC 28621

GILLESPIE, JANE, lawyer; b. Cin., Aug. 18, 1935; d. William Pembroke and Elizabeth (Biermann) G. Student, Vassar Coll., 1953-55; cert. Polit. Sci. U. Strasbourg, France, 1956; B.A., Northwestern U., 1958; LL.B., Yale U., 1962. Bar: N.Y. 1964, U.S. Dist. Ct. (so. and ea. dists.) N.Y. 1972. with McLanahan, Merritt, Ingraham, N.Y.C., 1964-69, Olwine, Connelly, Chase, O'Donnell & Weyher, N.Y.C., 1969-78; atty. Interpublic Group Cos., Inc., N.Y.C., 1978—, sec., asst. sec. various advt. agys. including McCann-Erickson, Inc., Campbell-Ewald Mktg. Inc., McCann Direct Inc., N.Y.C. Mem. Darien Representative Town Meeting, Conn., 1980-84, Five Mile River Commn., 1981—. Mem. ABA (subcom. on fed. regulation securities 1969—), Assn. Bar City N.Y. Club: Yale (N.Y.C.). General corporate, Securities, Private international. Office: Interpublic Group Cos Inc 1271 Ave of Americas New York NY 10020

GILLESPIE, WILLIAM TYRONE, judge; b. Great Falls, Mont., Mar. 7, 1916; s. William G. and Alma (McBride) G.; A.B., J.D., D.C.L., Willamette U., 1939; LL.D., Hillsdale Coll., 1957; m. Eleanor Johnson, Aug. 31, 1941; 1 son, William Tyrone. Admitted to Oreg., Wash. bars, 1939, Mich. bar, 1948; spl. agt. FBI, 1939-42; partner Pope & Gillespie, Salem, Oreg., 1946-48; mem. legal dept. Dow Chem. Co., Midland, Mich., 1948-54, asst. to pres., 1954-66; partner firm Gillespie, Riecker & George, Midland, Mich., 1966-76; judge Mich. 42d Jud. Circuit, 1977—. Trustee Hillsdale Coll., 1957-72, chmn., 1972-75, chmn. emeritus, 1975—. Served from 2d lt. to lt. col. AUS, 1942-46. Mem. State Bar Mich., Oreg., Wash., Midland County (past pres.) bar assns., Am. Legion, Michigan C. of C. (v.p.), 40 and 8, Blue Key, Beta Theta Pi. Republican. Methodist. Clubs: Masons (33 deg.), Rotary. Jurisprudence, State civil litigation. Home: 1200 W Sugnet Rd Midland MI 48640 Office: Courthouse Midland MI 48640

GILLETTE, W. MICHAEL, judge; b. Seattle, Dec. 29, 1941; s. Elton George and Hazel Irene (Hand) G.; children: Kevin, Saima. AB in German, Polit. Sci., Whitman Coll., 1963; LLB, Harvard U., 1966. Bar: Oreg. 1966, U.S. Dist. Ct. Oreg. 1966, U.S. Ct. Appeals (9th cir.) 1966, Samoa 1969, U.S. Supreme Ct. 1970, Vt. 1973. Assoc. Rives & Rochers, Portland, Oreg., 1966-67; dept. dist. atty. Multnomah County, Portland, 1967-69; asst. atty. gen. Govt. of Am. Samoa, 1969-71, State of Oreg., Salem, 1971-77; judge Oreg. Ct. Appeals, Salem, 1977-86; assoc. justice Oreg. Supreme Ct., Salem, 1986—. Avocation: officiating basketball and baseball. Office: Oregon Supreme Court 1147 State St Salem OR 97310

GILLIAM, CARROLL LEWIS, lawyer; b. Union, S.C., Sept. 25, 1929; s. D. Few and Cynthia Carolyn (Stone) G.; m. Margaret Clark Eagan, May 7, 1960; 1 dau., Cynthia Clark. A.B. cum laude, U. S.C., 1949, M.A. magna cum laude, 1950; J.D. with highest honors, George Washington U., 1957. Bar: D.C. 1957. Practice law Washington, 1957—; partner Grove, Jaskiewicz, Gilliam & Cobert, 1964—; mem. adv. com. on revision of rules Fed. Energy Regulatory Commn., 1978-81; mem. U.S. Dept. Edn. Appeal Bd., 1976-82. Served with USAF, 1950-53. Recipient Beaufort Watts Ball award U. S.C., 1949; John Bell Larner award George Washington U., 1957. Mem. Fed. Power Bar Assn. (pres. 1975-76), Am. Bar Assn. (chmn. natural resources law sect. 1977-78, chmn. standing com. environ. law 1978-80, ho. of dels. 1980—, council adminstrv. law sect. 1974-75), D.C. Bar Assn., Blue Key, Phi Beta Kappa, Delta Theta Phi, Order of the Coif. Democrat. Episcopalian. Clubs: University (Washington); Beach and Racquet (Isles of Palms, S.C.). Administrative and regulatory, FERC practice. Home: 4101 Aspen St Chevy Chase MD 20015 Office: 1730 M St NW Washington DC 20036

GILLIAM, CHARLES PHILLIPS, lawyer; b. Thomasville, N.C., July 25, 1950; s. Maurice Elliott and Elizabeth (Phillips) G. BS, U. N.C., 1972, MBA, 1976; JD summa cum laude, Detroit Coll. Law, 1982. Bar: Mich. 1982, U.S. Dist. Ct. (ea. dist.) Mich. 1982, U.S. Dist. Ct. (no. dist.) Tex. 1986. Branch mgr. First Fed. Savs. and Loan, Thomasville, 1973-76; fin. analyst Ford Motor Co., Dearborn, Mich., 1977-82; atty.office gen. counsel Xerox Corp., Stamford, Conn., 1982—. Mem. ABA, Am. Corp. Counsel Assn. Republican. Labor, General corporate. Home: 304 Mountain Rd Wilton CT 06897 Office: Xerox Corp Office of Gen Counsel PO Box 1600 Stamford CT 06904

GILLIAM, EARL BEN, federal judge; b. Clovis, N.Mex., Aug. 17, 1931; s. James Earl and Lula Mae G.; m. Barbara Jean Gilliam, Dec. 6, 1956; children—Earl Kenneth, Derrick James. B.A., Calif. State U., San Diego, 1953; J.D., Hastings Coll. Law, 1957. Bar: Calif. 1957. Dep. dist. atty. San Diego, 1957-62; judge San Diego Mcpl. Ct., 1963-74, Superior Ct. Calif., San Diego County, 1975-80, U.S. Dist. Ct. (so. dist.) Calif., San Diego, 1980—. Judicial administration. Office: US Courthouse 940 Front St San Diego CA 92189 *

GILLIES, DONALD ALLASTAIR, lawyer; b. Evanston, Ill., Sept. 15, 1931; s. Allastair and Alice (Brown) G.; m. Judith Bonnie Seepe, Aug. 19, 1961; 1 dau., Elizabeth Anne. B.A., Denison U., 1953; J.D., Northwestern U., 1956. Bar: Ill. 1956, U.S. Dist. Ct. (no. dist.) Ill., U.S. Ct. Appeals (7th cir.), U.S. Tax Ct. Assoc. Winston & Strawn, Chgo., 1956-61; assoc. Altheimer & Gray, Chgo., 1961-66, ptnr., 1966—. Contbr. articles to profl. jours. Trustee U. Chgo., 1977-83; trustee Bapt. Theol. Union, 1965—, pres., 1974—; bd. govs. Ill. St. Andrew Soc., 1978—, pres., 1986—; bd. dirs. Bapt. Retirement Home, 1964—. Served with U.S. Army, 1956-58. Mem. ABA, Ill. Bar Assn., Am. Coll. Probate Counsel (Ill. chmn. 1983—), Chgo. Bar Assn. (chmn. fed. tax com. 1978-79). Republican. Baptist. Clubs: University (Chgo.); Skokie Country (Glencoe, Ill.). Corporate taxation, Estate planning. Office: 333 W Wacker Dr Chicago IL 60606

GILLIN, MALVIN JAMES, JR., lawyer; b. Norfolk, Va., Apr. 28, 1946; s. Malvin James Gillin and Jacqueline A. (Howell) Kyslowsky; m. Judith Ann Fernie, July 3, 1967 (div. June 1978); children: Christine Lynn, Malvin James III, Craig Dean. BA, U. Hawaii, 1969; JD, U. Denver, 1974. Bar: Hawaii 1975, U.S. Dist. Ct. Hawaii 1975, U.S. Ct. Appeals (9th cir.) 1983, U.S. Supreme Ct. 1983, Colo. 1984. Atty. gen. State of Hawaii, Honolulu, 1975-76; sole practice Honolulu, 1976—. Mem. ABA, Hawaii Bar Assn., Assn. Trial Lawyers Am. Roman Catholic. Avocations: scuba diving, sailing. Personal injury, Criminal, Family and matrimonial. Office: 841 Bishop St Suite 924 Honolulu HI 96813

GILLIS, LUCIAN, JR., lawyer; b. Memphis, Feb. 4, 1952; s. Lucian Sr. and Betsy Virginia (Barham) G. BS in Comml. and Bus. Adminstrn., U. Ala., 1974, JD, 1977. Bar: Ala. 1977. Dep. dist. atty. Birmingham, Ala., 1977-80; assoc. Reams, Vollmer, Philips, Killion, Brooks & Schell, Mobile, Ala., 1980—. Mem. ABA, Ala. Bar Assn., Mobile Bar Assn., Birmingham Bar Assn., Mobile Jaycees, U.S. Powerlifting Fedn. (chmn. law and legis. com. 1984—). Republican. Avocation: weightlifting. Federal civil litigation, State civil litigation, Insurance. Home: 128 E Du Rhu Dr Mobile AL 36608 Office: Reams Vollmer Philips et al 3662 Dauphin St Mobile AL 36608

GILLMARTEN, MARY DEL REY, lawyer; b. Washington, Nov. 27, 1956; d. James Francis and Marie Lucille (Cherry) Marten; m. David Michael Gillmarten, Aug. 2, 1980; 1 child, Charles Peter. AB, U. Notre Dame, 1979; JD, Georgetown U., 1982. Bar: Va. 1982, U.S. Dist. Ct. (ea. dist.) Va. 1982. Assoc. Hart, Nugent & Ahearn, Alexandria, Va., 1982-84; atty. dept. treasury IRS, Washington, 1984—. Mem. ABA (tax sect.), Va. Bar Assn. (young lawyers div.). Roman Catholic. Avocations: needlework, poetry. Corporate taxation, Real property, General practice. Office: IRS 1111 Constitution Ave NW Washington DC 20224

GILLMORE, ALVER JAMES, lawyer; b. Newton, Kans., May 25, 1947; s. Alver James Jr. and Orva Rachel (Buller) G.; m. Mary Elizabeth Green, Oct. 13, 1984; children: Jeffrey Don, Erin Rachel. BA, Wichita State U., 1969; JD, U. Kans., 1972; LLM in Econ. Regulation, George Washington U., 1975. Bar: Kans. 1972, U.S. Dist. Ct. Kans. 1972. Assoc. Smith, Rushfelt, Mueller & Lamar, Overland Park, Kans., 1972-74; atty. ICC, Washington, 1974-76; ptnr. Speir, Stroberg & Sizemore, Newton, 1976—; bd. dirs. Sedgwick (Kans.) State Bank, Northview Devel. Services, Newton, Wenz Kennel Service, Newton. Editor: Kans. Law Rev., 1971-72. Mem. Kans. Legislature, 1976-79; chmn. Harvey County Rep. Party, Newton, 1980-86. Mem. ABA, Kans. Bar Assn., Harvey County Bar Assn. Mennonite. Probate, General corporate, Contracts commercial. Home: 215 SW 7th Newton KS 67114 Office: Speir Stroberg & Sizemore 809 Main Newton KS 67114

GILLUM, FORREST EARL, law educator, municipal court judge; b. Casper, Wyo., Sept. 21, 1945; s. Forrest H. and Goldie P. (Keck) G.; m. Sandra R. Nollmann, June 11, 1966; children—Shawn Michael, Shem Shalom. A.A. in Psychology, Casper Coll., 1969; B.A. in Criminal Justice, Chadron State Coll., 1975; M.P.A., U. Wyo., 1981. Patrolman Casper Police Dept., 1967-70, investigator, 1970-72; prof. criminal justice Casper Coll., 1972—; cons. Profl. Polygraph Services, Casper, 1972—; mcpl. judge Town of Evansville, Wyo., 1975—. Chmn. CSC, Casper, 1980—. Mem. Wyo. Assn. Minor Ct. Judges (sec.-treas. 1976-79), Pacific and Western Assn. Criminal Justice Educators (pres. 1982-83), Wyo. Polygraph Assn. (pres. 1984-85), Acad. Criminal Justice Scis. Republican. Criminal, Legal education, Judicial administration. Home: 3903 E 19th Ave Casper WY 82609 Office: Evansville Mcpl Ct PO Box 158 Evansville WY 82643

GILLY, K.J., corporate lawyer. AB, Tulane U., LLB. V.p., gen. counsel, corp. sec. McDermott Internat. Inc., New Orleans. Office: McDermott Inc 1010 Common St New Orleans LA 60035 *

GILMAN, ANDREW D., lawyer; b. N.Y.C., June 1, 1951; s. Harry and Phyllis (Margulies) G.; m. Dianne S. Rudo, June 9, 1985. BA, U. Pa., 1972, MS in Edn., 1973; JD, Fordham U., 1980. Bar: N.Y. 1981. Tchr. Springfield (Pa.) High Sch., 1973-74; assoc. Andrew Gilman Law Offices, N.Y.C., 1981—; pres. CommCore Inc., N.Y.C., 1985—. Contbr. articles to N.Y. Times and profl. jours. Mem. ABA (young lawyers div.). General practice, Entertainment. Home: 684 Broadway New York NY 10012 Office: CommCore Inc 156 Fifth Ave New York NY 10010

GILMAN, CHARLES ALAN, lawyer; b. Mineola, N.Y., Nov. 18, 1949; s. Manuel A. and Margaret (Werber) G.; m. Nancy Beinbrink, Sept. 14, 1974; children: Peter Hitchcock, Douglas Bowne, Katharine Walker. BS in Econs., U. Pa., 1971; JD, U. Va., 1974. Bar: N.Y. 1975, U.S. Dist. Ct. (ea. and so. dists.) N.Y. 1975, U.S. Ct. Appeals (2d cir.) 1975, U.S. Supreme Ct. 1980. Assoc. Cahill, Gordon & Reindel, N.Y.C., 1974-82, ptnr., 1982—. Mem. ABA, N.Y. State Bar Assn. Federal civil litigation, Securities, State civil litigation. Home: 8 Park Dr Plandome NY 11030 Office: Cahill Gordon & Reindel 80 Pine St New York NY 10005

GILMAN, CLAUDIA JANE, lawyer; b. N.Y.C., May 15, 1952; d. Albert and Josephine G.; m. Harry Eisenbaum, May 2, 1982; children: Mara, David, Arielle. BA, Cornell U., 1974; JD, Columbia U., 1977. Bars: N.Y. 1978, U.S. Dist. Ct. (so. dist.) N.Y. 1978. Assoc. Baker & McKenzie, N.Y.C., 1977-79, Taipei, Republic of China, Hong Kong and Beijing, 1979-81; sr. internat. atty. for Asia and Australia Warner Lambert Co., Morris Plains, N.J., 1982-85; asst. internat. counsel Capsugel div. Warner Lambert Co., Morris Plains, 1985—; lectr. Chinese law, overseas distbr. laws, and laws governing Arab boycott of Israel, 1981—. Contbr. articles on Chinese law to profl. jours. Private international, Contracts commercial, Health. Home: 7 Fieldstone Ct Randolph NJ 07869 Office: Warner Lambert Co 201 Tabor Rd Morris Plains NJ 07950

GILMAN, SHELDON G., lawyer; b. Cleve., July 20, 1943. B.B.A., Ohio U., 1965; J.D., Case Western Res. U., 1967. Bar: Ohio 1967, Ky. 1971, Ind. 1982, Fla. 1984, D.C. 1985, Tenn. 1985. Mem. staff accts. tax dept. Arthur Andersen & Co., Cleve., 1967-68; assoc. Handmaker, Weber & Meyer, Louisville, 1971-74, ptnr., 1974-78; ptnr. Barnett & Alagia, Louisville, 1984-87; ptnr. Lynch, Cox & Gilman, 1987—; gen. counsel Louisville Assn. Life Underwriters, 1977, 78. Bd. dirs., chmn. Louisville Minority Bus. Resource Ctr., 1975—; pres. Congregation Adath Jeshuran, 1986—; bd. dirs., v.p., sec. Louisville Orch., 1982-85; bd. dirs. City of Devondale (Ky.), 1976. Served with JAGC, AUS, 1968-71. Mem. Ky. Bar Assn. (ethics com. 1982-86), Louisville Employee Benefit Council (pres. 1980). Pension, profit-sharing, and employee benefits, Probate, Corporate taxation. Office: 444 S 5th St Louisville KY 40202

GILMORE, HORACE WELDON, U.S. dist. judge; b. Columbus, Ohio, Apr. 4, 1918; s. Charles Thomas and Lucille (Weldon) G.; m. Mary Hays, June 20, 1942; children—Lindsay Gilmore Lasser, Frances Gilmore Hayward. A.B., U. Mich., 1939, J.D., 1942. Bar: Mich. bar 1946. Law clk. U.S. Ct. Appeals, 1946-47; practiced in Detroit, 1947-51; spl. asst. U.S. atty., Detroit, 1951-52; mem. Mich. Bd. Tax Appeals, 1954; dep. atty. gen. State of Mich., 1955-56; circuit judge 3d Jud. Circuit, Detroit, 1956-80; judge U.S. Dist. Ct., 1980—; adj. prof. law Wayne State U. Law Sch., 1966—; lectr. law U. Mich. Law Sch., 1969—; faculty Nat. Coll. State Judiciary, 1966—; mem. Mich. Jud. Tenure Commn., 1969-76; chmn. Mich. Com. To Revise Criminal Code, 1965—, Mich. Com. To Revise Criminal Procedure, 1971-79; trustee Inst. for Ct. Mgmt. Author: Michigan Civil Procedure Before Trial, 2d edit, 1975; contbr. numerous articles to legal jours. Served with USNR, 1942-46. Mem. Am. Bar Assn., State Bar Mich., Am. Judicature Soc., Am. Law Inst., Nat. Conf. State Trial Judges. Office: US Dist Ct US Courthouse 231 W Lafayette Blvd Room 802 Detroit MI 48226

GILMORE, JOHN ALLEN DEHN, lawyer; b. Boston, Mar. 18, 1947; s. Myron Piper and Sheila (Dehn) G.; children: Dehn, Thomas. BA, Harvard U., 1970, JD, 1974. Bar: Mass. 1974. Assoc. Hill & Barlow, Boston, 1974-81, ptnr., 1981—, hiring ptnr., 1982—; bd. dirs. Mass. Correctional Legal Services, Boston. Fiske fellow, 1970-71. Mem. ABA, Mass. Bar Assn., Boston Bar Assn. Democrat. Federal civil litigation, State civil litigation. Home: 47 Reservoir St Cambridge MA 02138 Office: Hill & Barlow One Internat Pl Boston MA 02110

GILMORE, WEBB REILLY, lawyer; b. Lake Forest, Ill., Dec. 9, 1944; s. Durward Wilson and Dorothy Angeline (DeField) G.; m. Denise Regina Dever, May 9, 1970; children—Kara Anne, Kimberly Erin, Katharine Reilly. B.S., U.S. Naval Acad., 1966; J.D., U. Mo.-Columbia, 1973. Bar: Mo. 1973. Assoc. firm Stinson Mag & Fizzell, Kansas City, Mo., 1973-77, ptnr., 1977-79; ptnr. firm Gaar & Bell, Kansas City, Mo., 1979—; dir. Glasgow Savs. Bank, Mo., 1970—; dir. Oran State Bank, 1984—. Mem. Mo. Lottery Commn., 1985—. Served with USN, 1966-70. Mem. ABA, Mo. Bar Assn., Nat. Assn. Bond Lawyers. Democrat. Roman Catholic. Local government, Securities, Municipal bonds. Home: 833 Westover Rd Kansas City MO 64113 Office: Gaar & Bell 1600 City Centre Square 1100 Main St Kansas City MO 64105

GILSON, RONALD J., law educator; b. 1946. AB, Washington U., St. Louis, 1968; JD, Yale U., 1971. Ptnr. Steinhart, Goldberg, Feigenbaum & Ladar, San Francisco, 1972-79; assoc. prof. Stanford (Calif.) U., 1979-83, prof., 1983—. Office: Stanford Law Sch Stanford CA 94305 *

GILSTER, PETER STUART, lawyer; b. Carbondale, Ill., Dec. 10, 1939; s. John Sprigg and Ruth E. (Robinson) G.; m. Carol Clevenger, June 30, 1968; children—John F., Thomas B. B.S., U. Ill., 1962, J.D., 1965. Bar: Ill. 1965, Mo. 1968, U.S. Dist. Ct. (ea. dist.) Mo. 1969, U.S. Patent Office 1970, U.S. Ct. Appeals (8th cir.) 1980, U.S. Supreme Ct. 1980, U.S. Ct. Customs and Patent Appeals 1980, U.S. Ct. Appeals (Fed. cir.) 1982. Assoc. Koenig, Senniger, Powers & Leavitt, St. Louis, 1967-71, ptnr., 1971-72; patent atty. Monsanto Co., St. Louis, 1972-77; ptnr. Kalish & Gilster, St. Louis, 1977—; seminar lectr. U. Mo.-St. Louis, 1976-83. Merit badge counselor and troop committeeman St. Louis Area council Boy Scouts Am., 1980—. Served to capt. USAR, 1966-67. Decorated Army Commendation medal. Mem. Am. Intellectual Property Law Assn., Ill. Bar Assn., Mo. Bar Assn., Lawyer Pilots Bar Assn., Fed. Cir. Bar Assn., Bar Assn. Met. St. Louis (chmn. patent sect. 1975-76), Assoc. Pilots St. Louis (v.p. 1977-83, bd. dirs. 1975-87), World Affairs Council St. Louis, Phi Delta Phi. Club: Mo. Athletic (St. Louis). Patent, Trademark and copyright, Federal civil litigation. Office: Kalish & Gilster 818 Olive St Saint Louis MO 63101

GILYEART, STEVEN CRAIG, lawyer; b. Des Moines, Apr. 17, 1951; s. Russell Merlin and Bonnie Bernice (Hutzell) G.; m. Judith Kriz, Jan. 24, 1981. B.A. with honors, Okla. State U., 1974; J.D. with honors, U. Tex., 1977. Bar: Wash. 1977, U.S. Dist. Ct. (we. dist.) Wash. 1977, U.S. Dist. Ct. (ea. dist.) Wash. 1985. U.S. Tax Ct. 1982. Assoc. Williams, Lanza, Kastner & Gibbs, Seattle, 1977-81; sole practice, Seattle, 1981-82; ptnr. Torbenson, Thatcher, Yund, Blacklow & Gilyeart, Seattle, 1982-85; prin. Dempey & Braley, P.S., 1985—; vol. atty. N.W. Women's Law Ctr., Seattle, 1981—, Wash. Vol. Lawyers for the Arts, Seattle, 1981—. Contbr. articles to profl. jours. Mem. Mayor's Small Bus. Task Force, Seattle, 1982-84, past pres. Denny Regrade Bus. Assn., Seattle; bd. dirs. Health Info. Network, Seattle, 1981-84, Neighborhood Bus. Council, Seattle, 1982-84, Ewajo Dance Workshop, Seattle, 1984—. Mem. ABA, Nat. Vehicle Leasing Assn. (chmn. lawyers com. group 1984—), Am. Assn. Equipment Lessors, Western Assn. Equipment Lessors (dir. 1984-85, chmn. lawyers com. 1983-84, chmn. govt. affairs com. 1985—), Wash. Bar Assn., Wash. Assn. Equipment Lessors, Puget Sound Lessor's Group, Seattle-King County Bar Assn. (chmn. young lawyers sect. legis. com. 1982-84), Phi Delta Phi, Phi Kappa Phi, Omicron Delta Epsilon. Equipment leasing, Contracts commercial, General corporate. Home: 4617 Lake Washington Blvd S Seattle WA 98118 Office: Dempey & Braley PS Times Sq Bldg Suite 400 414 Olive Way Seattle WA 98101

GIMMY, DANIEL PATRICK, lawyer; b. Detroit, Apr. 4, 1946; s. Wilbur Warren and Helen Claire (Wallace) G.; m. Linda Carole Grande, June 4, 1971; children: Laura, Nicholas, Sara. BSME, Gen. Motors Inst., Flint, Mich., 1968; JD, Wayne State U., 1972. Bar: Mich. 1983, U.S. Dist. Ct. (so. dist.) Mich. 1974, Fla. 1977. With Gen. Motors Corp., Warren, Mich., 1972-73; atty. and counsellor Plunkett Cooney, Detroit, 1973-78; sr. atty. Am. Motors Corp., Southfield, Mich., 1978-84; v.p. law, sec. Yale Materials Handling Corp., Flemington, N.J., 1984—; arbitrator Am. Arbitration Assn., Detroit, 1974-84, Mich. Dist. Ct., Southfield, 1983-84. Served to sgt. USAR, 1968-74. Mem. ABA (antitrust sect.), Am. Corp. Counsel Assn.(sole practioner com. N.Y. chpt.), N.J. Corp. Counsel Assn. (bd. dirs. 1986—). Roman Catholic. Antitrust, General practice, Private international. Home: 23 Pleasant View Way Flemington NJ 08822 Office: Yale Materials Handling Corp Rts 523 and 31 Flemington NJ 08822

GINDIN, WILLIAM HOWARD, lawyer, judge; b. Perth Amboy, N.J., Sept. 1, 1931; s. Jac Paul and Belle Ruth (Steinberg) G.; m. Jane Hersh, June 24, 1954; m. Emily Shimkin, Dec. 25, 1965; children—Thomas L., Janine Drucker Gordon, Suzanne B., Geoffrey A. Drucker. A.B., Brown U., 1953; J.D., Yale U., 1956. Bar: N.J. 1956, U.S. Supreme Ct. 1965, U.S. Ct. Appeals (3d cir.) 1980. Assoc., Gindin & Gindin, Plainfield, N.J., 1956-62, ptnr., Plainfield and Bridgewater, N.J., 1962-82; adminstrv. law judge, Newark, 1982-85; U.S. bankruptcy judge, Trenton, 1985—; lectr. Inst. Continuing Legal Edn., Profl. Edn. Systems, Inc. Mem. Plainfield (N.J.) Human Relations Commn., 1965-72, chmn., 1968-72; pres. Temple Sholom, Plainfield, 1979-81; regional v.p. Union Am. Hebrew Congregations, 1983-86. Mem. Plainfield Bar Assn., Union County Bar Assn., Mercer County Bar Assn., N.J. Bar Assn., ABA. Club: Plainfield Rotary (pres. 1974-75). Bd. editors N.J. Bar Assn. Jour., 1962-72. Administrative and regulatory, Bankruptcy. Home: 30 James Ct Princeton NJ 08540 Office: 402 E State St Trenton NJ 08607

GINGELL, ROBERT ARTHUR, lawyer; b. Alexandria, Va., July 23, 1923; s. Reginald Jennings and Elizabeth Regina (Stoddard) G.; m. Grace Noffsinger, Oct. 28, 1950 (div. Dec. 1980); children—Robert Arthur, Gentry N.; m. Marianne B. McConnaughey, Dec. 10, 1980. A.B., George Washington U., 1947, J.D., 1949. Bar: D.C. 1949, Md. 1949, U.S. Dist. Ct. D.C. 1949, U.S. Ct. Appeals (D.C. cir.) 1949. Assoc., Harry J. Daly, Washington, 1949-50; sole practice, Washington and Silver Spring, Md., 1952-60; ptnr. Ritterpusch & Gingell, Rockville and Silver Spring, Md., 1960-80; sr. ptnr. Gingell & Prescott Law Offices, Silver Spring, 1980—. Served to capt. USMCR, 1943-46, 50-52. Fellow Am. Coll. Real Estate Lawyers; mem. Washington, D.C. Estate Planning Council. Democrat. Episcopalian. Clubs: Chevy Chase Country (Md.); Kenwood Country. Lodge: Rotary (pres. local club 1964-65, Paul Harris fellow 1980—). Real property, Probate, Estate planning. Home: 5220 Parkway Dr Chevy Chase MD 20815 Office: Gingell & Prescott 11151 Veirs Mills Rd Silver Spring MD 20902

GINGERICH, FLORINE ROSE, lawyer; b. Lowville, N.Y., Nov. 25, 1951; d. Beryl J. and Marion A. (Jantzi) G. BA in History, Goshen Coll., 1973; JD, U. Mich., 1976. Bar: Wash. 1976, U.S. Dist. Ct. (we. dist.) Wash. 1976. Assoc. Davis, Wright & Jones, Seattle, 1976-83; v.p., corp. counsel Seattle Trust and Svgs., 1983-85, v.p., sec., corp. counsel, 1985—. Mem. planning and allocations conf. panel United Way of King-Seattle County, 1979-82; bd. dirs. Consumer Credit Counseling Services of Seattle, 1982-83, Friends of Youth, Renton, Wash., 1986—. Mem. ABA, Wash. State Bar Assn., Seattle-King County Bar Assn. Clubs: Seattle, Columbia Tower (Seattle). Banking, Consumer commercial, General corporate. Office: Seattle Trust and Savs Bank 1000 2d Ave Seattle WA 98104

GINGISS, RANDALL JON, lawyer; b. Chgo., May 9, 1945; s. Benjamin J. and Rosalie (Eisenschiml) G.; m. Helene Milenbach, Mar. 21, 1976. A.B. cum laude, Amherst (Mass.) Coll., 1966; J.D., U. Mich., 1969; LL.M. in Taxation, DePaul U., Chgo., 1980. Bar: Ill. 1969, U.S. Ct. Mil. Appeals 1972, U.S. Tax Ct. 1974. Pvt. practice, Chgo., 1974-77; 2d v.p. Continental Ill. Nat. Bank & Trust Co., Chgo., 1977-82; ptnr. Levenfeld, Eisenberg, Janger, Glassberg & Samotny, Chgo., 1982—; adj. prof. Loyola U., 1982-84; prof. DePaul U., 1985 . Bd. dirs. USO of Chgo., 1978—, Chgo. Boys' Clubs, 1979—; mem. Animal Care and Control Commn. City of Chgo., 1980—; pres. Mental Health Assn. Chgo., 1982-83. Served with U.S. Navy, 1969-74. Mem. ABA, Ill. Bar Assn., Chgo. Bar Assn., Ill. C.P.A. Soc. Clubs: Tavern, Carleton (Chgo.). Contbr. articles to profl. jours. Estate planning, Estate taxation, Probate. Office: 33 W Monroe St Chicago IL 60603

GINGOLD, DENNIS MARC, lawyer; b. Plainfield, N.J., June 23, 1949; s. Michael Richard and Sally (Weiss) G.; m. Anne Carol Pearson, Sept. 4, 1970; children: Stacy Michele, Samantha Anne. BA, Rollins Coll., 1971; JD, Seton Hall U., 1974; LLM in Internat. Legal Studies, NYU, 1975. Bar: N.J. 1974, U.S. Dist. Ct. N.J. 1974, Colo. 1981, U.S. Dist. Ct. Colo. 1981, U.S. Ct. Appeals (10th cir.) 1984, U.S. Supreme Ct. 1985. Atty., advisor U.S. Comptroller Currency, Washington, 1976-79; counsel 12th Nat. Bank Region U.S. Comptroller Currency, Denver, 1979-80; ptnr. Gorsuch, Kirgis, Campbell, Walker & Grover, Denver, 1980-82, Kirkland & Ellis, Denver and Washington, 1982-85, Squire, Sanders & Dempsey, Washington, 1985—; adj. prof. law U. Denver, 1981-82. Named one of the Top 20 Banking Lawyers in U.S. Nat. Law Jour., 1983; Regianld Heber Smith fellow, 1975-76. Mem. Colo. Bar Assn., N.J. Bar Assn., Denver Bar Assn., Banking Law Inst. (adv. council 1983). Democrat. Jewish. Clubs: Denver Athletic; Bethesda (Md.) Country. Avocations: basketball, tennis, hiking. Banking, General corporate. Home: 8712 Crider Brook Way Potomac MD 20854 Office: Squire Sanders & Dempsey 1201 Pennsylvania Ave NW Washington DC 20004

GINGOLD, IRVING, lawyer; b. Bklyn., Mar. 7, 1930; s. Samuel and Ida (Gans) G.; m. Marcia Schalet, Mar. 31, 1951; children: Robin Elizabeth, Jodilynn, Valerie, Hilary. LLB, Bklyn. Law Sch., 1952. Bar: N.Y. 1952, U.S. Supreme Ct. 1957, U.S. Dist. Ct. (so. and ea. dists.) N.Y. 1958. Sole practice Roosevelt, N.Y., 1958—. Mem. Nassau County Bar Assn. (chmn. plaintiff's roundtable 1986, 87), Assn. Am. Trial Lawyers, N.Y. State Trial Lawyers Assn. Republican. Jewish. Avocation: photography. Personal injury, Products liability. Office: 529 Nassau Rd Roosevelt NY 11575

GINOTTI, JAMES DOMINICK, lawyer; b. Modesto, Calif., June 14, 1931; s. James Dominick and Margarete (Conant) G.; m. Peggy RoJean Cook, Aug. 30, 1950 (div. 1972); children: Deborah, James Dominick III, Theresa Marie, Sheryl Ann; m. Deborah Gail Van Pelt; 1 child, Leaha. JD, U. Pacific, 1967. Bar: Calif. 1967, Ala. 1970. Sr. ptnr. Dillon & Ginotti, Sacremento, 1967-71; sole practice Carmichael, Calif., 1971-74; dist. ct. judge

Alaska Ct. System, Anchorage, 1975-76; sr. ptnr. Ginotti & McAlpine, Valdez, Alaska, 1976-80; sole practice Wasilla, Alaska, 1980—; legis. adviser Alaska Legis., Juneau, 1974-75. Contbr. articles to profl. jours. Served with USN, 1948-50. Mem. ABA, Alaska Bar Assn., Calif. Bar Assn., Wasilla Bar Assn., Wasilla C. of C. Democrat. Roman Catholic. Club: Toastmaster Internat. (Wasilla). Avocations: writing, flying, sailing. Home and Office: Box 872642 Wasilla AK 99687

GINSBERG, ERNEST, lawyer, banker; b. Syracuse, N.Y., Feb. 14, 1931; s. Morris Henry and Mildred Florence (Slive) G.; m. Harriet Gay Scharf, Dec. 20, 1959; children: Alan Justin, Robert Daniel. B.A., Syracuse U., 1953, J.D., 1955; LL.M., Georgetown U., 1963. Bar: N.Y. 1955, U.S. Supreme Ct. 1964. Pvt. practice law Syracuse, 1957-61; mem. staff, office chief counsel IRS, 1961-63; tax counsel Comptroller of Currency, Washington, 1964-65; assoc. chief counsel Comptroller of Currency, 1965-68; v.p. legal affairs, sec. Republic Nat. Bank N.Y., U.S.A., N.Y.C., 1968-74; sr. v.p. legal affairs, sec. Republic Nat. Bank N.Y., U.S.A., 1975-86, exec. v.p., gen. counsel, sec., 1984-86, vice chmn. bd., gen. counsel, 1986—; sr. v.p., sec. legal affairs Republic New York Corp., N.Y.C., 1975-84, exec. v.p., gen. counsel, sec., 1984-86, vice chmn. bd., gen. counsel, 1986—; dir. SafraBank, Miami., Safra Bank II N.A., Pompano Beach, Fla., Safra Bank (Calif.), Los Angeles, Colonial Savs. Bank, N.A., Ocala, Fla. Served with AUS, 1955-57. Mem. ABA, N.Y. State Bar Assn., Phi Sigma Delta, Phi Delta Phi. Banking, General corporate, Administrative and regulatory. Office: Republic Nat Bank 452 Fifth Ave New York NY 10018

GINSBERG, EUGENE STANLEY, lawyer; b. Bklyn., Dec. 11, 1929; s. Joseph J. and Rose (Epstein) G.; m. Barbara A. Proskauer, May 31, 1953; (dec.); children—Debra, Mara; m. 2d, Estelle Strauss, June 29, 1980; stepchildren—William, Robert, Steven. B.B.A., CCNY, 1951; J.D., NYU, 1954. Bar: N.Y. 1955, U.S. Dist. Ct. (ea. and so. dists.) N.Y. 1957, U.S. Ct. Appeals (2d cir.) 1966, U.S. Supreme Ct. 1966. Ptnr. Krainin & Ginsberg, N.Y.C., 1958-62; sole practice, Bklyn. and Mineola, N.Y., 1962-73; ptnr. Ginsberg, Ehrlich, Reich & Hoffman and predecessors, Garden City, N.Y., 1973-83; ptnr. Jaspan, Ginsberg, Ehrlich, Reich & Levin, Garden City, 1983—. Arbitrator Nassau County Dist. Ct., 1980—; mem. nat. panel arbitrators Am. Arbitration Assn., 1966—; arbitrator Better Bus. Bur., 1982—. Served with U.S. Army, 1953-55. Mem. ABA (co-chmn. subcom. on profl. responsibility in labor arbitration 1977-83, subcom. on publ. of labor arbitration awards 1984-86 , labor arbitration and law of collective bargaining agreements com. 1975—), N.Y. State Bar Assn., Nassau County Bar Assn. (labor law com. 1973—, arbitration law com. 1973—, chmn. 1985—, grievance com. 1983—). General practice, General corporate. Home: 30 Parkway Dr Roslyn Heights NY 11577 Office: 300 Garden City Plaza Garden City NY 11530

GINSBERG, JEROME MAURICE, lawyer; b. Bklyn., May 8, 1939; s. Frank Ralph and Minnie (Altwerger) G.; m. Carol Elaine Cordover, Aug. 9, 1964; children: Andrew Ian, Lynn Ellen, Peter Ross. BA, CCNY, 1960; JD, NYU, 1963. Bar: N.Y. 1963, U.S. Dist. Ct. (so. and ea. dists.) N.Y. 1969, U.S. Supreme Ct. 1967. Assoc. Panken & Panken, N.Y.C., 1963-64; ptnr. Sakona, Ginsberg & Katsorhis and predecessor Sakona & Ginsberg, N.Y.C., 1964-83, Ginsberg & Katsorhis, N.Y.C., 1983—; lectr. U. Md., 1980, Criminal Cts. Bar Assn., Queens, N.Y., 1983. Author: Prepaid Legal Plan Primer, 1980; also articles. Editor Queens Bar Bull., 1966-74. Pres. Young Dems. Queens County, N.Y., 1959, Independence Dem. Club, Jamaica, N.Y., 1974; v.p. Plainview Jewish Ctr., 1984, pres., 1986. Served with U.S. Army, 1956-61. Recipient award of Honor, Queens Lawyers Club, 1981. Mem. ABA, Queens County Bar Assn. (pres. 1980-81, award of Meritorious Service 1982), Brandeis Assn. (pres. 1979-80), Network Bar Leaders (chmn. 1984—), N.Y. State Bar Assn. (ho. of dels. 1987—), N.Y. State Trial Lawyers, Network of Bar Leaders (chmn. 1984-86). Jewish. Lodge: K.P. State civil litigation, Family and matrimonial, Personal injury. Office: Ginsberg & Katsorhis 77-53 Main St Flushing NY 11367

GINSBERG, LARRY FLOYD, lawyer; b. Providence, Apr. 13, 1951; s. Irving and Adeline (Karman) G.; m. Rhonda L. Jacobs, Nov. 24, 1977; children: Jonathan Daniel, Spencer Jaron. BA in Psychology, SUNY, Stony Brook, 1973; JD, SUNY Buffalo, Amherst, 1976. Bar: N.Y. 1977, U.S. Dist. Ct. (so. and ea. dists.) N.Y. 1979, Conn. 1983, U.S. Dist. Ct. Conn. 1984. Legal editor Matthew Bender and Co., N.Y.C., 1977; assoc. Alosco & Patterson, N.Y.C., 1978-79, Berger & Assocs., N.Y.C., 1979-83; assoc., mgr. Jacoby & Meyers, Norwalk, Conn., 1984-85; sole practice Stamford, Conn., 1985—. Legal editor Administrative Law, 1977. Bd. dirs., v.p., gen. counsel Stamford Jewish Hist. Soc., 1983—; county committeeman Democratic Council, N.Y.C., 1978-79. Mem. ABA, Conn. Bar. Assn., Stamford-Darien Bar Assn. Club: Israel Task Force (chmn. 1982-84). Lodge: Masons, B'nai B'rith Nutmeg (pres. 1984-86. Avocations: travel, reading, sports, public speaking, art. Real property, General corporate, General practice. Home: 7 Russet Rd Stamford CT 06093 Office: 5 Hillandale Ave Stamford CT 06902

GINSBERG, LEWIS ROBBINS, Lawyer; b. Chgo., May 7, 1932; s. Maurice Jesse and Zelda (Robbins) G.; m. Linda Cox, June 16, 1973; children: Aaron, Brenda, Stephen. A.B., U. Chgo., 1953, J.D., 1956. Bar: Ill.; 1956. Assoc. firm Lederer, Livingston, Kahn & Adsit, Chgo., 1956, 60-63; corp. atty. Maremont Corp., Chgo., 1963-66; assoc. firm McDermott, Will & Emery, Chgo., 1966-69, ptnr., 1969—. Bd. dirs. Ravenswood Hosp. Med. Ctr., Chgo., 1981—. Served to capt. U.S. Army, 1957-60. Mem. Chgo. Bar Assn., Order of Coif. Democrat. Jewish. Club: University (Chgo.). General practice. Home: 5530 S Kimbark Ave Chicago IL 60637 Office: McDermott Will & Emery 111 W Monroe St Chicago IL 60603

GINSBERG, ROBERT MICHAEL, lawyer; b. N.Y.C., June 25, 1935; s. David A. and Paula (Daniels) G.; m. Judy Ann Haworth, Dec. 19, 1969 (div. Dec. 1978); m. Annette Elizabeth Hult, June 6, 1982; 1 child, Simon. B.A., U. Mich., 1956; LL.D., Yale U., 1959. Bar: N.Y. 1961, U.S. Dist. Ct. (so. dist.) N.Y. 1963, U.S. Dist. Ct. (ea. dist.) N.Y., 1974, U.S. Ct. Appeals (2d cir.) 1974, U.S. Supreme Ct. 1983. Sole practice, N.Y.C., 1963-68, 79-84; ptnr. Fuchsberg & Fuchsberg, 1968-79; ptnr. Ginsberg & Broome, N.Y.C., 1984—. Democratic dist. leader, N.Y.C., 1969-71, state committeeman, 1974—. Served with U.S. Army, 1959. Mem. Am. Trial Lawyers Assn., N.Y. State Trial Lawyers Assn., N.Y. County Bar Assn. Democrat. Jewish. Personal injury. Home: 225 W 106th St New York NY 10025 Office: Ginsberg & Broome 225 Broadway New York NY 10007

GINSBURG, BRUCE MARTIN, lawyer; b. Phila., Feb. 13, 1949; s. Paul and Evelyn (Greenberg) G.; m. Lisa Rubin, June 18, 1977; children: Aaron, Lauren. Student, Wroxton (Eng.) Coll., 1969; BA, Fairleigh Dickinson U., 1971; postgrad., Internat. Sch. Comparative Law, Paris, 1972; JD, U. San Diego, 1975. Bar: Pa. 1975, Calif. 1975, N.J. 1976, U.S. Ct. Appeals (3d cir.) 1983, U.S. Supreme Ct. 1984. Assoc. Sher, Moses, Zuckerman et al, Norristown, Pa.; sole practice Phila., 1977-80; ptnr. Ginsburg & Assocs., Phila., 1980—; solicitor Soc. Hill Savs. and Loan, Phila., 1981—. Mem. fin. com. Hon. Robert Borski, U.S. Congress, Phila., 1983—, Senator H. Salvatore, Phila., 1985, Dist. Atty. Ron Castille, Phila., 1985-86. Fellow Am. Acad. Advocacy; mem. Pa. Bar Assn., Phila. Bar Assn., Assn. Trial Lawyers Am., Phila. Trial Lawyers Assn. (bd. dirs. 1982—), Am. Friends Haifa U. (bd. dirs. 1983—). Republican. Jewish. Club: Locust (Phila.). Avocations: sailing, tennis, snow skiing, water skiing. Personal injury, Federal civil litigation, Insurance. Office: Ginsburg & Assocs 117 S 17th St Suite 608 Philadelphia PA 19103

GINSBURG, CHARLES DAVID, lawyer; b. N.Y.C., Apr. 20, 1912; s. Nathan and Rae (Lewis) G.; m. Marianne Laïs; children by previous marriage: Jonathan, Susan, Mark. A.B., W.Va. U., 1932; LL.B., Harvard U., 1935. Atty. for public utilities div. and office of gen. counsel SEC, 1935-39; law sec. to Justice William O. Douglas, 1939; asst. to commr. SEC, 1939-40; legal adviser Price Stblzn. Div., Nat. Def. Adv. Com., 1940-41; gen. counsel Office Price Adminstrn. and Civilian Supply, 1941-42, OPA, 1942-43; pvt. practice law Washington, 1946—; partner firm Ginsburg, Feldman & Bress; adminstrv. asst. to Senator M.M. Neely, W.Va., 1950; adj. prof. internat. law Georgetown U. (Grad. Sch. Law), 1959-67; Dep. commr. U.S. del. Austrian Treaty Commn., Vienna, 1947; adviser U.S. del. Council Fgn. Ministers, London, 1947; Mem. Presdl. Emergency Bd. 166 (Airlines), 1966; mem. Pres.'s Commn. on Postal Orgn., 1967; chmn. Presdl. Emergency Bd. 169 (Railroads), 1969; exec. dir. Nat. Adv. Commn. Civil Disorders, 1967. Author: The Future of German Reparations; Contbr. to legal jours. Bd. mem., chmn. exec. com. Nat. Symphony Orch. Assn., 1960-69; bd. govs. Weizmann Inst., 1965 (hon. fellow 1972); mem. vis. com. Harvard-Mass. Inst. Tech. Joint Center on Urban Studies, 1969; trustee St. John's Coll., 1969-75, chmn. bd., 1974-76; overseers com. Kennedy Sch. Govt. Harvard, 1971—; mem. council Nat. Harvard Law Sch. Assn., 1972—. Served from pvt. to capt. AUS, 1943-46; dep. dir. econs. div. Office Mil. Govt., 1945-46, Germany. Decorated Bronze Star medal, Legion of Merit; recipient Presdl. Certificate of Merit. Mem. Am. Law Inst., Council on Fgn. Relations, Phi Beta Kappa. Democrat. Clubs: Metropolitan, F Street, Federal City, Army and Navy. Administrative and regulatory, General corporate, Federal civil litigation. Home: 619 S Lee St Alexandria VA 22314 Office: 1250 Connecticut Ave NW Washington DC 20036

GINSBURG, DOUGLAS HOWARD, lawyer, educator; b. Chgo., May 25, 1946; s. Maurice and Katherine (Goodmont) G.; m. Claudia De Secundy, May 31, 1968 (div. Sept. 1980); 1 child, Jessica DeSecundy; m. 2d, Hallee Perkins Morgan, May 9, 1981; 1 child, Hallee Katherine Morgan. Diploma, Latin Sch. Chgo., 1963; B.S., Cornell U., 1970; J.D., U. Chgo., 1973. Bar: Ill. 1973, Mass. 1982, U.S. Supreme Ct. 1984, U.S. Ct. Appeals (9th cir.) 1986. Intern Covington & Burling, Washington, 1972; law clk. U.S. Ct. Appeals, Washington, 1973-74, U.S. Supreme Ct., Washington, 1974-75; prof. Harvard U., 1975-83; dep. asst. atty. gen. for regulatory affairs, Antitrust div. U.S. Dept. Justice, Washington, 1983-84, asst. atty. gen., Antitrust div., 1985-86; adminstr. for Info. and Regulatory Affairs Exec. Office Pres., Office Mgmt. and Budget, Washington, 1984-85; judge U.S. Ct. Appeals (D.C. cir.), 1986—; vis. prof. law Columbia U., N.Y.C., 1987—; lectr. law Harvard U., Cambridge, Mass., 1987—. Author: Regulation of Broadcasting: Law and Policy Towards Radio, Television and Cable Communications, 1979; Antitrust, Uncertainty, and Technological Innovation, 1980. Editor: (with W. Abernathy) Government, Technology and the Future of the Automobile, 1980. Contbr. articles to profl. jours. Recipient Mecham prize scholarship U. Chgo. Law Sch., 1970-73; Casper Platt award U. Chgo. Law Sch., 1972. Mem. Am. Econs. Assn., ABA (ex officio exec. council antitrust sect. 1985-86), Ill. State Bar Assn., Mass. Bar Assn., Boston Bar Assn., Fed. Bar Assn. (exec. council banking com. 1983—), Order of Coif, Phi Kappa Phi. Republican. Avocations: historic preservation; antiques. Office: US Ct Appeals 3d and Constitution Ave NW Washington DC 20001

GINSBURG, MARCUS, lawyer; b. Marietta, Ohio, Feb. 16, 1915; s. Louis and Dora (Brachman) G.; m. Martine Heilbron, Feb. 23, 1949; children: Harold Heilbron, Robert L. Student, Marietta Coll., 1932-33; A.B., U. Mich., 1936; J.D., Harvard U., 1939. Bar: Md. 1939, Tex. 1940. Assoc. Simon & Wynn, 1939-42; ptnr. Simon, Wynn, Sanders & Jones, 1945-51; mng. ptnr. McDonald, Sanders, Ginsburg, Gibson & Webb, 1951—; bd. dirs., vice chmn. exec. com. MBank Fort Worth, N.A. Pres. United Fund and Community Services, Fort Worth, 1962, Tarrant Council Community Council, 1966-67, Traveller's Aid Soc., Fort Worth, 1953-54; vice chmn. city solicitations commn., 1963-67; trustee Am. Jewish Congress; past v.p. Nat. Community Relations Adv. Council; mem. U.S. nat. commn. UNESCO, 1959-64, exec. com., 1963-64, steering com., 1964, chmn. pub. info. com., 1962-64; past v.p., treas. Children's Mus. Fort Worth; mem. Nat. Budget and Consultation Com., 1966—; mem. exec. com. Community Trust Fund of Tarrant County; trustee Retina Research Found.; bd. dirs. Fort Worth Art Assn. Served to 2d lt. USAAF, 1942-45. Decorated Army Commendation medal; recipient award excellency United Fund Fort Worth, award Fort Worth Traveller's Aid Soc. Fort Worth Community Council. Mem. Harvard Law Sch. Assn. (life mem., pres. Tex. 1955-56, nat. v.p. 1956-57, dir. 1978), Assn. Life Ins. Council, Tex. Assn. Bank Attys., Nat. Assn. Coll. and Univ. Attys., Newcomen Soc. N.Am., Confrerie des Chevaliers du Tastevin (commandeur N.Tex. chpt.), Pi Lambda Phi. Jewish (v.p. temple). Clubs: City, Fort Worth, Petroleum, Shady Oaks Country (Fort Worth). Banking, General corporate, Real property. Home: 3860 Bellaire Circle Fort Worth TX 76109 Office: McDonald Sanders Ginsburg Gibson & Webb 1300 Continental Plasza 777 Main St Fort Worth TX 76102

GINSBURG, RUTH BADER, federal judge; b. Bklyn., Mar. 15, 1933; d. Nathan and Celia (Amster) Bader; m. Martin David Ginsburg, June 23, 1954; children: Jane Carol, James Steven. A.B., Cornell U., 1954; postgrad., Harvard Law Sch., 1956-58; LL.B. Kent scholar, Columbia Law Sch., 1959; LL.D., Lund (Sweden) U., 1969, Am. U., 1981, Vt. Law Sch., 1984, Georgetown U., 1985, DePaul U., 1985, Bklyn. Law Sch., 1987. Bar: N.Y. 1954, D.C. 1975, U.S. Supreme Ct. 1967. Law sec. to judge U.S. Dist. Ct. (So. Dist. N.Y.), 1959-61; research assoc. Columbia Law Sch., N.Y.C., 1961-62; assoc. dir. project internat. procedure Columbia Law Sch., 1962-63; asst. prof. Rutgers U. Sch. Law, Newark, 1963-66; assoc. prof. Rutgers U. Sch. Law, 1966-69, prof., 1969-72; prof. Columbia U. Sch. Law, N.Y.C., 1972-80; U.S. Circuit judge U.S. Ct. Appeals, D.C. Circuit, Washington, 1980—; Phi Beta Kappa vis. scholar, 1973-74; fellow Center for Advanced Study in Behavioral Scis., Stanford, Calif., 1977-78; lectr. Salzburg Seminar, Austria, 1984; Bd. dirs. Am. Bar Found., 1979—, exec. com., 1981—, sec., 1987—. Author: (with Anders Bruzelius) Civil Procedure in Sweden, 1965, Swedish Code of Judicial Procedure, 1968, Sex-Based Discrimination, 1974, supplement, 1978; contbr. numerous articles to legal jours.; vol. editor: Business Regulation in the Common Market Nations, vol. 1, 1969. Mem. ABA, Am. Law Inst. (council mem. 1978—), Council on Fgn. Relations., Am. Acad. Arts and Scis. Office: US Court of Appeals US Courthouse 3rd & Constitution Ave NW Washington DC 20001

GINSKY, MARVIN H., corporate executive, lawyer; b. N.Y.C., Aug. 2, 1930; married. LL.B., NYU, 1955. Bar: N.Y. 1955. Atty. Paramount Pictures, N.Y.C., 1955-60; assoc. Marvin Rosenman, N.Y.C., 1960-61; asst. gen. counsel Champion Internat. Corp., Stamford, Conn., 1961-65, sec., 1965-67, assoc. counsel, 1967-69, gen. counsel, 1969-73, v.p., gen. counsel, 1973-81, sr. v.p., gen. counsel, 1981—. Mem. ABA. General corporate. Office: Champion Internat Corp One Champion Plaza Stamford CT 06921

GIOFFRE, ANTHONY BRUNO, lawyer, accountant; b. Port Chester, N.Y., Oct. 10, 1907; s. Bruno and Anna (Messina) G.; m. Louise M. Giorno, Sept. 17, 1933; children: Bruno J., Anthony B. Jr., Donald B., Anna G. BS in Acctg., Syracuse U., 1929; JD, Bklyn. Law Sch., 1967. Bar: N.Y. 1937, U.S. Dist. Ct. (so. dist.) N.Y. 1944. Ptnr. Gioffre & Gioffre, Port Chester, 1937—; head auditor Reconstrn. Fin., Washington, 1941-43; treas. Village of Port Chester, 1944-54, mayor, 54-56; estate tax atty. State of N.Y., Westchester County, 1958-59; assemblyman State of N.Y., Albany, 1960-65, senator, 1966-72. Chmn. Rye Town Rep. Com., N.Y., 1957-60. Mem. West Chester County Bar Assn., Port Chester-Rye Bar Assn., N.Y. State Soc. CPA's, Sons of St. Joseph (Outstanding Service award 1964), Sons of Italy (Outstanding Legis. award 1964, Dedicated Service award 1966, Outstanding Citizen award 1967, Man of Yr. award 1968), Long Island League Salt Water Sportsman (Distinguished Service award 1965), Port Chester Old Timers Athletic Assn. (Outstanding Civic award 1967), Builders Inst. Westchester and Putnam Counties (Recognition and Achievement award 1968), Calabria Mut. Aid Soc. New Rochelle (Outstanding Citizen award 1970), County Club (Man of Yr. award 1972). Roman Catholic. Real property, Probate, Criminal. Home: 20 Magnolia Dr Rye Brook NY 10573 Office: Gioffre & Gioffre PC 220 Westchester Ave Port Chester NY 10573

GIOFFRE, BRUNO JOSEPH, lawyer; b. Port Chester, N.Y., June 27, 1934; s. Anthony B. and Louise (Giorno) G.; m. Kathleen M. Bartlik, Nov. 14, 1959; children—Kathleen, Lisa, Michael, Christopher, B. Scott, David, Kerry. B.A., Cornell U., 1956, J.D., 1958. Bar: N.Y. 1958, U.S. Dist. Ct. (so. dist.) N.Y. 1973. Sr. mem. Gioffre & Gioffre, P.C., Port Chester, N.Y., 1958—; mem. adv. bd. First Am. Title Ins. Co.; justice Town of Rye (N.Y.), 1965—; dir., trustee Sound Fed. Savs. & Loan Assn. Bd. dirs., trustee United Hosp., Port Chester Pub. Library. Mem. Port Chester-Rye Bar Assn., Westchester Bar Assn., N.Y. Bar Assn., ABA, Westchester County Magistrate's Assn., N.Y. Magistrate's Assn. Clubs: Elks, KC. Real property, Probate. Home: 18 Beechwood Blvd Rye Brook NY 10573 Office: 220 Westchester Ave Port Chester NY 10573

GIORDANO, PAUL GREGORY, lawyer; b. Indpls., July 6, 1956; s. Albert G. and Marie Jacqueline (Duffey) G. BA summa cum laude, Coll. Notre Dame, Belmont, Calif., 1978; JD, U. Santa Clara, 1981. Bar: Nev. 1981, U.S. Dist. Ct. Nev. 1981, Calif. 1982, U.S. Dist. Ct. (no. dist.) Calif. 1982, U.S. Tax Ct. 1982, U.S. Ct. Appeals (9th cir.) 1982. Assoc. Hall & Haveson, Reno, 1981-83; dep. dist. atty. Churchill County, Fallon, Nev., 1983-84; dep. atty. gen. State of Nev., Carson City, 1984—. Treas. Associated Students Coll. of Notre Dame, Belmont, Calif., 1977. Mem. ABA, Washoe County Bar Assn. Republican. Roman Catholic. Avocations: sports, camping, fishing, hunting, skiing. Administrative and regulatory, Antitrust, State civil litigation. Home: 6012 Plumas St Apt G Reno NV 89509 Office: Nev Atty Gen's Office Capitol Complex Carson City NV 89710

GIORZA, JOHN C., lawyer; b. Lexington, Mo., May 25, 1950; s. Alphonso Ceno and Iris (Polla) G.; m. Jane Ray Dempsy, Sept. 5, 1981. BA, Westminster Coll., 1972; MBA, U. Mo. 1974, 1974; JD, U. Mo., 1978. Bar: U.S. Dist. Ct. (we. dist.) Mo. 1978. Assoc. Aull, Sherman & Worthington, Lexington, 1978-83; ptnr. Aull, Sherman, Worthington & Giorza, Lexington, 1983—. Mem. ABA, Mo. Bar Assn., Mo. Assn. Trial Attys., Kansas City Bar Assn., Lafayette County Bar Assn. (pres. 1979-80). Club: Shirkey Golf (Richmond, Mo.) (pres. 1982-85). Lodge: Lions (v.p. local chpt.1983-84). Avocations: travel, golf, collecting stamps, sporting events. General practice, Probate, Consumer commercial. Home: 604 Glenn Dr Lexington MO 64067 Office: Aull Sherman et al PO Box 280 Lexington MO 64067

GIPPIN, ROBERT MALCOLM, lawyer; b. Cleve., Feb. 3, 1948; s. Morris and Helena (Weil) G.; children—Sarah, Joshua, Rebecca. A.B., Dartmouth Coll., 1969; J.D., Harvard U., 1973. Bar: Ohio 1973. Asst. to dir. Ohio Dept. Commerce, Columbus, 1973; exec. sec. Ohio Real Estate Commn., Columbus, 1974-75; prosecutor Municipal Ct., Cuyahoga Falls, Ohio, 1975; ptnr. Buckingham, Doolittle & Burroughs, Akron, Ohio, 1975—. Active exec. com. Summit County Democratic Party, Akron, 1976—; pres. Summit County Council, 1982-84. Mem. Akron Bar Assn., Ohio Bar Assn., Phi Beta Kappa. Jewish. Avocations: reading; tennis; cooking. Federal civil litigation, State civil litigation, Administrative and regulatory. Home: 737 Merriman Rd Akron OH 44303 Office: Buckingham Doolittle & Burroughs 50 S Main St PO Box 1500 Akron OH 44309

GIRARD, LEONARD ARTHUR, lawyer; b. Chgo., Nov. 4, 1942; s. Oscar Lawrence and Ruth (Alpern) G.; m. Linda K. Grove (div. May 1980); children: Kimberly, Allison. BS in Econs., U. Oreg., 1964; LLB, Stanford U., 1967. Bar: Oreg. 1967, U.S. Dist. Ct. Oreg. 1967. Assoc. Rives, Bonyhadi & Smith, Portland, Oreg., 1967-73; ptnr. Stoel, Rives, Boley, Fraser & Wyse (merger Rives, Bonyhadi & Smith and Davies, Biggs, Strayer, Stoel & Boley), Portland, 1974—. Bd. dirs. Sunshine Div., Portland, 1973—. Mem. Oreg. Bar (dir. edn. 1973, bd. bar examiners 1975-78), Multnomah Bar Assn. (pres., v.p., sec. 1978-82, award merit 1978). Clubs: Portland City (chmn. study com. 1985—), Multnomah Athletic (Portland). Avocations: tennis, hiking, cross-country skiing, reading. Administrative and regulatory, Public utilities, State and local taxation. Office: Stoel Rives Boley Fraser & Wyse 900 SW 5th Ave Suite 2300 Portland OR 97204

GIRARD, NETTABELL, lawyer; b. Riverton, Wyo., Feb. 24, 1938; d. George and Arranetta (Bell) Girard. Student, Idaho State U., 1957-58; B.S., U. Wyo., 1959, LL.B., 1961. Bar: Wyo. 1961, U.S. Supreme Ct. 1969, D.C. 1969. Practiced in Riverton, 1963-69; atty.-adviser on gen. counsel's staff HUD; assigned Office Interstate Land Sales Registration, Washington, 1969-70; sect. chief interstate land sales Office Gen. Counsel, 1970-73; ptnr. Larson & Larson, Riverton, 1973-85; sole practice Riverton, 1985—; guest lectr. at high schs.; condr. seminar on law for layman Riverton br. A.A.U.W., 1965; condr. course on women and law; lectr. equal rights, job discrimination, land use planning. Editor: Wyoming Clubwoman, 1966-68; bd. editors Wyo. Law Jour, 1959-61; writer Obiter Dictum column Women Lawyers Jour; also articles in legal jours. Chmn. fund drive Wind River chpt. ARC, 1965; chmn. Citizens Com. for Better Hosp. Improvement., 1965; chmn. sub-com. on polit., legal rights and responsibilities Gov.'s Commn. on Status Women, 1965-69, adv. mem., 1973—; rep. Nat. Conf. Govs. Commn., Washington, 1966; local chmn. Law Day, 1966, 67; mem. state bd. Wyo. Girl Scouts U.S.A., sec., 1974—, mem. nat. bd., 1978-81 ; state vol. adviser Nat. Found., March of Dimes, 1967-69; legal counsel Wyo. Women's Conf., 1977; Riverton Civic League. Recipient Spl. Achievement award HUD, 1972, Disting. Leadership award Girl Scouts U.S.A., 1973, Franklin D. Roosevelt award Wyo. chpt. March of Dimes, 1985; named outstanding woman Wonder Woman and Girl Scouts U.S.A., 1982. Mem. Wyo., Fremont County, D.C. bar assns., Women's Bar Assn. for D.C., Internat. Fedn. Women Lawyers, Am. Judicature Soc., Am. Trial Lawyers Assn., Nat. Assn. Women Lawyers (del. Wyo., nat. sec. 1969-70, v.p. 1970-71, pres. 1972-73), AAUW (br. pres.), Wyo. Fedn. Womens Clubs (state editor, pres. elect 1968-69, treas. 1974-76), Progressive Women's Club, Kappa Delta, Delta Kappa Gamma (hon. mem. state chpt.). Club: Riverton Chautauqua (pres. 1965-67). Bankruptcy, Contracts commercial, General practice. Home: 224 W Sunset St PO Box 687 Riverton WY 82501 Office: 513 E Main St Riverton WY 82501

GIRARD, ROBERT A., law educator; b. 1931. LLB, Harvard U., 1956. Prof. law Stanford (Calif.) U. Office: Stanford Law Sch Stanford CA 94305 *

GIRARD-DICARLO, DAVID FRANKLIN, lawyer; b. Bryn Mawr, Pa., Jan. 20, 1943; s. John J. Girard-DiCarlo and Elizabeth (Patton) Ward; m. Constance Jean Bricker, Apr. 5, 1973. B.S., St. Joseph's U., 1970; J.D., Villanova U., 1973. Bar: U.S. Dist. Ct. (ea. dist.) Pa. 1973, Pa. 1973, U.S. Ct. Appeals (3d cir.) 1973, U.S. Supreme Ct. 1978. Assoc., Wolf, Block, Schorr & Solis-Cohen, Phila., 1973-74; assoc. Dilworth, Paxson, Kalish, Levy & Kauffman, Phila., 1974-78, ptnr., 1979; ptnr. Fell, Spalding, Goff & Rubin, Phila., 1979-82; ptnr. Blank, Rome, Comisky & McCauley, Phila., 1982—, chmn. labor and employment law sect., 1982-86, adminstrv. ptnr., 1986—; mem. hearing com. Disciplinary Bd. of Supreme Ct. of Pa., Phila., 1981-84, chmn. hearing com., 1984—; faculty mem. Workshop on Urban Mass Transp., Practicing Law Inst., San Francisco and Washington, 1978. Editor-in-chief Villanova Law Rev., 1972, Transit Law Rev., 1977-81; contbr. articles to legal jours. Chmn. bd. Southeastern Pa. Transp. Authority, 1979-82; mem. transp. taxation task force Tax Commn. of Commonwealth of Pa., 1981-82; mem. Pa. Rep. State Fin. Com., 1982—; bd. dirs. Greater Phila. Partnership, 1981-83, Urban Affairs Partnership, 1983-85, Hermitage Homeowners Assn., 1982-86; mem. World Affairs Council, Phila. Mem. ABA, Pa. Bar Assn., Phila. Bar Assn., Am. Pub. Transit Assn. (bd. dirs. 1979-82, chmn. bd. dirs. 1982, mem. exec. com. 1980-82). Episcopalian. Clubs: Union League of Phila., Urban, Vesper (Phila.); Waynesborough Country (Paoli, Pa.). Labor, General practice, General corporate. Home: 1126 St Andrews Rd Bryn Mawr PA 19010 Office: Blank Rome Comisky & McCauley 4 Penn Ctr Plaza Philadelphia PA 19103

GIRE, MICHAEL KENT, lawyer; b. San Francisco, Jan. 25, 1947; s. Milburn Arthur and Opal May (Lump) G.; m. Marguerite Bird Farrow, Jan. 26, 1980; children: Ann Gramza, Lyn Gramza. BS, Ohio State U., 1970; JD, Am. U., 1977. Bar: Ohio 1977, D.C. 1978. Analyst HHS, Washington, 1971-77; assoc. Bricker & Eckler, Columbus, Ohio, 1977-83, ptnr., 1983—. Trustee Community Health & Nursing Services, Columbus, Art for Community Expression, Columbus. Served with Ohio Air N.G., 1969-70. Mem. ABA (forum com. on health law), Ohio Bar Assn., Columbus Bar Assn., D.C. Bar Assn., Nat. Health Lawyers Assn., Am. Acad. Hosp. Attys., Ohio Soc. Hosp. Attys. (bd. dirs. 1984—). Democrat. Club: Capital (Columbus). Health.

GISLASON, DANIEL ADAM, lawyer; b. New Ulm, Minn., Oct. 13, 1944; s. Sidney Payson and Marjorie Louise (Fleck) G.; m. Margaret M. Hinke, Mar. 13, 1971; children—Adam Payson, Eirik David, Travis Arthur. B.A., U. Minn., 1966, J.D., 1969. Bar: Minn., U.S. Ct. Appeals (8th cir.), U.S. Dist Ct. Minn. Assoc., Gislason, Dosland, Hunter & Malecki, New Ulm, 1972-75, ptnr., 1975—. Served to capt. U.S. Army, 1969-72. Decorated Army Commendation medal. Mem. ABA, Def. Research Inst. (state chmn. 1982-85), Assn. Ins. Attys., Internat. Assn. Ins. Counsel, Minn. Bar Assn. (chmn. ct. rules com. 1986—), 9th Dist. Bar Assn. (pres. 1983-84), Minn. Def. Lawyers Assn. (bd. dirs. 1982-86). Republican. State civil litigation, Family and matrimonial, Federal civil litigation. Home: 48 Woodland Dr New Ulm MN 56073 Office: 1 S State St New Ulm MN 56073

GISLER, GEORGE LOUIS, lawyer; b. Indpls., Aug. 28, 1909; s. Benjamin Harrison and Anna Marie (Twente) S.; m. m. Georgia Helenanna Umscheid, Apr. 21, 1946; children—John Case, James Robert. A.B., Butler U., 1930;

J.D., U. Mich., 1933. Bar: Ind. 1933, Mo. 1934, U.S. Dist. Ct. (we. dist.) Mo. 1934, U.S. Ct. Appeals (8th cir.) 1950, U.S. Supreme Ct. 1950. Assoc., Michaels, Blackmar, Newkirk, Eager & Swanson, 1933-39; ptnr. Sebree, Shook & Gisler, Kansas City, Mo., 1939-42; regional atty. War Prodn. Bd., 1942-43; ptnr. Reeder, Gisler, Griffin & Dysart, Kansas City, Mo., 1947-58; sole practice, Kansas City, 1958—; dir. Dean Research Corp. Bd. dirs. Don Bosco Community Ctr., Kansas City, 1963-85; bd. dirs., sec. corp. Park Lane Med. Ctr., 1980—; chmn. Ind. Voters Assn., 1960; v.p. Kansas City Philharm. Assn., 1960-65; pres. Kansas City Careers Found., 1959-64; trustee Kansas City Conservatory Music, 1957-59; trustee Kansas City Lyric Opera, 1957-72. Served to lt. USNR, 1943-46 Mem. ABA, Mo. Bar Assn., Kansas City Bar Assn., Lawyers Assn. Kansas City. Clubs: Arrowhead Yacht, Carriage (pres. 1960-61). Contbr. articles to profl. jours. General practice, State civil litigation, General corporate. Address: 420 Winnebago Dr Lake Winnebago MO 64034

GISSBERG, JOHN GUSTAV, government official; b. Juneau, Alaska, May 6, 1943; s. Gustav Helmer and Claudia Katherine (Kearney) G.; m. Christie Yoshihara, Dec. 23, 1967; children—Eron Thomas, Christena Katherine Akiko. B.S. cum laude, U. Wash., 1965; postgrad. Stanford U. Interuniv. Ctr. (Tokyo U.), 1967; J.D., U. Mich., 1970, Ph.D. in Fisheries, 1971. Bar: Alaska 1971, Mich. 1971, U.S. Sup. Ct. 1980. Guest investigator Marine Policy Affairs and Ocean Mgmt. program Woods Hole (Mass.) Oceanographic Instn., 1971; extramural lectr. Faculty Law U. Singapore, 1972; assoc. Cole, Hartig, Rhodes & Norman, Anchorage, 1972-74; cons. The Conservation Found. and Rockefeller Found., Tokyo, 1974-76; asst. atty. gen. Fisheries Affairs sect. Dept. Law, State of Alaska, Anchorage, 1976-83, Juneau, 1982-83; commr. Gov.'s Comm. on Conf. of Law of the Sea, 1974, acting exec. sec., 1983; mem. ocean policy com. Nat. Acad. Sci., 1979-82; mem. com. scientists and experts Internat. North Pacific Fisheries Commn., 1979-80, 82, 85; Mem. editorial adv. bd. Marine Fisheries Mgmt. Law Reporter, 1982. Contbr. articles to profl. jours. Bd. dirs. Eaglecrest Ski Area, 1982-83. Ford Found. fellow, 1966-67, NDEA fellow, 1967-69. Mem. Am. Soc. Internat. Law, ABA, Alaska Bar Assn., Assn. Internat. Lawyers in Japan, Am. Fisheries Soc. (cert. fisheries scientist), Phi Eta Sigma. Roman Catholic. Club: Pioneers of Alaska. Environment. Office: Regional Fisheries Attache Am Embassy APO Box 217 San Francisco CA 96503

GITELMAN, MORTON, legal educator; b. Chgo., Feb. 7, 1933; s. Jack and Molly (Sponke) G.; m. Norma C. Linkow, Dec. 23, 1956 (dec. Feb. 1976); children: Neil, Eliot, Ronald; m. Marcia L. McIvor, May 15, 1977. Cert. in personnel adminstrn., Roosevelt U., 1954; JD, DePaul U., 1959; LLM, U. Ill., 1965. Bar: Ill. 1959, U.S. Ct. Appeals (10th cir.) 1963, Ark. 1972, U.S. Dist. Ct. (ea. and we. dists.) Ark. 1972, U.S. Ct. Appeals (8th cir.) 1972, U.S. Supreme Ct. 1974. Teaching fellow U. Ill., Urbana, 1959-60; research assoc. Duke U., Durham, N.C., 1960-61; assoc. prof. law U. Denver, 1961-65; prof. law U. Ark., Fayetteville, 1965—; chmn. Ark. Adv. Com. U.S. Commn. Civil Rights, 1972-82, mem., 1966—. Author: Unionization Attempts in Small Enterprises, 1963; co-editor Land Use, 1976, 3d rev. edition, 1983. Chmn. Fayetteville Planning Commn., 1972-76, mem., 1967-76; nat. bd. dirs. ACLU, 1969-72, pres. Ark. chpt., 1969-70. Served with U.S. Army, 1954-56. Recipient Disting. Teaching award U. Ark. Alumni Assn., 1978. Mem. Ill. Bar Assn., Ark. Bar Assn. Jewish. Legal education, Legal history, Real property. Home: 1229 W Lakeridge Fayetteville AR 72703 Office: U Ark Sch Law Fayetteville AR 72701

GITLIN, RICHARD ALAN, lawyer; b. Hartford, Conn., May 26, 1942; s. Max and Mary (Kaminsky) G.; m. Nancy Bobrow, Aug. 22, 1964; children—Jeffrey, David, Michael. B.A., U. Conn., 1964, J.D., 1967. Bar: Conn. 1967. Ptnr. Hebb & Gitlin, Hartford, 1973—; mem. Bankruptcy and Creditors' Rights Adv. Com., Practising Law Inst., 1981—; chmn., panelist, moderator, lectr. seminars. Author, co-author outlines for Practising Law Inst. Book, 1980-81, also articles. Mem. ABA (bus. bankruptcy com. of corp., banking and bus. law sect. 1981—, chmn. subcom. on internat. bankrupcy 1981—), Practising Law Inst., Hartford County Bar Assn., Conn. Bar Assn. (asst. treas. 1978-79, bd. govts. 1978-79). Bankruptcy, Corp fin. Office: Hebb & Gitlin 1 State St Hartford CT 06103

GITTENS, JAMES P., lawyer, consultant; b. Somerville, N.J., July 18, 1952; s. George Edward and Olivia (Thomas) G. BA, Rutgers U., New Brunswick, N.J., 1974; JD, Rutgers U., Newark, 1977; LLM, Georgetown U., 1985. Bar: Pa. 1977, D.C. 1981, U.S. Dist. Ct. D.C., U.S. Dist. Ct. Md. Asst. to commr. N.J. Dept. of Corrections, Trenton, 1977-78; congl. liaison HUD, Washington, 1978-79, asst. gen. counsel, 1979-81; spl. asst. atty. U.S. Atty.'s Office, Washington, 1981-82; sole practice Washington, 1982—. co-chmn. Cancer Soc., Washington, 1984. Mem. ABA, Nat. Bar Assn., Assn. Trial Lawyers Am., Nat. Conf. Black Lawyers (treas. 1981). Avocations: tennis, swimming, travel. General corporate, Federal civil litigation, Entertainment. Home: 114 14th St SE Washington DC 20003 Office: 1330 G St SE Washington DC 20003

GITTER, ALLAN REINHOLD, lawyer; b. Yonkers, N.Y., Aug. 26, 1936; s. George Reinhold and Katherine (Allan) G.; m. Barbara Ann Caudle, Sept. 6, 1958; children: Alison, Ryne, Kent. BA, Washington & Lee U., 1958; LLB, U. Mich., 1961. Bar: N.C. 1963, U.S. Dist. Ct. (mid., ea. and we. dists.) N.C. 1964, U.S. Ct. Appeals (4th cir.) 1964. From assoc. to ptnr. Womble, Carlyle, Sandridge & Rice, Winston-Salem, N.C. Fellow Am. Coll. Trial Lawyers; mem. Am. Bd. Trial Advs., Am. Counsel Assn., N.C. Assn. Def. Attys., Assn. Trial Lawyers Am. (assoc.), Internat. Assn. Ins. Counsel, Def. Research Inst. Federal civil litigation, State civil litigation, Insurance. Home: 1067 E Kent Rd Winston-Salem NC 27104 Office: Womble Carlyle Sandridge & Rice PO Drawer 84 Winston-Salem NC 27102

GITTER, MAX, lawyer; b. Samarkand, USSR, Nov. 17, 1943; came to U.S., 1950; s. Wolf and Paula (Nissenbaum) G.; m. Elisabeth Karla Gesmer, June 22, 1969; children: Emily F., Michael A. AB, Harvard U., 1965; LLB, Yale U., 1968. Bar: N.Y., D.C., U.S. Dist. Ct. (so. and ea. dists.) N.Y., U.S. Ct. Appeals (2d, 4th and 9th cirs.), U.S. Supreme Ct. Instr. U. Chgo. Law Sch., 1968-69; assoc. Paul, Weiss, Rifkind, Wharton & Garrison, N.Y.C., 1969-76, ptnr., 1976—; vis. lectr. law Yale U., 1986-87. Spl. counsel Mayor of N.Y.C. to Investigate Office of Chief Medical Examiner, 1985; bd. dirs. Mozartean Players Inc., N.Y.C., 1980—. Mem. Fed. Bar Council, Assn. of Bar of City of N.Y. (vice chmn. com. on profl. and jud. ethics 1985-86), Am. Law Inst. (speaker, panelist 1985—), Practicing Law Inst. (speaker, panelist 1983-85). Federal civil litigation, State civil litigation. Office: Paul Weiss Rifkind Wharton & Garrison 1285 Ave of Americas New York NY 10019

GIULIANI, RUDOLPH W., lawyer, government official; b. N.Y.C., May 28, 1944. A.B., Manhattan Coll.; J.D., NYU. Law clk. U.S. Dist. Ct. Judge, N.Y.C., 1968-70; asst. U.S. atty. So. Dist. N.Y.; exec. asst. U.S. atty., chief narcotics sect., and chief spl. prosecutions sect. Dept. Justice; assoc. dep. atty. gen. 1975-77, assoc. atty. gen., 1981-83; U.S. atty. N.Y., 1983—; mem. firm Patterson, Belknap, Webb and Taylor, N.Y.C., 1977-81; lectr. in field. Mem. Order of Coif. Office: US Atty's Office 1 St Andrews Plaza New York NY 10007

GIUSTI, WILLIAM ROGER, lawyer; b. N.Y.C., Oct. 27, 1947; s. John Eletto and Rita Marie (Lucarini) G.; m. Ingrid Gerke, Dec. 12, 1980. AB, Columbia Coll., 1969; postgrad., Oxford U., 1969-71; JD, Yale U., 1974. Bar: N.Y. 1975. Law clk. to judge U.S. Ct. Appeals (2d cir.), N.Y.C., 1974-75; assoc. Cravath, Swaine & Moore, N.Y.C., 1975-80; assoc. Shearman & Sterling, N.Y.C., 1980-82, ptnr., 1983—. Roman Catholic. Club: Yale (N.Y.C.). Banking, General corporate. Office: Shearman & Sterling 153 E 53rd St Citicorp Ctr New York NY 10005

GIVAN, RICHARD MARTIN, associate justice state supreme court; b. Indpls., June 7, 1921; s. Clinton Hodell and Glee (Bowen) G.; m. Pauline Marie Haggart, Feb. 28, 1945; children: Madalyn (Mrs. Larry R. Hesson), Sandra (Mrs. Michael O. Chenoweth), Patricia (Mrs. Thomas Siwek), Elizabeth. LL.B., Ind. U., 1951. Bar: Ind. bar 1952. Partner firm Bowen, Myers, Northam & Givan, 1960-69; justice Ind. Supreme Ct., 1969-74, chief justice., 1974-87, assoc. justice, 1987—; dep. pub. defender Ind., 1952-53, dep. atty. gen., 1953-64; dep. pros. atty. Marion County, 1965-66; Mem. Ind. Ho. Reps., 1967-68. Served to 2d lt. USAAF, 1942-45. Mem. ABA, Ind. Bar Assn., Indpls. Bar Assn., Ind. Soc. Chicago, Newcomen Soc. N.Am., Internat. Arabian Horse Assn. (past dir., chmn. ethical practices rev. bd.), Ind. Arabian Horse Club (pres. 1971-72), Sigma Delta Kappa., Soc. of Friends. Lodge: Lions. Jurisprudence. Office: Supreme Ct Ind 324 State House Indianapolis IN 46204

GIVENS, RICHARD AYRES, lawyer; b. N.Y.C., June 16, 1932; s. Meredith Bruner and Ruth Wheelock (Ayres) G.; m. Janet Eaton, Aug. 24, 1957; children—Susan Ruth, Jane Lucile. A.B., Columbia U., 1953; M.S. in Econs., U. Wis., 1954; LL.B., Columbia U., 1959. Bar: N.Y. 1959, U.S. Dist. Ct. (so. and ea. dists.) N.Y. 1960, U.S. Ct. Appeals (2d cir.) 1962, U.S. Supreme Ct. 1966, U.S. Ct. Claims 1980, U.S. Ct. Appeals (4th cir.) 1981. Assoc. Hughes, Hubbard, Blair & Reed, N.Y.C., 1959-61; asst. U.S. atty. So. Dist. N.Y., 1961-71; regional dir. FTC, N.Y., 1971-77; ptnr. Botein, Hays, & Herzberg, N.Y.C., 1977—; chmn. program on mktg. and distbn. Practising Law Inst., 1978, chmn. program on drafting documents in plain lang., 1981. Served with U.S. Army, 1954-56. Recipiend Ordronaux prize Columbia Law Sch., 1959. Mem. ABA, N.Y. State Bar Assn. (chmn. task force on simplification 1985—, legis. com., antitrust sect. 1980-83), Assn. Bar City N.Y., N.Y. County Lawyers Assn. (chmn. com. fed. legis. 1983—). Democrat. Unitarian. Author: Advocacy: The Art of Pleading a Cause, 1980, 2d rev. edition, 1985; Legal Strategies for Industrial Innovation (Best Law Book of 1982 award Assn. Am. Pubs.), 1982; Antitrust: An Economic Approach, 1983; contbr. articles to profl. jours. Antitrust, Federal civil litigation, Legislative. Home: 147-11 68th Rd Flushing NY 11367 Office: 200 Park Ave Suite 3014 New York NY 10166

GLAD, EDWARD NEWMAN, lawyer; b. Polk, Nebr., June 30, 1919; s. Lewis Olaf and Esther Ruth (Newman) G.; m. Suzanne Watson Lockley, Nov. 7, 1953; children: Amy Lockley, Lisanne Watson Lantz, William Edward. Student, U. Omaha, 1938-41; J.D., U. Mich., 1948. Bar: N.Y. 1949, Calif. 1959, D.C. 1964. Assoc. Barnes, Richardson & Colburn, N.Y.C., 1948-59; sr. ptnr. Glad & Tuttle, Los Angeles, San Francisco, 1959-71, Glad, Tuttle & White, 1971-79, Glad & White, 1979-81, Glad, White & Ferguson, 1981-84, Glad Ferguson, 1984—; lectr. customs law seminars ABA, IIT Conf., Tex. A & I, Laredo.; pres. Fgn. Trade Assn. So. Calif., 1965; v.p. Japan Am. Soc., 1969-73; pres. British-Am. C. of C., 1963-64, 70-72, Spain-U.S. C. of C., 1977-81; dir. Swedish-Am. C. of C., 1976-78, 82-84 ; chmn. adv. council Calif. State World Trade Commn., 1983-86, mem., 1986—. Author articles on U.S. customs law. Trustee St. George's Episcopal Nursery and Ungraded Sch., 1968-72. Served to lt. comdr. USNR, 1941-46, ETO. Decorated Order Brit. Empire. Mem. State Bar Calif., Bar Assn. D.C., N.Y. State Bar. Import and export law, and customs, Private international. Home: 519 Meadow Grove St Flintridge CA 91011 Office: 606 S Olive St Los Angeles CA 90014 also: 625 Market St 13th Floor San Francisco CA 94105

GLADDEN, JAMES WALTER, JR., lawyer; b. Pitts., Feb. 23, 1940; s. James Walter and Cynthia Unice (Hales) G.; m. Dianne Moore, Sept. 3, 1961; children—James, Thomas, Robert. A.B., DePauw U., 1961; J.D., Harvard U., 1964. Bar: Ill. 1964, U.S. Sup. Ct. 1978. Ptnr., Mayer, Brown & Platt, Chgo., 1964—. Mem. ABA. Labor, Environment, Federal civil litigation. Home: 324 Vernon Ave Glencoe IL 60022 Office: Mayer Brown & Platt 231 S LaSalle St Chicago IL 60604

GLADSON, GUY ALLEN, JR., lawyer; b. Chgo., May 14, 1928; s. Guy Allen and Martha Gertrude (Huffman) G.; m. Nancy McDonald Gladson, Jan. 7, 1956; children—Nancy, Guy, Kathryn, Carolyn, Patricia, William. B.A., Northwestern U., 1949; LL.B., U. Mich., 1952. Bar: Ill. 1952, Fla. 1956. Assoc., Winston, Strawn & Shaw, Chgo., 1952-56, Dixon, DeJarnette, Bradford, Williams, McKay & Kimbrell, Miami 1956-62; ptnr. Gladson and Sullivan, and predecessors, Miami, 1963—. Mem. ABA, Fla. Bar Assn., Dade County Bar Assn. Roman Catholic. Clubs: Coral Gables Country. Workers' compensation. Home: 5395 SW 80th St Miami FL 33143 Office: 7600 Southwest 57th Ave Suite 309 Miami FL 33143

GLADSTONE, MICHAEL HARPER, lawyer; b. Ahoskie, N.C., Sept. 12, 1957; s. John Lee and Peggy (Harper) G. BS in Commerce, U. Va., 1979; JD, U. Richmond, 1982. Bar: Va. 1982, U.S. Dist. Ct. (ea. dist.) Va. 1982, U.S. Dist. Ct. (we. dist.) Va. 1984. Assoc. Seawell, Dalton, Hughes & Timms, Richmond, Va., 1982-86, ptnr., 1987—. Editor, bd. dirs. The Local Litigator, 1985-86. Vol. Young Life Orgn., Richmond, 1983—. Mem. Va. Bar Assn. (law day com. 1985—), Richmond Bar Assn., Norfolk/Portsmouth Bar Assn., Va. Assn. Def. Attys., Def. Research Inst. Avocations: hunting, fishing, flying. State civil litigation, Federal civil litigation, Construction. Home: 3911 Ellwood Ave Richmond VA 23221 Office: Seawell Dalton Hughes & Timms 707 Mutual Bldg Richmond VA 23219

GLANTZ, DOUGLAS GENE, lawyer; b. Ridgway, Pa., May 6, 1949; s. Eugene Martin and Shirley Delena (Swope) G.; m. Darla JoAnne Black, June 23, 1973; 1 child, Amanda Susanne. BS in Chem. Engring., Pa. State U., 1971; MS, Rensselaer Poly. Inst., 1974; JD, Temple U., 1981. Bar: U.S. Patent Office 1979, Pa. 1981, U.S. Ct. Appeals (fed. cir.) 1983, U.S. Dist. Ct. (we. dist.) Pa. 1984, U.S. Supreme Ct. 1985. Tech. writer, editor Gen. Electric Co., Pittsfield, Mass., 1972-76; patent atty. Air Products and Chems., Inc., Allentown, Pa., 1976-82, Aluminum Co. Am., Pitts., 1982—; patent examiner U.S. Patent and Trademark Office, 1971-72. Patent, Real property, Government contracts and claims. Home: 138 Alleyne Dr Pittsburgh PA 15215 Office: Aluminum Co Am Legal Dept Alcoa Ctr PA 15069

GLANTZ, RONALD PAUL, lawyer, consultant; b. Fairfield, Conn., Mar. 4, 1953; s. Max and Estelle (Einbund) G.; m. Wendy Newman, Dec. 29, 1983. BS, U. Bridgeport, 1976; JD, Nova Law Ctr., 1980. Bar: Fla. 1981, U.S. Dist. Ct. (so. dist.) Fla. 1982. Sole practice Ft. Lauderdale, Fla., 1981-84; ptnr. Kern, Augustine & Glantz, Ft. Lauderdale, 1984-86, Glantz & Glantz, Ft. Lauderdale, 1986—; negotiator, cons., Ft. Lauderdale, 1984—. Mem. ABA, Broward County Bar Assn., Assn. Trial Lawyers Am., Plantation C. of C. Jewish. Lodge: B'nai B'rith (justice chpt.). Avocations: backgammon, racketball. Negotiations, State civil litigation, Real property.

GLANVILLE, ROBERT EDWARD, lawyer; b. Binghamton, N.Y., Aug. 1, 1950; s. Robert S. and Betty J. (Garlick) G.; m. Susan Anne Kime, Sept. 3, 1970. BA magna cum laude, SUNY, Binghamton, 1972; JD magna cum laude, Cornell U., 1976. Bar: N.Y. 1977, U.S. Dist Ct. (we. dist.) N.Y. 1978, U.S. Supreme Ct. 1981, U.S. Ct. Appeals (2d cir.) 1985. Law clk. to presiding judge Appellate Div., 4th Dept., Rochester, 1976-78; from assoc. to ptnr. Phillips, Lytle et al, Buffalo, N.Y., 1978-85; ptnr. Prahl & Glanville, Buffalo, 1986—. Mem. ABA, N.Y. State Bar Assn., Erie County Bar Assn., Am. Gas Assn. Avocations: whitewater kayaking, sailing, mountaineering, flying. Federal civil litigation, State civil litigation, Public utilities. Home: 66 Deer Run Glenwood NY 14069 Office: Prahl & Glanville 2300 Rand Bldg Buffalo NY 14203

GLANZMAN, SCOTTY LYNN, legal educator; b. Mondoui, Wis., Oct. 28, 1950; s. Oliver Henry and Phyllis Lillian (Moy) G. Student, U. Ibadan, Nigeria, 1972-73; BS, U. Wis., Eau Claire, 1974; JD, U. Minn., 1982. Bar: Minn. 1982. Research fellow Ctr. for Computer Assisted Legal Instruction, Mpls., 1982-84, systems analyst, applications mgr., 1984—; cons. U. Minn. Law Sch., 1984—. Mem. ABA (computer law sect.), Minn. Bar Assn., Hennepin County Assn. Avocations: experimental aircraft, golf, welding. Computer. Office: Ctr for Computer Assisted Legal Instruction 229 19th Ave S Minneapolis MN 55455

GLASER, PATRICIA L., lawyer; b. Charleston, W.Va., Sept. 15, 1947; d. Richard Stanley and Tilda Jane (Rosen) G.; m. Samuel Hunter Mudie, May 19, 1978; stepchildren: Heather and Jason Mudie. BA, Am. U., 1969; JD, Rutgers U., 1973. Bar: Calif. 1973, U.S. Dist. Ct. (no. and cen. dists.) Calif. 1973, U.S. Dist. Ct. (so. dist.) 1976, U.S. Ct. Appeals (9th cir.), U.S. Supreme Ct. Law clk. to presiding justice U.S. Dist. Ct.; from assoc. to ptnr. Wyman, Bautzer, Rothman, Kuchel & Silbert, Los Angeles, 1973—; judge pro tem West br. Los Angeles Mcpl. Ct., panelist legal continuing edn. programs. Mem. fund-raising com. Deukmejian for Gov. of Calif.; participant Parole-Aide program. Mem. Los Angeles County Bar Assn. (fed. cts. and practices com.). Avocations: travel, skiing, tennis, reading. Federal civil litigation, State civil litigation, Personal injury. Office: Wyman Bautzer Kuchel & Silbert 2049 Century Park E Los Angeles CA 90067

GLASGOW, JAMES MONROE, lawyer; b. Dresden, Tenn., Feb. 17, 1920; s. William Ayers and Mary Catherine (Dismukes) G.; m. Jo Evelyn Burkleen, Sept. 17, 1943; children: Carol Ann Kirkland, James Monroe Jr., Linda Sue Graham. JD, U. Tenn., 1948. Bar: Tenn. 1947, U.S. Ct. Appeals (6th cir.) 1956, U.S. Supreme Ct. 1956. Sole practice Dresden, 1948-52; asst. atty. gen. State of Tenn., Nashville, 1952-61; atty. Nat. Life & Accident Ins. Co., Nashville, 1961-63; ptnr. Elam, Glasgow, Tanner & Acree, Union City, Tenn., 1963—. Pres. Obion County United Way, Union City, 1974-75, Union City Arts Council, 1976-77. Fellow Am. Bar Found., Tenn. Bar Found., Am. Coll. Trial Lawyers; mem. ABA (ho. dels. 1977-78), Tenn. Bar Assn (bd. govs. 1975-78), Tenn. Def. Lawyers Assn., Tenn. Bar Foundation (chmn. elect), Obion County C. of C. (past pres.). Democrat. Methodist. Lodges: Rotary (past pres. Union City), Elks, Moose. General practice, Personal injury, Federal civil litigation. Home: 1212 Armstrong Rd Union City TN 38261 Office: Elam Glasgow Tanner & Acree PO Box 250 Union City TN 38261

GLASGOW, NORMAN M., lawyer; b. Washington, Aug. 14, 1922; children—Norman M., Heather Glasgow Harris, Glenn. B.S., U. Md., 1943; LL.B., George Washington U., 1949. Bar: D.C. 1949, U.S. Supreme Ct. 1956, Md. 1960. Assoc. Wilkes, McGarraghy & Artis, 1947-56; ptnr. Wilkes & Artis; mem. firm Wilkes, Artis, Hedrick & Lane. Bd. dirs., mem. econ. devel. com. Met. Washington Bd. Trade; mem. Citizens Tech. Adv. Com. for Drafting Bldg. Code and Zoning Regulations, Washington; mem. Commrs. Citizens Adv. Com. on Zoning, Washington. Mem. Urban Land Inst., Am. Soc. Planning Ofcls., Washington Bldg. Congress, Lambda Alpha. Club: Barristers (Washington). Real property, Local government, Land use, historic preservation. Home: 9012 Brickyard Rd Potomac MD 20854 Office: Wilkes Artis Hedrick & Lane 1666 K St Suite 600 NW Washington DC 20006

GLASGOW, ROBERT EFROM, lawyer; b. Portland, Oreg., Nov. 13, 1944; s. Joseph and Lee (Friedman) G.; m. Lesley G. Veltman, June 16, 1968; children—Jordan Robert, Emily Samantha. B.A., George Washington U., 1966, J.D., 1969. Bar: Oreg. 1969. Assoc., Dusenbery, Martin, Beatty, Bischoff & Templeton, Portland, 1969-72; ptnr. Martin, Bischoff, Templeton & Biggs, Portland, 1973-76, Glasgow & Kelly, Portland, 1977-79; ptnr. Glasgow & Kelly, P.C., 1980-85, pres., 1982-85; pres. Glasgow & Wight, P.C., 1985—. Trustee Multnomah County Legal Aid Service, 1974-76, chmn., 1976; trustee Jewish Family and Child Service, 1972-77, treas., 1976; trustee Jewish Community Ctr., 1975-76; trustee Oreg. Legal Services Corp., 1980—; Dem. precinctman, 1986—. Mem. ABA, Oreg. Bar Assn., Multnomah Bar Assn. Club: West Hills Racquet (Portland). Contracts commercial, General corporate, Family and matrimonial. Office: 506 SW 6th St Suite 1111 Portland OR 97204

GLASGOW, WILLIAM JACOB, lawyer; b. Portland, Oreg., Sept. 29, 1946; s. Joseph Glasgow and Lena (Friedman) Schiff; m. Renée Vonfeld, Aug. 30, 1969; children: Joshua, Andrew. BS magna cum laude, U. Pa., 1968; JD magna cum laude, Harvard U., 1972. Bar: Oreg. 1972, U.S. DIst. Ct. Oreg. 1972, U.S. Ct. Appeals (9th cir.) 1978. Assoc. Rives, Bonghadi & Drummond, Portland, 1972-76, ptnr., 1976-79; ptnr. Stoel, Rives, Boley, Fraser & Wyse, Portland, 1979-83; mng. ptnr. Perkins Coie, Portland, 1983—. Pres. bd. trustees Oreg. Mus. Sci. and Industry, Portland, 1981; pres. NW Fin. Symposium, Portland, 1985. Mem. ABA, Oreg. Bar Assn., Portland C. of C. (bd. dirs. 1983), Harvard Law Sch. Alumni Assn. (pres. Oreg. chpt. 1981). Democrat. Jewish. General corporate, Corporate taxation, Leveraged leasing. Home: 3725 SW Mt Adams Dr Portland OR 97201

GLASS, BEVERLY ELAINE, lawyer; b. Copiague, N.Y., Sept. 10, 1952; d. J. Leon Lazarowitz and Jennie Glass. BA, Calif. State U., 1974; JD, Southwestern U., Los Angeles, 1977. Bar: D.C. 1979, Calif. 1984. Prof. U. Balt., 1978-79, Marymount Coll., Arlington, Va., 1979-81; mng. ptnr. Sanders & Sanders, Washington, 1980-84; corp. counsel Genstar Corp., San Francisco, 1984-85; asst. v.p., asst. gen. counsel Fireman's Fund Ins. Co., Novato, Calif., 1985—. Democrat. Jewish. Securities, Pension, profit-sharing, and employee benefits, General corporate. Office: Firemans Fund Ins Co 777 San Marin Dr Novato CA 94998

GLASS, FRED STEPHEN, lawyer; b. Asheboro, N.C., Oct. 17, 1940; s. Emmett Frederick and Colene F. (Foust) G.; m. Gloria A. Grant, June 12, 1964; 1 child, Elizabeth Foust; m. Martha G. Daughtry, June 9, 1982. BA, Wake Forest U., 1963, JD, 1966. Bar: N.C. 1966, U.S. Dist Ct. (ea. dist.) N.C. 1966. Research asst. presiding justice N.C. Supreme Ct., 1966-67; ptnr. Miller, Beck, O'Briant and Glass, Asheboro, N.C., 1971-77; exec. dir. and legal counsel N.C. Democratic Party, 1977-78; dep. commr. N.C. Indsl. Commn., 1978; spl. Congl. asst. 4th Congl. Dist. N.C., 1979; ptnr. Harris, Cheshire, Leager and Southern, Raleigh, N.C., 1979-86; ptnr. Poyner and Spruill, Raleigh, 1987—; prof. law and govt. Asheboro Jr. Coll. Bus., 1973-76. Contbr. articles to profl. jours. Basketball coach and fitness instr. Randolph County YMCA; pub. chmn., United Appeal; bd. dirs., Randolph County Emergency Med. Technician Bd.; active Dem. campaigns, Gen. Greene, Old Hickory, Narragansett, San Diego County and Occoneechee councils Boy Scouts Am., council commr. for Roundtables, 1980—, asst. dist. commr. 1979-84; asst. scoutmaster nat. com. Boy Scouts of Am., dist. newsletter editor, council ex. bd., council commr., chancellor, council commrs. coll., 1980-83. Served with JAGC USN, 1967-71, capt. Res. Recipient Scouters tng. award Boy Scouts Am., Scouters Key, Den Leaders Tng. award, Dist. award of Merit, Silver Beaver, Young Man of the Year award City of Asheboro. Mem. Randolph County Bar Assn. (pres. 1971-74), 19th Jud. Dist. Bar Assn. (pres. 1974-75), N.C. Bar Assn. (chmn. young lawyer sect. Randolph County), Dist. Criminal Law Symposium (chmn. 1976). Democrat. Methodist. Medical. Home: 1003 Cindy St Cary NC 27511 Office: PO Box 10097 Raleigh NC 27605-0097

GLASS, JOEL, lawyer; b. N.Y.C. Nov. 17, 1942; s. Sam and Ruth (Neselrod) G.; m. Sheila Zolenge, Apr. 30, 1983. B.A., U. Buffalo, 1965; J.D., Bklyn. Law Sch., 1968. Bar: N.Y. 1968. Assoc., Ackerman, Salwen & Linzer, N.Y.C., 1968-74; ptnr. Ackerman, Salwen & Glass, N.Y.C., 1974—; lectr. Mt. Sinai Sch. Medicine, Emergency Care Inst., Sch. for Continuing Edn. Montefiore Hosp. and Med. Center, N.J. Hosp. Assn., Acad. Medicine, Hosp. Edn. and Research Fund, United Hosp. Fund.; cons. N.Y. State Assembly Ins. Com.; vol. hosp. rep. McGill Commn. on Malpractice and other med. hearings; mem. med. malpractice task force Am. Hosp. Assn. Served with USNG, 1970. N.Y. State Regents scholar, 1961; Nat. Merit scholar, 1961. Mem. ABA (med. legal com., health com.), N.Y. State Bar Assn., Assn. of Bar of City Of N.Y. (liabilty ins. com., medicine and law com., med. malpractice com.), Greater N.Y. Hosp. Assn. (legal com. study of arbitration and malpractice), Non-Profit Coordinating Com. N.Y. (liability ins. com.). Author: (with Gallet, Glass & Minkowitz) Rent Stabilization and Control Laws of New York, 1972. Health, Personal injury, Insurance. Office: Ackerman Salwen & Glass 605 3d Ave New York NY 10158

GLASS, JOHN D., JR., lawyer, independent oil and gas producer, rancher; b. Oklahoma City, Aug. 17, 1931; s. John D. and Gertrude (Coumbe) G.; m. Joanne Miller, June 7, 1958; children—John Duel, III, Kenneth Neen, Sharah Coumbe, Joel Murphy. B.B.A., U. Tex.-Austin, 1952, J.D., 1955. Bar: Tex. 1955, U.S. Dist. Ct. (ea. dist.) Tex. Ptnr., Glass & Glass, Tyler, Tex., 1955-75; sole practice, Tyler, 1975—; rancher. Served with U.S. Army, 1955-57. Mem. State Bar Tex., Smith County Bar Assn., Tex. and Southwestern Cattle Raisers Assn., Tex. Ind. Producers and Royalty Owners Assn. Republican. Episcopalian. Oil and gas leasing. Office: 917 InterFirst Plaza Bldg Tyler TX 75702

GLASS, ROY LEONARD, lawyer; b. Littleton, N.H., Jan. 27, 1947; s. Jack Irving and Noreen (Leiuthwait) Kline; m. Suzanne Schmidt Goldstein, May 20, 1967 (div. Oct. 1978); 1 child, Shannon Renee; m. Patricia Lee Wimbish, Dec. 9, 1978; 1 child, Ashley Leigh. A.A. with honors, St. Petersburg Jr. Coll., Fla., 1971; B.A., U. South. Fla., 1972; J.D., Fla. State U., 1975. Bar: Fla. 1976, U.S. Dist. Ct. (mid. dist.) Fla. 1977, U.S. Dist Ct. (no. dist.) Fla. 1978, U.S. Supreme Ct. 1979, U.S. Ct. Appeals (11th cir.) 1983. Assoc., Meyers, Mooney & Adler, Orlando, Fla., 1976-78; assoc. Barrett, Boyd & Bajoczky, Tallahassee, Fla., 1978-79; sole practice, Tallahassee, 1979-81; ptnr. Deserio & Glass, St. Petersburg, Fla., 1981-82; assoc. Battaglia, Ross, Hastings, Dicus & Andrews, St. Petersburg, 1982-85, sole practice, St.

Petersburg, 1985—; lectr., Floridians Against Constl. Tampering, Fla., 1984. Served to capt. U.S. Army, 1966-70, Vietnam. Mem. ABA, Am. Trial Lawyers Assn., Am. Arbitration Assn., Am. Soc. Law & Medicine, Acad. Fla. Trial Lawyers, Fla. Bar Assn. (health law com. 1984—, chmn. health care profls., subcom. 1984—), St. Petersburg Bar Assn. (legis. com. 1983-85, chmn. health care profls. subcom. 1983—, liaison med. soc. 1985—med. relations com. 1985—), St. Petersburg C. of C. (urban solutions task force 1983-84), Phi Delta Phi, Phi Kappa Phi, Beta Gamma Sigma. Clubs: Suncoast Tiger Bay (St. Petersburg, Fang & Claw award 1983), Breakfast Sertoma (Cert. of Appreciation 1984). Personal injury, State civil litigation, Administrative and regulatory. Home: 255 Capri Circle North Apt 11 Treasure Island FL 33706 Office: 3000 66th St N Suite B Saint Petersburg FL 33710

GLASS, STANFORD LEE, lawyer; b. Collinsville, Ill., May 6, 1934; s. Jere and Valma (Yawitz) G.; m. Rebecca Jean Koelling, June 23, 1957; children—Karyn, Linda, Steven. B.A., U. Ill., 1955; J.D., Harvard U., 1959. Bar: Ill. 1961. With Holleb & Coff, Inc., Chgo., 1962—, v.p., ptnr., 1983—; spl. counsel Adlai E. Stevenson, III, State Treas., 1966-70; gen. counsel Stevenson for Governor, 1982. Bd. dirs. Home Investments Fund, 1980-87, Met. Leadership Council, 1980-87; chmn. Ill. Health Facilities Authority, 1973-79. Mem. ABA, Ill. State Bar Assn., Chgo. Bar Assn. Estate planning, Personal income taxation, General corporate. Home: 853 Prospect St Winnetka IL 60093 Office: 55 E Monroe Suite 4100 Chicago IL 60603

GLASSER, IRA SAUL, civil liberties organization executive; b. Bklyn., Apr. 18, 1938; s. Sidney and Anne (Goldstein) G.; m. Trude Maria Robinson, June 28, 1959; children—David, Andrew, Peter, Sally. B.S. in Math., Queens Coll., 1959; M.A. in Math., Ohio State U., 1960. Instr. math. Queens Coll., N.Y.C., 1960-63; lectr. math. Sarah Lawrence Coll., Bronxville, N.Y., 1962-65; assoc. editor Current Mag., N.Y.C., 1962-64, editor, 1964-67; assoc. dir. N.Y. Civil Liberties Union, N.Y.C., 1967-70, exec. dir., 1970-78; exec. dir. ACLU, 1978—; cons. U. Ill.-Champaign-Urbana, 1964-65; dir. Asian Am. Legal Def. and Edn. Fund., N.Y.C., 1974—. Contbr. articles to profl. jours. Chmn. St. Vincents Hosp, N.Y.C., Community Adv. Bd., N.Y.C., 1970-72. Recipient Martin Luther King, Jr. award N.Y. Assn. Black Sch. Suprs., 1971, Gavel award ABA, 1972. Avocation: sports. Office: ACLU Inc 132 W 43d St New York NY 10036

GLASSER, ISRAEL LEO, judge; b. N.Y.C., Apr. 6, 1924; s. David and Sadie (Krupp) G.; m. Grace Gribetz, Aug. 24, 1952; children—Dorothy, David, James, Marjorie. LL.B., Bklyn. Law Sch., 1948; B.A., CUNY, 1976. Bar: N.Y. 1948. Fellow Bklyn. Law Sch., 1948-49, instr., 1950-52, asst. prof. law, 1952-53, asso. prof., 1953-55, prof., 1955-74, adj. prof., 1974, dean, 1977-82; judge U.S. Dist. Ct. N.Y., 1982—; judge N.Y. State Family Ct., N.Y.C., 1969-77. Mem. Am. Bar Assn. Legal education. Office: US District Court 225 Cadman Plaza East Brooklyn NY 11201

GLASSER, MATTHEW DAVID, lawyer; b. Chgo., Nov. 19, 1952; s. Robert Gene and Marcia (Wilson) G.; m. Becky Lee Nothnagel, Aug. 18, 1985. BA cum laude, U. Colo., 1974; JD, Cornell U., 1977. Bar: Colo. 1977, U.S. Dist. Ct. Colo. 1977. Assoc. Tallmadge, Tallmadge, Wallace & Hahn, P.C., Denver, 1977-81; atty. City of Broomfield, Colo., 1981—. Mem. Colo. Bar Assn., Denver Bar Assn., Boulder Bar Assn., Assn. Trial Lawyers Am., Met. City Attys. Assn. (pres. 1984), Colo. Mcpl. League (chmn. attys. sect. 1983-84), Cornell Law Club Colo. (pres. Denver chpt. 1985—). Local government, Government contracts and claims, Condemnation. Office: City of Broomfield 6 Garden Ctr Broomfield CO 80020

GLASSER, ROBERT, lawyer; b. Rego Park, N.Y., Oct. 30, 1949; s. Louis and Sally (Feld) G.; m. Lynne Listiak, Aug. 29, 1975. BA, U. Bridgeport, 1970, MA, 1973; JD, U. Akron, 1974; LLM, McGill U., 1981. Bar: N.Y. 1975, D.C. 1976, U.S. Supreme Ct. Asst. gen. counsel Air Transport Assn., Washington, 1975-84; counsel Kilpatrick & Cody, Washington, 1984-86, ptnr., 1986—. Mem. ABA. Clubs: Aero, Wings, Internat. Aviation. Lodge: Rotary. General corporate, Administrative and regulatory. Home: 5901 Munson Ct Falls Church VA 22041 Office: Kilpatrick & Cody 2501 M Street NW Washington DC 20037

GLASSMAN, CAROLINE DUBY, state justice; b. Baker, Oreg., Sept. 13, 1924; d. Charles Ferdinand and Caroline Marie (Colton) Duby; m. Harry Paul Glassman, May 21, 1953; 1 son, Max Avon. LL.B. summa cum laude, Williamette U., 1944. Bar: Oreg. 1944, Calif. 1952, Maine 1969. Title ins. atty. Title Ins. & Trust Co., Salem, Oreg., 1944-46; assoc. mem. firm Belli, Aske & Pinney, San Francisco, 1952-58; ptnr. firm Glassman, Beagle & Ridge, Portland, Maine, 1978—; judge Maine Supreme Ct., Portland; lectr. Sch. Law, U. Maine, 1967-68, 80. Author: Legal Status of Homemakers in State of Maine, 1977. Mem. ABA, Oreg. Bar Assn., Calif. Bar Assn., Maine Bar Assn., Maine Trial Law Assn. Roman Catholic. Judicial administration. Home: 56 Thomas St Portland ME 04102 Office: Maine Supreme Ct 142 Federal St Portland ME 04112 *

GLAUBERMAN, MELVIN L., lawyer; b. Bklyn., Nov. 3, 1927; s. Sam and Beatrice (Jacobs) G.; m. Maxine Dvorsetz, Dec. 25, 1955 (div.); children—David J., Nancy J., Jane C.; m. Naomi Alexander, Jan. 6, 1980. B.A., Bklyn. Coll., 1948; J.D., Harvard U., 1951. Bar: N.Y. 1951, U.S. Dist. Ct. (so. dist.) N.Y. 1953, U.S. Dist. Ct. (ea. dist.) N.Y. 1954, U.S. Supreme Ct. 1972. Sole practice, N.Y.C., 1951-56, 73-74; ptnr. Berman & Glauberman, N.Y.C., 1957-60, Berman, Glauberman & Raives, N.Y.C., 1960-72; sr. ptnr. Berman, Glauberman & Bernstein, N.Y.C., 1975—; mediator under N.Y. State Alternative Dispute Resolution Procedures. Contbr. to book Manual for Theatre Owners, 1955; contbr. NYU Tax Law Rev. Vice-pres. League in Aid of Crippled Children, Inc., N.Y.C., 1969; mem. Ins. Industry Ednl. Adv. Com. Mem. N.Y. State Trial Lawyers Assn. (lectr. 1984), Am. Arbitration Assn. (master arbitrator, lectr. 1982—). Personal injury, Probate, Real property. Home: 209 St Johns Ave Yonkers NY 10704 Office: Berman Glauberman & Bernstein 253 Broadway New York NY 10007

GLAVIN, A. RITA CHANDELLIER, lawyer; b. Schenectady, May 11, 1937; d. Pierre Charles and Helen C. (Fox) Chandellier; m. James H. Glavin, III, June 1, 1963; children—Helene, James, Rita, Henry. A.B. cum laude, Middlebury Coll., 1958; J.D., Union U. Albany Law Sch., 1961. Bar: N.Y. 1961, U.S. Dist. Ct. (no. dist.) N.Y. 1961, U.S. Tax Ct. 1965, U.S. Supreme Ct. 1978. Assoc. Eugene Steiner, Albany, N.Y., 1961-64, Helen Fox Chandellier, Schenectady, 1965-76; mem. Glavin and Glavin, Waterford, Schenectady, and Albany, N.Y., 1965-86, 87—; del. 4th Jud. Dist. Nominating Conv., 1966-67; confidential law clk. presiding justices N.Y. State Ct. Claims, 1968-71; surrogate judge Saratoga County, 1986. Bd. dirs., chmn. fin. com. Schenectady YWCA, 1979-81; tech. advisor HSA of Northeastern N.Y. Maternity and Pediatric Com., 1976; bd. dirs. Schenectady Jr. League, 1974, 76; del. N.Y. State Jr. League Pub. Affairs Com., 1976; bd. dirs., sec. Bellevue Maternity Hosp., Inc., 1966-83, bd. advisers, 1984—; trustee Middlebury Coll., 1978—, chmn. law com., 1982—, vice chmn. bd. dirs., 1986—. Mem. N.Y. State Bar Assn. (del. ho. of dels. 1987—), Saratoga County Bar Assn. (exec. com. 1981—, v.p. 1985, pres. 1986), Schenectady County Bar Assn., Phi Beta Kappa, Kappa Kappa Gamma. Mem. editorial bd. Albany Law Rev., 1960-61. General practice. Office: 69 2d St Waterford NY 12188

GLAVIN, JAMES HENRY, III, lawyer; b. Albany, N.Y., Oct. 6, 1931; s. James Henry, Jr. and Elizabeth Mary (Gibbons) G.; m. A. Rita Chandellier, June 1, 1963; children—Helene Elizabeth, James C., Rita Marie, James Henry IV. A.B., Villanova U., 1953; J.D., Albany Law Sch., 1956. Bar: N.Y. 1956, U.S. Dist. Ct. (no. dist.) N.Y. 1957, U.S. Supreme Ct. 1959, U.S. Dist. Ct. (mid. dist.) Tenn. 1959, U.S. Ct. Appeals (D.C. cir.) 1976, U.S. Ct. Mil. Appeals 1959. Mem. Glavin and Glavin, Waterford, N.Y., 1960—; mem. regional bd. Key Bank, N.A., 1968—, chmn., 1976—. County chmn. Democratic Party, Saratoga County, N.Y., 1964-68; bd. dirs. Bellevue Maternity Hosp., 1968—, Waterford Central Catholic Sch., 1969—; trustee St. Mary's Ch., Waterford, 1974—, Waterford Rural Cemtery. Served to capt. JAGC, USAF, 1957-60. Mem. Assn. Trial Lawyers Am., Am. Soc. Law and Medicine, Am. Acad. Polit. and Social Sci., ICC Practitioners Assn., Am. Psychology-Law Soc., N.Y. Trial Lawyers Assn., Am. Acad. Hosp. Attys., Transp. Lawyers Assn., Judge Advocates Assn., Nat. Health Lawyers Assn., Am. Acad. Polit. and Social Sci., ABA, Fed. Bar Assn., N.Y. State Bar Assn., Estate Planning Council Eastern N.Y., Saratoga County Bar Assn., Albany County Bar Assn., Rensselaer County Bar Assn., Internat. Soc. Gen. Semantics, Mystery Writers Am. Roman Catholic. Clubs: Nat. Lawyers, Air Force Assn.; Lions (past pres.), KC. Author: The Tour Broker and the Interstate Commerce Commission, 1977. General practice. Home: 66 Saratoga Ave Waterford NY 12188 Office: 69 2d St Waterford NY 12188

GLAVIN, JOHN JOSEPH, lawyer; b. Albany, N.Y., Sept. 11, 1905; s. James Edward and Anna Catherine (Rechmond) G.; m. Lilian Christine Slattery, Sept. 11, 1929 (dec. May 1984); children: John J., William F., Joanne M., Barbara E., Francis E. BA, Georgetown U., 1926; LLD, Albany Law Sch., 1929. Bar: N.Y. 1929, U.S. Dist. Ct. (no. dist.) N.Y. 1930. Sole practice Albany, 1929—; v.p., sec. Lexington Glass Inc., Albany, 1960-68; pres., treas. Saratoga (N.Y.) Restaurant Inc., 1980-85. Mem. ABA, N.Y. State Bar Assn., Albany County Bar Assn. Republican. Roman Catholic. Club: Albany Country (Guilderland, N.Y.). Lodge: KC. Family and matrimonial, Probate, Real property. Home: 100 High Meadow Ln Voorheesville NY 12186 Office: 9 Elk St Albany NY 12207

GLAZER, DONALD WAYNE, lawyer, educator; b. Cleve., July 26, 1944; s. Julius and Ethel (Goldstein) G.; m. Ellen S. Sarasohn, July 11, 1968; children: Elizabeth M., Mollie S. A.B. summa cum laude, Dartmouth Coll., 1966; J.D. magna cum laude, Harvard U., 1969; LL.M., U. Pa., 1970. Bar: Mass. 1970. Assoc. Ropes & Gray, Boston, 1970-78, ptnr., 1978—; instr. corp. fin. Boston U. Law Sch., 1975; lectr. law Harvard U., Cambridge, Mass., 1978—. Co-editor First Ann. Inst. on Securities Regulation, 1970; contbr. articles to legal jours. Trustee, treas. Hillel Found. Greater Boston; trustee Cowen Found., Santa Fe Neurol. Scis. Inst. Fellow Salzburg Seminar in Am. Studies, 1975. Mem. Am. Law Inst., ABA (co-chmn. subcom. on employee benefits and exec. compensation fed. securities law com.), Boston Bar Assn. (chmn. corp. sect., past chmn. securities law com.). Jewish. Securities, General corporate. Home: 47 Huntington Rd Newton MA 02158 Office: Ropes & Gray 225 Franklin St Boston MA 02110

GLAZER, JACK HENRY, lawyer; b. Paterson, N.J., Jan. 14, 1928; s. Samuel and Martha (Merkin) G.; m. Zelda d'Angleterre, Jan. 14, 1979. B.A., Duke U., 1950; J.D., Georgetown U., 1956; postgrad. U. Frankfurt (W.Ger.), 1956-57; S.J.D. U. Calif.-Berkeley, 1978. Bar: D.C. 1957, Calif. 1968. Atty., GAO and NASA, 1958-60; mem. maritime div. UN Internat. Labour Office, Geneva, Switzerland, 1960; spl. legal adv. UN Internat. Telecommunication Union, Geneva, 1960-62; atty. NASA Washington, 1963-66; chief counsel NASA-Ames Research Center, Moffett Field, Calif., 1966—; asst. prof. Hastings Coll. Law, dir. Hastings/NASA/NOAA research project. Served to capt. JAGC, USNR. Mem. White's Inn, San Francisco Bar Assn., Am. Inst. Aeronautics and Astronautics, Astrolaw Soc. Contbr. articles on internat. law to profl. jours. Public international, Government contracts and claims, Military. Home: 1110 Taylor St San Francisco CA 94108 Office: Whites Inn 37 White St San Francisco CA 94109

GLAZER, PETER KENDALL, lawyer; b. Eugene, Oreg., July 7, 1952; s. Howard Leonard and Jean (Kendall) G.; m. Karen Kay Painter, June 16, 1974; children: Peter Jr., Steven Scott. BA, U. Oreg., 1975, JD, 1978. Bar: Oreg. 1978, U.S. Dist. Ct. Oreg. 1981. Dep. dist. atty. Clackamas County, Oregon City, Oreg., 1978-82; ptnr. Kay & Glazer P.C., Lake Oswego, Oreg., 1982-84, Maurer, Glazer & Withers P.C., Lake Oswego, 1984—. Chmn. adv. com. Gov.'s DUII, Salem, Oreg., 1982—; treas. Victims Rights Com., Portland, Oreg., 1985—; bd. dirs. Oreg. Lifebelt Com., Tualatin, 1985—. Mem. Oreg. Bar Assn. (uniform civil jury instrs. com.), Clackamas County Bar Assn. (treas. 1983), Assn. Trial Lawyers Am., Oreg. Trial Lawyers Assn. Democrat. Lodge: Rotary. Avocation: tennis. Personal injury, State civil litigation, Family and matrimonial. Office: Maurer Glazer & Withers PC 4500 Kruse Way #390 Lake Oswego OR 97035

GLAZIER, JONATHAN HEMENWAY, lawyer; b. Hartford, Conn., May 14, 1949; s. Orman Hemenway and Susan (Micka) G.; m. Susan Gayle Davis, Dec. 12, 1983; 1 child, Martin Hemenway. Student, Australian Nat. U., Canberra, 1969; BA, Rice U., 1972; JD, George Washington U., 1980. Bar: Tex. 1980, U.S. Dist. Ct. (so. dist.) Tex. 1981, U.S. Ct. Appeals (5th cir.) 1981, U.S. Ct. Appeals (D.C. and Fed. cirs.) 1984, U.S. Ct. Internat. Trade 1984, D.C. 1986. Assoc. Chamberlain, Hrdlicka, White, Johnson and Williams, Houston, 1980-84, Busby, Rehm and Leonard, Washington, 1984—. Thomas J. Watson fellow, 1972-73. Mem. ABA, Fed. Cir. Bar Assn. Avocations: sailing, bicycling. International tax, International trade. Office: Busby Rehm and Leonard 1330 Connecticut Ave NW Suite 200 Washington DC 20036

GLAZIER, KENNETH CHARLES, lawyer; b. Pitts., Oct. 26, 1949; s. Edwin M. and Margaret A. (Waller) G. BSE, Princeton U., 1971; MBA, JD, Harvard U., 1979. Bar: Tex. 1979. Engr. Procter & Gamble, Balt., 1971-72; assoc. Vinson & Elkins, Houston, 1979-87; v.p. land and legal Newmont Oil Co., Houston, 1987—. Deacon Meml. Dr. Presbyn. Ch., Houston, 1986—. Served to lt. USNR, 1972-75. Mem. ABA, Houston Bar Assn. Republican. Avocations: swimming, raquetball, reading. General corporate, Securities, Oil and gas leasing. Home: 2100 Tanglewilde 217 Houston TX 77063 Office: Newmont Oil Co 600 Jefferson Ninth Floor Houston TX 77002

GLEASON, CHARLES SAPPINGTON, lawyer, consultant; b. Libertytown, Md., Sept. 30, 1924; s. James K. and Anne Gleason; m. Mary Ann Roberts, Sept. 17, 1949; children: Charles Thomas, Joseph John, Richard Paul, Robert Scott. Student, Georgetown U., 1949-51; JD, Ind. U., 1967. Bar: Ind. 1967, U.S. Dist. Ct. (so. and no. dists.) Ind., U.S. Ct. Claims 1972, U.S. Ct. Appeals (7th cir.) 1972, U.S. Supreme Ct. 1972, U.S. Dist. Ct. D.C., 1976, U.S. Ct. Appeals (fed. cir.) 1976. Mgr. Marine Office of Am., Indpls., 1951-71; ptnr. Gleason, Hay & Gleason, Indpls., 1967—; gen. counsel Profl. Ins. Agts., Indpls., 1967—. Served with USNR, 1942-47. Mem. Indpls. Bar Assn., Maritime Law Assn. U.S. (proctor). Democrat. Roman Catholic. Avocation: sailing. Admiralty, Insurance, General practice. Home: RR 4 Box 152 Woodland Lake IN 46160 Office: Gleason Hay & Gleason 939 N Alabama PO Box 44194 Indianapolis IN 46244

GLEASON, GERALD WAYNE, lawyer; b. Springfield, Mo., May 22, 1911. A.B., Drury Coll., 1933; postgrad U. Mo., 1938. Bar: Mo. 1938. Asst. pros. atty. Greene County (Mo.), 1947-48, 50-51; city atty. Springfield, 1952-56; acting city mgr. Springfield, 1953; mcpl. judge, Springfield, 1956-73; ptnr. Tucker & Gleason, Springfield, 1938—. Served to capt. U.S. Army, 1941-45, ETO. Mem. Greene County Bar Assn., Mo. Bar Assn. General practice, Probate, Local government.

GLEASON, JAMES MARNE, manufacturing and service company executive; b. Detroit, Sept. 9, 1935; s. James Ambrose and Mabel Ann (Johnston) G.; m. Marion Dustin Auerbach, Sept. 8, 1962; children—Stewart Hart, Jane Hart, Mary Carolyn; m. Ellen Jane O'Hara, July 4, 1981; children: James Marne, Sarah Wood. B.A., Mich. State U., 1958; J.D., Duke U., 1962. Bar: N.Y., U.S. Supreme Ct. Assoc. Donovan Leisure Newton & Irvine, N.Y.C., 1962-66; counsel aircraft engine group Avco Corp., Greenwich, Conn., 1966-75; sec. Carte Blanche Corp., Los Angeles, 1968-75; dir. Avco Records Corp and subs., N.Y.C., 1970-75; sr. group counsel metal and fabrications ops. NL Industries, Inc., N.Y.C., 1975-77, v.p., sec., gen. counsel, 1977-82, mem. ops. com., 1979-82; v.p., gen. counsel Burroughs Corp., Detroit, 1982—, also mem. exec. com.; dir. Oenoke Corp., New Canaan, Conn., pres., 1980-82. Mem. personnel bd. New Canaan Town Council, 1975-82, vice chmn., 1976-82; bd. govs. New Canaan Hist. Soc., 1972-82, sec., 1972-75, pres., 1975-76; dir. NL Industries Found., 1977-82; trustee Detroit Hist. Soc., 1983—, v.p. mus. com., 1985—; asst. Republican Nat. Conv., 1964, 68, 76, 80; dist. leader Republican Congl. Campaign, 1974-76; del. Conn. Rep. State Conv., 1982. Served to 1st lt. U.S. Army, 1959. Recipient Nathan Burkan award ASCAP, 1961; Mary Reynolds Babcock internat. law fellow, 1961. Mem. Am. Corp. Counsel Assn. (bd. dirs. 1982—, chmn. policy com. 1982-84), Mich. Gen. Counsel Assn. (chmn. 1983-86), Westchester-Fairfield Corp. Counsel Assn. (pres. 1975), Catalina Island Mus. Soc. Club: Recess (Detroit). Home: Old Lahser Rd Bloomfield Hills MI 48013 Office: Burroughs Corp Detroit MI 48232

GLEASON, JAMES MULLANEY, lawyer, insurance executive; b. Sioux City, Iowa, Sept. 27, 1948; s. Harry H. and Dorothy (Mullaney) G. B.A., Briar Cliff Coll., Sioux City, 1973; J.D., Creighton U., 1976. Bar: Iowa 1976, Nebr. 1976. Asst. counsel Woodmen of the World, Omaha, 1976-80, asst. gen. counsel, 1980—. Served with U.S. Army, 1968-69. Fellow Life Office Mgmt. Assn., Life Mgmt. Inst.; mem. Assn. Fraternal Benefit Counsel, Internat. Claims Assn. (edn. com.). Democrat. Roman Catholic. Insurance, Civil rights, Personal injury. Office: Woodmen of World Life Ins Soc 1700 Farnam St Omaha NE 68102

GLEASON, JEAN WILBUR, lawyer; b. St. Louis, Oct. 31, 1943; d. Ray Lyman and Martha (Bugbee) W.; m. Gerald Kermit Gleason, Aug. 28, 1966; children—C. Blake, Peter Wilbur. B.A., Wellesley Coll., 1965; LL.B. cum laude, Harvard U., 1968. Bar: Calif. 1969, D.C. 1978. Assoc. Brobeck, Phleger & Harrison, San Francisco, 1969-72; spl. counsel to dir. div. corp. fin. SEC, 1972-76, assoc. dir. div. investment mgmt., 1976-78; of counsel Fulbright & Jaworski, Washington, 1978-80; ptnr. Fulbright & Jaworski, 1980—. Mem. ABA (chmn. subcom. on securities and banks, bus. sect.), D.C. Bar Assn. (chmn. steering com. bus. sect.), Fed. Bar Assn. (exec. council, securities com.), Am. Bar Retirement Assn. (bd. dirs.), Phi Beta Kappa. General corporate, Banking. Home: 3411 Woodley Rd NW Washington DC 20016 Office: 1150 Connecticut Ave NW Washington DC 20036

GLEASON, JOSEPH HOWARD, lawyer; b. Boston, Sept. 13, 1933; s. Bernard Frederick Sr. and Margaret Elizabeth (Sullivan) G.; m. Barbara Anne Pedini, June 15, 1957; children: Paula Anne, Peter Joseph, Pamela Jean. AS in Mech. Engring. with honors, Wentworth Inst., 1958; BS in Indsl. Mgmt., Northeastern U., 1964; JD, New Eng. Sch. of Law, 1976. Bar: Mass. 1977; registered profl. engr., Mass. Sales engr. The Foxboro (Mass.) Co., 1960-63, systems engr., 1963-74, mgr. contracts, 1974-80, cons. legal bus., 1980-84, officer govt. bus. compliance, 1981—, atty., 1984—. Served with USCG, 1952-56. Mem. Mass. Bar Assn. Democrat. Roman Catholic. Avocations: gardening, handyman. Computer, Contracts commercial, Government contracts and claims. Home: 250 Cliff Dr North Attleboro MA 02760 Office: The Foxboro Co 33 Commercial St Foxboro MA 02035

GLEATON, FREDERICK NEAL, lawyer; b. Warwick, Ga., Nov. 30, 1952; s. Hugh Elbert and Mildred (Daniel) G.; m. Susanne Margaret Schiveree, June 14, 1975; children: Sarah Elizabeth, Amelia Anne. AB, U. Ga., 1973; JD, U. Va., 1976. Bar: Ga. 1976, U.S. Dist. Ct. (no. dist.) Ga. 1976, U.S. Ct. Appeals (5th cir.) 1976, U.S. Ct. Appeals (11th cir.) 1981. Assoc. Hurt, Richardson, Garner, Todd & Cadenhead, Atlanta, 1976-82, ptnr., 1983—. Bd. dirs. Ansley Park Civic Assn., Atlanta, 1984. Mem. ABA, Ga. Bar Assn., Atlanta Bar Assn., Ga. Def. Lawyers Assn., Lawyer's Club Atlanta, Def. Research Inst. Club: Ansley Golf (Atlanta). Federal civil litigation, State civil litigation, Personal injury. Home: 1642 Johnson Rd NE Atlanta GA 30306 Office: Hurt Richardson Garner Todd & Cadenhead 233 Peachtree St Suite 1100 NW Atlanta GA 30043

GLEAVES, CURT B., lawyer; b. Portland, Oreg., Feb. 20, 1957; s. Vernon Dale and Virginia Fay (Hawley) G.; m. Patricia Mary Gianelli, Dec. 18, 1977; children: John Thomas, Kristen Mary. BA, Stanford U., 1979; JD, U. Calif., San Francisco, 1982. Bar: Oreg. 1982. Assoc. Schwabe, Williamson, Wyatt, Moore & Roberts, Portland, 1982—. Mem. study com. Portland City Club, 1985. Named Future First Citizen, Eugene (Oreg.) Jaycees, 1975. Mem. ABA, Oreg. Bar Assn. (exec. com. securities regulation sect. 1984—), Multnomah Bar Assn., Am. Electronics Assn. (lawyers com. 1985—). Republican. Roman Catholic. Club: Multnomah Athletic (Portland). Avocations: skiing, backpacking, racquetball. Securities, General corporate, Trademark and copyright. Home: 7830 SW Raintree Beaverton OR 97005 Office: Schwabe Williamson Wyatt et al 1211 SW 5th Ave Portland OR 97204

GLEESON, PAUL FRANCIS, lawyer; b. Bronx, N.Y., June 20, 1941; s. William Francis and Julia Anne (Dargis) G.; children: Kevin F., Sean W., Brendan J., Colleen J. AB in History, Fordham U., 1963; JD, U. Chgo., 1966. Bar: Ill. 1966, U.S. Dist. Ct. (no. dist.) Ill. 1969, U.S. Ct. Appeals (6th cir.) 1972, U.S. Ct. Appeals (7th cir.) 1973. Assoc. Vedder, Price, Kaufman & Kammholz, Chgo., 1966-73, ptnr., 1973—. Author: (with Day, Green and Cleveland) The Equal Employment Opportunity Compliance Manual, 1978. Served to capt. U.S. Army, 1966-68, Vietnam. Decorated Bronze Star; Floyd Russell Mechem scholar, 1963-66. Mem. ABA, Assn. Trial Lawyers Am., Chgo. Bar Assn., VFW (post comdr. Northbrook, Ill. 1971-73), Order of Coif, Phi Beta Kappa. Roman Catholic. Club: Chgo. Athletic Assn. Labor. Office: Vedder Price Kaufman & Kammholz 115 S LaSalle St Chicago IL 60603

GLEGHORN, LINDA BON LIPE, lawyer; b. Clarksdale, Miss., Jan. 10, 1948; s. William Ray and Gwendolyn (Strickland) Lipe; m. Larry L. Gleghorn, Feb. 15, 1983. BBA in Accountancy, U. Miss., 1970, JD, 1971. Bar: Miss. 1971, Ark. 1976, U.S. Dist. Ct. (no. dist.) Miss. 1971, U.S. Dist. Ct. (ea. dist.) Ark. 1976, U.S. Ct. Appeals (8th cir.) 1985. Sr. tax acct. Arthur Young & Co., San Jose, Calif., 1971-74, A.M. Pullen & Co., Knoxville, Tenn., 1975; legal counsel to gov. State of Ark., Little Rock, 1975-79; dep. pros. atty. 6th Jud. Dist. Ark., Little Rock, 1979-80; chief counsel Ark. Public Service Commn., Little Rock, 1980-83; asst. U.S. atty. Eastern Dist. Ark., Dept. Justice, Little Rock, 1983—. Mem. ABA, Miss. State Bar, Ark. State Bar Assn. Episcopalian. Criminal. Office: US Atty's Office 600 W Capitol PO Box 1229 Little Rock AR 72203

GLEIM, MICHAEL ALAN, lawyer; b. San Francisco, Jan. 30, 1953. BA, U. Calif., Riverside, 1974; MA, U. Calif., 1975; JD, U. San Francisco, 1978; LLM in Taxation, U. San Diego, 1987. Bar: Calif. 1979. Sole practice San Francisco, 1979-81; tax analyst CCH Computax, Inc., El Segundo, Calif., 1981-84, dir. Tax systems devel., 1985-86, tax specialist TSD, 1986—; bd. dirs. Internat. Commerce Ops., Inc., Helena, Mont., 1976—. Mem. ABA, Am. Soc. Internat. Law. Club: Wig & Pen (London). Lodge: Elks. Avocations: sailing, bag pipes, wine tasting, dancing. Personal income taxation, Estate planning, Public international. Home: 607 S Prospect #206 Redondo Beach CA 90277 Office: CCH Computax Inc PO Box 92938 Los Angeles CA 90009

GLEIN, RICHARD JERIEL, lawyer; b. Los Angeles, Aug. 20, 1929; s. Henry Carl Glein and Elsie B. (Drummond) Schurman; divorced; children: Valerie, Kimberley, Richard Jr., Stacy. Student, U. Wash., 1953-58. Bar: Wash. 1963, U.S. Dist. Ct. (ea. and we. dists.) Wash. 1963, U.S. Ct. Appeals (9th cir.) 1963. Dep. pros. atty. King County, Wash., 1963-65; from assoc. to ptnr. Clinton, Fleck & Glein, Seattle, 1965—. Served to sgt. USAF, 1946-49, served to sgt. 1st class U.S. Army, 1950-51. Mem. ABA, Wash. State Bar Assn., Fed. Bar Assn., Seattle-King County Bar Assn., Internat. Footprint Assn. (pres. Seattle chpt. 1969-70, grand pres. 1982-83), Wash. State Def. Attys., Assn. Trial Lawyers Am., Wash. State Trial Lawyers Assn. Republican. Lodges: Elks, Eagles, Masons (master 1946-49, 73). General practice, State civil litigation, Federal civil litigation. Home: 12300 28th NE #104 Seattle WA 98125 Office: Clinton Fleck & Glein 2112 3d Ave Suite 500 Seattle WA 98121

GLEISS, HENRY WESTON, lawyer; b. Detroit, Nov. 22, 1928; s. George Herman and Mary Elizabeth (Weston) G.; m. Joan Bette Christopher, July 23, 1955; children—Kent G., Keith W. B.A., Denison U., 1951; J.D., U. Mich., 1954. Bar: Mich. 1955, U.S. Dist. Ct. (ea. dist.) Mich. 1955, U.S. Dist. Ct. (we. dist.) Mich. 1960, U.S. Ct. Appeals (6th cir.) 1964, U.S. Supreme Ct. 1967. Sole practice, Benton Harbor, Mich., 1957-61; ptnr. Globensky, Gleiss & Bittner, St. Joseph, 1961—; spl. asst. atty. gen. Mich., 1960—. Officer Jaycees, Mich.; bd. dirs. United Fund. Served with U.S. Army, 1955-57. Mem. ABA, Mich. Bar Assn., Berrien County Bar Assn. (pres. 1974), Assn. Trial Lawyers Am., Twin Cities C. of C. (v.p. 1975). Congregationalist. Clubs: Kiwanis, Moose (Benton Harbor); Economic of S.W. Mich.; Elks (St. Joseph). Condemnation, State civil litigation, Malpractice. Home: 1224 Miami Benton Harbor MI 49022 Office: 610 Ship St PO Box 290 Saint Joseph MI 49085

GLEISSER, MARCUS DAVID, author, lawyer, journalist; b. Buenos Aires, Argentina, Feb. 14, 1923; s. Ben and Riva (Kogan) G.; m. Helga Marianne Rothschild, Oct. 23, 1955; children: Brian Saul, Julia Lynne, Hannah Tanya, Ellyn Ruth. B.A. in Journalism, Case Western Res. U., 1945, M.A. in Econs., 1949; J.D., Cleve. State U., 1958. Bar: Ohio 1958, U.S. Supreme Ct.

1962, U.S. Dist. Ct. (no. and ea. dists.) Ohio 1981. Police reporter Cleve. Press, 1942-44, copy editor, 1944-47; advt. copy writer McDonough-Lewy, Inc., 1947-50; copy editor Cleve. Plain Dealer, 1950-52, gen. assignment reporter, 1952-57, courthouse reporter, 1957-63, real estate editor, 1963-81, fin. writer and investment columnist, 1981—. Author: The World of Cyrus Eaton, 1965, Juries and Justice, 1968; also articles.; editor-in-chief: Cleve.-Marshall Law Rev., 1956, 57. Trustee Cleve. Coll. Alumni Assn., 1968, Euclid Mayor's Exec. Council, 1973-76, Euclid Charter Commn., 1975-76. Recipient Nat. Bronze medal Am. Newspaper Pubs. Assn., 1944; Nat. Silver Gavel award ABA, 1958; Bronze medal Nat. Legal Aid and Defender Assn., 1963; Loeb award for disting. bus. and fin. writing U. Conn., 1966; cert. of recognition NCCJ, 1967; Silver Medal award consistently outstanding spl. feature columns Nat. Headliners Club, 1969; award Ohio Bar Assn., 1957, 58, 59, 60, 61, 62; award pub. service Cleve. Newspaper Guild, 1959; award for best column Cleve. Newspaper Guild, 1976; award Nat. Assn. Real Estate Editors, 1965, 71, 72, 73, 80, 81; award Nat. Assn. Real Estate Bds., 1966, 67, 68, 69, 70, 71, 73; award Nat. Assn. Home Builders, 1970; 1st prize Nat. Assn. Realtors, 1980; Bus.-Fin. Writing award Press Club Cleve., 1969; Disting. merit award Cleve. Assn. Real Estate Brokers, 1976; Excellence in Bus. Journalism award Press Club Cleve., 1983, 85, Fin. Writing award Pannell, Kerr & Forster, 1985. Mem. Am. Newspaper Guild, Sigma Delta Chi. Club: City (Cleve.). Landlord-tenant, Real property, Investments. Home: 575 Hemlock Dr Euclid OH 44132 Office: 1801 Superior Ave Cleveland OH 44114

GLEISSNER, JOHN DEWAR, lawyer; b. Greenwich, Conn., Jan. 11, 1952; s. Bruce Dewar and Ella Wilhelmina (Machetanz) G.; m. Katherine Lynn Thomaston, June 14, 1986. BA with honors, Auburn U., 1973; JD, Vanderbilt U., 1977. Bar: Ala. 1977, U.S. Ct. Appeals (11th cir.) 1977. Assoc. Davies, Williams and Wallace, Birmingham, Ala., 1977—. Chancellor St. Anne's Home Inc., Birmingham, 1982-86. Mem. ABA, Birmingham Bar Assn. (chmn. unauthorized practice of law com. 1983), Legal Aid Soc. Birmingham (pres. 1983). Episcopalian. Avocations: hunting, running, chess. Insurance, General practice. Home: 2420 Cahaba Rd Birmingham AL 35223 Office: Davies, Williams & Wallace 308 Jefferson Federal Bldg Birmingham AL 35203

GLEIT, ERNEST AARON, lawyer; b. N.Y.C., June 19, 1931; s. Nathan and Dora (Katz) G.; m. Sandra Barbara Perlman, Apr. 4, 1959; 1 child, Neil. AB, NYU, 1952; LLB, Columbia U., 1955. Bar: N.Y. 1956, U.S. Dist. Ct. (so. dist.) N.Y. 1960, U.S. Dist. Ct. (ea. dist.) N.Y. 1963. Assoc. Rosenman, Colin, Kaye, Petschek & Freund, N.Y.C., 1958-66; atty. Western Electric Co., N.Y.C., 1966-77, dir. regulatory matters, 1977-83; gen. atty. AT&T Technologies, Berkeley Heights, N.J., 1983-85, AT&T, Berkeley Heights, 1986—. Served with U.S. Army, 1956-58. Mem. ABA, Assn. of Bar of City of N.Y. Antitrust, Public utilities. Home: 467 Valley St Maplewood NJ 07040 Office: AT&T One Oak Way Berkeley Heights NJ 07922

GLEKEL, JEFFREY IVES, lawyer; b. N.Y.C., Apr. 8, 1947; s. Newton and Gertrude (Burr) G. A.B., Columbia U., 1969; J.D., Yale U., 1972. Bar: N.Y. 1973, U.S. Supreme Ct. 1981, U.S. Ct. Appeals (2d cir.) 1974, U.S. Dist. Ct. (so. dist.) N.Y. 1974. Law clk. to judge U.S. Dist. Ct. (so. dist.) N.Y., 1972-73; asst. U.S. atty. So. Dist. N.Y., 1973-77; law clk. to justice Byron R. White, U.S. Supreme Ct., Washington, 1977-78; ptnr. Skadden, Arps, Slate, Meagher and Flom, N.Y.C., 1980—; Editor, contbr.: Federal Litigation Practice, 1986; Business Crimes, 1982; note and comment editor Yale Law Jour., 1971-72. Contbr. articles to law jours. Mem. Assn. Bar City of N.Y. (chmn. com. fed. legislation 1984-87), ABA. Federal civil litigation, Criminal. Office: Skadden Arps Slate Meagher 919 3d Ave New York NY 10022

GLENN, CLETA MAE, lawyer; b. Clinton, Ill., Sept. 24, 1921; d. John and Mattie Sylvester (Anderson) Glenn; B.S., U. Ill., 1947; J.D., DePaul U. Coll. Law, 1976; m. Rex Eugene Loggans, Sept. 3, 1948 (div.); 1 dau., Susan. Real estate builder, developer, 1959-69; communications dir. Transp. Research Center, Northwestern U., Evanston, Ill., 1969-72; admitted to Ill. bar, 1977; practice law, Chgo., 1977—; lectr. Assn. Trial Lawyers Am., John Marshall Law Sch. Served with USN, 1943-59. Recipient Real Estate Humanitarian award Kislak Co., Miami, Fla., 1962. Mem. ABA, Ill. Bar Assn. (assembly rep., mem. standing com. on traffic laws and cts., family law sect. council), Chgo. Bar Assn., Assn. Trial Lawyers Am., Ill. Trial Lawyers Assn., Lex Leggio, Phi Alpha Delta. Editor: Collective Bargaining and Technological Change in American Transportation, 1979; contbr. articles to profl. publs. Family and matrimonial, General practice, Personal injury. Home: 200 E Delaware Pl Chicago IL 60611 Office: Glenn Law Offices Loggans Bldg 615 N Wabash Ave Chicago IL 60611

GLENN, EVERETT LAMAR, management firm executive, lawyer; b. Cleve., Sept. 6, 1952; s. Herschel and Callella Virginia (Sands) G. BA, Oberlin Coll., 1974; JD, Case Western Res. U., 1977. Bar: Ohio 1977, Calif. 1979. Assoc. Guren, Merritt, Sogg & Cohen, Cleve., 1977-79; dist. counsel SBA, San Francisco, 1979-80; assoc. Heller, Ehrman et al, San Francisco, 1980-83; pres. Sports Plus, Inc., Oakland, Calif., 1983—. Telethon worker United Negro Coll. Fund, Los Angeles, 1984; contbr. NAACP, 1985, Bay Area Black United Fund, Oakland, 1985. Recipient Image Builders award Coll. Bounders, 1984. Mem. ABA, Calif. Bar Assn., Ohio Bar Assn., Sports Lawyers Assn., Forum Com. on Sports and Entertainment. Democrat. Baptist. Club: Charles Houston Bar (San Francisco). Avocations: reading, athletics, writing, church, children. Entertainment, General corporate, Real property. Home: 3093 Broadmoor View Oakland CA 94605

GLENN, ROBERT EASTWOOD, lawyer; b. Catlettsburg, Ky., Dec. 24, 1929; s. Albert Sidney and Pauline Elizabeth (Eastwood) G.; m. Clydenne Reinhard, Mar. 16, 1956; children: Pauline Eastwood, Robert Eastwood Jr. BS cum laude, Washington and Lee U., 1951, JD cum laude, 1953. Bar: Va. 1952, U.S. Dist. Ct. (we. dist.) Va. 1958, U.S. Ct. Appeals (4th cir.) 1974, U.S. Supreme Ct. 1975. Assoc. Eggleston & Holton, Roanoke, Va., 1957-60; ptnr. Glenn, Flippin, Feldmann & Darby, Roanoke, 1960—; mem. Va. Bd. Bar Examiners, Richmond, 1982—. Mem. State Council for Higher Edn. for Va., 1980-84; rector Radford (Va.) Coll., 1975-79, bd. of visitors, 1972-79; chmn. Roanoke City Rep. Com., 1968-70, Roanoke Valley ARC, 1974-76. Served to 1st lt. (JAGC) USAF, 1953-57. Mem. ABA, Va. Bar Assn., Roanoke Bar Assn. (pres. 1980-81). Roman Catholic. Clubs: Hunting Hills Country, Shenandoah (Roanoke) (v.p. 1981), Commonwealth (Richmond). General corporate, Contracts commercial, Real property. Home: 3101 Allendale St SW Roanoke VA 24014 Office: Glenn Flippin Feldmann & Darby 315 Shenandoah Bldg Roanoke VA 24001

GLENNON, CHARLES EDWARD, judge, lawyer; b. Monticello, Ill., Apr. 5, 1942; s. William Edward and Beatrice Jane (Pierson) G.; m. Sylvia Ann McClintock, Aug. 24, 1965 (div. Aug. 1972); children—David, Caroline; m. Victoria Louise Pearre, Oct. 26, 1974; 1 child, Andrew. B.A., U. Ill., 1964, J.D., 1966. Bar: Ill. 1966, U.S. Supreme Ct. 1974. Assoc. Fellheimer & Fellheimer, Pontiac, Ill., 1968-73; ptnr. Gomien & Glennon Ltd., Dwight, Ill., 1973-75; cir. judge State of Ill., Pontiac, 1976—; lectr., author domestic relations, joint custody and mediation Ill. Jud. Conf. Village atty., Dwight, 1973-75; chmn. Salvation Army Adv. Bd., Pontiac, 1976; mem. Regional Youth Planning Commn., Livingston County Commn. on Children and Youth. Served as SP-5 U.S. Army, 1966-68. Fellow Ill. Bar Found.; mem. Livingston County Bar Assn., Ill. Bar Assn., Ill. Judges Assn., Am. Assn. Juvenile and Family Ct. Judges, Ill. Council Juvenile and Family Ct. Judges, Dwight C. of C. (bd. dirs. 1974-75). Republican. Episcopalian. Lodges: Lions, Rotary, Elks. Home: R R 1 Pontiac IL 61764 Office: 11th Cir Livingston County Courthouse Pontiac IL 61764

GLICK, BRIAN JAY, lawyer, contract advisor; b. Bklyn., Nov. 22, 1954; s. Merton and Vivian (Schwartz) G.; m. Susan Fern Sorgenstein, Aug. 22, 1981; 1 child, Justin Joshua. B.A. in History and English, Fordham U., 1977; J.D., Southwestern U., 1981. Bar: Fla. 1981, U.S. Dist. Ct. (so. dist.) Fla. 1982, U.S. Supreme Ct. 1984, U.S. Tex Ct. 1982. Supr. Credit Exchange, Inc., N.Y.C., 1973-77; sales rep. Hollingsworth, Co., Pottstown, Pa., 1977-78; pres. Legal Researchers, Los Angeles, 1978-81; sole practice, West Palm Beach, Fla., 1981-82, Boca Raton, Fla., 1982—; contract advisor Nat. Football League Players Assn., Washington, 1984. Author short stories, poetry. Advisor West Boca Community Council, 1983; bd. dirs. Estada Homeowners Assn., Boca Raton, 1984. Personal injury, Insurance, Family and matrimonial. Office: 900 N Federal Hwy Suite 300-340 Boca Raton FL 33432

GLICK, CYNTHIA SUSAN, lawyer; b. Sturgis, Mich., Aug. 6, 1950; d. Elmer Joseph and Ruth Edna (McCally) G. A.B., Ind. U., 1972; J.D., Ind. U.-Inpls., 1978. Bar: Ind. 1978, U.S. Dist. Ct. (so. dist.) Ind. 1978, U.S. Dist. Ct. (no. dist.) Ind. 1981. Adminstrv. asst. Gov. Otis R. Bowen, Ind., 1973-76; law clk. Ind. Ct. Appeals, 1976-79; dep. pros. atty. 35th Jud. Cir., LaGrange County, Ind., 1980-82, pros. atty., 1983—. Campaign aide Ind. Rep. State Cen. Com., Indpls., 1972-73. Named Hon. Speaker, Ind. Ho. of Reps., 1972, Sagamore of the Wabash, Gov. Ind., 1974. Fellow Ind. Bar Found.; mem. ABA, Am. Judicature Soc., Ind. State Bar Assn., LaGrange County Bar Assn. (pres. 1983-86), DAR, Delta Zeta. Republican. Methodist. Lodge: Eastern Star. General practice. Home: 113 W Spring St LaGrange IN 46761 Office: Office of Prosecuting Atty LaGrange County Ct House LaGrange IN 46761

GLICK, RICHARD MYRON, lawyer; b. Los Angeles, Mar. 16, 1952; s. Benjamin Ramon and Shirlee (Sabath) G.; m. Barbara Beckerman, July 23, 1972; children: Megan Hilary, Justin Scott. BA, U. Calif., Berkeley, 1973; JD, U. So. Calif., 1976. Bar: Calif. 1976, Oreg. 1979, U.S. Dist. Ct. Oreg. 1980, U.S. Ct. Appeals (9th cir.) 1984. Staff counsel Calif. Water Resources Control Bd., Sacramento, 1976-79; dep. city atty. City of Portland, Oreg., 1979-83; assoc. Rankin, McMurry et al., Portland, 1983-84, Ragen, Roberts, O'Scannlain, Robertson & Neill, Portland, 1984-85; ptnr. Ragen, Tremaine, Krieger, Schmeer & Neill, Portland, 1985—; instr. water rights law U. Calif., 1978. Bd. dirs., v.p. Portland Symphonic Choir, 1981-84; chair City of Portland Energy Commn., 1985—. Mem. ABA (alt. energy subcom.), Multnomah County Bar Assn., Northwest Small Hydrolectric Assn. (bd. dirs., gen. counsel), Oreg. Water Resources Congress, Phi Beta Kappa. Administrative and regulatory, FERC practice, Environment. Office: Ragen Tremaine et al First Interstate Ctr 23d Floor Portland OR 97201

GLICKMAN, JULIUS, lawyer; b. Big Spring, Tex., Mar. 19, 1940; s. Oscar and Bobbie (Peach) G.; m. Suzan Clark, Aug. 10, 1968; children: O.L. Clark, Jennifer Leone. BA with honors, U. Tex., 1962, LLB, 1966. Bar: Tex. 1966, U.S. Dist. Ct. (so. and ea. dists.) Tex., U.S. Ct. Appeals (5th cir.). Assoc. Brown, Kronzer et al, Houston, 1966-68; adminstrv. and legis. asst. to Congressman Bob Eckhardt U.S. Ho. of Reps., Washington, 1968-70; ptnr. Glickman, Perkinson & Cooksey, Houston, 1970-71; sole practice Houston, 1971-83; sr. ptnr. Glickman & Barnett, Houston, 1983—; adj. prof. U. Houston, 1985-86. Past bd. dirs. Houston chpt. U.S. Com. for UN, Bill of Rights Found., Children's Resource Info. Service, Houston; del. 5th Cir. Jud. Conf., Austin, 1985, Houston, 1986.Jt. Mem. ABA (co-chmn. ann. meeting 1983, chmn. Tex. small firm com. 1984, litigation sect.), Tex. Bar Assn., Houston Bar Assn. (Pres.'s award 1979, 82), Tex. Assn. Civil Trial Specialists (Houston pres., v.p., sec., treas.). Clubs: Cotillion (pres. 1980), Briar, Houston Ctr., Metro. Racquet (Houston), University. Federal civil litigation, State civil litigation, Antitrust. Office: Glickman & Barnett 1460 1st City Tower Houston TX 77002

GLICKMAN, RONNIE CARL, government official, lawyer; b. Junction City, Kans., Feb. 6, 1956; s. Lawrie Burton and Ruth Lael (Singer) G. AB, Duke U., 1977; MS in Pub. Adminstrn., Fla. State U., 1980, JD, 1981. Bar: Fla. 1981, U.S. Dist. Ct. (mid. dist.) Fla. 1981. Asst. states atty. Hillsborough County, Tampa, Fla., 1981-85, county commr., 1985-86; rep. Fla. Ho. of Reps., Tallahassee and Tampa, 1986—. Speaker sch. enrichment resource Vols. in Edn., Tampa, 1986; active Project Graduation Celebrity Auction, Tampa, 1986, celebrity bowlathon Big Bros./Big Sisters, Tampa, 1986, Say No To Drugs March, Tampa, 1986. Recipient Martin Luther King Leadership award Starting Together on Progress, 1986. Mem. ABA, Hillsborough County Bar Assn., Phi Beta Kappa, Order of Coif. Democrat. Jewish. Legislative, Local government. Home: 4526 La Capri Ct Tampa FL 33611 Office: 4302 Henderson Blvd Austin Bldg Suite 113 Tampa FL 33629

GLICKSMAN, ELLIOT BORIS, educator, lawyer; b. Detroit, Jan. 25, 1942; s. B.H. and Sylvia (Bier) G.; m. Thea Schwartz, Dec. 27, 1970. B.A., Eastern Mich. U., 1964; M.A., Wayne State U., 1966; J.D., U. Detroit, 1969. Bar: Mich. 1969. Practice, Detroit, 1969-70; asst. pros. atty. Wayne County (Mich.), 1970-72; staff atty. Burroughs Corp., Detroit, 1972-75; assoc. prof. law Thomas H. Cooley Law Sch., Lansing, Mich., 1975-80, prof. law, 1980—; ad hoc hearing referee Mich. Dept. Civil Rights, 1975—; vis. reseach fellow, faculty of law U. Birmingham (Eng.), 1984-85 . Bd. dirs. Pub. Radio, East Lansing, Mich., Opera Bd. Greater Lansing, Greater Lansing Symphony Council. Recipient Faculty award Mich. Jud. Inst., 1981, Disting. Men of Achievement award Cambridge U., 1986. Mem. Mich. Bar Assn., Ingham County Bar Assn., ABA, Assn. Trial Lawyers Am., Scribes, Thomas M. Cooley Law Sch. Faculty Writers Assn. (charter). Contbr. chpts. to books, articles to profl. jours. Office: Thomas M Cooley Law Sch 217 S Capitol Ave PO Box 13038 Lansing MI 48933

GLICKSMAN, ELLIOTT AARON, lawyer; b. Milw., Aug. 23, 1954; s. David Arthur and Nancy Norma (Schwartz) G.; m. Lorraine Frieders, June 22, 1985; 1 child, Benjamin Joseph. BA, U. Wis., 1976; JD with high distinction, U. Ariz., 1979. Bar: Ariz. 1979. Assoc. Law offices of Robert J. Hirsch, P.C., Tucson, 1979-81; ptnr. Messing & Glicksman, Tucson, 1981-83, Messing, McCrory & Glicksman, Tucson, 1983-84, Glicksman & Awerkamp, Tucson, 1985—. Chmn, Citizen Police Adv. Com., Tucson, 1980-81. Mem. Ariz. Bar Assn. (employment practice com.). Civil rights, State civil litigation, General practice. Office: Glicksman & Awerkamp PC 177 N Church Suite 1105 Tucson AZ 85701

GLICKSTEIN, STEVEN, lawyer; b. Bklyn., Jan. 3, 1952; s. Alexander and Esther (Camhi) G. BA, Lehigh U., 1973; JD, Columbia U., 1976. Assoc. Kaye, Scholer, Fierman, Hays & Handler, N.Y.C., 1976-84, ptnr., 1985—. Mem. ABA, D.C. Bar Assn., Fla. Bar Assn., N.Y. State Bar Assn. Antitrust, Federal civil litigation. Home: 1619 3d Ave Apt 9AE New York NY 10128 Office: Kaye Scholer Fierman Hays & Handler 425 Park Ave New York NY 10022

GLIDDEN, RICHARD MARK, lawyer; b. Broken Bow, Nebr., Dec. 17, 1955; s. James Clair and Norma Jean (Lane) G.; m. Cheryl I. Warkenthien, Aug. 22, 1981; children: Sara Mae, Alison Rae. BA, Kearney State U., 1977; JD, U. Nebr., 1981. Bar: Nebr. 1981, U.S. Dist. Ct. Nebr. 1986. Assoc. Hines & Hines, Benkelman, Nebr., 1981-84; sole practice Benkelman, 1984—; atty. County of Dundy, Nebr., 1984—, City of Benkelman. Treas., bd. dirs. Southwest Area Devel. Corp., Benkelman, 1983—. Mem. ABA, Nebr. Bar Assn. (cert. commendation 1985). Republican. Lutheran. Lodges: Lions (sec. 1985—), Masons (sr. warden 1986—). Avocations: hunting, fishing. General practice, Local government, Probate. Home: 514 6th Ave W Benkelman NE 69021 Office: 522 S Chief Benkelman NE 69021

GLIEGE, JOHN GERHARDT, lawyer; b. Chgo., Aug. 3, 1948; s. Gerhardt John Gliege and Jane Heidke; m. Carol Ann Simpson, Apr. 25, 1981; children: Gerhardt, Stephanie, Kristine. BA, Ariz. State U., 1969, MPA, 1970, JD, 1974. Bar: Ariz. 1974. Sole practice Scottsdale, Ariz., 1974-81, Flagstaff, Ariz., 1981—; prof. law No. Ariz. U., Flagstaff, 1981-83. Mem. Nat. Assn. of Bond Law. Municipal bonds, Administrative and regulatory, Land use and planning law. Home and Office: 10 Mt Elden Lookout Rd RR4 Box 722B Flagstaff AR 86001

GLINES, JACK HOLLOWAY, lawyer; b. Los Alamos, Calif., Aug. 22, 1911; s. John Thomas and Dora Beatrice (Holloway) G.; m. Francis Ruth Baril, July 24, 1938; children—Pamela Glines Jordan, Patrica Glines Rees. B.A. U. Calif., Berkeley, 1931, LL.B. 1934. Bar: Calif. 1934. Sole practice, Santa Maria, Calif., 1935-80; ptnr. Glines and Hardy, Santa Maria, 1980—; city atty., Santa Maria, 1942-46; dir. Santa Maria Savs. & Loan, 1959-74, Bill Loeper Ford, 1961-84. Mem. Santa Maria Public Library Bd., 1956—, pres., 1978-87 ; pres. Santa Maria Pioneer Assn., 1939-40. Mem. Calif. State Bar Assn., Santa Barbara County Bar Assn., No. Santa Barbara County Bar Assn. Democrat. Episcopalian. Clubs: Kiwanis, Santa Maria Country, Automobile of So. Calif. (adv. bd. 1977-83), Elks. Probate, Contracts commercial, Estate taxation. Home: 1125 S Speed St Santa Maria CA 93454 Office: 311 W Church St Santa Maria CA 93454

GLINKA, GLEB, lawyer; b. Brussels, Feb. 10, 1948; came to U.S., 1954.; s. Gleb Sr. and Elizabeth (Golinsky) G. BA, Reed Coll., 1972; MA, Yale U., 1975; JD, Temple U., 1981. Bar: Vt. 1981, U.S. Dist. Ct. Vt. 1982, U.S. Ct. Mil. Appeals 1984, U.S. Ct. Appeals (2d cir.) 1984. Reginald Heber Smith fellow Vt. Legal Aid Soc., St. Johnsbury, 1981-82; gen. counsel Vt. Sec. State, Montpelier, 1982-85; confidential law clk. to presiding justice U.S. Bankruptcy Ct., Rutland, Vt., 1985-87; sole practice Lyndon Center, Vt., 1987—; clk. com. Pa. Criminal Procedure Rules, Phila., 1979-81. Contbr. articles to profl. jours. Founder Conn. chpt. Gray Panthers, Stamford, 1977. Fellow Soc. Law and Medicine; mem. Vt. Bar Assn. (chmn. publs. com. 1985—), Assn. Trial Lawyers Am., Nat. Lawyers Guild, Phi Beta Kappa. Mem. Eastern Orthodox Ch. Avocations: mycology, semiotics, chess, computers, horseback riding. Administrative and regulatory, Bankruptcy, Criminal. Home: RD #1 Cabot VT 05647 Office: PO Box 117 Lyndon Center VT 05850

GLINN, FRANKLYN BARRY, lawyer; b. Newark, Oct. 22, 1943; s. Dave and Gertrude (Weinstein) G.; m. Sandra Lee Scales, Nov. 3, 1943; children—MacAdam Jordan, Dara Elisabeth, Daniel Garrett. B.A.E., U. Fla., 1965, J.D., 1968. Bar: Fla. 1969, U.S. Ct. Appeals (5th cir.) 1969, U.S. Dist. Ct. (so. dist.) Fla. 1970. Assoc. Ser, Greenspahn & Keyfetz, Miami, Fla., 1969-70, Ser & Keyfetz, Miami, 1970-72, Rabin, Sassoon, & Ratiner, Miami, 1972-74; ptnr. Ratiner & Glinn, Miami, 1974—. Mem. ABA, Am. Judicature Soc., Am. Trial Lawyers Assn., Acad. Fla. Trial Lawyers, Am. Arbitration Assn. Democrat. Jewish. State civil litigation, Personal injury, Workers' compensation. Office: Ratiner & Glinn 60 SW 13th St Miami FL 33130

GLOBER, GEORGE EDWARD, JR., lawyer; b. Edwards AFB, Calif., Aug. 10, 1944; s. George Edward and Catharine (Crain) G.; m. Deirdre Denman, May 22, 1971; children—Denman, Nancy King. A.B., Cornell U., 1966; J.D., Harvard U., 1969. Bar: Tex. 1969, U.S. Sup. Ct. 1976. Assoc., Vinson & Elkins, Houston, 1969-77; dir. Houston Dept. Pub. Service, 1977-78; mem. law dept. Exxon Prodn. Research Co., Houston, 1978—, asst. gen. csl., 1981-82, gen. csl., 1982—. Served with Air N.G., 1969-75. Mem. Am. Intellectual Property Law Assn., Houston Intellectual Property Law Assn. (bd. of govs. 1985—), Internat. Law Assn., Tex. Bar Assn., Houston Bar Assn., Assn. Corp. Patent Counsel (sec-treas. 1985-87). General corporate, Patent, Antitrust.

GLOSBAND, DANIEL MARTIN, lawyer; b. Salem, Mass., July 3, 1944; s. Leon Glosband and Ruth Pauline (Wentworth) Glosband School; m. Merrily Cotton, Dec. 23, 1967; children—Alexander, Gabriel, Oliver. B.A., U. Mass., 1966; J.D., Cornell U., 1969. Bar: Mass. 1969, U.S. Dist. Ct. Mass. 1970, U.S. Ct. Appeals (1st cir.) 1971, U.S. Dist. Ct. Conn. 1971, U.S. Dist. Ct. Vt. 1974, U.S. Supreme Ct. 1982. Assoc., then ptnr., firm Widett & Widett, Boston, 1969-75; ptnr. firm Goldstein & Manello, Boston, 1976—. Contbr. numerous articles on bankruptcy to profl. jours. Fellow Mass. Bar Found.; mem. Mass. Bar Assn. (chmn. bankruptcy com. 1980-83), Boston Bar Assn. (chmn. bankruptcy com. 1977-80), ABA (sect. on corps.). Democrat. Jewish. Bankruptcy. Home: 34 Atlantic Ave Swampscott MA 01907 Office: Goldstein & Manello 265 Franklin St Boston MA 02110

GLOSSER, JEFFREY MARK, lawyer; b. 1936; married; 1 child. BS in Econs. with distinction, U. Pa., 1958; JD, Harvard U., 1961. Bar: D.C. 1962. Law clk. to presiding justice U.S. Ct. Claims, 1963-64; assoc. Emery & Wood, Washington, 1965-69; ptnr. Jeffrey M. Glosser, P.C., Washington, 1969-86; counsel Whiteford, Taylor & Preston, Washington, 1986—; instr. continuing legal edn. courses sponsored by D.C. Bar, 1976—. Mem. ABA (adminstrv. law sect., mem. various coms.), D.C. Bar Assn. (mem., numerous coms.), Fed. Bar Assn. (U.S. Ct. Claims com.), Fed. Cir. Bar Assn. (rules com. 1985—). Federal civil litigation, Administrative and regulatory, Legislative. Office: Whiteford Taylor & Preston 888 17th St NW Washington DC 20006

GLOVER, DURANT MURRELL, lawyer; b. Wilmington, N.C., Mar. 6, 1951; s. Murrell Kelso and Erma Elizabeth (Williams) G.; m. Carol Ann Marquett, Dec. 16, 1978. AB, Duke U., 1973; JD with honors, U. N.C., 1976. Bar: N.C. 1976, U.S. Dist. Ct. (mid. dist.) N.C. 1976, U.S. Ct. Appeals (4th cir.) 1977, U.S. Supreme Ct. 1980. Assoc. Frassineti & Shaw, Greensboro, N.C., 1976-77; ptnr. Frassineti & Glover, Greensboro, 1977—. Mem., counsel Tarheel Triad Girl Scout Council Inc., Colfax, N.C., 1980—. Mem. ABA, N.C. Bar Assn., Greensboro Bar Assn. (editor Greensboro Bar News 1983-87, bd. dirs. 1987—), Order of Coif. Republican. Presbyterian. Probate, Real property, Consumer commercial. Home: 2011 Medhurst Dr Greensboro NC 27410 Office: Frassineti & Glover PO Drawer 1799 Greensboro NC 27402

GLOVER, WILLIAM HUDSON, JR., lawyer; b. Zebulon, Ga., Oct. 8, 1950; s. William Hudson and Sibyl (Williams) G.; m. Marsha Brooks, May 24, 1975; children: William Daniel, James Peter. BBA, U. Miss., 1973, JD, 1976. Bar: Miss. 1976, U.S. Dist. Ct. (no. dist.) Miss. 1976, U.S. Dist. Ct. (so. dist.) Miss. 1977, U.S. Ct. Appeals (5th cir.) 1983. Assoc. Wells, Wells, Marble & Hurst, Jackson, Miss., 1976-79, ptnr., 1979—; v.p. G&G Foods, Inc., Jackson, 1973-85. Elder Riverwood Bible Ch., Jackson, 1980-83, deacon, 1984—. Mem. ABA, Miss. Bar Assn. Avocations: karate, jogging. Labor, Real property, General corporate. Home: 151 Glenside Dr Jackson MS 39211 Office: Wells Wells Marble & Hurst PO Box 131 Jackson MS 39205

GLOVSKY, SUSAN G. L., lawyer; b. Boston, Apr. 16, 1955; d. Leonard B. and Marilyn S. (Shapiro) Loitherstein; m. Steven M. Glovsky, May 25, 1980. BS in Chemistry, U. Vt., 1977; JD, Boston U., 1980. Bar: Mass. 1980, Mich. 1980, N.Y. 1982, U.S. Dist. Ct. (ea. dist.) Mich. 1980, U.S. Patent Office 1981, U.S. Dist. Ct. Mass. 1982, U.S. Ct. Appeals (1st cir.) 1982. Assoc. Levin, Levin, Garvett & Dill, Southfield, Mich., 1980-81, Ladas & Parry, N.Y.C., 1981-82, Dahlen & Gatewood, Boston, 1982-83; ptnr. Dahlen & Glovsky, Boston, 1983-85; sole practice Boston and Salem, Mass., 1985—. Mem. ABA (litigation sect.), Mass. Bar Assn., Boston Bar Assn. (alt. dispute resolution com.), Boston Patent Law Assn. (chmn. litigation sect.), Maritime Law Assn. (assoc.), Am. Arbitration Assn. (panel arbitrators 1985—). Jewish. Avocations: swimming, cross-country skiing. Federal civil litigation, State civil litigation, Construction. Home: 131 Federal St Salem MA 01970 Office: 197 Portland St Boston MA 02114

GLOWACKI, THOMAS ROBERT, lawyer; b. Milw., Jan. 15, 1950; s. Thadeus Ralph and Grace Marcella (Krzeminski) G.; m. Martha Jane Appleyard, Aug. 19, 1972. BA with honors, U. Wis., 1972, JD, 1975. Bar: Wis. 1975, U.S. Dist. Ct. (we. dist.) Wis. 1975, U.S. Supreme Ct. 1981. Assoc. Harris & Hill, Madison, Wis., 1975-77; ptnr. Harris, Hill & Glowacki, Madison, 1977—; vis. lectr. law U. Wis., 1984, 86; lectr. Wis. Bar Assn., 1980, 83; com. mem. Bd. Atty.'s Profl. Responsibility, Madison, 1980. Author: (with others) The Guardian ad Liten in Wisconsin, 1986. Mem. Dane County Bar Assn. (exec. com. 1980-84, del. at large 1983-85). Republican. Avocations: antiques, Naval history. General practice, Consumer commercial, State civil litigation. Home: 2325 Oakridge Madison WI 53704 Office: Harris Hill & Glowacki 2037 Winnebago Madison WI 53704

GLOWINSKI, ROBERT WILLIAM, lawyer, educator; b. Paterson, N.J., Oct. 29, 1954; m. Devra Fader, June 30, 1979. BA, Rutgers U., 1976; JD, U. Balt., 1982. Bar: Md. 1982, D.C. 1984, U.S. Dist. Ct. Md. 1985, U.S. Dist. Ct. D.C. 1986. Atty. Nat. Forest Products Assn., Washington, 1978-86, Cunningham & Assocs., Washington, 1986—. Mem. ABA (chmn. arson com.), ASTM, Md. Bar Assn., Bar Assn. D.C., Soc. Fire Protection Engrs., Internat. Assn. Arson Investigators. Insurance, State civil litigation, Fire protection law. Office: Cunningham & Assocs 5039 Connecticut Ave NW Bldg 2 Washington DC 20008

GLUCK, ROBIN BEVERLY, lawyer; b. N.Y.C., Oct. 5, 1943; d. Irving and Rhoda (Ross) G. Student, Columbia U., 1962; BA, Fla. Atlantic U., 1974; JD, U. Miami, 1978. Bar: Fla. 1979, U.S. Dist. Ct. (so. dist.) Fla. 1980, U.S. Ct. Appeals (5th and 11th cirs.) 1980, U.S. Dist. Ct. (so. dist.) Fla. 1983, U.S. Supreme Ct. 1984. Assoc. Broad & Cassell, Bal Harbour, Fla., 1979, Meyer, Weiss et al, Miami Beach, Fla., 1980; sole practice Miami, Fla., 1980—. Mem. Ctr. Fine Arts, Miami, 1984—, Women's YMCA Network, Miami, 1985—. Mem. ABA, Fla. Bar Assn. (standing com. of unauthorized

practice law 1984—), Dade County Bar Assn. (arbitrator 1984—), Fla. Assn. Women Lawyers, Assn. Trial Lawyers Am., Dade County Trial Lawyers Assn., Nat. Inst. Trial Advocacy, Miami Bus. and Profl. Women's Orgn., Atty.'s Title Guarantee Fund, Acad. Fla. Trial Lawyers. Democrat. Jewish. Club: Tiger Bay. State civil litigation, Personal injury, Family and matrimonial. Office: 75 SW 8th St Suite 401 Miami FL 33130

GLUCKSMAN, JOYCE FRANCINE, lawyer; b. N.Y.C., Apr. 30, 1952; s. Jerome Orin and Theresa Anita (Roman) G. BA, Skidmore Coll., 1973; JD, Emory U., 1976. Bar: Ga. 1976, Fla. 1977, U.S. Ct. Appeals (5th cir.) 1976, U.S. Dist. Ct. (no. dist.) Ga. 1976, U.S. Ct. Appeals (11th cir.) 1981, U.S. Dist. Ct. (so. dist.) Fla. 1981. Legal asst. Ga. Dept. Human Resources, Atlanta, 1977; asst. counsel Nat. Treasury Employees Union, Atlanta, 1977-85; assoc. Sekulow & Roth P.C., Atlanta, 1985; sole practice Atlanta, 1986—; spl. master Ga. Office Fair Employment Practices, Atlanta, 1984—. Bd. dirs. Spina Bifida Assn. Atlanta, 1976—, Spina Bifida Assn. Am., Chgo., 1977-82, Atlanta Jewish Community Ctr., 1984—; mem. profl. adv. bd. Spina Bifida Assn. Am., Chgo., 1982-85. Mem. ABA, Ga. Bar Assn., Fla. Bar Assn., Atlanta Bar Assn., Indsl. Relations Research Assn. Labor, State civil litigation, Federal civil litigation. Home: 969 Los Angeles Ave NE Atlanta GA 30306 Office: 2505 Chamblee Tucker Rd Suite 303 Atlanta GA 30341

GLYNN, STEPHEN MICHAEL, lawyer; b. St. Louis, Sept. 5, 1944; s. James Edward Sr. and Marjorie (Murphy) G.; m. Pamela M. Brown, Aug. 7, 1965 (div. sept. 1975); children: S. Michael, T. Benson; m. Kathleen Walsh, Mar. 17, 1981. BS, U. Wis., Milw., 1967; JD with honors, U. Wis., Madison, 1970. Bar: Wis. 1970, U.S. Dist. Ct. (ea. and we. dists.) Wis. 1970, U.S. Ct. Appeals (7th cir.) 1971, U.S. Supreme Ct. 1973, U.S. Tax Ct. 1976, U.S. Ct. Appeals (10th cir.) 1979, U.S. Ct. Appeals (6th cir.) 1982, U.S. Ct. Appeals (11th cir.) 1984, U.S. Ct. Appeals (8th cir) 1985. Law clk. to presiding judge U.S. Dist. Ct., Madison, Wis., 1970-71; assoc. Shellow & Shellow, Milw., 1971-75, ptnr., 1975-81; ptnr. Shellow, Shellow & Glynn S.C., Milw., 1981—; pres. Legal Aid Soc., Milw., 1979—, bd. dirs. Named Best of the Bar-Criminal Def. Milw. Mag., 1985. Mem. ABA (criminal laws sect.), Wis. Bar Assn. (chmn. criminal law sect. 1978-79), Milw. Jr. Bar Assn. (exec. bd. 1974-76), Nat. Assn. Criminal Def. Lawyers, Wis. Jud. Council (insanity def. and preliminary hearing coms. 1979), Am. Soc. Safety Engrs. (criminal liability seminar 1986—). Democrat. Club: Milw. Athletic. Avocations: tennis, biking, swimming. Criminal, Civil rights. Home: 929 N Astor St Milwaukee WI 53202 Office: Shellow Shellow & Glynn SC 222 E Mason St Milwaukee WI 53202

GLYWASKY, DONALD STEVEN, lawyer; b. Amityville, N.Y., Feb. 24, 1955; s. Daniel Anthony and Margaret Elizabeth (Meyers) G.; m. Kristin Mary Zimmermann, Aug. 16, 1980. BA, SUNY, Buffalo, 1978; JD, Cleve. Marshall Law Sch., 1982. Bar: Ohio 1982, Tex. 1984, U.S. Dist. Ct. (no. dist.) Ohio 1982, U.S. Dist. Ct. (so. dist.) Tex. 1986. Assoc. Herbert Palkovitz Co. LPA, Cleve., 1982-83; atty. U.S. Corps of Engrs., Galveston, Tex., 1983-85; asst. county atty. Galveston County, 1985—. Mem. Tex. Trial Lawyers Assn. Democrat. Roman Catholic. Workers' compensation, State civil litigation, Local government.

GNESIN, MARK MEREDITH, lawyer; b. Long Branch, N.J., Apr. 19, 1952; s. Oscar and Sylvia (Katz) G.; m. Joan M. Campbell. BA, Rutgers U., 1974; JD, Southwestern U., Los Angeles, 1977. Bar: Calif. 1977, U.S. Dist. Ct. (cen. dist.) Calif. 1982. Spl. rep. Travelers Ins. Co., Los Angeles, 1978-80; assoc. Morgan, Wenzel & McNicholas, Los Angeles, 1980-83, Beam, DiCaro, D'Antony & Brobeck, Santa Ana, Calif., 1983-86, Callahan, McCune & Willis, Tustin, Calif., 1986—; judge pro tem Orange County Superior Ct., Santa Ana, 1985—, arbitrator, 1985—. Mem. Orange County Bar Assn., Assn. Southern Calif. Def. Counsel, Lex Romana. Avocations: sailing, scuba diving, skiing, weight lifting. Personal injury, Insurance, State civil litigation. Office: Callahan McCune & Willis 111 Fashion Ln Tustin CA 92680

GNOCCHI-FRANCO, CLAUDIO, lawyer; b. Rome, Mar. 1, 1949; came to P.R., 1951; s. Guido and Rosina (Di Franco) G.; m. Mayra Sanchez, June 12, 1975; 1 child, Paolo Alessandro. BA, U. P.R., 1974; JD, InterAm. U. Sch. Law, P.R., 1978. Bar: P.R. 1978, U.S. Dist. Ct. P.R. 1979, U.S. Ct. Appeals (1st cir.) 1979, U.S. Ct. Mil. Appeals 1981, U.S. Ct. Claims 1983, U.S. Supreme Ct. 1986, D.C. 1987. Capt. U.S. Army JAGC, Ft. Stewart, Ga., 1980; advanced through grades to maj. U.S. Army JAGC; procurement atty. U.S. Army JAGC, Ft. Stewart, 1980-81; appellate def. atty. U.S. Army Legal Services Agy. U.S. Army JAGC, 1981-85; post judge advocate U.S. Army Health Services Command U.S. Army JAGC, Frederick, Md., 1986—. Mem. Assn. Trial Lawyers Am. Republican. Roman Catholic. Fluent in Spanish and Italian langs. Avocations: jogging, photography, short-wave radio, pistol target shooting. Probate, Military, Administrative and regulatory. Home: 8843 Stauffer Rd Walkersville MD 21793 Office: US Army Health Services Command Fort Detrick Frederick MD 21701

GOANS, JUDY WINEGAR, lawyer; b. Knoxville, Tenn., Sept. 27, 1949; d. Robert Henry and Lula Mae (Myers) Winegar; m. Ronald Earl Goans, June 18, 1971; children: Robert Henson, Ronald Earl Jr. Student, Sam Houston State U., 1967-68; BS in Engring. Physics, U. Tenn., 1971, postgrad., 1971-74, JD, 1978. Bar: Tenn. 1978, U.S. Dist. Ct. (ea. dist.) Tenn. 1979, U.S. Patent Office 1980, U.S. Ct. Appeals (Fed. cir.) 1980, U.S. Supreme Ct. 1983. Instr. legal rights Knoxville Women's Ctr., 1977-78; patent analyst nuclear div. Union Carbide Corp., Oak Ridge, Tenn., 1978-79; patent atty. U.S. Dept. Energy, Washington, 1979-82; legis. and internat. intellectual property specialist Patent and Trademark Office, Washington, 1982—; judge Moot Ct. competition, Washington, 1984. Del. Nat. Women's Conf., Houston, 1977; bd. dirs. Nat. Orgn. for Women, Washington, 1977-79; mem. Knox County Rep. Exec. Com., Tenn., 1978-79, legal adv. bd. Knoxville Rape Crisis Ctr., 1979. Mem. ABA, Tenn. Bar Assn., Am. Intellectual Property Law Assn., Gov. Patent Lawyers Assn. (sec. 1981-83). Methodist. Patent, Public international, Legislative. Home: 2233 Pinefield Rd Waldorf MD 20601 Office: Patent and Trademark Office Office Legis and Internat Affairs Washington DC 20231

GOBBEL, LUTHER RUSSELL, lawyer, business executive; b. Durham, N.C., May 17, 1930; s. Luther and Marcia R. (Russell) G.; m. Jean M. Mollison, Apr. 4, 1959; children—Robert R., Katharine S. A.B., Duke U., 1952; J.D., Harvard U., 1955. Bar: Tenn. 1955, Md. 1972. Asst. counsel Bur. Ordnance, Navy Dept., Washington, 1955-59, asst. counsel Bur. Naval Weapons, San Diego, 1959-65; sr. atty. elec. div. Gen. Dynamics Corp., Rochester, N.Y., 1965-70; counsel Amecon div. Litton Systems, Inc., College Park, Md., 1970—; adv. bd. Bur. Nat. Affairs Fed. Procurements Report, Washington, 1968-79. Mem. Harper's Choice Village Bd., Columbia, Md., 1972-75; chmn. Columbia Combined Bds., 1973; Mem. Howard County Criminal Justice Task Force, Md., 1975-76; mem. Howard County Police Tng. Adv. Bd., 1976; mem. Howard County Charter Rev. Com., 1979, Md. Gen. Assembly Compensation Commn., 1984—, Prince Georges County Econ. Devel. Adv. Commn. Mem. ABA, Md. Bar Assn., Fed. Bar Assn. (nat. council 1962-71, nat. v.p. for 9th dist. 1963-64, pres. San Diego chpt. 1962-63), Am. Arbitration Assn. (panel of arbitrators 1969—). Democrat. Methodist. Government contracts and claims, General corporate. Home: 10931 Swansfield Rd Columbia MD 21044 Office: Litton Systems Inc 5115 Calvert Rd College Park MD 20740

GODARD, RANDY EUGENE, lawyer, consultant; b. Cedar City, Utah, Dec. 16, 1952; s. Gerald Eugene and Fern (Jones) G.; m. Linda Anne Fulks, May 9, 1975; children: Joanne Marie, Jacob Eugene, Benjamin James, Daniel Kinsey, Andrew Ross. BA in English, Portugese and Chemistry, Brigham Young U., 1977, MBA, JD, 1980. Bar: Tex. 1982, U.S. Dist. Ct. (so. dist.) Tex. 1982, Ill. 1986. Law clk. to presiding justice Utah State 8th Cir. Ct., Provo, Utah, 1978-79; assoc. Gray, Cary et al, San Diego, 1981; atty., sec. Rapada Corp., Houston, 1982-83; atty. Allied-Signal, Inc., Morristown, N.J., 1983-87, Borden, Inc., Columbus, Ohio, 1987—; cons. Nautilus Planning and Copygraphics, St. George, Utah, 1981—; legal advisor Tex. State Senator William Sarpalius, 1982. Contbr. articles to profl. jours. Advisor Boy Scouts Am., Fox Valley, Ill., 1985—; youth advisor, coach YMCA, Houston, 1982-85. Mem. ABA (internat. bus. banking and corp. law sect.), Tex. Bar Assn., Ill. Bar Assn., Phi Delta Phi. Mormon. Avocations: bicycling, hiking, skiing, golf, geneal. research. Private international, Contracts commercial, General corporate.

GODBOLD, GENE HAMILTON, lawyer; b. Mullins, S.C., June 14, 1936; s. John Dalton and Mildred (Stalvey) G.; m. Janice Louise McKay, June 24, 1960; children—Lori McKay, Scott Hamilton, Stephanie Louise. B.A., Furman U., Greenville, S.C., 1958; LL.B., Tulane U., 1963. Bar: Fla. 1963, U.S. Dist. Ct. (mid. dist.) Fla. 1964, U.S. Ct. Apls. (5th cir.) 1964. Assoc., Maguire, Voorhis & Wells, Winter Park, Fla., 1963-68, ptnr., 1968-84, pres., 1978-84; pres. Godbold, Allen, Brown and Builder, P.A., Winter Park, 1984—. Served to 1st lt. U.S. Army, 1958-60. Mem. Fla. Bar, Orange County Bar Assn. (mem. exec. com. 1968-72, pres. 1971-72), Orlando Area C. of C. Democrat. Club: Winter Park Racquet. Real property, State civil litigation. Address: 359 Carolina Ave Suite A Winter Park FL 32789

GODBOLD, JOHN COOPER, judge; b. Coy, Ala., Mar. 24, 1920; s. Edwin Condie and Elsie (Williamson) G.; m. Elizabeth Showalter, July 18, 1942; children: Susan, Richard, John C., Cornelia, Sally. B.S., Auburn U., 1940; J.D., Harvard U., 1948; LL.D. (hon.), Samford U., 1981. Bar: Ala. 1948. With firm Richard T. Rives, Montgomery, 1948-49; partner firm Godbold, Hobbs & Copeland (and predecessors), 1949-66; U.S. circuit judge Ct. Appeals 5th Circuit, 1966-81, chief judge, 1981; chief judge U.S. Ct. Appeals 11th Circuit, 1981-86. Bd. dirs. Fed. Jud. Center, 1976-81. Served with F.A. AUS, 1941-46. Mem. ABA, Fed., Ala., Montgomery County bar assns., Alpha Tau Omega, Omicron Delta Kappa, Phi Kappa Phi. Episcopalian. Club: Montgomery Country. Office: US Court Appeals PO Box 1589 Montgomery AL 36102 also: US Ct of Appeals Courthouse Atlanta GA 30303

GODEY, LAURENCE RINGGOLD, lawyer; b. Balt., July 21, 1929; s. Thomas R. and Helen E. (Moran) G.; m. Leonna Jean Hinnant, Apr. 12, 1959; children: Laurence R. Jr., John T., Elizabeth L. PhB, Loyola U., Balt., 1951; JD, U. Md., 1955. Bar: Md. 1955. Asst. trust officer Md. Trust Co., Balt., 1957-64; corp. trust officer Md. Nat. Bank, Balt., 1964-71; asst. counsel Monumental Gen. Ins. Co., Balt., 1971-75, asst. sec., gen. counsel, 1975—; bd. dirs. Coastline Ins. Co., Balt. Served to sgt. U.S. Army, 1955-57. Mem. ABA, Md. Bar Assn., Balt. Bar Assn., Balt. Stock Transfer Assn. (pres. 1959-71). Democrat. Roman Catholic. Insurance, Banking. Home: 211 Gaywood Rd Baltimore MD 21212 Office: Monumental Gen Ins Co 1111 N Charles St Baltimore MD 21201

GODFREY, CULLEN MICHAEL, lawyer; b. Fort Worth, Apr. 8, 1945; s. Cullen Aubrey and Agnes (Eiland) G.; m. Melinda McDonald, Sept. 4, 1970. B.A., U. Tex., 1968, J.D., 1970. Bar: Tex. 1969, U.S. Dist. Ct. (we. dist.) Tex. 1971, U.S. Ct. Appeals (5th cir.) 1979, U.S. Ct. Appeals (11th cir.) 1981. Ptnr. Sloan, Muller & Godfrey, Austin, Tex., 1969-72; staff atty. Hunt Oil Co., Dallas, 1972-74; staff atty. Tesoro Petroleum Corp., San Antonio, 1974-75, sr. atty., 1975-78, asst. gen. counsel, 1978-82; asst. gen. counsel Am. Petrofina, Inc., Dallas, 1982—. Served wtih USNG, 1968-74. Mem. ABA (chmn. subcom. on fgn. investment reporting, internat. law sect. 1984—), Dallas Bar Assn., Bd. of Legal Specialization (bd. cert. oil, gas and mineral law), San Antonio Bar Assn. (sec. corp. counsel sect. 1980-82). Republican. Methodist. Lodge: Kiwanis. General corporate, Oil and gas leasing, Private international. Office: Am Petrofina Inc PO Box 2159 Dallas TX 75221

GODFREY, PAUL BARD, lawyer; b. Denver, Jan. 10, 1927; s. Thurman A. and Florence B. (Bard) G.; m. Gwen Davenport, Aug. 21, 1928; children—Brett, Scott. B.A., U. Wyo., 1949, J.D., 1955. Bar: Wyo. 1955, U.S. Ct. Appeals (10th cir.) 1955, U.S. Dist. Ct. Wyo. 1955, Colo. 1987. Ptnr. Henderson, Thomson & Godfrey, 1955-60, Cheyenne, Wyo., ptnr., Henderson & Godfrey, 1960-67; ptnr. Godfrey & Sundahl, 1975-86, Godfrey, Sundahl & Jorgenson, 1986—. Chmn. Young Republicans, 1957-58; Rep. committeeman, 1964-66. Served with U.S. Army, 1945-46. Mem. Internat. Acad. Trail Lawyers, Bd. Trial Advs., ABA, Wyo. Bar Assn., Laramie County Bar Assn., Am. Legion, C. of C. (pres. 1961-62). Episcopalian. Lodges: Elks, Shriners, Masons. State civil litigation, Public utilities, Environment. Home: PO Box 328 Cheyenne WY 82001

GODFREY, RICHARD CARTIER, lawyer; b. Harvey, Ill., Sept. 25, 1954; s. Richard L. and Rosemary (Cartier) G.; m. Alice Bacon Woolsey, Aug. 27, 1983; 1 child, John Cartier. BA, Augustana Coll., 1976; JD, Boston U., 1979. Bar: Ill. 1979, U.S. Dist.Ct. (no. dist.) Ill. 1979, U.S. Ct. Appeals (7th cir.) 1983. Assoc. Kirkland & Ellis, Chgo., 1979-85, ptnr., 1985—. Mem. ABA, Ill. Bar Assn., Chgo. Bar Assn. Admiralty, Administrative and regulatory, Litigation relating to the oil industry. Home: 517 W Roscoe St Chicago IL 60657 Office: Kirkland & Ellis 200 E Randolph Dr Chicago IL 60601

GODFREY, THOMAS GRANT, lawyer; b. Milw., Mar. 4, 1921; s. Alfred L. and Helen H. (Humphery) G.; children—Thomas, Peter, William, Sarah, John, Katherine. B.A., U. Wis., 1942, J.D., 1947. Bar: Wis. 1947, U.S. Supreme Ct. 1960. Mem. Godfrey, Pfeil & Neshek, Elkhorn, Wis., 1947—, chmn. bd., 1983—. Mem. city council City of Elkhorn, 1949-72. Served with U.S. Army, 1943-46. Decorated Army Commendation medal. Mem. Am. Judicature Soc., Wis. Bar Assn., Walworth County Bar Assn. Club: Masons. Personal injury, Probate.

GODINER, DONALD LEONARD, lawyer; b. Bronx, N.Y., Feb. 21, 1933; s. Israel and Edith (Rubenstein) G.; m. Caryl Mignon Nussbaum, Sept. 7, 1958; children: Clifford, Kenneth. AB, NYU, 1953; JD, Columbia U., 1956. Bar: N.Y. 1956, Mo. 1972. Gen. counsel Stromberg-Carlson, St. Louis, 1965-73; assoc. gen. counsel Gen. Dynamics Corp., St. Louis, %; v.p., gen. counsel Permaneer Corp., St. Louis, 1973-75; ptnr. Gallop, Johnson, Godiner, Maoganstern & Crebs, St. Louis, 1975-80; v.p., gen. counsel Laclede Gas Co., St. Louis, 1980—. Editor Columbia U. Law Rev., 1955-56. Served with U.S. Army, 1956-58. Mem. ABA, N.Y. State Bar Assn., Met. St. Louis Bar Assn., Assn. of Bar of City of N.Y. Club: Noonday (St. Louis). Contracts commercial, General corporate, Public utilities. Home: 157 Trails West Dr Chesterfield MO 63017 Office: Laclede Gas Co 720 Olive St Saint Louis MO 63101

GODOFSKY, HARVEY JOSEPH, lawyer; b. Columbus, Ohio, Mar. 13, 1953; s. Arthur A. and Peggy B. (Pozinsky) G.; m. Joanne W. Godofsky, June 1, 1980; children: Dillon, Carlton, Jamie, Evan. BS, La. State U.; JD, Loyola U., New Orleans. Bar: La. 1979, U.S. Dist. Ct. La. Assoc. O'Keefe Law Firm, New Orleans, 1979-82, McGlinchey Law Firm, New Orleans, 1982-84; ptnr. Hebert, Mouledox & Bland, New Orleans, 1984—; adj. faculty Tulane U. New Orleans, 1983. Admiralty, Federal civil litigation, State civil litigation. Home: 127 Golden Pheasant Slidell LA 70461 Office: Hebert Mouledoux & Bland 601 Poydras St Suite 1650 New Orleans LA 70130

GODOFSKY, STANLEY, lawyer; b. N.Y.C., May 24, 1928; s. Eli and Lily (Deutsch) G.; m. Elaine Gloria Weiss, Dec. 15, 1951; children: Janice, David. A.B., Columbia U., 1949, J.D., 1951. Bar: N.Y. 1951, U.S. Supreme Ct. 1961. Assoc. Rogers & Wells, and predecessors, N.Y.C., 1951-64, ptnr., 1965—; spl. asst. counsel N.Y. State Crime Commn., 1952. Mem. bd. editors Columbia U. Law Rev., 1950, revising editor, 1951. Trustee Jewish Community Ctr. White Plains, N.Y., 1983—; mem. comm. on law and social action Am. Jewish Congress, 1986—. Mem. Am. Law Inst., ABA, N.Y. State Bar Assn., Assn. Bar City N.Y., Fed. Bar Council, Am. Judicature Soc., Internat. Bar Assn., Union Internationale des Avocats, World Assn. Lawyers, Internat. Assn. Jewish Lawyers and Jurists. Home: 22 Holbrooke Rd White Plains NY 10605 Office: Rogers & Wells Pan Am Bldg 200 Park Ave New York NY 10166

GODWIN, ELVA COCKRELL, lawyer; b. Houston, Sept. 15, 1949; d. Charles Franklin and Yvonne (Bownds) Cockrell; m. Edward Reddin Godwin Jr., June 25, 1977; children: Edward Reddin III, Charles C. BA in Sociology, Psychology, Southwestern U., 1971; JD, South Tex. Coll. Law, 1981. Bar: Tex. 1982, U.S. Dist. Ct. (so. dist.) Tex. 1986. Research technologist Baylor Coll. Medicine, Houston, 1971-72; social worker Dept. Welfare, Houston, 1972-79; assoc. Strong, Heyburn, Cockrell & Witherspoon, Houston, 1981-86, ptnr., 1986—. Mem. ABA, Tex. Bar Assn., Houston Bar Assn. Republican. Methodist. Avocations: fishing, boating, gardening. General practice, Probate, Family and matrimonial. Office: Strong Heyburn Cockrell & Witherspoon 4605 Post Oak Pl Houston TX 77027

GODWIN, ROBERT ANTHONY, lawyer; b. Phila., Apr. 24, 1938; s. Robert Anthony and Mary (MacElderry) G.; m. Isabel A. Tumelty, Jan. 20, 1941; children—Cara G., Marisa A., Elise D. B.S., Villanova U., 1960, J.D., 1963. Bar: Pa. 1964, U.S. dist. ct. (ea. dist.) Pa. 1964, U.S. Ct. Appeals (3d cir.) 1964, U.S. Supreme Ct. 1981. Vol. defender, Phila., 1964; assoc. Eastburn & Gray, Doylestown, Pa., 1968-70; asst. pub. defender Bucks County (Pa.), 1969-71; sole practice Newtown, 1971-73; ptnr. Timby & Godwin, Newtown, 1973-75; owner Robert A. Godwin & Assocs., Newtown, 1975—. Served with JAGC, USMC, 1964-68 Mem. Assn. Trial Lawyers Am., Mem. Pa. Trial Lawyers Assn., Bucks County Bar Assn. Club: Exchange. General practice, Federal civil litigation, State civil litigation. Office: Box J 110 S State St Newtown PA 18940

GOEBEL, WILLIAM HORN, lawyer; b. N.Y.C., Dec. 7, 1941; s. Harry H. and Maxine (Hamburger) G.; m. Barbara Golden, July 30, 1966; children: Jason, Pamela. AB, Columbia U., 1963; JD, NYU, 1966. Bar: N.Y. 1966. Assoc. Bernard Trencher, N.Y.C., 1966-69; real estate atty. J.C. Penney Co., Inc., N.Y.C., 1969-71; assoc. gen. counsel N.K. Winston Corp., N.Y.C., 1971-72, Teachers Ins. and Annuity Assn. Am./Coll. Retirement Equities Fund, N.Y.C., 1972—; lectr. NYU Sch. Continuing Edn., 1985—. Mem. Assn. Bar City of N.Y., N.Y. State Bar Assn. Real property, Contracts commercial. Office: Tchrs Ins & Annuity Assn Am 730 3d Ave New York NY 10017

GOEKJIAN, SAMUEL VAHRAM, lawyer, business executive; b. Syra, Greece, Aug. 22, 1927; s. Vahram K. and Aznive (Bagdassarian) G.; came to U.S., 1948, naturalized, 1954; B.A. (scholar), Syracuse U., 1952; J.D. (scholar), Harvard U., 1957; m. Jean Alison MacLeod, July 6, 1957; children—Kenneth Samuel, Christopher Allan, Peter Gregory, Lisa Dorothy. Admitted to N.Y. bar, 1958, D.C. bar, 1960; practiced in N.Y.C., 1957-58, Washington, 1958-68, Beirut, 1968-70, Paris, 1970-78, Washington, 1978-83; assoc. atty. Chase Manhattan Bank, N.Y.C., 1957-58; counsel Devel. Loan Fund, Dept. State, Washington, 1958-60; asso. firm Surrey, Karasik, Gould and Greene, Washington, 1960-62, mng. partner, 1962-68; sr. resident partner firm Surrey, Karasik and Greene, Beirut, 1968-70; sr. resident partner firm Surrey, Karasik, Morse & Goekjian, Paris, 1970-78; sr. partner firm Surrey & Morse, 1978-83; chmn., chief exec. officer Consol. Westway Group Inc., Englewood Cliffs, N.J., 1983—; cons. UN, 1962, 78—, AID, 1963; professorial lectr. Grad. Sch. Pub. Law, George Washington U., 1963-68; lectr. Internat. Law Inst., Georgetown U. Law Sch., Washington, 1974-83, adj. prof. law, 1979-83; counsel, mem. exec. com. Egypt-U.S. Bus. Council; mem. Council Fgn. Relations. Served with AUS, 1953-55. Mem. Am. (vice chmn. com. on African law 1966-67, chmn. 1967-68), Fed. (vice chmn. com. on internat. devel. 1964-67), Inter-Am., D.C. bar assns., Am. Law Inst. (spl. adv. com. on law governing internat. transactions 1960-62), Phi Beta Kappa. Author articles and book chpts. on internat. law and fin. Private international. Home: 1 Horizon Rd Fort Lee NJ 07024 Office: 464 Hudson Terr Englewood Cliffs NJ 07632

GOELZER, DANIEL LEE, government official, lawyer; b. Milw., Feb. 14, 1947; s. Gerald Howard and Roberta (Hart) G.; m. Kathryn Anne Oberly, July 13, 1974; 1 child, Michael W. B.B.A., U. Wis., 1969, J.D., 1973; LL.M., George Washington U., 1979. Bar: Wis. 1973, U.S. Dist. Ct. (we. dist.) Wis. 1973, U.S. Ct. Appeals (7th cir.) 1974, U.S. Ct. Appeals (2d, 9th and D.C. cirs.) 1975, U.S. Supreme Ct. 1976, D.C. 1979. Auditor, Touche, Ross & Co., Milw., 1969-70; law clk. to presiding justice U.S. Ct. Appeals, Chgo., 1973-74; atty. SEC, Washington, 1974-78, exec. asst. to chmn., 1978-83, gen. counsel, 1983—. Contbr. articles to law jours. Served with U.S. Army, 1969-70. Mem. ABA, Fed. Bar Assn., Am. Inst. C.P.A.s. Republican. Congregationalist. General corporate, Securities, Administrative and regulatory. Home: 5617 Namakagan Rd Bethesda MD 20816 Office: SEC 450 5th St NW Washington DC 20549

GOERING, ALAN CLYDE, lawyer; b. Halstead, Kans., June 17, 1951; s. Kenneth W. and Dorothy M. (Krehbiel) G.; m. Virginia J. Clausen, Dec. 30, 1972 (div. Aug. 1984); children: Christian, Gabriel; m. Sharon A. Shellenberger, Mar. 8, 1986. BS, U. Kans., 1973; JD, Washburn U., 1976. Bar: Kans. 1976, U.S. Dist. Ct. Kans. 1976. Assoc., ptnr. Chapin, Penny & Goering, Medicine Lodge, Kans., 1976-83; sole practice, Medicine Lodge, 1983—; city atty. City of Medicine Lodge, 1978-79, City of Kiowa, Kans., 1977—. Treas. Dem. County Com., Medicine Lodge, 1977-84, chmn., 1984—; Cubmaster Kanza council Boy Scouts Am., 1982-83. Mem. ABA, Assn. Trial Lawyers Am., Kans. Trial Lawyers Assn. (bd. govs. 1983-84), Kans. Bar Assn. (pres. Young Lawyers 1984-85, sec.-treas. family law sect. 1985—, Outstanding Service award 1985), S.W. Kans. Bar Assn., Order of Barristers. Lodge: Lions (pres. 1981-82). General practice. Home: 201 S Oak Medicine Lodge KS 67104 Office: 201 S Main St Medicine Lodge KS 67104

GOETHALS, RICHARD BERNARD, JR., lawyer; b. Glendale, Calif., Sept. 21, 1950; s. Richard Bernard Sr. and Mary Elizabeth (Moen) G.; m. Christine Marie Schmuck, Aug. 19, 1972; children: Joseph, Margaret, James, Catherine. BA, Santa Clara U., 1972, JD, 1975. Ptnr. Walkup, Shelby, Bastian, Melodia, Kelly & O'Reilly, San Francisco, 1975—. Personal injury. Home: 219 Aragon Blvd San Mateo CA 94402 Office: Walkup Shelby Bastian et al 650 California Ave Suite 3030 San Francisco CA 94108

GOETHEL, STEPHEN B., lawyer; b. Grand Rapids, Mich., Apr. 10, 1953; S. Warren B. Goethel and Beverly (Hendrick) Barrett; m. Lisa B. Chapple, July 29, 1978; children: Dana, Erica. BA, Mich. State U., 1975; JD, Detroit Coll. Law, 1979. Bar: Mich. 1979, U.S. Dist. Ct. (ea. dist.) Mich. 1979. Asst. prosecutor Oakland County, Mich., 1979-80; ptnr. Carlin, Ranno & Goethel, Southfield, Mich., 1980-83; sole practice Pontiac, Mich., 1983; assoc. Stein, Moran & Westerman, Ann Arbor, Mich., 1983—. Bd. dirs. Old West Side Assn., Ann Arbor, 1984-86. Mem. Mich. Trial Lawyers Assn., State Bar of Mich., Washtenaw County Bar Assn. Personal injury, Criminal, Insurance. Office: Stein Moran & Westerman 320 N Main St Ann Arbor MI 48104

GOETSCH, CHARLES CARNAHAN, lawyer, legal historian; b. New Haven, Nov. 9, 1950; s. John Black and Miriam (Finkeldey) G.; m. Cecilia Cartwright Moffitt, Mar. 31, 1980; childrren: Benjamin John, Megan Elizabeth. AB magna cum laude, Brown U., 1973; JD, U. Conn., 1976; LLM, Harvard U., 1977; postgrad. Yale Law Sch., 1978-79. Bar: Conn. 1978, N.Y. 1984, U.S. Dist. Ct. Conn. 1978, U.S. Dist. Ct. (so. dist.) N.Y. 1982, U.S. Ct. Appeals (2d cir.) 1982, U.S. Supreme Ct. 1984. Law clk. to judge U.S. Dist. Ct. Conn., 1978-79, to judge U.S. Ct. Appeals 2d Cir., 1979-80; assoc. Tyler, Cooper & Alcorn New Haven, 1980-81; ptnr. Cahill, Goetsch & DiPersia, P.C., New Haven, 1982—. Am. Bar Found. fellow, 1978; Nat. Endowment Humanities fellow, 1979. Mem. Am. Trial Lawyers Assn., ABA, Conn. Bar Assn., (fed. practice com.), Am. Soc. Legal History, Phi Beta Kappa. Congregationalist. Club: Harvard, Brown (N.Y.C.). Author: Essays on Simeon E. Baldwin, 1981, The Autobiography of Thomas L. Chadbourne, 1985; contbr. articles to legal jours.; editor Conn. Law Rev., 1974-76, Conn. Bar Jour., 1983—. Federal civil litigation, Legal history, Labor. Home: 99 Peck Hill Rd Woodbridge CT 06525 Office: 43 Trumbull St New Haven CT 06511

GOETTEL, GERARD LOUIS, federal judge; b. N.Y.C., Aug. 5, 1928; s. Louis and Agnes Beatrice (White) G.; m. Elinor Praeger, June 4, 1951; children: Sheryl, Glenn, James. Student, The Citadel, 1946-48; B.A., Duke U., 1950; J.D. (Harlan Fiske Stone scholar), Columbia U., 1955. Bar: N.Y. 1955. Asst. U.S. atty. So. Dist. N.Y., N.Y.C., 1955-58; dep. chief atty. gen.'s spl. group on organized crime Dept. Justice, N.Y.C., 1958-59; asso. firm Lowenstein, Pitcher, Hotchkiss, Amann & Parr, N.Y.C., 1959-62; counsel N.Y. Life Ins. Co., N.Y.C., 1962-68; with Natanson & Reich, N.Y.C., 1968-69; asso. gen. counsel Overmyer Co., N.Y.C., 1969-71; asst. counsel N.Y. Ct. on the Judiciary, 1971; U.S. magistrate U.S. Dist. Ct., So. Dist. N.Y., 1971-76, U.S. dist. judge, 1976—; adj. prof. law Fordham U. Law Sch., 1978—; mem. com. on criminal justice act U.S. Jud. Conf., 1981—; mem. com. on pretrial phase of civil litigation 2d Circuit Conf., 1984—; chmn. com. on criminal justice act So. Dist. N.Y., 1982—, chmn. com. on discovery,

1983—. Mem. council Fresh Air Fund, N.Y.C., 1961-64; bd. dirs. Community Action Program, Yonkers, N.Y., 1964-66. Served to lt. (j.g.) USCG, 1951-53. Mem. ABA. Club: Greenwoods Country (Winsted, Conn.). Jurisprudence. Home: 76B Heritage Hills Somers NY 10589 also: 232 Lakeridge Torrington CT 06790 Office: US Dist Ct 101 E Post Rd White Plains NY 10601

GOETTEMOELLER, DUANE A., lawyer; b. Sidney, Ohio, Feb. 21; s. Harold A. and Dolores (Eilerman) G.; m. Melody Campbell, Aug. 11, 1984. BA, St. Joseph's Coll., 1976; postgrad., Cath. Theological Union, 1976-77; 005, U. Salzburg, Austria, 1974-75; JD, U. Cin., 1982. Bar: Ohio, U.S. Dist. Ct. (so. and we. dists.) Ohio. Law clk. to presiging justice U.S. Dist. Ct. (so. dist.), Cin., 1980-82; assoc. Norman P. Smith Co., Sidney, 1982-85; ptnr. Kerrigan, Boller & Stevenson, Sidney, 1985—. Pres. Shelby County Health Found., Sidney, 1984—. Mem. ABA, Ohio Bar Assn., Shelby County Bar Assn. Roman Catholic. Lodge: Kiwanis (dir. local chpt. 1984—). Real property, Estate planning, Consumer commercial. Home: 13540 McCartyville Rd Anna OH 45302 Office: Kerrigan Boller & Stevenson 500 E Court St Sidney OH 45302

GOETZ, MAURICE HAROLD, lawyer; b. N.Y.C., Mar. 29, 1924; s. Morton M. and Elsie (Klein) G.; m. Pearl Goldberg, Sept. 12, 1948; children—Susan Goetz Zwirn, Janet L., Jill K. B.S.S., CCNY, 1947; J.D., Harvard U., 1950. Bar: N.Y. 1951. Assoc. Bandler Haas & Kass, N.Y.C., 1951-57; ptnr. Bandler Kass & Goetz, N.Y.C., 1957-66, Friedlander, Gaines, Ruttenberg & Goetz, N.Y.C., 1966-74, Rosenman & Colin, N.Y.C., 1974—; lectr. on labor law. Contbr. articles to Nat. Law Jour., Fed. Publs., Inc., others. Mem. ABA, N.Y. State Bar Assn. Labor, General corporate. Office: Rosenman & Colin 575 Madison Ave New York NY 10022

GOFF, BETSY KAGEN, lawyer, international management group executive; b. York, Pa., July 3, 1948; d. Kenneth Stanford Kagen and Charlotte (Senn) Isen; m. William Miller Goff, Mar. 8, 1973; 1 child, Kenneth Steven. B.S. in Econs., U. Pa., 1970; J.D., Temple U., 1974. Bar: N.Y. 1975. Asst. exec. dir. Writers Guild of Am., N.Y.C., 1974-75; contract atty. ABC Sports, N.Y.C., 1975-78, asst. gen. atty. ABC News, N.Y.C., 1978-81; N.Y. v.p. Internat. Mgmt. Group Trans World Internat., N.Y.C., 1981—; atty.-on-call Vol. Lawyers for the Arts, N.Y.C., 1974—, NOW, N.Y.C., 1975-79; dir. Living Arts, Inc., N.Y.C. Mem. Voters for Choice, Women in Sports. Entertainment, Sports, General corporate. Office: Internat Mgmt Group 22 E 71st St New York NY 10021

GOFF, MICHAEL HARPER, lawyer; b. Hartford, Conn., Aug. 4, 1927; s. Charles Weer and Fern (Harper) G.; m. Katharine Lyman Bliss, Feb. 11, 1949 (div.); children—Carlin Weer, Peter Lyman; m. Patricia Darilyn King, Apr. 20, 1984. Student, Loomis Sch., Conn., 1942-45, Bethany Coll., 1945, Trinity Coll., Conn., 1949; B.A., Swarthmore Coll., 1950; LL.B., Columbia U., 1953. Bar: N.Y. 1953. Asst. to dir. Legis. Drafting Research Fund Columbia, summer 1953; assoc. Debevoise & Plimpton, 1953-60, ptnr., 1961—; lectr. Banking Law Inst., 1966; cons. Atty. Gen. State of N.Y., 1977; spl. cons. Temp. Commn. to Study Orgnl. Structure City N.Y., 1953-54. Served with USNR, 1945-46; to 2d lt. F.A., AUS, 1946-48. Harlan Fiske Stone Scholar, Columbia U., 1951; Robert Noxon Toppan prize, Columbia U., 1952; E. B. Convers Prize, Columbia U., 1953. Fellow Am. Coll. Investment Counsel; mem. ABA (mem. com. devels. in bus. financing 1979—), N.Y. State Bar Assn., Assn. Bar City N.Y., Phi Delta Phi, Kappa Sigma. Democrat. Episcopalian. Clubs: Metropolitan, Canadian, Citicorp Ctr. (N.Y.C.); Bay Head Yacht (N.J.). General corporate, Securities. Home: 167 E 61st St New York NY 10021 Office: Debevoise & Plimpton 875 3d Ave New York NY 10022

GOFFE, WILLIAM ARTHUR, judge; b. Sulphur, Okla., Aug. 30, 1929. B.B.A., U. Okla., 1951, LL.B., 1956. Bar: Okla. 1956. Atty. Office Chief Counsel, IRS, 1956-60; mem. Martin, Logan, Moyers, Martin & Conway, Tulsa, 1960-71; judge U.S. Tax Ct., Washington, 1971—. Mem. ABA, Okla. Bar Assn., Phi Alpha Delta. Jurisprudence. Office: 400 2d St NW Washington DC 20217 *

GOFFSTEIN, JOHN HOWARD, lawyer; b. St. Louis, Aug. 25, 1942; s. Harry and Naomi (Schreiber) G.; m. Margaret Ann Michael, Jan. 26, 1966; children—Adam, Ann. B.A., U. Mo., 1964, J.D., 1966. Bar: Mo. 1966, U.S. Dist. Ct. (ea. dist.) Mo. 1967, U.S. Ct. Appeals (7th and 8th cirs.) 1968, U.S. Supreme Ct. 1975. Assoc., John H. Martin Law Offices, 1967-68, Levin & Weinhaus, 1968-69; ptnr. Bartley & Goffstein, 1970-71; ptnr. Bartley, Goffstein, Bollato and Lange, and predecessor, St. Louis, 1971—; mem. LCC adv. bd. AFL-CIO. Bd. dirs. Legal Aid Soc. St. Louis, 1972. Mem. St. Louis Met. Bar, St. Louis Bar Assn. (chmn. labor law com. 1977-78, mem. exec. com. 1979), ABA, Mo. Bar, Lawyers Assn. St. Louis, St. Louis County Bar Assn. (chmn. group legal services com. 1972-75, pres. 1980-81; (Outstanding Young Lawyer of St. Louis County, Essen award 1977), Sigma Rho Sigma, Phi Delta Phi. Assoc. editor Developing Labor Law, 1970-86. Labor, Pension, profit-sharing, and employee benefits, General practice. Office: Suite 604 130 S Bemiston Saint Louis MO 63105

GOFORTH, WILLIAM CLEMENTS, lawyer; b. Danville, Va., July 10, 1937; s. Henry Earl and Naomi Rivers (Hill) G.; m. Bonita May Karlstrom, Dec. 4, 1971. BA, U. S.C., 1959, MA, 1960; JD, Am. U., 1978. Bar: Va. 1979, N.C. 1979, U.S. Dist. Ct. (ea. dist.) Va. 1979, U.S. Ct. Appeals (4th cir.) 1979, U.S. Supreme Ct. 1982, U.S. Ct. Mil. Appeals 1984. Commd. 2d lt. USAF, 1959, advanced through grades to lt. col., 1980; spl. agt. USAF Office Spl. Investigation, Washington, 1960-80; mem. staff exec. def. privacy bd. Sec. of Def., Washington, 1980-84; sole practice Alexandria, Va., 1984—; cons. office of Sec. of Def., Washington, 1985, N.G. Bur., 1986. Mem. ABA (chmn. govt. access/privacy com. adminstrv. law sect. 1984—), Fed. Bar Assn., Va. Bar Assn. (com. legal edn. and admission to bar 1985—), N.C. Bar Assn., Am. Soc. Access Profls. (v.p. 1982-83, Outstanding Achievement award 1982), Assn. Fed. Investigators (cert.), Assn. Record Mgrs. (award 1976), U. S.C. Alumni Assn., Am. Legion, The Retired Officers Assn. Democrat. Club: Athletic Roundtable (Spokane). Lodges: Masons, Shriners.. Avocations: coin collecting, stamps. General practice, Administrative and regulatory, Government contracts and claims. Home: 5405 Duke St #503 Alexandria VA 22304 Office: 4600 Duke St Suite 427 Alexandria VA 22304

GOFRANK, CATHERINE ANN, lawyer; b. Detroit, May 8, 1951; d. Frank Louis and Helen Julia (Rzeznik) G. BA, U. Mich., 1972; JD, Ill. Inst. Tech., 1976. Bar: Mich. 1976, Fla. 1978, D.C. 1979. Mng. ptnr. Gofrank & Kelman, Southfield, Mich., 1979—. Mem. Gov.'s Citizens Com. on Consumer Affairs, 1981-82; hearing referee Mich. Civil Rights Commn., 1981—. Mem. ABA, Detroit Bar Assn., Oakland County Bar Assn., Women Lawyers Assn. Mich., Bar and Gavel Soc. Insurance, Personal injury, State civil litigation. Office: Gofrank & Kelman 26555 Evergreen Rd Suite 322 Southfield MI 48075

GOGO, GREGORY, lawyer; b. Varos, Lemnos, Greece, Oct. 6, 1943; came to U.S., 1946; s. Soterio and Christina (Choleva) G. BA, U. Chgo., 1966; MA, Rutgers U., 1972; JD, Seton Hall U., 1980. Bar: N.J. 1980, U.S. Dist. Ct. N.J. 1980. Reporter The Trentonian, Trenton, N.J., 1968-69; asst. project dir. Trenton Health Ctr., 1969-71; dir. planning UPI, Trenton, 1973-77; instr. sociology Trenton State Coll., 1973-77; assoc. Merlino, Rottkamp, Trenton, 1980-83; sole practice Trenton, 1983—. Exec. bd dirs. ARC, Trenton, 1972-77; spl. advisor to Pres. NAACP, Trenton, 1973-74; mem. parish council St. George Orthodox Ch., Hamilton Twp., N.J., 1984—. Recipient Archon Politis award Am. Hellenic Ednl. Prog. Assn., 1981, Cert. Merit, ARC, Trenton, 1977. Mem. ABA, N.J. Bar Assn., Mercer County Bar Assn., N.J. Assn. Trial Lawyers. Democrat. Contracts commercial, Personal injury, State civil litigation. Home: 1571 Lawrenceville Rd Lawrenceville NJ 08648 Office: 1542 Kuser Rd Suite B-1 Mercerville NJ 08619

GOHN, JACK LAWRENCE BENOIT, lawyer; b. London, July 13, 1949; s. Emile Benoit and Mary Louise (Mincher) Gohn; m. Sandra Ann Pomerantz, May 26, 1971 (div. 1986); children: Elizabeth Clare, Andrew Mark Benoit. BA, U. Pa., 1971; MA, Johns Hopkins U., 1973, PhD, 1975; JD, U. Md., Balt., 1981. Bar: Md. 1981, U.S. Dist. Ct. Md. 1982, U.S. Ct. Appeals (4th cir.) 1982. Law clk. to judge U.S. Dist. Ct. Md., Balt., 1981-82; assoc. Melnicove, Kaufman, Weiner, Smouse & Garbis, P.A., Balt., 1982—. Editor: Kingsley Amis: A Checklist, 1975, Progress and Survival, 1980. Contbr. articles to profl. jours. Mem. Md. Humanities Council, Balt., 1986—. Mem. ABA, Md. Bar Assn., Bar Assn. Balt. City, Order of Coif. Democrat. Roman Catholic. Transportation, Litigation, General practice. Home: 745 McHenry St Baltimore MD 21230 Office: Melnicove Kaufman Weiner Smouse & Garbis PA 36 S Charles St Suite 600 Baltimore MD 21201

GOLBERT, ALBERT SIDNEY, lawyer, educator; b. Denver, Nov. 26, 1932; s. George M. Golbert and Celia (Berenbaum) G.; m. Miriam Judith Goldman, Aug. 25, 1963; 1 child, Rebecca Leah. B.S., U. So. Calif., 1954; LL.B., U. Denver, 1956; LL.M., U. Mich., 1964; D.es Sc. (jur. candidate), U. Geneva, 1968. Bar: Colo. 1957, U.S. Dist. Ct. Colo. 1957, Calif. 1958, U.S. Dist. Ct. (cen. dist.) Calif. 1958, U.S. Ct. Mil. Appeals 1958, U.S. Supreme Ct. 1964, Mich. 1970, U.S. Dist. Ct. (ea. dist.) Mich. 1970, U.S. Customs Ct. 1972, U.S. Tax Ct. 1972, U.S. Ct. Appeals (9th cir.) 1974. Assoc. Oxman & Snyder, Denver, 1956-57; sr. internat. atty. Chrysler Corp., Chrysler Internat., S.A., Taranto, Italy, Izmir, Turkey, Geneva, Switzerland, Sidney, Australia, all 1961-70; of counsel Paul and Gordon, and Diamond, Tilem, Colden & Emery, Los Angeles, 1970-73; ptnr. Forry Golbert Singer & Gelles, Los Angeles, San Francisco, 1974-80; sr. ptnr. Bryan, Cave, McPheeters & McRoberts, Los Angeles, St. Louis, Washington, N.Y.C., Phoenix and London, Ryadh, Saudi Arabia, 1980—; prof. law Southwestern U. Sch. Law, 1970-74, adj. prof., 1974—. Lectr. Grad. Sch. Mgmt., UCLA, 1972-78, U. So. Calif. Law Ctr., 1974—. Contbr. articles to profl. jours. Bd. dirs. Los Angeles Opera Repertory Theatre, 1980-82. Served to capt. JAGD, USAF, 1958-61. Mem. ABA, Internat. Bar Assn., Am. Soc. Internat. Law, Calif. Calif. Bar Assn. (founding mem., internat. practice com., bus. law sect. 1986—), Los Angeles Country Bar Assn. (chmn. sect. internat. law 1984-85, sec. fgn. tax com. of taxation sect. 1986—), Calif. Bar (founding mem., Internat. Practice Com. Bus. Law sect. 1986—), Los Angeles Ctr. for Internat. Comml. Arbitration (v.p., bd. dirs. 1986—). Democrat. Jewish. Taxation international, Public international, Immigration, naturalization, and customs. Home: 301 Conway Ave Los Angeles CA 90024 Office: Bryan Cave McPheeters McRoberts 500 N Broadway St Louis MO 63102

GOLD, DAVID MARCUS, lawyer; b. Monticello, N.Y., Aug. 31, 1950; s. Harold Lewis and Pearl (Cutler) G.; m. Patricia Sue DeVries, June 21, 1981; 1 child, Marc Barnet. BA, SUNY, Binghamton, 1972; JD, Ohio State U., 1976, MA, 1977, PhD, 1982. Bar: Ohio 1978, N.Y. 1986. Lectr. hist. Ohio State U., Columbus, 1982-83; atty. Ohio Legis. Service Commn., Columbus, 1983-85; assoc. Baum & Shawn, Monticello, N.Y., 1985-87; sole practice Monticello, 1987—. Contbr. articles to profl. jours. Nat. Def. Fgn. Lang. fellow, 1975-76, Presidential fellow Ohio State U., 1981. Mem. N.Y. State Bar Assn., Orgn. Am. Historians, Maine Hist. Soc., Sullivan County Hist. Soc. (bd. dirs. 1985—), Phi Beta Kappa, Pi Sigma Alpha, Phi Kappa Phi. Republican. Jewish. Lodge: B'nai B'rith. Avocations: hist., sports. General practice, Legal history. Home: PO Box 658 South Fallsburg NY 12779 Office: 11 Hamilton Ave PO Box 1493 Monticello NY 12701

GOLD, GEORGE MYRON, lawyer, editor, writer; b. Bklyn., June 28, 1935; s. Harry and Rose Miriam (Meyerson) G.; m. Bunny Winters, Dec. 24, 1960; 1 child, Seth Harris. A.B., U. Rochester, 1956; J.D., NYU, 1959. Bar: N.Y. 1960. Practice N.Y.C., 1960-64, 67-78; legal editor Prentice-Hall, Inc., Englewood Cliffs, N.J., 1960-62; assoc. Speiser, Shumate, Geoghan & Law, N.Y.C., 1962-64; assoc. editor Research and Review Service Am., Inc., Indpls., 1964-67; dir. publs., mng. editor Estate Planners Quar./Farnsworth Pub. Co., Inc., Rockville Centre, N.Y., 1967-69; editor-in-chief Trusts & Estates, N.Y.C., 1969-75; editor, house counsel Ronald Press, N.Y.C., 1975-76; mng. editor Trust News, N.Y.C., 1976-78; dir. news publs. and info ABA, Chgo., 1978-83; sr. assoc. editor and dir. book div. ABA Jour., Chgo., 1984—; asst. to research counsel N.Y. Temp. State Commn. Estates, 1962-64. Author: The Propriety, Procedure and Evidentiary Effect of a Jury View, 1959, Investments by Trustees, Executors and Administrators, 1961, What You Should Know About Intestacy, 1962, What You Should Know About the Common Disaster, 1962, The Powers of Your Trustee, 1962, What You Should Know About the Antenuptial Agreement, 1963, Who May Be the Beneficiary of Your Will, 1963, What You Should Know About The Spendthrift Trust, 1963, Comprehensive Estate Analysis, 1966, You're Worth More Than You Think, 1966, Medicare Handbook, 1966, The ABCs of Administering Your Estate, 1966, The Will: An Instrument for Service and Sales, 1966, A Tax-Sheltered Pension Plan for the Close-Corporation Stockholder, 1968, Social Security Law in Nutshell, 1968, What You Should Know About Custodial Gifts to Minors, 1968, The Short-Term Trust and Estate Planning, 1976, The Importance of a Will, 1976, The Need for an Experienced Executor, 1976, Tax Tips-99 Ways to Reduce the Bite, 1976, Investment Management: No Job for the Amateur, 1971, Who Manages Your Securities, 1972, A Woman's Need for Financial Planning, 1972, The Lawyer's Role in the Search for Peace, 1982, True Counselors: Helping Clients Deal with Loss, 1983; editor: Fundamentals of Federal Income Estate and Gift Taxes, 1965-67, The R & R Tax Handbook, 1967, Tax-Free Reorganizations, 1968, Guide to Pension and Profit Sharing Plans, 1968, A Life Underwriter's Guide to Equity Investments, 1968, The Tired Tirade, 1968, A Handbook of Personal Insurance Terminology, 1968, The 15th Anniversary Edition of Estate Planners Quar., 1968, You, Your Heirs and Your Estate, 1968, The Furnsworth Letter for Estate Planners, 1968-69, How to Use Life Insurance in Business and Estate Planning, 1969, Human Drama in Death and Taxes, 1970, Don't Bank on It, 1970, The Feldman Method, 1970, Directory of Trust Instns. (ann.), Law Talk, 1986, The Supreme Court and Its Justices, 1987. Mem. citizens curriculum and fin. coms. Sch. Dist. #303, St. Charles, Ill. Mem. Soc. Law Writers (dir. 1972-75), ABA (dir. news publs. and info. 1978—, sr. assoc. editor, dir. book div. jour. 1984—), N.Y. State Bar Assn., Assn. Bar City N.Y., Chgo. Bar Assn., Estate Planning Council N.Y.C., Soc. Bus. Press Editors, Kappa Nu, Pi Alpha Lambda. Club: KP. Jurisprudence, Probate, Estate taxation. Home: 412161 Colson Dr Saint Charles IL 60174 Office: 750 N Lake Shore Dr Chicago IL 60611

GOLD, GERALD SEYMOUR, lawyer; b. Cleve., Feb. 2, 1931; s. David N. and Geraldine (Bloch) G.; m. Suzanne Kravitz, July 10, 1954; 1 dau., Anne. A.B., Case-Western Res. U., 1951, LL.B., 1954. Bar: Ohio 1954, U.S. Supreme Ct. 1961. Practiced in Cleve., 1954-60; chief asst. legal aid defender Cuyahoga County, Cleve., 1960-61; chief legal aid defender Cuyahoga County, 1961-65; assoc. firm Ulmer, Byrne, Laronge, Glickman & Curtis, Cleve., 1965-66; partner firm Gold, Rotatori, Schwartz & Gibbons, Cleve., 1966—; instr. in law Case-Western Res. U., 1965-66, Cleve. State Law Sch., 1968-69, Case-Western Res. Law-Medicine Center, 1961-77; lectr. to bar assns. commr. Cuyahoga County Pub. Defender, 1977-81. Contbg. author: American Jurisprudence Trials, 1966; Contbr. articles to law revs. Fellow Am. Coll. Trial Lawyers, Ohio State Bar Found., Internat. Soc. Barristers; mem. Case-Western Res. U. Law Alumni (pres. 1974-75, Soc. of Benchers), Cuyahoga County Criminal Ct. Bar Assn. (chmn.), ABA (criminal justice council), Ohio State Bar Assn. (chmn. criminal law sect. 1974-78, ho. of dels. 1986—), Greater Cleve. Bar Assn. (Merit award 1974, trustee 1978—, pres. 1982-83), Nat. Assn. Criminal Def. Lawyers (Merit award 1975, pres. 1977), Ohio Acad. Trial Lawyers (chmn. criminal law sect. 1970-75). Clubs: Court of Nisi Prius, Cleve. Skating. Criminal, Federal civil litigation, State civil litigation. Home: 2750 Claythorne Rd Shaker Heights OH 44122 Office: 1600 Leader Bldg Cleveland OH 44114

GOLD, I. RANDALL, lawyer; b. Chgo., Nov. 2, 1951; s. Albert Samuel and Lois (Rodrick) G.; m. Marcey Dale Miller, Nov. 18, 1978; children—Eric Matthew, Brian David. B.S. with high honors, U. Ill., 1973, J.D., 1976. Bar: Ill. 1976, U.S. Dist. Ct. (no. dist.) Ill. 1976, Fla. 1979, U.S. Dist. Ct. (so. dist.) Fla. 1979, U.S. Ct. Appeals (5th and 7th cirs.) 1979, U.S. Tax Ct. 1979, U.S. Ct. Appeals (11th cir.) 1981, U.S. Supreme Ct. 1982; C.P.A., Ill., Fla. Tax staff Ernst & Ernst, Chgo., 1976-77; asst. state atty. Cook County, Ill., 1977-78, Dade County, Miami, Fla., 1978-82; spl. atty. Miami Strike Force, U.S. Dept. Justice, Fla., 1982-87; sole practice, Miami, 1987—; lectr. Roosevelt U., Chgo., 1976-77; vice chmn. fed. practice com. on criminal sect. Fla. Bar 1986-87. mem. com. on relations between Fla. Bar and Fla. Inst. CPA's. Adviser Jr. Achievement, Chgo., 1976-78, Miami, 1982-84; coach, judge Nat. Trial Competition, U. Miami Law Sch., 1983—. Mem. ABA (govt. litigation counsel com.), Ill. Bar Assn., Chgo. Bar Assn., Dade County Bar Assn. (mem. fed. ct. com.), Decalogue Soc. Lawyers, Fed. Bar Assn., Assn. Trial Lawyers Am., Am. Inst. CPA's, Ill. Soc. CPA's, Fla. Inst. CPA's (com. on relations with Fla. Bar 1985-86), Am. Assn. Atty.-C.P.A.s (com. on relations with Fla. bar 1985-86), Internat. Platform Assn., Delta Sigma Pi. Jewish.Club: Tiger Bay Criminal. Office: 1401 Brickell Ave Suite 910 Miami FL 33131

GOLD, JOSEPH, lawyer; b. Blkyn., Nov. 13, 1927; s. Murray Lewis and Shirley (Ganson) G.; m. Gladys Ann Guss, Mar. 27, 1948; children—Sherry, Steven, Richard, Lauren. Student St. John's U.; LL.B., Bklyn. Law Sch., 1950. Bar: N.Y. 1950, U.S. Dist. Ct. (so. dist.) N.Y. 1951, U.S. Supreme Ct. 1961, U.S. Dist. Ct. (ea. dist.) N.Y. 1969, U.S. Dist. Ct. (no. dist.) N.Y. 1982. Assoc. Louis Dubow, N.Y.C., 1950-52; sole practice, N.Y.C., 1952-65, Great Neck, N.Y., 1965-70, Woodridge, N.Y., 1982—; mem. Goldstein & Goldstein, Monticello, N.Y., 1970-74, Kesten, Gerstman, Ledina, Monticello, 1974-82. Contbr. book revs. for law jour. Southwestern Law Sch., 1976. Served with AUS, 1945-47. Mem. N.Y. State Trial Lawyers, Assn. Trial Lawyers Am., Sullivan County Bar Assn. (bd. dirs. 1977-81, v.p. 1978-79, pres. 1979-80), N.Y. State Bar Assn. (ho. of dels. 1979-82), Gamma Eta Sigma (chmn. chpt. 1945). Chmn. Cub Scouts, Boy Scouts Am., Great Neck, 1960-64. Lodge: Elks. Personal injury, State civil litigation, Criminal. Home: 15 Cedar Park Commons Monticello NY 12701 Office: Joseph Gold Profl Bldg PO Box 456 Woodridge NY 12789

GOLD, LAURENCE STEPHEN, lawyer; b. N.Y.C., Dec. 2, 1936; s. Benjamin and Alice (Perse) G.; m. Carolyn Mondshein, Sept. 21, 1961; children: Elizabeth, Matthew. AB, Princeton U., 1958; LLB, Harvard U., 1961, LLM, 1962. Bar: N.Y. 1961, U.S. Supreme Ct. 1965, D.C. 1966. Law clk. to presiding justice U.S. Dist. Ct., Houston, 1962-63; atty. Gen. Counsel's Office, NLRB, Washington, 1963-65; assoc. Woll & Mayer, Washington, 1965-70; ptnr. Woll, Mayer & Gold, Washington, 1970-74; spl. counsel. AFL-CIO, Washington, 1974-84, gen. counsel, 1984—; lectr. George Washington U. Law Sch., Washington, 1970-79; vis. prof. Georgetown U. Law Sch., Washington, 1979-81. Mem. Inst. Civil Justice (bd. overseers 1983-87). Federal civil litigation, Labor. Home: 4822 Woodway Ln NW Washington DC 20016 Office: AFL-CIO 815 16th St NW Washington DC 20006

GOLD, MICHAEL ALLAN, lawyer; b. Binghamton, N.Y., Dec. 6, 1949; s. Tobias and Gertrude (Dubin) G.; m. Paula Ann Kane, July 16, 1982. BA, U. Conn., 1971; JD, Southwestern U., 1979. Bar: Calif. 1979, U.S. Dist. Ct. (cen. dist.) Calif. 1980, U.S. Ct. Appeals (9th cir.) 1984. Assoc. Stuart B. Walzer P.L.C., Los Angeles, 1980-82, Sheppard, Mullin, Richter & Hampton, Los Angeles, 1982-85; gen. counsel Hanseatic Corp., Long Beach, 1985-86; assoc. Jeffer, Mangels & Butler, Los Angeles, 1987—. Mem. ABA, Los Angeles County Bar Assn. Federal civil litigation, State civil litigation, General corporate. Office: Jeffer Mangels & Butler 1900 Ave of Stars 4th Floor Los Angeles CA 90067

GOLD, NEIL D., lawyer; b. N.Y.C., Jan. 28, 1948; s. Henry and Rose (Siegel) G.; m. Ellen Toff, Aug. 24, 1969; children: Jeffrey, Jason. BA, U. Rochester, 1969; JD, Harvard U., 1972. Assoc. Rosenman, Colin, Freund, Lewis & Cohen, N.Y.C., 1972-81, ptnr., 1981-86; ptnr. Gelberg & Abrams, N.Y.C., 1986—. Mem. ABA, Assn. of Bar of City of N.Y. General corporate, Securities. Office: Gelberg & Abrams 711 3d Ave New York NY 10017

GOLD, PAUL NICHOLAS, lawyer; b. Corpus Christi, Mar. 18, 1953; s. Sammy Gold and Emily (Benjamin) G.; m. Susan Katz, May 25, 1975; children: Jordan Lindsey, Alexander David. B.A. magna cum laude, U. Tex., 1974; J.D., So. Meth. U., 1977. Bar: Tex. 1977, U.S. Dist. Ct. (no., ea. and we. dists.) Tex. 1978. Asst. dist. atty. Dallas County, 1977-78; assoc. Law Offices of Frank L. Branson, P.C., Dallas, 1978-84, ptnr., 1984—; lectr. in field. Mem. ABA, Tex. Bar Assn. (continuing legal edn. com., lectr.), Dallas Bar Assn., Am. Trial Lawyers Assn. (continuing legal edn. com. 1986—), Tex. Trial Lawyers Assn. (assoc. dir. 1980—, co-chmn. med. malpractice litigation com. 1986—), Dallas Trial Lawyers Assn. (dir. 1979-85, treas. 1986, v.p. 1987—), Phi Beta Kappa, Phi Kappa Phi. Personal injury, Federal civil litigation, State civil litigation. Office: Law Offices of Frank L Branson PC 2178N Tower Plaza/Americas Dallas TX 75201

GOLD, RONALD THEODORE, lawyer; b. Bklyn., July 21, 1948; s. Solomon and Ann (Wolf) G.; m. Kay K. King, Dec. 5, 1977. BA in Polit. Sci. magna cum laude, St. John's U., 1970; JD, Washington and Lee U., 1973; LLM in Taxation, Emory U., 1984. Bar: Fla. 1973, Ga. 1976. Assoc. Carter, Ansley, Smith & McLendon, Atlanta, 1977-79, Birnbrey & Kresses, Atlanta, 1979-84, Alembik, Fine & Callner, Atlanta, 1984—. Active DeKalb County (Ga.) Homeowner's Assn., 1977-80, Hearthstone Civic Assn., DeKalb County, 1977-80, Tally Green Homeowner's Assn., Cobb County, Ga., 1980—. Served to capt. JAGC, USMC, 1973-77. Mem. Ga. Bar Assn., Fla. Bar Assn., Atlanta Bar Assn., Cobb C.of C. Republican. Avocations: tennis, water skiing, reading. Real property, Corporate taxation, Personal income taxation. Home: 5257 Amberbrook Ct Marietta GA 30067

GOLD, STEPHEN HOWARD, lawyer; b. Chester, Pa., Dec. 23, 1947; s. George and Rya Gold. BA, Franklin & Marshall Coll., 1969; JD with honors, George Washington U., 1972. Bar: Pa. 1972, U.S. Dist. Ct. (ea. dist.) Pa., 1973. Staff atty. Legal Assistance Assn. Del. County, Chester, 1972-73; asst. pub. defender County of Del., Media, Pa., 1974-78; sole practice Media, 1978—. Mem. Assn. Trial Lawyers Am., Pa. Trial Lawyers Assn., Pa. Bar Assn., Del. County Bar Assn. Republican. Personal injury. Office: 105 W 3rd St Media PA 19063

GOLD, STEVEN MICHAEL, lawyer; b. Bklyn., Sept. 19, 1953; s. Joseph and Gladys (Guss) G.; m. Susan Schwartz, Jan. 9, 1977; children: Rachel, David. BA, Hobart Coll., 1975; JD, Cornell U., 1978. Bar: Conn. 1979, N.Y. 1979, U.S. Dist. Ct. Conn. 1979, U.S. Dist. Ct. (no. dist.) N.Y. 1979. Confidential law asst. 3d dept. appellate div. N.Y. Supreme Ct., Albany, 1978-79; assoc. Schatz & Schatz, Ribicoff & Kotkin, Hartford & Stamford, Conn., 1979-86; ptnr. Schatz & Schatz, Ribicoff & Kotkin, Stamford, 1987—; mem. Conn. Venture Group. Treas. Community Council Westport (Conn.)/Weston, 1985, 2d v.p., 1986, bd. dirs., 1985-86; bd. dirs. Urban League Greater Bridgeport, 1987—;. Mem. ABA, N.Y. State Bar Assn., Conn. Bar Assn., Stamford/Darien Bar Assn., Nat. Assn. Transp. Practitioners (treas. Conn. chpt. 1983-85), Phi Delta Phi, Pi Gamma Mu. Democrat. Jewish. Avocation: squash. General corporate, Contracts commercial, Banking. Office: Schatz & Schatz Ribicoff & Kotkin One Landmark Sq Stamford CT 06901

GOLD, STUART WALTER, lawyer; b. N.Y.C., Mar. 3, 1949; s. Morris I. and Barbara (Walters) G.; m. Michele M. Cardella, June 26, 1983. BA in Polit. Sci., Bklyn. Coll., 1969; JD, NYU, 1972. Bar: N.Y. 1973, U.S. Supreme Ct. 1983, U.S. Ct. Appeals (2d, 8th, 9th and D.C. cirs.). Law clk. to presiding justice U.S. Dist. Ct. (so. dist.) N.Y., 1972-73; assoc. Cravath, Swaine & Moore, N.Y.C., 1973-80, ptnr., 1980—. Bd. dirs. N.Y. Lawyers for Pub. Interest, N.Y.C., 1982—. Mem. ABA, N.Y. State Bar Assn., Assn. of Bar of City of N.Y. (communications com.). Democrat. Avocations: tennis, travel. Federal civil litigation, Libel, Antitrust. Office: Cravath Swaine & Moore One Chase Manhattan Plaza New York NY 10005

GOLDBERG, ALAN JOEL, lawyer, commercial real estate developer; b. Bklyn, Jan. 22, 1943; s. Ralph and Dorothy (Rolnick) G.; 1 son, Cary Adam. B.A., U. Miami, 1965, J.D., 1968. Bar: Fla. 1968, U.S. Supreme Ct., U.S. Ct. Appeals (4th cir.). Ptnr. Goldberg, Young, Goldberg & Borkson, P.A., Ft. Lauderdale, Fla., 1968-82; atty. City of Margate (Fla.), 1969-70, City of Tamarac (Fla.), 1970-71; sole practice, Ft. Lauderdale, 1982—; pres. Proprty Systems, Inc.; chmn. bd. CulCon Systems, Inc. Mem. Citizen's Task Force on Transp., State of Fla.; vice chmn. Broward County Planning Council. Mem. ABA, Fla. Bar Assn. Republican. Real property. Office: 5100 N Federal Hwy Suite 412 Fort Lauderdale FL 33308

GOLDBERG, AVRUM M., lawyer; b. Pitts., Oct. 18, 1943; s. Bernard D. and Sylvia Ann (Marcus) G.; m. Constance L. Carnecchia, Jan. 12, 1967; children: Jason F., Morgan E. BS, Pa. State U.; JD, Villanova U. Bar: D.C. Atty. appellate sect. NLRB, Washington, 1969-73; assoc. Morgan, Lewis & Backius, Washington, 1973-76; ptnr. Wald, Harkrader & Ross, Washington, 1976-82, Akin, Gump, Strauss, Hauer & Feld, Washington, 1982—. Labor. Home: 9020 Belcourt Castle Pl Great Falls VA 22066 Office: Akin Gump

Strauss Hauer & Feld 1333 New Hampshire Ave NW #400 Washington DC 20036

GOLDBERG, CHARLES, lawyer; b. Denver, July 28, 1939; s. Max and Miriam (Harris) G.; m. Honey L. Weinstock, Aug. 27, 1961; children: Todd Adlai, Gregory Eban, Dianna Lynn. BA, U. Colo., 1961; JD, U. Denver, 1964. Bar: Colo. 1964, U.S. Dist. Ct. Colo. 1964, U.S. Ct. Appeals (10th cir.) 1964. Ptnr. Goldberg & Pred, Denver, 1964-65, Schmidt & Van Cise, Denver, 1965-74; judge Denver Dist. Ct., 1974-78; ptnr. Rothgerber, Appel, Powers & Johnson, Denver, 1978—. Mem. Colo. Bar Assn. (bd. govs.), Denver Bar Assn. (bd. trustees, outstanding young lawyer award 1969), Nat. Diocesan Attys. Assn. Federal civil litigation, State civil litigation, Matters peculiar to the Roman Catholic Church. Home: 677 Gilpin St Denver CO 80218 Office: Rothgerber Appell Powers & Johnson 1200 17th St #2800 Denver CO 80202

GOLDBERG, CHARLES, lawyer; b. Abington, Pa., Aug. 18, 1955; s. Herbert and Jeanette Goldberg; m. Arleen Folkes. BA, U. Mich., 1977; JD, U. Pa., 1980. Bar: Tex. 1980, U.S. dist. Ct. (so. dist.) Tex. 1981, U.S. Ct. Appeals (5th and 11th cir.) 1981, La. 1983, U.S. Dist. Ct. (mid. dist.) La. 1983. Lawyer Exxon Co., Baton Rouge, 1980—. Contbr. articles to profl. jours. Dist. chmn. Boy Scouts Am.; counsel La. Safety Belt Use Coalition. Mem. ABA, State Bar Assn. Tex., La. State Bar Assn., Baton Rouge Bar Assn. Club: Mich. Univ. (chmn. scholarship com.). Environment, Labor. Home: 9226 Kindletree Dr Baton Rouge LA 70817 Office: Exxon Baton Rouge Refinery Law Dept PO Box 551 Baton Rouge LA 70821

GOLDBERG, CHARLES L., lawyer; b. Los Angeles, June 7, 1940; . William M. and Mary S. (Schuster) G.; m. Diane Gail Walker, Dec. 18, 1966; children: Cori lynn, Julie Karen, Robert Yale. BA, UCLA, 1964, JD, 1967. Bar: Calif. 1968, U.S. Dist. Ct. (so., cen. and ea. dists.) Calif., U.S. Ct. Appeals (9th cir.), U.S. Supreme Ct. Ptnr. Goldberg & Frant, San Diego, 1968—; instr. criminal law Grossmont Coll., San Diego, 1978-79. Fellow Am. Bd. Criminal Lawyers (bd. dirs.); mem. San Diego Trial Lawyers Assn. (bd. dirs. 1983-85), Calif. Trial Lawyers Assn. (lectr.),Calif. Attys. for Criminal Justice, Nat. Assn. Criminal Defense Lawyers, San Diego Criminal Lawyers Club (founding mem.). Criminal. Office: Goldberg & Frant 303 W A St San Diego CA 92101

GOLDBERG, CHARLES NED, lawyer; b. San Antonio, Dec. 6, 1941; s. Harry and Mamie G.; children—Donald Harris, Allison Beth, William Korash. B.B.A., U. Tex., 1963, J.D., 1966. Bar: Tex. 1966, U.S. Dist. Ct. (so. dist.) Tex. 1969, U.S. Ct. Appeals (5th cir.) 1972. Mng. ptnr. Goldberg Kusin & Brown, Houston, 1980—; sec., dir. Affiliated Capital Corp., Houston, 1968-80. Mem. Southwest regional bd. Anti Defamation League, Houston, 1978—, mem. nat. commn., N.Y.C., 1982—; bd. govs. Houston Grand Opera, 1983-85. Served to capt. U.S. Army, 1966-68. Real property, Banking, Bankruptcy. Home: 1310 Chardonnay St Houston TX 77077 Office: Goldberg Kusin & Brown 5444 Westheimer Suite 1750 Houston TX 77056

GOLDBERG, FREDRIC NORMAN, lawyer; b. N.Y.C., July 2, 1954; s. Bernard and Phyllis (Schneider) G.; m. Holly Ann Perkins, June 13, 1981; 1 child, Brett Perkins. Bar: Mich. 1978, U.S. Dist. Ct. (we. dist.) Mich. 1978. Assoc. Mika, Meyers, Beckett and Jones, Grand Rapids, Mich., 1978-83, ptnr., 1984—. Mem. Mich. Bar. Assn. (antitrust law and corp. law sects.). Republican. Jewish. Avocations: fishing, sailing, baseball, computers. General corporate, Antitrust, Securities. Home: 6900 Oak Brook St SE Grand Rapids MI 49506 Office: Mika Meyers Beckett Jones 500 Frey Bldg Grand Rapids MI 49503

GOLDBERG, HAROLD P., lawyer; b. N.Y.C., Apr. 23, 1939; s. Samuel and Naomi (Freedman) G.; m. Ann Benyes, Feb. 4, 1961 (div.); m. Mary Ciccone, Aug. 28, 1982; children: William, Michele. BA, U. Vt., 1960; JD, Syracuse U., 1963. Bar: N.Y. 1963, U.S. Dist. Ct. (no. and we. dists.) N.Y. Ptnr. Crystal, Mantes & Rifken, Syracuse, 1965-74, Goldberg & Sanders, Syracuse, 1974-84; pres. Goldberg, Harding & Talev, Syracuse, 1984—; trustee U.S. Bankruptcy Ct (no. dist.), Syracuse, 1973—; bd. dirs. Consumer Credit Counselling Services Cen. N.Y. Lodge: B'nai B'rith (pres. 1968-69). Bankruptcy, Consumer commercial, State civil litigation. Office: Goldberg Harding & Talev 217 S Salina St Suite 500 Syracuse NY 13202

GOLDBERG, JAMES S., lawyer; b. Louisville, Feb. 4, 1950; s. Fred. M. Goldberg; m. Barbara Goldberg. BS, Ind. U., 1972; JD, U. Louisville, 1976. Bar: Ky., U.S. Dist. Ct. (ea. and we. dists.) Ky., U.S. Ct. Appeals (6th cir.). Asst. atty. gen. State of Ky., Louisville, 1976-77; ptnr. Goldberg & Simpson, Louisville, 1977—. Mem. ABA, Ky. Bar Assn., Louisville Bar Assn. Bankruptcy, Real property. Home: 710 Cadogan Ct Louisville KY 40222 Office: Goldberg & Simpson PSC 2800 1st Nat Tower Louisville KY 40202

GOLDBERG, JOEL HENRY, lawyer; b. Lewiston, Maine, Feb. 7, 1945; s. George and Evelyn Anne (Mackin) G. B.A., Brandeis U., 1967; J.D., Columbia U., 1970. Bar: N.Y. 1971, D.C. 1980. Atty. CAB, Washington, 1970-73; atty. SEC, Washington, 1973-77; assoc. csl. for fiduciary responsibility Office of Solicitor, U.S. Dept. Labor, Washington, 1977-79; assoc. dir. div. investment mgmt. SEC, Washington, 1979-81, dir. div. investment mgmt., 1981-83; ptnr. Shereff, Friedman, Hoffman & Goodman, N.Y.C., 1983—. Mem. Fed. Bar Assn., ABA (com. on securities regulation). Democrat. Jewish. Securities. Home: 360 E 72nd St New York NY 10021

GOLDBERG, JONATHAN D., lawyer; b. Louisville, July 9, 1951. BA, Ind. U., 1973; JD, U. Louisville, 1976. Bar: Ky. 1976. Assoc. Goldberg & Simpson P.S.C., Louisville, 1976—. Mem. Ky. Bar Assn. Office: Goldberg & Simpson 2800 1st Nat Tower Louisville KY 40202

GOLDBERG, LEONARD M., lawyer; b. Jersey City, N.J., Mar. 21, 1937; s. Jack Geddy and Ida Reva (Steinberg) G.; m. Susan Lee Horstein, Aug. 7, 1960; children—Mark Jay, Philip Seth. A.B. magna cum laude, Tufts U., 1957; J.D. magna cum laude, Harvard U., 1960. Bar: N.J. 1960, N.Y. 1966, U.S. Tax Ct. 1964. Trial atty. tax div. Dept. Justice, Washington, 1960-64; assoc. Roberts & Holland, N.Y.C., 1964-70; ptnr. Clapp & Eisenberg, Newark, N.J., 1970-79; sr. ptnr. Goldberg, Mufson & Spar (formerly Goldberg & Stark), West Orange, N.J., 1979—; lectr. Practicing Law Inst., N.J. Inst. Continuing Legal Edn., Fairleigh Dickinson U. Tax Inst., Seton Hall U. Tax Inst., Estate Planning Councils; N.J. del. to lawyers' liaison com. Mid-Atlantic region IRS, 1973-76. Chmn. West Orange public edn. com., 1976-77, mem. Am. Jewish Com. Fellow Am. Coll. Probate Counsel; mem. ABA, N.J. Bar Assn. (chmn. taxation sect. 1973-75), N.Y. State Bar Assn., Essex County Bar Assn., Estate Planning Council No. N.J., Internat. Assn. Jewish Lawyers and Jurists. Contbr. articles to profl. jours. Taxation, General corporate, Probate. Home: 6 Huntington Rd Livingston NJ 07039 Office: 200 Executive Dr West Orange NJ 07052

GOLDBERG, NEIL A., lawyer; b. N.Y.C., Dec. 24, 1947; s. Bernard G.; m. Susan C. Ginsberg; children: Jane Hana, Robert Saul. BA cum laude, SUNY, Stony Brook, 1967; JD cum laude, SUNY, Buffalo, 1973. Bar: N.Y. 1974, U.S. Dist. Ct. (we. dist.) N.Y. 1974. St. ptnr. Saperston & Day P.C., Buffalo, also bd. dirs. Contbr. articles to profl. jours. Mem. ABA, N.Y. State Bar Assn. (co-editor in chief Trying a Civil Suit 1987, chmn. product liability com. ins. negligence compensation law sect. 1986—), Erie County Bar Assn., Internat. Assn. Def. Counsel, Def. Research Inst., Am. Arbitration Assn. (bd. dirs. 1985—). State civil litigation, Insurance, Personal injury. Home: 93 Morris Ave Buffalo NY 14214 Office: Saperston & Day PC One Fountain Plaza Goldome Ctr Buffalo NY 14203-1486

GOLDBERG, PAUL JOSEPH, lawyer; b. N.Y.C., July 18, 1937; s. Simon and Grace (Feder) G.; m. Susan M. Gutman, June 16, 1968; 1 son, Scott Barry. A.B., Brown U. 1959; LL.B., Columbia U., 1962. Bar: N.Y. 1963, U.S. Dist. Ct. (so. and ea. dists.) N.Y. 1964, U.S. Tax Ct. 1964, U.S. Ct. Appeals (2d cir.) 1964, U.S. Ct. Appeals (9th cir.) 1985. Assoc. Chester C. Davis, N.Y.C., 1962-68; ptnr. Davis & Cox, N.Y.C., 1968-71, Lea, Goldberg & Spellun, P.C., N.Y.C., 1971-77, Kissam, Halpin & Genovese, N.Y.C., 1977-84, Golenbock and Barell, 1985—; mem. departmental disciplinary com. 1st Jud. Dept. 1979-81, chmn. hearing panel 1980-81. Mem. ABA (com. on depreciation and investment tax credit tax sect.), N.Y. State Bar Assn. (com. on continuing legal edn.). Corporate taxation, Estate taxation, General corporate. Home: 28 W Horseshoe Dr East Hills NY 11577 Office: 645 5th Ave New York NY 10022

GOLDBERG, ROBERT M., lawyer; b. Chgo., Jan. 23, 1941; s. Arthur Joseph and Dorothy (Kurgans) G.; m. Barbara Sproston, Feb. 13, 1966; children—Esther Fiona, Angus Ephraim, Duncan Abraham. B.A. with honors, Amherst Coll., 1963; postgrad. London Sch. Econs., 1964; J.D., Harvard U., 1967. Bar: Alaska 1969, Ill. 1969, U.S. Ct. Appeals (9th cir.) 1973, U.S. Ct. Appeals D.C. Cir. 1978, U.S. Sup. Ct. 1978, D.C. 1979. Law clk. presiding justice U.S. Ct. Appeals for D.C., 1967-68; assoc. Kay, Miller & Libby, Anchorage, 1969-70; assoc. prof. law sea grant program U. Alaska, 1970-72, adj. prof., 1980—; ptnr. Goldberg & Elliott, Anchorage, 1976-78, Goldberg, Breckberg, & Gottstein, Anchorage, 1978-80, Goldberg & Gottstein, Anchorage, 1980-82, Robert M. Goldberg & Assocs., Anchorage, 1982—; adj. prof. law U. Denver, 1973-75; adj. prof. govt. and econs. Alaska Pacific U., Anchorage, 1970-73. Trustee, Alaska Pacific U., 1975—; del. Democratic Nat. Conv., 1974, 76; chmn. Alaska Assn. for Hist. Preservation, 1981-85. Recipient Best Non-Fiction Book award Alaska Press Club, 1970. Mem. ABA, Ill. State Bar Assn., D.C. Bar Assn., Alaska Bar Assn., Fed. Bar Assn., Am. Soc. Internat. Law. Jewish. Editor: Alaska Survey & Report, Vols. I and II, 1970-72. Civil rights, Labor, General corporate. Home: 1130 S St Anchorage AK 99501 Office: 1107 W 7th St Anchorage AK 99501

GOLDBERG, STANLEY ZELIG, lawyer, banker; b. Pitts., May 22, 1937; s. Emanuel and Jeannette C. (Rosenbloom) G.; m. Marlou Synder, June 15, 1960; children—Jennifer J., David C. A.B., U. Pitts., 1959; J.D., Harvard U., 1962; postgrad. U. Paris, 1962-63. Bar: Pa. 1964, U.S. Dist. Ct. (we. dist.) Pa. 1964, U.S. Supreme Ct. 1967. Ptnr., Markel, Markel, Levenson & Schafer, Pitts., 1964-76; v.p. Pitts. Nat. Bank, 1976—. Pres. bd. dirs. Craig House-Technoma Workshop, Pitts., 1979-81. Mem. Internat. Bar Assn., ABA, Pa. Bar Assn., Allegheny County Bar Assn., U. Pitts. Coll. Alumni Assn. (pres. 1980-81). Democrat. Unitarian. Private international. Home: 1869 Swallow Hill Rd Pittsburgh PA 15220 Office: Pitts Nat Bank Pitts Nat Bldg 5th Ave and Wood St Pittsburgh PA 15265

GOLDBERG, STEPHEN B., legal educator; b. 1932. A.B., Harvard U., 1954, LL.B., 1959; postgrad. London Sch. Econs., 1959-60. Bar: Calif. 1961, Ill. 1967. Teaching fellow Harvard U., 1960-61; supervisory atty. NLRB, Washington, 1961-65; assoc. prof. U. Ill. Law Sch., 1965-68, prof., 1968-73, assoc. Ctr. Advanced Study, 1969-70; prof. Northwestern U. Law Sch., Chgo., 1975—; vis. scholar Am. Bar Found., 1973-74. Spl. cons. to chmn. NLRB, 1965-67; spl. labor cons. to U.S. Senator Burdick of N.D., 1968-71; cons. Pres.'s Commn. on Coal, 1979. Author: (with Getman and Herman) Union Representation Elections: Law and Reality, 1976. Mem. Nat. Acad. Arbitrators. Legal education. Office: Northwestern U Law Sch 357 E Chicago Ave Chicago IL 60611 *

GOLDBERG, STEVEN CHARLES, lawyer; b. Newburgh, N.Y., Sept. 16, 1949; s. Paul Maurice Goldberg and Lila (Sturm) Flusfeder. BA in Polit. Sci., Rutgers U., 1971, JD, 1974. Bar: N.J. 1975, D.C. 1975, U.S. Supreme Ct. 1980, N.Y. 1981, Ohio 1986. Counsel to chmn. Occupational Safety and Health Rev. Commn., Washington, 1974-76; dep. asst. chief hearing counsel Nuclear Regulatory Commn., Washington, 1976-83; sr. assoc. Newman & Holtzinger, Washington, 1983-85; asst. gen. counsel Battelle Project Mgmt. Div., Columbus, Ohio, 1985—. Mem. D.C. Bar Assn., Ohio Bar Assn. Jewish. Avocations: tennis, travel, film, art. Nuclear power, Environment, Transportation. Home: 136 Antelope Way #2B Worthington OH 43185 Office: Battelle Project Mgmt Div 505 King Ave Columbus OH 43201

GOLDBERG, VICTOR PAUL, law educator; b. 1941. BA, Oberlin (Ohio) Coll., 1963, MA, 1964; PhD, Yale U., 1970. From asst. to full prof. U. Calif., Davis, 1967-83; prof. Northwestern U., Evanston, Ill., 1983—; assoc. prof. U. Calif., Berkeley, 1977; prof. U. Va., Charlottesville, 1981; mem. Inst. for Advanced Studey, Princeton, N.J., 1978-79. Fellow Ctr. for Study of Pub. Choice, Blacksburg, Va., 1975-76. Office: Northwestern U Sch Law 357 E Chicago Ave Chicago IL 60611 *

GOLDBERG, WILLIAM JEFFREY, accountant; b. Chgo., Jan. 18, 1950; s. Harry and Bernice Dorothy (Benson) G. m. Brenda Liebling; children—Leslie Claire, Hollis Melissa. B.A., Knox Coll., 1971; J.D., Cornell U., 1974; postgrad. U. Chgo., 1976-78. Bar: Ill. 1974, U.S. Dist. Ct. (no. dist.) Ill. 1974. Fin. counseling officer Continental Ill. Nat. Bank, Chgo., 1974-79; supr. Peat Marwick Mitchell & Co., Houston, 1979-80, mgr., 1980-82, ptnr., 1982—; nat. dir. Personal Fin. Planning Services, 1984—; instr. law Ill. Inst. Tech. Chgo. Kent Coll. Law, 1977-78. Chmn. deferred giving Mus. Fine Arts, Houston, 1984—; com. chmn. United Jewish Campaign, 1984; trustee Jewish Fedn. of Greater Houston, 1985—. Mem. Am. Inst. C.P.A.s (personal fin. planning div., exec. com.), Tex. Soc. C.P.A.s, Houston Estate and Fin. Forum, Houston Bus. and Estate Planning Council, Knox Coll. Club Houston (pres. 1981-82). Clubs: Plaza (gov. 1984-86), Westwood Country. Personal income taxation, Estate taxation, Estate planning. Office: Peat Marwick Mitchell & Co PO Box 4545 Houston TX 77210

GOLDBERGER, ALAN STEVEN, lawyer; b. Newark, Jan. 31, 1949; s. Milton Howard and Miriam (Kaplan) G.; m. Carole Selikowitz, Oct. 13, 1985. AB, Franklin and Marshall Coll., 1971; JD, Rutgers U., 1974. Bar: N.J. 1975, U.S. Dist. Ct. N.J. 1975, N.Y. 1985. Ptnr. Goldberger & Goldberger, Clifton, N.J., 1975—. Author: Sports Officiating: A Legal Guide, 1984. Mem. ABA, N.J. Bar Assn., N.Y. Bar Assn., Internat. Assn. Approved Basketball Ofcls. Jewish. Avocations: officiating basketball, baseball and football. Consumer commercial, Insurance, Sports law. Home: 123 Grove St Clifton NJ 07013 Office: Goldberger & Goldberger 1373 Broad St PO Box 447 Clifton NJ 07015

GOLD-BIKIN, LYNNE Z., lawyer; b. N.Y.C., Apr. 23, 1938; d. Herbert Benjamin Zapoleon and Muriel Claire (Wimpheimer) Sarnoff; m. Roy E. Gold, Aug. 20, 1956 (div. July 1976); children—Russell, Sheryl, Lisa, Michael. B.A. summa cum laude, Albright Coll., 1969-73; J.D., Villanova Law Sch., 1973-76. Bar: Pa. 1976, U.S. Dist. Ct. (ea. dist.) Pa. 1976, U.S. Supreme Ct. 1979. Assoc. Pechner, Dorfman, Wolffe, Rounick & Cabot, Norristown, Pa., 1976-81; ptnr. Olin, Neil, Frock & Gold-Bikin, Norristown, 1981-82; pres. Gold-Bikin Devlin & Assocs., Norristown, 1982—. Author: Pennsylvania Marital Agreements, 1984; course planner for 12 manuals on continuing legal edn., 1978—. Mem. Albright Coll. Pres.'s Council, Reading, Pa., 1982—. Fellow Am. Acad. Matrimonial Lawyers; mem. ABA (family law sect. council mem. 1981—), Pa. Bar Assn. (family law sect. council mem. 1980—), Montgomery County Bar Assn. (chmn. family law com. 1984-86). Family and matrimonial. Home: 307 Hughes Rd King of Prussia PA 19406 Office: Gold-Bikin Devlin & Assocs One Montgomery Plaza Norristown PA 19401

GOLDBLATT, MICHAEL L., lawyer; b. New Orleans, Apr. 22, 1949; s. Bernard and Recille (Miller) G.; m. Ann Lynn Goldberg, July 7, 1970; children: Brian, Scott, Kevin, Justin, Tracy. AB, Washington U., St. Louis, 1970; JD, Tulane U., 1974. Bar: La. 1974, Tenn. 1984. Assoc. Deutsch, Kerrigan & Stiles, New Orleans, 1974-76; assoc. gen. counsel Tidewater Inc., New Orleans, 1976—; bd. advisors Am. Inst. for Law Training in Office, Phila., 1986. Editor: Management for In-House Counsel, 1985. Mem. ABA (com. chmn.), Am. Corp. Counsel Assn. (bd. dirs. 1986), Am. Soc. Corp. Secs. Securities, General corporate. Home: 4709 Folse Dr Metairie LA 70006 Office: Tidewater Inc 1440 Canal St New Orleans LA 70112

GOLDBLUM, A. PAUL, lawyer; b. N.Y.C., July 26, 1925; s. Meyer and Rebecca (Glassman) G.; m. Chantal Mona Laurent, Sept. 2, 1951. B.S. cum laude, Harvard U., 1947, LL.B., 1950. Bar: N.Y. 1951, U.S. Dist. Ct. (ea. and so. dists.) 1952, U.S. Ct. Appeals (2d cir.) 1973. Trial atty. Liberty Mutual Ins. Co., N.Y.C., 1950-55, sr. trial atty., 1962-76, N.Y. div. gen. atty., appellate counsel, 1977—; ptnr. Dent, Goldblum & Witschieben, N.Y.C., 1956-62. Chmn. law com. N.Y. Com. for Dem. Voters, 1956-60, 2d and 11th Jud. Dists. grievance com., 1974-82; bd. dirs. Greater Jamaica Devel. Corp., 1981—; vice chmn. adv. bd. Paralegal Inst. Queens Coll., 1980—; mem. exec. com. Flushing Meadows-Corona Park Corp., 1987—. Served to lt. (j.g.) USN, 1943-46, PTO. Fellow N.Y. Bar Found.; mem. Queens County Bar Assn. (pres. 1979-80, chmn. com. profl. ethics 1984—), N.Y. State Bar Assn. (del. 1981-87, v.p. 11th Jud. Dist. 1987—, chmn. Com. on Profl. Discipline 1978-81, vice chmn. Com. to Improve Ct. Facilities 1983—), Assn. of Bar of City of N.Y. Club: Harvard (N.Y.C.); Huguenot Yacht (New Rochelle, N.Y.). State civil litigation, Personal injury, Professional Responsibility. Home: 34-21 80th St Jackson Heights NY 11372

GOLDBRENNER, RONALD STEVEN, lawyer; b. Bronx, N.Y., Apr. 2, 1942; s. Harold and Fannie (Cohen) G.;m. Ellen Georgia Rattner, Mar. 20, 1965; children: David H., Rachel A. BA, CUNY, 1962; LLB, NYU, 1965, LLM, 1968. Bar: N.Y. 1966. Assoc. Zelby & Bustein, Esq., N.Y.C., 1965-66; with Schering-Plough Corp., Kenilworth, N.J., 1967-74; assoc. gen. counsel Lorillard, Inc., N.Y.C., 1974—. Pres. NYU Bus. Forum; bd. dirs. City Coll. Fund. Mem. ABA, Assn. of Bar of City of N.Y., N.Y.C. Bar Assn., Am. Corp. Counsel Assn., NYU Alumni Assn. (bd. dirs. grad. sch.). Contracts commercial, Administrative and regulatory, Trademark and copyright. Office: Lorillard Inc 666 Fifth Ave New York City NY 10103

GOLDEN, ALVIN JOSEPH, lawyer; b. Dallas, Oct. 30, 1940; s. Saul H. and Helen Frances (Hafter) G.; m. Mary Ann Geisler, Feb. 5, 1966; children: Phillip Travis, Pamela Elaine. Student So. Meth. U., 1958-60; BBA with honors, U. Tex., 1962, LLB, 1965. Bar: Tex. 1965, U.S. Dist Ct. (we. dist.) Tex. 1973, U.S. Ct. Claims 1979, U.S. Tax Ct. 1970; cert. estate planning and probate law, Tex. Bd. Legal Specialization. House counsel, comptroller Sta. KXYZ, Houston, 1965-66; assoc. William B. Hilgers, Austin 1966, 68-71; ptnr. Hilgers, Daugherty, Fielder, Golden & Kuperman, Austin, 1971-74, Daugherty, Kuperman, Golden & Morehead, P.C., 1974—. Bd. dirs. Tex. Assembly of Arts Council, 1978-84, pres., 1979-81; bd. dirs. Paramount Theatre, 1980—, pres., 1985-87. Served with U.S. Army, 1966-68. Decorated Commendation medal. Mem. ABA, Tex. Bar Assn. (council real property probate and trust sect.), Am. Coll. Probate Counsel. Jewish. Probate, Real property, General corporate. Office: Daugherty Kuperman Golden & Morehead MBank Tower Suite 1500 Austin TX 78701

GOLDEN, BRUCE PAUL, lawyer; b. Chgo., Dec. 4, 1943; s. Irving R. and Anne K. (Eisenberg) G. S.B. in Elec. Sci. and Engring., MIT, 1965, S.M. in Elec. Engring., 1966; J.D., Harvard U., 1969. Bar: Ill. 1969, U.S. Dict. Ct. (no. dist.) Ill. 1970. Assoc. McDermott, Will & Emery, Chgo., 1970-75, ptnr., 1976—; officer, dir. various corps.; speaker bank law, securities law, venture capital seminars. Contbr. articles to Banking Law Jour., contbg. editor, 1979—. Chmn. MIT Enterprise Forum Chgo.; bd. dirs. Entrepreneurship Inst. Chgo., Chgo. chpt. U.S. Entrepreneurs Network, Ill. Small Bus. Devel. Ctr. Clubs: MIT Alumni of Chgo., Union League (Chgo.). Banking, Securities. Home: 2800 N Lakeshore Dr Chicago IL 60657 Office: 111 W Monroe St Chicago IL 60603

GOLDEN, CHRISTOPHER ANTHONY, lawyer; b. N.Y.C., Sept. 24, 1937; s. Christopher A. and Helen (Foley) G.; m. Maureen A. Fitzpatrick, May 30, 1964; children: Colleen, Laureen. BA, St. John's Coll., Jamaica, N.Y., 1955; LLB, St. John's U., Jamaica, N.Y., 1967; M.B.A., St. John's U., 1977. Bar: N.Y. 1967, U.S. Dist. Ct. (so. and ea. dists.) N.Y. 1969, U.S. Ct. Appeals (2d cir.) 1969, U.S. Supreme Ct. 1974, U.S. Ct. Appeals (D.C. cir.) 1982. Mem. firm Flood, Conway, Walsh, Stahl & Farrell, N.Y.C., 1964-77; asst. gen. counsel Dry Dock Savs. Bank, N.Y.C., 1977-82; ptnr. Golden, Upton & Wexler P.C., Lynbrook, N.Y., 1982—; trustee Dry Dock Savs. Bank, 1982-83. Served with U.S. Army, 1960-61. Mem. ABA, N.Y. State Bar Assn., Coll. Mortgage Attys., Nat. Mortgage Inst. (trustee 1986—). Banking, Real property. Office: Golden Upton & Wexler PC 300 Merrick Rd 2d Floor Lynbrook NY 11563

GOLDEN, DANIEL LEWIS, lawyer; b. N.Y.C., May 7, 1913; s. Louis and Rose (Rosen) G.; m. Evelyn Shayevitz, July 9, 1941 (dec.); children—Roger M., Leslie Rosemary. B.S., Lafayette Coll., 1934; J.D., Rutgers U., 1938. Bar: N.J. 1939, D.C. 1976, U.S. Supreme Ct. 1957. Practice, South River, 1940—; mem. Golden, Shore, Zahn; co counsel, dir. United Jersey Bank/Mid State, Mt. Holly Water Co.; active survey legal systems USSR, East Europe for State Dept. Exchanges Programs, also for ABA, N.J. Bar Assn., 1961-75. Chmn. Middlesex County Ethics Com., 1967; mem. N.J. Gov.'s Commn. on Individual Liberty and Personal Privacy, 1977-84; chmn. lawyers sect. March of Dimes, 1961-81 ; trustee Lafayette Coll., 1975-80. Served to lt. USAAF, 1942-45. Recipient Kidd hon. citation for law Lafayette Coll., 1970, Rutgers Law award, 1971, Edison council award Boy Scouts Am. Fellow Am. Bar Found. (state chmn. 1986—), Am. Acad. Matrimonial Lawyers (bd. govs., counsel N.J. chpt. 1981—); mem. ABA (ho. of dels. 1972—, chmn. adv. commn. on election law and voter participation 1980-84), N.J. Bar Assn. (pres. 1970-71, editorial bd. jour. 1969—), Middlesex County Bar Assn. (pres. 1960-61, award 1961), Assn. Trial Lawyers Am., Trial Attys. N.J. (trustee 1969—, award 1986), Am. Judicature Soc., Pi Lambda Phi. Contbr. articles to profl. jours. General practice, Family and matrimonial. Office: 141 Main St South River NJ 08882

GOLDEN, DONALD ALAN, lawyer; b. Olean, N.Y., Aug. 31, 1953; s. Clayton Alexander and Dorothea Ann (Pfeil) G.; m. Patricia Ann Podgorniak, June 15, 1976 (div. Dec. 1981); m. Carol Anne Metz, Jan. 1, 1982; 1 child, Allyson Michelle. BS, SUNY, Brockport, 1975; JD, U. Miami, 1978. Bar: Fla. 1979. Asst. counsel Am. Title Ins. Co., Miami, Fla., 1980; assoc. corp. counsel Burger King Corp., Miami, 1980-82; ho. counsel Senior Corp., Miami Beach, Fla., 1982-86; assoc. Blackwell, Walker, Fascell & Hoehl, Miami, 1986—. Mem. ABA, Fla. Bar Assn., Am. Corp. Counsel Assn., Corp. Counsel Assn. of South Fla. Avocation: golf. Contracts commercial, General corporate, Real property. Home: 22043 SW 103d Ave Miami FL 33189 Office: Blackwell Walker Fascell & Hoehl 1 SE 3d Ave Miami FL 33131

GOLDEN, E(DWARD) SCOTT, lawyer; b. Miami, Fla., Sept. 25, 1955; s. Alvan Leonard and Fay Betty (Gray) G.; m. Jane Eileen DeKlavon, June 9, 1979; children: Daniel Bryan, Kimberly Michelle. Student, So. Fla. Christian Coll., 1975-76; BS, MIT, 1978; JD, Harvard U., 1981. Bar: Fla. 1981, U.S. Dist. Ct. (so. dist.) Fla. 1982, U.S. Tax. Ct. 1982. Assoc. Roberts and Holland, Miami, 1981-82, Valdes-Fauli, Richardson, Cobb & Petrey, P.A., Miami, 1982-83; v.p., shareholder Buck and Golden, P.A., Ft. Lauderdale, Fla., 1983—. Editor in chief Harvard Jour. of Law and Pub. Policy, 1980-81; contbr. articles to profl. jours. Chmn. deacons West Lauderdale Bapt. Ch., Broward County, Fla., 1984-86, tchr., 1983—, legal cons., 1983—; del. Fla. Rep. Grassroots Conv., Kissimmee, 1986; mem. Rep. Exec. Com., Broward County, 1984—; legal cons. Organizational Model for Elimination of Genocide in Am., Ft. Lauderdale, 1983—. Grantee Western Electric, 1972-74. Mem. ABA, Broward County Bar Assn., Christian Lawyers Assn. (pres. 1985-86), Christian Legal Soc., Order of Silver Knight, Zeta Beta Tau. Lodge: Optimists (treas. Dade County Carol City High Sch., 1971-72). Avocations: sports, politics, Bible study. General corporate, Real property, Securities. Home: 5410 Buchanan St Hollywood FL 33021 Office: Buck and Golden PA 499 NW 70th Ave Suite 220 Fort Lauderdale FL 33317

GOLDEN, GREGG HANNAN STEWART, lawyer; b. N.Y.C., Nov. 24, 1953; s. Edmond Jerome and Alvia Grace (Weinberger) G. AB with honors, Grinnell Coll., 1975; JD cum laude, Georgetown U., 1980. Bar: Pa. 1980, U.S. Dist. Ct. (mid. dist.) Pa. 1980, U.S. Ct. Appeals (3d and D.C. cirs.) 1981, Calif. 1982, N.J. 1983, D.C. 1984, U.S. Supreme Ct. 1984. Dep. atty. gen. State of Pa., Harrisburg, 1980-83; assoc. Hogan & Hartson, Washington, 1983-86; atty. Fed. Home Loan Bank Bd., Washington, 1986—; mem. div. IV com. on ct. rules, representation for needy civil litigants, D.C. Bar; trustee, sec. InterFuture, N.Y.C., 1979—. Fellow Johnson Found., 1972, Thomas J. Watson Found., 1975. Democrat. Jewish. Club: Nat. Lawyers (Washington). Federal civil litigation, Administrative and regulatory, Banking. Office: Fed Home Loan Bank Bd Office of Enforcement 1700 G St NW STOP 9-1 Washington DC 20552

GOLDEN, H. BRUCE, lawyer; b. Columbus, Ohio, Sept. 14, 1949; s. Louis H. and Rose (Breman) G.; m. 1 child, Blakely Anne. AB, Ind. U., 1971; JD, Emory U., 1974. Bar: Tex. 1974, U.S. Dist. Ct. (so. dist.) Tex. 1975, U.S. Ct. Appeals (5th cir.) 1976, U.S. Supreme Ct. 1978, U.S. Ct. Appeals (11th cir.) 1980, U.S. Dist. Ct. (no. dist.) Tex. 1986. Assoc. Bracewell & Patterson, Houston, 1974-80, ptnr., 1980-83; ptnr. Childs, Fortenbach, Beck & Guyton, Houston, 1983-84, Mayer, Brown & Platt, Houston, 1984—. Mem. ABA, Tex. Bar Assn., Houston Bar Assn., Order of Barristers, Phi Delta Phi. Federal civil litigation, State civil litigation. Home: 5000 Montrose Blvd

#13H Houston TX 77006 Office: Mayer Brown & Platt 700 Louisiana St Suite 3600 Houston TX 77002

GOLDEN, JOSEPH AARON, lawyer; b. Detroit, MI, Oct. 27, 1940; s. Milton and Sally (Schweitzer) G.; m. Frances Miriam Rubenstein, Aug. 16, 1965 (div. Apr. 1973); children: Manine Rosa, Jay Dylan, Nicholas Michael, Estuardo Golden; m. Cynthia Ann Sisson, June 24, 1979. BBA, Wayne State U., 1962; JD, U. Detroit, 1967. Bar: Mich. 1968, U.S. Ct. Appeals (6th cir.) 1974. Supervising atty. Wayne County Neighborhood Legal Services, Ecorse, Mich., 1968-70; ptnr. Craig, Fieger & Golden, Southfield, Mich., 1970-73, Fieger, Golden & Cousens, Southfield, 1973-78; sole practice Southfield, 1978-85; assoc. Sommers, Schwartz, Silver & Schwartz, Southfield, 1985—; adj. prof. labor law U. Detroit, 1987—. Co-author: Wrongful Termination Litigation in Mich., 1986; contbrg. author: Employee Dismissal Law: Forms and Procedures, 1986. Mem. ABA (pub. co-chmn. employee rights and responsibilities com.), Assn. Trial Lawyers Am., Mich. Trial Lawyers Assn., Plaintiff Employment Lawyers Assn. (nat. exec. bd. 1984—). Civil rights, Labor, Wrongful discharge. Office: Sommers Schwartz Silver & Schwartz 26555 Evergreen Rd Suite 1800 Southfield MI 48076

GOLDEN, LAWRENCE JAMES, lawyer; b. Norwalk, Conn., Feb. 9, 1947; s. Malcolm Harris and Jean Annabelle (Pohs) G.; m. Paula Marie Konon, May 17, 1986; 1 child, Matthew. BA, U. Va., 1969, JD, 1973. Bar: Conn. 1973. Research dir. Nat. Legal Research Group, Charlottesville, Va., 1973-84; assoc. Byrne, Slater, Sandler, Shulman & Rouse, Hartford, Conn., 1985—. Author: Equitable Distribution of Property, 1983; mem. editorial bd. Equitable Distbn. Jour., 1984—. Mem. ABA, Conn. Bar Assn., Hartford County Bar Assn. Public utilities, FERC practice. Home: 330 Main St Norwich CT 06360 Office: Byrne Slater et al 111 Pearl St Hartford CT 06103

GOLDEN, MARC ALAN, investment banker; b. Phila., Dec. 26, 1953; s. Mano Robert and Sue E. (Aronsohn) G. B.A., Yale Coll., 1975; M.B.A., J.D., Harvard U., 1980. Bar: N.Y. 1981, U.S. Dist. Ct. (so. and ea. dists.) N.Y. 1984, U.S. Supreme Ct. 1985. Legis. asst. U.S. Senator Richard Stone (Fla.), Washington, 1975; legis. aide, issues analyst U.S. Rep. William Green (Pa.), Washington, 1975-76; legis. counsel U.S. Senate Com. on Vets. Affairs, Washington, 1976; asst. to dep. dir. Fed. Jud. Ctr., Washington, 1978; assoc. Cravath, Swaine & Moore, N.Y.C., 1981-86; v.p. Goldman, Sachs & Co., N.Y.C., 1986—. Active N.Y. chpt. Lawyers' Alliance for Nuclear Arms Control, 1983—. Mem. ABA, N.Y. State Bar Assn., Assn. Bar City N.Y. Office: Goldman Sachs & Co 85 Broad St New York NY 10004

GOLDEN, MICHAEL PATRICK, lawyer; b. San Diego, Oct. 3, 1946; s. Thomas Parnell and Jane Marcella (Collins) G. BS in Bus. Adminstrn., Creighton U., 1971, MBA, 1974; JD, Calif. Western Sch. Law, 1977. Bar: Nev. 1979, U.S. Dist. Ct. Nev. 1980. Sole practice Reno, Nev., 1979-84; dep. city atty. Sparks, Nev., 1984; dep. dist. atty. Nye County, Tonopah and Pahrump, Nev., 1984-85; adminstrv. law judge State of Nev., Las Vegas, 1985—; instr. Clark County Community Coll., Pahrump, 1984-85; bd. dirs. Nev. Indian and Rural Legal Services, Reno, 1979-87. Mem. ABA, Nev. Bar Assn., Assn. Trial Lawyers Am. Club: Mission Bay Yacht (San Diego). Avocations: sailing, golfing, swimming. Administrative and regulatory, Bankruptcy, Family and matrimonial. Home: 4114 Yakima Ave Las Vegas NV 89121 Office: Nev Dept Adminstrn 2770 S Maryland Pkwy #102 Las Vegas NV 89102

GOLDEN, THOMAS FULLER, lawyer; b. New Orleans, May 24, 1942; s. Albert Courter and Thelma Loyce (Fuller) G.; m. Beverly Bost, Feb. 15, 1944; children: Dathel Elizabeth, Laura LeAnne, Julianne Candice. BA in Econs., Okla. State U., 1965; JD, Tulsa U., 1968. Bar: Okla. 1968, U.S. Supreme Ct. 1972. Ptnr. Hall, Estill, Hardwick, Gable, Callingsworth & Nelson, Tulsa, 1971—; gen. counsel Williams Bros. Overseas Co. Ltd., Toronto, Ont., Can., 1971-75; gen. counsel Williams Realty Corp., Tulsa, 1973—, River Ctr. Assoc., San Antonio, Tex., 1984—; gen. counsel Arctic Constructors, Fairbanks, Alaska, 1974-79; mem. U.S. Jud. Nominating Commn., Okla., 1980—. Pres. Tulsa Boys Home, 1980-82; bd. dirs. United Way, Tulsa, 1980-82; chmn. elect Downtown Tulsa, Unltd., 1987—. Recipient Okla. Gov. award, 1982. Republican. Methodist. Clubs: Pensacola Country (Fla.); Tulsa, Southern Hills Country (Tulsa). Mng. editor: Tulsa Law Jour., 1967-68. Real property, General corporate, Contracts commercial. Home: 2826 E 48th St Tulsa OK 74105 Office: 4100 Bank of Oklahoma Tower Tulsa OK 74172

GOLDEN, WILSON, lawyer; b. Holly Springs, Miss., Feb. 15, 1948; s. Woodrow Wilson and Constance Annette (Harris) G.; m. Pamela Wells; children: Wilson Harris, Lewis Hamilton. BPA, U. Miss., 1970, JD, 1977. Bar: Miss. 1977, U.S. Dist. Ct. (no. and so. dists.) Miss. 1977, U.S. Ct. Appeals (5th cir.) 1977,. Pub. affairs journalist Miss. authority for Ednl. TV, Jackson, 1970-72; asst. sec. Miss. State Senate, Jackson, 1972-76; assoc. Lane & Henderson, Greenville, Miss., 1977-80; ptnr. Watkins Ludlam & Stennis, Jackson, 1980—. Mem. Dem. State Exec. Com., 1976-84, Gov.'s Constl. Study Commn., 1985-86. Served to maj. USAR, 1970—. Recipient Disting. Reporting award Am. Polit. Sci. Assn. 1971, U.S. Law Week award Bur. Nat. Affairs, Inc., Washington, 1978. Mem. ABA, Miss. Bar Assn. (chmn. legis. com. 1984-86), Hinds County Bar Assn., Nat. Assn. Bond Lawyers. Democrat. Presbyterian. Lodge: Kiwanis (bd. dirs. Greenville 1978-80). Municipal bonds, Local government, Legislative. Home: 715 Arlington St Jackson MS 39202 Office: Watkins Ludlam & Stennis 633 N State St Jackson MS 39202

GOLDENHERSH, JOSEPH HERMAN, justice state supreme court; b. East St. Louis, Ill., Nov. 2, 1914; s. Benjamin and Bertha (Goldenberg) G.; m. Maxyne Zelenka, June 18, 1939; children: Richard, Jerold. LL.B., Washington U., St. Louis, 1935; LL.D. (hon.), John Marshall Law Sch., Chgo., 1972. Bar: Ill. 1936. Pvt. practice law East St. Louis, 1936-64; judge Appellate Ct. Ill., 1964-70; justice Supreme Ct. Ill., 1970-78, 82—, chief justice, 1979-82. Chmn. Initial Gifts United Fund East St. Louis, 1952-53; dir. Mississippi Valley council Boy Scouts Am., 1952-58; pres. Jewish Fedn. So. Ill., 1949-51; Trustee emeritus Christian Welfare Hosp., East St. Louis. Recipient Disting. Alumnus award Washington U. Law Sch., St. Louis, 1985. Mem. Appellate Judges Conf. (exec. com. 1969-70), East St. Louis Bar Assn. (pres. 1962-63), ABA, Ill. Bar Assn. Clubs: Mason (St. Louis) (33 deg., Shriner), Missouri Athletic (St. Louis). Home: 7510 Claymont Ct Belleville IL 62223 Office: Supreme Court Office 6464 W Main St Suite 3A Belleville IL 62223 *

GOLDENHERSH, MURRAY JACOB, lawyer; b. St. Louis, May 2, 1953; s. Marvin W. and Tamar T. (Altman) G.; m. Lisa Ruth Dordek, July 2, 1978; children: Benjamin F., Isaiah M., Pearl S., Louis E. BA, Northwestern U., 1976; MS in Acctg., Roosevelt U., 1979; JD, UCLA, 1982. Bar: Calif. 1982, Ill. 1983, U.S. Dist. Ct. (no. dist.) Calif. 1983, Mo. 1984, U.S. Dist. Ct. (ea. dist.) Mo. 1984, U.S. Dist. Ct. (so. dist.) Ill. 1984; CPA, Ill.; ordained rabbi, 1979. Assoc. Irell & Manella, Los Angeles, 1982-84; ptnr. Goldenhersh & Goldenhersh, Belleville, Ill., 1984—. Lectr. on Talmud Young Israel Synagogue, St. Louis, 1984—. Mem. ABA, St. Clair County Bar Assn., Bar Assn. Met. St. Louis, Assn. Trial Lawyers Am., Ill. Trial Lawyers Assn., Order of Coif. Democrat. Avocations: Talmudic studies, tennis. Personal injury, Workers' compensation. Home: 8157 Stanford Ct Saint Louis MO 63130 Office: Goldenhersh & Goldenhersh 6464 W Main St Belleville IL 62223

GOLDER, FREDERICK THOMAS, lawyer, educator; b. Brookline, Mass., July 5, 1943; s. Michael and Ida Shirley (Gropman) G.; Caron Sue Cohen, Oct. 8, 1966; children: Rachel Beth, David Ross, Naomi Lea. BA in English, U. Mass., 1965; JD, Suffolk Sch. Law, 1968; spl. student, Harvard U., 1968; LLM in Labor, NYU, 1969. Bar: Mass. 1968, U.S. Dist. Ct. Mass. 1969, U.S. Ct. Appeals (1st cir.) 1970, U.S. Supreme Ct. 1972. Ptnr. Golder & Shubow, P.A., Boston, 1968—; adj. faculty Northeastern U., Boston, 1972—; writer Callaghan & Co., Wilmette, Ill., 1982—. Author: Fair Employment Law, 1979, Wage and Hour Law, 1983, Health, Safety, etc., 1984, Legal Compliance Checkups: Business Clients, 1985, Labor and Employment Law: Compliance and Litigation, 1986. Legal counsel Rep. Comm. Peabody, Mass., 1972-75, Lynnfield, Mass., 1976—; commr. Lynnfield Soccer Assn., 1980—. Recipient Disting. Service award Harbor Area Community Devel., 1974. Fellow Mass. Bar Found.; mem. Fed. Bar Assn. (disting. service award 1984), Mass. Bar Assn., Assn. Trial Lawyers Am., Mass. Acad. Trial Attys. (disting. faculty award 1984, 86), Plaintiff Employment Lawyers Assn. (bd. dirs. 1986—). Avocations: reading, writing, tennis, basketball, photography. Labor, Civil rights, Federal civil litigation. Office: Golder & Shubow PA 59 Temple Pl Boston MA 02111

GOLDFARB, ALEXANDER A., b. Hartford, Conn., Oct. 27, 1925; s. Max and Bella (Kaplan) G. B.S., Trinity Coll., 1946; LL.B., Cornell U., 1949; postgrad. Yale U., 1950-51. Bar: Conn. 1949, U.S. Tax Ct. 1952, U.S. Supreme Ct. 1959, U.S. Ct. Appeals (2nd cir.) 1980. Instr. U. Nebr., 1949-50; counsel Democratic State Central Com., 1954-80, Greater Hartford Flood Commn., Conn., 1956-72; sole practice, Hartford; counsel credentials com. Dem. Nat. Conv., 1980; asst. corp. counsel City of Hartford, 1953-55, corp. counsel, 1972-76, 80-82. Mem. Wadsworth Atheneum, 1951—. Served with AUS, 1944. Mem. Pi Gamma Mu. Clubs: Yale, Cornell, Trinity, University (Hartford). General practice, Local government, Personal injury. Home: 73 Pearl St Middletown CT 06457 Office: Bushnell II Hartford CT 06103

GOLDFARB, BERNARD SANFORD, lawyer; b. Cleve., Apr. 15, 1917; s. Harry and Esther (Lenson) G.; m. Barbara Brofman, Jan. 4, 1966; children—Meredith Stacey, Lauren Beth. A.B., Case Western Res. U., 1938, J.D., 1940. Bar: Ohio bar 1940. Since practiced in Cleve.; sr. partner firm Goldfarb & Reznick, 1967—; spl. counsel to atty. gen. Ohio, 1950, 71-74; mem. Ohio Commn. Uniform Traffic Rules, 1973—. Contbr. legal jours. Served with USAAF, 1942-45. Mem. Am., Ohio, Greater Cleve. bar assns. General practice, Federal civil litigation, Labor. Home: 39 Pepper Creek Dr Pepper Pike OH 44124 Office: 1800 Illuminating Bldg Cleveland OH 44113

GOLDFARB, PHYLLIS, law educator; b. Sandusky, Ohio, Dec. 9, 1955; s. Charles Lewis and Jean Ann (Abram) G. BA, Brandeis U., 1978; EdM, Harvard U., 1979; JD, Yale U., 1982; LLM, Georgetown U., 1985. Bar: D.C. 1982, U.S. Ct. Appeals, U.S. Dist Ct. (D.C.). Asst. prof. No. Ill. U. Coll. Law, DeKalb, 1984-86, Boston Coll. Law Sch., Newton, Mass., 1986—; vis. prof. Georgetown U. Law Ctr., Washington, 1985; mem. adv. bd. women's studies program No. Ill. U., DeKalb, 1985-86. E. Barrett Prettyman fellow Georgetown U. Law Ctr., 1982-84. Mem. ABA (criminal justice sect., def. services subcommittee), Nat. Legal Aid and Defender Assn. (def. counsel competency com.). Legal education, Criminal, Jurisprudence. Home: 4 Chiswick Rd #2 Brookline MA 02146 Office: Boston Coll Law Sch 885 Centre St Newton MA 02159

GOLDFARB, RONALD CARL, lawyer; b. Bklyn., Apr. 20, 1947; s. Abe and Minnie (Sowalsky) G.; m. Marianne Kelleher, Apr. 10, 1983; 1 child, Rachel. B.A., Richmond Coll., 1971; J.D., New York Law Sch., 1975. Bar: N.Y. 1976, U.S. Dist. Cts. (so. and ea. dists.) N.Y. 1976, U.S. Ct. Appeals (2d cir.) 1976; N.J. 1977, U.S. Supreme Ct. 1979. Assoc. Rothblatt, Seijas & Peskin, N.Y.C., 1975-78; ptnr. Goldfarb & Bate, N.Y.C., 1978—. Contbg. author: Criminal Law Library. Jud. selection conv. chmn. Liberal Party of Richmond County, S.I., N.Y., 1976; arbitrator N.Y. Civil Ct., 1978—. Mem. ABA (com. on condominiums and coops. 1983—), N.Y. State Bar Assn., N.J. Bar Assn., Bergen County Bar Assn. (sec. coop. and condo. com. 1983), N.Y. County Lawyers Assn., Phi Delta Phi (magister-pres. 1974-75). Jewish. Real property, General corporate, General practice. Office: Goldfarb & Bate 15 Park Row New York NY 10038 also: 580 Sylvan Ave Englewood Cliffs NJ 07024

GOLDFARB, WILLIAM, legal educator, consultant; b. N.Y.C., Aug. 7, 1937; s. Herman and Yetta (Schlossberg) G.; m. Illse E. Heacox, June 18, 1983. B.A., Colgate U., 1959; LL.B., Yale U., 1962; M.A., Columbia U., 1966, Ph.D., 1974. Bar: N.Y. 1963, N.J. 1976. Assoc. Goldwater and Flynn, N.Y.C., 1963-65, Pomerantz, Levy, Haudek and Block, N.Y.C., 1965; ptnr. Schacter, Abuza and Goldfarb, N.Y.C., 1966-76; instr., asst. prof. humanities Stevens Inst. Tech., Hoboken, N.J., 1969-74; assoc. prof. environ. law Cook Coll., Rutgers U., New Brunswick, N.J., 1974-78, prof., 1979—; spl. cons. div. water resources N.J. Dept. Environ. Protection mem. N.J. Gov.'s Sci. Adv. Com.; pres. N.J. Environ. Lobby; judge environ. law essay contest Assn. Trial Lawyers Am. Recipient cert. of appreciation region II, EPA, 1976, outstanding service award Pollution Engring. mag., 1977. Mem. Am. Water Resources Assn., Fedn. Flyfishers. Clubs: Theodore Gordon Flyfishers (N.Y.C.); Trout Unltd. (Cross Fork, Pa.). Contbg. editor: Water Resources Bull.; author: Water Law, 1984; mem. editorial adv. bd. Resource Mgmt. and Optimization; contbr. articles to legal jours., articles on fly-fishing to mags., also chpts. to books. Environment. Home: 174 Pennington-Harbourton Rd Pennington NJ 08534 Office: Rutgers U Dept Environ Resources Cook Coll New Brunswick NJ 08903

GOLDHIRSCH, LAWRENCE BERTRAM, lawyer; b. N.Y.C., May 11, 1942; s. Max and Anne (Marshall) G.; m. Kathleen Louise McGough, Dec. 22, 1968; children—Elizabeth, Kendra. B.S. in Physics, CCNY, 1963; J.D., Bklyn. Law Sch., 1969. Bar: N.Y. 1942, U.S. Dist. Ct. (so. and ea. dists.) N.Y. 1971, U.S. Dist. Ct. Conn. 1975, U.S. Supreme Ct. 1975, U.S. Tax Ct. 1975, U.S. Ct. Appeals (2d cir.) 1975, U.S. Customs Ct. 1978, U.S. Ct. Appeals (3d cir.) 1982. Assoc., Harry H. Lipsig, P.C., N.Y.C., 1970-75; lectr. comparative law, consumers rights U. Dijon (France) also U. Montpellier (France), 1975-76; trial atty., counsel to firm Speiser & Krause, P.C., N.Y.C., 1976-87; assoc., Fuchsberg & Fuchsberg, N.Y.C., 1987—; mem. med. malpractice panel N.Y. County, 1978—, Kings County, 1978—; spl. master N.Y. County Supreme Ct., 1978—; lectr. air law, U.Nice, France, 1985-86. Mem. Assn. of Bar of City N.Y., Bklyn. Bar Assn. (mem. spl. com. on tort law 1973-76, mem. com. on criminal procedure 1973-76, chmn. com. on aerospace law 1973-76), Internat. Bar Assn. (vice-chmn. coms. on consumer affairs advt., unfair competition and products liability, gen. practice, mem. coms. on aero. law, civil procedures), ABA (com. on internat. litigation, mem. internat. law sect.), N.Y. State Trial Lawyers Assn., World Assn. Lawyers, World Peace Through Law Ctr., Assn. Trial Lawyers Am., Am. Phys. Soc. Personal injury, Private international, Federal civil litigation. Office: Fuchsberg & Fuchsberg 100 Church St New York NY 10007

GOLDIE, RAY ROBERT, lawyer; b. Dayton, Ohio, Apr. 1, 1920; s. Albert S. and Lillian (Hayman) G.; student U. So. Calif., 1943-44, J.D., 1957; student San Bernardino Valley Coll., 1950-51; m. Dorothy Roberta Zafman, Dec. 2, 1941; children—Marilyn, Deanne, Dayle, Ron R. Elec. appliance dealer, 1944-54; teaching asst. U. So. Calif. Law Sch., 1956-57; admitted to Calif. bar, 1957; dep. atty. gen. State of Calif., 1957-58; individual practice, San Bernardino, 1958—. Pres., Trinity Acceptance Corp., 1948-53. Mem. World Peace Through Law Center, 1962—; regional dir. Legion Lex, U. So. Calif. Sch. Law, 1959-75; chmn. San Bernardino United Jewish Appeal, 1963; v.p. United Jewish Welfare Fund San Bernardino, 1964-66, Santa Anita Hosp., Lake Arrowhead, 1966-69. Bd. dirs. San Bernardino Med. Arts Corp. Served with AUS, 1942-43. Fellow Internat. Acad. Law and Sci.; mem. Am., San Bernardino County bar assns., State Bar Calif., Am. Judicature Soc., Am. Soc. Hosp. Attys., Calif. Trial Lawyers Assn. (v.p. chpt. 1965-67, pres. 1967-68), Am. Arbitration Assn. (nat. panel arbitrators), Order of Coif, Nu Beta Epsilon (pres. 1956-57). Club: Lake Arrowhead Country (pres. 1972-73, 80-81), Lake Arrowhead Yacht, Club at Morningside. State civil litigation, General corporate, Real property. Home: 1 Hampton Ct Rancho Mirage CA 92270 Office: 432 N Arrowhead Ave San Bernardino CA 92401 also: 1111 Tahquitz E Palm Springs CA 92262

GOLDIE, RON ROBERT, lawyer; b. San Bernardino, Calif., Apr. 6, 1951; s. Ray R. and Dorothy R. (Zafman) G.; m. Betty J. Cooper, June 13, 1983; children: Meghan Ann, Rand R. Diploma, U. Paris, 1970; BA, U. So. Calif., 1972, MBA, JD, 1975. Bar: Calif. 1975, U.S. Dist. Ct. (cen., no. and so. dists.) Calif., U.S. Ct. Appeals (9th cir.). Atty. Goldie Law Corp., Los Angeles and San Bernardino, 1975-82; sole practice Los Angeles, 1982-86; prin. Law Offices of Ron R. Goldie, Los Angeles, 1986—. Republican. Jewish. Avocations: skiing, racquetball. Real property, General corporate, State civil litigation. Home: 762 Latimer Rd Rustic Canyon CA 90402 Office: 12100 Wilshire Blvd Suite 1100 Los Angeles CA 90025

GOLDIN, ARNOLD B., lawyer; b. Richmond, Va., July 28, 1949; s. David and Roslyn Goldin; m. Shara L. Burson, Nov. 22, 1973; children: Joshua, Rebecca. BA, U. Va., 1971; JD, Memphis State U., 1974. Bar: Tenn. 1974. Assoc. Dann, Blackburn & Smith, Memphis, 1974-76; ptnr. Dann, Blackburn & Goldin, Memphis, 1976-78, Goldin & Bloomfield, Memphis, 1978—. Mem. Assn. Trial Lawyers Am. (admiralty law sect.), Tenn. Trial Lawyers Assn. (v.p. 1983-85, pres. elect 1985-86, pres. 1986—, sustaining). Admiralty, Personal injury, Workers' compensation. Office: Goldin & Bloomfield PA PO Box 3165 Memphis TN 38173

GOLDLUST, PERRY FELIX, lawyer; b. N.Y.C., May 15, 1942; s. Sigmund J. and Jessie (Stein) G.; m. Sheila E. Gainen, June 13, 1965; children—Johanna, Joshua. B.B.A., CUNY, 1964; J.D., Bklyn. Law Sch., 1966. Bar: N.Y. 1966, Del. 1973. Personnel asst. indsl. relations Corning Glass, Inc., 1966-67; labor relations specialist indsl. relations ICI Ams., Inc., Tamaqua, Pa. and Wilmington, Del., 1967-73; 1st asst. city solicitor City of Wilmington, 1973-77; mem., dir. Levin, Goldlust & Clark, P.A., Wilmington, 1978-84; sole practice, Greenville, Del., 1984—. Mem. ABA, Del. Bar Assn., Del. Trial Lawyers Assn., Del. C. of C. Club: Ardensingers (Arden, Del.). Labor. Office: 126A Senatorial Dr Greenville DE

GOLDMAN, BARBARA LYNN, lawyer; b. N.Y.C., Jan. 3, 1958; d. Milton and Frieda (Altman) Katz; m. Lee Goldman, Sept. 3, 1982. BA with honors, SUNY, Binghamton, 1978; JD magna cum laude, Boston U., 1981. Bar: N.Y. 1982, U.S. Dist. Ct. (ea. dist.) Mich. 1983, Mich. 1984, Fla. 1986, U.S. Ct. Appeals (6th cir.) 1986. Trial atty. Bur. of Competition, FTC, Washington, 1981-83; assoc. Honigman Miller Schwartz & Cohn, Detroit, 1983-85, Epstein Becker Borsody & Green, Tallahassee, 1985-86, Dykema Gossett Spencer Goodnow & Trigg, Detroit, 1986—. Mem. ABA. Antitrust, Federal civil litigation, Health.

GOLDMAN, BRIAN A., lawyer, accountant; b. Balt., June 30, 1946; s. Marvin L. and Edythe R. Goldman; m. Eileen G. Safro, Aug. 22, 1970; children—Jonathan S., Evan M. B.S. in Real Estate Planning, Am. U., 1968; J.D., U. Md., 1971. Bar: Md. 1972, U.S. Dist. Ct. Md. 1972, U.S. Tax Ct. 1977, U.S. Supreme Ct. 1977, Acct., Balt., 1974—; mem. Burke, Gerber & Wilen, 1972-77, Sapero & Sapero, 1977-78; sole practice, 1978-83; ptnr. firm Goldman and Fedder, P.A., Balt., 1983-85, Fedder & Garten, P.A., 1986—; asst. prof. income taxation U. Balt., 1974-75. Mem. ABA, Md. Bar Assn., Balt. City Bar Assn., Md. Assn. C.P.A.s. Clubs: Center, Suburban (Balt.). Consumer commercial, General corporate, Real property. Office: Fedder & Garten PA 36 S Chalres St Suite 2300 Baltimore MD 21201

GOLDMAN, DAVID HARRIS, lawyer; b. Des Moines, Apr. 3, 1942; s. Harold A. and Kate (Marsh) G.; m. Catherine F. Fajen, June 3, 1984; 1 child, Jessica Ariel. AB, Brandeis U., 1964; postgrad., Oxford U., Eng., 1964-67; JD, U. Iowa, 1977. Bar: Iowa 1977, U.S. Dist. Ct. (so. dist.) Iowa 1977, U.S. Ct. Appeals (8th cir.,) 1977, U.S. Dist. Ct. (no. dist.) Iowa 1978, U.S. Ct. Claims 1980, U.S. Suprem Ct. 1986. Instr. philosophy Upsala Coll., East Orange, N.J., 1967-69; exec. dir. Community Improvement Inc., Des Moines, 1969-70; v.p., pres. Iowa Paint Mfg. Co., Inc., Des Moines, 1970-75; from assoc. to ptnr. Rogers, Phillips & Swanger, Des Moines, 1977-82; sr. ptnr. Black, Reimer & Goldman, Des Moines, 1982—. V.p. Iowa Civil Liberties Union, Des Moines, 1972-73; pres. Jewish Community Relations Commn., Des Moines, 1985—; bd. dirs. Iowa Children's and Family Services, Des Moines, 1971-75, Am. Soc. for Technion-Israel Inst. of Tech. Inc., N.Y.C., 1985—. Recipient Founders award Am. Soc. for Technion-Israel Inst. for Tech., 1985. Mem. ABA, Iowa Bar Assn., Polk County Bar Assn. Democrat. Club: Des Moines. Avocations: sailing, reading. Civil rights, Labor, Jurisprudence. Home: 692 48th St Des Moines IA 50312 Office: Black Reimer & Goldman 550 39th St Suite 300 Des Moines IA 50312

GOLDMAN, GARY CRAIG, lawyer; b. Phila., Dec. 28, 1951; s. Ronald Walter and Connie Sylvia (Stein) G.; m. Diane Rose Lane, Oct. 1, 1977; children—Justin Edward, Gregory David. B.A. magna cum laude, Temple U., 1973; J.D., Villanova U., 1976. Bar: Pa. 1976, U.S. Dist. Ct. (ea. dist.) Pa. 1981. Jud. law clk. Common Pleas Ct., Northampton County, Pa., 1976-77; asst. atty. gen. Pa. Dept. Pub. Welfare, Phila., 1977-81, asst. counsel, 1981-84; staff counsel CDI Corp., Phila., 1984-86, assoc. corp. counsel, 1986—. Assoc. editor Villanova Law Rev., 1974-76; contbr. articles to legal jours. Mem. Am. Corp. Counsel Assn., ABA, Phila. Bar Assn. Jewish. General corporate, Labor, Landlord-tenant. Home: 119 Fox Hollow Dr Langhorne PA 19047 Office: CDI Corp 10 Penn Ctr 12th Floor Philadelphia PA 19103

GOLDMAN, JERRY ALAN, lawyer; b. Rochester, N.Y., June 28, 1956; s. Harry and Estelle (Levy) G. BA, U. Rochester, 1976; JD, Albany Law Sch., N.Y., 1979. Bar: N.Y. 1980, Fla. 1980, U.S. Dist. Ct. (we. dist.) N.Y. 1980. Assoc. Wegman, Mayberry, Burgess & Feldstein & Mayberry, Kurlander, Licht & Lunn, Rochester, 1980-82; ptnr. Mayberry, Licht & Goldman, Rochester, 1982—. Treas. Rochester (N.Y.) Area Hillel Found., 1984—, sec., 1986—. N.Y. State Regents scholar, 1973. Mem. ABA, N.Y. State Bar Assn., Monroe County Bar Assn. (vice chmn. Fla. practice com. 1982-83, sec. mcpl. com. 1985—). Jewish. Lodge: B'nai B'rith (sec. 1984-85; bd. dirs. 1983, 86). Avocations: racquetball, tennis, nautilus. Environment, Local government, Real property. Home: 55 French Woods Circle Rochester NY 14618 Office: Mayberry Licht & Goldman 47 S Fitzhugh St Suite 800 Rochester NY 14614

GOLDMAN, JERRY STEPHEN, lawyer; b. Bklyn., Sept. 7, 1951; s. Bernard and Charlotte (Emerling) G.; m. Lisa Steinberg, Mar. 28, 1981; 1 child, Rachel Dawn. B.A., NYU, 1973; J.D., Boston U., 1976; LL.M. in Taxation, Temple U., 1983. Bar: Mass. 1977, N.Y. 1977, U.S. Dist. Ct. (ea. and so. dists.) N.Y. 1980, U.S. Supreme Ct. 1981, Pa. 1982, U.S. Tax Ct. 1983, U.S. Ct. Appeals (3d cir.) 1983, U.S. Dist. Ct. (ea. dist.) Pa. 1983, U.S. Ct. Appeals (2d cir.) 1987. Sr. asst. dist. atty. Kings County Dist. Atty.'s Office, Bklyn., 1976-82; sole practice, N.Y.C. and Phila., 1982—. Trustee Citizen's Crime Commn., Delaware Valley, 1983—, Tay Sacks of Delaware Valley, Phila., 1983—; vice chmn. Upper Southampton Planning Commn., 1985—. Mem. ABA, N.Y. State Bar Assn., Mass. Bar Assn., Pa. Bar Assn., Phila. Bar Assn. Jewish. Corporate taxation, Probate, General corporate. Office: 1411 Walnut St Suite 615 Philadelphia PA 19102 also: 396 Broadway 9th Floor New York NY 10013

GOLDMAN, JOEL J., lawyer; oil and gas drilling co. exec.; b. N.Y.C., Sept. 7, 1940; s. Myron and Pearl (Jacobs) G.; m. Jane I. Stalker, July 23, 1973; children—Elizabeth Ann, Rebecca Lynn. B.S., U. Va., 1962, J.D., Syracuse U., 1965. Bar: N.Y. 1966, U.S. Dist. Ct. (we. dist.) N.Y. 1966. Law clk. Myron Goldman, N.Y.C., 1965; staff atty., chief trial counsel Legal Aid Soc. Rochester (N.Y.), 1966-73; ptnr. Kaman, Berlove, Marafioti, Jacobstein & Goldman, Rochester, 1973—; lectr. family law; spl. investigator N.Y. State Spl. Commn. on Attica, 1972; mem. panel arbitrators Am. Arbitration Assn.; mem. faculty Nat. Bus. Inst., 1985—. Referee, Eastern Assn. Inter-Collegiate Football Ofcls., 1974—. Fellow Am. Acad. Matrimonial Lawyers; mem. ABA, N.Y. State Bar Assn. (exec. com. family law sect. 1982, mem. exec. com. 1981-86), Monroe County Bar Assn. (chmn. family law sect. 1982, exec. com. 1981—), Assn. Trial Lawyers Am. Jewish. Author continuing edn. materials. Contbg. editor Bender's Forms for Civil Practice, 1986, Medina's Bostwick, 1986. Family and matrimonial. Home: 67 Mountain Rd Rochester NY 14625 Office: 13 S Fitzhugh St Suite 400 Rochester NY 14614

GOLDMAN, JOEL L., lawyer; b. Bklyn., July 26, 1930; s. William and Henrietta (Schwartz) G.; m. Muriel Coplan, Aug. 14, 1955 (div. Dec. 1974); children: Alan, Audrey, Stephen. BBA, U. Fla., 1952, JD, 1954. Bar: Fla., U.S. Dist. Ct. (mid. and so. dists.) Fla., U.S. Ct. Appeals (5th and 11th cirs.). Ptnr. Goldman, Presser & Nussbaum, Jacksonville. Chmn. Jacksonville United Jewish Welfare Fund Campaign, 1969; pres. Jacksonville Jewish Fedn., 1972-73, bd. dirs., 1958-73; trustee River Garden Hebrew Home for Aged, 1969-71; bd. dirs. Jacksonville Jewish Ctr., 1970-71, Lawyers' Title Services Inc. of Duval County, 1968-72. Served with U.S. Army, 1954-56. Fellow Am. Acad. Matrimonial Lawyers; mem. Fla. Bar Assn. (trial and family law sects., continuing legal edn. com.), Jacksonville Bar Assn. (chmn. marital and family law sect. 1980-81), Acad. Fla. Trial Lawyers. Democrat. Clubs: University, No. Fla. Cruising. Lodge: B'nai B'rith. Avocation: sailing. Family and matrimonial, State civil litigation, Federal civil litigation. Home: 9439 San Jose Blvd 255 Jacksonville FL 32257 Office: Goldman Presser & Nussbaum 900 First Union Bldg Jacksonville FL 32202

GOLDMAN, JOEL S., lawyer; b. N.Y.C., Feb. 20, 1942; s. Abraham Goldman and Gertrude (Katz) Kohn; m. Barbara Davis; children: Romy,

Andrew, Jessica. BEE, NYU, 1962; JD, Fordham U., 1977. Staff engr. IBM, Armonk, N.Y., 1962-77; assoc. Darby & Darby P.C., N.Y.C., 1977-85; patent counsel Sci.- Atlanta Inc., Atlanta, 1985—. Contbr.: Commercial Damages, 1985. Mem. Am. Intellectual Property Law Assn., Atlanta Bar Assn., Assn. Corp. Counsel. Lodge: B'nai B'rith (bd. dirs. Atlanta 1985-86). Avocation: tennis. Computer, Patent, Trademark and copyright. Home: 780 Old Creek Trail Atlanta GA 30328 Office: Sci-Atlanta Inc 1 Technology Pkwy PO Box 105600 Atlanta GA 30348

GOLDMAN, LOUIS BUDWIG, lawyer; b. Chgo., Apr. 11, 1948; s. Jack Sydney and Lorraine (Budwig) G.; m. Barbara Marcia Berg, Oct. 2, 1983; 1 child, Jacqueline Ilyse. AB magna cum laude, U. Calif., Berkeley, 1970; JD cum laude, U. Chgo., 1975. Bar: Calif. 1975, U.S. Dist. Ct. (no. dist.) Calif. 1975, U.S. Ct. Appeals (9th cir.) 1975, N.Y. 1976, U.S. Dist. Ct. (so. and ea. dists.) N.Y. 1976, U.S. Ct. Appeals (2d cir.) 1976. Law clk. U.S. Dist. Ct., San Francisco, 1974-75; assoc. Cleary, Gottlieb, Steen & Hamilton, N.Y.C. and Paris, 1975-81; assoc. Edwards & Angell, N.Y.C., 1981-83, ptnr., 1986—; ptnr. Wald, Harkrader & Ross, N.Y.C., 1983-86; mng. dir. Abacus & Assocs. Inc., N.Y.C. Mem. ABA, Calif. Bar Assn., N.Y. State Bar Assn., Assn. of Bar of City of N.Y., N.Y. County Lawyers Assn., Order of Coif, Phi Beta Kappa. Private international, Securities, General corporate. Office: Edwards & Angell 430 Park Ave New York NY 10022

GOLDMAN, MARSHALL STANLEY, lawyer; b. White Plains, N.Y., May 10, 1938; s. David and Mary Goldman; m. Jessica Darilyn Goldman, July 26, 1964; children: Renee, Andrew. BA, Johns Hopkins U., 1960, JD, Syracuse U., 1963. Bar: N.Y., 1964, U.S. dist. ct. (so. dist.) N.Y., 1973, U.S. Tax Ct., 1976, U.S. Sup. Ct., 1970. Income, estate and gift tax examiner IRS, U.S. Treasury Dept., 1963-65; ptnr. Kahn & Goldman and predecessors, 1965-80; sole practice, White Plains, 1981—; panel arbitrators Am. Arbitration Assn. Bd. dirs. Yorktown Jewish Center; asst. dist. commr. Boy Scouts Am. Served to sgt. USAF, 1964-70. Recipient Achievement award U.S. Treasury Dept., 1965. Fellow Am. Acad. Matrimonial Lawyers; mem. ABA (bd. mgrs. 1986—), N.Y. State Bar Assn. (dir. 1980-82), Westchester Bar Assn. (dir. 1978-81, vice-chmn. family law sect. 1980-81), No. Westchester Bar Assn., White Plains Bar Assn., Yorktown Bar Assn. (pres. 1979), N.Y. State Trial Lawyers Assn., Estate Planning Council Westchester County. Editor Family Law Jour., 1980-81; contbr. chpts. in books. Family and matrimonial. Home: 410 Rutledge Dr Yorktown Heights NY 10598 Office: 175 Main St White Plains NY 10601

GOLDMAN, MARTHA ANN, law librarian; b. N.Y.C., Jan. 2, 1952; d. Alan W. and Naomi S. (Schur) G. BA, SUNY, Cortland, 1973; MLS, CUNY, 1976; postgrad., Pace U. Asst. librarian Milbank, Tweed, Hadley & McCloy, N.Y.C., 1976-78; reference librarian Cravath, Swaine & Moore, N.Y.C., 1978-79; head librarian Kelley Drye & Warren, N.Y.C., 1979-85; mgr info. services law dept. CBS Inc., N.Y.C., 1985-87; head librarian Jones, Day, Reavis & Pogue, N.Y.C., 1987—. Mem. Am. Assn. Law Libraries, Spl. Libraries Assn., Assn. Records Mgrs. and Adminstrs., Law Library Assn. of Greater N.Y. (bd. dirs. 1981-83). Librarianship. Office: Jones Day Reavis & Pogue 599 Lexington Ave New York NY 10022

GOLDMAN, MATTHEW RALPH, lawyer; b. N.Y.C., May 27, 1952; s. Marty and Ida (Breslow) G.; m. Elizabeth Ann Pearson, Jan. 8, 1982. BA in History magna cum laude, SUNY, Buffalo, 1974, BA in Am. Studies, 1975; JD, U. Pa., 1978. Bar: N.Y. 1979, U.S. Dist. Ct. (so. and ea. dists.) N.Y. 1980, U.S. Dist. Ct. (no. dist.) Ohio 1981, Ohio 1982. Assoc. Beinhauer, Rouhana & Pike, N.Y.C., 1979-80, Hammond & Morton P.C., N.Y.C., 1980-81; staff atty. AmeriTrust Co. Nat. Assn., Cleve., 1981-84, assoc. counsel, group head, 1984-87; with firm Baker & Hostetler, Cleve., 1987—. Mem. ABA, Phi Beta Kappa. Avocations: sports, nature activities, history. Banking, Bankruptcy, Consumer commercial.

GOLDMAN, RICHARD HARRIS, lawyer; b. Boston, June 17, 1936; s. Charles M. and Irene M. (Marks) G.; m. Patricia Grollman, June 21, 1959; children—Elaine, Stephen. B.A., Wesleyan U., 1958; LL.B., NYU, 1961. Bar: Mass. 1961, U.S. Dist. Ct. Mass. 1961. Mem. Slater & Goldman, Boston, 1961-76, Widett, Slater & Goldman, P.C., Boston, 1976—; dir. UST Capital Corp.; trustee, chmn. audit com. Grove Hall Savs. Bank. Trustee, v.p. Temple Israel; former chmn. Newton (Mass.) Human Rights Commn. Mem. ABA, Mass. Bar Assn., Boston Bar Assn., Mass. Conveyancers Assn. Club: Belmont Country (sec.). Real property, General corporate, Probate. Office: Widett Slater & Goldman PC 60 State St Boston MA 02109

GOLDMAN, ROBERT HURON, lawyer; b. Boston, Nov. 24, 1918; s. Frank and Rose (Sydeman) G.; m. Charlotte R. Rubens, July 5, 1945; children: Wendy Eve, Randolph Rubens. A.B., Harvard U., 1939, LL.B., 1943. Bar: N.Y. State 1945, Mass. 1951. Practiced in N.Y.C., 1945-50, Lowell, Mass., 1951—; law clk. Judge Learned Hand, U.S. Ct. Appeals, 1943-44; partner firm Goldman and Curtis (and predecessor firms), 1951—; columnist Lowell Sunday Sun Daily, 1954-78; v.p., asso. pub. Malden (Mass.) Evening News, 1969-86, Medford (Mass.) Daily Mercury, 1969-86, Melrose (Mass.) Evening News, 1969-86; mem. adv. bd. Baybank Middlesex., 1966-84; Radio commentator on internat. affairs, 1954-86. Author: A Newspaperman's Handbook of the Libel Law of Massachusetts, 1966, rev., 1974, The Law of Libel—Present and Future, 1969; Editor: Harvard Law Review, 1943. Chmn. Greater Lowell Civic Com., 1952-55, Lowell Hist. Soc., 1957-60, Lowell Devel. and Indsl. Commn., 1959-60; Del. Republican State Conv., 1960-62; Bd. dirs. Boston World Affairs Council, 1960-82. Named Citizen of Year Greater Lowell Civic Com., 1956. Mem. ABA (mem. nat. com. on consumer protection 1972-73, Sherman Act com. 1973—), Mass. Bar Assn. (chmn. bar-press com. 1973-76), Middlesex County Bar Assn., Lowell Bar Assn., Phi Beta Kappa. Club: Harvard (dir. Lowell 1968—). Antitrust, Libel, Federal civil litigation. Home: 8 Rolling Ridge Rd Andover MA 01810 Office: 4th Floor 144 Merrimack St Lowell MA 01852 Office: 1 Faneuil Hall Marketplace Boston MA 02109

GOLDMAN, ROY LAWRENCE, lawyer; b. N.Y.C., Nov. 11, 1954; s. Walter M. and Mildred (Schoemann) G.; m. Jacqueline A. Dzaluk, Sept. 4, 1983. BA, SUNY, Binghamton, 1976; JD, Georgetown U., 1979. Bar: D.C. 1979, N.Y. 1981, U.S. Dist. Ct. (so. dist.) N.Y. 1981. Law clk. to presiding justice U.S. Dist. Ct. (so. dist.), N.Y.C., 1979-81; assoc. Reavis & McGrath, N.Y.C., 1981-85; v.p., gen. counsel Internat. Healthcare Corp., Bethesda, Md., 1985-87; assoc. Reavis & McGrath, N.Y.C., 1987—. Pres. SUNY Met. Alumni Club, Binghamton, N.Y., 1982-83, chmn., 1983-84. Mem. ABA, N.Y. Bar Assn., D.C. Bar Assn. Health, General corporate, Securities. Office: Reavis & McGrath 345 Park Ave New York NY 10134

GOLDMAN, THOMAS LAVERNE, lawyer; b. Meridian, Miss., Dec. 2, 1929; s. James Samuel and Mattie (Privett) G.; m. Shirley Ann Stokes, Nov. 11, 1958; children: Charles Samuel, Lee Nicole. BA, U. Miss., 1954, JD, 1955. Assoc. Temple & Compton, Meridian, 1955-56; ptnr. Pigford & Goldman, Meridian, 1956-60, Holyfield & Goldman, Meridian, 1960-64, Goldman, Self & Goldman, Meridian, 1964-67, Goldman & Goldman, Meridian, 1967-81, Goldman, Dreyfus & Primeaux, Meridian, 1981—; atty. City of Meridian (Miss.), 1960-64, 85—, Town of Marion (Miss.), 1983-85. Vice chmn. Choctaw Heritage Council, Phila., Lauderdale County Econ. Devel. Authority, Meridian, 1984—; bd. dirs. Miss. Hist. Soc., Jackson, Miss., 1984-85, Miss. Natural Resources Bd., Jackson, 1986—. Served to maj. USAF, 1950-65. Mem. Miss. Bar Assn., Lauderdale County Bar Assn. (sec., treas. 1962-63, v.p. 1963-64, pres. 1964-65). Democrat. Baptist. Avocations: archaeology, hunting, fishing, historical research. Local government, Real property, General practice. Home: Rt 12 Box 410 Meridian MS 39305 Office: Goldman Dreyfus & Primeaux 1920 6th St Meridian MS 39301

GOLDNER, LEONARD HOWARD, lawyer; b. N.Y.C., June 18, 1947; s. Adolph and Florence (Cohen) G.; m. Jacqueline Slotnik, Apr. 1, 1969; children: Claudia Mara, Benjamin Micah. BA, U. Wis., 1969; JD, Harvard U., 1972. Bar: N.Y. 1974, U.S. Dist. Ct. (so. dist.) N.Y. 1974, U.S. Ct. Appeals (2d cir.) 1975. Law clk. U.S. Ct. Appeals (9th cir.) Honolulu, 1972-73; assoc. Simpson Thacher & Bartlett, N.Y.C., 1973-76; assoc. Shereff, Friedman, Hoffman & Goodman, N.Y.C., 1976-79, ptnr., 1979—. Trustee Soc. for Advancement of Judaism, N.Y.C., 1974-85; chmn. West End Synagogue, N.Y.C., 1985—. Mem. ABA, Assn. Bar of City of N.Y., N.Y. County Lawyers Assn. Securities, General corporate. Office: Shereff Friedman Hoffman & Goodman 919 3rd Ave New York NY 10022

GOLDSCHEIDER, SIDNEY, lawyer; b. Balt., Mar. 27, 1920; s. Harry and Esther Goldscheider; m. Sylvia Glick, June 13, 1943; children: Judith, Alan, Eileen (dec.). JD summa cum laude, U. Balt., 1942. Bar: Md. 1942, U.S. Ct. Appeals (4th cir.) 1942. Sole practice Balt., 1942—; with enforcement div. Office of Price Adminstrn., Balt., 1943-45; bd. dirs. Budget Rent-a-Car of N.Y.C. Bd. dirs. Beth Jacob Congregation, Balt., Safety First Club of Md.; sec. One Slade Condominium Council of Co-owners, Balt.; co-chmn. Shaare Zedek Med. Ctr. in Jerusalem, com. mem. Israel Bonds Ambassador's Ball; mem. Civic Assn. Honoree, Beth Jacob Congregation, 1973, 86, State of Israel Bonds, 1976; recipient citations Gov. Md., 1982, 86; City of Balt., 1982; Sidney Goldscheider Day proclaimed by Baltimore County and by City of Balt., Jan. 29, 1986; Disting. Service resolution Md. Ho. of Dels., 1986. Mem. Balt. City Bar Assn., Md. State Bar Assn., Md. Trial Lawyers Assn., U. Balt. Alumni Assn., Balt. C. of C., Associated Jewish Charities and Welfare Fund (lawyer's div.), Israel Prime Minister's Club, Am. Philatelic Soc., Heuisler Honor Soc., Phi Delta Tau. Lodge: Schreter B'nai B'rith (Outstanding Citizen award 1982). Avocations: visual and performing arts, music, philately, numismatics, sports. Personal injury, Workers' compensation. Home: 1 Slade Ave Baltimore MD 21208 Office: 218 E Lexington St Baltimore MD 21202

GOLDSCHMID, HARVEY JEROME, legal educator; b. N.Y.C., May 6, 1940; s. Bernard and Rose (Braiker) G.; m. Mary Tait Seibert, Dec. 22, 1973; children: Charles Maxwell, Paul MacNeil, Joseph Tait. A.B., Columbia U., 1962, J.D., 1965. Bar: N.Y. 1965, U.S. Supreme Ct. 1970. Law clk. to judge 2d Circuit Ct. Appeals, N.Y.C., 1965-66; assoc. firm Debevoise & Plimpton, N.Y.C., 1966-70; asst. prof. law Columbia U., 1970-71, assoc. prof., 1971-73, prof., 1973-84, Dwight prof. law, 1984—, dir. Center for Law and Econ. Studies, 1975-78; cons. in field to public and pvt. orgns.; mem. planning and program com. 2d Cir. Jud. Conf., 1982-85. Author: (with others) Cases and Materials on Trade Regulation, 1975, 2d edit., 1983; editor: (with others) Industrial Concentration: The New Learning, 1974, Business Disclosure: Government's Need to Know, 1979, (with others) The Impact of the Modern Corporation, 1984. Mem. ABA, Am. Law Inst. (dep. chief reporter 1980-84, reporter part IV corp. governance project), N.Y. State Bar Assn., Assn. Bar City N.Y. (v.p. 1985-86, chmn. exec. com. 1984-85, chmn. com. on antitrust and trade regulation 1971-74, nominating com.), Assn. Am. Law Schs. (chmn. sect. antitrust and econ. regulation 1976-78), Am. Assn. Internat. Commn. Jurists (bd. dirs.), Phi Beta Kappa. Clubs: Century Assn, Riverdale Yacht. Antitrust, General corporate, Federal civil litigation. Office: 435 W 116th St New York NY 10027

GOLDSMITH, ALAN EVANS, lawyer; b. Washington, Apr. 4, 1951; s. John Alan and Rosemarie (Mullany) G. BA cum laude, Kenyon Coll., 1973; JD, Cath. U., 1976. Bar: D.C., U.S. Ct. Mil. Appeals. Reference asst. Library of Congress, Washington, 1977-78; atty., advisor Bd. for Correction of Naval Records, Washington, 1982-84, supervisory atty., advisor, 1984—. Bd. dirs. Saxony Sq. Condominium Unit Owners Assn., Alexandria, Va., 1984—. Served to capt. (judge advocate) USAF, 1978-82. Mem. ABA, Fed. Bar Assn. Avocations: swimming, reading. Military. Home: 503 N Armistead St #T2 Alexandria VA 22312 Office: Bd Correciton Naval Records Dept of Navy Washington DC 20370

GOLDSMITH, JAMES ARTHUR, lawyer; b. Toledo, Apr. 10, 1955; s. Robert H. and Betty (Stotter) G.; m. Nancy Shaw, Sept. 10, 1983. BSBA in Mgmt., U. Denver, 1977; JD, Case-Western Res. U., 1980. Bar: Ohio 1980, Fla. 1981. Tax acct. Arthur Anderson & Co., Cleve., 1980-82; assoc. Ulmer, berne, Laronge, Glickman & Curtis, Cleve., 1982—. Mem. ABA, Ohio Bar Assn., Fla. Bar Assn., Cleve. Bar Assn. Jewish. Club: Oakwood (Cleve.) (trustee 1985—). Estate planning, Probate, Pension, profit-sharing, and employee benefits. Home: 19220 Lomond Blvd Shaker Heights OH 44122 Office: Ulmer Berne Laronge Glickman & Curtis 900 Bond Ct Bldg Cleveland OH 44114

GOLDSMITH, KAREN LEE, lawyer; b. Bridgeport, Conn., Jan. 10, 1946; d. James Joseph and Marjorie (Crowley) M.; m. Michael Goldsmith, Oct. 12, 1968 (dec. May 1979); children: Pamela S., Neil J.; m. Jeffery S. Hooie, June 13, 1980. AA summa cum laude, Seminole Jr. Coll., 1969; BA summa cum laude, U. Cen. Fla., 1975; JD cum laude, U. Fla., 1978. Bar: Fla. 1979, U.S. Dist. Ct. (mid. dist.) Fla. 1979, U.S. Dist. Ct. (so. and no. dists.) Fla. 1981, U.S. Ct. Appeals (11th cir.) 1981. Assoc. Pitts, Eubanks & Ross P.A., Orlando, Fla., 1978-80; assoc. Dempsey & Slaughter P.A., Orlando, 1980-83, ptnr., 1983; ptnr. Dempsey & Goldsmith P.A., Orlando, 1984—; lectr. Interhome '86, Ft. Lauderdale, Fla., 1986—, health care related legal issues various orgns., 1982—. Sr. editor U. Fla. Law Rev., 1978; contbr. articles to profl. jours. Bereavement coordinator, family life com. St. Margaret Mary Ch., Winter Park, Fla., 1985—. Mem. ABA, Fla. Bar Assn. (chmn. state law week 1985, 86), Orange County Bar Assn. (outstanding chmn. 1982), Nat. Health Lawyers Assn. (speaker 1982, 87), Assn. Trial Lawyers Am., Acad. Fla. Trial Lawyers, Order of Coif, Phi Kappa Phi. Democrat. Roman Catholic. Clubs: Horizon (Orlando), Citrus (Orlando). Avocations: raising and breeding dogs. Administrative and regulatory, State civil litigation, Health. Home: 208 Atherstone Ct Longwood FL 32779 Office: Dempsey & Goldsmith PA 605 E Robinson St Suite 500 Orlando FL 32801

GOLDSMITH, LEE SELIG, lawyer, physician; b. N.Y.C., Nov. 18, 1939; s. Isidore L. and Elsie (Friedman) G.; m. Arlene F. Applebaum, June 10, 1962; children: Ian Lance, Helena Ayn, Jordan Seth. B.S. with honors, N.Y. U., 1960, M.D., 1964, LL.B., 1967. Bar: N.Y. 1968, N.J. 1974. Assoc. clk. Speiser, Shumate, Geoghan Krause & Rheingold, 1965-70; individual practice law 1970-72; mem. firm Lea, Goldberg, Goldsmith & Spellen, N.Y.C., 1972-74; of counsel Newark, 1974-77; mem. firm Goldsmith, Cohen & Simon, 1976-77, Goldsmith & Cohen, 1977-80, Greenstone, Greenstone, Naishuler & Goldsmith, Newark, 1981, Goldsmith & Tabak, P.C., N.Y.C., 1981—, Goldsmith & Tabak, P.A., Englewood, N.J., 1981—; adj. prof. law Fordham U., 1976—; spl. counsel N.Y. State Senate health com., 1971; lectr. Practicing Law Inst.; chmn. Am. Bd. Law in Medicine, 1984-85. Author: Malpractice Made Easy, 1976, Hospital Liability Law, 1972, 2d edit. 1979; editor: Jour. Legal Medicine, 1978-81, Legal Aspects of Med. Practice, 1981—, Medical Malpractice (6 vols.), Guide to Medical Issues (6 vols.), 1986; contbr. articles to various publs. Fellow Am. Coll. Legal Medicine (bd. govs. 1982, pres.-elect 1986-87, pres. 1987-88, chmn. com. legis. rev.), N.Y. Acad. Medicine; mem. AMA, N.Y. Med. Soc., N.Y. County Med. Soc., Assn. of Bar of City of N.Y. (sec. sci. and law com. 1985—), N.Y. Trial Lawyers Assn., N.J. Trial Lawyers Assn. (bd. govs. 1984—), ABA, N.Y. Bar Assn., N.J. Bar Assn. Home: 1 Boulder Brook Rd Scarsdale NY 10583 Office: Goldsmith & Tabak PC 747 3d Ave New York NY 10017 also: 165 N Dean St Englewood NJ 07631

GOLDSMITH, MARY ANN, lawyer, consultant, small business owner; b. San Antonio, Dec. 12, 1952; d. John Robert and Mary Dean (Stephens) G.; m. Ronald Hollis Faulkner, Dec. 30, 1978; 1 child, Morgan Dean. BA with spl. honors, U. Tex., 1974, JD, 1979. Bar: Calif. 1979, U.S. Dist. Ct. (no. and cen. dists.) Calif. 1979, Tex. 1982. Assoc. Sheppard, Mullin, Richter & Hampton, Los Angeles, 1979-81; assoc. gen. counsel Tex. Energy Petroleum Corp., Houston, 1981-82, v.p., 1982-84, gen. counsel, 1983-86; sole practice Port Aransas, Tex., 1986—; owner Island Book Store, Port Aransas, 1986—. Articles editor U. Tex. Law Rev., 1978-79. Mem. Planning and Zoning Commn., Port Aransas, 1986—. Mem. ABA, Tex. Bar Assn., Calif. Bar Assn. Democrat. Club: Island Moorings Yacht (Port Aransas). General practice, Contracts commercial, Real property. Office: 315 S Alister PO Box 1896 Port Aransas TX 78373

GOLDSMITH, STEPHEN ERNEST, lawyer; b. N.Y.C., Dec. 25, 1944; s. Ernest and Charlotte Caroline Marie (Krohn) G.; m. Susan Diane Oberg, June 26, 1982. B.A., Marietta Coll., 1967; J.D., Oklahoma City U., 1976. Bar: Hawaii 1977, U.S. Dist. Ct. Hawaii 1977, U.S. Ct. Appeals (9th cir.) 1977. Assoc. atty. James Kruager, atty. at law, a law corp., Wailuku, Hawaii, 1977-81; sole practice, Wailuku, Maui, 1981—. Bd. dirs. Maui Philharm., Soc., Hawaii, 1984-85. Mem. ABA, Assn. Trial Lawyers Am. (state del. 1984-86), Hawaii Bar Assn., Maui County Bar Assn. (bd. dirs. 1984, adminstrv. v.p., pres. elect 1984-85, pres. 1986-87), Phi Delta Phi. Personal injury, State civil litigation, Workers' compensation. Office: 2158 Main St Suite 102 Wailuku Maui HI 96793

GOLDSMITH, WILLIS JAY, lawyer; b. Paris, Feb. 21, 1947; came to U.S., 1949; s. Irving and Alice (Rosenfeld) G.; m. Marilynn Jacobson, Aug. 12, 1973; children—Andrew Edward, Helene Sara. A.B., Brown U., 1969; J.D., NYU, 1972. Bar: N.Y. 1973, U.S. Ct. Appeals (2d cir.) 1975, D.C. 1978, U.S. Ct. Appeals (4th cir.) 1979, U.S. Ct. Appeals (D.C. cir.) 1979, U.S. Supreme Ct. 1980, U.S. Ct. Appeals (6th. cir.) 1985. Att. Dept. Labor, Washington, 1972-74; assoc. Guggenheimer & Untermyer, N.Y.C., 1974-77; assoc. Seyfarth, Shaw, Fairweather & Geraldson, Washington, 1977-79, ptnr., 1979-83; ptnr. Jones, Day, Reavis & Pogue, Washington, 1983—. Contbg. editor Employee Relations Law Jour., 1983—. Mem. ABA (sect. labor and employment law, com. on occupational safety and health law 1978—), D.C. Bar Assn. Democrat. Jewish. Clubs: University (Washington); Kenwood Golf and Country (Bethesda, Md.). Labor. Home: 6409 Elmwood Rd Chevy Chase MD 20815 Office: Jones Day Reavis & Pogue 655 15th St NW Washington DC 20005

GOLDSON, AMY ROBERTSON, lawyer; b. Boston, Jan. 16, 1953; d. Irving Edgar and E. Emily (Lippman) Robertson; m. Alfred Lloyd Goldson, June 29, 1974. BA magna cum laude, Smith Coll., 1973; JD, Cath. U., 1976. Bar: D.C. 1976, U.S. Dist. Ct. D.C. 1976, U.S. Ct. Appeals (D.C. and 4th cirs.) 1976. Atty. office of chief counsel, tax ct. litigation div. IRS, Washington, 1976-77; assoc. Smothers, Douple, Gayton & Long, Washington, 1977-82; sole practice Washington, 1982—. Gen counsel Congl. Black Caucus Found., Inc., Washington, 1977—. Mem. ABA, Nat. Bar Assn., Washington Bar Assn., D.C. Bar Assn., Phi Beta Kappa. Democrat. Roman Catholic. Club: Links (Washington). Avocations: swimming, skiing, tennis. General practice, Entertainment, General corporate. Home and Office: 4015 28th Pl NW Washington DC 20008

GOLDSTEIN, ABRAHAM S., lawyer, educator; b. N.Y.C., July 27, 1925; s. Isidore and Yetta (Crystal) G.; m. Ruth Tessler, Aug. 31, 1947; children: William Ira, Marianne Susan. B.B.A., CCNY, 1946; LL.B., Yale U., 1949, M.A. (hon.), 1961; M.A. (hon.), Cambridge (Eng.) U., 1964; LL.D. (hon.), N.Y. Law Sch., 1979, DePaul U., 1987. Bar: D.C. bar 1949. Law clk. to judge U.S. Ct. Appeals, 1949-51; partner firm Donohue & Kaufmann, Washington, 1951-56; mem. faculty Yale Law Sch., 1956—, prof. law, 1961—, dean, 1970-75, Sterling prof. law, 1975—; vis. prof. law Stanford Law Sch., summer 1963; vis. fellow Inst. Criminology, fellow Christ's Coll. Cambridge U., 1964- 65; faculty Salzburg Seminar in Am. Studies, 1969, Inst. on Social Sci. Methods in Legal Edn., U. Denver, 1970-72; vis. prof. Hebrew U., Jerusalem, 1976, UN Asia and Far East Inst. for Prevention Crime, Tokyo, 1983, Tel Aviv U., 1986; Cons. Pres.'s Com. Law Enforcement, 1967; mem. Conn. Bd. of Parole, 1967-69, Conn. Commn. Revise Criminal Code, 1966-70; mem. of the Conn. Planning Com. on Criminal Adminstrn., 1967-71; sr. v.p. Am. Jewish Congress, 1977-84, mem. exec. com., 1977—. Author: The Insanity Defense, 1967, The Passive Judiciary, 1981, (with L. Orland) Criminal Procedure, 1974, (with J. Goldstein) Crime, Law and Society, 1971; contbr. numerous articles and revs to profl. jours. Served with AUS, 1943- 46. Guggenheim fellow, 1964-65, 75-76. Criminal, Legal education. Office: Yale Law Sch New Haven CT 06520

GOLDSTEIN, ALVIN, lawyer; b. N.Y.C., Nov. 21, 1929; s. Abraham and Florence (Bruckner) G.; m. Eleanor Kronish, Dec. 27, 1959; children—Eric, Michael, Eileen. B.S.S., Coll. City N.Y., 1950; LL.B., Bklyn. Law Sch., 1953, S.J.D. magna cum laude, 1960. Bar: N.Y. State bar 1953. Asso. firm Levine & Berman, N.Y.C., 1955-59; partner Levine & Berman, 1963; practiced in N.Y.C., 1960-62; partner firm Berman, Paley, Goldstein & Berman, N.Y.C., 1964—. Contbr. articles to profl. publs. Served with AUS, 1953-55. Mem. N.Y. State Bar Assn., Assn. Bar City of N.Y., N.Y. Fencers Club (dir.). General practice. Home: 1 Chester Terr Hastings-on-Hudson NY 10706 Office: Berman Paley Goldstein & Berman 500 Fifth Ave New York NY 10110

GOLDSTEIN, BENNETT HOWARD, lawyer; b. Phila., Aug. 6, 1950; s. George and Rae (Manis) G. BA, Reed Coll., 1972; JD cum laude, Lewis & Clark U., 1980. Bar: Oreg. 1980, U.S. Dist. Ct. Oreg. 1980, U.S. Ct. Appeals (9th cir.) 1980. Assoc. Stoel, Rives, Boley, Fraser & Wyse, Portland, Oreg., 1980—, ptnr., 1986—. Mem. ABA, Oreg. Bar Assn. (ethics com.), Reed Coll. Alumni Assn. (bd. dirs. 1983-84). Republican. Jewish. Avocation: musician. State civil litigation, Federal civil litigation, Bankruptcy. Office: Stoel Rives Boley Fraser & Wyse 900 SW 5th Ave Portland OR 97204

GOLDSTEIN, CANDICE, lawyer; b. Chgo., Mar. 11, 1955; d. Alvin and Sheila Rose (Lefkowitz) G. AB, U. Mich., 1976; JD, U. Ill., 1980. Bar: Ill. 1980, U.S. Dist. Ct. (cen. dist.) Ill. 1980. Atty. Land of Lincoln Legal Assistance Found., Inc., Springfield, Ill., 1980-81; asst. pub. defender Champaign County, Urbana, Ill., 1982-83; sr. atty. Am. Judicature Soc., Chgo., 1984-86; asst. dir. research Def. Research Inst., Chgo., 1986—. Vol. mediator Neighborhood Justice Chgo., 1985—. Mem. ABA, Chgo. Council Lawyers, Am. Judicature Soc. Jewish. Club: Carlton (Chgo.). Insurance, Personal injury, Jurisprudence. Office: Def Research Inst 750 N Lake Shore Dr Chicago IL 60611

GOLDSTEIN, CHARLES ARTHUR, lawyer; b. N.Y.C., Nov. 20, 1936; s. Murray and Evelyn V. Goldstein; m. Judith Stein, Sept. 29, 1962 (div. 1982); 1 child, Deborah Ruth. A.B., Columbia U., 1958; J.D. cum laude, Harvard U., 1961. Bar: N.Y. 1962. Law clk. U.S. Ct. Appeals (2d cir.), 1961-62; assoc. Fried, Frank, Harris, Shriver & Jacobson, N.Y.C., 1962-69; ptnr. Schulte Roth & Zabel, N.Y.C., 1969-79; ptnr. Weil, Gotshal & Manges, N.Y.C., 1979-83, counsel, 1983-85; ptnr. Shea & Gould, N.Y.C., 1985—; lectr. Columbia U. Law Sch.; mem. real estate adv. bd. Real Estate Inst. of NYU. Gen. counsel to Citizens Budget Commn.; mem. Temp. Commn. on City Finances, 1975-77; mem. Gov.'s Task Force on World Trade Ctr. Mem. ABA, Assn. Bar City N.Y., Am. Coll. Real Estate Lawyers. Democrat. Jewish. Club: Harvard. Real property. Home: 475 Park Ave New York NY 10022 Office: Shea & Gould 330 Madison Ave New York NY 10017

GOLDSTEIN, DEBRA HOLLY, lawyer; b. Newark, Mar. 11, 1953; d. Aaron and Erica (Schreier) Green; m. Joel Ray Goldstein, Aug. 14, 1983; children: Stephen Michael, Jennifer Ann. BA, U. Mich., 1973; JD, Emory U., 1977. Bar: Ga. 1977, Mich. 1978, D.C. 1978, Ala. 1984. Tax analyst atty. Gen. Motors Corp., Detroit, 1977-78; trial atty. U.S. Dept. Labor, Birmingham, Ala., 1978—. Chairperson Women's Coordinating Bur., Birmingham, 1983-85; active United Way, Birmingham, 1983, Temple Beth-El Adult Edn., 1985-86; scholarship chairperson Nat. Council Jewish Women, 1986. Mem. ABA, Ga. Bar Assn., D.C. Bar Assn., Mich. Bar Assn., Birmingham Bar Assn. (law day com.), Ala. Bar Assn., Orgn. Rehab. Through Tng. (ORT). Jewish. Lodges: B'nai B'rith Women (chairperson S.E. region 1984-86, counselor 1986—, recipient Women's Humanitarian award 1983), Zonta (v.p. 1983-84), Hadassah (local bd. dirs. 1979-83). Labor, Federal civil litigation. Office: US Dept Labor Office of Solicitor Suite 201 2015 2d Ave N Birmingham AL 35203

GOLDSTEIN, E. ERNEST, lawyer; b. Pitts., Oct. 9, 1918; s. Nathan E. and Annie (Ginsberg) G.; m. Peggy Janet Rosenfeld, June 22, 1941; children: Susan M. Goldstein Lipsitch, Daniel F. A.B. cum laude, Amherst Coll., 1939; student, U. Chgo. Law Sch., 1940-42; LL.B., Georgetown U., 1947; S.J.D., U. Wis., 1956. Bar: D.C. 1947, Tex. 1958, U.S. Supreme Ct. 1967, conseil juridique, France 1973-79. Pvt. practice Washington, 1947; with Dept. Justice, also War Claims Commn., 1947-50; assoc. counsel crime com. U.S. Senate, 1950-51; gen. counsel antitrust subcom. for com. jud. Ho. of Reps., 1951-52; restrictive trade practices specialist Office U.S. Spl. Rep., Paris; also U.S. rep. productivity and applied research com. OEEC, 1952-54; prof. law U. Tex., 1955-65; counsel Coudert Freres, Paris, 1966-67; partner Coudert Freres, 1969-79; cons. CBS, Inc., 1980-85; lectr. Inst. Advanced European Studies, U. Nice, France, 1967, Free U. Brussels, 1967, Europa Inst., Amsterdam, 1970; vis. prof. U. P.R. Law Sch., 1962; prof. Am. seminar, Salzburg, Austria, 1963, 79; internat. law cons. Naval War Coll., 1962, 64; spl. asst. to pres. U.S., 1967-69; chmn. Internat. Lawyers Ann. Conf. Mgmt. Center Europe, 1971-79. Author: Trademark and Copyright Law, 1959, American Enterprise and Scandinavian Antitrust Law, 1962; contbr. author: LBJ: To Know Him Better, 1986; mem. adv. bd. Tex. Internat. Law Jour., 1983—. Chmn. S.W. regional adv. bd. Anti Defamation League, 1964-65; bd. dirs. Am. C. of C. in France, 1970-79, Centre Internat.

de Formation Européenne, 1971—; bd. govs., sec. Am. Hosp. Paris, 1972-79, sec., 1974-79; chmn. fund raising Democratic Party Com. in, France, 1973-77; mem. nat. com. Lyndon B. Johnson Meml. Grove, 1972-74; mem. nat. finance council Democratic Nat. Com., 1975-77. Served with AUS, 1942-46. Decorated Legion of Merit; chevalier Légion d'Honneur, 1971; chevalier Ordre des Arts et des Lettres, 1981; recipient Carl Fulda Internat. Law award U. Tex., 1978; Medal of Honor, Am. C. of C., Paris, 1984; Carnegie Found. fellow, 1954-55; Ford Found. Internat. Studies fellow, 1959-60. Mem. Order of Coif, Phi Delta Phi. Clubs: Travellers (Paris); Am. of Paris (pres. 1976-78). Antitrust, Private international, Patent. Home: Armorial II-2, La Residence CH 1884, Villars-s-Ollon Switzerland

GOLDSTEIN, HARVEY M., lawyer; b. Pitts., June 20, 1937; s. Louis and Ethel (Joseph) G.; m. Dale Harris, Sept. 4, 1963; m. Caron Balkany, Sept. 16, 1976; children—Anne Ellen, Lee Katherine. B.A., St. John's Coll., Annapolis, Md., 1959; J.D., Yale U., 1962. Bar: D.C. 1965, Fla. 1966. Cert. civil trial lawyer. Assoc., Frates, Fay, Floyd & Pearson, 1966-70; ptnr. Tobin, Fisch & Goldstein, P.A., 1970-73; sole practice, Miami, 1973-74; sr. ptnr. Goldstein & Goldstein, P.A., Miami, 1974-78; sr. ptnr. Goldstein P.A., Miami, 1978—. Dep. nat. fin. chmn. Nat. Democratic Party Bus. Council, 1983; bd. visitors and govs. St. John's Coll., Annapolis, Santa Fe, 1982—. Served as 1st lt. U.S. Army, 1963-66. Mem. ABA, Fed. Bar Assn., Acad. Fla. Trial Lawyers, Assn. Trial Lawyers Am., Am. Judicature Soc., Am. Arbitration Assn., Dade County Bar Assn., Alumni Assn. St. Johns Coll. (dir. 1982—). Author: Attorney's Handbook to Video-Tape Depositions, 1976. State civil litigation, Federal civil litigation, Personal injury. Home: 850 San Pedro Coral Gables FL 33156 Office: 1540 NW 15th St Rd Miami FL 33125

GOLDSTEIN, HOWARD SHELDON, lawyer; b. Bklyn., Apr. 22, 1952; s. Jerome Harold and Goldie (Goldsmith) G.; m. Amy Ruth Grossman, Aug. 24, 1980. B.A., CUNY-Queens Coll., 1974; J.D., Bklyn. Law Sch., 1977. Bar: N.Y. 1978, U.S. Dist. Ct. (so. and ea. dists.) N.Y. 1978. Assoc. Loew & Cohen, Esquires, N.Y.C., 1976-82, ptnr., 1982—. Contbr. articles to profl. jours. Mem. N.Y. State Bar Assn. (family law com., legis. com., condominium and coop. com.), N.Y. County Lawyers Assn. Republican. Jewish. Family and matrimonial, General corporate, Real property. Office: Loew & Cohen Esquires 32 Broadway New York NY 10004

GOLDSTEIN, HOWARD WARREN, lawyer; b. N.Y.C., Mar. 29, 1949; s. Murray and Claire (Millrod) G.; m. Wendy Jo Zacharius, Sept. 9, 1973; children: Lindsay Rebecca, Amanda Mikael. BA, Northwestern U., 1970; JD, NYU, 1973. Bar: N.Y. 1974, U.S. Dist. Ct. (so. and ea. dists.) N.Y. 1974, U.S. Ct. Appeals (2d cir.) 1975, U.S. Ct. Appeals (10th cir.) 1984, U.S. Supreme Ct. 1984, U.S. Ct. Appeals (6th cir.) 1985. Law clk. to judge U.S. Dist. Ct. (ea. dist.) N.Y., 1973-74; assoc. Cravath, Swaine & Moore, N.Y.C., 1974-76; asst. U.S. atty. Office of U.S. Atty. (so. dist.) N.Y., N.Y.C., 1976-80; assoc. Mudge, Rose, Guthrie, Alexander & Ferdon, N.Y.C., 1980-81, ptnr., 1982—. Co-author: The Rights of Crime Victims, 1985. Mem. Fed. Bar Council, N.Y. State Bar Assn., Assn. of Bar of City of N.Y., Order of Coif, Phi Beta Kappa. Jewish. Criminal, Federal civil litigation. Office: Mudge Rose Guthrie Alexander & Ferdon 180 Maiden Ln New York NY 10038

GOLDSTEIN, JOSEPH, legal educator; b. Springfield, Mass., May 7, 1923; s. Nathan E. and Anna (Ginsberg) G.; m. Sonja Lambek, Aug. 3, 1947; children: Joshua, Anne, Jeremiah, Daniel. A.B., Dartmouth Coll., 1943; Ph.D., London Sch. Econs., 1950; LL.B., Yale U., 1952; grad., Western New Eng. Inst Psychoanalysis, 1968. Bar: Va. 1953. Law clk. to judge U.S. Ct. Appeals D.C., 1952-53; acting asst. prof. Stanford Law Sch., 1954-56; Russell Sage resident, vis. scholar Harvard Law Sch., 1955-56; assoc. prof. Yale Law Sch., 1956-59, prof., 1959—, Justus S. Hotchkiss prof. law, 1968, Walton Hale Hamilton prof. law, sci. and social policy, 1970, prof. Child Study Center, Med. Sch., 1976—, Sterling prof. law, 1978—; exec. sec., research dir. Gov. Conn. Prison Study Com., 1956-57; cons. devel. neighborhood legal service Community Progress, Inc., New Haven, 1963-64; mem. U.S. atty. gen. com. poverty and adminstrn. criminal justice, 1962-63; cons. Legal Assistance Assos., Inc., New Haven, 1964-73; pres., bd. dirs. Friends of Legal Services South Central Conn., 1981—; bd. dirs. Vera Inst. Justice, 1966—, Sigmund Freud Archives, 1968—; mem. life scis. and social policy com. NRC, 1968; on legal services Office Econ. Opportunity, 1965, Council on Biology in Human Affairs, Salk Inst., 1969. Author: The Government of a British Trade Union, 2d edit, 1953, (with others) Criminal Law, 1962, The Family and the Law, 1965, Psychoanalysis, Psychiatry, and Law, 1967, Crime, Law and Society, 1971, (with Anna Freud and Albert J. Solnit) Beyond the Best Interests of the Child, 1973, 2d edit., 1979, Criminal Law-Theory and Process, 1974, Before the Best Interests of the Child, 1979, (with Burke Marshall and Jack Schwartz) The My Lai Massacre and Its Coverup: Beyond the Reach of Law, 1976, (with Anna Freud, Albert J. Solnit and Sonja Goldstein) In the Best Interests of the Child, 1986. Served with AUS, 1943-46. Fulbright scholar, 1949-50; law fellow U. Wis., 1958; Fulbright sr. lectr., 1973; Guggenheim fellow, 1982. Fellow Am. Acad. Arts and Scis.; mem. New Haven Legal Assistance Assn. Office: Yale U Law Sch New Haven CT 06520

GOLDSTEIN, KENNETH B., lawyer; b. Bklyn., Sept. 16, 1949; s. Nathan and Isabella (Solow) G. BA, Tulane U., 1973, JD, 1974; postdoctoral, Fordham U., 1979. Bar: N.Y. 1977, U.S. Dist. Ct. (so. and ea. dist.) N.Y. 1980, U.S. Ct. Appeals (D.C. cir.) 1981. Gen. mgr., v.p. Middletown (N.Y.) Window Cleaning Co., Inc., 1974; tchr. various schs., Middletown and Chester, N.Y., 1975-77; asst. sr. v.p., dir. mktg. Saks Fifth Ave, N.Y.C., 1977-79; sr. asst. dist. atty. Orange County, Goshen, N.Y., 1979-81; assoc. Zola & Zola, N.Y.C., 1981-83, Freedman, Weisbein & Samuelson P.C., Garden City, N.Y., 1983-85, Jaffe & Asher, N.Y.C., 1985—; bd. dirs. Middletown Window Cleaning Co., Inc. Bd. dirs. New Orleans Jazz and Heritage Found., 1972-74. Named one of Outstanding Young Men in Am., 1980. Mem. ABA, N.Y. State Bar Assn., Middletown Bar Assn., Orange County Bar Assn., Order of DeMolay. Republican. Jewish. Avocations: swimming, art, dance, opera. Family and matrimonial, Landlord-tenant, State civil litigation. Home: 145 E 35th St Apt 2ME New York NY 10016 Office: Jaffe & Asher 489 5th Ave New York NY 10017

GOLDSTEIN, M. ROBERT, lawyer, judge; b. N.Y.C., Nov. 18, 1927; s. Samuel and Dorothy (Kliban) G.; m. Susan Wallach, Nov. 17, 1932; children—Ellen Iris Goldstein Wasserson, Ivan. A.B., Pa. State U. 1947; J.D., NYU, 1949. Bar: N.Y. 1949, U.S. Dist. Ct. (so. and ea. dists.) N.Y. 1956, U.S. Supreme Ct. 1959, U.S. Ct. Appeals (2d cir.) 1969. Ptnr. Samuel Goldstein & Sons, N.Y.C., 1949—; judge Village Ct., Great Neck, N.Y., 1977—. Columnist, Condemnation, Certiorari in N.Y. Law Jour., 1972—. Chmn. Great Neck Planning Bd., 1966-69, Great Neck Bd. Zoning and Appeals, 1969-73; trustee, dep. mayor Village of Great Neck, 1973-77; past pres. Couple's Club, Temple Beth El, Great Neck, United Community Fund, Great Neck; past bd. dirs. Men's Club, Temple Beth El. Mem. Assn. Bar City N.Y., Nassau County Bar Assn., N.Y. County Lawyers' Assn. (chmn. real property com. 1979-84, sec. and bd. dirs. 1982—), N.Y. State Bar Assn., Pi Lambda Phi (pres. nat. council 1970s, pres. endowment fund 1972—). Democrat. Jewish. Club: Glen Head Country (v.p. 1983-85) (N.Y.). Condemnation, State and local taxation. Home: 12 Kings Pl Great Neck NY 11024 Office: Samuel Goldstein & Sons 30 Vesey St New York NY 10007

GOLDSTEIN, MARCIA LANDWEBER, lawyer; b. Bklyn., Aug. 7, 1952; d. Jacob and Sarah Ann (Danovity) Landweber; m. Mark Lewis Goldstein, June 3, 1973. AB, Cornell U., 1972, JD, 1975. Bar: N.Y. 1976, U.S. Dist. Ct. (so. and ea. dists.) N.Y., U.S. Ct. Appeals)2d and 9th cirs.). Assoc. Weil, Gotshal & Manges, N.Y.C., 1975-83, ptnr., 1983—. Mem. ABA (com. on creditors' rights, corp. counsel com.), Assn. of Bar of City of N.Y. (bankruptcy and reorgn. com.), Nat. Bankruptcy Conf., Practicing Law Inst. (panel 1985). Bankruptcy, Contracts commercial, Banking. Office: Weil Gotshal & Manges 767 Fifth Ave New York NY 10153

GOLDSTEIN, MARGARET FRENKEL, lawyer; b. La Ceiba, Honduras, Oct. 22, 1944; came to U.S., 1946; d. Lawrence and Helga (Nygaard) Frenkel; m. Larry S. Goldstein, June 12, 1966; children: Avram, Akiva. BA, CCNY, 1966; JD, NYU, 1976. Bar: N.Y. 1977, U.S. Dist. Ct. (so. and ea. dists.) N.Y. 1977. Assoc. von Maltitz, Derenberg, Kunin & Janssen, N.Y.C., 1976-79; assoc. Weiss, Dawid, Fross, Zelnick & Lehrman, N.Y.C., 1979-83, ptnr., 1983—. Editor Jour. of the Copyright Soc. of USA, 1973, NYU Jour. Internat. Law and Politics, 1974-76. Recipient Stephen P. Ladas Meml. award, 1977. Mem. ABA, Assn. Bar of City of N.Y., Nat. Commn. on Law and Pub. Affairs. Democrat. Jewish. Trademark and copyright. Home: 74-10 175th St Flushing NY 11366 Office: Weiss Dawid Fross Zelnick & Lehrman PC 750 Third Ave New York NY 10017

GOLDSTEIN, MARK HAROLD, lawyer; b. St. Louis, Dec. 20, 1955; s. Robert and Gay (Swartz) G. BBA, U. Wis., 1978, JD, 1981. Bar: Wis. 1981, Nev. 1982, U.S. Ct. Appeals (9th cir.) 1982. Ptnr. Lionel, Sawyer & Collins, Las Vegas, Nev., 1981—. Contbr. articles to profl. jours. Mem. ABA, Wis. Bar Assn., Nev. Bar Assn. (com. on bus. law 1985—). Democrat. Jewish. General corporate, Real property. Home: 2483 Whippoorwill Las Vegas NV 89121 Office: Lionel Sawyer & Collins 300 S 4th #1700 Las Vegas NV 89101

GOLDSTEIN, MICHAEL GERALD, lawyer; b. St. Louis, Sept. 21, 1946; s. Joseph and Sara G. (Finklestein) G.; m. Ilene Marcia Ballin, July 19, 1970; children—Stephen Eric, Rebecca Leigh. B.A., Tulane U., 1968; J.D., U. Mo., 1971; LL.M. in Taxation, Washington U., 1972. Bar: Mo. 1971, U.S. Dist. Ct. (ea. dist.) Mo. 1972, U.S. Tax Ct. 1972, U.S. Ct. Appeals (8th cir.) 1974, U.S. Supreme Ct. 1976. Atty. Morris A. Shenker, St. Louis, 1972-78; ptnr. Lashly, Caruthers, Baer & Hamel, and predecessor, St. Louis, 1979-84, Suelthaus & Kaplan, P.C. and predecessors, St. Louis, 1984—; dir. Anchor Floor Co., Maritz Inc.; mem. planning com. Mid-Am. Tax Confs.; lectr. taxation field. Bd. dirs. Jewish Family and Children's Service St. Louis, 1980—, pres., 1986—; bd. dirs. Jewish Fedn. of St. Louis; trustee United Hebrew Temple; grad. Jewish Fedn. St. Louis Leadership Devel. Council; co-chmn. lawyers div. Jewish Fedn. St. Louis Campaign, 1981-82. Served to capt. USAR, 1970-78. Mem. Am. Law Inst., ABA, Mo. Bar Assn., Bar Assn. Met. St. Louis, St. Louis County Bar Assn. Jewish. Author: BNA Tax Mgmt. Portfolios; contbr. numerous articles to profl. jours. Corporate taxation, Personal income taxation, Municipal Bonds. Home: 26 Log Cabin Dr Saint Louis MO 63124 Office: 8000 Maryland St 9th Floor Saint Louis MO 63105

GOLDSTEIN, MORT, lawyer, industrial engineer; b. N.Y.C., Apr. 13, 1942; s. Morris and Sarah (Elbaum) G.; children—Scott, Janice, Annette. BS in Indsl. Engring., Mont. State U., 1964; JD, U. Mont., 1969. Bar: Mont. 1970, Calif. 1970, U.S. Dist. Ct. (no. dist.) Calif. 1970, U.S. Supreme Ct. 1973, U.S. Dist. Ct. (cen. dist.) Calif. 1974, U.S. Dist. Ct. Mont. 1975, U.S. Dist. Ct. (ea. dist.) Calif. 1981. Assoc., Mintz, Giller, Himmelman & Minz, Oakland, Calif., 1969-75; ptnr. Hauge, Ober, Thompson & Goldstein, Havre, Mont., 1975-80; pres. Goldstein Law Firm, P.C., Havre, 1980—. Recipient award Am. Soc. Composers, Authors and Pubs., 1969. Mem. ABA, Calif. Bar Assn., Mont. Trial Lawyers Assn., Assn. Trial Lawyers Am. Lutheran. Probate, Personal injury, Probate. Office: PO Box 706 Havre MT 59501

GOLDSTEIN, NEAL, lawyer; b. Phila., Oct. 11, 1947; s. Norman and Helen (Ettinger) G.; m. Marilyn K. Zatz, June 8, 1969; children: Matthew, Benjamin. BA, Temple U., 1969, JD, 1973. Bar: Pa. 1973, U.S. Dist. Ct. (ea. dist.) 1973, U.S. Ct. Appeals (3d cir.) 1973. Law clk. to presiding justice Pa. Ct. Commons Pleas, Phila., 1973-74; assoc. Markowitz & Kirschner, Phila., 1974-78; ptnr. Gafni & Goldstein, Phila., 1979-80, Freedman & Lorry, P.C., Phila., 1981—. Labor. Home: 206 Drakes Drum Dr Bryn Mawr PA 19010 Office: Freedman & Lorry PC 800 Lafayette Bldg Philadelphia PA 19106

GOLDSTEIN, PAUL, lawyer, educator; b. Mount Vernon, N.Y., Jan. 14, 1943; s. Martin and Hannah (Shimberg) G.; m. Jan Thompson, Aug. 28, 1977. B.A., Brandeis U., 1964; LL.B. Columbia U., 1967. Bar: N.Y. 1968, Calif. 1978. Asst. prof. law SUNY-Buffalo, 1967-69, assoc. prof., 1969-71, prof., 1972-75; vis. assoc. prof. Stanford U., Calif., 1972-73, prof. law, 1975—, Stella W. and Ira S. Lillick prof. law, 1985—. Author: Changing the American Schoolbook-Law, Politics and Technology, 1978, Real Estate Transactions-Cases and Materials on Land Transfer, Development and Finance, 1980, 2d edit., 1985, Copyright, Patent, Trademark and Related State Doctrines-Cases and Materials on the Law of Intellectual Property, 2d edit., 1981, Real Property, 1984; also articles. Trademark and copyright, Real property.

GOLDSTEIN, PAUL E., corporate lawyer. BS, U. Ill., 1957; LLB, Yale U., 1961. Ptnr. Ross, Hardies, O'Keefe, Babcock & Parsons, 1962-72; gen. atty. People's Gas Co., Chgo., 1972-75, asst. gen. counsel, 1975-81; asst. gen. counsel MidCon Corp., Lombard, Ill., 1981-84, v.p., gen. counsel, 1984—. Office: Midcon Corp 701 E 22nd St Box 1207 Lombard IL 60148 *

GOLDSTEIN, RICHARD JAY, lawyer; b. Bklyn., Feb. 18, 1941; s. Hyman Lawrence and Helen Shirley G.; m. Rona S. Ruderman, June 25, 1961; children—Howard, Marcia. Student Menlo Coll., 1958-59; B.A., Stanford U., 1962; LL.B., UCLA, 1965. Bar: Calif. 1966, U.S. Dist. Ct. Calif., U.S. Ct. Appeals (9th cir.). Sole practice, Los Angeles, 1966-68; asst. sec. and ops. counsel Budget Fin. Plan, Los Angeles, 1968-72; v.p., gen. counsel, corp. sec. Nationwide Fin. Services subs. Citicorp, St. Louis, Mo., 1972-73; assoc. Buchalter, Nemer, Fields and Savitch, Los Angeles, 1973-76; ptnr. Buchalter, Nemer, Fields, Chrystie and Younger, P.C., Los Angeles, San Francisco, San Jose and Orange County, 1976—; lectr. Practising Law Inst., 1980—, Continuing Edn. of the Bar, Fin. Lawyers Conf., bd. dirs. Univ. Synagogue, Los Angeles; mem. adv. bd. Calif. Sec. of State's Citizens Adv. Bd.; pres. booster club Pacific Palisades High Sch., 1981-84. Mem. State Bar Calif., Los Angeles County Bar Assn. (comml. law and bankruptcy sect.), Internat. Bar Assn. (aero. law and comml. banking coms.), ABA (uniform comml. code com. sect. corp. banking and bus. law), Fin. Lawyers Conf. (treas. 1970-72, pres. 1975-76, bd. govs.), Nat. Comml. Fin. Assn., Am. Assn. Equipment Lessors (lawyers com.), Los Angeles C. of C. (aerospace com.). Democrat. Jewish. Club: Los Angeles Athletic. Contbr. articles to profl. jours., chpts. to books. Banking, Bankruptcy, Contracts commercial. Office: 700 S Flower St Suite 700 Los Angeles CA 90017

GOLDSTEIN, RICHARD M., lawyer; b. Chgo., June 30, 1952. B.S. in Accountancy, U. Ill.-Urbana, 1974; J.D. with honors, Ill. Inst. Tech.-Chgo.-Kent Coll. Law, 1977. Bar: Ill. 1977, U.S. dist. ct. (no. dist.) Ill. 1977, U.S. Supreme Ct. 1983. Founding ptnr. Benson & Goldstein, Chgo., 1977-80; ptnr. Benson, Goldstein & Stengel, Chgo., 1980-84; sole practice, 1984—. Chmn. housing com. Lakeview Citizens Council, 1976-78. Decalogue Soc. Lawyers acad. scholar, 1975; vol. atty. Lawyers for the Creative Arts, 1978—. Mem. ABA, Ill. State Bar Assn. (family law sect. council), Chgo. Bar Assn. (com. on matrimonial law), Chgo. Council Lawyers, Am. Judicature Soc., Lincoln Park C. of C., Bar and Gavel Soc. Assoc. editor Goldstein Trial Technique, 2d edit., 1977. Family and matrimonial, Probate, Entertainment. Address: 33 N Dearborn St Suite 2400 Chicago IL 60602

GOLDSTEIN, STEVEN, lawyer; b. St. Louis, Sept. 8, 1950; s. Alexander Julius and Dorothy Lea (Matier) G.; m. Laura Lou Staley, July 20, 1980. BS in Speech, Northwestern U., Evanston, Ill., 1972; JD, U. Mich., 1975. Bar: Mo. 1975. Ptnr. Husch, Eppenberger, Donohue, Cornfeld & Jenkins, St. Louis, 1975—. Mem. ABA, Mo. Bar Assn. (chmn. bankruptcy com. 1983-85), Bar Assn. of Met. St. Louis. Banking, Bankruptcy, Contracts commercial. Home: 5560 Waterman 1W Saint Louis MO 63112 Office: Husch Eppenberger Donohue Cornfeld & Jenkins 100 N Broadway 18th Floor Saint Louis MO 63102

GOLICK, TOBY BARBARA, lawyer, consultant; b. Boston, Apr. 9, 1945; d. Albert David and Sara (Sharaf) G.; m. Telford Taylor, Aug. 9, 1974; children—Benjamin W. Taylor, Samuel B. Taylor. B.A., Barnard Coll., 1966; J.D., Columbia U., 1969. Bar: N.Y. 1969, U.S. Supreme Ct. 1971, U.S. Ct. Appeals (2d cir.) 1971, U.S. Dist. Ct. (so. and ea. dists.) N.Y. 1970, Atty., then mng. atty. Queens Legal Services, N.Y.C., 1969-71; atty. Columbia Ctr. on Social Welfare Policy and Law, N.Y.C., 1971-72; sr. atty. Legal Services for Elderly, N.Y.C., 1976-85; clin. prof. Carduzo Sch. of Law, 1985—; dir. Cardozo Bet Tzedek Legal Services, 1985—; cons. Legal Services Corp., Washington, 1983. Contbr. articles to profl. publs. Mem. Assn. of Bar City of N.Y. Democrat. Jewish. Civil rights, Health, Pension, profit-sharing, and employee benefits. Home: 54 Morningside Dr New York NY 10025 Office: Cardozo Sch of Law 55 Fifth Ave New York NY 10003

GOLIN, MARGERY S., lawyer; b. New Brunswick, N.J., June 6, 1933; d. Jack C. and Dorothy (Kranz) Sosin; m. Hugo L. Golin, Sept. 4, 1955; children: Lise, Daniel. BS, Columbia U., 1955; MEd, Rutgers U., 1970, JD, 1979. Bar: N.J. 1979, U.S. Dist. Ct. N.J. 1979. Dep. pub. adv. N.J. Dept. Pub. Adv., Newark, 1980-86, dep. dir., 1984-86; prosecutor Edison Twp., N.J., 1987—. Councilwoman Edison Twp., N.J., 1975-83; chmn. planning bd. Edison Twp., 1974-75, mem. planning bd., 1973-74. Mem. ABA, N.J. Bar Assn. Public utilities. Office: William J Hamilton Jr 92 Bayard St New Brunswick NJ 08903

GOLKO, ANDREW ALBIN, lawyer; b. Weston Supermare, Eng., Oct. 9, 1945; came to U.S., 1951; s. Jerzy and Zdzislawa Anna (Inglot) G. B.S. in Fin., U. Ill.-Chgo., 1971; J.D., John Marshall Law Sch., 1975. Bar: Ill. 1972, U.S. Dist. Ct. (no. dist.) Ill. 1975, U.S. Ct. Internat. Trade 1982, U.S. Ct. Appeals 1983, U.S. Supreme Ct. 1979. Lic. real estate broker, Ill. Bldg. mgr. Cir. Campus Library, U. Ill., Chgo., 1969; real estate salesman and mgmt. C.B. Zeller Real Estate, Chgo., 1969-75; assoc. Chgo. Vol. Legal Services Found., 1974; vis. lectr. U. Ill.-Chgo., 1975-82; sole practice, Chgo., 1975—; pres. Golko Internat. Trade and Investment Group, Ltd., Brok, Poland, 1983—; cons. Polish law, 1979—; vis. lectr. Inst. Internat. Law, Warsaw U., Poland, 1980, Mem. ABA, Ill. Bar Assn., Chgo. Bar Assn., Nat. Advocate Soc., Cook County Advocate Soc., North Side Real Estate Bd., Am. Legion. General practice, Real property, Private international. Office: 1457 W Belmont Ave Chicago IL 60657

GOLOMB, DAVID BELA, lawyer; b. Bklyn., Apr. 19, 1949; s. Maurice and Rita (Pick) G.; m. Lisa Ann Cutler, June 17, 1984. B.A., Cornell U., 1970; J.D., St. John's U., 1974. Bar: N.Y. 1975, U.S. Dist. Ct. (so. dist.) N.Y. 1977, U.S. Dist. Ct. (ea. dist.) N.Y. 1978, U.S. Ct. Appeals (2d cir.) 1979, U.S. Supreme Ct. 1979. Trial atty. N.Y.C. Legal Aid Soc., 1974-77; adminstr. N.Y.C. Office of Dep. Mayor, 1977-78; spl. asst. atty. gen. N.Y. State Office of Medicaid Fraud Control, 1978-80; trial atty. Fuchsberg and Fuchsberg, N.Y.C., 1980-83; trial atty. Paul D. Rheingold, P.C., N.Y.C., 1983-85; ptnr. Rheingold & Golomb, P.C., N.Y.C., 1985—. Mem. ABA, N.Y. County Lawyers Assn., Assn. Bar City N.Y. (mem. tort litigation com.), Assn. Trial Lawyers Am., N.Y. State Trial Lawyers Assn. (mem. med. malpractice com.), N.Y. State Bar Assn. Democrat. Personal injury, Federal civil litigation, State civil litigation. Home: 552 La Guardia Pl New York NY 10012 Office: Rheingold and Golomb PC 113 E 37th St New York NY 10016

GOLOMB, GEORGE EDWIN, lawyer; b. Newark, Jan. 28, 1947; s. Max and Elizabeth (Epstein) G.; m. Cynthia Lifson, June 3, 1984. BA, Yale U., 1968; JD, U. Pa., 1972. Bar: N.Y. 1974, N.J. 1977, D.C. 1985, Md. 1985. Assoc. Weil, Gotshal & Manges, N.Y.C., 1972-74; law clk. to presiding judge U.S. Dist. Ct. (ea. dist.) N.Y., Bklyn., 1974-76; assoc. Donovan, Leisure, Newton & Irvine, N.Y.C., 1976-80; trial atty. civil div. U.S. Dept. Justice, Washington, 1980-84; assoc. Ellin & Baker, Balt., 1985; sole practice Balt., 1986—. Contbr. articles to profl. jours. Ford Found. fellow, 1975, Phelps Assn. fellow, 1967. Mem. ABA (govt. litigation com. 1984—), Balt. City Bar Assn. (exec. com. mem. 1986—), Md. State Bar Assn. Lodges: Rotary, B'nai B'rith. Federal civil litigation, State civil litigation. Home: 5602 Gulf Stream Row Columbia MD 21044 Office: 2 N Charles St Baltimore MD 21201

GOLPER, JOHN BRUCE, lawyer; b. El Paso, Tex., Sept. 6, 1950; s. Marvin Norman and Jean Rose (Becker) G.; m. Leslie Ann Lawry, Mar. 21, 1981; children: Matthew Brent, Brian Yale. BA with honors, Ind. U., 1972; JD, UCLA, 1975. Bar: Calif. 1975, U.S. Dist. Ct. (cen. dist.) Calif. 1975, U.S. Ct. Appeals (9th cir.) 1977, U.S. Dist. Ct. (no. and so. dists.) Calif. 1981, U.S. Supreme Ct. 1981, U.S. Ct. Appeals (3d cir.) 1982, U.S. Dist. Ct. (ea. dist.) Calif. 1986. Extern law clk. Calif. Ct. Appeal 1st Dist., San Francisco, 1974; assoc. Bodkin, McCarthy, Sargent & Smith, Los Angeles, 1975-78; ptnr. Parker Milliken, Clark, O'Hara & Samuelian, Los Angeles, 1978-86, Ballard, Rosenberg & Golper, Los Angeles, 1986—. Mem. Calif. Comparable Worth Task Force, Sacramento, 1984-86. Grable Meml. scholar Ind. U., 1968, Ind. State scholar, 1968, Honors Div. Merit scholar, 1971-72; recipient cert. of Recognition, Compensation Practices Assn. San Diego County, 1983, 84. Mem. ABA, Calif. Bar Assn., Los Angeles County Bar Assn., Indsl. Relations Research Assn., Electronic Salary and Wage Assn. Republican. Jewish. Club: Jonathan. Labor, Federal civil litigation, State civil litigation. Office: Ballard Rosenberg & Golper 1900 Ave of Stars Suite 2300 Los Angeles CA 90076

GOLSONG, HERIBERT, consultant, lawyer; b. Oberhausen, Germany, Oct. 23, 1927; s. Willibald B. and Paula A. (Friesenhahn) G.; m. Christine M. Vanneste, Oct. 12, 1954; children—Dominique, Thomas, Anne Sophie. Student Law Faculty U. Cologne (Germany), U. Wuerzberg (Germany); LL.D., U. Bonn (W.Ger), 1950; postgrad. Coll. of Europe, Belgium, 1951-52; diplomate Hague (Netherlands) Acad. Internat. Law, 1953; LL.D. (hon.), U. Edinburgh (Scotland), 1970. Dep. sec. European Commn. on Human Rights, 1954-57, sec. parliamentary legal com., 1957-59, sec. polit. com., 1959-60; dep. registrar European Ct. Human Rights, 1960-63, registrar, 1963-68; head legal services Council on Europe, 1963-68, head human rights directorate, 1977-79; legal adv. European Resettlement Fund, Paris, 1961-79; sec. gen. Arbitration Ctr., ICSID, IBRD, Washington, 1979-83; arbitrator ICSID and Am. Arbitration Assn.; Mem. investment Com. Nat. Fgn. Trade Council; adv. Arent, Fox, Kintner, Plotkin & Kahn, Washington; hon. prof. law U. Heidelberg (W.Ger.); adj. prof. law Washington Coll. Law. Decorated Order of Merit (W.Ger.); grand comdr. Order Merit (Liechtenstein); comdr. Order King Leopold (Belgium); comdr. Order St. Olav (Norway); comdr. Order of Merit (Austria). Mem. German Soc. Internat. Law, Max Planck Inst. Internat. Law (Kuratorium), French Soc. Internat. Law, Am. Soc. Internat. Law, Brit. Inst. Internat. and Comparative Law, German Soc. Procedural Law, Internat. Legal Materials (adv. bd.). Clubs: Oxford, Cambridge, London. Author numerous books in German, French and English on internat. pub. law and internat. fin. law; contbr. numerous articles to profl. jours. Private international, Public international, Contracts commercial. Office: 1818 H St NW Washington DC 20433

GOLTZER, GEORGE R., lawyer; b. N.Y.C., Oct. 15, 1945; s. Albert and Doris (Delman) G. BA, Syracuse U., 1966; JD, St. John's U., 1972. Bar: N.Y. 1973, U.S. Dist. Ct. (so. dist.) N.Y. 1975, U.S. Dist. Ct. (ea. dist.) N.Y. 1980, U.S. Ct. Appeals (2d cir.) 1980, U.S. Ct. Appeals (1st and 4th cirs.) 1985. Trial atty. criminal def. div. and law adv. bur. N.Y. City Legal Aid Soc., N.Y.C., 1972-76; ptnr. Goltzer & Adler, N.Y.C., 1976—; mem. faculty trial adv. program Legal Aid Soc., 1985-86; bd. dirs. The Toscanini Assns., Inc., N.Y.C. Vol. U.S. Peace Corps., Micronesia, 1966-68; mem. cen. screening com. 1st Jud. Dept., N.Y.C, 1985-86. Mem. ABA, N.Y.C. Criminal Bar Assn., Assn. Trial Lawyers Am., N.Y. State Defender's Assn., Nat. Assn. Criminal Def. Lawyers. Avocations: swimming, hiking, classical music. Criminal. Office: Goltzer & Adler 90 Broad St New York NY 10004

GOLUB, MARTIN JOSEPH, lawyer; b. New Bedford, Mass., Dec. 31, 1947; s. Harry I. and Avis E. (Radovsky) G.; m. Melinda Vickrey, Sept. 8, 1968; Elisabeth, Joseph. AB cum laude, Princeton U., 1969; JD cum laude, Boston Coll., 1977. Bar: Mass. 1977, U.S. Ct. Appeals (1st cir.) 1978, U.S. Dist. Ct. Mass. 1978, D.C. 1980, U.S. Dist. Ct. D.C. 1980, U.S. Ct. Claims 1980, U.S. Ct. Appeals (D.C. cir.) 1980, U.S. Supreme Ct. 1981. Assoc. Vom Baur, Coburn et al, Boston, 1977-79; assoc. Seyfarth, Shaw, Fairweather & Geraldson, Washington, 1979-85, ptnr., 1985—. Contbr. articles to profl. jours. Served to lt. (j.g.) USCG, 1971-74. Mem. ABA (internat. procurement com. pub. contract law sect.), Boston Bar Assn., D.C. Bar Assn., Nat. Contract Mgmt. Assn., Fedn. Pour L'Etude Du Droit Et Des Usages Du Commerce Internat. Club: Univ. (Washington). Government contracts and claims, Private international, Public international. Office: Seyfarth Shaw Fairweather & Geraldson 1111 19th St NW Washington DC 20036

GOMEZ, DAVID FREDERICK, lawyer; b. Los Angeles, Nov. 19, 1940; s. Fred and Jennie (Fujier) G.; m. Kathleen Holt, Oct. 18, 1977. BA in Philosophy, St. Paul's Coll., Washington, 1965, MA in Theology, 1968; JD, U. So. Calif., 1974. Bar: Calif. 1975, U.S. Dist. Ct. (cen. dist.) Calif. 1975, U.S. Dist. Ct. (ea. dist.) Calif. 1977, Ariz. 1981, US. Dist. Ct. Ariz. 1981, U.S. Ct. Claims 1981, U.S. Ct. Appeals (9th cir.) 1981, U.S. Supreme Ct. 1981; ordained priest Roman Cath. Ch., 1969. Staff atty. Nat. Labor Rela-

tions Bd., Los Angeles, 1974-75; ptnr. Gomez, Paz, Rodriguez & Sanora, Los Angeles, 1975-77, Garrett, Bourdette & Williams, San Francisco, 1977-80, Van O'Steen & Ptnrs., Phoenix, 1981-85; pres. David F. Gomez, PC, Phoenix, 1985—. Author: Somos Chicanos: Strangers in Our Own Land, 1973. Mem. ABA, Maricopa County Bar Assn., Los Abogados Hispanic Bar Assn., Plaintiff Employment Lawyer's Assn. Democrat. Labor, Federal civil litigation, State civil litigation. Office: 2111 E Highland Ave Suite 175 Phoenix AZ 85016

GONDELMAN, HAROLD, lawyer; b. Pitts., Dec. 16, 1922; s. Samuel and Mollie (Frishman) G.; m. Ruth G. Mullen, Aug. 14, 1949; children—Larry S., Kathy M. Gondelman Oklin, Richard F., Nancy B. A.B., U. Pitts., 1943, LL.B., 1949. Bar: Pa. 1950, U.S. Dist. Ct. (we. dist.) Pa. 1950, U.S. Ct. Appeals (3d cir.) 1951, U.S. Supreme Ct. 1973. Adminstrv. law asst. to presiding judge U.S. Dist. (we. dist.) Pa. 1950-53; law clk. to presiding judge Superior Ct. of Pa., 1954; ptnr. Jacobson & Gondelman, Pitts., 1954-68; sr. ptnr. Baskin, Boreman, Wilner, Sachs, Gondelman & Craig, Pitts., 1968-78; mem. Gondelman Baxter Mc Verry Smith Yatch & Trimm, P.C., Pitts., 1979—, mng. dir.; asst. county solicitor Allegheny County, Pa., 1962-65. Pres. Jewish Community Ctr. of Pitts., 1973-76. Served to 1st lt. U.S. Army, 1943-46; PTO. Recipient Man of Yr. award State of Israel, 1981, Histadrut, 1978. Mem. ABA, Pa. Bar Assn., Allegheny County Bar Assn., Acad. Trial Lawyers Allegheny County, Assn. Trial Lawyers Am., Nat. Assn. Criminal Def. Lawyers. Democrat. Jewish. Clubs: Green Oaks, Concordia; Boca Lago Country (Boca Raton, Fla.). Mem. staff U. Pitts. Law Rev., 1947-49. Federal civil litigation, State civil litigation, Criminal. Home: 1182 Beechwood Blvd Pittsburgh PA 15206 Office: 718 5th Ave Pittsburgh PA 15219

GONNELLA, LOUIS GREGORY, lawyer, educator; b. Newark; s. Angelo Michael and Eleanor (Fabbo) G. BA, Upsala Coll., 1973; JD, Coll. William and Mary, 1976. Bar: N.J. 1976, U.S. Dist. Ct. N.J. 1976, N.Y. 1982, U.S. Supreme Ct. 1980. Law clk. to presiding justice N.J. Superior Ct., Newark, 1976-77; assoc. Pub. Defender's Office, Bergen County, N.J., 1978—; instr. Am. Inst. Paralegal Studies, Essex County, N.J., 1984—. Vice pres. Upsala Coll. Alumni Council, East Orange, N.J., 1982-87, pres., 1987—; trustee Bergen County Legal Services, Hackensack, N.J., 1982-85. Mem. ABA, Phi Delta Phi. Roman Catholic. Avocations: hiking, chess, writing. Office: Office of Pub Defender 190 Main St 4th Fl Hackensack NJ 07601

GONSER, THOMAS HOWARD, lawyer, bar association executive; b. Berkeley, Calif., May 8, 1938; s. William Adam and Alice Gertrude (Lease) G.; m. Stephanie Jane Griffiths, Nov. 27, 1960; children: Thomas Howard, Catherine Ruth. A.A., U. Calif., Berkeley, 1958, B.A. in Polit. Sci., 1960, J.D., 1965. Bar: Calif. 1965, Idaho 1970. Atty. S.P. Co., San Francisco, 1965-68; asst. gen. counsel Boise Cascade Corp., Idaho, 1969-72; assoc. gen. counsel Boise Cascade Corp., 1972-81, asst. sec., 1972-81; exec. dir. Am. Bar Assn., Chgo., 1981—. Author: The Bar Foundation, 1979. Served with U.S. Army, 1960-62. Fellow Am. Bar Found.; mem. Idaho Law Found. (pres. 1977-80), Calif. Bar Assn., Am. Law Inst., Idaho State Bar, Nat. Conf. Bar Founds. (pres. 1980-81), Internat. Bar Assn. (dep. sec. gen. 1982—), Inter-Am. Bar Assn. dep. sec. gen. 1983-84). Methodist. General corporate. Office: Am Bar Assn 750 N Lake Shore Dr Chicago IL 60611 *

GONSON, S. DONALD, lawyer; b. Buffalo, June 13, 1936; s. Samuel and Laura Rose (Greenspan) G.; m. Dorothy Rose, Aug. 28, 1960; children—Julia, Claudia. A.B., Columbia U., 1958; J.D., Harvard U., 1961; postgrad., U. Bombay, India, 1961-62. Bar: Mass. 1962. With Hale and Dorr, Boston, 1962—, sr. ptnr., 1972—; lectr. Fin. Times (U.K.), Instl. Investrs, New Eng. Law Inst., Mass. Soc. C.P.A.s; co-chmn. Speech-Tech., N.Y.C., 1987—; instr. in law Boston U., 1963-65, bd. trustees Boston Five Cents Savs. Bank, 1973-83, bd. advisors 1983—; bd. dirs. Colonial Penn Group, Inc. Chmn. Mass. Community Devel. Fin. Corp., 1976-82; pres. Cambridge Ctr. for Adult Edn. Fulbright scholar, 1961-62. Mem. Internat. Bar Assn., ABA, Mass. Bar Assn., Boston Bar Assn. Clubs: Bay (Boston); Harvard Faculty, Cambridge Tennis (Cambridge). General corporate, Contracts commercial, Private international. Home: 32 Hubbard Park Cambridge MA 02138 Office: 60 State St Boston MA 02109

GONSOULIN, DEWEY JUDE, lawyer; b. Houston, Dec. 27, 1929; s. Robert Frederic and Elma (Bourgeois) G.; m. Jean Johnson, Apr. 25, 1959; children: Jean delaHoussaye Gonsoulin, Anne, Dewey Jr. BA, Rice Inst., 1951; LLB, U. Tex., 1954. Bar: Tex. 1954, U.S. Ct. Appeals (5th cir.) 1954. Assoc. Mehaffy, Weber & Keith, Beaumont, Tex., 1956-62; ptnr. Mehaffy, Weber, Keith & Gonsoulin, Beaumont, 1962—. Chmn. Beaumont (Tex.) Civil Service Commn., 1970—. Served to 1st lt. U.S. Army, 1954-56, CBI. Fellow Am. Coll. Trial Lawyers, Tex. Bar Found.; mem. ABA, Tex. Bar Assn., Tex. Assn. Def. Counsel (pres. 1978-79), Assn. Ins. Attys., Internat. Assn. Def. Counsel. Federal civil litigation, Personal injury, Labor. Home: 8185 Evangeline Ln Beaumont TX 77706 Office: Mehaffy Weber Keith & Gonsoulin 2615 Calder Beaumont TX 77701

GONYA, DONALD ALAN, lawyer; b. Berlin, N.H., Aug. 13, 1934; s. Joseph Wilson and Winifred (Devlin) G.; m. Suzanne DuRant, Nov. 28, 1959; children—Jeffrey Keenan, Karen Roof, Gail Elizabeth. B.A., U. N.H., 1957; LL.B., Boston U., 1963. Bar: N.H. 1963. Asst. regional atty. Office of Gen. Counsel, HEW, Charlottesville, Va., 1963-70, regional atty. Office of Gen. Counsel, Phila., 1970-73, dep. asst. gen. counsel Office of Gen. Counsel, Social Security Div., Balt., 1973-77, acting asst. gen. counsel Office of Gen. Counsel, Insp. Gen.'s Div., Washington, 1977-78, dep. asst. gen. counsel Social Security Div., Balt., 1978-79; acting assoc. commr. Office Hearings and Appeals, Social Security Adminstrn., Arlington, Va., 1979; asst. gen. counsel Office of Gen. Counsel, Social Security Div., HHS, Balt., 1979-86, chief counsel, Social Security Div., 1986—. Served as 1st lt. USAF, 1957-60. Named Outstanding Younger Fed. Lawyer, HEW, 1969; recipient Superior Service award HEW, 1975, Spl. citation Insp. Gen., 1977, Spl. citation Sec. HEW, 1977, Commr.'s citation Social Security Adminstrn., 1979, Meritorious Service award Pres. U.S., 1980. Administrative and regulatory, Pension, profit-sharing, and employee benefits. Office: 6401 Security Blvd Baltimore MD 21235

GONZALES, JEFFREY CHARLES, lawyer; b. Portland, Oreg., June 5, 1954; s. Edward Llamas and Lourdes (Durano) G.; m. Loida Fernando Lumba, Mar. 19, 1977; children: Jonathan, Jerilynn. BS, Portland State U., 1977, MBA, 1979; JD, U. Wash., 1982. Bar: Oreg. 1982, Wash. 1983, U.S. Dist. Ct. (we. dist.) Wash. 1984. Supr. United Parcel Service, Portland, 1977-79; contracts specialist Wash. State Lottery, Olympia, 1982-83; adminstr. contracts and regulations Wash. State Employment Security Dept., Olympia, 1983—. Precinct person Portland Dems., 1982. Mem. ABA, Wash. State Bar Assn., Oreg. Bar Assn., Oreg. Trial Lawyers Assn., Filipino-Am. Assn., Asian Law Assn. (steering com. 1979-84). Democrat. Roman Catholic. Avocations: coaching and playing basketball, tennis, piano. Immigration, naturalization, and customs, Personal injury, State civil litigation.

GONZALES, RICHARD JOSEPH, lawyer; b. Tucson, Mar. 5, 1950; s. Diego D. and Helen O. (Olivas) G.; m. Melinda K. Chamness, Dec. 21, 1974; children: Adrianne Dee, Laura Renee. BA, U. Ariz., 1972, JD, 1975. Bar: Ariz. 1976, U.S. Dist. Ct. Ariz. 1976, U.S. Ct. Appeals 1976. Asst. pub. defender Pima County Pub. Defenders Office, Tucson, 1976-77; dep. atty. criminal div. Pima County Atty.'s Office, Tucson, 1977-80; ptnr. Gonzales & Villarreal, P.C., Tucson, 1980—; assoc. instr. bus. law Pima Community Coll.,Tucson, 1977, criminal law, 1978-80; judge pro tem Pima County Superior Ct., 1983—; magistrate City of South Tucson, 1982-85; spl. magistrate City of Tucson, 1982-85. Mem. Tucson Tomorrow, 1984—, citizen's adv. council sunnyside Sch. Dist. #12, 1986—; chmn. com. Udall for Congress Ariz. 2d Congl. Dist., United Way Hispanic Leadership Devel. Program, 1984-86, Hispanic Profl. Action Com., 1984-85, vice-chairperson, 1983-84, chairperson, 1984-85; bd. dirs. Girls Club of Tucson, Inc., 1980-81, Teatro Carmen, Inc., 1981—, Sunnyside Devilaides, Inc., 1982-83, Alcoholism Council of Tucson, 1982-83, Crime Resisters, 1984-85, La Frontera Ctr., Inc., 1985—, Crime Prevention League, 1985-75; gen. counsel U. Ariz. Hispanic Alumni, 1984—, Accion 80's, 1983—. Named one of Outstanding Young Men of Am. U.S. Jaycee's, 1980; recipient Vol. of Yr. award United Way Greater Tucson, 1985. Mem. ABA, Ariz. Bar Assn., Pima County Bar Assn., Assn. Trial Lawyers Am., Ariz. Trial Lawyers Assn., Nat. Orgn. on Legal Problems of Edn., Supreme Ct. Hist. Soc., Phi Delta Phi. Democrat. Roman Catholic. Lodge: Optimists (Optimist of Yr. 1981). Personal injury, Criminal, General practice. Home: 7330 N Sonya Way Tucson AZ 85704 Office: Gonzales & Villarreal PC 261 N Court Ave Tucson AZ 85701

GONZALEZ, JOSE ALEJANDRO, JR., judge; b. Tampa, Fla., Nov. 26, 1931; s. Jose A. and Luisa Secundina (Collia) G.; m. Frances Frierson, Aug. 22, 1956 (dec. Aug. 1981); children—Margaret Ann, Mary Frances; m. Mary Sue Copeland, Sept. 24, 1983. B.A., U. Fla., 1952, J.D., 1957. Bar: Fla. 1958, U.S. Dist. Ct. (so. dist.) Fla. 1959, U.S. Ct. Appeals 1959, U.S. Supreme Ct. 1963. Practice in Ft. Lauderdale, 1958-64; claim rep. State Farm Mut., Lakeland, Fla., 1957-58; assoc. firm Watson, Hubert and Sousley, 1958-61, ptnr., 1961-64; asst. state atty. 15th Circuit Fla., 1961-64; circuit judge 17th Circuit Ft. Lauderdale, 1964-78, chief judge, 1970-71; assoc. judge 4th Dist. Ct. Appeals, West Palm Beach; U.S. dist. judge So. Dist. Fla., 1978—. Bd. dirs. Arthritis Found., 1962-72; bd. dirs. Henderson Clinic Broward County, 1964-68, v.p., 1967-68. Served to 1st lt. AUS, 1952-54. Named Broward County Outstanding Young Man, 1967; one of Fla.'s Five Outstanding Young Men Fla. Jaycees, 1967; Broward Legal Exec. of Yr., 1978. Mem. Fla. Bar, ABA, Am. Judicature Soc., Fed. Bar Assn., Broward County Bar, Ft. Lauderdale Jaycees (dir. 1960-61), Fla. Blue Key, Sigma Chi, Phi Alpha Delta. Democrat. Club: Kiwanian (pres. 1971-72). Home: 316 SE 17th Ave Fort Lauderdale FL 33301 Office: 205D US Courthouse 299 E Broward Blvd Fort Lauderdale FL 33301

GONZALEZ, RAUL A., judge; b. Weslaco, Tex., Mar. 22, 1944; s. Raul G. and Paula (Hernandez) G.; m. Dora Blanca Champion, Dec. 22, 1963; children—Celeste, Jaime, Marco, Sonia. B.A. in Govt., U. Tex., Austin, 1963; J.D., U. Houston, 1966; M. Jud. Process, U. Va., 1986. Bar: Tex. 1966. Asst. U.S. atty. U.S. Dist. Ct. (so. dist.) Tex., Brownsville, 1969-73; atty. Gonzalez & Hamilton, Brownsville, 1973-78; judge 103d Dist. Ct. Tex., Brownsville, 1978-81; assoc. justice U.S. Dist. Ct. Appeals (13th cir.), Corpus Christi, Tex., 1981-84; justice Tex. Supreme Ct., Austin, 1984—. Bd. dirs. Brownsville Boy's Club, Brownsville Community Devel. Corp., So. Tex. Rehab. Ind. Sch. Dist.; U.S. coordinator Worldwide Marriage Encounter in Spanish. Recipient Outstanding Performance Rating award Dept. Justice, 1972. Mem. Christian Legal Soc., Christian Conciliation Service, ABA, Tex. Bar Found. Lodge: Rotary. Avocations: jogging; racquetball. Home: 2300 Pebble Beach Austin TX 78747 Office: Supreme Ct Tex 14th and Colorado Sts PO Box 12248 Austin TX 78711

GONZALEZ-DIAZ, RAUL E., lawyer; b. Yabucoa, P.R., Nov. 7, 1939; s. Isais Gonzalez and Tomasa Diaz; m. Carmen L. Reyes, June 20, 1969; 1 son, Raul E. Gonzalez-Reyes. B.S., U. P.R., 1961, LL.B., 1964, M.P.A., 1964. Bar: P.R. 1964, U.S. Dist. Ct. P.R. 1969, U.S. Ct. Apls. (1st cir.) 1980, U.S. Sup. Ct. 1978. Law clk. P.R. Sup. Ct., 1964-65; exec. dir. Civil Rights Commn. P.R., 1965-67; dir. Office Indsl. Tax Exemption P.R., 1967-69; sole practice, San Juan, P.R., 1969-72; ptnr. O'Neill & Borges, San Juan, 1972-79; ptnr. Gonzalez, Bennazar & Colorado, San Juan, 1979—; lectr. civil rights, legis. process U. P.R., 1967-72; prof. civil procedure Cath. U. P.R. Sch. Law, 1983—, lectr. grad. program, 1983—. Recipient medal Inter-Am. Bar Assn., 1979. Mem. P.R. Bar Assn., Inter-Am. Bar Assn., ABA, Assn. Trial Lawyers Am., Sup. Ct. Hist. Soc. State civil litigation, Contracts commercial, Real property. Office: Gonzalez Bennazar & Colorado Banco Popular Ctr Bldg 1501 Hato Rey PR 00918

GONZALEZ-PITA, J. ALBERTO, lawyer; b. Havana, Cuba, Aug. 20, 1954; came to U.S., 1960; s. Benigno Jesus and Maria Modesta (Diaz) G.-P.; m. Suzanne J. Martin, Apr. 7, 1984. AA, Miami-Dade Community Coll., 1973; BA, U. Miami, 1974; JD, Boston U., 1977. Bar: Fla. 1977, U.S. Dist. Ct. (so. dist.) Fla. 1977, U.S. Ct. Appeals (5th cir.) 1977, U.S. Ct. Appeals (11th cir.) 1981. Assoc. Walton, Lantaff, Schroeder & Carson, Miami, Fla., 1977-80; assoc. Patton & Kanner, Miami, 1980-82, ptnr., 1982—. Mem. Acad. for Community Edn., Miami, 1980; bd. dirs. Inst. Innovative Intervention, Miami, 1980—. Mem. ABA, Internat. Bar Assn., Inter-Am. Bar Assn., Internationale des Avocats, Cuban-Am. Bar Assn., Assn. Trial Lawyers Am., Maritime Law Assn. U.S. Roman Catholic. Club: Bankers (Miami). Private international, Admiralty, Contracts commercial. Office: Patton & Kanner 150 SE 2d Ave Miami FL 33131

GOO, COLIN KIM KEONG, lawyer; b. Honolulu, June 30, 1952; s. Donald Tin Fui and Agnes Wong (Wong) G.; m. Eugenie C. Chock, Aug. 9, 1980; children: Cecily J.A., Brian Y.S. BA, U. Hawaii, 1975; JD, DePaul U., 1982. Bar: Hawaii 1982, U.S. Dist. Ct. Hawaii 1982. Assoc. Law Offices Bruce G. Jackson, Honolulu, 1982—; bd. dirs. Christian Vision Inc., Honolulu. Mem. adv. council Sr. Companion and Respite Services Program, Honolulu, 1985—, planned giving com. United Ch. Christ, Hawaii, 1985—. Mem. Hawaii Bar Assn. (estate and gift tax com. tax sect., real estate and fins. sect.), Hawaii Estate Planning Council, Hawaii Chinese Jaycees, Phi Alpha Delta. Democrat. Congregationalist. Avocation: racquetball, softball, basketball. Estate planning, Probate, Estate taxation. Home: 4154-3 Keanu St Honolulu HI 96816 Office: Law Offices Bruce G Jackson 1001 Bishop St 1132 Pacific Tower Honolulu HI 96813

GOOCH, ANTHONY CUSHING, lawyer; b. Amarillo, Tex., Dec. 3, 1937; s. Cornelius Skinner and Sidney Seale (Crawford) G.; m. Elizabeth Melissa Ivanoff, May 27, 1963 (div. Nov. 1983); children—Katherine C., Jennifer C., Melissa G., Andrew E. B.A., U. of South, 1959; diploma, Coll. of Europe, 1960; J.D., NYU, 1963, M.Comp.Law, 1964. Bar: N.Y. 1963. Assoc. Cleary, Gottlieb, Steen & Hamilton, N.Y.C., Paris, Brussels, Rio de Janeiro, 1963-72; ptnr. Cleary, Gottlieb, Steen & Hamilton, 1973—. Co-author: Loan Agreement Documentation, 1986, Swap Agreement Documentation, 1987; articles editor NYU Law Rev., 1962-63. Mem. ABA, N.Y. State Bar Assn., New York County Lawyers Assn., Assn. Bar City N.Y., Am. Soc. Internat. Law, Inter-Am. Bar Assn., Internat. Law Assn., Phi Beta Kappa, Order of Coif, Phi Delta Phi. Democrat. Episcopalian. Clubs: Stage Harbor Yacht (Chatham, Mass.); Rocky Point (Old Greenwich, Conn.). Private international, Banking, Contracts commercial. Office: Cleary Gottlieb Steen & Hamilton 1 State St Plaza New York NY 10004

GOOCH, ROBERT FRANCIS, lawyer; b. San Bernardino, Calif., May 1, 1918; s. Elmer Nicholas and Genevieve Agnes (Rodczweicz) G.; m. Virginia M. Gerardi, July 26, 1947; children—Patrick, Mary Gooch Wallis, Teresa Gooch, Melissa Gooch, Stevens. B.A., UCLA, 1939; LL.B., Stanford U., 1942. Bar: Calif. 1946. Sole practice, Hawthorne, Calif., 1946-54, Los Angeles, 1968-84; sr. ptnr. Gooch & Barrett, Hawthorne, 1954-64, Gooch & Jones, Hawthorne, 1965-68, Gooch & Feingold, Los Angeles, 1984—; mem. adv. com. Los Angeles Dist. Atty. Office, 1964; mem. arbitration panel Am. Arbitration Assn., Los Angeles, Bd. dirs. St. Anne's Found., Los Angeles, 1951—, pres., 1971-72. Served with USAF, 1942-45. Mem. Am. Judicature Soc., ABA, Los Angeles County Bar Assn., Calif. State Bar Assn. Republican. Roman Catholic. General corporate, Probate, Real property. Office: Gooch and Feingold 11340 W Olympic Blvd #303 Los Angeles CA 90064

GOOD, ADRIAN J., lawyer; b. Bellevue, Ohio, Nov. 29, 1924; s. Adrian E. and Ruth S. (Mitchell) G.; m. Nina E. Carver, June 8, 1946; children: Terrence, Anne, Linda. BS in Chemistry, Heidelberg U., 1948; MS in Organic Chemistry, Case Western Res. U., 1960; JD, Ind. U., 1975. Bar: Ind. 1975, Ohio 1975, U.S. Dist. Ct. (no. dist.) Ind. 1975, Tenn. 1977, U.S. Ct. Appeals (fed. cir.) 1986. Assoc. John A. Young P.C., Ft. Wayne, Ind., 1975-77; patent atty. Great Lakes Carbon, N.Y.C., 1977-83, patent counsel, 1983—; cons. Valspar, Ft. Wayne, 1972-73. Mem. Friends of Pub. Library, Elizabethton, Tenn., 1983. Served to tech. sgt. USAAF, 1943-45, PTO. Decorated Air medal; recipient Excellence in Devel. award Minn. Paint Co., 1968. Mem. ABA, Tenn. Bar Assn., Carter County Bar Assn., Am. Intellectual Property Law Assn., Am. Corp. Counsel Assn., Am. Chem. Soc. (chmn. 1970), Am. Legion. Democrat. Presbyterian. Club: Toastmasters (Warsaw, Ind.) (dist. gov. 1964) Lodges: Kiwanis (pres. 1980, bd. dirs. 1980-86), Elks. Avocations: photography, hiking, gardening, ham radio. Patent, Trademark and copyright. Home: 1906 W G St Elizabethton TN 37643

GOOD, CARL SOREN, lawyer; b. Detroit, May 25, 1951. BA, U. Mich., 1973; JD, Wayne State U., 1976, LLM, 1982. Bar: Mich. 1976. Staff assoc. St. Paul Title, Troy, Mich., 1979-81; staff assoc. Nat. Bank of Detroit, 1981-82, sr. assoc., 1982-86, asst. dir. law dept., 1986. Mem. ABA, Mich. State Bar Assn., Detroit Bar Assn. Banking, Consumer commercial, Real property. Office: Nat Bank Detroit 200 Renaissance Ctr Suite 2612 Detroit MI 48243

GOOD, RICHARD FEDERICK, lawyer; b. Akron, Ohio, Jan. 18, 1954; s. John Ferderick and Vivian (Semler) G. BBA, Miami U., Oxford, Ohio, 1976; JD, U. Colo., 1980. Bar: Colo. 1980, U.S. Supreme Ct. 1986. Assoc. E. Gregory Martin, P.C., Boulder, Colo., 1980-81; dep. dist. atty. Jefferson County Dist. Atty.'s Office, Boulder, 1981, Boulder County Dist. Atty.'s Office, Boulder, 1981-86; interim dir. prosecutional clinic U. Ga. Sch. of Law, Athens, 1986—. Mem. ABA, Assn. Trial Lawyers Am., Order of Coif. Democrat. Presbyterian. Avocations: skiing, golf, tennis, jogging, sailing. Criminal. Home: 1688 Prince Ave #207 Athens GA 30606

GOODALE, JAMES CAMPBELL, lawyer; b. Cambridge, Mass., July 27, 1933; s. Robert Leonard and Eunice (Campbell) G.; m. Toni Krissel, May 3, 1964; children: Timothy Fuller, Ashley Krissel; guardian: Joseph Clayton Akiwenzie. Grad., Pomfret Sch., 1951; B.A., Yale U., 1955; J.D., U. Chgo., 1958. Bar: N.Y. 1960. Assoc. Lord, Day & Lord, N.Y.C., 1959-63; gen. atty. N.Y. Times Co., 1963-67, gen. counsel, 1967-72, v.p., 1969-72, sr. v.p., 1972-73, exec. v.p., 1973-79, vice-chmn., 1979-80; mem. Debevoise & Plimpton, 1980—; with Community Law Office, East Harlem, 1968-70; vis. lectr. Yale U. Law Sch., 1977-80; adj. prof. NYU Sch. Law, 1983-86, Fordham Law Sch., 1986—; mem. N.Y. State Privacy and Security Com., 1976-79; adv. bd. Communications and the Law, 1980—; pres. Midtown Skating Corp., 1981—. Compilor, editor: The New York Times Company vs. U.S, 1971; co-founder, bd. editors: Media Law Reporter; bd. editors Nat. Law Jour., 1983—; columnist nat. and N.Y. law jours.; contbr. articles on communications law to profl. jours. Past bd. dirs. N.Y. Times Neediest Cases Fund, N.Y. Times Found.; past trustee Pomfret Sch., Gunnery Sch., St. Bernard's Sch., Boys' Club N.Y., Salzburg Seminar, Fed. Bar Council; mem. vis. com. U. Chgo. Law Sch., 1977-80; chmn. bd. Cable TV Law and Fin., 1983—. Served with AUS, 1959. Named one of 200 Rising Leaders in U.S. Time mag., 1974; William Brinckerhoff Jackson scholar, 1954-55; Nat. Honor scholar U. Chgo. Law Sch., 1955-58. Fellow N.Y. State Bar Assn. (chmn. spl. com. on pub. access to info. and proc. 1979-84, spl. com. on media law 1985—); mem. N.Y.C. Bar Assn. (chmn. communications law com. 1978-83, mem. corp. law com. 1977-81), ABA (governing bd. communications law forum, commn. on pub. understanding about law 1979-82), Columbia U. Seminars on Media and Society. Clubs: Yale (gov. 1964-67), Century Assn, Economic, St. Elmo, Elihu (gov. 1966-70), Washington Conn. (gov. 1972-78). Libel, General corporate. Office: Debevoise & Plimpton 875 Third Ave New York NY 10022

GOODE, DAVID RONALD, lawyer; b. Vinton, Va., Jan. 13, 1941; s. Otto and Hessie M. (Maxey) G.; m. Susan Skiles, June 22, 1963; children: Christina, Martha. AB, Duke U., 1962; JD, Harvard U., 1965. Bar: Va. 1965. Tax atty. Norfolk & Western Ry., Roanoke, Va., 1965-66, asst. gen. tax atty., 1967, gen. tax atty., 1968-70, dir. taxation, 1971-81; asst. v.p. taxation Norfolk So. Corp., Roanoke, 1982-85, v.p. taxation, 1985—. Mem. Va. Commn. for Arts, Richmond, 1984—; mem. steering com. Gov.'s Arts Awards, Richmond, 1985; dir., treas. Ctr. in the Sq., Roanoke. Mem. ABA (past chmn. depreciation com. tax sect.), Va. Bar Assn., Roanoke Bar Assn. (tax policy com.). Democrat. Methodist. Clubs: Hunting Hills Country, Jefferson (Roanoke). Avocations: golf, tennis. Corporate taxation, State and local taxation, Pension, profit-sharing, and employee benefits. Home: 2344 Woodcliff Rd Roanoke VA 24014 Office: Norfolk So Corp 8 N Jefferson St Roanoke VA 24042-0028

GOODE, KENNETH GEORGE, lawyer; b. Winnsboro, S.C., Aug. 7, 1950; s. Marshall Smith and Doris M. (LeGrand) G.; m. Betty Gail Massey, Dec. 19, 1970; children: Marshall, Taylor, Kenneth Jr. BA in Econs., Bus. Adminstrn., Furman U., 1973; JD, U. S.C., 1976. Bar: S.C. 1976. Assoc. Hyatt & Elliott, Columbia, S.C., 1976-78; sole practice Winnsboro, 1978-85; ptnr. Goode & Mueller, Winnsboro, 1985—; atty. Fairfield County, 1980—. Bd. dirs. Council Child Abuse and Neglect, 1981-83, U.S. Selective Service, 1984—, Winnsboro Downtown Devel. Assn., 1986—. Named Boss of Yr., Bus. and Profl. Women Assn., 1981; recipient Merit award Nat. Child Safety Council, 1983. Mem. ABA, S.C. Bar Assn., Assn. Trial Lawyers Am., S.C. Trial Lawyers Assn. Democrat. Clubs: Winnsboro Country (bd. dirs. 1983—), Winnsboro Pine Tree Players (v.p. 1984—). Lodge: Masons. Avocations: flying, trail riding, open wheel auto racing, sports cars. Personal injury, Family and matrimonial, Real property. Home: 309 Old Camden Rd Winnsboro SC 29180 Office: Goode & Mueller 229 S Congress St Winnsboro SC 29180

GOODFRIEND, MARK F., lawyer; b. Bklyn., Sept. 2, 1948; s. Isaac and Leah (Hamburger) G.; married, Aug. 4, 1974; children—Daniel, Janna. B.A. cum laude, U. Mass., 1970; J.D., Northeastern U., 1974. Bar: N.Y. 1975, U.S. Dist. Ct. (so. and ea. dists.) N.Y. 1975. Assoc. Windhelm, Bernard & Prindle, Nyack, N.Y., 1975-76; ptnr. Shapiro & Goodfriend, New City, N.Y., 1976—; justice Village of Spring Valley, N.Y., 1977—; mem. Family Ct. Adv. Com., Rockland County, N.Y., 1978—. Mem. Rockland County Magistrates Assn. (pres. 1980-81), Assn. Trial Lawyers Am. N.Y. Bar Assn., ABA. Democrat. State civil litigation, Family and matrimonial, Personal injury. Office: Shapiro & Goodfriend 75 N Middletown Rd Nanuet NY 10954

GOODFRIEND, ROBERT EDWARD, lawyer; b. N.Y.C., July 8, 1941; s. David Goodfriend and Pearl (Goldman) Blair; 1 child, Sharon Barbara. BA, Dartmouth Coll., 1963; MA, Stanford U., 1965, LLB, 1968. Bar: Tex. 1969, U.S. Ct. Appeals (5th cir.) 1969, U.S. Supreme Ct. 1974, U.S. Ct. Appeals (11th cir.) 1981. Law clk. to presiding justice U.S. Ct. Appeals (5th cir.), Dallas, 1968-69; ptnr. Akin, Gump, Strauss, Hauer & Feld, Dallas, 1969—. Mem. adv. council Sch. Gen. Studies U. Tex., Dallas, 1984—. Mem. ABA, Tex. Bar Assn. (client security fund com.), Dallas County Bar Assn. (chmn. continuing legal edn. com. 1981). Federal civil litigation, State civil litigation. Office: Akin Gump Strauss Hauer & Feld 1700 Pacific Ave Suite 4100 Dallas TX 75201-4618

GOODIN, EILEEN SUE, lawyer; b. Newark, Ohio, Jan. 29, 1955; d. Raymond L. and Joan (Green) G. B.A. cum laude, Kent State U., 1977; J.D., Ohio State U., 1980. Bar: Ohio 1980, U.S. Dist. Ct. (so. dist.) Ohio 1981, U.S. Ct. Appeals (6th cir.) 1981, U.S. Ct. Appeals (11th cir.) 1982, La. 1985, U.S. Dist. Ct. (ea. dist.) La. 1985, Tex. 1986. Law clk. Ohio Pub. Defender, Columbus, summer 1978; assoc. Barkan & Neff Co., L.P.A., Columbus, 1978-84, ptnr., 1984—. Assoc. adult Girl Scouts U.S.A., 1973—; active Friends of Library, Columbus, 1980—, Baseball Boosters Central Ohio, Columbus, 1982—; tutor Columbus Literary Council. Mem. ABA, Am. Trial Lawyers Assn., Ohio State Bar Assn., La. Bar Assn., Columbus Bar Assn., Ohio Trial Lawyers Assn., Women Lawyers Franklin County, NOW, Ohio State U. Alumni Assn. (life). Democrat. Methodist. Avocations: bicycling, sports, reading. Workers' compensation, Pension, profit-sharing, and employee benefits. Home: 1847 Misty Way Columbus OH 43232 Office: Barkan & Neff Co LPA 50 W Broad St #15151 PO Box 1969 Columbus OH 43216

GOODING, TOM, circuit judge; b. San Francisco, May 21, 1933; s. John Russell and Cecilia Marie (Kirsch) G.; m. Jill F. Gellerman, Dec. 27, 1955 (div. Mar. 1981); m. Charlotte Ann Snethen, Jan. 12, 1984. Student, U. Idaho, 1951-52, Boise State Coll., 1952-53; BA, Willamette U., 1955, LLB, 1958. Bar: Oreg. 1958, U.S. Dist. Ct. Oreg. 1958, U.S. Supreme Ct. 1972. Law clk. to presiding justice Oreg. Supreme Ct., Salem, 1958-59; sole practice La Grande, Oreg., 1959-84; cir. judge State of Oreg., La Grande, 1984—. Author: Law Office Economics and Management, 1967. Mem. adv. com. Oreg. Legis. Probate Revision, 1964-72. Recipient Florian Von Eschen Scholastic award, 1954. Mem. ABA (torts and ins. practice sects.), Oreg. State Bar Assn., Union-Wallowa County Bar Assn. (pres. 1973-74). Avocations: bird gaming, bird dog training. Office: PO Box 2950 LaGrande OR 97850

GOODLOE, WILLIAM CASSIUS, III, state justice; b. Lexington, Ky., Sept. 19, 1919; s. Green Clay and Helen Stuart (Wilson) G.; m. Phyllis Clarke, Sept. 19, 1941; children—William Cassius IV, Gwendolyn Ruth Goodloe Smith, Mary Michelle Goodloe Pahlman, Janette Jeanne Goodloe Lake, Richard Clay, Gerald Clarke, David Marshal. B.S. in Law, U. Wash., 1946, LL.D., 1948. Bar: Wash. 1948. Ptnr. Todd & Goodloe, Seattle, 1948-

72; judge King County Superior Ct., Seattle, 1972-84; justice Wash. State Supreme Ct., Olympia, 1984—; mem. Wash. State Senate, Olympia, 1951-59; cons. in field; faculty adviser Nat. Jud. Coll., Reno, Nev., 1976-84. Author: Jury Selection Manual for Bench and Bar, 1976. Wash. State Republican chmn., 1959-61. Served to lt. USNR, 1939-45; PTO, NATOUSA, MTO. Recipient award for watercolor Fox's Gem Shop, 1982. Mem. Seattle-King County Bar. Avocations: painting; amateur radio. Judicial administration. Home: 13190 Edgewater Ln NE Seattle WA 98125 Office: Wash Supreme Ct Temple of Justice Olympia WA 98504

GOODMAN, ALFRED NELSON, lawyer; b. N.Y.C., Jan. 21, 1945; s. Bernard R. and Mildred (Schlanger) G. B.S. in Mech. and Aerospace Scis., U. Rochester, 1966; J.D., Georgetown U., 1969. Bar: N.Y. 1970, D.C. 1971, U.S. Supreme Ct. 1974. Patent examiner U.S. Patent Office, Washington, 1969-71; assoc. Roylance, Abrams, Berdo & Goodman, Washington, 1971-74, ptnr., 1975—. Mem. Am. Patent Law Assn., ABA, D.C. Bar Assn. (chmn. patent, trademark and copyright law sect. 1984-85, bd. dirs. 1985-86), Bar Assn. D.C. Patent, Trademark and copyright, Antitrust. Home: 4948 Sentinel Dr Bethesda MD 20816 Office: Roylance Abrams Berdo & Goodman Suite 204 1225 Connecticut Ave NW Washington DC 20036

GOODMAN, BRUCE DENNIS, lawyer; b. Los Angeles, Mar. 4, 1954; s. Harold Stanton and Jane (Yaker) G.; m. Patricia J. Pokorski, Oct.1, 1983; 1 child, Emily. AB in Politics with high honors, Princeton U., 1975; JD, Stanford U., 1979. Bar: Ill. 1979. Extern to assoc. justice Calif. Supreme Ct., 1978-79; assoc. Sonnenschein, Carlin, Nath, & Rosenthal, Chgo., 1979-82; ptnr. Nagelberg & Resnick P.C., Chgo., 1982—; adj. prof. Kent Coll. Law Ill. Inst. Tech., Chgo., 1982—. Mem. ABA, Chgo. Bar Assn., Phi Beta Kappa. Real property, Probate, Estate planning. Home: 612 Concord Pl Barrington IL 60010 Office: Nagelberg & Resnick PC 200 S Wacker Chicago IL 60606

GOODMAN, EDWARD WILLIAM, lawyer; b. Jersey City, May 16, 1948; s. Benjamin and Eleanor Rene (Moss) G.; m. Janice Patricia Gary, Feb. 27, 1971; children—Tamara Alise, Derek Edward. B.Engring., Stevens Inst. Tech., 1969; J.D., Seton Hall Sch. Law, 1977. Bar: N.J. 1977, U.S. Dist. Ct. N.J. 1977. Project engr. Singer-Kearfott div., Wayne, N.J., 1969-75; patent engr. Singer Co., Elizabeth, N.J., 1975-77, patent atty., 1977-79; patent atty. U.S. Philips Corp., Tarrytown, N.Y., 1979-86, Toren, McGeady & Assocs. P.C., N.Y.C., 1986—. Mem. N.J. State Bar Assn. Democrat. Baptist. Patent, Trademark and copyright, General corporate. Home: 56 Campeau Pl Bergenfield NJ 07621 Office: 521 Fifth Ave New York NY 10175

GOODMAN, FRANK I., law educator, lawyer; b. 1932. A.B., Harvard U., 1954, LL.B., 1959; B.A., Oxford (Eng.) U., 1956. Bar: D.C. 1959, Calif. 1960. Assoc. Berlenson, Meyer, Rosenfeld & Sussman, Beverly Hills, Calif., 1960-62; spl. asst. to gen. counsel FPC, Washington, 1962; asst. to solicitor gen. U.S., Washington, 1962-65; acting prof. U. Calif.-Berkeley, 1965-72; research dir. Adminstrv. Conf. U.S., Washington, 1972-73, cons., 1973-74; vis. prof. U. Pa., 1973-76, prof., 1976—. Mem. Am. Law Inst. Past mem. editorial bd. Harvard Law Rev. Legal education. Office: U PA Law Sch 3400 Chestnut St Philadelphia PA 19104 *

GOODMAN, HELEN GEYH, lawyer; b. Bridgeport, Conn., Jan. 4, 1941; d. Charles Phillip and Helen Gladys (Anthony) Geyh; m. Jerome Goodman, Nov. 11, 1967; children: Johanna Claire, Ethan Michael. BA cum laude, Barnard Coll., 1964; MA, Columbia U., 1966, JD, 1979. Bar: N.Y. 1980. Assoc. Milbank, Tweed, Hadley & McCloy, N.Y.C., 1979-83; asst. gen. counsel Tambrands Inc., Lake Success, N.Y., 1983—. Mem. ABA, N.Y. State Bar Assn., Assn. of Bar of City of N.Y. General corporate. Office: Tambrands Inc 1 Marcus Ave Lake Success NY 11042

GOODMAN, HENRY A., lawyer; b. Boston, Sept. 4, 1940; s. Samuel and Sylvia (Galvin) G.; m. Julie Renee Fenster, May 30, 1968; 1 child, Dana Lyn. AB, Boston U., 1962, LLB, 1966. Bar: Mass. 1966, U.S. Dist. Ct. Mass. 1967, U.S. Ct. Appeals (1st cir.) 1967. Sole practice Boston and Norwood/Canton, Mass., 1966-71, 74-82; assoc. Backman, Katz & Goodman, Boston, 1971-74, Goodman & Novinsky, Brockton, Mass., 1982-85, Levitz, Lyons, Kesselman, Modiste, Levy & Goodman, Stoughton, Mass., 1986—. Contbr. articles to profl. jours. Active various polit. campaigns, 1964-72. Mem. Mass. Bar Assn. (intermittent pres.), Community Assn. Inst. (pres. New England chpt. 1981, bd. dirs.). Personal injury, Real property, Litigation. Home: 140 Copperwood Dr Stoughton MA 02072 Office: Levitz Lyons Kesselman et al Two Cabot Pl Stoughton MA 02072

GOODMAN, HERBERT RAYMOND, lawyer; b. El Paso, Tex., Oct. 31, 1932; s. Herbert Hatton and Hattie (Crosby) G.; m. Shirley Lumpkin, Sept. 4, 1957; 1 child, Paul Lumpkin. BA, U. Miss., 1957, JD, 1975; MDiv, Va. Seminary, 1960. Bar: Miss. 1975, U.S. Dist. Ct. Miss. 1975, U.S. Ct. Appeals (5th cir.) 1976. Curate Ch. Ascension, Lafayette, La., 1960-61; vicar St. David's Ch., Rayville, La., 1961-66; rector St. Paul's Ch., Jesup, Ga., 1966-69, All Saints Ch., Tupelo, Miss., 1969-73; ptnr. Carr & Goodman, Tupelo, 1976—. Served with USNR, 1949-54. Episcopalian. Lodge: Rotary. General practice, Probate, Federal civil litigation. Home: 1202 Belledeer Tupelo MS 38801

GOODMAN, JOHN PETER, lawyer; b. N.Y.C., Apr. 9, 1945; s. Morton Frederick and Immaculata (Ferrara) G.; m. Virginia Ann Furstenburg, June 3, 1978; 1 child, Aislinn Kate. BA in Am. Studies, Bard Coll., 1967; JD, N.Y. Law Sch., 1972, LLM in Taxation, 1974. Bar: N.Y. 1973, U.S. Dist. Ct. (ea. dist.) N.Y. 1976. Mgr. spl. projects J.P. Stevens & Co. Inc., N.Y.C., 1973-74; sr. tax atty Pfizer Inc., N.Y.C., 1974-76, tax counsel, 1981-84; sole practice N.Y.C., 1976-81; dir. taxes Alcon Labs. Inc., Ft. Worth, 1984-85, v.p. taxes, 1986—. Mem. Sec. Regan's Unitary Tax Task Force, 1983-84. Mem. Tax Execs. Inst., Internat. Fiscal Assn., Pharm. Mfrs. Assn. (tax. subcom.). Avocations: golf, tennis, carpentry, vegatable gardening, mil. miniature. Corporate taxation, General corporate, Public international. Home: 401 Big Creek Rd Weatherford TX 76086 Office: Alcon Labs Inc 6201 S Freeway Fort Worth TX 76134

GOODMAN, LOUIS ALLAN, lawyer; b. Providence, Nov. 13, 1943; s. Jacob and Frieda (Feldman) G.; m. Phebe Silver, June 9, 1968; children: Jonathan J., Rebecca A. AB, Columbia U., 1965; MA, Harvard U., 1966, JD, 1969. Bar: N.Y. 1970, Mass. 1973. Assoc. Skadden, Arps, Slate, Meagher & Flom, Boston, 1970-72, 73-77, ptnr., 1978—. Securities, General corporate. Home: 59 North St Newtonville MA 02160 Office: Skadden Arps Slate Meagher & Flom One Beacon St Boston MA 02108

GOODMAN, MARGUERITE RUTH, lawyer; b. Bklyn.; d. Samuel S. and Minnie (Bleckschmidt) G.; children: Katherine Petty, Ethan Petty. BA, CUNY, 1961; postgrad., Oxford U., Eng., 1961; MA, Cornell U., 1963; JD, Dickinson Sch. Law, 1978. Bar: Pa. 1978, U.S. Dist. Ct. (ea. dist.) Pa. 1978, U.S. Ct. Appeals (3d cir.) 1979. Assoc. Pepper, Hamilton & Scheetz, Phila., 1978-81, Kohn, Savett, Klein & Graf, P.C., Phila., 1986—; asst. city solicitor Phila. Law Dept., 1981, dep. city solicitor, 1981-83, div. dep. city solicitor, 1984-86. Mem. ABA, Phila. Bar Assn. 1st Pl. Nat. Moot Ct. Competition, 1977. Federal civil litigation, State civil litigation. Office: Kohn Savett Klein & Graf PC 1101 Market St 24th Floor Philadelphia PA 19107

GOODMAN, MARK N., lawyer; b. Phoenix, Jan. 16, 1952; s. Daniel H. and Joanne G.; m. Gwendolyn A. Langfeldt, Oct. 24, 1982; 1 child, Zachary A. BA, Prescott Coll., 1973; JD summa cum laude, Calif. Western Sch. Law, 1977; LL.M., U. Calif.-Berkeley, 1978. Bar: Ariz. 1977, Calif. 1977 U.S. Dist. Ct. (no. dist.) Calif. 1977, U.S. Dist. Ct. Ariz. 1978, U.S. Ct. Appeals (9th cir.) 1978, U.S. Dist. Ct. (so. dist.) Calif. 1981, U.S. Supreme Ct. 1981, U.S. Dist. Ct. (ce. dist.) Calif., 1982, Nebr. 1983, U.S. Dist. Ct. Nebr. 1983. Practice Law Offices Mark N. Goodman, Prescott, Ariz., 1978-79, 81-83, Mark N. Goodman, Ltd., Prescott, 1983-86; ptnr. Alward and Goodman, Ltd., Prescott, 1979-81; ptnr. Perry, Goodman, Drutz & Musgrove, Prescott, 1986-87, Goodman, Drutz & Musgrove, 1987—. Author: The Ninth Amendment, 1981. Contbr. articles to profl. jours. Bd. dirs. Yavapai Symphony Assn., Prescott, 1981-84. Notes and comments editor Calif. Western Law Review, 1976. Mem. ABA, Am. Trial Lawyers Assn. Yavapai County Bar Assn. (v.p. 1981-82). State civil litigation, Consumer commercial, Real property. Office: Goodman Drutz & Musgrove PO Box 2720 Prescott AZ 86302-2720

GOODMAN, MORTIMER, lawyer, consultant; b. N.Y.C., June 11, 1910; s. Nathan and Millie (Rein) G.; m. Estelle Helen Blumenthal, Dec. 25, 1935; 1 dau., Susan B. Campbell. Sc.B., NYU, 1931, J.D., 1933. Bar: N.Y. 1933, U.S. Dist. Ct. (so. dist.) N.Y. 1940, U.S. Dist. Ct. (ea. dist.) N.Y. 1941, U.S. Ct. Appeals (2d cir.) 1945, U.S. Supreme Ct. 1959. Assoc., Rosston, Hort & Brussel, 1940-47; sr. ptnr. Grandefeld & Goodman, 1948-78; counsel Grandefeld & Goodman, N.Y.C., 1978-80; cons. atty., N.Y.C., 1980—; pub. mem. Securities Industry Conf. on Arbitration, 1977—; mem. bd. arbitration N.Y. Stock Exchange, 1982—. Founder, State of Israel Bond Orgn., 1951; chmn. United Jewish Appeal, Flushing, N.Y., 1958; bd. dirs. YM-YWHA Greater Flushing, 1957—, v.p., 1979—; bd. dirs. N.Y. Fedn. Reform Synagogues, 1972-82, sec., 1982-86, assoc. treas. 1986—; pres. Free Synagogue of Flushing, 1953-56, hon. pres., 1967—. Mem. ABA, N.Y. County Lawyers Assn. (arbitration com.), Queens County Bar Assn. (surrogate ct. and real property coms.), Am. Arbitration Assn. (panel). Probate, Real property, Consultant securities arbitration. Home and Office: 47-62 Utopia Pkwy Flushing NY 11358

GOODMAN, WILLIAM FLOURNOY, III, lawyer; b. Aberdeen Miss., June 8, 1952; s. William Flournoy, Jr. and Edwina (McDuffie) G.; m. Nancy C. Graves, July 31, 1976; children: William Flournoy, Nancy Elizabeth. BA cum laude, Millsaps Coll., 1974; JD, U. Miss., 1977. Bar: Miss. 1977, U.S. Dist Ct. (so. and no. dists.) Miss. 1977, U.S. Ct. Appeals (5th cir.) 1977, U.S. Ct. Appeals (11th cir.) 1981. Assoc. Watkins & Eager, Jackson, Miss., 1977-81; ptnr., 1982—. Mem. ABA, Hinds County Bar Assn., Miss. Bar Assn., Miss. Def. Lawyers Assn., Def. Research Inst., Internat. Assn. Def. Counsel, Omicron Delta Kappa. Methodist. Lodge: Rotary. Federal civil litigation, State civil litigation. Home: 1609 Ivy St Jackson MS 39202 Office: Watkins & Eager PO Box 650 Jackson MS 39205

GOODMAN, WILLIAM HARRY, lawyer; b. Detroit, Apr. 26, 1940; s. Ernest and Freda (Kesler) G.; m. Jane Saxe, Oct. 19, 1963 (div. Mar. 1983); children: Amy Laura, Michael Alan, David Paul; m. Julie Hurwitz, Dec. 15, 1985; 1 child, Jacob Desmond. AB, U. Chgo., 1961, JD, 1964. Bar: Mich. 1965, U.S. Dist. Ct. (ea. and we. dists.) Mich. 1965, U.S. Dist. Ct. (no. dist.) Ohio 1965, U.S. Dist. Ct. (we. dist.) N.Y. 1965, U.S. Ct. Appeals (6th cir.) 1965, U.S. Dist. Ct. (no. dist.) Ala. 1985. Assoc. Goodman, Eden, Millander & Bedrosia, Detroit, 1965-70, ptnr., 1970—; bd. dirs. Mich. Legal Services, Detroit. Contbr. articles to profl. jours. Mem. Detroit Pub. Health Commn., 1981—, ACLU (Disting. Service award, Detroit, 1984). Recipient Disting. Service award ACLU, Detroit, 1984. Mem. Mich. Bar Assn., Nat. Lawyers Guild (pres. Detroit chpt. 1971-75, nat. pres. 1976-77), Mich. Trial Lawyers Assn., NAACP (Pres.'s award Detroit chpt. 1986). Civil rights, Federal civil litigation, Personal injury. Office: Goodman Eden et al 3000 Cadillac Tower Detroit MI 48226

GOODNER, DONALD SCOTT, lawyer; b. Ft. Smith, Ark., Feb. 24, 1942; s. Norman Duff and Dorothy Naomi (Greene) G.; m. Sherry Lee Frazier, Aug. 19, 1966; children—Douglas, Bethany, Nicholas. B.S., U. Ark., 1965, J.D., 1968. Bar: Ark. 1968, U.S. Dist. Ct. Ark. 1968, U.S. Ct. Appeals, (8th cir.) 1971, U.S. Supreme Ct. 1972. Sole practice, Waldron, Ark., 1968—; city atty. City of Waldron, 1977-82; mcpl. judge, 1987—; dep. prosecutor Scott County, Waldron, 1977-80. Mem. Ark. Bar Assn. (ho. of dels. 1976-79, vice chmn. real estate sect. 1986—), Waldron C. of C. (bd. dirs.). Democrat. Methodist. Lodge: Lions (v.p. 1978). Real property, Family and matrimonial, Computer. Office: 315 Washington St Waldron AR 72958

GOODRICH, JOHN BERNARD, lawyer; b. Spokane, Wash., Jan. 4, 1928; s. John Casey and Dorothy (Koll) G.; m. Therese H. Vollmer, June 14, 1952; children—Joseph B., Bernadette M., Andrew J., Philip M., Thomas A., Mary Elizabeth, Jennifer H., Rosanne M. J.D., Gonzaga U., 1954. Bar: Ill. bar 1955, Wash. bar 1954. Indsl. traffic mgr. Pacific N.W. Alloys, Spokane, 1950-54; asst. to gen. counsel Cromium Mining & Smelting Corp., Chgo., 1954-56; with Monon R.R., 1956-69, atty., gen. solicitor, 1956-66, sec., 1957-69, treas., 1959-66, v.p. law, 1966-69; also dir.; sec.-treas. I.C.G.R.R., Chgo., 1970-79; sec., gen. atty. I.C.G.R.R., 1979-85; gen. counsel Ill. Devel. Fin. Authority, Chgo., 1985—. Mem. Park Forest, Traffic and Safety Commn., 1963-66; mem. Park Forest Recreation Bd., 1966-77, chmn., 1969-70; trustee Village of Park Forest, 1977-80; mem. bd. Sch. Dist. 163, 1984—. Served with AUS, 1946-48. Mem. Wash. State Bar Assn., Chgo. Bar Assn. Republican. Roman Catholic. Lodges: KC, Elks. Club: Olympia Fields Country. Securities, Legislative, General corporate. Home: 47 Apple Ln Park Forest IL 60466 Office: 2 N LaSalle St Suite 980 Chicago IL 60602

GOODRIDGE, GEORGE SIDNEY, lawyer; b. Morristown, N.J., Sept. 6, 1945; m. Janellen Haber, Aug. 24, 1968; 3 children. BA, U. Rochester, 1967; JD, Case Western Res. U., 1972. Bar: N.Y. 1973, Conn. 1983. Assoc. Johnson, Rief & Mullan, P.C., Rochester, N.Y., 1972-76; asst. gen. counsel Schelegal Corp., Rochester, 1976-77; group counsel Emhart Corp., Hartford, Conn., 1977—. Commr. Farmington (Conn.) Planning and Zoning Commn., 1983—. Served with U.S. Army, 1968-70. Mem. ABA, Antique Auto Club of Am. Avocation: antique auto restoration. General corporate, Environment, Contracts commercial. Home: 21 Cedar Ridge Dr Farmington CT 06032 Office: Emhart Corp PO Box 2730 Hartford CT 06101

GOODRUM, WAYNE LOUIS, lawyer; b. Ft. Worth, Dec. 8, 1934; s. A.L. and Lillian E. (Thompson) G.; m. Betty C. McNiece, June 2, 1957 (div. 1973); children: Carolyn D. Goodrum Jones, Bryan W.; m. Arvella S. Powell, Nov. 23, 1973; 1 child, Whitney. BBA, Hardin-Simmons U., 1958; JD, U. Tex., 1971. Bar: Tex. 1972, U.S. Dist. Ct. (no. dist.) Tex. 1976, Ky. 1977, U.S. Dist. Ct. (ea. dist.) Ky. 1977, N.C. 1985. Div. mgr. Gen. Telephone of the Southwest, San Angelo, Tex., 1963-69, sr. atty., 1972-76; gen. counsel Gen. Telephone of Ky., Lexington, 1976-81; assoc. gen. counsel Gen. Telephone of the South, Durham, N.C., 1981—. Republican. Baptist. Administrative and regulatory, General corporate, Public utilities. Home: 5540 Inverness Dr Durham NC 27712 Office: Gen Telephone of the South 4100 N Roxboro Rd Durham NC 27702

GOODSON, ROBERT WADE, lawyer; b. Washington, Nov. 18, 1950; s. James Roy and Rita Theresa (Koontz) G.; m. Erin Patricia Donovan, Sept. 14, 1985. BA cum laude, U. Notre Dame, 1972, JD, 1976. Bar: Md. 1976, D.C. 1977. Law clk. to presiding judge U.S. Ct. Cir. Ct., Upper Marlboro, Md., 1976-77; assoc. Carr, Jordan, Coyne & Savits, Washington, 1977-83; ptnr. Carr, Goodson & Lee, Washington, 1983—. Mem. ABA, Montgomery County Bar Assn., Prince George's County Bar Assn., Md. Assn. Def. Trial Counsel, Md. Assn. Compensation Ins. Attys. Federal civil litigation, State civil litigation, Insurance. Office: Carr Goodson & Lee PC 1919 Penn Ave NW Suite 700 Washington DC 20006

GOODSTEIN, BARNETT MAURICE, lawyer; b. Dallas, Oct. 1, 1921; s. Arthur Louis and Viola Esther (Levy) G.; m. Mira Brodsky, Jan. 26, 1947; children—Pamela Renee, Heather Ann, Robin Leslie. Student, Rice Inst., 1938-40; B.A., U. Tex., Austin, 1942, M.A., 1942; postgrad., U. Wis., 1949-51; J.D., So. Meth. U., 1957. Bar: Tex. 1957, U.S. Dist. Ct. (no. dist.) Tex. 1957, U.S. Supreme Ct. 1971. Acting dir. case analysis Wage Stblzn. Bd., Dallas, 1951-53; practice of law Dallas, 1957—; pres. Goodstein & Starr, P.C., 1977—; lectr. econs. So. Meth. U., Dallas, 1946-48, 51-60; lectr. Massey Realty Coll., Real Estate Inst., Dallas; labor arbitrator, 1953—; former permanent arbitrator City of San Antonio, Police Officers' Assn. Hearing officer work suspensions appeals bd., City of Dallas, 1981-83; mem. Dallas County Sch. Bd., 1981—. Served with USAAF, 1942-46. Mem. ABA, Tex. Bar Assn., Dallas Bar Assn., Nat. Acad. Arbitrators, Am. Arbitration Assn. Real property, Labor, Arbitration. Home: 5022 DeLoache Ave Dallas TX 75220 Office: 4230 LBJ Freeway Suite 121 Dallas TX 75244

GOODWIN, ALFRED THEODORE, judge; b. Bellingham, Wash., June 29, 1923; s. Alonzo Theodore and Miriam Hazel (Williams) G.; m. Marjorie Elizabeth Major, Dec. 23, 1943 (div. 1948); 1 son, Michael Theodore; m. Mary Ellin Handelin, Dec. 23, 1949; children—Karl Alfred, Margaret Ellen, Sara Jane, James Paul. B.A., U. Oreg., 1947; J.D., 1951. Bar: Oreg. bar 1951. Newspaper reporter Eugene (Oreg.) Register-Guard, 1947-50; practiced in Eugene until, 1955; circuit judge Oreg. 2d. Jud. Dist., 1955-60; assoc. justice Oreg. Supreme Ct., 1960-69; U.S. dist. judge Dist. Oreg., 1969-71; judge U.S. Ct. Appeals 9th Circuit, 1971—. Contbr.: articles to Oreg. Law Rev, 1949-51; student editor articles to, 1950-51. Bd. dirs. Central Lane YMCA, Eugene, 1956-60, Salem (Oreg.) Art Assn., 1960-69; adv. bd. Eugene Salvation Army, 1956-60, chmn., 1959. Served to capt., inf. AUS, 1942-46, ETO. Mem. Am. Judicature Soc., Am. Law Inst., ABA (ho. of dels. 1986-87), Order of Coif, Phi Delta Phi, Sigma Delta Chi, Alpha Tau Omega. Republican. Presbyn. Club: Multnomah Athletic (Portland, (Oreg.). Jurisprudence. Home: 311 E Glenarm St #6 Pasadena CA 91106 Office: US Court of Appeals PO Box 91510 Pasadena CA 91109-1510

GOODWIN, HYMAN S., lawyer; b. Worcester, Mass., Aug. 30, 1907; s. Harry Louis and Ida (Tupper) G.; m. Ruth K. Klein, July 5, 1942 (dec. 1975); children: Felice G., Allan M. LLB, Boston U., 1931, JD, 1981. Bar: Mass. 1932, U.S. Dist. Ct. R.I. 1953, R.I. 1959, U.S. Supreme Ct. 1961. Ptnr. Macksound, Vacca & Goodwin, Providence, R.I. Mem. Tercentenary Commn., Worcester, Mass., 1935; pres. Young Dems., Worcester, 1948, Temple Beth El Brotherhood, Providence, 1950-52; chmn. Temple Beth El Sch. Com., 1953; chmn. Worcester County Infantile Paralysis campaign, 1947. Served with Counter Intelligence Corps U.S. Army, 1942-46, maj. Res. ret. Mem. R.I. Bar Assn. (ins. com. 1985-87), Assn. Trial Lawyers Am., R.I. Trial Lawyers Assn., Mil. Intelligence Assn. of New Eng. (v.p., bd. dirs.). Jewish. Club: Turks Head (Providence). Lodge: Masons. Avocations: photography, military history. Personal injury, Insurance. Home: 2 Jackson Walkway Regency W 1101 Providence RI 02903 Office: Macksound Vacca & Goodwin 740 Hosp Trust Bldg Providence RI 02903

GOODWIN, JAMES JEFFRIES, lawyer; b. San Juan, P.R., Aug. 24, 1949; s. David Badger and Elizabeth Ann (Ryan) G.; m. Mary Ann Schweikert, Nov. 29, 1981; 1 child, David Charles. B.A., U. Ky., 1971; M.P.A., Golden Gate U., 1977; J.D., U. Pacific, Sacramento, 1981. Bar: Calif. 1981, U.S. Dist. Ct. (ea. dist.) Calif. 1981, U.S. Ct. Appeals (9th cir.) 1983, U.S. Supreme Ct. 1984. Atty. Sacramento Pub. Defender's Office, 1980-82; sole practice, Sacramento, 1982—; legis. advocate Aircraft Owners and Pilots Assn., Washington, 1982—; legal counsel Emergency Med. Services, Sacramento, 1984. Served to capt. U.S. Army, 1971-77. Mem. Assn. Trial Lawyers Am., Calif. Trial Lawyers Assn. Episcopalian. Federal civil litigation, State civil litigation, Personal injury. Office: 2300 Bell Executive Ln Sacramento CA 95825

GOODWIN, ROBERT CRONIN, lawyer, consultant; b. Cleve., Mar. 17, 1941; s. Robert Clifford and Marion (Schmadel) G.; m. Judith Mary Baxter, June 7, 1968; children: Anne, Helen, Sharon, Katherine. AB, Fordham U., 1963; JD, Georgetown U., 1969. Bar: D.C. 1970. Vol., Peace Corps, Thailand, 1964-65; asst. community devel. advisor AID, Thailand, 1965-66; atty. advisor Office Gen. Counsel, Dept. Commerce, 1969-74; dep. asst. gen. counsel internat. and resource devel. programs Fed. Energy Adminstrn., Washington, 1974-77, asst. gen. counsel internat. conservation and resource devel. programs, 1977; asst. gen. counsel internat. trade and emergency preparedness Dept. Energy, 1977-79; ptnr. Thompson, Hine & Flory, 1979-82; v.p., gen. counsel China Energy Ventures, Washington, 1982-86; ptnr. Goodwin & Soble, 1986—; guest lectr. internat. petroleum contracts East China Petroleum Inst. Beijing, 1985; lectr. internat. contracts, Chinese law and trade law, Hong Kong, Singapore, Kuala Lumpur, Taipei, Jakarta, 1983. Editor-in-chief Law and Policy in International Business, 1968-69; contbr. articles to profl. jours. Mem. pvt. sch. bd. 1980-83. Recipient cert. of Merit Fed. Energy Adminstrn., 1974, cert. Spl. Achievement, 1974, 76. Mem. ABA, D.C. Bar Assn., Am. Soc. Internat. Law. Contracts commercial, Administrative and regulatory, Private international. Home: 3710 Bradley Ln Chevy Chase MD 20815 Office: 1300 19th St NW Washington DC 20036

GOOGASIAN, GEORGE ARA, lawyer; b. Pontiac, Mich., Feb. 22, 1936; s. Peter and Lucy (Chobanian) G.; m. Phyllis Elaine Law, June 27, 1959; children—Karen Ann, Steven George, Dean Michael. B.A., U. Mich., 1958; J.D., Northwestern U., 1961. Bar: Mich. Assoc. Marentay, Rouse, Selby, Fischer & Webber, Detroit, 1961-62; asst. U.S. Atty. U.S. Dept. Justice, Detroit, 1962-64; assoc. Howlett, Hartman & Beier, Pontiac and Bloomfield Hills, Mich., 1964-81; ptnr. Googasian, Hopkins, Rogers, Carlson & Hohauser and predecessor firms, Bloomfield Hills, 1981—; dir. Oakland Law Library Found., Pontiac, 1983—. Author: Trial Advocacy Manual, 1984. Pres. Oakland Parks Found., Pontiac, 1984; chmn. Oakland County Democratic party, Pontiac, 1964-70; state campaign chmn. Philip A. Hart, Detroit, 1970; bd. dirs. Big Bros. Oakland County. 1968-73. Fellow Am. Bar Found., Am. Coll. Trial Lawyers; mem. ABA, State Bar Mich., Assn. Trial Lawyers Am., Oakland County Bar Assn. (pres. 1985-86), Mich. State Bar Found. (commr. State Bar 1986—). Presbyterian. Club: U. Mich. Club Greater Detroit. Personal injury, Federal civil litigation, State civil litigation. Home: 3750 Orion Rd Rochester MI 48064 Office: Googasian Hopkins Rogers Carlson & Hohauser 300 E Long Lake Rd Suite 380 Bloomfield Hills MI 48013

GOOLRICK, ROBERT MASON, lawyer, consultant; b. Fredericksburg, Va., Mar. 25, 1934; s. John T. and Olive E. (Jones) G.; m. Audrey J. Dippo (div.); children—Stephanie M., Meade A. B.A. with distinction, U. Va., 1956; J.D., 1959. Bar: Va. 1959, D.C., 1959, U.S. Dist. Ct. D.C. 1961, U.S. Ct. Appeals (D.C. cir.) 1961. Assoc. Steptoe & Johnson, Washington, 1959-65, ptnr., 1965-79; sole practice, Alexandria, Va., 1979-83; cons. bus., oil and gas fin.; instr. U. Va. Law Sch. Mem. ABA (corps. sect.), Jefferson Soc., Raven Soc., Order of Coif, Phi Beta Kappa. Author: Public Policy Toward Corporate Growth, 1978; Corporate Mergers and Acquisitions under Federal Securities Laws, 1978. General corporate, Business finance, Oil and gas leasing. Home: 3320 Woodburn Village Dr #22 Annandale VA 22003-1255 Office: 6720 Curran St McLean VA 22101

GOORMAN, PERRY LEE, lawyer; b. Denver, June 19, 1951; s. Louis Henry and Irene Ruth (Thompson) G.; m. Patricia Ann Gibson, Dec. 31. 1976 (div. Oct. 1981); 1 child, Heather Ann; m. Julie Beth Furnish, Mar. 8, 1984. BA, Colo. State U., 1973; JD, U. Denver, 1977. Bar: Colo. 1977, U.S. Dist. Ct. Colo. 1977, U.S. Ct. Appeals (10th cir.) 1981, U.S. Supreme Ct. 1984. Assoc. DeMuth, Eiberger, Kemp & Backus, Denver, 1977-79; ptnr. Eiberger, Stacy & Smith, Denver, 1979-86; sole practice Englewood, Colo., 1986—. Mem. ABA, Colo. Bar Assn., Colo. Trial Lawyers Assn., Colo. Contractors Assn., Assn. Gen. Contractors, Colo. Assn. Commerce and Industry, Internat. Arabian Horse Assn., Colo. Arabian Horse Club. Avocations: golf, sailing, skiing, fishing, photography. Labor, Workers' compensation, Construction. Office: Plaza Marin 3 Suite 300 A 5600 S Quebec Englewood CO 80111

GOOSTREE, ROBERT EDWARD, educator; b. nr. Clarksville, Tenn., Sept. 23, 1923; s. William Lee and Lucy (Frech) G.; m. Jane Rogers, July 16, 1955; children—Laura, Frederic, Samuel. A.B., Southwestern at Memphis, 1943; M.A., State U. Ia., 1948, Ph.D., 1950; J.D., Am. U., 1962. Instr. polit. sci. U. Ia., 1946-50, U. Md., 1951-53; asst. prof. Am. U., 1953-56, asso. prof., 1956-60, prof., 1960-71; asst. dean Am. U. (Sch. Govt.), 1958-62, acting dean, 1962-63, prof. law and govt., 1963-71, acting dean law sch., 1970-71; prof. Capital U. Law Sch., Columbus, Ohio, 1971—; dean Capital U. Law Sch., 1971-79; cons. John F. Kennedy Center for Performing Arts, Washington, 1964-71; pres. League of Ohio Law Schs., 1984-85. Contbr. articles to legal jours. Mem. Reynoldsburg (Ohio) City Charter Commn., 1978-79; pres. League of Ohio Law Schs., 1984-85. Served with AUS, 1943-46. Mem. D.C., Supreme Ct. bars, Am., Fed. bar assns., Am. Polit. Sci. Assn., Am. Trial Lawyers Assn. Club: Nat. Lawyers (Washington). Legal education, Legal history, Local government. Home: 999 Matterhorn Dr Reynoldsburg OH 43068

GOOTEE, JANE MARIE, lawyer; b. Jasper, Ind., July 5, 1953; d. Thomas H. and Anne M. (Dreifke) G. BA, Ind. U., 1974; JD cum laude, St. Louis U., 1977. Bar: Ind. 1977, Mo. 1978, Mich. 1980, Ohio 1983, U.S. Dist. Ct. (so. dist.) Ind. 1977, U.S. Dist. Ct. (ea. dist.) Mich. 1980, U.S. Ct. Appeals (7th cir.) 1978, U.S. Supreme Ct. 1980, U.S. Ct. Appeals (6th cir.) 1982, U.S. Ct. Appeals (4th cir.) 1986. Dep. atty. gen. Ind., Indpls., 1977-79; corp. atty. Dow Chem. Co., Midland, Mich., 1979-81, ea. div. counsel, 1981-84, sr. atty., 1984-86, Mich. div. counsel, 1986—; mem. issue mgmt. team Dow Chem. Groundwater, 1986—, adv. com. Nat. Chamber Litigation Ctr. Environ. Law, 1985—; chair Dow Epidemiology Instl. Rev. Bd., 1984—; probono def. Midland Cir. Ct., 1980-81; adj. prof. Saginaw Valley State Coll.,

University Center, Mich., 1979-80. Bd. dirs. Big Sisters Midland, 1979-81, 84—, Big Bros./Big Sisters Midland, 1986—. Mem. ABA, Mo. Bar, Ohio Bar Assn., Mich. Bar Assn., Bar Assn. Greater Cleve. (corp. sec. gov.'s com. 1983), Assn. Trial Lawyers Am. Republican. Roman Catholic. Federal civil litigation, Environment. Home: 1412 Brentwood Dr Midland MI 48640 Office: Dow Chem Legal Dept Michigan Div 47 Bldg Midland MI 48667

GORAL, BRIAN HAROLD, lawyer; b. Chgo., Feb. 6, 1927; s. Bernard William and Lydia (Bloomquist) G.; m. Verna Marie Moriarity, Nov. 12, 1927; children—Bruce C., Bradley D., Diana L., Alan C. B.S., U. Denver, 1951, LL.B., 1951, J.D., 1970. Bar: Colo. 1951, U.S. Dist. Ct. Colo. 1952, U.S. Ct. Appeals (10th cir.) 1953, U.S. Supreme Ct. 1981. Asst. city atty., Denver, 1953-84, acting city atty., 1980, 81, 82, 83. Committeeman, Denver County Dem. Com., 1957, Jefferson County Dem. Com., 1966; pres. Baseball Assn. Applewood-Clear Creek, Golden, Colo., 1970-73. Served to lt. j.g. USNR, 1945-46. Mem. Lambda Chi Alpha, Phi Delta Phi. Republican. Baptist. General corporate, State civil litigation, Real property. Home: 14075 Crabapple Rd Golden CO 80401 Office: 5500 W 44th Ave Suite 200 Denver CO 80212

GORDAN, VICKI JOLENE TRIPP, lawyer; b. Portland, Maine, Mar. 14, 1956; d. Charles Herbert and Rosemary (Simmons) Tripp. BA, Bates Coll., 1977; JD, U. Maine, 1980; MBA, U. New Hampshire, 1986. Bar: Maine 1980. Asst. counsel UNUM Life Ins. Co., Portland, 1980—. Real property. Office: UNUM Life Ins Co 2211 Congress St Portland ME 04122

GORDESKY, MORTON, lawyer; b. Egg Harbor, N.J., Apr. 11, 1929; s. Benjamin and Rose (Suskin) G.; m. Marcelline D. Fallick, June 8, 1952 (div. 1982); children: Benjamin Todd, Nancy Hope Hafuta. BS, Temple U., 1950; JD, Rutgers U., 1954. Bar: Pa. 1955, U.S. Dist. Ct. (ea. dist.) Pa. 1958, U.S. Ct. Appeals (3rd cir.) 1983, U.S. Supreme Ct. 1983. Sole practice, Phila., 1954—. Mem. Phila. Dem. Com., 1956-68, mem. lawyer's com., fundraiser. Served with U.S. Army, 1954-56. Mem. Phila. Bar Assn., Amvets (judge adv. 1961-64), Greater Phila. C. of C. (internat. platform com.). Jewish. Lodges: KP, B'nai B'rith. State civil litigation, Criminal, Personal injury. Office: 2820 PSFS Bldg 12 S 12th St Philadelphia PA 19107

GORDLEY, JAMES RUSSEL, law educator; b. 1946. BA, U. Chgo., 1967, MBA, 1968; JD, Harvard U., 1970. Fellow U. Florence Inst. Law, Italy, 1970-71; assoc. Foley, Hoag & Eliot, Boston, 1971-72; fellow community law Harvard U., Cambridge, Mass., 1973-78; acting prof. U. Calif., Berkeley, 1978-81, prof., 1981—. Fellow Inst. Medieval Canon Law, U. Calif., Berkeley, 1978. Office: U of Calif Sch Law Boalt Hall Berkeley CA 94720 *

GORDON, BARRY L., lawyer; b. Chgo., Feb. 14, 1942; s. Philip and Dorothy (Pollack) G.; m. Janice Kozin, Apr. 8, 1967; children—Sandra, Paul. B.S., U. Ill., 1963; J.D., Ill. Inst. Tech.-Kent Coll. Law, 1967. Bar: Ill. 1968, U.S. Dist. Ct. (no. dist.) Ill. 1968, U.S. Supreme Ct. 1979; lic. real estate broker, Ill. Assoc. law firm Brody & Gore, Chgo., 1969-71, Heller & Morris, Chgo., 1971-73; pres. Barry L. Gordon & Assocs., P.C., Chgo., 1973—. Mem. Am. Arbitration Assn. (arbitrator 1974—), Chgo. Bar Assn., Ill. Trial Lawyers Assn. Family and matrimonial, Personal injury. Office: Barry L Gordon & Assocs PC 7 S Dearborn St Chicago IL 60603

GORDON, BURTON, lawyer; b. Bronx, N.Y., June 26, 1931; s. Howard H. and Jean (Seidman) G. BS, NYU, 1951; JD, Harvard U., 1954. Bar: N.Y. 1956, U.S. Dist. Ct. (so. and ea. dists.) N.Y. 1956, U.S. Ct. Appeals (2d cir.) 1974, U.S. Supreme Ct. 1974. Assoc. Manes, Sturim, Donovan & Laufer, N.Y.C., 1957-59; ptnr. Kaufman, Gordon & Kessler, N.Y.C., 1959-65; assoc. McLaughlin, Fiscella & Biancheri, N.Y.C., 1965-67, Harry H. Lipsig, N.Y.C., 1967-70, Bower & Gardner, N.Y.C., 1970-74; ptnr., pres. Gordon & Silber P.C., N.Y.C., 1974—; lectr. Am. Soc. Advancement of Anesthesia in Dentistry, 1984, NYU Coll. of Dentistry, 1985; mem. med. malpractice mediation panel 1st Jud. Dept., 1977—. Columnist, Physicians Med. Law Letter. Mem. med. malpractice mediation panel 1st jud. dept., 1977—. Served to cpl. U.S. Army, 1954-56. Mem. ABA (medicine and law com.), Assn. of Bar of City of N.Y., N.Y. State Bar Assn. (ins., negligence and compensation law sect., profl. liability ins. com.), Putnam County Bar Assn., Westchester County Bar Assn., Am. Soc. Law and Medicine, Inc., Soc. Med. Jurisprudence, Assn. Trial Lawyers Am., Manhattan Trial Counsel Assn., Def. Assn. of N.Y., Def. Research Inst. (econs. of def. practice com., med.-legal com., Internat. Soc. Barristers, Am. Arbitration Assn. (panel of arbitrators), Bklyn. Manhattan Trial Counsel Assn. Avocation: tennis. Personal injury, Insurance. Home: Cloud Bank Rd Garrison NY 10524 Office: Gordon & Silber PC 99 Park Ave New York NY 10016

GORDON, CHARLES, lawyer; b. N.Y.C., Oct. 12, 1905; s. Louis and Sarah (Tannenbaum) G.; m. Anne Chachanowsky, Mar. 17, 1940; children: Michael, Ellen. Student, CCNY, 1923-26; LL.B., NYU, 1927. Bar: N.Y. 1929, D.C. 1974, U.S. Supreme Ct. 1949. Atty. N.Y.C., 1929-39; with U.S. Immigration and Naturalization Service, 1939-74, dep. gen. counsel, 1962-66, gen. counsel, 1966-74; practice law Washington, 1974—; Adj. prof. law Georgetown U., 1963—, U. San Diego, 1974—; lectr. immigration law symposiums Practicing Law Inst., also various bar assns. and law schs. Author: (with Rosenfield) Immigration Law and Procedure, rev. edit, 1966, also ann. supplements and revisions; (with Ellen Gittel Gordon) Immigration and Nationality Law, student edit, 1979, Immigration Law and Procedure, desk edit, 1980. Active local civic orgns. and P.T.A. Recipient Annual Authorship award Fed. Bar Assn., 1965; Vicennial award Georgetown U., 1985, Outstanding Contbns. award Nat. Ctr. for Immigrants Rights, 1987. Mem. ABA (vice chmn. com. immigration and nationality 1967-73, chmn. 1973-81), Am. Immigration Lawyers Assn. (Outstanding Contbns. award 1983). Immigration, naturalization, and customs. Home: 11810 Seven Locks Rd Potomac MD 20854 Office: 1511 K St NW Washington DC 20005

GORDON, COREY LEE, lawyer; b. Mpls., Aug. 22, 1956; s. Jack I. and LaVerne (Shedlov) G.; m. Ciel Schaeffer, Aug. 29, 1982. BA, Macalester Coll., 1976; JD cum laude, U. Minn., 1980. Bar: Minn. 1980, U.S. Dist. Ct. Minn. 1981, U.S. Ct. Appeals (8th cir.) 1983, U.S. Supreme Ct. 1983. Assoc. Fried, Frank, Harris, Shriver & Jacobson, N.Y.C., 1980-81; ptnr. Shapiro, Lavintman & Gordon P.A., Mpls., 1982-85; assoc. Robins, Zelle, Larson & Kaplan, St. Paul, 1986—. Treas. The H.H.H. Fund, Minn., 1984—; active Dem. Farm Labor Party. Mem. ABA, Fed. Bar Assn., Minn. Bar Assn., Assn. Trial Lawyers Am. Jewish. Avocation: breeding dogs. Personal injury. Home: 2745 Aquila Ave S Saint Louis Park MN 55426 Office: Robins Zelle Larson & Kaplan 345 Saint Peter St Saint Paul MN 55102

GORDON, DANIEL R., lawyer; b. Bluffton, Ind., Aug. 30, 1951; s. Alfred R. and Gloria E. (Stoffel) G.; m. Elizabeth A. Berghoff, Sept. 10, 1983. BA, Ball State U., 1973; JD, Harvard U., 1976. Bar: Ind. 1976, U.S. Dist. Ct. (so. dist.) Ind. 1976, U.S. Dist. Ct. (no. dist.) Ind. 1981. Assoc. Cadick, Burns, Duck & Peterson, Indpls., 1976-80; ptnr. Dale, Gordon & Huffman, Bluffton, 1980—. Majority atty. Ind. Ho. of Reps., Indpls., 1979-80; pres. trustees Bluffton Wells County Pub. Library; mem. Indpls. Police Merit Bd., 1980; pres. St. Joseph's Parish Council, Bluffton, 1982-84; bd. dirs. Maumee Valley Legal Services, Ft. Wayne, Ind., 1981-84, Adams Wells Assn. for Retarded Citizens, Bluffton, Wells COunty United Way, 1981-83, Greater Indpls. Housing Devel. Corp., 1979-80. Mem. ABA, Ind. Bar Assn. (council probate , real property and trust sect. 1983—), Wells County Bar Assn. (pres. 1983-84), Ft. Wayne Estate Planning Council. Lodge: KC. Probate. Home: 1607 E 350 N Bluffton IN 46714 Office: Dale Gordon & Huffman PO Box 492 Bluffton IN 46714

GORDON, DAVID ELIOT, lawyer; b. Santa Monica, Calif., Mar. 8, 1949; s. Sam and Sylvia (Zerner) G.; m. Mary Debora Lane, Mar. 5, 1978. BA, Harvard U., 1969, JD, 1972. Bar: Calif. 1972. Ptnr. O'Melveny & Myers, Los Angeles, 1972—. Contbr. articles on tax and employee benefits to profl. jours. Fellow Los Angeles County Bar Found. (life, pres. 1984-85, bd. dirs. 1980-86); mem. ABA (employee benefits com. 1986—), Los Angeles County Bar Assn. (chmn. employee benefits com. 1986-87), Nat. Assn. Bond Lawyers (bd. dirs. 1982-84). Republican. Avocations: squash, racquetball. Pension, profit-sharing, and employee benefits, Corporate taxation, Personal income taxation. Office: O'Melveny & Myers 400 S Hope St Los Angeles CA 90071-2899

GORDON, EDGAR GEORGE, lawyer, banker; b. Detroit, Feb. 27, 1924; s. Edgar George and Verna Florence (Hay) G.; m. Alice Irwin, Feb. 4, 1967; children—David A., J. Scott. A.B., Princeton U., 1947; J.D., Harvard U., 1950. Bar: Mich. 1951, U.S. Supreme Ct. 1953. Assoc., Poole, Warren & Littell, Detroit, 1950-54; ptnr. Poole, Warren, Littell & Gordon, Detroit, 1953-63; gen. counsel Hygrade Food Products Corp., Detroit, 1963-69, sec., 1966-69, v.p., 1968-69; v.p., sec., counsel City Nat. Bank of Detroit, 1969-81; v.p., sec., gen. counsel No. States Bancorp., 1970-81; v.p., sec., counsel First of Am. Bank Corp., Kalamazoo, 1981-84, also ptnr. Howard & Howard, Kalamazoo, 1981—; pres., chmn. bd. First of Am. Mortgage Co., Kalamazoo, 1974-85. Served to lt. (j.g.), USNR, 1943-46. Mem. ABA, Mich. Bar Assn., Kalamazoo Bar Assn. Republican. Presbyterian. Clubs: Country of Detroit (Grosse Pointe, Mich.); Kalamazoo Country, Park (Kalamazoo). General corporate, Banking. Home: 4339 Lakeside Dr Kalamazoo MI 49008 Office: 400 Kalamazoo Bldg Kalamazoo MI 49007

GORDON, FRANK X., JR., judge; b. Chgo., Jan. 9, 1929; s. Frank X. and Lucille (Gburek) G.; m. Joan C. Gipe, Sept. 17, 1950; children: Frank X., Candace Gordon Lander. BA, Stanford U., 1951; LLB, U. Ariz., 1954. Bar: Ariz. 1954. Assoc. Gordon and Gordon, Kingman, Ariz., 1954-62; atty. City of Kingman, 1955-57; judge Superior Ct. Mohave County (Ariz.), Kingman, 1962-75; justice Ariz. Supreme Ct., Phoenix, 1975—, now chief justice; mem. various coms. Ariz. State Bar; Ariz. rep. to Council for State Ct. REps., Nat. Ctr. State Cts. Bd. visitors U. Ariz. Law Sch., 1972-75; trustee Chester H. Smith Meml. Scholarship Fund; past bd. dirs., pres. Mohave County Mental Health Clinic, Inc.; past mem. Gov.'s Commn. Mental Health; state bd. dirs. Ariz. Heart Assn.; active Boulder Dam Area council Boy Scouts Am. Mem. ABA, Ariz. Bar Assn. Maricopa County Bar Assn., Am. Judicature Soc., Mohave County C. of C. (past pres.). Democrat. Methodist. Lodges: Rotary, Elks. Office: Ariz Sup Ct State Capitol Bldg Phoenix AZ 85007

GORDON, HARRISON J., lawyer; b. Newark, Aug. 21, 1950; s. Carl and Rose (Katz) G.; m. Alice S. Belsky, Nov. 21, 1982; 1 child, Caryn Rachel. BS, U. Bridgeport, 1972; JD, U. Miami, 1975. Bar: N.J. 1976, U.S. Dist. Ct. N.J. 1976, U.S. Supreme Ct. 1980. Sole practice West Orange, N.J., 1976-78, Montclair, N.J., 1978-83; ptnr. Gordon & Gordon, West Orange, 1983—; adj. prof. Montclair State Coll., Upper Montclair, N.J., 1979-80; legal cons. Am. Title Ins. Co., Bryn Mawr, Pa., 1985—. Mem. allocations com. United Way of Northwest Essex, Montclair, 1981, Montclair Spl. Environ. Counsel, 1984—. Mem. N.J. State Bar Assn. (exec. com. young lawyers div. 1981-83), Assn. Trial Lawyers Am., N.J. Trial Lawyers Assn. (bd. govs. 1987—), Am. Arbitration Assn. (arbitrator), Soc. of Bar and Gavel, Psi Chi, Phi Alpha Theta. Lodge: Optimists (v.p. 1980-81, pres. 1981-82). Personal injury, Federal civil litigation, State civil litigation. Home: 143 Konner Ave Pine Brook NJ 07058 Office: Gordon & Gordon PA 80 Main St West Orange NJ 07052

GORDON, IRVING A., university dean, law educator, lawyer; b. 1917. B.A., U. Chgo., 1938; Hebrew Theol. Coll.; J.D., Northwestern U., 1947. Bar: Ill. 1947; ordained rabbi, 1941; C.P.A., Ill. Clk. Justice S. Minton, U.S. Ct. Appeals, 1948-49; assoc. Healy and Stickler, Chgo., 1949-51; gen. counsel Internat. Rolling Mills Corp., Chgo., 1951-60; assoc. Arnstein, Gluck, Weitzenfeld et al., Chgo., 1964-66; prof. Northwestern U., 1966—; vis. prof. Garrett Theol. Sem., 1971-74; mem. Ill. Gov.'s Constn. Research Group. Mem. Chgo. Bar Assn. (chmn. subcom. on urban housing), Am. Law Inst., Phi Beta Kappa. Past assoc. editor Ill. Law Rev. Legal education. Office: Northwestern U Law Sch 357 Chicago Ave Chicago IL 60611 *

GORDON, J. HOUSTON, lawyer; b. Camden, Tenn., Sept. 16, 1946; s. Houston Darnal and Frances Jane (Culvahouse) G.; 1 son, Houston Nathaniel. B.S. cum laude, U. Tenn., Martin, 1968; J.D., U. Tenn., Knoxville, 1970; LL.M., George Washington U., 1973. Bar: Tenn. 1970, D.C. 1978. Asst. dist. atty. 16th Jud. Cir. Tenn., 1974-75; ptnr. Gordon, Forrester & Whitaker, Covington, Tenn., 1974—. Mem. dean's alumni adv. council U. Tenn. Coll. Law. Served as capt. JAGC, U.S. Army, 1970-74. Mem. Tenn. Bar Assn., Am. Trial Lawyers Assn., Tenn. Trial Lawyers Assn. (bd. govs.), Memphis-Shelby County Bar Assn., Tipton County Bar Assn., Am. Judicature Soc. Federal civil litigation, State civil litigation, Criminal. Office: 114 W Liberty Ave PO Box 865 Covington TN 38019

GORDON, JACK ELLIOTT, JR., lawyer; b. Apr. 10, 1944; Tulsa; s. Jack Elliott and Janelle (Stallings) G.; m. Sandra Lee Fuller, Jan. 15, 1972; children—Casey Lee, Jacob Elliott. B.A., U. of South, Sewanee, Tenn., 1966; J.D., U. Ark., 1969. Bar: Okla. 1969, U.S. Dist. Ct. (no. dist.) Okla. 1969. Assoc., Bassmann, Gordon, Mayberry & Scarth, Claremore, Okla., 1972-76; ptnr. Gordon & Gordon, Claremore, 1976—. Mng. editor: U. Ark. Law Rev., 1968-69. Served to 1st lt. AUS, 1969-72. Mem. Assn. Trial Lawyers Am., Okla. Trial Lawyers Assn., Okla. Criminal Def. Lawyers Assn. Democrat. Episcopalian. General practice, Criminal, Civil litigation. Home: 502 E 4th St Claremore OK 74017 Office: Gordon & Gordon 212 S Missouri Ave Claremore OK 74017

GORDON, JAMES EDWARD, lawyer; b. Lincoln, Nebr., Sept. 5, 1946; s. Robert Merle and Sarah Ida (Reingold) G.; m. Pegi O. Pepper, July 20, 1974; children: Micala Renee, Shannon Leigh. BA, U. Nebr., 1972, JD, 1974. Bar: Nebr. 1974, U.S. Dist. Ct. Nebr. 1974. Ptnr. Ginsburg, Rosenberg, Ginsburg, Cathcart, Curry & Gordon, P.C., Lincoln, 1974-84, Erickson & Sederstrom, Lincoln, 1984—. Mem. Jud. Nominating Commn., Lincoln, 1982-86, City of Lincoln Charter Revision Commn., 1986—; v.p., bd. dirs. Folsom Children's Zoo Bd., Lincoln, 1985—, pres. 1987—. Served to sgt. U.S. Army, 1966-69, Vietnam. Rhodes scholar Rhodes Trust Fund, 1972. Mem. ABA, Assn. Trial Lawyers Am., Nebr. Assn. Trial Attys., Lincoln Univ. Club (bd. dirs. 1983-87, pres. 1985-86), Nebr. State Bar Assn. (family law com.), VFW, Am. Legion, DAV. Democrat. Jewish. Lodge: Elks. Avocations: tree planting, bicycling. State civil litigation, Family and matrimonial, Personal injury. Office: Erickson & Sederstrom PC 301 S 13th St Cornhusker Plaza Suite 400 Lincoln NE 68508

GORDON, JAMES S., lawyer; b. N.Y.C., Feb. 15, 1941; s. George S. and Sylvia A. (Wolfson) G.; m. Marcia G. Gordon, Dec. 22, 1968; children—Daniel, Sarah. B.A. with high honors, U. Fla., 1962; LL.B., Yale U., 1965. Bar: Ill. 1965, Fla. 1966, U.S. Supreme Ct. 1974. Asst. prof. Ind. U. Sch. Law, Bloomington, 1967-68, assoc. prof., 1969; ptnr. Feiwell, Galper & Gordon, Chgo., 1970-72; sole practice Chgo., 1972-80; pres. James S. Gordon, Ltd., Chgo., 1981—; dir. Instrumentalist Co., Northfield, Ill. Mem. Winnetka Caucus, 1981-82. Ford Found. grantee, 1965-66. Mem. ABA, Ill. State Bar Assn., Chgo. Bar Assn., Yale U. Law Alumni Assn. (exec. com. 1987—), Order of Coif, Phi Beta Kappa, Phi Alpha Delta, Clubs: Legal, Mid-Day (Chgo.); Birchwood (Highland Park, Ill.). Editor Yale Law Jour., 1963-65. Contbr. articles to profl. jours. Federal civil litigation, Antitrust, Administrative and regulatory. Office: 140 S Dearborn St Suite 404 Chicago IL 60603

GORDON, JEFFREY NEIL, law educator; b. Richmond, Va., June 18, 1949; s. Irving Leonard and Viola Anne (Clayman) G. BA, Yale U., 1971; JD, Harvard U., 1975. Bar: N.Y. 1977, D.C. 1981, U.S. Dist. Ct. (so. and ea. dists.) N.Y. 1978, U.S. Ct. Appeals (2d cir.) 1979. Reporter Rocky Mount News, Denver, 1971-72; law clk to presiding judge U.S. Ct. Appeals (10th cir.), Denver, 1975-76; assoc. Cleary, Gottlieb, Steen & Hamilton, N.Y.C., 1976-78; spl. asst. to gen. counsel, atty. advisor U.S. Treasury, Washington, 1978-81; prof. law NYU, N.Y.C., 1982—. Contbr. articles to profl. jours. Bd. dirs. employees fed. credit union NYU, 1983-86. Recipient Exceptional Service award U.S. Dept. Energy, 1982. Mem. ABA, Assn. of Bar of City of N.Y.; Phi Beta Kappa. Democrat. Jewish. Clubs: Harvard (N.Y.C.); Mory's (New Haven). General corporate, Banking. Home: 2 Washington Sq Village Apt 6N New York NY 10012 Office: NYU Law Sch 40 Washington Sq S New York NY 10012

GORDON, JOHN BENNETT, lawyer; b. Des Moines, Nov. 21, 1947; s. Bennett and Mary (Adelman) G.; m. Joanne Dunbar Westgate, Jan. 17, 1976; children—Anne Dunbar, Bennett Westgate, Susan Julia. A.B., Princeton U., 1969; J.D., Harvard U., 1973. Bar: Minn. 1974, U.S. Dist. Ct. Minn. 1974, U.S. Ct. Appeals (8th cir.) 1974, U.S. Supreme Ct. 1985. Clk., U.S. Ct. Appeals (5th cir.), Newnan, Ga., 1973-74; assoc. law firm Faegre & Benson, Mpls., 1974-80, ptnr., 1981—. Mem. Minn. State Bar Assn., Hennepin County Bar Assn. (pres. 1985-86), Minn. Def. Lawyers Assn. (bd. dirs.), Internat. Assn. Def. Counsel. Federal civil litigation, State civil litigation, Environment. Office: Faegre & Benson 2300 Multifoods Tower Minneapolis MN 55402

GORDON, KENNETH, newspaper executive; b. Trinidad, West Indies, Feb. 24, 1930; m. Marguerite Gordon; children—Roger, Rhett, Patricia, Lesley, Douglas, Nikki. Sr. Cambridge, St. Mary's Coll., Port of Spain, Trinidad. Program dir. Radio Trinidad, 1951-61, Trinidad TV, 1961; gen. mgr. Trinidad C. of C., 1962-69; mng. dir. Trinidad Express Newspapers Ltd., Port of Spain, 1969—; past pres. Caribbean Pub. and Broadcasting Assn.; former chmn. CANA; dir. Barbados Nation, Voice of St. Lucia, Dominica Chronicle; senator, minister Industry and Enterprises, 1987—. Recipient Premio SIP-Pedro Joaquin Chamorro award Inter Am. Press Assn., 1982, Gold medal Maria Moors Cabot award Columbia U., 1984, Astor award Commonwealth Press Union, 1985. Real property, General corporate, Municipal bonds. Office: Trinidad Express Newspapers Ltd, 35 Independence Sq, Port of Spain Trinidad

GORDON, MICHAEL, lawyer; b. Newark, Oct. 12, 1953; s. Carl and Rose (Katz) G. BA, Columbia U., 1975; JD, Rutgers U., 1979. Bar: N.J. 1980, U.S. Dist. Ct. N.J. 1980, U.S. Ct. Appeals (3d cir.) 1984. Adj. prof. Montclair State Coll., Upper Montclair, N.J., 1978-79; atty. N.J. Dept. of Environ. Protection, Trenton, 1979-80; sole practice Montclair, 1980-83; ptnr. Gordon & Gordon, P.A., West Orange, N.J., 1983—; spl. environ. counsel cities of Ridgefield, Montclair and Lafayette, N.J.; vis.lectr. Rutgers U., Newark, 1985. Vol. atty. Legal Services of Essex, Newark, 1984—. Recipient Cert. of Achievement, Ironbound Com. Against Toxic Waste, Newark, 1985, Outstanding Vol. award Essex Newark Legal Services, 1985. Mem. Assn. Trial Lawyers Am., N.J. State Bar Assn., N.J. Assn. Trial Lawyers (chmn. environ. law com.). Club: Columbia (North Jersey). Environment, Federal civil litigation, State civil litigation. Office: 80 Main St West Orange NJ 07052

GORDON, MICHAEL DAVID, lawyer; b. Kansas City, Mo., Mar. 17, 1941; s. Morris and Helen Grace (Ozar) G.; m. Susan David Driscoll, Apr. 2, 1963; children—Scott David, Ann David. B.S. with honors, U. Wis.-Madison, 1963; J.D., U. Mich., 1966. Bar: Mo. 1966, U.S. Dist. Ct. (we. dist.) Mo. 1970, U.S. Ct. Appeals (8th cir.) 1974, U.S. Ct. Appeals (3d cir.) 1976, U.S. Ct. Appeals (2d cir.) 1977, U.S. Ct. Appeals (7th cir.) 1984. Trial atty. 17th region NLRB, 1966-69; ptnr. Jolley, Walsh, Hager and Gordon, and predecessors, Kansas City, Mo., 1969—; lectr. Rockhurst Coll., 1971-73. Mem. ABA, Mo. Bar Assn. (labor law com. chmn. 1983-84), Kansas City Bar Assn., Indsl. Relations Research Assn., Soc. Labor Law and Social Security. Labor, Civil rights, Federal civil litigation. Home: 801 Greenway Terr Kansas City MO 64113 Office: 1300 Traders Bank Bldg Kansas City MO 64106

GORDON, MICHAEL MACKIN, lawyer; b. Boston, Apr. 15, 1950; s. Lawrence H. and Gladys (Mackin) G. AB, Vassar Coll., 1972; JD, Columbia U., 1976. Bar: N.Y. 1977, U.S. Dist. Ct. (so. and ea. dists.) N.Y. 1977, D.C. 1980, U.S. Ct. Appeals (2d cir.) 1985, U.S. Supreme Ct. 1985. Assoc. Seward & Kissel, N.Y.C., 1977-79; assoc. Cadwalader, Wickersham & Taft, N.Y.C., 1979-85, ptnr., 1985—. Mem. ABA, N.Y. State Bar Assn., N.Y. County Lawyers Assn. Club: Vassar (N.Y.C.). Federal civil litigation, State civil litigation, Environment. Home: 12 W 72d St New York NY 10023 Office: Cadwalader Wickersham & Taft 100 Maiden Ln New York NY 10038

GORDON, NEAL, lawyer; b. Bklyn., July 21, 1941; s. William and Pearl (Fenster) G.; m. Carole Marcia Harris; children—Rachel, Ilyse. B.A., U. Pa., 1963; J.D., N.Y.U., 1966. Bar: N.Y. 1967, U.S. Dist. Ct. (ea. dist.) N.Y. 1973, U.S. Dist. Ct. (so. dist.) N.Y. 1973. Assoc., Ladas Parry, N.Y.C., 1966-74, ptnr., 1975-77; trademark atty. Am. Home Products, 1977-82; gen. counsel, v.p., sec. Cartier Internat., Inc., N.Y.C., 1982—. Mem. U.S. Trademark Assn. (dir.), ABA, N.Y. Patent Assn. Office: Cartier Internat Inc 653 5th Ave New York NY 10022

GORDON, NORMAN JAMES, lawyer; b. Chgo., Dec. 24, 1945; s. Meyer and Alice (Vetzner) G.; m. Cheryl Bisk, June 8, 1969; children—David Benjamin, Joshua. B.A., U. Ill., 1967, J.D., 1970. Bar: Ill. 1970, Tex. 1974, U.S. Dist. Ct. (we. dist.) Tex. 1974, U.S. Ct. Appeals (5th cir.) 1974, U.S. Supreme Ct. 1974. Asst. states atty. Mclean County (Ill.), 1970; assoc. Diamond, Rash, Leslie & Smith, El Paso, Tex., 1974-76, ptnr., 1976—. Vice Pres. El Paso Jewish Community Center, 1980-82, pres., 1983-86; sec. El Paso Jewish Fedn., 1986—; treas. Hospice of El Paso, 1982-83; bd. dirs. Congregation B'nai Zion, El Paso. Served to capt. JAGC, U.S. Army, 1970-74. Recipient New Leadership award Nat. Jewish Welfare Bd., 1982. Mem. ABA, Ill. Bar Assn., State Bar Tex., Assn. Trial Lawyers Am., Tex. Bd. Legal Specialization (cert. civil trial law), Tex. Trial Lawyers Assn., El Paso Bar Assn. Public utilities, State civil litigation, Personal injury. Office: 725 First City Nat Bank El Paso TX 79901

GORDON, RICHARD WARREN, lawyer; b. Boston, Apr. 8, 1950; s. Raymond Lloyd and Mary Catherine (Lauro) G.; m. Kathleen Louise Carey, Oct. 9, 1982; children: Laura Catherine, Caitlin Marie. B.A. in Social Sci., Thomas Edison State Coll., 1975; J.D. cum laude, New Eng. Sch. Law, 1975; C.S.S. in Adminstrn. and Mgmt., Harvard U., 1983. Bar: Mass. 1975, U.S. Dist. Ct. Mass. 1976, U.S. Ct. Appeals (1st and fed. cirs.) 1977, U.S. Ct. Claims 1977, U.S. Tax Ct. 1977, U.S. Ct. Mil. Appeals 1977, U.S. Supreme Ct. 1979. Legal intern U.S. Dept. Justice, U.S. Atty., Boston, 1974-75; clk. to U.S. adminstrv. law judge, Boston, 1975-76; sr. staff atty. U.S. Office Hearings and Appeals, HHS, Boston, 1976-83; chief dep. clk. U.S. Ct. Appeals (1st cir.), Boston, 1983—; lectr. in field; moot ct. judge New Eng. Sch. Law. Acting chmn., mem. City of Somerville Youth Resources Commn., Mass., 1969-73. Served with USAF, 1971; to lt. (j.g.) USNR, 1973-77; to capt. USAR, 1982—. Decorated Nat. Def. Service medal; recipient Superior Performance award HHS Office Hearings and Appeals, 1981. Mem. ABA, Fed. Bar Assn., Mass. Bar Assn., Boston Bar Assn., Assn. Staff Attys. in HHS (v.p. 1979, pres. 1980), Mensa. Democrat. Roman Catholic. Club: Harvard of Boston. Lodge: Ancient and Hon. Arty. Co. Mass. Federal civil litigation, Criminal, Military. Home: 380 Lawrence Rd Medford MA 02155 Office: US Ct Appeals 1st Circuit 1606 John McCormack Bldg Boston MA 02109

GORDON, ROBERT ALLEN, lawyer; b. Evanston, Ill., Sept. 14, 1951; s. Robert A. and Elizabeth (Bergman) G.; m. Ellen Slater Guba, Feb. 2, 1985; 1 child, Robert A. III. BA, Yale U., 1973; JD, U. Va., 1976. Bar: Calif. 1976, U.S. Dist. Ct. (no. dist.) Calif. 1977, U.S. Dist. Ct. (ea. and cen. dists.) Calif. 1978, U.S. Ct. Appeals (9th cir.) 1978. Law clk. to chief judge U.S. Ct. Appeals (9th cir.), San Francisco, 1976-77; assoc. Pillsbury, Madison & Sutro, San Francisco, 1977-83, ptnr., 1984—. Mem. Order of Coif. Federal civil litigation, State civil litigation. Office: Pillsbury Madison & Sutro 225 Bush St San Francisco CA 94104

GORDON, ROBERT JAY, lawyer, educator; b. Miami, Fla., May 10, 1956; s. Jerome B. and Florence (Lipschitz) G.; m. Leslie C. Gottlieb, Sept. 5, 1982. B.A. with distinction, U. Mich., 1977; J.D. with honors, George Washington U., Washington, 1980. Bar: Pa. 1980, U.S. Dist. Ct. (ea. dist.) Pa. 1981, U.S. Ct. Appeals (3d cir.) 1984, N.J. 1985, U.S. Dist. Ct. N.J. 1985, U.S. Supreme Ct., 1986. Asst. dist. atty. Phila. Dist. Atty.'s Office, 1980-84; assoc. Greitzer & Locks, Phila., 1984—; adj. prof. Temple U., Phila., 1983-85. Contbr. articles to profl. jours. Mem. Assn. Trial Lawyers Am., ABA, Pa. Trial Lawyers Assn., Pa. Bar Assn., Phila. Bar Assn. Democrat. Jewish. State civil litigation, Federal civil litigation, Criminal. Home: 603 Revere Rd Merion PA 19066 Office: Greitzer & Locks 1500 Walnut St Philadelphia PA 19102

GORDON, ROBERT JAY, lawyer; b. Pontiac, Mich., Dec. 22, 1949; s. Irving Edward and Bertha Mae (Finkelstein) G.; m. Barbara Lynn Tobias, June 25, 1972; children—Arianna Lea, Zachary Issac Eli. B.A. with honors, U. Mich., 1971; J.D. cum laude, Boston U., 1974. Bar: Mich. 1974. Assoc. Jaffe, Snider, Raitt & Hauer, P.C., Detroit, 1974-80, ptnr., 1980—. V.p. Anti-Defamation League, Detroit, 1980-87, pres., 1987—; assoc. commr. Anti-Defamation League Nat. Commn., 1986—. Mem. ABA, Mich. Bar

Assn. Jewish. General corporate, Contracts commercial, Real property. Office: Jaffe Snider Raitt & Heuer PC 1800 First National Bldg Detroit MI 48226

GORDON, ROBERT P., lawyer; b. Los Angeles, Jan. 16, 1935; s. James B. and Ethel N. (Rosenstein) G.; m. Joanne Phillips; children—Leslie, Bruce, Michael, Julie. B.S., UCLA, 1956; J.D., U. So. Calif., 1959. Bar: Calif. 1960, U.S. Ct. Appeals (9th cir.) 1960, U.S. Supreme Ct. 1971. Ptnr. Goldman, Gordon & Lipstone, Los Angeles, 1977—; judge pro tem Beverly Hills Mcpl. Ct., 1972-80 mem. arbitration panel Los Angeles Superior Ct., 1979—. Served with USCGR, 1960-65. Mem. ABA, Los Angeles County Bar Assn., Def. Research Inst., Assn. So. Calif. Def. Counsel, Comml. Law League Am., Am. Arbitration Assn. (panel arbitrators), Surety Claims Assn. Los Angeles, Am. Bankruptcy Inst., Century City Bar Assn., Nu Beta Epsilon, Zeta Beta Tau. Clubs: Masons, Shriners. Bankruptcy, State civil litigation, Contracts commercial. Office: 1801 Century Park E #810 Los Angeles CA 90067

GORDON, ROBERT W., law educator; b. 1941. AB, Harvard U., 1967, JD, 1971. Asst. prof. SUNY, Buffalo, 1971-74, assoc. prof., 1974-77; assoc. prof. U. Wis., Madison, 1977-80, prof., 1980-83; prof. Stanford (Calif.) U., 1983—; vis. prof. Harvard U., Cambridge, Mass., 1979-80, Stanford U., 1982-83. Office: Stanford Law Sch Stanford CA 94305 *

GORDON, STEPHEN JACOB, lawyer; b. Worcester, Mass., Oct. 25, 1950; s. Jacob and Dorothy (Vickers) G.; m. Elaine H. Fagelman, Nov. 4, 1984; 1 child, Kimberly. BA, Assumption Coll., 1972; JD, John Marshall Law Sch., 1977. Bar: U.S. Dist. Ct. Mass. 1977, U.S. Ct. Appeals (1st and 4th cirs.) 1978, U.S. Customs Ct. N.Y. 1978. Law clk. to judge U.S. Dist. Ct. Ill., Chgo., 1976-77; atty. advisor Adminstrv. Office, U.S. Supreme Ct., Washington, 1977-78; sole practice Worcester, 1979—; past instr. bus. law Fisher Jr. Coll., Worcester; atty.-human rights com. Coop. Human Services, Worcester, 1982-84; atty. Com. for Pub. Counsel, Worcester, 1985—. Cons. various polit. candidates, Worcester, 1974-78. Mem. Mass. Bar Assn., Worcester Bar Assn., Am. Trial Lawyers Assn. Avocations: musician, skiing, swimming, tennis. Federal civil litigation, State civil litigation, Personal injury. Office: 500 Main St Worcester MA 01608

GORDON, TED HOWARD, lawyer; b. Oakland, Calif., May 2, 1946; m. Sharon J. Gordon, July 2, 1972; 1 child, Matthew. BS, San Jose State U., 1969, MBA, 1971; JD, Hastings Coll., 1973. Title asst. Transam. Title Ins. Co., 1967; mortgage clk. Commonwealth Mortgage Corp., 1968; research analyst Boise Cascade Bldg. Co., 1969; real estate broker Van Vleck Realtors, 1970; assoc. Graham, Gordon, McFarlan & Stewart, San Rafael, Calif., 1974-79, Gordon, McFarlan, Stewart & Blecher, San Rafael, 1979-86, Gordon, McFarlan & Blecher, San Rafael, 1987—; instr. Ju-Jitsu, San Francisco, 1964-71, Golden Gate U., San Francisco, 1976—; profl. lectr. Golden Gate U., 1985—. Author: California Real Estate Law: Text & Cases, 2d edit., 1985; co-author: Real Estate Principles in California, 5th ed., 1987. Recipient Disting. Person's award San Jose State U.; Real Estate Personality of Week, San Jose Mercury News. Mem. Nat. Real Estate Fraternity (pres. 1967-68, named Mem. of Yr.), Soc. Advancement Mgmt. (asst. to pres. 1969), Fin. Mgmt. Assn. (asst. to pres. 1969). Office: Gordon McFarlan & Blecher 1050 Northgate Dr Suite 475 San Rafael CA 94903

GORDON, THEODORA, lawyer; b. N.Y.C., Nov. 4, 1923; d. Samuel and Rose (Perlstein) G. BA, Hunter Coll., 1945; JD, U. Chgo., 1947. Bar: Ill. 1948. Collection atty. Chgo. Assn. Credit Men, 1949-51, Spiegel, Inc., Chgo., 1951-53; product liability atty. Toni Co. div. Gillette Co., Chgo., 1953-74; sole practice Chgo., 1974—; cons. Gillette Co., Boston, 1974-85; arbitrator Am. Arbitration Assn., Chgo., 1985-86. Contbr. articles to profl. jours. Pres. Elaine Settler Found., 1960-62, bd. dirs., 1960—; bd. dirs. Levinson Ctr. for Mentally Handicapped, 1975-81. Mem. Women's Bar Ill. (pres. 1964-65), Chgo. Bar Assn., Decalogue Soc., Ill. State Bar Assn., Am. Assn. Trial Lawyers. Democrat. Jewish. Avocations: reading, knitting, theater, opera. General practice, Personal injury, Probate. Home: 6033 N Sheridan Rd Apt 16K Chicago IL 60660 Office: 8 S Michigan Ave Chicago IL 60603-1575

GORDON, THOMAS NAPIER, lawyer; b. Columbia, Tenn., July 31, 1951; s. William Bradshaw and Jayne Alston (Napier) G. B.A., Vanderbilt U., 1973, J.D., 1976. Bar: Tenn. 1977, U.S. Dist. Ct. (mid. dist.) Tenn. 1977. Assoc., ptnr. Courtney, Fleming, Holloway & Gordon, Columbia, 1977-84; sole practice, Columbia, 1984—; adv. dir. First Farmers & Mchts. Nat. Bank, Columbia, 1984-86, dir., 1986—; chmn. bd. dirs., sec., treas. Gorham Co., Columbia; bus. and industry chmn. March of Dimes, Maury County, Tenn., 1978; chmn. attys. div. United Givers Fund, Maury County, 1979; bd. dirs. Kings Daughters Sch., Columbia, 1981—, treas., 1985—, Zion Christian Acad., Columbia, 1982-87. Mem. Tenn. Bar Assn., Maury County Bar Assn. Presbyterian. Real property, Probate, General corporate. Office: PO Box 1526 Columbia TN 38402

GORELICK, JAMIE SHONA, lawyer; b. N.Y.C., May 6, 1950; d. Leonard and Shirley (Fishman) G.; m. Richard E. Waldhorn, Sept. 28, 1975. BA, Radcliffe Coll., 1972; JD, Harvard U., 1975. Bar: D.C. 1975, U.S. Dist. Ct. D.C. 1976, U.S. Tax Ct. 1976, U.S. Ct. Claims 1976, U.S. Ct. Appeals (D.C. cir.) 1976, U.S. Ct. Appeals (5th cir.) 1977, U.S. Supreme Ct. 1979, U.S. Ct. Appeals (Fed. cir.) 1982, U.S. Ct. Internat. Trade 1984, U.S. Dist. Ct. Md. 1985, U.S. Ct. Appeals (4th cir.) 1986. Assoc. Miller, Cassidy, Larroca & Lewin, Washington, 1975-79, 80, ptnr., 1981—; asst. to sec., counselor to dep. sec. U.S. Dept. Energy, Washington, 1979-80; teaching mem. trial advocacy workshop Harvard Law Sch., Cambridge, Mass., 1982, 84; vice chmn. task force evaluation of audit investigative inspection components Dept. Def., Washington, 1979-80; mem. sec.'s transition team Dept. Energy, Washington, 1979. Bd. editors Corp. Criminal Liability Reporter, 1986—, Rico Litigation Reporter, 1986—; adv. bd. RICO Law Reporter, Corp. Criminal Liability Reporter; contbr. articles to profl. jours. Fellow Am. Bar Found.; mem. ABA (chmn. complex crimes litigation com. litigation sect. 1984—, vice chmn. complex crimes litigation com. 1983-84), D.C. Bar Assn. (bd. govs. 1982—, sec. bd. govs. 1981-82, bar found. bd. advisors 1985—, legal ethics com.), Womens Bar Assn. Federal civil litigation, Criminal, Libel. Office: Miller Cassidy Larroca & Lewin 2555 M St NW Washington DC 20037

GOREY, THOMAS MICHAEL, lawyer; b. Chgo., Dec. 10, 1953; s. Walter D. and Joan F. (Loftus) G.; m. Lorena A. Strobel, June 24, 1978. BA in Psychology, U. Ill., 1975; JD, DePaul U., 1978. Bar: Ill. 1978, U.S. Dist. Ct. (no. dist.) Ill. 1981. Law clk. to presiding justice Ill. Supreme Ct., Bloomington, 1978-79; assoc. Zukowski, Poper & Rogers, Crystal Lake, Ill., 1979-80; law clk. to presiding justice Ill. Appellate Ct., Rockford, 1980-81; legis. atty. AMA, Chgo., 1981-83, dir. dept. physician practice services, 1983-86, dir. dept. long range policy analysis, 1986—. Mem. ABA, Ill. Bar Assn., Nat. Health Lawyers Assn. Health. Home: 355 Cumberland Ln Crystal Lake IL 60014

GORIN, ROBERT SEYMOUR, lawyer; b. Cambridge, Mass., Oct. 4, 1935; s. Hyman and Ann L. (Pinciss) G.; m. Natalie Kirschner, June 26, 1960; 1 child, Bethel Stacy. BA, Wesleyan U., Middletown, Conn., 1957; JD, Columbia U., 1961. Bar: Va. 1962, U.S. Tax Ct. 1965, U.S. Supreme Ct. 1971, N.Y. 1973, U.S. Dist. Ct. (ea. and so. dists.) N.Y. 1975. Sr. trial atty. tax ct. office chief counsel IRS, N.Y.C., 1961-68; assoc. Silverman & Kalnick, N.Y.C., 1968-71; assoc. gen. counsel J.C. Penney Co., Inc., N.Y.C., 1971—. Fellow N.Y. Bar Found.; mem. ABA, N.Y. State Bar Assn. (chairperson elect corp. counsel sect.), Va. Bar Assn. Club: Columbia (N.Y.C.). General corporate, Private international, Corporate taxation. Office: JC Penney Co Inc Legal Dept 1301 Ave of Americas New York NY 10019

GORINSON, STANLEY M., lawyer; b. Bklyn., May 30, 1945; s. Rubin and Lena (Shulman) G.; m. Barbara Jorgenson, Jan. 28, 1983; children: Ross Evan, Hunter Lloyd. BA cum laude, Bklyn. Coll., 1967; JD with honors, Rutgers U., 1973. Bar: N.Y. 1974, U.S. Dist. Ct. (so. dist.) N.Y. 1976, U.S. Supreme Ct. 1979, Md. 1984, D.C. 1984, U.S. Dist. Ct. D.C. 1984. Atty. judgements sect. U.S. Dept. Justice, Washington, 1973-76, asst. chief transp. sect., 1977-79; chief spl. regulation industries U.S. Dept. Justice, N.Y.C., 1980-84; assoc. Wachtell, Lipton, Rosen & Katz, N.Y.C., 1976-77; chief counsel Pres. Com. on Three Mile Island, Washington, 1979; ptnr. Pillsbury, Madison & Sutro, Washington, 1984—. Contbg. author: Reporting on Regulatory Reform, 1985; also articles. Cons. NSF, Washington, 1982-83. Mem. ABA (bd. editors Antitrust Law Devels. 1984—, chmn. communications subcom. antitrust sect. 1985—, chmn. criminal pracitce subcom. litigation sect. 1985—, adminstrv. law sect.), Fed. Bar Assn., D.C. Bar Assn., Md. Bar Assn. Antitrust, Federal civil litigation, Administrative and regulatory. Office: Pillsbury Madison & Sutro 1667 K St NW Washington DC 20006

GORLA, MICHAEL JOSEPH, lawyer; b. St. Louis, Apr. 25, 1952; s. Joseph Charles and Agnes Loretta (Colombo) G.; m. Nancy Lyn Hutchison, July 9, 1982. BA, U. Mo., 1974; JD, St. Louis U., 1977. Bar: Mo. 1977, U.S. Dist. Ct. (ea. dist.) Mo. 1978, U.S. Ct. Appeals (8th cir.) 1979, U.S. Supreme Ct. 1981. Asst. pub. defender Mo. 21st Jud. Cir., St. Louis, 1978-79; sole practice St. Louis, 1979—. Basketball coach St. Ambrose Grade Sch., St. Louis, 1974—; bd. dirs. St. Ambrose Athletic Assn., St. Louis, 1982—. Mem. ABA, St. Louis County Bar Assn., Bar Assn. Met. St. Louis (vice chmn. criminal law sect. 1986—), Mo. Assn. Criminal Def. Attys. Avocations: softball, volleyball. Criminal, Personal injury, Workers' compensation. Home: 5426 Daggett Ave Saint Louis MO 63110 Office: 111 S Bemiston #211 Saint Louis MO 63105

GORLAND, SCOTT LANCE, lawyer; b. N.Y.C., Nov. 14, 1949; s. Emanuel and Gertrude (Friedman) G.; m. K. Roxanne McKee, Mar. 24, 1984; 1 child. BA, U. Mich., 1971; JD cum laude, U. Detroit, 1977. Bar: Mich. 1977, U.S. Dist. Ct. (ea. dist.) Mich. 1977, D.C. 1980, U.S. Dist. Ct. (we. dist.) Mich. 1984. Trial atty. U.S. Dept. Justice, Washington, 1977-83; assoc. Pepper, Hamilton & Scheetz, Detroit, 1983-86, ptnr., 1986—. Served to capt. USMCR, 1971-76. Mem. ABA, Fed. Bar Assn., Mich. Bar Assn., Detroit Bar Assn. Federal civil litigation, State civil litigation. Office: Pepper Hamilton & Scheetz 100 Renaissance Ctr 36th Floor Detroit MI 48243

GORLIN, CATHY ELLEN, lawyer; b. Shields Twp., Ill., July 25, 1953; d. Robert James and Marilyn (Alpern) G.; m. Marshall Howard Tanick, Feb. 20, 1982; 1 child, Lauren Gorlin. B.A. magna cum laude, Wesleyan U., 1975; J.D., U. Minn., 1978. Bar: Minn. 1978. Law clk. Minn. Atty. Gen.'s Office, St. Paul, summer 1976, Mpls. and Bloomington City Atty.'s Office, 1977-78; assoc. Mullin, Weinberg & Daly, Mpls., 1978; law clk. to judges Hennepin County Family Ct., Mpls., 1979-80, temp. referee, summer 1980; assoc. Larkin, Hoffman, Daly & Lindgren, Ltd., Mpls., 1980-84; ptnr. Best & Flanagan, 1984—; chairperson family law dept.; sec. Hennepin Lawyer Mag., 1983-85; chmn. Minn. Women Lawyers Appointments Com., Mpls., 1983—. Contbr. articles to legal publs.; guest appearances radio. Advance person Vice-Pres. Mondale, 1979, vol. various polit. candidates; del. 3d dist. conv., Minn., 1980-84. Named Atty. of Month, Larkin, Hoffman, Daly & Lindgren, Ltd., 1983. Mem. ABA, Minn. Bar Assn. (chmn. 1985-86), Hennepin County Bar Assn. (rep. to child support task force 1982, chmn. exec. com. family law sect., chmn. sect. 1982-84), Minn. Trial Lawyers Assn., Jewish Bus. and Profl. Women's Group (dir., support group coordinator), Minn. Women's Network (dir.), Jewish Family and Children Service Counseling Com., West Suburban C. of C. Democrat. Jewish. Family and matrimonial. Home: 1230 Angelo Dr Golden Valley MN 55422 Office: Best & Flanagan 3500 IDS Tower Minneapolis MN 55402

GORMAN, GERALD PATRICK, lawyer; b. Buffalo, Oct. 6, 1948; s. Gerald Joseph and Ellen Patricia (Lynch) G.; m. Julia Lucille Pericek, Aug. 21, 1971; children—Jonathan G., Jillian L., Jared P. B.A. in English, Canisius Coll., Buffalo, 1970; J.D., SUNY-Buffalo, 1973. Bar: N.Y. 1974, U.S. Supreme Ct. 1978, U.S. Dist. Ct. (we. dist.) N.Y. 1980, U.S. Ct. Apls. (2d cir.). Asst. dist. atty. Erie County, Buffalo, 1974-77; ptnr. Manz & Gorman Buffalo, 1977-83, Lankes, Semple, Waible & Gorman, Buffalo, 1983—. Mem. ABA, N.Y. State Bar Assn., Am. Trial Lawyers Assn., Erie County Bar Assn. (Trial Lawyers award 1973). Democrat. Roman Catholic. Club: Young Am. Soccer (v.p. 1984—), Southtowns Exchange. Federal civil litigation, State civil litigation, Criminal. Office: Lankes Semple Waible & Gorman 237 Main St Suite 300 Buffalo NY 14203

GORMAN, GERALD WARNER, lawyer; b. North Kansas City, Mo., May 30, 1933; s. William Shelton and Bessie (Warner) G.; m. Anita Belle McPike, June 26, 1954; children—Guinevere Eve, Victoria Rose. A.B. cum laude, Harvard U., 1954, LL.B. magna cum laude, 1956. Bar: Mo. 1956. Assoc. firm Dietrich, Davis, Dicus, Rowlands, Schmitt & Gorman, Kansas City, 1956-62; ptnr. Dietrich, Davis, Dicus, Rowlands, Schmitt & Gorman, 1963—; dir. North Kansas City State Bank, 1967-83, Musser-Davis Land Co., 1970—. Bd. govs. Citizens Assn. Kansas City, 1962—; trustee Harvard/Radcliffe Club Kansas City Endowment Fund, chmn. bd., 1977-83, trustee Kansas City Mus., 1967-82, Avondale Meth. Ch., 1969—, Citizens Bond Com. of Kansas City, 1973—, chmn. 7th jud. cir. citizens com., 1983—, chmn. Downtown Council Allis Plaza Reconstrn., 1983-85; bd. dirs. Spofford Home for Children, 1972-77. Served with U.S. Army, 1956-58, capt. USAR, 1958-64. Mem. Lawyers Assn. Kansas City (exec. com. 1968-71), ABA, Mo. Bar Assn., Kansas City Bar Assn., Clay County Bar Assn., Harvard Law Sch. Assn. Mo. (pres. 1973). Republican. Clubs: Harvard (pres. 1966), University (dir. 1983—), Kansas City, 611, Old Pike County. General corporate, Corporate taxation, Probate. Home: 917 E Vivion Rd Kansas City MO 64118 Office: 1700 City Center Sq Kansas City MO 64105

GORMAN, JAMES EDWARD, lawyer; b. Summit, Ill., Nov. 11, 1930; s. James Edward and Mae Catherine (Jiracek) G.; m. Beverly Ann Fink; children—Gregory, Stephen, Robert, William Mudge, Ann, James, Mary. B.A., St. Ambrose Coll., 1952; J.D., U. Ill., 1955. Bar: Ill. 1956, U.S. Dist. Ct. (so. dist.) Ill. 1958, U.S. Ct. Appeals 1979, U.S. Supreme Ct. 1980. Assoc., Heyl, Royster, Voelker and Allen, Peoria, Ill., 1957-59, Bernard, Gorman, Davidson, Edwardsville, Granite City, Ill., 1959-61; ptnr. Reed, Armstrong, Gorman & Coffey, Edwardsville, Ill., 1961—. Served with U.S. Army, 1955-57. Mem. ABA, Ill. Bar Assn., Am. Coll. Trial Lawyers, Ill. Trial Lawyers Assn., Am. Trial Lawyers Assn., Madison County Bar Assn. Roman Catholic. Club: KC. Insurance, Personal injury. Office: PO Box 467 Edwardsville IL 62025

GORMAN, JOSEPH THOMAS, JR., lawyer; b. Detroit, July 24, 1957; s. Joseph Thomas and Dolores Joan (Robillard) G.; m. Coleen Cay McCulley, Nov. 27, 1982; 1 child, Joseph Thomas III. BBA, So. Meth. U., 1978, JD, 1981. Bar: Tex. 1981. Assoc. Payne & Vendig, Dallas, 1981—. Mem. ABA, State Bar of Tex., Dallas Bar Assn. Roman Catholic. Real property, Banking, Representation of savings and loans associations. Home: 1409 Flintwood Richardson TX 75081 Office: Payne & Verdig 2355 Stemmons Freeway Suite 401 Dallas TX 75207

GORMAN, JOSEPH TOLLE, manufacturing executive; b. Rising Sun, Ind., 1937; m. Bettyann Gorman. B.A., Kent State U., 1959; LL.B., Yale U., 1962. Assoc. Baker, Hostetler & Patterson, Cleve., 1962-67; with legal dept. TRW Inc., Cleve., 1968-69, asst. sec., 1969-70, sec., 1970-72, v.p. sr. counsel automotive worldwide ops., 1972-73, v.p., asst. gen. counsel, 1973-76, v.p., gen. counsel, 1976-80, acting head communications function, 1978, exec. v.p. indsl. and energy sector, 1980-85, asst. pres., 1984-85, pres., chief operating officer, 1985—, mem. policy group, 1975—, also bd. dirs.; bd. dirs. Soc. Corp., Soc. Nat. Bank Cleve., Standard Oil Co. Trustee Univ. Circle, Inc., Govtl. Research Inst., Cleve. Play House, Cleve. Inst. Art, Leadership Cleve., United Way Services, Cleve. Council on World Affairs, Musical Arts Assn.; past trustee Cleve. Fedn. Community Planning; past mem. exec. com. Ctr. of Pub. Resources Project on Dispute Resolution; bd. advisors Yale Law Sch. Urgent Issues Program. Mem. ABA, Assn. Gen. Counsel (emeritus), Ohio Bar Assn., Cleve. Bar Assn., Yale Law Sch. Assn. (exec. com.), Greater Cleve. Growth Assn. (trustee, exec. com.), U.S. C. of C. (past chmn. corp. governance and policy com.), Council on Fgn. Relations. General corporate. Office: TRW Inc 1900 Richmond Rd Cleveland OH 44124

GORMAN, JOYCE JOHANNA, lawyer; b. N.Y.C., Aug. 23, 1952; d. Peter J. and Jane M. (Kelly) G. Student, Williams Coll., 1972-73; BA, Smith Coll., 1974; JD, U. Md., 1977. Bar: Md. 1977. Assoc. Miles & Stockbridge, Balt., 1977-84, ptnr., 1984—. Mem. Md. Bar Assn. (sec. corp. banking and bus. sects. 1983-84, vice chmn. 1984-85, chmn. 1985-86). Democrat. Roman Catholic. Club: Merchants (Balt.) (bd. dirs. 1980-87). Avocations: swimming, horseback riding, gourmet cooking, knitting. Municipal bonds, Real property. Home: 1926 Broadway Rd Lutnerville MD 21093 Office: Miles & Stockbridge 10 Light St Baltimore MD 21202 also Office: 1701 Pennsylvania Ave NW Suite 500 Washington DC 20006

GORMAN, ROBERT A., legal educator; b. 1937. A.B., Harvard U., 1958, LL.B., 1962. Bar: N.Y. 1963. Law clk. to judge U.S. Ct. Appeals (2d cir.), 1962-63; assoc. Proskauer, Rose, Goetz & Mendelsohn, N.Y.C., 1963-64; asst. prof. U. Pa., 1965-67, assoc. prof., 1967-69, prof., 1969—, assoc. dean, 1976—. Fulbright scholar Oxford U., 1958-59. Mem. Am. Law Inst., Am. Assn. Law Schs. (exec. com. 1975-76), AAUP (exec. com. 1975-77). Legal education. Office: U Pa Law Sch 3400 Chestnut St Philadelphia PA 19104 *

GORMAN, ROBERT JAMES, lawyer; b. Hartford, Conn., Dec. 19, 1950; s. Thomas Howard and Marguerite Jane (Clifford) G.; m. Catherine Elizabeth Kiernan, Oct. 15, 1970; children: Robert Jr., James, Shawn, Alane. BA, Coll. Holy Cross, 1972; JD, U. Conn., 1975. Bar: Conn. 1975, U.S. Dist. Ct. Conn. 1976, Fla. 1976, U.S. Dist. Ct. (so. dist.) Fla. 1978, U.S. Dist. Ct. (mid. dist.) Fla. 1985. Assoc. Rabinovitz, Gasner & Nassau, Hartford, 1975-77, Brennan, McAliley & Hayskar, Ft. Pierce, Fla., 1977-81; ptnr. Brennan, McAliley, Hayskar, McAliley & Jefferson, Ft. Pierce, 1982-85, Brennan, Hayskar, Jefferson & Gorman, P.A., Ft. Pierce, 1985—. Mem. St. Lucie County Dem. Club, Ft. Pierce, 1986. Mem. ABA, Fla. Bar Assn., St. Lucie County Bar Assn., Acad. Fla. Trial Lawyers, Fla. Def. Lawyers Assn. Episcopalian. Lodges: Rotary, Lions. State civil litigation, Federal civil litigation, Real property. Office: Brennan Hayskar Jefferson Gorman 515 S Indian River Dr Fort Pierce FL 33450

GORNICK, ALAN LEWIS, lawyer; b. Leadville, Colo., Sept. 23, 1908; s. Mark and Anne (Grayhack) G.; m. Ruth L. Willcockson, 1940 (dec. May 1959); children: Alan Lewis, Diana Willcockson (Mrs. Lawrence J. Richard, Jr.), Keith Hardin; m. Pauline Martoi, 1972. AB, Columbia U., 1935, JD, 1937. Bar: N.Y. 1937, Mich. 1948. Assoc. Baldwin, Todd & Young, N.Y.C., 1937-41, Milbank, Tweed, Hope & Hadley, 1941-47; asso. counsel charge tax matters Ford Motor Co., Dearborn, Mich., 1947-49; dir. tax affairs, chmn. tax com., tax counsel Ford Motor Co., 1949-64; lectr. tax matters NYU, Inst. Fed. Taxation, 1947-49, ABA and Practicing Law Inst. (courses on fundamentals in fed. taxation), 1946-55, Am. Law Inst. (courses in continuing legal edn.), 1950; spl. lectr. sch. bus. adminstrn. U. Mich., 1949, 53. Author: Estate Tax Handbook, 1952, Arrangements for Separation or Divorce, Handbook of Tax Techniques, 1952, Taxation of Partnerships, Estates and Trusts, rev. edit, 1952; adv. editor Nat. Tax Jour., 1952-55; contbr. articles on tax matters to profl. jours. Exec. bd. Detroit area council Boy Scouts Am., chmn. fin. com., 1960; pres. Mich. Assn. Emotionally Disturbed Children, 1962-65; v.p. Archives of Am. Art; mem. Mich. Heart Assn., Columbia Coll. council Columbia U., N.Y.C., Founder's Soc. Detroit Inst. Art; trustee Council on World Affairs, Detroit; pres. Detroit Hist. Soc.; mem. Bd. Zoning Appeals City Bloomfield Hills, 1980—. Recipient Gov.'s Spl. award State Colo., 1952. Mem. ABA (council tax sect. 1957-58), Detroit Bar Assn., N.Y. City Bar Assn. (chmn. subcom. estate and gift taxes 1943-47), Am. Law Inst., Tax Inst. Inc. (pres. 1954-55), U.S. C. of C., Empire State C. of C., Council on Fgn. Relations, Nat. Tax Assn. (exec. com.), Internat. Fiscal Assn. (council, nat. reporter 6th Internat. Congress Fiscal Law, Brussels 1952), Internat. Law Assn., Assn. Ex-Mems. Squadron A, Nat. Fgn. Trade Council (mem. com. taxes 1950), Automobile Mfrs. Assn. (chmn. com. on taxation 1960-62), Tax Execs. Inst. (pres. 1956-57), Fedn. Alumni Columbia (bd. dirs. 1946), Class 1935 Columbia Coll. (permanent pres.), N.Y. Adult Edn. Council (bd. dirs. 1939-45), Detroit Hist. Soc. (trustee, pres. 1083-85), Phi Delta Phi. Clubs: Bloomfield Hills (Mich.) Country, Detroit, Detroit Athletic, Columbia U., Church (N.Y.C.); Lawyers of U. of Mich., Columbia U. Alumni of Mich. (pres. 1950—), Otsego Ski (Gaylord, Mich.). Corporate taxation, Estate taxation, Personal income taxation. Home: 150 Lowell Ct Bloomfield Hills MI 48013 Office: 1565 Woodward Ave Suite 8 PO Box 957 Bloomfield Hills MI 48013

GORNISH, GERALD, lawyer; b. Phila., July 14, 1937; s. Edward H. and Sylvia (Elkan) G.; m. Rochelle Schildkraut, Mar. 5, 1961; children—Karen, Edward H. B.A. with honors, U. Pa., 1958; LL.B., Harvard U., 1961. Bar: Pa. 1962. Sole practice, Phila., 1962-66; asst. city solicitor City of Phila., 1964-66; with Goodis, Greenfield, Henry, Shaiman & Levin, Phila., 1966-71; dep. atty. gen., then atty. gen. Pa. Dept. Justice, 1971-78; with Wolf, Block, Schorr and Solis-Cohen, Phila., 1979—; atty. gen. Pa., 1978; dir. Office Civil Law, Pa. Dept. Justice, 1975-78; mem. Supreme Ct. Adv. Com. on Appellate Ct. Rules, 1974-85. Mem. ABA, Pa. Bar Assn. (council pub. utility law sect. 1984—), Phila. Bar Assn. (chmn. appellate cts. com. 1987, treas. campaign for qualified judges 1986—). Administrative and regulatory, Public utilities, State and local taxation. Home: 511 Anthwyn Rd Merion Station PA 19066 Office: Wolf Block Schorr & Solis-Cohen 12th Floor Packard Bldg Philadelphia PA 19102

GOROCHOW, VERA ZINA, lawyer; b. Rochester, N.Y., Mar. 2, 1955; s. Gabriel and Wanda (Shpakovsky) G. BS, St. John Fisher Coll., 1977; JD, Ohio State U., 1982. Bar: Ohio 1982, U.S. Dist. Ct. (no. dist.) Ohio 1984. Assoc. Thomas E. Ray and Assocs., Cardington, Ohio, 1982-85; sole practice Delaware, Ohio, 1985—. Mem. ABA, Ohio Bar Assn., Am. Quarter Horse Assn., Ohio Quarter Horse Assn. Estate planning, Probate, Estate taxation.

GORRELL, FRANK CHEATHAM, lawyer; b. Russellville, Ky., June 20, 1927; s. Lilburn D. and Vandalia Van Dyke (Strudwick) G.; m. Bette Jamison, June 14, 1947; children: Frank C. III, Jamison R. B.S., Vanderbilt U., 1949, LL.B., 1952. Bar: Tenn. 1952. Partner firm Bass, Berry & Sims, Nashville, 1952—; dir. Jamison Bedding Co., Franklin, Tenn., Downs, Inc., Nashville.; Mem. Tenn. Senate, 1963-70, speaker and lt. gov. Tenn., 1966-70; chmn. Tenn. Appellate Ct. Nominating Com., 1982-83. Trustee Acquinas Jr. Coll., Mills Sch. Mem. Am., Tenn., Nashville bar assns., Am., Tenn. trial lawyers assns., Am. Judicature Soc., Am. Coll. Trial Lawyers, Beta Theta Pi, Omicron Delta Kappa. Club: Elk. Federal civil litigation, State civil litigation, Legislative. Home: 319 Lynnwood Blvd Nashville TN 37205 Office: 2700 First Am Center Nashville TN 37238

GORRIN, EUGENE, lawyer; b. Irvington, N.J., Apr. 22, 1956; s. Harry and Ruth (Goldberg) G. BA, Rutgers U., 1978; JD, George Washington U., 1981; LLM in Taxation, NYU, 1982. Bar: N.J. 1981, U.S. Dist. Ct. N.J. 1981, U.S. Tax Ct. 1982, U.S. Supreme Ct. 1985. Assoc. Ozzard, Rizzolo, Klein, Mauro & Savo, Somerville, N.J., 1982-83, Levine, Furman & Davis, East Brunswick, N.J., 1984—. Mem. ABA (taxation sect.), N.J. Bar Assn. (taxation and young lawyers sects.), Middlesex County Bar Assn. (taxation sect.), U.S. Supreme Ct. Hist. Soc., Phi Alpha Delta. Democrat. Jewish. Probate, Corporate taxation, Personal income taxation. Home: 2607 Frederick Terr Union NJ 07083 Office: Levine Furman & Davis 3 Brier Hill Ct East Brunswick NJ 08816

GORSKE, ROBERT HERMAN, lawyer, arbitrator; b. Milw., June 8, 1932; s. Herman Albert and Lorraine (McDermott) G.; m. Antonette Dujick, Aug. 28, 1954; 1 child, Judith Mary (Mrs. Charles H. McMullen). Student, Milw. State Tchrs. Coll., 1949-50; B.A. cum laude, Marquette U., 1953, J.D. magna cum laude, 1955; LL.M. (W.W. Cook fellow), U. Mich., 1959. Bar: Wis. bar 1955, D.C. bar 1968, U.S. Supreme Ct. bar 1970. Assoc. firm Quarles, Spence & Quarles, Milw., 1955-56; atty. Allis-Chalmers Mfg. Co., West Allis, Wis., 1956-62; instr. law U. Mich. Law Sch., Ann Arbor, 1958-59; lectr. law Marquette U. Law Sch., Milw., 1963; assoc. firm Quarles, Herriott & Clemons, Milw., 1962-64; atty. Wis. Electric Power Co., Milw., 1964-67, gen. counsel, 1967—, v.p., 1970-72, 76—; mem. firm Quarles & Brady, Milw., 1972-76. Contbr. articles to profl. jours.; Editor-in-chief: Marquette Law Rev, 1954-55. Bd. dirs. Guadalupe Children's Med. Dental Clinic, Inc., Milw., 1976-86; trustee Ronald McDonald House, Wauwatosa, Wis., 1987—. Mem. State Bar Wis., Am. Bar Assn., Edison Electric Inst. (vice chmn. legal com. 1975-77, chmn. 1977-79), Am. Arbitration Assn. (panelist comml. arbitrators 1985—). Administrative and regulatory, General corporate, Public utilities. Home: 12700 Stephen Pl Elm Grove WI 53122 Office: Wis Electric Power Co 231 W Michigan St Box 2046 Milwaukee WI 53201

GORSKI, WALTER J., lawyer, insurance company executive; b. New Britain, Conn., Jan. 11, 1943; s. Walter J. and Jayne D. (Kancewicz) G.; m. Joan Pernal, Aug. 20, 1967; 1 child, Walter. B.S., U. Conn., 1964; J.D., U. Conn.-West Hartford, 1967. Bar: Conn. 1967, U.S. Ct. Appeals (2d cir.).

With Phoenix Mut. Life Ins. Co., Hartford, Conn., then assoc. firm Januszewski, Mc Quillan & Denigris, New Britain, 1967-73; sr. v.p., gen. counsel Conn. Mut. Life Ins. Co., Hartford, Conn., 1973—; Co-author: Connecticut Law of Zoning, 1967. Mem. Am. Corp. Counsel Assn. (bd. dir., v.p. Hartford chpt. 1984—), Assn. Life Ins. Counsel, Conn. Bar Assn. General corporate, Insurance. Office: Conn Mut Life Ins Co 140 Garden St Hartford CT 06105

GORSUCH, NORMAN CLIFFORD, law educator; b. Pitts., Oct. 3, 1942; s. Clifford Lee and Helen (Berzac) G.; m. Marjorie Jean Menzi, Sept. 10, 1966 (div. Sept. 1985); children—Elizabeth, Kieth, Jennifer, Deborah, David; m. Lenore W. Boston, Oct. 18, 1985. B.A. with honors, U. N.C., 1964; J.D., Columbia U., 1967. Bar: Alaska 1968, U.S. Dist. Ct. Alaska 1968, U.S. Ct. Internat. Trade 1968, U.S. Ct. Appeals (9th cir.) 1969, U.S. Supreme Ct. 1973. Assoc. Ely, Guess & Rudd, Anchorage, 1967-70, ptnr., 1970-71; ptnr. Ely, Guess & Rudd, Juneau, Alaska, 1974-82; dep. atty. gen. State of Alaska, Juneau, 1971-73, atty. gen., 1973-74, 82-85; assoc. prof. law and pub. adminstrn. U. Alaska, Juneau, 1985—; of counsel Guess & Rudd, Juneau, 1986—. Contbr. articles to profl. jours. Trustee Alaska Permanent Fund, Juneau, 1982—, 85; mem. Alaska Democratic Central Com., 1982; commr. Alaska Fed.-State Land Use Planning Commn., 1977-79. Mem. Alaska Bar Assn., Alaska C. of C. (bd. dirs. 1980-81, Juneau C. of C. (bd. dirs. 1979-82), Phi Beta Kappa. Democrat. Methodist. Lodge: Rotary. Legal education, Administrative and regulatory, Legislative. Office: U Alaska Sch Bus and Pub Adminstrn Ray Center Juneau AK 99801

GOSE, RICHARD VERNIE, lawyer; b. Hot Springs, S.D., Aug. 3, 1927; s. Vernie O. and Mame K. (Thompson) G.; B.S., U. Wyo., 1950; M.S. in Engring., Northwestern U., 1955; LL.B., George Washington U., 1967; J.D., George Washington U., 1968; children—Beverly Marie, Donald Paul, Celeste Marlene. Bar: N.Mex. 1967, U.S. Supreme Ct. 1976, Wyo. 1979. Exec. asst. to U.S. Senator Hickey, Washington, 1960-62; mgr. E.G. & G., Inc., Washington, 1964-66; asst. atty. gen. State of N.Mex., Santa Fe, 1967-70; sole practice law, Santa Fe, 1967—; assoc. prof. engring. U. Wyo., 1957-60; owner, mgr. Gose & Assocs., Santa Fe, 1967-78; sole practice law, Casper, Wyo., 1978-83; co-chmn. Henry Jackson for Pres., M.Mex., 1976, Wyo. Johnson for Pres., 1960. Served with U.S. Army, 1950-52. Registered profl. engr., N.Mex., Wyo.; Mem. 1st Jud. Dist. Bar Assn. (past pres.), N.Mex. Bar Assn., Wyo. Bar Assn., Phi Delta Theta, Pi Tau Sigma, Sigma Tau. Methodist. Lodge: Masons. General practice, Real property, Oil and gas leasing. Home and Office: PO Box 8301 Santa Fe NM 87504

GOSLAWSKI, LEONARD STEPHEN, lawyer; b. Chgo., Oct. 21, 1945; s. Stanley Leonard and Adeline Mary (Laskowski) G.; m. Marcia Jean Borla, Sept. 1, 1968; children—Jennifer, Mark. B.A., St. Mary's Coll., 1967; J.D., U. Notre Dame, 1970. Bar: Ind. 1970, U.S. Dist. Ct. (no. dist.) Ind. 1970, Ill. 1972, U.S. Dist. Ct. (no. dist.) Ill. 1972, U.S. Ct. Appeals (7th cir.) 1975, U.S. Supreme Ct. 1978, U.S. Tax Ct. 1981. Assoc., Jones, Obenchain, Johnson, Ford, Pankow & Link, South Bend, Ind., 1970-72; assoc. Lewis, Overbeck & Furman, Chgo., 1972-76, ptnr., 1976—; arbitrator Am. Arbitration Assn., Chgo., 1974—. Examiner, St. Joseph County Bd. Notary Examiners, South Bend, 1971; mem. bd. St. Raphael's Sch., Naperville, Ill., 1977-80. Served to capt. U.S. Army, 1978. Mem. Chgo. Bar Assn. Federal civil litigation, Labor, Pension, profit-sharing, and employee benefits. Office Lewis Overbeck & Furman: 135 S LaSalle St Suite 1000 Chicago IL 60603

GOSS, COLLEEN FLYNN, lawyer; b. Youngstown, Ohio, Mar. 26, 1955; d. William John and Amanda Elizabeth (Young) Flynn; m. Richard Ingersoll Goss, Jr., June 28, 1986. BA in Econs., Tufts U., 1977; JD, Case Western Res. U., 1980. Bar: Ohio 1980. Assoc. Benesch, Friedlander, Coplan & Aronoff, Cleve., 1980-85; atty. Midland Ross Corp., Cleve., 1985—. Mem. Jr. League of Cleve. Inc., 1980—; trustee, founder The Pacific Found. for the Advancement of Sci. and Medicine, Cleve.; trustee Camp Ho-Mita-Koda, Cleve. Mem. ABA, Ohio Bar Assn., Cleve. Bar Assn., Andover Alumni Council. Club: Cleve. Raquet. Avocations: tennis, squash, horseback riding, furniture refinishing. General corporate, Securities, Contracts commercial. Home: 18514 Winslow Rd Shaker Heights OH 44122 Office: Midland-Ross Corp 20600 Chagrin Blvd Cleveland OH 44122

GOSS, MICHAEL MAYER, lawyer; b. Phila., Dec. 26, 1942; s. Albert and Betty (Leibowitz) G.; m. Marlene Kohn, Aug. 20, 1967; children: Erica, Kimberly. BA, Pa. State U., 1964; JD, Villanova U., 1967. Bar: Pa. 1967, U.S. Dist. Ct. (ea., mid. and we. dists.) Pa. 1967. Ptnr. Weinstein, Goss & Katzenstein, Assocs., P.C., Phila., 1967—. V.p. Upper Moreland Bi-Centennial Commn., 1976; pres. Sands Condominium Assn., Ventnor, N.J., 1977. Mem. ABA, Phila. Bar Assn., Assn. Trial Lawyers Am., Pa. Trial Lawyers Assn., Am. Arbitration Assn., Lawyers Alliance Nuclear Arms Control, Jaycees (pres. 1972). Republican. Jewish. Lodge: B'nai B'rith (pres. Phila. 1971). Avocations: tennis, racquetball, reading. Contracts commercial, General corporate, Real property. Home: 3883 Mettler Ln Huntingdon Valley PA 19006 Office: Weinstein Goss & Katzenstein Assocs PC 1112 Ave of Arts Bldg Philadelphia PA 19107

GOSS, THOMAS MARKS, lawyer; b. Raleigh, N.C., Jan. 9, 1952; s. Russell E. and Louise (Marks) G.; m. Barbara Strong, June 11, 1977. AB, U. N.C., 1974; JD, Cath. U., 1981. Bar: Md. 1981, D.C. 1982, U.S. Dist. Ct. Md. 1982, U.S. Dist. Ct. D.C. 1983, U.S. Ct. Appeals (4th cir.) 1986. Assoc. Semmes, Bowen & Semmes, Balt., 1981—. Production editor Cath. U. Law Rev., 1980-81. Mem. ABA (torts and ins. practice sect., chmn.-elect rules and procedures com. 1986—), Fed. Bar Assn., Md. Bar Assn., D.C. Bar Assn., Balt. City Bar Assn., Md. Assn. Defense Counsel (chmn. legis. com. 1985-86). Insurance, Products liability, Civil litigation, federal and state. Office: Semmes Bowen & Semmes 250 W Pratt St Baltimore MD 21201

GOSSAGE, ROZA, lawyer, educator; b. Landreis Celle Lohheide, Germany, Mar. 21, 1947; came to U.S., 1949; d. Abram and Lola (Strubel) Berlinski; m. David Jordan, Gossage, Feb. 21, 1970; children—Brenda, Sara, Leah. B.A., U. Ill., 1968; J.D., DePaul Sch. Law, 1971. Bar: Ill. 1971, Fla. 1972, Mo. 1981, U.S. Dist. Ct. (no. dist.) Ill. 1971, U.S. Dist. Ct. (so. dist.) Ill. 1978, U.S. Ct. Appeals (7th cir.) 1972. Law clk. U.S. Dist. Ct. (no. dist.) Ill., Chgo., 1971-72; atty. State's Atty.'s Office of Cook County, Ill., 1972-74; atty State's Atty.'s Office of St. Clair County, Belleville, Ill., 1974-78; ptnr. Hutnick & Gossage, Belleville, 1978—; atty. Commn. to Revise and Rewrite Pub. Aid Code of Ill., Springfield, 1978-80; atty. Village of Summerfield, Ill., 1983—; arbitrator Better Bus. Bur., St. Louis, 1982—. Bd. dirs. YWCA, St. Clair County, Ill., 1981. Mem. St. Clair County Bar Assn., Met. Women's Bar Assn. (bd. dirs. 1981—), Ill. Bar Assn., Mo. Bar Assn., Fla. Bar Assn., So. Ill. Network of Women. Consumer commercial, Family and matrimonial, Personal injury. Office: 209 S Jackson Belleville IL 62221

GOSSELINK, MARGARET LAVIDGE, lawyer; b. Chgo., May 25, 1948; d. Robert James and Margaret Mary (Zwigard) Lavidge; m. Paul Gerard Gosselink, Aug. 9, 1975; children: Todd Lavidge, Robert Scott. BA, DePauw U., 1970; JD, So. Meth. U., 1974. Bar: Tex. 1974, U.S. Dist. Ct. (no. dist.) Tex. 1975, U.S. Dist. Ct. (we. dist.) Tex. 1979, U.S. Ct. Appeals (5th cir.) 1982. Fellow/atty. HEW/Tarrant County Legal Aid, Ft. Worth, 1974-75; hearings officer Tex. Health Facilities Commn., Austin, 1976-77; staff atty. Seton Med. Ctr., Austin, Tex., 1977-82, legal counsel, 1979-82, gen. counsel, 1982—; judge City of West Lake Hills, Tex., 1979-85. Bd. dirs. League House, Austin, 1981-83, treas., 1986—; precinct chmn., Travis Country Dem. Exec. Com., Austin, 1980-85. Reginald Heber Smith fellow HEW, Washington, 1974-75. Mem. State Bar Tex. (dir. health law 1980-82, sec.-treas. 1984-85, chmn. 1986-87), Travis Bar Assn. (bd. dirs. 1986—). Administrative and regulatory, General corporate, Health. Home: 923 Wild Basin Ledge Austin TX 78746 Office: Seton Med Ctr 1201 W 38th St Austin TX 78705

GOTCHER, JAMES RONALD, lawyer; b. Dallas, Jan. 18, 1947; s. James Bentley and Elga Audra (Dye ss) G.; m. Satoko Hata, June 20, 1970; 1 son, James Kensuke. B.A. magna cum laude in History, Calif. State U.-Long Beach, 1972; postgrad. U. Hawaii, 1972-73; J.D., Loyola U., Los Angeles, 1976. Bar: Calif. 1976, U.S. Supreme Ct. 1980. Assoc. Gruber & Kelman, 1976-77; ptnr. Gotcher & Shapiro, 1977-81; ptnr. Aberson, Lynes & Gotcher, 1982—. Mem. Town Hall of Los Angeles. Served with USAF, 1965-68. Decorated Bronze Star. Mem. Los Angeles County Bar Assn. (chmn. immigration law sect. 1983-84), Am. Immigration Lawyers Assn., ABA. Republican. Clubs: University (Los Angeles). Author: Comprehensive guide to U.S. Nonimmigrant Visas, 1983; contbr. articles to legal jours. Immigration, naturalization, and customs. Address: 15303 Ventura Blvd 9th Floor Sherman Oaks CA 91403

GOTIMER, HARRY ALBERT, lawyer, educator; b. N.Y.C., May 20, 1947; s. John Cornelius and Catherine Agnes (McDermott) G.; m. Patricia Mary Shaughnessy, Aug. 14, 1971; children—Susan Eileen, Kevin Patrick, Matthew Brendan. B.S., U.S. Mcht. Marine Acad., 1969; J.D., Georgetown U., 1973. Bar: N.Y. 1974, U.S. Dist. Ct. (so. dist.) N.Y. 1974, U.S. Dist. Ct. (ea. dist.) N.Y. 1974, U.S. Ct. Appeals (2d cir.) 1975, U.S. Ct. Claims 1975, U.S. Ct. Internat. Trade 1984, U.S. Supreme Ct. 1983. Atty. Gen. Counsel's Office, Maritime Adminstrn., U.S. Dept. Commerce, Washington, 1973-74; assoc. Kirlin, Campbell & Keating, N.Y.C., 1974-78, ptnr., 1978—; adj. asst. prof. law N.Y. Law Sch. Mem. sch. bd. Borough of Hopatcong, N.J., 1978-80, v.p., 1980-82; councilman Borough of Hopatcong, 1983-85; recruiting rep. U.S. Mcht. Marine Acad., 1979—. Served to comdr. USNR. Mem. ABA, Maritime Law Assn. U.S. Democrat. Roman Catholic. Clubs: West Shore Democratic (pres. 1983, exec. bd. 1984-85), Whitehall. Admiralty, Government contracts and claims, Insurance. Home: 123 Durban Ave Hopatcong NJ 07843 Office: Kirlin Campbell & Keating 14 Wall St New York NY 10005

GOTTESMAN, DAVID MARK, lawyer; b. Phila., Feb. 3, 1948; s. Milton Louis and Dorothy (Blumner) G.; m. Jean Corey, Nov. 4, 1972; children: Eric J., Marc D., Michael D. BA in Econs., U. N.H., 1970; JD, Suffolk U., 1973. Bar: N.H. 1973, Mass. 1973, U.S. Dist. Ct. N.H. 1973, U.S. Dist. Ct. Mass. 1974. Assoc. Leonard Profl. Assn., Nashua, N.H., 1973-75; sole practice Nashua, 1975-78; ptnr. Gottesman & Hollis, Nashua, 1978-82; sr. ptnr. Gottesman & Hollis P.A., Nashua, 1982—. Bd. dirs. Nashua Boys Club, 1979, Nashua Arts and Sci. Ctr., 1979. Mem. ABA, N.H. Bar Assn., Assn. Trial Lawyers Am., N.H. Trial Lawyers Assn. Republican. Jewish. Lodge: Rotary (pres. 1980-81). Avocations: sailing, golf, tennis, windsurfing. State civil litigation, Real property, Banking. Office: Gottesman & Hollis PA 39 E Pearl St Nashua NH 03060

GOTTFRIED, THEODORE ALEXANDER, lawyer; b. Chgo., Nov. 4, 1940; s. Theodore and Estelle (Foryst) G.; m. Nancy Ann Ringer, May 11, 1973; children: William Theodore, Nicole Diane. B.A., Roosevelt U., 1963; J.D., John Marshall Law Sch., 1966. Bar: Ill. 1966, U.S. Ct. Appeals (7th cir.) 1967, U.S. Dist. Ct. (no. dist.) Ill. 1967, U.S. Supreme Ct. 1970. Asst. pub. defender Cook County Pub. Defender's Office, Chgo., 1966-70; dist. defender Ill. Defender Project, Springfield, 1970-71, exec. dir., 1971-72; state appellate defender Office of State Appellate Defender Ill., Springfield, 1972—; lectr. in field; profl. instr. scuba diving. Recipient Meritorious Service award Gov. of Ill., 1972. Mem. ABA, Nat. Legal Aid and Defender Assn., Ill. State Bar Assn., Sangamon County Def. Bar Assn., Criminal Def. Consortium Cook County, Ill. Pub. Defender Assn., Ill. Defender Project, Ill. Attys. for Criminal Justice, Nat. Assn. Criminal Def. Lawyers, ACLU, Central Ill. Divers (pres. 1979-80), Big Bros.-Big Sisters Sangamon County. Author article series Chgo. Bar Jour., 1976-77. Criminal. Home: Rural Rt 3 Box 22 Sherman IL 62684 Office: 300 E Monroe Suite 100 Springfield IL 62701

GOTTLIEB, DANIEL SETH, lawyer; b. Los Angeles, Sept. 19, 1954; s. Seymour and Blanche Joyce (Kaufman) G.; m. Marilynn Jeanne Payne, July 21, 1985. BA summa cum laude, Columbia U., 1976; JD, Harvard U., 1980. Bar: Wash. 1980, U.S. Dist. Ct. (we. dist.) Wash. 1980. Ptnr. Riddell, Williams, Bullitt & Walkinshaw, Seattle, 1980—; coordinator S.E. Legal Clinic, Seattle, 1984-86. Mem. ABA, Nat. Assn. Bond Lawyers, Wash. State Bar Assn., Seattle-King County Bar Assn. (chmn. legal info. and referral clinics com. 1986—). Jewish. Avocations: tuba, hiking, bicycling. Municipal bonds. Home: 4428 Greenwood Ave N Seattle WA 98103 Office: Riddell Williams et al 1001 4th Ave Plaza Suite 4400 Seattle WA 98154

GOTTLIEB, GIDON ALAIN GUY, legal educator; b. Paris, Dec. 9, 1932. LLB with honors, London Sch. Econs., 1954; LLB, Trinity Coll., Cambridge (Eng.) U., 1956; diploma in comparative law, Cambridge (Eng.) U., 1958; LLM, Harvard U., 1957, JSD, 1962. Bar: Called to bar Lincoln Inn 1958. Lectr. govt. Dartmouth Coll., 1960-61; assoc. firm Shearman & Sterling, N.Y.C., 1962-65; mem. faculty N.Y. U. Law Sch., 1965-76; Leo Spitz prof. internat. law U. Chgo. Law Sch., 1976—; UN rep. Amnesty Internat., 1966-72; mem. founding com. World Assembly Human Rights, 1968; adv. bd. Internat. League Rights of Man; cons. in field. Author: The Logic of Choice: An Investigation of the Concepts of Rule and Rationality, 1968. Mem. U.S. Inst. Human Rights, Internat. Law Assn. (chmn. com. humanitarian law Am. chpt.), Am. Soc. Internat. Law., Council on Fgn. Relations. Club: Century Assn. (N.Y.C.). Public international, Jurisprudence. Office: U Chgo Law Sch 1111 E 60th St Chicago IL 60637

GOTTLIEB, PAUL MITCHEL, lawyer; b. N.Y.C., Mar. 30, 1954; s. Henry Gottlieb and Thelma Ethal (Friedman) Miller; m. Helene Manya Roiter, Apr. 3, 1982; 1 child, Jordan Seth. BA, Hobart Coll., 1976; JD, MBA, Washington U., St. Louis, 1980. Bar: Ill. 1980, U.S. Dist. Ct. (no. dist.) Ill. 1980. Assoc. Rudnick & Wolfe, Chgo., 1980-81; ind. trader Chgo. Bd. of Trade, 1981-83; staff atty. Chgo. Merc. Exchange, 1983-84, v.p. market regulation, 1984—. Contbr. articles to profl. jours. Mem. ABA (futures law com.), Chgo. Bar Assn. (futures regulation com., co-chmn. subcom. self regulatory orgns.). Jewish. Avocations: tennis, golf. Commodities, Administrative and regulatory. Home: 705 Mallard Ln Deerfield IL 60015 Office: Chgo Merc Exchange 30 S Wacker Dr Chicago IL 60606

GOTTSCHALK, ROBERT, lawyer, cons.; b. N.Y.C., Jan. 10, 1911. B.Sc. in Elec. Engring., McGill U., 1931; LL.B. cum laude, St. Lawrence U., 1934. Bar: N.Y. 1935, Ill. 1946, U.S. Supreme Ct. 1973, D.C. 1974, U.S. Ct. Appeals (Fed. cir.). Assoc., von Briesen & Schrenk, N.Y.C., 1934-41; patent and trademark counsel CPC Internat., 1941-46; asst. mgr. devel. and patent dept. Standard Oil Co. Ind., 1946-58, dir. contract and legal matters, 1958-61; gen. patent counsel Canteen Corp., 1961-64; dir. patents GAF Corp., 1965-70; dep. commr. U.S. Patent and Trademark Office, Washington, 1970-71, commr. patents, 1971-73; sole practice, Winnetka, Ill., 1974—; chmn. patent policy com. Nat. Acad. Scis., 1962-67; cons. to indsl. adv. bd. AEC, 1946-47; mem. univ. patent policy com. NRC, 1948-60; cons. to chmn. U.S. Govt. Patents Bd., 1950-55, White House Office Telecommunications Policy, 1976; cons. to dir. gen. Iranian Nat. Petrochem. Co., 1976; mem. adv. bd. Patent Trademark and Copyright Jour., 1974—; lectr. in field. Mem. ABA (patent, antitrust, sci. and tech. sects., chmn. atomic energy com. 1946, NSF com. 1946, govt. patent policy com. 1956), Chgo. Bar Assn., Fed. Bar Assn., Am. Patent Law Assn., Chgo. Patent Law Assn., N.Y. Patent Law Assn., NAM (vice chmn. patents and research com. 1944-49, chmn. patent law revision com. 1946-51, chmn. govt. interests com. 1963-64), Licensing Execs. Soc., Internat. Bus. Council, Am. Arbitration Assn. (panel of arbitrators). Clubs: Nat. Lawyers (Washington), Chemists (N.Y.C.). Contbr. articles to profl. jours. Patent, Trademark and copyright. Home: 183 Dickens Rd Northfield IL 60093 Office: 545 Lincoln Ave PO Box 8436 Winnetka IL 60093

GOUAUX, EUGENE GODFREY, lawyer; b. Lockport, La., Apr. 5, 1920; s. Francois Theophile and Mathilde (Robichaux) G.; m. Mary Catherine Harang, Sept. 19, 1949; children—Catherine Gouaux Duplantis, Eugene Godfrey, Patricia Gouaux Simpson, Mary Frances, James W. B.A., La. State U., 1942; J.D., Loyola U., New Orleans, 1949. Bar: La. 1949, U.S. Dist. Ct. (ea. dist.) La. 1950, U.S. Ct. Appeals (5th cir.) 1979, U.S. Supreme Ct. 1974. Practice, Lockport, 1949—; city atty. Town of Lockport, 1952—; dir. Raceland Bank & Trust Co., Assumption Land Co., Inc., Assumption Energy Co., Inc., Willswood Plantation, Inc.; pres. Willswood Energy Co., Inc. State rep. Parish of Lafourche, 1956-60; trustee La. State Colls. and Univs. Served to lt. USN, 1942-46. Named Outstanding Citizen of Yr. Lockport Lions Club, 1986. Mem. La. State Bar Assn., Lafourche Parish Bar Assn., Delta Theta Phi. Democrat. Roman Catholic. Clubs: Rotary, K.C. (4 deg.). State civil litigation, General practice, Probate. Home: 115 Lafourche St PO Box 338 Lockport LA 70374 Office: 111 Barataria St PO Box 338 Lockport LA 70374

GOUDE, CHARLES REUBEN, lawyer, public defender; b. Hemingway, S.C., Apr. 17, 1950; s. Bethel Oliver and Miriam Helena (Joye) G. BA in History magna cum laude, U. S.C., 1975, JD, 1979. Bar: S.C. 1979, U.S. Ct. Mil. Appeals 1980, U.S. Dist. Ct. S.C. 1984. Sole practice Georgetown, S.C., 1984—; dep. pub. defender Georgetown County, 1984-85, pub. defender, 1985—; adj. faculty Horry Georgetown Tech. Coll., 1986—. Served to sgt. USMC, 1968-72; served to capt. JAG USAF, 1980-84. Mem. Am. Trial Lawyers Assn., S.C. Bar Assn., Georgetown County Bar Assn., Phi Beta Kappa. General practice, State civil litigation, Family and matrimonial. Home: Route 3 Box 269A Hemingway SC 29554 Office: PO Box 706 Georgetown SC 29442

GOUGELMAN, PAUL REINA, lawyer; b. Chgo., Mar. 16, 1951; s. Paul Reina Gougelman and Jayne Bohus; m. Maureen S. Sikora, 1984. BA, Fla. Internat. U., Miami, 1975; JD, Nova Law Sch., Ft. Lauderdale, 1980. Bar: Fla. 1981, U.S. Dist. Ct. (so. dist.) Fla. 1981, U.S. Ct. Appeals (11th cir.) 1981, U.S. Dist. Ct. (mid. dist.) Fla. 1983. Atty. 1st Dist. Ct. Appeals, Tallahassee, 1980-83; assoc. Broad & Cassel, Maitland, Fla., 1984-87, Reinman, Harrell, Silverhorn & Graham, Melbourne, Fla., 1987—; spl. counsel for land use and growth mgmt. City of Maitland, 1984—; spl. counsel for code enforcement bd. City of Longwood, Fla., 1985-87; cons. growth mgmt. City of Lake Mary, Fla., 1985—; gov's appointee East Cen. Fla. Regional Planning Council. Mem. Orange County Bar Task Force, 1985. Mem. ABA, Fla. Bar (local govt. law sect., elected exec. council environ. and land use law sect.), Orlando C. of C. (project 2000 governance task force 1985-86), Maitland C. of C., Sierra Club. Democrat. Presbyterian. Local government, Real property, Land use and planning. Office: Reinman Harrell Silberhorn & Graham 1825 S Riverview Dr Melbourne FL 32901

GOUGH, AIDAN RICHARD, legal educator, consultant; b. Los Angeles, May 22, 1934; s. James Albert and Marian (Ford) G. AB, Stanford U., 1952, AM, 1957; JD, Santa Clara U., 1962; LLM, Harvard U., 1966. Bar: Calif. 1963, U.S. Dist. Ct. (no. dist.) Calif. 1963, U.S. Supreme Ct. 1966. Dep. probation officer Santa Clara County Juvenile Ct., San Jose, Calif., 1956-60; prof. law Santa Clara U., 1962—; alt. referee, judge pro tem Juvenile div. Santa Clara County Superior Ct., 1963—; reporter juvenile justice standards Nat. Joint Commn., N.Y.C.; active Dist. VII med. quality com. Calif. State Bd. Med. Quality Assurance, San Mateo, Calif., 1976-84; cons. emergency legal medicine Stanford (Calif.) Med. Ctr., 1978—, San Francisco Gen. Hosp. Med. Ctr., 1982—; legal advisor Calif. State Council Emergency Nurses Assn., Long Beach, Calif., 1980—; bd. dirs. Lifeguard HMO, Campbell, Calif., 1982—. Co-author, editor: Beyond Control: Status Offenders in the Juvenile Court, 1977. Co-chmn. bioethics com. Santa Clara County Med. Soc., San Jose, 1968; mem. profl. standards com. Santa Clara County Med. Soc., 1968—. Ford Found. fellow, 1965; recipient Outstanding Service to Medicine, Santa Clara County Med. Soc., 1978. Mem. ABA, Calif. Bar Assn., Santa Clara County Bar Assn., Am. Coll. of Legal Medicine, Internat. Soc. on Family Law (exec. council), Nat. Health Lawyers Assn. Republican. Roman Catholic. Avocations: fly fishing, golf, birding. Health, Family and matrimonial, Juvenile. Home: 2320 Park Ave Santa Clara CA 95050 Office: Santa Clara U School of Law Santa Clara CA 95053

GOULD, DIRK SAMUEL, lawyer; b. N.Y.C., Jan. 18, 1933; s. Joseph and Helen (Garey) G.; m. Libby Tombacher, Aug. 20, 1959; children: Michael, Peter. B.A., Queens Coll., N.Y.C., 1955; J.D., NYU, 1960, LL.M., 1964. Bar: N.Y. 1960. Asso. Sereni, Herzfeld & Rubin, N.Y.C., 1960-61, Squadron, Alter & Weinrib, N.Y.C., 1962-65; mem. Alter, Lefevre, Raphael, Lowry & Gould and predecessor Pross, Halpern, Lefevre, Raphael & Alter, N.Y.C., 1966-74; sec. Alter, Lefevre, Raphael, Lowry & Gould and predecessor Pross, Halpern, Lefevre, Raphael & Alter, 1974-78; mem. Arnow, Brodsky Bohlinger Einhorn & Alter, N.Y.C., 1979-83; sr. v.p., gen. counsel Van Wagner Communications, Inc., N.Y.C., 1983—; lectr. constl. law, pub. opinion, and propaganda Queens Coll., N.Y.C., 1961-64. Served as pilot USAF, 1955-58. Mem. ABA (labor law sect.), N.Y. County Lawyers Assn. (law of space com. 1966-73, mem. aero. law com. 1966-74), Am. Arbitration Assn. (nat. panel labor arbitration), Am. Corp. Counsel Assn. Club: Country of Torrington (Conn.). General corporate, Communication litigation. Office: 420 Lexington Ave New York NY 10017

GOULD, HAROLD I., lawyer; b. San Francisco, Feb. 19, 1929; s. Gene D. Evans and Beatrice C. (Altman) Bierer; m. Elizabeth Goldberg, Jan. 22, 1956; children: Helen N., William T., Lauren B. BA, UCLA, 1950, JD, 1955. Bar: Calif. 1956, U.S. Dist. Ct. (cen. dist.) Calif. 1956, U.S. Ct. Appeals (9th cir.) 1966. Sole practice Los Angeles, 1956-72, 86—, Beverly Hills, Calif., 1974-79; assoc. Bernfeld & Cohen, Los Angeles, 1973-74; sr. ptnr., pres. Gould & Merritt, Los Angeles, 1980-85, Gould, Merritt & Burke, Los Angeles, 1985-86. Served with U.S. Army, 1950-52, Korea. Mem. Los Angeles West C. of C. Democrat. Jewish. Avocations: travel, furniture refinishing and restoration, gardening, cooking, reading. State civil litigation, General corporate, General practice. Home: 1442 Lindacrest Dr Beverly Hills CA 90210 Office: 1900 Ave of Stars #250 Los Angeles CA 90067

GOULD, KENNETH B., lawyer; b. Boston, Oct. 26, 1955; s. Sidney Maurice Gould and Barbara (Michaelson) Shapiro; m. Judith E. Sklare, Aug. 31, 1980. BA magna cum laude, Harvard U., 1977; JD, Columbia U., 1980. Bar: Mass. 1980, U.S. Dist. Ct. Mass. 1981, U.S. Ct. Appeals (1st cir.) 1981. Assoc. Gaston Snow & Ely Bartlett, Boston, 1980—; mem. steering com. Cooperative Housing Task Force of New Eng., Boston, 1985—. Co-author: Industrial and Mixed Use Condominiums, Cooperatives and Time-Shares, 1985. Mem. ABA (real property probate and trust sect., author Condominiums, Cooperatives and Homeowner Assns. Com.), Mass. Bar Assn. (real property sect.), Mass. Conveyancers Assn., Boston Bar Assn. Real property, Landlord-tenant, Environment. Home: 35 Everett St Newton Centre MA 02159 Office: Gaston Snow & Ely Bartlett One Federal St Boston MA 02110

GOULD, TERRY ALLEN, lawyer, financial executive; b. St. Louis, Sept. 30, 1942; s. Courtney A. and Dorothy (Bitker) G.; m. Patricia Ann Wolf, July 21, 1968; children: Kristine Ann, Bradford Allen. BS, Miami U., Oxford, Ohio, 1965; postgrad. in bus. adminstrn., Washington U., St. Louis, 1966; JD cum laude, St. Louis U., 1981. Bar: Mo. 1981, U.S. Dist. Ct. (we. dist.) Mo. 1981, U.S. Dist. Ct. (ea. dist.) Mo. 1983, Wis. 1987, U.S. Supreme Ct. 1987. Security analyst Merc. Trust Co., St. Louis, 1965-66; mgmt. trainee Misco-Shawnee, Inc., St. Louis, 1966-68, br. mgr., 1969-72, v.p., 1972-73, exec. v.p. adminstrn., 1973-78, sec./treas., 1975-78, dir., 1976-79; trustee Misco-Shawnee Profit Sharing Trust, 1975-78; v.p., dir. GORA Investment Co., St. Louis, 1975-78; gen. ptnr. Tera Investment Assocs., 1978—; sole practice law, 1981-85; of counsel Morganstern, Soraghan, Stockenberg, McKitrick & Spoeneman, St. Louis, 1985-86, ptnr., 1986; ptnr. Morganstern, Soraghan, Stockenberg, McKitrick & Gould, 1986—; dir. Tera Mgmt. Corp., 1980—; dir. Suburban Nat. Bank Elk Grove (Ill.), 1972-77. Mem. bd. mgrs., vice chmn. fin. com., mem. membership com., downtown br. Greater St. Louis YMCA, 1976-82; bd. dirs. Wis. Music Network, 1982—, Clef, Inc., 1982—, St. Louis Charitable Found., 1984—. Mem. ABA, Met. St. Louis Bar Assn. (chmn. real estate and devel. com. 1983-84, chmn. bus. law sect. 1985-86), Delta Sigma Pi, Beta Theta Pi. General corporate, Real property, Securities. Office: Morganstern Soraghan et al 1750 Interco Corp Tower 101 S Hanley Saint Louis MO 63105

GOULD, WILLIAM BENJAMIN, law educator, lawyer; b. 1936. A.B., U.R.I., 1958; LL.B., Cornell U., 1961; postgrad. London Sch. Econs., 1962-63. Bar: Mich. 1962. Asst. gen. counsel UAW, AFL-CIO, Detroit, 1961-62; atty. NLRB, Washington, 1963-65; assoc. Battle, Fowler, Stokes & Kheel, N.Y.C., 1965-68; prof. Wayne State U., 1968-71; vis. prof. Harvard U., 1971-72; now prof. Stanford U. Law Sch.; overseas fellow and vis. prof. Churchill Coll., Cambridge, Eng., 1975; vis. scholar U. Tokyo, 1975; vis. scholar, 1978; Fulbright-Hays Disting. lectr. Kyoto Am. Studies Summer Seminar; mem. adv. council N.Y. State Sch. Indsl. and Labor Relations; cons. fgn. policy council Rockefeller Found., N.Y.C. Rockefeller Found. fellow, 1975; guggenheim fellow, 1978. Mem. Nat. Acad. Arbitrators (chmn. com. on law and legis.), ABA (sec.-elect labor and employment law sect.). Legal education. Office: Stanford U Law Sch Stanford CA 94305 *

GOULDER, DIANE KESSLER, lawyer; b. Columbus, Ohio, Apr. 27, 1950; d. Berry Lester and Shirley Lorraine (Goldstein) Kessler; m. Eric Alan Goulder, June 30, 1974; children—Jeremy, Joel, Anna Lisa. B.A., Ohio State U., 1972; J.D., Cornell U., 1975. Bar: Ohio 1975. Assoc., Mayer Terakedis & Weed, Columbus, 1975-76, Mayer, Terakedis & Blue Co. L.P.A., Columbus,

1976-79; sole practice, Worthington, Ohio, 1979-85; prin. Martin, Eichenberger & Baxter Co., L.P.A., 1985—; of counsel James J. Tansey & Assocs., Washington, 1984-85. Active Twig 173, Women's Aux. of Children's Hosp., Worthington, 1980-85. Mem. ABA (adj. mem. taxation com. 1979—), Ohio Bar Assn., Columbus Bar Assn. (employee benefits com. 1984—), Women Lawyers of Franklin County, Mortar Board. Pension, profit-sharing, and employee benefits, Estate planning, Corporate taxation. Home: 6636 Plesenton Dr W Worthington OH 43085 Office: 6641 N High St Suite E Worthington OH 43085

GOULDIN, DAVID MILLEN, lawyer; b. Binghamton, N.Y., Mar. 8, 1941; s. Paul C. and Virginia M. G.; m. Deborah A., Aug. 20, 1966; children—Robert, Michael, Lauryn, Derek. A.B., Princeton U., 1963; J.D., Cornell U., 1966. Bar: N.Y., U.S. Dist. Ct. N.Y. Ptnr. Levene, Gouldin & Thompson, Binghamton, 1966—. Pres., Broome County (N.Y.) Arena, 1979; chmn. Broome County Health Fair, 1986-87; gen. chmn. ministry endowment campaign Broome County Council of Chs., 1986-87, United Way Broome County, 1980, pres., 1982-84; bd. dirs. Roberson Ctr. for Arts, N.Y. State United Way, 1984—; trustee Wyo. Sem. Named to Sect. Four Hall of Fame, 1977, Outstanding Young Men Am., U.S. Jaycees, 1975. Mem. Broome County Bar Assn., N.Y. State Bar Assn. (Root-Stimson award 1987), Fedn. Bar 6th Dist. (pres. 1975). Republican. Methodist. Lodge: Rotary. State civil litigation, Personal injury. Home: 85 Highland Ave Binghamton NY 13905 Office: 902 Press Bldg Binghamton NY 13902

GOULDING, J(OHN) MICHAEL, lawyer; b. Whittier, Calif., June 27, 1953; s. Lavar O. Goulding and Lillie (Metcalf) Clark; m. Joan Williams, May 27, 1975; children: Jared, Melanie, Devin, Corey. BA magna cum laude, Brigham Young U., 1975; JD, U. Utah, 1978. Bar: Ariz. 1978, U.S. Dist. Ct. Ariz. 1979, U.S. Tax Ct. 1980, Calif. 1984. Assoc. Udall, Shumway et al, Mesa, Ariz., 1978-82, Snell and Wilmer, Phoenix, 1982-84; assoc. Thelen, Marrin, et al, San Francisco, 1984-85, ptnr., 1986—; adj. prof. Ariz. State U., Tempe, 1983-84. Mem. ABA (employee benefits com. sect. of taxation 1984—). Republican. Mormon. Pension, profit-sharing, and employee benefits. Office: Thelen Marrin Johnson & Bridges 2 Embarcadero Ctr San Francisco CA 94111

GOULET, LIONEL JOSEPH, lawyer, labor arbitrator; b. Chgo., June 27, 1922; s. Lionel Joseph and Myrtle Julia (Breen) G.; m. Victoria Teresa Makarczyk, Dec. 10, 1949; children—Lionel Joseph III, Vicky Lynne. B.A., U. Ill., 1943; LL.B., Georgetown U., 1954, postgrad. in labor law, 1964-66. Bar: U.S. Dist. Ct. (D.C.) 1954, Ill. 1967, U.S. Ct. Appeals (7th cir.) 1970, U.S. Dist. Ct. (no. dist.) Ill. 1975. Commd. ensign U.S. Navy, 1944, advanced through grades to comdr., 1959; ret., 1965; labor counsel Universal Oil Products Co., Des Plaines, Ill., 1966-71; v.p. corp. relations Sunbeam Corp., Oak Brook, Ill., 1971-82; atty. City of Chgo., 1983-85; sole practice, Chgo., 1985—. Sr. assoc. editor Georgetown Law Jour., 1954. Mem. N.W. Suburban council Boy Scouts Am., 1969-71. Mem. Soc. Profls. in Dispute Resolution (assoc.), ABA, Fed. Bar Assn., Indsl. Relations Research Assn., Ill. Bar Assn., Assn. Trial Lawyers Am., Phi Delta Phi. Republican. Roman Catholic. Lodges: Elks, Lions (bd. dirs. 1968-70). Labor, Workers' compensation, Labor arbitrator and mediator. Home and Office: 720 S Kaspar Ave Arlington Heights IL 60005-2322

GOUNLEY, DENNIS JOSEPH, lawyer; b. Phila., Jan. 29, 1950; s. George Gerard and Elizabeth Mary (Maggioncalda) G.; m. Martha Ann Zatezalo, Sept. 25, 1976. B.A., St. Joseph's Coll., Phila., 1971; J.D., Dickinson Sch. Law, 1974. Bar: Pa. 1974, U.S. Ct. Appeals (3d cir.) 1976, U.S. Supreme Ct. 1977. Sole practice, Greensburg, Pa., 1974-83; ptnr. Gounley & O'Halloran, Greensburg, 1984—. Council mem. Franklin Towne Condominium Assn., Murrysville, Pa., 1976-79; mem. Western Pa. Conservancy, Pitts., Westmoreland County Mus. Art, Greensburg. Mem. ABA, Pa. Bar Assn., Westmoreland Bar Assn. Republican. Roman Catholic. Lodges: Kiwanis, Elks. State civil litigation, Real property, Landlord-tenant. Home: 105 Crosswinds Ct Murrysville PA 15668 Office: Gounley & O'Halloran 15 E Otterman St Greensburg PA 15601

GOURLEY, ROBERT VAUGHN, lawyer; b. Spanish Fork, Utah, June 19, 1951; s. Robert Losee and Shirley Roberta (Pace) G.; m. Karol Lee Sheeley, May 16, 1974; children: Ryan Brent, Stephanie Dianne, Justin Scott, Ashley Nicole. BA, Brigham Young U., 1975, MA, 1978; JD, U. Puget Sound, 1982. Bar: Utah 1982, U.S. Dist. Ct. Utah 1982, Nev. 1984, U.S. Dist. Ct. Nev. 1984, U.S. Ct. Appeals (9th and 10th cirs.) 1984, U.S. Supreme Ct. 1985. Law clk. to judge U.S. Dist. Ct. Nev., Las Vegas, 1982-84; assoc. Beckley, Singleton, DeLanoy, Jemison & List, Las Vegas, 1987—. Mem. Boulder Dam council Boy Scouts Am., Las Vegas. Mem. ABA, Utah Bar Assn., Nev. Bar Assn., Clark County Bar Assn., Salt Lake Bar Assn., Assn. Trial Lawyers Am., Nev. Trial Lawyers Assn., Phi Delta Phi, Kappa Tau Alpha. Republican. Mormon. Avocations: reading, fly fishing, outdoor sports, backpacking. Bankruptcy, Banking, Water law, natural resource law. Home: 1305 Bittersweet Circle Las Vegas NV 89128

GOURVITZ, ELLIOT HOWARD, lawyer; b. Lewistown, Pa., Sept. 21, 1945; s. Louis and Irene (Brass) G.; m. Bonnie S. Hirsch; children—Evan, Amy, Ross, Ari. B.A., Rutgers U., 1966, J.D., 1969. Bar: N.J. 1969, N.Y. 1985, U.S. Dist. Ct. N.J. 1969, U.S. Tax Ct. 1970, U.S. Ct. Claims 1970, U.S. Ct. Appeals (3d cir.) 1972, U.S. Supreme Ct. 1973 U.S. Dist. Ct. (ea. dist.) Wis. 1985, U.S. Ct. Internat. Trade 1985, U.S. Ct. Appeals (2d, 4th, 5th, 7th, 8th, 9th, 10th and fed. cirs.) 1985; cert. civil trial atty., N.J. Sole practice, Union, N.J., 1969—; counsel Execs. Assn. N.J., 1976—; chmn. Supreme Ct. Rules Com., N.J., 1985. Contbr. articles to jours. on matrimonial law and taxation. Chmn. Early Settlement Panel of Essex Middlesex Union Counties. Named Man of Yr., United Cerebral Palsy League Union County, 1980. Fellow Am. Acad. Matrimonial Attys. (bd. mgrs., chmn. divorce mediation com. N.J.). Family and matrimonial. Office: 2424 Morris Ave Union NJ 07083

GOVER, ALAN SHORE, lawyer; b. Lyons, N.Y., Sept. 5, 1948; s. Norman Marvin and Beatrice L. (Shore) G.; m. Ellen Rae Ross, Dec. 4, 1976; children: Maxwell Ross, Mary Trace. AB, Tufts U., 1970; JD, Georgetown U., 1973. Bar: Tex. 1973, U.S. Dist. Ct. (so. dist.) Tex. 1974, U.S. Ct. Appeals (5th cir.) 1974, U.S. Supreme Ct. 1976, U.S. Ct. Appeals (D.C. cir.) 1977, U.S. Dist. Ct. (we. dist.) 1979, U.S. Ct. Appeals (2d cir.) 1979, U.S. Ct. Appeals (9th and 11th cirs.), U.S. Ct. Appeals (8th cir.) 1981. Assoc. Baker & Botts, Houston, 1973-80, ptnr., 1981-85; ptnr. Weil, Gotshal & Manges, Houston, 1985—. Editor, chmn. editorial bd.: Oil and Gas and Bankruptcy Laws, 1985. Trustee Congregation Beth Israel, Houston, 1980-86; adv. trustee Houston Ballet, 1986. Mem. ABA. Jewish. Club: Houston. Bankruptcy. Office: Weil Gotshal & Manges 1600 Republic Bank Ctr Houston TX 77002

GOWA, ANDREW J., lawyer; b. N.Y.C., Nov. 6, 1949; s. Everett M. and Louise (Friedman) G.; m. Joanne S. Gowa, Oct. 21, 1974; 1 child, Catherine J. AB magna cum laude, Tufts U., 1971; JD, U. Pa., 1974. Bar: Pa. 1974, N.Y. 1982. From assoc. to ptnr. Blank, Rome, Comisky & McCauley, Phila., 1974-84; sole practice West Chester, Pa., 1984—; v.p. N. Atlantic Investment Corp., Phila., 1984-85; chmn., chief exec. officer 1st Equity Cos., West Chester, Pa., 1985—; bd. dirs. Equitrust Real Estate Corp., West Chester. Mem. Tufts U. Alumni Council, Medford, Mass., 1983—; bd. dirs. Kaiserman Ctr. Jewish Community Ctrs. Phila, 1982—. Recipient Disting. Service medal Tufts U., 1982. Mem. Pa. Bar Assn. (ho. dels. 1983—), Phila. Bar Assn. (bd. govs. 1985, chmn. real estate sect. 1985, exec. bd. real estate sect. 1983—), Chester County Bar Assn. Club: Locust (Phila.). General practice, Real property. Home: 1358 Arbordale Rd Philadelphia PA 19151 Office: 1546 McDaniel Dr West Chester PA 19380-6670

GOWDY, FRANKLIN BROCKWAY, lawyer; b. Burlington, Iowa, Dec. 27, 1945; s. Franklin Kamm and Dorothy Faye (Brockway) G.; m. Jennifer June McKenrick, Nov. 27, 1982; stepchildren: Jeffrey F. Hammond, Tracy Hammond, Jonathan R. Hammond, Julie E. Hammond. BA in Polit. Sci., Stanford U., 1967; JD, U. Calif., Berkeley, 1970. Bar: U.S. Dist. Ct. (no. dist.) Calif. 1971, U.S. Ct. Appeals (9th cir.) 1971, U.S. Supreme Ct. 1979, U.S. Dist. Ct. (cen. dist.) Calif. 1984. Assoc. Brobeck, Phleger & Harrison, San Francisco, 1971-78, ptnr., 1978—. Mem. ABA, Calif. Bar Assn., San Francisco Bar Assn. Antitrust, Federal civil litigation, State civil litigation. Home: 3915 Happy Valley Rd Lafayette CA 94549 Office: Brobeck Phleger & Harrison 1 Market Plaza Spear St Tower San Francisco CA 94105

GOWEN, GEORGE W., lawyer; b. Leghorn, Italy, Sept. 14, 1929; s. Franklin and May G.; m. Marcia F. Fennelly, Jan. 17, 1959; children: Cynthia, Lee. AB, Princeton U., 1952; JD, U. Va., 1957. Bar: N.Y. 1958. Assoc. Dunnington, Bartholow & Miller, N.Y.C., 1957-66, ptnr., 1966-85; Fryer, Ross & Gowen, 1986—; bd. dirs. N.Am. Royalties, Inc., Paine Webber Cashfund, Inc., RMA Funds, Inc.; adj. prof. NYU Grad. Sch. Bus. Adminstn.; gen. counsel U.S. Tennis Assn.; assoc. counsel U.S. Olympic Com.; alt. mem. subcom. on prevention of discrimination and protection of minorities UN, 1970-74. Chmn. bd. ASPCA; bd. dirs. Nat. Park Found.; chmn. bd. Scenic Hudson, Inc. Served to 1st lt. U.S. Army, 1952-54. Mem. ABA. Republican. Episcopalian. Clubs: River (N.Y.C.); Metropolitan (Washington). General corporate, Probate, Sports. Home: 122 E 76th St New York NY 10021 Office: 551 Fifth Ave New York NY 10176

GOWEN, THOMAS LEO, JR., lawyer; b. Phila., June 22, 1949; s. Thomas L. and Jacqueline Gowen; m. Michele F. Charrier, Sept. 25, 1971; children: Christopher, Jonathan. BA, Haverford Coll., 1971; JD, Villanova U., 1977. Bar: Pa. 1977, U.S. Dist. (ea. dist.) Pa. 1977. Securities analyst Continental Bank, Phila., 1971-74; ptnr. Caiola, Caiola & Gowen, Norristown, Pa., 1977—; v.p., counsel Phila. Tennis Patrons, 1977—; bd. dirs. WHRC Radio Corp., Haverford, Pa., Phila. Internat. Tennis Corp. Mem. Montgomery County Bar Assn. (continuing legal edn. com.), Assn. Trial Lawyers Am. (exchange com. 1985—), Pa. Trial Lawyers Assn. (chmn. headtrauma seminar 1986), Nat. Jr. Tennis League of Phila. (v.p., chmn. bd. 1972—), Phila. Tennis Assn. (Seymour Coren award 1976). Personal injury, State civil litigation, Federal civil litigation. Home: 36 Glenbrook Rd Ardmore PA 19003 Office: Caiola Caiola & Gowen 506 Swede St Norristown PA 19401

GRAAE, STEFFEN WILLIAM, judge; b. Copenhagen, Denmark, Sept. 25, 1940; came to U.S., 1951; s. Soren Julius Winkel Graae and Madge Hilda (Jopson) Wells; m. Cynthia Margaret Norris, Aug. 13, 1966; 1 child, Jessica Winkel. BA, Yale U., 1962; MA, Oxford U., 1969; JD, Georgetown U., 1973. Bar: D.C., 1974, U.S. Dist. Ct. (D.C. cir.), 1974. Ptnr. Clarke & Graae, Washington, 1974-76; sole practice Washington, 1976-80; ptnr. Mirel & Graae P.C., Washington, 1980-82; judge D.C. Superior Ct., Washington, 1982—; adj. prof. law Georgetown U., 1975-76.. Author: D.C. Statutory and Case Law Annotation to Federal Rules of Evidence, 1975. Mem. ABA. Home: 150 N Carolina Ave SE Washington DC 20003 Office: Superior Ct DC 500 Indiana Ave NW Washington DC 20001

GRABAREK, WILLIAM CHRISTIAN, lawyer; b. Chgo., Apr. 19, 1939; s. Edward Thomas and Edith Viola (Christenson) G.; m. Marie Madeline Zimmerman, June 12, 1965 (div. Mar. 1986); children: Scott E., Heidi L., Svea K., Paul W. BA, Roosevelt U., 1968; JD, John Marshall Law Sch., 1975. Bar: Ill. 1975, U.S. Dist. Ct. (no. dist.) Ill. 1975, U.S. Patent Office 1980, U.S. Ct. Appeals (7th cir.) 1982. Chemist Armour Industrial Chem. Co., McCook, Ill., 1964-70; mgr. tech. service Daubert Chem. Co., Chgo., 1970-76; assoc. Kolar & Conte, Chgo., 1976-77; staff atty. Richardson Co., Des Plaines, Ill., 1977-81; sr. atty. Witco Corp., Melrose Park, Ill., 1981-85; house counsel midwest region Witco Corp., Melrose Park, 1985—; lectr. Ill. Inst. Continuing Legal Edn., 1984. Founding mem. Elburn and Countryside Community Ctr., Elburn, Ill., 1985—; trustee Village Willow Springs, Ill., 1976-77. Mem. ABA, Ill. Bar Assn., Chgo. Bar Assn., Patent Law Assn. Chgo., Chem. Industries Council Ill. (bd. dirs. 1984—). Democrat. Lutheran. Avocations: reading, bicycling, scouting. Environment, Patent, General corporate. Office: Witco Corp 2701 Lake St Melrose Park IL 60160

GRABEMANN, KARL W., lawyer; b. Chgo., Apr. 27, 1929; s. Karl H. and Trude (Stockram) G.; m. Mary Darr, Dec. 6, 1958; children: Robert S., Lisa D. B.S., Northwestern U., 1951, J.D., 1956. Bar: Ill. 1957, U.S. Supreme Ct. 1960, U.S. Ct. Appeals for D.C. 1957, U.S. Ct. Appeals for 7th Circuit 1957, U.S. Ct. Appeals for 5th Circuit 1967, U.S. Dist. Ct. for D.C. 1957, U.S. Dist. Ct. for No. Dist. Ill. 1957. Atty. NLRB, Chgo., 1956-60; ptnr. firm Turner, Hunt & Woolley, Chgo., 1960-69, Keck, Mahin & Cate, Chgo., 1969-79, McDermott, Will & Emery, Chgo., 1979—. Mem. ABA, Ill. Bar Assn., Chgo. Bar Assn. Republican. Club: Metropolitan (Chgo.). Labor, Federal civil litigation. Office: McDermott Will & Emery 111 W Monroe St Chicago IL 60603

GRABOW, RAYMOND JOHN, mayor; b. Cleve., Jan. 27, 1932; s. Joseph Stanley and Frances (Kalata) G.; B.S. in Bus. Adminstrn., Kent State U., 1953; J.D., Western Res. U., 1958; m. Margaret Jean Knoll, Nov. 27, 1969; children—Rachel Jean, Ryan Joseph. Bar: Ohio 1958. Counsel, No. Ohio Petroleum Retailers Assn., Cleve., 1965—; counsel, trustee Alliance of Poles Fed. Credit Union, 1972, also gen. counsel Alliance of Poles of Am.; councilman City of Warrensville Heights (Ohio), 1962-68, mayor, 1969—; sec. Sam's Investment Inc. Cleve., 1965—, Atlas Sewer & Pipe Cleaning Corp., Cleve., 1962—, Wick Restaurant Inc., Cleve., 1962—, Ohio Awning Co., Space Comfort Co., Wagner Awning & Mfg. Co. Mem. exec. com. Democratic party Cuyahoga County, 1966—, precinct com., 1966-80; trustee Brentwood Hosp.; bd. dirs. Polonia Found. Recipient award Polonia Found., 1970, other groups. Mem. Ohio State, Cuyahoga County, Greater Cleve. bar assns., Nat. Advs. Soc., Am. Judicature Soc., Assn. Trial Lawyers Am., Ohio Trial Lawyers Assn., Am. Legion, PLAV Vets., Cath. War Vets., Cleve. Soc., Warrensville Heights C. of C. (trustee), Nat. League Cities, Ohio Assn. Pub. Safety Dirs., Mcpl. Treas. Assn., Ohio Service Dirs. Assn., Ohio Jud. Conf., Cuyahoga County Safety Dirs. Assn., Ohio Mayors Assn., Ohio Mcpl. League, numerous ethnic orgns. Lodge: Order of Alhambra. State civil litigation, Probate, General corporate. Home: 20114 Gladstone Rd Warrensville Heights OH 44122 Office: Suite 815 Superior Bldg Cleveland OH 44114

GRACE, BRIAN GUILES, lawyer; b. Lawrence, Kans., Dec. 26, 1942; s. Bernard and Theola Avida (Guiles) G.; m. Carol Diane Seaver, June 9, 1967; children: Kevin A., Jeff S., Brady A. BBA, U. Kans., 1964, JD, 1967. Bar: Kans. 1967, U.S. Dist. Ct. Kans. 1967, U.S. Ct. Appeals (10th cir.) 1974. Assoc., ptnr. Curfman, Harris, Stallings, Grace & Snow and predecessor firm, Wichita, Kans., 1967-84; ptnr. Law Office of Brian G. Grace, Wichita, 1984—; mediator U.S. Dist. Ct. Kans., Wichita, 1984—. Bd. dirs. Leukemia Soc. of Kans., Inc., Wichita, 1974—. Mem. ABA (vice chmn. constn. litigation com. 1974-76—), Kans. Bar Assn., Kans. Trial Lawyers Assn., Assn. Trial Lawyers Am. Avocations: golf, tennis, bridge. Federal civil litigation, State civil litigation, Insurance. Home: 7735 Killarney Ct Wichita KS 67206 Office: 701 First National Bank Wichita KS 67202

GRACE, DAVID ALLEN, lawyer; b. El Dorado, Ark., Nov. 5, 1951; s. William Allen and Willie Saline (Franks) G.; m. Lucinda Elizabeth Forgy, Aug. 17, 1974; 1 child, Darby Allison. BA in Polit. Sci. and History, Hendrix Coll., 1973; JD with honors, U. Ark., 1976. Bar: Ark. 1976, U.S. Dist. Ct. Ark. 1977. Staff atty. Ark. Tax Revision Commn., Little Rock, 1976-77; assoc. Napper, Hardin & Wood, North Little Rock, 1977-78; ptnr. Napper, Wood, Hardin, Grace et al, North Little Rock, 1978-81, Grace, Napper, Allen & East, Little Rock, 1981-84, Hardin & Grace, Little Rock, 1984—. Co-author: Arkansas Construction Law, 1985. Mem. ABA, Am. Trial Lawyers Assn., Ark. Bar Assn., Bar Assn. Cen. Ark. (debtor-creditor com. 1983—), Pulaski County Bar Assn. Construction, Contracts commercial, Bankruptcy. Office: Hardin & Grace 410 W 3d St Suite 200 Little Rock AR 72203

GRACE, DAVID JOSEPH, lawyer; b. Dubuque, Iowa, Nov. 11, 1946; s. Joseph C. and Theresa F. (Pfiffner) G.; m. Mary Helen Meder, Sept. 7, 1968; children: Joseph, Michael, Elizabeth. BA, Loras Coll., 1968; JD, U. Iowa, 1972. Bar: Iowa, U.S. Dist. Ct. (no. and so. dists.) Iowa, 1972. Assoc. Davis, Grace, Harvey, Horvath, Gonnerman & Rouwenhorst, Des Moines, 1973—. Bd. dirs. Raccoon Valley Little League, Des Moines, 1985—. Served with U.S. Army, 1970-71. Mem. Polk County Bar Assn. (bd. dirs. 1984—). Democrat. Roman Catholic. Lodge: Lions (pres. Des Moines club 1982-83). State civil litigation, Federal civil litigation, Family and matrimonial. Home: 314 Glenview Des Moines IA 50312 Office: Davis Grace et al 212 Equitable Bldg Des Moines IA 50309

GRACE, EUGENE PETER, lawyer; b. N.Y.C., Sept. 19, 1951; s. John Peter and Gladys Elsie (Toellner) G.; m. Barbara Anne Gellella, July 8, 1973; children: Nicholas P., Andrew P. BA, MA, U. Pa., 1973; JD, Villanova U., 1976. Bar: Pa. 1976, N.J. 1977. Asst. counsel United Jersey Banks, Princeton, N.J., 1977-80; v.p., assoc. gen. counsel Provident Nat. Bank, Phila., 1980—. Co-author: (guide) Wire Transfer Customer Agreements, 1985. Mem. ABA, Pa. Bar Assn., Phila. Bar Assn., N.J. Bar Assn. Roman Catholic. Avocations: gardening, travel, reading, sports. Banking, Computer, Securities. Home: 1 Kent Ln Paoli PA 19301 Office: Provident Nat Bank Broad and Chestnut Sts Philadelphia PA 19110

GRACIN, HANK, lawyer; b. Massapequa Park, N.Y., Jan. 27, 1957; s. Bernard Tobias and Ada (Rosenberg) G.; m. Milette Shanon, June 9, 1985. BA with honors, SUNY, Binghamton, 1978; JD cum laude, NYU, 1981. Bar: N.Y. 1982, U.S. Dist. Ct. (so. dist.) N.Y. 1982. Assoc. Sullivan & Cromwell, N.Y.C., 1981-83, Schulte Roth & Zabel, N.Y.C., 1983-86, Reavis & McGrath, N.Y.C., 1986—. Editor: Private Placements and Restricted Securities, 1981. Mem. ABA (corp. banking, bus. law and internat. law sects.), Assn. of the Bar of the City of N.Y., Order of the Coif (NYU chpt.). Jewish. Avocations: bicycling, reading, piano. General corporate, Private international, Securities. Home: 50 Brompton Rd Apt 3Y Great Neck NY 11021 Office: Reavis & McGrath 345 Park Ave New York NY 10154

GRAD, FRANK PAUL, law lawyer; b. Vienna, Austria, May 2, 1924; came to U.S., 1939, naturalized, 1943; s. Morris and Clara Sophie (Scher) G.; m. Lisa Szilagyi, Dec. 6, 1946; children: David Anthony, Catharine Ann. B.A. magna cum laude, Bklyn. Coll., 1947; LL.B., Columbia U., 1949. Bar: N.Y. 1949. Assoc. in law Columbia U. Law Sch., 1949-50, asst. dir. Legis. Drafting Research Fund, 1953-55; assoc. dir. Legis. Drafting Research Fund, Columbia U. Law Sch., N.Y.C., 1956-68, dir., 1969—; mem. faculty Columbia U. Law Sch., 1954—; prof. law 1969—; Joseph P. Chamberlain prof. legis. Columbia U. Law Sch., 1982—; asso. firm House, Grossman, Vorhaus & Hemley, N.Y.C., 1950-53; mem. legal adv. com. U.S. Council Environ. Quality, 1970-73; mem. N.Y. Deptl. Com. Ct. Adminstrn., Appellate Div., 1st Dept., 1970-74; counsel N.Y. State Spl. Adv. Panel Med. Malpractice, 1975; legal counsel Nat. Mcpl. League, 1967—; cons. in field, 1955—; reporter U.S. Super fund Study group, 1981-82; dir. research N.Y.C. Charter Revision Commn., 1982-83; dir. research N.Y. State-City Commn. on Integrity in Govt., 1986. Author: Public Health Law Manual, 7th edit, 1981, The Drafting of State Constitutions, 1963, Environmental Law: Sources and Problems, 3d edit, 1985, Treatise on Environmental Law, 5 vols, 1973-87; co-author other legal reports; contbr. legal jours.; draftsman mcpl. codes and state legislation. Served with AUS, 1943-46. Mem. Am. Bar Assn., Am. Public Health Assn., Assn. Bar City N.Y., Am. Law Inst. Legal education, Environment, Legislative. Office: 435 W 116th St New York NY 10027

GRAD, JOHN DAVID, lawyer; b. N.Y.C., Sept. 8, 1947; s. James and Thelma (Lewis) G.; m. Rae Krohn, June 14, 1970; children: Arlen, Rebecca, Aaron. BA, Hamilton Coll., 1969; JD, NYU, 1972. Bar: N.Y. 1973, Va. 1973, D.C. 1974, U.S. Ct. Claims 1976, U.S. Supreme Ct. 1976. Law clk. to presiding judge U.S. Dist. Ct. (ea. dist.), Richmond, Va., 1972-73; assoc. Philip Hirschkop & Assoc., Alexandria, Va., 1973-77; ptnr. Hirschkop & Grad, P.C., Alexandria, 1977-86, John D. Grad & Assocs., P.C., Alexandria, 1986—; mem. Va. Med. Malpractice Review Bd., 1980—. Editor Jour. Internat. Law and Politics, 1971-72, contbr. articles to profl. jours. Bd. dirs. Residential Youth Services, Inc. 1981-83. Root-Tilden scholar. Mem ABA, Am. Soc. Law and Medicine (bd. dirs. 1982-85), Assn. Trial Lawyers Am., D.C. Bar Assn., Va. Bar Assn. (medico-legal liaison com. 1980—), Va. Trial Lawyers Assn., Va. Coll. of Criminal Def. Attys., Alexandria Bar Assn. (chmn. lawyer/physician com. 1982—, bd. dirs. 1985—), Phi Beta Kappa. Office: John D Grad & Assocs PC 112 N Columbus St Alexandria VA 22313

GRAD, NEIL ELLIOTT MARSHALL, lawyer; b. Los Angeles, Apr. 24, 1954; s. Harry S. and Clara B. (Goldstein) G.; m. Sherri Lynn Bonnet, Dec. 2, 1984; children: Amber Lynn, Sarah Lynn. BA, UCLA, 1975; JD, Calif. Western U., 1978. Bar: Nev. 1979, U.S. Dist. Ct. Nev. 1979, U.S. Ct. Appeals (9th cir.) 1979, U.S. Ct. Mil. Appeals 1980. Dep. dist. atty. Washoe County, Reno, 1979-80; sole practice Reno, 1980—; judge pro tem Reno Mcpl. Ct., 1982—, Sparks (Nev.) Mcpl. Ct., 1983—; counsel First Western Savs, Bank, Reno, 1982—; spl. counsel Nev. Bar, Reno, 1983; local counsel Electro Lux div. Consol. Foods, Reno, 1983-84, Longs Drug Stores, Reno, 1984—. Co-author: Indigency Law Handbook, 1977. Trustee Washoe County Library, Reno, 1983—. Mem. ABA, ALA, Nev. Bar Assn., Washoe County Bar Assn., UCLA Alumni Assn. (v.p., gen. counsel Sierra Nev. Bruins 1985—). Avocations: photography, racquetball, classical music. General practice, Family and matrimonial, Criminal. Office: 336 W Liberty St Reno NV 89501

GRADDICK, CHARLES ALLEN, lawyer; b. Mobile, Ala., Dec. 10, 1944; s. Julian and Elvera (Smith) G.; m. Corinne Whiting, Aug. 19, 1966; children: Charles Allen, Herndon Whiting, Corinne. J.D., U. Ala., 1970. Bar: Ala. 1970. Clk. Ala. Supreme Ct., 1970; asst. dist. atty. Mobile County, Ala., 1971-75; dist. atty. Mobile County, 1975-79; atty. gen. State of Ala., Montgomery, 1979-87; ptnr. Thorton, Farish and Gaunt, Montgomery, 1987—. Served with USNG, 1969—. Named Outstanding Young Man of Mobile Mobile Jaycees, 1976; recipient cert. appreciation Ala. Peace Officers, 1978, Appreciation award Optimists, 1978. Mem. Nat. Assn. Attys. Gen., Am. Trial Lawyers Assn., Am. Bar Assn., Ala. Bar Assn., Ala. Dist. Attys. Assn., Nat. Dist. Attys. Assn. Democrat. Episcopalian. Office: Thorton Farish and Gaunt 515 S Perry St Montgomery AL 36104

GRADY, JOHN F., federal judge; b. Chgo., May 23, 1929; s. John F. and Lucille F. (Shroder) G.; m. Patsy Grady, Aug. 10, 1968; 1 son, John F. B.S., Northwestern U., 1952, J.D., 1954. Bar: Ill. 1955. Practice law Chgo., 1955; asst. U.S. atty. for no. dist. Ill., 1956-61; practice law Waukegan, Ill., 1961-76; judge U.S. Dist. Ct. (no. dist.) Ill., Chgo., 1976-86, chief judge, 1986—. Assoc. editor: Northwestern U. Law Rev. Mem. Phi Beta Kappa. Judicial administration. Office: US Dist Ct 219 S Dearborn St Chicago IL 60604

GRAETZ, MICHAEL J., law educator; b. 1944. BBA, Emory U., 1966; LLB, U. Va., 1969. Advisor tax policy Asst. Sec. Treas., Washington, 1969-72; asst. prof. U. Va., Charlottesville, 1972-74, assoc. prof., 1974-77, prof., 1977-79; prof. U. So. Calif., Los Angeles, 1979-83, Yale U., New Haven, 1983—; adj. prof. Georgetown U., Washington, 1971-72; vis. prof. U. So. Calif., 1976-78, Calif. Inst. Tech., Pasadena, 1977-78. Office: Yale Law Sch Drawer 401A Yale Station New Haven CT 06520 *

GRAF, BAYARD MAYHEW, lawyer; b. West Grove, Pa., Jan. 17, 1926; s. Charles Earl and Elisabeth Helen (Mayhew) G.; m. Ruthann Hemphill, June 17, 1950; children—Bayard H., Evan M., Beverly R. B.S., Northwestern U., 1946, M.A., U. Pa., 1949; LL.B., Temple U., 1953. Bar: Pa. 1953, U.S. Dist. Ct. (ea. dist.) Pa. 1955, U.S. Ct. Appeals (3d cir.) 1955, U.S. Ct. Appeals (7th cir.) 1965, U.S. Ct. Appeals (D.C. cir.) 1976, U.S. Tax Ct. 1974, ICC bar 1971, U.S. Supreme Ct. 1967. Law clk. to justice Pa. Supreme Ct., 1953-55; assoc. Rawle & Handerson, 1955-57, J. Willison Smith, Jr., 1957-71, Harold E. Kohn, P.A., 1971-76; asst. v.p. Kohn, Savett, Klein & Graf, P.C., Phila., 1976—; lectr. fin. Temple U.; sec., dir. Melmark Home, Inc., Sherwood Hall, Inc.; dir., sec.-treas. Arronson Found., Lavine Found. Past bd. dirs., 2d vice chmn. Presbyn. Children's Village; mem. pres.'s council USO Phila.; mgr. championship Little League baseball team. Served to capt. Supply Corps, USNR, 1973-78. Mem. ABA, Pa. Bar Assn., Phila. Bar Assn., Lawyers Club Phila., D.C. Bar Assn., Am. Acad. Hosp. Attys., Nat. Health Lawyers Assn., Pa. Trial Lawyers Assn., Presbyn. Social Union (past pres.), Navy League U.S. (treas. Phila. council), Phi Kappa Psi (atty. gen.), Phi Alpha Delta (former justice). Republican. Presbyterian (ruling elder, clk. of session). Clubs: Union League (Phila.); Waynesborough Country. Probate, General corporate, Family and matrimonial. Home: 162 Beaumont Rd Devon PA 19333 Office: 2400 One Reading Ctr 1101 Market St Philadelphia PA 19107

GRAF, CARL NORVAL, JR., lawyer; b. Chgo., Apr. 19, 1942; s. Carl N. and Ruby D. (Moore) G.; m. Kathleen M. Oldacre, Aug. 5, 1967; children—Katherine L., Carl Norval III. B.S., Parsons Coll., 1966; J.D., Loyola

U., Chgo., 1969. Bar: Ill. 1969, U.S. Dist. Ct. (no. dist.) Ill. 1969. Mem. firm McDermott, Will & Emery, 1969-75; ptnr. Graf & Gulbrandsen, Morton Grove, Ill., 1975-77, Schneider, Graf & Trio, Morton Grove, 1977-81, Schneider & Graf, Morton Grove, 1982—; atty. tech. and zone bd. Home Builders Assn. Greater Chgo., 1976-81. Adv. bd. Morton Grove Crime Prevention Commn., 1977-81; atty. Lincolnshire Drug Awareness Bd., 1982—, North Shore Realtors Assn., 1982—. Trustee Dist. 103 Sch. Bd., Lake County, Ill., 1983; sec. Spl. Edn. Dist., Lake County, 1985. Mem. Chgo. Bar Assn., Ill. Bar Assn., ABA. Lutheran. Clubs: Morton Grove Lions, Masons, Shriners. General practice. Address: 65 Oak Ln Lake Forest IL 60045

GRAFF, DEBRA JO, lawyer; b. Chgo., May 26, 1951; d. Richard B. and Gail G. (Wineberg) G. BA magna cum laude, UCLA, 1973; cert. in teaching, Humboldt State Coll., 1974; JD cum laude, Southwestern U., 1981. Bar: Calif. 1982. Coordinator coop advt. Columbia Pictures, Burbank, Calif., 1980-82; contract title adminstr. Paramount Pictures, Hollywood, Calif., 1982-84; dir. bus. affairs Producers Sales Orgn., Los Angeles, 1984-86; sole practice Los Angeles, 1986—. Contbr. articles to profl. jours. Mem. Los Angeles Olympic Organizing Com., 1981-84; vol. Harriet Buhai Family Law Ctr., Los Angeles, 1982-86; active polit. fundraising. Mem. ABA, Los Angeles County Bar Assn., Beverly Hills Bar Assn. (symposium coordinator com. for the arts 1984-86). Avocations: aerobics, piano, puppetry. Entertainment, Family and matrimonial, Trademark and copyright.

GRAFSTEIN, JOEL M., lawyer; b. N.Y.C., May 27, 1948; s. Max G. and Elaine (Weisner) G.; m. Andree M. Clement, Aug. 4, 1974; 1 son, Michael Louis. B.S., U. Bridgeport, 1970; J.D., N.Y. Law Sch., 1973; LL.M., NYU, 1974. Bar: N.Y. 1973, Conn. 1973, U.S. Dist. Ct. Conn. 1973, U.S. Tax Ct. 1973. Assoc. Rome & Case, Bloomfield, Conn., 1974-82, Albrecht, Zelman, Hartford, Conn., 1982-83; ptnr. Lublin, Wolfe, Kantor & Silver, East Hartford, Conn., 1984—. Author: Connecticut Collection Law 1982, 83; Connecticut Foreclosure Law, 1984; Bankruptcy: A Primer, 1984; The Connecticut Unfair Trade Practices Act, 1986. Chmn. Republican Town Com., Barkhamstead, Conn., 1980-82; region chmn. Disaster Relief Com., Hartford, 1978-83. Mem. ABA, Conn. Bar Assn. (exec. com. 1978-83), Hartford County Bar Assn. Club: Lions (treas. 1976-80) (Bloomfield, Conn.). Bankruptcy, General corporate. Home: 2 Chiswick Ln North Canton CT 06059 Office: Lublin Wolfe Kantor & Silver 546 Burnside Ave East Hartford CT 06108

GRAHAM, ANDREW ALAN, lawyer; b. Lansing, Mich., Oct. 28, 1944; s. William A. and C. Pauline (DeVinney) G. BA, U. Cen. Fla., 1973; JD, Fla. State U., 1976. Bar: Fla. 1976, U.S. Dist. Ct. (mid. dist.) Fla. 1977, U.S. Ct. Appeals (5th cir.) 1977, U.S. Ct. Appeals (11th cir.) 1981, U.S. Supreme Ct. 1986. Sole practice Cocoa, Fla., 1976-79; sr. ptnr. Reinman, Harrell, Silberhorn & Graham, Melbourne, Fla., 1979—; lectr. Bar/Bri Fla. Bar Rev., Tallahassee, 1979—. Author: Florida Appellate Rules, 1977. Served with USN, 1963-71. Recipient Humanitarian award Am. Assn. Med. Preventics, 1981; Richmond I. Burge scholar Cen. Fla. U., 1972. Democrat. Club: Coast (Melbourne). State civil litigation, Personal injury, Insurance. Home: 4813 Union Cypress Pl West Melbourne FL 32904 Office: Reinmann Harrell et al 1825 S Riverview Dr Melbourne FL 32901

GRAHAM, ARNOLD HAROLD, legal educator; b. N.Y.C., Dec. 29, 1917; s. Julius E. and Rose Goldstein; m. Roselle Lesser, Dec. 23, 1939; children: Stuart R., Joel M., Jul E. B.S. with honors, NYU, 1945; LL.B., J.D. with honors, N.Y. Law Sch., 1952. Bar: N.Y. 1952, U.S. Supreme Ct. 1959, also U.S. Internat. Trade 1959, U.S. Tax Ct. 1959, U.S. Ct. Appeals for 2d Circuit 1959, U.S. Dist. Ct. for Hawaii 1959; C.P.A., N.Y. Practice pub. acctg. N.Y.C., 1945-52, individual practice law, 1952-76; dep. atty. gen. N.Y., 1952-54; cons. N.Y. Law Sch., N.Y.C., 1952-76; asst. dean, prof., treas. N.Y. Law Sch., 1976-77, vice dean, prof., treas., 1977—, cons., 1985—; cons., arbitrator Am. Arbitration Assn., 1952—; examiner of attys., N.Y.C.; law cons. exam. div. Am. Inst. C.P.A.s, 1976—; bd. visitors Appellate div., 1st dept. Supreme Ct. N.Y.; mem. jud. screening panel bankruptcy div. U.S. Dist. Ct. for So. Dist. N.Y., 1983-84; numerous guardianship appointments N.Y. State Supreme Ct., Surrogate's Ct.; mem. ind. screening panel Civil Ct. of City of N.Y., 1984. Trustee Ave R Temple, Kings Hwy. Bd. Trade; bd. advisers United Jewish Appeal; mem. exec. com. trusts and estates div. United Jewish Appeal-Fedn. Jewish Philanthropies. Recipient Ira Stone award for prof. of yr. N.Y. Law Sch., 1981. Fellow Am. Bar Found.; mem. ABA, Am. Law Inst., Am. Assn. Attys.-C.P.A.s (founder), Am. Trial Lawyers Assn., N.Y. Trial Lawyers Assn., Consular Law Soc., Fed. Bar Assn., Am. Bar Assn., Inst. Jud. Adminstrn., N.Y. State C.P.A. Soc., Fed. Bar Council, N.Y. County Lawyers Assn., Am. Arbitration Assn., Jewish Lawyers' Guild, Phi Delta Phi (hon., Disting. Alumnus award Dwight Inn). Jewish. Club: Merchants. Legal education, Probate, Estate taxation. Home: 2223 Ave T Brooklyn NY 11229 Office: New York Law Sch 57 Worth St New York NY 10013

GRAHAM, CHARLES BENJAMIN, JR., lawyer; b. Ft. Jackson, S.C., July 15, 1954; s. Charles Benjamin Sr. and Martha Jane (Glaze) G.; m. Beverly Ann Smith, Mar. 18, 1978; children: Charles Benjamin III, Mallory Kristen, Matthew Ryan. BA magna cum laude, U. Ga., 1976, JD, 1979. Bar: Ga. 1979, U.S. Dist. Ct. (no. dist.) Ga. 1979, U.S. Ct. Appeals (5th cir.) 1979, U.S. Ct. Appeals (11th cir.) 1981, U.S. Supreme Ct. 1983, U.S. Dist. Ct. (mid. dist.) Ga. 1984. Assoc. Glaze, McNally & Glaze, Jonesboro, Ga., 1979-81; sr. assoc. Glaze & McNally, Jonesboro, 1981-82; assoc. ptnr. Glaze & McNally P.C., Jonesboro, 1982-84; sr. ptnr. Graham & Ashby, Stone Mountain, Ga., 1984—; asst. atty. Fayette County, Fayetteville, Ga. 1979-82; asst. to the asst. atty. Clayton County, Jonesboro, 1979-82; asst. atty. Coll. Park, Ga., 1982-84, Hapeville, Ga., 1979-84, Riverdale, Ga., 1982-84, Union City, Ga., 1979-82, Fairburn, Ga., 1979-84, Palmetto, Ga., 1979-84, Lake City, Ga., 1979-84. Asst. atty. Clayton County Housing Authority, Jonesboro, Ga., 1982-84, Clayton County Water Authority, Jonesboro, 1982-84, Union City (Ga.) Downtown Devel. Authority, 1981-82; cons. subcom. on zoning Ga. Ho. of Reps., Atlanta, 1983; mediator Christian Conciliation Service Atlanta, Inc., 1984—; mem. Ga. Heart Assn., 1982—. Recipient Outstanding Service award Ga. Heart Assn., 1983. Mem. ABA, Ga. Bar Assn. (chmn. zoning task force 1980-83, am. planners assoc. joint zoning com.; Outstanding Service award 1982), Decatur/DeKalb Bar Assn., Assn. Trial Lawyers Am., Ga. Trial Lawyers Assn., Ga. Assn. Zoning Adminstrn. (founder, v.p. 1981-82), Atlanta C. of C., DeKalb C. of C., City and County Attys. Inst. (faculty 1983), Continuing Legal Edn. for Superior Ct. Judges (faculty 1985). Baptist. Lodges: Rotary (Stone Mountain, Ga.) (com. chmn. 1985); Optimist (Stone Mountain). Avocations: backpacking, photography. General corporate, Local government, General practice. Home: 587 Fond du Lac Dr Stone Mountain GA 30088 Office: Graham & Ashby 5405 Memorial Dr Suite I-2 Stone Mountain GA 30083

GRAHAM, DAVID ANTONY, lawyer; b. N.Y.C., Feb. 3, 1953; s. Lorenz Bell Jr. and Adele (Hersher) G.; m. Olga Pedroza, May 5, 1971; children: Xochitl, Joaquin, Esmeralda, Erica, Julian. AA, Community Coll., Denver, 1976; BA in Econs., U. Denver, 1978; JD, U. N.Mex., 1981. Bar: Colo. 1981, U.S. Dist. Ct. Colo. 1981, U.S. Ct. Appeals (10th cir.) 1981, N.Mex. 1982, U.S. Dist. Ct. N.Mex. 1982. Ptnr. Graham & Graham, Denver, 1981-82, San Luis, Colo., 1982-85; ptnr. Lopez, Chavez & Graham, Taos, N.Mex., 1985—; city atty. Municipality of San Luis, 1983—; bd. dirs. Quemado Corp., Chacon, N.Mex., Condor Inc., Albuquerque. Fellow HEW, 1978-81; grantee U. Denver, 1976-78. Mem. ABA, Assn. Trial Lawyers Am., Colo. Trial Lawyers Assn., N.Mex. Trial Lawyers Assn., Aircraft Owners and Pilots Assn., Campbell's List. State civil litigation, Criminal, Personal injury. Office: Lopez Chavez & Graham 706 Paseo de Pueblo Sur PO Box 6185 Taos NM 87571

GRAHAM, DONALD LYNN, lawyer; b. Salisbury, N.C., Dec. 15, 1948; s. Ernest Jethro and Mildred (Donald) G.; m. Brenda Joyce Savage, Sept. 27, 1969; 1 child, Sherrian Lynne. BA magna cum laude, W.Va. State Coll., 1971; JD, Ohio State U., 1974. Bar: Ohio 1974, U.S. Ct. Mil. Appeals, 1974, Fla. 1980, U.S. Dist. Ct. (so. dist.) Fla. 1980, Supreme Ct. 1980, U.S. Ct. Appeals (5th and 11th cirs.) 1981. Asst. U.S. atty. U.S. Dist. Ct. (so. dist.) Fla., Miami, 1979-84; ptnr. Raskin & Graham, Miami, 1984—; instr. U. Md., Hanau, Fed. Republic Germany, 1977-78, Embry Riddle U., Homestead, Fla., 1978-79. Served to Maj., asst. staff judge adv. U.S. Army, 1974-79. Recipient Arthur S. Fleming award Washington Jaycees, 1982, Superior Performance award U.S. Dept. Justice; named One of Outstanding Young Men of Am.,, 1984. Mem. Assn. Trial Lawyers Am., Nat. Bar Assn., Fed. Bar Assn. (so. Fla. pres. 1984-85, treas. 1982-83), Fla. Bar Assn., N.Y. Bar Assn., Ohio Bar Assn., NAACP, Alpha Phi Alpha. Democrat. Baptist. Avocation: fishing, reading. Federal civil litigation, State civil litigation, Criminal. Office: Raskin & Graham PA 744 NW 12 Ave Miami FL 33189

GRAHAM, HAROLD STEVEN, lawyer; b. Kansas City, Mo., Feb. 1, 1950; s. Martie Sydney and Elsie Helen (Bradford) G.; m. Deborah Ruth Glick, Apr. 8, 1973; children: Elizabeth, Jonathan, Joshua, Lauren. BS with distinction, U. Wis., 1972; JD, U. Chgo., 1976. Bar: Mo. 1976, U.S. Dist. Ct. (we. dist.) Mo. 1976. Assoc. Lathrop, Koontz & Norquist, Kansas City, 1976-81, ptnr., 1982—. Dir. fin. devel. Arthritis Found., Kansas City, 1983-84; mem. exec. com. Hyman Brand Hebrew Acad., Kansas City, 1985—; bd. dirs. Beth Shalom Synagogue, Kansas City, 1983—. Mem. ABA (subcom. real estate fin.), Mo. Bar Assn. (property law com.), U. Chgo. Alumni Assn. (pres. 1983-84). Avocations: tennis, running. Real property, Contracts commercial, General corporate. Office: Lathrop Koontz & Norquist 2345 Grand Ave Suite 2600 Kansas City MO 64108

GRAHAM, JUL ELIOT, lawyer, educator; b. Bklyn., June 14, 1953; s. Arnold Harold and Roselle (Lesser) G.; m. Sherry Robin Goldberg, Nov. 2, 1980. B.A. in Polit. Sci. cum laude, NYU, 1975; J.D. magna cum laude, N.Y. Law Sch., 1978. Bar: N.Y. 1979, U.S. Supreme Ct. 1984. Cons. Consumer Law Tng. Ctr., N.Y. Law Sch., 1976, mem. adj. faculty, 1980—; appellate law research asst. appellate div. 1st Dept., Supreme Ct. of State of N.Y., N.Y.C., 1978-79, staff atty., 1979-82, assoc. atty., 1982-83, law asst. to the justices, 1983—, exec. sec. deptl. adv. com. to family ct., 1979-82, editor criminal trial advocacy handbook, 1980—. Assoc. editor N.Y. Law Sch. Law Rev., 1976-78, contbg. author, 1975. Guest lectr. Joe Franklin Show, WOR-TV, 1982—. Mem. N.Y. County Lawyers Assn. (com. on communications and entertainment law 1980—, com. on penal and correctional reform 1980—, spl. com. on practical legal edn. 1979—), Am. Arbitration Assn. (arbitrator 1985—), Internat. Radio and TV Soc., Am. Film Inst., Phi Delta Phi, Phi Sigma Alpha. State civil litigation, Criminal, Legal education. Home: 249 Adelaide Ave Staten Island NY 10306 Office: NY State Supreme Ct Appellate Div 1st Jud Dept 41 Madison Ave New York NY 10010

GRAHAM, KEITH EVERETT, lawyer; b. Phila., Sept. 19, 1956; s. Eric Earl and Eleanor Lucille (Branche) G. BA, Yale U., 1978; JD, U. Chgo., 1982. Bar: Ill. 1982, U.S. Dist. Ct. (no. dist.) Ill. 1982. Assoc. Gardner, Carter & Douglas, Chgo., 1982-84, Hinshaw, Culbertson et al, Chgo., 1984—. Mem. ABA, Ill. Bar Assn., Chgo. Bar Assn. Federal civil litigation, State civil litigation, Contracts commercial.

GRAHAM, KENNETH ALBERT, lawyer, educator; b. Bridgeport, Conn., Aug. 15, 1948; s. Albert Charles and Rosemary (Farrell) G. B.A., U. Bridgeport, 1971; M.A., Northeastern U., 1974; J.D., Suffolk U., 1977. Bar: Conn. 1977, U.S. Dist. Ct. Conn. 1979, U.S. Ct. Appeals (2d cir.) 1980, U.S. Supreme Ct. 1981. Sole practice, Stratford, Conn., 1977-78; asst. clk. Conn. Superior Ct., Norwich, 1978; staff atty. Conn. Dept. Consumer Protection, Hartford, 1978-81; asst. atty. gen. Conn. Atty. Gen.'s Office, Hartford, 1981—; asst. prof. history Sacred Heart U., 1979—. Pres., Stratford Tennis Assn., 1983—. Served with U.S. Army, 1970-73. Mem. ABA, Bridgeport Bar Assn., Conn. Bar Assn. (exec. com. adminstrv. law sect. 1983—; exec. com. consumer law sect. 1978-84), Conn. Health Lawyers Assn., Am. Assn. Pub. Welfare Attys., Nat. Health Lawyers Assn., Stratford Hist. Soc., New Eng. Hist. Assn., Am. Hist. Assn., Delta Theta Phi (vice dean 1976-77, Scholarship Key 1976), Phi Alpha Theta. Administrative and regulatory, Health. Home: 280 Stratford Rd Stratford CT 06497 Office: Conn Atty Gens Office 90 Brainard Rd Hartford CT 06114

GRAHAM, KENNETH W., law educator; b. 1935. BA, U. Mich., 1957, JD, 1962. Prof. law UCLA. Office: UCLA Sch Law 405 Hilgard Ave Los Angeles CA 90024 *

GRAHAM, LAWRENCE EDWARD, lawyer, insurance company executive; b. Tomah, Wis., Dec. 7, 1936; s. Francis Michael and Theresa Mae (Snyder) G.; m. Helen Eva Damiano, Mar. 23, 1963; children—Damian, Mary, Helen, Amanda, Lawrence, Johnathan. A.B., Catholic U., 1958; J.D., NYU, 1969. Bar: N.J. 1969. Contract analyst N.Y. Life Ins. Co., N.Y.C., 1962-63; sr. underwriter N.Am. Reassurance Co., N.Y.C., 1963-69; group counsel Guardian Life Ins. Co., N.Y.C., 1969-76; assoc. counsel USLIFE Corp., N.Y.C., 1976-81, v.p.-counsel, 1981—. Served with U.S. Army, 1958-62. Mem. ABA (life ins. law com., pub. regulation, com.), N.J. Bar Assn. Republican. Episcopalian. Avocations: home rehabilitation; reading philosophy and history. Office: USLIFE Corp 125 Maiden Ln New York NY 10038

GRAHAM, MICHAEL PAUL, lawyer; b. Leavenworth, Kans., May 15, 1948; s. K.L. and Norma D. (Whiteside) G.; m. Pamela Jeanne Haymes, Feb. 21, 1976; children—Sarah Kathryn, Patrick Edward. A.B., Dartmouth Coll., 1970; J.D., Harvard, 1973. Bar: Tex. 1973. Assoc., Baker & Botts, Houston, Tex., 1973-80, ptnr., 1981—. Mem. Houston Bar Assn., Houston Bar Found. Federal civil litigation, State civil litigation. Office: Baker & Botts 3000 One Shell Plaza Houston TX 77002

GRAHAM, PAUL EUGENE, lawyer; b. Newark, Sept. 12, 1949; s. Hugh Joseph and Mildred Rose (Walz) G. BA, U. Rochester, 1971; JD, Seton Hall U., 1975. Bar: N.J. 1975, U.S. Dist. Ct. N.J. 1975, U.S. Dist. Ct. (ea. dist.) Mich. 1980. Dep. atty. gen. State of N.J., Trenton, 1975-77; assoc. Pitney, Hardin, Kipp & Szuch, Morristown, N.J., 1977-81, ptnr., 1982—. Mem. ABA, N.J. Bar Assn., Def. Research Inst. (product liability com.). Product liability, Personal injury. Home: 48 Tara Dr Belle Mead NJ 08502 Office: Pitney Hardin Kipp & Szuch 163 Madison Ave Morristown NJ 07960

GRAHAM, PETER JEFFREY STUART, lawyer; b. North Bay, Ont., Can., Aug. 3, 1954; s. Peter MacDonald and Rose (Monsour) G. B Comm., McGill U., Montreal, Can., 1975, BCL, LLB, 1979; LLB, Cambridge U., England, 1981; LLM, Columbia U., 1982. Bar: Que. 1982, Ont. 1983, D.C. 1983. Assoc. Borden & Elliot, Toronto, Ont., Can., 1979-80; fgn. lawyer Lovell, White & King, London, 1981; assoc. Phillips & Vineberg, Montreal, 1982-83, Hogan & Hartson, Washington, 1983—; bd. advisors Can. Bus. Roundtable, 1984—. Mem. editorial bd. Trade Law Topics, 1985—; contbr. articles to legal jours. Mem. Internat. Bar Assn., ABA, Can.-Am. Bar Assn. (bd. dirs.), Young Lawyers Internat. Assn. Anglican. Avocations: internat. travel, recreational athletics. General corporate, Securities, Public international. Home: 1600 N Oak St #1001 Arlington VA 22209 Office: Hogan & Hartson Columbia Sq 555 13th St NW Washington DC 20004-1109

GRAHAM, ROBERT CLARE, III, lawyer; b. Albuquerque, Mar. 24, 1955; s. Robert C. Jr. and Helen (Hoagland) G.; children: Jennifer, Jessica, Kourtney. BA, DePauw U., 1977; JD magna cum laude, Pepperdine U., 1980. Bar: Mo. 1980, Ill. 1981, U.S. Dist. Ct. (ea. dist.) Mo. 1981. Assoc. Shephard, Sandberg & Phoenix, St. Louis, 1980-82, Suelthaus & Kaplan, PC and predecessors, St. Louis, 1982—. Chmn. Kirkwood (Mo.) Greentree Festival, 1985. Named one of Outstanding Young Men in Am. Jaycees, 1981. Mem. ABA, Ill. Bar Assn., Mo. Bar Assn., Bar Assn. Met. St. Louis, St. Louis County Bar Assn. Republican. Presbyterian. Banking, General corporate, Real property. Office: Suelthaus & Kaplan PC 8000 Maryland 9th Floor Saint Louis MO 63105

GRAHAM, ROBERT LEE, lawyer; b. Balt., Sept. 10, 1940; s. Robert Lee and Elizabeth Keyser (Thom) G.; m. Sandra Williams; children: Samantha Stewart, Cameron Williams. BA, Colo. Coll., 1963; JD, Loyola U., Los Angeles, 1971. Bar: Calif. 1972, U.S. Dist. Ct. (cen. dist.) Calif. 1972, U.S. Dist. Ct. (so. dist.) Calif. 1980. Assoc. Edward S. Mack, Los Angeles, 1972-76; ptnr. McKay, Byrne, Graham & VanDam, Los Angeles, 1976—; judge pro tem Los Angeles Mcpl. Ct., 1983-84, Los Angeles Small Claims Ct., 1982—; arbitrator Los Angeles Superior Ct. Pres. Residents of Beverly Glen Inc., Los Angeles, 1971. Served with U.S. Army, 1963-67. Mem. ABA, Calif. Bar Assn., Los Angeles County Bar Assn., Assn. Southern Calif. Def. Counsel. Episcopalian. State civil litigation, Insurance, Personal injury. Home: 17015 Adlon Rd Encino CA 91436 Office: McKay Byrne Graham & VanDam 3250 Wilshire #603 Los Angeles CA 90010

GRAHAM, ROBERT WESTON, lawyer; b. Payette, Idaho, Apr. 17, 1915; m. Margaret Jane Trzcinski; children: Robert W. Jr., Douglas F., Priscilla Wyckoff, Malcolm S., Laura R. BA magna cum laude, Whitman Coll., 1936; LLB, Columbia U., 1939. Bar: U.S. Dist. Ct. (ea. and we. dists.) Wash. 1981, U.S. Ct. Appeals (9th cir.)1981, U.S. Supreme Ct. 1981. Assoc. Bogle & Gates, Seattle, 1839-49, ptnr., 1949—; lectr. law U. Wash.; lectr. in field; mem. U.S. Presdl. Del. to the Dem. Republic Madagascar on Occasion 25th Anniversary Malagasy Independence, June, 1985. Contbr. articles to profl. jours. Chmn. Citizens Conf. Wash. Cts. 1967, Western Inst. for Spl. Edn.; mem. Seattle King County Social Welfare Council, Puget Sound Econ. Devel. Council, Bob Packwood Fin. Com., 1985; mem. fin. com. Tim Hill for King County Exec.; mem. northwest dist. export council U.S. Dept. State; mem. nat. adv. council Ctr. for Study of the Presidency; mem. steering com. Wash. State Internat. Trade Ctr., 1985; co-chmn. Wash. State Rep. Fin. Com., 1985, Wash. State Rep. Fall Dinner, 1982; chmn. bd. overseers Whitman Coll., 1977-81; counselor Reagan-Bush Campaign; co-founder, 1st v.p. World Affairs Council Seattle; trustee Wash. State Internat. Trade Fair; nat. bd. dirs. Am. Cancer Soc., 1962-66. Recipient Harlan Fiske Stone award, 1939; James Kent scholar, 1939. Mem. ABA (ho. of dels. 1960-62, council antitrust sect. 1958-62), Wash. State Bar Assn., Seattle King County Bar Assn., Am. Judicature Soc. (bd. dirs. 1960-63), 9th Cir. Jud. Conf. (exec. com. 1976-80), Seattle C. of C. (pres. 1981-82), Social Hygiene Assn., Doctors Hosp. Assn., Wash. Pub. Ports Assn., Japan-Am. Soc., Japan-Am. Conf. Mayors and C. of C. Pres., Pub. Mems. Assn., Am. Fgn. Service Officers Assn., Phi Beta Kappa, Tau Kappa Epsilon, Phi Delta Phi. Clubs: Seattle Yacht, World Trade. Lodge: Rotary (dist. giv. Alaska, Yukaon Territory and Western Wash. 1984-85). Home: 5143 NE Laurelcrest Ln Seattle WA 98105 Office: US Embassy Vienna, Austria SECDEFREP/MBFR APO NY 09108

GRAHAM, SELDON BAIN, JR., lawyer, engineer; b. Franklin, Tex., Apr. 14, 1926; s. Seldon Bain and Lillian Emma (Struwe) G.; m. Patricia Gene Noah, Feb. 14, 1953; children—Seldon Bain, Kyle, Laurie. B.S., U.S. Mil. Acad., 1951; J.D., U. Tex., 1970. Registered profl. engr., Tex. Bar: Tex. 1970, U.S. Dist. Ct. (so. dist.) Tex. 1980, U.S. Ct. Appeals (5th cir.) 1983; cert. in oil, gas and mineral law Tex. Bd. Legal Specialization. Commd. 2d lt. U.S. Army, 1946; advanced through grades to col., 1979; with Office of Dep. Chief of Staff for Personnel, 1979; ret., 1979; area reservoir engr. ARCO, Okla., 1954-60; div. regulatory engr. Mobil Oil Co., Corpus Christi, 1961-67; counsel Exxon Co. USA, Houston, 1970-85; mem. legal com. Interstate Oil Compact Commn. Decorated Legion of Merit. Mem. ABA, Soc. Petroleum Engrs. Methodist. Oil and gas leasing. Home: 4713 Palisade Dr Austin TX 78731 Office: 309 Westgate Bldg Colorado at 12th St Austin TX 78701

GRAHAM, STEPHEN MICHAEL, lawyer; b. Houston, May 1, 1951; s. Frederick Mitchell and Lillian Louise (Miller) G.; m. Joanne Marie Sealock, Aug. 24, 1974; children: Aimee Elizabeth, Joseph Sealock, Jessica Anne. BS, Iowa State U., 1973; JD, Yale U., 1976. Bar: Wash. 1977. Assoc. Perkins Coie, Seattle, 1976-83, ptnr., 1983—. Bd. dirs. Wash. Spl. Olympics, Seattle, 1979-83, pres., 1983; mem. Seattle Bd. Ethics, 1982—, chmn., 1983-87, Seattle Fair Campaign Practices Commn., 1982—; trustee Cornish Coll. of the Arts, 1986—, Epiphany Sch., 1987—. Mem. ABA, Wash. State Bar Assn., Seattle-King County Bar Assn. Episcopalian. Clubs: Wash. Athletic, Columbia Tower. Securities, Contracts commercial, Banking. Office: Perkins Coie 1900 Washington Bldg Seattle WA 98101

GRAHAM, WILLIAM ARTHUR, educator, lawyer; b. Astoria, Oreg., Nov. 17, 1947; s. James Whitford and Wilma Louise (Perry) G.; m. Jean M. Van Buskirk, Sept. 9, 1972; children: Kristi Ann, Danelle Marie. BA, U. Mont., 1973, JD, 1977. Bar: Mont. 1977, U.S. Dist. Ct. Mont. 1977. Assoc. Sias & Ranstrom, Chinook, Mont., 1977-80; prof. U. Mont., Missoula, 1980-86; sole practice Missoula, 1987—; atty. The Fed. Land Bank Spokane, Wash., 1981—; faculty rep. Nat. Collegiate Athletic Assn. U. Mont., 1985-86. Trustee sch. bd. Chinook Pub. Schs., 1979-80; Served as communication technician USN, 1966-70, Vietnam. Recipient Emmett C. Anglin award U. Mont., 1977; named one of Outstanding Young Men in Am., 1978. Mem. ABA, Am. Bus. Law Assn., Mont. Bar Assn. (panelist seminars continuing legal edn., 1982-83, 85), Am. Bankruptcy Inst., Mont. Bankers Assn., Mont. Assn. Def. Counsel, Phi Delta Phi, Grizzly Athletic Assn., Missoula Road and Track Club. Methodist. Avocations: running, gardening. Bankruptcy, Contracts commercial, Consumer commercial. Home: 436 Fairview Missoula MT 59801 Office: 210 E Pine Suite 200 Missoula MT 59801

GRAHAM, WILLIAM B., pharmaceutical company executive; b. Chgo., July 14, 1911; s. William and Elizabeth (Burden) G.; m. Edna Kanaley, June 15, 1940 (dec.); children: William J., Elizabeth Anne, Margaret, Robert B.; m. Catherine Van Duzer, July 23, 1984. S.B. cum laude, U. Chgo., 1932, J.D. cum laude, 1936; LL.D., Carthage Coll., 1974, Lake Forest Coll., 1983; L.H.D., St. Xavier Coll. and Nat. Coll. Edn., 1983. Bar: Ill. 1936. Patent lawyer Dyrenforth, Lee, Chritton & Wiles, 1936-40; mem. Dawson & Ooms, 1940-45; v.p., mgr. Baxter Travenol Labs., Inc., Deerfield, Ill., 1945-53; pres., chief exec. officer Baxter Travenol Labs., Inc., 1953-71, chmn. bd., chief exec. officer, 1971-80, chmn. bd., 1980-85, sr. chmn., 1985—, also dir.; dir., mem. exec. com. 1st Nat. Bank, Chgo.; dir. Deere & Co.; prof., chairperson Weizmann Inst., 1978. Bd. dirs., pres. Lyric Opera Chgo.; vice chmn. bd. dirs. Nat. Park Fedn.; bd. dirs. Chgo. Hort. Soc., Nat. Council U.S.-China Trade; trustee Orchestral Assn., U. Chgo., Evanston (Ill.) Hosp. Recipient V.I.P. award Lewis Found., 1963; Disting. Citizen award Ill. St. Andrew Soc., 1974; Decision Maker of Yr. award Am. Statis. Assn., 1974; Marketer of Yr. award AMA, 1976; Found. award Kidney Found., 1981; Chicagoan of Yr. Chgo. Boys Club, 1981; Bus. Statesman of Yr. award Harvard Bus. Sch. Club Chgo., 1983; Achievement award Med. Tech. Services, 1983; Disting. Fellows award Internat. Ctr. for Artificial Organs and Transplantations, 1982; Chgo. Civic award DePaul U., 1986; recognized for pioneering work Health Industry Mfrs. Assn., 1981; inductedJr. Achievement Chgo. Bus. Hall of Fame, 1986. Mem. Am. Pharm. Mfrs. Assn. (past pres.), Ill. Mfrs. Assn. (past pres.), Pharm. Mfrs. Assn. (past chmn., award for spl. distinction leadership 1981), Phi Beta Kappa, Sigma Xi, Phi Delta Phi. Clubs: Chicago (past pres.), Commonwealth, Mid-Am., Commercial, Indian Hill, Casino (Chgo.); Old Elm (Lake Forest, Ill.); Seminole, Everglades, Bath & Tennis (Fla.); University, Links (N.Y.C.). General corporate. Home: 40 Devonshire Ln Kenilworth IL 60043 Office: Baxter Travenol Labs Inc One Baxter Pkwy Deerfield IL 60015

GRAHAM, W(ILLIAM) THOMAS, III, lawyer; b. Cleve., Nov. 9, 1950; s. William Thomas Jr. and Ilah M. (Kotts) G.; m. Teresa Marie Pillarelli, Oct. 7, 1984. BA, Johns Hopkins U., 1973; JD, U. Toledo, 1976. Bar: Mich. 1976, U.S. Dist. Ct. (ea. dist.) Mich. 1976, Ohio 1977, U.S. Dist. Ct. (no. dist.) Ohio 1982. Assoc. Krawetz & Spiros, Lambertville, Mich., 1976-80; ptnr. Lennard & Graham, Monroe, Mich., 1980—; asst. atty. Bedford Twp., Mich., 1976-80, atty., 1985—; atty. Erie Twp., Mich., 1982—. Mem. ABA, Mich. Bar Assn., Ohio Bar Assn., Monroe County Bar Assn., Mich. Trial Lawyers Assn. Presbyterian. Local government, Probate, Personal injury. Home: 7581 Dartmouth Dr Lambertville MI 48144 Office: Lennard & Graham 222 Washington St Monroe MI 48161

GRAHAM, WILLIAM THOMAS, lawyer; b. Waynesboro, Va., Oct. 24, 1933; s. James Monroe and Margaret Virginia (Goodwin) G.; m. Kent Hill, Feb. 1, 1958; children: Ashton Cannon, William Thomas Jr. AB in Econs., Duke U., 1956; JD, U. Va., 1962. Bar: N.C. 1962, Va. 1962, D.C. 1970, U.S. Supreme Ct. 1970. Assoc. Craige, Brawley and predecessor firms, Winston-Salem, N.C., 1962-64; ptnr. Craige, Brawley, Horton & Graham, Winston-Salem, 1965-69; assoc. gen. counsel HUD, Washington, 1969-70, Billings & Graham, Winston-Salem, 1971-75; judge N.C. Superior Ct., 1975-79; ptnr. Graham, Glenn, Crumpler & Habegger, Winston-Salem, 1979-81; sole practice Winston-Salem, 1981—. Chmn. Forsyth County Reps., Winston-Salem, 1966-69, 73-75, Forsyth County Bd. Elections, Winston-Salem, 1985-86. Served with U.S. Army, 1957-58. Methodist. Clubs: Old Town, Piedmont (Winston-Salem). Avocation: travel. General practice. Home: 1261 Kent Pl Winston-Salem NC 27104 Office: 102 S Cherry St Winston-Salem NC 27101

GRAHAME, ORVILLE FRANCIS BOOTH, lawyer, business executive; b. Palo, Iowa, Apr. 2, 1904; s. Samuel G. and Dawn (Booth) G.; m. Paula

Patton, Nov. 3, 1923; 1 dau., Sarah Jane (Cairns). B.A., U. Iowa, 1925; J.D., 1929. Bar: Iowa 1929, N.Y. 1932, Mass. 1940, U.S. Supreme Ct. 1954. Assoc. Guardian Life Ins. Co., 1929-39, asst. sec., 1936-39; cons., former v.p., dir. gen. counsel Paul Revere Life Ins. Co., Worcester, Mass., Paul Revere Variable Annuity Ins. Co., Paul Revere Corp., Avco Corp. and several affiliated cos.; dir. Thompson Steel Co., Inc.; corporator Worcester Devel. Corp., Worcester County Instn. for Savs.; Mem. nat. adv. com. White House Conf. Aging, 1959-61, tech. com. on income, 1971-72; Exec. com. Health and Accident Underwriters Conf., 1954-55; author, sponsor concept of guaranteed renewable adjustable premium accident and sickness ins., 1948; mem. Mass. Pension Study Commn., 1953-55, Mass. Variable Annuity Study Commn., 1956-60, Zoning Appeals Bd., Worcester, 1958-63; mem. com. on employment and retirement Nat. Council Aging; mem. U.S. Bus. Com. for Tax Reduction, 1963-64; lectr. N.Y. Coll. Ins., 1938-39. Author: (with others) The Life Insurance Contract, 1953; also legal articles.; Mem. editorial bd. Insurance Decisions, 1933-37. Bd. dirs. Worcester Red Cross, 1957-63, 66-74, U. Iowa Found., 1969-74, Iowa Law Sch. Found., 1970-73; Mem. N.Y. County Rep. com., 1934-36, George Bush com., 1987—; organizer Thomas E. Dewey for Pres. Club, 1940; asst. mgr. campaign Lt. Gov. S.G. Whittier, 1952, 56; coordinator campaign Lt. Gov. E.L. Richardson, 1964. Served with inf. U.S. Army Res., 1925-39. Recipient Distinguished Service award U. Iowa, 1964; donor U. Iowa Law Sch. Orville and Paula Grahame Courtyard, 1986. Fellow Ins. Inst. Am.; mem. ABA, Mass., Worcester County bar assns., AAAS, Assn. Bar City N.Y., N.Y. County Lawyers Assn., Acad. Polit. Sci., Am.-Scottish Found., Nat. Hist. Soc., Nat. Trust Historic Preservation, Assn. Nat. Archives, Assn. Life Counsel, Ins. Econs. Soc. Am. (pres. 1954-55), Worcester Hist. Soc., Am. Bar Found., Mass. Bar Found., Worcester Music Festival Assn., Am. Arbitration Assn. (arbitrator), Sierra Club, Newcomen Soc., Phi Alpha Delta, Order of Coif. Republican. Unitarian. Club: Worcester. Lodges: Mason, Shriner, Rotary. General corporate, Insurance. Home: 6 Bancroft Tower Rd Worcester MA 01609

GRALEN, DONALD JOHN, lawyer; b. Oak Park, Ill., Mar. 18, 1933; s. Oliver Edwin and Rosalie Marie (Buskens) G.; m. Jane Walsh, Dec. 29, 1956; children: Alana, Mark, Paul, Ann, Sarah. B.S., Loyola U., Chgo., 1956; J.D. with honors, Loyola U., 1957. Bar: Ill. 1958. Assoc. Sidley & Austin, Chgo., 1959-66; ptnr. Sidley & Austin, 1967—. Co-author (chpt. in book). Trustee Village LaGrange, Ill., 1973-77; chmn. LaGrange Zoning Bd., 1971-73, LaGrange Econ. Devel. Com., 1982; bd. dirs. Carson Pirie Scott Found., Chgo., 1980—, Jr. Achievement, 1978—, Met. Housing and Planning Council, 1982—, Community Family Service and Mental Health Assn., 1983-86. Served to 1st lt. U.S. Army, 1957-59. Mem. Chgo. Bar Assn., Ill. State Bar Assn., ABA, Am. Coll. Real Estate Lawyers. Clubs: Univ, Law; Legal (Chgo.); LaGrange Country. Real property. Home: 338 S Waiola LaGrange IL 60525 Office: Sidley & Austin 1 First Nat Plaza Chicago IL 60603

GRALNEK, DONALD D., lawyer; b. Chgo., July 24, 1945; m. Ann Gralnek, Apr. 15, 1972. BA, Stanford U., 1967; JD, U. Calif., Berkeley, 1970, M in City Planning, 1971. Bar: Calif. 1971. Ptnr. Ball, Hunt, Hart, Brown, Baerwitz, Long Beach, Calif., 1975-79, Rogers & Wells, Long Beach, 1979-83, Jones, Day, REavis & Pogue, Los Angeles, 1983—. Mem. ABA, Calif. Bar Assn., Los Angeles County Bar Assn., Urban Land Inst., Environ. Law Inst. Real property, Environment. Office: Jones Day Reavis & Pogue 333 S Grand Ave Suite 1400 Los Angeles CA 90071

GRAMES, CONAN PAUL, lawyer; b. Cedar City, Utah, Dec. 21, 1946; s. Lloyd Marion and JaLene (Heywood) G.; m. Cynthia Lynn Homer, May 30, 1972; children: Kerilee, Allison, Chase, Lauren, Christian. BA with honors, U. Utah, 1972; JD, Harvard U., 1975. Bar: Calif. 1975, U.S. Dist. Ct. (no. dist.) Calif. 1975. Assoc. Baker & McKenzie, San Francisco, 1975-76, Law Office of Tokyo Aoyama, 1976-82; ptnr. Baker & McKenzie, Tokyo, 1980-82; counsel Pacific div. Bristol-Myers Co., Tokyo, 1982-85; v.p., counsel Asia and Australasia div. Bristol-Myers Co., N.Y.C., 1985—. Coach Bantam Baseball, 1986. Served to ensign USAR, 1974-80. R.C. Gibbs scholar, 1973. Mem. ABA, Am. Corp. Council Assn., Japan Soc. N.Y., Am. C. of C. (chmn. 1981, President's Leadership award 1981), Phi Kappa Phi. Mormon. Avocations: tennis, trumpet, Japanese language. Private international, General corporate. Office: Bristol-Myers Co 345 Park Ave Suite 4170 New York NY 10154

GRAMLICH, CHARLES J., lawyer; b. Springfield, Ill., July 20, 1938; s. Harold J. and Caroline F. (Jallas) G.; m. Corinne M. Lee, Dec. 31, 1978; children—Ann, Brant, Libby. B.S., Bradley U., 1963; J.D., John Marshall Law Sch., 1966. Bar: Ill. 1967. Asst. state's atty. Sangamon County, Ill., 1967-68; state's atty. Edgar County, Ill., 1968-70; assoc. Pefferle, Maddox and Gramlich, Springfield, Ill., 1970-78; sole practice, Charles J. Gramlich Law Offices, P.C., Springfield, 1978-80; ptnr. Gramlich and Morse, P.C., Springfield, 1980-85; pres. Gramlich Law Offices, P.C., 1985—. Trustee Springfield Park Dist., 1976-80. Mem. Ill. Bar Assn., Sangamon County Bar Assn. (past pres.), Ill. Trial Lawyers Assn., Assn. Trial Lawyers Am. Republican. Roman Catholic. Personal injury, State civil litigation, Insurance. Office: 227 S 7th St Suite 204 Springfield IL 62701

GRAMM, JOANN LEIGH, lawyer; b. N.Y.C., Mar. 22, 1950; d. Vincent Joseph and Frances Adeline (Desio) G. BA, CUNY, 1975; postgrad. Law Sch. St. John's U., 1976-77; JD, Rutgers U., 1979; LLM in Taxation, Temple U., 1983. Bar: N.J. 1979, U.S. Dist. Ct. N.J. 1979, Pa. 1983. Law clk. Superior Ct. N.J., Atlantic City, 1979-80; assoc. Tort, Jacobs, Gross, Rosenberger & Todd, Atlantic City, 1980-82, Vasser, Spitalnick, Bloom, Mazin & Stein, P.A., Northfield, N.J., 1982-84; counsel Corbel & Co., Jacksonville, Fla., 1984-85; sole practice, Northfield, N.J., 1985—. Mem. N.J. Bar Assn., ABA, Atlantic County Assn. Women Lawyers, Phi Alpha Theta. Democrat. Roman Catholic. Pension, profit-sharing, and employee benefits, Probate. Office: 1200 Mill Rd PO Box 12 Northfield NJ 08225

GRAMMER, DAVID ALLEN, JR., lawyer; b. Albuquerque, Sept. 28, 1926; s. David A. Sr. and Allie Maurine (Parker) G.; m. Mary Elizabeth Johnson, Sept. 27, 1952; children: David A. III, Margaret, Mary Katherine, Patricia. BBA, Tex. U., 1947; JD, George Washington U., 1953. Bar: N.Mex. 1953, U.S. Dist. Ct. N.Mex. 1953. Pres. Grammer & Grammer P.A. and predecessor firms, Albuquerque, 1952—. Served with USN, 1944-46, as lt. Signal Corps., USN, 1949-51. Mem. Albuquerque Bar Assn. (pres. 1968), Assn. Trial Lawyers Am. Republican. Episcopalian. Club: Albuquerque Lawyers (pres. 1970). Lodge: Elks. Contracts commercial, Real property, Probate. Office: Grammer & Grammer PA 501 Tijeras NW Albuquerque NM 87102

GRAMMER, ELISA JOAN, lawyer; b. Dover, N.J., Feb. 5, 1952; d. Frank Allen and Wilma Elizabeth (Horster) G.; m. Fredric Davis Chanania, May 17, 1981; 1 child, Andrew Grammer Chanania. AB summa cum laude, Lafayette Coll., 1973; JD, Coll. of William and Mary, 1976; LLM with highest honors, George Washington U., 1980. Bar: Va. 1976, D.C. 1976, U.S. Ct. Appeals (5th and D.C. cirs.), U.S. Supreme Ct. 1983. Atty. U.S. Gen. Acctg. Office, Washington, 1976-78, Nuclear Regulatory Commn., Washington, 1978-80; atty., analyst U.S. Dept. Energy, Washington, 1980; assoc. Pierson, Semmes & Finley, Washington, 1981-84, ptnr., 1985-86; ptnr. Baller, Hammett, Williams & Grammer P.C., Washington, 1987—. Mem. ABA, Fed. Bar Assn., Fed. Energy Bar Assn., Women in Govt. Relations, Phi Beta Kappa. Administrative and regulatory, FERC practice, Environment. Office: Baller Hammett Williams & Grammer PC 1726 M St NW Suite 1001 Washington DC 20036

GRANADE, CALLIE VIRGINIA SMITH, lawyer; b. Lexington, Va., Mar. 7, 1950; d. Milton Hannibal and Callie Dougherty (Rives) Smith; m. Fred King Granade, Oct. 9, 1976; children: Taylor Rives, Milton Smith, Joseph Kee. BA, Hollins Coll., 1972; JD, U. Tex., 1975. Bar: Tex. 1975, Ala. 1976, U.S. Ct. Appeals (5th cir.) 1976, U.S. Dist. Ct. (so. dist.) Ala. 1977, U.S. Supreme Ct. 1980, U.S. Ct. Appeals (11th cir.) 1981. Law clk. to chief judge U.S. Ct. Appeals (5th cir.), Montgomery, Ala., 1975-76; asst. U.S. atty. U.S. Dept. Justice, Mobile, Ala., 1977—. Mem. ABA, Fed. Bar Assn., Ala. State Bar Assn., Tex. State Bar Assn., Mobile Bar Assn. Presbyterian. Criminal, Federal civil litigation. Home: PO Box 469 Bay Minette AL 36507 Office: US Attys Office PO Drawer E Mobile AL 36601

GRANADE, FRED KING, lawyer; b. Mobile, Ala., Mar. 3, 1950; s. Joe C. and Lucille (Williams) G.; m. Callie Virginia Smith, Oct. 9, 1976; children: Taylor Rives, Milton Smith, Joseph Kee. BA, Auburn U., 1972; JD, Washignton and Lee U., 1975. Bar: Ala. 1975, Fla. 1976, U.S. Dist. Ct. (so. dist.) Ala, 1977, U.S. Supreme Ct. 1979, U.S. Ct. Appeals (11th cir.) 1981. Law clk. to presiding justice Ala. Ct. of Criminal Appeals, Montgomery, 1975-76; assoc. Stone & Partin, Bay Minette, Ala., 1977-81; ptnr. Stone, Granade, Crosby & Blackburn, Bay Minette, 1981—. Mem. Ala. Bar Assn., Fla. Bar Assn., Baldwin County Bar Assn. Presbyterian. Office: Stone Granade Crosby & Blackburn 11 Pine St Bay Minette AL 36507

GRANAT, RICHARD STUART, lawyer, educator; b. N.Y.C., Nov. 11, 1940; s. George and Judith G.; m. Nancy Ruth Wruble, Dec. 23, 1962; children—Lisa, Hilary, Peter, David. B.A., Lehigh U., 1962; J.D. (Harlan Fiske Stone scholar), Columbia U., 1965. Bar: Md. 1966, D.C. 1977. Asst. counsel U.S. OEO, Washington, 1965-67, dir. housing programs 1967-78; asst. dir. Model Cities Agy., Office of Mayor, Balt., 1968-69; dir. Community Planning and Evaluation Inst. 1970-71; pres. Univ. Research Corp. Mgmt. Services Corp., 1970-77; sole practice, Washington, 1969—; pres. Automated Legal Systems, Inc., Phila., 1984—; dir. M.A. in Legal Studies Program, Antioch Sch. Law, 1979-83; pres., chmn. bd. Ctr. for Legal Studies, Washington, 1979—; pres. Inst. Paralegal Tng., Inc., Phila., 1982—. Chmn. bd. Ctr. Sch., Rockville, Md., pres. Nat. Ctr. for Edn. Testing Inc., 1986—, Inst. for Employee Benfits Tng., 1986—. Mem. ABA, Md. Bar Assn. Civil rights, Legal education, Jurisprudence. Home: 606 Greythorne Rd Wynnewood PA 19096 Office: 1926 Arch St Philadelphia PA 19103

GRAND, RICHARD D., lawyer; b. Danzig, Feb. 20, 1930; came to U.S., 1939, naturalized, 1944; s. Morris and Rena G.; m. Marcia Kosta, Jan. 27, 1952; 1 dau., Cindy. B.A., N.Y. U., 1951; J.D., U. Ariz., 1958. Bar: Ariz. bar 1958, Calif. bar 1973, U.S. Supreme Ct. bar 1973. Dep. atty. Pima County, Ariz., 1958-59; pvt. practice trial law Tucson, 1959—; founder, 1st pres. Inner Circle Advocates, 1972-75; founder 1966; now chmn. Richard Grand Found. Legal Research and Edn. Contbr. articles to legal publs. Mem. bd. visitors Ariz. State U. Law Sch.; mem. nat. adv. bd. Touro Law Sch. Recipient citation of honor Lawyers Coop. Pub. Co., 1964. Fellow Am. Acad. Forensic Scis., Internat. Soc. Barristers; asso. mem. Internat. Med. Soc. Paraplegia, Am. Coll. Legal Medicine; mem. Assn. Trial Lawyers Am. (gov. 1964-66), ABA (vice-chmn. com. govtl. liability law, sect. of tort and ins. practice 1986-87), Pima County Bar Assn., N.Y. State, Calif., , San Francisco, Los Angeles trial lawyers assns., Am. Bd. Trial Advs., Brit. Acad. Forensic Scis., Lawyers Club San Francisco, President's Club of U. Ariz. Personal injury. Address: 127 W Franklin St Tucson AZ 85701

GRANEY, MICHAEL PROCTOR, lawyer; b. Ashland, Ky., June 2, 1943; s. Mike Latelle and Irene (Sparks) G.; m. Kathleen Marie Riell, Oct. 15, 1980; children: Noelle, Michael W. BA, Duke U., 1965; JD, Ohio State U., 1968. Bar: Ohio 1968, D.C. 1976, U.S. Supreme Ct. 1976. Assoc. Porter, Stanley, Treffinger & Platt, Columbus, Ohio, 1968-74; ptnr. Porter, Stanley, Platt & Arthur, Columbus, 1974-80, Simpson, Thacher & Bartlett, Columbus, 1980—. Mem. ABA, D.C. Bar Assn., Ohio Bar Assn., Columbus Bar Assn., Franklin County Law Library Assn. (trustee). Administrative and regulatory, Antitrust, Federal civil litigation. Office: Simpson Thacher & Bartlett 1 Riverside Plaza Columbus OH 43215

GRANGE, GEORGE ROBERT, II, lawyer; b. Alexandria, Va., Apr. 14, 1947; s. George Robert and Lucille (Bell) G.; m. Kathy McPeek, Aug. 21, 1971; children—Stephen John, George Robert III, Sarah Ruth, Peter Mark. B.A. with honors, U. Va., 1969; postgrad. Div. Sch., Yale U., 1970-71; J.D., Harvard U., 1974. Bar: Mass. 1975, D.C. 1975, U.S. Supreme Ct. 1980, U.S. Dist. Ct. D.C. 1984, U.S. Ct. Appeals (D.C. cir.) 1984. Assoc. Zuggert, Scoutt & Rasenberger, Washington, 1975-77; ptnr. Gammon & Grange, Washington, 1977—; dir. East-West Services, Washington. Bd. dirs. Evang. Council for Fin. Accountability, Washington, 1980—; seminar speaker Christian Legal Soc., Christian Ministries Mgmt. Assn. and other non-profit groups. Mem. Christian Legal Soc. (nat. bd. dirs. 1983—), D.C. Bar Assn., ABA, Fed. Communications Bar Assn., Phi Beta Kappa. Republican. Administrative and regulatory, Corporate taxation, Nonprofit, communications.. Home: 18828 Cross Country Ln Gaithersburg MD 20879

GRANIER, KIRK RAYMOND, lawyer; b. Big Spring, Tex., Apr. 8, 1955; s. Vernon R. and Sylvia (de Bautte) G.; m. Jeannine Shoemaker, May 21, 1983. BA, Nicholls State U., 1972-76; JD, Loyola U., New Orleans, 1976-79. Bar: La. 1979, U.S. Ct. Mil. Appeals 1980, U.S. Dist. Cts. (ea. and mid.) La. 1984. Commd. as judge adv. USAF, Whiteman AFB, Mo., 1979, advanced through grades to capt., 1979-83; assoc. Fisher Fisher & Irby, Boutte, La., 1983-85; sole practice Luling, La., 1985—; judge adv. 834 combat support group USAFR, Hurlburt AFB, Fla., 1983—. Mem. La. Bar Assn., La. Trial Lawyer's Assn. Republican. Catholic. Lodges: KC (Luling), Kiwanis (com. chmn. West St. Charles chpt.). Personal injury, Criminal, State civil litigation. Home: 304 Maryland Dr Luling LA 70070 Office: 308 S River Rd Luling LA 70070

GRANNIS, VANCE BURNS, lawyer; b. South St. Paul, Sept. 3, 1908; s. David L. and Macha Lucinda (Vance) G.; m. Margrete Louise, June 7, 1934; children: Vance B., Macha Joy, Linda. BA, Carleton Coll., 1929; LLD, U. Minn., 1932. Bar: Minn. 1932, U.S. Supreme Ct. 1965, U.S. Dist. Ct. Minn., U.S. Ct. Appeals. Ptnr. Grannis and Grannis, South St. Paul, 1932-75; pres. Grannis and Grannis, P.A., 1975-80, Grannis, Grannis, Farrell and Knutson, 1980—; dir. Twin City Testing and Engring. Lab., Inc., St. Paul. Bd. dirs. Dakota County Ctr. for Arts, 1981-82, Dakota County Referral and Transp. for Srs., 1978-82. Mem. Minn Bar Assn. (sr. counselor 1982), U. Minn. Alumni Assn. (pres. 1960-61), South St. Paul C. of C. (pres. 1948). Clubs: St. Paul Athletic, Pool and Yacht (St. Paul); Silver Bay Country, Southview Country (South St. Paul). General practice. Office: 403 Northwestern Bank Bldg 161 N Concord Exchange S Saint Paul MN 55075

GRANOFF, GAIL PATRICIA, lawyer; b. Phila., July 25, 1952; s. Jerome Claymont and Jean (Kessler) G. A.B., Temple U., 1973; J.D., U. Pa., 1976. Bar: Pa. 1976, U.S. Dist. Ct. (ea. dist.) Pa. 1977, U.S. Ct. Appeals (3d cir.) 1977, U.S. Supreme Ct. 1981. Law clk. U.S. Ct. Appeals, 3d Circuit, Phila., 1976-77; assoc. Pepper Hamilton & Scheetz, Phila., 1977-84; counsel Rohm and Haas Co., Phila., 1984-86, sr. counsel, 1987—. Mem. ABA, Phila. Bar Assn. (exec. com. young lawyers sect. 1983—, sec. 1984—, commn. on jud. selection and retention investigative div. 1985—), Am. Corp. Counsel Assn. General corporate, Federal civil litigation, Antitrust. Office: Rohm and Haas Co Independence Hall West Philadelphia PA 19105

GRANT, CHARLES RANDALL, JR., judge; b. Washington, Mar. 30, 1945; s. Charles Randall and June (Morrill) G.; m. Joanne Mierzwinski, Apr. 10, 1971; 1 child, Kathryn. AB, Earlham Coll., 1967; JD, Washington U., 1970. Bar: D.C. 1972, Md. 1972. Adjudicator, land law examiner bur. land mgmt. U.S. Dept. Interior, Silver Spring, Md., 1970-73; atty., advisor bd. land appeals U.S. Dept. Interior, Arlington, Va., 1975-81, adminstrv. justice bd. land appeals, 1981—; sole practice Montgomery County, Md., 1973-75. Mem. ABA (natural resources sect.), Kensington-Wheaton Jaycees (pres. 1975-76). Unitarian. Avocations: jogging, fishing, tennis. Oil and gas leasing, Environment, Administrative and regulatory. Home: 8700 Camille Dr Potomac MD 20854 Office: US Dept Interior Office of Hearings and Appeals Arlington VA 22203

GRANT, EUGENE L., lawyer; b. Twin Falls, Idaho, May 11, 1953; s. Junior Lavar Grant and Helen Louise (Hart) Hyde; m. Janet K. Green, Aug. 16, 1974; children: Daniel, Amber, Jay, Kyle. BA in History with honors, U. Oregon, 1976, JD, 1979. Bar: Oreg. 1979, U.S. Dist. Ct. Oreg. 1979. From assoc. to ptnr. Schwabe, Williamson & Wyatt, Portland, Oregon, 1979—. Mem. advisory bd. Columbia Pacific council Boy Scouts Am., Oregon, 1985—; vice chmn. Wy-East district Boy Scouts Am., Portland, 1986—. Recipient Eagle Scout award Boy Scouts Am., 1968. Mem. ABA, Oreg. Bar Assn. (chmn. real estate leg. com. 1984-85, exec. com. real estate and land use sect. 1985—, speaker continuing legal edn. programs 1984—), Portland Jaycees (legal counsel, bd. dirs. 1980-82), Oreg. Jaycees (legal counsel, bd. dirs. 1902-82), Order of Coif. Republican. Mormon. Avocations: reading, backpacking, camping, youth work. Real property, General corporate, Landlord-tenant. Home: 8420 SE Clatsop Ct Portland OR 97266 Office: Schwabe Williamson & Wyatt 1211 SW 5th Portland OR 97204

GRANT, KARLEEN ANN, lawyer; b. Bethesda, Md., Jan. 20, 1950; d. Thomas Vincent and Caroline (Reiser) G. Student, U. Pitts., 1967-69; BS, U. Miami, 1971, JD cum laude, 1981; MA, Pepperdine U., 1978. Bar: Fla. 1981, U.S. Dist. Ct. (so. dist.) Fla. 1981, U.S. Ct. Appeals (11th cir.) 1981. Tchr. Monroe County Sch. Bd., Key West, Fla., 1971-72; corp. counsel Intervel Internat., Coral Gables, Fla., 1981; ptnr. Edwards & Grant, South Miami, Fla., 1981-82; div. counsel Burger King Corp., Miami, 1982-85; assoc. Stuzin & Camner P.A., Miami, 1985—. Bd. dirs. Miami Ballet Co., South Miami, 1985—. Served to capt. USAF, 1972-78. Mem. ABA, Fla. State Bar Assn., Dade County Bar Assn., Key West Panhellenic Alumni Assn. Roman Catholic. Avocation: classical ballet. Real property. Home: 8201 SW 81st Ct Miami FL 33143 Office: Stuzin & Camner PA 999 Brickell Ave Suite 400 Miami FL 33131

GRANT, LOUIS Z., lawyer, lecturer; b. Chgo., Oct. 17, 1907; s. Morris and Rebecca (Spector) G.; m. Ruth Kaplan, June 16, 1935; children—Burton, Cary. B.A., DePaul U., 1929; J.D., John Marshall Law Sch., Chgo., 1932. Bar: Ill. 1933. Sole practice, Chgo., 1933-69; ptnr. Burton F. Grant Ltd., and predecessor, Chgo., 1968—; lectr. matrimonial law; cons., reconcilor in domestic relations; founder, mem. Conciliation Cts. of Cook County (Ill.); acting judge U. Chgo. Moot Ct. Republican jud. candidate, 1958; founder Knesset Israel Nusach Sfard Congregation; incorporator Our Children of Cook County. Recipient award Knesset Israel Nusach Sfard Congregation, Chgo., 1955. Mem. Assn. Conciliation Cts., Am. Acad. Matrimonial Lawyers (founder 1965, cert. of recognition 1974), Decalogue Soc. Lawyers, North Suburban Bar Assn., N.W. Suburban Bar Assn., Chgo. Bar Assn. (matrimonial com.), Ill. Bar Assn., ABA (matrimonial com., conciliation commn., jud. adminstrv. div.). Republican. Jewish. Author: Child Custody and Child Visitation, 1945. Family and matrimonial. Office: 180 N La Salle St Suite 2400 Chicago IL 60601

GRANT, M. DUNCAN, lawyer; b. Madison, Wis., Apr. 22, 1950; s. David Evans and Margaret Jane (Bloomfield) G.; m. Marcia Joan Cox, Sept. 18, 1970 (div. Dec. 1975); 1 child, Thomas David. AB, Princeton U., 1972; JD, U. Pa., 1975. Bar: Pa. 1975, U.S. Dist. Ct. (ea. dist.) Pa. 1976, U.S. Ct. Appeals (3d cir.) 1977, U.S. Supreme Ct. 1980, U.S. Ct. Appeals (10th cir.) 1986. Law clk. to judge U.S. Ct. Appeals (3d cir.), Phila., 1975-76; assoc. Pepper, Hamilton & Scheetz, Phila., 1976-83, ptnr., 1983—. Am. fellow Salzburg Seminar, 1986. Mem. ABA, Pa. Bar Assn., Phila. Bar Assn. Democrat. Avocations: baseball, photography, jazz. Federal civil litigation, Antitrust, Libel. Home: 221 W Allens Ln Philadelphia PA 19119 Office: Pepper Hamilton & Scheetz 123 S Broad St Philadelphia PA 19109-1083

GRANT, MERWIN DARWIN, lawyer; b. Safford, Ariz., May 7, 1944; s. Darwin Dewey and Erma (Whiting) G.; m. Charlotte Richey, June 27, 1969; children: Brandon, Taggart, Christian. BA in Econs., Brigham Young U., 1968; JD, Duke U., 1971. Bar: Ariz. 1971, U.S. Dist. Ct. Ariz., U.S. Dist. Ct. (we. dist.) Tex., U.S. Ct. Appeals (5th, 8th, 9th and 10th cir.), U.S. Tax Ct., U.S. Supreme Ct. Sole practice Phoenix, 1977—; ptnr. Beus, Gilbert, Wake & Morrill, Phoenix, 1984—. Founding mem. Ronald Reagan Republican Task Force, Washington, 1984—; pres., bd. dirs. Golden Gate Settlement, Phoenix, 1975—. Mem. ABA (tax section), Assn. Trial Lawyers Am. Lodge: Kiwanis (bd. dirs. Phoenix chpt. 1972-79). Federal civil litigation, State civil litigation, Private international. Home: 4950 E Red Rock Phoenix AZ 85018 Office: Beus, Gilbert, Wake & Morrill 3300 N Central Ave Phoenix AZ 85012

GRANT, PATRICK ALEXANDER, lawyer, state representative; b. Denver, Nov. 14, 1945; s. Edwin Hendrie and Mary Belle (McIntyre) G.; m. Carla Clyde Yancey, Aug. 16, 1975; children: Mary Cameron, Sara Mansur, Alexis Hendrie. BA, Colgate U., 1967; MBA, Denver U., 1973; JD, Drake U., 1976. Bar: Colo. 1977. Law clk. to judge Colo. Ct. Appeals, Denver, 1976-77; assoc. Grant, McHendrie, Haines & Crouse, P.C., Denver, 1977-83, ptnr., v.p., 1984—, also bd. dirs.; state rep. Colo. Gen. Assembly, Denver, 1984—; mem. Colo. com. elected ofcls. for Soviet Jewry, Denver, 1985—, Colo. spl. task force tort liability and ins., Denver, 1985. Mem. Denver Community Mental Health Commn., 1985-86; exec. council, planning com. St. Joseph Hosp., Denver, 1985—; vestry person, jr. warden St. Barnabas Parish, Denver, 1979-84. Served as lt. USNR, 1967-71, Vietnam. Gates Found. fellow, 1985; recipient Outstanding Alumni award Kent Denver Country Day Sch., 1986; named one of Outstanding Young Men in Am. U.S. Jaycees, 1980. Mem. ABA, Colo. Bar Assn., Denver Bar Assn., Cherry Creek Improvement Assn. (former v.p., bd. dirs. 1981—), Western Stock Show Assn. (exec. com., bd. dirs. 1984—). Republican. Episcopalian. Club: Denver. Avocations: squash, wood chopping. Environment, Real property, Transportation. Home: 100 High St Denver CO 80218 Office: Grant McHendrie Haines & Crouse PC 1700 Lincoln St Suite 3000 Denver CO 80202

GRANT, PATRICK GERARD, lawyer; b. Shreveport, La., June 1, 1954; s. Henry Lowry and Patricia McIntosh (Nelson) G.; m. Rebecca Suzanne Rodgers, Feb. 7, 1981. BA in English, La. State U., 1972-76, JD, 1976-79. Bar: La. 1979, Tex. 1980. Atty. Dresser Industries, Inc., Houston, 1979-84, The M.W. Kellogg Co., Houston, 1984-86; asst. gen. counsel CRS Sirrine, Inc., Houston, 1986—; v.p., gen. counsel Grant Investments, Inc., Houston, 1986—. Mem. Houston Heights Assn., 1980, Vol. Lawyers and Accts. for The Arts, Houston, 1984. Mem. Tex. Bar Assn., Houston Bar Assn., La. State Bar Assn. Republican. Roman Catholic. Avocations: hunting, fishing, music. Contracts commercial, Private international, Real property. Office: CRS Sirrine Inc 1177 W Loop Smith Houston TX 77227

GRANT, ROBERT ALLEN, judge; b. Marshall County, Ind., July 31, 1905; s. Everett F. and Margaret E. (Hatfield) G.; m. Margaret Anne McLaren, Sept. 17, 1933; children—Robert A., Margaret Ann Soderberg. A.B., U. Notre Dame, 1928, J.D., 1930. Bar: Ind. bar 1930, U.S. Supreme Ct. bar 1940. Practiced in South Bend, Ind.; dep. pros. atty. St. Joseph County, 1935-36; mem. 76th-80th congresses from 3d Ind. Dist.; U.S. dist. judge No. Dist. Ind., 1957—, chief judge, 1961-72, sr. judge, 1972—; apptd. to Temp. Emergency Ct. Appeals U.S., 1976. Trustee U. Indpls., 1976—; mem. nat. council representing No. Ind., Boy Scouts Am., 1967. Mem. Am., Ind. bar assns. SAR. Republican. Methodist. Clubs: Masons (33 deg.), K.T., Shriners, Rotary, Elks, Order DeMolay (internat. supreme council, past grand master), Columbia (Indpls.); Summit (South Bend); Union League (Chgo.). Home: 98 Schellinger Sq Mishawaka IN 46544 Office: U S Dist Ct 308 Fed Bldg 204 S Main St South Bend IN 46601

GRANT, STEPHEN ALLEN, lawyer; b. N.Y.C., Nov. 4, 1938; s. Benton H. and Irene A. Grant; m. Anne. B. Grant, Feb. 11, 1961 (div. Nov. 1975); children: Stephen, Katharine, Michael; m. Anne-Marie Laignel, Dec. 8, 1975; children: Natalie, Elizabeth, Alexandra. AB, Yale U., 1960; LLB, Columbia U., 1965. Bar: N.Y. 1965, U.S. Supreme Ct. 1969. Law clk. to judge U.S. Ct. Appeals (2d cir.), N.Y.C., 1965-66; assoc. Sullivan & Cromwell, N.Y.C., 1966-73; ptnr. Sullivan & Cromwell, N.Y.C., 1973—. Served to lt. USN, 1960-62. Mem. ABA, N.Y. State Bar Assn., Assn. of Bar of City of N.Y., Council Fgn. Relations. Clubs: Down Town, Links. Private international, Securities, General corporate. Home: 1021 Park Ave New York NY 10028 Office: Sullivan & Cromwell 125 Broad St New York NY 10004

GRANT, SUSAN IRENE, lawyer; b. N.Y.C., Apr. 27, 1953; d. Walter Arnold and Beatrice L. (Thalheimer) G. BA, NYU, 1974; JD, Columbia U., 1977. Bar: N.Y. 1978, U.S. Dist. Ct. (ea. dist.) N.Y. 1978. Assoc. Law Offices of Rita Eredics, Esq., Flushing, N.Y., 1977-78; staff atty. The Dreyfus Corp., N.Y.C., 1978-85; asst. gen. counsel Prudential-Bache Securities Inc., N.Y.C., 1985—, asst. v.p., 1986—. Mem. ABA, N.Y. State Bar Assn., Am. Corp. Counsel Assn. Securities, General corporate. Home: 106-15 Queens Blvd Forest Hills NY 11375 Office: Prudential Bache Securities Inc One Seaport Plaza New York NY 10292

GRANT, WALTER MATTHEWS, lawyer, communications company executive; b. Winchester, Ky., Mar. 30, 1945; s. Raymond Russell and Mary Mitchell (Rees) G.; m. Ann Carol Straus, Aug. 5, 1967; children—Walter Matthews II, Jean Ann, Raymond Russell II. A.B.J., U. Ky., Lexington, 1967; J.D., Vanderbilt U., Nashville, 1971. Bar: Ga. 1971. Assoc. Alston & Bird, Atlanta, 1971-76, ptnr., 1976-83; v.p., gen. counsel, sec. Contel Corp. (formerly Continental Telecom Inc.), Atlanta, 1983—. Editor-in-chief Vanderbilt Law Rev., 1970-71, Ga. State Bar Jour., 1979-82. Recipient

Founder's Medal Vanderbilt Law Sch., 1971. Mem. State Bar Ga., ABA, Am. Soc. Corp. Secs., Atlanta Bar Assn. Baptist. Clubs: Commerce, Lawyers (Atlanta). General corporate. Home: 1422 Hanover West Dr NW Atlanta GA 30327 Office: Contel Corp 245 Perimeter Center Pkwy NE Atlanta GA 30348

GRASLIE, THOMAS ERIC, lawyer; b. Rapid City, S.D., Oct. 28, 1950; s. Orville Thomas and Helen Maxine (Knipfer) G. BA, S.D. State U., 1973; student Schiller Coll., Fed. Republic Germany, 1972; JD, U. S.D., 1976. Bar: S.D. 1976. States atty. Harding County, Buffalo, S.D., 1976—; city atty. Town of Buffalo, 1976—. Mem. Bd. Water and Natural Resources S.D. 1977-80, Bd. Minerals and Environment S.D., 1980—; pres. Harding County Reps., 1978-82. Mem. ABA, S.D. Bar Assn., S.D. Trial Lawyers Assn., Am. Trial Lawyers Assn., Am. Judicature Soc., S.D. Mcpl. Attys. Assn. (pres. 1986-87), Harding County C. of C. (pres. 1979-85). Lodges: Lions (pres. 1979-80), Masons, Shriners. General practice, Oil and gas leasing, Probate. Home: PO Box 427 Buffalo SD 57720 also: Graslie Law Office 100 Main St Buffalo SD 57720

GRASSIA, THOMAS C., lawyer; b. Westfield, Mass., Aug. 26, 1946; s. Thomas C. and Assunta (Abatiell) G.; m. Judith Chace Cranshaw, Aug. 15, 1970; children—Susan C., Joseph C. B.A., Boston U., 1968; J.D., Suffolk U., 1974. Bar: Mass. 1974, U.S. Dist. Ct. Mass. 1976, U.S. Supreme Ct. 1980. Asst. v.p. Plymouth Rubber Co., Canton, Mass., 1969-71; ptnr., P.T.S. Computer Services, Waltham, Mass., 1971-81; ptnr. D'Angio & Grassia, Waltham, 1974-85, Grassia & Mariolis, Wellesley, Mass., 1985—; agt. Indsl. Valley Title Ins. Co., Phila., 1980—, 1st Am. Title Ins. Co., N.Y.C., 1980—, Lawyers Title Ins. Co., Richmond, Va., Am. Title Ins. Co., Miami, Fla.; dir. of many regional corps. including Sytron Corp., Mcpl. Guard Rail Corp., Framingham, Mass., Fortune Guaranty Savs. Bank, Windham, N.H.; dir., asst. treas. Granite Subaru, Milford, Mass.; pres., treas., dir. Lender's Title & Abstract Co., Ltd., Wellesley; Contbr. articles to profl. publs., lectr. on law, pub. interest subjects. Mem. Bd. Health, Sherborn, Mass., 1976-81, Bd. Selectmen, Sherborn, 1981-85; trustee Leonard Morse Hosp., Natick, Mass., 1981-84; mem. Met. Boston Hosp. Council, Burlington, Mass., 1983-84; mem., team leader Sherborn Fire and Rescue Dept., 1974—; former mem. Sherborn Sch. Bd. Long Range Planning com., Sherborn Land Maintenance Study com., Sherborn Police Chief Selection com., Sherborn Emergency Med. Study com. Mem. ABA, Mass. Bar Assn., Mass. Conveyances Assn., Am. Arbitration Assn. (comml. arbitration bd.), Nat. Registry Emergency Med. Technicians. General corporate, Real property. Home: 75 Nason Hill Rd PO Box 178 Sherborn MA 01770 Office: Grassia & Mariolis 40 Grove St Wellesley MA 02181

GRATE, MARSHALL WARREN, lawyer; b. Garrett, Ind., Dec. 29, 1955; s. B. Gene and Jenyce (Likens) G.; m. Lanette M. Lawrence, Dec. 16, 1977; children: Rhodora, Keturah. BS in Am. Studies, Harding U., 1974-78; JD, Ind. U. at Purdue, Indpls., 1981. Bar: Ind. 1981, U.S. Dist. Ct. (we. dist.) Mich. 1981, Mich. 1985, U.S. Dist. Ct. (no. and so. dists.) Ind. 1985. Assoc. Livingston, Dildine, Halprie & Yoder, Ft. Wayne, Ind., 1981-85, Clary, Nantz & Wood, Grand Rapids, Mich., 1985—. Mem. ABA, Mich. State Bar Assn. Republican. Mem. Ch. Christ. Avocation: running. Labor, Federal civil litigation, State civil litigation. Office: Clary Nantz Wood et al 500 Calder Plaza Grand Rapids MI 49503

GRATTAN, S. AMY, lawyer; b. Englewood, N.J., Apr. 4, 1957; d. James A. and Joan Stephanie (Wareing) Arbucho; m. Richard H. Grattan, Sept. 7, 1985. BA, Lehigh U., 1979; JD, Washington & Lee U., 1982. Bar: Va. 1982, Md. 1986, D.C. 1987. Assoc. Cranwell, Flora & Moore, Roanoke, Va., 1982-86, Lord Whip Coughlan & Green, PA, Balt., 1986-87, Whiteford, Taylor & Preston, Balt., 1987—. Mem. ABA, Va. Bar Assn., Am. Trial Lawyers Assn., Va. Trial Lawyers Assn., Md. Bar Assn., Balt. Bar Assn. Episcopalian. Federal civil litigation, State civil litigation, Construction. Home: 1427 William St Baltimore MD 21230 Office: Whiteford Taylor & Preston Suite 1400 7 St Paul St Baltimore MD 21202-1626

GRAUBERT, JOHN DAVID, lawyer; b. N.Y.C., Apr. 16, 1956; s. David N. Graubert and Dorothy (McGuire) Greene. BA cum laude, Williams Coll., 1978; JD, Georgetown U., 1981. Bar: N.Y. 1982, D.C. 1983, U.S. Dist. Ct. D.C. 1983, U.S. Dist. Ct. 1986, U.S. Supreme Ct. 1986. Law clk. U.S. Ct. Appeals (5th cir.), Houston, 1981-82; assoc. Steptoe & Johnson, Washington, 1982—. Contbr. articles to profl. jours. Mem. ABA (antitrust and litigation sects.). Democrat. Federal civil litigation. Home: 2301 Cathedral Ave NW #406 Washington DC 20008 Office: Steptoe & Johnson 1330 Connecticut Ave Washington DC 20036

GRAUER, ALLAN L., lawyer; b. Marcus, Iowa, Apr. 8, 1930; s. Albert J. and Esther C. (Stowater) G.; m. Julie M. Fargo, June 15, 1952; children: Dr. G.F. Grauer, Valerie J. Grauer Cairns. BS in Econs., Iowa State U., 1952; JD, U. S.D., 1956. Bar: Nebr. 1956, S.D. 1956, N.Y. 1963, Minn. 1966. Atty. N.W. Bell Telephone Co., Omaha, 1956-61; atty. N.W. Bell Telephone Co., Mpls., 1966-84, v.p., gen. counsel, corp. sec., 1984—; atty. AT&T, N.Y.C., 1961-66; bd. dirs. Northwestern Bell Telephone Co., Omaha, Edison Sault Electric Co., Sault Ste. Marie, Mich. Bd. dirs. Henry Doorly Zoo, Omaha, 1983—, Western Heritage Mus., Omaha, 1984—. Mem. ABA, Nebr. Bar Assn., N.Y. Bar Assn., S.D. Bar Assn., Minn. Bar Assn. Republican. Lutheran. Home: Rural Rt #2 Omaha NE 68122 Office: Northwestern Bell Telephone Co 1314 Douglas On-the-Mall Omaha NE 68102

GRAVEL, CAMILLE FRANCIS, JR., lawyer; b. Alexandria, La., Aug. 10, 1915; s. Camille F. and Aline Delvaille G.; m. Katherine Yvonne David, Nov. 26, 1939 (dec. 1979); children—Katherine Ann Gravel Vanderslice, Mary Eileen Gravel Cappel, Martha Louise Antoon, Camille Francis, Grady David, Eunice Holloman Gravel, Virginia Maureen Gravel Carbo, Margaret Lynn, Mark Alan, Charles Gregory, Richard Alvin (dec.); m. Evelyn Giafala, 1980. Student U. Notre Dame, 1931-35, La. State U., 1935-37, Cath. U. Am., 1937-39; LL.D. (hon.), Loyola U., New Orleans, 1976. Bar: La. 1940, U.S. dist. ct. La. 1940, U.S. Ct. Appeals (5th cir.) 1953, U.S. Supreme Ct. 1954. Asst. dist. atty. 9th Jud. Dist., Rapides Parish, La., 1942; atty. State Inheritance Tax Collector, Rapides Parish, 1943-45; asst. city atty. Alexandria (La.), 1946-48; atty. La. Tax Commn., 1948-52; sr. ptnr. Gravel & Brady, Alexandria and Baton Rouge, 1952—. Mem. Gov.'s Commn. on Higher Edn. Services, 1978—; mem. Gov.'s Adv. and Rev. Commn. on Asst. Dist. Attys., 1979—; mem. bd. suprs. La. State U. and A&M Coll., 1975—, chmn. bd., 1981-82. Mem. U.S. Capitol Police Force, 1937-39. Hon. fellow Harry S. Truman Library Inst., 1975. Fellow Internat. Acad. Trial Lawyers, Internat. Soc. Barristers, Law Sci. Acad.; mem. ABA, Am. Judicature Soc., Am. Trial Lawyers Assn., Nat. Assn. Criminal Def. Lawyers, Nat. Diocesan Attys. Assn., La. Bar Assn., Alexandria Bar Assn. (pres. 1949-50), Notre Dame Law Assn., La. Trial Lawyers Assn., AAUP, Lamar Soc., Am. Assn. Ret. Persons, Am. Heart Assn., Cath. U. Am. Alumni Assn. (nat. bd. govs. 1977—), Alexandria-Pineville C. of C., Am. Legion, Phi Delta Phi, Kappa Sigma. Roman Catholic. Clubs: Elks (past exalted ruler), KC. Criminal, Legislative, Personal injury. Office: Gravel & Brady 711 Washington St PO Box 1792 Alexandria LA 71309

GRAVEL, JOHN COOK, lawyer; b. Burlington, Vt., Dec. 8, 1947; s. Clarke Albert and Phyllis Jean (Cook) G.; m. Mary Ann Luchini, June 14, 1969; children: Judson Christopher, Jamie Lee. BA in History, St. Michael's Coll., Winooski, Vt., 1969; JD, Boston Coll., 1972. Bar: Vt. 1972, U.S. Dist. Ct. Vt. 1973, U.S. Ct. Appeals (2d cir.) 1977. Assoc. Gravel, Shea & Wright, Burlington, 1972-79; ptnr. Bauer & Gravel, Burlington, 1980—; sec. Burlington Internat. Games, Inc., 1975—. apptd. mem. Vt. Statutory Revision Com., Montpelier, 1979—; trustee emeritus Burlington Coll., 1980-83; bd.dirs. Lyric Theatre, Inc., 1975-80, past pres.; bd. dirs. Flynn Theatre for Performing Arts, Ltd., Burlington, 1980— (past pres.), Vt. Cath. Charities, Inc., Burlington, 1976-85 (past pres.), Chittenden County United Way, Burlington, 1985—. Served to lt. U.S. Army, 1970-72. Mem. ABA, Vt. Bar Assn. Republican. Roman Catholic. Club: Ethan Allen (Burlington). Avocations: acting, musical theatre, jogging, basketball. Consumer commercial, General corporate, Probate. Home: 50 Prospect Hill Burlington VT 05401 Office: Bauer & Gravel 350 Main St PO Box 607 Burlington VT 05402

GRAVELEY, CHARLES ALLAN, lawyer; b. Bremerton, Wash., Oct. 28, 1944; s. John Gordon and Zita Leone (Zimmerman) G.; m. Julie Rae Toney, Feb. 18, 1984; children: Kenneth, Chad, Morgan. BBA, Carroll Coll., 1966; JD, U. Mont., 1973. Bar: Mont. 1973, U.S. Dist. Ct. Mont. 1973. Dep. atty. Lewis & Clark County, Helena, Mont., 1973-77; atty. Lewis & Clark County, Helena, 1977-83; sole practice Helena, 1983—; bd. dirs. Survivco, Inc., Kirkland, Wash., 1978—. Served with USN, 1966. Mem. Mont. Bar Assn., First Jud. Dist. Bar Assn., Young Lawyers of Helena (pres. 1975). Republican. Roman Catholic. State civil litigation, Real property, Family and matrimonial. Office: Bedford Ct Office 1111 N Rodney 1 Helena MT 59601

GRAVER, NANCY J., lawyer; b. Buffalo, Jan. 4, 1951; d. Hyman H. and Charlotte (Poler) G.; m. Stuart L. Smith, May 16, 1976 (div. Nov. 1979). BA in English with honors, Clark U., 1972; JD, John Marshall Law Sch., 1975, LLM in Taxation, 1985. Bar: Ill. 1976, U.S. Dist. Ct. (no. dist.) Ill. 1976. Sr. research atty. Callaghan & Co., Chgo., 1975-79; assoc. John H. Hoffman, P.C., Chgo., 1979-86; tax mgr. Goldberg Geiser & Co. Ltd., Chgo., 1987—. Mem. ABA, Ill. Bar Assn., Chgo. Bar Assn. Avocations: sailboat racing, stained glass artisan, miniaturist. Estate planning, Estate taxation, Personal income taxation. Home: 4221 N Paulina Ave Chicago IL 60613 Office: Goldberg Geiser & Co Ltd 29 N Wacker Dr Chicago IL 60606

GRAVES, HERBERT MAC, lawyer; b. Blackwell, Okla., Feb. 29, 1940; s. Carl Lee and Althea Dorothy (McCoy) G.; m. Virginia Beth Long, Aug. 14, 1971; children: Betsy Lynn, John Howard. BS, U. Okla., 1963, JD, 1969. Bar: Okla. 1969, U.S. Dist. Ct. (we. dist.) Okla. 1970, U.S. Ct. Appeals (10th cir.) 1970. Assoc. Love & Sullivan, Oklahoma City, 1969-71; ptnr. Sullivan, Graves & Densmore P.C., Oklahoma City, 1971—. Mem. Alcoholic Beverage Lic. Rev. Bd., Oklahoma City, 1978-81. Served to 1st lt. U.S. Army, 1963-66. Mem. ABA, Okla. Bar Assn. (sec. legal internship com. 1970-71, chmn.-elect bankruptcy sect.) Okla. County Bar Assn., Assn. Trial Lawyers Am., Okla. Trial Lawyers Assn., Am. Bankruptcy Inst., Phi Alpha Delta. Bankruptcy, State civil litigation, Consumer commercial. Office: Sullivan Graves & Densmore PC 3711 Classen Blvd Oklahoma City OK 73118

GRAVES, RAY REYNOLDS, U.S. Bankruptcy Ct. judge; b. Tuscumbia, Ala., Jan. 10, 1946; s. Isaac and Olga Ernestine (Wilder) G.; m. Lola Larice, July 27, 1974; 1 child, Claire Elise. B.A., Trinity Coll., Hartford, Conn., 1967; J.D., Wayne State U., 1970. Bar: Mich. 1971, U.S. Dist. Ct. (ea. dist.) Mich. 1971, U.S. Ct. Appeals (6th cir.) 1972, U.S. Supreme Ct. 1976, D.C. 1977. Defender, Legal Aid and Defender Assn., Detroit, 1970-71; assoc. Liberson, Fink, Feiler, Crystal & Burdick, 1971-72, Patmon, Young & Kirk, 1972-73; ptnr. Lewis, White, Clay & Graves, 1974-81; mem. legal dept. Detroit Edison Co., 1981; judge U.S. Bankruptcy Ct., Eastern Dist. Mich., Detroit, 1982—; mem. U.S. Ct. Com., State Bar Mich. Bd. dirs. Mich. Cancer Found.; bd. trustees Mich. Opera Theatre, 1986—, Mt. Clemens Gen. Hosp., 1987—. Mem. Nat. Conf. Bankruptcy Judges (bd. govs. 1984—), World Assn. Judges, World Peace Through Law Conf., Assn. Black Judges Mich., Wolverine Bar Assn., Detroit Bar Assn., D.C. Bar Assn., Delta Kappa Epsilon. Episcopalian. Bankruptcy, Banking. Office: US Bankruptcy Judge 1063 US Courthouse Detroit MI 48226

GRAY, ALVIN L., lawyer; b. Cleve., Feb. 3, 1928; s. Reuben Abraham and Lottie (Weingarden) G.; m. Anita Marie Belsito, Nov. 30, 1975; children—Lottie Mara, Rachel Evan. Student, Denison U., 1945, Union Coll., Schenectady, 1945-46; A.B., Western Res. U., 1949, LL.B., 1951. Bar: Ohio, U.S. Ct. Mil. Appeals, U.S. Supreme Ct. Sole practice Cleve., 1951-76; sr. ptnr. Gray, Luria & Belkin, Attys., Cleve., 1976-86, of counsel, 1986—; v.p., dir. Media-Com, Inc., Kent, Ohio, 1971-87. Author: A Visit to the Soviet Refuseniks, 1978 (spl. achievement award 1978); editor The Catalyst jour. of polit. thought, 1974-80 (spl. achievement award 1981). V.p. Am. Jewish Congress, N.Y.C., 1974-87, Jewish Welfare Bd., N.Y.C., 1987—; pres. Jewish Vocat. Service, Cleve., 1977-78, Jewish Community Ctr., Cleve., 1979-82, Am. Orgn. for Rehab. Through Tng., N.Y.C., 1983-86; v.p. World ORT Union, London, 1983-86, sec. 1986-87; assoc. treas. Jewish Community Fedn., Cleve., 1985-86, treas. 1987. Served with USN, 1945-46. Recipient Man of Yr. award Am. Orgn. for Rehab. Through Tng., 1976. Mem. Ohio Bar Assn., Cleve. Bar Assn., Cuyahoga County Bar Assn. (chmn. liaison com. 1975-79), Assn. Trial Lawyers Am., U.S. Supreme Ct. Bar Assn., U.S. Ct. Mil. Appeals Bar Assn. Democrat. Club: Oakwood (Cleve.). Avocations: photography; foreign travel; communal activism. Civil rights, State civil litigation, Personal injury. Home: 16800 Parkland Dr Shaker Heights OH 44120 Office: Gray Luria and Belkin 1920 Superior Bldg Cleveland OH 44114

GRAY, CHESTER L., JR., corporate executive, lawyer; b. Birmingham, Ala., Dec. 3, 1932; s. Chester L. and Louise (Cagle) G.; m. Barbara J. Robohm, June 19, 1954; children—Chester L. III, Scott D., Evan W. A.B. cum laude, Harvard U., 1954, J.D., 1960. Bar: N.Y. 1961, U.S. Dist. Ct. (so. dist.) N.Y. 1963, U.S. Dist. Ct. (ea. dist.) N.Y. 1963, Mass., 1967. Assoc., Simpson, Thacher & Bartlett, N.Y.C., 1960-66; mem. law dept. GTE and subs. GTE Sylvania, Inc., 1966-80, v.p., gen. counsel GTE Products Corp., 1980-83; v.p., assoc. gen. counsel GTE Corp., 1983—. Served to lt. (j.g.), USNR, 1954-57. Mem. ABA. Antitrust, General corporate, Private international. Address: 57 Highline Trail Stamford CT 06902

GRAY, FRANCIS IGNACY, lawyer; b. Ithaca, N.Y., Sept. 14, 1939; s. Frank S. Gray and Grace Switzer (Van Wagonen) Hall; m. Kay Effie Hurtt, Aug. 8, 1964 (div. Jan. 1974); m. Judith Ann Look, Feb. 1, 1974; children: Eric Allen, Erin Jae Sook, Sean Leslie. BEE, Cornell U., 1962; JD, Santa Clara U., 1970. Bar: Calif. 1971, U.S. Dist. Ct. (no. dist.) Calif. 1971, U.S. Ct. Appeals (9th cir.) 1971, U.S. Patent Office 1975, Oreg. 1986. Assoc. Romero, Weger & Gray, San Jose, Calif., 1971-75; patent adviser Office of Naval Research, San Francisco, 1975-80, patent counsel Naval Ocean Research and Devel. Activity and Nat. Space Tech. Lab., 1980-84; sr. patent atty. Tektronix, Inc., Beaverton, Oreg., 1984—. Pres., sec. Santa Clara (Calif.) Players, 1974-75. Served to 1st lt. USAF, 1962-65. Mem. Oreg. Patent Law Assn., Bay St. Louis Soccer Club (sec. 1982-84), Tibetan Terrier Club of No. Calif. (pres. 1973-75). Republican. Avocations: soccer, tennis, community theatre, show dogs, sailing. Patent, Trademark and copyright, General corporate. Office: Tektronix Inc Y3-121 PO Box 500 Beaverton OR 97077

GRAY, FRANKLIN DINGWALL, lawyer; b. Mpls., July 19, 1904; s. William Irving and Isabelle Wenonah (Welles) G.; m. Laura Erf, June 18, 1932; 1 dau., Ellen Gray. B.A. magna cum laude, U. Minn., 1925; B.A. in Jurisprudence (Rhodes scholar), Oxford (Eng.) U., 1927, B.C.L., 1928, M.A., 1953. Bar: Minn. 1929. Ptnr. firm Gray, Plant, Mooty, Mooty & Bennett, and predecessors, Mpls., 1942—; lectr. bus. law Sch. Bus. Adminstrn., U. Minn., 1937-45. Fellow Am. Coll. Trial Lawyers; mem. ABA, Minn. Bar Assn., Am. Arbitration Assn. (Twin Cities council), U. Minn. Alumni Assn. (pres. 1963-64), Phi Beta Kappa, Theta Delta Chi, Phi Delta Phi. Club: Rotary (pres. Mpls. 1965-66). Home: 5253 Richwood Dr Minneapolis MN 55436 Office: 3400 City Ctr Minneapolis MN 55402

GRAY, FRED DAVID, lawyer; b. Montgomery, Ala., Dec. 14, 1930; s. Abraham and Nancy G.; m. Bernice Hill, June 17, 1956; children: Deborah R., Vanessa L., Fred D., Stanley F. BS, Ala. State U., 1951; JD, Case Western Res. U., 1954. Bar: Ala. 1954, Ohio 1954, U.S. Dist. Ct. (mid. dist.) Ala. 1955, U.S. Supreme Ct. 1956, U.S. Ct. Appeals (5th cir.) 1958, U.S. Dist. Ct. (no. dist.) Ala. 1963, U.S. Tax Ct. 1968, U.S. Ct. Appeals (11th cir.) 1982. Sr. ptnr. Gray, Langford, Sapp, Davis & McGowan and predecessor firm, Montgomery and Tuskegee, Ala., 1983—. City atty. City of Tuskegee, 1965—; county atty. Macon County, Ala., 1970—; cooperating atty. NAACP Legal Def. Fund, Inc.; local gen. counsel Tuskegee U.; spl. asst. to atty. gen. State of Ala., 1975; past mem. Ala. Adv. Com. U.S. Commn. on Civil Rights; mem. Tuskegee Civic Assn. (life, award 1981); elder Tuskegee Ch. of Christ; bd. dirs. Southwestern Christian Coll., Terrell, Tex. Recipient Constl. Law award Ala. Civil Liberties Union, 1968, Disting. Alumni award Ala. State U., 1974, Social Engr.'s citation, 1975, Martin Luther King, Jr. Meml. Drum Major award So. Christian Leadership Conf., 1980, Black Achievers award, 1981, Fletcher Reed Andrews Grad. Yr. award Case Western Res. U., 1985, Man Yr. award Southwestern Christian Coll., 1986, Charles Hamilton Medallion of Merit, Washington Bar Assn., 1986. Mem. ABA, Assn. Trial Lawyers Am., Ala. Trial Lawyers Assn., Nat. Bar Assn. (pres., 1st Ann. Equal Justice award 1977), Macon County Bar Assn. (pres.), Nat. Bar Inst., NAACP (life), Soc. Benchers, Omega Psi Phi, Sigma Pi Phi. Office: Gray Langford Sapp Davis & McGowan PO Box 239 Tuskegee AL 36083 Office: 352 Dexter Ave Montgomery AL 36104

GRAY, GEORGE CLYDE, lawyer; b. Indpls., Dec. 27, 1944; s. Clyde and Rosemary (Oeftering) Zins G.; m. Martha Kidd, June 15, 1968 (div. Jan. 1972). B.A., Notre Dame U., 1966; J.D., Georgetown U., 1969. Bar: Ind. 1970, D.C. 1969, U.S. Dist. Ct. (so. and no. dists.) Ind. 1970, U.S. Ct. Claims 1983, U.S. Ct. Mil. Appeals 1970, U.S. Ct. Appeals (7th cir.) 1976, U.S. Ct. Appeals (D.C. cir.), U.S. Supreme Ct. 1976. Ptnr. Gray & Maple, Indpls., 1973-77; owner George Clyde Gray, P.C., Indpls., 1977-83; sr. ptnr. Gray, Robinson Eckert Ryan & Schreiber, Indpls., 1983-86, Gray, Robinson, Eckert & Ryan, 1986—. Contbr. article to profl. jour. Served to capt. U.S. Army, 1969-73. Decorated Army Commendation medal. Mem. ABA, Am. Trial Lawyers Assn., Ind. Trial Lawyers Assn. (legis. com. 1983-85, chmn. legis. com. 1986—, dir. 1986—), Indpls. Bar Assn., Johnson County Bar Assn. Democrat. Roman Catholic. Clubs: Notre Dame (Indpls.); Porsche of Am. Personal injury. Home: 521 Ashbourne Ln Greenwood IN 46142 Office: Gray Robinson Eckert et al 8130 S Meridian St Indianapolis IN 46217

GRAY, HERBERT HAROLD, III, lawyer; b. Chattanooga, Apr. 5, 1953; s. Herbert H. Jr. and Mary Ellen (Parsons) G.; m. Leah Reynolds Dickie, Nov. 8, 1986. AB, U. N.C., 1975; JD, Emory U., 1978. Bar: Ga. 1978, U.S. Supreme Ct. 1982. Assoc. Powell, Goldstein, Frazer & Murphy, Atlanta, 1978-80; assoc. Varner, Stephens, Wingfield, McIntyre & Humphries, Atlanta, 1980-85, ptnr., 1986—. Mem. ABA, Ga. Bar Assn., Atlanta Bar Assn., Lawyers Club (treas. 1986-87, exec. com. 1986—), Phi Delta Phi. Democrat. Episcopalian. Club: Atlanta City. Construction, Federal civil litigation, Real property. Home: 825 Starlight Dr NE Atlanta GA 30342 Office: Varner Stephens Wingfield et al 44 Broad St NW 1000 Grant Bldg Atlanta GA 30303

GRAY, J. CHARLES, lawyer, cattle rancher; b. Leesburg, Fla., Mar. 26, 1932; s. G. Wayne and Mary Evelyn (Albright) G.; m. Saundra Hagood, Aug. 18, 1955; children: Terese Ren, John Charles, Lee Jerome. BA, U. Fla., 1955, JD, 1958. Bar: Fla. 1958, U.S. Dist. Ct. (mid. dist.) Fla. 1958. County atty. Orange County (Fla.), 1978-85; pres. Gray, Harris & Robinson, P.A.; chmn. Fla. Turnpike Authority, 1965-67; city solicitor City of Orlando (Fla.), 1960-61; gen. counsel S.E. Bank of Orlando (Fla.); owner Gemini Springs Farms; pres. Santa Gertrudis Breeders Internat., 1981-83, Fla. Santa Gerudis Assn., 1976-78, Nat. Polled Santa Gertrudis Assn., 1975-77. Chmn. Pres.'s Council Advisors, U. Central Fla., 1978-84; v.p. U. Central Fla. Found., 1986—; mem. Commn. on Future of Fla.'s Pub. Univs.; dir. Internat. Cultural Ctr.; past pres. Orange County U. Fla. Alumni Assn., Pi Kappa Alpha Alumni Assn.; past dist. v.p. U. Fla. Alumni Assn.; mem. U. Fla. Pres.'s Council; past dir. Orlando C. of C.; past mem. Fla. Council of 100; mem. Com. of 100, Com. of 1000; founding bd. dirs. Fla. Epilepsy Found.; bd. dirs. Deseret Farms Wild Turkey Hunt; vice chmn. Indsl. Devel. Commn. Central Fla. Mem. U. Fla. Hall of Fame. Mem. ABA, Orange County Bar Assn., Fla. Bar Assn., Fla. Blue Key, Phi Alpha Delta, Pi Kappa Alpha. Republican. Episcopalian. Clubs: University (past dir.), Citrus (Orlando). Real property, Local government. Home: 37 Dirksen Dr DeBary FL 32713 Office: 201 E Pine St Suite 1200 Orlando FL 32801

GRAY, JAN CHARLES, lawyer; b. Des Moines, June 15, 1947. s. Charles Donald and Mary C. Gray; m. Anita Marie Ringwald, June 6, 1987. B.A. in Econs., U. Calif.-Berkeley, 1969; M.B.A., Pepperdine U., 1986, J.D., Harvard U., 1972. Bar: Calif. 1972, D.C. 1974. Law clk. Kindel & Anderson, Los Angeles, 1971-72; assoc. Halstead, Baker & Sterling, Los Angeles, 1972-75; sr. v.p., gen. counsel external affairs Ralphs Grocery Co. div. Federated Dept. Stores, Inc., Los Angeles, 1975—; judge pro tem Los Angeles Mcpl. Ct., 1977—; instr. bus. UCLA, 1976—, Pepperdine MBA Program, 1985—; arbitrator Am. Arbitration Assn., 1977—; media spokesman So. Calif. Grocers Assn., Calif. Grocers Assn.; real estate broker, Los Angeles, 1973—. Trustee, South Bay U. Coll. Law, 1978-79; mem. bd. visitors Southwestern U. Sch. Law, 1983—; mem. Los Angeles County Pvt. Industry Council, 1982—, exec. com. 1984—, chmn. econ. devel. task force, 1986—; mem. Los Angeles County Martin Luther King, Jr. Gen. Hosp. Authority, 1984—; mem. Los Angeles County Aviation Commn, 1986—; Los Angeles Police Crime Prevention Adv. Council, 1986—; Los Angeles Plaza Adv. Bd., 1983—; bd. dirs. RecyCAL of So. Calif., 1983—; bd. trustees Santa Monica Hosp., 1986—; mem. Los Angeles County Democratic Central Com., 1980-82 ; del. Dem. Nat. Conv., 1980. Recipient So. Calif. Grocers Assn. award for outstanding contbns. to food industry, 1982; Calif./Nev. Soft Drink Assn. appreciation award for No on 11 Campaign, 1983. Mem. ABA, Calif. Bar Assn., Los Angeles County Bar Assn. (exec. com. corp. law depts. sect. 1974-76, 79—, exec. com. barristers sect. 1974-75, 79-81, treas. 1986—), San Fernando Valley Bar Assn. (chmn. real property sect. 1975-77, Los Angeles Pub. Affairs Officers Assn., Los Angeles World Affairs Council, Calif. Retailers Assn. (supermarket com.), Food Mktg. Inst. (govt. relations com., govt. affairs council), So. Calif. Businessmen's Assn. (bd. dirs. 1981—, mem. exec. com. 1982—, sec. 1986—), Town Hall Los Angeles, U. Calif. Alumni Assn., Ephebian Soc. Los Angeles, Phi Beta Kappa. Club: Harvard of So. Calif. Contbg. author: Life or Death, Who Controls?, 1976; contbr. articles to legal jours. General corporate. Home: PO Box 407 Beverly Hills CA 90213 Office: PO Box 54143 Los Angeles CA 90054

GRAY, JOHN CARTER STEWART, lawyer; b. Louisville, Ky., Apr. 27, 1953; s. Downey Milliken and Elizabeth (Stewart) G.; m. Virginia Goodwin, June 24, 1986. BA, Dartmouth Coll., 1975; JD, U. Ky., 1978. Bar: Ky. 1978, Tenn. 1979. Law clk. to presiding justice Ky. Ct. Appeals, Owensboro, 1978-80; sec., counsel Earth Indsl. Waste Mgmt., Inc., Millington, Tenn., 1980—. Environment. Office: Earth Indsl Waste Mgmt Inc 3536 Fite Rd Millington TN 38053

GRAY, JOHN WALKER, JR., lawyer; b. Atlanta, June 25, 1930; s. John Walker Gray Sr. and Nell (Sears) Wornham; m. Nancy Valentine Lumpkin, Dec. 27, 1952; children: John Walker III, Burton Sears, David Bradley. BS, Va. Poly. Inst., 1952; LLB, U. Va., 1957. Bar: Va. 1957, D.C. 1957, N.Y. 1963. Assoc. Covington & Burling, Washington, 1957-59; solicitor N&W Ry. Co., Roanoke, Va., 1959-61; atty. C&P Telephone Co., Washington, 1961, atty. N.Y.C. area, 1961-65, 73-74; asst. v.p., atty. AT&T, Washington, 1965-83, corp. v.p., 1984—. Mem. adv. council Brookings Inst. Ctr. Pub. Policy Edn., Washington, 1983—. Served to capt. USAF, 1952-54. Mem. ABA, Fed. Bar Assn., Fed. Communications Bar Assn., Va. Bar Assn., D.C. Bar Assn., Fairfax Hosp. Assn. (trustee 1982—, vice chmn. 1984—). Episcopalian. Clubs: Metropolitan, International (Washington); Belle Haven Country (Alexandria). Avocations: tennis, sailing. General corporate, Private international, Government contracts and claims. Home: 1003 Danton Ln Alexandria VA 22308 Office: AT&T 1120 20th St NW Washington DC 20036

GRAY, KATHLEEN ANN, lawyer; b. Reading, Pa., May 16, 1947; d. Sebastian and Helen Mary (Zajac) Vespico; m. George A. Gray, Oct. 22, 1966 (dec. 1968). BSBA, Drexel U., 1971, MBA, 1978; JD, Wake Forest U., 1977. Bar: Pa. 1977. Computer programmer Ednl. Testing Service, Princeton, N.J., 1971-73, dir. EDP tng., 1973-74; assoc. Barley, Snyder, Cooper & Barber, Lancaster, Pa., 1977-83, ptnr., 1983—. Mem. Wake Forest Law Rev., 1975-77. Bd. dirs. Hist. Preservation Trust of Lancaster County, 1978—, v.p., 1984; sec. bd. dirs. Lancaster Integrated Specialized Transp. System, 1981-85; bd. dirs. Am. Lung Assn. of Lancaster County, 1982—, Leadership Lancaster; sec., treas. Found. Lancaster Chamber, 1985—; mem. arbitration panel Better Bus. Bur. Mem. ABA, Pa. Bar Assn., Lancaster County Bar Assn., Pa. Sch. Bd. Solicitors Assn., Nat. Assn. of Bond Lawyers. Republican. General corporate, Local government, Municipal bonds. Office: Barley Snyder Cooper & Barber 126 E King St Lancaster PA 17602

GRAY, LINDA (LOU), lawyer; b. Oklahoma City, July 15, 1951; d. Ongal Lafayette and Esther Florine (Moulden) G. Student, Okla. U., 1969-70; BA, Oklahoma City U., 1973, JD, 1975. Bar: Okla. 1975, U.S. Dist. Ct. (we. dist.) Okla. 1975, U.S. Ct. Appeals (10th cir.) 1978, U.S. Dist. Ct. (ea. and no. dists.) Okla. 1984, U.S. Supreme Ct. 1984. Assoc. Haynes & Singerman, Oklahoma City, 1975-78, Whitten & Pankey, Oklahoma City, 1978-81, Buck, Merritt & Hoyt, Oklahoma City, 1981-82; ho. counsel United Equity Life Ins., Oklahoma City, 1983-84; asst. atty. gen. Office of Atty. Gen., Oklahoma City, 1984-87, auditor, insp., 1987—; cons. atty. Dept. of Human

Services, Oklahoma City, 1979-81. Mem. exec. com. state Dems., Oklahoma City, 1979-87, 5th dist. sec., 1979-80, chmn., 1981-82, co-chmn., 1982-87; vol. Pub. Inebriate Alternative, Oklahoma City, 1975-78. Served as capt. (JAG) USAR, 1978—. Mem. Okla. Bar Assn., Res. Officers Assn., Iota Tau Tau. Democrat. Baptist. Club: High Noon Inc. (Oklahoma City) (sec. 1982). State civil litigation, Civil rights, Military. Home: 4609 NW 12th Oklahoma City OK 73127 Office: Office of State Auditor and Insp State Capitol Bldg Room 50 Oklahoma City OK 73105

GRAY, MERYL BENJAMIN, lawyer; b. Warren County, Ohio, Dec. 9, 1907; s. Albert W. and Fleeta V. (Crane) G.; m. Harriet J. Spencer, June 15, 1941 (dec. Oct. 1985); 1 dau., Judith Gray Fisher. B.A., Miami U., Oxford, Ohio, 1932; LL.B., Salmon B. Chase Law Sch., 1936. Bar: Ohio 1936. Pros. atty. Warren County, 1941-45; sr. mem. Gray & Duning, Lebanon, Ohio, 1974—. Served from pvt. to 1st lt. JAGC, U.S. Army, 1942-46; NATOUSA. Mem. ABA, Ohio Bar Assn., Am. Security Council, VFW, Am. Legion, Delta Upsilon. Democrat. Clubs: Pres., Eagles. Lodge: Elks. Estate planning, Probate, Estate taxation. Home: 305 S Mechanic St Lebanon OH 45036 Office: 4 S Broadway Lebanon OH 45036

GRAY, OSCAR SHALOM, lawyer; b. N.Y.C., Oct. 18, 1926. A.B., Yale U., 1948, J.D., 1951. Bar: Md. 1951, D.C. 1952, U.S. Supreme Ct. 1952. Atty.-adviser legal adviser's office U.S. Dept. State, Washington, 1951-57; sec. Nuclear Materials and Equipment Corp., Apollo, Pa., 1957-64, treas., 1957-67, v.p., 1964-71, dir., 1964-67; spl. counsel Presdl. Task Force on Communications Policy, Washington, 1967-68; cons. U.S. Dept. Transp., Washington, 1967-68, acting dir. office environ. impact, 1968-70; sole practice Washington, 1970—, Balt., 1971—; adj. prof., professorial lectr. Law Ctr. Georgetown U., Washington, 1970-71; lectr. Cath. U. Am., Washington, 1970-71; assoc. prof. U. Md., Balt., 1971-74, prof., 1974—; vis. prof. U. Tenn., 1977. Author: Cases and Materials on Environmental Law, 1970, 2d edit., 1973, supplements, 1974, 75, 77; (with F. Harper and F. James, Jr.) The Law of Torts, 2d edit., 1986; (with H. Shulman and F. James, Jr.) Cases and Materials on the Law of Torts, 3d edit., 1976; contbr. articles to legal jours. Mem. Am. Law Inst., D.C. Bar Assn., Selden Soc., Order Coif, Phi Beta Kappa. Legal education, Insurance, Torts. Office: 500 W Baltimore St Baltimore MD 21201

GRAY, RICHARD EDWARD, lawyer; b. Phila., May 19, 1944; s. Robert G.; 1 dau., Carson Margit. B.S., U. Pa., 1966, M.B.A., 1966; LL.B., U. Pa., 1969. Bar: N.Y. 1970. Assoc. Mudge Rose Guthrie & Alexander, N.Y.C., 1970-73, Satterlee & Stephens, N.Y.C., 1973-76; sr. ptnr. Gray & Richardson, N.Y.C., 1976—. chmn. Chariot Holdings, Ltd.; chmn. bd. dirs. Sandusky Plastics, Inc., Eastmet Corp. Bd. dirs. N.Y. Lyric Opera Co., 1980-82, AM. Friends of Vatican Library; chmn. bd. dirs. internat. exhibition com. Vatican Library Exhibitions. Mem. ABA. Republican. Episcopalian. Club: New York Yacht (N.Y.C.), Doubles. General corporate, Private international. Office: Eastern Stainless Steel Co PO Box 1957 Baltimore MD 21203

GRAY, VERONICA MERYL, lawyer; b. N.Y.C., Nov. 25, 1948; d. Hyman and Adeline (Levine) Moskowitz. BA magna cum laude, SUNY, Buffalo, 1970; MA, Syracuse U., 1973; JD, Pepperdine U., 1976. Bar: Calif. 1976. Atty. Inland Counties Legal Services, Riverside, Calif., 1976-79; assoc. Blumenthal, Grossman & Avis, Riverside, 1979-80; ptnr. Reid & Hellyer, San Bernardino, Calif., 1980—. Mem. Calif. Bar Assn. (bd. dirs. litigation and pub. affairs sects. 1985—), Inland Counties Women at Law Assn. (pres. 1984-85), Phi Beta Kappa. Federal civil litigation, State civil litigation. Office: Reid & Hellyer PO Box 6086 San Bernardino CA 92412

GRAY, WHITMORE, law educator, lawyer; b. 1932. A.B., Principia Coll., 1954; J.D., U. Mich., 1957; postgrad. U. Paris, 1957-58, U. Munich (W.Ger.), 1962. Bar: Mich. 1958. Assoc. Casey, Lane & Mittendorf, N.Y.C., 1958-60; asst. prof. U. Mich., 1960-63, assoc. prof., 1963-66, prof., 1966—; assoc. Cleary, Gottlieb, N.Y.C., 1981; mem. adv. bd. Soviet Law and Govt. and Soviet Statues and Decision. Japan Found. fellow U. Tokyo, 1977-78; lectr. contract law Chinese Acad. Social Scis., 1982; summer faculty Jilin U., People's Republic of China, 1985. Mem. Am. Assn. Law Schs. (past chmn. comparative law sect.), Internat. Acad. Comparative Law (assoc.), Assn. Asian Studies. Contbr. articles on comml. arbitration and alternative dispute resolution to profl. jours. Translator Russian Republic Civil Code, General Principles of Civil Law of People's Republic of China. Past editor-in-chief Mich. Law Rev.; bd. editors Am. Jour. Comparative Law. Legal education. Home: S 4th Ave Ann Arbor MI 48104 Office: U Mich Law Sch 621 S State St 333 Hutchins Hall Ann Arbor MI 48109

GRAY, WILLIAM OXLEY, lawyer; b. Iowa Falls, Iowa, Nov. 23, 1914; s. Clarence O. and Hazel (Oxley) G.; m. Mary Florence Comstock, Oct. 19, 1940; children—William Scott, John Steven, Mary Ellen Gray Hart, James C. B.A., Coe Coll., 1936; J.D., U. Iowa, 1938. Bar: Iowa 1938, U.S. Dist. Ct. (no. and so. dists.) Iowa 1938. Ptnr. Silliman & Gray, Cedar Rapids, Iowa, 1938-42; spl. agt. FBI, 1942-46; ptnr. Silliman, Gray & Stapleton, Cedar Rapids, 1946-85, Gray, Stefani & Mitvalsky, 1986— ; v.p., dir. Kwik-Way Mfg. Co., Marion, Iowa, 1952—; dir. Brenton Bank & Trust Co., Cedar Rapids, Iowa Electric Light & Power Co., Cedar Rapids. Chmn. Iowa Hwy. Commn., 1969-73; chmn. bd. trustees Coe Coll., Cedar Rapids, 1964-84. Mem. ABA, Iowa State Bar Assn., Linn County Bar Assn., Ex-Agts. FBI (pres. 1970-71), Cedar Rapids C. of C. (bd. dirs. 1968). Republican. Congregationalist. Club: Union League (Chgo.). Lodge: Masons. General corporate, Estate taxation, Family and matrimonial. Office: Gray Stefani & Mitvalsky 200 American Bldg Cedar Rapids IA 52401

GRAY, WILLIAM PATTON, JR., lawyer; b. Tuscaloosa, Ala., Mar. 13, 1943; s. William Patton and Ruth Herndon (Turner) G.; m. Rebecca Story Wright, Apr. 9, 1966; children—Stacy Elaine, Susan Meridith, Ashley Rebecca, John David. B.S. in Acctg., U. Ala.-Tuscaloosa, 1965, J.D., 1968. Bar: Ala. 1968, U.S. Dist. Ct. (no. dist.) Ala. 1972, U.S. Ct. Appeals (5th cir.) 1972, U.S. Ct. Appeals (11th cir.) 1983. Mem. trust dept. staff City Nat. Bank, Tuscaloosa, 1968; judge adv. U.S. Air Force, Columbus, Ohio, 1968-72; assoc. Hubbard & Waldrop, Tuscaloosa, 1972-73; ptnr. Tucker, Gray & Thigpen, Tuscaloosa, 1973-77, Tucker, Gray & Espy, Tuscaloosa, 1977-82, Gray, Espy & Nettles, Tuscaloosa, 1982—; lectr. law U. Ala.-Tuscaloosa, 1982—. Bd. dirs. Mental health Assn., 1983—; co-chmn. Mother's March, March of Dimes, 1973. Mem. Ala. Bar Assn., Ala. Trial Lawyers Assn. (exec. com.), Tuscaloosa C. of C. (subcom. chmn.). Democrat. Presbyterian. State civil litigation, Personal injury, Real property. Home: 5 Riverdale Rd Tuscaloosa AL 35406 Office: Gray Espy & Nettles 2728 8th St Tuscaloosa AL 35401

GRAYCK, MARCUS DANIEL, lawyer; b. N.Y.C., Aug. 28, 1927; s. Jack and Gertrude (Seeman) G.; children from previous marriage—Howard Alexander, Amelia Beth, Joshua Avram, David Louis. A.B., Bklyn. Coll., 1948; LL.B., Harvard U., 1951; LL.M., NYU, 1958. Bar: N.Y., Ill., U.S. Supreme Ct. Partner firm Baker & McKenzie, Chgo., 1973—; mem. adj. faculty, grad. tax program N.Y. U. Law Sch., 1959-75; adj. prof. law Loyola U. Law Sch., 1976—. Editor: Compensation and fringe benefits column Jour. Corp. Taxation; contbr. articles to profl. jours. Served with USN, 1945-46. Mem. ABA, Chgo. Bar Assn. Jewish. Club: Mid-America. Pension, profit-sharing, and employee benefits, Corporate taxation. Office: Baker and McKenzie 2800 Prudential Plaza Chicago IL 60601

GRAYLOW, RICHARD VERNON, lawyer; b. Sept. 4, 1940. BS, U. Wis., Milw., 1965; JD, U. Wis., 1969. Bar: Wis. 1969. Assoc. Lawton & Cates, Madison, Wis., 1969-74, ptnr., 1974—; lectr. ad hoc U. Wis. Sch. for Workers. Served to sgt. USMC, 1958-61. Mem. Wis. Bar Assn., Dane County Bar Assn., Assn. Trial Lawyers Am., Wis. Acad. Trial Lawyers. Avocation: sports. Labor, Civil rights, Workers' compensation. Office: Lawton & Cates SC 214 W Mifflin St Madison WI 53703

GRAYSON, EDWARD DAVIS, manufacturing company executive; b. Davenport, Iowa, June 20, 1938; s. Charles E. and Isabelle (Davis) G.; m. Alice Ann McLaughlin, Oct. 8, 1966; children: Alice Ann, Maureen Isabelle, Edward Davis, Charles Timothy. B.A., U. Iowa, 1964, J.D., 1967. Bar: Mass. 1967. Atty. Goodwin, Procter & Hoar, Boston, 1967-74; v.p., gen. counsel Wang Labs, Inc., Lowell, Mass., 1974-83, sr. v.p., 1983—, corp. sec., clk., 1976—; sec. Wang Inst. Grad. Studies, Tyngsboro, Mass., 1979—; trustee Wang Ctr. for Performing Arts, Boston, 1982—. Trustee U. Lowell, (Mass.), 1981—, chmn. bd. tustees, 1982—; trustee Pregnancy Help of Greater Boston, 1973—; advisor Weston Sch. Theology, 1984—. Served to capt. USAF, 1964-67. Mem. Mass. Bar Assn. (bd. dels. 1977-80), Boston Bar Assn., ABA (com. on corp. law depts.). Democrat. Roman Catholic. Club: The Skating of Boston. General corporate. Home: 33 Audubon Ln Belmon MA 02178 Office: Wang Labs Inc One Industrial Ave Lowell MA 01851

GRAZIANO, CRAIG FRANK, lawyer; b. Des Moines, Dec. 7, 1950; s. Charles Dominic and Corrine Rose (Comito) G. B.A. summa cum laude, Macalester Coll., 1973; J.D. with honors, Drake U., 1975. Bar: Iowa 1976, U.S. Dist. Ct. (no. and so. dist.) Iowa 1978, U.S. Ct. Appeals (8th cir.) 1977. Law clk. to sr. circuit judge M.D. Van Oosterhout, U.S. Ct. Appeals for 8th Circuit, Sioux City, Iowa, 1976-78; assoc. Dickinson, Throckmorton, Parker, Mannheimer & Raife, Des Moines, 1978-82, ptnr., 1982—. Mem. ABA, Iowa Bar Assn., Polk County Bar Assn., Nat. Health Lawyers Assn., Order of Coif, Phi Beta Kappa. Health, General corporate, Insurance. Office: Dickinson Throckmorton et al 1600 Hub Tower Des Moines IA 50309

GRAZIANO, RONALD ANTHONY, lawyer; b. N.Y.C., Aug. 13, 1948; s. Charles and Anna (DiPasquale) G.; m. Helen Ann McFadden, Aug. 4, 1973. B.A. in Polit. Sci., Fordham U., 1970; J.D., Rutgers-Camden Sch. Law, 1973. Bar: N.Y. 1974, N.J. 1974, U.S. Dist. Ct. N.J. 1974, U.S. Ct. Appeals (2d and 3d cirs.) 1975, U.S. Ct. Appeals (D.C. cir.) 1978, U.S. Supreme Ct. 1979; cert. civil trial atty Supreme Ct. of N.J. Law clk. to presiding judge U.S. Dist. Ct., N.J., 1973-74; assoc. Tomar, Parks, Seliger, Simonoff & Adourian, Haddonfield, N.J., 1974-79, ptnr., 1979—. Assoc. editor Rutgers-Camden Law Jour., 1972-73. Bd. dirs. Camden Regional Legal Services, 1977-80; mem. Planning Bd., Mount Laurel, N.J., 1981, 83, 84; councilman Mount Laurel Twp., 1981-83, mayor, 1984. Mem. Rutgers-Camden Law Sch. Alumni Assn. (chancellor 1976-77), Am. Arbitration Assn. (nat. panel 1979—), Camden County Bar Assn., N.J. State Bar Assn., ABA, Assn. Trial Lawyers Am. (exec. com. N.J. chpt. 1975). Democrat. Roman Catholic. Personal injury, Family and matrimonial, Civil rights. Office: Tomar Parks Seliger Simonoff & Adourian 41 S Haddon Ave Haddonfield NJ 08033

GREANIAS, GEORGE CONSTANTINE, lawyer, legal educator; b. Decatur, Ill., Apr. 20, 1948; s. Gus George and Katherine (Papadogianis) G. BA in History, Rice U., 1970; JD, Harvard U., 1973. Bar: Tex. 1973. Assoc. Liddell, Sapp & Zivley, Houston, 1973-74; sole practice Houston, 1977-81; assoc. prof. Rice U., Houston, 1977-86; of counsel Wood, Lucksinger & Epstein, Houston, 1986—. Trustee Mus. Fine Arts, Houston, 1982—, Annunciation Sch., Houston, 1982-84, 86—, Lighthouse of Houston, 1983—; bd. dirs. Houston Youth Ballet and Symphony, 1984—, Art League of Houston, 1984—, Girls Club of Houston, 1985—, Westbury Hosp., Houston, 1986—. Named one of ten Outstanding Young Men of Houston Jaycees, 1983. Mem. Tex. Bar Assn., Houston World Trade Assn. (bd. dirs. 1986—), Harvard U. Alumni Assn. Eastern Orthodox. Avocations: racquetball, running, reading. General corporate, Local government, Legislative. Office: City of Houston PO Box 1562 Houston TX 77251

GRECH, ANTHONY PAUL, law librarian; b. N.Y.C., July 16, 1930; s. Annibale H. and Anna Jane (Cassar) G. B.B.A., Manhattan Coll., 1952; M.L.S., Columbia U., 1961. Asst. reference librarian Assn. Bar City N.Y., 1958-65, reference librarian, 1965-67, librarian, 1967-84, librarian, curator, 1984—; mem. library com. of Eastman Arbitration Library, Am. Arbitration Assn., 1984-85. Mem. Am. Assn. Law Libraries (Joseph L. Andrews Bibliog. award 1967, chmn. micro fascimiles com. 1965-67, chmn. publs. com. 1975-76, exec. bd. 1980-83), Assn. Law Libraries Upstate N.Y. (treas. 1976-77), Bibliog. Soc. Am., Spl. Libraries Assn., Am. Arbitration Assn., Law Library Assn. Greater N.Y. (pres. 1967-68), ALA, Bibliog. Soc. U. Va., Internat. Assn. Law Libraries, Am. Printing History Assn., Nat. Micrographics Assn., Supreme Ct. Hist. Soc., Beta Phi Mu. Librarianship, Legal history. Home: 15 W 72d St New York NY 10023 Office: 42 W 44th St New York NY 10036

GRECO, JOSEPH DOMINIC, JR., lawyer; b. Jersey City, Aug. 22, 1955; s. Joseph Dominic Sr. and Bernice Amelia (Tamburello) G.; m. Sharon K. Hayes, Apr. 17, 1982. BS in Bus. Mgmt. cum laude, St. Peters Coll., Jersey City, 1977; JD, Fordham U., 1980. Bar: N.J. 1980, U.S. Dist. Ct. N.J. 1980. Law clk. to presiding judge Bergen County Courthouse, Hackensack, N.J., 1980-81; ptnr. Carluccio & Carluccio, Hoboken, N.J., 1981—. Chmn. issues com. to elect Tom Hynes N.J. senator, Maywood, 1982. Benjamin Darling scholar. Mem. ABA, N.J. Bar Assn., Hudson County Bar Assn., Courtsmen. Democrat. Roman Catholic. Real property, Estate taxation, State civil litigation. Home: 5 David Scott Dr Wayne NJ 07470 Office: Carluccio & Carluccio 96 Hudson St PO Box 230 Hoboken NJ 07030

GRECO, MICHAEL S., lawyer; b. Rende, Cosenza, Italy, Nov. 22, 1942; came to U.S., 1950; s. Raphael and Rose (Fellicetti) G.; m. Donna K. Green, Aug. 23, 1968; children—Christian Raphael, Jordan Phillip, Elizabeth Elena. A.B. in English, Princeton U., N.J., 1965; J.D., Boston Coll., 1972. Bar: Mass. Clk. U.S. Ct. Appeals for 2d Circuit, N.Y.C., 1972-73; assoc. Hill & Barlow, Boston, 1973-79, ptnr., 1979—; mem., Mass. Bd. Bar Overseers, 1978-81, vice chmn., 1980-81. Editor-in-Chief Boston Coll. Law Rev., 1971-72. Mem., Wellesly Permanent Sch. Accomodations Com., Mass., 1980-83; chmn. Mass. Gov.'s Bar Commn. on Alcoholic Clients, 1984-87; founder Mass. Gov.'s Commn. on Unmet Legal Needs of Children, 1986—. Inst Comparative Law fellow, U. Florence, Italy, 1974. Fellow Am. Bar Found., Mass. Bar Found. (treas., trustee 1980—); mem. ABA (del. 1985—), New Eng. Bar Assn. (v.p. 1985-86, pres. 1986-87), Mass. Bar Assn. (pres. 1985-86). Democrat. Club: Princeton (N.Y.C.). Federal civil litigation, State civil litigation. Home: 65 Livermore Rd Wellesley Hills MA 02181 Office: Hill & Barlow One International Pl Boston MA 02110

GREELEY, PAUL DAVID, lawyer; b. Elizabeth, N.J., July 19, 1957; s. Robert Patrick and Mary Lou (Johnson) G.; m. Nancy Wilson, Sept. 7, 1985. BA in Chemistry, Conn. Coll., 1979; JD, Gonzaga U., 1982. Bar: D.C. 1982, U.S. Dist Ct. D.C. 1984, U.S. Ct. Appeals (Fed. cir.) 1984. Legal intern Univ. Legal Assistance, Spokane, Wash., 1981-82; assoc. atty. Antonelli, Terry and Wands, Washington, 1982-85; atty. Standard Oil Co., Cleve., 1985-87; ptnr. Law Office of Paul D. Greeley, Cleve., 1987—; bd. dirs. Greelco, Newark, 1980—. Assoc. editor Can.-Am. Law Jour., Spokane, 1981-82. mem. exec. bd. Conn. Coll. Club of Washington, 1983-85; admissions aid Conn. Coll., New London, 1983—, Gonzaga U. Sch. Law, Spokane, 1984—; vol. atty. Legal Counsel for Elderly, Washington, 1983-85. Mem. ABA, D.C. Bar Assn., Conn. Patent Law Assn., U.S. Patent and Trademark Office, Westchester-Fairfield Corp. Counsel Assn., Inc. Roman Catholic. Club: Conn. Coll. Club of Fairfield County. Avocations: golf, tennis, snow skiing. Patent, General corporate, Private international. Home and Office: 12 Brookfield Dr Huntington CT 06484

GREELISH, THOMAS W., lawyer; b. 1939. BA, Rutgers U.; JD, Seton Hall U. U.S. atty. State of N.J., Newark. Office: Fed Bldg 970 Broad St Room 502 Newark NJ 07102 *

GREELY, MICHAEL TRUMAN, attorney general of Montana; b. Great Falls, Mont., Feb. 28, 1940; s. Myril Jay and Laura Harriet (Haugh) G.; m. Marilyn Jean Myhre, Dec. 1, 1972; children: Winston Truman, Morgen. B.A., Yale U., 1962; J.D., U. Mont., 1967. Bar: Mont. 1967. Tchr. pub. schs. Oklahoma City, 1962-63; asst. atty. gen. Mont., 1968-70; atty. gen. 1977—; chmn. Mont. Justice Project, 1975; dep. county atty. Cascade County, Mont., 1970-74. Mem. Mont. Ho. of Reps., 1971-74; mem. Mont. Senate, 1975-77; Pres. 8th Dist. Youth Guidance Home, Great Falls, 1971-72. Mem. Nat. Assn. Attys. Gen. (pres. 1983-84), Mont., Cascade County bar assns. Democrat. Criminal. Office: Justice Bldg 215 N Sanders St Helena MT 59620

GREEN, CARL JAY, lawyer; b. N.Y.C., Oct. 12, 1939; s. Irving and Ruth (Rispler) G.; m. Judith Lynn Slomoff, May 24, 1964; m. 2d, Pamela Carol Wattenberg, Sept. 21, 1975; children—Adam Mitchell, Brian Jeffrey, Anthony Loeb. A.B. magna cum laude, Harvard U., 1961; postgrad. U. Hong Kong, 1961-62; J.D., Yale U., 1965; postgrad. Japan Research Ctr., Tokyo (Stanford U.), 1973-74. Bar: N.Y. 1965, D.C. 1969, U.S. Supreme Ct. 1981. Assoc. Baker & McKenzie, N.Y.C., 1965-68; atty./advisor U.S. Dept. Transp., Washington, 1968-69; assoc. Caplin & Drysdale, Washington, 1969-72; program officer Ford Found., N.Y.C., 1973-75, rep. for Japan and E. Asia, Tokyo, 1975-80; ptnr. Wender Murase & White, Washington, 1980-86; ptnr. Milbank, Tweed, Hadley & McCloy, Washington, 1986—; research assoc. East Asian Legal Studies, Harvard Law Sch., 1981-83; Bd. dirs. Korea Econ. Inst. U.S. Nat. Com. Pacific Econ. Cooperation; trustee Asia Study Japan Am. Soc. of Washington, Lingnan U.; advisor U.S.-Japan Econ. Relations (Wise Men) Group, 1980-81. Fulbright fellow, 1961; Harvard U. travelling fellow, 1961-62. Mem. ABA (coms. internat. trade, China, Far Eastern law), Am. Soc. Internat. Law, Assn. Bar City N.Y., D.C. Bar Assn., Council Fgn. Relations, Asia Soc. (trustee 1983—), Phi Beta Kappa. Democrat. Jewish. Clubs: Cosmos, (Washington); University (N.Y.C.). Contbr. articles to publs. in field. Private international, Public international. Office: McKenna Conner & Cuneo 1575 Eye St NW Washington DC 20005

GREEN, CAROL H., lawyer, journalist; b. Seattle, Feb. 18, 1944; B.A. summa cum laude in History and Journalism, La. Tech. U., 1965; L.L.M. (Ford Found. fellow), Yale U., 1977; J.D., U. Denver, 1979. Intern, Shreveport (La.) Times, 1964, reporter, 1965-66; reporter Guam Daily News, 1966-67; city editor Pacific Jour., Agana, Guam, 1967-68; reporter, editorial writer, Denver Post, 1968-75, legal affairs reporter, 1977-79, asst. editor editorial page, 1979-81, house counsel, 1980-83, labor relations mgr., 1981-83; assoc. Holme Roberts & Owen, 1983-85; v.p. human resources and legal affairs Denver Post, 1985—; mem. corrections task force Colo. Criminal Justice Standards and Goals, 1985 speaker for USIA, India, Egypt. Bd. dirs. YWCA, Trans. Council, Denver C. of C. Recipient McWilliams award for juvenile justice, Denver, 1971; award for interpretive reporting Denver Newspaper Guild, 1979. Mem. ABA (forum on communications law), Colo. Women's Bar Assn., Colo. Bar Assn. (bd. govs. 1985-86, chairperson BAR-press com. 1980), Denver Bar Assn. (co-chairperson jud. selection and benefits com. 1982-85, 1st v.p. 1986), Alliance Profl. Women (exec. com.), Women's Forum, Leadership Denver. Clubs: Denver Press, Denver Athletic. Episcopalian. Labor, General corporate, Libel. Office: The Denver Post 650 15th St Denver CO 80202

GREEN, CLARENCE ARTHUR, lawyer; b. Ware, Mass., Mar. 14, 1938; s. Clarence Janes and Nellie (Mazik) G.; m. Bonnie Louise Bauer, Oct. 17, 1969; children: Christopher Jon, Jennifer Lynn. BSME, U. Mass., 1962; JD, Boston U., 1965. Bar: Mass. 1966, N.Y. 1967, Conn. 1986, U.S. Patent Office, U.S. Dist. Ct. (we., ea. and so. dists.) N.Y., U.S. Dist. Ct. Conn. Patent atty. Xerox Corp., Rochester, N.Y., 1966-70, patent counsel, 1972-76, mng. patent atty., 1976-80; atty. licensing Xerox Corp., Stamford, Conn., 1970-72; ptnr. Perman & Green, Fairfield, Conn., 1980—. Bd. dirs. Fairfield YMCA, 1985—. Mem. ABA, N.Y. State Bar Assn., Conn. Patent Law Assn. Patent, Trademark and copyright. Home: 105 Horseshoe Ln Fairfield CT 06430 Office: Perman & Green 425 Post Rd Fairfield CT 06430

GREEN, CLIFFORD SCOTT, judge; b. Phila., Apr. 2, 1923; s. Robert Lewis and Alice (Robinson) G.; m. Mabel Wood, June 20, 1959; children—Terri Alice, David Scott. B.S., Temple U., 1948, J.D., 1951. Bar: Pa. 1952. Practiced law Phila., 1952-64; dep. atty. gen. State of Pa., 1954; judge County Ct., Phila., 1964-68, Ct. Common Pleas, 1968-71, U.S. Dist. Ct. for Eastern Dist. Pa., Phila., 1971—; lectr. in law Temple U. Bd. dirs. Children's Aid Soc. of Pa., Crime Prevention Assn. Phila.; mem. bd. mgrs. Children's Hosp., Phila. Served with USAAF, 1943-46. Recipient Judge William Hastie Community and Country Service award, 1985, awards for community service Women's Christian Alliance, awards for community service Health and Welfare Council, awards for community service Opportunities Industrialization Center. Mem. Sigma Pi Phi. Presbyterian. Office: 15613 US Courthouse Independence Mall West 601 Market St Philadelphia PA 19106

GREEN, GERALD PATRICK, lawyer; b. Oklahoma City, Jan. 22, 1952; s. James Leonard and Patricia Jenean (Kinny) G.; m. Randi Dawn Parker, Aug. 1, 1980; children: Kimberly Parker, Hailey Madison. Grad., USAF Acad., 1972; BA, U. Okla., 1973; JD, Okla. U., 1976. Bar: Okla. 1976, U.S. Dist. Ct. (we., no. and ea. dists.) Okla. 1977, U.S. Ct. Appeals (10th cir.) 1977. Asst. mcpl. counselor City of Oklahoma City, 1976-77; assoc. Pierce, Couch, Hendrickson, Johnston & Baysinger, Oklahoma city, 1977-81, ptnr., 1982—. Mem. ABA, Def. Research Inst., Okla. Assn. Def. Counsel. Avocations: soccer, family. State civil litigation, Personal injury, Insurance. Office: Pierce Couch Hendrickson et al 1109 N Francis Oklahoma City OK 73106

GREEN, JAMES SAMUEL, lawyer; b. Berwick, Pa., May 24, 1947. AB, Princeton U., 1969; JD, Villanova U., 1972. Bar: Del. 1972, Pa. 1973, U.S. Dist. Ct. Del. 1973, U.S. Ct. Appeals (3d cir.) 1981. Assoc. Connolly, Bove, Lodge & Hutz, Wilmington, Del., 1972-74, ptnr., 1977—; dep. atty. gen. State of Del., Wilmington, 1975-76. Mem. ABA, Del. State Bar Assn. (treas. 1980-81), Assn. Trial Lawyers Am., Del. Assn. Trial Lawyers. Club: Ivy (Princeton). Federal civil litigation, State civil litigation, Libel. Home: 2603 W 17th St Wilmington DE 19806 Office: Connolly Bove Lodge Hutz 1220 Market St Wilmington DE 19801

GREEN, JEFFREY STEVEN, lawyer; b. N.Y.C., July 7, 1943; s. Morris and Fannie (Mandel) G.; m. Sydell Joan Loewenthal, Nov. 1, 1964; children—Robin Janet, Philip Peter. B.A. in Polit. Sci., CCNY, 1965; J.D., N.Y. U., 1969; A.M.P., Harvard U., 1982. Bar: N.Y. 1969, U.S. Dist. Ct. (so. dist. N.Y.) 1983, U.S. Dist. Ct. (ea. dist. N.Y.) 1983. Atty., Port Authority of N.Y. and N.J., N.Y.C., 1969-77, asst. chief fin. div. law dept., 1977-78, dep. chief fin. div. law dept., 1978-79, chief fin. div. law dept., 1979-85, asst. gen. counsel, 1985— . Contbr. articles to profl. publs. Trustee Pearl River Pub. Library, 1985—, Pearl River Sch. Bd., 1975-84, pres., 1977-80; exec. com. Rockland County Sch. Bds. Assn., 1976-84, pres., 1980-82. Mem. ABA, Nat. Assn. Bond Lawyers, N.Y. State Bar Assn., N.Y. County Lawyers Assn., Rockland County Bar Assn., Govt. Fin. Officers Assn. (chmn. com. of govtl. debt. and fiscal policy, 1984—), Mcpl. Forum N.Y., N.Y. State Govt. Fin. Officers Assn. Municipal bonds, Legislative, Administrative and regulatory. Office: Port Authority NY & NJ Law Dept 1 World Trade Ctr 67E New York NY 10048

GREEN, JOAN WHITESIDE, lawyer; b. Aug. 9, 1944; d. George Jr. and Viola W.; 1 child, Paul. BA, Calif. State U., Los Angeles, 1965, MA, 1968; JD, Whittier Coll., 1979. Bar: Calif. 1979, U.S. Dist. Ct. (cen. dist.) Calif. 1979, U.S. Ct. Appeals (9th cir.) 1985. Sole practice Los Angeles, 1979-84; ptnr. Lomax & Green, Los Angeles, 1984-87, Joan Whiteside Green & Assocs., Los Angeles, 1987—. Mem. ABA, Calif. Bar Assn. (commn. jud. nominees evaluation 1985—, del. state bar conv. 1983—), Nat. Bar Assn. (bd. dirs. region IX 1985-87), Black Women Lawyers So. Calif. (pres. 1983-84), Calif. Assn. Black Lawyers (bd. dirs. 1982), Calif. Women Lawyers (bd. govs. 1983-84), Langston Bar Assn. (bd. govs.), Nat. Assn. Securities Profls., Women Lawyers Los Angeles, Coalition of 100 Black Women, Women Aware, Jack and Jill of Am. (pres. Los Angeles chpt. 1986—), Ebony Guild of The Florence Crittenton Ctr. of Young Women and Infants (v.p. 1983-84). Office: Joan Whiteside Green & Assocs 3550 Wilshire Blvd Suite 800 Los Angeles CA 90010

GREEN, JONATHAN DAVID, lawyer; b. N.Y.C., Nov. 1, 1946; s. Daniel and Helen (Born) G.; m. Sally A. Sickles, Oct. 4, 1984. BA, Lafayette Coll., 1968; JD, NYU, 1975. Bar: N.Y. 1976, U.S. Dist. Ct. (so. dist.) N.Y. 1976. Assoc. Thacher, Proffitt & Wood, N.Y.C., 1975-80; asst. v.p. Rockefeller Group Inc., N.Y.C., 1980-83, v.p., sec., gen. counsel, 1983—. Served to 1st lt. USNR, 1969-72. Mem. ABA, N.Y. State Bar Assn., Assn. of Bar of City of N.Y. Democrat. Avocations: golf, fishing. Real property, General corporate, Entertainment. Office: Rockefeller Group Inc 1230 Ave of Americas New York NY 10020

GREEN, JOSEPH BENJAMIN, lawyer; b. N.Y.C., Oct. 23, 1947; s. Hank Green and Ruth (Finley) Lein; m. Carol Shasha, June 6, 1976; children: Jeffrey Scott, Ariana Carlyn. BA, Yale U., 1969; JD, Harvard U., 1976. Bar: Mass. 1977, U.S. Dist. Ct. Mass. 1978. Assoc. Hutchins & Wheeler, Boston, 1976-79; chief dist. ct. prosecutor Essex County Dist. Atty.'s Office, Salem, Mass., 1979-85, dir. of policy, 1985—; patrolman Met. Police Dept.,

Washington, 1970-73; clin. law supr. Harvard Law Sch., Cambridge, 1983—; speakers bur. Nat. Ctr. for Missing and Exploited Children. Contbr. articles to profl. jours. Mem. Child Support Commn., Boston, 1985, adv. bd. Gov.'s Alcohol Servers Awareness, Boston, 1985; commr. Commn. on Unmet Legal Needs of Children, Boston, 1986—. Younger Humanist fellow NEH, 1973-74. Mem. Mass. Bar Assn. (trial de novo task force 1985). Criminal, Juvenile, Missing Children. Office: Dist Attys Office 70 Washington St Salem MA 01970

GREEN, JOYCE HENS, federal judge; b. N.Y.C., Nov. 13, 1928; d. James S. and Hedy (Bucher) Hens; m. Samuel Green, Sept. 25, 1965 (dec. Oct. 23, 1983); children: Michael Timothy, June Heather, James Harry. B.A., U. Md., 1949; J.D., George Washington U., 1951. Bar: D.C. 1951, Va. 1956, U.S. Supreme Ct. 1956. Practice law Washington, 1951-68, Arlington, Va., 1956-68; ptnr. Green & Green, 1966-68; judge Superior Ct., D.C., 1968-79, U.S. Dist. Ct. for D.C., 1979—. Trustee D.C. div. Am. Cancer Soc., 1963-76. Named Woman Lawyer of Yr., 1979. Fellow Am. Acad. Matrimonial Lawyers, Am. Bar Found.; mem. Fed. Judges Assn. (bd. dirs.), ABA, Va. Bar Assn., Bar Assn. D.C., D.C. Bar, D.C. Women's Bar Assn. (pres. 1960-62), Exec. Women in Govt. (chmn. 1977), Kappa Beta Pi, Phi Delta Phi (hon.). Club: Nat. Lawyers (Washington). Office: US Dist Ct US Courthouse 3rd & Constitution Ave NW Washington DC 20001 Other Address: US District Court 844 King St Lockbox 12 Wilmington DE 19801

GREEN, KENNETH NORTON, lawyer, law educator; b. Chgo., Mar. 18, 1938; s. Martin and Sarah (Owens) G.; m. Joan Nemer, Oct. 17, 1968 (div. July 1974); 1 child, Joey. A.A., Wright Jr. Coll., 1960; B.A., Calif. State U.-Los Angeles, 1963; postgrad. Southwestern U., 1965-67; J.D., U. San Fernando Valley, 1968; Cert. (hon. teaching) Los Angeles Unified Sch. Dist., 1979. Bar: Calif. 1970, U.S. Dist. Ct. (cen. dist.) Calif. 1970, U.S. Supreme Ct. 1973. Tchr. Los Angeles, Calif., 1964-70; dep. pub. defender Los Angeles County, Calif., 1970-73, 75—; ptnr. Green & Pirosh, Los Angeles, 1973-75; head dept., pub. defender instr. Paralegal dept. U. Calif., Los Angeles, 1975—; judge pro tem Los Angeles Municipal Ct., 1978. Contbr. articles to legal publs. Ex officio mem. Prison Preventers, Calif. Dept. of Parole; mayor's com. Project Heavy; bd. dirs. City of Hope; Vista Del Mar; legal adv. panel Jewish Family Service; vol. atty. for indigents UCLA Law Sch.; vol. in Parole Program, com. chmn. Research Prejudice-Pvt. Clubs (Disting. Service award 1971). Served with U.S. Army, 1957-58, Korea. Mem. Pub. Defender Assn. (dir. 1971-74, chief wage 1973-75) ABA, Los Angeles County Bar Assn. (vice chmn. drug abuse 1975, exec. com. criminal justice 1977). Democrat. Jewish. Lodge: Justice (bd. dirs. 1971-72). Criminal, Juvenile, Legal education. Office: Pub Defender Los Angeles County 210 W Temple St Los Angeles CA 90012

GREEN, LAWRENCE JAMALIAN, lawyer; b. Lake City, S.C., May 18, 1945; s. James Abram and Gertrude Camelia (Porter) G.; m. Helen Louise Hinkle, April 22, 1967; 1 child, Patricia Ann. BS, N.C. A&T State U., 1966; JD, U. Denver, 1978. Bar: Colo. 1979, U.S. Dist. Ct. Colo. 1979, U.S. Ct. Appeals (10th cir.) 1979. Sr. contract adminstr. Martin Marietta Corp., Denver, 1978-85; sole practice Denver, 1985—. Inventor in field. Mem. archl. com. Ridgeview Hills Homeowners Assn., Littleton, Colo., 1979-82; chmn. accountability com. Sch. Dist. #6, Littleton, 1973-76. Served to capt. USAF, 1966-70. Named one of Outstanding Young Men in Am., 1981. Mem. ABA, Sam Cary Bar Assn., Littleton Jaycees. Democrat. Avocations: crossword puzzles, acrostics, art collecting, antiques, genealogical research. Construction, Government contracts and claims, Contracts commercial. Office: 1490 Lafayette St Suite 400 Denver CO 80218-2394

GREEN, LYNNE KNIGHT, lawyer; b. Eupora, Miss., June 15, 1954; d. James Aubrey and Mary Sue (McKee) Knight; m. Walter Galloway Green III, July 11, 1981; 1 child, Joseph Stone. BBA, U. Miss., 1975, JD, 1978. Bar: Miss. 1978, Tenn. 1985. Acct. tax dept. Ernst & Whinney, Memphis, 1978-84; counsel Associated Housing Developers, Inc., Memphis, 1984-85; assoc. Wildman, Harrold, Allen, Dixon & McDonnell, Memphis, 1985—. Mem. ABA, Am. Inst. CPA's, Tenn. Soc. CPA's, Am. Soc. Women Accts. (bd. dirs. Memphis chpt. 1985—), Estate Planning Council. Mem. Disciples of Christ. Avocations: water skiing, reading, golf, gardening. Estate planning, Personal income taxation, Contracts commercial. Home: 3384 Dell Glade Dr Memphis TN 38111 Office: Wildman Harrold et al 6060 Primary Pkwy Suite 328 Memphis TN 38119-5738

GREEN, MARSHALL MUNRO, lawyer; b. Staten Island, N.Y., Feb. 23, 1938; s. Thomas Marshall and Mary (Tibbitts) G.; m. Lucy Featherstone Abbott, June 15, 1959; children: Eleanor Thurston, John Marshall, Lucy Gatewood. AB, Harvard U., 1959, LLB cum laude, 1965. Bar: N.Y. 1965, Conn. 1976, Fla. 1976, U.S. Dist. Ct. Conn. 1984. Assoc. Breed, Abbott & Morgan, N.Y.C., 1965-72; ptnr. Williamson & Green, N.Y.C., 1972-76, Bisset, Atkins & Green, N.Y.C., 1976-82, LeBoeuf, Lamb, Leiby & MacRae, N.Y.C., 1982—. Trustee Childrens Aid Soc., N.Y.C., 1972—, Fedn. Protestant Welfare Agys., N.Y.C., 1980—, United Charities Inc., N.Y.C., 1983—. Fellow Am. Coll. Probate Counsel. Democrat. Episcopalian. Clubs: Harvard (N.Y.C.), Pequot Yacht (Southport, Conn.). Probate. Home: 900 Catamount Rd Fairfield CT 06430 also: 411 Pequot Ave Southport CT 06490

GREEN, MICHAEL AARON, lawyer; b. Newark, Oct. 21, 1950; s. Walter P. and Shirley (Cohen) G.; m. Susan L. Feinstein, June 28, 1981; 1 child, Rebecca. BA, Brandeis U., 1972; MA, U. Denver, 1978; JD, Yale U., 1980. Assoc. Paul, Weiss, Rifkind, et al, N.Y.C., 1980-83, Washington, 1983-84; assoc. Shereff, Friedman et al, N.Y.C., 1984-86, ptnr., 1987—. Mem. ABA. Securities, General corporate, Contracts commercial. Office: Shereff Friedman et al 919 Third Ave New York NY 10022

GREEN, PAUL, lawyer; b. Detroit, May 7, 1939; s. Manning Samuel and Ellen (Dicker) G.; m. Elizabeth Ann Elias, Sept. 12, 1962; children: Jacqueline, Robert. BA, Wayne State U., 1962, LLB, 1964. Ptnr. Gordon & Green P.C., Birmingham, Mich., 1964—. Mem. ABA, Mich. Bar Assn. Democrat. Avocations: piano, reading, jogging. Home: 677 Plum Ridge Dr Rochester Hills MI 48063 Office: Gordon & Green PC 280 N Woodward Suite 407 Birmingham MI 48011

GREEN, PAUL ANDREW, lawyer, educator; b. Washington, Sept. 8, 1957; s. Robert Norman and Elinor (Friedman) G; m. Julia Lillie Dolan, Aug. 16, 1981; 1 child, Sarah. BA, U. Chgo., 1978; JD with honors, U. Md., 1982. BarL Md. 1982, D.C. 1984. Law clk. to judge Md. Ct. Appeals, Annapolis, 1982-83; atty. Pension Benefit Guaranty Corp., Washington, 1983-85; assoc. Beins, Axelrod & Osborne, P.C., Washington, 1985—; adj. prof. law Cath. U., Washington, 1986—. Co-author: SEPPAA: An Overview, 1986; contbr. articles to profl. jours. Mem. ABA, Md. Bar Assn., D.C. Bar Assn. (chmn. employee benefits com. labor relations sect.). Democrat. Pension, profit-sharing, and employee benefits, Bankruptcy, Legal education. Home: 10105 Kindly Ct Gaithersburg MD 20879 Office: Beins Axelrod & Osborne PC 1200 15th St NW Suite 505 Washington DC 20005

GREEN, PHILIP BURTON, lawyer; b. Chgo., Aug. 2, 1947; s. Floyd Burton and Helen Marie (Krick) G. B.A. in Econs., Duke U., 1969; J.D., U. Ill., 1973. Bar: Ill. 1973, Colo. 1973, U.S. Dist. Ct. Colo. 1973, U.S. Dist. Ct. (no. dist.) Ill. 1973, U.S. Ct. Appeals (9th cir.) 1982, U.S. Supreme Ct. 1980. Staff atty. VISTA, ACTION, Denver, 1973-74; sole practice, Denver, 1974-80; sr. ptnr. Green & Josefiak, Denver, 1981—; counsel Catholic Community Services, Inc., Denver, 1974—. Mem. ABA, Am. Trial Lawyers Assn., Colo. Bar Assn., Colo. Trial Lawyers Assn. State civil litigation, Federal civil litigation, Juvenile. Office: Green & Josefiak 1888 Sherman St Suite 780 Denver CO 80203

GREEN, RANDALL WAYNE, lawyer; b. St. Louis, May 15, 1951; s. Jesse Brittain and Della (Highley) G.; m. Laura Deneke, July 3, 1971; children: Jason, Karl. BBA, U. Mo., St. Louis, 1977; JD, Harvard U., 1980. Bar: Wash. 1981, Hawaii 1985. Fin. analyst Boatmen's Nat. Bank, St. Louis, 1977; law clk. Minn. Supreme Ct., St. Paul, 1980-81; assoc. Foster, Pepper & Riviera, Seattle, 1981-83; legal cons. Kim & Chang, Seoul, Republic of Korea, 1983-85; assoc. Torkildson, Katz, Jossem, Fonseca & Moore, Honolulu, 1985-86; mng. dir. Apex Ltd., Kailua, Hawaii, 1986—. Co-chmn. taxation and U.S. govt. com. Am. C. of C. in Korea, Seoul, 1984-85. Served with USCG, 1970-74. Mem. Pacific and Asian Affairs Council. Private international, Contracts commercial. Home: 71 Aikahi Loop Kailua HI 96734 Office: Apex Ltd PO Box 1988 Kailua HI 96734

GREEN, RAY EUGENE, lawyer; b. San Antonio, Oct. 1, 1954. BA, Stanford U., 1975; JD, U. Tex., 1978. Bar: Tex. 1978, U.S. Dist. Ct. (no. dist.) Tex. 1978, U.S. Tax Ct. 1978, U.S. Ct. Appeals (5th cir.) 1978. Sole practice Dallas, Tex., 1978—; lectr. in field. Mem. ABA, Tex. Bar Assn., Dallas. Bar Assn., Dallas Assn. Young Lawyers, Coll. Bar Tex. Presbyterian. Avocations: tennis. Family and matrimonial, Contracts commercial, Real property. Office: 1333 Two Turtle Creek Village Dallas TX 75219

GREEN, RAYMOND BERT, lawyer; b. Hartford, Conn., July 12, 1929; s. William Gottlieb and Mayme Pauline (Judatz) G.; m. Barbara Louise Miller, Jan. 31, 1955; children: Elizabeth Hollister, William Goodrich. BA, Yale U., 1951, LLB, 1954. Bar: Conn. 1954, U.S. Dist. Ct. Conn. 1959, U.S. Supreme Ct. 1962, U.S. Ct. Appeals (2d cir.) 1966, U.S. Ct. Mil. Appeals 1974, U.S. Dist. Ct. (so. dist.) N.Y. 1976, U.S. Dist. Ct. (ea. dist.) N.Y. 1976. Assoc., Camp, Williams & Richardson, New Britain, Conn., 1954-55; assoc. Day, Berry & Howard, Hartford, Conn., 1958-65, ptnr., 1966—; dir. New Britain Herald; trustee Collinsville Savs. Soc. (Conn.); judge of probate Dist. of Canton, Conn., 1962—. Pres. bd. dirs. Am. Friends of Coll. Cevenol (France); bd. dirs. YMCA Met. Hartford, 1963-84, 86—; sec., bd. trustees Children's Mus. Hartford, 1977-85, Sci. Mus. of Conn., 1985-86. Served with USNR, 1955-58; comdr. JAGC, Res., 1958-79. Mem. Hartford County Bar Assn., ABA, Conn. Bar Assn. (chmn. ins. com. 1978-85), Judge Advs. Assn., Def. Research Inst., Conn. Def. Lawyers Assn. (bd. dirs. 1985—), Assn. Trial Lawyers Am., Nat. Coll. Probate Judges, Phi Beta Kappa. Republican. Congregationalist. Clubs: Univ. (Hartford), Officers of Conn., Naval Res. Officers Luncheon (N.Y.C.), Assn. Ex-Mems. Squadron A (N.Y.C.). State civil litigation, Federal civil litigation, Probate. Home: 120 West Rd Collinsville CT 06022 Office: Cityplace 2500 Hartford CT 06103

GREEN, RICHARD GEORGE, lawyer; b. N.Y.C., Dec. 13, 1913; s. Louis and Kate G. (Gottler) G.; m. Lynn Estelle Gold, Nov. 15, 1940 (div. 1954); m. Ruth D. Davis, July 2, 1954; children: Anna, Jennifer, Nancy, Richard Jr. BA, CUNY, 1932; LLB, Bklyn. Law Sch., 1936, JD, 1967. Bar: N.Y. 1937, U.S. Dist. Ct. (so. dist.) N.Y. 1940, U.S. Ct. Internat. Trade 1951, U.S. Ct. Appeals (2d cir.) 1951, U.S. Dist. Ct. (ea. dist.) 1964, U.S. Supreme Ct. 1967, U.S. Ct. Appeals (Fed. cir.) 1982. Asst. corp. counsel City of Long Beach,, N.Y., 1937; assoc. Irving Ribman Esq., N.Y.C., 1938-39; mng. atty. Hays, St. John, Abramson & Schulman, N.Y.C., 1939-40; house counsel Newspaper PM Inc., N.Y.C., 1940-48; sole practice N.Y.C., 1948-76; ptnr. Green & Hillman, N.Y.C., 1976—; adj. prof. SUNY, Stony Brook, 1974-75; lectr. Rutgers Law Sch., Newark, 1975-77, NYU Law Sch., N.Y.C., 1975-77; arbitrator Civil Ct., N.Y.C., 1980—. Editor Jour. Assn. for Psychiat. Treatment Offenders, 1963-66. park commr. Village Lloyd Harbor, N.Y., 1969-73; pres. Cold Spring Harbor Youth Ctr., N.Y., 1969-73; chmn. bd. dirs., trustee Inst. Advancement Med. Communication, N.Y.C. and Phila., 1965-80; bd. dirs., pres. Harry Futterman Fund Inc., N.Y.C., 1950-85. Served to 1st lt., U.S. Army, 1943-46. Mem. ABA (various coms.), Bar Assn. of City of N.Y., N.Y. County Lawyers Assn., Copyright Soc. U.S. (editorial bd. 1985—), ACLU (chmn. free speech and assn. com. 1980-86), Nat. Press Club, Overseas Press Club. Clubs: Nat. Press (Washington), Overseas Press (N.Y.C.). Avocations: swimming, fishing, reading. Entertainment, Libel, Trademark and copyright. Home: 37 W 12th St New York NY 10011 Office: Green & Hillman 1270 Ave of Americas New York NY 10020

GREEN, ROBERT LAMAR, JR., lawyer; b. East Lansing, Mich., May 4, 1951; s. Robert Lamar and Frances (Cowan) G.; m. Susan Clifton, Nov. 5, 1983. BS, U. Pa., 1973; JD, U. Md., 1976. Bar: Md. 1976, D.C. 1977. Clk. to presiding judge U.S. Dist. Ct. Md., Balt., 1976-77; assoc. Howrey & Simon, Washington, 1977-83; ptnr. Howry & Simon, Washington, 1984—. Club: Army Navy (Washington). Antitrust, Federal civil litigation, Administrative and regulatory. Office: Howrey & Simon 1730 Pennsylvania Ave NW Washington DC 20006

GREEN, THOMAS ANDREW, law and history educator, lawyer; b. 1940. A.B., Columbia U., 1961; A.M., 1962; Ph.D., 1970; J.D., Harvard U., 1972. Asst. prof. Bard Coll., Annandale, N.Y., 1967-69; now prof. law and history U. Mich. Law Sch. Mem. Selden Soc., Am. Hist. Assn., Am. Soc. Legal History. Legal education. Office: U Mich Law Sch 621 S State St 304 Hutchins Hall Ann Arbor MI 48109 *

GREEN, WILLIAM PORTER, lawyer; b. Jacksonville, Ill., Mar. 19, 1920; s. Hugh Parker and Clara Belle (Hopper) G.; m. Rose Marie Hall, Oct. 1, 1944; children: Hugh Michael, Robert Alan, Richard William. B.A., Ill. Coll., 1941; J.D., Northwestern U., 1947. Bar: Ill. 1947, Calif. 1948, U.S. Dist. Ct. (so. dist.) Tex. 1986, Ct. Customs and Patent Appeals 1948, U.S. Patent and Trademark Office 1948, U.S. Ct. Appeals (fed. cir.) 1982, U.S. Ct. Appeals (5th and 9th cirs.), U.S. Supreme Ct. 1948, U.S. Dist. Ct. (cen. dist.) Calif., U.S. Dist. Ct. (so. dist.) Tex., 1986. Practice patent, trademark and copyright law Los Angeles, 1947—; mem. firm Wills, Green & Mueth, 1974-83; of counsel Nilsson, Robbins, Dalgarn, Berliner, Carson & Wurst, Los Angeles, 1984—; del. Calif. State Bar Conv., 1982-87, delegation chair 1986. Bd. editors Ill. Law Rev, 1946. Mem. Los Angeles World Affairs Council, 1975—; del., chmn. Calif. State Bar Conv., 1986 Served lt. USNR, 1942-46. Mem. ABA, Calif Bar Assn., Los Angeles County Bar Assn (trustee 1986-87), Am. Intellectual Property Law Assn., Los Angeles Patent Law Assn. (past sec.-treas., bd. govs.), Lawyers Club Los Angeles (past treas., past sec., bd. govs., pres.-elect 1983 84, pres. 1985-86), Los Angeles County Bar Assn (trustee 1986-87), Am. Legion (past post comdr.), Phi Beta Kappa, Phi Delta Phi, Phi Alpha. Republican. Presbyn. (deacon 1961-63). Clubs: Big Ten of So. Calif, Northwestern U. Alumni of So. Calif, Phi Beta Kappa Alumni of So. Calif, Town Hall of Calif. Patent, Trademark and copyright. Home: 3570 E Lombardy Rd Pasadena CA 91107 Office: Nilsson Robbins Dalgarn Berliner Carson & Wurst 201 N Figueroa St 5th Floor Los Angeles CA 90012

GREENAN, THOMAS J., lawyer; b. Great Falls, Mont., July 13, 1933; s. Phil G. and Ada E. (Collins) G.; m. Helen Louise Shepard, June 1, 1957; children: Gregory, Kathleen, Timothy, Maureen, Daniel. Grad., Gonzaga U., 1953, JD, 1957. Bar: Wash. 1957, U.S. Dist. Ct. (we. dist.) Wash. 1959, U.S. Ct. Appeals (9th cir.) 1961, U.S. Supreme Ct. 1970. Asst. atty. gen. State of Washington, 1957-60, 62-63; assoc. Ferguson & Burdell, Seattle, 1963-68, ptnr., 1968—; lectr. on antitrust and civil practice and procedure. Trustee Gonzaga U., Spokane, Wash., 1984—. Recipient Civic Leadership Div. award Sta. KIRO Variety Club Telethon, 1980. Fellow Am. Coll. Trial Lawyers; mem. ABA, Washington State Bar Assn. (chmn. antitrust sect. 1980-81, chmn. disciplinary bd. 1983-84), Seattle-King County Bar Assn., Fed. Bar Assn. (pres. we. dist. Wash. 1982-83), Am. Judicature Soc. Democrat. Roman Catholic. Clubs: Wash. Athletic, Broadmoor Golf (Seattle). Lodge: KC. Antitrust, Federal civil litigation, Condemnation. Office: Ferguson & Burdell 2900 One Union Sq Seattle WA 98101

GREENAWALT, WILLIAM SLOAN, lawyer; b. Bklyn., Mar. 4, 1934; s. Kenneth William and Martha Frances (Sloan) G.; m. Jane DeLano Plunkett, Aug. 17, 1957 (div. May 1986); children: John DeLano, David Sloan, Katherine Downs. A.B., Cornell U., 1956; LL.B., Yale U., 1961. Bar: N.Y. 1962, U.S. Dist. Ct. (so. and ea. dists.) N.Y. 1962, U.S. Ct. Apls. (2d cir.) 1962, U.S. Supreme Ct. 1966. Assoc., Sullivan & Cromwell, N.Y.C., 1961-65; northeast regional legal services dir. U.S. Office Econ. Opportunity, N.Y.C., 1965-68; assoc. Rogers & Wells, N.Y.C., 1968-69, ptnr., 1969-77, sr. ptnr., 1977-81; sr. ptnr. Halperin, Shivitz, Eisenberg, Schneider & Greenawalt, N.Y.C., 1981-86, sr. ptnr. Eisenberg, Honig & Fogler, N.Y.C., 1986—; lectr. in field. Chmn., Applied Resources Inc., N.Y.C., 1968-70; state chmn. Community Aid Employment Ex-Offenders, Westchester, N.Y., 1971; pres. Westchester Legal Services, 1971-74; bd. dirs, 1975—; mem. N.Y. State Gov.'s Task Force Elem. and Secondary Edn., 1974-75; mem. Pres. Carter's Task Force Criminal Justice, 1976; panel comml. arbitrators Am. Arbitration Assn., 1977—, adv. council N.Y. State Senate Dems., 1978—; mem. Greenburgh Recreational Commn., 1976-83; pres. Westchester Crime Victims Assistance Agy., 1981-82; commr. Taconic State Parks, Recreation and Historic Preservation Commn., 1984—. Served to lt. comdr. U.S. Navy, 1956-58, Res., 1961-68. Fellow N.Y. Bar Found.; mem. ABA, N.Y. State Bar Assn. (chmn. com. on availability of legal services 1968-70, chmn. action unit #3 1979-81, chmn. spl. commn. on alternatives to jud. resolution of disputes 1981-85), Assn. Bar City N.Y., Nat. Legal Aid and Defenders Assn., Phi Alpha Delta. Democrat. Congregationalist. Clubs: County Tennis of Westchester (pres. 1979-80) (Scarsdale, N.Y.); Yale. Bd. editors: Yale Law Jour., 1959-61; contbr. articles in field to profl. jours. Federal civil litigation, State civil litigation, Antitrust. Address: Stevens Pl Hartsdale NY 10530

GREENBACKER, JOHN EVERETT, lawyer; b. Meriden, Conn., Oct. 4, 1917; s. Charles and Isabel Alice Francis G.; m. Carolyn Robertson Perrow, July 25, 1942; children—Susan Brown, John Everett, Florence Linn, Christopher F. Student, U. Conn., 1935-36; B.S., U.S. Naval Acad., 1940; J.D., Georgetown U., 1949, LL.M., 1969; M.A., George Washington U., 1964, U.S. Naval War Coll., 1964. Bar: D.C. 1949, Md. 1970, Va. 1976, U.S. Dist. Ct. (we. dist.) Va. 1979. Commd. ensign U.S. Navy, 1940, advanced through grades to capt., 1960; comdg. officer subchaser 1942-43, comdg. officer destroyer escorts, 1943-46, comdg. officer destroyer, 1955-57, comdg. officer attack transport, 1962-63, comdr. destroyer div. 262, 1961-62, comdr. destroyer squadron 6, 1965-66, ret., 1969; sr. atty. legal dept. Balt. Gas & Electric Co., 1969-72, mem. finance dept., 1972-74, treas., 1974-76; practice law Halifax, Va., 1976—; mem. firm J.E. Greenbacker & Son, 1978—. General practice, State and local taxation, Probate. Home: Route 1 Box 614 Halifax VA 24558 Office: 15 S Main St PO Box 488 Halifax VA 24558

GREENBAUM, ARTHUR FRANKLIN, lawyer; b. Toledo, Nov. 17, 1951; s. Meyer Louis and Isabel Marion (Goldwater) G.; m. Lorraine S. Latek, May 24, 1980. BA cum laude, Yale U., 1973; JD, U. Va., 1976. Assoc. Hogan & Hartson, Washington, 1976-80; prof. law Ohio State U., Columbus, 1980—; adj. faculty mem. Am. U., Washington, 1979-80. Contbr. articles to profl. jours. Mem. ABA (Ohio reporter state adminstrv. law project 1984—), Va. Bar Assn., D.C. Bar Assn., Order of Coif. Democrat. Avocations: softball, basketball, cooking, mysteries. Legal education. Home: 382 W 4th Ave Columbus OH 43201

GREENBAUM, MAURICE C., lawyer; b. Detroit, Apr. 3, 1918; s. Henry and Eva (Klayman) G.; m. Beatrice Wiener, May 31, 1919. B.A., Wayne State U., 1938; J.D., U. Mich. U., 1941; L.L.M., NYU, 1948. Bar: Mich. 1941, Conn. 1948, N.Y. 1947. Assoc. Herman H. Copelon, New Haven, Conn., 1948-50; ptnr. Greenbaum, Wolff & Ernst, N.Y.C., 1950-82; sr. ptnr. Rosenman & Colin, N.Y.C., 1982—. Co-author: Estate Tax Techniques. Village Justice Village Kings Point, Kings Point, N.Y., 1985—. Served to maj. U.S. Army, 1941-45. Democrat. Jewish. General corporate, Estate planning, Literary and copyright. Home: 24 Cow Ln Kings Point NY 11024 Office: Rosenman & Colin 575 Madison Ave New York NY 10022

GREENBAUM, SHELDON MARC, lawyer; b. Bklyn., July 1, 1950; s. Emil and Edith (Greenbaum) G.; m. Susan M. Weisberg, May 27, 1971; children—Diana, Elizabeth. B.S. magna cum laude, NYU, 1971, J.D., 1974. Bar: N.Y. 1975, U.S. Dist. Ct. (so. and ea. dists.) N.Y. 1975, U.S. Ct. Appeals (2d cir.) 1975, U.S. Supreme Ct. 1978. Law clk. Parker, Chapin, Flattau & Klimpl, N.Y.C., 1968-70; litigation atty., 1974-77; acct. Berkowitz & Brody, N.Y.C., 1971-72; asst. controller WaSko Gold Products Corp., N.Y.C., 1972-73; litigation atty. Hess, Segall, Guterman, Pelz & Steiner, N.Y.C., 1978-81; ptnr. Goldman and Greenbaum, P.C., N.Y.C., 1981-84, Goldman , Greenbaum & Milner, P.C., N.Y.C., 1984—. adj. asst. prof. law Grad. Sch. Bus. Adminstrn. and Coll. Bus. and Pub. Adminstrn., NYU, 1978-82. Mem. bd. appeals Village of Port Washington North, N.Y., 1980—. Served with USAR, 1970-76. Mem. ABA, N.Y. State Bar Assn., Assn. Bar City NY. Federal civil litigation, State civil litigation, Family and matrimonial. Home: 89 Radcliff Ave Port Washington NY 11050 Office: Goldman Greenbaum & Milner PC 1180 Ave of the Americas New York NY 10036

GREENBAUM, WILLIAM I., lawyer; b. Albany, N.Y., Dec. 12, 1950; s. Robert I. and Inez L. (Warshaw) G.; m. Elyse Robin Gellman, Oct. 19, 1985. Cert. de scolarité, L'Institut d'Etudes Politiques, Strasbourg, France, 1972; AB, Dartmouth Coll., 1973; JD, Cornell U., 1976. Bar: N.Y., U.S. Dist. Ct. (so., no. and ea. dists.) N.Y., U.S. Ct. Appeals (D.C. and 2d cirs.), U.S. Supreme Ct. Assoc. Chadbourne and Parke, N.Y.C., 1976-84; counsel EEO affairs Warner-Lambert Co., Morris Plains, N.J., 1984—. Mem. ABA (com. on employment law), Assn. of the Bar of the City of N.Y. (com. on sex and law 1983-86). Labor, Federal civil litigation. Home: 60 Cambridge Ct Madison NJ 07940 Office: Warner-Lambert Co 201 Tabor Rd Morris Plains NJ 07950

GREENBERG, DAVID HERBERT, lawyer; b. Bennington, Vt., July 21, 1948; s. Norman Howard and Selma Beverly (Goldberg) G.; m. Jane C. Kremer; children: Gabrielle, Lee. BA, U. Pa., 1970; JD, George Washington U., 1973. Bar: D.C. 1974, Vt. 1975, U.S. Dist. Ct. Vt. 1975, U.S. Ct. Appeals (2d cir.) 1976. Law clk. to presiding judge D.C. Superior Ct., Washington, 1973-75; asst. atty. gen. State of Vt., Montpelier, 1975-78; sole practice Burlington, Vt., 1978—; mem. com. Human Research U. Vt., Burlington, 1979-85, com. on Med. Research U. Vt., Burlington, 1986—; hearing officer Vt. Woodside Juvenile Rehab. Facility. Bd. dirs. Temple Sinai Reform Jewish Congregation, South Burlington, 1980—, pres. 1982-84, chmn. bldg. com., 1984—; bd. dirs. Baird Children's Ctr., Burlington, 1978-84. Mem. ABA, D.C. Bar Assn., Vt. Bar Assn., Chittenden County Bar Assn., Phi Delta Phi. Lodge: Lions (treas. 1982, sec. 1983, v.p. 1984, pres. 1985 Burlington chpt.). Avocation: sports. General practice, State civil litigation, Contracts commercial. Home: 28 N Williams Burlington VT 05401 Office: 2 Church St Suite 3G PO Box 201 Burlington VT 05402

GREENBERG, HAROLD, lawyer; b. Phila., Jan. 9, 1939; s. Saul and Sadie (Edelstein) G.; m. Frances Tint, Oct. 8, 1961 (div. Jan. 1984); children: Sheryl Jo, Gayle Tracy; m. Susan Youngblood, Mar. 11, 1984. BA, Pa. State U., 1961; JD, Temple U., 1965. Bar: Pa. 1965, Calif. 1967, U.S. Supreme 1974. Commd. 2d lt. U.S. Army, 1956, advanced through grades to capt., 1964, resigned, 1968; dep. pub. defender Los Angeles County, 1968, dep. dist. atty., 1968-71; sole practice Los Angeles, 1971—; prof. law Glendale (Calif.) U., 1968—; instr. Calif. State U., Los Angeles, 1970-82, U. So. Calif., Los Angeles, 1980. Mem. Los Angeles Dems., 1975-81, Calif. Dem. Council, 1978; pres. Reseda Dem. Club, Los Angeles, 1975; bd. dirs. West Park Jewish Community Ct., Canoga Park, Calif., 1972-75. Mem. ABA, Calif. Trial Lawyers Assn., Los Angeles Trial Lawyers Assn., Assn. So. Calif. Def. Attys., Phi Beta Kappa, Phi Kappa Phi. Democrat. Jewish. Criminal, State civil litigation, Family and matrimonial. Home: 2263 S Harvard Blvd Los Angeles CA 90018 Office: 2263 S Harvard Blvd Los Angeles CA 90018

GREENBERG, HOWARD RALPH, lawyer; b. N.Y.C., Nov. 12, 1939; s. Abraham and Elizabeth (Grossman) G.; m. Chaia K. Wishnia, June 20, 1965; children—Tami, Daniella. B.E.E., CCNY, 1962; J.D., Bklyn. Law Sch., 1970. Bar: N.Y. 1971, U.S. Patent Office 1972, U.S. Ct. Customs and Patent Appeals 1980. Engr. Am. Electric Power Service Corp., N.Y.C., 1962-71; patent atty. Stromberg-Carlson, Rochester, N.Y., 1971-73; sr. patent counsel Rockwell Internat. Corp., Dallas, 1973—. Mem. Am. Intellectual Property Law Assn., ABA, Licensing Execs. Soc., Zionist Orgn. Am., Eta Kappa Nu. Democrat. Jewish. Lodge: K.P. Patent, Trademark and copyright, Technology licensing. Home: 6801 Southpoint Dr Dallas TX 75248 Office: Rockwell Internat Corp PO Box 10462 Dallas TX 75207

GREENBERG, IRA GEORGE, lawyer; b. N.Y.C., May 8, 1946; s. Julius M. and Florence Greenberg; m. Linda Sharon Padell, Apr. 29, 1979; 1 child, Amanda. AB, Harvard U., 1968, JD, 1971. Bar: N.Y. 1972, D.C. 1980. Asst. to gen. counsel Office of Sec. of Army, Washington, 1971-74; assoc. Dewey Ballantine, N.Y.C., 1974-81; assoc. Summit Rovins & Feldesman and predecessor firm Burns Summit Rovins & Feldesman, N.Y.C., 1981-83, ptnr., 1983—; cons. atty. ACLU, N.Y.C., 1976—. Mem. class com. Harvard Coll. Fund, Cambridge, Mass., 1968—. Served to capt. U.S. Army, 1971-74. Mem. ABA, Assn. Bar City N.Y. Democrat. Federal civil litigation, State civil litigation, Antitrust. Office: Summit Rovins & Feldesman 445 Park Ave New York NY 10022

GREENBERG, JAMES, lawyer; b. Phila., Feb. 21, 1939; s. Abraham and Tillie (Gold) G.; m. Sarilee Greenberg, Aug. 26, 1961; children—Suellen,

Jonathan, Janet. B.S.E., Princeton U., 1961; J.D. cum laude, U. Pa., 1964. Bar: N.J. 1964, Pa. 1977, U.S. Supreme Ct. 1969. Clk., Superior Ct. N.J., 1964-65; assoc., then ptnr. Greenberg, Shmerelson, Weinroth & Etish, P.A., and predecessors, Camden, N.J. and Phila., 1965—; asst. prosecutor Camden County (N.J.), 1969-70; mcpl. prosecutor Cherry Hill Twp. (N.J.), 1971-73, mcpl. judge, 1973-81; mem. N.J. Supreme Ct. Com. on N.J. Dist. Cts. and N.J. Mcpl. Cts. Mem. Camden County Bar Assn. (trustee 1977-80, Peter J. Devine, Jr. award 1981), N.J. Bar Assn., Pa. Bar Assn., ABA, Trial Attys. N.J., Nat. Dist. Attys. Assn., Am. Judicature Soc. Clubs: B'rith Sholom, B'nai B'rith (Cherry Hill, N.J.). Consumer commercial, State civil litigation, Personal injury. Other: Land Title Bldg Broad and Chestnut Sts Suite 2226 Philadelphia PA 19110

GREENBERG, JOSHUA F., lawyer, law educator; b. Bklyn., Feb. 27, 1933; s. Emil and Betty (Fierer) G.; m. Reva Frances Messeloff, June 28, 1959; children: Elizabeth, James, Anne. B.A., Columbia U., 1954, LL.B., 1956. Bar: N.Y. 1956. Assoc. firm Kaye, Scholer, Fierman, Hays & Handler, N.Y.C., 1956-65; ptnr. Kaye, Scholer, Fierman, Hays & Handler, 1966—; chmn. advanced antitrust workshop Practising Law Inst., N.Y.C., 1969—; adj. prof. NYU Law Sch., N.Y.C., 1970—. Pres. Camp Ella Fohs, N.Y.C., 1965-85; trustee Beth Israel Med. Ctr., 1986—. Mem. ABA (council antitrust law sect. 1981-85), N.Y. State Bar Assn. (chmn. antitrust law sect. 1971). Jewish. Environment. Office: Kaye Scholer Fierman Hays & Handler 425 Park Ave New York NY 10022

GREENBERG, LORRAINE M., lawyer; b. N.Y.C., Dec. 1, 1952; d. Milton J. and Henrietta (Weinrib) G. BA, U. Colo., 1974; JD, John Marshall Law Sch., 1981. Bar: Ill. 1981, U.S. Dist. Ct. (no. dist.) Ill. 1981, U.S. Ct. Appeals (7th cir.) 1982. Assoc. Law Offices of Peter F. Geraci, Chgo., 1981-84; ptnr. Greenberg & Breyer, P.C., Chgo., 1984-85; sole practice Chgo., 1985—. Mem. Assn. Trial Lawyers Am., Ill. Trial Lawyers Assn., Ill. Bar Assn., Chgo. Bar Assn. Bankruptcy, Personal injury, Family and matrimonial. Office: 127 N Dearborn Suite 1444 Chicago IL 60602

GREENBERG, MARTIN JAY, lawyer, educator, author; b. Milw., Aug. 5, 1945; s. Sol and Phyllis (Schunder) G.; m. Beverly L. Young, Apr. 29, 1969; children—Kari, Steven. B.S., U. Wis., 1967; J.D., Marquette U., 1971. Bar: Wis. 1971. Assoc. Hoyt, Greene & Meissner, Milw., 1971-74, Weiss, Steuer, Berzowski & Kriger, Milw., 1974-76; ptnr. Greenberg & Boxer, Milw., 1976-78; sole practice, Milw., 1978—; asst. prof. law Marquette U., Milw., 1976-79, adj. prof., 1979—; bd. dirs., pres. Law Projects, Inc.; mem. book revisions com. Wis. Real Estate Examining Bd., 1978—. Mem. brotherhood bd. Congregation Emanu-El B'ne Jeshurun, Milw., 1976-78, treas., 1979—; bd. dirs. Community Coordinated Child Care, Milw., 1976-77, Jewish Nat. Fund, Project Re-Unite; mem. Shorewood (Wis.) Bd. Rev., 1977-81. Served with Wis. N.G., 1968-74. Morris Guten Vets. scholar, 1965; I.E. Goldberg scholar, 1966; Carnegie grantee, 1966; Wis. Student Assn. scholar, 1967; Thomas More scholar, 1969; Francis X. Swietlik scholar, 1971. Mem. ABA, Wis. Bar Assn., Milw. Bar Assn., Wis. Bar Found. (lectr. Project Inquiry 1980-81, Lawyer's Pro Bono Publico award 1978), Marquette U. Law Alumni Assn. (trustee), Jewish Vocat. Service (corp.), Woolsack Soc., Scribes, Tau Epsilon Rho (chancellor grad. chpt. 1972-73). Lodge: Masons. Author: Real Estate Practice, 1976, rev. edit., 1977; Wisconsin Real Estate, 1982; Mortgages and Real Estate Financing, 1982; editor Marquette Law Rev., 1969-71. Real property, Personal income taxation. Home: 9429 N Broadmoor Bayside WI 53217 Office: 1139 E Knapp St Milwaukee WI 53202

GREENBERG, MAXWELL ELFRED, lawyer; b. Los Angeles, Mar. 11, 1922; s. Abe Lewis and Annette Friedman G.; m. Marcie Caplan, Mar. 27, 1945; children: Jan Greenberg LeVine, Richard E., David J., Jonathan A. A.B. cum laude, UCLA, 1941; LL.B. magna cum laude, Harvard U., 1949. Bar: Calif. 1950, Ill. 1959. Practiced law Los Angeles, 1950—; research atty. Justice Roger Traynor, Calif. Supreme Ct., San Francisco, 1949-50; sr. mem. Greenberg, Bernhard, Weiss, Rosin, Inc., Los Angeles, 1954-84, Jeffer Mangels & Butler, Los Angeles, 1985—; pres. Greater Ariz. Savs. & Loan Assn., Phoenix, 1961-66, chmn. bd., 1966-72, chmn. exec. com., 1972-73; adj. prof. law UCLA, 1972-74. Author, editor, pub.: various legal outlines Calif. Bar Rev. Course, 1953-73. Nat. chmn. Anti-Defamation League, 1978-82; hon. chmn., 1983—; pres. Anti-Defamation Found., 1984—; chmn. community relations com., v.p. Jewish Fedn.-Council Greater Los Angeles, 1975-77; chmn. bd. Rural Devel. Corp., 1969-70; v.p. Los Angeles Police Commn., 1980-84; chmn. state adv. com. to U.S. Commn. on Civil Rights, 1985-87. Served to 1st. lt. AUS, 1942-46. Mem. State Bar Calif., Ill., Am. bar assns., Phi Beta Kappa, Pi Gamma Mu, Pi Lambda Phi. Democrat. Banking, Real property, Corporate taxation. Home: 10701 Wilshire Blvd Los Angeles CA 90024 Office: Jeffer Mangels & Butler 1900 Ave of Stars Los Angeles CA 90067

GREENBERG, MORTON PAUL, lawyer, insurance broker, advanced underwriting consultant; b. Fall River, Mass., June 2, 1946; s. Harry and Sylvia Shirley (Davis) G.; m. Louise Beryl Schindler, Jan. 24, 1970; 1 dau., Alexis Lynn. BSBA, NYU, 1968; JD, Bklyn. Law Sch., 1971; chartered life underwriter Am. Coll., 1975. Bar: N.Y. 1972. Atty., Hanner, Fitzmaurice & Onorato, N.Y.C., 1971-72; dir., counsel, cons. on advanced underwriting The Mfrs. Life Ins. Co., Toronto, Ont., Can., 1972—; mem. sales ideas com. Million Dollar Roundtable, Chgo., 1982-83; speaker on law, tax, and advanced underwriting to various profl. groups, U.S., Can. Author: (tech. jour.) ManuBriefs. Mem. ABA, N.Y. State Bar Assn., Assn. for Advanced Life Underwriting, Internat. Platform Assn., NYU Alumni Assn., Nat. Assn. of Life Underwriters, Denver Assn. Life Underwriters, Am. Soc. CLU. Estate planning, Corporate taxation, Personal income taxation. Office: 7617 E Sunrise Trail Parker CO 80134

GREENBERG, MYRON SILVER, lawyer; b. Los Angeles, Oct. 17, 1945; s. Earl W. and Geri (Silver) G.; m. Shlomit Gross; children—David, Amy. B.S. in Bus. Adminstrn., UCLA, 1967, J.D., 1970. Bar: Calif. 1971, U.S. Dist. Ct. (cen. dist.) Calif. 1971, U.S. Tax Ct. 1977; CPA, Calif. Staff acct. Touche Ross & Co., Los Angeles, 1970-71; assoc. Kaplan, Livingston, Goodwin, Berkowitz, & Selvin, Beverly Hills, 1971-74; ptnr. Dinkelspiel, Steefel & Levitt, San Francisco, 1975-80; ptnr. Steefel, Levitt & Weiss, San Francisco, 1981-82; pres. Myron S. Greenberg, Larkspur, Calif., 1982—; professorial lectr. tax. Golden Gate U. Mem. San Anselmo Planning Commn., 1976-77; bd. dirs. Bay Area Lawyers for Arts, 1979-80, Marin chpt. Am. Heart Assn. (bd. dirs., sec. 1984—). Mem. ABA, Marin County (Calif.) Bar Assn., Am. Inst. C.P.A.s, Calif. Soc. C.P.A.s, Real Estate Tax Inst. of Calif. Continuing Edn. Bar (planning com.), Larkspur C. of C. (bd. dirs. 1985-87). Democrat. Jewish. Author: California Attorney's Guide to Professional Corporations, 1977, 79; bd. editors, UCLA Law Rev., 1969-70. Corporate taxation, Personal income taxation, Estate taxation. Office: 80 E Sir Frances Drake Blvd Larkspur CA 94939

GREENBERG, RONALD DAVID, lawyer, educator; b. San Antonio, Sept. 9, 1939. s. Benjamin and Sylvia (Ghetlzer) G. BS, U. Tex., 1957; MBA, Harvard U., 1961, JD, 1964. Bar: N.Y. 1966, U.S. Dist. Ct. (ea. and so. dists.) N.Y. 1970, U.S. Ct. Appeals (2d cir.) 1975, U.S. Supreme Ct. 1975. Engr., bus. analyst Exxon Corp., N.Y.C., 1957-64; atty., engr. Allied Corp., N.Y.C., 1964-67; assoc. Arthur, Dry, Kalish, Taylor & Wood, N.Y.C., 1967-69, Valicenti, Leighton, Reid & Pine, N.Y.C., 1969-70; faculty Columbia U., N.Y.C., 1970—, prof. bus. law and taxation, 1982—; of counsel Delson & Gordon, N.Y.C., 1973—; lectr., cons. Citibank, Mfrs. Hanover Trust Co., Harcourt, Brace, Jovanovich, Inc., Prudential-Bache, Drexel, Burnham & Lambert, E.F. Hutton; vis. prof. Stanford U., Palo Alto, Calif., 1978, Harvard U., Boston, 1981. Author: Business Income Tax Materials, 1986; contbr. chpt. to book, articles to profl. jours. Cons. council City of N.Y., 1971-72, Manhattan Community Coll., 1974-76. Served to lt. USNR, 1957-59. Recipient Outstanding Prof. award Columbia U. Grad. Sch. Bus., 1973. Mem. ABA (chmn. com. on taxation gen. practice sect. 1978-83, chmn. com. on corp. banking and bus. law gen. practice sect. 1985—), NSPE, N.Y. State Bar Assn. (gen. practice sect., chmn. tax law com. 1983—, bus. law com. 1985—), Assn. Bar City of N.Y., N.Y. Acad. Scis., Mensa. Clubs: Harvard (N.Y.C.); Rye Golf (N.Y.). Corporate taxation, General corporate, Legal education. Home: 55 Morton St New York NY 10014 Office: Columbia Univ 625 Uris Hall New York NY 10027

GREENBERG, STEVEN MOREY, lawyer; b. Jersey City, N.J., Apr. 9, 1949; s. Joseph and Rhoda (Weisenfeld) G. A.B. cum laude, Syracuse U., 1971; J.D., U. Pa., 1974. Bar: N.J. 1974, U.S. Dist. Ct. N.J. 1974, N.Y. 1980. U.S. Dist. Ct. (so. dist.) N.Y., 1986, U.S. Dist. Ct. (ea. dist.) N.Y., 1986. Assoc. firm Carpenter, Bennett & Morrissey, Newark, 1974-77; assoc. firm Cole, Berman & Belsky, Rochelle Park, N.J., 1977-79; sole practice, Hackensack, N.J., 1979—; atty. Bergenfield (N.J.) Rent Leveling Bd., 1985—; trustee, chmn. youth activities com. Jewish Ctr. of Teaneck, 1978—; pres., trustee, v.p. Group Care Home for Sr. Adults, Bergenfield, 1983—, mem. gov. bd., 1986—, past sec.; adv. bd. dirs. Jewish Hosp. and Rehab. Ctr. of N.J., Jersey City and River Vale, 1982—; trustee Jewish Family Service Inc. of Bergen County, 1986—, The Solomon Schechter Day Sch. of Bergen County, 1986-87; mem. Jewish Community Relations Council No. N.J., 1986—. Mem. ABA, N.J. Bar Assn., Bergen County Bar Assn., Assn. Transp. Practitioners, Phi Kappa Phi, Pi Sigma Alpha. State civil litigation, Contracts commercial, General corporate. Home: 96 Westminster Ave Bergenfield NJ 07621 Office: 2 University Plaza Hackensack NJ 07601

GREENBERG, SUSAN ANN, lawyer; b. Bklyn., Mar. 15, 1957; d. Irving Arthur and Betty (Mayo) G. BA in Econs., Boston U., 1978; JD, Bklyn. Law Sch., 1981; LLM in Labor Law, NYU, 1986. Bar: N.Y. 1982, U.S. Dist. Ct. (ea. and so. dists.) N.Y. 1982. Assoc. Law Offices of Bert W. Subin P.C., N.Y.C., 1981-82; atty. N.Y. Life Ins. Co., N.Y.C., 1982-83, asst. counsel, 1982, assoc. counsel, v.p., 1982—; sec., bd.dirs. N.Y. State Adv. Council Employment Law, N.Y.C., 1985—, mem. Equal Employment Adv. Council, 1983—. Bus. editor Bklyn. Jour. Internat. Law, 1980-81. Mem. ABA. Labor, Immigration, naturalization, and customs, Federal civil litigation.

GREENBERGER, ERNEST, lawyer; b. Sarospatak, Hungary, Mar. 16, 1923; came to U.S., 1939, naturalized, 1944; s. Solomon and Esther (Weinberger) G.; m. Stacia Pleva, May 17, 1956; children—James J., Daniel A. B.A., Roosevelt U., 1945; J.D., U. Chgo., 1947. Bar: Ill. 1948, U.S. Supreme Ct. 1959. Assoc. firm Lawrence, Goldberg, Lawrence & Lewin, Chgo., 1947-55; ptnr. Antonow & Fink, Chgo., 1955-62; mem. firm Greenberger, Krauss & Jacobs, Chgo., 1962—; lectr. law U. Chgo. Downtown Center, 1960-61. Editor: U. Chgo. Law Rev, 1946-47. Bd. dirs. Am. Found. for Continuing Edn., 1953-65; bd. dirs. Jewish Community Centers Chgo., 1959-81, v.p., 1964-81; mem. Evanston Econ. Devel. Com., 1975-76. Mem. Am., Ill., Chgo. bar assns., Am. Arbitration Assn. (mem. nat. panel arbitrators 1962-75), Am. Coll. Real Estate Lawyers, Order of Coif. Democrat. Jewish. Club: Standard (Chgo.). Real property, Construction, General corporate. Office: Greenberger Krauss & Jacobs 180 N LaSalle St Suite 2700 Chicago IL 60601

GREENBERGER, I. MICHAEL, lawyer; b. Scranton, Pa., Oct. 30, 1945; s. David and Betty (Kabatchnick) G.; m. Marcia Devins, July 19, 1969; children—Sarah Devins, Anne Devins. A.B., Lafayette Coll., 1967; J.D., U. Pa., 1970. Bar: D.C. 1971, U.S. Dist. Ct. D.C. 1971, U.S. Ct. Appeals (D.C. cir.) 1971, U.S. Supreme Ct. 1975, U.S. Dist. Ct. Md. 1985, U.S. Ct. Appeals (fed. cir.) 1986. Law clk. U.S. Ct. Appeals for D.C. Circuit, Washington, 1970-71; legis. asst. to U.S. Congresswoman Elizabeth Holtzman, 1972-73; atty., advisor Office of Criminal Justice, Office U.S. Atty. Gen., 1973; assoc. Shea & Gardner, Washington, 1973-77, ptnr., 1977—; mem. D.C. Circuit Adv. Com. on Procedures, 1983—; legal cons. Software Engring. Inst., Carnegie-Mellon U. Editor-in-chief U. Pa. Law Rev., 1969-70; contbr. articles to profl. jours. Mem. M.I.T. Enterprise Forum, Washington, bd. dirs., 1984—; bd. dirs. Advanced Tech. Assn. Md., 1985—. Mem. Am. Law Inst., ABA, D.C. Bar Assn. (chmn. adminstrv. law sect. steering com. 1980-82), Phi Beta Kappa. Computer, Federal civil litigation, Government contracts and claims. Address: 2757 Brandywine St NW Washington DC 20008

GREENBLATT, EDWARD LANDE, lawyer; b. Augusta, Ga., Mar. 16, 1939; s. Robert B. and Gwendolyn (Lande) G.; m. Sherry Agoos, June 1, 1967; 1 dau., Susan. Student Duke U.; B.A., Birmingham So. Coll., 1961; LL.B., Emory U., 1964; LL.M., NYU, 1965. Bar: Ga. 1963, D.C. 1966, U.S. Supreme Ct. 1971. Atty., U.S. Dept. Treasury, Washington, 1965-66; assoc. Lipshutz, Frankel, Greenblatt, King and Cohen, and predecessors, Atlanta, 1967-71, ptnr., 1971—. Bd. dirs. Atlanta Legal Aid Soc., Atlanta Community Ctr., Paces Battle Assn.; bd. dirs., chmn. Atlanta B'nai B'rith Youth Orgn.; pres. temple, 1985—. Mem. ABA, State Bar Ga., Atlanta Bar Assn., Lawyers Club Atlanta, Am. Judicature Soc. Jewish. General corporate, Bankruptcy, Federal civil litigation. Home: 4417 Paces Battle NW Atlanta GA 30327 Office: 2300 Harris Tower Peachtree Ctr 233 Peachtree St NE Atlanta GA 30043

GREENBLATT, MORTON HAROLD, assistant attorney general; b. Waterbury, Conn., Oct. 31, 1916; s. Samuel F. and Dorothy K. (Katz) G.; m. Evelyn Lipman, Oct. 26, 1947; children: Sarah Beth, Ruth, David. BA, Yale U., 1937; LLB, Harvard U., 1940. Bar: Conn. 1941, U.S. Dist. Ct. Conn. 1947, U.S. Supreme Ct. 1961, U.S. Ct. Appeals (7th cir.) 1971. Vice pres., of counsel Ellmore Silver Co., Meriden, Conn., 1946-61; sole practice, Meriden, 1961-67; asst. pros. atty. 7th Cir. Ct., Meriden, 1962-66; asst. corp. counsel City of Meriden, 1966-81; asst. atty. gen. State of Conn., Hartford, 1982-86; of counsel Pomeranz, Orayton and Stabnich, Hartford, 1986—. Sec. Meriden Planning Commn., 1953-55; pres. Meriden Bd. Edn., 1955-61, Temple B'nai Abraham, 1977-79; chmn. Solid Waster Mgmt. Commn. of Branford, 1986—. Served to maj. USAAF, 1942-46. Mem. Meriden-Wallingford Bar Assn., Conn. Bar Assn., Am. Arbitration Assn., Conn. Assn. Mcpl. Attys. (treas.). Jewish. Local government, Workers' compensation. Home: 50 Turtle Bay Dr Branford CT 06405

GREENBLATT, RAY HARRIS, lawyer; b. Milw., June 29, 1931; s. Charles and Ethel (Harris) G.; m. Betty Goldsmith, July 11, 1955 (dec. Mar. 1967); children: Walter, Robert, Edward; m. Helen Judith Pick, Mar. 29, 1969 (div. Dec. 1969). B.S. in Econs., U. Pa., 1953; J.D. magna cum laude, Harvard U., 1956. Bar: Ill. 1956. Assoc. Mayer, Brown & Platt, 1956-64, ptnr., 1965—; arbitrator Am. Arbitration Assn., 1970—; lectr. U. Wis. Sch. for Bankers, Madison, 1964, 73, Ill. Inst. Continuing Legal Edn., 1973. Contbr. articles to profl. jours. Pres. Winnetka Bd. Edn., Ill., 1974-75, mem., 1969-74. Mem. ABA, Chgo. Bar Assn., Chgo. Council Lawyers. Jewish. Clubs: Economic (Chgo.), Cliff Dwellers (Chgo.), Union League (Chgo.); Lake Shore Country (Glencoe, Ill.). General corporate, Contracts commercial, Banking. Home: 1003 Westmoor Rd Winnetka IL 60093 Office: Mayer Brown & Platt 190 S LaSalle St Chicago IL 60603

GREENBLATT, RUSSELL EDWARD, lawyer, consultant; b. Chgo., Jan. 7, 1952; s. Abraham Abel Greenblatt and Freda (Katz) Leader. B.S., Ind. U., 1973; J.D., Northwestern U., 1978. Bar: Ill. 1978, Calif. 1983, U.S. Dist. Ct. (no. dist.) Ill. 1979. Acct., Arthur Andersen & Co., Atlanta, 1973-75; atty.-advisor Office of Chief Counsel, IRS, Washington, 1978-80; cons. Russell E. Greenblatt Cons. Co., Newport Beach, Calif. and Chgo., 1982-86; ptnr. Katten, Muchin, Zavis, Pearl, Greenberger & Galler, Chgo., 1980—; speaker fed. taxation NYU Inst., N.Y.C., 1982, U.S.C. Fed. Tax Inst., Los Angeles, 1984, 85; witness Ways and Means Com., U.S. Ho. Reps., Washington, 1984. Contbr. articles to profl. jours. Mem. ABA (sect. taxation), Ill. State Bar Assn. (sect. taxation). Office: Katten Muchin Zavis et al 525 W Monroe St Suite 1600 Chicago IL 60606

GREENBURG, G. SCOTT, lawyer; b. Santa Monica, Calif., Mar. 9, 1955; s. Phillip Harold and Ruth Elaine (Williams) G.; m. Shannon T. Harkins, Apr. 13, 1985. BBA cum laude, Wash. State U., 1977; JD cum laude, U. Puget Sound, 1980. Bar: Wash. 1980, U.S. Dist. Ct. (we. dist.) Wash. 1980. Clk. to judge U.S. Dist. Ct. (we. dist.) Wash., Seattle, 1980-81; ptnr. Shidler, McBroom, Gates & Lucas, Seattle, 1981—. Editor U. Puget Sound Law Rev., 1980. U. Puget Sound scholar 1979. Mem. ABA, Wash. Bar Assn. (planning com., co-chmn. Pacific Rim Computer Law Inst.1984-86, chmn. 1987—), Seattle-King County Bar Assn. (chmn. protecting intellectual property for new technology bus. 1983, continuing legal edn. com. 1984-86), Am. Electronics Assn. Avocations: snow skiing, basketball. Computer, General corporate, Private international. Office: Shidler McBroom Gates & Lucas 3500 First Interstate Ctr Seattle WA 98104

GREENE, ADDISON KENT, lawyer, accountant; b. Cardston, Alta., Can., Dec. 23, 1941; s. Addison Allen and Amy (Shipley) G.; m. Janice Hanks, Aug. 30, 1967; children: Lisa, Tiffany, Tyler, Darin. BS in Acctg., Brigham Young U., 1968; JD, U. Utah, 1973. Bar: Utah 1973, Nev. 1974, U.S. Tax Ct. 1979. Staff acct. Seidman and Seidman, Las Vegas, Nev., 1968-69, Peat Marwick Mitchell, Los Angeles, 1969-70; atty. Clark Greene & Assocs., Ltd., Las Vegas, 1973—; instr. Nev. Bar Rev., Las Vegas, 1975-78; bd. dirs. Cumorah Credit Union. Mem. Citizen's for Responsible Gov't, Las Vegas, 1979—; asst. dist. com. mem. Boy Scouts Am., Las Vegas, 1985—. Mem. ABA, Utah Bar Assn., Nev. Bar Assn., Nev. Soc. CPA's (assoc.), Am. Assn., Pension Actuaries (assoc.). Republican. Mormon. Avocations: golf, snow skiing. Pension, profit-sharing, and employee benefits, Probate, Personal income taxation. Office: Clark Greene & Assocs Ltd 5606 S Eastern Las Vegas NV 89119

GREENE, BARRY TODD, lawyer; b. N.Y.C., Sept. 17, 1955; s. Murray Arthur and Eileen Sally (Smolkin) G.; AB Yeshiva U., 1977; JD, Columbia U., 1982. Bar: N.Y. 1984, U.S. Dist. Ct. (so. and ea. dists.) N.Y. 1984. Law clk. to Justice Harold Rothwax, N.Y. State Supreme Ct., fall 1981; assoc. Finley, Kumble, Wagner, Heine, Underberg, Manley & Casey, N.Y.C., 1982-83; law clk. to Judge Irving R. Kaufman, U.S. Ct. Appeals (2nd cir.), 1983; sole practice, N.Y.C., 1984 -; lectr. in law analysis and writing Pace U. Sch. Law, White Plains, N.Y.; 1987 -; founding sponsor Civil Justice Found. Assoc. editor Columbia Jour. Environ. Law, 1981-82. Harlan Fiske Stone scholar Columbia U., Harold P. Seligson scholar (drafting comml. agreements, real estate practice and investment) Practicing Law Inst., 1984. Mem. ABA (litigation sect., corp., banking and bus. law sect., criminal justice sect., gen. practice sect., econs. of law practice sect., real property, probate and trust law sect.), N.Y. State Bar Assn. Assn. Bar City N.Y., Assn. Trial Lawyers Am., N.Y. State Trial Lawyers Assn., N.Y. County Lawyers Assn. (ethics com. 1985 -), Columbia U. Law Sch. Alumni Assn. (life, publs. com., class council). Jewish. Avocations: opera, reading, music, tennis. General practice, Federal civil litigations, State civial litigation. Office: 228 W 71st 8D New York NY 10023

GREENE, BERNARD HAROLD, lawyer; b. Bklyn., Sept. 21, 1925; s. Max and Clara (Pasweg) G.; m. Magda C. Schwartz, Sept. 19, 1948; children: Michael, Edith, Susan, Jonathan, David. B.B.A. magna cum laude, CCNY, 1948; LL.B. cum laude, Yale U., 1951. Bar: N.Y. 1952. Assoc. Paul, Weiss, Rifkind, Wharton & Garrison, N.Y.C., 1951-60; ptnr. Paul, Weiss, Rifkind, Wharton & Garrison, 1960—; vis. lectr. Yale Law Sch., New Haven, Ct., 1972-78, 81-83; dir. First Sterling Corp., N.Y.C.; adj. prof. N.Y. Law Sch., N.Y.C., 1985—. Chmn. deferred giving and estate planning com. Community Service Soc., N.Y.C., 1975-82. 1st lt. U.S. Army, 1943-47. Mem. Assn. Bar City N.Y. (mem. surrogate's ct. com. 1958-61). State civil litigation, Probate, Estate taxation. Home: 153 Union St Montclair NJ 07042 Office: Paul Weiss Rifkind Wharton and Garrison 1285 Ave of the Americas New York NY 10019

GREENE, BERNARD WILBURN, lawyer; b. Columbia, S.C., May 26, 1949; s. Frederick Bernard and Sylvesta (Singleton) G.; m. Ellen Elaine Pinderhughes, Sept. 1, 1984. BA, Swarthmore Coll., 1971; JD, Boston Coll., 1981. Bar: Ohio 1981, U.S. Dist. Ct. (no. dist.) Ohio 1982, U.S. Ct. Appeals (6th cir.) 1982. Assoc. Calfee, Halter & Griswold, Cleve., 1981—. Mem. bd. edn. Cleveland Heights-University Heights City Sch. Dist., 1986—. Mem. ABA, Ohio State Bar Assn., Cleve. Bar Assn., Ohio Sch. Bds. Assn. Democrat. Avocations: golf, swimming. Contracts commercial, Municipal bonds, Real property. Office: Calfee Halter & Griswold 1800 Society Bldg Cleveland OH 44114-2688

GREENE, EDWARD FRANK, lawyer; b. N.Y.C., Oct. 18, 1941; s. Foster Comings and Marjorie (Brier) G.; m. Diana Barton Harding, Aug. 5, 1967; children: Anna Tucker, Mary Barclay. BA, Amherst Coll., 1963; LLB, Harvard U., 1966. Bar: N.Y., D.C., U.S. Dist. Ct. (so. dist.) N.Y. Asst. prof. Wayne State Law Sch., Detroit, 1967-68; assoc. Willkie, Farr & Gallagher, N.Y.C., 1968-71, ptnr., 1972-78; dep. dir. corp. fin. div. SEC, Washington, 1978-79, dir. corp. fin. div., 1979-81, gen. counsel, 1981-82; ptnr. Cleary, Gottlieb, Steen & Hamilton, Washington, 1982—; adj. prof. law Georgetown U., Washington, 1982-84, U. Pa., Phila., 1984—. Contbr. articles to profl. jours. Bd. dirs. Washington Area Lawyers for Arts, 1984—. Teaching fellow Boston Coll. Law Sch., 1966-67. Mem. Fed. Bar Assn. (exec. mem. fed. securities com. 1983—), U. Calif. Securities Regualtion Inst. (exec. com. 1983—), Inst. SEC and Fin. Reporting (exec. com. 1983—). Democrat. Home: 633 E St SE Washington DC 20003 Office: Cleary Gottlieb Steen & Hamilton 1752 N St NW Washington DC 20036

GREENE, GORDON CHRISTOPHER, lawyer; b. Cin., Aug. 2, 1935; s. Thomas Rea and Letha (Cavendish) G.; m. Caroline McGinnis, June 13, 1956; children—Gordon Christopher, Daniel Wilkins. B.A. in Econs., U. Cin., 1957, J.D., 1960. Bar: Ohio 1960, U.S. Dist. Ct. (so. dist.) Ohio 1961, U.S. Dist. Ct. (ea. dist.) Ky. 1961, U.S. Ct. Appeals (6th cir.) 1962. Assoc. Milton M. Bloom, Cin., 1960-65; ptnr. Bloom, Greene, Thurman & Uible, Cin., 1965-72; prin. Bloom & Greene Co., L.P.A., Cin., 1972—, pres., 1977—; participant seminars on admiralty, malpractice, others. Mem. Indian Hill (Ohio) Recreation Commn., 1974—, chmn., 1977-78. Served with USAR, 1960-66. Fellow Am. Coll. Trial Lawyers, Ohio Bar Found.; mem. Cin. Bar Assn., Ohio Bar Assn., ABA, Internat. Assn. Ins. Counsel, Ohio Assn. Civil Trial Attys., Cin. Assn. Civil Trial Attys. (pres. 1984—), Am. Judicature Soc. Presbyterian. Club: Cin. Athletic. Contbr. articles to profl. jours. State civil litigation, Insurance, Personal injury. Office: 201 E 5th St Cincinnati OH 45202

GREENE, HAROLD H., judge; b. 1923. B.S., George Washington U., 1949, J.D., 1952. Asst. U.S. Atty. D.C., 1953-57; with Office Legal Counsel and Civil Rights Div. Dept. Justice, 1957-65; judge D.C. Ct. Gen. Sessions, 1965-66, chief judge, 1966-71; chief judge Superior Ct. of D.C., 1971-78; judge U.S. Dist. Ct. for D.C., 1978—. Mem. ABA, Bar Assn. D.C., Am. Judicature Soc. Judicial administration. Office: US Dist Ct 3d and Constitution Ave NW Washington DC 20001 *

GREENE, HERMAN FORTESCUE, lawyer; b. Raleigh, N.C., Sept. 21, 1945; s. Robert E. L. and Lucy (Fortescue) G.; m. Joy Warner, Sept. 1, 1968 (div. May 1986); children: Nathanael, Brendan. BA, U. Fla., 1966; MA, Stanford U., 1967; MTh, U. Chgo., 1969; JD, U. N.C., 1979. Bar: N.Y. 1980, Colo. 1983. Specialist community devel. Fifth City Redevel. Corp., Chgo., 1967-70; regional dir. Ecumenical Inst., Chgo., 1970-74; nat. co-dir. Town Meeting '76, Chgo., 1974-75; mgr. bus. Area Alcoholism Programs, Raleigh, 1975-76; assoc. Shearman & Sterling, N.Y.C., 1979-83; ptnr. Mayer, Brown & Platt, Denver, 1983-86, N.Y.C., 1987—; legal advisor Westwood Housing Inc., Denver, 1986. Research editor U. N.C. Law Rev., 1978-79; contbr. articles to profl. jours. Mem. bus. and econ. council Denver Dems., 1985. Served to 1st lt. U.S. Army, 1966-71. Woodrow Wilson fellow, 1966; named one of Outstanding Young Men in Am. U.S. Jaycees, 1977. Mem. ABA, N.Y. Bar Assn., Amnesty Internat. (lawyers com. 1986—), Order of Coif, Phi Kappa Phi. Democrat. Congregationalist. Avocations: running, music, tennis. Banking, General corporate. Home: 211 W 56th St Apt 16K New York NY 10019 Office: Mayer Brown & Platt 520 Madison Ave New York NY 10022

GREENE, JAMES S., JR., lawyer; b. Varilla, Ky., Sept. 9, 1917; s. James S. and Lucy Fuson (Smith) G.; m. Elizabeth B. Howard, Dec. 9, 1939; children: James S. III, Martha Letitia. Student, U. Tenn., 1934-37; LLB, U. Ky., 1939. Bar: Ky. 1938, U.S. Dist. Ct. (ea. dist.) Ky. 1940, U.S. Ct. Appeals (6th cir.) 1940, U.S. Dist. Ct. (we. dist.) Va. 1959, U.S. Ct. Appeals (4th cir.) 1961, U.S. Supreme Ct. 1963. Sole practice Harlan, Ky., 1939—. Served to sgt. U.S. Army, 1943-46. Mem. ABA, Ky. Bar Assn., Am. Judicature Soc., Am. Coll. Trial Lawyers. Federal civil litigation, State civil litigation, General practice. Home and Office: PO Box 995 205 1/2 Central St Harlan KY 40831

GREENE, JOHN JOSEPH, lawyer; b. Marshall, Tex., Jan. 19, 1946; William Henry and Camille Anne (Riley) G.; BA., U. Houston, 1969, M.A., 1974; postgrad. Oxford (Eng.) U., 1976, U. Okla., 1976; J.D., South Tex. Coll., 1978. Bar: Tex. 1978, U.S. Supreme Ct., 1982. Asst. atty. City of Amarillo, Tex., 1978-79; asst. atty. Harris County, Tex., 1979-83; sole practice, 1983—; city atty. City of Conroe (Tex.), 1983-84. Served to capt. USAR, 1969-76. Decorated Bronze Star, Air Medal. Mem. ABA, Houston Bar Assn., Res. Officers Assn., Assn. for Computing Machinery. Democrat. Roman Catholic. State and local taxation. Office: 505 W Davis Conroe TX 77301

GREENE, JOHN THOMAS, JR., judge; b. Salt Lake City, Nov. 28, 1929; s. John Thomas and Mary Agnes (Hindley) G.; m. Kay Buchanan, Mar. 31, 1955; children: Thomas B., John B., Mary Kay. B.A., U. Utah, 1952, J.D., 1955. Bar: Utah 1955. Law clk. Supreme Ct. Utah, Salt Lake City, 1954-55; asst. U.S. atty. Dist. Utah, Salt Lake City, 1957-59; partner firm Marr, Wilkins & Cannon, Salt Lake City, 1959-69, Cannon, Greene & Nebeker, Salt Lake City, 1969-74, Greene, Callister & Nebeker, Salt Lake City, 1974-85; judge U.S. Dist. Ct. Utah, 1985—; spl. asst. atty. gen. State of Utah, 1965-69; spl. grand jury counsel Salt Lake County, 1970; pres. Utah Bar Found., 1971-74, trustee, 1971—. Author: sect. on mining rights American Law of Mining, 1965; contbr. articles to profl. jours. Pres. Community Services Council, Salt Lake City area, 1971-73; Republican chmn. Voting Dist. 47, Salt Lake County, 1969-73; chmn. Utah Bldg. Authority, 1980-85; mem. Utah State Bd. Regents, 1983-86. Mem. Utah Bar Assn. (pres. 1970-71, chmn. judiciary com. 1971-76, chmn. com. post. law sch. tng. 1985—), ABA (Utah del. to ho. of dels. 1975-81, 82—, mem. spl. com. delivery legal service 1975-81, council gen. practice sect. 1974-82, chmn. spl. com. on environ. law 1971-75, mem. adv. com. Nat. Legal Service Corp. 1975-81, mem. standing com. on jud. selection, tenure and compensation 1985—), Am. Inn Ct. II (pres. 1983-84), U. Utah Alumni Assn. (dir. 1968-69), Order of Coif, Phi Beta Kappa, Phi Kappa Phi. Mormon. Clubs: Ft. Douglas Country, Salt Lake Tennis. Office: Fed Bldg 350 S Main St #222 Salt Lake City UT 84101

GREENE, MICHAEL ALAN, lawyer; b. Chgo., Sept. 18, 1946; s. Richard J. and Joan D. (Larrahee) G.; m. Alice M. Radcliffe, June 1, 1974; children: Adam R., Amy R. AB in History, Stanford U., 1968, JD, 1971. Bar: Calif. 1972, Idaho 1972, U.S. Dist. Ct. Oreg. 1972, U.S. Dist. Ct. (no. dist.) Calif. 1972, U.S. Ct. Appeals (9th cir.) 1972, U.S. Supreme Ct. 1975, Oreg. 1980, U.S. Dist. Ct. Oreg. 1980. Assoc. Eberle & Berlin, Boise, Idaho, 1972-80; ptnr. Rosenthal & Greene P.C., Portland, Oreg., 1980—; adj. prof. Boise State U., 1976-79. Contbr. articles to profl. jours. Bd. dirs., v.p., pres. Oreg. affiliate Am. Diabetes Assn., Portland, 1984—. Criminal Law Teaching fellow Stanford U., 1971-72. Mem. ABA, Assn. Trial Lawyers Am., Oreg. Trial Lawyers Assn. (gov. 1985—). Avocations: author, fly fishing. Personal injury, Legal malpractice, State civil litigation. Office: Rosenthal & Greene PC #1907 1001 SW 5th Ave Portland OR 97204

GREENE, MICHAEL ROY, lawyer; b. Little Rock, Mar. 26, 1949; s. Hugh Williamson and Betty Jo (Baker) G.; m. Donna K. Greene, Aug. 21, 1971; children: Christopher, Jessica. BA, Ark. State U.; JD, U. Ark. Bar: Ark. 1974, Tex. 1974, N.J. 1979. Atty. Southwestern Bell, Dallas, 1974-78, AT&T, Basking Ridge, N.J., 1978-81; v.p., gen. counsel, sec. Advanced Mobile Phone Service, Inc., Basking Ridge, 1981-83, pres., 1983; gen. atty. AT&T Information Systems, Parsippany, N.J., 1984; asst. gen. counsel AT&T Techs., Berkeley Heights, N.J., 1984—. Mem. Ark. Bar Assn., N.J. Bar Assn., Tex. Bar Assn., Fed. Communications Bar Assn., Assn. Trial Lawyers Am. General corporate, Public international, Government contracts and claims. Office: AT&T Technologies One Oak Way Berkeley Heights NJ 07922

GREENE, RALPH VERNON, lawyer; b. Cleve., Apr. 5, 1910; s. Charles R. and Pauline J. (Desch) G.; m. Martha F. Burwell, Aug. 12, 1939; 1 dau., Betsy. student Cleve. Coll., Western Res. U., 1942; J.D., John Marshall Law Sch., 1946. Bar: Ohio 1946, U.S. Dist. Ct. (no. dist.) Ohio 1954, U.S. Supreme Ct. 1960. With Cleve. Trust Co., 1929-43, Land Title Guarantee & Trust Co., Painesville, Ohio, 1945-46; sole practice, Willoughby, Ohio, 1946-62, 64-77; ptnr. Greene & Tulley, Willoughby, 1962-64, Greene, Tulley & Jurjans, 1977—; sec., dir. Feedall, Inc. Mem. Willoughby Hills (Ohio) Charter Commn., 1970-71; trustee Lake County Bd. Mental Retardation, 1971-73, Willoughby Sch. Fine Arts, 1967-75; bd. mgrs. YMCA, 1968-79, trustee, 1975-79; advisor to registrants SSS, 1950-75. Served with U.S. Army, 1943-45; ETO. Recipient Corpus Juris Secundum award, 1945; Am. Jurisprudence award, 1945; award SSS, 1975; named Man of Yr., YMCA, 1975. Mem. ABA, Ohio State Bar Assn., Lake County Bar Assn. (pres. 1956), Cleve. State U. Law Sch. Alumni Assn. Republican. Baptist. Club: Ohio Grange (Willoughby Hills). General corporate, Probate, Estate taxation. Office: 38021 Euclid Ave Willoughby OH 44094

GREENE, RICHARD FRANCIS, law educator; b. Omaha, Mar. 27, 1956; s. Roger F. and Shirley A. (Moore) G.; m. Patricia A. Glaze, Oct. 10, 1981; children: Christine, Jennifer. BS in Bus. Adminstrn., U. Nebr., Omaha, 1978, M in Profl. Acctg., 1985; JD, U. Nebr., Lincoln, 1981. Bar: Nebr. 1981, U.S. Tax Ct. 1982, U.S. Ct. Appeals (8th cir.) 1982. Tax specialist Peat, Marwick, Mitchell et al, Omaha, 1980-82; controller KV Internat., Omaha, 1982-84; asst. prof. tax acctg. U. Nebr., Omaha, 1984—; cons. Harz Sports, Omaha, 1983—, U.S. Inventory and Consulting, Omaha, 1983—. Cons. Nebr. Bus. Devel. Council, Omaha, 1986—. Mem. ABA, Nebr. Bar Assn., Am. Inst. CPAs, Nebr. Soc. CPAs. Republican. Roman Catholic. Avocations: reading, golf. Personal income taxation, Estate taxation, Corporate taxation. Home: 2683 N 129 Circle Omaha NE 68164

GREENE, RICHARD LAWRENCE, lawyer; b. Los Angeles, Oct. 16, 1938; s. Robert and Mildred (Dorfman) G.; m. Lorrie Lee Levin, Jan. 27, 1963; children: Dana Michele, Julie Alyson, Elisa Suzanne. AA, U. Calif., Berkeley, 1958, BS, 1960, LLB, 1963. Bar: Calif. 1964. Ptnr. Bronson, Bronson & McKinnon, San Francisco, 1964-84, Greene, Radovsky, Maloney & Share, San Francisco, 1984—; adj. prof. law U. Calif., Berkeley, 1984; lectr. tax insts. Contbr. articles to profl. jours. Bd. dirs. Koret Found., San Francisco, 1981—, San Francisco Hearing and Speech Cen., 1982—. Served with USAR, 1963-69. Mem. Calif. Bar Assn. (V. Judson Kelin award taxation sect. 1981), Order of Coif, Phi Beta Kappa. Jewish. Club: Concordia (San Francisco). Avocations: tennis, sports, kachina dolls, contemporary art. Corporate taxation, Estate planning, Personal income taxation. Office: Greene Radovsky Maloney & Share One Market Plaza 42d Floor San Francisco CA 94105

GREENE, STEPHEN CRAIG, lawyer; b. Watertown, N.Y., Apr. 27, 1946; s. Harold Adelbert and Mildred Esther (Baker) G.; A.B., Syracuse U., 1967, J.D., 1970; m. Nancy Jean Adams, Mar. 28, 1965; children—Kathryn, Stephen, Hilary. Admitted to N.Y. bar, 1971, U.S. Tax Ct. bar, 1977; asst. to pres. SUNY, Oswego, 1970-73; assoc. firm Leyden E. Brown, Oswego, 1973-75; partner firm Brown and Greene, 1976-81; individual practice law, 1981—; dir. Found. Corp. Legal Studies, Inc., 1968-70; town atty. Oswego, 1972—; counsel Oswego County Bd. Realtors, 1978—. Mem. Oswego County Republican Com., 1974-85, counsel, 1980-83; bd. dirs. Oswego Hosp., 1981—, mem. exec. com. 1985—, 1st v.p. Recipient Ins. Counsel Jour. award Internat. Assn. Ins. Counsel, 1970. Mem. Am., N.Y., Oswego County bar assns., Greater Oswego C. of C. (dir. 1980—), Phi Delta Phi. Episcopalian. Clubs: Oswego Country (counsel 1977-81). Masons (32 deg.), Shriners. Home: 611 W 1st St Oswego NY 13126 Office: 87 W Bridge St Oswego NY 13126

GREENE, THOMAS J., corporate lawyer; b. 1938. AB, U. Notre Dame, 1960; LLB, U. Mich., 1963. Sole practice 1964-69; atty. corp. law Western Airlines, Los Angeles, 1969-71, dir. law, 1971-72, asst. sec., dir. law, 1972-77, asst. v.p. corp. law, asst. sec., 1977-81, acting v.p., sec., gen. counsel, 1981-82, v.p., sec., gen. counsel, 1982—. Office: Western Air Lines Inc Box 92005 World Way Postal Ctr Los Angeles CA 90009 *

GREENE, THURSTON, lawyer; b. N.Y.C., Nov. 10, 1907; s. Richard Thurston and Charlotte Louise G.; m. Eileen Bingham Booker, Oct. 2, 1937; children—Marilyn Greene Rork, Jonathan, Eileen Greene Stentiford; m. 2d, Marta Brodie, Dec. 26, 1970. B.A., Williams Coll., 1929; LL.B., Harvard U., 1932. Bar: N.Y. 1933, Conn. 1947, U.S. Supreme Ct. 1947. Employee, Greene & Hurd, 1932-35; asst. dist. atty., staff Thomas E. Dewey, N.Y. County, 1935-37; ptnr. Greene & Greene, N.Y.C., 1937-42; sole practice, Torrington, Conn., 1946-52; ptnr. Greene & Cook, Torrington, 1952-63; counsel to Ebersol, Roraback & Brower, Torrington, 1963-69; ptnr. Greene & Rork, Torrington, 1969-82, Greene, Horan & Rork, Torrington, 1982—. Served to maj. USAF, 1942-45. Decorated Order of Cloud and Banner (Chinese). Mem. N.Y. State Bar Assn., Conn. Bar Assn., ABA, Assn. of Ex-Mems. of Squadron A (N.Y.), Internat. Order of Grizzly Riders (U. Mont. Found.). Clubs: University, Church. General practice, Probate, Real property. Office: 24 Mason St Torrington CT 06790

GREENEBAUM, LEONARD CHARLES, lawyer; b. Langgoens, Germany, Feb. 6, 1934; came to U.S. 1937, naturalized, 1952; s. Norbert and Henny Lisa (Greenbaum) G.; m. Barbara Rosendorf, Feb. 10, 1957; children—Beth Lynn, Cathy Sue, Steven I. B.S. cum laude in Commerce, Washington and Lee U., 1956, J.D. cum laude, 1959. Bar: D.C. 1959, Va. 1959., Md. 1965 Atty., Sachs, Greenebaum & Tayler and predeccessor firms, Washington, 1959-64, ptnr. 1964-75, mng. ptnr., 1975—; arbitrator Am. Arbitration Assn., Washington, 1975—. Chmn. bd. Davis Meml. Goodwill Industries, Washington, 1979-82; bd. dirs. Council for Ct. Excellenc. Served to capt. U.S. Army, 1957. Recipient Service to Handicapped People award Davis Meml. Goodwill Industries 1982. Fellow Am. Bar Found., mem. D.C. Bar Assn., Md. Bar Assn., Assn. Trial Lawyers Am., Internat. Platform Assn., Jud. Conf. D.C. Cir., Order of Coif, Phi Delta Phi. Jewish. Clubs: University (Washington); Bethesda Country (Md.); Wild Dunes (Charleston, S.C.). Federal civil litigation, General practice, Criminal. Home: 6121 Shady Oak Ln Bethesda MD 20817 Office: Sachs Greenebaum & Tayler 1140 Connecticut Ave NW Washington DC 20036

GREENEBURG, THOMAS MICHAEL, lawyer; b. Hammond, Ind., Dec. 15, 1948; s. Arthur and Molly Gertrude (Bush) G.; m. Susan Ione Drummond, Oct. 20, 1975; children: David Arthur, Rebecca Lynn. BA in Physics, Ind. U., 1970; JD, Northwestern U., 1973. Bar: Ind., Ill., U.S. Dist. Ct. (no. and so. dists.) Ind. 1973. Assoc. Lucas, Clifford & Holcomb, Merrillville, Ind., 1973-79, ptnr., 1979-81; ptnr. Walker, Fleming, Corbin & Greeneburg, Merrillville, Ind., 1981—; city atty. Hobart, Ind., 1974-75; atty. Independence Hill Conservancy Dist., Merrillville, 1978—. Fellow: Ind. Bar Found.; mem. ABA, Ind. Bar Assn., Ill. Bar Assn., Lake County Bar Assn., South Lake County Bar Assn. Jewish. Avocations: racquetball, softball, bowling. Pension, profit-sharing, and employee benefits, Local government, Contracts commercial. Home: 1900 W 99th Pl Crown Point IN 46307 Office: Walker Fleming Corbin & Greeneburg 99 E 86th Ave Merrillville IN 46410

GREENFIELD, JAMES MILTON, lawyer; b. Meadville, Pa., Feb. 5, 1951; s. Milton H. Greenfield and Alice M. (Mickle) Heald; m. Rosemary D. DePhilip, Dec. 28, 1974; 1 child, Amy E. BBA, U. Wis., 1973; JD, U. Pitts., 1977. Bar: Pa. 1977, U.S. Dist. Ct. (we. dist.) Pa. 1981, U.S. Ct. Appeals (3d cir.) 1983; CPA, Ill., Pa. Ptnr. Dale, Woodward, Montgomery & White, Franklin, Pa., 1977—; solicitor Franklin Indsl. and Comml. Devel. Authority, Franklin, 1985—. Officer Community Ambulance Service, Inc., Franklin, 1978—, Vis. Nurses Assn. Mem. ABA, Pa. Bar Assn., Venango County Bar Assn, Franklin Area C. of C. (chmn.). Republican. Methodist. Club: The Franklin (bd. dirs. 1983-84). Lodge: Elks. Probate, Bankruptcy, Contracts commercial. Home: Rosemont Farm Franklin PA 16323 Office: Dale Woodward Montgomery & White 1030 Liberty St Franklin PA 16323

GREENFIELD, JAMES ROBERT, lawyer; b. Phila., Mar. 31, 1926; s. Milton and Katherine E. (Rosenberg) G.; m. Phyllis Chaplowe, Aug. 17, 1947 (dec. May 1978); m. Joyce MacDonald Koehler, Mar. 22, 1980. B.S., Bates Coll., 1947; J.D., Yale U., 1950. Bar: Conn. 1950, U.S. Supreme Ct. 1959. Prin. firm Greenfield, Krick & Jacobs (P.C.), New Haven, 1958—; dir. So. New Eng. Telephone Co.; lectr. U. Conn. Law Sch., 1966-67, 71-72, 75-76. Mem. editorial bd.: Conn. Bar Jour, 1963-77. Pres. New Haven Symphony, 1976-78, Conn. Bar Found., 1976-77; bd. dirs. Nat. Jud. Coll., 1978-84. Served with USNR, 1944-46. Fellow Am. Bar Found.; mem. ABA (state del. 1975-78, bd. govs. 1978-81, ho. of dels. 1972-83, spl. com. on governance 1983-84, chmn. com. on scope and correlation 1985-86), Conn. Bar Assn. (pres. 1973-74), New Haven County Bar Assn. (pres. 1969-70), Judicature Soc. (bd. dirs. 1983—), Yale Law Sch. Assn. (sec. 1977-80). Clubs: Graduate, Quinnipiack, New Haven Lawn, Yale of N.Y.C. General practice, Family and matrimonial, State civil litigation. Home: 230 Blake Rd Hamden CT 06517 Office: 205 Church St New Haven CT 06510 *

GREENFIELD, JAY, lawyer; b. N.Y.C., Oct. 28, 1932; s. Benjamin Joseph and Sali (Sackler) G.; m. Judith Carol Kweskin, Sept. 8, 1957; children: Susan, Mark, Benjamin. AB with distinction, Cornell U., 1954; LLB magna cum laude, Harvard U., 1960. Bar: N.Y. 1961, U.S. Dist. Ct. (so. dist.) N.Y. 1964, U.S. Ct. Appeals (5th cir.) 1964, U.S. Supreme Ct. 1965, U.S. Ct. Appeals (3d cir.) 1972, U.S. Ct. Appeals (4th cir.) 1973, U.S. Ct. Appeals (2d cir.) 1975, U.S. Ct. Appeals (9th cir.) 1982, U.S. Dist. Ct. (no. dist.) 1983, U.S. Ct. Appeals (fed. cir.) 1985. Trial atty. antitrust Dept. Justice, Washington, 1960-61; assoc. Paul, Weiss, Rifkind, Wharton & Garrison, N.Y.C., 1961-70, ptnr., 1970—; instr. law Columbia U., Harvard U., N.Y. Law Jour., Nat. Inst. Trial Adv.; lectr. in field. Served to 1st lt. U.S. Army, 1955-57. Mem. ABA (chmn. econs. com. antitrust sect. 1980-84), Assn. of Bar of City of N.Y., Am. Coll. Trial Lawyers. Democrat. Jewish. Federal civil litigation, State civil litigation, Antitrust. Home: 539 Oakhurst Rd Mamaronek NY 10543 Office: Paul Weiss Rifkind Wharton & Garrison 1285 Ave of the Americas New York NY 10019

GREENFIELD, JOHN FREDERIC, lawyer; b. Washington, Dec. 8, 1943; s. George Albert and Virginia Louise (Sandtner) G.; m. Robin Gene Reid, Dec. 2, 1977; children: Mary, John Francis, Jennifer, Patrick. BA, Seattle U., 1968; JD, U. Idaho, 1973. Bar: Idaho 1974, U.S. Dist. Ct. Idaho 1974, U.S. Ct. Appeals (9th cir.) 1983, U.S. Supreme Ct. 1983. Asst. atty. gen. State of Idaho, Boise, 1974-75; gen. counsel Idaho Dept. Labor and Indsl. Services, Boise, 1975-76; sole practice Boise, 1976—. Mem. Gov.'s Adv. Com. on Workmen's Compensation, Boise, 1983—; chmn. Idaho Dem. Party, Boise, 1977-78. Served with U.S. Army, 1968-70, Vietnam. Mem. Am. Trial Lawyers Assn., Idaho Bar Assn., Idaho Trial Lawyers Assn. Workers' compensation, Labor, Personal injury. Home: 1119 Warm Springs Ave Boise ID 83712 Office: PO Box 854 Boise ID 83701

GREENFIELD, LARRY STUART, lawyer; b. New Brunswick, N.J., July 11, 1950; s. Bernard Herman and Natalie Harriet (Rosene) G.; m. Sharon Helene Foster, June 24, 1973; children: Daniel Evan, Nicole Sara. AB, Cornell U., 1972; JD, NYU, 1975. Bar: N.J. 1975, N.Y. 1976, U.S. Dist. Ct. N.J. 1975, U.S. Dist. Ct. (so. and ea. dists.) N.Y. 1977, Calif. 1980, U.S. Dist. Ct. (cen. dist.) Calif. 1980, U.S. Ct. Appeals (9th cir.) 1982, U.S. Dist. Ct. (so. dist.) Calif. 1984, U.S. Dist. Ct. (no. and ea. dists.) Calif. 1985, U.S. Supreme Ct. 1986. Law clk. to presiding justice N.J. State Ct., Jersey City, 1975-76; assoc. Hart and Hume, N.Y.C., 1976-77, Hardee, Barovick, Konecky and Braun, N.Y.C., 1977-80; assoc. Wyman, Bautzer, Kuchel and Silbert, Los Angeles, 1980-85, ptnr., 1985—. Judge pro tem West Los Angeles (Calif.) Mcpl. Ct., 1985—. Mem. ABA (sects. on litigation, forum com. on entertainment and sports industries) Assn. of the Bar of City of N.Y., Calif. State Bar Assn. Federal civil litigation, State civil litigation, Entertainment. Home: 4612 Via Apuesta Tarzana CA 91356 Office: Wyman Bautzer Kuchel and Silbert 2049 Century Park E Los Angeles CA 90067

GREENFIELD, MICHAEL C., lawyer; b. Chgo., May 4, 1934. B.A., U. Ill., 1955; J.D., Northwestern U., 1957. Bar: Ill. 1957, U.S. Supreme Ct. 1974. Asst. states atty. Cook County (Ill.), 1957-59; ptnr. Asher, Pavalon, Gittler & Greenfield, Ltd., Chgo., 1959—; mem. inquiry bd. Ill. Supreme Ct. Disciplinary Commn., 1973-77, mem. hearing bd., 1978—, vice chmn., 1984, chmn., 1985. Mem. Internat. Found. Employee Benefit Plans (bd. dirs. 1977-80, 85—), ABA, Ill. Bar Assn., Chgo. Bar Assn. Pension, profit-sharing, and employee benefits, Labor. Office: Two N LaSalle St Chicago IL 60602

GREENHALGH, STEPHEN IRVING, lawyer; b. Pontiac, Mich., Sept. 22, 1952; s. Joseph Robert and Margaret Elizabeth (Corwin) G.; m. Susan Marie Brochu, Aug. 28, 1982; 1 child, Meghan Margaret. BA, Albion Coll., 1974; JD, Washington and Lee U., 1977. Bar: U.S. Dist. Ct. (ea. dist.) Mich. 1977, U.S. Dist. Ct. (We. dist.) Mich. 1979, U.S. Ct. Appeals (6th cir.) 1981, U.S. Supreme Ct. 1982. Assoc. Hill, Lewis, Adams, Goodrich & Tait, Detroit, 1972-83, ptnr., 1984—. Martin P. Burks scholar Washington and Lee U., 1976. Republican. Methodist. Club: Detroit Athletic. Contracts commercial, Real property, Securities. Office: Hill Lewis Adams Goodrich & Tait 100 Renaissance Ctr 32d Floor Detroit MI 48243

GREENHILL, IRA JUDD, lawyer; b. N.Y.C. Nov. 17, 1921; s. Joseph and Sara (Hoffman) G.; m. Elaine Diane Maltzman, Dec. 2, 1951; children—Jonathan, Zachary, Lincoln. A.B. with high honors, Swarthmore Coll., 1943; J.D. (Harlan Fiske Stone Scholar), Columbia U., 1948. Bar: N.Y. 1948, U.S. Dist. Ct. (so. dist.) N.Y. 1950, U.S. Dist. Ct. (ea. dist.) N.Y. 1954, U.S. Ct. Appeals (2nd cir.) 1954. Sole practice, N.Y.C., 1948-83; sr. ptnr. Greenhill and Rubin, N.Y.C., 1983—. Served to maj. U.S. Army, 1943-46, 51-52. Club: Princeton (N.Y.C.) Insurance, State civil litigation, General practice. Home: 8 Sunset Rd Rye NY 10580 Office: 500 Fifth Ave New York NY 10110

GREENLEAF, WALTER FRANKLIN, lawyer; b. Griffin, Ga., Sept. 21, 1946; s. Walter Helmuth and Vida Mildred (Goheen) G. B.A., Mich. State U., 1968; M.A., U. N.C., 1970, J.D., U. Ala., 1973. Bar: Ala. 1973, Fla. 1974, U.S. Dist. Ct. (no. dist.) Ala. 1973, U.S. Ct. Appeals (5th cir.) 1974, U.S. Dist. Ct. (so. dist.) Fla. 1977, U.S. Ct. Appeals (11th cir) 1981. Law clk. U.S. Dist. Ct., Birmingham, Ala., 1973-74; assoc. Sirote, Permutt, et al, Birmingham, Ala., 1975-76; assoc., ptnr. Welbaum Zook, Jones, Williams, Miami, 1976—. Editor, Ala. Law Rev., 1972-73. Mem. ABA, Dade County Bar Assn., Am. Arbitration Assn. (panel of arbitrators), Order Coif, Phi Beta Kappa, Phi Kappa Phi, Phi Delta Phi, Omicron Delta Kappa. Insurance, Construction, Probate. Home: 417 Madeira Ave Coral Gables FL 33134 Office: Welbaum Zook Jones & Williams 2701 S Bayshore Dr P-H Miami FL 33133

GREENLEY, BEVERLY JANE, lawyer, educator; b. Cleve., Sept. 24, 1947; d. Gaylord H. and Joan C. (Gurklis) G. B.A., Principia Coll., 1969; J.D., U. Mo., 1976; LL.M., Washington U., 1981. Bar: Mo. 1976, Ill. 1977, U.S. Dist. Ct. (we. dist.) Mo. 1976, U.S. Tax Ct. 1979. Ptnr., McCarter & Greenley, St. Louis, 1976-81, McCarter Snyder & Greenley, St. Louis, 1981-85; assoc. prof. law Stetson U. Coll. Law, St. Petersburg, Fla., 1981-85; ptnr. Gage & Tucker, St. Louis, 1985—. Co-author: Missouri Lawyer's Guide, 1984. Mem. Mo. Bar Assn., Ill. Bar Assn. Estate taxation, Corporate taxation, Probate. Office: Gage & Tucker 7733 Forsyth Blvd Suite 2100 Saint Louis MO 63105

GREENMAN, FREDERICK FRANCIS, lawyer; b. N.Y.C. Feb. 22, 1933; s. Frederick F. and Mildred (Liebman) G.; m. Angela Lancieri; 1 son, Paul Rudolph. B.A., Harvard U., 1954, LL.B., 1961, LL.M., 1963. Bar: N.Y. 1962. Assoc. Hays, Sklar & Herzberg, N.Y.C., 1962-66; asst. U.S. atty. U.S. Atty.'s Office, So. Dist. N.Y., N.Y.C., 1966-69; assoc. Linden and Deutsch, N.Y.C., 1969-70, ptnr., 1971—. Mem. Assn. Bar City N.Y., ABA. Jewish. Civil Litigation, Administrative and regulatory. Office: Linden and Deutsch 110 E 59th St New York NY 10022

GREENMAN, KARL, lawyer; b. Boston, Jan. 4, 1933; s. Magnus and Evelyn (Alpert) G.; m. Karen B. Myhren, June 21, 1964; children: Heidi M., Katrina L. BA, U. Vt., 1954; LLB, Harvard U., 1957. Bar: Mass. 1957, U.S. Dist. Ct. Mass. 1962. Ptnr. Greenman, Grossman & Duffy, Boston, 1961—; Bd. dirs. Mt. Cranmore, Inc., North Conway, N.H. Mem. fin. com. Town of Westwood, Mass. Served to lt. comdr. USN, 1957-61. Mem. Mass. Bar Assn., New. Eng. Conveyancer's Assn., New Eng. Lawn Tennis Assn. (gen. counsel). Real property. Office: Greenman Grossman & Duffy 77 Summer Boston MA 02110

GREENOUGH, WALTER CROAN, lawyer; b. Port Washington, N.Y., Feb. 3, 1951; s. Walter Croan and Doris (Decker) G.; m. Nan Sedergren, Sept. 6, 1975. BA, Amherst Coll., 1972; JD, U. Chgo., 1975. Bar: Ill. 1975. Assoc. Schiff, Hardin & Waite, Chgo., 1975-81, ptnr., 1982—. Mem. ABA, Chgo. Bar Assn. Club: East Bank, Metropolitan (Chgo.). Federal civil litigation, State civil litigation. Office: Schiff Hardin & Waite 7200 Sears Tower Chicago IL 60606

GREENSPAN, ABRAHAM ALCON, company executive, lawyer; b. Mexico City, Oct. 1, 1933; came to U.S., 1950, naturalized, 1955; s. Nathan Citroen and Tanya (Alcon) G.; m. Hannah Goren, June 17, 1954 (div. 1962); 1 dau., Karen Elise; m. 2d, Laura Veronica Perez, May 14, 1971; children—Jacob, Ruth, Natalie. B.A., U. Tex., 1954, J.D., 1956; LL.M., U. Mex., 1957. Bar: Tex. 1956, U.S. Dist. Ct. (so. dist.) Tex. 1958, U.S. Ct. Appeals (5th cir.) 1958. Jr. ptnr. Sharpe, Cunningham & Garza, Brownsville, Tex., 1958-60; ptnr. Cunningham, Garza, Yznaga & Greenspan, Brownsville, 1960-62, Wood, Greenspan & Livingston, Ft. Worth, 1978-80; v.p. fin. Playas del Novillero, S.A., Guadalajara, Mex., 1965-76; pres. Saco Title, Inc., San Angelo, Tex., 1977-78; chief exec. officer Sanmark Internat., Inc., Houston, 1980—, also dir.; cons. Roymex Corp., Ft. Worth, 1980-82; chmn. bd. La Cima Resources, Inc., Houston, 1983—. Author: Treatise on Comparative Law, U.S.-Mexico, 1957. Served to capt. U.S. Army, 1962-65. Mem. Brownsville Jaycees (pres. 1959). Jewish. Club: Toastmasters (bd. dirs. 1961). Lodge: Kiwanis (bd. dirs. 1960). General corporate, FERC practice, Public international. Home: 61 Pipers Walk Sugarland TX 77479 Office: Sanmark Internat Inc 2909 Hillcroft St Suite 500 Houston TX 77057

GREENSPAN, JEFFREY DOV, lawyer; b. Chgo., July 19, 1954; s. Philip and Sylvia (Haberman) G.; m. Eleanor Helen Goldman, Aug. 28, 1983. BS in Econs., U. Ill., Urbana, 1976; JD, Ill. Inst. Tech., 1979. Bar: Ill. 1979, U.S. Dist. Ct. (no. dist.) Ill. 1979, U.S. Ct. Appeals (7th cir.) 1979. Atty. Govs. Office Consumer Services, Chgo., 1978-80; asst. pub. defender Cook County Pub. Defenders Office, Chgo., 1980-81; asst. corp. counsel Village of Skokie, Ill., 1981—; sec., treas. Polit. Cons., Inc., Skokie, 1984—. Author polit. computer software Master Campaigner, 1984. Mem. Niles (Ill.) Twp. Dem. Orgn., 1976-85; chmn. Niles Twp. Com. on Youth, 1982-85, TRY-Citizens for Drug Awareness, Niles, 1983-84. Mem. ABA, Ill. Bar Assn., Chgo. Bar Assn., Assn. Trial Lawyers Am., Decalouge Soc. Local government, State civil litigation, Land use and planning. Home: 9445 N Keeler Ave Skokie IL 60076 Office: Village of Skokie 5127 Oakton Skokie IL 60077

GREENSPAN, LEON JOSEPH, lawyer; b. Phila., Feb. 10, 1932; s. Joseph and Minerva (Podolsky) G.; m. Irene Greenspan, Nov. 2, 1958; children: Marjorie, David, Michael, Lisa. AB, Temple U., 1955, JD, 1958. Bar: N.Y. 1959; Fla. 1985. Sole practice, White Plains, N.Y., 1959-64; ptnr. Greenspan and Aurnou, White Plains, 1964-77; ptnr. Greenspan and Jaffe, White Plains, 1978-87; ptnr. Greenspan, Jaffe & Rosenbltt, Whiteplains, 1987—; counsel Brown, Boston; atty. Tarrytown (N.Y.) Housing Authority. Pres. Hebrew Inst., White Plains; vice chmn. ann. dinner NCCJ. Recipient Pres.'s award Union Orthodox Synagogues, 1982; Hebrew Inst. honoree, White Plains, 1983. Mem. ABA, Westchester County Bar Assn., White Plains Bar Assn., N.Y. State Trial Lawyers Assn., Criminal Cts. Bar Assn. Westchester County. Federal civil litigation, Antitrust, Personal income taxation. Home: 14 Pinebrook Dr White Plains NY 10605 Office: 180 E Post Rd White Plains NY 10601

GREENSPAN, RICHARD MATHEW, lawyer; b. Bklyn., Apr. 20, 1949; s. Harry and Ida Greenspan; m. Janet K. Greenspan; children: Russell, Lisa. BA cum laude, SUNY, Buffalo, 1971; JD, U. San Diego, 1974; LLM, N.Y.U., 1978. Bar: Calif. 1974, U.S. Ct. Appeals (9th cir.) 1980, N.Y. 1976, U.S. Ct. Appeals (2d cir.) 1976, N.J. 1978, U.S. Ct. Appeals (3d cir.) 1979, U.S. Supreme Ct. 1980. Assoc. Law Offices Charles R. Katz P.C., N.Y.C., 1975-86; sole practice N.Y.C., 1986—; adj. prof. grad. sch. mgmt. New Sch. for Social Research, N.Y.C., 1979—. Mem. ABA (labor arbitration sect.), N.Y. Bar Assn. (labor and employment law sect.), N.Y. County Lawyers Assn. (labor law com.). Labor, Pension, profit-sharing, and employee benefits. Office: 360 Lexington Ave New York NY 10017

GREENSPON, ROBERT ALAN, lawyer; b. Hartford, Conn., Apr. 17, 1947; s. George Arthur and Shirley Jean (Shelton) G.; m. Claire Alice Stone, Aug. 21, 1971; children: Colin Haynes, Alison Shelton. AB, Franklin and Marshall, 1969; JD, Columbia U., 1972. Bar: Conn. 1973, U.S. Dist. Conn. 1973, U.S. Ct. Appeals (2d cir.) 1983. Assoc. Robinson & Cole, Hartford, Conn., 1972-78; ptnr. Robinson & Cole, Hartford, 1978-81, Stamford, Conn., 1981-86; sr. v.p., gen. counsel Guinness Peat Aviation Corp., Stamford, 1985—. Mem. ABA (comml. fin. services, aircraft fin.), Conn. Bar Assn., Internat. Bar Assn., Southwestern Legal Found. (bd. advisors internat. and comparative law ctr.). Private international, Contracts commercial, Federal civil litigation. Home: 6 Weeds Landing Darien CT 06820 Office: Guinness Peat Aviation Corp 110 Harbor Plaza Dr Stamford CT 06902

GREENSTEIN, MARLA NAN, lawyer; b. Chgo., Jan. 20, 1957; d. Charles Allen and Lenore (Gould) G. Cert., Oxford U., Eng., 1978; AB, Georgetown U., 1979; JD, Loyola U., 1982. Bar: Ill. 1982, U.S. Dist. Ct. (no. dist.) Ill. 1982, U.S. Ct. Appeals (7th cir.) 1983. Sr. staff atty. Am. Judica-

ture Soc., Chgo., 1982-85; staff atty. Alaska Jud. Council, Anchorage, 1985—; cons. Com. on Cts. and Justice, Chgo., 1985. Author: Handbook for Judicial Nominating Commissioners, 1984. Mem. ABA, Pi Sigma Alpha. Avocations: photography, drawing. Judicial administration, Jurisprudence, Legislative. Office: Alaska Jud Council 1031 W 4th Ave Anchorage AK 99501

GREENSTEIN, MARTIN RICHARD, lawyer; b. Boston, Dec. 29, 1944; s. Paul and Sarah Greenstein; m. Laura H., May 28, 1978; children—Stacey, Marc, Seth, Andrew; stepchildren—Erick and April Hachenburg. B.S.E.E., Tufts U., 1965; M.S.E.E., Princeton U., 1966; J.D., John Marshall Law Sch., 1971. Bar: Ill. 1971, U.S. Patent Office 1971, N.Y. 1982, Calif. 1982. Mem. tech. staff Bell Telephone Labs., Naperville, Ill., 1965-70, mem. patent staff, 1970-71; assoc. firm Baker & McKenzie, Chgo., 1971-78, ptnr., 1978—; instr. John Marshall Law Sch., Chgo., 1972-76. Editorial bd. The Trademark Reporter, 1976—. Trustee Village of Lisle, 1980-83; bd. dirs. Ill. Software Assn. and Ctr., 1984—. Mem. ABA, Ill. Bar Assn., Am. Patent Law Assn., Chgo. Bar Assn., Patent Law Assn. Chgo. Trademark and copyright, Private international, Computer. Home: 2125 Neff Ct Lisle IL 60532 Office: Baker & McKenzie 2800 Prudential Plaza Chicago IL 60601

GREENSTEIN, NEIL DAVID, lawyer; b. Boston, Nov. 16, 1954; s. Paul and Sarah Greenstein; m. Karen Dale Turkanis, July 16, 1978; children: Michael, Cyndi. BSEE, Tufts U., 1976; JD, Am. U., 1979; ML in Taxation, Georgetown U., 1982. Bar: Va. 1979, Wis. 1982, Calif. 1986. Trademark atty. U.S. Patent and Trademark Office, Washington, 1979-82; assoc. Whyte and Hirschboeck S.C., Milw., 1982-86, Pillsbury, Madison and Sutro, San Francisco, 1986—. Trademark and copyright, Patent. Office: Pillsbury Madison and Sutro 235 Montgomery St PO Box 7880 San Francisco CA 94120

GREENSTEIN, ROBERT STANLEY, lawyer, microcomputer consultant; b. N.Y.C., Sept. 10, 1955; s. Jerome Irving and Sylvia Miriam (Kahan) G.; m. Cassandra Gutierrez, Oct. 10, 1982. BA, Cornell U., 1974; postgrad., Coll. Rec. Arts, 1977; JD, Southwestern U., 1981. Bar: Calif. 1981, U.S. Dist. Ct. (cen. dist.) Calif. 1981, U.S. Ct. Appeals (9th cir.) 1982. Sole practice Los Angeles, 1981—; pres. Perfect Match Computer Cons., Los Angeles, 1983—. Mem. ABA (legal tech. adv. counsel 1985—), Calif. Bar Assn., Los Angeles County Bar Assn. (computer users com. 1986—), Century City Bar Assn., Beverly Hills Bar Assn. (computer use com. 1985—), Nat. Acad. Rec. Arts & Scis. Avocations: computers, skiing, photography, audio and video tech. Entertainment, General corporate, Personal injury. Office: 2049 Century Park E 11th Floor Los Angeles CA 90067

GREENSTEIN, RUTH LOUISE, corporation executive, lawyer; b. N.Y.C., Mar. 28, 1946; d. Milton and Beatrice (Zutty) G.; m. David Seidman, May 19, 1972. B.A., Harvard U., 1966; M.A., Yale U., 1968; J.D., George Washington U., 1980. Bar: D.C. 1980. Fgn. service info. officer USIA, Washington and Tehran, Iran, 1968-70; adminstrv. asst. Export-Import Bank U.S., Washington, 1971-72; asst. dean Woodrow Wilson Sch. Pub. and Internat. Affairs, Princeton U., 1972-75; budget examiner U.S. Office Mgmt. and Budget, Washington, 1975-79; budget coordinator U.S. Internat. Devel. Coop. Agy., 1979-81; dep. gen. counsel NSF, 1981-84; assoc. counsel, then v.p. Genex Corp., Gaithersburg, Md., 1984—; mem. academic adv. panel to com. on exchanges, CIA, 1983—. Mem. D.C. Bar Assn., Nat. Acad. Scis. (panel on impact of nat. security controls on internat. tech. transfer 1985-87), AAAS (com. on sci. freedom and responsibility 1987—). General corporate, Administrative and regulatory. Home: 2737 Devonshire Pl NW Apt 511 Washington DC 20008 Office: Genex Corp 16020 Industrial Dr Gaithersburg MD 20877

GREENWALD, STEVEN JEFFREY, lawyer; b. Detroit, Jan. 7, 1954; s. Norbert E. Greenwald and Phyllis (Margoles) Greenwald Fershtman. BA in Philosophy and Pre-Law with highest honors, Mich. State U., 1976; JD, U. Detroit, 1980. Bar: Fla. 1980. Ptnr. Oconnor, Baylor, Elliott & Greenwald, Palm Beach Gardens, Fla., 1981-83; sole practice West Palm Beach, Fla., 1983—. Mem. ABA (trial lawyers sect.), Fla. Bar Assn. (trial lawyers sect.), Palm Beach County Bar Assn., Assn. Trial Lawyers Am., Acad. Fla. Trial Lawyers, Attys. Title Fund. Republican. Personal injury, Insurance, State civil litigation. Home: 3000 N Ocean Blvd Singer Island FL 33404 Office: 324 Datura Suite 210 West Palm Beach FL 33401

GREENWELL, LINDA LAMPING, lawyer; b. Clarksville, Tenn., Jan. 13, 1953. BA cum laude, Ind. U., 1975, JD, 1980cer. Bar: Ind. 1980, Ky. 1980. Assoc. Goldberg & Simpson P.S.C., Louisville, 1980. Mng. editor Ind. U. Law Rev., 1979-80. Mem. ABA (tort and ins. sect.), Ind. Bar Assn., Ky. Bar Assn., Louisville Bar Assn., Ky. Acad. Trial Lawyers. Office: Goldberg & Simpson PSC 2800 1st Nat Tower Louisville KY 40202

GREENWOOD, CLARENCE HENRY, lawyer; b. Glasgow, Mont., Dec. 9, 1947; s. Henry and Sophie (Birkoski) G.; m. Myrtle Rae Wilson, Aug. 14, 1976; 1 child, Chad Henry. BA with high honors, U. Mont., 1970, JD with honors, 1975; LLM in Taxation, NYU, 1977. Bar: Mont. 1975, U.S. Dist. Ct. Mont. 1975, Oreg. 1979, U.S. Dist. Ct. Oreg. 1979, U.S. Ct. Claims 1979, U.S. Tax Ct. 1979, U.S. Ct. Appeals (9th cir.) 1984. Sole practice Helena, Mont., 1975-76; law clk. to presiding justice U.S. Ct. Claims, Washington, 1977-79; assoc. Black & Helterline, Portland, Oreg., 1979-84; ptnr. Rappleyea, Beck, Helterline, Spencer & Roakie, Portland, 1985—. Mem. ABA, Mont. Bar Assn., Oreg. Bar Assn., Am. Judicature Soc. Corporate taxation, Estate taxation, Personal income taxation. Home: 2026 SW Vermont Portland OR 97219 Office: Rappleyea Beck Helterline et al 707 SW Washington 1200 Bank Calif Portland OR 97205

GREENWOOD, MYRTLE RAE, lawyer; b. Great Falls, Mont, May 11, 1950; s. Ray Charles and Miherva Euphemia (Henion) Wilson; m. Clarence Henry Greenwood, Aug. 14, 1976; 1 child, Chad. BA with high honors, U. Mont., 1972, JD, 1975; LLM, NYU, 1977. Bar: Mont. 1975, U.S. Ct. Appeals (4th cir.) 1978, Oreg. 1980, U.S. Dist. Ct. Oreg. 1982. Assoc. Gene Huntley Law Offices, Baker, Mont., 1975-76; staff atty. U.S. Dept. Labor, Washington, 1977-79; adminstrn. asst. U.S. Nat. Bank, Portland, Oreg., 1980-81; assoc. Kell, Alterman & Rumstein, Portland, 1981-85; counsel Willamette Savings, Portland, 1985—. Mem. Columbia Shores Chapter Community Assn., Portland, 1981-85; bd. dirs. Forest Park Children's Ctr., Portland, 1983-85. Mem. ABA, Oreg. Bar Assn., Mont. Bar Assn., Multnomah Bar Assn., Internat. Network Bus. and Profl. Women (registered agt.), Assn. Profl. Women. Avocation: family activities. Real property, Banking, Consumer commercial. Office: Willamette Savings Legal Dept 100 SW Market St Portland OR 97205

GREENWOOD, STEVEN MATLIN, lawyer; b. Los Angeles, Jan. 31, 1950; s. Lewis Greenwood and Arlyn (Matlin) Goldsby; m. Debra Vogel, July 31, 1977; children: Jamie, Laura. BA in Econs., U. Calif., Berkeley, 1972; JD, San Fernando Valley Coll., 1978. Bar: Calif. 1979, U.S. Dist. Ct. (cen. dist.) Calif. 1979; cert. real estate broker, Calif. Legal v.p. Hopkins Fin. Corp., Oxnard, Calif., 1979-80; sole practice Oxnard, 1980—. Editor: The Appeal: SFVC of Law, 1986; columnist The Reporter, 1983. Mem. Ventura County Bar Assn., Oxnard Jaycees (pres. 1983-84). Jewish. Lodge: Optimists (bd. dirs. Oxnard club 1984—). Avocations: music, singing, community service. Entertainment, Real property. Home and Office: 309 S A St Oxnard CA 93030

GREER, ALAN GRAHAM, lawyer; b. El Dorado, Ark., May 31, 1939; s. Arthur W. and Marie (Ross) G.; m. Patricia A. Seitz, Aug. 14, 1981. B.S., U.S. Naval Acad., 1961; J.D., U. Fla., 1969. Mem., Floyd Pearson Stewart Richman Greer Weil & Zack, Miami, Fla., 1969—; dir. Trade Nat. Bank of Miami. Chmn. Dade County Council Arts and Scis.; mem. Fla. State Task Force on Water Issues, Gov.'s Bus. Adv. Council on Edn. Served with USN, 1961-67. Fellow Internat. Soc. Barristers; mem. ABA, Fla. Bar Assn. (cert.), Assn. Trial Lawyers Am. Antitrust, Federal civil litigation, State civil litigation. Home: 224 Ridgewood Rd Coral Gables FL 33133 Office: Floyd Pearson et al 1 Biscayne Tower 25th Floor Miami FL 33131

GREER, CHARLES EUGENE, lawyer; b. Columbus, Ohio, Mar. 28, 1945; s. Earl E. Greer and Margaret I. Cavanass; m. Margaret G. Gaffney, July 22, 1978; 1 child, Erin Elizabeth. BS, Ind. U., 1972, JD, 1976. Ptnr. Ice, Miller, Donadio & Ryan, Indpls., 1976—. Served to sgt. USAF, 1965-68, Vietnam. Mem. ABA, Ind. Bar Assn., Indpls. Bar Assn., Order of Coif, Phi Eta Sigma, Beta Gamma Sigma. Club: Indpls. Athletic. Lodge: Rotary. Contracts commercial, Federal civil litigation, State civil litigation. Office: Ice Miller Donadio & Ryan 1 Am Sq Indianapolis IN 46282

GREER, DAVID CARR, lawyer; b. Dayton, Ohio, Feb. 14, 1937; s. Rowan A. and Janet (Carr) G.; m. Barbara Bennett, June 27, 1959 (div. Oct. 1985); m. Diane J. Sanford, Oct. 11, 1985; children: Thomas C., James H., Katherine A. BA summa cum laude, Yale U., 1959, LLB cum laude, 1962. Bar: Ohio 1962, U.S. Dist. Ct. (so. dist.) Ohio, U.S. Ct. Appeals (6th cir.), U.S. Supreme Ct. Assoc. Bieser, Greer & Landis, Dayton, 1962-67, ptnr., 1967—. Trustee Dayton area chpt. United Way, 1975-81; pres., 1979-81; trustee Dayton area chpt. ARC, 1970-75. Fellow Am. Coll. Trial Lawyers; mem. Def. Research Inst., ABA, Ohio Assn. Trial Attys., Assn. Trial Lawyers Am., Ohio State Bar Assn., Dayton Bar Assn. (pres. 1981-82), Internat. Assn. of Jazz Records Collectors (pres. 1982-83), Fretted Instruments Guild Am. Republican. Episcopalian. Avocations: leader and banjo player for Classic Jazz Stompers, collector of early jazz music and records. Federal civil litigation, State civil litigation, Personal injury. Home: 12 Tecumseh St Dayton OH 45402 Office: Bieser Greer & Landis 400 Gem Plaza 3d and Main Sts Dayton OH 45402

GREER, GORDON BRUCE, lawyer; b. Butler, Pa., Feb. 17, 1932; s. Samuel Walker and Winifred (Fletcher) G.; m. Nancy Linda Hannaford, June 14, 1959; children—Gordon Bruce, Alison Clark. B.A., Harvard U., 1953, J.D. cum laude, 1959. Bar: Wis. 1959, Mass. 1961. Assoc. Foley, Sammond & Lardner, Milw., 1959-61; assoc. Bingham, Dana & Gould, Boston, 1961-67, ptnr., 1967—. dir. The Colonial Group, Inc. Served to maj. USAFR. Mem. ABA, Mass. Bar Assn., Boston Bar Assn. Republican. Clubs: Brae Burn Country; Federal, Harvard (Boston). Editor Harvard Law Rev., vols. 71, 72. General corporate, Private international. Home: 45 Fieldmont Rd Belmont MA 02178 Office: 100 Federal St Boston MA 02110

GREER, RAYMOND WHITE, lawyer; b. Port Arthur, Tex., July 20, 1954; s. Mervyn Hardy Greer and Eva Nadine (White) Swain; m. Charlotte Ann Greer, Apr. 17, 1976; 1 child, Emily Ann. BA magna cum laude, Sam Houston State, 1977; JD, U. Houston, 1981. Assoc. Hoover, Cox & Shearer, Houston, 1980-83, Hinton & Morris, Houston, 1983-85; sole practice Houston, 1985-86; prin. Morris & Greer, P.C., Houston, 1986—. Mem. ABA, State Bar Tex., Houston Bar Assn., Fort Bend County Bar Assn., Assn. Trial Lawyers Am., Tex. Assn. Bank Counsel. Avocations: golf, water skiing, reading. State civil litigation, Federal civil litigation, Insurance. Office: Morris & Greer PC 952 Echo Ln Suite 110 Houston TX 77024

GREGG, JOHN RALPH, lawyer; b. Ann Arbor, Mich., Jan. 12, 1951; s. Ralph E. and Elizabeth (Palmer) G.; m. Peggy Jane Parkman, Aug. 6, 1977; 1 child, Katharine Ann. BA, U. Mich., 1973; JD, U. N.D., 1976. Bar: N.D. 1976, Minn. 1976, U.S. Dist. Ct. N.D. 1979. Ptnr. Gregg & McLean Law Office, Rugby and Bottineau, N.D., 1976—; asst. state's atty. Pierce County, Rugby, 1976-78; tribal judge Turtle Mountain Tribal Ct., Belcourt, N.D., 1979-80; state's atty. Bottineau County, N.D., 1983-86. Criminal, Real property, Oil and gas leasing. Home: 604 Jay Bottineau ND 58318 Office: Gregg & McLean Law Office PO Box 26 Bottineau ND 58318

GREGG, JON MANN, lawyer; b. Louisville, Oct. 22, 1943; s. James Willard and Margaret Josephine (Mann) G.; m. Jeanette Ruth Brandner, June 18, 1966 (div. Oct. 1980); children: Heather Suzanne, Douglas Robert; m. Carol Ruth Slonneger, July 9, 1983; 1 child, Catherine Marie. BS, U. Ill., 1965; LLB, Harvard U., 1968. Bar: Ill. 1968. Assoc. Sidley & Austin, Chgo., 1968-74, ptnr., 1974—. Securities, General corporate, Contracts commercial. Home: 344 W Wisconson Unit D Chicago IL 60614 Office: Sidley & Austin 1 First Nat Plaza Chicago IL 60603

GREGG, RICHARD, lawyer; b. Cananea, Mex., May 24, 1946; came to U.S., 1949; s. Enrique Francisco and Carolina (Rivas) G.; m Jean Ann Pharris, June 2, 1973; 1 child, Jessica Raquel. B.A., Calif. State U.-Dominquez Hills, 1972; J.D., U. Calif.-Davis, 1977. Bar: Calif. 1977, U.S. Dist. Ct. (ea. dist.) Calif. 1977, U.S. Dist. Ct. (no. dist.) Calif. 1984. Adminstrv. analyst City of Redondo Beach, Calif., 1972-74; ct. interpreter Yolo County Cts., Calif., 1975-79; legal asst. Calif. Dept. Motor Vehicles, Sacramento, 1976-77; ct. probate investigator Yolo County, 1978-83, ct. commr., 1983; ptnr. Lauricella & Gregg, Woodland, Calif., 1978-83; assoc. Boccado Law Firm, San Jose, Calif., 1983—. Editor Yolo County Bar Newsletter, 1981-83, Santa Clara County La Raza Lawyers Newsletter, 1984. Chmn. Safe Harbor Crisis House, Davis, Calif., 1982; TV moderator Raza Lawyers Assn., Sacramento, 1982. Served to 1st lt. U.S. Army, 1966-69, Vietnam. Decorated Army Commendation medal, Air medal. Mem. Yolo County Bar Assn. (pres. 1983), La Raza Lawyers Assn. (pres. Santa Clara County chpt. 1986), Calif. State Bar, Calif. Trial Lawyers Assn., Assn. Trial Lawyers Am., Santa Clara County Bar Assn, Santa Clara County La Raza Lawyers Assn (pres. 1986). Democrat. Club: Toastmasters (pres. Sacramento 1982, pres. Woodland 1981, Dist. Toastmaster of Yr. 1982). Personal injury, State civil litigation, Federal civil litigation. Office: Boccardo Law Firm 111 W St John St San Jose CA 95115

GREGG, TOM WILL, JR., lawyer; b. San Angelo, Tex., Dec. 31, 1939; s. Tom W. and Hazel V. (Williams) G.; m. Frances Preston, Oct. 16, 1965; children: Thomas Preston, Walter Parke. B.B.A., U. Tex., 1961, J.D., 1964. Bar: Tex. 1964, U.S. Dist. Ct. (no. dist.) Tex. 1966, U.S. Supreme Ct. 1968, U.S. Ct. Mil. Appeals 1968. Assoc. Kerr, Gayer & Lyons, San Angelo, 1966-69; ptnr. Kerr, Gayer & Gregg, 1969-74, Gregg & Sterling, 1974-81; sole practice, 1981—(all San Angelo). Chmn. lawyers com. Nat. Rural Electric Coop. Assn., 1984-86; chmn. bd. Ft. Concho Mus. Served with USAF, 1965-69. Mem. ABA, Tom Green County Bar Assn. Episcopalian. Contbr. articles to profl. jours. Club: Bentwood Country. Public utilities, Real property, Probate. Office: Box 1032 San Angelo TX 76902

GREGORY, DAVID LAWRENCE, law educator, lawyer, labor arbitrator; b. Detroit, Nov. 17, 1951; s. David Tallog and Anne Beverly (Klimchalk) G. BA, Cath. U., 1973; MBA, Wayne State U., 1977; JD, U. Detroit, 1980; LLM, Yale U., 1982. Bar: Mich. 1981, U.S. Dist. Ct. (ea. dist.) Mich. 1981. EEO counselor U.S. Postal Service, Detroit, 1974-77; labor relations rep. Ford Motor Co., Redford, Mich., 1977-80; assoc. Clark, Hardy & Lewis, Birmingham, Mich., 1980-82; prof. law St. John's U., Jamaica, N.Y., 1982—. Author numerous articles and book revs. Mem. ABA, Fed. Bar Assn., Am. Arbitration Assn. (labor panel 1983—), Indsl. Relations Research Assn., Soc. Profl. in Dispute Resolution. Democrat. Roman Catholic. Office: St John's Univ Law Sch Utopia Pkwy Jamaica NY 11439

GREGORY, GARY HUGH, lawyer; b. London, Ky., Aug. 18, 1955; s. Joe T. and Mary R. (Ruth) G.; m. Betty Sue Baker, Aug. 14, 1977; children: Jonah Ryan, Lindsey Marie. BS, Western Ky. U., 1978; JD, No. Ky. U., 1981. Bar: Ky. 1981, U.S. Dist. Ct. (ea. dist.) Pa. 1985. Sole practice Manchester, Ky., 1981—; atty. City of Manchester, 1984—. Gen. counsel Ky. State Young Rep. Club, Manchester, 1984; pres. Clay County Rep. Club, Manchester, 1983. Mem. ABA, Ky. Bar Assn., Assn. Trial Lawyers Am. Baptist. Lodges: Masons (trustee Manchester 1985—), Kiwanis (pres. Manchester 1985—). Avocations: tennis, fishing. Personal injury, General practice. Home: PO Box 461 Manchester KY 40962

GREGORY, GEORGE TILLMAN, JR., justice S.C. Supreme Ct.; b. McConnellsville, S.C., Dec. 13, 1921; s. George T. and Inez Anderson G.; m. Willie Mae Elliott, Dec. 27, 1951; children: George Tillman III, William Elliott. A.B., U. S.C., 1943, LL.B., 1944. Bar: S.C. 1944. U.S. commr. 1945-46; city recorder Chester, 1946-50; judge S.C. Circuit Ct., 6th Jud. Circuit, 1956-75; assoc. justice S.C. Supreme Ct., 1975—. Mem. S.C. Ho. of Reps., 1951-52, 55-56; Trustee Furman U., 1968-72. Mem. ABA, Law Fedn. and Euphradian Library Soc. (pres.). Jurisprudence. Office: Supreme Ct Bldg PO Box 11330 Columbia SC 29211 *

GREGORY, HARDY, JR., justice Georgia Supreme Court; b. Vienna, Ga., Aug. 11, 1936; s. Hardy and Mary Wood (Gaither) G.; m. Carolyn Burton, June 14, 1959; children: Hardy III, Elizabeth Marywood. B.S., U.S. Naval Acad., 1959; LL.B., Mercer U., 1967; LLM, U. Va., 1986. Bar: Ga. 1966. Atty. Adams & O'Neal, Macon, Ga., 1966-71, Davis & Gregory, Vienna, Ga., 1971-76; judge Superior Cts., Cordale Cir., Ga., 1976-81; justice Ga. Supreme Ct., Atlanta, 1981—. Chmn. Democratic Exec. Com. Dooly County, Ga., 1971-76; mem. Bd. Edn. Dooly County, 1972; trustee Mercer U., 1986—. Served to capt. USAF, 1959-64; served to capt. USN, 1955-59. Mem. Am. Law Inst. Democrat. Methodist. State civil litigation, Criminal. Office: Supreme Ct Ga Judicial Bldg Atlanta GA 30334

GREGORY, JOHN LUNSFORD, III, lawyer; b. Winston-Salem, N.C., May 26, 1947; s. John L. Jr. and Lou Dillard (Nissen) G.; m. Gail Doyle, Sept. 28, 1974; children: John L. IV, Elizabeth Doyle. Student, Vanderbilt U., 1965-67; BA, Lynchburg Coll., 1970; JD, U. Richmond, 1973. Bar: Va. 1973, U.S. Dist. Ct. (we. dist.) Va. 1974, U.S. Supreme Ct. 1978, U.S. Ct. Appeals (4th cir.) 1981. Ptnr. Young, Haskins, Mann & Gregory P.C., Martinsville, Va., 1973—. Editorial bd. U. Richmond Law Rev., 1972-73. Mem. ABA, Va. Bar Assn., Va. Trial Lawyers Assn. Contracts commercial, Real property, General corporate. Office: Young Haskins Mann & Gregory PC 60 W Church St Martinsville VA 24114-0072

GREGORY, JULIAN ARTHUR, JR., lawyer; b. East Orange, N.J., Dec. 16, 1912; s. Julian Arthur Sr. and Virginia (Evans) G.; m. Margaret P. Gregory, July 7, 1955; 1 child, Julian A. Jr. AB, Princeton U.; JD, Mich. U. Bar: N.Y. 1939, Conn. 1947, U.S. Supreme Ct. 1960, U.S. Dist. Ct. Conn. 1964. Assoc. Davies Auerbach, N.Y.C., 1938-39, Gregory, Stewart & Montgomery, N.Y.C., 1939-40, Davies Auerbach, N.Y.C., 1946-53; sole practice N.Y.C., 1954-60; sr. ptnr. Gregory & Adams, Wilton, Conn., 1960—. Selectman Bd. of Selectmen, Wilton, Conn., 1949-53. Served to capt. U.S. Army, 1941-46, PTO, Korea. Mem. ABA, Conn. Bar Assn., Assn. of Bar of City of N.Y., Norwalk-Wilton Bar Assn. Democrat. Congregationalist. Club: Princeton (N.Y.C.). Estate planning, Probate, Estate taxation. Office: Gregory & Adams PO Box 190 Wilton CT 06897

GREGORY, RICK DEAN, lawyer; b. Edmond, Okla., Feb. 22, 1954; s. Jerry D. and Elaine (Hall) G. B.A. in History, Central State U., 1977; J.D., Oklahoma City U., 1981. Bar: Okla. 1982, U.S. Dist. Ct. (ea. and we. dist.) Okla. 1982, U.S. Ct. Appeals (10th cir.) 1982. Juvenile parole officer dept. human services State of Okla., Oklahoma City, 1977-81; law clk. Jess Horn, Inc., Oklahoma City, 1981-82; atty. in sole practice, Oklahoma City, 1982—. Editor: Policy Options on Political Reform, 1974; author: A Historical, Legal and Moral Analysis of Unauthorized Audio Duplication in the United States, 1975. Mem. ABA, Am. Trial Lawyers Assn., Am. Judicature Soc., Okla. Bar Assn., Okla. Trial Lawyers Assn., Okla. County Bar Assn., Can. County Bar Assn., Okla. Criminal Defense Lawyers Assn. Democrat. Methodist. Avocations: skiing, tennis, swimming. Criminal, Personal injury, Insurance.

GREGORY, WILLIAM DAVID, lawyer; b. Mt. Vernon, Ky., July 9, 1939; s. David and Evelyn (Mason) G.; m. Mary Todd Gregory; children: Bill, Joe, Cindy. AB, U. Ky., 1961; LLB, U. Tenn., 1967. Bar: Ky. 1967, U.S. Dist. Ct. (ea. dist.) Ky., U.S. Ct. Appeals (6th cir.), U.S. Supreme Ct. Sole practice Mt. Vernon, 1967—; atty. Rockcastle County, Mt. Vernon, 1970-74; bd. dirs. Bank of Mt. Vernon. Served with U.S. Army, 1962-64. Republican. Baptist. Avocations: fishing, hunting. General practice. Office: Gregory Bldg Mount Vernon KY 40456

GREIG, BRIAN STROTHER, lawyer; b. Austin, Tex., Apr. 10, 1950; s. Ben Wayne Greig and Virginia Ann (Strother) Higgins; m. Jane Ann Sentilles, June 17, 1972; children: Travis Darden, Grace Hanna. BA, Washington and Lee U., 1972; JD, U. Tex., 1975. Bar: Tex. 1975, U.S. Dist. Ct. (ea. dist.) Tex. 1976, U.S. Ct. Appeals (5th cir.) 1976, U.S. Dist. Ct. (so. dist.) Tex. 1977, U.S. Dist. Ct. (we. dist.) Tex. 1980, U.S. Supreme Ct. 1980, U.S. DIst. Ct. (no. dist.) Tex. 1984, U.S. Ct. Appeals (11th cir.) 1984. Law clk. to chief judge U.S. Dist. Ct., Beaumont, Tex., 1975-76; ptnr. Fulbright & Jaworski, Austin, 1976—. Pres. Austin Lawyers and Accts. for Arts, 1981; trustee Laguna Gloria Art Mus., Austin, 1983—; bd. dirs. Zachary Scott Theater Ctr., Austin, 1981. Mem. ABA, Tex. Bar Assn., Travis County Bar Assn. Methodist. Clubs: Tarry House, Headliners (Austin). Avocations: hunting, fishing. Labor, Civil rights, Construction. Office: Fulbright & Jaworski 600 Congress Ave Austin TX 78701

GREIG, WILLIAM HAROLD, lawyer; b. Fayetteville, Ark., Nov. 15, 1951; s. James Kibler Greig and Betty Sue (Hamm) G.; m. M. Francine Stuckey, May 16, 1976; children: Elizabeth Anne, William David. BS, Kans. State U., 1973; JD, Washburn U., 1976; MBA, Eastern N.Mex. U., 1982. Bar: N.Mex. 1976, Kans. 1977, U.S. Dist. Ct. Kans. 1977, U.S. Dist. Ct. N.Mex. 1977. Ptnr. Van Soelen, Greig & Gutierrez Law Firm, Clovis, N.Mex., 1976—. Contbr. numerous articles to profl. jours. Bd. dirs. YMCA, Clovis, 1986—. Mem. ABA, Assn. Trial Lawyers Am., N.Mex. Trial Lawyers Assn. (state bar and supreme ct. coms.), Curry County Bar Assn. (v.p. 1976-77, pres. 1980-81). Democrat. Methodist. Avocation: writing. State civil litigation, Personal injury, Criminal. Home: PO Box 423 Clovis NM 88101 Office: Van Soelen Greig & Gutierrez PO Box 1080 Clovis NM 88101

GREIGG, RONALD EDWIN, lawyer; b. Washington, June 29, 1946; s. Edwin E. and Helen Marie (Marcy) G.; m. Patricia Anne Crowe, June 5, 1968; children: Elizabeth, Rebecca. BBA, Am. U., 1969, MBA in Fin., 1971; JD, Stetson U., 1976. Bar: Fla. 1976, U.S. Dist. Ct. (mid. dist.) Fla. 1976, D.C. 1978, U.S. Ct. Appeals (D.C. cir.) 1979, U.S. Supreme Ct. 1980, Va. 1985. Assoc. David E. De Serio, St. Petersburg, Fla., 1977-78, Edwin E. Greigg, Washington, 1979-82, Harris, Barrett & Dew, St. Petersburg, Fla., 1982-84; sole practice Arlington, Va., 1984—; sec. Anti-Pollution Indsl. Research Ltd., Wilmington, Del., 1985—. Author: A Guide to the FTC Franchise Disclosure Rule, 1979. Mem. search com. St. Dunstan's Ch., McLean, Va., 1986—. Served with USAR, 1969-75. Mem. Soc. Automotive Engrs., ABA, D.C. Bar Assn., Fla. Bar Assn., Va. Bar Assn., U.S. Trademark Assn., Fairfax C. of C., Washington Area Lawyers for the Arts, Phi Alpha Delta. Democrat. Episcopalian. Avocations: sailing, classic cars. Trademark and copyright, Patent, Computer. Office: 1201 S Eads St Arlington VA 22202

GREILSHEIMER, JAMES GANS, lawyer; b. N.Y.C., Oct. 14, 1937; s. Jerome J. and Lillian (Gans) G.; m. Louise B. Steiner, Aug. 11, 1974; children: Lauren, Julie, Michael, Jeremy. A.B. cum laude, Princeton U., 1959; LL.B., Harvard U., 1962. Bar: N.Y. 1963, D.C. 1969. Asst. U.S. atty. So. Dist. N.Y., 1963-68; litigating asst. corp. counsel City of N.Y., 1974-77, 1st asst. corp. counsel, 1978-80; ptnr. Stroock, Stroock & Lavan, N.Y.C., 1980—. Mem., sec. N.Y.C. Charter Rev. Commn., 1982-83; pres. N.Y. chpt. Am. Jewish Com., 1981-84; v.p. Jewish Community Relations Council of N.Y., 1981-85; bd. dirs. Non-profit Coordinating Commn. of N.Y., 1985—; dir. Vol. Cons. Group, Inc., 1986—. Mem. N.Y. County Lawyers Assn. (bd. dirs. 1981—, chmn. fed. cts. com. 1977-80), Assn. Bar City N.Y. (mcpl. affairs com. 1979-81), N.Y. State Bar Assn. (spl. com. on cts. and community 1975-81). Federal civil litigation, State civil litigation, Condemnation. Address: 7 Hanover Sq New York NY 10004

GREIMAN, GERALD PHILLIP, lawyer; b. Chgo., Jan. 7, 1950; s. Irvin and Era (Magill) G.; m. M. Susan Carlson, May 2, 1982; children: David, Nora. AB, Washington U., St. Louis, 1971, JD, 1975. Bar: Mo. 1975, D.C. 1977. Law clk. U.S. Ct. Appeals (8th cir.) Mo., St. Louis, 1975-77; assoc. Edward Greensfelder Jr., P.C., Washington, 1977-78; ptnr. Greensfelder & Greiman, P.C., Washington, 1978-86, Green, Kanefield, Hoffmann & Dankenbring, St. Louis, 1986—. Commr. Adv. Neighboorhood Commn. 3F, Washington, 1985-86. Mem. D.C. Bar Assn. (div. IV, mem. steering com, 1985—, co-chmn. com. on ct. rules, 1983—, mem. legis. com., 1985—), Order of the Coif. Democrat. Jewish. Avocations: bridge, golf, travel. Federal civil litigation, State civil litigation, General practice. Home: 7042 Westmoreland Dr Saint Louis MO 63130 Office: Green Kanefield Hoffman & Dankenbring 7733 Forsyth Blvd Saint Louis MO 63105

GRENIER, EDWARD JOSEPH, JR., lawyer; b. N.Y.C., Nov. 26, 1933; s. Edward Joseph and Jane Veronica (Farrell) G.; m. Patricia J. Grenier, June 22, 1957; children: Victoria-Anne, Edward Joseph, III, Peter C. B.A. summa cum laude, Manhattan Coll., N.Y.C., 1954; LL.B. magna cum laude, Harvard U., 1959. Bar: D.C. 1959, U.S. Ct. Apls. (D.C. cir.) 1959, U.S. Ct. Mil. Apls. 1960, U.S. Ct. Apls. (3d cir.) 1966, U.S. Sup. Ct. 1966, U.S. Ct. Apls. (9th cir.) 1973, U.S. Ct. Apls. (10th cir.) 1977, U.S. Ct. Apls. (5th cir.)

1982. Law clk. U.S. Ct. Apls. D.C. Cir., 1959-60; assoc. Covington & Burling, Washington, 1960-68; ptnr. Sutherland, Asbill & Brennan, Washington, 1968—; speaker in field of energy related issues to profl. orgns. Chmn. bd. trustees, mem. exec. com. Connelly Sch. Holy Child, Potomac, Md., 1976—; bd. dirs. D.C. Recording for the Blind, Washington, 1977—. Served to 1st lt. USAF, 1954-56. Mem. D.C. Bar Assn., Bar Assn. D.C., ABA, Fed. Energy Bar Assn., Fed. Communications Bar Assn., Fed. Bar Assn., Computer Law Assn., Internat. Council Computer Communications. Club: Met. (Washington). Contbr. articles in field to legal jours. FERC practice. Office: Sutherland Asbill & Brennan 1666 K St NW Washington DC 20006 *

GRESHAM, TIMOTHY WARD, lawyer; b. McKinney, Tex., Nov. 22, 1953; s. Charles Russell and Virginia Ruth (Smith) G.; m. Alice Marie Raynor, May 11, 1985; children: Whitney Verges, Jordan Leann. AB, Morehead State U., 1976; JD, U. Tenn., 1979. Bar: Tenn. 1980, Va. 1982, U.S. Dist. Ct. (we. dist.) Va. 1983. Assoc. Hamrick & Assocs., Bristol, Tenn., 1979-81; staff atty. Legal Services, Johnson City, Tenn., 1981; atty. The Pittston Co., Lebanon, Va., 1981-82; asst. atty. gen. State of Va., Abingdon, 1983-87; atty. Penn, Stuart, Eskridge and Jones, Abingdon, 1987—. Mem. Va. Bar Assn. (sec. bd. govs. 1986—, environ. law sect. 1985—), Va. State Bar. Administrative and regulatory, Environment, Workers' compensation. Home: PO Box 456 Abingdon VA 24210 Office: Penn Stuart Eskridge & Jones PO Box 2288 Abingdon VA 24210

GRESHAM, WAYNE EDGAR, lawyer; b. Louisville, Ky., Dec. 8, 1947; s. Edgar Lee and Alma W. (Weihe) G. BA in Internat. Studies, Miami U., Oxford, Ohio, 1969; JD, Ind. U., 1975. Bar: Ind. 1975, U.S. Dist. Ct. (no. and so. dists.) Ind. 1975, U.S. Ct. Appeals (7th cir.) 1976. Law clk. to presiding judge U.S. Dist. Ct. (no. dist.) Ind., Ft. Wayne, 1975-76; assoc. Ice, Miller, Donadio & Ryan, Indpls., 1976-82; sr. atty. AMAX Coal Co., Indpls., 1982-83, asst. gen. counsel, 1983-85, gen. counsel, 1985-87, v.p. law and govtl. affairs, 1987—. Bd. dirs. Cathedral Arts Inc., Indpls., 1978-86, Indpls. Opera Co., 1982. Mem. ABA, Ind. Bar Assn., Indpls. Bar Assn., Rocky Mountain Mineral Law Inst., Eastern Mineral Law Inst. Democrat. Lutheran. Club: Columbia, Skyline. Avocations: golf, swimming, bridge. General corporate.

GREVE, GUY ROBERT, lawyer; b. Bay City, Mich., Oct. 25, 1947. BA, U. Mich., 1970; postgrad., U. Kent, Canterbury, Eng., 1974; JD, Detroit Coll. of Law, 1975. Bar: Mich. 1975, U.S. Dist. Ct. (ea. dist.) Mich. 1975. Ptnr. Patterson & Greve, Bay City, 1975-78; asst. atty. City of Bay City, 1975-76, atty., 1976-78; sole practice Bay City, 1978—. Bd. dirs. Women's Crisis Ctr., Bay City, 1977-79, Am. Cancer Soc., 1975—, pres. 1982-83; pres. Muse-Hopper Mobile Mus., Eastern Mich., 1980-82. Mem. ABA, Mich. Bar Assn., Bay County Bar Assn., Assn. Trial Lawyers Am., Mich. Trial Lawyers Assn., Bay City C. of C., Bay City Jaycees (Dist. Service award 1981). Lodge: Optimists (pres. Bay City 1979-80, lt. gov. Bay City 1985-86). State civil litigation, Family and matrimonial, Personal injury. Home: 194 Athlone Beach Bay City MI 48706 Office: 919 Washington Ave PO Box 851 Bay City MI 48707

GREW, ROBERT RALPH, lawyer; b. Metamora, Ohio, Mar. 25, 1931; s. Edward Francis and Coletta Marie G.; m. Anne Gano Bailey, Aug. 2, 1958; 1 son, Christopher Adam. A.B., U. Mich., 1953, J.D., 1955. Bar: Mich. 1955, N.Y. 1958. Assoc., Carter, Ledyard & Milburn, N.Y.C., 1957-68, ptnr., 1968—; lectr. legal problems in banking and in venture capital investments Practising Law Inst. Mem. Internat. Bar Assn., ABA, N.Y. State Bar Assn. (chmn. health law com. 1986—), Assn. Bar City N.Y. Republican. Clubs: Union, Down Town Assn. Banking, General corporate, Real property. Office: Carter Ledyard & Milburn 2 Wall St New York NY 10005

GREY, THOMAS C., law educator, lawyer; b. 1941. B.A., Stanford U., 1963; B.A., Oxford (Eng.) U., 1965; LL.B., Yale U., 1968. Bar: D.C. 1969. Law clk. U.S. Ct. Appeals (D.C. cir.), 1968-69; law clk. Hon. Thurgood Marshall, U.S. Supreme Ct., 1969-70; staff atty. Washington Research Project, 1970-71; asst. prof. Stanford U. Law Sch., 1971-74, assoc. prof., 1974-78, prof., 1978—. Mem. Order of Coif. Past note and comment editor Yale Law Jour. Legal education. Office: Stanford U Law Sch Stanford CA 94305 *

GRIBBON, DANIEL MCNAMARA, lawyer; b. Youngstown, Ohio, Jan. 27, 1917; s. James Edward and Loretta (Hogan) G.; m. Jane Retzler, Sept. 13, 1941; children: Diana Jane Gribbon Motz, Deborah Ann Gribbon Alt. A.B., Western Res. U., 1938; J.D., Harvard U., 1941. Bar: D.C. 1946. Law clk. Judge Learned Hand, 1941-42; assoc. firm Covington & Burling, Washington, 1946-50; partner Covington & Burling, 1950—; dir. 1st Am. Bank N.A.; chmn. adv. com. on procedures U.S. Ct. Appeals (D.C. cir.). Served with USN, 1942-46; to lt. comdr. Res. Fellow Am. Bar Found.; mem. Am. Coll. Trial Lawyers, D.C. Bar Assn. (chmn. bd. profl. responsibility 1976-79). Roman Catholic. Clubs: Metropolitan, Chevy Chase; Harvard (N.Y.C.). Antitrust, General corporate, Federal civil litigation. Office: Covington & Burling 1201 Pennsylvania Ave NW Washington DC 20004

GRIBBS, PAULA REWALD, lawyer; b. Detroit, July 31, 1955; d. Roman Stanley and Katherine (Stratis) G.; m. Roman Rewald, Sept. 7, 1985. Student, Wayne State U., 1973-75; BA in Anthropology, U. Mich., 1976; postgrad., U. San Diego, 1977-78; JD, Detroit Coll. of Law, 1981. Bar: Mich. 1981, U.S. Dist. Ct. (ea. dist.) Mich. 1981. Assoc. Lopatin & Miller P.C., Detroit, 1982-85; sole practice Hamtramck, Mich., 1985—. Mem. ABA, Helenic Bar Assn., Advs. Bar Assn. (treas. 1986—), Women Lawyers Assn. of Mich. (state rep. 1986—), Mich. Trial Lawyers Assn. Criminal, Probate, Family and matrimonial.

GRIBOK, STEPHAN PAUL, lawyer; b. Washington, July 13, 1949; s. Peter and Catherine (O'Grady) G.; m. Eleanor Shaw, Nov. 29, 1975; children: Brian, Laura. BEE, Ga. Inst. Tech., 1971; JD, Rutgers U., 1980. Bar: U.S. Patent Office 1979, N.J. 1980, Pa. 1980, U.S. Dist. Ct. N.J. 1980, U.S. Dist. Ct. (ea. dist.) Pa. 1983, U.S. Ct. Appeals (D.C. cir.) 1983. Sr. control engr. Corning (N.Y.) Glass Works, 1973-77; assoc. Steele, Gould & Fried, Phila., 1980-86, ptnr., 1986—. Atty. Phila. Vol. Lawyers for the Arts, 1981—. Served with U.S. Army 1971-73. Mem. ABA, N.J. Bar Assn., Pa. Bar Assn., Phila. Bar Assn., Camden County Bar Assn., Phila. Patent Law Assn. Club: Sterling String band (Lindenwood, N.J.) (sgt. at arms 1986). Avocation: music. Patent, Trademark and copyright, Entertainment. Home: 7042 Campbell Ave Pennsauken NJ 08109 Office: Steele Gould & Fried 1700 Market St 3232 IVB Philadelphia PA 19103

GRIER, JOHN CUMMINGS, lawyer; b. Ft. Collins, Colo., Nov. 4, 1947; s. John Cummings III and Joyce (Mead) G.; m. Cherie Rose Johnston, Aug. 15, 1982; children: Genevieve R. Johnston-Grier, Kendrick Johnston-Grier. BA, Colo. State U., 1971; JD, Western State U., San Diego, 1978. Bar: Calif. 1979, U.S. Dist. Ct. (so. dist.) Calif. 1979, U.S. Ct. Appeals (5th cir.) 1980. Jr. ptnr. Mathews, Bergen & Potash, San Diego, 1979-81; ptnr. Mathews, Bergen, Potash & Grier, San Diego, 1981—. Mem. Calif. Bar Assn., Calif. Trial Lawyers, San Diego Trial Lawyers, San Diego County Bar Assn. Avocations: flying, racquetball. Personal injury, State civil litigation, Insurance. Home: 7485 Goodwood St San Diego CA 92134 Office: Mathews Bergen Potash & Grier 121 Broadway Suite 652 San Diego CA 92101

GRIER, JOSEPH WILLIAMSON, JR., lawyer; b. Charlotte, N.C., Aug. 5, 1915; s. Joseph Williamson and Beulah Mae (Wallace) G.; m. Catherine Langdon Smart, Oct. 28, 1949; children—Joseph Williamson, III, Catherine Witherspoon, Susan Grier Phillips, Roy Smart, Bruce Taliaferro, Robin Wallace. A.B. in Econs, U. N.C., Chapel Hill, 1937; J.D., Harvard U., 1940. Bar: N.C. bar 1940, U.S. Supreme Ct. bar 1947. Law clk. 4th Circuit Ct. Appeals, 1941-42; sr. partner firm Grier, Parker, Poe, Thompson, Bernstein, Gage and Preston, Charlotte, 1946-83; ptnr. Grier & Grier, 1984—; chmn. Charlotte Charter Revision Com.; vice chmn. Charlotte-Mecklenburg Consol. Commn. Mem. N.C. Bd. Higher Edn., 1964-65; chmn. bd. trustees Queens Coll., Charlotte, 1974—, chmn. emeritus 1982—; chmn. permanent jud. commn. Presbyterian Ch., 1966-71; trustee Presbyn. Found., 1972-78, v.p., 1973-76, pres. 1977-78; chmn. Charlotte Parks and Recreation Commn., 1959-63; pres. Charlotte-Mecklenburg YMCA, 1968-70, trustee, 1986—; bd. dirs. Community Sch. Arts; Ginter Found., trustee Edward C. Giles found. Served with U.S. Army, 1942-45. Decorated Bronze Star; recipient Man of Yr. award Civitan Club of Charlotte, 1967. Fellow Am. Bar Found., Am. Law Inst.; mem. N.C. Bar Assn. (bd. govs., v.p. 1983), ABA, Am. Judicature Soc., 26th Jud. Dist. Bar Assn. (pres. 1956), Am. Legion (dept. comdr. N.C. 1948-49), Phi Delta Theta. Democrat. Clubs: Charlotte Country, Charlotte City. General practice, Federal civil litigation, State civil litigation. Home: 1869 Queens Rd W Charlotte NC 28207 Office: Grier & Grier 1 Independence Ctr Suite 1240 Charlotte NC 28246

GRIER, PHILLIP MICHAEL, lawyer, association executive; b. Quitman, Ga., Aug. 31, 1941; s. Phillip Moore Grier and Helen Dale (Parrish) Cottingham. B.A., Furman U., 1963; J.D., U. S.C., 1969. Bar: S.C. 1969, U.S. Dist. Ct. S.C. 1969, U.S. Ct. Appeals (4th cir.) 1972, U.S. Supreme Ct. 1978, U.S. Ct. Appeals (fed. cir.) 1985. Asst. to pres. U. S.C., Columbia, 1969; assoc. Haynsworth, Perry, Bryant, Marion & Johnstone, Greenville, S.C., 1969-70; asst. dean for campus relations, staff counsel Univ. S.C., 1970-72, univ. counsel and ombudsman, 1972-74, univ. counsel, 1974-79; exec. dir. Nat. Assn. Coll. and Univ. Attys., Washington, 1979—; mem. adv. bd. Ctr. for Constl. Studies, U. Notre Dame and Mercer U., 1981—, Desegregation Support Ctr., Inst. for Services to Edn., Washington, 1980-82; mem. secretariat of nat. higher edn. orgns. Nat. Ctr. for Higher Edn., Washington, 1979—, mem. higher edn. inter-assn. legal adv. com., 1979—; mem. adv. bd. Acad. Collective Bargaining Info. Service, Washington, 1979—, Inst. for Higher Edn. Law and Governance, U. Houston, 1984—. Author: (with Joseph P. O'Neill) Financing in a Period of Retrenchment: A Primer for Small Private Colleges, 1984. Editor: The Corporate Counsellors Deskbook (Non-Profit Organizations Supplement), 1983; editor, contbg. author: Legal Deskbook for Administrators of Independent Colleges and Universities, 1982, 83, 84. Editor Coll. Law Digest, 1980—; mem. editorial adv. com. West Pub. Co., St. Paul, 1980—; editorial bd. Jour. Coll. and Univ. Law, Morgantown, W.Va., 1979—. Bd. dirs. Greenville Symphony, S.C., 1970. Served to capt. M.I., U.S. Army, 1963-66, USAR, 1966-74. Mem. ABA, Nat. Assn. Bar Execs., S.C. Bar Assn., Am. Assn. for Higher Edn., Furman U. Alumni Assn. (bd. govs. 1970-74), Entomological Soc. Am., U.S. Supreme Ct. Hist. Soc., Soc. Colonial Wars, Mil. Order Fgn. Wars, Columbia Hist. Soc., Omicron Delta Kappa, Phi Delta Phi. Clubs: City Tavern, Cosmos (Washington). General corporate, Administrative and regulatory, Federal civil litigation. Home: 2141 P St NW Washington DC 20037 Office: Nat Assn of Coll and Univ Attys One Dupont Circle NW Washington DC 20036

GRIESA, THOMAS POOLE, U.S. district judge; b. Kansas City, Mo., Oct. 11, 1930; s. Charles Henry and Stella Lusk (Bedell) G.; m. Christine Pollard Meyer, Jan. 5, 1963. A.B. cum laude, Harvard U., 1952; LL.B., Stanford U., 1958. Bar: Wash. 1958, N.Y. 1960. Atty. Justice Dept., 1958-60; with firm Symmers, Fish & Warner, N.Y.C., 1960-61, Davis Polk & Wardwell, N.Y.C., 1961-72; partner Davis Polk & Wardwell, 1970-72; judge U.S. Dist. Ct. So. Dist. N.Y., 1972—. Mem.: Stanford Law Rev., 1956-58. Bd. visitors Stanford Law Sch., 1982-84. Served to lt. (j.g.) USCGR, 1952-54. Mem. Bar Assn. City N.Y. Christian Scientist. Clubs: Union (N.Y.C.), Harvard (N.Y.C.). Jurisprudence. Office: US Ct House Foley Sq New York NY 10007

GRIFF, HARRY, lawyer; b. Worcester, Mass., May 27, 1952; s. Joseph J. and Dorothy J. (Goldsmith) G.; m. Joan G. Garovoy, May 27, 1973; children—Joshua, Jordana. B.A. with high distinction, U. Mich., 1973, J.D. with distinction, 1977. Bar: Mich. 1977, Colo. 1982. Legal counsel Social Security Adminstrn., HHS, Balt., 1978-79; trial atty. U.S. Dept. Justice, Washington, 1979-81; assoc. Dufford, Waldeck, Ruland, Wise & Milburn, Grand Junction, Colo., 1981-83; atty. Harmon & Griff, P.C., Grand Junction, 1983-86; ptnr. Williams, Larson, Foster & Griff, 1986—; bd. dirs. Partners, Inc.; legal counsel Grand Junction br. NAACP, 1983-84, Walker Field, Colo. Pub. Airport Authority, Grand Junction, 1984—. Mem. organizing com. pro bono program for Western Colo., Grand Junction, 1982-84; bd. dirs. Paradise Hills Homeowners Assn., Grand Junction, 1984—, Grand Junction Jewish Community Ctr., 1984—. Mem. Assn. Trial Lawyers Am., ABA, Colo. Bar Assn., Mesa County Bar Assn. (bd. dirs. legal aid program 1984—). Democrat. General practice. Home: 2697 Caribbean Dr Grand Junction CO 81501 Office: Williams Larson Foster & Griff 1354 E Sherwood Dr Grand Junction CO 81501

GRIFF, MARVIN T., lawyer; b. Boston, Oct. 1, 1955. BA, Brandeis U., 1978; JD, Tulane U., 1981. Bar: Mass. 1981, La. 1984. Atty., advisor FERC, Washington, 1982-84; atty. Mid La. Gas Co., New Orleans, 1984-85; assoc. Kadison, Pfaelzer, Woodard, Quinn & Rossi, Washington, 1985—. Contbr. articles to profl. jours. Mem. ABA, Fed. Bar Assn., La. Bar Assn., Mass. Bar Assn., Fed. Energy Bar Assn., Am. Gas Assn. Administrative and regulatory, FERC practice, Public utilities. Home: 2831 28th St Apt 11 Washington DC 20008 Office: Kadison Pfaelzer Woodard Quinn & Rossi 2000 Pa Ave NW Suite 7500 Washington DC 20006

GRIFFETH, RONALD CLYDE, lawyer; b. Athens, Ga., Jan. 5, 1935; s. Alton White and Lilly Clyde (Silvey) G.; m. June Mellosan Duffie, Feb. 16, 1963; children: Robin Audrey, Elaine Lilly. AB, U. Ga., 1957; JD, Augusta Sch. Law, 1972. Bar: Ga. 1972, U.S. Dist. Ct. (so. dist.) Ga. 1973, U.S. Ct. Appeals (11th cir.) 1973, U.S. Supreme Ct. 1983. Br. mgr., adjuster Gen. Adjustment Bur., Inc., West Palm Beach, Fla. and Augusta, Ga., 1958-66; v.p., claims counsel First of Ga. Ins. Group, Augusta, 1966-77; sole practice Augusta, 1977—. Chmn. adminstrv. bd. Grace United Meth. Ch., North Augusta, S.C., 1980-81. Served to capt. U.S. Army, 1957-65. Mem. ABA, Ga. Bar Assn., Augusta Bar Assn., Assn. Trial Lawyers Am., Ga. Trial Lawyers Assn. Methodist. Insurance, Personal injury, General practice. Home: 1848 Bolin Rd North Augusta SC 29841 Office: PO Box 1895 Augusta GA 30903

GRIFFIN, BRYANT WADE, judge; b. New Brunswick, N.J., Nov. 19, 1915; s. Bryant Wade and Maurine (McPherson) G.; m. Dorothy Thauwald, Sept. 2, 1939; children—Nancy Schaul, Bryant W., Georgia Lee Griffin Peterson. A.B., U. Cin., 1937, LL.B., 1939. Bar: Ohio 1939, N.J. 1940. Assoc. McCarter & English, Newark, 1939-40; with legal dept. Central R.R. N.J., 1940; ptnr. Hauck & Griffin, Clinton, N.J., 1940-43; sr. ptnr. Moser, Griffin, Kerby & Cooper, 1946-75; judge Superior Ct. N.J., Elizabeth, 1975—; lectr. Practicing Law Inst., N.Y. and N.J. Served to lt. USNR, 1943-46. Mem. ABA, N.J. Bar Assn., Union County Bar Assn. (pres. 1963), Summit Bar Assn. (pres. 1960). Republican. Clubs: Beacon Hill, Down Town Assn. (Summit), Loantaka Skeet (Florham Park), Amwell Valley Conservancy. Home: RD 1 Box 449 Stockton NJ 08559 Office: Hunterdon County Courthouse Flemington NJ 07306

GRIFFIN, CAMPBELL ARTHUR, JR., lawyer; b. Joplin, Mo., July 17, 1929; s. Campbell Arthur and Clara M. (Smith) G.; m. Margaret Ann Adams, Oct. 19, 1958; children: Campbell A., Laura Ann. B.A., U. Mo., 1951, M.A. in Acctg., 1952; J.D., U. Tex., 1957. Bar: Tex. 1957. Assoc. firm Vinson & Elkins, Houston, 1957-68, ptnr., 1968—; mem. mgmt. com. Vinson & Elkins, 1982—, mng. ptnr. Dallas office, 1986—. Mem. ofcl. bd. Bethany Christian Ch., Houston, 1962-65, 66-69, chmn. bd. elders, 1968; bd. dirs., sec. Houston Pops Orch., 1983—. Mem. ABA, Tex. Bar Assn., Houston Bar Assn., Dallas Bar Assn., State Bar Tex. (chmn. sect. corp. banking and bus. law 1974-75). General corporate, Securities. Office: 2020 LTV Ctr 2001 Ross Ave Dallas TX 75201

GRIFFIN, HARRY LEIGH, lawyer; b. Charlotte, N.C., May 1, 1935; s. Harry Leigh and Irma (Waters) G.; m. Brenda Raudenbush, June 6, 1960; children: Harry L. III, David W., Heather L., Andrea B. BA magna cum laude, Harvard U., 1957; LLB, Duke U., 1963. Bar: N.C. 1963, Ga. 1964. Law clk. to judge U.S. Ct. Appeals (4th cir.), Charlotte, 1963-64; from assoc. to ptnr. Smith, Currie & Hancock, Atlanta, 1964-77; ptnr. Trotter, Bondurant, Griffin, Miller & Hishon, Atlanta, 1977-80, Griffin, Cochrane & Marshall, Atlanta, 1980—; lectr. constl. law various edn1. insts. and profl. assns., 1964—. Author: Practical Construction Law, 1976; also articles. Served with U.S. Army, 1960-63. Mem. ABA, Ga. Bar Assn., Atlanta Bar Assn., N.C. Bar Assn., Nat. Duke Law Alumni Council, Duke Nat. Fund Council. Roman Catholic. Clubs: Ansley (Atlanta), Commerce (Atlanta). Avocations: trout fishing, reading. Construction. Home: 1981 Garraux Rd NW Atlanta GA 30327 Office: Griffin Cochrane & Marshall 100 Peachtree St NW Atlanta GA 30303

GRIFFIN, J. KENNETH, lawyer; b. Abilene, Tex., Dec. 1, 1945; s. Leo J., Jr. and Lucille L. (Ellison) G. B.A., Northeastern U., 1968; J.D., Suffolk U., 1971. Bar: Mass. 1971, U.S. Dist. Ct. Mass. 1977, U.S. Ct. Appeals (1st cir.) 1980. Dist. ct. prosecutor Middlesex County Dist. Atty., Cambridge, Mass., 1971; gen. counsel, exec. dir. Cambridge Rent Bd., 1972-78; asst. v.p. Comml. Union Ins. Co., Boston, 1978-82; sr. ptnr. Semenza, Lutfy & Griffin, Boston and Las Vegas, 1982-83; mng. ptnr. Lutfy, Griffin & Goulka, Boston, 1984—. Contbr. articles to profl. jours. Mem. ABA, Mass. Bar Assn., Mass. Def. Lawyers Assn., Am. Judicature Soc., Def. Research Inst., Nat. Inst. for Trial Advocacy (advocate). Insurance, State civil litigation, Federal civil litigation. Office: Lutfy Griffin & Goulka Two Oliver St Boston MA 02109

GRIFFIN, JOHN FRANCIS, JR., lawyer; b. Washington, Aug. 8, 1955; s. John F. and Janice B. (Palmer) G.; m. Joanne M. Conlon, Oct. 11, 1981. B.A., St. Michael's Coll., 1977; J.D., New Eng. Sch. Law, 1980. Bar: Mass. 1980, N.H. 1981, U.S. Dist. Ct. Mass. 1984, U.S. Ct. Appeals (1st cir.) 1981, U.S. Dist. Ct. N.H. 1981. Assoc. Fryer, Boutin & Warhall, Londonderry, N.H., 1981-83; sole practice, Merrimack, N.H., 1984—; adj. faculty Rivier Coll., Nashua, N.H., 1984—. Mem. Am. Trial Lawyers Assn., ABA, Nashua Bar Assn., N.H. Bar Assn. (young lawyers and continuing legal edn. coms.). Democrat. Roman Catholic. State civil litigation, General corporate, Real property. Home: 14 Ravine Rd Amherst NH 03031 Office: 1 Overlook Park Amherst NH 03031

GRIFFIN, JOSEPH RUBLE, justice; b. Woodland, Miss., July 4, 1923; s. Virgil H. and Martha E. (Davis) G.; m. Ruth M. Lollar, Feb. 18, 1946; children: Joseph Patrick, Martha Ruth. JD, U. Miss., 1936. Asst. atty. gen. State of Miss., Jackson, 1955-65; judge 2d cir. Ct. Miss. Bay, St. Louis, 1973-86; justice Miss. Supreme Ct., Jackson, 1986—; chmn. MIss. Confs. of Cir. Judges, 1983-85. Served to sgt., U.S. Army, 1943-46, ETO. Mem. Miss. Bar Assn. Democrat. Baptist. Avocation: fishing. General practice. Home: 509 Sunset Bay Saint Louis MS 39520 Office: Supreme Ct of Miss Gartin Bldg PO Box 117 Jackson MS 39205

GRIFFIN, L. ROBERT, lawyer; b. Elmira, N.Y., May 17, 1943; s. Leo Robert and Frances Irene (Johnson) G. B.S., LeMoyne Coll., 1965; LL.B., Harvard U., 1968; LL.M. NYU, 1974. Bar: Mass. 1968, N.Y. 1970, D.C. 1979, U.S. Dist. Ct. (so. dist.) N.Y. 1972, U.S. Dist. Ct. (ea. dist.) N.Y., 1972, U.S. Ct. Appeals (5th cir.) 1980, U.S. Ct. Appeals (6th cir.) 1982, U.S. Ct. Appeals (10th cir.) 1980, U.S. Ct. Appeals (D.C. cir.) 1979, U.S. Dist. Ct. (D.C.) 1984, U.S. Supreme Ct., 1980. Law clk. Mass. Supreme Jud. Ct., 1968-69; assoc. Willkie Farr & Gallagher, N.Y.C., 1969-78; sr. trial atty. Office of Comptroller of Currency, Washington, 1978-85, asst. dir. litigation, 1985—. Recipient Dept. Treasury Spl. Achievement award, 1982. Mem. ABA (com. on banking law), D.C. Bar Assn. Roman Catholic. Banking, Federal civil litigation, Labor. Home: Apt A 1010 1400 S Joyce St Arlington VA 22202 Office: 490 L'Enfant Plaza Washington DC 20219

GRIFFIN, RICHARD EARL, lawyer; b. El Dorado, Ark., Mar. 13, 1939; s. Ervin Earl and JoEllen (Posey) G.; m. Betty Marilyn Cutrer, Jan. 1, 1959; children—Richard Gregory, Robert Edward. B.S. in Pub. Adminstrn., U. Ark., 1963, J.D., 1963. Bar: Ark. 1963, U.S. Dist. Ct. (we. and ea. dists.) Ark. 1963, U.S. Ct. Appeals (8th cir.) 1973, U.S. Supreme Ct. 1970. Ptnr., Switzer & Griffin, Crossett, Ark., 1963-70, Griffin, Rainwater & Draper, Crossett, 1970—; chmn. First State Bank, Crossett, 1973—. Mem. Ark. State Senate, Little Rock, 1967-70; chmn. Ark. Dept. Corrections, Pine Bluff, Ark., 1972-84. Fellow Am. Coll. Trial Lawyers; mem. Am. Bd. Trial Advocates, Assn. Trial Lawyers Am., ABA, Ark. Bar Assn., Ark. Trial Lawyers Assn. General practice, Federal civil litigation, State civil litigation. Home: 1001 Elm St Crossett AR 71635 Office: Griffin Rainwater & Draper PO Box 948 310 Main St Crossett AR 71635

GRIFFIN, ROBERT WOOTEN, lawyer; b. Kinston, N.C., Feb. 27, 1952; s. Thomas Battle and Emma Britt (Davis) G.; m. Nancy Montez Hall, July 19, 1980 (div. Nov. 1982); m. Elizabeth Odette Baker, June 28, 1986. AB, U. N.C., 1974, JD, 1977. Bar: N.C. 1977, U.S. Dist. Ct. (ea. dist.) N.C. 1979, U.S. Supreme Ct. 1982, U.S. Ct. Appeals (4th cir.). 1984. Ptnr. Griffin & Griffin, Kinston, 1977—; instr. bus. law Lenoir Community Coll., Kinston, 1978. Chmn. Lenoir County Dems., Kinston, 1983—, precinct #3 Dems., Kinston, 1979-81, legacy Lenoir County chpt. Am. Cancer Soc., Kinston, 1977—; co-chmn. Lenoir County div. United Way, Kinston, 1985; pres. Young Dems. Lenoir County, 1979-81. Recipient Dem. of Yr. award Lenoir County Dems., 1983, Freedom Guard award N.C. Jaycees, 1983; named one of Outstanding Young Men in Am., 1983. Mem. ABA, N.C. Bar Assn., Lenoir County Bar Assn. (sec., treas. 1978-79, pres. 1979-80), 8th Jud. Dist. Bar Assn. (sec., treas. 1982-83), N.C. Acad. Trial Lawyers, Kinston Jaycees (pres. 1986—, jaycee of yr. award 1986), Phi Beta Kappa. Methodist. Avocation. running. General practice, Real property, Criminal. Home: 2204 Greenbriar Rd Kinston NC 28501 Office: Griffin & Griffin PO Box 3062 213 E Gordon St Kinston NC 28501

GRIFFIN, RONALD CHARLES, law educator; b. Washington, Aug. 17, 1943; s. Roy John and Gwendolyn (Points) G.; m. Vicky Treadway, Nov. 26, 1967; children—David Ronald, Jason Roy, Meg Carrington. B.S., Hampton Inst., 1965; postgrad. Harvard U., summer 1965; J.D., Howard U., 1968; LL.M., U. Va., 1974. Bar: D.C. 1970, U.S. Supreme Ct. 1973. Asst. corp. counsel Govt. of D.C., 1970; asst. prof. law U. Oreg., 1974-78; assoc. prof. law Washburn U., Topeka, 1978-81, prof., 1981—; vis. prof. U. Notre Dame, 1981-82; dir. Council on Legal Ednl. Opportunity, Summer Inst., Great Plains Region, 1983; grievance examiner Midwest region EEOC, 1984-85; arbitrator consumer protection complaints Northeast Kans. Better Bus. Bur., 1986-87. Served to capt. JAGC, U.S. Army, 1970-74. Named William O. Douglas Outstanding Prof. of Yr. 1985-86; Rockefeller Found. grantee Howard U., 1965-68; fellow Parker Sch. Fgn. and Comparative Law, Columbia U., summer 1981; Kline sabbatical research and study, Japan, 1985. Mem. ABA, Cen. States Law Sch. Assn. (pres.-elect 1987—). Contbr. articles to legal jours. Private international, Contracts commercial, Legal education. Home: 2031 Bowman Ct Topeka KS 66604 Office: Washburn U Sch Law Topeka KS 66621

GRIFFIN, THOMAS PATRICK, lawyer; b. Tulsa, Mar. 5, 1948; s. Josephine (Tague) G.; m. Marsha A. Mason, June 11, 1983. BA, U. Calif., 1970; JD, U. Ariz., 1973. Bar: Ariz. 1973, U.S. Dist. Ct. Ariz. 1973, U.S. Ct. Appeals (9th cir.) 1975, U.S. Supreme Ct. 1977. Exec. v.p. Union Bank, Tucson, 1973-78; assoc. Miller & Pitt, Tucson, 1978-82, ptnr., 1982—. Real property, Securities, General corporate.

GRIFFITH, BENJAMIN ELMO, lawyer; b. Cleve., Miss., Nov. 19, 1952; s. L. Ellis and Gloria Judson (Smith) G.; m. Kathy Orr, May 26, 1974; children: Benjamin Clark, Julie Faulkner. Cert., U. Salzburg, Austria, 1972; BA in Eng., German, U. Miss., 1973, JD, 1975. Bar: Miss. 1975, U.S. Dist. Ct. (no. dist.) Miss. 1975, U.S. Dist. Ct. (so. dist.) Miss. 1981, U.S. Ct. Appeals (5th cir.) 1981, U.S. Supreme Ct. 1984. Ptnr. Jacobs, Griffith, Eddins et al, Cleve., 1975-86, Griffith & Griffith, Cleve., 1986—; instr. local govt. Delta State U., Cleve., 1983; atty. Bd. of Suprs., Bolivar County, Miss., 1983—. Scoutmaster Troop 2 Boy Scouts Am., Cleve., 1976-82; chmn. bd. of deacons 1st Presbyn. Ch., Cleve., 1981, Presbyn. Day Sch., Cleve., 1984-85. Mem. ABA (litigation sect., torts and ins. sect.), Fed. Bar Assn., Miss. Bar Assn., Nat. Assn. County Civil Attys. (bd. of trustees 1985—), Miss. Def. Lawyers Assn., Assn. Trial Lawyers Am., Miss. Trial Lawyers Assn. (continuing legal edn. com. 1984-85), Miss. Assn. County Bd. Attys. (edn. com. 1986—), Bar Assn. of 5th Fed. Cir., Def. Research Inst. (product liability com., govtl. liability com.), Phi Delta Phi, Omicron Delta Kappa. Republican. Lodge: Lions (pres. Cleve. chpt. 1981-82, sec., treas. Dist. 30-0 1982-83). Avocations: jogging, fishing, skiing. Federal civil litigation, Local government, Personal injury. Home: 701 Maple St Cleveland MS 38732 Office: Griffith & Griffith PO Drawer 1680 Cleveland MS 38732

GRIFFITH, D. KENDALL, lawyer; b. Aurora, Ill., Feb. 4, 1933; s. Walter George and Mary Elizabeth Griffith; m. Susan Smykal, Aug. 4, 1962; children—Kay, Kendall. B.A., U. Ill., 1955, J.D., 1958. Bar: Ill. 1958, U.S. Supreme Ct. 1973. Assoc. Hinshaw, Culbertson, Moelmann, Hoban &

Fuller, Chgo., 1959-65, ptnr., 1965—; spl. asst. atty. gen. Ill., 1970-72; lectr. Ill. Inst. Continuing Legal Edn., 1970—. Trustee, Lawrence Hall Sch. for Boys, 1967—, v.p. for program, 1969-74; bd. dirs. Child Care Assn. Ill., 1970-73; mem. Lake Forest High Sch. Bd. Edn., 1983-84. Served to 2d lt. USAF, 1956. Mem. ABA (chmn. appellate advocacy com. 1983-84), Ill. Bar Assn., Chgo. Bar Assn., Appellate Lawyers Assn. Ill. (pres. 1973-74), Def. Research Inst., Ill. Def. Counsel, Chgo. Trial Lawyers Club. Club: University of Chgo. Mem. editorial bd. Ill. Civil Practice After Trial, 1970; co-editor The Brief, 1975-83; contbr. author Civil Practice After Trial, 1984; contbr. article to legal jour. State civil litigation, Federal civil litigation, Insurance. Office: Hinshaw Culbertson Moelmann et al 69 W Washington St Suite 2700 Chicago IL 60602

GRIFFITH, EMLYN IRVING, lawyer; b. Utica, N.Y., May 13, 1923; s. William A. and Maud A. (Charles) G.; m. Mary L. Kilpatrick, Aug. 13, 1946; children: William L., James R. AB, Colgate U., 1942; JD, Cornell U., 1950; also hon. degrees. Bar: N.Y. 1950, U.S. Supreme Ct. 1954. Gen. practice Lockport, N.Y., 1950-52, Rome, N.Y., 1952—; bd. dirs. various corporations. Contbr. articles on law and edn. to profl. jours. Mem. N.Y. State Bd. Regents, 1973—, Gov.'s Com. on Libraries, 1976-78, State Conf. on Professions, 1974-77, Intergovtl. Adv. Council on Edn., 1982-86; trustee, Aerospace Edn. Found., 1979—, Phi Gamma Delta Edn. Found., 1986—, pres. bd. internat. trustees, 1982-86; pres. Nat. Assn. State Bds. Edn., 1979-80, Nat. Welsh-Am. Found., 1982-84; chmn. State Conf. on Professions, 1975-78; mem exec. com. Bd. Pensions United Presbyn. Ch., 1966-72. Served to maj. U.S. Army, 1942-46. Recipient Alumni Disting. Service award Colgate U., 1975, Exceptional Service citation Air Force Assn., 1980. Fellow Am. Bar Found., N.Y. State Bar Found.; mem. ABA (com. pub. edn. 1975—), N.Y. State Bar Assn. (ho. of dels. 1974-77, com. lawyer competency 1986—, mem. bd. editors Bar Jour. 1986—, Root-Stimson award 1986), Oneida County Bar Assn. (pres. 1974-75), State Conf. County Bar Officers (chmn. 1975-77). Clubs: Rome, Fort Orange of Albany, Colgate of N.Y.C. General practice, Probate, Real property. Office: 225 N Washington St Rome NY 13440

GRIFFITH, JAMES LEWIS, lawyer; b. Phila., Sept. 13, 1940; s. Lewis Kenneth and Mary G. (Connors) G.; m. Eleanor May Hazlin, Feb. 27, 1965; children—Mary Eleanor, James Lewis, Anne Elisabeth; m. 2d, Linda Lee Ramsey, Sept. 16, 1978. B.A., St. Francis Coll., Loretto, Pa., 1962; J.D., Villanova U., 1965. Bar: Pa. 1965, D.C., U.S. Supreme Ct. Assoc., Liebert, Short, Fitzpatrick & Lavin, Phila., 1965-69, Obermayer, Rebmann, Maxwell & Hippel, Phila., 1969-79; pres., prin. trial counsel Griffith & Burr, P.C., Phila., 1979—; lectr. Villanova U., 1969-73; mem. com. standard jury trial instrns. for Commonwealth of Pa., Pa. Supreme Ct.; lectr. conf. on civil litigation Phila. Ct. Common Pleas. Served to lt., USAR, 1966-72. Mem. ABA, Phila. Bar Assn., Pa. Bar Assn., Pa. Trial Lawyers Assn., Assn. Trial Lawyers Am., Def. Research Inst., Internat. Assn. Ins. Counsel. Contbr. articles profl. jours. Insurance, State civil litigation, Personal injury.

GRIFFITH, MARY CORNWALL, lawyer; b. Denver, Nov. 29, 1915; d. Noah Hayden and Ida (Lindsey) G. B.A., U. Colo., 1938, J.D., 1941. Bar: Colo. Sole practice, Denver, 1941—. Gen. chmn. WAVE reunion, 1953; mem. Colo. Commn. on Status of Women, 1965-75; mem. Colo. Com. on Vets. Affairs, 1947-52; mem. Jud. Council of Colo., 1957-58; mem. women's adv. com. on def. manpower Dept. Labor, 1951-53; apptd. bd. ethics City Employees Denver, 1971-83. Served to comdr. USNR, ret. Mem. Am. Legion (judge adv. 1952, vice-comdr. 1956-57), Delta Delta Delta, Delta Sigma Rho. Clubs: Altrusa (2d v.p. 1970-73), P.E.O. Estate planning, Probate. Home: 1471 High St Denver CO 80218 Office: 1465 High St Denver CO 80218

GRIFFITH, STEPHEN LOYAL, lawyer; b. Washington, Dec. 8, 1945; s. Ernest Stacey and Margaret Dyckman (Davenport) G.; m. Christine Lynne Dickey, Aug. 16, 1981; children: David Michael Dickey-Griffith, Margaret Louise Dickey-Griffith. BA, Harvard U., 1967; M in Philosophy, Oxford U., Eng., 1969; JD, Stanford U., 1977. Bar: Oreg., U.S. Dist. Ct. Oreg., U.S. Ct. Appeals (9th cir.), U.S. Supreme Ct. Law clk. to presiding judge U.S. Dist. Ct., Portland, Oreg., 1977-78; assoc. Stoel, Rives, Boley, Fraser & Wyse, Portland, 1979-80, 82-85, ptnr., 1985—; counsel judiciary com. Ho. of Reps., Salem, Oreg., 1981; sole practice Salem, 1981-82; chmn. sentencing task force joint judiciary com. Oreg. Legislative Assembly, 1982; vice chmn. bd. bar examiners Oreg. State Bar, 1984—. Chmn. adv. com. 1,000 Friends of Oreg., Portland, 1982-84; mem. bd. edn. Portland Sch. Dist. #1, 1987—; bd. dirs. Metro Crisis Intervention Services, Portland, 1983—; mem. Portland Opera Chorus, 1979-84. Mem. Wilderness Soc. Republican. Presbyterian. Clubs: City, Harvard (Portland). Federal civil litigation, State civil litigation, Legal education. Home: 6220 SW 47th Place Portland OR 97221 Office: Stoel Rives Boley Fraser & Wyse 900 SW 5th AVe Portland OR 97204

GRIFFITH, STEPHEN MURRAY, JR., lawyer; b. Chgo., Oct. 26, 1953; s. Stephen Murray Sr. and Anne (McNamara) G.; m. Jane Cronin, June 11, 1977. BA, Northwestern U., 1975; JD, Coll. William and Mary, 1981. Bar: Ohio 1981, U.S. Dist. Ct. (so. dist.) Ohio 1981. Assoc. Taft, Stettinius & Hollister, Cin., 1981-82, 85—. Served to capt. JAGC, U.S. Army, 1982-85. Mem. ABA, Ohio Bar Assn., Cin. Bar Assn., Order of Coif. Republican. Roman Catholic. Real property, Military. Office: Taft Stettinius & Hollister 425 Walnut St Cincinnati OH 45202

GRIFFITH, STEVE CAMPBELL, JR., lawyer; b. Newberry, N.C., June 14, 1933; s. Steve Campbell and Bertie (Hambright) G.; m. Mary Stanley Salley, Dec. 22, 1962 (div. 1975); children: Mary Salley, Elizabeth Jane; m. Elizabeth Earhardt, May 22, 1976. B.S., Clemson U., 1954; LL.B., U. S.C., 1959. Ptnr. Blease & Griffith Attys., Newberry, 1959-64; asst. gen. counsel Duke Power Co., Charlotte, N.C., 1964-71; sec., assoc. gen. counsel Duke Power Co., 1971-74, gen. counsel, 1975-77, v.p., gen. counsel, 1977-82, sr. v.p., gen. counsel, 1982—, dir., mem. exec. com., 1982—. Mem. S.C. Gen. Assembly, 1961-62. Served to 1st lt. U.S. Army, 1955-57. Mem. ABA, N.C. Bar Assn., S.C. Bar Assn., Mecklenberg Bar Assn. Democrat. Episcopalian. Clubs: Charlotte City, Charlotte Country. Lodge: Masons. General corporate. Office: Duke Power Co 422 S Church St Charlotte NC 28242

GRIFFITH, STEVEN FRANKLIN, SR., lawyer, real estate title insurance agent and investor; b. New Orleans, July 14, 1948; s. Hugh Franklin and Rose Marie (Teutone) G.; m. Mary Elizabeth McMillan Frank, Dec. 9, 1972; children—Steven Franklin, Jason Franklin. B.B.A., Loyola U. of the South, 1970, J.D., 1972. Bar: La. 1972, U.S. Dist. Ct. (ea. dist.) La. 1975, U.S. Ct. Appeals (5th cir.) 1975, U.S. Supreme Ct. bar 1976. Law offices Senator George T. Oubre, Norco, La., 1971-75; sole practice, Destrehan, La., 1975—. Served to 1st lt. U.S. Army, 1970-72. Mem. ABA, La. Bar Assn., Assn. Trial Lawyers Am., La. Trial Lawyers Assn., New Orleans Trial Lawyers Assn., Fed. Bar Assn. Democrat. Club: Lions. Real property, Personal injury, Insurance. Office: 9001 River Rd Destrehan LA 70047

GRIFFITHS, DAVID, lawyer, educator; b. N.Y.C., Sept. 27, 1945; s. Daniel Joseph and Genevieve Patricia (Wilson) G. AB, Fordham U., 1969; JD, N.Y. Law Sch., 1975. Bar: N.Y. 1976, U.S. Dist. Ct. (ea. and so. dists.) 1976, N.J. 1979, U.S. Dist. Ct. N.J. 1979, U.S. Supreme Ct. 1979, U.S. Ct. Appeals (2d cir.) 1983. Asst. dist. atty. Bronx (N.Y.) Dist. Atty., 1975-78; ptnr. Griffiths & O'Connell, White Plains, N.Y., 1979—; asst. prof. Pace U. Sch. of Bus., Pleasantville, N.Y., 1978—; instr. Pace U. Law Sch., White Plains, 1981-83. Served to sgt. USMC, 1966-72. Mem. Westchester County Bar Assn., Assn. Trial Lawyers Am. Roman Catholic. Personal injury, Real property. Office: Griffiths & O'Connell 2 University Plaza Hackensack NJ 07601

GRILL, STEVEN ERIC, lawyer; b. N.Y.C., May 7, 1955; s. Harold and Ethel (Katz) G. BA magna cum laude, St. Lawrence U., 1977; JD, Cornell U., 1980. Bar: N.Y. 1981, U.S. Dist. Ct. (so. and ea. dists.) N.Y. 1981. Assoc. Cullen & Dykman, Brooklyn Heights, N.Y., 1980-84, Walsh, Sullivan & Mercurio and predecessor firm Walsh & Frisch, N.Y.C., 1984—. Prosecutor Village of Garden City Inc., N.Y., 1983, 84. Mem. ABA (litigation sect., comml. banking and fin. transactions litigation com., forum com. on entertainment and sports industries), N.Y. State Bar Assn. (civil practice law and rules com. 1984—), Assn. Bar of City of N.Y. Avocations: music, automobiles, skiing. Federal civil litigation, State civil litigation, Entertainment. Home: 250 First Ave New York NY 10009 Office: Walsh Sullivan & Mercurio 250 Park Ave New York NY 10177

GRILLI, PETER JOHN, lawyer; b. Westover AFB, Mass., Dec. 7, 1951; s. Thomas Guy and Margaret Filomena (Scarpelli) G.; m. Elizabeth Taggart Fisher, June 9, 1984; 1 child, David Thomas. BA in Am. Studies, Yale U., 1973; JD, Georgetown U., 1977. Bar: Fla. 1977, U.S. Dist. Ct. (mid. dist.) Fla. 1977, U.S. Ct. Appeals (5th cir.) 1979, U.S. Ct. Appeals (11th cir.) 1982. Law clk. to judge U.S. Dist. Ct., Tampa, Fla., 1977-79; atty Shackleford, Farrior, Stallings & Evans, Tampa, 1979-81; atty. Allen, Dell, Frank & Trinkle, Tampa, 1982-86; ptnr. Alpert, Josey, Freemon & Grilli, Tampa, 1986—. Mem. Yale Bay Area Alumni Schs. Com. (chmn. 1981—), Yale U. Alumni Assn. (del. 1986). Club: Yale (Tampa) (v.p. 1984—). Federal civil litigation, State civil litigation, Personal injury. Home: 3317 W Sevilla Circle Tampa FL 33629

GRILLOT, TIMOTHY JOSEPH, lawyer; b. Coffeyville, Kans., Mar. 27, 1958; s. Francis Albert Jr. and Mary Ellen (Haley) G.; m. Janette Kay Sawyer, May 27, 1977; children: Jared, Nicholas, Joel, Morgan, Thomas. Student, Labette Community Coll., 1976; BBA, U. Kans., 1979, JD, 1982. Bar: Kans. 1982, U.S. Dist. Ct. Kans. 1982. Assoc. Patton & Kerbs, Dodge City, Kans., 1982-85, Richard G. Tucker, Parsons, Kans., 1985—. Mem. ABA, Kans. Bar Assn., Labette County Bar Assn., Beta Gamma Sigma. Republican. Roman Catholic. Avocations: reading, golf. General practice. Office: Richard G Tucker PO Box 875 Parsons KS 67357

GRIM, DOUGLAS PAUL, lawyer; b. Bellingham, Wash., May 12, 1940; s. Paul R. and Vivian I. (McMillen) G.; m. Catherine Powers, Dec. 28, 1968; children—Caryn, Devin. B.A., Lawrence Coll., 1962; LL.B., Stanford U., 1965; LL.M., N.Y.U., 1966. Bar: Calif. 1966, U.S. Supreme Ct. 1985. Assoc. Hanna and Morton, Los Angeles, 1966-72; of counsel Harris, Noble, Uhler & Gallop, Los Angeles, 1972-75; ptnr. Nicholas, Kolliner, Myers, D'Angelo and Givens, Los Angeles, 1975; sole practice, Los Angeles, 1975—; instr. Golden Gate U. Sch. Law, 1975; dir. Am. Internat. Seaview Properties, Inc., 1976—; chmn. bd. Agri-Feeds, Inc., 1981—. Chmn. exec. com. Troop 35 Los Angeles Area Council Boy Scouts Am., 1967-72; v.p., dir. Los Angeles Jaycees, 1966-75. Recipient Michael F. Tobey award Los Angeles Jr. C. of C., 1972; named Outstanding Young Man of Am., 1972. Mem. State Bar of Calif., Los Angeles County Bar Assn., ABA. Methodist. Clubs: Jonathan, Riviera Tennis (Los Angeles), Wilshire Kiwanis (bd. dirs.), Uptown Investment (pres. 1978). Author: Drafting a 1244 Plan; Medical Reimbursement Plans. Corporate taxation, Real property, Probate. Home: 247 S Lorraine Blvd Los Angeles CA 90004 Office: 523 W Sixth St Los Angeles CA 90014

GRIMAUD, GERALD C., lawyer; b. Concord, N.H., July 27, 1942; s. James F. Grimaud and Elizabeth O. Walter; m. Helen Powe, Apr. 30, 1967; children: Rebecca, Gretchen, Gerald, Barbara. BA, Atlantic Union Coll., 1965, LLB, York U., 1971. Bar: Pa. 1971, U.S. Dist. Ct. 1973, N.Y. 1985. Asst. atty. gen. for environ. protection State of Pa., 1971-74; public defender Wyoming and Sullivan Counties, Pa., 1974-78; sole practice Tunkhannock, Pa., 1974—. bd. dirs. Pa. Environ. Council, 1974-80, United Services Agy., 1974-76, Home Health Services of N.E. Pa., 1974-76, Wyoming County Heart Soc., 1974-78; mem. rules com. Environ. Hearing Bd., 1982—. Mem. Pa. Bar Assn., Wyoming-Sullivan Counties Bar Assn. (sec. 1985-86, pres. 1986—, chmn. We The People Com. 1986—). Environment, Personal injury, Criminal. Office: 69 Putnam St Tunkhannock PA 18657

GRIMBALL, WILLIAM HEYWARD, lawyer; b. Charleston, S.C., Feb. 6, 1917; s. William Heyward and Panchita (Heyward) G.; m. Frances Lucas Ellerbe, Aug. 9, 1944; children—William Heyward, Henry E., Arthur, Francis E. A.B., Coll. of Charleston, 1938; LL.B., U. Va., 1941. Bar: S.C. bar 1941. Since practiced in Charleston; asso. firm Mitchell & Horlbeck, 1941-50; individual practice law 1950-59, 63-64; mem. firm Figg, Gibbs & Grimball, 1959-63; partner firm Grimball, Cabaniss, Vaughan & Guerard, 1964-80, Grimball, Cabaniss, Vaughan & Robinson, 1981-83; Grimball & Cabaniss, 1983—. Pres. Preservation Soc., Charleston, 1974-75; mem. S.C. Legislature, 1952-58; chmn. Charleston County del., 1955-58; alderman City of Charleston, 1960-72, mayor pro tem, 1969; mem. Charleston County Election Commn., 1978-81. Served with USNR, 1942-46; to lt. comdr. 1962. Fellow Am. Coll. Trial Lawyers, Am. Bar Found.; mem. Am. Law Inst., Am. Bar Assn., S.C. Bar Assn., Charleston County Bar Assn. (past pres.), Maritime Law Assn., Alumni Assn. Coll. of Charleston (pres. 1953), S.C. Bar Found. (v.p. 1985-86), Soc. of Cin., S.C. Soc., St. Andrews Soc., St. Cecilia Soc. Republican. Episcopalian. Club: Carolina Yacht. Lodges: Masons (past grand master S.C., 33 deg.), Shriners. Federal civil litigation, State civil litigation. Home: 107 Chadwick Dr Charleston SC 29407 Office: Liberty Nat Bank Bldg 151 Meeting St Charleston SC 29402

GRIMM, STANLEY ARNOLD, circuit court judge; b. Macon, Mo., Apr. 28, 1933; s. Victor Hugo and Anna Katherin (Arnold) G.; m. Dorothy Jane Morgan, Feb. 1, 1957; children: David, Mark, John. BS, Northeast Mo. State U., 1954; LLB, U. Mo., 1959. Bar: Mo. 1959. Assoc. Oliver & Oliver, Cape Girardeau, Mo., 1959-63; ptnr. Rader and Grimm, Cape Girardeau, 1963-72; circuit ct. judge State of Mo., Cape Girardeau, 1973—; chmn. Presiding Judges Commn., State of Mo., 1979-80, Supreme Ct. Com. on Criminal Instrns., 1981—; pres. Mo. Council of Juvenile Ct. Judges, State of Mo., 1977-78. Pres. Southeast Mo. Hosp. Assn., Cape Girardeau, 1983-85. Served with U.S. Army, 1954-56. Mem. Mo. Trial Judges Assn. (pres. state trial judges sect. 1981-82). Democrat. Lutheran. State civil litigation, Judicial administration. Home: 1251 Normal Cape Girardeau MO 63701 Office: Common Pleas Courthouse 44 N Lorimer Cape Girardeau MO 63701

GRIMM, WILLIAM THOMAS, lawyer; b. Phila., Feb. 23, 1940; s. Joseph L. and Evelyn (Gleason) G.; m. Sonja N. Grimm-Lied, Jan. 17, 1977; children: Emily Susan, Lars Johannes Lied, Nils Carstens Lied. AB, Lafayette Coll., 1961; LLB, U. Va., 1964. Bar: N.J. 1965, N.Y. 1970, Fla. 1973, Calif. 1980. Assoc. Archer, Greiner, Hunter & Read, Haddonfield, N.J., 1965-68; sr. assoc. Shearman & Sterling, N.Y.C., 1969-72; v.p., legal and corp. sec. Investment Corp. Fla., Ft. Lauderdale, 1972-75; chief counsel Westinghouse Electric Corp., Coral Springs, Fla., 1975-86, v.p., 1986—; chief counsel Westinghouse Communities Inc., Coral Springs, 1986—. Served with Air N.G., 1968-69, Korea. Mem. Fla. Bar Assn., Calif. Bar Assn., Assn. of Bar of City of N.Y. Republican. Methodist. Clubs: Windermere Island (Eleuthera, Bahamas); Ocean Colony (Half Moon Bay, Calif.). General corporate, Real property. Office: Westinghouse Communities Inc 3300 University Dr Coral Springs FL 33065

GRINDAL, HARALD THEODORE, lawyer; b. Rugby, N.D., Dec. 16, 1953; s. Harald Kivle and Jonette Torbjur (Tinseth) G.; m. Michele Kay Haskins, Sept. 22, 1979. BA, Augsburg Coll., 1976; JD, U. Minn., 1979. Bar: Minn., U.S. Dist. Ct. (Minn.) 1980. Communication analyst Dayton Hudson Corp., Mpls., 1979-80; spl. asst. atty. gen. Minn. Atty. Gen.'s Office, St. Paul, 1980-83; assoc. Opperman & Paquin, Mpls., 1983—; pres. Pol. Sci., Inc., Mpls., 1984—. Asst. treas. Growe for Sen. Com., Mpls., 1983-85; asst. fin. dir. Perpich Vol. Com., Mpls., 1986—; campaign mgr. Spannaus Vol. Com., Mpls., 1981-82; council mem. Hope Eng. Evang. Luth. Ch., Mpls., 1986—. Recipient alumni scholarship Augsburg Coll., Mpls., 1978. Mem. ABA, Minn. Bar Assn., Hennepin County Bar Assn., Nat. Health Lawyers Assn., Soc. Med. Assn. Counsels, Minn. Govt. Affairs Council. Mem. Democratic Farm Labor Party. Lutheran. Club: Greenway Athletic (Mpls.), Flagship Athletic (Eden Prairie). Avocations: racquetball, singing, classical and jazz music. Administrative and regulatory, Health, Legislative. Home: 5237 Woodlawn Blvd Minneapolis MN 55417 Office: Opperman & Paquin 100 Washington Ave S Minneapolis MN 55401

GRINDLE, JOHN, JR., lawyer; b. Washington, Aug. 24, 1916. B.A., Harvard U., 1939; LL.B., 1947. Bar: D.C. 1947. Washington rep. Milbank, Tweed, Hadley & McCloy, N.Y.C. and Washington, 1947-53, 54-74; gen. asst. to sec. HEW, 1953-54; of counsel Watson, Cole, Grindle & Watson, Washington, 1974—. Mem. Health and Welfare Council of D.C., 1955-65; vice chmn. bus. com. Nat. Symphony Orch. Sustaining Fund, 1957-59. Mem. ABA, D.C. Bar Assn., Harvard Law Sch. Assn. (nat. v.p. 1964-65, pres. D.C. assn. 1962-63), English Speaking Union (bd. govs. Washington br. 1958—), Harvard Alumni Assn. (dir. 1970-72). Probate and taxation, Estate planning. Home: 4215 7th St NW Washington DC 20011 Office: 1400 K St NW Washington DC 20005

GRINDLE, ROBERT PAUL, lawyer; b. Springfield, Ohio, Mar. 3, 1929; s. Harold J. and Elma C. (Beatty) G. BA, Wittenburg U., 1951; JD, Ohio State U., 1954. Bar: Ohio 1954, N.Y. 1963. Clk. claims dept. Allstate Ins. Co., Dayton and Cin., Ohio, 1954-62; patent atty. Firm of Greer Marechal, N.Y.C., 1962-68, M&T Chems. Inc., Rahway, N.J., 1968-71, Mandeville & Schweitzer, N.Y.C., 1971-80; sr. patent atty. Becton Dickinson & Co., Franklin Lakes, N.J., 1980—. Bd. Mgrs. Park Theater Performing Arts Ctr., Union City, N.J. Republican. Lutheran. Patent, Trademark and copyright. Home: 5 Acorn Pl North Caldwell NJ 07006 Office: Becton Dickinson & Co One Becton Dr Franklin Lakes NJ 07417-1880

GRINPAS, ROBERT MARK, lawyer; b. Chgo.; s. Joseph Edward and Edna Rose (Cooper) G.; m. Esther Ruth Duss, Dec. 23, 1980; children: Ginger Dania, Nile Kealoha. BS in Bus. and Econs., U. Ariz., 1965, JD, 1968. Bar: Hawaii 1982, U.S. Tax Ct. 1982, U.S. Dist. Ct. Hawaii 1982, U.S. Ct. Appeals (9th cir.) 1982. V.p. R&D Cartage Co., 1961-65; pres. Rovan Daisy, Inc., Kansas City, Mo., 1971-72, Zalinda Farms, Inc., Encinitas, Calif., 1974-78, Windsurfing Waikiki, Ltd., Honolulu, 1978-81; sole practice Lihue, Hawaii, 1982—; pres. Kauai Wind, Inc., Kauai, Hawaii, 1984—. Patentee windsurfing equipment. Bd. dirs. Kauai Ocean Rescue Council, Lihue, Kauai, Hawaii, 1983—. Mem. Hawaii Bar Assn., Kauai Bar Assn. (treas. 1986-87, v.p. 1987—), Assn. Trial Lawyers Am., Hawaii Jud. Conf. Lodge: Rotary (bulletin editor 1985-86). Avocations: windsurfing, jogging. Personal injury, General corporate, Real property. Office: 3016 Umi St Suite 211B Lihue HI 96766

GRISHAM, ALVIN MACRANDLE, lawyer; b. Knoxville, Tenn., Nov. 23, 1945; s. Arthur Clyde Sr. and Isabelle Waller (Goodwin) G.; m. Margaret Shaffer (div. Jan. 1981); children: Tony, Melanie; m. Stephanie Lynne Ourth, Aug. 28, 1982. BA, U. Tenn., 1967; JD, Nashville YMCA Law Sch., 1973. Bar: Tenn. 1973, U.S. Dist. Ct. (mid. dist.) Tenn. 1974, U.S. Dist. Ct. (ea. dist.) Tenn. 1982. Legal counsel State of Tenn., Nashville, 1974-81; assoc. Smith & Grisham, Chattanooga, 1982-84; sole practice Kingston, Tenn., 1984—; bd. dirs. Dunn Diversified Industries, Kingston. Chmn. Historic Zoning Commn., Kingston, 1985—; mem. Child Abuse Rev. Team, Roane County, Tenn., 1984—, title 20 council Tenn. Dept. Human Services, Knoxville, 1984—, com. Gov.'s 3 Star Program, Kingston, 1985—. Named one of Outstanding Young Men in Am., 1977, 79-80. Mem. ABA, Tenn. Bar Assn. (del. 1984—, long range planning and pub. relations coms.), Roane County Bar Assn. Methodist. Lodge: Rotary. General practice, State civil litigation, Family and matrimonial. Home: 231 New Shackle Island Rd Q-122 Hendersonville TN 37075 Office: 354 Cordell Hull Bldg Nashville TN 37219

GRISHAM, ARTHUR C., JR., lawyer; b. Knoxville, Tenn., Feb. 3, 1943; s. Arthur Clyde and Isabelle Waller (Goodwin) G.; m. Marian Elaine Cobb, Sept. 2, 1967; 1 son, Shane. B.S. in Indsl. Mgmt., U. Tenn.-Knoxville, 1965, J.D., 1971. Bar: Tenn. 1972, U.S. Dist. Ct. (ea. dist.) Tenn., U.S. Ct. Apls. (6th cir.). Staff atty. Chattanooga-Hamilton County Air Pollution Control Bur., 1971-73; ptnr. Goins, Gammon, Baker, Robinson & Grisham, Chattanooga, 1973-79; ptnr. Smith & Grisham, Chattanooga, 1979-86; ptnr. Grisham & Knight, Chattanooga, 1986— ; lectr. in field. Chmn. Chattanooga Wastewater Regulations Bd., 1978—; bd. dirs. Bethel Bible Village, 1981-85, mem. exec. com., 1983-85, chmn. bd., 1985. Served to capt. U.S. Army, 1965-69. Decorated Disting. Service medal. Mem. ABA, Tenn. Bar Assn. (mem. sessions ct. com. 1979-84), Chattanooga Bar Assn. (gov. 1978-80, pres. 1981-82), Christian Legal Soc. Baptist. Bankruptcy, State civil litigation, Consumer commercial. Office: 700 1st Tenn Bldg Chattanooga TN 37402

GRISSOM, GARTH CLYDE, lawyer; b. Syracuse, Kans., Jan. 24, 1930; s. Clyde and Bernice Minnie (Eddy) G.; m. Elena Joyce Kerst, Aug. 17, 1958; children: Colin, Grady, Cole, Kent. B.S., Kans. State U., 1951; LL.B., Harvard U., 1957. Ptnr. Sherman & Howard, Denver, 1963—; dir. Colo. State Bank, Denver. Sec., counsel, trustee Mile High United Way, Denver, 1985—; trustee Kans. State U. Found., Manhattan, 1962—. Mem. ABA, Colo. Bar Assn., Denver Bar Assn. (pres. 1985-86). Lodge: Rotary (sec. 1983-84, bd. dirs. 1983-86) (Denver). Securities, General corporate, Health. Home: 23 Skyline Dr Denver CO 80215 Office: Sherman & Howard 633 17th St Suite 2900 Denver CO 80202

GRISWOLD, ERWIN NATHANIEL, lawyer; b. East Cleveland, Ohio, July 14, 1904; s. James Harlen and Hope (Erwin) G.; m. Harriet Allena Ford, Dec. 30, 1931; children: Hope Eleanor Griswold Murrow, William Erwin. A.B., A.M., Oberlin Coll., 1925; LL.B., Harvard U., 1928, S.J.D., 1929; L.H.D. (hon.), Tufts Coll., 1949, Case Inst. Tech., 1950; LL.D. (hon.), U. B.C., 1949, Brown U., 1950, U. Sidney, U. Melbourne, 1951, Dalhousie U., 1952, Harvard, Amherst Coll., 1953, Columbia U., U. Richmond, 1954, Brandeis U., 1956, U. Mich., 1959, Northwestern U., 1960, Notre Dame U., Allegheny Coll., 1961, U. Toronto, 1962, Williams Coll., 1966, Tulane U., Boston Coll., Princeton U., 1968, Ripon Coll., 1972, Suffolk U., 1973, N.Y. Law Sch., 1978, U. Bridgeport, 1982, Oberlin Coll., 1982; D.C.L. (hon.), U. Western Ont., 1961, U. Toronto, 1962, U. Edinburgh, Georgetown U., 1963, Oxford U., 1964; D.Litt. (hon.), Western Res. U., 1967. Bar: Ohio 1929, Mass. 1935, D.C. 1973. With Griswold, Green, Palmer & Hadden, Cleve., 1929; atty. office solicitor gen., spl. asst. to atty. gen. Washington, 1929-34; asst. prof. law Harvard U., 1934-35, prof., 1935-46, dean, Charles Stebbins Fairchild prof. law, 1946-50, dean, Langdell prof. law, 1950-67; solicitor gen. U.S. 1967-73; partner Jones Day Reavis & Pogue, Washington, 1973—; mem. Alien Enemy Hearing Bd. for Mass., 1941-45; cons. expert U.S. Treasury Dept., 1942; mem. U.S. Civil Rights Commn., 1961-67; trustee Oberlin Coll., Bradford Jr. Coll., 1942-49, Tchrs. Ins. and Annuity Assn., 1942-46, Harvard Law Rev. Assn., 1938-67; bd. dirs. Am. Bar Found., pres., 1971-74; pres. Assn. Am. Law Schs., 1957-58. Author: Spendthrift Trusts, 1936, 2d edit., 1947, Cases on Federal Taxation, 1940, 6th edit., 1966, (with others) Cases on Conflict of Laws, 1941, rev. edit., 1964, The Fifth Amendment Today, Law and Lawyers in the United States. Fellow Am. Acad. Arts and Sci. (v.p. 1946-48), Brit. Acad. (corr.); hon. bencher Inner Temple; mem. ABA (ho. of dels. 1957-85, gold medal 1978), Mass. Bar Assn., Am. Law Inst., Am. Coll. Trial Lawyers, Am. Philos. Soc., Phi Beta Kappa. Clubs: Harvard (N.Y.C.); Burning Tree, Cosmos, Metropolitan (Washington); Century Assn. (N.Y.); Charles River Country. Federal civil litigation, Corporate taxation, Estate taxation. Home: 36 Kenmore Rd Belmont MA 02178 Office: 655 15th St NW Suite 600 Washington DC 20005

GRITCHEN, LYLE STEVEN, lawyer; b. Chgo., Nov. 13, 1949. AB, U. Ill., 1971; JD, Northwestern U., 1974. Bar: Ill. 1974, U.S. Dist. Ct. (no. dist.) Ill. 1974. Assoc. Kirkland & Ellis, Chgo., 1974-80, ptnr., 1980—. Mem. ABA, Ill. Bar Assn. General corporate, Securities. Office: Kirkland & Ellis 200 E Randlph Dr Chicago IL 60601

GRODD, LESLIE ERIC, lawyer; b. N.Y.C., Feb. 18, 1946; s. Abe and Celia G.; m. Judith Cota, June 18, 1967; children—Elissa, Katharine, Matthew. B.A. U. Vt., 1966; J.D., St. John's U., 1969; M.B.A., NYU, 1971. Bar: N.Y. 1969, Conn. 1974, D.C. 1982, U.S. dist. Ct. Conn. 1975, U.S. Tax Ct. 1980, U.S. Sup. Ct. 1975. With tax dept. Coopers & Lybrand, N.Y.C., 1969-74; sr. ptnr. Blazzard, Grodd & Hasenauer, Westport, Conn., 1974—. Mem. Am. Inst. C.P.A.s, Conn. Soc. C.P.A.s, Conn. Bar Assn., N.Y. Bar Assn., D.C. Bar Assn. Jewish. Corporate taxation, Estate taxation, Personal income taxation. Office: Blazzard Grodd & Hasenauer 943 Post Rd E PO Box 5108 Westport CT 06881

GRODNIK, CHARLES HUBERT, lawyer; b. Mpls., Sept. 7, 1944; s. Jacob and Lillian (Miller) Grodnik; m. Janice K. Slama, Mar. 15, 1969; children: Ann J., Carl J. BA, U. Minn., 1966, JD, 1969. Bar: Ind. 1970. Staff atty. Lincoln Nat. Corp., Ft. Wayne, Ind., 1969-71; assoc. Thorne & Yoder, Elkhart, Ind., 1971-75; ptnr. Thorne, Grodnik & Ransel, Elkhart, 1976—. Mem. Elkhart County Election Bd., 1984-85; del. Ind. Rep. Conv., 1976-83, 85—. Mem. Ind. Bar Assn. (family law sect.), Elkhart City Bar Assn., Am. Trial Lawyers Assn., Elkhart County Estate Planning Council (past pres.). Clubs: Elkhart Concert, Breakfast Optimist. Lodges: Masons, Shriners. General corporate, Family and matrimonial, Personal injury. Office: Thorne Grodnik & Ransel 228 W High St Elkhart IN 46516-3176

GROENKE, THEODORE A., lawyer; b. Maywood, Ill., Jan. 30, 1921; s. Theodore Otto and Selma R. (Struckmeyer) G.; m. Martha G. Groenke, July 5, 1947; children: Theodore A., Frederick John, Hans Robert. AB with honors, DePauw U., 1942; JD, Northwestern U., 1947. Bar: Ill., U.S. Dist. Ct. (no. dist.) Ill., U.S. Dist. Ct. (ea. dist.) Wis., U.S. Ct. Appeals (7th cir.), U.S. Supreme Ct. Assoc. Snyder, Chadwell & Fagerburg, Chgo., 1947-52, ptnr., 1952-61; mng. ptnr. antitrust and trial dept. McDermott, Will & Emery, Chgo., 1961—. Contbr. articles to profl. jours. Pres. Child Care Assn., Ill.; v.p. 46th Ward Regular Rep. Orgn., Ill., 1947-52; vestry Ch. of Holy Spirit, Ill. Served with U.S. Army, 1942-45, PTO. Mem. ABA (chmn. Robinson-Patman com., litigation sect.), Ill. Bar Assn. (chmn. antitrust div.), Cir. Ct. Bar Assn., Chgo. Bar Assn., Assn. Trial Lawyers Am., Am. Jud. Soc., Law Club, Legal Club, Am. Arbitration Assn. (comml. arbitration panel), Phi Beta Kappa. Episcopalian. Clubs: Lake Forest (Ill.) (charter); Exmoor Country; University; Mid-Day. Avocations: skiing, fishing, backpacking. Antitrust, Federal civil litigation, Administrative and regulatory. Home: 742 Exmoor Oaks Highland Park IL 60035 Office: McDermott Will & Emery 111 W Monroe St Chicago IL 60603

GROETHE, REED, lawyer; b. Indpls., Mar. 21, 1952; s. Alfred Phillip and Kathryn (Skerik) G.; m. Nancy Jayne Radefeld, June 2, 1977; children: Jacob Peter, Eric Alfred. BA, St. Olaf Coll., 1974; JD, U. Chgo., 1977. Bar: Wis. 1977. Law clk. to judge U.S. Ct. Appeals (5th cir.), Montgomery, Ala., 1977-78; assoc. Foley & Lardner, Milw., 1978—, ptnr., 1986—. Mem. ABA (tax sect.), Nat. Asn. Bond Lawyers, Wis. Bar Assn. Lutheran. Municipal bonds. Office: Foley & Lardner 777 E Wisconsin Milwaukee WI 53202-5367

GROFMAN, BERNARD NORMAN, political science educator, consultant; b. Houston, Dec. 2, 1944; s. Dave and Fannie (Pachter) G. BS in Math., U. Chgo., 1966, PhD in Polit. Sci., 1972. Asst. prof. polit. sci. SUNY, Stony Brook, 1970-76; assoc. prof. polit. sci. U. Calif., Irvine, 1976-80, prof., 1980—. Editor: (with others) Representation and Redistricting Issues, 1982, Choosing an Election System, 1984, Electoral Laws and Their Political Consequences, 1986. Research grantee NSF 1974-76, 77-79, 84-85, 85-86; Fellow Ctr. for Advanced Study in the Behavioral Scis., Stanford, Calif., 1985-86. Mem. Am. Polit. Sci. Assn., Pub. Choice Soc., Law and Soc. Assn. Avocations: ping-pong. Civil rights, Law and social science. Office: U Calif Sch of Social Scis Irvine CA 92717

GROGAN, MICHAEL KEVIN, lawyer, negotiator; b. Chgo., Sept. 26, 1951; s. William P. and Margaret (Campbell) G.; m. Nancy Ann Wilson, July 24, 1974; children—Margaret Lindsay, Kathryn Eileen, Michael Patrick. B.S., MacMurray Coll., 1972; J.D., Mercer U., 1976. Bar: Fla. 1976, Ga. 1976, U.S. Ct. Appeals (5th cir.) 1976, U.S. Ct. Appeals (11th cir.) 1982. Assoc., Coffman, Coleman, Andrews & Grogan P.A. and predecessors, Jacksonville, Fla., 1976-81, ptnr., 1981—; labor law research specialized legal reseach Little, Brown & Co., 1987—; legal counsel Riverside Avondale Preservation, Jacksonville, 1978—. Mng. editor Mercer Law Rev., Macon, Ga., 1975-76. Mem. Republican Nat. Com., Washington, 1980—; chmn. Fla. Pub. Employment Labor Relations Forum, 1985—. Ill. State scholar, 1969-72, Gov.'s intern, 1971. Mem. ABA, Fla. Bar Assn. (exec. council bor law and local govt. sects. 1982—, co-chmn. pub. employee relations com. 1985—), Ga. Bar Assn., Assn. Trial Lawyers Am. Roman Catholic. Clubs: River, Fla. Yacht (Jacksonville). Labor, Local government, Civil rights. Office: Coffman Coleman Andrews & Grogan PA PO Box 40089 Jacksonville FL 32203

GROMAN, ARTHUR, lawyer; b. Los Angeles, Sept. 13, 1914; s. Lou and Tinnie (Lurie) G.; m. Sally Buchalter, Apr. 27, 1941 (dec. 1968); children: Richard, Steven; m. Miriam Ginsberg, Aug. 14, 1969. AB, U. So. Calif., 1936; JD, Yale U., 1939. Bar: Calif. 1939. Atty. U.S. Dept. Treasury, 1939-41, IRS, 1942-44; assoc. Mitchell, Silberberg & Knupp, Los Angeles, 1944-48, ptnr., 1948-65, sr. ptnr., 1965—; bd. dirs. Occidental Petroleum Corp. Contbr. articles to profl jours. Past pres. Calif. Inst. Cancer Research UCLA, Los Angeles Jewish Community Found.; past. chpt. pres., nat. v.p. Am. Jewish Community; bd. visitors UCLA Med. Sch.; bd. counselors U. So. Calif. Law Sch.; bd. dirs. Armand Hammer Found., Armand Hammer Ctr. for Advanced Study of Nuclear Energy. Mem. ABA, Calif. Bar Assn., Los Angeles Bar Assn. Club: Hillcrest Country. Federal civil litigation, State civil litigation, General practice. Home: 520 Stonewood Dr Beverly Hills CA 90210 Office: Mitchell Silberberg & Knupp 11377 W Olympic Blvd Los Angeles CA 90064

GROMAN, TOD PHILIP, lawyer; b. Bklyn., June 22, 1951; s. Louis and Sylvia (Nussbaum) G.; m. Naomi Sandra Zlotnick, July 12, 1981; 1 child, NIcole Mallory. BA, CUNY, 1972; JD, St. John's U., 1975. Bar: N.Y. 1976, Fla. 1977, U.S. Dist. Ct. (so. and ea. dists.) N.Y. 1977, D.C. 1978. Asst. dist. atty. Kings County, Bklyn., 1975-79; assoc. Morris & Duffy, N.Y.C., 1979-85; ptnr. Belair, Klein, Groman & Evans, N.Y.C., 1985—. Personal injury, Insurance, State civil litigation. Home: 2166 Broadway New York NY 10024 Office: Belair Klein Groman & Evans 61 Broadway New York NY 10006

GRONER, BEVERLY ANNE, lawyer; b. Des Moines, Jan. 31, 1922; d. Benjamin L. and Annabelle (Miller) Zavat; m. Jack Davis, Dec. 31, 1940; children—Morrilou Davis Morell, Lewis A. Davis, Andrew G. Davis; m. 2d, Samuel Brian Groner, Dec. 17, 1962. Student Drake U., 1939-40, Catholic U., 1954-56; J.D., Washington Coll. Law, Am. U., 1959. Bar: Md. 1959, U.S. Supreme Ct. 1963, D.C. 1965. Sole practice, Bethesda, Md., 1963—; chmn. Md. Gov.'s Commn. on Domestic Relations Laws 1977—; trustee Montgomery-Prince George's Continuing Legal Edn. Inst.; lectr. to lay, profl. groups; participant continuing legal edn. programs, local and nat.; participant trial demonstration films Am. Law Inst., ABA Legal Consortium; participant numerous TV, radio programs; seminar leader Harvard Law Sch., 1987. Named One of Leading Matrimonial Practitioners in U.S., Nat. Law Jour., 1979, Best Divorce Lawyer in Md., Washingtonian Mag., 1981, One of Best Matrimonial Lawyers in U.S., Town and Country mag., 1985; recipient Disting. Service award Va. State Bar Assn., 1982. Fellow Am. Acad. Matrimonial Lawyers; mem. Bar Assn. Montgomery County (exec. com., chmn. family law sect. 1976, chmn. fee arbitration panel 1974-77, legal ethics com.), Md. State Bar Assn. (gov., chmn. family law sect. 1975-77, vice chmn. com. continuing legal edn., ethics com.), ABA (sec. Family Law Sect. 1983-84, vice chmn. 1984-86, chmn. 1986—, sect. council 1982-83, co-chmn. sect. marital property com., assn.'s adv. to Nat. Conf. of Commrs. on Uniform State Laws Drafting Com. on Uniform Marital Property Act), Phi Alpha Delta. Contbr. numerous articles to legal publs. Family and matrimonial.

GRONER, ISAAC NATHAN, lawyer; b. Buffalo, Oct. 22, 1919; s. Louis and Lena (Blinkoff) G.; m. Estelle Kaye, Sept. 14, 1941; children—Phyllis Gross, Robert, Lois Kanter. B.A. in econs. and gen. studies with distinction, Cornell U., 1939; M.A., NYU, 1942; LL.B. cum laude, Yale U., 1948. Bar: N.Y. 1948, U.S. Supreme Ct. 1953, D.C. 1954, U.S. Ct. Appeals (D.C. cir.) 1954, Md. 1955. Law clk. Chief Justice Fred M. Vinson, U.S. Supreme Ct., Washington, 1948-50; atty. Dept. Justice, Washington, 1950-51; chief counsel Wage Stabilization Bd., Washington, 1951-53; sole practice, Washington, 1953-64; ptnr. Cole and Groner, P.C., Washington, 1964—. Contbr. articles to law jours. Mem. ABA (co-chmn. com. on law govt. employee relations sect. labor relations law 1962-64), Order of Coif, Phi Beta Kappa, Phi Kappa Phi. Administrative and regulatory, Federal civil litigation, Labor. Home: 3304 Wake Dr Kensington MD 20895 Office: Cole and Groner PC 1615 L St NW Washington DC 20036

GRONER, SAMUEL BRIAN, judge; b. Buffalo, Dec. 27, 1916. AB, Cornell U., 1937, JD, 1939; MA in Econs., Am. U., 1950. Bar: N.Y. 1939, D.C. 1952, Md. 1953, U.S. Supreme Ct. 1944. Sole practice Buffalo, 1939-40; atty.-adviser U.S. Dept. Justice, Washington, 1946-53; sole practice Md. and Washington, 1953-63; ptnr. Groner, Stone & Greiger, Washington, 1955-57, Groner & Groner, Silver Spring and Bethesda, Md., 1962—; adminstrv. law judge U.S. Dept. Labor, Washington, 1979—; asst. to commr. FCC, Washington, 1953; asst. counsel Naval Ship Systems Command, Washington, 1963-73; trial atty. Office Gen. Counsel, Dept. Navy, Washington, 1973-74, assoc. chief trial atty., 1974-79; instr. Terrell Law Sch., Washington, 1948; mem. faculty USDA Grad. Sch., 1972—; reporter Md. Gov.'s Commn. on Domestic Relations Laws, 1977—; participant in continuing legal and jud. edn. Author: Modern Business Law, 1983, (with others) The Improvement of the Administration of Justice, 6th edit., 1981; assoc. editor Fed. Bar Jour., 1948-55; contbr. articles to profl. jours. Active PTA, civic assns., Jewish Community Council, Community Chest. Mem. ABA (vice chmn. pub. contract com. on adminstrv. claims and remedies law sect. 1976-79, chmn. 1979-80, mem. liaison commn. on professionalsim, 1985—, adv. to standing com. on lawyer competence, 1986—, jud. adminstrn. div.), Fed. Bar Assn., Montgomery County Bar Assn., Md. Bar Assn., D.C. Bar Assn., Cornell Law Assn. (pres. D.C. chpt. 1947-54), Govt. Adminstrv. Trial Lawyers Assn., Am. Law Inst., Inst. Jud. Adminstrn., Am. Judicature Soc., Supreme Ct. Hist. Soc., Nat. Lawyers Club, Phi Beta Kappa. Home: 6710 Western Ave Chevy Chase MD 20815 Office: 1111 20th St NW Washington DC 20036

GRONOWSKI, JOSEPH EDWARD, lawyer; b. Milw., Mar. 10, 1918; s. Joseph F. and Mary (Jeske) G.; m. Betty J. Andracki, Nov. 13, 1945; children—Joseph F., John F., Mary F. J.D., Marquette U., 1942. Bar: Wis. 1942, U.S. Ct. Appeals (7th and Fed. cirs.) 1977. Claims adjustor, claims supr., asst. claim mgr. Royal Globe Ins. Co., 1947-55; claims supr. compensation and bonding claims Am. Auto Ins. Co., 1955-60; atty. in charge Milw. Claim Office, Fidelity & Deposit Co. Md., 1960-73; assoc. Gronowski & Kirschnik, Brookfield, Wis., 1982-86; ptnr. Walther & Halling, S.C., Milw., 1986—. Served to 2d lt. JAGC, USAF, 1943-47; staff judge adv. AirNG, Wis.; lt. col. USAFR, ret. Mem. ABA (mem. forum com., tort and ins. sect., fidelity and surety subsect.), Milw. Ins. Claims Assn., Milw. Claims Mgrs. Council (pres. 1972), Fed. Cir. Bar Assn. Roman Catholic. Club: Wisconsin (Milw.). Fidelity and surety. Office: Gronowski & Kirschnik 625 E St Paul Ave Milwaukee WI 53202

GRONSO, WENDELL E., lawyer; b. Westport, S.D., Apr. 5, 1922; s. Dale and Gertrude (Jaekel) G.; m. Patricia M. Murphy, Jan 25, 1944; 1 child, Mark A. JD, U. Oreg., 1949. Bar: Oreg. 1949, U.S. Dist. Ct. Oreg. 1950. Sole practice Lebanon and Burns, Oreg., 1949-54, 74—; ptnr. Gill & Gronso, Lebanon, 1954-57, Cramer & Gronso, Burns, 1958-74. Mem. Burns High Sch. Bd., 1969-74, chmn., 1974. Served as lt. (j.g.) USN, 1942-45. Fellow Am. Coll. Trial Lawyers; mem. Oreg. Bar Assn. (bd. dirs 1964-67, v.p. 1966-67), Am. Bd. Trial Advocates (diplomat). Democrat. Episcopalian. Lodges: Lions, Elks, Mason, Shriner. State civil litigation. Home: Highland Ranch Estates Hines OR 97738 Office: 709 Ponderosa Village Burns OR 97720

GROPPER, ALLAN LOUIS, lawyer; b. N.Y.C., Jan. 25, 1944; s. Jerome F. and Susan M. (Weingarten) G.; m. Jane Evangelist, Aug. 10, 1968; 1 child, Andrew. B.A., Yale U., 1965; J.D., Harvard U., 1969. Bar: N.Y. 1969, U.S. Dist. Ct. (so. and ea. dists.) N.Y. 1971, U.S. Ct. Appeals (2d cir.) 1971, U.S. Supreme Ct. 1974. Atty. Civil Appeals Bur., Legal Aid Soc., N.Y.C., 1969-71; assoc. White & Case, N.Y.C., 1972-77, ptnr., 1978—. Bd. dirs. Community Action for Legal Services, Inc., 1986—. Mem. ABA (bus. bankruptcy com.), Assn. Bar City N.Y. (bankruptcy law com. 1984—, chmn. com. legal assistance 1985—), N.Y. State Bar Assn. Bankruptcy. Home: 115 Central Park W New York NY 10023 Office: White & Case 1155 Ave of the Americas New York NY 10036

GROSH, SUSAN ELLEN, lawyer; b. N.Y.C., Sept. 1, 1958; d. Thomas Bayard and Eleanor Louise (Wangerin) Grosh. B.A. summa cum laude, Fordham U., 1979; J.D., Coll. William and Mary, 1982. Bar: Pa. 1982. Dir., Post Conviction Assistance Project, Williamsburg, Va., 1980-82; assoc. Wenger, Byler & Thomas, 1982-86, Blakinger, Byler, Thomas and Chillas, P.C., Lancaster, Pa., 1982, 86—. Mem. ABA, Pa. Bar Assn., Lancaster Bar Assn. Republican. Presbyterian. Federal civil litigation, State civil litigation, Family and matrimonial. Office: Blakinger Byler Grove Thomas and Chillas PC 8 N Queen St Lancaster PA 17603

GROSMAN, ALAN M., lawyer; b. Newark, Mar. 13, 1935; s. Charles M. and Grace (Fishman) G.; m. Bette Bloomenthal, Dec. 27, 1967; children—Ellen, Carol. B.A., Wesleyan U., 1956; M.A., Yale U., 1957; J.D., N.Y. Law Sch., 1965. Bar: N.J. 1965, U.S. Dist. Ct. N.J. 1965, U.S. Sup. Ct. 1969. Ptnr., Grosman & Grosman and predecessors, Short Hills, N.J., 1965—; asst. prosecutor Essex County, N.J., 1968-69; mem. family part practice com. N.J. Supreme Ct., 1984—; lectr. in field. Mem. ABA (chmn. alimony, maintenance and support com. family law sect. 1983—), N.J. State Bar Assn. (exec. editor N.J. Family Lawyer, mem. exec. com. family law sect. 1980—, chmn. sect. 1987—), Am. Acad. Matrimonial Lawyers (pres. N.J. chpt. 1983-85, nat. bd. govs. 1984—), Essex County Bar Assn. (chmn. family law com. 1970-72), Phi Beta Kappa. Contbr. articles to profl. jours. Family and matrimonial. Address: PO Box 615 512 Millburn Ave Short Hills NJ 07078

GROSS, DAVID ANDREW, lawyer; b. Mineola, N.Y., Sept. 24, 1954; s. Robert A. and Elee (Kauffmann) G.; m. Elizabeth Gifford, July 30, 1978; 1 child, Robert Henry. BA, U. Pa., 1976; JD, Columbia U., 1979. Bar: D.C. 1979, U.S. Dist. Ct. D.C. 1980, U.S. Ct. Appeals (D.C. cir.) 1980. Assoc. Sutherland, Asbill & Brennan, Washington, 1979-87, ptnr., 1987—. Harlan Fiske Stone scholar Columbia U., 1978-79. Mem. ABA, Fed. Communications Bar Assn. Jewish. Communications and Telecommunications, Administrative and regulatory, Public utilities. Home: 1396 Canterbury Way Rockville MD 20854 Office: Sutherland Asbill & Brennan 1275 Pennsylvania Ave NW Washington DC 20007

GROSS, EDMUND SAMUEL, lawyer; b. Kansas City, Kans., Nov. 17, 1950; s. Michael and Eileen (Davis) G.; m. Michiko Miyamori, July 26, 1981. Student, U. Coll. Wales, 1970-71; BA cum laude, Tulane U., 1972; JD, MBA, Kansas U., 1980. Bar: Kans. 1980, U.S. Dist. Ct. Kans. 1980. Assoc. Weeks, Thomas & Lysaught, Kansas City, 1980-86, ptnr., 1986-87; atty. Farmland Industries, Inc., Kansas City, 1987—. Chmn. profl. div. United Way Campaign, Wyandotte County, Kans., 1980; treas. Kansas City Recruiting Dist. Assistance council, 1984—; pres. Santa Fe Trail chpt. USNR Assn., Kansas City, 1985—. Served to lt. USN, 1972-76, with Res. 1976—. Mem. ABA, Kans. Bar Assn., Wyandotte County Bar Assn. Avocations: water and snow skiing, sailing. Personal injury, Federal civil litigation, State civil litigation. Home: 6742 Fontana Prairie Village KS 66208 Office: Farmland Industries Inc PO Box 7305 Kansas City KS 64416

GROSS, JACK, lawyer; b. N.Y.C., Feb. 28, 1910; s. Henry S. and Anna (Rosenberg) G.; married; children: Stephen, Deborah, Jeffrey. BA, NYU, 1930, JD, 1932. Bar: N.Y. 1933, U.S. Dist. Ct. (so. dist.) N.Y. 1943, U.S. Ct. Appeals (2d cir.) 1951, U.S. Dist. Ct. (ea. dist.) N.Y. 1975, U.S. Supreme Ct. 1975. Assoc. Shaine & Weinrib, N.Y.C., 1936-43; ptnr. Shaine, Weinrib, Mallin & Gross, N.Y.C., 1946-57, Krause, Hirsch & Gross, N.Y.C., 1957-80; sr. ptnr. Stroock & Stroock & Lavan, N.Y.C., 1980—. Served to lt. USN, 1943-46. Mem. ABA, Assn. of Bar of City of N.Y., Bankruptcy Bar Assn. Democrat. Jewish. Clubs: Fairview Country (Greenwich, Conn.) (v.p.), Princeton, Merchants (bd. govs.) (N.Y.C.), Delaire Country (Fla.). Bankruptcy, Contracts commercial. Home: 15 Knollwood Dr Greenwich CT 06830 also: 16821 Rose Apple Dr Delray Beach FL 33445 Office: Stroock & Stroock & Lavan 7 Hanover Sq New York NY 10004

GROSS, JUSTIN ARTHUR, lawyer; b. Berkeley, Calif., Sept. 9, 1932; s. Andrew and Bess (Boyarsky) G.; m. Barbara Diamond, June 21, 1953 (div. Dec. 1982); children: Denise J. Kennedy, Robert D.; m. Julia Lynn McClendon, Sept. 23, 1983. LLB, Golden Gate U., 1960. Bar: Calif. 1961, U.S. Supreme Ct. 1969. Atty. Kaiser Ind. Corp., Oakland, Calif., 1961-69; dir. trusts Pacific Maritime Assn., San Francisco, 1969-79; counsel employee relations Consol. Freightways Inc., Palo Alto, Calif., 1979—. Served with U.S. Army, 1954-56. Avocation: photography. Labor, Pension, profit-sharing, and employee benefits, General corporate. Office: Consol Freightways Inc PO Box 10340 Palo Alto CA 94303

GROSS, MALCOLM JOSEPH, lawyer, association executive; b. Allentown, Pa., Oct. 2, 1940; s. John Tilghman and Agnes Amelia (Lieberman) G.; m. Lona Mae Farr, Aug. 24, 1963 (div.); m. Sally Lorensen Oeler, Apr. 9, 1976; children—Andrea, Stacey, John, Peter; stepchildren—Kurt, Rolf, Paula Oeler. A.B. cum laude, Muhlenberg Coll., 1962; J.D., Villanova U., 1965. Bar: Pa. 1965, U.S. dist. ct. (ea dist.) Pa. 1965. Law clk. to chief justice Pa. Supreme Ct., 1966; ptnr. Brennen & Gross, Allentown, 1966-72, Gross & Brown, Allentown, 1972-76; sr. ptnr. Gross, McGinley & McGinley, Allentown, 1976-83, Gross, McGinley & LaBarre, Allentown, 1983—; sr. ptnr. Gross, McGinley, LaBarrre, & Eaton ; asst. pub. defender Lehigh County, 1969-72; disciplinary com. Pa. Sup. Ct., 1975-79; solicitor Lehigh Valley Child Care, Inc., 1971-83, Lehigh County Office Children and Youth Services, 1972—, Head Start Lehigh Valley, 1980—, Wiley House, 1981—; pres. Grandview Cemetery Assn., Allentown, 1966—; law lectr. Muhlenberg Coll., 1972—; chmn., sec., treas. sta. WLVT-TV 39, 1969—. Chmn. collections com Muhlenberg Coll. Exec. Com Bd. Assocs., Allentown Art Mus. Lectr. in field. Pres., Cause, 1969-71; bd. dirs. Lehigh Valley Conservancy, 1969-72; mem. Gov.'s Council on Alcohol and Drug Abuse, 1969-75; bd. dirs. YMCA, 1971-76; pres., dir. Lehigh Valley Child Care, 1971-79; chmn. parish council Cathedral of St. Catherine of Siana, 1968-70; mem. Pa. state Democratic exec. fin. com., 1981—. Dubach scholar, 1961; recipient Phi Alpha Theta prize Muhlenberg Coll., 1962, Rinaldi prize Villanova Law Sch., 1964, YMCA disting. service award, Allentown, 1976. Mem. ABA, Pa. Bar Assn. (constl. law and child abuse coms.), Lehigh County Bar Assn. (orphan ct. rules and juvenile ct. coms.), Pa. Trial Lawyers Assn. (bd. govs.), Sigma Phi Epsilon. Bd. editors Villanova Law Rev., 1964-65; contbr. articles to legal and social work publs. General practice, Juvenile, Libel. Home: PO Box 1398 Allentown PA 18104 Office: 137 N 5th St PO Box 1398 Allentown PA 18105

GROSS, MONNYE R., lawyer; b. St. Louis, Apr. 1, 1957; s. Lester and Evelyn Ruth (Gold) G.; m. Kenneth Solomon, Mar. 20, 1983. Student, Hebrew U., Jerusalem, 1976-77; BA in English Lit., Northwestern U., 1978; JD, Ill. Inst. Tech., 1981; LLM in Taxation, DePaul U., 1983. Bar: Ill. 1981, U.S. Tax Ct. 1981, Pa. 1983, Mo. 1984. Assoc. Fordyce & Mayne, St. Louis, 1984-86, Newman, Goldfarb, Freyman & Stevens, St. Louis, 1986—; adj. faculty Webster U. Sch. Bus. Co-chairperson 9th constl. conf. Washington U., 1986; bd. dirs. Am. Jewish Congress, St. Louis, 1986—, Mo. Coalition Against Censorship, St. Louis, 1986—. Mem. ABA (tax sect.), St. Louis Bar Assn., ACLU. Democrat. Avocations: reading, writing, theater, tennis. General corporate, Estate planning, Personal income taxation. Office: Newman Goldfarb Freyman & Stevens 7777 Bonhomme Ave Suite 1724 Saint Louis MO 63105

GROSS, RICHARD ARTHUR, lawyer; b. Bremerton, Wash., Nov. 21, 1951; s. Ernest Arthur and Jean Rose (Lirette) G. BS in Polit. Sci., Whitman Coll.; JD, U. Puget Sound. Bar: Wash. 1978, U.S. Dist. Ct. (we. dist.) Wash. 1981. Assoc. Perrine, Casey & Davis, Port Orchard, Wash., 1978-81; ptnr. Casey & Gross P.S., Port Orchard, 1981-83; sole practice Port Orchard, 1983—. Mem. Wash. State Bar Assn., Kitsap County Bar Assn., Assn. Trial Lawyers Am., Wash. State Trial Lawyers Assn., Kitsap C. of C. (bd. dirs. 1981-85). General practice, Probate, Real property. Home: 7119 Richards Ave SE Port Orchard WA 98366 Office: 720 Prospect St Port Orchard WA 98366

GROSS, SEYMOUR, lawyer; b. Cleve., Nov. 11, 1927; s. Edward and Dora (Gitler) G.; m. Lois Henden, Apr. 30, 1956; children: Michael, Steven, Pamela. BBA, Case Western Res. U., 1949, JD, 1952. Bar: Ohio 1952, U.S. Dist. Ct. (no. dist.) Ohio 1955, U.S. Ct. Appeals (6th cir.) 1973, U.S. Supreme Ct. 1973, U.S. Ct. Claims 1983. Sole practice Cleve., 1952—. Fellow Ohio Acad. Trial Attys., Cleve. Acad. Trial Attys. (pres. 1978); mem. Assn. Trial Lawyers Am., Ohio Bar Assn., Cleve. Bar Assn. Personal injury, Probate, State civil litigation. Home: 5437 Bluebell Dr Lyndhurst OH 44124 Office: 436 Engineers Bldg Cleveland OH 44114

GROSS, STEVEN ROSS, lawyer; b. N.Y.C., June 15, 1946; s. Alexander and Lola (Mandelbaum) G.; m. Georgette Francine Kleinhaus, Dec. 14, 1968; children: Amy, Jillian. BA, Columbia U., 1968, MA, 1969; LLB, Cambridge U., 1971; JD, Yale U., 1973. Bar: U.S. Dist. Ct. (ea. and so. dists.) N.Y. 1974. Assoc. Debevoise & Plimpton, N.Y.C., 1973-80, ptnr., 1981—. Contbr. articles to profl. jours. Mem. ABA, Assn. of Bar of City of N.Y. Jewish. Bankruptcy. Home: 230 E 79th St New York NY 10021 Office: Debevoise & Plimpton 875 3d Ave New York NY 10022

GROSS, SUSAN LARKY, lawyer; b. Allentown, Pa., Mar. 14, 1957; d. Arthur Irving Larky and Georgia (Stonehill) Block; m. Steven Ronald Gross, Nov. 13, 1982. BS, George Washington U., 1978; JD, Western New England Coll., 1981. Bar: Conn. 1981, Mass. 1982, U.S. Dist. Ct. Conn. 1982, U.S. Dist. Ct. Mass. 1983, U.S. Ct. Appeals (1st cir.) 1983. Assoc. Winer & Sulzbach, New Haven, Conn., 1981-83; assoc. Morrison, Mahoney & Miller, Boston, 1983-84, mng. assoc., 1984—. Contbr. articles to bi-monthly mag. Norhteast Update , 1983—. Mem. ABA, Hampden County Bar Assn., Phi Beta Kappa. Avocations: sailing, knitting, needlepoint, swimming. Insurance, Federal civil litigation, State civil litigation. Home: 12D Byrne Ct Farmington CT 06032 Office: Morrison Mahoney & Miller 31 Elm St Springfield MA 01103

GROSS, TERENCE ALAN, lawyer; b. Asheville, N.C., Apr. 6, 1954; s. Leroy and Leah June (Vigodsky) G.; m. Cindy Lee Hoover, Sept. 25, 1983; 1 child, Kiel Arin. BA in Polit. Sci., Washington U., 1976; JD, Fla. State U., 1979. Bar: Fla. 1979, U.S. Dist. Ct. (no. dist.) Fla. 1979. Assoc. Pensacola, Fla., 1979-81; sole practice Pensacola, 1981—. Mem. Assn. Trial Lawyers Am. Jewish. Club: Myokis (Pensacola). Avocations: tennis, fishing, basketball, outdoor activities. Personal injury, Insurance, Criminal. Home: 3872 Paradise Bay Dr Gulf Breeze FL 32561 Office: 917 N Palafox St Pensacola FL 32501

GROSSBERG, DAVID, lawyer; b. N.Y.C., Sept. 14, 1925; s. Meyer and Ethel Grossberg; m. Miriam Weissner, Mar. 22, 1959; children: Amy, Robert. BS, CCNY, 1947; LLB, Harvard U., 1950. Bar: N.Y. 1951. With Berlack, Israels & Liberman, N.Y.C., 1951-54, Cohen & Grossberg, N.Y.C., 1954—. Served with U.S. Army, 1943-45, ETO. Mem. Assn. of Bar of City of N.Y., N.Y. County Bar Assn. Entertainment, Advertising, General practice. Office: Cohen & Grossberg 635 Madison Ave New York NY 10022

GROSSGOLD, NATHAN, lawyer; b. N.Y.C., Aug. 25, 1913; s. Joseph and Anna (Feit) G.; m. Helen Meisner, Aug. 26, 1939 (div. Feb. 1948); 1 child, Janet; m. Charlotte Bornstein, Mar. 12, 1949; children—Stuart, Minda, Jodi. J.D., Bklyn. Law Sch., 1939. Bar: N.Y. 1941, U.S. Dist. Ct. (so. and ea. dists.) N.Y. 1950, U.S. Supreme Ct. 1951, U.S. Dist. Ct. D.C. 1962, Ill. 1962. Assoc., M&N Grossgold, Flushing, N.Y., 1941-62; pres. N. Grossgold, Ltd., Skokie, Ill., 1962—; atty. Republic Chem. Co., Flushing, 1942-49; legal cons., dir. Telephone Radio Transport Corp., 1955-59; def. atty. Allstate Ins. Co., Chgo., 1962-71, Nat. Union Ins. Co., Chgo., 1965-74, Am. Home Ins. Co., Chgo., 1966-74; instr. Lawyers Postgrad. Clinic, Chgo., 1965-68. Committeeman, Boy Scouts Am., Chgo., 1948-52; pres. United Civic Council Queens, N.Y., 1956-59; active Leukemia Orgn., Skokie, 1975—. Mem. Ill. State Bar Assn., N. Suburban Bar Assn. Democrat. Jewish. Lodge: Masons. Personal injury. Home: 8042 N Kenton Skokie IL 60076

GROSSMAN, GARRY S., lawyer; b. Cleve., Aug. 13, 1950; s. Ely H. and Lee (Feinberg) G.; m. Susan Sonnenschein, July 20, 1980; children: Elyse, Julie. AB, U. Mich., 1973; MS, U. Toronto, Can., 1977; JD with high honors, George Washington U., 1982. Bar: D.C. 1982. Research assoc. Toronto Gen. Hosp., 1977-78; systems analyst HHS, Rockville, Md., 1979-81; assoc. Fried, Frank, Harris, Shriver & Jacobson, Washington, 1982—. Mem. ABA (pub. contract law and sci. and tech. sects.), D.C. Bar Assn., IEEE Computer Soc., Assn. for Computing Machinery, Computer Law Assn., D.C. Computer Law Forum, George Washington Law Alumni Assn. (D.C. chpt. treas. 1985-86, v.p. 1986—), Nat. Contract Mgmt. Assn., Order of Coif, Phi Eta Sigma. Government contracts and claims, Computer. Office: Fried Frank Harris Shriver & Jacobson 1001 Pennsylvania Ave NW Washington DC 20004

GROSSMAN, GEORGE STEFAN, law librarian, lawyer; b. Poltar, Czechoslovakia, May 31, 1938; m. Suzi Herczeg, 1960; 1 child, Zoltan. B.A., U. Chgo., 1960; LL.B., Stanford U., 1966; M.A. in Library Sci., Brigham Young U., 1971. Bar: Calif. 1966, Minn. 1974. Tech. processes law librarian U. Pa., 1966-68; assoc. prof. law, law librarian U. Utah, 1968-70, prof., law librarian, 1970-73; prof., dir. law library U. Minn., 1973-79, Northwestern U., Chgo., 1979—; cons. to univs. Contbr. articles to legal jours. Mem. Indian rights com. ACLU, 1973—, pres. Utah affiliate, 1972-73, bd. dirs. Ill. affiliate, 1982—. Mem. Am. Assn. Law Libraries,

Internat. Assn. Law Libraries, ABA. Librarianship, Legal education. Office: Northwestern U Sch Law Library 357 E Chicago Ave Chicago IL 60611 *

GROSSMAN, JAMES STUART, lawyer; b. Bklyn., Nov. 12, 1948; s. Harold H. and Shirley (Kempner) G.; m. Susan Victoria Smallwood, July 11, 1971; children—Douglas, Rebecca, Harold. B.A., Hobart Coll., 1970; J.D. cum laude, Bklyn. Law Sch., 1973. Bar: N.Y. 1974, U.S. Dist. Ct. (we. dist.) N.Y. 1975, U.S. Dist. Ct. (no. dist.) N.Y. 1982, U.S. Ct. Appeals (2d cir.) 1983, U.S. Supreme Ct. 1987. Assoc. Mousaw Vigdor Reeves Heilbronner Kroll, Rochester, N.Y., 1975-79, ptnr., 1980—. Articles editor Bklyn. Law Rev., 1973. Chmn. Mary Cariola Childrens Ctr., Rochester, 1984-85; treas., bd. dirs. Epilepsy Assn. Greater Rochester, 1984-85; v.p. Epilepsy Assn. of Greater Rochester, 1986—; v.p. Advocacy for Developmentally Disabled, 1986—, bd. dirs. 1985—; pres., bd. dirs. Al Sigl Ctr. for Rehabilitation Services Inc., 1985—; mem. Town of Penfield Zoning Bd. Appeals, 1984-85. Mem. N.Y. State Bar Assn., Monroe County Bar Assn., (com. chmn.), N.Y. State Epilepsy Assn. (bd. dirs. 1985—). Democrat. Jewish. Clubs: Hobart of Rochester (v.p. 1984, pres. 1985), Penfield Country. Real property, Condemnation. Home: 1704 Jackson Rd Penfield NY 14526 Office: Mousaw Vigdor et al 600 1st Fed Plaza Rochester NY 14614

GROSSMAN, JEROME KENT, lawyer, accountant; b. St. Louis, Apr. 15, 1953; s. Marvin and Myra Lee (Barnholtz) G.; m. Debbie Ada Kogan, Aug. 7, 1977; children: Hannah Felicia, Marni Celeste. AB cum laude, Georgetown U., 1974, JD, 1977. Bar: Mo. 1977, D.C. 1977, U.S. Ct. Claims 1979, U.S. Tax Ct. 1979, Del. 1980, U.S. Dist. Ct. Del. 1982; CPA, Mo. Acct., controller U.S. Dept. State, Washington, 1974-77; acct. Arthur Andersen & Co., St. Louis, 1977-79; ptnr. Bayard, Handelman and Murdoch, P.A., Wilmington, Del., 1979—, also bd. dirs. Co-author: ALI-ABA Course of Study on the Reform Act of 1984, 86. V.p. Jewish Community Ctr., Wilmington, 1986; bd. dirs. Congregation Beth Shalom, Wilmington, 1984—; mem. Del. State steering com. State of Israel Bonds. Mem. ABA (taxation sect., vice chmn. com. on tax acctg. problems 1986—, chmn. inventories subcom. 1982-86), Del. Bar Assn., Del. Tax Inst. (planning com. 1985-86), Del. Soc. CPA's (chmn. tax com. 1980-85, council 1985—), Alpha Sigma Nu. Democrat. Club: Rodney Sq. (Wilmington). Avocations: choir, opera, bridge. Corporate taxation, Personal income taxation, Estate taxation. Home: 803 Westover Rd Wilmington DE 19807 Office: Bayard Handelman and Murdoch PA PO Box 25130 Wilmington DE 19899

GROSSMAN, JOANNE BARBARA, lawyer; b. Brookline, Mass., Oct. 23, 1949; d. Bernard R. and Beatrice G. (Quint) G.; m. John H. Seesel, Dec. 30, 1973; children: Benjamin P., Rebecca A. AB, Radcliffe Coll., 1971; JD, U. Calif., Berkeley, 1975. Bar: Calif. 1975, D.C. 1976, U.S. Dist. Ct. D.C. 1976, U.S. Ct. Appeals (D.C. cir.) 1976, U.S. Supreme Ct. 1979. Assoc. Covington & Burling, Washington, 1975-83, ptnr., 1983—. Federal civil litigation, Antitrust, Administrative and regulatory. Office: Covington & Burling 1201 Pennsylvania Ave NW PO Box 7566 Washington DC 20044

GROSSMAN, MARK DONALD, lawyer; b. Niagara Falls, N.Y., Oct. 14, 1955; s. Stanley and Carolyn (Jaffe) G. BS in Bus. Adminstrn., SUNY, Buffalo, 1977; JD, Pace U., 1980. Bar: N.Y. 1981, U.S. Dist. Ct. (we. dist.) N.Y. 1982. Assoc. Grossman, Levine & Civiletto, Niagara Falls, 1981—; active supervisory com. Niagara Falls Hebrew Fed. Credit Union, 1984—. Mem. Niagara Falls Bar Assn., Western N.Y. Trial Lawyers Assn. Personal injury, State civil litigation, Criminal. Home: 710-4th St Niagara Falls NY 14302 Office: Grossman Levine & Civiletto 331 Buffalo Ave Niagara Falls NY 14303

GROSSMAN, RICHARD ALAN, lawyer, cons.; b. Detroit, Oct. 26, 1939; s. Moses M. and Alice May (Aronson) G.; m. Bemely Comtes; children—Justine Rebecca, Adam Douglas. B.A., Wayne State U., 1963; J.D. with honors, U. Mich., 1969. Bar: Calif. 1970, U.S. Ct. Apls. (9th cir.), 1970, U.S. Tax Ct., 1971, U.S. Sup. Ct. 1973. Assoc. Gang, Tyre & Brown, Hollywood, Calif., 1970-71; ptnr. Grossman & Levinthal, Los Angeles, 1973-75; prin. Richard A. Grossman, P.C., Beverly Hills, Calif., 1975—; staff, chief csl. NASA, 1967; vis. prof. Claremont Grad. Sch., 1974-75; judge pro tem Beverly Hills Mcpl. Ct., 1975-79, Los Angeles Super. Ct., 1980-82; cons. on internat. law, bus. and security transactions to industry, govt., 1975—; pres., pub. csl. Pub. Interest Law Office of Los Angeles County and Beverly Hills Bar, 1980-81; chmn. Fed. Jud. Survey, 1977. Mem. campaign staff Senator Robert F. Kennedy, 1968. Served to capt. USMC, 1957-60. Recipient Children's Med. Relief award Republic South Viet Nam, 1973. Mem. ABA. Democrat. Jewish. Contbr. articles to various legal publs.; author: I Am A Young Man (poetry), 2 vols., 1979. Federal civil litigation, Trademark and copyright, Private international. Office: 9601 Wilshire Blvd Suite 200 Beverly Hills CA 90210

GROSSMAN, SANFORD, lawyer; b. N.Y.C., July 4, 1929; s. Philip and Irene (Hare) G.; m. Barbara Rothman, May 23, 1951; children: Daniel J., Donna A. Student, NYU, 1947-49; LL.B., Bklyn. Law Sch., 1952. Bar: N.Y. 1953, U.S. Supreme Ct. 1964. Pvt. practice law N.Y.C., 1954-79; ptnr. Simpson Thacher & Bartlett, N.Y.C., 1979—; dir. Bellemead Devel. Corp., Roseland, N.J., Christiania Gen. Ins. Corp. of N.Y., Tarrytown. Served with U.S. Army, 1952-54. Mem. N.Y. County Lawyers Assn., Westchester Bar Assn. Clubs: India House (N.Y.C.), Princeton (N.Y.C.). Office: Simpson Thacher & Bartlett 1 Battery Park Plaza New York NY 10004

GROSSO, ROBERT JOHN, lawyer; b. Bronxville, N.Y., July 24, 1947; s. Nicholas P. and Mary (MacKay) G.; m. Carolyn R. Hersey, Nov. 22, 1969; children: Alissa Carin, Emily Kim. BS in Indsl. Engring., Newark Coll. Engring., 1969; MBA, Monmouth Coll., West Long Branch, N.J., 1973; JD, Seton Hall U., 1977. Bar: N.J., N.Y. Project engr. Naval Weapons Ctr. Earle, Colts Neck, N.J., 1969-74; legal asst., staff atty. Kidde, Inc., Clifton, N.J., 1974-79; sec., gen. counsel Lesney Products Corp., Moonachie, N.J., 1979-80, 81-83; asst. gen. counsel Goody Products, Inc., Kearny, N.J., 1980-81; sr. v.p., sec., gen. counsel Bevill, Bresler & Schulman, Inc., Livingston, N.J., 1983-85; asst. counsel First Investors Corp., N.Y.C., 1985—. Deacon First Presbyn. Ch., Ramsey, N.J., 1983-86; mem. planning bd. Byram Twp., 1987—. Mem. Assn. MBA Execs., ABA, N.Y. State Bar Assn., N.J. Bar Assn., Tau Kappa Epsilon (historian 1968-69). General corporate, General practice. Home: 4 Ross Rd Stanhope NJ 07874 Office: First Investors Corp 120 Wall St New York NY 10005

GROTTENDIECK, WILLIAM JOSEPH, III, lawyer; b. Fairmont, W.Va., July 31, 1943; s. William Joseph II and Mary Catherine (Farrell) G.; m. Virginia Ann Randolph, Sept. 16, 1969; 1 child, Virginia Ann. BA in Polit. Sci., W.Va. U., 1970, JD, 1973. Bar: W.Va. 1973, U.S. Dist. Ct. (so. dist.) W.Va. 1973, U.S. Ct. Mil. Appeals 1973. Commn. JAGC U.S. Army, 1973-80; advanced through grades to major USAR, 1983; gen. counsel Trio Petroleum Corp., Glenville, W.Va., 1980—. Bd. dirs. Summit Ctr. for Human Devel., Clarksburg, W.Va., 1981—, pres. 85-86, Glenville (W.Va.) Utility Commn., 1982-86. Mem. W.Va. State Bar, W.Va. Bar Assn. Democrat. Roman Catholic. Lodges: Rotary (pres. 1986—), Masons. Avocations: cross-country skiing, jogging. Oil and gas leasing. Home: 212 Johnson St Glenville WV 26351 Office: Trio Petroleum Corp Rt 76 Box 35E Glenville WV 26351

GROUSSMAN, RAYMOND G., diversified utility and energy company executive; b. Price, Utah, Dec. 15, 1935; s. Raymond K. and Gene E. (Goetzman) G.; m. Marilyn Kaye Jensen, Mar. 16, 1964; children: Katherine Anne, Laura Kaye, Daniel Ray, Adam J. B.S., U. Utah, 1961, J.D., 1966. Bar: Utah 1965, U.S. Supreme Ct. 1978. Police officer Salt Lake City Police Dept., 1962-66; mem. firm Amoss & Groussman, Salt Lake City, 1966-69; staff atty. Utah Legal Services, 1969-70; chief dep. Salt Lake County atty., 1970-71; assoc. Pugsley, Hayes, Watkiss, Campbell & Cowley, Salt Lake City, 1971-74; gen. counsel Mountain Fuel Supply Co., Salt Lake City, 1974-84; v.p. Mountain Fuel Supply Co., 1977-84; v.p., gen. counsel Questar Corp., 1984—; dir. Wexpro Co. Bd. dirs. Children's Service Soc. Utah, 1976-77; trustee Ft. Douglas Mil. Mus., 1976-84 ; bd. advisers Energy Law Center, U. Utah Coll. Law, 1978—; mem. criminal law revision com. Utah Legis. Council; bd. dirs. Utah Legal Services, 1970-78, United Way of Salt Lake City, 1982—. Served with U.S. Army, 1957-60; lt. comdr. USCGR, 1967—. Mem. Am. Bar Assn., Fed. Energy Bar Assn., Am. Gas Assn., Pacific Coast Gas Assn. (chmn. legal adv. council 1979-80), Salt Lake County Bar Assn., Salt Lake Legal Defenders Assn. (dir. 1978—), Salt Lake City C. of C., Sigma Alpha Epsilon, Delta Theta Phi. General corporate, Oil and gas leasing, Public utilities. Office: Mountain Fuel Supply Co 180 E 100 S St Salt Lake City UT 84139

GROVE, JACK FREDERICK, lawyer, educator; b. Hamilton, Ohio, Aug. 31, 1953; s. James Edward and Eleanor Katherine (Schlichter) G.; m. Susan Kathleen Flick, July 24, 1976; 1 child, Adam Nathaniel. B.S. in Agr., Ohio State U., 1975; J.D., U. Dayton, 1979. Bar: Ohio 1979, U.S. Dist. Ct. (so. dist.) Ohio 1979, U.S. Supreme Ct. 1984. Law clk. to Judge Fred B. Cramer, Hamilton, Ohio, 1979-80; asst. pros. atty. Butler County, Hamilton, 1980-87 ; instr. fin. Miami U., Oxford, Ohio, 1981-84; ptnr. Grove & Matre, Fairfield, Ohio, 1979—; bd. dir. adv. council Hamilton Tool Co., 1982-86. Mem. exec. com. Butler County Reps., Hamilton, Ohio, 1980-81; propr. Copper Fox Stables, Silverwood Farm. Mem. ABA, Ohio State Bar Assn., Butler County Bar Assn., Cin. Bar Assn., Sierra Club, Nat. Snaffle Bit Assn., Gamma Sigma Delta. Republican. Clubs: New London Hills, Hamilton City; Am. Ohio Quarter Horse Assn., Ohio Quarter Horse Assn., Tex. Quarter horse Assn. State civil litigation, Real property. Home: 1093 Davis Rd Hamilton OH 45013 Office: 1251 Nilles Rd Suite 10 Fairfield OH 45014

GROVE, LAD, lawyer; b. Corydon, Iowa, Aug. 22, 1948; s. Clifford E. and Mildred J. (Boyd) G.; m. Patricia S. Nogel, Mar. 6, 1976. BS, Iowa State U., 1970; JD, Drake U., 1973. Bar: Iowa 1973, US. Dist. Ct. (so. dist.) Iowa 1974, U.S. Dist. Ct. (no. dist.) Iowa 1979. Ptnr. Nigut & Grove P.C., Corydon, 1974-75; sole practice Ames, Iowa, 1976—; asst. atty. Story County, Iowa, 1976-78. Mem. ABA, Story County Bar Assn., Assn. Trial Lawyers Am., Iowa Trial Lawyers Assn. Republican. Methodist. Clubs: Story Cyclone (v.p. 1985-86, pres. elect 1986-87). Avocations: rugby, skiing, water sports. Personal injury, Real property. Home: 1505 Little Bluestem Ct #111 Ames IA 50010 Office: 218 SE 16th St Ames IA 50010

GROVE, RUSSELL SINCLAIR, JR., lawyer; b. Marietta, Ga., Dec. 25, 1939; s. Russell Sinclair and Miriam (Smith) G.; m. Charlotte Mariam Glasscock, Jan. 9, 1965; children—Farion Smith Whitman, Arthur Owen Sinclair. B.S., Ga. Inst. Tech., 1962; LL.B. with distinction, Emory U., 1964; postgrad., U. Melbourne Faculty Law, Australia, 1965. Bar: Ga. 1965, U.S. Supreme Ct. 1971, U.S. Ct. Appeals (11th cir.) 1983. Assoc. Smith, Currie & Hancock, Atlanta, 1966-67; assoc. Hansell & Post, Atlanta, 1968-72, ptnr., 1972—; mem. adv. com. Ctr. for Legal Studies; mem. exec. com. real property law sect. State Bar Ga. Author: Word Processing and Automatic Data Processing in the Modern Law Office, 1978, Legal Considerations of Joint Ventures, 1981, Structuring Endorsements and Affirmative Insurance, 1981, Management's Perspective on Automation, 1981, Mineral Law: Current Developments and Future Issues, 1983; co-author: The Integrated Data and Word Processing System, 1981, Georgia Partnership Law: Current Issues and Problems, 1982; editor-in-chief Jour. Pub. Law, 1963-64. Mem. Central Atlanta Progress, Inc.; bd. dirs. Caribbean Mission, Inc. Served with USMCR, 1960-65. Mem. ABA, Ga. Bar Assn., Atlanta Bar Assn., Bryan Soc., U.S. Marine Corps Assn. Ga. Lawyers, Eastern Mineral Law Found., Am. Coll. Mortgage Attys., Am. Coll. Real Estate Lawyers, Ga. Oil and Gas Assn., Ga. Cattlemen's Assn., Nat. Cattlemen's Assn., Am. Scotch Highland Breeders Assn., Can. Highland Cattle Soc., Highland Cattle Soc. U.K., Phi Delta Phi, Omicron Delta Kappa. Episcopalian. Clubs: Dunwoody Country, Commerce, Lawyers of Atlanta, Ashford. Real property, Contracts commercial, Oil and gas leasing. Office: 56 Perimeter Ctr E NE Suite 500 Atlanta GA 30346

GROVES, MARY LYNETT, lawyer; b. Queens, N.Y., Apr. 29, 1952; d. Philip Matthew and Jeanne Elizabeth (Vincent) Lynett; m. James Ernest Groves, Dec. 29, 1973; children: Matthew Charles, Mark Philip, Ellen Catherine. BA, U. Colo., 1974; JD, U. Denver, 1978. Bar: Colo. 1978, U.S. Ct. Appeals (10th cir.) 1978, Tex. 1984. Assoc. Kutak, Rock & Campbell, Denver, 1978-82, Calkins, Kramer, Grimshaw & Harring, Denver, 1982, McCall, Parkhurst & Horton, Dallas, 1982-83; ptnr. Wood, Lucksinger & Epstein, Dallas, 1983—. Mem. ABA, Tex. Bar Assn., Colo. Bar Assn., Nat. Assn. Bond Lawyers. Democrat. Roman Catholic. Municipal bonds. Office: Wood Lucksinger & Epstein 2121 San Jacinto St #1740 Dallas TX 75201

GROWE, GARY ALAN, lawyer; b. St. Louis, Jan. 12, 1952; s. Leonard Robert and Hortense (SMith) G.; m. Bethe Meryl, May 28, 1978; children: Jennifer Dawn, Jason Brett. BA in Polit. Sci., Ind. U., 1974; JD, George Washington U., 1977. Bar: Mo. 1977, U.S. Dist. Ct. (ea. and we dists.) Mo. 1977, U.S. Ct. Appeals (8th cir.) 1980. Assoc. Chused, Strauss et al, St. Louis, 1977-78; ptnr. Blumenfeld & Sandweiss, St. Louis, 1978-86, Law Offices of Donald Schlapprizzi, St. Louis, 1986—. Contbr. legal articles to profl jours. Bd. dirs., v.p. Young Audiences, St. Louis, 1985—; mem. steering com. Big Brothers/Big Sisters, St. Louis, 1981-83; mem. Leadership St. Louis Program, 1986-87. Mem. Am. Trial Lawyers Assn., Mo. Trial Lawyers Assn., Mo. Bar Assn. , Lawyers Assn. St. Louis, St. Louis County Bar Assn. (Outstanding Young Lawyer award). Avocations: politics, sports, reading. Federal civil litigation, State civil litigation, Personal injury. Office: Donald Schlapprizzi Law Offices 1015 Locust St Suite 914 Saint Louis MO 63101

GROWER, JOHN MARSHALL, lawyer; b. Hattiesburg, Miss., Sept. 24, 1924; s. John A. and Mary L. (LaGrone) G.; m. Mary C. Steinriede, Aug. 17, 1945; children—Mary Katherine, John M., Judith Ann, Janet Elizabeth, Patrick William, Michael Anthony. Student, Miss. State U., 1942-43; J.D., U. Miss., 1950. Bar: Miss. 1950. Assoc. Brunini, Grantham, Grower & Hewes, Jackson, Miss., 1951-56, ptnr., 1956—. Served with USN, 1942-46. Decorated knight of St. Gregory, Pope Paul VI 1965; knight of Equestrian Order of Holy Sepulchre, Pope Paul VI, 1977; named Lion of Yr., North Jackson Lions, 1964-65. Mem. ABA, Am. Petroleum Inst., Hinds County Bar Assn., Ind. Petroleum Assn. Am., Mid-Continent Oil and Gas Assn. (dir. and mem. exec. com. Miss.-Ala. div.), Miss. Bar Assn., Miss. Oil and Gas Lawyers Assn., Newcomen Soc. N.Am., U.S. Golf Assn. Democrat. Roman Catholic. Clubs: KC, Capital City Petroleum (bd. govs.), Country of Jackson, Miss. State U. Bulldog, Nat. Travel, Patio. Oil and gas leasing, Federal civil litigation, State civil litigation. Address: PO Drawer 119 Jackson MS 39205

GRUBB, KITTY GOLDSMITH, lawyer; b. Bennettsville, S.C., July 29, 1952; d. Harry Simon and Carolyn (Davis) Goldsmith; m. Lawrence Logan Grubb, Aug. 6, 1972. A.B., U. Ala.-Tuscaloosa, 1974; J.D. cum laude, Cumberland Sch. Law, 1977; LL.M. in Taxation, NYU, 1981. Bar: Ala. 1977, U.S. Ct. Appeals (5th cir.) 1979, Tenn. 1981, U.S. Ct. Claims 1981, U.S. Tax Ct. 1981, U.S. Ct. Appeals (4th cir.) 1980, U.S. Dist. Ct. (ea. dist.) Tenn. 1982, U.S. Ct. Appeals (6th and Fed. cirs.) 1984, U.S. Ct. Mil. Appeals 1984. Staff atty. TVA, Knoxville, 1977-79; assoc. Lockridge & Becker, P.C., Knoxville, 1981-82; ptnr. Dunaway, Harrell, Grubb, Van Hook & Cotton, LaFollette, Tenn., 1982-85; assoc. Wagner & Myers, P.C., Knoxville, 1985-86; prin. ptnr., McGehee & Grubb; P.C., Knoxville, 1986—; lectr. St. Mary's Hosp., Knoxville, Knoxville Women's Ctr., various other orgns.; mem. So. Pension Conf., Atlanta, 1981-82, Am. Pension Conf., N.Y.C., 1981-82. Assoc. editor Cumberland Law Rev., 1975-77. Chmn. fund drive, eastern Tenn. region Cumberland Sch. Law, 1979-80. Recipient Curia Honoris award Cumberland Sch. Law, 1978, cert. merit Cumberland Sch. Law chpt. Phi Delta Phi, 1977, cert. appreciation Knoxville Women's Ctr., 1983-86, Annie P. Selwyn award, 1986. Mem. Knoxville Bar Assn. (continuing legal edn. 1982—), ABA (Tenn. membership chmn. Young Lawyer's Conf. div. 1984-86), Ala. Bar Assn., Tenn. Bar Assn., Assn. Trial Lawyers Am., Cumberland Law Sch. Alumni Assn., NYU Law Sch. Alumni Assn., U. Ala. Alumni (v.p. eastern Tenn. chpt. 1983, pres. chpt. 1984, merit awards eastern Tenn. chpt. 1982, 83, 84, nat. award 1984), AAUW, Knoxville Assn. Women Execs., Nat. Assn. Women Execs., Knoxville Zool. Soc., Polit. Button Collectors (Dixie chpt., Am. chpt.), Century Club of U. Ala. Alumni (eastern Tenn. chpt.), Am. Platform Soc., Omicron Delta Epsilon, Pi Sigma Alpha. Democrat. Methodist. Corporate taxation, Personal income taxation, Labor. Office: McGehee Grubb & Currier 1634 Plaza Tower Knoxville TN 37929

GRUBBS, DONALD SHAW, JR., actuary; b. Bellvue, Pa., Dec. 15, 1929; s. Donald Shaw and Zora Fay (Craven) G.; m. Margaret Helen Crooke, Dec. 27, 1969; children: David, Deborah, Daniel, Dawson, Dwight, Douglas. AB, Tex. A&M U., 1951; postgrad., Los Angeles State Coll., 1953-54, Fresno State Coll., 1954-55, Boston U., 1955-57, Princeton Theol. Sem., 1959-60, Westminster Theol. Sem., 1960-61; JD, Georgetown U., 1979. Bar: D.C. 1979. Actuarial asst. New Eng. Mut. Life Ins. Co., Boston, 1955-58, Warner Watson, Inc., Boston, 1958-59; cons. actuary John B. St. John, Penllyn, Pa., 1959-65, Grubbs & Co., Phila., 1965-72; v.p. actuary Nat. Health and Welfare Retirement Assn., N.Y.C., 1972-74; dir. actuarial div. IRS, Washington, 1974-76; cons. actuary Buck Cons., Inc., Washington, 1976-86; pres. Grubbs and Co., Inc., Silver Spring, Md., 1986—; chmn. Joint Bd. for Enrollment Actuaries, Washington, 1975-76. Author: (with G.E. Johnson) The Variable Annuity, 1967. V.p. Ambler (Pa.) NAACP, 1961-61; chmn. Warminster (Pa.) Child Day Care Assn., 1962-64. Served to 1st lt. U.S. Army 1951-53, Korea. Decorated Bronze Star with V U.S. Army, 1953; recipient Employee Benefits Outstanding Achievement award Pension World, 1986. Fellow Soc. of Actuaries (sec. 1983-84), Conf. Actuaries in Pub. Practice; mem. Middle Atlantic Actuarial Club. (pres. 1981-82), ABA. Democrat. Unitarian. Pension, profit-sharing, and employee benefits. Home and Office: 10216 Royal Rd Silver Spring MD 20903

GRUBER, WILLIAM MICHAEL ONDREY, lawyer; b. Cleve., Oct. 17, 1955; s. Roman Frederick and Mary Margaret (Moriarty) G.; m. Lynn Frances Ondrey, June 16, 1984. BA, Georgetown U., 1977; JD, Case Western Res. U., 1982. Bar: Ohio 1982, U.S. Dist. Ct. (no. dist.) Ohio 1982. Asst. dir. law City of Cleve., 1982—. Chmn. bd. dirs. Cleve. Recycling Ctr.; chmn. adv. bd. Cleve. Waterfront Coalition. Mem. ABA, Clevel. Bar Assn., Sierra Club (chmn. lakefront com. northeast Ohio group). Local government, Public utilities, Consumer commercial. Home: 2655 Haddam Rd Cleveland OH 44120 Office: City of Cleve Dept Law City Hall Rm 106 Cleveland OH 44114

GRUCCIO-THORMAN, LILLIAN JOAN, lawyer; b. Camden, N.J., Jan. 30, 1927; d. Joseph and Millie Gruccio. grad. Steelman Bus. Sch., 1945; A.A., Rutgers U., 1947, LL.B., 1951, LL.D., 1968. Bar: N.J. 1952, U.S. Dist. Ct. N.J. 1952, U.S. Supreme Ct. 1960. Ptnr., Frank C. Propert, Camden, 1952-55; asso. Lewis & Hutchinson and successors, Camden, 1956-61; with legal dept. Campbell Soup Co., 1955; sole practice Pennsauken, N.J., 1961-73, Medford, N.J., 1973—. Mem. Camden City Juvenile Conf. Com., 1957-62; mem. Burlington County council Girl Scouts USA, 1975, chmn. by-laws com., 1975; bd. dirs. Camden County Health and Welfare Council, 1957-61, YWCA Camden, 1959-67, chmn. adult program com. 1957-67; mem. budget com. United Fund, 1968. Mem. ABA, N.J. Bar Assn., Burlington County Bar Assn., Camden County Bar Assn., Rutgers U. Law Sch. Alumni Assn. (chancellor South Jersey div. 1962). Republican. Baptist. General corporate, Probate, Real property. Home: 63 Sheffield Pl Vincentown NJ 08088 Office: Cedarbrook Bldg Taunton Blvd Medford NJ 08055

GRUEN, MICHAEL STEPHAN, lawyer; b. Los Angeles, Mar. 25, 1942; s. Victor and Elsie Caroline (Krummeck) G.; m. Susanna Lloyd, July 18, 1964; m. 2d, Vanessa Elisabeth Ahlfors, Jan. 3, 1976; children—Madeleine, Alexis, Viveca; stepchildren—Stefan, Sebastian. B.A. cum laude, Harvard Coll., 1963; LL.B., UCLA, 1966. Bar: Calif. 1966, N.Y. 1967, U.S. Ct. Appeals (2d cir.) 1975, U.S. Supreme Ct. 1975, U.S. Dist. Ct. (so. and ea. dists) N.Y. 1986. Assoc. Paul, Weiss, Rifkind, Wharton & Garrison, N.Y.C., 1966-69, Gilinsky, Stillman & Mishkin, N.Y.C., 1969-70, Wolf, Popper, Ross, Wolf & Jones, N.Y.C., 1970-74; gen. counsel Bio-Med. Scis., Inc., Fairfield, N.J., 1974-75; sole practice, N.Y.C., 1975-80; mem. Gruen & Muskin, N.Y.C., 1980, Gruen, Muskin & Thau, N.Y.C., 1981—. Bd. dirs. Boys' Athletic League, 1966-82; dir., sec. N.Y. Landmarks Conservancy, 1972—; bd. advisors Prep. Div. of Bklyn. Coll. Ctr. for Performing Arts, 1980-83; v.p., bd. dirs. Columbia Land Conservancy, 1986—; pres. Riverside Democrats, N.Y.C., 1971-72. Mem. ABA (bus. law, taxation, anti-trust sects.), N.Y. State Bar Assn. (bus. law sect.), Assn. Bar City of N.Y. Contbr. articles to legal publs. Federal civil litigation, State civil litigation, General corporate. Office: 500 Fifth Ave Suite 5225 New York NY 10110

GRUENBERGER, PETER, lawyer; b. Czechoslovakia, May 19, 1937; came to U.S., 1941; s. Leslie and Olga (Zollman) G.; m. Judy Ann Herz, June 7, 1959 (dissolved); children: Karen, Richard, Lauren. AB, Columbia U., 1958, LLB, 1961. Bar: N.Y. 1962, U.S. Dist. Ct. (so., ea. and no. dists.) N.Y. 1962, U.S. Ct. Appeals (1st and 2d cirs.) 1963, U.S. Supreme Ct. 1964. Assoc. Hughes, Hubbard & Reed, N.Y.C., 1962-69; ptnr. Weil, Gotshal & Manges, N.Y.C., 1970—. Contbr. articles on real estate law and litigation to profl. jours. Served as 1st lt. U.S. Army, 1961-62. Harlan Fiske Stone scholar, 1959-61. Mem. ABA (chmn. various coms. 1973-75, 79-86, spl. com. on class actions and discovery 1977-86, governing council 1975-78, litigation sect.), Assn. of Bar of City of N.Y. (grievance com. 1975-77). Club: Sunningdale Country (Scarsdale, N.Y.). Real property. Office: Weil Gotshal & Manges 767 Fifth Ave New York NY 10153

GRUENSTEIN, DEBRA LYNNE, lawyer; b. Phila., Apr. 12, 1953; d. Bernard and Shirley (Shapson) Horowitz; m. Jack L. Gruenstein, Aug. 19, 1974; children: Maris, Kyra. BA, Temple U., 1974, JD, 1977. Bar: Pa. 1977, U.S. Dist. Ct. (ea. dist.) Pa. 1977. Assoc. Wolf, Block, Schorr & Solis-Cohen, Phila., 1977-83; sole practice Phila., 1984—. Bd. dirs. Bus. Women's Network, Phila., 1985-86. Mem. ABA (bankruptcy com.), Pa. Bar Assn., Nat. Assn. Women Bus. Owners (v.p. membership Phila. chpt.). Avocations: reading, biking, swimming, piano, skiing. General corporate, Contracts commercial, Bankruptcy. Office: 1 E Penn Sq Bldg Suite 800 Juniper and Market Sts Philadelphia PA 19107

GRUMBINE, DAVID LEE, lawyer; b. Connersville, Ind., Aug. 31, 1951; s. Walter Klee and Dorothy Lee (Twigg) G.; m. Sally Ann Tippett, Aug. 23, 1975; children: Kristin, Kara, Andrew. BS, U. Evansville, 1974; JD, Thomas M. Cooley Law Sch., 1977. Bar: Mich. 1978, U.S. Dist. Ct. (we. dist.) Mich. 1979. Law clk. to presiding justice 2d Jud. Cir. Ct., St. Joseph, Mich., 1978-79; assoc. Seymour Zaban, St. Joseph, 1979-81, Small, Small & Dettman, P.C., Benton Harbor, Mich., 1981-82; ptnr. Small, Small, Dettman & Grumbine, P.C., Benton Harbor, 1982-84; atty., counselor Whirlpool Corp., Benton Harbor, 1984—; bd. dirs. Whirlpool Employees Fed. Credit Union, St. Joseph; instr. bus. law Cen. Mich. U., Benton Harbor, 1986. Pres. Child and Family Services Southwest Mich., St. Joseph, 1984—; bd. dirs. ARC, Berrien County Chpt., Benton Harbor, 1984—. Mem. ABA, Mich. Bar Assn., Berrien County Bar Assn. (sec. 1983-84). Republican. Congregationalist. Avocations: baseball, jogging. Personal injury, General corporate. Home: 2930 S Bluffwood Terr Saint Joseph MI 49085 Office: Whirlpool Corp Law Dept Benton Harbor MI 49022

GRUNBLATT, DAVID MICHAEL, lawyer; b. N.Y.C., Jan. 17, 1953; s. Joseph and Esther Vera (Unger) G.; m. Henna Rosenberg, July 3, 1978; 1 child, Meir. BA in Psychology, Bklyn. Coll., 1973; JD, NYU, 1977, LLM in Taxation, 1983. Bar: N.Y. 1978, U.S. Dist. Ct. (so. and ea. dists.) N.Y. 1978, U.S. Ct. Appeals (2d cir.) 1980. Assoc. Wildes & Weinberg, N.Y.C., 1977-85, ptnr., 1985—. Mem. Nat. Jewish Commn. of Law and Pub. Affairs, N.Y.C., 1980—. Mem. ABA, Am. Immigration Lawyers Assn., N.Y. County Lawyers Assn. (chmn. immigration and naturalization com.1985—). Immigration, naturalization, and customs. Office: Wildes & Weinberg 515 Madison Ave New York NY 10022

GRUND, JAMES ARTHUR, lawyer; b. Logansport, Ind., Jan. 8, 1919; s. Arthur Mack Grund and Charlotte Lillian (Crismond) Guthrie; m. Constance Hurst, June 27, 1942; children: James H, Jeffrey A., Jane Anne. LLB, Ind. U., 1949. Bar: Ind. 1949, U.S. Supreme Ct. 1973. Ptnr. Grund & Grund, Peru, Ind.; judge City of Peru, 1960-68; dep. prosecutor Miami County (Ind.), Peru, 1968-70, 79-82, pros. atty., 1970-79. Chmn. fund drive Miami County United Fund, Peru, 1963; mem. adv. bd. Salvation Army, Peru, 1955-85. Served as sgt. USAAF, 1941-45, CBI. Mem. Miami County Bar Assn. (past pres.), Sigma Alpha Epsilon. Republican. Lodge: Elks. Probate, Contracts commercial, Criminal. Home: 126 E Main Peru IN 46970 Office: Fern Grund & Grund 13 E Main Peru IN 46970

GRUNDAHL, JOHN ALVIN, lawyer; b. Sept. 3, 1946; s. Alvin T. and June Grundahl; m. Karen K. Kolpack, Nov. 27, 1971; children: Rachel Kay, Aaron John, Sarah Kaye. BS, St. Olaf Coll., 1968; JD, Marquette U., 1975. Bar: U.S. Dist. Ct. (ea. and we. dists.) Wis. Atty. Ct. Commr., West Bend, Wis., 1975-77; sole practice West Bend, 1977—. Served to lt. USN, 1969-71. Mem. Wis. Bar Assn., Washington County Bar Assn. (pres. 1986). Lodge:

Kiwanis. Family and matrimonial, Juvenile, Real property. Home: 1050 Terrace Dr West Bend WI 53095 Office: 123 S 6th Ave West Bend WI 53095

GRUNDFEST, JOSEPH ALEXANDER, lawyer, economist; b. N.Y.C., Sept. 8, 1951; s. Michael A. and Esther Grundfest: m. Carol Chia-Ming Hsu, Aug. 6, 1978. MSc Program, London Sch. Econs., 1972; BA, Yale U., 1973; JD, PhD (ABD) in Econs., Stanford U., 1978. Bar: Calif. 1978, D.C. 1979. Economist, cons. Rand Corp., Santa Monica, Calif., 1973-78; assoc. Wilmer, Cutler & Pickering, Washington, 1979-84; counsel, sr. economist Council Econ. Advisers, Washington, 1984-85; commr. SEC, Washington, 1985—. Contbr. articles to profl. jours. Research fellow Brookings Inst., 1978-79. Mem. ABA, SEC and Fin. Reporting Inst. (adv. council). Securities, Administrative and regulatory, Antitrust. Office: SEC 450 5th St NW Washington DC 20549

GRUNDMEYER, DOUGLAS LANAUX, lawyer, editor; b. New Orleans, Nov. 6, 1948; s. Raymond Wallace and Eva Myrl (Lanaux) G.; m. Elaine Ann Toscano, Jan. 19, 1977; 1 child, Sarah Elaine. BA, Tulane U., 1970, JD, 1976; MA in English, U. New Orleans, 1974. Bar: La. 1976, Calif. 1980, U.S. Dist. Ct. (no. dist.) Calif. 1980. Law clk. to presiding judge La. State Ct. Appeals (4th cir.), New Orleans, 1976-78, sr. law clk. to presiding judge, 1980—; assoc. legal editor Bancroft-Whitney Co., San Francisco, 1978-80, contract editor, 1981—. Contbr. editor American Jurisprudence Second Criminal Law, 1981; contbg. author La. Apellate Practice Handbook, 1986. Mem. ABA, State Bar Calif., La. Bar Assn. Democrat. Roman Catholic. State civil litigation, Jurisprudence, Criminal. Home: 5438 Vermillion Blvd New Orleans LA 70122 Office: Louisiana State Ct of Appeal 421 Loyola Ave New Orleans LA 70112

GRUNDSTEIN, NATHAN DAVID, lawyer, management science educator, management consultant; b. Ashland, Ohio, Sept. 19, 1913; s. Samuel Lewis and Rose J. (Kolinsky) G.; m. Dorothy Deborah Davis, Nov. 12, 1938; children: Miriam R. (Mrs. Bruce R. Levin), Margaret Judith, Leon D., Robert H. B.A., Ohio State U., 1935, M.Sc., 1936; Ph.D., Syracuse U., 1943; LL.B., George Washington U., 1951. Bar: Mich. 1954, Ohio 1981, U.S. Dist. Ct. Ohio, U.S. Dist. Ct. Mich. Legal research asst. Office Head Atty., Dept. Agr., 1939-40; adminstrv. asst. to asst. commr. FDA, 1940-41; adminstrv. officer, exec. asst. to vice chmn. for labor prodn. WPB, 1941-47; prof. pub. law and adminstrn. Wayne State U., 1947-58; prof. adminstrn. Grad. Sch. Pub. and Internat. Affairs, U. Pitts., 1958-64; prof. mgmt. policy, dir. grad. program pub. mgmt. sci. Case Western Res. U., 1964-84, prof. emeritus, 1984-85; mgmt. cons. Van Dresser Corp. and Ctr. for Minority Entrepreneurs, Inc., 1984—; gen. counsel Luminar Inc., Ohio, 1984—; sr. vis. scholar Canberra Coll. Advanced Edn., Canberra, Australia, 1979; cons. to govt. and industry; lectr. in field. Author: Administrative Practice and procedure Under the Federal Plant Quarantine Act, 1940, Administrative Practice and Procedure Under the Federal Food, Drug and Cosmetic Act, 1941, Industrial Mobilization for War, Vol. I, Part III, 1947, Cases and Readings on Administrative Law, (with J.F. Davison), 1952, Administrative Law and the Regulatory System, 1966, Presidential Delegation of Authority in Wartime, 1961, Ethical Concerns and the City Managers Code of Ethics, 1967, Administrative Law and the Regulatory System, rev. edit, 1968, The Managerial Kant, 1982, Futures of Prudence, 1984; Donor book collection to, Memphis State U. Chmn. Citizens Com. for Cleveland Heights Progress, 1979-81, 83-84. Mem. ABA, Inst. Mgmt. Sci. (exec. com. Coll. Philosophy 1980-84), Mich. Bar Assn., Ohio Bar Assn., Order of Coif, Phi Beta Kappa, Beta Gamma Sigma. Jewish. Administrative and regulatory, General corporate, Jurisprudence. Home: 2872 Washington Blvd Cleveland Heights OH 44118 Office: Case Western Res U Sears Bldg Sch Mgmt Cleveland OH 44106

GRUNING, DAVID WILLIAM, law educator; b. Orange, N.J., May 16, 1951; s. Herman William and Jane (Gedney) G.; m. Martha Fauver Scott, Nov. 6, 1976; 2 children. BA in Linguistics, Wesleyan U., 1973; MA in French, Middlebury Coll., 1975; JD magna cum laude, Tulane U., 1982. Bar: La. 1982. Assoc. Stone, Pigman, Walther, Wittmann & Hutchinson, New Orleans, 1982-86; asst. prof. sch. law Loyola U., New Orleans, 1986—; lectr. law sch. Tulane U., New Orleans, 1983-84. Mem. Bur. of Govtl. Research, New Orleans, 1985—, Agenda for Children, New Orleans, 1986, New Orleans Estate Planning Council; mem. com. New Orleans Parish Sch. Bd., 1986—. Mem. ABA, La. Bar Assn. (chmn. youth edn. com. young lawyers sect.), New Orleans Bar Assn., La. State Law Inst. (com. on revision of law of sale). Avocations: music, lit., running. Contracts commercial, Legal education, Probate. Home: 7927 Oak St New Orleans LA 70118 Office: Loyola U Sch Law Broadway Campus New Orleans LA 70118

GRUSH, JULIUS SIDNEY, lawyer; b. Los Angeles, Dec. 4, 1937; s. Rose (Ida) Yankovitz; m. Eileen, June 14, 1963 (div.); children: Robin, Randi, Ronna, Rodney. BS, UCLA, 1960; postgrad., U. Calif., San Francisco, 1960-62; LLB, Southwestern U., 1964. Bar: Calif. 1965. Dep. city atty. City of Los Angeles, 1965-67; sole practice Los Angeles, 1967—; prof. Bar-Bri Harcourt Brace Pubs. Bar Course, Los Angeles, 1986—. Pres. Lockhurst Booster Club; mem. City of Hope (past pres.). Mem. ABA, Los Angeles Bar Assn., Beverly Hills Bar Assn., Century City Bar Assn., Phi Alpha Delta. Republican. Lodge: Money of Brotherhood. State civil litigation, General corporate, Real property. Office: 1880 Century Park E Suite 1400 Los Angeles CA 90067

GRZECA, MICHAEL (GERARD), lawyer; b. Milw., Aug. 5, 1949; s. Leonard George and Katherine Anne (Lewis) G.; m. Linda Gail Schultz, Aug. 15, 1970; children—Amy Marie, Laura Elizabeth. B.A., Marquette U., 1971, J.D., 1974. Bar: Wis. 1974, U.S. Dist. Ct. (ea. and we. dists.) Wis. 1974, U.S. Supreme Ct., 1977. Assoc., Everson, Whitney, Everson & Brehm, S.C., Green Bay, Wis., 1974-80, shareholder, 1980-86; prin. Grzeca & Stanton, S.C., 1986—; Spl. counsel Wis. Bd. Attys. Profl. Responsibility, 1983—. Bd. dirs. Big Bros.-Big Sisters of Northeastern Wis., Green Bay, 1977—, pres., 1979-81, 85. Served as officer USAR, 1974-80. Mem. ABA, Def. Research Inst., Order of Barristers. Insurance, State civil litigation, Personal injury. Office: Grzeca & Stanton SC 2200 Riverside Dr Green Bay WI 54301

GUARINI, FRANK J., congressman; b. Jersey City, Aug. 20, 1924; s. Frank J. and Caroline (Critelli) G. Student, Columbia U.; B.A., Dartmouth Coll., 1947; LL.B., NYU, 1950, LL.M., 1955; postgrad. advanced law program, Acad. Internat. Law, The Hague Netherlands. Bar: N.J., U.S. Supreme Ct., Ct. Internat. Trade, U.S. Ct. Appeals, U.S. Tax Ct. Partner firm Guarini & Guarini, Jersey City, 1951—; mem. 96th-100th Congresses from 14th N.J. Dist.; mem. ways and means com., subcom. on trade, budget com., select com. on narcotics abuse and control; mem. N.J. Senate, 1966-72, chmn. air and water pollution and pub. health com., appropriations com., 1967-68. Co-author: New Jersey Rules of Evidence; contbr. numerous articles to profl. publs. Mem. council on govt. Fairleigh Dickinson U.; mem. exec. com. Christ Hosp., Jersey City; fund chmn. Urban League Hudson County.; bd. dirs. Hudson County Mental Health Assn., Hudson County Health and Tb League; mem. nat. bd. govs. ARC, also pres. Jersey City chpt.; chmn. bd. regents St. Peter's Coll., Jersey City; trustee Hudson County Bar Found. Served to lt. (s.g.) USNR, World War II, PTO. Fellow ABA; mem. Fed. Bar Assn., Inter-Am. Bar Assn., Hudson County Bar Assn. (trustee), N.J. State Bar Assn. (gen. council), Hudson County C. of C. and Industry (exec. com.), Hague Acad. Internat. Law (trustee), Assn. Am. Trial Lawyers (nat. bd. govs.), N.J. Assn. Trial Lawyers (chmn. exec. com.), Dante Alighieri Soc., UNICO, Phi Delta Phi (pres.), Alpha Delta Phi. Clubs: Rotary (dir.), Columbus Citizens, Bergen Carteret; University, Hudson County (Jersey City) (bd. govs.). Corporate taxation, Pension, profit-sharing, and employee benefits, International trade. Office: US Ho of Reps 2458 Rayburn House Office Bldg Washington DC 20515

GUARNIERI, DONALD LEWIS, lawyer; b. Warren, Ohio, May 8, 1934; s. Albert Andrew and Elsie Katherine (McKay) G.; m. Sandra Arlene Alesky, 1970. AB, Hiram Coll., 1956; LLB, Cleveland State U., 1960, LLM, JD. Bar: Ohio 1960, U.S. Supreme Ct. 1968, D.C. 1975. Sole practice Warren, 1960—. Author: Eighth Day of May. Chmn. bd. Warren Civic Music Assn.

GUBLER, JOHN GRAY, lawyer; b. Las Vegas, June 16, 1942; s. V. Gray and Loreta N. (Newton) G.; m. Mollie Boyle, Jan. 10, 1987; children from previous marriage: Laura, Matthew. B.A., U.Calif.-Berkeley, 1964; J.D., U. Utah, 1971; LL.M. in Taxation, NYU, 1973. Bar: Nev. 1971, U.S. Dist. Ct. Nev. 1973, U.S. Tax Ct. 1974, U.S. Ct. Appeals (9th cir.) 1978. Dep. pub. defender Clark County, Nev., 1973-74; ptnr. Gubler & Gubler, Las Vegas, 1974—; instr. continuing edn. community coll. Mem. Las Vegas Republican Men's Club. Served with U.S. Army, 1966-68. Mem. Clark County Bar Assn., ABA, State Bar of Nev. (disciplinary com. 1979—). Mormon. Clubs: Las Vegas-Paradise Rotary (pres. 1981-82), Knife & Fork (pres. 1978-80). General corporate, Estate planning, Probate. Office: 302 E Carson Suite 601 Las Vegas NV 89101

GUEHL, ROBERT LEE, lawyer; b. Troy, Ohio, Dec. 2, 1946; s. John Joseph and Lucille (Spires) G.; m. Martha T. Thierwechter, Sept. 25, 1971 (div. Aug. 1981); children: Heidi, Jason. BA in History, Ohio State U., 1970, JD, 1973; LLM, George Washington U., 1979. Bar: Ohio 1973, Colo. 1974, U.S. Supreme Ct. 1979, U.S. Dist. Ct. (no. dist.) 1980. Staff atty. USAF, Washington, 1979-80; asst. pub. defender County of Columbiana (Ohio), Lisbon, 1980—; ptnr. Goll & Guehl, Salem, Ohio, 1980—. Trustee Forensic Ctr. of Salem, 1984—; pres. Salem Community Theatre Group, 1984. Served to capt. U.S. Army, 1973-79, with USAF Res., 1982-84. Named one of Outstanding Young Men of Am. U.S. Jaycees, 1981, 83. Mem. ABA, Ohio Bar Assn., Ohio Acad. Trial Lawyers, Columbiana County Bar Assn., Forensic Fellows Soc., Ohio State U. Alumni Assn. (life). Republican. Lodges: Kiwanis (pres. Salem chpt. 1986—), Elks. Personal injury, State civil litigation, General practice. Office: Goll & Guehl PO Box 588 Salem OH 44460

GUERNSEY, THOMAS F., law educator. BA with distinction, U. Mich, 1973; JD cum laude, Wayne State U., 1976; LLM, Temple U., 1980. Bar: N.H. 1976, Va. 1983. Instr. law Vt. Law Sch., Royalton, 1976-78; asst. gen. counsel Temple Legal Aid Office, Phila., 1978-80; asst. prof. law T.C. Williams Sch. Law, U. Richmond (Va.), 1980-83, assoc. prof., 1983-86, prof., 1986—; mediator Offender Aid and Restoration Community Mediation Project, 1984—. Sr. assoc. editor Wayne Law Rev., 1974-76; also articles. Mem. ABA (chmn. negotiation competition com. 1983—). Home: 12110 Diamond Hill Dr Midlothian VA 23113 Office: Univ Richmond TC Williams Sch Law Richmond VA 23173

GUEST, BRIAN MILTON, lawyer; b. Vineland, N.J., Mar. 18, 1948; s. Edmund James Jr. and Vivian D. Guest. AB in Polit. Sci. with distinction, Rutgers U., 1970; JD, Boston U., 1973. Bar: N.J. 1973, U.S. Dist. Ct. N.J. 1973, U.S. Supreme Ct. 1978, U.S. Ct. Appeals (3d cir.) 1981. Assoc. Hartman & Schlesinger, Mt. Holly, N.J., 1973-78; ptnr. Hartman & Schlesinger, Mt. Holly, 1978-82, Bookbinder & Guest, Burlington, N.J., 1982-83, Bookbinder, Guest & Domzalski, Burlington, 1983—; pres., trustee Raritan Sigma Phi Epsilon Corp., New Brunswuck, N.J., 1983—. Mem. ABA, Trial Attys. N.J., N.J. Bar Assn. (gen. counsel del. 1983-86), Burlington County Bar Assn. (trustee 1982-84), Burlington County C. of C. (bd. dirs. 1987—). Lodge: Masons (worshipful master Mt. Holly club 1982). General corporate, Environment, Real property. Office: Bookbinder Guest & Domzalski 235 High St PO Box 429 Burlington NJ 08016

GUEST, FLOYD EMORY, JR., lawyer; b. Oglethorpe, Ga., May 5, 1929; s. Floyd Emory and Eula Belle (Jones) G.; m. Mary E. Vick, Oct. 12, 1955 (div. 1959); 1 child, Victoria Elizabeth; m. Martha J. Roy, Oct. 12, 1963; children—Alyson Jane, Emory Roy. A.B. in Bus. Adminstrn., Duke U., 1952; J.D., U. Tex., 1962; M.S. in Fin. Services, Am. Coll., 1980. Bar: Tex. 1962. Vice pres., controller Cosmopolitan Life, Houston, 1952-59; trust officer Bank of Southwest, 1962-67, Capital Nat. Bank, 1967-69; pres. Profl. Businessmen Assn. Retirement Plans Co., Houston, 1969—; Pres., Southgate Civic Assn., Houston, 1967, 68. Served to capt. USAFR, 1952-67. Mem. SAR, ABA, Tex. Bar Assn., Houston Bar Assn., Houston Estate and Fin. Forum, Houston Estate Planning Council, Delta Theta Phi (pres. Houston alumni 1964). Republican. Lodges: Downtown Optimist (pres. 1982-83), Masons, K.T. Probate, Pension, profit-sharing, and employee benefits, Corporate taxation. Home: 815 Redleaf Ln Houston TX 77090 Office: PBA Retirement Plans Co 1233 West Loop S Suite 1470 Houston TX 77027

GUEST, KARL REED, lawyer; b. Jacksonville, Fla., Sept. 29, 1951; s. Karl Macon and Lois (Reed) G.; m. Patricia Ontiveros, Oct. 20, 1984. BA, Emory U., 1973; JD, U. of Pacific, 1980; MBA, Calif. State U., 1982. Bar: Calif. 1980, U.S. Dist. Ct. (no. and cen. dists.) Calif. 1980. Asst. controller Stone Container Corp., Atlanta, 1974-77; sole practice Sacramento, 1980-82; assoc. Sehr & O'Connor, Inc., Walnut Creek, Calif., 1982-83; ptnr. Sehr, Lamb & Guest, Walnut Creek, 1983—. Named one of Outstanding Young Men of Am., 1974. Mem. ABA, Calif. Bar Assn., Contra Costa County Bar Assn. Avocations: skiing, sailing, golf. General corporate, Estate planning, General practice. Office: Sehr Lamb & Guest 39 Quail Cts Suite 300 Walnut Creek CA 94596

GUETZ, BURTON WALTER, lawyer; b. Aberdeen, S.D., Apr. 30, 1951; s. Max U. and Edith S. (Nathan) G.; m. Julia Suzanne Van Cleave, Apr. 29, 1978; children: Evan P., Lauren M. BS, U. Wyo., 1973, JD, 1976. Bar: Wyo. 1976, U.S. Dist. Ct. Wyo. 1976, U.S. Ct. Appeals (10th cir.) 1980. Dep. atty. Natrona County, Casper, Wyo., 1976-79, pros. atty., county atty., 1979-83; ptnr. Burke & Brown P.C., Casper, 1983-86; sole practice Casper, 1986—. Mem. Assn. Trial Lawyers Am., Wyo. Bar Assn., Natrona County Bar Assn., Wyo. Pros. Attys. Assn. (pres. 190-81), Nat. Dist. Attys. Assn. (bd. dirs. 1981-83). Republican. Methodist. Banking, Contracts commercial, Personal injury. Home: 1521 Newport Casper WY 82609 Office: 111 S Durbin Suite 300 Casper WY 82601

GUGGENHIME, RICHARD JOHNSON, lawyer; b. San Francisco, Mar. 6, 1940; s Richard F. and Charlotte Guggenhime; m. Emlen Hall, June 5, 1965 (div.); children—Andrew, Lisa, Molly. A.B. in Polit. Sci. with distinction, Stanford U., 1961; LL.B., Harvard U., 1964. Bar: Calif. 1965, U.S. Dist. Ct. (no. dist.) Calif. 1965, U.S. Ct. Appeals (9th cir.) 1965. Assoc. Heller, Ehrman, White & McAuliffe, 1965-71, ptnr., 1972—; spl. asst. to U.S. Senator Hugh Scott, 1964; bds. dir. Comml. Bank of San Francisco, global Savings Bank, San Francisco. Mem. San Francisco Bd. Permit Appeals, 1978-86; bd. dirs. Marine World Africa USA, 1980-86; mem. San Francisco Fire Commn., 1986—; trustee San Francisco U. High School, St. Ignatius Prep. Sch., San Francisco. Mem. Am. Coll. Probate Counsel, San Francisco Opera Assn. (dir.). Clubs: Bohemian, University, Wine and Food Soc., Olympic, Chevaliers du Tastevin (San Francisco); Silverado Country (Napa, Calif.); Vintage (Palm Springs). Probate, Estate planning. Home: 115 Presidio Ave San Francisco CA 94115 Office: Heller Ehrman White & McAuliffe 333 Bush St San Francisco CA 91104

GUGLIELMINO, ROSARIO JOSEPH, lawyer; b. Buenos Aires, Argentina, Apr. 3, 1911; s. Rosario and Giuseppina (Lo Turco) G.; 1 son, Russell John. A.B. with honors, Cornell U., 1934, J.D., 1936. Bar: N.Y. 1936. Sole practice, Rochester, N.Y., 1936—; exec. dir. and counsel Police Adv. Bd., 1963-70; counsel Eye Bank Assn. Am., 1963-70, Assn. Blind of Rochester and Monroe County, Inc., 1975—; pres. Rochester Radio Reading Service, Inc., 1983—. Bd. visitors Albion State Tng. Sch. and Western Reformatory for Women, 1956-66; founder, pres. Rochester Eye and Human Parts Banks, Inc., 1952, pres. emeritus, 1954—; founder, pres. Eye Bank Assn. Am., 1961-63; pres. Children's Meml. Scholarship Fund, 1958-60; mem. Rochester Council State Commn. Against Discrimination, 1956-66; bd. dirs. Assn. Blind of Rochester and Monroe County, Inc., 1973—; bd. visitors Batavia Sch. Blind, 1979—. Named Citizen of Yr., Valguarnera Soc., 1977; recipient Heise award Eye Bank Assn. Am., 1975. Mem. ABA, N.Y. State Bar Assn., Monroe County Bar Assn. (pres. 1969), N.Y. State Trial Lawyers Assn., Am. Judicature Soc., Am. Arbitration Assn., Phi Beta Kappa, Phi Kappa Phi. General practice, Probate, Real property. Home: 68 Fairlane Dr Rochester NY 14626 Office: 134 S Fitzhugh St Rochester NY 14608

GUIDO, DIANA LYDIA, lawyer; b. Berkeley, Calif., July 8, 1954; d. Salvador J. and Antonietta (D'Lessandro) G.; m. Donald Charles Schwartz, Aug. 26, 1984. BA, U. Calif., Berkeley, 1976; MA, U. San Francisco, 1978; JD, U. Golden Gate, 1982. Bar: Calif. 1984, U.S. Dist. Ct. (no. dist.) Calif. 1984, U.S. Ct. Appeals (9th cir.) 1986. Assoc. Law Offices of James J. Duryea, San Francisco, 1982-85; assoc., mng. atty. Ericksen, Arbuthnot, Walsh, Paynter & Brown, San Jose, Calif., 1985-86; assoc. Tarkington, O'Connor & O'Neill, San Francisco, 1986—. Mem. ABA, San Francisco Bar Assn., Santa Clara Bar Assn., Assn. Trial Lawyers Am., Calif. Young Lawyers Assn. State civil litigation, Insurance, Personal injury. Office: Tarkington O'Connor & O'Neill One Market Plaza Spear St Tower 19th Fl San Francisco CA 94105

GUIDRY, GREGORY, lawyer; b. New Orleans, Apr. 1, 1951; s. Lou Ira and Shirley M. (Gautreaux) G.; m. Ramsey Marie Perron, Dec. 27, 1974; children: Stephen, Caroline. BA cum laude, La State U., 1973, JD, 1976. Bar: La. 1976, Tex. 1977, U.S. Dist. Ct. (so. dist.) Tex., U.S. Dist. Ct. (ea., mid. and we. dists.) La., U.S. Ct. Appeals (5th cir.), U.S. Supreme Ct. Assoc. Fulbright & Jaworski, Houston, 1976-79, Onebane, Donohoe, et. al., Lafayette, La., 1979-82; ptnr. Lafayette, La., 1982—. Editor, sr. assoc. La. State U. Law Rev., 1975-76; contbr. articles to profl. jours. Mem. ABA, La. Bar Assn., Tex. Bar Assn., Am. Soc. Hosp. Attys., La. Nursing Home Assn. (spl. labor counsel 1985—), Order of Coif, Phi Kappa Phi, Mu Sigma Rho, C. of C. Roman Catholic. Avocations: hunting, fishing, golf, tennis. Labor. Home: 105 Clipper Cove Lafayette LA 70508 Office: PO Drawer 3507 102 Versailles Blvd Lafayette LA 70502

GUIDRY, HERVIN A., lawyer; b. New Orleans, Dec. 20, 1955; s. Hervin J. Jr. and Mary Ann (Richards) G. BA, La. State U., 1977, JD, 1980. Bar: La. 1981, U.S. Dist. Ct. (ea. and mid. dists.) La. 1983, U.S. Dist. Ct. (we. dist.) La. 1985. Law clk. to presiding justice La. Supreme Ct., New Orleans, 1981, La. Ct. Appeals (1st cir.), Baton Rouge, 1981-83; assoc. Barham & Churchill, New Orleans, 1983—. La. State Law Alumni Assn. scholar, 1979, 80. Mem. ABA, Fed. Bar Assn., La. Bar Assn., New Orleans Bar Assn., New Orleans C. of C. Avocation: sailing. Federal civil litigation, State civil litigation. Home: 12961 Jeannee Ct New Orleans LA 70128 Office: Barham & Churchill 400 Lafayette Suite 300 New Orleans LA 70130

GUIER, LESTER BENNETT, lawyer; b. Cadiz, Ky., Aug. 8, 1955; s. Leslie Arthur and Jane Rhea (Herndon) G.; m. Kathy Marie Crawford, Aug. 23, 1980; children: Amanda Marie, Nathaniel Bennett, Samuel Crawford. AA, Hopkinsville Community Coll., 1975; BA, U. Ky., 1977, JD, 1980. Bar: Ky., U.S. Dist. Ct. (we. dist.) Ky. Ptnr. Rorie & Guier, Hopkinsville, Ky., 1980—. Coordinator Boy Scouts Am., Hopkinsville, 1982-83. Mem. ABA, Ky. Bar Assn., Christian County Bar Assn., Jaycees (named one of Outstanding Young Men of Am. 1984). Democrat. Baptist. Lodge: Mason (master 1984, sec. 1985—). General practice, State civil litigation, Family and matrimonial. Home: 317 Wayne Dr Hopkinsville KY 42240 Office: Rorie & Guier 7th and Main St. Hopkinsville KY 42240

GUILD, A. COURTNEY, JR., lawyer; b. Richmond, Va.; s. A. Courtney and Caroline (Huddle) G.; m. Linda Spencer; children: Courtney Lynne, John Spencer, Lindsay Allyn. B, Va. Poly. Inst. and State U., 1970; JD, U. Louisville, 1976. Bar: Ky. 1976, U.S. Dist. Ct. (we. dist.) Ky. 1978, U.S. Dist. Ct. (ea. dist.) Ky. 1985. Assoc. Goldberg & Simpson, Louisville, 1976—. Office: 2800 1st Nat Tower Louisville KY 40202

GUILD, ALDEN, life insurance company executive; b. Boston, July 3, 1929; s. Howard Redwood and Frances Allen (Warren) G.; m. Ruth Ineta Creighton, Sept. 14, 1957; 1 child, Heather Louise. B.A., Dartmouth Coll., 1952; J.D., U. Chgo., 1957; LL.D. (hon.), Norwich/Vt. Coll., 1977. Bar: Vt. 1958. With law dept. Nat. Life Ins. Co., Montpelier, Vt., 1957—; asst. v.p., counsel, corp. sec. Nat. Life Ins. Co., 1974-83, v.p., gen. counsel, 1983—. Contbr. legal jours. Trustee Norwich U., 1972—, Vt. Coll., 1967—, Kimball U. Acad., 1972-74, Wood Art Gallery, 1961-72; mem. Dartmouth Coll. Alumni Council, 1975-78. Served with USAF, 1950-53, Korea. Recipient Disting. Service award Montpelier Jr. C. of C., 1962. Mem. ABA, Vt. Bar Assn., Assn. Life Ins. Counsel, Am. Council Life Ins. (state v.p.), VFW, Phi Beta Kappa, Order of Coif, Theta Chi. Republican. Club: Lake Mansfield Trout (Stowe, Vt.). Lodges: Masons, Elks. General corporate, Insurance, Securities. Home: Murray Rd RD 1 Montpelier VT 05602 Office: Nat Life Ins Co National Life Dr Montpelier VT 05604

GUILD, CLARK JOSEPH, JR., lawyer; b. Yerington, Nev., May 14, 1921; s. Clark Joseph and Virginia Ellen (Carroll) G.; m. Elizabeth Ann Ashley, July 20, 1945 (div. 1977); children—Clark J., Jeffrey S., Daniel E., Jann Cademartori; m. Joan Kathleen Brown, Mar. 30, 1984. B.A., U. Nev., 1943; J.D., Georgetown U., 1948. Bar: Nev. 1948, U.S. Dist. Ct. (no. dist.) Nev. 1948, U.S. Ct. Appeals (D.C. cir.) 1948, U.S. Supreme Ct. 1959, U.S. Ct. Appeals (9th cir.) 1984. Ptnr. Guild, Hagen & Clark, Ltd., Reno, Nev., 1953—; dir. S.W. Gas Corp., Las Vegas. Pres. YMCA, Reno, 1954, 64; regent U. Nev. System, 1972. Served to capt. inf. U.S. Army, 1942-46. Fellow Am. Coll. Trial Lawyers; mem. ABA, State Bar Nev., Clark County Bar Assn., Washoe County Bar Assn. (pres. 1959-60) Democrat. Episcopalian. Lodges: Masons, Elks. State civil litigation, Federal civil litigation, General practice. Office: Guild Hagen & Clark Ltd 102 Roff Way Reno NV 89501

GUILFORD, ANDREW JOHN, lawyer; b. Santa Monica, Calif., Nov. 28, 1950; s. Howard Owens and Elsie Jennette (Hargreaves) G.; m. Loreen Mary Gogain, Dec. 22, 1973; children: Colleen Catherine, Amanda Joy. AB summa cum laude, UCLA, 1972, JD, 1975. Bar: Calif. 1976, U.S. Dist. Ct. (cen. dist.) Calif. 1976, U.S. Ct. Appeals (9th cir.) 1976, U.S. Supreme Ct. 1979, U.S. Dist. Ct. (so. dist.) Calif. 1981. Assoc. Sheppard, Mullin, Richter & Hampton, Los Angeles and Newport Beach, Calif., 1975-82; ptnr. Sheppard, Mullin, Richter & Hampton, Newport Beach, 1983—; lectr. The Rutter Group, Encino, Calif., 1983—; judge pro tem, arbitrator Calif. Superior Ct., 1983—. Mem. Amicus Publico, Santa Ana, Calif., 1986—, Ctr. 500. Regents scholar U. Calif., Berkeley, 1968-72. Mem. ABA, Assn. Bus. Trial Lawyers, Calif. Bar Assn. (lectr. continuing edn. of the bar 1978—), Fed. Bar Assn., Orange County Bar Assn. (bd. dirs. 1985—, chmn. bus. litigation sect. 1983, chmn. delegation to state bar convention 1986, 87), Phi Beta Kappa (sec., treas. 1978-80, v.p. 1980-84), Pi Gamma Mu (subdeacon, warden, del. 1976—), Sigma Pi. Republican. Episcopalian. Avocations: theater, photography, sports, gardening, poetry. State civil litigation, Federal civil litigation, Contracts commercial. Home: 24756 Scott Ln Lake Forest CA 92630 Office: Sheppard Mullin Richter & Hampton 4695 MacArthur Ct 7th Floor Newport Beach CA 92660

GUILLIOT, PAUL JEROME, lawyer; b. Lafayette, La., Feb. 20, 1950; s. Roy and Joyce (Blanchet) G.; m. Christine Simon, June 15, 1976 (div. 1980); m. Sandrea Lane Everett, May 31, 1984. Student, La. State U., 1969-72; JD, Loyola U., New Orleans, 1975; LLM, So. Meth. U., 1977. Bar: La. 1975. Law clk. to presiding judge U.S. Dist. Ct. (we. dist.) La., Lafayette, 1975-76; assoc. Law Offices of R. Kennedy, Lafayette, 1978-79, Law Offices of J. Piccione, Lafayette, 1979-82; sole practice Lafayette, 1982-85; ptnr. Guilliot, Skinner & Everett, Lafayette, 1985—; local counsel Patterson Ins. Agy., So. Security Ins. Co., Bossier City, La., 1984—. Mem. ABA, Assn. Trial Lawyers Am., La. Trial Lawyers Assn. (steering com. 1986—), Lafayette C. of C. Democrat. Roman Catholic. Avocations: tennis, astronomy. Admiralty, Personal injury, State civil litigation. Home: 33 Audubon Oaks Blvd Lafayette LA 70506

GUILLOT, ELAINE WOLFE, lawyer; b. New Orleans, Mar. 8, 1943; d. Arnold Raymond and Marie Louise (Blanchard) W.; m. Arthur Joseph Guillot Jr., June 16, 1962 (div. Sept. 1982); children: Janine Marie, Stacey Anne; m. John Lucien DiMiceli Jr., Dec. 22, 1984. BBA, Loyola U., New Orleans, 1967, MBA, 1971, JD, 1977. Bar: La. 1970. Ptnr., sec., treas. Alford & Guillot Ltd., Slidell, La., 1977—; instr. bus. law Delgado Coll., Slidell, 1981-83; contract atty. St. Tammany Office Human Devel., Covington, La., 1981-85; atty. City of Slidell, 1983—. Co-founder council St. Tammany Victims of Family Violence, Slidell, 1978; chmn. East St. Tammany March of Dimes, Slidell, 1978; bd. dirs. community action agy. St. Tammany Parish, Covington, La., 1983. Named one of Outstanding Young Women Slidell Jaycees, 1977. Mem. ABA, La. Bar Assn. (ho. of dels. 1981-82), Slidell Bar Assn. (pres. 1981-82), St. Tammany Bar Assn. (treas. 1982—), Slidell Bus. and Profl. Womens Club (v.p. 1980, Woman of Yr. 1982), La. City Attys. Assn., Slidell C. of C. (bd. dirs., treas. 1982-84), Beta Sigma Phi. Avocations: sailing, gardening, hunting. Government contracts and claims, Local government, Real property. Office: City of Slidell 2055 Second St PO Box 828 Slidell LA 70459

GUIMOND, ROBERT WILFRID, medical physiology educator, lawyer; b. Fall River, Mass., Sept. 4, 1939; s. Romeo A. and Jeannette (Boissoneault) G.; m. Elaine Brodie, July 13, 1963; children—Jefferson, Jameson. B.A. in

History, U. R.I., 1961, Ph.D. in Physiology, 1970; J.D., New Eng. Sch. Law, 1978. Bar: Mass. 1978. Asst. prof. zoology U. R.I., Kingston, 1970-71; prof. biology Boston State Coll., 1971-82; prof. biology U. Mass., Boston, 1982—; sole practice law, Boston and Fall River, 1978—. Mem. Am. Physiol. Soc., ABA, Am. Soc. Law and Medicine, Am. Forestry Assn., Nature Conservancy. Democrat. Roman Catholic. Personal injury, Real property, Estate planning. Home: 307 Montgomery St Fall River MA 02720 Office: U Mass Harbor Campus Biology Dept Boston MA 02125

GUIN, JUNIUS FOY, JR., judge; b. Russellville, Ala., Feb. 2, 1924; s. Junius Foy and Ruby (Pace) G.; m. Dorace Jean Caldwell, July 18, 1945; children: Janet Elizabeth Smith, Judith Ann Mullican, Junius Foy III, David Jonathan. Student, Ga. Inst. Tech., 1940-41; A.B. magna cum laude; J.D., U. Ala., 1947; LL.D., Magic Valley Christian Coll., 1963. Bar: Ala. bar 1948. Practiced in Russellville; sr. partner firm Guin, Guin, Bouldin & Porch, 1948-73; fed. dist. judge Birmingham, Ala., 1973—; commr. Ala. Bar, 1965-73, 2d v.p., 1969-70; Pres. Abstract Trust Co., Inc., 1958-73; sec. Iuka TV Cable Co., Inc., Haleyville TV Cable Co., Inc., 1963-73; former dir., gen. counsel First Nat. Bank of Russellville, Franklin Fed. Savs. & Loan Assn. of Russellville.; Lectr. Cumberland-Samford Sch. Law, 1974—, U. Ala. Sch. Law, 1977—. Chmn. Russellville City Planning Com., 1954-57; 1st chmn. Jud. Commn. Ala., 1972-73; mem. Ala. Supreme Ct. Adv. Com. (rules civil procedure), 1971-73; mem. adv. com. on standards of conduct U.S. Jud. Conf., 1980—, mem. subcom. on Fed.-State relations (ct. adminstrv. com.); Republican county chmn., 1954-58, 71-72, Rep. state fin. chmn., 1972-73; candidate for U.S. Senator from, Ala., 1954; Ala. Lawyers' Finance chmn. Com. to Re-elect Pres., 1972; trustee Ala. Christian Coll. Served to 1st lt., inf. AUS, 1943-46. Named Russellville Citizen of Year, 1973; recipient Dean's award U. Ala. Law Sch., 1977. Mem. Am. Radio Relay League, ABA (mem. spl. com. on residential real estate transactions 1972-73), Ala. Bar Assn. (com. chmn. 1965-73, award of Merit 1973), Jefferson County Bar Assn., Fed. Bar Assn., Am. Law Inst., Ala. Law Inst. (dir. 1969-73, 76—), Am. Judicature Soc., World Peace Through Law Center, Farrah Law Soc., Farrah Order Jurisprudence (now Order of Coif), Quarter Century Wireless Assn., Phi Beta Kappa, Delta Chi. Mem. Ch. of Christ (elder). Jurisprudence. Office: US District Court 619 Federal Courthouse Birmingham AL 35203 *

GULARTIE, LOUISE BAUR, lawyer; b. Munich, Mar. 24, 1953; came to U.S., 1955; d. John Kenneth and Irene Maria Gulartie; m. Gary Eugene Uhd, Dec. 1, 1983; 1 child, Justin Edward. BA, U. Calif., Berkeley, 1974; JD, Southwestern U., 1978. Bar: Calif. 1978. Sole practice Los Angeles, 1981-82; ptnr. Gulartie and Uhd, Pasadena, Calif., 1982—. Judge pro tem Los Angeles County Mcpl. Cts., 1982-86; com. chmn. Friends of Kevin Martin, Pasadena, 1986. Mem. Calif. Attys. for Criminal Justice, Calif. Pub. Defenders Assn., Pasadena Young Lawyers Assn. (treas. 1982, v.p. 1983), Pasadena Bar Assn. Democrat. Roman Catholic. Avocations: fishing, antiques. Criminal, Administrative and regulatory, Landlord-tenant. Office: Gulartie and Uhd 221 E Walnut #110 Pasadena CA 91101

GULDEN, SIMON, lawyer, foods and beverages company executive; b. Montreal, Que., Can., Jan. 7, 1938; s. David and Zelda (Long) G.; m. Ellen Lee Barbour, June 12, 1977. B.A., McGill U., Montreal, 1959; LL.L., U. Montreal, 1962. Bar: Que. Ptnr. Genser, Philips, Friedman & Gulden, Montreal, 1963-68; sec., legal counsel Pl. Bonaventure, Inc., 1969-72; legal counsel real estate Steinberg Inc., Montreal, 1972-74; solicitor, prime atty. Bell Can., Montreal, 1975-76; v.p., gen. counsel, sec. Nabisco Brands Ltd, Toronto, 1976—. Mem. Internat. Assn. Lawyers and Jurists, Internat. Fiscal Assn., Can. Bar Assn., Internat. Bar Assn., Lord Reading Law Soc. Que., Toronto Bd. Trade, Assn. Conseils Franctization Que., Advt. and Sales Execs. Club, Am. Mgmt. Assn., Inst. Chartered Secs. and Adminstrs. (cert.), Osgoode Law Soc. Clubs: Island Yacht, Canadian, Cambridge (Toronto). General corporate. Home: 23 Danbury Ct, Unionville, ON Canada L3R 7S1 Office: 1 Dundas St W Suite 2900, Toronto, ON Canada M5G 2A9

GULEKE, JAMES O., II, lawyer; b. Amarillo, Tex., Sept. 5, 1948; s. James Seewald and Gaynor Norwood (Van Shaw) G.; m. Linda Kay Smith, Sept. 2, 1978; children—Martha Kathryn, Elizabeth Ann. B.A. with honors, U. Tex., 1970, J.D., 1974. Bar: Tex. 1974, U.S. Dist. Ct. (we. dist.) Tex. 1976. Assoc. Daugherty, Kuperman, Golden & Morehead, P.C., Austin, Tex., 1974-82, dir., 1982—; real estate broker, 1974—. Co-author article Tex. Bar Jour. (Tex. Bar Found. award 1981). Mayor, City of Rollingwood, Tex., 1980-84; bd. dirs. Child and Family Service of Austin, 1978-82; del. Tex. Democratic Conv., 1984; bd. dirs. Austin-Travis County Livestock Show, 1985—. Served to 1st. Air N.G., 1970-72, USAFR, 1972-80. Mem. ABA, Travis County Bar Assn., Tex. Assn. of Bank Counsel, Assn. Trial Lawyers Am., Tex. Trial Lawyers Assn. Presbyterian. State civil litigation, Federal civil litigation, General practice. Home: 5 Randolph Pl Austin TX 78746 Office: Daugherty Kuperman Golden et al 1500 Am Bank Tower Austin TX 78701

GULICK, PETER VANDYKE, lawyer; b. Honolulu, Feb. 15, 1930; s. Willard Clark and Harriet (Winch) G.; m. Kathryn Christen, June 23, 1952; children—Willard, Sarah, Scott. A.B., Princeton U., 1952; postgrad. Stanford U., 1952-53; LL.B., U. Wash., 1956. Bar: Wash. 1956, U.S. Dist. Ct. (we. dist.) Wash. 1956, U.S. Ct. Appeals (9th cir.) 1957. Mem. Foster, Pepper & Riviera, Seattle, 1956-78; sole practice, Bellevue, Wash., 1979—. Scoutmaster, dist. Round Table commr., chief Seattle council Boy Scouts Am., 1971-77; pres. Lake Heights Community Club, 1960; commr. Newport Hills Sewer Dist., 1966-72. Recipient dist. merit award Boy Scouts Am., 1976. Mem. ABA, Wash. State Bar Assn., Seattle-King County Bar Assn., East King County Bar Assn. Real property, Contracts commercial, General corporate.

GULINO, FRANK, lawyer; b. Bklyn., Aug. 14, 1954; s. Frank C. and Frances (Cataldo) G.; m. Donna Regina Cramer, June 30, 1984. BA, NYU, 1976; JD, Fordham U., 1979. Bar: N.Y. 1980, U.S. Dist. Ct. (no., so. ea. and we. dists.) N.Y. 1980, U.S. Tax Ct. 1980, U.S. Ct. Mil. Appeals 1980, U.S. Ct. Appeals (2d cir.) 1980, U.S. Ct. Internat. Trade 1982, U.S. Supreme Ct. 1983, U.S. Ct. Claims 1985, U.S. Ct. Appeals (8th and fed. cirs.) 1985, D.C. 1986, U.S. Dist. Ct. Nebr. 1986, U.S. Dist. Ct. Hawaii 1986, U.S. Ct. Appeals (3d, 5th, 6th, 7th, 9th, 10th and 11th cirs.) 1986. Law clk. to U.S. magistrate U.S. Dist. Ct. (so. dist.) N.Y., N.Y.C., 1979-80; assoc. Donovan, Leisure, Newton & Irvine, N.Y.C., 1980-83, Carro, Spanbock, Fass, Geller, Kaster & Cuiffo, N.Y.C., 1984-86; dep. gen. counsel N.Y.C. Housing Authority, 1986—; adj. assoc. prof. Fordham U. Sch. Law, N.Y.C., 1983—. Mem. ABA, Fed. Bar Assn., Fed. Bar Council, N.Y. State Bar Assn. (atty. advisor high sch. mock trial program 1980—), Fordham U. Alumni Assn. (bd. dirs. Urban Law Jour. 1982—, pres. 1984-85). Local government, State civil litigation, Administrative and regulatory. Office: NYC Housing Authority 250 Broadway New York NY 10007

GULKO, PAUL MICHAEL, insurance executive; b. Boston, Feb. 19, 1944; s. Jacob and Helen (Bornstein) G.; m. Judith Silbert, Sept. 20, 1970 (div. Mar. 1983); children—Harlan David, Brett Robert. B.A., Northeastern U., 1966; J.D., Suffolk U. Law Sch., 1970. Bar: Mass. 1971, U.S. Dist. Ct. Mass. 1971, U.S. Supreme Ct. 1978. Counsel Mass. Div. Ins., Boston, 1971-75; mgr., exec. sec. Mass. Insurers Insolvency Fund, R.I. Insurers Insolvency Fund, Conn., N.H., Wash., Vt., Maine, Va. Ins. Guaranty Assns., Boston, 1975; pres. Guaranty Fund Mgmt. Services, Boston, 1981—. Bd. dirs. Temple Israel, Swampscott, Mass., 1975-78, Jewish Rehab. Ctr. North Shore, Swampscott, 1976-80. Mem. ABA (chmn.-elect pub. regulation ins. law com.), Nat. Assn. of Ins. Commrs. (rehabilitators and liquidators task force, chmn. industry adv. com.), Nat. Com. of Ins. Guaranty Funds (task force mem. ops. com.). Democrat. Insurance. Office: 25 New Chardon St Boston MA 02114

GULLETT, B. BURTON, lawyer; b. Manchester, Tenn., Dec. 9, 1905; s. William Jefferson and Esta (Bryan) G.; m. Landis Shaw Bass; children—Virginia, Brenda. A.B., Cumberland U., Tenn., 1927, LL.B., 1927; postgrad., Vanderbilt U., Tenn., 1927-29. Bar: Tenn. 1927. Sole practice law Nashville, 1927-57; ptnr. White, Gullett, Phillips & Steele, Nashville, 1957-63, Gullett, Sanford & Robinson, Nashville, 1963—. Served to lt. col. USAF, 1942-46; ETO. Named Disting. Alumnus Cumberland Sch. Law, Samford U., 1970. Fellow Am. Bar Found., Tenn. Bar Found.; mem. ABA (ho. dels. 1968—, bd. govs. 1984—), Nashville Bar Assn. (pres. 1959-60), Tenn. Bar Assn. (pres. 1967-68), Jud. Conf. for Sixth Circuit (life), Am. Judicature Soc., Nashville C. of C., Kappa Sigma. Democrat. Methodist. Clubs: Exchange, Belle Meade Country, Nashville City, Cumberland (Nashville). Lodges: Masons (32 degree), Shriners (knight comdr. Ct. of Honor). Office: Gullett Sanford & Robinson PO Box 2757 Nashville TN 37219

GULLEY, DAVID WESLEY, state judge; b. Uvalde, Tex., Dec. 19, 1931; s. Titus David and Ola Elizabeth (Haygood) G.; m. Emma Jane Hampton, Aug. 13, 1966; 1 child, Cameron David. A.A., S.W. Tex. Jr. Coll., 1951; B.S. in Bus. Adminstrn., Trinity U., 1953; M.A. in Pub. Adminstrn., U. Tex., 1961, J.D., 1965; grad. Tex. Coll. Judiciary, 1977. Bar: Tex. 1965, U.S. Dist. Ct. no. dist.) Tex. 1966, U.S. Dist. Ct. (we. dist.) Tex. 1968, U.S. Ct. Appeals (5th cir.) 1967, U.S. Supreme Ct. 1970, U.S. Tax Ct. 1974, U.S. Ct. Appeals (11th cir.) 1981. Tchr. Sam Houston High Sch., San Antonio; research asst. Inst. Pub. Affairs, U. Tex. and State Comptroller's Office; adminstrv. analyst City Mgr.'s and Research and Budget Offices, Fort Worth; asst. city atty. City of Fort Worth, 1965-68; assoc. Witherspoon, Aikin, Langley, Woods & Gulley, Hereford, Tex., 1968-71, ptnr., 1971-76; gen. counsel, bus. mgr. George Warner Seed Co., Inc., 1976-77; dist. judge 222d Jud. Dist. of Tex., 1977—; mem. faculty Tex. Criminal Trial Advocacy Inst., Criminal Justice Ctr., Huntsville, Tex., 1980, 81, Tex. Regional Jud. Confs. Sems., 1987; mem. edn. com. Nat. Conf. State Trial Judges; mem. non-urban ct. com. Nat. Council Juvenile and Family Ct. Judges. Bd. dirs. Hereford chpt. Am. Cancer Soc., Hereford and vicinity YMCA, Hereford Community Concert Assn.; trustee Hereford Presbyn. Ch.; former gen. chmn. goals and progress com. Hereford and Deaf Smith County; chmn. troop com. Boy Scouts Am., exec. bd. Golden Spread Council. Fellow Tex. Bar Found.; mem. Am. Judicature Soc., ABA (jud. adminstrn. div., gen. practice sect., advocacy com., litigation sect.), Am. Judges Assn., Am. Polit. Sci. Assn. (law, cts. and jud. process sect.), Am. Legion, Blue Key, Phi Theta Kappa, Phi Sigma Alpha, Phi Delta Phi. Lodges: Masons, Shriners. Judicial administration, State civil litigation, Criminal. Home: 701 Country Club Rd Hereford TX 79045 Office: Room 305 County Courthouse Dist Judge 222d Jud Dist of Tex PO Box 1898 Hereford TX 79045

GULLEY, JACK HAYGOOD, lawyer; b. Uvalde County, Tex., Dec. 29, 1935; s. David and Elizabeth (Haygood) G. B.S., Trinity U., San Antonio, 1958; J.D., U. Tex.-Austin, 1962. Bar: Tex., U.S. Dist. Ct. (we. and so. dists.) Tex., U.S. Ct. Appeals (5th cir.), U.S. Supreme Ct. Assoc., Suttle & Kesser, Uvalde, Tex., 1964-65, George Red, Houston, 1965-66; ptnr. Doran, Gulley & Etzel, Del Rio, Tex., 1966—. Mem. Tex. Bar Assn., Val Verde County Bar Assn. Democrat. Clubs: Rotary (Del Rio), Mason (Uvalde). General practice, Federal civil litigation, State civil litigation. Address: PO Box 420248 Del Rio TX 78842

GULLEY, KENNETH GALEN, lawyer; b. Denver, May 29, 1950; s. Raymond Abraham and Carol Joan (Hess) G.; m. Barbara Ann Just, Nov. 30, 1974; children: Marne Christine, Meghan Kathleen. BS, Colo. State U., 1972; JD, Gonzaga U., 1977. Bar: Colo. 1977, U.S. Dist. Ct. Colo. 1977. Assoc. Weller, Friedrich, Hickisch & Hazlitt, Denver, 1978-80; sr. atty. Manville Corp., Denver, 1980-82; ptnr. Downey & Gulley P.C., Denver, 1982—. Pres. elect Faith Luth. Ch., Castle Rock, Colo., 1986—. Mem. ABA, Colo. Bar Assn., Denver Bar Assn., Colo. Def. Lawyers Assn. (pres. 1985-86). Republican. Avocations: racquetball, basketball. Insurance, Construction, State civil litigation. Home: 511 Coronado Dr Sedalia CO 80135 Office: Downey & Gulley PC 950 S Cherry St # 1210 Denver CO 80222

GULLEY, WILLIAM LOUIS, lawyer, insurance companies executive; b. Crozet, Va., Nov. 27, 1930; s. Julius Paul and Myrtle Kent (Moon) G.; m. Donna Marilyn Pearce, Sept 11, 1952; 1 son, Stuart Kent. J.D., T. C. Williams Sch. Law, U. Richmond, 1959. Bar: Va. 1959, Mich. 1983. Sole practice, town atty. and substitute county judge, Culpeper, Va., 1959-64; With Nationwide Ins., 1964-77, group claims atty., 1975-77; v.p., gen. counsel Mich. Life and Nat. Casualty Cos., subs. Nationwide Ins., Southfield, Mich., 1977-83, v.p. benefits, gen. counsel, 1983—; sr. v.p., gen. counsel Hickey Mitchell Agy., 1983—. Served to sgt. U.S. Army, 1952-55. Mem. Va. Bar, ABA, Internat. Claim Assn., Phi Alpha Delta. Lodge: Elks (Howell, Mich.). Insurance, General corporate. Office: Nat Casualty Co PO Box 8077 St Louis MO 63108

GULOTTA, FRANK ANDREW, JR., lawyer; b. N.Y.C., Nov. 2, 1939; s. Frank A. and Josephine M. (Giardina) G.; m. Joanne C. DeLessio, Jan. 29, 1966; children: Lisa, Frank A. BA, Trinity Coll., 1961; JD, Columbia U., 1964. Bar: N.Y. 1965, U.S. Dist. Ct. (ea. dist.) N.Y. 1972, U.S. Supreme Ct. 1970. Asst. dist. atty. Nassau County (N.Y.), 1965-69; prin. Gulotta & Stein, Mineola, N.Y., 1969—; dir. Am. Com. Italian Migration; counsel for Sen. Ralph Marino, Com. on Crime, 1979-82. Mem. ABA, Nat. Assn. Criminal Def. Attys., N.Y. State Sheriffs Assn. (grievance com. 10th jud. dist. 1986—), N.Y. State Bar Assn., Nassau County Bar Assn. (chmn. grievance com. 1983-85, bd. dirs. 1984—) Criminal Courts Bar Assn., Former Asst. Dist. Attys. Assn. (dir., past pres.), N.Y. State Dist. Atty. Assn., Nat. Dist. Attys. Assn., Am. Judicature Soc., Columbian Lawyers Assn. (dir.). Lodges: Elks, KC. Roman Catholic. General practice, Criminal, Family and matrimonial. Office: 1539 Franklin Ave Mineola NY 11501

GUNCKEL, STUART SQUIER, lawyer; b. Hays, Kans., Nov. 23, 1936; s. Clarence L. and Mary E. (Squier) G.; m. Patricia A. Painton, Aug. 28, 1959; children: Kristin L., Stephanie L. BS, U. Kans., 1958, LLB, 1961. Bar: Colo. 1963. Assoc. Kuraner & Freeman, Kansas City, Mo., 1961-63; ptnr. Akolt, Shepherd, Dick & Rovira, Denver, 1963-74; atty. Mountain Bell, Denver, 1974-79, gen. atty., 1979-83, assoc. gen. counsel, 1983-84, v.p., gen. counsel, sec., 1984—. Served with USAR, 1962-68. Mem. ABA, Colo. Bar Assn., Denver Bar Assn., Colo. Assn. Corp. Counsel. Republican. Clubs: University, Skyline Acres (Denver) (pres. 1980), Petroleum. Avocations: hiking, skiing, tennis. General corporate. Home: 4020 S Holly St Englewood CO 80111 Office: Mountain Bell 1801 California St #5100 Denver CO 80202

GUNDERSON, ELMER MILLARD, state justice; b. Mpls., Aug. 9, 1929; s. Elmer Peter and Carmaleta (Oliver) G.; m. Lupe Gomez, Dec. 29, 1967; 1 son, John Randolph. Student, U. Minn., U. Omaha, 1948-53; LL.B., Creighton U., 1956; LL.M., U. Va., 1982; LL.D., Calif. Western Sch. Law; student appellate judges seminar, N.Y. U., 1971; LL.D., U. Pacific. Bar: Nebr. bar 1956, Nev. bar 1958. Atty.-adviser FTC, 1956-57; pvt. practice Las Vegas, 1958-71; justice Nev. Supreme Ct., 1971—, now chief justice; instr. bus. law So. regional div. U. Nev.; lectr., author bulls. felony crimes for Clark County Sheriff's Dept.; counsel Sheriff's Protective Assn.; mem. legal staff Clark Council Civil Def. Agy.; legal counsel Nev. Jaycees. Compiler, annotator: Omaha Home Rule Charter; project coordinator: Jud. Orientation Manual, 1974. Chmn. Clark County Child Welfare Bd., Nev. central chpt. Nat. Multiple Sclerosis Soc.; hon. dir. Spring Mountain Youth Camp. Served with U.S. Army. Recipient A.J.S. Herbert Harley award. Mem. Am., Nebr., Nev. bar assns.; Mem. Inst. Jud. Adminstrn., Am. Law Inst., Am. Trial Lawyers Assn., Am. Judicature Soc., Phi Alpha Delta, Alpha Sigma Nu. Jurisprudence. Office: Supreme Ct Bldg Carson City NV 89710 *

GUNDERSON, MICHAEL ARTHUR, lawyer; b. Flint, Mich., Nov. 3, 1952; s. Robert Edward and Phyllis Elaine (Cronin) G.; m. Patricia Beatrice Holstein, Jan. 4, 1980; children: Eric Brendan, Ryan Dane. B.A., U. Mich., 1974; postgrad. Gonzaga U. Law Sch., 1974; J.D., Detroit Coll. Law, 1978. Bar: Mich. 1978, U.S. Dist. Ct. (ea. dist.) Mich. 1978, U.S. Dist. Ct. (we. dist.) Mich. 1980. Mem. firm Harvey, Kruse & Westen, P.C., Detroit, 1978-79, Fitgerald, Hodgman, Kazul, Rutledge, Cawthrone & King, P.C., Detroit, 1979-85; ptnr. Rutledge, Manion, Rabaut, Terry & Thomas, P.C., Detroit, 1986—; rep. assembly State Bar Mich., 1987—. Notes and comment editor Detroit Coll. Law Rev., 1976-77. Mem. ABA, Catholic Lawyers Soc. Detroit (pres. 1984-86, bd. dirs. 1981—), Mich. Bar Assn. , Detroit Bar Assn., Oakland County Bar Assn., Def. Research Inst., Am. Arbitration Assn. (arbitrator), Mich. Def. Trial Counsel, Incorp. Soc. Irish Am. Lawyers (bd. dirs. 1987—), Assn. Def. Trial Counsel, Delta Theta Phi. Republican. Roman Catholic. Personal injury, Insurance, State civil litigation. Home: 659 Rivard Blvd Grosse Pointe MI 48230 Office: Rutledge Manion Rabaut Terry & Thomas PC 2300 Buhl Bldg Detroit MI 48226

GUNDERSON, ROBERT VERNON, JR., lawyer; b. Memphis, Dec. 4, 1951; s. Robert V. and Suzanne (McCarthy) G.; m. Anne Durkheimer, May 15, 1982; children: Katherine Paige, Robert Graham. BA with distinction, U. Kans., 1973; MBA, U. Penn., 1974; MA, Stanford U., 1976; JD, U. Chgo., 1979. Bar: Calif. 1979, U.S. Dist. Ct. (no. dist.) Calif. 1979. Assoc. Cooley, Godward, Castro, Huddleson & Tatum, San Francisco and Palo Alto, Calif., 1979-84, ptnr., 1984—; panelist Venture Capital and Pub. Offering Negotiation, San Francisco and N.Y.C., 1981, 83, 85, Practicing Law Inst., N.Y.C. and San Francisco, 1986; moderator, panelist Third Ann. Securities Law Inst., 1985; sec. Dionex Corp., Sunnyvale, Calif., 1983—; visiting lectr. U. Santa Clara (Calif.) Law Sch., 1985. Exec. editor U. Chgo. Law Rev., 1978-79; contbr. articles to profl. jours. Mem. ABA (corps., banking and business law sects., various coms.), State Bar Calif. (panelist continuing legal edn. 1984), San Francisco Bar Assn., Am. Fin. Assn., Am. Soc. Corpoate Secs., Assn. Old Crows. Clubs: Wharton (San Francisco Bay Area). Avocations: contemporary art, music, travel. Securities, General corporate, Venture capital and emerging companies. Home: 243 Polhemus Ave Atherton CA 94025 Office: Cooley Godward et al 5 Palo Alto Sq Palo Alto CA 94306

GUNDLACH, NORMAN JOSEPH, lawyer; b. Belleville, Ill., May 23, 1907; s. Joseph E. and Bertha L. (Steudle) G.; m. Maxine Rain, Jan. 26, 1935; children: Gayle Gundlach McLean, Frank N. BS, U. Ill., 1928, LLB, 1931. Bar: Ill. 1931, Mo. 1931, U.S. Ct. Appeals (7th cir.) 1934, U.S. Ct. Appeals (8th cir.) 1934, U.S. Supreme Ct. 1946. Assoc., ptnr. Kramer, Campbell, Costello and Wiechert, Belleville, Ill., 1931; sr. ptnr. Gundlach, Lee, Eggmann, Boyle and Roessler, Belleville, 1954—; bd. dirs. various fin. institutions. Mem. U. Ill. Alumni Bd. Served with USNR, 1943-45. Mem. Ill. Bar Assn. (pres. 5th dist., chmn. various coms.), Mo. Bar (com.), Am. Coll. Trial Lawyers, Am. Bd. Trial Advs., East St. Louis Bar Assn. (pres.), St. Clair County Bar Assn. (pres.). Clubs: Media (St. Louis); St. Clair Country (Belleville); Garden of Gods (Colorado Springs, Colo.). Admiralty, Federal civil litigation, State civil litigation. Home: 19 S 78th St Belleville IL 62223 Office: Gundlach Lee et al 5000 W. Main St Belleville IL 62223

GUNN, ALAN, lawyer, legal educator; b. Syracuse, N.Y., Apr. 8, 1940; s. Albert Dale and Helen Sherwood (Whitnall) G.; m. Bertha Ann Buchwald, 1975; 1 child, William. B.S., Rensselaer Poly. Inst., 1961; J.D., Cornell U., 1970. Bar: D.C. 1970. Assoc. Hogan & Hartson, Washington, 1970-72; asst. prof. law Washington U., St. Louis, 1972-75, assoc. prof., 1975-76; assoc. prof. law Cornell U. Law Sch., Ithaca, N.Y., 1977-79, prof., 1979-84, J. duPratt White prof., 1984—. Author: Cases and Other Materials on Federal Income Taxation, 1981. Mem. ABA. Democrat. Personal income taxation, Corporate taxation, Personal injury. Home: 103 Midway Rd Ithaca NY 14850 Office: Cornell Law Sch Ithaca NY 14853

GUNN, MICHAEL PETER, lawyer; b. St. Louis, Oct. 18, 1944; s. Donald and Loretto Agnes (Hennelly) G.; m. Carolyn Ormsby Ritter, Nov. 27, 1969; children: Mark Thomas, Christopher Michael, John Ritter, Elizabeth Jane. JD, St. Louis U., 1968. Bar: Mo. 1968, U.S. Dist. Ct. (ea and we. dists.) Mo. 1968, U.S. Tax Ct. 1972. Assoc. Gunn & Gunn, St. Louis, 1968-81; ptnr. Gunn & Lane, St. Louis, 1981—. Chmn. lawyers sect. Archdiocese of St. Louis, 1976—. Served to sgt. U.S. Army, 1969-75. Mem. St. Louis County Bar, Bar Assn. Met. St. Louis (pres. 1987—), Lawyers Assn. St. Louis (pres. 1981-82). Roman Catholic. Probate, State civil litigation, Family and matrimonial. Home: 2232 Centeroyal Dr Des Peres MO 63131 Office: Gunn & Lane 818 Olive St Suite 660 Saint Louis MO 63101

GUNN, REBECCA LOUISE, lawyer, municipal judge; b. Ft. Dodge, Iowa, Mar. 16, 1951; d. Ralph Barnett and Margaret (Johnstone) G. Student, Kalamazoo Coll., 1969-71; B in Elected Studies, U. Minn., 1976; JD, Loyola U., Los Angeles, 1980; LLM in Tax Law, Denver U., 1986. Bar: Calif. 1980, Colo. 1981, U.S. Dist. Ct. Colo. 1981. Sole practice Loveland, Colo., 1981-85; ptnr. Weatherill & Gunn, Loveland, 1986—; asst. mcpl. judge City of Loveland, 1986—. Bd. dirs. Larimer County Vis. Nurses Assn. Mem. ABA, Colo. Bar Assn., Colo. Women's Bar Assn., Larimer County Women's Bar Assn. (treas. 1986). Avocations: volleyball, softball, camping, photography. Personal income taxation, Family and matrimonial, Bankruptcy. Home: 1105 W Shore Pl Loveland CO 80538 Office: Weatherill & Gunn 444 E 6th St Loveland CO 80537

GUNN, ROBERT RUSSELL, lawyer; b. Athens, Ga., Nov. 27, 1951; s. Uly S. and Margarett (Kallmeyer) G.; m. Brent Shuford, Aug. 24, 1974; children: Sam, Robert. BJ, U. Ga., 1974; JD, Mercer U., 1977. Bar: Ga. 1977, U.S. Dist. Ct. (mid. dist.) Ga. 1977, U.S. Ct. Appeals (11th cir.) 1977. Ptnr. Martin, Snow, Grant & Napier, Macon, Ga., 1977—. Mem. ABA, Ga. Bar Assn., Ga. Def. Lawyers Assn. Presbyterian. Insurance, State civil litigation, Federal civil litigation. Office: Martin Snow Grant & Napier PO Box 1606 Macon GA 31202

GUNNER, MICHAEL THOMAS, lawyer; b. Toledo, Jan. 20, 1948; s. Dale Clare and Rosemary (Hennessy) G.; m. Barbara Patrice Jones, Aug. 10, 1974; children—Lora P., Michelle N. Student U. Detroit, 1966-68; B.A., U. Toledo, 1970, J.D. cum laude, 1973. Bar: Ohio, 1973, U.S. Dist. Ct. (so. dist.) Ohio, 1974, U.S. Ct. Appeals (6th cir.) 1975, U.S. Supreme Ct. 1976. Asst. atty. gen. Ohio Atty. Gen. Office, Columbus, 1973-74; pub. defender City of Dayton (Ohio), 1974-76; assoc. Snyder, Hochman & Rakay, Dayton, 1976-78; ptnr. Smith & Gunner, Hilliard, Ohio, 1978-84; sole practice Columbus, 1984—; instr. Sinclair Community Coll., Dayton, 1975-78. Articles editor U. Toledo Law Rev., 1973. village solicitor Village of Plain City, Ohio, 1979-83; asst. law dir. Village of Dublin, Ohio, 1978-84; hearing officer Ohio Dept. Health, Columbus, 1979—; advisor Arthritis Found. of Columbus, 1981-82. Mem. ABA, Columbus Bar Assn. (ethics com.), Dayton Bar Assn., Ohio State Bar Assn., Ohio Trial Lawyers Assn. Democrat. Roman Catholic. Club: Daybreakers (Dublin) (trustee 1984—). Lodge: Kiwanis. Avocations: numismatics; sports; reading; art appreciation. Office: 31 E Whittier St Columbus OH 43206

GUNNING, DAVID HALL, lawyer; b. Cleve., May 30, 1942; s. Samuel David and Jane (Hall) G.; m. Robin Elizabeth Shumway, Aug. 6, 1965; children: David, Elizabeth, Paul. BA, Cornell U., 1964; JD, Harvard U., 1967. Bar: Ohio 1967, D.C. 1984, U.S. Ct. Appeals (D.C.) 1984. Assoc. Jones, Day, Reavis & Pogue, Cleve., 1967-72; staff asst. to pres. Washington, 1972-73; ptnr. Jones, Day, Reavis & Pogue, Cleve., 1973—, corp. group coordinator, 1982-84, coordinator firmwide corp. group, 1986—; regional mgn. ptnr. Jones, Day, Reavis & Pogue, Washington, 1984-86; bd. dirs. Devel. Alternatives Inc., Washington. Mem. Leadership Cleve., 1980; chmn. Council on Children and Families, Cleve., 1982, Child Day Care Planning Project, Cleve., 1983—; trustee, past pres. of bd. de Paul Sch., Cleve., 1982—; trustee Greater Cleve. Govt. Bus. Program, Cleve., 1984—, Univ. Circle, Inc., 1986—, New Cleve. Campaign, 1986—. Mem. ABA, D.C. Bar Assn., Ohio Bar Assn., Nat. Press Club. Clubs: Union, Tavern, Clevelander, Metropolitan, The Country. Avocations: tennis, reading, travel. General corporate, Private international. Home: 2571 N Park Blvd Cleveland Heights OH 44106 Office: Jones Day Reavis & Pogue 901 Lakeside Ave Cleveland OH 44114

GUNNING, FRANCIS PATRICK, lawyer, ins. assn. exec.; b. Scranton, Pa., Dec. 10, 1923; s. Frank Peter and Mary Loretta (Kelly) G.; m. Nancy C. Hill, Aug. 10, 1951; 1 son, Brian F. Student, City Coll. N.Y., 1941-43; LL.B., St. John's U., 1950. Bar: N.Y. bar 1950. Legal editor Prentice Hall Pub. Co., N.Y.C., 1950-51; legal specialist Tchrs. Ins. & Annuity Assn. Am., Coll. Retirement Equities Fund, N.Y.C., 1951-53; asst. counsel Tchrs. Ins. & Annuity Assn. Am., Coll. Retirement Equities Fund, 1953-57, asso. counsel, 1957-60, counsel, 1960-65, asst. gen. counsel, 1965-67, asso. gen. counsel, 1967, v.p., asso. gen. counsel, 1967-73, sr. v.p., gen. counsel, 1973-74, exec. v.p., gen. counsel, 1974—; mem. N.Y. adv. bd. Chgo. Title Ins. Co.; trustee, mem. exec. and audit coms. Mortgage Growth Investors. Contbr. articles on mortgage financing to profl. jours. Served with USAAF, 1943-46. Mem. ABA, N.Y. bar assns., Am. Land Title Assn., Am. Law Inst., Assn. Bar City of N.Y., Assn. Life Ins. Counsel, Nat. Assn. Coll. Univ. Attys., Am. Coll. Real Estate Lawyers. Republican. Roman Catholic. General corporate. Home: 32 Kewanee Rd New Rochelle NY 10804 Office: Tchrs Ins & Annuity Assn of Am 730 3rd Ave New York NY 10017

GUNTER, MICHAEL DONWELL, lawyer; b. Gastonia, N.C., Mar. 26, 1947; s. Daniel Cornelius and DeNorma Joyce (Smith) G.; m. Barbara Jo Benson, June 19, 1970; children: Kimberly Elizabeth, Daniel Cornelius III. BA in History with honors, Wake Forest U., 1969; JD with honors, U. N.C., 1972; MBA with honors, U. Pa., 1973. Bar: N.C., U.S. Dist. Ct. (mid. dist.) N.C. 1974, U.S. Tax Ct. 1975, U.S. Supreme Ct. 1979, U.S. Claims Ct. 1982, U.S. Ct. Appeals (D.C. cir.) 1985. Ptnr. Womble Carlyle Sandridge & Rice, Winston-Salem, N.C., 1974—; bd. dirs. G & J Enterprises Inc., Gastonia, Indsl. Belting Inc., Gastonia. Contbr. articles to profl. jours. Coach youth basketball Winston-Salem YMCA, 1981—; advisor Winston-Salem United Way Christmas Cheer Toy Shop, 1975; fund raiser Deacon Club, Wake Forest Univ.; bd. dirs. Centenary Meth. Ch., 1980, Goodwill Industries, Winston-Salem, 1985—. William E. Newcomble scholar U. Pa., 1972-73. Mem. ABA, So. Pension Conf., N.C. Bar Assn., Forsyth County Bar Assn.,Forsyth County Employee Benefit council, Winston-Salem Estate Planning Council (past bd. dirs.), Order of Coif. Democrat. Clubs: Forsyth Country, Twin City, Piedmont. Avocations: golf, fishing. Pension, profit-sharing, and employee benefits, Corporate taxation. Home: 128 Ballyhoo Dr Lewisville NC 27023 Office: Womble Carlyle Sandridge & Rice 1 Triad Park Winston-Salem NC 27101

GUNTHER, GERALD, lawyer, educator; b. Usingen, Germany, May 26, 1927; came to U.S., 1938, naturalized, 1944; s. Otto and Minna (Floersheim) Gutenstein; m. Barbara Kelsky, June 22, 1949; children: Daniel Jay, Andrew James. B.A., Bklyn. Coll., 1949; M.A., Columbia, 1950; LL.B., Harvard, 1953. Bar: N.Y. 1955. Law clk. Judge Learned Hand, 1953-54, Chief Justice Earl Warren, 1954-55; asso. firm Cleary, Gottlieb, Friendly & Hamilton, N.Y.C., 1955-56; asso. prof. law Columbia U., N.Y.C., 1956-59, prof., 1959-62; prof. law Stanford U., 1962-72, Wm. Nelson Cromwell prof., 1972—; lectr. polit. sci. Bklyn. Coll., 1949-50; vis. prof. Harvard Law Sch., 1972-73; mem. faculty Salzburg Seminar in Am. Studies, 1976, China Ctr. for Am. Law Study Beijing U., Peoples Republic of China, 1986; W.W. Crosskey Meml. lectr. U. Chgo., 1976; John A. Sibley Meml. lectr. U. Ga., 1979; Jerome W. Sidel Meml. lectr. Washington U., 1983; research dir. com. constl. simplification N.Y. Inter-law Sch., 1957-58; cons. Ford Found., 1974-80; dir. Columbia Fed. Cts. History Project, 1957-59; mem. bd. overseers com. to visit Harvard Law Sch., 1974-80; bd. overseers Harvard Law Rev., 1967-72; mem. steering com. Citizens for Constn., 1979-81; adv. com. on experimentation in law Fed. Jud. Ctr., 1978-81. Author: John Marshall's Defense of McCulloch versus Maryland, 1969, Constitutional Law, 11th edit, 1985, Individual Rights in Constitutional Law, 1970, 4th edit., 1986; mem. editorial bd. Found. Press, 1972—, Stanford Univ. Press, 1983-86; mem. adv. bd. and editorial bd. Ency. of Am. Constn., 1983-86; contbr. articles to profl. jours. Served with USNR, 1945-46. Recipient distinguished alumnus award Bklyn. Coll., 1961; Guggenheim fellow, 1962-63; Center Advanced Study in Behavioral Scis., fellow, 1969-70; Fulbright-Hays lectr. Ghana, 1970; Nat. Endowment Humanities fellow, 1980-81, 85-86. Fellow Am. Acad. Arts and Scis.; mem. Am. Philos. Soc., Am. Law Inst., Am. Hist. Assn. (mem. com. Littleton-Griswold Fund 1968-73), Orgn. Am. Historians. Legal education, Legal history, Constitutional law. Office: Stanford Law Sch Stanford CA 94305

GUREVITZ, MARK STUART, lawyer; b. Phila., Dec. 17, 1954; s. Emanuel and Lillian (Notis) G.; m. Christine Frances Inzerra, Oct. 27, 1984. BA in Polit. Sci., Pa. State U., 1975; JD, Temple U., 1979. Bar: Pa. 1979, U.S. Dist. Ct. (mid. dist.) Pa. 1980, U.S. Dist. Ct. (ea. dist.) Pa. 1985, U.S. Ct. Appeals (3d cir.) 1985. Assoc. McNees, Wallace & Nurick, Harrisburg, Pa., 1979-80; asst. dist. atty. State of Pa., Phila., 1980-85; assoc. White & Williams, Phila., 1985—. Editor: Temple Law Quarterly. Mem. ABA, Pa. Bar Assn., Phila. Bar Assn. Federal civil litigation, State civil litigation. Office: White & Williams 1234 Market St 17th Floor Philadelphia PA 19107

GURFEIN, RICHARD ALAN, lawyer; b. N.Y.C., Nov. 4, 1946; s. Jack and Ruth (Kronowitz) G.; m. Erica P. Temchin, Oct. 20, 1978; children—Jared L., Amanda, Jessica M. Wenger, Sarah R. B.E. in E.E., NYU, 1967; J.D., Bklyn. Law Sch., 1971. Bar: N.Y. 1972, U.S. Dist. Ct. (so. dist.) N.Y. 1973, U.S. Dist. Ct. (ea. dist.) N.Y. 1973, U.S. Supreme Ct. 1976. Assoc. atty. Mark B. Wiesen, P.C., N.Y.C., 1972-78; ptnr. Wiesen & Gurfein, N.Y.C., 1978-82, Wiesen, Gurfein & Jenkins, N.Y.C., 1982—; moderator, lectr. Nassau Acad. Law, N.Y. State Trial Lawyers Inst., 1985-87. Mem. Assn. Trial Lawyers Am., N.Y. State Trial Lawyers Assn. (bd. dirs. 1986—), N.Y. County Lawyers Assn., Nassau County Bar Assn. (chmn. com. on med. jurisprudence 1983-86). Personal injury, Insurance, State civil litigation. Office: Wiesen Gurfein & Jenkins 11 Park Pl New York NY 10007

GURICH, NOMA DIANE, lawyer; b. South Bend, Ind., Sept. 26, 1952; d. John and Ramona Belle (Brooks) G.; m. R. Steven Haught, Apr. 14, 1979. AB, Ind. State U., 1975; JD, U. Okla., 1978. Bar: Okla. 1978, U.S. Dist. Ct. (we. dist.) Okla. 1978, U.S. Ct. Appeals (10th cir.) 1978, U.S. Supreme Ct. 1983, U.S. Dist. Ct. (no. dist.) Okla. 1986. Assoc. Cheek, Cheek & Cheek, Oklahoma City, 1978-82; ptnr. Abowitz & Welch P.C., Oklahoma City, 1982—. Mem. ABA, Okla. Bar Assn., Oklahoma County Bar Assn., Def. Research Inst., Okla. Assn. Def. Counsel, Phi Alpha Delta. Republican. Methodist. Federal civil litigation, State civil litigation, Insurance. Office: Abowitz & Welch PC 15 N Robinson Suite 1000 Oklahoma City OK 73102

GURLEY, MICHAEL EDWARD, lawyer; b. Talladega, Ala., Mar. 19, 1947; s. Thomas E. and Annice (Davis) G.; m. Paula Avery, Mar. 17, 1982; children: Michael, Cassie, Lindy. BS, U. Ala., 1969, JD, 1972. Sole practice Centreville, Ala., 1972-80; asst. atty. gen. Atty. Gen. Ohio, Columbus, 1980-82; ptnr. Gurley, Rishel, Myers & Kopech, Columbus, 1982—; spl. asst. atty. gen. Ala. Atty. Gen.'s Office, Montgomery, 1976-80, Ohio Atty. Gen.'s Office, Columbus, 1982—; dist. atty. Bibb County, Centreville, 1977-80. Mem. Columbus Council on World Affairs, 1983—, Columbus Execs. Council, 1984—, Pres. Council, 1984—, Nat. Dem. Inst. Internat. Affairs, Nat. Fin. Council Dem. Nat. Com., U.S. Sen. Dem. Leadership Circle; del. People to People Program, China and Japan, 1986—. Fellow Roscoe Pound Found.; mem. ABA, Ohio Bar Assn., Ala. Bar Assn., Columbus Bar Assn., Ohio Assn. Trial Attys., Comml. Law League, Melvin Belli Soc. (trustee), Farrah Law Soc., Assn. Trial Lawyers Am. Democrat. Clubs: Capital, Athletic (Columbus). Lodge: Shriners. Avocations: reading, travel, tennis. Contracts commercial, Insurance, Government contracts and claims. Home: 4520 Carriage Hill Ln Columbus OH 43220 Office: Gurley Rishel Myers & Kopech 17 S High St Columbus OH 43215

GURNEY, JAMES THOMAS, lawyer; b. Ripley, Miss., Jan. 24, 1901; s. James Andrew and Mary Jane (Shepherd) G.; m. Blanche Johnson, Mar. 5, 1925; 1 son, J. Thomas. A.B., Miss. Coll., 1919, LL.D., 1972; student, U. Chgo., 1919-20, Columbia U., 1919; LL.B., Cumberland U., Lebanon, Tenn., 1922, J.D., 1968; LL.D., Stetson U., 1970; D.H.L., U. Fla., 1978. Bar: Fla. 1922. Mem. faculty Miss. Woman's Coll., Hattiesburg, 1919-21; and since practiced in Orlando; counsel Minute Maid Co. (div. Coca- Cola Co.); gen. counsel Orlando Utilities Commn., 1925—; dir. emeritus Beneficial Corp.; mem. Fla. Supreme Court com. for redrafting common law rules of procedure, 1945; mem. examining bd. Fla. Parole Commn., 1945; chmn. bd. control Fla. Insts. of Higher Learning, 1945-49, now bd. regents. Author: Life Insurance Law of Florida, 1934, Disability Claims Resort to Equity, 1940, World War II Construction of War clauses, 1946; contbr. articles to Fla. Bar Jour. Trustee New Orleans Bapt. Theol. Sem., 1960-67; former bd. dirs. Children's Home Soc. of Fla.; mem. Fla. Council of 100; sponsor for establishment J. Thomas Gurney Elem. Sch. of 1st Bapt. Ch. of Orlando, Fla. Recipient Cert. of Merit U. Fla., 1953; Distinguished Service award Stetson U., 1958; Distinguished Service citation New Orleans Bapt. Theol. Sem. and So. Bapt. Found., 1967; award Pres. Ind. Colls. Fla., 1970; Cert. of Appreciation Miss. Coll., 1984. Fellow Am. Bar Found., Am. Coll. Trial Lawyers; mem. ABA (com. on life ins. law, vice chmn. 1944-47, admissions 1944-48, ssn. and adv. spl. com. on pub. relations 1944-46, adminstrv. law 1945, chmn. Fla. membership com. on ins. sect. 1946-48), Fla. State Bar Assn. (pres. 1942-43), Orange County Bar Assn., Internat. Bar Assn., Am. Life Conv. (legal sect.), Assn. of Life Ins. Counsel (exec. com. 1946-48), Orange County Budget Commn. (chmn. 1935-42), Orlando Community Chest (gen. chmn.), Orlando C. of C. (pres. 1930, nat. council 1940-41, J. Thomas Gurney, Sr. ann. leadership award 1984), Internat. Platform Assn., Fla. Blue Key (hon.), Newcomen Soc., Alumni Assn. U. Fla. (hon.). Democrat. Baptist. Clubs: Lions (Orlando) (dist. gov. 35th dist. 1928), University (Orlando), Orlando Country (Orlando), Rotary (Paul Harris fellow) (Orlando). General practice, Probate, Federal civil litigation. Home: 1701 N Spring Lake Dr Orlando FL 32804 Office: 203 N Magnolia Ave The Gurney Bldg Orlando FL 32801

GURSKY, STEVEN RICHARD, lawyer; b. Bklyn., July 4, 1955; s. Milton and Edna (Krimko) Gursky; m. Ellen Kon, June 22, 1980; 1 child, Matthew Lawrence. BA, Bklyn. Coll., 1976; JD, Bklyn. Law Sch., 1979. Bar: N.Y. 1980, N.J. 1985, U.S. Dist. Ct. N.J. 1985. Sole practice N.Y.C., 1980—. Real property, General corporate, Contracts commercial. Office: 377 Broadway New York NY 10013

GURSTEL, NORMAN KEITH, lawyer; b. Mpls., Mar. 24, 1939; s. Jules and Etta (Abramowitz) G.; m. Jane Evelyn Golden, Nov. 24, 1984; children: Todd, Dana, Marc. BA, U. Minn., 1960, JD, 1962. Bar: Minn. 1962, U.S. Dist. Ct. Minn. 1963, U.S. Supreme Ct. 1980. Assoc. Robins, Zelle, Larson & Kaplan, Mpls., 1962-67; prin. Norman K. Gurstel and Assocs., Mpls., 1967—; arbitrator Hennepin County Dist. Ct.; lectr. U. Minn. Family Law Seminar. Mem. ABA (corp. banking and bus. law and family law sects.), Minn. Bar Assn. (co-chmn. family ct. com. bankruptcy law sect. 1966-67, family law and bankruptcy law), Hennepin County Bar Assn. (chmn. family law com. 1964-65, vice chmn. 1981-82, fee arbitration bd., creditors remedy com.), Fed. Bar Assn., Assn. Trial Lawyers Am., Minn. Trial Lawyers Assn., Am. Acad. Matrimonial Lawyers, Motor Carrier Lawyers Assn., Nat. Council Juvenile and Family Ct. Judges, Comml. Law League Am. (chmn. midwest region 1979-80, recording sec. 1980-81, sec. fund for pub. edn. 1981-83, bd. govs. 1983-86, pres.-elect 1986, pres. 1987), Phi Delta Phi. Jewish. Club: Oak Ridge Country (Mpls.). Lodges: Shriners, Masons. Contracts commercial, Family and matrimonial. Office: Norman K Gurstel and Assocs 431 S 7th St Minneapolis MN 55415

GUSMAN, ROBERT CARL, lawyer; b. N.Y.C., Nov. 17, 1931; s. Samuel and Esther (Zuckerman) G.; m. Harriet Wish, Aug. 21, 1955; children: Amy, Jennifer, Julie. BA, NYU, 1953; JD, Cornell U., 1956. Bar: N.Y. 1957, D.C. 1960, Calif. 1962. Asst. counsel Office Gen. Counsel, Dept. of Navy, Washington, 1956-58; spl. legal advisor fleet ballistic missile program USN, Washington, 1958-60; asst. gen. counsel Aerojet-Gen. Corp., El Monte, Calif., 1960-70, Lockheed Corp., Calabasas, Calif., 1970—; editorial cons. fed. contract reports Bur. Nat. Affairs, Washington, 1970-84, adv. bd. 1984—; spl. legal advisor Commn. on Govt. Procurement, Washington, 1970; instr. law Loyola U., Los Angeles, 1971-72; chmn. indemnification project group Aerospace Industries Assn., Washington, 1984-86, chmn. legal com., 1986. Contbr. articles to profl. jours. Mem. ABA (chmn. pub. contract law subcoms.), Fed. Bar Assn. (conf. chmn. 1985—), Am. Arbitration Assn. (arbitrator 1964—). Antitrust, Government contracts and claims, Legislative.

GUSSOW, IRVING BERNARD, lawyer; b. N.Y.C., Sept. 1; s. Abraham J. and Beatrice (Mardix) G.; m. Terryl J. Gralnik, June 20, 1971 (div. May 1985); children: Micah, Elena, Laurie, Jason; m. Shelly A. Angel, May 29, 1985. BA, Fla. State U., 1969; JD, U. Tenn., 1972. Bar: Fla. 1973, U.S. Supreme Ct. 1979, U.S. Ct. Claims 1980, U.S. Tax Ct. 1980, U.S. Ct. Appeals (5th and 11th cirs.) 1981. Assoc. Gordon V. Frederick, Sanford, Fla., Rosenblum & Pipkins, Fern Park, Fla.; sole practice Winter Park, Fla., 1977—. Mem. task force, arbitrator Seminole Juvenile Arbitration, Sanford, 1978-84; pres. Congregation Beth-Am, Altamonte Springs, Fla., 1978-80; del. Seminole Dems., Seminole City, Fla., 1980-84. Named Dir. Yr. Sanford-Seminole Jaycees, 1976. Mem. ABA, Seminole County Bar Assn., Orange County Bar Assn., Sanford-Seminole Jaycees (dir. yr. 1976). General practice, Criminal, Environment. Home: 95 Escondido Altamonte Springs FL 32701 Office: 861 W Morse Blvd Winter Park FL 32789

GUSSOW, JOHN ANDREW, lawyer; b. Bklyn., May 11, 1946; s. Emanuel M. and Jean M. (Gumpert) G.; children—Jerome A., Charles E. A.B., Dickinson Coll., 1967; J.D., Syracuse U., 1970. Bar: N.Y. 1971. Trial atty. civil div. Dept. Justice, N.Y.C., 1970-75; assoc. Melvin D. Kraft P.C., N.Y.C., 1975-76; asst. gen. counsel, asst. sec. M. Lowenstein Corp., N.Y.C., 1976-82, assoc. gen. counsel, asst. sec., 1982—; small claims arbitrator Civil Ct. Richmond County; mem. N.Y. State Cable TV Commn., 1984-86, ptnr. Hart and Gussow, 1986—; Law chmn., mem. exec. com. Richmond County (N.Y.) Republican Com.; Rep. candidate for dist. atty. Richmond County, 1983; commr. N.Y. State Cable TV Commn., 1984—; bd. dirs. Camelot Found. ; law chmn. Richmond County Rep. Com. Mem. ABA, Assn. Bar City N.Y., Textile Lawyers Assn., Customs Bar Assn., N.Y. State Bar Assn., Richmond County Bar Assn., Am. Arbitration Assn. (nat. panel). Jewish. Lodge: Richmond County Kiwanis. General corporate, State civil litigation, Contracts commercial. Home: 50 Yacht Club Cove Staten Island NY 10308 Office: 32 Narrows Rd S Staten Island NY 10305

GUST, GERALD NORMAN, lawyer; b. Amery, Wis., Dec. 26, 1946; s. Orville Edward and Lucille Clarice (Warner) G.; m. Susan Jean Dudding, Oct. 3, 1970; children: Shayne, Thomas, Betsy, Megan. BS, U. Wis., River Falls, 1969; JD, U. Wis., 1972. Bar: Wis. 1972, U.S. Dist. Ct. (we. dist.) Wis. 1972. Ptnr. Cwayna, Novitzke, Byrnes, Gust, Williams & Erspamer Ltd., Amery, 1972—; instr. U. Wis. Law Sch., Madison, 1983, 85, 87. Atty. City of Amery, 1975-80, Village of Deer Park, Wis., 1975-80; chmn. Polk County Dem. Party, Amery, 1977, DNR Appeal Panel, Amery, 1977; mem. Minn.-Wis. Boundary Area Commn., Amery, 1978-80; mem. Dist. Atty.'s Bd. Profl. Responsibility, 1982—. Mem. ABA, Wis. Bar Assn., St. Croix Valley Bar Assn., Assn. Trial Lawyers Am., Wis. Acad. Trial Lawyers (bd. dirs. 1982—). Democrat. Lutheran. State civil litigation, Personal injury, Workers' compensation. Office: Cwayna Novitzke Bynres et al PO Box 18 Amery WI 54001

GUSTAFERRO, BARBARA JEAN, lawyer; b. Richmond Heights, Ohio, Apr. 10, 1956; d. Roy E. and Florence D. (Dziedzicki) Thompson. BA, Lake Erie Coll., 1978; JD, Ohio State U., 1982. Bar: Ohio 1982, U.S. Dist. Ct. (no. dist.) Ohio 1985, U.S. Ct. Appeals (6th cir.) 1985, U.S. Ct. Appeals (fed. cir.) 1987, U.S. Supreme Ct. 1987. Assoc. Plate, Shapira et al, Erie, Pa., 1982-84, Dworken & Bernstein, Cleve., 1984—. Davison- Foreman grantee, Ohio State U., 1978. Mem. ABA, Ohio State Bar Assn., Lake County Bar Assn. Democrat. Roman Catholic. Avocations: music, sports, tennis, golf. Personal injury, State and federal civil litigation, Plantiff and defense. Home: 26670 Loganberry Dr Richmond Heights OH 44143 Office: Dworken Bernstein Co LPA 153 E Erie St Fainesville OH 44077

GUSTAFSON, ALBERT KATSUAKI, lawyer, engineer; b. Harimachida, Tokyo, Dec. 5, 1949; came to U.S., 1951; s. William A. and Akiko (Osada) G.; m. Helen Melissa Laird, July 31, 1971 (div. 1975); m. Karen Jane Ekblad, Dec. 31, 1978. B.A. with distinction, Stanford U., 1972; J.D., U. Wash., 1980. Bar: Wash. 1981, U.S. Dist. Ct. (we. dist.) Wash. 1981, U.S. Ct. Appeals (9th cir.) 1984. Acoustics analyst Boeing Co., Seattle, 1973-74, materiel buyer, 1974; legal editor, book pub. co., Seattle, 1975-76; research analyst Batelle Inst., Seattle, 1975-76; legal intern Office of U.S. Atty., Seattle, 1976; engr. U.P.R.R., 1977-85; corp. counsel Ansette Fin. Corp., Inc., Seattle, 1987—; pres. Albert K. Gustafson, P.S., Seattle, 1981—; corp. counsel Dorden, Inc., Centralia, Wash., 1984—, Ansette Fin. Corp., Inc., Seattle, 1987. Sec. local 117-E, United Transp. Union, 1984, local vice-chmn., 1984; Dem. precinct chmn., 1984. Kraft scholar, 1968; Calif. State scholar, 1968-72. Mem. Assn. Trial Lawyers Am., Wash. State Trial Lawyers Assn., ABA, Fed. Bar Assn., Seattle-King County Bar Assn., Seattle C. of C. Democrat. Presbyterian. Club: College. Lodges: Masons, Shriners, Order of DeMolay (master councilor 1968), Rotary. International, Contracts commercial, Admiralty. Home: 3971 Evanston Ave N Seattle WA 98103 Office: 804 First Interstate Ctr 999 Third Ave Seattle WA 98104 Office: Fuji Bldg 8F, 3-18-6 Hatchbori Chuo-ku, Tokyo 104, Japan

GUSTAFSON, DAVID EARL, lawyer; b. Chgo., May 6, 1950; s. Earl P. and Evelyn (Thue) G.; m. Deborah L. Berenter, Dec. 29, 1974 (div. June 1986); children: Danielle Andrea, Adam Marc. BA, No. Ill. U., 1972; post-grad., Ariz. State U., 1972-73; M in Social Work, U. Ill., 1975; JD, Southwestern U., 1978. Bar: Ariz. 1978, U.S. Dist. Ct. Ariz. 1978. Assoc. Johnson, Jessen, Dake & Oplinger, Phoenix, 1978-79, Moore, Demaree & Long, Phoenix, 1979-80, Bruce Demaree, PC, Phoenix, 1980-81; ptnr. Douglas & Gustafson, Phoenix, 1981-84, McCarthy, Marquardt & Gustafson, Phoenix, 1985—. Mem. ABA (trial, tort and ins., sects.), Assn. Trial Lawyers Am., Ariz. Trial Lawyers Assn., Phoenix Trial Lawyers Assn., Maricopa County Bar Assn. (trial practice section, med.-legal liaison com.). Democrat. Lodge: Elks. Avocation: snow and water skiing, scuba diving, hiking, camping, flying. Insurance, Personal injury, State civil litigation. Office: McCarthy Marquardt & Gustafson 13444 N 32nd St Suite 6 Phoenix AZ 85032

GUSTAFSON, LAWRENCE RAYMOND, lawyer; b. Florence, S.D., Aug. 16, 1918; s. Joseph Samuel and Olive Nora (Smith) G.; m. Anna Marie Paulsen, Feb. 20, 1943; children: Marjorie Ann Gustafson Haigh, Denice Marie Gustafson Jones. BS, U. S.D., 1941, JD, 1945. Bar: S.D. 1945, U.S. Dist. Ct. S.D. 1949, U.S. Ct. Appeals (8th cir.) 1963, U.S. Supreme Ct. 1974. Prin. Jefferson (S.D.) High Sch., 1941-42; tchr. Sr. High Sch., Watertown, S.D., 1942-43; supt. White River (S.D.) Sch., 1943-45; sole practice Britton, S.D., 1945—; states atty. Marshall County, Britton, S.D., 1947-51; atty. Veblen City, S.D., 1948—; tchr. Am. Bank Inst., Britton, 1960—; bd. dirs. Day County Bank, Webster, S.D. Mem. ABA, S.D. Bar Assn., Assn. Trial Lawyers Am., S.D. Trial Lawyers Assn., Delta Theta Phi. Republican. Lutheran. Lodges: Masons (master 1967-68, dist. master 1984-86), Oddfellow. Probate, Real property, Personal income taxation. Office: Box 202 Britton SD 57430

GUSTAFSON, RICHARD B., lawyer; b. Sault Ste. Marie, Mich., Apr. 4, 1940; s. Richard O. and Coralie (Booth) G.; m. Betty Lou Spangler, Apr. 25, 1964; children: Richard, Christopher. AB, Coll. William and Mary, 1962, JD, 1973. Bar: Mich., U.S. Dist. Ct. (ea. dist.) Mich., U.S. Ct. Appeals (6th cir.). Store mgr. Humble Oil and Refining Co., Norfolk, Va., 1963; asst. to LPG mgr. Humble Oil and Refining Co., Richmond, Va., 1967; dist. mgr. Unigas, Inc., Sacramento, Calif., 1967-69; exec. asst. Pargas, Inc., Waldorf, Md., 1969-70; assoc. Lambert & Leser, P.C., Bay City, Mich., 1973-76; ptnr. Skinner & Gustafson, Bay City, 1976-85; pres. Gustafson & Assocs., P.C., Bay City, 1985—; commentator Inst. Continuing Legal Edn., Ann Arbor, Mich., 1985—. Mem. Mich. Bar Assn., Hellenic Bar Assn., Mich. Trial Lawyers Assn., Am. Trial Lawyers Assn., Trout Unltd. Greek Orthodox. Club: Bay City Country. Lodge: Rotary. Avocation: fly fishing. Construction, Federal civil litigation, State civil litigation. Home: 2210 Groveland Rd Bay City MI 48708 Office: Gustafson & Assocs PC PO Box 876 Bay City MI 48707

GUSTE, WILLIAM JOSEPH, JR., lawyer, state ofcl.; b. New Orleans, May 26, 1922; s. William Joseph and Marie Louise (Alciatore) G.; m. Dorothy Schutten, Apr. 17, 1947; children: William Joseph III, Bernard Randolph, Marie Louise, Melanie Ann, Valerie Eve, Althea Marie, Elizabeth Therese, James Patrick, Anne Duchesne, John Jude (dec.). A.B., Loyola, New Orleans, 1942, LL.B., 1943, LL.D., 1974. Bar: La. bar 1943. Asso. firm Guste, Barnett & Redmann, 1943, 46-56, Guste, Barnett & Little, 1956-70, Guste, Barnett & Colomb, 1970-72; mem. La. Senate, 1968-72; atty. gen. State La., New Orleans, 1972—; Co-owner Antoine's Restaurant, New Orleans; chief counsel Housing Authority, New Orleans, 1957-71. Pres. New Orleans Cancer Assn., 1960-62; nat. pres. United Cancer Council, 1965-67; pres. Met. Crime Commn., 1956-57; Asso. Cath. Charities, 1960-62; chmn. Juvenile Ct. adv. com. Orleans Parish, 1961-63; Mem. City New Orleans Street Paving Study Com., 1965-66; Trustee Xavier U., 1967—, also chmn. bd. lay regents. Served with AUS, 1942-46, ETO. Named Outstanding Young Man City New Orleans, Nat. Jr. C. of C., 1951, comdr. Mil. and Hospitaller Order St. Lazarus of Jerusalem, 1978; recipient John F. Kennedy Leadership award Young Dems. La. State U., 1973; No. La. Polit. Action League award, 1975; Gautrelet award Springhill Coll., 1976; Housing Man of Yr. award Nat. Housing Conf., 1976; Nat. Penology award Am. Prison Ministry, 1979; Pelican award Ecology Center, 1980; Silver Torch award Anti-Defamation League; B'nai B'rith, 1980. Mem. Am. Assn. Small Bus. (dir.), Nat. Assn. Housing and Redevel. Ofcls. (dir.), Am. Judicature Soc., Legal Aid Bur., Am., La., New Orleans bar assns., St. Thomas More Cath. Lawyers Assn., Young Men's Bus. Club of Greater New Orleans (hon. life), Internat. House, Blue Key, Sigma Alpha Kappa, Phi Alpha Delta (hon.). Democrat. Roman Catholic. Clubs: Pickwick, Bienville. Criminal. *

GUTERMAN, JAMES HANS, lawyer; b. Ridgewood, N.J., Oct. 21, 1952; s. Hans L. and Dorothy C. (Nickel) G.; m. Wylly Morse, Aug. 17, 1974; 1 child, Lydia. AB with honors, Vassar Coll., 1974; JD with honors, U. N.C., 1978. Bar: N.C. 1978, Fla. 1983, U.S. Dist. Ct. (we. dist.) N.C. 1978, U.S. Ct. Appeals (4th cir.) 1979, U.S. Dist. Ct. (ea. dist.) N.C. 1980. Law clk. to presiding justice U.S. Dist. Ct. (we. dist.) N.C., Charlotte, 1978-79; assoc. Helms, Mulliss & Johnston, Charlotte, 1979-83; ptnr. Smith, Helms, Mulliss & Moore, Charlotte, 1984—; guest lectr. Robert Morris Assoc., Charlotte, 1985. Co-author: In the Opinion of the Bar: A National Survey of Bar Polling Practices, 1977; editor in chief U. N.C. Law Rev., 1977-78. Mem. allocations panel United Way, Charlotte, 1985—. Mem. ABA, N.C. Bar Assn. (lectr. contracts bar rev. course 1980-82), Fla. Bar Assn., Nat. Assn. Bond Lawyers. Democrat. Clubs: Olde Providence Racquet, Charlotte City. Avocation: tennis. Antitrust, Contracts commercial, Municipal bonds. Home: 4216 Carnoustie Ln Charlotte NC 28210 Office: Smith Helms Mulliss & Moore 227 N Tryon St Charlotte NC 28202

GUTH, PAUL C., lawyer; b. Vienna, Austria, Nov. 8, 1922; came to U.S., 1940; s. Alfred and Margaret (Haas) G.; m. Joan Margaret Totman, Mar. 28, 1962. B.A., Columbia U., 1943, LL.B., 1947. Bar: N.Y. 1948. Assoc. Cleary Gottlieb Friendly & Cox, N.Y.C., 1947-49; assoc. Lauterstein & Lauterstein, N.Y.C., 1950-51, ptnr., 1952-81; ptnr. Kelley Drye & Warren, N.Y.C., 1981—. Mem. editorial bd. Columbia Law Rev. Bd. dirs., officer Robert Lehman Found., Inc., N.Y.C., 1969—, Philip Lehman Found., Inc., N.Y.C., 1972—; pres., bd. dirs. Lutece Found., Inc., N.Y.C., 1983—; sec. Am. Ditchley Found., Inc., N.Y.C., 1983—; mem. fin. adv. bd. Victoria Home for Aged Men and Women, Ossining, N.Y., 1977—; asst. prosecutor war crimes trials Dachau and Mauthausen , 1945-46, chief investigator 3d. Army Intelligence Ctr., 1945. Served to 2d lt. AUS, 1943-46, ETO. Recipient Beck prize Columbia Law Sch., 1943. Mem. Am. Coll. Probate Counsel, Am. Judicature Soc., Assn. Bar City of N.Y., Fed. Bar Assn. Republican. Episcopalian. Clubs: Princeton (N.Y.C.); Lake (New Canaan, Conn.). Avocation: historical studies. Estate planning, Private international, Mergers and acquisitions. Home: 955 Fifth Ave New York NY 10021 Office: Kelley Drye & Warren 101 Park Ave New York NY 10178

GUTHALS, JOEL ERIC, lawyer; b. Santa Monica, June 11, 1945; s. Edward John and Ettie (Zamos) G.; m. Ann Magdalene Turner, Apr. 27, 1968; children: Jennifer, Joshua. BS, U. Calif., Los Angeles, 1967; MBA, U. Mont., 1970, JD, 1975. Bar: Mont. 1975, U.S. Dist. Ct. Mont. 1975, U.S. Ct. Appeals (10th cir.) 1980, U.S. Supreme Ct. 1982, U.S. Ct. Appeals (9th cir.) 1985. Law clk. to presiding justice U.S. Dist. Ct. Mont., Billings, 1975-76; from assoc. to ptnr. Moses, Tolliver & Wright, Billings, 1976-80; ptnr. Wright, Tolliver & Guthals, Billings, 1980—. Editor U. Mont. Law Rev., 1974-75; editor, annotator Montana Crininal Code Annotated, 1974. legal counsel Intermountain Planned Parenthood, Billings, 1983—; pres. Friends of KEMC, Inc., Billings, 1985—, bd. dirs. 1980—; bd. dirs. Billings Planned Parenthood, 1980-85, Billings Symphony, 1986—. Served to capt. USAF, 1967-71. Mem. ABA, Mont. Bar Assn., Am. Judicature Soc., Yellowstone County Bar Assn. Club: Briarwood Country (Billings). Avocations: music, reading, golf. Federal civil litigation, Contracts commercial, Bankruptcy. Home: Blue Creek Star Rt Billings MT 59101 Office: Wright Tolliver & Guthals 27 N 27th St Suite 2106 Billings MT 59103

GUTHMAN, JACK, lawyer; b. Cologne, Ger., Apr. 19, 1938; came to U.S., 1939, naturalized, 1945; s. Albert and Selma (Cahn) G.; m. Sandra Polk, Nov. 26, 1967. B.A., Northwestern U., 1960; LL.B., Yale U., 1963. Bar: Ill. bar 1963. Law clk. to dist. judge U.S. Dist. Ct. No. Ill., 1963-65; since practiced in Chgo.; partner firm Sidley & Austin, 1970—. Chmn. City Chgo. Zoning Bd. Appeals, 1975—. Democrat. Jewish. Club: Standard (Chgo.). Administrative and regulatory, Legislative, Real property. Office: 1 First Nat Plaza Chicago IL 60603

GUTHMANN, JOHN HOWARD, lawyer; b. St. Paul, Oct. 21, 1954; s. Howard Milton and Elizabeth Diane (Heimann) G.; m. Teresa Irene Wiggins, Aug. 25, 1984. BA in History, Polit. Sci., Cornell Coll., 1976; JD, William Mitchell Coll. of Law, 1980. Bar: Minn. 1980, U.S. Dist. Ct. Minn. 1980. Law clk. to presiding justice Minn. Supreme Ct., St. Paul, 1980-81; assoc. Hansen, Dordell, Bradt, Odlaug & Bradt, St. Paul, 1981—; adj. instr.

legal writing William Mitchell Coll. of Law, St. Paul, 1979-80, 81-82; lectr. Minn. Inst. of Legal Edn., St. Paul, 1986—. Editor-in-chief William Mitchell Law Rev., 1980; contbr. articles to law reviews. Advisor Boy Scouts Am., St. Paul, 1983—, cluster team chmn., 1984—. Mem. ABA, Minn. Bar Assn., Ramsey County Bar Assn., Minn. Def. Lawyers Assn. Republican. Mem. Unitarian Ch. State civil litigation, Insurance, Personal injury. Office: Hansen Dordell Bradt Odlaug & Bradt 1200 Conwed Tower Saint Paul MN 55101

GUTHRIE, DAN CALVIN, JR., lawyer; b. San Antonio, Nov. 19, 1948; s. Dan Calvin and Nova Jean (Sheppard) G.; m. Sherrill Reagan, Dec. 28, 1979; children—Reagan Jessica, Tiffany Amber, Chase Alexander. B.A., Rice U., 1971; J.D., U. Tex., 1974. Bar: Tex. 1974, U.S. Ct. Appeals (5th cir.) 1978, U.S. Ct. Appeals (11th cir.) 1981, U.S. Supreme Ct. 1979. Asst. dist. atty. Dallas County (Tex.), 1975-78; asst. U.S. atty. No. Dist. Tex., 1978-80; ptnr. Burleson, Pate & Gibson, Dallas, 1981—. People to People Del. to China, 1987. Mem. Nat. Assn. Criminal Def. Lawyers, Fed. Bar Assn., Assn. Trial Lawyers Am., ABA, State Bar Tex. (mem. penal code, code and criminal procedure com.), Tex. Criminal Def. Lawyers Assn., Tex. Trial Lawyers Assn., Dallas Bar Assn. Recipient Dean Hugh Scott Cameron Service award Rice U., 1971. Methodist. Criminal. Office: 2414 N Akard St 7th Floor Dallas TX 75201

GUTIERREZ, MAX, JR., lawyer; b. San Salvador, May 26, 1930; came to U.S., 1930, naturalized, 1959; s. Max J. and Elva (Sol) G.; m. Mary Juanita O'Hearn, Jan. 26, 1957; children—Michele M., Michael E., Paul F., William F., Laurelle M., Maxmillian J. A.B., U. Calif., Berkeley, 1953; J.D. cum laude, U. San Francisco, 1959; LL.M., Georgetown U., 1960. Bar: Calif. 1960. Assoc. firm Brobeck, Phleger & Harrison, San Francisco, 1960-67; mem. firm Brobeck, Phleger & Harrison, 1967—; lectr. U. San Francisco Sch. Law, 1963-72; dir. Dodge & Cox Stock Fund, Balanced Fund. Bd. dirs. Florence Crittenton Services. Served with AUS, 1953-55. Mem. ABA (subcouncil on real property, probate and trust law sect.), State Bar Calif. (family law com. 1967-69, chmn. 1969, chmn. probate and trust law com. 1973), Am. Bar Found., Am. Coll. Probate Counsel, Internat. Acad. Estate and Trust Law (pres. 1978-80), St. Thomas More Soc., Phi Delta Phi, Sigma Chi. Republican. Probate, Estate taxation, Family and matrimonial. Office: Brobeck Phleger & Harrison Spear St Tower One Market Plaza San Francisco CA 94105

GUTIN, IRVING, lawyer; b. N.Y.C., Apr. 12, 1932; s. Norman and Eva (Wilf) G.; m. Claire Rosenstein, Mar. 13, 1960 (div. 1974); m. Barbara C. Shannon, June 13, 1982; children: Nina J., Cheryl, Jeffrey A. Student, Bklyn. Coll., 1949-51, LLB, 1954, LLM, 1960. Bar: N.Y., U.S. Dist. Ct. (ea. and so. dists.) N.Y., U.S. Ct. Mil. Appeals, U.S. Supreme Ct. Assoc. Eckaus & Leader, N.Y.C., 1954-55; atty. Legal Aid Soc., N.Y.C., 1955-57; assoc. M.M. Friedman, N.Y.C., 1957-59; ptnr. Lotwin, Holdman & Gutin, N.Y.C., 1959-73; sr. v.p., gen. counsel Armin Corp., N.Y.C., 1974-81; v.p., gen. counsel Tyco Labs. Inc., Exeter, N.Y., 1981—; bd. dirs. Armin Corp., Jersey City, 1971—. Bd. dirs. N.Y.C. Assn. Help of Retarded, 1979-85, N.H. Charitiable Trust, Manchester, 1983—. Served with U.S. Army, 1954-56. General corporate, Securities. Office: Tyco Labs Inc Tyco Park Exeter NH 03833

GUTMAN, HARRY LARGMAN, law educator, lawyer; b. Phila., Feb. 23, 1942; s. I. Cyrus and Mildred B. (Largman) G.; m. Anne G. Aronsky, Aug. 28, 1971; children—Jonathan, Elizabeth. A.B. cum laude, Princeton U., 1963; M.A., Univ. Coll., Oxford, Eng., 1965; LL.B. cum laude, Harvard U., 1968. Bar: Mass. 1968, U.S. Tax Ct. 1969. Assoc., Hill & Barlow, Boston, 1968-75, ptnr., 1975-77; clin. assoc. Harvard U. Law Sch., 1971-77; instr. Boston Coll., 1974-77; atty.-advisor Office of Tax Legis. Counsel, U.S. Dept. Treasury, 1977-78, dep. tax legis. counsel, 1978-80; assoc. prof. law U. Va., Charlottesville, 1980-84; prof. U. Pa. Law Sch., 1984—; cons. Office Tax Policy, U.S. Dept. Treasury, 1980; cons. Am. Law Inst., 1980-84; vis. prof. U. Va. Law Sch., 1985—, Ill. Inst. Tech., 1986; reporter Am. Law Inst. Generation-Skipping Tax project; Am. Law Inst. Arden House III Conf. 1986—. Recipient Exceptional Service award U.S. Dept. Treasury, 1980. Author: Transactions Between Partners & Partnerships, 1973; Minimizing Estate Taxes: The Effects of Inter Vivos Giving, 1975; (with F. Sander) Tax Aspects of Divorce and Separation, 1985; (with D. Lubick) Treasury's New Views on Carryover Basis, 1979; Effective Federal Tax Rates on Transfers of Wealth, 1979; (with others) Federal Wealth Transfer Taxation: Cases & Materials, 1987; Federal Wealth Transfer Taxes After ERTA, 1983; Reforming Federal Wealth Transfer Taxes After ERTA, 1983. Personal income taxation, Estate taxation, Corporate taxation. Office: U Pa Law Sch 3400 Chestnut St Philadelphia PA 19104

GUTMAN, RICHARD MARTIN, lawyer; b. Chgo., Mar. 12, 1946; s. Raymond Tobias and Frieda (Garber) G. B.A. cum laude, Harvard U., 1967; J.D., U. Chgo., 1973. Bar: Oreg. 1973, Ill. 1974, U.S. Dist. Ct. (no. dist.) Ill. 1974, U.S. Ct. Appeals (7th cir.) 1977. Vol. Peace Corps, 1967-69; staff atty. ACLU Police Project, Chgo., 1973-74; sole practice, Chgo.; dir. Polit. Surveillance Litigation Project, Chgo., 1975—; investigator, writer Ralph Nader Congress project, Washington, 1972. Author: (with others) The Environment Committees, 1975. Contbr. numerous articles to prof. jours. Recipient 5th Anniversary award Alliance to End Repression, Chgo., 1975, Legal Eagle award Ind. Voters Ill.-Ind. Precinct Orgn., Chgo., 1981, Award of Distinction, 1st Unitarian Ch., Chgo., 1982. Civil rights, Political surveillance. Office: 407 S Dearborn St Chicago IL 60605

GUTNICK, H. YALE, lawyer; b. Phila., Mar. 20, 1942; s. Abraham L. and Irene (Grosflam) G.; m. Eleanor Stanton, June 10, 1968; m. 2d, Sally Meyers, Oct. 21, 1978 (div. Dec. 1986). children—Todd, Laura, Casey. B.A., Ohio Wesleyan U., 1964; J.D., U. Pitts., 1967. Bar: Pa. 1967, U.S. Dist. Ct. (we. and ea. dists.) Pa. 1967, U.S. Dist. Ct. D.C. 1969, U.S. Ct. Appeals (3d and D.C. cirs.) 1969, U.S. Ct. Appeals (5th cir.) 1976, U.S. Supreme Ct. 1978. Trial atty. U.S. Dept. Justice, Washington, 1967-69; ptnr. Rose, Schmidt, Dixon, Hasley, Whyte & Hardesty, Pitts., 1970-79, Strassburger McKenna Gutnick & Potter, Pitts., 1979—. Mem. ABA, Pa. Bar Assn., D.C. Bar Assn., Am. Trial Lawyers Assn., Pa. Trial Lawyers Assn. Jewish. Antitrust, Federal civil litigation, Entertainment. Office: 322 Blvd of Allies Suite 700 Pittsburgh PA 15222

GUTOF, RICHARD STEWART, lawyer; b. Chgo., July 30, 1940; s. Harry and Rose (Dreebin) G.; m. Anita L. Weiss, June 26, 1964; children—Daniel, Deborah. B.S., U. Ill., 1962; J.D., DePaul U., 1964. Bar: Ill. 1964, U.S. Dist. Ct. (no. dist.) Ill. 1964, U.S. Supreme Ct. 1971. Asst. state's atty. Cook County (Ill.), 1964-69; sole practice, Skokie, Ill., 1970—. Mem. ABA, Ill. Bar Assn., Chgo. Bar Assn., N.W. Suburban Bar Assn., North Suburban Bar Assn., Coalition Suburban Bar Assns. Cook County (past pres.), North Suburban Cook County Bar Assn. (past pres.). Criminal, Family and matrimonial, Personal injury. Home: 607 Lavergne Ave Wilmette IL 60091 Office: 9933 Lawler Ave #312 Skokie IL 60077

GUTOWSKI, MICHAEL FRANCIS, lawyer; b. Detroit, Oct. 23, 1950; s. John A. and Christine (Militti) G.; m. Susan M. Smith, Nov. 25, 1983; 1 child, Maria C. AB, U. Nebr., 1972; JD, Georgetown U., 1976. Bar: Nebr. 1976, U.S. Dist. Ct. Nebr. 1976. Asst. pub. defender Douglas County, Omaha, 1977-85; sole practice Omaha, 1985—. Mem. Nebr. Dem. Cen. Com., 1982-83, alt. mem., 1986—. Mem. ABA, Nebr. Bar Assn., Omaha Bar Assn. (newsletter com. 1985—), Nebr. Criminal Def. Attys. Assn., Nat. Assn. Criminal Def. Lawyers. Roman Catholic. General practice, Criminal. Office: 1823 Harney St #1009 Omaha NE 68102

GUTSHALL, FREDERICK RAYM, lawyer; b. Huntingdon, Pa., Sept. 28, 1946; s. Frederick Waldorf and Iva Oletha (Singer) G. BA in History, Juniata Coll., 1968; JD, Dickinson Sch. Law, 1976. Bar: Pa. 1976. Assoc. James E. Himes, Huntingdon, 1976—. Served with USN, 1968-72. Mem. ABA, Pa. Bar Assn., Huntingdon County Bar Assn. Democrat. Avocations: fishing, rafting, tennis, reading. State civil litigation, General practice, Probate. Home: 16 E Market St Mount Union PA 17066 Office: James E Himes 222 Penn St Huntingdon PA 16652

GUTSTEIN, SOLOMON, lawyer; b. Newport, R.I., June 18, 1934; s. Morris Aaron and Goldie Leah (Nussbaum) G.; m. Carol Feinhandler, Sept. 3, 1961; children—Jon Eric, David Ethan, Daniel Ari, Joshua Aaron. A.B. with honors, U. Chgo., 1953, J.D., 1956. Bar: Ill. 1956, U.S. Dist. Ct. (no. dist.) Ill. 1957, U.S. Ct. Appeals (7th cir.) 1958, U.S. Ct. Appeals (5th cir.) 1971, U.S. Supreme Ct. 1980; Rabbi, 1955. Assoc., Schradzke, Gould & Ratner, Chgo., 1956-60; ptnr. firm Schwartz & Gutstein, Chgo., 1961-65, Gutstein & Cope, Chgo., 1968-72, Gutstein & Schwartz, Chgo., 1980-83, Gutstein & Sherwin, Chgo., 1983-85; spl. asst. atty. gen. State of Ill., 1968-69; lectr. bus. law U. Chgo. Grad. Sch. Bus., 1973-82; lectr. in field, real estate broker, Author: Illinois Real Estate, 2 vols., 1983, rev. ann. updates, 1984—; co-author: Construction Law in Illinois, annually 1980-84; contbr. chpt. to Commercial Real Estate Transactions, 1962-76. Assoc. editor U. Chgo. Law Rev., 1954-56; editorial adviser Basic Real Estate I, also Advanced Real Estate II, 1960s-70s. Contbr. articles to profl. publs. Mem. Cook County Citizens Fee Rev. Com., 1965; alderman from 40th ward Chgo. City Council, 1975-79; mem. govt. affairs adv. com. Jewish Fedn., 1984—. Fuerstenberg scholar U. Chgo., 1950-56; Kosmerl fellow U. Chgo., 1953-56. Mem. Chgo. Bar Assn., Ill. State Bar Assn., Decalogue Soc. Lawyers (25 yr. cert. 1982). Democrat. Jewish. Lodge: B'nai B'rith. Real property, Probate, Health. Office: 180 N LaSalle St Chicago IL 60601

GUTTELL, STEVEN MICHAEL, lawyer; b. Boston, Mar. 10, 1947; s. Hyman Harold and Annette (Shuman) G.; m. Sharon Granek, Mar. 26, 1972; children: Adam Granek, Noah Daniel, Jess David. BSBA in Acctg., Northeastern U., 1969; JD cum laude, Suffolk U., 1974. Bar: Mass. 1974, U.S. Dist. Ct. Mass. 1975, U.S. Ct. Appeals (D.C. cir.) 1978, N.Y. 1980, U.S. Dist. Ct. (so. and ea. dists.) N.Y. 1980, Ariz. 1982, U.S. Dist. Ct. Ariz. 1982, U.S. Ct. Appeals (9th cir.) 1982. Atty. U.S. Dept. Labor, Washington, 1974-79, N.Y.C., 1979-81; ptnr. Gust, Rosenfeld, Divelbess & Henderson, Phoenix, 1982—. Served to 1st lt. U.S. Army, 1969-71, Vietnam. Mem. ABA (com. on employee rights and responsibilities, chmn. alternatives to litigation subcom.), Ariz. Bar Assn. (alternative dispute resolution com.), Maricopa County Bar Assn. Labor, Administrative and regulatory. Home: 9207 N 83d Way Scottsdale AZ 85258 Office: Gust Rosenfeld et al 201 N Central #3300 Phoenix AZ 85073-3300

GUTTENBERG, ARYEH, lawyer; b. N.Y.C., July 18, 1955; s. Jack and Eileen (Metzger) G.; m. Sandra Rochelle Lowy, June 25, 1978; children: Joel Gary, Seth Neal, Shana Jill, Rikki Elyse. BA, Yeshiva U., 1976; JD, Cardozo Law Sch., 1979; LLM in Taxation, NYU, 1981. Bar: N.Y. 1980, U.S. Dist. Ct. (so. and ea. dists.) N.Y. 1980, U.S. Tax Ct. 1982, Md. 1983, U.S. Dist. Ct. Md. 1983. Atty. and advisor to presiding justice U.S. Tax Ct., Washington, 1981-83; assoc. Frank, Bernstein, Conaway & Goldman, Balt., 1983—. Mem. editorial bd. The Rev. of Taxation of Individuals, 1983—; contbr. articles to profl. jours. Mem. ABA, Md. Bar Assn. Jewish. Avocations: basketball, tennis, softball. Corporate taxation, Personal income taxation, General corporate. Home: 2522 Willow Glen Dr Baltimore MD 21209 Office: Frank Bernstein Conaway & Goldman 300 E Lombard St Baltimore MD 21202

GUTTERMAN, ALAN J., lawyer; b. Bklyn., Nov. 21, 1942; s. Hyman and Madeline (Wolfe) G.; m. Emily Scharer, June 23, 1966; children—David, Andrew, Glenn, Jamie. B.A. with honors, U. Rochester, 1964; J.D., Rutgers U., 1967. Bar: N.J. 1967, U.S. Ct. Clms. 1970, U.S. Ct. Apls. (3d cir.) N.J. 1967, U.S. Sup. Ct. 1977. Law clk. U.S. Ct. Apls., 3d cir., 1967-68; assoc. Sills, Beck, Cummis, Radin & Tischman, Newark, N.J., 1968-71; sole practice, Union, N.J., 1972-75; ptnr. Gutterman, Wolkstein, Klinger & Yohalem and predecessor firm, Westfield, N.J., 1975—. Councilman, Westfield, N.J., 1979-83. Mem. N.J. State Bar Assn., Union County Bar Assn. Republican. Jewish. Editor: Rutgers Law Rev., 1966-67; contbr. N.J. Law Jour. General corporate, Real property, Probate. Office: Gutterman Wolkstein et al 240 E Grove St PO Box 2850 Westfield NJ 07091

GUTTLEIN, JORGE DE JESUS, lawyer; b. N.Y.C., Dec. 29, 1952; s. Pedro Guttlein and Rosa Lemus; m. Josephine Suarez, July 28, 1979; 1 child, Juan Carlos. BA, Columbia U., 1975, M in Internat. Affairs, JD, 1979. Bar: N.Y. 1980, U.S. Dist. Ct. (so. and ea. dists.) N.Y. 1980, U.S. Ct. Appeals (2d cir.) 1983. Atty. antitrust div. N.Y. Dept. Justice, N.Y.C., 1979-81; asst. U.S. atty. U.S. Dist. Ct. (so. dist.), N.Y.C., 1982—. Mem. ABA, N.Y. County Lawyers Assn., Puerto Rican Bar Assn., Met. Black Bar Assn. Democrat. Avocations: basketball, movies. Federal civil litigation, Estate taxation, Real property. Office: US Attys Office 1 St Andrews Plaza New York NY 10007

GUTTMAN, EGON, legal educator; b. Neuruppin, Germany, Jan. 27, 1927; came to U.S., 1958, naturalized, 1968; s. Isaac and Blima (Liss) G.; m. Inge Weinberg, June 12, 1966; children: Geoffrey David, Leonard Jay. Student, Cambridge U., 1945-47; LLB, U. London, 1950, LLM, 1952; postgrad., Northwestern U. Sch. Law, 1958-59. Barrister: Eng. 1952. Sole practice Eng., 1952-53; faculty Univ. Coll. and U. Khartoum Sudan, 1953-58, legal advisor to chief justice, 1953-58; founder, editor Sudan Law Jour. & Reports, 1956-57; researcher, lectr. Rutgers U. Sch. Law, Newark, 1959-60; asst. prof. U. Alta., Edmonton, Can., 1960-62; prof. Howard U. Law Sch., Washington, 1962-68, vis. adj. prof., 1968—; adj. prof. law Washington Coll. Law, Am. U., 1964-68, Louis P. Levitt scholar-prof., 1968—; lectr. Practicing Law Inst., 1964—; adj. prof. law Georgetown U. Law Ctr., 1972-74, Johns Hopkins U., Balt., 1973-81; vis. prof. Faculty of Law, Wolfson Coll., U. Cambridge, Eng., 1984; atty.-fellow SEC, 1976-79; cons. to various U.S. agys. and spl. commns. Author books including: Crime, Cause and Treatment, 1956, (with A. Smith) Cases and Materials on Domestic Relations, 1962, Modern Securities Transfers, 1967, 3d edit., 1987, (with R.G. Vaughn) Cases and Materials on Policy and the Legal Environment, 1973, rev., 1978, 3d edit., 1980; (with R.B. Lubic) Secured Transactions-A Simplified Guide, 1987; contbr. numerous articles, revs., briefs to profl. lit. Howard U. rep. Fund for Edn. in World Order, 1966-68; trustee Silver Spring Jewish Ctr., Md., 1976-79; mem. exec. com. Sha'are Tzedek Hosp., Washington, 1971-72. Leverhulm scholar, 1948-51; U. London studentship, 1951-52; Ford Found. grad. fellow, 1958-59, NYU summer workshop fellow, 1960, 61, 64; Louis P. Levitt Meml. scholar, 1982; recipient Outstanding Service award Student Bar Assn. Am. U., 1970, Law Rev. Outstanding Service award, 1981, Washington Coll. of Law Outstanding Contbn. to Acad. Program Devel. award, 1981. Mem. Am. Law Inst., ABA, Fed. Bar Assn. Assn. Trial Lawyers Am., Brit. Inst. Internat. and Comparative Law, Soc. Pub. Tchrs. Law (Eng.), Hon. Soc. Middle Temple, Hardwick Soc. of Inns of Ct., Sudan Philos. Soc., Assn. Can. Law Tchrs., Am. Soc. Internat. Law, Can. Assn. Comparative Law, Phi Alpha Delta (John Sherman Myers award 1972). Club: Largo. Lodge: B'nai B'rith. Contracts commercial, General corporate, Securities. Home: 930 Clintwood Dr Silver Spring MD 20902 Office: Am U Washington Coll Law 400 Massachusetts Ave NW Washington DC 20016

GUTTMAN, RUBIN, lawyer; b. Bklyn., June 22, 1952; s. Walter and Claire (Ferziger) G.; m. Eileen Jan Stewart, May 29, 1983. BA, Bklyn. Coll., 1974; JD, Cleve. State U., 1977. Bar: Ohi 1977, U.S. Dist. Ct. (no. dist.) Ohio 1978. Assoc. Dunn & Kraig, Cleve., 1977-80; ptnr. Dunn, Kraig & Guttman, Cleve., 1980-82; sole practice Cleve., 1983-85; prin. Rubin Guttman Co., L.P.A., 1985—. Mem. cabinet Jewish Community Fedn. Met. Cleve., 1984—; bd. dirs. Green Rd. Synagogue, Cleve., 1985—, Jewish Nat. Fund Cleve., 1986—; also others. Mem. Ohio Bar Assn., Assn. Trial Lawyers Am., Ohio Acad. Trial Lawyers. Avocations: model R.R.'s, toy train collecting. Personal injury, State civil litigation, General corporate. Office: 55 Pub Sq #2130 Cleveland OH 44113

GUY, JAMES MATHEUS, lawyer, realtor; b. Wichita, Kans., Aug. 26, 1945; s. Jesse Milton and Roberta Aldine (Housholder) G.; m. Cindy K. Sundell, Dec. 31, 1978. BA, U. Kans., 1967; JD, Washburn Coll., 1970. Bar: Kans. 1970, U.S. Dist. Ct. Kans. 1970. Assoc., Coombs & Brick, Wichita, Kans., 1970-71; atty. Fed. Land. Bank, Wichita, 1971-76, sr. atty., 1976-78, prin. atty., 1978-84, asst. gen. counsel litigation, 1985-86; realtor, gen. counsel and owner Consol. Realty, Inc., Wichita, 1986—. Founding mem. Kans. Preservation Alliance, Topeka, 1979—; pres. Midtown Citizens Assn., Wichita, 1984-85, mem MCA Exec. Bd., 1984—; bd. dirs., exec. com. Hist. Wichita-Sedgwick County, Inc., 1974—; mem. Wichita Hist. Landmarks Preservation Com., 1981—; bd. dirs., pres. Victorian Soc. in Am., Kans. chpt., Wichita, 1974-84, Skinner Lee Victorian House Mus., Wichita, 1976-84; mem., chmn. Wichita Hist. Landmarks Preservation Council, 1981—. Washburn U. law scholar, 1967, law research fellow, 1968-70. Mem. Wichita Area Corp. Counsels (sec. 1982-83), Washburn Law Sch. Assn., Kans. U. Alumni Assn. Lodges: Mason, Shriners. Real property, Bankruptcy, Banking. Home: 1116 Bitting Wichita KS 67203 Office: Consolidated Realty Inc 1107 N Broadway Wichita KS 67214

GUY, JOHN MARTIN, lawyer; b. Detroit, July 16, 1929; s. Alvin W. and Ann G. (Martin) G.; B.S., Butler U., 1958; J.D., Ind. U., 1961; children—Janice Lynn, Robert John. Bar: Ind. 1962. Practice law, Monticello, 1962—; atty. firm Siferd, Guy, Christopher, Loy & Guy, 1962—; mem. Ind. Ho. of Reps., 1971-74, house majority leader, 1973-74; mem. Ind. Senate, 1977-84, majority leader, 1979-80; dir. State and Savs. Bank. Pros. atty. 39th Jud. Circuit, 1963-67. Pres. White County Mental Health Assn., 1965-68. Trustee Monticello-Union Twp. Library Bd., pres., 1970-71. Served with USAF, 1951-55. Named Outstanding Republican Freshman Ind. Ho. of Reps., 1971, Ind. Senate, 1977. Mem. Am., Ind., Monticello bar assns., Am. Judicature Soc., Am. Trial Lawyers Assn., Monticello C. of C. (pres. 1975—), Am. Legion. Clubs: Masons, Shriners, Elks, Moose. Banking, Probate, Federal civil litigation. Office: 115 W Broadway PO Box 925 Monticello IN 47960

GUY, RALPH B., JR., judge; b. Detroit, Aug. 30, 1929; s. Ralph B. and Shirley (Skladd) G. AB, U. Mich., 1950, JD, 1953. Bar: Mich. 1953. Sole practice Dearborn, Mich., 1954-55; asst. corp. counsel City of Dearborn, 1955-58, corp. counsel, 1958-69; chief asst. U.S. Atty.'s Office (ea. dist.), Detroit and Mich., 1969-70, U.S. Atty., 1970-76; judge U.S. Dist. Ct. (ea. dist.) Mich., 1976-85, U.S. Ct. Appeals (6th cir.), 1985—; treas. Detroit-Wayne County Bldg. Authority, 1966-73; chmn. sch. study com. Dearborn Bd. Edn., 1973; mem. Fed. Exec. Bd., 1970—, bd. dirs., 1971-73. Recipient Civic Achievement award Dearborn Rotary, 1971; Distinguished Alumni award U. Mich., 1972. Mem. ABA (state chmn. sect. local govt. 1965-70), Fed. Bar Assn. (pres. 1974-75), State Bar Mich. (commr. 1975—), Detroit Bar Assn., Dearborn Bar Assn. (pres. 1959-60), Am. Judicature Soc., Nat. Inst. Municipal Law Officers (chmn. Mich. chpt. 1964-69), Mich. Assn. Municipal Attys. (pres. 1962-64), Mich. Municipal League, Out-County Suprs. Assn. (pres. 1965), Phi Alpha Delta, Lambda Chi Alpha. Club: U. Mich. Alumni (local pres. Dearborn 1961-62). Lodge: Rotary (local pres. 1973-74). Jurisprudence. Office: 200 E Liberty Suite 226 Ann Arbor MI 48104

GUYTON, ODELL, lawyer; b. Dublin, Ga., June 3, 1955; s. Clarence and Eleanor Jeanell (Graves) G.; m. Karen Boyer, May 19, 1979; children: Kiley Jeanell, Dana Laurel. BA, Moravian Coll., 1977; JD, Am. U., 1981. Bar: Pa. 1981. Chief asst. dist. atty. Phila., 1981—; chmn. Justice Ops. Task Force, Phila., 1986—; co-chmn. Victim Witness Task Force, Phila., 1986—; mem. supervisory bd. Phila. Adult Probation Intensive Supervison Program. Chmn. Community Safety Program Northwest Interfaith Movement, Phila., 1983-85. Named one of Outstanding Young Men of Am., U.S. Jaycees, 1981. Mem. ABA, Pa. Dist. Atty's. Assn., Phi Alpha Delta. Avocations: English history, biking, camping. Criminal, Crime victim's rights.. Office: Phila Dist Attys Office 1300 Chestnut St Philadelphia PA 19107

GUYTON, SAMUEL PERCY, lawyer; b. Jackson, Miss., Mar. 20, 1937; s. Earl Ellington and Eulalia (Reynolds) G.; m. Jean Preston, Oct. 11, 1959; children—Tamara Reynolds, William Preston, David Sage. B.A., Miss. State U., 1959; LL.B., U. Va., 1965. Bar: Colo. 1965, U.S. Dist. Ct. Colo. 1965, U.S. Tax Ct. 1977, U.S. Ct. Appeals (10th cir.) 1965, U.S. Ct. Appeals (5th cir.) 1981. Ptnr., Holland & Hart, Denver, 1965—; faculty Am. Law Inst. ABA, 1976-86. Sec., trustee Colo. Hist. Found., 1971-86, pres., 1983-86; trustee Music Assn. Aspen and Aspen Music Festival, 1980-86; precinct com. chmn. Democratic party, 1968-70. Served as capt. USAF, 1959-62. Fellow Am. Coll. Tax Counsel (mem. bd. of regents); mem. ABA (sect. taxation 1967-86, chmn. sect.'s com. on agr. 1980-82), Colo. Bar Assn. (tax council 1983-86, sec. 1983, chmn. 1985-86), Denver Bar Assn., Rocky Mountain Estate Planning Council, Greater Denver Tax Csls. Assn. (chmn. 1978), Law Club of Denver. Mem. United Ch. of Christ. Co-author: Cattle Owners Tax Manual, 1984, Supplement to Federal Taxation of Agriculture, 1983, Colorado Estate Planning Desk Book, 1984; contbr. articles to jours., mags.; bd. advs. Agrl. Law Jour., 1978-82; mem. editorial bd. Jour. Agrl. Tax and Law, 1983-86. Estate planning, Probate, Personal income taxation. Office: Holland & Hart PO Box 8749 Denver CO 80201

GUZZETTI, WILLIAM LOUIS, lawyer, oil company executive; b. Chgo., May 22, 1943. BA, Harvard U., 1964; JD with high honors, U. Fla., 1972. Bar: Fla. 1973, Tex. 1983. Assoc. Maguire, Yoorhis & Wells P.A., Orlando, Fla., 1972-76; sr. v.p., gen. counsel Saxon Oil Co., Dallas, 1976-85, pres., 1985—. Served to capt. U.S. Army, 1966-70, Vietnam. Mem. Fla. Bar Assn. (chmn. out of state practioners com. 1986—, bd. govs. 1987—), Tex. Bar Assn., Order of Coif. Roman Catholic. Club: Petroleum (Dallas). General corporate, Corporate taxation, Securities. Home: 2818 Welborn Dallas TX 75219 Office: Saxon Oil Co 717 N Harwood Suite 1300 Dallas TX 75201

HAAG, GERALD DEAN, lawyer; b. Hutchinson, Kans., Nov. 28, 1944; s. Harley F. and Frances O. (Bateman) H.; m. J. Diane Weirauch, July 16, 1966; children—Ashley, Brandon. B.A., Wichita State U., 1966; J.D., U. Kans., 1969. Bar: Kans. 1969, U.S. Dist. Ct. Kans. 1969, U.S. Ct. Appeals (10th cir.) 1969. Ptnr. Jochems, Sargent & Blaes, Wichita, Kans., 1969-77, Sargent, Klenda, Haag & Mitchell, Wichita, 1977-86, Wisdom & Haag, P.A., Wichita, 1986—; Mem. ABA, Kans. Bar Assn., Wichita Bar Assn., Order of Coif. Republican. Securities. Office: 200 E First Suite 100 Wichita KS 67202

HAAKE, CATHARINE ANN, lawyer; b. St. Joseph, Mo., Apr. 29, 1954; d. Henry Elmer and Mary Catharine (Growney) H. BS, U. Ill., 1976; JD, Northwestern U., 1979. Bar: Ill. 1979, U.S. Dist. Ct. (no. dist.) Ill. 1979, Colo. 1981, U.S. Dist. Ct. Colo. 1984. Assoc. Mayer, Brown & Platt, Chgo., 1979-81; assoc. Mayer, Brown & Platt, Denver, 1981-85, ptnr., 1986—. Mem. ABA, Ill. Bar Assn., Colo. Bar Assn., Denver Bar Assn. Banking, Contracts commercial, Bankruptcy. Office: Mayer Brown & Platt 600 17th St Suite 2800 S Denver CO 80202

HAAR, CHARLES MONROE, lawyer, educator; b. Antwerp, Belgium, Dec. 3, 1920; s. Benjamin and Dora (Eisner) H.; came to U.S., 1921; A.B., N.Y. U., 1940; LL.B., Harvard, 1948; M.A., U. Wis., 1941; LL.D., Lake Erie U., 1968; m. Natalie Zinn, 1946; children—Jeremy, Susan Eve, Jonathan. Bar: N.Y. 1949, U.S. Dist. Ct. (so. dist.) N.Y. 1950, U.S. Supreme Ct. 1968, Mass. 1978. Practice law, N.Y.C., 1949-52; asst. prof. law Harvard, 1952-54, prof., 1954-66, 69—, Louis D. Brandeis prof. law, 1972—; chmn. Joint Center for Urban Studies, Mass. Inst. Tech. and Harvard, 1969—, chmn. land policy roundtable Lincoln Inst. Land Policy; dir. Charles River Assos.; asst. sec. met. devel. Dept. Housing and Urban Devel., Washington, 1966-69. Chief reporter Am. Land Inst. project model code land devel., 1964-66; mem. Cambridge Redevel. Authority, Met. Area Planning Council, Mass. Gov.'s Com. on Resource Mgmt., 1974, Fin. Adv. Bd., 1978—, Uniform Commn. State Laws, 1979—, Jerusalem Com., 1970—; chmn. Pres.'s Task Force Preservation Natural Beauty, Task Force on Model Cities, on Suburban Problems; chmn. com. on met. governance RFF, 1970-72. Cons. White House, AID, HHFA, U.S. Senate Subcom. Govtl. Ops., World Bank, OTA, state and city agys.; mem. U.S. del. to UN Conf. on Habitat, 1976. Pres. Regional and Urban Planning Implementation, Inc.; bd. dirs. Zelda Zinn Found.; trustee Mass. Gen. Hosp., 1979—. Served to lt. (j.g.), USNR, 1942-46. Fellow Urban Land Inst.; mem. Am. Acad. Arts and Scis., Am. Inst. Planners, Brit. Town Planning Inst., Am. Bar Assn., Am. Law Inst., Phi Beta Kappa. Author: Land Planning Law in a Free Society; Land-Use Planning, 3d edit., 1977, Federal Credit and Private Housing, 1960, Law and Land, 1964, Golden Age of American Law, 1966, The End of Innocence, 1972, Housing the Poor in Suburbia, 1973, Suburban Problems, 1973, Property and Law, 1977, 2d edit., 1985, (with others) The Wrong Side of the Tracks, 1986. Editor: Beacon Classics of the Law. Contbr. articles to law, econs. and planning jours. Real property, Government contracts and claims. Office: Harvard Law Sch Cambridge MA 02138

HAARMANN, BRUCE DONALD, corporate lawyer; b. Milw., Jan. 14, 1952. BA, U. Wis., 1974, JD, 1978. Bar: Wis. 1978. Legal counsel Legis. Audit Bur., State of Wis., 1978-84; asst. counsel Wausau (Wis.) Ins. Cos., 1984—. Mem. ABA (corp., banking and bus. law sect.). Insurance, Commercial collections, Real property. Office: Wausau Ins Cos 2000 Westwood Dr Wausau WI 54401

HAAS, DOUGLAS ERIC, lawyer; b. Cleve., Mar. 22, 1950; s. Alvin Nelson and Barbara Hermene (Amster) H.; m. Judith Ann Conroy, Aug. 20, 1977; children: Amelia Rachel, Elizabeth Rebecca. B.A., Tufts U., 1973; J.D., M.B.A., Washington U., St. Louis, 1977. Bar: Ohio 1977, U.S. Dist. Ct. (no. dist.) Ohio 1977, D.C. 1980, U.S. Ct. Appeals (6th cir.) 1980, U.S. Supreme Ct. 1981. Ptnr. Benesch, Friedlander, Coplan & Aronoff, Cleve., 1977—; dir. Bud Industries, Inc., Willoughby, Ohio. Mem. ABA, Ohio State Bar Assn., Greater Cleve. Bar Assn., D.C. Bar Assn. Securities, General corporate, Labor. Home: 15709 Fernway Rd Shaker Heights OH 44120 Office: Benesch Friedlander Coplan & Aronoff 1100 Citizens Bldg Cleveland OH 44114

HAAS, JOHN HOWARD, real estate executive; b. Torrington, Conn., Nov. 20, 1948; s. Howard William and Helene Irma (Henschke) H.; m. Judith Ann Hyman, Nov. 20, 1971; children: Jason M., Justin A. BA in Econs., U. Conn., 1970; JD, U. Balt., 1975. Bar: Md. 1975. Assoc. Callahan, Calwell & Laudeman, Balt., 1975-76; asst. counsel McCormick & Co. Inc., Hunt Valley, Md., 1976-78; assoc. gen. counsel McCormick Properties, Hunt Valley, 1978-81, gen. counsel, 1981-84; pres. Huntington Realty Interests Ltd., Hunt Valley, 1984-86; exec. v.p. McCormick Properties Inc., Hunt Valley, 1986—; mem. exec. com. and bd. dirs. McCormick Properties, Inc.; bd. dirs. McCormick Constrn. Co. Inc., Hunt Valley. Served to 1st lt. U.S. Army, 1970-72. Mem. ABA, Nat. Assn. Realtors, Nat. Assn. Indsl. and Office Parks, Real Estate Syndication and Securities Inst., Md. Bar Assn. Avocations: sailing, golf. Real property, Securities, Personal income taxation. Home: 6 Clynmalira Ct Phoenix MD 21131 Office: McCormick Properties Inc 1101 McCormick Rd Hunt Valley MD 21031

HAAS, RICHARD, lawyer; b. Glens Falls, N.Y., Sept. 1, 1924; s. Marc and Henrietta (Vogelsanger) H.; m. Dorothy J. Walz, Aug. 2, 1946; children—Eric, Marco, Gregory. A.B., UCLA, 1946; LL.B., U. Calif.-Berkeley, 1950. Bar: Calif. 1951, U.S. Dist. Ct. (no., cen., ea. and so. dists.) Calif. 1951, U.S. Supreme Ct. 1970. Ptnr. Brobeck, Phleger & Harrison, San Francisco, 1959-79; mem. Lasky, Haas, Cohler & Munter, San Francisco, 1979—. Served to lt. USNR, 1941-46. Fellow Am. Coll. Trial Lawyers; mem. ABA, Order of Coif. Republican. Clubs: St. Francis Yacht (San Francisco); Claremont Country (Oakland, Calif.); Berkeley Tennis. Antitrust, Federal civil litigation, General practice. Home: 2901 Forest Ave Berkeley CA 94705 Office: Lasky Haas Cohler & Munter 505 Sansome St 12th Floor San Francisco CA 94111

HAAS, WILLIAM LAMBERT, investment co. exec., lawyer; b. Framingham, Mass., Jan. 23, 1940; s. Joseph L. and Helen C. (Mulcahy) H.; m. Mary Ann Slaker, Oct. 30, 1976. AB, Princeton U., 1961; LLB, Boston Coll., 1964; MST, Bentley Coll., 1979; LLM, Boston U., 1983. Bar: Mass. 1964, Ill. 1968, N.J. 1972, U.S. Ct. Appeals (7th cir.) 1972, U.S. Supreme Ct. 1972; CLU U.S. Dept. Treasury, 1968-69; mem. tax law staff Met. Life, N.Y.C., 1969-74; v.p. AIMS Group, Inc., N.Y.C., 1974-75; cons. U.S. Boston Corp., Burlington, Mass., 1975-81; pres. Tax & Investment Group, Lexington, Mass., 1981—. Mem. curriculum adv. council Bently Coll; trustee Leonard Morse Hosp., Natick, Mass.; bd. legal advs. Small Bus. Council Am.; mem. selection com. Am. Field Service. Served to lt. comdr. JAGC, USNR, 1964-67. Mem. ABA (chmn. subcom. on ins. and investments for profls. tax sect.), Mass. Bar Assn., Ill. State Bar Assn., Internat. Assn. Fin. Planners. Roman Catholic. Clubs: Princeton (N.Y.C.); Harvard (Boston); Toastmasters (Concord, Mass.). Author: The Professional Corporation, 1972; Tax Planning for Individuals, 1981; Employee Fringe Benefits, 1982. Personal income taxation, Insurance, Pension, profit-sharing, and employee benefits. Home: 41 Allen Farm Ln Concord MA 01742

HAASE, M. CRAIG, lawyer; b. Evanston, Ill., Mar. 3, 1943. Student U. Wis.-Madison, 1961-64; B.A. in Geology, Northwestern U., 1965; J.D., U. Ill., 1971. Bar: Nev. 1972. Instr. bus. law U. Ill., 1970-71; law clk. to Judge Bruce R. Thompson, U.S. Dist. Ct., Reno, 1971-72; assoc. Adams, Reed, Bowen & Murphy, Reno, 1972-73, Sanford, Sanford, Fahrenkopf & Mousel, Reno, 1973-75; ptnr. Hawkins, Rhodes, Sharp, Barbagelata, Haase, Reno, 1976-81; sole practice M. Craig Haase, P.C., Reno, 1981-84; ptnr. Haase, Harris & Morrison, 1984-86, Haase & Harris, 1986—; spl. dep. atty. gen. State of Nev., 1972-73; lectr.-in-chief Nev. Bar Rev., 1973; instr. real estate law U. Nev., Reno, 1973-74; faculty adv. Nat. Coll. State Judiciary, Reno, 1974. Mem. Rocky Mountain Mineral Law Found., Geol Soc. Am., Am. Inst. Mining Engrs., Ninth Cir. Jud. Conf. (del. 1976). Contbr. articles to legal jours.; assoc. editor Law Forum, U. Ill. Coll. Law. Mining and minerals, Real property, Contracts commercial. Office: 6121 Lakeside Dr Suite 240 Reno NV 89511

HAASE, WILLIAM XAVIER, lawyer; b. Cleve., Jan. 1, 1926; s. William Herman and Mary Veronica (McGurren) H.; m. Shirley Rickert, July 7, 1951 (div.); children—William Warren, Nancy Jane, Christian Douglas. A.B., Kent State U., 1949; J.D., Case Western Res. U., 1951. Bar: Ohio, U.S. Dist. Ct., Ohio. Assoc. Griswold and Leeper, Cleve., 1951-59; ptnr. Ford, Whitney & Haase, Cleve., 1960-75, Haase & Dempsey, Cleve., 1975-79, Arter & Hadden, Cleve., 1979—; dir. Reliable Spring and Wire, Cleve. Contbr. articles to profl. jours. Bd. dirs. Cleve. Suburban YMCA, 1968; trustee Cleve. Legal Aid Soc., 1971; law sch. del. Case Western Res. U., Cleve., 1977-78, vis. com. bd. overseers, 1978-80. Served with USN, 1944-46. Mem. ABA, Ohio Bar Assn. (vice-chmn. com. 1986-87), Am. Arbitration Assn., Cleve. Bar Assn. (chmn. com. 1983-84), Newcomen Soc. N.Am., Case Western Res. U. Alumni Assn. (pres. 1972-73). Republican. Unitarian. Clubs: Union, City (Cleve.). General corporate, Pension, profit-sharing, and employee benefits, Mergers, acquisitions & leveraged buyouts. Home: 12700 Lake Rd Apt #1103 Lakewood OH 44107 Office: Arter & Hadden 1100 Huntington Bldg Cleveland OH 44115

HABER, RICHARD JEROME, lawyer; b. Bethlehem, Pa., Aug. 29, 1939; s. Seymour and Sophie Haber; m. Rosemary Murdy, Dec. 22, 1983; children: Spencer B., Jennifer P. BA, Pa. State U., 1961; JD, U. Pa., 1964. Bar: Pa. 1964, U.S. Dist. Ct. (ea. dist.) Pa. 1965. Ptnr. Haber & Corriere, Bethlehem, 1968—. Mem. Pa. Boro Solicitors Assn. (pres. 1984-87). Democrat. Avocation: raising orchids. Estate planning, Local government, Real property. Home: Sharswood W Macada Rd Bethlehem PA 18017 Office: Haber & Corriere 433 E Broad St PO Box 1217 Bethlehem PA 18016

HABERBUSCH, CARL ARTHUR, lawyer; b. Rochester, N.Y., Jan. 15, 1946; s. Franklin A. and Helen J. (Murphy) H.; m. June M. Carey, Apr. 11, 1970; children: Robert, Margaret, Thomas, Timothy, Katherine. BA, Fairfield U., 1967; JD, Fordham U., 1970. Bar: N.Y. 1971, U.S. Supreme Ct. 1980, N.J. 1982. Assoc. Cahill, Gordon & Reindel, N.Y.C., 1970-83; asst. counsel Pan Am. World Airways Inc., N.Y.C., 1983-86; sr. atty. Burns and Roe Enterprises Inc., Oradell, N.J., 1986—. Mem. ABA (litigation and antitrust sects.), Am. Law Inst.-ABA (lectr. com. on continuing profl. edn.), N.Y. State Bar Assn. (lectr. com. on continuing legal edn.), Fordham U. Law Rev. Assn. (gov. 1973—). Club: Montclair (N.J.) United Soccer (v.p., trustee 1984—). Federal civil litigation, State civil litigation, Construction. Home: 104 Summit Ave Upper Montclair NJ 07043 Office: Burns and Roe Enterprises Inc 700 Kinderkamack Rd Oradell NJ 07649

HABIAN, BRUCE GEORGE, lawyer; b. Rockville Centre, N.Y., Nov. 23, 1947; s. George and Doris Marie (Cipollina) H. A.B., Boston Coll., 1969; J.D., Villanova U., 1972. Bar: N.Y. 1973, N.J. 1974, U.S. Dist. Ct. (so. and ea. dists.) N.Y. 1975, U.S. Ct. Appeals (2d cir.) 1975, U.S. Supreme Ct. 1976. Asst. corp. counsel Office Corp. Counsel N.Y.C., 1972-73; assoc. Martin, Clearwater & Bell, N.Y.C., 1973-79, ptnr., 1979—, sr. ptnr., 1983—; lectr. Practicing Law Inst., N.Y.C., 1981; lectr. in risk mgmt. Hosp. Fin. Mgmt. Assn., Hartford, Conn., 1981; cons. N.Y. State Commr. Health, N.Y.C., 1983; mem. Med. Malpractice Mediation Panel, Nassau County, N.Y., 1983-84. Mem. Assn. Bar City N.Y., ABA (litigation sect.). Republican. Roman Catholic. Club: University (N.Y.C.). Personal injury, Federal civil litigation, State civil litigation. Home: 993 Park Ave Apt 1-B New York NY 10028 Office: Martin Clearwater and Bell 220 E 42d St New York NY 10017

HABICHT, FRANK HENRY, II, lawyer; b. Oak Park, Ill., Apr. 10, 1953; s. Frank Henry and Jeanne Ellen (Patrick) H.; m. Wendy Louise Wilson, June 14, 1980; children—Jennifer Alane, Caroline Lesher. A.B., Princeton U., 1975; J.D., U. Va., 1978. Bar: D.C. 1978, U.S. Supreme Ct. 1983. Assoc. Kirkland & Ellis, Washington, 1978-81; spl. asst. to atty. gen. U.S., Dept. Justice, Washington, 1981-83; dep. asst. atty. gen. for natural resources Dept. Justice, Washington, 1982-83, asst. atty. gen. for land and natural resources, 1983—; mem. faculty Am. Law Inst. ABA Continuing Edn., 1983. Editor: Va. Jour. Internat. Law, 1977-78. Mem. transition team Dept. Justice, 1980. Dillard Legal Writing fellow, 1977-78; Nat. Merit scholar, 1971; recipient Edmund Randolph award 1984. Mem. ABA, U. Va. Alumni Assn. Republican. Presbyterian. Club: Princeton Rugby (pres. 1974-75). Environment, Oil and gas leasing, General corporate. Office: Dept Justice 10th and Constitution Ave NW Washington DC 20530

HABICHT, JAMES ROBERT, lawyer; b. Worthington, Minn., Oct. 31, 1946; s. Graydon Joshua and Dorothy Carolyn (Klas) H.; m. Valerie Ann Calvin, Aug. 24, 1968; children: Jane, Jennifer, Jeff. AA, Worthington Community Coll., 1966; BA, U. Minn., Morris, 1968; JD, U. Minn., Mpls., 1974. Bar: Minn. 1974, U.S. Ct. Appeals (11th cir.) 1974. Atty. Minn. Power and Light Co., Duluth, 1974-78, sr. atty., 1978-83, gen. counsel, sec., 1983-84, v.p., gen. counsel and sec., 1984—; active legal com. Edison Electric Inst., 1983—. Bd. dirs. St. Mary's Med. Ctr., Deluth, 1986—. Served to sgt. U.S. Army, 1969-71. Methodist. Club: Kitchi Gammi. Administrative and regulatory, General corporate. Office: Minn Power and Light Co 30 W Superior St Duluth MN 55802

HABLUTZEL, NANCY ZIMMERMAN, lawyer, educator; b. Chgo., Mar. 16, 1940; d. Arnold Fred Zimmerman and Maxine (Lewison) Zimmerman Goodman; m. Philip Norman Hablutzel, July 1, 1980; children—Margo Lynn, Robert Paul. B.S., Northwestern U., 1960; M.A., Northeastern Ill. U., 1972; J.D., Ill. Inst. Tech. Chgo.-Kent Coll. Law, 1980; Ph.D., Loyola U., Chgo., 1983. Bar: Ill. 1980, U.S. Dist. Ct. (no. dist.) Ill. 1980. Speech therapist various pub. schs. and hosps., Chgo. and St. Louis, 1960-63, 65-72; audiologist U. Chgo. Hosps., 1963-65; instr. spl. edn. Chgo. State U., 1972-76; asst. prof. Loyola U., Chgo., 1981-87; adj. prof. Ill. Inst. Tech. Chgo.-Kent Coll. Law, 1982—; legal dir. Legal Clinic for Disabled, Chgo., 1984-85, exec. dir., 1985—. Mem. Ill. Gov.'s Com. on Handicapped, 1972-75; mem. Council for Exceptional Children, faculty moderator student div., 1982-87. Loyola-Mellon Found. grantee, 1983. Mem. ABA, Ill. Bar Assn. (sec. standing com. on juvenile justice, 1986—, Inst. Pub. Affairs 1985—), Chgo. Bar Assn. (exec. com. of corp. law com. 1984—), Am. Ednl. Research Assn. Republican. Juvenile, Legal education, Disability law. Office: Legal Clinic for Disabled Rehab Inst of Chgo Room 1172 345 E Superior St Chicago IL 60611

HABLUTZEL, PHILIP NORMAN, law educator; b. Flagstaff, Ariz., Aug. 23, 1935; s. Charles Edward and Electa Margaret (Cain) H.; m. Nancy Zimmerman, July 1, 1980; children—Margo Lynn, Robert Paul. B.A., La. State U., 1958; postgrad. U. Heidelberg, W.Ger., 1959-60, 60-62; M.A., U. Chgo., 1960, J.D., 1967. Bar: Ill. 1967, U.S. Dist. Ct. (no. dist.) Ill. 1967. Research atty. Am. Bar Found., Chgo., 1967-68, sr. research atty., 1968-71; asst. prof. law Chgo.-Kent Coll. Law, Ill. Inst. Tech., 1971-73, assoc. prof., 1973-79, prof., 1979—, dir. grad. program in fin. services law, 1985—; cons. OEO Legal Services Program, 1967-69; reporter Ill. sec. state's com. on revision of not-for-profit corp. act, 1984-86. Pres., trustee, Chgo. Sch. Profl. Psychology, 1979-83; reporter Ill. Sec. of State's corp. laws adv. com., 1986—. Rotary Found. Advanced Study fellow, 1959-60. Mem. ABA (chmn. subcom. on adoption of Uniform Trade Secrets Act 1984-86), Ill. State Bar Assn., Chgo. Bar Assn. (chmn. com. on sci., tech. and law 1971-72, sec. corp. law com. 1986-87). Republican. Episcopalian. Author: (with R. Garrett, W. Scott) Model Business Corporation Act Annotated, 2d edit., 3 vols., 1971, (with J. Levi) Model Residential Landlord-Tenant Code, 1969. Avocations: travel, sailing, photography. General corporate, Legal education, Banking. Office: IIT Chgo-Kent Coll Law 77 S Wacker Dr Chicago IL 60606

HABUSH, ROBERT LEE, lawyer; b. Milw., Mar. 22, 1936; s. Jesse James and Beatrice (Liebenberg) H.; m. Miriam Lee Friedman, Aug. 25, 1957; children—Sherri Ellen, William Scott, Jodi Lynn. B.B.A., U. Wis., 1959, J.D., 1961. Bar: Wis. 1961, U.S. Dist. Ct. (ea. and we. dists.) Wis. 1961, U.S. Ct. Appeals (7th cir.) 1965, U.S. Supreme Ct. 1986. Pres. Habush, Habush & Davis, Milw., 1961—; lectr. U. Wis. Law Sch., Marquette U. Law Sch., State Bar Wis., other legal orgns. Author: Cross Examination of Non Medical Experts, 1981. Contbr. articles to legal jours. Served to capt. U.S. Army, 1959-75. Mem. ABA, Wis. Bar Assn., Wis. Acad. Trial Lawyers (pres. 1968-69), Am. Trial Lawyers Assn. (nat. parliamentarian, sec. 1971-73, bd. govs. 1983-86, pres. 1986—), Internat. Acad. Trial Lawyers (bd. dirs. 1983—), Am. Bd. Trial Advocates, Internat. Soc. Barristers, Inner Circle Advocates. Federal civil litigation, State civil litigation, Personal injury. Office: Habush Habush & Davis SC 777 E Wisconsin Ave Milwaukee WI 53202

HACK, LINDA, lawyer; b. Chgo., Nov. 30, 1949; d. Paul K. and Lorraine B. (Johnston) H.; m. Thomas E. Barnes, Nov. 30, 1967 (div. May 1977); m. Gary J. Derer, Aug. 15, 1979. MA, Roosevelt U., 1975; JD, DePaul U., 1979. Bar: Ill. 1979, Tex. 1980, U.S. Dist. Ct. (no. dist.) Ill. 1980, U.S. Dist. Ct. (no. dist.) Tex. 1981, U.S. Ct. Appeals (5th cir.) 1981, U.S. Ct. Internat. Trade 1982, U.S. Supreme Ct. 1983. Judge adminstrv. law Ill. Dept. Labor, 1979-80; assoc. Law Offices F. Ward Steinbach, 1981-83; ptnr. Hack & Derer, Dallas, 1983—; of counsel Hicks, Gillespie, James & Lesser, 1983-84; arbitrator Chgo. Mercantile Exchange. Mem. subcom. med. and legal ctrs. Goals for Dallas, 1984-85, steering com. CHOICE, 1984-86, polit. action com. Oak Lawn Dems., 1984-85, voter registration com. Dallas Area Women's Polit. Caucus, 1984, vice chmn. 1985-86, bd. dirs. 1984-85; bd. dirs. Tex. Abortion Rights Action League, 1985-86. Mem. ABA (various coms.), Ill. Bar Assn., Tex. Bar Assn. (various coms.), Dallas Bar Assn. (various coms.), Nat. Conf. Women's Bar Assns. (speakers bur. 1984-85, chmn. directory 1984-85, sec. 1985-86, v.p. 1986-87), Nat. Assn. Women Judges, Am. Judicature Soc., Tex. Young Lawyers Assn. (co-chmn. alt. dispute resolution com. 1984-86, liaison alt. dispute resolution com. 1983-84), Dallas Assn. Young Lawyers (chairperson alt. dispute resolution com. 1984-85), Dallas Women Lawyers Assn. (v.p. 1982-83, pres. 1983-84, pub. relations liaison 1984, liaison nat. conf. women's bar assn. 1984-86), Women's Bar Assn. Ill., Assn. Trial Lawyers Am., Ill. Trial Lawyers Assn., Tex. Trial Lawyers Assn., Acad. Family Mediators (full), Mediation Council Ill., Tex. Assn. Family Mediators, Inc. (founding mem.), Soc. Profls. in Dispute Resolution, Indsl. Relations Research Assn., Chgo. Mercantile Exchange, Nat. Fedn. Bus. and Profl. Women's Club (del. nat. convention 1983), Tex. Fedn. Bus. and Profl. Women's Club (chmn. pub. relations convention 1984-85, treas. 1984-85, chmn. individual devel. 1983-84, chmn. pub. relations 1983-84, recipient Tex. Nat. Program award 1983), White Rock Bus. and Profl. Women's Club (chmn. individual devel. 1983-84, chmn. goals com. 1984-85, pres. 1985-86), Bus. and Profl. Women, Dallas, Inc. (program chmn. 1982-83), Nat. Futures Assn., Nat. Panel Arbitrators, Am. Arbitration Assn. Lodge: Zonta. Avocations: travel, public speaking, soap operas. Alternate dispute resolution, State civil litigation, Real property. Home: 1650 N Humboldt Blvd Chicago IL 60647-5018 Office: 2800 Logan Blvd Chicago IL 60647

HACKER, JERRY WILLIAM, lawyer; b. Decatur, Ill., Jan. 5, 1944; s. William Henry and Alma Lee (Puckett) H.; m. Lois Fay Hetzler, Aug. 29, 1965; children: Justin Thomas, Travis William. BS in Mgmt., U. Ill., 1967; JD, U. Tenn., 1973. Bar: Tenn. 1973. Trial atty. FPC, Washington, 1975, FAA, Ord, Okla., 1975—. Served to capt. U.S. Army, 1967-70. Mem. ABA, Tenn. Bar Assn., Order of Coif, Phi Kappa Phi. Republican. Administrative and regulatory, Federal civil litigation, Condemnation. Home: 5504 NW 115th St Oklahoma City OK 73132 Office: FAA PO Box 25082 Oklahoma City OK 73125

HACKETT, KEVIN R., lawyer; b. Atlantic City, N.J., Apr. 16, 1949. Real property, Contracts commercial, Landlord-tenant. Office: Milbank Tweed Hadley & McCloy 1 Chase Manhattan Plaza New York NY 10005

HACKETT, ROBERT JOHN, lawyer; b. N.Y.C., Feb. 6, 1943; s. John P. and Marie S. (Starace) H.; m. Anita Carlile, Apr. 19, 1969; children: Robert J., John Peter, Kathryn Marie. AB, Rutgers U., 1964; JD, Duke U., 1967. Bar: N.Y. 1967, Ariz. 1972. Assoc. Milbank, Tweed, Hadley, McCloy, N.Y.C., 1967-71; ptnr. Evans, Kitchel & Jenckes, Phoenix, 1971—; sec., counsel Ariz. Fueling Facilities Corp., 1982-83. Editorial bd. Duke Law Jour. Mem. ABA, State Bar Ariz. (securities regulation sect., chmn. com. rules, regulations and legis.), Maricopa County Bar Assn., Pi Sigma Alpha. Republican. Roman Catholic. Club: Phoenix Duke U. Law Alumni (pres.). Securities, General corporate. Home: 1834 Palmcroft Dr NE Phoenix AZ 85007 Office: 2600 N Central Ave Phoenix AZ 85004

HACKETT, SYLVIA LAVADA, lawyer; b. Hagerstown, Md., Mar. 22, 1938; d. Alfred Mobray and Hazel Virginia (Sard) H. BA, Wake Forest U., 1959; JD, U. Balt., 1972. Bar: Md. 1972, D.C. 1981. Caseworker Dept. of Social Services, Towson, Md., 1959-67; probation officer Cir. Ct., Towson, 1967-72; atty., supr. support & custody div. Balt. County Cir. Ct., Towson, 1972—; sole practice Balt., 1972—; Bd. dirs. Samuel Ready Scholarships, Inc., Balt. Mem. adv. com. on adoption State of Md., Balt.; regional del. diocesan council, Episcopal Diocese Md., 1983-86, chmn. program and budget, 1985-86; mem. Gov.'s Task Force to Study Adoption Laws, 1985-87. Fellowship Nat. Endowment for the Humanities, U. Iowa, 1978. Mem. ABA, Md. Bar Assn., Women's Bar Assn. Md., D.C. Bar Assn., Assn. Family and Conciliation Courts, Iota Tau Tau. Republican. Family and matrimonial, Probate. Home and office: 113 Montrose Ave Catonsville MD 21228

HACKMAN, KAREN LEE, lawyer; b. Ephrata, Pa., Aug. 2, 1956; d. Robert L. Hackman and Florence M. Vaitl. BA, Susquehanna U., 1978; JD, Dickinson U., 1981. Bar: Pa. 1981, U.S. Dist. Ct. (mid. dist.) Pa. 1981. Assoc. Tive, Hetrick & Pierce, Harrisburg, Pa., 1981-83; ptnr. Rudnitsky & Hackman, Selinsgrove, Pa., 1983—; solicitor Snyder County, Pa., 1984—; lectr. Pa. Planning Assn., Pa. Dept. Community Affairs, Harrisburg, 1981—; adj. prof. bus. law Susquehanna U., Selinsgrove, 1985—; bd. dirs. SEDA Found., Inc. V.p. SUN Contact, Selinsgrove, 1984—; mem. State Dem. Com.; bd. dirs. Am. Cancer Soc., Middleburg, Pa., 1985—. Mem. ABA, Pa. Bar Assn., Snyder County Bar Assn., Selinsgrove Area C. of C. (v.p. 1986—), Cen. Susquehanna Valley C. of C. Mem. United Ch. of Christ. Lodge: Soroptomist (local bd. dirs. 1985—). Avocations: running, reading, photography. General practice, Local government, Real property. Home: 604 N Orange St Selinsgrove PA 17870 Office: Rudnitsky & Hackman PC The Courtyard Offices PO Box 9 Selinsgrove PA 17870

HACKMAN, MARVIN LAWRENCE, lawyer; b. Jasper, Ind., Jan. 29, 1934; s. Theodore Peter and Sarah Rose (Bellner) H.; m. Jane Marie Sermersheim, Aug. 23, 1958; children: Stephen J., Anne M., Michael A., Daniel T. AB summa cum laude, St. Joseph Coll., 1956; JD, magna cum laude, Ind. U., 1959. Bar: Ind. 1959, U.S. Dist. Ct. (so. dist.) Ind. 1959, U.S. Ct. Appeals (7th cir.) 1960. Law clk. to chief judge U.S. Dist. Ct., Indpls., 1959-61; mem. Hackman McClarnon & McTurnan, Indpls., 1961—. Mem. ABA, Ind. State Bar Assn., Indpls. Bar Assn., Phi Delta Phi, Order of Coif. Real property, General corporate, Landlord-tenant. Home: 4021 Royal Pine Blvd Indianapolis IN 46250 Office: Hackman McClarnon & McTurnan 1900 One Indiana Sq Indianapolis IN 46204

HACKMAN, RICHARD PAUL, lawyer; b. Brighton, Mass., May 30, 1946; s. Howard Thomas and Catherine Ann (Russell) H.; m. Martha Jane Craig, Sept. 29, 1973 (div. Aug. 1986); children: Mary, Brooke, Charles. BA, Holy Cross Coll., 1968; JD, William & Mary Coll. of Law, 1974. Bar: Va. 1974, U.S. Dist. Ct. (ea. dist.) Va. 1975, Pa. 1976, U.S. Dist. Ct. (ea. dist.) Pa. 1976. Assoc. Delk & Barlow, Smithfield, Va., 1974-76, Robert & Stuart, Exton, Pa., 1976; div. counsel Litton Industries, Inc., Clifton Heights, Pa., 1976-79; counsel RCA Corp., Camden, N.J., 1979—. Served to maj. (JAGC), Pa. Army Nat. Guard, 1979—. Mem. ABA, Pa. Bar Assn., Va. Bar Assn. Democrat. Roman Catholic. Government contracts and claims, General corporate. Home: 264 Hilldale Rd Villa Nova PA 19085 Office: RCA Corp Front and Cooper Camden NJ 08102

HACKMANN, FRANK H(ENRY), lawyer; b. St. Louis, Jan. 22, 1945; s. Sterling W. and Mary Elizabeth (Morrow) H.; m. Helen Susan Kurz, Dec. 28, 1968; children—Emily, Frederick, Meredith, Richard. B.S. in Chem. Engring., U. Ill., 1967, J.D., St. Louis U., 1972. Bar: Mo. 1972, Ill. 1973. Engr., Monsanto Co., St. Louis, 1967-73; dir. environ. affairs, environ. atty. Ralston Purina Co., St. Louis, 1973, environ. and energy counsel, 1973-85; assoc. counsel, 1985—; lectr., speaker on environ., energy and regulatory topics. Mem. Clayton (Mo.) Sch. Bd., 1976-86, pres., 1982-85. Mem. ABA, Mo. Bar, Bar Assn. Met. St. Louis (house counsel steering com., past chmn. environmental law com.), Environ. Law Inst. (assoc.), Am. Inst. Chem. Engrs., U.S. C. of C. (com. on environ.). Roman Catholic. Environment, FERC practice, Utility rate intervention. Office: Ralston Purina Co Checkerboard Square Saint Louis MO 63164

HACKMANN, KATHY ALENE, lawyer; b. Alton, Ill., Dec. 15, 1952; d. Alvin Harrison and Mildred Evelyn (Talbert) Petitt; m. William Sterling Hackmann, Dec. 22, 1973. B.A., U. Ill., 1973, M.S., 1974; J.D., Stanford U., 1980. Bar: Calif. 1980, Minn. 1983. Indsl. engr. Sears, Roebuck & Co., Chgo., 1974-77; research asst. Stanford U. (Calif.), 1978-80; law clk. Pacific Telephone Co., San Francisco, 1979, atty., 1980-85; atty. Pacific Telesis Group, 1985—. Mem. ABA, Calif. Bar Assn., Minn. Bar Assn., Bar Assn. San Francisco. Republican. Antitrust, Public utilities. Office: Pacific Telesis Group 140 New Montgomery #1622 San Francisco CA 94105

HADDAD, FRED, lawyer; b. Waterbury, Conn., Sept. 14, 1946; s. Fred Melad and Nancy Anne (Crean) H.; m. Julia Hester, Aug. 2, 1980; 1 dau., Allison Hester; children by previous marriage—Tonja, Tristan, Matthew. Student U. Conn., 1964; B.A., U. New Haven, 1971; J.D., U. Miami (Fla.), 1974. Bar: Fla. 1974, U.S. Dist. Cts. (so. and mid. dists.) Fla. 1975, U.S. Cts. Appeals (4th, 5th, 6th, 11th cirs.) 1975, U.S. Supreme Ct. 1977, U.S. Dist. Ct. (we. dist.) Tenn. 1982, U.S. Ct. Appeals (10th cir.) Ptnr. Sandstrom & Haddad (changed to Sandstrom & Haddad, Fort Lauderdale, Fla., 1974—. Mem. Fla. Bar (criminal law, reverse sting coms.), Broward County Criminal Def. Attys. Assn., Fed. Bar Assn. (exec. com.), Nat. Fla. Criminal Def. Attys. Assn., Assn. Trial Lawyers Am., Assn. Criminal Def. Lawyers. Democrat. Criminal, Civil rights. Office: Sandstrom & Haddad 429 S Andrews Ave Fort Lauderdale FL 33301

HADDAD, JAMES BRIAN, law educator, lawyer; b. 1942. B.A., U. Notre Dame, 1964; J.D., 1967; LL.M., Northwestern U., 1969. Bar: Ill. 1967. Asst. state's atty. Cook County (Ill.), 1967-69; first asst. state's atty., 1973-74; now prof. Northwestern U. Sch. Law; lectr. Nat. Coll. Dist. Attys., Houston, 1971—; prof.-reporter Ill. Jud. Conf. Seminars for Judges, 1971—; mem. Ill. Law Enforcement Commn., 1973-77; mem. Ill. Pattern Jury Instrn. Com., 1975—; mem. Ill. Criminal Sentencing Commn., 1978-80. Mem. Order of Coif. Author: (with others) Cases and Comments on Criminal Procedure, 1974. Legal education. Office: Northwester U Law Sch 357 E Chicago Ave Chicago IL 60611 *

HADDOCK, BRADLEY EUGENE, lawyer; b. Wichita, Kans., Jan. 4, 1955; s. Kenneth Eugene and Genevieve M. Haddock; m. Terri Sue Hannon, Jan. 7, 1978. Student, Am. U., 1976; BS, Phillips U., 1977; JD cum laude, Washburn U., 1980. Bar: Kans. 1980. Coordinator govt. relations Koch Industries Inc., Wichita, 1980-81, atty., 1981-84, sr. atty. chem. tech. group, 1985—. V.p. Quivira Council Boy Scouts Am., Wichita, 1982—, mem. nat. com. Order of Arrow, Dallas, 1982—, mem. North Cen. Region Adv. Bd., Kansas City, Kans., 1986—. Recipient Silver Beaver award, Boy Scouts Am., 1977; named Outstanding Young Alumnus, Phillips U., 1985. Mem. ABA, Kans. Bar Assn., Wichita Bar Assn., Wichita C. of C. (chmn., trustee, Leadership 2000, 1984-86). Republican. Evangelical. Avocations: tennis, camping, bicycling. Contracts commercial, General corporate, Environment. Home: 1541 Woodridge Dr Wichita KS 67206-3605 Office: Koch Industries Inc PO Box 2256 Wichita KS 67201

HADDON, PHOEBE ANNIESE, law educator, consultant; b. Washington, Aug. 29, 1950; d. Wallace James and Ida (Bassette) H.; m. Thurman N. Northcross, Dec. 16, 1972 (div. Dec. 1983); m. Frank M. McClellan, Dec. 31, 1985. BA with honors, Smith Coll., 1972; JD cum laude, Duquesne U., 1977; LLM, Yale U., 1985. Bar: Pa. 1977, U.S. Dist. Ct. (we dist.) Pa. 1977, D.C. 1979, U.S. Ct. Appeals (3d cir.) 1979, U.S. Dist. Ct. (ea. dist.) Pa. 1983. Field examiner Nat. Labor Relations Bd., Cin. and Pitts., 1972-74; law clk. to presiding justice U.S. Ct. Appeals (3d cir.), Pitts., 1977-79; assoc. Wilmer, Cutler & Pickering, Washington, 1979-81; asst. prof. law Temple U., Phila., 1981-84, assoc. prof. law, 1984-87, 88—; pres. Phila. Mortgage Assistance

Corp., 1987-88; hearing examiner Water Commn., Phila., 1985; cons. Redevel. Authority, Phila., 1985—, chmn. mortgage com., 1987-88. Editor in chief Duquesne U. Law Rev., 1977; editor Pitts. Legal Jour., 1978-79. Mem. Big Bros.-Big Sisters of Phila., 1984—. Mem. ABA, Pa. Bar Assn., Phila. Bar Assn., Soc. Am. Law Tchrs. (bd. govs. 1985—), Assn. Am. Law Schs. (exec. bd. minority sect.), Barristers Assn., Smith Coll. Alumnae Assn. (bd. dirs. 1986—, bd. counselors 1973—), Coalition 100 Black Women. Club: Phila. Girl Friends (co-pres. 1985—). Avocations: reading, swimming, aerobics. Personal injury, Constituional law, Legal education. Office: Temple Law Sch 1719 N Broad St Philadelphia PA 19122

HADDOX, JEROME B., lawyer; b. Cedar Falls, Iowa, Apr. 19, 1933; s. Homer Carroll and Helen Mary (Daum) H.; m. Donna Marie Doyle, Sept. 13, 1958; children: Jeffrey, Stephen, Michelle, Amy, Owen, Eric. BS, Ohio State U., 1955, JD, 1959. Bar: Ohio 1960; CLU, CPCU. Atty. Nationwide Ins., Columbus, 1960-64, Accuray Corp., Columbus, 1964-65, Western-Southern Life, Cin., 1965-68; v.p., sec., gen. counsel J.C. Penney Casualty Ins. Co., Westerville, Ohio, 1968-86; also bd. dirs. J.C. Penney Ins. Co., Westerville, Ohio; sr. atty. Jones, Day, Reavis & Pogue, Columbus, 1986—; bd. dirs. J.C. Penney of Ohio, Columbus, J.C. Penney Agy., Inc., J.C. Penney Inc. Agy. of Ky., J.C. Penney Inc. Agy. of Oreg. Bd. dirs. Upper Arlington Boosters Club. Served to 1st lt. USMC, 1955-57. Recipient Merit award Ohio Legal Ctr. 1965, 66, 67, 68. Inst. Chartered Property Cert. of Appreciation Soc. Casualty Underwriters. Mem. ABA, Ohio Bar Assn., Columbus Bar Assn. (chmn.), Ins. Fedn. of Ohio (chmn.), Fedn. Ins. and Corp. Council (chmn.). Roman Catholic. Clubs: Lawyers, Roadrunners (Columbus). Avocations: marathon running, travel. Insurance, General corporate, Administrative and regulatory. Home: 3744 Romnay Rd Columbus OH 43220 Office: Jones Day Reavis & Pogue 1900 Huntington Ctr 41 S High St Columbus OH 43215

HADEN, CHARLES H., II, judge; b. Morgantown, W.Va., Apr. 16, 1937; s. Charles H. and Beatrice L. (Costolo) H.; m. Priscilla Ann Miller, June 2, 1956; children: Charles H., Timothy M., Amy Sue. B.S., W.Va. U., 1958, J.D., 1961. Partner Haden & Haden, Morgantown, W.Va., 1961-69; state tax commr. W.Va. 1969-72; justice Supreme Ct. Appeals W.Va., 1972-75, chief justice, 1975; judge U.S. Dist. Ct. No. and So. Dists. W.Va., Parkersburg, 1975-82; chief judge U.S. Dist. Ct. So. Dist. W.Va., 1982—; mem. W.Va. Ho. of Dels., 1963-64; asst. prof. Coll. Law, W.Va. U., 1967-68; mem. com. adminstrn. probation system Jud. Conf., 1979-86. Mem. Bd. Edn., Monongalia County, W.Va., 1967-68. Fellow Am. Bar Found.; mem. ABA, W.Va. Bar Assn., W.Va. State Bar Assn., Bar Assn., Am. Judicature Soc. Office: US District Court PO Box 1139 Parkersburg WV 26102 *

HADJI, SERGE BASIL, lawyer; b. Salonica, Greece, Sept. 25, 1942; came to U.S., 1961; s. Basil Hadji-Mihaloglou and Katherine Hadji-Toliou; m. Yanna Mariolopoulou, Oct. 29, 1976; children: Alexios, Philip, Andreas. BA, U. Buffalo, 1965; JD, Detroit Coll. Law, 1968; LLM in Internat. Law, NYU, 1970. Bar: Mich. 1968, N.Y. 1970, U.S. Supreme Ct. 1974, Ohio 1980. Assoc. Rogers, Hoge & Hills, N.Y.C., 1970-78; trademark counsel TRW Inc., Cleve., 1978-82, sr. counsel, 1982—; adj. asst. prof. law NYU, 1974-78; vis. prof. Temple U., Athens, Greece, 1981. Trustee Anatolia Coll., Thessaloniki, Greece. Mem. Am. Soc. Internat. Law, Assn. of Bar of City of N.Y., U.S. Trademark Assn., Licensing Execs. Soc., Hellenic U. Grads. Assn. (trustee, counsel). Private international, Public international, Trademark and copyright. Home: 22149 Westchester Rd Shaker Heights OH 44122 Office: TRW Inc 1900 Richmond Rd Cleveland OH 44124

HADLOW, EARL BRYCE, lawyer; b. Jacksonville, Fla., July 29, 1924; s. Earl and Emily (Hadlow) Chrichton; m. Nancy Ann Petway, Apr. 5, 1969; children: Richard B., Janet V., Bryce P., Erin. BS, Duke U., 1947, JD, 1950, JD with high honors, 1950. Bar: Fla. 1950. Asst. solicitor Duval County, Jacksonville, 1952-53; ptnr. Mahoney, Hadlow & Adams, Jacksonville, 1953-84; gen. counsel, vice chmn. Barnett Banks Fla. Inc., Jacksonville, 1984—, also bd. dirs.; bd. dirs. Barnett Bank Jacksonville. Contbr. articles to profl. jours. Trustee Jacksonville U.; bd. dirs. Children's Home Soc., Fla., 1960-69. . Served with U.S. Army, 1943-46. Fellow Am. Coll. Probate Counsel; mem. ABA, Fla. Bar Assn. (bd. of govs. 1967-72, pres. 1973-74), Jacksonville Bar Assn. (pres. 1966), Am. Bankers Assn. (govt. relations council), Associated Industries Fla. (bd. dirs. 1985—), Fla. Assn. Bank Holding Cos. (pres.), C. of C., Order of Coif, Phi Delta Phi, Alpha Tau Omega. Republican. Episcopalian. Administrative and regulatory, Banking, Contracts commercial. Office: Barnett Banks Fla Inc 100 Laura St Jacksonville FL 32203

HADZI-ANTICH, THEODORE CIRILO, lawyer; b. Chgo., June 2, 1951; s. Cirilo Hadzi-Antich and Irene (Borovsky) Orlovsky; m. Diana Bahanovich, June 25, 1978; children: Theodore Jr., Vera. BA in English with high honors, U. Conn., 1973; JD, U. Okla., 1976. Bar: Md. 1976, D.C. 1978. Atty., advisor U.S. EPA, Washington, 1976-78; assoc. Dechert, Price & Rhoads, Washington, 1978-81; asst. prof. So. Meth. U. Law Sch., Dallas, 1981-83; counsel Gen. Electric Corp., Schenectady, N.Y., 1983-85, N.Y. State Environ. Facilities Corp., Albany, 1985—; adj. assoc. prof. Rensselaer Poly. Inst., Troy, N.Y., 1986—. Contbr. articles to profl. jours. Pres. bldg. fund com. Ch. of the Nativity, Albany, N.Y., 1985—. Recipient U.S. Law Week award Bur. Nat. Affairs, 1976. Mem. ABA, D.C. Bar Assn., U.S. Supreme Ct. Bar Assn., Md. Bar Assn., Nashville Songwriters Assn. Internat. Republican. Russian Orthodox. Avocations: composer, lyricist. Office: NY State Environ Facilities Corp 50 Wolf Rd Albany NY 12205

HADZIMA, JOSEPH GEORGE, JR., lawyer; b. Ft. Belvoir, Va., Oct. 21, 1951; s. Joseph George Sr. and Katharine (O'Meara) H.; m. Margaret Darasz, Sept. 29, 1973; children: Elizabeth, Jeffrey. BS, MIT, 1973, SM in Mgmt., 1977; JD, Harvard U., 1979. Bar: Mass. 1979. Assoc. Ropes & Gray, Boston, 1979-83, Sullivan & Worcester, Boston, 1983—; clk. South Boston Neighborhood Ho., 1979-84; lectr. MIT Sloan Sch. of Mgmt., Cambridge, Mass., 1984—. Mem. ABA, Boston Bar Assn., Boston Patent Law Assn. Computer, General corporate, Securities. Office: Sullivan & Worcester One Post Office Square Boston MA 02109

HAFER, JOSEPH PAGE, lawyer; b. Harrisburg, Pa., June 28, 1941; s. George Horace and Betty (Page) H.; m. Sandra M. McKee, June 29, 1963; children: Bradford G., Susan P., David E. AB, Lafayette Coll., 1963; JD with distinction, U. Mich., 1966. Bar: Pa. 1966, U.S. Dist. Ct. (mid. dist.) Pa. 1966, U.S. Supreme Ct. 1969, U.S. Ct. Appeals (3d cir.) 1976. Assoc. Metzger, Hafer, Keefer, Thomas & Wood, Harrisburg, 1966-77; ptnr. Thomas & Thomas, Harrisburg, 1977—; adj. prof. law Dickinson Coll., Carlisle, Pa. Pres. Cumberland Valley Sch. Bd., Mechanicsburg, Pa., 1976-85; pres. Hampden Twp. Rep. Assn., Camp Hill, Pa. Mem. Pa. Bar Assn., Assn. Trial Lawyers Am., Pa. Trial Lawyers Assn., Dauphin County Bar Assn. (court relations com., minority participation com.), Def. Research Inst., Pa. Def. Inst. Methodist. Insurance, Personal injury, Workers' compensation. Home: 235 E Lauer Ln Camp Hill PA 17011 Office: Thomas & Thomas 212 Locust St Harrisburg PA 17108

HAFFNER, ALFRED LOVELAND, JR., lawyer; b. Bklyn., Sept. 11, 1925; s. Alfred Loveland and Mary Ellen (Myers) H.; m. Mary Dolores Hyland, July 10, 1965; children: Mary Elizabeth, Anne Dolores, Jeanne Marie, Catherine Dianne. B.S. in Engring, U. Mich., 1950, J.D., 1956. Bar: N.Y. 1958, U.S. Patent and Trademark Office, 1958, U.S. Dist. Ct. (so. and ea. dists.) N.Y. 1959, U.S. Ct. Claims 1959, U.S. Ct. Appeals (fed. cir.) 1961, U.S. Supreme Ct. 1961, U.S. Ct. Appeals (2d cir.) 1962. Draftsman-engr., indsl. engr., asst. plant engr. Owens-Ill. Glass Co., Bridgeton, N.J., 1950-53, Streator, Ill., 1953-54; since practiced N.Y.C.; asso. firm Kenyon & Kenyon, N.Y.C., 1957-60, Ward, McElhannon, Brooks & Fitzpatrick, N.Y.C., 1960-61; partner Ward, McElhannon, Brooks & Fitzpatrick, 1961-71, Brooks Haidt Haffner & Delahunty, N.Y.C., 1971—; Chmn. Nat. Council Patent Law Assns., 1973-74, councilman, 1971—; bd. dirs. Nat. Inventors Hall of Fame Found., 1972—, pres., 1973-74, sec., 1980—. Served with USNR, 1943-46. Mem. ABA, N.Y. State Bar Assn., Am. Intellectual Property Law Assn., N.Y. Patent Trademark and Copyright Law Assn. (sec. 1964-68, dir. 1968-70, 71-72, pres. 1970-71), Strathmore Assn. Westchester (treas. 1976-79, v.p. 1980-82, pres. 1982-83, exec. com. 1983—), Phi Gamma Delta, Phi Alpha Delta. Club: Westchester Country. Patent, Trademark and copyright. Home: 1 Gainsborough Rd Scarsdale NY 10583 Office: 99 Park Ave New York NY 10016

HAFNER, THOMAS MARK, lawyer; b. Evansville, Ind., Aug. 8, 1943; s. Theodore Paul and Josephine Margaret (Herpolsheimer) H.; m. Joy Ruth Roller, June 10, 1967; children—Mark, Sharon, Matthew, Michael, Martin. B.A. with distinction, Valparaiso U., 1965, J.D., 1968. Bar: Ind. 1968, Tenn. 1980. Asso., Nieter, Smith, Blume, Wyneken & Dixon, Ft. Wayne, Ind., 1968-70; atty. Magnavox Co., Ft. Wayne, 1970-73, group counsel, 1973-77; sr. counsel N.Am. Philips Corp., Ft. Wayne, 1977-80, Knoxville, Tenn., 1980—. Author: Legal Guidelines for Regional Managers, 1978, The Bankruptcy Code: An Outline for Creditors, 1980, A Checklist for Distribution Agreements, 1985. Mem. ABA (chmn. subcom. counseling the mktg. function com. corp. counsel 1982—), Electronic Industries Assn. (chmn. govt. and consumer affairs council 1981-86, vice chmn. law com. 1986, chmn. 1987—), Am. Corp. Counsel Assn. (dir. at large Tenn. chpt. 1986—). Antitrust, Contracts commercial, Private international.

HAFTER, JEROME CHARLES, lawyer; b. Orlando, Fla., May 16, 1945; s. Jerome Sidney and Mary Margaret (Fugler) H.; m. Jo Cille Dawkins, July 18, 1976; 1 child, Jerome Bryan. BA summa cum laude, Rice U., 1967; BA with first class honors, Oxford U., Eng., 1969, MA, 1976; JD, Yale U., 1972. Bar: Miss. 1974, U.S. Ct. Appeals (5th cir.) 1974, U.S. Dist. Ct. (no. and so. dists.) Miss. 1974. Law clk. to presiding judge U.S. Ct. Appeals (5th cir.), Jackson, Miss., 1972-73; assoc. Lake, Tindall, Hunger & Thackston, Greenville, Miss., 1973-76, ptnr., 1976—; chmn. Miss. Bd. Bar Admissions, Jackson, 1979—; sec., treas. Hafter Realty Inc., Greenville, 1969—; mem. gov.'s constn. commn., Jackson, 1985-87. Author: Family History of Peter Quin, 1964, 2d. rev. edit., 1970. Pres. Downtown Improvement Assn. Greenville, 1980—, Common Cause/Miss., 1976-78; mem. Greenville City Election Commn., 1978—; chmn. com. on tax Miss. Econ. Council, Jackson, 1985, 87. Served to 1st lt., C.E., U.S. Army, 1972, maj., USAR, 1972—. Marshall scholar, 1967-69; Leadership Miss. Program fellow, 1976-77. Fellow Miss. Bar Found.; mem. ABA (vice chmn. com. on issues affecting legal profession, young lawyers div., 1980-82), Miss. Bar Assn. (bd. dirs. young lawyers div. 1976-79), Fed. Bar Assn. (v.p. no. Miss. 1977-78, 81-82), Nat. Conf. Bar Examiners, Am. Judicature Soc., Greenville C. of C. (bd. dirs. 1984-85, 87), Washington County Hist. Soc. (pres. Greenville chpt. 1981), Phi Beta Kappa. Episcopalian. Clubs: Greenville Golf and Country (v.p. 1977-79); Huntercombe Golf (Nuffield, Eng.); Vincents (Oxford, Eng.). Lodge: Kiwanis (Greenville pres. 1978-79, lt. gov. 1982-83). Federal civil litigation, General corporate, Bankruptcy. Home: 316 S Broadway Greenville MS 38701 Office: Lake Tindall Hunger & Thackston 127 S Poplar PO Box 918 Greenville MS 38702

HAGAN, CHARLES CURTIS, JR., lawyer; b. Louisville, Jan. 25, 1951; s. Charles Threatt and Eva Belle Hagan. BA, U. Louisville, 1972, JD, 1975. Bar: Ky. 1979, U.S. Dist. Ct. (we. dist.) Ky. 1980, U.S. Supreme Ct. 1986. Project dir., program developer Presbyn. Community Ctr., Louisville, 1976-78; asst. mgr. Citizens Fidelity Bank, Louisville, 1978-79; staff atty. Jefferson Dist. Pub. Defender, Louisville, 1979-80; sr. ptnr. Hagan & Osterholt, Louisville, 1980-84; sole practice Louisville, 1984—; speaker 24th and 25th Nat. Inst. on Crime Delinquency, 1977, 78. Mem. Jefferson Community Improvement Dist. Bd., Ky., 1979-83; official Jefferson County Surveyor, Ky., 1986—; exec. dir. Midwest Missionary Bapt. Youth Conf., 1984—. Earl Warren Legal Tng. Found. fellow, 1972-74, Council on Legal Edn. Opportunity fellow, 1972-74; named one of Outstanding Young Men of Am., Bd. Advisors, 1982. Mem. Ky. Bar Assn. (bd. dirs. inmate grievance mechanism bd. 1980-82), Nat. Bar Assn. (sec. 1983-84). Democrat. Baptist. Avocations: reading, photography, travel. Personal injury, Criminal, Probate. Office: 730 W Main St Suite 480 Louisville KY 40202

HAGAN, CHARLES F., corporate lawyer; b. 1923. BS, Georgetown U., 1946; LLB, Fordham U., 1949; LLM, NYU, 1957. Atty. Kerlin, Campbell & Keating, 1949-55; asst. gen. counsel Pfizer Inc., N.Y., 1955-74; gen. counsel Am. Home Products Corp., N.Y.C., 1974-78, v.p., gen. counsel, 1978—. Served to 2d lt. AUS, 1943-45. Office: Am Home Products Corp 685 3rd Ave New York NY 10017 *

HAGAN, PETER, lawyer; b. Staten Island, N.Y., Nov. 30, 1947; s. Peter Anthony and Frances Theresa (Golumb) H.; m. Barbara Ann Sibulski, Apr. 29, 1973; children: Mary Grace, Patrick. AB, Fordham U., 1969; JD, St. John's U., 1972; MLS, Pratt Inst., 1978; LLM, NYU, 1983. Bar: N.Y. 1973, U.S. Dist. Ct. (ea. and so. dists.) N.Y., U.S. Ct. Appeals (2nd cir.) 1977. Staff atty Consol. Edison, N.Y.C., 1973—; atty. Pax Christi, N.Y.C., 1983. Served to lt. USMC, 1969-73. Mem. Ctr. for Immigrant Rights, Phi Beta Kappa. Roman Catholic. Criminal, State civil litigation, Immigration, naturalization, and customs. Home: 134 Greeley Ave Staten Island NY 10306 Office: Consolidated Edison 4 Irving Pl New York NY 10003

HAGBERG, CHRIS ERIC, lawyer; b. Steubenville, Ohio, Dec. 19, 1949; s. Rudolf Eric and Sara (Smith) H.; m. Viola Louise Wilgus, Feb. 19, 1978. B.S., Duke U., 1975; J.D., U. Tulsa, 1978; postgrad. Nat. Law Ctr., George Washington U. Bar: Va. 1979, Okla. 1978, U.S. Ct. Appeals (4th cir.), Calif. 1986. Law clk. to presiding justice U.S. Dist. Ct. (no. dist.) Okla.; asst. counsel ADP Selection Office, Dept. Navy, Navy Regional Contracting Ctr., Washington; counsel Naval Supply Ctr., Pearl Harbor, Hawaii; Pacific area counsel Naval Supply Systems Command, Dept. Navy, Makakilo, Hawaii, assoc. counsel Naval Supply Systems Command, Washington; now atty. Pettit & Martin, Los Angeles. Served to lt. USN, 1970-74. Recipient David I. Milsten award, 1978, 7 Am. Jurisprudence awards, 1976-78, First prize Dept. Navy Legal Writing Contest, 1981. Mem. ABA, Fed. Bar Assn., Nat. Contract Mgmt. Assn., Order of Coif. Democrat. Presbyterian. Contbr. articles to legal jours. Government contracts and claims, Labor, Administrative and regulatory. Address: 4200 Ironwood Ave Seal Beach CA 90740

HAGBERG, VIOLA WILGUS, lawyer, contracting officer; b. Salisbury, Md., July 3, 1952; d. William E. and Jean Shelton (Barlow) Wilgus; m. Chris Eric Hagberg, Feb. 19, 1978. B.A., Furman U., Greenville, S.C., 1974; J.D., U. S.C., 1978, U. Tulsa, 1978; DOD Army Logistics Sch. honor grad. basic mgmt. def. acquisition, def. small purchase, advanced fed. acquisition regulation, Fort Lee, Va., 1981-82. Bar: Okla. 1978, Va. 1979, U.S. Ct. Appeals (8th cir.). With Lawyers Com. for Civil Rights, Washington, 1979; pub. utility specialist Fed. Energy Regulatory Commn., Washington, 1979-80; contract specialist U.S. Army, C.E., Ft. Shafter, Hawaii, 1980-81; contract officer/supervisory contract specialist Tripler Army Med. Ctr., Hawaii 1981-83; supervisory procurement analyst and chief policy sect. Procurement Div. U.S. Coast Guard, Washington, 1983; contract officer and chief Avionics Engring Branch sect. engring., 1984; procurement analyst office of sec. Dept. Transp., 1984-85. Mem. Nat. Contract Mgmt. Assn., ABA (law student div. liaison 1977-78), Va. State Bar Assn., Okla. Bar Assn., Phi Alpha Delta, Kappa Delta Epsilon. Government contracts and claims. Home: 4200 Ironwood Ave Seal Beach CA 90740 Office: USN NRCC Bldg 53 Long Beach CA 90822-5095

HAGEL, JAMES A., lawyer; b. Seattle, Jan. 28, 1943; s. Jon Hubbard and Alice Arlene (Zink) H.; m. Mary Louise Snowden. BS in Fin., Calif. State U., Long Beach, 1966, MBA in Mgmt. Ops. Research, 1968; JD, Southwest U., 1973. Bar: Calif. 1974, U.S. Dist. Ct. (cen. dist.) Calif. 1974; cert. coll. instr., Calif., 1977. Sole practice Torrance, Calif., 1974-75, Long Beach, 1978; atty. Pass & Fainsbert, Torrance, 1975-78; sr. ptnr. Hagel & Coulter, Seal Beach, Calif., 1979—; bd. dirs. Corrugated Components, Inc., Santa Fe Springs, Calif.; chief exec. officer Snowden Studios, Long Beach, 1983—; bus. cons. Seal Beach, 1985—. Bd. dirs., house counsel Cedar House (child abuse ctr.), Long Beach, 1983—; So. Calif. Early Music Soc., 1983-84. Recipient Judge Protem Service award Los Angeles Mcpl. Ct., 1983, 1984, Family Law Mediation Service award Los Angeles Superior Ct., Los Angeles, 1984. Mem. Delta Theta Phi. Republican. Episcopalian. Avocations: tennis, snow skiing. Real property, Contracts commercial, General practice. Office: Hagel & Coulter 323 Main St Seal Beach CA 90740

HAGEL, THOMAS LEO, lawyer; b. Ainsworth, Nebr., Nov. 2, 1948; s. Charles Dean and Elizabeth (Dunn) H.; m. Carol Marie Finn, Dec. 28, 1973 (div. Feb. 1975); m. Janice Marie Stucke, Sept. 28, 1986. BS, U. Nebr., Omaha, 1972; postgrad., Ohio U., 1972-73; JD, U. Nebr., Lincoln, 1976; LLM, Temple U., 1982. Bar: Nebr. 1976, U.S. Ct. Appeals (6th cir.) 1976, U.S. Supreme Ct. 1980, Ohio 1983, D.C. 1984. Dep. pub. defender State of Nebr., Lincoln, 1976-80; asst. prof. law U. Dayton, Ohio, 1982-86, assoc. prof. law, 1986—; lectr. U. Nebr., 1978-80, continuing legal edn. Nebr. Bar Assn., 1980, Temple U., 1980, Fed. Bar Exam., 1984—; instr. Temple U., 1980-82. Author: Dealing with the System: Handbook of Juvenile Rights and Responsibilities, 1977; also articles. V.p. Nebr. Civil Liberties Union, 1976-78; mem. exec. com. Juvenile Detention Ctr., Lincoln, 1977-79; legal counsel Freeway Sta., Lincoln, 1978-80, Head Start Policy Council, Dayton, 1983; bd. dirs. ACLU, Dayton, 1983; mem. Task Force for Mentally Disabled Offenders, Lincoln, 1979. Served to sgt. U.S. Army, 1967-69, Vietnam. Decorated Purple Heart, with 2 oak leaf clusters; Cross of Gallantry Republic of Vietnam, Bronze Star; Fellow Law and Humanities, Temple U., 1980-82. Mem. Dayton Bar Assn. Roman Catholic. Avocations: camping, fishing, reading. Legal education, State civil litigation, Criminal. Office: U Dayton Sch Law 300 College Park Dayton OH 45469-0001

HAGELIN, MICHAEL THOMAS, lawyer; b. Buffalo, Aug. 7, 1955; s. Howard James and Rita (Kent) H.; m. Marguerite Ann Molke. BA, U. Buffalo, 1977; JD, Pace U., 1980. Bar: N.Y., U.S. Dist. Ct. (we. dist.). Assoc. Gannon, Gannon & Sullivan, Buffalo, 1980-81, Dixon, DeMarie & Schoenborn P.C., Buffalo, 1982—. Mem. ABA, Erie County Bar Assn., Assn. Trial Lawyers Am. Personal injury, Insurance, Federal civil litigation. Office: Dixon DeMarie & Schoenborn PC 930 Convention Tower Buffalo NY 14202

HAGEMAN, JOHN ASHLEY, lawyer; b. Hays, Kans., July 17, 1954; s. E. Charles and Beverly J. (Harris) H.; m. Cynthia J. Turnbull, Aug. 30, 1980; 1 child, Lindsey Brooke. BS in Acctg. and Bus. Adminstrn., Kans. U., 1976; JD, Washburn U., 1980. Tax acct. Arthur Young & Co., Wichita, Kans., 1980-81; assoc. atty. Sargent, Klenda et al, Wichita, 1981-85. Mem. ABA, Kans. Bar Assn., Wichita Bar Assn., Phi Delta Theta (pres. 1985—). Republican. Congregationalist. Avocations: golf, fishing, hunting, skiing. Securities, General corporate, Real property. Home: 412 S Crestway Wichita KS 67218 Office: Sargent Klenda Austerman & Mitchell 100 W Main St Suite 1000 Wichita KS 67202

HAGEN, CHRISTOPHER DONALD, lawyer; b. Des Moines, Feb. 11, 1943; s. Charles Donald and Helen Elizabeth (Twombley) H.; m. Sherry Flores; children: Courtney, Matthew. BA, U. Iowa, 1965, JD, 1968. Bar: Iowa, U.S. Dist. Ct. Iowa, U.S. Ct. Appeals (8th cir.), U.S. Supreme Ct. Trial atty. HEW, Washington, 1968-78; asst. U.S. atty. Dept. Justice, Des Moines, 1978-86, U.S. atty., 1986—. Chmn. Combined Fed. Campaign, Des Moines, 1985. Mem. ABA, Iowa Bar Assn., Polk County Bar Assn., Fed. Exec. Council. Democrat. Methodist. Avocations: tennis, swimming. Home: 4927 Grand Ave Des Moines IA 50312 Office: US Attys Office 115 US Cthouse E 1st & Walnut Sts Des Moines IA 50309 *

HAGEN, GLENN W(ILLIAM), lawyer; b. Detroit, July 8, 1948; s. William A. and Lilian (Abrolat) H.; m. Cynthia Winn, July 21, 1984. BS in Chemistry, U. Ala., 1970; JD, Valparaiso U., 1973. Bar: Mich. 1973, U.S. Dist. Ct. (we. dist.) Mich. 1974, Colo. 1981, U.S. Dist. Ct. Colo. 1982. Ptnr. Peters, Seyburn & Hagen, Kalamazoo, Mich., 1973-76; dir. legal services City of Battle Creek, Mich., 1976-79; staff atty. CF&I Steel Corp., Pueblo, Colo., 1979-81; gen. counsel Commonwealth Investment Properties Corp., Littleton, Colo., 1981-82; assoc. Berkowitz & Brady, Denver, 1982-83, Zarlengo, Mott, Zarlengo & Winbourn, Denver, 1983—. Del. Colo. Rep. Party, 1986. Mem. ABA (young lawyers exec. council 1978-81, membership com. 1976-82, gen. practice sect., chmn. small bus. enterprises 1986), Mich. Bar Assn. (young lawyer's exec. council, 1976-80), Colo. Bar Assn. (chmn. long range planning com. 1983-86, gen. practice exec. council 1985—, budget com. 1986—), Denver Bar Assn., Colo. Def. Lawyers Assn., Colo. Lawyers for Arts, Nat. Fedn. Ind. Bus., Am. Arbitration Assn. (mem. panel). Lutheran. Avocations: skiing, travel, photography. General practice, Real property, State civil litigation. Home: 7562 S Monaco Way Englewood CO 80112 Office: Zarlengo Mott Zarlengo & Winbourn 300 S Jackson St Suite 570 Denver CO 80209

HAGENDORF, STANLEY, lawyer, writer; b. Bklyn., Mar. 1, 1930; s. David and Fanny (Hammer) H.; m. Tilbeth Greene, Nov. 18, 1962; children—Lauren, Wayne, Richard. B.S. in Econs., U. Pa., 1953, J.D. cum laude, Harvard U., 1956, LL.M. in Taxation, N.Y.U. 1961. Bar: N.Y. 1956, Fla. 1975. Assoc. Hellerstein, Rosier & Brudney, N.Y.C., 1957-59; sole practice N.Y.C., 1960-70; ptnr. Karow & Hagendorf, N.Y.C., 1970-75, Hagendorf & Schlesinger, N.Y.C., Coral Gables, Fla., 1975-84, Hagendorf, Deason & Frank, 1984-85, Stanley Hagendorf, 1985—; assoc. prof. law U. Miami Law Sch., Coral Gables, 1975-80; dir.-lectr. Hagendorf-Chaykin Tax Workshop, N.Y.C.; mem. Fin. & Estate Planning Adv. Bd., Commerce Clearing House. Served with U.S. Army, 1948-51. Recipient Disting. Lectr. award Nat. Soc. Public Accts. Scholarship Found., 1980; cert. of appreciation N.Y. County Lawyers Assn., 1982. Mem. ABA, N.Y. State Bar Assn., Fla. Bar Assn. (cert. tax lawyer). Author: Tax Guide for Buying and Selling a Business, 6th edit., 1986; Tax Manual for Corporate Liquidations, Redemptions and Estate Planning Recapitalizations, 1978; Liquidations, Redemptions and Recapitalizations: Taxation and Planning, 1986; contbr. numerous articles on taxation to profl. jours. Corporate taxation, Estate taxation, Personal income taxation. Office: 4563 Central Ave Saint Petersburg FL 33713 also: 575 Fifth Ave Suite 19D New York NY 10017

HAGENGRUBER, DONALD LLEWELLYN, lawyer, educational administrator; b. Wausau, Wis., Dec. 3, 1949; s. Roy Arthur and Virginia (Morgan) H.; m. Claire Ann Szablinski, Aug. 23, 1975; 1 child, Dana Dorothea. BA with honors, U. Wis., 1972, MA, 1973, JD cum laude, 1977; LLM, Georgetown U., 1981. Bar: Wis. 1977, U.S. Dist. Ct. (we. dist.) Wis. 1977, U.S. Ct. Mil. Appeals 1978. Asst. chief legal service Nat. Naval Med. Ctr., Bethesda, Md., 1978-81; spl. asst. to pres. Uniformed Services U., Bethesda, 1981—; exec. sec. bd. regents Uniformed Services Univ., Bethesda, 1983—; spl. asst. to pres. Uniformed Services U., Bethesda, 1981-86, gen. counsel, 1987—; mem. panel advisors regents/ alumni fund Henry M. Jackson Found. Advancement Mil. Medicine, Bethesda, Md., 1985—. Served to lt. USNR, 1977-81. Mem. ABA, Am. Soc. Law and Medicine, Wis. Bar Assn., Naval Res. Assn., Judge Advs. Assn., Res. Officers Assn., Uniformed Services U. Alumni Assn., Inc. (exec. bd. dirs. 1981-87). Office: USUHS Room A1013 Uniformed Services U of Health Scis Bethesda MD 20814-4799

HAGER, ORVAL O., lawyer; b. Lincoln, Nebr., Nov. 18, 1918; s. Ora Orval and Marie Katherine (Schaefer) H.; m. Margaret Anne Ambrose, Nov. 21, 1985; 1 dau., Nancy Ellen (dec.). B.S., U. Nebr., 1940; J.D. cum laude, Willamette U., 1949. Bar: Oreg. 1949, U.S. Dist. Ct. Oreg. 1949. Assoc. Miller, Nash, Wiener, Hager & Carlsen, Portland, Oreg., 1949-53, ptnr., 1953—. Past bd. dirs. Oreg. Ind. Coll. Found., YMCA of Columbia-Willamette; trustee Willamette U.; trustee, sec. U. Portland; past pres. Oreg. Heart Assn., 1968. Served to lt. col. USAR, 1940-67. Mem. Nat. Assn. Estate Planning Councils (past bd. dirs.), Estate Planning Council of Portland (past pres.), Am. Coll. Probate Counsel, Oreg. State Bar (past chmn. corps. and partnerships, real property, client security fund coms.). Republican. Clubs: Arlington (dir., pres.), Waverley Country (past pres.); Portland Golf (past pres.), Multnomah Athletic, Rotary (treas. Portland chpt.). Probate, Estate planning, General corporate. Home: 6237 SW Round Hill Way Portland OR 97221 Office: 111 SW Fifth Ave Suite 3500 Portland OR 97204

HAGERMAN, JOHN DAVID, lawyer; b. Houston, Aug. 1, 1941; s. David Angle and Noima L. (Clay) H.; m. Linda J. Lambright; children: Clayton Robert, Holly Elizabeth. BBA, So. Meth. U., 1963; JD, U. Tex., Austin, 1966. Bar: Tex. 1966, U.S. Dist. Ct. (so. dist.) Tex. 1967, U.S. Ct. Appeals (5th cir.) 1967, U.S. Supreme Ct. 1969. Pres., ptnr. Hagerman & Seureau, Inc., Spring, Tex., 1966—; condr. legal econs. seminars. Contbr. articles to profl. jours. Res. dep. sheriff, Montgomery County, Tex.; com. mem. Montgomery County Fair Assn., 1978—. Mem. ABA, Tex. Bar Assn., Houston Bar Assn., Houston Outdoor Advt. Assn., Beta Sigma Phi. Republican. Club: Petroleum (Houston). Avocations: swimming, shooting. Banking, State civil litigation, Contracts commercial. Office: Hagerman & Seureau Inc 24800 Interstate 45 #100 Spring TX 77373

HAGGARD, CARL DOUGLAS, lawyer; b. San Diego, May 13, 1948; s. Carl Newton and Norma (Brabham) H.; m. Charlene, Oct. 15, 1977; chil-

dren—Stephanie, Peter, Jarrett. Student U. of Miami, 1966-67; B.A., U. Houston, 1970; J.D., South Tex. Coll. Law, 1973. Bar: Tex. 1973, U.S. Dist. Ct. (so. dist.) 1984, U.S. Ct. Appeals (5th cir.) 1984, U.S. Dist. Ct. (we. dist.) Tex. 1985, U.S. Dist. Ct. (ea. dist.) Tex. 1985, U.S. Dist. Ct. (no. dist.) Tex. 1985. Sole practice, Houston, 1973-76; asst. dist. atty. Harris County, Houston, 1976-84; with legal dept. Phillips Petroleum Co., Houston, 1984-86, Conoco, Inc. 1986—; lectr. Abilene Christian Coll., 1974-75, U. Houston, 1974-75, Bates Coll. Law, 1980-82. Named Outstanding Young Man Jaycees, 1980. Mem. Houston Bar Assn. (dir. juvenile justice sect. 1983-84), Order Barristers, Phi Alpha Delta. Federal civil litigation, State civil litigation, Personal injury. Home: 7702 Candlegreen Ln Houston TX 77071 Office: Conoco Inc Legal Dept PO Box 2197 Houston TX 77252-2197

HAGGARD, JOEL EDWARD, lawyer; b. Portland, Oreg., Oct. 10, 1939; s. Henry Edward and Kathryn Shirley (O'Leary) H.; m. Mary Katherine Daley, June 8, 1968; children: Kevin E., Maureen E., Cristin E. BSME, U. Notre Dame, 1961; M in Nuclear Engring., U. Okla., 1963; JD, U. Wash., 1971. Bar: Wash. 1971, U.S. Dist. Ct. (we. dist.) Wash., U.S. Ct. Appeals (9th cir.), U.S. Supreme Ct. Nuclear engr. Westinghouse Corp. Bettis Atomic Power Lab., Pitts., 1963-67; research engr. aerospace div. The Boeing Co., Seattle, 1968; engr., mgmt. cons. King County Dept. Pub. Works, Seattle, 1969-71; assoc. Houghton, Cluck, Coughlin & Riley, Seattle, 1971-74, ptnr., 1975-76; sole practice Seattle, 1977, 85—; ptnr. Haggard, Tousley & Brain, Seattle, 1978-84; judge marriage tribunal, Archdiocese of Seattle; chmn. Columbia River Interstate Compact Commn., 1975—. Contbr. articles to profl. jours. Sec., bd. trustees Seattle Symphony;. Mem. ABA, Wash. Bar Assn. (environ. law sect., rules of profl. conduct com.), Seattle-King County Bar Assn., Am. Arbitration Assn. (nat panel.), Am. Nuclear Soc., Am. Pub. Works Assn. Clubs: Rainier, Wash. Athletic, Astoria Golf and Country, Magnolia Community (past. pres., bd. dirs.). Land use, Real property, Environment. Office: 1215 4th Ave Suite 2426 Seattle WA 98161

HAGGART, VIRGIL JAMES, JR., lawyer; b. Omaha, Dec. 31, 1929; s. Virgil James and Mildred Elizabeth (Weston) H.; m. Barbara Barnum, June 26, 1954; m. 2d, Helen Shoemaker, Nov. 17, 1978. Student Stanford U., 1947-49; BBA, Northwestern U., 1951; JD, U. Mich., 1954. Bar: Nebr. 1954, U.S. Dist. Ct. Nebr. 1954, U.S. Ct. Appeals (8th cir.) 1974, U.S. Supreme Ct. 1976. Ptnr. King and Haggart, Omaha, 1954-63, Lane, Baird, Pedersen & Haggart, Omaha, 1963-70, Baird, Holm, McEachen, Pedersen, Hamann & Haggart, Omaha, 1970-81, Gaines, Otis, Haggart, Mullen & Carta, Omaha, 1981-85, Daub & Haggart, 1985—; bd. dirs. Nebr. Nat. Bank, Omaha, Western Printing Co. Dir. Nat. Audubon Soc., 1972-78, exec. com., 1974-78, pres.'s adv. council, 1979—. Served with U.S. Army, 1955-57. General practice, Banking, Probate. Address: Suite 1 10801 Pacific St Omaha NE 68154

HAGGERTY, JAMES CHARLES, lawyer; b. Omaha, Sept. 11, 1930; s. Clarence Edward and Sarah C. (Neary) H.; m. Marlene M. Segrich, July 4, 1956; children: Marianne, Marguerite, Thomas, Sally, Terrence, Nancy, James Jr., John. BA, Seton Hall U., 1955; LLB, Georgetown U., 1958. Assoc. Marley, Winkelreid & Hillis, Newark, 1959-61; ptnr. Haggerty & Donohue, Union, N.J., 1961—; judge N.J. Mcpl. Ct. Served to sgt. USAF, 1948-52. Mem. ABA, Am. Judges Assn., Am. Arbitration Assn., Internat. Soc. Barristers. Republican. Roman Catholic. Avocation: golf. Office: Haggerty & Donohue 2204 Morris Ave Union NJ 07083

HAGGERTY, WILLIAM FRANCIS, lawyer; b. Orange, N.J., June 4, 1943; s. Francis Anthony and Grace Agnes (Cullen) H.; m. Emily Catherine Giacobazzi, Sept. 3, 1965; 1 child, Erin Catherine. AB, U. Detroit, 1965, JD, 1979; MA, Eastern Mich. U., 1970. Bar: Mich. 1980, U.S. Dist. Ct. (ea. dist.) Mich. 1980. Assoc. Greenbaum & Greenbaum, Southfield, Mich., 1979-80; legal editor Mich. Supreme Ct., Lansing, 1980-81, sr. legal editor, 1981-82, asst. reporter of decisions, 1982-84, acting reporter of decisions, 1984-85, reporter of decisions, 1985—; adj. prof. Thomas M. Cooley Law Sch., Lansing, 1983—; cons. Ceramica Mirage S.pA., Pavullo, Italy, 1985. Mem. ABA, Fed. Bar Assn., Inc. Soc. Irish/Am. Lawyers, Nat. Assn. Reporters of Decisions, Mich. Bar Assn. (com. on libraries, legal research and publ.), Legal Authors Soc. Reporter of judicial decisions, Legal education, Contracts commercial. Office: Mich Supreme Ct PO Box 30052 Lansing MI 48909

HAGGLUND, CLARANCE EDWARD, lawyer, computer company executive; b. Omaha, Feb. 17, 1927; s. Clarence Andrew and Esther May (Kelle) H.; m. Dorothy S. Hagglund, Mar. 27, 1953; children—Laura, Bret, Katherine; m. Merle Patricia Hagglund, Oct. 28, 1972. B.A., U. S.D., 1949; J.D., William Mitchell Coll. Law, 1953. Bar: Minn. 1955, U.S. Ct. Appeals (8th cir.) 1974, U.S. Supreme Ct. 1963. Diplomate Am. Bd. Profl. Liability Attys. Ptnr. Hagglund & Johnson and predecessor firms, Mpls., 1973—; ptnr. Hagglund, Oskie, Priesz and Jefferson, to present; pres. Internat. Control Systems, Inc., Mpls., 1979—, Hill River Corp., Mpls., 1976—; gen. counsel Minn. Assn. Profl. Ins. Agts., Inc., Mpls., 1965-86. Contbr. articles to profl. jours. Served to lt. comdr. USNR, 1945-46, 50-69. Fellow Internat. Soc. Barristers; mem. Minn. Bar Assn., ABA, Lawyer Pilots Bar Assn., U.S. Maritime Law Assn. (proctor), Acad. Cert. Trial Lawyers Minn. (dean 1983-85), Nat. Bd. Trial Advocacy (cert. in civil trial law). Roman Catholic. Clubs: Ill. Athletic (Chgo.); Edina Country (Minn.); Calhoun Beach (Mpls.). Personal injury, Federal civil litigation, State civil litigation. Home: 3719 Xerxes Ave S Minneapolis MN 55410 Office: 4000 Olson Memorial Hwy Suite 501 Golden Valley MN 55422

HAGMEIR, THOMAS EDMISTON, lawyer, educator; b. Buffalo, Jan. 30, 1933; s. Edmiston L. and Bertha (Fruauff) H.; m. Susan F. Reis, May 16, 1968; 1 child, Catherine Jennie. B.S. in Bus. Adminstrn., SUNY-Buffalo, 1954, J.D., 1956, M.Ed. in Vocat. Edn., 1969. Bar: N.Y. 1958, U.S. Dist. Ct. (we. dist.) N.Y. 1959. Assoc. Brown Kelly Turner Hassett & Leach, Buffalo, 1958-69; sole practice, Lancaster-Depew, N.Y., 1970—; prof. law Erie Community Coll., Williamsville, N.Y., 1970—; evaluator real estate Empire State Coll., Buffalo, 1979—; acting village justice Village of Lancaster, N.Y., 1973-81, Village of Sloan, N.Y., 1974-85. Served with U.S. Army, 1956-58. Mem. ABA, Am. Vocat. Assn., N.Y. State Bar Assn., N.Y. State Magistrates Assn. Probate, Legal education. Home: 45 Burwell Ave Lancaster NY 14086 Office: 33 Central Ave Lancaster NY 14086

HAHN, JOHN S., lawyer; b. Sikeston, Mo., July 30, 1952. AB, Duke U., 1974; JD, Yale U., 1977. Bar: D.C. 1977. Ptnr. Kirkland & Ellis, Washington. Office: Kirkland & Ellis 655 Fifteenth Sts NW Washington DC 20005 *

HAHN, MICHAEL JAMES, lawyer; b. Miami Beach, Fla., Dec. 24, 1949; s. Hubert P. and Elizabeth (Silcox) H. AB, U. Ga., 1971; JD, U. Miss., 1974; LLM in Taxation, Emory U., 1975. Bar: Miss. 1974, U.S. Supreme Ct. 1975. Atty., tax advisor dept. treasury IRS, Washington, 1982—. Mem. ABA, Fed. Bar Assn., Miss. Bar Assn., Am. Judicature Soc., Res. Officer Assn. U.S. Corporate taxation, Public utilities. Home: 4201 S 31st St #1035 Arlington VA 22206

HAHN, PAUL BERNARD, lawyer; b. Prague, Czechoslovakia, Aug. 13, 1947; came to U.S. 1949, naturalized, 1954; s. George and Edith (Blum) H.; m. Denise Szabo, Aug. 7, 1976; 1 child, Aaron. BA, Queens Coll., 1969; MS, L.I.U., 1971; JD, Bklyn. Law Sch., 1976. Bar: N.Y. 1977, U.S. Dist. Ct. (ea., so. dists.) N.Y. 1977. Tchr. Bklyn. Pub. Schs., 1969-77; assoc. J.V. Salierno Law Firm, Middle Village, N.Y., 1977-78; dist. office counsel SBA, N.Y.C., 1978-82; sr. assoc. Goldman, Horowitz & Cherno, Mineola, N.Y., 1982-83; sr. atty. Heller Fin., Inc., N.Y.C., 1983—; spl. asst. U.S. Atty. U.S. Atty.'s Office, so. dist., N.Y.C., 1981-82. Contbr. articles to profl. jours. Mem. ABA, Assn. of Bar of City of N.Y., Assn. Comml. Fin. Attys. Bankruptcy, Contracts commercial. Office: Heller Financial Inc 101 Park Ave New York NY 10178

HAHN, RICHARD FERDINAND, lawyer; b. Chgo., May 20, 1909; s. Ernest Theodore and Emily (Sattler) H.; m. Grace Elizabeth Jepsen, Sept. 1, 1935; children—Nancy (Mrs. Noel G. Fischer), Lawrence. B.S., U. Ill., 1930, J.D., 1933. Bar: Ill. bar 1933. Since practiced in Chgo.; mem. firm Halfpenny, Hahn & Roche, Chgo. and Washington. Mem. Woodstock (Ill.) City Council, 1965-67, 73-79; mem., sec. Woodstock Police Commn., 1968-71; mem. Woodstock Indsl. Devel. Commn., 1967-69, Woodstock City Planning Commn., 1957-62, 79-85; mem. Woodstock Community High Sch. Bd., 1952-55, 56-62, pres., 1958-62; Bd. dirs. Woodstock Fine Arts Assn., 1963-67. Mem. Am., Ill., Chgo. bar assns., Am. Judicature Soc., Phi Alpha Delta. Republican. Lodge: Masons. General corporate, Antitrust, Probate. Home: 415 Laurel Ave Woodstock IL 60098 Office: 20 N Wacker Dr Chicago IL 60606

HAIDRI, AMIRALI YUSUFALI, lawyer; b. Mwanza, Tanzania, July 10, 1947; came to U.S., 1972; s. Yusufali Kaderbhai and Aminabai Haji (Hassanbhai) Hons. BS, U. Leeds, Eng., 1971; JD cum laude, N.Y. Law Sch., 1980; MS, NYU, 1983. Bar: U.S. Patent Office 1978, N.Y. 1981, N.J. 1983, U.S. Dist. Ct. N.J. 1983. Assoc. W.P. Thompson & Co., Liverpool, Eng., 1971-72, Haseltine, Lake & Waters, N.Y.C., 1972-81; patent atty. Texaco Devel. Corp., Harrison, N.Y., 1981-82, Lever Bros. Co., Edgewater, N.J., 1982-84; ptnr. Haidri, Glazer & Kamel, Union, N.J., 1984—. Mem. ABA, Union County Bar Assn., Essex County Bar Assn. Muslim. Club: British Schs. and Univs. (N.Y.C.) (bd. dirs. 1987). Lodge: Masons (jr. steward Montclair, N.J.). Personal injury, Workers' compensation, Trademark and copyright. Home: 16 Harper Terr Cedar Grove NJ 07009 Office: Haidri Glazer & Kamel Ideal Profl Park 2333 Morris Ave Suite C14 Union NJ 07083

HAIG, ALEXANDER P., lawyer; b. Ft. Knox, Ky., Apr. 9, 1952. BA, Georgetown U., 1974, JD, 1977. Bar: D.C. 1977. Ptnr. Finley, Kumble, Wagner et al, Washington. Office: Finley Kumble Wagner et al 1120 Connecticut Ave NW Washington DC 20036 *

HAIGHT, CHARLES SHERMAN, JR., federal judge; b. N.Y.C., Sept. 23, 1930; s. Charles Sherman and Margaret (Edwards) H.; m. Mary Jane Peightal, June 30, 1953; children: Nina E., Susan P. B.A., Yale U., 1952, LL.B., 1955. Bar: N.Y. State 1955. Trial atty., admiralty and shipping dept. Dept. Justice, Washington, 1955-57; assoc. firm Haight, Gardner, Poor & Havens, N.Y.C., 1957-68; partner Haight, Gardner, Poor & Havens, 1968-76; judge U.S. Dist. Ct. for So. Dist. N.Y., 1976—. Bd. dirs. Kennedy Child Study Center; adv. trustee Am.-Scandinavian Found., chmn., 1970-76; bd. mgrs. Havens Fund. Mem. Maritime Law Assn., U.S., N.Y. State Bar Assn., Bar Assn. City N.Y., Fed. Bar Council. Episcopalian. Jurisprudence. Office: US Courthouse Foley Sq New York NY 10007

HAIGHT, EDWARD ALLEN, lawyer; b. Rockford, Ill., July 2, 1910; s. John T. and Augusta (Granger) H.; m. Valerie E. Haight, Jan. 1, 1935; children—Edward Allen, George Ives II, Edith Diane, Stephen Holmes. B.A., U. Wis., 1931; LL.B., Harvard U., 1934. Bar: Ill. bar 1934. Since practiced in Chgo.; ptnr. Haight & Hofeldt and predecessor firm Haight, Hofeldt, Davis & Jamor, Chgo., 1956—. Served as lt. USNR, 1943-46. Mem. Am., Ill., Chgo., 7th Circuit bar assns., Am., Chgo. patent law assns., Am. Coll. Trial Lawyers. Clubs: Union League (Chgo.); Skokie Country. Federal civil litigation, Patent, Trademark and copyright. Home: 364 Central Ave Highland Park IL 60035 Office: 55 E Monroe St Chicago IL 60603

HAIGHT, GREGORY DALE, lawyer; b. Washington, June 21, 1943; s. Chester Dale and Virginia (Gardner) H.; m. Karen Marta Taylor, May 6; children—Jeffrey Allen, Shannon Marie, Cameron Matthew, Taylor Nicole. A.B. in Math., Boston Coll., 1965; J.D., Georgetown U., 1968. Bar: D.C. 1968, Va. 1969, Md. 1973, U.S. Dist. Ct. (ea. dist.) Va. 1972, U.S. Ct. Appeals (4th cir.) 1972. Assoc., Gosnell, Durkin & Cappello, Washington, 1969-70; asst. commonwealth and county atty. Arlington County (Va.), Arlington, 1969-72; ptnr. Belli & Keilp, Washington, 1972-73; ptnr. Haight, Tramonte & Siciliano, Falls Ch., Va., 1973—. Recipient award Am. Arbitration Assn., 1976. Mem. Va. Bar Assn., Fairfax County Bar Assn., Assn. Trial Lawyers Am., Va. Trial Lawyers Assn., Plaintiffs Bar (pres. 1985—). Episcopalian. Club: Westwood Country. Personal injury, State civil litigation, Criminal. Office: Haight Tramonte & Siciliano 210 E Broad St Falls Church VA 22046

HAILE, JOHN SANDERS, lawyer, accountant; b. Jacksonville, Fla., July 26, 1956; s. John Jr. and Waltress (Sanders) H.; m. Audrey Lee Cryan, Apr. 17, 1982; children: Jay John, Jenifer Leigh, Christina Janel. AA, Fla. State U., 1975, BS magna cum laude, 1977, JD, 1980; JD, Oxford U., Eng., 1980. Bar: Fla. 1982, U.S. Tax Ct. 1984. Tax acct. Coopers & Lybrand, Ft. Lauderdale, Fla., 1978-79; asst. state's atty. Broward County, Ft. Lauderdale, 1979-80; tax specialist Peat, Marwick & Mitchell, Ft. Lauderdale, 1980-82; sr. ptnr. Haile & Co., CPA's, Boca Raton, Fla., 1981—; pres. John S. Haile, P.A., Boca Raton, 1982—; trustee City of Deerfield Beach, Fla., 1983-86. Charter mem. Estate Planning Council, 1984—; mem. Boca Raton Income, Estate and Gift Tax Council, 1984—; active Gulf Stream council Boy Scouts Am.; trustee City of Deerfield Beach (Fla.), 1983-86. Bd. of Regents scholar State of Fla., 1974. Mem. ABA, Palm Beach County Bar Assn., Am. Inst. CPA's, Fla. Inst. CPA's, Am. Assn. Attys.-CPA's, Am. Judicature Soc., Tax Practitioners Roundtable, Am. Water Ski Assn., Beta Gamma Sigma, Beta Alpha Psi, Phi Delta Phi. Republican. Presbyterian. Clubs: Gold Coast Ski (Delray Beach, Fla.); Am. Barefoot (Winter Haven, Fla.). Avocations: slalom and barefoot waterskiing, scuba diving, spearfishing, swimming. Corporate taxation, Estate planning, Real property. Home: 5129 E Lakes Dr Pompano Beach FL 33064 Office: Royal Palm Towers 1700 S Dixie Hwy Boca Raton FL 33432

HAIMBAUGH, GEORGE DOW, JR., lawyer, educator; b. Rochester, Ind., Nov. 21, 1916; s. George Dow and Agnes Elizabeth (Sharp) H.; m. Katharine Louise Draper, Aug. 20, 1960. A.B., DePauw U., 1938; postgrad. Georgetown U., 1938-40; J.D., Northwestern U., 1952; J.S.D., Yale U., 1962. Bar: Ill. 1953, S.C. 1973, U.S. Dist. Ct. (no. dist.) Ohio 1962, U.S. Supreme Ct. 1969. Asst. prof. U. Akron Coll. Law, 1960-63; assoc. prof. law U. S.C., Columbia, 1963-70; prof. U. S.C., 1970—, David W. Robinson prof. law, 1979—, assoc. Inst. Internat. Studies, 1967—, mem. Byrnes Internat. Ctr. Adv. Council, 1984—; spl. master U.S. Dist. Ct. (no. dist.) Ohio, 1962-63; mem. adv. bd. Nat. Inst. Justice, 1982-85; assoc. Belle W. Baruch Inst. Marine Biology and Coastal Research, 1978—. Mem. Ga.-S.C. Boundary Commn., 1978—; deacon 1st Presbyterian Ch., Columbia. Served to maj. USMC, 1940-46. Mem. Am. Law Inst., ABA (chmn. adv. com. to standing com. on law and nat. security 1979-82), S.C. Bar Assn., Richland County Bar Assn., Am. Soc. Internat. Law, Assn. Am. Law Schs. (chmn. sect. coustitutional law 1975-77), Order of the Coif, Phi Delta Phi, Delta Phi Epsilon, Sigma Delta Chi Soc. Profl. Jooumalsits, Order of Coif, Order of Palmetto, Phi Gamma Delta. Republican. Club: Mil. Order World Wars. Legal education, Public international, Libel. Office: Univ SC Law Sch Columbia SC 29208

HAIMS, ARNOLD BRODY, lawyer; b. N.Y.C., June 19, 1931; s. David Richard and Helen (Brody) H.; m. Toni Robb, June 1, 1963; children: Charles, Sally, Kitty. BA, Stanford U., 1953, LLB, 1959. Bar: Calif. 1960, U.S. Dist. Ct. (no. dist.) Calif. 1960, U.S. Ct. Appeals (9th cir.) 1960. Law clk. to presiding justice Calif. Dist. Ct. Appeal, San Francisco, 1960-61; trial lawyer So. Pacific Co., San Francisco, 1961-63, Berry, Davis & McInerney, Oakland, Calif., 1963-76; ptnr. Haims, Johnson, MacGowan & McInerney, Oakland, 1976—. Served to capt. USMC, 1956-59. Mem. ABA, Calif. Bar Assn. (pub. relations com. 1970-71), Nat. Assn. Trial Lawyers, Internat. Assn. Ins. Counsel. Republican. Clubs: Olympic (San Francisco), Harbor Bar Isle (Alameda, Calif.). State civil litigation, Insurance, Personal injury. Home: 1234 Caroline Alameda CA 94501 Office: Haims Johnson MacGowan & McInerney 490 Grand Ave Oakland CA 94610

HAIMS, BRUCE DAVID, lawyer; b. N.Y.C., Nov. 25, 1940; s. Samuel Harold and Judith (Feller) H.; m. Judith Herman (dissolved); children: Carolyn, Daniel, Nolan. BS in Econs., U. Pa., 1962; LLB magna cum laude, Harvard U., 1965; LLM in Taxation, NYU, 1972. Bar: Conn. 1965, N.Y. 1967, U.S. Ct. Appeals (2d cir.) 1968, U.S. Tax Ct. 1972. Assoc. Debevoise & Plimpton, N.Y.C., 1967-72, ptnr., 1973—; bd. dirs. Axe Houghton Mgmt. Co., Tarrytown, N.Y. Bd. dirs. Equity Library Theatre, N.Y.C., 1986—. Served to capt. U.S. Army, 1965-67. Mem. N.Y. State Bar Assn., Assn. of Bar of City of N.Y., Internat. Fiscal Assn. Corporate taxation, Personal income taxation, Entertainment. Home: 470 West End Ave Apt 14A New York NY 10024 Office: Debevoise & Plimpton 875 3d Ave New York NY 10022

HAINES, JOHN ALDEN, lawyer; b. Merrill, Mich., July 26, 1934; s. John Alden and Pearl Ann (Bader) H.; m. Esther Catherine Mueller, Aug. 25, 1956; children—Kimberly Ann, Kathryn Sue, John Alden III. A.A., Bay City Jr. Coll., 1953; B.A., U. Mich., 1955; J.D., Detroit Coll., 1958. Bar: Mich., 1959. Sole practice law, Bridgeport, Mich., 1959-67; sr. ptnr. Haines & Marti, 1968—; justice of peace Bridgeport Twp., 1961-68. Pres., bd. dirs. Bridgeport Civic Assn., 1963, 1966; dist. chmn. Boy Scouts Am., Saginaw. 1969; county del. Saginaw Republican Party, 1964, 84. Mem. Saginaw Bar Assn. (sec. 1980-82, dir. 1983-85, v.p. 1985-86, pres. 1986-87, Meritorious Service award, 1979, cert. commendation 1985), Mich. Bar Assn., Am. Judicature Soc., Bridgeport C. of C., (pres., dir. 1962-63), Delta Theta Phi. Lutheran. Clubs: Bridgeport Country, Bridgeport Gun. Avocations: golf, skiing. Real property, Probate, Personal injury. Home: 4030 Jordan Dr Saginaw MI 48601 Office: Haines & Marti 6221 Dixie Hwy Bridgeport MI 48722

HAINES, MARTHA MAHAN, lawyer; b. Detroit, Feb. 4, 1952; d. Albert F. and Martha M. (Sager) Mahan; m. Richard L. Haines, Dec. 22, 1973; children: Ella Catherine, Emily Martha. Student, U. Utah, 1970-72; BA, Wayne State U., 1974; JD, U. Mich., 1977. Bar: Ill. 1978, U.S. Dist. Ct. (no. dist.) Ill. 1982. Jr. ptnr. Chapman and Cutler, Chgo., 1978-86; of counsel Altheimer & Gray, Chgo., 1986—. Mem. Chgo. Bar Assn. (vice chmn. local govt. law com. 1984-85), Nat. Assn. Bond Lawyers. Democrat. Presbyterian. Municipal bonds, Local government. Home: 1236 Lake Ave Wilmette IL 60091 Office: Altheimer & Gray 333 W Wacker Dr Chicago IL 60606

HAINES, MICHAEL ANTHONY, lawyer; b. Hamilton, Ontario, Can., Nov. 11, 1942; s. Arthur B. and Nora (Regan) H.; m. Eugenia DeMeo, July 1, 1977; children: Jennifer Christine, Jonathan Patick. AB, UCLA, 1964; JD, U. Calif., Berkeley, 1971. Bar: Calif. 1972, U.S. Dist. Ct. (no., cen. and so. dists.) Calif. 1972, U.S. Supreme Ct. 1979. Assoc. Tuttle & Taylor, Los Angeles, 1971-73, Morrison & Foerster, San Francisco, 1973-77; sole practice San Francisco, 1977-82; ptnr. Shartsis, Friese & Ginsburg, San Francisco, 1982-84, Carroll, Weller & Haines, San Francisco, 1984-85, Carroll & Haines, San Francisco, 1985-86; of counsel Jeffer, Mangels & Butler, San Francisco, 1986—. Bd. dirs. Tiburon (Calif.) Fire Protection Dist., 1979-83; treas. Tiburon Vol. Fire Dept., 1984—. Served to lt. USNR, 1965-68. Mem. ABA (bus. law sect., real estate law sect.), Calif. Bar Assn., San Francisco Bar Assn. Clubs: San Francisco Yacht (Belvedere, Calif.), Tiburon (Calif.) Peninsula. Avocations: sailing, flying, golf, tennis, running. Real property, General corporate, Banking. Office: Jeffer Mangels & Butler 44 Montgomery St Suite 2785 San Francisco CA 94104

HAINES, MICHAEL CURTIS, lawyer; b. Batavia, N.Y., Feb. 8, 1949; s. Paul Robert and Dorothy Grace (Ludington) H.; m. Patricia Yvonne Van Dyken, May 22, 1982; children: Daniel Curtis, Mark Timothy. A.B., U. Mich., 1971, J.D., 1974. Bar: Mich. 1974, U.S. Dist. Ct. (we. dist.) Mich. 1974. Assoc., Mika, Meyers, Beckett & Jones, Grand Rapids, Mich., 1974-79, ptnr., 1980—; mem. securities law adv. com. Mich. Corp. and Securities Bur., Lansing, Mich., 1977-85; commr. City of Adrian Gas Rate Commn., Mich., 1983-84, 86; lectr. in field. Mem. Grand Rapids Bar Assn., State Bar Mich., ABA, Mich. Oil and Gas Assn. (chmn. legal and legis. com. 1977—), Order of Coif, Phi Beta Kappa. Republican. Mem. Reformed Ch. Am. Public utilities, Oil and gas leasing, General corporate. Office: Mika Meyers Beckett & Jones 500 Frey Bldg Grand Rapids MI 49503

HAINES, RICHARD MCKINNEY, lawyer; b. Cin., Feb. 2, 1950; s. Robert Andrew and Dorothy (Brown) H.; m. Susan Dessoir; 1 child, Colleen Dessoir. BA, Denison U., 1972; LLM, U. Cin., 1976. Bar: Ohio 1976. Assoc. Cors, Hair & Hartsock, Cin., 1976-81; ptnr. Hartsock, Harris & Schneider, Cin., 1982-83, Porter, Wright, Morris & Arthur, Cin., 1986—; bd. dirs. Brown Pub. Co., Urbana., Ohio. Local chmn. Brown for Gov. Com., Cin., 1982. Mem. ABA, Cin. Bar Assn., Ohio Bar Assn. Clubs: Mt. Lookout Civic, Cin. Athletic. Banking, Consumer commercial, Bankruptcy. Office: Porter Wright Morris & Arthur 1650 Atrium One Cincinnati OH 45202

HAINLINE, FORREST ARTHUR, JR., retired automotive company executive, lawyer; b. Rock Island, Ill., Oct. 20, 1918; s. Forrest Arthur and Marian (Pearson) H.; m. Nora Marie Schrot, July 7, 1945; children—Forrest III, Jon, Patricia, Judith, Brian, David, Nora. A.B., Augustana Coll., Rock Island, Ill., 1940; J.D., U. Mich., 1947, LL.M., 1948. Bar: Ill. 1942, Mich. 1943, Fla. 1970, U.S. Supreme Ct. 1946. Mem. firm Cross, Wrock, Miller & Vieson and predecessor, Detroit, 1948-71, ptnr., 1957-71; v.p., gen. counsel Am. Motors Corp., Detroit, 1971-84, sec., 1972-84, ret. Chmn., Wayne County Regional Interagy. Coordinating Com. for Developmental Disabilities, Mich., 1972-76; chmn. grievance com. U.S. Tennis Assn., 1970-85, mem. exec. com., 1972-74, 83-85, chmn. constn. and rules, 1983-86, v.p. So. region, 1985-86; arbitrator Men's Internat. Profl. Tennis Council, 1977-85; pres. Cath. Social Services Oakland County, Mich., 1972-75; mem. exec. com. Western Tennis Assn., 1964—, pres., 1972-73, chmn. constn. and rules com., 1976-84; mem. Men's Internat. Profl. Tennis Council, 1985—; pres. Western Improvement Assn., 1969-75; bd. dirs. Augustana Coll., 1974-82, sec., 1975-82; bd. dirs. Providence Hosp., Southfield, Mich., 1975-84, sec. 1980, vice chmn., 1981, chmn., 1982, chmn. exec. com., 1983-84. Served to 1st lt. AUS, 1942-46. Named (with family) Tennis Family of Yr., U.S. Tennis Assn., 1974; recipient Outstanding Service award Augustana Coll., 1977; named to Rock Island High Sch. Sports Hall of Fame, 1977, Mich. Amateur Sports Hall of Fame, 1978, Augustana Coll. Sports Hall of Fame, 1980. Mem. ABA, Fed. Bar Assn., Mich. Bar. Assn., Ill. Bar Assn., Fla. Bar Assn., Am. Judicature Soc., Augustana Coll. Alumni Assn. (pres. bd. dirs. 1973-74), Phi Alpha Delta. Clubs: Suntide Condominiums, Kenmore Golf, Detroit Tennis, Squash. Lodge: KC. Home: 1357 NE Ocean Blvd Stuart FL 33494 address: Kenmore Villa 46 Flat Rock NC 28731

HAINSFURTHER, A. MICHAEL, lawyer; b. Jacksonville, Ill., Aug. 13, 1956; s. Albert F. and Nancy Sue (McNeeley) H.; m. Lauri Ann Patterson, Aug. 7, 1981; children: Albert Nicholas, Meredith Ann. BS in Bus., Centenary Coll., 1978; JD, Washington U., 1981. Bar: Tex., U.S. Dist. Ct. (no. dist.) Tex. Assoc. Geary, Stahl & Spencer, Dallas, 1981—. Pres. Hillside Homeowners Assn., Dallas, 1985; mem. Pub. Safety Com., Dallas, Dallas Crime Commn., Adminstrv. Bd. Meth. Ch., Dallas. Mem. ABA, Tex. Bar Assn., Dallas Bar Assn., U.S. Dist. Ct. (no. dist.) Tex., Dallas Assn. Young Lawyers (bd. dirs. 1984—), Real Estate Securities Syndicates Inst. (bd. dirs. 1985—), Order of Coif, Omicron Delta Kappa, Alpha Chi. Republican. Avocations: softball, golf, tennis, basketball. Securities, General corporate, Construction. Home: 6104 Yellow Rock Tr Dallas TX 75248 Office: Geary Stahl & Spencer 6400 InterFirst Pl 901 Main St Dallas TX 75202

HAISCH, ANTHONY ALBERT, lawyer; b. Detroit, Oct. 5, 1939; s. Albert and Helen (Czata) H.; m. Estelle F. Zuchlewski, Mar. 2, 1963. BS in Bus. Adminstrn., Wayne State U., 1968, MBA, 1970, JD, 1972. Bar: Mich. 1972, Fla. 1973. Atty. Cross, Wrock, Miller & Vieson, Detroit, 1972-79; asst. v.p., gen. atty. Mich. Bell Telephone Co., Detroit, 1979-85; of counsel Buessee, Buesser et al, Detroit, 1985—; sole practice Detroit. Served with U.S. Army, 1958-60. Mem. Am. Arbitration Assn., Indsl. Relations Research Assn. Republican. Lutheran. Club: Renaissance (Detroit). Avocation: Golf. Labor, State civil litigation, Federal civil litigation. Home: 477 Chalfonte Grosse Point Farms MI 48236 Office: 100 Renaissnace Ctr Suite 2707 Detroit MI 48243

HAJEK, FRANCIS PAUL, lawyer; b. Hobart, Tasmania, Australia, Oct. 21, 1958; came to U.S., 1966; s. Frank Joseph and Kathleen Beatrice (Blake) H. BA, Yale U., 1980; JD, U. Richmond, 1984. Bar: Va. 1984, U.S. Dist. Ct. (ea. dist.) Pa. 1984, U.S. Ct. Appeals (4th cir.) 1986. Law clk. to presiding magistrate U.S. Dist Ct., Norfolk, Va., 1984-85; assoc. Seawell, Dalton, Hughes & Timms, Norfolk, 1985-87, Weinberg & Stein, Norfolk, 1987—. Mem. ABA (exec. com. young lawyers' sect.), Assn. Trial Lawyers Am., Va. Bar Assn., Norfolk-Portsmouth Bar Assn. Roman Catholic. Avocations: squash, tennis. Federal civil litigation, State civil litigation, Civil rights. Home: 543 W 20th St Norfolk VA 23517 Office: Weinberg & Stein 1510 1st Va Bank Tower 101 Saint Paul's Blvd PO Box 3789 Norfolk VA 23514

HAJEK, ROBERT J., lawyer, real estate broker, commodity broker, nursing home owner; b. Berwyn, Ill., May 17, 1943; s. James J., Sr., and Rita C. (Kalka) H.; m. Maris Ann Enright, June 19, 1965; children—Maris Ann,

Robert J., David, Mandie. B.A., Loras Coll., 1965; J.D., U. Ill., 1968. Bar: Ill. 1968, U.S. Tax Ct. 1970, U.S. dist. ct. (no. dist.) Ill. 1971, U.S. Ct. Appeals (7th cir.) 1972, U.S. Supreme Ct. 1972. Lic. real estate broker, Ill., Nat. Assn. Securities Dealers; registered U.S. Commodities Futures Trading Commn. ptnr. Hajek & Hajek, Berwyn, Ill., 1968-76; pres., bd. chmn. Hajek, Hajek, Koykar & Heytag, Ltd., Westchester, Ill., 1976-85; pres., chief exec. officer Land of Lincoln Ptnrs. Real Estate, Inc., Glendale Heights, Ill., 1985—; ptnr., owner Camelot Manor Nursing Home, Streator, Ill., 1978—, Ottawa Care Ctr., Ill., 1981—, Law Centre Bldg., Westchester, 1976—; owner Garfield Ridge Real Estate, Chgo., 1973-78, Centre Realty, Westchester, 1976-85; ptnr. Westbrook Commodities, Chgo., 1983; v.p., bd. mem., gen. counsel DeHart Gas and Oil Devel., Ltd., 1970-73; prin. Northeastern Okla. Oil and Gas Prodn. Venture, Tulsa, 1982—; exec. v.p., gen. counsel Garrett Plante Corp., 1978—, Ottawa Long Term Care, Inc., 1982—; bd. dirs. Land of Lincoln Savs. and Loan, 1981—, Home Title Services of Am., Inc., 1981—, Land of Lincoln Ins. Agy., Inc., 1982—, Medema Builders, Inc., 1983—, Land of Lincoln Ptnrs. Real Estate of Ill., Inc., 1984—, Land of Lincoln Ptnrs. Real Estate, Inc., 1984—, The Ill. Co., 1984—, Ill. Co. Properties, Inc., subs. of Ill. Co., 1984—, Ottawa Long Term Care, Inc., 1982—, Garrett Plante Corp., 1978—. Sr. boys' basketball coach Roselle Recreation Assn., Ill., 1981-83. Mem. ABA, Ill. Bar Assn., Ill. Health Care Assn., Phi Alpha Delta. Republican. Roman Catholic. Clubs: Amateur Radio, No. Ill. Dx Assn. Banking, Construction, Real property. Office: Hajek Hajek Koykar & Heying Ltd Law Centre Bldg Mannheim at Roosevelt Rd Westchester IL 60153

HAKEN, JACK EDWARD, lawyer; b. N.Y.C., Feb. 22, 1944; s. Herman R. and Doris (Rosenblatt) H.; m. Georgia M. Williams, Nov. 21, 1965; 1 child, Carl. B.E.E., Rensselaer Poly. Inst., 1964, M.Engr., 1968; J.D., Union U., 1974. Bar: N.Y. 1975, U.S. Ct. Appeals (Fed. cir.) 1976, U.S. Patent and Trademark Office 1974; registered profl. engr., N.Y. Engr., Rensselaer Poly. Inc., Troy, N.Y., 1964-70; patent atty. Gen. Electric Co., Schenectady, 1974-77; patent counsel U.S. Philips Corp., Tarrytown, N.Y., 1977-81, group patent counsel, 1981—. Patentee in area of computer equipment. Active Environ. Commn., Poestenkill, N.Y., 1973-77. Patent, Computer. Home: 5 Old Neversink Rd Danbury CT 06810 Office: US Philips Corp 580 White Plains Rd Tarrytown NY 10591

HAKODA, HARVEY NOBUO, lawyer; b. Kona, Hawaii, Nov. 8, 1943; s. Konao and Doris Harumi (Mori) H. BA, U. Hawaii, 1965; MS, U. So. Calif., 1973; JD, U. San Francisco, 1980. Bar: Hawaii 1980, U.S. Dist. Ct. Hawaii, 1980, U.S. Ct. Appeals (9th cir.) 1982. Pres. Spaces, Ltd., Honolulu, 1972-76, house counsel, 1983—; sole practice Honolulu, 1980-81; lawyer Office of Pub. Defender, Kona, 1981-82; bd. dirs. Spaces Ltd., Honolulu, 24 Hawaii, Inc., Honolulu, Space Travel, Inc., Honolulu. Served to capt. USAF, 1966-72. Mem. Phi Delta Phi. Buddhist. General practice, Private international, Construction. Office: 1522 Makaloa St Suite 206 Honolulu HI 96814

HAKOLA, DAVID BROWN, federal agency administrator; b. Albertsville, Ky., May 19, 1944; s. Jack Arvid and Virginia Almeda (Brown) H.; m. Edith Elaine Dinneen, Mar. 27, 1970; children: Nelo Arvid, Emily Virginia. BS, George Mason U., 1975; grad., Va. Bar Reading Program, 1979. Bar: Va. 1982, U.S. Ct. Appeals (4th cir.) 1982. Pres. Tru-Life Color, Jacksonville, Fla., 1964-65; asst. mgr. Capital Credit Corp., Washington, 1966-72; asst. computer op. Am. Enterprise Inst., Washington, 1972-82; sole practice Falls Church, Va., 1982-84; atty. adminstrv. rev. task force U.S. Dept. of Edn., Washington, 1984-85, staff asst. fed real property adminstrn., 1985—; mem. staff postal rate transition team commn. Pres. Ronald Reagan, Washington, 1980-81; bd. dirs. Am. Edn. Found., Alexandria, 1980-82. Sec. Ravenwood Civic Assn., Falls Church, Va., 1984—. Mem. ABA, Va. Bar Assn., Nat. Lawyers Club. Republican. Club: City Tavern (Georgetown). Avocation: upland game and waterfowl shooting competitions. Administrative and regulatory, Real property, General practice. Office: US Dept Edn 400 Maryland Ave SW Washington DC 20202

HALBACH, EDWARD CHRISTIAN, JR., legal educator; b. Clinton, Iowa, Nov. 8, 1931; s. Edward Christian and Lewella (Sullivan) H.; m. Janet Elizabeth Bridges, July 25, 1953; children: Kristin Lynn, Edward Christian III, Kathleen Ann, Thomas Elliot, Elaine Diane. B.A., U. Iowa, 1953, J.D., 1958; LL.M., Harvard U., 1959; LL.D., U. Redlands, 1973. Assoc. prof. Sch. Law, U. Calif. at Berkeley, 1959-62, prof., 1963—, dean, 1966-75. Co-author: Materials on Decedents' Estates and Trusts, 1965, 73, 81, 87, California Will Drafting, 1965; reporter Uniform Probate Code, 1969, Materials on Future Interests, 1977, Death, Taxes and Family Property, 1977; author: Use of Trusts in Estate Planning, 1975, Income Taxation of Estates and Trusts, 1978, 81, 84, 86; Fundamentals of Estate Planning, 1983, 86, 87, also articles in legal publs. Served from 2d to 1st lt. USAF, 1954-56. Mem. ABA (chmn. various coms. sect. individual rights and responsibilities and sect. real property probate and trust law, dir. probate and trust div., sect. chmn.), Iowa Bar Assn., Am. Law Inst. (advisor restatement 2d property), Am. Acad. Polit. and Social Scis., Am. Bar Found., Am. Coll. Probate Counsel, Am. Coll Tax Counsel, Internat. Acad. Estate and Trust Law (v.p., exec. com., pres.). Probate. Home: 679 San Luis Rd Berkeley CA 94707

HALBACH, JOSEPH JAMES, JR., lawyer; b. Balt., Aug. 13, 1956; s. Joseph James Sr. and Mary Louise (Mortensen) H.; m. Susan Lu Tuatay, may 5, 1984. BA, U. Tex., 1978, JD, 1982. Bar: Tex. 1982, U.S. Ct. Appeals (5th cir.) 1982, U.S. Dist. Ct. (so. dist.) Tex. 1983, U.S. Supreme Ct. 1986. Assoc. Bonham, Carrington & Fox, Houston, 1982-86; ptnr. Wilshire & Scott, P.C., Houston, 1986—. Mem. ABA, Assn. Trial Lawyers Am., Tex. Trial Lawyers Assn., Houston Trial Lawyers Assn., Am. Judicature Soc., Houston Young Lawyers Assn. (chmn. com. for arts 1982—, dir. 1986—). Club: Texas (Houston). Avocations: golf, tennis, snow skiing, water skiing, outdoor activity. Federal civil litigation, State civil litigation. Home: 4063 Merrick Houston TX 77025

HALBACH, PATRICE HALEY, lawyer; b. St. Paul, Aug. 11, 1953; d. Thomas Joseph and Catherine (Young) Haley; m. Gerald Patrick Halbach; children: Julia, Kelly. BA, U. Minn., 1975, JD, 1980. Bar: Minn. 1980, U.S. Dist. Ct. Minn. 1980. Atty. Fredrikson & Byron, Mpls., 1980-83; tax atty. Cargill Inc., Mpls., 1983—. Mem. ABA, Minn. Bar Assn., Phi Beta Kappa. Corporate taxation, Private international. Home: 1074 Lake Oaks Dr Shoreview MN 55440 Office: Cargill Inc PO Box 9300 Minneapolis MN 55440

HALBERSTAM, MALVINA GUGGENHEIM, legal educator, lawyer; b. Kempno, Poland, May 2, 1937; d. Marcus and Pearl (Halberstam) H.; children—Arye, Achiezer. B.A. cum laude, Bklyn. Coll., 1957; J.D., Columbia U., 1961, M.I.A., 1964. Bar: N.Y. 1962, U.S. Dist. Ct. (so. dist.) N.Y. 1963, U.S. Ct. Appeals (2d cir.) 1965, U.S. Supreme Ct. 1966, Calif. 1968. Law clk. Judge Edmund L. Palmieri, Fed. Dist. Ct. (so. dist.) N.Y., 1961-62; research assoc. Columbia Project on Internat. Procedure, 1962-63; asst. dist. atty. N.Y. County, 1963-67; with Rifkind & Sterling, Los Angeles, 1967-68; sr. atty. Nat. Legal Program on Health Problems of the Poor, Los Angeles, 1969-70; prof. Loyola U. Sch. Law, Los Angeles, 1970-76, Benjamin N. Cardozo Sch. Law, Yeshiva U., N.Y.C., 1976—; vis. prof. Gould Law Ctr., U. So. Calif., Los Angeles, 1972-73, U. Va. Sch. Law, 1975-76, U. Tex. Sch. Law, summer 1974; vis. prof. Hebrew U. Jerusalem, 1984-85; counselor on internat. law Dept. State, 1985-86; cons. Dept. State, 1986—; mem. Columbia U. Seminar on Human Rights; cons. U.S. Dept. State, 1986—. Articles and rev. editor Columbia Law Rev., 1960-61; contbr. articles, commentary, book revs. to profl. publs. Kent Scholar, Stone Scholar; recipient Jane Marks Murphy prize. Mem. Am. Law Inst. (reporter model penal code project 1977-79), Am. Soc. Internat. Law (program com. 1987), Internat. Law Assn. Am. Br. (exec. com. human rights com. 1987), Columbia Law Sch. Alumni Assn., Phi Beta Kappa. Criminal, Public international, Federal civil litigation. Home: 160 Riverside Dr New York NY 10024 Office: Yeshiva U Benjamin N Cardozo Sch Law 55 Fifth Ave New York NY 10003

HALBRITTER, MARC ALAN, lawyer; b. Morgantown, W.Va., Mar. 21, 1955; s. Robert Carl and Waneila (Chloe) H.; m. Debora Diane Whetsell, July 10, 1982; 1 child, Ashlee Brooke. BBA cum laude, W.Va. U., 1977, JD, 1980. Bar: W.Va. 1980, U.S. Dist. Ct. (no. and so. dists.) W.Va. 1980; CPA, W.VA. Hearing examiner Pub. Service Commn. of W.Va., Charleston, 1980-83; gen. counsel Strategic Ventures, Inc., Charleston, W.Va., 1983-84; gen. atty. Hope Gas, Inc., Clarksburg, W.Va., 1984—. Football official W.Va. Secondary Schs. Athletic Assn., Parkersburg, 1984-86; trustee St. Barnabas Episc. Ch., Bridgeport, W.Va., 1986—. Mem. ABA, W.Va. Bar Assn., Am. Gas Assn. Republican. Avocations: snowskiing, golfing, hunting, fishing. Public utilities, General corporate. Home: 33 Clubview Dr Bridgeport WV 26330 Office: Hope Gas Inc PO Box 2868 Clarksburg WV 26302

HALBROOK, STEPHEN PORTER, lawyer; b. Greenwood, Miss., Sept. 12, 1947; s. James Porter and Nelwyn Lola (Nason) H.; m. Marsha Jean Quarterman, July 22, 1947; children: Lisa Cherie, Stephen Che, Patrick Nason. AA, Fla. Coll., 1967; BS, Fla. State U., 1969, PhD, 1972; JD, Georgetown U., 1978. Bar: Va. 1978, U.S. Supreme Ct. 1981, D.C. 1984, U.S. Ct. Appeals (4th, 5th and 7th cirs.). Asst. prof. Tuskegee (Ala.) Inst., 1972-74, Howard U., Washington, 1974-79; sole practice Fairfax, Va., 1978—; asst. prof. George Mason U., Fairfax, 1980-81. Author: That Every Man Be Armed, 1984; also articles. Mem. ethics com. Fairfax Hosp., 1982—; chmn. zoning com. Mantua Civic Assn., Fairfax, 1982-85. Law & Liberty fellow Inst. for Humane Studies, 1981. Mem. ABA, Va. Bar Assn. (pub. info. com.), Fairfax Bar Assn., Assn. Trial Lawyers Am., Va. Trial Lawyers Assn., SAR (chancellor 1984—), Nat. Rifle Assn. (bylaws com.). Avocation: marathon running. Federal civil litigation, Criminal, Jurisprudence. Office: 10605 Judicial Dr Suite B-3 Fairfax VA 22030

HALDANE, MARK THOMAS, lawyer; b. Beverly, Mass., July 5, 1955; s. Robert and Marian Jennie (Jordan) H.; m. Susan Marian Briggs, Aug. 25, 1978. BA in History, U. Mich., 1977; JD, New Eng. Sch. Law, 1980. Bar: Mass. 1980, U.S. Dist. Ct. Mass. 1981, U.S. Ct. Appeals (1st cir.) 1981, U.S. Tax Ct. 1983. Counsel in-house Sentry Protective Systems, East Boston, Mass., 1981—; bd. dirs. Creative Systems Engring., Brookline, Mass. Moderator Wilmington (Mass.) Congl. Ch., 1986; mem. Wilmington Rep. Town Com., 1986; exec. bd. dirs. council 7th Congl. Dist. Reps., Everett, Mass., 1985. Mem. ABA, Assn. Trial Lawyers Am., Mich. Alumni Assn. Club: U. Mich. M. Avocations: golf, racquetball, basketball, baseball, football. Consumer commercial, Family and matrimonial, Personal injury. Home: 41 Brentwood Ave Wilmington MA 01887 Office: Sentry Protective Systems Corp PO Box 525 East Boston MA 02128

HALDEMAN, GEORGE PAUL, lawyer; b. York, Pa., Dec. 10, 1941; s. George Greybill and Lillian Doris (Shepp) H.; m. Elizabeth Anne Breckinridge, Feb. 20, 1962 (div. Apr. 1976); children: Paul Nelson, Alexander David; m. Kathryn Margaret Rashleigh, May 16, 1976. BA, Am. U., 1965; JD, Georgetown U., 1969. Bar; Md. 1969, D.C. 1970, U.S. Dist. Ct. D.C. 1970, U.S. Ct. Appeals (4th cir.) 1970, U.S. Supreme Ct. 1974. Ptnr. Brault, Graham et al, Rockville, MD, 1970-79, Lambert, Furlow et al, Rockville, 1981-84, Adelman & Haldeman, Rockville, 1985—. Pres. Carter Hill Homeowners Assn., Rockville, 1973; vice chmn. Unitarian Ch. Rockville, 1978. Mem. ABA, Md. Bar Assn., Montgomery County Bar Assn. (exec. com. 1979), Assn. Trial Lawyers Am., Def. Research Inst. Democrat. State civil litigation, Insurance, Personal injury. Home: 1089 Larkspur Terr Rockville MD 20850 Office: Adelman & Haldeman 200A Monroe St Rockville MD 20850

HALE, CANDACE, lawyer; b. N.Y.C., Mar. 16, 1953; d. Thomas Shaw and Geraldine Evelyn (Murphy) H. BA, Sarah Lawrence Coll., 1974; JD cum laude, Harvard U., 1982. Bar: Calif., U.S. Dist. Ct. (no., cen., and ea. dists.) Calif. 1983. Assoc. Brobeck, Phleger & Harrison, San Francisco, 1982-85, Landels, Ripley & Diamond, San Francisco, 1985—. Mem. ABA, San Francisco Bar Assn., Calif. Women Lawyers Assn., San Francisco Women Lawyers Assn. Federal civil litigation, State civil litigation. Home: 44 Cazneau Ave Sausalito CA 94965 Office: Landels Ripley & Diamond 450 Pacific Ave San Francisco CA 94113

HALE, CHARLES RUSSELL, lawyer; b. Talpa, Tex., Oct. 17, 1916; s. Charles L. and Exa (Evans) H.; m. Clementine L. Moore, Jan. 5, 1946; children: Robert R., Norman B. A.B., Stanford U., 1939; J.D., Fordham U., 1950. Bar: N.Y. 1950, Calif. 1953. Supr., United Geophys. Co., Pasadena, Calif., 1940-46; mem. patent staff Bell Telephone Labs., N.Y.C., 1947-48, Sperry Gyroscope Co., Great Neck, N.Y., 1948-51; practiced in Pasadena 1951-54; mem. firm Christie, Parker & Hale, Pasadena, 1954—. Mem. ABA, Los Angeles Bar Assn., Pasadena Bar Assn. (v.p. 1960-61), Am. Patent Law Assn., AAAS, Am. Soc. Internat. Law, IEEE. Clubs: University (Pasadena); Rancho Santa Fe (Calif.) Golf. Patent, Trademark and copyright, Federal civil litigation. Home: PO Box 616 Rancho Santa Fe CA 92067 Office: 350 W Colorado Blvd Pasadena CA 91105

HALE, DANIEL CUDMORE, lawyer; b. Denver, Nov. 5, 1944; s. George Ellis and Dorothy Ann (Cudmore) H.; children—Brad, Tessa. B.S. in Mktg., U. Colo., 1967, J.D., 1971. Bar: Colo. 1971, U.S. Dist. Ct. Colo. 1971, U.S. Ct. Appeals (10th cir.) 1971, U.S. Supreme Ct. 1979. Clk. to judge U.S. Dist. Ct., Denver, 1971-72; chief trial dep. Boulder Dist. Atty.'s Office Colo., 1973-76; atty. Miller, Gray & Hale, Boulder, 1976-84; ptnr. Miller, Hale & Harrison, Boulder, 1984—; cert. instr. search and seizure State of Colo., 1980—; instr. trial advocacy U. Colo., 1987. Bd. dirs. Boulder County Bd. of Developmental Disabilities, Boulder, 1982—, pres., 1984-85. Mem. Boulder County Bar Assn. (sec., treas. 1977-79, bd. govs. 1985—, lectr. 1986), Colo. Bar Assn., Nat. Assn. Criminal Def. Lawyers, Am. Trial Lawyers Assn, Colo. Criminal Def. Bar. Democrat. Criminal, Personal injury. Home: 1225 Kalmia Boulder CO 80302 Office: Miller Hale & Harrison 2305 Broadway Boulder CO 80302

HALE, JOSEPH ROBERT, lawyer; b. Ridgway, Ill., June 12, 1927; s. Everett Lee and Grace (Jackson) H.; m. Marie Katherine Everhart, Dec. 5, 1983; children: Susan Lee, Sally Jo, Joseph Robert Jr. BS, U. Ill., 1950, LLB, 1952. Sole practice Shawneetown, Ill., 1952—; judge County of Gallatin, Shawneetown, 1954-62; mem. 59th dist. Ho. of Reps., State of Ill., 1962-64; chief of staff Ill. Atty. Gen., Springfield, 1981-83; ombudsman Gov. of Ill., Springfield, 1983-84; chief legal counsel Dept. Conservation, Springfield, 1984-86. Sec. Ill. Rep. State Cen. Com., Springfield, 1982-86; mem. 22d Dist. Rep. State Cen. Com., Shawneetown, 1966-86. Served with U.S. Army, 1945-47. Mem. ABA, Ill. Bar Assn., Tri County Bar Assn., Am. Judicature Soc. Presbyterian. Home: 500 N Marshall St Shawneetown IL 62984 Office: 1st Nat Bank Bldg PO Drawer L Shawneetown IL 62984

HALEY, CHARLES FREDERICK, lawyer; b. Florence, Ala., Jan. 5, 1945; s. Joseph Logan and Martha Louise (Horst) H.; m. Barbara Ann Richard, Apr. 13, 1968 (div. Jan. 1987); children: Deron Joseph, Ryan Patrick, Shannon Rose; m. Carla June Morris, Feb. 14, 1987. Student, Mich. State U., 1966-68; BA, U. Pitts., 1970, JD, 1973. Bar: Pa. 1973, U.S. Dist. Ct. (we. dist.) Pa. 1973, U.S. Supreme Ct. 1980. Sole practice Butler, Pa., 1973-85; labor counsel Heck's Inc., Nitro, W.Va., 1985—; 1st asst. pub. defender County of Butler, 1973-83; referee appeals Commonwealth of Pa., Pitts., 1983-85; instr. Indiana U. of Pa., 1976; solicitor Fraternal Order Police, Butler, 1978-83, Adams Twp., Mars, Pa., 1981-83. Served with U.S. Army, 1966-68. Mem. ABA, Pa. Bar Assn. (del. 1981-82), Phi Alpha Delta. Republican. Roman Catholic. Lodges: Mensa, Moose. Avocations: acting, rugby. Labor, General corporate. Home: 1009 Dartmouth Ave Charleston WV 25302 Office: Heck's Inc PO Box 158 Nitro WV 25143

HALEY, WILLIAM PATRICK, lawyer; b. Chateauroux, France, July 18, 1955; came to U.S., 1955; s. William and Sue Earnestine (Martin) H.; m. Paula June McGuire, June 7, 1980. AA, Labette Community Coll., 1975; BA summa cum laude, Wichita State U., 1977; JD, U. Kans., 1980. Bar: Kans. 1980, U.S. Dist. Ct. Kans. 1980. Law clk. to presiding judge U.S. Dist. Ct. Kans., Topeka, 1980—. Mem. ABA, Kans. Bar Assn., Order of Coif. Democrat. Methodist. Avocations: sports, reading. Home: 3230 SW 30th Terr Topeka KS 66614 Office: US Dist Ct Kans 444 SE Quincy Topeka KS 66683

HALFERTY, JAMES BURKHARDT, lawyer; b. Lancaster, Wis., Oct. 9, 1930; s. Clay E. and Leone F. (Burkhardt) H.; m. Jo Anne M. Bullock, Sept. 14, 1964; children—Matthew C., Susan E., Laura E. B.A., U. Wis., 1952, LL.B., 1956. Bar: Wis. 1956, U.S. Dist. Ct. (we. dist.) Wis. 1956. Assoc. I.E. Rasmus, Chippewa Falls, Wis., 1956-61; sole practice Lancaster, Wis., 1961—; dist. atty. Grant County (Wis.), 1962-72; city atty. City of Lancaster, 1975-80; instr. criminal evidence and procedure U. Wis.-Platteville, 1968—. Bd. dirs. Lancaster Meml. Hosp., 1975—; trustee Congl. Ch., Lancaster, 1982-84. Mem. Wis. State Bar, Grant County Bar. Republican. Club: Masons. General practice. Home: 515 W Pine St Lancaster WI 53813 Office: 108 S Madison St Lancaster WI 53813

HALICZER, JAMES SOLOMON, lawyer; b. Ft. Myers, Fla., Oct. 27, 1952; s. Julian and Margaret (Shepard) H. BA in English Lit., U. So. Fla., 1976, MA in Polit. Sci., 1978; JD, Stetson U., 1981. Bar: Fla. 1982. Assoc. Conrad, Scherer & James, Ft. Lauderdale, Fla., 1982-86, 86—, Bernard & Mauro, Ft. Lauderdale, 1986. Mem. Phi Kappa Phi, Pi Sigma Alpha, Omicron Delta Kappa. Methodist. Avocations: reading, jogging. Personal injury, State civil litigation, Health. Home: 3031 N Ocean Blvd #8 Fort Lauderdale FL 33308 Office: Conrad Scherer and James 633 S Federal Hwy Fort Lauderdale FL 33301

HALIW, ANDREW JEROME, III, lawyer, engineer; b. Ansbach, Fed. Republic of Germany, Aug. 8, 1946; came to U.S., 1950; s. Ilko and Sophie (Kindrat) H.; m. Adrianne Olena Leheta, July 21, 1979; children: Larissa Andrea, Andrea Stephanie. BEE, Wayne State U., 1968, JD, 1972. Bar: Mich. 1973, U.S. Dist. Ct. (ea. dist.) Mich. 1973, U.S. Supreme Ct. 1982. Divisional elec. engr. J & L div. LTV, Warren, Mich., 1968-72; assoc. Sullivan & Leavitt P.C., Northville, Mich., 1972-79, ptnr., 1979—, also bd. dirs.; bd. dirs. Dibrova, Inc., Warren, Four Seasons, Inc., Royal Oak, Mich., Metric Tool, Inc., Detroit, Am. Supplier Inst., Dearborn, Mich., Advanced Systems and Designs, Inc., Dearborn, Am. Quality Services, Dearborn. Atty. Ukrainian Cultural Ctr., Warren, 1984; del. Farmington Hills Reps., 1986—. Mem. ABA, Detroit Bar Assn., Oakland County Bar Assn., Detroit Engring. Soc. Republican. Roman Catholic. General corporate, State civil litigation, Federal civil litigation. Home: 38250 W Nine Mile Rd Northville MI 48167 Office: Sullivan & Leavitt PC 22375 Haggerty Rd PO Box 400 Northville MI 48167

HALL, ALAN, lawyer; b. N.Y.C., June 21, 1939; s. Glen Robert and Mary (Cook) H.; m. Joanna Moatz, Aug. 26, 1961; children—Beth Alison, Brian Matthew; m. Maureen Hamilton Beggs, Dec. 29, 1977; 1 son, Glen Douglas. B.A., Pa. State U., 1962; J.D., NYU, 1966. Bar: N.H. 1966, U.S. Dist. Ct. N.H. 1966, U.S. Ct. Appeals (1st cir.) 1969. Trust and estate adminstr. Chase Manhattan Bank, N.Y.C., 1963-66; assoc., Wadleigh, Starr, Peters, Dunn & Chiesa, Manchester, N.H., 1966-69, ptnr., 1970—; adj. prof. U. N.H., 1981; instr. bus. law N.H. Coll. Acctg. and Commerce, 1969. Clk., Manchester Police Found.; trustee, clk. Roscoe A. Ammon Charitable Found. Mem. ABA, Am. Arbitration Assn., N.H. Bar Assn., Manchester Bar Assn. Congregationalist. Labor. Address: 95 Market St Manchester NH 03101

HALL, BETSY, lawyer; b. Marietta, Ohio, Aug. 2, 1952; d. Benjamin Franklin Hall and Betty Lou (Fogle) Smith; m. Fred O. Williams, Feb. 7, 1981 (div. Aug. 1985); children: Jackson Hall-Williams, Olivia Hall-Williams. BJ, U. Tex., 1974; postgrad., St. Mary's U., San Antonio, 1974-75; JD, So. Meth. U., 1977. Bar: Tex. 1977, U.S. Dist. Ct. (we. dist.) Tex. 1979, U.S. Dist. Ct. (no. dist.) Tex. 1980, U.S. Ct. Appeals (5th cir.) 1980, Ark. 1981, U.S. Dist. Ct. (we. dist.) Ark. 1981, U.S. Ct. Appeals (8th cir.) 1981, U.S. Dist. Ct. (ea. dist.) Okla. 1983, U.S. Ct. Appeals (10th cir.) 1983, U.S. Dist. Ct. Minn. 1985, U.S. Supreme Ct. 1985, U.S. Dist. Ct. (ea. dist.) Tex. 1986. Briefing atty. U.S. Dist. Ct. (we. dist.) Tex., El Paso, 1977-79; assoc. Robbins, Zelle, Larson & Kaplan, Dallas, 1979-81; ptnr. Hardin, Jesson & Dawson, Ft. Smith, Ark., 1981—. Mem. Southwestern Law Jour.; contbr. articles to profl. jours. Mem. Sebastian County Young Dems., 1982—; bd. dirs. United Cerebral Palsy Western Ark., Fort Smith, 1982-85, Comprehensive Juvenile Services Western Ark., Ft. Smith, 1981—, Sebastian County Law Library Bd., Ft. Smith, 1984, chmn. 1986-87. Mem. ABA, Tex. Bar Assn., State Bar of Ark., Am. Judicature Soc., Assn. Trial Lawyers Am., Sebastian County Bar Assn., Phi Delta Phi. Methodist. Lodge: Zonta (bd. dirs., past pres. Ft. Smith club 1981—). Federal civil litigation, State civil litigation. Office: Hardin Jesson & Dawson PO Drawer 968 Fort Smith AR 72902

HALL, BETTY JEAN, public interest group executive, lawyer; b. Richmond, Ky., July 12, 1946; d. James Russell and Lillian (Guy) Hall; m. Thomas Michael Burke, Oct. 6, 1979; children—Tiffany Michelle and Timothy Michael (twins). BA, Berea Coll., 1968; JD, Antioch Sch. Law, 1976. Bar: D.C. 1977, Va. 1977, Tenn. 1979, U.S. Dist. Ct. D.C. 1977, U.S. Ct. Appeals (D.C. cir.) 1977. Assoc. Law Offices of James Lawson, Washington, 1976-77; exec. dir. and gen. counsel Coal Employment Project, Oak Ridge, Tenn. and Dumfries, Va., 1977—; bd. dirs. Highlander Ctr., New Market, Tenn., S.E. Women's Employment Coalition, Versailles, Ky.; chmn. bd. dirs. So. Appalachian Leadership Devel. Program, Lexington, Ky. Recipient Rockefeller Pub. Service award, 1981; Berea Coll. Service award, 1985; named Ms. Mag. Woman to Watch in the 80's, 1980; Nat. Women's Health Network Health Advocate of Yr., 1980; John Hay Whitney fellow, 1978-80. Mem. ABA, D.C. Bar Assn., Va. Bar Assn., Tenn. Bar Assn. Civil rights. Home: 16221 Sunny Knoll Ct Dumfries VA 22026

HALL, CARLYLE WASHINGTON, JR., lawyer; b. N.Y.C., Feb. 6, 1943; s. Carlyle Washington and Anzonette Marguerite (Asmussen) H.; Aug. 28, 1964 divorced; 1 son, Carlyle Washington III; m. Joanne Jackson, Jan. 1, 1977; children: Christopher Jackson, Andrew Jackson. B.A., Yale U., 1963; J.D. magna cum laude, Harvard U., 1966. Bar: Calif. Tchr. law, adminstr. Internat. Legal Center, Sudan, Uganda, 1966-69; asso. firm O'Melveny and Myers, Los Angeles, 1969-71; co-founder, staff atty. Center for Law in Pub. Interest, Los Angeles, 1971—; commr. Tahoe Regional Planning Agy., 1981-83. Bd. dirs. Pub. Counsel Inc., 1977-79, Calif. Common Cause, 1980-81, League to Save Lake Tahoe, 1984—. Recipient Environ. Activist of Year award Ventura County Environ. Coalition, 1975; Clean Air award Calif. Lung Assn., 1978; Durfee award for Contbn. to Advancement of Human Dignity, Durfee Found., 1982; Vivian Stimson vis. fellow Cambridge U., fall 1983; Donald Hagman Meritorious award, Am. Planning Assn., 1985. Litigated pub. interest cases in Calif. Environment, Civil rights, Local government. Home: 2711 Anchor Ave Los Angeles CA 90064 Office: 10951 W Pico Blvd Los Angeles CA 90064

HALL, CHARLES MARTIN, lawyer; b. South Charleston, W.Va., May 20, 1949; s. Charles Everett and Betty Ruth (Harrison) H. BA, Washington and Lee U., 1971; JD, Emory U., 1975. Bar: Ga. 1975, U.S. Dist. Ct. (no. dist.) Ga. 1975, U.S. Ct. Appeals (11th cir.) 1981. Assoc. Lainer, Elliot & Price, Atlanta, 1975-77, Law Offices of Leon L. Rice, III, Atlanta, 1977-80; ptnr. Rice, Hall & Keene, Atlanta, 1980-82; sole practice Atlanta, 1982—; trustee and sec.-treas. Annandale at Suwanee (Ga.), Inc., Atlanta, 1982—. State chmn. Hugh O'Brian Youth Found., Atlanta, 1984-86; bd. dirs. Ga. Dental Edn. Found., Inc., 1987. Served to capt. USAR. Mem. State Bar Ga., Ga. Trial Lawyers Assn., Atlanta Bar Assn., Atlanta Jaycees (legal counsel 1985-86, Chmn. of Yr. award 1977, 85, 86), Psi Upsilon (bd. dirs., treas. 1974—). Methodist. Club: Atlanta City. Lodge: Civitan (local pres. 1980-81). Avocations: scuba diving, weight lifting. General corporate, Contracts commercial, State civil litigation. Home: 19 Stratford Hall Pl Atlanta GA 30342 Office: 900 Pharr Ctr 550 Pharr Rd Atlanta GA 30305

HALL, CHRISTOPHER PATRICK, lawyer; b. Elizabeth, N.J., Jan. 23, 1954; s. James Mathew and Catherine Ann (Cagney) H.; m. Britt Mixer, June 23, 1979. BA, Dartmouth Coll., 1976; BA in Law, Oxford U., Eng., 1978; JD, U. Chgo., 1980. Bar: Wash. 1980, N.Y. 1982. Assoc. Perkins Coie, Seattle, 1980-81; spl. dep. prosecutor King County, Seattle, 1981-82; assoc. Donovan, Leisure, Newton & Irvine, N.Y.C., 1982-86, Jones, Day, Reavis & Pogue, NYC, 1986—. Aide, speaker U.S.I.S. Dept. of State, London, 1976-78; coordinator Hollings for U.S. Pres., N.Y.C, 1983-84. Rhodes scholar, 1976-78. Mem. ABA (litigation sect., editor jour. 1986—, corp., bus. and banking sect., antitrust sect.), N.Y. State Bar Assn., Assn. of Bar of City of N.Y. Roman Catholic. Club: N.Y. Athletic (social com.). Securities, Federal civil litigation, Libel. Home: 198 Blvd Pelham NY 10803 Office: Jones Day Reavis & Pogue 599 Lexington Ave New York NY 10022

HALL, CYNTHIA HOLCOMB, judge; b. Los Angeles, Feb. 19, 1929; d. Harold Romeyn and Mildred Gould (Kuck) Holcomb; m. John Harris Hall,

June 6, 1970 (dec. Oct. 1980); 1 child, Harris Holcomb; 1 child by previous marriage, Desma Letitia. A.B., Stanford U., 1951, J.D., 1954; LL.M., NYU, 1960. Bar: Ariz. 1954, Calif. 1956. Law clk. to judge U.S. Ct. Appeals 9th Circuit, 1954-55; trial atty. tax div. Dept. Justice, 1960-64; atty.-adviser Office Tax Legis. Counsel, Treasury Dept., 1964-66; mem. firm Brawerman & Holcomb, Beverly Hills, Calif., 1966-72; judge U.S. Tax Ct., Washington, 1972-81, U.S. Dist. Ct. for central dist. Calif., Los Angeles, 1981-84; U.S. circuit judge 9th Circuit, Pasadena, Calif., 1984—. Served to lt. (j.g.) USNR, 1951-53. Office: 125 S Grand PO Box 91510 Pasadena CA 91109-1510

HALL, DAVID WAYNE, lawyer; b. Ashland, Ky., Feb. 24, 1946; s. Ersie L. and Margie (Franz) H.; m. Nikki Charlene Swanson, Dec. 15, 1979; children: Ashley, Laura, Jonathan, Scott. BS, U. Ky., 1969, JD, 1973. Bar: Ky. 1975. Real estate rep. Phillips Petroleum Co., Columbus, Ohio, 1973-77; real estate atty. Wendy's Internat. Inc., Columbus, 1977-82; Corp. Counsel Orange Co. Inc., Columbus, 1982-84; regional corp. counsel Am. Diversified Capital, Tampa, Fla., 1984-86; gen. counsel, sec. Hardy Devel. Corp., Orlando, Fla., 1986—. Mem. ABA, Ky. Bar Assn., Internat. Council Shopping Ctrs. Republican. Presbyterian. Avocations: golf, softball. General corporate, Real property, Banking. home: 1877 E Crowley Circle Longwood FL 32779 Office: Hardy Devel Corp 2170 W State Rt 434 Longwood FL 32779

HALL, DAVID WINSTON, lawyer; b. Washington, May 27, 1939; s. Loren Boyd and Winona Elizabeth (Bringhurst) H.; m. Sally Mary Cooper, Apr. 15, 1967; children: Matthew Loren, Samuel Kaeo Taylor. BA in Polit. Sci., Yale U., 1961; JD, George Washington U., 1971. Bar: Hawaii 1971, U.S. Dist. Ct. Hawaii 1971. Dep. pub. defender Honolulu, 1971; ptnr. Hart, Sherwood, Leavitt, Blanchfield & Hall, Honolulu, 1971, Hart, Leavitt & Hall, Honolulu, 1976-78, Edmunds & Hall, Honolulu, 1979-80, Hall & Wong, Honolulu, 1980-82; sole practice Honolulu, 1982—; mem. Jud. Conf., Hawaii, 1985—; arbitrator Ct. Annexed Arbitration, Hawaii, 1985—. Pres. Nuuanu Neighborhood Assn., Honolulu, 1981—. Served to lt. comdr. USNR, 1961-66. Mem. ABA, Hawaii Bar Assn., Assn. Trial Lawyers Am., Nat. Assn. Criminal Def. Lawyers. Methodist. Avocations: tennis, hiking, biking. Federal civil litigation, State civil litigation, Criminal. Home: 3462 Kahawalu Dr Honolulu HI 96817 Office: 733 Bishop St Suite 1280 Honolulu HI 96813

HALL, DENISE PAGE, lawyer; b. Indpls., Aug. 27, 1952; d. Russell Winston and Deronda (Bird) Page; married; 1 child, Paige Meredith. BA, Ind. U., 1974; JD, U. Notre Dame, 1977. Bar: Ind. 1977, U.S. Dist. Ct. (so. dist.) Ind. 1977. Assoc. Hilgedag, Johnson, Secrest & Murphy, Indpls., 1977-80, Meils, Zink, Thompson, Dietz & Bole, Indpls., 1980—; prof. Ind. Vocat. Tech. Coll., Indpls., 1977-80; mem. Marion County Jud. Nominating com., Indpls., 1986—. Dir. children's choir N. United Meth. Ch., Indpls., 1976—, mem. adminstrv. bd., 1983-84, music com., 1985—; singer Indpls. Opera Co., Ind. Opera Theatre; solosit Indpls. Cathedral Arts Series, Indpls. Area Chs. Named one of Outstanding Young Women Am., 1983. Mem. Indpls. Bar Assn. (chmn. law studies com., ct. liasion, speaker bur., career day, law in pub. sch. seminar, exec. com. young lawyers' sect. 1982-83, bd. mgrs. 1985-86). Club: Riviera (Indpls.). Avocation: tennis. Office: Meils Zink Thompson Dietz & Bole 2 Market Sq #830 Indianapolis IN 46204

HALL, DONALD J., law educator; b. 1943. BS, Fla. State U., 1965; JD, U. Fla., 1968. Assoc. Icord, Merrill et al, Sarasota, Fla., 1968-70; assoc. dean Sch. Law Vanderbilt U., Nashville, 1979-84, prof., 1979—. Office: Vanderbilt Univ Sch of Law Nashville TN 37240 *

HALL, FRANK DAWSON, lawyer, cattle rancher; b. Fort Lauderdale, Fla., Oct. 14, 1927; s. Miles Lewis and Mary Francis (Dawson) H.; m. Mildred Doyle, May 8, 1960; 1 child, Laurie. B.A., Duke U., 1949; J.D., U. Fla., 1951; diploma in comparative law, City of London Coll. Law, 1950. Bar: Fla. 1951, U.S. Dist. Ct. (so. dist.) Fla. 1951, U.S. Supreme Ct. 1970. Ptnr. Hall & Hedrick, Miami, Fla., 1951-77; ptnr. Hall & Swann, Coral Gables, Fla., 1977-79, 86—, Gaston Snow & Ely Bartlett, Hall & Swann, Coral Gables, Fla., 1979-86; rancher; cattle rancher; hon. consul gen. for Thailand, 1978—; v.p., gen. counsel Howard Johnson Co., N.Y.C., Boston, Miami, Fla., 1967-71; mem. adv. council Practicing Law Inst., 1970-71; mem. jud. nominating commn. Fla. Supreme Ct., 1975-79. Editorial staff U. Fla. Law Rev., 1950; contbr. articles, chpts. to profl. publs. Mem. bd. mgmt. Miami YMCA. Served to capt. JAGC, U.S. Army, 1952-54. Fellow Am. Bar Found., Fla. Bar Found.; mem. ABA (exec. council gen. practice sect. 1972-76, chmn. real estate transaction com. 1972-79, chmn. franchise law com. 1983—), Dade County Bar Assn., Inter-Am. Bar Assn., Fla. Bar (exec. council and bd. dirs. real property div. 1958-62, vice chmn. internat. law com. 1971-75, chmn. agri-bus. law com. 1976-77, exec. council gen. practice sect. 1986—, steering com. Fla. Bar Manual on Franchise Law and Practice), Am. Judicature Soc., U.S. C. of C., World Assn. Lawyers, Am. Counsel Assn. (bd. dirs. 1984-86), Am. Coll. Real Estate Lawyers, Phi Delta Phi. Methodist. Club: University (past pres.), Riviera Country. General corporate, Real property, General practice. Home: 1119 Hardee Rd Coral Gables FL 33146 Office: Gaston Snow & Ely Bartlett 2801 Ponce de Leon Blvd 6th Floor Coral Gables FL 33134

HALL, FRANKLIN PERKINS, lawyer, banker, state official; b. Amelia, Va., Dec. 12, 1938; s. Perkins Lee and Lois E. Hall; m. Phoebe Ann Poulterer, July 26, 1969; children—Kimberly Ann, Franklin P. Jr. B.S., Lynchburg Coll., 1961; M.B.A., Am. U., 1964, J.D., 1966. Bar: Va. 1966. Aide to U.S. Senate, Washington, 1964; aide to v.p. U.S., Washington, 1964-67; spl. asst. sec. Dept. HUD, Washington, 1968-69; sr. ptnr. Hall & Hall, Richmond, 1969—; chmn. bd. Cardinal Savs. and Loan Assn., Richmond, Va., 1979-84; chmn. bd. Commonwealth Bank, Richmond, 1984—; spl. counsel Va. Gen. Assembly, Richmond, 1970-75. Del. Va. House of Dels.; active Va. Gen. Assembly, 1976—; bd. dirs. Central Richmond Assn., 1974-75, Richmond Jaycees, 1972-73. Recipient Disting. Service award Richmond Jaycees, 1972; Outstanding Young Man of Va. award, 1973; Va. Jaycees award, 1974; Disting. Citizen award Nat. Mcpl. League, 1976. Mem. Va. Trial Lawyers Assn. (bd. govs. 1982-84), Richmond Bar Assn. (exec. com. 1973-76), Soc. Advancement Mgmt., Newcomen Soc. Democrat. Presbyterian. Clubs: Willow Oaks, Downtown. Federal civil litigation, Administrative and regulatory, General corporate. Office: Hall & Hall 700 E Main St Suite 1 Richmond VA 23219

HALL, GORDON R., state supreme court chief justice; b. Vernal, Utah, Dec. 14, 1926; s. Roscoe Jefferson and Clara Maud (Freestone) H.; m. Doris Gillespie, Sept. 6, 1947; children: Rick Jefferson, Craig Edwin. B.S., U. Utah, 1949, LL.B., 1951. Bar: Utah 1952. Sole practice Tooele, Utah, 1952-69; city atty. City of Grantsville, Utah, 1954-69; town atty. Town of Wendover, Utah, 1955-69, Town of Stockton, Utah, 1955-69; legal adviser Tooele Army Depot, 1953-58; county atty. Tooele County, 1958-69; judge 3d Jud. Dist. Utah, 1969-77; assoc. justice Supreme Ct. Utah, 1977-81, chief justice, 1981—; pres. Utah Assn. Counties, 1965; mem. Pres.'s Adv. Com. OEO, 1965-66. Served with U.S. Maritime Service, 1944-46. Mem. ABA, Utah Bar Assn. Office: Supreme Ct Utah 332 State Capitol Salt Lake City UT 84114

HALL, JACQUELINE YVONNE, lawyer, administrative law judge; b. Detroit, Jan. 8, 1953; d. William Hamilton and Evelyn Virginia (Callaway) H. B in Indsl. Adminstrn., Gen. Motors Inst., 1976; JD, Detroit Coll. Law, 1980. Bar: Mich. 1980. Corp. selection coordinator Ford Motor Co., Dearborn, Mich., 1978-80, position evaluation analyst, 1980-81, staff atty., 1981-84; adminstrv. law judge Mich. Dept. Labor, Detroit, 1984—; magistrate Worker's Compensation Bd. Magistrates. Named one of Top Ladies of Distinction Trade Union Leadership. Mem. Nat. Bar Assn., Women Lawyers Assn., Internat. Assn. Personnel Women, Nat. Assn. Women Judges, Mich. Assn. Adminstrv. Law Judges, Assn. Black Judges Mich., NAACP, Wolverine Bar Assn., Founders Soc., U. Detroit Black Alumni Assn. (bd. advisors 1983—), Delta Sigma Theta. Workers' compensation. Office: Mich Dept Labor 1200 Sixth St Mich Plaza Bldg Detroit MI 48226

HALL, JAMES ALEXANDER, lawyer; b. Garrett, Ky., Oct. 26, 1946; s. Elmer and Ellen (Moore) H.; m. Marie N. DiLauro, Apr. 28, 1984. BS in Edn., Ohio State U., 1973; JD, Samford U., 1979. Bar: Ohio, 1979. Sole practice Columbus, Ohio, 1979—. Atty., cons. Franklin Twp., Columbus, 1984—. Served as cpl. USMC, 1966-68, Vietnam. Mem. Assn. Trial Lawyers Am., Franklin County Trial Lawyers Assn., Ohio State Bar Assn., VFW (atty., cons. Ohio Chpt. 1985—), Mensa. Family and matrimonial, Criminal. Home: 4038 Old Poste Rd Columbus OH 43220 Office: 555 City Bank Columbus OH 43215

HALL, JOAN M., lawyer; b. Inman, Nebr., Apr. 13, 1939; d. Warren J. and Delia E. (Allyn) McClurg; m. Wesley G. Hall, Aug. 3, 1967 (dec.); children—Colin Michael, Justin Allyn. B.A., Nebr. Wesleyan U., 1961; J.D., Yale U., 1965. Bar: Ill. 1965, U.S. Dist. Ct. (no. dist.) Ill. 1965, U.S. Ct. Appeals (7th cir.) 1965. Assoc. Jenner & Block, Chgo., 1965-71; ptnr. Jenner & Block, 1971—; vice chmn. com. character and fitness Ill. Supreme Ct. Mem. exec. com. Yale Law Sch. Assn., 1976—, treas., 1982-85; bd. dirs. Yale Law Sch. Fund, 1978—, chmn., 1984-86; bd. dirs. Chgo. Lawyers' Com. Civil Rights Under Law, 1978—, chmn., 1983-84; bd. dirs. Legal Assistance Found. Chgo., 1979-82; trustee Nat. Coll. Edn., 1984—, Rush-Presbyn.-St. Luke's Hosp., 1984—; mem. Gannon-Proctor Commn., 1982-84; trustee, bd. govs. Nebr. Wesleyan U., 1983—; bd. dirs. Goodman Theatre; mem. vis. com. Northwestern U. Sch. Law, 1987—. Fellow Am. Coll. Trial Lawyers; mem. ABA (chmn. litigation sect. 1982-83, mem. fed. judiciary com. 1985—, mem. resource devel. council 1984—), Ill. Bar Assn., Chgo. Bar Assn., Bar Assn. 7th Fed. Circuit, Chgo. Council Lawyers, Law Club Chgo. Clubs: Chicago (dir.) Economic (Chgo.). Federal civil litigation, State civil litigation. Office: Jenner & Block One IBM Plaza Chicago IL 60611

HALL, JOHN HOPKINS, lawyer; b. Dallas, May 10, 1925; s. Albert Brown and Eleanor Pauline (Hopkins) H.; m. Marion Martin, Nov. 23, 1957; children—Ellen Martin, John Hopkins. Student, U. Tex., 1942, U. of South, Sewanee, Tenn., 1942-43; LL.B., So. Meth. U., 1949. Bar: Tex bar 1949. Partner firm. Strasburger & Price, Dallas, 1957—. Served with U.S. Army, 1943-45. Fellow Tex. Bar Found., Am. Bar Found., Internat. Acad. Trial Lawyers, Am. Coll. Trial Lawyers; mem. Am. Bar Assn., Tex. Bar Assn., Dallas Bar Assn., Tex. Assn. Def. Counsel, Def. Research Inst. Episcopalian. Clubs: City Club, Royal Oaks Country, Fin and Feather. Federal civil litigation, State civil litigation. Office: Strasburger & Price 4300 Interfirst Plaza Dallas TX 75202

HALL, JOHN WESLEY, JR., lawyer; b. Watertown, N.Y., Jan. 28, 1948; s. John Wesley and Mary Louise (Hodge) H.; m. Rebecca B. Bane, Nov. 22, 1947; children—Justin William, Mark Daniel. B.A., Hendrix Coll., 1970; J.D., U. Ark., 1973. Bar: Ark. 1973, D.C. 1975, U.S. Dist. and Circuit Cts. 1973, U.S. Supreme Ct. 1976; cert. criminal trial adv. Nat. Bd. Trial Advocacy. Dep. pros. atty., Little Rock, 1973-79, head career criminal div., 1978-79; trial advocacy instr. Ark. Prosecuting Attys. Assn., 1977-79; law clk. Ark. Supreme Ct., 1974; sole practice law, Little Rock, 1979—; lectr. law U. Ark., Little Rock, 1985—, criminal lawyer seminars. Mem. Ark. Bar Assn. (ho. of dels. 1976-79), Assn. Trial Lawyers Am., Am. Bd. Criminal Lawyers, Nat. Assn. Criminal Def. Lawyers, Ark. Assn. Criminal Def. Lawyers (pres. 1987—), First Amendment Lawyer's Assn. Episcopalian. Author: Search and Seizure, 1982, Professional Responsibility of the Criminal Lawyer, 1987; Trial Handbook for Arkansas Lawyers, 1986; editor, author: Arkansas Prosecutor's Trial Manual, 1976-77; Arkansas Extradition Manual, 1978; contbr. articles to profl. jours. Criminal, Federal Constl. litigation, Civil rights. Home: 12920 Southridge Dr Little Rock AR 72212 Office: 523 W 3d St Little Rock AR 72201

HALL, LUTHER EGBERT, JR., lawyer; b. New Orleans, Nov. 14, 1926; s. Luther Egbert and Louisiana (Heard) H.; m. Marie Grehan, Aug. 5, 1950; children—Wendel, Patricia, Terrell, Clayton, Robert. B.B.A., Tulane U., 1950, LL.B., 1952. Bar: La. 1952, U.S. Supreme Ct. 1971. Assoc. Curtis, Foster & Dillon, New Orleans, 1952-54; asst. city atty. City of New Orleans, 1954-56; atty. Pan Am. Petroleum Corp., 1956-62; assoc. Jones, Walker, Waechter, Poitevent & Carrere & Denegre, 1962-67, ptnr., 1967—; pres. Biloxi Marshlands Corp., 1980—. Served with USN, 1944-46. Mem. ABA, Am. Judicature Soc., La. Mineral Law Inst., Phi Delta Phi. Republican. Roman Catholic. Club: Boston. Oil and gas leasing, Real property. Home: 6037 Perrier St New Orleans LA 70118 Office: Jones Walker Waechter Poitevent Carrere & Denegre 201 St Charles Ave New Orleans LA 70170

HALL, MARC GREGORY, lawyer; b. Annapolis, Md., June 3, 1957; s. Paul Harris and Doris Olivia (Wilburn) H. Student, U. London, 1977; BA, Am. U., 1978; JD, Loyola U., New Orleans, 1981. Bar: Md. 1981, U.S. Dist. Ct. Md. 1982, U.S. Ct. Appeals (4th cir.) 1982, D.C. 1985. Asst. states atty. Prince Georges County, Upper Marlboro, Md., 1982-84, Montgomery County, Rockville, Md., 1984—. Mem. Nat. Dist. Attys. Assn., Nat. Ry. Assn. Avocations: model railroading, classical music. Criminal. Office: States Atty Office 151 Courthouse Sq PO Box 151 Rockville MD 20850

HALL, MILES LEWIS, JR., lawyer; b. Fort Lauderdale, Fla., Aug. 14, 1924; s. Miles Lewis and Mary Frances (Dawson) H.; m. Muriel M. Fisher, Nov. 4, 1950; children: Miles Lewis III, Don Thomas. A.B., Princeton U., 1947; J.D., Harvard U., 1950. Bar: Fla. 1951. Since practiced in Miami; ptnr. Hall & Hedrick, 1953—; dir. Gen. Portland, Inc., 1974-81. Author: Election of Remedies, Vol. VIII, Fla. Law and Practice, 1958. Chmn. 3d Appellate Dist. Ct. Nominating Commn., State Fla., 1972-75; pres. Orange Bowl Com., 1964-65, dir., 1950-84, sec., treas. 1984-86, dir. 1986—; vice-chmn., dir. Dade County (Fla.) ARC, 1961-62, chmn., 1963-64, dir., 1967-73; nat. fund cons. ARC, 1963, 66-68, trustee, 1985—; bd. pres. Ransom Sch. Parents Assn., 1966; chmn. South Fla. Gov.'s Scholarship Ball, 1966; mem. exec. bd. South Fla. council Boy Scouts Am., 1966-67; citizens bd. U. Miami, 1961-66; mem. Fla. Council of 100, vice chmn., 1961-62; mem. Coral Gables (Fla.) Biltmore Devel. Com., 1972-73; mem. bd. visitors Coll. Law, Fla. State U., 1974-77; bd. dirs. Coral Gables War Meml. Youth Ctr., 1967—, pres., 1969-72, bd. dirs; bd. dirs. Salvation Army, Miami, 1968-83, Am. Found., Inc., 1985—, Fla. Citizens Against Crime 1984—. Served to 2d lt. USAAF, 1943-45. Mem. ABA (Fla. co-chmn. membership com. sect. corp., banking and bus. law 1968-72), Dade County Bar Assn. (dir. 1964-65, pres. 1967), Fla. Bar, Am. Judicature Soc., Miami-Dade County C. of C. (v.p. 1962-64, dir. 1966-68), Harvard Law Sch. Assn. Fla. (dir. 1964-66), Alpha Tau Omega. Methodist (bd. stewards). Clubs: Kiwanis, Cottage, Harvard, The Miami, City of Miami (Miami); Princeton of So. Fla. (past pres., dir.). State civil litigation, General corporate, Estate planning. Home: 2907 Alhambra Circle Coral Gables FL 33134 Office: Suite 1400 Republic Nat Bank Bldg 150 SE 2d St Miami FL 33131

HALL, RAYMOND PERCIVAL, III, lawyer; b. N.Y.C., Dec. 30, 1943; s. Raymond P. Jr. and Mae (Williams) H. BA, Howard U., 1966, JD, 1969. Bar: N.J. 1972, U.S. Tax Ct. 1981. Atty. Essex County Legal Services, Orange, N.J., 1970-72; legal advisor state taxation Office of Newark Studies, 1972-73; sole practice Jersey City, 1974—; assoc. Louis E. Saunders, Jersey City, 1974-78; editor Prentice-Hall, Paramus, N.J., 1974-86; founder, bd. dirs. Inst. Poverty and Law, Jersey City; legal advisor Ethnic Community Ctr., Jersey City, 1977-79. Author: Law and Poverty in America, 1978; editor: All States Tax Guide 1974. Mem. Film Forum, N.Y.C., 1986. Recipient Cert. of Achievement, Reginald Huber Smith Fellow, 1971, Cert. of Achievement, Nat. Urban Fellows, Yale U., 1972. Mem. ABA, Nat. Bar Assn., Afro-Am. Arbitration Orgn., NAACP. Avocations: poetry, film, jazz music. State and local taxation, Poverty and law, General practice. Office: 286 Summit Ave Jersey City NJ 07306

HALL, REED STANLEY, lawyer; b. Idaho Falls, Idaho, July 29, 1929; s. Reed LeRoy and Melba (Stevens) H.; m. Dorothy Stuart, Apr. 26, 1955; children—John, Christopher, Gary, Suzanne, Elizabeth, Andrew. B.S., Brigham Young U., 1951; M.A., U. Ill., 1953; J.D., Harvard U., 1958. Bar: Calif. 1959, U.S. Dist. Ct. (cen. dist.) Calif. 1959. Assoc. Price, Postel & Parma, Santa Barbara, Calif., 1960-68; atty. Sears, Roebuck and Co., Alhambra, Calif. and Chgo., 1968—; sec., dir. Pacific Installers, Inc., Alhambra, 1976-85. Editor Yearbook Brigham Young U., 1951. Chmn. campaign for sch. tax rate election, Whittier, Calif., 1970. Mem. State Bar Calif. (com. on history of law in Calif. 1980-83, chmn. 1982-83), ABA. Republican. Mormon. Club: University (Whittier). Consumer credit, Legal history. Office: Sears Roebuck and Co Legal Dept Sears Tower Chicago IL 60684

HALL, REX ANDREW, lawyer, investor; b. Yuma, Ariz., Nov. 3, 1950; s. Andrew Calvin and Theda Bernice (Weatherby) H.; m. Elizabeth Janann Powell, Mar. 28, 1975; 1 child, Christina Rexanne. BS with honors, N.Mex. State U., 1972; JD, So. Meth. U., 1975. Bar: N.Mex. 1976, Tex. 1976, U.S. Dist. Ct. N.Mex. 1976, U.S. Ct. Appeals (10th cir.) 1986. Ptnr. Hall & Hill, Deming, N.Mex., 1976—; v.p. Sun Meadows Inc., Deming, 1983—. Sec. Deming Airport Commn., 1985—. Mem. ABA, Tex. Bar Assn., N.Mex. Bar Assn. Democrat. Methodist. Club: Rio Mimbres Country (Deming) (bd. dirs. 1982—). Lodges: Rotary, Sun Rise Lions. Avocations: golf, history, tennis. Bankruptcy, Federal civil litigation, State civil litigation. Home: PO Box 68 Deming NM 88031 Office: PO Box 1599 Deming NM 88031

HALL, ROBERT HOWELL, U.S. district judge; b. Soperton, Ga., Nov. 28, 1921; s. Instant Howell, Jr. and Blanche (Mishoe) H.; m. Janice Kay Wren, July 15, 1982; children: Carolyn C., Patricia A., Howell A. B.S. in Commerce, U. Ga., 1941; LL.B., U. Va., 1948; LL.D. (hon.), Emory U., 1973. Bar: Ga. bar 1948, also U.S. Supreme Ct 1948. Prof. law Emory U., 1948-61; asst. atty. gen. Ga., 1953-61; head criminal div. Ga. Law Dept., 1959-61; judge Ga. Ct. Appeals, Atlanta, 1961-74; justice Ga. Supreme Ct., Atlanta, 1974-79; judge U.S. Dist. Ct. (no. dist.) Ga., 1979—; Chmn. Jud. Council Ga., 1973-74, Gov.'s Commn. on Jud. Processes, 1971-73. Author 3 legal texts, also articles. Served with AUS, 1942-46; lt. col. Res. ret. Recipient Leadership award Harvard Law Sch. Assn. Ga., 1971; Golden Citizenship award Fulton Grand Jurors Assn., 1975. Fellow Am. Bar Found.; mem. ABA (ho. dels. 1971-73, chmn. com. Nat. Inst. Justice 1976-80), Am. Judicature Soc. (dir. 1964—, pres. 1971-73, Harley award 1974), Nat. Center State Cts. (adv. council 1971-77, dir. 1977-80), Inst. Ct. Mgmt. (trustee 1976-86), Atlanta Lawyers Club, Delta Tau Delta, Delta Sigma Phi, Phi Delta Phi. Jurisprudence. Office: 2188 U S Courthouse 75 Spring St SW Atlanta GA 30303

HALL, ROBERT TURNBULL, III, lawyer; b. Norfolk, Va., Aug. 25, 1945; s. Robert Turnbull and Mary Evelyn H.; m. Colleen Coffee, Aug. 17, 1968; children—Meghan, Robert. B.S., Washington and Lee U., 1967; J.D., Georgetown U., 1971. Bar: U.S. Dist. Ct. D.C. 1971, D.C. Ct. Appeals 1971, U.S. Ct. Appeals (D.C. cir.) 1972, U.S. Ct. Appeals (5th cir.) 1972, U.S. Supreme Ct. 1975, U.S. Ct. Appeals (11th cir.) 1981, U.S. Ct. Appeals (9th cir.) 1982, U.S. Ct. Appeals (8th cir.) 1983. Assoc. Reid & Priest, N.Y.C., 1971-77, ptnr., 1978—. Mem. ABA, D.C. Bar Assn., Fed. Energy Bar Assn. Administrative and regulatory, FERC practice. Home: 162 Mercer St Princeton NJ 08540 Office: Reid & Priest 40 W 57th St New York NY 10019

HALL, SAM BLAKELEY, JR., judge, former congressman; b. Marshall, Tex., Jan. 11, 1924; s. Sam Blakeley and Valerie (Curtis) H.; m. Madeleine Segal, Feb. 9, 1946; children—Linda Rebecca Hall Palmer, Amanda Jane Hall Wynn, Sandra Blake. Student, Coll. Marshall, 1942; LL.B., Baylor U., 1948. Bar: Tex. 1948. Practice law Marshall, 1948-76; mem. 94th-98th Congresses, 1st Dist Tex.; judge U.S. Dist. Ct. (ea. dist.) Tex., 1985—. Past mem. bd. dirs. East Tex. Area council Boy Scouts Am.; past trustee Wiley Coll., Marshall; past chmn. Marshall Bd. Edn.; past chmn. bd. dirs. Harrison County Hosp. Assn., Marshall; mem. bd. devel. Baylor U. Served with USAAF, 1943-45. Recipient Boss of Yr. award Harrison County Legal Secs. Assn., 1965. Mem. Am. Bd. Trial Advocates, ABA, Tex. Bar Assn., N.E. Tex. Bar Assn. Harrison County Bar Assn. (past pres.), Marshall C. of C. (past pres.; Outstanding Citizen award 1970). Democrat. Mem. Ch. of Christ. Lodge: Kiwanis. Office: US Dist Ct 500 State Line Ave Room 309 Texarkana TX 75501 *

HALL, SUSAN MEDBURY, lawyer; b. Stamford, Conn., Sept. 29, 1947; d. Eben Clarke and Jane Elizabeth (Terhune) H.; m. Samuel G. Mygatt, June 11, 1977; children: Elizabeth, Jenny, Catherine. BA, Smith Coll., 1969; JD, Boston U., 1977. Bar: Mass. 1977. Adminstrv. asst. HUD, Washington, 1969-73; exec. asst. Urban Devel. Corp., N.Y.C., 1973-74; ptnr. Goodwin, Procter & Hoar, Boston, 1977—. Mem. ABA, Mass. Bar Assn. Real property, Contracts commercial, Banking. Office: Goodwin Procter & Hoar Exchange Pl Boston MA 02109

HALL, TERRENCE LYON, lawyer; b. Jackson, Mich., Oct. 24, 1949; s. Kenneth F. and Jean (Lyon) H. B.A., Stanford U., 1972; J.D., Detroit Coll. Law, 1978. Bar: Mich. 1978, U.S. Dist. Ct. (ea. dist.) Mich. 1978, U.S. Ct. Appeals (6th cir.) 1982. Ptnr., Terrence L. Hall & John W. Isgrigg, P.C., Pontiac, Mich., 1978—. Sec., Oakland County Br. ACLU Mich., 1982—. Mem. Assn. Trial Lawyers Am., Mich. Bar Assn., Mich. Orgn. Social Security Claimants' Reps., Mich. Trial Lawyers Assn., Nat. Orgn. Social Security Claimants' Reps., Oakland County Bar Assn., Oakland Trial Lawyers' Assn. Unitarian. Personal injury, Social security disability appeals. Office: Terrence L Hall & John W Isgrigg 4519 Highland Rd (M-59) Pontiac MI 48054

HALL, WALTER RANDALL, II, lawyer; b. Washington, May 30, 1948; s. Walter Randall and Geneva (Bowman) H.; m. Jean Louise Galloway, Aug. 15, 1970; children: Walter R. III, Stephen M., Lindsey A. BA, U. Pa., 1970; JD, U. Va., 1973. Bar: Pa. 1973. Assoc. Morgan, Lewis & Bockius, Phila., 1973-80, ptnr., 1980—. Served to 2d lt. USAF, 1973. Mem. ABA, Pa. Bar Assn., Phila. Bar Assn., Order of Coif. Presbyterian. Public utilities, FERC practice, Nuclear power. Office: Morgan Lewis & Bockius 2000 One Logan Sq Philadelphia PA 19103

HALL, WILLIAM BRYAN, JR., lawyer, retired military officer; b. Elmore County, Ala., Jan. 31, 1939; s. William Bryan Sr. and Gola B. (Still) H.; m. Margaret Priscilla Wideman, June 9, 1963 (div. Feb. 1978); children: Margaret Ceilon Bedwell Hall, Priscilla Jean; m. Kathryn Diane Gray, Jan. 1, 1982. BS in Commerce, U. Md., 1968; JD, U. Md., Balt., 1980. Bar: Md. 1980. Commd. U.S. Army, 1958, advanced through grades to, ret., 1980; assoc. Sullivan & Sullivan, Cumberland, Md., 1980-82; ptnr. Sullivan & Hall, Cumberland, 1982-84; sole practice Cumberland, 1985—. Decorated Bronze Star, Legion of Merit. Mem. VFW (trustee 1982-85), Vietnam Vets Am. (pres. 1986-87), Am. Legion. Democrat. Lodge: Lions. Criminal, Family and matrimonial, General practice. Home and Office: 201 Fayette St Cumberland MD 21502

HALL, WILLIAM WENDELL, lawyer; b. San Antonio, Sept. 11, 1956; s. William Clifford and Mary McKay (Trevor) H.; m. Susan Davis, Apr. 19, 1986. BA, U. Tex., 1978; JD, St. Mary's U., San Antonio, 1981. Bar: Tex., U.S. Dist. Ct. (so. and we. dists.) Tex., U.S. Ct. Appeals (5th cir.), U.S. Supreme Ct. Briefing atty. to presiding justice Tex. Ct. Criminal Appeals, Austin, 1981-82; assoc. Fulbright & Jaworski, San Antonio, 1982—. Contbr. articles to profl. jours. Mem. San Antonio Mus. Assn., 1985, World Affairs Council, San Antonio, 1985; bd. dirs. Bexar County Mediation Ctr., San Antonio, 1985, South Tex. chpt. Nat. Multiple Sclerosis Soc., 1987—; Vol. Ctr., San Antonio, 1986—. Recipient Vol. of Yr. award Vol. Ctr., San Antonio, 1985; named one of Outstanding Young Men of Am., 1982-86. Fellow: State Bar Tex. Found., San Antonio Bar Found.; mem. Bar Assn. Tex. (various coms.), San Antonio Bar Assn. (various coms.), Tex. Young Lawyers Assn. (bd. dirs. 1985—, Outstanding Dir. award 1986, sec. 1987—), San Antonio Young Lawyers Assn. (member comm. chmn., bd. dirs. 1985—), Phi Alpha Delta, Lambda Chi Alpha. Republican. Episcopalian. Labor, Civil rights, Federal civil litigation. Office: Fulbright & Jaworski 2200 InterFirst Plaza 300 Convent St San Antonio TX 78205

HALLANAN, ELIZABETH V., U.S. district judge; b. Charleston, W.Va., Jan. 10, 1925; s. Walter Simms and Imogene (Burns) H. A.B., U. Charleston, 1946; J.D., W.Va. U., 1951; postgrad. U. Mich., 1964. Atty., Crichton & Hallanan, Charleston, 1952-59; mem. W.Va. State Bd. Edn., Charleston, 1955-57; mem. Ho. of Dels., W.Va. Legislature, Charleston, 1957-58; asst. commr. pub. instns., Charleston, 1958-59; mem., chmn. W.Va. Pub. Service Commn., Charleston, 1969-75; atty. Lopinsky, Bland, Hallanan, Dodson, Deutsch & Hallanan, Charleston, 1975-84; judge U.S. Dist. Ct. (so. dist.) W.Va., 1983—. Mem. White House Conf. on Children and Youth. Mem. ABA, W.Va. Bar Assn. Judicial administration. Office: US Dist Ct PO Drawer 5009 Beckley WV 25801

HALLE, JOHN JOSEPH, lawyer; b. Washington, Aug. 10, 1947; s. Louis Joseph and Barbara (Mark) H.; m. Barbara Weiss, Nov. 11, 1973; 1 child, Melissa. BA with honors, U. Oreg., 1968; MA, Tufts U., 1973; postgrad., Harvard U., 1977-78; JD, Suffolk U., 1978. Bar: Oreg. 1978, Wash. 1986.

Assoc. Gilbertson, Brownstein, Sweeney, Kerr & Grim, Portland, Oreg., 1978-81; from assoc. to ptnr. Stoel, Rives, Boley, Fraser & Wyse, Portland, 1981—. Served to lt. USNR, 1969-79. Mem. ABA, Oreg. Bar Assn. (bd. dirs. securities sect.), Pacific NW Internat. Trade Assn. (v.p. 1985—). Securities, General corporate, Private international. Office: Stoel Rives Boley Fraser & Wyse 900 SW 5th Ave Portland OR 97204

HALLE, MOLLIE JOHNSON, lawyer; b. Charleston, S.C., Dec. 7, 1954; d. William Kenneth and Martha Mathilda (Cotten) Johnson; m. Oliver Grant Halle, Aug. 10, 1985. BA, Clemson U., 1976; JD, U. S.C., 1979. Bar: S.C. 1979. Spl. agent FBI, Savannah, Ga., 1979-80, N.Y.C., 1980-84, Washington, 1984-85; spl. agent, prin. legal advisor FBI, Atlanta, 1985—; spl. asst. atty. U.S. Dist. Ct. (so. dist.) N.Y. 1982-84, instr. div. continuing edn. U. Va., 1984-85. Mem. S.C. Bar Assn., Kappa Kappa Gamma Alumni Assn., Phi Delta Phi. 1st FBI agt. to receive a cross designation as SAUSA. Criminal, Federal civil litigation, Government contracts and claims. Home: 2840 Hitchcock Mill Run Marietta GA 30068 Office: FBI 275 Peachtree St Suite 925 Atlanta GA 30303

HALLE, PETER EDWARD, lawyer; b. N.Y.C., Apr. 29, 1944; s. Edward and Georgia Elaine (Lindo) H.; m. Carolyn Lamm, Aug. 12, 1972; 1 child, Alexander Peter. Student, Oberlin Coll., 1962-64; BA in History, NYU, 1967; JD cum laude, U. Miami, 1973. Bar: Fla. 1973, D.C. 1975, U.S. Dist. Ct. (so. dist.) Fla. 1975, U.S. Dist. Ct. D.C. 1980, U.S. Ct. Appeals (5th and 11th cirs.) 1982, U.S. Supreme Ct. 1980, U.S. Ct. Appeals (D.C. cir.) 1984. Trial atty. antitrust div. U.S. Dept. Justice, Washington, 1973-79, asst. chief, trial sect. antitrust div., 1979-81; assoc. Milbank, Tweed, Hadley & McCloy, Washington, 1981-86; ptnr. Morgan, Lewis & Bockius, Washington, 1986—. Served to 1st lt. U.S. Army, 1968-70. Mem. ABA (chmn. fed. practice com. young lawyers div. 1978-80, exec. council young lawyers div. 1979, co-chmn. legis. com. litigation sect. 1985—), Fed. Bar Assn. (nat. council mem. 1981-82), Bar Assn. D.C. (chmn. D.C. affairs sect. 1981-82, bd. dirs. 1983-84, chmn. library com. 1984, com. chmn. yr. 1984). Avocations: running, skiing, tennis. Antitrust, Federal civil litigation, Criminal. Home: 2101 Connecticut Ave NW Washington DC 20008 Office: Morgan Lewis & Bockius 1800 M St NW Washington DC 20036

HALLECK, MICHAEL JOHNSTON, lawyer; b. N.Y.C., June 23, 1944; s. John Crane and Virginia (pierson) H.; m. Susan Leslie Gamble, June 24, 1966; children—Jeffrey Alexander, Andrew John. B.A., Muskingum Coll. and Exeter U. (Eng.), 1966; J.D., Ohio State U., 1971. Bar: Ohio 1971, U.S. Dist. Ct. (no. dist.) Ohio 1975. Assoc. Hahn, Loeser, Freedheim, Dean & Wellman, Cleve., 1971-73; ptnr. Halleck & Geer, Bowling Green, Ohio, 1976—. Past bd. dirs. Wood County Bd. Mental Health and Mental Retardation, Wood County Mental Retardation Bd., Home Health Adv. Bd. Mem. Ohio Bar Assn., Wood County Bar Assn. (pres. 1987), Ohio Acad. Trial Lawyers, Assn. Trial Lawyers Am., Wood County Law Library Assn. (past pres.). State civil litigation, Personal injury, General practice. Office: 105 N Main St Bowling Green OH 43402

HALLENBERG, ROBERT LEWIS, lawyer; b. Louisville, Oct. 21, 1948; s. Daniel Ward and Anna Mae (Lewis) H.; m. Susan Annette Shaffer, Nov. 29, 1980; children—Shea F., Jonathan E.R. Moore, Robert Lewis Jr. B.A., U. Ky., 1970, J.D., 1973; LL.M. in Taxation, U. Miami (Fla.), 1974. Bar: Ky. 1973, U.S. Dist. Ct. (we. dist.) Ky. 1975, U.S. Tax Ct. 1986. Ptnr. firm Woodward, Hobson & Fulton, Louisville, 1974—; adj. prof. U. Louisville Sch. Law, 1974-80. Bd. dirs. Louisville Theatrical Assocs., 1980—, v.p., sec., 1985—; bd. dirs. Goodwill Industries Ky. Mem. Louisville Estate Planning Council (pres. 1979-80), Employee Benefit Council of Louisville, Employee Benefit Council, Estate Planning Forum (bd. dirs. 1986—), ABA (subchpt. S com. 1974-77, real property, probate and trust com. 1985—), Ky. Bar Assn. (sec. tax com. 1984-85). Republican. Episcopalian. Clubs: Pendennis, Owl Creek Country (Anchorage, Ky.). Estate planning, Pension, profit-sharing, and employee benefits, General corporate. Office: Woodward Hobson & Fulton 2500 1st Nat Tower Louisville KY 40202

HALLER, ALBERT A., corporate lawyer; b. East Detroit, Mich., June 17, 1934; s. Albert Karl and Pauline (Bauhammer) H.; m. Ann Peacock, Dec. 30, 1964 (dec. 1974); children: David, Michael, Christopher; m. Eileen Patricia Hoye, Dec. 3, 1976. BA with honors, Mich. State U., 1955; JD with highest honors, U. Mich., 1959. Bar: Ohio 1959, Ill. 1964, Mich. 1985. Assoc. Fuller & Henry, Toledo, 1959-64; atty. Packaging Corp. of Am., Evanston, Ill., 1964-74, asst. gen. counsel, 1974-83, v.p., sec., gen. counsel, 1983—. Mem. ABA, Chgo. Bar Assn., Mich. Bar Assn., Order of Coif. Roman Catholic. Lodge: Elks. Home: 2334 Cowper Evanston IL 60201 Office: Packaging Corp of Am 1603 Orrington Ave Evanston IL 60204

HALLER, ALBERT JOHN, lawyer; b. N.Y.C., May 5, 1931; s. Karl C. and Louise M. (Rickli) H.; m. Karen S. Kratoville, Aug. 9, 1958; children: Christopher, Debra. BA, Washington U., St. Louis, 1953, JD, 1958. Bar: Mo. 1958, U.S. Supreme Ct., 1966. Ptnr. Cupples, Cooper & Haller, St. Louis, 1962-82; sr. ptnr. Haller, Leonard & Tripp, St. Louis, 1982—; bd. dirs. Langenbacher Data Systems, Gerhard Surgical and Med. Trustee Children's Home Soc., St. Louis, 1978—. Served to capt. USNR, 1953-55. Recipient Service to Scouting award Nat. Eagle Scout Assn., 1958; named Outstanding Citizen, Brentwood, Mo. Jr. C. of C., 1968. Mem. Mo. Bar Assn., Met. St. Louis Bar Assn. Republican. General corporate, Probate, General practice. Home: 618 Spring Meadows Manchester MO 63011 Office: Haller Leonard & Tripp PC 7751 Carondelet Saint Louis MO 63105

HALLETT, KENNETH VICTOR, lawyer; b. Milw., Feb. 19, 1956; s. Kenneth Jalane and Agnes (Jagiello) H. AB, U. Notre Dame, 1977; JD, Harvard U., 1980. Bar: Wis. 1980. Assoc. Quarles & Brady, Milw., 1980—; sec., lectr. in securities law Marquette U. Law Sch., Milw., 1984—. Sec. adv. com. Wis. Act 200, 1984-86; fin. chmn. community Milw. County Council Boy Scouts Am., 1984—. Mem. ABA, Wis. Bar Assn., Milw. Bar Assn., Milw. Young Lawyers Assn. Roman Catholic. Club: Milw. Athletic, Notre Dame. Avocations: travel, reading, sports. Securities, General corporate, Banking. Home: 4421 N Woodburn St Shorewood WI 53211 Office: Quarles & Brady 411 E Wisconsin Ave Milwaukee WI 53202

HALLIBURTON, JOHN ROBERT, lawyer; b. Shreveport, La., July 31, 1934; s. Ralph Eloe and Mary Katherine (Smith) H.; m. Julia Ella Bateman, Dec. 17, 1955; children—Cherie Ann, John Robert II, Rhonda Marie. B.S. in Math., Centenary Coll. La., 1955; J.D., So. Methodist U., 1964; postgrad. Grad. Sch. Am. and Fgn. Law, 1968-70; LL.M. in Internat. Law, George Washington U., 1974. Bar: Tex. 1964, U.S. Supreme Ct. 1967, U.S. Ct. Claims 1968, U.S. Ct. Appeals (former 5th cir.) 1968, U.S. Dist. Ct. (no. dist.) Tex. 1969, U.S. Dist. Ct. D.C. 1970, D.C. Ct. Appeals 1973, U.S. Ct. Appeals (D.C. cir.) 1976, U.S. Dist. Ct. (we. dist.) La. 1981, U.S. Ct. Appeals (5th and 11th cirs.) 1981, U.S. Ct. Claims 1982, U.S. Ct. Appeals (fed. cir.). Field support engr. Chrysler corp., Huntsville, Ala., 1959-60; with Rockwell Internat. Corp. (merged into Rockwell Internat. Corp./Collins Radio Co. 1973), 1960-80, dir. govt. relations and contract policy Collins Radio Co., Washington, 1969-74, gen. mgr. Collins Radio Limitada, Brazil, and v.p. Collins Radio Internat., Inc., also v.p. Collins Systems Internat., Inc., 1974-75, mgr. contracts and dealer adminstr., electronics internat. ops. Rockwell Internat. Corp., Dallas, 1975-76, dir. govt. relations electronic systems group Rockwell Internat. Corp., 1976-80; asst. U.S. atty. We. Dist. La., Dept. Justice, Shreveport, 1980—; mem. telecommunications tech. adv. com. Dept. Commerce, Washington, 1973-74. Author profl. reports. Composer, lyricist Absence, 1953. Mem. PAC good govt. com. Rockwell Internat. Corp., Dallas, 1978-80. Served to 1st lt. U.S. Army, 1955-59. Mem. State Bar Tex. (sec.-treas. internat. law sect. 1979-80, vice chmn. 1980-81, program chmn. 1979-81), D.C. Bar Assn. (internat. law and transaction div. com. on transfer of tech. 1977-81, govt. contracts and litigation div. 1977-81), Omicron Delta Kappa, Alpha Sigma Pi, Kappa Alpha (sec. 1954-55), Phi Delta Phi. Roman Catholic. Clubs: Nat. Aviation (Washington); Chandlers Landing Yacht (Rockwall, Tex.). Lodge: K.C. Federal civil litigation, Public international, Personal injury. Home: PO Box 278 7 Northcrest Circle Rockwall TX 75087 Office: US Attys Office Western Dist La 500 Fannin Suite 3B12 Shreveport LA 71101

HALLIDAY, LANA, lawyer; b. N.Y.C., Oct. 7, 1942; d. Samuel and Hilda (Mintz) Friestater; m. Robert Andrew Feinschreiber, July 30, 1967 (div. May 1979); children: Steven Andrew, Kathryn Ann; m. David Graham Halliday, June 21, 1980. AB, Barnard Coll., 1965; JD magna cum laude, Wayne State U., 1969; LLM, Yale U., 1970. Bar: N.Y. 1971, U.S. Tax Ct. 1979. Assoc. Pascus, Gordon & Hyman, N.Y.C., 1970; atty. CIT Fin. Corp., N.Y.C., 1971-73; sole practice N.Y.C., 1973-76; tax atty. Pfizer, Inc., N.Y.C., 1976—. Contbr. articles to profl. jours. Republican. Avocations: ice skating, piano playing, gardening. Corporate taxation, Pension, profit-sharing, and employee benefits. Home: 205 West End Ave Apt 8H New York NY 10023 Office: Pfizer Inc 235 E 42nd St New York NY 10017

HALLINAN, ROBERT EDWARD, laywer; b. N.Y.C., Sept. 25, 1952; s. Robert F. and Virginia Q. (Quigg) H.; m. Cornelia Ireland; children: Elizabeth, Tess. AB, Kenyon Coll., 1974; JD, SUNY, Buffalo, 1977. Bar: N.Y. 1978. Assoc. Harris, Beach, Wilcox, Rubin & Levey, Rochester, N.Y., 1977-82; asst. counsel Teachers Ins. and Annuity Assn., N.Y.C., 1982—. Mem. Phi Beta Kappa. Roman Catholic. Real property. Home: 69 High Way Chappaqua NY 10514 Office: Teachers Ins and Annuity Assn 730 3d Ave New York NY 10017

HALLISEY, JEREMIAH FRANCIS, lawyer; b. Boston, Jan. 15, 1939; s. Jeremiah Francis and Cecilia A. (Lucey) H.; children: Jeremy Michael, Sean Richard. AB, Boston Coll., 1960; MA, Cornell U., 1962; LLB, U. Calif., Berkeley, 1966. Bar: Calif. 1966, U.S. Ct. Appeals (9th cir.) 1966, U.S. Supreme Ct. 1983. Dep. dist. atty. Contra Costa Ct., Martinez, Calif., 1966-68; trial atty. SEC, San Francisco, 1968-70; ptnr. Hallisey & Johnson, San Francisco, 1971-86. Regent U. Calif., Berkeley, 1981-83; indsl. biotech. commr. Calif. Legis., Sacremento, 1982-83. Served with U.S. Army, 1963-68. Fellow Am. Bar Found.; mem. ABA, Calif. Bar Assn. Democrat. Roman Catholic. Clubs: Olympic. Legislative, Antitrust, State civil litigation. Home: 1824 Piedras Circle Danville CA 94526 Office: Hallisey & Johnson 1 California Suite 2235 San Francisco CA 94111

HALLMAN, LEROY, lawyer; b. Grandview, Tex., July 16, 1915; s. Ernest L. and Willa (Prestridge) H.; m. Martha Booker, Nov. 12, 1944; children—Martha B., Willa Anne, Samuel John. Diploma Hillsboro Jr. Coll., 1934; LL.B. with highest honors, U. Tex., 1939. Ptnr. Phinney Hallman & Coke, Dallas, 1946-84, Storey, Armstrong, Steger & Martin, 1984—; dir. Frozen Food Express Industries, Inc., Dallas, Hub Hill, Inc., Dallas. Contbr. articles to profl. jours. Mem. City of University Park Planning and Zoning Commn., Tex., 1972-80. Served to maj. USAAF, 1940-46, PTO. Fellow Tex. Bar Found.; mem. ABA, Dallas Bar Assn., State Bar Tex., Motor Carrier Lawyer Assn. (pres. 1970-71), Delta Theta Phi, Democrat. Baptist. Clubs: Northwood, Petroleum. Administrative and regulatory, General corporate. Home: 3212 Southwestern Dallas TX 75225 Office: Storey Armstrong Steger & Martin 3100 LTV Center 2001 Ross Ave Dallas TX 75201

HALLOCK, ROBERT WAYNE, lawyer; b. Sterling, Ill., Jan. 13, 1944; s. John O. and Jennie S. (Stauffer) H.; m. Patricia Ann Biron, Jan. 2, 1981. B.A., Eureka Coll., 1966; J.D. with very highest honors, U. Ill., 1971. Bar: Ill. 1971, U.S. Dist. Ct. (no. dist.) Ill. 1971, U.S. Supreme Ct. 1971. Assoc. Kirkland and Ellis, Chgo., 1971-76; ptnr. Kirkland and Ellis, 1977-84, Isham Lincoln & Beale, Chgo., 1985—. Mem. ABA, Ill. Bar Assn., Chgo. Bar Assn., Order of Coif. Bankruptcy, Federal civil litigation, State civil litigation. Home: 555 W Madison St Apt 4810-12-1 Chicago IL 60606 Office: Isham Lincoln & Beale Three First National Plaza Chicago IL 60602

HALLORAN, MICHAEL, lawyer; b. Berkeley, Calif., May 20, 1941. BS, U. Calif., Berkeley, LLB, 1965. Atty. Pillsbury, Madison & Sutro, San Francisco. Office: Pillsbury Madison & Sutro 225 Bush St San Francisco CA 94104 *

HALLORAN, ROBERT BARTLEY, lawyer; b. Stamford, Conn., Aug. 23, 1950; s. Robert M. and Eileen (Fahey) H.; m. Donna Anderson, Sept. 20, 1975; children: Kelly, Kyle, Kaitlin. BA in Econs., Georgetown U., 1972; JD, U. Conn., 1975. Bar: Conn. 1975, U.S. Dist. Ct. Conn. 1975, U.S. Ct. Appeals (2d cir.) 1975. Assoc. Feingold, Halloran & Mester, Hartford, Conn., 1975-81; ptnr. Alfano & Halloran, Hartford, 1981—. Mem. Conn. Bar Assn. (young lawyers sect.), Conn. Trial Lawyers Assn. (bd. govs. 1978—, pres. 1985—), Am. Bd. Trial Advs. Democrat. Roman Catholic. Club: Exchange (West Hartford) (treas. 1985). Avocations: skiing, reading. Personal injury, Workers' compensation. Home: 172 Stoner Dr West Hartford CT 06107 Office: Alfano & Halloran 89 Oak St Hartford CT 06106

HALLUIN, ALBERT PRICE, biotechnology executive, lawyer; b. Washington, Nov. 8, 1939; s. William Ord and Martha (Blundon) H.; m. Joanne Rita Forbes, Apr. 16, 1966; children—Marcus Anthony, Russell Price. B.A., La. State U., 1964; J.D., U. Balt., 1969. Bar: Md. 1970, U.S. Supreme Ct. 1976, U.S. Ct. Appeals (Fed. cir.) 1982. Examiner U.S. Patent and Trademark Office, Washington, 1965-69; assoc. Jones, Tullar & Cooper, Arlington, Va., 1969-71; sr. patent atty. CPC Internat. Inc., Englewood Cliffs, N.J., 1971-76; counsel Exxon Research and Engring. Co., Florham Park, N.J., 1976-83; gen. patent and trademark counsel, mem. mgmt. com. Cetus Corp., Emeryville, Calif., 1983—; lectr. in field. Chmn. troop com., asst. scoutmaster Westfield council Boy Scouts Am. Mem. ABA, Am. Intellectual Property Assn. (past chmn. chem. practice com., dir., sec.), AAAS, N.J. Patent Law Assn. (bd. mgrs., treas., 2d v.p.), Patent Office Soc., License Exec. Soc., Assn. Corporate Patent Counsel. Contbr. articles to profl. jours. Patent, Trademark and copyright, General corporate. Office: Cetus Corp 1400 53rd St Emeryville CA 94608

HALM, HOWARD LEE, lawyer; b. Honolulu, July 17, 1942; s. Gilbert and Mary A.S. (Kim) H.; m. Margaret Kurashita Halm, Dec. 19, 1964; children: David Gilbert, Eric Charles, Marisa Karin. BA, UCLA, 1965; JD, U. San Diego, 1968. Bar: Calif. 1969, U.S. Dist. Ct. (cen. dist.) Calif. 1969, U.S. Ct. Appeals (9th cir.) 1969. Dep. atty. gen. State's Atty.'s Office, Los Angeles, 1969-75; ptnr. Breidenbach, Swainston, Crispo & Way, Los Angeles, 1975—. Recipient Commendation award City of Los Angeles, 1986. Mem. ABA, Calif. Bar Assn. (various coms.), Los Angeles County Bar Assn. (various coms.), Def. Research Inst., Assn. Southern Calif. Def. Counsel, Japanese Am. Bar Assn. Avocations: golf, skiing. Office: Breidenbach Swainston Crispo & Way 611 W 6th St Suite 1300 Los Angeles CA 90017

HALPER, EMANUEL BARRY, lawyer, author, educator; b. Bronx, N.Y., June 24, 1933; s. Nathan N. and Molly (Rabinowitz) H.; m. Ilona Rubinstein, Mar. 5, 1961; children: Eve Brook, Dan Reed. AB, CCNY, 1954; JD, Columbia U., 1957. Bar: N.Y. 1958, D.C. 1981, Pa. 1982, Minn. 1982, Wis. 1982, N.D. 1984. House counsel Howard Stores Corp., Bklyn., 1960; assoc. Frederick Zissu, N.Y.C., 1960-65; ptnr. Zissu, Berman, Halper & Gumbinger, N.Y.C., 1965—; adj. prof. NYU, 1973—. Author: Wonderful World of Real Estate, 1975, Shopping Centers and Store Leases, 1979; columnist N.Y. Law Jour., 1982—; contbg. editor Real Estate Review, N.Y.C., 1973—; chmn. editorial policy com. Internat. Property Investment Jour., Hempstead, N.Y., 1982—. Served with USAR, 1957-63. Recipient Disting. Teaching award NYU, 1978. Mem. ABA (chmn. comml. leasing com. 1986—), World Assn. Lawyers (chmn. internat. real estate com. 1982—), Internat. Inst. Real Estate Studies (chmn. bd. 1980—). Jewish. Club: Atrium (N.Y.). Avocations: writing, painting, gardening, weight lifting, swimming. Real property, Construction, Bankruptcy. Office: Zissu Berman Halper & Gumbinger 450 Park Ave 12th Floor New York NY 10022

HALPERIN, THEODORE PHILIP, lawyer; b. N.Y.C., Apr. 12, 1927; s. Harry Joshua and Eva (Goodman) H.; m. Betty Ann Joseph, Mar. 26, 1953; children—Amy Sara Halperin Wood, Jonathan Joseph. B.A., U. Conn., 1948; J.D., NYU., 1951. Bar: N.Y. 1951, U.S. Supreme Ct., U.S. Dist. Ct. (so. and ea. dists.) N.Y., U.S. Ct. Appeals (2d cir.). Asst. atty. gen. State of N.Y., 1953-54; adminstrv. asst. U.S. Congress, Washington, 1954-55; ptnr. Halperin, Shivitz, Scholer & Steingut, N.Y.C., 1955-67, N.Y.C., 1968-78, Halperin & Marcus, N.Y.C., 1979-84, Halperin, Karow & Marcus, N.Y.C., 1985—; mem. Alexander fellows program Cardozo Sch. Law, N.Y.C., 1983—. Pres., bd. dirs. Riverdale Mental Health Assn., Bronx, 1960-70, trustee endowment fund, 1983—; chmn. citizens adv. com. MTA Mgmt. Study, N.Y.C., 1978-81; mem. com. on transp. law Nat. Research Council, Transp. Research Bd.; bd. dirs. Riverdale Sr. Ctr., Bronx, 1974—. Named Man of Yr., Riverdale Community Council, 1983. Mem. Assn. Bar City of N.Y. (chmn. transp. com. 1985—, chmn. spl. com. on energy 1974-75), Bronx Bar Assn. (chmn. civil rights com. 1961), N.Y. State Bar Assn. Democrat. Jewish. Clubs: City (trustee 1979—, v.p. 1984—), City Athletic, NYU. (trustee 1968-70, v.p.). Probate, Real property, General corporate. Office: Halperin Karow & Marcus 535 Fifth Ave New York NY 10017

HALPERN, ALEXANDER, lawyer; b. Tokyo, Aug. 13, 1948; came to U.S., Dec. 1948; s. Abraham Meyer and Mary (Fujii) H.; m. Carol Dreiling, May 12, 1973; children: Solomon J., Eve M., Peter N. BA in Sociology, Brandeis U., 1970; JD, U. Denver, 1976. Bar: Colo. 1976, U.S. Dist. Ct. Colo. 1976, U.S. Ct. Appeals (10th cir.) 1981, U.S. Supreme Ct. 1983. Ptnr. Caplan and Earnest, Boulder, Colo., 1976—. Pres. Ashoka Credit Union, Boulder, 1978—; dep. dir. Vajradhatu Ch., Boulder, 1986. Mem. ABA, Colo. Bar Assn., Colo. Assn. of Sch. Bd. Attys., Boulder County Bar Assn. Democrat. Buddhist. Local government, Federal civil litigation, State civil litigation. Office: Caplan and Earnest 1301 Spruce St Suite 300 Boulder CO 80302

HALPERN, BURTON, lawyer; b. Nashville, June 16, 1941; s. Nathan and Ethel (Seligman) H.; m. Virginia Carpenter, Dec. 27, 1968; children: Jeffrey, Elizabeth. BA, George Peabody Coll., 1964; JD, U. Tenn., 1968. Bar: Tenn. 1968, Mo. 1971, U.S. Dist. Ct. (we. dist.) Mo. 1971. Asst. gen. counsel Hussmann Corp., Bridgeton, Mo., 1971-85, gen. counsel, 1985—. Antitrust, General corporate, Contracts commercial. Home: 1531 Deerhorn Dr Chesterfield MO 63017 Office: Hussmann Corp 12999 St Charles Rock Rd Bridgeton MO 63044

HALPERN, JAMES BLADEN, lawyer; b. Buffalo, Apr. 20, 1936; s. Philip and Goldene P. (Friedman) H.; m. Jessie Malkoff, July 6, 1958 (div.); 1 child, Jennifer; m. Niesa N. Brateman, Aug. 26, 1979; 1 child, Sheri. B.A., Harvard U., 1958, J.D., 1961. Bar: N.Y. 1961, D.C. 1970. Atty. corp. fin. div. SEC, Washington, 1961-64; chief counsel-instns., instl. investor study 1969-70; asso. firm Proskauer Rose Goetz & Mendelsohn, N.Y.C., 1964-69, Arent, Fox, Kintner, Plotkin & Kahn, Washington, 1971-73; ptnr. Arent, Fox, Kintner, Plotkin & Kahn, 1974—. Mem. ABA, Fed. Bar Assn., N.Y. State Bar Assn., D.C. Bar Assn., Assn. Bar City N.Y., Am. Law Inst. Democrat. Jewish. Club: Harvard N.Y.C. General corporate, Securities. Home: 6904 Whittier Blvd Bethesda MD 20817 Office: 1050 Connecticut Ave Washington DC 20036

HALPERN, JOSEPH W., lawyer; b. Bklyn., June 12, 1954; s. Jacob and Helen (Bliss) H. BA, NYU, 1976, JD, 1979. Bar: Colo. 1979, U.S. Dist. Ct. Colo. 1979, U.S. Ct. Appeals (9th cir.) 1980, U.S. Ct. Appeals (10th cir.) 1985. Assoc. Holland & Hart, Denver, 1979-85, ptnr., 1985—. Trustee Colo. Hist. Found., Denver, 1984—. Mem. ABA, Colo. Bar Assn., Denver Bar Assn., Phi Beta Kappa. Federal civil litigation, State civil litigation, Communications. Office: Holland & Hart 555 17th St Suite 2900 Denver CO 80202

HALPERN, KENNETH JAY, N, lawyer; b. N.Y.C., Oct. 19, 1942; s. Harry and Toby (Casson) H.; m. Mishele I. Kay. July 22, 1967; children: Ian, Joshua. BS, U. Del., 1965; JD, Bklyn. Law Sch., 1968. Bar: N.Y. 1968, U.S. Dist. Ct. (ea. and so. dists.) N.Y. 1973, U.S. Ct. Appeals 1973, U.S. Supreme Ct. 1974. Mem. tax dept. Arthur Anderson and Co., N.Y.C., 1968-69; asst. dist. atty. Nassau County, Mineola, N.Y., 1969-75; ptnr. Hession, Halpern & Bekoff, Mineola, 1975—; mem. local rules com. U.S. Bankruptcy Ct. (ea. dist.) N.Y. Pres., bd. dirs. Harbor Green (N.Y.) Civic Assn. Mem. N.Y. State Bar Assn., Nassau County Bar Assn., Nassau/Suffolk Trial Lawyers Assn., Former Asst. Dist. Atty's. Assn. Avocations: skiing, basketball, coaching. General corporate, Bankruptcy, State civil litigation. Office: Hession Halpern & Bekoff 29 Roslyn Rd Mineola NY 11501

HALPERN, LINDA ANN, lawyer; b. Eau Claire, Wis., Feb. 24, 1954; d. Samuel A. Halpern and Margery W. (Zimmerman) Harris; m. Keith R. Fisher, Aug. 3, 1980. AB, Princeton U., 1976; JD, Georgetown U., 1979. Bar: D.C. 1979, U.S. Ct. Appeals (D.C. and 4th cirs.) 1981, U.S. Ct. Claims 1983, U.S. Dist. Ct. D.C. 1980. Assoc. Seyfarth, Shaw, Fairweather & Geraldson, Washington, 1979-83; trial atty. U.S. Dept. Justice, Washington, 1983-85; asst. U.S. atty. U.S. Atty's Office, Washington, 1985—. Named Best Oralist Am. Coll. Trial Lawyers, 1978. Mem. ABA. Avocations: skiing, horseback riding, classical music. Federal civil litigation, Labor, Medical malpractice. Home: 8 Scotch Mist Ct Rockville MD 20854 Office: US Atty's Office 555 4th St NW Washington DC 20001

HALPERN, PHILIP MORGAN, lawyer; b. Derby, Conn., Apr. 17, 1956; s. Edwin Vincent and Carol Veronica (Gallagher) H.; m. Arlene Bua, Mar. 29, 1981. BS magna cum laude, Fordham U., 1977; JD, Pace U., 1980. Bar: N.Y. 1981, U.S. Dist. Ct. (so. and ea. dists.) N.Y. 1981, U.S. Ct. Appeals (2d cir.) 1982, U.S. Tax Ct. 1984, U.S. Supreme Ct. 1985. Law clk. to sr. judge U.S. Dist. Ct. (so. dist.) N.Y., N.Y.C., 1980-82; assoc. litigation dept. Kimmelman, Sextet & Sobel, N.Y.C., 1982-83; ptnr. Quinn, Cohen, Shields & Bock, N.Y.C., 1983—. Chmn. Young Reps., Tuckahoe, N.Y., 1975-77; chmn. taxi commn. Village of Mamaroneck, N.Y., 1986-87, mem. planning bd., 1987—. Mem. ABA, N.Y. State Bar Assn. (com. on lawyer competency), Assn. of Bar of City of N.Y., Assn. Trial Lawyers Am., N.Y. Trial Lawyers Assn., N.Y. County Lawyers Assn., Fed. Bar Council. Roman Catholic. Club: Westchester Country. Federal civil litigation, State civil litigation. Office: Quinn Cohen Shields & Bock 545 Madison Ave New York NY 10022

HALPERN, RALPH LAWRENCE, lawyer; b. Buffalo, May 12, 1929; s. Julius and Mary C. (Kaminker) H.; m. Harriet Chasin, June 29, 1958; children: Eric B., Steven R., Julie B. LL.B. cum laude, U. Buffalo, 1953. Bar: N.Y. 1953. Teaching assoc. Northwestern U. Law Sch., 1953-54; assoc. firm Jaeckle, Fleischmann, Kelly, Swart & Augspurger, Buffalo, 1957-58; asso. firm Raichle, Banning, Weiss & Halpern (and predecessors), 1958-59, ptnr., 1959-86; ptnr. Jaeckle, Fleischmann & Mugel, Buffalo, 1986—. Pres. Buffalo Council World Affairs, 1972-74, Temple Beth Zion, Buffalo, 1981-83; chmn. Buffalo chpt. Am. Jewish Com., 1975-77; bd. govs. United Jewish Fedn., Buffalo, 1972-78. Served to capt. JAGC U.S. Army, 1954-57. Mem. ABA, N.Y. State Bar Assn. (chmn. com. profl. ethics 1971-76, chmn. com. jud. election monitoring 1983-86, chmn. spl. com. to consider adoption of ABA model rules of profl. conduct 1983-85), Erie County (N.Y.) Bar Assn., Am. Judicature Soc., Am. Law Inst. Antitrust, Federal civil litigation, General corporate. Home: 88 Middlesex Rd Buffalo NY 14216 Office: 800 Norstar Bldg Buffalo NY 14202

HALPERN, SAMUEL JOSEPH, lawyer; b. Passaic, N.J., May 30, 1946; s. Hyman and Ruth (Wechsler) H. BA, Susquehanna U., 1968; JD, Am. U., 1971. Bar: N.J. 1972, U.S. Supreme Ct. 1975. Law clk. to presiding judge N.J. Superior Ct., Newark, 1971-72; dep. atty. gen. State of N.J., Trenton, 1972-80; sole practice Paterson, N.J., 1980—. Mem. ABA, N.J. Bar Assn., Essex County Bar Assn., Passaic County Bar Assn. Democrat. Jewish. Avocation: coin collecting. Administrative and regulatory, State civil litigation, Pension, profit-sharing, and employee benefits. Office: 21 Lee Place Paterson NJ 07505

HALPIN, STEVEN EDWARD, lawyer; b. Houston, Sept. 22, 1948; s. Max Leon and Rosalie (Dubinski) H.; m. Sharon Helaine Goldstein, Sept. 6, 1970; children: Jennifer Leigh, Stephanie Erin. BS in Polit. Sci., U. Houston, 1970; JD, South Tex. Coll. Law, 1974. Bar: Tex. 1974, U.S. Dist. Ct. (so. dist.) Tex. 1974, U.S. Ct. Appeals (5th cir.) 1974, U.S. Supreme Ct. 1979. Sole practice Houston, 1974—. Mem. Tex. Bar Assn., South Tex. Coll. Law Alumni Assn., Order of Lytae. Democrat. Jewish. Lodge: B'nai Brith. Real property, Landlord-tenant. Home: 11623 Fieldbrook Houston TX 77077 Office: 5151 San Felipe Suite 860 Houston TX 77056

HALPRIN, HENRY S., lawyer, educator; b. N.Y.C., May 5, 1924; s. Abraham J. and Julia (Steiner) H.; divorced; children: Karen K. Sims, Bruce S. LLD, U. Va., 1949, JD, 1970. Bar: N.Y. 1949, U.S. Dist Ct. (ea. and so. dists.) N.Y. 1950, U.S. Supreme Ct. 1961, U.S. Dist. Ct. (so. and ea. dists.) Conn. 1963, Conn. 1967. Asst. dir. spl. programs U.S. Housing and Homes Agy., N.Y.C., 1955-61; sr. assoc. Demov & Morris, 1961-62, ptnr., 1962-64; sole practice N.Y.C., 1965-68; ptnr. Halprin & Goler, N.Y.C., 1968—; adj. asst. prof. NYU, 1979—; lectr. Baruch Coll., 1981—. Real property. Home: 24 Buena Vista Dr Westport CT 06880 Office: Halprin & Goler 60 E 42nd St New York NY 10165 also: 10 Middle St Bridgeport CT 06604

HALSEY, PATRICIA FREDERICK, lawyer, consultant; b. Los Angeles, May 11, 1948; d. Charles Jess and Jewel (Carter) Frederick; m. William C. Halsey, Jan. 20, 1972 (div. June 1980); m. Leslie Joseph Munroe, July 30, 1983; children: William Lionel, Mark F. Student, Chapman Coll., 1966; AA, Cerritos Coll., 1968; BA, UCLA, 1970; JD, Calif. Western Sch. of Law, 1975. Bar: Calif. 1975, U.S. Ct. Mil. Appeals 1976, U.S. Supreme Ct. 1980. Commd. USMC, Japan and Washington, 1974; advanced through grades to maj. USMC, 1981; judge adv. USMC, Japan and Washington, 1975-85; chief client services Dept. of the Army, San Francisco, 1986—; cons. U.S. Dept. Health and Human Services, Washington, 1978-80, U.S. Embassy, Berlin, 1983-85. Contbr. articles to profl. jours. Witness on domestic violence program U.S. Congl. Commn., Washington, 1980; speaker Calif. Atty. Gen. Conf. on Domestic Violence, 1979-80; keynote speaker Berlin's Fed. Women's Week, 1985; speaker Calif. Family Support Council, 1987. Recipient Cert. of Appreciation Berlin Brigade, 1985. Mem. ABA (family law com.), Internat. Women's Club (bd. dirs. 1984-85), San Diego Bar Assn., San Francisco Bar Assn. Avocations: snow skiing, long distance running. Family and matrimonial, General practice, Administrative and regulatory. Office: Chief Client Services Br Office of Staff Judge Adv San Francisco CA 94129-5900

HALSTEAD, HARRY MOORE, lawyer; b. Washington, Nov. 9, 1918; s. John Harry and Lucinda (Moore) H.; m. Carmella Ann LaRosa, Sept. 7, 1946; children—William, Lucinda, Christina, Concetta. A.B., Rutgers U., 1941; J.D., Yale U., 1948; LL.M., U. So. Calif., 1953. Bar: Calif. bar 1949. Pvt. practice Los Angeles, 1949—; sr. ptnr. firm Halstead, Baker & Olson, 1959—; lectr. taxation, estate and trust law. Author several books; contbr. articles to profl. jours. Trustee Linfield Coll., McMinnville, Oreg., 1973-82, S. Pasadena United Methodist Ch. Served to maj. AUS, 1941-46. Mem. Am. Bar Assn. (vice chmn. com. tax and estate planning 1967-77, vice chmn. com. state death taxes 1977-80), State Bar Calif., U. So. Calif. Alumni Assn., Phi Gamma Delta. Clubs: Rutgers So. Calif. (past pres.), Yale of So. Calif. (past pres.), San Marino City, Arcadia Tennis. Estate taxation, Estate planning, Probate. Home: 1400 Old Mill Rd San Marino CA 91108 Office: 615 S Flower St Los Angeles CA 90017

HALSTROM, FREDERIC NORMAN, lawyer; b. Boston, Feb. 26, 1944; s. Reginald F. and Margaret M. (Graham) H.; m. Mary Ann Joseph, Aug. 14, 1982; 1 dau., Ingrid Alexandra. Student Northeastern U., 1961-63, U.S. Air Force Acad., 1963-65; A.B., Georgetown U., 1967; J.D., Boston Coll., 1970. Bar: Mass. 1970, U.S. Dist. Ct. Mass. 1971, U.S. Dist. Ct. R.I. 1981, U.S. Tax Ct. 1981, U.S. Ct. Appeals (1st cir.) 1971. Assoc., Schneider and Reilly. P.C., Boston, 1970-73, ptnr. Parker, Coulter, Daley and White, Boston, 1973-78; prin. Frederic N. Halstrom, P.C., Boston, 1978—; spl. prosecutor Dist. Atty., Norfolk County, 1969-70; spl. asst. city solicitor City of Quincy, 1980. Fellow Boston Coll. Law Sch.; mem. Fed. Bar Assn., ABA (chmn. products liability com. gen. practice sect. 1980—, award of achievement young lawyers div. 1978, vice chmn. taxation on ins. cos. sect. 1986—), Assn. Trial Lawyers Am. (gov. 1984, state del. 1976-78, 86—), Am. Judicature Soc., Mass. Acad. Trial Attys. (co-chmn. tort law sect. 1980—, bd. of govs. 1976—), Mass. Bar Assn. (pres. young lawyers div. 1977-78, bd. of dels. 1978-80), Middlesex County Bar Assn. Roman Catholic. Clubs: Algonquin, University (Boston). Editor Mass. Law Quar., 1972; contbr. articles to profl. jours. Personal injury, Insurance, State civil litigation. Home: 483 River Rd Carlisle MA 01741 Office: 132 Boylston St Boston MA 02116

HALTOM, ELBERT BERTRAM, JR., U.S. district judge; b. Florence, Ala., Dec. 26, 1922; s. Elbert Bertram and Elva Mae (Simpson) H.; m. Constance Boyd Morris, Aug. 19, 1949; 1 dau., Emily m. Haltom Olsen. Student, Florence State U., 1940-42; LL.B., U. Ala., 1948. Bar: Ala. 1948. Practiced in Florence, 1948-80; mem. firm Bradshaw, Barnett & Haltom, 1948-58, Haltom & Patterson, 1959-80; U.S. dist. judge No. Dist. Ala., Birmingham, 1980—; bar commr. 11th Jud. Circuit Ala., 1976-80. Mem. Ala. Ho. of Reps., 1954-58; mem. Ala. Senate, 1958-62; candidate lt. gov. Ala., 1962; mem. Ala. Democratic Exec. Com., 1966-80. Served with USAAF, 1943-45. Decorated Air medal with four oak leaf clusters. Fellow Internat. Soc. Barristers, Am. Coll. Trial Lawyers; mem. ABA, Ala. Bar Assn., Am. Judicature Soc., Newcomen Soc. N.Am., Am. Legion, V.F.W., Phi Gamma Delta, Phi Delta Phi. Methodist. Office: 207 U S Post Office & Courthouse 101 Holmes Ave NE Huntsville AL 35801

HALVA, ALLEN KEITH, legal publications consultant; b. Willow River, Minn., Jan. 23, 1913; s. Edward and Frances R. (Allen) H.; m. Julia M. Halva, Oct. 25, 1941; children—Barbara Jo Halva Kachmarzinski, Kurt Edward. Student Pasadena Jr. Coll. and Los Angeles City Coll., 1931-32; LL.B. cum laude, Calif. Assoc. Colls., 1935; LL.M., Los Angeles U. Applied Edn., 1950, S.J.D., 1951. Bar: Calif. 1936, Minn. 1941. With West Pub. Co., 1942-82; law book editor; retired ; legal publs. cons. Mem. State Bar Calif., Minn. State Bar Assn., Ramsey County Bar Assn., Am. Judicature Soc., Am. Security Council, Nat. Taxpayers Union, Am. Assn. Retired Persons. Presbyterian. Club: Hospitaller Order of St. John of Jerusalem. Editing law books. Home: 253 S Warwick St Saint Paul MN 55105

HALVERSON, LOWELL KLARK, lawyer, writer; b. Tacoma, May 4, 1942; s. Sidney Lawrence and Jeannette (Thompson) H.; m. Diane Edna Vosburgh, June 13, 1964; children: Liana Kay, Ward Vosburgh. AB, Harvard U., 1964; JD, U. Wash., 1968. Bar: Wash. 1968, N.Y. 1981, U.S. Supreme Ct. 1979. Sr. ptnr. Halverson & Strong, Seattle, 1970—; bd. dirs. Pacific Family Law Found., Seattle, 1983—, Wash. Legal Found., 1984—. Author, editor: Washington Lawyer Practice Manual, 3 vols., 1972-78; author: (with others) Divorce in Washington-A Humane Approach, 1985; (with others) Divorce in New York, 1987. Fellow Am. Acad. Matrimonial Lawyers; mem. ABA, Wash. State Bar Assn. (gov. 7th congl. dist. 1977-80, Disting. Service award 1983, editor-in-chief Family Law Deskbook), N.Y. State Bar Assn., Seattle-King County Bar Assn. (trustee 1975-77, chmn. young lawyers sect. 1974-75, Disting. Service award 1986). Clubs: Harvard of Wash. (pres. 1974), Rainier. Family and matrimonial, Civil rights. Home: 3014 90th Pl SE Mercer Island WA 98040 Office: Halverson & Strong 900 Hoge Bldg 705 2d Ave Seattle WA 98104

HALVERSON, STEVEN THOMAS, lawyer; b. Enid, Okla., Aug. 29, 1954; s. Robert James Halverson and Ramona Mae (Ludke) Selenski; m. Diane Mary Schueller, Aug. 21, 1976; children: John Thomas, Anne Kirsten. BA cum laude, St. John's U., 1976; JD, Am. U., 1979. Bar: Va. 1979, Minn. 1980, U.S. Dist. Ct. Minn. 1980, U.S. Ct. Claims, U.S. Ct. Appeals (4th and 8th cirs.). Asst. project dir. ABA, Washington, 1977-79; with Briggs & Morgan, St Paul., 1980-83; ptnr. Hart & Bruner, Mpls., 1983-84; v.p., assoc. gen. counsel, dir. pub. affairs M.A. Mortenson Cos., Mpls., 1984—; adj. prof. William Mitchell Coll. Law, St. Paul;. 1980—. Co-author: Federal Grant Law, 1982; contbr. articles to profl. jours. Bd. dirs. Tandem Inc., Mpls., 1985—, Minn. Opera, Mpls., 1986—. Mem. ABA (pub. contract law sect. 1984—, chmn. construction com. 1985—), Minn. Bar Assn. (governing council civil litigation sect. 1985—), Am. Arbitration Assn. (arbitrator 1986—). Republican. Roman Catholic. Club: North Oaks Golf (Minn.). Construction, Government contracts and claims, Legislative. Home: 50 E Pleasant Lake Rd North Oaks MN 55110 Office: MA Mortenson Cos 700 Meadow Ln N PO Box 710 Minneapolis MN 55440

HALVORSON, NEWMAN THORBUS, JR., lawyer; b. Detroit, Dec. 17, 1936; s. Newman Thorbus and Virginia Westbrook (Markle) H.; m. Sally Clark Stone, May 3, 1969; children: Christina English, Charles Burgess Westbrook. AB, Princeton U., 1958; LLB, Harvard U., 1961. Bar: Ohio 1962, D.C. 1963, U.S. Supreme Ct. 1965. Assoc. Covington & Burling, Washington, 1962-70, ptnr., 1970-83, 85—; asst. U.S. atty. Office of U.S. Atty., Washington, 1983-85. Editor, author Harvard Law Rev., 1960-61. Sr. warden, vestryman Christ Ch. Georgetown, Washington, 1983-86; bd. dirs. Lupus Found. D.C., 1974-85; treas., bd. dirs. Eugene and Agnes E. Meyer Found., Washington, 1976—; chmn. bd. dirs., trustee Potomac Sch., McLean, Va., 1980-86. Mem. ABA, D.C. Bar Assn. Republican. Episcopalian. Clubs: Met. (Washington), Chevy Chase (Md.). General corporate, Federal civil litigation, Corporate taxation. Home: 3500 Lowell St NW Washington DC 20016 Office: Covington & Burling 1201 Pennsylvania Ave NW PO Box 7566 Washington DC 20044

HAMANN, H. FREDRICK, patent lawyer; b. Omaha, Nov. 6, 1924; s. Martin Lorenz and Alma (Harms) H.; m. Jean Van Fradenburg, June 5, 1949; children—Terry Jean Hamann McKown, H. Fredrick. Ph.B., U. Wis.-Madison, 1945; J.D. with honors, George Washington U., 1953; LL.M., U. So. Calif., 1968. Bar: U.S. Dist. Ct. D.C. 1953, N.Mex. 1954, Calif. 1962. Patent counsel Los Alamos Sci. Labs., 1953-58, ACF Industries, Riverdale, Md., 1958-59; asst. patent counsel Atomics Internat. div. Rockwell Internat., Canoga Park, Calif., 1959-63, Sci. Ctr. div., Thousand Oaks, Calif., 1963-69, patent counsel corp. electronics ops., Anaheim, Calif., 1969-80, corp. patent counsel, 1980—. Asst. editor Am. Intellectual Property Law Assn. quar. jour., 1973-86. Served with USN, 1943-46; PTO. Mem. ABA, Am. Intellectual Property Law Assn. (dir. 1975-78), Order of Coif. Republican. Patent, Trademark and copyright. Office: Rockwell Internat 3370 Miraloma Ave AF52 Anaheim CA 92803

HAMBLEN, LAPSLEY WALKER, JR., judge; b. Chattanooga, Tenn., Dec. 25, 1926; s. Lapsley Walker and Libby (Shipley) H.; m. Claudia Royster Terrell, Mar. 20, 1971; children by previous marriage—Lapsley Walker, Alien M., William Shipley. B.A., U. Va., 1949, LL.B., 1953. Bar: W.Va. 1954, Ohio 1955, Va. 1957. Trial atty. IRS, Atlanta, 1955; atty. advisor U.S. Tax Ct., 1956; ptnr. Caskie Frost Hobbs & Hamblen and predecessor firms, Lynchburg, Va., 1957-82; dep. asst. atty. gen. tax div. U.S. Dept. Justice, 1982; judge U.S. Tax Ct., Washington, 1982—; former trustee Fed. Tax Inst.; former co-dir. ann. Va. conf. on fed. taxation U. Va. Served with USN, 1945-46. Fellow Am. Coll. Tax Counsel, Am. Coll. Probate Counsel, Raven Soc., Order of Coif, Omicron Delta Kappa, Phi Alpha Delta. Presbyterian. Office: US Tax Ct 400 Second St NW Washington DC 20217

HAMBLET, MICHAEL JON, lawyer, former state official; b. Rapid City, S.D., Aug. 10, 1940; s. Herbert F. and Helen F. (Tice) H.; m. Maureen Anne Murphy, Nov. 26, 1966 (div. May 1986); children—Tracy Anne, Michael Jon. B.A., U. Ill., 1962; J.D., U. Mich., 1965. Bar: Ill. 1965, U.S. Dist. Ct. (no. dist.) Ill. 1965, U.S. Ct. Appeals (7th cir.) 1974, U.S. Tax Ct. 1980. Assoc. Mayer, Brown, Chgo., 1965-69; ptnr. Herrick, NcNeill, McElroy & Peregrine, Chgo., 1969-78, Greenberg, Keele, Lunn & Aronberg, Chgo., 1979-81; ptnr., pres. McNeill, Fick, Hamblet & Vacin, P.C., Chgo., 1982-83, Mathewson, Hamblet & Casey, Chgo., 1983—; mem. Ill. State Bd. Elections, Chgo. and Springfield, 1978—, chmn., 1979-81, 83-85, vice chmn., 1981-83, also mem. Fed. Election and Voting System Standards Coms, 1984-85; mem. Ill. Bldg. Authority, Chgo., 1973-78, chmn., 1977-78; dir., pres. Kent Culligan, Inc., Grand Rapids, Mich., 1968—; sec., dir. Indel Elec. Distbrs., Chgo., 1979—; mem. Gov.'s Election Reform Commn., 1984-85. Mem. Cook County Econ. Devel. Adv. Com., 1982—; bd. dirs. Com. on Ill. Govt., Chgo., 1968-78; mem. New Trier Democratic Orgn., Winnetka, Ill., 1972—, exec. com., 1972-78, v.p., 1974-78. Mem. Ill. State Bar Assn., Chgo. Bar Assn., Chgo. Council Lawyers. General corporate, Federal civil litigation, State civil litigation. Home: 1322 Sutton Pl Chicago IL 60610 Office: Mathewson Hamblet & Casey 36 W Randolph Suite 800 Chicago IL 60601

HAMBRICK, JACKSON REID, lawyer, educator, writer; b. Griffin, Ga., Nov. 14, 1917; s. Andrew Jackson and Susan Irene (Westmoreland) H.; m. Lucille Warden Rhudy, Sept. 6, 1941; children: Irene Frazier Olsen, Kenton Warden. A.B., Wofford Coll., 1938; LL.B., Duke U., 1942. Bar: N.Y. 1943, D.C. 1958. Practiced law N.Y.C., 1942-47; atty. Dept. Treasury, IRS, Washington, 1947-57; asso. prof. law George Washington U., Washington, 1957-61; prof. George Washington U., 1961-82; vis. prof. law Duke U., 1965; cons. on fed. taxation. Editor-in-chief: Duke U. Law Rev.; contbr. articles to law revs. Mem. N.Y. Bar Assn., D.C. Bar, Order of Coif. Democrat. Methodist. Corporate taxation, Estate taxation, Personal income taxation. Home: 6022 Oakdale Rd McLean VA 22101

HAMBURG, CHARLES BRUCE, lawyer; b. Bklyn., June 30, 1939; s. Albert Hamburg and Goldie (Blume) H.; m. Stephanie Barbara Steingesser, June 23, 1962; children—Jeanne M., Louise E. B.Ch. Engring., Poly. Inst. Bklyn., 1960; J.D., George Washington U., 1964. Bar: N.Y. 1964. Patent examiner U.S. Patent Office, 1960-63; patent atty. Celanese Corp. Am., N.Y.C., 1963-65; patent atty. Burns, Lobato & Zelnick, N.Y.C., 1965-67; patent atty. Nolte & Nolte, N.Y.C., 1967-75; prin. C. Bruce Hamburg, N.Y.C., 1976-79; ptnr. Jordan & Hamburg, N.Y.C., 1979—. Recipient Superior Service award (2) U.S. Patent Office, 1963, 63. Mem. ABA, Am. Patent Law Assn., N.Y. Patent Law Assn., Internat. Assn. Protection Intellectual Property, Queens Bar Assn., Bklyn. Bar Assn. Club: Masons. Author: Patent Fraud and Inequitable Conduct, 1972, 78; Patent Law Handbook, 1983-84, 84-85, 85-86; monthly columnist Patent and Trademark Rev., 1976-85, patents and licensing. Patent, Trademark and copyright. Office: 122 E 42d St New York NY 10168

HAMEL, MARK EDWIN, lawyer; b. Ontonagon, Mich., Apr. 9, 1953; s. Peter C. and Marian E. (Peterson) H.; m. Pamela Kay Jenkins, May 31, 1975; children: Nathan, Gregory. BA, Carroll Coll., 1975; JD, Harvard U., 1978. Bar: Minn. 1979, U.S. Dist. Ct. Minn. 1979. Law clk. to presiding justice Minn. Supreme Ct., St. Paul, 1978-79; assoc. Dorsey & Whitney, Mpls., 1979-85, ptnr., 1985—. Mem. Minn Bar Assn., Hennepin Bar Assn. (real property sect.). Presbyterian. Club: Mpls. Athletic. Real property, Landlord-tenant. Office: Dorsey & Whitney 2200 1st Bank Pl E Minneapolis MN 55402

HAMEL, RICHARD PAUL, lawyer; b. Quincy, Mass., May 1, 1943; s. Edmond Leo and Irene Marie (Hebert) H.; m. Patricia Mary Crawford, Sept. 17, 1966; children—Jennifer A., Michelle J., Suzanne P., Jeffrey R. A.B. cum laude, Harvard U., 1965; J.D. cum laude, Boston U., 1968. Bar: Mass. 1968. Assoc., MacGregor, MacGregor and Waldron, Haverhill, Mass., 1968-70, assoc. Kazarosian, Allison & Phillips, Haverhill, 1970-71; sr. ptnr. Hamel and Deshaies, Amesbury, Mass., 1971—. Contracts commercial, Probate, Real property.

HAMEL, RODOLPHE, drug company executive; b. Lewiston, Maine, June 3, 1929; s. Rodolphe and Alvina Melanie (Bilodeau) H.; m. Marilyn Vivian Johnsen, June 10, 1957; children—Matthew Edward, Anne Melanie. B.A., Yale U., 1950; LL.B., Harvard U., 1953. Bar: Maine bar, D.C. bar 1953, N.Y. bar 1957. Assoc. firm Shearman & Sterling, N.Y.C., 1956-66; internat. counsel Bristol Myers Co., N.Y.C., 1966-72, 73; v.p., counsel internat. div. Bristol Myers Co., 1974-81, assoc. gen. counsel co., 1978—; v.p. Bristol-Myers Co., 1983—; v.p., sec., gen. counsel Macmillan Inc., N.Y.C., 1972-73. Served to 1st lt. AUS, 1953-56. Mem. ABA, N.Y. State Bar Assn., N.Y.C. Bar Assn. Clubs: Board Room (N.Y.C.), Yale (N.Y.C.). General corporate, Private international. Home: 6 Stratford Ln Ho-ho-kus NJ 07423 Office: 345 Park Ave New York NY 10022

HAMERMESH, LAWRENCE ABRAHAM, lawyer; b. Harvey, Ill., June 14, 1952; s. Morton and Madeline (Goldberg) H.; m. Marion Yager, Aug. 7, 1983; 1 child, Simon E. BA, Haverford Coll., 1973; JD, Yale U., 1976. Bar: Del. 1976. From assoc. to ptnr. Morris, Nichols, Arsht & Tunnell, Wilmington, Del., 1976—; sec. Del. Bd. of Bar Examiners, 1982-86. Contbr. articles to profl. jours. Bd. dirs. Del. ACLU, 1986—. Mem. Am. Judicature Soc., Nat. Inst. Trial Adv. Democrat. Jewish. State civil litigation, General corporate. Home: 500 Milton Dr Wilmington DE 19802 Office: Morris Nichols Arsht & Tunnell PO Box 1347 Wilmington DE 19899

HAMES, LUTHER CLAUDE, JR., judge; b. Marietta, Ga., Nov. 18, 1917; s. Luther Claude and Patience (Owens) H.; m. Kathryn Johnson, Sept. 11, 1917; children—Kay, Lucia, Patricia. LL.B., Woodrow Wilson Coll. Law, 1939. Bar: Ga. 1939. Solicitor gen., prosecutor, 1953-68; judge Superior Ct., 1968-80; sr. judge Superior Cts. of Ga., Marietta, 1980—; vice chmn. pattern jury instrn. com. Criminal div. Council Superior Ct. Judges. Mem. Marietta City Council, mayor pro tem, 1948-50; past pres. Cobb C. of C. Served with AUS, World War II. Mem. ABA, Ga. Bar Assn., Cobb Bar Assn. (past pres.), Dist. Attys. Assn. Ga. (past pres.). Democrat. Baptist. Club: Masons. Jurisprudence, Criminal, Family and matrimonial. Home and Office: 335 Old Trace Rd Marietta GA 30064

HAMES, WILLIAM LESTER, lawyer; b. Pasco, Wash., June 21, 1947; s. Arlie Franklin and Nina Lee (Ryals) H.; m. Pamella Kay Rust, June 3, 1967; children: Robert Alan, Michael Jonathan. BS in Psychology, U. Wash., 1974; JD, Willamette U., 1981. Bar: Wash. 1981, U.S. Dist. Ct. (ea. dist.) Wash. 1982, U.S. Ct. Appeals (9th cir.) 1985, U.S. Dist. Ct. (we. dist.) Wash. 1985. Counselor Wash. Juvenile Ct., Walla Walla, Wash., 1974-76; reactor operator control rm. United Nuclear Inc., Richland, Wash., 1976-77; assoc. Sonderman, Egan & Hames, Kennewick, Wash., 1981-84, Timmons & Hames, Kennewick, 1984-86, Sonderman, Timmons & Hames, Kennewick, 1987—; bd. dirs. Hames-Rust, Inc., Kennewick, Columbia Industries; gov. affairs commn. Tridec, Kennewick, 1981—, mem. venture capital commn., 1986—. Bd. dirs. Planned Parenthood, Kennewick, 1984—, Ctr. Sci., Industry and Arts, Richland, 1984—. Mem. Am. Trial Lawyers Assn., Wash. State Bar Assn., Wash. State Trial Lawyers Assn., Benton- Franklin County Bar Assn. Democrat. Methodist. Club: Clover Island Yacht. Bankruptcy, Personal injury, Consumer commercial. Home: 410 W 21st St Kennewick WA 99337 Office: Sonderman Timmons & Hames PO Box 5498 Kennewick WA 99336-0498

HAMILTON, CLYDE H., federal judge; b. Edgefield, S.C., Feb. 8, 1934; s. Clyde H. and Edwina (Odom) H.; m. Mary Elizabeth Spillers, July 20, 1957; children—John C., James W. B.S., Wofford Coll., 1956; J.D. with honors, George Washington U., 1961. Bar: S.C. 1961. Assoc. J.R. Folk, Edgefield, 1961-63; assoc., gen. ptnr. Butler, Means, Evins & Browne, Spartanburg, S.C., 1963-81; judge U.S. Dist. Ct. S.C., Columbia, 1981—; reference asst. U.S. Senate Library, Washington, 1958-61; gen. counsel Synalloy Corp., Spartanburg, 1969-80. Mem. editorial staff Cumulative Index of Congl. Com. Hearings, 1955-58; bd. editors George Washington Law Rev., 1959-60. Pres., Spartanburg County Arts Council, 1971-73; pres. Spartanburg Day Sch., 1972-74, sustaining trustee, 1975-81; mem. steering com. undergrad. merit fellowship program and estate planning council Converse Coll., Spartanburg; trustee Spartanburg Methodist Coll., 1979-84; mem. S.C. Supreme Ct. Bd. Commrs. on Grievances and Discipline, 1980-81; del. Spartanburg County, 4th Congl. Dist. and S.C. Republican Convs., 1976, 80; mem., past chmn. fin. com. and adminstrv. bd. Trinity United Meth. Ch., Spartanburg, trustee, 1980-83. Served to capt. USAR, 1956-62. Mem. ABA, S.C. Bar Assn., Spartanburg County Bar Assn. Club: Piedmont (Spartanburg) (bd. govs. 1979-81). Judicial administration. Office: US Dist Ct 1845 Assembly St Columbia SC 29201

HAMILTON, ELWIN LOMAX, lawyer; b. Lubbock, Tex. Mar. 18, 1934; s. Elwin Louis and Mildred (Hunt) H.; m. Brenda Linzey; children—Lauren, Karen. A.S., Arlington State Coll., 1954; B.A., North Tex. State Coll., 1956; LL.B., U. Tex., Austin, 1959. Bar: Tex. 1959, U.S. Dist. Ct. (no. dist.) Tex. 1961, U.S. Dist. Ct. (we. dist.) Tex. 1972, U.S. Ct. Claims 1972, U.S. Ct. Appeals (5th cir.) 1961. Atty. Humble Oil Co., Corpus Christi, Tex., 1959-60; mem. firm Morton & Brownfield, Tex., 1960-66; mcpl. judge, Morton, Tex., 1960-61; county dist. atty., Terry County, 1963-66; asst. exec. dir. State Bar Tex., 1966-69; asst. atty. gen., State of Tex., 1969-73; atty. Tex. Securities Bd., Austin, 1973-74; asst. gen. counsel to Gov. of Tex., Austin, 1974-82; ptnr. Senterfitt & Childress, Hamilton & Shook, San Saba, Tex., 1982-86, sole practice, 1987—. Presbyterian. State civil litigation, Probate, Real property. Home: 1206 W Sunset St San Saba TX 76877 Office: Senterfitt & Childress 1502 W Wallace Box 547 San Saba TX 76877

HAMILTON, HERMAN LYNN, JR., lawyer; b. Prescott, Ark., Feb. 20, 1934; s. Herman L. Sr. and Esther N. (Haug) H.; m. Patti Alice Walsh, Sept. 4, 1954; children: H. Lynn III, David P., James A. BA, U. Ark., 1955, JD, 1957. Bar: Ark. 1957, U.S. Dist. Ct. Ark. 1957, U.S. Ct. Appeals (8th cir.) 1965. Ptnr. Arnold, Hamilton & Streetman, Hamburg, Ark., 1957—; atty. City of Hamburg, 1961-62, mcpl. judge 1962-82; spl. justice Ark. Supreme Ct., 1973, 77, 79; v.p. Ark. Law Rev. Bd., 1984—; 1st pres., Ark. Interest on Lawyers Trust Accounts Found., 1986, bd. dirs. V.p. De Soto Council Boy Scouts Am., 1981-82; chmn. adminstrv. bd. Hamburg United Meth. Ch., 1984-85; chmn. bd. dirs. Ashley Meml. Hosp., Crossett, Ark., 1985—. Recipient Silver Beaver award De Soto Council Boy Scouts Am., 1979; named Disting. Alumnus, U. Ala. Sch. Law, 1985. Fellow Ark. Bar Found.; mem. Ark. Bar Assn. (ho. of dels. 1971-77, 83-86, chmn. interest on lawyers trust accounts com. 1981-86), Assn. Trial Lawyers Am., Ark. Trial Lawyers Assn. Lodge: Masons. State civil litigation, Estate planning, Personal injury. Office: Arnold Hamilton & Streetman PO Box 71 Hamburg AR 71646

HAMILTON, JACKSON DOUGLAS, lawyer; b. Cleve., Feb. 5, 1949; m. Margaret Lawrence Williams, Dec. 19, 1971; children: Jackson Douglas Jr., William Schuyler Lawrence. BA, Colgate U., 1971; JD, U. Pa., 1974. Bar: Calif. 1974, U.S. Dist. Ct. (cen. dist.) Calif. 1974, U.S. Tax Ct. 1978. Ptnr. Kadison, Pfaelzer, Woodard, Quinn & Rossi, Los Angeles, 1986—; adj. prof. law U. San Diego, 1981, Golden Gate U., San Francisco, 1981-85; cons. Calif. Continuing Edn. Bar, 1983-84, select com. on sports Calif. Senate, 1983-85. Editor Entertainment Law Reporter, 1979—; contbr. articles to profl. jours. Mem. ABA (tax sect., internat. law sect.), Los Angeles County Bar Assn. (tax sect., internat. law sect.). Republican. Presbyterian. Corporate taxation, General corporate, Private international. Office: Kadison Pfaelzer Woodard Quinn & Rossi 707 Wilshire Blvd 40th Floor Los Angeles CA 90017

HAMILTON, JAMES, lawyer, author; b. Chester, S.C., Dec. 4, 1938; s. Herman Prioleau and Edith Muriel (Gilchrist) H.; m. Siri Kristina Hagglund, July 14, 1979; children—William James, Erik Gilchrist, Kathryn Heyward. A.B., Davidson Coll., 1960; LL.B., Yale U., 1963; LL.M., U. London, 1966. Bar: D.C. 1967, U.S. Ct. Appeals (9th cir.) 1977, U.S. Supreme Ct. 1978, U.S. Temporary Emergency Ct. Appeals, 1980, U.S. Ct. Claims 1981, U.S. Ct. Appeals (4th cir.) 1983, U.S. Ct. Appeals (11th cir.) 1985. Assoc. firm Covington & Burling, Washington, 1966-73; asst. chief counsel Senate Select Com. on Presdl. Campaign Activities (Watergate Commn.), U.S. Senate, Washington, 1973-74; mem. firm Ginsburg, Feldman & Bress, Washington, 1975—; chief counsel Spl. Joint Com. on Referendum Rev., Congress of Micronesia, 1978; spl. counsel human resources subcom. for briefing book investigation Ho. of Reps., Washington, 1983-84; dep. chief counsel Alaska Senate impeachment inquiry, 1985; mem. Jud. Conf. of U.S. Ct. Appeals for Fed. Cir., 1986, for D.C. Cir., 1978, 80; mem. GAO investigative task force, 1985. Author: The Power to Probe: A Study of Congressional Investigations, 1975; contbr. articles to profl. jours., articles to major newspapers. Issue coordinator, polit. organizer, advance man Presidential Campaign of Edmund S. Muskie, Washington, 1970-72. Served as 1st lt. U.S. Army, 1963-65. Decorated Army Commendation medal; Ford Found. travel and study grantee, 1974-75. Mem. ABA (individual rights subcom., litigation subcom.) D.C. Bar (com. on legal ethics 1983—), Am. Arbitration Assn. (panel of arbiters), Council for Ct. Excellence (dir.). Democrat. Presbyterian. Club: St Albans Tennis (Washington). Federal civil litigation, Legislative, Criminal. Home: 3321 Rowland Pl NW Washington DC 20008 Office: Ginsburg Feldman & Bress Chartered 1250 Connecticut Ave NW Washington DC 20036

HAMILTON, JAMES R., lawyer; b. Goodell, Iowa, Mar. 26, 1916; s. Steven S. and Agnes J. (Murphy) H.; m. Jean E. Edson, July 17, 1942; children: Martha, Steve, Willis, James, Theresa, Tim, Mary, Maggie. BA, Buena Vista Coll , 1937; JD, Creighton U., 1946. Bar: Iowa 1946, U.S. Dist. Ct. Iowa 1946. Ptnr. Hamilton Law Firm, Storm Lake, Iowa, 1946—. Chmn. Iowa Conservation Commn., 1968-69; aide to Gov. Harold Hughes, Iowa, 1965. Served to capt. U.S. Army, 1942-46. Named an Hon. Col., Gov. Harold Hughes, 1965. Mem. Internat. Soc. Barristers, Assn. Trial Lawyers Am., Iowa Acad. Trial Lawyers (pres. 1976-77). Lodges: Elks, Moose. Insurance, Personal injury, Workers' compensation. Office: 606 Ontario St PO Box 188 Storm Lake IA 50588

HAMILTON, JEFFREY SCOTT, lawyer; b. Noblesville, Ind., May 25, 1956; s. J.W. and Nancy Elizabeth (Hilton) H.; m. Carolyn Lynn Gilliam, June 30, 1979; children: Bethany Ann, Cara Michelle. BA, King Coll., 1978; JD, U. Tenn., 1981. Bar: Va. 1981, U.S. Dist. Ct. (we. dist.) Va. 1982, U.S. Ct. Appeals (4th cir.) 1984. Asst. commonwealth atty. Scott County, Gate City, Va., 1981-82; assoc. Quillen Law Offices, Gate City, 1982—. atty. Moccasin Gap Sanitation, Weber City, Va., 1983—; bd. dirs. Scott County Indsl. Authority, Gate City, 1985, Scott County Sch. Bd., Gate City, 1986—. Named Outstanding Young Man Am., 1984. Mem. ABA, Va. Bar Assn., Scott County Bar Assn. (pres. 1985-86), Scott County Jaycees (pres. 1982-83). Republican. Baptist. Personal injury, Insurance, Consumer commercial. Home: 105 N Dogwood Weber City VA 24251 Office: Quillen & Fulton PO Box 339 Gate City VA 24251

HAMILTON, JOHN ANTHONY, lawyer; b. Evansville, Ind., Aug. 8, 1951; s. Thomas William and Thelma Catherine (Miller) H.; m. Donna Faye Winstead, Apr. 22, 1971; children: Jason Christopher, Ashley Wynn. BS, U. So. Ind., 1975; JD, Ind. U., 1978. Bar: Ind. 1975, U.S. Dist. Ct. (so. dist.) Ind. 1978. Ptnr. Bunner, John, Heathcotte & Hamilton, Evansville, 1978-84; city redevel. atty. City of Evansville, 1980-84; sole practice Evansville, 1984—. Sec. Evansville Boys Club Alumni Assn., 1984-86; bd. dirs. Mater Dei Friends and Alumni, Evansville, 1986. Served with USAF, 1972-74. Mem. ABA, Ind. State Bar Assn., Assn. Trial Lawyers Am., Evansville Bar Assn. Roman Catholic. Avocations: running, horses. General corporate, Personal injury, Probate. Home: 415 S Peerless Evansville IN 47712 Office: 401 Court Bldg 123 NW 4th Evansville IN 47712

HAMILTON, JOHN RICHARD, lawyer; b. El Dorado, Kans., Jan. 8, 1940; s. Silas H. and Ora B. (Barker) H.; m. Shirley A. Tekamp, June 16, 1960 (div. July 1976); children: Michele L., Brian J.; m. Louise Brock, Dec. 22, 1984. BS, Union U., 1962; JD, Washburn Law Sch., 1965. Bar: Kans. 1965, U.S. Dist. Ct. Kans. 1965, U.S. Ct. Appeals (10th cir.) 1969. Ptnr. Crane, Martin, Claussen, Hamilton & Forbes, Topeka, 1965-84; sole practice, Topeka, 1985—. Mem. Kans. Bar Assn., Topeka Bar Assn., ABA, Kans. Trial Lawyers Assn. (bd. dirs., v.p. 1982-83). Republican. Club: Shawnee Country (Topeka). Federal civil litigation, State civil litigation, Condemnation. Home: 5637 SW Urish Rd Topeka KS 66610

HAMILTON, MARY JANE, legal educator. d. Raymond Edward and Mary Jane (Cannell) H.; m. David L. Reed, July 23, 1971. BA in History summa cum laude, Siena Heights Coll., 1960, LHD (hon.), 1986; MA, Cath. U., 1962, PhD in Medieval History and Latin Lit. with Honors, 1964; JD, U. Calif., Davis, 1974. Bar: Calif. 1975. Assoc. staff editor New Cath. Encyclopedia, Washington, 1963-65; prof. depts. history and criminal justice Calif. State U., Sacramento, 1965-79; asst. dean sch. law U. Calif., Davis, 1979—; lectr. various orgns.; pres.-elect Calif. State Univ. Sacramento Faculty Assn., 1978-79, v.p., 1977-78, pres. women's faculty, 1975-76. Contbr. articles to profl. jours. Bd. dirs. Calif. Inst. Clin. Soc. Workers, 1983-86. Fellow Calif. State U. and Colls. System Los Angeles, 1978-79, Woodrow Wilson fellow, 1960-61, Woodrow Wilson dissertation fellow, 1963, Nat. HEW fellow, 1979; research grantee Calif. State U. Sacramento, 1969-71, 77. Mem. ABA, Calif. Bar Assn., Sacramento County Bar Assn. (exec. bd. dirs. 1983-86), Women Lawyers Sacramento (pres. 1983, exec. bd. dirs. 1980-84), Calif. Women Lawyers Assn. (exec. bd. dirs. 1982), Am. Hist. Assn. (nat. com. on women 1972-75), Medieval Acad. Am., Medieval Assn. Pacific (exec. bd. dirs. 1983-86), Am. Soc. for Legal History. Legal education, Family and matrimonial, Legal history. Office: Univ Calif Davis Sch Law Davis CA 95616

HAMILTON, PALMER CLARKSON, lawyer, columnist; b. Mobile, Ala., Oct. 9, 1947; s. Clarkson Mazyck and Martha Henshaw (Pillans) H.; m. Amy Ross St. John, June 16, 1984. BA, U. Ala., 1970; JD, Duke U., 1973. Bar: Ala. 1974, U.S. Dist. Ct. (no. and so. dists) Ala. 1976. Dep. asst. Office Comptroller of Currency, Washington, 1974-76, chief new bank chartering, 1975-76; assoc. Hamilton, Butler, Riddick, Tarlton & Allen, Mobile, Ala., 1976-79; ptnr. Miller, Hamilton, Snider & Odom, Mobile, 1979—; mem. Ala. Banking Code Revision Com., 1978-79. Polit. columnist Azalea City News and Rev., 1978-84, Mobile Press Register, 1985—. Pres. Mobile br. and Nat. bd. English Speaking Union; pres. Mobile Hist. Homes Tour, 1979; vestry mem. Christ Episc. Ch., 1984—; chmn. bd. trustees Mobile Pub. Library, 1979-82. Recipient Best Original Column award Ala. Press Assn. 1984. Mem. ABA, Ala. Bar Assn., Maritime Law Assn., Mobile Mystic Soc. Democrat. Avocations: reading, writing. Banking, Admiralty, Administrative and regulatory. Home: 211 Rapier Ave Mobile AL 36604 Office: Miller Hamilton Snider & Odom PO Box 46 Mobile AL 36604

HAMILTON, PERRIN C., lawyer, state official; b. Phila., Oct. 15, 1921; m. Bette J. Shadle; children—Deborah, Maribeth, Perrin. LL.B., Dickinson Coll., 1948. Bar: D.C., PA. 1949. Spl. counsel U.S. Senate, 1953; ptnr. Hepburn Willcox Hamilton & Putnam, Phila.; commr. Crime Victims Bd., Delaware River Port Authority; dir. Maxim Healthcare Corp. Bd. dirs. Valley Forge Mil. Acad., Freedoms Found.; bd. advisers Dickinson Coll., Salvation Army. Served to lt. USNR, World War II. Decorated Order of Merit, Italy; Freedoms Found. award, 1970. Mem. ABA, Pa. Bar Assn., Phila. Lawyers Club (past pres.), Episcopalian. Clubs: Union League (pres.), Merion Cricket. Constitutional law, General practice. Home: 210 Glenn Rd Ardmore PA 19003 Office: Hepburn Willcox Hamilton & Putnam 1100 One Penn Center Plaza Philadelphia PA 19103

HAMILTON, PETER BANNERMAN, lawyer; b. Phila., Oct. 22, 1946; s. William George Jr. and Elizabeth Jane (McCullough) H.; m. Elizabeth Anne Arthur, May 8, 1982; children—Peter Bannerman, Jr., Brian Arthur. A.B., Princeton U., 1968; J.D., Yale U., 1971. Bar: D.C. 1972, Pa. 1972, Ind. 1985. Mem. staff Office Asst. Sec. Def. for Systems Analysis and Office Gen. Counsel, Dept. Def., Washington, 1971-74; mem. firm Williams & Connolly, Washington, 1974-77; gen. counsel Dept. Air Force, Washington, 1977-78; dep. gen. counsel HEW, Washington, 1979; exec. asst. to sec. HEW, 1979; spl. asst. to Sec. and Dep. Sec. Def., Washington, 1979-80; partner Califano, Ross & Heineman, Washington, 1980-82; v.p., gen. counsel, sec. Cummins Engine Co., Inc., 1983-86, v.p. law and treasury, 1987—. Articles editor: Yale Law Jour, 1970-71. Served to lt. USN, 1971-74. Recipient Exceptional Civilian Service decoration Dept. Air Force, 1978; Dept. Def. medal for Disting. Public Service, 1981. Democrat. Home: 2717 Riverside Dr Columbus IN 47201 Office: Cummins Engine Co Inc Box 3005 Columbus IN 47202

HAMILTON, PHILLIP DOUGLAS, lawyer; b. Pasadena, Calif., Oct. 16, 1954; s. Ivan and Annette O. (Brown) H.; m. Gerry Messner, Sept. 17, 1976 (div. Feb. 1984); m. Janet L. Hester, Apr. 22, 1984; children: Melissa, John. B.A., U. Pa., 1976; J.D., Pepperdine U., 1979. Bar: Calif. 1979, U.S. Dist. Ct. (cen. dist.) Calif. 1980. Assoc., Offices of James J. DiCesare, Santa Ana, Calif., 1979-84; sole practice, Newport Beach, Calif., 1984—. Recipient Am. Jurisprudence award, 1980. Mem. Assn. Trial Lawyers Am., Orange County Trial Lawyers Assn., Calif. Trial Lawyers Assn., Calif. Trial Lawyers Polit. Action Com., Orange County Bar Assn. Republican. Presbyterian. Personal injury, Insurance. Office: 610 Newport Center Dr Suite 300 Newport Beach CA 92660

HAMILTON, RICHARD ABBOTT, lawyer; b. Toledo, Feb. 14, 1932; s. Harry Abbott and Esther May (Gore) H.; m. Ann Elizabeth Davis, Jan. 24, 1958; children: Richard Abbott, Thomas Gore. BA in Econs., U. Mich., 1954, JD, 1957. Bar: Ohio 1957, U.S. Dist. Ct. (no. dist.) Ohio 1957, U.S. Ct. Appeals (6th cir.)1975, U.S. Supreme Ct. 1980. Sole practice Toledo, 1957—; instr. U. Toledo, 1984—. Scoutmaster Boy Scouts Am., Toledo; trustee 1st Congl. Ch., Toledo. Mem. Toledo Bar Assn., Assn. Trial Lawyers Am., Ohio Civil Trial Attys., Def. Research Inst. Republican. Clubs: Toledo, Sandusky (Ohio) Sailing. Avocation: skiing. State civil litigation, Federal civil litigation, Personal injury. Home: 2350 Drummond Rd Toledo OH 43606 Office: Metzger Hamilton & Cherry 520 Madison Ave 1003 Spitzer Bldg Toledo OH 43604

HAMILTON, ROBERT LOWERY, lawyer; b. Orlando, Fla., Jan. 24, 1942; s. Ben Lee and Madge (Highfield) H.; m. Ealnor Sue Hamilton, June 9, 1972; children: Thomas Lane, David Lee. BS, Stetson U., 1964, JD, 1967; LLM, U. Miami, 1971; MS, Rollins Coll., 1979. Bar: Fla. 1967, D.C. 1971. Asst. city atty. City of Orlando, 1971-72, chief asst. city atty., 1974-82, city pros./police legal adviser, 1971-72, city atty., 1982—; chief judge Mcpl. Ct., Orlando, 1972-74; prof. criminal justice Rollins Coll., 1979-84; sworn police res. officer, spl. dep. sheriff; pres. Cen. Fla. Criminal Justice Council, 1987. Sec.-treas. Orange County Criminal Justice Council, 1979. Served with U.S. Army, 1967-70. Decorated Bronze Star medal, Purple Heart, Army Commendation medal; recipient Steinhardt award, Stetson U., 1967; Parker Internat. Aviation Law award, U. Miami, 1971. Mem. Fla. Bar Assn., D.C. Bar Assn., Am. Judicature Soc., ABA, Orange County Bar Assn., Fla. Assn. Police Attys., Fla. Mcpl. Attys. Assn. (treas. 1986-87). Democrat. Episcopalian. Clubs: Rotary (pres. 1976-77), Masons (Shriner). Local government, Labor, State civil litigation. Home: 1212 Bahama Dr Orlando FL 32806 Office: City Hall 400 S Orange Ave Orlando FL 32801

HAMILTON, SUSAN OWENS, transportation company executive, lawyer; b. Birmingham, Ala., Aug. 7, 1951; d. William Lewis and Vonnette (Wilson) Owens; m. M. Raymond Hamilton, June 8, 1974. BA, Auburn U., 1973; JD, Cumberland/Samford U., 1977. Bar: Ala., Fla. Claim agt. Seaboard System R.R. and predecessor cos., Birmingham, Ala., 1977-78; atty. Seaboard System R.R. and predecessor cos., Louisville, 1978-80, claims atty., 1980-81; asst. gen. atty. Seaboard System R.R. and predecessor cos., Jacksonville, Fla., 1981-83, asst. gen. solicitor, 1983-84, gen. mgr. freight claim services, 1984-85; asst. v.p. casualty prevention Chessie System R.R.'s, Balt. and Jacksonville, 1985-86; asst. v.p. freight damage prevention and claims CSX Transp., Jacksonville, 1986—. Mem. ABA, Jacksonville Bar Assn., Bus. and Profl. Women (pres. Jacksonville chpt. 1984-85), Fla. Bus. and Profl. Women (outstanding young careerwoman 1982). Democrat. United Methodist. Lodge: Uptown Civitan (bd. dirs. Jacksonville club 1982-84). Avocations: music, reading, sports. Home: 12154 Hidden Hills Dr Jacksonville FL 32225 Office: CSX Transportation 500 Water St Jacksonville FL 32202

HAMM, COLEMAN DURDEN, JR., lawyer; b. Dothan, Ala., Jan. 19, 1947; s. Coleman D. Sr. and Tura H. Hamm; m. Janice McDuffie, Dec. 23, 1966; children: Coleman D. III, Elaine M. BS, U. Ala., Birmingham, 1975; JD, Birmingham So. Coll., 1980. Bar: Ala. 1980, U.S. Dist. Ct. (no. and mid. dists.) Ala. 1980, U.S. Ct. Appeals (11th cir.) 1980. Assoc. Costello & Stott, Birmingham, 1980-81; mng. ptnr. Amari & Hamm, Birmingham, 1981—. Sunday sch. tchr. Serves as maj. Ala. Air N.G., 1966—. Named one of Outstanding Young Men Am., 1982. Mem. ABA, Ala. Bar Assn., Assn. Trial Lawyers Am., Ala. Trial Lawyers Assn., Christian Legal Soc., U. Ala. Birmingham Nat. Alumni Assn. (nat. bd. dirs. 1982-84). Mem. Assembly of God Ch. Avocation: ch. activities. Personal injury, Family and matrimonial. Office: Amari & Hamm 9636 Parkway E Birmingham AL 35215

HAMM, DAVID BERNARD, lawyer; b. Bklyn., Oct. 6, 1948; s. Isidore I. and Sarah (Lamm) H.; m. Margaret Weiss, June 20, 1971; children: Jennifer A., Michael S. BA cum laude, CUNY, Bklyn., 1971; JD magna cum laude, N.Y. Law Sch., 1977. Bar: N.Y. 1978, U.S. Dist. Ct. (no. dist.) N.Y. 1978, U.S. Dist. Ct. (so. and ea. dists.) N.Y. 1979, U.S. Supreme Ct. 1981, U.S. Ct. Appeals (2d cir.) 1982. Law clk. to presiding judge N.Y. State Ct. Appeals, Albany, 1977-79; assoc. Herzfeld & Rubin P.C., N.Y.C., 1979-85, ptnr., 1986—. Mem. Commn. Legis. and Civic Action Agudath Israel of Am., N.Y.C., 1979—, Nat. Jewish Commn. Law and Pub. Affairs, N.Y.C., 1979—. Recipient Community Service award Agudath Israel of Am., 1986. Mem. ABA, N.Y. State Bar Assn. (com. civil practice law and rules), NYU Alumni Assn. (Prof. Vincent LoLordo award 1977). Democrat. Avocation: volleyball. Federal civil litigation, State civil litigation, Insurance. Home: 2015 E 22d St Brooklyn NY 11229 Office: Herzfeld & Rubin PC 40 Wall St New York NY 10005

HAMMEL, JOHN WINGATE, lawyer; b. Indpls., Dec. 25, 1943; s. Walter Francis and Mary Vivian (Patterson) H.; m. Linda Ann Yarling, Dec. 22, 1972; children: William Wingate II, Kathryn Christine, Rebecca Ann. BS, Butler U., 1967; postgrad., So. Ill. U., 1967-68; JD, Ind. U., 1975. Bar: Ind. 1975, U.S. Dist. Ct. (so. dist.) Ind. 1975, U.S. Ct. Mil. Appeals 1978, U.S. Ct. Appeals (7th cir.) 1983. Assoc. Yarling, Winter, Tunnell & Robinson, Indpls., 1975-83; ptnr. Yarling, Robinson, Hammel & Lamb, Indpls., 1983—. Served to capt. U.S. Army N.G., 1981. Mem. ABA, Ind. Bar Assn., Indpls. Bar Assn. Republican. Insurance, Consumer commercial, Personal injury. Home: 5242 Rucker Circle Indianapolis IN 46250 Office: Yarling Robinson Hammel & Lamb 729 N Pennsylvania St Indianapolis IN 46204

HAMMER, BILL C., lawyer, consultant, developer; b. Tucumcari, N.Mex., Sept. 2, 1947; s. William Glenn and Marguerite Louise (Keller) H.; m. Charmayne Stednick, Aug. 30, 1975. BS, U. Nev., 1969, MBA, 1970; JD, U. Houston, 1974. Bar: Tex. 1974, Nev. 1974, U.S. Dist. Ct. Nev. 1974, U.S. Ct. Appeals (5th cir.) 1974, U.S. Ct. Appeals (9th cir.) 1975, U.S. Dist. Ct. (so. dist.) Tex. 1975, U.S. Dist. Ct. (cen. dist.) Tex. 1980. Assoc. Haynes & Fullenweider, Houston, 1974, Morse, Foley & Wadsworth, Las Vegas, Nev., 1974-75; chief dep. dist. atty. Clark County Dist. Atty., Las Vegas, 1975-79; dep. and chief dep. atty gen. Nev. Atty. Gen., Las Vegas, 1979-81; assoc. Cromer, Barker, Michaelson, Gillock & Rawlings, Las Vegas, 1981; sole practice Las Vegas, 1981—; chmn. Clark County Ethical Standards Commn., Las Vegas, 1985—; mem. State Bar Nev. Fee Dispute Com., Las Vegas, 1977—. Gen. counsel West Oakey Bapt. Ch., Las Vegas, 1981—, First Bapt. Ch., Boulder City, Nev., 1974—. Mem. ABA, Nev. Bar Assn. (fee dispute com. 1977—, jud. selection com. 1984—), Nat. Assn. Gaming Attys., Assn. Trial Lawyers Am., Am. Judicature Soc., Nev. Trial Lawyers Assn. (sec. 1985—, pres. elect 1987—), U. Houston Law Alumni Assn., Alpha Tau Omega Alumni. Baptist. Avocations: car racing, fishing, camping, boating, shooting. Personal injury, Real property, Construction. Office: 610 S Ninth St Las Vegas NV 89101

HAMMER, BRUCE EDWARD, lawyer; b. San Antonio, Tex., Aug. 29, 1954; s. Bobby Joe and Bonnie Pearl (Reynolds) H.; m. Donna Ruth Owens, July 23, 1972; children: Travis Lee, Heather Renee. BME, Southwestern State U., 1976; JD, Tulsa U., 1979. Bar: Okla. 1979, U.S. Dist. Ct. (we. dist.) Okla. 1979. Sole practice Enid, Okla., 1979-82; house counsel Farmers Corp. Grain Dealers Assn., Enid, 1982-83; ptnr. Wiens & Hammer, Blackwell, Okla., 1983—. Bd. dirs. Troop 32 Boy Scouts Am., Blackwell, 1984—; elder First Christian Ch., Blackwell, 1986. Mem. ABA, Okla. Bar Assn., Kay County Bar Assn. Democrat. Mem. Christian Ch. Lodges: Lions, Ambucs. Avocations: backpacking, hunting, fishing, skiing, music. Consumer commercial, Oil and gas leasing, General practice. Home: 942 N 9th Blackwell OK 74631 Office: Wiens & Hammer 118 S 1st PO Box 352 Blackwell OK 74631

HAMMER, DAVID LINDLEY, lawyer; b. Newton, Iowa., June 6, 1929; s. Neal Paul and Agnes Marilyn (Reece) H.; m. Audrey Lowe, June 20, 1953; children—Julie, Lisa, David. B.A., Grinnell Coll., 1951; J.D., U. Iowa, 1956. Bar: Iowa 1956, U.S. Dist. Ct. (no. dist.) Iowa 1959, U.S. Dist. Ct. (so. dist.) Iowa 1969, U.S. Supreme Ct. 1977. Assoc. O'Connor & Thomas, Dubuque, Iowa, 1956-64, ptnr., 1964—; mem. grievance commn. Iowa Supreme Ct., 1973-85, adv. rules com., 1986—. Bd. dirs. Linwood Cemetery Assn., 1973—, pres., 1983-84; bd. dirs., past pres. Finley Hosp.; past campaign chmn., past pres. United Way; past bd. dirs. Carnegie Stout Pub. Library. Served with U.S. Army, 1951-53. Fellow Am. Coll. Trial Lawyers; mem. Young Lawyers Iowa (past pres.), Iowa Def. Counsel Assn. (dir.), Assn. Ins. Attys. (exec. council 1984—, chmn. Iowa chpt.), Fedn. Ins. Counsel, ABA, Iowa State Bar Assn. (past chmn. continuing legal edn. com.), Iowa Acad. Trial Lawyers, Dubuque County Bar Assn. (past pres.). Republican. Congregationalist. Author: The Game is Afoot, 1983, For the Sake of the Games, 1986. State civil litigation, Federal civil litigation, Insurance. Office: CyCare Plaza Suite 200 Dubuque IA 52001

HAMMER, DONALD GORDON, lawyer; b. Bklyn., Jan. 21, 1950; s. David Marshall and Doris Bernice (Tweten) H.; m. Mary Lynn Goff, Aug. 6, 1977; children: Marshall Kelly, William Andrew. BS, U. N.C., 1971, JD, 1974. Bar: Va. 1974. Ptnr. Burke, Graybeal & Hammer, Marion, Va., 1974—. Former bd. dirs. Smyth County Red Cross, Marion, Smyth County YMCA, Marion. Mem. ABA, Smyth County Bar Assn. (former pres.), Va. Trial Lawyers Assn. Club: Holston Hills Country (pres. 1984-85) (Marion). Lodge: Rotary. Avocations: sports, reading. Real property, Personal injury, Probate. Office: Burke Graybeal & Hammer 111 N Church St Marion VA 24354

HAMMER, HOWARD MARTIN, business law educator, lawyer; b. Indpls., Aug. 20, 1947; s. Wendell Delson and Anna Catherine (Flanagan) H.; m. Carol Louise Hartwell, May 25, 1974; children: Laura Elizabeth, Stephanie Lynn. BA in Philosophy, Wabash Coll., Crawfordsville, Ind., 1968; JD cum laude, Ind. U., Indpls., 1976; MA in Econ., Ball State U., 1980. Bar: Ind. 1976, U.S. Dist. Ct. (so. dist.) Ind. 1976. Sole practice Indpls., 1976, Muncie, Ind., 1976—; prof. bus. law Ball State U., Muncie, 1976—. Mem. Ball State U. Law Day Com., 1980—. Served with U.S. Army, 1968-70. Mem. ABA (1st place pub. service award 1984, 85, bus. law, tax sect., sci. and tech. sect.), Ind. Bar Assn. (bus. law sect., internat. law sect.), Muncie Bar Assn., Beta Gamma Sigma (sec. Ball State U. chpt. 1984-86), U.S. Chess Fedn., Am. Go Assn. Consumer commercial, Computer, Contracts commercial. Home: 8200 Ravenwood Dr Muncie IN 47303 Office: Ball State U Dept of Fin Muncie IN 47306

HAMMER, SANDRA NEIMAN, lawyer; b. N.Y.C., June 17, 1947; d. Melvin and Bernice (Lebowitz) N.; m. Otto R. Hammer, Aug. 25, 1969 (div.); m. Brandon Becker, May 20, 1978; children: Elliott M.N., Gabriel W. BA, CCNY, 1969; JD, U. San Diego, 1978; LLM, NYU, 1981. Bar: Calif. 1978, U.S. Dist. Ct. (so. dist.) Calif. 1979, U.S. Ct. Appeals (9th cir.) 1979. Adminstrv. analyst Consumer Affairs Unit, Syracuse, N.Y., 1973-75; atty. food and drug advt. FTC, Washington, 1978-79, atty. advt. practices div., 1984—; asst. prof. Cath. U. Law Sch., Washington, 1980-84. Mng. editor Food Drug Cosmetic Law Jour., Washington, 1981-85. Food and Drug fellow Food and Drug Law Inst., 1978-80. Administrative and regulatory, Food and drug. Home: 713 Lamberton Dr Silver Spring MD 20902 Office: FTC Advt Practices Div 6th St and Penn Ave NW Washington DC 20580

HAMMER, THOMAS JOHN, law educator; b. Milw., Mar. 14, 1949; s. John Joseph Hammer and Edna Rose (Doane) Winnemuller; Patricia K. Rutkowski, Oct. 8, 1983; 1 child, Matthew J. BA, Marquette U., 1971, JD, 1975. Bar: Wis. 1975, U.S. Dist. Ct. (ea. and we. dists.) Wis. 1975. Asst. dist. atty. Milw. County, 1975-81; vis. asst. prof. law Marquette, Milw., 1981-82, asst. prof. law, 1982—. Bd. dirs. Cath. Social Services, Milw., 1985—; commr. Fire and Police Commn., Shorewood, Wis., 1985—. Recipient 5 Yr. Teaching award Wis. Jud. Coll., Madison, Wis., 1985. Mem. ABA, Wis. Bar Assn. (bd. dirs. criminal law sect. 1981—). Roman Catholic. Criminal. Home: 4420 N Sheffield Ave Shorewood WI 53211 Office: Marquette U Law Sch 1103 W Wisconsin Ave Milwaukee WI 53233

HAMMERMAN, STEPHEN LAWRENCE, lawyer, financial services company executive; b. Bklyn., Apr. 18, 1938; s. David S. and Hannah (Chaimowitz) H.; m. Eleanor Draizen; children—Ira, Charles, Michael, Caryn. B.S. in Econs., U. Pa., 1959; LL.B., NYU, 1962. Assoc. Dewey and Ballantine, N.Y.C., 1962-64; asst. U.S. Atty. U.S. Attys. Office, N.Y.C., 1964-68; assoc. Paul and Weiss, N.Y.C., 1968-69; sr. v.p., gen. counsel White, Weld & Co., N.Y.C., 1969-78; mng. dir., gen. counsel Merrill Lynch-White Weld Capital Markets, N.Y.C., 1978-79; N.Y. regional adminstr. SEC, N.Y.C., 1979-81; asst. to pres., v.p., gen. counsel Merrill, Lynch, Pierce, Fenner & Smith Inc., N.Y.C., 1981-84; sr. v.p., gen. counsel Merrill Lynch & Co. Inc., N.Y.C., 1984-85, exec. v.p., chief adminstrv. officer, gen. counsel, 1985—; dir. Merrill Lynch & Co., N.Y.C., 1985—. Author: Securities Law Techniques, 1985. Mem. N.Y. Stock Exchange (legal adv. com.), Securities Industry Assn. (fed. regulation com), N.Y.C. Bar Assn. (investment com. chmn.). Home: 1495 Bay Blvd Atlantic Beach NY 11509 Office: Merrill Lynch & Co Inc 165 Broadway New York NY 10080 *

HAMMESFAHR, ROBERT WINTER, lawyer; b. Pittsfield, Mass., May 17, 1954; s. Frederick W. and Patricia Lue (Winter) H.; m. Susan J. Gardner. BA, Colgate U., 1975; JD, Northwestern U., Chgo., 1978. Bar: Ill. 1978, U.S. Dist. Ct. (no. dist.) Ill. 1978. From assoc. to ptnr. Peterson, Ross, Schloerb & Seidel, Chgo., 1978—. Mem. ABA, Chgo. Bar Assn. Club: University (Chgo.). Avocations: tennis, skiing. Insurance, State civil litigation, Environment. Office: Peterson Ross Schloerb & Seidel 200 E Randolph Dr Suite 7300 Chicago IL 60601

HAMMOND, JANE LAURA, librarian, lawyer; b. nr. Nashua, Iowa; d. Frank D. and Pauline (Flint) H. B.A., U. Dubuque, 1950; M.S., Columbia U., 1952; J.D., Villanova U., 1965. Bar: Pa. 1965. Cataloguer Harvard Law Library, 1952-54; asst. librarian Sch. Law, Villanova (Pa.) U., 1954-62, librarian, 1962-76, prof. law, 1965-76; law librarian, prof. law Cornell U., Ithaca, N.Y., 1976—; Adj. prof. Drexel U., 1971-74; mem. depository library council to pub. printer U.S. Govt. Printing Office, 1975-78. Mem. Am. Assn. Law Libraries (sec. 1965-70, pres. 1975-76), Council Nat. Library Assns. (sec.-treas. 1971-72, chmn. 1979-80), ALA, ABA (com. on accreditation 1982-87, chmn. com. on accreditation 1983-84, council sect. on legal edn. 1984—), PEO. Episcopalian. Legal education. Office: Cornell Law Library Myron Taylor Hall Ithaca NY 14853

HAMMOND, MARK BASHLINE, lawyer; b. Summit, N.J., Nov. 16, 1945; s. Eugene C. and Isabelle Irene (Bashline) H.; m. Joanne Louise Kugler, Aug. 4, 1973; 1 child, Brian C. BA, Dickinson Coll., 1968; JD, Dickinson Sch. Law, 1973; MBA, Shippensburg U., 1982. Bar: Pa. 1973. Mgmt. trainee Valley Bank & Trust Co., Chambersburg, Pa., 1973-74, asst. trust officer, 1974-77, in house counsel, 1977—. Bd. dirs. Presbyn. Homes, Inc., Camp Hill, Pa., 1975-81, vice chmn., 1978-81. Served with U.S. Army, 1968-70. Mem. Pa. Bar Assn., Franklin County Bar Assn., Am. Legion, VFW. Republican. Presbyterian. Lodge: Elks. Avocations: computers, running. Banking, Contracts commercial, Probate. Home: 1720 Wilson Ave Chambersburg PA 17201-1456 Office: Valley Bank & Trust Co PO Box 459 Chambersburg PA 17201-0459

HAMMONS, ALLEN JAMES, JR., lawyer; b. Houston, Aug. 16, 1958; s. Allen James and Irene Lillian (Harbour) H.; m. Rhonda Kim Welch, Mar. 5, 1983; children: James Richard, LaRhonda Jordan. AA, Brazosport Coll., 1978; BBA, Tex. Tech U., 1979, JD, 1982. Assoc. William A. Dyess, Brownfield, Tex., 1982-84; assoc. Hale & Dyess, Brownfield, 1984-85, ptnr., 1986. Pres. United Way Terry County, Brownfield, 1986—; bd. dirs. Terry County Child Welfare Bd., 1986. Mem. ABA, Tex. State Bar Assn., Terry County Bar Assn., Brownfield C. of C. (bd. dirs. 1986—). Methodist. Lodge: Optimists (sec., treas. 1985-86, pres. 1986—). Avocations: tennis, baseball. Family and matrimonial, Criminal, General practice. Home: PO Box 1051 Brownfield TX 79316 Office: Hale & Dyess 303 W Broadway Brownfield TX 79316

HAMNER, REGINALD TURNER, lawyer; b. Tuscaloosa, Ala., June 4, 1939; s. Raiford Samuel and Ellie Wells (Turner) H.; m. Anne Ellen Young, Nov. 8, 1969; children: Patrick Turner, William Christian. BS, U. Ala., 1961, JD, 1965. Bar: Ala. 1965, U.S. Dist. Ct. (mid. dist.) Ala. 1966, U.S. Ct. Appeals (5th cir.) 1966, U.S. Ct. Mil. Appeals 1968, U.S. Supreme Ct. 1968, U.S. Ct. Appeals (11th cir.) 1981. Law clk. Supreme Ct. Ala., 1965; dir. legal-legis. affairs, The Med. Assn., State of Ala., 1968-69; sec., exec. dir. Ala. State Bar, Montgomery, 1969—. Bd. dirs. SE br., YMCA, Montgomery, 1978-81; former legal counsel govtl. adv. panels investigating Ala. Prison System; vice chmn. State Child Welfare Com. Served with USAF, 1965-68, col. USAFR. Fellow Am. Bar Found.; mem. ABA (numerous coms., mem. ho. of dels.), Am. Judicature Soc., Nat. Assn. Bar Execs. (pres. 1978-79), Ala. Council Asn. Execs. (pres. 1984), Ala. Law Inst. (council), Jud. Conf. U.S. Ct. Appeals (11th cir. 1981—), Alpha Epsilon Delta, Phi Alpha Delta, Delta Tau Delta. Baptist. Club: Montgomery Country. Address: 3407 Drexel Rd Montgomery AL 36106 Office: 415 Dexter Ave PO Box 671 Montgomery AL 36101

HAMPSON, ALFRED AUBERT, lawyer; b. Portland, Oreg., Dec. 9, 1920; s. Alfred Aubert and Ethel (McQuaid) H.; m. Elizabeth Griffin, Sept. 23, 1944; children: Cuyler H. Kidney, Griffin S., Dirk McQ., Brooks S. H., Blair M. Student, Reed Coll., 1939-40; AB, Stanford U., 1943; LLB, Harvard U., 1946. Bar: Calif. 1948, Oreg. 1953. Assoc. Brobeck, Phleger & Harrison, San Francisco, 1948-53, Maguire, Shields, Morrison & Bailey, Portland, 1953-55; ptnr. Hampson & Weiss, Portland, 1955-66, Rives & Rodgers, Portland, 1966-68, Hampson, Bayless, Murphy & Stiner (and predecessor firm Hampson & McLean), Portland, 1968—; bd. dirs. The Irwin Hudson Co., Portland. Co-author Droit Des Affairs Des Estats-Unis D'Amerique, 1971. Mem. ABA, State Bar Calif., Oreg. State Bar. Republican. Unitarian. Clubs: Waverley Country (Portland), Bohemian (San Francisco). General corporate. Office: Hampson Bayless Murphy & Stiner 300 Bank of California Tower 707 W Washington St Portland OR 97205

HAMPSON, ROBERT GEORGE, lawyer; b. Elizabeth, N.J., Jan. 28, 1943; s. George Lyle and Barbara (Monkauskas) H.; m. Tamara Davis, Feb. 17, 1979; children: Christopher, Elizabeth. BA, Rutgers U., 1968; JD, Seton Hall U., 1971. Bar: N.J. 1972, U.S. Dist. Ct. N.J. 1972. Assoc. Richard F. Plechner, Metuchen, N.J., 1971-73, Burton & Quackenboss, South River, N.J., 1973-74, Robert T. Quackenboss, East Brunswick, N.J., 1974-75; sr. ptnr. Hampson & Millet, Somerset, N.J., 1975—; mcpl. prosecutor Helmetta,

N.J., 1972-73, Spotswood, N.J., 1972-73, Madison Twp., N.J., 1972-73, Somerville, N.J., 1975-82. Author: (with others) Industrial Revenue Bond Financing: a supplement, 1968. Served to 1st lt. USAF, 1968-72. Mem. Am. Trial Lawyers Assn., Def. Research Inst., N.J. Bar Assn., N.J. Def. Assn., Middlesex County Trial Lawyers Assn. (past officer), Somerset County Bar Assn. (trustee), Lawyers Encouraging Govt. and Law (sponsor). Democrat. Roman Catholic. Avocations: tennis, fishing, golf, skin diving, hi-fi, woodworking. Home: 3 Ledgewood Ct Warren Township NJ 08860 Office: Hampson & Millet 285 Davidson Ave Somerset NJ 08873

HAMPTON, CHARLES EDWIN, lawyer, mathematician, computer programmer; b. Waco, Tex., Oct. 22, 1948; s. Roy Mizell and Hazel Lucretia (Cooper) H.; m. Cynthia Torrance, Sept. 14, 1968; children: Charles Edwin, Adam Ethan. Student Baylor U., summer 1967, Rice U., 1967-68; BA with highest honors, U. Tex., Austin, 1971, JD with high honors, 1977; MA (NSF fellow 1971-74), U. Calif.-Berkeley, 1972, CP, 1975. Bar: Tex., 1977, U.S. Dist. Ct. (we. dist.) Tex., 1979, U.S. Dist. Ct. (no. dist.) Tex., 1980, U.S. Ct. Appeals (5th cir.) 1986. Research asst. U. Calif.-Berkeley, 1974-75; briefing atty. to justice Tex. Supreme Ct., 1977-78; assoc. Law Offices Don L. Baker, P.C., Austin, 1978-81; legal counsel Office Ct. Adminstrn., Tex. Jud. Council, Austin, 1981; staff atty. Supreme Ct. Tex., 1981-84; assoc. Rinehart & Nugent, 1984-87. Del. Travis County Dem. Conv., 1978, 80, 82, 84, 86. Moody Found. scholar. Mem. ABA, State Bar Tex., Travis County Bar Assn., Tex. Young Lawyers Assn. (co-recipient award for best law rev. article in Tex. 1979), Chancellors, Order of Coif, Phi Beta Kappa, Phi Kappa Phi, Phi Delta Phi. Mem. Ch. of Christ. Lodge: Lions. State civil litigation, Bankruptcy, Consumer commercial. Office: 1002 West Ave Suite 300 Austin TX 78701

HAMPTON, CLYDE ROBERT, lawyer; b. Worland, Wyo., May 10, 1926; s. Clyde E. and Mabel L. (Lasley) H.; m. Dorothy Laura Gaebelein, June 3, 1949; 1 dau.: Dorothy Norma. B.A., Columbia Coll., 1949; LL.B., U. Colo., 1952. Bar: Colo. 1952. Atty., then counsel, sr. counsel and now gen. atty. Conoco, Inc., Denver, 1952-85, ret., 1985—, sole practice, 1985—; lectr., educator in field. Republican committeeman; bd. dirs. Denver Baptist Theol. Sem.; ch. officer Presbyterian ch. Served to capt. USNR. Recipient numerous awards in energy-related fields. Mem. Am. Petroleum Inst. (past chmn. environ. law com.; Disting. Merit award 1982), ABA (past chmn. Natural Resources Law Sect.), Denver Bar Assn., Colo. Bar Assn., Sigma Chi, Phi Alpha Delta. Clubs: Petroleum, Columbia U. Alumni (Denver). Author: Landman's Legal Handbook, 1970; contbr. numerous articles on environ. law, natural resources to profl. jours. Environment, Oil and gas leasing, General corporate. Home and Office: 14830 E Jefferson Ave Aurora CO 80014

HAMPTON, ROBERT JOSEPH, lawyer; b. Tulsa, May 1, 1928; s. Heber Perry and Ora Della (Lamberson) H.; m. Norma Helen Spriggs, Aug. 5, 1951; children: Karen Ann, Lawrence Paul. BS, U. Tulsa, 1952, JD, 1980. Bar: Okla. 1980. Asst. to pres. Kendavis Industries, Tulsa, 1952-80; ptnr. Robert J. Hampton & Assocs., Tulsa, 1980—; owner Angel Arbor Children's Shop's, Tulsa, 1965-79. Author: Historical Highlights of the Past 20 Billion Years. Served with USN, 1946-48. Grantee Eugene Lorton Found., 1951. Mem. ABA, Okla. Bar Assn., Tulsa County Bar Assn., Soc. for Happiness and Contemplation (founder), Delta Sigma Pi, Sigma Nu, Tulsa Astronomy Club. Republican. Presbyterian. General practice, Personal injury, Probate. Home: 4821 S 69th E Ave Tulsa OK 74145 Office: Robert J Hampton & Assocs 420 S Main 1001 Mayo Bldg Tulsa OK 74102

HAMPTON, THURMAN BRUCE, lawyer; b. N.C., Feb. 5, 1949; s. Joseph Sam and Ernestine (Rodgers) H.; married. BS in Polit. Sci., N.C. Agrl. and Tech. State U., 1970; JD, State U. Iowa, 1973; diploma, JAG's, 1973, cert., 1983, diploma, 1984. Bar: Iowa 1973, Ct. Mil. Appeals 1973, N.C. 1978. Asst. prof. law N.C. Central U. Sch. of Law, Durham, N.C., 1976-79; sole practice Eden, N.C., 1979-82, 85-86; asst. dist. atty 17th Jud. Dist., Rockingham and Caswell Counties, N.C., 1982-85, dist. atty., 1986; bd. dirs. Eden br. Wachovia Bank. Trustee Morning Star Bapt. Ch., Eden, 1985—. Served to cap. JAGC, U.S. Army, 1973-76, maj. JAGC mil. judge Res. Mem. N.C. Bar Assn. Democrat. Baptist. Lodge: Kiwanis (bd. dir. 1985—). Avocations: running, weight lifting. Criminal, Military. Home: PO Box 3387 Eden NC 27288

HAMRA, SAM FARRIS, JR., lawyer, restaurateur; b. Steele, Mo., Jan. 21, 1932; s. Sam Farris and Victoria (Homra) H.; m. June Samaha, Apr. 1, 1956; children: Sam Farris III, Karen E., Michael K., Jacqueline K. BS in Bus., U. Mo., 1954, LLB, 1959. Bar: Mo. 1959. Assoc. Miller, Fairman, Sanford, Carr & Lowther, Springfield, Mo., 1959-65; sole practice Springfield, 1965—; pres., chmn. bd. Wendy's of SW Mo., Inc., Springfield, 1977—, Wendy's of Mo., Springfield, 1977—; vice chmn. Landmark Bank, Springfield; bd. dirs. Landmark Bancshares Corp., St. Louis; chmn. Law Day USA, 1960. Mem. vestry St. James Episcopal Ch., 1962-64, 69-71, lay reader, 1959-84; trustee Episcopal Diocese West Mo.'s Charitable Trust, 1984—; chmn. United Fund Kickoff Campaign, 1966; bd. dirs. devel. fund. U. Mo., 1981—; mem. boosters Southwest Mo. State U., Springfield; bd. dirs. Jr. Achievement of Middle Am., Inc., 1978-81; corp. chmn. Cerebral Palsy Telethon, 1981; bd. dirs. Lester E. Cox Med. Ctrs., Springfield, 1985—; bd. dirs., bd. govs. St. Jude Children's Research Hosp./ALSAC, Memphis, 1985—; mem. fin. com. Gephardt for Pres. Com., 1985—; chmn. elect Springfield area Sports Hall of Fame com., 1986—; active Dem. Nat. Com., various state and nat. polit. campaigns. Named Springfield's Outstanding Young Man of Yr., 1966, Mo.'s Outstanding Young Man of Yr., 1967. Mem. ABA, Mo. Bar Assn., Greene County Bar Assn. (treas. 1966-67, bd. dirs. 1974-77), Legal Aid Assn. Greene County (bd. dirs. 1976-78), Mo. Inst. for Justice, Inc. (bd. dirs. 1980), Springfield C. of C. (bd. dirs. 1971-77, chmn. city council liaison com. 1974-75), Springfield Jaycees (pres. 1963-64), U. Mo. Alumni Assn. (athletics com. 1981—), So. Fedn. Syrian and Lebanese Am. Clubs (chmn. bd. 1981-82, v.p. 1983-84, pres. 1984-85). Club: Tiger (U. Mo.), Hickory Hills Country (chmn. bldg. com. 1979-80), Cedars of the Ozarks (v.p. 1981). Lodge: Rotary (chpt. pres. Springfield Southeast 1967-68), Masons, Shriners. Real property, General corporate, General practice. Home: 3937 Saint Andrews Dr Springfield MO 65804 Office: Two Corp Ctr Suite 2-200 1949 E Sunshine Springfield MO 65804

HAMRICK, CLAUDE MEREDITH, transp. co. exec., lawyer; b. Rutherford County, N.C., July 27, 1926; s. Roland B. and Thelma H.; m. Lena Mae Lewis, July 6, 1957; children—Kent Lewis, Roland Mont. Student, Pfeiffer Jr. Coll., 1943-44; LL.B., Wake Forest U., 1950. Bar: N.C. bar 1950. Practiced law Winston-Salem, N.C., 1953-59; partner firm Spry and Hamrick, Winston-Salem, 1959-69, Hamrick Doughton and Newton Winston-Salem, 1969-77; v.p., gen. counsel McLean Trucking Co., Winston-Salem, 1977—; also dir. McLean Trucking Co. Mem. N.C. Ho. of Reps., 1961-67. Served with JAGC U.S. Army, 1944-46, 50-52. Mem. N.C., 21st Jud. Dist. bar assns., Motor Carrier Lawyers Assn. Democrat. Baptist. General corporate. Home: 360 Staffordshire Rd Winston-Salem NC 27104 Office: McLean Trucking Co 1920 W 1st St Winston-Salem NC 27102

HAMRICK, KAREN SUSAN, lawyer; b. Charleston, W.Va., Nov. 22, 1955; d. Roland Edward and Elizabeth Antoinette (Rohling) H. BA in Psychology, W.Va. U., 1977, MS in Indsl. Relations, 1979, JD, 1982. Bar: W.Va. 1982, U.S. Dist. Ct. (so. dist.) W.Va. 1982, U.S. Ct. Appeals (4th cir.) 1983. Assoc. Fred F. Holroyd, Charleston, 1982-83; ptnr. Holroyd & Hamrick, Charleston, 1983-85; sole practice Charleston, 1985—; instr. U. Charleston, 1983—; hearing examiner W.Va. Workers Compensation Fund, Charleston, 1986; v.p. Kanawha County Correctional Officers Commn., Charleston, 1985—. Mem. ABA, Kanawha County Bar Assn. Roman Catholic. Labor, Workers' compensation. Home: 125 Sheridan Circle Charleston WV 25314 Office: 405 Capitol St Suite 912 Charleston WV 25301

HAMROCK, MARK ANDREW, lawyer; b. Macomb, Ill., Sept. 25, 1954; s. Andrew John Hamrock and Ruby (Davis) Beresford. BA, Western Ill. U., 1976; JD, So. Ill. U., 1979. Bar: Ill. 1979. Assoc. Hendricks, Watt & Grace, Murphysboro, Ill., 1979-82; sole practice Murphysboro, 1982-85; ptnr. Wolff and Jones, Murphysboro, 1986—. Mem. Ill. Bar Assn., Assn. Trial Lawyers Am. Avocations: golf, bowling, softball. Criminal, Family and matrimonial, Personal injury. Office: Wolff and Jones 1013 Chestnut Murphysboro IL 62966

HANAWAY, DONALD JOHN, state attorney general; b. Stevens Point, Wis., Dec. 25, 1933; s. John Leo and Agnes Marie (Flatley) H.; B.B.A., U. Wis., 1958, LL.B., 1961; m. JoAnn R. Gaskell, June 21, 1958; children—Patrick James, Mary Kathleen, Michael John, Maureen Megan. Bar: Wis. 1961. Asst. dist. atty. Brown County, Green Bay, Wis., 1963-64, spl. prosecutor, 1967-78; city atty. City of De Pere (Wis.), 1964-72, 76-79, mayor, 1972-74; mem. firm Condon, Hanaway & Wickert, Ltd., Green Bay, 1969-84; mem. firm Hanaway, Kuehne & Dietz, Green Bay, 1984-86; mem. Wis. Senate, 1979-87, asst. minority leader, 1981-83; atty. gen. State of Wis., Madison, 1987—. Active various local govtl., civic and parish coms. Served with U.S. Army, 1954-56. Mem. ABA, Wis. Bar Assn., Brown County Bar Assn., Wis. Acad. Trial Lawyers, Wis. Sch. Attys. Assn. (charter), De Pere C. of C. (exec. sec. 1964-69). Republican. Club: Optimist (charter) (De Pere). Office: Office of Attorney Gen State Capitol Madison WI 53701

HANBURY, JOHN IRUINE, lawyer; b. Farmville, Va., Sept. 18, 1956; s. Burton Blanton and Jane Lee (Hutcheson) H.; m. Sally Munro Grumbles, Jan. 20, 1979; children: John Jr., Paul Blanton, David Burton. BA, Centre Coll. of Ky., 1978; JD, U. Ky., 1982. Bar: Ky. 1982, U.S. Dist. Ct. (ea. dist.) 1983, U.S. Ct. Appeals, (6th cir.) 1984. Bus. analyst Dun & Bradstreet, Louisville, 1978-79; assoc. Vanantwerp, Monge, Jones & Edwards, Ashland, Ky., 1982-85, ptnr., 1986—. Bd. dirs. Jr. Achievement of Ky.-Ohio Valley, Ashland, 1986—; capt. Boyd County Community Chest, Ashland, 1983—. Mem. ABA, Boyd County Bar Assn., Ky. Bar Assn., Ky. Def. Counsel, Inc. Republican. Methodist. Lodge: Lions. Avocations: boating, water skiing, bridge. State civil litigation, Contracts commercial, Insurance. Home: 2418 Central Pkwy Ashland KY 41101 Office: Vanantwerp Monge Jones & Edwards 1416 Winchester Ave Ashland KY 41101

HANCOCK, GEORGE LOUIS, JR., lawyer; b. Middletown, Ohio, June 8, 1953; s. George L. Sr. and Virginia B. (Ballard) H.; m. Dana R. Brennan, Sept. 2, 1978; 1 child, Ryan L. BA, U. Ky., 1971-75; JD, U. Toledo, 1978. Bar: Ohio 1979, U.S. Ct. Mil. Appeals 1979, U.S. Supreme Ct. 1982. Commd. as officer U.S. Army, 1979, advanced through grades to capt., 1979; legal officer U.S. Army, Fort Knox, Ky., 1979; trial def. counsel U.S. Army, Fort Knox, 1979-82, chief of legal assistance, 1982-83; post judge adv. U.S. Army, Ft. Detrick, Md., 1983—. Named Ky. Col. Mem. Assn. Trial Lawyers Am., Judge Adv. Assn. Democrat. Methodist. Avocations: horse racing, chess. Military, Labor, Criminal. Home: 2111 Michie Dr Apt #36 Charlottesville VA 22901

HANCOCK, JAMES H., lawyer; b. Phila., July 1, 1940; s. J. Howard and Martha M. (Johnson) H.; m. Judith A. Luther, Aug. 14, 1967; children—John D., David H. B.A., Ky. Wesleyan Coll., 1963; J.D., Vanderbilt U., 1966; LL.M., in Taxation, NYU, 1971. Bar: N.Y. 1966, U.S. Tax Ct. 1968, U.S. Ct. Claims 1969, D.C. 1978. Assoc. Seward & Kissel, and predecessor firm, Meyer, Kissel, Matz & Seward, N.Y.C., 1964-74, ptnr., 1974—; lectr. tax law Fordham Law Sch., Bronx, N.Y., 1972-77, World Trade Ctr. Inst., N.Y.C., 1978. Mem. ABA, N.Y. State Bar Assn., Assn. Bar City of N.Y., D.C. Bar Assn., Nat. Assn. Bond Lawyers, Phi Delta Phi. Club: India House (N.Y.C.). Contbr. articles to profl. fin. jours. Contracts commercial, Private international, Real property. Office: Wall St Plaza New York NY 10005

HANCOCK, JAMES HUGHES, judge; b. 1931. B.S., U. Ala., 1953, LL.B., 1957. Bar: Ala. Ptnr. firm Balch, Bingham, Baker, Hawthorne, Ward & Williams, Birmingham, Ala., 1957-73; judge U.S. Dist. Ct. (no. dist.) Ala., Birmingham, 1973—. Mem. Ala. Bar Assn. Judicial administration. Office: US District Court 357 Federal Courthouse Birmingham AL 35203 *

HANCOCK, S. LEE, lawyer; b. Knoxville, Tenn., Aug. 11, 1955; s. Melton Donald and Alma Helen (McDaniel) H.; m. Kathleen Ann Koll, July 26, 1986. BS summa cum laude, Southwest Mo. State U., 1975; JD cum laude, So. Meth. U., 1979. Bar: Mo. 1979, U.S. Dist. Ct. (we. dist.) Mo., U.S. Tax Ct. 1982, U.S. Ct. Claims 1983; CPA, Mo. Assoc. Blackwell, Sanders, Matheny, Weary & Lombardi, Kansas City, Mo., 1979-83, ptnr., 1984—. Mem. Mo. Council Econ. Edn., Kansas City, 1984-86. Mem. ABA, Mo. Bar Assn., Kansas City Bar Assn., Lawyer's Assn. Kansas City (pres. young lawyers sect. 1986—, bd. dirs. 1986—), Order of Coif, MENSA. Republican. Avocations: sailing, skiing, photography. Corporate taxation, General corporate, Securities. Home: 430 W Meyer Blvd Kansas City MO 64113 Office: Blackwell Sanders Matheny Weary & Lombardi 2480 Pershing Rd Suite 600 Kansas City MO 64108

HANCOCK, STEWART F. JR., state judge. Judge U.S. Ct. Appeals, Albany, N.Y., 1986—. Office: Ct Appeals Hall Eagle St Albany NY 12207 *

HANCOCK, WILLIAM GLENN, lawyer; b. Richmond, Va., June 3, 1950; s. William Cary and Doris (Glenn) H.; children: William Claiborne, James Cole, Caroline Carter. BS in Econs., U. Va., 1968-72; post-grad., Tulane U., 1972-73; JD, U. Richmond, 1973-75. Bar: Va. 1975. Assoc. Mays & Valentine, Richmond, 1975-81, ptnr., 1981—; bd. dirs. Home Beneficial Corp., Richmond; bd. dirs., counsel Home Beneficial Life Ins. Co., 1984—. Editor U. Richmond Law Rev., 1975. Fundraiser United Givers Fund YMCA, Richmond, 1978-80; bd. dirs. Richmond Tennis Patrons, 1978-80, Ronald McDonald House, Richmond, 1981-85. Mem. ABA, Va. Bar Assn. (chmn. young lawyers sect. 1985-86), St. Christopher's Alumni Assn. (pres. 1983-85). Real property, General corporate, Insurance. Office: Mays & Valentine 1111 E Main St Richmond VA 23219

HAND, JAMES S., member of congressional staff; b. Mt. Kisco, N.Y., Mar. 14, 1949; m. Gail Stewart; children: Jordan, Alison. BA, UCLA, 1971; JD, U. N.D., 1980. Bar: N.D. 1980, U.S. Dist. Ct. N.D. 1980, U.S. Ct. Appeals (8th cir.) 1983. Assoc. Anderson and Assocs., Grand Forks, N.D., 1980-82; sole practice Grand Forks, 1982-84; ptnr. Hand & Triplett, Grand Forks, 1984-87; state rep. for U.S. Senator Kent Conrad 1987—; adj. grad. faculty Embry-Riddle Aeronautical U., Grand Forks AFB, 1983; lectr. U. N.D., 1985-86. Pub. mem. N.D. Bd. of Nursing, Bismarck, N.D., 1986-87. Mem. N.D. Bar Assn., Greater Grand Forks County Bar Assn., Nat. Health Lawyers Assn. Legislative, Government contracts and claims. Office: 104 Fed Bldg 102 N 4th St Grand Forks ND 58201

HAND, WILLIAM BREVARD, federal judge; b. Mobile, Ala., Jan. 18, 1924; s. Charles C. and Irma W. H.; m. Allison Denby, June 17, 1948; children: Jane Connor Hand Dukes, Virginia Alan Hand Hollis, Allison Hand Peebles. B.S. in Commerce and Bus. Adminstrn, U. Ala., 1947, J.D., 1949. Bar: Ala. 1949. Mem. firm Hand, Arendall, Bedsole, Greaves & Johnston, Mobile, 1949-71; chief judge U.S. Dist. Ct. (so. dist.) Ala., 1971—. Chmn. Mobile County Republican Exec. Com., 1968-71. Served with U.S. Army, 1943-46. Decorated Bronze Star medal. Mem. Am., Fed., Ala., Mobile bar assns. Methodist. Jurisprudence. Office: US District Court PO Box 1964 Mobile AL 36633 *

HANDEL, RICHARD CRAIG, lawyer; b. Hamilton, Ohio, Aug. 11, 1945; s. Alexander F. and Marguerite (Wilks) H.; m. Katharine Jean Carter, Jan. 10, 1970. AB, U. Mich., 1967; MA, Mich. State U., 1968; JD summa cum laude, Ohio State U., 1974; LLM in Taxation, NYU, 1978. Bar: Ohio 1974, S.C. 1983, U.S. Dist. Ct. (so. dist.) Ohio 1975, U.S. Dist. Ct. S.C. 1979, U.S. Tax Ct. 1977, U.S. Ct. Appeals (4th cir.) 1979, U.S. Supreme Ct. 1979; cert. tax specialist. Assoc. Smith & Schnacke, Dayton, Ohio, 1974-77; asst. prof. U. S.C. Sch. Law, Columbia, 1978-83; ptnr. Nexsen, Pruett, Jacobs & Pollard, Columbia, 1983—. Contbr. articles to legal jours. Served with U.S. Army, 1969-70, Vietnam. Gerald L. Wallace scholar, 1977-78; recipient Outstanding Law Prof. award, 1980-81. Mem. ABA, S.C. Bar Assn., Richland County Bar Assn., Order of Coif. Corporate taxation, Personal income taxation, Estate planning. Home: 2704 Wheat St Columbia SC 29205 Office: Nexsen Pruet Jacobs & Pollard 1401 Main St 12th Floor PO Drawer 2426 Columbia SC 29202

HANDELMAN, WALTER JOSEPH, lawyer; b. New Rochelle, N.Y., Sept. 8, 1931; s. Edward and Blanche Edith (Berman) H.; m. Judith Helen Ashe, Oct. 12, 1958; children—David, Daniel, Matthew. A.B. magna cum laude, Harvard U., 1953, LL.B., 1958. Bar: N.Y. 1959, U.S. Dist. Ct. (so. dist.) N.Y. 1962, U.S. Dist. Ct. (ea. dist.) 1962. Assoc. Edward Handelman, N.Y.C., 1958-71; prin. Walter J. Handelman, N.Y.C., 1971-84, White Plains, N.Y., 1985—. Mem. Bd. Archtl. Rev. Scarsdale, 1965-68; pres. East Scarsdale Assn. 1969-71; trustee Scarsdale Pub. Library, 1974-77; mem. Bd. Appeals, 1980-87, Preservation League N.Y. State, 1986—. Served to lt. USNR, 1953-55. Mem. N.Y. County Lawyers Assn. (com. on profl. ethics). Republican. Jewish. Club: Town (pres. 1978-79). Church and ecclesiastical, Probate, General practice. Home: 260 Mamaroneck Rd Scarsdale NY 10583 Office: 1 N Broadway White Plains NY 10601

HANDELSMAN, LAWRENCE MARC, lawyer; b. N.Y.C., Jan. 17, 1945; s. David and Ruth (Litner) H.; m. Sara Pruzan, June 10, 1967; children: Sharon, Carolyn. BBA, CCNY, 1965; JD, NYU, 1968. Bar: N.Y. 1968, U.S. Ct. Mil. Appeals 1969, U.S. Dist. Ct. (so. and ea. dists.) N.Y. 1973, U.S. Ct. Appeals (2d cir.) 1973, Fla. 1978. Assoc. Stroock & Stroock & Lavan, N.Y.C., 1973-78, ptnr., 1979—. Served to capt. JAGC, U.S. Army, 1969-73. Mem. ABA (bus. bankruptcy com. 1969—), Assn. of Bar of City of N.Y. (bankruptcy com. 1974-77, 1985—). Bankruptcy, Federal civil litigation. Home: 22 Scarsdale Farm Rd Scarsdale NY 10583 Office: Stroock & Stroock & Lavan 7 Hanover Sq New York NY 10004

HANDLEMAN, AARON L., lawyer; b. Bridgeport, Conn., Mar. 31, 1946; s. Howard W. and Beatrice (Kaplan) H.; m. Sandra R. Landow, Aug. 31, 1969; children: Michelle, Jessica. BA, Marietta Coll., 1968; JD, George Washington U., 1971. Bar: D.C. 1971, U.S. Dist. Ct. D.C. 1971, Md. 1972, U.S. Supreme Ct. 1978. Assoc. Danzansky, Dickey, Tydings et al, Washington, 1971-78; ptnr. Finley, Kumble, Wagner, Heine, Underberg, Manley & Casey, Washington, 1978—. Gen. counsel, bd. dirs. Cultural Alliance Greater Washington, 1981—; bd. trustees Marietta Coll., Ohio, 1985—. Named Outstanding Young Alumni Marietta Coll., 1981. Democrat. Jewish. Federal civil litigation, State civil litigation, Insurance litigation--defense legal malpractice suits. Home: 11713 Le Havre Dr Potomac MD 20854 Office: Finley Kumble Wagner Heine et al 1120 Connecticut Ave NW Washington DC 20036

HANDLER, ALAN B., state justice; b. Newark, July 20, 1931; m. Rose Marie H.; 5 children. A.B., Princeton U., 1953; LL.B., Harvard U., 1956. Bar: N.J. bar 1956. Dep. atty. gen. 1961-64, 1st asst. atty. gen., 1964-68; justice Superior Ct., 1968-73; spl. counsel to gov. 1976-77; justice N.J. Supreme Ct., 1977—. Mem. Harvard Law Sch. Assn. of N.J. (past pres.), Phi Beta Kappa. Jurisprudence. Office: NJ Supreme Ct Richard J Hughes Justice Complex CN 979 Trenton NJ 08625 *

HANDLER, HAROLD ROBERT, lawyer; b. Jersey City, Aug. 24, 1935; s. Morris Sidney and Fan (Krieger) H.; m. Roberta Beryl Berg, Aug. 6, 1961; children: Maren, Jeremy, Jolyon. BS, Lehigh U., 1957; LLM, Columbia U., 1961. Bar: N.Y. 1961, U.S. Tax Ct. 1963, U.S. Ct. Appeals (2d cir.) 1980. Atty., advisor U.S. Tax Ct., Washington, 1961-63; assoc. Simpson, Thacher & Bartlett, N.Y.C., 1963-69, ptnr., 1970—; adj. assoc. prof. law NYU, 1978-80. Chmn. fin. com., citizens adv. com. Met. Transp. Authority, N.Y.C., 1975-79. Mem. ABA, N.Y. State Bar Assn. (chmn. subcom. tax sect. 1979-83), Assn. of Bar of City of N.Y. (chmn. tax. com. 1983-86), Am. Law Inst. Corporate taxation, Personal income taxation. Office: Simpson Thacher & Bartlett One Battery Park Plaza New York NY 10004

HANDLER, MILTON, lawyer; b. N.Y.C., Oct. 8, 1903; s. George and Ray (Friedman) H.; m. Marion W. Kahn, Dec. 21, 1932 (dec.); 1 dau., Carole Enid; m. Miriam Adler, Feb. 3, 1955. A.B., Columbia U., 1924, LL.B. Ordronaux prize, 1926; LL.D., Hebrew U., 1965. Bar: N.Y. 1927. On staff Columbia U., 1927-72, now prof. law emeritus; engaged in pvt. practice law specializing in antitrust, trademark la; sr. partner firm Kaye, Scholer, Fierman, Hays & Handler; pres. N.Y. Majestic Corp., 1937-48; Gen. counsel Nat. Labor Bd., 1933-34; spl. asst. to gen. counsel Treasury Dept., 1938-40; asst. gen. counsel Lend Lease Adminstrn., 1942-43; spl. counsel Fgn. Econ. Adminstrn., 1943-44; asso. pub. mem. Nat. War Labor Bd., 1944; adviser Am. Law Inst. Restatement of Torts and Restatement of Torts second; arbitrator numerous important labor and comml. disputes; Mitchell lectr. Buffalo Law Sch., 1956-57; lectr. U. Leyden, The Netherlands, 1963; Mem. atty. gen.'s nat. com. to study antitrust laws, 1953-55. Author: books, articles including Antitrust in Perspective, 1957; Cases and Materials on Trade Regulation, 4th edit., 1967; Cases and Materials on Business Torts, 1972, Twenty-Five Years of Antitrust, 1973, (with others) Cases and Materials on Trade Regulation, 1975; Editor: Columbia Law Rev, 1924-26. Hon. chmn. bd. dirs. Am. Friends of Hebrew U., Jerusalem; dep. chmn., bd. govs. Hebrew U. Recipient bicentennial silver medallion Columbia, 1954; Scopus award Am. Friends of Hebrew U., 1963; medal of excellence Columbia Law Alumni, 1976; Outstanding Research in Law and Govt. award Fellows of Am. Bar Found., 1977; Human Relations award lawyers div. Anti-Defamation League Appeal, 1979; Milton Handler chair in trade regulation established at Columbia Law Sch., 1974; Joseph M. Proskauer award lawyers div. United Jewish Appeal, 1980; Handler Auditorium on Mt. Scopus Campus of Hebrew U., dedicated 1975. Fellow Am. Coll. Trial Lawyers, Am. Bar Found., Fed. Bar Council; mem. ABA (council antitrust sec. 1961-64), Fed. Bar Assn., N.Y. State Bar Assn. (chmn. spl. com. to study state antitrust laws 1956-66), Assn. Bar City N.Y., N.Y. County Lawyers Assn. (dir. 1953-56). Democrat. Jewish religion. Clubs: Men's Faculty (Columbia); Harmonie. Antitrust, Trademark and copyright, Federal civil litigation. Home: 625 Park Ave New York NY 10021 Office: 425 Park Ave New York NY 10022

HANDLIN, JOSEPH JASON, lawyer; b. N.Y.C., Feb. 21, 1952; s. Nathan and Beatrice (Greenberg) H.; m. Laura Sara Ellin, Aug. 18, 1985. AB magna cum laude, Harvard U., 1973; JD, NYU, 1976. Bar: N.Y. 1977, U.S. Dist. Ct. (so. and ea. dists.) N.Y. 1977. Gen. counsel Muzak Corp., N.Y.C., 1977-78; assoc. Estroff, Frankel & Waldman, N.Y.C., 1978-80, Guggenheimer & Untermyer, N.Y.C., 1980-84, Dahan & Nowick, N.Y.C., 1984-86, Epstein, Becker, Borsody & Green P.C., N.Y.C., 1986—; adj. assoc. instr. Cardozo Law Sch., N.Y.C., 1983—. Recipient Lewis F. Powell, Jr. Medal for Excellence in Adv. Am. Coll. Trial Lawyers, 1975. Mem. ABA, N.Y. State Bar Assn., Assn. of Bar of City of N.Y., N.Y. County Lawyers Assn. Club: Harvard (N.Y.C.) (sec. admissions com. 1986-87). Real property. Home: 345 South End Ave Apt 7H New York NY 10280 Office: Epstein Becker Borsody & Green PC 250 Park Ave New York NY 10177

HANDMAKER, S.A., lawyer; b. Louisville, May 27, 1930; s. Sidney David Handmaker and Ethel (Baron) Emmergick; m. Muriel Beton, Aug. 30, 1953; children: Ellen H. Handmaker Grosovsky, David S., William B., Robert S. AB, Stanford U., 1952, JD, 1953. Ptnr. Handmaker, Weber & Rose and predecessor firms, Louisville, 1956-86, Handmaker, Saltsman & Webb, Louisville, 1986—. Pres. Jewish Community Fedn., Louisville, 1975-78; v.p. Nat. Jewish Community Relations Adv. Council, 1982-85, exec. com., 1985—, Council Jewish Fedns. Inc., N.Y., 1983—, exec. com., 1986—. Served to capt. JAGC, U.S. Army, 1953-56. Mem. ABA, Ky. Bar Assn., Louisville Bar Assn. Democrat. General corporate. Office: Handmaker Saltsman & Webb 2010 Ky Home Life Bldg Louisville KY 40202

HANDSCHUH, G. GREGORY, lawyer; b. Mineola, N.Y., Mar. 11, 1941; s. George and Anita Mary (Bracken) H.; m. Kristine Limbert, May 23, 1969; children: Thomas, Catherine, Caroline. BA, U. Detroit, 1962, MA, 1964; JD, St. John's U., N.Y.C., 1975. Bar: N.Y. 1976. Dist. mgr. Control Data Corp., N.Y.C., 1967-72; trial atty. FTC, Washington, 1975-79; atty. Amdahl Corp., Sunnyvale, Calif., 1979-82, mng. atty., 1982-84, corp. counsel, asst. sec., 1984—; mem. bd. dirs. Goodwill Industries Santa Clara. Pres. U. Detroit Young Reps., 1961-62, Saddler Oaks Home Owners Assn., Reston, Va., 1978-79. Mem. ABA, N.Y. State Bar Assn. Republican. Roman Catholic. Avocation: ice hockey. Antitrust, General corporate, Intellectual property law. Home: 4390 Corte De Boleyn San Jose CA 95118 Office: Amdahl Corp 1250 E Arques Ave Sunnyvale CA 94086

HANDWERKER, KEVIN, lawyer; b. Bklyn., Nov. 18, 1956; s. Sam and Sybil (Shapiro) H.; m. Debbie Cooper, Apr. 18, 1982; 1 child, Scott. BS in Acctg., SUNY, Albany, 1978; JD, Fordham U., 1981. Bar: N.Y. 1982, Fla. 1982. Sr. acct. Arthur Andersen & Co., N.Y.C., 1978-82; assoc. Shearman & Sterling, N.Y.C., 1982—. Bd. dirs. 336 E 50th St Tenants Corp., N.Y.C., 1982—, Saratoga Condominum Assn., N.Y.C., 1986—. Mem. ABA, Fla. Bar Assn., N.Y. State Bar Assn., N.Y. State Soc. Pub. Accts. Securities, Banking. Office: Shearman & Sterling 53 Wall St New York NY 10005

HANEMANN, JAMES, JR., lawyer; b. New Orleans, Dec. 31, 1935; s. James and Mary Rollins (Douglass) H.; m. Ann Mahorner, Aug. 7, 1965; children: James Douglas, Katherine Glennon. BS in Civil Engring., Tulane U., 1957, JD, 1963. Bar: La. 1963, U.S. Dist. Ct. (ea. dist.) La. 1963, U.S. Ct. Appeals (5th cir.) 1963, U.S. Supreme Ct. 1967. Assoc. Phelps, Dunbar, Marks, Claverie & Sims, 1963-64, 66-69, ptnr., 1969-74; assoc. Terriberry, Carroll, Yancey & Farrell, 1964-66; ptnr. Poitevent & Hanemann, 1974-81; sole practice 1981-82; ptnr. Hanemann & Little, 1982-83; prin. Hanemann & Assocs., 1983—. Adv. editor The Maritime Lawyer, 1975—; contbr. articles to profl. jours. Bd. dirs. Boys Club Greater New Orleans, 1977-81; chmn. U.S. Blind Golfers' Championship, 1980. Served to lt. USN, 1957-63. Mem. ABA, Fed. Bar Assn., La. Bar Assn. (ho. of dels. 1980—), New Orleans Bar Assn., Maritime Law Assn. (com. on arrangements, chmn. Ladies' and Mens' golf tournaments 1976, 84), Gulf Steamship Claims Assn. (pres. 1970), Order of Coif, Omicron Delta Kappa, Kappa Delta Phi, Phi Delta Phi. Roman Catholic. Clubs: Bienville (New Orleans) (pres. 1975-76), New Orleans Country (bd. dirs. 1974-75). Lodge: Rotary (pres. New Orleans chpt. 1976-77). Federal civil litigation, State civil litigation, Admiralty. Home: 5528 Hurst St New Orleans LA 70115 Office: Henemann & Assocs 812 Gravier Suite 910 New Orleans LA 70112

HANEN, ANDREW SCOTT, lawyer; b. Elgin, Ill., Dec. 10, 1953; s. Eugene Edward Hanen and Phyllis Jean (VanderWorker) Fee; m. Diane Dillard, Jan. 5, 1980. BA, Denison U., 1975; JD, Baylor U., 1978. Bar: Tex. 1978, U.S. Dist. Ct. (no., so., ea., and we. dists.) Tex. 1978, U.S. Ct. Appeals (5th and 11th cirs.) 1978, U.S. Supreme Ct. 1978. Briefing atty. Supreme Ct. Tex., Austin, 1978-79; ptnr. Andrews & Kurth, Houston, 1979—. Gen. counsel Sunshine Kids, Houston, 1983—; mem. Harris County Jud. Qualifications Com., Houston, 1984—. Fellow Tex. BarFound., Houston Bar Found.; mem. ABA, Houston Bar Assn. (chmn. com. 1984—, Pres. award 1985), Houston Young Lawyers Assn. (treas. 1986, Outstanding Service award 1982, 83, 85). Club: Tex. (Houston). Federal civil litigation, State civil litigation, Personal injury. Office: Andrews & Kurth 4200 Tex Commerce Tower Houston TX 77002

HANES, JAMES HENRY, consulting business executive, lawyer; b. Houston, Dec. 23, 1922; s. Ralph Davis and Mable Mae (Anderson) H.; m. Doris Marilyn Hall, Sept. 1950; children: Douglas, Stephen, Barbara, Constance. B.S. with honors, Rose-Hulman Inst., 1944; J.D., U. Mich., 1951. Bar: Mich. 1951, Okla. 1955, Colo. 1974, U.S. Supreme Ct. 1976. With Dow Chem. Co., U.S.A., 1946-48, 51-86; dir. indsl. relations Dow Chem. Co., 1968-72; gen. mgr. Dow Chem. Co. (Rocky Flats div.), Golden, Colo., 1972-74; gen. counsel Dow Chem. Co. U.S.A., Midland, Mich., 1974-86; v.p. Dow Chem. Co. U.S.A., 1976-86, also mem. public issues com., retirement bd.; exec v.p., gen. counsel, dir. Omni Tech Internat. Ltd., 1986—; dir. Dorinco Reins. Co., First Nat. Bank, Boulder, Colo., 1973-74. Mem. gen. fund com. Saginaw Valley State Coll., 1976—, Rose Hulman Inst., 1985—; class agt. Rose-Hulman Inst., 1985—; bd. dirs. Mid Mich. Health Care Systems, 1984—, Midland Hosp. Center, 1975-84, chmn., 1977-79, chmn. fin. com., 1979-82, chmn. personnel com., 1982-85; bd. dirs. Midland United Way, 1970-72; active local Boy Scouts Am.; chmn. Bd. Stratford Pines Nursing Home, 1986—. Served to lt. (j.g.) USNR, 1944-46. Recipient Individual Contbns. award Soc. Mfg. Engrs., 1974, Safety award Life is Fragile Club, 1974. Mem. NAM, Mich. Bar Assn., Colo. Bar Assn., Okla. Bar Assn., Midland County Bar Assn. (past pres.), Chem. Mfrs. Assn. (gen. counsel com.), Nat. Legal Center Public Interest (lawyers adv. com.). Presbyterian (elder). Lodges: Rotary, Masons (32 deg.). General corporate, Labor, Real property. Home: 4455 Arbor Dr Midland MI 46840 Office: 2715 Ashman St Midland MI 48640

HANES, LEIGH B., JR., lawyer; b. Roanoke, Va., Apr. 4, 1918; s. Leigh Buckner and Lillian Lee (Thompson) H.; m. Frances Hulda Hilton, Nov. 1, 1945; children—Katherine W. Hanes Feldmann, Leigh Thompson, David Hilton. B.A. cum laude, Hampden-Sydney Coll., 1940; LL.B., U. Md., 1948. Bar: Va. 1951, U.S. Supreme Ct. 1970. Spl. agt. FBI, 1943-49; ptnr. Hanes & Hanes, Roanoke, Va., 1951-56; asst. U.S. atty. Western Dist. Va., 1956-59, U.S. atty., 1969-75; commonwealth's atty. Botetourt County, Va., 1976-79; town atty., Troutville, Va., 1981-86; mem. jud. conf. 4th Cir. Ct. Appeals; mem. City Council Roanoke, 1953-56; vice mayor, Roanoke, 1953-56. Mem. State Scenic River adv. bd., Va. State Bar Med. Malpractice Arbitration Panel; dir. Regional Partnership Roanoke Valley; mem. arbitration panel Better Bus. Bur. Western Va., exec. com. Pvt. Industry Council 5th Dist. Employment and Tng. Consortium; chmn. bd. dirs. League of Older Ams. Found., Western Va. Served with AUS, 1944-46. Mem. Fed. Bar Assn., Roanoke Bar Assn., Botetourt County Bar Assn., Va. Local Govt. Attys. Assn., Botetourt County C. of C. (pres. 1983), Omicron Delta Kappa, Tau Kappa Alpha, Chi Beta Phi, Sigma Upsilon. Republican. Presbyterian. Clubs: Buchanan Rotary; Masons (Roanoke). Real property, Criminal.

HANFORD, TIMOTHY LLOYD, lawyer; b. San Francisco, Oct. 24, 1955; s. Lloyd David Jr. and Noel (Straus) H.; m. Terry Goss, Aug. 29, 1981; children: Megan, Daniel. BS, Stanford U., 1977; JD cum laude, Harvard U., 1980. Bar: Calif. 1980, U.S. Dist. Ct. (no. dist.) Calif. 1980. Assoc. Cooley, Godward et al, San Francisco, 1980-87; asst. tax counsel minority com. on ways and means U.S. Ho. of Reps., Washington, 1987—. Mem. ABA. State and local taxation, Corporate taxation, Legislative. Home: 5802 Lone Oak Dr Bethesda MD 20814 Office: Minority Com Ways and Means US Ho of Reps 1106 Longworth House Office Bldg Washington DC 20515

HANFT, NOAH JONATHAN, lawyer; b. N.Y.C., Jan. 12, 1953; s. Edwin and Gladys (Potash) H.; m. Cecile B. Strauss, Aug. 8, 1976; children: Alexandra Julia, Elizabeth Anna. BA in Govt. and Pub. Adminstrn., Am. U., 1973; JD, Bklyn. Law Sch., 1976; LLM in Trade Regulations, NYU, 1982. Sr. trial atty. Legal Aid Soc., N.Y.C., 1977-81; assoc. Ladas & Parry, N.Y.C., 1982-84; sr. atty. Mastercard Internat., N.Y.C., 1984-87, v.p., counsel, 1987—; instr. Cordoza Inst. of Trial Advocacy, N.Y.C., 1982—. General corporate, Trademark and copyright, Labor. Home: 11 Columbia Pl Brooklyn Heights New York NY 11201

HANGER, CHARLES ERNEST, lawyer; b. Oakland, Calif., Feb. 23, 1924; s. Samuel McLean and Mae Claudia (Stanifer) H.; m. Ann Folger, Sept. 4, 1948 (div.); children: Dean C., Susan S.; m. Faye Ellene Williams, Sept. 5, 1953; 1 dau., Julie; stepchildren: Gilbert Foerster, Deborah Clemmer. B.A., U. Calif.-Berkeley, 1948, LL.B., 1950. Bar: Calif. 1951, U.S. Supreme Ct. 1968. Assoc. Steinhart Office, San Francisco, 1951-59; assoc. Brobeck, Phleger & Harrison, San Francisco, 1959-61, ptnr., 1962—. Served to 1st lt. U.S. Army, 1943-45. Decorated Purple Heart. Fellow Am. Coll. trial Lawyers (state chmn. 1981-83), Am. Coll. Trial Lawyers (regent 1983—); mem. ABA, Calif. Bar Assn., San Francisco Bar Assn. Republican. Episcopalian. Clubs: St. Francis Yacht (San Francisco), Merchants Exchange (San Francisco). Antitrust, Federal civil litigation, State civil litigation. Home: 12 Woodside Way PO Box 1344 Ross CA 94957 Office: Brobeck Phleger & Harrison Spear St Tower San Francisco CA 94105

HANGER, WILLIAM JOSEPH, lawyer; b. Louisville, Mar. 18, 1943; s. Jesse Morris and Georgia Lee (Clifford) H.; m. Leilani Ella Kenney, Aug. 29, 1964; children: Amy, Jesse. BS in Bus., Ind. U., 1965; JD, U. Louisville, 1968. Bar: Ind. 1968, U.S. Dist. Ct. (so. dist.) Ind. 1968. Ptnr. Hanger & Allen, Clarksville, Ind., 1968-77, Hanger, Engebretson & Mayer, Clarksville, 1977-87, Hanger, Engebretson, Mayer & Vogt, Clarksville, 1987—; bd. dirs. United Bank of Ind., Clarksville. Counsel Clark County Community Action, Jeffersonville, Ind, 1969; pres. Clark County Heart Assn., Jeffersonville, 1971-74; commr. Clark County Air Bd., Jeffersonville, 1983—. Mem. Ind. Bar Assn., Clark County Bar Assn. Republican. Roman Catholic. Avocations: boating, golf. Contracts commercial, Family and matrimonial, Real property. Office: Hanger Engebretson et al 501 Eastern Blvd Clarksville IN 47130

HANGLEY, WILLIAM THOMAS, lawyer; b. Long Beach, N.Y., Mar. 11, 1941; s. Charles Augustus and Faustine Charmillot Hangley; m. Mary Dupree Hangley, July 24, 1965; children—Michele Dupree, William Thomas, Katherine Charmillot. B.S. in Music, SUNY-Coll. at Fredonia, 1963; J.D. cum laude, U. Pa., 1966. Bar: Pa. 1966, U.S. Ct. Appeals (3d cir.) 1966, U.S. Dist. Ct. (ea. dist.) Pa. 1966. Assoc. Schnader, Harrison, Segal & Lewis, Phila., 1966-69; mem., pres. Hangley Connolly Epstein Chicco Foxman & Ewing (fomerly Goodman & Ewing), Phila, 1969—; dir. Pub. Interest Law Ctr. Phila. Mem. ACLU; dir. Ams. for Democratic Action, 1972-81. Mem. ABA, Pa. Bar Assn. (corp. and litigation coms., securities and antitrust subcoms.), Phila. Bar Assn., Order of Coif. Roman Catholic. Club: Racquet (Phila.). Contbr. articles to profl. publs. Federal civil litigation, Securities. Office: Hangley Connolly Et Al 1429 Walnut St Philadelphia PA 19102

HANIG, LYNN, lawyer; b. N.Y.C., Nov. 23, 1946; d. Philip and Florence (Lerner) Tropper; m. Joel Dennis Hanig, July 25, 1971; children: Sara Elizabeth, Matthew Adam. BA, Russell Sage Coll., 1967; JD, Boston U., 1971. Bar: N.Y. 1972, U.S. Dist. Ct. (so. and ea. dists.) N.Y. 1975, U.S. Supreme Ct. 1978. Atty. Legal Aid Soc., N.Y.C., 1971-73; sole practice Poughkeepsie, N.Y., 1974—; instr. paralegal program NYU, 1974; legal cons. Welfare Research, Inc., Troy, N.Y., 1977-78; atty. Dept. Social Services, Dutchess County, N.Y., 1976-86. Mem. N.Y. State Bar Assn., N.Y. State Women's Bar Assn., Mid-Hudson Women's Bar Assn. (corr. sec. 1983-84, judiciary com. 1982), Dutchess County Bar Assn. (chairperson judiciary com. 1986-87, jud. legal com. 1986-87). Lodge: B'nai B'rith (Women's club). Avocations: riding, reading, gardening. Family and matrimonial, General practice.

HANINGTON, PAULA KAY, lawyer; b. Colquitt, Ga., May 20, 1956; s. Buford Lavon and India R. (Lofton) Taylor; m. John Foster Hanington, May 3, 1986. BA cum laude, Valdosta State Coll., 1978; JD, U. Ga., 1981. Bar: Ga., U.S. Dist. Ct. (mid. dist.) Ga., 1983, U.S. Ct. Appeals (11th cir.), 1983. Assoc. Law Offices of John H. Hayes, Albany, Ga., 1982-84, Gilberg & Kraselsky, Albany, 1984-85; sole practice Albany, 1985—; pub. defender City of Albany, 1984—; spl. asst. atty. gen. Ga. Atty. Gen.'s Office, 1986—. Mem. ABA, Ga. Bar Assn., Dougherty County Bar Assn. (lectr. 1983—), Assn. Trial Lawyers Am., Assn. Ga. Trial Lawyers, Soc. Outstanding Youmng Women Am., Women in Network. Avocations: horseback riding, gourmet cooking, boating. Juvenile, Criminal, Family and matrimonial. Office: 505 N Jackson St Albany GA 31701

HANKIN, MITCHELL ROBERT, lawyer; b. Phila., May 16, 1949; s. Samuel and Harriet (Cohen) H. BA, Trinity Coll., Hartford, Conn., 1971; JD, Columbia U., 1974. Bar: Pa. 1974, U.S. Dist. Ct. (ea. dist.) Pa. 1975, U.S. Ct. Appeals (3d cir.) 1975. Assoc. Blank, Romeklaus, Comisky, Phila., 1974-75; asst. U.S. atty. U.S. Atty.'s Office, Phila., 1975-76; ptnr. Hankin Enterprises, Willow Grove, Pa., 1976—; bd. dirs. Bank of Old York, Bank of King of Prussia (Pa.), Royal Bank of Pa. Mem. ABA, Pa. Bar Assn., Montgomery County Bar Assn., Phila. Bar Assn., Phi Beta Kappa. State civil litigation, Contracts commercial, Real property. Home: 22 Latham Park Melrose Park PA 19126

HANKINS, GALE WILLIAM, lawyer; b. Mobridge, S.D., Dec. 15, 1955; s. Gale C. and Joyce (Spiry) H.; m. Jo Ellen Hensley, Nov. 25, 1983; children: Megan C., Jonathan C., William M. BA, U. Mo., 1978; JD, U. Kans., 1981. Bar: Kans. 1982, U.S. Ct. Appeals (10th cir.), 1982. Sole practice Spring Hill, Kans., 1982—; mgr. adminstrn. Am. Carriers Inc., Overland Park, Kans., 1986—. V.p. Spring Hill Community Arts Counsel, 1984. Mem. ABA, Kans. Bar Assn., Assn. Trial Lawyers Am., Kans. Trial Lawyers Assn., Spring Hill Jaycees. Lutheran. Lodge: Ruitans (bd. dirs. Spring Hill 1986, v.p. 1987). Avocation: sports. Pension, profit-sharing, and employee benefits, General practice, Real property. Home: 401 N Webster PO Box 96 Spring Hill KS 66083 Office: Am Carriers Inc 9393 W 110th St Overland Park KS 66210

HANKINS, MITCHELL DALE, lawyer; b. Anahuac, Tex., Jan. 11, 1957; s. Cecil Wayne and Joyce (Deviller) H.; m. Karla Lynn Babcock, Aug. 12, 1978; children: Katherine Michelle, Mary Elizabeth. BA cum laude, Southwestern U., 1978; JD, U. Tex., 1981. Bar: Tex. 1981, U.S. Dist. Ct (no. dist.) Tex., 1981, U.S. Ct. Appeals (5th cir.), 1985. Assoc. Carr, Evans, Fouts & Hunt, Lubbock, Tex., 1981-84, Curry, Curry & Robinson, Lubbock, 1984-86; sole practice Lubbock, 1986—. Bd. dirs. Leadership Lubbock, 1986, Am. Heart Assn., Lubbock, 1986. Mem. Bar Assn. Tex., Lubbock County Bar Assn., Tex. Assn. Def. Counsel, Lubbock County Young Lawyers. Methodist. Lodge: Rotary (bd. dirs. 1986). State civil litigation, Personal injury, Insurance. Home: 4309 94th St Lubbock TX 79423 Office: Box 53572 Lubbock TX 79453

HANKINS, TIMOTHY HOWARD, lawyer; b. Tazewell, Va., Jan. 25, 1956; s. Ralph Arnold and Phyllis Ann (Belcher) H.; m. Debra Lynn, Sept. 5, 1981; children: Tamra Lynn, Amanda Rae. BS in Bus., Va. Commonwealth U., 1978; JD, U. Richmond, 1981. Bar: Va. 1981. Sole practice Newport News, 1981—. Counsel Gosnold Canal Com., Hampton, Va., 1986, Langley Sch., Hampton, 1986. Mem. ABA, Va. Bar Assn., Newport News Bar Assn., Va. Trial Lawyers Assn., Assn. Trial Lawyers Am. Republican. Baptist. Personal injury, Criminal, Family and matrimonial. Home: 22 W Riverpoint Dr Hampton VA 23669 Office: 306 Main St Newport News VA 23601

HANKS, MAJA KRISTIN, lawyer; b. San Francisco, Nov. 7, 1950; s. Sigrid Felicia (Seppala) Hanks. BA, Calif. Poly. U., 1971; postgrad. U. of Uppsala, Sweden, 1972; JD, LaVerne Law Sch., 1977. Bar: Calif. 1977. Assoc. Lewis, Rouda & Lewis, San Francisco, 1977-79; sole practice, San Francisco, 1979—; lectr. for various groups, 1980—; instr. trial advocacy Hastings Coll. of Law, Nat. Coll. of Advocacy. Co-author: Third Party Civil Damages for Rape, 1984. Named one of 10 Most Successful Women Lawyers in U.S. Time mag., 1983. Mem. Calif. Women Lawyers, Queen's Bench, Calif. Lawyers for Individual Freedom, Assn. Trial Lawyers Am., Calif. Trial Lawyers Assn. (bd. govs. 1982—, pres.-elect 1986), San Francisco Trial Lawyers (bd. govs., officer 1978-87). Democrat. Personal injury, State civil litigation. Office: 390 Hayes St Suites 3 and 4 San Francisco CA 94102

HANKS, STEPHEN GRANT, lawyer; b. Rexburg, Idaho, June 7, 1950; s. Grant E. and Elaine (Stephens) H.; m. Debra Joan Dyrr, Aug. 6, 1975; children: Adrianne, Brandon, Tiffany. BS, Brigham Young U., 1974; MBA, U. Utah, 1975; JD, U. Idaho, 1978. Bar: Idaho 1978, U.S. Dist. Ct. Idaho 1978. Counsel Morrison-Knudsen Co., Inc., Boise, Idaho, 1978-82, asst. gen. counsel, 1982-85; asst. gen. counsel Morrison Knudsen Corp., Boise, 1985-86, assoc. gen. counsel, 1986—; chmn. Idaho Corp. Takeover Law Com., Boise, 1985-86. Mem. ABA, Fed. Bar Assn., Am. Corp. Counsel Assn., Am. Inst. CPA's, Idaho Soc. CPA's. General corporate, Construction, Securities. Home: 3130 Terra Dr Boise ID 83709 Office: Morrison Knudsen Corp PO Box 73 Boise ID 83707

HANLEY, DANIEL E., lawyer; b. Palo Alto, Calif., Aug. 25, 1945; s. Lydon J. and Annette Hanley; m. Judith A. Hanley, Oct. 28, 1972; children: Brian C., Sean A. BA, U. Santa Clara, 1967, MBA, 1969, JD, 1974. Bar: Calif. 1974, U.S. Supreme Ct. 1978. Corp. counsel AMI, Inc., Sunnyvale, Calif., 1974; sole practice San Jose, Calif., 1975—. Served to sgt. USMC, 1969-75. Republican. State civil litigation, Federal civil litigation, Estate planning. Office: Mariani & Hanley 1091 Lincoln Ave San Jose CA 95125

HANLEY, DAVID BURRIS, lawyer; b. Balt., May 18, 1954; s. N. Burris and Magaret Lureta (Cox) H. BA, Johns Hopkins U., 1976; JD, U. Balt., 1979. Bar: Md. 1979; CPA Md. Med. coder Johns Hopkins Sch. of Hygiene, Balt., 1976-80; contracts mgmt. rep. Westinghouse Electric Corp., Balt., 1980-85, div. contracts advisor, 1985—, (of counsel), 1984-85. Mem. ABA, Md. Bar Assn., Westinghouse Jaycees (of counsel). Democrat. Methodist. Government contracts and claims, Personal income taxation, Probate. Home: 1719 Hartsdale Rd Baltimore MD 21239

HANLEY, ROBERT FRANCIS, lawyer, educator; b. Spokane, Wash., June 26, 1924; s. Richard E. and Ada E. (St. Peter) H.; m. Margaret Lungren, June 12, 1947 (div.); children: Kathleen Hanley Creore, Marcia Hanley Hoover, Elizabeth; m. Joan McLaughlin, Mar. 26, 1982. BS, Northwestern U., 1947, JD, 1950. Bar: Ill. 1950, Colo. 1983. Asst. atty. gen. State Ill., Chgo., 1952-55; ptnr. Isham Lincoln & Beale, Chgo., 1959-68, Jenner & Block, Chgo., 1968-82, Morrison & Foerster, Denver, 1982—; mem. faculty Northwestern U., Chgo., 1960-82, U. Colo., 1986—. Contbr. articles to profl. jours. Served to lt. col. USMC, 1942-64. Fellow Am. Coll. Trial Lawyers, Internat. Soc. Barristers; mem. Nat. Inst. Trial Advocacy (chmn. bd. 1981-82), ABA (chmn. sect. litigation 1975-76, ho. of dels. 1977—; Ali Francis Rawle award 1986). Democrat. Clubs: University (Denver); Saddle and Cycle (Chgo.). Federal civil litigation, Antitrust, State civil litigation. Home: 2552 E Alameda #41 Denver CO 80209 Office: Morrison & Foerster 1670 Broadway Suite 3100 Denver CO 80202

HANLEY, ROBERT LEE, JR., lawyer; b. Balt., May 22, 1956; s. Robert Lee Sr. and Bernadette Marie (Gahan) H.; m. Kathleen Michelle Riley, June 16, 1979; 1 child, Zachary Andrew. BS magna cum laude, Towson State U., 1978; JD with honor, U. Md., 1982. Bar: Md. 1982, U.S. Dist. Ct. Md. 1983. Assoc. Nolan, Plumhoff & Williams, Towson, Md., 1982-86, ptnr., 1987—. Coach Parkville Recreation Lacrosse, Balt., 1982—. Mem. ABA, Md. Bar Assn., Balt. County Bar Assn., Assn. Trial Lawyers Am., Md. Trial Lawyers Assn., Soc. Friendly Sons St. Patrick. Republican. Episcopalian. Clubs: Advocate (Towson); Latshaw Lacrosse (Balt.) (pres., bd. dirs. 1983—). Personal injury, State civil litigation, Federal civil litigation. Home: 8651 Tower Bridge Way Lutherville MD 21093 Office: Nolan Plumhoff & Williams 204 W Pennsylvania Ave Towson MD 21204

HANLEY, THOMAS FRANCIS, III, lawyer; b. Santa Monica, Calif., Oct. 30, 1951; s. Thomas F. Jr. and Beverly Greene (Goodrich) H.; m. Susan Laurie Glasser, July 20, 1974; children: Kristen, Sean, Erin. BBA, Loyola U., Los Angeles, 1974; JD cum laude, Southwestern U., 1978. Bar: Calif. 1979, U.S. Dist. Ct. (cen. dist.) Calif. 1979. Assoc. Thorpe, Sullivan, Workman & Thorpe, Los Angeles, 1979-84, Jones, Day, Reavis & Pogue, Los Angeles, 1984—. Editor Southwestern U. Law Rev., 1978; asst. editor Constitutional Government in America, 1980. Chmn. Douglas A. Salem Meml. Scholarship fund Southwestern U., 1982, 85-86. Mem. ABA, Los Angeles County Bar Assn. Democrat. Roman Catholic. Club: Los Angeles Athletic. Real property, General corporate, Construction. Home: 1650 Braeburn Rd Altadena CA 91001 Office: Jones Day Reavis & Pogue 355 S Grand Ave Suite 3000 Los Angeles CA 90071

HANNA, JOHN PAUL, lawyer, writer; b. N.Y.C., July 12, 1932; s. Paul Robert and Jean (Shuman) H. BA, Stanford U., 1954, JD, 1959. Bar: Calif. 1960. Ptnr. Hanna & Wagner, Palo Alto, Calif., 1960-78; sole practice Palo Alto, 1978—; lectr. in law Stanford U., 1983. Author: Teenagers and the Law, 1967, The Complete Layman's Guide to the Law, 1975, The California Condominium Handbook, 1976, Residential and Commercial Common Interest Law & Practice, 1986. Trustee Castilleja Sch., Palo Alto, 1974—. Served to 1st lt. U.S. Army, 1954-56. Named One of Outstanding Young Men of Calif., U.S. Jaycees, 1967. Mem. ABA, Calif. Bar Assn. (lectr. real property sect.). Club: Menlo Circus (Atherton, Calif.). Lodge: Elks. Real property. Office: 525 University Ave Palo Alto CA 94301

HANNA, JOSEPH JOHN, JR., lawyer; b. Portland, Oreg., Aug. 14, 1938; s. Joseph John Sr. and Amelia (Rask) H.; m. Judith K. Grischaw. BBA, U. Portland, 1960; JD, Georgetown U., 1963; LLM in Taxation, NYU, 1964. Bar: Oreg. 1963. Ptnr. Hanna, Urbigkeit, Jensen, Goyak & O'Connell, P.C., Portland, 1987—; adj. prof. law in fed. taxation Northwestern Sch. Law, Portland, 1975—. Author: Contemporary Trust and Will Forms, 1982. Judge protem Oreg. Tax Ct. 1977—; spl. asst. atty. gen. State of Oreg., 1979—. Fellow Am. Coll. Probate Counsel (state chmn. 1981-85, bd. regents 1986—); mem. Oreg. Bar Assn. (chmn. taxation sect. 1983), Portland Estate Planning Council (past chmn.), Internat. Bar Assn. Corporate taxation, Estate taxation, Personal income taxation. Office: Hanna Urbigkeit Jensen et al 1211 SW Fifth Ave Portland OR 97204-3797

HANNA, KATHERINE MERRITT, lawyer; b. Keene, N.H., Sept. 5, 1953; d. George R. and Shirley (Garfield) H.; m. R. Shep Melnick, Jan. 24, 1981. BA, Mt. Holyoke Coll., 1975; JD, Boston Coll., 1979. Bar: N.H. 1979, U.S. Dist. Ct. N.H. 1979, U.S. Ct. Appeals (1st cir.) 1982. Legis. asst. U.S. Senate, Washington, 1975-77; law clk. to presiding justice U.S. Dist. Ct. of N.H., Concord, 1979-81; assoc. Wadleigh Law Firm, Manchester, N.H., 1981-85; ptnr. Castaldo, Hanna & Malmberg, Concord, 1985—; incorporator N.H. Charitable Fund, Trustee, Concord, 1982—, Robert Frost Farm, Derry, N.H., 1982—. Del. Dem. Nat. Conv., 1972, 76, 84, N.H. Constitution Conv., 1974; rep. N.H. House Reps., 1975-77; legal counsel N.H. Dems., 1984-86. Mem. N.H. Bar Assn. (com. cooperation with cts. 1984—). Federal civil litigation, State civil litigation, Construction. Office: Castaldo Hanna & Malmberg 14 South St Concord NH 03301

HANNA, MARTIN SHAD, lawyer; b. Bowling Green, Ohio, Aug. 4, 1940; s. Martin Lester and Julia Loyal (Moor) H.; m. Sharon Ann Higgins, Feb. 10, 1969; children—Jennifer Lynn, Jonathan Moor, Katharine Anne. Student, Bowling Green State U.; B.S., Purdue U., 1962; J.D., Am. U., 1965. Bar: Ohio 1965, D.C. 1967, U.S. Supreme Ct. 1969. Ptnr. Hanna, Middleton & Roebke, 1965-70; ptnr. Hanna & Hanna, Bowling Green, 1971—; spl. counsel for atty. gen. Ohio, 1969-71, 82-85, Ohio Bd. Regents, 1974; instr. Bowling Green State U., 1970, Ohio Div. Vocat. Edn., 1970—, Ohio Peace Officer Tng. Council, 1968; legal adviser NW Ohio Vol. Firemen's Assn., 1970—. Contbr. articles to profl. publs. Elder, lay minister Presbyterian Ch.; state chmn. Ohio League Young Republican Clubs, 1972-73; nat. vice chmn. Young Rep. Nat. Fedn., 1973-75, counselor to chmn., 1975-77; vice chmn. Wood County Rep. Exec. Com., Ohio, 1972-80, precinct committeeman, 1968-80; trustee Bowling Green State U., 1976-86; mem. Ohio State Fire Commn., 1979—. Recipient George Washington honor medal award Freedoms Found. at Valley Forge, 1969, award of merit Ohio Legal Ctr. Inst., 1973, Robert A. Taft Disting. Service award, 1974, James A. Rhodes Leadership award, 1975; named one of 10 Outstanding Young Men, Ohio Jaycees, 1968. Mem. ABA, D.C. Bar Assn., Ohio Bar Assn., Northwest Ohio Bar Assn., Wood County Bar Assn., Toledo Bar Assn., Am. Trauma Soc. (trauma and law com.), Phi Delta Phi, Pi Kappa Delta, Omicron Delta Kappa. State civil litigation, Criminal, Personal injury. Home: 506 Knollwood Dr Bowling Green OH 43402 Office: 700 N Main St Bowling Green OH 43402

HANNA, RICHARD WHITMAN, lawyer, consultant; b. Bethel, Conn., Apr. 21, 1930; s. William and Elaine H.; m. Rosella Ross, Mar. 5, 1955 (div. 1968); children: William, Katherine, Susan. BA, Conn. U., 1950, JD, 1953. Bar: Conn. 1953. Ptnr. Wanderer, Hanna & Talarico, Danbury, Conn., 1957—; corporator Union Savings Bank, Danbury, 1968—. Rep. Conn. State Legisl., 1960; bd. dirs. Danbury Cemetery Assn., 1960—; bd. dirs., sec. Found. for Community Encouragement, Knoxville, Tenn., 1984—, Neustadt Mus. Tiffauv Art, N.Y.C., 1985—. Served to capt. USAF, 1954-57. Mem. ABA, Conn. Bar Assn., Danbury Bar Assn. Clubs: Danbury, Ridgewood Country (Danbury). Avocation: duplicate bridge. Home: 6 Juniper Ridge Dr Danbury CT 06811 Office: 142 Deer Hill Ave Danbury CT 06810

HANNA, ROBERT CECIL, lawyer, construction company executive; b. Albuquerque, July 28, 1937; s. Samuel Gray and Orvetta (Cecil) H.; B.A., U. N.Mex., 1959, J.D., 1962. Admitted to N.Mex. bar, 1962; practiced in Albuquerque, 1962-70, 72—; organizer, dep. dir. Micronesian Legal Services Corp., Trust Ter. Pacific Islands, 1970-71; practiced in Hilo; Hawaii, 1974; partner Cotter, Atkinson, Kelsey & Hanna, Ortega, Snead, Dixon & Hanna, Albuquerque, 1975-77; owner, pres., prin. Robert C. Hanna & Assocs., Albuquerque, 1978-80; pres. Sedco Internat. USA, Inc., Albuquerque, 1977-79, Suncastle Builders, Inc., Albuquerque, 1978—; pres. Am. Legal Consortium, 1984—; N.Mex. Real Estate Consortium Ltd., 1986—; mem. Bd. Bar Commrs., Trust Ter. Pacific Islands, 1971-72. Recipient award Rocky Mountain Mineral Law Found., 1962; Public Service award Micronesian Legal Services Corp. Bd. Dirs., 1972. Mem. Hawaii Bar Assn., N.Mex. Bar Assn., Albuquerque Bar Assn. Real property, Entertainment, Private international. Home: 310 Rio Grande Blvd SW Albuquerque NM 87104 Office: Am Legal Consortium 1840 Lomas Blvd NE Albuquerque NM 87106 also: 150 Lahainaluna Rd Lahaina Maui HI 96761

HANNAN, EDWIN YORK, lawyer; b. Grenada, Miss., Apr. 15, 1958; s. William Owen Roberts Jr. and Lillian Perry (York) H.; m. Cindy Leigh Bloodworth, May 21, 1978; children: Abigail Leigh, Kimberly Claire. BPA magna cum laude, U. Miss., 1979, JD, 1982. Bar: Miss. 1982, La. 1982, U.S. Dist. Ct. (no. dist.) Miss. 1982, U.S. Dist. Ct. (ea. dist.) La. 1982, U.S. Ct. Appeals (5th cir.) 1982, U.S. Dist. Ct. (so. dist.) Miss. 1983, U.S. Dist. Ct. (we. Dist.) La. 1985. Assoc. McCalla, Thompson, Pyburn & Ridley, New Orleans, 1982-83; assoc. Satterfield & Allred, Jackson, Miss., 1983-86, ptnr., 1987—. Named one of Outstanding Young Men in Am., 1985. Mem. ABA (litigation sect.), Miss. Bar Assn., La. Bar Assn., Hinds County Bar Assn., Miss. Def. Lawyers Assn., Jackson Young Lawyers Assn. Roman Catholic.

Lodge: Kiwanis. Avocations: sports, reading. Federal civil litigation, State civil litigation, Insurance. Home: 230 Meadowlane Madison MS 39110 Office: Satterfield & Allred PO Drawer 1120 Jackson MS 39215-1120

HANNAWALT, WILLIS DALE, lawyer; b. Delaware, Ohio, Apr. 28, 1928; s. Othello Erwin and Dorothy (Sherbourne) H.; m. Vivian Nina Chaya, Sept. 8, 1950; children: Nina Jo, James Frederick, Rachel Beth. A.B., U. Chgo., 1950, J.D., 1954. Bar: Calif. 1955, U.S. Supreme Ct. 1970. Teaching fellow Stanford U., Palo ALto, Calif., 1954-55; assoc. Pillsbury, Madison & Sutro, San Francisco, 1955-65, ptnr., 1965—; mem. faculty Golden Gate Law Sch., San Francisco, 1958-68; cons. Hudson Inst., Tarrytown, N.Y., 1964. Chmn. State Bar Jour. Com., 1964. Served with USCG, 1946-47, 51-53. Fellow ABA; mem. Calif. Bar Assn., San Francisco Lawyer's Club. Democrat. Club: Olympic (San Francisco). Office: Pillsbury Madison & Sutro 225 Bush St San Francisco CA 94104

HANNON, GREGORY JOHN, lawyer, b. N.Y.C., July 26, 1953; s. Gerard John and Ann Veronica (Mitchell) H.; m. Linda Denyse Tausz, Aug. 20, 1977. B.S., Mt. St. Mary's Coll., 1975; J.D., Temple U., 1978. Bar: Pa. 1978, U.S. Dist. Ct. (ea. dist.) Pa. 1979, U.S. Dist. Ct. (mid. dist.) Pa. 1983, U.S. Ct. Appeals (3rd cir.) 1984; cert. U.S. fed. ct. arbitrator, 1985, U.S. Supreme Ct. 1986. Law clk. to presiding justice, Flemington, N.J., 1978-79; ptnr. Brobyn & Forceno, Phila., 1979—. Asst. scoutmaster Troup 114, Boy Scouts Am., 1977—. Mem. Assn. Trial Lawyers Am., Pa. Bar Assn., Phila. Bar Assn., Phila. Trial Lawyers Assn., Pa. Trial Lawyers Assn. Roman Catholic. Personal injury. Office: Brobyn Forceno & Arangio 1000 The Phila Bourse Philadelphia PA 19106

HANNON, TIMOTHY PATRICK, lawyer; b. Culver City, Calif., Nov. 29, 1948; s. Justin Aloysius and Ann Elizabeth (Ford) H.; m. Patricia Ann Hanson, May 1, 1976; children—Sean Patrick, James Patrick. Student U. Vienna, 1968-69; B.A., U. Santa Clara, 1970, J.D. cum laude, 1974. Bar: Calif. 1974, U.S. Dist. Ct. (no. dist.) Calif. 1974, U.S. Dist. Ct. (so. and ea. dists.) Calif. 1978, U.S. Ct. Appeals (9th cir.) 1978, Ct. Mil. Appeals, 1979, D.C. 1981, U.S. Tax Ct. 1983, U.S. Ct. Claims, 1983; cert. trial and def. lawyer; Uniform Code Mil. Justice. Mem. law office N. Perry Moerdyke, Jr., Palo Alto, Calif., 1975-81; ptnr. Moerdyke & Hannon, Palo Alto, Calif., 1982-84, Atwood, Hurst, Knox & Anderson, 1984-86; sole practice Campbell, Calif., 1986—; instr. San Jose State U., 1985—; instr. extension courses U. Calif., Santa Cruz, 1982-83; arbitrator Santa Clara County Superior Ct., Santa Clara County Mcpl. Ct.; judge pro tem Santa Clara County Mcpl. Ct. Chmn., Menlo Park Housing Commn., 1979-81, v.p., 1983—. Served with Army N.G., 1970-76. Mem. ABA, Santa Clara County Bar Assn., U. Santa Clara Law Alumni Assn. (bd. dirs. 1980-81, sec. 1981-83, v.p. 1983-85, pres. 1985—). Roman Catholic. Real property. Home: 806 Buckwood Ct San Jose CA 95120 Office: 1901 S Bascom Ave Suite 1440 Campbell CA 95008

HANRAHAN, KATHLEEN SUSAN, lawyer; b. Tallahassee, Mar. 5, 1957; s. Edward Brackett and Dorothy Helen (Breen) H.; m. Richard Burton Capek Jr., Sept. 5, 1981. BA cum laude, Colo. Coll., 1979; JD, U. Denver, 1982. Bar: Colo. 1982, U.S. Dist. Ct. Colo. 1983, U.S. Ct. Appeals (10th cir.) 1983. Assoc. Richard E. Mishkin, P.C., Denver, 1983-84; bankruptcy trustee U.S. Dept. Justice, Denver, 1984—; assoc. Cortez & Friedman, P.C., Englewood, Colo., 1985—. Mem. ABA, Colo. Bar Assn., Colo. Women's Bar Assn., Denver Bar Assn. (pub. interest com. young lawyers sect.). Republican. Presbyterian. Avocations: skiing, tennis, oil painting. Banking, General corporate, Real property. Office: Cortez & Friedman PC 5251 DTC Pkwy #700 Denver CO 80111

HANS, PETER E., lawyer; b. Madison, Wis., Aug. 31, 1954; s. Gunard E. and Irene M. Hans; m. Mary C. Hans, Aug. 26, 1978; children: Laura, Joel. BA, U. Wis., 1975, MA, 1977, JD, 1980. Bar: Wis. 1980, Minn. 1980, U.S. Dist. Ct. (we. dist.) Wis. 1980, U.S. Dist. Ct. Minn. 1981, U.S. Ct. Appeals (7th cir.) 1983. Assoc. Faegre & Benson, Mpls., 1980-81, Boardman, Suhr, Curry & Field, Madison, 1981-86; assoc. counsel The Rural Cos., Madison, 1986—. Note and comment editor U. Wis. Law Rev., 1979-80. Firefighter Shorewood Fire Dept., Wis.; mem. adminstrv. bd. 1st United Meth. Ch., Madison. Mem. ABA, Wis. Bar Assn., Dane County Bar Assn. State civil litigation, Insurance, Personal injury. Home: 2909 Columbia Rd Madison WI 53705 Office: The Rural Cos PO Box 5555 Madison WI 53705

HANSBURY, STEPHAN CHARLES, lawyer; b. Mt. Holly, N.J., Nov. 3, 1946; s. Charles Clark and Kathryn Irene (Meyer) H.; m. Donna Jean Leach, Nov. 6, 1971; children: Elizabeth Kathryn, Jillian Judith, Stephanie Clark. BA, Allegheny Coll., 1968; MBA, Fairleigh Dickinson U., 1973; JD, Seton Hall U., 1977. Bar: N.J. 1977, U.S. Dist. Ct. (no. dist.) N.J. 1977, U.S. Supreme Ct. 1982. Dir. spl. programs Bloomfield (N.J.) Coll., 1968-71; dir. fin. aid Monmouth Coll., West Long Beach, N.J., 1971-72; asst. adminstr. Morris View, Morris Plains, N.J., 1972-78; assoc. Harper, Hansbury & Martin, Morris Plains, 1978—; mem., gen. counsel Cheshire Home, Florham Park, N.J., 1978—, Ciba-Geigy Corp., Summit, N.J., 1980—. Aide Arthur Albohn, Morristown, N.J., 1980-83. Mem. ABA, N.J. Bar Assn., Morris County Bar Assn., Am. Trial Lawyers Assn. Republican. Episcopalian. Clubs: Rockaway River Country Club (Denville, N.J.), Kellogg (Morristown,). Lodge: Rotary (bd. dirs. Morris Plains 1981-83). Avocations: tennis, golf, reading. State civil litigation, Family and matrimonial, Real property. Home: Rt 3 Box 160 Twin Brooks Trail Chester NJ 07930 Office: Hansbury Martin & Knapp 736 Speedwell Ave PO Box 198 Morris Plains NJ 07930

HANSELL, EDGAR FRANK, lawyer; b. Leon, Iowa, Oct. 12, 1937; s. Edgar Noble and Celestia Delphine (Skinner) H.; m. Phyllis Wray Silvey, June 24, 1961; children—John Joseph, Jordan Burke. A.A., Graceland Coll., 1957; B.B.A., U. Iowa, 1959, J.D., 1961. Bar: Iowa 1961. Mem. Nyemaster, Goode, McLaughlin, Emery & O'Brien, P.C., Des Moines, 1964—; ptnr. Nyemaster, Goode, McLaughlin, Emery & O'Brien, P.C., 1968—; bd. dirs. Britt Tech. Corp., The Vernon Co. Mem. editorial adv. bd. Jour. Corp. Law, 1985—. Bd. dirs. Des Moines Child Guidance Ctr., 1972-78, 81—, pres., 1977-78; bd. dirs. Child Guidance Found., 1983—; trustee Iowa Law Sch. Found., 1975—, pres., 1983—; bd. dirs. Des Moines Community Playhouse, Inc., 1982—, Iowa Sports Found., 1986—. Served with USAF, 1961-64. Mem. ABA, Iowa Bar Assn. (pres. young lawyers sect. 1971-72, gov. 1971-72, 85—, mem. grievance commn. 1973-78, Merit award young lawyers sect. 1977, chmn. corp. and bus. law com. 1979-85), Polk County Bar Assn. General corporate, Contracts commercial. Home: 4001 John Lynde Rd Des Moines IA 50312 Office: Nyemaster Goode McLaughlin et al Hubbell Bldg Des Moines IA 50309

HANSELL, RONALD STEPHEN, lawyer; b. Lafayette, Ind., Aug. 20, 1948; s. Richard Grant and Regina Agnes (Minnicus) H.; m. Rosemarie Neimeyer, Aug. 21, 1971; 1 child Sarah Neimeyer. BSCE, Purdue U., 1972, MSCE, 1974; JD, Ind. U., Indpls., 1979. Bar: Ind. 1979, U.S. Dist. Ct. (so. dist) Ind. 1979, U.S. Patent Office 1981, U.S. Supreme Ct. 1983; registered profl. engr. Ind., Ohio, Ky. Engr. transp. regional planning commn. Allen County, Lima, Ohio, 1974-75; sr. project engr. RQAW & Assocs., Inc., Indpls., 1975-80; counsel regulatory affairs AMAX Coal Co., Indpls., 1980-83; assoc. Rocap, Rocap, Sceeset & Young, Indpls., 1984, Burris, Burris & Margerum, Indpls., 1985—; chmn. infiltration-inflow and drainage subcom. Combined Sewer Overflow, citizens adv. com. Indpls. Dept. Pub. Works, 1980—. Served with USMC, 1968-70, Vietnam. Mem. ASCE, ABA, Ind. Bar Assn., Indpls. Bar Assn. Republican. Roman Catholic. Avocations: tae kwon do karate, guitar, choral music; registered land surveyor, Ind., Ohio. State civil litigation, Consumer commercial, Patent. Home: Beech Bank 1205 W 64th St Indianapolis IN 46260-4409 Office: Burris Burris & Margerum 5 E Market St Indianapolis IN 46204-3080

HANSEN, CAROL M., judge; b. Oklahoma City, July 3, 1929; d. Albertis and Elizabeth Marie (Cheney) M.; m. Paul N. Hanson, Oct. 20, 1951; children: Elizabeth, Patti, Judith, Mary, Heidi. BA, Oklahoma City, 1950, JD, 1974. Bar: Okla. 1975, U.S. Dist. Ct. (we. dist.) Okla. 1977. Asst. to presiding justice Okla. Supreme Ct., Oklahoma City, 1975-80; marshal Okla. Supreme Ct., 1984-85; mng. atty. Legal Aid of Western Okla., Stillwater, 1980-83; mcpl. judge City of Stillwater, 1983-84; judge Okla. Ct. Appeals, Oklahoma City, 1985—. Mem. Stillwater Dispute Resolution Com.; vol. Hospice; sec. Payne County Linking Agy.; Stillwater League of Women Voters. Mem. ABA, Okla. Bar Assn. (chmn. correctional instn. com. 1983-85, atty. impairment com.), Humane Soc., Stillwater C of C, Phi Delta Phi. Presbyterian. Avocations: tennis, water skiing, snow skiing, reading. Judicial administration, Poverty law. Home: 333 N W 5th 2214 Oklahoma City OK 73102 Office: Oklahoma Ct Appeals 1915 N Stiles Suite 357 Oklahoma City OK 73105

HANSEN, CHRISTOPHER AGNEW, lawyer; b. Yakima, Wash., Dec. 10, 1934; s. Raymond Walter and Christine F.M. (Agnew) H.; m. Sandra Ridgely Pindell, Aug. 4, 1959; Anne Ridgely, Christopher Agnew Jr., Eric Bruce. BS, Cornell U., 1957; JD, U. Md., 1963. Bar: Md. 1963, U.S. Supreme Ct. 1973, U.S. Ct. Appeals (4th cir.) D.C. 1978. Law clk. Cir. Ct. for Balt. County, Towson, Md., 1960-63; assoc. Piper & Marbury, Balt., 1963-74; sole practice Towson, 1974-83; of counsel Casey, Scott & Canfield, Washington, 1982—; ptnr. Constable, Alexander & Skeen, Towson, 1984-86, Parks, Hansen & Ditch, Towson, 1986—. Served to cpl. U.S. Army, 1957-60. Mem. ABA, D.C. Bar, Md. State Bar Assn., Bar Assn. Balt. County, Balt. City Bar Assn., Md. Assn. Def. Trial Counsel, Phi Alpha Delta. Episcopalian. Federal civil litigation, State civil litigation, Insurance. Office: Parks Hansen & Ditch 409 Washington Ave Suite 1012 Towson MD 21204

HANSEN, MAX A., lawyer; b. Dillon, Mont., Apr. 11, 1949; s. Fred A. and Patricia A. (Daugharty) H. BS, Carroll Coll., 1971; JD, U. San Diego, 1976. Bar: Mont. 1976, Calif. 1977, U.S. Dist. Ct. Mont. 1981, Utah 1986, U.S. Dist. Ct. Utah 1986. Assoc. W.G. Gilbert, Jr., Dillon, 1976-79; dep. county atty. County of Beaverhead, Mont., 1978-79; sole practice Dillon, 1980—; mem. Supreme Ct. Commn. on Admission to Bar, Helena, Mont., 1985-87. Chmn. City of Dillon Police Commn., 1982—. Mem. ABA, Calif. State Bar Assn., Utah Bar Assn., Mont. Bar Assn. (trustee 1980-87, chmn. bd. dirs. 1986-87, pres.-elect 1987—), Mont. Trial Lawyers Assn., Western Mont. Coll. Found. (vice-chmn. 1985-87), Beaverhead County C. of C. (bd. dirs. 1983—). Lodge: Elks. Avocations: reading, skiing, backpacking, cycling, traveling. General practice, Contracts commercial, Probate. Home: 3725 Flynn Ln Dillon MT 59725 Office: PO Box 1301 Dillon MT 59725

HANSEN, RICHARD KING, lawyer; b. Modesto, Calif., May 28, 1938; s. Robert and Gretchen (King) H.; m. S. Loretta Young, Dec. 31, 1971; 1 dau., Kymberly Joy. B.S. in Bus. and Tech, Oreg. State U, 1961; J.D., U. So. Calif., 1969. Bar: Calif. bar 1971. With mktg./contracts Bendix Corp., North Hollywood, Calif., 1962-68; mgr. contracts Electonic Memories, Inc., Hawthorne, Calif., 1969; atty., contracts Pertec Computer Corp., Los Angeles, 1970-73; sec., gen. counsel Pertec Computer Corp., 1973-81, v.p., 1975-81; of counsel Riordan, Caps, Carbone & McKinzie, P.C., Los Angeles, 1981-82; sole practice Torrance, Calif., 1982—. Mem. Am. Bar Assn., Calif. Bar Assn., Los Angeles County Bar Assn., Phi Alpha Delta, Phi Kappa Tau. Republican. Congregationalist. General corporate, Contracts commercial. Office: 2360 Plaza Del Amo Suite 105 Torrance CA 90501

HANSEN, ROYAL IVORY, lawyer; b. Salt Lake City, Aug. 26, 1948; s. Charles N. and Lois (Ivory) H.; m. Laura Cowley, Aug. 10, 1970; children: Royal II, Elizabeth, Julie, Christine, Allison. BS cum laude, U. Utah, 1972, JD, 1975. Bar: Utah 1975, U.S. Ct. Appeals (D.C. cir.) 1976, D.C. 1977, U.S. Ct. Appeals (10th cir.) 1977, U.S. Ct. Appeals (9th cir.) 1979, U.S. Supreme Ct. 1979. Field rep. U.S. Ho. of Reps., Washington, 1971-72; law clk. Office of Utah Atty. Gen., Salt Lake City, 1973-75; atty., law clk. D.C. Ct. Appeals, 1975-76; assoc. Moyle & Draper P.C., Salt Lake City, 1976-80, ptnr., 1980—; advisor Salt Lake City Ct. Misdemeants, Salt Lake City, 1976-78. Minister Mormon Ch., Reading, Eng., 1967-69; chmn. voting dist., county and state del. Utah Reps., Salt Lake County, 1972-82; coach Youth soccer, baseball and basketball, Salt Lake City, 1979—; unit commr. Boy Scouts Am., 1985—. Presdl. Merit scholar U. Utah, 1974, Merlin J. Norton scholar, 1975. Mem. ABA, Fed. Bar Assn. (chmn. pub. lands 1981), Utah Bar Assn. (chmn. law day 1977-79, asst. editor jour. 1973-75), D.C. Bar Assn., Salt Lake County Bar Assn., Assn. Trial Lawyers Am. (assoc.), Def. Research Inst., Skull and Bones, Am. Judicature Soc. Club: Salt Lake Swimming and Tennis. Lodge: Rotary. Federal civil litigation, State civil litigation, Insurance. Office: Moyle & Draper PC 600 Deseret Plaza Salt Lake City UT 84111-1901

HANSHAW, A. ALAN, lawyer; b. Kankakee, Ill., June 23, 1926; s. Armand E. and Deborah Bertine (Sanborn) H.; m. Emma H. Hernandez, Sept. 1, 1951; children: Mark A., John W., David M., Deborah L., A. Andrew. Bar: Ariz. 1955, U.S. Dist. Ct. Ariz. 1956, U.S. Supreme Ct. 1964. Law clk. Ariz. Supreme Ct., 1955-56; asst. city atty. City of Tucson, 1956-58; assoc., then ptnr. Godard, Gin, Hanshaw & Gianas, Tucson, 1958-69; gen. counsel U.S. V.I. Corp., 1964-65; sole practice, Tucson, 1969-72; shareholder, bd. dirs. Waterfall, Economidis, Hanshaw & Villamana, P.C., Tucson, 1972—. Pres. United Way of Tucson, 1977; bd. dirs. La Frontera Mental Health Ctr., 1981—, pres., 1983-84. Served with U.S. Mcht. Marine, 1944-46. Mem. Ariz. Bar Assn., State Bar Ariz. (cert. real property specialist), Nat. Health Lawyers Assn. Episcopalian. Clubs: Rotary (Tucson); Mission Bay Yacht (San Diego). General corporate, Health, Real property. Home: 802 N Corinth Ave Tucson AZ 85710 Office: Williams Centre 5210 W Williams Circle Suite 800 Tucson AZ 85711

HANSHER, DAVID ALLEN, lawyer; b. Milw., Mar. 13, 1944; s. Irving L. and Pearl L. (Hiken) H.; m. Adriane S. Rubenstein, Sept. 20, 1970; children—Beth, Bradley, Scott. B.S., U. Wis., 1965, J.D., 1968. Bar: Wis. 1968, U.S. Dist. Ct. (ea. dist.) Wis. 1973, U.S. Ct. Appeals (7th cir.) 1975, U.S. Supreme Ct. 1977. Asst. city atty. City of Milw., 1968-72; ptnr. Deutch, Hansher & Grodsky, Milw., 1972—; ct. commr. Milw. County Circuit Ct., 1978—. Mem. Am. Arbitration Assn. (arbitrator 1975—), Assn. Trial Lawyers Am., Wis. Acad. Trial Lawyers, ABA, Wis. Bar Assn., Milw. Bar Assn., U. Wis. Alumni Assn. State civil litigation, Personal injury, Transportation. Home: 9450 N Fairway Circle Milwaukee WI 53217 Office: Deutch and Hansher 161 W Wisconsin Suite 5170 Milwaukee WI 53203

HANSMANN, HENRY BAETHKE, law educator; b. Highland Park, Ill., Oct. 5, 1945; s. Elwood Hansmann and Louise Frances (Baethke) Hansmann Moore; m. Margaret Williams Ferguson, June 17, 1984. J.D., Yale U., 1974, Ph.D., 1978. Asst. prof. law U. Pa. Law Sch., Phila., 1975-81, assoc. prof. law, econs. and pub. policy, 1981-83; prof. law Yale U., New Haven, 1983—. Contbr. articles to profl. jours. John Simon Guggenheim Found. fellow, 1985-86. Mem. Am. Econ. Assn. Legal education. Home: 7 Burns St New Haven CT 06511 Office: Yale U Law Sch Box 401A Yale Sta New Haven CT 06520

HANSON, ARNOLD PHILIP, JR., lawyer, publishing company executive; b. Boston, Nov. 24, 1949; s. Arnold Philip and Della Ann (Lavernoich) H.; m. Barbara Jean Davis, Oct. 19, 1974; children: Christopher, Stephanie, Jonathan. AB, Dartmouth Coll., 1971; JD, Boston U., 1974; M. in Mgmt., Yale U., 1982. Bar: N.H. 1974, U.S. Dist. Ct. N.H. 1974. Assoc., Bergeron & Hanson, Berlin, N.H., 1974-78, ptnr., 1978-80; teaching asst. Yale U., New Haven, 1980-82; asst. to chmn. Insilco Corp., Meriden, Conn., 1982-83; pub. Taylor Pub., Dallas, 1983—; bd. dirs. Berlin Coop. Bank, 1977-81; cons. in field. Active numerous civic orgns. Mem. ABA, Assn. MBA's, N.H. Bar Assn. (bd. govs. 1979-80), N.H. Trial Lawyers Assn. (bd. govs. 1978-80). Republican. Roman Catholic. General corporate. Home: 1528 Harrington Dr Plano TX 75075 Office: Taylor Pub Co PO Box 597 Dallas TX 79221

HANSON, BRUCE EUGENE, lawyer; b. Lincoln, Nebr., Aug. 25, 1942; s. Lester E. and Gladys (Diessner) H.; m. Peggy Pardun, Dec. 25, 1972. B.A., U. Minn., 1965, J.D., 1966. Bar: Minn. 1966, U.S. Dist. Ct. Minn. 1966, U.S. Tax Ct. 1973, U.S. Ct. Appeals (8th cir.) 1973, U.S. Ct. Appeals (fed. cir.) 1983, U.S. Supreme Ct. 1970. Ptnr., Doherty, Rumble & Butler, St. Paul, 1966—. Mem. Ramsey County Bar Assn., Minn. State Bar Assn., Am. Acad. Hosp. Attys., Minn. Soc. Hosp. Attys. (bd. dirs.), Assn. Trial Lawyers Am. Order of Coif, Phi Delta Phi. Clubs: St. Paul Athletic; North Oaks Golf (Minn.). Health, Federal civil litigation, State civil litigation. Home: 23 Evergreen Rd North Oaks MN 55110 Office: Doherty Rumble & Butler 1500 1st Nat Bank Bldg Saint Paul MN 55101

HANSON, EUGENE NELSON, lawyer, educator; b. Iola, Wis., Sept. 27, 1917; s. Harris Gilbert and Delia (Nelson) H.; m. Katie Lou Craft, June 29, 1950; children: P. Louise (Mrs. Ronald F. Gossard), Jennifer Lou (Mrs. Kyle M. Wilhelm). B.A., Luther Coll., Decorah, Iowa, 1939; M.A., U. Wis., 1940, J.D., 1946; LL.M., U. Mich., 1948; LLD, Ohio No. U., 1985. Bar: Wis. 1946, Ohio 1954. Asst. prof. law Ohio No. U., Ada, 1947-51; asso. prof. Ohio No. U., 1951-54, prof., 1954-75, 76-84, prof. emeritus, 1984—, dean, 1958-73; Fulbright prof. U. Iceland, 1960; distinguished vis. prof. McGeorge Sch. Law, U. of Pacific, 1974-75, prof., 1975-76; judge Hardin County Ct., 1983—. Pres. Village Council, 1960-61; Sec. Nat. Lutheran Campus Ministry, Luth. Ch. Am., 1964-67; mem. exec. bd. Ohio Synod, 1969-71. Recipient Distinguished Service award Luther Coll., 1966. Mem. Am., Ohio bar assns., Order of Coif. Democrat. Legal education, Personal injury, Jurisprudence. Home: 604 Merrie Monte Ln Ada OH 45810

HANSON, FRANK OSCAR, JR., lawyer; b. Salt Lake City, Jan. 24, 1950; s. Frank Oscar Sr. and Frances Odelia (Pitts) H.; m. Billie Kane Joyce, Aug. 12, 1972; children: Frank III, Vince, Rebecca, Lenora. BA, Wake Forest U., 1972; JD, Samford U., 1975. Bar: Ala. 1975, U.S. Ct. Appeals (11th cir.), U.S. Dist. Ct. (no. dist.) Ala. 1976, U.S. Supreme Ct. 1981. Mem. Hall, Parker & Hanson, Birmingham, Ala., 1975-79; assoc. Emond & Vines, Birmingham, 1979-85, ptnr., 1986—; mcpl. ct. judge Springville, Ala., 1976-86, Odenville, Ala., 1976-86, Margaret, Ala., 1976-86, White's Chapel, Ala., 1985-86. Deacon Centercrest Bapt. Ch., Birmingham, 1978-86. Mem. ABA, Assn. Trial Lawyers Am., Ala. Trial Lawyers (bd. govs.), Ala. Bar Assn. Republican. Baptist. Avocations: tennis, handball, carpentry. Federal civil litigation, State civil litigation, Personal injury. Home: 732 Valley Dr Birmingham AL 35206 Office: 1900 Daniel Bldg Birmingham AL 35233

HANSON, FRED B., lawyer; b. Glenview, Ill.; s. August Theodore and Flora Alice (Kays) H.; m. Jane Roberts, Oct. 24, 1934 (dec. Jan. 1971); m. Lucy Merrick, Dec. 10, 1971; children: Linscott, Per, Marta. Student, DePauw U., 1924-26, Northwestern U., 1927-28; LLB, Ill. Inst. Tech., 1932. Bar: Ind. 1925, Ill. 1932, U.S. Dist. Ct. (no. dist.) Ill. 1932. Ptnr. Ross, Berchem & Hanson, Chgo., 1932-34; sole practice Chgo., 1934-37, 52—; atty. Standard Oil Co., Chgo., 1937-46; ptnr. Hanson & Doyle, Chgo., 1946-52; gen. counsel., bd. dirs. various banks and cos. Author: Claim Handling, 1956; contbr. articles to profl. jours. atty. Village of Glenview, 1950-54, judge, 1946-50; trustee Bethany Brethern Hosp., Chgo., 1960-71, Maryhaven, Glenview, 1946-72. Served to lt.comdr. USN, 1943-46, PTO. Mem. ABA, Ill. Bar Assn., Chgo. Bar Assn. Democrat. Clubs: Chgo. Yacht, The Attic; Riverside Country (Menominee, Mich.). Avocations: yachting, fishing. Banking, General corporate, Probate. Office: 1000 Skokie Blvd Willmette IL 60091

HANSON, GARY A., lawyer, legal educator; b. Santa Fe, Sept. 30, 1954; s. Norman A. Hanson and Mary Gene (Moore) Garrison; m. Tracey J. Tannen, Mar. 11, 1982. BS magna cum laude, U. Utah, 1976; JD, Pepperdine U., 1980. Bar: Calif. 1980, U.S. Dist. Ct. (cen. dist.) Calif. 1980, U.S. Ct. Appeals (9th cir.) 1980. Sole practice Westlake Village, Calif., 1980-82; assoc. gen. counsel Pepperdine U., Malibu, Calif., 1982-83, acting gen. counsel, 1983-84, univ. gen. counsel, 1984—; adj. prof. law Pepperdine U., Malibu, 1982—; atty. pro bono San Fernando Valley Christian Sch., Los Angeles, 1982-83. Recipient Pres.'s award San Diego Christian Found., 1984. Mem. ABA, Los Angeles County Bar Assn., Nat. Assn. Coll. and Univ. Attys., Pro Bono Estate Adv. Service. Republican. General corporate, Legal education, College and university law. Office: Office of Gen Counsel Thornton Adminstrv Ctr 24255 Pacific Coast Hwy Malibu CA 90265

HANSON, JEAN ELIZABETH, lawyer; b. Alexandria, Minn., June 28, 1949; d. Carroll Melvin and Alice Clarissa (Frykman) H.; m. H. Barndt Hauptfuhrer, May 15, 1982; children: Catherine Jean, Benjamin Colman (twins). BA, Luther Coll., 1971; JD, U. Minn., 1976. Bar: N.Y. 1977, U.S. Dist. Ct. (so. dist.) 1977. Probation officer Hennepin County, Mpls., 1972-73; law clk. Minn. State Pub. Defender, Mpls., 1975-76; assoc. Fried, Frank, Harris, Shriver & Jacobson, N.Y.C., 1976-83, ptnr., 1983—. Named one of People to Watch Fortune Mag., 1985, Big Deals Savvy Mag., 1986. Mem. ABA, N.Y. State Bar Assn., N.Y. Women's Bar Assn., U. Minn. Law Alumni Assn. Democrat. Lutheran. General corporate, Securities, Mergers and acquisitions. Office: Fried Frank Harris Shriver & Jacobson One New York Plaza New York NY 10004

HANSON, JOHN J., lawyer; b. Aurora, Nebr., Oct. 22, 1922; s. Peter E. and Hazel Marion (Lounsbury) H.; m. Elizabeth Anne Moss, July 1, 1973; children from their previous marriages—Mark, Eric, Gregory. A.B., U. Denver, 1948; LL.B. cum laude, Harvard U., 1951. Bar: N.Y. bar 1952, Calif. bar 1955. Asso. firm Dewey, Ballantine, Bushby, Palmer & Wood, N.Y.C., 1951-54; partner firm Gibson, Dunn & Crutcher, Los Angeles, 1954—; mem. exec. com. Gibson, Dunn & Crutcher, 1978—. Contbr. articles to profl. jours. Trustee Palos Verdes (Calif.) Sch. Dist., 1969-73. Served with U.S. Navy, 1942-45. Fellow Am. Coll. Trial Lawyers; mem. Am. Bar Assn., Los Angeles County Bar Assn. (chmn. antitrust sect. 1979-80). Clubs: Bel Air Country (Los Angeles); Mission Hills Country (Rancho Mirage, Calif.); Fox Acres Country (Red Feather Lakes, Colo.). Home: 953 Linda Flora Dr Los Angeles CA 90049 Office: 333 S Grand Ave Los Angeles CA 90017

HANSON, KENNETH HAMILTON, lawyer; b. Chgo., Sept. 10, 1919; s. Clinton H. and Della (Bonson) H.; student North Park Coll., 1939-40; B.S., Northwestern U., 1943, J.D., 1949; m. Elaine F. Bleck, May 19, 1951; children—Christine E., Karen D., Kenneth Hamilton. Admitted to Ill. bar, 1949; practiced law, Chgo., 1949-53; atty. bus. devel. dept. First Nat. Bank Chgo., 1953-61; trial atty. Antitrust div. U.S. Dept. Justice, Chgo., 1961-83; mem. firm Brace & O'Donnell, Chgo., 1983—. Mem. edit. bd. law review. Served to lt. (j.g.) USNR, 1943-46. Mem. ABA (antitrust, litigation and corp. sects.), Ill. State Bar Assn., 7th Circuit Bar Assn., Am., Fed., Chgo. bar assns.(former chmn. Fed. Civil Procedure com.), Beta Theta Pi, Phi Delta Phi. Republican. Presbyn. Antitrust, Federal civil litigation, Securities. Home: 955 Melody Rd Lake Forest IL 60045 Office: 332 S Michigan Ave Suite 1858 Chicago IL 60604

HANSON, KENT BRYAN, lawyer; b. Litchfield, Minn., Sept. 17, 1954; s. Calvin Bryan and Muriel (Wessman) H.; m. Barbara Jane Elenbaas, Aug. 24, 1974; children: Lindsay Michal, Taylor Jordan, Chase Philip. AA with high honors, Trinity Western Coll., 1974; BA, U. B.C., Vancouver, 1976; JD magna cum laude, U. Minn., 1979. Bar: Minn. 1979, U.S. Dist. Ct. Minn. 1980, U.S. Ct. Appeals (8th cir.) 1980, U.S. Dist. Ct. (we. dist.) Wis. 1983, Wis. 1985. Assoc. Grossman, Karlins, Siegel & Brill, Mpls., 1979-81, Gray, Plant, Mooty, Mooty & Bennett, Mpls., 1981-85; ptnr. Bowman & Brooke, Mpls., 1985—. Dir. Inner City Boys Club; bd. dirs. Cen. Free Ch., Mpls., 1979-81; 12th ward del. Mpls. Dem. Farmer Labor Party Conv., 1982; mem. exec. bd. Cen. Free Ch., Mpls., 1986. Mem. ABA, State Bar Wis., Minn. Def. Lawyers Assn., Minn. State Bar Assn., Hennepin County Bar Assn. Mem. Evang. Free Ch. of Am. Avocations: classical music, tennis. Product liability litigation, Federal civil litigation, State civil litigation. Office: Bowman and Brooke 600 Midwest Plaza W 801 Nicollet Mall Minneapolis MN 55402

HANSON, RONALD WILLIAM, lawyer; b. LaCrosse, Wis., Aug. 3, 1950; s. Orlin Eugene and Irene Agnes (Yeske) H.; m. Sandra Kay Cook, Aug. 21, 1971; 1 child, Alec Evan. B.A. summa cum laude, St. Olaf Coll., 1972; J.D. cum laude, U. Chgo., 1975. Bar: Ill. 1975, U.S. Dist. Ct. (no. dist.) Ill. 1975, U.S. Ct. Appeals (7th cir.) 1978. Assoc. Sidley & Austin, Chgo., 1975-83, ptnr., 1983—; official advisor to Nat. Conf. of Commrs. on Uniform State Laws; lectr. Ill. Inst. Continuing Legal Edn., Springfield, 1979—, Am. Bankruptcy Inst., Washington, 1984—, Banking Law Inst., 1985. Contbr. articles to profl. jours. Mem. ABA, Ill. Bar Assn., Chgo. Bar Assn., Order of Coif, Phi Beta Kappa. Republican. Lutheran. Club: Monroe (Chgo.). Bankruptcy, Federal civil litigation. Home: 664 58th St W Hinsdale IL 60603 Office: Sidley & Austin 1 1st National Plaza Chicago IL 60603

HANSON, STEVEN ALLEN, lawyer; b. Valley City, N.D., Dec. 13, 1949; s. Allen Roger and Evelyn Edna (Schlader) H.; m. Linda Mae Moen, Dec. 27, 1969; children: Jenna, Karl. BA, Concordia Coll., Moorhead, Minn., 1972; JD, U. N.D., 1979. Bar: N.D. 1979, Minn. 1979, U.S. Dist. Ct. Minn. 1979. Sole practice Brainerd, Minn., 1979-80, 85—; ptnr. Hanson & Krueger, Ltd., Brainerd, 1980-81, Gustafson, Hanson & Krueger, Ltd.,

Brainerd, 1981-85. Bd. dirs., v.p. Brainerd Area Arts Alliance, 1984—; bd. dirs., treas. Minn. Equine Research Found. Mem. ABA, Assn. Trial Lawyers Am., Minn. Trial Lawyers Assn., Minn. State Bar Assn., Internat. Arabian Horse Assn., YMCA. Republican. Lutheran. Lodge: Elks. Avocations: racquetball, endurance horse racing. State civil litigation, Family and matrimonial, General corporate. Home: 5531 Ebinger Rd N Brainerd MN 56401 Office: 510 Maple St Brainerd MN 56401

HANTLA, GEORGE BRADLEY, lawyer; b. Litchfield, Ill., Aug. 24, 1947; s. George Wesley and Marjorie Jean (Christen) H.; m. Anne E. McNamara, Nov. 28, 1969; children—Christopher Bradley, Elizabeth Suzanne. B.B.A., U. Miss., 1969; J.D., St. Louis U., 1973. Bar: Ill. 1973, U.S. Dist. Ct. Ill. 1973, U.S. Supreme Ct. 1980. Assoc. LeChien & Hantla, Belleville, Ill., 1973-76; sole practice, Litchfield, 1976—; dir. Litchfield Nat. Bank; city atty. City of Litchfield, 1981-84. Mem. ABA, Trial Lawyers Assn. Am., Ill. Bar Assn., Montgomery County Bar Assn. (pres. 1981-83). Roman Catholic. Lodge: Elks. General practice, Banking, State civil litigation. Home: 12 Pinewood Rd Litchfield IL 62056 Office: 413 N State St Litchfield IL 62056

HANZLIK, RAYBURN DEMARA, lawyer, executive recruiter; b. Los Angeles, June 7, 1938; s. Rayburn Otto and Ethel Winifred (Membery) H. B.S., Principia Coll., 1960; M.A., Woodrow Wilson Sch. Fgn. Affairs, U. Va., 1968; J.D., U. Va., 1974. Bar: Va. 1975, D.C. 1977. Staff asst. to Pres. U.S., Washington, 1971-73; asso. dir. White House Domestic Council, 1975-77; of counsel firm Danzansky Dickey Tydings Quint & Gordon, Washington, 1977-78, Akin Gump Hauer & Feld, Washington, 1978-79; individual practice law Los Angeles, 1979-81; adminstr. Econ. Regulatory Adminstrn., Dept. Energy, Washington, 1981-85; ptnr. Heidrick and Struggles, Inc., 1985—. Contbg. author: Global Politics and Nuclear Energy, 1971, Soviet Foreign Relations and World Communism, 1965. Alt. del. Republican Nat. Conv., 1980; dir. Calif. Rep. Victory Fund, 1980; trustee Hastings Coll., Nebr. Served to lt. USN, 1963-68, Vietnam. Mem. ABA, Va. Bar Assn., D.C. Bar Assn., Nat. Petroleum Council. Republican. Christian Scientist. Club: Los Angeles Petroleum. Attorney recruiting, FERC practice, Legislative. Home: 30371 Via Chico Place Laguna Niguel CA 92677 Office: Heidrick & Struggles 445 S Figueroa St Suite 2330 Los Angeles CA 90071

HAPKE, DANIEL S., JR., lawyer; b. St. Louis, Aug. 12, 1946; s. Daniel S. Sr. and Nancy Conway (Anderson) H.; m. Pamela Candice Turner, Jan. 10, 1981; children: J. Derek Nolen, Daniel S. III, Kevin G. BS, St. Louis U., 1968, JD, 1974. Bar: Mo. 1974, U.S. Dist. Ct. (ea. dist.) Mo. 1975. Assoc. Klamen, Summers & Compton, St. Louis, 1973-75; atty. Sverdrup Corp., St. Louis, 1975-84; asst. gen. counsel Gen. Dynamics Corp., St. Louis, 1984—; lectr. sch. architecture Washington U., St. Louis, 1981-84. Contbr. articles to profl. jours. Served to lt. USN, 1968-71. Mem. ABA, Mo. Bar Assn., Met. St. Louis Bar Assn. (chmn. com . 1978-79), Am. Corp. Counsel Assn. (pres. St. Louis chpt. 1987—). General corporate, Private international, Construction. Office: Gen Dynamics Corp 7733 Forsyth Blvd Saint Louis MO 63105

HARAB, ELLIOT PETER, lawyer; b. Cheverly, Md., May 5, 1948; s. Israel Jerry and Dorothy (Klein) H. B.A., Fairleigh Dickinson U., 1970; J.D., Case Western Res. U., 1974. Bar: Pa. 1975, U.S. Ct. Appeals (Fed. cir.) 1975. Trademark atty., examiner U.S. Patent and Trademark Office, Washington, 1974-80, editor Trademark Manual of Examining Procedure, 1980-81, mng. atty. examining operation, 1983-84; trademark atty. Am. Home Products Corp., N.Y.C., 1984—; chmn. Ann. Nat. Trademark Expn., 1983-84, mem. coordinating com. Nat. Inventors Day Program, 1976-84. Mem. Fed. Bar Assn., ABA, U.S. Trademark Assn. (patent and trademark office com.), N.J. Patent Law Assn., N.Y. Patent, Trademark and Copyright Law Assn., Case Western Res. U. Sch. Law Alumni Assn. (bd. govs.), Phi Alpha Delta. Lodges: Masons, B'nai B'rith. Trademark and copyright. Home: 200 Westgate Dr Edison NJ 08820 Office: Am Home Products Corp Trademark Legal Sect 685 3d Ave New York NY 10017

HARALSON, DALE, lawyer; b. Colorado City, Tex., Aug. 7, 1937; m. Betty L. Haralson; children—Wendy, Kristi. B.B.A., Hardin-Simons U., 1959; J.D., U. Ariz., 1963. Bar: Ariz. 1963, U.S. Dist. Ariz., 1976, U.S. Dist. Ct. (we. dist.) Tex. 1976, U.S. Ct. Appeals (5th, 9th and 10th cirs.) 1976, U.S. Surpeme Ct. 1975. Ptnr., Haralson, Kinerk & Morey, P.C., Tucson; lectr. in field. Trustee, Tucson Gen. Hosp., 1968-74, chmn. exec. com., 1969-71, chmn., 1971-72. Fellow Internat. Soc. Barristers, Internat. Acad. Trial Lawyers; mem. Assn. Trial Lawyers Am. (nat. v.p. 1981-81, nat. treas. 1978-81), Ariz. Trial Lawyers Assn. (pres. 1969-70), Western Trial Lawyers Assn. (gov. 1976—, v.p. 1986—), So. Ariz. Trial Lawyers Assn. (pres. 1968-69), Am. Bd. Trial Advs., Ariz. Bar Assn., Tex. Trial Lawyers Assn., Practising Law Inst., Law-Sci. Acad., Am. Arbitration Assn., ABA. Personal injury. Address: 82 S Stone Tucson AZ 85701

HARBESON, ROBERT G., lawyer; b. Camden, N.J., Aug. 18, 1946; s. James Page III and Eleanor (Taylor) H.; m. Karen Shivers, Oct. 27, 1973; 1 child, Lee Page. BA, Gettysburg U., 1968; JD, Rutgers U., 1971. Bar: N.J., U.S. Dist. Ct. N.J., U.S. Ct. Appeals (3d cir.). Ptnr. Archer & Greiner, Haddonfield, N.J., 1971—; Editor Rutgers Law Rev., 1970. Pres. Planned Parenthood, Camden County, 1977-79, 83-86. Served to capt. USAR. Mem. ABA, N.J. Bar Assn. (chmn. exec. com. civil practice 1984-86), Camden County Bar Assn. Episcopal. Avocations: skiing, golf, reading. Insurance, Personal injury, State civil litigation. Office: Archer & Greiner PO Box 331 Haddonfield NJ 08033

HARBISON, JAMES WESLEY, JR., lawyer; b. Mooresville, N.C., Aug. 30, 1934; s. James Wesley and Ola Mae (Bonney) H.; m. Margaret Geddes Morgan, Apr. 15, 1961; children: Anne, James. AB, Duke U., 1956; LLB, Yale U., 1959. Bar: N.C. 1959, N.Y. 1960, U.S. Dist. Ct. (so. and ea. dists.) N.Y. 1961, U.S. Ct. Appeals (2d cir.) 1962, U.S. Supreme Ct. 1968, U.S. Ct. Appeals (7th cir.) 1970, U.S. Ct. Appeals (5th cir.) 1975. Assoc. Simpson, Thacher & Bartlett, N.Y.C., 1960-73; ptnr. Wickes, Riddell, Bloomer, Jacobi & McGuire, N.Y.C., 1973-78, Morgan, Lewis & Bockius, N.Y.C., 1979—. Served to capt. USAF, 1959-60, N.Y. A.N.G., 1960-68. Mem. ABA, N.C. Bar Assn., N.Y. State Bar Assn., Assn. of Bar of City of N.Y., Fed. Bar Council, Am. Judicature Soc. Democrat. Methodist. Clubs: Met., Yale (N.Y.C.). Federal civil litigation, State civil litigation, Antitrust. Home: 30 East End Ave New York NY 10028 Office: Morgan Lewis & Bockius 101 Park Ave New York NY 10178

HARBISON, WILLIAM JAMES, state judge; b. Columbia, Tenn., Sept. 11, 1923; s. William Joshua and Eunice Elizabeth (Kinzer) H.; m. Mary Elizabeth Coleman, June 14, 1952; children: William Leslie, Mary Alice. Student, The Citadel, 1943-44; B.A., Vanderbilt U., 1947, J.D., 1950. Bar: Tenn. 1950. Pvt. practice law Nashville, 1950-74; spl. justice Tenn. Supreme Ct., Nashville, 1966-67; justice Tenn. Supreme Ct., 1974—, chief justice, 1980-82; adj. prof. law Vanderbilt Law Sch., Nashville, 1950—; chmn. civil rules com. Tenn. Supreme Ct., 1965-74. Editor-in-chief: Vanderbilt Law Review, 1949-50. Mem. Metro Nashville Bd. Edn., 1970-74. Served with AUS, 1943-46. Mem. ABA, Tenn. Bar Assn., Nashville Bar Assn. (pres. 1970-71), Order of Coif, Phi Beta Kappa. Democrat. Methodist. Clubs: Cedar Creek, Cumberland, Rotary. Jurisprudence. Home: 1031 Overton Lea Rd Nashville TN 37220 Office: 311 Supreme Ct Bldg Nashville TN 37219

HARBOTTLE, ANN WOODLEY, lawyer; b. Greenville, S.C., July 23, 1956; d. Donald Robert Woodley and Elizabeth Van Dyke; m. Scott Allan Harbottle, Aug. 6, 1983. BA in Polit. Sci. and Journalism summa cum laude, U. Ariz., 1978; JD cum laude, Ariz. State U., 1981. Bar: Ariz. 1981, U.S. Dist. Ct. Ariz. 1981, D.C. 1983, U.S. Dist. Ct. D.C. 1984, U.S. Ct. Appeals (D.C. and 9th cirs.) 1984, U.S. Ct. Appeals (7th cir.) 1986, U.S. Supreme Ct. 1987. Law clk. to chief judge U.S. Dist. Ct. Ariz., Phoenix, 1981-83; assoc. Winston & Strawn, Washington, 1983—. Mem. ABA, Am. Trial Lawyers Assn., Ariz. Bar Assn., D.C. Womens Bar Assn. Democrat. Presbyterian. Federal civil litigation, State civil litigation, Administrative and regulatory. Office: Winston & Strawn 2550 M St NW Suite 500 Washington DC 20037

HARBUR, NATHAN CLAYTON, lawyer; b. Kansas City, Mo., Oct. 27, 1951; s. Clayton Joseph and Mildred Louise (Neumeyer) H.; m. Kathleen Pearce, Sept. 5, 1981. AB, Lafayette Coll., 1974; JD, U. Kans., 1977. Bar: Kans. 1977, U.S. Ct. Appeals (10th cir.) 1983. Assoc. then ptnr. Gardner and Davis, Olathe, Kans., 1977-84; ptnr. Watson, Ess, Marshall and Enggas, Olathe, 1985, Miller and Bash, PC, Overland Park, Kans., 1985—; instr. real estate law Johnson County Community Coll., Overland Park, 1979. Mem. ABA (dist. rep. young lawyers div. 1982-84), Kans. Bar Assn. (pres. young lawyers sect. 1981-82, Service awards 1984, 85), Johnson County Bar Assn., Assn. Trial Lawyers Am. Baptist. Lodge: Rotary. Avocations: weight tng., golf, basketball. Federal civil litigation, State civil litigation, Real property. Home: 8680 W 102d Terr Overland Park KS 66212 Office: Miller and Bash PC 9401 Indian Creek Pkwy PO Box 25405 Overland Park KS 66225

HARDEE, DAVID WYATT, lawyer; b. Greensville, N.C., Jan. 7, 1947; s. David Wyatt and Anne Lee (Hooker) H. BS, Washington and Lee U., 1969; JD, Duke U., 1972. Bar: N.C. 1972, D.C. 1985. Ptnr. Caudle, Underwood & Kinsey, Charlotte, N.C., 1973-82; minority tax counsel fin. com. U.S. Senate, Washington, 1982-84; ptnr. Akin, Gump, Strauss, Hauer & Feld, Washington, 1984—. Mem. ABA, N.C. Bar Assn., D.C. Bar Assn. Corporate taxation. Home: 1004 22d St NW Washington DC 20037 Office: Akin Gump Strauss Hauer & Feld 1333 New Hampshire Ave NW Washington DC 20036

HARDEGREE, ARTHUR LEE, III, lawyer; b. Ashland, Ala., Apr. 7, 1956; s. Arthur Lee and Ann Martha (Harris) H.; m. Sharon Ann Bougrand, May 26, 1979; children: Wendy Nicole, Meredith Lane. BS, U. Ala., 1977, JD, 1980. Bar: Ala. 1980. Atty. So. Farm Bur. Life, Jackson, Miss., 1980-82, asst. counsel, 1982-83; asst. counsel AmSouth Bank N.A., Birmingham, Ala., 1983-86, sr. asst. counsel, 1986—. Chmn. bd. editors Jour. of the Legal Profession, 1980. Mem. ABA, Mortgage Bankers Assn. Lawyers Group. Avocations: water and snow skiing. Real property, Banking, Consumer commercial. Home: 5504 Heath Row Dr Birmingham AL 35243 Office: Am South Bank NA Legal Dept PO Box 11007 Birmingham AL 35288

HARDEN, GARY MARTIN, lawyer; b. Detroit, Jan. 12, 1955; s. Arthur E. and Julia C. (Butcko) H.; m. Sherrie M. Larberg, May 12, 1984. BBA in Acctg., U. Notre Dame, 1977; JD cum laude, U. Toledo, 1980; LLM in Taxation, NYU, 1981. Bar: Ohio 1980, U.S. Dist. Ct. (no. dist.) Ohio 1983, U.S. Tax Ct. 1983. Assoc. Frank D. Jacobs P.A., Toledo, 1981-84, Eastman & Smith, Toledo, 1984—; speaker numerous seminars; adj. prof. U. Toledo, 1986—. Kenneson fellow, 1980-81. Mem. ABA (tax sect.), Ohio Bar Assn., Toledo Bar Assn. Roman Catholic. Corporate taxation, General corporate. Office: Eastman & Smith 240 Huron Toledo OH 43604

HARDEN, RICHARD LEE, lawyer; b. Miami, Fla., Oct. 31, 1945; s. O.L. and Mable Estelle (McPherson) H.; m. Margaret Joan May, Apr. 7, 1973; children—Meredith, William, Richard. B.A., Washington and Lee U., 1967, J.D. magna cum laude, 1973. Bar: N.Y. 1974, Tex. 1983. Assoc. Winthrop, Stimson, Putnam, & Roberts, N.Y.C., 1973-81, ptnr., 1982; ptnr. Moore & Peterson, Dallas, 1982—. Contbr. articles to legal jours. Served with U.S. Army, 1969-71; ETO. Mem. ABA, Assn. Bar City N.Y., Dallas Bar Assn., Order of Coif. Republican. Club: Downtown Assn. (N.Y.C.). Securities, General corporate, Public utilities. Home: 4926 Swiss Ave Dallas TX 75214 Office: Moore & Peterson 2800 First City Ctr Dallas TX 75201

HARDGROVE, JAMES ALAN, lawyer; b. Chgo., Feb. 20, 1945; s. Albert John and Ruth (Noonen) H.; m. Kathleen M. Peterson, June 15, 1968; children: Jennifer Anne, Amy Kristine, Michael Sheridan. BA, U. Notre Dame, 1967; cert. English law, U. Coll. Law, 1969; JD, U. Notre Dame, 1970. Bar: Ill. 1970, U.S. Ct. Appeals (7th cir.) 1970, U.S. Dist. Ct. (no. dist.) Ill. 1970, U.S. Dist. Ct. (cen. dist.) Ill. 1978, U.S. Supreme Ct. 1980. Law clk. to presiding justice U.S. Ct. Appeals (7th cir.), Chgo., 1970-71; assoc. Sidley & Austin, Chgo., 1971-76, ptnr., 1977—. Mem. ABA, Ill. Bar Assn., Chgo. Bar Assn., Legal Club. Federal civil litigation, State civil litigation, Antitrust. Home: 948 Ridge Ave Evanston IL 60202 Office: Sidley & Austin One First Nat Plaza Chicago IL 60603

HARDIG, MARK NELSON, lawyer; b. Cin., Apr. 13, 1955; s. William Lucuis and Elizabeth Carol (Nelson) H.; m. Carrie Ellen Alvis, Apr. 9, 1983; children: Olivia Brooke, Cara Lindsay. BA, U. Notre Dame, 1977; JD, No. Ky. U., 1981. Bar: Ohio 1981, U.S. Dist. Ct. (so. dist.) Ohio 1981, U.S. Dist. Ct. (no. dist.) Ind. 1983. Law clk. to presiding justice Ohio Ct. Appeals (12th dist.), Middletown, 1981-82; assoc. Baden, Jones, Scheper & Crehan Co. L.P.A., Hamilton, Ohio, 1982—. Rep. precinct exec. Hamilton County, 1980. Mem. ABA, Ohio Bar Assn., Butler County Bar Assn., Cin. Bar Assn. Roman Catholic. Avocation: basketball. Criminal, Personal injury, Family and matrimonial. Home: 138 Monitor Ave Cincinnati OH 45233 Office: Baden Jones Scheper & Crehan Co LPA 222 High St Hamilton OH 45211

HARDIN, ADLAI S., JR., lawyer; b. Norwalk, Conn., Sept. 20, 1937; s. Adlai S. and Carol (Moore) H. BA, Princeton U., 1959; LLB, Columbia U., 1962. Bar: N.Y. 1963, U.S. Dist. Ct. (so. and ea. dists.) N.Y. 1965, U.S. Supreme Ct. 1967, U.S. Ct. Appeals (2d, 3d, 4th, 5th, 9th and D.C. cirs.). Assoc. Milbank, Tweed, hadley & McCloy, N.Y.C., 1963-70, ptnr., 1971—. Trustee Spence Sch., 1981—; former elder, trustee, Madison Ave Presbyn. Ch. Served with USAR, 1962-68. Mem. ABA (former chmn. N.Y. State membership com., antitrust sect.), Fed. Bar Council (bd. trustees 1983—, v.p. 1986—, chmn. winter bench and bar conf. 1986, chmn. membership com.), N.Y. State Bar Assn. (com. on profl. ethics, jud. election monitoring com.), Assn. of Bar of City of N.Y. (sec. 1979-82, exec. com. 1979-82, sec. com. profl and jud. ethics 1967-70, chmn. 1970-73, spl. com. lawyer's role in securities transactions, spl. com. to cooperate with ABA in revision of Canons of Ethics, nom. com.). Clubs: River, Univ., Down Town, Blue Hill Troupe, Amateur Ski N.Y., Old Lyme Country, Old Lyme Beach. Antitrust, Federal civil litigation, State civil litigation. Office: Milbank Tweed Hadley & McCloy 1 Chase Manhattan Plaza New York NY 10005

HARDIN, GEORGE TIMOTHY, lawyer; b. Greeneville, Tenn., Feb. 1, 1947; s. James Neal and Ina (Anderson) H.; m. Maxie Duran, May 3, 1980; children: James Donaghey, William Ross. BA, U. Va., 1969; JD, N.Y. Law Sch., 1974. Bar: N.Y. 1975, Tex. 1978. Asst. to gen. counsel U.S. Life Title Ins. Co. of N.Y., N.Y.C., 1975-78; v.p. and sr. escrow officer Safeco Land Title of Dallas, 1978-80; v.p. and closing atty. Dallas Title Co., 1980-83; sole practice Dallas, 1983—. Co-Author: Tax Deferred Property Exchanges Under Section 1031 of the Internal Revenue Code, 1980; contbr. articles on real estate devel. and non-jud. foreclosures to profl. jours. Mem. administrv. bd. 1st United Meth. Ch. Dallas, 1985. Mem. ABA (title ins. com. 1985—), Tex. State Bar Assn. (legal forms com. 1983—), Dallas Bar Assn. (real estate sect. 1978—), N.Y. County Lawyers Assn. Democrat. Methodist. Avocations: sports car racing, music, tennis. Real property. Office: 866 Tex Commerce Bank Tower Plaza of Americas Lockbox 150 Dallas TX 75201

HARDIN, HAL D., lawyer, former United States attorney; b. Davidson County, Tenn., June 29, 1941. B.S., Middle Tenn. State U., 1966; J.D., Vanderbilt U., 1968; attended, State Jud. Coll., Reno, 1976. Bar: Tenn. 1969, U.S. Supreme Ct. 1973, U.S. Claims Ct., U.S. Ct. Mil. Appeals, U.S. Tax Ct. 1978, D.C. 1983. Fingerprint technician FBI, 1961; dir. St. Louis Job Corps Ctr., 1968; asst. dist. atty. Nashville, 1969-71; mem. firm Jack Norman & Assocs., Nashville, 1970-75, Gracey and Maddin, Nashville, 1975; presiding judge Nashville Trial Cts., 1976-77; U.S. atty. Middle Dist. Tenn., 1977-81; practice law Nashville, 1981—; of counsel firm Gracey, Maddin, Cowan & Bird, Nashville, 1985-87; prof. govt. Aquinas Coll., 1975-76. Bd. dirs. Leadership Nashville Alumni Assn., 1985—. Served in Peace Corps, 1963-65. Mem. Nashville Bar Assn. (dir., v.p.), Tenn. Bar Assn. (gen. counsel), ABA, D.C. Bar, Tenn. Criminal Def. Attys., Am. Bd. Trial Advs. Federal civil litigation, State civil litigation, Criminal. Office: 219 2d Ave N Nashville TN 37201

HARDIN, PATRICK HENRY, law educator; b. Birmingham, Ala., Aug. 14, 1940; s. Charles A. and Mary I. (Rocks) H.; m. Julia Wells Demerath, June 13, 1964; children: Rebecca, Katherine. AB, U. Ala., 1962; JD, U. Chgo., 1965. Bar: Ill. 1966, Tenn. 1977, U.S. Ct. Appeals (5th cir.) 1970, U.S. Ct. Appeals(6th cir.) 1973, U.S. Ct. Appeals (9th, D.C. cirs.) 1974, U.S. Supreme Ct., 1972. Assoc. Pope, Ballard et al, Chgo., 1965-67; trial atty. civil rights div. U.S. Dept. Justice, Washington, 1967-70; chief counsel to chmn. NLRB, Washington, 1970-72, assoc. gen. counsel, 1972-75; assoc. prof. law coll. U. Tenn., Knoxville, 1975-80, prof. law, 1980—, assoc. dean coll. law, 1986—. Contbr. articles to profl. jours. Recipient Younger Fed. Lawyer award Fed. Bar Assn., 1974. Mem. ABA (officer, sec. labor law sect. 1983-84), Nat. Academy Arbitrators, Soc. Profls. in Dispute Resolution (officer, parliamentarian 1972-73). Unitarian. Labor. Home: 3521 Talahi Dr Knoxville TN 37919 Office: Univ Tenn Law Coll 1505 Cumberland Ave Knoxville TN 37919-1800

HARDING, MARC STEVEN, lawyer; b. Des Moines, Nov. 8, 1947; s. John Henry and Marilyn Gloria (Anderson) H.; m. Kay Ellan Zimmerman, June 21, 1980; stepchildren—Jodi, Tory. B.A., U. Iowa, 1970, J.D., 1973. Bar: Iowa 1973, U.S. Dist. Ct. (no. and so. dists.) Iowa 1973, U.S. Ct. Appeals (8th cir.) 1974, U.S. Ct. Claims 1976, U.S. Tax Ct. 1976, U.S. Supreme Ct. 1976. Sole practice, Des Moines, 1973—. Mem. Iowa State Bar Assn., ABA, Assn. Trial Lawyers Iowa, Assn. Trial Lawyers Am., S. Des Moines C. of C. (bd. dirs. 1987—). Lodges: Lions, Masons. Family and matrimonial, Personal injury. Home: 387 Hoover Prole IA 50229

HARDING, RAY MURRAY, JR., lawyer; b. Logan, Utah, Nov. 23, 1953; s. Ray M. Sr. and Martha (Rasmussen) H.; m. Rebecca Joan, May 26, 1973; children: Michelle, Nicole, Justin. BS, Brigham Young U., 1975; JD, J. Reuben Clark Law Sch., 1978. Bar: Utah 1978. Ptnr. Harding & Harding, American Fork and Pleasant Grove, Utah, 1978-85; owner Harding & Assoc., American Fork and Pleasant Grove, 1986—; atty. Lindon City and Pleasant Grove City, Utah, 1983—, Alpine City and American Fork, Utah, 1985—. Named Businessman of Yr., Future Bus. Leaders of Am., 1983. Mem. ABA, Utah State Bar Assn., Utah Trial Lawyers Assn., Utah County Bar Assn., Pleasant Grove C. of C. (pres. 1983). Republican. Mormon. Club: Utah Governor's (Salt Lake City). Lodge: Kiwanis (local bd. dirs. 1982-83). Banking, General practice, Personal injury. Home: 1630 E 480 S Pleasant Grove UT 84003 Office: Harding & Assoc 110 S Main St Pleasant Grove UT 84062 also: 306 W Main St American Fork UT 84003

HARDING, SAMUEL ARLON, lawyer; b. Lawton, Okla., Mar. 28, 1945; s. Curtis Arlon and Margaret Louise (Caruthers) H.; m. Sheila Beth Borochoff, May 5, 1968; children—Rochelle Anne, Jennifer Lynne. B.A., Okla. State U., 1967; M.B.A., U. So. Ill., 1972; J.D., U. Okla., 1974. Bar: Nev. 1975, U.S. Dist. Ct. Nev. 1976. Assoc. Beckley, Singleton, Delanoy, Jemison & Reid, Las Vegas, 1974-76; dep. atty. Clark County Pub. Defender, Las Vegas, 1976; ptnr. Burleigh, Zervas & Harding, Las Vegas, and Harding & Zervas, Las Vegas, 1976-77, Harding & Dawson, Las Vegas, 1977—. Served to capt. USAF, 1968-72. Decorated D.F.C. Insurance, Personal injury, State civil litigation. Home: 3129 Desmond St Las Vegas NV 89121 Office: 626 S 3d St Las Vegas NV 89101

HARDING, WILLIAM ALAN, lawyer; b. Lincoln, Nebr., Sept. 1, 1944; s. J. Max and Eileen A. (Gordon) H.; m. Nancy J. Neubauer, Dec. 19, 1970; children: Tiffany, Jeffrey. BA, U. Nebr., 1966, JD, 1969. Bar: Nebr. 1969, U.S. Dist. Ct. Nebr. 1969, U.S. Ct. Appeals (5th, 8th, and 10th cirs.) 1969, U.S. Ct. Appeals (2d cir.) 1970, U.S. Ct. Appeals (4th, 11th and D.C. cirs.) 1971, U.S. Supreme Ct. 1972. Mem. Nelson & Harding, P.C., Lincoln, 1969—; instr. legal writing Coll. Law U. Nebr., Lincoln, 1971-74, instr. legal research Lincoln Sch. Commerce, 1974-75; lectr. numerous orgns. and assns. on labor and employment law; mem. payroll costs session White House Conf. on Small Bus., 1986. Co-chmn. citizens adv. com. City-County, implementation com., 1975; pres. bd. dirs. Cosmopolitan Charities Found., 1973-76; sec. Nebr. Fedn. Young Reps., 1967-68, conv. chmn., 1965, 75; chmn. constitution com. Lancaster County Reps., 1973-76, resolutions com. chmn., 1976-86. Mem. Nebr. Assn. Commerce and Industry (chmn. labor relations council 1983-86). Republican. Roman Catholic. Clubs: University (pres. 1984-85), Hillcrest Country (Lincoln). Labor. Home: 5415 Trotter Rd Lincoln NE 68516 Office: Nelson & Harding PC 1200 N St 500 The Atrium Lincoln NE 68501-2028

HARDMAN, CHRISTOPHER RAY, lawyer; b. Salem, Oreg., Oct. 10, 1954; s. Joseph McClain and Margaret Alice (Smith) H.; m. Britt Lynn Nelson, Jan. 11, 1986. BS in Polit. Sci., Hanover Coll., 1976; JD, Willamette U., 1979. Bar: Oreg. 1979, U.S. Dist. Ct. Oreg. 1980, U.S. Supreme Ct. 1983. Clk. typist U.S. Dept. Commerce, Washington, 1972-77; law clk. Legis. Counsel, Salem, Oreg., 1978-80; dep. dist. atty. Multnomah County Dist. Atty's Office, Portland, 1980—; bar counsel Oreg. State Bar, Portland, 1983—. Caretaker, bd. dirs. Friends of Deepwood, Oreg., 1978-81; committeeman Portland Marathon, 1984—, Dem. Party of Oreg., Portland, 1985—, Neil Goldschmidt for Gov., Portland, 1986. Mem. ABA (young lawyers div. 1985), Oreg. Young Atty.s Assn. (bd. dirs. 1983-85, v.p. 1985—, pres. 1986), Oreg. Bar Assn. (detention and corrections com.), Beta Theta Pi (treas. 1974-75). Episcopalian. Avocations: marathon running, backpacking, politics. Criminal. Home: 3327 NE 20th Portland OR 97212 Office: Multnomah County Dist Atty 1021 SW 4th Rm 600 Portland OR 97204

HARDTNER, QUINTIN THEODORE, III, lawyer; b. Shreveport, La., Mar. 5, 1936; s. Quintin Theodore and Jane (Owen) H.; m. Susan Mayer, June 30, 1962; children—Susan Owen, Quintin Theodore IV, George Jonathan. B.B.A., Tulane U., 1957, J.D. 1961. Bar: La. 1961. Assoc. Jones, Walker, Waechter, Poitevent, Carrere & Denegre, New Orleans, 1961-62; ptnr. Hargrove, Guyton, Ramey and Barlow, Shreveport, 1962—; dir. 1st Nat. Bank Shreveport. Past mem. adv. bd. Salvation Army; past trustee, past chmn. bd. All Sts. Episcopal Sch., Vicksburg, Miss.; past trustee, past chmn. St. Mark's Day Sch.; past trustee Southfield Sch.; vestryman St. Mark's Episcopal Ch.; past bd. dirs., v.p. Shreveport Assn. for Blind; past bd. dirs. Family and Children's Services; past co-chmn. Centenary Coll. Fund. Served to lt. USMC, 1957-59. Fellow Am. Coll. Probate Counsel; mem. ABA, La. State Bar Assn. (past mem. ho. of dels.), Ark.-La.-Tex. Tax Inst. (bd. dirs.), Shreveport Bar Assn. (past pres.), Estate Planning Council Shreveport (past dir., past pres.). Clubs: Boston (New Orleans); Shreveport, Cambridge. Lodge: Rotary (pres., bd. dirs.). Probate, General corporate, Estate planning. Home: 910 Ockley Dr Shreveport LA 71106 Office: 700 First Fed Plaza 505 Travis St PO Box B Shreveport LA 71161

HARDY, ASHTON RICHARD, lawyer; b. Gulfport, Miss., Aug. 31, 1935; s. Ashton Maurice and Alice (Baumbach) H.; m. Katherine Ketelsen, Sept. 4, 1959; children: Karin K., Katherine B. BBA, Tulane U., 1958, JD, 1962. Bar: La., 1962, FCC, 1976. Ptnr. Jones, Walker, Waechter, Poitevent, Carrere & Denegre, New Orleans, 1962-74, 76-82; gen. counsel FCC, Washington, 1974-76; ptnr. Fawer, Brian, Hardy, Zatzkis, New Orleans, 1982-86, Hardy & Popham, 1986—; gen. counsel La. Assn. Broadcasters, 1976-86, Greater New Orleans Assn. Broadcasters, 1976—, La. Assn. Advt. Agys., 1982-86; lectr. advance rep. to Pres. U.S., 1971-74. Served to lt. USN, 1958-60. Mem. Fed. Bar Assn., La. Bar Assn. (del. ho. of dels. 1987—), FCC Bar Assn., Christian Legal Soc. Republican. Evangelical Christian. Clubs: Bienville, Metairie Country. Administrative and regulatory, Contracts commercial, General corporate. Home: 306 Cedar Dr Metairie LA 70005 Office: 700 Camp St New Orleans LA 70130

HARDY, CHARLES LEACH, U.S. district judge; b. Los Angeles, Jan. 24, 1919; s. Charles Little and Dorothy (Leach) H.; m. Jean McRae, Jan. 26, 1947; children: Charles M., Caroline, Catherine, John L. Julianne, Eileen, Sterling A., Steven W., Janette. B.S., U. Ariz., 1947, LL.B., 1950. Bar: Ariz. 1949. Pvt. practice Phoenix, 1949-66; dep. county atty. Maricopa County, Ariz., 1952-55; asst. atty. gen. State of Ariz., 1956-59; judge Ariz. Superior Ct., 1966-80; U.S. dist. judge Ariz. Dist., Phoenix, 1980—. Pres. Young Democratic Clubs Ariz., 1956-57, nat. committeeman, 1957-58; chmn. Maricopa County Dem. Central Com., 1958-59; mem. Ariz. Bd. Crippled Children's Services, 1965. Served with F.A. AUS, 1941-45. Decorated Bronze Star. Mem. ABA, Am. Judicature Soc., State Bar Ariz., Maricopa County Bar Assn. Mormon. Jurisprudence. Office: US Courthouse Bldg 230 N 1st Ave Room 6031 Phoenix AZ 85025 *

HARDY, HARVEY LOUCHARD, lawyer; b. Dallas, Dec. 2, 1914; s. Nat L. and Winifred H. (Fouraker) H.; m. Edna Vivian Bedell, Feb. 14, 1948; children—Victoria Elizabeth Hardy Pursch, Alice Anne Hardy Gannon. Bar: Tex. 1936, U.S. Dist. Ct. (so. and we. dists.) Tex. 1946, U.S. Ct. Appeals (5th cir.) 1946, U.S. Supreme Ct. 1949. First asst. dist. atty. Bexar County, San Antonio, 1947-50, acting dist. atty., 1950-51; city atty., San Antonio, 1952-53, Castle Hills, Tex., 1959—, Leon Valley, Tex., 1967—, Garden

Ridge, Tex., 1972—, Roma, Tex., 1973—, Helotes, Tex., 1984—, Cibolo, Tex., 1986— ; legal advisor bd. trustees Firemen and Policemen's Pension Fund of San Antonio, 1956—; legal advisor Grey Forest Utilities, 1986— . Served to 1st lt. inf. U.S. Army, 1941-45. Decorated Bronze Star. Fellow Tex. Bar Found.; mem. Nat. Inst. Mcpl. Legal Officers, ABA, Tex. Bar Assn., San Antonio Bar Found., Tex. Assn. City Attys., San Antonio Bar Assn. Methodist. Local government, Probate. Home: 215 Atwater Dr San Antonio TX 78213 Office: 560 GPM South Tower San Antonio TX 78216

HARDY, MICHAEL LYNN, lawyer; b. St. Louis, Aug. 28, 1947; s. William Frost and Ruth (Shea) H.; m. Martha Bond, Sept. 2, 1972; children: Brian M., Kevin S. AB, John Carroll U., 1969; JD, U. Mich., 1972. Bar: Ohio 1972. Assoc. Guren, Merritt, et al, Cleve., 1972-77, ptnr., 1977-84; ptnr. Thompson, Hine & Flory, Cleve., 1984—. Bd. advisors Harvard Environ. Law Rev., 1976-78. Served to capt. U.S. Army, 1969-74. Mem. ABA (litigation sect., nat. resources sect.), Ohio State Bar Assn. (sec. environ. law com. 1983-84, vice-chmn. 1984-86, chmn. 1987—), Def. Research Inst. Club: Canterbury Golf (Shaker Heights, Ohio). Administrative and regulatory, Environment, Federal civil litigation. Home: 3330 Dorchester Rd Shaker Heights OH 44120 Office: Thompson Hine & Flory 629 Euclid Ave Cleveland OH 44114

HARDY, WILLIAM ROBINSON, lawyer; b. Cin., June 14, 1934; s. William B. and Chastine M. (Sprague) H.; m. Barbro Anita Medin, Oct. 11, 1964; children: Anita Christina, William Robinson. AB magna cum laude, Princeton U., 1956; JD, Harvard U., 1963. Bar: Ohio 1963, U.S. Supreme Ct. 1975. Life underwriter New Eng. Mut. Life Ins. Co., 1956-63; assoc. Graydon, Head & Ritchey, Cin., 1963-68, ptnr., 1968—; mem. panel comml. and constrn. industry arbitrators Am. Arbitration Assn., 1972—; reporter joint com. for revision of rules of U.S. Dist. Ct. for So. Dist. Ohio, 1975, 80, 83. Bd. dirs. Cin. Union Bethel, 1968—, pres., 1977-82; bd. dirs. Ohio Valley Goodwill Industries Rehab. Ctr., Cin., 1970—, pres., 1981—; mem Cin. Bd. Bldg. Appeals, 1976—, vice chmn., 1983, chmn., 1983—. Served to capt. USAR, 1956-68. Recipient award of merit Ohio Legal Ctr. Inst., 1975, 76. Mem. ABA, Ohio Bar Assn., Cin. Bar Assn., Am. Judicature Soc., Assn. Trial Lawyers Am., Ohio Acad. Trial Lawyers, 6th Circuit Jud. Conf. (life), AAAS, Ohio Soc. Colonial Wars (gov. 1979), Phi Beta Kappa. Mem. Ch. of Redeemer. Clubs: Princeton (N.Y.C.); Racquet (Cin.). Federal civil litigation, State civil litigation, Antitrust. Home: 1339 Michigan Ave Cincinnati OH 45208 Office: Graydon Head & Ritchey 1900 Fifth Third Ctr 511 Walnut St Cincinnati OH 45202

HARE, GLENN PATRICK, lawyer; b. Washington, May 22, 1948; s. Walter Joseph and Elizabeth Flora (Brown) H.; m. Karen Elizabeth Roesky, June 28, 1969; children: Owen G., Erin M. BS cum laude, U. Balt., 1971; MBA, Tulane U., 1973; JD, Loyola U., New Orleans, 1979. Bar: La. 1979, U.S. Dist. Ct. (ea. dist.) La. 1979, U.S. Dist. Ct. (mid. dist.) 1981, U.S. Ct. Appeals (5th and 11th cirs.) 1981, U.S. Dist. Ct. (we. dist.) La. 1983, U.S. Dist. Ct. Md. 1986, Md. 1987. Sr. rep. indsl. relations Kaiser Aluminum & Chem. Corp., Chalmette, La., 1973-79; assoc. McGlinchey, Stafford, Mintz, Cellini & Lang P.C., New Orleans, 1979-86, Kruchko & Fries, Balt., 1986—. Mem. ABA, La. Bar Assn., Md. Bar Assn., Balt. County Bar Assn., St. Thomas Moore Soc. Md. Inc., Beta Alpha. Republican. Roman Catholic. Avocations: tennis, boating, reading, family. Labor, Federal civil litigation, State civil litigation. Office: Kruchko & Fries 28 W Allegheny Ave 606 Towson Towers Baltimore MD 21204

HARFF, CHARLES HENRY, diversified industrial company executive, lawyer; b. Wesel, Fed. Republic Germany, Sept. 27, 1929; s. Philip and Stephanie (Dreyfuss) H.; m. Marion Haines MacAfee, July 19, 1958; children—Pamela Haines, John Blair, Todd Philip. B.A., Colgate U., 1951; LL.B., Harvard U., 1954; postgrad., U. Bonn, Fed. Republic Germany, 1955. Bar: N.Y. 1955, Pa. 1985. Assoc. Chadbourne & Parke, N.Y.C., 1955-64, ptnr., 1964-84; sr. v.p., gen. counsel, sec. Rockwell Internat. Corp., Pitts., 1984—. Trustee Christian Johnson Endeavor Found., N.Y.C., 1984—. Fulbright scholar U. Bonn, Fed. Republic Germany, 1955. Mem. ABA, N.Y. State Bar Assn., Pa. State Bar Assn., Machinery and Allied Products Inst. (law council 1984—), The Assn. of Gen. Counsel. Clubs: Econ. of N.Y., Harvard, Hemisphere (N.Y.C.); Duquesne, Allegheny Country (Pitts.); Farm Neck (Martha's Vineyard, Mass.). General corporate, Securities. Home: Blackburn Rd Sewickley PA 15143 Office: Rockwell Internat Corp 600 Grant St Pittsburgh PA 15219

HARGESHEIMER, ELBERT, III, lawyer; b. Cleve., Jan. 4, 1944; s. Elbert and Agnes Mary (Heckman) H.; m. Cheryl H. Schroeder, July 9, 1966; children—Heather Leigh, Elbert IV, Jon-Erik, Piper Elizabeth. A.B., Cornell U., 1966; J.D., SUNY-Buffalo, 1969. Bar: N.Y. 1970, U.S. Dist. Ct. (we. dist.) N.Y. 1971. Assoc. Miller, Bouvier, O'Connor & Cegielski, Buffalo, 1970-73, ptnr., 1973-74; ptnr. Godinho & Hargesheimer, Hamburg, N.Y., 1974-84; sole practice, Hamburg, 1984—. Chief counsel Joint Legis. Commn. to Revise Bus. and Corp. Law, N.Y. State Assembly and Senate, 1974-75; prosecutor Village of Blasdell (N.Y.), 1978-80, 83-87, village atty. 1980-82; fund chmn. South Towns Hosp. Found., Inc., 1973-76, fin. chmn., bd. dirs., 1976-77, v.p., 1978-82; chmn. Hamburg Town Republican Com., 1978—; coordinator Erie County Pretrial Services Program, 1987—; counsel Erie County Rep. Com., 1980—; mem. Erie County Bd. Ethics, 1979—, chmn. 1983.; charter mem., counsel S.W. Hamburg Taxpayers Assn. Named Mr. Republican, Town of Hamburg Rep. Club, 1982. Mem. N.Y. State Bar Assn., Western N.Y. County Bar Assn., Erie County Trial Lawyers Assn., Theta Chi. Methodist. General practice, General corporate, Family and matrimonial. Home: 2920 South Creek Rd Hamburg NY 14075 Office: 12 Main St Hamburg NY 14075

HARGIS, DAVID MICHAEL, lawyer, writer; b. Warren, Ark., Feb. 10, 1948; s. James Von Hargis and Noma Lee (Anderson) Watkins; m. Carolyn Jane Sangster (div. 1981); children—Michelle Leigh, Michael Bradley; m. Linda Jane Huckelbury, Jan. 8, 1981; 1 child, Christopher Key. B.S.B.A. with honors, U. Ark., 1970, J.D., 1973. Bar: Ark. 1973, U.S. Dist. Ct. (ea. and we. dists.) Ark. 1974. Assoc. Williamson Law Firm, Monticello, Ark., 1973-74; asst. U.S. atty. Eastern Dist. Ark., Little Rock, 1974-75; assoc. House, Holmes & Jewell, Little Rock, 1975-79; ptnr. House, Holmes & Jewell, P.A., Little Rock, 1979-85; founder Wilson, Wood & Hargis, 1985—; atty. Legal Services Corp., Little Rock, 1977; county atty. Pulaski County, Ark., 1980-82; atty. Pulaski County Quorum Ct., 1980-82; spl. circuit judge Pulaski County Circuit Ct., 1982; atty. Office of Spl. Prosecutor, Pulaski County Grand Jury, 1983-84; spl. counsel Ark.Ins. Dept., 1984. Editor-in-chief Ark. Law Rev., 1972-73; guest columnist Ark. Gazette, 1984. Contbr. articles to legal jours. Co-author: Quality Assurance in Health Test, American College of Pathologists, 1986. Recipient spl. commendation Legal Services Corp., 1977, Ark. Edn. Assn., 1984. Mem. ABA (legal edn. sect., corp. sect.), Ark. Bar Assn., Omicron Delta Kappa, Beta Gamma Sigma. Methodist. Federal civil litigation, State civil litigation, Contracts commercial. Home: 36 River Ridge Circle Little Rock AR 72212 Office: Hargis Wood & Lawrence 1st Comml Bldg 23d Floor Little Rock AR 72201

HARGIS, JAMES RICHARD, lawyer; b. Victoria, Tex., Aug. 23, 1951; s. Aureleus Vaden and Rosalie Wilson (Burns) H.; m. Holly Patricia Green, Oct. 20, 1973; 1 child, Jennifer Burns. BA, U. Tex., 1973; JD, George Mason U., 1980. Bar: Va. 1980, U.S. Dist. Ct. (ea. dist.) Va. 1980, U.S. Ct. Appeals (4th cir.) 1980, Tex. 1982, U.S. Ct. Appeals (5th cir.) 1982. Legis. asst. to senator Henry Bellmon U.S. Senate, Washington, 1975-80; assoc. Dawson Riddell, Washington, 1980-81; mgr. fed. pub. affairs Aminoll, Inc., Washington, 1981-84; assoc. Babb & Hanna, P.C., Austin, Tex., 1985—. Mem. ABA, Va. Bar Assn., Tex. Bar Assn. Episcopalian. Avocations: golf, skiing, sailing. Legislative, Administrative and regulatory, Real property. Office: Babb & Hanna PC 905 Congress Ave Austin TX 78701

HARGRAVE, RUDOLPH, judge Oklahoma Supreme Court; b. Shawnee, Okla., Feb. 15, 1925; s. John Hubert and Daisy (Holmes) H.; m. Madeline Hargrave, May 29, 1949; children: Cindy Lu, John Robert, Jana Sue. LL.B., U. Okla., 1949. Began legal practice at, Wewoka, 1949; asst. county atty. Seminole County, 1951-55; judge Seminole County Ct., 1964-67, Seminole County Superior Ct., 1967-69; dist. judge Okla. Dist. Ct., Dist. 22, 1969-79; assoc. justice Okla. Supreme Ct., 1979—. Mem. Seminole County Bar Assn., Okla. Bar Assn., ABA. Democrat. Methodist. Lodges: Lions; Masons. Office: Okla Supreme Ct Okla State Capitol Lincoln Blvd Oklahoma City OK 73105 *

HARGROVE, JOHN R., federal judge. Judge, U.S. Dist. Ct. Md., Balt. Judicial administration. Office: US Dist Ct 101 W Lombard St Baltimore MD 21201 *

HARGROVE, JOSEPH LEONARD, JR., lawyer; b. Beeville, Tex., May 5, 1949; s. Joseph Leonard Sr. and Martha (Dean) H.; m. Nancy Katherine Green, May 22, 1971; children: Robert Green, Reginald Joseph. BA in History, U. Tex., 1971; JD, La. State U., 1975. Bar: La. 1975, U.S. Dist. Ct. (we. dist.) La. 1975, U.S. Ct. Appeals (5th cir.) 1975, U.S. Supreme Ct. 1975. Assoc. Hargrove, Guyton, Ramey & Barlow, Shreveport, La., 1975-79; ptnr. Hargrove, Guyton, Ramey & Barlow, Shreveport, 1979—. Mem. La. Bar Assn., Shreveport Bar Assn. (grievance and ethics com.). Clubs: Shreveport, Shreveport Country. Oil and gas leasing, Bankruptcy. Home: 9639 Norris Ferry Rd Shreveport LA 71106 Office: Hargrove Guyton Ramey & Barlow 700 First Federal Plaza Shreveport LA 71101

HARGROVE, ROBERT CLYDE, lawyer; b. Shreveport, La., Dec. 13, 1918; s. Reginald Henry and Hallie (Ward) H.; m. Marjorie Clare Chinski, Sept. 29, 1920; 1 son, Reginald Henry II. B.A., Rice U., 1939; LL.B., Yale U., 1942. Bar: La. 1946, D.C. 1975. Ptnr., Hargrove, Guyton, Van Hook & Hargrove, Shreveport, La., 1946-58; v.p. Bechtel Internat. Corp., San Francisco, 1958-61; sole practice, Shreveport, 1961—; of counsel Casey, Lane & Mittendorf, Washington, 1975-80, Hargrove, Guyton, Ramey & Barlow, Shreveport, 1976-78; ptnr. Hargrove Oil & Gas Co., Shreveport, 1948—. Past trustee U. South, Sewanee, Tenn.; mem. vestry St. Mark's Episcopal Ch., Shreveport; mem. Met. Opera Nat. Council, N.Y.C.; past pres. Southfield Sch., Shreveport; past officer, bd. dirs. YMCA, Opera Assn.; exec. v.p., dir. Shreveport Opera; pres. Shreveport Bridge Assn. lifetime assoc. Rice U. Served to capt. U.S. Army, 1942-46. Decorated D.S.C., Purple Heart, Combat Infantryman's Badge, others. Named One of Top 20 Energy Practitioners, Nat. Law Jour. Mem. ABA Fed. Energy Bar Assn., La. Bar Assn., D.C. Bar Assn., Shreveport Bar Assn. Democrat. Episcopalian. Clubs: Shreveport Bridge (past pres.), Shreveport Club (La.); Metropolitan (Washington); Hawkeye Hunting (Center, Tex.), Cambridge. FERC practice, Federal civil litigation. Office: 1217 Commercial Nat Bank Bldg 333 Texas Suite 1217 Shreveport LA 71101-3677

HARIRI, RONALD DAVID, lawyer; b. Forest Hills, N.Y., May 31, 1957; s. Mansour and Angela (Bonilla) H. AB, Columbia U., 1978, JD, 1981. Bar: N.Y., U.S. Dist. Ct. (so. and ea. dists.) N.Y. Assoc. Finley, Kumble, Wagner, Heine, Underberg & Casey, N.Y.C., 1981-85, Pryor, Cashman, Sherman & Flynn, N.Y.C., 1985-86, Kleinberg, Kaplan, Wolff & Cohen P.C., N.Y.C., 1986—. Democrat. Jewish. Avocation: sailing. General corporate. Home: 66-36 Yellowstone Blvd Forest Hills NY 11375 Office: Kleinberg Kaplan Wolff & Cohen PC 522 Fifth Ave New York NY 10001

HARKAWAY, AARON ABRAHAM, judge; b. Nashua, N.H., Dec. 24, 1917; s. Joseph and Jennie (Frank) H.; m. Ada B. Winarsky, May 29, 1947; children—Jill, Barry. B.A., U. N.H., 1938; J.D., Columbia U., 1941. Bar: N.Y. 1942, N.H. 1946, U.S. Dist. Ct. N.H. 1947, U.S. Supreme Ct. 1967. Ptnr., Harkaway, Gall & Shapiro and predecessors, Nashua, 1946-72; ptnr. Leonard & Harkaway, Nashua, 1972-73; chief justice Nashua Dist. Ct., 1973-84; mem. jud. planning com. N.H. Supreme Ct., chmn. juvenile justice subcom.; pres. Corp. for Improvement of Justice in N.H.; mem. adv. bd. Nashua Hosp. Assn.; mem. N.H. Commn. on Children and Youth. Mem. N.H. Bar Assn., ABA., N.H. Judges Assn. (pres. 1977). Republican. Jewish. Author: N.H. Juvenile Justice Code of 1979. Juvenile, General practice, State civil litigation. Home: 4 White Gate Dr Nashua NH 03060 Office: Office of Barry L. Harkaway 3 Water St Nashua NH 03060

HARKEY, HENRY AVERILL, lawyer; b. Charlotte, N.C., June 17, 1949; s. Henry Lee and Elizabeth (Averill) H.; m. Catherine Ward, Aug. 6, 1977; children—Jonathan Henry, Christopher Harris. B.A., Washington and Lee U., 1971; J.D., Wake Forest U., 1975. Bar: N.C. 1975, U.S. Dist. Ct. (we. dist.) N.C. 1975. Asst. dist. atty. Office Dist. Atty., Charlotte, N.C., 1975-76; ptnr. Harkey, Fletcher & Lambeth, Charlotte, 1976—. Asst. scout master Mecklenburg County council Boy Scouts Am., 1975—; bd. dirs. Double Oaks Day Care Ctr., Charlotte, 1977—; mem. Charlotte Cert. Devel. Corp., 1981—. Recipient Disting. Service award Charlotte Jaycees, 1982. Mem. N.C. Acad. Trial Lawyers, N.C. Bar Assn., N.C. Coll. Advocacy, ABA, Wake Forest U. Sch. Law Lawyer Alumni Assn. (pres.). State civil litigation, Personal injury, Criminal. Home: 3901 Abingdon Rd Charlotte NC 28211 Office: Harkey Fletcher & Lambeth 200 Queens Rd Suite 200 Charlotte NC 28204

HARKEY, HENRY LEE, lawyer; b. Mt. Pleasant, N.C., Aug. 23, 1916; s. Frederick Lee and Carrie Mae (Heilig) H.; m. Elizabeth Averill, Dec. 13, 1941; children: Henry Averill, Averill Currie. AB cum laude, Davidson Coll., 1938; JD cum laude, U. N.C., 1947. Bar: N.C. 1947. Sr. ptnr. Harkey, Fletcher and Lambeth, Charlotte, N.C., 1950—. Served to col. USAR, 1938-58. Mem. ABA, N.C. Bar Assn. Presbyterian. Clubs: Charlotte City, Myers Park Country (Charlotte). Lodges: Masons, Shriners. General corporate, Condemnation, General practice. Home: 3807 Foxcroft Rd Charlotte NC 28211 Office: 200 Queens Rd Suite 200 Charlotte NC 28204

HARKEY, JOHN NORMAN, lawyer; b. Russellville, Ark., Feb. 25, 1933; s. Olga John and Margaret (Fleming) H.; m. Willa Moreau Charlton, May 24, 1959; children—John Adam, Sarah Leigh. A.S., Marion (Ala.) Inst., 1952; LL.B., U. Ark., 1959, B.S., 1959, J.D., 1969. Bar: Ark. bar 1959. Since practiced in Batesville; pros. atty. 3d Jud. Dist. Ark., 1961-65; Ins. commr. Ark., 1967-68; chmn. Ark. Commerce Commn., 1968-69. Served to 1st lt. USMCR, Korea. Mem. ABA, Ark. Bar Assn., Am. Assn. Trial Lawyers, Am. Judicature Soc., Am. Bar Register, Am. Bar Found., ACLU, Ark. Council Human Relations, U.S. Marine Corps League, Am. Checker Fedn., Delta Theta Phi. Personal injury, Federal civil litigation, State civil litigation. Home: Route 4 Batesville AR 72501 Office: PO Box 2535 Batesville AR 72501

HARKEY, PAUL, administrative law judge; b. Idabel, Okla., Mar. 4, 1920; s. John Paul and Jessie Ruth (Elliott) H.; m. Lucille Roy, June 1, 1942; children—Cheryl Annette Harkey Nordstrom, Roy Lee, John Paul III. B.A., Southeastern Okla. Coll., 1950; LL.B., U. Okla., 1961, J.D., 1970. Bar: Okla. 1948, U.S. Dist. Ct. (no., ea. and we. dists.) Okla., Tex. 1966, U.S. Dist. Ct. (ea., no. and we. dists.) Tex., U.S. Dist. Ct. (ea. dist.) Pa., Hawaii, also others. Pvt. practice law, Idabel and Norman, Okla., 1948-64; U.S. adminstrv. law judge HEW/HHS, Dallas, 1964—. Mem. Okla. Ho. of Reps., 1946-54. Served to capt. USN, from 1940, ATO, PTO. Mem. ABA. Administrative and regulatory, Pension, profit-sharing, and employee benefits, Judicial administration. Home: PO Box 22-2122 Dallas TX 75222 Office: Office Hearings & Appeals DHHS Suite 252 10830 N Central Pkwy Dallas TX 75231

HARKINS, FRANCIS JOSEPH, JR., lawyer; b. N.Y.C., June 20, 1949; s. Francis Joseph Sr. and Winifred E. (Daly) H.; m. Mary Manning, May 9, 1981. BA, Fairfield U., 1971; JD, N.Y. Law Sch., 1974. Bar: N.Y., U.S. Dist. Ct. (so. and ea. dists.) N.Y. Corp. counsel City of N.Y., 1974-75; corp. atty. W.R. Grace & Co., N.Y.C., 1975—. Vol. The Legal Aid Soc., N.Y.C., 1986—. Mem. N.Y. State Bar Assn., Assn. of Bar of City of N.Y., N.Y. County Lawyers Assn. (corp. law dept. com.). Club: N.Y. Athletic. Avocations: sailing, trapshooting, reading, golf. General corporate, Private international, Administrative and regulatory. Home: 28 Prospect Park SW Brooklyn NY 11215 Office: W R Grace & Co 1114 Ave of the Americas New York NY 10036

HARKINS, KENNETH R., federal judge; b. Cadiz, Ohio, Sept. 1, 1921; m. Helen Mae Dozer, Dec. 26, 1942; children—M. Elaine, Richard A. B.A. in Econs., Ohio State U., 1943, LL.B., 1948, J.D., 1967. Bar: Ohio 1949. Atty. U.S. Housing and Home Fin. Agy., 1949-51; trial atty. antitrust div. U.S. Dept. Justice, Washington, 1951-55; co-counsel Antitrust subcom. Judiciary Com. Ho. of Reps., Washington, 1955-60; gen. counsel Stromberg Carlson div. and electronics div. Gen. Dynamics Corp., 1960-64; chief counsel Antitrust subcom. Judiciary Com. Ho. Reps., Washington, 1964-71; commr. U.S. Ct. Claims, Washington, 1971-82, judge, 1982—. Served to 1st lt. U.S. Army, 1943-46. Office: US Ct Claims 717 Madison Pl NW Washington DC 20005 *

HARKINS, PATRICK NICHOLAS, III, lawyer; b. Jackson, Miss., Apr. 27, 1941; s. Patrick Nicholas and Mary Ruth (Gammon) H.; m. Mary Elizabeth Wilson, Apr. 12, 1969; children—Elizabeth Glenn, DeMatt Henderson. B.B.A., U. Notre Dame, 1963; J.D., U. Miss., 1965. Bar: Miss. 1965, U.S. Dist. Ct. (no. and so. dists.) Miss. 1965, U.S. Ct. Appeals (5th cir.) 1965, U.S. Supreme Ct. 1968. Legis. asst. U.S. Congressman G.V. Montgomery, 1967-68; assoc. atty. Watkins, Pyle, Ludlam, Winter & Stennis, Jackson, 1969; atty. Watkins & Eager, Jackson, 1970—, ptnr., 1973—. Served to capt. U.S. Army, 1965-67. Mem. Internat. Assn. Ins. Counsel, ABA, Miss. Bar Assn., Miss. Def. Lawyers Assn., Hinds County Bar Assn. Roman Catholic. Clubs: Capital City, Country (Jackson). Federal civil litigation. Home: 2060 Sheffield Dr Jackson MS 39211

HARL, NEIL EUGENE, economist, lawyer, educator; b. Appanoose County, Iowa, Oct. 9, 1933; s. Herbert Peter and Bertha Catherine (Bonner) H.; m. Darlene Ramona Harris, Sept. 7, 1952; children: James Brent, Rodney Scott. B.S., Iowa State U., 1955, Ph.D., 1965; J.D., U. Iowa, 1961. Bar: Iowa 1961. Field editor Wallace's Farmer, 1957-58; research assoc. U.S. Dept. Agr., Iowa City and Ames, Iowa, 1958-64; assoc. prof. econs. Iowa State U., Ames, 1964-67; prof. Iowa State U., 1967—, Charles F. Curtiss Disting. prof., 1976—; frequent lectr. in field; mem. adv. group Commr. IRS, 1979-80. Author: Farm Estate and Bus. Planning, 1973, 9th edit., 1984, Legal and Tax Guide for Agricultural Lenders, 1984; Agricultural Law, 15 vols., 1980-81, Agricultural Law Manual, 1985; co-author: Farmland, 1982; contbr. articles to profl. jours.; author/actor films and videotape programs. Trustee Iowa State U. Agrl. Found., 1969—. Served to 1st lt. AUS, 1955-57; capt. USAR. Recipient Outstanding Tchr. award Iowa State U., 1973, Disting. Service to Agr. award Am. Soc. Farm Mgrs. and Rural Appraisers, 1977, Faculty Service award Nat. Univ. Extension Assn., 1980, Disting. Service award Am. Agrl. Editors Assn., 1984, Disting. Service award Iowa State U. Extension, 1984, Disting. Achievement citation, Iowa State U., 1985, Henry A. Wallace award 1987, Disting. Service to State Govt. award., Nat. Gov.'s Assn., 1986, Disting. Service award, State of Iowa, 1986, Superior Service award, USDA, 1987. Fellow Am. Agrl. Econs. Assn. (exec. bd. 1979-85, pres. 1983-84, Outstanding Extension Program award, 1970, Excellence in Communicating Research Results award, 1975, Disting. Undergrad. Tchr. award, 1976, Farm Leader of Yr. Des Moines register, 1986); mem. ABA, Iowa Bar Assn., Am. Agrl. Law Assn. (pres. 1980-81, Disting. Service award 1984). Agricultural law, Estate planning, Estate taxation. Home: 2821 Duff Ave Ames IA 50010 Office: Dept Econs Iowa State U Ames IA 50011

HARLAN, NANCY MARGARET, lawyer; b. Santa Monica, Calif., Sept. 10, 1946; d. William Galland and Betty M. (Miles) Plett; B.S. magna cum laude, Calif. State U., Hayward, 1972; J.D., U. Calif., Berkeley, 1975; m. John Hammack, Dec. 1, 1979; children—Laryssa Maria Rebello, Leea Elyce Harlan. Admitted to Calif. bar, 1975, Fed. bar, U.S. Dist. Ct. for Central Dist., 9th Circuit, 1976; assoc. firm Poindexter & Doutré, Los Angeles, 1975-80; residential counsel Coldwell Banker Residential Brokerage Co., Fountain Valley, Calif., 1980-81; sr. counsel for real estate subs. law dept. Pacific Lighting Corp., Santa Ana, Calif., 1981—. Exec. v.p. student body U. Calif., Berkeley, 1974-75; bd. dirs. La Casa. Mem. State Bar Calif., Am. Bar Assn., Los Angeles County Bar Assn., Orange County Bar Assn. (dir. corp. counsel sect. 1982—), Calif. Women Lawyers Assn., Orange County Women Lawyers Assn., Los Angeles Women Lawyers Assn., Nat. Assn. Female Execs., Bus. and Profl. Women. Real property, General corporate. Office: Pacific Lighting Corp 48 Brookhollow Dr Santa Ana CA 92705

HARLESS, FRED STAPEL, judge; b. Montgomery, Ala., July 9, 1919; s. O.L. and Lillian E. (Stapel) H.; m. Ruth Wilkinson, Dec. 27, 1946; children: Rexanne, Stacey. LLB, So. Meth. U., 1950. Sole practice Dallas, 1950-70; dist. judge 14th Dist. Ct., Dallas, 1971-80, 116th Dist. Ct., Dallas, 1982-86. Served with USNR, 1942-45. Mem. Tex. Bar Assn., Dallas Bar Assn. Republican. Presbyterian. Home: 16738 Lauder Ln Dallas TX 75248

HARLESTON, JOHN, lawyer; b. Charleston, S.C., Oct. 8, 1954; s. William and Isabel (Rapier) H.; m. Kathleen McMahon, June 8, 1985; 1 child, Elizabeth Ann. BA with distinction, U. Va., 1976; JD cum laude, U. S.C., 1981. Bar: S.C. 1981, U.S. Dist. Ct. S.C. 1981, U.S. Ct. Appeals (4th cir) 1982, U.S. Ct. Appeals (D.C. cir.) 1986. Staff atty. dept. health and environ. control State of S.C., Columbia, 1981—; faculty S.C. Bar Continuing Legal Edn. on Environ. Law, Columbia, 1985. Mem. S.C. Interagy. Task Force on Marinas/Shellfish, Columbia, 1984. Mem. ABA, Order of Wig and Robe, Order of Coif. Roman Catholic. Administrative and regulatory, Environment. Office: SC Dept Health and Environ Control 2600 Bull St Columbia SC 29201

HARLEY, HALVOR LARSON, banker, lawyer; b. Atlantic City, Oct. 7, 1948; s. Robison Dooling and Loyde Hazel (Gauhnauer) H. B.Sc., U. S.C., 1971, M.A., 1973; J.D., Widener U., 1981. Bar: Pa. 1982. Staff psychologist Columbia Area Mental Health Ctr., S.C., 1971-73; dir. Motivational Research Consultants, Columbia, 1973-79; psychologist Family Ct. Del., Wilmington, 1979, sole practice law, Phila., 1982; v.p. investment banking Union Bank, Orange, Calif., 1982—. Author: Herpes Sufferers Get Help, 1982; also articles. Fundraiser Orange County Performing Arts Ctr., 1983-84; mem. chair circle Calif. Democratic Party, 1983-84; vol. Hosp. Ship HOPE, Sri Lanka, 1968-69; bd. dirs. Lido Sands Homeowners Assn., Newport Beach, Calif., 1984—. Mem. Orange County Bankers Assn., Assn. Trial Lawyers Am., Am. Judicature Soc., Indsl. League Orange County (membership com. 1983-84), Am. Bankers Assn., World Trade Ctr. Assocs. Orange County (directing com. 1983—), Psi Chi (chpt. pres. 1971-73). Democrat. Theosophist. Banking, General corporate, Securities. Home: 5015 Lido Sands Dr Newport Beach CA 92663 Office: Union Bank 445 S Figueroa St Los Angeles CA 90071

HARLEY, ROBISON DOOLING, JR., lawyer, educator; b. Ancon, Panama, July 6, 1946; s. Robison Dooling and Loyde Hazel (Gochenauer) H.; m. Suzanne Purviance Bendel, Aug. 9, 1975; children—Arianne Erin, Lauren Loyde. B.A., Brown U., 1968; J.D., Temple U., 1971; LL.M., U. San Diego, 1985. Bar: Pa. 1972, U.S. Ct. Mil. Appeals 1972, Calif. 1976, N.J. 1978, U.S. Supreme Ct. 1980, D.C. 1981, U.S. Dist. Ct. N.J., U.S. Dist. Ct. (cen. and so. dists.) Calif., U.S. Ct. Appeals (9th cir.) 1982. Cert. criminal law specialist Calif. Bd. Legal Specialization; cert. criminal trial adv. Nat. Bd. Trial Advocacy. Asst. agy. dir. Safeco Title Ins. Co., Los Angeles, 1975-77; ptnr. Cohen, Stokke & Davis, Santa Ana, Calif., 1977-85; sole practice, Santa Ana, Calif., 1985—; instr. Orange County Coll. Trial Advocacy, paralegal program U. Calif.; judge pro-tem Orange County Cts. Bd. dirs. Orange County Legal Aid Soc. Served to lt. col. JAGC, USMCR, 1971—; trial counsel, def. counsel, mil. judge, asst. staff judge adv. USMC, 1971-75, asst. regional def. counsel Western Region, 1986—. Mem. Orange County Bar Assn. (judiciary com., criminal law sect., adminstrn. of justice com.), Orange County Trial Lawyers Assn., Calif. Trial Lawyers Assn., Assn. Trial Lawyers Am., Calif. Attys. for Criminal Justice, Calif. Pub. Defenders Assn., Nat. Assn. for Criminal Def. Attys., Assn. Specialized Criminal Def. Advs., Orange County Criminal Lawyers Assn. (found. com.), Res. Officers Assn., Marine Corps Reserve Officers Assn. Republican. Criminal, Military, Juvenile. Home: 12 Bayberry Way Irvine CA 92715 Office: 825 N Ross St Santa Ana CA 92701

HARLIN, MAXEY BARLOW, JR., lawyer; b. Bowling Green, Ky., Oct. 13, 1915; s. Maxey Barlow Sr. and Margaret Harlin; m. Nancy Helm Moore, Aug. 24, 1935; children: Maxey B., John M. (dec.), Nancy Elizabeth Harlin Tyrie. LLB, U. Louisville, 1938. Bar: Ky. 1938. Ptnr. Harlin, Parker & Rudloff, Bowling Green, 1938—. Mem. Constn. Revision Assembly, Frankfort, Ky., 1964-66, bd. of regents We. Ky. U. Mem. ABA, Ky. Bar Assn. (pres. 1951-52, bd. govs. 1940-51, 56-64), Am. Coll. Trial Lawyers. Home: 1508 Chestnut St Bowling Green KY 42101

HARLOW, EUGENE MARCHANT, lawyer; b. Clarksdale, Miss., July 11, 1957; s. William Gadsberry Harlow and Betty (Cobb) Townsend; m. Jan Baird; children: Daphne Baird, Meacham Ann. BBA, U. Miss., 1979, JD,

1982. Assoc. Gibbes, Graves, Mullins, Bullock & Ferris, Laurel, Miss., 1982—. Chmn. Jones County Unit Am. Cancer Soc., 1985-86, consumer protection com. Econ. Devel. Authority, 1986—; bd. of trustees St. John's Day Sch., Laurel, Miss., 1986—; vestryman St. John's Episc. Ch. Mem. ABA, Miss. Bar Assn. (code profl. responsibility com., long range planning com., chmn. local affiliates com. young lawyers sect.), Jones County Bar Assn. (pres. young lawyers div. 1985-86). Episcopalian. Avocations: gardening, hunting, fishing. Insurance, Real property, Workers' compensation. Home: 734 Oak Dr Laurel MS 39440 Office: Gibbes Graves Mullins Bullok & Ferris 1107 W 6th St PO Drawer 1409 Laurel MS 39441-1409

HARMAN, CHARLES DALE, JR., lawyer; b. Bluefield, W.Va., Mar. 21, 1934; s. C. Dale Sr. and Bernardine Elizabeth (Cassidy) H.; m. Katherine Anne Ross, Apr. 4, 1964; children: Charles D. III, Allan Ross, Sayers French II. BS, Va. Tech. U., 1956; LLB, U. Va., 1962. Bar: Ga. 1962. Assoc. Jones, Bird & Howell, Atlanta, 1962-67, ptnr., 1968-73; ptnr. Harman, Asbill & Roach, Atlanta, 1973-84, Harman, Owen, Saunders & Sweeney, Atlanta, 1984—. Served to 1st lt. U.S. Army, 1956-59. Mem. ABA, Ga. Bar Assn., Atlanta Bar Assn. Clubs: Capital City, Piedmont Driving (Atlanta). Home: 615 Tuxedo Pl NW Atlanta GA 30342 Office: Harman Owen Saunders & Sweeney 229 Peachtree St NE Atlanta GA 30303

HARMAN, JOHN ROYDEN, lawyer; b. Elkhart, Ind., June 30, 1921; s. James Lewis and Bessie Bell (Mountjoy) H.; m. Elizabeth Rae Crosier, Dec. 12, 1943; 1 child, James Richard. B.S., U. Ill., 1943; J.D., Ind. U., 1949. Bar: Ind. 1949. Since practiced in Elkhart; asso. Proctor & Proctor, 1949-52; partner Cawley & Harman, 1960-65, Thornburg, McGill, Deahl, Harman, Carey & Murray, 1965-82, Barnes & Thornburg, 1982—; atty., City of Elkhart, 1952-60. State del. Ind. Republican Com., 1962-70; Pres., bd. dirs. Crippled Childrens Soc.; bd. dirs. United Community Services Elkhart County. Served to 1st lt., F.A. AUS, 1943-46, PTO. Mem. ABA, Ind. Bar Assn. (council 3d dist. corp. counsel sect.), Elkhart County Bar Assn. (pres. 1977), Elkhart Bar Assn. (pres. 1970), Elkhart C. of C. (pres. 1977, bd. dirs. 1972-75), Phi Kappa Psi, Alpha Kappa Psi, Phi Delta Phi. Presbyterian. Clubs: Rotary (pres. 1977-78), Elcona Country (dir. 1981-83) (Elkhart). Contracts commercial, General corporate, Probate. Home: 54905 Shorelane Elkhart IN 46514 Office: First Nat Bank Bldg Elkhart IN 46514

HARMON, E(VERETT) GLENN, lawyer; b. Port Orchard, Wash., Jan. 5, 1914; s. Eben G. and Emma Ruth (Meyer) H.; m. Jean P. Sargent, Feb. 2, 1940; children—Rondi Lee Ellis, Nadine Kay Sherman, E. Gil, Douglas W. B.A. in English-Journalism, Wash. State U., 1940, LL.B., Gonzaga U., 1953. Bar: Wash. 1953, U.S. Dist. Ct. (ea. dist.) Wash. 1955, U.S. Dist. Ct. (we. dist.) Wash. 1957, U.S. Ct. Apls. (9th cir.) 1960, U.S. Sup. Ct. 1972. Law clk., Wash. Sup. Ct. 1954; bill drafter Wash. Legislature, 1955; assoc. Witherspoon, Kelly, Davenport, Toole, Spokane, 1955-59, ptnr., 1959—; counsel Wash. State Tax Control Council, 1961-66, Lake Coeur D'Alene (Idaho) Property Owners & Taxpayers Assn., 1964—; gen. counsel Norwest Lakes and Rivers Legal Found., 1984—. Pres., Spokane Mcpl. League 1967. Served with U.S. Army, 1944-46. Mem. ABA, Wash. State Bar Assn. (recipient award of merit 1964), Spokane County Bar Assn. Club: Spokane. Libel, Labor, Trademark and copyright. Office: Old National Bank Bldg Spokane WA 99201

HARMON, GAIL MCGREEVY, lawyer; b. Kansas City, Kans., Mar. 15, 1943; d. Milton and Barbara (James) McGreevy; m. John W. Harmon, June 11, 1966; children: James, Eve. BA cum laude, Radcliffe Coll., 1965; JD cum laude, Columbia U., 1969. Bar: Mass. 1970, D.C. 1976, U.S. Dist. Ct. D.C. Assoc. Gaston Snow & Ely Bartlett, Boston, 1970-75, Steptoe & Johnson, Washington, 1975-76, Roisman, Kessler & Cashdan, Washington, 1976-77; ptnr. Harmon & Weiss, Washington, 1977—. Democrat. Episcopalian. Corporate taxation, General corporate. Office: Harmon & Weiss 2001 S St NW #430 Washington DC 20011

HARMON, MELINDA FURCHE, lawyer; b. Port Arthur, Tex., Nov. 1, 1946; d. Frank Cantrell and Wilma (Parish) Furche; m. Frank G. Harmon III, Oct. 16, 1976; children: Mary Elizabeth, Phelps, Francis. AB, Harvard U., 1969; JD, U. Tex., 1972. Bar: Tex. 1973, U.S. Dist. Ct. (so. dist.) Tex. 1974, U.S. Dist. Ct. (no. dist.) Tex. 1975, U.S. Dist. Ct. (ea. dist.) Tex. 1978, U.S. Ct. Appeals (5th and 11th cirs.) 1981, U.S. Supreme Ct. 1982, U.S. Ct. Claims 1987. Law clk. to presiding judge U.S. Dist. Ct. (so. dist.) Tex., Houston, 1973-75; atty. Exxon Co., Houston, 1975—. Mem. ABA, Tex. Bar Assn., Houston Bar Assn. Republican. Roman Catholic. Club: Harvard Radcliffe. Federal civil litigation, State civil litigation. Home: 2165 Dryden Rd Houston TX 77030 Office: Exxon Co USA PO Box 2180 Room 1825 Houston TX 77001

HARMON, ROBERT LON, lawyer; b. Saginaw, Mich., Jan. 27, 1938; s. Homer W. and Vena M. (Moore) H.; m. Ruth Susan Schaberg, Aug. 25, 1962; children—Matthew Moore, Daniel Palmer. B.S.E. in Elec. Engring., U. Mich., 1960, J.D. with distinction, 1963. Bar: D.C. 1964, Ill. 1965, Wis. 1983. Law clk. to assoc. judge U.S. Ct. Customs and Patent Appeals, Washington, 1963-65; ptnr. Hume, Clement, Brinks, Willian & Olds, Ltd., Chgo., 1965-83, Willian, Brinks, Olds, Hofer, Gilson & Leone, Ltd., Chgo., 1983—. Mem. ABA, Ill. Bar Assn., Chgo. Bar Assn., Am. Patent Law Assn., Chgo. Patent Law Assn. Club: Anglers (Chgo.). Co-author: Patent Law, 1965; contbr. articles to legal pubis. Patent, Federal civil litigation. Home: 814 Woodbine Ln Northbrook IL 60062 Office: One IBM Plaza Suite 4100 Chicago IL 60611

HARMS, EDWARD CLAIR, JR., lawyer, educator; b. Roseburg, Oreg., Sept. 21, 1924; s. Edward Clair Sr. and Gleneva (McClain) H.; m. Patricia Honeywood Walker, Dec. 21, 1946; children: Kathleen P., Kerry E., Kimberly L. Harms Miller. BS, U. Oreg., 1947, JD, 1949. Bar: Oreg. 1949, U.S. Dist. Ct. Oreg. 1950, U.S. Supreme Ct. 1965, U.S. Ct. Appeals (9th cir.) 1983. Sole practice Springfield, Oreg., 1949-68; ptnr. Harms & Harold, Springfield, 1968-78, Harms, Harold & Leahy, Springfield, 1978-86; sr. ptnr. Harms, Harold, Leahy & Pace, Springfield, 1986—; adj. prof. law U. Oreg., Eugene, 1958-75. Mayor City of Springfield, 1953-61; vice chmn. environ. quality commn. State of Oreg., 1959-73; pres. League of Oreg. Cities, Salem, 1959-60, Oreg. State Bd. Higher Edn., 1975-85, pres. 1980-82. Served to lt. USN, 1942-46, PTO. Mem. ABA, Lane County Bar Assn., Sprinfield C. of C. (First Citizen award 1957), Springfield Jaycees (Jr. 1st Citizen award 1956, Youn Man of Yr. 1956), Phi Alpha Delta. Democrat. Baptist. Clubs: Oreg. (Eugene-Springfield) (pres. 1969), Eugene Country. Avocations: mountain climbing (holder Obsidians Oreg. Cascades award), golf. Local government, General practice, Probate. Home: 845 Willacade Ct Springfield OR 97477 Office: Harms Harold Leahy & Pace 223 North A Suite D Springfield OR 97477

HARMS, STEVEN ALAN, lawyer; b. Detroit, Feb. 15, 1949; s. Herbert Rudolph and Elsa Jane (McClelland) H.; m. Nancy Gayle Banta, June 26, 1971; children—Jennifer Elizabeth, Heather Lynn, Robin Ann. B.A., Hope Coll., 1970; J.D., Detroit Coll. Law, 1975. Bar: Mich. 1975, U.S. Dist. Ct. (so. dist.) Mich. 1975, U.S. Ct. Appeals (6th cir.) 1982. Ptnr. Muller, Muller, Richmond, Harms, Myers & Sgroi, P.C., Birmingham, Mich.; sec. gen. practice session State Bar Mich., 1982-83; lectr. in field. Author: Successful Collection of a Judgement, 1981; Rights of Commercial Creditors, 1982; editor General Practitioner, State Bar Mich., 1978-82. Mem. adminstrv. bd. St. Paul's United Meth. Ch., Rochester, Mich., 1984—. Mem. ABA, Detroit Bar Assn. Republican. Club: Pearson Yacht Owners Assn., Hunter Sailing Assn. (vice commodore 1985-86). Consumer commercial, Contracts commercial. Office: Muller Muller Richmond Harms & Sgroi PC 1880 S Woodward Birmingham MI 48011

HARNACK, DON STEGER, lawyer; b. Milw., June 19, 1928; s. Benjamin John and Katherine (Steger) H.; m. Rose Marie Ball, Oct. 17, 1959; children: Christopher Wallen, Gretchen Marie, Pamela Ann. BS, U. Wis., 1950; LLB, Harvard U., 1953. Bar: Wis. 1953, U.S. Dist. Ct. (ea. dist.) Wis. 1955, U.S. Tax Ct. 1957, Ill. 1959, U.S. Dist. Ct. (no. dist.) Ill. 1962, U.S. Ct. Appeals (6th and 7th cirs.) 1963, U.S. Ct. Claims 1966, U.S. Ct. Appeals (8th cir.) 1971, U.S. Supreme Ct. 1972. Assoc. Quarles, Spence & Quarles, Milw., 1955-57; trial atty. regional counsel IRS, Chgo., 1957-61; assoc. Dixon, Todhunter, Knouf & Holmes, Chgo., 1961-65; ptnr. McDermott, Will & Emery, Chgo., 1965—. Contbr. articles to profl. jours. Mem. Winnetka Zoning Bd., Ill., 1971-75; park bd. atty. Winnetka Park Dist., 1978-83; pres. North East Ill. Council Boy Scouts Am., North Shore, Ill., 1982-83; trustee ULC Boys Club, Chgo., 1974—, Village of Winnetka, 1984—. Served to lt. USNR. Recipient Silver Beaver award Boy Scouts Am., 1984. Mem. ABA, Ill. Bar Assn., Wis. Bar Assn. Republican. Club: Union League (Chgo.) (bd. dirs., officer, v.p. 1981—, pres. 1987). Avocations: fishing, tennis, golf, reading. Corporate taxation, State and local taxation, Federal civil litigation.

HARNESS, WILLIAM WALTER, lawyer; b. Ottumwa, Iowa, Apr. 14, 1945; s. Walter W. and Mary E. (Bukowski) H.; m. Carolyn Margaret Barnes, Jan 4, 1969; children—Matthew William, Michael Andrew. B.A., U. Iowa, 1967; J.D., Cleve. State U., 1974. Bar: Ohio 1975, U.S. Dist. Ct. (no. dist.) Ohio 1975, D.C. 1976, U.S. Dist. Ct. D.C. 1976, U.S. Ct. Appeals (D.C. cir.) 1976, U.S. Ct. Appeals (5th cir.) 1981, U.S. Dist. Ct. (we. dist.) N.C. 1979, U.S. Ct. Appeals (1st cir.) 1980, U.S. Ct. Appeals (4th cir.) 1981, U.S. Ct. Appeals (11th cir.) 1981. Mem. labor relations staff Monogram Industries, Cleve., 1970-75; asst. counsel Nat. Treasury Employees Union, Washington, 1975-77, nat. counsel, Atlanta, 1977—; lectr. Emory U., Atlanta, 1978—; participant various seminars Ga. State U. Pres. Spring Mill-Kingsborough Ct. Corp., Atlanta. Served to 1st lt. U.S. Army, 1967-70. Mem. ABA (com. on fed. labor-mgmt. 1981-84), D.C. Bar Assn. (bd. dirs.), Soc. Fed. Labor Relations Profls., Indsl. Relations Research Assn. Labor, Federal civil litigation, Civil rights. Home: 1285 Mile Post Dr Dunwoody GA 30338 Office: Nat Treasury Employees Union 2801 Buford Hwy Suite 430 Atlanta GA 30329

HARNEY, DAVID MORAN, lawyer; b. Marysville, Calif., June 30, 1924; s. George Richard and Eileen M. (Daly) H.; m. Evelyn Brint Turner, Mar. 17, 1945; children—Brian Patrick, David Turner. Student Loyola U., Los Angeles, 1942-43, Ariz. State U., 1943-44, Southwestern La. U., 1944; J.D., U. So. Calif., 1948. Bar: Calif. 1949. Ptnr. Harney, Wolfe, Pagliuso, Shaller & Carr and predecessor firms, Los Angeles, 1950—. Served to 1st lt. USMC, 1942-45. Mem. Internat. Acad. Trial Lawyers (pres.-1983-84). Democrat. Roman Catholic. Club: Jonathan (Los Angeles). State civil litigation. Home: 880 W 1st St 705 Los Angeles CA 90012 Office: 201 N Figueroa St #1300 Los Angeles CA 90012

HAROLDSON, JEFFREY DAVID, lawyer; b. Ann Arbor, Mich., May 15, 1957; s. Olaf Haroldson and Arlys Ann (St. Clair) Button; m. Jacquelyn Joyce Peterson, June 6, 1982; 1 child, James St. Clair. BA, U. Mich., 1978; JD, Cornell U., 1981. Bar: N.Y. 1982, U.S. Dist. Ct. (so. dist.) N.Y., 1982. Assoc. Milbank, Tweed, Hadley & McCloy, N.Y.C., 1981—. Editor Cornell Law Rev. 1980-81, assoc., 1979-80. Mem. ABA (fed. regulation securities com., banking law com., sub-com. for comml. lending), N.Y. State Bar Assn., Assn. of the Bar City of N.Y. Republican. Episcopalian. Banking, Municipal bonds, Securities. Home: 546 Hillcrest Rd Ridgewood NJ 07450 Office: Milbank Tweed Hadley & McCloy 1 Chase Manhattan Plaza New York NY 10005

HARON, DAVID LAWRENCE, lawyer; b. Detroit, Sept. 24, 1944; s. Percy Hyman and Bess (Holland) H.; m. Pamela Kay Colburn, May 25, 1969; children: Eric, Andrea. BA, U. Mich., 1966, JD, 1969. Bar: Mich. 1969, U.S. Dist. Ct. (ea. dist.) Mich., 1969, U.S. Supreme Ct. 1974. Law clk. to chief judge Mich. Ct. Appeals, Detroit, 1969-70; assoc. Barris, Sott, Denn & Driker, Detroit, 1970-74; sr. ptnr. Josephson, Tennen & Haron, Southfield, Mich., 1974—; cons. Universe Computer Software, 1985; pres., bd. dirs. S&H Licensing Corp., Southfield. Mem. editorial bd. Prospectus Jour. Law Reform, 1969, (newsletter) Atty.'s Mktg. Report, 1986—. Counsel to treas. Com. to Re-elect Senator Riegle, Troy, Mich., 1981-82; bd. dirs. Forest Elem. Sch. PTO, Farmington Hills, Mich., 1983; v.p. North Farmington (Mich.) Baseball for Youth, 1984; mem. WTVS Auction, Detroit, 1985-86; trustee Temple Israel, West Bloomfield, Mich., 1987—, also tchr. Sunday sch. Recipient Outstanding Alumnus award Mumford High Sch., Detroit, 1985, Cert. recognition City of Farmington Hills, 1986. Mem. ABA, Assn. Trial Lawyers Am., Am. Arbitration Assn. (arbitrator), Mich. Bar Assn. (chmn. com. 1977-78), Detroit Bar Assn., Oakland County Bar Assn., Southfield Bar Assn., U. Mich. Alumni Assn., Tau Delta Phi. Democrat. Jewish. Club: Renaissance. Lodge: B'Nai Brith Barristers. General corporate, Real property, Personal injury. Home: 34685 Old Timber Rd Farmington Hills MI 48018 Office: Josephson Tennen & Haron 24800 Northwestern Southfield MI 48075

HARPER, ALFRED JOHN, II, lawyer; b. El Paso, Tex., Aug. 11, 1942; s. Mosely Lloyd and Marion M. (McClintock) H.; m. Cynthia Newkam; children—A. John, Leslie J. B.A., North Tex. State U., 1964; LL.B. cum laude, So. Meth. U., 1967. Bar: Tex. 1967, U.S. Ct. Appeals (5th cir.) 1968, U.S. Supreme Ct. 1971, U.S. Dist. Ct. (no. dist.) Tex. 1975, U.S. Ct. Appeals (9th cir.) 1976, U.S. Dist. Ct. (we. dist.) Tex. 1976, U.S. Ct. Appeals (11th cir.) 1982, U.S. Ct. Appeals (10th cir.) 1984, U.S. Dist. Ct. (so. dist.) Tex. 1967; cert. labor law specialist State Bar Tex. bd. labor specialization. Assoc. Fulbright & Jaworski, Houston, 1967-74, ptnr., 1974—. Editor Jour. Air Law and Commerce, 1966-67; contbr. articles to profl. jours. Served with USMCR, 1960-66. Mem. ABA (past mgmt. co-chmn. com. on devel. of law under Nat. Labor Relations Act, labor law sect.), Tex. Bar Assn. Order of Coif. Republican. Methodist. Club: Briar. Labor, Civil rights. Office: 1301 McKinney 47th Floor Houston TX 77010

HARPER, CONRAD KENNETH, lawyer; b. Detroit, Dec. 2, 1940; s. Archibald Leonard and Georgia Florence (Hall) H.; m. Marsha Louise Wilson, July 17, 1965; children: Warren Wilson, Adam Woodburn. B.A., Howard U., 1962; LL.B., Harvard U., 1965. Bar: N.Y. 1966. Law clk. NAACP Legal Def. and Edni. Fund, N.Y.C., 1965-66; staff lawyer NAACP Legal Def. and Ednl. Fund, 1966-70; asso. firm Simpson Thacher & Bartlett, N.Y.C., 1971-74; ptnr. Simpson Thacher & Bartlett, 1974—; lectr. law Rutgers U., 1969-70; vis. lectr. law Yale U., 1977-81; cons. HEW, 1977; chmn. admissions and grievances com. U.S. Ct. Appeals (2d cir.), 1987—. Trustee N.Y. Pub. Library, Lawyers' Com. for Civil Rights under Law, Mus. City of N.Y.; vestryman Ch. of St. Barnabas, Irvington, N.Y., 1982-85. Fellow Am. Bar Found., Am. Coll. Trial Lawyers; mem. ABA (bd. editors Jour. 1980-86), Nat. Bar Assn., N.Y. State Bar Assn., Assn. Bar City N.Y. (chmn. exec. com. 1979-80), Am. Law Inst. (council 1985—), Am. Assn. for Internat. Commn. Jurists (bd. dirs.), Council Fgn. Relations., Phi Beta Kappa. Democrat. Episcopalian. Clubs: Harvard, India House (N.Y.C.). Office: 1 Battery Park Plaza New York NY 10004

HARPER, GREGORY LIVINGSTON, lawyer; b. Jackson, Miss., June 1, 1956; s. C. Douglas and Lois (Livingston) H.; m. Sidney Hancock, Aug. 11, 1979. BS in Chemistry, Miss. Coll., 1978; JD, U. Miss., 1981. Bar: Miss. 1981, U.S. Dist. Ct. (no. and so. dists.) Miss. 1981, U.S. Ct. Appeals (5th cir.) 1981. Assoc. Law Offices James W. Nobles Jr., Jackson, 1981-83; sole practice Jackson, 1983—. Mem. Assn. Trial Lawyers Am., Miss. Bar Assn., Miss. Trial Lawyers Assn., Hinds County Bar Assn., Hinds County Trial Lawyers Assn. Baptist. Personal injury, Family and matrimonial, Criminal. Home: 5 Spring Lake Point Jackson MS 39208 Office: 515 Court St Jackson MS 39201

HARPER, LINDA WALKER, lawyer; b. Davenport, Iowa, Dec. 14; d. Frank Barton and Golda (Schultz) Walker; m. Timothy W. Harper; 1 son, Jesse. B.S., U. Mich., 1978; J.D., Thomas Cooley Law Sch., Lansing, Mich., 1982. Bar: Mich. 1982, U.S. Dist. Ct. (ea. dist.) Mich. 1982. Vice pres. Twp. Zoning Bd., Gregory, Mich., 1977-81; law clk. Livingston County Cir. Ct., Mich., 1980-82; sole practice, Fowlerville, Mich., 1982—. Mem. ABA, Assn. Trial Lawyers Am., Women Lawyers Mich., Women Lawyers Livingston County. Republican. Family and matrimonial, Probate, General practice. Office: 309 E Grand River Fowlerville MI 48836

HARPER, MONICA LAFFERTY, lawyer; b. Cologne, Fed. Republic Germany, Sept. 14, 1942; came to U.S., 1954; d. William Joka and Josephine (Foerster) Breckenridge; m. Richard William Lafferty, Jan 9, 1965 (div. Jan 1979); children: Peter William, Elliot Richard; m. Albert Buckner Harper, June 4, 1982; 1 child, Jacob Joka. BA, Chestnut Hill Coll., 1964; student, Villanova U., 1972-73; JD, U. Conn., 1976. Bar: Conn. 1978, U.S. Dist. Ct. Conn. 1978. Tchr. French Archdiocese of Phila., 1964-68; assoc. Rome, Case, Kennelly & Klebanoff P.C., Bloomfield, Conn., 1978-84, ptnr., 1984-85; sole practice Hartford, Conn., 1985—. Mem. town com. Simsbury Dems., Conn., 1971; alternate Simsbury Planning Commn., 1973. Mem. ABA, Conn. Bar Assn. (exec. com. family law sect.), Hartford County Bar Assn. (family law com.), Conn. Trial Lawyers Assn., Hartford Women Attys. Assn. (co-chairperson program com.), Conn. Council Divorce and Family Mediators, Inc., Hartford Women's Network. Democrat. Avocations: gardening, racquetball. Family and matrimonial, Personal injury. Home: 4001 South St Coventry CT 06106 Office: 60 Washington St Hartford CT 06106

HARPER, STEVEN JAMES, lawyer; b. Mpls., Apr. 25, 1954; s. James Henry and Mary Margaret (Fischer) H.; m. Kathy Joseph Loeb, Aug. 21, 1976; children: Benjamin James, Peter William. BA with highest distinction, MA in Econs., Northwestern U., 1976; JD magna cum laude, Harvard U., 1979. Bar: Ill. 1979, U.S. Dist. Ct. (no. dist.) Ill. 1979. Assoc. Kirkland & Ellis, Chgo., 1979-85, ptnr., 1985—. Mem. ABA. Club: University (Chgo.). Federal civil litigation, State civil litigation. Office: Kirkland & Ellis 200 E Randolph Dr Chicago IL 60601

HARPER, WILLIAM BRUCE JR., lawyer; b. Columbia, S.C., Aug. 10, 1945; s. William Bruce and Sarah Ellen (Poston) H.; m. Melinda Crow, Jan. 11, 1946; children: William, Jackson, Sarah. BA, U. of the South, 1967; JD, U. S.C., 1971. Bar: S.C. 1971, Fla. 1972, U.S. Dist. Ct. (so. dist.) Fla. 1974, U.S. Supreme Ct. 1974, U.S. Ct. Appeals (5th cir.) 1981, U.S. Ct. Appeals (D.C. cir.) 1983. Law clk. to presiding justice U.S. Dist. Ct., Miami, 1971-72; ptnr. Floyd Pearson Stewart Richman Greer & Will, Miami, 1972-81, Harper & Hewitt PA, Miami, 1981—. Served with USNG, 1968-70, USAFR, 1970-74. Mem. Fla. Bar Assn. (bd. govs. young lawyers sect. 1977-78, bd. govs. 1977-79), ABA, Assn. Trial Lawyers Am., Acad. Fla. Trial Lawyers (bd. dirs. 1978-82). Democrat. Episcopalian. Clubs: University, Bankers, Grove Isle, Riviera, Tiger Bay. Office: 44 W Flagler St Suite 2550 Courthouse Tower Miami FL 33130

HARPSTER, JAMES ERVING, lawyer; b. Milw., Dec. 24, 1923; s. Philo E. and Pauline (Daanen) H.; Ph.B., Marquette U., 1950, LL.B., 1952. Bar: Wis. 1952, Tenn. 1953; dir. info. services Nat. Cotton Council Am., Memphis, 1952-55; dir. public relations Christian Bros. Coll., 1956; mgr. govt. affairs dept. Memphis C. of C., 1956-62; exec. v.p. Rep. Assn. Memphis and Shelby County, 1962-64; individual practice law, Memphis, 1965; ptnr. Rickey, Shankman, Blanchard, Agee & Harpster, and predecessor firm, Memphis, 1966-80, Harpster & Baird, 1980-83; pvt. practice, 1984—. Mem. Shelby County Tax Assessor's Adv. Com., 1960-61; editor, asst. counsel Memphis and Shelby County Charter Com., 1962; mem. Shelby County Election Commn., 1968-70; mem. Tenn. State Bd. Elections, 1970-72, sec., 1972; mem. Tenn. State Election Commn., 1973-83, chmn., 1974, sec., 1975-83; a founder Lions Inst. for Visually Handicapped Children, 1954, chmn. E. H. Crump Meml. Football Game for Blind, 1956; pres. Siena Student Aid Found., 1960; bd. dirs. Memphis Public Affairs Forum; mem. Civic Research Com., Inc., Citizens Assn. Memphis and Shelby County; Republican candidate Tenn. Gen. Assembly, 1964; v.p. Nat. Council Rep. Workshops, 1967-69; pres. Rep. Workshop Shelby County, 1967, 71, 77, 78, Rep. Assn. Memphis and Shelby County, 1966-67; chmn. St. Michael the Defender chpt. Catholics United for the Faith, 1973, 75. Served as sgt. USAAF, 1942-46. Mem. Am., Tenn., Wis. bar assns., Navy League U.S., Am. Conservative Union, Conservative Caucus, Cardinal Mindszenty Found., Am. Security Council, Am. Cause, Am. Legion, Latin Liturgy Assn. Roman Catholic. Home: 3032 E Glengarry Rd Memphis TN 38128 Office: 100 N Main Bldg Suite 3217 Memphis TN 38103

HARPSTER, LINDA MARIE, lawyer, educator; b. Washington, Mar. 11, 1945; d. John Thomas and Marie (Jones) H. BA in English, U. Tex., 1968, MA in English, 1972; JD, No. Ky. U., 1978. Bar: Ky. 1978, Ohio 1980. Tchr. english Boone County High Sch., Florence, Ky., 1972-76; instr. No. Ky. U., Highland Heights, 1976-78, dir. spl. services and devel. studies, 1978-80; dir. legal services St. Francis-St. George Hosp., Cin., 1980-85, Sisters of Charity Health Care Systems Inc., Cin., 1985—; adj. faculty Mt. St. Joseph Coll., Cin., 1984—; speaker various health assns., 1983—. Editor: No. Ky. U. Law Rev., 1977-78. Adminstr. Linton Chamber Music Series, Cin., 1983—; arbitrator Better Bus. Bur., Cin., 1984—; trustee Mental Health Services NW, Cin., 1985—, DES Action, Cin., 1985—. NEH grantee, 1981. Mem. Am. Soc. Hosp. Risk Mgrs., Ohio Soc. Hosp. Risk Mgrs. (sec. 1983-85, v.p. 1985—), Am. Coll. Healthcare Execs., Woman's City Club (counsel 1985—). Avocations: contra dancing, Scottish country dancing, bicycling. Health, General corporate, Personal injury. Home: 2605 Eden Ave #8 Cincinnati OH 45219 Office: Sisters Charity Health Care Systems 345 Neeb Rd Cincinnati OH 45238-5198

HARRAL, JOHN MENTEITH, lawyer; b. Ancon, Panama Canal Zone, June 25, 1948; s. Brooks Jared and Sara (Mumma) H.; m. Marjorie Van Fosson, Aug. 15, 1970; children: Alyse, Jessica. BBA, U. Miss., 1971, JD, 1974. Bar: Miss. 1974, U.S. Dist. Ct. (so. dist.) Miss. 1974, U.S. Ct. Appeals (5th cir.) 1977. Law clk. to judge U.S. Ct. Appeals (5th cir.), New Orleans, 1978-79; ptnr. White & Morse, Gulfport, Miss., 1979—. Chmn. Episc. Services for Aging, Miss. Gulf Coast, 1981—, bd. dirs.; lay reader St. Mark's Episc. Ch., Gulfport, 1980—, chalice bearer, vestryman. Served to lt. JAGC, USNR, 1974-78.78. Mem. ABA, Miss. Young Lawyer Div. (bd. dirs. 1982-84), Harrison County Young Lawyers (pres. 1984), Harrison County Bar Assn. (v.p. 1986), Gulf Coast Law Inst. (bd. dirs. 1983—), Phi Delta Phi. Republican. Clubs: Bayou Bluff Tennis, Gulfport Yacht. Banking, Bankruptcy, Insurance. Home: 12 Old Oak Ln Gulfport MS 39503 Office: White & Morse One Hancock Plaza Gulfport MS 39502

HARREL, ALAN DAVID, lawyer; b. Miami, Fla., Nov. 12, 1947; s. Nicholas David and Geraldine Betty (Stolz) H.; m. Jeanne Lynn Burroughs, Dec. 29, 1970; children: Julie Elizabeth, Nicholas David III. BA, Westminster Coll., 1969; JD, U. Ark., Little Rock, 1978. Bar: Ark 1978, U.S. Dist. Ct. (we. dist.) Ark. 1978, Tex. 1979, U.S. Dist. Ct. (ea. dist.) Tex. 1979, U.S. Ct. Appeals (5th cir.) 1981. Assoc. Young, Patton & Folsom, Texarkana, Ark., 1978-81; ptnr. Atchley, Russell, Waldrop & Hlavinka, Texarkana, 1981—. Bd. dirs. Bowie County Child Welfare Bd., Texarkana, 1979-81. Served to capt. USAF, 1969-76. Mem. ABA, Tex. Bar Assn., Ark. Bar Assn., Tex. Young Lawyers Assn. (dir. 1983-85), Phi Alpha Delta. Methodist. Avocations: tennis, flying, racquetball. Personal injury, State civil litigation, Federal civil litigation. Home: 3507 Richwood Dr Texarkana TX 75503 Office: Atchley Russell Waldrop & Hlavinka 803 Spruce St PO Box 1049 Texarkana TX 75504

HARRELL, LIMMIE LEE, JR., lawyer; b. Jackson, Tenn., Aug. 15, 1941; s. Limmie Lee Sr. and Mary Benthal (Nowell) H.; m. Judy F. Lynchard, Sept. 3, 1964; children: Limmie Lee III, Mary Kimberly. BS, Memphis State U., 1963, JD, 1966. Bar: Tenn. 1966, U.S. Dist. Ct. (we. dist.) Tenn. 1968, U.S. Supreme Ct. Ptnr. Harrell, Harrell & Agee, Trenton, Tenn., 1966—. Pres. Gibson County Young Dems., Trenton, Tenn., 1968. Named one of Outstanding Young Men in Am. Mem. ABA, Tenn. Bar Assn., Gibson County Bar Assn., Assn. Trial Lawyers Am., Tenn. Trial Lawyers Assn., Memphis State Alumni Assn. (pres. 1984-85). Baptist. Club: Pinecrest Country Club (Trenton, Tenn.) (pres. (2) terms). Lodges: Elks (exalted ruler 1971-72), Moose. Avocations: golf, fishing, hunting, water skiing. General practice, Personal injury, Criminal. Home: 100 Rosemont Dr Trenton TN 38382 Office: Harrell Harrell & Agee Court Sq Trenton TN 38382

HARREN, KEVIN HUGH, lawyer; b. Greenwich, N.Y., Oct. 3, 1951; s. James and Mary (Feely) H.; m. Judith Greene, Sept. 9, 1978; children: Jeffrey, Gregory, Bethany. BS, Georgetown U., 1973; JD, Union U., 1977. Bar: N.Y. 1978, U.S. Dist. Ct. (no. and we. dists.) N.Y. 1978, U.S. Ct. Appeals (2d and D.C. cirs.) 1979. Field atty. Nat. Labor Relations Bd., Albany, N.Y., 1977-78; assoc. sr. counsel N.Y. State United Tchrs., Albany, 1978—. Contbg. editor: Developing Labor Law, 1983. Mem. ABA (labor and employment law sect.), N.Y. State Bar Assn. Labor. Home: 4 Capitol Ave Delmar NY 12054 Office: NY State United Tchrs 159 Wolf Rd Box 15-008 Albany NY 12212-5008

HARRIGAN, NANCY STAFFORD, lawyer; b. Albany, N.Y., Apr. 15, 1941; d. John Henry and Anne Ernestine (Stafford) H. B.A., Marymount Coll., 1963; J.D., Albany Law Sch., 1966. Bar: N.Y. 1966, U.S. Dist. Ct. (no. dist.) N.Y. 1966. Asst. counsel SUNY-Albany, 1966-70, assoc. counsel, 1970-74, asst. to chancellor, 1974-77, sr. assoc. counsel, 1977-79, dep. univ. counsel, 1979—; mem. com. on character and fitness N.Y. Supreme Ct.,

appellate div., 3d dept., Albany, 1981—. Mem. ABA, Nat. Assn. Coll. and Univ. Attys., Am. Soc. Pub. Adminstrn., N.Y. State Bar Assn., N.Y. State Women's Bar Assn. Administrative and regulatory, General corporate. Office: SUNY State University Plaza Albany NY 12246

HARRING, MICHAEL ADRIAN, lawyer; b. Oak Park, Ill., June 1, 1950; s. Ronald James and Helen Jane (Young) H.; m. Lois Diana Dal Santo, July 20, 1974; children—James Adrian, Victoria Helen. B.A., U. Ill., 1972; student Georgetown U., 1976; J.D., Loyola U., Chgo., 1975. Bar: Ill. 1975, D.C., 1979, U.S. Supreme Ct. 1979. Atty., SEC, Washington, 1975-76, sr. atty., 1976-80; assoc. Pope, Ballard, Shepard & Fowle, Chgo., 1980-84; atty. Deere & Co., Moline, Ill., 1984-86, sr. atty., 1986—. Contbr. articles to law revs. Mem. Ill. Bar Assn., ABA, Phi Alpha Delta. Methodist. Securities, General corporate. Office: Deere & Co John Deere Rd Moline IL 61265

HARRINGTON, ARTHUR JOHN, lawyer; b. Kenosha, Wis., Apr. 7, 1950; s. Arthur Matthew and Lorreta (Bitautis) H.; m. Julie Beth Chier; children: Jordan and Emily. BA in Econs., U. Wis., 1972, JD, 1975. Bar: Wis. 1975, U.S. Dist. Ct. (ea. and we. dists.) Wis., U.S. Ct. Appeals (7th cirs.) 1978, U.S. Ct. Appeals (D.C. cir.) 1982. Assoc. Charne & Glassner, Milw., 1975-81, ptnr., 1981—. Editor-in-chief The Milwaukee Lawyer, 1983—; contbr. articles to law revs. Mem. Police and Fire Commn., Grafton, Wis., 1984—; treas. Matt Flynn for Congress Com., Fox Point, Wis., 1978. Mem. 7th Cir. Bar Assn., Milw. Young Lawyer's Assn. (Outstanding Lawyer award 1982), Milw. Bar Assn., ABA, Assn. Trial Lawyers Am. Democrat. Roman Catholic. Avocations: drawing, running. Bankruptcy, Environment, Federal civil litigation. Home: 3619 Marseilles 126N Mequon WI 53092 Office: Charne & Glassner 211 W Wisconsin Ave Milwaukee WI 53203

HARRINGTON, BRUCE MICHAEL, lawyer; b. Houston, Mar. 12, 1933; s. George Haymond Harrington and Doris (Gladden) Maginnis; m. Anne Griffith Lawhon, Feb. 15, 1958; children—Julia Griffith, Martha Gladden, Susan McIver. B.A., U. Tex., 1960, J.D. with honors, 1961. Bar: Tex. 1961, U.S. Dist. Ct. (so. dist.) Tex. 1962, U.S. Ct. Appeals (5th cir.) 1962, U.S. Supreme Ct. 1973. Assoc. Andrews & Kurth and predecessor firm, Houston, 1961-73, ptnr., 1973-84; sole practice Houston, 1984—; dir. Offenhauser Co., Houston, Allied Metals, Inc., Houston. Trustee, St. John's Sch., Houston, 1981—, chmn. bd., chief exec. officer, 1986—; trustee St. Luke's Episcopal Hosp., Tex. Med. Ctr., Houston, 1983—; bd. dirs. YMCA Bd. Mgmt. Mem. ABA, Tex. Bar Assn., Houston Bar Assn., Order of Coif, Phi Delta Phi. Republican. Episcopalian. Clubs: Houston Country, Petroleum, Houston. General corporate, Banking. Home: 3608 Overbrook Ln Houston TX 77027 Office: 4212 San Felipe Suite 415 Houston TX 77027

HARRINGTON, C. MICHAEL, lawyer; b. Borger, Tex., Oct. 6, 1946. BA, Yale U., 1969; diploma in devel. econs., Cambridge U., Eng., 1970; JD, Harvard U., 1973. Bar: Tex. 1973. Ptnr. Vinson & Elkins, Houston. Address: Vinson & Elkins 3300 First City Tower 1001 Fannin Houston TX 77002 *

HARRINGTON, CHARLES FREDERICK, lawyer; b. Buffalo, Apr. 24, 1923; s. Henry Bassett and Emilie (Fuller) H.; m. Virginia Hornbarger, June 14, 1952; children: William, Richard, Susan, Charlotte. BA, U. Rochester, 1947; LLB, Harvard U., 1950. Bar: N.Y. 1950. Ptnr. Harrington & Harrington, Buffalo, 1950-73; sole practice Buffalo, 1973-77; sr. ptnr. Harrington & Klaasesz, Buffalo, 1977—. V.p. Orchard Park (N.Y.) Sch. Bd., 1974-76; chmn. bd. ethics, Town of Orchard Park, 1966—; pres. Orchard Park Symphony, 1981-84. Served with U.S. Army, 1943-46. Fellow Am. Coll. Probate Counsel; mem. ABA, N.Y. State Bar Assn. (lectr. 1980-83), Erie County Bar Assn. (past chmn. surrogates ct. com., lectr. 1980-83), Estates Analysts of Western N.Y.(Pres. 1983). Republican. Presbyterian. Probate, Estate taxation. Home: 205 Forest Dr Orchard Park NY 14127 Office: Harrington & Klaasesz 290 Main St Room 610 Buffalo NY 14202

HARRINGTON, DONALD JOSEPH, lawyer; b. Detroit, Nov. 4, 1925; s. Francis J. and Marjorie H. (Kenna) H.; m. Monica L. O'Callaghan, Sept. 10, 1949; children: Gloryann, Donna, Robert, Rosemary. BS in Aero. Engring., U. Mich., 1946; JD, U. Detroit, 1951; LLM, George Washington U., 1953. Bar: Mich. 1952, D.C. 1953. Research engr. Ford Motor Co., Dearborn, Mich., 1947-50, patent atty., 1956—; research engr. Jered Industries, Birmingham, Mich., 1950-51; patent examiner U.S. Patent Office, Washington, 1951-53; patent atty. Chrysler Corp., Detroit, 1953-56. Served to lt. USN, 1943-46. Mem. Mich. Bar Assn. (patent and trademark council 1983—), Mich. Patent Law Assn. (pres. 1980-81). Roman Catholic. Clubs: Birmingham Athletic, Cranbrook Indoor Tennis (Birmingham). Avocations: tennis, woodworking, gardening. Patent, Trademark and copyright. Home: 17330 Locherbie Birmingham MI 48009 Office: Ford Motor Co Office Gen Counsel 911 Parklane Towers E Dearborn MI 48126

HARRINGTON, JAMES PATRICK, lawyer; b. Butte, Mont., Jan. 31, 1942; s. James Patrick and Mary Ellen (Harrington) H.; m. Joan Evelyn Lucas, Feb. 1, 1964 (div. Feb. 1977); children—Jeanette, James, Donna, Diana, Laura. B.A., Carroll Coll., Helena, Mont., 1964; M.A., U. Wyo., 1967; J.D., Notre Dame, 1970. Bar: Ind. 1970, Mont. 1975, U.. Dist. Ct. (no. dist.) Ind. 1970, U.S. Dist. Ct. (so. dist.) Ind. 1970, U.S. Dist. Ct. Mont. 1975, U.S. Ct. Appeals (7th cir.) 1975, U.S. Tax Ct. 1975. Assoc., Thronburg, McGill, Deahl, Harman, Carey & Murray, South Bend, Ind., 1970-75; atty. Mont. Power Co., Butte, 1975-77; ptnr. Poore, Roth & Robinson, Butte, 1977-81; sole practice, Butte, 1981-83, 84—; hearing examiner Mont. Workers Compensation Ct., Helena, 1983-84; sole practice, Butte, 1984—. Mem. Mont. Trial Lawyers Assn., ABA, Silver Bow County Bar Assn. (pres. 1987), Mont. Assn. Def. Counsel, Greys Inn, Delta Epsilon Sigma, Beta Gamma Sigma, Omicron Delta Esilon. Democrat. Roman Catholic. State civil litigation, Workers' compensation, Personal injury. Home: 106 Pintlar Ln Butte MT 59701 Office: 106 W Granite Butte MT 59701

HARRINGTON, PENNY NANCY, lawyer; b. Jackson, Tenn., Nov. 21, 1945; d. Joseph Lawrence Jr. and Nancy (Griffin) H. BS, Mid. Tenn. State. U., 1967; JD, Vanderbilt U., 1982. Bar: Tenn. 1982, U.S. Dist. Ct. (mid. dist.) Tenn. 1982, U.S. Ct. Appeals (6th cir.) 1984, U.S. Ct. Appeals (11th cir.) 1985. Editor The Tenn. Report, Nashville, 1970-72; asst. to house speaker Tenn. Gen. Assembly, Nashville, 1972-74, asst. to lt. gov., 1974-79; ptnr. Thompson & Bussart, Nashville, 1982-87; gen. counsel Tenn. Dept. Conservation, Nashville, 1987—; participant law seminar, Caen, France, 1985. Founding mem. CABLE, Nashville, 1978; treas. State Campaign Pub. Service Com., Nashville, 1986—. Mem. ABA, Nat. Criminal Def. Lawyers Assn., Tenn. Bar Assn., Tenn. Criminal Def. Lawyers Assn. (exec. dir. 1982—), Nashville Bar Assn. (chmn. legis. com. 1986—). Democrat. Roman Catholic. Clubs: Nashville City, Capitol Hill (Nashville). Avocations: tennis, history. Legislative, Criminal, Administrative and regulatory. Office: Office of Gen Counsel Tenn Dept Conservation 701 Broad Nashville TN 37219-5237

HARRINGTON, RICK ALAN, lawyer; b. Columbus, Ohio, Jan. 17, 1945; s. Richard Lee and Mary Elizabeth (Klein) H.; m. Suzan Gay Davis, Mar. 20, 1971; children: Richard Tucker, Timothy Alan. BA with highest honors, U. Kans., 1967; JD cum laude, Harvard U., 1970. Bar: U.S. Dist. Ct., 1971, D.C., U.S. Ct. Appeals (D.C. and 5th cirs.), 1975. Assoc. Arent, Fox, Kintner, Plotkin & Kahn, Washington, 1970-77, ptnr., 1978-79; sr. atty. Du Pont De Nemours & Co., Wilmington, Del., 1979-83, mng. counsel, 1983—. Republican. Federal civil litigation, State civil litigation, Personal injury. Home: 1120 Dorset Dr West Chester PA 19382 Office: Du Pont De Nemours & Co Legal Dept 1007 Market St Wilmington DE 19898

HARRINGTON, TRAVERS ROUNTREE, JR., lawyer; b. Norfolk, Va., Nov. 6, 1949; s. Travers Rountree Sr. and Mary Francis (Dyer) H. BA, Hampden-Sydney Coll., 1971; JD, U. S.C., 1975. Bar: S.C. 1975, W.Va. 1976. Staff atty., hearing examiner W.Va. Pub. Service Commn., Charleston, 1975-76; ptnr. Jesser & Harrington, Fayetteville, W.Va., 1977—; atty. W.Va. Legislature, Charleston, 1978, Town of Gauley Bridge, W.Va., 1978—, Town of Meadow Bridge, W.Va., 1977—; assoc. adj. prof. polit. sci. W.Va. Tech. U., Montgomery, 1977-78. Mem. Dem. Senatorial Exec. Com., Fayetteville, 1982—; chmn. Dem. Del. Senatorial Exec. com., Fayettville, 1982—; bd. dirs. W.Va. Civil Liberties Union, 1982. Mem. W.Va. Bar Assn., Assn. Trial Lawyers Am. Presbyterian. Clubs: Edgewood Country (Charleston), White Oak Country (Oak Hill, W.Va.). State civil litigation, Local government, Family and matrimonial. Office: Jesser & Harrington PO Drawer 450 Fayetteville WV 25840

HARRIS, ALLAN MICHAEL, lawyer, judge; b. N.Y.C., Sept. 30, 1940; s. Lawrence Cecil and Shirley Etta (Jaffe) H.; m. Linda Paula Licker, June 21, 1964 (dec. Oct. 1981); children: Lauren Ivy, Leslie Eden; m. Lillian S. Levin, May 8, 1985 (div. May 1986). BS in Acctg., Temple U., 1965; JD, U. Pa., 1965. Bar: N.J. 1965, N.Y. 1984, U.S. Supreme Ct. 1969. Ptnr. Rubenstein, Albert & Loukedis, Paterson, N.J., 1970, Fontanella, Shashaty, Harris & Lalomia, Paterson, 1971-81; prosecutor City of Fair Lawn, N.J., 1974, judge Mcpl. Ct., 1975—; assoc. Ravin, Greenberg & Zackin, Roseland, N.J., 1981—; atty. Paterson Zoning Bd., 1970-72; mem. con. on mcpl. cts. N.J. Supreme Ct., 1983—. Mem. Fair Lawn Environ. Commn., 1974. Mem. N.J. Bar Assn., Passaic County Bar Assn., Bergen County Bar Assn., Beta Gamma Sigma. Jewish. Bankruptcy, Contracts commercial, General corporate. Home: 7 Ashburn Place Fair Lawn NJ 07410 Office: Ravin Greenberg & Zackin PA 101 Eisenhower Pkwy Roseland NJ 07068

HARRIS, ALLEN, lawyer, educator; b. Bklyn., Feb. 3, 1929; s. Edward and Minnie (Herzog) H.; m. Susanne T. Berger, Sept. 1, 1957. B.A., N.Y.U., 1949; J.D., Columbia U., 1954. Bar: N.Y. 1954, Mo. 1968, U.S. Sup. Ct. 1966, U.S. Ct. Mil. Appeals 1956, U.S. Tax Ct. 1954, U.S. Ct. Appeals (2d cir.) 1955, U.S. Dist. Ct. (so. dist.) N.Y. 1955, (ea. dist.) N.Y. 1957. Assoc. Newman and Newman, N.Y.C., 1954-55, Garey and Garey, N.Y.C., 1955-56; asst. dist. atty. New York County, 1956-59; 1st asst. counsel, trial counsel, coordinating com. on discipline First Jud. Dept., N.Y. State Sup. Ct., 1959-62; law sec. to justice N.Y. State Sup. Ct., 1962-63; gen. counsel, labor negotiator United Board and Carton Corp., N.Y.C., 1963; asst. counsel N.Y. State Commn. on Investigation, 1963-65; assoc. dir. Inst. Jud. Adminstrn., N.Y.U., 1965-67; prof. law, dir. community legal edn., dir. legal research, dir. legal assistance to inmates clinic, dir. public service project in law enforcement U. Mo., Kansas City, 1967-69; prof. law Bklyn. Law Sch., 1969-72; counsel N.Y. State Study Commn. for N.Y.C., 1972; spl. asst. atty. gen. N.Y. State, 1972-76; sole practice, N.Y.C., 1976-79; sr. law asst., appellate div. First Jud. Dept., N.Y. State Sup. Ct., N.Y.C., 1979—; cons. for legal matters N.Y. State Select Com. on Correctional Instns., 1971-72; dir. spl. projects N.Y.C. Patrolmen's Benevolent Assn., 1978; cons. to police in Kansas City, 1968-69; mem. faculty appellate judges seminars N.Y. U., 1965-67; involved in numerous hearings. Served as 1st lt., inf. U.S. Army, 1951-53; col. JAGC. Decorated Combat Infantryman's badge; recipient N.Y. State Conspicuous Service cross. Mem. ABA, N.Y. State Bar Assn., Nat. Dist. Attys. Assn., N.Y. State Dist. Attys. Assn., Assn. Bar City N.Y., N.Y. County Lawyers Assn., Fed. Bar Council, Richmond County Bar Assn., Kansas City Bar Assn., Mil. Order World Wars, Res. Officers Assn. U.S., AAUP, Internat. Assn. Chiefs Police. Jewish. Club: City. Contbr. articles to encys. and legal jours. Federal civil litigation, State civil litigation, Criminal. Home: 700 Victory Blvd 18D Staten Island NY 10301 Office: 25th St and Madison Ave New York NY 10010

HARRIS, BENJAMIN HARTE, JR., lawyer; b. Mobile, Ala., Sept. 12, 1937; s. Ben H. and Mary Cade (Aldridge) H.; m. Martha Elliott Lambeth, Aug. 26, 1961; children—Benjamin Harte, Wayt. A.B., Davidson Coll., 1959; J.D., U. Ala., 1962. Bar: Ala. 1962, U.S. Dist. Ct. (so. dist.) Ala. 1964, U.S. Ct. Appeals (5th cir.) 1981, U.S. Supreme Ct. 1971, U.S. Ct. Appeals (11th cir.) 1981. Assoc. Johnstone, Adams, Bailey, Gordon & Harris (formerly Johnstone, Adams, May, Howard & Hill), Mobile, Ala., 1964-70, ptnr., 1971—. Past pres., bd. dirs. Boys' Club; chmn., trustee UMS Prep Sch. Mem. Mobile County Bar Assn. (exec. com.), Ala. State Bar (bd. commrs., mem. exec. com., trustee bar found., pres.-elect, past chmn. disciplinary commn.), Ala. Def. Lawyers Assn., Am. Arbitration Assn. Episcopalian. Club: Athelstan. Personal injury, Workers' compensation, Real property. Office: PO Box 1988 Mobile AL 36633

HARRIS, BRIAN CRAIG, lawyer; b. Newark, Sept. 8, 1941; s. Louis W. and Lillian (Frankel) H.; m. Ellen M. Davis, Aug. 20, 1978; children—Andrea, Keith. B.S., Boston U., 1963; J.D., Rutgers U., 1966. Bar: N.J., 1968, D.C. 1968, U.S. Ct. Appeals (3d cir.) 1968, N.Y. 1984, U.S. Ct. Appeals (2d cir.) 1985. Asst. corp. counsel Newark, 1968-70; assoc. Braff, Litvak & Ertag, East Orange, N.J., 1970-72; ptnr. Braff, Litvak, Ertag, Wortmann & Harris, East Orange, 1972-85, Braff, Ertag, Wortmann, Harris & Sukoneck, Livingston, N.J., 1985—. adj. lectr. law and medicine Seton Hall U., South Orange, N.J., 1982-83, trial preparation Rutgers U., Newark, 1983, strategy of def. United Tech. Corp., Chgo., 1986. Chmn. Essex County Heart Assn., East Orange, 1972-73; contbg. mem. Nat. Ileitis Found., N.Y.C., 1983—. Mem. ABA, N.Y. State Bar Assn., N.J. Bar Assn., Essex County Bar Assn., Essex County Trial Lawyers Assn., Middlesex County Trial Lawyers Assn., Assn. Trial Lawyers Am., Def. Research Inst., N.J. Trial Lawyers Assn. Jewish. Club: Water Mill Country (N.Y.). Avocations: running, basketball, theater, study of mil. strategy of land forces in World War II. Personal injury, Product liability, Federal civil litigation. Home: 2 Ashley Rd Llewellyn Park West Orange NJ 07052-4915 Office: Braff Ertag Wortman Harris & Sukoneck 570 W Mt Pleasant Ave Livingston NJ 07039 Office: 475 Fifth Ave Suite 1614 New York NY 10017

HARRIS, CHARLES DICK, lawyer; b. Ballinger, Tex., Sept. 29, 1951; s. William R. and Artie Bell (Corbett) H. BA, Tex. Tech U., 1974, JD, 1976. Bar: U.S. Dist Ct. (no. dist.) Tex. 1982. Assoc. O. Henry Young, Jr., Abilene, Tex., 1977-80; ptnr. Young & Harris, Abilene, 1980-86, Harris & McBeath, Abilene, 1986—; seminar speaker U. Tex. Bankruptcy Conf., 1983. Mem. ABA, Tex. Bar Assn., Abilene Bar Assn. (v.p. 1980-81, sec.-treas. 1981-82), Jaycees. Avocations: golf, sailing, skiing. Bankruptcy, Banking, Federal civil litigation. Home: 3218 Woodlake Abilene TX 79606 Office: Harris & McBeath PO Box 3835 Abilene TX 79604

HARRIS, CHARLES EDISON, lawyer; b. Ft. Lauderdale, Fla., Sept. 16, 1946; s. Thomas Edison and Margaret (Bailey) H.; m. Jeanne Dammas, June 17, 1969; children: David Edison, Ginger Suzanne, Brian Charles. BA, U. Fla., 1969; JD, Harvard U., 1972. Bar: Fla. 1972, U.S. Dist. Ct. (mid. dist.) Fla. 1978, U.S. Supreme Ct. 1978. Assoc. Maguire, Voorhis & Wells PA, Orlando, Fla., 1972-73; gen. counsel, sec. Sun Banks, Inc., Orlando, 1973-75; sr. v.p. adminstrn., sr. v.p. legal affairs and sec. Sun Bank, Inc., Orlando, 1976-81; asst. prof. law U. Fla., Gainesville, 1975-76; sole practice Orlando, 1981-84; pres. Sunscape Internat., Inc., Orlando, 1981—; ptnr. Arky, Freed, Stearns, Watson, Greer, Weaver & Harris PA, Orlando, 1984-85, Smith, Mackinnon, Mathews, Harris & Christiansen, PA, Orlando, 1985—. Author: Business Negotiating Power: Optimizing Your Side of the Deal, 1983; (with others) Major Equipment Procurement, 1983, Computer Contract Negotiations, 1981. Served to capt. U.S. Army, 1969-77. Mem. ABA, Fla. Bar Assn. Securities, General corporate, Computer. Home: 3339 Northglenn Dr Orlando FL 32806 Office: Smith Mackinnon Mathews et al 255 S Orange Ave Suite 850 Orlando FL 32801

HARRIS, CHRISTY FRANKLIN, lawyer; b. Greensboro, N.C., Dec. 8, 1945; s. Luther Franklin and Rebecca Ann (Bluster) H.; m. Judy Irene Yielding, May 6, 1967; children: Stacey Lynn, Aubrey Leigh. BA, U. Fla., 1967, JD with honors, 1970. Bar: Fla. 1970, U.S. Dist. Ct. (mid. dist.) Fla. 1970, U.S. Ct. Mil. Appeals 1971, U.S. Ct. Appeals (11th cir.) 1984. Assoc. Holland & Knight, Lakeland, Fla., 1970, 1973-74; pres. Canan & Harris P.A., Lakeland, 1974-76; pres., sr. atty. Harris, Midyette & Clements P.A., Lakeland, 1976—; Mem. 10th cir. Grievance Com., Lakeland, 1976-79, 83-86, chmn. 1979, vice chmn., 1986; mem. Unauthorized Practice of Law Com., 1983—. Bd. dirs. Program to Aid Drug Abusers, Lakeland, 1975-76, Campfire, 1979—. Served to capt. USMC, 1970-73. Named to Hon. Order of Ky. Cols., 1974. Mem. ABA, Fla. Bar Assn., Lakeland Bar Assn., Attys. Title Ins. Fund, Order of Coif, Phi Beta Kappa, Phi Kappa Phi. Democrat. Club: Lakeland Yacht and Country. Avocations: tennis, golf, sports car activities. State civil litigation, Contracts commercial, General corporate. Home: 1429 Fairhaven Dr Lakeland FL 33803 Office: Harris Midyette & Clements PA 2012 S Florida Ave PO Box 2451 Lakeland FL 33803

HARRIS, D. ALAN, lawyer; b. Oak Park, Ill., Mar. 4, 1949; s. E.B. and M.A. (Solberg) H.; m. Marcella Ruble, July 13, 1985. AB, U. Ill., Urbana, 1970, JD, 1973. From assoc. to ptnr. Freeman, Freeman & Salzman, Chgo., 1974-81; sole practice Chgo., 1981—; spl. dep. atty. gen. Commonwealth of Pa., 1981—. Mem. ABA, Ill. Bar Assn., Chgo. Bar Assn. Club: Union League (Chgo.). Antitrust, Bankruptcy, Federal civil litigation. Office: 507 N Wells St Chicago IL 60610

HARRIS, DALE HUTTER, judge, lecturer; b. Lynchburg, Va., July 10, 1932; d. Quintus and Agnes (Adams) Hutter; m. Edward Richmond Harris Jr., July 24, 1954; children—Mary Fontaine, Frances Harris Russell, Jennifer Harris Haynie, Timothy Edward. B.A., Sweet Briar Coll., 1953; M.Ed. in Counseling and Guidance, Lynchburg Coll., 1970; J.D., U. Va., 1978. Bar: Va. 1978, U.S. Dist. Ct. (we. dist.) Va. 1978, U.S. Ct. Appeals (4th cir.) 1978. Admissions asst. Sweet Briar Coll. (Va.), 1953-54; caseworker Winchester/Frederick Dept. Welfare, Va., 1954-55; vis. lectr. Lynchburg Coll. (Va.), 1971; assoc. Davies & Peters, Lynchburg, 1978-82; substitute judge 24th Dist. Gen. Dist. and Juvenile and Domestic Relations Dist. Cts. Va., 1980-82; judge Juvenile and Domestic Relations Dist. Ct., Lynchburg, 1982—; lectr. law U. Va. Law Sch., 1986—. Vice chmn. bd. dirs. Sweet Briar Coll., 1976-86; vol. coordinator vols. in probation with Juvenile and Domestic Ct., 1971-73; chmn. steering com. for establishment Youth Service Bur., Lynchburg, 1972-73; chmn. bd. dirs. Lynchburg Youth Services, 1973-75; mem. adv. bd. Juvenile Ct., 1957-60, 62-68, sec., 1966-68; bd. dirs. Family Service Lynchburg, 1967-69; Lynchburg Fine Arts Ctr., 1965-67, Seven Hills Sch., 1966-73, Greater Lynchburg United Fund, 1963-65, Lynchburg Assn. Mental Health, 1960-61, Miller Home, 1980-82, Lynchburg Gen.-Marshall Lodge Hosps., Inc., 1980-82; v.p. Lynchburg Mental Health Study Commn., 1966; bd. dirs. Lynchburg Sheltered Workshop for Mentally Retarded Young Adults, 1965-69; bd. dirs. Lynchburg Guidance Ctr., 1959-61, v.p., 1970, pres., 1961; bd. dirs. Hist. Rev. Bd. Lynchburg, 1978-82. Mem. Nat. Council Juvenile and Family Ct. Judges, ABA, Va. State Bar, Va. Trial Lawyers Assn., Va. Bar Assn., Lynchburg Bar Assn., Phi Beta Kappa. Home: 1309 Crenshaw Ct Lynchburg VA 24503 Office: Juvenile and Domestic Relations Dist Ct PO Box 757 Lynchburg VA 24505

HARRIS, DALE RAY, lawyer; b. Crab Orchard, Ill., May 11, 1937; s. Ray B. and Aurelia M. (Davis) H.; m. Toni K. Shapkoff, June 26, 1960; children—Kristen Dee, Julie Diane. B.A. in Math., U. Colo., 1959; LL.B., Harvard U., 1962. Bar: Colo. 1962, U.S. Dist. Ct. Colo. 1962, U.S. Ct. Appeals (10th cir.), 1962, U.S. Supreme Ct. 1981. Assoc. Davis, Graham & Stubbs, Denver, 1962-67, ptnr., 1967—, chmn. mgmt. com., 1982-85; speaker, instr. various antitrust seminars. Mem. cabinet Mile High United Way campaign, 1986-87; mem. devel. council U. Colo. Arts and Scis. dept., 1985—; trustee The Spaceship Earth Fund, 1986—; area chmn. Harvard Law Sch. Fund, 1978-81. Served with USAR, 1962-68. Fellow ABA, Am. Bar Found.; mem. Colo. Bar Assn. (chmn. antitrust com. 1980-84; council corp. banking and bus. law sect. 1978-83), Denver Bar Assn., Colo. Assn. Corp. Counsel (pres. 1973-74), Denver Law Club (pres. 1976-77), Phi Beta Kappa. Clubs: University, Union League (Chgo.). Lodge: Denver Rotary. Antitrust, Federal civil litigation. Home: 2032 Bellaire St Denver CO 80207 Office: 370 17th St Denver CO 80201

HARRIS, DANIEL MARK, lawyer; b. Chgo., May 23, 1951; s. Irving David and Tobie Gertrude (Zion) H.; m. Faith Bressler, Sept. 2, 1978; children: David, Rachel, Joseph, Talia, Tobie. BA, Johns Hopkins U., 1972; JD, Harvard U., 1977. Bar: Ill. 1978, D.C. 1980, Calif. 1980, U.S. Dist. Ct. (no. dist.) Ill. 1981. Law clk. to presiding justice U.S. Ct. Appeals (9th cir.), 1977-78; law clk. to assoc. justice Brennan U.S. Supreme Ct., Washington, 1978-79; assoc. O'Melveney & Myers, 1979-80; asst. atty. gen. State of Ill., 1980-82; from assoc. to ptnr. Mayer, Brown & Platt, Chgo., 1982—. Mem. nat. legal affairs com. Anti Defamation League. Mem. ABA, Ill. Bar Assn. Republican. Jewish. Lodge: B'nai B'rith (anti defamation league). Civil rights, Federal civil litigation, General corporate. Office: Mayer Brown & Platt 190 S LaSalle St Chicago IL 60603

HARRIS, DAVID B., lawyer; b. N.Y.C., 1946. BA with high honors, Rutgers U., 1968, MA, 1969, JD, 1975. Bar: N.J. 1975, U.S. Dist. Ct. N.J. 1975, U.S. Ct. Appeals (3d cir.) 1982, U.S. SUpreme Ct. 1984. Asst. dir. fact finding dept. Anti-Defamation League, N.Y.C., 1969-70; criminal justice planner City of Newark, 1970-72; dep. atty. gen. Office Atty. Gen., Trenton, 1976-80; asst. dep. pub. advocate Dept. Pub. Adv., Trenton, 1980-85, supervising atty., 1985—. Mem. police accountability project Greater Newark Urban Coalition, 1975-76; mem. police practice com. N.J. ACLU, 1978-80. Eagleton Inst. Rutgers U. fellow, 1968-69. Mem. ABA, N.J. Bar Assn. (lawyers in pub. employment com.), Phi Beta Kappa. Environment, Civil rights, Administrative and regulatory. Office: Dept Pub Advocate CN 850 Trenton NJ 08625

HARRIS, DAVID NEIL, lawyer; b. Jasper, Ala., Mar. 24, 1951; s. I.W. and Doris Jean (East) H.; m. Vecie Michele Sowell; children: David, Amy, Anna. BA, U. So. Miss., 1973; M Church Music, New Orleans Bapt. Sem., 1976; JD, U. Miss., 1981. Bar: Miss. 1982, U.S. Dist. Ct. (no. and so. dists.) Miss. 1982, U.S. Ct. Appeals (5th cir.) 1982. Ptnr. Fonedren & Harris, Pascagoula, Miss., 1982-84; sole practice Pascagoula, 1984—. Mem. ABA, Miss. Bar Assn., Assn. Trial Lawyers Am., Miss. Trial Lawyers Assn. Democrat. Baptist. Lodge: Rotary. Avocations: golf, gardening, travel. Personal injury, Family and matrimonial, Criminal. Home: 126 Watersedge Ocean Springs MS 39564 Office: PO Box 306 Pascagoula MS 39567

HARRIS, DON VICTOR, JR., lawyer; b. Nottingham Twp., Ind., Jan. 16, 1921; s. Don Victor and Nellie Florence (Dukes) H.; m. Joan Elliott Haffler, Aug. 15, 1959; children: Leigh Elliott, Meghan St. Clair. A.B., DePauw U., 1943; J.D., Harvard U., 1945. Bar: D.C. 1947. Law clk. to judge U.S. Ct. Appeals 2d Circuit, 1945-46; assoc. firm Covington & Burling, Washington, 1946-57; partner Covington & Burling, 1957—; lectr. in law George Washington U., 1963-64; lectr. tax insts.; mem. IRS Commr.'s Adv. Group, 1976. Contbr. articles to law jours.; Case editor: Harvard Law Rev. Bd. dirs. Tudor Pl. Found., Oak Hill Cemetery Co.; past bd. dirs. Nat. Eye Found. Fellow Am. Coll. Tax Counsel, Am. Bar Found. (life); Mem. Am. Law Inst. (life), ABA (chmn. sect. taxation 1976-77), D.C. Bar Assn., Fed. Bar Assn., Phi Beta Kappa, Beta Theta Pi, Am. Camellia Soc. (judge). Episcopalian. Clubs: Met, Chevy Chase, City Tavern. Corporate taxation, Estate taxation, Personal income taxation. Home: 2803 P St NW Washington DC 20007 Office: 1201 Pennsylvania Ave NW Washington DC 20044

HARRIS, DONALD RAY, lawyer; b. Lake Preston, S.D., Apr. 21, 1938; s. Raymond H. and Nona (Trousdale) H.; m. Shirley J. Rothenberger, July 2, 1962; children—Beverly, Scott; m. Sharon K. Brown, Sept. 4, 1982. B.A., State U. Iowa, 1959; J.D., U. Iowa, 1961. Bar: Iowa 1961, Ill. 1963, U.S. Dist. Ct. (no. dist.) Ill. 1963, U.S. Ct. Appeals (3d, 4th 6th and 7th cirs.) 1976, U.S. Supreme Ct. 1977. Assoc. firm Jenner & Block, Chgo., 1963-70, ptnr., 1970—. Served to 2d lt. U.S. Army, 1961-63. Mem. ABA, Ill. Bar Assn., Chgo. Bar Assn., Bar Assn. 7th Cir., Chgo. Council Lawyers, Am. Coll. Trial Lawyers, Chgo. Legal Club, Chgo. Law Club. Federal civil litigation, State civil litigation, Criminal. Office: Jenner & Block 1 IBM Plaza Chicago IL 60611

HARRIS, EARL DOUGLAS, lawyer; b. Athens, Ga., Apr. 9, 1947; s. Roland Russell and Martha Sue (Davis) H.; m. Jean Wright, Dec. 26, 1975; children—Jeannette, Stephanie. B.S.A.E., U. Ga., 1970, M.B.A., J.D., 1973. Bar: Ga. 1973, U.S. Dist. Ct. (mid. dist.) Ga. 1973, U.S. Ct. Appeals (5th cir.) 1973, U.S. Ct. Claims 1977, U.S. Tax Ct. 1977, U.S. Patent Office 1977, U.S. Customs Ct. 1977, U.S. Supreme Ct. 1977, U.S. Ct. Customs and Patent Appeals 1980, U.S. Ct. Internat. Trade 1981, U.S. Ct. Appeals (11th cir.) 1981. Sole practice, Watkinsville, Ga., 1973-76, 1986—; city atty. Town of Bogart, 1974-75, 85—; sr. ptnr. Harris & Rice, Watkinsville, 1977-78; mem. Harris, Rice & Alford, P.A., Watkinsville, 1978-80; ptnr., pres. Harris & Alford, P.A., Watkinsville, 1980-85; pres. Fed. Title Corp., 1978—; county atty. Oconee County (Ga.), 1978-80; atty. Town of Bishop, 1980—; corp. sec. Lawlog Corp., 1980—. Bd. dirs. Clarke County unit Am. Cancer Soc., 1970-72; mem. Oconee County Dem. Exec. Com., 1976—, treas., 1976-82. Served with USCMR, 1965-68; with USAF, 1968. Mem. Ga. Trial Lawyers Assn., ABA, Western Cir. Bar Assn., Gridirion Secret Soc., AGHON, U. Ga. Agrl. Alumni Assn. (pres. young alumni div. 1975-76), Oconee County C. of C. (dir., sec. 1976-78), Blue Key, Sphinx, Omicron Delta Kappa, Sigma Iota Epsilon, Alpha Zeta. Presbyterian (ruling elder). Clubs: Masons (sr. grand warden 1986-87), Order of Eastern Star, Shriners, KT, Tall Cedars of

Lebanon, Royal Order of Scotland, Red Cross of Constantine. Patent, General practice, Real property. Home: 8700 Macon Rd Athens GA 30606 Office: PO Box 498 Main St Watkinsville GA 30677

HARRIS, EDWARD MONROE, JR., office equipment comany executive; b. Phila., June 5, 1923; s. Edward Monroe and Grace Ida (Wilson) H.; m. Marion Hoyt Stevens, Sept. 16, 1950; children—Edward Monroe, Marion Olney, Peter Duncan. B.A., Yale U., 1943; LL.B., U. Pa., 1949. Bar: N.Y. 1949. Assoc., Sullivan & Cromwell, N.Y.C., 1949-57; assoc. counsel Kennecott Copper Corp., N.Y.C., 1957-62; corp. counsel, sec. MacMillan Inc., N.Y.C., 1963-67; sec., gen. counsel Pitney Bowes Inc., Stamford, Ct., 1967—, v.p., 1969—. Dir., Conn. Joint Council on Econ. Edn., 1974—; trustee Conn. Pub. Expenditure Council, 1979-85, exec. com., 1983-85; dir. Stamford Mus. and Nature Ctr. Inc., 1980—, treas., 1982-84, first v.p., 1984-86, pres., 1986— ; trustee Edward W. Hazen Found., 1981—. Served to 1st lt. USMCR, 1943-46. Presbyterian. Club: Wee Burn Country (Darien). General corporate. Office: Pitney Bowes Inc Walter H Wheeler Jr Dr Stamford CT 06926

HARRIS, GORDON H., lawyer; b. Atlanta, May 7, 1938; s. Huie H. Harris and Elizabeth (McBrayer) Stroud; m. Dorothy Laing, Dec. 6, 1960; children: Sarah Katherine, Bruce McBrayer. BA in Math., U. Fla., 1961, JD with honors, 1965. Bar: Fla. 1966, U.S. Dist. Ct. (mid. dist.) Fla., U.S. Ct. Appeals (5th and 11th cirs.), U.S. Supreme Ct. 1966. Instr. legal writing and research U. Fla. Law Sch., Gainesville, 1965-66; assoc. Holland and Knight, Bartow, Fla., 1966-69; ptnr. Gray, Harris & Robinson, Orlando, Fla., 1969—; asst. atty. Orange County, 1978-84; guest instr. Valencia Community Coll., 1978-80; atty. Tourist Devel. Council, 1977—; asst. prosecutor Orange County, 1969-71. Exec. editor U. Fla. Law Rev., 1964-65. Mem. East Ctl. Fla. Regional Planning Council, Orlando, 1976-77; sr. warden St. Michael's Episc. Ch., 1980, lay reader 1966—; chmn. bd. trustees Trinity Prep. Sch., 1984—; exec. com. Fla. Citrus Bowl, 1982—, bd. dirs. 1980—; bd. dirs. March of Dimes 1977-82, Parents Anonymous of Fla., Inc., 1982—, Valencia Community Coll. Found., 1978—. Mem. ABA, Fla. Bar Assn., Orange County Bar Assn., Assn. Trial Lawyers Am., Acad. Fla. Trial Lawyers, U. Fla. Alumni Assn. (nat. pres. 1981, chmn. bd. 1982, dir. Gator boosters 1973-83, life), Am. Judicature Soc., Fla. Shrine Assn. (pres. 1982-83), Order of Coif, Fla. Blue Key, Phi Kappa Phi, Phi Delta Pi, Kappa Alpha. Republican. Clubs: Touchdown, Country, University (Orlando); Citrus, Downtown Athletic. Lodge: Shriners (potentate 1983), Masons. Construction, Condemnation, General practice. Office: Gray Harris & Robinson PA PO Box 3068 Orlando FL 32802

HARRIS, HARVEY ALAN, lawyer; b. St. Louis, Nov. 5, 1936; s. Irvin S. and Sylvia Zelda (Goodman) H.; m. Gloria G. Zelizer, Aug. 14, 1960; children—Stephen, David A., Linda A.; m. 2d, Linda Ruth Everett, Mar. 17, 1977. A.B. magna cum laude, Harvard U., 1958, J.D., 1961. Bar: Mo. 1961, U.S. dist. ct. (ea. dist.) Mo. 1963, U.S. Ct. Appeals (8th cir.) 1979, U.S. Supreme Ct. 1979. Ptnr. The Stolar Partnership, and predecessors, St. Louis, 1961—; cons. Office Policy Devel. and Research, HUD. Bd. dirs., v.p. Jewish Fedn. St. Louis; bd. dirs. Jewish Hosp., St. Louis, Juvenile Diabetes Assn., St. Louis, Grand Ctr. Assn., St. Louis, Am. Jewish Com., St. Louis; commr. St. Louis Sci. Ctr. Mem. ABA, Mo. Bar, St. Louis Bar Assn., Phi Beta Kappa. Democrat. Clubs: Westwood, Noonday, Harvard of St. Louis (v.p. 1983) (St. Louis). Author: Schumpeter's Theory of Innovation, 1958. Real property, General corporate, Contracts commercial. Home: 31 Westmoreland Pl Saint Louis MO 63108 Office: 515 Olive 17th Floor Saint Louis MO 63101

HARRIS, ISAAC RON, lawyer; b. Haifa, Israel, Oct. 1, 1954; came to U.S., 1955; s. Lee B. and Leah (Jacobson) H.; m. Shari E. Shapiro, Sept. 6, 1981. BA, Brown U., 1976; JD, Georgetown U., 1980. Bar: N.Y. 1981, U.S. Dist. Ct. (so. and ea. dists.) N.Y. 1981. Asst. dist. atty. Kings County, Bklyn., 1980-84; assoc. Hall, Dickler, Lawler, Kent & Friedman, N.Y.C., 1984-85, Marcus, Rippa & Gould, White Plains, N.Y., 1985—. Mem. ABA, N.Y. State Bar Assn., Westchester County Bar Assn., White Plains Bar Assn. General practice, Real property. Home: 5 Ledgewood Commons Millwood NY 10546 Office: Marcus Rippa & Gould 4 Cromwell Pl White Plains NY 10601

HARRIS, JAMES ALAN, lawyer; b. Pocatello, Idaho, Nov. 19, 1957; s. Wesley M. and Myrtle L. (Taggart) H.; m. Catherine Ann Bennett, Aug. 16, 1985. BA, Idaho State U., 1979; JD, U. Wash., 1982; LLM in Taxation, Georgetown U., 1985. Bar: Wash. 1982, U.S. Tax Ct. 1985, D.C. 1986, U.S. Dist. Ct. D.C. 1986. Atty.-advisor U.S. Tax Ct., Washington, 1982-85; assoc. Zuckert, Scoutt, Rasenberger & Johnson, Washington, 1985—. Mem. ABA, Wash. State Bar Assn., D.C. Bar Assn. Avocations: music, sailing, bicycling, tennis. Corporate taxation, Personal income taxation, Probate. Office: Zuckert Scoutt Rasenberger & Johnson 888 17th St NW Suite 600 Washington DC 20006

HARRIS, JAMES MICHAEL, lawyer; b. Evanston, Ill., Aug. 13, 1951. BA, Brown U., 1973; JD, U. Chgo., 1976. Bar: D.C. 1976, U.S. Ct. Appeals (D.C. cir.) 1977, U.S. Ct. Appeals (4th, 5th and 9th cirs.) 1979, U.S. Ct. Appeals (2d cir.) 1980, Calif. 1981, U.S. Dist. Ct. (no., cen., ea. and so. dists.) Calif. 1981, U.S. Supreme Ct. 1983. Law clk. to presiding justice Washington, 1976-77; assoc. Bredhoff & Maisse, Washington, 1977-81; assoc. Sidley & Austin, Los Angeles, 1981-83, ptnr., 1983—; vis. lectr. U. Va., Charlottesville, 1978. Editor-in-chief U. Chgo. Law Rev., 1975-76. Federal civil litigation, State civil litigation. Office: Sidley & Austin 2049 Century Park E Los Angeles CA 90067

HARRIS, JANINE DIANE, lawyer; b. Akron, Jan. 12, 1948; s. Russell Burton and Ethel Harriet (Smith) H.; m. Robert I. Coward, Sept. 14, 1968 (div. 1977); m. 2d John Richard Ferguson, Feb. 1, 1980; children—Brigit Grace, Rachel Anna. A.B., Bryn Mawr Coll., 1970; J.D., Georgetown U. Law Sch., 1975. Bar: Va. Supreme Ct. 1975, U.S. Dist. Ct. D.C. 1976, U.S. Ct. Appeals (D.C. cir.) 1976, D.C. Ct. Appeals 1976, U.S. Supreme Ct. 1978, U.S. Ct. Appeals (6th cir.) 1981, U.S. Ct. Appeals (8th cir.) 1981. Assoc. firm Baker & Hostetler, Washington, 1975-78, Pettit & Martin, Washington, 1978-79, Peabody, Lambert & Meyers, Washington, 1979-82, ptnr., 1983-84; sole practice law, Washington, 1984—. Contbr. articles to legal jours. Mem. Nat. Conf. Women's Bar Assns. (bd. dirs. 1984-87, v.p. 1986—), Nat. Found. for Womens' Bar Assn. (pres. 1985-87), Women's Bar Assn. D.C. (pres. 1984—), D.C. Bar Assn. (bd. govs. 1984—), ABA (com. on specialization) Va. Women Attys. Assn. Club: Bryn Mawr. Administrative and regulatory, Federal civil litigation, General corporate. Office: 113 W Franklin St Baltimore MD 21201

HARRIS, JERALD DAVID, lawyer; b. Cin., July 14, 1947; s. Donald W. and Dorothy (Botwin) H.; m. Carol Sue Fohlen, Mar. 25, 1972; children—Alyse, Jeffrey, Danielle. B.A., Miami U., Oxford, Ohio, 1969; J.D., U. Cin., 1972. Bar: Ohio 1972, U.S. Dist. Ct. (so. dist.) Ohio 1972, U.S. Ct. Appeals (6th cir.) 1977, U.S. Dist. Ct. (ea. dist.) Ky. 1978, U.S. Supreme Ct. 1978. Assoc. Kondritzer Gold & Frank, Cin., 1972-75, ptnr., 1975-79; sole practice, Cin., 1979-81; sr. ptnr. Harris and Katz Co. L.P.A., Cin., 1982—; lectr. U. Cin. Coll. of Law, 1986—. Author Ohio Workers' Compensation Handbook, 1986; editor Workers' Compensation Jour. Ohio. Co-chmn. young profl. div. Jewish Welfare Fund; bd. dirs. Hillel; vice chmn. Isaac M. Wise Temple Bldg. Fund campaign; mem. Young Leadership Council of Jewish Fedn. of Cin.; v.p., bd. dirs. Jewish. Vocat. Service; bd. dirs. Bonds for Israel; mem. Jewish Community Relations Council-WCET; active Jerry Springer for Gov. campaign; county chmn. Supreme Ct. campaign; bd. dirs. ARC, 1975-79. Mem. Cin. Bar Assn. (past chmn. workers compensation com. 1983-86, other coms.), Ohio Bar Assn., Assn. Trial Lawyers Am., Ohio Acad. Trial Lawyers (chmn. social security and adminstrv. law sect., vice chmn. worker compensation com., regional coordinator workers compensation com., Service to Legal Profession award 1981, Disting. Service award 1985), Nat. Orgn. Social Security Claimants Reps. (Ohio chmn. 1981-83), Am. Soc. Law and Medicine, Phi Alpha Theta. Democrat. Workers' compensation, Personal injury. Home: 10592 Cinderella Dr Cincinnati OH 45253 Office: Harris & Katz Co LPA 1212 Bartlett Bldg 36 E 4th St Cincinnati OH 45202

HARRIS, JOEL B(RUCE), lawyer; b. N.Y.C., Oct. 15, 1941; s. Raymond S. and Laura (Green) H.; m. Barbara J. Rous, June 13, 1965 (div.); 1 child, Clifford S.; m. Deborah Sherman, Apr. 1, 1986. A.B., Columbia U., 1963; LL.B., Harvard U., 1966; LL.M., U. London, 1967. Bar: N.Y. 1968, U.S. Dist. Ct. (so. dist.) N.Y. 1970, U.S. Ct. Appeals (2d cir.) 1970, U.S. Dist. Ct. (ea. dist.) N.Y. 1975, U.S. Supreme Ct. 1976, U.S. Ct. Appeals (3d cir.) 1980, U.S. Dist. Ct. (we. dist.) N.Y. 1981. Assoc. Simpson, Thacher & Bartlett, N.Y.C., 1967-70; asst. U.S. atty. So. Dist. N.Y., 1970-74, chief civil rights unit, 1973-74; assoc. Weil, Gotshal & Manges, N.Y.C., 1974-76, ptnr., 1976-86; ptnr. Thacher, Proffitt & Wood, N.Y.C., 1986—; speaker, panelist, moderator confs. Contbr. articles to profl. jours. Knox Meml. fellow, 1966-67. Mem. ABA (chmn. com. internat. litigation 1981-84, chmn. com. personal rights litigation 1984—), N.Y. State Bar Assn., Assn. Bar City N.Y., Inter-Am. Bar Assn., Fed. Bar Council, Am. Soc. Internat. Law, Internat. Law Assn., Am. Judicature Soc. Federal civil litigation, Private international, State civil litigation. Home: 152 Remsen St Apt 3 Brooklyn Heights NY 11201 Office: Thacher Proffitt Wood 2 World Trade Ctr New York NY 10148

HARRIS, JOHN CLINTON, JR., lawyer; b. Scottsboro, Ala., Mar. 13, 1946; m. Carolyn Wilson, June 3, 1967. BA, Washington & Lee U., 1969; JD, U. Ala., 1972. Bar: Ala. 1973. Ptnr. Harris & Hasseltine, Florence, Ala., 1978—. Mem exec. com. Lauderdale County Dems., Florence, 1978—. Mem. Lauderdale Bar Assn. (pres. 1981). Lodge: Kiwanis (pres. Florence 1980). Probate, Real property. Home: 217 Forest Hills Dr Florence AL 35630 Office: Harris & Hasseltine 407 S Court St Florence AL 35630

HARRIS, JOHN PAUL, III, lawyer; b. Fredericksburg, Va., May 18, 1941; s. John Paul Jr. and Ruby (Cook) H.; m. Rebecca Ann Fox, Aug. 5, 1966; 1 child, Katherine McNeal. BS, U.S. Nava. Acad., 1965; JD, Samford U., 1977. Bar: Va. 1977, U.S. Dist. Ct. (ea. dist.) Va. 1977, U.S. Ct. Appeals (4th cir.) 1978, U.S. Supreme Ct. 1986. Commn. 2d lt. USN, 1965, naval avaitor, 1961-74, resigned, 1978; atty. Commonwealth of Va., King George County, 1978-80; ptnr. Harris & Harris, Fredericksburg, 1977—. Mem. Assn. trial Lawyers Am. (nat. bd. trial advocacy 1986), Va. Trial Lawyers Assn. Personal injury. Office: Harris & Harris PC 1619 Jeff Davis Hwy Fredericksburg VA 22401

HARRIS, LEE S., lawyer; b. Phila., Oct. 14, 1952; s. Nelson S. and Betty (Loewy) H.; m. Alison Lurie, Jan. 4, 1976; children: Jennifer, Aaron. AB, Harvard U., 1974; JD, U. San Francisco, 1977. Bar: Calif. 1977, U.S. Dist. Ct. (no. dist.) Calif. 1977. Ptnr. Cartwright, Sucherman & Slobodin, Inc., San Francisco, 1980—; instr. Hastings Coll. Advocacy U. Calif., San Francisco, 1984—. Mem. Assn. Trial Lawyers Am., U. San Francisco Alumni Assn. (bd. dirs. 1985—). Club: Harvard (San Francisco). Real property, State civil litigation, Personal injury. Office: Cartwright Sucherman & Slobodin Inc 101 California St 26 Floor San Francisco CA 94111

HARRIS, MICALYN SHAFER, lawyer; b. Chgo., Oct. 31, 1941; d. Erwin and Dorothy (Sampson) Shafer. AB, Wellesley Coll., 1963; JD, U. Chgo., 1966. Bar: Ill. 1966, Mo. 1967, U.S. Dist. Ct. (ea. dist.) 1967, U.S. Supreme Ct. 1972, U.S. Ct. Appeals (8th cir.) 1974, N.Y. 1981. Law clk. U.S. Dist. Ct., St. Louis, 1967-68; atty. The May Dept. Stores, St. Louis, 1968-70, Ralston-Purina Co., St. Louis, 1970-72; atty., asst. sec. Chromalloy Am. Corp., St. Louis, 1972-76; sole practice, St. Louis, 1976-78; div. counsel, gen. counsel S.B. Thomas, Inc.; div. counsel CPC N.Am., 1978—; corp. counsel and asst. sec. CPC Internat., Englewood, Cliffs, N.J., 1978—. Mem. ABA (co-chmn. subcom. counseling the mktg. function, securities law com., tender offers and proxy statements subcom.), Ill. Bar Assn., N.Y. State Bar Assn. (securities regulation com.), Bar Assn. Met. St. Louis (chmn. TV com.), Mo. Bar Assn. (chmn. internat. law com.), Am. Corp. Counsel Assn. N.J. (bd. dirs.). Antitrust, Securities. Address: 625 N Monroe Ridgewood NJ 07450

HARRIS, MICHAEL GENE, optometrist, educator, lawyer; b. San Francisco, Sept. 20, 1942; s. Morry and Gertrude Alice (Epstein) H.; B.S., U. Calif., 1964, M. Optometry, 1965, D. Optometry, 1966, M.S., 1968; J.D., John F. Kennedy U., 1985; m. Andrea Elaine Berman, Nov. 29, 1969; children—Matthew Benjamin, Daniel Evan. Bar: Calif., U.S. Dist. Ct. (no. dist.) Calif. Assoc. practice optometry, Oakland, Calif., 1965-66, San Francisco, 1966-68; instr., coordinator contact lens clinic Ohio State U., 1968-69; asst. clin. prof. optometry U. Calif., Berkeley, 1969-73, dir. contact lens extended care clinic, 1969-83, chief contact lens clinic, 1983—, assoc. clin. prof., 1973-76, asst. chief contact lens service, 1970-76, assoc. chief contact lens service, 1976—, lectr., 1978-80, sr. lectr., 1980—, vice chmn. faculty Sch. Optometry, 1983—, prof. clin. optometry, 1984-86; clin. prof. optometry, 1986—; John de Carle vis. prof. City U., London, 1984; pvt. practice optometry, Oakland, Calif., 1973-76; lectr., cons. in field; mem. regulation rev. com. Calif. State Bd. Optometry; cons. hypnosis Calif. Optometric Assn., Am. Optometric Assn.; cons. Nat. Bd. Examiners in Optometry, Soflens div. Bausch & Lomb, 1973—, Barnes-Hind Hydrocurve Soft Lenses, Inc., 1974—, Contact Lens Research Lab., 1976—, Wesley-Jessen Contact Lens Co., 1977—, Palo Alto VA, 1980—, Primarius Corp., Cooper Vision Optics-Alcon, 1980—; Planning commr. Town of Moraga, Calif., 1986; founding mem. Young Adults div. Jewish Welfare Fedn., 1965—, chmn. 1967-68; commr. Sunday Football League, Contra Costa County, Calif., 1974-78. Charter Mem. Jewish Community Ctr. Contra Costa County; founding mem. Jewish Community Mus. San Francisco, 1984; life mem. Bay Area Council for Soviet Jews, 1976; bd. dirs. Jewish Community Relations Council of Greater East Bay, 1979—, Campolindo Homeowners Assn., 1981—; pres. student council John F. Kennedy U. Sch. Law, 1984-85. Fellow U. Calif., 1971; Calif. Optometric Assn. Scholar 1965, George Schneider Meml. scholar, 1964. Fellow Am. Acad. Optometry (diplomate contact lens sect.; chmn. contact lens papers; mem. contact lens com. 1974—, vice chmn. contact lens sect. 1980-82, chmn. 1982-84, 84-86), Assn. Schs. and Colls. Optometry (council on acad. affairs), AAAS; mem. Assn. for Research in Vision and Ophthalmology, Am. Optometric Assn. (proctor 1969—), Calif. Optometric Assn., Assn. Optometric Contact Lens Educators, Am. Optometric Found., Mexican Soc. Contactology (hon.), Internat. Soc. Contact Lens Research, Calif. State Bd. Optometry (regulation rev. com.), Calif. Acad. Scis., U. Calif. Optometry Alumni Assn. (life), ABA, Assn. Trial Lawyers Am., Calif. Trial Lawyers Assn., Calif. Young Lawyers Assn., Contra Costa Bar Assn., Mus. Soc., Mensa. Democrat. Lodge: B'nai B'rith. Editor current comments sect. Am. Jour. Optometry, 1974-77; editor Eye Contact, 1984—; contbr. chpts. to books; author various syllabuses; contbr. articles to profl. pubs. Health, Personal injury, Personal income taxation. Home: 43 Corte Royal Moraga CA 94556 Office: Univ Calif Sch Optometry Berkeley CA 94720

HARRIS, PATRICIA SKALNY, lawyer; b. Detroit, Mar. 28, 1949; d. John Francis and Sophie Skalny. B.A., U. Mich., 1970, J.D., 1974. Bar: Mich. 1974, U.S. Dist. Ct. (ea. dist.) Mich. 1976. Atty. Gen. Motors Corp., Detroit, 1974—. Mem. ABA, Mich. Bar Assn., Women Lawyers Assn., Soc. Automotive Engrs. Federal civil litigation, State civil litigation, Personal injury. Office: Gen Motors Corp 3044 W Grand Blvd Detroit MI 48202

HARRIS, PHILLIP LLOYD, lawyer; b. Kansas City, Mo., July 6, 1923; s. Lloyd Virgil and Emma Nancy (Manes) H.; m. Nancy Jane Whitnell, Mar. 31, 1945; children—Mark Lloyd, Mary Janet. B.S. in Bus., U. Colo., 1949, J.D., 1949. Bar: Kans. 1949, Mo. 1949. County atty. Geary County (Kans.), 1954-56; U.S. commr. Dist. Kans., 1956-60; mcpl. judge City of Junction City (Kans.), 1960-66; city atty. City Junction City, 1966-73, City Overland Park (Kans.), 1973-85 ; dir. Urban Law Ctr., Kansas City. Served to maj. USMC, 1942-45, 52-53. Mem. ABA, Kans. Bar Assn., Johnson County Bar Assn., Geary County Bar Assn. (past pres.), Cent. Kans. Bar Assn. (past pres.), Nat. Inst. Mcpl. Law Officers (Kans. chmn.), Kansas City Attys. Assn. (past pres.). Episcopalian. Local government, Municipal bonds. Home: 11101 W 99th St Overland Park KS 66214 Office: 14 Corporate Woods 8717 W 110th St Suite 640 Overland Park KS 66212

HARRIS, RICHARD BATES, lawyer; b. Boston, Mar. 12, 1932; s. Robert S. and Ruth (Horsfall) H. BA, U. Rochester, 1954; JD, New England Sch. Law, 1964. Bar: Mass. 1964, U.S. Dist. Ct. Mass. 1964. Sole practice Boston, 1964-69; atty. Cen. Mass. Legal Services, Fitchburg, 1969-73; sole practice Leominster, Mass. Mem. ABA, Assn. Trial Lawyers Am., Mass. Acad. Trial Attys., Mass. Bar Assn., Interamerican Bar Assn., Armenian Law Soc. Workers' compensation, Personal injury, Criminal. Home: 171 Bolton Rd Harvard MA 01451 Office: 11 Park St Leominster MA 01453

HARRIS, RICHARD EUGENE VASSAU, lawyer; b. Detroit, Mar. 16, 1945; s. Joseph S. and Helen Harris; m. Milagros A. Brito; children: Catherine, Byron. AB, Albion Coll., 1967; JD, Harvard U., 1970; postdoctoral, Inst. Advanced Legal Studies, London, 1970-71. Bar: Calif. 1972. Assoc. Orrick, Herrington, Rowley & Sutcliffe, San Fancisco, 1972-77; ptnr. Orrick, Herrington & Sutcliffe, San Francisco, 1978—. Mem. Christian Edn. Bd., Piedmont (Calif.) Community Ch., 1983-86. Knox fellow Harvard U., 1970-71. Mem. ABA (council urban state and local govt. sect. 1983—, vice chmn. govt. liability com. 1982-84, antitrust law sect. franchising com. 1978-81, state action subcom. 1981—, BOULDER task force 1983-84, litigation sect. corp. counsel com., subcom. chmn. 1980-82, 83—, vice chmn. 1982-83, co-chmn. Nat. Insts. Antitrust Liability 1983, 85), Bar Assn. San Francisco (fed. cts. com. 1977—, appellate cts. com. 1987—, ethics com. 1987—), Calif. Bar Assn. (bus. law sect., antitrust sect., intellectual property sect., tax sect.). Federal civil litigation, State civil litigation, Antitrust. Office: Orrick Herrington & Sutcliffe 600 Montgomery St San Francisco CA 94111

HARRIS, RICHARD FOSTER, III, lawyer; b. Charlotte, N.C., Apr. 10, 1942; s. Richard Foster and Frances Virginia (McCurdy) H.; m. Jacqueline Kaplan; children—Richard Foster, IV, John Walter Rodney. A.B. in English, Duke U., 1964; J.D., U. N.C., Chapel Hill, 1967. Bar: N.C. 1967, U.S. Dist. Ct. (we. dist.) N.C. 1971, U.S. Ct. Appeals (4th cir.) 1973. Assoc. Eugene C. Hicks III, Charlotte, 1968-70; ptnr. Hicks, Harris & Sterrett and predecessor Hicks & Harris, Charlotte, 1970-81; sole practice, Charlotte, 1982—. Served with Air N.G., 1967-73. Mem. ABA, N.C. State Bar, N.C. Bar Assn. (Outstanding Young Lawyer award 1977, chmn. Young Lawyers Sect. 1977-78), Assn. Trial Lawyers Am., N.C. Acad. Trial Lawyers, Mecklenburg County Bar Assn. (chmn. young lawyers sect. 1976-77). Democrat. Lutheran. Club: Myers Park Country (Charlotte). Family and matrimonial, Personal injury, Probate. Home: 329 Cherokee Pl Charlotte NC 28207 Office: 757-B Providence Rd Charlotte NC 28207

HARRIS, ROBERT JAMES, lawyer, mediator; b. Boston, Oct. 5, 1930; s. Louis S. and Bertha (Herman) H.; m. Zelma Jean Porter, Feb. 8, 1953; children: David, Elizabeth, Katherine. BA, Wesleyan U., Middletown, Conn., 1953; LLB, Yale U., 1956. Bar: Conn. 1956, U.S. Dist. Ct. Conn. 1956, Mich. 1974, U.S. Dist. Ct. (ea. dist.) Mich. 1975, U.S. Ct. Appeals (6th cir.) 1986. Assoc. Goldstein & Peck, Bridgeport, Conn., 1957-58; asst. prof. law George Washington U., Washington, 1958-59; from asst. prof. to prof. law U. Mich., Ann Arbor, 1959-74; ptnr. Harris, Lax, Guenzel & Dew, Ann Arbor, 1974—; cons. New Detroit Com., 1967-68; adj. prof. polit. sci. U. Mich., Ann Arbor, 1975—, adj. prof. law, 1981-85. Contbr. articles to profl. jours. Mayor City of Ann Arbor, 1969-73; bd. dirs. ACLU Fund of Mich., Detroit, 1970—, bd. dirs. Legal Services S.E. Mich.; 1st v.p. S.E. Mich. Council of Govts., Detroit, 1972-73. Rhodes scholar, 1951. Mem. ABA, Mich. Bar Assn. (real property sect., legal aid com.), Nat. Health Lawyers Assn., Mich. Health Care Lawyers Assn., Lawyers Alliance Nuclear Arms Control. Democrat. Jewish. Real property, General corporate, Health. Home: 3904 Tubbs Ann Arbor MI 48103 Office: Harris Lax Guenzel & Dew 320 City Ctr Bldg Ann Arbor MI 48103

HARRIS, ROBERT LEWIS, lawyer; b. Arkadelphia, Ark., Mar. 4, 1944; s. Benjamin F. and Lucy L. (Luster) H.; m. Glenda Newell, Mar. 17, 1984; children: Anthony, Regina. AA, Merritt Coll., 1963; BA, San Francisco State U., 1965; JD, U. Calif., Berkeley, 1972. Bar: Calif. 1972, U.S. Dist. Ct. (no. dist.) Calif. 1972, U.S. Ct. Appeals (91th cir.) 1972, U.S. Supreme Ct. 1978, U.S. Ct. Appeals (11th cir.) 1986. Dep. probation officer Alameda County, Oakland, Calif., 1965-69; atty. Pacific Gas & Electric Co., San Francisco, 1972—; bd. dirs. Blue Shield Calif., San Francisco. Contbr. articles to profl. jours. Fellow Am. Bar Found.; mem. ABA, Nat. Bar Assn. (pres. 1979-80, C. Francis Stradford award 1982), Calif. Assn. Black Lawyers (founder 1977, Loren Miller award 1986), Charles Houston Bar Assn. (pres. 1976-79), NAACP, Kappa Alpha Psi, Sigma Pi Phi. Avocation: fishing. Corportate free speech-first amendment. Home: 6137 Arlington Blvd Richmond CA 94805

HARRIS, ROBERT THOMAS, lawyer, real estate broker; b. Union City, Tenn., Dec. 17, 1943; s. Thomas Vernell and Rebecca Maye (Rice) H.; m. Lenore Ethel Zobel, June 19, 1966; children—Rebecca Louise, Grant Thomas. B.A., Calif. Western U., 1965; J.D., Stanford U., 1968. Bar: Calif. 1969, U.S. Dist. Ct. (so. dist.) Calif. 1969, U.S. Ct. Appeals (9th cir.) 1969, U.S. Supreme Ct. 1972, U.S. Dist. Ct. (cen. and ea. dists.) Calif. 1976. Dep. city atty., San Diego, 1969-70; ptnr. Wiza, Harris & Reed, San Diego, 1971-73; asst. city atty., Imperial Beach, Calif., 1971-73; asst. county counsel Ventura County, Calif., 1973-86; city atty. City of Stockton, Calif., 1986—; litigation lectr. Calif. County Counsel, Assn., 1979. Co-author: Misdemeanor Prosecution Manual, 1969; author, lectr. local jurisdiction on fed. lands, 1979. Mem. State Calif. Bar (litigation sect.), San Diego County Bar Assn., Ventura County Bar Assn. (bd. dirs. 1981-83), San Joaquin County Bar Assn., Phi Delta Phi. Local government, State civil litigation, Federal civil litigation. Office: City Atty Office City Hall Stockton CA 95202

HARRIS, ROGER KING, lawyer; b. Moscow, Idaho, June 6, 1947; s. Dee Miekle and Betty Jean (Kinghorn) H.; m. Merla Rose Ashby, Mar. 17, 1972; children: Aaron Ashby, Jonathan Dee, Amanda Jean, Benjamin Nathaniel, Timothy James. BS, Oreg. State U., 1973; JD, Lewis and Clark U., 1977. Bar: Oreg. 1978, U.S. Dist. Ct. Oreg. 1984, U.S. Ct. Appeals (9th cir.) 1984. Dep. dist. atty. Multnomah County, Portland, Oreg., 1977-78, Linn County, Albany, Oreg., 1978-82; v.p. legal affairs Evergreen Internat. Aviation, Inc., McMinnville, Oreg., 1982-84; asst. gen. counsel Portland (Oreg.) Gen. Electric Co., 1984—; instr. law Linn-Benton Community Coll., Albany, 1979-82. Mem. Albany Community Choral, 1980-81, legis. rev. com. ODAA, Salem, Oreg., 1981; com. chmn. Boy Scouts Am., Albany and Tualatin, Oreg., 1980—; community dir. White House Conf. on Families, Albany, 1979. Mem. ABA, Oreg. Bar Assn. (sec. ethics com.), Multnomah Bar Assn., Blue Key. Republican. Federal civil litigation, State civil litigation, General corporate. Home: 445 W Division St Sherwood OR 97140 Office: Portland Gen Electric Co 121 SW Salmon St Suite 1300 Portland OR 97204

HARRIS, SCOTT BLAKE, lawyer; b. N.Y.C., June 18, 1951; s. Stanley Robert and Adele Jean (Ganger) H.; m. Barbara Straughn Harris, Aug. 5, 1978. AB magna cum laude, Brown U., 1973; JD magna cum laude, Harvard U., 1976. Bar: D.C. 1977, U.S. Ct. Appeals (D.C. cir.) 1978, U.S. Ct. Appeals (5th and 7th cirs.) 1979, U.S. Ct. Appeals (3d cir.) 1981, U.S. Ct. Appeals (4th cir.) 1982, U.S. Supreme Ct. 1983. Law clk. to presiding justice U.S. Dist. Ct., Washington, 1976-77; assoc. Williams & Connolly, Washington, 1977-84, ptnr., 1984—; mem. com. on pro-bono representation, Jud. Conf. D.C. Cir., 1981, 83—, 84—, Media Com. D.C. Cts.,1983-85, council fgn. relations, 1986—; nat. adv. bd. Ctr. for Nat. Policy, 1986—. Legal advisor Carter-Mondale Com., Inc., Washington, 1979-80, Mondale for Pres., Washington, 1982-84; mem. Dems. for Def., 1981—; bd. dirs. Brown U. Associated Alumni, Providence, R.I., 1980—. Mem. Phi Beta Kappa. Federal civil litigation, Contracts commercial, Private international. Home: 3409 Fulton St NW Washington DC 20007 Office: Williams & Connolly 839 17th St NW Washington DC 20006

HARRIS, STANLEY SUTHERLAND, federal judge; b. Washington, Oct. 19, 1927; s. Stanley Raymond and Elizabeth (Sutherland) H.; m. Rebecca Ashley, Aug. 1, 1964; children—Scott Sutherland, Todd Ashley, Mark Ashley. B.S., U. Va., 1951, J.D., 1953. Bar: D.C. 1953, U.S. Supreme Ct. 1964. Assoc., then ptnr. Hogan & Hartson, Washington, 1953-70; judge Superior Ct. D.C., 1971-72, D.C. Ct. Appeals, 1972-82; U.S. atty. for D.C. Dept. Justice, 1982-83; judge U.S. Dist. Ct. D.C., 1983—. Served with U.S. Army, 1945-47. Recipient Judiciary award Assn. Fed. Investigators, 1982. Mem. ABA, Bar Assn. D.C. (bd. dirs. 1970-72, Lawyer of Yr. award 1982). Republican. Methodist. Home: 9621 Weathered Oak Ct Bethesda MD 20817 Office: US Courthouse 3rd and Constitution Ave, NW Washington DC 20001

HARRIS, STEPHEN JAMES, lawyer; b. Ann Arbor, Mich., June 26, 1954; s. James R. and Mary Lee (Pellerin) H.; m. Madeline S. Kinney, Aug. 12, 1978; children: Alison W., Daniel P. BS, LeMoyne Coll., 1976; JD, U. Detroit, 1979. Bar: Mich. 1979, U.S. Dist. Ct. (ea. dist.) Mich. 1979. Ptnr. Plunkett & Cooney, Detroit, 1979—. Mem. ABA, Mich. Bar Assn., Detroit Bar Assn., Macomb County Bar Assn. Avocations: model ship building,

jogging. Contracts commercial, Bankruptcy, General corporate. Office: Plunkett & Cooney 900 Marquette Bldg Detroit MI 48226

HARRIS, STEVEN MARK, lawyer; b. Detroit, July 8, 1954; s. Merle Alan and Shirley Joyce (Barnett) H. BA, Brandeis U., 1976; JD, U. Mich., 1979. Bar: D.C. 1979, U.S. Supreme Ct. 1983. Assoc. Schnader, Harrison, Segal & Lewis, Phila. and Washington, 1977-81; legal asst. to gen. counsel FCC, Washington, 1981-82, legal asst. to commr., 1982-83; exec. dir., fed. regulatory relations Pacific Telesis Group, Washington, 1983—. Editor in chief Michigan Yearbook International Legal Studies, 1980. Trustee Golden Jubilee Commn. Telecommunications, Washington, 1984—. Mem. ABA, Am. Soc. Internat. Law. Administrative and regulatory. Office: Pacific Telesis Group 444 N Capitol St Suite 718 NW Washington DC 20001

HARRIS, THOMAS V., lawyer; b. N.Y.C., Apr. 6, 1948; s. Bernard V. and Miriam (Sullivan) H.; m. Marcia Elizabeth Vogler, Aug. 11, 1979; children: Stephen Charles, Laura Jane. A.B. cum laude, Harvard U., 1970; J.D., Cornell U., 1973. Bar: Wash. 1973, U.S. Dist. Ct. (we. dist.) Wash. 1973, U.S. Dist. Ct. (ea. dist.) Wash. 1980, U.S. Ct. Appeals (9th cir.) 1973. Shareholder, dir. Merrick, Hofstedt & Lindsey, P.S., Seattle, 1973—; moot ct. judge U. Wash., 1981—. Contbr. articles to profl. jours. Mem. ABA, Internat. Assn. Ins. Counsel. Roman Catholic. Club: Wash. Athletic. Personal injury, Insurance, Federal civil litigation. Home: 8860 SE 74th Pl Mercer Island WA 98040-5765 Office: Merrick Hofstedt & Lindsey PS 710 9th Ave Seattle WA 98104 *

HARRIS, THORNE D., III, lawyer; b. New Orleans, Nov. 5, 1950; s. Thorne D. and Myra (Banister) H. Jr.; m. Mary Margaret Hattier, June 18, 1971. B.A. in English, U. New Orleans, 1972; J.D., La. State U., 1974. Bar: La. 1974, U.S. Dist. Ct. (ea. dist.) La. 1974, U.S. Dist. Ct. (mid. and we. dists.) La. 1976, U.S. Ct. Appeals (5th cir.) 1974, U.S. Ct. Appeals (11th cir.) 1981. with Sessions, Fishman, et al, New Orleans, 1974-81, Monroe & Lemann, New Orleans, 1981-82, McNulty, O'Conner, et al, New Orleans, 1982-84; sole practice, New Orleans, 1984—; cons. computer law and law office computer systems. Author: Legal Guide to Computer Software Protection: A Practical Handbook on Copyrights, Trademarks, Publishing and Trade Secrets, 1984; Contbr. articles to profl. jours. Mem. La. State U. Law Rev. Chmn. U. New Orleans Awards and Scholarship Com., 1980-86; mem. Civitan, New Orleans, 1977-78. Named one of Outstanding Young Men of Am., Jaycees, 1984, 86. Mem. La. Bar Assn. (sects. on litigation, mineral law, ins., bus. and antitrust 1974—), New Orleans Bar Assn., ABA (sects. on sci. and tech., patent, copyrights and trademarks, corps. 1975—, chmn. software subcom. of copyright and new technology com. 1984—, chmn. subcom. piracy, 1986—), Vol. Lawyers for Arts, Order of Coif, Phi Eta Sigma. Republican. General practice, Federal civil litigation, Computer. Office: 326 S Broad St New Orleans LA 70119

HARRIS, TYREE BRYSON, lawyer; b. Nashville, Feb. 26, 1921; s. Tyree B. and Mattie (Duncan) H.; m. Temesia Dilleka, June 9, 1944; children: Tyree B. IV, Temesia H. JD, U. Tenn., 1943. Bar: Tenn. 1942, U.S. Dist Ct. (mid. dist.) Tenn. 1942, U.S. Ct. Appeals (6th cir.) 1943. Assoc. Walker & Hooker, Nashville, 1943-47, ptnr., 1948-51; ptnr. Hooker, Keeble, Dodson & Harris, Nashville, 1951-74, Dodson, Harris, Robinson & Aden, Nashville, 1974-87, Trahue, Sturdivant & DeWitt, Nashville, 1987—. Fellow Internat. Acad. Trial Lawyers (pres. 1980-81), Am. Coll. Trial Lawyers; mem. ABA, Fedn. of Ins. Counsel, Nashville Bar Assn. (pres. 1961-62). Democrat. Prebyterian. Clubs: Richland Country, Nashville City. Federal civil litigation, State civil litigation, Personal injury. Home: 6666 Brookmont Terr Nashville TN 37205 Office: Trahue Sturdivant & DeWitt L & C Towers 27th Floor Nashville TN 37219

HARRIS, WARREN LOUIS, lawyer; b. N.Y.C., July 14, 1952; s. Herman and Estelle Harris; m. Joy Gail Dunn, Sept. 3, 1977; children: Isaac A., Jared M. BA, U. So. Fla., 1974; JD, U. Fla., 1977. Bar: Fla. 1978. Assoc. Albritton, Sessums et al, Tampa, Fla., 1977-83; ptnr. Cheeseman, Harris & Phillips, Tampa, 1983—. Bd. dirs. Northside Community Mental Health Ctr., Tampa, 1984—. Mem. Fla. Bar Assn., Hills County Bar Assn., Assn. Trial Lawyers Am., Fla. Trial Lawyers Assn. Personal injury, Workers' compensation, Family and matrimonial. Home: 4106 Leona Tampa FL 33629 Office: Cheeseman Harris & Phillips 700 Twiggs St Suite 105 Tampa FL 33601

HARRIS, WAYNE MANLEY, lawyer; b. Pittsford, N.Y., Dec. 28, 1925; s. George H. and Constance M. Harris; m. Diane C. Quigley, Sept. 30, 1979; children—Wayne, Constance, Karen, Duncan, Claire. LL.D., Albany Law Sch., U. Rochester, 1951. Bar: N.Y. 1952. Ptnr., Harris, Maloney, Horwitz, Evans & Fox, and predecessors, Rochester, N.Y., 1958—. Pres. Delta Labs., Inc. (non-profit environ. lab.), 1971—, pres. friends of Bristol Valley Playhouse Found., 1984-87, Monroe County Conservation Council Inc., 1985-87. Served with AUS, 1944-46. Decorated Bronze Star. Recipient Sportsman of Yr. award Genesee Conservation League, Inc., 1960, Conservationist of Yr. award Monroe County Conservation Council, Inc., 1961, Kiwanian of Yr. award, Kiwanis Club, 1965, Livingston County Fedn. of Sportsmen award, 1966, N.Y. State Conservation Council Nat. Wildlife Fedn. Water Conservation award, 1967, Rochester Acad. of Sci. award, 1970, Am. Motors Corp. Conservation award, 1971, Rochester C. of C. award, 1972. Drafter 5 laws passed into law in N.Y. State. State civil litigation, General corporate, Probate. Home: 60 Mendon Center Rd Honeoye Falls NY 14472 Office: 700 First Fed Plaza Rochester NY 14614

HARRISON, CHARLES MAURICE, lawyer, communications company executive; b. Anderson, S.C., Aug. 30, 1927; s. Emmitte Smallwood and Jessie Maysel (Hawkins) H.; m. Lorna Jean Tomalty, June 27, 1970; children: Suzanne Elizabeth, Linda Jean. A.B., Marshall U., 1949; J.D., W.Va. U., 1952. Bar: W.Va. 1952, D.C. 1958, N.Y. 1965, N.J. 1972. Legal asst. W.Va. Dept. Ins., Charleston, 1952-54; hearing examiner Public Service Commn., Charleston, 1954-57; atty. Chesapeake and Potomac Telephone Co., Washington and Charleston, 1957-64, Western Electric Co., N.Y.C., 1964-69; gen. atty., sec., treas. Bellcomm, Inc., Washington, 1969-71; asst. gen. counsel, asst. sec. Bell Telephone Labs., Murray Hill, N.J., 1971-75; gen. atty., sec. Bell Telephone Labs., 1975-76, sec., gen. counsel corporate matters, 1976-84; asst. sec., asst. gen. counsel AT&T Bell Labs, 1985—. Trustee Family Counseling Service Somerset County, N.J., pres., 1978-81; chmn. Research and Devel. Council N.J.; bd. dirs. Martin Luther King Youth Ctr., 1984—; chmn. Bridgewater (N.J.) Commn. on Drug Abuse, 1986—; commr. Bridgewater-Raritan Youth Services, 1986—. Served with AC U.S. Army, 1945-46. Mem. ABA (co-chmn. subcom. practical ethical considerations, com. corp. counsel litigation sect.), N.J. Assn. Corp. Counsel, W.Va. State Bar, D.C. Bar Assn., N.J. State Bar Assn. Republican. General practice, Federal civil litigation, State civil litigation. Office: AT&T Bell Labs 101 John F Kennedy Pkwy Short Hills NJ 07078

HARRISON, CLARENCE BUFORD, JR., oil company executive, lawyer; b. Dallas, Sept. 27, 1944; s. Clarence Buford and Clara Janie (Jones); m. Kate Butler, July 19, 1969; children: Amy Elizabeth, Patrick Buford, Amanda Mae. BBA in Fin., U. Tex.-Austin, 1967; JD, U. Tex., 1970. Bar: Tex. 1970. Tax staff Touche Ross & Co., Dallas, 1970-71; assoc. Diamond Goodner Winkle, Wells & Harrison, Dallas, 1971-72; gen. counsel, gen. mgr., dir. Scoggins Petroleum Corp., Dallas, 1972-75; pres. Interam. Oil & Minerals Inc., successor corp., 1981—; ptnr. firm Harrison Vernon & Clark, Dallas, 1975—; speaker profl. seminars including Tri State Oil & Gas, Ind., Ill., Ky., Ind. Oil Producers. Roman Catholic. Club: Dallas Petroleum, Univ. (Dallas). Oil and gas leasing, Banking. Home: 1138 Wilderness Trail Richardson TX 75080 Office: 12221 Merit Dr Suite 960 Dallas TX 75251

HARRISON, DAVID GEORGE, lawyer; b. Albany, Oreg., Apr. 6, 1945; s. Russell Benjamin and Altha Edna (Green) H.; m. Katherine Scott Crockett, Jan. 2, 1971; children—Elizabeth, Scott. B.S., Oreg. State U., 1967; M.B.A., Am. U., 1973; J.D., U. Oreg., 1973. Bar: Oreg. 1973, D.C. 1974, Tenn. 1975, Va. 1978, U.S. Dist. Ct. (ea. dist.) Tenn. 1975, U.S. Dist. Ct. (we. dist.) Va. 1978, U.S. Dist. Ct. (ea. dist.) Va. 1982, U.S. Ct. Appeals (4th cir.) 1978. Legal counsel, sec. Tenn. Forging Steel Corp., Harriman, Tenn., 1974-77; atty. Martin, Hopkins & Lemon, Roanoke, Va., 1977-81, Wetherington & Melchionna, Roanoke, 1981—. Bd. dirs. Family Service of Roanoke Valley, 1982-84, mem. exec. com., 1983-84. Served with U.S. Army, 1968-71. Mem. ABA (mem. antitrust and labor relations com. of labor and employment law sect. 1978), Va. State Bar, Va. Bar Assn., Roanoke Bar Assn., D.C. Bar, Oreg. State Bar. Presbyterian. Club: Kiwanis. Contracts commercial, General corporate, Securities. Office: Weatherington & Melchionna 1100 United Va Bank Bldg Roanoke VA 24011

HARRISON, DONALD, lawyer; b. N.Y.C., Mar. 2, 1946; s. David and Arlene Beverly (Johnson) H.; m. Ellen Louise Kroll, Aug. 30, 1970; children: Matthew Austin, Margaret Wynne. BA magna cum laude, Harvard U., 1967, JD magna cum laude, 1971. Bar: D.C. 1973, U.S. Ct. Internat. Trade 1975, U.S. Ct. Appeals (Fed. cir.) 1982, U.S. Supreme Ct. 1979. Law clk. to presiding judge Francis L. Van Dusen U.S. Ct. Appeals 3d circuit, Phila., 1972-73; assoc. Covington & Burling, Washington, 1973-79; ptnr. Leva, Hawes & Symington, Washington, 1979-83, Miller & Chevalier, Chartered, Washington, 1983—. Editor Harvard Law Rev., 1969-71. Private international, Environment. Office: Miller & Chevalier Chartered 655 15th St NW Metropolitan Sq Washington DC 20005

HARRISON, EARL DAVID, lawyer, real estate executive; b. Bryn Mawr, Pa., Aug. 25, 1932; m. Lisa Philippa Wanderman, Oct. 25, 1981; 1 son, H. Jason. BA, Harvard U., 1954; JD, U. Pa., 1960. Bar: D.C. 1960. Sole practice, Washington; exec. v.p. Washington Real Estate Corp., 1986—. Served to capt. U.S. Army, 1954-57. Decorated Order of Rio Branco (Brazil); Order of Merit (Italy). Mem. ABA, D.C. Bar Assn., Washington, D.C. Assn. Realtors. Real property, Private international, Contracts commercial. Home: 336 Constitution Ave NE Washington DC 20002 Office: 777 14th St NW Suite 305 Washington DC 20005

HARRISON, FREDERICK JOSEPH, lawyer; b. Cheyenne, Wyo., Dec. 31, 1951; s. Gerald Lee and Bessie (Ferro) H.; m. Loris Ann Engstrom, May 14, 1977; children: Kimberly, Jared, Kathryn, Jane. BA in Polit. Sci and Am. Studies with high honors, U. Wyo., 1974, JD, 1977. Bar: Wyo. 1977, U.S. Dist. Ct. Wyo. 1977, U.S. Ct. Appeals (10th cir.) 1977. Sole practice Rawlins, Wyo., 1977—; asst. pub. defender 1981-86; rep. Wyo. Legislature, Cheyenne, 1982—; dep. atty. Carbon County, Rawlins, 1977-80, asst. pub. defender, 1981—; asst. mcpl. judge, Rawlins, 1977-79; gen. counsel Carbon Power & Light, Saratoga, Wyo., 1983—; town atty., Encampment and Riverside, Wyo., 1979—. Chmn. Carbon County Dem. Party, 1978-80, Dem. caucus, 1986—; state committeeman, 1980-82. Fellow Wyo. Def. Lawyers Assn., Comml. Law League; mem. Wyo. Bar Assn. (law and reform com.) Wyo. Trial Lawyers Assn. Roman Catholic. Lodges: Elks, Lions. Avocation: history. Insurance, Personal injury, Real property. Home: 715 W Maple St Rawlins WY 82301 Office: 1st Wyo Bank Bldg 4th & Buffalo Sts Rawlins WY 82301

HARRISON, GRESHAM HUGHEL, lawyer; b. Johnson County, Ga., June 19, 1924; s. James Wheeler and Geneva Frances (Jordan) H.; m. Leslie Powell, June 22, 1924; 1 son, Samuel Hughel. LL.B., Mercer U., 1954, J.D., 1964. Bar: Ga. 1955, U.S. Supreme Ct. 1961. Asst. atty. gen. State Ga., 1956-63; sole practice, Lawrenceville, Ga., 1963—; judge Recorders Ct. Gwinnett County, Ga., 1972-78; judge State Ct. Gwinnett County, 1978-79. Served with USN, 1942-46, 50-52; ETO. Mem. ABA, Am. Judicature Soc., Ga. Bar Assn., Gwinnett Bar Assn. Democrat. Presbyterian. Club: Kiwanis (lt. gov.) (Lawrenceville, Ga.). General practice, Criminal. Office: Hughel Harrison Law Firm Box 88 Lawrenceville GA 30245

HARRISON, JAMES JOSHUA, JR., lawyer, corporate executive; b. Balt., Sept. 5, 1936; s. James Joshua and Marion Elizabeth (Thompson) H.; m. Mary English Darden, June 14, 1957; children—James Joshua III, William Darden, Mary Withers, John Theodore, Robert English, Elizabeth Ann. B.C.E., Cornell U., 1960; J.D., U. Balt., 1963; M.B.A., Loyola Coll., Balt., 1976. Bar: Md. 1963, U.S. Supreme Ct. 1975, U.S. Dist. Ct. Md. 1975, U.S. Ct. Appeals (4th cir.) 1975. Engr., Whiting-Turner, Balt., 1960-61; engr., sr. contracts specialist Martin Marietta Corp., Balt., 1962-66; assoc. gen. counsel, asst. sec. McCormick & Co., Inc., Hunt Valley, Md., 1966-73, sec., gen. counsel, 1973—, v.p., 1980—, also dir.; sec., dir. McCormick Properties, Inc., Hunt Valley; dir. McCormick Constrn. Co., Hunt Valley. Mem. adv. com. U. Balt. Law Sch., 1982—; fund raiser Loyola Coll., 1981; mem. vestry Trinity Episcopal Ch., Towson, Md., 1983—; com. chmn. Lutherville Community Assn., Md., 1978-81. Mem. ABA, Md. Bar Assn., Am. Soc. Corp. Secs. Democrat. General corporate, Real property. Home: 302 Melanchton Ave Lutherville MD 21093 Office: McCormick & Co Inc 11350 McCormick Rd Hunt Valley MD 21031

HARRISON, JOHN CONWAY, state justice; b. Grand Rapids, Minn., Apr. 28, 1913; s. Francis Randall and Ethglyn (Conway) H.; widowed; children—Nina Lyn, Robert Charles, Molly M., Frank R., Virginia Lee. LL.D., George Washington U., 1940. Bar: Mont. 1947, U.S. Dist. Ct. 1947. County atty. Lewis and Clark County, Helena, Mont., 1934-60; justice Mont. Supreme Ct., Helena, 1961—. Pres. Mont. TB Assn., Helena, 1951-54; Am. Lung Assn., N.Y.C., 1972-73, local council Boy Scouts Am., Great Falls, Mont., 1976-78. Served to col. U.S. Army. Lodge: Kiwanis (pres. 1953). Jurisprudence. Home: 516 N Park St Helena MT 59601 Office: Mont Supreme Ct Justice Bldg Helena MT 59601

HARRISON, JOHN EDWARDS, lawyer, real estate executive; b. Arlington, Va., Aug. 15, 1946; s. Hunter Creycroft and Margaret (Edwards) H.; m. Sally Hart Jones, July 23, 1969; children—Lucy Love, Sally Hart. Student U. N.C., 1964-66; B.S. in Fgn. Service, Georgetown U., 1971, J.D., 1977. Bar: Va. 1977, U.S. Ct. Appeals (4th cir.) 1977, D.C. 1980, U.S. Ct. Appeals (D.C. cir.). Assoc. Tolbert, Smith Fitzgerald & Ramsey, Arlington, 1977-79, Melrod, Redman & Gartlan, Washington, 1979-81; ptnr. Light & Harrison, P.C., McLean, Va., 1981—; chmn. bd. George H. Rucker Realty, Arlington, 1981—, McLean Fin. Corp., 1981—; dir. McLean Savs. and Loan. Served to 1st lt. U.S. Army, 1966-69, Vietnam. Decorated Silver Star, Bronze Star with V and cluster, Purple Heart. Mem. ABA, Va. Bar Assn., D.C. Bar Assn., Nat. Assn. Realtors. Episcopalian. Clubs: Army Navy (Washington); Farmington Country (Charlottesville, Va.). Federal civil litigation, State civil litigation, Construction. Home: 6341 Georgetown Pike McLean VA 22101 Office: Light & Harrison PC 6849 Old Dominion Dr McLean VA 22101

HARRISON, KEITH MICHAELE, law educator; b. Washington, Nov. 6, 1956; s. Charles Thomas Harrison Sr. and June Earlene (Bell) Harrison-Russ; m. Karen Marie Anderson, Aug. 21, 1982. BA, St. John's Coll., Sante Fe, 1977; JD, U. Chgo., 1981. Bar: Ill. 1981, D.C. 1982, N.Y. 1985. Clin. teaching fellow Antioch Sch. Law, Washington, 1985-86; asst. prof. law No. Ill. U., DeKalb, 1986—; legal cons. United Planning Orgn., Washington, 1985. Served to lt. USCG, 1981-85. Mem. ABA, Ill. Bar Assn., D.C. Bar Assn. Legal education, Criminal, Immigration, naturalization, and customs. Office: No Ill U Coll Law DeKalb IL 60115

HARRISON, MARION EDWYN, lawyer; b. Phila., Sept. 17, 1931; s. Marion Edwyn and Jessye Beatrice (Cilles) H.; m. Carmelita Ruth Deimel, Sept. 6, 1952; children: Angelique Harrison Bounds, Marion Edwyn III, Henry Deimel. B.A., U. Va., 1951; LL.B., George Washington U., 1954, LL.M., 1959. Bar: Va. 1954, D.C. 1958, Supreme Ct. 1958. Spl. asst. to gen. counsel Post Office Dept., 1958-60, assoc. gen. counsel, 1960-61, mem. bd. contract appeals, 1958-61; ptnr. firm Harrison, Lucey & Sagle (and predecessors), Washington, 1961-78, Barnett & Alagia, 1978-84; ptnr. Scott, Harrison & McLeod, 1984-86, Law Offices Marion Edwyn Harrison, Washington, 1986—; Mem. council Adminstrv. Conf. U.S., 1971-78, sr. conf. fellow, 1984—. mem. D.C. Law Revision Commn., 1975—; lectr. Nat. Jud. Coll., Reno, 1979. Author articles, manuals.; Editor-in-chief: Fed. Bar News, 1960-63; mem. editorial bd.: Adminstrv. Law Rev, 1976—. Trustee AEFC Pension Fund, 1986—; pres. Young Rep. Fedn. Va., 1954-55; mem. Va. Rep. Cen. Com., 1954-55; bd. visitors Judge Adv. Gen. Sch., Charlottesville, Va., 1976-78; chmn. Wolf Trap Assn., 1984-87; bd. dirs. Wolf Trap Found., 1984—; pub. mem. USIA Inspection Mission, Argentina, 1971. Served as officer AUS, 1955-58. Decorated Commendation medal. Fellow Am. Bar Found. (life); mem. ABA (chmn. sect. adminstrv. law 1974-75, ho. of dels. 1978—, bd. govs. 1982-86, chmn. com. on fgn. and internat. orgns. 1986-87, chmn. lawyers in govt. 1980-82), Fed. Bar Assn. (nat. council 1966-82), Inter-Am. Bar Assn., Bar Assn. D.C. (chmn. adminstrv. law sect. 1970-71, bd. dirs. 1971-72), George Washington U. Law Assn. (pres. 1974-77). Episcopalian (vestry). Clubs: Washington Golf and Country, Metropolitan, Nat. Lawyers (Washington); Farmington Country (Charlottesville, Va.). Home: 4111 N Ridgeview Rd Arlington VA 22207 Office: 3105 NE 28th St Fort Lauderdale FL 33308 Office: S Folkenstrosse 14 2d Floor, Zurich 8008, Switzerland

HARRISON, MARK I., lawyer; b. Pitts., Oct. 17, 1934; s. Coleman and Myrtle (Seidenman) H.; m. Ellen R. Gier, June 15, 1958; children: Lisa, Jill. A.B., Antioch Coll., 1957; LL.B., Harvard U., 1960. Bar: Ariz. 1961. Law clk. to justices Ariz. Supreme Ct., 1960-61; partner Harrison & Lerch, Phoenix, 1966—. Co-author: Arizona Appellate Practice, 1966; editorial bd. ABA/BNA Lawyers Manual on Profl. Conduct, 1983-86; contbr. articles to legal jours. Bd. dirs. Careers for Youth, 1963-67, pres., 1966-67; vice chmn. Maricopa County Democratic Central Com., 1967-68; vice chmn. Ariz. Dem. Com., 1969-70, legal counsel, 1970-72; del. Dem. Nat. Conv., 1968; chmn. Phoenix City Bond Adv. Commn., 1976-79; pres. Valley Commerce Assn., 1978. Fellow Am. Bar Found.; mem. ABA (chmn. commn. pub. understanding law 1984-87, standing com. profl. discussion, 1976-84, chmn., 1982-84, chmn. coordinating com. on professionalism, 1987—), Maricopa County Bar Assn. (pres. 1970), Am. Bd. Trial Advocates, State Bar Ariz. (bd. govs. 1971-77, pres. 1975-76), Nat. Conf. Bar Pres. (exec. council 1971-73, 75-79, pres. 1977-78), Western States Bar Conf. (pres. 1978-79), Am. Judicature Soc. (exec. com. 1983-86, bd. dirs. 1983-87), Ariz. Civil Liberties Union, Harvard Law Sch. Assn. (nat. exec. council 1980-84). Federal civil litigation, State civil litigation, Antitrust. Home: 33 E State Ave Phoenix AZ 85020 Office: 1001 N Central Ave Suite 900 Phoenix AZ 85004

HARRISON, NANCY JANE, lawyer; b. Madison, Ind., Oct. 12, 1934; d. Roy Denny and Mary Kathryn (Hall) Holwager; m. James Wesley Cone, July 22, 1956 (div. 1968); 1 child, Heather Lynn; m. Russell Francis Harrison, Nov. 28, 1969. A.B in Chemistry, Ind. U., 1956; J.D., Ind. U.-Indpls., 1980. Bar: Ind. 1980, U.S. Dist. Ct. (so. dist.) Ind. 1980, U.S. Ct. Appeals (fed. cir.) 1982. Assoc. organic chemist Eli Lilly & Co., Indpls., 1956-58, organic chemist, 1958-66, 68-70, patent technician, 1971-74, patent agt., 1974-80, patent atty., 1980—. Contbr. articles to profl. jours. Mem. ABA, Ind. State Bar Assn. (patent, trademark and copyright sect. sec.-treas. 1983-84, vice-chmn. 1984-85, chmn.-elect 1985-86, chmn. 1986-87), Am. Intellectual Property Law Assn., Am. Chem. Soc. Mem. Christian Ch., Disciples of Christ. Patent, Trademark and copyright. Home: 5325 Ohmer Ave Indianapolis IN 46219 Office: Eli Lilly & Co Lilly Corp Ctr Indianapolis IN 46285

HARRISON, ORRIN LEA, III, lawyer; b. Dallas, July 1, 1949; s. Orrin Lea Jr. and Annie Bell (Lassig) H.; m. Paula Diane Wagnon, May 29, 1971; children: Orrin IV, Erin, Lindsey. BA cum laude, U. of South; JD with honors, So. Meth. U. Bar: Tex. 1974, U.S. Dist. Ct. (no., so. and we. dists.) Tex., U.S. Ct. Appeals (5th and 11th cirs.), U.S. Supreme Ct. From assoc. to ptnr. Locke, Purnell, Boren, Laney & Neely, Dallas, 1974—. Sec. 500 Inc., Dallas, 1981, treas. 1982; chancellor Ch. Incarnation, Dallas, 1985—; bd. dirs. Dallas Econ. Devel. Council, 1986—. Served to lt. JAGC, USN, 1971-75. Fellow Tex. Bar Assn.; mem. ABA, Dallas Bar Assn. (bd. dirs. 1983—), Tex. Young Laywers Assn. (bd. dirs. 1981-83), Dallas Young Lawyers Assn. (pres. 1980-81). Republican. Episcopalian. Club: Town (Dallas). Avocations: jogging, racquetball. Federal civil litigation, Antitrust, State civil litigation. Home: 3624 Normandy Dallas TX 75205 Office: Locke Purnell Boren Laney & Neely 3600 Republic Bank Tower Dallas TX 75201

HARRISON, REESE LENWOOD, JR., lawyer; b. San Antonio, Jan. 5, 1938; s. Reese Lenwood and Ruth Leona (Fischer) H.; m. Judith Karen Scott, Oct. 9, 1964; children: Judith Karen Scott Jr., Tiffany Farrah Lynn. BBA, Baylor U., 1959, MS, 1965; JD, So. Meth. U., 1962. Bar: Tex. 1962, U.S. Dist. Ct. (we. dist.) Tex. 1964, U.S. Ct. Appeals (5th cir.) 1964, U.S. Ct. Claims 1968, U.S. Supreme Ct. 1968, U.S. Ct. Appeals (fed. cir.) 1968, U.S. Tax Ct. 1972, U.S. Ct. Internat. Trade 1973, U.S. Dist. Ct. (no. dist.) Tex. 1976, U.S. Dist. Ct. (so. dist.) Tex. 1978, U.S. Ct. Mil. Appeals 1979, U.S. Ct. Appeals (11th cir.) 1981. Asst. U.S. atty. Dept. Justice, San Antonio, 1964-72, spl. asst. to U.S. Atty., 1972-73; ptnr. Oppenheimer, Rosenberg, Kelleher & Wheatley, Inc., San Antonio, 1972—; mem. criminal justice com. Alamo Area Council of Govts., San Antonio, 1966-71; advisor local bds. SSS, San Antonio, 1972-75. Bd. dirs. San Antonio Livestock Expn. and Rodeo, 1971—, v.p., dir. San Antonio Charity Horse Show, 1975-78. Served to lt. col. USAFNG, 1963—. Named Outstanding Young Man of San Antonio, San Antonio C. of C., 1973. Mem. ABA, Fed. Bar Assn. (pres. San Antonio chpt. 1971-72), Tex. Bar Assn., San Antonio Bar Assn, InterAm. Bar Assn., Nat. Dist. Atty's Assn., Judge Advocate's Assn., Am. Judicare Assn., Am. Trial Lawyers Assn., Tex. Trial Lawyers Assn., San Antonio Trial Lawyers Assn., Tex. Assn. Civil Trial Lawyers, San Antonio Bar Found., Am. Econ. Assn., So. Econ. Assn., Nat. Assn. Bus. Economists, Soc. Govt. Economists. Democrat. Baptist. Club: Town (San Antonio). Lodge: Shriners, Masons (Grand Master 1982-83). Avocation: equistrian sports. Federal civil litigation, State civil litigation, Antitrust. Office: Oppenheimer Rosenberg et al 711 Navarro Suite 600 San Antonio TX 78205

HARRISON, RICHARD WAYNE, lawyer; b. Marfa, Tex., June 23, 1944; s. George Willis and Mildred Irene (Rooks) H. AA with honors, Schreiner Inst., Kerrville, Tex., 1964; BBA, U. Tex.-Austin, 1966, JD, 1968. Bar: Tex. 1968, U.S. Dist. Ct. (ea. dist.) Tex. 1968, U.S. Dist. Ct. (so. dist.) Tex. 1973, U.S. Dist. Ct. (we. dist.) Tex. 1974, U.S. Supreme Ct. 1975, U.S. Ct. Appeals (5th cir.) 1977, U.S. Dist. Ct. (no. dist.) Tex. 1983. Ptnr. Florence & Harrison, Hughes Springs, Tex., 1968-69; sole practice Hughes Springs, Tex., 1969-73; asst. atty. gen. Atty. Gen.'s Office of Tex., Austin, 1973-74, chief tax div., 1974-76, spl. asst. atty. gen., 1976-78; ptnr. McGinnis, Lochridge & Kilgore, Austin, Tex., 1978—. Precinct chmn. Cass County Dem. Com., 1969-73; pres. Hughes Springs Indsl. Found., 1970; Cass County chmn. Salvation Army, 1970-72; area coordinator Lloyd Bentsen for Senate Com., 1970; chmn. Hughes Springs United Fund Drive, 1972; mem. Austin Convocation Cursillo Steering Com., 1983-86, chmn., 1985-86; sr. warden St. Luke's-on-the-Lake Episcopal Ch., 1984. Mem. State Bar of Tex. (mem. fed. jud. com. 1980-83, bar jour. com. 1980-83), Travis County Bar Assn., Cass County Bar Assn. (past pres.), Schreiner Coll. Former Student Assn. (bd. dirs. 1985—). Democrat. Clubs: Austin, Horseshoe Bay Country.Lodge: Masons. Federal civil litigation, State civil litigation, State and local taxation. Home: 6202 Shadow Mountain Dr Austin TX 78731 Office: McGinnis Lochridge & Kilgore 1300 Capitol Ctr 919 Congress Ave Austin TX 78701

HARRISON, ROBERT WAYNE, lawyer; b. Phoenix, Ariz., Dec. 26, 1950; s. Robert Joseph and Nora Ann (Mullane) H.; m. Deborah Ann Sheldon, Nov. 14, 1981; children: Tyler, Colin, Jennifer. BS, U.S. Naval Acad., 1972; postgrad., Bklyn. Law Sch., 1978-79; JD, U. San Diego, 1981. Bar: Calif. 1982, U.S. Dist. Ct. (so. dist.) Calif. 1982. Commd. ensign USN, 1972, advanced through grades to lt., 1976, resigned, 1978; assoc. Hollywood & Neil, San Diego, Calif., 1982—. Served to comdr. USNR, 1978—. Mem. ABA, San Diego County Bar Assn., Assn. S. Calif. Def. Counsel, San Diego County Barristers Club (pres. 1986—), San Diego Def. Lawyers, Friendly Sons of St. Patrick (v.p. 1987—), U. San Diego Alumni Assn. (bd. dirs.). Republican. Roman Catholic. Clubs: Old Mission Beach, Cuyumaca (San Diego). Avocations: sailing, running, tennis. Personal injury, Insurance, State civil litigation. Home: 3565 Jewell St San Diego CA 92109 Office: Hollywood & Neil 1010 2d Ave Suite 1712 San Diego CA 92101-4959

HARRISON, RODDY L., lawyer; b. Sacramento, Feb. 3, 1939; s. Tom C. and Viola H. (Dedrick) H; children—Amy, Perry. B.S., Tex. A&M U., 1961; J.D., Baylor U. Bar: Tex. 1963, U.S. Dist. Ct. (we. dist.) Tex. 1964, U.S. Ct. Appeals (10th cir.), U.S. Ct. Appeals (5th cir.) 1970, U.S. Ct. Appeals (11th cir.) 1981. Dist. atty. 143d Jud. Dist., 1969-72; chief prosecutor Dist. 6-A for greivance com. State Bar Tex., 1972-76; practice law, Pecos, Tex. First v.p. Tex. Bighorn Soc. Found. N.Am. Wild Sheep. Mem. Tex. Trial Lawyers Assn. (exec. counsel criminal sect. 1976-77), State Bar Tex., Trans-Pecos Bar Assn., Reeves County Bar Assn., Assn. Trial Lawyers Am. State civil litigation, Federal civil litigation, Criminal.

HARRISON, SAMUEL HUGHEL, lawyer; b. Atlanta, Jan. 12, 1956; s. Gresham Hughel and Leslie (Powell) H.; m. Margaret Mary Carew, June 24, 1978; 1 child, Peter James. Student, Mercer U., 1974-75; BA magna cum laude, Washington & Lee U., 1978; JD cum laude, U. Ga., 1981. Bar: Ga. 1981, U.S. Dist. Ct. (no. dist.) Ga. 1981, U.S. Ct. Appeals (11th cir.) 1981, U.S. Dist. Ct. (mid. dist.) Ga. 1985. Ptnr. Harrison & Harrison, Lawrenceville, Ga., 1981-86, 87—; solicitor state ct. Guinnett County,

Lawrenceville, 1986. Mem. vestry St. Edward the Confessor Episcopal Ch., Lawrenceville, 1983—; del. council Episcopal Diocese Atlanta, Athens, Ga., 1986—. Mem. Ga. Bar Assn. (family law and criminal law sects.), Ga. Assn. Criminal Def. Lawyers, Pros. Attys. Council Ga., Nat. Assn. Criminal Def. Lawyers, Gwinnett County C. of C. Democrat. Avocations: photography, hiking, books. Criminal, Legal history, Family and matrimonial. Office: Harrison & Harrison 151 Pike St PO Box 88 Lawrenceville GA 30246-0088

HARRISON, TERESA HARSHMAN, lawyer; b. Louisville, Apr. 11, 1953; d. John Burnett Harshman and Billye Ruth (Braly) August; m. Lee David Harrison, Sept. 2, 1978; 1 child, Samantha M. BFA, New Coll., 1975; JD, Stetson U., 1979. Bar: Fla. 1979. Ptnr. de Manio, Harrison & Assocs. P.A., Sarasota, Fla., 1980-85; sole practice Sarasota, 1985—. Coeditor: The Docket. Mem. ABA, Fla. Bar Assn., Sarasota County Bar Assn. (young lawyers sect.), Fla. Assn. Women Lawyers (treas. Sarasota County chpt. 1985—). Democrat. Jewish. Contracts commercial, State civil litigation. Home: 3353 Higel Sarasota FL 34242

HARRISON, WILLIAM K., lawyer; b. Cin., Apr. 3, 1933; s. William K. and Genevieve (Poor) H.; m. Nancy Darling, May 28, 1960; children: Susan, Janet, Lissa. BA, Vanderbilt U., 1954; JD, U. Va., 1959. Bar: Ohio 1959, U.S. Dist. Ct. (so. dist.) Ohio 1960, U.S. Dist. Ct. Ga. 1965. Assoc. Frost and Jacobs, Cin., 1959-64; atty. Gulf Oil Corp., Atlanta, 1964-65; sr. counsel, asst. sec. Merrell Dow Pharms. Inc., Cin., 1965—. Trustee Mental Health Service N. Cen., Cin., 1982—; pres. Reading C. of C., 1975-78. Served to 1st lt. U.S. Army, 1954-56. Mem. ABA (anti trust sect. 1965—), Ohio State Bar Assn. (product liability sect. 1980—), Cin. Bar Assn. (corp. counsel com. 1965—). Roman Catholic. Club: O'Bannon Creek Golf (Loveland, Ohio). Avocation: golf. Personal injury, Antitrust, Administrative and regulatory. Home: 8230 Hopewell Rd Cincinnati OH 45242 Office: Merrell Dow Pharm Inc 10123 Alliance Rd Cincinnati OH 45242

HARROCH, RICHARD DAVID, lawyer; b. Casablanca, Morocco, June 15, 1953; s. Roger and Laury (Gabay) H.; m. Mona E. Lessing, Oct. 26, 1985. BA, U. Calif., Berkeley, 1974; JD, UCLA, 1977. Bar: Calif. 1977. Atty. Chickering & Gregory, San Francisco, 1977-80, Morrison & Foerster, San Francisco, 1980-83; ptnr. Orrick, Herrington & Sutcliffe, San Francisco, 1983—; v.p. No. Calif. Real Estate Securities and Syndication Inst., San Francisco, 1984—. Co-author: Private Real Estate Syndications, 1983; co-author, planner, editor: Start-Up Companies, 1985; contbr. articles to profl. jours. Mem. ABA, Calif. Bar Assn. (chmn. com. on partnerships 1984-85), San Francisco Bar Assn.(co-chmn. corps. com. 1984—). Avocations: basketball, writing. General corporate, Securities, Real property. Home: 2327 Bay St San Francisco CA 94123 Office: Orrick Herrington & Sutcliffe 600 Montgomery St San Francisco CA 94123

HARROLD, BERNARD, lawyer; b. Wells County, Ind., Feb. 5, 1925; s. James Delmer and Marie (Mounsey) H.; m. Kathleen Walker, Nov. 26, 1952; children—Bernard James, Camilla Ruth, Renata Jane. Student, Biarritz Am. U., 1945; A.B., Ind. U., 1949, LL.B., 1951. Bar: Ill. 1951. Since practiced in Chgo.; assoc., then mem. firm Kirkland, Ellis, Hodson, Chaffetz & Masters, 1951-67; sr. partner Wildman, Harrold, Allen & Dixon, 1967—. Note editor: Ind. Law Jour, 1950-51; contbr. articles to profl. jours. Mem. Winnetka Caucus Com., 1967-68. Served with AUS, 1944-46, ETO. Fellow Am. Coll. Trial Lawyers; mem. ABA, Ill. Bar Assn. (chmn. evidence program 1970), Chgo. Bar Assn., Law Club, Soc. Trial Lawyers, Internat. Bus. Council Mid-Am., German Am. C. of C., Order of Coif, Phi Beta Kappa, Phi Eta Sigma. Clubs: Chicago Curling, University; Executives (Chgo.). State civil litigation, Federal civil litigation, General practice. Home: 809 Locust St Winnetka IL 60093 Office: One IBM Plaza Chicago IL 60611

HARROLD, DENNIS EDWARD, lawyer; b. Los Angeles, Nov. 7, 1947; s. Edward Adron and Helen Lucille (Morrison) H.; m. Mary Ann Padgett, Oct. 21, 1972; children—Teresa Lauren, Derek Christopher. B.S., Ind. U., 1969; J.D., 1972. Bar: Ind. 1972, U.S. Dist. Ct. (so. dist.) Ind. 1972, U.S. Ct. Mil. Appeals 1972, U.S. Ct. Appeals (7th cir.) 1982, U.S. Supreme Ct. 1986. Pub. defender Shelby Superior Ct., Shelbyville, Ind., 1976-77; assoc. Adams & Cramer, Shelbyville, 1976-78; sec. Soshnick, Bate and Harrold, P.C., 1979-85; sec. Bate, Harrold & Meltzer, P.C., Shelbyville, 1985—; sch. bd. atty. Shelbyville Central Schs., Ind., 1978—; atty. Shelby County dept. pub. welfare, 1987—. Mem. adv. bd. Salvation Army, Shelbyville, 1982—. Served to capt. U.S. Army, 1972-76, Korea. Named Hon. Mem. Bar Republic of Korea, Ministry of Justice, Seoul, 1975. Fellow Ind. Bar Found.; mem. ABA, Ind. State Bar Assn. (ho. of dels. 1982-85), Shelby County Bar Assn., Indpls. Bar Assn., Assn. Trial Lawyers Am., Nat. Sch. Bds. Assn. Council Sch. Attys., Internat. Legal Soc. Korea, Ind. Trial Lawyers Assn., Ind. Pub. Defender Council. Republican. Roman Catholic. Lodges: Lions, Elks. Personal injury, State civil litigation, Family and matrimonial. Home: Rural Rt 2 Box 405 Shelbyville IN 46176 Office: Bate Harrold & Meltzer PC 505 S Harrison PO Box 477 Shelbyville IN 46176

HARROP, R(OBERT) DANIEL, lawyer; b. Providence, Dec. 27, 1950; s. Robert James and V. Madeline (Durand) H.; m. Denise Gagnon, June 3, 1972 (div. Aug. 1984); children: Sean Daniel, Eileen Bridgett; m. Marcia Feole, Oct. 20, 1985. BS, Providence Coll., 1972; JD, St. John's U., 1975. Bar: R.I. 1975, U.S. Dist. Ct. R.I. 1975. Ptnr. Harrop & Harrop, West Warwick, R.I., 1975-79, Harrop & Pollock, West Warwick, 1980—; solicitor Town of West Warwick, 1981—. Mem. R.I. Bar Assn. Democrat. Roman Catholic. Lodge: Lions (v.p. West Warwick chpt. 1984). Avocations: photography, scuba diving, restoring classic autos. Local government, Real property, Probate. Home: 17 Sunset Ave West Warwick RI 02893 Office: PO Box 455 45 Providence St West Warwick RI 02893

HARROW, BARRY RICHARD, lawyer, mathematician; b. N.Y.C., Mar. 20, 1949; s. Hyman and Hannah (Bersson) H.; m. Nettie Peña, Oct. 25, 1975 (div. Aug. 1985). BS, SUNY, Stony Brook, 1970, MA, 1971, MS, 1974; JD, U. West Los Angeles, 1980. Bar: Calif. 1980, U.S. Dist. Ct. (no. dist.) Calif. 1980, U.S. Dist. Ct. (cen. dist.) Calif. 1982. Prof. math. Suffolk County Community Coll., Selden, N.Y., 1975, Los Angeles Community Coll., 1976-78, Calif. State U., Northridge, 1976-78; statistician Jet Propulsion Lab., Pasadena, Calif., 1977-80; atty. David M. Hollingsworth, Monterey, Calif., 1980-83; sole practice Carmel, Calif., 1983—. Mem. ABA, Calif. Bar Assn. Republican. Avocation: piano. General practice, Real property, Probate. Home: Box 222234 Carmel CA 93922 Office: 26615 Carmel Ctr Pl Carmel CA 93923

HARSHMAN, MICHAEL STUART, lawyer; b. Youngstown, Ohio, June 14, 1940; s. Max and Shirley (Grossman) H.; m. Roslyn C. Teitelbaum, Dec. 23, 1964 (div. July 1975); children: Cheri, Vicki, Tracy, Kimberly; m. Joy Cushwa, Aug. 24, 1985. BA, Ohio State U., 1963; JD, U. Tex., 1966. Bar: Ohio 1966, Tex. 1966, U.S. Dist. Ct. (no. dist.) Ohio 1967, U.S. Supreme Ct. 1976, U.S. Tax Ct. 1982, Pa. 1986. Ptnr. McLaughlin, DiBlasio & Harshman, Youngstown, 1970-83, Harshman, Waldman & Gervelis, Youngstown, 1983—. Chmn. legal com. ACLU, Youngstown, 1970—. Fellow Roscoe Pound Am. Trial Lawyers Found. (lifetime); mem. ABA, Ohio Bar Assn., Tex. Bar Assn., Ohio Acad. Trial Lawyers (sustaining), Ohio State U. Bar Assn., Assn. Trial Lawyers Am. (sustaining). Democrat. Jewish. Federal civil litigation, State civil litigation, Personal injury. Office: Harshman Waldman & Gervelis 105 E Boardman St Youngstown OH 44503

HART, BROOK, lawyer; b. N.Y.C., Aug. 24, 1941; s. Walter and Julie H.; m. Barbara Ingersoll, Nov., 1980; children—Morgan M., Lauren L., Ashley I. Grad. Johns Hopkins U., 1963; LL.B., Columbia U., 1966. Bar: N.Y. 1966, U.S. Ct. Appeals (9th cir.) 1967, Hawaii 1968, U.S. Supreme Ct. 1972, Calif. 1973. Law clk. to chief judge U.S. Dist. Ct. Hawaii, 1966-67; assoc. counsel Legal Aid Soc. Hawaii, 1968; assoc. Greenstein and Cowan, Honolulu, 1968-70; chief pub. defender State of Hawaii, 1970-72; co-founder, ptnr. Hart, Leavitt and Hunt, Honolulu, 1972-80; co-founder, ptnr. Hart and Wolff, Honolulu, 1980—; instr. course U. Hawaii, 1972-73, lectr. Sch. Law, 1974—; apptd. Nat. Commn. on Study Def. Services, 1974, Planning Group for U.S. Dist. Ct. Hawaii, 1975; spl. counsel City Council of City and County of Honolulu, 1976-77, spl. investigative counsel to trustee in bankruptcy THC Fin. Corp., 1977; mem. Jud. Council State of Hawaii com. on revision state penal codes, 1984—; lectr. schs., profl., civic groups; mem. com. to select Fed. Pub. Defender Dist. of Hawaii, 1981. Recipient Reginald Heber Smith award Nat. Legal Aid and Defender Assn., 1971; named Bencher, Am. Inn of Ct., Hawaii, 1982—. Fellow Am. Bd. Criminal Lawyers; mem. ABA, Hawaii Bar Assn., State Bar Calif., Am. Judicature Soc., Nat. Legal Aid and Defender Assn., Nat. Assn. Criminal Def. Lawyers, Calif. Attys. for Criminal Justice. Contbr. chpts. to books, articles to profl. publs. Federal criminal litigation, State criminal litigation. Office: Hart and Wolff 333 Queen St Suite 610 Honolulu HI 96813

HART, CLIFFORD HARVEY, lawyer; b. Flint, Mich. Nov. 12, 1935; s. Max S. and Dorothy H. (Fineberg) H.; m. Alice Rosenberg, June 17, 1962; children—Michael F., David E., Steven A. A.B., U. Mich., 1957, J.D., 1960. Cert. civil trial advocate, Nat. Bd. Trial Advocacy. Bar: Mich. 1960, U.S. Dist. Ct. (ea. and we. dists.) Mich. 1962. Assoc. Stevens & Nelson, Flint, Mich., 1960-62; ptnr. White, Newblatt, Nelson & Hart, Flint, 1962-64; shareholder Dean, Dean, Segar, Hart & Shulman, P.C., and predecessor firms Leitson, Dean, Dean, Segar & Hart, Leitson, Dean, Dean, Abram & Segar, Flint, 1965—; adjunct assoc. prof. U. Mich. Sch. Mgmt.; lectr. Inst. Continuing Legal Edn., Mich.; lectr. Mich. Jud. Inst. Pres. Vis. Nurse Assn., Flint, 1967; pres. Temple Beth El, 1973-75; trustee United Way Genesee County, 1981—; mem. Roscoe Pound Found. Mem. ABA, Mich. State Bar Assn. (chmn. Negligence Law sect. 1981-82, rep. assembly 1975-81), Mich. Trial Lawyers Assn. (pres. 1977-78, lectr.), Genesee County Bar Assn. (pres. 1975-76), Assn. Trial Lawyers Am. (bd. govs. 1979—, lectr., home office and budget com. 1980-84, exec. com. 1984-85, chmn. elections com. 1984-87), Am. Judicature Soc., Nat. Bd. Trial Advocacy (cert. 1980, 85). Democrat. Lodge: B'Nai B'rith (past pres.). Personal injury, Insurance. Office: 1616 Genesee Towers Suite 1616 Flint MI 48502

HART, DAVID CHURCHILL, lawyer; b. Galesburg, Ill., Mar. 5, 1940; s. Herbert Edward and Florence (Butterweck) H.; m. Beth Rubinstein, Aug. 11, 1963; children: Melissa, Katherine. BA, Northwestern U., 1962; LLB, Harvard U., 1965. Bar: Ill. 1965, U.S. Dist. Ct. (no. dist.) Ill. 1965. Assoc. Ross & Hardies, Chgo., 1965-69; atty. R.R. Donnelley & Sons Co., Chgo., 1969-85; gen. counsel R.R. Donnelly & Sons Co., Chgo., 1985-86, v.p., gen. counsel, 1986—. Served to 1st lt. USAR, 1966-71. Mem. ABA (com. on corp. law depts.), Chgo. Bar Assn. Club: Univ. (Chgo.). General corporate. Office: R R Donnelley & Sons Co 2223 Martin Luther King Dr Chicago IL 60616

HART, DEBORAH DIANE, lawyer; b. Tampa, Fla., Feb. 1, 1955; d. Donald Stanley and Lois Frances (Snyder) H. AA, Fla. State U., 1974; BA in Acctg., U. South Fla., 1976; JD with honors, U. Fla., 1980. Bar: Fla. 1980, U.S. Dist. Ct (mid. dist.) Fla. 1981, U.S. Ct. Appeals (11th cir.). Assoc. Moffitt, Hart & Miller, Tampa, 1980-83; counsel house jud. com. State of Fla., Tallahassee, 1983-84; asst. atty. gen. Fla. Dept. Legal Affairs, Tallahassee, 1984—. Mem. Fla. Govt. Bar Assn. Presbyterian. Avocations: reading, needlework, music. Administrative and regulatory, Health, Legislative. Office: Dept Legal Affairs Capitol Bldg Room 1601 Tallahassee FL 32301

HART, DOUGLAS EDWARD, lawyer; b. Richmond, Ind., Sept. 10, 1958; s. James Edward and Janet Marie (Keiser) H. BA, Ind. U., 1979; JD, U. Mich., 1982. Bar: Ohio 1982, U.S. Dist. Ct. (so. dist.) Ohio 1982, U.S. Ct. Appeals (6th cir.) 1983, U.S. Ct. Appeals (5th cir.) 1987. Assoc. Frost & Jacobs, Cin., 1982—. Mem. ABA, Ohio Bar Assn., Cin. Bar Assn., Order of Coif. Republican. Federal civil litigation, State civil litigation. Office: Frost & Jacobs 2500 Central Trust Ctr Cincinnati OH 45202

HART, JOHN CLIFTON, lawyer; b. Chgo., Apr. 29, 1945; s. Clifton Edwin and Eleanor (Zielinski) H.; m. Dianne Lynn Wenzel, Jan. 18, 1969; children—David Clifton, Steven Philip, Kristin Dianne. B.S., Loyola U., Chgo., 1967; postgrad. Northwestern U. Sch. Law, 1967-69; J.D., U. N.D., 1972. Bar: Minn. 1973, U.S. Dist. Ct. Minn. 1973, Tex. 1979, U.S. Dist. Ct. (no. dist.) Tex. 1979, U.S. Ct. Appeals (8th cir.) 1980, U.S. Ct. Appeals (5th cir.) 1980, U.S. Dist. Ct. (we. and so. dists.) Tex. 1981, U.S. Dist. Ct. (ea. dist.) Okla. 1983, U.S. Dist. Ct. (ea. dist.) Tex. 1984. Ptnr. Robins, Zelle, Larson & Kaplan, Mpls., 1973-81; v.p. Gollaher & Hart, Dallas, 1981-84; pres. Hart & Engen, Dallas, 1984—. Mem. N.D. Law Rev., 1971-72. Contbr. articles to profl. publs. Served to capt. USAF, 1969-73. Mem. Minn. State Bar Assn., State Bar Tex., ABA. Tex. Assn. Def. Counsel, Dallas Bar Assn., Dallas Assn. Def. Counsel. Republican. Lutheran. Insurance, Federal civil litigation, State civil litigation. Office: Hart & Engen 9330 LBJ Freeway Suite 525 Dallas TX 75243

HART, KARL VANCE, lawyer, horse farm owner; b. Mayo, Fla., June 25, 1937; s. Lester C. and Ouida P. (Perry) H.; m. Roxann Ravlin, Aug. 17, 1968; 1 child, John Ravlin. BS in Polit. Sci., Fla. State U., 1960; postgrad., U. N.C., 1960-61; JD, Harvard U., 1964. Bar: Fla. 1964, U.S. Dist. Ct. (mid. dist.) Fla. 1964, U.S. Dist. Ct. (so. dist.) Fla. 1965, U.S. Ct. Appeals (5th cir.) 1965, U.S. Dist. Ct. (no. dist.) Fla. 1973, U.S. Supreme Ct. 1976, U.S. Ct. Appeals (11th cir.) 1981. Law clk. to presiding justice U.S. Dist. Ct. (mid. dist.) Fla., 1964-65; assoc. Shutts & Bowen, Miami, Fla., 1965-68; ptnr. Shutts & Bowen, Orlando, Miami, West Palm Beach and Ocala, Fla., 1969—; atty. Dade County Delegation to Fla. Legislature, 1967. Mem. Harvard Law Sch. Assn., Cambridge; sponsor GOPvictory fund Nat. Rep. Congr. Com., Washington. Served to sgt. USAF, 1955-58. Mem. ABA, Fed. Bar Assn., Fla. Bar Assn. (agricultural law com. 1983-84, clients security fund com. 1983-84), Assn. Trial Lawyers Am., Acad. Fla. Trial Lawyers, Am. Judicature Soc., Internat. Arabian Horse Assn. (bd. dirs. 1976-80), Am. Horse Shows Assn. (bd. dirs. 1983—). Republican. Clubs: Univ., Bankers (Miami) (founding mem. 1979). Arabian horse farm owner. Antitrust, Federal civil litigation, Construction. Home: PO Box 110 Orange Lake FL 32681 Office: Shutts & Bowen 20 N Orange St Suite 1000 Orlando FL 32801

HART, LARRY CALVIN, lawyer; b. Lawton, Okla., Dec. 24, 1942; s. Clifford C. and Evelyn M. (Dupler) H.; m. Leslie K. Bolek, April 1986. A.B.A., Otero Coll., 1963; B.S., Colo. State U., 1967; J.D., Loyola U., Los Angeles, 1974. Bar: Calif. 1974, U.S. Dist. Ct. (cent. dist.) Calif. 1974, U.S. Ct. Appeals (9th cir.) 1979, U.S. Dist. Ct. (ea. and no. dists.) Calif. 1980. Assoc., Ned Good, Los Angeles, 1974-76, Hagenbaugh & Murphy, Los Angeles, 1976-77; ptnr. Hart & Michaelis, Los Angeles, 1977-84; Brill, Hunt & Hart, Los Angeles, 1984-86; Musick, Peeler & Garrett, Los Angeles, 1987—; instr. Inst. Safety and Systems Mgmt., Univ. So. Calif., Los Angeles, 1982—; hearing officer Los Angeles Superior Ct., 1982—. Mem. Assn. So. Calif. Def. Counsel (bd. dirs. 1980-83), Aviation Ins. Assn. Calif. (v.p. 1983-84, pres. 1986-87), Def. Research Inst., Calif. Bar Assn., Lawyer Pilots Bar Assn. Federal civil litigation, State civil litigation, Insurance. Office: Musick Peeler & Garrett One Wilshire Blvd Los Angeles CA 90017

HART, LYNN PATRICIA, lawyer; b. Schenectady, N.Y., Sept. 12, 1954; d. H. Philip Hart and M. Patricia (Dinsmore) Hart-Franco; m. Frederick T. Muto, Sept. 8, 1979; children: Daniel Frederick, Christopher Hart. BA cum laude, Westmont Coll., 1976; JD, U. Calif., Berkeley, 1979. Bar: U.S. Dist. Ct. (so. dist.) Calif. Law clk. to presiding justice U.S. Dist. Ct., San Diego, 1979-80; assoc. Heller, Ehrman, White & McAuliffe, San Francisco, 1980-83, Howard, Rice, et al, San Francisco, 1983—. Author: Property not Subject to Probate Administration, 1986, Decedent Estate Practice CEB, 1986. Mem. estate planning councils of San Francisco and East Bay; bd. dirs. Dwight House, Berkeley, 1982. Mem. ABA (real property, probate and trust law sect., com. spl. problems of bus. owners sect.), San Francisco Bar Assn. (probate and trust law sect., outstanding pro bono atty. 1982, 83), Calif. Women Lawyers, Women Tax Lawyers, Queen's Bench. Democrat. Presbyterian. Avocations: tennis, skiing. Probate, Estate planning, Estate taxation. Office: Howard Rice et al 3 Embarcadero Ctr San Francisco CA 94611

HART, MICHAEL DAVID, lawyer; b. St. Louis, June 8, 1951; s. Michael Joseph and Jane Teresa (Feld) H.; m. Elizabeth A. Bearly, Aug. 19, 1978; children: Michael Jay, Paul William. BA in Econs., U. Mo., St. Louis, 1973; JD, U. Mo., Kansas City, 1978. Bar: Mo. 1979, U.S. Dist. Ct. (ea. dist.) Mo. 1980, U.S. Ct. Appeals (8th cir.) 1980. Assoc. E.J. McElligott, Independence, Mo., 1979-80; assoc. Peper, Martin, Jensen, Maichel & Hetlage, St. Louis, 1980-85, ptnr., 1986—; substitute lectr. Laclede Sch. Law, St. Louis, 1981-86. Rep. ward pres., St. Louis, 1971-73; del. Mo. Rep. Conv., 1972; active various local campaigns; pres. Hadley Twp. Rep. Club, 1987—. Served with USN, 1973-76, with Res. 1977—. Mem. ABA, Mo. Bar Assn., St. Louis Bar Assn. (chmn. courts com. young lawyers sect. 1982-83, chmn. consumer law com. 1983-84, legis. com. 1985—), VFW, Am. Legion (vice comdr. St. Louis chpt. 1984—). Roman Catholic. State civil litigation, Federal civil litigation, Legislative. Home: 7015 Maryland Saint Louis MO 63130 Office: Peper Martin Jensen Maichel & 720 Olive St 24th Floor Saint Louis MO 63101

HART, RICHARD BANNER, life insurance company executive, lawyer; b. Winston-Salem, N.C., Apr. 9, 1932; s. Samuel Bruce and Cordia M. (Lamb) H.; m. Jean Elizabeth Shinn, Apr. 28, 1956; 1 dau., Fabra. A.B. in Polit. Sci, U. N.C., Chapel Hill, 1957, J.D., 1959. Bar: N.C. 1959, Tenn. 1970; C.L.U., 1970. Assoc. counsel Jefferson Standard Life Ins. Co., Greensboro, N.C., 1959-70; with NLT Corp. and Nat. Life and Accident Ins. Co., Nashville, 1970-85; asst. v.p., counsel NLT Corp. and Nat. Life and Accident Ins. Co., 1973-75, sec., counsel, 1975-84; v.p., sec., assoc. gen. counsel Am. Gen. Ins. Cos., Nashville, 1982—; v.p., sec., gen. counsel Intereal Co., 1984-85, also dir.; sec., counsel, dir. Nat. Property Owners Ins. Co.; sec. NLT Mktg. Services Co., Guardsman Life Ins. Co.; lectr. in field. Bd. editors U. N.C. Law Rev., 1958-59. Mem. budget com. Guilford County United Fund, N.C., 1968-69; mem. Guilford County Mental Health Assn., 1968-69; bd. dirs. Phi Kappa Sigma Found. Served with AUS, 1953-55. Mem. N.C. Bar Assn., Tenn. Bar Assn., Nashville Bar Assn., Assn. Life Ins. Counsel, Am. Corp. Counsel Assn., Nashville Area C. of C., Am. Soc. Corp. Secs. (exec. com., pres. S.E. region 1979—), Nashville Com. Fgn. Relations, Eng. Speaking Union, U.S. Phi Delta Phi, Phi Kappa Sigma (nat. officer, exec. bd. 1971-77). Methodist. Clubs: Exchange (Nashville) (bd. dirs.); YMCA Fitness Ctr. Home: 2815 Kenway Rd Nashville TN 37215 Office: Am Gen Center-Nashville Nashville TN 37250

HART, ROBERT M., lawyer; b. N.Y.C., Nov. 7, 1944; s. Charles John and Helen Ann (Hammond) H.; m. Dale Elizabeth McConaughy, Nov. 2, 1970; 3 children. BA, Marist Coll., 1966; JD, Duke U., 1969. Bar: N.Y. 1969, U.S. Ct. Appeals (2d cir.) 1970, U.S. Dist. Ct. (so. dist.) N.Y. 1979. Assoc. Donovan, Leisure, Newton & Irvine, N.Y.C., 1969-71, 74-77, London, 1972-73; ptnr. Donovan, Leisure, Newton & Irvine, N.Y.C., 1977-84, Dorsey & Whitney, N.Y.C., 1984—; lectr. law Duke U., Durham, N.C., 1986—. Contbr. articles to profl. jours. Sr. Fellow Duke U., 1983—. Mem. ABA (securities regulation com. 1981—), N.Y. State Bar Assn., Assn. of Bar of City of N.Y. (securities regulation com. 1979-82). General corporate, Securities. Address: Dorsey & Whitney 350 Park Ave NY NY 10022

HART, RONALD ALTON, judge; b. Lewiston, Maine, July 11, 1932; m. Jeanette T. Bennett, Mar. 1, 1952. Cert., Auburn Maine Sch. of Commerce, 1955; JD, U. Maine, 1958. Bar: Maine 1958, U.S. Dist. Ct. Maine 1959. Assoc. judge Bath (Maine) Mcpl. Ct., 1959-62; dist. atty. Sagadahoc County, Bath, Maine, 1964-68; probate judge Sahadahoc County, Bath, Maine, 1968—; chmn. adv. bd. Key Bank of Maine, Bath br., 1974—. Past mem. Maine Small Bus. Adv. Council; mem. Maine State Jud. Council, 1972-78, Maine Probate Law Revision Commn., chmn. Maine Rules of Probate Procedure, 1973-78; bd. dirs. Morse High Boosters, Bath, 1968-78, YMCA, Bath, 1969-79; chmn. March of Dimes, Bath, 1964-69. Served with USAF, 1951-53. Mem. Sagadahoc County Bar Assn. (pres. 1980-82), Maine Bar Assn. (bd. dirs. 1972-80), Assn. Trial Lawyers Am., Maine Trial Lawyers Assn. (bd. dirs. 1974-82), Maine Probate Judges Assembly (chief judge 1978). Home: 20 Foreside Common Dr Falmouth ME 04105 Office: County Courthouse 37 Court Bath ME 04530

HART, STEPHEN STRONG, lawyer; b. Salt Lake City, June 25, 1952; s. William Glenn Napier and Ethel Cleone (Stonrg) H.; m. Kathleen Ann Pickens, June 15, 1971; children: Ryan Jay Strong, Brandon Lee, Justin William, Trenton Joseph. BS in Polit. Sci. magna cum laude, U. Utah, 1973, JD, 1976. Bar: Idaho 1976. Dep. pros. atty. Bonneville County, Idaho Falls, Idaho, 1976-78; sole practice Idaho Falls, 1979-81; ptnr. Law Offices of Hart & Hart, Idaho Falls, 1981—; pub. defender Bonneville County, 1980—. Editor Jour. of Contemporary Law, 1973-74. Candidate, pros. atty. Idaho Falls Reps., 1978; committeeman precinct, Bonneville County, 1980; coach youth soccer and basketball, Idaho Falls, 1980-85; coach, officer East Bonneville Little League, 1981—; scoutmaster Boy Scouts Am., Idaho Falls, 1982. Mem. ABA, Idaho Bar Assn., Assn. Trial Lawyers Am., Idaho Trial Lawyers Assn., 7th Dist. Bar Assn., Soc. Bar and Gavel, Phi Beta Kappa, Phi Kappa Phi, Pi Sigma Alpha. Mormon. Mormon. Avocations: hunting, fishing, collecting stamps, reading. Family and matrimonial, Criminal, Consumer commercial. Home: 4080 Dixie Idaho Falls ID 83401 Office: Law Offices of Hart & Hart 482 C St Suite 313 Idaho Falls ID 83402-3537

HART, WILLIAM THOMAS, judge; b. Joliet, Ill., Feb. 4, 1929; s. William Michael and Geraldine (Archambeault) H.; m. Catherine Motta, Nov. 27, 1954; children: Catherine Hart Fornero, Susan Hart DeMario, Julie Hart Boesen, Sally, Nancy. J.D., Loyola U.-Chgo., 1951. Bar: Ill. 1951, U.S. Dist. Ct. 1957, U.S. Ct. Appeals 7th cir. 1954, U.S. Ct. Appeals D.C. 1977. Asst. U.S. atty. No. Dist. Ill., Chgo., 1954-56; spl. asst. atty. gen. State of Ill., 1957-58; spl. asst. state's Cook County, Ill., 1960; judge U.S. Dist. Ct., Chgo., 1982—; mem. firm Defrees & Fiske, 1956-59; ptnr. Schiff, Hardin & Waite, 1959-82. Pres. adv. bd. Mercy Med. Ctr., Aurora, Ill., 1980-81; v.p. Aurora Blood Bank, 1972-77; trustee Rosary High Sch., 1981-82; bd. dirs. Chgo. Legal Assistant Found., 1974-76. Served with U.S. Army, 1951-53. Decorated Bronze Star. Mem. 7th Cir. Bar Assn., Law Club, Legal Club, Soc. Trial Lawyers, Union League Club of Aurora, Calif. (hon.). Jurisprudence. Office: US Dist Ct 219 S Dearborn St Chicago IL 60604

HARTE, JOHN WILLIAMS, lawyer; b. Montgomery, Ala., Dec. 8, 1945; s. John Williams and Cecil (Lunsford) H.; m. Rachel Ellen Shaw, Apr. 22, 1972; 1 child, Charles Arthur. BS in Commerce, Bus. Adminstrn., U. Ala., 1967; JD, U. S.C., 1971. Instr. in history St. Angela Acad., Aiken, S.C., 1968-69; sole practice Aiken, 1971—; prof. bus. law Aiken Tech. Coll., 1973-75; city atty. New Ellenton, S.C., 1974-78, 1985—; pub. defender Aiken County, 1975-78; spl. cir. judge State of S.C., 1979-82; recorder ct. judge Jackson, S.C., 1974-78; family ct. judge State of S.C., 1978-82. Mem. State of S.C. Bd. of Jud. Standards, 1980-82, State of S.C. Bd. of Grievences, 1982-85. Mem. ABA, Am. Trial Lawyers Assn., S.C. Trial Lawyers Assn. Clubs: Whiskey Rd. Fox Hounds, Palmetto Golf (Aiken). Personal injury, Family and matrimonial, Criminal. Office: 231 Pendleton St Aiken SC 29802

HARTEL, STEPHEN CAMILLE, lawyer; b. New Orleans, Feb. 8, 1904; s. Theodore Frederick and Mary (Briede) H.; m. Rosary Vera Nix, July 2, 1942; children: Stephen C. Jr., Mary Brent, Rosary Hartel O'Neill, Joseph Francis. JD, Loyola U., New Orleans, 1926. Bar: La. 1927, U.S. Dist. Ct. La. 1930, U.S. Ct. Appeals 1932, U.S. Supreme Ct. 1935. Ptnr. Hartel & Kenny, New Orleans, 1926—. Past pres. New Orleans Legal Aid Bur. Served to lt. USN, 1942-45. Recipient Bishops Cross, Cath. Bishop Diocese Biloxi, 1985. Mem. Loyola U. Alumni Assn. (past. pres.), St. Thomas More Law Soc. (past pres.). Democrat. Roman Catholic. Clubs: New Orleans Country, Bienville, Round Table. Consumer commercial, General practice, Real property. Home: 54 Fontainebleau Dr New Orleans LA 70125 Office: Hartel & Kenny 150 Baronne St 412 Pere Marquette Bldg New Orleans LA 70112 also: 204 S Beach Blvd Waveland MS 39576

HARTEL, STEPHEN CAMILLE, JR., lawyer; b. New Orleans, Sept. 24, 1945; s. Stephen Camille and Rosary (Nix) H.; m. Conchita Garcia, Mar. 25, 1970; children: Genevieve, Rosary Nicole, Stephanie. BA, U. Notre Dame, 1967; JD, Tulane U., 1970. Assoc. Hartel & Kenny, New Orleans, 1970-71, ptnr., 1971-76; ptnr. Hartel, Kenny & Dimitry, New Orleans, 1976-84; pres. Hartel & Kenny, P.L.C., New Orleans, 1984—; pres. Legal Aid Bur., New Orleans, 1983-85; adv. dir. Delta Homestead, New Orleans, 1979-82, First City Bank, New Orleans, 1982-85. Pres. adv. bd. St. Elizabeth's Girls Home, New Orleans, 1977-79. Named Dist. Dir. of Yr. Ark.-La. Exchange Club, 1979-80. Mem. ABA, La. Bar Assn., New Orleans Bar Assn., Comml. Law League. Republican. Roman Catholic. Club: Exchange (New Orleans) (Exchangite of Yr. 1974-75). Home: 4101 Vendome Pl New Orleans LA 70125 Office: Hartel & Kenny PLC 150 Baronne St 412 Pere Marquette Bldg New Orleans LA 70112

HARTELIUS, CHANNING JULIUS, lawyer; b. Gt. Falls, Mont., Oct. 2, 1946; s. Chester Werner and Hildegarde Margaret (Kelm) H.; m. Judith Irene Bromlie, Aug. 2, 1977; children—Rhonda, Kerry, Chanin. B.A. with

honors, U. Mont., 1968, J.D. with honors, George Washington U., 1971. Bar: Va. 1971, Mont. 1971. Asst. atty. gen. Mont., 1971; ptnr. Wuerthner & Hartelius, Gt. Falls, 1972-73, Hartelius & Lewin, Gt. Falls, 1973-78, Hartelius & Assocs., P.C., Gt. Falls, 1978—; asst. city atty., Gt. Falls, 1972-76; instr. Coll. Gt. Falls, 1980. Participant Leadership Gt. Falls, 1983. Served to capt. Q.M.C., USAR, 1971-82. Recipient presdl. award of excellence U.S. Jaycees, 1976. Mem. ABA, Am. Trial Lawyers Assn., Mont. Bar Assn., Cascade County Bar Assn., Great Falls Jaycees (pres. 1976), Mont. Hist. Soc. Republican. Lutheran. Clubs: Toastmasters (pres. 1975), Meadow Lark Country. Contbr. articles to legal jours.; author: Understanding Bankruptcy, A Guide, 1981; Montana Handbook on Contract for Deeds, 1982; co-author: Law and the Municipal Ecology, 1971. Personal injury, Real property, General practice. Home: 315 4th Ave N Great Falls MT 59401 Office: 600 Central Plaza Suite 408 Great Falls MT 59401

HARTHUN, LUTHER ARTHUR, lawyer; b. Lansing, Ill., Apr. 25, 1935; s. Herbert and Martha (Loeber) H.; m. Ann Elizabeth Brose, Sept. 24, 1961; children—Matthew James, Nancy Lynn, Jill Marie, Laura Ann. B.A., Valparaiso U., 1957; J.D., U. Chgo., 1960; LL.M., U. Calif., Berkeley, 1961. Bar: Ill. 1961, Calif. 1961, Va. 1985. Assoc. Hopkins, Sutter Owen, Mulroy & Davis, Chgo., 1961-66; gen. counsel, sec. A-T-O Inc. (now Figgie Internat. Inc.), Cleve., 1966-70; v.p., gen. counsel, sec. A-T-O Inc. (now Figgie Internat. Inc.), Willoughby, Ohio, 1970; sr. v.p., internat. gen. counsel Figgie Internat., Inc., Richmond, Va., 1970—. Mem. ABA, Ill. Bar Assn., Calif. Bar Assn., Am. Soc. Corp. Secs., Ohio Bar Assn., Va. Bar Assn. Lutheran. Jurisprudence. Office: 1000 Virginia Center Pkwy Richmond VA 23295

HARTIGAN, JOHN M., lawyer; b. Chgo., May 6, 1932; m. Mary K. Carroll; 4 children. BS, U. Notre Dame, 1955; JD, Northwestern U., 1958. Bar: Ill. 1958. Ptnr. Carroll, Hartigan & McCauley, Ltd., Chgo., 1959—. General corporate, Banking. Home: 600 Greenwood Ave Kenilworth IL 60043 Office: Carroll Hartigan & McCauley 1 N LaSalle St 3100 Chicago IL 60602

HARTIGAN, MICHAEL DAVID, lawyer; b. Boston, Sept. 24, 1956; s. Joseph Anthony and Lillian Marie (McGowan) H.; m. Susan Michele Lawrence, June 8, 1986. BSBA, Stonehill Coll., 1978; JD, U. Notre Dame, 1981; LLM, Boston U., 1983. Bar: Mass. 1981, U.S. Dist. Ct. Mass. 1982, U.S. Tax Ct. 1986, U.S. Ct. Appeals (1st cir.) 1986. Assoc. Bradley, Barry and Tarlow, P.C., Boston, 1981-82; tax mgr. Peat Marwick Main and Co., Boston, 1983—. Contbr. articles to profl. jours. John Dorwin scholar U. Notre Dame, 1980. Fellow Mass. Soc. CPA's; mem. ABA, Am. Inst. CPA's. Corporate taxation, Estate taxation, Insurance. Office: Peat Marwick Mitchell & Co One Boston Pl Boston MA 02108

HARTIGAN, NEIL F., attorney general Illinois, lawyer. former lieutenant governor Illinois; b. Chgo., May 4, 1938; S. David and Colletta Hogan; m. Marge Hartigan, June 9, 1962; children: John, Elizabeth, Laura, Bridget. Grad. social scis., Georgetown U., 1958; J.D., Loyola U., Chgo., 1961; LL.D. (hon.), Lincoln Coll., 1975. Bar: Ill. bar 1962. Formerly dep. adminstrv. officer City of Chgo.; legis. counsel City of Chgo. in Ill. 75th Gen. Assembly; then chief legal counsel Chgo. Park Dist.; lt. gov. Ill., 1973-77; pres., chief exec. officer Real Estate Research Corp., Chgo., 1977-79; dir. Real Estate Research Corp., 1977; sr. v.p. 1st Nat. Bank Chgo., 1977-83; sr. v.p., area head Western Hemisphere, 1979-83; atty. gen. State of Ill., 1983—; lectr. former mem. faculty John Marshall Law Sch. Active Am. Cancer Soc. drives; chmn. Nat. Conf. Lt. Govs., 1976; former mem. exec. com. Council State Govts.; bd. dirs. Georgetown U.; mem. vis. com. on public policy U. Chgo.; bd. dirs. Chgo. Conv. and Tourism Bur., TRUST, Inc., Lincoln Park Zool. Soc.; mem. exec. com. March of Dimes; chmn. Super-walk, 1978. Named One of 200 Hundred Young Ams. Most Likely To Provide New Generation of Leadership Time mag.; among Ten Outstanding Young Men of Yr. Chgo. Jr. C. of C., 1967; Man of Year Loyola U. Alumni Assn. and Chgo. Bar Assn., 1982; hon. pres. Spanish-speaking div. Jr. C. of C., Chgo. Mem. Am. Bar Assn., Ill. Bar Assn., Chgo. Bar Assn., Chgo. Assn. Commerce and Industry (v.p. urban affairs), Chgo. Council on Fgn. Relations, Young Presidents Orgn., Nat. Council on Aging, Irish Fellowship Club. Clubs: Economic, Executive, Rotary, K.C, Hundred of Cook County.

HARTLEY, GLENN HENRY, lawyer; b. Waukon, Iowa, Apr. 2, 1947; s. Grant R. and Esther (Beneke) H.; m. Barbara Jean Rambo, Feb. 28, 1981; children: Mariah, Grant. BS, U. Wis., LaCrosse, 1969; JD, U. Wis., Madison, 1974. Bar: Wis. 1974, U.S. Dist. Ct. (we. dist.) Wis. 1974, U.S. Dist. Ct. (ea. dist.) Wis. 1978, U.S. Supreme Ct. 1980. Ptnr. Schmitt, Hartley & Arndorfer S.C., Merrill, Wis., 1974—. Mem. ABA, Wis. Bar Assn. (bd. govs. 1982-86), Lincoln County Bar Assn. (pres. 1979), Assn. Trial Lawyers Am., Wis. Acad. Trial Lawyers, Def. Research Inst. Avocations: hunting, fishing. Personal injury, State civil litigation, General practice. Home: N 2163 County Hwy G Merrill WI 54452 Office: Schmitt Hartley & Arndorfer SC 1029 E Main St Merrill WI 54452

HARTMAN, BURTON ARTHUR, lawyer; b. Bklyn., Oct. 11, 1924; s. Irving I. and Esther (Kramer) H.; m. Florence Greenstein, Oct. 24, 1944; children—Helen L. Hartman Owens, Cathy I. Hartman Edwards. Student, Allegheny Coll., 1940-42; A.B., NYU, 1947, LL.B., 1950. Bar: N.Y. 1950, U.S. Dist. Ct. (so. and ea. dists.) N.Y. 1957, Fla. 1976. Sole practice N.Y.C., 1950-58; assoc. Otterbourg, Steindler, Houston & Rosen, N.Y.C., 1958-63; asst. gen. counsel N.Y. Life Ins. Co., N.Y.C., 1963-77; ptnr. Morgan, Lewis & Bockius, Miami, Fla., 1978-82, Squire, Sanders & Dempsey, Miami, 1982—; lectr. Eastern Sch. Real Estate, N.Y.C., 1968-73; adj. lectr. Real Estate Inst., NYU, 1975-76. Served as 1st lt. USMC, 1943-46. Mem. ABA (editorial bd. Real Estate Fin. Newsletter), Am. Coll. Real Estate Lawyers, Am. Coll. Mortgage Attys., Am. Land Title Assn. Republican. Clubs: Calusa Country, Bankers. Real property, General corporate. Office: Suite 3000 100 Chopin Plaza Miami FL 33131

HARTMAN, GEORGE EDWARD, marketing scientist, lawyer, educator; b. Newton, Kans., Oct. 20, 1926; s. Albert J. and Ellen (Pawlick) H. B.S., Kans. U., 1950; M.B.A., Ind. U., 1951; Ph.D., U. Ill., 1958; J.D., U. Cin., 1964. Bar: Ohio bar 1964. Instr. in mktg. Tex. A. and M. U., 1951-52; asst. prof. U. N.D., Grand Forks, 1952-55; instr. U. Ill., Urbana, 1955-58; prof. U. Cin., 1958—; practice law Cin., 1964—; cons. mktg. Contbg. author: Handbook of Modern Marketing, 1970, 86, Business and Its Environment, 1974, Fundamentals of Management Finance, 1981, 84; bd. editors legal devel. sect. Jour. Mktg, 1965-83; columnist Mktg. News, 1965-83. Mem. regional export council Dept. Commerce, 1969-74; mem. bd. mgrs. U. Cin. YMCA; bd. dirs. U. Cin., 1978-80, S.W. Ohio Consumer Assn. Served with Adj.-Gen.'s Office AUS, 1945-46. Mem. World Trade Club (chmn. edn. com. 1974-75), Cin. C. of C., Am. Mktg. Assn., Am., Ohio bar assns., Acad. Internat. Bus., Am. Council Consumer Interests, AAUP, Beta Gamma Sigma, Delta Sigma Pi, Phi Delta Phi, Lambda Chi Alpha. Democrat. Presbyterian. Club: Masons. Antitrust, General practice. Home: 310 Bryant St Cincinnati OH 45220

HARTMAN, GREGORY CALVIN, lawyer; b. Reading, Pa., Aug. 16, 1946; s. Calvin and Marie Ann (Bachman) H.; m. Patricia Ann Dougherty, Feb. 1, 1969; children: Erika Maude, Colleen Ann. BA, Dickinson Coll., 1968, JD, 1974; LLM in Estate Planning, U. Miami, 1981. Bar: Pa. 1974, Fla. 1980, U.S. Dist. Ct. (so. dist.) Fla. 1980, U.S. Dist. Ct. (ea. dist.) Pa. 1980, U.S. Tax Ct. 1980, U.S. Ct. Appeals (3d, 5th and 11th cir.) 1980. Sole practice Camp Hill, Pa., 1975-80; assoc. Guren, Merritt et al, Miami, Fla., 1980-82, Roland & Schlegel, Reading, Pa., 1982—. Host/creator TV show Fin. Forum, 1983, 85. Served to sgt. U.S. Army, 1968-71, ETO. Mem. ABA, Fla. Bar Assn., Pa. Bar Assn., Berks County Bar Assn., C. of C. (chmn. small bus. com. 1986—). Republican. Corporate taxation, Estate taxation, General corporate. Home: 8 E 35th St Reading PA 19606 Office: Roland & Schlegel PC 627 N 4th St Reading PA 19603

HARTMAN, JOHN IVES, JR., lawyer; b. Lancaster, Pa., Oct. 22, 1919; s. John Ives and Loneita Eckert (Straub) H.; m. Mary Elizabeth Johnson, Jan. 27, 1945; 1 son, Thomas Hartman; m. Phyllis Mary Eshelman, Aug. 26, 1967; stepchildren—Barbara Shea, Constance Page, Christopher Quinn. A.B. summa cum laude, Princeton U., 1941; J.D., U. Pa., 1948. Bar: Pa. 1949. Assoc. Windolph and Johnston, Lancaster, 1949-55; ptnr. Windolph, Burkholder & Hartman, Lancaster, 1956-75, Hartman & Underhill, Lancaster, 1975-77, sr. ptnr. Hartman Underhill & Brubaker, 1978—; adj. prof. Franklin and Marshall Coll., Lancaster, 1950-67. Chmn. Assocs. in Downtown Lancaster, 1982. Served to lt. comdr. USNR, 1941-46. Mem. Am. Law Inst. Republican. Episcopalian (past chancellor Diocese of Central Pa.). Probate, Family and matrimonial. Home: 202 E Marion St Lancaster PA 17602 Office: 221 E Chestnut St Lancaster PA 17602

HARTMAN, MARSHALL J., lawyer, educator; b. Chgo., Mar. 9, 1934; s. Paul and Anna Lily (Rose) H.; m. Patricia Gail Henig, July 30, 1961; children—Ann, Judy, Danny. A.B., U. Chgo., 1954; B.Hebrew Letters, Coll. Jewish Studies, Chgo., 1954; J.D., U. Chgo., 1957. Bar: Ill. 1958, U.S. Dist. Ct. (no. Dist.) Ill., U.S. Ct. Appeals (7th cir), U.S. Supreme Ct. 1962. Youth dir. South Side Hebrew Congregation, Chgo., 1958-61; asst. pub. defender, Cook County, Chgo., 1963-70; probation officer Cook County Juvenile Ct., 1958-60, asst. to presiding judge, 1960-63; nat. dir. defender services Nat. Legal Aid and Defender Assn., 1970-76; vis. assoc. prof. U. Ill., Chgo., 1978—; exec. dir. Criminal Def. Consortium of Cook County, Chgo., 1976-78; treas., gen. counsel Nat. Defender Inst., Chgo., 1978—; chief pub. defender 19th jud. cir. Lake County, Ill. Author: Hartman's Handy Guide, 1968, Constitutional Criminal Procedure Handbook, 1986; contbr. articles to profl. jours. Mem. Am. Jewish Congress. Served to 1st lt. USAR, 1961-62. Recipient Reginald Heber Smith award, Nat. Legal Aid and Defender Assn., 1978; Silver Circle award U. Ill., 1982, 85. Mem. Ill. Pub. Defender Assn. (pres.), Ill. Acad. Criminology (v.p., pres.), ABA (ho. of dels.), Chgo Bar Assn. Democrat. Criminal, Jurisprudence, Legal education. Home: 6554 N Spaulding Lincolnwood IL 60645 Office: Nat Defender Inst 1620 Central Evanston IL 60201

HARTMANN, KENNETH, lawyer; b. Chgo., Apr. 2, 1950; s. Orvel Arthur and Anita (Everding) H.; m. Carol Beth Draeger, Aug. 5, 1978; children—Elizabeth Ann, Kristen Carol. B.A. with high honors, U. Ill., 1971; J.D., U. Chgo., 1977. Bar: Ill. 1977, U.S. Dist. Ct. (no. dist.) Ill. 1977. Assoc., Sonnenschein, Carlin, Nath & Rosenthal, Chgo., 1977-79, Coffield, Ungaretti, Harris & Slavin, Chgo., 1979-81; ptnr. Rudnick & Wolfe, Chgo., 1981-85; pres. Cen. Chgo. Distributing Co., 1985—. Mem. Phi Beta Kappa. Republican. Lutheran. General corporate, Banking, Real property. Office: Rudnick & Wolfe 555 N Tripp Ave Chicago IL 60624

HARTNETT, THOMAS ROBERT, III, lawyer; b. Sioux City, Iowa, July 19, 1920; s. Thomas R. and Florence Mary (Graves) H.; m. Betty Jeanne Dobbins, Mar. 3, 1943; children—Thomas Robert Joseph, Jeanine Elizabeth, Dennis Edward, Glenn Michael. Student Trinity Coll., 1937-39; LL.B., U. So. Calif., 1948. Bar: Tex. 1948, U.S. Dist. Ct. (no. dist.) Tex. 1949, U.S. Ct. Appeals (5th cir.) 1954, U.S. Ct. Appeals (10th cir.) 1955, U.S. Supreme Ct. 1957, U.S. Ct. Appeals (11th cir.) 1983. Sole practice law, Dallas, 1948—. Served with USAAF, 1939-45. Mem. State Bar Tex., Dallas Bar Assn. Republican. Roman Catholic. State civil litigation, Federal civil litigation. Home: 5074 Matilda St #224 Dallas TX 75206 Office: 2320 South Tower LB 174 Plaza of the Americas Dallas TX 75201

HARTNETT, WILL FORD, lawyer; b. Austin, Tex., June 3, 1956; s. James Joseph and Emily (High) H. BA, Harvard U., 1978; JD, U. Tex., 1981. Bar: Tex. 1981, U.S. Ct. Appeals (5th cir.) 1985, U.S. Supreme Ct. 1985; cert. in Estate Planning and Probate Law Tex. Bd. Legal Specialization. Assoc. Turner, Hitchins, Dallas, 1981-82, Law Office James J. Hartnett, P.C., Dallas, 1982—; bd. dirs. Allied Bank Mockingbird, Dallas; Tex. Guaranteed Student Loan Corp., Austin. Mem. ABA, Dallas Bar Assn., Dallas Assn. Young Lawyers. Republican. Roman Catholic. Club: Harvard Dallas (treas. 1984-86). Probate, Condemnation, State civil litigation. Home: 4591 Elsby Ave Dallas TX 75209 Office: Law Office James J Hartnett PC 2800 MBank Bldg Dallas TX 75201

HARTSEL, NORMAN CLYDE, lawyer; b. San Diego, Sept. 25, 1944; s. Norman E. and Margaret (Vaughan) H.; m. Molly E. Atherholt, June 14, 1969; children—Christian, Bennett. A.B., Kenyon Coll., 1967; J.D., Case Western Res. U., 1970. Bar: Ohio 1970, Mich. 1979, Fla. 1982, U.S. Ct. Appeals (6th cir.) 1984, U.S. Tax Ct. 1982. Assoc. Shumaker, Loop & Kendrick, Toledo, 1971-76, ptnr., 1977-85; pres. Norman C. Hartsel Co. LPA, Toledo, 1985-87, ptnr. Watkins & Bates, 1987—. Recipient Disting. Alumni award Kenyon Coll., 1981. Mem. ABA, Ohio Bar Assn., Mich. Bar Assn., Fla. Bar Assn., Toledo Bar Assn. Episcopalian. Clubs: Carranor Hunt and Polo, Belmont Country. Estate planning, Probate, Estate taxation. Home: 113 Holly Ln Perrysburg OH 43551

HARTSHORN, ROLAND DEWITT, lawyer; b. Cordele, Ga., May 27, 1921; s. George DuBois and Nola Nancy (Redwine) H.; m. Mildred Stromick, Aug. 15, 1953; children—Marie Anne Hartshorn Kuhn, Elizabeth Lee, Roland David. J.D., Emory U., 1948. Bar: Va. 1956, D.C., 1956, Ga. 1948. Sole practice, Atlanta, 1948-50; sole practice, 1956-70; ptnr. Thomas, Thomas & Hartshorn, Springfield, Va., 1970-75; ptnr. Holst & Hartshorn, Arlington and Falls Church, Va., 1975—. Served to capt. U.S. Army, 1950-56. Mem. D.C. Bar Assn., Va. State Bar Assn., Fairfax County Bar Assn. (mem. legis. com.). Republican. Presbyterian. Lodges: Lions, Moose. General practice, Personal injury, Probate. Home: 3103 Sleepy Hollow Rd Falls Church VA 22042 Office: Holst & Hartshorn 6400 Arlington Blvd Falls Church VA 22042

HARTWELL, CHRISTOPHER LYNN, lawyer; b. Dallas, Aug. 30, 1950; s. Roy A. and Grace M. (Fomby) H.; m. Sandra H. Ferdman, Apr. 20, 1979. BA, U. Tex., 1972; JD, Yale U., 1975. Bar: Tex. 1975, D.C. 1976, Calif. 1980. Research assoc. Sch. Law Yale U., New Haven, Conn., 1975-76; assoc. Webster & Chamberlain, Washington, 1976-80; ptnr. Wilson, Sonsini, Goodrich & Rosati, Palo Alto, Calif., 1980—. Contbr. articles to profl. jours. Mem. ABA. Democrat. Corporate taxation, Personal income taxation, General corporate.

HARTWELL, JANE BARRY, lawyer; b. Milton, Mass., Feb. 19, 1956; s. John E. and Marjorie A. Barry; m. Davis Hartwell, Oct. 8, 1983; 1 child, Thomas. AB, Dartmouth Coll., 1978; JD, Yale U., 1981. Law clk. to presiding justice Mass. Supreme Ct., Boston, 1981-82; assoc. atty. Murray, Plumb & Murray, Portland, Maine, 1982—. Mem. ABA, Maine Bar Assn., Am. Trial Lawyers Assn., Maine Trial Lawyers Assn. Federal civil litigation, State civil litigation, Public utilities. Office: Murray Plumb & Murray 75 Pearl St Portland ME 04101

HARTY, JAMES Q., lawyer; b. Phila., Dec. 10, 1925. AB, La Salle Coll., 1949; MBA, U. Pa., Phila., 1952, LLB, 1959. Bar: Pa. 1961. Ptnr. Reed, Smith, Shaw & McClay, Pitts. Address: Reed Smith Shaw & McClay James H Reed Bldg Mellow Sq 435 6th Ave & William Penn Way Pittsburgh PA 15219 *

HARTZ, STEVEN EDWARD MARSHALL, lawyer, educator; b. Cambridge, Mass., July 11, 1948; s. Louis and Stella (Feinberg) H.; m. Janice Lindsay, June 12, 1976. A.B. magna cum laude, Harvard Coll., 1970; J.D. U. Chgo., 1974. Bar: N.Y. 1975, U.S. Dist. Ct. (so. and ea. dists.) N.Y. 1975, Fla. 1979, U.S. Dist. Ct. (so. dist.) Fla. 1979, U.S. Ct. Appeals (2d cir.) 1975, U.S. Tax Ct. 1979, U.S. Ct. Appeals (5th cir.) 1979, U.S. Ct. Appeals (11th cir.) 1981, U.S. Supreme Ct. 1979, U.S. Dist. Ct. (mid. dist.) Fla. 1984. Assoc. Cleary, Gottlieb, Steen & Hamilton, N.Y.C., 1974-79; asst. U.S. atty. U.S. Dept. Justice, Miami, Fla., 1979-82, dep. chief criminal div., chief fraud and pub. corruption sect. 1981-82; sole practice, Miami, Fla., 1982—; of counsel David B. Van Kleeck, P.A., Boca Raton, Fla., 1982—; lectr. dept. English, U. Miami 1984, adj. assoc. prof., 1985—. Co-author: Housing, A Community Handbook, 1973. Vol. atty. M.F.Y. Legal Services, N.Y.C., 1978. Recipient Dirs.' award U.S. Dept. Justice, 1981; Fulbright Hays scholar, 1970. Mem. ABA, Fla. Bar, Assn. Bar City N.Y., N.Y. State Bar Assn., Fed. Bar Assn., Dade County Bar Assn., Nat. Assn. Criminal Def. Lawyers, Phi Beta Kappa. Criminal, Consumer commercial. Office: 2600 SW 3d Ave Suite 700 Miami FL 33129

HARTZELL, ANDREW CORNELIUS, JR., lawyer; b. Balt., Nov. 5, 1927; s. Andrew Cornelius and Mary Frances (Milholland) H.; m. Mary Leontine McPhillips, July 31, 1954; children: Andrew Cornelius III, Stephen Carroll, James Francis, Mary Leontine, John Michael, Peter Milholland. B.A., Yale U., 1950, LL.B., 1953. Bar: N.Y. 1953, Ohio 1955, U.S. Supreme Ct. Law clk. Fed. Judge Irving R. Kaufman, N.Y.C., 1953-54; assoc. Thompson, Hine & Flory, Cleve., 1954-63, Debevoise, Plimpton, Lyons & Gates, N.Y.C., 1963-65; ptnr. Debevoise and Plimpton and predecessor firms, 1966—. Contbr. articles to legal jours. and to Antitrust Advisor, McGraw-Hill Pub. Co., 1971, 78; Note and Comment editor Yale Law Jour, 1952-53. Mem. bd. archtl. rev. Village of Scarsdale, N.Y., 1965-67; mem. Adv. Council on Environ. Conservation, 1986—, chmn., 1987—. Served with U.S. Army, 1946-48, Japan. Fellow Am. Coll. Trial Lawyers; mem. Assn. Bar City N.Y., N.Y. State Bar Assn., ABA, Am. Law Inst. Roman Catholic. Clubs: Village of N.Y., Fox Meadow; Town (Scarsdale). Antitrust, Federal civil litigation, State civil litigation. Home: 7 Eastwoods Ln Scarsdale NY 10583 Office: 875 3d Ave New York NY 10022

HARTZELL, FRANKLIN MACVEAGH, lawyer; b. Carthage, Ill., Aug. 24, 1923; s. Franklin MacVeagh and Mary Glenn (Ferris) H.; m. Eleonore Emma Gaebe, May 18, 1946; children: Susan L. (dec.), Thomas F., Phoebe M. Hartzell Wear. BS, U. Ill., 1948, LLB, 1950. Bar: Ill. 1950, U.S. Tax Ct. 1955. Sole practice Carthage, 1950; assoc. Hartzell, Glidden, Tucker, Neff & O'Neal and predecessor firms, Carthage, 1952-55, ptnr., 1956—; chmn. bd. dirs. Marine Trust Co., Carthage, 1st Fed. Savings and Loan of Colchester, Ill.; bd. dirs. Pioneer Lumber Co., Dallas City, Ill. atty. City of Carthage, 1955-69; bd. dirs. Meml Hosp. Assocs., Carthage, 1958-72, Hancock Nursing Home 1967-72. Served to 1st lt. U.S. Army, 1943-46, 50-52, PTO. Mem. ABA, Ill. Bar Assn., Hancock County Bar Assn., Am. Coll. Probate Counsel, Soc. Hosp. Attys., Phi Delta Phi, Delta Kappa Epsilon. Democrat. Presbyterian. Banking, Probate, Estate taxation. Home: 306 S Madison St Carthage IL 62321 Office: Hartzell Glidden Tucker Neff & O'Neal 608 Wabash Carthage IL 62321

HARUTUNIAN, ALBERT THEODORE, III, lawyer; b. San Diego, May 15, 1955; s. Albert Theodore Jr. and Elsie Ruth (Tomboulian) H. BA, Claremont Men's Coll., 1977; JD, U. Calif., Berkeley, 1980. Bar: Calif. 1980, U.S. Dist. Ct. (so. dist.) Calif. 1980, U.S. Ct. Apppeals (9th cir.) 1982, U.S. Supreme Ct. 1984. Law clk. to presiding judge U.S. Dist. Ct., San Diego, 1980-81; assoc. Luce, Forward, Hamilton & Scripps, San Diego, 1982—; spl. counsel standing com. on discipline U.S. Dist. Ct. Calif., San Diego, 1983-85; judge pro tem San Diego Mcpl. Ct., 1986—; mem. com. fed. cts. Calif. State Bar, 1986—. Vol. Combined Health Agys. Drive, San Diego, 1983; bd. govs. Muscular Dystrophy Assn., San Diego, 1985; mem. LEAD Inc., San Diego, 1986—. Named one of Outstanding Young Men of Am., 1983; recipient Outstanding Service award 9th Jud. Cir. Conf., 1986. Mem. ABA (labor and employment sect.), Calif. Bar Assn. (labor sect.), San Diego Bar Assn. (fed. ct. com.), Calif. State Bar Ct. (referee 1985—), Am. Arbitration Assn. (arbitrator 1986—), U. Calif. Alumni Assn. (class rep. 1985—), Claremont McKenna Coll. Alumni Assn. (founding dir., San Diego chpt., 1984—). Republican. Avocations: music, basketball, tennis. Labor, Federal civil litigation, State civil litigation. Office: Luce Forward Hamilton & Scripps 110 West A St Suite 1700 San Diego CA 92101

HARVEY, ALAN CHRISTOPHER, lawyer; b. Atlanta, Aug. 4, 1951; s. Ernest Christopher and Vivian May (Hoenstine) H.; m. Camille Cunningham, June 21, 1975; children: Allison, Erica, Katherine. BA, Furman U., 1973; JD, Emory U., 1977. Bar: Ga. 1977, U.S. Dist. Ct. (no. dist.) Ga. 1977. Assoc. Harvey, Willard, Elliott & Olsen, Decatur, Ga., 1977-85; sole practice Decatur, 1985—; adj. assoc. judge Magistrate Ct. DeKalb County, 1985—. Mem. Donor Resource Devel. com. ARC, DeKalb, DeKalb/Rockdale adv. com. Met. Atlanta chapter ARC, Ga. Vol. Lawyers Arts, Airplane Noise task force, City of Decatur. Mem. ABA, Ga. Bar Assn., Decatur-DeKalb Bar Assn., DeKalb Vol. Lawyers, Ga. Trial Lawyers Assn. Baptist. Avocation: racewalking. State civil litigation, Family and matrimonial, General practice. Home: 1051 Lakeshore Dr Avondale Estates GA 30002 Office: 309 Sycamore St Decatur GA 30030

HARVEY, ALEXANDER, II, judge; b. Balt., May 3, 1923; s. Fred B. and Rose (Hopkins) H.; m. Mary E. Williams, Feb. 24, 1951; children—Elizabeth H., Alexander IV. B.A., Yale U., 1947; LL.B., Columbia U., 1950. Bar: Md. 1950. Assoc. firm Ober, William, Grimes & Stinson, Balt., 1950-66; partner Ober, William, Grimes & Stinson, 1953-66; asst. atty. gen. Md., 1957-58; judge U.S. Dist. Ct. for Md., 1966-86, chief judge, 1986—; Mem. Gov. Md. Com. to Study Blue Sky Law of Md., 1961; mem. character com. Ct. Appeals Md. 8th Jud. Circuit. Bd. dirs. Balt. Symphony Assn., 1966-68; pres., dir. Balt. Opera Guild, 1960; bd. dirs. Balt. Council Social Agys., 1957-63; trustee Ch. Home and Hosp., Balt., 1952-71. Served to 1st lt. AUS, World War II, ETO. Mem. Am., Md., Balt. bar assns., Phi Beta Kappa. Episcopalian (vestry 1967-70). Jurisprudence. Home: 7300 Brightside Rd Baltimore MD 21212 Office: 101 W Lombard St Baltimore MD 21201

HARVEY, BARBARA, lawyer, legal educator; b. N.Y.C., Feb. 19, 1946; d. William and Sylvia (Abramson) Masin. Student Antioch Coll., 1962-65; B.A., Wayne State U., 1968, J.D., 1975. Bar: Mich., 1975. Law clk. to C.W. Joiner, U.S. dist. judge, Detroit, 1975-77; assoc. firm Barris, Sott, Denn & Driker, Detroit, 1977-79; asst. prof. Law Sch., Wayne State U., Detroit, 1979-82, adj. prof., 1982—; legal dir. ACLU of Mich., Detroit, 1983-86; practice labor law, Detroit, 1982—; mem. nat. adv. bd. Assn. for Union Democracy, N.Y.C., 1981—; mem. lawyers adv. com. Teamsters Rank and File Def. and Edn. Fund, Detroit, 1981-83. Article and book rev. editor Wayne Law Rev., 1975; contbr. articles to publs. Dir. Met. Detroit br. ACLU of Mich., 1977—, mem. lawyers com., 1979—, exec. sec., 1981-85, v.p., 1985—; hearing referee Mich. Civil Rights Commn., Lansing and Detroit, 1983—. Clin. program grantee U.S. Dept. Edn., 1980, 81; editor's scholar Wayne Law Sch., 1974-75; Law Sch. Fund scholar, 1973-75. Mem. ABA, State Bar Mich., Detroit Bar Assn., Assn. Trial Lawyers, Am., Mich. Trial Lawyers Assn. Labor, Civil rights, Federal civil litigation. Office: 925 Ford Bldg Detroit MI 48226

HARVEY, CHARLES ALBERT, JR., lawyer; b. Beverly, Mass., Sept. 28, 1949; s. Charles A. and Phyllis B. (O'Rourke) H.; m. Whitney Ann Neville, Sept. 21, 1985; 1 child, John Whitney. AB, Assumption Coll., 1971; JD, U. Maine, 1974. Bar: Maine 1974, Mass. 1974, U.S. Supreme Ct. 1979. Assoc. Verrill & Dana, Portland, Maine, 1974-79, ptnr., 1979—; assoc. chief counsel Pres.'s Commn. on the accident at Three Mile Island, Washington, 1979; mem. adv. com. on civil rules U.S. Supreme Jud. Ct., 1978—; chmn. adv. com. on local rules for U.S. Dist. Ct. Maine, 1985—. Trustee Portland Symphony Orch., 1982—, Portland Stage Co., 1984—. Republican. Clubs: Cumberland (Portland), Portland Yacht (Falmouth, Maine). Federal civil litigation, State civil litigation. Office: Verrill & Dana 2 Canal Plaza PO Box 586 Portland ME 04112

HARVEY, GREGORY M., lawyer. AB, Harvard U., 1959, JD, 1962. Bar: Pa. 1963. Ptnr. Morgan, Lewis & Bockius, Phila. Address: Morgan Lewis & Bockius 2000 One Logan Sq Philadelphia PA 19103 *

HARVEY, JAMES MARTIN, JR., lawyer; b. Fairfax, S.C., Aug. 4, 1956; s. James Martin and Barbara Joan (Smith) H.; m. Mary Elizabeth Geddings, June 23, 1979; children: James Martin III, Rodney Daniel. BA cum laude, U. S.C., 1978, JD, 1981. Bar: S.C. 1981, U.S. Dist. Ct. S.C. 1982. Law clk. to presiding justice 2d Jud. Cir. Ct. S.C., Barnwell, 1981-82; assoc. Blatt & Fales, Barnwell, 1982—. Bd. dirs. City Zoning Commn., Barnwell, 1986, Barnwell County United Way, 1983, Crystal Jenkins Life Fund for Children, 1985; coach Dixie Youth Baseball. Mem. ABA, S.C. Bar, S.C. Trial Lawyers Assn., Am. Trial Lawyers Assn., Am. Bankruptcy Inst. Democrat. Baptist. Clubs: Sweetwater Country (bd. dirs. 1985—), Winton Investors (Barnwell). Lodge: Masons. Avocations: fishing, golf. Personal injury, Bankruptcy, General practice. Home: 1801 Pinehaven Dr Barnwell SC 29812

HARVEY, JONATHAN PAUL, lawyer, real estate developer; b. Albany, N.Y., Oct. 9, 1941; s. Arthur Joseph and Alice (Dryfach) H.; m. Margaret Steele, July 19, 1969; children—Johns Hopkins, Caroline Rose. B.A., U. Pa., 1963; LL.B. Union U., 1966. Bar: N.Y. 1967, U.S. Supreme Ct. 1978. Sr. ptnr. Harvey and Harvey, Mumford & Kingsley, Albany, N.Y.; chmn. State of N.Y. Com. on Profl. Standards 3d Jud. Dept. 1977, mem. 1980—; mem. Com. on Character and Fitness 3d Jud. Dist., 1980—. Mem. adv. counsel N.Y. State Commn. for Human Rights, 1970-74; pres., bd. dirs. Urban League of Albany, 1974-76. Mem. Am. Arbitration Assn. (panel arbitrators), Albany County Bar Assn. (dir. 1977-79, chmn. grievance com. 1979—), Rensselaer County Bar Assn., N.Y. State Bar Assn. (Ho. of Dels. 1981-85), Capital Dist. Trial Lawyers Assn., Assn. Trial Lawyers Am. (sustaining).

Clubs: Ft. Orange (Albany); Royal Corinthian Yacht, Island Sailing (Cowes, Eng.). Author: The Doctrine of Informed Consent; also articles. General practice, Personal injury, Real property. Home: 38 Cameron Rd Troy NY 12180 Office: 29 Elk St Albany NY 12207

HARVEY, LEIGH KATHRYN, lawyer; b. Abilene, Tex.; d. Jasper Elliott and Kathryn E. (McDaniel) H.; m. Bert Gubbels, Oct. 1983. BA cum laude, U. Tex., 1971, JD, 1974. Bar: Tex. 1975. Asst. atty. City of San Angelo, Tex., 1974-77; asst. dist. atty. County of Fort Bend, Richmond, Tex., 1978; sole practice various cities, Tex., 1977—; bd. dirs. Tex. Coca-Cola Bottling Co., Abilene. Bd. dirs. Tom Green County Community Action Council, San Angelo, 1975-77, pres. 1976; vol. judge bd. advs. U. Tex. Law Sch., Austin, 1980; mem. Met. Austin 2000, 1982. Recipient Young Careerist award Dist. 7 Bus. and Profl. Women's Club, 1977. Mem. ABA, Tex. Bar Assn. (legal forms com. manual for Real Estate Transactions rev. edit. 1986—), Travis County Bar Assn., Bell Lampasas Mills County Young Lawyers Assn. (sr. citizen project 1986—). Episcopalian. General practice. Office: PO Box 948 Lampasas TX 76550

HARVEY, MARK WAYNE, lawyer; b. Clovis, N.Mex., Feb. 20, 1954; s. Tom L. and Mary J. Harvey; m. Politcia A. Matzoll, July 20, 1976; children: Mike, John, Katie, Jessica. BS, U.S. Mil. Acad., 1976; JD, George Washington U., 1981. Bar: W.Va. 1981. Commd. 2d lt. U.S. Army, 1976, advanced through grades to capt., 1980; trial def. counsel U.S. Army, Ft. Belvoir, Va., 1981-83; appellate counsel U.S. Army, Washington, 1983-84; sr. def. counsel U.S. Army, San Antonio, 1984—. Co-editor Advocate mag., 1983-84. Mem. ABA (litigation sect.), Nat. Assn. Criminal Def. Lawyers. Republican. Roman Catholic. Avocation: running. Criminal, Federal civil litigation. Office: US Army Trial Def Service Health Services Command Fort Sam Houston TX 78234

HARVEY, MORRIS LANE, lawyer; b. Madisonville, Ky., Apr. 22, 1950; s. Morris Lee and Margie Lou (Wallace) H.; m. Judith Kay French, May 27, 1972; children: Morris Lane Jr., John French, Laura Kathleen. BS, Murray State U., 1972; JD, U. Ky., 1974. Bar: Ill. 1975, U.S. Dist. Ct. (so. dist.) 1979. Assoc. Hanagan & Dousman, Mt. Vernon, Ill., 1975-77; ptnr. Feigner, Quindry, Molt & Harvey and successor firms, Fairfield, Ill., 1977-85; sole practice Fairfield, 1986—; instr. Frontier Community Coll., Fairfield, 1977-79; spl. asst. atty. gen. State of Ill., Fairfield, 1977-82; Ill. pres. Woodman of World Life Ins., 1985. Recipient Outstanding Young Man Am. U.S. Jaycees, 1978, 81. Mem. ABA, Ill. Bar Assn., Assn. Trial Lawyers Am., Ill. Trial Lawyers Assn., Am. Judicature Soc. State civil litigation, Family and matrimonial, Personal injury. Home: 10 Park Ln Fairfield IL 62837 Office: 215 SE 3d St Fairfield IL 62837

HARVEY, WILLIAM BRANTLEY, JR., lawyer, former state lieutenant governor; b. Walterboro, S.C., Aug. 14, 1930; s. William Brantley and Thelma (Lightsey) H.; m. Helen Coggeshall, Dec. 30, 1952; children: Eileen L., William Brantley, III, Helen C., Margaret D., Warren C. A.B. in Polit. Sci, The Citadel, 1951, LL.D. (hon.), 1978; J.D. magna cum laude, U. S.C., 1955. Bar: S.C. 1955. Since practiced in Beaufort; sr. partner firm Harvey & Battey; mem. S.C. Ho. of Reps. from Beaufort County, 1958-74, chmn. rules com., mem. constl. revision com.; lt. gov. State of S.C., 1974-78; local dir. C & S Nat. Bank of S.C.; dir. Tidewater Investment and Devel. Corp.; pres. S.C. Bar. Commr. S.C. Parks, Recreation and Tourism Commn.; v.p. Coastal Carolina council Boy Scouts Am.; vice chmn. Citadel Devel. Found. Served to lt. AUS, 1952-54. Mem. Am., S.C., Beaufort County bar assns., Phi Beta Kappa, Kappa Alpha, Phi Delta Phi. Presbyterian (elder). General practice, Administrative and regulatory, General corporate. Home: 501 Pinckney St Beaufort SC 29902 Office: 1001 Craven St PO Box 1107 Beaufort SC 29902

HARVEY, WILLIAM BRANTLEY, III, lawyer; b. Columbia, S.C., Sept. 1, 1955; s. William Brantley Jr. and Helen (Coggeshall) H.; m. Wendy Bergfeldt, Dec. 30, 1978; 1 child, William Brantley IV. BA, Duke U., 1977; JD, U. S.C., 1980. Bar: S.C. 1980, U.S. Dist. Ct. S.C. 1980, U.S. Ct. Appeals (4th cir.) 1986. Assoc. Nelson, Mullins, Grier & Scarborough, Columbia, 1980-83; ptnr. Harvey & Battey P.A., Beaufort, S.C., 1983—. Deacon 1st Presbyn. Ch., Beaufort, 1983-86; county chmn. Phil Lader for Gov., Beaufort, 1986—. Mem. ABA, S.C. Bar Assn. (exec. com. young lawyers div.), S.C. Def. Trial Lawyers, Def. Research Inst. Democrat. Presbyterian. Lodges: Sertoma (bd. dirs. 1986—), Rotary. Avocations: tennis, golf, boating, fishing, hunting. State civil litigation, General corporate, Federal civil litigation. Home: 302 Federal St Beaufort SC 29902 Office: Harvey & Battey PA PO Drawer 1107 Beaufort SC 29901

HARVIN, DAVID TARLETON, lawyer; b. Houston, Feb. 15, 1945; s. William Charles and Ruth Helen (Beck) H.; m. Sarah Ann Hartman, Apr. 21, 1973; children—Kimberly Kate, William Hartman, John Andrew. B.A., Yale U., 1967; J.D., U. Tex., 1970. Bar: Tex. 1970, U.S. Supreme Ct. 1977, U.S. Ct. Appeals (5th cir.) 1971, U.S. Dist. Ct. (no., so. and ea. dists.) Tex. Law clk. U.S. Ct. Appeals (5th cir.), 1970-71; assoc. Vinson & Elkins, Houston, 1971-77, ptnr., 1977—. Chmn. bd. trustees Stehlin Found. for Cancer Research. Fellow Tex. Bar Found., Houston Bar Found.; mem. ABA. Episcopalian. Club: Houston Country, Galveston Country. Antitrust, Federal civil litigation, State civil litigation. Home: 911 Old Lake Houston TX 77057 Office: Vinson & Elkins 1001 Fannin Houston TX 77002

HARVIN, WILLIAM CHARLES, lawyer; b. San Francisco, Feb. 15, 1919; s. William Charles and Irma Beth (Hawkins) H.; m. Ruth Helen Beck, Nov. 30, 1942; children: David Tarleton, Susan Elizabeth Harvin Lawhon, Andrew Richard. B.A., U. Tex., 1940, LL.B., 1947. Bar: Tex. 1946. Sr. ptnr. Baker & Botts, mng. ptnr., chmn. exec. com., 1972-84; bd. dirs. Tex. Commerce Bancshares, Inc.; chmn. U.S. Circuit Judge Nominating Commn. 5th Circuit; lectr. legal insts. and law schs. Contbr. articles to legal periodicals. Chmn. bd. dirs. Houston C. of C., Tex. Med. Center, Inc.; bd. dirs. U. Tex. Health Scis. Ctr. Houston, San Jacinto History Mus.; vice chmn. bd. dirs. St. Luke's Episcopal Hosp. ; trustee St. John's Sch., Houston, Episc. Theol. Sem. of S.W., Austin; chmn. bd. trustees Kelsey-Seybold Found.; pres. Greater Houston Community Found.; chmn. bd. govs. The Forum Club of Houston. Served with USN, 1941-45. Fellow Am. Coll. Trial Lawyers, Am., Tex. bar founds.; mem. Council on Fgn. Relations, Philos. Soc. Tex., Am. Law Inst., Am. Bar Assn., Fedn. Ins. Counsel (pres. 1969-70), Def. Research Inst. (dir. 1969-72), Phi Delta Theta, Phi Delta Phi. Episcopalian (vestry). Clubs: Houston Country, Ramada. Federal civil litigation, State civil litigation, General corporate. Office: Baker & Botts One Shell Plaza Houston TX 77002

HARVITT, ADRIANNE STANLEY, lawyer; b. Chgo., May 15, 1954; d. Stanley and Maryln (Loye) H.; m. Donald Martin Heinrich, Aug. 27, 1977. AB, U. Chgo., 1975, MBA, 1976; JD with honors, Ill. Inst. Tech./Kent Coll. Law, 1980. Bar: Ill. 1980, U.S. Dist. Ct. (no. dist.) Ill. 1983, U.S. Ct. Appeals (7th cir.) 1985, U.S. Supreme Ct. 1985. Fin. analyst Bell & Howell Co., Chgo., 1976-77; staff atty. U.S. Commodity Futures Trading Commn., Chgo., 1980-83; assoc. Hannafan & Handler, Chgo., 1983-85; ptnr. Harvitt & Gekas, Ltd., Chgo., 1985—. Mem. ABA, Ill. Bar Assn. (hon. mention received for article 1982), Chgo. Bar Assn., U. Chgo. Women's Bus. Group, Art Inst. Chgo. Avocations: flying, skiing, swimming. Federal civil litigation, Commodities, Bankruptcy. Office: Harvitt & Gekas Ltd 1355 LaSalle S #1254 Chicago IL 60603

HARWELL, DAVID WALKER, state justice; b. Florence, S.C., Jan. 8, 1932; s. Baxter Hicks and Lacy (Rankin) H.; divorced; children—Robert Bryan, William Baxter. LL.B., J.D., U. S.C., 1958. Bar: S.C. Partner firm Harwell & Harwell; circuit judge S.C., 1973-80; justice S.C. Supreme Ct., 1980—. Mem. S.C. Ho. of Reps., 1962-73. Served with USNR, 1952-54. Mem. Am. Bar Assn., Am. Trial Lawyers Assn., S.C. Bar Assn., S.C. Trial Lawyers Assn. Democrat. Presbyterian. Jurisprudence. Address: City-County Complex Drawer X Florence SC 29501

HARWICK, ROBERT DEAN, JR., lawyer; b. N.Y.C., May 8, 1953; s. Robert D. and Elaine L. (Crandall) H. BA, Cornell U., 1975; JD, George Washington U., 1978. Bar: D.C. 1978, Md. 1979, U.S. Dist. Ct. Md. 1980, U.S. Dist. Ct. D.C. 1981, U.S. Ct. Appeals (4th cir.) 1981. Law clk. to presiding judge Anne Arundel County State of Md. Cir. Ct., Annapolis, 1978-79; atty. Allen, Thieblot & Alexander, Balt., 1979—. Mem. Md. Bar Assn., Bar Assn. Balt. City, D.C. Bar Assn. Democrat. Unitarian. Bankruptcy, Consumer commercial, State civil litigation. Home: 7023 F Lachlan Circle Baltimore MD 21239 Office: Allen Thieblot & Alexander The World Trade Ctr 4th floor Baltimore MD 21202

HARWOOD, BRUCE ALAN, lawyer; b. Chgo., Oct. 31, 1955; s. Richard C. Harwood and Harriet K. Bernstein; m. Lucy J. Karl, Sept. 5, 1982; 1 child, Alexander. BA, Northwestern U., 1978; JD, Washington U., St. Louis, 1981. Bar: Ill. 1981, U.S. Dist. Ct. (no. dist.) Ill. 1981, U.S. Ct. Appeals (7th cir.) 1984, U.S. Supreme Ct. 1985. Ptnr. Schwartz, Cooper, Kolb & Gaynor Chtd., Chgo., 1981—; lectr. Ill. Inst. Continuing Legal Edn. Bankruptcy, Banking, Federal civil litigation. Home: 656 Buckingham 3W Chicago IL 60657 Office: Schwartz Cooper Kolb & Gaynor Chtd 33 N LaSalle St Suite 2222 Chicago IL 60602

HARWOOD, DENNIS WESTCOTT, lawyer; b. Orange, Calif., Oct. 8, 1938; s. Donald Dorsey and Beth E. (Westcott) H.; m. Carol Louise New, Feb. 1, 1962; children: Darah, Cynda, David. BA, Pomona Coll., 1960; JD, U. So. Calif., 1964. Bar: Calif. 1965, U.S. Dist. Ct. (cen. dist.) Calif., U.S. Ct. Appeals (9th cir.), U.S. Supreme Ct. Ptnr. Harwood & Adkinson and predecessor, Newport Beach, Calif., 1965—; councilman City of Fountain Valley, Calif., 1967-68; judge pro-tem Orange County Superior Ct., Calif., 1982—. Mem. Rep. State Cen. Com., Calif., 1968-72; bd. dirs. Orange County Law Library, Calif., 1978-86, pres., 1980-81. Club: Big Canyon Country (Newport Beach). Avocations: golf. Real property, General corporate, Banking. Office: Harwood & Adkinson PO Box 1907 Newport Beach CA 92663

HASAK, JANET ELINORE, patent lawyer; b. Rochester, N.Y., Oct. 12, 1952; d. Charles Milton and June Charlotte (Raymond) Baird; m. James Philip Hasak, Oct. 4, 1975; children: John Clifford, Andrew Charles. BA, Hartwick Coll., 1974; MS, U. Rochester, 1976; JD, Seton Hall U., 1983. Bar: U.S. Patent Office 1977, N.J. 1983, U.S. Dist. Ct. N.J. 1983, U.S. Ct. Appeals (D.C. cir.) 1984, Calif. 1986, U.S. Dist. Ct. (no. dist.) Calif. 1986. Tutor, teaching fellow Hartwick Coll., Oneonta, N.Y., 1973-74; teaching asst., fellow U. Rochester, 1974-76; patent agt. Nat. Starch & Chem. Corp., Bridgewater, N.J., 1976-81; legal trainee Exxon Research & Engrng. Co., Florham Park, N.J., 1981-83; sr. patent agt. Cetus Corp., Emeryville, Calif., 1983, sr. patent atty., 1984-86, asst. intellectual property counsel, 1986—. Mem. Seton Hall Law Rev., 1981-83. Sherman Clark fellow in chemistry U. Rochester, 1974-75. Mem. ABA, Am. Intellectual Property Law Assn., AAAS, Peninsula Intellectual Property Law Assn., Alameda Victorian Preservation Soc., San Francisco Patent and Trademark Law Assn., Alameda Swim Assn. Patent, Trademark and copyright. Office: Cetus Corp 1400 53d St Emeryville CA 94608

HASENAUER, JUDITH ANNE, lawyer; b. Rochester, N.Y., Sept. 28, 1946; d. William F. and Arline (Burns) H. A.A., Monroe Community Coll., Rochester, N.Y., 1966; A.B., U. Rochester, N.Y., 1969; J.D., Golden Gate U., 1973; C.L.U., American Coll., Bryn Mawr, Pa., 1978. Bar: Calif. 1974, Conn. 1974, U.S. Dist Ct. Conn. 1975, N.Y. 1983, D.C. 1983. Ptnr., Blazzard, Grodd & Hasenauer, Westport, Conn., 1974—. Contbr. articles to profl. jours. Bd. dirs. Friends of Norwalk Community Coll., Conn., 1977-83; sec. Fairfield County C.L.U.s, Conn., 1983-85. Securities, Insurance. Office: Blazzard Grodd & Hasenauer 943 Post Rd E Westport CT 06880

HASKEL, JULES J., lawyer; b. Bklyn., Sept. 9, 1929; s. Manny and Sadie H.; m. Arlene Haskel, Apr. 19, 1957; children—Lynn S. Haskel Lancaster, Barbara I. Haskel Weiner, Carol S. B.S. in Journalism, Medill Sch. Journalism, Northwestern U., 1951; J.D., NYU, 1954. Bar: N.Y. 1955, U.S. Dist. Ct. (so. and ea. dists.) N.Y. 1957, U.S. Tax Ct. 1958, U.S. Ct. Apls. (2d cir.) 1981, U.S. Supreme Ct. 1962. Assoc. Grossman & Grossman, N.Y.C., 1954-55; exec. dir. membership campaign ABA, N.Y.C., 1955-56; assoc. Otterbourg, Steindler, Houston & Rosen, N.Y.C., 1956-57, Newman & Bisco, N.Y.C., 1957-59; ptnr. Koopersmith & Haskel, Jamaica, N.Y., 1960-77, Durben & Haskel, Garden City, N.Y., 1977—. Mem. law com. Fedn. Jewish Philanthropies of N.Y., 1978—; bd. dirs. Queens Legal Services Corp., 1970-73. Fellow Am. Coll. Probate Counsel; mem. ABA, N.Y. State Bar Assn. (ho. of dels. 1975—, chmn. trusts and estates law sect. 1982, nominating com. 1981-84, v.p. 1984-85, exec. com. 1986—), N.Y. State Bar Found. (bd. dirs. 1986—), Queens County Bar Assn. (pres. 1973-74, chmn. judiciary com. 1978-79, editor bar bull. 1964-66), Jamaica Lawyers Club (pres. 1968-69), Nassau County Bar Assn., NYU Law Alumni Assn. (v.p. 1970-73, 77-81). Jewish. Probate, General corporate, Real property. Office: Durben & Haskel 200 Garden City Plaza Garden City NY 11530

HASKELL, WYATT RUSHTON, lawyer; b. Birmingham, Ala., May 15, 1940; s. Preston Hampton and Mary Wyatt (Rushton) H.; m. Susan Porter Nabers, June 1, 1968; children: John Howze, Henry Devereux, Samuel Drayton. AB, Amherst Coll., 1961; LLB, Yale U., 1965. Bar: Ala. 1965. Assoc. Bradley, Arant, Rose & White, Birmingham, 1966-71; staff atty. So. Natural Gas Co., Birmingham, 1971-73; ptnr. Haskell, Slaughter & Young, Birmingham, 1973—; vis. research asst. U. Muenster, Fed. Republic Germany, 1965-66; vis. prof. U. Ala. Law Sch., 1970-73; bd. dirs. CKM Realty Inc., Birmingham. Contbr. articles to profl. jours. Bd. dirs. City Museum Birmingham, 1980—. Mem. ABA, Ala. Bar Assn., Birmingham Bar Assn. Presbyterian. Club: Mountain Brook. Municipal bonds. Home: 2964 Cherokee Rd Birmingham AL 35223 Office: Haskell Slaughter et al 800 First Nat Southern Nat Bldg Birmingham AL 35223

HASKETT, MARTIN CARLATON, lawyer, judge; b. Robstown, Tex., May 16, 1932; s. Martin Carlaton and Laura Belle (Womack) H.; m. Della Pitt (div.); 1 son, George Martin; m. 2d Gloria Faye Spiegelhauer, May 25, 1958; children—DeAnna Dale, Cynthia LaRae, Carla Malane. B.A., Tex. A&I U., 1954; LL.B., U. Tex.-Austin, 1958. Bar: Tex. 1958, U.S. Dist. Ct. (so. dist.) Tex. 1959, U.S. Ct. Mil. Appeals 1979. Sole practice law, Aransas Pass, Tex., 1958—; city atty., Ingleside, Tex., 1969—, Gregory, Tex., 1982—; justice of the peace San Patricio County, Aransas Pass, Tex., 1964—. Mem. Aransas Pass C. of C. Democrat. Lodges: Masons, Rotary. General practice, Judicial administration, Military. Home: 623 S 11th St Aransas Pass TX 78336 Office: Box 478 Aransas Pass TX 78336

HASKINS, GEORGE LEE, lawyer, educator; b. Cambridge, Mass., Feb. 13, 1915; s. Charles Homer and Clare (Allen) H.; m. Anstiss Crowninshield Boyden, July 15, 1944 (dec. 1978). Classical diploma, Phillips Exeter Acad., 1931; AB summa cum laude, Harvard U., 1935, JD, 1942; Henry fellow, Merton Coll., Oxford U., 1935-36; MA (hon.), U. Pa., 1971. Bar: Mass. 1943, ICC 1951, Pa. 1952, Maine 1968, U.S. Supreme Ct. 1952, various fed. cts. in 1st and 3d circuits. Jr. fellow Soc. of Fellows, Harvard U., 1936-42, lectr. dept. sociology, 1937-38; Lowell lectr. Boston, 1938; assoc. Herrick, Smith, Donald & Farley, Boston, 1942; with office of spl. asst. to sec. of state 1946; asst. prof. law U. Pa., 1946-48, assoc. prof., 1948-49, prof., 1949—, Algernon Sydney Biddle prof., 1974-85, Algernon Sydney Biddle prof. emeritus, 1985—, mem. faculty arts and scis., 1976—; sole practice Pa., 1986—; vis. prof. law Rutgers Law Sch., Camden, N.J., 1987; ofcl. observer War Dept.; rep. U.S. delegation to UN Conf., San Francisco, 1945; spl. atty. legal dept. Pa. R.R., 1951-54, cons. counsel, 1954-70; apptd. by Pres. Eisenhower to Permanent Com. on Oliver Wendell Holmes Devise, 1956; asst. reporter for Supreme and Superior Cts. Pa., 1970-72; univ. seminar assoc. Columbia, 1971-73, 77—; U.S. Supreme Ct. Hist. Soc. lectr., 1981; permanent mem. Jud. Conf. U.S. Third Circuit; vice chmn. com. on legal history fellowships Am. Bar Found., 1978-83; dir., v.p. Pa. Mut. Fund, N.Y.C., 1961-68; mem. nat. adv. com. U.S. Constn., N.Y. Pub. Library, 1985-87. Author: The Statute of York and the Interest of the Commons, 1935, The Growth of English Representative Government, 1948, (with others) American Law of Property, 1952, A History of the U.S. Supreme Court, vol. 2, part 1: John Marshall Foundations of Power, 1981, (with M.P. Smith) Pennsylvania Fiduciary Guide, 1957, 2d edit., 1962, Law and Authority in Early Massachusetts, 1960, 2d edit., 1977, A History of the Town of Hancock, Maine, 1978; also numerous articles in U.S., fgn. periodicals; contbr. to Ency. Brit.; mem. panel of authors preparing: History of U.S. Supreme Ct. (authorized by Congress), 1958; editor: Death of a Republic (John Dickinson), 1963, Phi Beta Kappa series, 1934-37; adv. bd. editors Speculum, 1949-69; bd. editors William and Mary Quar., 1969-70, Papers of John Marshall, Williamsburg, Va., Justice Bradley papers, Studies in Legal History. Mem. Hancock (Maine) 1976 Bicentennial Commn., 1978, Sesquicentennial History Commn., Internat. Commn. for History of Rep. Instns.; mem. humanities council Sta. WHYY-TV, Phila., Wilmington, Del., 1976—. Served with CAC AUS, 1942-43; from 1st lt. to capt. War Dept. Gen. Staff, 1943-46; from 1st lt. to capt. Gen. Staff Corps, 1945; maj. Res., 1946-54. Decorated Army Commendation medal with oak leaf clusters, various merit citations U.S. Army and sec. of state, 1946; recipient Demobilization award Social Sci. Research Council, 1946; elected Consejero del Instituto Internacional para Unificacion del Derecho Publico, 1956; John Simon Guggenheim fellow, 1957; Am. Bar Found. affiliated scholar, 1985—. Fellow Royal Hist. Soc., Am. Soc. for Legal History (hon.), Medieval Acad. Ireland; mem. ABA, Mass. Bar Assn., Maine Bar Assn., Pa. Bar Assn., Phila. Bar Assn., Assn. Bar City of N.Y., Hancock County Bar Assn., Swedish Colonial Soc., Am. Judicature Soc., Am. Arbitration Assn. (nat. panel arbitrators 1968—), C.H. Haskins Soc. Anglo-Norman Studies (hon.), Société Internationale pour l'Histoire du Droit (council 1970, 75—), Am. Soc. for Legal History (pres. 1970-74, bd. dirs. 1977-80), Am. Antiquarian Soc., Internat. Law Soc., Soc. Colonial Wars, Am. Acad. Polit. Sci., Am. Hist. Assn., Am. Law Inst. (hon. life mem.), Assn. ICC Practitioners, Juristic Soc., Brit. Records Assn., Mediaeval Acad. Am. (council 1958-60), Soc. Comparative Legis., Colonial Soc. Mass., Mass. Hist. Soc. (corr. mem.), Maine Hist. Soc., Va. Hist. Soc., Colonial Soc. Pa. (gov.'s council 1977), Art Alliance Phil Selden Soc. (corr. sec. Pa.), Am. Geneal. Soc., Geneal. Soc. Pa., Inst. Early Am. History and Culture (council, editorial bd.), Société Jean Bodin Pour l'Histoire Comparative des Institutions, Société Internationale pour l'Etude de Philosophie Mediévale (membre titulaire), Academie d'Histoire Européenne (hon. corr.), S.R., Mayflower Descs., Boston Athenaeum, Library Co. Phila., U.S. Ct. Tennis Assn., Am. Soc. Ancient Instruments, Am. Soc. 18th Century Studies, Internat. Soc. St. Thomas Aquinas, Mil. Order Fgn. Wars U.S. (companion), Soc. War 1812, New. Eng. Land Title Assn., Hancock Hist. Soc. (bd. dirs. 1979-80), Century Assn., Order of Coif (award for scholarly writing Pa. chpt. 1982), Phi Beta Kappa. Clubs: Somerset (Boston); Legal, Racquet, Harvard (Phila.); Met. (Washington); Brit. Schs. and Univs., Pilgrims of U.S., Century Assn. (N.Y.C.); Royal Automobile, Athenaeum (London). Legal history, Probate, Public utilities. Home: PO Box 760 Paoli PA 19301 Office: U Pa Law Sch 3400 Chestnut St Philadelphia PA 19104

HASKINS, GUY HALIFAX, JR., lawyer; b. N.Y.C., June 19, 1922; s. Guy Halifax and Augusta Louise (Gerhardt) H.; m. Elizabeth Crosby Runyan, Nov. 20, 1943; children: Karen Elizabeth, Linda Runyan, Wendy Noel. BSCE, Va. Mil. Inst., 1943; JD, Rutgers U., 1949. Bar: N.J. 1950, U.S. Dist. Ct. N.J. 1950, U.S. Supreme Ct. 1966, U.S. Tax Ct. 1970, U.S. Ct. Appeals (3d cir.) 1982, N.Y. 1986. Assoc. Guy H. Haskins, Jr., Bloomfield, N.J., 1950-56, Skeffington, Haskins & Skeffington, Bloomfield, 1956-60, Skeffington, Haskins & Robottom, 1960-66, Haskings, Robottom & Hack, Bloomfield, 1966-78, Haskins, Hack, Piro & O'Day, P.A., West Orange, N.J., 1978-86; mem. Supreme Ct. Ethics Com. Trustee V.M.I. Found., Inc., Presbyn. Homes, Job Haines Home; elder, pres. bd. trustees Presbyn. Ch. Served to 1st lt. U.S. Army, 1943-46. Mem. ABA, Fedn. Ins. and Corp. Counsel, Internat. Assn. Def. Counsel, Am. Judicature Soc., N.J. Bar Assn., Essex County Bar Assn., Va. Mil. Inst. Alumni Assn. (dir.). Republican. Presbyterian. Club: Essex Fells Country (N.J.). Lodges: Rotary (past pres.), Masons (past master). Assoc. editor Rutgers Law Rev. Federal civil litigation, State civil litigation. Office: Haskins Hack Piro O'Day Merklinger & Wallace PA 200 Executive Dr West Orange NJ 07052

HASKINS, PATRICK DEAN, lawyer; b. Miami, Fla., Aug. 21, 1956; s. Jimmy and Lorraine (Murphy) H.; m. Arlene Elizabeth Muller, June 30, 1985; 1 child, Alexander Sean. Student, Doane Coll., 1974-75; BA in History, St. Mary's Coll. Md., 1978; JD, U. Md., 1981. Bar: Md. 1981, U.S. Dist. Ct. Md. 1982, U.S. Bankruptcy Ct. 1982. Law clk. to presiding justice Harford County Cir. Ct., Bel Air, Md., 1981-82; assoc. Law Office Greg Rapisarda, Bel Air, 1983-85; ptnr. Rapisarda, Stevenson & Haskins, P.A., Bel Air, 1985—. St. Mary's scholar, 1978. Mem. ABA, Md. State Bar Assn., Harford County Bar Assn. Republican. Baptist. Avocations: golf, basketball, reading. General practice, Family and matrimonial. Home: 1815 Twin Oak Rd Jarrettsville MD 21084 Office: Rapisarda Stevenson & Haskins PA 38 E Broadway PO Box 543 Bel Air MD 21014

HASKINS, TERRY EDWARD, lawyer, politician; b. Pontiac, Mich., Jan. 31, 1955; s. Charles Edward and Dorothy Mae (Bushfield) H.; m. Gloria Esperanza Arias, June 3, 1978; children: David Edward, Bryan Scott. BS, Bob Jones U., 1976, MA, 1978; JD, U. S.C., 1981. Bar: S.C. 1982. Corp. atty. Liberty Corp., Greenville, S.C., 1981-82; sole practice Greenville, 1982-86; ptnr. Haskins & Patton, Greenville, 1986—. Councilman City of Greenville, 1983-86; mem. S.C. Ho. of Reps., 1986—. Republican. Baptist. Real property, General corporate, Personal injury. Home: 2 Iverson St Greenville SC 29615 Office: 1809 Wade Hampton Blvd Greenville SC 29609

HASKINS, THOMAS MARSTON, lawyer; b. Bryn Mawr, Pa., July 20, 1950; s. Jefferson Porterfield and Alice Marston (Sloan) H.; m. Margo L. Witt, Feb. 3, 1971 (div. Feb. 1986); children: William E., David M., Nicole L. BA in Philosophy, Dickinson Coll., 1972, JD cum laude, 1975. Bar: Va. 1975, U.S. Dist. Ct. (ea. dist.) Va. 1975, U.S. Ct. Appeals (4th cir.) 1975. Assoc. Kellam, Pickrell & Lawler, Norfolk, Va., 1975-79, Breeden, Mac Millan & Green, Norfolk, 1983-87; sole practice Virginia Beach, Va., 1979-83; v.p., gen. counsel 1st Fed. Savs. and Loan Assn. of Colorado Springs, Colo., 1987—. Mem. ABA, Virginia Beach Bar Assn., Norfolk-Portsmouth Bar Assn., Aircraft Owners and Pilots Assn. (legis. council), Toastmasters (pres. 1981), Virginia Beach Jaycees (v.p. 1979-81). Republican. Methodist. Avocations: flying, fishing, jogging. Bankruptcy, Contracts commercial, Federal civil litigation. Office: 1st Fed Savs and Loan Assn 5225 N Academy Blvd Colorado Springs CO 80907

HASKINS, WALTER DEWEY, lawyer; b. Kansas City, Kans., Apr. 1, 1956; s. Walter Dewey and Margaret Bell (Follett) H. BA magna cum laude, Drury Coll., 1977; JD, U. Kans., 1980. Bar: Okla. 1980, U.S. Dist. Ct. (no., ea. and we. dists.) Okla. 1980, U.S. Ct. Appeals (10th cir.) 1981. Ptnr. Best, Sharp, Thomas & Glass, Inc., Tulsa, 1980—. Mem. Def. Research Inst., Okla. Assn. Def. Counsel, Okla. Bar Assn., Tulsa County Bar Assn. Republican. Avocations: aviation, golf. Personal injury, Insurance, Federal civil litigation. Home: 1116 E 21st Pl Tulsa OK 74114 Office: Best Sharp et al 525 S Main 1500 Park Centre Bldg Tulsa OK 74103

HASL, HANNELORE VERA MARGARETE, lawyer; b. Hersbruck, Bavaria, Fed. Republic Germany, June 13, 1955; came to U.S., 1956; d. Siegfried C. and Gunda (Aures) H. AB, Duke U., 1976; MBA, Cornell U., 1978; JD, Rutgers U., 1981. Bar: N.J. 1982, D.C. 1982, U.S. Dist. Ct. N.J 1982, U.S. Dist. Ct. D.C. 1982, U.S. Ct. Appeals (5th cir.) 1982, U.S. Ct. Internat. Trade 1984, U.S. Ct. Appeals (fed. cir.) 1984. Assoc. Duncan, Allen & Mitchell, Washington, 1981-83; atty., advisor U.S. Internat. Trade Commn., Washington, 1983-84; v.p., gen. counsel IML Tech. Inc., North Branch, N.J., 1984—. Editor-in-chief JD/MBA Quarterly, 1983. Mem. ABA, N.J. Bar Assn., D.C. Bar Assn., Soc. Plastics Engrs., Nat. Assn. JD/MBA Profls. (incorporating dir. 1983, trustee 1984—). General corporate, Private international, Public international. Office: IML Tech Inc 200-A Meister Ave North Branch NJ 08876-1301

HASLINGER, JOHN EDWARD, lawyer; b. Buffalo, Apr. 5, 1949; s. Edward Joseph and Rose Dolores (Hoak) H.; m. Catherine Lee Johnston, June 29, 1974; children: Jarod Thomas, Joshua Adam. BA, Canisius Coll., 1971; JD, SUNY, Buffalo, 1974. Bar: N.Y. 1975, U.S. Dist. Ct. (we dist.) N.Y. 1975. Ptnr. Hellings, Morey, Kresse, Rickers & Whissel, Buffalo, 1975—. Mem. Erie County Bar Assn. (recording sec. practice and procedure surrogate ct. com. 1975-86). Roman Catholic. Avocations: raquetball, fishing. Probate, Real property, General practice. Office: Hellings Morey et al 1320 Liberty Bldg 420 Main St Buffalo NY 14202

HASS, WILLIAM RALPH, lawyer; b. Springfield, Mo., Jan. 28, 1936; s. Ralph Levaga and Angie Veleta (Morse) H.; m. Helen Jeanne Best, Jan. 10, 1959; children—Mary, Melissa, William T. B.S., Southwest Mo. State U., 1958, J.D., U. Ark., 1962. Bar: Ark. 1962, Mo. 1969, U.S. Supreme Ct. 1967. Ptnr., Niblock and Hass, Fayetteville, Ark., 1964-66; asst. atty. gen., Ark., 1966-68; sole practice, Thayer, Mo., 1969—; asst. pros. atty. Washington County, (Ark.), 1965-66; city atty. City of Mammoth Spring Ark., 1970-86; atty. City of Thayer, Mo., 1970—. Served with AUS, 1962-64. Mem. Mo.

Bar Assn., Ark. Bar Assn. Club: Thayer-Mammoth Spring Rotary (pres. 1982). Real property, Probate, General corporate. Home: 320 N 10th St Thayer MO 65791 Office: 211 Chestnut St Thayer MO 65791

HASSAN, ALLEN C., lawyer, physician, surgeon, educator; b. Red Oak, Iowa, Mar. 29, 1936; s. Oman Diab Hassan and Dorothea Tuttle. DVM, Iowa State U., 1962; MD, U. Iowa, 1966; JD, Lincoln U., 1978. Bar: Calif. 1981, U.S. Dist. Ct. (ea. dist.) Calif. 1981, U.S. Supreme Ct. 1981; diplomate Am. Bd. Psychiatry and Neurology. Intern Mt. Zion Hosp., San Francisco, 1966-67; residency Mendolino State Hosp. Psychiatry, 1967-70; sole practice Sacramento, Calif., 1981—; clin. instr. family practice, U. Calif., Davis, 1976-86. Served as cpl. USMC, 1954-57. Fellow Coll. of Legal Medicine; mem. AMA, Am. Acad. Family Physicians (program chmn. 1973-76, sec., treas. 1974, 75, pres. 1975-76), Calif. Bar Assn., Calif. Trial Lawyer Assn., Calif. Med. Assn. Avocations: reading, jogging, golf, flying, scuba diving. Personal injury, Workers' compensation, Professional negligence. Home: 401 Bret Harte Sacramento CA 95822 Office: 2933 El Camino Sacramento CA 95821

HASSELL, MORRIS WILLIAM, judge; b. Jacksonville, Tex., Aug. 9, 1916; s. Alonzo Seldon and Cora Lee (Rainey) H.; m. Mauriete Watson, Sept. 3, 1944; children—Morris William, Charles Robert. A.A., Lon Morris Coll., 1936; J.D., U. Tex., Austin, 1942. Bar: Tex. 1941, U.S. Dist. Ct. 1948, U.S. Supreme Ct. 1973. County atty. Cherokee County, Tex., 1943-47; mem. Norman Hassell Spiers & Thrall of Rusk and Jacksonville, Tex., 1948-78; judge 2d Jud. Dist. Tex., 1978—; chmn. bd. Swift Oil Co., 1964-77, H & I Oil Co., 1968-77; dir. First State Bank, Rusk, Tex., 1959-78. Mayor, City of Rusk, Tex., 1959-63, 73-78; trustee Rusk Ind. Sch. Dist., 1967-73; trustee, chmn. exec. com. Lou Morris Coll., Jacksonville; chmn. bd. trustees Tex. conf. United Methodist Ch.; vice-chmn. bd. trustees Lakeview Meth. Assembly; trustee Tex. ann. conf. United Meth. Found. Mem. State Bar Tex., ABA; fellow Tex. Bar Found., Am. Bar Found. Democrat. Clubs: Kiwanis (lt. gov. 1964), Masons, Odd Fellow. Judicial administration. Home: 1300 Copeland St Rusk TX 75785 Office: 2d Jud Dist Ct PO Box 196 Rusk TX 75785

HASSELQUIST, MAYNARD BURTON, lawyer; b. Amador, Minn., July 1, 1919; s. Harry and Anna F. (Froberg) H.; m. Lorraine Swenson, Nov. 20, 1948; children—Mark D., Peter L. B.S.L., U. Minn., 1941; J.D.L., U. Minn., 1947. Bar: Minn. 1948. Asst. mgr. taxation Gen. Mills Inc., Mpls., 1947-53; chmn. internat. dept. Dorsey & Whitney, Mpls., 1953-81, sr. ptnr.; dir. Graco Inc., Mpls., McLaughlin Gormley King Co., Mpls., ADC Telecommunications, Inc., Mpls., Wesco Resources, Billings, Mont., Soprea S.A., Paris. Gen. counsel, bd. dirs. Swedish Council Am.; past chmn. Japan-Am. Soc. Minn.; bd. dirs., counsel James Ford Bell Library; chmn. Fairview Hosps. Internat., Ltd., Cayman Islands. Served with USN, 1941-46. Mem. ABA, Minn. Bar Assn., Internat. Bar Assn., Am. Soc. Internat. Law. Republican. Lutheran. Club: Mpls. Private international, General corporate, Corporate taxation. Office: Dorsey & Whitney 2200 First Bank Place East Minneapolis MN 55402

HASSOLD, ROBERT WILKINSON, JR., lawyer; b. Phila., Dec. 16, 1953; s. Robert Wilkinson Sr. and Ann Mitchell (Crane) H.; m. Kimbrough Anne Harper, June 10, 1978; children: Anne Crane, Robert Wilkinson III. BA, U. N.C., 1976; JD, U. S.C., 1979. Bar: S.C. 1979. Ptnr. Haynsworth, Marion, McKay & Guerard, Greenville, S.C., 1979—. Bd. dirs. Speech, Hearing and Learning Ctr., Greenville, 1985—, sec., 1985-86. Mem. ABA (forum com. on constrn. industry), S.C. Bar Assn., Greenville County Bar Assn., Christ Ch. Epis. Sch. Alumni Assn. (v.p. 1981-82, pres. 1982-83). Republican. Avocations: tennis, squash, running, soccer. Construction. Office: Haynsworth Marion McKay & Guerard 75 Beattie Pl Two Shelter Ctr 11th Floor Greenville SC 29602

HASSON, JAMES KEITH, JR., lawyer, law educator; b. Knoxville, Tenn., Mar. 3, 1946; s. James Keith and Elaine (Biggers) H.; m. Jayne Young, July 27, 1968; 1 son, Keith Samuel. B.A., Duke U., 1967, J.D., 1970. Bar: Ga. 1971, D.C. 1971. Assoc. Sutherland, Asbill & Brennan, Atlanta, 1970-76, ptnr., 1976—; prof. law Emory U., Atlanta, 1976—; dir. House-Hasson Hardware Co., Knoxville, 1971—. Contbr. articles to profl. jours. Chmn. Met. Atlanta Crime Commn., 1986-87, also trustee; mem. Atlanta Civilian Review Bd.; mem. Leadership Atlanta, 1981-82. Served to 1st lt. U.S. Army, 1970-71. Mem. ABA (com. chmn. 1983-85), Atlanta Bar Assn. (counsel 1977-80, Pres's. Disting. Service award 1980). Presbyterian. Club: Lawyers. Corporate taxation, Estate planning, Health. Home: 3185 Chatham Rd NW Atlanta GA 30305 Office: Sutherland Asbill & Brennan 3100 First Atlanta Tower Atlanta GA 30383

HASSON, KIRKE MICHAEL, lawyer; b. East St. Louis, Ill., Oct. 25, 1949; s. David S. and Audrey (Leber) H.; m. Nancy Lyons, Apr. 25, 1981. B.A., Yale U., 1971; J.D., Harvard U., 1974. Bar: Calif. 1974, U.S. Dist. Ct. (no. dist.) Calif. 1974. Assoc., Pillsbury, Madison & Sutro, San Francisco, 1974-81, ptnr., 1982—; mem. Am. Arbitration Commn., Internat. Found. Employee Benefit Plans. Bd. dirs., chmn. Bread and Roses, Mill Valley, Calif., 1983-85. Federal civil litigation, State civil litigation, Pension, profit-sharing, and employee benefits. Office: Pillsbury Madison & Sutro 235 Montgomery St PO Box 7880 San Francisco CA 94120

HASTERT, DIANE DESKINS, lawyer; b. Tacoma, May 11, 1944; d. John William and M. Helene (Willoughby) Deskins; m. Mark Hallet Hastert, Sept. 24, 1965; children: Shanna Kathleen, Hallet Anne. BA, U. Wash., 1964; JD, U. Hawaii, 1978. Bar: Hawaii 1978, U.S. Dist. Ct. Hawaii 1978, U.S. Ct. Appeals (9th cir.) 1979. Dir. Damon, Key, Char & Bocken, Honolulu, 1978—. Mem. transp. com. Oahu Devel. Conf., Honolulu, 1983-87; appointee Traffic Safety Commn., Honolulu, 1985—; bd. dirs. Goodwill Industries, Honolulu, 1980—; Hawaii del. 9th cir. Jud. Conf., Honolulu, 1986—. Mem. ABA, Hawaii Bar Assn. (sec., bd. dirs. 1986—), Assn. Trial Lawyers Am. Club: Honolulu. Federal civil litigation, State civil litigation, Personal injury. Office: Damon Key Char & Bocken 1001 Bishop St Pauahi Tower Suite 1600 Honolulu HI 93618

HASTINGS, ALCEE LAMAR, judge; b. Altomonte Springs, Fla., Sept. 5, 1936; s. Julius C. and Mildred L. H.; 1 child. B.A., Fisk U., 1958; postgrad., Howard U. Sch. Law, 1958-60; J.D., Fla. A&M U., 1963. Bar: Fla. 1963. Mem. firm Allen and Hastings, Ft. Lauderdale, 1963-66; sole practice Ft. Lauderdale, 1966-77; judge Circuit Ct. Broward County, Fla., 1977-79; judge U.S. Dist. Ct. So. Dist. Fla. 1979—; adj. prof. criminal justice dept. Nova U.; lectr. So. Regional Council on Black Am. Affairs; lectr., cons. Internat. Juvenile Officers Assn., Peace Corps Vols. in Avon Park, Fla., 1966; legal counsel Community Action Migrant Program, Broward County Classroom Tchrs.; mem. Gov.'s Conf. on Criminal Justice, State of Fla.; lectr., cons. to elem. and secondary public and pvt. schs., chs., synagogues, social orgns., civic orgns., colls. and univs. in U.S.; co-propr. Tri-City News. Host TV program: Pride, Sta. WPLG; columnist: West Side Gazette. Atty. various civic assns., Broward County and State of Fla.; mem. Bi-Racial Adv. Commn., Broward County Personnel Adv. Commn.; sec. Fla. Council on Aging; chmn. Broward Youth Services Task Force; mem. State of Fla. Edn. Commn., Task Force on Crime, Democratic Exec. Com; candidate for Fla. Ho. of Reps., Fla. Senate, U.S. Senate, Fla. Public Service Commn.; bd. dirs. Urban League of Broward County, Child Advocacy, Inc., The Starting Place, Broward County Sickle Cell Anemia Found., Fla. Voters League, Broward County Council on Human Relations; trustee Mt. Hermon A.M.E. Ch., Ft. Lauderdale, Broward Community Coll., Bethune Cookman Coll. Recipient numerous awards and honors including; Humanitarian award Broward County Young Democarts, 1978; Citizen of Year award Zeta Phi Beta, 1978; Sam Delevoe Human Rights award Community Relations Bd. of Broward County, 1978; Glades Festival of Afro Arts award Zeta Phi Beta, 1981; named Man of Year, Com. Italian Am. Affairs, 1979-80. Mem. ABA (standing com. profl. discipline), Nat. Bar Assn. (Chmn.'s award 1981), Am. Trial Lawyers Assn., Fla. Bar Assn., U.S. Dist. Judges Council., A.M.E. Ch. Clubs: Elks, KP. Judge Alcee Hastings Day proclaimed for City of Daytona Beach in his honor on Dec. 14, 1980. Jurisprudence. Office: US Dist Ct South Fed Courthouse Sq 301 N Miami Ave 5th Floor Miami FL 33128-7788 *

HASTINGS, EDWIN HAMILTON, lawyer; b. Yonkers, N.Y., Jan. 2, 1917; s. Edwin H. Jr. and Emily (Clark) H.; m. Mabel Hurst, July 12, 1941 (div. June 1957); children: Judy H. Hastings Johnson, Jill S. Hastings Appleby; m. Suzanne Saul, July 1, 1957; 1 child, Andrew C. AB, Amherst Coll., 1938; LLB, Columbia U., 1941. Bar: N.Y. 1941, R.I. 1946, U.S. Dist. Ct. R.I. 1947, U.S. Ct. Appeals (1st cir.) 1950, Mass. 1951. Assoc. Larkin, Rathbone & Perry, N.Y.C., 1941-42, Tillinghast, Collins & Tanner, Providence, 1946-53; ptnr. Tillinghast, Collins & Graham, Providence, 1953—; bar examiner State of R.I., 1968-74, chmn. of bd., 1972-74; chmn. com. on future of criminal law R.I. Supreme Ct., 1973-75; bar examiner U.S. Dist. Ct. R.I., 1981-84. Served to 1st lt. U.S. Army, 1942-46, 51-52, Korea. Mem. ABA, R.I. Bar Assn., Lawyers Alliance Nuclear Arms Control. Baptist. Avocation: bird watching. Estate planning, Probate, Federal civil litigation. Home: 210 Payton Ave Warwick RI 02889 Office: Tillinghast Collins & Graham 1 Old Stone Sq Providence RI 02903

HASTINGS, LAWRENCE VAETH, physician, lawyer; b. Flushing, N.Y., Nov. 23, 1919; s. Henry Luftman and Lillian (Vaeth) H.; m. Doris Lorraine Erickson, Dec. 11, 1971; children: Wilhelmina Streeton and Laura Thynne (twins). Student, Columbia U., 1939-40, student Law Sch., 1949-50; student, U. Mich. Engring. Sch., 1942-43, Washington U., 1943-44, U. Vt., 1943; M.D., Johns Hopkins U., 1948; J.D., U. Miami, 1953. Bar: Fla. 1954, U.S. Supreme Ct. 1960, D.C. 1976; cert. Am. Bd. Legal Medicine. Intern, U.S. Marine Hosp., S.I., N.Y., 1948-49; asst. surgeon, sr. asst. surgeon USPHS, 1949-52; asst. resident surgery Bellevue Hosp. Med. Ctr., 1951; med. legal cons., trial atty. Miami, Fla., 1953—; sr. ptnr. Hastings & Goldman; asst. prof. medicine U. Miami, 1964—, lectr. law, 1966; adj. prof. St. Thomas of Villanova Law Sch., Biscayne Coll., Miami, Fla. Contbr. articles to profl. publs. Bd. dirs. Miami Heart Inst.; trustee Barry Coll., Miami, 1976—, Fla. Internat. U., 1979—. Served with AUS, 1943-46. Fellow Acad. Fla. Trial Lawyers, Am. Coll. Legal Medicine, Law-Sci. Acad. Found. Am.; mem. Am. Acad. Forensic Scis., Assn. Trial Lawyers Am., Fla. Bar (vice chmn. med. legal com. 1957, vice chmn. trial tactics com. 1963-65, chmn. steering com. trial tactics and basic anatomy seminars), Pitts. Inst. Legal Medicine, AMA, Fla., Dade County med. assns., Johns Hopkins Med. and Surg. Assn., Pithotomy Club, Assn. Mil. Surgeons, U. Miami Law Alumni Assn. (pres. 1967), ABA, Fla., Dade County bar assns., Acad. Psychosomatic Medicine, Com. of 100 Miami Beach, Alpha Delta Phi, Phi Eta Sigma, Phi Alpha Delta. Roman Catholic. Clubs: Two Hundred, Bankers, Jockey, Palm Bay, Miami; Bal Harbour (Fla.); LaGorce Country, Bath, Surf (bd. govs. 1976—, chmn. bd. 1978-82, pres. 1978-80), Com. 100, Indian Creek Country, Miami Beach, River of Jacksonville; N.Y. Athletic, Metropolitan, Princeton (N.Y.C.). Admiralty, Federal civil litigation, State civil litigation. Home: 229 Bal Cross Dr Bal Harbour FL 33154 Office: 530 City National Bank Bldg 300 71st St Miami Beach FL 33141

HASTINGS, MICHAEL LYNN, lawyer; b. Huntington Park, Calif., Apr. 29, 1944; s. James William and Jane Ellen (Shields) H.; m. Shannon Regina Quill, Oct. 18, 1969; children—Damon, Ryan. Student Calif. State Coll., 1963; B.S., Fla. State U., 1966; J.D., Stetson U., 1969. Bar: Fla. 1969, D.C. 1971, U.S. Dist Ct. (mid. and no. dists.) Fla., U.S. Ct. Appeals (5th and 11th cirs.) 1973, U.S. Supreme Ct. 1976. Law clk. to justice Supreme Ct. Fla., 1971-73; ptnr. Battaglia, Ross, Hastings, Dicus & Andrews, St. Petersburg, Fla., 1973—. Mem. Com. of 100, Contractors and Builders Assn., 1982—. Served to capt. U.S. Army, 1969-71. Decorated Bronze Star; recipient Vietnamese award for Service, 1971—; Pinellas Park C. of C. Cert. of Appreciation, 1979. Mem. St. Petersburg C. of C., D.C. Bar, St. Petersburg Bar Assn., ABA, Fla. Bar, Pinellas County Trial Lawyers Assn. Democrat. Roman Catholic. Clubs: Bardmoor Country, Seminole Lake Country. State civil litigation, Family and matrimonial, Environment. Address: PO Box 41100 980 Tyrone Blvd Saint Petersburg FL 33743

HASTINGS, ROBERT WILLIAM, II, lawyer; b. Afton, Wyo., Aug. 8, 1946; s. Robert William and Norma (Call) H.; m. Judy Lynn Throssell, Aug. 1, 1973; children: Robert III, Whitney, Christian, Courtney. BA with honors, U. Wyo., 1968; JD, U. Mich., 1977. Bar: Hawaii 1977, U.S. Dist. Ct. Hawaii 1977. Assoc. Torkildson, Katz, Jossem, Fonseca & Moore, Honolulu, 1977-81, ptnr., 1981-83; ptnr. Torkildson, Katz, Jossem, Fonseca & Moore, Kailua-Kona, Hawaii, 1983—. Vice chmn. Rep. Senatorial Dist. North Hawaii, 1985-86; mem. West Hawaii com., Kailua-Kona, 1984—; trustee North Hawaii Hospice, Kamuela, 1985—. Served to lt. USNR, 1968-74. Mem. ABA (mem. sects. taxation, probate, property and trust law), Hawaii State Bar Assn., Phi Beta Kappa. Mormon. Lodge: Rotary (vocat. service 1985—). Avocations: hiking, skiing, snorkeling. Probate, Estate taxation, Estate planning. Home: PO Box 628 Kamuela HI 96743 Office: Torkildson Katz Jossem Fonseca et al 75-5751 Kuakini Hwy 105 Kailua-Kona HI 96740

HASTINGS, WILLIAM CHARLES, state supreme ct. judge; b. Newman Grove, Nebr., Jan. 31, 1921; s. William C. and Margaret (Hansen) H.; m. Julie Ann Simonson, Dec. 29, 1946; children—Pamela, Charles, Steven. B.Sc., U. Nebr., 1942, J.D., 1948. Bar: Nebr. bar 1948. With FBI, 1942-43; mem. firm Chambers, Holland, Dudgeon & Hastings, Lincoln, 1948-65; judge 3d jud. dist. Nebr., Lincoln, 1965-79, Supreme Ct. Nebr., Lincoln, 1979—. Pres. Child Guidance Center, Lincoln, 1962, 63; v.p. Lincoln Community Council, 1968, 69; vice chmn. Antelope Valley council Boy Scouts Am., 1968, 69; pres. 1st Presbyn. Ch. Found., 1968—. Served with AUS, 1943-46. Mem. Am. Bar Assn., Nebr. Bar Assn., Lincoln Bar Assn., Nebr. Dist. Judges Assn., Phi Delta Phi. Republican. Presbyterian (deacon, elder, trustee). Club: East Hills Country (pres. 1959-60). Jurisprudence. Home: 1544 S 58th St Lincoln NE 68506 Office: Nebr Supreme Ct State House Lincoln NE 68509

HASTY, FREDERICK EMERSON, III, laywer; b. Coral Gables, Fla., Oct. 21, 1950; s. Frederick and Rose (Irwin) H.; m. Deborah Thornton, Oct. 20, 1979; 1 son, Frederick Emerson, IV. B.A., U. Fla., 1973; J.D., Mercer U., 1976. Bar: Fla., Ga. Legal advisor City Macon, Ga., 1976-79; asst. state atty. 11th Jud. Circuit, Miami, Fla., 1979; assoc. Thornton & Herndon, Miami, 1979-83; ptnr. Schwartz & Hasty, Miami, 1983-85, Wicker, Smith Blomquist, Tutan, O'Hara, McCay, Graham & Lane, 1985—. Bd. dirs. Admirals of Fleet Fla., Miami, 1983. Democrat. Roman Catholic. State civil litigation, Health, Personal injury. Home: 601 Gondoliere Coral Gables FL 33134 Office: Wicker Smith 2900 SW 28th Terr 5th Floor Grove Plaza Miami FL 33133

HASTY, GERALD RICHARD, political science educator, retired army officer; b. Pekin, Ill., Apr. 12, 1926; s. Leslie Parke and Bernice Arthene (Brown) H.; B.S., Bradley U., 1952; M.B.A., 1954; postgrad. Harvard, 1961; M.A., Am. U., 1962; Ph.D., Northwestern U., 1963; LL.B., Blackstone Sch. Law, 1968; postgrad. summers U. Toledo, 1958, U. Maine, 1963, State U. N.Y. at Buffalo, 1963, Armed Forces Staff Coll., 1968, Air War Coll., 1965, Harvard Law Sch., 1976; D.D. (hon.), Am. Fellowship Ch., 1977; m. Betty Anne Osmundson, June 23, 1951; children—Grant Rutledge, Mark Osmund, Deborah Anne. Commd. 2d lt. U.S. Army, 1954, advanced through grades to lt. col., 1966; chief Q.M. Supply div. 7th Logistical Command, Korea, 1961-62; comdg. officer 34th Supply and Service Bn., Vietnam, 1966, also dir. adminstrn. 58th Field Depot; exec. asst. joint logistics rev. bd. Office Sec. Def., Washington, 1969-70; comdg. officer Charleston (S.C.) Army Depot, 1970-72; joint logistics plans officer on staff comdr.-in-chief UN Command, 1972-73; logistics staff officer Joint and Strategic Forces Directorate, Army Concepts Analysis Agy., Bethesda, Md., 1973-74, ret.; asst. prof. pub. adminstrn. George Washington U., Washington, 1964-65, 67, assoc. prof., 1968-69, 73; vis. prof. polit. sci. Bapt. Coll., Charleston, 1970-72, now prof.; tchr., lectr., various colls., U.S. Korea, Vietnam; vis. prof. Central Mich. U., 1974—. Counselor, Boy Scouts Am., 1968—; mem. citizen's adv. and action council to gov. Coastal Carolina Community Prerelease Center, S.C. Dept. Corrections; bd. dirs. Charleston Safety Council; apptd. spl. envoy by gov. for Commonwealth of Pa., 1970; del. S.C. Republican Conv., 1978, 80, 82, 84, 86; pres. 20th Rep. Precinct, S.C., 1978-86. Served AUS, 1944-50. Decorated Legion of Merit with oak leaf cluster, Purple Heart with oak leaf cluster; recipient Presdl. Achievement award Pres. Ronald Reagan, 1982; Nat. Endowment for Humanities fellow U. Ga., summer 1978; Freedoms Found. at Valley Forge fellow, summers 1984-86. Mem. Charleston Trident C. of C., La. Societe Francaise deBienfaisance de Charleston, Navy League, Mil. Order Purple Heart, Fed. Exec. Assn. (com. on govt.-wide policy areas), Armed Forces Mgmt. Assn., S.C. Law Enforcement Officers Assn., Nat. Def. Transp. Assn., Am. Bar Assn., S.C. Polit. Sci. Assn. (exec. council, pres.), Mensa, Pi Sigma Alpha, Tau Kappa Epsilon, Pi Gamma Mu. Lutheran. Mason (32 deg., Shriner), Kiwanian. Address: Sandhurst-on-the-Ashley 1282 Winchester Dr Charleston SC 29407 Office: Baptist Coll Wingo Hall Suite F PO Box 10087 Charleston SC 29411

HATCH, DENISON HURLBUT, JR., lawyer; b. Greenwich, Conn., Sept. 7, 1949; s. Denison Hurlbut and Louise (Bingham) H.; m. Wendy Ann Swanson, Sept. 4, 1971;children: Denison H. III, Erica Swanson. AB, Cornell U., 1971; JD, Northwestern U., 1980. Bar: Del. 1980, U.S. Dist. Ct. Del. 1980, U.S. Ct. Appeals (3rd cir.) 1983, U.S. Ct. Claims 1984, U.S. Tax Ct. 1984, U.S. Supreme Ct. 1983. Atty. Morris, Nichols, Arsht & Tunnell, Wilmington, Del., 1980—. Mem. ABA (taxation sect.), Del. Bar Assn. (asst. to pres. 1983-84), Richard Rodney Inn of Ct., Wilmington, 1985—. Republican. Corporate taxation, Contracts commercial, Pension, profit-sharing, and employee benefits. Home: 2100 Kentmore Pkwy Wilmington DE 19806 Office: Morris Nichols Arsht & Tunnell 12th and Market Sts PO Box 1347 Wilmington DE 19899

HATCH, SUMNER JONES, lawyer; b. Salt Lake City, July 14, 1920; s. Sumner and Heloise (Jones) H.; m. Shirley Bunnell, Dec. 26, 1950; children—Julia Lee, Michael B. J.D., U. Utah, 1948. Bar: Utah 1949, U.S. Ct. Appeals (10th cir.) 1949. Mem. firm Banks & Hatch, Salt Lake City, 1949-50, McCarty & Hatch, Salt Lake City, 1955-63, Hatch McRae & Richardson, Salt Lake City, 1963-76; ptnr. Hatch & McCaughey, Salt Lake City, 1976—. Served with field arty. Signal Corps, U.S. Army 1942-46, to capt., 1950-52. Mem. Am. Bd. Trial Advocates, Utah Bar Assn., Salt Lake County Bar Assn., Phi Alpha Delta. Club: Ambassador. Criminal, Personal injury, Probate. Office: 72 East 400 South Suite 330 Salt Lake City UT 84111

HATCHER, JOHN LESLIE, lawyer, former justice; b. Tohula, Miss., July 1, 1930; s. John Leonard and Virginia R. (Moore) H.; m. Wendy Dorothy Burrage, May 23, 1954; (div.) children—John L., Wendy H. Duke, Glynis H., William L. B.B.A., U. Miss., 1952, J.D., 1957. Bar: Miss. 1957, U.S. Dist. Ct. (no. and so. dists.) Miss. 1957. Sole practice, Cleveland, Miss., 1957—; county ct. judge Bolivar County (Miss.) Cleveland, 1975-76, 77-83; justice 11th Cir. Ct. Dist. Miss., 1969; spl. asst. atty. gen. Milk Commn., and commr. Agr. and Commerce, Miss., 1960-70. Former pres. Bolivar County Sch. Dist. 4, sch. bd., 1968-78; bd. dirs. Miss. Sch. Bd. Assn., 1974-78; former deacon 1st Presbyn. Ch., Cleveland; mem. Miss. Econ. Council, County Farm Bur. Served to lt. USN, 1952-55. Recipient Outstanding Service award Bolivar County (Miss.) County Sch. Dist 4, 1968-78. Mem. Miss. Trial Lawyers Assn., Miss. State Bar Assn., Bolivar County Bar Assn. (pres. 1965-66, 84-85), C. of C., Miss. Delta Council. Clubs: Cleveland (Miss.) Country, Masons. Administrative and regulatory, State civil litigation, Personal injury. Office: Box 1495 Cleveland MS 38732

HATCHETT, JOSEPH WOODROW, judge; b. Clearwater, Fla., Sept. 17, 1932; s. John Arthur and Lula Gertrude (Thomas) H.; m. Betty Lue Davis, Aug. 20, 1956; children—Cheryl Nadine, Brenda Audrey. A.B., Fla. A. and M. U., 1954; J.D., Howard U., 1959; J.D. certificate mil. judge course, U.S. Naval Justice Sch., Newport, R.I., 1973. Bar: Fla. bar 1959. Practice in Daytona Beach, 1959-66; asst. U.S. atty. Dept. Justice, Jacksonville, Fla., 1966-70; U.S. magistrate U.S. Cts., Jacksonville, 1971-75; justice Supreme Ct. Fla., Tallahassee, 1975-79; judge U.S. Ct. of Appeals, Fifth Circuit, 1979—; Cooperating atty. N.A.A.C.P. Legal Def. Fund, 1960-66; gen. counsel Masons of Fla., 1963-66; cons., mem. staff dept. urban renewal, Daytona Beach, 1963-66, spl. asst. to city atty., 1964; Mem. com. selection for Jacksonville Naval Res. Officer Tng. Corps, 1971. Contbr. articles to profl. jours. Mem. John T. Stocking Meml. Trust, med. sch. scholarships, 1961-66; Co-chmn. United Negro Coll. Fund of Volusia County, Fla., 1962; bd. dirs. Jacksonville Opportunities Industrialization Center, 1972-75. Served to 1st lt. AUS, 1954-56, Germany. Recipient Mary McCloud Bethune medallion for community service Bethune-Cookman Coll., 1965, medallion for human relations, 1975. Mem. Am., Nat., Fla., Jacksonville, D. W. Perkins, Fed. bar assns., Am. Judicature Soc., Nat. Council Fed. Magistrates, V.F.W., Omega Psi Phi. Baptist (trustee). Club: Fla-Jax (Jacksonville) (Man of Year 1974). Jurisprudence. Home: PO Box 981 Tallahassee FL 32302 Office: US Court of Appeals First Fla Bank Bldg Suite 810 PO Box 10429 Tallahassee FL 32302

HATFIELD, HARRY MAXWELL, lawyer; b. Charleston, W.Va., July 24, 1947; s. Morris Maxwell and Dorothy Anne (Hill) H.; m. Marcia Kaye Ellis, Aug. 5, 1972; children: Matthew, Amanda, William. BS, W.Va. U., 1969, MBA, 1970, JD, 1973. Bar: W.Va. 1973, U.S. Dist. Ct. (so. dist.) W.Va. 1973. Sole practice Madison, W.Va., 1973-86; ptnr. Hatfield & Bentley, Madison, 1986—; bd. dirs. Boone Nat. Bank, Madison. Active with Little League, Madison; chmn. bd. deacons Madison Bapt. Ch., 1985; trustee Coal River Recreation Found., Madison, 1986. Mem. ABA, W.Va. Bar Assn., W.Va. Trial Lawyers Assn., Boone County Bar Assn. (past pres.). Democrat. Lodges: Rotary, Masons (32 degree). Personal injury. Home: PO Box 598 (Hatfield Farm) Madison WV 25130 Office: 55 Ave B PO Box 598 Madison WV 25130

HATFIELD, PAUL GERHART, lawyer, judge; b. Great Falls, Mont., Apr. 29, 1928; s. Trueman LeRoy and Grace Lenore (Gerhart) H.; m. Dorothy Ann Allen, Feb. 1, 1958; children—Kathleen Helen, Susan Ann, Paul Allen. Student, Coll. of Great Falls, 1947-50; LL.B., U. Mont., 1955. Bar: Mont. bar 1955. Asso. firm Hoffman & Cure, Gt. Falls, Mont., 1955-56, Jardine, Stephenson, Blewett & Weaver, Gt. Falls, 1956-58, Hatfield & Hatfield, Gt. Falls, 1959-60; chief dep. county atty. Cascade County, Mont., 1959-60; dist. ct. judge 8th Jud. Dist., Mont., 1961-76; chief justice Supreme Ct. Mont., Helena, 1977-78; U.S. Senator from Mont., 1978-79; U.S. dist. judge for Dist. of Mont., Gt. Falls, 1979—; Vice chmn. Pres.'s Council Coll. of Great Falls. Author: standards for criminal justice, Mont. cts. Served with U.S. Army, 1951-53. Korea. Mem. Am., Mont. bar assns., Am. Judicature Soc. Roman Catholic. Jurisprudence. Office: US Dist Ct PO Box 1529 Great Falls MT 59403

HATHAWAY, GARY RAY, lawyer; b. Liberal, Kans., July 5, 1942; s. Addison E. and Helen M. (Nix) H.; m. Sonja J. Brewer, Aug. 6, 1977. BA, Southwestern Coll., Winfield, Kans., 1964; JD, Washburn U., 1969. Bar: Kans. 1969, U.S. Dist. Ct. Kans. 1969, U.S. Supreme Ct. 1978, U.S. Ct. Appeals (10th cir.) 1979. County atty. Grant County, Ulysses, Kans., 1971-72, 80-84; ptnr. Hathaway and Kimball, Ulysses, 1972—; city atty. City of Ulysses, 1972-76. Pres. Sta. KANZ Pub. Radio, Garden City, Kans.; mem. bd. pension Meth. Ch., Wichita, Kans. Mem. Am. Legion, Phi Alpha Delta. Republican. Lodges: Elks, Kiwanis. Oil and gas leasing, State civil litigation, Federal civil litigation. Home: 218 N Wilson St Ulysses KS 67880 Office: Hathaway and Kimball 123 N Glenn St Ulysses KS 67880-0527

HATHAWAY, GERALD THOMAS, lawyer; b. Frankfurt, Fed. Republic of Germany, Aug. 5, 1954; came to U.S., 1955; s. Robert Ernest Hathaway and Jacqueline Anne (Hughes) Gouin; m. Kathleen Ann McCauley, Dec. 27, 1980; children: Michael, Anne. BA, LaSalle U., 1976; JD, U. Pitts., 1979. Bar: Pa. 1979, N.J. 1980, N.Y. 1983, U.S. Dist. Ct. (ea. dist.) Pa. 1980, U.S. Dist. Ct. N.J. 1980, U.S. Ct. Appeals (3d cir) 1980, U.S. Dist. Ct. (cen. dist.) Ill. 1981, U.S. Dist. Ct. (so. and ea. dists.) N.Y. 1984., Assoc. Cunniff, Bray & McAleese, Phila., 1979-82; assoc. Holtzmann, Wise & Shepard, N.Y.C., 1982-86, ptnr., 1987—. Author: (musical play) Ire, 1984; contbg. editor (2d edit.): Second Supplement The Developing Labor Law, 1987; contbr. articles to profl. jours. Vol. dir. NYU Grad. Sch. Bus., 1983—; asst. sec. Riverside Opera Ensemble, N.Y.C., 1984—. Mem. ABA, N.Y. State Bar Assn., Pa. Bar Assn., Assn. Bar of City of N.Y. Republican. Roman Catholic. Club: Corinthian Yacht (Cape May, N.J.). Avocations: theatre, photography, sailing. Labor, Federal civil litigation, Entertainment. Home: 384 Clinton St Brooklyn NY 11231 Office: Holtzmann Wise & Shepard 745 Fifth Ave New York NY 10151

HATHAWAY, STANLEY KNAPP, lawyer; b. Osceola, Nebr., July 19, 1924; s. Franklin E. and Velma Clara (Holbrook) H.; m. Roberta Louise Harley, Nov. 26, 1948; children—Susan Garrett, Sandra D'Amico. A.B., U. Nebr., 1948, LL.B., 1950; LL.D., U. Wyo., 1975. Bar: Nebr. 1950, Wyo., 1950, U.S. Dist. Ct. Wyo., Nebr., Mont. 1950, U.S. Supreme Ct. 1964. Sole practice, Torrington, Wyo., 1950-66; gov. Wyo., 1967-75; assoc. Hathaway, Speight & Kunz, Cheyenne, Wyo., 1975—; dir. Pacific Power & Light Co., Nerco, Inc., Portland, Oreg., Apache Corp., Mpls., Firt Wyo. Bancorp.,

Cheyenne, Wyo.; county atty. Goshen County (Wyo.), 1955-62; sec. U.S. Dept. Interior, 1975. Served with USAAF, 1943-45. Decorated Air medals with 5 clusters. Mem. ABA, Wyo. State Bar Assn. Republican. Anglican Orthodox. Clubs: Lions, Masons (Cheyenne); Shriners (Rawlins, Wyo.). Administrative and regulatory, General corporate, General practice. Office: Hathaway Speight and Kunz 1 Pioneer Center Cheyenne WY 82001

HATHCOX, VALINDA, lawyer; b. Sulphur Springs, Tex., Dec. 14, 1947; d. Bill Jack and Margie Dale (Parkins) H.; m. Charles Edward Mueller, Jan. 2, 1971 (div. Dec. 1979). Student, Alliance for Internat. Studies, Leysin, Switzerland, 1967; BA with high honors, East Tex. State U., 1969, MA, 1969; JD, U. Tex., 1975. Bar: Tex. 1974, U.S. Dist. Ct. (no. dist.) Tex. 1979, U.S. Tax Ct. 1980. Hearings examiner Tex. Comptroller Pub. Accts., Austin, 1975-79; assoc. Golden, Potts, Boeckman & Wilson, Dallas, 1979-80; dir. programs Tex. Bar Assn., Austin, 1980-83; asst. atty. gen., dir. legis. resources Atty. Gen. of Tex., Austin, 1983-84; dir. govtl. affairs Tex. Assn. of Counties, Austin, 1984-86; sole practice Austin, 1986—; instr. bus. law Austin Community Coll., 1983, law for sr. citizens Lifetime Learning Inst., Austin, 1980-83; continuing edn. inst. U. Tex., Austin, 1983-84. Columnist County Progress mag., Tex. Dist. and County Clk. mag.; contbr. articles to profl. jours. Mem. steering com. The Women's Fund, Austin, 1986—, nat. com. explorers div. Boy Scouts Am., Irving, Tex., 1983—; chmn. friends of scouting Lone Star Council, Austin, 1984-85; bd. of trustees Travis County Lawyer Referral, Austin, 1983-86. Fellow Tex. Bar Found. (dist. nominating com.); ABA (chmn. com.), Tex. Bar Assn. (pres. women and the law sect. 1982, council gen. practice sect. 1983—), Tex. Bar Coll., Travis County Bar Assn. (bd. dirs. 1981-82), Travis County Women Lawyers Assn. (chartered), Tex. Young Lawyers Assn. (chmn. com. 1976—), Austin Young Lawyers Assn. (pres. 1981-82), Women's Art Guild, Order of Rainbow Girls. Democrat. Baptist. Avocation: scuba diving. Legislative, Administrative and regulatory, State and local taxation. Office: PO Box 12824 Austin TX 78711

HATT, DONALD GREGORY, lawyer; b. Albany, N.Y., Sept. 18, 1917; s. George J. II and Eleanore J. (Jones) H.; m. Cynthia H. Worthington, Oct. 12, 1943; children: Gregory R., Barent S., George J. III, Schuyler W., Elizabeth E. BA, Williams Coll., 1940; LLB cum laude, Union U., Albany, 1947. Bar: N.Y. 1947, U.S. Dist. Ct. (no. dist.) N.Y. 1947. Assoc. law offices of George J. Hatt II, Albany, 1947-58; sole practice Albany, 1958-62, 75—; ptnr. Morris, Sanford & Hatt and successor firms, Albany, 1962-75; lectr. bankruptcy Albany Law Sch., 1963-71. Past pres. Northeastern N.Y. Speech Ctr., Family and Children Service, Inc., Council Community Services; mem. Vestry St. Peter's Episc. Ch.; sec. standing com. Episc. Diocese Albany; bd. dirs. ARC. Served to lt. col. USAR, 1942-64. Mem. ABA, N.Y. State Bar Assn., Albany County Bar Assn., Comml. Law League Am., Am. Arbitration Assn., Albany Execs. Assn. (past pres.). Republican. Clubs: University (Albany), Albany Country. Lodge: Rotary (past pres. Albany chpt.). Avocations: sports, bridge. Bankruptcy, Consumer commercial, General corporate. Home: 31 Constitution Dr Glenmont NY 12077 Office: 11 N Pearl St Albany NY 12207

HATTER, TERRY JULIUS, JR., judge; b. Chgo., Mar. 11, 1933. A.B., Wesleyan U., 1954; J.D., U. Chgo., 1960. Bar: Ill. 1960, Calif. 1965, U.S. Dist. Ct. 1960, U.S. Ct. Appeals 1960. Adjudicator VA, Chgo., 1960-61; asso. Harold M. Calhoun, Chgo., 1961-62; asst. public defender Cook County Chgo., 1961-62; asst. U.S. atty. No. Dist. Calif., San Francisco, 1962-66; chief counsel San Francisco Neighborhood Legal Assistance Found., 1966-67; regional legal services dir. Exec. Office Pres. OEO, San Francisco, 1967-70; exec. dir. Western Center Law and Poverty, Los Angeles, 1970-73; exec. asst. to mayor, dir. criminal justice planning City of Los Angeles, 1974-75; spl. asst. to mayor, dir. urban devel. 1975-77; judge Superior Ct. Calif., Los Angeles, 1977-80, U.S. Dist. Ct. Central Dist. Calif., Los Angeles, 1980—; assoc. clin. prof. law U. So. Calif. Law Center, 1970-74; prof. law Loyola U. Sch. Law, Los Angeles, 1973-75; mem. faculty Nat. Coll. State Judiciary, Reno, 1974; lectr. Police Acad., San Francisco Police Dept., 1963-66, U. Calif., San Diego, 1970-71, Colo. Jud. Conf., 1973. Vice pres. Northbay Halfway House, 1964-65; vice chmn. Los Angeles Regional Criminal Justice Planning Bd., 1975-76; mem. Los Angeles Mayor's Cabinet Com. Econ. Devel., 1976-77, Mayor's Policy Com., 1973-77, chmn. housing econ. and community devel. com., City Los Angeles, 1975-77, chmn. housing and community devel. tech. com., 1975-77; vice chmn. Young Democrats Cook County, 1961-62; chmn. bd. Real Estate Coop; bd. dirs. Bay Area Social Planning Council, Contra Costa, Black Law Center Los Angeles, Nat. Fedn. Settlements and Neighborhood Centers, Edn. Fin. and Governance Reform Project, Mexican Am. Legal Def. and Ednl. Fund, Nat. Health Law Program, Nat. Sr. Citizens Law Center, Calif. Law Center, Los Angeles Regional Criminal Justice Planning Bd.; mem. exec. com. bd. dirs. Richmond chpt. NAACP, Constl. Rights Found.; trustee Wesleyan United Meth. Ch. Mem. Nat. Legal Aid and Defender Assn. (dir., vice chmn.), Los Angeles County Bar Assn. (exec. com.), Am. Judicature Soc., Charles Houston Law Club, Order of Coif, Phi Delta Phi. Office: US District Court US Courthouse 312 N Spring St Los Angeles CA 90012 *

HAUBEN, RONALD BRUCE, lawyer; b. N.Y.C., Aug. 15, 1957; s. Robert Irving and Ruth Thelma (Meyerowitz) H.; m. Vicki Marlene Berger, Aug. 10, 1980; 1 child, Andrea Lynne. BA, SUNY, Binghamton, 1978; JD, NYU, 1981. Bar: N.Y. 1982, Pa. 1983, U.S. Dist. Ct. (ea. dist.) Pa. 1983, U.S. Ct. Appeals 1985. Law clk. to presiding justice U.S. Dist. Ct. (mid. dist.), Williamsport, Pa., 1981-83; assoc. Morgan, Lewis & Bockius, Phila., 1983—. Bd. dirs. project area com. Washington Sq. West, Phila., 1985. Mem. ABA, Phila. Bar Assn. (fed. cts. com., computer law com.). Democrat. Jewish. Computer, Federal civil litigation, State civil litigation. Office: Morgan Lewis & Bockius 2000 1 Logan Sq Philadelphia PA 19103

HAUBOLD, SAMUEL ALLEN, lawyer; b. Watertown, S.D., July 29, 1938; s. Gustuv Herman and Leone Marjorie (York) H.; m. Caroline V. Thompson. Sept. 27, 1969; 1 child, Caroline A. BS in Engring., Northwestern U.; JD, Harvard U. Bar: Ill. 1966, U.S. Dist. Ct. (no. dist.) Ill. 1966, U.S. Ct. Appeals (7th cir.) 1970, U.S. Supreme Ct. 1974, U.S. Ct. Appeals (9th cir.) 1979. Assoc. Kirkland & Ellis, Chgo., 1966, ptnr., 1972—. Served to lt. USN, 1960-63. Mem. ABA. Presbyterian. Clubs: Mid Am., Saddle and Cycle Club (Chgo.). Federal civil litigation, Antitrust, Nuclear power. Home: 1242 N Lake Shore Dr Chicago IL 60610 Office: Kirkland & Ellis 200 E Randolph Dr Chicago IL 60601

HAUGER, HAROLD KEITH, lawyer; b. Pitts., May 28, 1945; s. Harold N. and Ruth A. (Irwin) H. B.S., U. Pitts., 1968; J.D., Duquesne U., 1973. Bar: Pa. 1973, Fla. 1977, U.S. Dist. Ct. (we. dist.) Pa. 1974, U.S. Supreme Ct. 1979, U.S. Patent Office 1982, U.S. Trademark Office 1982, Calif. 1986. Assoc., Martin and Finnegan, Monroeville, Pa., 1974-77; sole practice, Pitts., 1977—. agt. Lawyers Title Ins. Co. Past bd. dirs. Turtle Creek Valley Mental Health/Mental Retardation, Inc.; v.p. Greenridge Civic Assn.; active Greater Irwin Bd. Realtors. Mem. Greater Irwin C. of C. (Ambassador), ABA (real estate, intellectual property, legal econs. sects.), Pa. Bar Assn., Fla. Bar Assn. (by-laws com), Allegheny County Bar Assn., Westmoreland County Bar Assn., Assn. Trial Lawyers Am., Pa. Trial Lawyers Assn., Patent Law Assn. Pitts., Calif. Bar Assn., Am. Patent Law Assn., Delta Theta Phi, Jaycees (pres. 1977-78, exhausted rooster), Pitts. Ski Club, Western Pa. Corvette Club. Lodge: Rotary (past bd. dirs., coms.). General practice, Patent, Trademark and copyright. Home: 209 Colony Dr Irwin PA 15642 Office: H Keith Hauger 28 Fairwood Dr Irwin PA 15642

HAUGHEY, THOMAS MALCOLM, lawyer; b. Cin., Aug. 19, 1945; s. John Hirt and Ruth (Littinger) H.; m. Marcia Wiepking, Aug. 23, 1970; children: Douglas Bernard, Christine Michelle, Katherine Elizabeth. BBA, Miami U., Oxford, Ohio, 1967; JD, Boston U., 1971; postgrad. fed. securities law Haverford Coll., 1973. Bar: Mass. 1971, N.H. 1972, U.S. Dist. Ct. Mass. 1971, U.S. Dist. Ct. N.H. 1972, U.S. Ct. Appeals (1st cir.) 1979, U.S. Supreme Ct. 1979. Pub. relations rep. Fisher Body div. Gen. Motors Corp., Detroit, 1967-68; assoc. Winer, Lynch & Pillsbury, Mashua, N.H., 1971-72; assoc. counsel Nashua Corp., 1972-75; ptnr. Haughey & Philpot, Laconia, N.H., 1975-81; ptnr. Haughey, Philpot & Laurent, P.A., Laconia, 1981—; real estate closing atty. U.S. Farmers Home Adminstrn., Citicorp Mortgage Co., Homeowners Fed. Mortgage Corp., The Boston Fine Mortgage Corp., Lakes Region Gen. Hosp., Laconia, 1982; state chmn. Com. For A Sensible Govt., 1981; pres. The Taylor Home, Laconia, 1983—. Mem. ABA, Mass. Bar Assn., N.H. Bar Assn., Belknap County Bar Assn. (v.p.), Comml. Law League of Am. Democrat. Unitarian. Clubs: Laconia Country (sec. 1982—, bd. dirs.), N.H. Chess Assn. (incorporator 1983). Real property, General corporate, Contracts commercial. Home: 27 Wentworth Ave Laconia NH 03246 Office: Haughey Philpot & Laurent PA 816 Main St Laconia NH 03246

HAUGHT, ROBERT STEVEN, lawyer; b. Norman, Okla., Mar. 20, 1953; s. Robert Lester and Mary Sue (Fuchs) H.; m. Noma Diane Gurich, Apr. 14, 1979. AB, Georgetown U., 1974; JD, U. Okla., 1978. Bar: Okla. 1978, U.S. Dist. Ct. (we. dist.) Okla. 1978, U.S. Ct. Appeals (10th cir.) 1978, U.S. Dist. Ct. (ea. dist.) Okla. 1980, U.S. Dist. Ct. (no. dist.) Okla. 1981, U.S. Supreme Ct. 1983. Assoc. Ames, Daugherty, Oklahoma City, 1978-82, ptnr., 1982-85; ptnr. Daugherty, Bradford, Fowler and Moss, Oklahoma City, 1986—. Contbr. articles to Am. Indian Law Rev. Mem. ABA, Okla. Bar Assn., Def. Research Inst., Order of Barristers. Republican. Federal civil litigation, State civil litigation. Office: Daugherty Bradford Fowler and Moss 900 First City Pl Oklahoma City OK 73102

HAUHART, ROBERT CHARLES, lawyer, educator; b. St. Louis, Dec. 17, 1950; s. Shields and Naomi (Allen) H. BS, So. Ill. U., 1972; MA, Washington U., St. Louis, 1973; JD, U. Balt., 1981; PhD, U. Va., 1982. Bar: Md. 1982, Pa. 1984, U.S. Dist. Ct. (mid. dist.) Pa. 1984, U.S. Ct. Appeals (3d cir.) 1984, U.S. Dist. Ct. (no. dist.) N.Y. 1987, U.S. Ct. Appeals (2d cir.) 1987. Sole practice Balt., 1982-84; assoc. Rieders, Travis Law Firm, Williamsport, Pa., 1985-86; atty. Lewisburg (Pa.) Prison Project, 1984-86, Prisoners Legal Services N.Y., 1986—; vis. assoc. prof. Towson (Md.) State U., 1980-84. Author: Paralegal Manual for Prisoner Advocacy, 1985, Prisoners' Civil Actions in Federal Court, 1986, Due Process Administration Reviews, 1986. Mem. ABA, Am. Sociol. Assn., Balt. City Bar Assn. (dir. speaker's bur. 1982-83). Civil rights, Federal civil litigation, Personal injury. Home: 53 Johnson Ave #15 Plattsburgh NY 12901 Office: Prisoners Legal Services NY 22 Broad St Plattsburgh NY 12901

HAUPTLY, DENIS JAMES, lawyer; b. Jersey City, Nov. 6, 1945; s. John James and Genevieve Elaine (Dunt) H.; m. Elizabeth M. Howard, Dec. 21, 1968; 1 child, Matthew Howard. BA, St. Michael's Coll., 1968; JD, Notre Dame U., 1972. Bar: Oreg. 1972. Law clk. to presiding judge U.S. Ct. Appeals (9th cir.), Portland, Oreg., 1972-73; atty. U.S. Dept. Justice, Washington, 1973-78, assoc. dir. Office of Legislation, 1978-81; sr. staff atty. U.S. Ct. Appeals (1st cir.), Boston, 1981-87; gen. counsel U.S. Sentencing Commn., Washington, 1985-86, Office Legislative Affairs, Adminstrv. Office U.S. Cts., Washington, 1987—. Author: Journey From the Past, 1982, In Vietnam, 1985, A Convention of Delegates, 1986. Mem. ABA. Criminal, Judicial administration. Home: 4615 44th St NW Washington DC 20016 Office: Adminstrv Office US Cts Washington DC 20004

HAURY, JOHN CARROLL, lawyer; b. Louisville, Aug. 24, 1948; s. Harry Clay and Louise (Rose) H.; m. Ellen Louise Fatout, Nov. 24, 1967 (div. Oct. 1983); children: Amanda, Jonas Dylan. BA, Wesleyan U., 1970; JD, Ind. U., 1975. Bar: Ind. 1975, U.S. Dist. Ct. (so. dist.) Ind. 1975. Chief dep. Lawrence County Prosecutor's Office, Bedford, Ind., 1975-78; ptnr. Robbins & Haury, Bedford, 1975-83, Haury & Nelson, Bedford, 1983—. past bd. dirs., pres. Lawrence County United Way, 1980-84; past pres. Lawrence county Park Bd., past Ind. Legal Services Orgn. Mem. Ind. State Bar Assn., Lawrence County Bar Assn. (past pres. and sec.), Assn. Trial Lawyers Am. Avocations: tennis, golf, basketball, running. Personal injury, Criminal, Family and matrimonial. Home: Rural Rt 11 Box 127 Bedford IN 47421 Office: 1534 I St Bedford IN 47421

HAUSEN, STANLEY SHERMAN, lawyer; b. N.Y.C., July 3, 1928; s. Edward H. and Anna (Mendelsohn) H.; m. Nina G., Nov. 26, 1953; children—Harris, Scott. LL.B., N.Y. Law Sch., 1953. Bar: N.Y. 1953, U.S. Supreme Ct. 1960, U.S. Dist. Ct. (ea. and so. dists.) N.Y. 1968. Atty., Allstate Ins. Co., Queens, N.Y.C., 1955-57; assoc. Harry Lipsig, N.Y.C., 1957-58; sole practice, Flushing, N.Y., 1958-80, Mineola, N.Y., 1980—. Arbitrator, Civil Court, N.Y.C., 1974—, Am. Arbitration Assn., N.Y.C. and Garden City, 1974—. Mem. Democratic Com. Bronx and Nassau, 1955—; pres. New Ridge Civic Assn., Woodbury, N.Y., 1968—. Served with AUS, 1953-55. Mem. Nassau County Bar Assn., Queens County Bar Assn., N.Y. State Assn. Trial Lawyers. Jewish. Lodge: Masons. Insurance, Personal injury. Home: 55 Orchard Ct Woodbury NY 11797 Office: 204 Old Country Rd Mineola NY 11501

HAUSER, GREGORY FRANCIS, lawyer; b. Canandaigua, N.Y., Sept. 20, 1954; s. Joseph J. and Margaret M. (Krott) H. BS with high honor, Mich. State U., 1975, MS, 1977; JD cum laude, NYU, 1981. Bar: N.Y. 1982, U.S. Dist. Ct. (so. and ea. dists.) N.Y. 1983, U.S. Ct. Appeals (2d cir.) 1985, U.S. Dist. Ct. (ea. dist.) Wis. 1986, U.S. Tax Ct. 1987. Assoc. litigation Paul, Weiss, Rifkind, Wharton & Garrison, N.Y.C., 1981-83, Walter, Conston, Alexander & Green, P.C., N.Y.C., 1983—. Mem. legis. com. Citizens Union, N.Y.C., 1984—. Mem. ABA, Assn. of Bar of City of N.Y., Delta Chi. Democrat. Roman Catholic. Club: St. Bartholomews (N.Y.C.). Federal civil litigation, State civil litigation, Private international. Home: 331 W 76th St Apt 4A New York NY 10023 Office: Walter Conston Alexander & Green PC 90 Park Ave New York NY 10016

HAUSER, HARRY RAYMOND, lawyer; b. N.Y.C., July 12, 1931; s. Milton I. and Lillian (Perlman) H.; m. Deborah Marlowe, Aug. 6, 1954; children: Mark Jeffrey, Joshua Brook, Bradford John, Matthew Milton. AB, Brown U., 1953; JD, Columbia U., 1959. Bar: N.Y. 1959, Mass. 1963, Wash. 1972. Practice in N.Y.C., 1959-61, Boston, 1962—; atty. Sperry Rand Corp., 1959-61, Hotel Corp. Am., N.Y.C., 1961-62; v.p., sec., gen. counsel Hotel Corp. Am., 1962-70; mem. firm Gadsby & Hannah, 1971—; bd. dirs. FRU-CON Corp., Warren Corp. Trustee, v.p., mem. bd. of property mgrs. Temple Israel, Boston. Served to lt. comdr. USNR, 1954-57. Mem. ABA, N.Y. State Bar Assn., Mass. Bar Assn., D.C. Bar Assn., Brown U. Club. Home: 37 Claremont St Newton MA 02158 Office: One Post Office Sq Boston MA 02109

HAUSER, RITA ELEANORE ABRAMS, lawyer; b. N.Y.C., July 12, 1934; d. Nathan and Frieda (Litt) Abrams; m. Gustave M. Hauser, June 10, 1956; children—Glenvil Aubrey, Patricia. A.B. magna cum laude, Hunter Coll., 1954; Dr. Polit. Economy with highest honors (Fulbright grantee), U. Strasbourg, France, 1955; Licence en Droit, U. Paris, 1958; student law sch., Harvard U., 1955-56; L.L.B. with honors, NYU, 1959; LL.D. (hon.), Seton Hall U., 1969, Finch Coll., 1969, U. Miami, Fla., 1971. Bar: D.C. 1959, N.Y. 1961, U.S. Supreme Ct. 1967. Sole practice N.Y.C., 1961—; ptnr. Moldover, Hauser, Strauss & Volin, 1968-72; sr. ptnr. Stroock & Stroock & Lavan, 1972—; Handmaker lectr. Louis Brandeis Lectr. Series, U. La. Law Sch.; lectr. on internat. law Naval War Coll. and Army War Coll.; Mitchell lectr. in Law SUNY Buffalo; USIA lectr. constl. law Egypt, India, Australia, New Zealand; bd. dirs. Wickes Cos., Inc., Israel Investors Corp. Contbr. articles on internat. law to profl. jours. U.S. rep. to UN Commn. on Human Rights, 1969-72; mem. U.S. del. to Gen. Assembly UN, 1969; vice chmn. U.S. Adv. Com. on Internat. and Cultural Affairs, 1973-77; mem. N.Y.C. Bd. Higher Edn., 1974-76, Stanton Panel on internat. info., edn., cultural relations to reorganize USIA and Voice of Am., 1974-75, Mid. East Study Group Brookings Inst., 1975, U.S. del. World Conf. Internat. Women's Yr., Mexico City, 1975; co-chmn. Com. for Re-election Pres., 1972; co-chair Presdl. Debates project LWV, 1976; adv. bd. Nat. News Council, 1977-79; bd. dirs. March of Dimes of N.Y., Bd. for Internat. Broadcasting, 1977-80; trustee N.Y. Philharm. Soc.; adv. bd. Ctr. for Law and Nat. Security, U. Va. Law Sch/. 1978-84; vis. com. Ctr. Internat. Affairs Harvard U., 1975-81; co-chmn. Coalition for Reagan/Bush; bd. govs.; v.p. Am. Jewish Com.; chmn. adv. panel Internat. Parliamentary Group for Human Rights in Soviet Union, 1984-86; U.S. pub. del. Vienna follow-up meeting Conf. on Security and Cooperation in Europe, 1986—; mem. spl. refugee adv. panel Dept. State, 1981, mem. adv. panel on internat. law, 1986—; former trustee Internat. Legal Ctr., Legal Aid Soc. N.Y., Freedom House. Intellectual Exchange fellow, Japan Soc. Fellow ABA (life, standing coms. on law and nat. security, 1979-85, on world order under law 1969-78, on judicial selection, tenure, compensation, 1977-79, council sect. on individual rights and responsibilities, 1970-73, adv., bd. jour., 1973-78); mem. Assn. Bar City N.Y., Am. Soc. Internat. Law (exec. com. 1971-76), Am. Fgn. Law Assn. (dir.), Am. Arbitration Assn. (past dir.), Am. Soc. Internat. Law (past exec. com.), Inst. East-West Security Studies (bd. dirs., exec. com.), Council on Fgn. Relations, Harvard Law Sch. Assn. N.Y.C. (trustee), Friends of The Hague Acad. Internat. Law (bd. dirs.). Republican. Banking, Private international, Public international. Home: 700 Park Ave New York NY 10021 Office: 7 Hanover Sq New York NY 10004

HAUSMANN, EDWIN DAVID, lawyer; b. Evanston, Ill., July 14, 1941; s. Louis and Ella (Wolf) H.; m. Sue Sullivan, July 4, 1969; children: Elizabeth, Neil. BS in Chem. Engring., Northwestern U., 1963; MS in Chem. Engring, U. Calif., Berkeley, 1965, JD, 1972. Bar: Calif. 1972, U.S. Dist. Ct. (cen. and so. dists.) Calif. 1972, U.S. Ct. Appeals (9th cir.) 1980. Trial atty. antitrust div. U.S. Dept. Justice, Los Angeles, 1972-77; ptnr. Silverberg, Rosen, Los Angeles, 1977-83; chief counsel Fred Sand Realtors, Los Angeles, 1983-87; ptnr. Levinson & Lieberman, Beverly Hills, Calif., 1987—. Mem. ABA, Los Angeles Bar Assn. (del. to state bar 1983), Beverly Hills Bar Assn., Assn. Bus. Trial Lawyers (seminar com.). Federal civil litigation, State civil litigation, Real property. Home: 315 S Highland Ave Los Angeles CA 90036 Office: Levinson & Lieberman 9401 Wilshire Blvd Suite 1250 Beverly Hills CA 90212

HAUSNER, JOHN HERMAN, judge; b. Detroit, Oct. 31, 1932; s. John E. and Anna (Mudrak) H.; m. Alice R. Kieltyka, Aug. 22, 1959. Ph.B. cum laude, U. Detroit, 1954, M.A., 1957, J.D. summa cum laude, 1966. Bar: Mich. 1967, U.S. Ct. Appeals (6th cir.) 1968, U.S. Supreme Ct. 1971, U.S. Tax Ct. 1976, U.S. Ct. Claims 1976, U.S. Ct. Mil. Appeals 1976. Tchr., Detroit Pub. Schs., 1954, 56-59, 61-67; teaching fellow U. Cin., 1959-61; instr. U. Detroit, 1961-74; sole practice, Detroit, 1967-69; asst. U.S. atty., 1969-73; chief asst. U.S. atty. Eastern Dist. Mich., 1973-76; judge 3d Jud. Circuit Mich., Wayne County, 1976—; lectr. Law Sch.; faculty adviser Nat. Jud. Coll., 1978-79. Active Civic Searchlight. Served with U.S. Army, 1954-56. Mem. Fed. Bar Assn. (mem. exec. bd. Detroit chpt. 1976—), ABA, State Bar Mich., Mich. Judges Assn., Detroit Bar Assn., Steuben Soc., Blue Key, Alpha Sigma Nu. Republican. Roman Catholic. Author: Sebastian, The Essence of My Soul, 1982; contbr. articles to Detroit Advertiser. State civil litigation, Criminal, Family and matrimonial. Office: 144 Lafayette St Suite 406 Detroit MI 48226

HAUSSER, ROBERT LOUIS, lawyer; b. Cin., Apr. 3, 1914; s. Oscar and Alma J. (Ebel) H.; m. Dorothy Ann Oakes, Aug. 17, 1940; children: George Louis, Robert Oakes, Julia Janet Hausser Guffey and Joel Severin (twins). AB, DePauw U., 1936; LLB, Columbia U., 1939. Bar: Ohio 1939, N.Y. 1940, U.S. Dist. Ct. (so. dist.) Ohio 1942. Assoc. Baldwin, Todd & Young, N.Y.C., 1939-41; ptnr. Hausser & Zimmer, Marietta, Ohio, 1941—; bd. dirs., v.p. Ohio Bar Title Ins. Co., Dayton; instr. Wash. Tech. Coll., 1973. Author: Ohio Real Property, 5 vols., 1952-58, (with William R. Van Aken) Ohio Real Estate Transactions, 3 vols., 1964, Ohio Real Estate Law and Practice, 1985, (with Allen B. Diefenbach) Ohio Estate Planning and Probate Adminstration, 2 vols., 1969, (with William R. Van Aken) Ohio Real Estate Law and Practice, 1985. Pres. Wash. County Hist. Soc., 1964; judge Marietta Police Ct., 1946-57; mem. Marietta City Civil Service Commn., 1967—; pres. Marietta City Bd. of Edn., 1963; past elder Presbyn. Ch., clk. of session. Served to sgt. U.S. Army, 1944-45, ETO. Decorated Purple Heart with oak leaf cluster; recipient Outstanding Research in Law and Govt. award Ohio State Bar Found., 1985. Fellow Am. Coll. Probate Counsel; mem. ABA (real property, probate and trust law com.), Ohio Bar Assn. (exec. com. 1956-59, chmn. real property sect. 1970-72, editor quar. bulletin of real property sect. 1973-76), Ohio Land Title Assn. (editor "Title Topics" 1967—), Am. Legion, Phi Beta Kappa. Democrat. Clubs: Marietta Sr. Reading (pres. 1961-62), Marietta Country. Lodges: Lions (pres. Marietta chpt. 1948), Masons. Avocations: golf, bowling. Probate, Real property, General corporate. Home: 507 8th St Marietta OH 45750 Office: Hausser & Zimmer 406 Dime Bank Bldg Marietta OH 45750

HAUTZINGER, JAMES EDWARD, lawyer; b. Omaha, Apr. 15, 1936; s. Julius M. and Iva (Beach) H.; m. Susan Jean O'Brien, June 20, 1959; children: Peter Grattan, Sarah Jean, Andrew Beach; m. 2d, Leslie Ann Walker, Apr. 21, 1979. BA, Grinnell Coll., 1958; JD, U. Chgo., 1961. Bar: Colo. 1961, U.S. Dist. Ct. Colo. 1961, U.S. Supreme Ct. 1972, U.S. Ct. Appeals (10th cir.) 1961, U.S. Ct. Appeals (5th cir.) 1981, U.S. Ct. Appeals (9th cir.) 1980. Assoc. Sherman & Howard, Denver, 1961-67, ptnr., 1967—, also mem. exec. com.; lectr. Legal counsel People for Haskell campaign, 1972-78, Hart for Senate campaign, 1980; alt. del. Dem. Nat. Conv., 1968; mem. vis. com. U. Chgo. Law Sch., 1978-80. Mem. ABA, Colo. Bar Assn. (labor law com.), Denver Bar Assn., Indsl. Relations Research Assn., Phi Beta Kappa, Order of Coif. Clubs: Denver Athletic, Pinehurst Country, Law (Denver). Mng. editor Chgo. Law Rev., 1960. Labor, Antitrust. Office: 633 17th St Suite 2900 Denver CO 80202

HAUVER, TERENCE LEE, lawyer; b. Hagerstown, Md., July 14, 1947; s. Arthur Leroy and Anne (Larkin) H.; m. Cheryl Santa Cruz, Dec. 19, 1971; children: Terence Lee II, Erin Leigh. AA, Strayer Bus. Coll., 1967; BS, La. State U., 1971; MBA, Monmouth Coll., 1976; JD, Tulane U., 1980. Ptnr. Sessions, Fishman, Rosenson, Boisfontaine, Nathan & Winn, New Orleans, 1980-87, Lowe, Stein, Hoffman & Allweiss, New Orleans, 1987—. Served to capt. U.S. Army, 1972-77. Decorated D.S.M. Mem. ABA, La. Bar Assn., New Orleans Bar Assn. Family and matrimonial, General practice. Home: 2511 Hudson Place New Orleans LA 70114 Office: Lowe Stein Hoffman & Allweiss 650 Poydras St Suite 2450 New Orleans LA 70130

HAVIGHURST, CLARK CANFIELD, law educator; b. 1933. A.B., Princeton U., 1955; J.D., Northwestern U., 1958. Bar: Ill. 1958, N.Y. 1962. Research assoc. Duke U., 1960-61; assoc. Debevoise, Plimpton, Lyons & Gates, N.Y.C., 1961-64; assoc. prof. Duke U., 1964-68, prof., 1968-86,William Neal Reynolds prof., 1986—; vis. assoc. prof. Stanford U., 1968; vis. prof. Northwestern U., 1970, U. Mich., 1983; scholar-in-residence Inst. Medicine, Nat. Acad. Scis., 1972-73; dir. Program on Legal Issues in Health Care, Duke U., 1969—; adj. scholar in law and health policy Am. Enterprise Inst. for Pub. Policy Research, 1976—; cons. FTC, Washington, 1978-79. WHO fellow, summer 1976. Mem. Nat. Acad. Scis., Inst. Medicine, Order of Coif. Author: Deferred Compensation for Key Employees, 1964; Deregulating the Health Care Industry, 1982; editor: Regulating Health Facilities Construction, 1974; editor Law and Contemporary Problems, 1965-70; past comment editor Northwestern U. Law Rev. Legal education. Office: Duke U Law Sch Durham NC 27706

HAVILAND, CAMILLA KLEIN, lawyer; b. Dodge City, Kans., Sept. 13, 1926; d. Robert Godfrey and Lelah (Luther) Klein; m. John Bodman Haviland, Sept. 7, 1957. A.A., Monticello Coll., 1946; B.A., Radcliffe Coll., 1948; J.D., Kans. U., 1955. Bar: Kans. 1955. Assoc. Calver & White, Wichita, Kans., 1955-56; sole practice, Dodge City, 1956—; probate, county and juvenile judge Ford County (Kans.), 1955-77; mem. Jud. Council Com. on Probate and Juvenile Law. Mem. adv. bd. Salvation Army, U. Kans. Sch. Religion. Recipient Nathan Burkan award ASCAP, 1955. Mem. Ford County Bar Assn. (pres. 1980), S.W. Kans. Bar Assn. (pres. 1968), Kans. Bar Assn., ABA, C. of C., Order of Coif, PEO, Phi Delta Delta. Democrat. Episcopalian. Clubs: Prairie Dunes Country (Hutchinson, Kans.); Soroptimists. Contbr. articles to profl. jours. Real property, General practice. Home: 2006 E Lane Dodge City KS 67801 Office: 203 W Spruce Box 17 Dodge City KS 67801

HAVILAND, JAMES MORRISON, lawyer; b. Washington, Oct. 12, 1942; s. John G. and Mary Harwood (Lyman) H.; m. Catherine Daniel, Sept. 12, 1967; children: John, Grant, Mary Catherine. BA, Westminster Coll., 1964; JD, U. Mich., 1967. Bar: Mo. 1967, W.Va. 1969. Law clk. to presiding judge U.S. Ct. Appeals, 4th Cir., 1967-68; vol. lawyer VISTA, Princeton, W.VA., 1968-69; atty. Appalachia Research and Def. Fund, Charleston, W.VA., 1969-71; assoc. Dietrich, Davis, Burrell, Dicus & Rowlands, Kansas City, Mo., 1971-74; atty. United Mine Workers of Am., Charleston, 1974-78; ptnr. McIntyre, Haviland & Jordan, Charleston, 1978—; adj. prof. W.Va. Inst. of Tech., Montgomery, 1976-77. Mem. W.Va. Bar Assn., AFL-CIO (lawyers coordinating com.). Democrat. Episcopalian. Club: Charleston Tennis. Labor, Federal civil litigation, State civil litigation. Office: McIntyre Haviland & Jordan 124 Capitol St Charleston WV 25301

HAVILAND, JAMES THOMAS, II, lawyer; b. Chgo., Jan. 6, 1931; s. F. Hobert and Anita Moselle (Lyndon) H.; m. Barbara Marie James, June 29,

1957; children: James III, Richard, Mary, Elizabeth, Anne. BA, Middlebury Coll., 1957; JD, U. Conn., 1964. Bar: U.S. Dist. Ct. Conn. 1965, U.S. Supreme Ct. 1969. Asst. atty. gen. State of Conn., Hartford, 1964-65; from assoc. to ptnr. Howard, Kohn, Sprague & FitzGerald, Hartford, Conn., 1965—; pub. defender State of Conn., New London, 1970; atty. Town of Groton, Conn., 1971-77. Served to pvt. 1st class U.S. Army, 1952-55, Korea. Mem. ABA, Conn. Bar Assn., New London County Bar Assn., Hartford County Bar Assn., Assn. Trial Lawyers Am., Conn. Trial Lawyers Assn. Republican. Roman Catholic. Club: Groton Long Point (Conn.) Yacht (treas. 1972-76). Lodge: Lions (pres. Groton chpt. 1974-75), Elks. State civil litigation, Federal civil litigation. Home: Club House Point Box 3277 Groton Long Point CT 06340-1603 Office: Howard Kohn Sprague & FitzGerald 603 Poquonnock Rd Groton CT 06340

HAWES, DOUGLAS WESSON, lawyer; b. West Orange, N.J., Nov. 17, 1932. B.A., Principia Coll., 1954; J.D., Columbia U., 1957; M.B.A., N.Y. U., 1961. Bar: N.Y. 1958, U.S. Supreme Ct. 1961. Assoc., then ptnr. LeBoeuf, Lamb, Leiby & MacRae, N.Y.C., 1958—; adj. prof. law Vanderbilt U., 1972—, NYU, 1976—; dir. Colson, Inc., Friteco, Inc., Hackensack Water Co., Nat. Bank Washington, Petersburg Group, Ltd., United Water Resources Inc., Washington Bancorp. Contbr. articles to legal publs. Trustee Principia Coll. Mem. ABA (fed. securities law, exec. com. fed. regulation securities coms., pub. utility holding co., internat. securities matters sects.), N.Y. State Bar Assn., Bar Assn. City N.Y. (corp. law com.), Am. Law Inst., Internat. Faculty for Corp. and Capital Market Law. General corporate, Public utilities, Securities. Home: 755 Park Ave New York NY 10021 Office: 520 Madison Ave New York NY 10022

HAWKINS, ARMIS EUGENE, judge; b. Natchez, Miss., Nov. 11, 1920; s. Charles Mayfield and Lela (Hill) H.; m. Patricia Burrow, Aug. 20, 1948; children: Janice Hawkins Shrewsbury, Jean Ann, James Charles. Student, Wood Jr. Coll., 1938-39, Millsaps Coll., 1943; LL.B., U. Miss., 1947. Bar: Miss. Individual practice law Houston, Miss., 1947-51; dist. atty. 3d Circuit Ct. Dist. Miss., 1951-59; assoc. justice Miss. Supreme Ct., 1981—. Served with USMC, 1942-46, PTO. Mem. ABA, Am. Judicature Soc., Miss. Trial Lawyers Assn., Miss. State Bar. Baptist. Office: Supreme Court Office PO Box 117 Jackson MS 39205 *

HAWKINS, BARRY CURTIS, lawyer; b. Portland, Maine, Oct. 7, 1943; s. Guy Curtis and Veronica (Whelan) H.; m. Lilyan Ferrazzano, Jan. 29, 1966; children: Kevin, Christopher, Stefanie, Kirsten. BA, Bowdoin Coll., 1965; JD, U. Va., 1968. Bar: Conn. 1968, U.S. Dist. Ct. Conn. 1970, U.S. Ct. Appeals (2d cir.) 1970. From assoc. to ptnr. Tyler, Cooper & Alcorn, New Haven, Stamford, Conn., 1970—. Chmn. Impact Civic Group, West Haven, Conn., 1972-75; pres. Savin Park Condominium Assn., West Haven, 1972-74. Served to capt. U.S. Army, 1968-70, Vietnam. Decorated Bronze Star. Mem. ABA, Conn. Bar Assn. (exec. com. real property sect.), Stamford Bar Assn., Am. Coll. Real Estate Lawyers, Community Assns. Inst. (founding mem., v.p. Conn. chpt. 1980-81), New Eng. Land Title Assn. Democrat. Roman Catholic. Real property, Banking, General corporate. Home: 4 Rainey Ln Westport CT 06880 Office: Tyler Cooper & Alcorn 3 Landmark Sq Stamford CT 06901

HAWKINS, CARL S., law educator, lawyer; b. 1926. A.B., Brigham Young U., 1948; J.D., Northwestern U., 1951. Bar: Ill. 1951, Washington, 1951, Mich. 1965, Utah 1977. Fellow U. Chgo., 1951; practice, Washington, 1951-52; clk. U.S. Supreme Ct., 1952-53; practice, Washington, 1953-57; asst. prof. U. Mich., 1957-61, assoc. prof., 1961-65, prof., 1965-73; prof. Brigham Young U. J. Reuben Clark Law Sch., 1973—, dean, 1981-85; chmn. Civil Procedure Commn., State Bar Mich., 1965-69; reporter Mich. Supreme Ct. Commn. Standard Jury Instrn., 1964-72; exec. sec. Mich. Law Rev. Com., 1970-72; mem. Jud. Nomination Com. 10th Cir., 1977-78; mem. rules civil procedure Utah Supreme Adv. Commn., 1985—; exec. dir. Fla. Academic Task Force for Rev. of Ins. and Tort Systems, 1986—; chmn. Utah Atty. Gen. Adminstrv. Law Adv. Commn., 1981—. Mem. Order of Coif, Phi Kappa Phi. Author: (with Honigman) Michigan Court Rules Annotated, 6 vols., 1962-72; (with Green and others) Cases on Torts, 1977; (with Green and others) Cases on Advnaced Torts, 1977; past editor-in-chief Ill. Law Rev. Legal education. Office: Brigham Young U J Reuben Clark Law Sch Provo UT 84602

HAWKINS, CARMEN DOLORAS, lawyer; b. Los Angeles, Sept. 17, 1955; d. Lenell Herman Hawkins and Doloras Mondy. BA, U. Calif., 1977; JD, Georgetown U., 1981. Bar: D.C. 1981, Calif. 1982, U.S. Dist. Ct. (cen. dist.) Calif. 1982, U.S. Ct. Appeals (9th cir.),1982. Atty. Law Offices of Thomas G. Neusom, Los Angeles, 1982-84; sole practice Los Angeles, 1984—; atty. Los Angeles Community Coll., 1984, Wilson & Becks, 1986; gen. counsel Los Angeles Trade Tech. Coll. Found., Los Angeles, 1985—. Bd. dirs. Calif. Dems. for New Leadership, Los Angeles, 1985—; mem. New Frontier Dem. Club, Los Angeles, 1984—, New Dem. Channel, Los Angeles, 1984—; commr. City of Los Angeles Commn. on Bicentennial of U.S. Constitution, 1976. Recipient Community Service award Los Angeles City Council, 1985, Community Service award Calif. State Senator Diane Watson, 1985. Mem. ABA, Los Angeles County Bar Assn., Los Angeles County Bar Barristers Assn. (exec. com. 1986—), NAACP, Black Women Lawyers of Los Angeles (parliamentarian 1985—), John M Langston Bar Assn., Black Women's Forum, Phi Alpha Delta. Democrat. African Methodist Episcopalian. Avocations: bicycling, tennis. State civil litigation, Insurance, Probate. Office: 117 E 8th St Suite 515 Long Beach CA 90813

HAWKINS, CYNTHIA RAYBURN, lawyer; b. Chgo., June 7, 1957; d. Norman La Hugh and Hilda Jeanette (Duke) H.; m. J. Daniel Rayburn Jr., Oct. 10, 1981. BA, U. Fla., 1977, JD, 1980. Bar: Fla. 1980, U.S. Ct. Mil. Appeals 1981, La. 1985, U.S. Dist. Ct. (ea. dist.) La. 1985, U.S. Ct. Mil. Appeals, U.S. Ct. Appeals (5th cir.) 1986. Atty. VA, New Orleans, 1984-85; asst. U.S. atty. U.S. Dept. Justice, New Orleans, 1985—. Served with JAGC, USAF, 1981-84, capt. Res. 1984—. Mem. ABA, Fla. Bar Assn., La. Bar Assn., Res. Officers Assn. Avocations: jogging, bicycling. Criminal, Military. Office: US Dept Justice Office US Atty 500 Camp St New Orleans LA 70130

HAWKINS, ELDRIDGE THOMAS ENOCH, lawyer; b. East Orange, N.J., Sept. 4, 1940; s. Eldridge and Agnes (Goode) H.; m. Linda Cofer, Sept. 5, 1976; children: Eldridge Thomas Enoch II, Hillary Alicia. BA, Rutgers U., 1962; JD, Seton Hall U., 1966. Staff atty. EEOC, Washington, 1966-67, Newark Legal Services, 1967; exec. dir. Monmouth Legal Services Orgn., Red Bank, N.J., 1968-69; prosecutor East Orange Mcpl. Ct., 1970-72; ptnr. Hawkins & Rossi, East Orange, 1970-77; sole practice East Orange, 1977—; mem. Essex (N.J.) County Ethics Com., 1979. Legis. sponsor, drafter New Jersey Code of Criminal Justice, 1974-75. N.J. State Assemblyman, Trenton, 1973-77; trustee Hosp. Ctr. Orange, N.J. Recipient Thurgood Marshall award Seton Hall Law Sch., Newark, 1976, Pub. Service award Rutgers U., 1975; named one of Outstanding Young Men in Am., 1976, East Orange Jaycee of Yr., 1972. Mem. Nat. Bar Assn., Garden State Bar Assn. (founding pres. 1971). Democrat. Avocation: track and field. Home: Llewellyn Park West Orange NJ 07052 Office: 110 S Munn Ave East Orange NJ 07018

HAWKINS, ELIOT DEXTER, lawyer; b. N.Y.C., May 6, 1932; s. Dexter Clarkson and Evelyn Byrd (Eliot) H.; m. Margaret O. Childers, Jan. 13, 1962 (div. 1976); children: Robert E.D., Ruthanna C. B.A., Harvard U., 1954, J.D., 1960; B.A., Oxford U., Eng., 1956; M.A., Oxford U., 1960. Bar: N.Y. 1960. Assoc. Winthrop, Stimson, Putnam & Roberts, N.Y.C., 1960-69, Milbank, Tweed, Hadley & McCloy, N.Y.C., 1969-73; ptnr. Milbank, Tweed, Hadley & McCloy, 1974—. Mem., trustee Community Service Soc. of N.Y., 1962-78, 80—. Served to 1st lt. U.S. Army, 1956-58. Mem. ABA, Assn. of Bar of City of N.Y., N.Y. State Bar Assn. Club: Harvard (N.Y.C.). Estate planning, Probate, Estate taxation. Office: Milbank Tweed Hadley & McCloy 1 Chase Manhattan Plaza New York NY 10005

HAWKINS, FALCON BLACK, judge; b. Charleston, S.C., Mar. 16, 1927; s. Falcon Black and Mae Elizabeth (Infinger) H.; m. Jean Elizabeth Timmerman, May 28, 1949; children—Richard Keith, Daryl Gene, Mary Elizabeth Hawkins Eddy, Steely Odell II. B.S., The Citadel, 1958; LL.B., U. S.C., 1963, J.D., 1970. Bar: S.C. bar 1963. Leadingman electronics Charleston (S.C.) Naval Shipyard, 1948-60; salesman ACH Brokers, Columbia, S.C., 1960-63; from assoc. to sr. ptnr. firm Hollings & Hawkins and successor firms, Charleston, 1963-79; U.S. dist. judge Dist. of S.C., Charleston, 1979—. Bd. visitors Med. U. S.C. Served with Mcht. Marines, 1944-45; Served with AUS, 1945-46. Mem. Jud. Conf. 4th Jud. Circuit, ABA, S.C. Bar Assn., Charleston County Bar Assn., Am. Trial Lawyers Assn., S.C. Trial Lawyers Assn. Democrat. Methodist. Clubs: Carolina Yacht, Hibernian Soc. Charleston. Lodge: Masons. Jurisprudence. Office: US Courthouse PO Box 835 Charleston SC 29402

HAWKINS, HOWARD R., JR., lawyer; b. Tarrytown, N.Y., July 3, 1950. AB, Harvard U., 1972; JD, Fordham U., 1975. Bar: N.Y. 1976. Law clk. to presiding justice U.S. Dist. Ct. N.Y., N.Y.C., 1975-77; ptnr. Cadwalader, Wickersham & Taft, N.Y.C., 1977—. Address: Cadwalader Wickersham & Taft 100 Maiden Ln New York NY 10038 *

HAWKINS, JOHN CLAIBORNE, JR., lawyer, justice of peace; b. Shreveport, La., Sept. 3, 1941; s. John Claiborne and Dorothy Marie (Chauvet) H.; m. Mary Idalee Raffaelli June 5, 1965; children—Johnette, Mark, Virginia. Student Centenary Coll., 1959-61; B.S.B.A. in Acctg., U. Ark., 1963, J.D., 1966. Bar: Tex. 1966, Ark. 1966, U.S. Dist. Ct. (we. dist.) Ark. 1966, U.S. Dist. Ct. (ea. dist.) Tex. 1969, U.S. Ct. Appeals (5th cir.) 1972, U.S. Supreme Ct. 1982; cert. law enforcement instr., cert. law enforcement officer, cert. hypnotist-investigator. Ptnr. Raffaelli & Hawkins, Texarkana, Tex., 1968-74, Hitt & Pesek, Texarkana, 1974-76; sole practice, Texarkana, 1977—; justice of peace Bowie County (Tex.), Texarkana, 1985—; city atty. Wake Village (Tex.), 1971—; substitute mcpl. judge City of Texarkana, 1979-84; instr. East Tex. State U., Texarkana, 1979. Pres. Texarkana Sheltered Workshop, 1968-73; bd. dirs. Texarkana Youth Baseball, 1968, 83; cubmaster pack 86 Caddo Council Boy Scouts Am., 1978-79; mem. Leadership Texarkana, 1983—. Served to capt. U.S. Army, 1964-68, lt. col. JAGC Res. Mem. Texarkana Bar Assn., Tex. Bar Assn., Ark. Bar Assn., Texas City Attys. Assn., Ark. Trial Lawyers Assn., ABA, Assn. U.S. Army (nat. adv. bd. 1982—, exec. com. Ark-O-Tex chpt. 1977—), Res. Officers Assn., Sheriff's Assn. Tex., Am. Security Council, Mensa, Mil. Mensa, Tex. Narcotics Officer Assn., Texarkana C. of C. Democrat. Roman Catholic. State civil litigation, General practice, Judicial administration. Office: PO Box 5969 312 W 4th St Texarkana TX 75505

HAWKINS, JOHN DONALD, JR., lawyer; b. Bronxville, N.Y., Dec. 30, 1956; s. John Donald and Lucille Phyllis (Sassano) H.; m. Alice Sherron Harward, May 17, 1980; children: Alison Lyn, Megan Leigh. BA in Polit. Sci. and English with honors, Lehigh U., 1977; JD with honors, U. N.C., 1980. Bar: N.Y., U.S. Dist. Ct. (so. dist.) N.Y. Assoc. Mudge, Rose, Guthrie, Alexander & Ferdon, N.Y.C., 1980—. Mem. N.Y. State Bar Assn., Assn. of Bar of City of N.Y., Phi Beta Kappa. Roman Catholic. General corporate, Securities, Leverage lease financing. Home: 1253 Post Rd Scarsdale NY 10583 Office: Mudge Rose Guthrie Alexander & Ferdon 180 Maiden Ln New York NY 10038

HAWKINS, KAREN L(EE), lawyer; b. Central Falls, R.I., Oct. 17, 1945; d. Everett Yale Jr. and Kathryn Mary (Zagar) H. BA, U. Mass., 1967; MEd, U. Calif., Davis, 1976; JD, Golden Gate U., 1979, MBA in Tax, 1981. Bar: Calif. 1979, U.S. Dist. Ct. (no. dist.) Calif. 1979, U.S. Tax Ct. 1984, U.S. Dist. Ct. (ea. dist.) Mich. 1986. Resident dir. U. Mass., Amherst, 1967-69; communications cons. Pacific Telephone Co., San Francisco, 1969-73; asst. dean U. Calif., Davis, 1973-76; sr. tax cons. Touche Ross & Co., San Francisco, 1979-83; sole practice San Francisco, 1983-84; ptnr. Berger & Taggart, San Francisco, 1984-86, Taggart & Hawkins, San Francisco, 1986—; lectr. Golden Gate U., San Francisco, 1978-79, 83-84; panelist Rutter Group, San Francisco, 1986. Mem. Nat. Women's Polit. Caucus, San Francisco. Mem. ABA (taxation and litigation sects.), Calif. Bar Assn., San Francisco Bar Assn. (chmn. jud. appointments com. 1986), Bay Area Women Tax Lawyers (pres. 1986—). Avocations: golf, jogging, scuba diving.. Tax litigation, Corporate taxation, Taxation partnership. Office: Taggart & Hawkins 100 Bush St 20th Floor San Francisco CA 94104

HAWKINS, RICHARD MICHAEL, lawyer; b. Nevada City, Calif., July 23, 1949; s. Robert Augustus and Virginia June (Hawke) H.; m. Linda Lee Chapman, Sept. 27, 1975; children: Ryan, Alexandra Michelle. BS in Math., U. Calif., Davis, 1971; JD, Calif. State U., San Francisco, 1974; LLM in Taxation, U. Pacific, 1983. Bar: Calif. 1974, U.S. Dist. Ct. (ea. dist.) Calif. 1974, U.S. Dist. Ct. (no. dist.) Calif. 1982, U.S. Ct. Claims 1982, U.S. Tax Ct. 1982, U.S. Ct. Appeals (9th cir.) 1982, U.S. Supreme Ct. 1982. From assoc. to ptnr. Larue & Francis, Nevada City, 1974-76; ptnr. Larue, Roach & Hawkins, Nevada City, 1977-78; of counsel Berliner & Ellers, Nevada City; ptnr. Berliner, Spiller & Hawkins, Nevada City, 1981; sole practice Grass Valley, Calif., 1981—. Bd. dirs. 49'ers Fire Dist., Nevada City, 1977-81, asst. fire chief, 1981-83, fire chief, 1983—; bd. dirs. Nevada City Edn. Fund, 1985—. Mem. ABA, Nevada County Bar Assn. (v.p. 1976), Order of Coif, Phi Kappa Phi. Democrat. Roman Catholic. Avocations: skiing, bicycling, sailing, marathon running. Probate, Estate taxation, Personal income taxation. Home: 14762 Banner Quaker Hill Rd Nevada City CA 95959 Office: 10563 Brunswick Suite 2 Grass Valley CA 95945

HAWLEY, ROBERT CROSS, lawyer; b. Douglas, Wyo., Aug. 7, 1920; s. Robert Daniel and Elsie Corienne (Cross) H.; m. Mary Elizabeth Hawley McClellan, Mar. 3, 1944; children—Robert Cross, Mary Virginia, Laurie McClellan. B.A. with honors, U. Colo., 1943; LL.B., Harvard U., 1949. Bar: Wyo. 1950, Colo. 1950, U.S. Dist. Ct. Colo. 1950, U.S. Dist. Ct. Wyo. 1954, U.S. Ct. Appeals (10th cir.) 1955, Tex. 1960, U.S. Ct. Appeals (5th cir.) 1960, U.S. Supreme Ct. 1960, U.S. Dist. Ct. (so. dist.) Tex. 1961, U.S. Ct. Appeals (D.C. cir.) 1961, U.S. Ct. Appeals (8th cir.) 1979, U.S. Ct. Appeals (11th cir.) 1981. Assoc. Barrister Weller & Friedrich, Denver, 1949-50; sr. atty. Continental Oil Co., Denver, 1952-58, counsel, Houston, 1959-62; ptnr., v.p. Ireland, Stapleton & Pryor, Denver, 1962-81; ptnr. Dechert Price & Rhoads, Denver, 1981-83, Hawley & VanderWerf, Denver, 1983—; pres. Highland Minerals, Denver; dir. Yorker Mfg., Denver, Bank of Denver, Calvin Exploration, Sante Fe. Contbr. articles to Oil & Gas Bd. dirs. Am. Cancer Soc., Denver. Recipient Alumni Recognition award U. Colo., Boulder, 1958, Meritorious Service award Monticello Coll., Godfrey, Ill., 1967; Sigma Alpha Epsilon scholar, 1941-43. Mem. Denver Assn. Oil and Gas Title Lawyers (pres. 1983-84), Denver Petroleum Club (pres. 1978-79), Harvard Law Sch. Assn. Colo. (pres. 1980-81), Associated Alumni U. Colo. (pres. and bd. dirs. 1956-57), Law Club, Denver (pres. 1958-59), ABA, Colo. Bar Assn., Denver (pres. 1958-59), Bar Assn., Tex. Bar Assn., Wyo. Bar Assn., Fed. Energy Bar Assn. (legal and lands com.), Interstate Oil Compact Comn., Rocky Mt. Oil and Gas Assn., Chevaliers du Tastevin. Republican. Episcopalian. Clubs: Denver Country, Petroleum, Gyro, Univ. (Denver); Colo. Arlberg (Winter Park). Oil and gas leasing, FERC practice. Office: Hawley & VanderWerf 730 17th St Suite 730 Denver CO 80202 Home: 4401 E 3d Ave Denver CO 80220

HAWLEY, WILLIAM LEE, lawyer; b. Cleve., Sept. 15, 1954; s. Donald Wade and Jane Louise (Lee) H.; m. Monica Oberlin, July 5, 1980; children: Rachel, Douglas. BA, Baldwin-Wallace Coll., 1976; JD, Ohio State U., 1979. Bar: Ohio 1979, U.S. Dist. Ct. (no. dist.) Ohio 1979, U.S. Ct. Appeals (5th and 6th cirs.) 1979. Assoc. Hoppe, Frey, Hewitt & Milligan, Warren, Ohio, 1979-85; ptnr. Hoppe, Frey, Hewitt & Milligan, Warren, 1986—. Mem. ABA, Ohio State Bar Assn., Ohio Assn. Civil Trial Attys., Trumbull County Bar Assn. Republican. Lutheran. State civil litigation, Insurance, Personal injury. Office: Hoppe Frey et al 500 Second Nat Tower Warren OH 44481

HAXBY, LEONARD JAMES, lawyer; b. Whitehall, Mint., Oct. 30, 1938; LL.B., LaSalle U., 1962. Bar: Mont. 1964, U.S. Dist. Ct. Mont. 1965, U.S. Ct. Appeals (9th cir.) 1965, U.S. Supreme Ct. 1980. Ptnr., Holland, Holland & Haxby, Butte, Mont., 1965-74; asst. staff stty. Silver Bow County Legal Services, 1966-68; sr. counsel metall. div. Anaconda Mining Co., 1974-75; hearing officer Mont. Dept. Instns., Butte, 1975—; pub. defender, Silver Bow County, 1975-77. Pres., Silver Bow Humane Soc., 1969-72, Butte Catholic Community Council, 1982-83; bd. dirs. Big Brothers Am., 1966-67, United Givers, 1974-76, S.W. Mont. Alcoholic Abuse Ctr.; adviser Butte Silver Bow Child Abuse Team. Mem. Assn. Trial Lawyers Am., Mont. Trial Lawyers Assn., Am. Judicature Soc., ABA, Silver Bow County Bar Assn. (v.p. 1976-77). Recipient cert. achievement Law Day Preparation, 1969; Club: Kiwanis (outstanding club pres. award 1977; lt. gov. Mont. 1979-80, disting. found. chmn. of Mont., 1985-86). Personal injury, Probate, General practice. Home: 2720 Wharton St Butte MT 59701

HAY, CHARLES RICHARD, lawyer; b. Clay Center, Kans., Oct. 5, 1950; s. Carl August and Margaret Jean (Cook) H.; m. Deanne Kay Watts, Aug. 8, 1971; 1 child, Bryan Richard. BJ, U. Kans., 1972, JD, 1974. Bar: Kans. 1974, U.S. Dist. Ct. Kans. 1974, U.S. Ct. Appeals (10th cir.) 1980. Assoc. Goodel, Stratton, Edmonds & Palmer, Topeka, 1974-79, ptnr., 1979—; adj. asst. prof. law Washburn U., Topeka, 1980—. Chmn. crusade Am. Cancer Soc., Topeka, 1977-78; pres., bd. dirs. Topeka Hospice, 1978—. Mem. ABA, Kans. Bar Assn. (pres. young lawyers sect. 1983-84, Outstanding Service award 1984), Topeka Bar Assn., Kans. Assn. Def. Counsel, Kans. Hosp. Attys. Assn. (bd. dirs. 1985—), Topeka Lawyers Club. Democrat. Methodist. Club: Top of the Tower (Topeka). Avocations: reading, bicycling, gardening, travel. Health, Pension, profit-sharing, and employee benefits, Bankruptcy. Home: 5991 SW 24th Terr Topeka KS 66614 Office: Goodell Stratton Edmonds & Palmer 215 E 8th St Topeka KS 66603

HAY, GEORGE ALAN, law and economics educator; b. N.Y.C., Feb. 4, 1942; s. George N. and Marjorie H. (Prote) H.; m. Eleanor Mary McCarthy. BS, Le Moyne Coll., 1963; MA, Northwestern U., 1967, PhD, 1969. From asst. to assoc. prof. econs. Yale U., New Haven, 1967-74; dir. econs. antitrust div. U.S. Dept. Justice, Washington, 1973-79; prof. law and econs. Cornell U., Ithaca, N.Y., 1979—. Contbr. articles on antitrust to profl. jours. Fulbright scholar Oxford U., 1984-85. Mem. ABA, Am. Econ. Assn., Assn. Am. Law Schs. (chmn. antitrust sect. 1985-87). Antitrust. Office: Cornell Law Sch Ithaca NY 14853

HAY, JOHN LEONARD, lawyer; b. Lawrence, Mass., Oct. 6, 1940; s. Charles Cable and Henrietta Dudley (Wise) H.; m. Millicent Victoria, Dec. 16, 1967; 1 child, Ian. A.B. with distinction, Stanford U., 1961; J.D., U. Colo., 1964. Bar: Colo. 1964, Ariz. 1965, D.C. 1971. Assoc. Lewis and Roca, Phoenix, 1964-69, ptnr., 1969-82; ptnr. Fannin, Terry & Hay, 1982-87, Allen, Kimerer & LaVelle, 1987—; dir. Ariz. Life and Disability Ins. Guaranty Fund, 1983—, Ariz. Licensors and Franchisors Assn., 1985—. Mem. Democratic Precinct Com., 1966-78; Ariz. State Dem. Com., 1968-78; chmn. Dem. Legis. Dist., 1971-74; mem. Maricopa County Dem. Central Com., 1971-74; bd. dirs. ACLU, 1973-78, Community Legal Services, 1983—. Mem. ABA, Maricopa County Bar Assn. (bd. dirs. 1972-85), State Bar of Ariz., Ariz. Licensors and Franchisors Assn. (bd. dirs. 1985—), Ariz. Civil Liberties Union (recipient disting. citizen award 1979, bd. dirs. 1967-84, pres. 1973-77). General corporate, Franchising, Insurance. Home: 201 E Hayward Ave Phoenix AZ 85020 Office: 2715 N 3d St Phoenix AZ 85004

HAY, PETER HEINRICH, college dean, lawyer; b. Berlin, Sept. 17, 1935; came to U.S., 1953, naturalized, 1969; s. Edward Arthur and Margot Hedwig (Tull) H.; m. Norma M. Gossman, 1958 (div. 1973); m. Grazina O. Parokas, Jan. 26, 1974; children: Cedric, Tomas, Tadas. B.A., U. Mich., 1958, J.D., 1958; postgrad., univs. Göttingen and Heidelberg, Ger., 1959-60. Asst. prof. law U. Pitts., 1961-63; asst. prof. law U. Ill., Urbana, 1963-64; assoc. prof. U. Ill., 1964-66, prof., 1966—, assoc. dean Coll. Law, 1974-80, dean, 1980—; hon. prof. U. Freiburg, Ger., 1975—; cons. U.S. Dept. State, 1974-77. Mem. editorial bd. Am. Jour. Comparative Law, 1961, Cahiers de Droit Européen, Brussels, 1969—; author: (with Stein) Law and Institutions of the Atlantic Area, 1963, 67, Federalism and Supranational Organizations, 1966, (with LaFave) International Trade, Investment and Organizations, 1967, Symposium on International Unification of Law, 1968, Einführung in das amerikanische Recht, 1975, 2d edit., 1987, An Introduction to U.S. Law, 1976, Chinese translation by Beijing U., 1983, (with Stein and Waelbroeck), European Community Law in Perspective, 1976, supplement, 1985, Ungerechtfertigte Bereicherung im internationalen Privatrecht, 1976, (with Rotunda) The American Federal System, 1982, (with Scoles) Conflict of Laws, 1982, 84, supplement, 1986; also numerous articles. Mem. Internat. Acad. Comparative Law (assoc.), AAUP, Société de Legislation Comparée (Paris), Am. Fgn. Law Assn., ABA (assoc.), Am. Law Inst., Am. Soc. Internat. Law, Am. Acad. Fgn. Law. Roman Catholic. Club: Rotary. Federal civil litigation, State civil litigation, Private international. Home: 2302 Shurts Circle Urbana IL 61801 Office: 209 Law Bldg 504 E Pennsylvania Ave Champaign IL 61820

HAY, THOMAS HAROLD, lawyer; b. Detroit, June 17, 1946; s. Raymond Harold and Marion (Jay) H.; m. Donna Erma Hebert, Aug. 16, 1968; children—Jennifer, Ivan, Timothy. B.A., No. Mich. U., 1968; J.D., U. Mich., 1971. Bar: Mich. 1971, U.S. Dist. Ct. (we. dist.) Mich. 1973, U.S. Ct. Appeals (6th cir.) 1975, U.S. Supreme Ct. 1976; cert. civil trial advocate Nat. Bd. Trial Advocacy. Law clk. presiding justice 30th Circuit Ct., Lansing, Mich., 1971-72; assoc. Church, Wyble, Kritselis & Tesseris, Lansing, 1972-82; ptnr. Anderson, Hay & Wonch, Lansing, 1982—. Mem. Assn. Trial Lawyers Am. (Mich. state del. 1986), Mich. Trial Lawyers Assn. (lectr. People's Law Sch. 1983-84, exec. bd. dirs. 1982-87, chmn. no fault task force 1982-85), ABA. Democrat. Club: Gaelic (Detroit) Personal injury, Federal civil litigation, State civil litigation. Office: 1300 N Waverly Lansing MI 48917

HAYASHI, YOSHIMI, justice state supreme court; b. Honolulu, Nov. 2, 1922; s. Shigeo and Yuki H.; m. Eleanor Hayashi, Aug. 8, 1953; 1 child, Scott K. B.A., U. Hawaii, 1950; LL.B., George Washington U., 1958. Bar: Hawaii 1958. Practice of law Lihue, Kauai, Hawaii, 1958-61; asst. U.S. atty. 1961-67, U.S. atty. for Hawaii, 1967-69; judge Hawaii Dist. Ct. 1st Circuit, 1974-80; chief judge Hawaii Intermediate Ct. Appeals, 1980-82; assoc. justice Hawaii Supreme Ct., Honolulu, 1982—. Served to sgt. U.S. Army, 1943-46. Democrat. Buddhist. Judicial administration. Office: Hawaii Supreme Court 417 S King St Honolulu HI 96813 *

HAYCRAFT, CHARLES ARTHUR, lawyer; b. Madelia, Minn., July 19, 1930; s. Beryl Edmund and Iola Gladys (Anderson) H.; m. Lois Marlene Mosel, Apr. 5, 1953 (div. 1969); children: Jon Arthur, Jeffrey Charles, James Ray, Lorna Sue; m. Jean Alyce Deman, Sept. 15, 1973. BA in History, U. Md., 1960; JD, Jackson Sch. Law, 1975. Bar: Miss. 1978, U.S. Dist. Ct. (no. dist.) Ala. 1986. Mgr. personnel Gen. Foods Corp., 1949-50; spl. agt. office spl. investigations USAF, 1950-62; spl. investigator VA Hdqrs., 1962-67; chief investigations and security, Chgo. area office FAA, 1967-69; various positions EEOC, Memphis, Washington, Jackson, Miss. and New Orleans, 1969-85; sole practice Birmingham, Ala., 1985—; pro bono arbitrator Better Bus. Bur., Birmingham, Ala., 1983—. Mem. ABA, Fed. Bar Assn., Miss. Bar Assn., Assn. Fed. Investigators, Soc. Profls. in Dispute Resolution, Am. Arbitration Assn. (panelist), Better Bus. Bur. (arbitration panelist). Republican. Avocations: genealogical research, reading, jogging. Administrative and regulatory, Civil rights, Labor. Home: 102 Ventura Ave Birmingham AL 35209 Office: 2107 5th Ave N Birmingham AL 35203

HAYDEN, RAYMOND PAUL, lawyer; b. Rochester, N.Y., Jan. 15, 1939; s. John Joseph and Orpha (Lindsay) H.; m. Suzanne Saloy, Sept. 1, 1962; children—Thomas Gerard, Christopher Matthew. B.S. in Marine Transit, SUNY Maritime Coll., 1960; LL.B., Syracuse U., 1963. Bar: N.Y. 1963, U.S. Ct. Appeals (2d cir.) 1963, U.S. Dist. Ct. (ea. and so. dists.) N.Y. 1964, U.S. Supreme Ct. 1967. Assoc. Haight Gardner Poor & Havens, N.Y.C., 1963-70; asst. gen. counsel Commonwealth Oil Co., N.Y.C., 1970-71; ptnr. Hill Rivkins Carey Loesberg O'Brien & Mulroy, N.Y.C., 1971—. Mem. Coll. Council, SUNY Maritime Coll., 1977—, chmn., 1983—. Served to lt. j.g. USNR, 1960-70. Mem. ABA (chmn. standing com. on admiralty and maritime law 1982-86), Maritime Law Assn. U.S. (chmn. com. on admissions 1974-82). Clubs: India House, Downtown Athletic (N.Y.C.); Brookville Country (N.Y.). Admiralty. Office: Hill Rivkins Carey Loesberg O'Brien & Mulroy 21 West St New York NY 10006

HAYEK, CAROLYN JEAN, judge; b. Portland, Oreg., Aug. 17, 1948; d. Robert A. and Marion L. (DeKoning) H.; m. Steven M. Rosen, July 21, 1974; 1 child, Jonathan David. BA in Psychology, Carleton Coll., 1970; JD, U. Chgo., 1973. Bar: Wash. 1973. Assoc. firm Jones, Grey & Bayley, Seattle, 1973-77; sole practice law, Federal Way, Wash., 1977-82; judge Federal Way Dist. Ct., 1982—. Task force mem. Alternatives for Wash., 1973-75; mem. Wash. State Ecol. Commn., 1975-77; bd. dirs. 1st Unitarian Ch. Seattle, 1986—. Mem. ABA, Wash. Women Lawyers, Wash. State Bar Assn., AAUW (br. pres. 1978-80, chmn. state level conf. com. 1986-87), King County Dist. Ct. Judges Assn. (treas., exec. com., com. chmn.), Elected

Wash. Women (dir. 1983-87), Nat. Assn. Women Judges (nat. bd. dirs., dist. bd. dirs. 1984-86), Federal Way Women's Network (bd. dirs. 1984-87, pres. 1985), Greater Federal Way C. of C. (dir. 1978-82, sec. 1980-81, v.p. 1981-82). Republican. Office: Federal Way Dist Ct 33506 10th Pl S Federal Way WA 98003

HAYERS, PAUL HUGH, lawyer; b. Wichita Falls, Tex., Dec. 2, 1942; s. Carl Edward and Emogene (Wagoner) H.; m. Jannis Baker, Aug. 16, 1964; children—Stephanie Laura, Christopher Mark. B.B.A., So. Meth. U., 1964; J.D., Georgetown U., 1967. Bar: Tex. 1967, U.S. Dist. Ct. (no. dist.) Tex. 1968, U.S. Ct. Appeals (5th cir.) 1975, U.S. Ct. Appeals (11th cir.) 1981. Ptnr. McKelvey & Hayers, Electra, Tex., 1967-84, mng. owner, 1984—. Commr. City of Electra, 1972-75, 80-86, mayor pro-tem, 1974, 75, 85, city atty., 1976-80, 86; chmn. Wichita County Tax Appraisal Dist., Wichita Falls, Tex., 1980—; bd. dirs. Tex. Assn. Appraisal Dists., 1985—; chmn. Wichita County Child Welfare Bd., 1979-84. Mem. State Bar Tex., Wichita County Bar Assn., Electra C. of C. Democrat. Methodist. Clubs: Rotary (pres. 1984), Lions (pres. 1971-72). Probate, Real property, Personal income taxation. Home: 200 Southland Electra TX 76360 Office: McKelvey & Hayers 109 N Main Electra TX 76360

HAYES, BURGAIN GARFIELD, lawyer; b. Ft. Ord, Calif., May 20, 1948; s. Sybil (Cain) H.; children: Christine, Katherine. BA, Am. U. Sch. Internat. Studies, 1969; JD, U. Tex., 1975. Bar: Tex. 1975, U.S. Dist. Ct. (we. dist.) Tex. 1976, U.S. Ct. Appeals (5th cir.) 1981, U.S. Dist. Ct. (so. dist.) Tex. 1983, U.S. Dist. Ct. (ea. dist.) Tex. 1984, U.S. Dist. Ct. (no. dist.) Tex. 1985, U.S. Supreme Ct. 1985, U.S. Dist. Ct. (we. dist.) Okla. 1986. Trial prosecutor, chief civil sect. County Atty.'s Office, Austin, Tex., 1974-77; assoc. Clark, Thomas, Winters and Shapiro, Austin, 1977-82; ptnr. Clark, Thomas, Winters and Newton, Austin, 1982—. Editor: Tex. Internat. Law Jour., 1973-74. Served to 1st lt. U.S. Army, 1969-72. Mem. ABA, Fed. Bar Assn., Tex. State Bar Assn., Travis County Bar Assn., Internat. Assn. Ins. Counsel, Tex. Assn. Ins. Counsel, Def. Research Inst., Assn. Ins. Attys. Club: Capital (Austin). Avocations: fishing, sports. Federal civil litigation, State civil litigation. Home: PO Box 1148 Austin TX 78767 Office: Clark Thomas Winters and Newton 700 Lavaca Austin TX 78701

HAYES, BYRON JACKSON, JR., lawyer; b. Los Angeles, July 9, 1934; s. Byron Jackson and Caroline Violet (Scott) H.; m. DeAnne Saliba, June 30, 1962; children—Kenneth Byron, Patricia DeAnne. Student, Pomona Coll., 1952-56; B.A. magna cum laude, Harvard U., LL.B. cum laude, 1959. Bar: Calif. 1960, U.S. Supreme Ct. 1963. Assoc., McCutchen, Black, Verleger & Shea, Los Angeles, 1960-68, ptnr., 1968—. Trustee, Los Angeles Ch. Extension Soc. United Methodist Ch., 1967-77, pres., 1974-77; Dir., pres. Pacific and S.W. United Methodist Found., 1978-83, chancellor annual conf., 1979-86. Served to capt. U.S. Army, 1959-65. Named layperson of yr. Pacific and S.W. Annual Conf., United Methodist Ch., 1981. Mem. Am. Coll. Mortgage Attys., Calif. Bar Assn., ABA, Am. Judicature Soc., Assn. Real Estate Attys., Los Angeles County Bar Assn. (chmn. real property sect. 1982-83), Pomona Coll. Alumni Assn. (pres. 1984-85). Club: Lakeside Golf (Toluca Lake, Calif.). Real property, Contracts commercial, General corporate. Office: 600 Wilshire Blvd 9th Floor Los Angeles CA 90017

HAYES, DAVID GREENE, lawyer, district attorney general Tenn.; b. Cookeville, Tenn., Aug. 22, 1943; s. O. W. and Marguerite (Green) H.; m. Georgiana Scott, Oct. 10, 1973; children—Scott, Julie, David. B.S., U. Tenn., 1964; J.D., U. Miss., 1970. Bar: Miss. 1971, U.S. Dist. Ct. (no. dist.) Miss. 1971, Tenn. 1972, U.S. Dist. Ct. (we. dist.) Tenn. 1972, U.S. Ct. Appeals (6th cir.) 1974. Mem. staff legal dept. Exxon Corp., Houston, 1972-73; ptnr. firm Maness, Conley & Hayes, Union City, Tenn., 1972-78; dist. atty. gen. State of Tenn., 1978—; lectr. U. Tenn., 1982; mem. exec. com. Tenn. Dist. Atty.'s Gen. Conf., 1982-84, pres. conf., 1984-85. Mem. Obion County Bar Assn. (past pres.), Tenn. Bar Assn. (bd. govs. 1984-85, past chmn. state membership com.), ABA, Union City C. of C., Delta Theta Phi, Pi Sigma Alpha. Democrat. Criminal. Office: Dist Atty Gen's Office Union County Courthouse Union City TN 38261

HAYES, DAVID JOHN ARTHUR, JR., association executive; b. Chgo., July 30, 1929; s. David J.A. and Lucille (Johnson) H.; m. Anne Huston, Feb. 20, 1963; children—David J.A. III, Cary. A.B., Harvard U., 1952; J.D., Ill. Inst. Tech.-Kent Coll. Law, 1961. Bar: Ill. Trust officer, asst. sec. First Nat. Bank of Evanston, Ill., 1961-63; gen. counsel Ill. State Bar Assn., Chgo., 1963-66; asst. dir. ABA, Chgo., 1966-68, div. dir., 1968-69, asst. exec. dir., 1969—; exec. dir. Naval Res. Lawyers Assn., 1971-75; asst. sec. gen. Internat. Bar Assn., 1978-80. Contbr. articles to profl. jours. Served to capt. JAGC, USNR. Fellow Am. Bar Found.; mem. ABA, Ill. State Bar Assn. (ho. of dels. 1972-76), Interam. Bar Assn. (asst. sec. gen. 1984—), Nat. Orgn. Bar Counsel (pres. 1967), Chgo. Bar Assn. Club: Michigan Shores. Legal association executive, Military, Probate. Home: 908 Pontiac Rd Wilmette IL 60091 Office: 750 N Lake Shore Dr Chicago IL 60611

HAYES, DAVID MICHAEL, lawyer; b. Syracuse, N.Y., Dec. 2, 1943; s. James P. and Lillie Anna (Wood) H.; m. Elizabeth S. Tracy, Aug. 26, 1972; children: Timothy T., Ann Elizabeth S. A.B., Syracuse U.; LL.B., U. Va., 1968. Bar: N.Y. 1969, Va. 1968. Assoc. Hiscock & Barclay, Syracuse, 1968-72; asst. gen. counsel Agway Inc., Syracuse, 1972-81, gen. counsel, 1981—; sec. counsel to bd. dirs. Texas City City Refining Inc., 1978—. Bd. dirs. Syracuse Boys Club, 1980. Served with U.S. Army N.G., 1968-74. Mem. ABA; mem Onondaga County Bar assn.; mem. N.Y. State Bar Assn., Va. State Bar. Democrat. Club: Skaneateles Country. General corporate. Office: Agway Inc PO Box 4933 Syracuse NY 13221-4933

HAYES, DEWEY NORMAN, JR., lawyer; b. Douglas, Ga., May 7, 1955; s. Dewey N. and Margaret Harrell (Haley) H.; m. Clara June Carver, Mar. 10, 1984. AB, U. Ga., 1976; JD, Mercer U., 1979. Bar: U.S. Dist. Ct. (so. and mid. dists.) Ga. 1979, U.S. Ct. Appeals (5th and 11th cirs.) 1979. Sole practice Douglas, 1979—; city atty. Ambrose, Ga., 1980—; soliciter State Ct., Coffee County, Ga., 1985—. V.p. Coffee County ARC, Douglas, 1980-85, Ga. Assn. Dem. County Chmn., 1985; mem. Dem. Exec. Com., Atlanta, 1985—. Mem. Ga. Assn. Dems. (v.p., co-chmn. 1985—). Democrat. Methodist. Lodge: Lions (v.p. Douglas 1983—, pres. 1987). State civil litigation, Federal civil litigation, Workers' compensation. Home: 504 N College Ave Douglas GA 31533 Office: 105 S Madison Ave PO Box 933 Douglas GA 31533

HAYES, DEWEY NORMAN, lawyer; b. Ga., July 27, 1923; s. J.C. and Mary (Walsh) H.; m. Margare Haley, June 16, 1951; children: Dewey Jr., Franklin, Candy. AB, Mercer U., JD, 1949. Bar: Ga. 1949, U.S. Supreme Ct. 1966. Mem. Ga. Ho. of Reps., 1953-56; dist. atty. Waycross Jud. Cir., Ga., 1957-80; sole practice Douglas, Ga., 1980—; instr. law South Ga. Coll., 1973. Author: You and the Law, 1970, Georgia Warrants, 1972; Miranda, 1973; Search and Seizure, 1973. Mem. Ga. State Crime Commn., 1973-74. Served with U.S. Army, 1942-46, ETO, PTO. Mem. Nat. Dist. Atty.'s Assn., Dist. Attys. Assn. Ga. (pres. 1972), Am. Legion, V.F.W., Douglas Bar Assn. (pres. 1962—), Delta Theta Phi (pres. 1949), Kappa Sigma. Methodist. Lodges: Elk, Lion, Woodman of World. Pension, profit-sharing, and employee benefits, Insurance, Personal injury. Office: PO Box 766 Douglas GA 31533

HAYES, GEORGE NICHOLAS, lawyer; b. Alliance, Ohio, Sept. 30, 1928; s. Nicholas John and Mary Irene (Fanady) H. B.A., U. Akron, 1950; M.A., Western Res. U., 1953, LL.B., 1955. Bar: Ohio 1955, U.S. Dist. Ct. Alaska 1957, Alaska 1959, U.S. Ct. Appeals (9th cir.) 1958, U.S. Supreme Ct. 1964, Wash. 1972. Mcpl. ct. prosecutor, asst. county prosecutor Portage County, Ravenna, Ohio, 1955-57; asst. U.S. atty. Fairbanks and Anchorage (Alaska), 1957-59; dep. atty. gen. State of Alaka, 1959-62; dist. atty. 3d Jud. Dist., Anchorage, 1960-62; atty. gen., Juneau, Alaska, 1962-64; spl. counsel to Gov., State of Alaska on earthquake recovery program at Washington, 1964; ptnr. Delaney, Wiles, Hayes, Reitman & Brubaker, Inc., Anchorage, 1964—. Mem. ABA, Alaska Bar Assn., Ohio Bar Assn., Anchorage Bar Assn., Am. Coll. Trial Lawyers (state chmn.). Democrat. Personal injury, Federal civil litigation, State civil litigation. Office: 1007 W 3d Ave Anchorage AK 99501

HAYES, GERALD JOSEPH, lawyer; b. Bronx, N.Y., July 24, 1950; s. James Joseph and Gladys (Guest) H.; m. Diane Elizabeth Willoughby, July 21, 1984; 1 child, Erin Jane. BA, U. Mass., 1972; JD, U. Miami, 1978. Bar: N.Y. 1979, U.S. Dist. Ct. (so. dist.) N.Y. 1979. Assoc. Baker & McKenzie, N.Y.C., 1978-85, ptnr., 1985—. Mem. ABA (atomic energy com. pub. utility law sect.), Assn. of Bar of City of N.Y. (com. on nuclear tech. and law, com. on ins. law). Insurance, Private international, Nuclear power. Office: Baker & McKenzie 805 3d Ave New York NY 10022

HAYES, KENNETH THOMAS, lawyer; b. Grand Rapids, Mich., Oct. 18, 1913; s. Thomas Rutherford and Emma Amelia (Engel) H.; m. Caroline Mary Woodford, June 21, 1941 (dec. Nov. 1968); children: Ronald, Jain, Patrick, Kenneth T. Jr.; m. Barbara Nancy Lovingfoss, Nov. 26, 1970. LLB, Ind. U., 1937. Bar: Mich. 1938. Music detective Allaben & Wiarda, Grand Rapids, 1937-43; police prosecutor City of Grand Rapids, 1946-48; ptnr. A-W Hayes & Hewitt, Grand Rapids, 1948-52, Hayes, Davis & Dellenbusch, Grand Rapids, 1952-85. Pres. Better Films Council, Grand Rapids, 1948-50. Served to lt. JAGC, USAF, 1943-46, CBI, with Res. 1946-73. Mem. ABA, Fed. Bar Assn., Mich. Bar Assn. (chmn. mil.), Grand Rapids Bar Assn., Assn. Trial Lawyers Am., Res. Officers Assn. (pres. 1950), Air Force Assn. (pres. 1948). Republican. Episcopalian. Avocations: philatelist, piano. State civil litigation, Personal injury, Insurance. Home: 2945 Woodcliff Circle Grand Rapids MI 49506 Office: Hayes Davis & Dellenbusch 535 Fountain NE Grand Rapids MI 49503

HAYES, LEWIS MIFFLIN, JR., lawyer; b. Mpls., May 5, 1941; s. Lewis Mifflin and Helen Camille (Vail) H.; m. Patricia Louise Schwab, June 3, 1967; m., Roberta Jane Hobson, Dec. 29, 1977; m. Diana Amorosino, Mar. 31, 1983; children: Rhoda Margaret, Lewis Mifflin, III, Robert Nelson. AB cum laude in Polit. Sci., Kenyon Coll., Gambier, Ohio, 1963; LLB with distinction, Duke U., 1966. Bar: N.Y. 1967, N.J. 1974, U.S. Sup. Ct. 1974, U.S. Tax Ct. 1978, U.S. Dist. Ct. (so. and ea. dist.) N.Y. 1968, U.S. Dist. Ct. N.J. 1974, U.S. Ct. Apls. (2d cir.). Assoc. Mudge Rose Guthrie & Alexander, N.Y.C., 1966-73, Gifford, Woody, Carter & Hays, N.Y.C., 1973-76; ptnr. Hayes and Jenkins, N.Y.C. and Elizabeth, N.J., 1976-80; sole practice, N.Y.C. and Elizabeth, 1980—. Trustee The Vail-Deare Sch., 1979-83. Served with U.S. Navy, 1966-68. Mem. N.J. State Bar Assn. Presbyterian. Clubs: Seaside Park (N.J.) Yacht; Elizabeth Town & Country. Federal civil litigation, Contracts commercial, Probate. Home: 310 Pearl Pl Scotch Plains NJ 07076 Office: 24-52 Rahway Ave Elizabeth NJ 07202

HAYES, MARGARET MARY, lawyer; b. Southington, Conn., Oct. 26, 1957; d. Michael Francis and Ann Theresa (Draper) H. BA magna cum laude, Tufts U., 1979; JD, U. Conn., 1982. Bar: Conn. 1982, U.S. Dist. Ct. Conn. 1982. Assoc. Anderson & Alden, Bristol, Conn., 1982-86, ptnr., 1986—. 1st v.p. Bristol Girls' Club Family Ctr., 1986—. Mem. ABA, Conn. Bar Assn., Bristol Bar Assn. (treas. 1986—), Assn. Am. Trial Lawyers, Conn. Trial Lawyers Assn. Democrat. Roman Catholic. State civil litigation, Criminal, Personal injury. Office: Anderson & Alden 238 Main St Bristol CT 06010

HAYES, MARK STEPHEN, lawyer; b. Oakland City, Ind., July 5, 1946; s. Daniel J. and Helen M. (Koenig) H.; m. Janice S. Hougland, Aug. 4, 1968; children: Meredith A., Matthew D. BS, Ind. State U., 1967, MBA, 1972; MA, Mich. State U., 1968; JD, Ind. U., 1976; PhD, Ohio U., 1981. Bar: Ind. 1976, D.C. 1978, U.S. Supreme Ct. 1979. Instr. Ind. State U., Terre Haute, 1968-72; atty. FCC, Washington, 1976-84; sr. atty. Storer Communications, Inc., Miami, Fla., 1984—. General corporate, Libel, Communications. Office: Storer Communications Inc 12000 Biscayne Blvd Miami FL 33181

HAYES, MICHAEL AUGUSTINE, JR., lawyer; b. N.Y.C., June 14, 1934; s. Michael Augustin and Mary Rita (Ross) H.; m. Sheila Mary Hagan, May 26, 1962; children—Laura Marie, Allison Mary, Susannah Rachel. A.B., Fordham U., 1955, LL.B., 1961. Bar: N.Y. 1961, U.S. Dist. Ct. (so. dist.) N.Y. 1967, U.S. Dist. Ct. (no. dist.) N.Y. 1983. Mem. firm Hayes & Hayes, N.Y.C., 1961-63; assoc. Joyce, Campbell & Paluso, N.Y.C., 1963-65; ptnr. Wilson, Bave & Hayes, Yonkers, N.Y., 1965-82, McCabe & Mack, Poughkeepsie, N.Y., 1982—. Mem. Westchester County Bd. Suprs., 1963-67. Served to capt. USAF, 1955-58. Mem. Assn. Trial Lawyers Am., Assn. Ins. Attys., ABA, N.Y. State Bar Assn., Westchester County Bar Assn., Dutchess County Bar Assn. Republican. Roman Catholic. State civil litigation, Insurance, Personal injury. Home: 17 Deer Hill Ln Briarcliff Manor NY 10510 Office: McCabe & Mack 42 Catharine St Poughkeepsie NY 12602

HAYES, NEIL JOHN, lawyer; b. N.Y.C., Nov. 16, 1951; s. John T. and Marion G. (Watson) H.; m. Rebecca W. Wisner, Dec. 8. 1985. BA, Villanova U., 1973; JD, Stetson U., 1981. Bar: Fla. 1982, U.S. Dist. Ct. (so. and mid. dists.) Fla. 1982, U.S. Supreme Ct. 1986. Detective Mt. Laurel (N.J.) Police Dept., 1974-79; law clk. to chief judge Fla. 5th Dist. Ct. Appeals, Daytona Beach, 1982-83; assoc. Jones & Foster P.A., W. Palm Beach, Fla., 1983—. Assoc. editor Stetson U. Law Rev., 1981. Mem. ABA, Fla. Bar Assn., Palm Beach County Bar Assn., Palm Beach County Claims Assn., Fla. Def. Lawyers Assn. Republican. Roman Catholic. Lodge: Rotary. Avocations: golf, racquetball. State civil litigation, Insurance, Contracts commercial. Home: 2558 Lochmore Rd West Palm Beach FL 33407 Office: Jones & Foster PA 505 S Flagler Dr West Palm Beach FL 33402

HAYES, NORMAN ROBERT, JR., lawyer; b. Schenectady, N.Y., Apr. 12, 1948; s. Norman Robert Sr. and Ethel May (Blair) H.; m. Alice S. Margitan, Oct. 14, 1972; children: Robert, Charles. BS, Clarkson U., 1970; JD, Union U., 1973. Bar: N.Y. 1974, U.S. Dist. Ct. (no. dist.) N.Y. 1974, U.S. Supreme Ct. 1978. Assoc. Wemple, Daly, Casey, Hayes, Watkins & Harter, Schenectady, 1973-86; ptnr. Hayes, Watkins & Casey, Schenectady, 1986—; pres. S.P.B. Industries, Clifton Park, N.Y., 1979—; bd. dirs. Saratoga Econ. Devel. Corp., Saratoga Springs, N.Y., Home Funding Finders Inc., Clifton Park, N.Y. Pres. County Knolls South Civic Assn., Clifton Park, 1975-76. Served to capt. U.S. Army, 1973-74. Mem. ABA, N.Y. State Bar Assn., Schenectady County Bar Assn. Republican. Banking, Real property, General corporate. Home: 19 Turnberry Ln Clifton Park NY 12065 Office: Hayes Watkins & Casey 1745 Rt 9 Clifton Park NY 12065

HAYES, RICHARD JOHNSON, association executive, lawyer; b. Chgo., May 25, 1933; s. David John Arthur and Lucille Margaret (Johnson) H.; m. Mary R. Lynch, Dec. 2, 1961; children: Susan, Richard, John, Edward. B.A., Colo. Coll., 1955; J.D., Georgetown U., 1961. Bar: Ill. 1961. Assoc. firm Barnabas F. Sears, Chgo., 1961-63, Peterson, Lowry, Rall, Barber and Ross, Chgo., 1963-65; staff dir. Am. Bar Assn., Chgo., 1965-70; exec. dir. Internat. Assn. Ins. Counsel, Chgo., 1970—; instr. various legal programs 1966—, Ins. Counsel Trial Acad., 1973—. Editor: Antitrust Law Jour, 1969—. Served to 1st lt. AUS, 1955-57. Mem. Am., Chgo. socs. assn. execs., ABA (chmn. prepaid legal services 1977-78), Ill. Bar Assn., Chgo. Bar Assn., Jr. Bar (chmn. 1965), Nat. Conf. Lawyers and Ins. Cos. (bd. dirs. 1983—), Phi Alpha Delta, Beta Theta Pi. Clubs: Rotary/One (Chgo.), Tower (Chgo.); Mich. Shores (Wilmette, Ill.). Federal civil litigation, State civil litigation, Insurance. Home: 1920 Thornwood St Wilmette IL 60091 Office: 20 N Wacker Dr Chicago IL 60606

HAYES, ROY C., lawyer; b. 1940. AB, Notre Dame U.; JD, U. Detroit. Bar: Mich. 1986. U.S. atty. ea. dist. State of Mich., Detroit. Office: 817 Fed Bldg 231 W Lafayette Detroit MI 48226 *

HAYES, WEBB COOK, III, lawyer; b. Toledo, Ohio, Sept. 25, 1920; s. Webb Cook and Martha (Wilder) H.; m. Betty Frost, May 14, 1945; children: Webb Cook, Burke Frost, Stephen Austin, Jeffrey Kent. B.A., Yale U., 1942; LL.B., George Washington U., 1948. Bar: D.C. 1948, U.S. Ct. Claims 1951, U.S. Ct. Mil. Appeals 1951, U.S. Supreme Ct. 1951. Ptnr. Frost & Towers, Washington, 1948-73, Baker & Hostetler, Washington, 1973—; dir. Textron Inc., Providence, mem. exec., audit, nominating coms. Pres. trustee Rutherford B. Hayes Presdl. Ctr., Fremont Ohio, 1952—; trustee Washington Hosp. Ctr., 1962-72, James Johnston Trust, 1970-78. Served to lt. USN, 1942-46. Mem. ABA, D.C. Bar Assn., Bar Assn. D.C., Barristers, Lawyers Club D.C. Republican. Clubs: Chevy Chase, Burning Tree, Met. Home: 4401 Boxwood Rd Bethesda MD 20816 Office: 1050 Connecticut Ave NW Washington DC 20036

HAYGOOD, JOHN WARREN, lawyer; b. Richmond, Tex., Sept. 16, 1924; s. Claude Culberson and Jessie Hurley (Scott) H.; m. Mary Forea McGill, Aug. 25, 1946 (div.); children—Scott McGill, Reid Alexander (dec.), Holly Mary. A.B., Centenary Coll. of La., 1947; LL.B., Tulane U. of La., 1950. Bar: La. 1950, U.S. Dist. Ct. (we. dist.) La. 1952, U.S. Supreme Ct. 1959, U.S. Ct. Appeals (5th cir.) 1960, U.S. Dist. Ct. (ea. and mid. dists.) La. 1966, U.S. Dist. Ct. (so. dist.) Miss. 1968. Atty. legal dept. Ark.-Fuel Oil Corp., Shreveport, La., 1953-58; ptnr. Stagg, Cady, Haygood & Beard, Shreveport, 1958-65, Jones, Walker, Waechter, Poitevent, Carrere & Denegre, New Orleans, 1965—. Served as 2d lt. USAAF, 1943-45; 1st lt. USAF, 1950-52. Mem. La. State Bar Assn., ABA, Fed. Power Bar Assn. Republican. Methodist. Clubs: Plimsoll, City (New Orleans). Administrative and regulatory, Federal civil litigation, State civil litigation. Office: Jones Walker Waechter Poitevent Carrere & Denegre 201 St Charles Ave New Orleans LA 70170

HAYHURST, RICHARD ALLEN, lawyer; b. Parkersburg, W.Va., Dec. 28, 1948; s. Blake and Jane (Collinson) H.; m. Abigail Jane Seaman, Mar. 29, 1975. Student, Coll. William and Mary, 1965-66; AB in Econs., W.Va. U., 1969; JD, U. Mich., 1972. Bar: W.Va. 1972, U.S. Supreme Ct. 1977. Sole practice Parkersburg, 1972-77, 87—; ptnr. Davis, Davis, Hall & Clavis, Parkersburg, 1977-83, Davis, Bailey, Pfalzgraf & Hall, Parkersburg, 1983-87; judge Mcpl. Ct., Pennsboro, W.Va., 1980—. Disting. Service award W.Va. U. Sch. Law, 1983. Mem. ABA, Def. Research Inst., Nat. Assn. R.R. Trial Counsel, Eastern Mineral Law Found., W.Va. Bar Assn. (v.p. 1981-82). Republican. Presbyterian. Club: Bankers (Cin.). Banking, Insurance, Admiralty. Home: 1117 Juliana St Parkersburg WV 26102 Office: 410 Market St PO Box 86 Parkersburg WV 26102

HAYNES, GEORGE CLEVE, lawyer, author; b. St. Louis, Jan. 15, 1946; s. George Cave and Helen Marie (Cleve) H. B.A., So. Ill. U., Edwardsville, 1969; J.D., Ill. Inst. Tech., 1974. Bar: Wash. 1977, U.S. Dist. Ct. (we. dist.) Wash. 1977, U.S. Ct. Appeals (9th cir.) 1978, U.S. Supreme Ct. 1982. Ptnr. Puro & Haynes, Seattle, 1977-79; sole practice, Seattle, 1979-84, 86—; ptnr. Fligeltaub & Haynes, Seattle, 1984-86; judge pro tem Seattle Mcpl. Ct., 1977-84, King County Superior Ct., 1980; instr. Edmonds Community Coll., Wash., 1983-84; gen. counsel Alternative Intervention Resources King County, Seattle, 1984—. Mem. Wash. State Bar Assn., Sherlock Holmes Soc. of London, La Società Dante Alighieri. Club: Diogenes. Criminal, General practice, Legal history. Office: 1318 Joseph Vance Bldg 1402 3d Ave Seattle WA 98101

HAYNES, JEAN REED, lawyer; b. Miami, Fla., Apr. 6, 1949; d. Oswald Birnam and Arleen (Weidman) Dow; m. William Rutherford Reed, Apr. 15, 1974 (div. Sept. 1981); m. Thomas Beranek Haynes, Aug. 7, 1982. A.B. with honors, Pembroke Coll., 1971; M.A., Brown U., 1971; J.D., U. Chgo., 1981. Bar: Ill. 1981, U.S. Dist. Ct. (no. dist.) Ill. 1983, U.S. Ct. Appeals (7th cir.) 1982. Tchr. grades 1-4 Abbie Tuller Sch., Providence, 1971-72; tchr./facilitator St. Mary's Acad., Riverside, R.I., 1972-74; tchr./head lower sch. St. Francis Sch., Goshen, Ky., 1974-78; law clk. U.S. Ct. Appeals (7th cir.), Chgo., 1981-83; assoc. Kirkland & Ellis, Chgo., 1983—. Sustaining fellow Art Inst. Chgo., 1982—, mem. aux. bd. 1986—. Mem. ABA (litigation sect.), Chgo. Bar Assn., Ill. Bar Assn. (life), Am. Judicature Soc. (life). Federal civil litigation. Home: 179 East Lake Shore Dr Chicago IL 60611 Office: Kirkland & Ellis 200 E Randolph Dr Chicago IL 60611

HAYNIE, GILMORE SMITH, JR., lawyer; b. Bluffton, Ind., May 1, 1947; s. Gilmore Smith and Mary Ann (Kunkel) H.; m. Susan J. Higgins, Nov. 13, 1976; children: Devon Ann, Gilmore Smith III. BS, Ind. U., 1969, JD, 1973. Bar: Ind. 1973, U.S. Dist. Ct. (no. and so. dists.) Ind. 1973, U.S. Ct. Appeals (7th cir.) 1975. Assoc. Livingston, Dildine, Haynie & Yoder, Ft. Wayne, Ind., 1973-79, ptnr., 1979—. Active United Way of Allen County, Ft. Wayne, 1980—; bd. dirs. Jr. Achievement No. Ind., 1986—. Served with USAR, 1969-75. Mem. ABA, Ind. Bar Assn., Allen County Bar Assn. (exec. com. trial lawyers sect. 1983, chmn. civil procedure 1980-81). Democrat. Presbyterian. Clubs: Ft. Wayne Country (bd. dirs. 1984-86), Friars (Ft. Wayne). State civil litigation, Federal civil litigation, Insurance. Home: 6136 Devils Hollow Rd Fort Wayne IN 46804 Office: Livingston Dildine Haynie & Yoder 1400 One Summit Sq Fort Wayne IN 46802

HAYNIE, HOWARD EDWARD, lawyer; b. Chgo.; s. Howard Edward and Jean Potter (Faller) H.; m. Charlotte Ruth Monson, Sept. 25, 1954; children—Roy Faller, Guy Howard, Robin Ruth Haynie Schnettler. Student, Colo. U., 1946-48; B.S.B.A. with highest distinction, Northwestern U., 1951; J.D. cum laude, Loyola U.-Chgo., 1959. Bar: Ill. 1959. Ptnr. Sidley & Austin, Chgo., 1969. Bd. dirs. Chgo. Assn. Retarded Citizens, 1970—, Wilmette Camp Property, Inc., Ill., Wilmette Forum, 1976—, New Trier Twp. Citizens League, 1980—; trustee MacMurray Coll., 1987—; mem. Wilmette Zoning Bd., 1970-80, chmn., 1975-80; trustee MacMurray Coll., 1987—. Served to 1st lt. USMCR, 1951-53. Mem. Chgo. Mortgage Attys. Assn., Blue Key, Phi Alpha Delta, Beta Gamma Sigma, Sigma Chi. Republican. Clubs: Union League, Shriners, Westmoreland Country, Sheridan Shores Yacht, Mid Day, Legal, Law. Real property. Office: Sidley & Austin One First National Plaza Chicago IL 60603

HAYNSWORTH, KNOX LIVINGSTON, JR., lawyer; b. Greenville, S.C., Jan. 10, 1934; s. Knox Livingston and Elizabeth (Goldsmith) H.; m. Priscilla Barrett, July 2, 1960; children—Knox L., Priscilla B., Clement F. LL.B., U. S.C., 1959. Bar: S.C. 1959, D.C. 1974. Assoc. Haynsworth, Perry, Bryant, Marion & Johnstone, Greenville, 1959-64; ptnr. Thompson, Ogletree, and Haynsworth, Greenville, 1964-72; sr. ptnr. Haynsworth, Baldwin, Miles, Johnson, Greaves & Edwards, and predecessors, Greenville, 1972—; bd. govs. S.C. Bar, 1975, 77-80, mem. ho. of dels. 1975-77, 80-81, sec., 1981-82, pres.-elect, 1982-83, pres., 1983-84. Mem. ABA (labor relations law sect.), 4th Cir. Jud. Conf., Am. Judicature Soc., Am. Bar Found. (fellow), S.C. Bar Found. (fellow), Greater Greenville C. of C. Episcopalian. Clubs: Poinsett, Commerce, Greenville (Greenville); Summit (Columbia, S.C.). Labor, Workers' compensation. Home: 20 Woodland Way Circle Greenville SC 29601 Office: Haynsworth Baldwin Miles et al 918 S Pleasantburg Dr PO Box 10888 Greenville SC 29603 also: 1034 Riverside Ave Jacksonville FL 32204

HAYS, JACK D.H., state supreme court justice; b. Lund, Nev., Feb. 17, 1917; s. Charles Harold and Thelma (Savage) H.; children by previous marriage—Eugene Harrington, Rory Cochrane, Bruce Harvey, Victoria Wakeling. Grad., So. Meth. U., 1941. Bar: Ariz. 1946. Since practiced in Phoenix, asst. city atty., 1949-52; U.S. atty. Dist. Ariz., 1953-60; superior ct. judge Maricopa County, 1960-69; justice Ariz. Supreme Ct., 1969—, chief justice, 1972-74; Mem. 21st Ariz. Legislature, 1952; mem. Young Republican Exec. Com., 1948-50, Rep. State Central Com., 1948-53; vice chmn. Maricopa Rep. Com., 1949-53; Ariz. chmn. Eisenhower for Pres., 1952. Mem. State Justice Planning Governing Bd., 1969-74; mem. adv. bd. Roosevelt council Boy Scouts Am.; awards juror Freedoms Found., Valley Forge, 1973; Bd. dirs. Maricopa Legal Aid Soc. Served as maj. F.A. AUS, 1941-46. Recipient Big Brother of Year award, 1966; Outstanding State Appellate Judge award Assn. Trial Lawyers Am., 1984. Mem. Am. Judicature Soc. (Herbert Lincoln Harley award 1974), Am. Law Inst., Fed. Bar Assn., ABA, Inter-Am. Bar Assn., Ariz. Judges Assn. (pres. 1965-66), Inst. Jud. Administrn., Ariz. Acad., Assn. Trial Lawyers Am. (Outstanding State Appellate Judge award 1984), Lambda Chi Alpha, Phi Alpha Delta. Episcopalian. Lodge: Rotary. Jurisprudence. Office: 221 West Wing State Capitol Phoenix AZ 85007

HAYS, LARRY WELDON, lawyer; b. Houston, Feb. 8, 1936; s. Weldon Edgar and Clara Elizabeth (Carney) H. B.A., U. Tex., 1958; J.D., U. Houston, 1968. Bar: Tex. 1968. Asst. county atty. Harris County (Tex.), 1969-81, 83—; counsel Stewart Title Co., Houston, 1981-83. Mem. Harris County Hist. Commn. Served to capt. U.S. Army, to 1972. Mem. Houston Bar Assn., Tex. State Hist. Assn., Sons Republic of Tex., SAR, SCV, Phi Alpha Delta. Real property, State and local taxation, Condemnation. Office: 1001 Preston Room 634 Houston TX 77002

HAYS, RICHARD MARTIN, steel company executive, lawyer; b. Pitts., Dec. 19, 1927; s. Clarence Martin and Anne (Darby) H.; m. Barbara Ann Gerlit, Sept. 5, 1953; children—Richard Martin, Jr., David Willis, Carol Ann, Virginia Louise. A.B., Bucknell U., 1949; J.D., Cornell U., 1952. Bar:

Pa. 1952. Asst. atty. law dept. U.S. Steel Corp., Pitts., 1954-58, asst. sec., gen. atty., N.Y.C., 1964-76, asst. sec., sr. gen. atty.-corp., Pitts., 1976-83, sec., asst. gen. counsel, 1983—; sec., atty. Que. Cartier Mining Co., Port Cartier, Can., 1958-64. Served with U.S. Army, 1952-54. Mem. ABA, Pa. Bar Assn., Allegheny County Bar Assn., Am. Soc. Corp. Secs. (bd. dirs. 1978-85, chmn. 1983-84). Republican. Presbyterian. Clubs: Duquesne, Saint Clair Country (Pitts.). General corporate. Home: Two Mission Dr Pittsburgh PA 15228 Office: USX Corp 600 Grant St Pittsburgh PA 15230

HAYS, ROBERT ALEXANDER, lawyer; b. Westerly, R.I., June 20, 1944; s. William Henry and Margaret Elizabeth (Tefft) H.; m. Norma Marie Camerlin, Aug. 23, 1969; children—Stephanie Rebecca, Gregory Alexander. Assoc. Sci., Mitchell Coll., 1967; B.S., NYU, 1969, M.S., 1970; J.D., Del. Law Sch., 1976. Bar: N.J. 1976, U.S. Dist. Ct. N.J. 1976, U.S. Patent Office 1974, U.S. Ct. Appeals (fed. cir.) 1982. Mem. tech. staff RCA, Moorestown, N.J., 1970-73, patent atty., Princeton, N.J., 1973-78, resident patent counsel, Cherry Hill, N.J., 1978-80; group patent counsel Perkin-Elmer, Norwalk, Conn., 1980-84; patent counsel ITT, Shelton, Conn., 1984-86, patent atty. Pitney Bowes, Stamford, Conn., 1986—. Mem. Conn. Patent Law Assn., Tau Beta Pi, Eta Kappa Nu. Patent.

HAYS, ROBERT D., lawyer; b. Pitts., Apr. 12, 1927; s. Robert R. and Almeda (Davies) H.; m. Eloise Ruth Edwards, July 1, 1950; children: Janice L., Robert E. BBA, Ohio State U., 1950, JD, 1952. Bar: Ohio, U.S. Dist. Ct. (so. dist.) Ohio. Assoc. Alexander, Ebinger & Wenger, Columbus, Ohio, 1952-56; gen. counsel, sr. v.p. White Castle System, Inc., Columbus, 1956—. Bd. dirs. Better Bus. Bur. cen. Ohio, 1977—; sec., trustee Edgwar W. Ingram Found., Columbus, 1976—; bd. of trustees Julian Marcus Sr. Citizens Placement Bur., 1987—. Served with USNR, 1945-46. Mem. ABA, Ohio Bar Assn., Columbus Bar Assn., Am. Corp. Counsel Assn., Cen. Ohio Corp. Counsel Assn. (bd. dirs. 1983—), Foodservice and Lodging Inst. (bd. dirs. 1980—, pres. 1984-85), Ohio Council Retail Mchts. Chain Restaurants (chmn. 1984—, bd. dirs. 1984—), Columbus Jaycees (pres., bd. dirs. 1961, Outstanding Dir. 1959, Disting. Service award 1961). Republican. Clubs: Scioto Country (Columbus); Imperial Golf (Naples, Fla.). Avocations: golf, sports, reading. Labor, General corporate, Pension, profit-sharing, and employee benefits. Office: White Castle System Inc 555 Goodale St Columbus OH 43215

HAYS, SAMUEL SPARTAN, lawyer, consultant; b. Fairfield, Ala., Apr. 15, 1920; s. Samuel Spartan and Mabel (Vines) H.; m. Edwina Mallette Pringle, Jan. 26, 1942; children—Mary Mallette, Sally Ellen. B.S., U. Ala., 1942, J.D., 1952; M.S. in Govt. Mgmt., U. Denver, 1944. Bar: Ala. 1952, U.S. Supreme Ct. 1965. Tax research assoc. Tax Found., N.Y.C., 1944; rep. Tax Assn. Md., 1944-45; research dir. Tax Assn. Mo., 1945-46; exec. dir. Tax Assn. Ark., 1946-50; cons. Tax Assn. Pa., summer 1952; ptnr. law firm, Birmingham, Ala., 1952-59; tax and fiscal adv. Dept. State to Govt. of Iran, 1959-65, Govt. of Jordan, 1965, also intermittent cons. to other nations; sole practice, Mountain Brook, Ala., 1965—; cons. internat. bus. and taxes. Served with USN, 1943. Alfred P. Sloan Found. grantee, 1942-44. Episcopalian. Club: Masons. Editor Ala. Law Rev., 1952. Private international, General corporate, Corporate taxation.

HAYS, STEELE, judge; b. Little Rock, Mar. 25, 1925; s. L. Brooks and Marion (Prather) H.; m. Peggy Wall, July 12, 1980; children: Andrew Steele, Melissa Louise, Sarah Anne. B.A., U. Ark., 1948; J.D., George Washington U., 1951. Bar: Ark. 1951. Adminstrv. asst. to Congressman Brooks Hays, 1951-53; practice in Little Rock, 1953-79; mem. firm Spitzberg, Mitchell & Hays, 1953-79; circuit judge 6th Jud. Circuit Ark., Little Rock, 1969-70; judge Ark. Ct. Appeals (1st cir.), 1979-81; assoc. justice Ark. Supreme Ct., 1981—; chmn. Bd. Law Examiners, 1968-70. Mem. Ark. com. U.S. Civil Rights Commn.; Del. Presbyn. Ch. Consultation on Ch. Union, 1968-70; Trustee Presbyn. Found. Mem. ABA, Ark. Bar Assn. (past sec.-treas.), Sigma Chi, Delta Theta Phi. Jurisprudence. Home: 3515 Hill Rd #4 Little Rock AR 72205 Office: Justice Bldg Little Rock AR 72201

HAYS, THOMAS CLYDE, lawyer; b. Franklin, Ind., Mar. 3, 1951; s. Clyde Gilbert and Anna Marie (Hill) H.; m. Mary Linda Lux, June 19, 1976; children: Thomas Clyde Jr., Lindsay Marie. AB, Ind. U., 1973; JD, Woodrow Wilson Sch. Law, 1977. Bar: Ga. 1977, Ind.1979, U.S. Dist. Ct. (no. dist.) Ga. 1977, U.S. Dist. Ct. (so. dist.) Ind. 1979. Assoc. Spence, Garrett & Spence, Alpharetta, Ga., 1977-78, Reeves and Collier, Atlanta, 1978-79, Kitley and Schreckengast, Beech Grove, Ind., 1979-82; ptnr. Schreckengast and Hays, Indpls., 1982-85; assoc. Lewis, Bowman, St. Clair & Wagner, Indpls., 1985—. Pres. Briar Ln. Homeowners Assn., 1984. Mem. ABA, Ind. State Bar Assn., Ga. State Bar Assn., Indpls. Bar Assn. (litigation sect.), Ind. Def. Lawyer's Assn., Carmel (Ind.) Dad's Club. Republican. Roman Catholic. Lodges: Optimist (pres. Southside club 1984-85), Masons. Avocations: golf, bicycling. Insurance, State civil litigation, Personal injury. Home: 3491 Bridger N Dr Carmel IN 46032 Office: Lewis Bowman St Clair & Wagner 5101 Madison Ave Indianapolis IN 46227

HAYWARD, EDWARD JOSEPH, lawyer; b. Springfield, Mo., Dec. 4, 1943; s. Joseph Hunter and Rosemary (Barber) H.; m. Ellinor Duffy, Aug. 30, 1968; children: Jeffrey, Stephen, Susan. Student, U. d'Aix Marseille, Aix-en-Provence, France, 1963-64; AB, Stanford U., 1965; JD, Harvard U., 1971. Bar: N.Y. 1972, Minn. 1980. Assoc. Cleary, Gottlieb, Steen & Hamilton, N.Y.C. and Brussels, 1971-75, Oppenheimer Wolff & Donnelly, Brussels, 1975-79; ptnr. Oppenheimer Wolff & Donnelly, Mpls., 1979—; pres. Twin Cities Fgn. Trade Zone Inc., Mpls., 1983-84. Chmn. legis. com. Minn. World Trade Assn., Mpls., 1984—. Served to capt. U.S. Army, 1965-68. Mem. Minn. Bar Assn. (councillor internat. law sect. 1983—, sec. 1986—), French-Am. C. of C. (pres. 1985—). Republican. Episcopalian. Club: Mpls. Athletic. Avocations: languages, sports. Private international, General corporate, Immigration, naturalization, and customs. Office: Oppenheimer Wolff & Donnelly 4800 IDS Ctr Minneapolis MN 55402

HAYWARD, GEORGE JOHN, lawyer; b. Kingston, Pa., Dec. 30, 1944; s. Ralph R. and Martha P. (Tamkus) H.; m. Nancy E. Goldsmith, 1967 (div. 1974); children: Benjamin G., Jennifer R., Christopher D.; m. Jennifer M. Jordan, Feb. 23, 1985. BA, Kings Coll., 1966; JD, Harvard U., 1969. Bar: Pa. 1970, N.Y. 1980. Assoc. Montgomery, McCracken, Walker & Rhoads, Phila., 1969-71, Wolf, Block, Schorr & Solis-Cohn, Phila., 1971-73; gen. counsel AAMCO Industries, Inc., Bridgeport, Pa., 1973-78; asst. counsel, sec., dir. DeLorean Motor Co., N.Y.C., 1979-83; gen. counsel Internat. Distribution Ctrs., North Bergen, N.J., 1983—. Mem. ABA, Pa. Bar Assn., N.Y. State Bar Assn. Club: Harvard (N.Y.C.). General corporate, Contracts commercial, General practice. Home: 55 Stonewall Circle White Plains NY 10607 Office: Internat Distribution Ctrs Inc 2424 Railroad Ave North Bergen NJ 07047

HAYWARD, THOMAS ZANDER, JR., lawyer; b. Evanston, Ill., Arp. 21, 1940; s. Thomas Z. and Wilhelmina (White) H.; m. Sally Madden, June 20, 1964; children: Thomas Z., Wallace M., Robert M. BA, Northwestern U., 1962, JD, 1965; MBA, U. Chgo., 1970. Bar: Ill. 1966, Ohio, 1966, U.S. Dist. Ct. (no. dist.) Ill. 1966, U.S. Supreme Ct. 1970. Assoc. Defrees & Fiske, Chgo., 1965-69, ptnr., 1969-81; ptnr. Boodell, Sears, Giambalvo & Crowley, Chgo., 1981—. Trustee Northwestern U., 1980-84. Recipient Northwestern U. Alumni Service award, 1973. Mem. ABA (ho. of dels. 1984—), Ill. State Bar Assn., Chgo. Bar Assn. (pres. 1983-84). Republican. Presbyterian. Clubs: Chicago, Barrington Hills Country. General corporate, Real property. Home: 8 W County Line Rd Barrington Hills IL 60010 Office: 69 W Washington St Suite 500 Chicago IL 60602

HAYWOOD, EDMUND BURKE, lawyer; b. Raleigh, N.C., Mar. 22, 1953; s. Hubert Benbury Jr. and Virginia Louise (Allison) H.; Terri Elizabeth Starritt, May 16, 1981; 1 child, Edmund Burke Jr. BA in French, U. N.C., 1976, JD, 1979; postgrad., N.C. State U., 1979-80. Bar: N.C. 1980, U.S. Dist. Ct. (ea. dist.) N.C. 1980, U.S. Ct. Appeals (4th cir.) 1981, U.S. Supreme Ct. 1983. Assoc. Jordan, Brown, Price & Wall, Raleigh, N.C., 1980-83; ptnr. Bass, Haywood & Powell (and predecessor firms), Raleigh, 1984—. Mem. Capital Area Community Chorus, Raleigh, 1985—; bd. dirs. Raleigh YMCA, 1985—. Mem. ABA, N.C. Bar Assn., Wake County Bar Assn. (pres. young lawyers div. 1986—), Mensa, English-Speaking Union (pres. Raleigh-Durham-Chapel Hill br. 1986—), Phi Delta Theta, Phi Delta Phi, Phi Eta Sigma. Democrat. Episcopalian. Clubs: Raleigh Execs., Terpsichorean, Milburnie Fishing, Soc. of the Cin. Lodge: Rotary. Avocations: running, weight lifting, singing. Real property, Consumer commercial, General practice. Home: 2704 Kittrell Dr Raleigh NC 27608 Office: Bass Haywood & Powell 1204 BB&T Bldg Raleigh NC 27602

HAZARD, GEOFFREY CORNELL, JR., law educator; b. Cleve., Sept. 18, 1929; s. Geoffrey Cornell and Virginia (Perry) H.; m. Elizabeth O'Hara; children—James G., Katherine W., Robin P., Geoffrey Cornell III. B.A., Swarthmore Coll., 1953; LL.B., Columbia U., 1954. Bar: Oreg. 1954, Calif. 1960, Conn. 1982. Asso. firm Hart, Spencer, McCulloch, Rockwood & Davies, Portland, Oreg., 1954-57; exec. sec. Oreg. Legis. Interim Com. Jud. Adminstrn., 1957-58; asso. prof. law, then prof. U. Calif. at Berkeley, 1958-64; prof. law U. Chgo., 1964-71; prof. law Yale U., 1971—, prof. mgmt., 1979-83, Sterling prof. law, 1986—, acting dean Sch. Orgn. and Mgmt., 1980-81; dir. Am. Law Inst., 1984—; exec. dir. Am. Bar Found., Chgo., 1964-70; reporter Am. Law Inst. Restatement of Judgments, 1974-82; mem. Adminstrv. Conf. U.S., 1971-78. Author: (with David W. Louisell and Colin Tait) Pleading and Procedure, 1962, 5th edit., 1983, Research in Civil Procedure, 1963, (with Fleming James) Civil Procedure, 3d edit, 1985, Ethics in the Practice of Law, 1978, (with W. William Hodes) Law of Lawyering, 1985, also articles.; Editor: Law in a Changing America, 1968, (with Deborah Rhode) Legal Profession: Responsibility and Regulation, 1985. Served with USAF, 1948-49. Mem. ABA (reporter Spl. Commn. to Evaluate Profl. Standards 1978-83, Commn. on Standards of Jud. Adminstrn., 1971-77, cons. Spl. Commn. Standards of Ind. Conduct, 1970-72), Calif. State Bar, Conn. Bar Assn., Assn. Bar City N.Y., Phi Beta Kappa. Episcopalian. Club: Century Assn. (N.Y.C.). Civil Procedure, Jurisprudence, Legal ethics. Home: 207 Armory St New Haven CT 06511

HAZARD, JOHN NEWBOLD, retired public law educator; b. Syracuse, N.Y., Jan. 5, 1909; s. John Gibson and Ada Bosarte (DeKalb) H.; m. Susan Lawrence, March 8, 1941; children: John Gibson, William Lawrence, Nancy, Barbara Peace. Ed., The Hill Sch., 1926; A.B., Yale U., 1930; LL.B., Harvard U., 1934; certificate, Moscow Juridical Inst., 1937; J.S.D., U. Chgo., 1939; LL.D., U. Freiburg, 1969, Lehigh U., 1970, Leiden U., 1975, U. Paris, 1977, U. Louvain, 1979, U. Sydney, 1986. Bar: N.Y. bar, U.S. Supreme Ct. bar. Fellow Inst. of Current World Affairs (student of Soviet law), 1934-39; asso. with law firm Baldwin, Todd & Young, N.Y.C., 1939-41; dep. dir. U.S.S.R. br. Fgn. Econ. Adminstrn. (and predecessor agys.), 1941-45; adv. on state trading Dept. State, 1945-46; prof. public law Columbia, 1946-77, Nash prof. law, 1976-77, Nash prof. law emeritus, 1977—; adviser on Soviet law to U.S. chief of counsel for prosecution of Axis criminality, 1945; lectr. Soviet law U. Chgo., 1938-39; lectr. Soviet polit. instns. Columbia U., 1940-41; lectr. internat. politics Fgn. Service Ednl. Found., 1944-46; vis. prof. law Yale U., spring 1949, 50, 52, 54, 56; vis. Fulbright prof. U. Cambridge, London Sch. Econs., 1952-53, U. Louvain, Belgium, 1979; vis. prof. U. Tokyo, summer 1956, Grad. Sch. Internat. Studies, Geneva, 1959-60; prof. Luxembourg Comparative Law Faculty, summers 1958-60, Strasbourg Comparative Law Faculty, summers 1962-87; vis. prof. U. Teheran, fall 1966, U. Sydney, 1978, summer 1986; Goodhart prof. Cambridge U., 1981-82; prof. European U. Inst., 1984-85; sr. specialist East-West Center Hawaii, spring 1967; fellow Center for Advanced Study in the Behavioral Scis., 1961-62. Author: Soviet Housing Law, 1939, Law and Social Change in the USSR, 1953, The Soviet System of Government, 1957, Settling Disputes in Soviet Society, 1960, (with I. Shapiro) The Soviet Legal System, 1962, Communists and Their Law, 1969, Managing Change in the USSR, 1983; Recollections of a Pioneer Sovietologist, 1983; Editor: Soviet Legal Philosophy, 1951; Bd. editors: Am. Slavic and East European Rev; mng. editor, 1951-59; bd. editors: Am. Polit. Sci. Rev, 1950, Am. Jour. Internat. Law, 1956-72, hon. editor, 1974—; bd. editors: Am. Jour. Comparative Law, 1952—. Dir. and sec. Am. Assn. for the Advancement of Slavic Studies, 1948-60, treas., 1961-65. Recipient Pres.'s Certificate of Merit, 1947. Mem. ABA (vice chmn. internat. and comparative law 1951-58), Assn. of Bar of City of N.Y. (chmn. com. fgn. law 1947-50), Am. Polit. Sci. Assn., Am. Soc. Internat. Law (exec. council 1946-49, 51-54, v.p. 1971-73, hon. v.p. 1973-84, hon. pres. 1984-86), Am. br. of Internat. Law Assn. (chmn. exec. com. 1958-59, v.p. 1957-73, pres. 1973-79), Internat. Acad. Comparative Law (pres. 1984—), Internat. Assn. Legal Sci. (pres. 1968-70), Am. Philos. Soc., Am. Acad. Arts and Scis., World Assn. Law Profs. (co-chmn. 1975-84), Consular Law Soc. (pres. 1986-87), Am. Fgn. Law Assn. (pres. 1973-76), Brit. Acad. (corr.), Phi Alpha Delta, Alpha Delta Phi. Democrat. Episcopalian. Clubs: Century (N.Y.); University (Washington); Wolf's Head. Legal education, Jurisprudence, Soviet Law. Home: 20 E 94th St New York NY 10128 Office: 435 W 116th St New York NY 10027

HAZELWOOD, KEITH WILLIAM, lawyer; b. Granite City, Ill., Feb. 27, 1947; s. Everett Henry and Mabel Marie (Tilley) H.; m. Nancy Ann Keith, Jan. 12. 1973; children: Royce William, Robert Spencer. AB, Dartmouth Coll., 1967; JD, Washington U., 1970. Bar: Mo. 1970, U.S. Dist. Ct. (ea. and we. dists.) Mo. 1970, U.S. Ct. Appeals (8th cir.) 1970, U.S. Supreme Ct. 1972. Assoc. Shaw & Howlett, Clayton, Mo., 1970-74; sole practice St. Charles, Mo., 1974-75; assoc. Bruere & Rollings, St. Charles, 1975-77; ptnr. Rollings, Gerhardt & Hazelwood, St. Charles, 1977-80, Hazelwood, Barklage & Barklage, St. Charles, 1981—. Bd. dirs. St. Charles County YMCA, 1983—, Leadership St. Louis; v.p., sec., bd. dirs. Providence Program, St. Louis, 1985—; chmn., bd. overseers Lindenwood Coll., St. Charles, 1986—. Served to 1st lt. USMC, 1968. Mem. Mo. State Bar Assn., St. Charles County Bar Assn., St. Charles C. of C. (bd. dirs., treas. 1987—). Republican. Episcopalian. Lodges: Jaycees (local pres., state legal counsel, region legal counsel St. Louis 1974—). Real property. Office: Hazelwood Barklage & Barklage PC 1053 Cave Springs Rd Suite 201 Saint Charles MO 63303

HAZEN, JAMES MICHAEL, lawyer; b. Erie, Pa., Dec. 17, 1948; s. John M. and Anne M. (Musser) H.; m. Catherine S. Cline, June 10, 1972 (div. Aug. 1983); m. Ann M. O'Donnell, Nov. 26, 1983; 1 child, Elizabeth. AB, Columbia U., 1970, JD, 1973. Bar: N.Y. 1974, U.S. Dist. Ct. (so. and ea. dists.) N.Y. 1974, U.S. Ct. Appeals (2d cir.) 1974, N.J. 1984, U.S. Dist. Ct. (no. dist.) N.Y. 1985, U.S. Ct. Appeals (3d cir.) 1985. Assoc. Haight, Gardner, Poor & Havens, N.Y.C., 1973-80; ptnr. McHugh, Leonard & O'Conor, N.Y.C., 1980-84, Leonard, Kenny & Stearns, N.Y.C., 1984—. Mem. ABA, N.Y. State Bar Assn., N.J. Bar Assn., Maritime Law Assn. Republican. Roman Catholic. Federal civil litigation, State civil litigation. Home: 700 Victory Blvd Staten Island NY 10301 Office: Leonard Kenny Stearns 26 Broadway New York NY 10004

HAZEN, WILLIAM HARRIS, finance executive; b. Salem, Mass., Jan. 6, 1931; s. Julius Elijah and Dorothy (Harris) H.; m. Judith Ettl, Feb. 22, 1959; children: Cordelia, Alexes. A.B., Bowdoin Coll., 1952; J.D., Harvard U., 1958. Bar: N.Y. 1959. With firm Pell, Butler, Hatch, Curtis & LeViness, N.Y.C., 1959-61; exec. asst. to N.Y. supt. banks, 1962-64; with J.W. Seligman & Co., N.Y.C., 1964-68, partner, 1969-80, mem. mng. com., 1981—, also bd. dirs.; pres., chief exec. officer Seligman Securities, Inc., N.Y.C., 1981-83, J. & W. Seligman Trust Co., 1983—; v.p. Seligman Mut. Funds, 1969-81, Tri-Continental Corp., N.Y.C., 1969-81. Adv. mem. Joint Legislative Com. Revise Banking Laws, N.Y. State, 1964; bd. overseers Bowdoin Coll., 1981—Served to lt. USNR, 1952-55, Korea. Mem. Zeta Psi. Congregationalist (trustee). Club: Heights Casino (Bklyn.). Home: 55 Remsen St Brooklyn Heights NY 11201 Office: One Bankers Trust Plaza New York NY 10006

HEAD, CHRISTOPHER ALAN, lawyer; b. Buffalo, Nov. 28, 1951; s. Alan S. and Mary Ellen (Carrig) H.; m. Kathleen Rosemarie Meosky, Aug. 22, 1976; children: Matthew, David, Maribeth & Sally. BA, Canisius Coll., 1974; JD, U. Akron, 1977. Bar: Ohio 1977, N.Y. 1978, U.S. Dist. Ct. (we. dist.) N.Y. 1979. Adminstr. contracts Comptek Research Inc., Buffalo, 1977-78, corp. counsel, 1978-82, gen. counsel, 1983-85, v.p., gen. counsel, 1985—; corp. counsel Barrister Info. System Corp., Buffalo, 1982-83; bd. dirs. Goldome N.Y. Capital Corp., Wilmington, Del. Mem. ABA, N.Y. State Bar Assn., Erie County Bar Assn., Niagara Frontier Corp. Counsel Assn. (pres. 1984-85). Democrat. Roman Catholic. General corporate, Government contracts and claims, Securities. Home: 124 Crosby Ave Kenmore NY 14217 Office: Comptek Research Inc 110 Broadway Buffalo NY 14203

HEAD, HAYDEN W., JR., federal judge; b. Sherman, Tex., Nov. 12, 1944; s. Hayden W. Head and Marshall (Elmore) Skinner; m. Barbara J. Lewis, July 19, 1969; children—Hayden W. III, Rebecca Louise, Jennifer Ruth. Student, Washington and Lee U., 1962-64; B.A., U. Tex., 1966, LL.B., 1968. Bar: Tex. Assoc. Head & Kendrick, Corpus Christi, Tex., 1972-76, ptnr., 1976-81; U.S. dist. judge U.S. Dist. Ct., Corpus Christi, 1981—. Served to lt. JAGC, USN, 1969-72. Fellow Tex. Bar Found.; mem. ABA, State Bar Tex. Republican. Episcopalian. Avocations: fishing, hunting, skiing. Office: US Dist Ct 521 Starr St Corpus Christi TX 78401 *

HEAD, HAYDEN WILSON, lawyer; b. Sherman, Tex., Feb. 6, 1915; s. Hayden Wilson and Ruth (Bulloch) H.; m. Marshall Elmore, July 2, 1938 (divorced); 1 child, Hayden W. Jr.; m. Annie Blake Morgan, June 15, 1950. B.A., Austin Coll., 1934; LL.B., U. Tex., 1937. Bar: Tex. 1937. Sr. ptnr. Head & Kendrick and predecessor firms, Corpus Christi, 1955—; adv. dir. First City Bank, Corpus Christi, chmn. trust com., 1963-78. Pres. Nueces County chpt. ARC, 1948-49, United Community Services of Corpus Christi, 1962; chmn. Airport Adv. Bd. City Corpus Christi, 1956-86, chmn. Joint Airport Zoning Bd. City Corpus Christi and Nueces County, 1979-81; trustee Spohn Hosp., 1970—; mem. exec. com. Coastal Bend Council Govts., 1970—, chmn., 1973. Served to capt. USSAF, 1941-45. Decorated D.F.C., Air medal with 9 oak leaf clusters; recipient Disting. Alumnus award Austin Coll., 1977, U. Tex. 1984. Fellow Tex. Bar Found., Am. Bar Found.; mem. ABA, Nueces County Bar Assn., State Bar of Tex. (chmn. mineral law sect. 1954-55), Corpus Christi C. of C. (chmn. area devel. com. 1982—). General practice, Oil and gas leasing, Real property. Office: Head & Kendrick 1020 First City Bank Tower Corpus Christi TX 78477

HEAD, HUGH GARLAND, III, lawyer; b. Norfolk, Va., Jan. 22, 1929; s. Hugh Garland and Jessie (Grover) H.; m. Edith Jackson, June 30, 1959 (div. 1967); 1 child, Garland Grover; m. 2d, Vickie Murrill, Mar. 2, 1968; 1 child, Hugh Wickstrom. A.B., U. South, Sewanee, Tenn., 1950; student U. Grenoble, France, 1949; LL.B., U. Ga., 1958. Bar: Ga. 1958; U.S. Supreme Ct. 1964. Sole practice, Atlanta, 1958-68, Roswell, Ga., 1969—; farmer, Woodstock, Ga, 1971—. Mgr., Little League Baseball, Roswell, 1969-73. Served to lt. U.S. Navy, 1951-55; Korea. Mem. State Bar Ga. (mem. edn. com. 1981-84), North Fulton Bar Assn. (dir. 1982-84). Republican. Episcopalian. Club: Burns (dir. 1967-69). Probate, Estate planning. Home: 8705 Wheeler Rd Woodstock GA 30188 Office: 825 Mimosa Blvd Roswell GA 30075

HEAD, HUGH GARLAND, JR., lawyer; b. Atlanta, Dec. 3, 1905; s. Hugh Garland Sr. and Carrie Lulla (Morse) H.; m. Jessie Ella Grover, Mar. 13, 1928; children: Hugh Garland III, William LeVert, Douglas Arthur. LLB, Atlanta Law Sch., 1937; postgrad., Oxford (Eng.) U., 1943. Bar: Ga. 1937, U.S. Dist. Ct. (so., mid. and no. dists.) Ga., 1937; U.S. Supreme Ct., 1956. Asst. city atty. Atlanta, 1945-46, sole practice, 1945—; Contbr. articles to legal jours. Served to maj. U.S. Army, 1942-45, lt. col. Res. ret. Decorated Mem. British Empire. Recipient Bronze medal Inst. Continuing Legal Edn., Ga., 1973. Fellow Internat. Acad. Trial Lawyers (hon., bd. govs. 1971-72); mem. Am. Trial Lawyers Assn. (lifetime faculty, bd. govs. 1975-81, Disting. Lectr. citation 1965), Ga. Trial Lawyers Assn. (pres. 1958, named life mem. bd. govs. 1974), ABA (speaker nat. conv. 1968), Ga. Bar Assn. (Honor Roll award 1980), Atlanta Bar Assn. (exec. com. 1958), SAR (nat. trustee 1960-64, Good Citizenship Bronze medal 1963), The Belli Soc. (trustee). Clubs: Atlanta Athletic, Ft. McPherson Golf, Lawyers. Lodge: Masons. Personal injury, Probate. Home: 154 Laurel Forest Circle NE Atlanta GA 30342 Office: 250 Lenox Plaza 3384 Peachtree Rd NE Atlanta GA 30326

HEAD, PATRICK JAMES, lawyer; b. Randolph, Nebr., July 13, 1932; s. Clarence Martin and Ellen Cecelia (Magirl) H.; m. Eleanor Hickey, Nov. 24, 1960; children: Adrienne, Ellen, Damian, Maria, Brendan, Martin, Sarah, Daniel, Brian. A.B. summa cum laude, Georgetown U., 1953, LL.B., 1956, LL.M. in Internat. Law, 1957. Bar: D.C. 1956, Ill. 1966. Asso. firm John L. Ingolsby (and predecessor firm), Washington, 1956-64; gen. counsel internat. ops. Sears, Roebuck & Co., Oakbrook, Ill., 1964-70; counsel midwest ter. Sears, Roebuck & Co., Skokie, Ill., 1970-72; v.p. Montgomery Ward & Co., Inc., Washington, 1972-76; v.p., gen. counsel, sec. Montgomery Ward & Co., Inc., Chgo., 1976-81; v.p., gen. counsel FMC Corp., Chgo., 1981—. Mem. Chgo. Crime Commn.; bd. regents Georgetown U., Washington. Mem. D.C. Bar Assn., Chgo. Bar Assn., ABA. Democrat. Roman Catholic. Clubs: Met. (Washington); Chgo, Internat. General corporate, Administrative and regulatory, Federal civil litigation. Office: FMC Corp 200 E Randolph St Chicago IL 60601

HEAD, WILLIAM CARL, lawyer, real estate developer; b. Columbus, Ga., Mar. 4, 1951; s. Louis Bernice and Betty June (Vickery) H.; m. Sandra Earle, Sept. 3, 1972 (div. 1979); m. Kathleen Crenshaw, Aug. 8, 1981; 1 stepchild, Stephanie A. Hansen. BA cum laude, U. Ga., 1973, JD, 1976. Bar: Ga. 1976, U.S. Dist. Ct. (mid. dist.) Ga. 1976, U.S. Ct. Appeals (5th and 11th cirs.) 1979. Ptnr. Galis, Timmons, Andrews & Head, Athens, Ga., 1977-79, Andrews & Head P.C., Athens, 1979-82; sole practice Athens, 1982-85; ptnr. McDonald, Head, Carney & Haggard, Athens, 1985—; real estate developer, Athens, 1979—. Pres. Joseph Henry Lumpkin Found., Inc., Athens, 1979; chmn. Bridge the Gap seminar, Atlanta, 1980. Awardee Athens-Clarke Heritage Found. Inc., Athens, 1983. Mem. ABA, Assn. Trial Lawyers Am., Ga. Trial Lawyers Assn., Am. Bankruptcy Inst., Order of Barristers. Democrat. Baptist. Club: Pres's. (U. Ga.). Bankruptcy, Real property, General corporate. Home: 125 Longview Dr Athens GA 30605 Office: McDonald Head Carney & Haggard 345 W Hancock Ave Athens GA 30603

HEADMAN, ARLAN OSMOND, JR., lawyer; b. Salt Lake City, Utah, Oct. 22, 1952; s. Arlan O. and Ione (Ficklin) H.; m. Debra Card, Aug. 20, 1973; 1 child, Alexander Oliver. B.S., U. Utah, 1974, J.D., 1977. Bar: Utah 1977, U.S. Dist. Ct. Utah 1977. Cons., Ra-Tek Investment, Denver, 1981-82; sole practice, Salt Lake City, 1982-84; ptnr. Smith & Headman, Salt Lake City, 1984—; mem. rule change com. Ad Hoc Com., Utah State Securities Div., 1984. Del., Utah Democratic Conv., 1972, state and county Dem. Conv., 1986. U. Utah scholar, 1971. Mem. Mt. West Venture Capital Club, Phi Eta Sigma, ABA. Mormon. Securities, General corporate, Real property. Office: Smith & Headman 420 E S Temple Suite 334 Salt Lake City UT 84111

HEADRICK, STIRMAN RUSSELL, lawyer; b. Dallas, Dec. 15, 1951; s. Hal Stirman and Dorothy (Dooley) H.; m. Margaret Monroe Lawson, Aug. 16, 1975; children: Stirman Russell Jr., Henry Claiborne. BA, Rhodes Coll., 1973; JD, U. Tenn., 1977. Bar: Tenn. 1977, U.S. Dist. Ct. (we. dist.) Tenn. 1978, U.S. Ct. Appeals (6th cir.) 1980, U.S. Supreme Ct. 1981. Law clk. to presiding justice U.S. Dist. Ct., Memphis, 1977-78; assoc. Armstrong, Allen, Braden, Goodman, McBride & Prewitt, Memphis, 1978-85, ptnr., 1985—. Federal civil litigation, State civil litigation, Libel. Office: Armstrong Allen Braden Goodman et al 1900 One Commerce Sq Memphis TN 38103

HEADRICK, THOMAS EDWARD, lawyer, educator; b. East Orange, N.J., June 28, 1933; s. Lewis Barnard and Marian Elizabeth (Rogers) H.; m. Mary Margaret Shontz, June 27, 1957; children—Trevor, Todd. B.A., Franklin and Marshall Coll., 1955; B.Litt., Oxford (Eng.) U., 1958; LL.B., Yale U., 1960; Ph.D., Stanford U., 1975. Bar: Conn. 1960, Calif. 1962. Asst. dir. Ansonia (Conn.) Redevel. Agy., 1959-60; law clk. to justice Wash. State Supreme Ct., Olympia, 1960-61; assoc. firm Pillsbury, Madison & Sutro, San Francisco, 1961-64; mgmt. cons. Emerson Cons., London, 1964-66, Baxter, McDonald & Co., Berkeley, Calif., 1966-67; asst. dean Stanford U. Law Sch., 1967-70; v.p. acad. affairs Lawrence U., 1970-76; dean SUNY at Buffalo Law Sch., 1976-85, prof. law, 1976—; cons. Nat. Endowment for Humanities, NSF; legal commentator Sta. WKBW-TV, 1978-80. Author: The Town Clerk in English Local Government, 1962; co-editor Law and Policy. Mem. Am. Polit. Sci. Assn., Law and Soc. Assn., Erie County Bar Assn., Policy Studies Orgn., Phi Beta Kappa. Real property, General corporate. Office: SUNY at Buffalo Law Sch 624 O'Brian Hall Buffalo NY 14260

HEAFEY, EDWIN AUSTIN, JR., lawyer; b. Oakland, Calif., Nov. 1, 1930; s. Edwin Austin Sr. and Florence (Jochim) H.; divorced; children: Ryan, Matthew, Alison. AB, U. Santa Clara, 1952; LLB, Stanford U., 1955. Bar: Calif. 1955, U.S. Dist. Ct. (no. and cen. dists.) Calif. 1955, U.S. Supreme Ct. 1984, U.S. Dist. Ct. (ea. dist.) Wis. 1986. Sr. ptnr. Crosby, Heafey, Roach & May, Oakland, 1955—; instr. law U. Calif., Berkeley, 1963-78. Author: California Trial Objections, 1967. Mem. Am. Bar Found., Assn. Trial Lawyers Am., Calif. Trial Lawyers Assn., Am. Bd. Trial Advs., Am. Coll. Trial Lawyers, Nat. Assn. R.R. Trial Counsel, Assn. Def. Counsel Northern

Calif., Calif. Bar Assn., Alameda County Bar Assn., San Francisco Bar Assn., Internat. Soc. Barristers. Republican. Roman Catholic. Club: Claremont Country (Oakland) (mem. comm. 1986—). Federal civil litigation, State civil litigation. Office: Crosby Heafey Roach & May 1999 Harrison St Oakland CA 94612

HEALEY, ARTHUR H., state supreme court justice; b. New Haven, May 5, 1920; s. Arthur and Agnes (Hannon) H.; m. Frances T. Murphy, Apr. 24, 1954; children: Theresa A., Monica F., Moira A., Arthur T., Alicia M., Francis J., Michael K., Matthew M., Anne E. BA, Trinity Coll., 1944; LLB, Harvard U., 1947. Bar: Conn. 1948. Mem. Conn. Senate, 1955-61, minority leader, 1957-59, majority leader, 1959-61; judge Ct. Common Pleas, 1961-65; judge Superior Ct., Hartford, Conn., 1965-79, chief judge, 1977-78; presiding judge appellate session Superior Ct., 1977-79; assoc. justice Conn. Supreme Ct., Hartford, 1979—; chmn. State Legis. Council, 1959-61; mem. Jud. Rev. Council, 1978-79; co-chmn. Conn. Justice Commn., 1978-79. Mem. State Library Bd., 1979. Served with AUS, World War II. Mem. Conn. Bar Assn., New Haven County Bar Assn. Judicial administration. Office: Conn Supreme Ct Supreme Ct Bldg 231 Capitol Ave Hartford CT 06106

HEALY, GEORGE WILLIAM, III, lawyer; b. New Orleans, Mar. 8, 1930; s. George William and Margaret Alford H.; m. Sharon Saunders, Oct. 26, 1974; children: George W. IV, John Carmichael, Floyd Alford, Hyde Dunbar, Mary Margaret. B.A., Tulane U., 1950, J.D., 1955. Bar: La. bar 1955, U.S. Supreme Ct. bar 1969. Asso. firm Phelps, Dunbar, Marks, Claverie & Sims, New Orleans, 1955-58; partner Phelps, Dunbar, Marks, Claverie & Sims, 1958—; mem. U.S. del. Comite Maritime Internat., Tokyo, 1969, Lisbon, 1985; lectr. in field. Served with USN, 1951-53. Fellow Am. Coll. Trial Lawyers, Maritime Law Assn. U.S. (exec. com.), Am. Bar Assn.; mem. La. State Bar Assn., New Orleans Bar Assn. (1st v.p. 1987), La. Assn. Def. Counsel, New Orleans Assn. Def. Counsel, Internat. Assn. Def. Counsel. Republican. Episcopalian. Clubs: Boston, La, Stratford, Plimsoll, Whitehall, Yale, Recess (pres. 1978), Pinfeathers Hunting, New Orleans Lawn Tennis, Propeller, Mariners. Admiralty. Home: 6020 Camp St New Orleans LA 70118 Office: 30th Floor Texaco Bldg 400 Poydras St New Orleans LA 70130

HEALY, HAROLD HARRIS, JR., lawyer; b. Denver, Aug. 27, 1921; s. Harold Harris and Lorena (Isom) H.; m. Elizabeth A. Debevoise, May 24, 1952; 1 son, Harold Harris III. A.B., Yale U., 1943, LL.B., 1949. Bar: N.Y. 1949, U.S. Supreme Ct 1957. Now mem. firm Debevoise & Plimpton, N.Y.C.; resident partner Debevoise & Plimpton (European office), Paris, 1964-66; exec. asst. to U.S. atty. gen., 1957-58; Mem. Am. adv. council Ditchley Found., 1972—; Bd. dirs. Legal Aid Soc., 1968—, chmn., 1975-79. Bd. dirs. Met. Opera Guild, 1975—, ; trustee Vassar Coll., 1977-86 . Served from 2d lt. to capt. F.A. AUS, 1943-46, ETO. Decorated Bronze Star medal, chevalier de la Legion d'Honneur. Mem. Am., N.Y. State bar assns., Assn. Bar City N.Y. (sec. 1959-61), Am. Law Inst., Order of Coif, Am. Soc. Internat. Law (mem. exec. council 1977-80), Internat. Law Assn., Internat. Bar Assn., Union Internationale des Avocats (pres. 1979-81), Am. Coll. Investment Counsel, Council Fgn. Relations, France-Am. Soc., Pilgrims U.S., Yale Law Sch. Assn. (exec. com. 1974-82, v.p. 1980-82), Phi Beta Kappa, Zeta Psi, Phi Delta Phi. Republican. Episcopalian. Clubs: University (N.Y.C.), Century Assn. (N.Y.C.); Travellers (Paris), Cercle de l'Union Interallié e (Paris); Metropolitan (Washington). Contracts commercial, General corporate, Private international. Home: 1170 Fifth Ave New York NY 10029 Office: 875 3d Ave New York NY 10022

HEALY, JOAN MCDONOUGH, lawyer, nurse; b. Pitts., Aug. 7, 1955; d. Aloysius G. and Julia Ann (Connolly) McDonough; m. Patrick Kevin Healy, May 9, 1981. B.S. in Nursing, Georgetown U., 1977; J.D., Cath. U. Am., 1980. Bar: N.C. 1981, D.C. 1981. R.N. Staff nurse Georgetown U. Hosp., Washington, 1977-78; law clk. Aaron M. Levine, P.A., Washington, 1978-80, firm Jackson, Campbell & Parkinson, Washington, 1980-81; gen. counsel Forsyth Meml. Hosp. Found., Winston-Salem, N.C., 1981-84, corp. sec., 1981-84; gen. counsel, asst. sec. Carolina Medicorp Enterprises, Inc., 1984-86; corp. sec. Salem Health Services, Inc., Winston-Salem, 1982—, Found. Health Systems Corp., Winston-Salem, 1982-84; v.p. legal affairs Carolina Medicorp, 1985—. Mem. ABA, D.C. Bar Assn., N.C. Bar Assn., N.C. Acad. Trial Lawyers, N.C. Soc. Hosp. Attys., Nat. Health Lawyers Assn., Sigma Theta Tau. Office: Carolina Medicorp Inc 3333 Silas Creek Pkwy PO Box 15025 Winston-Salem NC 27103

HEALY, JOSEPH FRANCIS, JR., lawyer, airline executive; b. N.Y.C., Aug. 11, 1930; s. Joseph Francis and Agnes (Kett) H.; m. Patricia A. Casey, Apr. 23, 1955; children: James C., Timothy, Kevin, Cathleen M., Mary, Terence. B.S., Fordham U., 1952; J.D., Georgetown U., 1959. Bar: D.C. 1959. With gen. traffic dept. Eastman-Kodak Co., Rochester, N.Y., 1954-55; air transp. examiner CAB, Washington, 1955-59; practiced in Washington, 1959-70, 80-81; asst. gen. counsel Air Transport Assn. Am., 1966-70; v.p. legal Eastern Air Lines, Inc., N.Y.C. and Miami, Fla., 1970-80; ptnr. Ford, Farquhar, Kornblut & O'Neill, Washington, 1980-81; v.p. legal affairs Piedmont Aviation, Inc., Winston Salem, N.C., 1981-84, sr. v.p., gen counsel, 1984—. Served to 1st lt. USAF, 1952-54. Mem. ABA, Fed. Bar Assn., Internat. Bar Assn., Am. Soc. Corp. Secs., Am. Irish Hist. Soc., Nat. Aero. Assn., Beta Gamma Sigma, Phi Delta Phi. Clubs: Univ., Internat. Aviation (Washington); Wings (N.Y.C.); Piedmont (Winston-Salem). General corporate. Home: 236 Heatherton Way Winston-Salem NC 27104 Office: Piedmont Aviation Inc One Piedmont Plaza Winston-Salem NC 27156

HEALY, JOSEPH ROBERT, lawyer; b. Troy, N.Y., Apr. 15, 1939; s. Thomas Francis and Isabel Kathryn (Eagle) H.; m. Sylvia Anne Tuccillo, May 14, 1976; 1 child, Daniel Joseph. B.A. in Sociology, Siena Coll., 1961; J.D., Albany Law Sch., 1965. Bar: N.Y. 1973, U.S. Dist. Ct. (no. dist.) N.Y. 1973. Claims examiner Social Security Adminstrn., Glens Falls, N.Y., 1961-62; personnel examiner N.Y. State Dept. Civil Service, Albany, 1965-69, sr. legal examiner, 1969-71, atty., 1971-75, sr. atty., 1975-82, assoc. atty., 1982—, dir. civil service security ops., 1983—. Author newsletter N.Y. State Orgn. Mgmt. Confidential Employees News Network. Active Woodland Hills Homeowners Assn., Clifton Park, N.Y. Republican. Roman Catholic. Administrative and regulatory. Home: 5 George Dr Clifton Park NY 12065 Office: NY State Dept Civil Service 1220 Washington Ave Albany NY 12223

HEALY, MARY JACQUELINE, lawyer; b. Covington, Ky., Nov. 8, 1952; d. Jack Martin and Gloria Ann (Iasillo) Fausz; m. James Patrick Healy, Mar. 20, 1982; 1 child, Ann Marie. BA with honors, U. Cin., 1974; JD, No. Ky. U., 1978. Bar: Ohio 1978. Trust assoc. 1st Nat. Bank of Cin., 1974-76; assoc. Paxton & Seasongood, Cin., 1976—; adj. prof. U. Cin., 1982-84. Mem. exec. council Cancer Control Council, Cin., 1979—; trustee Cin. Estate Planning Council, 1979—. Mem. ABA, Ohio Bar Assn., Cin. Bar Assn., Delta Theta Phi. Republican. Mem. United Ch. of Christ. Club: Cin. Lawyers. Avocations: decorating, cooking, knitting, traveling, running. Estate planning, Probate, Estate taxation. Home: 22 Fairfield Fort Thomas KY 41075 Office: Paxton & Seasongood 1700 Central Trust Tower Cincinnati OH 45202

HEALY, NICHOLAS JOSEPH, lawyer, educator; b. N.Y.C., Jan. 4, 1910; s. Nicholas Joseph and Frances Cecilia (McCarthy) H.; m. Margaret Marie Ferry, Mar. 29, 1937; children: Nicholas, Margaret Healy Parker, Rosemary Healy Bell, Mary Louise Healy White, Donall, Kathleen Healy Hamon. A.B., Holy Cross Coll., 1931; J.D., Harvard U., 1934. Bar: N.Y. 1935, U.S. Supreme Ct. 1949. Pvt. practice N.Y.C., 1935-42, 48—; mem. Healy & Baillie (and predecessor law firms), 1948—; chmn. bd. dirs. Victory Carriers, Inc. (and affiliated cos.); spl. asst. to atty. gen. U.S., 1945-48; tchr. admiralty law NYU Sch. Law, 1947-86, adj. prof., 1960-86; Niels F. Johnsen vis. prof. maritime law Tulane Maritime Law Ctr., 1986. Contbr.: chpts. on admiralty to Annual Survey Am. Law, 1948—; author: (with Sprague) Cases on Admiralty, 1950, (with Currie) Cases and Materials on Admiralty, 1965, (with Sharpe), Cases and Materials on Admiralty, 1974, 2d edit., 1986; editor: Jour. Maritime Law and Commerce; assoc. editor: American Maritime Cases; mem. bd. editors: Il Dirittimo Marittimo; contbr. to Ency. Brit. Chmn. USCG adv. panel on Rules of the Road, 1966-72; mem. permanent adv. bd. Tulane Admiralty Inst. Served to lt. (s.g.) USNR, 1942-45. Mem. Maritime Law Assn. U.S. (pres. 1964-66), Assn. Average Adjusters U.S. (chmn. 1959-60), ABA (ho. dels. 1964-66), N.Y. State Bar Assn., Comité Maritime Internat. (exec. council 1972-79, v.p. 1985—), Assn. Bar City N.Y., Soc. Friendly Sons St. Patrick. Democrat. Roman Catholic. Clubs: Harvard (N.Y.C.), India House (N.Y.C.), Downtown Athletic (N.Y.C.). Admiralty. Home: 132 Tullamore Rd Garden City NY 11530 Office: Healy & Baillie 29 Broadway New York NY 10006

HEARN, SHARON SKLAMBA, lawyer; b. New Orleans, Aug. 15, 1956; d. Carl John and Marjorie C. (Wimberly) Sklamba; m. Curtis R. Hearn. B.A. magna cum laude, Loyola U., New Orleans, 1977; J.D. cum laude, 1980. Bar: La. 1980, Tex. 1982. Law clk. to presiding judge U.S. Ct. Appeals Fed. Cir., Washington, 1980-81; assoc. Johnson & Swanson, Dallas, 1981-84, Kullman Inman Bee & Downing, New Orleans, 1984—. Recipient Am. Legion award, 1970; Tulane Law Sch. Merit award, 1978, 79. Mem. ABA, La. State Bar Assn. (bd. cert.), Tex. State Bar Assn., Dallas Women Lawyers Assn. Democrat. Roman Catholic. Pension, profit-sharing, and employee benefits, Labor. Home: 44 Swallow Ln New Orleans LA 70124 Office: Kullman Inman Bee & Downing 615 Howard Ave New Orleans LA 70130

HEARSCH, JANIS CAMILLE BROWN, lawyer; b. Glendale, Calif., Dec. 23, 1943; d. Kenneth W. and Goldie O. (Schnuerle) Brown; m. Robert R. Hearsch, July 4, 1976; 1 child, Hirshol Pheir. JD, Whittier Coll., 1981. Bar: Calif. 1981. Assoc. Marvin M. Mitchelson, Los Angeles, 1981-82; sole practice Los Angeles, 1983—; directing atty., mediator, lawyer Family Law Mediation Group, Los Angeles, 1983—. Mem. ABA, Calif. Bar Assn., Los Angeles County Bar Assn., Beverly Hills Bar Assn., Century City Bar Assn., Women Lawyers Calif., Am. Acad. Mediators. Clubs: Bus. and Profl. Women of Beverly Hills, The Inside Edge. Avocations: whitewater rafting, reading, ultralight aircrafting. Mediation business and family law, Family and matrimonial. Home: 8246 Redbush Ln Panorama City CA 91402 Office: Family Law Mediation Group 2049 Century Park East #1100 Los Angeles CA 90067

HEARST, JAMES HENRY, lawyer; b. Wheeling, W.Va., Jan. 26, 1946; s. David S. and Sally (Recht) H.; m. Nancy Louise Sierawski, Jan. 25, 1976; children: Beth, Debbie, David. BS, Syracuse U., 1967; JD, W.Va. U., 1975. Bar: W.Va. 1976, U.S. Dist. Ct. (so. dist.) W.Va. 1976, U.S. Dist. Ct. (no. dist.) W. Va. 1982. Asst. prosecuter Nicholas County, Summersville, W.Va., 1976-80; ptnr. Hearst & Merrifield, Fairmont, W.Va., 1981-84; sole practice Fairmont, 1984—; instr. Fairmont State Coll., 1983—. Mem. City of Fairmont Bd. Adjustments, 1985—, Dep. Sheriff Civil Service Commn., Fairmont, 1985—; chmn. Nicholas County Heart Assn., Summersville. Served with USN, 1968-72, Vietnam. Democrat. Jewish. General practice, Criminal, State civil litigation. Office: 309 Cleveland Ave Profl Bldg Suite 416 Fairmont WV 26554

HEATH, CHARLES DICKINSON, lawyer, telephone company executive; b. Waterloo, Iowa, June 28, 1941; s. George Clinton and Dorothy (Dickinson) H.; m. Carilyn Frances Cain, June 3, 1972. B.B.A., U. Iowa, 1962, J.D., 1966; M.B.A., U. Ariz., 1963. Bar: Iowa 1966, Pa. 1969, Ind. 1970, U.S. Supreme Ct. 1971, Wis. 1973, Ariz. 1975, Mich. 1979, Fla. 1979. Asst. gen. counsel Kohler Co. (Wis.), 1973-79; securities and tax counsel Kellogg Co., Battle Creek, Mich., 1979-81; assoc. gen. counsel Universal Telephone Inc., Milw., 1981—. Securities, Public utilities, Corporate taxation.

HEATH, JOSEPH JOHN, lawyer; b. Watertown, N.Y., Mar. 19, 1946; s. Robert Edward and Lucille Frances (Ferringer) H.; 1 child, Travis Jackson. B.A., Syracuse U., 1968; J.D., SUNY-Buffalo, 1974. Bar: N.Y. 1975, U.S. Dist. Ct. (no. dist.) N.Y. 1976. Trial atty. Attica Bros. Legal Def., Buffalo, 1975-76; ptnr. Heath, Rosenthal & Weissman, Syracuse, 1976—; adj. prof. SUNY-Oswego, 1982-83; clin. prof. Syracuse U., 1982; sec. bd. dirs. G.C. Hanford Co., Syracuse, 1986, Allflex Mfg. Co., Syracuse, 1986. Bd. dirs. Hiscock Legal Aid Soc., 1984. Served with USN, 1968-70. Mem. Nat. Lawyers Guild, Onondaga County Bar Assn., N.Y. State Bar assn., N.Y. State Defenders Assn. Democrat. Roman Catholic. Criminal, Civil rights, Family and matrimonial. Office: Heath Rosenthal & Weissman 472 S Salina St Syracuse NY 13202

HEATON, GERALD LEE, lawyer; b. Detroit, Feb. 28, 1952; s. Gerald and Bernice Johanna (Cromp) H.; m. Ilene Renee Mann, Oct. 25, 1975. AA, North Cen. Mich. Coll., 1972; BA, Albion Coll., 1974; JD, Ohio No. U., 1976. Bar: Ohio 1977, U.S. Dist. Ct. (so. dist.) Ohio 1977. Ptnr. Lile & Heaton, Bellefontaine, Ohio, 1977-79, MacGillivray & Heaton, Bellefontaine, 1979—; asst. pros. atty. Logan County, Bellefontaine, 1977-84; soliciter Village of BellCtr., Ohio, 1982—, Village of De Graff, Ohio, 1982—. Pres. United Way, Bellefontaine, 1984, bd. dirs., 1982—. Mem. ABA, Ohio Bar Assn., Logan County Bar Assn., Logan County C. of C. Republican. Roman Catholic. Lodges: Lions, Masons. Avocations: golf, tennis, crossword puzzles. Personal injury, State civil litigation, Criminal. Home: 4671 State Rt 274 W Huntsville OH 43324 Office: MacGillivray & Heaton 325 N Main Bellefontaine OH 43311

HEATON, JOSEPH EDWARD, JR., lawyer; b. Galesburg, Ill., Dec. 19, 1949; s. Joseph E. and Mary Elizabeth (Elmer) H.; m. Mary Jo Schock, Aug. 26, 1972; children: Jon, Elizabeth, Sarah, Ellen. BS, Ind. U., 1972; JD, John Marshall Law Sch., 1975. Bar: Ill. 1975, U.S. Dist. Ct. (no. dist.) Ill. 1975. Assoc. Dixon, Devine, Ray & Morin, Dixon, Ill., 1975-78, Ward, Murray, Pace & Johnson, Sterling, Ill., 1978—; bd. dirs., sec., treas., Riverview Mgmt. Services, Inc., Dixon. Trustee, 1st v.p. Katherine Shaw Bethea Hosp., Dixon, 1980-86; elder First Presbyn. Ch., Dixon, 1982-84; bd. dirs. Jr. Achievement, Dixon, 1982-86; bd. dirs., v.p. Sauk Valley Med. Services Corp., Dixon, 1985-86. Mem. ABA, Assn. Trial Lawyers Am., Ill. Bar Assn., Ill. Trial Lawyers Assn., Lee County Bar Assn., Whiteside County Bar Assn. Club: Dixon Country (greens chmn. 1983-86). State civil litigation, Insurance, Personal injury. Home: Rock Bend Farm 918 Bend Rd Dixon IL 61021 Office: Ward Murray Pace & Johnson PC 202 E Fifth St Sterling IL 61081

HEATON, ROGER LAURENCE, lawyer; b. Rockville Centre, N.Y., Sept. 18, 1949; s. Gordon W. and Anne (Davis) H.; m. Susan J. W. Heaton, May 20, 1983; 1 child, W. Bradford. Student, Wesleyan U., 1967-68; BS, Denison U., 1971; JD, U. San Diego, 1981. Bar: Calif. 1982, U.S. Dist. Ct. N.D. 1982, U.S. Dist. Ct. (no. dist.) Tex. 1982, U.S. Dist. Ct. S.D. 1983, U.S. Dist. Ct. (so. dist.) Calif. 1983, U.S. Dist. Ct. Hawaii. Assoc. Ungerman, Hill et al, Dallas, 1982-83, Shigemura and Ching, Honolulu, 1983, McInnis, Fitzgerald et al, San Diego, 1983—; instr. in legal research and writing U. San Diego , 1981-82. Mem. ABA, Calif. Bar Assn., So. Calif. Def. Counsel Assn., San Diego Bar Assn., San Diego Def. Counsel Assn. Avocations: athletics, family activities. State civil litigation, Insurance, Personal injury. Office: McInnis Fitzgerald 1320 Columbia St San Diego CA 92101

HEBL, THOMAS LEE, SR., lawyer; b. Madison, Wis., Nov. 14, 1945; s. Francis R. and Janet E. (Miller) H.; m. Christine DeCelles, Aug. 23, 1975; children: Allison DeCelles, Thomas Lee Jr., Ashley Miller. BBA, U. Wis., Whitewater, 1968; JD, John Marshall Law Sch., 1975. Bar: Wis. 1975, U.S. Dist. Ct. (we. dist.) Wis. 1979. Sole practice Sun Prairie, Wis., 1975-76; ptnr. Hebl & Hebl, Sun Prairie, 1976-84, Hebl, Hebl, Hebl & Desmond-Hebl, Sun Prairie, 1984—; bd. dirs. Commonwealth C.U., Sun Prairie. Chmn. Sun Prairie Tax Incremental Fin. Dist. #1, 1980-85; pres. Sun Prairie C. of C., 1981-82. Mem. Dane County Bar Assn. Club: Colonial (Sun Prairie) (bd. dirs. 1985—). Lodge: Rotary (pres. 1980). Probate, Real property, General practice.

HECHT, BARBARA ELIZABETH ROBERTS, lawyer; b. Kansas City, Mo., Oct. 29, 1946; d. Ralph Thomas and Margaret Naomi (Owen) Henderson. B.A. in History and Govt., U. Mo.-Kansas City, 1969, J.D., 1971. Bar: Mo. 1971. Asst. counsel, asst. sec. Oppenheimer Industries, Inc., Kansas City, 1971-72, corp. counsel, sec., 1972-76, corp. counsel, sec., asst. v.p., 1976-81, counsel, 1981—; v.p., dir. Gunsight, Inc., 1979-81; v.p., sec. Ft. McRae Corp., 1983—; pres. Sera II Corp., 1985—; Kansas City. Named Vol. of 1978, N.W. Mo. Probation and Parole Citizens Adv. Bd.; bd. dirs. Engle Water Users Assn., 1985. Mem. ABA (real estate and probate sect., fgn. investments in U.S. real estate 1986—), Kansas City Bar Assn. (chmn. real estate com.), Phi Alpha Delta. Republican. Real property, General corporate, Private international.

HECHT, CHARLES JOEL, lawyer; b. N.Y.C., Mar. 15, 1939; s. Charles Maurice and Jane Ann Hecht; m. Deborah Carole Herman, Sept. 2, 1963; children: Stacey Ann, Eric Simon. BA, Cornell U., 1961, LLB, 1963. Bar: N.Y. 1965, U.S. Dist. Ct. (ea. and so. dists.) N.Y. 1971, U.S. Supreme Ct. 1971, U.S. Ct. Appeals (2d cir.) 1975, U.S. Ct. Appeals (5th and 7th cirs.) 1979, U.S. Ct. Appeals (6th cir.) 1985. Atty. SEC, Washington, 1966-69; assoc. Mermelstein, Burns & Lesser, N.Y.C., 1969-71; sole practice N.Y.C., 1971—. Contbr. articles to profl. jours. Served to 1st lt. U.S. Army, 1963-65. Mem. ABA (commodities regulation com.), N.Y. State Bar Assn. Club: Lotos (N.Y.C.) (fin. com. 1983—, membership com. 1985—, bd. dirs. 1986—). Avocations: bicycle racing, stamp collecting. Securities, General corporate, Administrative and regulatory. Office: 60 E 42nd St New York NY 10165

HECHT, FRANK THOMAS, atty.; b. Ann Arbor, Mich., June 18, 1944; s. Hans H. and Ilse (Wagner) H. AB, Stanford U., 1966; postgrad., Johns Hopkins U., 1966-68, U. Chgo., 1968; JD, U. Chgo., 1975. Bar: Ill. 1975, U.S. Dist. Ct. (no. dist.) 1975, U.S. Ct. Appeals (7th cir.) 1975, U.S. Supreme Ct. 1981. With Migrant Farmworker Litigation Project, Chgo., 1978-81, dir., 1981-82; assoc. Levy & Erens, Chgo., 1982-85; ptnr. Erens & Miller, Chgo., 1985-86, Hopkins & Sutter, Chgo., 1986—; cooperating atty. ACLU, Union, Ill., 1983—, bd. dirs. 1985—; bd. dirs. Cook County Legal Assistance Found., 1984-85, Nat. Inst. for Trial Advocacy, 1978. Contbr. Civil Rights Law Reporter. Exec. dir. New Univ. Conf., 1970-72. Reginald Heber Smith fellow, 1975-78. Mem. ABA, Assn. of Trial Lawyers of Am., Chgo. Council of Lawyers, Nat. Lawyers Guild. Federal civil litigation, State civil litigation, Civil rights. Home: 240 Maplewood Rd Riverside IL 60546 Office: Hopkins & Sutter 3 First Nat Plaza Chicago IL 60602

HECHT, ISAAC, lawyer; b. Balt., Dec. 28, 1913; s. Lee I. and Miriam D. Hecht; m. Catharine Straus, Mar. 26, 1941; children: Eleanor Hecht Yuspa, Henry L., Marjorie Hecht Kaplan. BS in Econs., Johns Hopkins U., 1936; LLB, U. Md., 1938. Bar: Md. 1938, U.S. Dist. Ct. Md. 1938, U.S. Tax Ct. 1940, U.S. Ct. Appeals (4th cir.) 1940, U.S.Supreme Ct. 1960. Ptnr. Hecht & Chapper, Balt. Pres. Oheb Shalom Congregation Balt. City, 1958-61, life hon. trustee; mem. bd. Jewish Edn., 1962-68; past bd. dirs. Balt. chpt. Am. Jewish Com. and Jewish Welfare Fund. Fellow Md. Bar Found., Am. Coll. Probate Counsel; mem. ABA (mem. standing com. on lawyers' responsibility for client protection 1984—, active various coms.), Md. Bar Assn. (bd. govs. 1978-79, active various coms.), Clients' Security Trust Fund of the Bar of Md. (trustee 1966—, treas. 1967—), Bar Assn. of Balt. City, Judicial Conf. of the 4th Cir., Assn. Life Ins. Counsel, Balt. Estate Planning Council (exec. com. 1964-69, sec. 1964-66, v.p. 1966-67, pres. 1967-68), Jud. Conf. 4th Cir., Balt. Assn. Tax Counsel, Phi Epsilon Pi. Democrat. Club: Johns Hopkins, Suburban of Balt. County (bd. govs. 1970-72). Probate, General corporate, Estate planning. Home: Eleven Slade Apts #307 Baltimore MD 21208 Office: Hecht & Chapper 1111 Fidelity Bdlg Baltimore MD 21201

HECHT, MERVYN LEONARD, lawyer; b. Freeport, Ill., Apr. 24, 1938; s. Max and Dorothy H.; m. Elizabeth Anne Fink, Jan. 31, 1960; children: Matthew Lynd, Micah Spencer, Rachel Eleanor. Student, Sorbonne, U. Paris, 1959; BA, U. Calif., Los Angeles, 1960; LLD, Harvard U., 1963. Contract reviewer N. Am. Aviation, Los Angeles, 1963-64; sr. ptnr. Hecht, Diamond & Greenfield, Pacific Palisades, Calif., 1963—; prof. law W. Los Angeles Sch. Law, 1974-86. Co-author: Landslide and Subsidence Liability, 1974; contbr. articles on TV, electronics to profl. publs., also tax articles and med. risk issues. Avocations: amateur radio, sailing, tennis. Office: Hecht Diamond & Greenfield Inc 15415 Sunset Blvd Pacific Palisades CA 90272

HECHT, NATHAN LINCOLN, judge; b. Clovis, N.Mex., Sept. 15, 1949; s. Harold Lee and Mary Loretta (Byerly) H. BA, Yale U., 1971; JD cum laude, So. Meth. U., 1974. Bar: Tex. 1974, D.C. 1975, U.S. Dist. Ct. D.C. 1975, U.S. Ct. Appeals (D.C. cir.) 1975, U.S. Dist. Ct. (no. and we. dists.) Tex. 1976, U.S. Ct. Appeals (5th cir.) 1976, U.S. Supreme Ct. 1979. Law clk. to presiding judge U.S. Appeals (D.C. cir.), 1974-75; assoc. Locke, Purnell, Boren, Laney & Neely, Dallas, 1976-81; dist. judge 95th Dist. Ct., Dallas, 1981-86; justice U.S. Ct. Appeals (5th cir.), Tex., 1986—. Contbr. articles to profl. jours. Bd. visitors So. Meth. U., Dallas, 1984-87; bd. trustees Children's Med. Found., Dallas, 1983; bd. dirs. Children's Med. Ctr. N., Dallas, 1985—; elder Valley View Christian Ch., Dallas, 1981—. Served to lt. USNR, 1971-79. Named Outstanding Young Lawyer of Dallas, Dallas Assn. of Young Lawyers, 1984. Fellow Tex. Bar Found., Am. Bar Found.; mem. ABA, Dallas Bar Assn., D.C. Bar Assn. Republican. Avocations: piano, organ. Judicial administration. Home: 1107 Terrace Trail Carrollton TX 75006 Office: US Ct of Appeals 600 Commerce St Dallas TX 75202

HECHT, ROBERT D., lawyer; b. Seneca, Kans., Oct. 17, 1934; s. Jesse J. and Flossie Isabel (Ridgeway) H.; children—Lisa Fay, Julia Paige. B.B.A., Washburn U., 1956, J.D., 1958. Bar: Kans. 1958, U.S. Dist. Ct. Kans. 1958, U.S. Ct. Appeals (10th cir.) 1969, U.S. Supreme Ct. 1969. Asst. county atty. Shawnee County, Kans., 1961-65, county atty., 1965-69, county counselor, 1969-75; ptnr. Gray, Freidberg & Davis, Topeka, 1965-69, Scott, Quinlan & Hecht, Topeka, 1969—; past adj. prof. Washburn U. Sch. Law, Topeka; dir. Benchmark Securities, Topeka; sch. atty. Unified Sch. Dist. 345, Topeka, 1979—; Contbr. articles to Kans. Trial Lawyers Jour. Co-chmn. Shawnee County March of Dimes, 1963; candidate for atty. gen. State of Kans., 1968. Served as capt. JAGC, USAF, 1958-61. Mem. ABA, Kans. Bar Assn., Assn. Trial Lawyers Am., Kans. Trial Lawyers Assn. (bd. govs. 1974—, v.p. 1981-82), Am. Judicature Soc. Republican. Federal civil litigation, Administrative and regulatory, Criminal. Office: Scott Quinlan & Hecht 3301 Van Buren Topeka KS 66611

HECK, GRACE FERN, lawyer; b. Tremont City, Ohio, Nov. 13, 1905; d. Thomas J. and Mary Etta (Maxson) H.; m. Leo H. Faust, May 25, 1977. B.A. cum laude, Ohio State U., 1928, J.D. summa cum laude, 1930. Bar: Ohio 1930, U.S. Dist. Ct. (so. dist.) Ohio 1932, U.S. Supreme Ct. 1960. Researcher, Nat. Commn. Law Observance and Enforcement, U.S. Dist. Ct. (so. dist.) Ohio, 1930-31, Ohio Judicial Council and Law Inst. Johns Hopkins U., 1931-32; prosecuting atty. Champaign County, Urbana, Ohio, 1933-37; sole practice, Urbana, 1937-43, 73-85, Springfield, 1947-73; assoc. Corry, Durfey & Martin, Springfield, 1943-47; mcpl. judge Champaign County, 1954-58. Exec. sec. War Price and Rationing Bd., Urbana, 1941-43; bd. trustees Spring Grove Cemetery Assn., 1954—; sec. bd. trustees Magnetic Springs Found., Ohio, 1957-62; pres. Ohio State U., Coll. Law Alumni Assn., Columbus, 1971-72; charter mem. Friends of Libraries Ohio State U., Friends of Hist. Costume and Textile Collection; mem. Nat. Council Coll. Law, Ohio State U. Columbus, 1971—; mem. Springfield Art Assn.; trustee Champaign County Arts Council, 1987—. Recipient Disting. Service award Ohio State U., 1971. Mem. Ohio State Bar Assn. (com. mem.), Champaign County Bar and Law Library Assn. (pres. 1965), Springfield Bar and Law library Assn. (sec. 1946-59, pres. 1963), ABA, Ohio State U. Alumni Assn. (2d v.p. 1956-58, adv. bd. 1962-73, Alumni Centennial award 1970), Order of Coif, Phi Beta Kappa, Zeta Tau Alpha, Kappa Beta Pi, Delta Theta Tau (nat. v.p. 1938-40, nat. pres. 1941-42, bd. trustees 1942-45). Democrat. Methodist. Clubs: Springfield Country (Ohio); Troy Country (Ohio); Altrusa. Lodge: Order of Eastern Star. Avocations: fishing, hunting, travel, photography, gravestone rubbings. State civil litigation, Probate, General practice. Home: 134 W Church St Urbana OH 43078

HECKEMEYER, ANTHONY JOSEPH, circuit court judge; b. Cape Girardeau, Mo., Jan. 20, 1939; s. Paul Q. and Frances G. (Goetz) H.; m. Elizabeth Faye Littleton, Feb. 13, 1964; children: Anthony Joseph, Matthew Paul, Mary Elizabeth, Andrew William, Sarah Kathryn. BS, U. Mo., 1962, JD, 1972; grad., Nat. Judicial Coll., 1980, Juvenile Coll., 1984. Bar: Mo. Mem. Mo. Ho. Reps., Jefferson City, 1964-72; sole practice Sikeston, Mo., 1972-80; cir. judge Benton, Mo., 1980—. Named Outstanding Conservation Legislator Sears, 1968, Found. Mo. Wildlife Fed., 1968. Home: 654 Park Sikeston MO 63801 Office: Office of Cir Judge PO Box 256 Benton MO 63736

HECKENBACH, DAVID W., lawyer; b. Denver, Oct. 17, 1954; s. William E. and Phylliss (Brandt) H.; m. Diana M. Watson, July 12, 1980; 1 child, Rachel Marie. BA, Washington & Lee U., 1976; JD, U. Colo., 1979. Bar: Colo. 1979, U.S. Dist. Ct. Colo. 1979, U.S. Ct. Appeals (10th cir.) 1984. Dep. dist. atty. Denver Dist. Atty.'s Office, 1979-84; assoc. Halaby & McCrea, Denver, 1984-85; chief dep. dist. atty. complex prosecutions Denver

Dist. Atty.'s Office, 1985—; lobbyist Colo. Dist. Atty.'s Council, Denver, 1984—. Vol. Colo. Heart Assn., Denver, 1985. Mem. ABA, Colo. Bar Assn., Denver Bar Assn., Colo. Dist. Atty.'s Council, Nat. Dist. Atty.'s Assn. Office: Denver Dist Atty's Office 303 W Colfax Suite 1300 Denver CO 80204

HECKER, ROBERT J., lawyer; b. White Plains, N.Y., July 10, 1937; s. Hyman and Rose (Marcus) H.; m. Barbara L. Cott, June 28, 1959; children: Douglas M., Stacey L. AB, Brandeis U., 1959; JD, Fordham U., 1962. Bar: N.Y. 1962, U.S. Dist. Ct. (so. and ea. dists.) N.Y., U.S. Supreme Ct. Sole practice White Plains, 1962—; assoc. judge City Ct., White Plains, 1977-81. Mem. N.Y. State Bar Assn., Westchester County Bar Assn., White Plains Bar Assn. (pres. 1971), N.Y. State Magistrates Assn. Republican. General corporate, Real property, Contracts commercial. Office: 202 Mamaroneck Ave White Plains NY 10601

HECKMAN, DONALD REX, II, lawyer; b. St. Joseph, Mich., May 30, 1946; s. Donald Rex Sr. and Betty Ann (Blakeman) H.; m. Lisa B. Heckman, May 30, 1981; 1 child, Hilary Allison. BS with honors, U. Calif., Berkeley, 1968, JD, 1973. Bar: Calif. 1973, U.S. Dist. Ct. (ea. dist.) Calif. 1973, U.S. Tax Ct. 1973. Process engr. Shell Chem. Co., Martinez, Calif., 1968-70; ptnr. Wilke, Fleury, Hoffelt, Gould & Birney, Sacramento, Calif., 1973—; instr. grad. tax program Golden Gate U., Sacramento, 1979-81; lectr. continuing edn. programs Calif. CPA Found. for Edn. and Research, Palo Alto, Calif., 1981—; sec. Sacramento Estate Planning Council, 1986—. Exec. bd. dirs. Sacramento/San Joaquin chpt. Muscular Dystrophy Assn., 1979-82. Mem. ABA (tax sect.), Calif. Bar Assn. (tax sect., lectr. continuing edn. 1984—), Sacramento County Bar Assn. (tax sect.), Phi Beta Kappa, Tau Beta Pi. Republican. Congregationalist. Club: 20/30 (Sacramento). Avocations: stamps, cross-country skiing, racquetball, golf. Probate, Corporate taxation, General corporate. Home: 570 34th St Sacramento CA 95816 Office: Wilke Fleury Hoffelt Gould & Birney 300 Capitol Mall Suite 1300 Sacramento CA 95814

HECKT, PAUL NORMAN, lawyer; b. Mpls., Apr. 12, 1953; s. Melvin Dean and Dorothy M. (Simons) H.; m. Kathleen Jean Martin, Aug. 22, 1980; 1 child, Ann Hye. BA, Gustavus Adolphus Coll., 1975; JD, U. Minn., 1978. Bar: Minn. 1978, U.S. Dist. Ct. Minn. 1978, U.S. Ct. Appeals (8th cir.) 1979. Spl. asst. atty. gen. antitrust div. State of Minn., St. Paul, 1978-81, spl. asst. atty. gen. utilities div., 1981-83, spl. asst. atty. gen. unemployment div., 1983-84; legal counsel H.B. Fuller Co., St. Paul, 1984—. Mem. ABA, Minn. Bar Assn., Ramsey County Bar Assn. Lutheran. Avocations: pvt. pilot (instrumented), hockey, carpentry, fishing, golf. Antitrust, Banking, Real property. Home: 7444 13th Ave S Richfield MN 55423 Office: HB Fuller Co 2400 Energy Park Dr Saint Paul MN 55108

HECTOR, BRUCE JOHN, lawyer; b. Newark, Feb. 18, 1950; s. Henry Francis and Doris Mary (Campbell) H.; m. Carol Ann Seely, Aug. 10, 1974. BA in English, Coll. of the Holy Cross, 1971; JD, NYU, 1974. Bar: N.J. 1974, U.S. Dist. Ct. N.J. 1974, N.Y. 1976, U.S. Dist. Ct. (ea. and so. dists.) N.Y. 1976, U.S. Ct. Appeals (4th cir.) 1977, U.S. Ct. Appeals (3d cir.) 1981. Assoc. Podvey & Sachs, Newark, 1974-75, Hill, Rivkins et al, N.Y.C., 1975-81; atty. Becton Dickinson & Co., Franklin Lakes, N.J., 1981—. Leader explorer law post Boy Scouts Am., Glen Rock, N.J., 1985—. Mem. Maritime Law Assn. U.S.(proctor on admirality 1981—). Democrat. Roman Catholic. Avocations: jazz and classical guitar. Federal civil litigation, General corporate, Environment. Home: 121 Belvidere Rd Glen Rock NJ 07452 Office: Becton Dickinson & Co 1 Becton Dr Franklin Lakes NJ 07417

HEDGE, CYNTHIA ANN, lawyer; b. LaPorte, Ind., June 7, 1952; d. John S. and Edith Rae (Badkey) H. A.B., Ind. U., 1975; J.D., Valparaiso U., 1978. Bar: Ind. 1978, U.S. Dist Ct. (no. dist., so. dist.) Ind. 1978. Staff writer Ind. Dept. Commerce, Indpls., 1975; pub. relations asst. Ravinia Festival, Chgo., 1976; free-lance writer, LaPorte County, Ind., 1978—; dep. pros. atty. LaPorte County, 1978—; sole practice, Michigan City, Ind., 1978—; dir. Michiana Industries, LaPorte County. Chairperson, Child Abuse Adv. Team, LaPorte County, 1982—; bd. dirs., chairperson Parents and Friends of the Handicapped, Inc., 1986—; mem. bd. Bethany Lutheran Ch., LaPorte, 1982—, United Way, Michigan City, 1987—. Mem. ABA, Ind. Bar Assn., LaPorte County Bar Assn., Michigan City Bar Assn., Christian Legal Soc., Ind. U. Alumni Assn., AAUW, Michigan City C. of C. Home: 2912 N Regal Dr LaPorte IN 46350 Office: 601 Franklin Sq Michigan City IN 46360

HEDLAND, JOHN SIGURD, lawyer; b. Sioux Falls, S.D., Aug. 12, 1940; s. Sigurd and Olga (Rustad) H.; m. Karen A. Halvorson, July 13, 1963; children: Katherine, Rebecca, Eric. BA, Augustana Coll., 1962; LLB cum laude, U. Minn., 1965. Bar: Minn. 1965, Alaska 1969, U.S. Dist. Ct. Alaska 1969, U.S. Ct. Appeals (9th cir.) 1971. Trial atty. U.S. Dept. of Justice, Washington, 1965-68; dir. litigation Alaska Legal Services, Anchorage, 1968-70; ptnr. Hedland, Fleischer, Friedman, Brennan & Cooke, Anchorage, 1970—. Chmn. Alaska Local Boundary Commn., 1971-73. Served with USAR, 1959-65. Lutheran. Avocations: tennis, fishing, sports. Federal civil litigation, State civil litigation, Local government. Home: 1726 Laurence Ct Anchorage AK 99501 Office: Hedland Fleischer Friedman Brennan & Cooke 1227 W 9th Suite 300 Anchorage AK 99501

HEDRICK, DAVID WARRINGTON, lawyer; b. Jacksonville, Fla., Oct. 25, 1917; s. Frederic Cleveland and Edith (Warrington) H.; m. June Nicholson, Apr. 23, 1949; children—John Warrington, Stephen Brian. B.A. with honors, U. Fla., 1940, J.D. with honors, 1947. Bar: Fla. 1947, U.S. Supreme Ct. 1962. Assoc. LeRoy B. Giles, 1947-52; ptnr. Giles, Hedrick & Robinson, Orlando, Fla., 1953—, chmn. bd.; savs. dir. Comint Corp., 1963-79, sec., 1966—; dir. Indsl. Devel. Commn. of Mid-Fla., 1978-79; pres. Attys. Title Services, 1963-64. Legal counsel, bd. dirs. Central Fla. Council Boy Scouts Am., 1970—; bd. dirs. Holiday Hosp. of Orlando, 1966-69; mem. Orange County Human Planning Council, pres., 1973-75, bd. dirs., 1973—; mem. Orlando Mayor's Interracial Adv. Commn., 1967; chmn. United Appeal Drive of Orange County (Fla.), 1967, pres., 1970, chmn. bd. dirs., 1971, chmn. social planning com., 1973-76, bd. dirs. and legal counsel, 1975—; chancellor Diocese of Central Fla., Winter Park, 1970—. Served to capt. AUS, 1941-46; ETO; to col. USAR, 1946-67. Decorated Bronze Star; Belgian Fourragere. Recipient Disting. Eagle Scout award Boy Scouts Am., 1972, Silver Beaver award, 1976. Mem. Orange County Bar Assn. (pres. 1959-60, past pres. council 1976—), ABA, Fla. Bar, Am. Judicature Soc., Am. Legion, VFW, Fla. Blue Key, Assn. of U.S. Army, Res. Officers Assn., Phi Kappa Phi, Phi Delta Phi, Alpha Tau Omega. Democrat. Episcopalian. Clubs: Country of Orlando, Univ. (Orlando), River (Jacksonville); Kiwanis of North Orlando. General corporate, Probate, Real property. Home: 1729 Reppard Rd Orlando FL 32803 Office: Giles Hedrick & Robinson 109 E Church St Suite 301 Orlando FL 32801

HEDRICK, JOHN RICHARD, lawyer; b. Lubbock, Tex., May 15, 1952; s. Earl Ralph Jr. and Ella Fay (Groves) H. BBA, Tex. Tech U., 1974; JD, St. Mary's U., San Antonio, 1976. Bar: Tex. 1977, U.S. Dist. Ct. (no. dist.) Tex. 1977, U.S. Tax Ct. 1977, U.S. Dist. Ct. (so. dist.) Tex. 1979, U.S. Ct. Appeals (5th cir.) 1979, U.S. Supreme Ct. 1980. Sole practice Austin, Tex., 1977-78; gen. counsel Pan Am. U., Edinburg, Tex., 1978-80; asst. univ. counsel U. Houston System, 1980-82; corp. counsel Lifemark Corp., Houston, 1982-84; gen. counsel HealthStar Corp., Houston, 1984—; lectr. Pan Am. U., Edinburg, 1979, U. Houston, 1981; mem. fed. jud. appointment adv. com. Tex. Bar Assn., Austin, 1980—. Local bd. dirs. SSS, Houston, 1981—. Named one of Outstanding Young Men in Am., 1984. Mem. ABA, Tex. Bar Assn., Nat. Health Lawyers Assn., Am. Acad. Hosp. Attys., Sigma Alpha Epsilon, Phi Alpha Delta. Democrat. Presbyterian. Club: Plaza (Houston). Avocation: golf. General corporate, Health, Corporate taxation. Home: 5000 Milwee Unit 53 Houston TX 77092 Office: HealthStar Corp 3555 Timmons Ln 700 Houston TX 77027

HEEBE, FREDERICK JACOB REGAN, U.S. district judge; b. Gretna, La., Aug. 25, 1922; s. Bernhardt and Marguerite (Reagan) H.; m. Doris Stewart, Oct. 6, 1984; children by previous marriage: Frederick Riley, Adrea Dee. B.A., Tulane U., 1943, LL.B., 1949. Bar: La. 1949. Practice in Gretna, 1949-60; dist. judge div. B, 24th Jud. Dist. Ct., Jefferson Parish, La., 1960-66; U.S. dist. judge Eastern Dist. La., 1966—, now chief judge. Mem. Community Welfare Council Jefferson Parish, from 1957; chmn. Jefferson Parish Bd. Pub. Welfare, 1953-55; Mem. Jefferson Parish Council, 1958-60, vice chmn., 1958-60; Bd. dirs. Social Welfare Planning Council New Orleans, New Orleans Regional Mental Center and Clinic, W. Bank Assn. for Retarded. Served to capt., inf. AUS, World War II. Decorated Purple Heart, Bronze Star. Mem. Am., La., New Orleans, Fed. bar assns., Am. Judicature Soc., Phi Beta Kappa. Office: US Courthouse Chambers C-525 500 Camp St New Orleans LA 70130

HEEGE, ROBERT CHARLES, judge; b. Independence, Iowa, Feb. 4, 1922; s. Harold Spring and Esther Louisa (Roberts) H.; m. Grace Anne Chamberlain, June 3, 1945; children: Peter James, Catherine Elizabeth, John Haines. BS, U. Iowa, 1943; JD, 1947. Bar: Iowa, S.D., U.S. Ct. Appeals (8th cir.). Ptnr. Davenport, Evans, Hudwitz & Smith, 1947-79; presiding judge 2d Jud. Cir. Ct., Sioux Falls, S.D., 1979-86. Pres. Community Playhouse, Singing Legionnaires. Served with USN, 1943-45. Mem. ABA, Iowa Star Bar Assn., S.D. State Bar Assn. Republican. Presbyterian. Jurisprudence. Office: 2d Judicial Circuit 415 N Dakota Ave Sioux Falls SD 57102

HEENAN, MICHAEL TERENCE, lawyer; b. Pitts., Jan. 28, 1942; s. Paul Joseph and Helen (Chemas) H.; m. Maryte Victoria Narkevicius, Feb. 12, 1970; children: Garrett, Leslie, Suzanne. BS, Mount St. Mary's Coll., Emmitsburg, Md., 1964; JD, U. Pitts., 1967. Bar: Pa. 1967, D.C. 1972, U.S. Supreme Ct. 1974, U.S. Ct. Mil. Appeals 1974, U.S. Ct. Claims 1975, U.S. Customs Ct. 1975. Atty. adviser Bd. Vets. Appeals, Washington, 1971-73; trial atty. div. mine safety and health Office of Solicitor Dept. of Interior, 1973-74; assoc. Webster, Kilcullen & Chamberlain, 1974-76; ptnr. Kilcullen, Smith & Heenan, 1976-80, Smith, Heenan & Althen, Washington, 1980—; instr. internat. law U.S. Navy Res. Officers Sch., 1971-72. Author: Understanding MSHA, 1981, Enforcement, Administrative and Judicial Review, Coal Law and Regulation, 1983; co-author: (with Ronald E. Meisburg) Federal Regulation of Mine Safety and Health, Administration, Practice and Procedure, 1986. Served to lt. USNR, 1968-71. Mem. ABA, Fed. Bar Assn., Pa. Bar Assn., D.C. Bar Assn., Interam. Bar Assn., Internat. Bar Assn. Administrative and regulatory, Federal civil litigation, Labor. Office: 1110 Vermont Ave NW Suite 400 Washington DC 20005

HEENE, FRED LEWIS, JR., lawyer; b. N.Y.C., June 19, 1946; s. Fred Lewis and Ruth Caroline (Pilchard) H.; m. Cheryl Lee, June 1, 1968; children: Alison Nicole, Cindy. B.A. in Polit. Sci., Ariz. State U., 1968; J.D., Western State U., 1977. Bar: Calif. 1978. Police officer City of Orange, Calif., 1972-73; claims adjuster Global Van Lines, 1973-74; supr. VA, 1974-78; sr. ptnr. Couwenberg & Heene, Pomona, Calif., 1978-86, sole practice, 1987—; tchr. edn. law Calif. State U.; tchr. bus. law Pacific Christian Coll.; asst. prof. law New Port Coll. Law. Commr. airports San Bernardino County, Calif., 1980-86; trustee Chino Unified Sch. Dist. Bd. Edn., 1979—, pres. 1982-83, 86-87. Served to capt., USAF, 1968-72. Mem. Pomona Trial Lawyers Assn., Calif. Trial Lawyers Assn., Calif. Pub. Defenders Assn., ABA, Pomona Estate Planning Council. Republican. Club: Chino Lions. Criminal, Estate planning, Probate. Office: 666 N Park Ave Pomona CA 91768

HEERWAGEN, ELWOOD J., JR., lawyer; b. East Orange, N.J., Mar. 17, 1934; s. Elwood J. and Grace S. (Stager) H.; m. Dorothy A. Heerwagen, July 4, 1959; children: Christopher E., Valerie A. BA, Rutgers U., 1955; JD, U. Pa., 1958. Bar: U.S. Dist. Ct. D.C. 1958, Calif. 1961, U.S. Dist. Ct. (so. dist.) Calif. 1961, N.J. 1964, U.S. Dist. Ct. N.J. 1964. Assoc. Pelton, Gunther & Gudmanson, San Francisco, 1962-63, Toner, Crowley, Wolper & Vanderbilt, Newark, 1963-67; asst. counsel Thomas A. Edison Industries subs. McGraw-Edison Co., West Orange, N.J., 1967-71; atty. Nuclear Fuel Services subs. Getty Oil Co., Rockville, Md., 1971-73; assoc. Apruzzese & McDermott, P.A., Springfield, N.J., 1973-80, ptnr., 1980-85; ptnr. Schenck, Price, Smith & King, Springfield, 1986—; sec. Syncro Machine Co., Whittaker, Clark & Daniels Internat. Sales Co. Inc. Served to lt. USN, 1958-61. Mem. ABA (bus. law sect., labor law sect.), D.C. Bar Assn., Calif. Bar Assn. Club: Morristown. General corporate, Environment, Real property. Home: 3A4 Suzan Ct West Orange NJ 07052 Office: Schenck Price Smith & King 10 Washington St Morristown NJ 07960

HEFFERAN, HARRY HOWARD, JR., lawyer; b. Norwalk, Conn., Dec. 20, 1925; s. Harry H. and Madeleine C. (Lee) H.; m. Catherine Sharon, Mar. 31, 1951; children: Paul, Lee, Sharon, Michael, Stephen, Matthew, Timothy. BS, Georgetown U., 1948, JD, 1950. Bar: Conn. 1951, U.S. Supreme Ct. 1961, D.C. 1966, U.S. Ct. Appeals (2d cir.) 1973. Assoc. Atty. W. Whitton, Norwalk, 1951-52; ptnr. Sibal, Hefferan & Griffin, Norwalk, 1952-62, Hefferan & Rimer, Norwalk, 1962-78, Lovejoy, Hefferan, Rimer & Cuneo, P.C., Norwalk, 1978—; assoc. bd. dirs. Union Trust Co., Norwalk. Chmn. Norwalk Hosp., 1971-73, Mother's March on Polio, Norwalk, 1955, Ward A Dem. Com., Norwalk, 1953-55; pres. Norwalk United Way, 1975. Mem. ABA (local chmn. 1971-73), Conn. Bar Assn. (bd. dirs. 1971-73), Norwalk/Wilton Bar Assn. (pres. 1980-81). Roman Catholic. Lodge: Kiwanis (pres. 1955-56). Avocations: golf, spectator sports, reading, amateur historian. Real property, Administrative and regulatory, Health. Office: Lovejoy Hefferan Rimer & Cuneo PC 637 West Ave PO Box 390 Norwalk CT 06852

HEFFERNAN, MICHELE OLGA, lawyer; b. Buffalo, Apr. 1, 1949; d. John J. and Rita (DeSpirt) H. BA, Coll. New Rochelle, 1971; JD, SUNY, Buffalo, 1974. N.Y. 1975, U.S. Dist. Ct. (we. dist.) N.Y. 1975. From assoc. to ptnr. Jaeckle, Fleischmann & Mugel, Buffalo, 1974—; bd. dirs. Artpark & Co., Inc., Lewiston, N.Y. Mem. ABA, N.Y. State Bar Assn., Erie County Bar Assn. (bd. dirs. 1985—). Pension, profit-sharing, and employee benefits, Personal income taxation. Office: Jaeckle Fleischmann & Mugel 800 Norstar Bldg Buffalo NY 14202

HEFFINGTON, JACK GRISHAM, lawyer, bank executive, insurance company executive, horse breeder; b. Lawrenceburg, Tenn., Mar. 8, 1944; s. Charles Alexander and Kathlyn (Grisham) H.; m. Nancy Caroline Heffington, Sept. 29, 1979; 1 dau., Jacquelyn Elliott. B.S., Memphis State U., 1967; J.D., U. Ark., 1971. Bar: Tenn. 1971, Ala., 1972. Ptnr., Heffington & Thomas, Murfreesboro, Tenn., 1972—; pres., chmn. Middle Tenn. Mortgage Co., Murfreesboro, 1973—; pres., chmn. Keg Life Ins. Co. of S.C., Columbia, 1977—; owner Tan Oak Farms, Murfreesboro; dir. 1st Nat. Bank of Rutherford County, Murfreesboro. Mem. ABA, Ala. Bar Assn., Tenn. Bar Assn., Sigma Delta Chi. Mem. Ch. of Christ. General corporate. Home: 634 E Main St Murfreesboro TN 37130 Office: 209 N Spring St Murfreesboro TN 37130

HEFFINGTON, JOSEPH ROBERT, lawyer, rancher; b. Terrell, Tex., Dec. 24, 1940; s. Joseph Elard and Elsie Alvoy (Crane) H.; m. Dierdre Ann Furmenger, Oct. 24, 1959 (div.); children—Wendy Heffington Waymire, Keith Robert, Derek James. Student North Tex. State U., 1961-65; J.D., U. Tex.-Austin, 1968. Bar: Tex. 1968, U.S. Dist. Ct. (we. dist.) Tex. 1968. Securities investigator Tex. State Securities Bd., Austin, 1968-69; sole practice, Austin, 1969—. Founder Travis County Childrens Fund, Austin, 1976—; mem. citizens adv. com. Juvenile Bd. of Travis County, Austin, 1976-80. Mem. Tex. Trial Lawyers. General practice, State and local taxation, General corporate. Home: Westgate Bldg Austin TX 78701 Office: Littlefield Bldg Suite 416 Austin TX 78701

HEFFLER, PAUL MARK, lawyer; b. N.Y.C., Nov. 22, 1953; s. Abraham Solomon and Selma (Cohen) H.; m. Jacqueline Louise McDowell Ethredge, July 9, 1986; children: L. Paul Ethredge, Amanda Michelle Heffler. BS in Social Work, U. Ala., 1975; JD, Samford U., 1979. Bar: Ala. 1979, U.S. Dist. Ct. (no. dist.) Ala. 1980, U.S. Ct. Appeals (5th cir.) 1980, U.S. Ct. Appeals (11th cir.) 1981, U.S. Tax Ct. 1983. Social worker Ala. Dept. Pensions and Security, Birmingham, 1975-76; sole practice Birmingham, 1979-81, Jasper, Ala., 1984—; asst. atty. gen. surface mining commn. State of Ala., Jasper, 1981-84. Mem. ABA, Ala. Bar Assn., Walker County Bar Assn., Am. Arbitration Assn. (panel comml. arbitrators), U.S. Naval Inst. (assoc.), Phi Alpha Delta. Democrat. Jewish. General practice, Criminal, Juvenile. Home: 1410 W 8th St Jasper AL 35501 Office: 2028-A 3d Ave PO Box 3494 Jasper AL 35502-3494

HEFFRON, JONATHON KENNETH, lawyer, bank executive; b. Austin, Minn., Nov. 2, 1952; s. Kenneth A. and Eva (Johnson) H.; m. Barbara Ann Demchyk, Oct. 18, 1980; 1 child, Lindsay Ann. BA magna cum laude, U. Minn., 1974; JD, Southwestern U., 1977; LLM, George Washington U., 1981. Bar: Calif. 1978, U.S. Dist. Ct. (cen. dist.) Calif. 1978, D.C. 1982, U.S. Ct. Appeals (D.C. cir.) 1982, Tex. 1985. Staff atty. Fed. Home Loan Bank Bd., Washington, 1978, trial atty., 1979-83, gen. counsel, corp. sec., 1983, sr. v.p., gen. counsel, 1984-85, exec. v.p., gen. counsel, 1985—. Pres. Snowden's Mill Homeowners Assn., Silver Spring, Md., 1981-83; mem. task force Montgomery County Homeowners Assn., Rockville, Md., 1982-83. Mem. ABA, Calif. Bar Assn., Tex. Bar Assn., Dallas County Bar Assn. Democrat. Roman Catholic. Club: Prestonwood Country. Banking, General corporate, Administrative and regulatory. Office: Fed Home Loan Bank 500 E Carpenter Freeway Irving TX 75062

HEFNER, ARCHIE, lawyer; b. Gridley, Calif., Dec. 4, 1922; s. Robert Emmet and Caroline Vida (Sheppard) H.; m. Barbara Bowler, June 2, 1945; children—William R., Madeline, Mark D. Student Calif. State U., Chico, 1940-43, U. of Pacific, 1943; J.D., U. Calif.-Hastings Coll. Law, 1949. Bar: Calif. 1950. Assoc., Hoberg & Finger, San Francisco, 1950-51; ptnr. Hefner, Stark & Marois and predecessor, Sacramento, 1951—; sr. ptnr., pres. Archie Hefner, Inc., Sacramento, 1981—. Bd. dirs. Sacramento Tree Found., 1982—; trustee Sacramento Pioneer Found., 1972—, Sacramento Regional Found., 1986—, Sacramento Symphony Found., 1984-87; chmn. Sacramento Host Commn., 1983-84, Sacramento Opera Assn. Adv. Bd., 1985—; dir. Sacramento Symphony Assn., 1968-80, pres. 1974-76. Served to lt. (j.g.) USNR, 1942-46, PTO. Mem. ABA, Am. Judicature Soc., Sacramento Jr. C. of C. (pres. 1955), Sacramento Met. C. of C. (pres. 1966), Sacramento Execs. Assn. (pres. 1957), Order of Coif. Republican. Lodges: Scottish Rite, Masons, Shriners, Rotary. Real property, Probate, Contracts commercial.

HEFTER, DANIEL S., lawyer; b. Chgo., Mar. 4, 1956; s. David and Terese Roslyn (Fenig) H.; m. Nancy Carole Slack, June 10, 1979; 1 child, Laurelin Joy. BS, U. Ill., 1977; JD, U. Mich., 1980. Bar: Ill. 1980, U.S. Dist. Ct. (no. dist.) Ill. 1980, U.S. Ct. Appeals (7th cir.) 1981, U.S. Ct. Appeals (D.C. cir.) 1983, U.S. Supreme Ct. 1987. Assoc. Isham, Lincoln & Beale, Chgo., 1980—. Mem. ABA. Libel, Federal civil litigation. Home: 4253 N Avers Chicago IL 60618 Office: Isham Lincoln & Beale 3 1st National Plaza Chicago IL 60602

HEFTER, LAURENCE ROY, lawyer; b. N.Y.C., Oct. 13, 1935; s. Charles S. and Rose (Postal) H.; m. Jacqulyn Maureen Miller, June 13, 1957; children—Jeffrey Scott, Sue-Anne. B.M.E., Rensselaer Poly. Inst., 1957, M.S. in Mech. Engring., 1960; J.D. with honors, George Washington U., 1964. Bar: Va. 1964, N.Y. 1967, D.C. 1973. Instr. Rensselaer Poly. Inst., Troy, N.Y., 1957-59; patent engr. Gen. Electric Co., Washington, 1959-63; sr. patent atty. Atlantic Research Corp., Alexandria, Va., 1963-66; assoc. firm Davis, Hoxie, Faithfull & Hapgood, N.Y.C., 1966-69; mem. firm Ryder, McAulay & Hefter, N.Y.C., 1970-73, Finnegan, Henderson, Farabow, Garrett & Dunner, Washington, 1973—; profl. lectr. trademark law George Washington U., 1981—. Mem. ABA (chmn. patent com. adminstrv. law sect. 1975-76, chmn. patent office affairs com. patent, trademark and copyright sect. 1976-80, unfair competition com. 1980-81), N.Y. State Bar Assn., D.C. Bar Assn., Va. Bar Assn. (dir. patent, trademark and copyright sect. 1976-78), Internat. Bar Assn. (chmn. trademark com. 1986—), Am. Patent Law Assn. (chmn. trademark com. 1979-81, dir. 1981-84), U.S. Trademark Assn. (dir. 1982-84), Internat. Assn. Advancement of Teaching and Research in Intellectual Property, Order of Coif, Alpha Epsilon Pi. Trademark and copyright, Patent, Federal civil litigation. Home: 7405 Pinehurst Pkwy Chevy Chase MD 20815 Office: 1775 K St NW Washington DC 20006

HEGARTY, MARY FRANCES, lawyer; b. Chgo., Dec. 19, 1950; d. James E. and Frances M. (King) H. B.A., DePaul U., 1972, J.D., 1975. Bar: Ill. 1975, U.S. Dist. Ct. (no. dist.) Ill. 1976, U.S. Supreme Ct. 1980. Ptnr. Lannon & Hegarty, Park Ridge, Ill., 1975-80; sole practice, Park Ridge, 1980—; dir. Legal Assistance Found. Chgo., 1983—. Mem. revenue study com. Chgo. City Council Fin. Com., 1983; mem. Sole Source Rev. Panel, City of Chgo., 1984; pres. Hist. Pullman Found., Inc., 1984-85. Mem. Ill. State Bar Assn. (real estate council 1980-84), Chgo. Bar Assn., Women's Bar Assn. Ill. (pres. 1983-84), NW Suburban Bar Assn., Park Ridge Women Entrepreneurs. Democrat. Roman Catholic. Club: Chgo. Athletic Assn. Real property, Probate, General corporate. Office: 301 W Touhy Park Ridge IL 60068

HEGARTY, TERRENCE K., lawyer; b. Chgo., June 8, 1944; s. Dennis L. P. and Katharine B. (Foster) H.; m. Judith J. Palace, Aug. 27, 1967; children: Kimberly, Kristen, Jessica; m. Maureen Allice McPartlin, June 15, 1985; 1 child, Katherine. BS, Loyola U., Chgo., 1966, JD, 1969. Bar: Ill. 1969, U.S. Dist. Ct. (no. dist.) Ill. 1969, U.S. Supreme Ct., 1973. Trial atty. Law Office of Tim J. Harrington, Chgo., 1970-72; sr. atty. Terrence K. Hegarty and Assocs., Ltd., Chgo., 1972—; bd. dirs. David Pusch Dance Studios, Chgo.; alumni cons. Gestalt Inst. Chgo. Assoc. editor Ill. Trial Lawyers Jour., 1985—. Mem. Ill. Soc. Nat. Bd. Trial Advocates (founding), Soc. Trial Lawyers, Ill. State Bar Assn. (bd. govs. 1986-88). Democrat. Personal injury, State civil litigation, Civil rights. Office: 77 W Washington St Suite 1306 Chicago IL 60602

HEGARTY, WILLIAM EDWARD, lawyer; b. N.Y.C., Nov. 18, 1926; s. William Alfred and Mary Johanna (Condon) H.; m. Barbara Meade Fischer, Oct. 26, 1950; children: Katharine Hegarty Bouman, Mary Hegarty Colombo, William, Amanda. AB, Princeton U., 1947; LLB, Yale U., 1950. Bar: N.Y. 1951, D.C. 1973, U.S. Supreme Ct. 1962. With Cahill, Gordon & Reindel (and predecessors), N.Y.C., 1950—; ptnr. Cahill, Gordon & Reindel (and predecessors), 1962—, sr. ptnr., 1969—. Bd. dirs. Florence J. Gould Found., French Inst./Alliance Française, Mcpl. Art Soc.; mem. Greenwich Inland Wetlands and Watercourses Agy. Served with USNR, 1944-46. Mem. ABA, Am. Bar Found., Assn. Bar City N.Y., Am. Law Inst., Am. Coll. Trial Lawyers., N.Y.C. Legal Aid Soc. (bd. dirs.). Clubs: Indian Harbor Yacht (bd. dirs.), India House, Coffee House, Cercle de l'Union Interallie. Civil litigation. Home: Mead's Point Greenwich CT 06830 Office: 80 Pine St New York NY 10005

HEGGY, RODNEY JOE, lawyer; b. St. Louis, Aug. 26, 1955; s. Tom L. Heggy and Helen C. Shadid; m. Suzanne Julia Parker, May 24, 1980. BA, Southeastern Okla. State U., 1977; MS, U. Southwestern La., 1978; JD, U. Houston, 1981. Bar: Tex. 1981, Okla. 1982, U.S. Dist. Ct. (we. dist.) Okla. 1982, U.S. Ct. Appeals (10th cir.) 1985. Assoc. Cheek, Cheek & Cheek, Oklahoma City, Okla., 1982—. Mem. ABA, Okla. County Bar Assn., Okla. Assn. Def. Counsel. Insurance, Personal injury, Federal civil litigation. Office: 311 N Harvey Oklahoma City OK 73102

HEID, DANIEL BRIAN, lawyer; b. San Diego, Jan. 5, 1949; s. Thomas Louis and Mary Kay (Smith) H.; m. Cheryl Lynn Winchester, Dec. 16, 1972; children: Lisa, Andrea, Brenda, Steven. BS, Western State U., 1974, JD, 1975. Bar: Calif. 1976, U.S. Dist. Ct. (so. dist.) Calif, 1976, Wash. 1978, U.S. Dist. Ct. (we. dist.) Wash. 1978, U.S. Dist. Ct. (ea. dist.) Wash. 1983. Dep. pros. atty. Lewis County Prosecutor's Office, Chehalis, Wash., 1978-79; assoc. Hall & Roewe, Chehalis, Wash., 1979-83; atty. City of Toppenish, Wash., 1983-85; prosecutor City of Mabton, Wash., 1985—; atty. City of Sunnyside, Wash., 1983—; instr. bus. law, criminal justice Centralia (Wash.) Coll., 1979-83, Heritage Coll., Toppenish, 1983—; lectr. Chehalis Police Res. Training, 1982-83, Yakima Valley Police Res. Acad., Sunnyside and Toppenish, 1983—. Del., parliamentarian Lewis County, State of Wash. Rep. Convs., 1980. Served with USMC and USNR, 1969-71, Vietnam. Mem. ABA, Calif. State Bar Assn., Wash. State Bar Assn., Wash. Assn. Mun. Attys., Yakima County Bar Assn. Republican. Mem. Nazarene Ch. Lodge: Kiwanis (bd. dirs. Sunnyside club 1985—). Avocations: reading, photography, woodworking. Criminal, Labor, Local government. Home: PO Box 692 Sunnyside WA 98944 Office: City of Sunnyside 818 E Edison Ave Sunnyside WA 98944

HEIDRICH, ROBERT WESLEY, lawyer; b. Chgo., Aug. 1, 1927; s. Carl G. and Harriet B. (Butzlaff) H.; m. Lennice L. Hubenbecker, June 19, 1948; children—John G., Robert G., Kimberly L. Student U. Wis., 1944-45, 47-48; J.D., DePaul U., 1951. Bar: Ill. 1951. Calif. 1974, Tenn. 1980. Atty., Brunswick Corp., Chgo., 1953-60, 65-69, v.p. Brunswick AG (Switzerland), 1960-61, dir. Brunswick Internat. Fin. A.G. (Switzerland), 1962-65; sec., corp. counsel Nat. Can Corp., Chgo., 1969-73; v.p., sec., gen. counsel, dir. Rohr Industries, Inc., Chula Vista, Calif., 1973-79, corporate v.p., gen. counsel

hotel group, 1979-85; counsel Kaiser Steel Corp., 1985—. Chmn. Riverside-Brookfield Community Caucus, 1972; bd. dirs. Am. Internat. Sch. of Zurich, 1964-65; chmn. Jr. Achievement, Chgo., 1970-75. Served with U.S. Army, 1945-47. Mem. Frederick Law Olmstead Soc. (founding pres. 1967-69). General corporate. Home: 5171 Parkfield Ln La Verne CA 91750 Office: 9400 Cherry Ave Fontana CA 92335

HEIER, DAVID SCOTT, lawyer; b. Phila., Sept. 15, 1953; s. Marvin Anthony and Donna (Stepp) H.; m. Patricia Elaine Wilkin, Aug. 27, 1977; children: Gregory Scott, Michelle Elaine. BA, U. Dayton, 1975, MA, JD, 1979. Bar: Ohio 1979, U.S. Mil. Ct. Appeals 1980, U.S. Ct. Claims 1982, U.S. Tax Ct. 1982, U.S. Dist. Ct. (so. dist.) Ohio 1984, U.S. Ct. Appeals (6th cir.) 1985, U.S. Supreme Ct. 1985. Asst. atty. City of Upper Arlington, Ohio, 1983-85; staff atty. Hyatt Legal Services, Columbus, Ohio, 1985-86; sole practice Columbus, 1986—. Mem. Upper Arlington City Council, 1986—, chmn. ins. com., 1986—, mem. safety com., 1986—, Zoning and Planning Bd., Upper Arlington, 1986—. Served to capt. USMC, 1980-83, with res. Mem. ABA, Ohio Bar Assn., Columbus Bar Assn., Marine Corps Assn., Civic Assn. Republican. Methodist. Family and matrimonial, General practice, Local government. Home: 2353 Bristol Rd Upper Arlington OH 43221 Office: 501 S High St Columbus OH 43215-5667

HEIFETZ, ALAN WILLIAM, judge; b. Portland, Maine, Jan. 15, 1943; s. Ralph and Bernice (Diamon) H.; m. Nancy Butler Stone, Aug. 11, 1968; children: Andrew Stone, Peter Stone. A.B., Syracuse U., 1965; J.D., Boston U., 1968. Bar: Maine 1968, Mass. 1968, U.S. Dist. Ct. Mass. 1969, U.S. Supreme Ct. 1972. Assoc. Chayet and Flash, Boston, 1968-70; trial atty. ICC, Washington, 1970-72, counsel to chmn., 1972-78, adminstrv. law judge, 1978-80; adminstrv. law judge Fed. Labor Relations Authority, Washington, 1980-82; chief adminstrv. law judge Dept. HUD, Washington, 1982—; mem. forum faculty Am. Arbitration Assn., Washington, 1983—; appointed mem. Adminstrv. Conf. U.S., 1986—; mem. Forum of U.S. Adminstrv. Law Judges, v.p. 1986-87. Mem. Fallsmead Civic Assn. (Md.). Mem. Fed. Adminstrv. Law Judges Conf. (mem. exec. com. 1982-85). Club: Potomac Tennis (Md.). Administrative and regulatory, Labor. Home: 23 Infield Ct N Potomac MD 20854 Office: US Dept HUD 451 7th St SW Washington DC 20410 *

HEIL, PAUL WILLIAM, lawyer; b. Pontiac, Mich., Dec. 11, 1940; s. William and Louise Pauline (Haefner) H.; m. Clarissa Afton Karle, Oct. 7, 1966; children—Bartholomew A., Hanns-Georg K., Maximilian. A.B., U.Mich., 1963; LL.B., U. Pa., 1966; postgrad. in law Ludwig-Maximilians Universitat, Munich, W.Ger., 1973-74. Bar: Mich. 1967, U.S. Dist. Ct. (ea. dist.) Mich. 1975. Assoc. Joslyn & Keydel, Detroit, 1966-73; atty. legal dept. Dow Chem. Co., Midland, Mich., 1974—, sr. atty., 1979-86, staff counsel, 1986—. Mem. ABA, Mich. Bar Assn., Detroit Bar Assn., Midland County Bar Assn., Am. Soc. Internat. Law. Democrat. Roman Catholic. Club: Princeton of N.Y. General corporate, Pension, securities and finance, Private international. Home: 1023 Balfour St Midland MI 48640 Office: 2030 Dow Center Midland MI 48674

HEILBRON, DAVID M(ICHAEL), lawyer; b. San Francisco, Nov. 25, 1936; s. Louis H. and Delphine A. (Rosenblatt) H.; m. Nancy Ann Olsen, June 21, 1960; children—Lauren Ada, Sarah Ann, Ellen Selma. B.S. summa cum laude, U. Calif., Berkeley, 1958; A.B. first class, Oxford U., Eng., 1960; LL.B. magna cum laude, Harvard U., 1962. Bar: Calif. 1963, U.S. Dist. Ct. (no. dist.) Calif. 1963, U.S Ct. Appeals (9th cir.) 1963, U.S. Ct. Appeals (D.C. cir.) 1972, U.S Dist. Ct. (ea. dist.) Calif. 1981, U.S. Dist. Ct. Nev. 1982, U.S. Dist. Ct. (cen. dist.) Calif. 1983. Assoc. McCutchen, Doyle, Brown & Enersen, San Francisco, 1962-69; ptnr. McCutchen, Doyle, Brown & Enersen, 1969-85, mng. ptnr., 1985—; vis. lectr. appellate advocacy U. Calif. Berkeley, 1981-82, 83-84; panelist arbitration program Continuing Edn. of Bar, 1982; mem. vis. com. Golden Gate U. Sch. Law, 1983. Bd. dirs. San Francisco Jewish Community Ctr., 1974—, Legal Aid Soc., 1974-78, Legal Assistance to Elderly, San Francisco, 1980, San Francisco Renaissance, 1982—; pres. San Francisco Sr. Ctr., 1972-75; co-chmn. San Francisco Lawyers' Com. for Urban Affairs, 1976. Rhodes scholar. Fellow Am. Bar Found.; mem. State Bar Calif. (chmn. com. cts. 1982-83, bd. govs. 1983-85, mem. commn. on discovery 1984—, pres. 1985-86), ABA, Bar Assn. San Francisco (chmn. conf. dels. 1975-76, pres. 1980), Calif. Acad. Appellate Lawyers, Am. Coll. Trial Lawyers, Am. Arbitration Assn. (bd. dirs. 1986—, adv. council No. Calif. chpt., 1982—, chmn. 1987—, jud. council 1987—). Democrat. Clubs: World Trade, Calif. Tennis. Federal civil litigation, State civil litigation, Construction. Office: 26th Floor 3 Embarcadero Ctr San Francisco CA 94111

HEILIGENSTEIN, CHRISTIAN ERICA, lawyer; b. St. Louis, Dec. 7, 1929; s. Christian A. and Louisa M. (Dixon) H.; m. Carol Ann Blust, Aug. 30, 1965 (div. Oct. 1978); children: Christie, Julie; m. Liselotte Warbanoff, Feb. 6, 1981. BS in Law, U. Ill., 1953, JD, 1955. Bar: Ill. 1955, U.S. Dist. Ct. (ea. dist.) Ill. 1955, U.S. Ct. Appeals (7th cir.) 1956, U.S. Dist. Ct. (so. dist.) Ill. 1960, U.S. Supreme Ct. 1982. Assoc. Listeman & Bandy, East St. Louis, Ill., 1955-61; sole practice, Belleville, Ill., 1962-84; ptnr. Heiligenstein & Badgley, Belleville, 1984—; dir., exec. com. 1st Nat. Bank of Belleville, dir. Magna Group, Inc. Recipient Alumni of Month award U. Ill. Law Sch., 1982. Mem. Ill. State Bar Assn., Internat. Acad. Trial Lawyers, St. Clair County Bar Assn., St. Louis Bar Assn., Inner Circle Advs., Am. Bd. Trial Advs., Am. Acad. Profl. Liability Attys., Assn. Trial Lawyers Am. (bd. govs. 1985-87), Ill. Trial Lawyers Assn. (bd. dirs. 1975—, v.p. 1986). Democrat. Clubs: Mo. Athletic (St. Louis); Union League (Chgo.); Beach (Palm Beach, Fla.). Personal injury, Workers' compensation. Home: Rural Rt 5 PO Box 231 Belleville IL 62222 Office: 30 Public Sq Belleville IL 62220

HEILMAN, CARL EDWIN, lawyer; b. Elizabethville, Pa., Feb. 3, 1911; s. Edgar James and Mary Alice (Bechtold) H.; m. Grace Emily Greene, Nov. 29, 1934 (div. 1952); children—John Greene, Elizabeth Greene; m. 2d, Claire Virginia Phelps, Oct. 10, 1952. B.A., Lafayette Coll., Easton, Pa., 1932, M.A., 1933; J.D. magna cum laude, U. Pa., 1939. Bar: N.Y. 1940, Pa. 1940, Mass. 1973, U.S. Supreme Ct. 1960. Tchr. English, Easton High Sch., 1934-36; assoc. Dwight, Harris, Koegel & Caskey, N.Y.C., 1939-42; atty. OPA, Washington, 1942-43; atty. N.Y. Gov.'s Commn. to Investigate Workmen's Compensation Law, N.Y.C., 1943-44; assoc. Dewey, Ballantine, Bushby, Palmer & Wood, N.Y.C., 1944-59, ptnr., 1959-73; counsel to firm Csaplar & Bok, Boston, San Francisco and Phila., 1973—. Trustee Upsala Coll., East Orange, N.J., 1970-73. Fellow Am. Bar Found.; mem. ABA, Boston Bar Assn., Order of Coif. Republican. Episcopalian. Clubs: Univ. (N.Y.C.); Down Town (Boston). General corporate, Real property, Private Financing. Home: One Devonshire Pl Apt 2605 Boston MA 02109

HEILMAN, PAMELA DAVIS, lawyer; b. Buffalo, July 2, 1948; d. George Henry and Natalie (Maier) Davis; m. Robert D. Heilman, June 27, 1970. AB, Vassar Coll., 1970; JD, SUNY, Buffalo, 1975. Bar: N.Y. 1976, Fla. 1980. Assoc. Hodgson, Russ, Andrews, Woods & Goodyear, Buffalo, 1975-84, ptnr., 1984—. Bd. dirs. United Way Buffalo, 1985—, D'Youville Coll. Ctr. for Women in Mgmt., Buffalo, 1985—. Mem. ABA, N.Y. State Bar Assn. (com. internat. trade and transactions 1985—), Fla. Bar Assn., Erie County Bar Assn. General corporate. Office: Hodgson Russ Andrews Woods & Goodyear 1800 One M&T Plaza Buffalo NY 14203

HEIM, ROBERT CHARLES, lawyer; b. Phila., Dec. 9, 1942; s. William Francis and Mary Elizabeth (Murray) H.; m. Jean Mary Ross, June 20, 1964; children: Karen Elizabeth, Christopher Robert. BS, U. Pa., 1964, JD, 1972; MBA, Coll. William and Mary, 1968. Bar: U.S. Dist. Ct. (ea. dist.) Pa. 1972, U.S. Ct. Appeals (3d cir.) 1974, U.S. Supreme Ct. 1985. Assoc. Dechert, Price and Rhoads, Phila., 1972-79, ptnr., 1979—; mem. lawyers adv. com. to U.S. Ct. Appeals (3d cir.), 1985—. Little league baseball coach, Wayne, Pa., 1984-86; mem. Shipley Sch. Fathers Assn., Bryn Mawr, Pa., 1984-86. Served to capt. USNR. Mem. Phila. Bar Assn. (bd. govs. 1984-86, chmn. fed. cts. com. 1986. Clubs: Lawyers, Racquet (Phila.). Federal civil litigation, State civil litigation, Administrative and regulatory. Office: Dechert Price & Rhoads 3400 Centre Square W Philadelphia PA 19102

HEIMAN, MAXWELL, lawyer; b. Hartford, Conn., Apr. 24, 1932; s. David and Mary (Berman) H.; m. Sylvia P. Dress, Aug. 18, 1957; children—Deborah J., Scott D. B.A., U. Conn., 1954; J.D., Boston Coll. Law, 1957. Bar: Conn. 1957, U.S. Dist. Ct. Conn. 1958, U.S. Ct. Appeals (2d cir.) 1961, U.S. Supreme Ct. 1963, U.S. Tax Ct. 1974. Assoc. Bracken and Burke, Hartford, 1957-65; ptnr. Furey, Donovan & Heiman, P.C., Bristol, Conn., 1965—. Editor Conn. Criminal Procedure; contbr. articles to profl. jours. Mem. Republican Town Com., Newington, Conn., 1963-73; mem. Newington Bd. Edn., 1969-73, 74-75; bd. dirs. Hartford Legal Aid Soc., 1979—. Fellow Am. Bar Found., Am. Coll. Trial Lawyers; mem. ABA (ho. of dels. 1980—, chmn. steering com., nominating com.), Conn. Bar Assn. (past pres.), Hartford County Bar Assn. (past pres.), Assn. Trial Lawyers Am., Am. Judicature Soc., Nat. Assn. Def. Lawyers in Criminal Cases. Jewish. Club: Chippanee Country (Bristol). Lodge: Masons. Criminal, State civil litigation, Federal civil litigation. Home: 210 Brookside Rd Newington CT 06111 Office: 43 Bellevue Ave Bristol CT 06010

HEIMANN, WILLIAM EMIL, lawyer; b. New Braunfels, Tex., Oct. 5, 1928; s. Emil Erno and Gladys Lorene (Cook) H.; m. Mary Elizabeth Welch, May 21, 1960; children—Martin Emil, David Phillips. LL.B., Okla. U., 1951. Bar: Okla. bar 1951. Partner Kerr-Davis-Roberts-Heimann-Irvine & Burbage, Oklahoma City, 1960-65; atty. Kerr-Conn & Davis, Oklahoma City, 1954-60; gen. atty., asst. sec. Kerr-McGee Corp., Oklahoma City, 1965-73; v.p., gen. counsel, asst. sec. Kerr-McGee Corp., 1973-75, v.p., gen. counsel, sec., 1975-86, v.p., sec., 1986—. Bd. editors: Okla. Law Rev, 1949-50. Served with U.S. Army, 1951-53. Mem. Am. Bar Assn., Am. Soc. Corp. Secs., Okla. Bar Assn., Okla. County Bar Assn., Order of Coif, Phi Delta Phi, Lambda Chi Alpha. Presbyterian. General corporate. Home: 836 NW 39th St Oklahoma City OK 73118 Office: PO Box 25861 Oklahoma City OK 73125

HEINDL, PHARES MATTHEWS, lawyer; b. Meridian, Miss., Dec. 14, 1949; s. Paul A. and Leila (Matthews) H.; m. Linda Ann Williamson, Sept. 21, 1985; 1 child, Lori Elizabeth. BS in Chem. Engring., Miss. State U., 1972; JD, U. Fla., 1981. Bar: Fla. 1981, Calif. 1982, U.S. Dist. Ct. (cen. dist.) Calif. 1983, U.S. Dist. Ct. (mid. dist.) Fla. 1983. Assoc. Lafollette, Johnson et al, Los Angeles, 1982-83, Sam E. Murrell & Sons, Orlando, Fla., 1983-84; sole practice Orlando, Fla., 1984—; cons. atty. Nat. Legal Found., Virginia Beach, Va., 1985—. Precinct coordinator Freedom Council, Orlando, 1986. Mem. Fla. Bar Assn., Calif. Bar Assn., Orange County Bar Assn., Assn. Trial Lawyers Am., Fla. Acad. Trial Lawyers, Tau Beta Pi. Republican. Mem. Assembly of God Ch. Avocations: sailing, tennis. Personal injury, State civil litigation, Workers' compensation. Home: 838 E Charing Cross Cirlce Lake Mary FL 32746 Office: 400 W Colonial Orlando FL 32804

HEINE, ANDREW NOAH, lawyer; b. Camden, N.J., Nov. 12, 1928; s. Aaron Heine and Miriam (Leventon) Heine Shindler; m. Barbara Fatt, June 28, 1950 (div. 1966); children—Nancy Virginia, Priscilla Joanne, Jonathan Roger; m. Joni Cherbo, Oct. 28, 1968; 1 child, Adam Merl Stefan. B.A., Amherst Coll., 1949; LL.B., Yale U., 1952. Bar: N.Y. 1953. Assoc. Sullivan & Cromwell, N.Y.C., 1953-59; assoc. Rosenman, Colin et al, N.Y.C., 1959-61; sr. ptnr. Marshall Bratter, et al, N.Y.C., 1961-73, Finley, Kumble, Wagner, Heine, Underberg, Manley, Myerson & Casey, N.Y.C., 1973—; dir. Citizens Utilities Co., Stamford, Conn., Olsten Corp., Westbury, N.Y., Bastian Industries, N.Y.C., Mcht. Bank of Calif., Los Angeles, 1st Peoples Bank N.J., Am. Bakeries Co., N.Y.C. Served to lt. USNR, 1953-56. Mem. Assn. Bar City N.Y. Club: Century Country (Purchase, N.Y.). General corporate, Real property, Securities. Home: 441 E 57th St New York NY 10022 Office: Finley Kumble Wagner Heine Underberg Manley & Casey 425 Park Ave New York NY 10022

HEINEMAN, BENJAMIN WALTER, JR., lawyer; b. Chgo., Jan. 25, 1944; s. Benjamin Walter and Natalie (Goldstein) H.; m. Jeanne Cristine Russell, June 7, 1975; children: Matthew R., Zachary R. B.A. magna cum laude, Harvard U., 1965; B.Letters, Balliol Coll., Oxford U., Eng., 1967; J.D., Yale U., 1971. Bar: D.C. bar 1973, U.S. Supreme Ct. bar 1973. Reporter Chgo. Sun Times, 1968; law clk. Assoc. Justice Potter Stewart, U.S. Supreme Ct., 1971-72; staff atty. Center for Law and Social Policy, 1973-75; with Williams Connolly and Califano, Washington, 1975-76; exec. asst. to sec. HEW, Washington, 1977-78; asst. sec. for planning and evaluation HEW, 1978-79; partner Califano, Ross & Heineman, Washington, 1979-82, Sidley & Austin, Washington, 1982—. Author: The Politics of the Powerless: A Study of the Campaign Against Racial Discrimination, 1972, Memorandum for the President: A Strategic Approach to Domestic Affairs in the 1980's, 1981; editor-in-chief: Yale Law Jour., 1970-71. Rhodes scholar, 1965-67. Mem. Phi Beta Kappa. Home: 4914 30th Pl NW Washington DC 20008 Office: 1722 Eye St NW Washington DC 20006

HEINEN, MARK LEE, lawyer; b. Sheboygan, Wis., Sept. 2, 1946; s. Lester William and Maude (Joosse) H.; m. Margaret A. Edwards, Aug. 26, 1967; children: Elizabeth, Anne. BA, Central Coll., Pella, Iowa, 1968; MA, U. Ariz., 1972; JD, Harvard U., 1978. Bar: Mich. 1978, U.S. Dist. Ct. (ea. dist.) Mich. 1978, U.S. Dist. Ct. (we. dist.) Mich. 1981, U.S. Ct. Appeals (2d and 6th cirs.) 1982. Assoc. Gregory, Van Lopik, Moore & Jeake, Detroit, 1978-83, ptnr., 1984—. Served with U.S. Army, 1970-72. Mem. ABA (labor sect.), Mich. Bar Assn. (labor sect.), Detroit Bar Assn. (library com. 1981—). Labor, Federal civil litigation. Home: 17510 Santa Barbara Detroit MI 48221 Office: Gregory Van Lopik Moore & Jeakle 2042 First Nat Bldg Detroit MI 48226

HEINEN, PAUL ABELARDO, lawyer, executive; b. Teaneck, N.J., Jan. 9, 1930; s. Paul and Encarnacion (Maestu) H.; m. Gloria Newman, Oct. 9, 1952; children—Heidi E., Paul C. B.B.A., U. Mich., 1954, J.D., 1956, M.B.A., 1957; S.M., MIT, 1963. Bar: Mich. 1957, Ill. 1982. Assoc. gen. counsel Chrysler Corp., Detroit, 1968-76, sec., 1969-81, v.p., 1974-81, v.p., gen. counsel, sec., 1976-81; v.p., gen. counsel GATX Corp., Chgo., 1981—. Bd. govs. Met. Planning Council, Chgo. Served to 1st lt. U.S. Army, 1951-53, Korea. Mem. ABA, Mich. Bar Assn., Ill. Bar Assn., Chgo. Bar Assn., Order of Coif, Beta Gamma Sigma. Clubs: Oakland Hills (Birmingham, Mich.); Chicago, Mid-Am. General corporate. Home: 1780 S Oak Knoll Dr Lake Forest IL 60045 Office: GATX Corp 120 S Riverside Plaza Chicago IL 60606

HEINES, MOLLY KATHLEEN, lawyer; b. Bklyn., July 29, 1953; d. William Joseph and Muriel Rita (Brown) H.; m. Thomas Joseph Moloney, Dec. 26, 1976. BA, Barnard Coll., 1975; JD, Columbia U., 1978. Bar: N.Y. 1979, U.S. Dist. Ct. (so. and ea. dists.) N.Y. 1979. Assoc. Simpson, Thacher & Bartlett, N.Y.C., 1978-83; assoc. counsel The Equitable Life Assurance Soc. of U.S., N.Y.C., 1983-85, asst. gen. counsel, 1985—. General corporate, Computer, Securities. Office: The Equitable Life Assurance Soc US 787 7th Ave New York NY 10019

HEININGER, ERWIN CARL, lawyer; b. Ann Arbor, Mich., Apr. 9, 1921. A.B., U. Mich., 1943, J.D., 1952. Bar: Mich. 1953, Ill. 1953, U.S. Dist. Ct. (no. dist.) Ill. 1954, U.S. Ct. Claims 1957, U.S. Ct. Appeals (7th cir.) 1962, U.S. Ct. Appeals (3d cir.) 1981, U.S. Ct. Appeals (2d cir.) 1983, U.S. Ct. Appeals (10th cir.) 1984, U.S. Supreme Ct. 1960. Trial atty. antitrust div. Dept. Justice, Chgo., 1953-55; asoc. Mayer, Friedlich, Spies, Tierney, Brown & Platt, Chgo., 1955-60; ptnr. Mayer, Brown & Platt, Chgo., 1960-86. Contbr. articles to profl. jours. Fellow Am. Coll. Trial Lawyers; mem. ABA, Fed. Bar Assn., Ill. Bar Assn., Chgo. Bar Assn., 7th Cir. Bar Assn., Chgo. Council Lawyers, Law Club Chgo., Legal Club Chgo., Assn. Trial Lawyers Am., Maritime Law Assn. U.S., Phi Delta Phi, Lambda Chi Alpha. Clubs: University, Metropolitan, (Chgo.); National Lawyers (Washington). Antitrust, Federal civil litigation. Office: Mayer Brown & Platt 190 S LaSalle St Chicago IL 60603

HEINS, SAMUEL DAVID, lawyer; b. Providence, May 31, 1947; s. Maurice Haskell and Hadassah (Wagman) H.; m. Dianne Claire Hogg, July 22, 1972; children: Madeleine Sarah, Nora Anne. BA, U. Minn., 1968, JD, 1972. Bar: Minn., 1973, U.S. Dist. Ct. Minn. 1973, U.S. Ct. Appeals (8th cir.). Law clk. U.S. Dist. Ct. Minn., Mpls., 1972-73; assoc. Firestone Law Firm, St. Paul, 1973-76; ptnr. Tanick & Heins, Mpls., 1976—; vis. asst. prof. Sch. Architecture, U. Minn.-Mpls., 1974—. Mem. Mpls. Charter Commn., 1983-84; pres. Minn. Lawyers Internat. Human Rights Com., Mpls., 1983—, Minn. Ctr. for Torture Victims, Mpls., 1985—. Mem. ABA, Minn. State Bar Assn. (bd. govs. 1978—). Federal civil litigation, State civil litigation.

HEINTZ, JEFFREY THEODORE, lawyer; b. Akron, Ohio, Nov. 9, 1949; s. Willard E. and Janet C. (Helmkamp) H.; m. Rose L. Rothman, Mar. 25, 1972; children: Michael E., Adam M. BA, Ohio U., 1972; JD, U. Akron, 1975. Bar: Ohio 1975, U.S. Dist. Ct. (no. dist.) Ohio 1975, U.S. Ct. Appeals (6th cir.) 1977. Assoc. Blakemore, Rosen, Meeker & Varian, Akron, 1975-80, ptnr., 1980-84; ptnr. Brouse and McDowell, Akron, 1984—. Case and comment editor U. Akron Law Rev., 1974-75. Chmn. Cuyahoga Falls (Ohio) Bd. Zoning Appeals, 1983-85. Mem. ABA, Ohio Bar Assn., Akron Bar Assn., Comml. Law League Am. Bankruptcy, Contracts commercial, Real property. Home: 3359 Purdue St Cuyahoga Falls OH 44221 Office: Brouse & McDowell 500 1st Nat Tower Akron OH 44308

HEINZ, JOHN PETER, lawyer, educator; b. Carlinville, Ill., Aug. 6, 1936; s. William Henry and Margaret Louise (Denby) H.; m. Anne Murray, Jan. 14, 1967; children: Katherine Reynolds, Peter Lindley Murray. A.B., Washington U., St. Louis, 1958; LL.B., Yale U., 1962. Bar: D.C. 1962, Ill. 1966, U.S. Supreme Ct. 1967. Teaching asst. polit. sci. Washington U., St. Louis, 1958-59, instr., 1960; asst. prof. law Northwestern U. Sch. Law, Chgo., 1965-68, assoc. prof., 1968-71, prof., 1971—, prof. law and urban affairs, 1972—, dir. program law and social scis., 1968-70, dir. research, 1973-74; affiliated scholar Am. Bar Found., Chgo., 1974—, vis. scholar, 1975-76, exec. dir., 1982-86. Author: (with A. Gordon) Public Access to Information, (with E. Laumann) Chicago Lawyers; contbr. articles to profl. jours. Served to capt. USAF, 1962-65. Grantee NIMH, 1970-72, NSF, 1970, 78-81, 84-86, CNA Found., 1972, Am. Bar Found., 1974—, Russell Sage Found., 1978-80. Fellow Am. Bar Found.; mem. Law and Soc. Assn., Am. Polit. Sci. Assn., ABA. Legal education, Criminal. Home: 525 Judson Ave Evanston IL 60202 Office: Northwestern U Sch Law 357 E Chicago Ave Chicago IL 60611

HEINZ, WILLIAM DENBY, lawyer; b. Carlinville, Ill., Nov. 26, 1947; s. William Henry and Margaret (Denby) H.; children—Kimberly, Rebecca, Elizabeth. B.S., Millikin U., 1969; J.D., U. Ill., 1973. Bar: Ill. 1973, U.S. Dist. Ct. (no. dist.) Ill. 1974, U.S. Ct. Appeals (3d cir.) 1982, U.S. Ct. Appeals (5th cir.) 1973, U.S. Ct. Appeals (7th cir.) 1976, U.S. Supreme Ct. 1979. Law clk. to judge U.S. Ct. Appeals (5th cir.), Tuscaloosa, Ala., 1973-74; assoc. Jenner & Block, Chgo., 1974-80, ptnr., 1980—. Mem. ABA, Ill. State Bar Assn., Chgo. Bar Assn., Order of Coif. General practice, Federal civil litigation, General corporate. Home: 2017 Grant St Evanston IL 60201 Office: Jenner & Block 1 IBM Plaza 37th Floor Chicago IL 60611

HEISE, JOHN IRVIN, JR., lawyer; b. Balt., Dec. 13, 1924; s. John Irvin and Ruby Belle (Carpenter) H.; m. Jacqueline Mosey Morley, Sept. 3, 1949; children—John Irvin III, Liane Des Roches, Jeff Howard, Suzanne. A.B., U. Md., 1947; J.D., U. Va., 1950. Bar: Md. 1950, D.C. 1953, U.S. Sup. Ct. 1962. Trial atty. civil div. Dept. Justice, Washington, 1950-52; assoc. Shea Greenman Gardner & McConnaughey, Washington, 1952-57; ptnr., pres. Heise Jorgensen & Stefanelli, P.A., Silver Spring, Md., 1957—. Committeeman, merit badge counselor, dist. chmn. sustaining mem. dr. Boy Scouts Am.; chmn. Md. Ednl. Found., Inc., 1972—. Served to maj. USAF, 1942-45. Recipient Gottwals award U. Md., 1978. Mem. Am. Bar Assn., Fed Bar Assn., Md. Bar Assn., D.C. Bar Assn., Montgomery County Bar Assn., Md. Alumni Assn. (pres. 1972-73), Omicron Delta Kappa, Phi Kappa Phi. Republican. Episcopalian. Clubs: M (pres. 1966-67), Terrapin (pres. 1961-62). Federal civil litigation, Administrative and regulatory, General corporate.

HEISERMAN, ROBERT GIFFORD, lawyer; b. El Paso, July 5, 1946; s. Robert Gifford and Nancy Mildred (Wardlow) H.; m. Nancy Fay Price, Oct. 20, 1973; 1 child, Laura. B.A., U. Oreg., 1968; J.D., U. Denver, 1971. Bar: Ct. Colo. 1972; U.S. Dist. Ct. Colo. 1972, U.S. Dist. Ct. N.Mex. 1972, U.S. Dist. Ct. D.C. 1972, U.S. Dist. Ct. (so. dist.) Ala. 1974, U.S. Ct. Appeals (10th cir.) 1975, U.S. Supreme Ct. 1976. Legis. draftsman N.Mex. Legislature, Santa Fe, 1972-73; sole practice, Santa Fe, 1973, Denver, 1974—. Mem. Emergency Med. Services Council, Denver, 1981-84. Mem. Am. Immigration Lawyers Assn. (nat. bd. govs., chmn. profl. ethics and grievances com. 1982-87, founder Colo. chpt., treas. Colo. chpt. 1978-81), ABA, Colo. Bar Assn., Denver Bar Assn., D.C. Bar Assn., Internat. Bar Assn., InterAm. Bar Assn. Democrat. Methodist. Immigration, naturalization, and customs. Home: 6378 S Far View Ln Evergreen CO 80439 Office: 1625 Broadway Suite 2780 Denver CO 80202

HEISINGER, JAMES GORDON, JR., lawyer; b. Carmel, Calif., Aug. 17, 1952; s. James Gordon Sr. and Rosemary F. (Walters) H.; m. Pamela Quinn, Mar. 24, 1979; children: Michael, Alexander. BA, U. Calif., Santa Cruz, 1974; JD, Lewis and Clark Coll., Portland, 1979. Bar: Calif. 1979, U.S. Dist. Ct. (no. dist.) Calif. 1979, U.S. Ct. Appeals (9th cir.) 1985, U.S. Supreme Ct. 1985. Sole practice Carmel, 1980-87; atty. City of Sand City, Calif., 1985—; ptnr. Buck, Heisinger, Perkins & Ernst, Carmel, Calif., 1987—; instr. Monterey (Calif.) Coll. of Law, 1983—. Chmn. Carmel chpt. ARC, 1985—; bd. dirs. Vols. in Action, Monterey, 1983-85. Mem. ABA, Calif. Bar Assn., Monterey County Bar Assn. Democrat. Roman Catholic. Lodge: Rotary (bd. dirs. 1985-86). Avocation: windsurfing. Real property, Administrative and regulatory, Local government. Office: Buck Heisinger Perkins & Ernst 26335 Carmel Rancho Blvd Carmel CA 93922

HEISLER, QUENTIN GEORGE, JR., lawyer; b. Jefferson City, Mo., June 30, 1943; s. Quentin George and Helen (Reynolds) H.; m. Susan Davis, Jan. 24, 1970; children—Sarah, Thomas, Margaret. A.B., Harvard U., 1965, J.D., 1968. Bar: Ill. 1968, U.S. Dist. Ct. (no. dist.) Ill. 1969, Fla. 1977. Assoc. McDermott, Will & Emery, Chgo., 1968-69, 70-75, ptnr., 1975—; legal counsel Office Minority Bus. Enterprise, Dept. Commerce, Washington, 1969-70; chmn. Exec. Compensation Group. Gen. editor: Trust Administration in Illinois, 1983. Chmn. Winnetka Caucus, Ill., 1983; mem. Winnetka Bd. Edn., 1985—. Mem. ABA, Ill. Bar Assn., Chgo. Council Estate Planning. Clubs: University, Harvard (bd. dirs.) (Chgo.). Estate taxation, Probate. Office: McDermott Will & Emery 111 W Monroe St Chicago IL 60603

HEITLAND, ANN RAE, lawyer; b. Marshalltown, Iowa, Feb. 5, 1950; d. Harry Benjamin and Vivian E. (Gissel) H. BA, U. Chgo., 1972, JD, 1975. Bar: Ill. 1975, U.S. Dist. Ct. (no. dist.) Ill. 1975, U.S. Ct. Appeals (7th cir.) 1977. Assoc. Schiff, Hardin & Waite, Chgo., 1975-82, ptnr., 1982—. Editor: U. Chgo. Law Rev., 1974-75. Trustee Downers Grove (Ill.) Pub. Library, 1983-85. Mem. ABA, Chgo. Bar Assn. Federal civil litigation, State civil litigation. Office: Schiff Hardin & White 7200 Sears Tower Chicago IL 60606

HEITNER, KENNETH HOWARD, lawyer; b. Jersey City, Apr. 1, 1948; s. Charles Fred and Molly (Vogelman) H.; m. Anne Barbara Siegel, June 14, 1970; children: Douglas, Andrew. BA, Rutgers U., 1969; JD, NYU, 1973, LLM, 1977. Bar: N.Y. 1974, U.S. Dist. Ct. (so. and ea. dists.) N.Y. 1975, U.S. Tax Ct. 1976. From assos. to ptnr. Weil, Gotshal & Manges, N.Y.C., 1973—. Served with U.S. Army, 1969-75. Mem. ABA, N.Y. State Bar Assn. (com. bankruptcy, corps., tax club, exec. com. tax sect.), Assn. of Bar of City of N.Y. Club: Fairview Country (Greenwich, Conn.) (bd. govs. 1983—). Corporate taxation, Personal income taxation. Office: Weil Gotshal & Manges 767 Fifth Ave New York NY 10153

HEITZ, BRUCE A., corporate lawyer. Sec., gen. counsel Tex. Am. Bancshares Inc., Ft. Worth. Office: Tex Am Bancshares Inc 500 Throckmorton Fort Worth TX 76102 *

HEJTMANEK, DANTON CHARLES, lawyer; b. Topeka, July 22, 1951; s. Robert Kieth and Bernice Louise (Krause) H.; m. Jenny Jordan, May 26, 1973; 1 child, Brian J. BBA in Acctg., Washburn U., 1973, JD, 1976. Bar: Kans. 1976, U.S. Dist. Ct. Kans. 1976, U.S. Tax Ct. 1976. Ptnr. Schroer, Rice, Bryan & Lykins, P.A., Topeka, 1975-86, Bryan, Lykins, Hejtmanek & Wulz, P.A., Topeka, 1986—. Mem. ABA (rep. young lawyers Kans. and Nebr.), Kans. Bar Assn. (pres. young lawyers 1985), Am. Trial Lawyers Assn., Kans. Trial Lawyers Assn. Republican. Presbyterian. Lodge: Sertoma (pres. 1983). Avocations: snow skiing, travel. Personal injury, Probate, Family and matrimonial. Home: 1422 Collins Topeka KS 66606 Office: 115 E Seventh St Topeka KS 66603

HEKTNER, CANDICE ELAINE, lawyer; b. Fargo, N.D., Apr. 22, 1948; d. Alfred G. and Hope E. Hektner; 1 child, Nicole A. BA, Concordia Coll., Moorhead, Minn., 1970; JD, Valparaiso U., 1975. Bar: Minn. 1975, N.D. 1975, U.S. Dist. Ct. Minn. 1975, U.S. Dist. Ct. N.D. 1975. Assoc. Ochs Larsen Law Firm, Mpls., 1975-80; ptnr. Chadwick, Johnson & Condon, P.A., Mpls., 1980—. Mem. ABA, Minn. Bar Assn., Minn. Def. Lawyers Assn. Lutheran. Workers' compensation, Personal injury, Insurance. Office: Chadwick Johnson & Condon PA 7235 Ohms Ln Edina MN 55431

HELBERT, MICHAEL CLINTON, lawyer; b. Wichita, Kans., Dec. 30, 1950; s. Robert Lee and Carrollyn Jean (Stull) H.; m. Sandra Sue Ziegler, Aug. 26, 1978; 1 son, Michael Ryan. A.B., U. Kans.-Lawrence, 1972, J.D., 1975. Bar: Kans. 1975, U.S. Dist. Ct. Kans. 1975, U.S. Supreme Ct. 1980, U.S. Ct. Appeals (10th cir.) 1984. Intern, Douglas County Legal Aid, Lawrence, 1974-75; assoc. law firm Atherton, Hurt & Sanderson, Emporia, Kans., 1975-77; ptnr. firm Guy, Helbert, Bell & Smith, and predecessor firm, Emporia, 1978-81, prin., 1981—. Treas. Lyon County Rep. Cen. Com., 1986—; mem. adv. bd. Kans. U. Endowment Assn., 1977-81; chmn. profl. div. United Way of Emporia, 1978. Mem. Kans. Trial Lawyers Assn., Kans. Bar Assn., Assn. Trial Lawyers Am., Lyon-Chase County Bar Assn. (treas. 1982, v.p. 1983, pres. 1984), Emporia C. of C. (past dir., past vice-chmn.), Emporia Jaycees (past dir.), Kans. Jaycees (past dir.). Presbyterian. State civil litigation, Real property, Workers' compensation. Home: 1721 Hammond Dr Emporia KS 66801 Office: Guy Helbert Bell & Smith Chartered 519 Commercial Emporia KS 66801

HELDMAN, VICTORIA C., lawyer; b. Dayton, Ohio, Aug. 28, 1949; d. Paul F. and Anne F. (Thomas) Schmitz; m. Louis M. Heldman, Sept. 21, 1971 (div. 1973); m. John Askins, Feb. 28, 1975 (div. 1977). B.A. in Journalism with distinction, Ohio State U., 1972; J.D., U. Detroit, 1975. Bar: Mich. 1975, U.S. Dist. Ct. (ea. and we. dists.) Mich. 1975, U.S. Ct. Appeals (6th cir.) 1977, U.S. Ct. Appeals (3d cir.) 1980, U.S. Supreme Ct. 1983, Colo. 1984, U.S. Ct. Appeals (10th Cir.) 1984. Assoc. Lopatin, Miller, Bindes & Freedman, Detroit, 1973-76; ptnr. Schaden, Heldman & Lampert, Detroit, 1977—; adj. prof. U. Detroit Sch. Law, 1982. Co-author: (with Richard F. Schaden) Product Design Liability, 1982; contbg. author: Women Trial Lawyers: How They Succeed in Practice and in the Courtroom, 1986. Mem. ABA, Mich. Bar Assn., Colo. Bar Assn., Assn. Trial Lawyers Am., Colo. Trial Lawyers Assn., Mich. Trial Lawyers Assn., Lawyer-Pilots Bar Assn. Personal injury, Aviation. Address: 1731 Emerson Denver CO 80218

HELDT, JEFFREY ALAN, lawyer; b. Sacramento, Calif., Mar. 31, 1948; s. Richard Franklin and Anne (Smalstis) H.; m. Annette Louise Hall, Aug. 15, 1970; children: Alainya, Abigail. BA, Johns Hopkins U., 1969; JD cum laude, Wayne State U., 1972. Bar: Mich. 1973, U.S. Dist. Ct. (ea. dist.) Mich. 1973, U.S. Ct. Appeals (10th cir.) 1982, U.S. Ct. Appeals (6th cir.) 1984, U.S. Supreme Ct. 1986. Asst. U.S. atty. Ea. Dist. Mich., Detroit, 1973-75; asst. v.p., gen. counsel Bank of Commonwealth, Detroit, 1976-78; mng. ptnr. Levin, Levin, Garvett & Dill, Southfield, Mich., 1984—; instr. in bus. law Walsh Coll., Troy, Mich., 1977-78, U.S. Atty. Gen.'s Advocacy Inst., Washington, 1976; cons. in litigation strategy, Southfield, 1982—. Mem. Mich. Bar Assn. Civil rights, Federal civil litigation, State civil litigation. Office: Levin Levin Garvett & Dill 3000 Town Ctr Suite 1800 Southfield MI 48075

HELFGOTT, SAMSON, lawyer; b. N.Y.C., May 10, 1939; s. Benjamin Wolf and Hannah (Stern) H.; m. Joyce Ann Miller, Feb. 21, 1965; children—Yaffa, Eliezer, Batsheva, David. B.E.E. cum laude, CCNY, 1961; M.E.E., NYU, 1963; J.D. cum laude, Fordham U., 1972; M.H.L., Yeshiva U., 1962, D.H.L., 1974. Bar: N.Y. 1973, U.S. Patent Office 1973, U.S. Supreme Ct. 1978, Patent agt. Eugene S. Lovette, N.Y.C., 1961-65, Leonard H. King, N.Y.C., 1965-67; patent engr. IBM Corp., Rockville, Md., 1967-69; patent atty. Western Electric Co., N.Y.C., 1971-74; patent counsel Gen. Electric Co., N.Y.C., 1969-71, 1974-86; ptnr. Helfgott & Karas, P.C., 1986—. Editor: Foreign Patent Litigation 1983. Contbr. articles to profl. jours. Patentee in communications systems. Vice pres. Jewish Community Council, West Lawrence, N.Y., 1980-84, Congregation Kneseth Israel, West Lawrence, 1982-83. Mem. ABA, Am. Patent Law Assn. (chmn. Japanese sub-com., harminization com.), N.Y. Patent Law Soc. (chmn. fgn. com.), Eta Kappa Nu. Jewish. Patent. Home: 611 Caffrey Ave W Lawrence NY 11691 Office: Helfgott & Karas 420 Lexington Ave Suite 2900 New York NY 10170

HELLAWELL, ROBERT, legal educator; b. Long Island, N.Y., Jan. 24, 1928; s. Edwin V. and Nora D. (Mahoney) H.; m. Jane Buck, June 16, 1951; 1 dau., Kathleen Abbott. A.B., Williams Coll., 1950; LL.B., Columbia U., 1953. Bar: N.Y. 1954, Ohio 1955. Law clk. U.S. Circuit Ct. judge, 1953-54; with firm Jones, Day, Cockley & Reavis, Cleve., 1954-61; partner Jones, Day, Cockley & Reavis, 1961; atty., adviser formation Peace Corps, 1961; dir. projects in Peace Corps, Tanganyika, 1961-63; dep. assoc. dir. Peace Corps, 1963-64; assoc. prof. law Columbia Law Sch., N.Y.C., 1964-67, prof. law, 1967—, vice dean, 1973-76, acting dean, 1976-77, dir. African Law Center, 1971-77, co-dir. Investment Negotiation Center, 1973-82, dir. Center for Law and Econs., 1978-79; vis. prof. U. Ghana, 1969; cons. admiralty law UN Commn. Internat. Trade Law, 1971. Co-author: Taxation of Business Enterprises, 1987, Taxation of Transnational Transactions, 1987; editor: United States Taxation and Developing Countries, 1980; co-editor: Competition in International Business, 1981, Negotiating Foreign Investments, 1982; notes editor: Columbia Law Rev, 1952-53. Bd. dirs. Internat. Law Inst., Georgetown U., 1973-85. Served with AUS, 1946-48, Korea. Mem. Delta Kappa Epsilon, Phi Delta Phi. Corporate taxation, Personal income taxation. Home: 560 Riverside Dr New York NY 10027 Office: Columbia Law Sch New York NY 10027

HELLDORFER, BERNARD GEORGE, law educator, lawyer; b. Bklyn., Aug. 4, 1955; s. Bernard John and Lillian Elizabeth (Stietz) H.; m. Linda Helen Sturm, June 14, 1980. BS, St. John's U., Jamaica, N.Y., 1977, JD, 1980. Bar: N.Y. 1981, U.S. Dist. Ct. (so. and ea. dists.) N.Y. 1981. Assoc. counsel Mobil Oil Corp., N.Y.C., 1979-81, counsel, 1981-83; instr. St. John's U., 1983-84, asst. prof., 1984—; arbitrator N.Y.C. Stock Exchange, 1983—, Am. Stock Exchange, N.Y.C., 1984—, N.Y.C. Civil Ct., 1984—; counsel Zemek, Puskuldjian & Frustaci, Bklyn., 1984—. Sect. editor The Bus. Lawyer jour., 1986; co-producer (film) Careers in Law, 1986. Pro bono counsel Our Lady of Hope Athletic Assn., Middle Village, N.Y., 1981—, German-Am. Dance Group, Ridgewood, N.Y., 1981—. Mem. ABA, N.Y. State Bar Assn. (Outstanding Service award 1984), Assn. Bar City of N.Y., Holy Name Soc., Phi Delta Phi. Republican. Roman Catholic. Lodge: KC. Avocations: music, fishing, boating, photography. Consumer commercial, General corporate. Home: 59-58 70th St Maspeth NY 11378 Office: St Johns U Grand Central & Utopia Pkwys Jamaica NY 11439

HELLER, DONALD HERBERT, lawyer; b. N.Y.C., June 1, 1943; s. Nathan and Sylvia (Wexler) H.; m. Lesley Siskin, July 24, 1976; children: Michael, Joshua, Alexandra. BA in Econs., Queens Coll., 1966; JD, Bklyn. Law Sch., 1969. Bar: N.Y. 1969, Calif. 1973, U.S. Dist. Ct. (cen., no. and ea. dists.) Calif. 1974, U.S. Ct. Appeals (9th cir.) 1974. Asst. dist. atty. N.Y. County, N.Y.C., 1969-73; asst. U.S. atty. Calif. Dist. Ct. (ea. dist.), Sacramento, 1973-77; sole practice Sacramento, 1977-86; judge pro tempore Sacramento County Superior Ct., 1986—. Mem. Sacramento County Bar Assn., Assn. Trial Lawyers Am., Calif. Trial Lawyers Assn. Democrat. Jewish. Club: North Ridge Country (Fair Oaks, Calif.); Arden Hills Country. Avocation: golf. Federal civil litigation, State civil litigation, Criminal. Home: 5160 Keane Dr Carmichael CA 95608 Office: 1000 G St Suite 300 Sacramento CA 95814

HELLER, FRED IRA, lawyer, legal consultant; b. Bklyn., July 3, 1945; s. Murray Joseph and Pearl (Epstein) H.; m. Lynne Sue Shusterman, June 9, 1968; children: Robert, Jason. BA, Hofstra U., 1968; JD, Bklyn. Law Sch., 1972. Bar: N.Y. 1974, U.S. Dist. Ct. (ea. dist.) N.Y. 1974, U.S. Ct. Appeals (2d cir.) 1975, U.S. Supreme Ct. 1977. Atty. Speiser & Krause PC, N.Y.C., 1974-80; pres. Heller Assoc. Ltd., Merrick, N.Y., 1980—; lectr. Practicing Law Inst., N.Y.C., 1981-82. Co-author: How to Use Video in Litigation, 1986. Mem. ABA, Assn. Trial Lawyers of Am. (lectr. 1981), N.Y. State Bar Assn., N.Y. State Trial Lawyers Assn., Nassau County Bar Assn. Avocations: photography, hiking. Video documentary production for litigation. Home: 33 Fox Blvd Merrick NY 11566 Office: Heller Associates Ltd 33 Fox Blvd Merrick NY 11566

HELLER, HANES AYRES, lawyer; b. New Orleans, Mar. 10, 1940; s. John Roderick and Susie Mae (Ayres) H.; B.A., Yale U., 1962; LL.B., Harvard U., 1965; m. Deborah Sheldon Lee, June 19, 1965; children—Hanes Ayres, Lee McGavock. Admitted to N.Y. bar, 1966; assoc. firm Dewey, Ballantine, Bushby, Palmer & Wood, N.Y.C., 1965-68; atty. CPC Internat., Englewood Cliffs, N.J., 1968-76, div. counsel Best Foods div., 1976-78, assoc. gen. counsel, 1978-80, gen. counsel N.Am. div., 1980-82, v.p., gen. counsel, 1982-84; asst. gen. counsel CPC Internat., 1982—. Mem. ABA, N.Y. State Bar Assn., Assn. Bar City N.Y. Home: 450 W Saddle River Rd Upper Saddle River NJ 07458 Office: CPC Internat Inc Internat Plaza Englewood Cliffs NJ 07632

HELLER, JACK ISAAC, lawyer; b. Passaic, N.J., July 12, 1932; s. Aaron and Ruth (Brown) H.; m. Naomi Heller, Mar. 8, 1959; children—Michael Adam, Daniel Noah, Rafael Gustav. A.B., U. Chgo., 1952; LL.B., Columbia, 1958. Teaching fellow, research asst. internat. program in taxation Harvard Law Sch., 1958-61; sr. tax adviser OAS, Washington, 1961-62; tax economist Latin Am. Bur., U.S. AID, 1962-65; with Office Gen. Counsel, AID, 1965-66; legal adviser AID, Brazil, 1966-67; asst. dir. AID, 1967-68; dir. Office of Devel. Programs, Latin Am. Bur., AID, 1969-72; atty., mgr. spl. projects Office Gen. Counsel, Gen. Electric Co., 1972-74; practice law Washington, 1974-79; partner firm Heller & Lloyd, 1979-86; ptnr. Kuder, Temple, Smollar & Heller P.C., Washington, 1986—; co-dir. spl. programs in Latin Am., U. Ill. Coll. Law, 1975-80, spl. programs in China, 1982-86. Author: Tax Incentives for Industry in Less Developed Countries, 1963. Served with AUS, 1953-55. Private international, General corporate, General practice. Home: 3431 Porter St NW Washington DC 20016 Office: Kuder Temple Smollar & Heller PC 1015 20th St NW Washington DC 20036

HELLER, JOHN RODERICK, III, lawyer, bus. exec.; b. Harrisburg, Pa., Aug. 14, 1937; s. John Roderick and Susie May (Ayres) H.; m. Nancy Ann Washburn, Aug. 18, 1962; children—Elizabeth, Carolynn, John. A.B. summa cum laude, Princeton U., 1959; A.M. in History, Harvard U., 1960, J.D. magna cum laude, 1963. Bar: D.C. 1964. Assoc. Wilmer, Cutler & Pickering, Washington, 1963-65, 68-71, ptnr., 1971-82, of counsel, 1982-85; spl. asst. to dir. for India, AID, New Delhi, 1966-67, regional legal adviser, Pakistan, 1967-68; pres. Bristol Compressors, Inc. (Va.), 1982-85; pres. Nat. Corp. for Housing Partnerships, 1985—, also bd. dirs.; bd. dirs. Auto-Trol Tech. Corp., Riggs Nat. Bank; prof. law George Washington U., 1976-81. Recipient Meritorious Honor award U.S. Dept. State, 1967. Mem. Am. Soc. Internat. Law, ABA, Soc. of Cincinnati, Supreme Ct. Hist. Soc. (dir.). Presbyterian. Clubs: Metropolitan (Washington); Chevy Chase (Md.). General corporate, Private international, Public international. Office: Nat Corp for Housing Partnership 1133 15th St NW Washington DC 20005

HELLER, PHILIP, lawyer; b. N.Y.C., Aug. 12, 1952; s. Irving and Dolores (Soloff) H.; divorced; 1 child, Howard Philip. Student, Harvard U., 1975; BA, Boston U., 1976, JD, 1979. Bar: Mass. 1979, N.Y. 1980, U.S. Ct. Appeals (1st and 9th cirs.) 1980, U.S. Supreme Ct. 1983, Calif. 1984, U.S. Dist. Ct. (no., so. and cen. dists.) Calif., U.S. Dist. Ct. (ea. and so. dists.) N.Y., U.S. Dist. Ct. Mass. Law clk. to judge U.S. Dist. Ct. (so. dist.) N.Y., N.Y.C., 1979; litigation assoc. Winthrop, Stimson, Putnam & Roberts, N.Y.C., 1980-81, Sullivan & Worcester, Boston, 1981-83, Paul, Hastings, Janofsky & Walker, Los Angeles, 1983—. Legis. aid Senator Edward M. Kennedy, Boston, Washington, 1969-71; mem. staff gov. Michael S Dukakis, Boston, 1974-75. Mem. ABA (litigation sect.), Calif. Bar Assn., Los Angeles County Bar Assn. (evaluation of profl. standards com.). Democrat. Club: Harvard of So. Calif. Federal civil litigation, State civil litigation. Home: 9950 Durant Dr Beverly Hills CA 90212 Office: Paul Hastings Janofsky & Walker 555 S Flower St 22d Floor Los Angeles CA 90071

HELLER, RICHARD MARTIN, lawyer, educator; b. Phila., Sept. 15, 1944; s. Leonard and Helen Heller. BEd, West Chester U., 1966; postgrad., U. Nev., Las Vegas, 1968, U. Md., 1970-71; JD, Villanova U., 1974. Bar: Pa. 1974, U.S. Dist. Ct. (ea. dist.) Pa. 1975, N.J. 1977, U.S. Dist. Ct. N.J. 1979, U.S. Ct. Appeals (3d cir.) 1979, U.S. Supreme Ct. 1979. Sole practice Norwood, Pa., 1975-77, Media, Pa., 1977-80, 81—; ptnr. Serini, Heller & Dilullo, Broomall, Pa., 1980; instr. Pa. State U., Media, 1978—, Delaware County Bd. Realtors, Springfield, Pa., 1985—. Recipient George Washington Honor medal Freedoms Found., Valley Forge, Pa., 1968. Republican. Roman Catholic. Real property, Probate. Office: 200 W Front St PO Box 498 Media PA 19063

HELLER, RICHARD STEWART, lawyer; b. N.Y.C., Sept. 14, 1952; s. Morris and Esther (Goldstein) H.; m. Nancy Barth. BA in History, Rutgers U., 1974; JD, Wake Forest U., 1978. Bar: N.Y. 1979. Assoc. Weisman, Celler et al, N.Y.C., 1978-80, Cahill, Gordon & Reindel, N.Y.C., 1980-83, Fried, Frank, Harris, Shriver & Jacobson, N.Y.C., 1983; ptnr. Krassy & Heller P.C., N.Y.C., 1983—. Contbr. articles to legal jours. Mem. ABA, N.Y. State Bar Assn. Securities. Office: Krassy & Heller PC 400 Madison Ave New York NY 10017

HELLER, ROBERT HENRY, JR., judge; b. Balt., Mar. 8, 1942; s. Robert Henry and Wanda Nettie (Mills) H.; divorced; children: Robert Henry III, Christopher Michael. BS, U. Md., 1964, JD with honors, 1972. Bar: Md., U.S. Dist. Ct. Md., U.S. Ct. Appeals (4th cir.), U.S. Supreme Ct. Salesman Xerox Corp., Balt., 1969-70; assoc. Turk, Manis & Duckett, Annapolis, Md., 1972-73; ptnr. Corbin, Warfield & Heller, Severna Park, Md., 1973-84; assoc. judge Anne Arundel County Cir. Ct., Annapolis, 1986—; instr. Md. Inst. for Continuing Profl. Edn. for Lawyers, Balt., 1985—, Md. Trial Lawyers Assn., 1985—. bd. dirs., pres. Woods Adult Day Care Ctr., Severna Park, 1973-79; bd. trustees, pres. Gibson Island (Md.) Country Schs., 1979-85; trustee Severn Sch., Severna Park, 1983—. Served to lt. comdr. USNR, 1964-73. Mem. ABA, Md. Bar Assn., Anne Arundel County Bar Assn., Am. Judicature Soc., Am. Judges Assn. Republican. Presbyterian. Avocations: tennis, skiing, sailing. Judiciary. Home: 32 Cornhill St Annapolis MD 21401 Office: Cir Ct for Anne Arundel County Church Circle Annapolis MD 21401

HELLER, RONALD GARY, manufacturing company executive, lawyer; b. N.Y.C., May 29, 1946; s. Max and Lucy (Weinwurm) H.; m. Joyce R. Mueller, May 29, 1969; children—Caren, Amy, Beth. B.A., CCNY, 1967; postgrad., U. Wis. Law Sch., 1967-68; J.D., Fordham U., 1972. Bar: N.Y. Assoc. Cahill Gordon & Reindel, N.Y.C., 1972-77; asst. sec. Cluett, Peabody & Co. Inc., N.Y.C., 1977-81, sec., 1981-86, v.p., sec., gen. counsel, 1986—. Served with USAR, 1969-75. Mem. Am. Soc. Corp. Secs. General corporate, Securities. Home: 14 Kershner Pl Fair Lawn NJ 07410 Office: Cluett Peabody & Co Inc 510 Fifth Ave New York NY 10036

HELLER, RONALD IAN, lawyer; b. Cleve., Sept. 4, 1956; s. Grant L. and Audrey P. (Lecht) H.; m. Shirley Ann Stringer, Mar. 23, 1986. AB with high honors, Univ Mich., 1976, MBA, 1979, JD, 1980. Bar: Hawaii 1980, U.S. Ct. Claims 1982, U.S. Tax Ct. 1981, U.S. Ct. Appeals (9th cir.) 1981; Trust Territory of Pacific Islands 1982, Republic of Marshall Islands 1982; CPA, Hawaii. Assoc. Hoddick, Reinwald, O'Connor & Marrack, Honolulu, 1980-84; ptnr. Reinwald, O'Connor & Marrack, 1984—; adj. prof. U. Hawaii Sch. Law, 1981; bd. dirs. Hawaii Women Lawyers Found., Honolulu, 1984-86, Hawaii Performing Arts Co., Honolulu, 1984—. Actor, stage mgr. Honolulu Community Theatre, 1983—, Hawaii Performing Arts Co., Honolulu, 1982—. Mem. Am. Inst. CPA's, ABA, Hawaii State Bar Assn., Hawaii Women Lawyers, Assn. Trial Lawyers Am. State and local taxation, Corporate taxation, General corporate. Office: Reinwald O'Connor & Marrack 733 Bishop St Suite 2400 Honolulu HI 96813

HELLER, THOMAS C., law educator; b. 1944. B.A., Princeton U., 1965; LL.B., Yale U., 1968. Bar: Wis. 1975. Fellow Internat. Legal Ctr., Bogotá, Colombia, 1968-70; fellow in law and modernization Yale U., 1970-71; asst., then assoc. prof. U. Wis., 1971-79; vis. prof. U. Miami, 1977-78; assoc. Yale Inst. Social Policy Studies, 1978-79; vis. assoc. prof. Stanford U., 1978-79, prof. law, 1979—; of counsel Rosen, Rencho & Henderson, 1980. Office: Stanford University Law School Stanford CA 94305 *

HELLERSTEIN, ALVIN KENNETH, lawyer; b. N.Y.C., Dec. 28, 1933; s. Max and Rose (Lichtenstein) H.; m. Mildred Markow, June 29, 1936; children—Dina, Judith, Joseph. A.B., Columbia U., 1954, LL.B., 1956. Bar: N.Y. 1956, U.S. Ct. Appeals (2d cir.) 1960, U.S. Supreme Ct. 1964, U.S. Ct. Appeals (D.C. cir.) 1978, U.S. Ct. Appeals (3d and 9th cirs.) 1980, U.S. Ct. Appeals (1st cir.) 1985. Ptnr. Stroock & Stroock & Lavan, N.Y.C., 1969—, also co-head litigation dept.; lectr. continuing legal edn. programs Am. Law Inst., Practicing Law Inst. Contbr. articles to profl. jours. Past chmn. Bd. Jewish Edn. Served to capt. JAGC, U.S. Army, 1957-60. Mem. Assn. Bar City N.Y. (exec. com., past chmn. com. on fed. cts., past mem. com. on judiciary, past mem. com. on securities regulations, past mem. com. profl. and jud. ethics), Fed. Bar Council (v.p.), ABA, N.Y. State Bar Assn. (standing com. of 2d cir. Ct. Appeals on improving civil litigation, past mem. 2d cir. coms. on pre-trial phase of civil cases and on civil appeals mgmt. plan). Democrat. Federal civil litigation, State civil litigation, Insurance. Office: Stroock & Stroock & Lavan 7 Hanover Sq New York NY 10004

HELLMAN, CHARLES DAVID, lawyer; b. N.Y.C., Mar. 29, 1955; s. Morton J. and Martha D. (Kaufman) H.; m. Leslie Faye Schwartz, Sept. 2, 1984. AB, Cornell U., 1976; JD, Rutgers U., 1981. Bar: N.J. 1981, U.S. Dist. Ct. N.J. 1981, U.S. Ct. Appeals (3d cir.) 1982, N.Y. 1986, U.S. Dist. Ct. (so. and ea. dists.) N.Y. 1986. Law clk. to presiding justice U.S. Dist. Ct. N.J., Newark, 1981-82; assoc. Lowenstein, Sandler, Brochin, Kohl, Fisher & Boylan, Roseland, N.J., 1982-86; assoc. counsel The Chase Manhattan Bank N.A., N.Y.C., 1986—. Editor Rutgers U. Law Rev., 1979-80, notes and comments editor, 1980-81. Mem. ABA, N.J. Bar Assn., N.Y. State Bar Assn. Banking, Federal civil litigation, State civil litigation. Home: 1992 Parkwood Dr Scotch Plains NJ 07076 Office: The Chase Manhattan Bank NA 1 Chase Manhattan Plaza 29th Floor New York NY 10081

HELLUMS, CLARENCE THEO, lawyer; b. Jasper, Ala., Oct. 10, 1941; s. Clarence Theo and Jean (Logan) H.; m. Sylvia Sardy, Jan. 13, 1967; children—Heidi Marie, Christopher Theo. B.S., U. Ala., 1963, LL.B., 1965. Bar: Ala. 1965, U.S. Dist. Ct. (no. dist.) Ala. 1967, U.S. Ct. Appeals (5th cir.) 1968, U.S. Ct. Appeals (11th cir.), U.S. Supreme Ct. 1975. Ptnr., Hellums & McDuff, Tuscaloosa, Ala., 1967-70; pres. First Res. Co., Inc., Tuscaloosa, 1970-72, Am. Guaranty & Trust Co., Tuscaloosa, 1972-73; sole practice, Tuscaloosa, 1973-81; sr. ptnr. Hellums & Meigs, Tuscaloosa and Centreville, Ala., 1982—; asst. prof. U. Ala., Tuscaloosa, 1968-72. Pres. Internat. Y's Men's Club, Tuscaloosa, 1970-72, Family Counseling Service, Tuscaloosa, 1973-75, Friends of Library, Tuscaloosa, 1976; bd. dirs. YMCA, Tuscaloosa, 1977. Served to capt. U.S. Army, 1964-67. Mem. Ala. Bar Assn., Ala. Trial Lawyers Assn., Tuscaloosa County Bar Assn., Phi Alpha Delta (state justice). Democrat. Baptist. Lodge: Masons. Federal civil litigation, Real property, General practice. Home: 4649 Woodland Forest Dr Tuscaloosa AL 35405 Office: Hellums & Meigs 2703 6th St Tuscaloosa AL 35401 also: PO Box 188 Centreville AL 35042

HELMAN, ROBERT ALAN, lawyer; b. Chgo., Jan. 27, 1934; s. Nathan W. and Esther (Weiss) H.; m. Janet R. Williams, Sept. 13, 1958; children—Marcus E., Adam J., Sarah E. Student, U. Ill., 1951-53; B.S.L., Northwestern U., 1954, LL.B., 1956. Bar: Ill. 1956. Asso. firm Isham, Lincoln & Beale, Chgo., 1956-64; partner Isham, Lincoln & Beale, 1965-66; partner firm Mayer, Brown & Platt, Chgo., 1967—; bd. dirs. No. Trust Corp., No. Trust Co., So. Pacific Transp. Co., VHA Ins. Services Co., Shorebank Corp. Co-author: Commentaries on 1970 Illinois Constitution, 1971; contbr. articles to legal jours. Mem. fin. planning com. Chgo. Crime Commn.; chmn. Citizens Com. on Juvenile Ct. Cook County, 1969-81; pres. Legal Assistance Found., Chgo., 1973-76; bd. dirs. United Charities Chgo., 1967-73; trustee Chgo. Council on Fgn. Relations, U. Chgo. Hosps., Aspen Inst. Served with AUS, 1956-58. Mem. ABA, Chgo. Bar Assn., Am. Law Inst., Chgo. Council Lawyers, Legal Club Chgo., Law Club Chgo., Order of Coif. Clubs: Commercial, Chicago, Cliffdwellers, Economics, Union League (Chgo.); Point-O-Woods Country (Mich.). General corporate, Public utilities, Securities. Home: 4940 S Kimbark Ave Chicago IL 60615 Office: 190 S LaSalle St Chicago IL 60604

HELMER, DAVID ALAN, lawyer; b. Colorado Springs, May 19, 1946; s. Horton James and Alice Ruth (Cooley) H.; m. Jean Marie Lamping, May 23, 1987. BA, U. Colo., 1968, JD, 1973. Bar: Colo. 1973, U.S. Dist. Ct. Colo. 1973. Assoc., Neil C. King, Boulder, Colo., 1973-76; mgr. labor relations, mining regulations Climax Molybdenum Co., Inc. div. AMAX, Inc., Climax, Colo., 1976-83; prin. Law Offices David A. Helmer, Frisco, Colo., 1983—; sec., bd. dirs. Z Comm. Corp., Frisco, 1983—. Editor U. Colo. Law Rev., 1972-73; contbr. articles to legal jours. Bd. dirs. Summit County Council Arts and Humanities, Dillon, Colo., 1980-865, Advs. for Victims Assault, Frisco, 1984—; bd. dirs., legal counsel, v.p. Summit County United Way, 1983—; bd. dirs., legal counsel Summit County Alcohol and Drug Task Force, Inc., 1984—. chmn. Summit County Reps., 1982—; chmn. 5th Jud. Dist. (Colo.) Rep. Com., 1982—; chmn. resolutions com. Colo. Rep. Conv., 1984—, del. Rep. Nat. Conv., 1984; chmn. chmn. reaccreditation com. Colo. Mountain Coll., Breckenridge, 1983—; founder, bd. dirs. Dillon Bus. Assn., 1983—; atty. N.W. Colo. Legal Services Project, Summit County, 1983—. Served to master sgt. USAR, 1969. Mem. Continental Divide Bar Assn., Colo. Bar Assn., ABA, Phi Gamma Delta. Presbyterian. Club: Dillon Corinthian Yacht (commodore 1987—). General practice, Real property, State civil litigation. Home: 121 Three Rivers Box 300 Dillon CO 80435 Office: 619 Main St Drawer E Frisco CO 80443

HELMHOLZ, R. H., law educator; b. Pasadena, Calif., July 1, 1940; s. Lindsay and Alice (Bean) H.; m. Marilyn P. Helmholz. AB, Princeton U., 1962; JD, Harvard U., 1965; PhD, U. Calif., Berkeley, 1970. Prof. law and hist. Washington U., St. Louis, 1970-81; prof. law U. Chgo., 1981—. Author: Marriage Litigation, 1975, Select Cases on Defamation, 1985. Guggenheim fellow, 1986. Mem. ABA, Selden Soc. (v.p. 1984—). Clubs: Univ. (Chgo.); Reform (London). Legal history, Oil and gas leasing, Real property. Home: 1222 E 49th Chicago IL 60615 Office: U Chgo Law Sch 1111 E 60th St Chicago IL 60637

HELMINSKI, FRANCIS JOSEPH, lawyer; b. Glen Cove, N.Y., Aug. 28, 1957; s. Frank Ralph and Catherine (Loughran) H. BA, Wayne State U., 1978, MA in History, JD, 1981; MPH, Harvard U., 1985. Bar: Mich. 1982, U.S. Dist. Ct. (ea. dist.) Mich. 1982, U.S. Ct. Appeals (6th cir.) 1983, Colo. 1985, U.S. Dist. Ct. Colo. 1985, U.S. Ct. Appeals (10th cir.) 1985, U.S. Supreme Ct. 1986. Atty. Harper-Grace Hosps., Detroit Med. Ctr., 1982-84, 1986—; interim adminstr., spl. counsel Atty. Discipline Bd. Mich., Detroit, 1985-86; assoc. in law Am. Coll. of Legal Medicine, 1984. Hearing panelist Atty. Discipline Bd. Mich., Wayne County, 1986—. Mem. ABA (former chmn. com. on legal problems in med. research, sci. and tech. sect.), Am. Soc. of Law and Medicine, Am. Soc. for Legal History, Phi Beta Kappa. Democrat. Avocation: baseball. Legal history, Health, General corporate. Office: Harper-Grace Hosps Detroit Med Ctr Dept Legal Affairs 3990 John R St Detroit MI 48201

HELMREICH, MARTHA SCHAFF, lawyer; b. Syracuse, N.Y., July 24, 1936; d. Lester and Anne J. (Aalfs) Schaff; m. Jonathan E. Helmreich, Aug. 1959; children: Anne, Dana, Douglas. Student, Swarthmore Coll., 1954-56; BA, Mt. Holyoke Coll., 1958; MA, Syracuse U., 1959; JD, U. Pitts., 1982. Bar: Pa. 1982, U.S. Dist. Ct. (we. dist.) Pa. 1982, U.S. Ct. Appeals (3d cir.) 1986. Law clk. to judge U.S. Dist. Ct (so. dist.) W.Va., Charleston, 1982-84; assoc. Litman, Litman, Harris, Brown & Watzman, Pitts., 1984—. Mem. Crawford Cen. Sch. Bd., Meadville, Pa., 1973-78; bd. dirs. Northwest TriCounty Intermediate Unit, Erie, Pa., 1975-78. Mem. ABA, Pa. Bar Assn., Allegheny County Bar Assn. Federal civil litigation, State civil litigation, General practice. Home: 844 Beech Ave Pittsburgh PA 15233 Office: Litman Litman Harris Brown & Watzman 1701 Grant Bldg Pittsburgh PA 15219

HELMS, DAVID ALONZO, lawyer; b. Evanston, Ill., July 5, 1934; s. Hugh Judson and Edna (Peterson-Holmes) H.; div.; children—Donald Anthony, Cybil Estelle. B.B.A., Northwestern U., 1956; J.D., U. Calif.-Berkeley, 1969. Bar: N.Y. 1972, Calif. 1973, Ill. 1974. With Matson Navigation Co., San Francisco, 1958-66, mgr. mktg. research, passenger ops., 1963-66; assoc. law firm Paul, Weiss, Rifkind, Wharton & Garrison, Esqs., N.Y.C., 1969-72; spl. asst. to mayor of Berkeley, Calif., 1972-73; dep. sec.

state, spl. asst. to gov. Calif., 1973-75; exec. sec. Civil Rights Bar Assn., San Francisco, 1975-80; asst. dean, mem. faculty Chgo.-Kent Coll. Law, Ill. Inst. Tech., Chgo., 1979-81; atty., regional counsel FAA, Des Plaines, Ill., 1982-84; vol. atty. Howard Area and Cabrini-Green Law Clinics, Chgo. Vol. Legal Services Found., 1981—; sole practice law, David A. Helms & Assocs., Evanston and Chgo., 1981—; legal advisor to nat. pres. op. Push, 1986; real estate broker. Editor: Civil Rights Law Jour., Vol. I & II, 1974-78. Bd. dirs. Pub. Advocates, San Francisco, 1977-79. Mem. ABA, Chgo. Council Lawyers, Cook County Bar Assn., Chgo. Bar Assn. Baptist (mem. legal com., law clinic 1984—). Administrative and regulatory, Labor, Real property.

HELPRIN, LISA KENNEDY, lawyer; b. Boston, Dec. 4, 1950; d. Eugene P. and Adelaide (Magowski) Kennedy; m. Mark H. Helprin, June 28, 1980; 1 child, Alexandria Morris. BA, Am. U., 1972; JD, U. Mich., 1975; LLM, NYU, 1983. Bar: N.Y. 1976, U.S. Dist. Ct. (so. and ea. dists.) N.Y. 1976. Assoc. Chadbourne Parke, N.Y.C., 1976-79; v.p. Chase Manhattan Bank, N.Y.C., 1979-86; sole practice Seattle, 1986—. Mem. N.Y. State Bar Assn. Repubican. Jewish. Corporate taxation.

HELVIE, KIRK RANDALL, lawyer; b. Chgo., July 13, 1956; s. DeVerle D. and Marjorie (Cox) H.; m. Linda Weis, July 19, 1980. BA with honors, Drake U., 1978, JD, 1981. Bar: Idaho 1981, U.S. Dist. Ct. Idaho 1981. Ptnr. Moffatt, Thomas, Barrett & Blanton, Boise, Idaho, 1981—. Mem. ABA, Idaho Bar Assn., Boise Bar Assn. State civil litigation, Insurance, Antitrust. Office: Moffatt Thomas Barrett & Blanton PO Box 829 Boise ID 83701

HELVIN, STEPHEN HOLLAND, judge; b. Charlottesville, Va., July 24, 1943; s. James Barkley and Elaine (Holland) H.; m. Frances Ann Mobley, July 22, 1967; 1 son, Stephen Holland. B.A., Hampden Sydney Coll., 1965; J.D., U. Richmond, 1968. Bar: Va. 1968, U.S. Dist. Ct. (ea. and we. dists.) Va., U.S. Ct. Appeals (4th cir.). Assoc. firm Gordon & Haugh, Charlottesville, 1968-72; ptnr. Haugh, Helvin & Treakle, Charlottesville, 1972-80; asst. commonwealth atty. Commonwealth of Va., Albemarle County, 1972-76; substitute judge 16th Jud. Dist. Commonwealth of Va., Charlottesville, 1976-80, judge, 1980—; dir. Charlottesville Legal Aid Soc., 1974-76; lectr. U. Va. Law Sch., Charlottesville, 1976. Mem. Scenic River Commn., Albemarle County, 1975; bd. dirs. James River Alcoholic Safety Com., 1983. Mem. ABA, Va. Bar Assn., Am. Judges Assn., Charlottesville-Albemarle Bar Assn. (pres. 1976), Am. Judicature Soc., Hampden Sydney Coll. Alumni Council. Club: Redland (Charlottesville). Home: RD 5 Box 220C Charlottesville VA 22901 Office: Albemarle Dist Ct Court Sq Charlottesville VA 22901

HEMING, CHARLES E., lawyer; b. N.Y.C., Mar. 1, 1926; s. Charles E. and Lucile (Wolf) H.; m. Olga Landeck, Sept. 21, 1949 (div.); children—Michael, Lucy, Amanda. Grad., Phillips Acad., Andover, 1944; A.B., Princeton U., 1948; LL.B., Columbia U., 1950. Bar; N.Y. 1950, U.S. Dist. Ct. (so. dist.) N.Y. 1951, U.S. Supreme Ct. 1954, U.S. Tax Ct. 1968, U.S. Ct. Appeals (2d cir.) 1962. Ptnr. Wormser, Kiely, Alessandroni, Hyde & McCann, N.Y.C., 1982—. Trustee Village of Scarsdale, N.Y., 1972-76. Served with USNR, 1944-46. Fellow Am. Bar Found., Am. Coll. Probate Counsel, N.Y. State Bar Found.; mem. ABA (ho. of dels.), N.Y. State Bar Assn. (pres. 1986-87), Assn. Bar City N.Y. (past chmn. com. lectures and continuing edn., com. trusts estates surrogate's cts.), Amateur Ski Club N.Y. (past pres.). Club: Scarsdale Town (pres. 1971-72). Estate planning, General practice. Office: Wormser Kiely Alessandroni Hyde & McCann 100 Park Ave New York NY 10017

HEMINGWAY, ALFRED HENRY, JR., lawyer; b. Leominster, Mass., Aug. 4, 1942; s. Alfred Henry and Therese Constance (Barriere) H.; m. Julie Ellen Murphy, June 10, 1967 (dec. May 1986); children: Kathryn Therese, Jessica Lee. BS, Worcester Poly. Inst., 1964; MS, U. Mass., 1970; JD, Stanford U., 1971. Bar: Calif. 1972, N.Y. 1973, U.S. Dist. Ct. (so. dist.) N.Y. 1974, U.S. Dist. Ct. (ea. dist.) N.Y. 1974, U.S. Dist. Ct. (ea. dist.) Mich. 1982, U.S. Ct. Appeals (2d cir.) 1975, U.S. Ct. Appeals (fed. cir.) 1973, U.S. Patent Office 1973, U.S. Supreme Ct. 1985, U.S. Dist. Ct. (ea. dist.) Wis. 1984. Assoc. Davis, Hoxie, Faithfull & Hapgood, N.Y.C., 1971-74, Morgan, Finnegan, Pine, Foley & Lee, N.Y.C., 1974-76, Bryan & Bollo, Stamford, Conn., 1976-79, Arthur, Dry & Kalish, N.Y.C., 1979-81, Offner & Kuhn, N.Y.C., 1981-82; mem. Felfe & Lynch, N.Y.C., 1982—. Contbg. author: Practicing Law in New York City, 1975. League dir., coach Wilton Soccer Assn., Conn. 1981—; select team coach Conn. Jr. Soccer Adminstrn., 1985. Served to capt. U.S. Army, 1966-68. Mem. Calif. Bar Assn. Federal civil litigation, Patent and trademark. Home: 221 Linden Tree Rd Wilton CT 06897 Office: Felfe & Lynch 805 3d Ave New York NY 10022

HEMKER, JOSEPH BERNARD, lawyer, educator; b. Delphos, Ohio, Mar. 1, 1952; s. Herman A. and Alvera C. (Lammers) H.; m. Diane Marie Przewozniak, Dec. 10, 1977; 1 child, Alexander Joseph. BBA magna cum laude, Western Mich. U., 1976; JD summa cum laude, Thomas M. Cooley Law Sch., 1980. Bar: Mich. 1981, Ind. 1986, U.S. Dist. Ct. (we. dist.) Mich. 1981, U.S. Dist. Ct. (so. dist.) Ind. 1986, U.S. Ct. Appeals (6th cir.) 1981. Intern Lansing (Mich.) City Attys. Office, 1979-80; pre-hearing atty. Mich. Ct. Appeals, Lansing, 1981-82, law clk. to chief judge, 1982-83; adj. instr. Kalamazoo Valley Community Coll., 1984-85; atty. Howard & Howard Attys., Kalamazoo, 1983—. Contbr. articles to legal jour. Recipient West Pub. Hornbook award 1979, Corpus Juris Secundum award West Pub. Co., 1980; Southfield Bar Assn. scholar, 1980. Mem. ABA (corp. communication law sects.), Mich. Bar Assn. (corp., banking and computer law sects. proprietary rights com.), Ind. Bar Assn. (corp., banking, tax and employment law sects.), Kalamazoo County Bar Assn. (computer law sect.), Ingham County Bar Assn., Kalamazoo Forum (chmn. tax abatement com.). Roman Catholic. Club: Gull Lake Country (Richland, Mich.). Lodge: Rotary (bd. dirs. Kalamazoo S. club). Avocations: golf, jogging. Contracts commercial, Computer, Estate planning. Office: Howard & Howard Attys 400 Kalamazoo Bldg Kalamazoo MI 49007

HEMMENDINGER, NOEL, lawyer; b. Bernardsville, N.J., Dec. 25, 1913; s. Max and Jeannette (Harris) H.; m. Marjorie Knebelman, Aug. 28, 1948; children: Eric, Lucy, John. AB, Princeton U., 1934; JD, Harvard U., 1937. Bar: D.C. 1937, N.Y. 1938, U.S. Dist. Ct. (so. dist.) N.Y. 1938, U.S. Supreme Ct. 1956. Law clk. U.S. Ct. Appeals (2d cir.), N.Y.C., 1937-38; asst. U.S. atty. S.D. and N.Y., 1938-40; spl. asst. to U.S. atty. gen. U.S. Dept. Justice, N.Y.C., 1940-42; staff official U.S. Dept. State, Washington, 1946-56; ptnr. Stitt & Hemmendinger and successor firms, Washington, 1957-77, Arter, Hadden & Hemmendinger, Washington, 1977-83, Wald, Harkrader & Ross, Washington, 1983-85; of counsel Willkie, Farr & Gallaher, Washington, 1985—; dep. dir. U.S. Japan Trade Council, Washington, 1957-77, bd. dirs. Trustee, counsel Japan Am. Soc. Washington, 1957—. Served to capt. U.S. Army, 1942-46, ETO. Decorated Bronze Star, 1945; named to Japanese Order of the Sacred Treasure 2d class, 1981. Mem. ABA, D.C. Bar Assn., Customs and Internat. Trade Bar Assn. Democrat. Clubs: Cosmos, Internat. (Washington); Princeton (N.Y.C.). Avocation: tennis. Private international, Public international. Home: 2007 Martha's Rd Alexandria VA 22307 Office: Willkie Farr & Gallagher 818 Connecticut Ave NW Washington DC 20006

HEMMER, JAMES P., lawyer; b. Oshkosh, Wis., Mar. 28, 1942; s. Joseph John and Margaret Louise (Nuernberg) H.; m. Francine M. Chamallas, June 4, 1967; children—James, Christopher, Sarah. A.B. summa cum laude, Marquette U., 1964; LL.B., Harvard U., 1967. Bar: Ill. 1967. Assoc. Bell, Boyd & Lloyd, Chgo., 1967-74, ptnr., 1975—; adj. prof. law Marquette U., 1985-86; lectr. Ill. Inst. Continuing Legal Edn.; bd. dirs. Constrn. Projects Mgmt. Inc., Holco Corp. Mem. Kenilworth (Ill.) Sch. Dist. 38 Bd. Edn., v.p. 1985—, Kenilworth Citizens Adv. Caucus; bd. dirs. Jos. Sears Sch. Devel. Fund. Wickersham fellow. Mem. ABA, Ill. Bar Assn. (editor banking and comml. law newsletter), Alpha Sigma Nu, Phi Theta Psi, Phi Sigma Tau, Sigma Tau Delta. Clubs: University, Law, Legal (Chgo.), Kenilworth. Contbr. articles to legal jours. General corporate, Banking, Contracts commercial.

HEMNES, THOMAS MICHAEL SHERIDAN, lawyer; b. Chgo., Nov. 10, 1948; s. Paul Gene and Dorothy Mary (Carl) H.; m. Carole Elizabeth Powers Dec. 20, 1970; children: Anna Ryan, Abigail Powers, Jonathan James. AB, Harvard U., 1970, JD, 1974. Bar: Mass. 1976, U.S. Dist. Ct. Mass., 1976, U.S. Dist. Ct. (no. dist.) N.Y. 1985. Law clk. U.S. Ct. Appeals (3d cir.), Phila., 1974-75; assoc. Foley, Hoag & Eliot, Boston, 1975-81, ptnr., 1981—; lectr. Northeastern U. Co-compilor: The Legal Word Book, 1978, rev. edit., 1982; contbr. articles on copyright, trademark, law firm mgmt. and other topics; editor, officer Harvard Law Rev., 1973-74. Corporator Handel & Hayden Soc., Boston, 1980-85, The Trademark Reporter, 1985—. Mem. ABA, Mass. Bar Assn., Boston Bar Assn., Boston Patent Law Assn., U.S. Trademark Assn. (assoc.). Trademark and copyright, Contracts commercial. Home: 49 Hammond Rd Belmont MA 02178 Office: Foley Hoag & Eliot One Post Office Sq Boston MA 02109

HEMPHILL, KATHRYN GLENN, lawyer; b. Hickory, N.C., Sept. 1, 1946; d. Samuel Mills and Mary Kathryn (Frye) H.; m. F. Gordon Cobb, Oct. 25, 1980. Student, U. Aberdeen, Scotland, 1966-67; BA, Sweet Briar Coll., 1969; MA in Clin. Psychology, Appalachian State U., 1974; JD, Wake Forest U., 1980. Bar: N.C. 1981. Sole practice Newland, N.C., 1981-85; ptnr. Hemphill & Gavenus, Newland, 1985—. Mem. ABA, N.C. Bar Assn., N.C. Acad. Trial Lawyers. Republican. Lutheran. Family and matrimonial, General practice, Probate. Office: Hemphill & Gavenus Sokossa St PO Box 758 Newland NC 28657

HEMPHILL, MEREDITH, JR., lawyer; b. Spring Lake, N.J., Oct. 12, 1931; s. Meredith and Katharine (Dilworth) H.; m. Beverly Bell, Feb. 6, 1960; children—Mary, M. Scott, Geoffrey G., Mark A. B.Chem. Engring., Rensselaer Poly. Inst., 1953; J.D., U. Mich., 1959. Bar: N.Y. 1960, Pa. 1976. Assoc. Cravath, Swaine & Moore, N.Y.C., 1959-67; atty., gen. atty. Bethlehem (Pa.) Steel Corp., 1967-73, asst. gen. counsel, 1973-79, asst. v.p. and asst. gen. counsel, asst. sec., 1979-85, asst. gen. counsel and asst. sec., 1985—. Served with USMCR, 1953-55. Mem. ABA, Pa. Bar Assn., Northampton County Bar Assn. Republican. Clubs: Saucon Valley Country, Bethlehem. General corporate, Federal civil litigation, State civil litigation. Home: 238 E Market St Bethlehem PA 18018 Office: Martin Tower Bethlehem PA 18016

HENDEL, MAURICE WILLIAM, lawyer, consultant; b. Holyoke, Mass., Feb. 24, 1909; s. Richard and Helen (Katz) H.; m. Evelyn F. Berger, Dec. 30, 1934; children—Richard C., Eugene L. Ph.B., Brown U., 1930; J.D., Harvard U., 1933. Bar: R.I. 1933, U.S. Dist. Ct. R.I. 1935. Counsel to Sec. of State of R.I., Providence, 1949-79, editor Pub. Laws, 1949-79; cons. to constl. convs. State of R.I., 1954, 62, 68-69, 86; cons. home rule charters cities and towns, 1960—, mem., sec. Statute Consolidation Commn., 1953-56; parliamentarian R.I. Senate, 1949-79. Mem. editorial bd. R.I. Bar Jour. Mem. Democratic City Com., Providence, 1940-60, Dem. Town Com., Lincoln, R.I., 1961—. Mem. R.I. Bar Assn., Pawtucket Bar Assn. Jewish. Clubs: Kirkbrae Country (Lincoln); Faculty of Brown U. (Providence). Lodge: Masons (past master, high priest). General corporate, Probate, Family and matrimonial. Home: 142 Jenckes Hill Rd Lincoln RI 02865 Office: McMahon Hendel McMahon 200 Main St Pawtucket RI 02860

HENDER, GEORGE SNOWDEN, lawyer; b. Jersey City, June 23, 1942; s. George P. and Maude (Snowden) H.; m. Mary Jane Nystrom, Mar. 18, 1967; children—Hope, Timothy, Amanda. B.A., Washington and Jefferson Coll., 1964; J.D., Am. U., 1967. Bar: Pa. 1969, U.S. Supreme Ct. Sr. v.p. Phila. Stock Exchange, 1969-76; exec. v.p. Tague Securities Corp., Bryn Mawr, Pa., 1976—, pres. 1986— ; pres. Bryn Mawr Corp., 1978—; exec. v.p. Bryn Mawr Group, 1978—, Banc Am. Options, Inc., 1983—; ptnr. Butler & Hender, Bryn Mawr, 1980—; bd. govs., exec. com., chmn. bus. conduct com. Phila. Stock Exchange, 1981—; dir. Bryn Mawr Group, Options Clearing Corp., Phila. Stock Clearing Corp., Phila. Depository Trust Co., Phila. Bd. of Trade, Tague Securities Corp., Bryn Mawr Corp. Elder, Swarthmore Presbyn. Ch., 1978-81; bd. dirs. South Media Fire Dept. Served with U.S. Army, 1967-73. Mem. Am. Bar Assn., Pa. Bar Assn., Phila. Bar Assn. Republican. Presbyterian. Clubs: The Club at World Trade Center (N.Y.C.); Peale (Phila.). General corporate, Administrative and regulatory, Contracts commercial. Office: 1811 Chestnut St Philadelphia PA 19103

HENDERSON, ALBERT JOHN, judge; b. Canton, Ga., Dec. 12, 1920; s. Albert Jefferson and Cliffie Mae (Cook) H.; m. Jenny Lee Medford, Feb. 24, 1951; children—Michael John, Jenny Lee. LL.B., Mercer U., 1947. Bar: Ga. bar 1947. Practiced law Marietta, Ga., 1948-60; judge Juvenile Ct. Cobb County, Ga., 1953-60, Superior Ct. Cobb County, 1961-68, U.S. Dist. Ct. for No. Dist. Ga., Atlanta, 1968-76; chief judge U.S. Dist. Ct. for No. Dist. Ga., 1976-79; judge U.S. Circuit Ct. of Appeals for 5th Circuit, 1979-81, U.S. Circuit Ct. Appeals for 11th Circuit, 1981—; asst. solicitor gen. Blue Ridge Jud. Circuit, 1948-52. Chmn. Cobb dist. Atlanta council Boy Scouts Am., 1964. Served with AUS, 1943-46. Fellow Am. Bar Found.; mem. State Bar Ga., Am., Atlanta, Cobb Jud. bar assns., Lawyers Club Atlanta, Am. Judicature Soc. Office: US Court Appeal 50 Spring St SW Atlanta GA 30303

HENDERSON, DAN FENNO, lawyer, educator; b. Chelan, Wash., May 24, 1921; s. Joe and Edna (Fenno) H.; m. Carol Drake Hardin, Sept. 14, 1957; children—Louis, Karen, Gail, Fenno. A.B., Whitman Coll., 1944, LL.D., 1983; A.B., U. Mich., 1945; J.D., Harvard U., 1949; Ph.D. in Polit. Sci, U. Calif., Berkeley, 1955. Bar: bar Wash 1949, Korea 1955, Japan 1955, Calif 1956. Movie, radio censor Dept. Def., Japan, 1946-47; teaching asst. polit. sci. dept. U. Calif., Berkeley, 1949-51; atty. firm Little, LeSourd, Palmer & Scott, Seattle, 1951-52; instr. ext. div. U. Calif., Berkeley, 1952-54; atty. firm Graham James & Rolph, San Francisco, 1955-57; ptnr. Graham James & Rolph, Tokyo, 1957-62; ptnr. firm Adachi, Henderson, Miyatake and Fujita, Tokyo, 1973—; Prof. law, dir. Asian Law Program, U. Wash. Sch. Law, 1962—; vis. prof. law Harvard U., 1968-69, Monash U., Melbourne, Australia, 1979, Cambridge (Eng.) U., 1980; cons. Asia Found., 1967—, Battelle Inst., 1969—. Author: Conciliation and Japanese Law, 1965, The Constitution of Japan, It's First Twenty Years, 1969, Foreign Enterprise in Japan, 1973, Village Contracts in Tokugawa, Japan, 1975, Civil Procedure in Japan, 1981, 2d edit., 1985; bd. editors Jour. Japanese Studies; contbr. articles to profl. jours. Trustee Seattle Art Mus.; overseer Whitman Coll., 1985—. Served to lt. AUS, 1943-46. Investment fellow Am. Soc. Internat. Law, 1962-64. Mem. Assn. Asian Studies, Am. C. of C. Japan (past sec., dir.), Japanese-Am. Soc. Legal Studies (pres.), Am. Assn. Comparative Study of Law (dir.). Clubs: Rainier, University (Seattle); Tokyo Lawn Tennis. Admiralty, Legal history. Home: 632 36th Ave E Seattle WA 98112 Office: U Wash Sch of Law Seattle WA 98105 also: CPO Box 96, Tokyo 100 Japan

HENDERSON, DANIEL ELI, JR., lawyer; b. Houston, Mar. 16, 1921; s. Daniel Eli Sr. and Retti Beatrice (Dotson) H.; m. Enza Palmisano, Feb. 3, 1946; children: Beatrice Carrico, Pamela, Daniel Eli III, Monique L. Henderson DeMaria. BA, Trinity U., San Antonio, 1950; JD, U. Tex., 1950; MA, George Washington U., 1962, LLM, 1963. Bar: Tex. 1950, U.S. Supreme Ct. 1956, Calif. 1966. Commd. 2d lt. USAF, 1942, advanced through grades to col., 1961, retired, 1966; ptnr. Henderson & Merenbach, Santa Barbara, Calif., 1966-68; assoc. Cavaletto, Webster et al, Santa Barbara, 1968-71; ptnr. Henderson, Goodwin et al, Santa Barbara, 1971-75, Henderson, Rogers et al, Santa Barbara, 1975-85, Henderson & Angle, Santa Barbara, 1986—. Mem. ABA, Santa Barbara County Bar Assn., Assn. So. Calif. Def. Counsel. Democrat. Insurance, Personal injury, State civil litigation. Home: 1127 N Patterson Ave Santa Barbara CA 93111 Office: Henderson & Angle 530 E Montecito St Santa Barbara CA 93140

HENDERSON, DANIEL LAMAR, lawyer; b. Ruleville, Miss., Nov. 24, 1955; s. Travis Daniel and Peggy Sue (Roberts) H. Grad., Lee Coll., Ga. Southern Coll., 1979; JD, Atlanta Law Sch. Bar: Ga., U.S. Dist. Ct. (no. dist.) Ga. Sole practice Marietta, Ga. Mem. Assn. Trial Lawyers Am. (criminal law sect.), Nat. Assn. Criminal Def. Lawyers, Ga. Law Assn. (criminal law sect.), Ga. Bar Assn. (criminal law sect., younger law sect.), Atlanta Bar Assn. (criminal law sect., internat. trans. sect.), Atlanta Council Young lawyers. Democrat. Avocations: reading, fishing, attending profl. sporting events. Criminal, Private international, Personal injury. Home: 160 Aviation Rd SE Marietta GA 30060 Office: 180 Roswell St Suite A Marietta GA 30060

HENDERSON, DAVID ALLEN, lawyer; b. Japan, Feb. 18, 1948; s. Frank David and Pauline Elizabeth (Patton) H. BA, Miami U., Oxford, Ohio, 1970; LLB, U. Cin., 1974. Bar: Calif. 1974, U.S. Ct. Appeals (9th cir.) 1975, U.S. Dist. Ct. (no. dist.) Calif. 1976, U.S. Dist. Ct. (ea. dist.) Calif. 1978, U.S. Supreme Ct. 1978, D.C. 1980, N.Y. 1981, U.S. Ct. Appeals (D.C. cir.) 1982, Ariz. 1983, U.S. Dist. Ct. Ariz. 1983. Law clk. to presiding justice U.S. Ct. Appeals (9th cir.), San Diego, 1974-75; adj. prof. U. San Diego Coll. Law, 1975; assoc. Pillsbury, Madison & Sutro, San Francisco, 1975-79, Chadburn, Park, Whiteside & Wolfe, N.Y.C. and Washington, 1981-82; dep. gen. counsel Pres.'s Council on Wage and Price Stability, Washington, 1979-81; ptnr. Brown & Bain, Phoenix and Palo Alto, Calif., 1983—; mem. adv. bd. St. Francis Meml. Hosp., 1978—, Ctr. Nat. Policy, Washington, 1981—, Corp. Pub. Broadcasting, Washington, 1969-70; counsel to Alfred Kahan, inflation advisor to Pres., Washington, 1979-81. Editor in chief U. Cin. Law Rev. Gov.'s council Dem. Nat. Com., Washington, 1981-82. Mem. ABA (litigation and anti-trust sects.), Order of Coif. Clubs: St. Francis Yacht, Olympic (San Francisco). Avocations: sailing, horseback riding, skiing. Antitrust, Federal civil litigation, Computer. Office: Brown & Bain PO Box 400 Phoenix AZ 85001

HENDERSON, DONALD BERNARD, JR., lawyer; b. Birmingham, Ala., June 27, 1949; s. Donald B. and Pauline V. (Szulinski) H.; m. Ruth Ann Jeffers, Sept. 12, 1981. B.S., U. Ala., 1971, J.D., 1974; LL.M. in Taxation, NYU, 1976. Bar: Ala. 1974, N.Y. 1983. Ptnr. Sirote, Permutt et al, Birmingham, 1976-83; sr. assoc. Rein, Mound & Cotton, N.Y.C., 1983-85, ptnr. Kroll, Tract, Harnett, Pomerantz & Cameron, N.Y.C., 1985—; lectr. Birmingham chpt. Am. Coll., Bryn Mawr, Pa., 1977-82. Contbr. articles to profl. jours. Mem. exec. com., sec. Lenox Hill Democratic Club, N.Y.C., 1983—, exec. com. N.Y. State New Dem. Coalition, N.Y.C., 1983—. Mem. ABA (tax sect.), N.Y. Bar Assn., N.Y. County Lawyers Assn., Ala. Bar Assn. (sec. tax sect. 1982-83). Corporate taxation, Insurance, General corporate. Home: 360 E 72d St Apt B206 New York NY 10021 Office: Kroll Tract Harnett Pomerantz & Cameron 500 Fifth Ave New York NY 10110

HENDERSON, ERSKINE DALE, lawyer; b. Aurora, Colo., Apr. 11, 1949; s. Dale Theodore and Anna (Darden) H.; m. Lillian T. Polite, Dec. 1, 1979. Student Stanford U., 1969; B.A. cum laude Wesleyan U., 1971; J.D., Columbia U., 1976. Bar: N.Y. 1977, D.C. 1978, U.S. Dist. Ct. (so. and ea. dists.) N.Y. 1980, U.S. Ct. Appeals (D.C. cir.) 1982, U.S. Supreme Ct. 1982, U.S. Ct. Claims 1983, U.S. Ct. Internat. Trade, 1983, U.S. Tax Ct. 1983, U.S. Ct. Appeals (2d, 3d, 4th, 6th, 7th, 8th, 9th, 10th, 11th cirs.) 1983, U.S. Dist. Ct. D.C. 1983, U.S. Dist. Ct. (we. and no. dists.) N.Y. 1983. Assoc., Rein, Mound & Cotton, N.Y.C., 1976-77, Skadden Arps et al., N.Y.C., 1977—; pres. The PH Fund, Inc., N.Y.C., 1986—; mng. ptnr., gen. counsel PH Enterprises, N.Y.C., 1984—, pres., 1986—; counsel The Bryce-Templeton Group, N.Y.C., 1985—; cons. Hughes Investments, Denver, 1983-84. Contbr. poetry to New Voices in Am. Poetry, 1985, 86. Co-founder Black African Relief Com., N.Y.C., 1984; life mem. Africare, Washington, 1983. Recipient Woodbury Medal, 1967; named one of Outstanding Young Men of Am., 1985. Mem. ABA, Nat. Assn. Securities Profls., Nat. Assn. Broadcasters. Federal civil litigation, State civil litigation, Securities. Office: Skadden Arps Slate Meagher & Flom 919 3d Ave New York NY 10022

HENDERSON, EUGENE LEROY, lawyer; b. Columbus, Ind., July 21, 1925; s. Harry E. and Verna (Guffey) H.; m. Mary Louise Beatty, Sept. 6, 1948; children—Andrew, Joseph, Carrie Henderson Walkup. B.A., Franklin Coll., 1950; J.D., Harvard U., 1953. Bar: Ind. 1953. Assoc. Baker & Daniels, Indpls., 1953-59; ptnr. Baker & Daniels, 1959-65; sr. ptnr. Henderson, Daily, Winthrow & DeVoe and predecessor firms, Indpls., 1965—; bd. dirs. Maplehurst Group, Inc., Maplehurst Farms, Maplehurst Deli-Bake, Inc., PHD Venture Capital Corp.; sec. Ind. Fin. Investors, Inc. Mem. Ind. State Bd. Edn., 1984—; pres. Hoosier Art Salon; trustee Franklin Coll., Lacy Found.; bd. dirs. Indpls. Boys' Club. Served with U.S. Maritime Service, 1943-44, AUS, 1944-46. Mem. Indpls. Bar Assn., Ind. Bar Assn., ABA, Internat. Law Assn., Indpls. Mus. Art. Democrat. Clubs: Indpls. Athletic, Meridian Hills Country, Skyline, Venture, Lawyers, Econ. Lodge: Rotary. Contracts commercial, General corporate, Private international. Home: 6225 Sunset Ln Indianapolis IN 46260 Office: Henderson Daily Winthrow & DeVoe 2450 One Indiana Sq Indianapolis IN 46204

HENDERSON, FRANK ELLIS, state supreme court justice; b. Miller, S.D., Apr. 2, 1928; s. Frank Ellis and Hilda (Bogstad) H.; m. Norma Jean Johnson, Dec. 27, 1956; children: Frank Ellis, III, Kimberly, Patrick, Andrea, Eric, John, Anastasia, Matthew. LL.B., U. S.D., 1951. Bar: Fed. Dist. Ct. bar for Dist. S.D 1954. Practiced law Pennington County, S.D., 1953-74; judge 7th Jud. Circuit, State of S.D., 1975-78; justice S.D. Supreme Ct., 1979—; mem. S.D. Senate, 1965-66, 69-70. Served to 1st lt. inf. U.S. Army, 1951-53, Korea. Bronze Star, Korean Service medal, United Nations medal. Mem. Pennington County Bar Assn., S.D. State Bar Assn., Am. Legion, VFW (nat. legal staff 1960-61), DAV (state staff judge adv. 1963-64, post comdr. 1962), Phi Delta Theta. Republican. Roman Catholic. Office: Supreme Ct State Capitol Bldg Pierre SD 57501

HENDERSON, GEORGE ERVIN, lawyer; b. Pampa, Tex., June 7, 1947; s. Ervin L. and Elizabeth (Yoe) H.; m. Linda D. Dalrymple, Aug. 22, 1970; children: Andrew, Elizabeth. BA, Tex. Christian U., 1969; JD, Yale U., 1972. Bar: Tex. 1972, U.S. Dist. Ct. (so. dist.) Tex. 1974, U.S. Dist. Ct. (we. dist.) 1978. Assoc. Fulbright & Jaworski, Houston and Austin, 1972-79; ptnr. Fulbright & Jaworski, Austin, 1983—, Sneed & Vine, Austin, 1979-82; adj. instr. law U. Tex., Austin, 1983-85. Contbr. articles to profl. jours. Served to capt. USAR, 1972-78. Mem. Tex. Bar Assn. (chmn. corp., banking and bus. law sect. 1983), Tex. Assn. Bank Counsel (pres. 1985-86). Clubs: Austin, Austin Yacht, Metropolitan, Capitol. Banking, Bankruptcy. Office: Fulbright & Jaworski 600 Congress Suite 2400 Austin TX 78701

HENDERSON, GORDON DESMOND, lawyer; b. Oakland, Calif., May 25, 1930. A.B. magna cum laude, Harvard U., 1951, J.D. magna cum laude, 1957. Bar: D.C. 1957, N.Y. 1965. Ptnr. Barrett, Smith, Schapiro, Simon & Armstrong, N.Y.C., 1965-79, Weil, Gotshal & Manges, N.Y.C., 1979—; spl. counsel to SEC, 1962-64; chmn. policy adv. group. N.Y. Joint Legis. Commn. to Study N.Y. State Tax Law, 1982—; mem. N.Y.C. Tax Study Commn., 1986—. Mem.: Harvard Law Rev, 1955-57. Mem. Scarsdale Planning Commn., 1975-77; pres. Civic Assn. Hollin Hills, Alexandria, Va., 1962. Mem. Assn. Bar City N.Y. (chmn. com. on corp. law 1969-72), N.Y. State Bar Assn. (chmn. tax sect. 1979), ABA, Am. Coll. Tax Counsel, Am. Law Inst., Phi Beta Kappa. Corporate taxation, Personal income taxation. Home: 16 Sunset Ln Rye NY 10580

HENDERSON, HAROLD RICHARD, lawyer; b. Washington, Nov. 5, 1942; s. Harold Richard and Channie (Catlett) H.; m. Franzine Moore, Dec. 31, 1965; children: Kimberly Michele, Jessica Nicole, Harold R. III. BS, Mich. State U., 1972; JD, Harvard U., 1976. Bar: D.C. 1976, U.S. Dist. Ct. D.C. 1977, U.S. Ct. Appeals (D.C. cir.) 1977, U.S. Supreme Ct. 1985. Assoc. Margan. Lewis & Bockius, Washington, 1976-80; asst. gen. counsel Amtrak, Washington, 1980-82, dep. gen. counsel, 1982-84, gen. counsel, 1984-86, v.p. law, 1986—. Bd. dirs. Rosemont Daycare Ctr., Washington, 1978—, Homemakers Health Aid Service Inc., Washington, 1982—. Mem. ABA, Nat. Bar Assn., Com. Ry. and Airline Labor Lawyers. Baptist. Avocations: biking, fishing, running, photography. General corporate, Labor, Federal civil litigation. Home: 432 Orchard St NW Vienna VA 22180 Office: AMTRAK 400 N Capitol St NW Washington DC 20001

HENDERSON, JAMES RUTLEDGE, IV, lawyer; b. Raleigh, N.C., Mar. 12, 1949; s. James Rutledge III and Anna Lunda (Slack) H.; 1 child, James Rutledge V; m. Felicia Helen de Courcy; 1 child, Felicia Gabrielle de Courcy. BA, Old Dominion U., 1971; JD, U. Va., 1974. Bar: Va. 1974, D.C. 1975, U.S. Ct. Appeals (4th cir.) 1980, U.S. Supreme Ct. 1984. Assoc. Mayer, Brown & Platt, Washington, 1975-81, Mullins & Mullins, Tazewell, Va., 1981-82; ptnr. Mullins & Henderson, Tazewell, 1982—. Mem. Assn. Trial Lawyers Am., Va. Trial Lawyers Assn. Democrat. Presbyterian. Avocations: photography, angling. Civil rights, Federal civil litigation, Family and matrimonial. Home: 409 Marion Ave Tazewell VA 24651 Office: Mullins & Henderson 227 W Main St PO Box 843 Tazewell VA 24651

HENDERSON, JOHN RICHARD, lawyer; b. Oshkosh, Wis., Jan. 25, 1953; s. John Vernon and Audrey Lorraine (Erban) H.; m. Vicki Lyn Nahman, May 28, 1983. BBA, U. Wis., 1975; JD, U. Colo., 1978. Bar:

Colo. 1978, U.S. Dist. Ct. Colo. 1978, U.S. Ct. Appeals (10th cir.) 1981. Assoc. Vranesh, Raisch & Schroeder, Boulder, 1978-80; assoc. Vranesh & Raisch, Boulder, 1980-83, ptnr., 1983—. Committeeman Boulder County Rep. Party, 1984—, area coordinator 1985—. Mem. ABA (hard minerals com.), Colo. Bar Assn., Boulder County Bar Assn. (chmn. natural resources com. 1983-85), Colo. Mining Assn. (bd. dirs.), Boulder County Metal Mining Assn., Boulder County Horseman's Assn. Clubs: Colo. Classics. Avocations: tennis, horseback riding, skiing, travel, reading. Real property, Mine and minerals, State civil litigation. Office: PO Box 871 Boulder CO 80306

HENDERSON, JOHN ROBERT, lawyer; b. Ft. Worth, Apr. 21, 1950; s. Julius Adrian and Jane Marie (Fitts) H.; m. Cynthia Lynn Wendland, May 27, 1972; 1 child, Michael Robert. B.B.A., U. Tex., 1972; J.D. with honors, Tex. Tech. U., 1975. Bar: Tex. 1975, U.S. Dist. Ct. (no. dist.) Tex. 1976, U.S. Dist. Ct. (ea. dist.) Tex. 1981, U.S. Ct. Appeals (5th and 11th cirs.) 1981, U.S. Dist. Ct. (so. dist.) Tex. 1982, U.S. Dist. Ct. (we. dist.) Tex. 1983. Briefing atty. 12th Dist. Tex. Ct. Appeals, Tyler, 1975-76; assoc. Stalcup, Johnson, Meyers & Miller, Dallas, 1976-78, Meyers, Miller & Middleton, Dallas, 1978-80; assoc. Jones, Day, Reavis & Pogue, Dallas, 1981-83, ptnr., 1984—. Bd. dirs. The 500 Inc., Dallas, 1982-83, sponser, 1984, 85; bd. dirs. Dallas Opera, 1982-84, Dallas Repertory Theater, 1983-84, Dallas Civic Music Assn., 1987—. Mem. ABA (litigation sect., young lawyers div. liaison to forum com. on constrn. industry 1985—), Dallas Assn. Def. Counsel, Tex. Assn. Def. Counsel, Tex. Bd. Legal Specialization (cert.), Dallas Bar Assn. (council constrn. law sect. 1983-85), Order of Coif. Episcopalian. Club: Argyle. Federal civil litigation, State civil litigation, Construction. Office: Jones Day Reavis & Pogue 2300 LTV Ctr 2001 Ross Ave Dallas TX 75201

HENDERSON, KEVIN JAMES, lawyer; b. Seattle, Apr. 29, 1944; s. Paul Wesley and Margaret Mary (Papke) H.; m. Ardis Jean Jahnke, Sept. 11, 1965; children: Sean James, Timothy Walter, Joseph Paul. BA, Seattle U., 1966; JD, Loyola U., Los Angeles, 1972; MBA, Seattle U., 1985. Bar: Wash. 1972, U.S. Dist. Ct. (we. dist.) Wash. 1973, U.S. Ct. Appeals (9th cir.) 1983, U.S. Dist. Ct. (ea. dist.) Wash. 1985. Ptnr. McNair & Henderson, Seattle, 1973-79; sole practice Seattle, 1979-82; gen. counsel Am. Discount Corp., Seattle, 1982-85; counsel Skippers, Inc., Bellevue, Wash., 1985—. Officer, mem. Magnolia Recreational Council, Seattle, 1983—; officer, bd. dirs. Northwest Ctr. for the Retarded, Seattle, 1981—. Served to sgt. U.S. Army, 1966-69, Vietnam. Mem. ABA (forum com. on franchising, corps. and banking sect.), Wash. State Bar Assn., Seattle-King County Bar Assn. Roman Catholic. Avocations: reading, skiing. General corporate, Real property, Franchising. Office: Skippers Inc 14450 NE 29th Pl Suite 200 Bellevue WA 98007

HENDERSON, THELTON EUGENE, federal judge; b. Shreveport, La., Nov. 28, 1933; s. Eugene M. and Wanzie (Roberts) H.; 1 son, Geoffrey A. B.A., U. Calif.-, Berkeley, 1956, J.D., 1962. Bar: Calif. 1962. Atty. U.S. Dept. Justice, 1962-63; assoc. firm FitzSimmons & Petris, 1964, assoc., 1964-66; directing atty. San Mateo County (Calif.) Legal Aid Soc., 1966-69; asst. dean Stanford (Calif.) U. Law Sch., 1968-76; ptnr. firm Rosen, Remcho & Henderson, San Francisco, 1977-80; judge U.S. Dist. Ct. No. Dist. Calif., San Francisco, 1980—; asso. prof. Sch. Law, Golden Gate U., San Francisco, 1978-80. Served with U.S. Army, 1956-58. Mem. Nat. Bar Assn., Charles Houston Law Assn. Jurisprudence. Office: US Dist Ct 450 Golden Gate Ave Room 19042 San Francisco CA 94102 *

HENDERSON, THOMAS, lawyer; b. Des Moines, May 17, 1955; s. Clarence Henry and Elizabeth (Myers) H. BA, Drake U., 1977, JD, 1980. Bar: Iowa 1980, U.S. Dist. Ct. (so. dist.) 1980. Assoc. Hopkins and Huebner, Des Moines, 1980-85, Whitfield, Musgrave, Selvy, Kelly & Eddy, Des Moines, 1985—; adj. prof. law Drake U., Des Moines, 1983-84. Mem. Iowa State Bar Assn. (young lawyers sect., sec. 1985-86, pres.-elect 1986-87, pres. 1987—). Episcopalian. Personal injury, Workers' compensation, Insurance. Home: 3422 Clark Des Moines IA 50311 Office: Whitfield Law Firm 1300 First Interstate Bank Bldg Des Moines IA 50309

HENDERSON, WILLIAM NELSON, lawyer; b. Marion, Ill., May 1, 1940; s. William S. and Adriana (Nelson) H.; m. Elaine H. Huddleston, May 21, 1981; children: Wesley, Theodore, Marshall, Darla, Donald. BA, N.Mex. Highlands U., 1962; JD, U. Utah, 1974. Bar: N.Mex. 1974, U.S. Dist. Ct. N.Mex. 1974, U.S. Ct. Appeals (10th cir.) 1981. Mng. atty. Gallagher & Ruud, Albuquerque, 1974-75; sole practice Albuquerque, 1975-80; mng. atty. Atkinson & Kelsey P.A., Albuquerque, 1980-81; ptnr. Franchini, Henderson, Wagner & Oliver, Albuquerque, 1981—; vis. lectr. U. N.Mex. Law Sch., Albuquerque, 1976-81. Author: New Mexico Probate Manual, 1976. Bd. dirs. Christian Conciliation Service, Albuquerque, 1986—. Mem. Assn. Trial Lawyers Am., N.Mex. Bar Assn., N.Mex. Trial Lawyers Assn., Albuquerque Bar Assn. Democrat. Presbyterian. Avocations: handball, softball, tennis, fishing, backpacking. Family and matrimonial, Probate. Office: Franchini Henderson Wagner & Oliver 707 Broadway NE Suite 100 Albuquerque NM 87102

HENDIN, ROY ALLEN, lawyer; b. St. Louis, Jan. 23, 1956; s. Aaron and Lillian Hendin; m. Ellen Jaffe, Aug. 31, 1986. BJ, U. Mo., 1977; JD, George Washington U., 1981. Bar: Mo. 1981, Ill. 1982. Assoc. Lewis & Rice, St. Louis, 1981-83; sole practice St. Louis, 1984-85; mem. ITT Comml. Fin. Corp., St. Louis, 1985—. Avocation: sports. Contracts commercial, Bankruptcy. Home: 403 Country Oak Chesterfield MO 63017 Office: ITT Comml Fin Corp 11477 Olde Cabin Rd Saint Louis MO 63141

HENDRICKS, EDWIN FRANCIS, lawyer; b. Oak Park, Ill., Oct. 2, 1941; s. Edwin F. and Kathleen (Enright) H.; m. Genevieve Wilmer, Aug. 31, 1963; children: Elizabeth, Kathleen, Edwin, Genevieve. BA, Santa Clara U., 1963; JD, U. Ariz., 1969. Bar: Ariz. 1969, U.S. Dist. Ct. Ariz. 1969, U.S. Ct. Appeals (9th cir.) 1975, U.S. Supreme Ct. 1976. Assoc. Snell & Wilmer, Phoenix, 1969-71; ptnr. Meyer, Hendricks, Victor, Osborn & Maledon, Phoenix, 1971—; judge pro tem Maricopa County Superior Ct., Phoenix, 1980—, Ariz. Ct. Appeals, Phoenix, 1986—; mem. nomination commn. Superior Ct., 1986—, 9th Cir. Merit Screening Com. for Bankruptcy Judges Dist. Ariz. Bd. trustees Xavier High Sch., Phoenix, 1980-83, pres. 1983; bd. regents Brophy College Preparatory, Phoenix, 1984—; bd. dirs. Boys Clubs of Metro Phoenix, 1980—; mem. bd. visitors U. Ariz. Coll. Law, 1984-86, Ariz. State U. Coll., 1986—. Served to 1st lt. U.S. Army, 1963-66. Fellow Ariz. and Maricopa County Bar Found.; mem. ABA, Ariz. Bar Assn. (bd. govs. 1986—), Maricopa County Bar Assn. (bd. dirs. 1980—, pres. 1985-86, bd. dirs. vol. lawyers adv. bd. 1981-86, chmn. 1986—), Assn. Trial Lawyers Am., Am. Judicature Soc., Nat. Inst. Trial Advocacy (faculty 1984—). Democrat. Roman Catholic. Clubs: Phoenix Country, Mansion (Phoenix). Avocations: sports, hunting, fishing. Federal civil litigation, State civil litigation, Personal injury. Home: 317 E Glenn Dr Phoenix AZ 85020 Office: Meyer Hendricks Victor Osborn & Maledon 2700 North 3rd St Suite 4000 Phoenix AZ 85004

HENDRICKS, JOHN CHARLES, lawyer; b. Sellersville, Pa., Oct. 26, 1941; m. Linda Ann Sauerland, Aug. 28, 1965; children—Karl Erik, Kirstin Ann. A.B. with honors in Polit. Sci. cum laude, Dickinson Coll., Carlisle, Pa., 1963; J.D., George Washington U., 1966, LL.M. in Taxation, 1973. Bar: U.S. Dist. Ct. D.C. 1967, U.S. Ct. Appeals (D.C. cir.) 1970, U.S. Tax Ct. 1970, U.S. Supreme Ct. 1973, U.S. Ct. Claims 1974, Md. 1978. Assoc., Ash, Bauersfeld, Burton & Mooers, Washington, 1969-74, ptnr., 1975-77; ptnr. Ash, Bauersfeld, Burton, Hendricks & Tyrrell and predecessor, Washington, 1977—; speaker profl. seminars; bd. dirs. various corps. Bd. dirs. Lutheran Social Services of Met. Washington, 1975-78, 80-86, pres. 1976, 84-86, chmn. fin. com., 1977-78, 80-83. Served to capt. U.S. Army, 1967-69. Mem. ABA, Md. Bar Assn., D.C. Bar Assn., Contbr. articles to profl. jours. Personal income taxation, General corporate, Estate planning and administration. Home: 21414 Davis Mill Rd Germantown MD 20874 Office: 4520 East-West Hwy #505 Bethesda MD 20814

HENDRICKS, KATHERINE, lawyer; b. Logan, Utah, Apr. 12, 1949; d. Charles Durrell and Leah Grace (Funk) H.; m. O. Yale Lewis, Jr., Sept. 7, 1985. BS, MS, MIT, 1972; JD, Boston U., 1975. Bar: Mass. 1976, Colo. 1982, Wash. 1984, U.S. Dist. Ct. Mass. 1979, U.S. Dist. Ct. (no. dist.) N.Y., U.S. Dist. Ct. Colo., U.S. Dist. Ct. Wash., U.S. Ct. Appeals (1st cir.), 1978, U.S. Ct. Appeals (9th cir.), 1984. Assoc. Palmer & Dodge, Boston, 1975-81, Garfield & Hecht, Aspen, Colo., 1981-84, Wickwire, Lewis, Goldmark & Schorr, Seattle, 1984-86; ptnr. Hendricks & Lewis, Seattle, 1986—. Fellow Delta Gamma Found.; mem. ABA. Federal civil litigation, State civil litigation. Home: 1516 Federal Ave E Seattle WA 98102 Office: Hendricks & Lewis 2675 First Interstate Ctr Seattle WA 98104

HENDRICKS, RANDAL ARLAN, lawyer; b. Kansas City, Mo., Nov. 18, 1945; s. Clinton H. and Edith T. (Anderson) H.; m. Suann Rose, June 1, 1965 (div. 1976); children—Kristin Lee, Daehne Lynn; m. Jill Edith Duke, Mar. 22, 1982; 1 child, Bret Larson-Hendricks. Student, U. Mo.-Kansas City, 1963-65; B.S. with honors, U. Houston, 1968, J.D. with honors, 1970. Bar: Tex. 1970, U.S. Dist. Ct. (so. dist.) Tex. 1970. Assoc. Baker & Botts, Houston, 1970-71; sole practice, Houston, 1971—; ptnr. Hendricks Sports Mgmt., Houston, 1977-81; pres. Hendricks Mgmt. Co., Inc., Houston, 1981—. Dir. profl. div. Excellence Campaign, U. Houston, 1971; bd. dirs. Cypress Creek Christian Ch., Spring, Tex., 1979—; expert witness U.S. Senate Subcom. on Antitrust and Monopoly, 1972. Mem. Houston Bar Assn., Assn. Reps. Profl. Athletes (bd. dirs. 1978—, mem. at large 1978-79, treas. 1979-80, v.p. 1980-81, pres. 1981-82, chmn. ethics com. 1978-80, chmn. baseball com. 1981—), Order of Barons (chancellor 1969-70), Phi Kappa Phi, Phi Delta Phi. Sports, Real property, Personal income taxation. Home: PO Box 296 Tomball TX 77375 Office: 400 Randal Way Suite 106 Spring TX 77388

HENDRICKSON, RAY, lawyer; b. Valley City, N.D., Nov. 10, 1937; s. David John and Ragna S. (Olson) H. BS, N.D. State U., 1962; postgrad., U. Wash., 1962-68; JD, Western State U., 1973; MA in Psychology, Pepperdine U., 1981. Bar: Calif. 1973, U.S. Dist. Ct. (no., ea., so., and cen. dists.) Calif. 1973, U.S. Ct. Appeals (9th cir.) 1976, U.S. Supreme Ct. 1976. Chemist Deft, Inc., Torrance, Calif., 1971-73; sole practice Newport Beach, Calif., 1973—; judge pro tem Orange County (Calif.) Superior and Mcpl. Cts., 1980—. Counsel Libertarian Party, Newport Beach, 1975—; bd. dirs. Irvine (Calif.) Community Theater, 1975—, Western State U. Coll. Legal Clinic, Fullerton, Calif., 1984—. Served with U.S. Army, 1955-58, Korea. Recipient YMCA award, 1960. Mem. ABA, Orange County Bar Assn., Calif. Trial Lawyers Assn., Phi Kappa Phi, Phi Lambda Upsilon, Blue Key. Avocations: skiing, scuba diving, running. Family and matrimonial, Personal injury, State civil litigation. Office: 4000 Mac Arthur Blvd Newport Beach CA 92660

HENDRICKSON, ROBERT AUGUSTUS, lawyer; b. Indpls., Aug. 9, 1923; s. Robert Augustus and Eleanor Riggs (Atherton) H.; m. Virginia Reiland Cobb, Feb. 3, 1951 (div. 1980); m. Zita Davisson, May 12, 1981; children—Alexandra Kirk, Robert Augustus III. Cert., Yale U., 1943, U. Besancon, France, 1945, U. Sorbonne, France, 1946; J.D., Harvard U., 1948. Bar: N.Y. 1949, Ind. 1948, Fla. 1971, U.S. Supreme Ct. 1959, U.S. Ct. Internat. Trade 1978. Assoc. Lord, Day & Lord, N.Y.C., 1948-52; law asst. to Surrogates of N.Y. County, 1952-54; assoc. Breed, Abbott & Morgan, 1954-67; ptnr. Lovejoy, Wasson, Lundgren & Ashton, 1967-76; counsel Coudert Bros., N.Y.C., 1977-78, ptnr., 1979-86; counsel Citibank N.A., 1986—; chmn., dir. Republic Aerospace Co., Inc.; bd. dirs. Sebring Lakes Inc., St. Martin's Press, Inc., Grove's Dictionaries of Music Inc.; chmn., bd. dirs. Republic Aerospace Co., Inc., 1987—; vis. prof. U. Miami, Coral Gables, Fla., 1976; mem. sec. of State's Adv. Group on Trusts, 1983—; trade rep. U.S. Sec. of Commerce Industry Sector Adv. Com. on Services in Trade, 1985—. Author: The Future of Money, 1970; The Cashless Soc., 1972; Hamilton I 1757-1789; Hamilton II 1789-1804; The Rise and Fall of Alexander Hamilton, 1981; others. Contbr. articles to profl. jours. Bd. dirs., sec. Mental Health Assn. of N.Y.C. and Bronx Counties, 1964-74; trustee, v.p. Friendly Homes Inc., 1960-80; trustee Hosp. Chaplaincy, 1960-85, Internat. Ctr. Disabled, 1968—, St. Hilda's and St. Hugh's Sch., 1968-81; trustee Carl Duisberg Soc., 1976—, chmn., chief exec. officer, 1983—. Served to 1st lt. U.S. Army, 1951. Decorated Bronze Star, Purple Heart with oak cluster; Yale U. regional scholar, 1941-42; Phelps Assn. scholar, 1942. Mem. ABA, N.Y. State Bar Assn., Ind. Bar Assn., Bar Assn. City N.Y., Fla. Bar, Consular Law Soc. (pres. 1982-83, chmn. 1983-85), Am. Fgn. Law Assn. (v.p. 1982, pres. 1983—), Internat. Acad. Estate and Trust Law (exec. council), Am. Soc. Internat. Law, Am. br. Internat. Law Assn., Maritime Law Assn. of U.S., Bankruptcy Lawyers Bar Assn., N.Y. Commerce and Industry Assn. (chmn. com. on trusts 1964-68), Union Internat. des Avocats. Republican. Episcopal. Clubs: Century Assn., Union, Racquet and Tennis, Sky, Colonial Wars, Pilgrims of U.S., The Church (pres. 1977-79). Estate planning, Private international, Estate taxation. Office: 641 Lexington Ave 9th Floor New York NY 10022

HENDRICKSON, ROBERT CHARLES, lawyer; b. Sacramento, Apr. 22, 1952; s. Milton C. and Elizabeth (Anderson) H.; m. Carola E. Ingram, June 26, 1982; 1 child, David Logan. BSCE, U. Calif., Berkeley, 1974, MSCE, 1975, JD, 1979. Bar: Calif. 1979, U.S. Dist. Ct. (no. dist.) Calif. 1979, U.S. Ct. Appeals (9th cir.) 1979, U.S. Tax Ct. 1986; registered profl. engr. Assoc. Thelen, Marrin, Johnson & Bridges, San Francisco, 1979-86, Hancock, Rothert & Bunshoft, San Francisco, 1986—. Construction, Contracts commercial, Federal civil litigation. Office: Hancock Rothert & Bunshoft 4 Embarcadero Ctr 10th Floor San Francisco CA 94111

HENDRICKSON, THOMAS ATHERTON, lawyer; b. Indpls., May 12, 1927; s. Robert Augustus and Eleanor Riggs (Atherton) H.; m. Sandra Bly Shepard, Feb. 6, 1960; children—Thomas Shepard, Heidi Bly, Melanie Parke. B.A., Yale U., 1949; LL.B., Ind. U., 1952. Bar: Ind. 1952, U.S. Dist. Ct. (so. dist.) Ind. 1952, U.S. Tax Ct. 1956, U.S. Ct. Mil. Appeals 1956, U.S. Supreme Ct. 1956, U.S. Ct. Appeals (7th cir.) 1958, U.S. Dist. Ct. (no. dist.) Ind. 1986. Assoc. Buschmann, Krieg, Devault & Alexander, 1952-53; ptnr. Purvis & Hendrickson, 1953-56, Royse, Travis, Hendrickson & Pantzer, Indpls., 1956-83, Hendrickson, Travis, Pantzer & Miller, 1983—; dep. prosecutor Marion County (Ind.), 1954-57. Mem. Indpls. Hist. Preservation Commn., 1982-83; mem. Marion County/Indpls. Hist. Soc., pres., 1984-85; mem. adv. bd. Fund for Landmark Indpls. Properties, 1984-85, Cath. Sem. Found. Indpls., Inc., 1985—; former Marion County lay rep. planning com. Central Ind. Library Services Authority, recipient Outstanding Service award; former council pres. Indpls. Great Books. Served to lt. (s.g.) USNR, 1945-56. Mem. Indpls. Bar Assn. (v.p. 1972), Ind. Bar Assn. (ho. of dels.), Fed. Bar Assn., 7th Circuit Bar Assn., Indpls. Lawyers Assn., Indpls. Lawyers Club, Ind. U. Alumni Assn. (life mem.), Beta Theta Pi, Phi Delta Phi. Clubs: Indpls. Ski (past pres.), Columbia, Indpls. Sailing, Indpls. Literary, Dramatic, Mud Creek Players. Bankruptcy, Federal civil litigation, Corporate taxation. Home: 7979 Lantern Rd Indianapolis IN 46256 Office: 120 Monument Circle 240 Indianapolis IN 46204

HENDRY, ROBERT RYON, lawyer; b. Jacksonville, Fla., Apr. 23, 1936; s. Warren Candler and Evalyn Marguerite (Ryon) H.; m. Lee Comstock, June 21, 1956; children: Lorraine Evalyn, Lynette Comstock, Krista Ryon. BA. in Polit. Sci., U. Fla., 1958, JD, 1963. Bar: Fla. 1963. Assoc. Harrell, Caro, Middlebrooks & Wiltshire, Pensacola, Fla., 1963-66; assoc. Helliwell, Melrose & DeWolf, Orlando, Fla., 1966-67, ptnr., 1967-69; ptnr., pres. Hoffman, Hendry, Parker & Smith and predecessor Hoffman, Hendry & Parker, Orlando, 1969-77, Hoffman, Hendry & Stoner and predecessor, Orlando, 1977-82, Hendry, Stoner, Sims & Sawicki, Orlando, 1982—. Mem. Dist. Export Council, 1977—, vice chmn., 1981; bd. dirs. World Trade Ctr. and predecessor, Orlando, 1979—, pres., 1980-82, 84; chmn. Fla. Gov.'s Conf. on World Trade, 1983; mem. internat. fin. and mktg. adv. bd. U. Miami Sch. Bus., Fla. Commn. on Internat. Edn., 1986—. Served to 1st lt. U.S. Army, 1958-60, to capt. Army N.G., 1960-70. Mem. Fla. Council Internat. Devel. (bd. dirs. 1972-85, chmn. 1977-79, adv. bd. 1985—), Fla. Bar (vice chmn. internat. law com. 1974-75, chmn. com. 1976-77, mem. exec. council internat. law sect. 1982—, v.p. Fla. Assn. Voluntary Agys. for Caribbean Action 1987—), Orange County Bar Assn. (treas. 1971-74), Brit.-Am. C. of C. (bd. dirs., sec. 1984-85). Club: University (Orlando). Private international, General corporate, Real property. Office: 215 E Central Blvd Orlando FL 32801

HENEGAN, JOHN CLARK, lawyer; b. Mobile, Ala., Oct. 14, 1950; s. Virgil Baker and Marie (Fife) Gunter; m. Morella Lloyd Kuykendall, Aug. 5, 1972; children: Clark, Jim. BA in English and Philosophy, U. Miss., 1972, JD, 1976. Bar: Miss. 1976, U.S. Dist. Ct. (no. dist.) Miss. 1976, N.Y. 1979, U.S. Dist. Ct. (so. dist.) N.Y. 1979, U.S. Ct. Appeals (5th and 11th cir.) 1981, U.S. Dist. Ct. (so. dist.) Miss. 1984, U.S. Ct. Appeals (2d cir.) 1985. Law clk. to judge U.S. Ct. Appeals (5th cir.), N.Y.C., 1976-77; atty. Dewey, Ballantine, Busby, Palmer & Wood, N.Y.C. and Washington, 1977-81; exec. asst., chief of staff Gov. William Winter, Jackson, Miss., 1981-84; atty. Butler, Snow, O'Mara, Stevens & Cannada, Jackson, 1984—; lectr. U. Miss. Ctr. Continuing Legal Edn., 1985, Miss. Jud. Coll., Oxford, 1982. Editor in chief Miss. Law Jour., 1976; editor Miss. Lawyer, 1985. Bd. dirs. Mississippians for Ednl. Broadcasting, Jackson, 1983—; mem. State Ethics Commn., Jackson, 1984—. Mem. ABA, Miss. Bar Assn. (chmn. Law Day U.S.A., 1983), N.Y. State Bar Assn., Miss. Def. Lawyers Assn., Miss. Law Jour. Alumni Assn. (bd. dirs. 1985—), Fed. Bar Assn., Jackson C. of C., Phi Kappa Phi, Phi Delta Phi, Omicron Delta Kappa. Democrat. Presbyterian. Avocations: reading, running. Antitrust, Federal civil litigation, Libel. Home: 4025 Kings Hwy Jackson MS 39216 Office: Butler Snow O'Mara et al Deposit Guaranty Plaza Suite 1700 Jackson MS 39205

HENG, DONALD JAMES, JR., lawyer; b. Mpls., July 12, 1944; s. Donald James and Catharine Amelia (Strom) H.; m. Kathleen Ann Bailey, Sept. 2, 1967; 1 child, Francesca Remy. B.A. cum laude, Yale U., 1967; J.D. magna cum laude, Minn., 1971. Bar: Calif. 1971, U.S. Dist. Ct. (no. dist.) Calif. 1971, U.S. Ct. Appeals (9th cir.) 1971. Assoc. Brobeck, Phleger & Harrison, San Francisco, 1971-73, ptnr., 1978—; atty.-adviser Office Internat. Tax Counsel, Dept. Treasury, Washington, 1973-75; lectr., writer on tax-related subjects. Note and comment editor Minn. Law Rev., 1970-71. Co-recipient award for outstanding performance Am. Lawyer Mag., 1981; Fulbright scholar, Italy, 1967-68. Mem. ABA, Calif. Bar Assn., Oakland Mus. Assn. (pres. 1985-87, bd. dirs. 1983—), Order Coif. Republican. Congregationalist. Personal income taxation, Private international. Office: Brobeck Phleger & Harrison Spear St Tower One Market Plaza San Francisco CA 94105

HENICAN, CASWELL ELLIS, lawyer; b. New Orleans, Feb. 10, 1905; s. Joseph Patrick and Alice (Boning) H.; m. Elizabeth Cleveland, June 18, 193O; children: Alice (Mrs. Claude V. Perrier, Jr.), Caswell Ellis Jr., Margaret (Mrs. F. Gordon Wilson, Jr.), Dorothy (Mrs. Charles E. Heidingsfelder), Joseph Patrick III. LL.B., Tulane U., 1926. Bar: La. 1926. Since practiced in New Orleans; assoc. Lemle, Moreno & Lemle, 1926-33; sr. partner Henican, Carriere & Cleveland, 1933-40, Henican, James & Cleveland, 1940—. Chmn. La. State Bd. Pub. Welfare, 1940-47; pres. New Orleans Community Chest, 1940, Council Social Agencies, 1939, Assoc. Cath. Charities New Orleans, 1938; chmn. bd. Mercy Hosp.; mem. exec. com., pres. Magnolia Sch. Bd. Named Most Outstanding Young Man New Orleans Jr. C. of C., 1940; Most Outstanding Alumnus Jesuit High Sch., 1960; named to Tulane U. Hall of Fame, 1978, Greater New Orleans Hall of Fame, 1980; decorated Knight St. Gregory, Knight St. Louis. Mem. New Orleans Bar Assn., La. Bar Assn., ABA, Soc. Hosp. Attys. of Am., Hosp. Assn. (charter), Nat. Assn. Honest Lawyers. Federal civil litigation, State civil litigation, Real property. Home: 1401 Nashville Ave New Orleans LA 70115 Office: Henican James & Cleveland 111 Veterans Blvd Suite 1200 Metairie LA 70005

HENINGER, STEPHEN DON, lawyer; b. Flora, Ill., June 23, 1950; s. Donald Dan and Bernadette (Murphy) H.; m. Karen Lou Rice, Apr. 3, 1971; children: Erik, Jill, Sean. BA in English, U. Ill., 1972; JD summa cum laude, Cumberland Sch. Law, 1977. Bar: Ala. 1977, U.S. Dist. Ct. (no. dist.) Ala. 1977, U.S. Ct. Appeals (D.C. and 11th cirs.) 1977, U.S. Supreme Ct. 1982. Law clk. to presiding judge U.S. Dist. Ct., Birmingham, Ala., 1977; ptnr. Hare, Wynn, Newell & Newton, Birmingham, 1980—; mem. adv. com. on appellate procedures Ala. Supreme Ct. Served to 1st lt. U.S. Army, 1972-74. Mem. Ala. Trial Lawyers Assn. (exec. com. 1983—), Am. Bd. Trial Advs. Office: Hare Wynn Newell & Newton City Fed Bldg Suite 700 Birmingham AL 35203

HENKE, RAYMOND LANGE, lawyer; b. Pomona, Calif., May 31, 1953; s. Burton Lehman and Wilma (Lange) H.; m. Cheryl Rene Harris, Oct. 20, 1984; 1 child, Cory Lehman. Ba, U. Hawaii, Honolulu, 1976; JD, U. San Francisco, 1979. Bar: Calif. 1979, U.S. Dist. Ct. (cen. and so. dists.) Calif. 1979. Assoc. Butler, Dan, Allis & Reback, Los Angeles, 1979—; judge pro tem Calif. Superior and Mcpl. Cts. Contbr. articles to profl. jours. Mem. Assn. Trial Lawyers Am., Calif. Trial Lawyers Assn., Los Angeles Trial Lawyers Assn. (contbg. editor Advocate). Democrat. Personal injury, Federal civil litigation, State civil litigation. Office: Butler Dan Allis & Reback 626 Wilshire Blvd Suite 914 Los Angeles CA 90017-3266

HENKE, ROBERT JOHN, lawyer, engineer; b. Chgo., Oct. 13, 1934; s. Raymond Anthony and May Dorothy (Driscoll) H.; m. Mary Gabrielle Handrigan, June 18, 1960; children—Robert Joseph, Ann Marie. B.S.E.E., U. Ill., 1956; M.B.A., U. Chgo., 1964; J.D., No. Ill. U., 1979, postgrad. John Marshall Law Sch. Bar: Ill. 1980, Wis. 1980, U.S. Dist. Ct. (no. dist.) Ill. 1980, U.S. Dist. Ct. (we. and ea. dists.) Wis. 1980, U.S. Supreme Ct. 1984; registered profl. engr., Ill., Wis. sr. elec. engr. Commonwealth Edison Co., Chgo., 1956-80; elec. engr. Peterson Builders, Sturgeon Bay, Wis., 1982-83; sr. elec., cost estimating engr. Sargent & Lundy Engrs., Chgo., 1985—; instr. econs. and criminal law NE Wis. Tech. Inst., 1981-82; asst. dist. atty. Door County, Wis., 1981, ct. commr., 1981-82; sole practice, Door County, 1981-84, Lake County, Ill., 1984—; dir. Scand, Door County. Vice chmn. Door County Bd. Adjustment, 1983-84; atty. coach Wis. Bar Found. High Sch. Moot Ct. Competition, Door County, 1984; vol. lawyers program, Lake County, Ill., 1985—. Served with USAR, 1958-63. Mem. ABA, Wis. Bar Assn., Door Kewaunee Bar Assn. (pres. 1983-84), Ill. Bar Assn. (vol. lawyers program Lake County chpt.), Chgo. Bar Assn., Lake County Bar Assn., Am. Judicature Soc., Ill. Soc. Profl. Engrs., Assn. Trial Lawyers Am., IEEE, NSPE, Am. Assn. Cost Engrs. Roman Catholic. General practice, Patent, Trademark and copyright. Home: 835 D Country Club Dr Libertyville IL 60048 Office: Sargent & Lundy Engrs 55 E Monroe St Chicago IL 60603

HENKEL, KATHRYN G., lawyer; b. West Columbia, Tex., Oct. 16, 1952; d. Louis Ory Jr. and Patricia Dolores (Fields) Gundy; m. David Richard Henkel, June 15, 1974. BA, Rice U., 1973; JD, Harvard U., 1976. Bar: Tex. 1976, U.S. Tax Ct. 1981, U.S. Dist. Ct. (no. dist.) Tex. 1982, U.S. Supreme Ct. 1983. Assoc. Coke & Coke, Dallas, 1976-78, Hughes & Hill, Dallas, 1978-82; ptnr. Hughes & Luce, Dallas, 1982—. Mem. Dallas Zoo, 1982—, Dallas Women's Ctr. 1986—, planned giving com. Dallas Women's Found., 1986—; adv. council Communities Found. Tex. Inc., 1982—, adv. panel Dallas Symphony Orch., 1987—;. Mem. ABA (selection com. estate and gift taxes, chairperson subcom. publs. and important devels. 1987—), Tex. Bar Assn. (com. chairperson taxation sect. 1982-86, council 1986—), Dallas Bar Assn. (sec, treas. taxation sect. 1985-86, vice chairperson 1986-87—, council 1983—). Roman Catholic. Avocations: reading, travel. Estate planning, Probate, Corporate taxation. Home: 4302 Glenleigh Dallas TX 75220 Office: Hughes & Luce 1000 Dallas Bldg Dallas TX 75201

HENKIN, LOUIS, educator, lawyer; b. Russia, Nov. 11, 1917; came to U.S., 1923, naturalized, 1930; s. Yoseph Elia and Frieda Rebecca (Kreindel) H.; m. Alice Barbara Hartman, June 19, 1960; children: Joshua, David, Daniel. A.B., Yeshiva Coll., 1937, L.H.D., 1963; LL.B., Harvard U., 1940. Bar: N.Y. 1941, U.S. Supreme Ct 1947. Law clk. to Judge Learned Hand, 1940-41, Justice Frankfurter, 1946-47; cons. legal dept. UN, 1947-48; with State Dept., 1945-46, 48-57; U.S. rep. UN Com. Refugees and Stateless Persons, 1950; adviser U.S. del. UN Econ. and Social Council, 1950, UN Gen. Assembly, 1950-53, Geneva Conf. on Korea, 1954; assoc. dir. Legis. Drafting Research Fund, lectr. law Columbia U., 1956-57, lectr. law, 1956-57; vis. prof. law U. Pa., 1957-58, prof. law, 1958-62; prof. internat. law and diplomacy, prof. law Columbia U., 1962, mem. Inst. War and Peace Studies, 1962—, Hamilton Fish prof. internat. law and diplomacy, 1963-78, Harlan Fiske Stone prof. constl. law, 1978-79, Univ. prof., 1979—; co-dir. Ctr. for Study of Human Rights, 1978—; U.S. mem. Permanent Ct. Arbitration, 1963-69; adviser U.S. Del. UN Conf. on Law of the Sea, 1972-80; mem. adv. panel on internat. law Dept. State, 1975-80; mem. Human Rights Com. U.S. Commn. for UNESCO, 1977-80; Carnegie lectr. Hague Acad. Internat. Law, 1965; Frankel lectr. U. Houston, 1969; Gottesman lectr. Yeshiva U., 1975; Lockhart lectr. U. Minn. Law Sch., 1976; Francis Biddle lectr. Harvard Law Sch., 1978; Univ. lectr. Columbia U., 1979; Sherrill lectr. Yale U. Law Sch., 1981; Jefferson lectr. U. Pa. Law Sch., 1983; Irvine lectr. Cornell U., 1986; cons. to govt.; pres. U.S. Inst. Human Rights, 1970—; bd. dirs. Lawyers Com. Internat. Human Rights, 1978—; trustee Cardozo Law Sch.; chief reporter Am. Law Inst. Restatement of Fgn. Relations Law of U.S., 1979-87. Author: Arms Control and Inspection in American law, 1958, The Berlin

Crisis and the United Nations, 1959, Disarmament: The Lawyer's Interests, 1964, Law for the Sea's Mineral Resources, 1968, Foreign Affairs and the Constitution, 1972, The Rights of Man Today, 1978, How Nations Behave: Law and Foreign Policy, 2d edit., 1979, (with others) Human Rights in Contemporary China, 1986; editor: Arms Control: Issues for the Public, 1961, (with others) Transnational Law in a Changing Society, 1972, World Politics and the Jewish Condition, 1973, 1980, The International Bill of Rights: The International Covenant of Civil and Political Rights, 1981, (with others) International Law, Cases and Materials, 2d. edit., 1987; bd. editors: Am. Jour. Internat. Law, 1967—, co-editor-in-chief, 1978-84; bd. editors Ocean Devel. and Internat. Law Jour., 1973—, Jerusalem Jour. Internat. Relations, 1976—; contbr. articles to profl. jours. Served with AUS, 1941-45. Decorated Silver Star; Guggenheim fellow, 1979-80; recipient Law Alumni Medal of Excellence, Columbia U. Sch. of Law, 1982; Friedmann Meml. award, 1986. Fellow Am. Acad. Arts and Scis.; mem. Council Fgn. Relations, Am. Soc. Internat. Law (v.p. 1974-75), Internat. Law Assn. (v.p. Am. br. 1973—), Am. Soc. Polit. and Legal Philosophy (pres. 1985-87), Institut de Droit Internat.(assoc.), Am. Polit. Sci. Assn., Internat. Assn. Constl. Law (v.p. 1982—), Am. Philos. Soc. Legal education, Human rights, Civil rights. Home: 460 Riverside Dr New York NY 10027

HENN, HARRY GEORGE, legal educator; b. New Rochelle, N.Y., Oct. 8, 1919; s. Harry Christian and Mollie (Malsch) H. B.A. summa cum laude, NYU, 1941, J.S.D., 1952; LL.B. with distinction, Cornell U., 1943. Bar: N.Y. 1944. Assoc. Whitman, Ransom & Coulson, N.Y.C., 1943-53; mem. faculty Cornell U. Law Sch., 1953-85, prof. law, 1957-85, Edward Cornell prof. law, 1970-85, prof. emeritus, 1985—, Donald C. Brace Meml. lectr., 1978; vis. prof. law Hastings Coll. Law, 1979, NYU, 1983; spl. counsel Cornell U., 1953-56; pres., dir. Cornell Daily Sun, 1966-73; guest lectr. NYU, 1953-78; acting village justice, Cayuga Heights, Ithaca, N.Y., 1965-74; trustee Copyright Soc. U.S., 1953—, pres., 1961-63; mem. UNESCO panel internat. copyright; also panel cons. gen. revision copyright law; cons. corp. law annotated project Am. Bar Found., 1959-60, 63-64, 68; research cons. N.Y. State Joint Legislative Com. to Study Revision Corp. Law; also Library of Congress. Author: Copyright Primer, 1979, 2d edit., 1987, Teaching Materials Agency, Partnership and Other Unincorporated Business Enterprises, 1972, 2d edit., 1985, Teaching Materials on the Laws of Corporations, 1974, supplement, 1980, 2d edit., 1986; co-author: Laws of Corporations and Other Business Enterprises, 3d edit., 1983, supplement, 1986, also articles.; contbr. to: Ency. Brit; Editor-in-chief: Cornell Law Quar, 1943. Pres. Ithaca Opera Assn., 1968-73, 79-81; trustee South Central Research Library, 1967-74. Mem. ABA (past chmn. copyright div.), AAUP (chpt. pres. 1968-70), Internat. Gesellschaft für Urheberrecht E.V., N.Y. State Assn. Magistrates, Phi Beta Kappa, Order of Coif, Delta Upsilon, Phi Kappa Phi (chpt. pres. 1964-65), Phi Delta Phi. Clubs: Statler (Cornell U.); Tower (Ithaca Coll.). Legal education, General corporate, Trademark and copyright. Home: Vanderbilt Towers II Apt 604 Three Bluebill Ave Naples FL 33963

HENNEGAN, JOHN OWEN, lawyer; b. Balt., Apr. 22, 1947; s. A. Owen and Catherine Louise (Hoffman) H.; m. Eileen O'Conner Stack, Feb. 10, 1973; 1 child, Brendan. BS, Loyola Coll., Balt., 1969; JD, U. Balt., 1974. Bar: Md. 1974, U.S. Dist. Ct. Md. 1974. Asst. states atty. State of Md., Balt., 1974-79; assoc. T. Bayard Williams, Balt., 1976-82; ptnr. Romadka, Gontrum, Hennegan & Foos, Balt., 1982—; instr. Essex Coll., Balt., 1974-78. Vol. Montebello Rehab. Hosp., Balt., 1986—; chmn. com. Elect Judge Page and Ensor, Balt., 1986—, Elect William Evans, Balt., 1986—. Mem. Assn. Trial Lawyers Am., Md. Trial Lawyers Assn., Balt. County Bar Assn. (law day com.), Md. Bar Assn. Democrat. Roman Catholic. Club: Loyola Coll. Greyhound (pres. Balt.). Lodge: Ancient Order Hibernians. Avocations: golf, racquetball. State civil litigation, Personal injury, Probate. Home: 5 White Wood Ct Baltimore MD 21236 Office: Romadka Gontrum Hennegan & Foos 809 Eastern Blvd Baltimore MD 21221

HENNEKE, DAVID CHARLES, lawyer; b. Enid, Okla., Nov. 30, 1955; s. Charles Dean and Betty Ann (Gregg) Henneke. BS in Polit. Sci., Okla. State U., 1978; JD, U. Tulsa, 1980; postgrad., Oxford U., Eng., 1980. Bar: Okla. 1981, U.S. Dist. Ct. (we. dist.) Okla. 1981, U.S. Ct. Appeals (9th cir.) 1983, U.S. Supreme Ct. 1986. Ptnr. Farrant & Henneke, Enid, 1981-83, Farrant, Henneke, Brown & Shirley, Enid, 1983-85, Blakley, Grey & Henneke, P.C., Enid, 1986—. Republican. Presbyterian. Avocations: flying, sports, hunting. Bankruptcy, State civil litigation, Personal injury. Home: 3622 Whippoorwill Ln Enid OK 73703 Office: Blakley Gray & Henneke 220 W Maple Enid OK 73701

HENNEMUTH, JEFFREY ALAN, lawyer; b. Cleve., Oct. 24, 1956; s. George Herman and Dorothy (Thomas) H.; m. Kathy Elizabeth Bryant. AA, Cuyahoga Community Coll., 1976; BA magna cum laude, Baldwin-Wallace Coll., 1978; JD, Ohio State u., 1981. Bar: Ohio 1981, U.S. Dist. Ct. (no. dist.) Ohio 1982, U.S. Ct. Appeals (6th cir.) 1982, U.S. Ct. Appeals (3d cir.) 1984, U.S. Ct. Appeals (9th cir.) 1985, U.S. Ct. Appeals (4th cir.) 1986, U.S. Supreme Ct. 1986. Instr. legal writing and law Ohio No. U., Ada, 1981-83; law clk. to sr. cir. judge U.S. Ct. Appeals (6th cir.), Akron, Ohio, 1983-84; staff atty. U.S. Dept. Labor, Washington, 1984—. Alt. del. Ohio Dem. Conv., Cleve., 1982. Mem. ABA, Ohio Bar Assn., Phi Delta Phi. Presbyterian. Avocations: reading, music, golf, photography. Federal civil litigation, Administrative and regulatory, Labor. Home: 9894 Burke Pond Ct Burke VA 22015 Office: US Dept Labor Office of Solicitor 200 Constitution Ave NW Washington DC 20210

HENNENBERG, MICHAEL CHAIM, lawyer; b. Weiden, Fed. Republic Germany, Sept. 23, 1948; came to U.S., 1949; s. Jacob and Hildegard (Hohenleitner) H.; m. Susan Spitz, Mar. 7, 1982; children: Julia Esther, Deborah Pearl. B.S. in Bus. Adminstrn., Ohio State U., 1970; J.D., Cleve. State U., 1974. Bar: Ohio 1974, U.S. Dist. Ct. (no. dist.) Ohio 1974, U.S. Ct. Appeals (6th cir.) 1977, U.S. Supreme Ct. 1978. Dep. clk. Cuyahoga County Juvenile Ct., Cleve., 1972; law clk. Law Students Civil Rights Research Council, Cleve. Marshall Coll. Law, Cleve. State U., 1972-73; legal intern Pub. Defender's Office, Cuyahoga County, Cleve., 1973-74; ptnr., trial lawyer Greene & Hennenberg Co., L.P.A., Cleve., 1974—; panel chmn. Cuyahoga County Common Pleas Ct. Arbitration Commn., 1974—; guest lectr. profl. meetings; panelist legal topics, radio and TV shows. Contbr. articles to legal publs. Mem. Simon Wisenthal Ctr. for Holocaust Studies; bd. dirs. Hebrew Free Loan Assn., 1979-83; Citizens League Greater Cleve.; vice chmn. ann. fund raising drive Jewish Community Fedn. Mem. Ohio Acad. Trial Lawyers (criminal law standing com.), Cleve. Bar Assn. (mem. criminal law sect. 1974—, chmn.; 1981-82, legis. liaison 1983-85 , mem. steering com. task force on violent crime 1982—, mem. jud. selection com. 1982-85, trustee 1985—), Cuyahoga Criminal Def. Lawyers Assn. (founder, editor quar. newsletter, pres. 1986-87), Ohio State Bar Assn., Assn. Trial Lawyers Am., Nat. Assn. Criminal Def. Lawyers, ABA, U.S. Supreme Ct. Hist. Soc., Cleve. State U. Law Alumni Assn. Criminal. Home: 29200 Shaker Blvd Pepper Pike OH 44124 Office: Greene & Hennenberg Co LPA 801 Bond Court Bldg Cleveland OH 44114

HENNER, PETER WILLIAM, lawyer; b. N.Y.C., July 4, 1952. BA, Rutgers U., 1972, M in City and Regional Planning, 1979, JD, 1980. Bar: N.Y. 1980, N.J. 1980, U.S. Dist. Ct. N.J. 1980, U.S. Dist. Ct. (so. dist.) N.Y. 1982, U.S. Dist. Ct. (no. dist.) N.Y. 1984, U.S. Dist. Ct. (we. dist.) N.Y. 1986. Bus. mgr., organizer Textile Workers Union Am., Hudson, N.Y., 1975-76; asst. counsel N.Y. State Assembly, Albany, 1980-81; gen. counsel security employees council AFSCME, Albany, 1981-84; sole practice Albany, 1984—; spl. counsel Village of Canajoharie, 1986—; instr. labor law Cornell U. Sch. Indsl. and Labor Relations, 1984—; hearing officer N.Y. State Bd. Equalization and Assessment, 1985—. Columnist Point of Law, 1984-85. Chmn. planning and zoning com. N.Y.C.-Bronx Community Planning Bd., 1977. Mem. ABA, N.Y. State Bar Assn., Albany County Bar Assn. Democrat. Club: Adirondack Mountain (outing com.). Avocations: chess, mountaineering. Labor, Environment, Criminal. Home: 529 2d St Albany NY 12206 Office: 424 New Scotland Ave Albany NY 12208

HENNESSEY, EDWARD FRANCIS, state supreme ct. justice; b. Boston, Apr. 20, 1919; s. Thomas M. and Winifred C. (Tracey) H.; m. Elizabeth Ann O'Toole, Oct. 15, 1945; 1 dau., Beth Ann. B.S. cum laude, Northeastern U., 1941, LL.D., 1976; LL.B. cum laude, Boston U., 1949, LL.D., 1976; LL.D., Suffolk U., 1974, New Eng. Sch. Law, 1974. Bar: Mass. bar 1949. Partner firm Martin, Magnuson & Hennessey, Boston, 1950-66; judge Mass. Superior Ct., 1967-71; asso. justice Supreme Jud. Ct. of Mass., 1971-76, chief justice, 1976—; lectr. on trial practice Boston U., 1956-64. Author: (with Martin) Trial Practice, 2 vols, 1954. Served to capt. U.S. Army, 1941-45. Decorated Bronze Star; recipient Distinguished Pub. Service award Boston U., 1975, St. Thomas More Pub. Service award Diocese of Worcester, 1975. Fellow Am. Bar Assn.; mem. Boston Bar Assn., Mass. Bar Assn., Nat. Conf. of Chief Justices (pres. 1985-86), Nat. Ctr. for State Cts. (pres. 1985-86). Home: 29 Rosalie Rd Needham MA 02192 Office: Supreme Judicial Ct Courthouse Boston MA 02108

HENNESSEY, GILBERT HALL, JR., lawyer; b. El Paso, Ill., Nov. 30, 1916; s. Gilbert Hall and Moneta R. (Raisch) H.; m. Charlotte M. Mayfield, Oct. 5, 1940; children: Gilbert H., John R., Jane K. Hennessey Palia. BS, U. Ill., 1938, JD with honors, 1940. Bar: Ill. 1940, U.S. Dist. Ct. (no. dist.) Ill. 1941, U.S. Ct. Appeals (7th cir.) 1942, U.S. Supreme Ct. 1949. Assoc. Jenner & Block and predecessors, Chgo., 1940-42, 1946-50, ptnr., 1950—. Contbr. articles to legal jours. Trustee Lewis U., 1976—. Served to lt. USN, 1942-46. Mem. ABA, Ill. State Bar Assm., Chgo. Bar Assn. Republican. Clubs: Legal of Chgo. (pres. 1971-72), Law of Chgo., Union League (Chgo.). Real property, Banking. Home: 356 Cottage Ave Glen Ellyn IL 60137 Office: Jenner & Block One IBM Plaza Suite 3800 Chicago IL 60611

HENNESSEY, JOHN WILLIAM, lawyer, title company executive; b. Anadarko, Okla., Aug. 9, 1922; s. Martin Francis and Eva Nevada (Kelly) H. Student Loyola U., New Orleans, 1941; J.D., St. Mary's U., San Antonio, 1947. Bar: Tex. 1947, U.S. Dist. Ct. (so. dist.) Tex. 1957, U.S. Dist. Ct. (we. dist.) Tex. 1958, U.S. Dist. Ct. (we. dist.) Okla. 1960. Sole practice, San Antonio, 1947-57, Corpus Christi, Tex., 1957—; pres., chief counsel First Title Co. of Corpus Christi, 1972—. Served in U.S. Army; ETO. Mem. Assn. Trial Lawyers Am., Am. Judicature Soc., State Bar Tex., San Antonio Bar Assn., Nueces County Bar Assn., ABA. Roman Catholic. General practice, Real property, State civil litigation. Home: 638 Moray Pl Corpus Christi TX 78411 Office: Everhart Profl Bldg 4658 Everhart Corpus Christi TX 78411

HENNESSY, DEAN MCDONALD, lawyer, manufacturing company executive; b. McPherson, Kans., June 13, 1923; s. Ernest Weston and Beulah A. (Dunn) H.; m. Marguerite Sundheim, Sept. 6, 1946 (div. Sept. 1979); children—Joan Hennessy Wright, John D., Robert D., Scott D.; m. 2d, Darlene MacLean, Apr. 4, 1981 (dec.). A.B. cum laude, Harvard U., 1947, LL.B., 1950; M.B.A., U. Chgo., 1959. Bar: Ill. 1951; assoc. Carney, Crowell & Leibman, Chgo., 1950-53; atty. Borg-Warner Corp., Chgo., 1953-62; with Emhart Corp., Hartford, Conn., 1962—, asst. sec., 1964-67, sec., gen. counsel, 1967-74, v.p., sec., gen. counsel, 1974-76, v.p., gen. counsel, 1976-86; sr. v.p., gen. counsel, 1986—; dir. Emhart Industries, Inc., Emhart Internat. Corp., USM Corp. Trustee West Hartford Bicentennial Trust, Inc., 1976-77, Friends and Trustees of Bushnell Meml., Hartford, 1978—. Served to lt. (j.g.) USNR, 1943-46. Sheldon fellow. Mem. ABA, Am. Soc. Corp. Secs., Machinery and Allied Products Inst. (vice chmn. law council 1984—). Republican. Presbyterian. General corporate. Home: 410 Lovely St Avon CT 06001 Office: Emhart Corp 426 Colt Hwy PO Box 2730 Farmington CT 06032

HENNESSY, ELLEN ANNE, lawyer, educator; b. Auburn, N.Y., Mar. 3, 1949; d. Charles Francis and Mary Anne (Roan) H.; m. Frank Daspit, Aug. 27, 1974. BA, Mich. State U., 1971; JD, Cath. U., 1978; LLM in Taxation, Georgetown U., 1983. Bar: D.C. 1978, U.S. Ct. Appeals (D.C. cir.) 1978, U.S. Supreme Ct. 1984. Various positions Nat. Endowment for Humanities, Washington, 1971-74; atty. office chief counsel IRS, Washington, 1978-80; atty.-advisor Pension Benefit Guaranty Corp., Washington, 1980-82; assoc. Stroock & Stroock & Lavan, Washington, 1982-85; ptnr. Willkie Farr & Gallager, Washington, 1985—; adj. prof. law Georgetown U., Washington, 1985—. Mem. ABA (supervising editor taxation sect. newsletter 1984—), Women in Employee Benefits (pres. 1987—). Democrat. Avocation: whitewater canoeing. Pension, profit-sharing, and employee benefits, Bankruptcy. Home: 1926 Lawrence St NE Washington DC 20018 Office: Willkie Farr & Gallagher 818 Connecticut Ave NW Washington DC 20006

HENNING, JOEL FRANK, lawyer, author, publisher, consultant; b. Chgo., Sept. 15, 1939; s. Alexander M. and Henrietta (Frank) H.; m. Grace Weiner, May 24, 1964; children: Justine, Sarah-Anne, Dara. A.B., Harvard U., 1961, J.D., 1964. Bar: Ill. 1965. Assoc. firm Sonnenschein, Levinson, Carlin, Nath & Rosenthal, Chgo., 1965-70; fellow, dir. program Adlai Stevenson Inst. Internat. Affairs, Chgo., 1970-73; nat. dir. Youth Edn. for Citizenship, 1972-75; dir. profl. edn. Am. Bar Assn., Chgo., 1975-78; asst. exec. dir. communications and edn. Am. Bar Assn., 1978-80; sr. ptnr. Joel Henning & Assocs., 1980—; pres., pub. LawLetters, Inc., 1980—; pub. Lawyer Hiring and Training Report, 1980—, Almanac of Fed. Judiciary, 1984—; editor Bus. Lawyer Update, 1980—; mem. faculty Inst. on Law and Ethics, Council Philos. Studies; chmn. Fund for Justice, Chgo., 1979-85. Author: Law-Related Education in America: Guidelines for the Future, 1975, Holistic Running: Beyond the Threshhold of Fitness, 1978, Mandate for Change: The Impact of Law on Educational Innovation, 1979, Improving Lawyer Productivity: How to Train, Manage and Supervise Your Lawyers, 1985, Law Practice and Management Desk Book, 1987; contbr. articles and criticism to nat. mags. and legal publs. Chmn. Gov.'s Commn. on Financing Arts in Ill., 1970-71; bd. dirs. Ill. Arts Council, 1971-81, Columbia Coll., Chgo.; bd. dirs., v.p., mem. exec. com. ACLU of Ill.; trustee S.E. Chgo. Commn.; mem. Joseph Jefferson Theatrical Awards Com. Fellow Am. Bar Found. (life); mem. Am. Law Inst., ABA (ho. of dels.), Chgo. Bar Assn., Chgo. Council Lawyers (co-founder), Social Sci. Edn. Consortium. General corporate, Legal education, General practice. Office: 332 S Michigan Ave Suite 1460 Chicago IL 60604

HENNINGSEN, DAVID SEAN, lawyer; b. Omaha, Oct. 25, 1949; s. Raymond F. and Gertrude (Markey) H.; m. Jane Ellen Christy, Mar. 25, 1972; children: Christy, Erin. BA, U. Santa Clara, 1971; JD, U. Puget Sound, 1975. From assoc. to ptnr. Robinson & Wood, San Jose, Calif., 1975—; freelance cons. ins., Bay Area, Calif., 1975—; judge pro tem Santa Clara Supreme Ct., San Jose, 1980—; arbitrator various fed. and state cts., Bay Area, 1980—. Mem. ABA, Calif. Bar Assn., Northern Calif. Assn. Def. Counsel, Def. Research Inst. Lodge: Elks. Avocation: golf. Insurance, Personal injury.

HENRY, ANGELA LOUISE, lawyer, nurse; b. Toronto, Ont., Can., Feb. 17, 1953; came to U.S., 1964; d. Fredrick Charles and Joan Shirley (Webb) H. RN, Ga. Bapt. Nursing Sch., Atlanta, 1973; BS, U. S.C., 1977, JD, 1981. Bar: S.C. 1981, U.S. Dist. Ct. S.C. 1982, U.S. Ct. Appeals (4th cir.) 1982; RN. Staff nurse Richland Meml. Hosp., Columbia, S.C., 1974-75, spl. procedures nurse, 1975-78; estate adminstr. bankruptcy div. U.S. Dist. Ct. S.C., Columbia, 1981-83; assoc. McKay, McKay, Grubbs & Nunn, Columbia, 1983-85; ptnr. McKay, McKay & Henry, Columbia, 1985—; lectr. on legal implications in medicine various locations, 1985—. Mem. Columbia Action Council. Mem. ABA, Def. Lawyers Assn., Comml. Law League, S.C. Bar Assn., Richland CountyBar Assn., Am. Coll. Obstetrics and Gynecology (legis. rep. nursing div. 1986—), S.C. Investors Club. Clubs: TIP (Columbia). Bankruptcy, Insurance, Personal injury. Home: 3004 Prentice Ave Columbia SC 29205 Office: McKay McKay & Henry 1919 Gadsden St PO Box 7217 Columbia SC 29202

HENRY, ARTHUR WAYNE, lawyer; b. Newport, Tenn., Feb. 1, 1957; s. Arthur and Norma Jean (Bryant) H.; m. Deborah Jean Puckett, June 7, 1980. BBA, Memphis State U., 1978; JD, U. Tenn., 1981. Bar: Tenn. 1981, U.S. Dist. Ct. (ea. dist.) Tenn. 1981, U.S. Ct. Appeals (6th cir.) 1986. Assoc. Hailey, Waters, Sykes, & Sharp, Sevierville, Tenn., 1981-82; ptnr. Fowler and Gibson, Loudon, Tenn., 1982—; bd. dirs. Knoxville (Tenn.) Legal Aide Soc. Bd. dirs. Loudon Mchts. and Property Owners, 1985—; vestry Ch. Resurrection, 1985—, sr. warden, 1987—. Mem. ABA, Trial Lawyers Am., Tenn. Bar Assn., Loudon County Bar Assn. (pres. 1984-85), Loudon C. of C. (pres. 1984-85). Republican. Episcopalian. Lodge: Rotary. Avocations: sports, sports cars. Banking, Contracts commercial, State civil litigation. Home: Upper Lakeview Dr Loudon TN 37774 Office: Fowler and Gibson 322 Grove St Loudon TN 37774

HENRY, EDWIN MAURICE, JR., lawyer, electrical engineer, consultant; b. Cambridge, Md., June 26, 1930; s. Edwin Maurice Henry Sr. and Emma Lee (Wilson) Clayton; m. Barbara Ann Brittingham, Feb. 2, 1952; children: Barbara Jo, Kim M. Student, U.S. Naval Acad., 1949-51; BSEE, John Hopkins U., 1957; JD, U. Balt., 1972. Bar: Md. 1974, U.S. Dist. Ct. Md. 1974; registered profl. engr., Md. Assoc. Pairo & Pairo, Balt., 1973-76; ptnr. Pairo & Henry, Ellicott City, Md., 1976-86; sole practice Ellicott City, 1986—; mem. Md. Atty. Grievance Rev. Bd., 1980-83. Author: Defense of Speeding Vascar, 1974. Served with USN, 1947-51. Mem. ABA, Md. Bar Assn., Howard County Bar Assn., Md. Trial Lawyers Assn., Am. Legion. Democrat. Methodist. Clubs: Eastern Shore Soc., Saints and Sinners (Balt.); Cambridge Yacht. Lodges: Masons, Shriners, Jesters. Avocations: travel, boating. Personal injury, Family and matrimonial, State civil litigation. Home: 9035 Overhill Dr Ellicott City MD 21043 Office: 8433 Main St PO Box 309 Ellicott City MD 21043

HENRY, FORREST ALFRED, lawyer; b. Detroit, Sept. 9, 1951; s. Forrest Alfred Sr. and Maxine Delores (Knoblock) H. BA in Econs. and German, U. Mich., 1973; JD, Wayne State U., 1976. Bar: Mich. 1976, U.S. Dist. Ct. (ea. dist.) Mich. 1976. Assoc. Logan, Huchla & Wycoff, Riverview, Mich., 1976-77; asst. dir. labor relations Detroit Chpt., Associated Gen. Contractors of Am., Inc., 1977-86, dir. labor relations, 1986—. Author: Work Assignment Disputes Under National Labor Relations Act, 1985. Mem. Mich. Bar Assn. Labor. Office: Associated Gen Contractors Am Detroit Chpt 18100 Schaefer Hwy Detroit MI 48235

HENRY, FREDERICK EDWARD, lawyer; b. St. Louis, Aug. 28, 1947; s. Frederick E. and Dorothy Jean (McCulley) H.; m. Vallie Catherine Jones, June 7, 1969; children—Christine Roberta, Charles Frederick. A.B., Duke U., 1969, J.D. with honors, 1972. Bar: Ill. 1972, U.S. Dist. Ct. (no. dist.) Ill. 1972, Calif. 1982. Assoc. Baker & McKenzie, Chgo., 1972-79, ptnr., 1979—. Bd. dirs. Lincoln Park Conservation Assn., Chgo., 1983-85, Old Town Triangle Assn., Chgo., 1980-83, pres., 1984. Recipient Willis Smith award Duke U. Law Sch., 1972. Mem. ABA, Chgo. Bar Assn., Calif. State Bar, Order of Coif. Private international, Corporate taxation. Home: 164 W Eugenie St Chicago IL 60614 Office: Baker & McKenzie 2800 Prudential Plaza Chicago IL 60601

HENRY, JAMES R., lawyer. BA, SUNY, Potsdam, 1976; JD, Yale U., 1979. Bar: N.Y. 1980. Assoc. White & Case, N.Y.C. and Washington, 1979-81, Luster & Salk, Groton, N.Y., 1982-84; ptnr. Luster, Salk & Henry, Groton, 1984—. Mem. ABA, N.Y. State Bar Assn., Tompkins County Bar Assn., Groton Bus. Assn. Real property, Probate, General practice. Office: Luster Salk & Henry PO Box 95 Groton NY 13073

HENRY, JOHN ALFRED, lawyer; b. Westbrook, Maine, Feb. 11, 1931; s. Donald M. and Josephine M. (Perry) H.; children—James Richard, Jeffrey Alan. B.A. cum laude, Bowdoin Coll., 1952, J.D. with honors, George Washington U., 1960. Bar: Va. 1960, Mass. 1961, Ariz. 1968. Tax law specialist Rulings div. Nat. Office IRS Washington 1959-61; assoc. Ropes & Gray, Boston, 1960-68, Lewis & Roca Phoenix, 1968-70; founding ptnr. Henry, Kimerer & La Velle, 1970-84; of counsel Allen, Kimerer & LaVelle, Phoenix, 1985—. Chmn. bd. Legal Profls. Credit Union; mem. exec. com. Am. Cancer Soc. Ariz. Div., Inc., 1969—, pres., 1976-77, chmn. bd., 1977-79, chmn. legacy com., 1979-83; vice chmn. ann. dinner NCCJ, 1983, 84. Served with USAF, 1952-56. Recipient Am. Cancer Soc. Annual Nat. Divisional award, 1978, 83. Mem. ABA, State Bar Va., State Bar Mass., State Bar Ariz. Republican. Clubs: Univ., Mansion, Plaza (Phoenix). Contbr. to legal jours. Corporate taxation, Contracts commercial, Real property. Home: 4936 E Arroyo Verde Dr Paradise Valley AZ 85253 Office: Allen Kimerer & LaVelle 2715 N 3d St Phoenix AZ 85004

HENRY, PETER YORK, lawyer; b. Washington, Apr. 28, 1951; s. David Howe II and Margaret (Beard) H.; m. Rebecca Jo Csajka, Aug. 1976; children—Ryan York, Zachary Price. B.B.A., Ohio U., 1973; J.D. St. Mary's U., San Antonio, 1976. Bar: Tex. 1976. Sole practice, San Antonio, 1976—. Mem. Tex. Bar Assn., Am. Trial Lawyers Assn., Tex Trial Lawyers Assn., San Antonio Trial Lawyers Assn., San Antonio Bar Assn., Phi Delta Phi. Personal injury, Insurance, Workers' compensation. Home: 6806 Forest Haven San Antonio TX 78240 Office: 224 Casa Blanca San Antonio TX 78215

HENRY, ROBERT H., state official. Atty. gen. State of Okla., Oklahoma City, 1987—. Office: Atty Gen's Office 112 State Capitol Bldg Oklahoma City OK 73105 *

HENRY, ROBERT JOHN, lawyer; b. Chgo., Aug. 1, 1950; s. John P. and Margaret P. (Froelich) H.; m. Sharon A. Tyma, June 3, 1972; children: Cherylyn, Deanna, Laurin. BA cum laude, Loyola U., Chgo., 1973, JD cum laude, 1975. Bar: Ill 1975, U.S. Dist. Ct. (no. dist.) Ill. 1975. Atty. Continental Ill. Nat. Bank, Chgo., 1975-77; atty. Allied Van Lines, Inc., Chgo., 1977-81, assoc. gen. counsel, 1981—. Alt. scholar Weymouth Kirkland Found., 1971. Mem. ABA, Chgo. Bar Assn., Am. Corp. Counsel Assn. Contracts commercial, General corporate, Securities. Office: Allied Van Lines Inc PO Box 4403 Chicago IL 60680

HENRY, RONALD GEORGE, lawyer, executive; b. Beaver Falls, Pa., May 14, 1949; s. Ronald S. and Alice (Ross) H.; m. Linda Callahan, Aug. 28, 1976. AB with honors, Georgetown U., 1971, JD, 1974. Bar: Pa. 1974, U.S. Supreme Ct. 1977, D.C. 1978. Asst. atty. gen. Pa. Dept. Commerce, Harrisburg, Pa., 1974-76; counsel to lt. gov. State of Pa., Harrisburg, 1976-79; assoc. Ballard, Spahr, Andrews & Ingersoll, Phila., 1979-83; v.p. pub. fin. Prudential Bache, Inc., Phila., 1983-85, Smith Barney, Harris Upham & Co., Phila., 1985—. Author: (with others) Financing Colleges and Universities, 1983. Mem. ABA, Pa. Bar Assn., D.C. Bar Assn., Phila. Bar Assn. Municipal bonds, Legislative, Local government. Office: Smith Barney Harris Upham & Co Inc 3100 Centre Sq W Philadelphia PA 19102

HENRY, ROXANN ELIZABETH, lawyer; b. Westover AFB, Mass., June 24, 1953; d. William and Elizabeth (Stretch) H.; m. George J. Nolfi Jr.; 1 child, Katherine Elizabeth. AB, Vassar Coll., 1975; JD, Rutgers U., 1978. Bar: Pa. 1979, N.J. 1980, U.S. Dist. Ct. N.J. 1980, D.C. 1981, U.S. Ct. Appeals (11th cir.) 1981, U.S. Ct. Appeals (6th cir.) 1982, U.S. Dist. Ct. D.C. 1984, U.S. Ct. Appeals (D.C. cir.) 1984, U.S. Supreme Ct. 1984. Law clk. to presiding justice U.S. Ct. Appeals (8th cir.), Kansas City, Mo., 1978-80; assoc. Howrey & Simon, Washington, 1980-85, ptnr., 1986—. Recipient Armitage award, 1977; C. Wallace Vail scholar, N.J. Bar Found., 1977. Mem. ABA, N.J. Bar Assn., Pa. Bar Assn., Women's Bar Assn. Washington, Washington Bar Assn. Club: Vassar (Washington). Antitrust, Federal civil litigation, Administrative and regulatory. Office: Howrey & Simon 1730 Pennsylvania Ave NW Washington DC 20006

HENSCHEL, GEORGE LIPMAN, lawyer; b. Bronx, N.Y., Oct. 1, 1949; s. Herbert and Ida Sarah (Goldstein) H.; m. Lucille Carol Mitchell, May 23, 1976; children—Sarah Ann, Rebecca Elise. A.B., Cornell U., 1971; J.D., Duke U., 1974. Bar: N.H. 1974, U.S. Dist. Ct. N.H. 1974, Fla. 1975. Atty. Office of Solicitor, U.S. Dept. Labor, Washington, 1975-78, asst. counsel for OSHA safety standards, 1978—. Vol. Prince George's County Spl. Olympics, Md., 1981-83; bd. dirs. Congregation Adat Reyim, Springfield, Va., 1982—, pres., 1987—. Recipient Spl. Achievement award Office of Solicitor, U.S. Dept. Labor, 1979, 82, 85. Mem. ABA (adminstrv. law, labor relations sects.), Fla. Bar, N.H. Bar Assn. Jewish. Clubs: Washington Capitals Fan (pres. 1979-80, 81-82) (Lanham, Md.); Nat. Hockey League Boosters (pres. 1981-82) (St. Louis). Avocation: competitive crossword puzzles. Labor, Administrative and regulatory. Home: 8910 Tailcoat Ct Springfield VA 22153 Office: Office of Solicitor Div OSHA US Dept Labor 200 Constn Ave NW Room S-4004 Washington DC 20210

HENSHAW, SIGRID MARGUERITE, lawyer, accountant; b. Des Moines, Aug. 19, 1932; d. Hadar Oscar and Marguerite (Gonda) Ortman; m. Harold W. Henshaw, Apr. 2, 1977. B.B.A. with distinction, Northwestern U., 1963; J.D., South Tex. Coll. Law, 1978. Bar: Okla. 1978; C.P.A., Ill., Tex., Okla. Managerial positions with C.P.A. firms and various corps., Phoenix, Chgo. and Los Angeles, 1955-71; asst. sec., dir. corporate tax Cordura, Inc., Los Angeles, 1971-73, Geosource, Inc., Houston, 1973-76; C.P.A. in individual practice, Tulsa, 1977—; sole practice law, Tulsa, 1978-80; mng. atty. Henshaw & Leblang, Tulsa, 1980—. Mem. ABA (tax sect.), Fla. Bar Assn.,

Okla. Bar Assn., Tulsa County Bar Assn., Assn. Am. Trial Lawyers (sustaining), Okla. Soc. C.P.A.s Tex. Soc. C.P.A.s, Phi Alpha Delta. Corporate taxation, Personal income taxation, Estate taxation. Office: Henshaw & Leblang 7661 E 61st St Suite 251 Tulsa OK 74133

HENSLEY, WILLIAM MICHAEL, lawyer; b. Fresno, Calif., Apr. 25, 1954; s. Goldia Reeves and Allene (Watson) H.; 1 child, Gilliann Mar. BA, U. So. Calif., 1976; JD, Rutgers U., 1979. Bar: Calif., U.S. Dist. Ct. (no., ea. and cen. dists.) Calif., U.S. Ct. Appeals (9th cir.). Research atty. 5th dist. ct. appeals State of Calif., Fresno, 1979-81; assoc. Kadison, Pfaelzer, Woodard, Quinn & Rossi, Los Angeles, 1981—. Mem. ABA, Los. Angeles County Bar Assn., Wilshire Bar Assn., Los Angeles Bar Commn. on Appellate Cts., Assn. Bus. Trial Lawyers, Lawyers Club Los Angeles, Fed. Bar Assn. Los Angeles. Democrat. Mem. Ch. of Christ. Club: Demolay (Fresno) (chaplain 1971-72). Avocations: skiing, tennis, music, journalism. Federal civil litigation, State civil litigation, Antitrust. Home: 435 S LaFayette Park Pl #208 Los Angeles CA 90057 Office: Kadison Pfaelzer Woodard et al 707 Wilshire Blvd 40th Floor Los Angeles CA 90017

HENSON, HOWARD KIRK, lawyer; b. Chgo., Apr. 28, 1956; s. Howard I. and Constance M. (Evanhoff) H. BA, Ga. State U., 1979; JD, U. Ga., 1982. Bar: Ga. 1982, U.S. Dist. Ct. (no. dist.) Ga. 1983, U.S. Dist. Ct. (mid. dist.) Ga. 1986. Sole practice Atlanta, 1982-86; of counsel Corlew, Smith & Wright, Atlanta, 1984-86; house counsel Am. States Ins. Co., Atlanta, 1986—. Committeeman DeKalb County Dems., Decatur, Ga., 1985. Mem. ABA, Ga. Bar Assn., Atlanta Bar Assn., Def. Research Inst. State civil litigation, Insurance, Workers' compensation. Home: 2249 Virginia Pl Apt B Atlanta GA 30305 Office: Am States Ins Co Stanford Bldg 2960 Brandywine Rd Suite 110 Atlanta GA 30341

HENTHORN, CHARLES REX, lawyer; b. Crawfordsville, Ind., Oct. 7, 1937; s. Albert C. and Mildred P. (Lough) H.; m. Sandra Jo Templeton; children: Charles Mark, Douglas Alan, David Christopher. AB, Wabash Coll., Crawfordsville, 1959; JD, Ind. U., 1962. Bar: Ind. 1962, U.S. Dist. Ct. (so. dist.) Ind. 1962, U.S. Tax Ct. 1962, U.S. Supreme Ct. 1962. Assoc. atty. Harding & Henthorn, Crawfordsville, 1963-68, ptnr., 1968-72; ptnr., officer Harding & Henthorn PC, Crawfordsville, 1972-85, Harding, Henthorn & Harris PC, Crawfordsville, 1985—; pros. atty. 22d Jud. Cir. of Ind., 1967-70; asst. judge adv. 38th Infantry Div., Indpls., 1966-69; bd. dirs. Montgomery Savings Assn., Crawfordsville, 1981—. Bd. dirs. Montgomery County United Fund, Crawfordsville, 1967-68, Montgomery County Mental Health Assn., 1966-68. Served to capt. N.G., 1962-69. Mem. ABA, Am. Arbitration Soc., Assn. Ins. Attys., Ind. State Bar Assn., Ind. Def. Counsel, Montgomery County Bar Assn. (pres. 1964-65). Republican. Mem. Disciple of Christ Ch. Lodges: Masons. Avocations: water sports, cross country skiing. Personal injury, State civil litigation, General practice. Office: Harding Henthorn & Harris PC 122 East Main St Crawfordsville IN 47933

HEPNER, CHARLES EDWARD, lawyer; b. Oakland, Calif., July 29, 1925; s. Edward and Mabel (Marsh) H.; m. Anne Hoyt, Sept. 26, 1956; children—Robert Marsh, Elizabeth Sterrett. Student Calif. Inst. Tech., 1942-44; B.S., U. Calif.-Berkeley, 1948; M.S., MIT, 1950; LL.B., Yale U., 1968. Bar: N.Y. 1968, Conn. 1977. Research engr. Gen. Dynamics Corp., Groton, Conn. and Barden Corp., Danbury, Conn., 1954-65; assoc. Kenyon and Kenyon, N.Y.C., 1968-84, ptnr., 1984—. Served to lt. USNR, 1943-46, 52-54. Mem. ABA, Conn. Bar Assn., N.Y. Patent Law Assn., Phi Beta Kappa, Sigma Xi, Tau Beta Pi. Patent, Trademark and copyright. Office: Kenyon & Kenyon 1 Broadway New York NY 10004

HEPPENHEIMER, HARRY, lawyer, accountant, educator; b. N.Y.C., Aug. 14, 1922; s. Morris and Hermine (Sussman) H.; m. Julianne M. Forgash, June 16, 1946; children: Mitchell R., Lee B., Jill Ann. BS, NYU, 1947; JD, U. Notre Dame, 1952. Bar: Ill. 1952, Ind. 1952, U. S. Dist. Ct. (no. dist.) Ind. 1952. adj. prof. Ind. U., South Bend, 1953-80; lectr. various law and bus. seminars throughout midwest, 1955-85. Dem. precinct committeeman, South Bend, 1975-80. Served to sgt. U.S. Army, 1943-46. Mem. ABA, Am. Inst. CPA's, Ind. CPA's, Ind. Bar Assn. Jewish. Lodge: Elks. Personal income taxation, State civil litigation, Probate. Home: 2902 Miami St South Bend IN 46614 Office: 704 W Washington South Bend IN 46601

HEPPLEWHITE, DAVID WILSON, lawyer; b. Cleve., Sept. 10, 1951; s. James Wilson and Helen Louise (Boyd) H.; m. Anne-Marie E. Rhodes, Nov. 23, 1984. BA, Colo. Coll., 1973; MA, Drake U., 1978, JD, 1981. Bar: Ill. 1981, U.S. Dist. Ct. (no. dist.) Ill. 1981, U.S. Ct. Appeals (7th cir.) 1981. Assoc. Burditt & Calkins, Chgo., 1981-84, Burditt, Bowles & Radzuns, Ltd., Chgo., 1984-85, Kasdin & Nathanson, Chgo., 1985—. Contbr. articles on med. device regulation to profl. jours., 1984—. Mem. ABA, Chgo. Bar Assn. (co-chmn. com. 1985-86), Beta Beta Beta, Pi Gamma Mu. Republican. Congregationalist. Federal civil litigation, State civil litigation, Personal injury. Office: Kasdin & Nathanson 135 S LaSalle St Chicago IL 60603

HERALD, JOHN PATRICK, lawyer; b. Latrobe, Pa., Sept. 27, 1947; s. John P. and Doris Faye (Galvin) H.; m. Bridget Grace Tobin, Aug. 17, 1973; children: Brian Michael, Matthew Patrick, Molly Bridget, John Francis. AB in History, John Carroll U., 1969; JD, U. Notre Dame, 1972. Bar: Ill. 1972, U.S. Dist. Ct. (no. dist.) Ill. 1972, U.S. Ct. Appeals (7th cir.) 1975, U.S. Supreme Ct. 1978. Assoc. Baker & McKenzie, Chgo., 1972-79, ptnr., 1979—. Mem. ABA, Ill. Bar Assn., Chgo. Bar Assn., 7th cir. Bar Assn., Chgo. Trial Lawyers Club (pres. 1982-85), Soc. Trial Lawyers, Internat. Assn. Ins. Counsel. Roman Catholic. Federal civil litigation, State civil litigation, Personal injury. Home: 1721 N Normandy Chicago IL 60635 Office: Baker & McKenzie 130 E Randolph Suite 2700 Chicago IL 60601

HERAUF, WILLIAM ANTON, lawyer; b. Dickinson, N.D., Feb. 26, 1957; s. Herbert Henry and Nancy Dann (Rabe) H.; m. Joan Thompson, May 17, 1986. BSBA, U. N.D., 1979, JD, 1982. Bar: N.D. 1982, Minn. 1982, U.S. Dist. Ct. N.D. 1982. Assoc. Mackoff, Kellogg, Kirby & Kloster, Dickinson, 1982-84; corp. atty. Multi Nat. Diving Eduators Assn., Marathon, Fla., 1984—; states atty. City of Dickinson, 1985-87, asst. city atty., 1985—; assoc. Ficek Law Office, Dickinson, 1985—; Asst. state Fla., 1985—. Fireman, Dickinson Vol. Fire Dept., 1985—; bd. dirs. Dickinson Underwater Search and Recovery Team, 1985—. Mem. ABA (recipient Bronze Key 1982, Bd. Govs cert. 1982), N.D. Trial Lawyers Assn. (bd. dirs. 1985—), Assn. Trial Lawyers Am., Stark County Bar Assn. Lutheran. Lodge: Elks. Avocations: skiing, scuba diving, running, swimming, reading. Personal injury, State civil litigation, General practice. Home: Rural Rt 2 Box 112 Dickinson ND 58601 Office: Ficek Law Office 41 1st Ave W Dickinson ND 58601

HERB, FRANK STEVEN, lawyer; b. Cin., Nov. 9, 1949; s. Frank X. and Jean M. (Zurcher) H.; m. Jean L. Jeffers, June 21, 1971; children: Tracy Lynn, Jacquelyn Anne. BS, Bowling Green U., 1971; JD, U. Cin., 1974. Bar: Ohio 1974, Fla. 1978. Bd. dirs. Centergate Property Owners Assn., Sarasota, Fla., 1979-80, home/sch. com. Incarnation Sch., Sarasota, 1983-84, Brock Wilson Found., Sarasota, 1983—, Riegels Landing Assn., Sarasota, 1986—. Served to capt. JAGC USAF, 1975-78. Mem. Ohio Bar Assn., Fla. Bar Assn. (chmn. 12th Jud. cir. unauthorized practice of law com. 1986—), Sarasota Bar Assn. Republican. Roman Catholic. Avocations: boating, woodworking, skiing. General corporate. Office: Nelson Hesse Cyril Smith et al 2070 Ringling Blvd Sarasota FL 34242

HERBERS, JOHN A., lawyer; b. St. Louis, Oct. 3, 1957; s. Vincent T. and Mary Janette (Buescher) H.; m. Norma Jeanne Hinz, Aug. 13, 1983; children: J. Andrew, Daniel P. BS in Fgn. Service, Georgetown U., 1979; JD, Boston Coll., 1982. Bar: Wis. 1982, U.S. Tax Ct. 1983, U.S. Ct. Appeals (7th cir.) 1986. Sales rep. Taylor Assocs. Inc., St. Louis, 1979-80; assoc. Reinhart, Boerner et al, Milw., 1982—; lectr. ATS-continuing legal edn. Wis. State Bar, Madison, 1986—. Mem. ABA, Milw. Bar Assn. Lodge: Rotary. Avocations: reading, cycling, camping, traveling. Probate, Estate taxation, Personal income taxation. Home: 1562 E Hampton Milwaukee WI 53217 Office: Reinhart Boerner et al 111 E Wisconsin Suite 1800 Milwaukee WI 53202

HERBERT, DAVID LEE, lawyer, author; b. Cleve., Oct. 1, 1948; s. William Clayton and Virginia Margaret (Battersby) H.; m. Lynda Jane Rosenkranz, Aug. 23, 1970; children—Laurance, Jason, Meredith. B.B.A., Kent State U., 1971; J.D., U. Akron, 1974. Bar: 1974, U.S. Dist. Ct. (no. dist.) Ohio 1974, U.S. Ct. Appeals (6th cir.) 1984. Asst. prosecutor Stark County Prosecutor's Office, Canton, Ohio, 1974-80; ptnr. Herbert, Treadon, Benson & Frieg, Canton, 1975—; pres. Profl. Reports Corp., 1986—; assoc. prof. Kent State U. (Ohio), 1980—; pres., turstee Lake Twp. Trustees, Hartville, Ohio, 1983—; mem., sec., asst. chmn. Ohio Gov.'s Organized Crime Law Enforcement Cons. Com., Columbus, 1976-78; comml. arbitrator Am. Arbitration Assn., 1983—; mem., sec. Stark County Pub. Defender Com., Canton, Ohio, 1982—. Author: Attorneys' Master Guide to Psychology, 1980; Legal Aspects of Preventive and Rehabilitative Exercise Programs, 1984; Corporations of Corruption: The Systematic Study of Organized Crime, 1984; others; editor: The Exercise Standards and Malpractice Reporter, 1986—; contbr. articles to profl. jours. Bd. dirs. Stark County Jr. Achievement, Canton, Ohio, 1983; mentor, pupil enrichment program Lake Local Sch. Bd., Hartville, Ohio, 1981-83. Recipient Continuing Legal Edn. award ABA/Am. Law Inst., 1975. Mem. ABA (liaison to jud. adminstrn. div. 1972-73), Def. Research Inst., Am. Coll. Sports Medicine, Stark County Trustees and Clks. Assn., Stark County Bar Assn. (exec. com. 1984, grievance com. 1979-82), Akron/Canton Def. Lawyers Assn., Ducks Unltd., North Canton Jaycees (com. chmn. 1975-76). Republican. General corporate, Insurance, State civil litigation. Home: 1055 Clearvale St NE Hartville OH 44632 Office: Herbert Treadon Benson & Frieg 4665 Douglas Circle NW Canton OH 44718

HERBERT, DONALD ROY, lawyer, business exec.; b. Mpls., Nov. 4, 1935; s. Roy Patrick and Bertha Lydia (Mathre) H.; m. Carol A. Elofson, June 28, 1958; children—Karen, James, Phillip. B.S.L., U. Minn., 1957, LL.B. cum laude, 1959. Mem. firm Dorsey, Owen, Barker, Scott & Barber, Mpls., 1959-62; corp. lawyer Peavey Co., Mpls., 1962-77, v.p., gen. counsel, sec., 1977-85; sr. v.p., gen. counsel, sec. Gelco Corp., Eden Prairie, Minn., 1985—. Mem. ABA, Minn. State Bar Assn. (bd. govs. 1976-77), Corp. Counsel Assn. Minn. (pres. 1975-76). Republican. Lutheran. Club: Mpls. Athletic. Home: 1500 16th Terr NW New Brighton MN 55112 Office: Gelco Corp 1 Gelco Dr Eden Prairie MN 55344

HERBERT, JAMES KELLER, lawyer; b. Titusville, Pa., Feb. 16, 1938; s. James Keller and Mary Louise (Carey) H.; m. Carol Sellers, Nov. 13, 1980; children—Michael Brendan, Mary Frances. B.S., Stanford U., 1959; LL.B., U. Calif., Berkeley, 1962. Bar: Calif. bar 1963. Asso. McCutchen, Black, Verleger & Shea, Los Angeles, 1962-64; asst. prof. Loyola U. Law Sch., Los Angeles, 1964-68; partner firm Richards, Watson, Dreyfuss & Gershon, Los Angeles, 1968-84; acad. dir. Barpassers, div. Barrister Project, 1985—; exec. dir. Harcourt, Brace, Jovanovich Legal, Inc., Los Angeles, 1966-85; adj. prof. McGeorge Sch. Law, UCLA, 1973-74. Served with Calif. Army N.G., 1956-62. Mem. Calif. Bar Assn., Los Angeles County Bar Assn. Club: Jonathan (Los Angeles). Legal education, Federal civil litigation, State civil litigation. Office: 1231 Santa Monica Mall Santa Monica CA 90401

HERBERT, JOHN CAMPBELL, lawyer; b. Erie, Pa., Dec. 3, 1950; s. John Wallace and Elizabeth (Campbell) H.; m. Janet Ruth Harder, Oct. 20, 1973; children: Jennifer, Vanessa. BS, Denison U., 1973; JD, Tulane U., 1977. Bar: D.C. 1977, La. 1978, U.S. Dist. Ct. (ea. dist.) La. 1978, U.S. Ct. Appeals (5th cir.) 1978, U.S. Dist. Ct. (mid. dist.) La. 1984, U.S. Ct. Claims 1984, U.S. Supreme Ct. 1984. Assoc. Deutch, Kerrigan & Stiles, New Orleans, 1978-79; ptnr. Simon, Peragine, Smith & Redfearn, New Orleans, 1979—. Mem. ABA (vice chmn. oil and gas production com. natural resources sect., La. del. young lawyers conv. 1982-84), La. Bar Assn. (sec. young lawyers sect. 1984), Fed. Energy Bar Assn. (bd. dirs. N.Y. chpt.). Democrat. Oil and gas leasing, Federal civil litigation. Office: Simon Peragine Smith & Redfearn 1100 Poydras 30th Floor New Orleans LA 70163

HERBERT, MICHAEL JOSEPH, law educator. BA summa cum laude, John Carroll U., 1974; JD magna cum laude, U. Mich., 1977. Bar: Wis. 1977, U.S. Dist. Ct. (ea. dist.) Wis. 1977, Ohio 1981, U.S. Dist. Ct. (no. dist.) Ohio 1981, Va. 1985. Assoc. Whyte & Hirschboeck, Milw., 1977-81, Buckingham, Doolittle & Burroughs, Akron, Ohio, 1981-82; asst. prof. law T.C. Williams Sch. Law, U. Richmond (Va.), 1982-85, assoc. prof., 1985—. Contbr. articles to profl. jours. Named Disting. Educator U. Richmond, 1985; recipient Program for Enhancing Teaching Effectiveness Summer award U. Richmond, 1986. Mem. ABA, Va. Bar Assn., Wis. Bar Assn., Am. Bankruptcy Inst., Order of Coif, Alpha Sigma Nu. Home: 1506 Westshire Ln Richmond VA 23233 Office: Univ Richmond TC Williams Sch Law Richmond VA 23173

HERBOLSHEIMER, ROBERT TILTON, lawyer; b. LaSalle, Ill., Mar. 9, 1954; s. George L. and Texie (Tilton) H.; m. Nancy Bruce, Sept. 4, 1983. BA, Carleton Coll., 1976; JD, Hamline U., 1980. Bar: Minn. 1980. Spl. asst., atty. advisor to dept. adminstr. EPA, Washington, 1981-83, spl. asst. to adminstr., 1983-85; assoc. Manatt, Phelps, Rothenberg & Evans, Washington, 1985—. Editor Jour. of Minn. Pub. Law, 1979-80. Pres. Minn. State Soc. of Washington, 1985-86; campaign mgr. Tom Trimarco for congress, Beverly, Mass., 1980; Minn. field dir. George Bush for Pres., Mpls., 1980. Mem. ABA (natural resources and family law sects.). Republican. Methodist. Environment, Legislative, Administrative and regulatory. Home: 2115 Westmoreland St Falls Church VA 22043 Office: Manatt Phelps Rothenberg & Evans 1200 New Hampshire Ave NW Washington DC 20036

HERBRUCK, JOHN HENRY, lawyer; b. Cleve., Jan. 12, 1944; s. Henry Alexander and Ione M. (Harsh) H.; m. Ann Eleizabeth Heil, Aug. 14, 1965; children: Matthew, Mary Ann. BS, Miami U., Oxford, Ohio, 1966; JD, Duquesne U., 1973. Bar: Pa. 1973, U.S. Dist. Ct. (we. dist.) Pa. 1973, U.S. Supreme Ct. 1985. Atty. Penn Cen.-Con-Rail, Pitts., 1973-77; atty., mgr. Crucible Steel Co., Midland, Pa., 1977-80; sole practice Beaver, Pa., 1980—; gen. counsel Beaver County Bd. Realtors, 1981—. V.p. Beaver Area Heritage Found., 1981-82; pres. Beaver Area Heritage Found., 1982-83; bd. dirs. Beaver Area Found., 1978—. Mem. ABA, Pa. Bar Assn., Allegheny County Bar Assn., Beaver County Bar Assn., Pa. Assn. Trial Lawyers. Republican. Episcopalian. Clubs: Connoquenissing Country Club (Ellwood City), Ft. McIntosh (Beaver, Pa.). Lodge: Elks (presiding justice 1981—). Avocation: golf. General practice, Family and matrimonial, Personal injury. Home: 540 River Rd Beaver PA 15009 Office: 647 3d St Beaver PA 15009

HERBST, PETER CALDWELL, lawyer; b. Northhampton, Mass., Mar. 21, 1948; s. John C. Jr. and Mildred C. (Caldwell) H.; m. Jane Butterworth; children: Peter, Nathaniel, Benjamin. BA, Washington Coll., Chestertown, Md., 1970; JD, U. Maine, 1973. Bar: Conn. 1973, U.S. Dist. Ct. Conn. 1975, U.S. Supreme Ct. 1978. Assoc. Catherine G. Roraback Law Offices, Canaan, Conn., 1973-76; ptnr. Febbroriello and Herbst, Torrington, Conn., 1976—; corporator Northwest Bank for Savings, Winsted, Conn., 1986—; adj. instr. real estate law, U. Conn., 1987—. Mem. bd. fin. Town of Goshen, Conn., 1979-85. Mem. Conn. Bar Assn. (exec. com. real property sect. 1985—). Democrat. Congregationalist. Lodge: Rotary. Real property. Home: North St Litchfield CT 06759 Office: Febbroriello and Herbst 355 Prospect St Torrington CT 06759

HERBST, TODD LESLIE, lawyer; b. N.Y.C., July 15, 1952; s. Seymour and Charlotte (Wolper) H.; m. Robyn Beth Kellman, June 3, 1979; children: Scott Marshall, Carly Nicole. BA, CUNY, 1974; JD, John Marshall Law Sch., 1977. Bar: N.Y. 1978. Assoc. Max E. Greenberg, Cantor & Reiss, N.Y.C., 1977-83, mng. ptnr., 1984—, ptnr., 1986—; bus. cons. Shimizu Am. Corp., N.Y.C., 1983—. Pres. Congregation Eitz Chaim Anshei Wolozon, N.Y.C., 1986. Mem. ABA, N.Y. State Bar Assn., N.Y. County Lawyers Assn. Jewish. Avocations: writing poetry, traveling, automobiles. Contracts commercial, Construction, Real property. Home: 2 Settlers Ct New City NY 10956 Office: Max E Greenberg Cantor et al 100 Church St New York NY 10057

HERCHENROETHER, HENRY CARL, JR., lawyer; b. Pitts., July 10, 1920; s. Henry C. and Edna M. (Meyer) H.; m. Nell Elizabeth Young, July 24, 1948; children: Richard H., Peter Y., Daniel D. BA, Westminster Coll., 1942; JD, U. Pitts., 1949. Bar: Pa. 1950. Assoc. Alter, Wright & Barron, Pitts., 1950-58, ptnr., 1958—. Bd. dirs., gen. counsel Pitts. Theol. Sem., Pitts., 1958—; mem. adv. bd. The Salvation Army, Pitts., 1960—; mayor Ben Avon Boro, Allegheny County, Pa., 1960-68. Served to lt. USNR, 1942-46. Recipient Disting. Alumni award Westminster Coll., New Wilmington, Pa., 1983. Mem. ABA, Nat. Assn. Coll. and Univ. Attys., Pa. Bar Assn., Allegheny County Bar Assn. Republican. Presbyterian. Club: Duquesne (Pitts.). Estate planning, Probate, Estate taxation. Home: 158 Dickson Ave Pittsburgh PA 15202 Office: Alter Wright & Barron 316 Fourth Ave Pittsburgh PA 15222-2002

HERCHENROETHER, PETER YOUNG, lawyer; b. Pitts., Apr. 14, 1954; s. Henry C. and Nell E. (Young) H.; m. Susan E. Suomi, Aug. 4, 1979; 1 child, Gregory A. BA, Westminster Coll., 1976; JD, Vanderbilt U., 1979. Bar: Pa. 1979, U.S. Dist. Ct. (we. dist.) Pa. 1979, U.S. Ct. Appeals (3d cir.) 1984, U.S. Supreme Ct. 1985. Assoc. Alter, Wright & Barron, Pitts., 1979-85, ptnr., 1986—. Mem. ABA, Pa. Bar Assn., Allegheny County Bar Assn. Republican. Presbyterian. General corporate, General practice, Probate. Office: Alter Wright & Barron 2000 Commonwealth Bldg 316 4th Ave Pittsburgh PA 15222-2002

HERD, HAROLD SHIELDS, state supreme ct. justice; b. Coldwater, Kans., June 3, 1918. B.A., Washburn U., 1941, J.D., 1942. Bar: Kans. bar 1943. Partner firm Rich and Herd, Coldwater, 1946-53; individual practice law Coldwater, 1953-79; justice Kans. Supreme Ct., 1979—; mayor, Coldwater, 1949-53, county atty., Comanche County, Kans., 1954-58; mem. Kans. Senate, 1965-73, minority floor leader, 1969-73. Bd. govs. Washburn Law Sch., 1974-78; mem. Kans. Com. for Humanities, 1975-80, chmn. 1980. Mem. S.W. Bar Assn. (pres. 1977), Kans. Bar Assn. (exec. council 1973-80). Office: Kans Jud Center 301 W 10th St Topeka KS 66612

HEREFORD, EARLE J., JR., lawyer; b. Richmond, Va., Apr. 16, 1944; s. Earle J. and Minnie (Spies) H.; m. Margaret Winsor, Aug. 25, 1979; 1 child, Elizabeth. BA, Yale U., 1968; JD, U. Wash., 1973. Bar: Wash. 1973, U.S. Dist. Ct. Wash. 1973, U.S. Ct. Appeals (9th cir.) 1973. Law clk. to judge U.S. Dist. Ct. (we. dist.) Wash., Seattle, 1973-76; asst. atty. gen. antitrust div. State of Wash., Seattle, 1977-81; assoc. Culp, Dwyer, Guterson & Grader, Seattle, 1981-84, ptnr., 1985—. Antitrust, Federal civil litigation. Home: 10576 15th Ave NW Seattle WA 98177 Office: Culp Dwyer Guterson & Grader One Union Sq 27th Floor Seattle WA 98101-3143

HERGE, J. CURTIS, lawyer; b. Flushing, N.Y., June 14, 1938; s. Henry Curtis and Josephine E. (Breen) H.; m. Joyce Dorean Humbert, Aug. 20, 1960; children: Cynthia Lynda, Christopher Curtis. Student, Cornell U., 1956-58; B.A., Rutgers U., 1961, J.D. (Sebastian Gaeta scholar), 1963. Bar: N.Y. 1964, U.S. Supreme Ct. 1970, U.S. Ct. Claims 1974, D.C. 1974, Va. 1976. Assoc. firm Mudge Rose Guthrie & Alexander, N.Y.C., 1963-71; spl. asst. to atty. gen. U.S. Dept. Justice, Washington, 1973; assoc. solicitor conservation and wildlife U.S. Dept. Interior, Washington, 1973-74; asst. to sec. and chief staff U.S. Dept. Interior, 1974-76; ptnr. Sedam & Herge, McLean, Va., 1976-85, Herge, Sparks, Christopher & Biondi, McLean, Va., 1985—; dir. Diversified Labs., Inc., Ann E.W. Stone & Assocs., Inc., Job Sharers, Inc., Palmer Tech. Services, Inc., Eaton Design Group, Inc., Savant Press, Inc., Nat. Bank No. Va., No. Va. Banking Corp. Bd. dirs. Nat. Conservative Polit. Action Com., Citizens United for Am., Am. Def. Lobby, Council Nat. Def., Renascence Found., The Am. Lobby Econ. Recovery Taskforce; mem. adv. bd. Washington Legal Found., Western Legal Found., Nat. Taxpayers Legal Fund, Va. Commonwealth escheator Loudoun County and City of Fairfax, 1979-83; co-dir. Presdl. Inaugural Com., 1973; dep. dir. spokesmen resources Com. for Reelection of Pres., 1971-72; mem. natural resources council Republican Nat. Com.; mem. Fairfax County Rep. Com.; mem. Office Pres.-Elect Fed. Election Commn. Transition Team, 1980; co-chmn. N.Y. Honor Am. Day, 1970; speaker fed. election laws. Mem. Am., N.Y. State, Va., D.C. bar assns., Phi Kappa Sigma. Club: Capitol Hill. Administrative and regulatory, General corporate, Probate. Home: 1102 Waynewood Blvd Alexandria VA 22308 Office: Herge Sparks Christopher & Biondi 8201 Greensboro Dr McLean VA 22102

HERIN, WILLIAM ABNER, judge; b. Macon, Ga., May 14, 1908; A.B., U. Fla., 1930, J.D., 1933. Bar: Fla. 1933. Assoc., Hudson & Cason, 1933-48; judge Circuit Ct. Fla. 11th circuit, Miami, 1948-84; ret. 1984; adminstrv. asst. to Congressman J. Mark Wilcox of Fla., 1936-38; legis. counsel Dade County Del., Fla. Legislature, 1939-41; legal adviser office Fgn. Liquidation Commn., Dept. State, Far East, 1946-47; asst. atty. County of Dade, Fla., 1938-47; of counsel Duff and Brown, Miami, 1986—; ofcl. ct. historian 11th Jud. Cir. Fla.; trustee Nat. Conf. Met. Cts., pres., 1969-70; mem. vis. com. Inst. for Ct. Mgmt. Founder, bd. dirs. Boys Club Greater Miami; bd. dirs. Met. YMCA; mem. adv. bd. South Fla. council Boy Scouts Am. Served to capt. USNR, 1941-68; ret. Mem. ABA, Fla. Bar (chmn. pub. relations com. 1941), Dade County Bar Assn. (v.p. 1941), Am. Law Inst., Am. Judicature Soc., Phi Beta Kappa, Phi Kappa Phi, Phi Delta Phi. Author: Trial Jurors' Handbook, 1952-82; Local Circuit Court Rules, 1957-82; Standard Grand Jury Charge, 1958-83; contbr. articles to legal jours. Jurisprudence. Home: 470 NE 51st St Miami FL 33137 Office: 14 SW 2d Ave Miami FL 33130

HERLIHY, EDWARD D., lawyer; b. Glens Falls, N.Y., May 4, 1947. BA, Hobart Coll., 1969; JD, George Washington U., 1972. Assoc. Wachtell, Lipton, Rosen & Katz, N.Y.C. Contbr. articles to profl. jours. Securities. Office: Wachtell Lipton Rosen & Katz 299 Park Ave New York NY 10171

HERLIHY, THOMAS MORTIMER, lawyer; b. N.Y.C., Apr. 8, 1953; s. John Wilfred and Mary Frances (O'Sullivan) H.; m. Janice Anne Lazzaro, Aug. 26, 1978; children: Carolyn Jane, John Wilfred II. BA in History, Columbia U., 1975; JD, Fordham U., 1978. Bar: Calif. 1978, U.S. Dist. Ct. (no. dist.) Calif. 1978, U.S. Dist. Ct. (ea. and so. dists.) Calif. 1979, U.S. Dist. Ct. (cen. dist.) Calif. 1984, U.S. Ct. Appeals (9th cir.) 1979. Assoc. Pettit & Martin, San Francisco, 1978-82; ptnr. Kornblum, Kelly & Herlihy, San Francisco, 1982—; lectr. Rutter Group, trial skills program Calif. Continuing Edn. of Bar, 1983-86. Mem. ABA (litigation sect., torts and ins. practice sect.), Calif. Bar Assn., San Francisco Bar Assn., Calif. Def. Counsel, Def. Research Inst. Republican. Roman Catholic. Clubs: Olympic, Commonwealth (San Francisco); Columbia. Insurance, Federal civil litigation, State civil litigation. Home: 1424 Cortez Ave Burlingame CA 94010 Office: Kornblum Kelly & Herlihy 445 Bush St San Francisco CA 94108

HERMAN, CHARLES JACOB, lawyer, accounting firm executive; b. Balt., May 31, 1937; s. Jacob and Edna M. (Hackett) H.; m. Frances L. Leonard, Oct. 25, 1958; children—Alison, Charles J., Leonard. B.A., U. Balt., 1958, J.D., 1961. Bar: Md. 1961. Atty. Fidelity & Deposit, N.Y.C., 1958-69, Aetna Ins. Co., Hartford, Conn., 1969-71, INA, Phila., 1971-76; officer Home Ins. Co., N.Y.C., 1976-80; nat. ptnr., dir. litigation support services Laventhol & Horwath, Phila., 1980—. Co-author: (manual) Bonds on Public Works, 1986. Past pres. St. John's Lutheran Ch., Morrisville, Pa; bd. dirs. Luth. Home, Germantown, Germantown Home. Served to sgt. U.S. Army, 1961-66. Mem. ABA, Internat. Assn. Ins. Counsel, Am. Arbitration Assn., Md. Bar Assn. Republican. Lutheran. Insurance, Contracts commercial, State civil litigation. Home: 957 Randolph Dr Yardley PA 19067 Office: Laventhol & Horwath CPAs 1845 Walnut St Philadelphia PA 19103

HERMAN, LEE MERIDETH, lawyer; b. Phila., Apr. 14, 1954; s. Frederick Reid and Jeanne (Spoont) H.; m. Patricia Foster Yusem, Apr. 28, 1985; 1 child, David Foster. BS in Econs. magna cum laude, Boston Coll., 1975, JD, 1978. Bar: Pa. 1978, N.J. 1978, U.S. Dist. Ct. Pa. 1978, U.S. Dist. Ct. N.J. 1978. Law clk. to presiding judge Ct. Common Pleas, Phila., 1978-79; ptnr. Bayer, Herman & Leizerowski, Phila., 1979-82, Needle, Feldman & Herman, Phila., 1982-85; sole practice Phila., 1985—. Assoc. editor Am. Jour. Law and Medicine, 1977-78. Counsel Dropsie Coll., Phila., 1978-82; bd. dirs. Temple Adath Israel, Merion. Pa., 1982—, pres. men's club, 1982-85, Future Leadership of Jewish Nat. Fund, Phila. Counsel. Republican. Jewish. Club: Golden Slipper. Lodge: Masons. Consumer commercial, Probate, State civil litigation. Home: 7446 Ruskin Rd Philadelphia PA 19151 Office: 3900 Ford Rd Suite 13 Philadelphia PA 19131 also: 75 Haddon Ave Suite 200 Haddonfield NJ 08033

HERMAN, RUSS MICHEL, lawyer; b. New Orleans, Apr. 26, 1942; s. Harry and Reba Nell (Hoffman) H.; m. Barbara Ann Kline, July 5, 1965; children—Stephen Jay, Penny Lynn, Elizabeth Rose. B.A., Tulane U., 1963, LL.B., 1966. Bar: La. 1966, U.S. Dist. Ct. (ea. dist.) La. 1966, U.S. Ct. Appeals (5th cir.) 1970, U.S. Supreme Ct., 1972. Law clk. U.S. Ct. Appeals (4th cir.), New Orleans, 1965-66; ptnr. Herman, Herman, Katz & Cotlar

(formerly Herman & Herman), New Orleans, 1966—; sec. Citizens for Justice, Inc., 1980; guest lectr. Loyola U. Law Sch., La. State U. Law Sch., Practising Law Inst.; adj. prof. law Tulane U. Law Sch., 1979—; spl. trial counsel New Orleans Aviation Bd., 1974-76; mem. adv. council La. chpt. Am. Arbitration Assn., 1976—; mem. Civil Dist. Ct. Commn. on Local Rules and Forms, 1979, U.S. Dist. Ct. Com. on Disciplinary Rules and Revision Local Rules, 1979-80; mem. disciplinary com. U.S. Dist. Ct. (ea. dist.) La., 1980—. Mem. New Orleans Bd. Zoning Appeals, 1974-80; bd. dirs. Jewish Welfare Fedn., New Orleans; trustee Jewish Family and Children's Services, New Orleans; campaign chmn. for Gov. David C. Treen in Greater Met. area, 1980, 84. Served with U.S. Air N.G., 1959-65. Named Boss of Yr., New Orleans Legal Secs. Assn., 1981-82; life fellow Roscoe Pound Found. Mem. Fed. Bar Assn., Assn. Trial Lawyers Am. (bd. govs. 1986—, parlimentarian 1987—), ABA, La. Bar Assn. (ho. of dels. 1980-81, 85-86, asst. bar examiner 1975-80), La. Bar Found. (trustee 1980—), La. Trial Lawyers Assn. (pres. 1980-81, Pres.'s award 1977, Leadership award 1981-82), Boge Doga Soc. of Barristers, Ky. Trial Lawyers Assn., N.Y. State Trial Lawyers Assn., Calif. Trial Lawyers Assn., Pa. Trial Lawyers Assn., Trial Lawyers for Pub. Justice, Civil Justice Found., La. Found. for Law and Soc. (trustee), Ariz. Trial Lawyers Assn., Roscoe Pound Soc., Coalition for Consumer Justice. Democrat. Jewish. Federal civil litigation, State civil litigation, Personal injury. Home: 5346 Chestnut St New Orleans LA 70115 Office: Herman Herman Katz & Cotlar 820 O'Keefe Ave New Orleans LA 70113

HERMAN, STEPHEN ALLEN, lawyer; b. Suffolk, Va., Nov. 27, 1943; m. Sally Jean Mansbach, Sept. 7, 1968; children: Braden, Andrew. BS, U. Pa., 1965; LLB, U. Va., 1968. Bar: Va. 1968, D.C. 1970, U.S. Ct. Appeals (D.C. cir.) 1970. Instr. law U. Chgo., 1968-70; assoc. Kirkland & Ellis, Washington, 1970-75, ptnr., 1975—. Author: FERC Practice and Procedure, 1984. Mem. ABA, Fed. Energy Bar Assn. FERC practice, Contracts commercial, Administrative and regulatory. Office: Kirkland & Ellis 655 15th St NW Washington DC 20005

HERMAN, STEPHEN CHARLES, lawyer; b. Johnson City, N.Y., Apr. 28, 1951; s. William Herman and Myrtle Stella (Clark) Keithline; m. Jeanne Ellen Nelson, Sept. 9, 1972; children—Neelie Kristine, Stefanie Anne, Christopher William. Student Cedarville Coll., 1969-72; B.A., Wright State U., 1973; J.D., Ohio No. U., 1976. Bar: Mo. 1977, Ill. 1977, U.S. Dist. Ct. (no. dist.) Ill. 1979, U.S. Dist. Ct. (ea. dist.) Mo. 1978, U.S. Ct. Appeals (D.C. cir.) 1979, U.S. Ct. Appeals (5th cir.) 1980, U.S. Ct. Appeals (7th cir.) 1979. Atty., Mo. Pacific Railroad Co., St. Louis, 1977-78; assoc. Belnap, McCarthy, Spencer, Sweeney & Harkaway, Chgo., 1978-82; ptnr. Belnap, Spencer & McFarland, Chgo., 1982-83, Belnap, Spencer, McFarland & Emrich, Chgo., 1983-84, Belnap, Spencer, McFarland, Emrich & Herman, Chgo., 1984—. Mem. ABA, Mo. Bar Assn., Ill. State Bar Assn., Chgo. Bar Assn., Met. Bar Assn. of St. Louis, Assn. of Transp. Practitioners. Club: Tower, (Chgo.). Transportation, Administrative and regulatory, Federal civil litigation. Home: 575 Ivy Ct Lake Forest IL 60045 Office: Belnap Spencer McFarland Emrich & Herman 20 N Wacker Dr Chicago IL 60606

HERMAN, STEVEN ROGER, lawyer; b. Glendale, Ariz., Nov. 10, 1952; s. Richard Edwin and Darlys Elaine (Steuber) H.; m. Barbara Ann Stoneman, June 9, 1979; children: Casey, Michael. BS in Econs., Ariz. State U., 1974; postgrad., Harvard U., 1978; JD, U. Calif., Berkeley, 1978. Bar: Ariz., 1978, Calif., 1978; CPA, Calif., 1980. Staff acct. Lester Witte & Co., Phoenix, 1973-75; assoc. Graham & James, San Francisco, 1978-80; jr. ptnr. O'Connor, Cavanagh, Anderson, Westover, Killingsworth & Beshears, Phoenix, 1980—; lectr. Golden Gate U., San Francisco, 1984. Vol. Talieson West Frank Lloyd Wright Sch. Architecture, Scottsdale, Ariz., 1986. Mem. Ariz. Bar Assn. (speaker 1982, chmn. com. on legis. tax sect. 1983-84). Lutheran. Avocations: skiing, reading, music, theatre. Real property, Securities, Taxation--partnerships.. Home: 4009 E Coolidge Phoenix AZ 85108 Office: O'Connor Cavanagh Anderson et al One E Camelback Suite 1100 Phoenix AZ 85012-1656

HERMAN, SUSAN N., legal educator; b. Bklyn., Feb. 16, 1947; d. Nathan H. and Frances (Pickus) H.; m. Paul A. Gangsei, June 16, 1978; 1 child, Erica Herman Gangsei. AB, Barnard Coll., 1968; JD, NYU, 1974. Bar: N.Y. 1975, U.S. Dist. Ct. (so., we. and no. dists.) N.Y. 1975, U.S. Ct. Appeals (2d cir.) 1975. Law clk. to presiding justice U.S. Ct. Appeals (2d cir.), N.Y.C., 1974-76; assoc. dir. Prisoners' Legal Services N.Y., N.Y.C., 1976-80; from asst. prof. to prof. Bklyn. Law Sch., 1980—; mem. criminal procedures com. U.S. Dist. Ct. (ea. dist.) N.Y., Bklyn., 1986, coordinator training program civil litigation fund, 1984. Contbr. articles to profl. jours. Mem. due process com. ACLU, 1982—, chmn., 1985—. Mem. ABA (corrections com.), Order of Coif. Criminal, Civil rights. Office: Bklyn Law Sch 250 Joralemon St Brooklyn NY 11201

HERMAN, WILLIAM CHARLES, lawyer; b. N.Y.C., Nov. 6, 1935; s. Milton and Hortense (Rosenthal) H.; m. Elizabeth Leitner; children: Howard, Sarah Jane. BA, CCNY, 1958; LLB, Columbia U., 1959. Bar: N.Y. 1960, U.S. Dist. Ct. (so. and ea. dists.) 1964, U.S. Ct. Appeals (2d cir.) 1964, U.S. Supreme Ct. 1964. Assoc. Howard H. Spellman, N.Y.C., 1960-61; sole practice N.Y.C., 1962-65; assoc. Gilbert S. Rosenthal, N.Y.C., 1965-70; ptnr. Rosenthal & Herman, N.Y.C., 1970-82, Rosenthal, Herman & Mantel, P.C., N.Y.C., 1982—. Bd. dirs., pres. Camphill Spl. Schs., Inc., Glenmoore, Pa., 1980—; bd. dirs., v.p. Camphill Found., Kimberton, Pa., 1982—; trustee Camphill Assn., N.Am., Copake, N.Y., 1982—. Served with U.S. Army, 1959-60. Fellow Am. Acad. Matrimonial Lawyers (chmn. matrimonial law com. 1982-84); mem. ABA, N.Y. State Bar Assn., N.Y. County Lawyers Assn. (bd. dirs. 1979-85). Avocations: charitable activities, fishing. Family and matrimonial, State civil litigation. Home: 95 Lord Kitchener Rd New Rochelle NY 10804 Office: 310 Madison Ave New York NY 10017

HERMANIES, JOHN HANS, lawyer; b. Aug. 19, 1922; s. John and Lucia (Eckstein) H.; m. Dorothy Jean Steinbrecher, Jan. 3, 1953. A.B., Pa. State U., 1944; J.D., U. Cin., 1948. Bar: Ohio 1948. Atty. Indsl. Commn. Ohio, 1948-50; asst. atty. gen. State of Ohio, 1951-57, asst. to gov., 1957-59; ptnr. Hermanies & Major (formerly Beall, Hermanies, Bortz & Major), Cin., 1976-82; mem. Ohio Supreme Ct., 1976-82; mem. Ohio Bd. Bar Examiners, 1963-68. Mem. Southwest Ohio Regional Transit Authority, 1973-76, trustee U. Cin., 1977—; bd. election Hamilton County, Ohio, 1984—; chmn. exec. com. Hamilton County Rep. Party, 1974—. Served with USMC, World War II. Mem. ABA, Ohio Acad. Trial Lawyers Assn., Am. Judicature Soc. Clubs: Bankers, Queen City, Highland Country. State civil litigation, Workers' compensation. Home: 2110 Columbia Pkwy Cincinnati OH 45202 Office: Hermanies & Major 30 Garfield Pl Suite 740 Cincinnati OH 45202

HERMANN, DONALD HAROLD JAMES, lawyer, educator; b. Southgate, Ky., Apr. 6, 1943; s. Albert Joseph and Helen Marie (Snow) H. A.B. (George E. Gamble Honors scholar), Stanford U., 1965; J.D., Columbia U., 1968; LL.M., Harvard U., 1974; M.A. (Univ. scholar), Northwestern U., 1979, Ph.D., 1981. Bar: Ariz. 1968, Wash. 1969, Ky. 1971, Ill. 1972, U.S. Supreme Ct. 1974. Mem. staff, directorate devel. plans Dept. Def., 1964-65; With Legis. Drafting Research Fund, Columbia U., 1966-68; asst. dean Columbia Coll., 1967-68; mem. faculty U. Wash., Seattle, 1968-71, U. Ky., Lexington, 1971-72; mem. faculty DePaul U., 1972—, prof. law and philosophy, 1978—, dir. acad. programs and interdisciplinary study, 1975-76, assoc. dean, 1975-78, dir. Health Law Inst., 1985—; lectr. dept. philosophy Northwestern U., 1979-81; counsel DeWolfe, Poynton & Stevens, 1984—; vis. prof. Washington U., St. Louis, 1974, U. Brazilia, 1976; lectr. law Am. Soc. Found., 1975-78, Sch. Edn. Northwestern U., 1974-76, Christ Coll. Cambridge (Eng.) U., 1977, U. Athens, 1980; vis. scholar U. N.D., 1983; mem. NEH seminar on property and rights Stanford U., 1981; participant law and econs. program U. Rochester, 1974; mem. faculty summer seminar in law and humanities UCLA, 1978; Bicentennial Fellow of U.S. Constitution Claremont Coll., 1986; bd. dirs. Council Legal Edn. Opportunity, Ohio Valley Consortium, 1972, Ill. Bar Automated Research Corp., 1975-81, Criminal Law Consortium Cook County, Ill., 1977-80; cons. Adminstrv. Office Ill. Cts., 1975—; reporter cons. Ill. Jud. Conf., 1972—; mem. Center for Law Focused Edn., Chgo., 1977—; faculty Instituto Superiore Internazionale Di Science Criminali, Siracusa, Italy, 1978—; bd. dirs. Horizons Community Services, 1985; cons. Commerce Fedn., State of São Paulo, Brazil, 1975. Editor: Hosp. Law. Bd. dirs. Ctr. for Ch.-State Studies, 1982—, Horizons Community Services, 1985—. John Noble fellow Columbia U., 1968; fellow U. Chgo, 1975-76, Harvard U., 1973-74, Northwestern U., 1978-82, Stanford U. 1981; NEH fellow Cornell U., 1982, Judicial fellow U.S. Supreme Ct., 1983-84, Bicentennial fellow of the U.S. Constitution, Claremont Coll., 1986. Mem. ABA, Ill. Bar Assn., Chgo. Bar Assn., Am. Acad. Polit. and Social Sci., Am. Law Inst., Nat. Health Lawyers Assn., Ill. Assn. Hosp. Attys., Ma. Soc. Law and Medicine, Am. Soc. Polit. and Legal Philosophy, Nat. Health Lawyers Assn., Am. Judicature Soc., Am. Philos. Assn., Soc. for Bus. Ethics, Soc. for Phenomenology and Existential Philosophy, Internat. Assn. Philosophy of Law and Soc., Soc. Writers on Legal Subjects, Internat. Penal Law Soc., Soc. Law and Med., Soc. Am. Law Tchrs., Am. Assn. Law Schs. (del., sect. chmn., chmn. sect. on jurisprudence), Am. Acad. Hosp. Attys., Ill. Assn. Hosp. Attys., Chgo. Hist. Preservation Soc., Evanston Hist. Soc., Northwestern U. Alumni Assn., Signet Soc. of Harvard. Episcopalian. Clubs: Hasty Pudding (Harvard); University, Quadrangle (Chgo.); Univ. (Evanston). Health, Jurisprudence, Criminal. Home: 1243 Forest Ave Evanston IL 60202 also: 880 Lakeshore Dr Chicago IL 60611 Office: De Paul Univ Coll Law 25 E Jackson St Chicago IL 60604

HERMANN, PHILIP J., lawyer; b. Cleve., Sept. 17, 1916; s. Isadore and Gazella (Gross) H.; m. Cecilia Alexander, Dec. 28, 1945; children: Gary, Ann. Student, Hiram Coll., 1935-37; B.A., Ohio State U., 1939; J.D., Western Res. U., 1942. Bar: Ohio 1942. Of counsel Hermann Cahn & Schneider (and predecessors), Cleve., 1946-86, 1986—; pres., then chmn. bd. Jury Verdict Research, Cleve. Author: Better Settlements Through Leverage, 1965, Do You Need a Lawyer?, 1980; contbr. legal articles to various publs. Served to lt. comdr. USNR, 1942-46, PTO. Mem. ABA (past vice chmn. casualty law com., past chmn. use of modern tech. com.), Ohio Bar Assn. (past chmn. ins. com., past chmn. fed. ct. com., past mem. ho. of dels.), Cleve. Bar Assn. (past chmn. membership com.), Am. Law Firm Assn. (past chmn. bd.), Fedn. Ins. Counsel. Club: Walden Golf and Tennis. Federal civil litigation, State civil litigation, Insurance. Home: 615 Acadia St Apt P7 Aurora OH 44202 Office: Hermann Cahn & Schnieder 1070 Huntington Bank Bldg Cleveland OH 44115

HERMANN, THOMAS GEORGE, lawyer; b. Cleve., June 15, 1935; s. George James and Elizabeth Virginia (Kreckel) H.; m. Maria Veres, Aug. 31, 1968 A.B., John Carroll U., Cleve., 1963; J.D., Cleve. State U., 1969. Bar: Ohio 1969, U.S. Dist. Ct. (no. dist.) Ohio, 1970, U.S. Ct. Appeals (6th cir.) 1971, N.Y. 1986, U.S. Dist. Ct. (so. dist.) N.Y. 1986. Atty., Legal Aid Soc. Cleve., 1969-70; assoc. Squire, Sanders & Dempsey, Cleve., 1970-79, ptnr., 1979—; lectr. seminars, Cleve. Advocacy Inst. Served with U.S. Army, 1954-57. Recipient Prize Project award ABA-AMA, 1982; Exceptional Performance citation Def. Research Inst., 1982; Merit Service award Bar Assn. Greater Cleve., 1981-82. Mem. ABA (chmn. law office tech. com. sect. sci. and tech., 1982—), Bar Assn. Greater Cleve. (chmn. med.-legal com., chmn. group travel com.), Cuyahoga County Bar Assn., Cleve. Assn. Civil Trial Attys. (pres. 1981-82). Republican. Club: Cleve. Athletic. State civil litigation, Federal civil litigation, Computer. Office: Squire Sanders & Dempsey 1800 Huntington Bank Bldg Cleveland OH 44115

HERMES, PAMELA JANE, lawyer; b. Breckenridge, Minn., Apr. 17, 1956; d. Claire Joseph and Evelyn Cecil (Geisen) H.; m. Frank Joseph Dooley, June 19, 1982. BS summa cum laude, U. N.D., 1978, JD with distinction, 1981. Bar: N.D. 1982, Idaho 1982, U.S. Dist. Ct. N.D. 1982, Minn. 1983, U.S. Ct. Appeals (8th cir.) 1986. Law clk. to presiding justice Idaho Supreme Ct., Boise, 1981-83; assoc. Vogel, Brantner, Kelly, Knudson, Weir & Bye, Fargo, N.D., 1983-84, shareholder, 1985—. Sr. editor N.D. Law Rev., 1980-81. Mem. City Election Bd. Resolutions, Fargo, 1985—; performer with Nativity Contemporary Singers, 1983—. Mem. ABA, N.D. State Bar Assn., Idaho State Bar Assn., Cass County Bar Assn., Order of Coif, Order of Barristers. Democrat. Roman Catholic. Clubs: Great Plains Bicycling, Lake Agassiz Pacers. Avocations: triathloning, running, knitting, skiing, reading. State civil litigation, Insurance, Personal injury. Home: 97 21st Ave N Fargo ND 58102 Office: Vogel Brantner et al 502 1st Ave N Fargo ND 58102

HERN, JOSEPH GEORGE, JR., lawyer; b. Long Branch, N.J., Apr. 13, 1956; s. Joseph George Sr. and Virginia Ann (Hertlein) H.; m. Francine Law, May 29, 1982. BA, Rutgers U., 1978; JD, Stetson Coll. Law, 1982. Bar: Fla. 1982, U.S. Dist. Ct. (mid. dist.) Fla. 1984, U.S. Ct. Appeals (11th cir.) 1984. Law clk. to presiding judge Commonwealth Ct. Pa., Harrisburg, 1982-84; assoc. Wendel & Chritton, Lakeland, Fla., 1984—. Mem. Hist. Preservation Bd., Lakeland, 1985—, chmn. 1986—; bd. dirs. Vols. in Service to Elderly, Lakeland, 1985—, Cath. Social Services Polk County, Lakeland, 1984—, vice chmn., 1986—. Charles A. Dana Stetson Coll. Law, 1981-82. Mem. ABA, Fla. Bar, Lakeland Bar Assn., Polk County Trial Lawyers Assn., Comml. Law League, Lakeland Jaycees (Jaycee of Yr. 1984-85, v.p., dir. 1984—). Democrat. Club: Lakeland Christina. Lodge: Rotary. Avocations: travel, sports, reading. State civil litigation, Consumer commercial, Family and matrimonial. Home: 3015 Willow Ave Lakeland FL 33813 Office: Wendel & Chritton 5300 S Florida Ave Lakeland FL 33807

HERNANDEZ, DANIEL MARIO, lawyer; b. Tampa, Fla., Sept. 26, 1951; s. Mario and Margaret (Alvarez) H.; m. Debra Sue Coleman, Dec. 6, 1980. BA, U. South Fla., 1972; JD, U. Fla., 1976. Bar: Fla. 1977, U.S. Dist. Ct. (middle dist.) Fla. 1977, U.S. Dist. Ct. (so. dist.) Fla. 1983. Asst. state atty. State Atty.'s Office, Tampa, 1977-82; assoc. Wilson and Sawyer P.A., Tampa, 1983; sole practice Tampa, 1983—. mem. steering com. Campaign for Judge Sam Pendino, Tampa, 1986. Mem. Criminal Def. Lawyers Assn., Hillsborough County Bar Assn. (ethics com., fee arbitration com.). Democrat. Baptist. Avocations: tennis, jogging. Criminal, Family and matrimonial, Personal injury. Office: 902 N Armenia Ave Tampa FL 33609

HERNANDEZ, DAVID N(ICHOLAS), lawyer; b. Albuquerque, Nov. 5, 1954; s. B.C. and Evangeline (C De Baca) H.; m. Alice A. McLish, June 7, 1975. BA, U. N.Mex., 1975, MBA, 1978, JD, 1979. Bar: N.Mex. 1979, U.S. Dist. Ct. N.Mex. 1979. Law clk. to presiding justice N.Mex. Supreme Ct., Santa Fe, 1979-80; assoc. Knight, Custer & Duncan, Albuquerque, 1980-82; sole practice Albuquerque, 1982—; mem. com. rules appellate ct. procedure N.Mex. Supreme Ct., 1984—; bd. dirs. Delta Dental N.Mex., Albuquerque. Mem. Environ. Planning Commn., Albuquerque, 1984-86, PHS assocs. Presbyn. Healthcare Found., 1985—. Named one of Outstanding Young Men Am., 1980. Mem. ABA, N.Mex. Bar Assn., Albuquerque Bar Assn., Am. Judicatur Soc., Greater Albuquerque C. of C. (bd. dirs. 1982-86, polit. action com. 1983-85). Avocations: tennis, golf, reading, fishing, politics. Contracts commercial, Probate, Real property.

HEROLD, KARL GUENTER, lawyer; b. Munich, Fed. Republic Germany, Feb. 3, 1947; s. Guenter K.B. and Eleonore E.E. (Arndt) H.; m. Helen Robinson, Sept. 14, 1968; children: Deanna, Donna, Nicole, Jessica, Christine. BS, Bowling Green State U., 1969; JD, Case Western Res. U., 1972. Bar: Ohio 1872, N.Y. 1985. Ptnr. Jones, Day, Reavis & Pogue, Cleve., 1972—; trustee Internat. and Comparative Law Ctr. Southwest Legal Found., Dallas, 1983; bd. dirs. Didier Taylor Refractories Corp., Cin., Redland Corp., San Antonio, v.p., Redland Credit Corp., San Antonio, v.p., Redland Fin. Inc., San Antonio, v.p., 1979-86. Trustee Cleve. Internat. Program, 1982—. Mem. ABA, Internat. Bar Assn., Order of Coif, Omicron Delta Kappa. Private international, General corporate. Home: 2212 Edgeview Dr Hudson OH 44236 Office: Jones Day Reavis & Pogue 1700 Huntington Bldg Cleveland OH 44115

HERON, JULIAN BRISCOE, JR., lawyer; b. Washington, Dec. 17, 1939; s. Julian B. Sr. and Doris S. (Strange) H.; m. Kathleen Ann Sweeney, Aug. 13, 1983; children: Kimberle, Melissa, Julian III, Kevin. BS, U. Ky., 1962, LLB, 1965. Bar: Ky. 1965, D.C. 1966, U.S. Dist. Ct. D.C. 1966, Md. 1968, U.S. Ct. Appeals D.C. cir.) 1968, U.S. Supreme Ct. 1968. Ptnr. Pope, Ballard & Loos, Washington, 1968-81, Heron, Burchette, Ruckert & Rothwell, Washington, 1981—. Pres. Washington Internat. Horse Show, 1984, 85. Served to capt. USAF, 1965-68. Mem. ABA (chmn. agri. com. of adminstrv. law sect.), D.C. Bar Assn. (chmn. ethics com.), Ky. Bar Assn., Md. Bar Assn., Bar Assn. of D.C. Republican. Roman Catholic. Clubs: Faquier Springs Country Club (Warrenton, Va.). Administrative and regulatory, Private international, Legislative. Office: Heron Burchette Ruckert & Rothwell 1025 Thomas Jefferson St Suite 700 Washington DC 20007

HERPST, ROBERT DIX, lawyer, optical company executive; b. Teaneck, N.J., Jan. 23, 1947; s. Harold Dix and Anita Augusta (Adams) H.; divorced; children: Katherine Elizabeth, Lauren Gabriel. BS, NYU, 1969; JD, Rutgers U., 1972. Bar: N.J., U.S. Supreme Ct. Assoc. Pitney, Hardin & Kipp, Morristown, N.J., 1972-77; assoc. BOC Group, Inc., Montvale, N.J., 1977-87, div. counsel, 1978-80, assoc. corp. counsel, 1980-82, corp. counsel, asst. sec., 1982—; pres. Internat. Crystal Labs., Inc., Garfield, N.J., 1982—. Mem. ABA (internat. bus. law com., overseas equity and joint venture investment subcom. of corp., banking and bus. law sect.). Avocations: golf, politics, stock market, graphic arts. General corporate, Private international, Mergers and acquisitions. Home: 1 Lincoln St Suffern NY 10901 Office: The BOC Group Inc 85 Chestnut Ridge Rd Montvale NJ 07645

HERR, MICHAEL JOSEPH, lawyer; b. Galesburg, Ill., Nov. 20, 1954; s. Robert Joseph and Theresa Lucille (Endres) H.; m. Lori Ann Nelson, Oct. 16, 1982. BS, Northwestern U., 1976; JD, U. Ill., 1980. Bar: Ill. 1980, U.S. Dist. Ct. (cen. dist.) Ill. 1981, U.S. Ct. Appeals (7th cir.) 1983. Assoc. Barney Olson II Ltd., Galesburg, 1980-81, Law Office Karl Bredberg, Aledo, Ill., 1981—; asst. pub. defender Mercer County, Aledo, 1981—; atty. City of New Boston, Ill., 1983-85. Mem. ABA, Ill. Bar Assn., Mercer County Bar Assn. (sec., treas. 1984—), Aledo C. of C. Roman Catholic. Lodge: Kiwanis. Avocations: jogging, reading, traveling, collecting mil. miniatures, baseball. General practice, Criminal, State civil litigation. Home: 1306 SW 3d Ave Aledo IL 61231 Office: Law Office Karl Bredberg 403 SE 3d Ave Aledo IL 61231

HERR, PHILIP MICHAEL, lawyer, tax consultant; b. N.Y.C., June 22, 1955; s. Norman and Grace (Sporn) H.; m. Lorrie Wiener, Nov. 23, 1978; children: Gabrielle Robyn, Nicole Dana, Adam Russell. BS, BA magna cum laude, Long Island U., C.W. Post Ctr., 1977; JD, Ohio No. U., 1980. Bar: N.Y. 1981, U.S. Tax Ct. 1982. Tax staff Ernst & Whinney, N.Y.C., 1980-82; tax sr. Arthur Young & Co., N.Y.C., 1982-83; tax supr. Wiss & Co., Livingston, N.J., 1983—; adj. prof. bus. Ohio No. U., Ada, 1978-80, Fairleigh Dickinson U., Rutherford, N.J., 1983-86; lectr. IRS, 1986—. Editor tax and financial Jour., 1985. Mem. ABA (tax, family and real property, probate and trust law sects.), N.Y. State Bar Assn., Pi Gamma Mu. Republican. Jewish. Avocations: racquetball, swimming. Pension, profit-sharing, and employee benefits, Estate planning, Taxation-estate, gift, trust, personal and corporate. Home: 8 Cross Ridge Circle Marlboro NJ 07746 Office: Wiss & Co 354 Eisenhower Pkwy Livingston NJ 07039

HERRELL, ROGER WAYNE, lawyer; b. Washington, July 29, 1938; s. Stanley D. and Lillian B. (Davis) H.; m. Eugenia M., June 11, 1960; children: Sharon, Julie, Roger. BEE, U. Va., 1960, JD, 1963. Bar: Va. 1963, Pa. 1964, U.S. Patent Office 1964. Assoc. Howson & Howson, Phila., 1963-70, ptnr., 1970-73; ptnr. Dann, Dorfman, Herrell & Skillman, P.C., Phila. and predecessor firm, 1973—; corp. sec. Leo Pharm. Products, Inc., Leo Labs. Ltd. subs. Leo Pharm. Products, 1980—. Contbr. articles to legal publs. Active Franklin Inst., 1964—; bd. dirs. Union League Phila., 1981-84. Mem. ABA (chmn. econs. com. PTC sect. 1983-85), Pa. Bar Assn. (ho. of dels. 1979—), Phila. Bar Assn. (chmn. econs. com. 1985), Va. State Bar, Am. Pat. Law Assn., Phila. Pat. Law Assn. (bd. govs. 1980-82), Nat. Council Pat. Law Assns. (council 1982-84). Republican. Presbyterian. Clubs: Merion Cricket (Haverford, Pa.); Phila. Country (Gladwyne, Pa.), Martin's Dam, Penn, Lawyers, Virginia (past pres.) (Phila.), Union League (Phila.) (bd. dirs. 1981-84, 86—). Patent, Trademark and copyright, Computer.

HERREN, THOMAS KELLY, lawyer; b. Lexington, Ky., July 10, 1954; s. Donald Ray and Patricia Ann (Eads) H.; m. Constance McGarry Kerr, Oct. 22, 1983. BA, U. Ky., 1976, JD, 1980. Bar: Ky. 1980, U.S. Dist. Ct. (ea. dist.) Ky. 1981. Assoc. Rosenbaum & Rosenbaum, Lexington, 1980-85, Law Offices of Peter Perlman, Lexington, 1985—; asst. county atty. Commonwealth of Ky., Lexington, 1984—. Candidate Lexington Urban County Council At Large, 1982; coach South Lexington Jr. Basketball Team, 1986—; bd. dirs. Met. Group Homes, Inc., Lexington, 1985—, Children's Services Bd., Lexington, 1986—. Mem. Ky. Bar Assn. (ins. com.), Fayette County Bar (pro bono com.), Assn. Trial Lawyers Am., Ky. Trial Lawyers Assn., Jaycees. Democrat. Methodist. Avocations: tennis, basketball. Personal injury, State civil litigation, Federal civil litigation. Home: 314 Glendover Rd Lexington KY 40503 Office: 388 S Broadway Lexington KY 40508

HERRICK, STEWART THURSTON, lawyer; b. Grenada, Miss., July 30, 1945; s. Samuel Thurston and Elizabeth Glenn (Stewart) H.; m. Gretchen Ann Schein, Sept. 9, 1967; children—Alisa, Craig, Ashlie. B.A., Syracuse U., 1967; J.D. cum laude, Suffolk U., 1974. Bar: Mass. 1974, U.S. Dist. Ct. Mass. 1975, U.S. Ct. Claims 1975, U.S. Ct. Appeals (1st cir.) 1976, U.S. Supreme Ct. 1984. Assoc. atty. Law Offices of F. Lee Bailey, Boston, 1974-76; ptnr. Harrison & Maguire, Boston, 1976-85, Catanzaro, Effron & Herrick, Ashland, Mass., 1985—. Mem. Ashland Democratic Town Com. (Mass.), 1982-83; troop leader Patriots Trail council Girl Scouts Am., 1984; bd. dirs., coach Ashland Youth Soccer, 1986—. Mem. Assn. Trial Lawyers Am., ABA, Mass. Bar, Boston Bar Assn., Mass. Assn. Bank Counsel. Federal civil litigation, State civil litigation, Personal injury. Office: Catanzaro Effren & Herrick 25 W Union St Ashland MA 01721

HERRICK, WILLIAM DUNCAN, lawyer; b. Claremont, N.H., June 27, 1941; s. Cedric Duncan and Rena (Beauman) H.; m. Patricia Susan Hoffman, Sept. 6, 1966; children: Christian, Kevin, Keely. BSChemE, Northeastern U., 1964; JD, George Washington U., Washington, 1967. Sr. patent atty. Kimberly-Clark Corp., Roswell, Ga., 1984-85, assoc. patent counsel, 1985-86, patent counsel, 1986—. Served as capt. U.S. Army, 1968-70. Patent. Office: Kimberly-Clark Corp B 200/1 1400 Holcomb Br Rd Roswell GA 30076

HERRING, CHARLES DAVID, lawyer, educator; b. Muncie, Ind., Mar. 18, 1943; s. Morris and Margaret Helen (Scherbaum) H.; children—David, Margaret, Christopher. B.A., Ind. U., 1965, J.D. cum laude, 1968. Bar: Ind. 1968, Calif. 1971, U.S. Dist. Ct. (so. dist.) Ind., U.S. Dist. Ct. (so. dist.) Calif. Research assoc. Ind. U., 1965-68; intern Office of Pros. Atty., Monroe County, Inc., 1967-68; ptnr. Herring, Stubel & Lehr, and predecessor Herring and Stubel, San Diego, 1972—; prof. law Western State U., 1972—. Vice chmn. Valle de Oro Planning Com., Spring Valley, Calif., 1972-75; chmn. Valle de Oro Citizens Exec. Com. for Community Planning, Spring Valley, 1975-78. Served with JAGC, U.S. Army, 1968-72. Mem. ABA (nat. best brief award 1968), Ind. Bar Assn., Calif. Bar Assn., San Diego County Bar Assn., Conf. Spl. Ct. Judges, Calif. Trial Lawyers Assn., Order of Coif. Author: (with Jim Wade) California Cases on Professional Responsibility, 1976. State civil litigation, Insurance, Real property. Home: 1968 Treseder Circle El Cajon CA 92021 Office: Herring Stubel & Lehr 101 W Broadway Suite 1670 San Diego CA 92101

HERRING, CHARLES EVANS, JR., lawyer; b. Lake Providence, La., Jan. 3, 1951; s. Charles Evans and Billie Icie (Lovelady) H.; m. Madeline Ann Nelson, Aug. 19, 1972; children: Hyland Charles, Amanda Madeline, Megan Ann. BA magna cum laude, Northwestern (La.) State U., 1973; JD, La. State U., 1976. Bar: La. 1976, U.S. Dist. Ct. (we. dist.) La. 1977, U.S. Supreme Ct. 1986. Ptnr. Rankin, Yeldell, Herring & Katz, Bastrop, La., 1976—. Mem. sch. bd. St. Joseph Cath. Sch., Bastrop, 1985—, pres. 1986. Mem. ABA, La. Bar Assn., Assn. Trial Lawyers Am., La. Trial Lawyers Assn. (bd. govs. 1983—), 4th Judicial Dist. Bar Assn. (ct. liason com. 1985—). Democrat. Roman Catholic. Lodge: Optimist (Bastrop) (dir. 1982-83, sec. treas. 1983-84). Family and matrimonial, Personal injury, General practice. Home: 712 Elmhurst St Bastrop LA 71220 Office: Rankin Yeldell Herring & Katz 411 S Washington Bastrop LA 71220

HERRING, GROVER CLEVELAND, lawyer; b. Nocatee, Fla., Dec. 9, 1925; s. Joseph I. and Martha (Selph) H.; m. Dorothy L. Blinn, Apr. 17, 1947; children: Stanley T., Kenneth Lee. JD, U. Fla., 1950. Bar: Fla. 1950. Assoc. Haskins & Bryant, 1950-52; sole practice West Palm Beach, Fla., 1952-60, 64—; ptnr. Blakeslee, Herring & Bie and predecessor firm, 1953-60, Warwick, Paul & Herring, 1964-70, Herring & Evans now Arnstein, Gluck,

Lehr & Milligan, 1970; atty. City of Atlantis, Fla., City of West Palm Beach, 1960-63, Town of Ocean Ridge, Fla., 1953-61, 64-66, Village of Royal Palm Beach, Fla., 1964-72, Town of South Palm Beach, Fla., 1966-72; spl. master-in-chancery 15th Jud. Cir. Palm Beach County, 1953-54; judge ad litem Mcpl. Ct., West Palm Beach, 1954-55; bd. dirs. Lawyers Title Services Inc., West Palm Beach. Contbr. legal articles to profl. revs. Active PTA, Family Service Agy., Palm Beach County Mental Health Assn.; chmn. profl. sect. ARC, 1960; mem. Charter Revision Com. West Palm Beach, 1960-65, Palm Beach County Resources Devel. Bd., 1959—, Dem. Exec. Com., 1965-70; apptd. mem. Govtl. Study Commn. by Fla. Legis.; bd. dirs. Community Chest. Served with USNR, 1944-46. Mem. ABA, Palm Beach County Bar Assn. (treas. 1960), John Marshall Bar Assn., Fla. Bar Assn., Am. Judicature Soc., Lawyers Title Guaranty Fund (field rep. 1955-60, 64—), East Coast Estate Planning Council, Nat. Inst. Mcpl. Law Officers, Law-Sci. Acad., Assn. Trial Lawyers Am. (assoc. editor 1960—), Lawyers Lit. Club, Nat. Mcpl. League, U. Fla. Law Ctr. Assn., World Peace Through Law Ctr., Fla. Sheriff's Assn. (hon.), U. Fla. Alumni Assn., VFW, Am. Legion, West Palm Beach C. of C., Civic Music Assn., Palm Beach County Hist. Soc. (pres. 1969-72), New Eng. Hist. Geneal. Soc. Boston. Clubs: West Palm Beach Country (hon.); Airways (N.Y.C.). Lodges: Eight Oaks River, Masons (32 deg.), Elks, Moose. Home: 3515 Australian Ave West Palm Beach FL 33407 Office: Forum III Bldg Tower B West Palm Beach FL 33401

HERRINGTON, ALVIN D., lawyer; b. Wellington, Kans., Sept. 23, 1930; s. Joseph M. and Ethel L. Herrington; m. Sally G. Herrington; children—Daniel, Mark, Tracy. A.B., U. Kans., LL.B., 1956. Bar: Kans., U.S. Dist. Ct. Kans., U.S. Ct. Appeals (10th cir.). Ptnr. Mcdonald, Tinker, Skaer, Quinn & Herrington, Wichita, Kans., 1956—; testimony and appearances before various legis. and govtl. agys. on various legal issues; speaker on workers' compensation and product liability. Active Boy Scouts Am., pres. Quirira council. Served with CIC, U.S. Army. Recipient Silver Beaver award Boy Scouts Am. Mem. Wichita Bar Assn., Kans. Bar Assn., ABA, Fedn. Ins. Counsel, Kans. Assn. Commerce and Industry, Order of Coif. Democrat. Contbr. articles on workers' compensation and products liability to profl. jours.; author legislation on workers' compensation and products liability; editor: (with others) Kansas Workers' Compensation Manual. Personal injury, Federal civil litigation, State civil litigation. Office: 300 W Douglas Ave Suite 530 Wichita KS 67202

HERRMANN, PHILIP ERIC, lawyer; b. Wilmington, Del., May 31, 1956; s. Jay J. and Myrtle Irene (Kennedy) H.; m. Cynthia Jean Longobardi, Sept. 6, 1980. BA, Emory U., 1978; JD, Widener U., 1981. Bar: Del. 1981, U.S. Dist. Ct. Del. 1982. Assoc. Schmittinger & Rodriguez P.A., Dover, Del., 1981-82, ptnr., 1982-84; resident atty. Schmittinger & Rodriguez P.A., Wilmington, Del., 1984—. Contbr. articles to Delaware Law Forum. Cofounder Injured Persons Adv. Com., Wilmington, 1986—. Mem. ABA, Del. Bar Assn., New Castle County Bar Assn., Kent County Bar Assn., Assn. Trial Lawyers Am., Del. Trial Lawyers Assn. (legis. Key Man com.), Am. Jurisprudence Soc., New Castle County C. of C. (chmn. ins. com. 1985—, leukemia fundraising fin. com. 1986), Phi Delta Phi. Democrat. Avocation: art collecting. Workers' compensation, Personal injury, Lobbying. Home: 313 Stonehurst Dr Wilmington DE 19804

HERROLD, RUSSELL PHILLIPS, JR., lawyer; b. Zanesville, Ohio, Mar. 17, 1924; s. Russell Phillips and Wilma (Lane) H.; m. Marcia Lucille Rafn, July 14, 1951; children: Russell P. III, Nancy Elizabeth, Richard Edward. AB, Yale U., 1948; JD, Harvard U., 1951. Bar: Ohio 1951, U.S. Dist. Ct. (so. dists.) Ohio, U.S. Supreme Ct. Assoc. Vorys Sater Seymour & Pease, Columbus, Ohio, 1951-57, ptnr., 1957—. Pres. Community Health and Nursing Assn., Columbus, 1968; bd. dirs. Vols. of Am., Columbus, 1975; chmn. Presbytery Major Mission Fund, Columbus, 1976; moderator Scioto Valley Presbytery, Columbus, 1980; sec. Friendship Village of Columbus, Friendship Village of Dublin; trustee Classic Car Club of Am. Mus. Mem. ABA, Ohio State Bar Assn., Columbus Bar Assn. Republican. Clubs: Columbus, Scioto Country Club. Lodge: Masons. Avocations: golf, classic cars, beekeeping. Workers' compensation, State civil litigation, Real property. Office: Vorys Sater Seymour & Pease 52 E Gay St Columbus OH 43215

HERRON, JAMES M., lawyer; b. Chgo., May 4, 1934; s. J. Leonard and Sylvia H.; m. Janet Ross, June 12, 1955; children: Kathy Lynn, Tracy Ellen, Andrew Ross. A.B., U. Mo., Columbia, 1955; postgrad., Northwestern U., 1958-59; J.D., Washington U., 1961; postgrad., Harvard Bus. Sch., 1982. Bar: Mo. 1961, Ohio 1971, Fla. 1975. Asst. gen. counsel, asst. sec. May Dept. Stores Co., St. Louis, 1961-70; asso. counsel Federated Dept. Stores, Inc., Cin., 1970-71; v.p., sec., gen. counsel Kenton Corp., N.Y.C., 1971-73; gen. counsel Ryder System, Inc., Miami, Fla., 1973-74; v.p., sec., gen. counsel Ryder System, Inc., 1974-78, sr. v.p., sec., gen. counsel, 1978-79, exec. v.p., gen. counsel, 1979—, sec., 1983-86. First v.p., bd. dirs., mem. exec. com. Greater Miami Opera Assn., chmn. corp. devel. com., 1981-82; bd. dirs. Am. Cancer Soc., 1985-87; trustee Ransom Everglades Sch. Served with USMC, 1955-58. Mem. ABA, Mo. Bar Assn., Bar Assn. Met. St. Louis, Assn. Bar City of N.Y., Am. Soc. Corp. Secs., Fla. Bar Assn., Dade County Bar Assn. Club: Royal Palm Tennis (dir.). Home: 3831 Estepona Ave Miami FL 33178 Office: Ryder System Inc 3600 NW 82d Ave Miami FL 33166

HERRON, JANET D., lawyer; b. Stoughton, Mass., Aug. 22, 1941; d. Thomas J. and Dorothy H. (Rogers) Herron; m. Gary Peacock, Apr. 23, 1966 (div. Apr. 1975); 1 child, Jefferson S. Student, Regis Coll., 1959-61; AB, Stonehill Coll., 1963; JD, Stetson U., 1977. Bar: Fla. 1978, U.S. Dist. Ct. (mid. dist.) Fla. 1979, U.S. Ct. Appeals (11th cir.) 1984. Assoc. Anderson & Spangler P.A., St. Petersburg, 1978-80; atty., advisor Social Security Adminstrn., Tampa, Fla., 1980-82; assoc. Law Offices of Julian L. Miller, Pinellas Park, Fla., 1982-83; sole practice Pinellas Park, 1983—. Mem. Nat. Orgn. Social Security Claimants Reps., Fla. Bar Assn., St. Petersburg Bar Assn. Disability benefits. Home: 11420-2 2d St N Saint Petersburg FL 33702 Office: 9700 Koger Blvd Suite 209 Saint Petersburg FL 33702

HERSH, ALVIN DAVID, lawyer; b. Newark, Mar. 14, 1932; s. Emanuel Harold and Fay Eileen (Goldberg) H.; m. Irma Joy Goldman, Oct. 12, 1957; children: Wendy Sue, Stephanie Jill, Melissa Ann. BA, Rutgers U., 1953, JD, 1956. Bar: N.J. 1957, U.S. Dist. Ct. N.J. 1957, U.S. Ct. Appeals (3d dist.) 1965, U.S. Supreme Ct. 1962. Ptnr. Shurkin, Hersh & Fershing, Newark and West Orange, N.J., 1964-76; sr. ptnr. Hersh, Leonard & Fenik, Morristown, N.J., 1976-82, Wacks, Hersh, Ramsey & Berman, Morristown, 1982—; judge N.J. Mcpl. Ct., Mine Hill, 1986—. Pres. Boys Club, Newark, 1962-64, Assn. for Retarded Citizens, Essex Unit, East Orange, N.J., 1982-84; bd. dirs., Somerset Unit, Manville, N.J., 1985-86. Served as capt. USCGR, 1956-83. Mem. ABA, N.J. Bar Assn., Morris County Bar Assn., Assn. Trial Lawyers Am. Republican. Jewish. Lodges: Lions, B'nai B'rith (pres. 1958-60). State civil litigation, General practice, Personal injury. Home: 48 N Maple Ave Basking Ridge NJ 07920 Office: Wacks Hersh Ramsey & Berman 222 Ridgedale Ave PO Box 2249-R Morristown NJ 07960

HERSH, ROBERT MICHAEL, life insurance company executive, lawyer; b. N.Y.C., Feb. 12, 1940; s. Isaac and Esther (Cohen) H.; m. Louise Hersh, Sept. 23, 1984; 1 dau., Lauren. B.A., Columbia U., 1960; J.D., Harvard U., 1963. Bar: N.Y. 1964. Assoc. Malcolm A. Hoffmann, 1964-66, Valicenti, Leighton, Reid & Pine, 1966-68; atty. Kraftco Corp., N.Y.C., 1968-74; assoc. counsel Equitable Life Assurance Soc. U.S., N.Y.C., 1974-76, asst. gen. counsel, 1976-78, v.p. and counsel, 1978-83, v.p. and assoc. gen. counsel, 1983—; dir. Ideal Mut. Ins. Co., 1972-74; chief announcer Madison Sq. Garden Track Meets, 1974—; chief athletics announcer 1984 Olympic Games. Mem. Assn. Bar City N.Y. (com. on profl. and jud. ethics 1978-81, consumer affairs com. 1984-85, ins. com. 1985—), Athletics Congress U.S.A. (dir. 1979—, chmn. records com. 1979—, chmn. grand prix com. 1982—), Internat. Amateur Athletic Fedn. (tech. com. 1984—), Assn. Track and Field Statisticians. Served with USAR, 1963-69. Columnist: Track and Field News, 1973—, sr. editor, 1974—; contrig. editor Runner mag., 1980-87. Contbr. articles on athletics to various mags. General corporate, Insurance, Securities. Home: 92 Club Dr Roslyn Heights NY 11577 Office: Equitable Life Assurance Soc USA 787 7th Ave New York NY 10019

HERSHATTER, RICHARD LAWRENCE, lawyer, novelist; b. New Haven, Sept. 20, 1923; s. Alexander Charles and Belle (Blenner) H.; B.A., Yale U., 1948; J.D., U. Mich., 1951; m. Mary Jane McNulty, Aug. 16, 1980; children by previous marriage—Gail Brook, Nancy Jill, Bruce Warren; 1 stepdau., Kimberly Ann Matlock. Bar: Conn. 1951, Mich. 1951, U.S. Supreme Ct. 1959. Sole practice law, New Haven, 1951-85, Clinton, Conn., 1985—; state trial referee, 1984—. Chmn., Clinton Republican Town Com. (Conn.), 1984—; Author: The Spy Who Hated Licorice, 1966; Fallout For a Spy, 1968; The Spy Who Hated Fudge, 1970. Mem. Branford (Conn.) Bd. Edn., 1963-71. Served with U.S. Army Air Corps, 1942-44, AUS, 1944-46. Mem. Conn. Sch. Attys. Council (pres. 1977), New Haven County Bar Assn., Conn. Bar Assn., Middlesex County Bar Assn., Mystery Writers Am., W. Haven C. of C. (pres. 1956). Lodge: Masons. General practice, Labor, Local government. Office: 2 Rt 81 Suite 1 Clinton CT 06413

HERSHBERG, DAVID STEPHEN, lawyer, business executive; b. N.Y.C., Nov. 22, 1941; s. Irving and Sophie (Esikoff) H.; m. Karen Jay Subow, July 29, 1965; children: Jared, Rachel. AB, NYU, 1962; JD, Harvard U., 1965. Bar: N.Y. 1966. Assoc. corp. Finley, Kumble, Wagner, N.Y.C., 1972-76; counsel Am. Express Co., N.Y.C., 1976-78, asst. gen. counsel, 1978-81, dep. gen. counsel, 1981-84, sr. exec. v.p., 1984-87, vice chmn., 1987—, also bd. dirs.; bd. dirs. SLB Inc., N.Y.C, Fin. Guaranty Ins. Co., N.Y.C. Spl. gifts chmn. Am. Cancer Soc., N.Y.C.; mem. budget com. Village of Larchmont, N.Y, 1985; bd. dirs., vice chmn. exec. com. Anti-Defamation League N.Y.C., 1982. Served with mil. Intelligence, 1966-67. Mem. ABA (fed. regulations of securities com., broker-dealer matters subcom.), Assn. of Bar of City of N.Y. (securities regulation com. 1986—), Phi Beta Kappa. Club: Orienta Beach (Mamaronek, N.Y.). General corporate, Securities. Office: Shearson Lehman Bros Inc 200 Vesey St New York NY 10048 Home: 20 Flint Ave Larchmont NY 10285

HERSHCOPF, GERALD THEA, lawyer; b. N.Y.C., Feb. 8, 1922; s. Paul and Rose (Thea) H.; m. Elaine Yeckes, June 10, 1950; 1 dau., Jane. A.B., Columbia U., 1943; cert. in French civilization, U. Paris, 1945; J.D., Harvard U., 1949. Bar: N.Y., 1949, U.S. Dist. Ct. (so. dist.) N.Y. 1960, U.S. Supreme Ct. 1981. Assoc. Marshall, Bratter, Greene, Allison & Tucker, N.Y.C., 1949-54; ptnr. Starr & Hershcopf, N.Y.C., 1954-56, Hershcopf & Graham and successor firms, N.Y.C., 1956-77; Hershcopf, Graham & Sloame, N.Y.C., 1977-81, Hershcopf, Sloame & Stevenson, N.Y.C., 1981-83; sr. ptnr. Hershcopf, Stevenson & McConnell, N.Y.C., 1983-84, Hershcopf, Stevenson, McConnell & Tannenbaum, N.Y.C., 1984-86, Hershcopf, Stevenson, Tannenbaum & Glassman, 1986—; gen. ptnr. Norfolk Realty Corp., N.Y.C., 1961-86; chmn. bd. N.Am. Planning Corp., N.Y.C., 1968-71; pres. Consortium Met. Law Schs., N.Y.C., 1983—. Served with U.S. Army, 1943-46; ETO. Mem. Assn. Bar City N.Y., N.Y. State Bar Assn. (gen. practice sect.), Judge Advs. Assn., French-Am. C. of C., Real Estate Bd. N.Y., Beta Sigma Rho. Republican. Jewish. Clubs: Harvard, City Athletic, Tennisport, Columbia U. Tennis, LeClub (N.Y.C.). Real property, Bankruptcy, Securities. Home: 737 Park Ave New York NY 10021 Office: Hershcopf Stevenson et al 230 Park Ave New York NY 10169

HERSHENSON, GERALD MARTIN, lawyer; b. Revere, Mass., May 14, 1941; s. Morris and Ida Rita (Engorn) H.; m. Sarah Shirley Knobel, June 15, 1969; children—David, Rachel. B.S. in B.A., Boston U., 1963, LL.B., 1966. Bar: Mass. 1966, Pa. 1969, U.S. Dist. Ct. (ea. dist.) Pa. 1970, U.S. Supreme Ct. 1976. Law clk. Judge E. Hettrick, Boston, 1966-67; ptnr. Curtin & Heefner, Morrisville, Pa., 1969—. Mem. Democratic Nat. Com., Washington, 1983, Mideast Trade Mission, 1983; officer Bucks County Dem. Com., Doylestown, Pa., 1984; mem. fin. com. Bob Edgar for Pa. Senate, 1986. Served as capt. U.S. Army, 1967-69. Decorated Army Commendation medal; recipient Young Leadership award Jewish Fedn., Bucks County, Pa., 1982. Mem. Assn. Trial Lawyers Am., Pa. Bar Assn., Pa. State Dem. Fin. Com., Am. Arbitration Assn., Pa. Trial Lawyers Assn., Bucks Bar Assn. (treas. 1980-82), Syda Found. Jewish. Club: Jewish Fedn. of Delaware Valley (Bucks County, Pa.) (v.p. 1980-86). State civil litigation, Consumer commercial, Contracts commercial. Home: 1431 Buford Dr Yardley PA 19067 Office: Curtin & Heefner 250 N Pennsylvania Ave PO Box 217 Morrisville PA 19067

HERSHEY, ADRIAN VERNON, lawyer; b. Steubenville, Ohio, Dec. 13, 1948; s. Melvin Arthur and Anna Ruth (Walsh) H.; m. Susan Louise Granatir, July 10, 1971; children: John Patrick, Brian Michael. BA, West Liberty (W.Va.) State Coll., 1972; JD, U. Akron, 1975. Bar: Ohio 1975, U.S. Dist. Ct. (so. dist.) Ohio 1976, U.S. Ct. Appeals (6th cir.) 1984. Ptnr. Blake, Hershey & Bednar, Steubenville, 1975—; criminal prosecutor City of Steubenville, 1976-80; asst. county prosecutor Jefferson County Prosecutor's Office, Steubenville, 1980-82; founder, legal cons. Victim's Aid Program, Steubenville, 1977-80; cons., bd. dirs. Ohio Legal Services, Columbus, 1982-85. Mem. exec. com. Jefferson County Dems., Steubenville, 1984—; cofounder, legal cons. Alternatives to Living in a Violent Environment, Steubenville, 1983—. Mem. Ohio Bar Assn., Jefferson County Bar Assn. (treas. 1980), Assn. Trial Lawyers Am., Comml. Law League Am. Lodge: Masons. Avocations: golf, hunting, fishing, kayaking, sailing. Personal injury, State civil litigation, Consumer commercial. Office: Blake Hershey & Bednar 4110 Sunset Blvd Steubenville OH 43952

HERSHEY, DALE, lawyer; b. Pitts., Mar. 24, 1941; s. Henry E. and Elizabeth (Loeffler) H.; m. Susanne W. Hershey, July 8, 1967; children—Lauren, Alex. B.A., Yale U., 1963; LL.B., Harvard U., 1966. Bar: Pa. 1966, U.S. Dist. Ct. (we. dist.) Pa. 1966, U.S. Ct. Appeals (3d cir.) 1971, U.S. Tax Ct. 1978, U.S. Supreme Ct. 1979. With Eckert, Seamans, Cherin & Mellott, Pitts., 1966—; now ptnr. Eckert, Seamans, Cherin & Mellott; adj. prof. indsl. adminstrn. and law, Carnegie Mellon U., 1986. Pres. Legal Aid Soc. Pitts.; bd. dirs. Gateway to Music, Inc.; fellow Carnegie Inst. Mus. Art. Mem. ABA, Pa. Bar Assn., Allegheny County Bar Assn., Am. Law Inst., Harvard Law Sch. Assn. Western Pa. (pres.). Unitarian. Clubs: Harvard-Yale-Princeton, Yale (N.Y.C.); Fox Chapel Racquet. Antitrust, Federal civil litigation, Private international. Home: 311 Dorseyville Rd Pittsburgh PA 15215 Office: Suite 4200 600 Grant St Pittsburgh PA 15219

HERSHMAN, MENDES, lawyer; b. Northampton, Pa., May 20, 1911; s. Joel and Rose (Grossman) H.; m. Frances Sybil Stackell, June 2, 1935; children: Jane, Martha. A.B., N.Y.U., 1929; LL.B., Harvard U., 1932. Bar: N.Y. 1933. Spl. counsel for housing N.Y. Life Ins. Co., N.Y.C., 1946-62; asst. gen. counsel N.Y. Life Ins. Co., 1962-64, assoc. gen. counsel, 1964-69, v.p., gen. counsel, 1969-72, sr. v.p., gen. counsel, 1972-77; sr. partner firm Rosenman & Colin and predecessor firm Rosenman Colin Freund Lewis & Cohen, N.Y.C., 1977—; lectr. joint com. on continuing legal edn. Am. Law Inst.-Am. Bar Assn., Practising Law Inst.; chmn. legal adv. com. to bd. dirs. N.Y. Stock Exchange, 1978-83, mem. ex officio, 1983—; vis. prof. Marshall-Wythe Law Sch., Coll. William and Mary, 1978-79; chmn. Mayor's Com. on Judiciary, 1972-77, N.Y. State Commn. on Jud. Nominations, 1978—, N.Y. State Commn. on Uniform State Laws. Bd. editors: N.Y. Law Jour, 1969—; Contbr. articles profl. jours. Bd. dirs. N.Y. Landmarks Conservancy, N.Y.C. Pub. Devel. Corp.; vice chmn. Citizens Union. Recipient N.Y. State award, certificate of Outstanding Pub. Service, 1960. Fellow Am. Bar Found.; mem. Assn. Bar City N.Y. (com. chmn., past v.p., chmn. exec. com.), Am. Bar Assn. (mem. council, sect. officer, chmn. ho. of dels. corp., banking and bus. law sects.), Am. Law Inst. (chmn. com. on continuing legal edn.), N.Y. County Lawyers Assn., Harvard Law Sch. Assn. N.Y.C. (trustee, pres.), Phi Beta Kappa. General corporate, Insurance, Real property. Home: 200 E 66th St New York NY 10021 Office: 575 Madison Ave New York NY 10022

HERSHMAN, MORRIS PAUL, lawyer; b. Phila., Nov. 12, 1951; m. Shirley P. Seiden, Mar. 7, 1982. BS, Haverford Coll., 1973; JD, U. Chgo., 1976. Bar: Pa. 1976, U.S. Ct. Appeals (3d cir.) 1976. Assoc. Wolf, Block, Schorr & Solis-Cohen, Phila., 1976-81, Fox, Rothschild, O'Brien & Frankel, Phila., 1981-86, Rudolf, Seidner, Goldstein, Rochestie & Salmon P.C., Phila., 1986—. Bd. dirs., corr. sec. Gershman YM-YWHA, Phila., 1978—. Mem. ABA, Pa. Bar Assn., Phila. Bar Assn. (condominium com.), Phi Delta Phi. Real property, Banking, Contracts commercial. Home: 825 Strawberry Ln Wynnewood PA 19096 Office: Rudolf Seidner et al 300 Lewis Tower Bldg 225 S 15th St Philadelphia PA 19102

HERSHMAN, MURRAY JOHN, lawyer; b. Bristol, Conn., May 1, 1951; s. Harry Herbert and Beverly Marie (Cohen) H.; m. Paula Lynn Loundy, Oct. 18, 1980; children: Adam Ross, Samantha Gayle. BA, George Washington U., 1974; JD, Thomas M. Cooley Law Sch., 1978. Bar: Pa. 1982, U.S. Tax Ct. 1982. Legis. asst. congressman James J. Delaney, Washington, 1974-75; assoc. Epstein, Becker, Borsody & Green, Washington, 1978-80; tax law specialist office of chief counsel IRS, Washington, 1980-83; tax mgr. KMG Main Hurdman, Salisbury, Md., 1983-85; prin. Faw, Casson & Co., Salisbury, 1985—; adj. prof. taxation Salisbury State Coll., 1984—. Contbr. articles on tax to local newspaper. Bd. dirs. Salisbury-Wicomico Arts Council, Salisbury, 1983—, adv. com. Wicomico County Bd. Edn., Salisbury, 1985—. Mem. ABA (taxation sect.), Pa. Bar Assn., Md. Bar Assn., Salisbury C. of C. Democrat. Jewish. Club: Exchange (Salisbury). Lodge: Masons. Avocations: stamp and coin collecting, tennis, basketball. Corporate taxation, Personal income taxation, General corporate. Home: 612 Douglas Rd Salisbury MD 21801 Office: Faw Casson & Co 117 E Market St Salisbury MD 21801

HERSRUD, LESLIE RAYMOND, retired judge; b. Petrel, N.D., Apr. 6, 1914; s. Martin H. and Luella (Hardy) H.; m. Mary Leone Smith, Oct. 5, 1942. BA, St. Olaf, North Field, Minn., 1935; JD, U. Minn., 1938. Bar: S.D. 1938. Sole practice Lemmon, S.D., 1938-55; judge U.S. Ct. Appeals (8th cir.), Lemmon, 1955-81; retired, sr. status State of S.D., Lemmon, 1981—; bd. dirs. Bank of Lemmon. Served with U.S. Army, 1942-45, ETO. Mem. ABA, S.D. Bar Assn. (editor jour. 1940-42), 8th Cir. Bar Assn., Luth. Hosp. and Homes Soc. (bd. dirs. Fargo, N.D., 1955-86). Republican. Criminal, Judicial administration. Home: 304 3d Ave W Lemmon SD 57638

HERTEL, THEODORE BERNHARD, JR., lawyer; b. Milw., Jan. 23, 1947; s. Theodore B. and Mabel (Cunningham) H.; m. Betty J. Karweick, Apr. 10, 1971 (div. Feb. 1985); m. Margaret M. Ley, July 1986. Student, Freie U. Berlin, 1967-68; BA, Carroll Coll., 1969; JD, U. Wis., 1972. Bar: Wis. 1972, U.S. Dist. Ct. (ea. and we. dists.) Wis. 1972, U.S. Ct. Appeals (7th cir.) 1977, U.S. Supreme Ct. 1977. Assoc. Gaines & Saichek S.C., Milw., 1972-79; ptnr. Saichek & Hertel S.C., Milw., 1979—; lectr. U. Wis. Law Sch., Madison, 1975—. Mem. ABA, Milw. Bar Assn. (fee arbitration com. 1980—, chmn. panel 1984-86, chmn. com. 1986-87), Bar Assn. of 7th Fed. Cir., Wis. Acad. Trial Lawyers, Assn. Trial Lawyers Am., Am. Judicature Soc. Avocations: travel, reading, theater. Real property, State civil litigation, General practice. Home: 4754 N Hollywood Ave Whitefish Bay WI 53211 Office: 161 W Wisconsin Ave Milwaukee WI 53203

HERTING, CLAIREEN LAVERN, personal financial planning executive; b. Chgo., Sept. 7, 1929; d. Ernst and Louise Caroline (Wagner) Molzan; m. Robert L. Herting, June 5, 1954; 1 son, Robert L., Jr. B.S., U. Ill.-Champaign, 1951; M.B.A., Northwestern U., Chgo., 1953; J.D., John Marshall Law Sch., 1960. Bar: Ill. 1960. C.P.A., Ill. With Cooper & Lybrands, Chgo., 1951—, dir. personal fin. planning, 1974—. Contbr. articles to profl. jours. Bd. dirs. Easter Seal Soc. Met. Chgo., 1974—, Chgo. Soc. Contemporary Composers, 1979-84; bd. trustees John Marshall Law Sch., Chgo., 1980—; com. mem. Ill. Dept. Registration and Edn., Springfield, 1984—. Recipient Disting. Service award John Marshall Alumni Assn., Chgo., 1983. Mem. Am. Inst. C.P.A.s, ABA, Ill. Bar Assn., Ill. C.P.A. Soc. (bd. dirs. 1974-76), Chgo. Estate Planning Council (past pres., bd. mem. 1976-84), Chgo. Bar Assn. Probate, Estate taxation. Home: 1281 N Northwest Hwy Chicago IL 60068

HERTZBERG, HAROLD JOEL, lawyer; b. Los Angeles, July 29, 1922; s. Irving J. and Clara (Goldinger) H.; m. Leona Garber, July 28, 1946; 1 child, Rita Campbell. BS, UCLA, 1943, LLB, 1958. Bar: Calif. 1959, U.S. Dist. Ct. (cen. dist.) Calif. 1959. Sole practice Beverly Hills, Calif., 1959-62; ptnr. Hertzberg, Childs & Miller and predecessor firms, Beverly Hills, 1962-85, Rosenfeld, Meyer, & Susman, Beverly Hills, 1985—. Author: Accounting for Fiduciaries. Mem. Pres. Beverly Hills Estate Planning Council, 1972. Served to lt. (j.g.) USN, 1943-46, PTO. Avocations: stamp collecting, golf. General corporate, Estate planning. Home: 1333 S Beverly Glen Blvd Los Angeles CA 90024 Office: Rosenfeld Meyer & Susman 9601 Wilshire Blvd 4th floor Beverly Hills CA 90210

HERTZBERG, ROBERT STEVEN, lawyer; b. Detroit, June 8, 1954; s. Stuart Earl and Marilyn Jean (Cohen) H.; m. Linda Bellows, Aug. 11, 1984. BS, Eastern Mich. U., 1976; JD, Thomas M. Cooley Law Sch., 1979. Bar: Mich. 1979, U.S. Dist. Ct. (ea. dist.) Mich. 1981, U.S. Ct. Appeals (6th cir.) 1982. Sole practice Southfield, Mich., 1979-82; ptnr. Hertzberg & Golden, P.C., Birmingham, Mich., 1982—; v.p., bd. dirs. Golden Title Ins. Agency Inc., Birmingham, 1985—; v.p., bd. dirs., Mill Investment Ltd., Birmingham, 1985—; mng. ptnr. WHF&L, Birmingham, 1985—; chmn. assn. of trustees Ea. Dist. Mich., Detroit, 1982—. Contbr. articles to profl. jours. Mem. ABA (bus. bankruptcy sect.), Fed. Bar Assn, Mich. Bar Assn., Oakland County Bar Assn. (young mem. bd. 1980-82), Detroit Bar Assn., Comml. Law League of Am. (patron, Midwest exec. council). Democrat. Jewish. Avocations: hockey, baseball, model building, travel, art. Bankruptcy, Banking, Federal civil litigation. Home: 31525 Nottingham Franklin MI 48025 Office: Hertzberg & Golden P C 344 N Woodward Birmingham MI 48011

HERWITZ, DAVID RICHARD, legal educator; b. Lynn, Mass., Dec. 8, 1925; s. Harry M. and Sarah (Shapiro) H.; student U. Wis., 1942-43; B.S., Mass. Inst. Tech., 1946; LL.B. magna cum laude, Harvard, 1949; m. Carla B. Cowett, Jan. 22, 1960; children—Andrew B., Juliet F. Admitted to Mass. bar, 1949; practiced in Boston, 1951-54; teaching fellow Harvard Law Sch., 1950-51, asst. prof. law, 1954-57, prof. law, 1957—, Austin Wakeman Scott prof. law, 1980; faculty supr. Harvard-Brandeis coop. research for Israel's legal devel., 1957-59; lectr. Northeastern Sch. Law, 1951-54. Cons., U.S. Treasury Dept., 1961-64. Author: Cases and Materials on Business Planning, 1966, temp. 2d edit., 1984; Corporations Course Game Plan, 1975; Materials on Accounting for Lawyers, 1980. Legal education. Home: Littles Point Swampscott MA 01907 Office: Harvard U Law Sch Cambridge MA 01907 *

HERZ, CHARLES HENRY, lawyer; b. Newark, Oct. 28, 1939; s. Henry and Margaret (Boa) H.; m. Barbara Jane Knapp; children—Amy, Katherine. A.B., Princeton U., 1961; LL.B., Yale U., 1967. Bar: D.C. 1968. Assoc. Covington & Burling, Washington, 1967-76; gen. counsel NSF, Washington, 1976—. Served to 1st lt. U.S. Army, 1962-64, W.Ger. Mem. Nat. Conf. Lawyers and Scientists (chmn. 1982-84), ABA, AAAS. Administrative and regulatory, Government contracts and claims, Corporate taxation. Office: Nat Science Found 1800 G St NW Washington DC 20550

HERZECA, LOIS FRIEDMAN, lawyer; b. N.Y.C., July 7, 1954; d. Martin and Elaine Shirley (Rapoport) Friedman; m. Christian Stefan Herzeca, Aug. 15, 1980. B.A. Harpur Coll., SUNY-Binghamton, 1976; J.D., Boston U., 1979. Bar: N.Y. 1980, U.S. Dist. Ct. (so. and ea. dist.) N.Y. 1980. Atty. antitrust div. U.S. Dept. Justice, Washington, 1979-80; assoc. Fried, Frank, Harris, Shriver & Jacobson, N.Y.C., 1980-86, ptnr., 1986—. Editor Am. Jour. Law and Medicine, 1978-79. Mem. ABA, N.Y.C. Bar Assn. Securities, General corporate. Office: Fried Frank Harris Shriver & Jacobson 1 New York Plaza New York NY 10004

HERZEL, LEO, lawyer; b. N.Y.C., Sept. 10, 1923; s. Salomon and Rose (Kalt) H.; m. Eileen Louise Engel, Feb. 2, 1946; children: David Franklin, Sarah Elizabeth. A.B., U. Iowa, 1947; postgrad., London Sch. Econs., 1947-48; M.A., U. Ill., 1949; J.D., U. Chgo., 1952. Bar: Ill. 1952. Assoc. Mayer, Brown & Platt, Chgo., 1952-61, ptnr., 1962—; dir. Brunswick Corp., Skokie, Ill. Contbr. articles to legal jours.; editor-in-chief: U. Chgo. Law Rev., 1951-52. Mem. ABA, Ill. Bar Assn., Chgo. Bar Assn., Chgo. Council of Lawyers, Phi Beta Kappa. Clubs: Chicago; Attic (Chgo.). General corporate, Banking, Securities. Home: 344 South Ave Glencoe IL 60022 Office: Mayer Brown & Platt 190 S LaSalle St Chicago IL 60603

HERZOG, BRIGITTE, lawyer; b. St. Sauveur, France, Jan. 11, 1943; came to U.S., 1970, naturalized, 1976; d. Roger and Berthe (Niobey) Ecolivet; m. Peter E. Herzog, June 29, 1970; children: Paul Roger, Elizabeth Ann. Licence en Droit, Law Sch. Pantheon, Paris, 1967, Diplomes d'Etudes Superieures in Internat. and Criminal Law, 1968; diploma Acad. Internat. Law, The Hague, Netherlands, 1969; JD Syracuse Coll. Law, 1975. Bar:

Paris, 1968, N.Y. 1976. Assoc. Chardenon Law Firm, Paris, 1968-70, Cleary, Gottlieb et al., Paris, 1976-77; staff atty. Carrier Corp., Syracuse, N.Y., 1977-83, sr. atty., 1983-84, asst. gen. counsel, 1984-86, counsel European and Transcontinental Ops., Surrey, Eng., 1986—. Contbr. to Harmonization of Laws in the EEC Fifth Sokol Colloquium, 1983; contbr. articles on French and internat. law to profl. jours. Bd. Dirs. Syracuse Stage Guild, 1974-77. Mem. ABA, N.Y. Bar Assn., Am. Fgn. Law Assn. Roman Catholic. General corporate, Private international. Home: 34 Ovington St, London SW3 2JB, England Office: Carrier Corp ETO, Goldvale House, Church St West, Woking GU2 1DH Surrey, England

HERZOG, JACOB HAWLEY, lawyer; b. Albany, N.Y., Jan. 6, 1911; s. Lester William and Ethel Louise Herzog; m. Madelon Pound, June 25, 1937; children—Jacob H., Madelon H. Miller, Scott P., Mary E.; m. Betty Warren, May 12, 1960. A.B., Princeton U., 1932; J.D., Albany Law Sch., 1935, LL.D. (hon.), 1982. Bar N.Y. 1935, U.S. Dist. Ct. (no. dist.) N.Y. 1935, U.S. Ct. Appeals (2d cir.) 1979, U.S. Tax Ct. 1950. Assoc. Randall J. LeBouef, Albany, 1935-37; ptnr. Herzog & Nichols, Albany, 1937-40; election commr. Albany County, 1939-40; ptnr. Pattison, Herzog, Sampson & Nichols, and predecessor firms, 1946-79; justice Albany City Ct., 1946-54; treas. Albany County, 1954-57; adj. gen. State of N.Y., 1957-59; pres., ptnr. Herzog, Nichols, Engstrom & Koplovitz, P.C., Albany, 1979—; trustee Home and City Savs. Bank. Trustee Hartwick Coll.; pres. bd. dirs. Meml. Hosp. of Albany; pres. Albany Local Devel. Corp.; trustee, pres. Albany Law Sch.; treas. Albany Pub. Library. Served to lt. col. U.S. Army, 1940-46, to brig. gen. Army NG, 1937-60. Decorated Silver Star, Bronze Star, Purple Heart, Combat Inf. badge. Fellow N.Y. Bar Found.; mem. ABA, N.Y. State Bar Assn., Albany County Bar Assn. Democrat. Lutheran. Clubs: Albany Country, Ft. Orange, University (Albany), Princeton (N.Y.C.), Masons (past master), Shriners. Estate planning, Probate, Estate taxation. Home: 76 Western Ave Albany NY 12203 Office: 99 Pine St PO Box 1279 Albany NY 12201

HERZOG, RICHARD BLUM, JR., lawyer; b. Atlanta, Aug. 6, 1948; s. Richard Blum Sr. and Jeanne (Henson) H.; m. Wendy Foster, Aug. 27, 1978 (div. June 1985). BA in Polit. Sci., U. Ga., 1970, JD cum laude, 1979. Bar: Ga. 1979, U.S. Dist. Ct. (no. dist.) Ga. 1979, U.S. Ct. Appeals (11th cir.) 1981. Law clk. to presiding judge U.S. Bankruptcy Ct., Atlanta, 1980-81; assoc. Hurt, Richardson, Garner, Todd & Cadenhead, Atlanta, 1981-83; ptnr. Bisbee, Parker & Rickertsen, Atlanta, 1983—. Author: Bankruptcy: A Concise Guide for Creditors and Debtors, 1983. Vol. United Way, Atlanta, 1983, group leader, 1984, div. leader, 1985. Served with USNR, 1970-76. Mem. ABA (bus. bankruptcy com., rules subcom.), Ga. Bar Assn., Atlanta Bar Assn., Am. Judicature Soc., Ga. Legal History Found. Democrat. Jewish. Clubs: Atlanta Lawn Tennis Assn., Atlanta Area Friends of Folk Music. Contracts commercial, Bankruptcy. Home: 614 Clairemont Ave Decatur GA 30030 Office: Bisbee Parker & Rickertsen 127 Peachtree St NE 400 Candler Bldg Atlanta GA 30303

HERZOG, RONALD STEVEN, lawyer; b. N.Y.C., Feb. 1, 1948; s. Henry and Ruth (Flegenheimer) H.; m. Karen Sue Schneider, July 4, 1976; children: Kimberley, Lindsey, Ashley. BS, Boston U., 1969; JD, Fordham U., 1973. Bar: N.Y. 1974, U.S. Dist. Ct. (so. and ea. dists.) N.Y. 1974, U.S. Ct. Appeals (2d cir.) 1974, U.S. Ct. Appeals (9th cir.) 1975. Assoc. Jackson & Nash, N.Y.C., 1973-78, Forsyth, Decker, Murray & Hubbard, N.Y.C., 1978-79; ptnr. Hall, McNicol, Hamilton & Clark, N.Y.C., 1980—; arbitrator Am. Arbitration Assn., N.Y.C., 1984, Nat. Futures Assn., Chgo., 1985. Federal civil litigation, State civil litigation. Home: 26 Wilputte Pl New Rochelle NY 10804 Office: Hall McNicol Hamilton & Clark 220 E 42d St New York NY 10017

HERZSTEIN, ROBERT ERWIN, lawyer; b. Denver, Feb. 26, 1931; s. Sigmund Edwards and Estelle Ruth (Borwick) H.; m. Priscilla Holmes, July 11, 1956; children: Jessica Anne, Emily Holmes, Robert Holmes. AB, Harvard U., 1952, LLB, 1955. Bar: Colo. 1956, D.C. 1959, U.S. Supreme Ct. 1962. Sr. ptnr., other positions Arnold & Porter, Washington, 1958-80, sr. ptnr., 1981—; undersec. for Internat. Trade U.S. Dept. Commerce, Washington, 1980-81; mem. exec. com., bd. dirs. Survival Tech., Inc., Betheda, Md., 1969—. Contbr. articles to profl. jours. Trustee Internat. Law Inst., Washington, 1974—; vice-chmn., bd. dirs. Internat. Human Rights Law Group, Washington, 1984—; mem. Mex./U.S. bus. Com., N.Y.C. and Mexico City, 1981—. Mem. ABA, Am. Soc. Internat. Law (exec. council 1981-84), Council on Fgn. Relations. Home: 4962 Quebec St NW Washington DC 20016 Office: Arnold & Porter 1200 New Hampshire Ave NW Washington DC 20036

HESLIN, JAMES MITCHELL, lawyer; b. San Mateo, Calif., Oct. 30, 1950; s. James Richard Heslin and Yvonne (Bise) Ludewick. BSChemE, U. Calif., Santa Barbara, 1973; JD, U. Calif., Berkeley, 1978. Bar: Calif. 1978, U.S. Dist. Ct. (no. dist.) Calif. 1978, U.S. Patent Office 1979, U.S. Ct. Appeals (fed. cir.) 1983. Patent atty. FMC Corp., Santa Clara, Calif., 1978-80; ptnr. Townsend & Townsend, Palo Alto, Calif., 1980—. Patent, Trademark and copyright. Office: Townsend & Townsend 5 Palo Alto Sq Palo Alto CA 94306

HESLOP, JOHN WILLIAM, JR., lawyer; b. Johnstown, Pa., Sept. 20, 1955; s. John W. Sr. and Rita Teresa (Dimond) H. BA, U. Pitts., 1977, JD, 1980. Bar: Pa. 1980, U.S. Dist. Ct. (we. and mid. dists.) Pa. 1983. Law clk. to presiding judge York (Pa.) County, 1980-81; assoc. Leopold, Eberhardt & Goldstein, P.C., Altoona, Pa., 1981-85; asst. sec. Leopold, Eberhardt & Goldstein, P.C., Altoona, 1985—. Bd. dirs. YMCA, Hollidaysburg, Pa., 1985. U. Pitts. scholar Johnstown, 1973-74. Mem. ABA, Assn. Trial Lawyers Am., Pa. Bar Assn. (workers' compensation sect., civil litigation sect.), Blair County Bar Assn. (bd. govs. rep. 1984—, social com. 1985—, membership com. 1986—). Republican. Roman Catholic. Club: Altoona Track. Avocations: competitive running, golf, softball, basketball, volleyball. State civil litigation, Insurance, Personal injury. Home: Rd 2 Box 254 Altoona PA 16601 Office: Leopold Eberhardt Goldstein PC 414 N Logan Blvd Altoona PA 16602

HESS, EMERSON GARFIELD, lawyer; b. Pitts., Nov. 13, 1914. A.B., Bethany Coll., 1936; J.D., U. Pitts., 1939. Bar: Pa. 1940. Sr. ptnr. Hess, Reich, Georgiades, Ray & Homyak and predecessor firm Emerson G. Hess & Assocs., Pitts., 1940—; solicitor Scott Twp. Sch. Bd., 1958-65; legal counsel Judiciary com. Pa. Ho. of Reps., 1967-69; solicitor Scott Twp., 1968-69, Crafton Borough, 1974-78, Authority for Improvements in Municipalities of Allegheny County, 1977-80. Bd. dirs. Golden Triangle YMCA, Pitts., 1945—, WQED Ednl. TV, Pitts., 1952-68; pres., dir. Civic Light Opera Assn., Pitts., 1967-68; mem. internat. com. YMCA World Service, N.Y.C., 1968-78; trustee, chmn. Central Christian Ch., Pitts., 1962-63; pres. Anesthesia and Resuscitation Found., Pitts., 1964—, Pa. Med. Research Found., 1960—. Mem. ABA, Pa. Bar Assn., Allegheny County Bar Assn. General corporate, Probate, Real property. Home: 43 Robin Hill Dr Pittsburgh PA 15136 Office: 1900 Koppers Bldg Pittsburgh PA 15219

HESS, FREDERICK J., U.S. attorney; b. Highland, Ill., Sept. 22, 1941; s. Fred and Matilda (Maiden) H.; m. Mary V. Menkhus, Nov. 13, 1976; children—Frederick, M. Elizabeth. B.S. in Polit. Sci., History, St. Louis U., 1963; J.D., Washburn Sch. Law, Topeka, 1971. Bar: Kans. 1971, Ill. 1975, U.S. Supreme Ct. 1975, D.C. 1977, U.S. Tax Ct. 1977. Asst. U.S. atty. Dept. Justice, East St. Louis, Ill., 1971-73, 1st asst. U.S. atty., 1973-76; ptnr. Stiehl & Hess, Belleville, Ill., 1977-82; U.S. Atty. So. Dist., Ill., East St. Louis, Ill., 1982—. Served to capt. USAF, 1964-68. Fellow Ill. Bar Assn.; mem. Kans. Bar Assn., D.C. Bar Assn. Republican. Clubs: MAC (St. Louis); Tamarac Golf (Shilo, Ill.). Federal civil litigation, State civil litigation, Criminal. Home: 325 S High Belleville IL 62220

HESS, GEORGE FRANKLIN, II, lawyer; b. Oak Park, Ill., May 13, 1939; s. Franklin Edward and Carol (Hackman) H.; m. Diane Ricci, Aug. 9, 1974; 1 son, Franklin Edward. B.S. in Bus., Colo. State U., 1962; J.D., Suffolk U., 1970; LL.M., Boston U., 1973. Bar: Pa. 1971, Fla. 1973, U.S. Tax Ct. 1974, U.S. Dist. Ct. (so. dist.) Fla. 1975. Assoc. Hart, Childs, Hepburn, Ross & Putnam, Phila., 1970-72; instr. Suffolk U. Law Sch., Boston, 1973-74; ptnr. Henry, Hess & Hoines, Ft. Lauderdale, Fla., 1974-79; sole practice George F. Hess II, P.A., (merged with Mousaw, Vigdor, Reeves, Heilbronner & Kroll., Rochester, N.Y., 1981, name now Mousaw, Vigdor, Reeves & Hess), Ft. Lauderdale, 1979—, now ptnr. Bd. dirs. Children's Home Soc., Ft. Lauderdale, 1985—, Nadeau Charitable Found.; Served to lt. USNR, 1963-66. Mem. ABA, Fla. Bar Assn., Broward County Bar Assn., SAR, Phi Alpha Delta. Episcopalian. Clubs: Tower, Logo Mar, Lauderdale Yacht (Ft. Lauderdale); U.S. Navy League. Estate planning, Probate, Personal income taxation. Home: 2524 Castilla Isle Fort Lauderdale FL 33301 Office: Mousaw Vigdor Reeves & Hess 1410 One Financial Plaza Fort Lauderdale FL 33394

HESS, JERRY JOHN, lawyer; b. Davenport, Iowa, Sept. 29, 1930; s. John Walter and Margaret Louise (Meisner) H.; m. Marilyn Mae Miller, Feb. 4, 1951; children: John J., Thomas R. BBA, Drake U., 1959; JD, U. Mo., Kansas City, 1967. Bar: Kans. 1967, U.S. Dist. Ct. Kans. 1967, U.S. Supreme Ct. 1972. Credit supr. Phillips Petroleum Co., Kansas City, 1951-70; sole practice Overland Park, Kans., 1970—. Mem. citizens com. Johnson County Criminal Justice Adv. Council, Olathe, Kans., 1984—. Mem. Kans. Bar Assn., Johnson County Bar Assn., Am. Judges Assn., Kans. Mcpl. Judges Assn., Phi Alpha Delta. Republican. Roman Catholic. Lodge: K.C. (adv.). Local government, Family and matrimonial, Probate. Home: 9732 W 89th Terr Overland Park KS 66212 Office: 6405 Metcalf Suite 100 Overland Park KS 66202

HESS, LAWRENCE EUGENE, JR., lawyer; b. Phila., Aug. 18, 1923; s. Lawrence Eugene and Charlotte (Engel) H.; m. Jane Strayer, June 11, 1949; children—Lawrence Edward, Charlotte Jane. Student Princeton U., 1942-43; B.S., U.S. Naval Acad., 1947; J.D. with honors, George Washington U., 1954. Bar: Pa. 1954, D.C. 1954, U.S. Supreme Ct. 1963. Commd. ensign U.S. Navy, 1946, advanced through grades to lt. comdr.; assigned to various ships and stas.; ret., 1966; house counsel Nat. Liberty Life Ins. Co., Valley Forge, Pa., 1966-67, Standard Computers, Inc., 1967-68; atty. Def. Personnel Support Center, Phila., 1968-69; counsel Am. Acceptance Corp., Phila., 1969-74; sole practice, Fort Washington, Pa., 1974—. Mem. Sch. Bd. Upper Dublin Sch. Dist. Montgomery County, Pa., 1981-85; pres. bd. trustees Glenside (Pa.) United Meth. Ch., 1973-76, trustee, 1987—. Mem. ABA, Fed. Bar Assn., Pa. Bar Assn., Phila. Bar Assn., Montgomery Bar Assn., Comml. Law League Am., Judge Advocates Assn., Pa. Trial Lawyers Assn., Montgomery Trial Lawyers Assn., Navy League U.S., U.S. Naval Acad. Alumni Assn. Phila. (past pres., dir.), Ret. Officers Assn. (life mem.; bd. dirs. Willow Grove chpt.), Am. Legion, Mil. Order World Wars. Republican. Clubs: Army-Navy (Arlington, Va.); Mfrs. Golf and Country (Oreland, Pa.); Princeton (N.Y.C.) Lodge: Masons. Mem. editorial bd. George Washington U. Law Rev., 1952-53. General practice, Probate, Family and matrimonial. Home: 515 Dreshertown Rd Fort Washington PA 19034

HESS, MICHAEL ANTHONY, lawyer; b. Roscrea, Tipperary, Ireland, July 5, 1952; came to U.S. 1955; s. A. Michael and Marjorie (Lane) H. BA, U. Notre Dame, 1974; JD, George Washington U., 1977. Bar: D.C. 1977, U.S. Dist. Ct. D.C. 1978, U.S. Ct. Appeals (D.C. cir.) 1978, U.S. Supreme Ct. 1982, U.S. Dist. Ct. (no. and ea. dists.) Calif. 1983, U.S. Ct. Appeals (9th cir.) 1983. Research dir., mng. editor Nat. Inst. Mcpl. Law Offices, Washington, 1977-80; staff atty. redistricting div. Rep. Nat. Com., Washington, 1981-83, dep. chief counsel, 1983—; cons. Internat. City Mgmt. Assn., Washington, 1980. Co-author: Defending Against the (Zoning) Taking Challenge, 1979, Federal Grant Conditions, 1979, Municipal Legal Departments: Administration and Finance, 1979; co-authorMunicipalities and Civil Rights Act Litigation, 1978, Proof of Legislative and Administrative Intent, 1979, The Law of Reapportionment and Redistricting, 1981-82, 1981. Mem. Rep. Nat. Lawyers Assn., Heritage Council Working Group on Bicentennial of Constitution, 1986-87, speaker's bur. Commn. on Bicentennial of U.S. Constitution, 1987. Mem. ABA, D.C. Bar Assn. Roman Catholic. Administrative and regulatory, Federal civil litigation, Election law reapportionment and redistricting law. Home: Quince Hill Farm Kearneysville WV 25430 Office: Republican National Com 310 1st St SE Washington DC 20003

HESS, ROBERT KENNEDY, lawyer; b. Pontiac, Mich., June 22, 1946; s. Howard Roy Hess; m. Rebecca Ann Johnson, June 22, 1972; children: Howard William, Adrianna Marie. AA with honors, Genesee Community Coll., 1971; BA with distinction, U. Mich., 1976; JD, Thomas M. Cooley Law Sch., 1980. Bar: Mich. 1981, U.S. Dist. Ct. (ea. dist.) Mich. 1981. Dep. pub. adv. State of Mich., Alpena, 1981-82; chief asst. pub. defender State of Mich., Bay City, 1985—; pros. atty. Alcona County, Harrisville, Mich., 1982-84. Served with USN, 1964-68. Mem. Mich. Trial Lawyers Assn. (criminal law com.). Republican. Lutheran. Criminal. Home: PO Box 569 Bay City MI 48707 Office: Bay County Pub Defender Office 812 N Jefferson Bay City MI 48708

HESSBERG, ALBERT, II, lawyer; b. Albany, N.Y., June 14, 1916; s. Rufus R. and Jeannette S. (Susholz) H.; m. Elisabeth F. Goold, May 9, 1948; children—Caroline E. Hessberg Smedvig, Albert III, Philip G. B.A., Yale U., 1938, LL.B., 1941; LL.D. (hon.), Coll. of St. Rose, 1982. Bar: N.Y. 1946. Asso., Arthur J. Harvey, Albany, 1946; asso. Poskanzer, Hessberg, Blumberg, Dolin, Barba, Greisler & Trombly, Albany, 1947-53, ptnr., 1953-84; ptnr. Hiscock & Barclay, 1985—; dir. Wytex Corp., Albany, Litchfield Investment, Albany. Bd. govs. Albany Med. Center Hospital; trustee Albany's Hosp. for Incurables. Served to lt. comdr. USNR, 1941-45. Mem. Albany County Bar Assn., N.Y. State Bar Assn., ABA, Am. Coll. Probate Counsel, N.Y. State Bar Found., Am. Legion, UN Assn. Clubs: Albany County, Fort Orange (Albany), Yale of N.Y.C. Jewish. Contbg. author: How to Live and Die with New York Probate. Probate, Estate taxation, General corporate. Home: 1635 New Scotland Rd Slingerlands NY 12159 Office: 60 State Suite 755 Albany NY 12207

HESSEL, MILDRED REDA, lawyer; b. St. Louis, Mar. 26, 1913; D. Abraham Aaron and Fanny (Wrobel) Margulis; m. Meyer Hessel, Dec. 30, 1941; children: Arthur Richard, Joan. BA, JD, Washington U., St. Louis, 1936. Sole practice St. Louis, 1936—. Bd. dirs., sec. Girl Scouts U.S. of Greater St. Louis; pres. Conf. of Jewish Orgns.; bd. dirs. Miriam Sch. (united order of true sisters). Mem. Mo. Bar Assn., Bar Assn. of Met. St. Louis, St. Louis County Bar Assn., Assn. Trial Lawyers Am. Jewish. Family and matrimonial, General practice, Personal injury. Office: 300 Hunter Ave Saint Louis MO 63124

HESSELBACH, BRUCE WILLIAM, lawyer; b. N.Y.C., Sept. 29, 1950; s. William Bruce and Margaret Loretta (Walsh) H.; m. Carol Louise Streeter, June 3, 1972; children: Erica Nancy, Brian Jeffrey. BA, Yale U., 1972; JD, Villanova U., 1975. Bar: N.Y. 1976, U.S. Dist. Ct. (so. dist.) N.Y. 1978. Assoc. Easton & Echtman P.C., N.Y.C., 1976—. Mem. ABA, N.Y. State Bar Assn., Assn. of Bar of City of N.Y. State civil litigation, Real property, Contracts commercial. Home: 145-14 33d Ave Flushing NY 11354 Office: Easton & Echtman PC 122 E 42d St New York NY 10168

HESSLINK, ROBERT MELVIN, JR., lawyer; b. Sheboygan, Wis., Nov. 7, 1945; s. Robert M. Sr. and Camilla Frances (Reisner) H.; m. Sue Ellen Schneider, Sept. 6, 1968 (div. Mar. 1981); m. Caryl F. Kappelman Welk, Oct. 18, 1986. BS, Lakeland Coll., 1968; LLD, U. Wis., 1972. Bar: Wis. 1973, U.S. Dist. Ct. (we. dist.) Wis. 1973, U.S. Dist. Ct. (ea. dist.) Wis. 1976, U.S. Ct. Appeals (7th cir.) 1983, U.S. Supreme Ct. 1983. Staff atty. TVA, Knoxville, 1972-73; asst. corp. counsel Dane County, Madison, Wis., 1973-76; assoc. atty. Mulcahy & Wherry S.C., Madison, 1976-78; ptnr. Dewitt, Sundby, Huggett, Schumacher & Morgan, Madison, 1978-84; prin. Hesslink Law Offices, Madison, 1984—. Editor: Urban Lawyer, 1983-84. Served with U.S. Army, 1969-71. Mem. ABA, (vice chmn. com. on pub. employee labor relations 1984—), Wis. Bar Assn., Dane County Bar Assn. Roman Catholic. Avocations: tennis, camping, running. Labor, Administrative and regulatory, Federal civil litigation. Home: 2513 Westbrook Ln Madison WI 53711 Office: 6200 Gisholt Dr Madison WI 53713

HESSON, WILLIAM M., JR., lawyer; b. Balt., Jan. 8, 1943; s. William M. and Ethel (Rau) H.; m. Sylvia Bushong, Sept. 11, 1965; children—Michael, Stephanie. B.A., Washington Coll., Chestertown, Md., 1964; J.D., Vanderbilt U., 1967. Bar: Md. 1968, U.S. Dist. Ct. Md. 1968, U.S. Ct. Appeals (4th cir.) 1977, U.S. Supreme Ct. 1977, D.C. 1984. Staff atty. Legal Aid Bur., Balt., 1967-69; assoc. Nolan, Plumhoff & Williams, Towson, Md., 1969-74, ptnr., 1975—. Mem. inquiry panel Atty. Grievance Commn., Annapolis, 1978—; mem. 3d Cir. Jud. Nomination Commn., 1983-87; chmn. panel Health Claims Arbitration Office, Balt.; trustee Franklin Sq. Hosp., 1986—, Friends Sch. of Balt., 1986—. Mem. ABA, Am. Arbitration Assn., Am. Judicature Soc., Fed. Bar Assn., Md. State Bar Assn., Balt. County Bar Assn. (exec. council), Md. Assn. Realtors (bd. dirs.), Greater Balt. Bd. Realtors (treas. 1987). Democrat. Lutheran. Club: Baltimore Country. General corporate, State civil litigation, Real property. Office: Nolan Plumhoff & Williams 204 W Pennsylvania Ave Towson MD 21204

HEST, BRUCE HENRY, lawyer, consultant; b. Bronx, N.Y., Apr. 27, 1953; s. Irving William and Rose June (Palmer) H.; m. Robin Sue Lopato, June 11, 1983; 1 child, Ivy Monica. BA, NYU, 1974; JD, Fordham U., 1977; LLM, Boston U., 1985. Bar: N.Y. 1978, Fla. 1978, D.C. 1979, Mass. 1984, U.S. Tax Ct. 1985, U.S. Supreme Ct. 1986. Atty. N.Y. State Supreme Ct., N.Y.C., 1977-79; assoc. Siegel & Gale, N.Y.C., 1979-82; atty. New England Mut. Life Ins. Co., Boston, 1982-87; assoc. Craif Donoff, P.A., Boca Raton, Fla., 1987—; cons. Chase Manhattan Bank, N.Y.C., 1981, Equitable Life Assurance Co., N.Y.C., 1981, Barnett Banks, Jacksonville, Fla., 1983-84. Editor: Bender's Corporations Forms, 1979. Mem. ABA, N.Y. State Bar Assn., Fed. Communications Bar Assn., Boca Raton Real Estate Planning Council. Avocations: computers, photography, music. Probate, Pension, profit-sharing, and employee benefits, Entertainment. Home: 8249 Severn Dr Boca Raton FL 33433 Office: Craig Donoff PA 2300 Corp Blvd NW Suite 137 Boca Raton FL 33431

HESTER, CHRISTOPHER SCOTT, lawyer; b. Big Spring, Tex., Oct. 3, 1956; s. Joseph P. and Majorie B. (Barnes) H.; m. Rhonda Lynn Mabry, Nov. 27, 1982; children: Christopher S. II, Stefan Mabry. Student, U. N.C., 1975-77; BA in Polit. Sci., U. Ga., 1979; JD, Wake Forest U., 1982. Bar: N.C. 1982, U.S. Dist. Ct. (ea. and mid. dists.) N.C. 1982, Fla. 1983, U.S. Dist. Ct. (ea. and mid. dists.) Fla. 1983. Law clk. to presiding justice U.S. Dist. Ct. (ea. dist.) N.C., New Bern, 1982-83; law clk. U.S. Dist. Ct. (mid. dist.) N.C., Greensboro, 1983-84; assoc. Lowndes, Drosdick et al, Orlando, Fla., 1984-85, Reinman, Harrell et al, Melbourne, Fla., 1985—. Avocations: golf, tennis, sailing. Federal civil litigation, State civil litigation, Admiralty. Home: 360 Carissa Dr Satellite Beach FL 32937 Office: Reinman Harrell et al 1825 S Riverview Dr Melbourne FL 32901

HESTER, JON LEE, lawyer; b. Eschwege, Hessen, Fed. Republic of Germany, Apr. 30, 1948; s. Louis Lee and Irmgard Mimi (Brussler) H.; m. Karen Kay Bohner, Jan. 17, 1969; children: Gregory Sean, Scott Adam, Michael David. BA, Alaska Meth. U., 1970; JD, U. Okla., 1972; cert., Nat. Jud. Coll., 1978. Gen. counsel USDA, Washington, 1973; sole practice Oklahoma City, 1973-76, 1982—; spl. dist. judge Oklahoma County, Oklahoma City, 1976-82; mem. faculty U. Okla., Norman, 1978—, Rose State Coll., Midwest City, Okla., 1978-83. Contbr. articles to profl. jours. Chmn. Dem. Precinct, Bethany, Okla., 1973-76. Fellow Am. Acad. Matrimonial Lawyers; mem. Okla. Bar Assn. (chmn. family law sect. 1983, 86), Okla. County Bar Assn. (bd. dirs. 1983-85). Lutheran. Avocations: soccer, playing, refereeing, volunteer coaching, horses. Family and matrimonial. Office: 5400 NW Grand Blvd #360 Oklahoma City OK 73112

HESTER, WORTH HUTCHINSON, lawyer; b. Bladenboro, N.C., Apr. 6, 1923; s. William Wade and Elizabeth (Penny) H.; m. Anne Sutton, Dec. 20, 1952 (dec. Aug. 1958); children: Elizabeth Anne, Henry Clifton, Emily Jean; m. Anna Ruth King, Dec. 18, 1961; children: Ruth Ellen, Worth Jr., Matthew Wade, Mark Anthony, Anita Lynette. BS, Wake Forest U., 1948, JD, 1950. Bar: N.C. 1950. Staff atty. gen. State of N.C., Raleigh, 1954-55; ptnr. Hester & Hester and predecessor firm Hester, Johnson, Johnson & Hester, Elizabethtown, N.C., 1955—. Served with Med. Service Corps, U.S. Army, 1943-46. Baptist. Lodge: Kiwanis (pres. Elizabethtown). Avocation: golf. Real property, Probate. Home: PO Box 127 Elizabethtown NC 28337 Office: Hester & Hester 115 Courthouse Dr Elizabethtown NC 28337

HESTERBERG, GREGORY XAVIER, lawyer; b. Bklyn., Dec. 3, 1950; s. Alexander G. and Ruth (Tooley) H. B.A., Georgetown U., 1972; J.D., Bklyn Law Sch., 1975. Bar: N.Y. 1976. Ptnr. Hesterberg & Keller, Bklyn., 1975—; lectr. Bklyn. archdiocese. Interviewer admissions com. Georgetown U.; bd. dirs., pres. Flatbush Boys' Club; bd. dirs. Emerald Assn. L.I. Mem. ABA, N.Y. State Bar Assn., Bklyn. Bar Assn. (treas.), Catholic Lawyers Guild (sec.). Clubs: Kiwanis (Garden City, L.I.); N.Y. Athletic (N.Y.C.). Contbr. articles to profl. jours. Probate, Real property, Estate taxation. Office: Hesterberg & Keller 32 Court St Brooklyn NY 11201 also: 170 Old Country Rd Mineola NY 11505

HETHERINGTON, JOHN JOSEPH, lawyer; b. Phila., Jan. 22, 1947; s. Jack Joseph and Josephine J. (Krawiec) H.; m. Janet Louise Erven; children: Wendy Lynn, John Joseph, Patrick John. BA, U. Pa., 1974; JD, Gonzaga U., 1977. Bar: Pa. 1977, U.S. Dist. Ct. (ea. dist.) Pa. 1979, U.S. Ct. Appeals (3d cir.) 1983. Staff atty. Legal Services Northeast Pa., Wilkes-Barre, 1977-79; sole practice Chalfont, Pa., 1979-82, Hilltown, Pa., 1986—; ptnr. Toll, Hetherington & Ghen, Doylestown, Pa., 1982-86; cons., lectr. pre-retirement workshops, Devon, Pa., 1984—; solicitor Hilltown (Pa.) Twp. Townwatch Assn., 1982—; legal counsel to pension miners orgn., Glen Lyon, Pa., 1977-79; bd. dirs. Pennswood Village, Newtown, Pa. Mem. Bucks County Adult Services Adv. Bd., Doylestown, 1981-84. Served with USAF, 1966-69. Mem. Pa. Bar Assn. (chmn. com. on legal affairs of older persons 1983-85, lectr. 1982—, lectr., author, course planner 1985, com. on legal affairs of elderly and social security law 1987), Bucks County Bar Assn. (com. on legal problems of elderly, panelist), Nat. Orgn. Social Security Claimants' Reps., Am. Soc. Law and Medicine. Republican. Roman Catholic. Avocations: horticulture, collecting contemporary music. General practice, Estate planning, Pension, profit-sharing, and employee benefits. Home: PO Box 229 Hilltown PA 18927 Office: Hilltown Pike PO Box 229 Hilltown PA 18927

HETHERWICK, GILBERT LEWIS, lawyer; b. Winnsboro, La., Oct. 30, 1920; s. Septimus and Addie Louise (Gilbert) H.; m. Joan Friend Gibbons, May 31, 1946 (dec. Aug. 1964); children—Janet Hetherick Pumphrey, Ann Hetherwick Lyons, Gilbert, Carol Hetherwick Sutton, Katherine Hetherwick Hummel; m. 2d, Mertis Elizabeth Cook, June 7, 1967. B.A. summa cum laude, Centenary Coll., 1942; J.D., Tulane U., 1949. Bar: La. 1949. With legal dept. Arkla, Inc., Shreveport, La., 1949-53; ptnr. Blanchard, Walker, O'Quin & Roberts, Shreveport, 1953—. Mem. Shreveport City Charter Revision Com., 1955; Shreveport Mcpl. Fire and Police Civil Service Bd., 1956, vice chmn., 1957-78, chmn., 1978—. Served with AUS, 1942-46. Recipient Tulane U. Law Faculty medal, 1949. Mem. La. Bar Assn., Shreveport Bar Assn. (pres. 1987), Fed. Energy Bar Assn., Order of Coif, Phi Delta Phi, Omicron Delta Kappa. Episcopalian. Club: Petroleum of Shreveport. General practice. Home: 4604 Fairfield Ave Shreveport LA 71106 Office: First Nat Bank Tower Shreveport LA 71101

HETKE, RICHARD L., lawyer; b. Monrovia, Calif., June 1, 1952; s. Richard Louis and Susan (Botschner) H.; m. Holly Susan Hansen, June 3, 1983. AB, Dartmouth Coll., 1973; JD, Harvard U., 1978. Bar: Calif. 1978, Ill. 1980. Assoc. Thelen, Marrin, Johnson, San Francisco, 1978-80, Mayer, Brown & Platt, Chgo., 1980-82; counsel Household Internat., Northbrook, Ill., 1982-84; sr. counsel Kraft, Inc., Glenview, Ill., 1984—. Mem. ABA, Ill. Bar Assn., Phi Beta Kappa. Clubs: Dartmouth (Chgo.) (v.p. 1980—), Tuscumbia (Green Lake, Wis.). Avocations: baseball memorabilia, golf, tennis. Antitrust, General corporate, Private international. Home: 211 E Ohio St Chicago IL 60611 Office: Kraft Inc Kraft Ct Glenview IL 60025

HETLAGE, ROBERT OWEN, lawyer; b. St. Louis, Jan. 9, 1931; s. George C. and Doris M. (Talbot) H.; m. Anne R. Willis, Sept. 24, 1960; children—Mary T., James C., Thomas K. A.B., Washington U., St. Louis, 1952, LL.B., 1954; LL.M., George Washington U., 1957. Bar: Mo. 1954, U.S. Dist. Ct. (ea. dist.) Mo. 1954, U.S. Supreme Ct. 1957. Ptnr., Hetlage & Hetlage, 1958-65, Peper, Martin, Jensen, Maichel & Hetlage, St. Louis, 1966—. Served to 1st lt. U.S. Army, 1954-58. Fellow Am. Bar Found.; mem. Bar Assn. Met. St. Louis (pres. 1967-68), Mo. Bar (pres. 1976-77), ABA (chmn. real property, probate and trust law sect. 1981-82), Am. Coll. Real Estate Lawyers (pres. 1985-86), Am. Bar Found. Am. Judicature Soc., Anglo-Am. Real Property Inst. (treas. 1982-83). Real property. Office: 24th Floor 720 Olive St Saint Louis MO 63101

HETLAND, JOHN ROBERT, lawyer, educator; b. Mpls., Mar. 12, 1930; s. James L. and Evelyn (Lundgren) H.; m. Mildred Woodruff, Dec. 1951 (div.); children: Lynda Lee, Robert John, Debra Ann.; m. Anne Kneeland, Dec. 1972; children: Robin T. Kneeland, Elizabeth J. Kneeland. B.S.L., U. Minn., 1952, J.D., 1956. Bar: Minn. bar 1956, Calif. bar 1962. Practice law Mpls., 1956-59; asso. prof. law U. Calif., Berkeley, 1959-60; prof. law U. Calif., 1960—; practice law Berkeley, 1959—; vis. prof. law Stanford U., 1971, 80, U. Singapore, 1972. Author: Hetland, California Real Property Secured Transactions, 1970, Hetland, Commercial Real Estate Transactions, 1972, Hetland, Secured Real Estate Transactions, 1974, Maxwell, Riesenfeld, Hetland and Warren, California Cases on Security Transactions in Land, 2d edit., 1975, 3d edit., 1984, Hetland, Secured Real Estate Transactions, 1977; contbr. articles to legal, real estate and fin. jours. Served to lt. comdr. USNR, 1953-55. Mem. state bars Calif. and Minn., Am. Bar Assn., Order of Coif, Phi Delta Phi. Republican. Federal civil litigation, State civil litigation, Real property. Home: 20 Redcoach Ln Orinda CA 94563 Office: 2600 Warring St Berkeley CA 94704

HETMAN, NICHOLAS WAYNE, lawyer; b. Reno, May 12, 1950; s. Walter and Anita Joyce (Eastwood) H.; m. Rebekah Marion Lundy, Mar. 10, 1972 (div. Aug. 1976); m. Alta Adams, June 12, 1977; 1 child, Andrea Nicole. BA in English, Emory and Henry Coll., 1971; JD, U. Tenn., 1977. Bar: Ky. 1978, U.S. Ct. Appeals (5th and D.C. cirs.) 1983, U.S. Supreme Ct. 1984. Atty. Tex. Gas Transmission Corp., Owensboro, Ky., 1977—; gen. counsel TXG Engring., Owensboro, 1986—; gen. counsel, asst. sec. TXG Alaska, Owensboro, 1986—. Served with USNR, 1971-74. Mem. ABA, Ky. Bar Assn. (chmn. corp. ho. counsel sect. 1984-85), Daviess County Bar Assn., Am. Corp. Counsel Assn., Assn. Interstate Commerce Commn. Practitioners. Democrat. Baptist. Avocation: sports. General corporate, FERC practice, Oil and gas leasing. Home: 1855 Aspenwood Ct A4 Owensboro KY 42301 Office: Tex Gas Transmission Corp 3800 Frederica St Owensboro KY 42301

HETSKO, CYRIL FRANCIS, retired lawyer, corporation executive; b. Scranton, Pa., Oct. 4, 1911; s. John Andrew and Anna (Lesco) H.; m. Josephine G. Stein, Nov. 12, 1932; children—Jacqueline V. (Mrs. Charles F. Kaufer), Cyril M., Cynthia F. (Mrs. William J. Rainey). Jeffery F. A.B., Dickinson Coll., 1933; J.D., U. Mich., 1936. Bar: Pa. 1937, N.Y. 1938, U.S. Supreme Ct. 1965. Assoc. Chadbourne, Parke, Whiteside & Wolff (name now Chadbourne & Parke), 1936-55, partner, 1955-64; gen. counsel Am. Brands, Inc.,, 1964-77, v.p., 1965-69, sr. v.p., 1969-77, also former dir.; former dir. Acme Visible Records, Inc., Acushnet Co., Am. Brands Export Corp., Am. Tobacco Internat. Corp., James B. Beam Distilling Co., James B. Beam Distilling Internat. Co., Duffy-Mott Co., Inc., Gallaher Ltd. (Gt. Britain), Master Lock Co., Master Lock Export, Inc., Swingline, Inc., Andrew Jergens Co., Sunshine Biscuits, Inc., Swingline Export Corp., Wilson Jones Co. Mem. ABA, Fed., N.Y. State bar assns., U.S. Trademark Assn. (dir. 1959-67, 68-72, 73-77, pres. 1965-66, hon. bd. chmn. 1966-67, mem. council past presidents 1977—), Order of Coif, Phi Beta Kappa, Phi Delta Theta, Delta Theta Phi. Republican. Presbyterian. Clubs: Intrepids, Explorers, Williams (N.Y.C.); Nat. Lawyers (Washington); Ridgewood (N.J.) Country. General corporate. Home: 714 Waverly Rd Ridgewood NJ 07450

HEUBEL, WILLIAM BERNARD, lawyer, internt. contract cons.; b. Sharon, Pa., Mar. 7, 1928; s. Herman J. and Margaret (Becker) H. Student Gannon U., 1948-49; B.S., Purdue U., 1952; J.D., Ind. U., 1954. Bar: Ind. 1955, U.S. Dist. Ct. (so. dist.) Ind. 1955. Mem. profl. mgmt. staff AT&T Long Lines, 1955-61; contract adminstr. nuclear and def. Westinghouse Electric Corp., Pitts., 1961-68, mgr. mktg. adminstrn. nuclear, 1968-73, contract mgmt. cons. corp. mktg., 1973-81, contract cons. internat. sales contracts-law dept., 1981—. Served with AUS, 1946-48. Mem. ABA, Internat. Bar Assn., Am. Mgmt. Assn. Roman Catholic. Contracts commercial, Private international, Government contracts and claims. Office: 123 Franklin Dr Greenburg PA 15601

HEUSSI, JONATHAN A., lawyer; b. Elizabethtown, N.Y., Apr. 6, 1951; s. Andre A. and Hope A. (Evenson) H.; m. Marsha K. Pleiss, July 31, 1978 (div. 1981); m. Deborah M. Collins, June 29, 1984; stepchildren: Erin Towne, Amy Towne. BA, U. N.H., 1976; JD, Creighton U., 1979. Bar: N.Y. 1981. Assoc. law offices of Patrick J. Carney, Ticonderoga, N.Y., 1980-82; sole practice Ticonderoga, 1982—. Committeeperson, treas. Essex County (N.Y.) Dems., 1985—; bd. dirs. Citizens' Domestic Violence & Criminal Justice Planning Corp. Essex County, Elizabethtown, 1984—. Mem. ABA (family law sect.), Essex County Bar Assn. Democrat. Family and matrimonial, Real property, Consumer commercial. Home: 75 Plank Rd Mineville NY 12956 Office: 14 Father Joques Pl Ticonderoga NY 12883

HEWES, RICHARD DAVID, lawyer; b. Biddeford, Maine, Aug. 16, 1926; s. Clyfton and Mary Frances (Libbey) H.; m. Betsey Shaw, Sept. 25, 1954; children: Nancy Hewes Barry, Richard N., James S., Anne K., Carolyn Hewes Smith. BA, U. Maine, Orono, 1950; LLB, Boston U., 1953. Bar: Maine 1953, Mass. 1954, U.S. Dist. Ct. Mass. 1955, U.S. Ct. Appeals (1st cir.) 1959, U.S. Dist. Ct. Maine 1960, U.S. Ct. Internat. Trade 1963. Assoc. Clyfton Hewes, Saco, Maine, 1953-54; atty. Liberty Mut. Ins. Co., Boston, 1954-60; ptnr. R. R. L. & Hewes, Portland, Maine, 1960-63, Thompson, W., Hewes & S., Portland, 1963-71, Hewes, Douglas, Whiting & Quinn, Portland, 1971—. Rep. Maine Ho. of Reps., Augusta, 1967-76; speaker Maine Ho. of Reps., 1973-74; senator Maine State Legis., Augusta, 1977-78, co-chmn. judiciary com., 1971-72; co-chmn. legal affairs com. Cumberland County Commrs., Portland, 1977-78, commr., 1984—, chmn. 1986-87; mem. exec. com. Greater Portland Council of Govts., 1986—. Served to capt. U.S. Army, 1945-60, Korea. Recipient Dist. Service to Youth award Maine State YMCA, 1983, Commendation award Maine Hwy. Safety Commn., 1971, Cert. of Appreciation Portland chpt. ARC, 1983. Mem. ABA, Maine State Bar Assn., Cumberland County Bar Assn. (pres. 1984), Northern New Eng. Def. Counsel (pres. 1973), Fedn. of Ins. and Corp. Counsel. Republican. Episcopalian. Clubs: Portland Country Club (Falmouth, Maine), Portland (pres. 1965, chmn. bd. dirs. 1966). Avocations: tennis, badminton. State civil litigation, Probate, Workers' compensation. Home: 15 Garden Ln Cape Elizabeth ME 04107 Office: Hewes Douglas Whiting & Quinn 103 Exchange St Portland ME 04112-7108

HEWIT, RUSSELL LYLE, lawyer; b. Santa Monica, Calif., Feb. 16, 1952; s. Oliver Hartley III and Patricia (Callender) H.; m. Nan Louise McGlennon, June 8, 1973; m. Meghan Elizabeth, Russell Lyle Jr., Grant McCabe, Alexander Goodfellow. BA, Washington & Lee U., 1974, JD cum laude, 1977. Assoc. Shanley & Fisher, Newark, 1977-79; ptnr. Dughi & Hewit, Cranford, N.J., 1979—. Editor Washington and Lee Law Rev., 1976-77. Trustee Wardlaw-Hartridge Sch., Edison. N.J., 1981—. Mem. ABA, Assn. Trial Lawyers Am., N.J. Bar Assn., Washington and Lee U. Alumni Assn. (pres. no. N.J. chpt. 1982—), Order of Coif. Presbyterian. Federal civil litigation, State civil litigation, Environment. Home: 58 Fairview Ave Chatham NJ 07928 Office: Dughi & Hewit 340 North Ave Cranford NJ 07016

HEWITT, EMILY CLARK, lawyer; b. Balt., May 26, 1944; d. John Frank and Margaret Genevieve (Gray) H. A.B., Cornell U., 1966; M.Phil., Union Theol. Sem., 1975; J.D., Harvard U., 1978. Bar: Mass. 1978, U.S. Dist. Ct. Mass. 1979, U.S. Ct. Appeals (1st cir.) 1984. Ordained priest Protestant Episcopal Ch., 1974. Adminstr. Cornell and Hofstra U. Upward Bound Programs, N.Y.C., 1967-69; asst. minister St. Mary's Episcopal Ch., Manhattanville, N.Y., 1972-73; lectr. Union Theol. Sem., N.Y.C., 1972-73, 74-75; asst. prof. Andover Newton Theol. Sch., Newton Centre, Mass., 1973-75; assoc. firm Hill & Barlow, Boston, 1978-85; ptnr. firm Hill & Barlow, Boston, 1985—. Co-author: Women Priests: Yes or No?, 1973; contbr. works in field. Bd. dirs. Mass. Found. for Humanities and Pub. Policy, South Hadley, 1983—. Mem. ABA, Mass. Bar Assn. (council mem. real property sect., 1983-86), Women's Bar Assn. Mass., New Eng. Women in Real Estate (bd. dirs. 1985—), Mass. Conveyancers Assn. Real property, Landlord-tenant, Contracts commercial. Office: Hill & Barlow One Internat Pl 100 Oliver St Boston MA 02110

HEWITT, JAMES WATT, lawyer; b. Hastings, Nebr., Dec. 25, 1932; s. Roscoe Stanley and Willa Manners (Watt) H.; student Hastings Coll., 1950-52; B.S., U. Nebr., 1954, J.D., 1956; m. Marjorie Ruth Barrett, Aug. 8, 1954; children—Mary Janet, William Edward, John Charles, Martha Ann. Bar: Nebr. 1956. Practice, Hastings, 1956-57, Lincoln, Nebr., 1960—; v.p., gen. counsel Nebco, Inc., Lincoln, 1961—; vis. lectr. U. Nebr. Coll. Law, 1970-71; adj. fellow univ. studies U. Nebr., 1978—; dir. Vistar Bank (formerly Gateway Bank), Lincoln. Mem. state exec. com. Rep. Party, 1967-70, mem. state central com., 1967-70, legis. chmn., 1968-70. Bd. dirs. Lincoln Child Guidance Center, 1969-72, pres., 1972; bd. dirs. Lincoln Community Playhouse, 1967-73, pres., 1972-73; trustee Bryan Meml. Hosp., Lincoln, 1968-74, 76-82, chmn., 1972-74; trustee U. Nebr. Found., 1979—. Served to capt. USAF, 1957-60. Mem. Am. (Nebr. state del. 1972-80, bd. govs. 1981-83), Nebr. State (chmn. ins. com. 1972-76, chmn. pub. relations com. 1982-84, pres. 1985-86), Fed., Lincoln bar assns., Newcomen Soc., Am., Nebr., Lincoln rose socs., Round Table, Beta Theta Pi, Phi Delta Phi. Congregationalist. Clubs: University, Country of Lincoln (Lincoln). General corporate. Home: 2990 Sheridan Blvd Lincoln NE 68502 Office: 1815 Y St PO Box 80268 Lincoln NE 68501

HEWITT, JOHN DAVID, criminal justice and criminology educator; b. Carmel, Calif., Oct. 8, 1945; s. Lester Eugene and Sarah Louise (Mann) H.; m. Avis Grey Davis, Sept. 5, 1970; children—Eben Mann, Sara Grey. B.A., Western Wash. State Coll., 1968; M.A., Ball State U., 1969; Ph.D., Wash. State U., 1975. Instr. Glenville State Coll., W.Va., 1969-70, Coll. Wooster, Ohio, 1970-72; asst. prof. Valparaiso U., Ind., 1975-76; asst. prof. dept. criminal justice and corrections Ball State U., Muncie, Ind., 1976-80, assoc. prof., 1980-84, prof. criminal justice and criminology, 1984—; sr. research assoc. sociology U. Va., 1977; vis. scholar U. Mich., 1983; cons. Nat. Ctr. for State Cts., Williamsburg, Va., 1977-79; assoc. dir. Ctr. for Middletown Studies, Muncie, 1984—. Co-author: Criminal Justice in America, 1985, The Impact of Sentencing Reform, 1983. Assoc. editor Social Sci. Jour., 1984—, Justice Quar., 1985—; contbr. articles to profl. jours. Pres. Bethel Home Place for Boys, Muncie, 1979; bd. dirs. Youth Service Bur., Muncie, 1978-80. Grantee Law Enforcement Assistance Adminstrn., 1978, Ind. Criminal Justice Planning Agy., 1977. Mem. Am. Soc. Criminology, Acad. Criminal Justice Scis., Social Sci. Assn. Democrat. Unitarian Universalist. Legal history, Legal education. Home: 1515 Kimberly Ln Muncie IN 47304 Office: Dept Criminal Justice Ball State U Muncie IN 47306

HEYCK, THEODORE DALY, lawyer; b. Houston, Apr. 17, 1941; s. Theodore Richard and Gertrude Paine (Daly) H. B.A., Brown U., 1963; J.D., N.Y. Law Sch., 1979. Bar: N.Y. 1980, Calif. 1984, U.S. Ct. Appeals (2nd cir.) 1984, U.S. Supreme Ct. 1984, U.S. Dist. Ct. (so. and ea. dists.) N.Y. 1980, U.S. Dist. Ct. (we. and no. dists.) N.Y. 1984, U.S. Dist. Ct. (ce. and so. dists.) Calif. 1984, U.S. Ct. Appeals (9th cir.) 1986. Paralegal dist. atty. Bklyn., 1975-79; asst. dist. atty. Bklyn. dist., Kings County, N.Y., 1979-85; dep. city atty., Los Angeles, 1985—; bd. dirs. Screen Actors Guild, N.Y.C., 1977-78. Mem. ABA, AFTRA, Bklyn. Bar Assn., Assn. Trial Lawyers Am., N.Y. Trial Lawyers Assn., N.Y. State Bar Assn., Calif. Bar Assn., Fed. Bar Council, Los Angeles County Bar Assn., Screen Actors Guild, Am. Fedn. TV and Radio Artists, Actors Equity Assn., Nat. Acad. TV Arts and Scis., Screen Actors Guild, Criminal, General practice, Federal civil litigation. Home: 11135 Calvert St North Hollywood CA 91606 also: 142 W 26th St New York NY 10001 Office: Office of City Atty City Hall East 200 N Main St Los Angeles CA 90012

HEYER, JOHN HENRY, II, lawyer; b. Rochester, N.Y., May 4, 1946; s. Joseph Lester and Margaret Mary (Darcy) H.; m. Charla Ann Prewitt; divorced; children: Thomas, William, John III, Richard, Mary. BA, U. Colo., 1969; JD, U. Denver, 1972. Bar: Colo. 1973, U.S. Dist. Ct. Colo. 1973, N.Y. 1976, Pa. 1979, U.S. Dist. Ct. (we. dist.) N.Y. 1980, U.S. Supreme Ct. 1982. Atty. Texaco, Inc., Denver, 1973-75; sole practice Olean, N.Y., 1975—; pres. NOrtheastern Land Services, Inc., Olean, N.Y., 1982—, Enertech Corp., Olean, 1983—; v.p. Vector Capital Corp., Rochester, N.Y., 1985—. Asst. dist. atty. Cattaraugus County, Olean, 1978-81. Mem. ABA (natural resources law sect.), N.Y. State Bar Assn. (real property law sect., real property devel. com., environ law sect.), Erie County Bar Assn., Cattaraugus County Bar Assn., Eastern Mineral Law Found. (trustee 1984—), Independent Oil and Gas Assn. of N.Y. Roman Catholic. Oil and gas leasing, Environment, Bankruptcy. Home: 4 Mile Rd Allegany NY 14706 Office: 201 N Union St Olean NY 14760

HEYLMAN, PAUL MONROE, lawyer; b. Cleve., Dec. 6, 1952; s. Martin Charles and Katherine (Monroe) H.; m. Susan Rae Greenbaum, Aug. 8, 1976; 1 child, Caroline Rae. BA, St. John's Coll., Annapolis, Md., 1974; JD, Am. U., 1978. Bar: D.C. 1978, U.S. Dist. Ct. D.C. 1979, U.S. Ct. Appeals (D.C. cir.) 1979, U.S. Ct. Appeals (10th cir.) 1982, U.S. Ct. Appeals (6th cir.) 1985, U.S. Ct. Appeals (9th cir.) 1985. Assoc. Carr, Jordan, Coyne & Savits, Washington, 1978-79; assoc. Schmeltzer, Aptaker & Sheppard P.C., Washington, 1979-83, ptnr., 1983—. Mem. ABA. Democrat. Lutheran. Labor, Pension, profit-sharing, and employee benefits. Home: 7106 Clarden Rd Bethesda MD 20814 Office: Schmeltzer Aptaker & Sheppard PC 1800 Massachusetts Ave NW Washington DC 20036

HEYMAN, IRA MICHAEL, university chancellor; b. N.Y.C., May 30, 1930; s. Harold Albert and Judith (Sobel) H.; m. Therese Helene Thau, Dec. 17, 1950; children—Stephen Thomas, James Nathaniel. AB in Govt., Dartmouth Coll., 1951; JD, Yale U., 1956; LLD (hon.), U. Pacific, 1981; LHD (hon.), Hebrew Union Coll., 1984; L.H.D. (hon.), U. Md., 1986. Bar: N.Y. 1956, Calif. 1961. Legis. asst. to U.S. Senator Ives, 1950-51; assoc. Carter, Ledyard & Milburn, N.Y.C., 1956-57; law clk. to presiding justice U.S. Ct. Appeals (2d cir.), New Haven, 1957-58; chief law clk. to Supreme Ct. Justice Earl Warren, 1958-59; acting assoc. prof. law U. Calif. at Berkeley, 1959-61, prof. law, 1961—, prof. city and regional planning, 1966—, vice chancellor, 1974-80, chancellor, 1980—; vis. prof. Yale Law Sch., 1963-64, Stanford Law Sch., 1971-72; bd. dirs. Pacific Gas & Electric Co., 1985—; counsel task force on demonstrations and protest Pres.'s Commn. on Violence, 1968-69; mem. Pub. Land Law Rev. Commn., 1968-70, Commn. on Isla Vista, U. Calif.-Santa Barbara, 1970; cons. various orgns. Editor Yale Law Jour.; contbr. articles to profl. jours. Sec. Calif. adv. com. U.S. Commn. Civil Rights, 1962-67; trustee Dartmouth Coll., 1982—, Lawyers' Commn. for Civil Rights Under Law, 1977—; chmn. exec. com. Nat. Assn. State Univs. and Land Grant Colls., 1986; chmn. Div. I subcom. Nat. Collegiate Athletic Assn. Pres.'s Commn., 1986—; chmn. Human Rights and Welfare Commn. City of Berkeley, 1966-68; chmn. acad. senate policy com. U. Calif., Berkeley, 1965-67, state-wide acad. assembly, 1964-66, 72-73; pres. Pres. and Chancellor group Pacific 10 Conf., 1984-85; mem. research adv. com. Oakland Inter-Agy. Project, 1964-65; bd. dirs. Am. Council on Edn., 1984-85. Served to 1st lt. USMC, 1951-53, to capt. USMCR, 1953-58. Named Chevalier de la Legion D'Honneur Govt. France, 1985. Mem. Am. Law Inst. (asst. reporter). Democrat. Legal education. Home: U Calif Univ House Berkeley CA 94720

HEYMANN, PHILIP B., educator, former govt. ofcl.; b. Pitts., Oct. 30, 1932. B.A., Yale U., 1954; LL.B., Harvard U., 1960. Bar: D.C., Mass. Trial atty. gen. Dept. Justice, Washington, 1961-65; asst. atty. gen. criminal div. Dept. Justice, 1978-81; dep. adminstr. Bur. Security and Consular Affairs, Dept. State, Washington, 1965; acting adminstr. Bur. Security and Consular Affairs, Dept. State, to 1967; dep. asst. sec. of state for Bur. Internat. Orgns., 1967, exec. asst. to under sec. of state, 1967-69; with Legal Aid Agy. of D.C., 1969; faculty law Harvard U., 1969-78, 81—; asso. prosecutor and cons. to Watergate Spl. Prosecution Force, summers 1973-75. Served with USAF, 1955-57. Office: Harvard Law Sch Cambridge MA 02138

HEYWOOD, BARBARA LORENTSON, lawyer; b. Bethesda, Md., Feb. 14, 1955; d. Adrian Vincent and Anna Mae (Paul) Lorentson; m. David Arms Heywood, Oct. 12, 1985. BS in Fgn. Service, Georgetown U., 1976; JD, Coll. William and Mary, 1981; LLM, U. Miami, 1982. Bar: Ohio 1981, Fla. 1983, Pa. 1985. Dep. trial clk. U.S. Tax Ct., Washington, 1976-78; assoc. McDonald, Hopkins & Hardy, L.P.A., Cleve., 1982-85, Drinker Biddle & Reath, Phila., 1985—. Mem. ABA, Pa. Bar Assn., Fla. Bar Assn., Phila. Bar Assn. Avocations: cross-country skiing, travel, bicycling. Pension, profit-sharing, and employee benefits, Estate planning, Personal income taxation. Office: Drinker Biddle & Reath 1100 PNB Bldg Philadelphia PA 19107

HEYWOOD, ROBERT GILMOUR, lawyer; b. Berkeley, Calif., May 18, 1949; s. Warren Zimri and Jean (Reinecke) H.; m. Carolyn Cox, June 10, 1972; children: Karen, Laura, John. AB with distinction, Stanford U., 1971; MA, U. Calif., Berkeley, 1972; JD cum laude, Santa Clara U., 1975. Bar: Calif. 1975, U.S. Dist. Ct. (no. and ea. dists.) Calif. 1975, U.S. Ct. Appeals (9th cir.) 1976, U.S. Supreme Ct. 1979. Assoc. Hanna, Brophy, MacLean, McAleer & Jensen, Oakland, Calif., 1976—; instr. Santa Clara U., 1975-77; faculty ctr. for trial and appellate adv. Hasting Coll. of Law, San Francisco; adj. prof. law U. Calif., Hastings, 1982-86; judge pro tem, arbitrator Alameda County Superior Ct. Bd. dirs. Alameda County Legal Aid Soc., Oakland, 1978-85. Mem. ABA, Calif. Bar Assn. (panelist continuing edn. of bar), Alameda County Bar Assn., Assn. Def. Counsel, Calif. Compensation Def. Attys. Assn. Personal injury, Workers' compensation, Insurance. Office: Hanna Brophy MacLean McAleer & Jensen 1970 Broadway Suite 1225 Oakland CA 94612

HIARING, ANNE, lawyer; b. Ross, Calif., Nov. 8, 1950; d. Phillip and Claire (Riebe) H.; m. Morgan Hall, July 29, 1978. BA, Reed Coll., 1972; JD, Hastings Coll. Law, U. Calif., 1979. Bar: Calif. 1979, U.S. Dist. Ct. (no. dist.) Calif. 1979, U.S. Dist. Ct. (so. dist.) Calif. 1986, U.S. Dist. Ct. (cen. dist.) Calif. 1987. Assoc. McCutchen, Doyle, Brown & Enersen, San Francisco, 1979-82, Graham & James, San Francisco, 1982-85; atty. Pacific Telesis Group, San Francisco, 1985—. Mem. Calif. Bar Assn. (mem. exec. com. intellectual property sect. 1986—, chmn. intellectual property com. 1982-83, pres. Barristers Club), Phi Beta Kappa. Club: Barristers. Trademark and copyright, Computer. Office: Pacific Telesis Group 140 New Montgomery St 10th Floor San Francisco CA 94105

HIBBERT, DAVID WILSON, lawyer; b. Atlanta, Nov. 21, 1950; s. George Wilfred and Dorothy Marie (Woodall) H.; m. Mary Frances Disco, June 21, 1975; children: Hector, Norman, Floyd. BA, Mercer U., 1972; JD, Emory U., 1972. Bar: Ga. 1975, U.S. Dist. Ct. (no. dist.) Ga. 1975. Sole practice Atlanta, 1975—. Mem. Ga. Bar Assn., Atlanta Bar Assn. (chmn. referral com. 1981—). Democrat. Baptist. Club: Lawyers of Atlanta, Atlanta Radio, Atlanta Bonsai (treas. 1982). Avocations: bonsai, amateur radio. Family and matrimonial, Personal injury, Workers' compensation. Home: 5255 Bowers Brook Dr Lilburn GA 30247 Office: 1720 First Fed Bldg Atlanta GA 30303

HIBBS, LOYAL ROBERT, lawyer; b. Des Moines, Dec. 24, 1925; s. Loyal B. and Catharine (McClymond) H.; children: Timothy, Theodore, Howard, Dean. B.A., U. Iowa, 1950, LL.B., 1952. Bar: Iowa 1952, Nev. 1958, U.S. Supreme Ct. 1971. Ptnr. Hibbs, Roberts, Lemons, Grundy, Eisenberg, Reno, 1972—. Fellow Am. Bar Found. (Nev. state chmn. of the fellows); mem. ABA (standing com. Lawyer Referral Service 1978-79, steering com. state dels. 1979-82, consortium on legal services and the public 1979-82, Nev. del. to Ho. of Dels. 1978—, bd. govs. 1982—85, mem. legal tech. adv. council 1985-86, com. on nat. conf. groups 1985—), Iowa Bar Assn., Nev. Bar Assn. (bd. govs. 1968-78, pres. 1977-78), Washoe County Bar Assn. (pres. 1967-68), Nat. Jud. Coll. (bd. dirs. 1986—), Greater Reno C. of C. (dir. 1970-73), Phi Alpha Delta. State civil litigation, Insurance, Probate. Home: 1489 Foster Dr Reno NV 89509 Office: 350 S Center St Reno NV 89501

HICKEL, GERARD FREDERICK, lawyer; b. Pitts., Sept. 28, 1946; s. Gerard Joseph and Marian Ann (Schluep) H.; m. Kathleen Ann Vaughn, Nov. 24, 1971; children: Gerard, Lauren, Jacqueline, Ashley, Deidra, Logan. BS, U. Dayton, 1968; JD, U. Toledo, 1971. Bar: Mich. 1972, Pa. 1973, U.S. Supreme Ct. 1977. Counsel Duquesne Light Co., Pitts., 1972—. Served to capt. USAR, 1971-84. Club: Oakmont Country (Pa.). Environment, General corporate, Nuclear power. Office: Duquesne Light Co 301 Grant St Pittsburgh PA 15279

HICKEY, JOHN HEYWARD, lawyer; b. Miami, Fla., Dec. 18, 1954; s. Weyman Park Hickey and Alice Joan (Heyward) Brown; m. Helen Hardie, Sept. 15, 1984. BA magna cum laude, Fla. State U., 1976; JD, Duke U., 1980. Bars: Fla. 1980, U.S. Dist. Ct. (so. dist) Fla. 1980, U.S. Dist. Ct. (mid. dist.) Fla. 1982, U.S. Ct. Appeals (5th cir.) 1982, U.S. Ct. Appeals (11th cir.) 1983, U.S. Supreme Ct. 1985. Trial lawyer Smathers & Thompson, Miami, 1980-85, Hornsby & Whisenand, Miami, 1985—; chmn. grievance com. Fla. Bar, 1984—, lectr. bridge-the-gap seminars, 1984-85, jud. evaluation com., 1985, mem. young lawyers div., 1986—. Interviewer of prospective undergrads. Duke U. Alumni Adv. Com., 1984—. Mem. ABA (litigation mgmt. and econs. com. 1986—, comml. transactions and banking com. 1986—), Dade County Bar Assn. (media relations com. 1982-83, membership com. 1982-83, legal edn. com. 1983-84, cir. ct. com. 1983-84, dir. 1984-86, chmn. young lawyers sect. meetings and programs com. 1985-86, chmn. lawyers sect. sports com. 1984-85, mem. exec. com. 1985—, cert. of merit 1985, chmn. profl. arbitration subcom. 1986—), Greater Miami C. of C., Phi Beta Kappa. Federal civil litigation, State civil litigation, Insurance. Home: 810 Palermo Ave Coral Gables FL 33134 Office: Hornsby & Whisenand 1110 Brickell Ave PH Suite Miami FL 33131

HICKMAN, DARRELL DAVID, state justice; b. Searcy, Ark., Feb. 6, 1935; s. James Paul and Mildred Margaret (Jackson) H.; m. Kerry Lee Hardcastle, Oct. 16, 1971; children: Dana, David, Torrie. Student, Harding Coll., Searcy, 1952-55; LL.B., U. Ark., 1958. Bar: Ark. 1958. Pvt. practice Searcy, 1964-70; dep. pros. atty. White and Woodruff counties, 1965; chancery judge 1st Chancery Circuit, 1972-76; asso. justice Ark. Supreme Ct., 1977—. Served with USN, 1958-64. Judge Freedoms Found. awards, 1977. Mem. Ark. Bar Assn. Mem. Ch. of Christ. Jurisprudence. Office: Supreme Court 3004 Painted Valley Little Rock AR 72212 *

HICKMAN, PAULA DIANE, lawyer, educator; b. Miami, July 24, 1947; d. Paul William Hickman and Eva Lena (McCampbell) Melvin; m. Arthur G. Wimer III, Apr. 1, 1973 (div. Apr. 1976); m. Charles J. Rojek, Jan. 2, 1987. Student Longwood Coll., 1965-67; B.A. with honors, U. Tenn., 1969. Bar: Pa. 1980, N.H. 1981, Maine 1981, N.J. 1983, Fla. 1986. Flight attendant Pan Am. World Airways, N.Y.C., 1972-77; law clk. N.J. Superior Ct., Burlington, N.J., 1979-80; atty. Pub. Defender Program, Exeter, N.H., 1981-83; dep. clk. Rockingham County Superior Ct., Exeter, 1983-86; sole practice, Marathon, Fla., 1986—; instr. McIntosh Coll., Dover, N.H., 1984-85. Past treas. bd. dirs. Rockingham Family Planning. Mem. ABA, N.H. Bar Assn., Fla. Keys Bar Assn., Rockingham County Bar Assn. (past v.p., past sec./treas.). Personal injury, Real property, General corporate. Office: PO Box 1368 Marathon FL 33050

HICKMAN, PAULA HAZELRIG, lawyer; b. Birmingham, Ala., Dec. 28, 1950; s. John William and Virginia (Cobb) Hazelrig; m. Kenneth Leslie Hickman, Jan. 29, 1972; children: Kenneth Brooks, William Hamilton. Student, Hollins Coll., 1968-70; BA, U. Ala., 1972; JD, La. State U., 1978. Bar: La. 1978, Ala. 1980, U.S. Ct. Appeals (5th cir.) 1985. Law clk. to presiding justice U.S. Ct. Appeals (5th cir.), Birmingham, 1978-79; assoc. Hargrove, Guyton, Ramey & Barlow, Shreveport, La., 1982—. Community v.p. Jr. League Shreveport, 1985-86; adv. bd. KDAQ Pub. Radio, Shreveport, 1986—; founder The Lighthouse: An Educational Enrichment Ctr. Inc., Shreveport, 1984; panelist Hugh O'Brien Youth Found. Seminar, Shreveport, 1986; chmn. bd. dirs. Pioneer Heritage Ctr., Shreveport, 1985; bd. dirs. La. Life Scis. Mus., Shreveport, 1985, Shreveport Rescue Mission Inc., 1985—. Mem. ABA, La. Bar Assn., Ala. Bar Assn., Shreveport Bar Assn. (legal services com. 1985-86). Republican.. Baptist. Probate, General practice. Home: 815 Unadilla St Shreveport LA 71106 Office: Hargrove Guyton Ramey & Barlow 505 Travis St Shreveport LA 71161

HICKS, CASSANDRA PAULINE, lawyer; b. Green Bay, Wis., Sept. 12, 1956; d. Paul Edward and Marjorie (Paine) H.; m. Jeffrey Stuart Weintraub, June 26, 1983. B.A. in Psychology and Polit. Sci., Ohio Wesleyan U., 1978; J.D., Am. U., 1981. Bar: Md. 1981, D.C. 1982. Assoc., Shapiro, Meiselman & Greene, Chtd., Rockville, Md., 1981—; dean's fellow LAWCOR, Washington Coll. Law, 1979-81. Mem. Md. Bar Assn., D.C. Bar Assn., Montgomery County Bar Assn. (chmn. Young Lawyers sect., council litigation sect., Chair of Yr. award 1986), Assn. Trial Lawyers Am. Democrat. Jewish. Club: Jewish Community Ctr. (Rockville). Personal injury, Family and matrimonial, State civil litigation. Office: Shapiro Meiselman & Greene Chtd 50 W Montgomery Ave Suite 230 Rockville MD 20850

HICKS, DEBORAH ANN WHITMORE, lawyer; b. New Orleans, Sept. 27, 1958; d. Warren Frederick and Shirley Ann (Tompkins) Whitmore; m.

Edgar Stennette Hicks, Aug. 8, 1982. AA, Lake-Sumter Community Coll., 1976; BA, U. Cen. Fla., 1978; JD, Mercer U., 1982. Bar: Ga. 1982, Fla. 1982, U.S. Ct. Appeals (11th cir.) 1983, U.S. Dist. Ct. (no. and mid. dists.) Ga. 1983, Ala. 1985, U.S. Dist. Ct. (mid. dist.) Ala. 1985, U.S. Dist. Ct. (no. dist.) Fla. 1986; lic. real estate broker, Fla. Sole practice Eufaula, Ala., 1982—; asst. county atty. Lamar Co., Barnesville, Ga., 1984. Mem. Assn. Trial Lawyers Am., Ga. Trial Lawyers Assn., Ala. Trial Lawyers Assn., Barbour County Bar Assn., Eufaula Jaycees, Eufaula C. of C. Republican. Baptist. Club: Morning Garden. General practice, Personal injury, Real property. Home and Office: Deborah Whitmore Hicks 244A Eufaula Office Park Eufaula AL 36027

HICKS, GEORGE GREGORY, lawyer; b. Boise, Idaho, Apr. 5, 1954; s. Francis Heubert and Barbara Jane (Nicholson) H.; m. Patti Park, Dec. 27, 1975; children: Emily Rae, Kaitlyn Elizabeth. BS in Polit. Sci., U. Idaho, 1976, JD, 1980. Bar: Idaho, 1980. Pub. defender Elmore County, Mountain Home, 1980-84; pres. Elmore County Bar Assn., Mountain Home, 1982-84; ptnr. Hicks Law Offices, Mountain Home, Idaho, 1984—. Trustee Sch. Dist. 193, Mountain Home, 1984—; bd. dirs. Parents Anonymous, Mountain Home, 1981-85, vice chmn. 1981-85; bd. dirs. Elmore County Youth Services, Mountain Home, 1985—. Mem. ABA (family law div.), Idaho Bar Assn., Idaho Trial Lawyers Assn. Democrat. Roman Catholic. Avocations: golf, intramural athletics, hunting, family outings. Criminal, Family and matrimonial, General practice. Home: 730 S 10th E Mountain Home ID 83647

HICKS, JAMES B(RADLEY), lawyer; b. Los Angeles, Mar. 28, 1959; s. John and Liane (Wolker) H.; m. Natalia A. Huryn, Oct. 15, 1983. BA, MA, Yale U., 1978; MBA, JD, Harvard U., 1982. Bar: Calif. 1982, U.S. Dist. Ct. (cen. dist.) Calif. 1982, U.S. Ct. Appeals (3d cir.) 1985. Assoc. Sullivan & Cromwell, N.Y.C., 1982, Paul, Hastings, Janofsky & Walker, Santa Monica, Calif., 1983-84, Loeb & Loeb, Los Angeles, 1984-87, White & Case, Los Angeles, 1987—. Contbr. articles to profl. jours. Mem. Los Angeles County Bar Assn. (bench and bar relations com. 1986—), Calif. Bar Assn. (history law in Calif. com. 1986—, chmn. Calif. Supreme Ct. Soc. subcom. 1987—). Clubs: Harvard (N.Y.C.); Pandits (New Haven, Conn.). Federal civil litigation, State civil litigation, Legal history. Office: White & Case 333 S Hope St Los Angeles CA 90071

HICKS, JAMES THOMAS, physician, lawyer; b. Brownsville, Pa., June 5, 1924; s. Thomas and Florence Julia (O'Donnell) H.; B.S., U. Pitts., 1945, A.B., 1946, M.S., 1946; Ph.D., George Washington U., 1950; M.D., U. Ark., 1956; J.D., DePaul U., 1975; m. Ellen Elliott, Aug. 25, 1950; children—Ellen, Mary Jo. Intern USPHS, Balt., 1958-60; resident VA Hosp., Pitts., 1958-60; admitted to Ill. bar, 1977, U.S. Ct. of Appeals, 1977, Pa. bar, 1977 U.S. Supreme Ct. Bar, 1980; practice medicine specializing in forensic and legal medicine, River Forest, Ill., 1964—; dir. labs. Oak Park (Ill.) Hosp., 1964—; pres. Oakton Service Corp., 1968—; Oakton Service Corp. of Pa. Served with USPHS, 1956-57. Fellow Nat. Cancer Inst., 1949-50. Fellow ACP, Internat. Coll. Surgeons; mem. AMA, ABA, Ill. Bar Assn., Pa. Bar Assn., Assn. Am. Trial Lawyers, Am. Assn. Hosp. Lawyers, Sigma Xi. Clubs: Univ., Whitehall, Oak Park Country, Carlton. Contbg. editor Hosp. Formulary Mgmt., 1966-70. Criminal, Health. Home: 7980 W Chicago Ave River Forest IL 60305 Office: 520 Maple Ave Oak Park IL 60304

HICKS, JOHN STANTON, lawyer; b. Fayetteville, N.C., May 24, 1943; s. Andrew R. and Barbara (Butterheim) H.; divorced; children: Deanna, Stephanie, Lisa; m. Judith Augustine, Feb. 15, 1980; children: Michael, Mark, Jeffrey. BA, Colgate U., 1965; JD, Albany Law Sch., 1976. Bar: N.Y. 1977. Corp. sec. Warwick (N.Y.) Savs. Bank, 1969-72; ptnr. Davis & Hicks, Chester, N.Y., 1978-85, Hicks & Myrow, Chester and Warwick, N.Y., 1986—. Bd. dirs. Community Ctr., 1976—, Arden Hill Hosp., Goshen, N.Y., 1982-85. Served to 1st lt. U.S. Army, 1966-69. Mem. ABA, N.Y. State Bar Assn., Orange County Bar Assn., Jaycees. Republican. Lodge: Rotary. General practice. Home: 29 Oakland Ave Warwick NY 10990 Office: Hicks & Myrow 11 Main St Chester NY 10918

HICKS, ROBERT DEHARDIT, lawyer; b. Richmond, Va., Mar. 24, 1956; s. Clarence Flippo and Miriam Patricia (DeHardit) H.; m. Nancy Jean Jacques, May 24, 1986. BA, U. Va., 1977, JD, 1981. Bar: Va. 1981, D.C. 1981, U.S. Dist. Ct. (ea. dist.) Va. 1981, U.S. Dist. Ct. D.C. 1982, U.S. Ct. Appeals (4th cir.) 1984. Assoc. Sherman, Meehan & Curtin, Washington, 1981-83, Martin, Hicks & Ingles, Gloucester, Va., 1983—. Mem. ABA, Assn. Trial Lawyers Am., Va. Trial Lawyers Assn. (bd. govs. 1984-85), Order of Coif. Democrat. Avocation: sailing. State civil litigation, Criminal, Family and matrimonial. Office: Martin Hicks & Ingles PO Box 708 Gloucester VA 23061

HICKS, ROSS HAMILTON, lawyer; b. Sweetwater, Tenn., July 24, 1946; s. Arthur Eugene and Lucille (Sherrill) H.; m. Nancy Kathryn Smith, Aug. 8, 1970; 1 child, Kathryn Suzanne. BA, Vanderbilt U., 1968; JD, U. Tenn., 1971. Bar: Tenn. 1972, U.S. Dist. Ct. (mid. dist.) Tenn. 1972. Assoc. Cunningham & Mitchell, Clarksville, Tenn., 1972-74; ptnr. Cunningham, Mitchell & Hicks, Clarksville, 1974—. Pres. Clarksville C. of C., 1979; mem. Austin Peay State U. Found., 1980—. Served to capt. USAR, 1970-78. Mem. ABA, Tenn. Bar Assn., Clarksville-Montgomery Bar Assn. (pres. 1979), Tenn. Council Sch. Attys. (v.p. 1986), Clarksville Jaycees (disting. service award 1980-81). Democrat. Presbyterian. Lodge: Kiwanis (pres. Clarksville 1979). Avocations: golf, gardening. General practice. Home: 2209 N Meadow Dr Clarksville TN 37043 Office: Cunningham Mitchell & Hicks 310 Franklin St PO Box 367 Clarksville TN 37041-0367

HICKS, WILLIAM ALBERT, III, lawyer; b. Welland, Ont., Can., Apr. 6, 1942; s. William Albert and June Gwendolyn (Birrell) H.; m. Bethany G. Galvin, May 21, 1982; children—James Christopher, Scott Kelly, Alexandra Elizabeth, Samantha Katherine. A.B., Princeton U., 1964; LL.B., Cornell U., 1967. Bar: N.Y. 1967, Ariz. 1972, U.S. Dist. Ct. Ariz. Assoc. Seward & Kissel, N.Y.C., 1967-68; assoc. Snell & Wilmer, Phoenix, 1972-75, ptnr., 1976—; instr. Ariz. State U. Sch. Law 1974-75. Bd. advisers Casino USA, Inc. 1981-84; bd. dirs. Scottsdale Arts Ctr. Assn., 1984—, v.p. devel., 1985-87. Served to. capt. JAG Corps, USAF 1968-72. Recipient DSM. Mem. ABA, Ariz. Bar Assn., Maricopa County Bar Assn., Nat. Assn. Bond Lawyers (vice chmn. com. on financing health care facilities 1982-83, chmn. com. on financing health care facilities 1983-86), Princeton U. Alumni Assn. Ariz. (pres. 1978-81, sec. 1981—). Clubs: Princeton (N.Y.C.), Paradise Valley (Ariz.) Country. Securities, Municipal bonds, General corporate. Office: 100 Valley Bank Ctr Phoenix AZ 85073

HIDALGO, EDWARD, lawyer, former secretary U.S. Navy Dept.; b. Mexico City, Oct. 12, 1912; came to U.S., 1918, naturalized, 1936; s. Egon and Domitila (Hidalgo) Kunhardt; children: Joanne, Edward, Richard, Tila. B.A. magna cum laude, Holy Cross Coll., 1933; J.D., Columbia U., 1936; civil law degree, U. Mexico Law Sch., 1959. Bar: N.Y. 1936, Mexico 1959, D.C. 1976. Law clk. 2d Circuit Ct. Appeals, N.Y., 1936-37; assoc. Wright, Gordon Zachry & Parlin, N.Y.C., 1937-42; mem. Eberstadt Com. on Unification of Mil. Services, Washington, 1945; spl. asst. to Sec. of Navy James Forrestal, Washington, 1945-46; partner Curtis, Mallet-Prevost, Colt & Mosle, 1946-48; founder, sr. partner Barrera. Siqueiros & Torres Landa, Mexico City, 1948-65; spl. asst. to Sec. of Navy Paul H. Nitze, Washington, 1965-66; partner Cahill, Gordon & Reindel, Paris, 1966-72; spl. asst. econ. affairs to dir. USIA, Washington, 1972; gen. counsel Congl. liaison USIA, 1973-76; asst. sec. for manpower, res. affairs and logistics U.S. Navy Dept., Washington, 1977-79; sec. U.S. Navy Dept., 1979-81. Served with USNR, 1942-46. Decorated Bronze Star, Royal Order of Vasa (Sweden); Order of Aztec Eagle (Mex.). Roman Catholic. Clubs: Chevy Chase, Met. Administrative and regulatory, Government contracts and claims, Private international. Office: 1828 L St NW Suite 1111 Washington DC 20036

HIDEN, ROBERT BATTAILE, JR., lawyer; b. Boston, May 8, 1933; s. Robert Battaile Sr. and Clotilda (Waddell) H.; m. Ann Eliza McCracken, Mar. 27, 1956; children: Robert B. III, Elizabeth Patterson, John Hughes. BA, Princeton U., 1955; LLB, U. Va., 1960. Bar: N.Y. 1961, U.S. Ct. Appeals (2d cir.) 1974, U.S. Dist. Ct. (so. dist.) N.Y. 1975. Assoc. Sullivan & Cromwell, N.Y.C., 1960-67, ptnr., 1968—. Articles editor and contbr. U. Va. Law Rev., 1959-60. Trustee Hampton (Va.) U. and Hampton Inst., 1984—; commr. Larchmont Little League, N.Y., 1964-68; chmn. Larchmont Jr. Sailing Program, 1977-78; vestry, jr. warden St. John's Episc. Ch., Larchmont, 1982—. Served to lt. (j.g.) USNR, 1955-57. Mem. ABA, N.Y. State Bar Assn., Assn. of Bar of City of N.Y., N.Y. County Bar Assn., Am. Judicature Soc., Raven Soc., Order of Coif, Omicron Delta Kappa. Democrat. Clubs: Larchmont U. (pres. 1976-77), Larchmont Yacht (trustee 1979-85); N.Y. Yacht (N.Y.C.); Scarsdale Golf (N.Y.). Avocations: skiing, golf, sailing, tennis. General corporate, Securities, Mergers and acquisitions. Home: 2 Walnut Ave Larchmont NY 10538 Office: Sullivan & Cromwell 250 Park Ave New York NY 10177

HIEKEN, CHARLES, lawyer; b. Granite City, Ill., Aug. 15, 1928; s. Samuel and Margaret (Isaacs) H.; m. Donna Jane Clanin, Jan. 6, 1961; children: Tina Jane, Seth Paul. SBEE, MIT, 1952, SMEE, 1952; LLB, Harvard U., 1957. Bar: Ill., 1957, Mass., 1958, U.S. Supreme Ct., 1960, U.S. Ct. Customs and Patent Appeals, 1961, U.S. Ct. Claims, 1963, U.S. Ct. Appeals (fed. cir.), 1982. Patent asst. Lab. Electronics, Boston, 1954-56, Fish, Richardson & Neave, Boston, 1956-57; assoc. Hill, Sherman, Meroni & Simpson, Chgo., 1957, Joseph Weingarten, Boston, 1957-58; assoc. Wolf, Greenfield & Hieken, Boston, 1958-61, ptnr., 1961-70; prin. Charles Hieken Law Offices, Waltham, Mass., 1970-87, of counsel, Fish & Richardson, Boston, 1987—. Mem. Boston Bar Assn. (mem. civil procedure com. 1959—), Mass. Bar Assn. (chmn. intellectual property com. 1977-80), Ill. State Bar Assn. Served with U.S. Army, 1952-54. Mem. Boston Patent Law Assn. (chmn. pub. relations com. 1965-66, chmn. antitrust law com. 1966-70, 78-80, treas. 1970-71, v.p. 1971-72, pres.-elect, 1972-73, pres. 1973-74), IEEE (sr.) (indsl. adv. com. to domestic policy rev. on indsl. innovation, patent and info. subcom 1978-79), Tau Beta Pi, Eta Kappa Nu. Club: MIT Faculty. Patent, Federal civil litigation, Trademark and copyright. Home: 193 Wilshire Dr Sharon MA 02067 Office: 470 Totten Pond Rd Boston MA 02154-1981

HIERING, JAMES G., lawyer; b. Seaside Park, N.J., Apr. 16, 1931; s. Albert C. and Phoebe M. (McGann) H.; m. Nancy Lee Newman, June 10, 1955 (div.); children—Lisa, Susan, Leslie; m. 2d, Cynthia C. Common, Apr. 17, 1970 (div.); children—Julie, Tricia; m. 3d, Mary C. Morrison, Dec. 13, 1986. A.B., Princeton U., 1953; LL.B., Harvard U., 1956. Bar: Ill. 1956. Ptnr., Keck, Mahin & Cate, Chgo., 1956—; dir. Schawk Inc., Barnegat Power & Cold Storage Co. Mem. ABA, Am. Judicature Soc., Ill. Bar Assn., Chgo. Bar Assn., Bar Assn. 7th Fed. Circuit. Republican. Presbyterian. Clubs: University, Metropolitan, Chicago Yacht, Economic, Executives (Chgo.). Antitrust, Federal civil litigation, General corporate. Home: 1440 N Lake Shore Dr Chicago IL 60610 Office: 8300 Sears Tower 233 S Wacker Dr Chicago IL 60606

HIERONYMUS, EDWARD WHITTLESEY, lawyer; b. Davenport, Iowa, June 13, 1943. B.A. cum laude, Knox Coll., 1965; J.D. with distinction, Duke U., 1968. Bar: Calif. 1969, Iowa 1968. Ptnr. O'Melveny & Myers, Los Angeles, 1974—. Contbr. articles on law to profl. jours. Exec. sec. Los Angeles Com. Fgn. Relations, 1975-86. Served with Judge Adv. Gen. U.S. Army, 1965-74. Mem. ABA (award for profl. merit 1968), Calif. Bar Assn. (co-chair natural resources subsect., real property sect. 1986—), Los Angeles County Bar Assn., Iowa Bar Assn. Oil and gas leasing, Real property, Contracts commercial. Office: 400 S Hope St Los Angeles CA 90071

HIGBE, CLIFTON MELTON HARVIN, lawyer, real estate broker, insurance company executive; b. Columbia, S.C., Sept. 13, 1932; s. William Wellington and Agnes Irene (Shaw) H.; m. Sally Marith Mehren, June 18, 1955; children—Clifton, Elizabeth Lynn, Randall John William; m. 2d, Anne Elizabeth Jensen, Feb. 14, 1980. A.A., Am. River Coll., 1962; J.D., U. of Pacific, 1970. Bar: Calif. 1971, U.S. Dist. Ct. (ea. dist.) Calif. 1971. Gen. mgr. Comstock Steel Co., Sacramento, 1958-64; prin. Higbe Co., Real Estate & Ins., Sacramento, 1964-66, 1971—; dist. sales mgr. Pacific Telephone Co., Sacramento, 1966-71; sole practice, Sacramento, 1971—; lectr. in field; mem. Steel Service Ctr. Inst., 1958-64. Served to 1st lt. USAF, 1950-58. Recipient Outstanding Adv. award Jr. Achievement, 1967; Am. Jurisprudence award McGeorge Sch. Law, 1967. Mem. Calif. State Bar, Sacramento County Bar, ABA. Republican. General corporate, Real property, Probate. Office: 1555 River Park Dr Suite 202 Sacramento CA 95815

HIGGINBOTHAM, A. LEON, JR., federal judge; b. Trenton, N.J., Feb. 25, 1928; m. Jeanne Foster; children: Stephen, Karen, Kenneth. Student, Purdue U., 1944-46; BA, Antioch Coll., 1949; LLB, Yale U., 1952. Asst. dist. atty. Phila. County, 1953-54; ptnr. Norris, Green, Harris & Higginbotham, Phila., 1954-62; spl. dep. atty. gen. State of Pa., Harrisburg, 1956-62; commr. FTC, Washington, 1962-64; judge U.S. Dist. Ct. (ea. dist.) Pa., 1964-77, U.S. Ct. Appeals, Phila., 1977—; spl. hearing officer conscientious objectors U.S. Justice Dept., Washington, 1960-62; commr. Pa. Human Relations Commn., 1961-62. Office: 22613 US Courthouse Independence Mall W 601 Market St Philadelphia PA 19106 *

HIGGINBOTHAM, JOHN TAYLOR, lawyer; b. St. Louis, Feb. 10, 1947; s. Richard Cann and Jocelyn (Taylor) H.; m. Lauren Flint Totty, Aug. 9, 1975 (div. 1979). B.A., UCLA, 1969; J.D., Columbia U., 1972. Bar: N.Y. 1975, Calif. 1976. Assoc., Kirlin, Campbell & Keating, N.Y.C., 1972-74; atty. Nat. Bank of N.Am., N.Y.C., 1974-76; atty., dir. real estate Korvettes Inc., N.Y.C., 1979-82; assoc. Leon Katz, Bklyn., 1983-84; assoc. Finley, Kumble, Wagner, Heine, Underberg, Manley & Casey, N.Y.C., 1984—. Editor: Safe Deposit Decisions and Practice, 1977—. Mem. ABA, Assn. Bar City N.Y. Real property.

HIGGINBOTHAM, PATRICK ERROL, judge; b. Ala., Dec. 16, 1938. Student, Arlington State Coll., 1956-57, North Tex. State U., 1958, U. Tex., 1958; B.A., U. Ala., 1960, LL.B., 1961. Bar: Ala. 1961, Tex. 1962, U.S. Supreme Ct. 1962. Partner firm Coke & Coke, Dallas, 1964-75; judge U.S. Dist. Ct. for No. Dist. Tex., Dallas, 1976-82, U.S. Ct. Appeals for 5th circuit, Dallas, 1982—; adj. prof. constl. law So. Meth. U. Law Sch., 1971—, adj. prof. constl. law, 1981—; mem. faculty Fed. Jud. Center, Washington, Columbia U. Trial Seminar, Nat. Inst. Trial Advocacy; conferee Am. Assembly, 1975, Pound Conf., 1976. Contbr. articles, revs. to profl. pubs.; note editor: Ala. Law Rev, 1960-61; narrator: one-hour video tape Law in Changing Soc, 1977. Chmn. bd. First United Methodist Ch., Richardson, Tex. Named Outstanding Alumnus U. Tex., Arlington, 1978, One of Nation's 100 Most Powerful Persons for the 80's Next Mag. Fellow Am. Bar Found.; mem. Am. Bar Assn. (chmn. com. to compile fed. jury charges antitrust sect., mem. council antitrust sect., bd. editors Jour.), Dallas Bar Assn. (dir., chmn. coms. legal aid, civic affairs), Dallas Bar Found. (dir.), Am. Law Inst., S.W. Legal Found., Am. Judicature Soc. (dir., trustee), Farrah Law Soc., Bench and Bar, Order of Coif, Omicron Delta Kappa. Jurisprudence. Office: 1100 Commerce St Room 13E23 Dallas TX 75242

HIGGINS, ANDREW JACKSON, state supreme ct. justice; b. Platte City, Mo., June 21, 1921; s. Andrew Jervy and Frances Beverly H.; m. Laura Joan Brown, Oct. 30, 1948; children: Susan Louise, Laura Frances. A.B., Central Coll., 1943; LL.B., Washington U., St. Louis, 1948. Bar: Mo. bar 1948. Practice law Platte City, 1948-60; former pros. atty. Platte County; former mayor Platte City; judge Jud. Circuit 6, 1960-64; commr. Mo. Supreme Ct., Jefferson City, 1964-81; assoc. justice Mo. Supreme Ct., 1981—. Past chmn. Platte County Democratic Central Com. Served with USN, 1943-46. Mem. Sigma Alpha Epsilon, Delta Theta Phi. Address: Mo Supreme Ct PO Box 150 Jefferson City MO 65102 *

HIGGINS, DANNY GLENN, lawyer, minister; b. Draper, N.C., Mar. 5, 1949; s. William Gentry and Nannie Evelyn (Powell) H.; m. Barbara Sue Sands, Aug. 3, 1975 (widowed Oct. 1979). BA in History, Pfeiffer Coll., 1972; JD, Wake Forest U., 1975. Bar: N.C. 1975, U.S. Dist. Ct. (mid. dist.) N.C. 1976; ordained to ministry Bapt. Ch., 1985. Sole practice Eden, N.C., 1975-78; asst. dist. atty. 17th Jud. Dist., Wentworth, N.C., 1979-81; sole practice Wake Forest, N.C., 1982-83; asst. dist. atty. 11th Jud. Dist., Lillington, N.C., 1984-85; sole practice Dunn, N.C., 1985-86; atty. Washington County, Plymouth, N.C., 1986—; minister Pleasant Memory Bapt. Ch., Coats, N.C., 1985-86; legis. intern Council on Christian Life and Pub. Affairs, Bapt. State Conv. of N.C., Raleigh, 1983, 85. Author newsletter Legis. Info. Network News, 1983, 85. Mem. ABA, N.C. State Bar Assn., Washington County Bar Assn., 2d Jud. Dist. Bar Assn. Democrat. Avocations: auto mechanics, reading, hiking, canoeing, preaching. Local government. Home: PO Box 276 Plymouth NC 27962 Office: Washington County Courthouse PO Box 1007 Plymouth NC 27962

HIGGINS, JOHN PATRICK, lawyer, insurance company executive; b. Beloit, Wis., Feb. 13, 1952; s. John Eugene and Catherine Marie (Beaudry) H. B.A. cum laude, St. Norbert Coll., 1973; postgrad. DePaul U. Law Sch., 1974-76; J.D., U. Wis.-Madison, 1977; MBA, Keller Grad. Sch. Mgmt., Milw., 1986. Bar: Wis. 1977, U.S. Dist. Ct. (ea. and we. dists.) Wis., U.S. Ct. Appeals (7th cir.), U.S. Supreme Ct. Assessment technician Kenosha County Assessor, Wis., 1973-75; law clk. various firms, Madison, 1976-77; claims atty. Employers Ins. of Wausau (Wis.), 1977-80, trial atty., Milw., 1980—; part-time instr. North Central Tech. Inst., Wausau, 1980; dir. and v.p.-legal John E. Higgins Appraisal Co., Kenosha; lectr., speaker various profl. and fraternal groups. Author articles and monographs. Bd. dirs., arbitrator Roman Cath. Archdiocese of Milw., 1983—; active Milw. Repertory Theater, 1983—, Holy Name Soc. Milw., 1983-85. Mem. State Bar Wis. (bd. dirs. young lawyers div. 1978—, sec. 1979-82, chmn. law reform com. 1984—, chmn. long range planning conf. young lawyers div. 1986, chmn. gavel awards com. 1985—, chmn. communications com. 1984—, chmn. and mem. various other coms.), ABA, Def. Research Inst., Thomas More Soc., State Bar Assn. Wis., Civil Trial Counsel Wis., Milw. Bar Assn., Waukesha County Bar Assn., St. Norbert Coll. Alumni Assn. (exec. bd. dirs. 1979—, chpt. liaison, editor chpt. newsletter), Am. Corp. Counsel Assn. Phi Alpha Delta. State civil litigation, Insurance, General corporate. Home: 3431 N 92d St Milwaukee WI 53222 Office: Employers Ins of Wausau 6620 W Capitol Dr Milwaukee WI 53216

HIGGINS, KENNETH DYKE, lawyer; b. Benton, Tenn., Aug. 21, 1916; s. Fredrick Dyke and Martha (Dunn) H.; m. Jane Blair Webb; children: Jane Webb, Kenneth Dyke. AA, Tenn. Wesleyan Coll., 1936, LLB (hon.), 1984; AB, Transylvania U., 1938; JD, Tulane U., 1942. Bar: Tenn. 1946. Ptnr. Higgins, Biddle & Chester, Athens, Tenn., 1946—. Served to lt. USN, 1942-46, PTO. Mem. ABA, Tenn. Bar Assn. Lodge: Kiwanis (sec.). General practice. Home: 1200 Woodacres Dr Athens TN 37303

HIGGINS, MARY CELESTE, lawyer, researcher; b. Chgo., Feb. 9, 1943; d. Maurice James and Helen Marie (Egan) H. A.B., St. Mary-of-the-Woods (Ind.) Coll., 1965; J.D., DePaul Univ., 1970; LL.M., John Marshall Law Sch., Chgo., 1976; certs. program for lawyers Harvard U., 1981, 82, M.P.A., 1982; M.Phil., U. Cambridge (Eng.), 1983. Bar: Ill. 1970, U.S. Dist. Ct. (no. dist.) Ill. 1970. Sole practice, Chgo., 1970-72, 79-80; atty. corporate counsel dept. Continental Bank, Chgo., 1972-76; asst. sec., asst. counsel Marshall Field & Co., Chgo., 1976-79; sr. atty. Mattel, Inc., Hawthorne, Calif., 1980-81; research in revitalization and adjustment of U.S. industries in U.S. and world markets, 1981-83; legal cons., 1983-85; Midwest regional officer Legal Services Corp., 1985-86, assoc. dir., 1986, acting dir. office of field services, 1986—. Recipient Am. Jurisprudence awards for academic excellence, 1966-70. Mem. ABA, Ill. Bar Assn. Clubs: Harvard (N.Y.C., Boston, Chgo.); United Oxford and Cambridge, Univ., Univ. Women's, Royal Commonwealth Soc., Am. Women's (London). General corporate, Private international, Public international. Home: 3432 S Wakefield Apt #B-2 Arlington VA 22206

HIGGINS, ROBERT GERARD, lawyer; b. Chgo., Feb. 22, 1952; s. William Edward and Catherine Mary (Smith) H.; m. Joellen Hartman, Aug. 14, 1976; children: Erin, Claire, William. BA, U. Notre Dame, 1973; JD, Loyola U., Chgo., 1977. Bar: Ill. 1977, U.S. Dist. Ct. (no. dist.) Ill. 1977, Minn. 1979, Tex. 1986, U.S. Dist. Ct. (no. dist.) Tex. 1986. Assoc. Hoffman & Davis, Chgo., 1977-82; ptnr. Ross & Block, Chgo., 1982-84; ptnr. Schwartz & Freeman, Chgo., 1984-86, Dallas, 1986—. Roman Catholic. Real property, Banking, General corporate. Home: 3521 Nancy Ct Plano TX 75023 Office: Schwartz & Freeman 14180 Dallas Pkwy Dallas TX 75240

HIGGINS, RONALD CLARENCE, lawyer; b. Gadsden, Ala., Nov. 6, 1946; s. Clarence E. and Jewel I. (Ford) H.; m. Angie Denice Castleberry, Dec. 23, 1976; 1 child, James Ronald. BA, U. Ala., 1967, MA, 1970; JD, Samford U., 1981. Bar: Ala. 1981, U.S. Dist. Ct. (no. dist.) Ala. 1981. Social worker Ala. Dept. Pensions and Security, LaFayette, 1971-76, Gadsden, 1976-78; sole practice Gadsden, 1981-82; domestic referee Etowah County Cir. Ct., Gadsden, 1982—; lectr. seminar Continuing Legal Edn., Gadsden, 1985. Research editor Am. Jour. Trial Advocacy, 1980-81. Mem. ABA, Ala. Bar Assn. (family law sect.), U. Ala. Alumni Assn. (bd. dirs. Etowah County chpt. 1985—), MENSA. Methodist. Lodge: Kiwanis. Avocations: fly fishing, fly tying, music, photography, ch. organist. Family and matrimonial, Juvenile. Home: 543 Haralson Ave Gadsden AL 35901 Office: Etowah County Cir Ct 800 Forrest Ave Gadsden AL 35999

HIGGINS, STEPHEN BOYD, lawyer; b. San Antonio, July 18, 1946; s. John William and Dorothy May (Summers) H.; m. Carol Ann Saye, Aug. 9, 1975; children: Margaret Saye, Elizabeth Boyd. BA, Yale U., 1968; JD, St. Louis U., 1976. Bar: Mo. 1976, U.S. Ct. Appeals (8th cir.) 1977, U.S. Supreme Ct. 1980, U.S. Dist. Ct. (ea. dist.) Mo. Asst. U.S. atty. U.S. Dept. Justice, St. Louis, 1976-80; assoc. Huson, Eppenberger et al, St. Louis, 1980-83, ptnr., 1983—; adj. prof. communications Webster U., St. Louis, 1986—. Bd. dirs. St. Louis Pub. Library. Served to capt. U.S. Army, 1968-70. Mem. ABA (Silver Gavel award 1973, Cert. of Merit 1974), Bar Assn. Met. St. Louis (chmn. med. communications com. 1984—). Republican. Roman Catholic. Club: Yale (St. Louis). Federal civil litigation, State civil litigation, General corporate. Home: 5265 Westminster Pl Saint Louis MO 63108 Office: Suite 1800 100 N Broadway Saint Louis MO 63102

HIGGINS, THOMAS A., federal judge; b. 1932. AA, Christian Bros. Coll., 1952; BA, U. Tenn., 1954; LLB, Vanderbilt U., 1957. Ptnr. Willis & Higgins, 1960-61; assoc. Cornelius, Collins, Higgins & White, 1961-66, ptnr., 1966-84; judge U.S. Dist. Ct. (mid. dist.) Tenn., Nashville, 1984—. Served with AUS, 1957-60. Office: A845 US Courthouse 801 Broadway Nashville TN 37203-3869 *

HIGGINS, WILLIS EDWARD, lawyer; b. Pitts., Aug. 7, 1940; s. Edward Nichols and Mildred Lucille (Engel) H.; m. Susan Laythe, Sept. 19, 1964; children—Frank, Edward. B.S. in Chem. Engring., U. Pitts., 1962; J.D., U. Chgo., 1965. Bar: Mich., 1966, Vt., 1968, Calif., 1978, Ariz. 1976, U.S. Pat. Off., 1966. Pat. atty. Dow Chem. Co., Midland, Mich., 1965-67; pat. atty. IBM' Essex Junction, Vt., 1967-73; sole practice, Bristol, Vt., 1973-74; pat. atty. Motorola Inc., Phoenix, 1974-75, sr. pat. atty., 1975-76; pat. csl. Nat. Semicondr. Corp., Santa Clara, Calif., 1976-77, dir. pats. and trademarks, 1977-78; assoc. Gregg, Hendricson, Caplan & Rosso, San Francisco, 1978; ptnr. Gregg, Caplan & Higgins, Menlo Park, Calif., 1978-86; assoc. Flehr, Hohbach, Test, Albriton & Herbert, Palo Alto, 1986—. Referee Am. Youth Soccer Orgn., Palo Alto, Calif., 1979—, Calif. Youth Soccer Assn., 1982—; assoc. referee U.S. Soccer Fedn., 1982-83, referee, 1983—; asst. scoutmaster Stanford Area council Boy Scouts Am., 1980—, explorer adviser, 1983—. Recipient Wood Badge, Boy Scouts Am., 1982. Mem. ABA, Vt. Bar Assn., State Bar Calif., State Bar Ariz., State Bar Mich., Peninsula Pat. Law Assn. (treas. 1981-82, sec. 1982-83, v.p. 1983-84, pres. 1984-85), San Francisco Pat. and Trademark Law Assn. Democrat. Unitarian. Lodge: Order of Arrow. Patent, Trademark and copyright, Federal civil litigation. Home: 3449 Thomas Dr Palo Alto CA 94303 Office: 200 Page Mill Rd Suite 200 Palo Alto CA 94306-2022

HIGGINSON, JAMES JACKSON, lawyer; b. N.Y.C., Dec. 10, 1921; s. James J. and Virginia (Mitchell) H. Grad., Groton (Mass.) Sch., 1940; B.A., Harvard U., 1943, LL.B., 1949. Bar: N.Y. bar 1949, U.S. Supreme Ct. bar 1957. Practiced in N.Y.C., 1949—; partner firm Appleton, Rice & Perrin, 1969—; Dir. F.H. Prince & Co., Inc. Served to capt. AUS, 1943-46, 50-52. Mem. N.Y. State Bar Assn., Assn. of Bar of City of N.Y. Probate, Family and matrimonial, Federal civil litigation. Home: 800 Fifth Ave New York NY 10021 Office: 444 Madison Ave New York NY 10022

HIGGINSON, THOMAS LEE, lawyer; b. N.Y.C., Jan. 2, 1920; s. James Jackson and Lucy Virginia (Mitchell) H.; m. Theodora Winthrop, Sept. 11, 1948 (div. 1984); children: Thomas Lee Jr., Elizabeth, Robert Winthrop; m. Shirley Foerderer Ames, June 30, 1984. Student, Groton Sch.; A.B., Harvard U., 1942, LL.B., 1949. Bar: N.Y. 1950. Since practiced in N.Y.C.; mem. firm Shearman & Sterling, 1957—; exec. com., bd. dirs. Fiduciary

Trust Co. of N.Y. Bd. dirs., sec. Nassau Hosp. Assn.; trustee, sec. The Frick Collection, Percival E. and Ethel Brown Foerderer Found. Served from 2d lt. to maj. AUS, 1942-46. Decorated Bronze Star. Mem. Am., N.Y. State bar assns., Assn. Bar City N.Y. Republican. Episcopalian. Clubs: Brook (N.Y.C.), Links (N.Y.C.), Downtown Assn. (N.Y.C.); Piping Rock (L.I.). General corporate. Office: 53 Wall St New York NY 10005

HIGGS, CRAIG DEWITT, lawyer; b. Coronado, Calif., Mar. 19, 1944; s. DeWitt Alexander and Florence (Fuller) H.; m. Yvonne De Necochea, May 22, 1976; children—Marisa DeWitt, Alexander Craig. B.S., U. Redlands, 1966; J.D., U. San Diego, 1969. Bar: Calif. 1971, U.S. Dist. Ct. (so. dist.) Calif. 1971. Dept. city atty. San Diego, 1970-71; assoc. Higgs, Fletcher & Mack, San Diego, 1971-76, ptnr., 1976—; dir. San Diego Law Ctr., 1983—. Bd. visitors U. San Diego Sch. Law, 1983—. Mem. San Diego Bar Found. (bd. dirs. 1983—), State Bar Calif. (chmn. commn. on jud. nominees evaluation 1981), San Diego County Bar Assn. (pres. 1984). Democrat. State civil litigation, Federal civil litigation, Personal injury. Home: 2840 Maple St San Diego CA 92104 Office: Higgs Fletcher & Mack 401 West A St Suite 2000 San Diego CA 92101

HIGGS, DAVID COREY, lawyer; b. Washington, Feb. 23, 1956; s. Roland Wellington and Mabel Ann (Corey) H.; m. Kathleen Marie Vanderwall, Apr. 5, 1986; children: Jenny, Jill. BA, U. Minn., 1978, JD, 1981. Bar: Minn. 1981, U.S. Dist. Ct. Minn. 1982. Assoc. Engebretson & Assocs., St. Paul, 1981-85; ptnr. Ostgard, Higgs & Warner, St. Paul, 1985—; tutor U. Minn. Minority Lawyers Assn., Mpls., 1984-85. Mem. ABA, Minn. Bar Assn., Ramsey County Bar Assn., Minn. Trial Lawyers Assn., Minn. Minority Lawyers Assn. Family and matrimonial, Personal injury, General practice. Office: Ostgard Higgs & Warner 444 Cedar St Suite 720 Saint Paul MN 55101

HIGH, DAVID ERWIN, lawyer; b. Nashville, Nov. 14, 1953; s. C. Allen and Mary Francis (McGhee) H. BA with high honors, U. Tenn., 1975; JD, YMCA Night Law Sch., 1980. Bar: Tenn. 1980, U.S. Dist. Ct. (mid. dist.) Tenn. 1980, U.S. Ct. Appeals (6th cir.) 1984, U.S. Supreme Ct. 1984. Law clk. to presiding judge Tenn. Ct. Criminal Appeals, Nashville, 1980-81; ptnr. Garfinkle, Wilson & High, Nashville, 1981—. Mem. Nashville Bar Assn. (co-chmn. criminal justice com. 1986), Assn. Trial Lawyers Am., Tenn. Trial Lawyers Assn. (bd. govs. 1983-85), Tenn. Assn. Criminal Def. Attys., Nat. Assn. Criminal Def. Attys., Coopers Inn Hon. Soc. Democrat. Episcopalian. Avocations: boating, fishing. Criminal, Personal injury. Home: 2539 Miami Ave Donelson TN 37214 Office: Garfinkle Gober Wilson & High 430 3d Ave N Suite 101 Nashville TN 37201

HIGH, SUZANNE IRENE, lawyer; b. Chgo., June 10, 1946; d. Jack G. and Irene (Sinko) H. A.B. cum laude, Syracuse U., 1968; M.A., Northwestern U., 1973; postgrad. Rosary Coll., 1974-75; J.D., DePaul U., Chgo., 1979. Bar: Ill. 1979, Fla. 1979, U.S. Sup. Ct. 1982. Tchr., Peace Corps, Wolisso, Ethiopia, 1968-70; researcher Compton's Ency., Ency. Brit., Chgo., 1970-72; ptnr. Renn & High, Chartered, Lisle, Ill, 1979—. Bd. dirs. Little Friends, Inc., 1985-86. Mem. ABA, Fla. Bar Assn., Ill. Bar Assn., DuPage County Bar Assn. (probate com. 1987—), Women's Bar Assn. Ill., Fla. Women's Bar Assn., Nat. Assn. of Women Lawyers, DuPage Assn. Women Lawyers, Ill. Trial Lawyers Assn., NOW, Lisle C. of C. Club: Women in Mgmt. (Oak Brook, Ill.). General corporate, General practice, Probate. Home: 4756 Main St Lisle IL 60532 Office: 2805 Butterfield Rd Suite 150 Oak Brook IL 60521

HIGHBERGER, WILLIAM FOSTER, lawyer; b. Suffern, N.Y., May 15, 1950; s. John Kistler and Helen Stewart (Foster) H.; m. Carolyn Barbara Kuhl, July 12, 1980. AB, Princeton U.; JD, Columbia U. Bar: Calif. 1976, U.S. Dist. Ct. (cen. dist.) Calif. 1976, U.S. Ct. Appeals (2d cir.) 1976, U.S. Ct. Appeals (9th cir.) 1977, U.S. Dist. Ct. (so. and ea. dists.) Calif. 1979, U.S. Supreme Ct. 1980, D.C. 1981, U.S. Dist. Ct. (no. dist.) Calif. 1981, U.S. Dist. Ct. D.C. 1982, U.S. Ct. Appeals (D.C. cir.) 1982, U.S. Ct. Appeals (3d cir.) 1983, N.Y. 1984, U.S. Dist. Ct. (so. dist.) N.Y. 1984, U.S. Dist. Ct. (ea. dist.) N.Y. 1985. Law clk. to judge U.S. Ct. Appeals (2d cir.), Bridgeport, Conn., 1975-76; assoc. Gibson, Dunn & Crutcher, Washington and Los Angeles, 1976-82, ptnr., 1983—. Notes and comments editor Columbia U. Law Rev., 1974. Mem. Nat. Trust for Hist. Preservation, Washington, 1980—, Nature Conservatory, Washington, 1981—, Pacific Palisades (Calif.) Presbyn. Ch., 1987—. James Kent scholar Columbia U., 1973. Mem. ABA (com. on individual rights and reponsibilities in workplace, labor sect., litigation sect.), Indsl. Relations Research Assn., Am. Judicature Soc., Internat. Soc. for Social Security and Labor Relations Law. Republican. Clubs: Princeton (N.Y.C.); Univ. Cottage (Princeton, N.J.). Labor, Pension, profit-sharing, and employee benefits, Federal civil litigation. Home: 11688 Picturesque Dr Studio City CA 91604 Office: Gibson Dunn & Crutcher 333 S Grand Ave Los Angeles CA 90071

HIGHFIELD, ROBERT EDWARD, lawyer; b. Indpls., Apr. 15, 1930; s. Edward Grant and Anna Elizabeth (Hawkins) H.; m. Carolyn Elizabeth Galle, Aug. 6, 1954; children: Paige Lynn, Tod Edward. AB, Ind. U., 1954, JD, 1960. Bar: Ind. 1960. Assoc. Barnes & Thornburg and predecessor firm, Indpls., 1960-67, ptnr., 1968—; mem. faculty ann. labor-mgmt. seminars NLRB, Ind. U.; lectr. on employment discrimination and affirmative action. Pres., bd. dirs. Indpls. Arts Chorale. Served to 1st lt. U.S. Army, 1955-57. Mem. ABA, Ind. State Bar Assn., Indpls. Bar Assn., Ind. C. of C. (personnel and labor relations com.). Republican. Presbyterian. Club: Columbia. Labor, Pension, profit-sharing, and employee benefits, Workers' compensation. Office: 1313 Merchants Bank Bldg Indianapolis IN 46204

HIGHSAW, JAMES LEONARD, JR., lawyer; b. Memphis, Jan. 6, 1914; s. James Leonard and May (Baker) H.; m. Jane Fillmore Dunlap, June 20, 1945; children: Rhoda Jane Highsaw Bush, James Leonard III, Carol Anne. A.B., Princeton U., 1935; J.D., Harvard U., 1941. Bar: Tenn. 1940, D.C. 1954. Staff atty. Nat. Home Loan Bd., 1941-44; staff atty. CAB, 1944-48, chief intercarrier relationship, 1948-51, chief litigation, 1951-55; ptnr. Mulholland, Hickey & Lyman, Washington, 1955-69; sr. ptnr. Highsaw & Mahoney, Washington, 1970-76; sr. partner Highsaw & Mahoney, P.C., Washington, 1976-87, of counsel, 1987—; lectr. aviation law Am. U. Law Sch. Chmn. Drummond (Md.) Citizens Com., 1966-76. Author articles in field. Mem. ABA (co-chmn. equal employment opportunity com. 1977-79), Fed. Bar Assn., D.C. Bar Assn., Phi Beta Kappa. Democrat. Presbyterian. Administrative and regulatory, Federal civil litigation, Labor. Home: 4601 Drummond Ave Chevy Chase MD 20815 Office: 1050 17th St NW Washington DC 20036

HIGHTOWER, GEORGE WILLIS, lawyer; b. Nacogdoches, Tex., Apr. 9, 1937; s. Harrison and Laura (Spencer) H.; married, Nov. 24, 1978; children: George B., Lorna, Jenny, Joan, Steven Todd. BEE, U. So. Calif., 1964, MS, 1969, JD, 1975. Bar: Calif. 1983. Sole practice Los Angeles, 1975—. Civil rights, Labor, Real property. Office: Box 4975 Culver City CA 90231

HILDEBRAND, CHARLES FREDERICK, lawyer; b. Sheboygan, Wis., Aug. 25, 1954; s. Frederick William and Patricia Joan (Schaffer) H.; m. Judith A. Scharfenberger, Mar. 17, 1984. AB in Econs., U. Calif., Davis, 1976; MBA in Fin., JD, Cornell U., 1980. Bar: Mich. 1980, Conn. 1981. Staff atty. Gen. Motors Corp., Detroit, 1980, United Techs. Corp., Hartford, Conn., 1980-81; sr. atty. Elliott Co. div. United Techs. Corp., Jeannette, Pa., 1981-84; counsel Internat. Aero Engines, East Hartford, Conn., 1984—. Acct. exec. United Fund, Greensburg, Pa., 1984; joint bd. dirs. Smithfield United Ch., Pitts., 1984; bd. dirs. Twin Lakes Condominium Assn., North Branford, Conn., 1986. Mem. Am. Corp. Counsel Assn., Internat. Laser Class Assn., Phi Beta Kappa, Phi Kappa Phi. Republican. Congregationalist. Avocations: sailing, skiing. Private international, Contracts commercial, General corporate.

HILDEBRAND, DANIEL WALTER, lawyer; b. Oshkosh, Wis., May 1, 1940; s. Dan M. and Rose Marie (Baranowski) H.; m. Bonnie E. Benedict, Aug. 25, 1964; children: Daniel G., Douglas P., Elizabeth A. BS, U. Wis., 1962, LLB, 1964. Bar: Wis. 1964, U.S. Dist. Ct. (we. dist.) Wis. 1964, N.Y. 1965, U.S. Dist. Ct. (so. and ea. dists.) N.Y. 1967, U.S. Ct. Appeals (2d cir.) 1968, U.S. Dist. Ct. (ea. dist.) Wis. 1970, U.S. Ct. Appeals (7th cir.) 1970, U.S. Supreme Ct. 1970, U.S. Tax Ct. 1986. Assoc. Willkie, Farr & Gallagher, N.Y.C., 1964-68; from assoc. to ptnr. Ross & Stevens, S.C., Madison, Wis., 1968—; lectr. U. Wis. Law Sch., Madison, 1972-84. Editor: U. Wis. Law Rev., 1963-64. Mem. Joint Survey Com. on Tax Exemptions, Wis., 1973-79; chmn. Code Profl. Responsibility Rev. Com., 1984-85. Mem. ABA (fed. cts. com. litigation sect.), Wis. Bar Assn. (bd. govs. 1981-85), N.Y. State Bar Assn., Dane County Bar Assn. (pres. 1980-81), 7th Cir. Bar Assn. Roman Catholic. Lodge: Kiwanis (past pres. Madison club). Federal civil litigation, State civil litigation. Office: Ross & Stevens S.C. 1 S Pinckney St Madison WI 53703

HILDER, PHILIP HARLAN, prosecutor; b. Highland Park, Ill., July 2, 1955. BA, U. Iowa, 1977; JD, Boston Coll., 1981. Bar: Ill. 1981, Tex. 1985, U.S. Dist. Ct. (so. dist.) Tex., U.S. Dist. Ct. (no. dist.) Ill., U.S. Ct. Appeals (5th and 7th cirs.). Assoc. Clausen, Miller, Gormon, Caffrey & Witous P.C., Chgo., 1981-84; asst. U.S. atty. Dept. Justice, Houston, 1984—. Mem. Ill. Bar Assn., Tex. Bar Assn., Chgo. Bar Assn., Houston Bar Assn., Assn. Trial Lawyers Am., Ill. Trial Lawyers Assn. Avocations: skiing, camping. Criminal, Federal civil litigation, Legislative. Office: US Attys Office 515 Rusk St Houston TX 77008

HILEMAN, RICHARD GLENN, JR., lawyer; b. Des Moines, Mar. 31, 1950; s. Richard Glenn Sr. and Margaret (Deahl) H.; m. Sara Kay Gaarde, Dec. 23, 1972; 1 child, Catherine Lynne. BA in Philosophy and English, St. Olaf Coll., 1972; MA in Philosophy, U. Iowa, 1978, JD, 1980. Bar: Iowa 1980, U.S. Dist. Ct. (no. dist.) Iowa 1980. From assoc. to ptnr. Simmons, Perrine, Albright & Ellwood, Cedar Rapids, Iowa, 1980—. Served to capt. USAF, 1972. Mem. ABA, Iowa Bar Assn., Linn County Bar Assn., Order of Coif. Republican. Club: Hillcrest Country (Mt. Vernon, Iowa). Avocation: golf. Federal civil litigation, State civil litigation, General practice. Home: 717 4th Ave N Mount Vernon IA 52314 Office: Simmons Perrine Albright & Ellwood 1200 Merchants Bank Cedar Rapids IA 52401

HILFIGER, ROGER HENRY, lawyer; b. Bradford, Pa., Sept. 24, 1945; s. Henry Bennett and Vivian (Rogers) H.; m. Sally Hewitt, Dec. 18, 1976; children: Heather Marie, James Henry, Ben Rogers, Andrew Michael. BS, Northeastern State U., Tahlequah, Okla., 1967; JD, U. Tulsa, 1972. Bar: Okla. 1972, U.S. Dist. Ct. (ea. dist.) Okla. 1972, U.S. Ct. Appeals (10th cir.) 1985. Ptnr. Jones, Jones, Hilfiger & Miller, Muskogee, Okla., 1972-85; U.S. atty. east dist. Okla. U.S. Dept. Justice, Muskogee, 1985—. Served with U.S. Army, 1967-69. Republican. Methodist. Office: US Dept Justice 333 Federal Bldg Fifth & Okmulgee Muskogee OK 74401

HILGENDORF, ROBERT NELSON, lawyer; b. Beaver Dam, Wis., June 5, 1942; s. Howard W. and Eleanor (Olson) H.; m. Lucy Moore, June 23, 1968; children: Matthew, Nathan. BA, Yale U., 1964; JD, Harvard U., 1967. Bar: Mass. 1967, Ariz. 1975, U.S. Dist. Ct. Ariz. 1975, U.S. Ct. Appeals (9th cir.) 1975, U.S. Supreme Ct. 1975, U.S. Dist. Ct. N.Mex. 1976, U.S. Ct. Appeals (10th cir.) 1976. Atty. DNA (Navajo Indian) Legal Services, Chinle, Ariz., 1968-74; sole practice law Chinle, 1975; dep. atty. gen. Office of Atty. Gen. N.Mex., Santa Fe, 1975-81; sole practice law Santa Fe, 1981—; bd. commrs. N.Mex. State Bar Assn., 1976-86, v.p., 1983-84, pres., 1984-85; bd. dirs. DNA Legal Services, Window Rock, Ariz. Avocations: music, athletics. Bankruptcy, State civil litigation, Consumer commercial. Office: PO Box 2768 226 Galisteo Santa Fe NM 87501

HILL, ALFRED, lawyer, educator; b. N.Y.C., Nov. 7, 1917; m. Dorothy Turck, Aug. 10, 1960; 1 dau., Amelia. B.S., Coll. City N.Y., 1937; LL.B., Bklyn. Law Sch., 1941; LL.D., 1986; S.J. D., Harvard U., 1957. Bar: N.Y. State bar 1943, Ill 1958. With SEC, 1943-52; prof. law So. Meth. U., 1953-56, Northwestern U., 1956-62; prof. law Columbia U., 1962-75, Simon H. Rifkind prof. law, 1975—. Contbr. articles on torts, conflict of laws, fed. cts. to legal jours. Mem. Am. Law Inst. Federal civil litigation, Private international, Personal injury. Home: 79 Sherwood Rd Tenafly NJ 07670 Office: Columbia Law Sch New York NY 10027

HILL, BARRY MORTON, lawyer; b. Wheeling, W.Va., Sept. 13, 1946; m. Jacqueline Sue Jackson, Aug. 12, 1967; children: Jackson Duff, Brandy. BS in Journalism, W.Va. U., 1968, JD, 1977. Bar: W.Va. 1977, U.S Dist. Ct. (no. and so. dists.) W.Va. 1977, Ohio 1978, U.S. Dist. Ct. (no. dist.) Ohio 1978, U.S. Ct. Appeals (3d, 4th, 6th and D.C. cirs.) 1984, U.S. Supreme Ct. 1984, U.S. Ct. Appeals (2d and 11th cirs.) 1986, Pa. 1986; cert. civil trial specialist Nat. Bd. Trial Adv. Ptnr. Zagula, Hill, Dittmar & Thomas and predecessor firms, Weirton, W.Va., 1977—; mem. W.Va. Pattern Jury Instrn. Panel, 1986. Served to 1st lt. U.S. Army, 1969-71. Mem. ABA, Assn. Trial Lawyers Am., Ohio Acad. Trial Lawyers, Pa. Trial Lawyers Assn., W.Va. Trial Lawyers Assn. (pres.-elect 1986, Outstanding mem. 1984), Acad. Fla. Trial Lawyers Assn., N.Y. Trial Lawyers Assn. Democrat. Avocations: golf, automobiles, audio/video equipment. Federal civil litigation, State civil litigation, Personal injury. Home: 934 Neptune Ave Chester WV 26034 Office: Zagula Hill Dittmar & Thomas 3334 Main St Weirton WV 26062

HILL, BRIAN DONOVAN, lawyer; b. Sanford, Fla., July 27, 1947; s. Herbert Charles and Catherine (Kinney) H.; m. Carol Ponton, Aug. 24, 1978; children: Erin, Chad, Michael, Matthew, Casey. BS, U. Fla., JD. Bar: Fla. 1975, U.S. Dist. Ct. (mid. dist.) Fla. Assoc. Maquire, Voorhis & Wells, Gainesville, Fla., 1974-80, Swann and Haddock, Orlando, Fla., 1980-82; ptnr. Taraska and Hill, Orlando, 1983-86, Hill and Hill, Orlando, 1986—. Served to lt. USN, 1969-74. Mem. Phi Beta Kappa, Phi Kappa Phi. State civil litigation, Federal civil litigation, Personal injury. Home: 1037 Lancaster Dr Orlando FL 32806 Office: Hill & Hill PA PO Box 2873 Orlando FL 32802

HILL, DENISE ANN, lawyer; b. Ames, Iowa, Dec. 18, 1954; d. Bruce Lloyd and Lee Ann (Johnson) H.; m. Robert E. McManigal, Jan. 17, 1986. BS, U. Nebr., 1976; JD, Creighton U., 1980. Bar: Nebr. 1980, U.S. Dist. Ct. Nebr. 1980, U.S. Ct. Appeals (8th cir.) 1980, U.S. Supreme Ct. 1985. Asst. city atty. law dept. City of Omaha, 1980-87; sole practice Omaha, 1987—. Bd. dirs. Omaha Zoological Soc., 1983-87. Mem. ABA, Nebr. Bar Assn., Omaha Bar Assn. Republican. Congregationalist. Lodge: Zonta (v.p. 1984-85, bd. dirs. 1985-86, pres. 1986—). Avocations: tennis, swimming, physical fitness, sewing. General practice. Home: 7724 Westgate Circle Omaha NE 68124 Office: 10810 Farnam Dr #434 Omaha NE 68154

HILL, EARL MCCOLL, lawyer; b. Bisbee, Ariz., June 12, 1926; s. Earl George and Jeanette (McColl) H.; m. Bea Dolan, Nov. 22, 1968; children—Arthur Charles, John Earl, Darlene Johnson, Tamara Gentry. B.A., U. Wash., 1960, J.D., 1961. Bar: Nev. 1962, U.S. Ct. Clms. 1978, U.S. Ct. Apls. (9th cir.) 1971, U.S. Sup. Ct. 1978. Law clk. Nev. sup. ct., Carson City, 1962; assoc. Gray, Horton & Hill, Reno, 1962-65, ptnr. 1965-73; ptnr. Hill Cassas de Lipkau and Erwin, Reno, 1974—, Sherman & Howard, Denver, 1982—; judge pro tem Reno mcpl. ct., 1964-70; lectr. continuing legal edn. Mem. Nev. Commn. on Jud. Selection 1977-84; trustee Rocky Mountain Mineral Law Found. 1976—. Mem. ABA, State Bar Nev. (chmn. Com. on Jud. Adminstrn. 1971-77), Washoe County Bar Assn., Am. Judicature Soc., Soc. Mining Law Antiquarians. Club: Prospectors. Contbr. articles to profl. publs. Public land and natural resources, Aviation. Office: 300 Holcomb Profl Ctr 333 Holcomb Ave PO Box 2790 Reno NV 89505

HILL, HENRY ALBERT, lawyer; b. Athens, Greece, Dec. 14, 1939; s. Henry A. and Priscilla (Capps) H. BA, Amherst Coll., 1961; JD, Stanford U., 1965. Bar: N.J. 1965, U.S. Ct. Appeals (3d cir.) 1965, U.S. Supreme Ct. 1969. Assoc. Mason, Griffin & Pierson (formerly Mason, Griffin & Moore) Princeton, N.J., 1965-72, ptnr., 1972-80; ptnr. Brener, Wallack & Hill, Princeton, N.J., 1980—; lectr. Rutgers Sch. Law, Newark, 1972-73; mem. N.J. Adv. Council Corrections, 1977-80, chmn., 1979-80. Mem. Gov.'s Task Force on Housing, 1981—. Mem. ABA, N.J. State Bar Assn. (chmn. correctional reform com. 1975-77, chair-elect land use law sect.), Princeton County Bar Assn., Mercer County Bar Assn., Somerset County Bar Assn., Assn. Trial Lawyers Am. Club: Nassau (Princeton, N.J.). Real property, Administrative and regulatory, Environment. Office: Brener Wallack & Hill 210 Carnegie Ctr 4th Floor Princeton NJ 08543

HILL, JANET WADSWORTH, lawyer; b. N.Y.C., Jan. 11, 1915; d. James P. and Florine P. (Hall) Hill; m. William J. Gordon, May 1, 1942 (dec.); 1 child, Gail Hill Gordon McCale. BFA, Syracuse U., 1935; LLB magna cum laude, Bklyn. Law Sch., 1940. Bar: N.Y. 1940, U.S. Dist. Ct. (no. dist.) N.Y. 1942. Ptnr. Gordon and Hill, Norwich, N.Y., 1941-67; sole practice, Norwich, 1973—; county atty. Chenango County, N.Y., 1944-46; legal research asst. Chenango County family, surrogates and county ct., 1973-75; commr. conciliation 6th jud. dist. N.Y. State Conciliation Bur., 1967-73; mem. Temporary N.Y. State Commn. To Recodify Family Ct. Act, 1979—; mem. N.Y. State Assembly, 1946-58, N.Y. State Senate, 1959-62; chmn. N.Y. State Joint Legis. Com. on Matrimonial and Family Laws, 1955-62, counsel, 1963-64; del. N.Y. State Constl. Conv., 1967; counsel N.Y. State Assembly Agr. Com., 1963-64; trustee David F. Follett Supreme Ct. Library, 1963—. Mem. N.Y. Statewide com. for 1970 White House Conf. on Children and Youth; mem. Mohawk Valley Regional Conf. on Children and Youth, 1970; del. N.Y. Gov.'s Conf. on Children and Youth, 1970, White House Conf. on Children, 1970; past pres., bd. trustees Knox Sch., St. James, N.Y.; past mem. adv. council N.Y. State Coll. Home Econs., Cornell U.; past bd. dirs. N.Y. State div. Am. Cancer Soc.; del. Churchmen's Internat. Consultation on Ch. and Industry; bd. dirs. Chanango County Soc. for Prevention Cruelty to Animals. Mem. ABA (vice chmn. com. on marriage and family counselling and conciliation family law sect. 1971-74), N.Y. State Bar Assn. (family law sect.), Chenango County Bar Assn. (pres. 1968), Phi Alpha Delta, Delta Kappa Gamma (hon. Pi State orgn.), Delta Kappa Gamma (hon. N.Y. State Sigma chpt.). Republican. Episcopalian. Mem. Bklyn. Law Rev., 1938-40. Family and matrimonial, Probate, Environment. Home: 91 E Main St Norwich NY 13815 Office: 39 Sheldon St PO Box 270 Norwich NY 13815

HILL, JAY, lawyer; b. Cin., Sept. 26, 1949; s. Malquin Bankston Hill and Norma Ann (Janke) Cartwright; m. Janet E. Greenlee, Sept. 6, 1968. BS, U. Cin., 1971, JD, 1977; cert., Nat. Coll. Criminal Def. Lawyers, Houston, 1978. Bar: Ohio 1977, U.S. Dist. Ct. (so. dist.) Ohio 1977, U.S. Tax Ct. 1981, U.S. Supreme Ct. 1981, U.S. Dist. Ct. (no. dist.) Ohio 1985. Project officer CORVA, Cin., 1977-78; staff atty. pub. defender div. Cin. Legal Aid Soc., 1978-79; assoc. Swain & Hardin, L.P.A., Cin., 1979—. Mem. Project Rev. Com. Cin. Symphony Assn., 1985—; bd. dirs. Williams YMCA, Cin., 1983-86. Served with U.S. Army, 1971-74. Mem. Ohio Bar Assn., Cin. Bar Assn. (domestic relations com., negligence law com.), Assn. Trial Lawyers Am., Kappa Delta Pi. Democrat. Mem. Unitarian Ch. Clubs: Cin. Revolver, Clifton Track (Cin.). Lodge: Masons. Avocations: running, fishing, hiking, shooting. Family and matrimonial, Personal injury, General corporate. Home: 2200 Victory Pkwy Apt 1107 Cincinnati OH 45206 Office: Swain & Hardin LPA 1529 Madison Rd Cincinnati OH 45206

HILL, JOHN, JR., Justice, Tex. Supreme Ct., Austin. Judicial administration. Office: Office of the Supreme Ct of Tex Box 12248 Capitol Station Austin TX 78711 *

HILL, JOHN EARLL, lawyer; b. Frankfurt, Fed. Republic Germany, Feb. 16, 1949; came to U.S., 1950; s. Raymond Dunlap and Ruth Berrien (Waller) H.; m. Marcia Searight Porter, Sept. 17, 1978; children: John Porter, Christopher Carpenter, Emily Berrien, Peterson Waller. BA in Govt., U. Va., 1971; JD, U. Ga., 1974; LLM in Taxation, Emory U., 1983. Bar: Ga. 1971. Assoc. Thomasson & Hardcastle, Atlanta, 1974-77, Gray, Gilliland & Gold, Atlanta, 1977-82; gen. counsel, v.p. Exec. Compensation Systems Inc., Atlanta, 1982—. Mem. ABA (subcom. exec. compensation 1983—), Ga. Bar Assn., Atlanta Bar Assn., Atlanta Hist. Soc. Avocations: tennis, golf, reading. Pension, profit-sharing, and employee benefits. Office: Exec Compensation Systems Inc 2 Peachtree St Suite 2612 Atlanta GA 30383

HILL, JOHN HOWARD, lawyer; b. Pitts., Aug. 12, 1940; s. David Garrett and Eleanor Campbell (Musser) H. B.A., Yale U., 1962, J.D., 1965. Bar: Pa. 1965, U.S. Dist. Ct. (we dist.) Pa. 1965, U.S. Ct. Appeals (3d cir.) 1965, U.S. Supreme Ct. 1982. Assoc. Reed, Smith, Shaw & McClay, Pitts., 1965-75, ptnr., 1975—. Mem. Travelers Aid Soc. Pitts., 1973—, treas., 1982—. Mem. ABA, Pa. Bar Assn., Allegheny County Bar Assn., Hosp. Assn. Pa., Pa. Soc., World Affairs Council, Pitts. Symphony Soc., Pitts Opera Assn., Phi Gamma Delta. Republican. Presbyterian. Clubs: Duquesne (Pitts.), Fox Chapel Golf (Pitts.); Rolling Rock (Ligonier, Pa.). Labor. Home: 4722 Bayard St Pittsburgh PA 15213 Office: Mellon Sq 435 6th Ave Pittsburgh PA 15219

HILL, MILTON KING, JR., lawyer; b. Balt., Nov. 29, 1926; s. Milton King and Mary Fusselbaugh (Hall) H.; m. Agnes Ciotti, June 11, 1949; children—Thomas Michael, Milton King, III, Susan Hill Voneiff. B.S. in Bus. and Pub. Adminstrn., U. Md., 1950, J.D., 1952. Bar: Md. 1952, U.S. Dist. Ct. Md. 1952, U.S. Ct. Appeals (4th cir.) 1952. Assoc., Smith, Somerville & Case, Balt., 1952-55, ptnr., 1955—; mem. faculty Md. Hosp. Ednl. Inst.; dir. Union Meml. Hosp.; mem. adv. bd. U. Balt. Law Sch. Served with USAF, 1944-46. Fellow Am. Coll. Trial Lawyers, Internat. Soc. Barristers; mem. Md. State Bar Assn., Nat. Conf. Commrs. Uniform State Laws (pres. 1981-83), Assn. Def. Trial Counsel (pres. 1964-65), Internat. Assn. Ins. Counsel, ABA (ho. of dels. 1981-83), Md. Bar Found., Am. Acad. Hosp. Attys. Clubs: Potapskut Sailing Assn., Center, Wednesday Law, Round Table. State civil litigation, Federal civil litigation, Insurance. Home: 106 Tunbridge Rd Baltimore MD 21212 Office: 100 Light St Baltimore MD 21202

HILL, OLIVER WHITE, SR., lawyer, consultant; b. Richmond, Va., May 1, 1907; s. William Henry White Jr. and Olivia (Lewis) White-Hill; m. Beresenia Ann Walker, Sept. 5, 1934; children—Oliver White Hill, Jr. A.B., Howard U., 1931, J.D., 1933; LL.D. (hon.), St. Paul's Coll., 1978, Va. State U., 1982. Bar: Va. 1934, U.S. Dist. Ct. (ea. dist.) Va. 1939, U.S. Ct. Appeals (4th cir.) 1940, U.S. Dist. Ct. (we. dist.) Va. 1947, U.S. Supreme Ct. 1950. Sole practice, Roanoke, Va., 1934-36, Richmond, Va., 1939-43, 59-61; ptnr. Hill, Martin & Robinson, Richmond, 1943-45, Hill Martin & Olphin, Richmond, 1955-59; asst. to commr. FHA, Washington, 1961-66; asst. to asst. sec. Mortgage Credit and Fed. Housing Commn., Washington, 1966; ptnr. Hill, Tucker, & Marsh, Richmond, 1966—; dir. So. Aid Life Ins. Co., Richmond, HTM, Inc., Richmond; mem. President's Commn. on Govt. Contract Compliance, Washington, 1951-53, Commn. on Constl. Revision for Commonwealth of Va., U. Va., 1968-69, Va. State Bar Disciplinary Bd., 1976-82. Bd. dirs. Richmond br. NAACP, 1940-61, Richmond Urban League, 1950-61; mem. City Council, Richmond, 1948-50, Richmond Citizens Assn., 1950-54, Richmond City Democratic Com., 1956-61, 67-72, Va. Regional Med. Program, 1969-76; chmn. legal com. Va. State Conf. of NAACP, 1940-61. Served to staff sgt. U.S. Army, 1943-45, ETO. Recipient Chgo. Defender Merit award, 1949, Howard U. Alumni award, 1950, Nat. Publ. Assn. Russwurm award, 1952, Disting. Service award Delver Women's Club, 1954, Va. State Conf. of NAACP award, 1957, Ann. Conv. award NAACP, 1964, Disting. Service award Va. Tchrs. Assn., 1964, Francis Ellis Rivers award NAACP Legal Def. and Edn. Fund, 1976, Charles Hamilton Houston Medallion of Merit award Washington Bar Assn., 1976, Outstanding Pub. Service award The Moles, 1977, Disting. Service award Va. Union U. Am. Black Soc. Workers, 1978, John Mercer Langston Outstanding Alumnus award Howard U. Student Bar Assn., 1980, William Robert Ming Advocacy award NAACP, 1980, Appreciation award Va. State U., 1981, William P. Robinson Meml. award Democratic Party Va., 1981, Alumnus of Yr. award Howard U. Alumni Assn., 1981, Disting. Service award Va. State U., 1981, Distinguished Scholar award Oliver W. Hill Black Pre-Law Assn. of U. Va., 1983, citation for Disting. Legal Service, Richmond chpt. Frontiers of Am., 1954, Cert. of Appreciation, Assn. for Study of Afro-Am. Life and History, 1974, Brotherhood citation NCCJ, 1982. Fellow Old Dominion Bar Assn. Found. (pres. 1985—); mem. Old Dominion Bar Assn. (pres. 1941-43, 46-56, recipient numerous awards), Va. Bar Found., Richmond Bar Assn., Nat. Bar Assn. (C. Francis Stradford award 1959), NAACP (legal def. fund The Simple Justice award 1986), James Madison Meml. Com., Global Assn. Liberation and Advancement of Civilized Human Earthlings and Devel. of Universalists (founder), Sigma Pi Phi (grand sire archon 1964-66), Omega Psi Phi (Omega Man of Yr. 1957). Baptist. Civil rights, General practice, Probate. Home: 3108 Noble Ave Richmond VA 23222 Office: Hill Tucker & Marsh 509 N 3d St Richmond VA 23219

HILL, PETER WAVERLY, lawyer; b. White River Junction, Vt., June 24, 1953; s. Richard Bert and Elaine Etta (Kimball) H.; m. Suzanne Miller, Nov. 21, 1983; 1 stepchild, Marshall Jackson Miller. BA in Philosophy and

Govt., U. Ariz., 1975, JD, 1978. Bar: Ariz. 1978, U.S. Dist. Ct. (no. dist.) N.Y. 1979, N.Y. 1980, U.S. Ct. Appeals (2d cir.) 1982. Staff atty. Legal Aid Soc. Mid N.Y., Utica, 1978-79, Oneonta, 1979-83; assoc. Law Offices of Paternoster & O'Leary, Walton, N.Y., 1983-84; sole practice Oneonta, 1985—; bd. dirs. OURS-Delaco Assn., Inc., Delhi, N.Y. Contbr. articles to profl. jours. Mem. N.Y. State com. Socialist Party, Syracuse. Mem. ABA, N.Y. State Bar Assn., Otsego County Bar Assn., Delaware County Bar Assn., Assn. Trial Lawyers Am., N.Y. State Trial Lawyers Assn., Nat. Lawyers Guild. Unitarian Universalist. State civil litigation, General practice, Workers' compensation. Home: 103 Elm St Oneonta NY 13820 Office: 37 Dietz St PO Box 823 Oneonta NY 13820

HILL, PHILIP, lawyer; b. East Saint Louis, Ill., Mar. 13, 1917; s. Nehemiah William and Lulu Myrtle (Johnson) H.; m. Betty Jean Stone, July 4, 1942; children—William Stone, Thomas Chapman, Nancy Layton, Mary Anne. A.B. in Chemistry, U. Ill., 1937; Ph.D. in Chemistry, Ohio State U., 1941; J.D., John Marshall Law Sch., Chgo., 1968. Bar: Ill. 1968, U.S. Patent Office 1969, U.S. Ct. Appeals (fed. cir.) 1982. With Standard Oil Co. Ind., 1941-78, patent atty., 1969-73, dir. petroleum and corp. patents and licensing, 1973-78; ptnr. Hill & Hill, Lansing, Ill., 1978-86, sole practice Philip Hill, P.C., 1987—; cons. Univ. Patents, Inc., Norwalk, Conn. Mem. ABA, Ill. State Bar Assn., Chgo. Bar Assn., Am. Intellectual Property Law Assn., Chgo. Patent Law Assn., Am. Chem. Soc., AAAS. Methodist. Clubs: Kiwanis (Lansing) (pres. 1959, 84), Lansing Country. Contbr. articles to profl. jours.; patentee in field. Patent, General corporate. Home: 3241 N Schultz Dr Lansing IL 60438 Office: 3256 Ridge Rd Suite 207 PO Box 187 Lansing IL 60438

HILL, RHONDA KENYON, lawyer; b. Des Moines, Oct. 16, 1955; d. Ronald Deforest and Margaret Louise (Quigley) Kenyon; m. James Derek Hill, Feb. 18, 1984. BFA, Drake U., 1979, JD, 1981. Bar: Iowa 1982, U.S. Dist. Ct. (no. dist.) Iowa 1982, U.S. Ct. Appeals (8th cir.) 1983, Ark. 1986, U.S. Dist. Ct. (ea. and we. dists.) Ark. 1987. Sole practice Des Moines, 1982-83; legal asst. Leisure Am. Resorts, Inc., Florence, Ala., 1982-84; asst. atty. gen. Little Rock, 1985—. Named one of Outstanding Young Women in Am., 1984. Mem. ABA, Iowa Bar Assn., Ark. Bar Assn., Phi Alpha Delta (dist. justice 1982-83, dep. internat. justice 1984-85). Methodist. Labor, General corporate, State Government/consumer protection. Home: 5409 N Hills Blvd North Little Rock AR 72116 Office: Ark Atty Gen 201 E Markham Heritage West Bldg Little Rock AR 72201

HILL, (GEORGE) RICHARD, lawyer; b. Chapel Hill, N.C., Oct. 22, 1951; s. Reuben Lorenzo and Marion (Ensign) H.; m. Karen Meehl, Oct. 5, 1974; children: Seth Jacob, Jonathan David, Spencer Thomas. BA, U. Minn., 1973, MA, 1975; JD, Yale U., 1978. Bar: Wash. 1978. Assoc. Foster, Pepper & Riviera, Seattle, 1978-84, ptnr., 1984—. Chmn. ch.-state com. ACLU Wash., Seattle, 1982-83, chmn. legal com., 1985—. Mem. ABA (chmn. landuse litigation and damages subcom. 1986—, hazardous waste subcom. 1985—, chmn. conditional use permit sect. 1983-84, land use planning and zoning com.), Wash. State Bar Assn. (land use and environ. law sect., editor sect. newsletter 1984-86). Environment, Real property, Zoning. Office: Foster Pepper & Riviera 1111 3d Ave Suite 3400 Seattle WA 98101

HILL, ROBERT CHARLES, foreign affairs policy adviser, lawyer; b. Greenwich, Conn., Mar. 28, 1952; s. George Urho and Martha Ilona (Nyburn) H.; m. Mary Anne Carroll, May 13, 1972; children: Robert, Kristin, Jessica, David, Elizabeth, Michael. BA cum laude, CUNY, 1974; JD, Georgetown U., 1980. Bar: Va. 1980. Tchr. The Heights Sch., Washington, 1977-79; dep. dir. presdl. correspondence The White House, Washington, 1981-83; spl. asst. to Asst. Sec. State Dept., Washington, 1983—. Republican. Roman Catholic. Public international, Legislative. Home: 14507 Briarwood Terr Rockville MD 20853 Office: Dept State Bur Internat Orgns 2201 C St NW Washington DC 20520

HILL, ROBERT DEAN, lawyer; b. Pueblo, Colo., Sept. 19, 1935; s. Hugh Boyd and Frances Evaline (Stubbs) H.; m. Marilyn A. Evans, Apr. 7, 1963; children—Andrea Lynn, Jeffrey Brian. B.S., U. Nebr., 1959; J.D., 1959; postgrad. U. Fla., 1979-80. Bar: Nebr. 1959, Colo. 1969, U.S. Tax Ct. 1980. Ptnr. Hill & Corrigan, Colorado Springs, 1977—. Mem. past pres. Pikes Peak Tax Counsel. Served with Nebr. N.G., 1959-65. Mem. Estate Planning Council Colorado Springs. Republican. Clubs: Country of Colo., Elks. Corporate taxation, Probate, Pension, profit-sharing, and employee benefits. Office: Holly Sugar Bldg Suite 400 Colorado Springs CO 80903

HILL, RUFUS SADLER, JR., civil servant, lawyer, writer; b. Anderson, S.C., June 30, 1935; s. Rufus Sadler and Lois (Pressly) H.; m. Carolyn Kennedy Wood, Nov. 27, 1968; children: Barbara Kennedy, John Justin. BS, Clemson U., 1957; LLB, Duke U., 1960. Bar: S.C. 1960, D.C. 1963, U.S. Supreme Ct. 1964. Atty. bd. govs. Fed. Res. System, 1960-63; atty., advisor ICC, Washington, 1963-68, advisor to commrs., 1968-73, rev. bd. mem., 1973-81, sr. atty., 1981-84; sr. adjudicator GAO, 1984—. Author short pieces. Mem. St. Columba's Episc. Serve the Needy, 1981—; former Sunday Club service chmn. Nat. Presbyn. Ch. Served with U.S. Army, 1960-61. S.C. Rhodes scholar nominee, 1956. Mem. Am. Soc. Pub. Adminstrn., Am. Polit. Sci. Assn. Episcopalian. Administrative and regulatory, Civil rights, Banking. Address: 3331 Legation St NW Washington DC 20015

HILL, STEPHEN A., lawyer; b. East Palestine, Ohio, June 1, 1954; s. George Alan and Nancy Lee (Brookhart) H. BA, Ohio No. U., 1976, JD, 1979. Bar: U.S. Dist. Ct. (no. dist.) Ohio 1982. Sole practice East Palestine, 1979—; contracted mng. staff atty. Northeast Ohio Legal Service, Lisbon, Ohio, 1980—; law dir. City of East Palestine, Ohio, 1987—. Bd. dirs. Community Action Agy., Lisbon, 1983. Mem. ABA, Ohio Bar Assn., Columbiana County Bar Assn. Republican. Presbyterian. Family and matrimonial, General practice, Probate. Office: 284 N North Market St East Palestine OH 44413

HILL, WILLIAM CHARLES, state justice; b. Newark, May 10, 1917; s. William Herbert and Alice Anna (de Groote) H.; m. Grace Giarratano, May 2, 1942; children: Carol, Pamela, Elizabeth. B.A., NYU, 1939, J.D., 1941; M.A., U. Vt., 1967. Bar: N.Y. bar 1942, Vt. bar 1947. Practiced in N.Y., Vt., 1942-59; judge Vt. Superior Ct., 1959-76, chief judge, 1972-76; justice Vt. Supreme Ct., 1976—; vis. lectr. polit. sci. Trinity Coll., Burlington, Vt., 1973—; vis. lectr. trial advocacy Franklin Pierce Law Sch., 1985—; mem. Vt. Ho. of Reps., 1953-57. Contbg. author: New Eng. Politics. Served with U.S. Army, 1942-46; lt. col. JAGC U.S. Army Res., 1946-72. Mem. Vt. Bar Assn. Republican. Club: Masons. Address: PO Box 680 RD 1 Hinesburg VT 05461

HILL, WILLIAM JAMES, III, lawyer; b. Shreveport, La., Dec. 2, 1946; s. William James Jr. and Blanche (Crumpler) H.; m. Constance K. Draughon, Dec. 8, 1967 (div. May 1975); 1 child, Courtney; m. Sandra Kay Weber, Apr. 10, 1981; children: Allyson, Kendal, Elyse, Jamey, Weber. BA, Vanderbilt U., 1968; MS, North Tex. State U., 1971; JD, La. State U., 1974. Bar: La. 1974, Tex. 1975. Assoc. Smitherman, Lunn, Hussey & Chastain, Shreveport, 1974-79; ptnr. Smitherman, Lunn, Chastain & Hill, Shreveport, 1979—. Bd. dirs. Shreveport Little Theater, 1980-81, Shreveport Opera, 1984—. Served to maj., USAR. Mem. ABA, Assn. Trial Lawyers Am., La. Trial Lawyers Assn., La. Def. Lawyers Assn., Ark.-La.-Tex. Tax Inst. (pres. 1981-82), La. Bar Assn., Tex. Bar Assn., Internat. Bar Assn., Shreveport Bar Assn. Republican. Methodist. Clubs: University (Shreveport), Shreveport Country, Pierremont Oaks. Lodge: Rotary (bd. dirs. Shreveport club 1985). Avocations: golf, tennis. Real property, Estate planning, Probate. Home: 1608 Gentilly Dr Shreveport LA 71105 Office: Smitherman Lunn Chastin & Hill 329 Texas St 800 CNB Bldg Shreveport LA 71101

HILLBERG, MARYLOU ELIN, lawyer; b. Chgo., Nov. 6, 1950; d. Harold Andrew Hillberg and Eunice Elin (Anderson) Peterson; m. Andrew Charles Lennox, Aug. 6, 1983; 1 child, Elin Elizabeth Lennox. BFA, San Francisco Art Inst., 1973; JD, U. Calif., San Francisco, 1979. Bar: Calif. 1979, U.S. Dist. Ct. (no. dist.) Calif. 1979. Dep. dist. atty. Sonoma County, Santa Rosa, Calif., 1980; sole practice Santa Rosa, 1981—; adj. prof. Sonoma State U., Rohnert Park, Calif., 1982—. Chmn. bd. dirs. Sonoma County Drug Abuse Alternatives Ctr., Santa Rosa, 1983-84; bd. dirs. ACLU, Santa Rosa, 1982-84. Mem. Sonoma County Women in Law (chairperson 1983-84). Democrat. Mem. United Christian Ch. Criminal, Juvenile. Office: 115 4th St Santa Rosa CA 95401

HILLER, ROBERT STANFORD, lawyer; b. Memphis, Dec. 19, 1951; s. Sigmund Felix Hiller and Marie Louise (Levy) Steuer; m. Jeannie Anne Fischer, Aug. 11, 1979; children: Robert Webster, Dean Stanford. BA, Ind. U., 1973; JD, U. Tenn., 1976. Bar: Ohio 1977, U.S. Dist. Ct. (so. dist.) Ohio 1977, U.S. Ct. Appeals (6th cir.) 1982. Assoc. Reisenfeld & Hiller, Cin., 1977-82; assoc. Rendigs, Fry, Kiely & Dennis, Cin., 1983-87, ptnr., 1987—. Jewish. Club: Cin. Athletic. Avocations: triathlons, photography. Insurance, Personal injury, State civil litigation. Office: Rendigs Fry Kiely & Dennis 900 Central Trust Tower Cincinnati OH 45202

HILLESTAD, CHARLES ANDREW, lawyer; b. McCurtain, Okla., Aug. 30, 1945; s. Carl Oliver and Aileen Hanna (Sweeney) H.; m. Ann Ramsey Robertson, Oct. 13, 1973. BS, U. Oreg., 1967; JD, U. Mich., 1972. Bar: Colo. 1972, U.S. Dist. Ct. Colo. 1972, U.S. Ct. Appeals (10th cir.) 1972. Clk. Colo. Supreme Ct., Denver, 1972-73; ptnr. DeMuth & Kemp, Denver, 1973-83, McGuire, Cornwell & Blakey, Denver, 1983—; licensed real estate broker, Denver, 1975—. Legal counsel Enterprise Hill Hist. Dist. Assn., council mem. Denver Art Mus.; former bd. dirs. Hist. Denver, Inc.; mem. Com. for Denver Arts, Leadership Denver Assn., ad hoc com. of Denver Real Estate Atty. Specialists. Served to staff sgt. U.S. Army, 1968-70, Vietnam. Mem. ABA, Colo. Bar Assn., Denver Bar Assn., Colo. Lawyers for the Arts, POETS. Avocations: photography, art collecting, historic and environmental preservation, history and architecture reading, rafting. Real property, Landlord-tenant, Contracts commercial. Home: 2151 Tremont Place Denver CO 80205 Office: McGuire Cornwell & Blakey 1225-17th St Suite 2650 Denver CO 80202

HILLIARD, DAVID CRAIG, lawyer; b. Framingham, Mass., May 22, 1937; s. Walter David and Dorothy (Shortiss) H.; m. Celia Schmid, Feb. 16, 1974. BS, Tufts U., 1959; JD, U. Chgo., 1962. Bar: Ill. 1962, U.S. Supreme Ct. 1966. Mng. ptnr. Pattishall, McAuliffe & Hofstetter, Chgo. and Washington, 1971—; adj. prof. law Northwestern U. Author: Trademarks, Trade Identity, and Unfair Trade Practices, 1974, Unfair Competition and Unfair Trade Practices, 1985, Trademarks, 1987; editor in chief Chgo. Bar Record, 1978-81. Trustee Art Inst. Chgo., also chmn. sustaining fellows, 1981-85, chmn. adv. com. dept. architecture, 1981—, pres. aux. bd., 1977-79; trustee Newberry Library; pres. Lawyers Trust Fund Ill.; mem. vis. com. Northwestern U. Sch. Law, DePaul U. law Sch., U. Chgo. Sch. of Law and Sch. of Social Services Adminstrn., Northwestern U. Assocs., 1985—; mem. profl. adv. bd. Atty. Gen. Ill. 1982-84; mem. Ill. Commn. on Rights of Women, 1983-85; bd. dirs. Ill. Inst. Continuing Legal Edn., 1980-82; pres. Planned Parenthood Assn. Chgo., 1975-77. Served to lt. JAGC, USN, 1962-66. Recipient Maurice Weigle award, 1974, Chgo. Council Lawyers award, 1983. Mem. ABA (chmn. trademark div. 1986-87), Ill. Bar Assn., Chgo. Bar Assn. (pres. 1982-83, founding chmn. young lawyers sect. 1971-72). Clubs: Economic, Law, Legal, University, Casino. Trademark and copyright, Federal civil litigation, Administrative and regulatory. Home: 1320 N State Pkwy Chicago IL 60610 Office: Pattishall McAuliffe & Hofstetter 33 W Monroe St Chicago IL 60603

HILLIARD, WILLIAM RAYMOND, JR., lawyer; b. Geneva, N.Y., Jan. 15, 1953; s. William R. and Mary (Edwards) H.; m. JoAnne Tiller, Sept. 13, 1980; children: Laura Lamon, Caroline Talbott. BS, Boston U., 1974; JD, U. Louisville, 1978. Bar: Ky. 1978, U.S. Dist. Ct. (ea. dist.) Ky. 1978. Assoc. Tarrent, Combs & Bullitt, Lexington, Ky., 1978-79; ptnr. Gess, Mattingly, Saunier & Atchison, Lexington, 1979—. Mem. ABA, Ky. Bar Assn., Fayette County Bar Assn., Am. Horse Council, Ky. Polo Assn. (bd. dirs. 1979—). Republican. Episcopalian. Equine law, Real property, Contracts commercial. Office: Gess Mattingly et al 201 W Short St Lexington KY 40507

HILLMAN, DOUGLAS WOODRUFF, federal judge; b. Grand Rapids, Mich., Feb. 15, 1922; s. Lemuel Serrell and Dorothy (Woodruff) H.; m. Sally Jones, Sept. 13, 1944; children: Drusilla W., Clayton D. Student, Phillips Exeter Acad., 1941; A.B., U. Mich., 1946, LL.B., 1948. Bar: Mich. 1948, U.S. Supreme Ct. 1967. Assoc. Lilly, Luyendyk & Snyder, Grand Rapids, 1948-53; partner Luyendyk, Hainer, Hillman, Karr & Dutcher, Grand Rapids, 1953-65, Hillman, Baxter & Hammond, 1965-79; U.S. dist. judge Western Dist. Mich., Grand Rapids, 1979—; chief judge Western Dist. Mich., 1986—; instr. Nat. Inst. Trial Advocacy, Boulder, Colo. Chmn. Grand Rapids Human Relations Commn., 1963-66; chmn. bd. trustees Fountain St. Ch., 1970-72; pres. Family Service Assn., 1967. Served as pilot USAAF, 1943-45. Decorated D.F.C., Air medal.; Recipient Annual Civil Liberties award ACLU, 1970. Fellow Am. Bar Found.; Mem. Am. Bar Assn., Mich. Bar Assn. (chmn. client security fund), Grand Rapids Bar Assn. (pres. 1963), Am. Coll. Trial Lawyers (Mich. chmn. 1979), 6th Circuit Jud. Conf. (life), Internat. Acad. Trial Lawyers, Fedn. Ins. Counsel, Internat. Assn. Ins. Counsel, Internat. Soc. Barristers (pres. 1977-78), Nat. Bd. Trial Advocacy. Clubs: M (U. Mich.); University (Grand Rapids); Rotary, Torch. Jurisprudence. Office: 110 Michigan St NW 682 Grand Rapids MI 49503

HILLMAN, JORDAN JAY, law educator; b. 1924. M.A. in Polit Sci., U. Chgo., 1947, J.D., 1950; S.J.D., Northwestern U., 1965. Bar: Ill. 1950. Mem. legal staff Ill. Commerce Commn., 1950-53; with Chgo. and Northwestern Ry., 1954-67, gen. counsel, 1963-67, v.p. law, 1966-67; prof. law Northwestern U., 1967—; sr. legal cons., gen. counsel U.S. Ry. Assn., 1974-76, spl. counsel, 1976-79; legal cons. Amtrak, 1978; mem. labor panel Nat. Mediation Bd. Mem. Constn. Study Commn., State of Ill., 1963-67; mem. Zoning Amendment Com., Evanston, Ill., 1963-68; mem. Bd. Edn., Dist. 202, Evanston Twp. High Sch., 1968-71; mem. Chgo. Transit Authority Bd., 1981—. Mem. Am. Arbitration Assn. (mem. labor panel), Chgo. Bar Assn. (bd. mgrs. 1970-72), Phi Beta Kappa Author: Competition and Railroad Price Discrimination, 1968; The Parliamentary Structuring of British Road-Rail Freight Coordination, 1973; The Export-Import Bank at Work; Promotional Financing in the Public Sector, 1982. Office: Northwestern University Law School 357 E Chicago Ave Chicago IL 60611

HILLMAN, ROBERT ANDREW, lawyer; b. N.Y.C., Dec. 23, 1946; s. Herman D. and Edith N. (Geilich) H.; m. Elizabeth Hall Kafka, Aug. 24, 1969; children: Jessica H., Heather D. BA, U. Rochester, 1969; JD, Cornell U., 1972. Bar: N.Y. 1973, Iowa 1976. Law clk. to judge U.S. Dist. Ct., N.Y.C., 1972-73; assoc. Debevoise & Plimpton, N.Y.C., 1973-74; prof. law U. Iowa, Iowa City, 1975-82, Cornell U., Ithaca, N.Y., 1982—. Author: (with others) Common Law and Equity Under The UCC, 1985, Law: Its Nature, Functions, and Limits, 1986, Contract and Related Obligation: Theory, Doctrine, and Practice, 1987; contbr. articles to profl. jours. Mem. Am. Arbitration Assn. (arbitrator 1980—). Avocations: tennis, basketball. Consumer commercial, Contracts commercial. Office: Cornell U Law Sch Ithaca NY 14853

HILLS, CARLA ANDERSON, lawyer, former secretary housing and urban development; b. Los Angeles, Jan. 3, 1934; d. Carl H. and Edith (Hume) Anderson; m. Roderick Maltman Hills, Sept. 27, 1958; children: Laura Hume, Roderick Maltman, Megan Elizabeth, Alison Macbeth. A.B. cum laude, Stanford U., 1955; student, St. Hilda's Coll., Oxford (Eng.) U., 1954; LL.B., Yale U., 1958; hon. degrees, Pepperdine U., 1975, Washington U., 1977, Mills Coll., 1977, Lake Forest Coll., 1978, Williams Coll., 1981. Bar: Calif. 1959, U.S. Supreme Ct. 1965. Asst. U.S. atty. civil div. Los Angeles, 1958-61; partner firm Munger, Tolles, Hills & Rickershauser, Los Angeles, 1962-74, Latham, Watkins & Hills, Washington, 1978-86, Weil, Gotshal & Manges, Washington, 1986—; asst. atty. gen. civil div. Justice Dept., Washington, 1974-75; sec. HUD, 1975-77; dir. IBM Corp., Corning Glass Works, Am. Airlines, Fed. Nat. Mortgage Assn., Allied Signal Corp., Rand Corp., Chevron Corp.; adj. prof. Sch. Law, UCLA, 1972; mem. Trilateral Commn., 1977-83, Am. Com. on East-West Accord, 1977-79, Internat. Found. for Cultural Cooperation and Devel., 1977—, Fed. Acctg. Standards Adv. Council, 1978-80; bd. dirs. Internat. Exec. Service Corps.; mem. corrections task force Los Angeles County Sub-Regional; adv. bd. Calif. Council on Criminal Justice, 1969-71; mem. standing com. discipline U.S. Dist. Ct. for Central Calif., 1970-73; mem. Adminstrv. Conf. U.S., 1972-74; mem. exec. com. law and free soc. State Bar Calif., 1973; bd. councillors U. So. Calif. Law Center, 1972-74; trustee Pomona Coll., 1974-79, U. So. Calif., Brookings Instn.; mem. at large exec. com. Yale Law Sch., 1973-78; mem. com. on Law Sch. Yale Univ. Council; Gordon Grand fellow Yale U., 1978; mem. Sloan Commn. on Govt. and Higher Edn., 1977-79; mem. advisory com. Princeton U., Woodrow Wilson Sch. of Pub. and Internat. Affairs, 1977-80. Co-author: Federal Civil Practice, 1961; co-author, editor: Antitrust Adviser, 1971, 3d edit., 1985; contbg. editor: Legal Times, 1978—; mem. editorial bd.: Nat. Law Jour, 1978—. Trustee U. So. Calif., 1977-79, Norton Simon Mus. Art, Pasadena, Calif., 1976-80, Lawyers Com. for Civil Rights under Law, 1978-84; trustee Urban Inst., 1978-80, chmn., 1983—; co-chmn. Alliance To Save Energy, 1977—; vice chmn. adv. council on legal policy Am. Enterprise Inst., 1977-84; bd. visitors, exec. com. Stanford U. Law Sch., 1978-81; bd. dirs. Am. Council for Capital Formation, 1978—; mem. adv. com. M.I.T.-Harvard U. Joint Center for Urban Studies, 1978-82. Fellow Am. Bar Found.; mem. Los Angeles Women Lawyers Assn. (pres. 1964), ABA (chmn. publs. com. antitrust sect. 1972-74, council 1974, 77-84, chmn. 1982-83), Fed. Bar Assn. (pres. Los Angeles chpt. 1963), Los Angeles County Bar Assn. (mem. fed. rules and practice com. 1963-72, chmn. issues and survey 1963-72, chmn. sub-com. revision local rules for fed. cts. 1966-72, mem. jud. qualifications com. 1971-72), Am. Bar Inst. Clubs: Yale of So. Calif. (dir. 1972-74); Yale (Washington). Antitrust. Office: Weil Gotshal & Manges 1615 L St NW Suite 700 Washington DC 20036

HILLSTROM, ROBERT ARTHUR, lawyer; b. Mpls., Aug. 20, 1932; s. Arthur Chester and Clara Myrtle (Amundson) H.; m. Patricia Louise Murray, June 16, 1951; children: Robyn Louise, Scott David, Shelley Karee, Bradley Harlan, Tamara Lane. BS, U. Minn., 1955; JD cum laude, William Mitchell Coll. Law, 1970. Bar: Minn., U.S. Dist. Ct. Minn. 1970, U.S. Ct. Appeals (8th cir.), U.S. Supreme Ct. 1979. Mng. ptnr. Hillstrom & Bale Ltd., Mpls., 1973-86; spl. counsel environ. law Met. Waste Control Commn., St. Paul, 1975-86; valuation cons. Mpls. Community Devel. Agy., 1974-80. Mem. capital long range improvements com. City of Mpls., 1976-77. Harvey J. Reid scholar William Mitchell Coll. Law, 1967. Mem. ABA, Minn. State Bar Assn., Hennepin County Bar Assn. (eminent domain com. 1975—), Am. Soc. Appraisers (sr. mem.). Presbyterian. Club: Riverside Country (Bozeman, Mont.). Lodge: Masons. Avocations: fly fishing, Tenn. walking horses, skiing. Condemnation, General practice, Environment. Office: Hillstrom & Bale Ltd 7900 Xerxes Ave S Minneapolis MN 55431

HILLYARD, LYLE WILLIAM, lawyer; b. Logan, Utah, Sept. 25, 1940; s. Alma Lowell and Lucille (Rosenbaum) H.; m. Alice Thorpe, June 24, 1964; children: Carrie, Lisa, Holly, Todd, Matthew. BS, Utah State U., 1965; JD, U. Utah, 1967. Bar: Utah 1967. Pres. Hillyard, Low & Anderson, Logan, 1967—; senator State of Utah, Salt Lake City, 1985—. Rep. chmn. Cache County, Logan, 1970-76; Utah State Rep., 1981-84; pres. Cache County C. of C., 1977. Named Oustanding Young Man, Utah Jaycees, 1972; recipient Disting. Service award, Logan Jaycees, 1972, Merit award Cache Valley council Boy Scouts Am., 1981. Mem. ABA, Utah State Bar Assn., Cache County Bar Assn., Assn. Trial Lawyers Am., Am. Bd. Trial Advocates. Mormon. Club: Big Blue (Logan). Lodge: Kiwanis. Family and matrimonial, Personal injury, Probate. Office: Hillyard Low Anderson 175 E First N Logan UT 84321

HILLYER, HAYWOOD HANSELL, III, lawyer; b. New Orleans, Sept. 30, 1937; s. Haywood Hansell, Jr. and Ellen Blair (Sinclair) H.; m. Brenda Clayton Edmonson, Apr. 1, 1961 (div.); children: Haywood Hansell IV, Richard Quin Edmonson. BA, Tulane U., 1959, JD, 1963. Bar: La. 1963, U.S. Dist. Ct. (ea. dist.) La. 1963, U.S. Ct. Appeals (5th cir.) 1963, U.S. Customs Ct. 1964, U.S. Supreme Ct. 1979, U.S. Ct. Appeals (11th cir.) 1981. Assoc. Milling, Benson, Woodward, Hillyer, Pierson & Miller and predecessor firms, New Orleans, 1963-68, ptnr., 1968—; prof. law corps., 1981—. Sec. Orleans Parish Rep. Exec. Com., 1963-67; mem. La. Rep. State Cen. Com., 1967—; bd. dirs. Info. Council of Ams., 1965—. Internat. Schoolboy fellow English Speaking Union, St. Bees Sch., Cumbria, Eng., 1954-55. Mem. ABA, Fed. Bar Assn. (pres. New Orleans chpt. 1982-83, nat. v.p. for 5th cir. 1984-85), La. Bar Assn. (chmn. sect. of labor relations law 1981-82), New Orleans Bar Assn. (3d v.p. 1985-87). Episcopalian. Clubs: Southern Yacht, New Orleans Lawn Tennis; Boston; Stratford (New Orleans). Labor, Federal civil litigation, Federal civil litigation. Office: Whitney Bldg Milling Benson Woodward Hillyer Pierson & Miller Suite 1100 New Orleans LA 70130

HILTEBRAND, STEPHEN MARK, lawyer; b. Cherry Hill, N.J., Jan. 9, 1951; s. John Henry and Margaret W. (Murphy) H.; m. Susan C. Vogel, Aug. 25, 1984. BA, Rutgers U., 1973; JD, Seton Hall U., 1978. Bar: N.J. 1978, U.S. Dist. Ct. N.J. 1978, U.S. Ct. Appeals (3d cir.) 1978, U.S. Supreme Ct. 1978. Legis. aide N.J. Assembly, 1981—; sole practice Cherry Hill; panelist Matrimonial Early Settlement Panel, Camden, N.J., 1985—. Treas. assemblyman Dennis L. Riley, N.J., 1982—. Mem. ABA, Camden County Bar Assn., Camden County Pro Bono Program, Assn. Trial Lawyers Am. Democrat. Roman Catholic. Avocations: writing, sports, music (profl. drumming). Criminal, Personal injury, Family and matrimonial. Office: 409 Rt 70 East Suite 218 Cherry Hill NJ 08034

HILTON, CLAUDE MEREDITH, federal judge; b. Scott County, Va., Dec. 8, 1940; s. Claude Swanson and Edna (Fletcher) H.; m. Joretta Cabaniss, June 16, 1963; children: John, Rachel. BS, Ohio State U., 1963; JD, Am. Univ., 1966. Dep. clk. of cts. Arlington County, Va., 1964-66, asst. commonwealth atty., 1967-68, commonwealth atty., 1974; sole practice Arlington, 1967-85; judge U.S. Dist. Ct. (ea. dist.) Va., Alexandria, 1985—; asst. commonwealth atty., Arlington, 1967-68, commonwealth atty., 1974; dep. clk. ct., Arlington, 1964-66; commr. in chancery U.S. Ct. Appeals (4th cir.), 1976-85; bd. govs. criminal law sect. Va. State Bar, 1979-84, chmn., 1982-83, mem. ins. com., 1981-85. Mem. ABA, Va. Bar Assn., Arlington County Bar Assn. Republican. Methodist. Lodges: Masons, Alexandria Lodge of Perfection, Kena Temple. Home: 3912 Upland St Arlington VA 22207 Office: US Courthouse 200 S Washington St Alexandria VA 22314 *

HILTS, EARL T., lawyer, government official; educator; b. Ilion, N.Y., Mar. 31, 1946; stepson Leon Thomas and Gertrude Annette (Daly) Butler; m. Mae Hwa Kim, Apr. 13, 1973; children—Troy Alan, Kimberly Michelle. B.S., St. Lawrence U., 1967; J.D., Albany Law Sch., 1970. Bar: N.Y. 1972. Gen. atty.-advisor Dept. Army, Watervliet Arsenal, N.Y., 1978-80, supervisory atty.-advisor, Watervliet 1980—; adj. prof. Schnectady Community Coll., 1985—. Pee Wee Football coach Shenendehowa Schs., Clifton Park, N.Y.; Pee Wee wrestling coach Shenendehowa Schs., Clifton Park; Little League coach West Crescent Halfmoon Baseball League, Clifton Park. Served as capt. JAGC, U.S. Army, 1972-76. Scholar St. Lawrence U., 1963-67, Albany Law Sch., 1967-70. Mem. N.Y. State Bar Assn., Am. Legion, Pi Mu Epsilon. Republican. Roman Catholic. Government contracts and claims, Labor, Legal education. Home: 28 Oakwood Blvd Clifton Park NY 12065 Office: Legal Office Watervliet Arsenal Watervliet NY 12189

HIMELEIN, LARRY M., lawyer; b. Buffalo, June 27, 1949; s. Levant Maurice and Barbara McKenzie (Neilson) H.; m. Julie Ann Peglowski, Mar. 20, 1982; children—Ryan Charles, Brendan Levant, Meghan Lee. B.A., Ithaca Coll., 1971; J.D., Suffolk U., 1975. Bar: N.Y. 1976. Sole practice, Gowanda, N.Y., 1977-79; assoc. Levant Himelein, Jr., Gowanda, 1979-82; dist. atty. Cattaraugus County, Little Valley, N.Y., 1982—; mem. Arson Task Force, Little Valley, 1982—, Traffic Safety Bd., 1982—, Cattaraugus County Police Chiefs, Little Valley, 1982—. Mem. Athletics Congress. Mem. N.Y. State Bar Assn., N.Y. State Dist. Attys. Assn., Cattaraugus County Bar Assn., Erie County Bar Assn., Am. Legion. Democrat. Episcopalian. Clubs; Pulaski (Olean, N.Y.); Slovenian (Gowanda). Criminal. Home: 167 W Main St Gowanda NY 14070 Office: Cattaraugus County Ctr 303 Court St Little Valley NY 14755

HIMELES, MARTIN STANLEY, JR., lawyer; b. Balt., Mar. 13, 1956; s. Martin Stanley and Betty Jean (Applebaum) H.; m. Paula Kilimnik, Aug. 26, 1984. BA summa cum laude, Yale U., 1978; JD magna cum laude, Harvard U., 1981. Bar: N.Y. 1982, U.S. Dist. Ct. (so. and ea. dists.) N.Y. 1982, U.S. Ct. Appeals (4th cir.) 1982, U.S. Dist. Ct. Md. 1986. Law clk. to judge U.S. Ct. Appeals (4th cir.), Balt., 1981-82; assoc. Parker, Auspitz, Neesemann & Delehanty P.C., N.Y.C., 1982-86; asst. U.S. atty. U.S. Atty's. Office, Balt., 1986—. Mem. ABA, Phi Beta Kappa. Democrat. Criminal, Federal civil litigation.

HIMELFARB, STEPHEN ROY, lawyer; b. Washington, Feb. 19, 1954; s. Jordan Sheldon and Marion (Soloman) H.; m. Anne Patricia Spille, June 26, 1983; 1 child, Kara Michelle. BS in Bus. Adminstrn., Am. U., 1976; JD, George Mason U., 1980. Bar: D.C. 1982, Md. 1982, U.S. Dist. Ct. D.C. 1982, U.S. Dist. Ct. Md. 1982, U.S. Ct. Appeals (D.C. and 4th cirs.) 1982, U.S. Supreme Ct. 1985. V.p. ECA Bus. Communications Network, Washington, 1982-85; ptnr. Himelfarb & Podryhula, Washington, 1985—; v.p. Video Shack Inc., Woodbridge, Va., 1984—. Mem. ABA, Fed. Bar Assn., Assn. Trial Lawyers Am., Phi Delta Phi. Democrat. Jewish. Avocations: electronics, tennis, stamp collecting. Contracts commercial, General corporate, Personal injury. Home: 5148 Linette Ln Annandale VA 22003 Office: Himelfarb & Podryhula 1000 Connecticut Ave NW Suite 1200 Washington DC 20036

HIMES, JAY L(ESLIE), lawyer; b. Milw., Sept. 27, 1948; s. Joseph and Sally (Liebman) H. BA, U. Wis., 1970, JD, 1972. Bar: Wis. 1972, U.S. Dist. Ct. (ea. and we. dists.) Wis. 1972, N.Y. 1974, U.S. Dist. Ct. (so. dist.) N.Y. 1975, U.S. Ct. Appeals (2d cir.) 1975, U.S. Dist. Ct. (ea. dist.) N.Y. 1978, U.S. Ct. Appeals (9th cir.) 1982, U.S. Supreme Ct. 1982. Assoc. Phillips, Hoffman & Bloch, Milw., 1972, Paul, Weiss, Rifkind, Wharton & Garrison, N.Y.C., 1973-82, 85—; ptnr. Snow, Becker et al, N.Y.C., 1983-85. Mem. ABA, Wis. Bar Assn., Assn. of Bar of City of N.Y., Phi Beta Kappa, Order of Coif. Federal civil litigation, State civil litigation, Antitrust. Office: Paul Weiss Rifkind Wharton Garrison 1285 Ave of the Americas New York NY 10019

HINCHEY, JOHN WILLIAM, lawyer; b. Knoxville, Tenn., June 18, 1941; s. Roy William and Ruth (Owenby) H.; m. Sherie Paulette, May 12, 1968; children—Paul William, Meredith Marie. A.B., Emory U., 1964, LL.B., 1965; LL.M., Harvard U., 1966; M.Litt., Oxford U., 1980. Bar: Ga. 1965, U.S. Dist. Ct. (no. dist.) Ga. 1968, U.S. Ct. Appeals (5th cir.) 1968, U.S. Supreme Ct. 1969. Asst. atty. gen. State of Ga., Atlanta, 1968-72; ptnr. McConaughey & Hinchey, Decatur, Ga., 1972-76, Phillips & Mozley, Atlanta, 1976-84, Phillips, Hinchey & Reid, Atlanta, 1984—. Mem. ABA, Am. Judicature Soc., Ga. Bar Assn., Atlanta Bar Assn. Republican. Methodist. Club: Druid Hills Golf. Contbr. articles to profl. jours. Construction, Federal civil litigation, Insurance. Office: Phillips Hinchey & Reid 340 Monarch Plaza 3414 Peachtree Rd NE Atlanta GA 30326

HINCHLIFF, JAMES, lawyer; b. Des Moines, Dec. 12, 1939; s. John William and Thursa Louise (Barger) H.; m. Margot Jane Barrett, June 28, 1986; children: Lauri Mason, John. BA in Music, Drake U., 1962; AM, Harvard U., 1965; JD, U. Chgo., 1972. Bar: Ill., U.S. Dist. Ct. (no. dist.) Ill. Atty. Peoples Energy Corp., Chgo., 1972-76, sr. counsel, 1976-79, asst. gen. counsel, 1979-84, v.p., gen. counsel, 1984—. Bd. dirs., officer Chase House Inc., Chgo., 1983—. Mem. ABA, Chgo. Bar Assn. Avocations: musicology, history. Home: 3200 N Lake Shore Dr #2110 Chicago IL 60657 Office: Peoples Energy Corp 122 S Michigan Ave Chicago IL 60603

HINDELANG, ROBERT LOUIS, lawyer; b. Detroit, Nov. 21, 1946; s. John Louis and Louise M. (Vantiem) H.; m. Paula Marie Hirzel, July 13, 1973; children: Marianne, Maureen, Michael, Matthew, Mark. BS, Wayne State U., 1968, MBA, 1970; JD, U. Detroit, 1975. Bar: Mich. 1975, U.S. Dist. Ct. Mich. 1975, U.S. Ct. Internat. Trade 1976, U.S. Supreme Ct. 1980; CPA, Mich. Sec., treas. Barry Steel Corp., Detroit, 1973-80, chief exec. officer, 1980-82; sole practice E. Detroit, Mich., 1982—. Mem. ABA, Mich. Bar Assn., Mich. Assn. CPA's. Roman Catholic. Private international, General corporate, Corporate taxation. Office: 18121 E Eight Mile Rd East Detroit MI 48021

HINDIN, MAURICE J., judge; b. Los Angeles, Oct. 10, 1910; s. Theodore J. and Ida (Fisch) H.; m. Dorothy Sweet, Aug. 11, 1938; children—Arthur, Carol. B.S. in Bus. Adminstrn., U. So. Calif., 1933, J.D., 1935. Bar: Calif. 1935, U.S. Supreme Ct. 1942. Sr. ptnr. Hindin, McKittrick & Marsh, Los Angeles, until 1972; judge Los Angeles Jud. Dist. Ct., 1972—. Mem. Calif. State Bar Assn., Los Angeles County Bar Assn., ABA. Office: Los Angeles County Courthouse 110 N Grand Ave Los Angeles CA 90012

HINDMAN, DENNIS MICHAEL, lawyer; b. Bellingham, Wash., Mar. 18, 1947; s. Everett F. and Lillian R. (Vaughn) H.; m. Mary Bell, Apr. 10, 1977 (div. Aug. 1978); 1 child, Brian K. BA in Econs., Western Wash. State Coll., 1969; JD, Willamette U., 1972. Bar: Wash. 1972, U.S. Dist. Ct. (we. dist.) Wash. 1973. Caucus atty. Wash. State Senate, Olympia, 1973; sole practice Bellingham, 1973-82; ptnr. Hindman & Tasker, Bellingham, 1982—; atty. Port of Bellingham, 1973-78. Rotary Internat. Exchange fellow, 1975. Mem. ABA, Wash. State Bar Assn., Assn. Trial Lawyers Am., Wash. State Trial Lawyers Assn. (sec. 1973-76, seminar chair 1977-78, bd. govs. 1978-84), B.C. Trial Lawyers Assn. (out-of-province). Federal civil litigation, Insurance, Personal injury. Office: 306 Flora St Bellingham WA 98225

HINDMARCH, THOMAS MICHAEL, lawyer; b. Easton, Pa., Oct. 3, 1950; s. Donald R. and Irene A. (Maloney) H.; m. Jane E. Condon; children: Matthew, Meghan. BA in Internat. Relations, Lafayette Coll., 1972; JD, Wake Forest U., 1978; LLM in Taxation, NYU, 1980. Bar: N.C. 1978. Assoc. Petree Stockton, Winston-Salem, N.C., 1980-82; tax atty. ICI Americas Inc., Wilmington, Del., 1982—. Served to 1st lt. U.S. Army, 1972-76. Mem. ABA (com. capital recovery and leasing tax sect.). Republican. Methodist. Corporate taxation, Pension, profit-sharing, and employee benefits, State and local taxation. Office: ICI Ams Inc Rt 202 and New Murphy Rd Wilmington DE 19810

HINDS, CAROLINE WELLS, lawyer; b. Mobile, Ala., Mar. 27, 1953; d. William Portman and Helen (McCrary) W.; m. Thomas M. Hinds, Apr. 27, 1985. BA, U. Ala., 1975, JD, 1978. Bar: Ala. 1978, U.S. Dist. Ct. (so. dist.) Ala. 1978, U.S. Supreme Ct. 1982. Ptnr. Gallalee, Denniston & Cherniak, Mobile, Ala., 1978-84, Brown, Hudgens, Richardson, P.C., Mobile, 1984—. Author Alabama Realtor mag. 1982. Bd. dirs. YWCA, Mobile, 1983—, Jr. League of Mobile, 1985—, Women's Council of Realtors, Mobile, 1982—; mem. Leadership Mobile, 1986. Named One of Outstanding Young Women of Am., Mobile, 1983. Mem. Ala. State Bar, Mobile Bar Assn., Phi Delta Phi. Methodist. Avocations: water sports, photography, golf, tennis, calligraphy. Real property, Probate, Contracts commercial. Home: 440 Brindlewood Dr Mobile AL 36608 Office: 1495 University Blvd PO Box 16818 Mobile AL 36616

HINDS, RICHARD DE COURCY, lawyer; b. Boston, Nov. 28, 1941; s. Lester DeCourcy and Patricia Marshall (Tate) H.; m. Pamela Dee, Aug. 20, 1969. B.A., Tufts U., 1964; LL.B., Columbia U., 1967. Bar: N.Y. 1967, D.C. 1973. Law clk. Judge Leonard P. Moore, 2d Cir., N.Y.C., 1967-68; assoc. Sullivan & Cromwell, N.Y.C., 1968-71; ptnr. Cleary, Gottlieb, Steen & Hamilton, Washington, 1973—. Mem. ABA, Am. Law Inst. Contbr. articles in field to profl. jours. Administrative and regulatory, Environment, Public international. Home: 2926 P St NW Washington DC 20007 Office: Cleary Gottlieb Steen & Hamilton 1752 N St NW Washington DC 20036

HINERMAN, PHILIP LEE, lawyer; b. Huntington, W.Va., Apr. 22, 1954; s. Robert Evan and Anna Marie (Conner) H.; m. Elizabeth Lewis, Aug. 22, 1981. AB, Marshall U., 1975; JD, Washington and Lee U., 1979. Bar: Va. 1979, W.Va. 1979, Ohio 1983, U.S. Ct. Appeals (4th cir.) 1980. Law clk. to presiding justice U.S. Ct. Appeals, Richmond, Va., 1979-80; assoc. McGuire, Woods & Battle, Richmond, 1980-82, Jenkins and Fenstermaker, Huntington, 1982-83; staff counsel Leaseway Transp. Co., Beachwood, Ohio, 1983-85; assoc. corp. counsel Leaseway Transp. Corp., Beachwood, Ohio, 1985-87, corp. counsel, 1987—. Mem. ABA, Ohio State Bar Assn., Va. Bar Assn., Am. Corp. Counsel Assn. (bd. dirs. N.E. region), Fernway Assn., Omicron Delta Kappa. Episcopalian. Environment, General corporate, Contracts commercial. Office: Leaseway Transp Corp 3700 Park East Dr Beachwood OH 44122

HINES, JOHN PRIDGEN, lawyer; b. Cordele, Ga., Feb. 28, 1945; s. John Pepper and Lucille (Pridgen) H.; m. Mary Alice Slemons, Aug. 24, 1968 (div. 1982); children—Hamilton Pepper, Elizabeth Alison. A.B., Emory U., 1967; J.D., U. Ga., 1970; LL.M. in Taxation, Georgetown U., 1975. Bar: Ga. 1970, U.S. Dist. Ct. (no. dist.) Ga. 1970, U.S. Supreme Ct. 1973, U.S. Tax Ct. 1973. Trial atty. tax div. U.S. Dept. Justice, Washington, 1970-75; assoc. Smith, Cohen, Ringle, Kohler & Martin, Atlanta, 1975-77; ptnr. Phillips, Hart & Mozley, Atlanta, 1977-79, Hines & Lowendick, P.C., Atlanta, 1979—. Served to capt. JAGC, U.S. Army, 1970-71. Mem. ABA, Ga. Bar Assn., Atlanta Bar Assn. Methodist. Club: Capital City (Atlanta). Corporate taxation, General corporate, Insurance. Office: 1800 Peachtree St NW Suite 600 Atlanta GA 30309

HINES, N. WILLIAM, law educator, administrator; b. 1936. A.B., Baker U., 1958; LL.B., U. Kans., 1961. Bar: Kans. 1961, Iowa, 1965. Grad. fellow Harvard U., 1961-62; law clk. U.S. Ct. Apls. 10th cir., 1960-61; teaching fellow Harvard U., 1961-62; asst. prof. law U. Iowa, 1962-65, assoc. prof., 1965-67, prof., 1967-73, disting. prof., 1973—, also dean; vis. prof. Stanford U., 1974-75; panelist Nat. Acad. Sci., 1975-76; cons. Argonne Lab; dir. Environ. Law Inst., 1978-83. Mem. ABA, Order of Coif. Notes and comments editor Kans. Law Rev. Office: University of Iowa College of Law Iowa City IA 52242

HINES, PAUL WILLIAM, lawyer; b. Detroit, Nov. 6, 1946; s. Lenford Hannis and Alma Wallace (Gray) H.; m. Suzanne Helen Hutchinson, Nov. 5, 1966 (div. Dec. 1978); children: Paul, Jeffrey; m. Carol Ann Sweeney, June 15, 1980; 1 child, Alexander. BA, Mich. State U., 1968; JD, Wayne State U., 1973. Bar: Mich. 1973, U.S. Dist. Ct. (ea. dist.) Mich. 1973, U.S. Dist. Ct. (we. dist.) Mich. 1979, U.S. Dist. Ct. (no. dist.) Ohio 1982. Assoc. Kitch & Suhrheinrich, Detroit, 1973-76; ptnr. Sommers & Schwartz, P.C. Mem. Detroit Bar Assn., Oakland County Bar Assn., Southfield Bar Assn., Assn. Trial Lawyers Am., Mich. Trial Lawyers Assn. Republican. Avocation: automobile racing. State civil litigation, Personal injury, Federal civil litigation. Office: Sommers & Schwartz PC 1800 Travelers Tower Southfield MI 48076

HINES, RODNEY ALAN, lawyer; b. Somerset, Ky., May 30, 1951; s. Robert Vernon and Mary June (Whitaker) H.; m. Melissa Francis Burns, June 10, 1978; children: John Robert, Kathryn Burns. BS, Auburn U., 1973; JD, U. Ala., Birmingham, 1981. Bar: Ala. 1981, U.S. Dist. Ct. (no. dist.) Ala. 1981. Claims adjuster Liberty Mut. Ins. Co., Louisville, 1974-75; owner, operator Linch's Magnavox, Columbus, Ga., 1975-77; sr. claims adjuster Am. Mut. Ins. Co., Birmingham, 1977-79; sr. claims adjuster Wausau Ins. Co., Birmingham, 1979—, claims atty., 1981—. Mem. ABA, Birmingham Bar Assn., Montgomery County Trial Lawyers Assn., Ala. Claim Assn., Ala. Workers Compensation Claim Assn., Theta Chi. Lutheran. Workers' compensation, State civil litigation, Personal injury. Home: 3449 Loch Ridge Dr Birmingham AL 35216 Office: Wausau Ins Cos 700 Century Park S Suite 216 Birmingham AL 35226

HINES, WILLIAM JOSEPH, lawyer; b. Lima, Ohio, Oct. 1, 1951; s. Cletus W. and Margaret Ann (Schüum) H.; m. Linda Sue Bennett, Feb. 8, 1986. BA in History, U. Cin., 1973; JD, Ohio No. U., 1976. Bar: Ohio 1976, Idaho 1978, U.S. Dist. Ct. Idaho 1978, U.S. Ct. Appeals (9th cir.) 1978. Atty. Franklin County (Ohio) Legal Aid, 1976-78; assoc. Imhoff & Lynch, Ltd., Boise, Idaho, 1978-83; sole practice Boise, 1983-86; atty. litigation Goicoechea Law Offices, Boise, 1986—. Mem. Idaho State Bar Assn., Idaho Trial Lawyers Assn. State civil litigation, Personal injury, Real property. Home: 5755 Collister Dr Boise ID 83703 Office: Goicoechea Law Offices 701 N Franklin St Boise ID 83702

HINGLE, GILMER PAUL, lawyer; b. Baton Rouge, July 19, 1946; s. Kriss Joseph and Marguerite (Gendrow) H.; m. Delilah DeBlieux, Oct. 19, 1969 (div. 1978); 1 child, Stephanie A. BA, La. State U., 1971, JD, 1975. Bar: La. 1975, U.S. Dist. Ct. (we. dist.) La. 1977, U.S. Dist. Ct. (no. dist.) Miss. 1977, U.S. Supreme Ct. 1980. Sole practice Monroe, La., 1975; assoc. Boles, Mounger, Halack & Olsen, Monroe, 1976, DeCelle & Smith, Monroe, 1977; ptnr. DeCelle, Smith & Hingle, Monroe, 1978, Smith & Hingle, Monroe, 1978—. Mem. ABA, La. Trial Lawyers Assn. Democrat. Roman Catholic. Lodges: Kiwanis, Optimists. Avocations: scuba diving, guitar, hunting. Real property, Criminal, General practice. Office: Smith & Hingle 2200 Forsythe Ave Monroe LA 71201

HINGSTON, ROBERT ALLEN, lawyer; b. Waukesha, Wis., Mar. 21, 1949; s. Allen Robert and Doris D. (Sivula) H. BA, Ripon Coll., 1971; JD, U. Fla., 1974. Bar: Fla. 1974, U.S. Dist. Ct. (so. dist.) Fla. 1975, U.S. Ct. Appeals (5th cir.) 1977, U.S. Dist. Ct. (mid. dist.) Fla. 1978, U.S. Ct. Appeals (11th cir.) 1981. Assoc. Welbaum, Zook, Jones & Williams, Miami, Fla., 1974-79, ptnr., 1979—. V.p. Howard-Palmetto Khoury League, Miami, 1986-87. Mem. ABA (fidelity and surety com. of tort and ins. practice sect. 1979—, constrn. com. of litigation sect. 1981—, forum com. on constrn. industry 1984—), Dade County Bar Assn., Am. Arbitration Assn. (arbitrator 1983—), Coconut Grove Jaycees. Republican. Episcopal. Lodge: Optimists (local v.p. 1982-86). Construction, State civil litigation, Federal civil litigation. Office: Welbaum Zook Jones & Williams Coconut Grove Bank-PH 2701 S Bayshore Dr Miami FL 33133

HINKLE, DONALD EARL, lawyer, tax executive; b. Linton, Ind., Feb. 13, 1952; s. A. Earl and Mary Ellen (Birt) H.; m. Mary Elizabeth Haag, Aug. 7, 1976; children: Lauren Rebecca, Gregory Earl. BS in Bus., Ind. U., 1974, JD, 1976. Bar: Ind. 1976, U.S. Dist. Ct. (so. dist.) Ind. 1976. Tax mgr. Arthur Andersen and Co., Indpls., 1976-83; dir. taxes Banc One Ind. Corp., Indpls., 1983—. Mem. ABA, Ind. State Bar Assn., Am. Inst. CPA's, Ind. CPA Soc., Tax Execs. Inst. Avocations: auto racing, photography. Corporate taxation. Home: 8914 Kirkham Rd Indianapolis IN 46260-1641 Office: Banc One Ind Corp 111 Monument Circle Indianapolis IN 46277-3066

HINKLE, ROBERT LEWIS, lawyer; b. Apalachicola, Fla., Nov. 7, 1951; s. Jene L. and Lena (Chauncey) H.; m. Marylou Bevis, June 8, 1974; children: Sarah N., Megan L. BA magna cum laude, Fla. State U., 1972; JD magna cum laude, Harvard U., 1976. Bar: Fla. 1976, Ga. 1977. Law clk. to judge U.S. Ct. Appeals (5th cir.), Atlanta, 1976-77; assoc. Sutherland, Asbill & Brennan, Atlanta, 1977-78; ptnr. Hinkle & Battaglia, Tallahassee, 1978-82, Wadsworth, Davis & Hinkle, Tallahassee, 1982-84, Holland & Knight, Tallahassee, 1984-85, Aurell, Fons, Radey & Hinkle, Tallahassee, 1985—; adj. prof. law Fla. State U., Tallahassee, 1981. Federal civil litigation, State civil litigation. Home: 2043 Quinn Ct Tallahassee FL 32308 Office: Avrell Fons Radey & Hinkle 101 N Monroe St PO Drawer 11307 Tallahassee FL 32302

HINMAN, HARVEY DEFOREST, lawyer; b. Binghamton, N.Y., May 7, 1940; s. George Lyon and Barbara (Davidge) H.; m. Margaret Snyder, June 23, 1962; children: George, Sarah, Marguerite. BA, Brown U., 1962; JD, Cornell U., 1965. Bar: Calif. 1965. Assoc. Pillsbury, Madison & Sutro, San Francisco, 1965-72, ptnr., 1973—. Bd. dirs., sec. Holbrook Palmer Park Found., 1977—; bd. dirs. Phillips Brooks Sch., 1978-84. Mem. ABA, San Francisco Bar Assn. Private international, Contracts commercial, Oil and gas leasing. Office: 225 Bush St San Francisco CA 94104

HINMAN, JAMES STUART, lawyer; b. Phila., Apr. 30, 1955; s. Herbert Stuart Hinman and Marion Dorothy (Bolton) Northrup; m. Joan Brenda Karas, Aug. 16, 1980; children: Joseph Stuart, Robert James. BA, Gettysburg Coll., 1976; JD, Syracuse U., 1980. Bar: N.Y. 1981, U.S. Dist. Ct. (we. dist.) N.Y. 1981. Assoc. Antell & Harris, Rochester, N.Y., 1980-82, ptnr., 1983-84; ptnr. Antell, Harris & Hinman, Rochester, N.Y., 1985-86, Antell & Hinman, Rochester, 1987—. Asst. scoutmaster Boy Scout Am., Irondequoit, N.Y., 1982—. Recipient Am. Jurisprudence awards Bancroft Whittney Lawyers Co-op, Rochester, N.Y., 1980. Mem. ABA, N.Y. Bar Assn., Assn. Trial Lawyers Am., N.Y. State Trial Lawyers Assn. Democrat. Congregationalist. General practice, State civil litigation, Family and matrimonial. Home: 103 Minocqua Dr Rochester NY 14617 Office: Antell & Hinman 19 W Main St 6th Fl Rochester NY 14614

HINOJOSA, RICARDO H., federal judge; b. 1950. BA, U. Tex., 1972; JD, Harvard U., 1975. Judge U.S. Dist. Ct. (so. dist.) Tex.; law clk. to presiding justice Tex. Supreme Ct., 1975-76; assoc. Ewers, Toothaker & McAllen, Tex., 1976-83; judge U.S. Dist. Ct. (so. dist.) Tex., Brownsville, 1983—. Office: US Dist Ct 311 U S Courthouse PO Box 2066 Brownsville TX 78520 *

HINSHAW, CHESTER JOHN, lawyer; b. Sacramento, Calif., Mar. 10, 1941; s. Chester Edward and Gertrude Lorraine (Miller) H.; m. Karen Forbes Breakey, Feb. 19, 1977. AB, Stanford U., 1963; JD, U. Calif., Berkeley, 1966. Bar: Calif. 1966, U.S. Dist. Ct. (no. dist.) Calif. 1967, U.S. Ct. Appeals (9th cir.) 1967, N.Y. 1968, U.S. Dist. Ct. (so. dist.) N.Y. 1972, U.S. Dist. Ct. (ea. dist.) N.Y. 1974, U.S. Ct. Appeals (2d cir.) 1974, U.S. Dist. Ct. (no. dist.) N.Y. 1980, U.S. Dist. Ct. (ea. dist.) Mich. 1982, U.S. Dist. Ct. (no. dist.) Tex. 1983, Tex. 1984, U.S. Ct. Appeals (5th cir.) 1984. Assoc. Chadbourne & Parke, N.Y.C., 1967-74, ptnr., 1974-83; ptnr. Jones, Day, Reavis & Pogue, Dallas, 1983—; lectr. U. Calif. Berkeley, 1966. Mem. ABA, Tex. Bar Assn., Calif. Bar Assn. Republican. Clubs: Met. (N.Y.C.), Tower (Dallas). Federal civil litigation, Antitrust, Private international. Office: Jones Day Reavis & Pogue 2300 LTV Ctr 2001 Ross Ave PO Box 660623 Dallas TX 75201

HINSHAW, DAVID LOVE, tax lawyer; b. Wichita, Kans., June 17, 1947; s. Wallace Bigham and Mary Elizabeth (Love) H.; m. Carol Lynn Green, Sept. 30, 1972; children—Cara Danielle, Derek Love. B.S. in Bus., U. Kans., 1969; J.D., U. Houston, 1972. Bar: Tex. 1972, U.S. Supreme Ct. 1979. Tax atty. Exxon Co., U.S.A., Houston, 1972-77, sr. tax atty., 1977-79, tax counsel, 1979-80; gen. tax counsel Reliance Electric Co., Cleve., 1980-82; asst. gen. tax counsel Esso Europe Inc., London, 1982-86, Exxon Co., Internat., Florham Park, N.J., 1986—. Mem. ABA (vice chmn. com. on state and local taxes, sect. taxation 1981-82, com. on taxation and fiscal policy), Internat. Fiscal Assn., Internat. C. of C. (com. on taxation). Republican. Corporate taxation, State and local taxation, Personal income taxation. Home: 14 Saddle Hill Rd Far Hills NJ 07931 Office: Exxon Co Internat 200 Park Ave Florham Park NJ 07932

HINSON, HILLORD HENSLEY, lawyer; b. Houston, May 2, 1940; s. Hillord and Mary B. (Hensley) H.; m. Michelle Gay Hall, Mar. 4, 1967; children—Michelle Lee, Travis Mark. B.B.A., U. Okla., 1962; J.D., U. Houston, 1972. Bar: Tex. 1972, U.S. Dist. Ct. (so. dist.) Tex. 1973, U.S. Ct. Appeals (5th cir.) 1975, U.S. Supreme Ct. 1979, U.S. Ct. Appeals (11th cir.) 1983. Assoc. David Berg & Assocs., Houston, 1972-73, Henley, Ryan & Driscoll, Houston, 1973-75; ptnr. Hinson & Hinson, Houston, 1975—. Bd. dirs., v.p. Houston Lawyer Referral Services, Inc., 1985—. Fellow Lawyers in Mensa; mem. ABA, Tex. Bar Assn. (sec. grievance com. 1982—), Houston Trial Lawyer Assn. (bd. dirs. 1980-84), Tex. Acad. Family Law Specialists (bd. cert. 1980), Gulf Coast Family Law Specialists, Houston Bar Assn. (family law sect.), Delta Theta Phi. Family and matrimonial. Office: Hinson & Hinson 400 Beltway 8 Suite 630 Houston TX 77060

HINTON, CHARLES FRANKLIN, lawyer; b. Des Moines, June 30, 1932; s. Charles Franklin and Wilma Pearl (Nuzum) H. B.A., U. Iowa, 1957, J.D., 1959. Bar: Iowa 1959. Ptnr., Hinton, Boller, Huisinga, Waterloo, Iowa, 1959-62; asst. county atty. Black Hawk County, Iowa, 1960-64; asst. city solicitor City of Waterloo, 1966-68; spl. prosecutor Black Hawk County, 1972—; atty. Heart Fund, 1966-70. Mem. Black Hawk County Rep. Com., 1962-64. Mem. ABA, N.Y. State Trial Lawyers Assn., Iowa Bar Assn., Black Hawk County (sec. 1966) Bar Assn., Assn. Trial Lawyers Am. Club: Sertoma (named dist. pres. 1968). Banking, General practice, Trademark and copyright. Home: 3908 Midway Dr Waterloo IA 50701 Office: 751 Progress Ave Waterloo IA 50701

HINTON, QUINCY THOMAS, JR., lawyer; b. Lake Charles, La., July 1, 1941; s. Quincy Thomas and Maxine Elaine (Brooks) H.; m. Glynda Guthrey, Aug. 24, 1963; children—Christopher, Benjamin, Catherine. B.A., McNeese State U., 1964; J.D., Loyola U., New Orleans, 1967. Bar: La. 1967, U.S. Dist. Ct. (ea. dist.) La. 1967, U.S. Ct. Appeals (5th cir.) 1967, U.S. Supreme Ct. 1979, Tex. 1984, U.S. Dist. Ct. (so. dist.) Tex. 1984. Landman, Shell Oil Co., New Orleans, 1969-76; land mgr.-onshore Aminoil USA Inc., Houston, 1976-77; sr. profl. landman Gen. Crude Oil Co., Houston, 1977-78; mgr. land and legal dept. Jones Exploration, Houston, 1978-83; ptnr. Broadhurst, Brook, Mangham & Hardy Houston, 1983—. Contbr. articles to profl. jours. Recipient Outstanding Service award Nat. Assn. Royalty Owners, 1984. Mem. Am. Assn. Petroleum Landmen, Tex. Bar Assn., La. Bar Assn., Houston Bar Assn., Houston Assn. Petroleum Landmen, Delta Theta Phi. Republican. Am. Baptist. Oil and gas leasing. Home: 3311 Riverlawn Dr Kingwood TX 77339 Office: Broadhurst Brook Mangham & Hardy 1st City Tower Suite 1511 1001 Fannin Houston TX 77002

HINTON, VIRGIL OTTERBEIN, lawyer, lecturer, educator; b. Canton, Ohio, Sept. 7, 1912; s. Charles G. and Julia A. (Hoover) H.; m. Charlotte H. Keller, June 21, 1941. A.B., Otterbein Coll., 1934, LL.D. (hon.), 1983; LL.B., William McKinley Sch. Law, 1938; postgrad. Case Western Res. U. Bar: Ohio 1938. Ptnr., Seiple, Hinton, Mylett & Zink, 1955-63; ptnr. Seiple, Hinton, Mylett & Klide, 1963-73; sr. ptnr. Hinton, Klide, Horowitz & DeLaCruz, Canton, 1973-83, sr. assoc. Hinton, DeLacruz, Holland & Poulos, 1983—; tchr., lectr. on probate law, estate planning, real estate. Trustee, mem. devel. bd. Otterbein Coll., 1962-85; chmn. Seran Found., Canton, 1968—; active Westbrook Park United Methodist Ch. Served in USAAF, 1942-45; ETO. Recipient Nat. Disting. Service award Canton Bd. Edn., 1962, Nat. Recreation Assn., 1962; Disting. Alumni award Otterbein Coll., 1973. Mem. Old Timers Basketball Orgn. (Hall of Fame). Republican. Clubs: Canton Athletic, Masons; Edgewood Golf (North Canton, Ohio); Kiwanis. Estate planning, Probate, Real property. Home: 2111 Amarillo Dr NW North Canton OH 44720 Office: 806 Ameritrust Bldg Canton OH 44702

HINUEBER, MARK ARTHUR, lawyer; b. Litchfield, Ill., May 22, 1952; s. Gustave C. and Rita (Ringenbach) H.; m. Maureen E. Archbold, Aug. 16, 1980. BA, Blackburn Coll., 1973; JD, John Marshall Law Sch., 1977. Bar: Ill. 1977, Calif. 1978. Assoc. Abrams, Mix & London, Chgo., 1977; counsel, asst. corp. sec. Scripps League Newspapers, Inc., San Mateo, Calif., 1978—. Named one of Outstanding Young Men Am. Mem. ABA, Calif. Bar Assn., Ill. Bar Assn. Avocations: golf, reading. Libel, General corporate. Office: Scripps League Newspapers PO Box 1491 San Mateo CA 94401

HIPPLE, ROBERT JOHN, lawyer; b. Pitts., Oct. 2, 1944; s. John A. and Eileen M. Hipple; m. Barbara Bates Croft; children: Shannon, Kristin, Bethann. BA, Wesleyan U., 1966; JD, Georgetown U., 1969, LLM in Taxation, 1971. Bar: Va. 1969, Ga. 1975, U.S. Dist. Ct. (no. dist.) Ga., U.S. Ct. Appeals (5th and 11th cirs.). Trial atty. tax div. U.S. Dept. Justice, Washington, 1968-73; prof., dir. grad. tax program Emory U., Atlanta, 1973-78; sole practice Atlanta, 1978—; adj. prof. law Georgetown U. Grad. Tax Program, Washington, 1972-73. Contbg. author: Norton-Bankruptcy Law Report; contbr. articles to profl. jours. Mem. ABA, Ga. Bar Assn., Atlanta Bar Assn., Lawyers Club Atlanta. Corporate taxation, Securities, Private international. Office: 44 Broad St Atlanta GA 30303

HIPSH, HARLENE JANET, lawyer; b. Kansas City, Mo., Aug. 7, 1950; d. Charles and Dorothy (Wengrover) H.; m. Harris H. Wilder, Aug. 16, 1981; children: Charly Hannah Wilder, Samuel Truman Wilder. BA, Columbia U., 1977; JD, Cardozo Sch. Law, 1980. Bar: N.Y. 1980, Mo. 1981, U.S. Ct. Appeals (8th cir.) 1981. Law clk. to presiding justice U.S. Ct. Appeals (8th cir.), Kansas City, 1980-82; atty. civil rights office U.S. Dept. Edn., Kansas City, 1984; sole practice Kansas City, 1985-87; ptnr. Wilder & Hipsh, Kansas City, 1987—. Editor Law Rev., 1979-80. Bd. dirs. Jewish Community Relations Bur., Kansas City, 1981—, Planned Parenthood of Kansas City, 1984—. Mem. ABA, Mo. Bar Assn., Assn. Women Lawyers, ACLU. Democrat. Club: Oakwood Country (Kansas City). Civil rights, Federal civil litigation, General practice. Office: 4901 Main St Suite 410 Kansas City MO 64112

HIPSHMAN, ANNE, lawyer; b. San Francisco, Aug. 3, 1951; d. Julius Streng and Ruth (Gross) H. AB, U. Calif., Berkeley, 1976; JD, Golden Gate U., 1980. Bar: Calif. 1980, U.S. Dist. Ct. (no. dist.) Calif. 1980, U.S. Ct. Appeals (9th cir.) 1982. Compliance officer U.S. Dept. Labor, San Francisco, 1978-81; assoc. William C. Gordon, San Francisco, 1981-83; ptnr. Montgomery & Hipshman, San Francisco, 1983-86; sole practice San Francisco, 1986—; cons. Instituto Laboral De La Raza, San Francisco, 1982—; supervising atty. Bay Area Sexual Harassment Clinic, San Francisco, 1984—. Walter Karabian scholar State of Calif., 1974. Mem. ABA, Calif. Bar Assn. (labor and employment sect.), San Francisco Bar Assn.

Democrat. Avocations: softball, tennis, dancing. Civil rights, State civil litigation, Labor. Office: 433 Turk St San Francisco CA 94102

HIRL, PATRICIA ANN, lawyer, law educator; b. Dubuque, Iowa, Aug. 24, 1948; d. James E. and Lois E. (Mesecher) H.; m. Elliot C. Rothenberg, Aug. 7, 1978 (div. Feb. 1981). BA in Social Sci., St. Cloud U., 1973; MA in Journalism, JD, U. Iowa, 1976. Bar: Iowa 1976, Minn. 1977, U.S. Dist. Ct. Minn. 1977. Atty. Minn. Pub. Interest Research Group, Mpls., 1976-77; sole practice St. Paul, 1977-82; assoc. gen. counsel Mpls. Star and Tribune, 1982—; adj. prof. William Mitchell Coll. Law, St. Paul, 1982—; pres. Minn. Newspaper Found., Mpls., 1986—; active com. on access to ct. files Minn. Supreme Ct., St. Paul, 1986—. Co-author: Media Law in the Midwest, 1983. Mem. Citizen's League, Mpls., 1981—; vol. announcer Minn. Pub. TV, St. Paul, 1984—; bd. dirs. Concepts for Family Living, Mpls., 1985—; co-founder Minn. Free Speech Com., Mpls., 1985—; mem. Mpls. Art Inst. Mem. Minn. Bar Assn. (chmn. publs. com. 1985—), Iowa Bar Assn., Hennepin County Bar Assn., Soc. Profl. Journalists, Minn. Hist. Soc., Am. Arbitration Assn. Avocations: writer (short stories and poetry), nature, photography. General corporate, Libel. Home: 11621 Live Oak Dr Minneapolis MN 55343 Office: Mpls Star and Tribune Legal Dept 425 Portland Ave Minneapolis MN 55488

HIRSCH, ALAN SETH, lawyer; b. Miami Beach, Fla., May 22, 1950; s. Morse Sable and Belle (Falk) H.; m. Marsha Fay Yellin, June 9, 1974; children: Melanie, Sara. B.A., U. N.C., 1971; J.D., Columbia U., 1974; program for sr. mgrs. in govt. John F. Kennedy Sch. Govt. Harvard U., 1984. Bar: N.C. 1974, U.S. Dist. Ct. (ea., we. and mid. dists.) N.C. 1975, U.S. Ct. Appeals (4th cir.) 1975. Assoc. atty. gen. N.C. Dept. Justice, Raleigh, 1974-75, asst. atty. gen., 1976—, chief counsel consumer protection div., 1976-85, environ. protection div., 1985—; adj. prof. polit. sci. N.C. State U., Raleigh, 1977-80. Mem. N.C. Bar Assn., Nat. Assn. Attys. Gen. (chmn. coop. enforcement com. 1982-84). Democrat. Jewish. Federal civil litigation, Environment, Legislative. Home: 6 Lacrosse Pl Chapel Hill NC 27514 Office: NC Dept Justice PO Box 629 Raleigh NC 27602

HIRSCH, BARBARA B., lawyer; b. Chgo., July 5, 1938; d. Maurice Louis and Ruth (Hartman) H.; m. Eugene Pekow, Mar. 16, 1980. LLB, DePaul U., 1966. Bar: Ill. 1966, U.S. Dist. Ct. (no. dist.) Ill. 1966, U.S. Supreme Ct. 1970. Assoc. Chadwell & Kayser, Chgo., 1966-70; sole practice Chgo., 1970—; instr. DePaul U. Law Sch., Chgo., 1970-71, Roosevelt U., Chgo., 1984—. Author: Divorce: What a Woman Needs to Know, 1973, Living Together, A Guide to the Law for Unmarried Couples, 1976. Bd. dirs. ACLU, Chgo., 1985—. Mem. ABA, Chgo. Bar Assn., Fed. Bar Assn., Assn. Trial Lawyers Am., Am. Judicature Soc., 7th Cir. Bar Assn. Office: 176 W Adams St Chicago IL 60603

HIRSCH, DANIEL, lawyer; b. Bklyn., Feb. 26, 1940; s. Burton and Lee (Roller) H.; m. Trina Lutter, July 15, 1965 (div.); children—Jessica Elyse, Jeremy Bram. B.S., U. Pa., 1960; J.D., Columbia U., 1963. Bar: N.Y. 1964. Assoc. Carter Ledyard & Milburn, N.Y.C., 1964-68; sole practice, N.Y.C., 1968-74; ptnr. Jones, Hirsch, Connors & Bull, N.Y.C., 1974—; bd. dirs. United Pacific Reliance Life Ins. Co. N.Y., Telemundo Group, Inc., SCOR U.S. Corp. Served to lt. USNR, 1965-75. Mem. Assn. Bar City N.Y., N.Y. State Bar Assn. Club: Univ. (N.Y.C.). General corporate, Insurance, Private international. Home: 85 East End Ave Apt 11F New York NY 10028 Office: 101 E 52d St New York NY 10022

HIRSCH, DAVID L., lawyer, corporation executive. B.A., Pomona Coll., 1959; J.D., U. Calif.-Berkeley, 1962. Bar: Calif. 1963. With NI (Industries), Inc., Long Beach, Calif., 1966—, now v.p., sr. counsel. Mem. Commn. on Govt. Procurement for U.S. Congress, 1971. Fellow Am. Bar Found.; mem. ABA (sec. pub. contract law sect. 1977-78, mem. council 1978-80, chmn. 1981-82), Calif. Bar (bd. advisors pub. law sect.), Los Angeles County Bar Assn., Fed. Bar Assn., Nat. Contract Mgmt. Assn. (nat. bd. advisors), Fin. Exec. Inst. (legal advisor com. on govt. bus.). Mem. editorial adv. bd. Bur. Nat. Affairs' Fed. Contracts Report. Contracts commercial, Government contracts and claims. Office: NI Industries Inc 1 Golden Shore PO Box 2960 Long Beach CA 90801

HIRSCH, JEFFREY ALLAN, lawyer; b. Chgo., June 14, 1950; s. Leo Paul And Dorthy (Seidman) H.; m. Lennie Sue Henderson, June 16, 1979; children: Lea, Ashley. BSBA, U. Fla., 1972, JD with honors, 1975. Bar: Fla. 1975, U.S. Dist. Ct. (so. and mid. dists.) Fla. 1975. Assoc. Swann & Glass, Coral Gables, Fla., 1975-76, Glass, Schultz, Weinstein & Moss, Coral Gables, 1976-80; ptnr. Holland & Knight, Ft. Lauderdale, Fla., 1980—; exec. dir. Govtl. Research Ctr., Gainesville, Fla., 1975. Active Leadership Broward, Ft. Lauderdale, 1986—. Mem. ABA, Fla. Bar Assn., Broward County Bar Assn. Mem. ABA, Fla. Bar Assn., Broward County Bar Assn. Avocations: reading, travel. Consumer commercial, Federal civil litigation, State civil litigation.

HIRSCH, JEROME SETH, lawyer; b. N.Y.C., Sept. 11, 1948; s. S. Richard and Lillian (Avenet) H.; m. Rosalie B. Hirsch; children: Cara, Rebecca. BA in Econs., SUNY, Binghamton, 1970; JD, Fordham U., 1974. Bar: N.Y. Assoc. Skadden, Arps, Slate, Meagher & Flom, N.Y.C., 1974-81, ptnr., 1982—. Mem. ABA (class action and derivative lawsuits subcom. 1982-85, vice chmn. 1983-84, corp. counsel com., vice chmn. subcom. on settlement of litigation 1987—), N.Y. State Bar Assn., Assn. of Bar of City of N.Y. Securities, Federal civil litigation, State civil litigation. Office: Skadden Arps Slate Meagher & Flom 919 Third Ave New York NY 10022

HIRSCH, MELVIN L., lawyer; b. N.Y.C., Jan. 20, 1923; s. Aaron and Henriette (Felberbaum) H.; m. Dorothy Thorner, Sept. 17, 1949; children—Susan Hirsch, Jon. B.A., Cornell U., 1944; J.D., Harvard U., 1948. Bar: N.Y., U.S. Supreme Ct. Sr. v.p., gen. counsel A J Armstrong Co., N.Y.C., 1954-73; sr. atty. United Mchts., N.Y.C., 1973-78; sole practice, N.Y.C., 1978—; chmn. Transp. Capital Corp., N.Y.C.; dir. Leucadia Nat. Corp., N.Y.C.; founder Continental Bank, Garden City, N.Y., 1974. Trustee Nat. Leukemia Assn., Garden City, 1976-81. Mem. Assn. Fin. Attys. (pres. 1971-73). Clubs; Harvard, Cornell (N.Y.C.). General corporate, Real property, Banking. Office: 60 E 42d St New York NY 10165

HIRSCH, MORRIS WAYNE, lawyer; b. San Francisco, Mar. 16, 1956; s. Robert Spencer and Lucille Ina (Sachs) H.; m. Dianne May Thompson, July 2, 1978. BA in English, U. Calif., Berkeley, 1977; JD cum laude, Harvard U., 1980. Bar: Calif. 1980, U.S. Dist. Ct. (no. dist.) Calif. 1980, U.S. Ct. Appeals (9th cir.) 1980, U.S. Dist. Ct. (cen. dist.) Calif. 1983, U.S. Dist. Ct. (ea. dist.) Calif. 1984, U.S. Ct. Appeals (11th cir.) 1986. Assoc. Pillsbury, Madison & Sutro, San Francisco, 1980—. Mem. ABA (corp., banking and bus. law sect., bus. bankruptcy com.), Calif. Bar Assn. (real property and bus. law sects., chmn. uniform comml. code com., anti-deficiency law com.), San Francisco Bar Assn. (comml. law and bankruptcy sect.), Barristers Club San Francisco (co-chair bankruptcy and comml. law com.), Phi Beta Kappa. Avocations: racquetball, reading, snorkeling. Bankruptcy, Contracts commercial. Office: Pillsbury Madison & Sutro 225 Bush St San Francisco CA 94120

HIRSCHFELD, MICHAEL, lawyer; b. Bronx, N.Y., July 4, 1950; s. Lawrence John and Ida (Miller) H.; m. Heidi P. Greenspan, June 17, 1973; children: Adam Lawrence, Philip Richard. BEE summa cum laude, CCNY, 1972; JD cum laude, U. Pa., 1975; LLM in Taxation, NYU, 1980. Bar: N.Y. 1976, U.S. Dist. Ct. (so. and ea. dists) N.Y. 1976, U.S. Tax Ct. 1978. Assoc. Shearman and Sterling, N.Y.C., 1975-80, Roberts and Holland, N.Y.C., 1980-83; ptnr. Carro, Spanbock, Kaster and Cuiffo, N.Y.C., 1983—; lectr. World Trade Inst., N.Y.C., 1985, NYU Inst. on Real Estate Taxation, 1986—; Crittenden Press, 1987—. Contbr. articles to profl. jours. Mem. ABA (mem. sect. on taxation, vice-chmn. real estate tax problems com. 1987—, chmn. syndications subcom. 1985-87, vice chmn. ACRS depreciation recapture subcom. 1983-85, task force on Pres.'s tax reform proposals minimum tax subcom. 1985—), N.Y. State Bar Assn. (tax sect. coms. on income from real property, U.S. Activities of fgn. taxpayers 1984—, mem. at large tax sect. exec. com. 1987—), Assn. of the Bar of the City of N.Y., Internat. Tax Assn., Internat. Fiscal Assn. Avocation: music (drum). Corporate taxation, Personal income taxation, International and real estate taxation. Office: Carro Spanbock Kaster and Cuiffo 1345 Ave of the Ams New York NY 10105

HIRSCHHORN, AUSTIN, lawyer; b. Detroit, Feb. 20, 1936; s. Herman and Dena Grace (Ufberg) H.; m. Susan Carol Goldstein, June 30, 1963; children—Laura Elsie, Carol Helen, Paula Gail. B.A. with honors, Mich. State U., 1957; LL.B., Wayne State U., 1960. Bar: Mich. bar 1960. Since practiced in Detroit; atty. Arnold M. Gold Law Offices, 1960-63; partner Gold & Hirschhorn, 1963-65; individual practice 1965-68, 79-80; partner firm Boigon, Hirschhorn & Winston, 1968-69, Boigon & Hirschhorn, 1969-78, Zemke & Hirschhorn (P.C.), 1980-83, Austin Hirschhorn, P.C., 1983—; lectr. Inst. Continuing Legal Edn., Mich. Trustee City Sch. Detroit. Served with AUS, 1960-62. Mem. Am., Detroit, Oakland County bar assns., State Bar Mich., Comml. Law League Am. Jewish. General practice. Home: 26903 York Huntington Woods MI 48070 Office: 26111 Evergreen Suite 310 Southfield MI 48076

HIRSCHHORN, JOEL, lawyer; b. Bklyn., Mar. 13, 1943; s. Leo S. and Thelma (Bassin) H.; m. Evelyn Ruth Finkelstein, Jan. 29, 1966; children—Bennett K., Douglas K. B.A., U. Conn., 1964; J.D., U. Wis.-Madison, 1967, LL.M., 1968. Bar: Fla. 1967, Wis. 1967, U.S. Ct. Appeals (5th cir.) 1969, U.S. Supreme Ct. 1972, U.S. Ct. Appeals (1st cir.) 1976, U.S. Ct. Appeals (4th cir.) 1977, U.S. Ct. Appeals (7th and 11th cirs.) 1981, U.S. Ct. Appeals (10th cir.) 1982, U.S. Ct. Appeals (6th cir.) 1983, U.S. Ct. Appeals (9th cir.) 1984, U.S. Ct. Appeals (3d cir.) 1986. Sole practice, Miami, Fla., 1967-69; assoc. Abramson, Rosenthal & Hirschhorn and predecessor Wilson, Abramson & Rosenthal, Miami, 1969-70, jr. ptnr., 1970-71; sole practice, Miami, 1971-75; sr. ptnr. Hirschhorn & Freeman, P.A., Miami, 1975-78; sole practice, Miami, 1978—; frequent lectr. bar assns., legal seminars, various law groups, univs. and colls. throughout U.S. Bd. trustees Hope Ctr. Retarded Citizens, Miami; active Miami chpt. Am. Jewish Committee. Mem. First Amendment Lawyer's Assn. (pres. 1974-75), Nat. Assn. Criminal Def. Lawyers (cert. for work in criminal def. 1979, cert. for work regarding opposition to cameras in courtrooms 1980, dir. 1980—), ABA, Fla. Bar Assn. (ethics com. criminal law sect. 1986-87), Dade County Bar Assn. (cert. appreciation 1975), Am. Judicature Soc., Assn. Trial Lawyers Am., Fla. Criminal Def. Lawyer's Assn. Democrat. Jewish. Clubs: Ocean Reef Yacht (Key Largo, Fla.); Bimini (Bahamas) Big Game and Fish; B'nai B'rith (Anti-Defamation League). Criminal. Office: 2766 Douglas Rd Miami FL 33133

HIRSCHMAN, SHERMAN JOSEPH, lawyer, accountant, educator; b. Detroit, May 11, 1935; s. Samuel and Anna (Maxmen) H.; m. Audrey Hecker, 1959; children—Samuel, Shari. B.S., Wayne State U., 1956, J.D., 1959, LL.M., 1968. Bar: Mich. 1959, Fla. 1983, Wis. 1984; C.P.A., Mich., Fla.; cert. tax lawyer, Fla. Practice, Mich., 1959—; instr. comml. law Detroit Coll. Bus., 1971—. Served with U.S. Army Res., 1959-62. Mem. Mich. Bar Assn., Fla. Bar Assn., Wis. Bar Assn. Corporate taxation, Personal income taxation, Pension, profit-sharing, and employee benefits. Office: 29870 Midlebelt St Farmington Hills MI 48018 also: 3101 W Buffalo Tampa FL 33557

HIRSH, LEONARD STEVEN, lawyer; b. Bklyn., July 17, 1951. BA, Yeshiva U., 1973; JD, NYU, 1976; M of Law in Taxation, Georgetown U., 1982. Bar: N.Y. 1977, D.C. 1982. Atty. office of chief counsel IRS, Washington, 1977-81; assoc. Patterson, Belknap, Webb & Tyler, Washington, 1981-85; ptnr. Parker, Chapin, Flattau & Klimpl, N.Y.C., 1985—. Mem. ABA, D.C. Bar Assn. Pension, profit-sharing, and employee benefits, Personal income taxation. Home: 1421 Hudson Rd Teaneck NJ 07666 Office: Parker Chapin Flattau & Klimpl 1211 Ave of Americas New York NY 10036

HIRSH, ROBERT JOEL, lawyer; b. Shamokin, Pa., May 18, 1935; s. David and Rose (Koplansky) H.; children—Christine, Jonathan, Thomas. B.S., U. Ariz., 1960, J.D., 1964. Bar: Ariz. 1964, U.S. Dist. Ct. Ariz. 1965, U.S. Ct. Appeals (9th cir.) 1965, U.S. Supreme Ct. 1971; cert. criminal specialist. Ptnr. firm Messing Hirsh & Franklin, Tucson, 1969-72, Hirsh & Hooker, Tucson, 1972-73, Hirsh, Shiner & Walker, Tucson, 1973-77, Hirsh & Bayles, Tucson, 1977-82, Hirsh & Fines, P.C., Tucson, 1982-84, Hirsh, Sherick & Murphy, P.C., 1985—. Mem. Ariz. Attys. for Criminal Justice (founder, v.p.), 9th Cir. Jud. Conf. (del.), Pima County Bar Assn. Ariz. State Bar Assn. (cert. criminal specialist), Nat. Assn. Criminal Def. Lawyers, Calif. Attys. for Criminal Justice, Am. Bd. Criminal Lawyers, Am. Coll. Trial Lawyers, ABA. Criminal. Mailing Address: PO Box 3024 Tucson AZ 85702-3024 Office: 110 S Church Ave #429 Tucson AZ 85701

HIRSHON, ROBERT EDWARD, lawyer; b. Portland, Maine, Apr. 2, 1948; s. Selvin and Gladys (Wein) H.; m. Roberta Lynn Miller, Aug. 16, 1969; children: Todd, Sara, Jason, Miriam. BA, U. Mich., 1970, JD, 1973. Bar: Maine 1973, U.S. Dist. Ct. Maine 1973, U.S. Ct. Appeals (1st cir.) 1977. Ptnr. Drummond, Woodsum, Plimpton & MacMahon P.A., Portland, 1973—; chairperson Continuing Legal Edn. Com., Augusta, Maine, 1977-83. Contbr. articles to profl. jours. Chairperson Breakwater Sch Bd., Portland, 1978-85; mem. Zoning Bd. Appeals, Cape Elizabeth, Maine, 1983—. Mem. ABA, Maine Bar Assn. (pres. 1986—, chairperson continuing legal education com.), Cumberland County Bar Assn., Assn. Trial Lawyers Am. Avocations: reading, tennis, skiing. Federal civil litigation, State civil litigation, Family and matrimonial. Home: 2 Oakhurst Rd Cape Elizabeth ME 04107 Office: Drummond Woodsum Plimpton & MacMahon PA 245 Commercial St Portland ME 04101

HIRSHON, SHELDON IRA, lawyer; b. Bklyn., Mar. 27, 1947; s. Jay and Jeanne (Benk) H.; 1 child, Jessica. BS, NYU, 1968, JD, 1972, LLM, 1978. Bar: N.Y. 1972. Assoc. Graubard, Moskovitz, McGoldrick, Dannett & Horowitz, N.Y.C., 1972-76, Windels, Marx, Davies & Ives, N.Y.C., 1976-78, Krause, Hirsch & Gross, N.Y.C., 1978-80; assoc., ptnr. Stroock & Stroock & Lavan, N.Y.C., 1980—. Bankruptcy, General corporate. Office: Stroock & Stroock & Lavan 7 Hanover Sq New York NY 10004

HISHON, ELIZABETH ANDERSON, lawyer; b. Cortland, N.Y., Aug. 26, 1944; d. Clarence Edward and Marion (Gleason) Anderson; m. Robert Harold Hishon, Apr. 30, 1977. BA, Wellesley Coll., 1966; JD, Columbia U., 1972. Bar: Ga. 1972. Ptnr. O'Callaghan, Saunders & Stumm, Atlanta, 1982—; bd. dirs. Ctr. for Rehab. Tech., Inc., Atlanta. Mem. ABA, Ga. Bar Assn., Atlanta Bar Assn., Atlanta Lawyers Club. Real property, Contracts commercial, Landlord-tenant. Office: O'Callaghan Saunders & Stumm 6201 Powers Ferry Rd Suite 330 Atlanta GA 30339

HITCH, HORACE, lawyer; b. Princeton, Ind., July 3, 1921; s. Horace and Edith Mae (Ervin) H.; m. Helen Tuttle, Oct. 7, 1943; children: Peter H., Thomas E. B.Sc., U. Minn., 1942, LL.B., 1947. Bar: Minn. 1947. Ptnr. Dorsey & Whitney, Mpls., 1947—. Chancellor Episcopal Diocese Minn., 1974—. Served with USNR, 1942-46, 51-52. Mem. Minn. Bar Assn., Am. Judicature Soc., ABA. Clubs: Minikada, Mpls. Pension, profit-sharing, and employee benefits, General corporate, Estate planning. Office: 2200 1st Bank Pl E Minneapolis MN 55402

HITCHCOCK, BION EARL, lawyer; b. Muscatine, Iowa, Oct. 9, 1942; s. Stewart Edward and Arlene Ruth (Eichelberger) H.; m. Adele Berry, June 11, 1966; children—Collin William, Amber Leigh. B.S.E.E., Iowa State U., 1965; J.D., U. Iowa, 1968. Bar: Iowa 1968, Okla. 1968, U.S. Ct. Customs and Patent Appeals 1973, U.S. Ct. Appeals (fed. cir.) 1982. Atty., Phillips Petroleum Co., Bartlesville, Okla., 1968-69, 73-76; mgr. licensing Phillips Petroleum Co. Europe-Africa, Brussels, 1977-80, sr. patent counsel Phillips Petroleum Co., Bartlesville, 1980-84, assoc. gen. patent counsel, 1984—. Pres. Bartlesville Symphony Orch., 1975-77, 82-84; bd. dirs. Bartlesville Allied Arts and Humanities Council, 1976-77, 80-86, 1st v.p., 1982-83; mem. Govt. and Fin. Goals for Bartlesville Com., 1974-75; bd. dirs. Bartlesville Community Concert Assn., 1982—, Okla. Assn. Symphony Orchs., 1983—. Served to lt. JAGC, USN, 1969-73. Mem. ABA, Okla. Bar Assn. (dir. patent trademark and copyright sect. 1980-86, sec. 1982-83, chmn. 1984-85), Iowa Bar Assn., Washington County Bar Assn. (pres. 1981-82), Am. Intellectual Property Law Assn., Am. Judicature Soc., Fed. Cir. Bar Assn., Licensing Execs. Soc., Eta Kappa Nu. Patent, Private international, Intellectual property. Home: 1200 SE Guinn Ln Bartlesville OK 74006 Office: Phillips Petroleum Co 236 PLB Bartlesville OK 74004

HITCHCOCK, J. GARETH, retired judge; b. Putnam County, Ohio June 10, 1914; s. Roy C. and Laura (Adam) H.; m. Helen M. Eck, June 10, 1941 (dec. Oct. 1972); children—James Edward, David Louis; m. 2d, Ruth E. Fessel, Aug. 18, 1973. LL.B., Ohio State U., 1939, J.D., 1969. Bar: Ohio 1939, U.S. Dist. Ct. (no. dist.) Ohio 1945, U.S. Dist. Ct. (no. dist.) Ind. 1960, U.S. Supreme Ct. 1960, U.S. Ct. Appeals (7th cir.) 1960. Sole practice, Paulding, Ohio, 1939-40; spl. agt. FBI, 1940-42; sole practice, Port Clinton, Ohio, 1946-51; protection chief Joseph Home Co., Pitts., 1951-57; investment sales Federated Investors Inc., Pitts., 1957-59; practice, Paulding, Ohio, 1959-60; judge Common Pleas Ct. Paulding County (Ohio), 1960-86. Served with AUS, 1942-46. Mem. Ohio Bar Assn. (bar activities com. 1963-80, com. jud. adminstrn. and legal reform 1981—), Paulding County Bar Assn., N.W. Ohio Bar Assn., Am. Judicature Soc., Judge Advocates Assn., Ohio Common Pleas Judges Assn., Soc. Former Spl. Agts. of FBI. Republican. Episcopalian. Club: Kiwanis (lt. gov. 1970-71). Contbr. articles to profl. jours. Administrative and regulatory, Legal history. Home: 733 N Cherry St Paulding OH 45879

HITCHCOCK, PAUL RICHARD, lawyer; b. Piqua, Ohio, Sept. 29, 1951; s. James Richard and Dorothy (Fletcher) H.; m. Virginia Marie Halabis, Oct. 19, 1983. BS in Physics, Ohio State U., 1973, JD summa cum laude, 1976. Bar: Ohio 1977, U.S. Dist. Ct. (no. dist.) Ohio 1977, U.S. Ct. Appeals (6th cir.) 1979, U.S. Ct. Appeals (6th cir.) 1981, U.S. Ct. Appeals (D.C. cir.) 1987. Atty. CSX Transp. and predecessor firm Chessie System R.R., Cleve., 1977-78, asst. gen. atty., 1979-80, asst. gen. solicitor, 1981-85; gen. atty. CSX Transp. and predecessor firm Chessie System R.R., Balt., 1986—. Mem. ABA, Ohio Bar Assn., Assn. Transp. Practitioners, Am. Corp. Counsel Assn. Administrative and regulatory, Antitrust, Transportation. Home: 90 E Padonia Rd Timonium MD 21093 Office: CSX Transportation 100 N Charles St Baltimore MD 21201

HITCHCOCK, STEPHEN JAY, lawyer; b. Mich., Dec. 16, 1946; s. Jay J. and Arlene (Force) H.; m. Eunice L. Dible, Sept. 6, 1969; children: Aaron, Heather. BA, Western Mich. U., 1969; JD, Detroit Coll. Law, 1973. Bar: Mich. 1973, Fla. 1973, U.S. Dist. Ct. (ea. and we. dists.) Mich. 1973. Ptnr. Nystrom, Nystrom & Hitchcock, Bloomfield Hills, Mich., 1973—. Mem. Zoning Bd. Appeals, Novi, Mich.; trustee Orchard United Meth. Ch., Farmington Hills, Mich., 1984—, Novi Bd. Edn., 1986—. Republican. Computer, Insurance, Pension, profit-sharing, and employee benefits. Home: 24551 Kings Pointe Novi MI 48050 Office: Nystrom Nystrom & Hitchcock 1400 N Woodward Ave Suite 203 Bloomfield Hills MI 48303-2015

HITE, HOLLIS MARIE, lawyer; b. Buffalo, May 8, 1952; d. James Neil and Nancy Jane (Burfield) H.; children: Matthew, Jonathan. B.S. summa cum laude, SUNY-Buffalo, 1973, J.D., 1977. Bar: U.S. Ct. Appeals (4th cir.) 1978, N.Y., U.S. Dist. Ct. (no. dist.) N.Y. Assoc. Cohen & Lombardo, Buffalo, 1977; tax atty. IRS, Syracuse, N.Y., Rochester, N.Y., 1977-81; of counsel Cohen, Lombardo et al, Buffalo, 1981-82; ptnr. James N. Hite & Assocs., Buffalo, 1983—; cons., mem. Child Care Coalition of N.Y., Buffalo, 1983—. Recipient Clifford C. Furnas award SUNY-Buffalo, 1973. Mem. Woman's Bar Assn. State of N.Y. (v.p. Western N.Y. chpt. 1983-84, pres. 1984-85, 85-86), Erie County Bar Assn., N.Y. State Bar Assn., Fed. Bar Assn., Assn. Trial Lawyers Am., N.Y. State Trial Lawyers Assn. Personal injury, Insurance, State civil litigation. Office: James N Hite & Assocs 257 Elmwood Ave PO Box 169 Buffalo NY 14222

HITE, RANDALL LEE, lawyer; b. Des Moines, May 17, 1957; s. Frederick Leebert and Wilda Jean (Lee) H.; m. Carol Ann Smith, Aug. 14, 1982. BA, U. Iowa, 1978; JD, Western State U., 1981. Bar: Calif. 1982. Assoc. Randall, Stewart et al, Santa Ana, Calif., 1982-83; ptnr. Hite & Assoc., Santa Ana, 1983—. Federal civil litigation, State civil litigation, Criminal. Office: Hite & Assoc 1502 N Broadway Santa Ana CA 92706

HITE, THOMAS ERSKINE, JR., lawyer; b. Greenwood, S.C., Feb. 22, 1953; s. Thomas Erskine and Mary (Harper) H.; m. Deabra Seal, Aug. 17, 1975; children: Heather, Thomas III, Merideth. BA, U. S.C., 1975, JD, 1978. Bar: S.C. 1978, U.S. Dist. Ct. S.C. 1978, U.S. Ct. Appeals (4th cir.) 1978, U.S. Supreme Ct. 1985. Assoc. Lowery & Vaughn, Anderson, S.C., 1975-77; ptnr. Day, Williams & Hite, Seneca, S.C., 1977-78, Hite & Pruitt, Abbeville, S.C., 1978—; atty. City of Abbeville, 1982—. Atty. Abbeville Sch. Dist., 1982—; mem. State Devel. Bd., Columbia, 1985—. Mem. ABA, Assn. Trial Lawyers Am., S.C. Trial Lawyers Assn., Abbeville C. of C. (founder 1978). Methodist. Avocation: hunting with bow and arrow. State civil litigation, Family and matrimonial, Real property. Home: 411 N Main St Abbeville SC 29620 Office: Hite & Pruitt 102 Pickens St Abbeville SC 29620

HITTLE, DAVID WILLIAM, lawyer; b. Medford, Oreg., Apr. 28, 1947; s. Merritt Lyle and Maryjane (Williams) H.; m. Sharon Lea Crowley, Sept. 27, 1969 (div. June 1975). BS, Oreg. State U., 1969; JD, Lewis & Clark Coll., 1974. Bar: Oregon 1974, U.S. Dist. Ct. Oreg. 1974, U.S. Ct. Appeals (9th cir.) 1976, U.S. Supreme Ct. 1977. Assoc. William Claussen PC, Salem, Oreg., 1974-75, Dye & Olson, Salem, 1975-79; ptnr. Olson, Hittle & Gardner, Salem, 1979-82, Callahan, Hittle & Gardner, Salem, 1982—; instr. Linfield Coll., McMinnville, Oreg., 1982-87; mcpl. judge pro tem City of Salem, 1978-85; dist. judge pro tem Oreg., 1982-85. Mem. Oreg. Trial Lawyers Assn. (legis. chmn. workers compensation 1985), Oreg. Bar Assn. (worker's compensation sect., sec. 1982, chmn. 1984, bd. govs. 1985—, contbr. author Bar book on Worker's Compensation 1980, 84, Real Property 1985, Legislation, 1985), Marion County Bar (bd. dirs. 1984-86, v.p. 1987), Oreg. Workers' Compensation Attys. (exec. com. 1978—), Oreg. Supreme Ct. Disciplinary Bd. 1984-85. Avocations: snow skiing, flying, mountain climbing, fly fishing. Workers' compensation, Personal injury, Pension, profit-sharing, and employee benefits. Home: 3365 Camellia Dr S Salem OR 97302 Office: Callahan Hittle & Gardner 2659 Commercial St SE Salem OR 97302

HIX, PHYLLIS MARIE, lawyer; b. Bloomfield, Iowa, Mar. 28, 1936. Student, U. Iowa, 1954-56; BS in Occupational Therapy cum laude, U. So. Calif., 1959, JD, 1962. Bar: Calif. 1963. Assoc. Lawler, Felix & Hall, 1963, Overton, Lyman & Prince, 1963-66, Dryden, Harrington & Swartz, 1967-74; sole practice 1974-76; ptnr. Kurlander & Hix, San Marino, Cailf., 1976—; mem. commn. on jud. nominees evaluation State of Calif., 1979-81, arbitration panel Los Angeles County Superior Ct.; Mcpl. Judge Pro Tem; Superior Ct. Settlement Officer. Co-author (column) Strange As It Seems. Mem. Calif. Bar Assn. (chmn. resolutions com. 1977, state bar ct., asst. presiding referee, exec. com. 1976-80, bd govs. 1981—), Los Angeles County Bar Assn. (exec. com. 1969-72, chmn. legal med. com. 1974-75, adv. com.), Assn. So. Calif. Def. Counsel (bd. dirs. 1973-75, 77-79), Am. Bd. Trial Advs. (mem. exec. com. 1975-76), Def. Research Inst., Calif. Women Lawyers (founding mem.), Am. Arbitration Assn. (nat. bd. dirs. 1976-80). Office: Kurlander & Hix 1455 San Marino Ave San Marino CA 91108

HJELLUM, JOHN, lawyer; b. Aurland, Sogn, Norway, Mar. 29, 1910; s. Olav Iversen and Belle (Ohnstad) H.; m. Helen Jeanette Fodness, May 12, 1935; children: Janice Ann, Joan Mae, John II. LL.B., J.D., U. N.D., 1934. Bar: N.D. 1934. Since practiced in Jamestown; mem. firm Hjellum, Weiss, Nerison, Jukkala, Wright & Paulson; investigator fed. violations Dept. Justice, 1934; asst. states atty. Stutsman County, N.D., 1943-45; states atty. 1948-50; sec. N.D. Broadcasting Co., 1950-62. Active community drives.; chmn. N.D. Eisenhower for Pres. group, also N.D. Citizens for Eisenhower-Nixon; vice chmn. Stutsman County Republican Orgn., 1955-58; mem. Stutsman County Central Com., 1958-62; del. Rep. Nat. Conv., 1952; trustee Jamestown Coll., 1967-75; chmn., trustee N.D. Ind. Coll. Fund, 1957-68. Served with CIC, AUS, 1944-45. Fellow Internat. Acad. Trial Lawyers (dir. 1969-75, 78-84); mem. ABA, Internat. Bar Assn., N.D. Bar Assn. (pres. 1957-58), 4th Jud. Dist. Bar Assn. (pres. 1949-50), Stutsman County Bar Assn. (pres. 1940-41, 49-50), Am. Legion, VFW, Order of Coif (hon.), Lambda Chi Alpha, Phi Delta Phi, Kappa Kappa Psi. Methodist (chmn. bd. 1946-76). Club: Masons. Home: 916 2d Ave NW Jamestown ND 58401 Office: PO Box 1900 Jamestown ND 58402

HJELMFELT, DAVID CHARLES, lawyer; b. Chgo., Nov. 25, 1940; s. Allen T. and Doris (Hauber) H.; m. Kendall L. Lawrence, Aug. 17, 1969; children—Trevor Christian, Rebecca Kirstan. A.B. cum laude, Kans. State U.-Manhattan, 1962; LL.B., Duke U., 1965. Bar: Kans. 1965, Colo. 1965,

D.C. 1973, U.S. Supreme Ct. 1978, U.S. Ct. Appeals (D.C. cir.) 1973, U.S. Ct. Appeals (5th and 11th cirs.) 1981, U.S. Ct. Appeals (10th cir.) 1982. Vis. prof. Sch. Law, U. Okla., Norman, 1970-71; staff atty. U.S. AEC, Albuquerque, 1971-73; ptnr. Goldberg, Fieldman & Hjelmfelt, Washington, 1973-78; sole practice, Fort Collins, Colo., 1978-81; ptnr. Hjelmfelt and Larson, Fort Collins, 1981—. Mem. council liberal edn. Kans. State U.; bd. dirs. Christian Conciliation Service, Fort Collins. Served to lt. JAGC, USNR, 1965-68. Mem. ABA, Christian Legal Soc., Colo. Bar Assn. Republican. Author: Antitrust and Regulated Industries, 1985; contbr. articles to profl. jours. Antitrust, Public utilities, Federal civil litigation. Office: 2629 Redwing Rd Fort Collins CO 80526

HJELMSTAD, WILLIAM DAVID, lawyer; b. Casper, Wyo., Apr. 4, 1954; s. Alvin Gordon and A. Thecla (Walz) H. A.A. in Social Sci., Casper Coll., 1974; B.S. in Psychology, U. Wyo., 1976, J.D., 1979. Bar: Wyo. 1979, U.S. Dist. Ct. Wyo. 1979. Dept. county pros. atty. Hot Springs County, Thermopolis, Wyo., 1979-80; asst. pub. defender Natrona County, Casper, Wyo., 1980-82; sole practice, Casper, 1981—. Mem. ABA (family law com. 1983-84, adoption com. 1983-84), Wyo. Trial Lawyers Assn., Assn. Trial Lawyers Am., Am. Judicature Soc. Lodges: Elks, Kiwanis. Family and matrimonial, Probate, General practice. Home: 2242 Thorndike Casper WY 82601

HLAVIN, JOSEPH RAYMOND, JR., lawyer; b. Chgo., Jan. 29, 1929; s. Joseph Raymond Sr. and Helen (Hanus) H.; m. Genrose Smith, Nov. 19, 1955. BS, Loyola U., Chgo., 1951, MS in Indsl. Relations, 1952; JD, DePaul U., Chgo., 1959. Bar: Ill. 1959, U.S. Dist. Ct. (no. dist.) Ill. 1959. Dir. labor relations Pullman Standard, Chgo., 1954-81; dir. employee relations Becor Western, South Milwaukee, Wis., 1982—. Served to 1st lt. USAF, 1952-53. Labor. Home: 5137 Grand Ave Western Springs IL 60558 Office: Becor Western Inc 1100 Milwaukee Ave South Milwaukee WI 53172

HOAG, JACK CARTER, lawyer; b. Chgo., May 25, 1952; s. Jack C. and Claire M. (Johnson) H.; m. Tamra Mary Potter, June 26, 1982. BA cum laude, Lawrence U., 1974; JD, U. Wis., 1978. Bar: Wis. 1978, U.S. Dist. Ct. (we. dist.) Wis. 1981, U.S. Ct. Appeals (7th cir.) 1982. Ptnr. Sedor & Hoag, S.C., Janesville, Wis., 1979—. Mem. program services com. YMCA, Janesville, 1980—, half marathon com., 1980—, chmn. membership drive 1983; basketball coach St. Matthews Luth. Sch., Janesville, 1982; mem. spl. com. on after sch. sports Janesville Bd. Edn., 1983; campaign leader Am. Heart Assn. Drive, Janesville, 1986; mem. adv. bd. Salvation Army, Janesville, 1984—; bd. dirs. Beginning Group Home, Janesville, 1985-86. Mem. ABA, Nat. Assn. Criminal Def. Lawyers, Wis. Bar Assn., Rock County Bar Assn. Lutheran. Lodge: Kiwanis. Avocations: basketball, running, water skiing, coaching, recreational sports. State civil litigation, Criminal, Family and matrimonial. Office: Sedor & Hoag SC 11 N Main PO Box 1145 Janesville WI 53547-1145

HOAG, MARY MOORE, lawyer; b. Raleigh, N.C., May 28, 1943; d. Charles Leonard and Mary Graham (Croom) H. AB, Wellesley Coll., 1965; MA, U. Wis., 1968; JD, Harvard U., 1976. Bar: N.Y. 1977, U.S. Dist. Ct. (so. and ea. dists.) N.Y. 1977, U.S. Ct. Appeals (3d cir.) 1977, Tex. 1987. Assoc. Davis, Polk & Wardwell, N.Y.C., 1976-79; staff atty. Sun Co., Inc., Phila., 1979-82, Pennzoil Co., Houston, 1982-83, Crown Cen. Petroleum Corp., Houston, 1983—. Author: The Social Aspects of ITV, ITV Model Implementation Plan, ITV Evaluation Model. Mem. cultural activities group Houston Combined Schs., 1986—, Hoston Internat. Edn. Inst., 1986—, Houston Ballet and Symphony Group, 1986—; tutor French Houston Ind. Sch. Dist., 1986—. Fulbright scholar, 1965-66; recipient Merit award U.S. Office Edn., 1972, White Ho. Citation Exec. Office of Pres., 1973. Mem. Phi Beta Kappa. Presbyterian. Clubs: Wellesley, Harvard (Houston); Combined Colls. Avocations: travel, scuba diving, skiing, politics. Antitrust, Contracts commercial, Oil and gas leasing. Home: 832 Fleetwood Pl Dr Houston TX 77079 Office: Crown Cen Petroleum Corp 4747 Bellaire Blvd Houston TX 77401

HOAGLAND, GRANT TAYLOR, lawyer; b. Los Angeles, June 21, 1949; s. Dallas Baram and Marydene (Oldham) H. BA cum laude, Calif. State U., 1974; JD, Western State U., 1978. Bar: Calif. 1979. Assoc. Law Offices of Erwin Sobel, Beverly Hills, Calif., 1979-80, Jacoby & meyers, San Francisco, 1980-85; sole practice South Gate, Calif., 1985—. Mem. South Gate Parks and Recreation Commn., Calif., 1980-84, chmn., 1983-84. Mem. ABA, Los Angeles Bar Assn., Assn. Trial Lawyers Am., Los Angeles Trial Lawyers Assn. Lodge: Elks. Family and matrimonial, Personal injury, Criminal. Home: 2882 W Rome Ave Annaheim CA 92804 Office: PO Box 1153 South Gate CA 90280

HOAGLAND, KARL KING, JR., lawyer; b. St. Louis, Aug. 21, 1933; s. Karl King and Mary Edna (Parsons) H.; m. Sylvia Anne Naranick, July 13, 1957; children: Elizabeth Parsons, Sarah Stewart, Karl King, III, Alison Thomson. B.S. in Econs, Wharton Sch., U. Pa., 1955; LL.B., U. Ill., 1958. Bar: Ill. 1958, U.S. Dist. Ct. (so. dist.) Ill. 1958. Of counsel Hoagland, Maucker, Bernard & Almeter, Alton, Ill., 1960—; gen. counsel Jefferson Smurfit Corp., Alton, 1963—, also bd. dirs.; gen. counsel Container Cooperation of Am., Alton, 1986—; bd. dirs. Millers' Mut. Ins. Assn. Ill. Asst. editor: U. Ill. Law Forum, 1957-58. Trustee, treas. Monticello Coll. Found., 1965—. Served to 1st lt. USAF, 1958-60. Mem. ABA, Ill. Bar Assn., Madison County Bar Assn., Alton-Wood River Bar Assn., Order of the Coif, Twin Rivers C. of C., Beta Gamma Sigma. Republican. Episcopalian. Clubs: Lockhaven Country (Alton); Mo. Athletic (St. Louis). Avocations: tennis, skiing, hunting, fishing. General corporate. Home: PO Box 130 Alton IL 62002 Office: 401 Alton St Alton IL 62002

HOAGLAND, SAMUEL ALBERT, lawyer, pharmacist; b. Mt. Home, Idaho, Aug. 19, 1953; s. Charles Leroy and Glenna Lorraine (Gridley) H.; m. Karen Ann Mengel, Nov. 20, 1976; children: Hiliary Anne, Heidi Lynne. BS in Pharmacy, Idaho State U., 1976; JD, U. Idaho, 1982. Bar: Idaho 1982, U.S. Dist. Ct. Idaho 1982, U.S. Ct. Appeals (9th cir.) 1984. Lectr. clin. pharmacy Idaho State U., Pocatello, 1976-78, lectr. pharmacy law, 1985—, dean's adv. council Coll. Pharmacy, 1987—; hosp. pharmacist Mercy Med. Ctr., Nampa, Idaho, 1978-79; retail pharmacist Thrifty Corp., Moscow, Idaho, 1980-82; assoc. Dial, Looze & May, Pocatello, 1982—; chmn. malpractice panel Idaho Bd. Medicine, Boise, 1983—, adminstrv. hearing officer, 1986—; bd. dirs. Phi Delta Chi, Inc., Pocatello. Mem. ABA, Idaho Trial Lawyers Assn., Sixth Dist. Bar Assn., Pocatello C. of C., Am. Pharm Assn., Am. Soc. Pharmacy Law. Health, Personal injury, Contracts commercial. Home: 256 S Johnson Pocatello ID 83204 Office: Dial Looze & May PO Box 370 Pocatello ID 83204

HOARE, JAMES JOSEPH, lawyer; b. Bronx, N.Y., Dec. 16, 1943; s. James Peter and Hanora Mary (LeHane) H.; m. Ethel Levitt, Dec. 15, 1960 (div.); 1 child, Adam Edward; m. Madelaine Patricia Lyda, July 5, 1979; children: Shawn David, Lindsey Svea. BA, NYU, 1974; JD, U. Detroit, 1978. Bar: Mich. 1978, N.Y. 1986, U.S. Dist. Ct. (ea. and so. dists.) Mich. 1978, U.S. Ct. Appeals (6th cir.) 1985, U.S. Supreme Ct. 1983. Assoc. Weinbaum, Willis & Abbo, Detroit, 1978-84; ptnr. Weinbaum, Willis, Abbo & Hoare, Southfield, Mich., 1984—. Fellow Nat. Bd. Trial Lawyers; mem. ABA, Nat. Assn. Criminal Def. Lawyers, Assn. Trial Lawyers Am., Southfield Bar Assn. Home: 1431 W Lake Dr Walled Lake MI 48088 Office: Weinbaum Willis Abbo & Hoare 18530 W 10 Mile Rd Southfield MI 48075-2615

HOBBS, CASWELL O., III, lawyer; b. Sherman, Tex., Aug. 25, 1941; s. Caswell Owen II and Marie Elizabeth (Bloomfield) H.; m. Anne Louise Simpson, June 7, 1968; children: Elizabeth Ellen, Emily Jane. BS, U. Kans., 1963; LLB, U. Pa., 1966. Bar: D.C. 1967, U.S. Ct. Appeals (4th cir.) 1975, U.S. Supreme Ct. 1972. Asst. to chmn., dir. Office of Policy Planning and Evaluation, FTC, Washington, 1970-73; assoc. Morgan Lewis & Bockius, Washington, 1973-76, ptnr., 1976—; lectr. Practising Law Inst. Contbr. articles to profl. jours. Trustee Legal Aid Soc. D.C., 1982—. Served to capt. JAG Corps, USAR, 1966-72. Fellow ABA (council, vice chmn. sect. antitrust law 1981-85); mem. Legal Aid Soc. D.C. (bd. dirs.), Antitrust, Administrative and regulatory, General corporate. Office: 1800 M St NW 6th Floor Washington DC 20036

HOBBS, FRANKLIN DEAN, III, lawyer; b. Huntington Park, Calif., May 30, 1952; s. Frank D. II and Bette J. (Little) H.; m. Victoria Shevlin, Mar. 6, 1987. BA, Claremont (Calif.) McKenna Coll., 1974; JD, UCLA, 1977. Bar: Calif. 1977, U.S. Supreme Ct. 1983. Assoc. Rutter, Ebbert & O'Sullivan, Los Angeles, 1977-82; ptnr. Rutter, O'Sullivan, Greene & Hobbs, Los Angeles, 1983—. Pres. Music Ctr. In the Wings, Los Angeles, 1986—; bd. dirs. Los Angeles Nagoya Sister City, 1986—. Mem. Assn. Trial Lawyers Am., Assn. Bus. Trial Lawyers. Republican. Federal civil litigation, State civil litigation, Real property. Office: Rutter O'Sullivan Greene & Hobbs 1900 Ave of the Stars Suite 2200 Los Angeles CA 90067

HOBBS, RICHARD WHITE, lawyer; b. West Eminence, Mo., July 24, 1912; s. James Richard and Mary Ellen (White) H.; m. Louise Ann Redus, July 5, 1942. Grad., Hill Mil. Acad., 1931; JD, U. Ark., 1942. Bar: Ark. 1942, U.S. Dist. Ct. (ea. dist.) Ark. 1946, U.S. Dist. Ct. (we. dist.) Ark. 1948, U.S. Supreme Ct. 1956. Sole practice Hot Springs, Ark., 1946-67; sr. ptnr. Hobbs, Longinotti, Bosson & Naramore and predecessor firms, Hot Springs, 1967—; chief dep. pros. atty. Garland County, Hot Springs, 1947-53. Pres. Hot Springs Pub. Facilities Bd., 1979—. Served to capt. Air Corps U.S. Army, 1942-46, PTO. Decorated 7 Bronze Stars. Fellow Ark. Bar Found.; mem. ABA, Ark. Bar Assn., Assn. Trial Lawyers Am., Am. Judicature Soc., Am. Soc. Law and Med., Law-Sci. Acad. of Am. Democrat. Anglican. Club: Exchange (Hot Springs) (pres. 1955-57). Lodges: Elks, Masons, Shriners. Avocation: travel. Personal injury, Family and matrimonial, Probate. Home: 115 Shelby Hot Springs AR 71901 Office: Hobbs Longinotti Bosson & Naramore 715 W Grand Ave Hot Springs AR 71913

HOBBS, TRUMAN MCGILL, lawyer, judge.; b. Selma, Ala., Feb. 8, 1921; s. Sam F. and Sarah Ellen (Greene) H.; m. Joyce Cummings, July 9, 1949; children—Emilie C. Reid, Frances John Rose, Dexter Cummings, Truman McGill. A.B., U. N.C., 1942; LL.B., Yale U., 1948. Bar: Ala. 1948. Practiced in Montgomery, 1951-80; law clk. U.S. Supreme Ct., 1948-49; partner Hobbs, Copeland, Franco & Screws, 1951-80; U.S. dist. judge Montgomery, 1980—; Chmn. Ala. Unemployment Appeal Bd., 1952-58. Pres. United Appeal Montgomery; pres. Montgomery County Tb Assn.; v.p. Ala. Com. for Better Schs.; Chmn. Montgomery County Exec. Democratic Com., 1970. Served to lt. USNR, 1942-46, ETO, PTO. Decorated Bronze Star medal. Fellow Am. Coll. Trial Lawyers; mem. Internat. Acad. Trial Lawyers, Ala. Plaintiffs Lawyers Assn. (past pres.), Ala. Bar Assn. (pres. 1970-71), Montgomery County Bar Assn. (past pres.). Home: 2301 Fernway Dr Montgomery AL 36111 Office: PO Box 4954 Montgomery AL 36101

HOBELMAN, CARL DONALD, lawyer; b. Hackensack, N.J., Dec. 26, 1931; s. Alfred Charles and Marion (Gerrish) H.; m. Grace Palumbo, Apr. 25, 1964. B.C.E., Cornell U., 1954; J.D., Harvard U., 1959. Bar: N.Y. 1960, D.C. 1980, U.S. Supreme Ct. 1975. Assoc. Leboeuf, Lamb, Leiby & MacRae, N.Y.C., 1960-64; ptnr. Leboeuf, Lamb, Leiby & MacRae, N.Y.C. and Washington, 1965—; dir. Adirondack Lakes Survey Corp., Albany, N.Y. Contbr. articles on energy-related topics to profl. jours. Served to 1st lt. U.S. Army, 1954-56. Mem. Fed. Energy Bar Assn. (pres. 1980-81), N.Y. State Bar Assn., Assn. Bar City N.Y. (chmn. atomic energy com.), ABA, D.C. Bar Assn. Republican. Clubs: Metropolitan (Washington); University (N.Y.C. and Washington). Avocations: travel, philately. General corporate, Administrative and regulatory. Home: 2420 Tracy Pl NW Washington DC 20008 Office: LeBoeuf Lamb Leiby & MacRae 1333 New Hampshire Ave NW Washington DC 20036

HOBLIN, PHILIP J., JR., securities company executive; b. S.I., N.Y., July 31, 1929; s. Philip J. and Mary A. (Brown) H.; m. Eileen P. Killilea, Jan. 10, 1959; children: Philip, Monica, Michael. B.S., Fordham U., 1951, LL.D., 1957. Bar: N.Y. 1957. Regional atty. Bache & Co., N.Y.C., 1958-63; exec. v.p., gen. counsel Shearson Lehman Bros. Inc., 1963—; co-chmn. Law Center, Inst. Finance, N.Y.C., 1972—; mem. Joint Industry Com. Securities Protection, 1969; mem. bd. arbitration N.Y. Stock Exchange; chmn. arbitration com. Chgo. Bd. Options Exchange, 1977-78, mem. conduct com., 1979-80; mem. exec. and nat. arbitration coms. Nat. Assn. Securities Dealers, also mem. bus. conduct com. dist. 12, 1974-77; mem. Securities Industry Conf. on Arbitration, 1977-81. Author: Arbitration Can Be Broker's Solution to Disputes, 1972, also law rev. articles. Bd. advisers Xavier High Sch., N.Y.C., 1969; pres. Sons of Xavier, 1977-79; trustee Village of Suffern, N.Y., 1985—. Served as spl. agt. USAF, 1951-53; col. Res. (ret.). Mem. Security Industry Assn. (pres. compliance div. 1970-72), ABA, N.Y. County Lawyers Assn., Am. Legion, Res. Officers Assn. (v.p. air N.Y. State chpt. 1973-74, sec. judge adv. gen. N.Y.C. chpt.), VFW, Military Order of World Wars, Air Force Assn. Clubs: Tuxedo Country (N.Y.), Skytop, Downtown Athletic. Lodges: KC, Elks. General corporate. Home: 15 Lancaster Dr Suffern NY 10901 Office: 14 Wall St New York NY 10005

HOBSON, BERNARD EDWARD, lawyer; b. Austin, Tex., July 24, 1953; s. Bernard and Vivian Claire (Moran) H.; m. Pam Standley, Oct. 1, 1983. BA, Knox Coll., 1974; MA, Rice U., 1976; JD, U. Houston, 1979. Bar: Tex. 1980, U.S. Dist. Ct. (so. dist.) Tex. 1980, U.S. Ct. Appeals (5th cir.) 1980, U.S. Ct. Appeals (11th cir.) 1981, U.S. Ct. Claims 1983, U.S. Supreme Ct. 1983, Colo. 1986, U.S. Dist. Ct. (we. dist.) Tex. 1986. Assoc. Pizzitola, Hinton & Sussman, Houston, 1979-80; 1st asst. dist. atty. Ft. Bend County Dist. Atty.'s Office, Richmond, Tex., 1980-83; asst. U.S. atty. U.S. Atty.'s Office Dept. of Justice, Houston, 1983-86, El Paso, Tex., 1986-87; with U.S Atty's. Office Organized Crime Drug Enforcement Task Force, Denver, 1987—; instr. Lamar U., Beaumont, Tex., 1983—, Atty. Gen.'s Adv. Inst., Washington, 1985—. Recipient Spl. Commendation award U.S. Dept. of Justice, 1984, Appreciation Cert. Gulf Coast Crime Prevention Assn., 1983, Commr.'s award U.S. Immigration and Naturalization Service, 1985. Mem. ABA, Fed. Bar Assn. (bd. dirs. 1985—), Tex. Bar Assn., Assn. Trial Lawyers Am., Nat. Dist. Attys. Assn., Am. Judicature Soc. Presbyterian. Avocations: tennis, racquetball. Criminal. Home: 807 Spruce Boulder CO 80302

HOBSON, DONALD LEWIS, judge; b. Detroit, Jan. 11, 1935; s. Oscar and Theresa H.; 1 dau., Donna Lynne. Student Ohio State U., 1951-55; B.S. in History, Eastern Mich. U., 1957; M.A., Mich. State U., 1960; J.D., Detroit Coll. Law, 1965; L.H.D. (hon.), Shaw Coll., 1977; postgrad. U. Mich., 1958, 59, Wayne State U. Law Sch., 1965-66, Hampton Inst., 1962, U.S. Naval Acad., 1974, 76, U. Nev.-Reno, 1978. Bar: Mich. 1965, Wis. 1965, U.S. Dist. Ct. (ea. dist.) Wis. 1965, U.S. Tax Ct. 1965, U.S. Dist. Ct. (ea. dist.) Mich. 1966, U.S. Ct. Appeals (6th cir.) 1966, U.S. Supreme Ct. 1968, U.S. Ct. Mil. Appeals 1981. Tchr. social scis. Detroit Pub. Schs., 1957-64; coordinator Detroit Bd. Edn. Job Upgrading Program, 1964-66; with U.S. atty's office, Washington, 1965; assoc., ptnr. Goodman, Eden, Millender, Goodman & Bedrosian, Detroit, 1966-72; judge Common Pleas Ct. City of Detroit, 1972-77; apptd. to Recorder's Ct. Detroit, 1977, elected judge, 1978—; assoc. prof. Detroit Coll. Law, 1974-77; adj. lectr. law dept. Walsh Coll. Acctg. and Bus. Adminstrn., 1968-71; vis. lectr. Shaw Coll. Detroit, 1971-79. Mem. nat. bd. Council on Legal Ednl. Opportunities; hearing referee Mich. Civil Rights Commn.; sec. income tax rev. bd. City of Detroit; mem. spl. com. on landlord-tenant problems Mich. Supreme Ct.; chmn. bd. trustees Shaw Coll.; bd. dirs. Mich. Youth Found. and Police Athletic League; mem. Urban Alliance; co-chmn. Concerned Citizens for Mental Health; exec. bd., v.p., life mem. Detroit NAACP. Served with U.S. Army, 1958-60; serving as comdr. JAGC USNR. Recipient Honors award Eastern Mich. U. Alumni, 1974. Mem. Am. Arbitration Assn. (arbitration panelist, mem. Detroit Regional Adv. Council), Nat. Lawyers Guild (nat. exec. bd.), Assn. Trial Lawyers Am. (exec. bd. Detroit chpt.), Nat. Bar Assn. (nat. bd.), State Bar Mich. (rep. assembly), Wolverine Bar Assn. (counsel grievance bd., pres., bd. dirs.), Nat. Assn. for Equal Opportunity in Higher Edn., Nat. Assn. Criminal Def. Lawyers (hon.), Mich. Assn. Criminal Def. Lawyers, Black Law Student Scholarship Fund (trustee). Home: 2136 Bryanston Crescent Detroit MI 38207 Office: Recorders Court 1441 St Antoine Detroit MI 48226

HOBSON, HENRY WISE, JR., lawyer; b. Worcester, Mass., Nov. 17, 1921; s. Henry Wise and Edmonia Taylor (Bryan) H.; m. Elizabeth Balch, Apr. 17, 1944; children: Henry W. III, Elizabeth Hobson Garrett, Susan Hobson Catlin, Sarah Hobson Landenwitsch, Anthony W. BA, Yale U., 1942; LLB, U. Cin., 1948; LLD (hon.), Xavier U., 1983. Bar: Ohio 1948, U.S. Dist. Ct. (so. dist.) Ohio, 1950. Assoc. Frost & Jacobs, Cin., 1948-55, ptnr., 1955-83, mng. ptnr., 1983-86, sr. ptnr., 1986—; bd. dirs., sec. Potter Shoe Co., Cin.; bd. dirs. Ohio Nat. Life Ins. Co., Cin.; bd. dirs., v.p. Cin., New Orleans & Tex. Pacific R.R., Cin. Active Boy Scouts, ARC, United Appeal, Community Chest, Cin. Inst. Fine Arts, Children's Home. Served to 1st lt. USAF, 1943-45, PTO. Decorated Air medal, D.F.C. Mem. ABA, Ohio Bar Assn., Cin. Bar Assn., Nat. Assn. of R.R. Trial Counsel. Republican. Episcopalian. Avocation: sports. Estate taxation, Estate planning, Corporate taxation. Home: 8545 Camargo Club Dr Cincinnati OH 45243 Office: Frost & Jacobs 2500 Central Trust Ctr Cincinnati OH 45202-4182

HOBSON, JAMES RICHMOND, lawyer; b. Atlanta, Sept. 13, 1937; s. Richmond Pearson and Alice Chambers (Carey) H.; m. Nancy Hulbert Saussy, Nov. 29, 1963; children—Kathleen Hunter, Caroline Richmond, Susan Saussy. B.A. in English, Cornell U., 1959; M.A. in Govt., Georgetown U., 1963; J.D., U. San Francisco, 1971. Bar: Calif. 1972, U.S. Ct. Appeals (9th cir.) 1972, U.S. Dist. Ct. (no. dist.) Calif. 1972, D.C., 1973, U.S. Ct. Appeals (D.C. cir.) 1973, U.S. Dist. Ct. D.C. 1973. Staff writer Charlotte Observer, N.C., 1963; researcher, writer Republican Nat. Com., Washington, 1964-65; info. officer Hoover Instn., Stanford, Calif., 1966-72; atty., mgr. FCC, Washington, 1972-78; asst. v.p. GTE Service Corp., Washington, 1978-81; Washington counsel GTE Corp., 1982—. Editor mag. pieces for Med. Econs., 1965. Bd. dirs. Mid-Peninsula Citizens for Fair Housing, Palo Alto, Calif., 1971-72; sr. warden Immanuel Ch. on the Hill, Alexandria, Va., 1977; mem. traffic and parking bd. City of Alexandria, Va., 1980-82. Served with U.S. Army, 1959-60. Mem. ABA, Fed. Bar Assn., Fed. Communications Bar Assn. (exec. com. 1984—), Corp. Counsel Assn. (bd. dirs. Washington Met. area 1983-86), Sigma Alpha Epsilon. Republican. Episcopalian. Clubs: Metropolitan (Washington). Administrative and regulatory, Legislative, Public utilities. Home: 3613 Trinity Dr Alexandria VA 22304 Office: GTE Corp 1850 M St NW Suite 1200 Washington DC 20036

HOCHBERG, JEROME A., lawyer; b. Newark, Jan. 22, 1933. B.A., Cornell U., 1954; J.D., Harvard U., 1959. Bar: N.Y. 1960, U.S. Supreme Ct. 1963, D.C. 1968. Law clk. U.S. Dist. Ct., Newark, 1959-61; trial atty. antitrust div. U.S. Dept. Justice, Washington, 1961-73; asst. chief N.Y. field office U.S. Dept. Justice, 1968-71; ptnr. Rowley & Scott, 1974-79, Arter & Hadden, 1979—. Editor: Merger Case Digest, 1967; contbr. articles to profl. jours. and chpts. to books. Served to 1st lt. U.S. Army, 1955-57, Korea. Mem. ABA (com. chmn. antitrust sect., officer jud. adminstrn. div. 1975-82), D.C. Bar Assn. (chmn. div. antitrust 1974-77). Antitrust, Federal civil litigation. Office: Arter & Hadden 1919 Pennsylvania Ave NW Washington DC 20006

HOCHBERG, ROBERT BOAZ, lawyer; b. N.Y.C., Aug. 31, 1953; s. Charles Bernard and Leah (Kay) H. B.A., NYU, 1974; J.D., N.Y. Law Sch., 1977. Bar: N.Y. 1977, Pa. 1978, U.S. Dist. Ct. (ea. dist.) Pa. 1978. Assoc. Kelley, Drye & Warren, Assocs., N.Y.C., 1977, Liebert, Short, Fitzpatrick & Lavin, Phila., 1978-83; ptnr. Silverstein & Kaufman, 1983-85, Hochberg & Safron, Phila., 1985—; dir. paralegal studies Inst. Career Devel., Phila., 1981—. Mem. Steering com. Democratic Party, Phila., 1983. Mem. Maritime Law Assn. of U.S., Assn. Trial Lawyers Am., Jewish. Admiralty, Federal civil litigation, Criminal. Home: 425 S 20th St Philadelphia PA 19103 Office: 2031 Locust Suite 1501 Philadelphia PA 19103

HOCHBERG, RONALD MARK, lawyer, legal educator; b. Bklyn., Apr. 3, 1955; s. Fred Stanley and Adele (Gunsberg) H.; m. Sharon Ann Berg, Aug. 11, 1985. BA, Rutgers U., 1977; JD, Bklyn. Law Sch., 1980; LLM, U. Miami, Coral Gables, 1982. Bar: N.J. 1980, Fla. 1981, N.Y. 1983. Assoc. Klatsky & Klatsky, Red Bank, N.J., 1980-81, Furst, Singer & Yusem, Somerville, N.J., 1982-83, Schanker & Puderbach, Melville, N.Y., 1983-86; ptnr. Schanker & Hochberg, Melville, N.Y., 1987—; adj. assoc. prof. Adelphi U., Garden City, N.Y., 1983—. Contbr. articles to profl. jours. Mem. ABA, N.Y. State Bar Assn., Fla. Bar Assn., N.J. Bar Assn., Internat. Assn. for Fin. Planning. Estate taxation, Estate planning, Pension, profit-sharing, and employee benefits. Office: 275 Broad Hollow Rd #217 Melville NY 11747

HOCHMAN, JAMES ALAN, lawyer; b. N.Y.C., July 8, 1949; s. Jacques Opper and Carol Louise (Schloss) H.; m. Linda Marie Legner, Sept. 5, 1982; 1 child, Jessica Ross. AB in English and Am. Lit. cum laude, Brown U., 1971; JD, Boston U., 1977. Bar: Ill. 1977. Atty Plotkin & Jacobs, Chgo., 1977-78; br. counsel Layers Title Ins. Corp., Chgo., 1978-79; gen. counsel Downs Mohl and Co., Chgo., 1979-80; sole practice Chgo., 1980-82; regional counsel Coldwell Banker Comml. Group Inc., Chgo., 1982—; lectr. Chgo. Kent Coll. Law, 1980-83. Served to comdr. USN, with res. 1970—. Mem. ABA, Chgo. Bar Assn. Club: DownTown Sports (Chgo.). Real property, Civil litigation. Office: Coldwell Banker Comml Group Inc 200 E Randolph Dr Suite 6509 Chicago IL 60601

HOCHMAN, JAMES BERTRAM, lawyer, judge; b. Springfield, Ohio; s. Jack Holiday and Ruth Janice (Schwartz) H.; m. Jeanne Mildred Krieger, Dec. 23, 1962; children: Jeffrey Lawrence, Marla Joy. BS, Ohio State U., 1963, JD, 1965. Bar: U.S. Dist. Ct. (so. dist.) Ohio 1966. Asst. atty. gen. State of Ohio, Columbus, 1966; asst. to city atty. City of Dayton, Ohio, 1966-69; ptnr. Knee, Snyder & Parks, Dayton, 1965-75, Hochman, Snyder, Rakaye & Schmidt, Dayton, 1975-79, Hochman & Horwitz, Dayton, 1979—; judge 2d cir. ct. Montgomery County, Dayton, 1970—. Mem. ABA, Am. Acad. Trial Lawyers, Montgomery County Trial Lawyers (trustee). Club: Ohio State U. (Montgomery) (pres. 1985—). Workers' compensation, Personal injury. Home: 4625 Tara Way Dayton OH 45426 Office: Hochman & Horwitz 650 Talbott Tower Dayton OH 45402

HOCHMAN, JEFFREY J., lawyer; b. Bklyn., July 13, 1952; s. Martin and Lenore Hochman. BS, U. Fla., 1974; JD, South Tex. Coll. Law, 1977. Bar: Fla. 1978, U. S. Dist. Ct. (so. dist.) Fla. 1978, U.S. Ct. Appeals (11th cir.) 1981, N.Y. 1985, U.S. Supreme Ct. 1985. Asst. atty. State of Fla., Ft. Lauderdale, 1979-81; legal advisor Ft. Lauderdale Police Dept., 1981—; lectr. various insts., 1981—. Author: Forfeiture Sting Operations and Procedure Manual for Law Enforcement Agencies. Mem. ABA, Fla. Bar Assn. (forfeitures and sting operations subcoms. criminal law sect.), Broward County Bar Assn., Fla. Assn. Police Attys. Criminal, State civil litigation, Legislative. Office: Ft Lauderdale Police Dept 1300 W Broward Blvd Legal Unit Fort Lauderdale FL 33312

HOCK, FREDERICK WYETH, lawyer; b. Newark, July 10, 1924; s. Herbert Hummel and Carol (Wyeth) H.; m. Alfeld Catherine Larsen, Mar. 4, 1945; children—Carolyn, Sandra, Rhonda; m. 2d, Ellen Barbara Weidner, June 28, 1975. A.A., Princeton U., 1944; B.A., Rutgers U., 1948, LL.B., 1950, J.D., 1968. Bar: N.J. 1949. Assoc. Stevenson, Willette & McDermott, 1949-51; sole practice, 1951-65; ptnr. Hock & Sharkey, East Orange, N.J., 1965-79; sr. ptnr. Hock, Silverlieb, & Kramer and predecessor, Livingston, N.J., 1979—; acting judge East Orange Mcpl. Ct., 1954-57; mem. adv. bd. Maplewood Bank and Trust Co., Livingston, 1987—. Chmn. Juvenile Conf. Com. 1958-62; trustee House of Good Shepherd 1970—; bd. dirs. Essex County chpt. ARC, 1987—. Served with USMC 1942-46. Mem. ABA, N.J. Bar Assn., Northwestern N.J. Estate Planning Council (dir. 1981—). Probate. Office: 70 S Orange Ave Livingston NJ 07039

HOCKER, DONALD BRUCE, lawyer; b. Waltham, Mass., Nov. 21, 1952; s. Donald B. and Iris Allene (Clark) H.; m. Susan Gayle Lindler. July 17, 1976; 1 child, Michael Thomas. BA in Psychology, Clemson U., 1975, MEd in Counseling, 1976; JD, U. S.C., 1981. Bar: S.C. 1981, U.S. Dist. Ct. S.C. 1981. Counselor Laurens (S.C.) County Family Ct., 1976-78; sole practice Laurens, 1981—. Mem. ABA, S.C. Bar Assn., Laurens County Bar Assn., S.C. Trial Lawyers Assn. Democrat. Lutheran. Lodges: Kiwanis (past bd. dirs. Lauren 1981). Avocations: golf, spectator sports. State civil litigation, Family and matrimonial, General practice. Home: 108 Barksdale Circle Laurens SC 29360 Office: 235 W Laurens St Laurens SC 29360

HODGE, JAMES EDWARD, lawyer; b. Alexander City, Ala., Sept. 24, 1936; s. William H. and Nellie (Greene) H.; m. Nancy Bates, Aug. 24, 1963; children: Stephanie, Christopher, Timothy, Michael. BA, Stetson U., 1958; JD, U. Fla., 1963. Bar: Fla. 1963, U.S. Dist. Ct. (mid. dist.) Fla. 1963, U.S. Ct. Appeals (5th cir.) 1963, U.S. Supreme Ct. 1972, U.S. Ct. Appeals (11th cir.) 1981. Ptnr. Jones, Foerster & Hodge, Jacksonville, Fla., 1966-74, Foerster & Hodge, Jacksonville, 1974-82, Milne, Hodge & Milne, Jacksonville,

1982-85; sole practice Jacksonville, 1985-86; ptnr. Blackwell, Walker, Fascell & Hoehl, Jacksonville, 1986—; Spl. counsel Gov. Fla. 1981-82. Pres. Cerebral Palsy Jacksonville, 1972; bd. dirs. Little League Baseball, Jacksonville, 1976-81, Bolles Sch. Dads Assn., Jacksonville, 1978-82; bd. dirs. Jacksonville Port Authority, 1980—, chmn., 1986—. Named one of Outstanding Young Men Am., 1968. Mem. ABA, Fla. Bar Assn., Jacksonville Bar Assn. (bd. govs. 1972-73), Stetson U. Alumni Assn. (pres. 1968), Phi Delta Phi. Episcopalian. Lodge: Rotary (pres. West Jacksonville club 1979-80). Avocations: tennis, reading biographies, spectator sports, walking. Banking, Contracts commercial, Real property. Home: 4984 Ortega Forest Dr Jacksonville FL 32210 Office: Blackwell Walker Fascell & Hoehl 4215 Southpoint Blvd Jacksonville FL 32216

HODGE, NICHOLAS SIM, lawyer; b. Alexandria, Va., Feb. 23, 1954; s. Carleton Taylor and Patricia (Sutcliffe) H. BA, U. Pa., 1976; JD, Yale U., 1981. Bar: Mass. 1981, U.S. Dist. Ct. Mass. 1982, U.S. Ct. Appeals (1st cir.) 1982. Assoc. Gaston Snow & Ely Bartlett, Boston, 1981—. Mem. ABA, Mass. Bar Assn., Boston Bar Assn. Securities, General corporate. Office: Gaston Snow & Ely Bartlett One Federal St Boston MA 02110

HODGE, WILSON EUGENE, lawyer; b. Waynesboro, Miss., Apr. 30, 1943; s. James Thurlow and Dollie Mae (Clark) H.; m. Peggy Jean Powell, July 17, 1977. BS, Miss. State U., 1966; JD, Samford U., 1972. Bar: Fla. 1972, Miss. 1972. Asst. research Miss. Supreme Ct., Jackson, 1972-73; asst. atty. tax com. State of Miss., Jackson, 1973-74; ptnr. Hutchinson & Hodge, Tupelo, Miss., 1974-78; sole practice Homestead, Fla., 1978—. Candidate city judge Tupelo Dems., 1977. Served to sgt. U.S. Army, 1966-69. Mem. ABA, Miss. Bar Assn., Fla. Bar Assn. (various coms.). Methodist. Avocations: tennis, jogging, reading, sports, gardening. Bankruptcy, Contracts commercial, State civil litigation. Home: 1135-B N Franklin Ave Homestead FL 33034

HODGES, CHARLES EDWARD, JR., lawyer; b. Portland, Oreg., Mar. 9, 1931; s. Charles Edward and Alice (Collins) H.; m. Marjorie Ann Burns, Sept. 4, 1954 (div. May 1975); children: Lynn, Charles E. III, Ann Michelle, Michael Rowe, Elizabeth Kay, Brenda; m. Raberta Mildred Mason, Oct. 18, 1975; 1 child, Stephen Edward. BA, St. Martin's Coll., 1956; LLB, Northwestern Coll. Law, 1960. Bar: Oreg. 1961, U.S. Dist. Ct. Oreg. 1961. Claims rep. Farmers Ins., Portland, 1956-61; sole practice Portland, 1961-86; ptnr. Hodges & Sipprell, Portland, 1986—; mem. Legal Aid, Portland, 1980—, Vol. Lawyers, Portland, 1984—. Mgr., coach Little League, Portland, 1968-73, 86—, Babe Ruth League, Portland, 1977 Served with USN, 1951-54, Korea. Mem. Multnomah County Bar Assn., Assn. Trial Lawyers Am., Oreg. Assn. Def. Counsel, Def. Research and Trial Lawyers Assn., Lewis and Clark Alumni Assn., Blue Goose. Roman Catholic. Club: Multnomah Athletic (Portland). Avocations: tennis, baseball, golf, basketball, football. State civil litigation, Insurance, Personal injury. Home: 3327 SW Heather Ln Portland OR 97229 Office: Hodges & Sipprell PC 708 SW 3d #205 Portland OR 97204

HODGES, JOT HOLIVER, JR., lawyer, business executive; b. Archer City, Tex. Nov. 16, 1932; s. Jot Holiver and Lola Mae (Hurd) H.; m. Virginia Cordray Pardue, June 11, 1955; children—Deborah, Jot, Darlene. BS, BBA, Sam Houston State U., 1954; JD, U. Tex.-Austin, 1957. Bar: Tex., U.S. dist. ct. (so. dist.) Tex., U.S. Ct. Appeals (5th cir.). Asst. atty. gen. State of Tex., 1958-60; gen. counsel Tex. Pharm., 1960-61; assoc. gen. counsel Tex. Med. Assn. and Tex. Hosp. Assn., 1960-61; founder, sr. ptnr. Hodges & Grant; chmn. bd. Presidio Devel. Corp.; bd. dirs., gen. counsel First Nat. Bank of Missouri City; gen. ptrs. Double Eagle Ranch, Ltd., Pinto Creek Ranch, Ltd. Served to capt. U.S. Army. Methodist. Club: Houston Contbr. articles to legal, med., pharm. and hosp. jours. General practice, Real property, General corporate. Home: 3527 Thunderbird Missouri City TX 77459 Office: Hodges & Grant 3660 Hampton Dr Suite 200 Missouri City TX 77459-3016

HODGES, RALPH B., state Supreme Court justice; b. Anadarko, Okla., Aug. 4, 1930; s. Dewey E. and Pearl R. (Hodges) H.; m. Janelle H.; children: Shari, Mark, Randy. B.A., Okla. Baptist U.; LL.B., U. Okla. Atty. Bryan County, Okla., 1956-58; judge Okla. Dist. Ct., 1959-65; justice Okla. Supreme Ct., Oklahoma City, 1965—. Judicial administration. Office: State Capitol Bldg Oklahoma City OK 73105 *

HODGES, ROBERT W., lawyer; b. Norway, Maine, Feb. 15, 1949; s. William Arther and Dorethy May (Pratt) H.; m. Darcy Jean Lunceford, June 1, 1974; children: Elizabeth, Matthew. BA, San Francisco State U., 1977; JD, U. Calif., San Francisco, 1980. Bar: Calif. 1980. Assoc. Siders Law Office, Danville, Calif., 1980-83, Craddick, Candland & Conti, Alamo, Calif., 1983—. Served to capt. U.S. Army, 1968-75, to maj. USAR, 1975—, Vietnam. Mem. ABA, Contra Costa Bar Assn., Alameda Bar Assn., Assn. Def. Counsel, Calif. Bar Assn. Republican. Avocations: golf, basketball, coin collecting. State civil litigation, Insurance, Personal injury. Office: Craddick Candland & Conti 915 San Ramon Valley Blvd #260 PO Box 810 Danville CA 94526

HODGES, WILLIAM TERRELL, judge; b. Lake Wales, Fla., Apr. 28, 1934; s. Haywood and Clara Lucy (Murphy) H.; m. Peggy Jean Woods, June 8, 1958; children: Judson, Daniel, Clay. B.S.B.A., U. Fla., 1956, J.D., 1958. Bar: Fla. 1959. Mem. firm Macfarlane, Ferguson, Allison & Kelly, Tampa, 1958-71; instr. bus. law U. South Fla., Tampa, 1961-66; judge U.S. Middle Dist. of Fla., Tampa, 1971—, chief judge, 1971—; Mem. Jud. Conf. Com. on Ops. of Jury System. Exec. editor, U. Fla. Law Rev., 1957-58. Mem. Am., Tampa-Hillsborough County bar assns., Fla. Bar (chmn. grievance com. 1967-70, chmn. uniform comml. code com. 1970-71), Dist. Judges Assn. 5th Circuit (co-chmn. com. on pattern jury instrn. 1977-81), Dist. Judges Assn. 11th Circuit (chmn. jury instrns. com. 1982—, pres. 1981-82) Am. Judicature Soc. Office: US Dist Ct PO Box 2908 Tampa FL 33601 *

HODGINS, DANIEL STEPHEN, lawyer; b. Scranton, Pa., June 21, 1939; s. Alva Daniel and Jane M. (Chupko) H.; m. Amalija Joan Flogl, June 17, 1965; children: Katharine, Dianne, Nicholas. BS in Chemistry, Elizabethtown Coll., 1961; PhD, U. Del., 1966; JD, Oklahoma City U., 1981. Bar: Okla. 1982, U.S. Patent Office 1983, Tex. 1985. Postdoctoral fellow Brandeis U., Waltham, Mass., 1965-67; prof. biochemistry dept. Okla. U. Sch. Medicine, Oklahoma City, 1967-81; assoc. Dunlap & Codding, Oklahoma City, 1981-84, Arnold, White & Durkee, Austin, Tex., 1984—. Contbr. articles to profl. jours. Mem. AAAS, Am. Soc. Biol. Chemistry, Am. Chem. Soc., Am. Intellectual Property Law Assn., Sigma Xi. Patent, Biotechnology. Office: Arnold White & Durkee 600 Congress Ave Suite 2300 Austin TX 78701

HODGSON, ARTHUR CLAY, lawyer; b. Little River, Kans., Aug. 22, 1907; s. Edward Howard and Flora Cleveland (Perry) H.; m. Annie Letitia Green, Jan. 5, 1939; children—Richard, David, Edward, Alice Anne, James. A.B., U. Kans., 1929; J.D., George Washington U., 1937. Bar: Kans. 1936, D.C. 1936, U.S. Supreme Ct. 1950. Sole practice, Washington, 1936-38; practice, Lyons, Kans., 1938—, ptnr. Hodgson & Kahler, 1969—. Pres. Lyons Jaycees; bd. dirs. Lyons C. of C. Served with USN, 1943-45. Mem. Kans. Trial Lawyers Assn., Assn. Trial Lawyers Am. (bd. govs. 1973-76), Rice County Bar, S.W. Kans. Bar, Kans. Bar Assn. (del., disting. service award 1985), ABA (ho. of dels. 1976-82). Democrat. Congregationalist. Clubs: Rotary (Lyons); Masons (Little River). General practice, State civil litigation, Personal injury. Home: Rural Route Little River KS 67457 Office: 119 1/2 W Main Lyons KS 67554

HODGSON, MORGAN DAY, lawyer; b. N.Y.C., May 14, 1947; d. Richard and Geraldine (Reed) H.; m. William T. Lake, Jan. 18, 1975; children: Devon, Spencer, Eve. BA, Harvard U., 1969; JD, Stanford U., 1973. Bar: D.C. 1973. Trial atty. FTC, Washington, 1973-75, asst. to dir. consumer protection, 1975-76; ptnr. Steptoe & Johnson, Washington, 1976—. Mem. Human Devel. Bur., Washington Bd. of Trade 1980—; mem. Stanford Law Sch. Bd. of Visitors, Palo Alto, Calif., 1981-84. Democrat. Federal civil litigation, Labor, Government contracts and claims. Home: 3235 R St NW Washington DC 20007 Office: Steptoe & Johnson 1330 Connecticut Ave NW Washington DC 20036

HODSON, THANE RAYMOND, lawyer; b. Ottawa, Kans., Oct. 30, 1953; s. Nova R. and Rose G. (Wedman) H.; m. Claudia A. Aiken. BA, U. Kans., 1975; JD, Washburn U., 1977; LLM, Georgetown U., 1979. Bar: Kans. 1978, U.S. Tax Ct. 1980, Colo. 1981. Atty. SEC, Washington, 1979-80; assoc. Keller, McSwain, Wing & Maxfield, Denver, 1980-81, Kutak, Rock & Campbell, Denver, 1981—. Summerfield scholar U. Kans., Lawrence, 1973. Mem. ABA, Kans. Bar Assn., Colo. Bar Assn. Republican. Club: Trout Unltd. (Denver). Avocations: fishing, intramural athletics, wine collecting. Corporate taxation, Personal income taxation. Office: Kutak Rock & Campbell 707 17th St 2500 Denver CO 80202

HOECKER, JAMES JOHN, lawyer; b. Rhinelander, Wis., July 12, 1945; s. Raymond Anton and Elizabeth Augusta (Kaiser) H. BA, Northland Coll., 1967; MA, U. Ky., 1970, PhD, 1975; JD, U. Wis., 1978. Bar: Wis. 1978, U.S. Dist. Ct. (we. dist.) Wis. 1978. Atty. office commr. ins. State of Wis., Madison, 1978; assoc. Bell & Fox, Madison, 1979; atty., advisor FERC, Washington, 1979-84, asst. gen. counsel rulemaking and legis. analysis, 1984-86, asst. gen. counsel gas and oil litigation, 1986—; advisor legal affairs to commrs. Holden and Sheldon, 1981-82. Author: Joseph Priestly and the Idea of Progress, 1987; contbr. articles to profl. jours. Mem. ABA, Fed. Energy Bar Assn., Wis. Bar Assn., Phi Delta Phi, Phi Alpha Theta. Democrat. Congregationalist. Avocations: etching, oil painting. Legislative, FERC practice, Public utilities. Home: 129 N Fillmore St Arlington VA 22201 Office: FERC 825 N Capitol St Washington DC 20426

HOEFFLIN, RICHARD MICHAEL, lawyer, judicial administrator, contractor; b. Los Angeles, Oct. 20, 1949; s. David Greenfield and Gloria (Harrison) H.; m. Susan J. Amoroso, Mar. 29, 1969; children—Alyssa, Jennifer, Richard, II. B.S. in Acctg. cum laude, Calif. State U.-Northridge, 1971; J.D., Loyola U., Los Angeles, 1974. Bar: Calif. 1974, U.S. Dist. Ct. (cen. dist.) Calif. 1974, U.S. Tax Ct. 1976, U.S. Dist. Ct. (no. and so. dists.) Calif. 1976, U.S. Supreme Ct. 1982. With Lewitt, Hackman, Hoefflin, Shapiro & Marshall, 1974—, ptnr., 1977—; judge pro tem Los Angeles Mcpl. Ct., 1982—; family law mediator Los Angeles Superior Ct., 1982-86. Co-founder Ventura County Homeowners For Equal Taxation, Westlake Village, Calif., 1978-79; pres., counsel Westlake Hills Homeowners Assn., 1975-77. Mem. Los Angeles Bar Assn., Ventura County Bar Assn., ABA, San Fernanado Valley Bar Assn. Republican. Roman Catholic. Club: North Ranch County (pres. tennis assn. 1984-85). Real property, State civil litigation, Family and matrimonial. Office: Lewitt Hackman Hoefflin et al 16633 Ventura Blvd Suite 1100 Encino CA 91436

HOEFLE, H. FREDERICK, lawyer; b. Cin., Apr. 7, 1938; s. Henry Alfred and Norma (Lambeck) H.; m. Joyce Ann Dreier, Aug. 21, 1965; children: Jennifer, Meredith. AB with high honors, U. Cin., 1960; JD, Chase Coll. Law, Cin., 1965. Bar: Ohio 1965, U.S. Supreme Ct. 1971, U.S. Ct. Appeals (5th and 6th cirs.), U.S. Dist. Ct. (so. dist.) Ohio, U.S. Dist. Ct. (ea. dist.) Ky. Assoc. Shea & McKay, Norwood, Ohio, 1966-71; asst. atty. gen. State of Ohio, Cin., 1971-79; sole practice, Cin., 1971—; sr. trial counsel Hamilton County Pub. Defender, Cin., 1979—; mem. death penalty task force U.S. Ct. Appeals (6th cir.). Contbg. author: Ohio Death Penalty Manual, 1981; Ohio Appellate Manual, 1983. Mem. Ohio Death Penalty Task Force, Columbus, 1981—. Mem. Cin. Bar Assn. (exec. com. 1976, spl. award of merit 1978), Ohio State Bar Assn., Order of Curia, Phi Beta Kappa, Phi Delta Theta. Democrat. Unitarian. Club: Cin. Athletic. Criminal, State civil litigation, General practice. Home: 4532 Runningfawn Dr Cincinnati OH 45247 Office: 1500 American Bldg 30 E Central Pkwy Cincinnati OH 45202

HOEFLING, VIRGINIA ANN, lawyer; b. N.Y.C., Aug. 1, 1931; d. Amerigo and Lucy S. (Mauriello) De Vito; m. Vincent R., Aug. 12, 1951; children: Richard, Raymond, Charles, Francis, Stephen, Jeannine. BA in Urban Studies, Bradford Coll., 1976; JD cum laude, Suffolk U., 1980. Bar: Mass. 1980, U.S. Dist. Ct. Mass. 1981, U.S. Ct. Appeals (1st cir.) 1981. Sole practice Boston, 1981-82; law clk. to presiding justice Mass. Superior Ct., Boston, 1981, 82-83, chief law clk. to presiding justices, 1983-84; asst. atty. gen. State of Mass., Boston, 1985—. Editor Suffolk Transnational Law Jour., 1979-80; also contbr. articles to profl. jours. Pres. St. John Neumann Guild, Roxbury, Mass., 1966—; mem. Town Meeting, Winchester, Mass., 1976—, Gov.'s Task Force on Presumptive Sentencing, 1984-85; liaison senate and house criminal justice coms. Superior Ct. Task Force, 1984-85; assoc. mem. Winchester Zoning Bd. Appeals, 1985—. Recipient St. John Neumann award, Neumann Ctr., Phila., 1980. Mem. ABA, Mass. Bar Assn. (justice task force 1984-85, chem. dependency com. 1985-), Mass. Assn. Women Lawyers (exec. bd. mem. scholarship found. 1983-, corr. sec. 1986-), Boston Bar Assn., Phi Delta Phi. Democrat. Roman Catholic. Avocations: internat. travel, collecting miniatures. Insurance, State civil litigation, Administrative and regulatory. Home: 156 Forest St Winchester MA 01890 Office: Dept Atty Gen One Ashburton Pl Boston MA 02108

HOEGLE, ROBERT LOUIS, lawyer; b. Pitts., Sept. 28, 1952; s. Theodore Lawrence and Esther Frances (Schneider) H.; m. Marsha Jean Benson, July 11, 1981. AB, Georgetown U., 1974, JD, 1977. Bar: D.C. 1977, U.S. Dist. Ct. D.C. 1978, U.S. Ct. Appeals 1978, U.S. Supreme Ct. 1981. Assoc. Olwine, Connelly, Chase, O'Donnell & Weyher, Washington, 1977-86, ptnr., 1986—. Mem. ABA. Republican. Roman Catholic. Club: International (Washington). Federal civil litigation, Administrative and regulatory, Antitrust. Home: 6314 Kellogg Dr McLean VA 22101 Office: Olwine Connelly Chase et al 1850 K St NW Suite 890 Washington DC 20006

HOEHN, ELMER L., lawyer; b. Memphis, Ind., Dec. 19, 1915; s. Louis and Agnes (Goss) H.; m. Frances Cory, June 10, 1943; children: Kathleen Gillmore, G. Patrick. B.S., Canterbury Coll., 1936, Northwestern U., 1937; J.D., U. Louisville, 1940. Bar: Ky. 1940, D.C. 1969, U.S. Supreme Ct. 1969, U.S. Ct. Appeals 1970, Ind. 1981. Prof. bus. and law Jeffersonville High Sch., Ind., 1937-41, Ind. U., 1940-41; with legal and personnel div. Am. Barge Lines, 1942-44; realtor Ind., 1949—; apptd. dir. by Gov. Ind. Oil and Gas, 1949-53; apptd. adminstr. by Pres. U.S. Oil Import Adminstrn., 1965-69; sec.-treas. Am. Assn. Oil Well Drilling Contractors, 1956-60; exec. sec. Ind. Oil Producers and Land Owners Assn., 1953-64; pvt. practice law Washington, 1969—; cons. petroleum, natural resources, energy and environment. Mem. Ind. Gen. Assembly, 1945- 49, minority floor leader, 1947, chief clk., 1949, Democratic chmn., Clark County, Ind., 1945-52; Ind. del. Dem. Nat. Conv., 1964, chmn. 8th Congl. Dist., 1952-58; mem. Ind. Dem. Exec. Com., 1952-58, Ind. and Midwest campaign mgr., LBJ campaign for president, 1960. Named hon. citizen Ind., Ky. Mem. ABA, Fed. Bar Assn., Ky. Bar Assn., D.C. Bar Assn., Ind. Bar Assn., Am. Petroleum Inst., Soc. History in the Fed. Govt., Sigma Delta Kappa. Roman Catholic. Clubs: Nat. Lawyers, Nat. Press (Washington); Ind. Legislators (Indpls); Elks Country (Jeffersonville). Administrative and regulatory. Home: 5914 Woodley Rd McLean VA 22101 also: 19 Blanchel Terr Jeffersonville IN 47130 Office: 1523 L St NW Washington DC 20005 also: 1415 S Clark Blvd Jeffersonville IN 47130

HOEKSTRA, KATHLYN B., lawyer; b. Chgo., June 9, 1952; d. Henry R. and Marilyn B. (Jordan) H. BA, Albion Coll., 1974; JD, John Marshall Law Sch., 1981. Bar: Ill. 1981, U.S. Dist. Ct. (no. dist.) Ill. 1981. Assoc. Kanter & Mattenson, Chgo., 1981-86; sole practice Chgo. and Rosemont, Ill., 1986—; atty. Swingmaster Corp., Chgo.; atty., exec. v.p., bd. dirs. Quartermain, Ltd., Chgo.; v.p. fin., legal counsel Tommy Lasorda Foods, Inc., Rosemont; pres. Microwave-Pac, Ltd. Mem. ABA, Chgo. Bar Assn. (com chmn. 1983-85, Cert. of Appreciation 1984, 85). Avocations: photography, sports. General corporate, Entertainment, Securities. Office: 5216 Wesley Terr Rosemont IL 60018

HOELLEN, JOHN JAMES, lawyer; s. John J. and Mame F. (Skellinger) H.; m. Mary Jane McMeans, Apr. 24, 1948; children—Elizabeth J. Hoellen Ward, Robert B. B.A., Northwestern U., 1935, J.D., 1938. Bar: Ill. 1938, U.S. Dist. Ct. (no. dist.) Ill. 1938, U.S. Ct. Appeals (7th cir.) 1966. Assoc., Willner & Horwitz, Chgo., 1938-46; atty. Ill. Dept. Registration and Edn., 1946-47; ptnr. Leonard, Hoellen & Raszus, Chgo., 1947-54, Hoellen & Willens, Chgo., 1954-68, John J. Hoellen and Assocs., Chgo., 1968-75, Hoellen, Lukes & Halper, Chgo., 1975—; spl. asst. atty. gen., 1969-75; dir., gen. counsel Bank of Ravenswood, Chgo., 1962—. Bd. dirs. Chgo. Transit Authority, 1979—, vice chmn. 1986— , vice chmn., 1986—; alderman City of Chgo., 1947-75; del. Republican Nat. Conv., 1972, 76, 80, 84; mem. Rep. Central Com. Cook County, 1964—, nominee for mayor of Chgo., 1975; pres. Sulzer Family Found., 1958—. Served to lt. U.S. Navy, 1941-46. Mem. ABA, Ill. Bar Assn., Chgo. Bar Assn., Am. Judicature Soc. Methodist. Clubs: Execs., Kiwanis, Chgo. Probate, Real property, Contracts commercial. Office: 1940 Irving Park Rd Chicago IL 60613

HOENICKE, EDWARD HENRY, lawyer, corporate executive; b. Chgo., Apr. 12, 1930; s. Edward Albert and Henrietta Christina (Hameister) H.; m. Janice Armande Gravel, Aug. 14, 1954; children—Jeanne E., Anne L. A.B., Cornell U., 1950; J.D., U. Mich., 1956. Bar: N.Y. 1956. Assoc. Cravath, Swaine & Moore, N.Y.C., 1956-59; div. counsel Olin Corp., N.Y.C., 1959-68; v.p., gen. counsel Beechnut, Inc., N.Y.C., 1968-69; pres. Beechnut Lifesavers Internat., N.Y.C., 1969-76; v.p., asst. gen. counsel Squibb Corp., N.Y.C., 1976-77; sr. v.p., gen. counsel, UAL, Inc. and United Airlines, Inc., Elk Grove Village, Ill., 1977—. Bd. dirs. Care, Inc., 1971—. Served with USAF, 1951-53. Mem. ABA. Club: Exmour Country (Highland Park, Ill.). General corporate. Office: Allegis Corp 1200 Algonquin Rd Elk Grove Village IL 60007

HOENS, CHARLES HENRY, JR., lawyer; b. Roselle Park, N.J., Apr. 2, 1922; s. Charles Henry and Helen Marguerite (Schreiber) H.; m. Mary Preston McLaren, May 31, 1952; children—Charles Henry, Helen E., John M., Thomas W. A.B., Cornell U., 1947; J.D. with honors, Rutgers U., 1950. Bar: N.J. 1950, N.Y. 1982. Assoc., Toner, Speakman & Crowley, Newark, 1950-53; asst. U.S. atty., chief civil div. Dist. N.J., Newark, 1953-61; assoc. Lum, Biunno & Tompkins, Newark, 1961-64, ptnr., 1965-83, Lum, Hoens, Abeles, Conant & Danzis, Newark, 1984—; dir. Damon G. Douglas Co., Cranford, N.J. Trustee, Masonic Charity Found. N.J., 1966-72, 79-82, pres., 1969; trustee Presbyn. Homes N.J., 1976-83, chmn. bd., 1983. Served to lt. col. U.S. Army, 1942-63. Mem. ABA (vice-chmn. fidelity and surety law com.), Fed. Bar Assn., N.J. State Bar Assn., Essex County Bar Assn. Republican. Presbyterian. Club: Essex. Lodge: Masons (Daniel Coxe medal 1979). Insurance, Federal civil litigation, Government contracts and claims. Home: 67 Kinnan Way Basking Ridge NJ 07920 Office: 103 Eisenhower Pkwy Roseland NJ 07068

HOERNER, ROBERT JACK, lawyer; b. Fairfield, Iowa, Oct. 12, 1931; s. John A. and Margaret (Simmons) H.; m. Judith Chandler, Apr. 11, 1954; children: John Andrew, Timothy Chandler, Blayne Marie, Michelle Margaret; m. Susan Priscilla Warren, Aug. 27, 1980. BA, Cornell U., 1953; JD, U. Mich., 1958. Bar: Ohio 1960, U.S. Supreme Ct. 1964. Law clk. to Chief Justice Earl Warren, U.S. Supreme Ct., Washington, 1958-59; chief evaluation sect. antitrust div. Dept. Justice, Washington, 1963-65; ptnr. Jones, Day, Reavis & Pogue, Cleve., 1967—. Contbr. articles to legal jours. Mem. ABA, Ohio Bar Assn., Cleve. Bar Assn. Antitrust, Patent, Consumer commercial. Office: Jones Day Reavis & Pogue 1700 Huntington Bldg Cleveland OH 44115

HOEVELER, WILLIAM M., judge; b. Aug. 23, 1922; m. Mary Griffin Smith, 1950; 4 children. Student, Temple U., 1941-42; B.A., Bucknell U., 1947; LL.B., Harvard U., 1950. Bar: Fla. bar 1951. Practice law Miami, Fla., 1951-77; firm individual practice law; judge U.S. Dist. Ct. for Fla. So. Dist., 1977—; mem. U.S. Dist. Ct. Com. for Rev. Local Rules; lectr. in field. Incorporator, bd. dirs. Youth Industries, Inc.; mem. vestry St. Stephens Episcopal Ch., 1973-75, chancellor, 1973. Served to lt. USMC, 1942-46. Mem. Am. Judicature Soc., Fla. Bar (personal injury and wrongful death adv. com. 1976), Phila. Bar Assn., Dade County (Fla.) Bar Assn. (chmn. charity drives com. 1966), Am. Bar Assn. (chmn. com. on products, profl. and gen. liability law 1972-73, program chmn. sec. ins., negligence and compensation law 1975, mem. sect. governing council 1975-78, mem. governing com. of forum com. on constrn. industry), Omicron Delta Kappa. Jurisprudence. Office: US Dist Ct PO Box 013660 Flagler Station Miami FL 33101 *

HOEY, JAMES DOUGLAS, III, lawyer; b. Palo Alto, Calif., Oct. 26, 1956; s. James Douglas II and Joyce (McLain) H.; m. Natalie Venezia, Aug. 13, 1983. BA, U. Calif., Santa Barbara, 1978; JD, U. Calif., San Francisco, 1981. Bar: Calif. 1981, U.S. Dist. Ct. (so. dist.) Calif. 1981. Assoc. Dorazio, Barnhorst, Goldsmith & Bonar, San Diego, 1981-85, Lillick, McHose & Charles, San Diego, 1985—. Mem. ABA, Calif. Bar Assn., San Diego County Bar Assn., Calif. Trial Lawyers Assn., Hastings Alumni Assn. (bd. dirs. 1983—), San Diego Jr. C. of C. Republican. Avocation: sports. Admiralty, Federal civil litigation, Personal injury. Home: 71 Antigua Ct Coronado CA 92118 Office: Lillick McHose & Charles 101 W Broadway Suite 1800 San Diego CA 92101

HOEY, WILLIAM EDWARD, lawyer; b. Mckeesport, Pa., Sept. 22, 1930; s. Edward Duane and Helen (Damm) H.; m. Shirley Morgan, Dec. 27, 1954; children—Gregory, Jonathan, Jessica, Christopher, Erica. A.B., Dickinson Coll., 1952, LL.B., 1954. Bar: Pa. 1957, U.S. Dist. Ct. (we. dist.) Pa. 1957, U.S. Supreme Ct. 1970, Fla. 1972, U.S. Dist. Ct. (so. dist.) Fla. 1975. Sole practice, Pitts., 1957-75, Miami, Fla., 1975—. Served with M.C., U.S. Army, 1954-56. Mem. ABA, Pa. Bar Assn., Allegheny County Bar Assn., Pa. Def. Inst., Am. Arbitration Assn., Fla. Bar, Dade County Bar Assn., Fla. Def. Lawyers Assn., Def. Research Inst., Internat. Assn. Def. Counsel, Phi Kappa Psi, Pi Delta Epsilon. State civil litigation, Federal civil litigation, Insurance. Home: 17701 SW 77th Ave Miami FL 33157 Office: 2398 S Dixie Hwy Miami FL 33133

HOFF, JONATHAN M(ORIND), lawyer; b. Chgo., July 4, 1955; s. Irwin S. and Ida (Indritz) H. AB, U. Calif., Berkeley, 1978; JD, UCLA, 1981. Bar: Calif. 1981, U.S. Dist. Ct. (no. and cen. dists.) Calif. 1981, N.Y. 1982, U.S. Dist. Ct. (so. dist.) N.Y. 1982, U.S. Ct. Appeals (4th, 5th, 7th, 8th, 9th, 10th cirs.) 1982. Assoc. Weil, Gotshal & Manges, N.Y.C., 1981—. Comment editor UCLA Law Rev., 1980-81; contbr. articles to law jours. Chmn. Coastal Heritage Found., San Francisco, 1975—; pres. Lake Merced Coastal Preservation Council, San Francisco, 1975-76; exec. dir. P.A.C.E., San Francisco, 1975-77. Mem. ABA, Calif. Bar Assn. Securities, Corporate commercial litigation, Mergers and acquisitions. Office: Weil Gotshal & Manges 767 Fifth Ave New York NY 10153

HOFF, RENAE, lawyer; b. Caldwell, Idaho, Feb. 23, 1951; d. Edwin Herbert Hoff and Agnes Mary (Stoltz) Feiling; m. Craig L. Gibson. BA, Coll. of Idaho, 1979; JD, Southwestern U., 1981. Bar: Idaho 1981, U.S. Dist. Ct. Idaho 1981, U.S. Ct. Appeals (9th cir.) 1986. Assoc. Gunn & Hoff, Caldwell, 1981—; referral atty. pro bono panel Idaho State Bar, 1983—; bd. dirs. Idaho Legal Aid Services, Inc., 1986—. Mem. ABA (career satisfaction com.), 3d Jud. Bar Assn. (ct. liaison), Assn. Trial Lawyers Am., Idaho Trial Lawyers Assn., Canyon County Lawyers Club. Democrat. Criminal, Family and matrimonial. Office: Gunn & Hoff PO Box 69 Caldwell ID 83606

HOFF, TIMOTHY, law educator, priest; b. Freeport, Ill., Feb. 27, 1941; s. Howard Vincent and Zillah (Morgan) H.; m. Virginia Nevill. A.B., Tulane U., 1963, J.D., 1966; student U. London, 1961-62; LL.M., Harvard U., 1970. Bar: Fla. 1967, Ala. 1973, U.S. Dist. Ct. (mid. dist.) Fla. 1967. Assoc., Williams, Parker, Harrison, Dietz & Getzen, Sarasota, Fla., 1966-69; asst. legal editor The Fla. Bar, 1969; asst. prof. U. Ala., 1970-73, assoc. prof., 1973-75, prof. law, 1975—; cons. Ala. Law Inst.; reporter Ala. Adminstrv. Procedure Act, 1977—; ordained priest Episcopal Ch. Vice-pres., founding dir. Hospice of West Ala.; founding dir. Community Soup Bowl, Inc.; Episc. priest assoc. Canterbury Chapel U. Ala. Recipient Hist. Preservation Service award, 1976. Mem. ACLU, Maritime Law Assn. U.S., AAUP, Council on Religion and Law, Episc. Soc. for Ministry in Higher Edn., Phi Beta Kappa, Order of Coif, Omicron Delta Kappa, Eta Sigma Phi. Democrat. Club: University. Author: Alabama Limitations of Actions, 1984; contbr. articles to profl. jours. Admiralty, State civil litigation, Jurisprudence. Home: 2601 Lakewood Circle Tuscaloosa AL 35405-2727 Office: U Ala Law Sch Box 1435 Tuscaloosa AL 35487-1435

HOFF, VALERIE MARGARET KNECHT, lawyer; b. Tacoma, Nov. 9, 1946; d. Norbert Francis and Dorothy Margaret (Fawcett) Knecht; m. Mack Harrison Shultz, May 15, 1971 (dec. Mar. 1974); 1 son, Mack Harrison, Jr.; m. 2d David Daniel Hoff, Nov. 25, 1978; stepchildren—James Bradley, Paula J., Deana L. B.A., U. Puget Sound, 1969; M.A., Purdue U., 1975;

J.D., U. Puget Sound, 1978. Bar: Wash. 1978, U.S. Dist. Ct. (we. dist.) Wash., U.S. Ct. Appeals (9th cir.). Assoc. Manza, Moceri & Messina, Tacoma, 1978-79; ptnr. Rydberg, Hoff & Gagley, Kent, Wash., 1979-82; sole practice, Seattle, 1982-87, ptnr. Nelson & Hoff, P.S., Inc., 1987—; speaker legal issues, 1983—. Mem. ABA, Wash. State Bar Assn., Seattle-King County Bar Assn., Women's Univ. Club, Wash. State Trial Lawyers Assn., Kappa Kappa Gamma Alumnae Assn. (pres. Seattle chpt.). Republican. Roman Catholic. State civil litigation, Family and matrimonial, General practice. Home: 4434 170th Ave SE Issaquah WA 98027 Office: Nelson & Hoff PS Inc 304 Onb Plaza 10800 NE 8th St Bellevue WA 98004

HOFF, WILLIAM BRUCE, JR., lawyer; b. Parkersburg, W.Va., Sept. 13, 1932; s. William Bruce and Edith Virginia (Stalnaker) H.; m. Catherine Louise McCue, Feb. 20, 1954; children: William Bruce, David Franklin, Jennifer, Catherine. A.B. with honors, W.Va. U., 1954; L.L.B., Harvard U., 1957. Bar: Ill. 1958, U.S. Supreme Ct. 1972. Assoc. Mayer, Brown & Platt, Chgo., 1957-66, ptnr., 1967—. Co-author Federal Litigation Guide (vols. 2 and 3), 1985. Chmn. Winnetka (Ill.) Caucus Com., 1969-70. Mem. Am. Coll. Trial Lawyers, ABA, Chgo. Bar Assn., 7th Circuit Bar Assn., Phi Beta Kappa. Federal civil litigation, State civil litigation, Nuclear power. Home: 1340 Scott Ave Winnetka IL 60093 Office: Mayer Brown & Platt 231 S LaSalle St Chicago IL 60604

HOFFHEIMER, DANIEL JOSEPH, lawyer; b. Cin., Dec. 28, 1950; s. Harry Max and Charlotte (O'Brien) H.; m. Sara Wood Elder, May 9, 1970 (div. 1979) 1 child, Rebecca Anne; m. Penny Friedman, June 7, 1981; 1 child, Rachel Friedman. AB cum laude, Harvard Coll., 1973; JD, U. Va., 1976. Bar: Ohio 1976, U.S. Dist. Ct. (so. dist.) Ohio 1976, U.S. Ct. Appeals (6th cir.) 1977, U.S. Ct. Appeals (D.C. and Fed. cirs.) 1986, U.S. Ct. Internat. Trade 1986, U.S. Supreme Ct. 1980. Assoc. Taft, Stettinius & Hollister, Cin., 1976-84, ptnr., 1984—; lectr. law Coll. Law, U. Cin., 1981-83. Editor in chief U. Va. Jour. Internat. Law, 1975-76; co-author: Practitioners' Handbook Ohio First District Court of Appeals, 1984, Practitioners Handbook U.S. 6th Circuit Court of Appeals, 1984; contbr. articles to profl. jours. Mem. Cin. Symphony Bus. Relations Com., 1977—; mem. adv. bd. for Consumer Protection, Cin., 1978-80; trustee Cin. Chamber Orch., 1977-80, Seven Hills Schs., Cin., 1980—, Internat. Visitors Ctr., Cin., 1980-84, Friends Coll. Conservatory of Music, Cin., 1985-86, Children's Psychiat. Ctr., Cin., 1986—. Named Outstanding Young Man, U.S. Jaycees, 1984. Mem. ABA, Fed. Bar Assn. (treas. 1984, sec. 1985, v.p. 1986—), Ohio State Bar Assn., Cin. Bar Assn. Democrat. Clubs: Harvard of Cin. (bd. dirs. 1980—, v.p., 1983-86, pres. 1986-87). Avocations: music, tennis, Chinese art. Federal civil litigation, State civil litigation, General practice. Home: 1125 Edwards Rd Cincinnati OH 45208 Office: Taft Stettinius & Hollister 1800 First Nat Bank Ctr Cincinnati OH 45202

HOFFMAN, ALAN CRAIG, lawyer, consultant; b. Chgo., Oct. 1, 1944; s. Morris Joseph and Marie E. H. B.A., Carthage Coll., 1968; J.D., John Marshall Law Sch., 1973. Bar: Fla. 1973, Ill. 1973, U.S. Dist. Ct. (no dist.) Ill. 1974, U.S. Dist. Ct. (mid. dist.) Fla. 1981, U.S. Ct. Appeals (7th cir.) 1974, U.S. Ct. Appeals (5th and 11th cirs.) 1981, U.S. Supreme Ct. 1977. Staff atty. Cook County Legal Assistance Found., Brookfield, 1973-74, Patient Legal Services, Chgo., 1974; sole practice, Chgo., 1973—, River Grove, Ill., 1973-86, Oak Brook, Ill., 1980-87—, Hinsdale, Ill., 1987—; with assocs., 1980—; spl. asst. atty. gen. Ill. Criminal Justice Div., Chgo., 1977-79, Ill. Condemnation Div., Chgo., 1980-87; pres. Almar, Ltd., 1986—; v.p. Marach, Ltd., 1986—; asst. prof. law Lewis U., 1974-79, vis. prof. Coll. Law Paraprofl. Center, 1974-76, adj. prof., 1979-80; assoc. prof. No. Ill. U., 1979-80; v.p. Adv. Adv. Service, Inc.; cons. med.-legal cases, 1982—. Mem. Oak Park Twp. (Ill.) Mental Health Bd., 1975-80, v.p. 1975, chmn. program com. 1975-77, pres. 1978. Mem. Am. Acad. Legal Medicine (assoc. in law), ABA, Ill. State Bar Assn. (chmn. standing com. on mentally disabled 1977-78), Chgo. Bar Assn., DuPage Bar Assn., West Suburban Bar Assn., Chgo. Acad. Law and Medicine, Am. Soc. Law and Medicine, Chgo. Acad. Legal Medicine, Mensa, Ill. Trial Lawyers Assn., Fla. Bar Assn., Assn. Trial Lawyers Am., Phi Alpha Delta. Author: (with F. Lane and D. Birnbaum) Lane's Medical Litigation Guide, 1981; contbr. articles to Med. Trial Technique Quar.; editorial bd. Jour. Legal Medicine, 1980—. Personal injury, State civil litigation, Workers' compensation. Address: 104 S Washington St Suite 2 Hinsdale IL 60521

HOFFMAN, BERNARD H., lawyer; b. Red Bank, N.J., Apr. 11, 1933; s. Louis Hoffman and Anna Mindlin; m. Selma Swirin, Nov. 26, 1961; children: Alan B., Marla L. BA, NYU, 1951, LLB, 1955. Bar: N.J. 1960. Assoc. George A. Gray, Red Bank, 1960-61, Arnone & Zager, Red Bank, 1961-70; sole practice Red Bank, 1970-74; ptnr. Hoffman & Schreiber, P.A., Red Bank, 1975—; mcpl. ct. judge Shrewsbury Borough. Mem. Red Bank Civil Rights Commn., 1966; chmn. Bd. Adjustment of Borough of Red Bank; mem. Bd. Mgmt. of YMCA, N.J. Selective Service Bd. Served with U.S. Army. Mem. ABA, N.J. Bar Assn. (past chmn. family law sect.), Monmouth Bar Assn. (past chmn. family law com.), Am. Acad. Matrimonial Lawyers (pres., pres-elect N.J. chpt.), Internat. Acad. Matrimonial Lawyers. Republican. Club: NYU. Lodges: B'nai Brith, Masons. Family and matrimonial, Probate, Real property. Office: Hoffman & Schreiber 199 Broad St PO Drawer 789 Red Bank NJ 07701

HOFFMAN, DANIEL S., lawyer. b. 1931. B.A., U. Colo., 1951; LL.B., U. Denver, 1958. Bar: Colo. 1958. Practice, Denver, 1958-63, 65-78; mgr. safety City and County of Denver, 1963-65; prof., dean U. Denver Coll. Law, 1978-84, dean and prof. emeritus, 1984—; ptnr. Holme Roberts & Owen, Denver, 1984—. Mem. Am. Coll. Trial Lawyers (state chmn. 1975-76), Colo. Bar Assn. (pres. 1976-77), Colo. Trial Lawyers Assn. (pres. 1961). Legal education. Office: 1700 Broadway Suite 1800 Denver CO 80290

HOFFMAN, DANIEL STEVEN, lawyer, educator; b. N.Y.C., May 4, 1931; s. Lawrence Hoffman and Juliette (Marbes) Ostrov; m. Beverly Mae Swenson, Dec. 4, 1954; children—Lisa Hoffman Ciancio, Tracy Hoffman Petersen, Robin Hoffman Black. B.A., U. Colo., 1951; LL.B., U. Denver, 1958. Bar: Colo. 1958. Assoc., ptnr. Fugate, Mitchem, Hoffman, Denver, 1951-55; mgr. of safety City and County of Denver, 1963-65; ptnr. Kripke, Hoffman, Carrigan, Denver, 1965-70, Hoffman, McDermott, Hoffman, Denver, 1970-78; of counsel Hoffman & McDermott, Denver, 1978-84; ptnr. Holme Roberts & Owen, Denver, 1984—; dean Coll. Law, U. Denver, 1978-84, dean emeritus, prof. emeritus, 1984—; bd. dirs. Continuing Legal Edn. in Colo., 1971-74; chmn., mem. Merit Screening Com. for Bankruptcy Judges, Denver, 1979-84; subcom. chmn. Dist. Atty.'s Crime Adv. Commn., Denver, 1984—. Contbr. chpts. to books. Mem. Rocky Mountain region, Anti-Defamation League, Denver, 1985; bd. dirs. Colo. chpt. Am. Jewish Com., 1985; mem. adv. com. Samaritan Shelter, Archdiocese of Denver, 1985; bd. dirs. Legal Ctr. for Handicapped Citizens, Denver, 1985—; chmn. Rocky Flats Blue Ribbon Citizens Com., Denver, 1980-83; bd. visitors Brigham Young U. J. Reuben Clark Law Sch., 1986—. Served with USAF, 1951-55. Recipient Humanitarian award Rocky Mountain chpt. Anti-Defamation League, 1984. Fellow Am. Coll. Trial Lawyers (state chmn. 1975-76), Internat. Soc. Barristers, Colo. Bar. Found., Am. Bar Found.; mem. Colo. Bar. Assn. (pres. 1976-77, Young Lawyer of Yr. award 1965), Colo. Trial Lawyers Assn. (pres. 1961-62), Assn. Trial Lawyers Am. (nat. com. mem. 1962-63), Am. Judicature Soc. (bd. dirs. 1977-81), Order of Coif (hon.). Democrat. Jewish. Avocation: platform tennis. Federal civil litigation, State civil litigation, Personal injury. Office: Holme Roberts & Owen 1700 Broadway Suite 1800 Denver CO 80290

HOFFMAN, DAVID GARY, lawyer, legal educator; b. Phila., Dec. 6, 1954; s. Carl Joseph and Martha Marie (Mehler) H.; m. Kathryn Jean Seyler, Aug. 6, 1977; 1 child, Kathryn Leigh. BA, St. Josephs Coll., Phila., 1977; JD, Cath. U., 1980. Bar: D.C. 1981, Va. 1983, U.S. Tax Ct. 1981, U.S. Ct. Appeals (4th cir.) 1983. Tax cons. Reznick, Fedder & Silverman CPA's, Bethesda, Md., 1980-81; sole practice Fairfax, Va., 1981—; instr. tax law and corp. law U. Md., College Park, Md., 1982—, real property law George Washington U., 1984—. Contbr. articles to legal jours. Mem. ABA, Phi Alpha Delta. Republican. Roman Catholic. Avocation: writing. Corporate taxation, Personal income taxation, General corporate. Office: 4101 Chain Bridge Rd Suite 311 Fairfax VA 22030

HOFFMAN, JAMES PAUL, lawyer, hypnotist; b. Waterloo, Iowa, Sept. 7, 1943; s. James A. and Luella M. (Prokosch) H.; m. Debra L. Malone, May 29, 1982; 1 dau., Tiffany K. B.A., U. No. Iowa, 1965, J.D. U. Iowa, 1967. Bar: Iowa 1967, U.S. Dist. Ct. (no. dist.) Iowa 1981, U.S. Dist. Ct. (so. dist.) Iowa 1968, U.S. Dist. Ct. (so. dist.) Ill, U.S. Tax Ct. 1971, U.S. Ct. Appeals (8th cir.) 1970, U.S. Supreme Ct. 1974. Sr. mem. James P. Hoffman, Law Offices, Keokuk, Iowa, 1967—; chmn. bd. Iowa Inst. Hypnosis. Fellow Am. Inst. Hypnosis; mem. ABA, Iowa Bar Assn., Lee County Bar Assn., Assn. Trial Lawyers Am., Ill. Trial Lawyers Assn., Iowa Trial Lawyers Assn. Democrat. Roman Catholic. Author: The Iowa Trial Lawyers and the Use of Hypnosis, 1980. Personal injury, Workers' compensation, State civil litigation. Home and Office: Middle Rd PO Box 1066 Keokuk IA 52632

HOFFMAN, JOHN DOUGLAS, lawyer; b. Easton, Pa., Jan. 9, 1939; s. John Douglas and Margaret Shirley (Kummer) H.; m. Lynne Ellen Campbell, Feb. 4, 1967; children—Alison, Mark. B.A. magna cum laude, Yale U., 1960, LL.B., 1964; Woodrow Wilson fellow, 1960; Fulbright scholar Free U. Berlin (Germany), 1960-61. N.Y. 1965, U.S. Ct. Appeals (2d cir.) 1966, Calif., 1967, U.S. Ct. Appeals (9th cir.) 1967, U.S. Dist. Ct. (so. and ea. dists.) N.Y. 1966, U.S. Dist. Ct. (no. dist.) Calif. 1967, U.S. Suprme Ct. 1972, U.S. Ct. Appeals D.C. cir.) 1975. Assoc. Cleary, Gottlieb, Steen & Hamilton, NYC, 1964-67, Cooley, Godward, Castro, Huddleson & Tatum, San Francisco, 1967-71; exec. dir., atty. Sierra Club Legal Def. Fund, Inc., San Francisco, 1972-77, trustee, gen. counsel, 1978—; mem. dir. Ellman, Burke & Cassidy, San Francisco, 1978—. Mem ABA, San Francisco Bar Assn., Sierra Club. Club: Yale (San Francisco). Real property, Civil litigation, Environment. Home: 14 Lincoln Ave Mill Valley CA 94941 Office: Suite 200 One Ecker Bldg San Francisco CA 94105

HOFFMAN, JOHN ERNEST, JR., lawyer; b. N.Y.C., May 1, 1934; s. John E. and Effe K. (Dooling) H.; m. Jean Wheeler, Aug. 13, 1955; children: Jean E., John E., Katherine P., Carolyn W., Christine D. A.B. cum laude, Princeton U., 1955; J.D., Harvard U., 1960. Bar: N.Y. 1961, U.S. Dist. Ct. (so. and ea. dists.) N.Y. 1962, U.S. Dist. Ct. (we. dist.) N.Y. 1963, U.S. Ct. Appeals (2d cir.) 1963, U.S. Supreme Ct. 1964, U.S. Ct. Appeals (3d cir.) 1974, U.S. Ct. Appeals (10th cir.) 1975, U.S. Ct. Appeals (6th cir.) 1986. Assoc. Shearman & Sterling, 1960-68, ptnr., 1968—. Co-author: American Hostages in Iran: The Conduct of a Crisis, 1985. Served to 1st lt. U.S. Army, 1955-57. Fellow Am. Coll. Trial Lawyers; mem. ABA, N.Y.C. Bar Assn., Am. Soc. Internat. Law. Congregationalist. Club: University (N.Y.C.). Federal civil litigation, Private international, Administrative and regulatory. Home: 300 Millwood Rd Chappaqua NY 10514 Office: Shearman & Sterling 153 E 53d St New York NY 10022

HOFFMAN, JOHN FLETHCER, lawyer; b. N.Y.C., May 22, 1946; s. George Fletcher and Helen (Gilbert) H.; m. Coralie Tallman, June 29, 1969; children: Julie Gilbert, William Delano. BS, St. Lawrence U., 1969; JD, Washington and Lee U., 1975. Bar: N.Y. 1976, U.S. Dist. Ct. (so. dist.) N.Y. 1976, U.S. Dist. Ct. (ea. dist.) N.Y. 1978, U.S. Supreme Ct. 1980, U.S. Ct. Appeals (2d cir.) 1982. Assoc. Cadwalader, Wickersham & Taft, N.Y.C., 1975-83, ptnr., 1983—. Trustee 1st Unitarian Congl. Soc. Bklyn, 1980-83, Bklyn. Childrens' Mus., 1985—. Mem. ABA, Fed. Bar Council, N.Y. County Lawyers Assn., Order of Coif, Omicron Delta Kappa. Antitrust, Federal civil litigation, State civil litigation. Office: Cadwalader Wickersham & Taft 100 Maiden Ln New York NY 10038

HOFFMAN, JOHN FREDERICK, lawyer; b. Rochester, Ind., Apr. 2, 1922; s. George Edgar and Ethel Lucille (Yoder) H.; m. Patricia Helen Bennett, July 1, 1950. B.A., U. Mich., 1941; LL.B., Harvard U., 1947, LL.D., 1947. Bar: Ill. 1948, U.S. Dist. Ct. (no. dist.) Ill. 1948, U.S. Ct. Mil. Appeals 1954; Ind. 1957, U.S. Dist. Ct. (no. and so. dists.) Ind. 1958, U.S. Supreme Ct. 1962. Assoc. Bohrer, Blackman & Loman, Chgo., 1947-49, Edward Blackman, Chgo., 1949-56; sole practice, Lafayette, Ind., 1957-68; mem. Hoffman & Melichar, Lafayette, 1969-79; ptnr. Hoffman, Melichar & Luhman, Lafayette, 1980-84, Hoffman & Luhman, 1985—; county atty. Tippecanoe County, 1971-82; dir. Farmers & Mchts. Bank, Rochester, Ind., 1958-85. Mem. Ind. Bar Assn., Ill. Bar Assn., Tippecanoe County Bar Assn., Am. Judicature Soc., Ct. of Appeals of 7th Cir. Assn. Republican. State civil litigation, Federal civil litigation, General practice. Office: 700 The Life Bldg PO Box 99 Lafayette IN 47902

HOFFMAN, JOHN HARRY, lawyer, accountant; b. Chgo., June 18, 1913; s. Dave and Rose (Gewirtzman) H.; J.D., John Marshall Law Sch., 1938; m. Gwen Zollo, Dec. 30, 1949; children—Alana Sue Glickson, Edward Jay, Gayle Beth Hoffman Olsen. Bar: Ill. 1938, U.S. Supreme Ct. 1956. Practice law, Chgo., 1938—; propr. John H. Hoffman & Co., 1952—, ptnr., 1966—; pres. John H. Hoffman, P.C., 1972. C.P.A., Ill. Mem. ABA, Ill. Bar Assn., Chgo. Bar Assn., Decalogue Soc., Am. Inst. C.P.A.s, Ill. Soc. C.P.A.s. Club: Twin Orchard Country (Long Grove, Ill.). Lodges: Masons (32d degree), Shriners, B'nai B'rith. Estate planning, Pension, profit-sharing, and employee benefits, Probate. Office: 221 N LaSalle St Chicago IL 60601

HOFFMAN, JOHN RAYMOND, lawyer; b. Rochester, N.Y., July 24, 1945; s. Raymond Edward and Ruth Emily (Karnes) H.; m. Linda Lee Moore, Aug. 22, 1970; 1 child, Heather Anne. B.A., Washburn U., 1967; J.D., U. Mo.-Kansas City, 1971. Bar: Mo. 1972, Tenn. 1976, Kans. 1980, U.S. Supreme Ct. 1975. Law clk. United Telecom, Kansas City, Mo., 1967-70, gen. atty., 1970-75; gen. counsel, sec. United Telephone System-Southeast Group, Bristol, Tenn., 1975-80; v.p., gen. counsel United Telephone System Inc., Kansas City, Mo., 1980-84; sr. v.p. legal, dir. US Telecom, Inc., Kansas City, Mo., 1984-86 ; sr. v.p. regulatory legis. affairs, US Sprint Communications Co., Kansas City, 1986—. Bd. dirs. Trinity Luth. Hosp., Kansas City, 1984—, Kansas City Young Audiences, Inc., 1981-85, Johnson County Fire Dist., Prairie Village, Kans., 1982-86, Kansas City/Coro Found., 1983-84. Mem. ABA, Mo. Bar Assn., Tenn. Bar Assn., Kans. Bar Assn., Kansas City Bar Assn., Competitive Telecommunications Assn. (pres. 1986—), Kappa Sigma, Phi Delta Phi. Club: Optimist. Public utilities, Administrative and regulatory, General corporate. Home: 6607 Willow Ln Mission Hills KS 66208 Office: US Sprint PO Box 11315 Kansas City MO 64112

HOFFMAN, JOSEPH ANTHONY, lawyer; b. St. Marys, Pa., May 11, 1956; s. Leander Anthony and Betty Jane (Hoffman) H. BA with highest honors, St. Vincent Coll., 1978; JD with honors, U. Tex., 1981. Bar: Tex. 1981, U.S. Dist. Ct. (no. dist.) Tex. 1981. Law clk. U.S. Dept. Justice, Washington, 1979; sr. assoc. Jenkens, Hutchison & Gilchrist, Dallas, 1981—. Mem. 500 Inc. Patron of the Arts, Dallas, 1986—, improvement of city services com. Goals for Dallas, 1986—; bd. dirs. Tex. New Years Com., Dallas, 1983—; co-chmn. social/recreation com. Highland Park Presbyn. Ch., Dallas, 1985—. James R. Dougherty scholar, U. Tex., 1979-80; recipient FAA Achievement award, 1978, Internat. Youth in Achievement award, 1980; named Outstanding Young Men Am. award, 1986. Mem. ABA (corp. banking bus. law sect.), Tex. Bar Assn. (corp. banking bus. law sect., fin. insts. com. 1985—), Dallas Bar Assn., Dallas Young Lawyers Assn. (liason 1986—). Avocations: photography, biking, softball, racquetball, travel. General corporate, Securities. Home: 7145 Bennington Dallas TX 75214 office: Jenkens & Gilchrist 3200 Allied Bank Tower Dallas TX 75202-2711

HOFFMAN, JOSEPH BOWYTZ, lawyer; b. Pitts., Apr. 3, 1957; s. William Lawrence and Barbara Esther (Bowytz) H. BS, U. Md., 1979; JD, George Washington U., 1982. Bar: D.C. 1982, U.S. Tax Ct. 1983; CPA, Md. Assoc. Ginsburg, Feldman & Bress, Washington, 1982—; seminar speaker Am. Horse Council, Washington, 1985. Mem. ABA (tax sect.), D.C. Bar Assn. (tax sect.). Democrat. Jewish. Avocations: horseback riding, tennis, golf, bicycling. Equine law, Personal income taxation, Private international. Home: 1318 22d St NW 301 Washington DC 20037 Office: Ginsburg Feldman & Bress 1250 Connecticut Ave NW 700 Washington DC 20036

HOFFMAN, KRIS, lawyer, shopping center development executive; b. Portland, Oreg., Jan. 5, 1941; s. Lee Hawley and Judith (Scott) H.; m. Elaine Croshier Whitaker; children—Leslie, Kristin, Eric, Carol, Adrienne. B.S., Stanford U., 1962, M.S., 1963, J.D., 1968. Bar: Calif. 1969, U.S. Dist. Ct. (no. dist.) Calif. 1969, U.S. Ct. Appeals (9th cir.) 1969. Assoc. Pettit & Martin, San Francisco, 1969-74; gen. counsel to Sutter Hill Ltd., Palo Alto, Calif., 1975; div. counsel to Kaiser Aetna, Oakland, Calif., 1976; corp. counsel, v.p. store devel. Pay Less Drug Stores, 1977-80; gen. counsel, v.p. store devel., corp. sec. Save Mart Stores, Modesto, Calif., 1980-84; ptnr. Orosco Hoffman, 1984—; lectr. in field. Trustee Meml. Hosp. Found., 1982-85. Stanford U. fellow, 1963. Mem. ABA, Calif. Bar Assn., Fresno County Bar Assn., Internat. Council Shopping Ctrs. General corporate, Landlord-tenant, Real property. Office: Orosco Hoffman 5380 N Fresno St Suite 101 Fresno CA 93710

HOFFMAN, LEONARD ELBERT, JR., retired judge; b. Little Rock, Oct. 16, 1919; s. Leonard Elbert and Fern (Weille) H.; m. Clara Graeber, Mar. 31, 1948; children: Leonard III, Paul F., Gretchen Devine, Sally H. Hurd. Student, Tyler Jr. Coll., 1938-39; LLB, U. Tex., Austin, 1947. Bar: Tex. 1947, U.S. Dist. Ct. (no. dist.) Tex. 1947, U.S. Supreme Ct. 1960. Sole practice Dallas, 1948-49, 54-70; assoc. Ungerman, Hill & Ungerman, Dallas, 1949-54; judge 160th Judicial Dist. Ct., Dallas, 1971-87. Contbr. articles to profl. jours. Mem. adv. bd. St. Philips Episcopal Sch. and Community Ctr.; past chmn. No. Dist. Circle 10 Council Boy Scouts Am., chmn. adv. bd. Mem. ABA, Tex. Bar Assn., Dallas Bar Assn., Am. Judicial Soc., Dallas County Criminal Bar Assn., World Assn. Judges (pres. 1985—), Nat. Congress Met. Courts (bd. dirs. 1985—), State Bar Assn. Tex. (judicial sect.), Nat. Conf. State Trial Judges, Am. Legion, Dallas Colony Mayflower Descendants, Tyler Jr. Coll. Alumni Assn. Republican. Episcopalian. Clubs: High Noon of Dallas; Rock Creek Barbeque. Lodges: Lions, Masons, Shriners. State civil litigation, Judicial administration, Federal civil litigation. Office: 160th Judicial Dist Ct Records Bldg 3rd Fl Dallas TX 75202

HOFFMAN, MARVIN, lawyer; b. Phila., Oct. 23, 1927; s. Samuel and Ann (Wolkin) H.; m. Silver R. Poetash, Dec. 23, 1957; children: Razelle, Eric, Sharon, Adam. BS, Syracuse U., 1949, JD, 1952. Bar: N.Y. 1952, U.S. Dist. Ct. (no. dist.) N.Y. 1952. System atty. Niagara Mohawk Power Corp., Syracuse, N.Y., 1974—. Served with U.S. Army, 1953-55. Mem. Onondaga County Bar Assn. Club: Jewish War Vets. (Syracuse). Avocations: boating, fishing. Environment, Administrative and regulatory, General practice. Home: 111 Cooper Ln Dewitt NY 13214 Office: Niagara Mohawk Power Corp 300 Erie Blvd W Syracuse NY 13202

HOFFMAN, MATHEW, lawyer; b. Bklyn., Mar. 9, 1954; s. S. David and Naomi B. (Brosterman) H.; m. Debra C. Zalkind, Sept. 3, 1978; children: Ari, Gavriel. BA, U. Mich., 1974; JD, Columbia U., 1977. Bar: N.Y. 1978, U.S. Dist. Ct. (so. dist., ea. dist.) N.Y. 1978, U.S. Ct. Appeals (2d cir.) 1980. Atty. Proskauer, Rose, N.Y.C., 1978-80, Gordon, Hurwitz, N.Y.C., 1980-85; ptnr. Koether, Harris & Hoffman, N.Y.C., 1985—. Contbr. articles on securities and products liability to profl. jours. Mem. Jewish Flame (trustee 1979—). Federal civil litigation, Securities, State civil litigation. Home: 41 Vivian Dr Scarsdale NY 10583 Office: Koether Harris & Hoffman 620 Fifth Ave New York NY 10020

HOFFMAN, MICHAEL HARRIS, lawyer; b. Phila., Nov. 29, 1952; s. Howard and Roberta (Birnbaum) H.; m. UnMi Kim, Feb. 27, 1981; children: Paula Kim, Albert Mark. BA in Chinese, Ohio State U., 1975; JD, So. Meth. U., 1978. Bar: Tex. 1978, Md. 1982, D.C. 1983, U.S. Dist. Ct. D.C. 1983, U.S. Dist. Ct. Md. 1984, U.S. Ct. Appeals (D.C. and 4th cirs.) 1985. Sole practice Annapolis, Md., 1982-85, Washington, 1985—; cons. Hoffman Assocs., Washington, 1982—. Legal history advisor Banneker-Douglas Mus., Annapolis, 1983-84; bd. dirs. Korean Social Services, Balt., 1985-86; legal advisor internat. sect. Balt. Red Cross, 1985-86, Balt. Refugee Adv. Team, 1986—. Served to capt. U.S. Army, 1979-82, Korea. Mem. ABA, Fed. Bar Assn., Res. Officers Assn., Civil Affairs Assn., Am. Soc.-Legal History. Republican. Jewish. Avocations: book collecting, travel. Administrative and regulatory, Immigration, naturalization, and customs, Private international. Home: 5925 Cherrywood Terr Apt 104 Greenbelt MD 20770 Office: 4201 Connecticut Ave NW Suite 402 Washington DC 20008

HOFFMAN, PAUL SHAFER, lawyer; b. Harrisburg, Pa., Dec. 12, 1933; s. Paul and Lucy Rose (Shafer) H.; m. Patricia Ann Rudisill, 1958; children: Eric, Kathryn, Julia, Margot. AB in Physics, Gettysburg Coll., 1957; JD, Harvard U., 1962. Bar: N.Y. 1963, U.S. Patent Office 1963, U.S. Dist. Ct. (so. dist.) N.Y. 1977, U.S. Ct. Appeals (2d cir.) 1977, U.S. Supreme Ct. 1977. Assoc. Kenyon & Kenyon, N.Y.C., 1962-63; application analyst IBM-ASDD, Yorktown, N.Y., 1963-66; dir. tech. research Matthew Bender Co., N.Y.C., 1966-68; v.p. Bowne and Co., Inc., N.Y.C., 1968-77; sole practice Croton-on-Hudson, N.Y., 1977—. Mem. Croton (N.Y.) Sch. Bd., 1972-75, pres. 1974-75; trustee Village of Croton-on-Hudson, 1977-81; bd. dirs. Croton Caring Com., Inc., 1982—. Served to cpl. U.S. Army, 1952-54. Mem. ABA (chmn. sci. and tech. sect. 1980-81), N.Y. State Bar Assn., Westchester County Bar Assn., Computer Law Assn. (bd. dirs. 1984—). Republican. Lutheran. Club: Harvard (N.Y.C.). Lodge: Masons. Computer, Trademark and copyright. Office: 139 Grand St PO Box 40 Croton-on-Hudson NY 10520

HOFFMAN, RICHARD BRUCE, lawyer; b. Columbus, Ohio, June 8, 1947; s. Marion Keith and Ruth Eileen (McLear) H.; m. Sandra Kay Schenkel, July 26, 1975; 1 child, Kipp Hunter. BS in Gen. Engring., U. Ill., 1970; JD, DePaul U., 1973; LLM, John Marshall Sch. of Law, 1981. Bar: Ill. 1973, U.S. Dist. Ct. (no. dist.) Ill. 1973, U.S. Patent and Trademark Office 1973, U.S. Ct. Appeals (7th cir.) 1979, U.S. Ct. Appeals (fed. and 9th cirs.) 1982. Assoc. McCaleb, Lucas & Brugman, Chgo., 1973-76, ptnr., 1976-84; ptnr. Tilton, Fallon, Lungmus & Chestnut, Chgo., 1984—. Mem. ABA, Ill. Bar Assn., Chgo. Bar Assn., Patent Law Assn. Chgo. (sec. 1980-82), Am. Intellectual Property Law Assn., U.S. Trademark Assn. Club: Legal, Union League (Chgo.). Avocations: bicycling, canoeing, antique furniture restoration. Patent, Trademark and copyright, Federal civil litigation. Office: Tilton Fallon Lungmus & Chestnut 100 S Wacker Dr #960 Chicago IL 60606

HOFFMAN, RICHARD (MELVIN), lawyer; b. N.Y.C., Oct. 22, 1942; s. Simon and Pearl (Lancet) H.; children—Mark, Michael. Grad., CCNY, 1964; LL.B., Bklyn. Sch. Law, 1967. Bar: N.Y. 1968. Law clk. to presiding judge U.S. Dist. Ct. (ea. dist.) N.Y., N.Y.C., 1967-69; assoc. Kramer, Lowenstein, Nessen & Kamin, N.Y.C., 1969-73; various positions legal dept. Gen. Instrument Corp., N.Y.C., 1973-82, v.p., gen. counsel, 1982-86, v.p. gen. counsel, sec., 1986—. Mem. N.Y.C. Bar Assn. (com. corp. law depts. 1981-84). General corporate, Securities, Private international. Home: 60 Brite Ave Scarsdale NY 10583 Office: Gen Instrument Corp 767 Fifth Ave New York NY 10153

HOFFMAN, ROBERT B., lawyer; b. Chgo., Oct. 11, 1938; s. Raphael and Maxine Lee (Marienthal) H.; m. Catherine Janda; children—David, Cynthia, Michael. B.S., U. Wis., 1960; J.D., Northwestern U., 1963. Bar: Calif. 1963, Ill. 1968, U.S. Supreme Ct. 1968, U.S. Ct. Appeals (5th cir.) 1968, U.S. Ct. Appeals (6th cir.) 1968, U.S. Ct. Appeals (7th cir.) 1968, (9th cir.) 1965. Atty., NLRB, San Francisco, 1963-68; sr. ptnr. Arnstein, Gluck, Lehr, Barron & Milligan, Chgo., 1968-86, chmn. labor dept., 1968-86, chmn. hiring com., 1977-82, mem. exec. com., 1979-81; ptnr. Laner, Muchin, Dombrow & Becker, Chgo., 1986—; arbitrator Ill. Labor Relations Bd., 1986—, Ill. Ednl. Labor Relations Bd., 1986—; hearing officer Ill. Bd. Edn., 1986—. Mem. ABA, Calif. Bar Assn., Chgo. Bar Assn., Am. Arbitration Assn. (labor arbitration panel 1969—). Club: Metropolitan (Chgo.). Contbr. articles to legal publs. Labor. Office: 350 N Clark St Chicago IL 60610

HOFFMAN, ROBERT DEAN, JR., lawyer; b. New Orleans, Dec. 15, 1954; s. Robert Dean Sr. and Ruth Ann (Wheelahan) H. BS, Auburn U., 1975; JD, Loyola U., New Orleans, 1978; LLM in Taxation, Emory U., 1980. Bar: La. 1978, U.S. Dist. Ct. (ea. dist.) La. 1978, U.S. Ct. Appeals (5th cir.) 1979, U.S. Tax. Ct. 1981, U.S. Ct. Appeals (11th cir.) 1981, U.S. Dist. Ct. (mid. dist.) La. 1982. Ptnr. Ballin & Hoffman, New Orleans, 1978—. Lanaza-Greco Meml scholar Loyola U., 1978. Mem. ABA, La. Bar Assn. Club: Over the Mountain Athletic (commr. 1985—, sportsmanship award 1986). Personal income taxation, Real property, Contracts commercial. Home: #2 Duckhook Dr New Orleans LA 70118 Office: Ballin & Hoffman 210 Baronne St Suite 920 New Orleans LA 70112

HOFFMAN, ROBERT JOSEPH, lawyer; b. Boston, June 16, 1928; s. Harry and Lauretta (Goldberg) H.; m. Phyllis Jane Elhady, Jan. 6, 1973; children: Daniel Nathan, Elizabeth Ann. AB magna cum laude, Harvard U., 1951, JD, 1954. Bar: Mass. 1954, U.S. Dist. Ct. Mass. 1955, U.S. Ct. Appeals (1st. cir.) 1957, U.S. Supreme Ct. 1962. Assoc. Hoffman & Hoffman, Boston, 1954-55, ptnr., 1958—; asst. U.S. atty. U.S. Dept. Justice,

Boston, 1955-58. Mem. Mass. Bar Assn., Boston Bar Assn., Mass. Assn. Bank Counsel (exec. bd.), Mass. Conveyancers Assn. (exec. bd., pres. 1986). Clubs: Harvard (Boston); Vineyard Haven Yacht (Martha's Vineyard, Mass.) (bd. govs. exec. com.). Avocations: music, reading, skiing, tennis. Real property, General practice. Office: Hoffman & Hoffman 44 School St 6th Floor Boston MA 02108

HOFFMAN, S. DAVID, lawyer; educator; b. N.Y.C., June 16, 1922; s. Joseph and Ida (Katz) H.; m. Naomi Barbara Brosterman, June 30, 1946; children—Mathew E., Robert Adam. B.E. in Elec. Engring., Yale U., 1945; J.D., St. John's U., N.Y.C., 1955. Bar: N.Y. 1955, Ill. 1981, U.S. Ct. Mil. Apls. 1961, U.S. Pat. Off. 1964, U.S. Sup. Ct. 1960. Engr., Western Electric Co., N.Y.C. and Newark, 1946-49; resident legal csl. Am. Nat. Standards Inst., N.Y.C., 1955-66, dir. contracts and cert., 1955-66, head elec. engr., 1949-66; v.p., gen. csl. Underwriters Labs. Inc., Northbrook, Ill., 1966—; adj. prof. div. of indsl. and systems engring. dept. mech. engring. U. Ill., Chgo., 1974—. Mem. indsl. adv. bd. U. Ill., Chgo. Served with USNR, 1942-46, 50-52. Recipient Joint award ASTM-Standards Engring. Soc., 1980. Fellow Standards Engring. Soc. (Leo B. Moore medal 1980); mem. Assn. Trial Lawyers Am., ABA, Def. Research Inst., N.Y. State Bar Assn., ASTM. Clubs: Yale, Internat. (Chgo.); Yale (N.Y.C.); Mission Hills Country (Northbrook). Contbr. numerous articles to profl. jours. General corporate, Federal civil litigation, Administrative and regulatory. Office: 333 Pfingsten Rd Northbrook IL 60062

HOFFMAN, STUART KENNETH, lawyer; b. Phila., Dec. 16, 1949; s. Isadore and Lorraine (Schwartz) H.; m. Stephanie R. Heckerling, July 31, 1977; children: Jarrett Reid, Darren Philip. BS, NYU, 1971; JD, Am. U., 1974. Bar: Fla. 1974. Assoc. Corrigan & Salas, Miami, Fla., 1975, Becker & Poliakoff, Miami, 1975-78, Schwartz & Nash, Miami, 1978-84; ptnr. Fine, Jacobson, Schwartz, Nash, Block & England P.A., Miami, 1984—. Democrat. Jewish. Real property. Office: Fine Jacobson Schwartz Nash Block & England PA 777 Brickell Ave Miami FL 33131

HOFFMAN, THOMAS JOSEPH, lawyer; b. Chgo., Aug. 15, 1956; s. James Walter and Carolyn June (Eckerty) H.; m. Cecelia Lynn Schwab, July 29, 1978; 1 child, Megan Amber. BS cum laude, Bradley U., 1977; JD with high distinction, John Marshall Sch. Law, 1981. Bar: Ill. 1981. Assoc. Claudon, Lloyd, Barnhart & Beal, Ltd., Canton, Ill., 1981-83, Drendel, Schanlaber, Horwitz & Tatnall, P.C. and predecessor firm Drendel, Schanlaber & Horwitz, P.C., Aurora, Ill., 1983—. Advisor Nat. Alliance for Energy Contingency Planning for Health Resources, Colorado Springs, Colo., 1984—. Mem. Ill. Bar Assn. (sec. Fulton County 1981-82), Order John Marshall. Lodge: Kiwanis (sec. Canton 1982-83). General corporate, Probate, Contracts commercial. Home: 18 Hawthorne Dr North Aurora IL 60542 Office: Drendel Schanlaber & Horwitz PC 520 Redwood Dr Aurora IL 60506

HOFFMAN, WALTER EDWARD, judge; b. Jersey City, July 18, 1907; s. Walter and Ella Adele (Sharp) H.; m. Evelyn Virginia Watkins, Apr. 6, 1939 (dec.); m. 2d Helen Caulfield, Nov. 6, 1971; children—Carole Hoffman Hancock, Walter Edward. B.S. in Econs., U. Pa., 1928; postgrad. Coll. William and Mary Law Sch., 1928-29, LL.D., 1985; LL.B., Washington and Lee U., 1931, LL.D., 1970. Bar: Va. 1929, U.S. Dist. Ct. (ea. dist.) Va. 1930, U.S. Supreme Ct. 1945; assoc. Rumble & Rumble, Norfolk, Va., 1931-35; ptnr. Breeden & Hoffman, Norfolk, 1935-54; judge U.S. Dist. Ct. Va., Norfolk, 1954-74, sr. judge 1974—; instr. Coll. William and Mary, 1933-40, asst. prof. law, 1940-42, vis. prof. law, 1977-78 chmn. adv. com. on criminal rules, 1978-84, mem. Standing com. on rules and practice, 1984—; chmn. Conf. Met. Chief Judges, 1977-86. Recipient Herbert Harley award Am. Judicature Soc., 1976; Devitt award for disting. service to cause of administrn. of justice, 1983. Mem. ABA, Va. State Bar Assn. Methodist. Clubs: Cosmopolitan of Norfolk (pres. 1953), Norfolk Yacht and Country; Princess Anne Country (Virginia Beach, Va.); Masons, Shriners (past potentate). Criminal, Admiralty, Federal civil litigation. Office: US Courthouse Room 314 Norfolk VA 23510

HOFFMANN, MALCOLM ARTHUR, lawyer; b. N.Y.C., Nov. 26, 1912; s. Abraham A. and Minna (Newmark) H.; m. Anna Frances Luciano, Apr. 13, 1939 (dec.); children—Gertrude Nina (Mrs. William Bolter), Jessica Ann (Mrs. William Merritt Davis). BA magna cum laude, Harvard U., 1934, JD, 1937. Bar: N.Y. 1938, U.S. Supreme Ct. 1943, U.S. Dist. Ct. (so. and ea. dist.) N.Y., U.S. Dist. Ct. Conn., U.S. Ct. Appeals (1st, 2d, 3d, 5th, 11th and D.C. cirs.). Sr. atty. NLRB, 1939-43; spl. atty. appellate sect. criminal div. Dept. Justice, 1943, spl. asst. to atty. gen. U.S. antitrust div., 1944-55; of counsel Greenbaum, Wolff and Ernst, N.Y.C., 1959-60; prin. Law Firm of Malcom A. Hoffman, N.Y.C., 1960—; lectr. Practising Law Inst.; mem. faculty Joint Com. on Continuing Legal Edn., Am. Law Inst., ABA, 1966; lectr. trade problems Am. Mgmt. Assn., 1967-71; lectr. antitrust sect. meeting ABA, Honolulu, 1967, lectr. litigation sect. meeting, San Francisco, 1976. Author: Government Lawyer, 1955; Lawyers Heritage, 1956, (with M. L. Ernst) Back and Forth, 1966; editor: Hoffmann's Antitrust Law and Techniques, 2 vols. 1963; co-editor: Monopolies, Markets and Mergers; contbr. articles to profl. jours. Chmn. bd. Hoffmann Sch., Inc. Fellow Am. Bar Found.; mem. World Assn. Lawyers (founder), Am. Judicature Soc., ABA (vice chmn. com.), Internat. Bar Assn., Fed. Bar Assn., N.Y. State Bar Assn. (past chmn. com., exec. com.), Assn. of Bar of City of N.Y. (past chmn. subcom.), Fed. Bar Council (past sec. trade regulation com.). Clubs: Harvard Talk (chmn.) (N.Y.C.). Antitrust, State civil litigation, Federal civil litigation. Home: 5440 Independence Ave Riverdale NY 10471 Office: 12 E 41st St New York NY 10017

HOFFMANN, MICHAEL RICHARD, lawyer; b. Des Moines, Apr. 26, 1947; s. Robert Wyman Hoffmann and Margaret Inez (Wagner) H., stepson Patricia Hilliard; m. Carol Elaine Tomb, July 29, 1973; children—Kurt Michael, Kristen Elaine, Kevin Richard. B.S. in Chemistry and Zoology, U. Iowa, 1969; J.D., Drake U., 1972; LL.M. in Patent and Trade Regulation, George Washington U., 1973. Bar: Iowa 1972, U.S. Ct. Customs and Patent Appeals 1972, U.S. Patent and Trademark Office 1973, U.S. Dist. Ct. (so. and no. dists.) Iowa 1974, U.S. Ct. Appeals (8th cir.) 1976, U.S. Supreme Ct. 1977. Clerk Jones, Hoffmann & Davison, Des Moines, 1970-73; assoc. Bacon and Thomas, Arlington, Va., 1973-74; assoc. Jones, Hoffmann & Davison, Des Moines, 1974-79, ptnr., 1979-83; pres. Michael R. Hoffmann, P.C., Des Moines, 1983—; mem. Iowa Def. Counsel, Def. Research Inst., Inc. Recipient Am. Jurisprudence award Bancroft-Whitney Co. and Lawyers Coop. Pub. Co., 1970-72. Mem. Iowa State Bar Assn., ABA (sci. and tech. sect.), Iowa Patent Bar Assn. (charter mem.), Am. Patent Law Assn., Am. Judicature Soc., Polk County Bar Assn., Iowa Assn. Workers' Compensation Lawyers. Phi Alpha Delta (dist. marshall 1970). Lutheran. Clubs: Prairie (Des Moines); Nat. Rifle (Washington). Workers' compensation, Personal injury, Insurance. Office: Jones Hoffmann & Davison 1000 Des Moines Bldg Des Moines IA 50309

HOFFMANN, ULRICH VICTOR, lawyer, airline company executive; b. Munich, Federal Republic Germany, Sept. 15, 1928; s. Rudolf F. and Amelie M. Hoffman; m. Barbara Anne Boyle, May 11, 1957; children: Michael U., Donald R., Kathleen A. B.S., Georgetown U., 1952, LL.B., 1956. Bars: D.C. 1956, U.S. Ct. Appeals (D.C. cir.) 1956, U.S. Supreme Ct. 1963. Atty. CAB, 1956-64; gen. atty. Trans World Airlines, Inc., N.Y.C., 1964-68; asst. gen. counsel Trans World Airlines, Inc., 1968-78, v.p., gen. counsel, 1978-82, sr. v.p. external affairs, gen. counsel, 1984—. Served with U.S. Army, 1952-54. Democrat. Roman Catholic. Home: 437 Belden Hill Rd Wilton CT 06897 Office: Trans World Airlines Inc 605 3d Ave New York NY 10158 *

HOFFMEYER, WILLIAM FREDERICK, lawyer; b. York, Pa., Dec. 20, 1936; s. Frederick W. and Mary B. (Stremmel) H.; m. Betty J. Hoffmeyer, Feb. 6, 1960 (divorced); 1 child, Louise C.; m. Karen L. Semmelman, 1985. AB, Franklin and Marshall Coll., 1958; JD, Dickinson Sch. Law, 1961. Bar: Pa. 1962, U.S. Dist. Ct. (mid. dist.) Pa. 1981. Sole practice, 1962-81; sr. ptnr. Hoffmeyer & Semmelman, 1982—; instr. York Coll., Pa. State U., York and Capitol Campuses. Author: The Abstractor's Bible, 1981, Pennsylvania Real Estate Installment Sales Contract Manual, 1981, Real Estate Settlement Procedures, 1982, Contracts of Sale, 1985, How to Plot a Deed Description, 1986; author and lectr. of Pa. Bar Inst.'s audio-cassette program: Recent and Recently Remembered Developments in Real Estate Financing, 1981, and numerous other programs. Mem. ABA, Pa. Bar Assn., York County Bar Assn., York County Bd. Realtors. Lodges: Lions; Masons. Real property, General practice. Address: 30 N George St York PA 17401

HOFFSTOT, HENRY PHIPPS, JR., lawyer; b. Pitts., Nov. 13, 1917; s. Henry Phipps and Marguerite (Martin) H.; m. Barbara Drew, Apr. 17, 1948; children: Thayer Drew Hoffstot Unterman, Henry Phipps, III. A.B., Harvard U., 1939, LL.B., 1942. Bar: Pa. bar 1942. Asso. firm Reed Smith Shaw & McClay, Pitts., 1946-55; partner Reed Smith Shaw & McClay, 1956—; pres., dir. Pennsgrove Water Supply Co., 1967-84; Adv. bd. Biltmore Co., 1985—. Active Commn. for Study of Common Body of Knowledge for C.P.A.s, N.Y., 1965-67, Nat. Parks Centennial Commn., 1971-73; trustee Carnegie Library, Pitts., 1966—, v.p., 1970—; trustee Carnegie Inst., 1966—, sec., 1968—; supervising com. Bellefield Boiler Plant, 1967—, chmn., 1978—; trustee Family and Children's Service, 1962-68, 69-75, 77-83, pres., 1964-66; trustee Pitts. Regional Library Center, 1967—; trustee St. Edmunds Acad., 1964-72, pres., 1968-70; bd. dirs. Community Chest of Allegheny County, 1962-68, exec. com., 1968-69; bd. dirs. Mendelssohn Choir, Pitts., 1958-85, treas., 1959-61; bd. dirs. Pitts. Chamber Music Soc., 1968—; bd. dirs. Vis. Nurse Assn. of Allegheny County, 1948—, pres., 1957-60, 66-67, 79-83; mem. council Am. Mus. in Britain, 1979—; trustee, v.p. Phipps Friends, 1985—; bd. dirs. Pitts. chpt. World Federalist Assn., 1967—. Served with inf. AUS, 1942-46. Fellow Am. Bar Found.; mem. ABA, Pa. Bar Assn., Allegheny County Bar Assn., Am. Coll. Probate Counsel, Am. Law Inst., SAR (pres. Pitts. chpt. 1978-79). Presbyterian. Clubs: Economic (Pitts.) (dir. 1978-79), Duquesne (Pitts.), Harvard-Yale-Princeton (Pitts.), Pitts. Golf (Pitts.); Rolling Rock, Harvard (N.Y.C.); Bath and Tennis, Everglades (Palm Beach). General corporate, Estate planning, Probate. Home: 5057 5th Ave Pittsburgh PA 15232 Office: Reed Smith Shaw & McClay Mellon Sq 6th Ave & William Penn Pittsburgh PA 15219-1886

HOFMANN, WILLIAM ECKHARDT, lawyer; b. Chicago Heights, Ill., Mar. 12, 1949; s. Charles Eckhardt and Frieda Marie (Bleichroth) H.; m. Maryellen Duffy, July 11, 1981. BA, Carleton Coll., 1971; JD, Washington U., St. Louis, 1974. Bar: Ill. 1974, U.S. Dist. Ct. (no. dist.) Ill. 1974, U.S. Tax Ct. 1977, U.S. Supreme Ct. 1980. Sole practice Chgo., 1976—. Trustee Chicago Heights Symphony Orch., 1976-80. Mem. ABA, Ill. Bar Assn., Chgo. Bar Assn. Republican. Presbyterian. Lodge: Rotary (past dir.). General corporate, Probate, Real property. Office: 36 W Randolph #500 Chicago IL 60601

HOFRICHTER, LAWRENCE S., lawyer; b. Bklyn., May 22, 1947; s. Norman and Ethel May (Isaacson) H.; m. Frima Fox, June 28, 1969; children: Michael Eli Fox, Lee Harris Fox. AB, NYU, 1968, JD, 1971. Bar: N.Y. 1972. Law asst. law dept. The Port Authority of N.Y. and N.J., N.Y.C., 1971-72; atty. fin. div., law dept. Port Authority of N.Y. and N.J., N.Y.C., 1972-79, asst. chief fin. div., law dept., 1979-80, dep. chief fin. div., law dept., 1980-86, chief fin. div., law dept., 1986—, also sec. adv. group, 1976, chairperson, 1977. Treas., pres. Alumni Assn. Lafayette High Sch., Bklyn., 1968-78. Mem. ABA (employment taxes com., taxation sect., state and local govt. bargaining com., labor and employment law sect.), N.Y. State Bar Assn. (tax exempt bonds com., employee benefits com. tax sect., life, health and accident ins. com., ins., negligence and compensation law sect., labor and employment law sect.), N.Y. County Lawyers Assn., Nat. Assn. Bond Lawyers. Lodge: K.P. Municipal bonds, Labor, Local government. Office: The Port Authority of NY and NJ One World Trade Ctr Room 66 E New York NY 10048

HOFSTADTER, SARAH KATHERINE, lawyer; b. N.Y.C., July 22, 1952; d. Richard and Beatrice (Kevitt) Hofstadter White. B.A. magna cum laude, Princeton U., 1974; J.D., Stanford U., 1978. Bar: Calif. 1978, U.S. Dist. Ct. (no. dist.) Calif. 1978, U.S. Ct. Appeals (9th cir.) 1978, U.S. Dist. Ct. (cen. dist.) Calif. 1981. Law clk. U.S. Ct. Appeals (9th cir.), San Francisco, 1978-80; law clk. to presiding justice U.S. Dist. Ct. (no. dist.), San Francisco, 1980-81; assoc. firm Howard, Rice, Nemerovski, Canady, Robertson & Falk, P.C., San Francisco, 1981—; instr. New Coll. Calif. Sch. Law, San Francisco, 1979-80; mem. bd. visitors Stanford (Calif.) Law Sch., 1985—. Bd. dirs. Bar Assn. San Francisco, 1987—, Stanford Pub. Interest Law Found., 1979-81. Mem. ABA, ACLU, Calif. Women Lawyers Assn., Bar Assn. San Francisco (state bar conf. of dels. 1985—), San Francisco Women Lawyers Alliance, Bay Area Lawyers for Individual Freedom, Phi Beta Kappa. Democrat. Federal civil litigation, State civil litigation. Office: Howard Rice Nemerovski et al 3 Embarcadero Ctr # 700 San Francisco CA 94111

HOGAN, CLAUDE HOLLIS, lawyer; b. Bishop, Calif., Mar. 2, 1920; s. Claude Hollis and Emma Janet (Slade) H.; m. June Cunningham, June 12, 1946; 1 child, Patricia. A.B., Coll. of Pacific, 1942; LLB., Yale U., 1948. Bar: Calif. 1949. Assoc. Pillsbury, Madison & Sutro, San Francisco, 1948-58, ptnr., 1959—. Contbr. articles to profl. jours. D. dirs. Ernest D. van Loben Sels- Eleanor Slate van Loben Sels Charitable Found., San Francisco, 1964—; pres. Ernest D. van Loben Sels-Eleanor Slate van Loben Sels Charitable Found., 1971—; mem. San Francisco Lawyers Com. on Urban Affairs, 1973—, com-chmn., 1978; bd. dirs. Legal Aid Soc. San Francisco, 1974—; trustee Lawyers Com. for Civil Rights under Law, 1980—; pres. Child Care Law Ctr., 1985-87, bd. dirs., 1985-87. Mem. State Bar Calif. (exec. com. taxation sect. 1975-76, bd. legal specialization 1981-85), ABA, Bar Assn. San Francisco (chmn. taxation sect. 1970, dir. 1978, pres. found. 1983-84), Internat. Fiscal Assn., Am. Judicature Soc., Calif. C. of C. (tax com. 1973-81). Corporate taxation, Personal income taxation, State and local taxation. Office: Pillsbury Madison & Sutro Standard Oil Bldg 225 Bush St San Francisco CA 94104

HOGAN, ROBERT B., lawyer; b. Cin., June 11, 1947; s. Robert G. and Mary (Ball) H.; m. Kathy Bradford, Aug. 9, 1980. BS, Georgetown U., 1969; JD, U. Cin., 1972; LLM in Taxation, NYU, 1974. Bar: Ohio 1972. Sole practice tax law Cin., 1974-81; tax supr. KMG Main Hurdman, Cin., 1981-83; atty. Union Cen. Life Ins. Co., Cin., 1983-85, tax counsel, 1985—; tax counsel Carillon Life Ins. Co., Cin., 1985—, Carillon Investments, Cin., 1986—. Served to 1st lt. USAF, 1973. Fellow Life Mgmt. Inst.; mem. Cin. Bar Assn., Tax Execs. Inst. Corporate taxation, State and local taxation, Insurance. Office: Union Cen Life Ins Co PO Box 179 Cincinnati OH 45201

HOGAN, THOMAS FRANCIS, district judge; b. Washington, May 31, 1938; s. Bartholomew W. and Grace (Gloninger) H.; m. Martha Lou Wyrick, July 16, 1966; 1 son, Thomas Garth. A.B., Georgetown U., 1960, J.D., 1966; postgrad., George Washington U., 1960-62. Bar: Md. 1966, U.S. Dist. Ct. D.C. 1967, D.C. 1967, U.S. Ct. Appeals (D.C. cir.) 1972, U.S. Dist. Ct. Md. 1973, U.S. Supreme Ct. 1973. Law clk. to presiding judge U.S. Dist. Ct. D.C., 1966-67; counsel Nat. Commn. on Reform of Fed. Criminal Laws, Washington, 1967-68; ptnr. McCarthy & Wharton, Rockville, Md., 1968-75, Kenary, Tietz & Hogan, Rockville, 1975-81, Furey, Doolan, Abell & Hogan, Chevy Chase, Md., 1981-82; U.S. dist. judge U.S. Dist. Ct. D.C., Washington, 1982—; asst. prof. Potomac Sch. Law, Washington, 1977-79. Pub. mem. Officer Evaluation Bd. U.S. Fgn. Service, 1973; chmn. Christ Child Inst. for Disturbed Children, 1975; bd. dirs. Providence Hosp., Washington. Recipient cert. recognition and appreciation for vol. services Montgomery County Govt., 1976; recipient cert. appreciation Christ Child Soc., 1976; St. Thomas More fellow Georgetown U. Law Ctr., 1965-66. Mem. ABA (Md. chmn. Drug Abuse Edn. Program, Young Lawyers sect. 1970-73, mem. Litigation sect.), Bar Assn. D.C. (mem. com. on D.C. cts.), Md. State Bar Assn. (Litigation sect.), Montgomery County Bar Assn. (chmn. legal ethics com. 1973-74, lawyer referral service com. 1974-75, adminstrn. justice com. 1979-82, bd. govs. 1977-78), Nat. Inst. for Trial Advocacy Assocs., Def. Research Inst., Md. Assn. Def. Trial Counsel, Md. Trial Lawyers Assn., Georgetown U. Alumni Assn., Smithsonian Assocs., John Carroll Soc. Clubs: Barristers, Chevy Chase. State civil litigation, Federal civil litigation, Probate. Office: US Dist Ct US Courthouse 3d and Constitution Ave NW Washington DC 20001 *

HOGEN, PHILIP NERE, U.S. attorney; b. Kadoka, S.D., Nov. 15, 1944; s. Marvis and Florence (Brown) H.; m. Marilyn J. Teupel, June 30, 1970; children—Vanya Sue, Herbert Hoover. B.S., Augustana Coll., 1967; J.D., U. S.D., 1970. Bar: S.D. 1970, U.S. Dist. Ct. S.D. 1970, U.S. Ct. Appeals (8th cir.) 1981. Ptnr. Larson & Hogen, Kennebec, S.D., 1970-72; adminstrv. asst. S.D. congressman James Abdnor, Washington, 1973-74; states atty. Jackson County States Atty.'s Office, Kadoka, S.D., 1975-81; U.S. atty. U.S. Dist. Ct. S.D., Sioux Falls, 1981—. Chmn., Lyman County Republican Central Com., S.D., 1972, Jackson County Rep. Central Com., S.D., 1975-81; chmn. platform com. S.D. Rep. Central Com., Pierre, 1978. Served with USAR, 1964-70. Mem. ABA, Fed. Bar Assn., S.D. Bar Assn., S.D. States Attys. Assn. (pres. 1979-81). Lutheran. Federal civil litigation, Criminal. Home: 4408 S Highland Sioux Falls SD 57103 Office: US Attys Office 400 S Phillips Sioux Falls SD 57102

HOGG, JESSE STEPHEN, lawyer; b. Whitesburg, Ky., Dec. 24, 1931; s. Doyle and Crystal (Eversole) H.; m. Lorella Joyce Graham, Jan. 26, 1957 (div. 1978); children: Laura Ellen, Stephen Graham. BSBA, Morehead State U., 1953; JD, U. Ky., 1958. Bar: Ky. 1958, Fla. 1962, U.S. Dist. Ct. (no., middle and so. dists.) Fla., U.S. Ct. Appeals (2d, 4th, 5th, 6th, 11th cirs.), U.S. Supreme Ct. Sole practice Winchester, Ky., 1958-62; assoc. Fowler, White, Collins, Gillan, Humkey and Trenam, Tampa, Fla., 1962-65, ptnr., 1965-68, head dept. labor law, 1968-69; sr. ptnr. Hogg, Allan, Ryce, Norton and Blue P.A., various locations, Fla., 1969—. Served with U.S. Army, 1954-55. Mem. ABA (lab law sect. 1962—), Fla. Bar Assn. (labor law com. 1962—), Ky. Bar Assn. Republican. Club: Ocean Reef. Avocations: boating, sport fishing. Labor, Federal civil litigation, State civil litigation. Home: 7701 Erwin Rd Coral Gables FL 33143 Office: Hogg et al 121 Majorca Ave Coral Gables FL 33134

HOGG, STEPHEN LESLIE, lawyer; b. Covington, Ky., Jan. 26, 1953; s. Floyd Byrd and Wanda Mae (Hill) H.; m. Juanita Rae Locke, Aug. 22, 1980; 1 child, Chelsea Marie Fletcher. BBA, U. Ky., 1976; JD, No. Ky. U., 1980. Bar: Ky. 1980, Fla. 1981, U.S. Dist. Ct. (ea. dist.) Ky. 1981, U.S. Ct. Appeals (6th cir.) 1983, U.S. Supreme Ct. 1987. Assoc. Stratton, May & Hays, Pikeville, Ky., 1980—. Democrat. Banking, Consumer commercial, Oil and gas leasing. Home: 153 Pem Friend Ln Pikeville KY 41501 Office: Stratton May & Hays PO Drawer 851 Pikeville KY 41501

HOGSHIRE, EDWARD LEIGH, lawyer; b. Norfolk, Va., Apr. 14, 1943; s. Russell Blake and Margaret Maria (Johnston) H.; m. Martha Alsop Kent, Aug. 29, 1970; children—Edward Carlisle, Charles Kent. B.A. in English, J.D., U. Va. Bar: Va. 1970, D.C. 1972. Staff atty. Council of Better Bus. Burs., Washington, 1971-72; dir. Student Legal Services, Charlottesville, Va., 1972-73; assoc. Lowe & Gordon, Ltd., 1973-76; ptnr. Paxson, Smith, Boyd, Gilliam & Gouldman, 1976-82, Buck, Hogshire & Gouldman, Ltd., Charlottesville, 1982—; lectr. in law U. Va. Sch. Law, 1980—. Chmn. Criminal Justice Adv. Council, Charlottesville, 1975-76; pres. Charlottesville/Albemarle Mental Health Assn., 1981-83. Served as 1st lt. U.S. Army, 1965-67. Recipient Scribner-Garnett award Charlottesville/Albemarle Mental Health Assn., 1981; Cert. of Merit, Criminal Justice Adv. Council, Thomas Jefferson Planning Dist. Com., 1978. Mem. Va. Bar Assn. (jud. com. 1977—, young lawyers conf., statewide coordinator inmate assistance project 1977-79, Citation for Significant Service), ABA, Va. Trial Lawyers Assn. Democrat. Episcopalian. State civil litigation, Criminal, Labor. Office: Buck Hogshire & Gouldman Ltd 400 Court Sq Charlottesville VA 22901

HOGUE, L(OUIS) LYNN, legal educator; b. Little Rock, Jan. 8, 1944; s. Benton and Maxine (Otey) H.; m. Carol Jane Rowland, May 28, 1966. AB magna cum laude, William Jewell Coll., 1966; MA, U. Tenn., 1968, PhD, 1972; JD, Duke U., 1974. Bar: N.C. 1974, Ark. 1979, U.S. Supreme Ct. 1979, Ga. 1983. Asst. prof. pub. law and govt. U. N.C. Inst. of Govt., Chapel Hill, 1974-76; vis. asst. prof. law U. Detroit, 1977; from asst. prof. to assoc. prof. U. Ark., Little Rock, 1977-82; prof. law Ga. State U., Atlanta, 1982-86, assoc. dean acad. affairs, 1986—. Editor: Public Health and the Law, 1980. Mem. Am. Soc. for Legal History (sec.). Democrat. Episcopalian. Legal education, Civil rights, Legal history. Home: 797 Cumberland Rd NE Atlanta GA 30306 Office: Ga State U Coll of Law University Plaza Atlanta GA 30303-3092

HOGUE, TERRY GLYNN, lawyer; b. Merced, Calif., Sept. 23, 1944; s. Glynn Dale and Lillian LaVonne (Carter) H.; m. Joanne Laura Sharples, Oct. 3, 1969; children: Morgan Taylor, Whitney Shannon. BA, U. Calif., Fresno, 1966, postgrad., 1967; JD, U. Calif., San Francisco, 1972. Bar: Calif. 1972, U.S. Dist. Ct. (cen. dist.) Calif. 1973, Idaho 1975, U.S. Dist. Ct. Idaho 1975, U.S. Supreme Ct. 1976. Assoc. Reed, Babbage & Coyle, Riverside, Calif., 1972-75; sole practice Hailey, Idaho, 1975-77; ptnr. Campion & Hogue, Hailey, 1977-80, Hogue & Speck, Hailey and Ketchum, Idaho, 1980-82, Hogue, Speck & Aanestad, Hailey and Ketchum, Idaho, 1982—. Bd. dirs. Blaine County Med. Ctr., Hailey, 1975—. Served to sgt. U.S. Army, 1969-71. Mem. ABA, Calif. Bar Assn., Idaho Bar Assn., Idaho Trial Lawyers Assn. (bd. govs. 1982—, treas. 1985-86, sec. 1986-87), Hailey C. of C. (bd. dirs. 1975-83). Lodge: Rotary (bd. dirs. Hailey club 1975-80). General practice. Home: PO Box 1259 Ketchum ID 83340 Office: Hogue Speck & Aanestad 120 East Ave Box 987 Ketchum ID 83340

HOHMAN, A.J., JR., lawyer; b. San Antonio, Dec. 19, 1934; s. A.J. and Helen (Stehling) H.; m. Mary C. Leonard, Aug. 30, 1958; children: Kristin Marie, Jonathan David. BA in Econs., St Mary's U., San Antonio, 1959, LLB, 1959. Bar: Tex. 1961, U.S. Dist. Ct. (we. and so. dists.) Tex. 1970, U.S. Ct. Appeals (5th cir.) 1971; U.S. Supreme Ct. 1971. Asst. dist. atty. Bexar County, San Antonio, 1961-64; ptnr. Hope, Hohman & Georges, San Antonio, 1964-87. Editor: Barrister News, 1958-59. Bd. dirs. St. Peter's and St. Joseph's Ch's Homes, San Antonio, 1974-87, pres. 1980-81, 86-87; pres. Ursuline Acad., San Antonio, 1982-84, bd. dirs. 1984-87. Served to 1st lt. U.S. Army, 1959-61. Fellow Am. Bd. Trial Advocates (pres. San Antonio chpt. 1983-84); mem. Tex. Trial Lawyers Assn. (assoc. dir. 1981-87), San Antonio Trial Lawyers Assn. (pres. 1980), Am. Trial Lawyers Assn. (1975-87). Democrat. Roman Catholic. Avocations: travel, all outdoor activities, reading. Personal injury, State civil litigation. Office: Hope Hohman & Georges 301 W Market St San Antonio TX 78205

HOHN, MICHAEL, lawyer; b. Columbus, Ohio, Dec. 27, 1948; s. Robert William and Esther (Day) H.; m. Sharon Ann Dickman, May 18, 1985. BA, Coll. Wooster, 1970; JD, Ohio State U., 1974. Bar: Ohio 1974, U.S. Dist. Ct. (so. dist.) Ohio 1976, U.S Tax Ct. 1984. Asst. gen. counsel Landmark Inc., Columbus, 1976-79; atty. Huffy Corp., Dayton, Ohio, 1979-81; mng. atty. Hyatt Legal Services, Cin., 1981-83; assoc. Mary G. Nash Law Office, Hamilton, Ohio, 1983-84; sole practice Cin., 1984—. Mem. Vol. Lawyers for the Poor, Cin., 1985—; ruling elder Immanuel Presbyn. Ch., Cin., 1986—. Mem. Cin. Bar Assn. Democrat. Avocations: choral music, gourmet cooking. Criminal, Estate planning, Personal injury. Home: 3420 Beaumont Pl Cincinnati OH 45205 Office: 229 E Court St #1 Cincinnati OH 45202

HOKE, GEORGE PEABODY, lawyer; b. St. Paul, Mar. 18, 1913; s. George Edward and Carolyn Grahfs (Peabody) H.; m. Carolyn Elizabeth Glass, May 25, 1940 (div. 1963); children—Carolyn G., George G. Jared Peabody. A.B. cum laude, Dartmouth Coll., 1935; J.D., Yale U., 1938. Bar: Minn. 1939, U.S. Dist. Ct. Minn. 1940, U.S. Dist. Ct. (so. dist.) Iowa 1965, U.S. Tax Ct. 1945, U.S. Ct. Appeals (8th cir.) 1970. Ptnr., Snyder Gale Hoke, Richard & Janes, Minneapolis, 1943-57, Wheeler, Fredriksen, Hoke & Larson, Minneapolis, 1957-61; sr. ptnr. Hoke, Roehrdenz, Bigelow & Chamberlain, Mpls., 1975-86; central U.S. counsel Inter-provincial Pipe Line Co., Can., 1950-54; sec. and chmn. bd. Velie Ryan, Inc., Rochester, Minn., 1940-70; trustee Shattuck Sch., Faribault, Minn., 1940-70. Vestryman St. David's Episc. Ch., Hopkins, Minn., 1940-65, St. Paul's Episc. Ch., Mpls., 1985—; chmn. Henn County Civil Def., Mpls. and Wayzata, 1942-45; campaign sec. Republican State Central Com. Minn., St. Paul, 1944-48; campaign chmn., 1948; mem. Minn. Rep. Central Com., 1940-48. Served to lt. j.g., USN, 1942-1943. Mem. Am. Law Inst. (life mem., mem. joint com. A.B.A./Am. Law Inst. 1940-50), ABA (Minn. state dir. jr. bar. conf. 1945-55), Hennepin County Bar Assn. (chmn. tax sect. and jr. bar sec. 1945-55), Minn. State Bar Assn., Am. Judicature Soc. (state dir. 1960), Phi Delta Phi (province pres. 1940-70), Beta Theta Pi. Republican. Episcopalian. Clubs: Minneapolis, Mory's Assn. (New Haven). General practice, Insurance, Probate. Home and Office: 1945 Kenwood Pkwy Minneapolis MN 55405

HOLBERG, RALPH GANS, JR., lawyer; b. Mobile, Nov. 5, 1908; s. Ralph G. and Lillian (Frohlichstein) H.; m. Amelia Schwarz, Feb. 16, 1938; children: Ralph G. III, Robert S. J.D., U. Ala., 1932. Bar: Ala. 1932. Since practiced in Mobile; former ptnr. Holberg, Tully, Holberg & Danley. Author: Mobile County Court House, 1979. Pres. Mobile County chpt. ARC, 1954-55; chmn. Southeastern area council, 1957-58; bd. mem. emeritus Mobile County chpt., Ala. nat. v.p., 1960-61, mem. nat. bd. govs., 1965-68,

68-71; chmn. bd. Mobile County Bd. Pensions and Security, 1947-77; bd. dirs. Mobile Gen. Hosp., 1963-67; chmn., 1965-67; mem. Ala. State Docks Adv. Bd., 1962-69, 3d Army Area Adv. Com., Gov. Ala. Com. Adult Edn. Negroes, 1949; chmn. Mobile Pub. Library Bd., 1954-55; past appeal agt. local selective service bd.; past pres. Estate Planning Council Mobile, 1971-72, Hon. Fellows Mobile Coll., 1972-73; mem. nat. adv. council Nat. Multiple Sclerosis Soc., 1973—; alt. Mobile Hist. Devel. Commn., 1973-76; pres. Old Shell Rd. PTA, 1954-55, Ala. Jr. C. of C., 1935; mem. bd. Mobile Community Chest and Council, 1965-71; trustee Mobile YWCA, 1978—; bd. dirs. Gordon Smith Ctr., 1973-85. Served to lt. USNR, 1944-46. Recipient Disting. Service Key Mobile Jr. C. of C., 1938; J.N. Carmichael Meml. award, 1984; named Mobilian of Year, 1963; ann. vol. service award named in his honor ARC, 1986. Fellow Am. Coll. Probate Counsel; mem. ABA, Ala. Bar Assn., Mobile Bar Assn. (pres. 1942), VFW, Ala. Hist. Assn. (exec. com. 1981-85), Ala. Jud. Coll. Faculty Assn. (hon.), SCV, Am. Legion (post comdr. 1947-48), Mobile Jaycees (pres. 1934), Mobile Area C. of C. (dir. 1962-65, 71-74, 81), Mobile Hist. Preservation Soc. (dir. 1974-77), Mobile's Azalea Trail (pres. 1934-35), Navy League, Am. Council Judaism (nat. adv. bd. 1955-85), Spring Hill Ave. Temple (past pres., mem. bd.), Zeta Beta Tau. Clubs: Exchange (charter, past pres.), Internat. Trade, Touchdown (past mem. bd.), Mobile Country. Probate, Estate planning. Home: Apt 216 217 Berwyn Dr W Mobile AL 36608 Office: Suite 701 Commerce Bldg Mobile AL 36602

HOLBROOK, DAN W., lawyer; b. Louisville, Feb. 10, 1948; s. Allie Arnold and Anna Jane (Day) H.; m. Mary Wells, Dec. 28, 1975; children: Christopher, Nathaniel Wells. BA, Rollins Coll., 1969, MBA, 1970; JD, Willamette U., 1977; LLM, U. Miami, 1978. Bar: Ky. 1977, Tenn. 1978, Fla. 1978, U.S. Dist. Ct. (ea. dist.) Tenn. 1978, U.S. Tax Ct. 1978. Cons. The Wyatt Co., Washington, 1970-74; mem. Egerton, McAfee, Armistead & Davis, P.C., Knoxville, Tenn., 1978—; mem. probate study com. Tenn., Nashville, 1986—; lectr. U. Tenn. Ann. Tax Conf., Knoxville, 1983—, other legal seminars. Mem. profl. adv. bd. Fort Sanders Hosp. Found., Knoxville, 1982—, East Tenn. Community Found., 1985—; bd. dirs. ARC, Knoxville, 1982—, Word for Living, Knoxville, 1984—, Marriage Alive, Knoxville, 1984—. Named Man of Yr. U.S. Jaycees, 1974. Mem. ABA, Knoxville Bar Assn. (tax sect., pres. 1987—), Knoxville Estate Planning Council, Knoxville Assn. Profls. (pres. 1981-82), Christian Legal Soc. Presbyterian. Avocations: running, skiing, reading. Estate planning, Probate, Estate taxation. Home: 1000 Nokomis Circle Knoxville TN 37919 Office: Egerton McAfee Armistead & Davis PC 500 1st American Ctr Knoxville TN 37902

HOLBROOK, DONALD BENSON, lawyer; b. Salt Lake City, Jan. 4, 1925; s. Robert Benson H.; m. Betty J. Gilchrist, Apr. 24, 1947; children—Mark, Thomas, Gregory, Mary. JD, U. Utah, 1952. Bar: Utah 1953. Pres. Jones Waldo, Holbrook and Mc Donough, Salt Lake City, 1973—; dir. Kearns-Tribune Corp.; bd. adv. Mountain Bell, 1974-84. Bd. dirs. Utah Assn. UN, 1963-64; bd. dirs. and exec. com. Utah Coop. Assn., 1962-82; vice chmn., chmn fin. com. bd. regents U. Utah, 1965-67, chmn. bd. 1965-67, 67-69, vice chmn., 1970-73, chmn., 1974-82, 83—; commr. Western Interstate Commn. Higher Edn., chmn. 1982—; pres. and chmn. bd. Ballet West, 1982-84; bd. dirs. Utah Democratic Party, exec. sec. 1955-65, exec. com. 1956-65; chmn. resolutions com. State Dem. Conv., 1958; chmn. antitrust and monopoly subcom. Western States Dem. Conf., 1962-66; campaign mgr. Gov. Calvin L. Rampton, 1964, 68; Dem. Conv., 1968; del. Dem. Nat. Conv., 1968; candidate for U.S. Senate, 1974. Recipient Disting. Alumni award U. Utah, 1985. Fellow Internat. Acad. Trial Lawyers, Am. Bar Found., mem. U. Utah Coll. Law Alumni Assn. (pres. 1957), ABA (gen. chmn. Rocky Mountain Region 1962, Utah chmn., mem. com. sect. corp., banking and bus. law 1962—), Salt Lake County Bar Assn. (chmn. com. continuing legal edn. 1961, chmn. com. World Peace Through Law, 1964, pres. 1964-65, chmn. com. jud. retirement 1968), Beta Theta Phi, Phi Kappa Phi, Delta Theta Phi (disting. alumni award 1967), Order of Coif (award for contbns. to law, scholarship and community service 1968). Clubs: Alta, Jeremy Ranch Country. Editor-in-chief Utah Law Rev., 1951-52. Antitrust, Administrative and regulatory, Federal civil litigation. Office: Suite 1500 First Interstate Bank Plaza Salt Lake City UT 84111

HOLBROOK, FRANK MALVIN, lawyer; b. Atlanta, Mar. 26, 1952; s. James David and Mary Linda (Fambrough) H.; m. Julie Melissa Holley, Aug. 30, 1975; children: Holley Marie, James Clinton. AA with honors, Brevard Community Coll., Cocoa, Fla., 1972; BS cum laude, Fla. State U., 1974; JD cum laude, U. Ga., 1979. Bar: Ga. 1979, Miss. 1979, U.S. Dist. Ct. (no. and so. dists.) Miss. 1979, U.S. Ct. Appeals (5th cir.) 1979, U.S. Ct. Appeals (11th cir.) 1982. Assoc. Fuselier, Ott & McKee, Jackson, Miss., 1979-83; assoc. Thompson, Alexander & Crews, Jackson, 1983-85, ptnr., 1985—. Mem. ABA, Fed. Bar Assn., Miss. State Bar Assn., State Bar Ga., Hinds County Bar Assn. Republican. Methodist. Avocations: photography, camping, canoeing. Federal civil litigation, Contracts commercial, Bankruptcy. Office: Thompson Alexander & Crews 118 N Congress Jackson MS 39201

HOLBROOK, JAMES MITCHELL, lawyer; b. Mineral Wells, Tex., Sept. 9, 1945; s. James R. and Gladys (Denman) H.; m. Robin Miller, Sept. 17, 1966; children—Holly, Tracy. B.A., U. Tex.-Austin, 1967; J.D., St. Mary's U., 1971. Bar: Tex. 1972, U.S. Dist. Ct. (we. dist.) Tex. 1972, U.S. Ct. Appeals (5th cir.) 1972; cert. in comml. and residential real estate. Ptnr. Sawtelle, Goode, Davidson & Troilo, San Antonio, 1971-82; ptnr. Holbrook, Kaufman & Becker, San Antonio, 1983; instr. Advanced Real Estate Course, Tex. State Bar, 1981. Mem. Alamo Hts. City Council, 1981-85. Mem. San Antonio Bar Assn. (pres. 1983-84). Presbyterian. Real property, Contracts commercial. Address: 300 Convent #2300 Interfirst San Antonio TX 78205-3724

HOLCOMB, LYLE DONALD, JR., lawyer; b. Miami, Fla., Feb. 3, 1929; s. Lyle Donald and Hazel Irene (Watson) H.; m. Barbara Jean Roth, July 12, 1952; children—Susan Holcomb Davis, Douglas J., Mark E. B.A., U. Mich., 1951; J.D., U. Fla., 1954. Bar: Fla. 1955, U.S. Supreme Ct. 1966, U.S. Ct. Appeals (5th and 11th cirs.) 1981. Ptnr. Holcomb & Holcomb, Miami, 1955-72; assoc. Copeland, Therrel, Baisden & Peterson, Miami Beach, Fla., 1972-75; ptnr. Therrel, Baisden, Stanton, Wood & Setlin, Miami Beach, 1967-85; ptnr. Therrel Baisden & Meyer Weiss, Miami Beach, 1985—; mem. organizing bd. Econ. Opportunities Legal Services Program (now Legal Services of Greater Miami, Inc.), 1965-75; pres. So. Fla. Migrant Legal Services Program (now Fla. Rural Legal Services), 1966-68. Mem. exec. council So. Fla. council Boy Scouts Am., 1958—; pres. Miami chpt., counselor state soc. Huguenot Soc. Fla. Served with USNR, 1947-53. Recipient Silver Beaver award So. Fla. council Boy Scouts Am., 1966. Fellow Am. Coll. Probate Counsel, Acad. Fla. Probate and Trust Litigation Attys.; mem. Dade County Bar Assn. (dir. 1960-71, sec. 1963-71), Miami Beach Bar Assn. (pres. 1980), Fla. Bar (exec. council Real Property, Probate and Trust Law Sect. 1979—), ABA, Am. Judicature Soc., Estate Planning Council Greater Miami., Soc. Mayflower Descs. (pres. Miami club, counselor state soc.). Republican. Mem. United Ch. of Christ. Club: Univ. Yacht. Probate, Real property. Home: 700 Malaga Ave Coral Gables FL 33134 Office: 1111 Lincoln Rd Suite 600 Miami Beach FL 33139

HOLDEN, CHARLES ST. GEORGE, lawyer; b. San Francisco, Sept. 19, 1949; s. St. George and Moira (Kennedy) H.; m. Roberta Ann Cohen, June 1, 1984. BA, U. Calif., Berkeley, 1972; JD, U. Calif., San Francisco, 1975. Bar: Calif. 1975, U.S. Dist. Ct. (no. dist.) Calif. 1975, Alaska 1976, U.S. Dist. Ct. Alaska 1977, U.S. Ct. Appeals (9th cir.) 1977, Hawaii 1979, U.S. Dist. Ct. (cen. dist.) Calif. 1986. Assoc. Kennedy & Azar, Fairbanks, Alaska, 1977-78; law. clk. to trial judge State of Hawaii, Wailuku, Maui, Hawaii, 1978-79; sole practice San Francisco, 1979—. Mem. Calif. Bar Assn., San Francisco Bar Assn. Clubs: Bohemian (San Francisco); Naval (London). Real property, Oil and gas leasing, State civil litigation. Office: 155 Montgomery Suite 1107 San Francisco CA 94104

HOLDEN, FREDERICK DOUGLASS, JR., lawyer; b. Stockton, Ca., Nov. 21, 1949; s. Frederick Douglass and Sarah Frances (Young) H.; m. Emily Kenyon, Nov. 30, 1974 (div. May 1985). BA, U. Calif., Santa Barbara, 1971; JD, U. Calif., Davis, 1974. Bar: Calif. 1974, U.S. Dist. Ct. (no., cen., ea. and so. dists.) Calif. 1974, U.S. Ct. Appeals (9th cir.) 1974. Assoc. Brobeck, Phleger & Harrison, San Francisco, 1974-81, ptnr., 1981—; speaker Calif. Continuing Legal Edn. of Bar, Calif., 1983-85. Mng. editor U. Calif. Davis Law Rev., 1974. Mem. ABA, Calif. Bar Assn. (cert. merit 1984), San Francisco Bar Assn. (cert. appreciation 1985). Democrat. Avocations: skiing, running, mountaineering, volleyball. Bankruptcy, Contracts commercial. Home: 80 Lyford Dr No 2 Tiburon CA 94920 Office: Brobeck Phleger & Harrison Spear St Tower One Market Plaza San Francisco CA 94105

HOLDEN, STEPHEN, III, lawyer; b. White Plains, N.Y., Feb. 27, 1939. B.A., Hamilton Coll., 1961; J.D., Cornell U., 1964. Bar: N.Y. 1965. chief exec. officer, Holden Bros., P.C., White Plains, 1965—. Mem. ABA, N.Y. Bar Assn., West County Bar Assn. (past dir., del.), White Plains Bar Assn. (past pres.). Probate, Real property, General practice. Office: 124 Court St White Plains NY 10601

HOLDENRIED, JOHN RICHARD, lawyer; b. Sioux City, Iowa, Jan. 11, 1950; s. Russell J. and Shirleymae (Zechman) H.; m. Lynne Reed, Oct. 10, 1980; children: Jake, Joseph. BSBA, Creighton U., 1972; JD, U. Mich., 1975. Bar: Nebr. 1975, U.S. Dist. Ct. Nebr. 1975, U.S. Ct. Appeals (8th cir.) 1975. Law clk. to presiding justice U.S. Dist. Ct. Nebr., Lincoln, 1975-77; assoc. Baird & Holm Law Offices, Omaha, 1977—; legal research writing instr. Creighton U. Law Sch., Omaha, 1980—. Bd. dirs. Big Bros.-Big Sisters of Midlands, Omaha, 1979-84, pres. 1984; active Leadership Omaha, 1983-84; vol. Lawyers in Schs., Omaha. Mem. ABA, Nebr. Bar Assn., Omaha Bar Assn., Am. Acad. Hosp. Attys., Nat. Health Lawyers Assn. Roman Catholic. Health, Labor. Office: Baird Holm Law Office 1500 Woodmen Tower Omaha NE 68102

HOLDER, ANGELA RODDEY, lawyer, educator; b. Rock Hill, S.C., Mar. 13, 1938; d. John T. and Angela M. (Fisher) Roddey; 1 child, John Thomas Roddey Holder. Student, Radcliffe Coll., 1955-56; B.A., Newcomb Coll., 1958; postgrad., Faculty of Law-King's Coll., London, 1957-58; J.D., Tulane U., 1960; LL.M., Yale U., 1975. Bar: La. 1961, S.C. 1960, Conn. 1981. Counsel Roddey, Sumwalt & Carpenter, Rock Hill, S.C., 1960—; atty. criminal div. New Orleans Legal Aid Bur., 1961-62; counsel York County Family Ct., S.C., 1962-64; asst. prof. polit. sci. Winthrop Coll., Rock Hill, 1964-74; research assoc. Yale Law Sch., 1975-77, exec. dir. program in law, sci. and medicine, 1976-77; lectr. dept. pediatrics Yale Med. Sch., 1975-77, asst. clin. prof. pediatrics and law, 1977-79, assoc. clin. prof., 1979-83, clin. prof., 1983—; counsel for medicolegal affairs Yale-New Haven Hosp. and Yale Med. Sch., 1977—. Author: The Meaning of the Constitution, 1968, 2d edit., 1987, Medical Malpractice Law, 1975, 2d edit. 1978, Legal Issues in Pediatrics and Adolescent Medicine, 1977, 2d edit., 1985; contbg. editor: Prism mag.; contbg. editor., AMA; mem. editorial bd.: IRB; Law, Medicine and Health Care, Jour. Philosophy and Medicine; contbr. articles to profl. jours. Mem. Rock Hill Sch. Bd., 1967-68; bd. dirs. Family Planning Clinic, chmn., 1970-73. Mem. ABA, S.C. Bar Assn. (medico-legal com. 1973—), La. Bar Assn., Soc. Med. Jurisprudence, Am. Soc. Hosp. Attys., Am. Soc. Law and Medicine (treas. 1981-83, sec. 1983-85, pres. 1986-87). Democrat. Episcopalian. Health, Legal education, Medical. Home: 23 Eld St Apt B New Haven CT 06511 Office: Yale-New Haven Hosp 20 York St New Haven CT 06504

HOLDERMAN, JAMES F., JR., federal judge; b. 1946. BS, U. Ill., 1968, JD, 1971. Judge U.S. Dist. Ct. (no. dist.) Ill., Chgo., 1985—; asst. U.S. atty. City of Chgo., 1972-78; assoc. Sonnenschein, Carlin et al, Chgo., 1978-85; judge U.S. Dist. Ct. (no. dist.) Ill., Chgo., 1985—; lectr. law U. Chgo., 1983—. Office: U S Dist Ct 219 S Dearborn St Room 2146 Chicago IL 60604 *

HOLLAND, FRED ANTHONY, lawyer; b. Wilmington, Del., Aug. 29, 1955; s. Bernard Allen and Rosalie May (Wellman) H.; m. Martha Jean Barry, July 29, 1978; 1 child, Maureen Patricia. BA, U. Del., 1977; JD, Coll. William and Mary, 1980. Bar: Pa. 1981, U.S. Dist. Ct. (mid. dist.) Pa. 1985. Law clk. to presiding judge Ct. Common Pleas, Williamsport, Pa., 1981-82; asst. dist. atty. Lycoming County, Williamsport, 1983; assoc. Kieser & Gahr, Williamsport, 1983-84, Liebert, Short, Fitzpatrick & Hirshland, Williamsport, 1985—; adj. instr. Pa. State U., State College, 1986—. Banking, Contracts commercial, Real property. Home: 508 Highland Terr Williamsport PA 17701 Office: Liebert Short Fitzpatrick & Hirshland 30 W 3d St Williamsport PA 17701

HOLLAND, H. RUSSEL, federal judge; b. 1936; m. Diane Holland; 3 children. BBA, U. Mich., 1958, LLB, 1961. With Alaska Ct. System, Anchorage, 1961, U.S. Atty.'s Office, Dept. Justice, Anchorage, 1963-65; assoc. Stevens & Savage, Anchorage, 1965-66; ptnr. Stevens, Savage, Holland, Erwin & Edwards, Anchorage, 1967-68; sole practice Anchorage, 1968-70; ptnr. Holland & Thornton, Anchorage, 1970-78, Holland, Thornton & Trefry, Anchorage, 1978, Holland & Trefry, Anchorage, 1978-84, Trefry & Brecht, Anchorage, 1984; judge U.S. Dist. Ct. Alaska, Anchorage, 1984—. Mem. ABA, Alaska Bar Assn., Anchorage Bar Assn. Judicial administration. Office: U S District Court 701 C St Box 54 Anchorage AK 99513 *

HOLLAND, LYMAN FAITH, JR., lawyer; b. Mobile, June 17, 1931; s. Lyman Faith and Louise (Windom) H.; m. Leannah Louise Platt, Mar. 6, 1954; children: Lyman Faith III, Laura. B.S. in Bus. Adminstrn, U. Ala., 1953; LL.B., 1957. Bar: Ala. 1957. Assoc. firm Hand, Arendall & Bedsole, Mobile, 1957-62; partner firm Hand, Ardendall, Bedsole, Greaves and Johnston, 1963—. Mem. Mobile Historic Devel. Com., 1965-69, v.p., 1967-68; Bd. dirs. Mobile Azalea Trail, Inc., 1963-68, chmn. bd., 1963-65; bd. dirs. Mobile Mental Health Center, 1969-76, v.p., 1972, pres., chmn. bd., 1973; bd. dirs. Mobile chpt. ARC, vice chmn., 1975-77, exec. vice chmn., 1978-80, chmn., 1980-82; bd. dirs. Deep South council Girl Scouts U.S.A., 1965-71, Gordan Smith Center Inc., 1973, Bay Area Council on Alcoholism, 1973-76, Community Chest and Council of Mobile County, Inc., 1976-81; bd. dirs. Greater Mobile Mental Health-Mental Retardation, 1975-81, pres., 1975-77. Served to 1st lt. USAF, 1953-55; lt. col. Res. ret. Mem. Am., Mobile County bar assns., Ala. State Bar (chmn. sect. corp., banking and bus. law 1978-80), Am. Coll. Probate Counsel, Ala. Law Inst. (council), Pi Kappa Alpha, Phi Delta Phi. Baptist (deacon; ch. trustee 1968-73, chmn. trustees 1971-73). Clubs: Lions (Mobile), Athleston (Mobile); Country Club of Mobile, Bienville. Probate, Banking, Real property. Home: 717 Westmoreland Dr W Mobile AL 36609 Office: Box 123 Mobile AL 36601

HOLLAND, PATRICIA MARCUS, lawyer; b. Pitts., July 29, 1952; d. E. Robert and Betty (Rosenfield) Marcus. BA in History and Polit. Sci., U. Rochester, 1974; JD, Case Western Res. U., 1977. Summer assoc. Jones, Day, Reavis & Pogue, Cleve., 1976; assoc. Schiff, Hardin & Waite, Chgo., 1977-82; assoc. Benesch, Friedlander, Coplan & Aronoff, Cleve., 1982-84, ptnr., 1984—. Mem. community relations com., strategic planning com. Jewish Community Fedn. Cleve., 1984; trustee NCCJ, Cleve. chpt. No. Ohio region, Anti-Defamation League, B'nai B'rith. Mem. ABA, Ohio Bar Assn., Cleve. Bar Assn., Case Western Res. U. Law Alumni Assn. (bd. govs.), Order of Coif. General corporate, Securities. Office: Benesch Friedlander et al 850 Euclid Ave Cleveland OH 44114

HOLLAND, RANDY JAMES, judge; b. Elizabeth, N.J., Jan. 27, 1947; s. James Charles and Virginia (Wilson) H.; m. Ilona E. Holland, June 24, 1972; B.A. in Econs., Swarthmore Coll., 1969; J.D. cum laude, U. Pa., 1972. Bar: Del. 1972. Ptnr., Dunlap, Holland & Rich and predecessors, Georgetown, Del., 1972-80; ptnr. Morris, Nichols, Arsht & Tunnell, Georgetown, 1980-86; justice Supreme Ct. Del., 1986—. mem. Del. Bd. Bar Examiners, 1978-86; mem. Gov.'s Jud. Nominating Commn., 1978-86, sec., 1982-85, chmn., 1985-86; mem. Del. Supreme Ct. Consol. Com., 1985-86. Pres. adminstrv. bd. Ave. United Methodist Ch., Milford, Del., trustee Peninsula Ann. Conf. Recipient Henry C. Loughlin prize for legal ethics U. Pa. 1972. Trustee Del. Bar Found.; mem. ABA, Assn. Trial Lawyers Am., Del. Trial Lawyers Assn. (bd. govs.), Del. Bar Assn., Am. Soc. Hosp. Attys., Am. Judicature Soc. Republican. Mem. editorial bd. Del. Lawyer Mag., 1981-85; contbr. chpt. Del. Appelate Handbook, 1985—. Health, Probate, State civil litigation.

HOLLAND, WILLIAM LOUIS, lawyer; b. North Tonawanda, N.Y., Sept. 11, 1935; s. Raymond F. and Margaret (Breitenbach) H.; m. Frances Kathryn McCreary, Aug. 28, 1963; children: Thomas Sean, Catherine Anne, William Kevin. BA, U. Rochester, 1957; MA, Yale U., 1960, PhD, 1965; JD, George Washington U., 1978. Bar: D.C. 1979, Va. 1982. Field rep., dist. supr. Regional Office Econ. Opportunity, Atlanta, 1966-70, chief plans budget and evaluation, 1970-74; cons. program evaluation Nat. Sci. Found., Washington, 1975, Performance Devel. Inst., Washington, 1982-84; program analyst HHS, Washington, 1976-81; gen. ptnr. Holland & Dockterman, Alexandria, Va., 1984—; asst. prof. Emory U., Atlanta, 1963-66; adj. faculty U. So. Calif., 1986, George Washington U., Washington, 1986. Treas., v.p. Worldwide Peace Found., Alexandria, 1985—; mem. Dowden Terr. Civic Assn., Alexandria. Fellow Yale U., 1959-62, Woodrow Wilson Found., 1957; grantee U. Rochester, 1956. Mem. ABA, D.C. Bar Assn., Alexandria Bar Assn., Alexandria C. of C. (vice chmn. health care com. 1986—), Phi Beta Kappa. Family and matrimonial, Administrative and regulatory, General practice. Home: 1901 Hawthorne Ave Alexandria VA 22311 Office: Holland & Dockterman 1513 King St Alexandria VA 22314

HOLLAND, WILLIAM MEREDITH, lawyer; b. Live Oak, Fla., Feb. 6, 1922; s. Isaac and Annie Elizaa (Williams) H.; m. Mamie Smith, June 3, 1947; children—William Meredith, Maurice, Gian, Gaelim, Shakira; m. 2d, Margaret Elizabeth Erving, Apr. 9, 1976. B.A., Fla. A. & M. U., 1947; J.D., Boston U., 1951. Bar: Fla. 1951, U.S. Dist. Ct. (so. dist.) Fla. 1952, U.S. Ct. Appeals (5th cir.) 1953, U.S. Supreme Ct. 1956, Ptnr., Holland & Smith, Lake Park, Fla., 1954—; mcpl. judge City of Riviera Beach, Fla., 1973-77. Served with AUS, 1943-46. Mem. Fla. Bar Assn., ABA, Nat. Bar Assn., Am. Judicature Soc., ACLU, NAACP, Council Human Relations, Urban League. Civil rights, Federal civil litigation, State civil litigation. Home: 611 W Kolmia Dr Lake Park FL 33403 Office: 611 Kalmia Dr Lake Park FL 33403

HOLLAND, WILLIAM RAY, diversified company executive; b. Ada, Okla., Dec. 19, 1938; s. Arthur Bruce and Artie Mary (Hood) H.; m. Donna Ruth Albright, Jan. 25, 1959; children—Donna Kristen, William Dallas, John Foster. B.S., U. Denver, 1960, J.D., 1962. Bar: Colo. bar 1963, Ark. bar 1964. With Met. Area Planning Commn. Little Rock, 1959-63; atty. Southwestern Bell Telephone, Little Rock, 1964-66; assoc. firm Bridges Young Matthews & Davis, Little Rock, 1966-73; with AMCA Internat. Ltd. (formerly Dominion Bridge Co. Ltd.) and AMCA Internat. Corp., Hanover, N.H., 1973—, exec. v.p., 1981-85, pres., chief exec. officer, 1986-87, chmn., chief exec. officer, 1987—. Served to capt., JAGC USAF, 1968. Mem. Am. Bar Assn., Ark. Bar Assn. Republican. Baptist. Home: 13 Pine Dr Hanover NH 03755 Office: AMCA Internat Ltd Dartmouth Nat Bank Bldg B Hanover NH 03755

HOLLANDER, BRUCE LEE, lawyer, business executive; b. Queens, N.Y., Aug. 16, 1943; s. I. Gerard and Argate (Polmer) H.; m. Beverly Ann Olund, Apr. 28, 1967; children—Aaron Gerard, Adam Robert. Student Cornell U., 1961-62; B.S. in Psychology, U. Miami, 1970; J.D. cum laude, 1973. Bar: Fla. 1973, U.S. Dist. Ct. (mid. and so. dists.) Fla. 1973, U.S. Ct. Appeals (5th cir.) 1973. Assoc. Snyder, Young, Stern & Tannenbaum, Miami, Fla., 1973-76; ptnr. Garlick, Cohn, Darrow & Hollander, Hollywood, Fla., 1976-82, Hollander & Assocs., P.A., Hollywood, 1982—; lectr. in field; mem. adv. bd. Broward Bank, 1982, mem. elect, 1983; pres. Automated Title Services, Hollywood. Contbr. articles to Mortgage Notes, Fla. Bar Jour. Bd. dirs. Broward County chpt. ARC, Fla., 1979-81. Mem. ABA, Broward County Bar Assn., Fla. Bar (rep. 17th jud. cir. for real property, probate and trust law sect. 1978—, exec. council real property, probate and trust law sect. 1979—, chmn. 2d mortgage law subcom. 1979—, also corp., banking and bus. law sect. and econs. and mgmt. law practice sect.), Nat. Second Mortgage Assn., Nat. Consumer Fin. Assn. (home equity sect.), Nat. Assn. Mortgage Brokers, Fla. Assn. Mortgage Brokers, Soc. Wig and Robe, Soc. Bar and Gavel (justice, honor council), Sports Car Club Am. (S.E. divisional champion 1968, 76-77, 86), Delta Theta Phi, Phi Kappa Phi. Jewish. Real property, General corporate, Contracts commercial. Office: Hollander & Assocs PA 1940 Harrison St Hollywood FL 33020

HOLLANDER, WILLIAM VICTOR, lawyer; b. N.Y.C., Nov. 18, 1918; s. Edmund and Mildred (Richter) H.; m. Annette Bendett, June 20, 1942; children—Maureen Linda, James Mark, Thomas Roy, Susan Karen, Carol Joyce, Nancy Sharon. B.E.E., Cooper Union, 1947; M.Ad.E., NYU, 1950; J.D., Cleve. State U., 1957. Bar: Ohio 1957, Conn. 1971, U.S. Dist. Ct. Conn. 1971, U.S. Ct. Appeals (2d cir.) 1971, U.S. Supreme Ct. 1972, U.S. Ct. Appeals (7th cir.) 1976. Cert. Bd. Cert. Safety Profls. Mgr. govt. contracts adminstrn. Bendix Corp., York, Pa., 1950-53; dir. corp. devel. Standard Products Co., Cleve., 1953-61; exec. asst. to pres. Gyrodyne Co., St. James, N.Y., 1961-62; dir. loss prevention Olin Corp., New Haven, 1963-81; ptnr. Hollander & Assocs., Hamden, Conn., 1981—. Served to maj. U.S. Army, 1940-46; ETO, Decorated Bronze Star. Mem. ABA (com. on occupational safety and health law 1974), Am. Soc. Safety Engrs. (profl. mem.), Nat. Safety Mgmt. Soc. (v.p. New Eng. 1975-76). General practice, Product Liability, Labor. Office: Hollander & Assocs 65 Wright Ln Hamden CT 06517

HOLLEB, MARSHALL MAYNARD, lawyer; b. Chgo., Dec. 25, 1916; s. A. Paul and Sara (Zaretsky) H.; m. Doris Bernstein, Oct. 15, 1944; children—Alan R., Gordon P., Paul D. B.A., U. Wis., 1937; M.B.A., Harvard U., 1939, I.A., 1941, J.D., 1942. Bar: Ill. 1947, U.S. Supreme Ct. 1960. Assoc. Levenson, Becker & Peebles, Chgo., 1947-51; ptnr. Yates & Holleb, Chgo., 1952-59, Holleb, Gerstein & Glass, Chgo., 1960-81; sr. ptnr. Holleb & Coff, Chgo., 1982—; dir. Acorn Fund; chmn. bd. dirs. Urban Assocs. Chgo., Inc. Trustee Hull House Assn., pres., 1980-82; trustee Nat. Bldg. Mus., Chgo. Inst. Psychoanalysis; trustee, gen. legal csl. Mus. Contemporary Art Chgo.; mem. adv. bd. Landmarks Preservation Council, Fair Housing Ctr. of Home Investments Fund, Citizens Sch. Com.; mem. vis. coms. Oriental Inst. and Visual Arts of U. Chgo.; bd. dirs. Internat. Visitors Ctr., Mostly Music, Inc.; mem. Ill. Internat. Trade and Port Promotion Adv. Com., 1982, Chgo.'s Future Project Com. of Trust, Inc., 1982; mem. nat. adv. bd. on internat. edn. programs U.S. Dept. Edn., 1981; pres. Chgo. Theater Preservation Group Ltd., sec., bd. dirs. The Arts Club Chgo.; bd. dirs. bd. dirs. Chgo. Maritime Soc.; mem. nat. adv. com. and del. White House Conf. on Aging 1971, 81; mem. Ill. Council on Aging, 1961-81, chmn., 1973-81; panel mem. Ill. Statewide Comprehensive Outdoor Recreation Plan; mem. weatherization adv. com. Ill. Dept. Bus. and Econ. Devel. 1975—; mem. Ill. appeal bd. SSS 1966-73; cons. Vt. research project HUD; mem. Chgo. Plan Commn., 1984—. Served from pvt. to 1st lt. Adj. Gen. Dept., U.S. Army 1943-46. Recipient Humanitarian of Yr. Henry Booth House award, Hull House Assn., 1979; Am. Heritage award Am. Jewish Com., 1986, Arts award Mostly Music Inc., 1986, City Brightener award Bright New City, Chgo., 1987. Mem. ABA, Ill. Bar Assn., Chgo. Bar Assn., Fed. Bar Assn., Am. Soc. Internat. Law, Am. Arbitration Assn. (nat. panel), Am. Inst. Planners, Nat. Assn. Housing and Redevel. Ofcls., Urban Land Inst., Lambda Alpha. Democrat. Clubs: Arts, University, Bryn Mawr Country, Executives (Chgo.). Contbr. articles to profl. jours. Real property, General corporate, Estate planning. Office: Suite 4100 55 E Monroe St Chicago IL 60603

HOLLEMAN, CARL PARTIN, lawyer; b. Wake County, N.C., Aug. 6, 1921; s. Aaron and Vera Maude (Holland) H.; m. Ruth Warren, Mar. 25, 1949; children—Carl P., Warren Lee. J.D., Wake Forest U., 1949. Bar: N.C. 1950. Sole practice, Apex, N.C., from 1950; now ptnr. Holleman & Stam; town atty. Town of Apex, 1953—; judge Recorders Ct., Apex, 1956. Mem. Wake County Bd. Elections, 1964-74, chmn., 1970-74; mem. Wake County Pub. Libraries, 1960-72, chmn., 1969-72; nat. bd. dirs. Boy Scouts Am., 1969-75; bd. dirs. Wake County Hist. Soc., 1976-82, pres., 1977-79, 80-81; mem. bd. assocs. Meredith Coll.,1985—; pres. Wake County Young Democratic Club, 1955; tchr. men's Bible class Bapt. Ch., 1960-84. Served with USAAC, 1942-46; PTO. Recipient Silver Beaver award Boy Scouts Am., 1962. Mem. ABA, N.C. Bar Assn., Wake County Bar Assn. (pres. 1981, chmn. legal aid com., 1982-84), 10th Jud. Dist. Bar (dir. 1964-67, 77-82, chmn. 1979, pres. 1981), N.C. Acad. Trial Lawyers, Phi Delta Phi. Democrat. Club: Lions. State civil litigation, General practice, Probate. Office: 106 Holloman St Apex NC 27502

HOLLEMAN, FRANK SHARP, III, lawyer; b. Seneca, S.C., May 19, 1954; s. Frances (Hull) H.; m. Anne Barker, July 31, 1976. BA, Furman U., 1976; JD, Harvard U., 1979; MS, London Sch. of Econs. and Polit. Sci., 1981. Bar: S.C. 1979, U.S. Ct. Appeals (4th cir.) 1980, D.C. 1982, U.S. Dist. Ct. S.C. 1982, U.S. Supreme Ct. 1985. Assoc. Wyche Law Firm, Greenville, S.C., 1982-86, ptnr., 1986—. Acct. exec. Greenville (S.C.) County United Way, 1983; fin. chmn. Greenville (S.C.) County Dems., 1983-84, chmn.,

1984—. Knox fellow Harvard U., 1979. Mem. ABA, S.C. Bar Assn., Greenville County Bar Assn., Phi Beta Kappa, Pi Gamma Mu. Presbyterian. Federal civil litigation, State civil litigation. Home: 52 E Tallulah Dr Greenville SC 29605 Office: Wyche Burgess Freeman & Parham PA 44 E Camperdown Way Greenville SC 29603

HOLLERAN, KEVIN JOSEPH, lawyer; b. Coatesville, Pa., Nov. 13, 1951; s. Richard Paul and Elizabeth Faller (Hufnagel) H. AB, Dickinson Coll., 1973; JD, Villanova U., 1976. Bar: Pa. 1976, U.S. Supreme Ct. 1985. Law clk. to presiding judge Commonwealth Ct. of Pa., Harrisburg, 1976-77; assoc. Gawthrop, Greenwood & Halsted, West Chester, Pa., 1978-83, ptnr., 1983—. V.p. Chester County chpt. United Way, Exton, Pa., 1983—; pres. Homemaker/Home Health Services Inc., Exton, 1985—. Mem. ABA, Pa. Bar Assn., Chester County Bar Assn. (chmn. young lawyers div. 1979). Republican. Roman Catholic. Club: Whitford Country (Exton); Cath. Philopatrian Lit. Inst. (Phila.). Probate, Health. Home: Adele Alley West Chester PA 19382 Office: Gawthrop Greenwood & Halsted 119 N High St PO Box 562 West Chester PA 19381-0562

HOLLEY, AUDREY RODGERS, lawyer; b. N.Y.C., Jan. 18, 1939; d. Mortimer W. and Susan K. Rodgers; m. George M. Holley Jr., July 30, 1964 (dec. Oct. 1983); 1 child, Stephen C.R. BA, Radcliffe Coll., 1961; JD, U. Detroit, 1981. Bar: Mich. 1982, U.S. Dist. Ct. (ea. dist.) Mich. 1982. Assoc. Rickel & Earle, Detroit, 1985—. Mem. ABA, Fed. Bar Assn., Mich. Bar Assn., Detroit Bar Assn. General practice, State civil litigation, General corporate. Office: Rickel & Earle 100 Renaissance Ctr Suite 1575 Detroit MI 48243

HOLLIDAY, JAMES SIDNEY, JR., lawyer; b. Baton Rouge, Mar. 6, 1941; s. James Sidney and Ione Grace (McKay) H.; m. Frances Broussard, June 19, 1965; children—Stephen James, Laurie Frances, Amy Eilleen, Jennie Inez. B.S. with honors, La. State U., 1962, J.D. with honors, 1965. Bar: La. 1965, U.S. Supreme Ct. 1971, U.S. Dist. Ct. (mid. and ea. dists.) La., D.C. 1977. Ptnr., McCollister, McCleary, Fazio & Holliday, 1965-87; ptnr. Anderson & Holliday, 1987—; instr. La. State U., Coll. Engring. Co-author: Louisiana Construction Law; Louisiana Corporation Law. Mem. exec. bd. Boy Scouts Am., La. Arts and Humanities Council. Mem. Fed. Bar Assn. (Treas. Baton Rouge chpt.), ABA, La. Bar Assn. (council, bd. govs., chmn.), Baton Rouge Bar Assn., Phi Alpha Delta, Phi Delta Phi. Clubs: Country (Baton Rouge); City; Camelot. Lodge: Rotary. Construction, General corporate. Office: 5555 Hilton Ave 5th Floor Baton Rouge LA 70808

HOLLIDAY, RONALD STURGIS, lawyer; b. Wichita, Kans., Dec. 11, 1947; s. Robert Dwight and Mary Irene (Smith) H.; m. Deborah June Winship, Aug. 29, 1975; children: Brian Joseph, Kathryn June. BA with honors, U. Kans., 1969; JD magna cum laude, U. Mich., 1972. Bar: Mich. 1972, U.S. Dist. Ct. (ea. dist.) Mich. 1972, U.S. Dist. Ct. (we. dist.) Mich. 1977, U.S. Ct. Appeals (6th cir.) 1982, Fla. 1986, U.S. Dist. Ct. (mid. dist.) Fla. 1987. Assoc. Dykema, Gossett, Spencer, Goodnow & Trigg, Detroit, 1972-80; ptnr. Dykema, Gassett, Spencer, Goodnow & Trigg, Detroit, 1980—. Served to lt. JAGC, USN, 1973-76. Recipient Leadership Detroit award Greater Detroit C. of C., 1980. Fellow Mich. State Bar Found. (mem. antitrust law sect.); mem. ABA, Mich. Bar Assn., Detroit Bar Assn., Fla. Bar Assn., Sarasota County Bar Assn. Banking, Federal civil litigation, General corporate. Office: Dykema Gossett et al 720 S Orange Ave Sarasota FL 33578

HOLLIN, SHELBY W., lawyer; b. Varilla, Ky., July 29, 1925; s. Herbert and Maggie Hollin; m. Martha Jane Fisch, Nov. 27, 1948; children—Sheila K, Henry T., Richard G., Roberta E., Nathan W., Jacob C. B.B.A., St. Mary's U., 1965, J.D., 1970. Bar: Tex. 1969, U.S. Supreme Ct. 1974, U.S. Claims, 1978, U.S. Ct. Appeals 1981. Sole practice, San Antonio, 1969—; mem. nat. bd. advisors Am. Biog. Inst. Served with USAF, World War II. Decorated Air medal, Air Force Commendation medal with oak leaf cluster; recipient award for fighting discrimination Govt. Employed Mejures, 1981, others. Mem. Tex. State Bar, San Antonio Bar Assn., Tex. Trial Lawyers Assn., Res. Officers Assn. (life), Air Force Assn. (life), VFW (life), DAV (life), Am. Legion, Mil. Order World Wars. Baptist. Civil rights, General practice, Labor. Home and Office: 7710 Stagecoach San Antonio TX 78227

HOLLINGSWORTH, JEFFREY ALAN, lawyer; b. Berkeley, Calif., May 7, 1951; s. Alan Merrill Hollingsworth and Barbara Marie (McGaffey) Peterson; m. Leslie Lizabeth Haines, June 18, 1977. BA with honors, Mich. State U., 1973; JD cum laude, U. Mich., 1981. Bar: Wash. 1981, U.S. Dist. Ct. (we. dist.) Wash. 1982, U.S. Ct. Appeals (9th cir.) 1983, U.S. Dist. Ct. (no. dist.) Calif. 1986. Assoc. Perkins Coie, Seattle, 1981—. Vol. atty. ad litem program King County, Seattle, 1983—. Mem. ABA, Wash. State Bar Assn., Seattle-King County Bar Assn. Democrat. Avocation: musician. Labor, Federal civil litigation, State civil litigation. Office: Perkins Coie 1900 Washington Bldg Seattle WA 98101

HOLLINGSWORTH, JOE GREGORY, lawyer; b. Indpls., Mar. 3, 1949; s. Don Roy and Marilyn Ann (Gregory) H.; m. Nancy Elaine Bartlett, Jan. 21, 1971; children: Gregory Bartlett, Grant Wagner. BA, De Pauw U., 1971; JD, Georgetown U., 1974. Bar: D.C. 1975. From assoc. to ptnr. McKenna, Conner & Cuneo, Washington, 1974-82; ptnr. Spriggs, Bode & Hollingsworth, Washington, 1982—. Presbyterian. Clubs: University (Washington), Kenwood Country (Bethesda, Md.). Avocations: tennis, running, golf, swimming. Administrative and regulatory, Federal civil litigation, Environment. Home: 5324 Portsmouth Rd Bethesda MD 20816 Office: Spriggs Bode & Hollingsworth 1015 15th St NW Suite 1100 Washington DC 20005

HOLLINGTON, RICHARD RINGS, JR., lawyer, banker; b. Findlay, Ohio, Nov. 12, 1932; s. Richard Rings and Annett (Kirk) H.; m. Sally Stecher, Apr. 4, 1959; children: Florence A., Julie A., Richard R. III. Peter S. B.A., Williams Coll., 1954; J.D., Harvard U., 1957. Bar: Ohio 1957. Spl. counsel Ohio Atty. Gen., Cleve., 1963-70; ptnr. Marshman, Hornbeck & Hollington, Cleve., 1958-67, McDonald, Hopkins, Hardy & Hollington, Cleve., 1967-69; law dir. City of Cleve., 1971-72; mng. ptnr. Baker & Hostetler, Cleve., 1969-71, 73—; chmn. bd. dirs., pres. Ohio Bank & Savs. Co. Mem. Ohio Gen. Assembly, 1967-70; mem. exec. com. Ohio Republican fin. Com., 1971—, Cuyahoga County Rep. Orgn., 1968—; mem. Cuyahoga County Rep. Central Com., 1962-66; trustee Cleve. State U., 1970-73, Greater Cleve. Hosp. Assn., 1976-82, Cleve. Mus. Natural History, 1969-81, Cleve. Zool. Soc., 1970—, N.E. Ohio Regional Sewer Dist., 1972-73, Cuyahoga County Hosp. Found., 1968-73, Greater Cleve. Growth Corp., 1972, Ohio Mcpl. League, 1972, others. Mem. ABA, Ohio Bar Assn., Cuyahoga Bar Assn., Greater Cleve. Bar Assn., Law Dirs. Assn., Sixth Cir. Jud. Conf. (life), Ct. of Nisi Prius. Clubs: Union (Cleve.), Tavern (Cleve.), Rowfant (Cleve.), Cleve. Athletic (Cleve.); The Country (Pepper Pike); Roaring Gap (N.C.); Rolling Park (Pa.). Home: 20020 Marchmont Rd Shaker Heights OH 44122 Office: 3200 National City Ctr Cleveland OH 44114

HOLLINS, MITCHELL LESLIE, lawyer; b. N.Y.C., Mar. 11, 1947; s. Milton and Alma (Bell) H.; m. Nancy Kirchheimer, Mar. 27, 1977; 1 child, Herbert K., II. B.A., Case Western Res. U., 1967; J.D., NYU, 1971. Bar: Ill. 1971, U.S. Dist. Ct. (no. dist.) Ill. 1971. Assoc., Sonnenschein Carlin Nath & Rosenthal, Chgo., 1971-78, ptnr., 1978—. Asst. sec. Jr. Achievement Chgo., 1980—; bd. dirs. Young Men's Jewish Council, 1973-75; bd. dirs. young people's div. Jewish United Fund Met. Chgo., 1972-76; bd. dirs. Med. Research Inst. Council, Michael Reese Hosp. and Med. Center, 1978—, mem. exec. com., 1979—, sec., 1981-82, gen. counsel, 1983-86, vice chmn., 1987—, chmn. jr. bd., 1978-79. Mem. ABA, Ill. State Bar Assn., Chgo. Bar Assn. Republican. Clubs: Standard, Lake Shore Country (mem. bd. govs. 1984—, sec. 1985—), Legal. Note and comment editor NYU Jour. Internat. Law and Politics, 1970-71. General corporate, Securities. Home: 994 Vernon Ave Glencoe IL 60022 Office: 8000 Sears Tower Chicago IL 60606

HOLLINSHEAD, EARL DARNELL, JR., lawyer; b. Pitts., Aug. 1, 1927; s. Earl Darnell and Gertrude (Cahill) H.; m. Sylvia Antion, June 29, 1957; children: Barbara, Kim, Earl III, Susan. AB, Ohio U., 1948; LLB, U. Pitts., 1951. Bar: Pa. 1952, U.S. Ct. Mil. Appeals 1954, U.S. Dist. Ct. (we. dist.) Pa. 1955, U.S. Supreme Ct. 1956, U.S. Ct. Appeals (3d cir.) 1959, U.S. Dist. Ct. (ea. dist.) Ohio 1978. Sole practice Pitts., 1955-70; ptnr. Hollinshead & Mendelson, Pitts., 1970—; mem. Pitts. Estate Planning Council; bd. dirs. Immutech, Inc., Rochester, N.Y. Contbr. articles to profl. jours. Served to lt. USNR, 1951-55. FellowPa. Bar Found. (life); mem. Pa. Bar Assn. (chmn. real property div. 1983-85, real property, probate and trust sects. 1985-86), Allegheny County Bar Assn. (chmn. real property sect. 1975-76), Pa. Bar Inst. (lectr., planner), Am. Coll. Real Estate Lawyers. Real property, Bankruptcy, Probate. Home: 2535 Windgate Rd Bethel Park PA 15102 Office: Hollinshead & Mendelson 230 Grant Bldg Pittsburgh PA 15219

HOLLIS, EVERETT LOFTUS, lawyer; b. Wilkes-Barre, Pa., Dec. 6, 1914; s. Frank E. and Mary C. (Loftus) H.; m. Marion Jennings, June 21, 1941; children—Nicholas, Mary, Benjamin; m. Jane Scholl Farrell, Apr. 17, 1974. B.S., U. Ill., 1936; LL.B., Harvard, 1939. Bar: Mass. 1939, N.Y. 1954, Ill. 1966, D.C. 1970. Law clk. to Justice H. T. Lummus, Mass. Supreme Jud. Ct., 1940; pvt. law practice Boston, 1941; atty. OPA, 1941-43; with Atomic Energy Commn., 1947-52, gen. counsel, 1951-52; formerly gen. corp. counsel Gen. Electric Co., N.Y.C.; now ptnr. firm Mayer, Brown and Platt (attys.), Chgo. and Washington; exec. dir. Commn. on Founds. and Pvt. Philanthropy.; Mem. Pres.'s Com. on Contract Compliance; mem. Nat. Commn. on Med. Profl. Liability. Co-author: Federal Conflict of Interest Laws, 1960. Mem. Rockefeller U. Council, N.Y.C. Served as lt. USNR, 1943-46. Mem. ABA, 7th Cir. Bar Assn., D.C. Bar Assn., N.Y.C. Bar Assn., Am. Law Inst., Chgo. Council Fgn. Relations, Beta Gamma Sigma. Clubs: Univ. (Chgo.), Met. (Chgo.); Harvard (N.Y.C.). General corporate, Legislative. Home: 1448 N Lake Shore Dr Chicago IL 60610 Office: 190 S LaSalle St Chicago IL 60603

HOLLIS, LOUIE ANDREW, lawyer; b. Enteprise, Ala., Nov. 10, 1942; s. Louie Andrew and Bonnie Ruth (Jones) H. m. Carol Duke, Dec. 20, 1979; m. Jean Virginia Grimes, Sept. 27 (div. 1976); children—Kelly, Allison. B.S., U. Ala., 1965, J.D., 1968. Bar: Ala. 1968, U.S. Dist. Ct. (so., mid. and no. dists.) Ala. Sole practice, Enterprise, Ala., 1970-76; assoc. Emond & Vines, Birmingham, Ala., 1976-81, Hardin & Hollis, 1981—. Contbr. articles to profl. jours. Served to capt. U.S. Army, 1968-78. Vietnam. Decorated Bronze Star; Vietnamese Commendation medal. Mem. Ala. Trial Lawyers Assn. (pres.-elect, treas., sec., 2d v.p. bd. govs., exec. com.), Assn. Trial Lawyers Am. ABA. Democrat. Methodist. Personal injury, Federal civil litigation, State civil litigation. Home: 1120 Beacon Pkwy E Suite 607 Birmingham AL 35209 Office: PO Box 11328 Birmingham AL 35201

HOLLIS, SHEILA SLOCUM, lawyer; b. Denver, July 15, 1948; d. Theodore Doremus and Emily M. (Caplis) Slocum; m. John Hollis, 1 dau., Windsong. B.S. cum laude with honors, U. Colo., 1971; J.D. (Law Sch. scholar), U. Denver, 1973. Bar: Colo. 1974, D.C. 1975, U.S. Supreme Ct. 1980. Trial atty. FPC, Washington, 1974-75; asso. firm Wilner & Scheiner, Washington, 1975-77; dir. office enforcement Fed. Energy Regulatory Commn., Washington, 1977-79; partner firm Butler & Binion, Washington, 1980-84; ptnr. Broadhurst, Brook, Mangham & Hardy, Washington, 1984-87 ; ptnr. Vinson & Elkins, 1987—; profl. lectr. in law Nat. Law Center, George Washington U., 1980-87. Co-author: Energy Decision Making, 1983; contbr. articles to profl. publs. Established and developed Enforcement Program of Fed. Energy Regulatory Commn. Mem. ABA (mem. council Natural Resources sect., coordinating group on energy law, liaison with Southwestern Legal Found.), Internat. Oil and Gas Ednl. Inst. (adv. bd.), Southwestern Legal Found., Nat. Gas Inst. (chmn. 1983-87), Fed. Energy Bar Assn., D.C. Bar. Club: National Press. FERC practice, Administrative and regulatory, Private international. Office: 1455 Pennsylvania Ave NW Washington DC 20004

HOLLOWAY, HILIARY HAMILTON, banker, lawyer; b. Durham, N.C., Mar. 7, 1928; s. Joseph Sim and Zelma (Slade) H.; m. Beatrice Gwen Larkin, Dec. 21, 1951; children: Hiliary H., Janis L. B.S.C., N.C. Central U., 1949; Ed.M., Temple U., 1956, J.D., 1964. Bar: Pa. 1965, U.S. Dist. Ct. (ea. dist.) Pa. 1965, U.S. Supreme Ct. 1965. Bus. mgr. St. Augustine's Coll., Raleigh, N.C., 1950-53; nat. exec. dir. Kappa Alpha Psi, Phila., 1953-65; mem. firm Hazell & Bowser, Phila., 1965-68; asst. counsel Fed. Res. Bank, Phila., 1968-72, v.p., gen. counsel, 1972-82, sr. v.p., gen. counsel, 1982—; arbitrator Am. Arbitration Assn. trustee emeritus N.C. Central U.; vice chmn. Met. YMCA, Phila., 1973—; trustee Lankenau Hosp., 1978—; bd. dirs. Phila. Mus. Art, 1980—. Recipient Disting. Community Service award Chapel of Four Chaplains, Phila., 1975; recipient Martin Luther King award Educator's Roundtable, Phila., 1977, Laurel Wreath award Kappa Alpha Psi, Detroit, 1982. Mem. ABA, Phila. Bar Assn., Nat. Bar Assn., Fed. Bar Assn. General corporate, Banking. Office: Fed Res Bank Phila Ten Independence Mall Philadelphia PA 19106

HOLLOWAY, JAN CHARLENE, lawyer; b. Houston, Nov. 6, 1957; d. Charles B. and Betty (Womack) H. BA, La. State U., 1978, JD, 1981. Bar: La. 1981, U.S. Dist. Ct. (we. dist.) La. 1983, U.S. Dist. Ct. (mid. dist.) La. 1984, U.S. Ct. Appeals (5th cir.) 1985. Law clk. to presiding justice U.S. Dist. Ct. (we. dist.), Alexandria, La., 1981-83; assoc. Gold, Simon, Weems, Bruser, Sharp, Sues & Rundell, Alexandria, 1983—. Chmn. bd. dirs. Cen. La. Chpt. ARC, Alexandria, 1987—. Mem. ABA, La. Bar Assn. (chmn. essay contest young lawyer's sect, 1985-86, young lawyer's sect. council 1987—), Alexandria Bar Assn. (chmn. law week 1985-86), 5th Cir. Bar Assn., Am. Judicature Soc. Republican. Baptist. Consumer commercial, Contracts commercial, Real property.

HOLLOWAY, WILLIAM J., JR., federal judge; b. 1923. A.B., U. Okla., 1947; LL.B., Harvard U., 1950. Mem. firm Halloway & Halloway, Oklahoma City, 1950-51; atty. dept. justice Washington, 1951-52; ptnr. Crowe, Dunleavy & Thaweat, 1952-68; judge U.S. Ct. Appeals 10th Circuit, Oklahoma City, 1968—, now chief judge. Served to 1st lt. AUS, 1943-47. Mem. ABA, Fed. Bar Assn., Okla. Bar Assn., Oklahoma County Bar Assn. Office: US Court Appeals PO Box 1767 Oklahoma City OK 73101 *

HOLLYER, A(RTHUR) RENE, lawyer; b. Wycoff, N.J., July 28, 1938; s. Richard W. and Florence (Vervaet) H.; m. Lauraine Dennis, Apr. 8, 1978; children—James Richard, Jennifer Ashley. B.A., Williams Coll., 1961; M.P.A., Woodrow Wilson Sch., Princeton, 1963; LL.B., Columbia U., 1966. Bar: N.J. 1966, N.Y. 1968, U.S. Dist. Ct. N.J. 1966, U.S. Dist. Ct. (so. and ea. dists.) N.Y. 1969, U.S. Ct. Appeals (3d cir.) 1970, U.S. Ct. Appeals (2d cir.) 1971, D.C. 1972, U.S. Supreme Ct. 1974. Law sec. to judge N.J. Superior Ct., Newark, 1966-67; assoc. Olwine, Connelly, Chase, O'Donnell & Weyher, N.Y.C., 1968-70, 72-74; asst. U.S. atty. Dist. N.J., 1970-71; ptnr. Hollyer, Jones, Pindyck, Brady & Chira and predecessor firms, N.Y.C., 1974—; spl. master N.Y. Supreme Ct., N.Y.C., 1979-82. Mem. N.Y. State Bar Assn., N.J. Bar Assn., Assn. Bar City N.Y., N.Y. County Lawyers Assn. Federal civil litigation, State civil litigation, General practice. Home: 50 Hamilton Rd Glen Ridge NJ 07028 Office: Hollyer Jones Pindyck Brady & Chira 342 Madison Ave New York NY 10173

HOLM, FLOYD W., lawyer; b. Panguitch, Utah, Nov. 17, 1953; s. Floyd S. and Hazel Agnes (Tippetts) H.; m. Sandra Jeanne Wangerin, Mar. 16, 1977; children: F. Andrew, Stephanie, Nathan, Rebecca. AS, Snow Coll., 1974; BS, U. Utah, 1978, JD, 1981. Bar: Utah 1981, U.S. Dist. Ct. Utah 1981. Assoc. Snow, Christensen & Martineau, Salt Lake City, 1981-83, Chamberlain & Higbee, Cedar City, Utah, 1984—. Topics editor U. Utah Law Rev., 1980-81. Mem. Cedar City Festival Celebration Com., 1985—. Mem. ABA. Democrat. Mormon. Club: Exchange (Cedar City) (bd. dirs. 1986—). Avocation: golf. Personal injury, State civil litigation, General practice. Office: Chamberlain & Higbee 250 S Main St PO Box 726 Cedar City UT 84720

HOLM, MELVIN EDWARD, lawyer; b. Syracuse, N.Y., Jan. 7, 1942; s. Melvin Carl and Beatrice (Fritcher) H.; m. Eugenia Mueller, June 16, 1962; children: Heather Anne, Michael Edward, Christian Frederic. BA, Syracuse U., 1965, JD, 1968. Bar: N.Y. 1969, U.S. Dist. Ct. (no. dist.) N.Y. 1969, U.S. Dist. Ct. (we. dist.) N.Y. 1971, U.S. Ct. Appeals (2d cir.) 1984. Assoc. Hancock and Espabrook, Syracuse, 1968-82; of counsel N.Y. Senate, Albany, 1974-84; sole practice Fayetteville, N.Y., 1983—; bd. dirs. Material Handling Products, McIntyre Paper Co., Adams Paper Co.; cons. McCormick Assn. Inc., Fayetteville, 1985—; prin./broker Century 21 Lymestone, Fayetteville, 1983—. Bd. dirs. Curry Coll., Milton, Mass., 1985—, Syracuse Symphony Orch., 1977-82; chmn. Town of Manlus (N.Y.) Rep. Com., 1980-84; mem. United Way, Syracuse, 1974. Mem. ABA, N.Y. Bar Assn., Onondaga County Bar Assn. Republican. Lodge: Mason. General corporate, Legislative, Real property. Office: 7030 E Genesee St Fayetteville NY 13066

HOLMAN, CHARLES F(REDRICK), III, lawyer, law educator; b. Lansing, Mich., Oct. 27, 1957; s. Charles F. Holman Jr. and Thelma J. (Smith) Trahan. B in Gen. Studies, U. Mich., 1977; JD, Wayne State U., 1980. Bar: Mich. 1981. Law clk. Mich. Dept. Civil Rights, Detroit, 1978-80; legal counsel Mich. Legis. Service Bur., Lansing, 1981-87; trial atty. U.S. EEOC, Detroit, 1987—; adj. prof. Cooley Law Sch., Lansing, 1984—. Asst. corp. counsel City of Detroit, 1983; state supt. spl. com. Minorities in Higher Edn., Lansing, 1983-86; cons. affirmative action City of Jackson, Mich., 1983-84. Regents Alumni scholar U. Mich., 1974; fianlist White House fellowship, 1983. Mem. ABA (vice chmn. young lawyers human rights com. 1985—, individual rights and responsibility sect., exec. council 1987, chmn., 1987—), Mich. Bar Assn. (chmn. high sch. speakers program 1984-85, mem. young lawyers sect. exec. council 1983—; Outstanding Service Citation 1985), NAACP (Spingarn medal selection com. 1981-84, nat. legal com. 1981-84, nat. officers com. 1982, personnel com. 1981-83, bd. dirs. 1977-79, 1981-83, Mitchell Leadership award 1982). Democrat. Avocations: genealogy, civil and human rights, pub. speaking. Legislative, Civil rights, Legal education. Office: 1540 McNamara Bldg 477 Michigan Ave Detroit MI 48226

HOLMAN, JOHN CLARKE, lawyer; b. Milw., Apr. 19, 1938; s. John Abner and Myrtle Vivian (Salter) H.; m. Jeanne Riba, Sept. 2, 1960 (div.1971); children: Lee Anne, Melaney Anne; m. Anne Elizabeth Wooster, Apr. 28, 1973; 1 child, Elizabeth Anne. BS, U. Wis., 1961; JD, Am. U., 1965; postgrad., Holborn Coll. Law, London, 1965-67. Bar: U.S. Dist. Ct. D.C. 1966, U.S. Ct. Appeals (D.C. and fed. cirs.) 1968, U.S. Supreme Ct. 1972. Examiner U.S. Patent Office, Washington, 1961-65; expert intellectual property Marks & Clerk, London, 1965-67; ptnr. Holman & Stern, Washington, 1967-77, pres., 1977—. Author: U.S. Patent Law, 1971. Mem. ABA, Licensing Execs. Soc., Assn. Internat. Patent Law Attys., Am. Inst. Mining Engrs., Internat. Fed. Indsl. Property Attys., Interam. Assn. Indsl. Property, Am. Intellectual Patent Law Assn., Internat. Assn. Protection Indsl. Property, U.S. Trademark Assn., Am. Soc. for Metals. Republican. Episcopalian. Patent, Trademark and copyright. Office: Holman & Stern Chtd 2401 15th St NW Washington DC 20009

HOLME, JOHN CHARLES, JR., lawyer; b. N.Y.C., Aug. 3, 1940; s. John Charles and Anne Robinson (Mackey) H.; m. Diane Louise Stover, July 24, 1965; children—Christopher Scott, Jennifer Anne. Student Washington Coll., 1958-60; B.A., U. Vt., 1962; LL.B., Cornell U., 1965. Bar: N.Y. 1966, U.S. Dist. Ct. (we. dist.) N.Y. 1966, Ohio 1974, U.S. Dist. Ct. (no. dist.) Ohio 1974, U.S. Ct. Appeals 1979, Vt. 1982, U.S. Dist. Ct. Vt. 1983. Assoc. Dutcher, Witt, Sidoti & Considine, Rochester, 1966-69; assoc. Antell Harris, Githler & Calleri, Rochester, 1968-69; trust adminstr. Marine Midland Bank, Rochester, 1969-70, asst. trust officer, 1970-73, trust officer, 1973-74; staff atty. Advocates for Basic Legal Equality, Toledo, 1974-82; assoc. William E. Dakin, Jr., Chester, Vt., 1982-83; v.p., sec. Dakin & Holme, P.C., Chester, 1984—. Mem. Chester Fire Dept., 1982—; v.p. Mental Health Services Southeastern Vt., Bellows Falls, 1983—. Mem. Vt. Bar Assn., Assn. Trial Lawyers Am. Democrat. Mem. United Ch. of Christ. State civil litigation, General practice, Real property. Home: PO Box 474 Chester VT 05143 Office: Dakin & Holme PC PO Box 499 Chester VT 05143

HOLMES, CHARLES EVERETT, lawyer; b. Wellington, Kans., Dec. 21, 1931; s. Charles Everett and Elizabeth Francis (Bergin) H.; m. Lynn Lacy, Jan. 2, 1954; children—Anne Lacy, Charles Everett, Rebecca. B.A., Wichita U., 1953; LL.B., U. Okla., 1961. Bar: Okla. 1961. Practice, Tulsa, after 1961; sec. Sinclair Oil & Gas Co., Sinclair Can. Oil Co., Mesa Pipeline Co., Border Pipe Line Co., Sinclair Transp. Co., Ltd.; ptnr. Rogers, Bell & Robinson, Tulsa, 1969-71; v.p. Nat. Bank of Tulsa, 1971-78; atty. Petro-Lewis Corp., Denver, 1978—. Served with USAF, 1954-56, 61-62. Mem. ABA, Okla. Bar Assn., Tulsa County Bar Assn. Roman Catholic. (del. Okla. Council Cath. Diocese 1966—, chmn. Cath. Parish Governing Body 1968—, bd. dirs. Youth Services, Travelers Aid, Com. Fgn. Relations). Oil and gas leasing, General corporate, Administrative and regulatory. Home: 4505 S Yosemite Apt 103 Denver CO 80237 Office: Energy Ctr I 717 17th St PO Box 2250 Denver CO 80201

HOLMES, CLIFTON LEE, (SCRAPPY), lawyer; b. Kilgore, Tex., Feb. 17, 1939; s. Clyde Frank and Ima Edith (Osborne) H.; m. Edwina McKellar, Jan. 19, 1960 (dec. 1979); children—Niki, Bryan, Lacy, Shelly. B.A., U. Tex.-Austin, 1961; J.D. with honors, George Washington U., 1966. Bar: Tex. 1967, U.S. Dist. Ct. (ea. dist.) Tex. 1973, U.S. Supreme Ct. 1974, U.S. Dist. Ct. (we. dist.) Tex. 1974, U.S. Ct. Appeals (5th cir.) 1974, U.S. Dist. Ct. (no. dist.) Tex. 1979, U.S. Ct. Appeals (11th cir.) 1981, U.S. Dist. Ct. (so. dist.) Tex. 1984. Regional rep. U.S. Dept. Labor, Austin, Tex., 1966-67; sole practice, Gilmer, Tex., 1967-68; asst. dir. Job Corps, Washington, 1968-70; editor State Bar Tex., Austin, 1970-71; sole practice, Austin, 1971-74, Kilgore/Longview, Tex., 1974—. Editor: Federal Criminal Practice Manual, 1975, Voice for the Defense, 1977-81, Capital Murder Defense, 1978. State del. Democratic Party, 1976, 80. Mem. Tex. Criminal Def. Lawyers Assn. (bd. dirs. 1974-81, v.p., 1982-83, pres.-elect 1983-84, pres. 1984-85; commendation award 1974, 77, 79, 82), Tex. Trial Lawyers Assn., Nat. Criminal Def. Lawyers Assn. Democrat. Criminal, Personal injury, Workers' compensation. Home: 3614 Danville Dr Kilgore TX 75662 Office: Holmes Law Office PO Drawer 3267 Longview TX 75606

HOLMES, DALLAS SCOTT, lawyer, educator; b. Los Angeles, Dec. 2, 1940; s. Donald Cherry and Hazel (Scott) H.; m. Patricia McMichael, Aug. 21, 1965; children—Mark Scott, Tobin John. A.B. cum laude, Pomona Coll., 1962; M.Sc., London Sch. Econs., 1964; J.D., U. Calif.-Berkeley, 1967. Bar: Calif. 1968. Assoc. Best, Best & Krieger, Riverside, Calif., 1968-74, ptnr., 1974—; exec. asst. to Assembly majority floor leader, Calif. State Legislature, Sacramento, 1969-70; asst. adj. prof. Grad. Sch. Mgmt., U. Calif.-Riverside, 1977—; city atty. Cities of Corona, Banning and Redlands (Calif.). Pres., Pomona Coll. Alumni Council, 1973-74, Century Club, Riverside, 1974-76, Citizens Univ. Com., 1983-85, Downtown Riverside Assn., 1987—. Named Man of Yr., Riverside Press-Enterprise, 1962, Young Man of Yr., Riverside Jr. C. of C., 1972. Mem. Riverside County Bar Assn. (pres. 1982), Calif. State Bar Assn. (exec. com. pub. law sect. 1983-86), ABA, Internat. Bar Assn. Republican. Presbyterian. Contbr. articles on mass transit, assessment of farmland in Calif., exclusionary zoning to profl. jours.; author proposed tort reform initiative for Calif. physicians. Local government, Labor, Legislative. Home: 4515 6th St Riverside CA 92501 Office: 3750 University Ave PO Box 1028 Riverside CA 92502

HOLMES, HAL, lawyer; b. Trenton, Tenn., Oct. 18, 1908; s. Victor Hal and Alice Mosely (Davidson) H.; m. Margarette Harrison, Oct. 31, 1937; 1 son, Hal. Student, Vanderbilt U., Nashville, 1930; LL.B., Cumberland U., Lebanon, Tenn., 1931. Bar: Tenn. 1931, U.S. Dist. Ct. (we. dist.) Tenn. 1936, U.S. Ct. Appeals (6th cir.) 1980. Sole practice, Trenton, 1931-34; ptnr. Holmes and Holmes, Trenton, 1934-67; assoc. Malone, Holmes and Gossum, Trenton, 1968—. Served with combat engrs., 1944-46. Mem. Gibson County Bar Assn. Methodist. Federal civil litigation, State civil litigation, General practice. Office: Malone Holmes Gossum PO Box 491 Trenton TN 38382

HOLMES, JAMES RICHARD, lawyer; b. Pittsfield, Mass., Jan. 6, 1955; s. John F. and Alice (Blaney) H. BA in History, Williams Coll., 1976; JD, Tulane U., 1979. Bar: La. 1979, U.S. Dist. Ct. (ea. dist.) La. 1979, U.S. Dist. Ct. (mid. dist.) La. 1981, U.S. Ct. Appeals (5th cir.) 1984. Assoc. Chaffe, McCall, Phillips, Toler & Sarpy, New Orleans, 1979-84, spl. ptnr., 1984-87; with Carmouche, Gray & Hoffman, New Orleans, 1987—; bd. dirs. Affiliated Marine Service Inc., Slidell, La., HarWin Inc., Slidell, Comml. Towing Inc., Kenner, La. Mem. ABA, La. Bar Assn., New Orleans Bar Assn., Maritime Law Assn. (procter), Assn. Transp. Practioners. Avocation: theatre. Admiralty, Insurance, Private international. Home: 5617 Marshall Foch New Orleans LA 70124 Office: 2100 Poydras Ctr 650 Poydras St New Orleans LA 70130-6121

HOLMES, KENNETH HOWARD, lawyer; b. St. Paul, June 13, 1936; s. John Turner and Beatrice Carolina (Johnson) H.; m. Karen Ruth Seeger,

Aug. 6, 1960; children: J. Scott, Mark, Michael. B.S. in Law, U. Minn., 1958, LL.B. magna cum laude, 1960. Bar: Minn. 1960, N.Y. 1962, U.S. Supreme Ct. 1969, Calif. 1986. Assoc. Dewey, Ballantine, Bushby, Palmer & Wood, N.Y.C., 1961-69, ptnr., 1969—. Mem. ABA, N.Y. State Bar Assn., Assn. Bar City N.Y., Order of Coif. Federal civil litigation, State civil litigation. Office: Dewey Ballantine Bushby Palmer & Wood 333 S Hope St Los Angeles CA 90071

HOLMES, MARIAN MCGRATH, lawyer; b. Chgo., Apr. 1, 1934; d. Harmon Webber and Margaret Helen (Goodman) McGrath; children—Margaret Etta, Karen Chandler. B.A., Wellesley Coll., 1956; M.Ed., Nat. Coll. Edn., 1970; postgrad. Northwestern U., 1975; J.D., Tex. Tech U., 1982. Bar: Tex. 1982. Pres., Hartzell Corp., Evanston, Ill., 1969-70; tchr. North Shore Country Day Sch., Winnetka, Ill., 1970-76; headmistress Trinity Sch., Midland, Tex., 1976-79; assoc. atty. Lemon, Close, Shearer, Ehrlich & Brown, Perryton, Tex., 1982-85; assoc. Bennett, Thomas & Feldman, Dallas, 1986—. Author, editor Tex. Tech Law Rev., 1980-82. Mem. steering com. for Panhandle br. Women's Advocacy Project, Inc., Austin, 1983—; elder Trinity Presbyn. Ch., 1984-86. Centennial Fund grantee, 1972; recipient Oil and Gas law award, 1982. Mem. ABA, Tex. Bar Assn., Dallas Bar Assn., Northeast Panhandle Bar Assn. (pres. 1984-86). Republican. Clubs: Bus. and Profl. Women's, Wheatheart Republican Women's (pres. 1983). Home: 3000 Amherst Dallas TX 75225

HOLMES, RICHARD WINN, state supreme ct. justice; b. Wichita, Kans., Feb. 23, 1923; s. Winn Earl and Sidney (Clapp) H.; m. Gwen Sand, Aug. 19, 1950; children—Robert W., David K. B.S., Kans. State U., 1950; J.D., Washburn U., 1953. Bar: Kans. bar 1953, U.S. Dist. Ct. bar 1953. Practice law Wichita, Kans., 1953-77; judge Wichita Mcpl. Ct., 1959-61; instr. bus. law Wichita State U., 1959-60; justice Kans. Supreme Ct., 1977—. Served with USNR, 1943-46. Mem. Kans., Topeka, Wichita bar assns., Am. Judges Assn. (founder, bd. govs. 1980—). Jurisprudence. Home: 2535 Granthurst Ave Topeka KS 66611 Office: Kansas Judicial Center Topeka KS 66612

HOLMES, ROBERT ALLEN, lawyer, educator, consultant, lecturer; b. Sewickley, Pa., Dec. 12, 1947; s. Lee Roy John and Nellie Ann (Kupits) H.; m. Linda Lee Freeman Aug. 16, 1969; children—Wesley Paige, Ashley Reagan. B.A. in Bus. Administrn., Coll. William and Mary, 1969, J.D., 1972. Bar: Md. 1972, U.S. Dist. Ct. Md. 1972, Va. 1973, U.S. Dist. Ct. (ea. dist.) Va. 1973. Assoc. Ober, Grimes & Shriver, Balt., 1972-73, Kellam, Pickrell & Lawler, Norfolk, Va., 1973-75; ptnr. Holliday, Holmes & Inman, Norfolk, 1975-77; asst. prof. law Bowling Green State U., Ohio, 1977-82, assoc. prof., 1982—; dir. Purchasing Law Inst., 1979—, EEO-Affirmative Action Research Group, 1978—; lectr. profl. seminars and workshops throughout country on discrimination and affirmative action law. Author: (books) (with others) Computers, Data Processing and the Law, 1984; numerous manuals on discrimination and affirmative action law. Contbg. editor, monthly columnist Midwest Purchasing, 1983-84. Recipient Outstanding Young Man award William and Mary Soc. Alumni, 1973. Mem. Md. Bar Assn., Va. Bar Assn., Am. Bus. Law Assn., Am. Soc. Personnel Adminstrs., Nat. Assn. Purchasing Mgmt., Mensa. Republican. Methodist. Contracts commercial, Labor. Home: 1034 Conneaut Ave Bowling Green OH 43402 Office: Bowling Green State U Legal Studies Dept Bowling Green OH 43403

HOLMES, ROBERT EDWARD, justice Ohio Supreme Ct.; b. Columbus, Ohio, Nov. 14, 1922; s. Harry Barclay and Nora Jane (Birney) H.; m. Jean Wren; children—Robert Edward, Hamilton Barclay. A.B., Ohio U., 1943, LL.B., 1949. Bar: Ohio bar. Practiced law 1949-69; mem. Ohio Ho. of Reps., 1960-69; judge 10th Dist. Ct. Appeals, Columbus, 1969-78; justice Ohio Supreme Ct., Columbus, 1979—. Pres. Columbus Area Internat. Program, Council Internat. Programs; founder Columbus Community Camp; bd. dirs. Boy Scouts Am., Salvation Army, Pilot Dogs, Inc. Served with USN, 1944-46. Mem. Columbus Bar Assn., Ohio Bar Assn., Am. Bar Assn. Republican. Office: Supreme Ct Ohio 30 E Broad St Columbus OH 43215 *

HOLMES, RONALD LOYD, lawyer; b. Tylertown, Miss., Dec. 30, 1948; s. Jamie Wendel and Mavis Mildred (Martin) H.; m. Janette Elizabeth Santos, Mar. 14, 1979; children: Karen, Shelley, Brandon. BBA, La. Tech. U., 1970; JD, La. State U., 1973. Assoc. Phelps, Dunbar, Marks, Claverie & Sims, New Orleans, 1973-77; ptnr. Winstead, McGuire, Sechrest & Minick, Dallas, 1977-84; pres. The Duke Cos., San Antonio, 1984-86; ptnr. Holmes and Millard, Dallas, 1986—. Trustee polit. action com. San Antonio Apt. Assn., 1986. Served with U.S. Army, 1973. Mem. ABA, Tex. Bar Assn., La. Bar Assn., Dallas Bar Assn., Baton Rouge Bar Assn. (mil. justice 1973), Order of Coif. Real property. Office: 1201 Elm St Suite 2200 Renaissance Tower Dallas TX 75270

HOLMQUEST, DONALD LEE, physician, astronaut, lawyer; b. Dallas, Apr. 7, 1939; s. Sidney Browder and Lillie Mae (Waite) H.; m. Ann Nixon James, Oct. 24, 1972. B.S. in Elec. Engring, So. Meth. U., 1962; M.D., Baylor U., 1967, Ph.D. in Physiology, 1968; J.D., U. Houston, 1980. Student engr. Ling-Temco-Vought, Dallas, 1958-61; electronics engr. Tex. Instruments, Inc., Dallas, 1962; intern Meth. Hosp., Houston, 1967-68; pilot tng. USAF, Williams AFB, Ariz., 1968-69; scientist-astronaut NASA, Houston, 1967-73; research assoc. MIT, 1968-70; asst. prof. radiology and physiology Baylor Coll. Medicine, 1970-73; dir. nuclear medicine Eisenhower Med. Ctr., Palm Desert, Calif., 1973-74; assoc. dean medicine, assoc. prof. Tex. A&M U., College Station, 1974-76; dir. nuclear medicine Navasota (Tex.) Med. Ctr., 1976—, Med. Arts Hosp., Houston, 1977—; ptnr. Wood Lucksinger & Epstein, Houston, 1980—. Contbr. articles to med. jours. Mem. Soc. Nuclear Medicine, Am. Coll. Nuclear Physicians, Tex. Bar Assn., Am. Fighter Pilots Assn., Sigma Xi, Alpha Omega Alpha, Sigma Tau. Health. Home: 3721 Tangley Rd Houston TX 77005

HOLMSTROM, GREGORY LEONARD, lawyer; b. Portland, Oreg., Mar. 5, 1948; s. Leonard and Louise (Sevland) H.; m. Lynn Marie Fischer, Dec. 19, 1970; children: Nathan, Matthew, Seth. BA, Hamline U., 1970; JD, U. Minn., 1974. Bar: Minn. 1974, U.S. Dist. Ct. Minn. 1974. Ptnr. Reishus & Holmstrom (and predecessor firms), Granite Falls, Minn., 1974—; bd. dirs. Citizens State Bank, Echo, Minn. atty. City of Granite Falls, 1976—, City of Echo, 1980—; bd. dirs. Ind. Sch. Dist. 894, Granite Falls, 1986—. Served to sgt. USAR, 1969-75. Named one of Outstanding Young Men Am., U.S. Jaycees, 1976. Mem. ABA, Minn. Bar Assn., 12th Dist. Bar Assn. (pres. 1985—), Granite Falls C. of C. (pres. 1976, bd. dirs. 1974—), Jaycees (pres. 1975). Lodge: Kiwanis (pres. 1985). Avocations: hunting, golfing, water activities, yard work, travel. General practice, Criminal, Local government. Office: Reishus & Holmstrom 685 Prentice St Granite Falls MN 56241

HOLOHAN, WILLIAM ANDREW, state justice; b. Tucson, June 1, 1928; s. Andrew S. and Dorothy L. (Bennett) H.; m. Kathryn Dewey, Dec. 12, 1953; 4 children. LL.B., U. Ariz., 1950. Bar: Ariz. 1950. Asst. U.S. atty., 1953-60; judge Superior Ct., 1963-72; justice Ariz. Supreme Ct., Phoenix, 1972—, chief justice, 1982-87. Served with U.S. Army, 1950-53. Decorated Bronze Star medal. Office: Ariz Supreme Ct 217 South-West Wing Phoenix AZ 85007

HOLSCHUH, JOHN DAVID, judge; b. Ironton, Ohio, Oct. 12, 1926; s. Edward A. and Helen (Ebert) H.; m. Carol Stouder, Aug. 13, 1927; 1 son, John David. B.A., Miami U., 1948; J.D., U. Cin., 1951. Bar: Ohio bar 1951. Law clk. U.S. Dist. Ct. judge, 1952-54; mem. firm Alexander, Ebinger, Holschuh, Fisher & McAlister, Columbus, Ohio, 1954-80; judge U.S. Dist. Ct. for so. dist. Ohio, 1980—; mem. com. on codes of conduct Jud. Conf. U.S., 1985—; adj. prof. law Coll. Law, Ohio State U., 1970. Pres. bd. dirs. Neighborhood House, 1969-70. Fellow Am. Coll. Trial Lawyers; mem. Order of Coif, Phi Beta Kappa, Omicron Delta Kappa. Jurisprudence. Home: 2630 Charing Rd Columbus OH 43221 Office: 85 Marconi Blvd Columbus OH 43215

HOLSINGER, CANDICE DOREEN, lawyer; b. Pitts., June 9, 1955; d. Edward P. and Myrtle-Jane (Atwood) H.; m. Barry Alan McClune, Nov. 23, 1984. BA, Westminster Coll., 1977; JD, Duquesue U., 1981. Bar: Pa., U.S. Dist. Ct. (we. dist.) Pa. Law clk. Child Advocacy Assn., Pitts., 1981; assoc. Tarasi & Tyle, Pitts., 1982-84, Metz, Cook, Hanna, Welsh Bluestone & Beamer, Pitts., 1984—. Mem. ABA, Pa. Bar Assn., Allegheny County Bar Assn., Am. Trial Lawyers Assn. General practice, State civil litigation. Home: 434 Caldwell Ave Wilmerding PA 15148 Office: Metz Cook Hanna et al 408 Grant Bldg Pittsburgh PA 15219

HOLST, DALE LAWSON, lawyer; b. Cedar Rapids, Iowa, Oct. 21, 1929; s. Paul Peter and Ruby (Bartlett) H.; m. Wilma Jacqualine Wilson, Jan. 10, 1954; m. 2d Patricia Lee Creech, Feb. 11, 1966; children—Susan B., Stephen W. Holst, Linda Lu Holst. B.S., U. Iowa, 1950; LL.B., U. Denver, 1955. Bar: Colo. 1956, U.S. Dist. Ct. Colo. 1956. Sole practice, Colorado Springs, Colo., 1956—. Committeeman, Republican Com., 1973—, chmn. 20th rep. dist., 1976-81. Served with AUS, 1951-53. Fellow Am. Coll. Probate Counsel; mem. ABA, Am. Judicature Soc., Colo. Bar Assn., El Paso County Bar Assn., Colorado Springs Estate Planning Council. Republican. Lutheran. Clubs: Colorado Mountain, Rotary, Masons, Shriners. State civil litigation, Personal injury. Office: 210 Holly Sugar Bldg Colorado Springs CO 80903

HOLSTEAD, JOHN BURNHAM, lawyer; b. Dallas, Mar. 5, 1938; s. J.B. and Maurice (Cook) H.; m. Marilyn Morris, Nov. 23, 1963; children: Will, Rand, Scott. B.A., La. Tech. U., 1959; LL.B., U. Tex.-Austin, 1962. Bar: Tex., U.S. Dist. Ct. Tex., 1965, U.S. Ct. Appeals (5th cir.), Colo., U.S. Ct. Appeals (10th cir.), U.S. Supreme Ct. Briefing clk. Tex. Sup. Ct., 1962-63; assoc. Culton, Morgan, Britain & White, Amarillo, Tex., 1963-65; assoc. Vinson & Elkins, Houston, 1965-72, ptnr., 1972—; speaker civil litigation and bus. disputes. Fellow Internat. Soc. Barristers, Tex. Bar Found.; mem. ABA, Tex. Bar Assn., Houston Bar Assn. Episcopalian. Clubs: Ramada, River Oaks Country. Federal civil litigation, State civil litigation. Office: 3228 First City Tower Houston TX 77002

HOLT, G. WOODROW, lawyer; b. Dayton, Ohio, Sept. 9, 1953; s. Gerald W. and Mabel Holt; m. Barbara A. Hoffman, Mar. 11, 1983; 1 child, Andrea. BBA, Ohio U., 1976; JD, Ohio State U., 1982. Bar: Ohio 1982; CPA, Ohio. Acct. Cooper & Lybrand, Columbus, Ohio, 1976-79; assoc. Schwartz, Kelm, Warren & Rubenstein, Columbus, 1982—. Mem. ABA, Ohio Bar Assn., Columbus Bar Assn., Am. Inst. CPAs. Democrat. General corporate, Securities, Contracts commercial. Home: 3191 Martin Rd Dublin OH 43017 Office: Schwartz Kelm Warren & Rubenstein 41 S High St Columbus OH 43215

HOLT, IVAN LEE, JR., former judge; b. Marshall, Mo., May 4, 1913; s. Ivan Lee and Leland (Burks) H.; m. Mary Edwards Depping, Dec. 26, 1945; children: Mary Diana Depping Hoxie, Janet Mildred Depping Resnik, Ivan Lee III; m. Rojena Joan Kabbaz, Feb. 7, 1986. Student, Princeton U., 1931-34; A.B., U. Chgo., 1935, J.D., 1937; LL.D. (hon.), McKendree Coll., 1962; D.C.L. (hon.), Central Meth. Coll., 1983. Bar: Mo. 1937. Assoc. Marion C. Early, St. Louis, 1937-40; asst. circuit atty. City of St. Louis, 1940-42; asst. prof. law Washington U. Law Sch., St. Louis, 1947-48; assoc. Jones, Hocker, Gladney & Grand, St. Louis, 1948-49; judge 22d Circuit Mo., 1949-83; spl. judge Supreme Ct. Mo., Mo. Ct. Appeals Eastern Dist.; mem. faculty Nat. Coll. State Trial Judges, 1967-70; mem. council judges Nat. Council on Crime and Delinquency, 1953-74, exec. com., 1970-73, chmn., 1973-74; Mo. del. Nat. Conf. State Trial Judges, 1967-70; mem. Mo. Commn. on Retirement, Removal and Discipline, 1972-82; mem. vis. com. Law Sch., U. Chgo., 1975-78; mem. Am. Judicature Soc., 1952-83, dir., 1962-64. Contbr. articles profl. publs. Bd. dirs. Barnes Hosp., 1951—, Goodwill Industries, 1952-82, Mo. Hist. Soc., 1972-78; bd. dirs. Methodist Children's Home Mo., 1948-74, pres., 1952-62. Served from lt. (j.g.) to comdr. USNR, 1942-46. Recipient Pub. Service award U. Chgo. Alumni Assn., 1955; fellow Inst. Jud. Adminstrn., 1966-70. Mem. ABA (council sect. jud. adminstrn. 1955-62, chmn. jud. adminstrn. 1962-63, ho. of dels. 1963-66, mem. spl. coms. standards criminal justice and standards jud. conduct), St. Louis Bar Assn. (Disting. Jud. and Pub. Service award 1963), Mo. Bar, Lawyers Assn. St. Louis (life), Am. Law Inst. (life), Law Library Assn. (mem. bd. 1962-72, pres. 1972-82), SR, Sons Confederate Vets, Sigma Alpha Epsilon, Phi Delta Phi. Democrat. Methodist (jud. council 1956-60). Clubs: University, Pike County Country. Lodge: Masons. Trial judge, Industrial. Home: Route 1, Box 165 Louisiana MO 63353

HOLT, JACK WILSON, JR., state chief justice; b. Harrison, Ark., May 18, 1929; s. Jack Wilson and Mary Margaret (Spikes) H.; m. Diane Kelley, Aug. 21, 1966 (div. 1985); children—Kelly, Candace; m. Molly Molitor, Feb. 9, 1985. J.D., U. Ark., 1952. Bar: Ark. 1952. Pros. atty. 16th Jud. Dist., Little Rock, 1955-60; chief asst. atty. State of Ark., Little Rock, 1960-62; sole practice law Little Rock, 1962-80; chief justice Ark. Supreme Ct., Little Rock, 1985—. Fellow Am. Coll. Trial Lawyers, Ark. Bar Found.; mem. Pulaski Bar Assn., ABA, Ark. Bar Assn. (Golden gavel award 1976). Democrat. Methodist. Lodge: Lions (v.p. 1980). Avocations: flying; quail hunting. Home: 7 Tanglewood St Little Rock AR 72202 Office: Ark Supreme Court 3004 Painted Valley Little Rock AR 72212

HOLT, JASON, lawyer; b. East Orange, N.J., July 1, 1953; s. Isaac and Demarest (Hawkin) H. BS, Cornell U.; JD, Rutgers U., Newark. Bar: Pa. 1980, U.S. Dist. Ct. Pa. 1981, U.S. Ct. Appeals (3d. cir.) 1981, N.J. 1983, U.S. Dist. Ct. N.J. 1983. Atty., personnel specialist Office of Essex County Exec., Newark, 1981-84; acting dir. Essex County Office Affirmative Action, Newark, 1983; legal counsel N.J. State Legislature, Trenton, 1984-85; sole practice East Orange, 1985—; asst. corp. counsel City of East Orange, 1986—. Dist. leader Essex County (N.J.) Com., 1984, 85; legal counsel East Orange Mcpl. County Com., 1986, Surrogate Elections, Essex County, 1986; bd. dirs. United Light of Hist. Developers, East Orange, 1981-83. Named one of Outstanding Young Men Am., 1980; recipient Honor Resolutions N.J. Senate, N.J. Assembly and Gov. of N.J., Trenton, 1985, Gov.'s Commendation (1st black atty. to receive this honor), Civilian Recognition Commendation East Orange Police Commrs. Mem. ABA, N.J. State Bar Assn., Garden State Bar Assn., NAACP, Cornell U. Alumni Assn., Rutgers U. Alumni Assn., Afro-Am. Hist. Soc. Club: Cornell U. (Essex County). Avocations: music, sports. Legislative, Municipal law, Bankruptcy. Office: Corp Counsel 44 City Hall Plaza East Orange NJ 07019

HOLT, MICHAEL BARTHOLOMEW, lawyer; b. Jersey City, July 10, 1956; s. William A. and Grace (Donohue) H.; m. Mary Patricia Butler, Aug. 14, 1982; children: Melissa Aislynn, Scott Michael. BA magna cum laude, Providence Coll., 1978; JD, Seton Hall U., 1982. Bar: N.J. 1982, U.S. Dist. Ct. N.J. 1982, U.S. Dist. Ct. (ea. and so. dists.) N.Y. 1985, U.S. Ct. Appeals (3d cir.) 1985, U.S. Supreme Ct. 1986. Assoc. Keane, Brady & Hanlon, Jersey City, 1982-84, Waters, McPherson, McNeill P.A., Secaucus, N.J., 1984-87; ptnr. O'Halloran, Holt and Assocs., Bayonne, N.J., 1987—. Mem. ABA, N.J. Bar Assn., Essex County Bar Assn., Hudson County Bar Assn., Assn. Trial Lawyers Am. Real property, General corporate, General practice. Home: 171 Overlook Ave Belleville NJ 07109 Office: O'Halloran Holt and Assocs 310 Broadway Bayonne NJ 07002

HOLT, ROBERT BLAINE, lawyer; b. Ft. Wayne, Ind., Dec. 26, 1956; s. Robert Elijah and Rowena (Stewart) H. BA, U. Denver, 1979; JD, Temple U., 1982. Bar: Tex. 1982, U.S. Dist. Ct. (no. dist.) Tex. 1982, U.S. Ct. Appeals (5th cir.) 1982. Briefing atty. Tex. Ct. Criminal Appeals, Austin, 1982-83; sr. staff atty. 5th Supreme Jud. Ct. Appeals, Dallas, 1983-85; sole practice Dallas, 1985—; lectr. on AIDS various schs. and orgns. Mem. Lambda Legal Def. Fund, N.Y.C.; dir. bd. of advs. Nat. Lawyers Guild AIDS Network, San Francisco, 1985—, AIDS Resource Ctr., Dallas, 1985—. Mem. ABA, Tex. Bar Assn., Dallas Young Lawyers Assn., Am. Judicature Soc., Phi Alpha Delta, U. Denver Alumni Assn. Republican. Methodist. Lodge: Masons. Criminal, Civil rights, Labor. Home: 4106 Newton St Dallas TX 75219 Office: 900 Jackson St Dallas TX 75202

HOLT, WAYLAND GARTH, retired judge; b. Gatesville, Tex., June 16, 1915; s. William Albert and Annie (Powell) H.; m. Margaret Rutherford, Mar. 29, 1942 (dec. 1971); children: Marguerette Shamburger, Anita March; m. Maxine Scott Westfall, June 3, 1972; stepchildren: Dana Huckle, June Williamson, Lesa Stephens. BA, Baylor U., 1948, JD cum laude, 1949. Bar: Tex. 1949, U.S. Dist. Ct. (no. dist.) Tex. 1950. County atty. Scurry County, Snyder, Tex., 1953-56; dist. atty. 132d Jud. Dist. Tex., Snyder, 1957-70, dist. judge, 1970-84; sr. judge (retired, serves by assignment), 1985—. Served to capt. U.S. Army, 1940-45, ETO. Mem. State Bar Tex. (chmn. criminal law sect. 1964-65, sunset com. 1982-83), Scurry County Bar Assn. (pres. 1951, 55), Snyder C. of C., Snyder Jaycees (v.p. 1949—), Western Tex. Coll. Booster Club (pres. 1979-80, 85-87). Democrat. Baptist. Clubs: Gold Coaters (Snyder) (pres. 1980-81). Lodges: Lions (pres. 1959—), Masons (33 degree) (dist. chmn. 1965—). Judicial administration, Criminal, State civil litigation. Home: 2905 Westridge Dr Snyder TX 79549 Office: PO Box 96 Snyder TX 79549

HOLTH, FREDRIK DAVIDSON, lawyer; b. New London, Conn., Dec. 31, 1940; s. Frederick Skarup and Louise (Davidson) H.; m. Constance Q. Holth, Oct. 8, 1966; children: Fredrik, Christina L. B.A., Providence Coll., 1962; J.D., Fordham U., 1967. Bar: Conn. 1967, U.S. Dist. Ct. Conn. 1976, U.S. Supreme Ct. Asst. atty. gen. State of Conn., 1967; assoc. C. Robert Satti, 1967-69; ptnr. Dreyfus & Holth, 1969-80; propr. Holth, Kollman & Fairlie, 1980—. Mem. 20th Dist. Central Republican Com. Conn., 1975—; mem. Lyme (Conn.) Rep. Town Com., 1970—; chmn. Lyme Conservation Commn., 1972—. Mem. Assn. Trial Lawyers Am., Conn. Trial Lawyers Assn., Conn. Bar Assn., New London County Bar Assn. Roman Catholic. Personal injury, Federal civil litigation, State civil litigation. Address: 58 Huntington St New London CT 06320

HOLTZ, EDGAR WOLFE, lawyer; b. Clarksburg, W.Va., Jan. 18, 1922; s. Dennis Drummond and Oleta (Wolfe) H.; m. Alberta Lee Brinkley, May 6, 1944; children: Diana Hilary, Heidi Johanna. B.A., Denison U., 1943; J.D., U. Cin., 1949. Bar: Ohio 1949, U.S. Supreme Ct. 1957, D.C. 1961. Assoc. firm Matthews & Matthews, Cin., 1949-53; asst. dean Chase Law Sch., Cin., 1952-55; asst. solicitor City of Cin., 1950-55; asst. chief office of opinions and rev. FCC, Washington, 1955-56; dep. gen. counsel FCC, 1956-60; mem. firm Hogan & Hartson, Washington, 1960—. Trustee Denison U., Granville, Ohio, 1974—. Served to 1st lt. USAAF, 1943-45. Decorated D.F.C., Air medal with 2 clusters. Fellow Am. Bar Found.; mem. Am. Bar Assn. (standing com. on gavel awards), Ohio Bar Assn., D.C. Bar Assn., Fed. Communications Bar Assn. (pres. 1977-78), Am. Judicature Soc., Newcomen Soc. N. Am., Nat. Communications Club. Republican. Methodist. Clubs: Metropolitan (Washington), George Town (Washington). Communications, Administrative and regulatory, General corporate. Office: Hogan & Hartson 555 13th St NW Washington DC 20004

HOLTZ, GREGORY THEODORE, lawyer, bank executive, legal educator; b. Cleve., Dec. 1, 1951; s. Theodore Stanley and Helen Barbara (Lewandowski) H.; m. Joan Alice Mate, Oct. 22, 1983. AB, Xavier U., 1974; JD, Case Western Res. U., 1977; MS, Cleve. State U., 1983. Bar: Ohio 1977, U.S. Dist. Ct. (no. dist.) Ohio 1979, D.C. 1979, Fla. 1980, U.S. Ct. Appeals (D.C. cir.) 1980, U.S. Ct. Appeals (6th and 11th cirs.) 1981, U.S. Supreme Ct. 1981, U.S. Ct. Appeals (6th cir.) 1983. Sole practice Garfield Heights, Ohio, 1977-79; asst. legal counsel United Savs. and Loan Assn., Cleve., 1978-80; ptnr. Holtz & Holtz, Garfield Heights, 1979-84; trust officer Cen. Nat. Bank, Cleve., 1984-86; sr. trust officer Soc. Nat. Bank, Cleve., 1986—; solicitor, prosecutor Village Bklyn. Heights, Ohio, 1980-84; instr. Am. Inst. for Paralegal Studies, 1982—. Mem. Bar Assn. of Greater Cleve., Estate Planning Council of Greater Cleve., Cuyahoga County Law Dirs. Assn., Order ofAlhambra, Alpha Sigma Nu. Roman Catholic. Lodges: Rotary (pres. Garfield Heights chpt. 1983-84). Probate, Estate planning. Home: 19840 Battersea Blvd Rocky River OH 44116 Office: Soc Nat Bank 800 Superior Ave Cleveland OH 44114

HOLTZMAN, ELIZABETH, lawyer, district attorney; b. Bklyn., Aug. 11, 1941; d. Sidney and Filia Holtzman. A.B. magna cum laude, Radcliffe Coll., 1962; J.D., Harvard U., 1965; L.D.S., Regis Coll., 1975, Skidmore Coll., 1980, Simmons Coll., 1981, Smith Coll., 1982. Bar: N.Y. Assoc. Wachtell, Lipton, Rosen, Kalz & Kern, N.Y.C., 1965-67; asst. to mayor N.Y.C., 1968-69; assoc. Paul, Weiss, Rifkind, Wharton & Garrison, 1970-72; mem. 93d-96th Congresses from 16th dist., N.Y.; vis. prof. NYU Law Sch. and Grad. Sch. Pub. Adminstrn., 1981; dist. atty. Kings County Bklyn., 1982—. N.Y. State Democratic committeewoman, 1970-72; del. Dem. Nat. Conv., 1972; mem. Select Commn. Immigration Policy, 1979-80; mem. Pres.'s Nat. Commn. on U.S. Observance Internat. Women's Yr.; Dem. nominee U.S. Senate, 1980; mem. Am. Jewish Commn. Holocaust; bd. overseers Harvard U., 1976-82; mem. Helsinki Watch Com., 1981—. Lawyers Com. Internat. Human Rights, 1981—. Recipient Nat. Council Jewish Women's Faith and Humanity award, YWCA Elizabeth Cutter Morrow award, Maccabean award N.Y. Bd. Rabbis, Alumni recognition award Radcliffe Coll. Alumnae Assn., 1973; N.J. and Los Angeles ACLU awards for contbns. to def. of Constn. and preservation of civil liberties, 1981; Am. Traditions award B'nai B'rith, 1984, Athena award N.Y.C. Commn. on Status of Women, 1985; Woman of Yr. award Bus. and Profl. Women, 1985, 5th Kent State Conf. on Holocaust, Humanitarian award, 1986, Queens B'nai B'rith Women's Humanitarian award, 1986, Jewish War Vets. Outstanding and Meritorious Service award, 1986, Child Abuse Prevention award Recognition of Committment to Children, 1986. Fellow N.Y. Inst. Humanities; mem. Nat. Women's Polit. Caucus, Bar Assn. City N.Y., NOW (Equality award for Overall Achievement L.I. chpt. 1987, N.Y.C. task force Cert. of Appreciation 1987), Phi Beta Kappa. Office: 210 Joralemon St Brooklyn NY 11201

HOLTZSCHUE, KARL BRESSEM, lawyer; b. Wichita, Kans., Mar. 3, 1938; s. Bressem C. and Josephine E. (Landsittel) H.; m. Linda J. Gross, Oct. 24, 1959; children—Alison, Adam, Sara. A.B., Dartmouth Coll., 1959; LL.B., Columbia U., 1966. Bar: N.Y. 1967, U.S. Dist. Ct. (so. and ea. dists.) N.Y. 1968. Assoc., Webster & Sheffield, N.Y.C., 1966-73, ptnr., 1974—. Trustee Soc. St. Johnland, 1980-86, Ensemble Studio Theatre, 1986—. Author: New York Practice Guide: Real Estate, Vol. 1 on Purchase and Sale, 1986. Served to lt. (j.g.) USN, 1959-62. Mem. ABA (mem. com. on condominiums, coops. and homeowners assns. 1981-83, mem. com. on creditors rights in real estate financing 1982, com. on real estate financing 1983-85), N.Y. State Bar Assn. (mem. com. on condominiums and coops. 1978-87), Real Estate Bd. N.Y. (law com. 1980—), Assn. Bar City N.Y. (mem. com. on real property law 1977-80, chmn. 1987—), Am. Coll. Real Estate Lawyers, Dartmouth Lawyers Assn. (founding mem.). Author: Real Estate Contracts, 1985. Episcopalian. Real property. Home: 122 E 82nd St Apt 3C New York NY 10028 Office: 237 Park Ave New York NY 10017

HOLZ, HARRY GEORGE, lawyer; b. Milw., Sept. 13, 1934; s. Harry Carl and Emma Louise (Hinz) H.; m. Nancy L. Heiser, May 12, 1962; children: Pamela Gretchen, Bradley Eric, Erika Lynn. BS, Marquette U., 1956, LLB, 1958; LLM, Northwestern U., 1960. Bar: Wis. 1958, Ill. 1960. Teaching fellow Northwestern U. Sch. Law, 1958-59; assoc. Sidley & Austin, Chgo., 1960; ptnr. Quarles & Brady, Milw., 1968—; lectr. law securities regulation U. Wis. Law Sch., 1971-74; adj. prof. securities regulation law Marquette U. Sch. Law, 1976—; mem. faculty program on antitrust law Wis. State Bar Advanced Tng. Seminars, 1975-82, mem. faculty program on securities law, 1975—. Bd. visitors Marquette U. Sch. Law, 1986. Served to capt. C.E. U.S. Army, 1960-67. Mem. ABA (Reform-Pathway com., corp. counsel com.), Wis. Bar Assn. (chmn. dir. corps., banking and bus. law sect. 1978-79, bd. dirs. 1978-83, corp. and bus. laws com. 1985—), Milw. Bar Assn., Bar Assn. 7th Fed. Circuit, Marquette U. Sch. Law Woolsack Soc. (bd. dirs.), Beta Gamma Sigma. Lutheran. Clubs: Milw. Athletic, Western Racquet. Antitrust, General corporate, Securities. Office: Quarles & Brady 411 E Wisconsin Ave Milwaukee WI 53202

HOLZER, RICHARD JEAN, lawyer; b. Easton, Pa., Jan. 31, 1940; s. J. A. and Ann C. (Carta) H.; B.A., Gettysburg Coll., 1961; M.B.A., U. Dayton, 1971; student N.Y. U., 1968-69; J.D., Salmon P. Chase Coll. Law, No. Ky. State U., 1975; m. Charlotte L. Branson, Aug. 15, 1964; children—Richard Jean, C. Christopher. Field rep. INA, Pitts., 1961-66; assoc. R. D. Griewahn & Assos., Erie, Pa., 1966-68; mgr. compensation and benefits Curtis-Wright Corp., Woodridge, N.J., 1968-69; mgr. personnel services, McCall Printing Co., Dayton, 1969-70; labor relations adminstr. City of Dayton, 1970-75; admitted to Ohio bar, 1975; atty. pub. sector labor and corp. law, ptnr. Pickrel, Schaeffer and Ebeling, Dayton, 1975—; law dir. City of Englewood (Ohio); asst. prof. U. Dayton, 1976-77, Wright State U., 1979-80. Com. chmn. Montgomery County Personnel Task Force, 1979—; soccer coach Northmont Bd. Edn., 1983—. Served with U.S. Army, 1962-64. Recipient Book award for labor law No. Ky. State U. Mem. Am. Soc. Personnel Adminstrs., Nat. Pub. Employers Labor Relations Assn., Ohio Pub. Employers Labor Relations Assn., Ohio League Mcpl. Attys., Ohio Council Sch. Bd. Attys. (vice chmn.), Ohio State Bar Assn., Fed. Bar Assn., Dayton Bar Assn., Scabbard and Blade, Phi Alpha Delta, Lambda Chi Alpha. Lutheran (council 1976—, pres. council 1978-79). Civil rights, Labor, Local government. Home: 10887 Putnam Rd Englewood OH 45322 Office: 2700 Kettering Tower Dayton OH 45423

HOLZMAN, JAMES L(OUIS), lawyer; b. Bklyn., Jan. 7, 1949; s. Robert Conrad and Muriel Claire (Smith) H.; m. Jonnie Irene Frisbie; children—James Casey, Meredith Claire, Jon Carroll. B.A., John B. Stetson U., 1970; J.D., U. Fla., 1972. Bar: Fla. 1973, Del. 1973, U.S. Dist. Ct. Del. 1974, U.S. Dist. Ct. (so. dist.) Fla. 1973, U.S. Tax Ct. 1973, U.S. Ct. Appeals (3d cir.) 1976, U.S. Ct. Appeals (fed. cir.) 1983. Assoc., Prickett, Ward, Burt & Sanders, Wilmington, Del., 1973-77, ptnr., 1977-79; ptnr. Prickett, Jones, Elliott, Kristol & Schnee, Wilmington, 1979—. Mem. Del. State Bar Assn. (mem. gen. corp. law com. 1979—), Assn. Bar City N.Y., ABA, Fla. Bar, Fed. Bar Assn. (speaker and participant securities law seminar program 1976-78). Democrat. Roman Catholic. Club: Rodney Square (Wilmington). General corporate, Federal civil litigation. Home: 3213 Fordham Rd Wilmington DE 19807 Office: Prickett Jones Elliot et al 1310 King St Wilmington DE 19899

HOLZMANN, JAMES CHARLES, lawyer; b. North Olmstead, Ohio, Sept. 24, 1947; s. Clarence Carl and Ruth Mina (Schultz) H.; m. Deborah Marie Buchanan, Dec. 21, 1985; children: Kirsten Marya, Loren Paige, Lara Nicole, Rachael Elizabeth. BA, Case Western Res. U., 1971; JD, Western State U., 1978. Bar: Calif. 1978, U.S. Dist. Ct. (so. dist.) Calif. 1978, U.S. Dist. Ct. (cen. dist.) Calif. 1982, U.S. Ct. Appeals (9th cir.) 1982, U.S. Supreme Ct. 1982. Ptnr. Wampler, Holzmann, Imhoff & Stone, San Diego, 1978-80, Holzmann, Imhoff & Stone, San Diego, 1980-85; sole practice San Diego, 1985—; cons. Burglar and Fire Alarm Assn. San Diego County, 1982-85. Editor in chief Criminal Justice Jour., 1977-78. Bd. dirs. Ramona (Calif.) Luth. Pre-Sch., 1985-86. Served to capt. USMC 1968-74. Decorated Silver Star; recipient Corpus Juris Secundum, West Pub. Co., 1978. Mem. Am. Trial Lawyers Assn., ABA, San Diego Trial Lawyers Assn., San Diego Bar Assn. Republican. Lutheran. Lodge: Elks. State civil litigation, Federal civil litigation, Personal injury. Office: 110 West C St Suite 2202 San Diego CA 92101

HOMER, BARRY WAYNE, lawyer; b. Junction City, Kans., Jan. 13, 1950. BA, U. Kans., 1972; JD, U. Chgo., 1975. Bar: Calif. 1975, U.S. Dist. Ct. (no. dist.) Calif. 1975, U.S. Tax Ct. 1980. Assoc. Brobeck, Phleger & Harrison, San Francisco, 1975-82, ptnr., 1982—. Co-author: Attorney's Guide to Pension and Profitcharing Plans, 1985; contbr. articles to profl. jours. Mem. ABA (employee benefits com. tax sect. 1978—), Western Pension Conf. Pension, profit-sharing, and employee benefits, Corporate taxation. Office: Brobeck Phleger & Harrison One Market Plaza San Francisco CA 94105

HON, DONALD ALLEN, lawyer; b. Pleasant Hill, Mo., Apr. 5, 1942; s. William Harris and Ella Frances (Raffurty) H.; m. Rita Ann Renner, Aug. 27, 1967 (div. 1976); children—Michael Thomas, Michelle Ann. A.A., Palomar Coll., 1966; B.S., San Diego State U., 1969; J.D., Western State U., 1973. Bar: Calif. 1973, U.S. Dist. Ct. (so. dist.) Calif. 1973, U.S. Ct. Appeals (9th cir.) 1983. Assoc. Greer, Popko, Miller & Forester, San Diego, 1974; sole practice, San Diego, 1974—; del. Calif. State Bar, 1984. Served to cpl. USMC, 1961-64. Mem. San Diego County Bar Assn., San Diego State U. Vets. Club (pres. 1966). Democrat. Roman Catholic. Club: United Comml. Travelers (San Diego) (sr. counselor 1974-75). Lodge: Optimists. Labor. Home: 8724 Van Horn La Mesa CA 92041 Office: 2232 El Cajon Blvd San Diego CA 92104

HONAKER, JIMMIE JOE, lawyer; b. Oklahoma City, Jan. 21, 1939; s. Joe Jack and Ruby Lee (Bowen) H.; m. Beverly Ruth Sargent, Aug. 20, 1960; children—Jay Jimmie, Kerri Ruth. B.A., Colo. Coll., 1963; J.D., U. Wyo., 1966. Bar: Colo. 1966, U.S. Dist. Ct. Colo. 1966, U.S. Ct. Appeals (10th cir.) 1982. Sole practice, Longmont, Colo., 1966—; mem. Atty.'s Title Guaranty Fund, Inc. Incorporator Longmont Boys Baseball, 1969; chmn. Longmont City Charter Commn., 1973; chmn. ch. bd. 1st Christian Ch., Longmont, 1975, 76; chmn. North Boulder County unit Am. Cancer Soc., 1978, 79. Recipient Disting. Service award Longmont Centennial Yr., 1971; named Outstanding Young Man, Longmont Jaycees, 1973. Mem. Colo. Bar Assn. (interprofl. com. 1972—), Boulder Bar Assn. (med./legal com. 1983—), Christian Legal Soc., Internat. Assn. Approved Basketball Ofcls. (cert., bd. dirs. Colo. bd. #4), Nat. Eagle Scout Assn. (vice chmn. Arapahoe Eagle Aerie), Phi Alpha Delta. Club: Buffalo (Boulder, Colo.). Real property, Probate, Contracts commercial. Office: 647 17th Ave Longmont CO 80501-2601

HONAKER, RICHARD HENDERSON, lawyer; b. Laramie, Wyo., Mar. 10, 1951; s. Hayward E. and Faola I. (Henderson) H.; m. Shannon Kathleen Casey, Dec. 24, 1978; children: Heather, Harmony, Dustin. BA cum laude, Harvard U., 1973; JD, U. Wyo., 1976. Bar: Wyo. 1976, U.S. Dist. Ct. Wyo. 1976, U.S. Ct. Appeals (10th cir.) 1977. Asst. atty. gen. State of Wyo., Cheyenne, 1976-79, state pub. defender, 1979-81; ptnr. Honaker & Hampton, Rock Springs, Wyo., 1981—. Press sec. to Gov. of Wyo., 1979-81; mem. Wyo. State Legis., Sweetwater County, 1987—. Mem. Wyo. Bar Assn., Wyo. Trial Lawyers Assn. (v.p. 1985-86, pres. 1986-87), Assn. Trial Lawyers Am., Nat. Assn. Criminal Def. Lawyers, Christian Legal Soc., Rutherford Inst. Democrat. Personal injury, Criminal, Civil rights. Office: 214 Winston Dr PO Box 1804 Rock Springs WY 82901

HONE, JAY R., lawyer; b. Lima, Ohio, Nov. 30, 1952; s. Lawrence Calvin and Miriam (Karch) H. BA, Otterbein Coll., 1974; JD, Duke U., 1977. Bar: Ohio 1977, N.Mex. 1980, D.C. 1980, U.S. Ct. Appeals (10th cir.) 1982. Area def. counsel Kirtland (N.Mex.) AFB, 1979-81; instr. law dept. USAF Acad., Colorado Springs, Colo., 1981-82; assoc. Rodey Law Firm, Albuquerque, 1982-86, Montgomery & Andrews, Albuquerque, 1986—; mem. Instl. rev. bd. Lovelace Med. Ctr., Albuquerque, 1985—. Served to capt. USAF, 1978-82. Republican. Methodist. Personal injury, Insurance, Juvenile. Home: 9220 Guadalupe Trail NW Albuquerque NM 87114 Office: Montgomery & Andrews PA PO Box 26927 Albuquerque NM 87125

HONEYCHURCH, DENIS ARTHUR, lawyer; b. Berkeley, Calif., Sept. 17, 1946; s. Winston and Mary Martha (Chandler) H.; m. Judith Ann Poliquin, Oct. 5, 1969; children: Sean, James, Thomas. BA, UCLA, 1968; JD, U. Calif., San Francisco, 1972. Bar: Calif. 1972, U.S. Dist. Ct. (no. dist.) Calif. 1972, U.S. Ct. Appeals (9th cir.) 1972. Dep. pub. defender Sacramento County Calif., Sacramento, 1973-75; supervising asst. pub. defender Solano County, Fairfield, Calif., 1975-78; ptnr. Honeychurch & Finkas and predecessor firm, Fairfield, 1978—. Bd. dirs. Fairfield-Suisun Unified Sch. Dist., Fairfield, 1979-83, Solano Community Coll., Fairfield, 1985—, Falls Sch. Found., Fairfield, 1985—; chmn. bd. dirs. Downtown Improvement Dist., Fairfield, 1980-82. Mem. Assn. Trial Lawyers Am., Nat. Assn. Criminal Def. Lawyers, Calif. Trial Lawyers Assn., Calif. Attys. Criminal Justice, Calif. Pub. Defenders Assn., Calif. Bd. Legal Specialization (cert.), Nat. Bd. Trial Adv. (cert.). Democrat. Criminal. Office: Honeychurch & Finkas 823 Jefferson St Fairfield CA 94533

HONEYMAN, ROBERT WAYNE, lawyer; b. Norristown, Pa., Feb. 11, 1918; s. Cornelius Voorhees and Mary (Wismer) H.; m. Mary Atkins, Aug. 13, 1942; children: Mary Beth Honeyman Leary, Kathleen Ann Honeyman Sellers, Gregory A., Robert W. Jr., Virginia L. Honeyman Kelley. AB, U. Pa., 1939, JD, 1942. Bar: Pa. 1942. Ptnr. Fox, Differ & Honeyman, Norristown, 1946-59; judge ct. common pleas Montgomery (Pa.) County, 1960-80; of counsel Fox, Differ, Callahan, Ulrich & O'Hara, Norristown, 1980—; bd. dirs. Bank and Trust Co. of Old York Rd., Willow Grove, Pa., 1980—. Mem. bd. consultors Villanova (Pa.) U. Law Sch., 1962—. Served to 1st lt. U.S. Army, 1942-45, PTO. Mem. ABA, Pa. Bar Assn., Montgomery Bar Assn. (past bd. dirs.), Am. Legion, Fraternal Order Police. Republican. Roman Catholic. Club: Commercial (Norristown). Lodge: KC. Probate, General practice. Home: 905 Cherry Circle Lansdale PA 19446 Office: Fox Differ Callahan Ulrich & OHara 317 Swede St Norristown PA 19401

HONIG, EMANUEL AARON, lawyer; b. Franklin Borough, N.J., Oct. 5, 1909; m. Ann F. Friedman, Mar. 7, 1940; children: Harvey J., Richard E. BA with honors, Lehigh U., 1931; LLB, Columbia U., 1934. Bar: N.Y. 1935, N.J. 1936, U.S. Supreme Ct. 1966. Assoc. George H. Rosenstein, Newark, 1936-40; sole practice Franklin, 1940-69; assoc. Honig & Kovach, Franklin, 1970; ptnr. Honig & Honig P.C., Franklin, 1971—; atty. Hardyston Twp. Mcpl. Ct., 1945-54, Franklin Borough Mcpl. Ct., 1962-74; sec. Franklin Lanes, Inc., 1963—, Sussex County Title Service, Co., Inc., 1969-75; mem. adv. bd. dirs. Nat. Community Bank. Mem. Franklin (N.J.) Recreation Commn., 1966-71; past pres. Franklin Little League; sec. Alexander Linn Hosp., Sussex, N.J., 1950-67, pres., 1967-76; chmn. Franklin Borough Indsl. Commn., 1960-65; atty. Sussex County Vocat. Bd. of Edn., 1966—, Vernon Twp. Planning Bd., 1977, Vernon Twp. Bd. Adj., 1977-83; v.p. Somerset-Sussex Legal Services Office, 1971-73, planning council Morris-Sussex Regional Health Facilities, 1967-73; trustee Wallkill Valley Health Care Corp., 1965-70, No. N.J. Comprehensive Health Planning Council, 1972-77, Am. Prepaid Legal Services Inst., 1980-83. Fellow Am. Bar Found.; mem. ABA (spl. com. on prepaid legal services, Ho. of Dels. 1978—, N.J. chmn. membership com. sr. lawyers 1986), N.J. Bar Assn. (soc. 1939-74, 2d v.p. 1974-75, 1st v.p. 1975-76, pres. 1977-78, spl. counsel litigation 1970, chmn. law and poverty com. 1965-69, chmn. availability of legal services com. 1969—, chmn. spl. com. on prepaid legal services 1972-75, chmn. membership com. 1986—), Sussex County Bar Assn. (chmn. ethics com. 1970-72, pres. 1965-66), Am. Arbitration Assn. (arbitrator). Republican. State civil litigation, Condemnation, General corporate. Home: 92 Mountain Rd Box 621 Hamburg NJ 07419 Office: Honig & Honig 83 Main St Franklin NJ 07416

HONNOLD, JOHN OTIS, JR., legal educator; b. Kansas, Ill., Dec. 5, 1915; s. John Otis and Louretta (Wright) H.; m. Annamarie Kunz, June 26, 1939; children: Carol Honnold Davidon, Heidi Honnold Spencer, Edward. B.A., U. Ill., 1936; J.D., Harvard U., 1939. Bar: N.Y. 1940, Pa. 1953, U.S. Supreme Ct 1953. Atty. firm Wright, Gordon, Zachry & Parlin, N.Y.C., 1939-41, SEC, 1941; chief ct. rev. br. OPA, 1942-46; mem. faculty U. Pa. Law Sch., 1946-69, 74-85, prof. law, 1952-69, 74-85, prof. emeritus, 1984—; Arthur Goodhart prof. sci. of law. U. Cambridge, 1982-83; mem. vis. faculty U. Beijing, 1984, U. Hawaii, 1986; Canterbury vis. fellow, N.Z., 1986; chief internat. trade law br. UN; sec. UN Commn. on Internat. Trade Law, 1969-74; mem. faculty law sessions Salzburg (Austria) Seminar Am. Studies, 1960, chmn., 1963, 66; chief counsel Miss. Office, Lawyer's Com. for Civil Rights under Law, 1965; U.S. del., mem. drafting com. diplomatic conf. preparing uniform law for internat. sales of goods, The Hague, Holland, 1964; U.S. del UN Commn. Internat. Trade Law, 1969, 77; U.S. del. diplomatic confs. Conv. Carriage of Goods by Sea, Hamburg, 1978, Contracts for Internat. Sale of Goods, Vienna, 1980; gen. reporter 12th Internat. Congress Comparative Law, 1986. Author: Sales and Sales Financing, 5th edit, 1984, The Life of the Law, 1964, (with E.L. Barrett, Jr. and P.W. Bruton) Cases and Materials on Constitutional Law, 3d edit, 1968, (with E. Allen Farnsworth) Commercial Law, 4th edit, 1985, Unification of the Law Governing International Sales of Goods, 1966, Uniform Law for International Sales under the 1980 UN Convention, 1982; Security Interests in Personal Property, 1985; also articles; bd. editors: Am. Jour. Comparative Law, 1959-70, 76-84. Guggenheim fellow, 1958; Fulbright sr. research scholar U. Paris, 1958; recipient The berge award for contbn. to Pvt. Internat. Law, ABA, 1986. Private international. Home: 524 Rutgers Ave Swarthmore PA 19081 Office: Law Sch U Pa 34th and Chestnut Sts Philadelphia PA 19104

HONSOWETZ, FRANK WILLIAM, lawyer; b. Bremerton, Wash., June 23, 1944; s. Frank William and Marguerite M. (McGilvray) H.; m. Marianne L. Davis, Aug. 20, 1977. B.A., Wash. State U., 1966; J.D., U. Oreg., 1972. Bar: Oreg. 1972, U.S. Dist. Ct. Oreg. 1972, U.S. Supreme Ct. 1984. Assoc. firm Sahlstrom, Starr & Vinson, Eugene, Oreg., 1972-73; ptnr. Cooley & Honsowetz, Eugene, 1973-75, Gardner & Honsowetz, Eugene, 1975-78, Lombard, Gardner, Honsowetz, Brewer & Schons, Eugene, 1978—; speaker masters program Los Angeles Trial Lawyers Assn., 1983. Pres. Lane County Fair Bd., 1977—; mem. Lane County Arbitration Com., Fast Track Com. Served to 1st lt. U.S. Army, 1966-68, Vietnam. Mem. Oreg. Trial Lawyers Assn. (officer 1980—, pres. 1982-83, columnist state mag. 1982-83, President's award 1983), Citizens of Oreg. Lawyers Trust (bd. dirs., legis. chmn. 1983—), Assn. Trial Lawyers Am., Phi Alpha Delta. Republican. Methodist. Lodge: Elks. Personal injury, Family and matrimonial, State civil litigation. Home: 379 Brae Burn Dr Eugene OR 97405 Office: Lombard Gardner Honsowetz Brewer & Schons 725 Country Club Rd Eugene OR 97401

HOOD, CHARLES DAVID, JR., lawyer; b. Ft. Polk, La., Apr. 24, 1954; s. Charles David Sr. and Vera Hook (Gettys) H.; m. Carolyn Marie Morgan, Aug. 21, 1976; 1 child, Charles David III. BA, U. S.C., 1975, JD, 1978. Bar: Fla., U.S. Dist. Ct. (mid. dist.) Fla., U.S. Ct. Appeals (5th cir.). Assoc. Cobb & Cole, Daytona Beach, Fla., 1978-83, ptnr., 1983—; instr. bus. law Daytona Beach Community Coll., 1985; arbitrator Juvenile Criminal Justice Program, 1980—; pres., bd. dirs. Act, Inc., 1984—. Coach football, basketball and baseball teams, Ormond Beach, Fla., 1979-85; team chmn. Meml. Hosp. Keystone campaign; county coordinator Steve Pajcic for Gov. campaign; mem. United Way Allocations Com.; lectr. on successful bd. dirs. United Way of Volusia County, Inc., 1986, bd. dirs. 1986, Volusia County Drug Council, 1982-83, Sunshine Health Plan, 1985—, Stewart Treatment Ctr., 1985—, bd. dirs. Leadership Council Daytona Beach, 1985—; v.p., bd. dirs. Human Resources Ctr., 1982-83; pres., bd. dirs. Big Pine Community Care, 1984—, Atlantic Treatment Ctr., 1984—, Easter Seals Soc., 1987—; pres. Greater Volusia Tennis League, 1982-84. Mem. Volusia County Bar Assn. (chmn. law week com. 1981), Acad. Fla. Trial Lawyers Assn., Volusia County C. of C. (better bus. com. 1981). Lodge: Kiwanis (treas. Ortona club 1983; chmn. Easter Seals auction, Bluegrass jamboree 1982-83, tennis tournament 1984—; bd. dirs. Ortona club 1982-83, Daytona Beach club 1983-85). State civil litigation, Insurance, Health. Home: 27 Riverridge Trail Ormond Beach FL 32074 Office: Cobb & Cole 150 Magnolia Ave Daytona Beach FL 32015

HOOD, HAROLD, judge; b. Hamtramck, Mich., Jan. 14, 1931; s. W. Sylvester and Lenore Elizabeth (Hand) H.; m. Laurann Harris, June 26, 1952; children—Harold Keith, Kenneth, Kevin, Karen; m. 2d, Lottie Vivian Jones, Jan. 29, 1977. Bar: Mich. 1960, U.S. Ct. Appeals (6th cir.) 1964, U.S. Supreme Ct. 1964, U.S. Ct. Appeals (7th cir.) 1966. Ptnr. Hood, Rice and Charity, 1960-61; asst. corp. counsel City of Detroit, 1961-69; chief asst. U.S. atty. Eastern Dist. Mich., 1969-73; judge Common Pleas Ct., Detroit, 1973-77, Recorders Ct., Detroit, 1977-78, 3d Jud. Cir. Ct. Mich., 1978-82, Mich. Ct. Appeals, 1982—; mem. com. on Standard civil jury instrns. Mich. Supreme Ct., also mem. com. to review and consolidate Mich. ct. rules; commr. Mich. Jud. Tenure Commn., 1986—. Vice pres. Nat. Council on Alcoholism, 1979—, bd. dirs. Greater Detroit Area chpt., 1976—. Served to 1st lt. Signal Corps, U.S. Army; Korea. Decorated Army Commendation medal; recipient commendation Fed. Exec. Bd., 1968, Assn. Black Judges, 1983, Achievement award No. Province Kappa Alpha Psi, 1972, Outstanding Citizen award Mich. Chronicle, 1975, NCA-OD Pres.'s award, 1985, NCA-OD Mich. Vol Yr. award, 1985. Mem. ABA, Mich. Bar Assn., Detroit Bar Assn., Fed. Bar Assn., Nat. Bar Assn. (jud. council), Wolverine Bar Assn., Am. Judges Assn., Mich. Judges Assn. (mem. exec. com.), Assn. Black Judges Mich. (founding chmn.), Mich. Assn. Professions, Old Newsboys Goodfellows of Detroit (bd. dirs. 1981—, pres. 1986-87), Kappa Alpha Psi (past polemarch). Jurisprudence, State civil litigation, Criminal. Office: 900 First Federal Bldg Detroit MI 48226

HOOD, JAMES CALTON, lawyer; b. Panama Canal Zone, Oct. 29, 1947; s. Robin Calton and Eleanor (Marquard) H.; m. Elise Joan Gregory, Aug. 16, 1969; children: Jamie, Molly. BA, U. N.H., 1969; JD, Georgetown U., 1972. Bar: N.H. 1972. Dir., v.p. McLane, Graf, Raulerson & Middleton, P.A., Manchester, N.H., 1972—. Bd. dirs. Manchester YMCA, 1976, chmn. 1986—; trustee St. Paul's Meth. Ch., Manchester, 1985. Served to 1st lt. U.S. Army, 1972-73. Mem. ABA, N.H. Bar Assn. (chmn. corp. sect. 1985), Phi Beta Kappa, Phi Kappa Phi. General corporate, Banking, Public utilities. Home: 85 Hemlock St Manchester NH 03104 Office: McLane Graf Raulerson & Middleton PA 40 Stark St Manchester NH 03105

HOOD, JAMES MICHAEL, lawyer; b. Des Moines, Mar. 27, 1945; s. James Vincent and Maybl (Rayburn) H.; m. Sherrie Elaine Lazar, Apr. 16, 1973; children—James Michael, Grace. B.A., Drake U., 1967, J.D., 1970. Bar: Iowa 1970, U.S. Dist. Ct. (so. dist) Iowa 1970, U.S. Dist. Ct. (no. dist.) Iowa 1972, U.S. Dist. Ct. (so. dist.) Ill. 1978, U.S. Supreme Ct. 1978. Sole practice, Davenport, Iowa, 1970—. Served with USN, 1970-72. Mem. ABA, Iowa Bar Assn., Scott County Bar Assn., Assn. Trial Lawyers Iowa, Assn. Trial Lawyers Am., Iowa Assn. Worker Compensation Lawyers. Personal injury, Workers' compensation. Office: 302 Union Arcade Davenport IA 52801

HOOD, LAWRENCE E., law librarian; b. Long Beach, Calif., Mar. 24, 1945; s. Ernest F. and Mary E. (Gale) H.; m. Noelle E. Marts, Aug. 30, 1973; children: Christian, Olivia, Ezra, Claire, Nicholas. BA, Brigham Young U., 1971, MLS, 1978. Serials librarian Brigham Young U. Law Library, Provo, Utah, 1973-78, acquisitions librarian, 1978-82, reference librarian, 1982-83; dir. Dallas County Law Library, 1983—. Founding editor (semi-monthly rev.) Abstracts of Book Reviews in Legal Periodicals, 1974-78. Mem. adv. com. El Centro Coll. Legal Asst. Program, Dallas, 1986-87. Mem. Am. Assn. Law Libraries, Southwestern Assn. Law Libraries, Dallas Assn. Law Librarians. Mormon. Librarianship, Legal history. Office: Dallas County Law Library Govt Ctr 2d Floor 600 Commerce St Dallas TX 75202-4606

HOOD, WILLIAM WAYNE, JR., lawyer; b. Tulsa, July 22, 1941; s. William Wayne and Alys (Charles) H.; m. Nancy Raynolds; children—W. Wayne III, Kristina L. B.A., U. Okla., 1963; LL.B., U. Tulsa, 1966. Bar: Okla. 1966, U.S. Dist. Ct. (no. dist.) Okla. 1966. Sole practice, Tulsa, 1966-70; pub. defender Tulsa County, 1966-68; ptnr. Hood & Lindsey, Tulsa, 1970—. Served to maj. JAGC, USAR, 1966—. Fellow Am. Acad. Matrimonial Lawyers (v.p. 1985—); mem. ABA, Okla. Bar Assn. (dir. continuing legal edn.-family law 1980-84, chmn. family law sect. 1975-77, 80-82), Tulsa County Bar Assn. (exec. com. 1979), Okla, Trial Lawyers Assn. (family law editor The Adv. 1979-84). Republican. Roman Catholic. Family and matrimonial. Office: Hood & Lindsey 1914 S Boston Tulsa OK 74119

HOOF, JAMES BRUCE, lawyer; b. Boston, May 25, 1948; s. Wayne and Mary Eleanor (English) H.; m. Lloydette Humphrey, Feb. 1, 1969; 1 child, Mary Lloyd. BA, U. N.C., 1970; JD, Vanderbilt U., 1973. Bar: N.C. 1973, U.S. Dist. Ct. (middle dist.) N.C. 1975, U.S. Dist. Ct. (ea. dist.) 1978. Assoc. Spears, Barnes, Baker & Boles, Durham, N.C., 1973-77; ptnr. Spears, Barnes, Baker, Hoof & Wainio, Durham, 1977—. V.p. agy. relations, bd. dirs. United Way of Durham, 1979-84; pres. bd. dirs. Assn. Am. Dance Festival, Durham, 1979-83; bd. dirs. Durham Child Adv. Commn., 1985—, Durham chpt. N.C. Symphony; exec. com. Durham County Dem. Party, 1985—. Mem. ABA, N.C. Bar Assn., N.C. Assn. Def. Attys. (bd. dirs. 1985—), Durham County Bar Assn., Phi Beta Kappa. Presbyterian. Lodge: Friendly City Sertoma (sec. Durham club 1974-75). State civil litigation, Personal injury, Insurance. Home: 3215 Banbury Way Durham NC 27707 Office: 433 W Main St PO Box 270 Durham NC 27702

HOOFMAN, ROBERT SIDNEY, lawyer; b. Birmingham, Ala., May 25, 1954; s. Sidney T. and Edna (Hoene) H.; 1 child, Jonathan Matthew. BA, U. Cen. Fla., 1976; JD, U. Fla., 1979. Bar: Fla. 1979. Law clk. Fla. Ct. Appeals (5th dist.), Daytona Beach, 1979-81; assoc. Dewolf, Ward & Morris, Orlando, Fla., 1981-85, ptnr., 1985—. Mem. ABA, Orange County Bar Assn. Republican. Presbyterian. Club: Citrus. Consumer commercial, State civil litigation. Office: Dewolf Ward & Morris PA 1475 Hartford Bldg 200 E Robinson St Orlando FL 32801

HOOG, PATRICK EDWARD, lawyer; b. Ft. Wayne, Ind., Mar. 30, 1954; s. Joseph Eugene and Frances (Clancy) H. BS in Bus., Ind. U., 1976, JD cum laude, 1979. Bar: Ind. 1979, Ariz. 1984. Assoc. Barrett, Barrett and McNagny, Ft. Wayne, 1979-84, Snell and Wilmer, Phoenix, 1984—; lectr. Am. Banking Inst., various seminars. Mem. ABA, Ariz. State Bar Assn., Maricopa County Bar Assn., Ind. State Bar Assn. (cert. bankruptcy specialist). Republican. Roman Catholic. Club: La Mancha Athletic (Phoenix). Bankruptcy, Consumer commercial, Landlord-tenant. Home: 6041 N 41st Paradise Valley AZ 85253 Office: Snell and Wilmer 3100 Valley Bank Ctr Phoenix AZ 85073

HOOK, GEORGE CLIVE, II, lawyer; b. Chgo., Nov. 30, 1938; s. George Clive and Mary (Swank) H.; m. Carol M. Petersen, May 11, 1968; children—Dana Valerie, George Clive III. A.B., Knox Coll., 1960; J.D., U. Chgo., 1963. Bar: Ill. 1963. Ptnr. Schiff, Hardin & Waite, Chgo., 1967-78; mem. Much Shelist Freed Denenberg, Ament & Eiger, P.C., Chgo., 1978-85; ptnr. McBride, Baker & Coles, Chgo., 1985—. mem. Sec. of State's Bus. Orgns. Com. Chmn. editorial bd. Illinois Corporation Law Annotated. Served to capt. JAGC U.S. Army, 1964-67. Decorated Bronze Star. Mem. ABA, Ill. Bar Assn., Chgo. Bar Assn. (chmn. corp. law com.), Scabbard and Blade, Phi Beta Kappa, Pi Sigma Alpha. General corporate, Insurance, Securities. Home: 1324 Hollywood Glenview IL 60025 Office: Three First Nat Plaza Chicago IL 60602

HOOK, MARY JULIA, lawyer; b. Kansas City, Mo., Oct. 31, 1947; d. Vernon Anthony and Dula Mariah (Wood) H.; m. David Lee Smith, Dec. 30, 1972. BA, So. Meth. U., 1967, MA, 1969, JD, 1972; LLM, Harvard U., 1975. Bar: Tex. 1972, Colo. 1975. Trial atty. U.S. Dept. Justice, Washington, 1972-74, 75-76; assoc. Holland & Hart, Denver, 1976-81, ptnr., 1981—. Contbr. chpts. to legal publs., 2d edit. Mem. ABA, Fed. Bar Assn. (chmn. natural reources com. energy, environ. and natural resources sect.), Tex. Bar Assn., Colo. Bar Assn., Denver Bar Assn., Assn. Trial Lawyers Am., Order of Coif, Phi Beta Kappa. Democrat. Methodist. Clubs: Denver, Denver Athletic. Oil and gas leasing, Environment, Mining and Minerals. Home: 2036 Dexter St Denver CO 80207 Office: Holland & Hart 555 17th St Suite 2900 Denver CO 80202

HOOKANSON, KATHRYN, lawyer; b. Oak Park, Ill., Sept. 19, 1948; d. Edward John Lundquist Hookanson and Nancy (Huntington) Francis. BA in Internat. Studies, Am. U., 1971; JD, Memphis State U., 1977. Bar: Tenn. 1977, U.S. Dist. Ct. (we. dist.) Tenn. Mgr., trainee GEICO, Chevy Chase, Md., 1971-72, Reliance Ins. Co., Nashville, 1973; assoc. Law Offices of Richard Glassman, P.C., Memphis, 1977-80; asst. prof. Memphis State U., 1980-83; sole practice Memphis, 1983-86; legal counsel Memphis State U., 1986—. Vol. Rape Crisis Ctr., Memphis, 1986—; mem., chmn. Draft Bd. #5, Memphis, 1986—; treas. Memphis Area Legal Services, Inc., 1986—. Recipient Service award Outstanding Young Women of Am., 1984, Service award Memphis Area Legal Services, Inc., 1985. Mem. ABA, Memphis Bar Assn., Memphis-Shelby County Bar Assn. Mem. Unitarian Ch. Club: Pilot Internat. (Memphis) (pres. 1986—). Avocations: aerobics, needlework, racquetball, reading. Legal education. Office: Memphis State U Office of Pres Memphis TN 38152

HOOPER, JOEL RANDALL, lawyer; b. Nashville, June 16, 1952; s. Sidney Larimore and Jaime Roberta (Schrader) H.; m. Mary Ann Whitley, Apr. 15, 1978; children: Mary Margaret, Jordan Roberta. BA, Vanderbilt U., 1974; JD, U. Fla., 1977. Bar: Fla. 1977, U.S. Dist. Ct. (no. dist.) Fla. 1978, U.S. Ct. Appeals (5th cir.) 1978, U.S. Dist. Ct. (so. and mid. dists.) Fla. 1981, U.S. Ct. Appeals (11th cir.) 1981. Assoc. Scruggs, Carmichael, Long, Tomlinson, Roscow, Pridgeon, Helping & Young, Gainesville, Fla., 1977-81; ptnr. Scruggs & Carmichael, P.A. and predecessor firm, Gainesville, 1981—. Mem. Assn. Trial Lawyers Am., Acad. Fla. Trial Lawyers, Bar Assn. 8th Jud. Cir. Fla. (treas. 1983-85, pres. 1986—). Republican. Mem. Ch. of Christ. Avocations: golf, reading novels. Personal injury, State civil litigation, Federal civil litigation. Office: Scruggs & Carmichael PA 1 SE 1st Ave PO Drawer C Gainesville FL 32602

HOOPES, TERENCE JAMES, lawyer; b. South Bend, Ind., Feb. 16, 1955; s. Charles Hollingsworth and Ruth (James) H.; m. Maureen Ann Donley, Nov. 13, 1982. BA, New Coll., 1976; JD, Georgetown U., 1980, LLM, 1985. Bar: Ohio 1980, U.S. Dist. Ct. (no. dist.) Ohio, 1980, D.C. 1982. Assoc. Buckingham, Doolittle & Burroughs, Akron, Ohio, 1980-82; sole practice Washington, 1982-84; editor Mark A. Stephens, Ltd., Silver Spring, Md., 1984-85; tax law specialist employee plans, tech. and actuarial div. IRS, Treasury Dept., Washington, 1985—. Served with USMC, 1973-74. Mem. Ohio Bar Assn., D.C. Bar. Avocations: numismatics, scuba. Pension, profit-sharing, and employee benefits, Personal income taxation, Estate taxation. Office: IRS 1111 Constitution Ave Room 6231 Washington DC 20224

HOOPINGARNER, JOHN MARTIN, lawyer, educator; b. Dover, Ohio, May 8, 1954; s. Dallas Stanley and Josephine (Agosti) H.; m. Susan Scott Hanhart, July 17, 1976; Children: Scott David, Katherine Ann. BA, Muskingum Coll., 1976; JD, Ohio No. U., 1979. Bar: Ohio 1979, U.S. Dist. (no. dist.) Ohio 1979, U.S. Dist. Ct. Appeals (6th. cir.) 1983, U.S. Supreme Ct. 1984. Assoc. Smith Rnner Hanhart Miller & Kyler, New Philadelphia, Ohio, 1979-85; ptnr. Hanhart Miller & Kyler, New Philadelphia, 1985—;

instr. real estate law Kent State U., New Philadelphia, 1986—. Bd. dirs. Tuscarawas County Bd. Mental Retardation and Devel. Disabilities, New Philadelphia, 1981—, chmn. 1983—, Tuscarawas County YMCA, 1982-85, Am. Cancer Soc., Tuscarawas County, 1985—, Tuscarawas County C. of C., 1981-85; bd. trustees, sec. Ohio Assn. County Bds. Mental Retardation & Devel. Disabilities, 1987—. Mem. ABA (real property, probate and trust law sect.), Ohio Bar Assn. (bd. govs. young lawyers sect.), Tuscarawas County Bar Assn. (pres. 1985-86), Dover Jaycees (bd. dirs. 1981-84). Democrat. Club: Union Country (Dover). Lodge: Elks. General practice, Real property, Probate. Home: 320 East 14th St Dover OH 44622 Office: Hanhart Miller & Kyler 405 Chauncey Ave PO Box 668 New Philadelphia OH 44663

HOOSER, EUGENE ALBERT, lawyer; b. Los Angeles, Apr. 25, 1948; s. Minnie (Verhuel) Hooser; m. Lisa Madsen, Mar. 2, 1985; children: Danielle Mirian, Lauren A. AA in Police Sci., Palomar Coll., 1973; BS in Law, We. State U. Coll. Law, San Diego, 1976, JD, 1978. Bar: Calif. 1979, U.S. Dist. Ct. (so. dist.) Calif. 1979. Sole practice San Diego, 1979—; judge pro tem Calif. Superior Ct., San Diego, 1983—; arbitrator County Superior Ct. San Diego, 1981-86. Contbr. articles to profl. jours. Served to sgt. U.S. Army, 1967-69, Vietnam. Decorated Bronze Star. Mem. ABA, Assn. Trial Lawyers Am., Calif. Trial Lawyers Assn. Republican. Avocations: family outings, buying cars, horses, weight lifting, helicopter pilot. State civil litigation, Insurance, Personal injury. Office: 2103 El Camino Real Oceanside CA 92054

HOOTMAN, GREGORY WAYNE, lawyer; b. Piqua, Ohio, Aug. 1, 1950; s. Wayne Franklin and Barbara Ruth (Baker) H.; m. Susan Lynne Rohel, Aug. 11, 1972; children: Robert Gregory, Daniel Christopher. BA, Ohio State U., 1971; JD, Capital U., 1978. Bar: Fla. 1980, U.S. Dist. Ct. (mid. dist.) Fla. 1980, U.S. Dist. Ct. (so. dist.) Fla. 1981, U.S. Ct. Appeals (11th cir.) 1982. Ptnr. Dickinson, O'Riorden, Gibbons, Quale, Shields & Carlton, Sarasota, Fla., 1980—. Served to lt. (j.g.) USN, 1971-75. Mem. Fla. Bar Assn. (trial sect., local govt. sect.). Republican. Avocations: golf, fishing. Federal civil litigation, State civil litigation, Local government. Home: 1860 Springwood Dr Sarasota FL 33582 Office: Dickinson O'Riorden Gibbons et al 1750 Ringling Blvd Sarasota FL 33577

HOOTON, MICHAEL EDWARD, lawyer; b. Des Moines, July 25, 1950; s. Court Madison and Helen Dean (Belding) H.; m. Margaret Ann Barnett, Aug. 26, 1972; children: Robert, Katherine, John, Christopher. BBA, U. Iowa, 1972; JD, U. San Diego, 1975; LLM, NYU, 1976. Bar: Calif. 1976, Va. 1976, U.S. Dist. Ct. (ea. dist.) Va. 1976, U.S. Ct. Appeals (4th cir.) 1976. Atty. Hunton & Williams, Richmond, Va., 1976-80; atty. H.J. Heinz Co., Pitts., 1980-85, sr. atty., 1985—. Contbr. articles to profl. jours. Mem. ABA, Calif. Bar Assn., Va. Bar Assn. Avocations: reading, tennis, squash. General corporate, Securities, Private international. Office: H J Heinz Co PO Box 57 Pittsburgh PA 15230

HOOVER, DAVID CARLSON, lawyer; b. Waterville, Maine, Apr. 22, 1950; s. Jack Cauldwell and Mary Elizabeth (Donavan) H.; m. Kathleen Delia Powell, June 28, 1981; 1 child, Maegan Elizabeth. BA, U. N.H., 1972; JD cum laude, Suffolk U., 1976. Bar: Mass. 1977, U.S. Dist. Ct. Mass. 1982, U.S. Supreme Ct. 1982, U.S. Ct. Appeals (1st cir.) 1983. Atty. advisor NOAA, Washington, 1976-79; gen. counsel Mass. Div. Marine Fisheries, Boston, 1979-83; spl. asst. atty. gen. Mass. Dept. Atty. Gen., Boston, 1980—; gen. counsel Mass. Dept. of Fisheries, Wildlife and Environ. Law Enforcement, Boston, 1983—; adminstrv. law magistrate Commonwealth of Mass., 1979—; lectr. Franklin Pierce Law Ctr., Concord, N.H., 1984. Contbr. articles to profl. jours. Mem. Mass. Bar Assn., Com. on Chemical Dependency, Lawyers Concerned for Lawyers. Avocations: miniaturist, woodworking, civil war history. Administrative and regulatory, Environment, Wildlife management. Home: 808 Watertown St West Newton MA 02165 Office: Dept Fisheries Wildlife and Environ Law Enforcement 100 Cambridge St Boston MA 02202

HOOVER, EARL REESE, savings association executive, lawyer; b. Dayton, Ohio, Nov. 19, 1904; s. John Jacob and Flora Maude (Brosier) H.; m. Alice Lorene Propst, Dec. 18, 1931; 1 child, Richard Wilson. A.B., Otterbein Coll., 1926, LL.D., 1955; J.D., Harvard U., 1929; LL.D., Salem Coll., 1961. Asst. atty. gen. State of Ohio, Columbus, 1930-31, 32; assoc. Mooney, Hahn, Loeser, Keough & Beam, Cleve., 1933-46; sole practice, Cleve., 1946-50; instr. bus. Fenn Coll. (now Cleve. State U.), 1950-51; law dir. Town of Aurora, Ohio, 1949-50; judge Common Pleas Ct. of Cuyahoga County, Cleve., 1951-69; sr. v.p. Shaker Savs. Assn., Shaker Heights, Ohio, 1969-80, mem. adv. bd. dirs., 1977-80; sr. v.p. Ohio Savs. Assn., 1980—; guest speaker numerous clubs, assns. Author: Cradle of Greatness: National and World Achievements of Ohio's Western Reserve, 1977. Bd. dirs. Cleve. Law Library, 1942-54, Citizens Bur., 1945-53; bd. dirs. Cleve. Roundtable of NCCJ, 1946-52, mem. exec. com., 1950-52, treas., 1950-52, chmn. food industry com Cleve. Health Council, 1942-46; trustee, mem. exec. com. Nationalities Services Ctr., 1953-56; mem. Cleve. Landmarks Commn., 1974-82; exec. bd. dirs. Greater Cleve. Bicentennial Commn., 1975-76; trustee Cleve. Masonic Library Assn., 1973-83; chmn. pub. relations com. Anti-Tv League of Cleve. and Cuyahoga County, Cleve., 1963-65; trustee Otterbein Coll., 1935-60, chmn. alumni relations and publicity com. of bd. trustees, 1945-60; mem. men's com. Cleve. Playhouse, 1950-57; bd. dirs. Neighborhood Settlement Assn., 1951-58; exec. bd. dirs. Greater Cleve. council Boy Scouts Am., 1956-59, chmn. council's Ct. of Honor, 1949-55, chmn. Newton D. Baker Dist., 1956-59, rep. to Nat. Council, 1957; bd. dir. Cleve. Ch. Fedn., 1955-58, Western Res. Hist. Soc., 1968—, Shaker Hist. Soc., 1969-81, v.p., 1970-71; bd. dirs. Religious Heritage of Am., 1958-59; v.p. Ripon Club (Rep. Club), 1949; mem. exec. Cleve. Civil War Round Table, 1969-70. Named Father of Hall of Fame Otterbein Coll., 1968; recipient Disting. Alumnus award Alumni Assn. of Otterbein Coll., 1970, award for Outstanding Service to Scouting Boy Scouts Am., Southwest Dist., 1972. Mem. Bar Assn. Greater Cleve., Cleve. Bar Assn. (rep. to Council of Dels. of Ohio State Bar Assn. 1937-38, chmn. coms.), Ohio State Bar Assn. (chmn. coms.), Cuyahoga County Bar Assn., Early Settlers Assn. of Western Res. (pres. 1971-72, bd. dirs. 1967—, mem. com. establishing Hall of Fame 1971), Harvard Alumni Assn. of Cleve., Harvard Law Sch. Alumni Assn., Otterbein Coll. Alumni Assn. (nat. pres.). Mem. United Ch. of Christ. Clubs: City (v.p. 1948, bd. dirs. 1946-48), Cleve. Shrine Luncheon (pres. 1959, bd. dirs. 1957-59), Cleve. Advt., Hundred Club (pres. 1938), Republic (bd. dirs. 1940-41, 44-48, pres. 1947). Lodges: Rotary (chmn. projects, emcee civic luncheons), Kiwanis of Cleve. (bd. dirs. Found. 1963-66, v.p. 1965-66), Masons, Shriners, Jesters. State civil litigation, Probate. Office: Ohio Savs Assn 13109 Shaker Sq Cleveland OH 44120

HOOVER, JAMES LLOYD, librarian, educator; b. Oklahoma City, June 15, 1945; s. Lloyd and Myrtle Marie (Blair) H. B.A., U. Okla., 1967, J.D., 1973; M.L., U. Wash., 1974. Cert. law librarian; bar: Mo. 1975. Asst. law librarian St. Louis U., 1974-75; assoc. law librarian U. Okla., Norman, 1975-78; asst. law librarian Columbia U., N.Y.C., 1978-82, law librarian, prof., 1982—. Editor: (with others) American Indian Legal Materials, 1980. Mem. Mo. Bar Assn., Am. Assn. Law Libraries, Am. Soc. Info. Sci., Assn. Am. Law Schs. Legal education, Legal history, Librarianship. Office: Columbia U 435 W 116th St New York NY 10027

HOOVER, RUSSELL JAMES, lawyer; b. Evanston, Ill., Apr. 27, 1940; s. Russell E and Grace M. (Nolan) H.; m. Judith Devine, Aug. 29, 1973; m. 2d JoAnn Dale Cloud, Sept. 15, 1979. A.B., U. Notre Dame, 1962; J.D. Georgetown U., 1965. Bar: Ill. 1968. Assoc. Jenner and Block, Chgo., 1968-75, ptnr. 1975—. Served to capt. U.S. Army, 1965-67. Decorated Army Commendation medal. Federal civil litigation, State civil litigation, Criminal. Home: 550 Monroe Ave River Forest IL 60305 Office: One IBM Plaza Suite 5300 Chicago IL 60611

HOPE, MARY, legal editor; b. Pasadena, Calif., Sept. 4, 1942; d. Louis Hunter and Roberta (Hope) Gwinn; children: Michael D. Wilson, Karen H. Wilson. BA, Cornell U., 1964; MLS, U. Md., 1970; JD, U. Denver, 1982. Bar: Colo. 1982. Librarian U. Colo., Colorado Springs, 1978; adminstrv. asst. Colo. Coll., Colorado Springs, 1978-79; assoc. Cross, Gaddis, Kin & Quicksall, Colorado Springs, 1982-83; in house author Shepards/McGraw-Hill, Colorado Springs, 1983-84; law editor Wiley Law Publs., Colorado Springs, 1984—. Bd. dirs. Colorado Springs Urban League, 1985. Mem. ABA, Colo. Bar Assn., Colo. Women's Bar Assn. (bd. del. 1983-85), El Paso County Bar Assn. Democrat. Lutheran. Clubs: Downton, Toastmasters (sec. 1984, pres. 1985) (Colorado Springs). Avocations: aerobics, skiing, sewing. Legal publishing. Office: Wiley Law Publs 711 N Tejon St PO Box 1777 Colorado Springs CO 80901

HOPE, THEODORE SHERWOOD, JR., lawyer; b. N.Y.C., Oct. 7, 1903; s. Theodore Sherwood and Winifred (Ayres) H.; m. Emily Louise Blanchard, June 28, 1934; 1 son, Peter Blanchard. A.B., Harvard U., 1925; LL.B., Columbia U., 1928. Bar: N.Y. 1931, U.S. Supreme Ct. 1936. Instr., Columbia U. Law Sch., N.Y.C., 1928-29; assoc. instr. Johns Hopkins U. Inst. Law, Balt., 1929-32; sole practice, N.Y.C., 1932-33; with Paramount Bankruptcy Trustees, N.Y.C., 1933-34; assoc. Donovan Leisure Newton & Lumbard, name changed to Donovan Leisure Newton & Irvine, N.Y.C., 1934-40, 1941-49, ptnr., 1949-86, counsel, 1986—; assoc. prof. law Cornell U. Law Sch., 1940-41. Mem., fellow council Pierpont Morgan Library. Mem. Assn. Bar City N.Y., N.Y. State Bar Assn., N.Y. County Bar Assn., Am. Soc. Internat. Law. Clubs: Lotos, Harvard of N.Y.C. Contbr. articles to legal jours. Antitrust, Corporate taxation, FERC practice. Home: 11 Fifth Ave New York NY 10003 Office: 30 Rockefeller Plaza New York NY 10012

HOPGOOD, TOM KOLSTAD, lawyer; b. Williston, N.D., Jan. 1, 1954; s. M. Theodore and Freddie Louise (Kolstad) H.; m. Loraine C. Crosby, June 4, 1977; children: Julie Marie, Amy Leigh. BA, Mont. State U., 1976; JD, Gonzaga U., 1979. Bar: Mont. 1979, U.S. Dist. Ct. Mont. 1979. Law clk. to presiding justice Mont. Supreme Ct., Helena, Mont., 1979; assoc. Lobe & Pauly P.C., Helena, 1980-82, ptnr., 1982—. Mem. ABA, Mont. Bar Assn., 1st Jud. Dist. Bar Assn. (sec., treas. 1984-85, v.p. 1985-86, pres. 1986—), Mont. Trial Lawyers Assn. General practice, State civil litigation, State and local taxation. Office: Lobe & Pauly PC PO Box 176 Helena MT 59624

HOPKINS, ALBEN NORRIS, lawyer; b. Ripley, Miss., Feb. 14, 1941; s. Lloyd Carter and Reba Genova (Norris) H.; m. Ruth Boyd, May 31, 1963; children—Ashley Anne, A. Norris. B.A., Delta State Coll., 1963; J.D., U. Miss., 1965; B.A., William Carey Coll., 1985; student Blue Mountain Coll., U. Pa. Bar: U.S. Dist. Ct. (so. dist.) Miss. 1966, U.S. Dist. Ct. (no. dist.) Miss. 1970, U.S. Ct. Appeals (5th cir.) 1972, U.S. Supreme Ct. 1972, U.S. Ct. Appeals (11th cir.) 1981, U.S. Ct. Mil. Appeals 1986. Assoc. Daniel, Coker & Horton, Jackson also Gulfport, Miss., 1965-67, ptnr., 1967-69, resident ptnr., 1969-77; sr. ptnr., mng. ptnr. Hopkins, Vaughn & Anderson, Gulfport, Miss., 1977—. Bd. dirs. Delta State U. Found., USO, 1974-75, 83—, Gulf Pines council Girl Scouts U.S.A., 1974-82, United Way Harrison County; bd. dirs., chmn. planned giving com., dist. dir. Am. Heart Assn.; asst. chmn. State Heart Fund, 1983, chmn., 1985. Served to col. U.S. Air N.G. Fellow Miss. Bar Found.; mem. Internat. Assn. Ins. Counsel, Fedn. Ins. Counsel, Maritime Law Assn. U.S., Southeastern Admiralty Assn., Hinds County Bar Assn., Harrison County Bar Assn. (v.p. 1976-77), Miss. Bar Assn. (mem. jud. selection com. 1978-79), ABA, Lamar Order, Fed. Bar Assn., Def. Research Inst., Miss. Trial Lawyers Assn., Am. Trial Lawyers Assn., Miss. Def. Lawyers Assn. (bd. dirs. 1979-82), Kappa Alpha, Pi Kappa Delta, others. Republican. Baptist. Clubs: Broadwater Country, Bayou Bluff Tennis, Gulfport Yacht, University, Masons, Shriners. Federal civil litigation, State civil litigation. Office: PO Drawer 1510 Gulfport MS 39502

HOPKINS, BRUCE RICHARD, lawyer, educator, author; b. Sault Ste. Marie, Mich., Apr. 25, 1941; s. Frederick Benton and Jane Doris (Carnahan) H.; m. Sharon Anne Holliday, Sept. 16, 1966; children—Natalie, Christopher. B.A., U. Mich., 1964; J.D., George Washington U., 1967, LL.M., 1971. Bar: D.C. 1969, U.S. Dist. Ct. D.C. 1969, U.S. Ct. Appeals (D.C. cir.) 1969, U.S. Tax Ct. 1970, U.S. Ct. Appeals (4th cir.) 1974, U.S. Ct. Claims 1975. Assoc., ptnr. Williams, Myers & Quiggle, Washington, 1969-76; ptnr. Baer, Marks & Upham, N.Y.C. and Washington, 1976-78; prin. Hewes & Hopkins, P.C., Washington, 1978-80; prin. Hewes, Hopkins & Morella, P.C., Washington, 1980-81; prin. Bruce R. Hopkins, P.C., Washington, 1981-85; ptnr. Baker & Hostetler, Washington, 1985—; lectr. law George Washington U. Nat. Law Ctr. Mem. ABA, D.C. Bar Assn., Nat. Assn. Coll. and Univ. Attys. (cert. for contbns. in higher edn. law 1980). Club: Congressional Country (Bethesda, Md.). Author: Charity Under Siege: Government Regulation of Fund Raising, 1980; Charitable Giving and Tax-Exempt Organizations; Impact of 1981 Tax Act, 1981; Law of Tax-Exempt Organizations, 5th edit. Corporate taxation, Personal income taxation, Administrative and regulatory. Office: Baker & Hostetler Suite 1100 1050 Conn Ave NW Washington DC 20036

HOPKINS, CHARLES PETER, II, lawyer; b. Elizabeth, N.J., June 16, 1953; s. Charles Peter Sr. and Josephine Ann (Battaglia) H.; m. Elizabeth Anna Altinger, Jan. 21, 1984; 1 child, Courtney Alexandra. AB summa cum laude, Boston Coll., 1975, JD, 1979. Bar: N.J. 1979, U.S. Dist. Ct. N.J. 1979, U.S. Ct. Supreme Ct. 1985. Assoc. Gagliano, Tucci & Kennedy, West Long Branch, N.J., 1980; sole practice West Long Branch, 1980-81; assoc. Sparks & Sauerwein, Shrewsbury, N.J., 1981—; arbitrator U.S. Dist. Ct. N.J., 1985—. Mem. West Long Branch Sch. Bd., 1980-82. Mem. ABA, N.J. Bar Assn., Monmouth Bar Assn., N.J. Def. Assn., Phi Beta Kappa. Republican. Roman Catholic. Avocations: landscaping, tennis, history. State civil litigation, Personal injury, Insurance. Office: Sparks & Sauerwein 655 Shrewsbury Ave Shrewsbury NJ 07701

HOPKINS, DONALD RAY, lawyer; b. Tulsa, Nov. 14, 1936; s. Stacy and Carrie (McGlory) H.; m. Ann Marie Ashmore, Dec. 24, 1967 (div. July 1972); 1 child, Yvonne Ann-Marie. BA, Kans. U., 1958; MA, Yale U., 1959; JD, U. Calif., Berkeley, 1965; LLM, Harvard U., 1969. Bar: Calif. 1981, U.S. Supreme Ct., U.S. Dist. Ct. (no. dist.) Calif. 1981, U.S. Ct. Appeals (9th cir.). Asst. dean of students U. Calif., Berkeley, 1965-67, asst. exec. chancellor, 1967-68; atty. legal def. fund NAACP, N.Y.C., 1969-70; exec. v.p. Pacific Cons., Berkeley, 1970-71; dist. adminstr. 8th Congl. Dist. Calif., Oakland, 1971—; sole practice Oakland, 1981—. Contbr. articles to mags. and newspapers. Mem. Equal Employment Opportunity Bd., Berkeley, 1966-68, Commn. on Met. Problems, Berkeley, 1967, African Film Soc. Bd., various cities, 1972-78, Charter Rev. Commn., Oakland, 1983; bd. dirs. Vols. on Parole, Oakland, 1983—, northern Calif., 1966-68. Fellow Woodrow Wilson Found., 1959. Mem. ABA, Charles Houston Bar Assn. (bd. dirs. 1985—), Assn. Trial Lawyers Am., Calif. Assn. Black Lawyers, Am. Acad. Polit. Sci., ACLU. Democrat. Baptist. Club: Lakeview (Oakland). Avocations: chess, auto clubs, photography. General practice, Personal injury, State civil litigation. Home: 1039 Amitor Dr Berkeley CA 94705 Office: 8th Congl Dist 201 13th St Oakland CA 94617

HOPKINS, GEORGE MATHEWS MARKS, lawyer, business executive; b. Houston, June 9, 1923; s. C. Allen and Agnes Cary (Marks) H.; m. Betty Miller McLean, Aug. 21, 1954; children: Laura McLean, Edith Cary. Student, Ga. Sch. Tech., 1943-44; B.S. in Chem. Engring, Ala. Poly. Inst., 1944; LL.B., J.D., U. Ala., 1949; postgrad., George Washington U., 1949-50. Bar: Ala. 1949, Ga. 1954; Registered profl. engr., Ga. registered patent lawyer, U.S., Can. qualified deep-sea diver. Instr. math. U. Ala., 1947-49; assoc. firm A. Yates Dowell, Washington, 1949-50, Edward T. Newton, Atlanta, 1950-62; asst. dir. research, legal counsel Auburn (Ala.) Research Found., 1954-55; partner firm Newton, Hopkins and Ormsby (and predecessor), Atlanta, 1962—; spl. asst. atty. gen. State of Ga., 1978; chmn. bd. Southeastern Carpet Mills, Inc., Chatsworth, Ga., 1962-77, Thomas-Daniel & Assocs., Inc., 1981—, Eastern Carpet Mills, Inc., 1983—; dir. Xepol Inc. Served as lt., navigator, Submarine Service USNR, 1944-46, 50-51. Mem. ABA, Ga. Bar Assn. (chmn. sect. patents 1970-71), Atlanta Bar Assn., Am. Intellectual Property Law Assn., Am. Soc. Profl. Engrs., Submarine Vets. World War II (pres. Ga. chpt. 1977-78), Phi Delta Phi, Sigma Alpha Epsilon. Episcopalian. Clubs: Nat. Lawyers (Washington); Atlanta Lawyers, Univ. Yacht, Phoenix Soc, Cherokee Town and Country, Atlanta City. Patent, Trademark and copyright. Home: 795 Old Post Rd NW Atlanta GA 30328 Office: Newton Hopkins & Ormsby Equitable Bldg 10th Floor 100 Peachtree St Atlanta GA 30303

HOPKINS, GROVER PREVATTE, lawyer; b. Jacksonville, Fla., Sept. 2, 1933; s. John Taylor and Capitola (Prevatte) H.; m. Ann Hutchinson, Oct. 16, 1965 (dec.); children—John, Corbin; m. 2d, Connie Jefferys, June 7, 1973. A.B., Fla. State U., 1958; J.D., U.N.C., 1971. Bar: N.C. 1971, U.S. Dist. Ct. (ea. dist.) N.C. 1971, Fla. 1972, U.S. Ct. Appeals (4th cir.) 1974, U.S. Supreme Ct. 1974, D.C. 1981. Announcer, Sta. WTAL, Tallahassee, 1951-54; pub. relations dir. Inter-Am. U., San Germá n, P.R., 1958-60; personnel mgr. Northridge Knitting Mills, San Germá n, 1960-62; cons. bus. and personnel, Mayagú ez, P.R., and Miami, Fla., 1963-69; mem. Weeks & Muse, Tarboro, N.C., 1971-73, Hopkins & Allen, Tarboro, 1973-. Served with U.S. Army, 1954-57. Mem. ABA, N.C. Bar Assn., D.C. Bar Assn., Inter-Am. Bar Assn. (council), N.C. Trial Lawyers Assn. Republican. Episcopalian. Personal injury, Family and matrimonial, Bankruptcy. Office: 212 Main St Tarboro NC 27886

HOPKINS, RANDOLPH BYRD, lawyer; b. Oakland, Calif., Dec. 16, 1951; s. Byrd and Mary Caroline (Reed) H.; m. Sarah Brown, Aug. 18, 1973; children: Frances, Beth, Cathy. BA, Guilford Coll., 1974; JD, U. Ark., 1977. Bar: Ark. 1977, U.S. Dist. Ct. (ea. dist.) Ark. 1977, U.S. Ct. Appeals (8th cir.) 1979. Assoc. Barber, McCaskill, Amsler, Jones & Hale, P.A., Little Rock, 1977—. Mem. Indian princesses YMCA, Little Rock. Mem. ABA, Ark. Bar Assn., Pulaski County Bar Assn. Club: Country Little Rock. Federal civil litigation, Contracts commercial, Insurance. Home: 221 S Ridge Rd Little Rock AR 72207 Office: Barber McCaskill Amsler Jones & Hale PA 1500 Union Nat Plaza Little Rock AR 72201

HOPKINS, SAMUEL, investment banker; b. Highland, Md., Oct. 18, 1913; s. Samuel Harold and Roberta (Smith) H.; m. Winifred Holt Bloodgood, Oct. 15, 1938 (dec. Oct. 1954); children: Samuel, Henry; m. Anne E. Dankmeyer, Oct. 21, 1955; children: Robert, Frederick. B.S., Johns Hopkins U., 1934; LL.B., U. Md., 1938. With Fidelity & Deposit Co. of Md., 1934-69, asst. to treas., 1934-50, asst. treas., 1950-54, sec., 1954-67, v.p., sec., dir., 1967-69; dir., mem. trust com. Equitable Trust Co., Balt., 1967-81; sec., dir. Md. Life Ins. Co., 1963-69; gen. partner Alex. Brown & Sons (investment bankers), Balt., 1970-75; ltd. partner Alex, Brown & Sons (investment bankers), 1976-86. Mem. adv. com. housing for elderly U.S. Housing and Finance Agy., 1956-60; mem. Balt. Bd. Recreation and Parks, 1965-77, pres., 1965-67, 74-77, v.p., 1968-74; Republican candidate for Congress, 1952; mem. Md. Ho. of Dels., 1950-54; Rep. candidate for mayor, Balt., 1955; del. Rep. Nat. Conv., 1976; trustee Balt. Mus. Art, Peale Mus.; vice-chmn. bd. trustees Sheppard and Enoch Pratt Hosp.; trustee, v.p. State Colls. Md., 1963-70; mem. Balt. City Planning Commn., 1985—. Served from ensign to lt. USNR, 1942-45. Mem. ABA, Balt. Security Analysts Soc., Md. Hist. Soc. (treas. 1956-69, pres. 1970-75, trustee), Inst. Chartered Security Analysts. Episcopalian. Banking, Local government, Admiralty. Home: 45 Warrenton Rd Baltimore MD 21210 Office: Alex Brown & Sons 135 E Baltimore St Baltimore MD 21202

HOPKINS, THOMAS ARSCOTT, lawyer; b. Cleve., June 29, 1931; s. Albert T. and Georgine Arscott (Robinson) H.; m. Ann Elizabeth White, Sept. 23, 1962; children: Ingrid O., Matthew W., Hannah R., Helen A. B.A., Yale U., 1953; LL.B., Harvard U., 1960. Bar: Ohio 1960, N.Y. 1961. Assoc. White & Case, N.Y.C., 1960-71, ptnr., 1972—; resident ptnr. White & Case, Brussels, 1976-79. Mem. ABA, N.Y. State Bar Assn., Assn. Bar City N.Y. (chmn. corp. law com. 1975-76). General corporate, Private international, Banking. Office: White & Case 1155 Ave of Americas New York NY 10036

HOPP, WALTER JAMES, lawyer; b. Longmont, Jan. 17, 1945; s. Conrad and Frieda (Gies) H.; m. Margaret Ann Warnock, June 17, 1965 (dec. July 1985); children: Elizabeth Ann, Walter David, William John, Martha Jean; m. Vicki S. Lake, Nov. 29, 1985; 1 child, Emily Jean. BA, U. Colo., 1967, JD, 1970. Bar: Colo. 1970, U.S. Dist. Ct. Colo. 1970, U.S. Ct. Appeals (10th cir.) 1970. Law clk. U.S. Dist. Ct., Denver, 1970-71; assoc. Schey & Schey, Longmont, 1971-73, ptnr., 1973-80; sole practice Longmont, 1980-81, Hopp & Assocs., Longmont, 1981-83; mng. ptnr. Hopp, Carson & Beckmann, P.C., Longmont, 1983—. Mem. ABA, Colo. Bar Assn., Boulder County Bar Assn., Assn. Trial Lawyers Am., Colo. Trial Lawyers Assn. Democrat. Lutheran. Real property, Probate, General practice. Home: 5021 Fox Hill Dr Langmont CO 80501 Office: Hopp Carlson & Beckmann PC 2130 Mountain View Ave Longmont CO 80501

HOPPE, CRAIG ALLEN, lawyer; b. Racine, Wis., Aug. 13, 1950; s. William Edward and Audrey Leone (Stephen) H.; m. Victoria S. Hoppe, Aug. 20, 1977; 1 child, Travis Aaron. BA in Journalism, U. Nev., 1972; JD, S. Tex. Coll. Law, 1977. Bar: Nev. 1978, U.S. Dist. Ct. Nev. 1984. Claims examiner Am. Hardware Mut. Ins. Co., Houston, 1973-77; assoc. Miles, Pico & Mitchell, Las Vegas, Nev., 1977-80; counsel Seisdata Services, Inc., Houston, 1980-83; assoc. Morse & Mowbray, Las Vegas, 1983-85, Bell & Young, Las Vegas, 1985—. Editor: (newsletter) Seismic Sunrise, 1980-83, Byline, 1986—. Founder Lone Mountain Town Bd., Las Vegas, 1984; N.W. Citizens Adv. Assn., Las Vegas, 1979. Mem. ABA, Assn. Trial Lawyers am., Def. Research Inst., Nev. Bar Assn., Clark County Bar Assn. Republican. Lutheran. Avocations: golf, antiques, landscaping. Insurance, Administrative and regulatory, Alternative dispute resolution--arbitration and mediation. Office: Bell & Young Ltd 601 S Rancho #D-31 Las Vegas NV 89106

HOPPEL, ROBERT GERALD, JR., lawyer; b. Scranton, Pa., Dec. 26, 1921; s. Robert Gerald and Ellen Amelia (Casey) H. B.S., U. Scranton, 1950; J.D., Georgetown U., 1954. Bar: D.C. 1955, U.S. Ct. Appeals (D.C. cir.) 1955, U.S. Supreme Ct. 1974. Supervising auditor GAO, Washington, 1950-57; ptnr. Coles & Goertner, Washington, 1957-82; ptnr. Hoppel, Mayer & Coleman, Washington, 1982-84; sole practice, 1984—. Served to cpl. USAAF, 1943-45. Mem. ABA, Maritime Adminstrv. Bar Assn., D.C. Bar, Bar Assn. D.C., Internat. Platform Assn., Am. Legion, Nat. Lawyers Club. Republican. Roman Catholic. Clubs: Propellor (Washington); Elks (Scranton, Pa.). Administrative and regulatory, Admiralty, Government contracts and claims. Office: 3600 Massachusetts Ave NW Washington DC 20007

HOPWOOD, HOWARD H., corporate lawyer; b. 1945. BA, Williams Coll., 1967; JD, Case Western Res. U., 1974. Asst. gen. counsel dept. adminstrv. services State of Ohio, 1974-75; sr. legal officer Bank One of Columbus, Ohio, 1975-80; sr. atty. First Wis. Corp., Milw., 1980-81, asst. counsel, 1981-82, v.p., 1982-83, 1st v.p., gen. counsel, 1983—. Office: 1st Wis Corp 777 E Wisconsin Ave Milwaukee WI 53202 *

HORAN, JOHN DONOHOE, lawyer; b. N.Y.C., Mar. 4, 1948; s. Michael Joseph, Jr. and Anna Patricia (Donohoe) H.; m. Judith R. Levinson, Aug. 8, 1976; children—Michael L., Emily L. B.A., Fordham Coll., 1970; J.D., Rutgers U., 1974. Bar: N.J. 1974, U.S. Dist. Ct. N.J. 1974, U.S. Ct. Appeals (3d cir.) 1980, U.S. Supreme Ct. 1981. Ptnr., Goodman, Stoldt, Breslin & Horan, Hackensack, N.J., 1974-84, Stoldt, Horan & Cino, 1984—. Bd. dirs. Research Fund for Cystic Fibrosis, Inc., 1985—. Mem. Bergen County Bar Assn. (com. on employment discrimination 1979—, founder, chmn. com. environ. law 1983—, chmn. subcom. on hazardous waste litigation 1983—), Trial Attys. N.J., ABA (litigation), N.J. State Bar Assn. (com. on environ. law). Federal civil litigation, State civil litigation, Environment. Office: Stoldt Horan & Cino 401 Hackensack Ave Hackensack NJ 07601

HORAN, JOHN PATRICK, lawyer; b. Wilkes-Barre, Pa., Sept. 13, 1952; s. John Joseph and Rosina Olivia (Giunta) H.; m. Joette Elizabeth Young, July 8, 1978; 1 child, John Ryan. AB cum laude, U. Notre Dame, 1974, JD, 1977. Bar: Fla. 1977, U.S. Dist. Ct. (so. dist.) Fla. 1977. Assoc. Kimbrell, Hamann et al, Miami, Fla., 1977-79, Smathers & Thompson, Miami, 1979-80, Myers, Kenin et al, Miami, 1980-83, Foley, Lardner, Van den Berg et al, Orlando, Fla., 1983—; lectr. Profl. Edn. Systems Inc., Eau Claire, Wis., 1982—, constrn. law Nat. Bus. Inst., 1987—. Author (handbook) Florida Collection Law, 1983—. Mem. ABA, Fla. Bar Assn., Orange County Bar Assn., U. Notre Dame Alumni Club (sec., treas. Miami chpt. 1981-83, pres. 1983). Federal civil litigation, State civil litigation, Construction. Home: 2250 King James Ct Winter Park FL 32792 Office: Foley Lardner Van den Berg et al PO Box 2193 Orlando FL 32802

HOREY, EDWARD MADIGAN, judge; b. Cameron Mills, N.Y., Dec. 19, 1921; s. Joseph Arthur and Florence Agnes (Madigan) H.; m. Marion Alice Weis, Jan. 2, 1954; children—Joseph Edward, Eirene Kathleen. B.A. magna cum laude, St. Bonaventure U., 1943; LL.B., Cornell U., 1949; student U. Glascow (Scotland), 1945-46. Bar: N.Y. 1949, U.S. Dist. Ct. (we. dist.) N.Y. 1951, U.S. Tax Ct. 1958, U.S. Supreme Ct. 1958. Assoc. Shane & McCarthy,

Olean, N.Y., 1949-51; spl. asst. atty. gen. Saratoga Investigation, State of N.Y., 1951-52; ptnr. Shane & McCarthy, Olean, N.Y., 1952-71; judge Surrogate Ct., Cattaraugus County, State of N.Y., 1971—. Contbr. law opinions to Official Reporter for the State of N.Y., 1971—. Mem., Olean Planning Bd. Served to capt. AUS, 1943-46. Decorated Bronze Star medal. Mem. Am. Legion (vice comdr.), N.Y. State Bar Assn., N.Y. State Trial Lawyers Assn., ABA, Surrogate Ct. Judges Assn. (past pres.), Cattaraugus County Bar Assn. (past pres.). Republican. Roman Catholic (parish council). Clubs: Exchange, St. Vincent DePaul. Lodge: Elks. Probate, Family and matrimonial, State civil litigation. Home: 414 Tyler Ave Olean NY 14760 Office: Surrogate Ct 600 Mfrs Hanover Bank Bldg Olean NY 14760

HORGAN, JOHN JOSEPH, lawyer; b. St. Louis, Sept. 3, 1921; s. Daniel Joseph and Mary Theresa (Moore) H.; m. Mary Frances King, June 21, 1929; children—John J. Jr., Mary C., Paul F., Patrick J., Thomas M. J.D., St. Louis U., 1951. Bar: Mo. 1951, U.S. Dist. Ct. (ea. dist.) Mo. 1951. Assoc. city counselor St. Louis, 1959-65; ptnr. Moser, Marsalek, Carpenter, Cleary, Jaeckel & Keaney, St. Louis, 1965—; instr. bus. law St. Louis U., 1959-71. Served with USAF, 1942-46. Mem. ABA, St. Louis Met. Bar Assn., Lawyers Assn. St. Louis, Assn. Def. Counsel St. Louis (pres. 1971), Internat. Bar Assn., Def. Research Inst., Delta Theta Phi, Delta Sigma Pi. Roman Catholic. Club: Media (St. Louis). Federal civil litigation, State civil litigation, Insurance. Home: 4 Meadow Acres Ln Saint Louis MO 63124 Office: 314 N Broadway Saint Louis MO 63102

HORKOVICH, ROBERT MICHAEL, lawyer; b. Kew Gardens, N.Y., June 11, 1954; s. Andrew Horkovich and Amelia (Rauba) Patti. BA in Econs. and Govt., Fordham U., 1976, JD, 1979. Bar: N.Y. 1980, U.S. Dist. Ct. (so. and ea. dists.) N.Y. 1980, U.S. Ct. Appeals (2d cir.) 1980, U.S. Ct. Mil. Appeals 1980. Aide to U.S. Senator James L. Buckley, N.Y., 1975-77; assoc. Skadden, Arps, Slate, Meagher & Flom, N.Y.C., 1979-80, Cadwalader, Wickersham & Taft, N.Y.C., 1984—; dir. ops. N.Y. State Polit. Action Com., 1977-79. Articles editor Fordham Urban Law Jour., 1978-79, bd. dirs. 1984—; contbr. articles to profl. jours. Served to capt. USAF, 1980-84. Named Co. Grade Officer of Yr. 1100 Air Base Wing, 1982, Eagle Scout Boy Scouts Am., 1972. Mem. Pi Sigma Alpha. Roman Catholic. Avocations: skiing, water sports, impressionist art. Federal civil litigation, State civil litigation, Antitrust. Office: Cadwalader Wickersham & Taft 100 Maiden Ln New York NY 10038

HORN, ANDREW WARREN, lawyer; b. Cin., Apr. 19, 1946; s. George H. and Belle (Collin) H.; m. Melinda Fink; children—Lee Shawn, Ruth Belle. B.B.A. in Acctg., U. Miami, 1968, J.D., 1971. Bar: Fla. 1971, U.S. Dist. Ct. (so. dist.) Fla. 1972, U.S. Tax Ct. 1974. Ptnr. Gillman & Horn P.A., Miami, Fla., 1973-74; sole practice Miami, 1974—. Bd. dirs. Young Democrats of Dade County. Recipient Am. Jurisprudence award Lawyers Coop. Pub. Co., 1970. Mem. ABA, Fla. Bar. Club: Tiger Bay. State civil litigation, Personal injury, Consumer commercial. Office: 111 SW 3d St 6th Floor Miami FL 33130

HORN, CHARLES LILLEY, lawyer; b. Mpls., May 12, 1927; s. Charles Lilley and Louise Eugenie (Brace) H.; m. Nancy Lou Taylor, Mar. 7, (dec. Feb. 1977); children—David Andrew, Louise Alicia; m. Barbara Allinson Teachout, Jan. 28, 1978. B.A., Princeton U., N.J., 1950; J.D., U. Minn., Mpls., 1953. Bar: Minn. 1953. Assoc. Faegre & Benson, Mpls., 1953-65, ptnr., 1965—. Author: The Iron Ore Industry of Minnesota and Problems of Depleted Reserves (Wolf Ballierson Meml. prize 1950), 1950. Trustee, sec. Minn. Chpt. of Nature Conservancy, Mpls., 1972—. Served with U.S. Army, 1945-47. Recipient Oak Leaf award The Nature Conservacy, 1978. Mem. Minn. State Bar Assn. Republican. Episcopalian. Clubs: Minikahda, Mpls. Athletic. Lodge: Masons. Avocations: birding; golf. Real property. Home: 9078 Hyland Creek Rd Bloomington MN 55437 Office: Faegre & Benson 33 S 6th St Minneapolis MN 55402

HORN, EVERETT BYRON, JR., lawyer; b. Newton, Mass., Aug. 18, 1927; s. Everett Byron and Ella Frances (Doody) H.; m. Patricia Ann Reusch, Sept. 10, 1949; children: Everett B. III, John M., Daniel J., Cynthia A. Whetten. AB, Harvard U., 1949; JD, Boston Coll., 1954. Bar: Mass. 1954, U.S. Dist. Ct. Mass. 1955, U.S. Supreme Ct. 1965. Asst. counsel Liberty Mut. Ins. Co., Boston, 1954-63; sr. v.p. and gen. counsel Mass. Indemnity and Life Ins. Co., Hyannis, 1964-75; counsel New Eng. Mut. Life Ins. Co., Boston, 1976-77; v.p. and gen. counsel Boston Mut. Life Ins. Co., Canton, Mass., 1977—; bd. dirs. Vt. Life and Health Ins. Guaranty Assn., Maine Life and Health Ins. Guaranty Assn., R.I. Life and Health Ins. Guaranty Assn. Pres. Seaside Park Taxpayers Assn., West Hyannis Port, Mass. 1961-64. Served as cpl. USAAF, 1945-46. Mem. ABA (vice chmn. life ins. law com. ins. law sect. 1985—), Mass. Bar Assn., Barnstable County Bar Assn., Norfolk County Bar Assn., Assn. Life Ins. Counsel, Soc. Corp. Ins. Litigators. Republican. Roman Catholic. Clubs: Hyannis Yacht; Harvard. Avocation: sailing. Insurance, General corporate. Home: 500 Ocean St Apt 120 Hyannis MA 02601 Office: Boston Mut Life Ins Co 120 Royall St Canton MA 02021

HORN, HERBERT, retired judge; b. Phila.; s. Michael and Mary (Petrosky) H.; m. Pauline Smith, Sept. 16, 1934; children—Leonard C., Rhoda M. Horn Steinberg. LL.B., Dickinson Sch. Law, 1932. Bar: N.J. 1934, U.S. Dist. Ct. N.J. 1934. Assoc. Thompson & Hanstein, Atlantic City, 1934-40; ptnr. Lloyd & Horn, Atlantic City, 1940-41, Lloyd, Horn & Perskie, Atlantic City, 1941-54, Lloyd, Horn, Megargee & Steedle, Atlantic City, 1954-65; judge N.J. Superior Ct., 1965-80. Served with AUS, 1944-45. Named Disting. Grad., Dickinson Sch. Law, 1979. Mem. Atlantic County Bar Assn., N.J. Bar Assn., ABA, Am. Coll. Trial Lawyers, Woolsack Hon. Soc. Jewish. Club: Linwood Country. Home: 1900 Consulate Pl West Palm Beach FL 33401

HORN, LAWRENCE ALAN, lawyer, business executive; b. Peoria, Ill., June 3, 1949; s. Joseph and Leila Joy (Waldman) H.; m. Carol Jan Shaskan, Nov. 27, 1976; children: Michael Brian, Jonathan Daniel. BA, Yale U., 1971; JD, Columbia U., 1974. Bar: D.C. 1975, U.S. Dist. Ct. (D.C. dist.) 1978, U.S. Ct. Appeals (1st, 2d, 5th, 8th, 9th, 10th and D.C. cirs.) 1978, U.S. Supreme Ct. 1978. Assoc. Melrod, Redman & Gartlan, Washington, 1974-75; atty. gen. counsel office SEC, Washington, 1975-78; assoc. gen. counsel Pub. Broadcasting Service, Washington, 1978-80, dep. gen. counsel, 1980-82, sr. v.p., gen. counsel, 1982-85; pres., gen. counsel HKM Corp., Washington, 1985—; adj. prof. Chinese law Georgetown U., Washington, 1974-75. Assoc. editor Columbia Jour. of Transnational Law, 1972-74. Mem. ABA. General corporate, Business start-up, acquisition and development. Office: HKM Corp Washington Sq Sta PO Box 65092 Washington DC 20035-5092

HORN, STEPHEN, lawyer; b. N.Y.C., Sept. 12, 1946; s. Leonard and Gladys (Blitz) H.; m. Kerry Corcoran, Oct. 9, 1977. B.S. in Indsl. Engring., Rutgers, 1968; J.D. cum laude, Seton Hall Sch., 1973. Bar: D.C. 1974, U.S. Dist. Ct. D.C. 1979, U.S. Ct. Appeals (D.C. cir.) 1979, Md. 1982. Trial atty. Dept. Justice, Washington, 1973-78; ptnr. Horn & Conroy, 1979-83, Schmeltzer, Aptaker & Sheppard, P.C., 1983—. Editor-in-chief Jour. Seton Hall Law Rev., 1972-73. Contbr. articles to profl. publs. Served to 1st lt. inf., U.S. Army, 1968-70, Vietnam. Recipient Spl. Achievement award U.S. Dept. Justice, 1976. Mem. ABA (chmn. com. 1981-85). Republican. Jewish. Federal civil litigation, Criminal. Office: Schmeltzer Aptaker & Sheppard P C 1800 Massachusetts Ave NW 500 Washington DC 20036

HORNBOSTEL, JOHN F., JR., lawyer; b. N.Y.C., Aug. 28, 1940; s. John F. and Clara Eunice (Mulvihill) H.; m. Elizabeth Jean Allen, Sept. 15, 1961; children: John Patrick, Victoria Lynn. BA, Middlebury Coll., 1962; JD, Fordham U., 1971. Bar: N.Y. 1971. Asst. sec., atty. Asarco, N.Y.C., 1967-72; asst. gen. counsel Comml. Solvents, N.Y.C., 1972-74; assoc. gen. counsel Nat. Distillers, N.Y.C., 1974-82; gen. counsel, sec. RMI Co., Niles, Ohio, 1982—; bd. dirs. Tradco, Sullivan, Mo., RMI Govt. Affairs; bd. dirs., gen. mgr. Micron, Salt Lake City. Div. head United Fund, Warren, Ohio, 1985—. Served to capt. U.S. Army, 1962-67. Mem. ABA, Assn. of Bar of City of N.Y., Corp. Counsel Assn., Westchester-Fairfield Counties Counsel Assn. Republican. Roman Catholic. Clubs: Youngstown (Ohio) Country; Darien (Ct.) Country. Antitrust, Contracts commercial, General corporate. Office: RMI Co 1000 Warren Ave Niles OH 44446

HORNE, MICHAEL STEWART, lawyer; b. Mpls., May 10, 1938; s. Owen Edward and Adeline (DiGeorgio) H.; m. Martha Brean, Sept. 11, 1965; children—Jennifer, Katherine, Sarah, Owen. B.A., U. Minn., 1959; LL.B., Harvard U., 1962. Bar: D.C. 1963, U.S. Ct. Appeals (D.C. cir.) 1964, U.S. Supreme Ct. 1968, U.S. Ct. Appeals (6th cir.), 1966, U.S. Ct. Appeals (4th cir.) 1979, U.S. Ct. Appeals (5th cir.), 1979, U.S. Ct. Appeals (2nd cir.) 1980, U.S. Ct. Appeals (11th cir.) 1983. Assoc. Covington & Burling, Washington, 1964-71, ptnr., 1971—. Mem. D.C. Bar Assn., ABA, FCC Bar Assn., Am. Judicature Soc. Democrat. Administrative and regulatory, Labor, Libel. Home: 9008 LeVelle Dr Chevy Chase MD 20815 Office: Covington & Burling 1201 Pennsylvania Ave NW PO Box 7566 Washington DC 20044

HORNE, TERRELL THOMAS, lawyer; b. Daytona, Fla., Mar. 28, 1956; s. Thomas Ansel and Mary Jo (Tyler) H.; m. Martha McElveen, May 21, 1983. BA, Vanderbilt U., 1977; JD, U. S.C., 1981; LLM in Taxation, U. Fla., 1986. Bar: S.C. 1982. Assoc. Bryan Law Firm, Sumter, S.C., 1982—; sec. Sumter Estate Planning Council, 1984-85. Mem. ABA, S.C. Bar Assn. (dist. rep. consumer law sect. 1985—), Order of Wig and Robe, Phi Beta Kappa. Lodge: Sertoma. Corporate taxation, Estate taxation, State civil litigation. Office: Bryan Bahnmuller King Golman & McElveen 17 E Calhoun St Sumter SC 29150

HORNE, THOMAS CHARLES, lawyer; b. Montreal, Que., Can., Mar. 28, 1945; s. George Marcus and Ludwika (Tom) H.; m. Martha Louise Presbry, June 25, 1972; children: Susan Christine, Mary Alice, David Charles, Mark Walter. BA magna cum laude, Harvard U., 1967, JD with honors, 1970. Bar: Mass. 1970, Ariz. 1972, U.S. Supreme Ct. 1974. Assoc. Donovan, Leisure, Newton & Irvine, N.Y.C.; sr. ptnr. Lewis & Roca, Phoenix; mng. ptnr. Horne, Kaplan & Bistrow P.C., Phoenix. Author: Arizona Construction Law, 1978. Chmn. Ariz. Air Pollution Control Hearing Bd., Phoenix, 1976-78; mem. Paradise Valley (Ariz.) Sch. Bd., 1978—, pres. 1981-82, 85—. Mem. Ariz. Bar Assn. (chmn. constrn. law com. litigation sect.). Democrat. Jewish. Office: Horne Kaplan & Pistrow 2480 Valley Bank Ctr 201 N Central Ave Phoenix AZ 85073

HORN EPSTEIN, PHYLLIS LYNN, lawyer; b. Phila., Sept. 10, 1955; d. Harold and Bernice H. BA, Temple U., 1977, JD, 1980, LLM, 1984. Bar: Pa. 1980, U.S. Dist. Ct. (ea. dist.) Pa., U.S. Ct. Appeals (3rd cir.). Assoc. Blumstein, Block & Vanore, Phila., 1980-81; assoc. Epstein, Beller & Shapiro, Phila., 1982-85, ptnr., 1985-86; ptnr. Epstein, Shapiro & Epstein, Phila., 1986—; instr. LaSalle Coll., Phila., 1980-82; vice chmn. Fee Dispute Com., Phila. 1985, chmn., 1986. Mem. Hadassah, Phila., 1986, Women for Greater Phila., 1986. Mem. ABA (tax sect., group editor newsletter 1982-85, editor Business Women's Network Tax Commentary 1986—, court procedure com. 1984—), Phila. Bar Assn., Pa. Trial Lawyers Assn. Office: Epstein Shapiro & Epstein 1515 Market St 15th Fl Three Penn Ctr Philadelphia PA 19102

HORNER, STEPHEN PULLAR, lawyer; b. New Rochelle, N.Y., Dec. 24, 1946; m. Briane Seaman, Aug. 21, 1971; children: Brinsley, Gregory. BA, Dickinson Coll., 1967; MBA, Temple U., 1969, JD, 1972. Bar: N.Y. 1974, Conn. 1987. Assoc. Cullen & Dykman, Bklyn., 1972-73, Jackson, Lewis, Manhattan, N.Y., 1973-75; ptnr. Arthur, Dry & Kalish, Manhattan, N.Y., 1975-84; labor counsel Uniroyal, Inc., Middlebury, Conn., 1984-86. Asst. scoutmaster Troop 125 Boy Scout Am., Wilton, Ct., 1985—; vice chmn. govt. relations com. Juvenile Diabetes Found. Internat., N.Y.C., 1984—, bd. dirs. 1983-85. Served to capt. U.S. Army, 1972-77. Mem. Westchester Fairfield County Corp. Counsel Assn. (vice chmn. equal employment opportunity, labor sect.). Labor. Home and Office: 43 Linden Tree Rd Wilton CT 06897

HORNER, TERRY DAVID, lawyer; b. Graz, Austria, Feb. 9, 1955; (parents Am. citizens); s. Dwight Burton Horner and Opal Ruth (Hoffman) Hamilton; m. Barbara Ellen Goodman, July 16, 1978. Student, McPherson Coll., 1973-75, Reed Coll., 1975-76; BA, NYU, 1978; JD, Bklyn. Law Sch., 1981. Bar: N.Y. 1981, U.S. Dist. Ct. (so. and ea. dists.) N.Y. 1983, U.S. Supreme Ct. 1986. Assoc. Siff, Newman, Rosen & Parker P.C., Poughkeepsie, N.Y., 1984-86; asst. pub. defender Dutchess County, Poughkeepsie, N.Y., 1986—. Mem. N.Y. State Bar Assn., Dutchess County Bar Assn. Democrat. Unitarian. Avocations: architecture, map collecting, antiques, classical music. Criminal. Home: 38 Parkwood Blvd Poughkeepsie NY 12603 Office: Dutchess County Pub Defender 28 Market St Poughkeepsie NY 12601

HORNISHER, MICHAEL, lawyer; b. San Antonio, June 25, 1949; s. Charles J. and Irene (Borbibly) H.; m. Mary Rita Jordan, July 15, 1974; children: David Michael, Sara Lorraine. BA, U. Ariz., 1971, JD, 1974. Bar: Ariz. 1974, U.S. Dist. Ct. Ariz. 1979. Assoc. Neighborhood Law Offices, Tucson, 1973-74, Law Offices Charles J. Rondelli, Tucson, 1975-79; sole practice Tucson, 1979—; dep. prosecutor Pima County, Tucson, 1974; bd. dirs. Tucson Savs. & Loan, Colorado Springs Savs. & Loan, Colo. Mem. ABA, Ariz. Bar Assn. (courthouse com. young lawyers sect., Pima County publicitiy com.), Fed. Bar Assn., Pima County Bar Assn., U. Ariz. Alumni Assn., U. Ariz. Law Coll. Alumni Assn., Greater Ariz. Bicycling Assn. (author articles 1985), Childbirth Edn. Assn. (cons. 1979—, author articles 1979), Nat. League Am. PenWomen (cons. 1979—), Nat. Rifle Assn. Avocations: competitive cycling, photography, camping. General practice, Real property, General corporate. Office: 2455 E Speedway #104 Tucson AZ 85719

HORNSBY, CYRUS EDWARD, III, lawyer; b. Birmingham, Ala., Feb. 6, 1943; s. Cryus Edward Jr. and Mary (Morrison) H.; m. Nancy Arnold, Sept. 21, 1962 (div. 1972); children: Cyrus E. VI, Spencer; m. Barbara Friedson, Jan. 1, 1983. BA, Princeton U., 1965; JD, Harvard U., 1968. Bar: Fla., Ga. Assoc. Jones, Bird & Howell, Atlanta, 1968-69; assoc. corp fin. Robinson-Humphrey Co., Atlanta, 1969-70; pres. Rutenberg Corp., Clearwater, Fla., 1970-74; sr. v.p., treas. Gen. Devel., Miami, 1974-76; mng. ptnr. Paul & Thompson, Miami, 1976-82, Hornsby & Whisenand, Miami, 1982—; Bd. dirs. 1st Nat. Bank Miami. Bd. dirs. Theatre Bd. Fla., Miami, 1983—; exec. com. New World Ctr. Action Com., Miami, 1979—. Mem. Fla. C. of C. (bd. dirs. 1979-85), Greater Miami C. of C. (trustee 1985—). Club: Miami, Grove Isle, Ocean Reef; Ivy (Princeton, N.J.). General corporate, Securities, Banking. Home: 1581 Brickell Ave #2001 Miami FL 33129 Office: Hornsby & Whisenand 1110 Brickell Ave Penthouse Miami FL 33131

HORNSTINE, LOUIS FOX, lawyer; b. Phila., May 24, 1950; s. Stanley M. and Doris G. (Fox) H.; m. Linda M. DeZolt, Nov. 25, 1979; children: Adam Joshua, Blair Leah. BA, Upsala Coll., 1972; JD, Temple U., 1977. Bar: N.J. 1983. Ptnr. Gorelick, Groon & Hornstine, Wildwood, N.J., 1977-82; sole practice Wildwood, 1982—. Republican. Jewish. General practice, State civil litigation, Criminal. Home: 9205 Seaview Ave Wildwood Crest NJ 08260 Office: 4004 Pacific Ave Wildwood NJ 08260

HORODAS, ERIC DAVID, lawyer; b. N.Y.C., Aug. 1, 1953; s. Bernard Stuart and Shirley (Handler) H.; m. Karen Heller, May 12, 1979; children: Kevin, Marc. BA, U. Rochester, 1975; JD, NYU, 1978. Bar: N.Y. 1979, Calif. 1980, U.S. Dist. Ct. (no. dist.) Calif. 1980, U.S. Tax Ct. 1981. Counsel Met. Life Ins. Co., N.Y.C., 1978-79, San Mateo, Calif., 1979-80; v.p., legal counsel Consol. Capital Cos., Emeryville, Calif., 1980-84, sr. v.p., asst. gen. counsel, 1985—; lectr. Calif. Edn. of Bar, U. Calif., Berkeley. Mem. ABA. Real property. Office: Consol Capital Cos 2000 Powell St Emeryville CA 94556

HOROHO, KENNETH JOSEPH, JR., lawyer; b. Johnstown, Pa., Oct. 22, 1955; s. Kenneth Joseph Sr. and Ann (Kazmer) H. BS, St. Francis Coll., 1977; JD, Duquesne U., 1980. Bar: Pa. 1980, U.S. Tax Ct. 1980. Tax atty. Touche Ross and Co., Pitts., 1980-82; assoc. Raphael, Gruener & Raphael P.C., Pitts., 1982—; bd. dirs. Nat. Communications, Inc., Dravosburg, Pa., Nat. Security Systems Corp., Dravosburg. Bd. of mgmt. Pitts. YMCA, 1982—, v.p., 1985—; chmn. Al Abrams sports banquet YMCA, 1985-86. Mem. ABA, Pa. Bar Assn. (co-chairperson local bar liaison young lawyers div.), Allegheny County Bar Assn. (chmn. elect young lawyers sect.). Democrat. Roman Catholic. Avocations: reading, sports, traveling. Family and matrimonial, General corporate, Estate planning. Home: 2088 Whited St Pittsburgh PA 15210 Office: Raphael Gruener & Raphael PC Grant Bldg 35th Floor Pittsburgh PA 15219

HOROWITZ, DONALD LEONARD, law educator, researcher, arbitrator, lawyer; b. N.Y.C., June 27, 1939; s. Morris and Yetta (Hibscher) H.; m. Judith Anne Present, Sept. 4, 1960; children—Marshall, Karen, Bruce. A.B., Syracuse U., 1959, LL.B., 1961; LL.M., Harvard U., 1962, A.M., 1965, Ph.D., 1967. Bar: N.Y. 1962, D.C. 1979, U.S. Ct. Appeals (D.C., 6th, 7th and 10th cirs.) 1970, U.S. Supreme Ct. 1969. Law clk. U.S. Dist. Ct. (ea. dist.) Pa., 1965-66; research assoc. Harvard U. Ctr. Internat. Affairs, 1967-69; atty. Dept. Justice, Washington, 1969-71; fellow Council on Fgn. Relations and Woodrow Wilson Internat. Ctr. for Scholars, Washington, 1971-72; research assoc. Brookings Instn., Washington, 1972-75; sr. fellow Research Inst. on Immigration and Ethnic Studies, Smithsonian Instn., Washington, 1975-81; prof. law Duke U., Durham, N.C., 1980—; cons. Ford Found., 1977-82; McDonald-Currie Meml. lectr. McGill U., Montreal, Que. Can., 1980; mem. labor, comml. and community dispute panels of arbitrators Am. Arbitration Assn.; mem. Council on Role of Cts., 1978-83. Guggenheim fellow, 1980-81; Nat. Humanities Ctr. fellow, 1984. Author: The Courts and Social Policy (Nat. Acad. Public Adminstrn. Louis Brownlow prize for best book in public adminstrn. 1977), 1977; The Jurocracy: Government Lawyers, Agency Programs and Judicial Decision, 1977; Coup Theories and Officers' Motives, 1980, Ethnic Groups In Conflict, 1985; mem. editorial bd. Ethnicity, 1974-82, Law and Soc. Rev., 1979-82, Law and Contemporary Problems, 1983-84. Labor, Criminal, Jurisprudence. Office: Duke U Sch Law Durham NC 27706

HOROWITZ, HAROLD A., lawyer; b. N.Y.C., May 7, 1950; s. Samuel and Gabriella (Feldman) H.; m. Judy Shulman, June 17, 1977; children: Shalom Yosef, Leah, Moshe David, Devorah, Pinchas. BA, Yeshiva U., 1971; MA, Columbia U., 1973, JD, 1976. Assoc. Shearman & Sterling, N.Y.C., 1976-78, Finley, Kumble, Wagner, Heine, Underberg, Manley & Casey, N.Y.C., 1978-82; ptnr. Booth, Lipton & Lipton, N.Y.C., 1982-86, Salon, Marrow & Dyckman, N.Y.C., 1986—. Securities, General corporate, Antitrust. Office: Salon Marrow & Dyckman 41 E 42d St New York NY 10017

HOROWITZ, HAROLD W., law educator; b. 1923. A.B., UCLA: 1943; LL.B., Harvard U., 1949, S.J.D., 1967; LL.M., So. Calif. U., 1954. Bar: Calif. 1950. Instr. law U. So. Calif., 1950-51, asst. prof. 1951-53, assoc. prof., 1953-56, prof. 1956-61; Thayer teaching fellow Harvard U., 1954-55; assoc. gen. counsel U.S. Dept. HEW, 1961-64; acting prof. UCLA, 1964-65, prof., 1965—, vice chancellor faculty relations, 1974—; dep. gen. counsel Gov.'s Commn. on the Los Angeles Riots, 1965; mem. nat. adv. com. to legal service program OEO, 1965-72. Bd. dirs. Western Ctr. on Law and Poverty, 1967-70; mem. Calif. State adv. com. U.S. Commn. on Civil Rights, 1966-71. Book rev. editor Harvard Law Rev. Office: University of California Law School 405 Hilgard Ave Los Angeles CA 90024 *

HOROWITZ, ILANA, lawyer; b. N.Y.C., Jan. 31, 1950; d. Philip and Sophia (Newman) H. BA, Goucher Coll., 1972; JD, N.Y. Law Sch., 1977. Bar: Ill. 1977, U.S. Dist. Ct. (no. dist.) Ill. 1978, U.S. Ct. Appeals (7th cir.) 1979, Ohio 1981, Fla. 1981, U.S. Dist. Ct. (no and ea. dists.) Ohio 1981. Assoc. Fohrman, Lorie, Holstein, Sklar, Cottle LPA, Chgo., 1977-78, Schwarzwald, Robiner, Wolf & Rock LPA, Cleve., 1982-84; sole practice Cleve., 1980-82, 84—; bd. of trustees Divorce Equity, Inc., Cleve., 1985—. Mem. Ohio Domestic Relations Task Force, 1986-87. Mem. ABA (family law sect. 1984—), Fla. Bar Assn. (family law sect. 1985—), Ohio Bar Assn. (family law sect. 1984), Cuyahoga County Bar Assn. (family law sect. 1985—), Cleve. Bar Assn. (program dir. family sect. 1984-85). Jewish. Family and matrimonial. Office: 23811 Chagrin Blvd Suite 310 Cleveland OH 44122

HOROWITZ, JAY STANLEY, lawyer; b. Phila., Feb. 17, 1943; s. David and Johanna (Backall) H.; m. Elizabeth Hardin Horowitz, Dec. 24, 1968; children—Alexandra, Damon. Student Dartmouth Coll. 1960-62; B.A. magna cum laude with distinction, U. Pa., 1964; LL.B., Harvard U., 1967. Bar: Pa. 1968, D.C. 1976, Colo. 1976. Sr. law clk. to judge U.S. Dist. Ct. (ea. dist.) Pa. 1967-69; asst. U.S. atty. So. Dist. N.Y. 1969-73; asst. spl. prosecutor Watergate Spl. Prosecution Force, Washington, 1973-76; ptnr. Horowitz & Assocs., P.C., Denver 1976—; lectr. in field. Mem. ABA, Colo. Bar Assn., Denver Bar Assn., Phi Beta Kappa. Club: Denver Athletic. Federal civil litigation, Criminal, State civil litigation. Home: 1516 Shooting Star Golden CO 80401

HOROWITZ, LOUISE SCHWARTZ, lawyer; b. N.Y.C., Jan. 24, 1932; d. Charles and Bertie (Grad) Schwartz; m. David H. Horowitz, June 20, 1951 (div. 1976); children—Marilyn, Roger, Diana. B.A., Smith Coll., 1953; M.A., Columbia U., 1955, Ph.D., 1969; J.D., N.Y. Law Sch., 1981. Bar: N.Y. 1982. Lectr., Bklyn. Coll., 1966-67; assoc. prof. L.I.U., 1967-75, asst. dir. Learning Ctr., 1975-76; research fellow Wagner Coll., 1976-78; legal intern U.S. Atty.'s Office, Ea. Dist. N.Y., 1980-81; asst. corp. counsel Law Dept. City of N.Y., 1982-86 ; assoc. Budd, Larner, Kent, Gross, Picillo & Rosenbaum, 1986—. Contbr. articles to profl. jours. Mem. N.Y. Woman's Bar Assn., Am. Philos. Assn., N.Y. State Bar Assn., Fed. Bar Council. Democrat. Jewish. General practice, Federal civil litigation, State civil litigation. Home: 12 W 72d St New York NY 10023 Office: Budd Larner Kent Gross Picillo & Rosenbaum 140 Cedar St New York NY 10006

HOROWITZ, STEVEN GARY, lawyer; b. Miami Beach, Fla., Sept. 4, 1950; s. Arthur R. and Bernice (Schwamm) H.; m. Susan Eve Haar, Dec. 7, 1985. BA, Yale U., 1972; JD and M in Pub. Policy, Harvard U., 1978. Bar: Mass. 1979, U.S. Dist. Ct. Mass. 1979. Asst. planner N.Y.C. Dept. Planning, 1972-74; law clk. to presiding justice U.S. Dist. Ct., Boston, 1978-79, ct. monitor, 1979-81; ptnr. Hill and Barlow, Boston, 1981-87; of counsel Cleary, Gottleib, Steen & Hamilton, N.Y.C., 1987—. Co-author: Primer on Transferable Development Rights, 1979. Bd. dirs. and gen. counsel Arts of Boston, 1983-87; cons. to Mayor of Jerusalem, 1981-83. Mem. Mass. Bar Assn. (pub. law sect. council 1985-87), Boston Bar Assn. Democrat. Jewish. Real property, Environment, Public law. Home: 32 Morton St New York NY 10014 Office: Cleary Gottleib Steen & Hamilton One State St Plaza New York NY 10004

HORRIGAN, ELIZABETH BRANDER, lawyer, bank executive; b. Cleve., Mar. 29, 1955; d. Daniel Leary and Gretchen Emilie (Brander) H.; m. Patrick G. Boylston, Nov. 21, 1986. BA, Carleton Coll., 1976; JD, Lewis & Clark U., 1980. Bar: Oreg. 1981. Assoc. Ragen, Roberts et al, Portland, Oreg., 1981-84, Bauer, Winfree et al, Portland, 1984-85; asst. v.p. U.S. Nat. Bank of Oreg., Portland, 1985—. Mem. Oreg. Bar Assn. (sec. exec. com. securities law sect. 1985-86). Bond and debt services for national bank. Office: US Nat Bank of Oreg 309 SW 6th Ave 5th Floor Portland OR 97204

HORSEY, HENRY RIDGELY, state supreme court justice; b. Lewes, Del., Oct. 18, 1924; s. Harold W. and Philippa (Ridgely) H.; m. Ann M. Baker, May 19, 1979; children: Robert Wolfe, Josephine Elizabeth; children by previous marriage: Henry Ridgely, Edmond P.V., Alexandra Therese, Philippa Ridgely, Randall Revell. A.B., Harvard Coll., 1949, LL.B., 1952. Bar: Del. 1953. With firm Berl, Potter & Anderson, Wilmington, Del., 1952-62, Wilmington Trust Co., 1962-65; individual practice law Dover, Del., 1965-69; mem. firm Morris, James, Hitchens & Williams, Wilmington, 1969-78; justice Supreme Ct. of Del., Dover, 1978—. Served with inf. AUS, 1943-46. Mem. ABA, Del. Bar Assn. Office: Supreme Ct Bldg 57 The Green Dover DE 19901

HORSLEY, GEORGE WILLIAM, lawyer; b. Creal Springs, Ill., July 15, 1910; s. Otto and Della Susan (Schafer) H.; m. Mary Pauline Surman, June 17, 1933 (dec. Sept. 1965); children: George William, Judy K. Lott; m. Anna Bell, June 1, 1979. Student, U. Ill.; LLB, Lincoln Coll. of Law. Bar: Ill. 1935, U.S. Supreme Ct. 1951, U.S. Ct. Appeals (7th, 8th and 10th cirs.), U.S. Dist. Ct. Sole practice Springfield, Ill., 1935—. Portrayed Abraham Lincoln for 100 consecutive performances with Abe Lincoln Players, Springfield, 1947-66. Mem. Ill. Ho. of Reps., Springfield, 1946-66, Ill. State Senate, Springfield, 1966-72. Served to lt. USN, 1943-45. Mem. ABA, Ill. State BAr Assn. Assn. Trial Lawyers Am., Ill. Trial Lawyers Assn., Amvets, VFW. Republican. Methodist. Clubs: Navy, Cosmos (adj. gen. 1941, 46). Avocations: boating, music. Personal injury, Labor, Probate. Home: 1402

W Lake Dr Springfield IL 62707 Office: 316 E Adams St Springfield IL 62701

HORSLEY, JACK EVERETT, lawyer, author; b. Sioux City, Iowa, Dec. 12, 1915; s. Charles E. and Edith V. (Timms) H.; m. Sallie Kelley, June 12, 1939 (dec.); children: Pamela, Charles Edward; m. Bertha J. Newland, Feb. 24, 1950 (dec.); m. Mary Jane Moran, Jan. 20, 1973; 1 child, Sharon. AB, U. Ill., 1937, JD, 1939. Bar: Ill. 1939. With Craig & Craig, Mattoon, Ill., 1939—, sr. counsel specializing in med. malpractice; vice chmn., bd. dirs. Cen. Nat. Bank, 1976—; mem. lawyers adv. council U. Ill. Law Forum, 1960-63; lectr. Practising Law Inst., N.Y.C., 1967-73, Ct. Practice Inst., Chgo., 1974—, U. Mich. Coll. Law Inst. Continuing Legal Edn., 1968; vis. lectr. Orange County (Fla.) Med. Soc., 1975, San Diego Med. Soc., 1970, U. S.C., 1976, Duquesne Coll., 1970; chmn. rev. com. Ill. Supreme Ct. Disciplinary Commn., 1973-76. Narrator: Poetry Interludes, Sta. WLBH-FM; author: Trial Lawyer's Manual, 1967, Voir Dire Examinations and Opening Statements, 1968, Current Development in Products Liability Law, 1969, Illinois Civil Practice and Procedure, 1970, The Medical Expert Witness, 1973, The Doctor and the Law, 1975, The Doctor and Family Law, 1975, The Doctor and Business Law, 1976, The Doctor and Medical Law, 1977, Testifying in Court, 1973, 2d edit., 1983, 3d edit., 1987, Anatomy of a Medical Malpractice Case, 1984; contbr. articles to profl. jours. including RN Mag. and Forensic Scis.; cons., contbr. Med. Econs., 1969—; legal cons. Mast-Head, 1972—. Pres. bd. edn. Sch. Dist. 100, 1946-48; bd. dirs. Moore Heart Research Fund, 1969—; vol. reader in recording texts Am. Assn. for Blind, 1970-72. Served to lt. col. U.S. Army, 1942-46. Fellow Am. Coll. Trial Lawyers; mem. ABA, Ill. Bar Assn. (exec. council ins. law 1961-63, lectr. law course for attys. 1962, 64-65, Disting. Service award 1982-83), Coles-Cumberland Bar Assn. (v.p. 1968-69, pres. 1969-70, chmn. com. jud. inquiry 1976-80, chmn. meml. com. 1981—), Am. Arbitration Assn. (nat. panel arbitrators), U. Ill. Law Alumni Assn. (pres. 1966-67, Alumni of Month Sept. 1974), Ill. Def. Counsel Assn. (pres. 1967-68), Soc. Trial Lawyers (chmn. profl. activities 1960-61, bd. dirs. 1966-67), Adelphic Debating Soc., Assn. Ins. Attys., Internat. Assn. Ins. Counsel, Am. Judicature Soc., Appellate Lawyers Assn., Scribes, Delta Phi (exec. com. alumni assn. 1960-61, 67-68), Sigma Delta Kappa. Republican. Lodge: Masons (32 degree). Medical, State civil litigation. Home: 50 Elm Ridge Mattoon IL 61938 Office: Craig & Craig 1807 Broadway PO Box 689 Mattoon IL 61938

HORSLEY, WALLER HOLLADAY, lawyer; b. Richmond, Va., July 2, 1931; s. John Shelton and Lilian (Holladay) H.; m. Margaret Stuart Cooke, Dec. 3, 1955; children—Margaret Terrell, Stuart W., John Garrett. B.A. with distinction, U. Va., 1953, LL.B., 1959. Bar: Va. 1959, U.S. Dist. Ct. (ea. dist.) Va. 1959, U.S. Tax Ct. 1959, U.S. Ct. Appeals (4th cir.) 1959, U.S. Supreme Ct. 1969. Ptnr. Hunton & Williams, Richmond, 1959—; lectr. taxation U. Va. Law Sch., 1961-65, 69. Mem. adv. council Sch. Bus., Va. Commonwealth U., 1983—; sr. warden St. Stephen's Episcopal Ch., 1977-79; gen. conv. dep. Diocese of Va., 1979, 85; pres. Richmond Tennis Patrons Assn., 1969. Served with USN, 1953-56; to lt. comdr. USNR, 1956-62. Recipient Algernon Sydney Sullivan award, 1953. Fellow Am. Bar Found.; mem. Va. State Bar (pres. 1982-83), ABA, Va. Bar Assn., Bar Assn. Richmond, Am. Coll. Probate Counsel (bd. regents), Internat. Acad. Estate and Trust Law (exec. council), Omicron Delta Kappa, Phi Beta Kappa, Order of Coif. Democrat. Episcopalian. Clubs: Country of Va., Bull & Bear, Westwood Racquet (Richmond). Mem. editorial bd. Taxation for Lawyers, 1975-86, Probate Lawyer, 1976—, Probate Notes, 1976—, editor, 1986-87; bd. advisors Va. Tax Rev., 1981—; contbr. articles to legal jours. Estate planning, Estate taxation, State and local taxation. Office: Hunton & Williams 707 E Main St PO Box 1535 Richmond VA 23212

HORTON, ANDREW MARCUS, lawyer; b. Washington, Aug. 28, 1949; s. John Ryder and Grace (Calhoun) H.; m. Peggy Louise, Jan. 20, 1973; children: Rachel, Joanna. AB, Harvard U., 1971; JD, Georgetown U., 1977. Bar: Va. 1977, Maine 1978. Law clk. to presiding justice U.S. Dist. Ct., Washington, 1977-78; assoc. Verrill & Dana, Portland, Maine, 1978-82, ptnr., 1983—; instr. law Suffolk U., Boston, 1985. Chmn. Maine Bd. of Arbitration and Conciliation, Augusta, 1985—. Mem. ABA, Maine Bar Assn., Cumberland County Bar Assn. Democrat. Congregationalist. Federal civil litigation, State civil litigation. Home: 25 Motley St Portland ME 04112 Office: Verrill & Dana 2 Canal Plaza Portland ME 04112

HORTON, JAMES WRIGHT, lawyer; b. Belton, S.C., Dec. 24, 1919; s. John Aiken and Emmae (Tate) H.; m. Eunice Rice, Nov. 20, 1948; children—James Wright, Max Rice, Rex Rice. B.A., Furman U., 1942; J.D., Harvard U., 1948. Bar: S.C. 1948. Ptnr. Nettles & Horton, Greenville, S.C., 1948-52; ptnr. Rainey, Fant & Horton, Greenville, S.C., 1952-70, Horton, Drawdy, Marchbanks, Ashmore, Chapman & Brown, Greenville, S.C., 1970-78, Horton, Drawdy, Hagins, Ward & Johnson, Greenville, S.C., 1978. Pres. United Fund Greenville County, 1959; mem. Greenville County Sch. Trustees, 1964-70, vice chmn., 1969; pres. Greenville Family and Children's Service, 1954-55, 68-70; bd. dirs. Salvation Army, 1969—, treas., 1970-71; bd. dirs. Family and Children's Service, Greenville Mental Health Clinic, 1956-59, Greater Greenville Community Found., 1981. Served with USMCR, 1942-46. Decorated Silver Star. Mem. Greenville County Bar Assn. (pres. 1981). Baptist (deacon 1964-69, 71-72, 86—). Home: 2 Osceola Dr Greenville SC 29605 Office: 307 Pettigru St Greenville SC 29602

HORTON, LUTHER WILLIAM, lawyer; b. Natchitoches, La., Aug. 30, 1947; s. James Adams and Ersula (Estes) H.; m. Shirley Ann Grasser, Dec. 30, 1977. B.S. in Polit. Sci., La. Tech. U., 1969; J.D., Tulane U., 1973. Bar: Calif. 1973, U.S. Dist. Ct. (so. dist.) Calif. 1973, U.S. Ct. Appeals (9th cir.) 1974. Law clk. U.S. Ct. Appeals (9th cir.), San Diego, 1973-74; ptnr. Luce, Forward, Hamilton & Scripps, San Diego, 1974—; lectr. in field. Mem. Calif. Bar Assn. (lectr. continuing edn. of the Bar), San Diego County Bar Assn. (chmn. ins. and negligence sect. 1978). Republican. Methodist. State civil litigation, Insurance, Personal injury. Home: 1036 Calle Mesita Bonita CA 92002 Office: Luce Forward Hamilton & Scripps 110 W A St Suite 1700 San Diego CA 92101

HORTON, PAUL BRADFIELD, lawyer; b. Dallas, Oct. 19, 1920; s. Frank Barrett and Hazel Lillian (Bradfield) H.; m. Susan Jeanne Diggle, May 19, 1949; children: Bradfield Ragland, Bruce Ragsdale. B.A., U. Tex., Austin, 1943, student Law Sch., 1941-43; LL.B., So. Methodist U., 1947. Bar: Tex. 1946. Ptnr. McCall, Parkhurst & Horton, Dallas, 1951—; lectr. mcpl. bond law and pub. finance S.W. Legal Found.; drafter Tex. mcpl. bonds legislation, 1963—. Mem. Gov.'s Com. Tex. Edn. Code, 1967-69. Served to lt. USNR, 1943-46. Mem. Am., Dallas bar assns., Nat. Water Resources Assn., Tex. Water Conservation Assn., Govt. Finance Officers Assn., The Barristers, Delta Theta Phi, Beta Theta Pi. Clubs: Dallas Country, Crescent, Tower, Chaparral, 2001 (Dallas); Austin. Municipal bonds. Home: 5039 Seneca Dr Dallas TX 75209 Office: McCall Parkhurst & Horton 900 Diamond Shamrock Tower Dallas TX 75201

HORTON, THOMAS DAVID, lawyer, publisher; b. Canton, Ohio, June 3, 1927; s. Edmund Earl and Stella (Jenks) H.; m. Jean Marie McArn, May 12, 1956; children—Laura, Robert, Stella. J.D., Washington Coll. Law, 1958. Bar: D.C. 1959, Va. 1959, Nev. 1965, U.S. Ct. Appeals (D.C. cir.) 1960, U.S. Ct. Appeals (9th cir.) 1960. Sole practice, Arlington, Va., 1959-61, Pioche, Nev., 1961-66, Battle Mountain, Nev., 1967-78, Carson City, Nev., 1978—; dist. atty. Lander County, Battle Mountain, 1967-74, pub. adminstr., 1967-74. Author: (with others) Republic: Decline and Future Promise, 1975, Emerging Struggle for State Sovereignty, 1980. Publisher: (book) Square Dollar Series, 1950—, Coke on Magna Carta, 1974. Radiological defense officer Lander County, Battle Mountain, 1967-78; comdr. Am. Legion, Dept. of Nev., 1975-76; chmn. exec. council Defenders of Am. Constitution, Washington, 1956—; legal counsel Com. to Restore the Constn., Ft. Collins, Colo. Served with USN, 1945-49. Recipient Liberty award Congress of Freedom, 1971; Liberty Bell award, Am. Legion, 1976; named Man of Yr., Wis. Legis. and Research Com., 1977. Mem. Battle Mountain C. of C. (dir. 1973), Sigma Nu Phi. Democrat. Presbyterian. Club: Sertoma. Personal injury, Mining, General practice. Office: 305 North Carson St PO Box 2107 Carson City NV 89702

HORTON, WILLIAM HARRISON, lawyer; b. N.Y.C., Sept. 4, 1942; s. James Robert and Elizabeth Juanita (Harrison) H.; m. Linda Elizabeth Diefenthaler, Aug. 8, 1964; 1 child, Jennifer Elizabeth. B.A., Bowdoin Coll., 1964; J.D., U. Chgo., 1967. Bar admittee: N.J. 1967, U.S. dist. ct. N.J. 1967, U.S. Ct. Mil. Apls. 1969, U.S. Ct. Apls. (3d cir.) 1982. Assoc. McCarter & English, Newark, 1967-68, 70-78, ptnr., 1978—. Mem. Bedminster Twp. Com., 1977-82, chmn. fin. com., 1977-82, chmn. mcpl. facilities com., 1980-82, 84—. Served as combat engr. U.S. Army, 1968-70; capt., legal adv. to comdg. gen. II Field Force Arty., 1969-70; Vietnam. Decorated Army Commendation medal, Bronze Star (2). Mem. ABA, N.J. Bar Assn., Essex County Bar Assn., Fed. Bar Assn., Assn. Trial Attys. N.J., Am. Arbitration Assn. (cert. arbitrator in comml. matters), Phi Delta Phi, Chi Psi. Clubs: Essex (Newark); Roxiticus Golf (Mendham, N.J.); Windows on the World, World Trade Center (N.Y.C.). Bankruptcy, Federal civil litigation, State civil litigation. Office: McCarter & English 550 Broad St Newark NJ 07102

HORTTOR, DONALD J., lawyer; b. Fort Scott, Kans., May 3, 1932; s. Elmer J. and Cleda C. (Cox) H.; m. Jane Ann Ausherman, Mar. 22, 1959; children—Daun Ann, Bretton J. A.B. in Econs., U. Kans., 1953, J.D., 1959; LL.M. in Taxation, NYU, 1961. Bar: Kans. 1959, U.S. Dist. Ct. Kans. 1959, U.S. Ct. Appeals (10th cir.) 1963, U.S. Supreme Ct. 1965, U.S. Tax Ct. 1965. Adj. prof. Washburn U. Law Sch., Topeka, 1965-76; Assoc. Cosgrove, Webb and Oman, Topeka, 1959-63, ptnr., 1963—. Served to capt. USAF, 1953-56. Mem. ABA, Topeka Bar Assn., Kans. Bar Assn. Republican. Congregationalist. Clubs: Topeka Country, Masons, Elks, Moose. Author: Estate Planning, Why a Will; Kansas Estate Administration. Estate taxation, State and local taxation, Probate. Office: Bank IV Tower Suite 1100 Topeka KS 66603

HORWIN, LEONARD, lawyer; b. Chgo., Jan. 2, 1913; s. Joseph and Jennie (Fuhrmann) H.; m. Ursula Helene Donig, Oct. 15, 1939; children—Noel Samuel, Leonora Marie. LL.D. cum laude, Yale U., 1936. Bar: Calif. 1936, U.S. Dist. Ct. (cen. dist.) Calif. 1937, U.S. Ct. Appeals (9th cir.) 1939, U.S. Supreme Ct. 1940. Assoc., Lawler, Felix & Hall, 1936-39; ptnr. Hardy & Horwin, Los Angeles, 1939-42; counsel Bd. Econ. Warfare, Washington, 1942-43; attache, legal adviser U.S. Embassy, Madrid, Spain, 1943-47; sole practice, Beverly Hills, Calif., 1948—; dir., lectr. Witkin-Horwin Rev. Course on Calif. Law, 1939-42; judge pro tempore Los Angeles Superior Ct., 1940-42; instr. labor law U. So. Calif., 1939-42. U.S. rep. Allied Control Council for Ger., 1945-47; councilman City of Beverly Hills, 1962-66, mayor, 1964-65; chmn. transp. Los Angeles Goals Council, 1968; bd. dirs. So. Calif. Rapid Transit Dist., 1964-66; chmn. Rent Stabilization Com., Beverly Hills, 1980. Fellow Am. Acad. Matrimonial Lawyers; mem. ABA, State Bar Calif., Order Coif. Clubs: Balboa Bay, Aspen Inst. Contbr. articles to profl. jours. Family and matrimonial, General practice, Real property. Office: 121 S Beverly Dr Beverly Hills CA 90212

HORWITCH, DANIEL B., lawyer; b. New Haven, Apr. 9, 1953; s. Eugene Lionel and Norma (Croog) H.; m. Cynthia Louise Tyler, Aug. 15, 1981. BA, U. Conn., 1975; JD, Suffolk U., 1981. Bar: Conn. 1981, U.S. Dist. Ct. (Conn.) 1983. Law clk. to presiding justice Conn. Superior Ct., New Haven, 1981-82, adminstrv. law clk., 1982-83; legal services counsel Conn. Jud. Dept., Hartford, Conn., 1983-84; jud. evaluation adminstr. Conn. Jud. Dept., Hartford, 1984-86, statewide bar counsel, 1986—. Broadcaster Conn. Radio Info. Service, Wethersfield, 1985-87. Mem. ABA, Conn. Bar Assn. Judicial administration. Office: Conn Jud Dept Drawer N Station A Hartford CT 06106

HORWITZ, CLIFFORD WOLF, lawyer; b. Chgo., May 25, 1959; s. Andrew J. and Donna (Magida) H. Student, U. Colo.; BS, U. Fla.; JD, Loyola U., Chgo.; postdoctoral, Northwestern U. Ptnr. Horwitz, Horwitz & Assocs., Chgo., 1977—. Mem. ABA, Fed. Bar Assn., Appellate Bar Assn., Chgo. Bar Assn., Assn. Trial Lawyers Am., Ill. Trial Lawyers Assn., Phi Kappa Phi. Personal injury. Home: 2650 Lakeview Chicago IL 60614 Office: Horwitz Horwitz & Assocs 180 N LaSalle Suite 2201 Chicago IL 60603

HORWITZ, DONALD PAUL, restaurant chain executive; b. Chgo., Feb. 5, 1936; s. Theodore J. and Lillian H. (Shlensky) H.; m. Judith Robin, Aug. 23, 1964; children—Terry Robin, Linda Diane, Gail Elizabeth. B.S., Northwestern U., 1957; J.D., Yale U., 1960. Bar: Ill. bar 1961, D.C. bar 1961, U.S. Supreme Ct 1966; C.P.A., Ill. With atty.'s gen. honors program Dept. Justice, 1961-63; atty. firm Gottlieb & Schwartz, Chgo., 1963-66; with Arthur Young & Co. (C.P.A.'s), Chgo., 1966-72; ptnr. Arthur Young & Co. (C.P.A.'s), 1971-72; exec. v.p., sec., dir. McDonald's Corp., Oak Brook, Ill., 1972—; dir. CML Labs.; lectr. Grad. Sch. Commerce, DePaul U., Chgo. Contbr. articles to profl. jours. Mem. caucus nominating com. Village of Glencoe, Ill., 1975-78; bd. dirs. Chgo. Med. Sch./U. Health Scis., Recordings for Blind; vice chmn., bd. dirs. Highland Park Hosp., Anti-Defamation League; hon. trustee St. Augustine's Coll., Chgo. Mem. Am. Bar Assn., Ill. Bar Assn., Chgo. Bar Assn., Am. Inst. CPA's, Ill. Soc. CPA's. Club: Briarwood Country (pres., dir.). Office: McDonalds Corp 1 McDonald Plaza Oak Brook IL 60521

HORWITZ, JOHN, lawyer; b. Cedar Falls, Iowa, Dec. 22, 1945; s. Marvin Lewis and Marian Francis (Diamond) H.; m. Diane Joan Steinberg, Aug. 24, 1969; children: Margo Stacey, Justin Alexander. BA, NYU, 1968; JD, Bklyn. Law Sch., 1972. Bar: N.Y. 1973, Ill. 1981, U.S. Dist. Ct. (so. and ea. dists.) N.Y., U.S. Ct. Appeals (2d cir.). Tchr. N.Y.C. Bd. Edn., 1968-72; asst. dist. atty. Kings County, Bklyn., 1972-74; sr. atty. Pan Am. Airways, N.Y.C., 1974-81; trademark counsel McDonald's Corp., Oak Brook, Ill., 1981—. Mem. ABA, Ill. Bar Assn., Chgo. Bar Assn., U.S. Trademark Assn. (bd. dirs. 1983-84). Democrat. Jewish. Clubs: International (Chgo.); Arrowhead Swim and Tennis (Wheaton, Ill.) (bd. dirs. 1985). Avocations: chess, hunting. Trademark and copyright, Private international, General corporate. Office: McDonalds Corp McDonalds Plaza Oak Brook IL 60251

HORWITZ, MITCHELL WOLF, lawyer; b. Chgo., July 3, 1954; s. Andrew J. Horwitz and Donna Magida. BA in Psychology, No. Ill. U., 1976; JD with honors, John Marshall Law Sch., 1979. Bar: Ill. 1979, U.S. Dist. Ct. (no. dist.) Ill. 1979, Fla. 1980, U.S. Ct. Appeals (7th cir.) 1986. Ptnr. Andrew J. Horwitz & Assoc., Chgo., 1979-83; v.p., sec. Horwitz, Horwitz & Assoc., Ltd., Chgo., 1983—. Mem. ABA, Assn. Trial Lawyers Am., Ill. Worker's Compensation Lawyers Assn., Ill. Trial Lawyers Assn., Ill. State Bar Assn., Fla. State Bar Assn. Workers' compensation, Personal injury. Office: Horwitz Horwitz & Assocs 180 N LaSalle St Chicago IL 60601

HORWITZ, MORTON J., law educator; b. 1938. A.B., CCNY, 1959, Ph.D., 1964; LL.B., Harvard U., 1967. Bar: Mass. 1970. Law clk. to judge U.S. Ct. Appeals D.C. Cir., 1967-68; Charles Warren fellow Harvard U., 1968-70, asst. prof. law, 1970-74, prof., 1974—. Author: The Transformation of American Law, 1780-1860, 1977. Mem. Selden Soc., Am. Soc. Legal History. Office: Harvard U Law Sch Cambridge MA 02138 *

HOSCHEIT, DALE HERBERT, lawyer; b. Peru, Ill., Jan. 8, 1928; s. John Herbert and Charlotte Elizabeth (Nothnagel) H.; m. Stephanie Bland, Aug. 12, 1961; children—Mary Susan, Anne Marie, James Herbert. B.S. in Chem. Engring., U. Ill., 1951; J.D., 1956. Bar: Ill. 1956, D.C. 1959. Patent counsel Internat. Minerals & Chem. Corp., 1961-67; ptnr. Banner, Birch, McKie & Beckett, Washington, 1967—. Bd. dirs. Washington Hearing and Speech Soc., Sibley Meml. Hosp., Washington. Mem. ABA, Am. Patent Law Assn., Licensing Execs. Soc. Patent, Trademark and copyright, Federal civil litigation. Office: One Thomas Circle NW Washington DC 20005

HOSEMAN, DANIEL, lawyer; b. Chgo., Aug. 18, 1935; s. Irving and Anne (Pruzansky) H.; m. Susan H. Myles, Aug. 7, 1960; children—Lawrence N., Joan E., Jonathan W. B.A., U. Ill., 1956, J.D., 1959. Bar: Ill. 1959, U.S. Dist. Ct. (no. dist.) Ill. 1960, U.S. Ct. Appeals (7th cir.) 1967, U.S. Supreme Ct. 1976. Sole practice, Chgo., 1959—; mem. panel pvt. atty. trustees U.S. Bankruptcy Ct. No. Dist. Ill., 1979—. Trustee Ill. Legal Services Fund, 1978—; v.p. Allied Jewish Sch. Bd. Met. Chgo., 1977—; v.p. United Synagogue Am., 1978—. Served with USAFR, 1959-65. Mem. Decalogue Soc. Lawyers (pres. 1981-82, award of merit 1979-80), Ill. Bar Assn. (sect. council on banking comml. and bankruptcy law), Lake County Bar Assn. (com. on bankruptcy 1980—), Chgo. Council Lawyers, Advocates Soc., Comml. Law League Am. Bankruptcy, Consumer commercial, Contracts commercial. Home: 2151 Tanglewood Ct Highland Park IL 60035 Office: 105 W Madison St Suite 704 Chicago IL 60602

HOSKINS, DAVID LEROY, lawyer; b. Burlington, Wis., May 24, 1945; s. Dwight LeRoy and Alice (Anderskow) H.; m. Martha Jane Pickens, June 6, 1968; children: Leah Scott, Micah Ward. BA, Centenary Coll., 1970; postgrad., Nat. U. Ireland, Dublin, 1970-71; JD, Tulane U., 1980. Bar: La. 1980, U.S. Ct. Appeals (5th and 11th cirs.) 1980, U.S. Dist. Ct. (we. dist.) La. 1981, U.S. Supreme Ct. 1986. Law clk. to presiding justice U.S. Ct. Appeals (5th cir.), New Orleans, 1980-81; assoc. Scofield, Bergstedt, Gerard, Mount & Veron, Lake Charles, La., 1981-84, ptnr., 1984—. Author numerous poems and fiction; contbr. articles to profl. jours. Served with U.S. Army, 1967-69, Vietnam. Mem. ABA, La. Bar Assn., S.W. La. Assn. Def. Counsel. Democrat. Avocation: creative writing. Federal civil litigation, State civil litigation, Jurisprudence. Office: Scofield Bergstedt Gerard Mount & Veron 1114 Ryan St PO Drawer 3028 Lake Charles LA 70601

HOSKINS, RICHARD JEROLD, lawyer; b. Ft. Smith, Ark., June 19, 1945; s. Walter Jerold and Emma Gladys (Gaither) H.; children: Stephen Weston, Philip Richard. B.A., U. Kans., 1967; J.D., Northwestern U., 1970. Bar: N.Y. 1971, Ill. 1976, U.S. Supreme Ct. 1982. Assoc. Davis Polk & Wardwell, N.Y.C., 1970-73; asst. U.S. atty., So. Dist. N.Y., 1973-76; assoc. Schiff Hardin & Waite, Chgo., 1976-77, ptnr., 1978—; lectr. U. Va. Law Sch., 1980-83. Contbr. articles to profl. jours. Mem. Chgo. Crime Commn.; mem. vis. com. U. Chgo. Div. Sch.; mem. bd. dirs. John Howard Assn.; mem. Fed. Def. Panel, N.D., Ill. Mem. ABA, Ill. Bar Assn., Chgo. Bar Assn., Chgo. Council Lawyers, 7th Circuit Bar Assn., Assn. Bar City of N.Y., Chgo. Council Fgn. Relations, Am. Arbitration Assn. (nat. panel arbitrators). Clubs: University, Law of Chgo., Metropolitan (Chgo.). Federal civil litigation, Antitrust, Criminal. Office: 7200 Sears Tower Chicago IL 60606

HOSSLER, DAVID JOSEPH, lawyer; b. Mesa, Ariz., Oct. 18, 1940; s. Carl Joseph and Elizabeth Ruth (Bills) H.; m. Gretchen Anne, Mar. 2, 1945; 1 child, Devon Annagret. B.A., U. Ariz., 1969; J.D., 1972. Bar: Ariz. 1972, U.S. dist. ct. Ariz. 1972, U.S. Supreme Ct. 1977. Legal intern to chmn. FCC, summer 1971; law clk. to chief justice Ariz. Supreme Ct., 1972-73; chief dep. county atty. Yuma County (Ariz.), 1973-74; ptnr. Hunt, Stanley, Hossler and Rourke, Yuma, Ariz., 1974—; instr. in law and banking, law and real estate Ariz. Western Coll.; instr. in bus. law Webster U. Mem. precinct com., Yuma County Rep. Cen. Com., 1974—, vice chmn., 1982; bd. dirs. Yuma County Assn. Behavior Health Services, also pres., 1981. Served with USN. Recipient Man and Boy award Boys Clubs Am., 1979; named Vol. of Yr., Yuma County, 1981-82. Mem. Assn. Trial Lawyers Am., Am. Judicature Soc., Yuma County Bar Assn. (pres. 1975-76), VFW, Am. Legion, U. Ariz. Alumni Assn. (nat. bd. dirs., past pres.). Episcopalian. Club: Rotary (pres. Yuma club 1987-88). Editor-in-chief Ariz. Adv., 1971-72. State civil litigation, Personal injury, Family and matrimonial. Home: 2802 Fern Dr Yuma AZ 85364 Office: Hunt Stanley Hossler & Rourke 330 W 24th St Yuma AZ 85364

HOSTER, CRAIG WILLIAM, lawyer; b. Ft. Worth, Apr. 11, 1946; s. Vernon Floyd and Ann (Claycomb) H.; m. Beverly Jeanne Drew, Nov. 15, 1969; children: Chistopher Drew, Ashley Ann. BBA, U. Okla., 1971, JD, 1973. Bar: Okla. 1973, U.S. Dist. Ct. (no. dist.) Okla. 1973, U.S. Ct. Appeals (10th cir.) 1975. Assoc. Conner, Winters, Ballaine, Barry & McGowen, Tulsa, 1973-78, ptnr., 1979-81; ptnr. Baker, Hoster, McSpadden, Clark & Rasure, Tulsa, 1981—. Mem. ABA, Okla. Bar Assn., Tulsa County Bar Assn., Order of Coif, Phi Delta Phi, Delta Tau Delta. Methodist. Avocation: snow skiing. Federal civil litigation, State civil litigation. Home: 2255 S Rockford Tulsa OK 74114 Office: Baker Hoster McSpadden Clark & Rasure 800 Kennedy Bldg Tulsa OK 74103

HOTCHKISS, NANCY, lawyer; b. Burns, Oreg., July 25, 1957; d. Richard Allen and Vera Lou (Mackenzie) H.; m. Jay Miller Smith, Nov. 29, 1980. BS, Oreg. State U., 1979; JD, U. Pacific, 1982. Bar: Calif. 1982, U.S. Dist. Ct. (ea. dist.) Calif. 1982, U.S. Dist. Ct. (no. dist.) Calif. 1986. Assoc. Charles W. Trainor, Sacramento, 1982-86; ptnr. Trainor, Robertson & Smits, Sacramento, 1986—. Mem. ABA, Sacramento County Bar Assn. (council 1985—, v.p. real property sect. 1983, bankruptcy and comml. law sect.), Barristers Club (local program chair 1984-85, v.p. 1985-86, pres. 1986—), Women Lawyers of Sacramento, Calif. Trustees Assn., Capitol City Trial Lawyers Assn., Sacramento C. of C., Kappa Kappa Gamma (v.p. 1984-85, pres. 1985-86). Republican. Lodge: Soroptimist (pres. Sacramento club 1985-86). Avocations: sports, gardening. Real property, Landlord-tenant, Bankruptcy. Office: Trainor Robertson & Smits 601 University Ave Suite 265 Sacramento CA 95825

HOTH, STEVEN SERGEY, lawyer; b. Olewein, Iowa, Jan. 30, 1941; s. Donald Leroy and Ina Dorothy (Barr) H.; m. JoEllen Maly, July 29, 1967; children: Andrew Steven, Peter Lindsey. AB, Grinnell Coll., 1962; JD, U. Iowa, 1966; postgrad. U. Pa., 1968, Oxford (Eng.) U., 1973. Bar: U.S. Ct. Appeals (8th cir.) 1966, U.S. Tax Ct. 1967, U.S. Ct. Claims 1967, U.S. Dist. Ct. Iowa 1968, U.S. Dist. Ct. N.D. 1968, U.S. Dist. Ct. S.D. 1968, U.S. Supreme Ct. 1973, U.S. Ct. Appeals (7th cir.) 1982. Law clk. to chief justice U.S. Ct. Appeals (8th cir.), Fargo, N.D., 1967-68; assoc. Hirsch, Adams, Hoth & Krekel, Burlington, Iowa, 1968-72, ptnr., 1972—; asst. atty. Des Moines County, Burlington, 1968-72, atty., 1972-83; alt. mcpl. judge, Burlington, 1968-69; lectr. criminal law Southeastern Community Coll., West Burlington, 1972—; assoc. prof. polit. sci. Iowa Wesleyan Coll., Mt. Pleasant, 1981-82; pres. Burlington Cablevision, Inc., Burlington Broadcasting, Ltd., Burlington Short Line RR. Inc.; bd. dirs. LaMont, Ltd., Sino-Am. Aviation Services Corp.; sec. Burlington Loading Co. Chmn. Des Moines County Civil Service Commn.; moderator 1st Congl. Ch., Burlington; bd. dirs. UN Assn.; chmn. commn. on ministry, mem. exec. com. Nat. Assn. Congl. Christian Chs.; moderator 1st Congl. Ch., Burlington; treas. 1st dist. Dem. Com.; bd. dirs. Legal Aid Soc. Planned Parenthood Des Moines County. Reginald Heber Smith fellow in legal aid Cheyenne River Indian Reservation, Eagle Butte, S.D., 1967-68; recipient chmn.'s award ARC, 1980. Mem. ABA (internat. sect., tax sect.), Iowa State Bar Assn., Des Moines County Bar Assn., Am. Judicature Soc., Agrl. Law Com., Iowa Def. Council, Grinnell Coll. Alumni Assn. (bd. dirs.), Burlington-West Burlington C. of C. (bd. dirs.). Clubs: Burlington Golf, New Crystal Lake (Burlington) (pres.). Lodges: Elks, Eagles, Masons, Rotary (Burlington). Contbr. numerous articles to profl. jours. General practice, General corporate, Private international. Address: 200 Jefferson St PO Box 1105 Burlington IA 52601

HOTTINGER, JOHN CREIGHTON, lawyer; b. Mankato, Minn., Sept. 18, 1945; s. Raymond Creighton and Hilda (Baker) H.; m. Miriam Jean Willging, Oct. 31, 1971; children: Julie, Creighton, Janna. BS, Coll. St. Thomas, 1967; JD, Georgetown U., 1971. Bar: Minn. 1972, U.S. Dist. Ct. Minn. 1977, U.S Dist Ct. (no. dist.) Ohio 1982. Legis. asst. Hon. Donald M. Fraser, Washington, 1968-69, Dem. Study Group, Washington, 1969-73; ptnr. Farrish, Johnson, Maschka & Hottinger, Mankato, 1973-85; sr. ptnr. Hottinger Law Offices, Mankato, 1985—; mem. Com. on Products Liability. Bd. dirs. United Way, Greater Mankato area, 1980-86; Dem. candidate for Minn. state senate, 1982. Mem. ABA, 5th Dist. Bar Assn., Minn. Bar Assn., Minn. Def. Lawyers. Roman Catholic. Avocation: computer operations. State civil litigation, Personal injury, Insurance. Office: Hottinger Law Offices 108 Hickory #200 PO Box 3183 Mankato MN 56001

HOTTLE, DARRELL RIZER, judge; b. Hillsboro, Ohio, Sept. 13, 1918; s. George Emmitt and Alice Reverda (Bishop) H.; m. Catherine Carpenter, Nov. 15, 1947; children—Kay, Larry. B.A., Ohio State U., 1940; LL.B., Western Res. U., 1947. Bar: Ohio 1947. Pros. atty. Highland County, Ohio, Hillsboro, 1949-52; solicitor City of Hillsboro, Ohio, 1950; judge Highland County Common Pleas Ct., Hillsboro, Ohio, 1955—. Contbr. articles to legal jours. Chmn. Highland County Dem. Exec. Com., 1952-54; past trustee Otterbein Home, Lebanon, Ohio. Recipient Silver Beaver award Cen. Ohio council Boy Scouts Am., 1967. Mem. ABA, Ohio Bar Assn. (exec. com.), Am. Judicature Soc., Highland County Bar Assn. (past pres.). Democrat. Methodist (lay leader 1968-75, conf. 1971). Lodges: Rotary (past pres. Hillsboro), Masons (master 1976, 33 deg.), Elks (exalted ruler 1957). Judicial administration. Home: 335 W Walnut St Hillsboro OH 45133 Office: PO Box 833 Hillsboro OH 45133

HOUCK, CHARLES WESTON, U.S. district judge; b. Florence, S.C., Apr. 16, 1933; s. William Stokes and Charlotte Barnwell (Weston) H.; m. Wana

Kaye Hutchinson, Mar. 28, 1980; children: Charles Weston, Charlotte Elizabeth. Grad., U. N.C., 1954; LL.B., U. S.C., 1956. Bar: S.C. Mem. firm Willcox, Hardee, Houck, Palmer & O'Farrell, 1956, 58-70;; partner firm Houck, Clarke & Johnson, 1971-79; U.S. dist. judge Dist. S.C., Florence, 1979—. Mem. S.C. Ho. of Reps., 1963-66; chmn. Florence City-County Bldg. Commn., 1968-76. Served with AUS, 1957-58. Mem. ABA, S.C. Bar Assn. Episcopalian. Jurisprudence. Office: PO Box 2260 Florence SC 29503 *

HOUCK, JOHN BURTON, lawyer; b. Mt. Clemens, Mich., Apr. 6, 1928; s. William Alfred and Louise Ann (Macey) H.; m. Wanda Jean Wright, Feb. 4, 1950; children: Lisa Karen, William Wright, Katherine Jane. A.B., U. Mich., 1949, M.A. in Econs., 1951, J.D., 1953. Bar: N.Y. 1955, Mich. 1957, Ohio 1960, Calif. 1979. Assoc. Milbank, Tweed, Hope & Hadley, N.Y.C., 1953-56; asst. sec. Ford Motor Co., Dearborn, Mich., 1956-59; assoc. Jones, Day, Reavis & Pogue, Cleve., 1959-63, ptnr., 1963—; ptnr. Jones, Day, Reavis & Pogue, Los Angeles, 1981—. Contbr. articles to profl. jours. Mem. ABA (Council, sect. internat. law and practice), State Bar of Calif., Los Angeles County Bar Assn. (exec. com. sect. internat. law), Am. Law Inst., Order of Coif. Clubs: Riviera Tennis (Los Angeles); Clevelander (Cleve.). General corporate, Private international, Banking. Home: 512 Moreno Ave Los Angeles CA 90049 Office: Jones Day Reavis & Pogue 355 S Grand Ave Suite 3000 Los Angeles CA 90071

HOUGER, L(EROY) WILLIAM, lawyer; b. Livingston, Mont., Jan. 27, 1939; s. Leroy G. and Lois H. Houger; m. Carolyn A.; children—Heidi, Lisa. Student Whitworth Coll., 1957-58; B.A., U. Wash., 1961, J.D. with honors, 1964. Bar: Wash. 1964, U.S. Dist. Ct. D.C. 1972, U.S. Supreme Ct. 1972. Law clk. Judge Frederick G. Hamley, U.S. Ct. Apls. 9th Cir., 1964-65; assoc. Perkins, Coie, Stone, Olson & Williams, Seattle, 1965-66; ptnr., co-founder Garvey, Schubert, Adams & Barer and predecessor, Seattle and Washington, 1966-81; ptnr., founder Houger, Miller & Stein, Seattle and Richland, Wash., 1981—. Mem. Wash. State Bar Assn. (past chmn. trial practice sect.), King, Benton and Franklin Counties Bar Assn., Federated Ins. Defense Council. Author: Highway Mail Transportation Contracting, 2 vols., 1973; editorial bd. U. Wash. Law Rev., 1962-64. State civil litigation, Insurance, Personal injury. Home: 16736 Shore Dr NE Seattle WA 98155 Office: 1319 Lee Blvd Richland WA 99352 also: 1100 Olive Way Suite 1800 Seattle WA 98101

HOUGH, THOMAS HENRY MICHAEL, lawyer; b. Midland, Pa., Aug. 4, 1933; s. Bert Patrick and Marguerite (Mullen) H.; m. Jocelyn Peltz, Aug. 20, 1956; children—Jocelyn, Thomas Henry Michael. A.B., Dickinson Coll., 1955; J.D., Dickinson Sch. Law, 1958. Bar: Pa. 1959, U.S. Ct. Appeals (3d cir.) 1975, U.S. Supreme Ct. 1970. Field atty. NLRB, Pitts., 1959-60; atty. United Steelworkers Am., 1960-68; ptnr. Lucchino, Gaitens & Hough, Pitts., 1968-79; ptnr. Hough & Gleason, P.C., Pitts., 1980—; adj. assoc. prof. pub. sector arbitration and pub. sector collective bargaining Grad. Sch. Pub. and Internat. Affairs, U. Pitts., 1970—. Mem. Pitts. Symphony Soc., Western Pa. Conservancy, Carnegie Inst. Mem. ABA, Pa. Bar Assn., Allegheny County Bar Assn. Democrat. Roman Catholic. Labor, Health. Home: 2370 Oakview Dr Pittsburgh PA 15237 Office: Suite 1200 Lawyers Bldg Pittsburgh PA 15219

HOULIHAN, DAVID PAUL, lawyer; b. Youngstown, Ohio, May 14, 1937; s. Paul V. and Delcie (Norman) H.; m. Marlene K. Betras, Aug. 13, 1960; children: Kevin, Rex, Laura, Brian. BS, Youngstown State U., 1959; postgrad., Purdue U., 1960; LLB, Georgetown U., 1964. Bar: D.C. 191965, U.S. Ct. Appeals (D.C. cir.) 1965, U.S. Supreme Ct. 1968, U.S. Ct. Internat. Trade 1976, U.S. Ct. Customs and Patent Appeals 1976, U.S. Ct. Appeals (Fed. dir.) 1982. Analyst U.S. Internat. Trade Commn., Washington, 1960-64; counsel U.S.-Japan trade council Stitt & Hemmendinger, Washington, 1964-68; ptnr. Daniels, Houlihan & Palmeter P.C., Washington, 1968-84, Mudge, Rose, Guthrie, Alexander & Ferdon, Washington, 1984—; lectr. Oxford U., Eng., 1972; bd. dirs. Internat. Bus. and Econ. Research Corp., Washington. Mem. ABA, D.C. Bar Assn., Assn. of Bar of City of N.Y., British-Am. C. of C. (bd. dirs. 1974—). Democrat. Roman Catholic. Avocations: sailing, music. Private international, Immigration, naturalization, and customs. Office: Mudge Rose Guthrie Alexander & Ferdon 2121 K St NW Washington DC 20037

HOULIHAN, F(RANCIS) ROBERT, JR., lawyer; b. Boston, May 27, 1944; s. F. Robert Sr. and Elizabeth A. (Mullen) H.; m. Susan M. Forti, June 11, 1977. AB, Bates Coll., 1966; MA, Northwestern U., 1967; JD, Boston U., 1972. Bar: Mass. 1972, U.S. Dist. Ct. Mass. 1983. Atty. Boston Legal Services, 1972-74; assoc. Kunen & Hart, Marlboro, Mass., 1974-77; asst. dist. atty. Middlesex County, Cambridge, Mass., 1977-81; ptnr. Heavey & Houlihan, P.C. and predecessor firm Heavey, Houlihan & Wynne, P.C., Brookline, Mass., 1981—. Mem. ABA, Mass. Bar Assn. Democrat. Roman Catholic. Clubs: Longwood Indoor Tennis (Chestnut Hill, Mass.). Avocations: amateur ice hockey, tennis. General practice, State civil litigation, Federal civil litigation. Office: Heavey & Houlihan 229 Harvard St Brookline MA 02146

HOUPT, ROBERT CAMPBELL, lawyer; b. Phila., June 22, 1948; s. Herman Lyle and Elizabeth Mitchell (MacAlpine) H.; m. Deborah Susan Richwine, Nov. 8, 1973; children: Matthew Campbell, Dana Leslie. BA, Covenant Coll., 1970; student, Oxford U., 1968; JD, Washington U., 1973. Bar: Pa. 1973, U.S. Dist. Ct. (ea. dist.) Pa. 1978, U.S. Supreme Ct. 1979. Asst. dist. atty. County of Chester, Pa., 1970-76, chief dep. dist. atty., 1976-79; ptnr. Kean & Houpt, West Chester, Pa., 1979-83, Portnoff & Houpt, Paoli, Pa., 1983—. Campaign chmn. Rep. Orgn., Chester County, 1977-78; fin. vol. Judicial Retention Campaign, Chester County, 1980; solicitor Chester County Sheriff, 1984—. Mem. Pa. Trial Lawyers Assn., Assn. Trial Lawyers Am. Republican. Presbyterian. Club: Radley Run (West Chester) (sec. 1984-85), West Chester County (handicap commn. 1986). Family and matrimonial, Real property. Office: Portnoff & Houpt 45 Darby Rd Paoli PA 19301

HOUSE, CALVIN RICHARD, lawyer, legal educator; b. St. Johnsbury, Vt., Sept. 14, 1951; s. Loren Gaylord and June Helen (Shipman) H.; m. Carol Ann Jablonski, May 8, 1976 (div. Dec. 1985). BA, Columbia U., 1973, JD, 1976. Bar: N.Y. 1977, U.S. Dist. Ct. (so. and ea. dists.) N.Y. 1977, U.S. Ct. Appeals (2d cir.) 1979. Assoc. Cravath, Swaine & Moore, N.Y.C., 1976-80; dep. commr. N.Y.C. Dept. Consumer Affairs, N.Y.C., 1980-82; ptnr. Ratner, House & Murch, N.Y.C., 1982-84; asst. prof. Western State U., Fullerton, Calif., 1984—. Mem. ABA, Assn. of Bar of City of N.Y. Democrat. Federal civil litigation, Legal education, Trademark and copyright. Office: Western State U 1111 N State College Blvd Fullerton CA 92631

HOUSEMAN, ALAN WILLIAM, lawyer; b. Colorado Springs, Colo., Apr. 23, 1943; s. Murl Clarence and Opal Juanita (Snyder) H.; m. Susan Hays Margolis, June 17, 1967; children: Alana Judith, Nora Suzanne. BA, Oberlin Coll., 1965; JD, NYU, 1968. Bar: Mich. 1968, U.S. Dist. Ct. (ea. dist.) Mich. 1969, U.S. Dist. Ct. (we. dist.) Mich. 1970, U.S. Ct. Appeals (6th cir.) 1973, U.S. Supreme Ct. 1976, D.C. 1979, U.S. Ct. Appeals (D.C. cir.) 1982, U.S. Ct. Appeals (3d cir.) 1982. Reginald Heber Smith fellow Wayne County Legal Services, Detroit, 1968-69; dir. Mich. Legal Services, Detroit, 1969-76; dir. research inst. Legal Services Corp., Washington, 1976-81; dir. Ctr. for Law and Social Policy, Washington, 1981—. Author: (with others) Legal Services History, 1984; contbr. articles to profl. jours. Chmn. Orgn. of Legal Services Back-Up Ctrs., N.Y.C., 1973-75; vice chmn. Project Adv. Group, Washington, 1974-76. Recipient Achievement award Project Adv. Group, 1979. Mem. ABA, Nat. Legal Aid and Defender Assn. (chmn. civil com. 1975-77, recipient spl. award 1973), Law and Soc. Assn., Soc. Am. Law Tchrs. Democrat. Mem. United Ch. Christ. Avocations: hiking, tennis, music. Administrative and regulatory, Civil rights, Health. Home: 1715 Crestwood DR NW Washington DC 20011 Office: Ctr for Law and Social Policy 1616 P St NW Washington DC 20036

HOUSTON, GORMAN, state judge. Judge Ala. Supreme Ct., Montgomery, 1986—. Office: Jud Bldg PO Box 218 Montgomery AL 36104 *

HOUSTON, WILLIAM MCCLELLAND, lawyer; b. Pitts., Jan. 19, 1923; s. Fred C. and Fame (Whiteside) H.; m. Josephine Simpson, Feb. 4, 1950; children: William McClelland Jr., Ann H. Houston Kelley, Barbara S. Houston Kinek. BS, Haverford Coll., 1943; JD with distinction, U. Mich., 1945. Bar: Pa. 1946. Ptnr. Houston, Houston & Donnelly, Pitts., 1946—; vice-chmn. decedents' estates adv. com. Pa. Joint State Govt. Commn.; past mem. Pa. Supreme Ct. Orphans' Ct. Rules Com. Past pres. Western Pa. Heart Assn. Served with AUS, 1945-46. Mem. ABA, Pa. Bar Assn. (past chmn. real property, probate and trust sect.), Allegheny County Bar Assn. (past. chmn. ethics com., probate and trust sect.), Am. Coll. Probate Counsel, Pitts. Estate Planning Council (past pres.). Republican. Presbyterian. Clubs: Duquesne (Pitts.); Edgeworth (Sewickley, Pa.). Office: Houston Houston & Donnelly 2510 Centre City Tower Pittsburgh PA 15222

HOVDE, F. BOYD, lawyer; b. Mpls., Aug. 7, 1934; s. Frederick L. and Priscilla L. (Boyd) H.; m. Alice Austell, Feb. 21, 1981; children by previous marriage—Frederick R., Debra L., Kristine L., Sarah L. A.B., Princeton U., 1956; J.D., U. Mich. 1959. Bar: Ind. 1959, U.S. Dist. Ct. (no. and so. dists.) Ind. 1959, U.S. Ct. Appeals (7th cir.) 1960, U.S. Supreme Ct. 1977. Assoc. Ice, Miller, Donadio & Ryan, Indpls., 1959-67, ptnr., 1967-69; ptnr. Townsend, Hovde, Townsend & Montross, Indpls., 1969-77; mem. Townsend, Hovde, Townsend & Montross, P.C., 1977-84; mem. Townsend, Hovde & Montross, P.C., 1984-85; mem. F. Boyd Hovde, P.C., 1985—; mem. com. on rules of practice and procedure Ind. Supreme Ct., 1980—. Mem. Indpls. Bar Assn. (treas. 1969, v.p. 1974, pres. 1979), ABA (del. 1980-83), Ind. Trial Lawyers Assn. (bd. dirs. 1970—, pres. 1976-77), Assn. Trial Lawyers Am., Am. Coll. Trial Lawyers, Internat. Acad. Trial Lawyers, Ind. Coll. Trial Lawyers, Indpls. Jaycees (pres. 1963-64), Ind. Golf Assn. (pres. 1974-75), Western Golf Assn. (dir. 1969-81, v.p. 1972-81). Clubs: Columbia (Indpls.); Crooked Stick Golf (Carmel, Ind.); Pine Valley Golf (Clementon, N.J.); Pine Tree Golf (Boynton Beach, Fla.). Personal injury, State civil litigation, Federal civil litigation. Office: 150 E Market St Indianapolis IN 46204

HOVDESVEN, ARNE, lawyer; b. Hagerstown, Md., May 17, 1928; s. E. Arne and Florence (Lesher) H.; m. Joan Tubbs, Dec. 22, 1956; children: Steven, Eric, Susan. B.A., North Tex. State Coll., Denton, 1947; J.D., U. Mich., Ann Arbor, 1956. Indsl. relations specialist Allis-Chalmers Mfg. Co., Milw., 1947-50; assoc. Shearman & Sterling, N.Y.C., 1956-65; ptnr. Shearman & Sterling, 1965—. 1st. lt. U.S. Army, 1950-53. Mem. ABA, N.Y. State Bar Assn. (chmn. bus. banking and corp. law sect. 1984-85), Assn. Bar City N.Y. Lutheran. Clubs: Sleepy Hollow Country (Scarborough, N.Y.); India House (N.Y.C.). Home: 680 Long Hill Rd W Braircliff Manor NY 10510 Office: Shearman & Sterling 53 Wall St New York NY 10005

HOVIS, RAYMOND LEADER, lawyer; b. Phoenixville, Pa., Jan. 13, 1934; s. Raymond Samuel and Mary Elizabeth (Leader) H.; m. Lorraine Catherine Baugher, Jan. 28, 1961; children: Michelle P., Michael D., Steven M. BS in Econs., U. Pa., 1955, JD, 1958. Bar: Pa. 1959, U.S. Dist. Ct. (mid. dist.) Pa. 1961, U.S. Ct. Appeals (D.C. cir.) 1973, U.S. Supreme Ct. 1979, U.S. Ct. Appeals (3d cir.) 1983. Assoc. Stock and Leader, York, Pa., 1959-66, ptnr., 1966—. Rep. Gen. Assmbly Commonwealth of Pa., Harrisburg, 1969-72; chmn. York County Govt. Study Commn., Pa., 1973-74; chmn. bd. Pa. affiliate Am. Heart Assn., Harrisburg, 1978-79. Recipient Charles E. Rohlfing Citizenship award U. Pa., 1955; Disting. Service award Pa. affiliate Am. Heart Assn., 1979. Mem. ABA, Pa. Bar Assn. (delegate 1983-84, v.p. statutory law com. 1983-85), York County Bar Assn. (pres. 1981), Assn. Trial Lawyers Am., Pa. Trial Lawyers Assn., Nat. Assn. Bond Lawyers. Democrat. Lutheran. Municipal bonds, Local government, State civil litigation. Home: RD #2 Box 260 Wrightsville PA 17368

HOVIS, ROBERT HOUSTON, III, lawyer; b. Washington, Apr. 19, 1942; s. Robert Houston and Lera Frances (Robbins) H.; m. Mary Ann Jennings, Dec. 27, 1965. B.S., U. Tenn., 1964, J.D., 1966. Bar: Tenn. 1967, Va. 1967, U.S. Dist. Ct. (ea. dist.) Va. 1973. Asst. commonwealth atty. Fairfax County, Va., 1969-71; pvt. practice law, Fairfax County, 1971—; prin. Hovis & Assocs., Annandale, Va.; commr. in chancery Circuit Ct. Fairfax County, 1969—. Mem. adv. council Salvation Army, Annandale, 1984—; bd. dirs. Annandale C. of C., 1984. Served with U.S. Army, 1967-69, Germany. Mem. Assn. Trial Lawyers Am. (cert. Nat. Coll. Advocacy 1981, cert. Med. Malpractice Advanced Coll. 1983), Va. Trial Lawyers Assn., Fairfax County Bar Assn., Va. State Bar. Democrat. Methodist. Lodge: Rotary (pres. 1983-84). Personal injury. Home: 3401 Hickory Hills Dr Oakton VA 22124 Office: Hovis and Assocs 4544 John Marr Dr Annandale VA 22003

HOVLAND, CARL MICHAEL, lawyer; b. Los Angeles, Dec. 26, 1941; s. Carl Oscar and Marie Kathreen (Toomey) H.; m. Lee E. Burroughs (div. July 1984); children: Ami, Carter, Michael. BA, U. Calif., Berkeley, 1964, JD, 1967. Bar: Calif. 1967, U.S. Ct. Appeals (9th cir.) 1967, U.S. Supreme Ct. 1972. From assoc. to ptnr. Shield & Smith, Los Angeles, 1967-74; sole practice Redondo Beach, Calif., 1974—; judge pro tem Los Angeles County Mcpl. Ct., 1972—; arbitrator Los Angeles County Superior Ct., 1974—. Mem. ABA, Calif. Bar Assn., Calif. Trial Lawyers Assn., Los Angeles Trial Lawyers Assn., Am. Bd. Trial Advs., Am. Arbitration Assn. Personal injury. Office: 1650 S Pacific Coast Hwy #300 Redondo Beach CA 90277

HOWARD, BARRY, real estate executive, lawyer; b. Pitts., Aug. 13, 1949; m. Elayne Beth Smith, Aug. 15, 1971. BS in Econs., U. Pa., 1971; JD, U. Chgo., 1974. Bar: Pa. 1974, U.S. Dist. Ct. (ea. dist.) Pa. 1974. Assoc. Dechert, Price & Rhoads, Phila., 1974-82, ptnr., 1982-84; v.p. Berwind Realty Services Inc., Phila., 1984-86, exec. v.p., 1986—; bd. dirs. Berks Ridge Corp., Phila. Mem. ABA (com. on partnerships 1984—), Ins. Fedn. Pa. Real property. Office: Berwind Realty Services Inc 3000 Centre Sq W Philadelphia PA 19102

HOWARD, DAGGETT HORTON, lawyer; b. N.Y.C., Mar. 20, 1917; s. Chester Augustus and Olive Ree (Daggett) H.; m. Patricia McClellan Exton, Sept. 1950; children: Daggett Horton Jr., Jeffrey, David, Patricia. B.A. magna cum laude, Yale U., 1938, J.D., 1941. Bar: N.Y. 1942, D.C. 1961. Legal staff Root, Clark, Buckner & Ballantine, N.Y.C., 1941-43, Lend Lease Adminstrn., Fgn. Econ. Adminstrn., 1943-44; exec. asst. to spl. counsel to Pres. White House, 1945; legal adviser Fgn. Econ. Adminstrn., also Dept. State, 1945-47; internat. atty., asst. chief internat. and rules div. CAB, 1947-52; asso. gen. counsel Dept. Air Force, 1952-56, dep. gen. counsel, 1956-58; gen. counsel FAA, 1958-62; partner Cox, Langford & Brown, Washington, 1962-66, Howard, Poe & Bastian, Washington, 1966-83, Howard & Law, Washington, 1983—. Bd. editors: Yale Law Jour. Past mem. policy com. Daniel and Florence Guggenheim Aviation Safety Center; corp. mem. Children's Hosp. D.C. Recipient Exceptional Civilian Service award Dept. Air Force, 1958; Disting. Service award FAA, 1962. Mem. Yale Law Sch. Assn. Washington, Corbey Ct., Fed., Am. bar assns., Phi Beta Kappa, Alpha Sigma Phi. Clubs: Yale (Washington), Metropolitan (Washington), Nat. Capital Democratic (Washington); Chevy Chase. General corporate, Real property, Arbitration. Home: 4319 Cathedral Ave Washington DC 20016 Office: 1701 Pennsylvania Ave NW Washington DC 20006

HOWARD, GEORGE, JR., U.S. dist. judge; b. Pine Bluff, Ark., May 13, 1924. Student, Lincoln U., 1951; B.S., U. Ark., J.D., 1954; LL.D., 1976. Bar: Ark. bar 1953, U.S. Supreme Ct. bar 1959. Pvt. practice law Pine Bluff, 1953-57; spl. asso. justice Ark. Supreme Ct., 1976, assoc. justice, 1977; justice U.S. Ct. Appeals, Ark., 1979-80; U.S. dist. judge, Eastern dist. Little Rock, 1980—; Mem. Ark. Claims Commn., 1969-77; chmn. Ark. adv. com. Civil Rights Commn.. Recipient citation in Recognition of Faithful and Disting. Service as mem. Supreme Ct. Com. on Profl. Conduct, 1980, Disting. Jurist award, Judicial Council Nat. Bar Assn., 1980; voted Outstanding Trial Judge for 1984-85, Ark. Trial Lawyers Assn. Mem. Am. Bar Assn., Ark. Bar Assn., Jefferson County Bar Assn. (pres.). Baptist. Office: US District Court PO Box 349 Little Rock AR 72203 *

HOWARD, GLEN SCOTT, lawyer; b. Birmingham, Ala., May 28, 1950; s. Jack and Bernice (Koffman) H.; m. Lauren Oldak, Sept. 2, 1978; 1 child, Gregory Alan. AB cum laude, Harvard Coll., 1971; JD, U. Chgo., 1974. Law clk. to chief judge U.S. Dist. Ct., Atlanta, 1974-76; assoc. Sutherland, Asbill & Brennan, Washington, 1976-81, ptnr., 1981—. Performer radio show and record album: Classics Illustrated, 1984; contbr. articles to profl. jours. Vol. United Jewish Appeal, Washington, 1983—; singer Choral Arts Soc. Washington, 1978—, pres., 1986—; bd. dirs. Am. Chamber Players, Washington, Choral Arts Soc. Washington. Mem. ABA, Fed. Bar Assn., Fed. Energy Bar Assn. (chmn. legis. com. 1986—), Nat. Energy Resources Orgn. Democrat. Avocations: singing, music, photography, tennis, cooking. FERC practice, Real property, Legislative. Home: 2746 Jenifer St NW Washington DC 20015 Office: 1275 Pennsylvania Ave NW Washington DC 20004

HOWARD, GREGORY CHARLES, lawyer, real estate developer; b. Cambridge, Mass., Jan. 20, 1947; s. Robert L. and Nonamae (Lawlor) H.; m. Kathy Arlene Steinbacher, Oct. 1, 1983. Student Clarkson Coll., 1965-67; BS, Boston U., 1969; JD, New Eng. Sch. Law, 1975. Bar: Mass. 1975, U.S. Dist. Ct. Mass. 1975, U.S. Supreme Ct. 1979. Assoc. Carmen L. Durso, Boston, 1975-77, Norris Kozodoy & Krasnoo, Boston, 1977-79; sole practice, Boston, 1979-80, 86—; ptnr. Hoff Ernstoff & Howard, Boston, 1980-86; mem. steering com. Mass. Bar Lawyer Referral, Boston, 1982-85. Real estate, Personal injury, State civil litigation. Home: 5 Eliot Ave Chestnut Hill MA 02167 Office: 7 Commerical Wharf W Boston MA 02110

HOWARD, JEFFREY HJALMAR, lawyer; b. N.Y.C., Aug. 23, 1944; s. Virgil Edward and Margaretta E. H.; m. Brenda H. Howard, June 19, 1966; children—Taggart Harrison, Brooke Kennedy. B.A. in Philosophy, Randolph-Macon Coll., 1966; postgrad. (English Speaking Union scholar) U. Edinburgh (Scotland), 1965; LL.B., U. Va., 1969. Bar: D.C. 1970, U.S. Sup. Ct. 1978, U.S. Ct. Apls. (10th cir.) 1980. Law clk. Circuit Ct., Montgomery County, Md., 1969-70; assoc. Covington & Burling, Washington, 1970-74; assoc. gen. counsel EPA, Washington, 1974-76; ptnr. Howard & Sizemore, Washington, 1976-77; assoc., Covington & Burling, Washington, 1977-80; ptnr. Davis, Graham & Stubbs, Washington, 1980—; lectr. antitrust and environ. law U. Va. 1976-86. Mem. ABA, D.C. Bar Assn., Internat. Bar Assn., Va. Soc. Fellows, Order Coif, Alpha Psi Omega, Alpha Epsilon Pi, Delta Sigma Rho-Tau Kappa Alpha, Omicron Delta Kappa. Presbyterian. Editorial bd. Va. Law Rev., 1967-69; contbr. chpts. to books and articles to profl. jours. Antitrust, Environment, Administrative and regulatory. Home: 1021 Duchess Ct McLean VA 22102 Office: 1001 22d St NW Suite 500 Washington DC 20037

HOWARD, JOEL MANNING, III, lawyer; b. Ogdensburg, N.Y., Mar. 22, 1947; s. Joel Manning II and Louise Craig (Olds) H.; m. Mary Ann Blase, June 30, 1973; children: H. Adam, Joel Manning IV. AB, St. Lawrence U., 1968; JD, Union U., Albany, N.Y., 1971. Bar: N.Y. 1972, U.S. Dist. Ct. (no. dist.) N.Y. 1972, U.S. Dist. Ct. (so., ea. and we. dists.) N.Y. 1982, U.S. Ct. Appeals (2d cir.) 1982, Fla. 1983, U.S. Dist. Ct. Vt. 1986. Atty. Gen. Bldg. Contractors of N.Y. State, Albany, 1971-73; assoc. Bryant, O'Dell & Basso, Syracuse, N.Y., 1973-75; sole practice Albany, 1975-77; assoc. DiFabio & Couch P.C., Albany, 1977-79; ptnr. Couch & Howard P.C., Albany, 1979—; sec. Air Ky. Air Lines, Inc., Owensboro, 1985—. Served to capt. U.S. Army, 1968-74. Mem. ABA, N.Y. State Bar Assn., Fla. Bar Assn., Albany County Bar Assn., Capital Dist. Trial Lawyers Assn. Republican. Presbyterian. Club: Schuyler Meadows (Loudonville, N.Y.); Ft. Orange (Albany). Construction, Real property, Contracts commercial. Home: 49 Princess Ln Loudonville NY 12211 Office: Couch & Howard PC 48 Howard St Albany NY 12207

HOWARD, JOHN WAYNE, lawyer; b. Newport, R.I., Dec. 17, 1948; s. Joseph Leon and Irene Elizabeth (Silver) H.; m. Kathleen Amanda Busby, Oct. 7. 1978. B.A., U. Calif.-San Diego, 1971; J.D. Calif. Western Sch. Law, 1976; postgrad. San Diego Inn of Ct., 1979, Hastings Coll. Advocacy, 1981. Bar: Calif. 1978, U.S. Dist. Ct. (so. dist.) Calif. 1978. Assoc. Robert T. Dierdorff, San Diego, 1978-79; sole practice, San Diego, 1979-82; ptnr. Howard & Neeb, San Diego, 1982-84; prin. John W. Howard and Assocs., San Diego, 1984-86; jud. arbitrator Superior Ct. Calif., 1983—; gen. counsel Ace Parking, Inc., 1986—; pres. HBE Western Properties, Inc., 1986—. Chmn., San Diego County Indigent Def. Adv. Bd., 1981-84, mem. subcom. on def. monitoring and budget for Office Defender Services of San Diego County; mem. select com. on small bus., Calif. State Assembly, 1983—; chmn. San Diego Pub. Arts Adv. Bd.; mem. San Diego County Council of Com. Chairs; chmn. precinct orgn. Roger Hedgecock for Supt. Campaign Com., 1976, mem. steering com., 1976; chmn. Muscular Dystrophy Telethon, San Diego, 1983; bd. govs. Muscular Dystrophy Assn., 1985—; vice chmn. San Diego Festival of Arts, 1983-84; pres. Bowery Theatre, San Diego, 1984; pres., bd. dirs. La Jolla Stage Co.; founder, bd. dirs. San Diego Theatre League; bd. dirs. San Diego Med. Oncology Research Found., Ilan-Lael Found.; bd. dirs., chmn. legal affairs subcom. Calif. Motion Picture Council; mem. adv. bd. dirs. San Diego Motion Picture Bur.; mem. pub. edn. com. Am. Cancer Soc.; bd. dirs. Am. Ballet Found.; founder, bd. dirs. San Diego Theatre Found., 1984—; founder, legal counsel San Diego Symphony Soc., 1986—, Combined Orgn. for the Visual Arts, 1986—; mem. 44th Congl. Dist. Adv. Com.; mem. Com. to Re-Elect Congressman Bill Lowery; mem. San Diego County 4th Dist. Adv. Com.; mem. steering com. Bill Cleaton for Mayor, 1976, city council campaigns for Marla Marshall, Neil Good and Robert Ottilie, 1987. Mem. ABA, Calif. State Bar, Assn. Trial Lawyers Am., U. Calif.-San Diego Alumni Assn. (past v.p., bd. dirs.), Calif. Western Sch. Law Alumni Assn., Friendly Sons of St. Patrick, Phi Alpha Delta. Republican. Lodge: Rotary. State civil litigation, Entertainment, General corporate. Office: PO Box 81889 San Diego CA 92138-1889

HOWARD, JOSEPH CLEMENS, judge; b. Des Moines, Dec. 9, 1922; m. Gwendolyn Mae London, Dec. 1954; 1 son. B.A., U. Iowa, 1950; LL.B., Drake U., 1955, M.A., 1957, J.D., 1968; postgrad., Washington and Lee U., Northwestern U. Law Sch., U. Nev.; postgrad. hon. degree, Morgan State Coll., 1972. Bar: Md. Probation officer Supreme Bench Balt. City, 1958-60; mem. firm Howard and Hargrove, 1960-64; asst. state's atty. 1964-66, chief of trial sec., 1966-67, asst. city solicitor, 1967-68; spl. cons. dept. edn.; asso. judge Supreme Bench of Balt. City, 1968-79; vis. prof. Grad. Sch. Nat. Coll. State Trial Judges, U. Nev., Reno, 1971; vis. lectr. Johns Hopkins U., Balt., 1971, 73; vis. prof. Nat. Coll. Dist. Attys., U. Houston, 1973; vis. lectr. Morgan State U., 1973-77; chief judge criminal ct. Supreme Bench of Balt. City, 1975-76; cons. communications dept. Nat. League Cities, 1978, Nat. Center for State Cts., 1978; chmn. exec. com. Md. Jud. Conf., 1977-78; judge U.S. Dist. Ct., Dist. Md., 1979—. Contbr. articles to legal jours. Mem. Mayor's Task Force on Community Relations, Balt.; chmn. Mayor's Task Force Juvenile Delinquency; bd. govs. Antioch Coll. Sch. Law, 1976-79; mem. Nat. Com. Black Elected Ofcls., 1972; mem. bd. govs. Citizens Planning and Housing Assn.; bd. dirs. Legal Aid Bur., Nat. Bar Found.; trustee Antioch Coll., 1974-75. Served with U.S. Army, 1944-47, PTO. Recipient Afro-Am. award, 1968; Police Community Relations award, 1971; Walter P. Carter award, 1971; Kappa Alpha Psi Achievement award, 1973; Benjamin Banneker Public Affairs award, 1975; Bicentennial Jud. award Black Am. Law Students Assn., 1976; Delta Sigma Theta Jud. award, 1977; Henry McNeill Turner Soc. award Bethel A.M.E. Ch., 1978; Man of Year award Nat. Assn. Negro Bus. and Profl. Women's Clubs, 1979; Women Behind the Community award, 1979; Spl. Jud. Service award Herbert M. Frisby Hist. Soc., 1980. Mem. ABA, Nat. Bar Assn., World Assn. Judges, Monumental City Bar Assn., Phi Alpha Delta. Office: Suite 540 US Courthouse 101 W Lombard St Baltimore MD 21201 *

HOWARD, KENYON B., lawyer, chemical engineer; b. 1918. BS, Calif. Inst. Tech., 1941; JD, Humphreys Coll., 1980. Bar: Calif. 1980, U.S. Dist. Ct. (no. and ea. dists.) Calif. U.S. Tax Ct., U.S. Ct. Appeals (9th cir.). Owner Tri-Dex Co., Visalia, Calif., 1949-78; prof. Coll. of the Sequoias, Visalia, 1968-83; sole practice Visalia, 1980—. Mem. ABA, Tulare County Bar Assn., AICHE, Am. Chem. Soc., Assn. for Computing Machinery. General practice, State civil litigation, Federal civil litigation. Office: PO Box 3958 Visalia CA 93278

HOWARD, MARK HALE, lawyer; b. Rexburg, Idaho, June 22, 1953; s. Merrill William and Joyce (Hale) H.; m. Sharon Elaine Baggs, Dec. 15, 1978; children: Mark Robert, David Merrill, Michael Scott. A in Bus., Ricks Coll., 1975; BS in Acctg., Brigham Young U., 1978, M in Acctg., 1978, JD, 1981. Bar: Utah 1981, Colo. 1983, U.S. Dist. Ct. Utah 1981, U.S. Dist. Ct. Colo. 1983, U.S. Tax Ct. 1981; CPA, Colo. Atty. IRS Dist. Counsel, Denver, 1981-85, Salt Lake City, 1985; spl. asst. U.S. Atty. for Dist. Utah, 1985—. Corporate taxation, Estate taxation, Personal income taxation. Home: 564 W 490 S Orem UT 84058 Office: IRS Dist Counsel 125 S State Room 1311 Salt Lake City UT 84138

HOWARD, ROBERT CAMPBELL, JR., lawyer; b. Bklyn., June 7, 1951; s. Robert Campbell and Helen (Buck) H.; m. Bonnie L. Bossert, Apr. 15, 1972; 1 child, Cordell Campbell. Ba in Polit. Sci., Ariz. State U., 1973, JD, 1976. Bar: Ariz. 1976, U.S. Dist. Ct. Ariz. 1976. Assoc. Combs & Foley, Phoenix, 1976-77, Paul Bradwell, P.C., Phoenix, 1977-78; ptnr. Jekel & Howard, Scottsdale, Ariz., 1978—; judge pro-tempore City of Scottsdale, Ariz. 1983—. Commr. City of Scottsdale Airport, 1985—; bd. dirs. Sereno Soccer League, Phoenix, 1986; mem. Scottsdale Charros, 1986. Mem. Ariz. Bar Assn., Maricopa County Bar Assn., Scottsdale Bar Assn. (pres. 1985—). Republican. Presbyterian. Avocations: tennis, slow pitch softball. State civil litigation, Consumer commercial, Family and matrimonial. Office: Jekel & Howard 4323 N Brown Suite E Scottsdale AZ 85251

HOWARD, ROBERT HENRY, lawyer; b. Port Huron, Mich., Apr. 13, 1913; s. William Joseph and Anna Grace (Carey) H.; m. Roberta Tresham, June 19, 1939; children: Lucy Jane Howard Seatter, Timothy Tresham. AB, U. Mich., 1934, LLB, 1936. Bar: Ill. 1936, U.S. Dist. Ct. (so. dist.) Ill. 1939, U.S. Ct. Appeals (7th cir.) 1956, U.S. Supreme Ct. 1963. Atty. City of Monmouth, Ill., 1942-46; asst. atty. gen. State of Ill., Monmouth, 1946-50; ptnr. Howard & Padella, Monmouth, 1950-77, Howard & Brinkmann, Monmouth, 1977—; chmn. bd. Western Stoneware, Monmouth; bd. dirs. Community Nat. Bank, Monmouth. Bd. dirs. Monmouth Hosp., 1948-52. Mem. ABA, Ill. Bar Assn. Republican. Club: Union League (Chgo.). Lodges: Rotary (pres. Monmouth 1958), Masons. Probate. Home: 1124 E Euclid Ave Monmouth IL 61462

HOWARD, ROBERT LAWRENCE, lawyer; b. Chgo., June 14, 1948; s. Sherwin G. and Patricia (Roth) H. BA, U. Tex., 1970, JD, 1971. Bar: Tex. 1972, N.Y. 1973, U.S. Dist. Ct. (so. and ea. dists.) N.Y., U.S. Ct. Appeals (2d cir.), U.S. Tax Ct. Staff atty. IRS, N.Y.C., 1972-73; assoc. Weil, Gotshal & Manges, N.Y.C., 1973-75; sole practice, N.Y.C., 1975-80; ptnr. Glass & Howard, P.C., N.Y.C., 1980-86; of counsel Labozzetta & Hass, N.Y.C., 1986-87, sole practice, 1987—; adj. prof. Pace U. Sch. Law, 1980—. Contbr. articles to profl. jours. Mem. ABA, Assn. of Bar of City of N.Y., Bankruptcy Lawyers Bar Assn. Bankruptcy. Home: 322 W 57th St New York NY 10019 Office: 275 Madison Ave 35th Floor New York NY 10016

HOWARD, SHARI IRENE, lawyer; b. Cleve., Sept. 20, 1953; d. J.M. and M. Irene (Dougan) Killen; m. Stanley Carson Howard, Oct. 4, 1975 (div. May 1982). Student, Miami U., Oxford, Ohio, 1971-72, Ohio State U., Lima and Columbus, 1972-76; BA, Ariz. State U., 1977, JD, 1980. Bar: Ariz. 1982, U.S. Dist. Ct. Ariz. 1982. Assoc. Meyer, Vucichevich & Cimala, Phoenix, 1980-86, Burch & Cracchiolo, Phoenix, 1986—. Mem. Ariz. Legis. Com. Lower Ct. Reform, Phoenix, 1981-82; fund raiser Liberty Wildlife Found., Phoenix, 1986. Mem. ABA, Ariz. Bar Assn., Ariz. State U. Law Coll. Bar Assn. (pres. 1978-79), Ariz. State U. Alumni Assn. (bd. dirs. 1980-83), Ariz. State U. Pre-Law Soc. (organizer, pres. 1976-77), Phi Alpha Delta (v.p. 1979-80). Family and matrimonial. Office: Burch & Cracchiolo 702 E Osborn Rd Phoenix AZ 85014

HOWARD, STEVEN GRAY, lawyer; b. Lafayette, Ind., Aug. 9, 1951; s. C. Warren and Joan Elizabeth (Gray) H.; m. Deborah F. Mooring, July 24, 1982; children: Jeremy, Jessica, Judd, Christopher, Adrienne. BA, Purdue U., 1973; JD with honors, U. Ark., 1977. Bar: Ark. 1977, U.S. Dist. Ct. (ea. and we. dists.) Ark. 1978. Assoc. Thaxton & Hout, Newport, Ark., 1977-86; ptnr. Thaxton, Hout, Howard & Nicholson, Newport, Ark., 1986—; mcpl. judge City of Tuckerman, Ark., 1979—; city atty. Campbell Sta., Ark., 1977—. Assoc. editor U. Ark. Law Rev., 1976-77. Bd. dirs. Northeast Ark. Legal Services, Inc., Newport, 1978-82, Legal Services of Ark., Little Rock, 1980-82. Mem. ABA, Ark. Bar Assn., Jackson County Bar Assn. (pres. 1979-80), Ark. Trial Lawyers Assn., Delta Theta Phi, Order of Barristers. Democrat. Methodist. Lodge: Rotary. Avocations: hunting, fishing. Real property, State civil litigation, General practice. Office: Thaxton Hout Howard & Nicholson 600 3d St Newport AR 72112

HOWARD, TIMOTHY JOHN, lawyer; b. Princeton, Ill., May 27, 1950; s. William Corbett Howard and Rosella (Elmblad) Willey; m. Patricia Marie Dwyer, Aug. 11, 1972; children: Rebecca, Thomas, Mary, James. AB, Princeton U., 1972; JD, U. Notre Dame, 1976. Bar: Ill. 1976, U.S. Dist. Ct. (cen. dist.) Ill. 1976, U.S. Ct. Appeals (7th cir.) 1981. Assoc. Kavanagh, Scully, Sudow, White & Frederick PC, Peoria, Ill., 1976-80, ptnr., 1981—. Commr. Peoria County Bd., 1982—; alt. del. 1984 Democratic Nat. Conv., San Francisco; pres. Peoria Area World Affairs Council, 1985-86. Mem. ABA, Peoria County Bar Assn., Ill. State Bar Assn.. Lutheran. Clubs: Creve Coeur, Willow Knolls Country (Peoria). State civil litigation, Consumer commercial, Banking. Office: Kavanagh Scully Sudow White & Frederick 700 Commercial Nat Bank Bldg Peoria IL 61602

HOWARD, TIMOTHY JON, lawyer; b. Washington, Aug. 22, 1952; s. Jonah S. and Virginia Inez (Price) H.; m. Janice Lynn Loock, July 15, 1979; children: Emily M., Mark P. BA in Philosophy, U. Mich., 1974; JD, Harvard U., 1977. Bar: Tex. 1977. Assoc. Johnson, Bromberg, Leeds & Riggs, Dallas, 1977-79; atty. Shell Oil Co., Houston, 1979—. Bd. dirs. Kingsbridge Mcpl. Utility Dist., Harris and Ft. Bend counties, Tex., 1986—. Mem. ABA (corp. banking and bus. law and internat. law sects.), Tex. Bar Assn. (corp. banking and bus. and internat. law sects.). Republican. General corporate, Securities, Corporate finance and structuring joint ventures. Home: 9223 Chesney Downs Dr Houston TX 77083 Office: Shell Oil Co Legal Orgn PO Box 2463 Houston TX 77252

HOWARTH, KIM A., lawyer; b. Rome, N.Y., July 6, 1955; s. Dean Arthur Howarth and Judith Ann (Henning) Grenawalt; m. Tracy Jo Biely, Nov. 21, 1981; 1 child, Adam Arthur. BBA, U. Wis., Whitewater, 1977; JD, U. Wis., Madison, 1980. Bar: Wis. 1980, U.S. Dist. Ct. (ea. and we. dists.) Wis. 1980, U.S. Ct. Appeals (7th cir.) 1980. Assoc. Godfrey, Pfeil & Neshek S.C., Elkhorn, Wis., 1982—; bd. dirs. Vocat. Industries, Elkhorn, Wis. Mem. ABA, Wis. Bar Assn., Walworth County Bar Assn., Assn. Trial Lawyers Am., Wis. Trial Lawyers Assn. Avocations: fishing, water skiing, snow skiing, racquetball, jogging. Personal injury, Contracts commercial, Bankruptcy. Office: Godfrey Pfeil & Neshek SC 11 N Wisconsin St Elkhorn WI 53121

HOWE, DRAYTON FORD, JR., lawyer; b. Seattle, Nov. 17, 1931; s. Drayton Ford and Virginia (Wester) H.; m. Joyce Arnold, June 21, 1952; 1 son, James Drayton. A.B., U. Calif.-Berkeley, 1953; LL.B., Hastings Coll. Law, 1957. Bar: Calif. 1958, C.P.A. Calif. Atty. IRS, 1958-61; tax dept. supr. Ernst & Ernst, San Francisco, 1962-67; ptnr. Bishop, Barry, Howe & Reid, San Francisco, 1968—; lectr. on tax matters U. Calif. extension, 1966-76. Mem. Calif. Bar Assn., San Francisco Bar Assn. (chmn. client relations com. 1977), Calif. Soc. C.P.A.s. State civil litigation, Corporate taxation, Estate planning.

HOWE, JAY EDWIN, lawyer; b. Omaha, Apr. 13, 1940; m. Anita González, May 4, 1968; children: Joseph E., Olivia G. BA, U. Iowa, 1963, JD, 1966. Bar: Iowa 1966, U.S. Dist. Ct. (so. dist.) Iowa 1966. Atty. Adair County, Iowa, 1973-79; ptnr. Howe & Olesen, Greenfield, Iowa, 1979—. Chmn. Adair County Dem. Cen Com., 1979—. Served with U.S. Army, 1966-68. Mem. Iowa Bar Assn. Methodist. Club: Chamber (Greenfield) (pres.). General practice. Office: Howe & Olesen Box 86 Greenfield IA 50849

HOWE, JONATHAN THOMAS, lawyer; b. Evanston, Ill., Dec. 16, 1940; s. Frederick King and Rosalie Charlotte (Volz) H.; m. Lois Helene Braun, July 12, 1963; children: Heather C., Jonathan Thomas Jr., Sara E. B.A. with honors, Northwestern U., 1963; J.D. with distinction, Duke U., 1966. Bar: Ill. 1966, U.S. Dist. Ct. (no. dist.) Ill. 1966, U.S. Ct. Appeals (7th cir.) 1967, U.S. Tax Ct. 1968, U.S. Supreme Ct. 1970, U.S. Ct. Appeals (D.C. cir.) 1976, U.S. Dist. Ct. (D.C.) 1976, U.S. Ct. Appeals (9th cir.) 1980, U.S. Ct. Appeals (4th, 5th, 11th cirs.) 1983. Ptnr. Jenner & Block, Chgo., 1966-85, sr. ptnr. in charge assn. and adminstrv. law dept., 1978-85; founding and sr. ptnr. Howe & Hutton, Chgo., 1985—; mem. exec. and adv. coms. to Ill. Sec. of State to revise the Ill. Area Not for Profit Act, 1983-86; dir. Pacific Mut. Realty Investors, Inc., 1985-86. Contbg. editor: Ill. Inst. for Continuing Legal Edn., 1973—, Sporting Goods Bus., 1977—, Meeting News, 1978—; contbr. articles to legal jours. Mem. Dist. 27 Bd. Edn., Northbrook, Ill., 1969—, sec., 1969-72, pres., 1973-84; chmn. bd. trustees Sch. Employee Benefit Trust, 1979-85; founding bd. dirs., pres. Sch. Mgmt. Found. Ill., 1976-84; mem. exec. com. Northfield Twp. Republican Orgn., 1967-71; bd. deacons. Village Presbyn. Ch. Northbrook, 1975-78, trustee, 1981-83; spl. advisor Pres.'s Council Phys. Fitness and Sports, 1983-85. Mem. ABA (antitrust sect., Nat. Inst. com., corp. banking and bus. law sect., sect. on litigation, adminstrv. law sect.; mem. internat. law com., continuing edn. com., tort and ins. practice, vice chmn. com. sports law 1986—), Ill. Bar Assn. (antitrust sec., civil practice sect., sch. law sect., adminstrv. law sect.; co-editor Antitrust Newsletter 1968-70), Chgo. Bar Assn. (def. of prisoners com. 1966-83, antitrust law com. 1971—, continuing edn. com. 1977—, chmn. assn. and profl. soc. law com. 1984—), Nat. Sch. Bds. Assn. (nat. bd. dirs.. 1979—, exec. com. 1981-82, 83—, sec.-treas. 1983-85, 2d v.p. 1985-86, pres.-elect 1986-87, chmn. devel. com. 1982-87, pres. 1987—), D.C. Bar Assn., Am. Judicature Soc., Ill. Assn. Sch. Bds. (pres. 1977-79, bd. dirs. 1971—), Am. Soc. Assn. Execs. (vice chmn. legal com. 1983-86), Order of Coif, Psi Upsilon. Clubs: Legal, Law, Mid-America, Barclay, Sunset Ridge Country, Tower. Administrative and regulatory, Antitrust, Federal civil litigation. Home: 3845 Normandy Ln Northbrook IL 60062 Office: 20 N Wacker Dr Suite 3550 Chicago IL 60606

HOWE, RICHARD RIVES, lawyer; b. Portland, Oreg., Dec. 21, 1942; s. Hubert Shattuck Jr. and Anna Gertrude (Moody) H.; m. Elizabeth Anne Crowell, Aug. 29, 1964; 1 child, Richard Rives Jr. BA, Yale U., 1964; JD, Harvard U., 1967. Bar: N.Y. 1968, U.S. Ct. Appeals (2d cir.) 1973, U.S. Dist. Ct. (so. and ea. dists.) N.Y. 1973, U.S. Supreme Ct. 1973. Assoc. Sullivan & Cromwell, N.Y.C., 1967-74, ptnr., 1974—. Pres. Short Hills Assn., N.J., 1986—; bd. dirs. Peoples' Symphony Concerts, N.Y.C., 1983—, Neighborhood Assn. Millburn Twp., N.J., 1985—.

HOWE, THOMAS RICHARD, district court judge; b. Beloit, Wis., Nov. 25, 1941; s. Richard and Margaret (Burns) H.; m. Joan Elizabeth Blair, June 17, 1967; children—Kathleen, Timothy, Shelly. B.A. in Polit. Sci., Coll. of St. Thomas, 1964; J.D., U. Minn., 1967. Bar: Minn. 1967, U.S. Dist. Ct. Minn. 1970. Instr. constl. law U.S. Coast Guard Acad., New London, Conn., 1967-70; ptnr. Melchert, Hubert & Howe, Waconia, Minn., 1970-79; county judge State of Minn., Chaska, 1979-83, dist. judge, Hastings, 1983—. Office, mem. Carver County Democrat-Farmer-Labor Party, Chaska, 1972-79. Served to lt. (j.g.), USCG, 1967-70. Mem. 8th Dist. Bar Assn., Minn. Dist. Judges Assn., Minn. County Judges Assn., Minn. Bar Assn. Roman Catholic. Lodge: Lions. Home and Office: PO Box 83 467 Lakeview Terr Waconia MN 55387

HOWELL, ALAN PETER, lawyer, company executive, arbitrator; b. Honolulu, Aug. 1, 1927; s. Hugh and Mavis Halcyon (Shawk) H.; m. Sara Grounds, Feb. 26, 1954; children: David Wallace, Brian Cochran. BA, Yale U., 1950; LLB, Cornell U., 1953. Bar: Hawaii 1954. Law clk. to chief justice Ter. Supreme Ct. Hawaii 1953-54; asst. pub. prosecutor City and County Honolulu, 1954-58; ptnr. Hogan & Howell, 1958-71; sole practice, 1971-86; magistrate 6th dist. Dist. Ct. Honolulu, 1964-68; arbitrator Am. Arbitration Assn., 1967—. Rep. precinct pres., Hawaii, 1956-58; pres. chpt. 184 Exptl. Aircraft Assn. Served with U.S. Army, 1946-48, to 1st lt. USAFR, 1950-58. Mem. Hawaii Bar Assn. Christian Scientist. Clubs: Pacific, Outrigger Canoe. Probate, Personal injury, General practice. Office: 733 Bishop St Suite 2515 Honolulu HI 96813-4057

HOWELL, ALLEN WINDSOR, lawyer; b. Montgomery, Ala., Mar. 10, 1949; s. Elvin and Bennie Merle (Windsor) H.; children—Christopher Darby, Joshua Darby. B.A., Huntington Coll., 1971; LL.B., Jones Law Sch., 1974. Bar: Ala. 1974, U.S. Supreme Ct. 1977, U.S. Ct. Appeals (fed. cir.) 1983, U.S. Ct. Appeals (11th cir.) 1981, U.S. Tax Ct. 1979, U.S. Claims Ct. 1982, U.S. Dist. Ct. (mid. dist.) Ala. 1975, U. Dist. Ct. (so. dist.) Ala. 1978. Archivist, Hist. Research Center, Air U., Maxwell AFB, Ala., 1972-75; sole practice, Montgomery, 1975-82, 83—; asst. atty. gen., chief legal sect. Ala. Medicaid Agy., Montgomery, 1982-83; adj. prof. Jones Law Sch., 1983—, Ala. Christian Coll., 1975— (both Montgomery). Hon. lt. col., aide de camp Gov. Ala., 1974. Mem. ABA, Assn. Trial Lawyers Am., Montgomery County Bar Assn. (newsletter editorial com. 1984-85). Republican. Mem. Ch. of Christ. Author Alabama Civil Practice Forms, 1986. Federal civil litigation, State civil litigation, Personal injury. Office: 416 E Grove St Montgomery AL 36104

HOWELL, ARTHUR, lawyer; b. Atlanta, Aug. 24, 1918; s. Arthur and Katharine (Mitchell) H.; m. Caroline Sherman, June 14, 1941; children: Arthur, Caroline, Eleanor, Richard, Peter, James; m. Janet Kerr Franchot, Dec. 16, 1972. A.B., Princeton U., 1939; J.D., Harvard U., 1942; LL.D. (hon.), Oglethorpe U., 1972. Bar: Ga. 1942. Assoc. F.M., 1942-45; ptnr. Alston & Bird (and predecessor firms), 1945—; dir., gen. counsel Atlantic Steel Co.; v.p., dir. Creomulsion Co.; dir. Alpha Fund, Inc., J.S. Tech., Inc.; past pres. Atlanta Legal Aid Soc. Pres. Met. Atlanta Community Services, 1956, dir., 1953—; pres. Community Planning Council, 1961-63; gen. chmn. United Appeal, 1955; spl. atty. gen. State Ga., 1948-55; spl. counsel Univ. System Ga., State Sch. Bldg. Authorities, 1951-70; adv. com. Ga. Corp. Code, 1967—; chmn. Atlanta Adv. Com. Parks.; Trustee Princeton, 1964-68, Atlanta Speech Sch.; trustee, past chmn. Oglethorpe U.; trustee Morehouse Coll., Westminister Schs., Atlanta, Episcopal High Sch., Alexandria, Va., Inst. Internat. Edn. (exec. com. 1969-72). Named hon. alumnus Ga. Inst. Tech. Fellow Am. Coll. Probate Counsel (chmn. com. on profl. standards 1982-85, regent 1984—); mem. Am. Law Inst., Am., Ga., Atlanta bar assns., Internat. Acad. of Estate and Trust Law (academician), Lawyers Club of Atlanta (past pres.), Am. Judicature Soc., Soc. Colonial Wars, Phi Beta Kappa. Presbyn. (elder, trustee, chmn. bd. trustees 1985—). Clubs: Mill Reef, Capital City, Piedmont Driving, Commerce, Homosassa Fishing; Nassau (Princeton, N.J.); Princeton (N.Y.C.). Probate, General corporate. Home: 33 Ivy Ridge Atlanta GA 30342 Summer home: Petit Ridge Dr Big Canoe GA 30143 Office: 1200 C & S Bank Bldg Atlanta GA 30335

HOWELL, BRIAN GRAHAM, lawyer; b. Phila., May 14, 1954; s. Richard Graham and Rita Gloria (Monastra) H.; m. Lisa Marguerite Maiale, June 6, 1982; children: Meredith, Carl. BA, Dickinson Coll., 1976; JD, Rutgers U., 1979. Bar: N.J. 1979, U.S. Dist. Ct. N.J. 1979. Assoc. Bertman, Johnson & Sahli, Hammonton, N.J., 1979-85; ptnr. Donio, Bertman, Johnson, Sahli & Greco, Hammonton, 1985, Donio, Olivo & Howell, Hammonton, 1986—. Pres. Hammonton Bd. Edn., 1985. Mem. ABA, N.J. State Bar Assn., Atlantic County Bar Assn. Lodge: Lions. General practice, Personal injury. Home: 728 Central Ave Hammonton NJ 08037 Office: Donio Olivo & Howell PC 24 Central Ave Hammonton NJ 08037

HOWELL, DONALD LEE, lawyer; b. Waco, Tex., Jan. 31, 1935; s. Hilton Emory and Louise (Hatchett) H.; m. Gwendolyn Avera, June 13, 1957; children—Daniel Liege, Alison Avera, Anne Turner. B.A. cum laude, Baylor U., 1956; J.D. with honors, U. Tex., 1963. Bar: Tex. 1963. Assoc. Vinson & Elkins, Houston, 1963-70, ptnr., 1970—, mem. mgmt. com., 1980—. Served to capt. USAFR, 1956-59. Woodrow Wilson fellow, 1959-60. Fellow Tex. Bar Found., Houston Bar Found.; mem. Am. Law Inst., Nat. Assn. Bond Lawyers (pres. 1981-82, bd. dirs. 1979-83), Order of Coif, Phi Delta Phi. Democrat. Baptist. Clubs: Ramada, Houston Ctr. (Houston). Municipal bonds.

HOWELL, HARLEY THOMAS, lawyer; b. Chgo., June 5, 1937; s. Harley W. and Geneva (Engelmann) H.; m. Aliceann A. McLaughlin, Apr. 23, 1983; children by previous marriage: Shelley A., Rebecca L., Emily S. A.B., Princeton U., 1959; J.D., Yale U., 1962. Bar: Md. 1962, U.S. Supreme Ct. 1966, D.C. 1972. Law clk. to chief judge U.S. Ct. Appeals (4th cir.) 1962-63; assoc. Semmes, Bowen & Semmes, Balt., 1966-72, ptnr., 1972—; mem. Gov.'s Commn. to Revise Annotated Code Md., 1975-85; mem. standing com. on rules of practice and procedure Ct. Appeals of Md., 1985—. Bd. dirs. Balt. Symphony Orch., 1975—; trustee Edn. Ctr. of Sheppard Pratt, 1986—. Served to capt. JAG Corps, U.S. Army, 1963-66. Decorated Army Commendation medal. Mem. ABA, Md. State Bar Assn., Balt. City Bar Assn., D.C. Bar Assn., Fed. Bar Assn. Democrat. Clubs: Center, Wine and Food Soc., Wranglers Law (Balt.). Libel, Federal civil litigation, State civil litigation. Home: 1012 Chestnut Ridge Dr Lutherville MD 21093 Office: 250 W Pratt St Baltimore MD 21201

HOWELL, JOEL WALTER, III, lawyer; b. Jackson, Miss., Dec. 25, 1949; s. Joel W. and Elizabeth (Harris) H.; m. Wilhelmina C. Pontus, June 25, 1983. BA, Millsaps Coll., 1971; JD, Columbia U., 1974. Bar: Tex. 1974, U.S. Ct. Appeals (5th cir.) 1974, Miss. 1975, U.S. Dist. Ct. (no. and so. dists.) Miss. 1975. Ptnr. Daniel, Coker, Horton, Bell & Dukes, Jackson, 1975-80; sole practice Jackson, 1981—. Contbg. editor, case notes and comments editor Columbia Jour. Transnat. Law, 1973-74. Mem. ABA, Tex. Bar Assn., Miss. Bar Assn., Hinds County Bar Assn., Assn. Trial Lawyers Am., Miss. Trial Lawyers Assn., Miss. Def. Lawyers Assn., Def. Research Inst., Miss. Bankruptcy Conf. Federal civil litigation, State civil litigation, Personal injury. Home: 4515 Parisian Dr Jackson MS 39206 Office: PO Box 16772 5446 Executive Pl Jackson MS 39236

HOWELL, KENNETH KENNEDY, lawyer; b. San Pedro, Calif., Dec. 30, 1931; s. Newton Price and Elaine (Kennedy) H.; m. Ann Glasscock, Apr. 7, 1961; 1 son, Kenneth K. Jr.; m. Gail Sager, Mar. 13, 1972; children: Adam K., Katherine K. B.A. U. Ala., 1956; J.D., U. Chgo., 1959. Bar: N.Y. 1960, Ala. 1961, Ill. 1964, Calif. 1971. Assoc. Sullivan & Cromwell, N.Y.C., 1959-61, Moore, Thomas, Taliaferro, Forman & Burr, Birmingham, Ala., 1961-63, Isham, Lincoln & Deale, Chgo., 1963-68; exec. dir. Legal Assistance Found., Chgo., 1968-76; ptnr. Sidley & Austin, Los Angeles, 1976—; assoc. prof. U. Ala., Birmingham, 1962-63, U. Chgo., 1970-71. Mem. Chgo. Counsel Lawyers (dir. 1972-76), Chgo. Bar Assn., Order of Coif. Home: 476 18th St Santa Monica CA 90402 Office: Sidley & Austin 2049 Century Park E Los Angeles CA 90067

HOWELL, MARK FRANKLIN, lawyer; b. El Paso, Tex., Nov. 19, 1934; s. Benjamin Randolph and Romaine (Safford) H.; m. Linda O'Reilly (div.); m. Jayne Upton (div.); m. Linda Way Howell; children: Madeline, Celia, Cara. BA in History, Stanford U., 1956; LLB, U. Tex., 1961. Bar: Tex. 1961, U.S. Ct. Customs and Patent Appeals 1967, U.S. Supreme Ct. 1971. Ptnr. Howell & Fields, El Paso, 1961-86; sole practice El Paso, 1986—. Contbr. articles to profl. jours. Chmn. Mayor's Com. on Housing, El Paso, 1970; vice chmn., commr. El Paso Housing Authority, 1970-72. Served to capt. U.S. Army, 1956-58. Mem. Tex. Bar Assn., El Paso County Bar Assn. (bd. dirs. 1984—), Assn. Trial Lawyers Am. (sustaining, state del. 1981-83), Tex. Trial Lawyers Assn. (bd. dirs. 1973-81, 86—), El Paso Trial Lawyers Assn. (pres. 1975, v.p. 1973-74, bd. dirs. 1972-75). Democrat. Episcopalian. Federal civil litigation, State civil litigation. Home: PO Box 1146 Santa Teresa NM 88008

HOWELL, MORTON BOYTE, lawyer; b. Nashville, July 17, 1919; s. Morton B. and Marie Lyle (Harwell) H.; m. Nancy Watkins, Sept. 25, 1943; children—Morton B., William W. B.A., Vanderbilt U., 1939; LL.B., Yale U., 1942. Bar: Tenn. 1941, U.S. Dist. Ct. (mid. dist.) Tenn. 1947, U.S. Supreme Ct. 1952, U.S. Ct. Appeals (6th cir.) 1966. Assoc. Price, Barksdale & Price, 1946-51; sole practice, Nashville, 1951-57, 64-65; ptnr. Howell, Neese & Tuck, 1957-62, Howell & Tuck, 1962-63; Howell & Fisher, 1966-82, Howell, Fisher, Branham & North, all Nashville, 1983—; city recorder City of Belle Meade (Tenn.), 1946-47, city atty., 1947-74, mayor, 1974-82. Served to capt. USAAF, 1942-46. Mem. Nashville Bar Assn., Tenn. Bar Assn., ABA, Phi Delta Theta. Presbyterian. Clubs: Cumberland, Exchange. Litigation, General corporate, Local government. Office: Suite 400 Court Square Bldg 300 James Robertson Pkwy Nashville TN 37201

HOWELL, WELDON ULRIC, JR., lawyer; b. Dallas, July 16, 1947; s. Weldon U. and Betty (Temple) H.; m. Barbara Molina, July 14, 1973; children—Benjamin, Sarah. B.A., U. Ariz., 1969; postgrad. City London Poly. Sch., 1971; J.D., U. Tex., 1973. Bar: Tex. 1973, Calif. 1974, U.S. Dist. Ct. (cen., no., so. and ea. dists.) Calif., U.S. Ct. Appeals (9th cir.) 1984, U.S. Tax Ct. 1981, U.S. Ct. Claims 1981. Briefing atty to assoc. justice Supreme Ct. Tex., Austin, 1973-74; assoc. Schramm & Raddue, Santa Barbara, Calif., 1974-77, sr. ptnr., chmn. bus. and tax dept., 1977—. mem. Santa Barbara County Bar Assn. (chmn. tax sect. 1984, bd. dirs. 1986-87), Barristers Club Santa Barbara (pres. 1977-78), Pi Kappa Alpha. Democrat. Clubs: Tennis of Santa Barbara (chmn., 1980), Birnam Wood Golf. General corporate, Securities, Personal income taxation. Home: 2525 Anacapa Santa Barbara CA 93105 Office: Schramm & Raddue 15 W Carrillo Santa Barbara CA 93101

HOWELL, WESLEY GRANT, JR., lawyer; b. Salt Lake City, Dec. 4, 1937; s. Wesley Grant and Mary (Schettler) H.; m. Kay Hayes, Sept. 7, 1961 (div. Apr. 1974); children: Elizabeth, Stephanie; m. Sonja Kropf, Aug. 14, 1982. BEE, U. Utah, 1962; LLB, Columbia U., 1965. Assoc. Gibson, Dunn & Cruthcer, Los Angeles, 1966-72; ptnr. Gibson, Dunn & Cruthcer, Los Angeles and Washington, 1972—. Mem. N.Y. State Bar Assn., D.C. Bar Assn., Calif. Bar Assn., Los Angeles Bar Assn. Republican. Mormon. Club: Alta (Salt Lake City). Securities, General communications litigation. Home: 3201 N Wakefield St Arlington VA 22207 Office: Gibson Dunn & Crutcher 1050 Connecticut Ave NW Washington DC 20036

HOWELL, WILLIAM ASHLEY, III, lawyer; b. Raleigh, N.C., Jan. 2, 1949; s. William Ashley II and Caroline Erskine Greenleaf; m. Esther Holland, Dec. 22, 1973. BS, Troy State U., 1972; JD, Birmingham Sch. Law, 1977; postgrad. U. Ala.-Birmingham. Bar: Ala. 1977, U.S. Dist. Ct. (no. dist.) Ala. 1977, U.S. Ct. Appeals (5th cir.) 1977, U.S. Supreme Ct. 1982, U.S. Ct. Appeals (11th cir.) 1983. Atty. pub. defender div. Legal Aid. Soc. of Birmingham, 1977-78, later civil div.; dist. office atty. SBA, Birmingham, 1980-82, dist. counsel Ala. Dist., 1982—. Bd. dirs. Hoover Homeowners Assn., 1977-81. Recipient Am. Jurisprudence Criminal Procedure Book award. Mem. ABA, Fed. Bar Assn. (sec. Birmingham chpt. 1980-81), Ala. Bar Assn. (com. on future of the profession 1978-81, 83-84), Birmingham Bar Assn., Comml. Law League, Sigma Delta Kappa (Outstanding Sr. award 1977). Episcopalian. Government contracts and claims, Consumer commercial, Contracts commercial. Home: 1439 Steven Circle Birmingham AL 35226 Office: US Small Bus Adminstrn 2121 8th Ave N Room 200 Birmingham AL 35203

HOWES, BRIAN THOMAS, lawyer; b. Sioux Falls, S.D., July 23, 1957; s. Thomas A. and Joyce L. (McFarland) H.; m. Robin Kay Schoonover, June 2, 1979; children: Phillip, Adam. BS in Bus. Adminstrn. and Acctg., BA in Polit. Sci., Kans. State U., 1979; JD, U. Kans., 1982. Bar: Mo. 1982, U.S. Dist. Ct. (we. dist.) Mo. 1982. Assoc. Shughart, Thomson & Kilroy, Kansas City, Mo., 1982-85; v.p., gen. counsel Tenenbaum-Hill Assocs., Inc., Kansas City, 1985—; speaker property tax appeals Continuing Legal Edn. in Colo., Inc. and Colo. Bar Assn., 1987. Contbg. mem. Dem. Nat. Com. Mem. ABA, Assn. Trial Lawyers Am., Kansas City Met. Bar Assn., Lawyers Assn. Kansas City, Internat. Assn. of Assessing Officers. Episcopalian. State and local taxation, Real property. Home: 222 W 66th Terr Kansas City MO 64113 Office: Tenenbaum-Hill Assocs Inc 4900 Main #1000 Kansas City MO 64112

HOWIE, BRUCE GRIFFITH, lawyer; b. Oceanside, Calif., Apr. 10, 1953; s. Donald Lynk and Virginia Mae (Farmer) H.; m. Robbyn L. Walsh, May 2, 1982. AB, Harvard U., 1975; JD, Boston U., 1978. Bar: Fla. 1978, U.S. Dist. Ct. (mid. dist.) 1979, U.S. Ct. Appeals (5th and 11th cirs.) 1979, U.S. Supreme Ct. 1982. Asst. pub. defender City of Clearwater, Fla., 1978-85; assoc. Tanney, Forde, Donahey, Eno & Tanney P.A., Clearwater, 1985—. Mem. ABA, St. Petersburg Bar Assn., Clearwater Bar Assn., Nat. Assn. of Criminal Def. Lawyers, ACLU (local v.p., counsel 1983—). Criminal, Civil rights. Office: Tanney Forde Donahey Eno & Tanney PA 13584 49th St N Clearwater FL 33520

HOWIE, JOHN ROBERT, lawyer; b. Paris, Tex., June 29, 1946; s. Robert H. and Sarah Francis (Caldwell) H.; m. Evelyn Eileen Yates, May 3, 1969; children—John Robert, Ashley Elizabeth. B.B.A., North Tex. State U., 1968; J.D., So. Meth. U., 1976. Bar: Tex. 1976, U.S. Dist. Ct. (no. dist.) Tex. 1976, U.S. Dist. Ct. (ea. dist.) Tex. 1984, U.S. Ct. Appeals (5th, 10th and 11th cirs.), U.S. Supreme Ct. 1985, U.S. Dist. Ct. (so. dist.) Tex. 1987; cert. in personal injury trial law Tex. Bd. Legal Specialization, 1982. Ptnr. Law Offices of Windle Turley, Dallas, 1976—. Editor The Verdict, 1981-86. Served to lt. comdr. USNR, 1968-77. Mem. Tex. Trial Lawyers Assn. (bd. dirs. 1983-87), Dallas Trial Lawyers Assn. (sec.-treas. 1984, v.p. 1985, pres. 1986), Assn. Trial Lawyers Am. (vice chmn. aviation sect. 1984-85, chmn. 1986), Am. Bd. Trial Advocates, ABA (vice chmn. aviation law sect. 1986-87), State Bar Tex., Dallas Bar Assn., Lawyer/Pilots Bar Assn. Democrat.

Presbyterian. Personal injury, Federal civil litigation, State civil litigation. Home: 4328 Livingston Dallas TX 75205 Office: Law Offices of Windle Turley PC 6440 N Central Expressway Suite 1000 Dallas TX 75206

HOWITT, IDELLE ANNE, lawyer; b. Providence, Dec. 4, 1949; d. Julius Harry and Shirley (Bertman) H. B.A., Boston U., 1971; J.D., Temple U., 1974; M.B.A., NYU, 1981. Bar: Pa. 1974, D.C. 1975, U.S. Supreme Ct. 1978, N.Y. 1983. Atty., Fed. Res. Bd., Washington, 1975-76; atty.-advisor U.S. Commn. on Civil Rights, Washington, 1976-79; mgr. pub. affairs Supermarkets Gen. Corp., Woodbridge, N.J., 1979-80; merger and acquisition assoc. Chase Manhattan Capital Markets Corp., N.Y.C., 1982-85; dir. bus. devel. Standard Research Cons., N.Y.C., 1985—; arbitrator Better Bus. Bur., N.Y.C., 1982-84. Bd. dirs. Mt. Vernon Coll. Sch. Bus., Washington, 1976-79. Recipient Silver Key award ABA, 1973. Mem. ABA, N.Y. Women's Bar Assn. (bd. dirs.), Nat. Assn. Women Bus. Owners (bd. dirs. 1976-79). General corporate, Pension, profit-sharing, and employee benefits, Estate planning.

HOWLAND, GARY MARVIN, lawyer; b. Abilene, Kans., Dec. 22, 1942; s. Marvin L. and Gladys Marie (Wetzel) H.; m. Joyce E. Ratliff; children: John Linly, Neal Patrick. BA in Sociology, Ft. Hays State U., 1966; M in Regional Community Planning, Kans. State U., 1970; JD, Washburn U., 1980. Bar: Kans. 1980, U.S. Dist. Ct. Kans. 1980, U.S. Supreme Ct. 1986. Constrn. engr. Hunter Constrn. Co., Hays, Kans., 1966-69; dir. state planning Dept. Community Devel., Jefferson City, Mo., 1970; asst. to gen. asst. sec. HUD, Washington, 1970-74; budget examiner OMB, Washington, 1974-77; asst. sec. Kans. Dept. Adminstrn., Topeka, 1981-84; sole practice Topeka, 1984—; cons. Kans. Dept. Econ. Devel., Topeka, 1973-74. Contbr. articles to profl. jours. Served with USAF, 1963-65. Mem. Kans. Bar Assn., Topeka-Kans. Bar Assn., Marshall County Bar Assn. (pres. 1980-81). Republican. Lutheran. General practice, Workers' compensation, Labor. Home: 2329 Ashworth Pl Topeka KS 66614 Office: 700 Jackson Suite 202 Topeka KS 66603

HOWLAND, RICHARD MOULTON, lawyer; b. Glen Cove, L.I., N.Y., Jan. 2, 1940; s. Richard Moulton and Natalie (Fuller) H.; m. Julie Rose Keschl, Sept. 28, 1974; children—Kimberly Merrill, Gillian Fuller. B.A., Amherst Coll., 1961; J.D., Columbia U., 1968. Bar: Mass. 1968. Assoc. firm Nutter, McLennen & Fish, Boston, 1968-69, DiMento & Sullivan, Boston, 1969-70; atty. for students U. Mass., Amherst, 1970-74; practice law, Amherst, 1974—; adj. prof. U. Mass., 1972-76; vis. lectr. Amherst Coll., 1983. Adv. bd. Art Inst. Boston; pres. Leverett PTO, 1981-85; bd. dirs. Leverett Craftsmen and Artists, Inc., 1986—. Served to lt. (j.g.) USNR, 1961-65. Mem. ABA (vice chmn. profl. liability com.), Boston Bar Assn., Mass. Bar Assn. (chmn. com. on chem. dependency), Franklin Bar Assn., Hampshire Bar Assn. (del. to Mass Bar Assn., sec., v.p. 1986—), Am. Trial Lawyers Assn., Mass. Acad. Trial Lawyers, Amherst C. of C. (pres. 1985-87). Club: Skating (v.p.) (Amherst). Co-editor: Lawyers Weekly, 1979—. State civil litigation, Personal injury, General practice. Home: 112 Depot Rd Leverett MA 01054 Office: 358 N Pleasant St Amherst MA 01004

HOWLETT, MICHAEL JOSEPH, JR., lawyer; b. Chgo., July 10, 1948; s. Michael Joseph and Helen (Geary) H.; m. Kathleen Fitzgerald, Oct. 2, 1970; children—Elizabeth, Melissa, Catherine. B.A., St. John's U., Collegeville, Minn., 1970; J.D., U. Notre Dame, 1973. Bar: Ill. 1973, U.S. Dist. Ct. (no. dist.) Ill. 1975, U.S. Ct. Appeals (7th cir.) 1975, Ind. 1980, U.S. Supreme Ct. 1980. Law clk. U.S. Dist. Ct., U.S. Ct. Appeals, Chgo., 1973-75; asst. U.S. atty. no. dist. Ill., Chgo., 1975; ptnr. firm Moriarty, Hultquist & Howlett, Chgo. and South Bend, Ind., 1980-83; assoc. judge Cir. Ct. Cook County (Ill.), Chgo., 1983-86; counsel, Hayes & Power, 1986-87; ptnr. Phelan, Pope & John, Ltd., Chgo., 1987—; pub. dir. Mid-Am. Commodity Exchange, Chgo., 1981-83; spl. dep. prosecutor St. Joseph County (Ind.), South Bend, 1981-83; dir., officer, treas., intervenor Lawyers Assistance Program, Chgo., 1984; panel atty. Fed. Defender Program, Inc., U.S. Dist. Ct. (no. dist.) Ill., 1977-83; adj. prof. trial practice and civil procedure John Marshall Law Sch., Chgo., 1977-79, 83-84; mem. fed. criminal jury instrns. com. 7th Cir. Ct. Appeals, Chgo., 1981—; lectr. profl. responsibility Loyola U. Law Sch., Chgo., 1984—; lectr. trial practice U. Chgo. Law Sch., 1985—. Candidate Ill. lt. gov. Adlai Stevenson Solidarity Party, 1986. Mem. Chgo. Bar Assn., Ill. Bar Assn., ABA, Ill. Judges Assn. (bd. dirs. 1984-86), Ill. Trial Lawyers Assn. Democrat. Roman Catholic. Judicial administration, State civil litigation, Legal education. Office: Phelan Pope & John Ltd 180 N Wacker Dr Suite 500 Chicago IL 60606

HOWLETT, ROBERT GLASGOW, lawyer; b. Bay City, Mich., Nov. 10, 1906; s. Lewis Glasgow and Anne Lucile (Hurst) H.; m. Barbara Withey, Sept. 19, 1936; children: Eleanor Howlett Burton, Craig G., Douglas W. BS, Northwestern U., 1929, JD, 1932. Bar: Ill. 1932, N.Y. 1940, D.C. 1944, Mich. 1947, Tenn. 1947. Ptnr. Varnum Riddering Schmidt & Howlett, Grand Rapids, Mich., 1949-83; of counsel Varnum Riddering, Schmidt & Howlett, Grand Rapids, Mich., 1983—; mem. Mich. Employment Relations Commn., 1963-76, chmn., 1964-76; chmn. Fed. Service Impasses Panel, 1976-78, 82-84, mem., 1984—; sec., bd. dirs. Light Metals Corp., Elston Richards Inc.; mem. Fgn. Service Impasse Disputes Panel, 1976-78, 81—; industry mem. shipbldg. commn. Nat. War Labor Bd., 1943-45; spl. asst. atty. gen., dept. aero. State of Mich., 1957-61; vis. prof. Mich. State U., East Lansing, 1972, 75. Contbr. articles to profl. jours. Chmn. Kent County Republican Com., 1956-61; del. Rep. Nat. Conv., 1960. Mem. ABA, Grand Rapids Bar Assn. (pres. 1962-63), State Bar Mich., Nat. Acad. Arbitrators, Indsl. Relations Research Assn. (pres. Detroit chpt. 1978-79), Soc. Profls. in Dispute Resolution (pres. 1974-75), Assn. Labor Relations Agys. (pres. 1977-78), Am. Arbitration Assn. (bd. dirs. 1975—, Disting. Service award 1982). Clubs: Kent Country, Peninsular (Grand Rapids). Labor. Home: 2910 Oak Hollow Dr SE Grand Rapids MI 49506 Office: Suite 800 171 Monroe St NW Grand Rapids MI 49503

HOWLEY, JOHN, lawyer; b. Jersey City, Apr. 18, 1908; s. Michael Emmet and Henrietta (Symes) H.; m. Gertrude Crumley Warner, Sept. 20, 1941. B.S. summa cum laude, Princeton U., 1929; LL.D., Harvard U., 1932. Bar: Ill. 1933, N.Y. 1937. Asso., Donovan, Leisure, Newton & Irvine, N.Y.C., 1934-46; ptnr. Crawford & Reed, N.Y.C., 1946-60; ptnr. Hall, Casey, Dickler & Howley, N.Y.C., 1960-76; of csl. McCabe & Mack, Poughkeepsie, N.Y., 1976—; organizer, exec. v.p. Assn. Investors in N.Y. Utilities, Inc. Served with USNR, 1943-45. Mem. Assn. Bar City N.Y. Republican. Episcopalian. Clubs: University, Millbrook Golf and Tennis. General practice. Home: Old Camby Rd Verbank NY 12585 Office: 63 Washington St PO Box 509 Poughkeepsie NY 12602

HOWLEY, LOREN BLACKMAN, lawyer; b. Washington, Jan. 13, 1953; d. Martin and Rena (Rottersman) Blackman; m. Bill Howley, Oct. 18, 1974; children: Jacob David, Isaac William. BA, Yale U., 1970; JD, W.Va. U., 1981. Bar: W.Va. 1981, U.S. Dist. Ct. (so. dist.) W.Va. 1981, U.S. Dist. Ct. (no. dist.) W.Va. 1984. Atty. W.Va. Legal Services Plan, Gassaway, 1981; sole practice Grantsville, W.Va., 1982—. Bd. dirs. Minnie Hamilton Health Care Ctr., Grantsville, W.Va., 1983-84, Heartwood Dance Ctr., Big Bend, W.Va., 1983—. Mem. ABA, W.Va. Bar Assn., Nat. Lawyers Guild. Democrat. Jewish. Avocations: dance, gardening. General practice, Family and matrimonial, Criminal. Office: PO Box 580 Grantsville WV 26147

HOWORTH, DAVID BISHOP, lawyer; b. Temple, Tex., Feb. 6, 1947; s. M. Beckett Jr. and Mary Hartwell (Bishop) H.; m. Martha Ellen Peacock, July 28, 1970; children: Katherine Somerville, Emily Hartwell. BA, Yale U., 1971; JD, U. Miss., 1975. Bar: N.Y. 1976, U.S. Dist. Ct. (so. and ea. dists.) N.Y. 1977, U.S. Ct. Appeals (2d cir.) 1984. Assoc. Dewey, Ballantine, Bushby, Palmer & Wood, N.Y.C., 1975-77, 78-83, ptnr., 1984—; asst. prof. law U. Miss., University, 1977-78. Mem. ABA, N.Y. State Bar Assn., Assn. of Bar of City of N.Y. Federal civil litigation, State civil litigation. Home: 3 Sherman St Brooklyn NY 11215 Office: Dewey Ballantine Bushby Palmer & Wood 140 Broadway New York NY 10005

HOY, CARLETON ROBERT, lawyer; b. Sioux City, Iowa, Dec. 12, 1928; s. Carl Blythe and Hazel Winnie (Bergeson) H.; m. Joan Eva Ary, June 26, 1954; children: Thomas Carleton, Scott Gregory, James Lester. BBA, U. S.D., 1950, JD, 1956. Bar: S.D. 1956, U.S. Dist. Ct. S.D. 1956, U.S. Ct. Appeals (8th cir.), U.S. SUpreme Ct. 1976. Law clk. to presiding justice U.S. Dist. Ct., Sioux Falls, 1956-57; assoc. Davenport, Evans, Hurwitz & Smith, Sioux Falls, 1957-59, ptnr., 1959—. Bd. dirs. YMCA, Sioux Falls, 1965—. Served to 1st lt. inf. U.S. Army, 1951-52, Korea. Fellow Internat. Soc. Barristers (bd. govs. 1980—, 2d v.p. 1986, 1st v.p. 1987), Am. Coll. Trial Lawyers; mem. Am. Bd. Trial Advs. (adv.), S.D. Bar Assn. (pres. 1979-80), S.D. Trial Lawyers Assn. (pres. 1968-69), Fedn. Ins. Counsel. Republican. Congregationalist. Club: Minnehaha Country (Sioux Falls) (pres. 1975). Lodge: Rotary (pres. local club 1971-72), Masons, Shriners. Federal civil litigation, State civil litigation, Personal injury. Home: 1209 Cedar Pl Sioux Falls SD 57103 Office: Davenport Evans Hurwitz & Smith 513 S Main Ave Sioux Falls SD 57102-0993

HOYNE, ANDREW THOMAS, lawyer; b. Urbana, Ill., Oct. 5, 1947; s. Robert M. and Avonne L. (Andrews) H.; m. Janet Watson, Apr. 11, 1970; children: Matthew, Benjamin, Emily. BA, Knox Coll., 1969; JD, Washington U., St. Louis, 1974, LLM, 1982. Bar: Mo. 1974, U.S. Supreme Ct. 1979. Assoc. gen. counsel, asst. sec. Seven-Up Co., St. Louis, 1974-87, Invitron Corp., St. Louis, 1987—. Participant Leadership St. Louis, 1984-85. Served to 1st lt. U.S. Army, 1969-71. Mem. ABA, Mo. Bar Assn., Bar Assn. Met. St. Louis (chmn. ho. counsel com. 1981-82, chmn. bus. law sect. 1983-84, treas. 1984-85, sec. 1985-86). General corporate, Real property, Corporate taxation. Office: Seven-Up Co 121 S Meramec Saint Louis MO 63105

HOYNE, SCOTT WILLIAM, lawyer; b. Evanston, Ill., Feb. 16, 1950; s. Thomas Maclay and Doris (Olson) H.; m. Melinda Smith, Dec. 5, 1981; children: Megan, Lindsey. BA, Northwestern U., 1972, JD, 1975. Bar: Ill. 1975, U.S. Dist. Ct. (no. dist.) Ill. 1975, U.S. Ct. Appeals (7th cir.) 1975. Assoc. Peterson, Ross, Schloerb & Seidel, Chgo., 1975-78, Conklin & Adler Ltd., Chgo., 1978-83, Crotty & Hoyne, Chgo., 1983—. Avocations: skiing, tennis. Insurance, Commercial, corporate, General practice. Home: 458 E Carpenter Dr Palatine IL 60067 Office: Crotty & Hoyne 30 S Wacker Dr Suite 2812 Chicago IL 60606

HOYNES, LOUIS LENOIR, JR., lawyer; b. Indpls., Sept. 23, 1935; s. Louis L. and Catharine (Parker) H.; m. Judith E. Kass, Oct. 12, 1958 (div. 1979); children: Thomas M., William D., Ellen B.; m. Virginia Devin, Dec. 9, 1979. AB, Columbia U., 1957; JD cum laude, Harvard U., 1962. Bar: N.Y. 1963, U.S. Supreme Ct. 1967, U.S. Dist. Ct. (so. dist.) N.Y., U.S. Ct. Appeals (2d cir.), U.S. Ct. Appeals (7th cir.) 1986. Assoc. Willkie, Farr & Gallagher, N.Y.C., 1962-68, ptnr., 1969—; lectr. law Columbia U., N.Y.C., 1982—. Served to lt. USNR, 1957-59, PTO. Mem. ABA, N.Y. State Bar Assn., Assn. of City of Bar of N.Y. Federal civil litigation, General corporate, Labor. Home: 47 Cornwells Beach Rd Sands Point NY 11050 Office: Willkie Farr & Gallagher One Citicorp Ctr 153 E 53rd St New York NY 10022

HOYT, MARCIA SWIGART, lawyer; b. Massillon, Ohio, Aug. 4, 1944; d. Robert William and Delores Jane (Swaney) Swigart; m. Kenneth Loyd Hoyt, Apr. 6, 1974. B.Ed., Ohio U., 1966, M.Ed., 1970; J.D., Ohio State U., 1979. Bar: Ohio 1979. Dir. Ohio State U., Columbus, 1970-76; assoc. firm Hahn, Loeser Freedheim, Dean & Wellman, Cleve., 1979-81; asst. counsel AmeriTrust Co., Cleve., 1981-84; atty. Roadway Services, Inc., Akron, Ohio, 1984-85; sole practice, Columbus, 1985—. Vice pres. Cleve. Independence Day Assn.; trustee Project Friendship, Inc., Cleve. Mem. ABA, Ohio Bar Assn., Bar Assn. Greater Cleve, Columbus Bar Assn. Republican. Lutheran. Contracts commercial, General corporate, Labor. Home: 8345 Greyrocks Way Worthington OH 43085 Office: 51 N High St Suite 481 Columbus OH 43215

HOYT, MONT POWELL, lawyer; b. Oklahoma City, Apr. 3, 1940; s. Lester Dean and Paula (Powell) H.; m. Alice Nathalie Ryan, June 15, 1974; children: Mont Powell Jr., Kathleen, Michael, Caroline. B.A., Northwestern U., 1962; J.D., Okla. Law Sch., 1965; M.C.L., U. Chgo., 1968. Bar: Okla., 1965, Tex., 1968. Law clk. U.S. Dist. Ct., Oklahoma City, 1965; stagiaire to French advocat Paris, 1967-68; assoc. Baker and Botts, Houston, 1968-75, ptnr., 1975—; adj. prof. U. Houston, 1970-76;. Contbr. articles to profl. jours. Bd. dirs. French Am. Found., N.Y.C., 1979-85; elder Memorial Drive Presbyterian Ch., 1973-76, 83-86; ann. giving chmn. Episcopal High Sch., 1985-86. Mem. ABA (chmn. sect. internat. law and practice 1984-85), Internat. Bar Assn. (counsil sect. of energy and nat. resources law), Am. Soc. Internat. Law, Am. Arbitration Assn., French Am., German Am. C. of C. (bd. dirs. 1978—), U. Chgo. Law Sch. Alumni Assn. (v.p. 1980—), Council on Fgn. Relations. Clubs: Houston Country, Coronado (Houston), Metropolitan (Washington). Avocations: golf, tennis, running, international affairs. Private international, General corporate, Contracts commercial. Office: Baker and Botts 3000 One Shell Plaza Houston TX 77006

HRITZ, GEORGE F., lawyer; b. Hyde Park, N.Y., Aug. 28, 1948; s. George F. and Margaret M. (Callahan) H.; m. Suzan Courtney Hritz, July 6, 1982. A.B., Princeton U., 1969; J.D., Columbia U., 1973. Bar: N.Y. 1974, D.C. 1978, U.S. Supreme Ct. 1979. Law clk. U.S. Dist. Ct. (ea. dist.) N.Y., N.Y.C., 1973; assoc. Cravath, Swaine & Moore, N.Y.C., 1974-77; counsel U.S. Senate Select Com. Ethics Korean Inquiry, Washington, 1977-78; ptnr. Moore & Foster, Washington, 1978-80, Davis, Markel & Edwards, N.Y.C., 1980—; assoc. ind. counsel, Washington, 1986—. Bd. dirs. Internat. Rescue Com. Mem. ABA (internat. law sect.), D.C. Bar Assn., Bar Assn. City of N.Y. Club: Princeton. Federal civil litigation, State civil litigation, Private international. Office: Davis Markel & Edwards 100 Park Ave Suite 3200 New York NY 10017

HRUSKA, ALAN J., lawyer; b. N.Y.C., July 9, 1933. B.A., Yale U., 1955, LL.B., 1958. Bar: N.Y. 1959, U.S. Supreme Ct. 1970. Assoc. firm Cravath, Swaine & Moore, N.Y.C., 1958-67; ptnr. Cravath, Swaine & Moore, 1968—; chmn. planning and program com. 2d Circuit Jud. Conf., 1974-80; co-chmn. 2d Circuit Commn. Reduction of Burdens and Costs in Civil Litigation, 1977-80; commr. N.Y. State Exec. Adv. Commn. on Adminstrn. of Justice, 1981-83. Author: Borrowed Time, 1984. Mem. ABA, Am. Coll. Trial Lawyers, N.Y. State Bar Assn., Assn. of Bar of City of N.Y. (sec. 1965-66), Fed. Bar Council (trustee 1976—, pres. elect 1983-84, pres. 1984-86), Inst. Jud. Adminstrn. (trustee 1978—, pres. 1982-85). Office: Cravath Swaine & Moore One Chase Manhattan Plaza New York NY 10005

HSU, ROGER Y. K., lawyer; b. Tientsin, China, Apr. 9, 1927; came to U.S., 1948, naturalized, 1962; s. Mary C. Hsu; m. Evangeline C. Chung, Aug. 12, 1950; children: Daphne, Jeffrey. B.S., St. John's U., Shanghai, China, 1948; M.S., U. Mass., 1951; Ph.D., Case Western Res. U., 1953, J.D., 1964. Bar: Ohio 1964. With Lubrizol Corp., Wickliffe, Ohio, 1952—; now sr. v.p. law Lubrizol Corp.; lectr. organic chemistry Cleve. State U. Mem. Am. Bar Assn., Am. Arbitration Assn., Union Internationale des Avocats, Sigma Xi. Home: 14445 Hartwell Novelty OH 44072 Office: The Lubrizol Corp 29400 Lakeland Blvd Wickliffe OH 44092

HUANG, THOMAS WEISHING, lawyer; b. Taipei, Taiwan, Feb. 1, 1941; arrived U.S., 1967; s. Lienden and Helen (Yen) H. B.A., Taiwan U., 1964; J.D. magna cum laude, Ind. U. Indpls., 1970; LL.M., Harvard U., 1971, S.J.D., 1975. Bar: D.C. 1975, Mass. 1976, U.S. Dist. Ct. Mass. 1976, U.S. Ct. Appeals (1st cir.) 1978, N.Y. 1980. Judge advocate Chinese Army, Taiwan, 1964-65; legal officer Treaty and Legal Dept., Ministry of Fgn. Affairs, Taiwan, 1966-67; assoc. Chemung County Legal Services, Elmira, N.Y., 1975-76; assoc. law firm Taylor Johnson & Wieschhoff, Marblehead, Mass., 1980; prin. Reiser & Rosenberg, Boston, 1982-86, Huang & Assocs., Boston, 1987—; exec. v.p. Excel Tech. Internat. Co., Brunswick, N.J., 1982—; legal counsel Nat. Assn. Chinese Ams., Washington, 1979-80. Mem. editorial bd. Ind. Law Forum, 1969-70; contbr. articles to legal jours. Bd. dirs. Chinese Econ. Devel. Council, Boston, 1978-80; mem. Gov.'s Adv. Council on Guangdong, 1984—. Mem. Boston Bar Assn. (mem. internat. law sect. steering com. 1979—, mem. ad hoc com. on code of profl. conducts), ABA, Nat. Assn. Chinese Ams. (v.p. Boston chpt. 1984-86, pres. 1986—). Democrat. Contracts commercial, Immigration, naturalization, and customs, Private international. Home: 30 Farrwood Dr Andover MA 01810 Office: 4 Longfellow Pl 37th Floor Boston MA 02114

HUBBARD, ELIZABETH LOUISE, lawyer; b. Springfield, Ill., Mar. 10, 1949; d. Glenn Wellington and Elizabeth (Frederick) H.; m. A. Jeffrey Seidman, Oct. 27, 1974 (div. May 1982). Student Millikin U., 1967-69; B.A., U. Ky., 1971; J.D. with honors, Ill. Inst. Tech.-Chgo. Kent Coll. Law, 1974. Bar: Ill. 1974, U.S. Dist. Ct. (no. dist.) Ill. 1974, U.S. Ct. Appeals (7th cir.) 1976, U.S. Supreme Ct. 1984. Atty. Wyatt Co., Chgo., 1974-75, Gertz & Giampietro, Chgo., 1975-76, Baum, Sigman, Gold, Chgo., 1976-81, Elizabeth Hubbard, Ltd., Chgo., 1981—; legal counsel NOW, Chgo., 1978—, sec., 1977. Editor Chgo. Kent Law Rev., 1970. Bd. dirs., mem. The Remains Theatre, 1985—. Mem. Chgo. Bar Assn. (fed. civil procedure com.), Ill. State Bar Assn., Women's Bar Assn. Democrat. Civil rights, General corporate, Family and matrimonial. Office: 55 E Monroe Chicago IL 60603

HUBBARD, GEORGE MORRISON, III, lawyer; b. Summit, N.J., Apr. 21, 1947; s. George Morrison and Elizabeth (Jones) H.; m. Mary Smith, Aug. 4, 1973; children—Samuel Morrison, Elizabeth Anne. B.S., U. Vt., 1970; J.D., U. Miss., 1974. Bar: Miss. 1974, Ga. 1974, U.S. Dist. Ct. (no. dist.) Miss. 1974, U.S. Dist. Ct. (so. dist.) Ga. 1974, U.S. Ct. Appeals (5th cir.) 1978, U.S. Ct. Appeals (11th cir.) 1981, U.S. Supreme Ct. 1984. Assoc. Calhoun Hubbard, Riddle & Cox., P.C., Savannah, Ga., 1974-84; sole practice, Savannah, 1985—; cons. Aero-Med Internat., Inc., Savannah, 1983—, Fields Life-Care, Inc., Savannah, 1979-85, Travel Health-Care Internat., 1985—. Mem. ABA, Am. Trial Lawyers Assn., Ga. Assn. Criminal Def. Lawyers, Ga. Trial Lawyers Assn., Plaintiff Trial Lawyers of Savannah (pres. 1982). Republican. Club: Marshwood Country (Savannah). Family and matrimonial, Criminal, Juvenile. Home: 1418 Dale Dr Savannah GA 31406 Office: 21 E York St Savannah GA 31401

HUBBARD, ROBERT DALE, lawyer; b. Jackson, Miss., Mar. 3, 1949; s. John William and Bobbie Nell (Vance) H.; m. Georgia Sue Gray, Mar. 13, 1971; children: Neilson Gray, Aubrey Claire. BS, Miss. State U., 1971; JD with distinction, Miss. Coll. of Law, 1981. Bar: Miss. 1981. Sole practice Jackson, 1981-83; ptnr. Ferrell & Hubbard, Jackson, 1983—. Served to capt. USAR, 1971-81. Named one of Outstanding Young Men in Am., 1985. Mem. ABA (constrn. and industry com., corp., banking and bus. law sect., liaison young lawyers div. to forum com. on air and space law 1983-84), Miss. Bar Assn. (membership services com.), Hinds County Bar Assn. (law day bar com.), Jackson Young Lawyers Assn. (legal line com.), Assn. Trial Lawyers Am., Miss. Trial Lawyers Assn. (chmn. brief bank com. 1984-85, 85-86). Avocations: golf, snow skiing. Personal injury, General practice, Construction. Office: Ferrell & Hubbard 405 Tombigbee St Jackson MS 39201

HUBBARD, THOMAS EDWIN (TIM), lawyer; b. Roseboro, N.C., July 10, 1944; s. Charles Spence and Mary Mercer (Reeves) H.; m. Leslie Howard, July 20, 1985; 1 child, Marvin Gannon. BS in Biomed. Engring., Duke U., 1970, postgrad., 1970-71; JD, U. N.C., 1973. Bar: N.C. 1973. Regulation writer, med. devices FDA, Washington, 1974-75; asst. dir. clin. affairs Zimmer USA, Warsaw, Ind., 1975, dir. regulatory affairs, 1975-76; house counsel Gen. Med. Corp., Richmond, Va., 1976-79; sole practice, Pittsboro, N.C., 1979—; pres. Chathamborough Research Group, Inc., Sanford, Ct., 1982—, Chathamborough Farms Inc., 1982—; sec., treas. Hubbard-Corry, Inc., Pittsboro, 1981—; chmn. Hubbard Bros., Inc., Chapel Hill, N.C., 1982-87; bd. dirs. No. State Legal Service, Hillsborough, N.C., 1980—, pres., 1986—. V.p. N.C. Young Dems. 4th Congl. Dist., 1970-71; mem. State Dem. Exec. Com., 1972-73. Served to sgt. USMC, 1963-67. Mem. ABA, N.C. Bar Assn., Assn. for Advancement Med. Instrumentation (govt. affairs com. 1976). Democrat. Methodist. Administrative and regulatory, Personal injury, Food and Drug. Office: Chathamborough Research Group Inc 105 West St Pittsboro NC 27312

HUBBELL, CALVIN KEITH, lawyer; b. Gary, Ind., Feb. 10, 1933; s. Charles Wagner Hubbell and Ora (Wyatt) Hoffman; m. Beverly Joyce Stephens, Feb. 29, 1956; children: Calvin Keith (dec.), Stephen Ross. BS, Ind. U., 1957, JD, 1960. Bar: Ill. 1960, U.S. Dist. Ct. (no. dist.) Ill. 1960, U.S. Ct. Appeals (7th cir.) 1963, U.S. Supreme Ct. 1965, Ind. 1972, U.S. Dist. Ct. (so. dist.) Ind. 1972, U.S. Dist. Ct. (no. dist.) Ind. 1974, U.S. Ct. Appeals (6th cir.) 1980. Asst. gen. solicitor Consol. Rail Corp., Chgo., 1960-71; assoc. James A. Dooley and Assocs., Chgo., 1971-73; sole practice Valparaiso, Ind., 1973—. Mem. Ind. U. Law Jour., 1959-60. Served with U.S. Army, 1951-54. Mem. ABA, Ill. Bar Assn., Ind. Bar Assn., Porter County Bar Assn., Nat. Assn. Criminal Def. Lawyers, Assn. Trial Lawyers Am., Ind. Trial Lawyers Assn., Ind. Assn. Criminal Def. Lawyers. Republican. State civil litigation, Criminal, Personal injury. Home: 610 Yellowstone Rd Valparaiso IN 46383 Office: 802 LaPorte Ave Valparaiso IN 46383

HUBBELL, ERNEST, lawyer; b. Trenton, Mo., Aug. 28, 1914; s. Platt and Maud Irene (Ray) H.; m. Nevah Smith, Apr. 25, 1943; 1 child, Platt Thorpe. AA, Trenton Jr. Coll., 1934; JD, Georgetown U., 1938. Bar: D.C. 1937, Mo. 1938, U.S. Supreme Ct. 1946. Practice Trenton, 1938-39, Jefferson City, Mo., 1939-42; sole practice Kansas City, Mo., 1947-52; ptnr. Hubbell, Sawyer, Peak & O'Neal (formerly Hubbell, Lane & Sawyer), Kansas City, Mo., 1952—; asst. atty. gen. Mo., 1939-42; first chmn. bench, bar com. 16th Jud. Cir. Ct., Kansas City, 1964-69, mem 16th Cir. Jud. Nominating Commn., 1970-75; mem. U.S. Cir. Judge Nominating Commn., 1977-80. Trustee Legal Aid and Defender Soc. Greater Kansas City, 1964-73; mem. Law Found. U. Mo. Kansas City, 1966-71; chmn. Nat. Council on Crime and Delinquency, 1966-76; pres. Hubbell Family Hist. Soc., 1981-85; mem. Soc. Fellows Nelson Art Gallery. Served with USAAF, 1942-44; to capt. AUS, 1944-46. Mem. ABA, Kansas City Met. Bar Assn. (pres. 1963-64, ann. Achievement award 1974, 1st ann. Litigator Emeritus award), Mo. Bar Assn., Assn. Trial Lawyers Am. (assoc. editor R.R. law sect. of jour. 1951—), Mo. Assn. Trial Attys. (pres. 1954, editor bull. 1955), Lawyers Assn. Kansas City, Lawyers Assn. St. Louis, Archeol. Inst. Am., SAR. Episcopalian. Democrat. Club: Kansas City. Personal injury, Federal civil litigation, State civil litigation. Home: 1210 W 63d St Kansas City MO 64113 Office: Hubbell Sawyer Peak O'Neal Power & Light Bldg 106 W 14th St 25th floor Kansas City MO 64105

HUBER, MELVYN JAY, lawyer; b. N.Y.C., May 18, 1929; s. Solomon and Gilda (Gochman) H.; m. Helen Elizabeth Ruth Talbert, Sept. 28, 1950; children—Michael Clay, David Talbert, Victoria Lynne. B.A. (Rector scholar 1947-49), DePauw U., 1949; J.D., Columbia U., 1954; M.S. in Fin. Services, Am. Coll., 1982. Bar: N.Y. 1955, U.S. Dist. Ct. (so. dist.) N.Y. 1980, U.S. Tax Ct., U.S. Supreme Ct. 1984, U.S. Dist. Ct. (ea. dist.) N.Y., 1986. Assoc. Paul Weiss, Rifkind, Wharton & Garrison, N.Y.C., 1954-56; supr. Mut. Benefit Life Ins. Co., N.Y.C., 1956-61, gen. agt., 1961-63; gen. agt. Mass. Mut. Life Ins. Co., N.Y.C., 1963-74; v.p. Manhattan Life Ins. Co., N.Y.C., 1975-76; sole practice, N.Y.C. and New Rochelle, N.Y., 1976—; faculty N.Y. Ctr. Fin. Studies. New Rochelle chmn. for Republican gubernatorial campaign, 1967; capt. Aux. Police, Scarsdale, N.Y. Served to capt. USMC, 1950-52. Mem. Am. Soc. C.L.U.s (pres. N.Y. chpt. 1971-72, bd. dirs. 1972-75, bd. dirs. jour. 1970-75, bd. dirs. Westchester chpt. 1986—), N.Y.C. Bar Assn., ABA, Lawyers in MENSA, Nat. Rifle Assn., Theodore Roosevelt Assn., Mensa, Marine Corps Officers Assn. Author in field. Probate, Pension, profit-sharing, and employee benefits, Insurance. Office: 60 E 42d St New York NY 10165

HUBER, RICHARD GREGORY, lawyer, educator; b. Indpls., June 29, 1919; s. Hugh Joseph and Laura Marie (Becker) H.; m. Katherine Elizabeth McDonald, June 21, 1950; children: Katherine, Richard, Mary, Elizabeth, Stephen, Mark. B.S., U.S. Naval Acad, 1942; J.D., U. Iowa, 1950; LL.M., Harvard U., 1951; LLD, New England Sch. Law, 1985. Bar: Iowa 1950. Instr. law U. Iowa, 1950; assoc. prof. law U. S.C., 1952-54; assoc. prof. Tulane U., 1954-57; assoc. prof. Boston Coll., 1957-59, prof., 1959—, dean, 1970-85. Contbr. articles and book reviews to profl. jours. Vice chmn. Mass. chpt. Multiple Sclerosis Soc.; pres. bd. trustees Beaver Country Day Sch. Served with USN, 1941-47, 51-52. Mem. ABA (del., mem. council legal edn., trustee law sch. admissions council), Mass. Bar Assn., Boston Bar Assn.; Am. Bar. Found. ; Mem. Soc. Am. Law Tchrs., Mass. Bar Found., Assn. Am. Law Schs. (pres. elect 1987-88), Council of Legal Edn. Opportunity (pres. 1975-79), Flaschner Jud. Inst., Am. Judicature Soc. Democrat. Roman Catholic. Condemnation, Legal education, Real property. Home: 406 Woodward St Newton MA 02168 Office: 885 Centre St Newton MA 02159

HUBERMAN, RICHARD LEE, lawyer; b. Lynn, Mass., Dec. 6, 1953; s. Irving Morris and Selma Edythe (Wolk) H. AB, Harvard U., 1975, JD, 1978. Bar: Mass. 1979, D.C. 1979. Atty. Office of Rail Pub. Counsel, Washington, 1978-80; counsel subcom. on commerce, consumer protection

and competitiveness (formerly commerce, transp. and tourism) U.S. Ho. of Reps., Washington, 1980—. Mem. ABA, Mass. Bar Assn., Harvard Law Sch. Assn. Democrat. Club: Harvard (Washington). Legislative, Administrative and regulatory. Home: 1316 New Hampshire Ave NW #204 Washington DC 20036 Office: Ho Subcom on Commerce Consumer Protection and Competitiveness Rm H2-151 Annex 2 Washington DC 20515

HUBSCHMAN, HENRY ALLAN, lawyer; b. Newark, N.J., Aug. 12, 1947; s. Morris and Esther (Weissman) H. B.A., Rutgers U., 1969; J.D., Harvard U., 1973, M.Public Policy, 1973. Bar: Mass. 1973, N.J. 1974, D.C. 1974. Law clk. to presiding justice U.S. Dist. Ct. Mass., Boston, 1973-74; assoc. Fried, Frank, Harris, Shriver & Jacobson, Washington, 1974-77, 79-80; partner 1980—; exec. asst. to Sec. HUD, Washington, 1977-79; dir. Fed. Nat. Mortgage Assn., 1979—. Henry Rutgers scholar, 1969; Recipient Outstanding Achievement award HUD, 1978, HUD Sec.'s award for excellence, 1979. Mem. Am. Bar Assn., Phi Beta Kappa. Democrat. Jewish. Federal civil litigation, Securities, Insurance. Home: 3832 Gramercy St NW Washington DC 20016 Office: 1001 Pennsylvania Ave NW Washington DC 20004

HUBSCHMAN, RICHARD ANTHONY, JR., lawyer; b. Englewood, N.J., Nov. 8, 1955; s. Richard A. and Mary Ann (Valentino) H.; m. Linda Ann Fitzsimmons, July 23, 1983. AA, U. Fla., 1975; BS, Fairleigh Dickinson U., 1977; JD, Nova U., 1981. Bar: N.J. 1981, Fla. 1981, U.S. Dist. Ct. N.J. 1981, U.S. Tax Ct. 1981, U.S. Ct. Appeals (3d cir.) 1981. Assoc. Panetta & Sassano, Ft. Lee, N.J., 1981-83; ptnr. Hubschman & Rotolo, Englewood Cliffs, N.J., 1983-86; sole practice Palisades Park, N.J., 1986—; prosecutor Borough of Ft. Lee, 1982; asst. county counsel Bergen County, Hackensack, N.J., 1986—. Councilman Englewood Cliffs, 1986—; mem. com. Bergen County, 1984-85. Mem. Ft. Lee Unico. Republican. Roman Catholic. Lodges: Lions, Rotary. Real property, Consumer commercial, Contracts commercial. Office: 318 Bergen Blvd Palisades Park NJ 07650

HUDDLESTON, JOSEPH RUSSELL, judge; b. Glasgow, Ky., Feb. 5, 1937; s. Paul Russell and Laura Frances (Martin) H.; m. Heidi Wood, Sept. 12, 1959; children: Johanna, Lisa, Kristina. Bar: Ky. 1962, U.S. Ct. Appeals (6th cir.) 1963, U.S. Supreme Ct. 1970. Ptnr. Huddleston Bros. & Duncan, Bowling Green, Ky., 1962-87; judge Warren Cir. Ct. Div. I, 1987—; mem. Adv. Com. for Criminal Law Revision, 1969-71; mem. exec. com. Ky. Crime Commn., 1972-77. Mem. ABA, Ky. Bar Assn. (ho. of dels. 1971-80), Assn. Trial Lawyers Am. (state del. 1981-82), Ky. Acad. Trial Attys. (bd. govs. 1975—, pres. 1978), Bowling Green Bar Assn. (pres. 1972), So. Ky. Estate Planning Council (pres. 1983), Bowling Green-Warren County C. of C. (bd. dirs. 1987), Phi Alpha Delta. Democrat. Episcopalian. Clubs: Port Oliver Yacht (Bowling Green); Jefferson (Louisville); Princeton (N.Y.C.). Home: 1704 Rollingwood Way Bowling Green KY 42101 Office: The Justice Ctr 925 Center St PO Box 3000 Bowling Green KY 42102-3000

HUDETZ, JOSEPH BERNARD, lawyer, accountant, printing company executive; b. Chgo., Aug. 27, 1947; s. John Francis and Gwendolyn M. (Palmer) H.; m. Patricia A. Kelleher, May 17, 1969; children: Joseph, Christopher, Sarah. BS, No. Ill. U., 1969; postgrad. in bus. adminstrn. Loyola U., Chgo., 1974; JD, Ill. Inst. Tech., 1978; CPA, U. Ill., 1974. Bar: Ill. 1979, U.S. Supreme Ct. 1979, U.S. Tax Ct. 1980. Acct., asst. controller SCM Corp., Chgo. and Cleve., 1970-75; owner, operator System 27, advt. firm, Oak Brook, Ill., 1975-82; ptnr. Hudetz Mindel & Assocs., Oak Brook 1978—, Savage & Assocs., CPA's, Oak Brook, 1979—; chief fin. officer, legal counsel Solar Press, Naperville, Ill., 1982—, also bd. dirs. Mem. ABA, Ill. Bar Assn., Am. Inst. CPA's. Republican. Roman Catholic. Lodge: Rotary (pres. Plainfield). General corporate, Corporate taxation, Pension, profit-sharing, and employee benefits. Office: Solar Press 1120 Frontenac Dr Naperville IL 60566

HUDIAK, DAVID MICHAEL, paralegal program administrator, lawyer, educator; b. Darby, Pa., June 27, 1953; s. Michael Paul and Sophie Marie (Glowaski) H.; m. Veronica Ann Barbone, Aug. 28, 1982; 1 child, David Michael Jr. BA, Haverford Coll., 1975; JD, U. Pa., 1978. Bar: Pa. 1979, U.S. Dist. Ct. (ea. dist.) Pa. 1979, N.J. 1981, U.S. Dist. Ct. N.J. 1981. Assoc. Jerome H. Ellis, Phila., 1978-79, Berson, Fineman & Bernstein, Phila., 1979-80; sole practice Aldan, Pa., 1980-81; dir. tng. paralegal program PJA Sch., Upper Darby, Pa., 1982—; mem. staff Nat. Ctr. Ednl. Testing, Phila., 1982—; instr. Villanova (Pa.) U., 1985. Mem. ABA, Pa. Bar Assn. Legal education, General practice. Office: PJA Sch 7900 W Chester Pike Upper Darby PA 19082

HUDNER, PHILIP, lawyer, rancher; b. San Jose, Calif., Feb. 24, 1931; s. Paul Joseph and Mary E. (Dooling) H.; m. Carla Raven, Aug. 6, 1966; children—Paul Theodor, Mary Carla, William Charles. B.A. with great distinction, Stanford U., 1952, LL.B., 1955. Bar: Calif. 1955. Atty. Pillsbury, Madison & Sutro, San Francisco, 1958—, ptnr., 1970—; rancher San Benito County, Calif., 1970—. Asst. editor: Stanford Law Rev., 1954-55; author articles on estate and trust law. Pres. Soc. Calif. Pioneers, 1976-78; bd. governance Coll. Notre Dame, Belmont, Calif., 1980-83, trustee, sec., 1983—; trustee, sec. Louise M. Davies Found., 1974—; trustee James A. Folger and Jane C. Folger Found., 1976—; bd. dirs., sec.,treas. Drum Found., 1983—. Served with U.S. Army, 1956-58. Fellow Am. Bar Found.; mem. Internat. Acad. Estate and Trust Law (steering com. 1974-75, exec. council 1980—), Attys. Probate Assn. San Francisco (1st v.p.), Am. Coll. Probate Counsel, San Benito County Saddle Horse Assn., Phi Beta Kappa. Democrat. Roman Catholic. Clubs: Pacific Union, Lagunitas Country, Frontier Boys, Rancheros Visitadores. Office: 225 Bush St San Francisco CA 94104

HUDNUT, STEWART, manufacturing company executive, lawyer; b. Cin., Apr. 29, 1939; s. William Herbert and Elizabeth Allen (Kilborne) H.; m. Penelope Pleger, June 15, 1963; children—Alexander, Andrew, Parker. A.B., Princeton U., 1961; postgrad., Oxford U., Eng., 1962; J.D., Harvard U., 1965. Bar: N.Y. 1965, U.S. Dist. Ct. (so. and ea. dists.) N.Y., U.S. Ct. Appeals (2d cir.). Assoc. Davis Polk & Wardwell, N.Y.C., 1965-73, Paris, 1968-70; v.p., asst. gen. counsel Bankers Trust Co., 1973-77; v.p., gen. counsel, sec. Scovill Inc., Waterbury, Conn., 1977—. Contb. editor Modern Banking Forms. Sec., trustee Assn. for Protection of Adirondacks; bd. dirs. Litchfield Land Trust, Conn.; tchr. Parent Effectiveness Tng.; bd. dirs., mem. exec. com. United Way of Naugatuck Valley Inc.; bd. dirs. ARC. Woodrow Wilson fellow, Keasbey fellow. Mem. ABA, Conn. Bar Assn., Greater Waterbury C. of C. (bd. dirs.). Republican. Episcopalian. Club: U. Western Conn. General corporate. Home: North St Litchfield CT 06759

HUDSON, CAROLYN ANNE, lawyer; b. Indpls., Nov. 25, 1944; d. Harry Albert and Nancy Bess (Ridge) Koss; m. Lucien Newport Hudson Jr., July 2, 1966; 1 child, Leigha Lynn. BE, U. Fla., 1970; JD, U. San Diego, 1980, LLM in Taxation, 1984. Bar: Calif. 1980, U.S. Dist. Ct. (so. dist.) Calif. 1981. Commd. 2d lt. USMC, 1974, advanced through grades to maj., 1986; major USMCR, 1986—; assoc. Littler, Mendelson, Fastiff & Tichy, San Diego, 1986—. Recipient Tribute to Women and Industry YMCA, 1984, Tribute to Women in Govt. Calif. Women in Govt., 1983; named one of Outstanding Young Women in Am., 1980. Mem. Calif. Bar Assn., San Diego County Bar Assn., San Diego Trial Lawyers Assn. Avocations: painting, interior design. Labor. Home: 6932 Jackson Dr San Diego CA 92119 Office: Littler Mendelson Fastiff & Tichy 701 B St San Diego CA 92101

HUDSON, DIRK LUDWIG, lawyer; b. Berkeley, Calif., Jan. 19, 1937; s. William Lester and Virginia Frances (Ludwig) H.; m. Sharon Jean Kuker, Feb. 15, 1969; children—Maura Ann, Deirdre Elizabeth, Holman Lester. B.A., San Francisco State U., 1964; J.D., U. Calif., Berkeley, 1967. Bar: Calif. 1968, U.S. Dist. Ct. (no. dist.) Calif. 1968, U.S. Dist. Ct. (cen. dist.) Calif. 1973, U.S. Ct. Appeals (9th cir.) 1973, U.S. Supreme Ct. 1980. Research asst. Dist. Atty., Contra Costa County, Martinez, Calif., 1966-67; dep. dist. atty. Los Angeles County, 1968—. Pres. Young Ams. for Freedom, San Francisco State U., 1964; mem. anti-pornography task force, Los Angeles County, 1986, com. to rev. recommendations of U.S. Atty. Gen.'s Commn. on Pornography, 1986. San Francisco State U. Scholar, 1963-64. Mem. Boalt Hall Alumni Assn., Nat. Dist. Atty.'s Assn., Calif. Dist. Atty.'s Assn., Phi Alpha Delta. Club: Commonwealth of Calif. State appellate litigation, Federal appellate litigation, Criminal. Office: Office of Dist Atty Los Angeles County 211 W Temple St Los Angeles CA 90012

HUDSON, GEORGE NAYLOR, lawyer; b. Lewes, Del., Sept. 17, 1944; s. John Wallace Jr. and Myrtle (Bunting) H.; m. Elizabeth Mamilton Lyon, June 11, 1966; children: Heather H., George N. Jr. BA, Davis and Elkins Coll., 1966; JD, Coll. of William and Mary, 1972. Bar: Va., Del. Commd. 2d lt. USAF, 1966, advanced through grades to lt. col., 1987, with Res., 1974—; chief mil. justice USAF, Dover, Del., 1972-74; ptnr. Vaughn & Hudson, Dover, 1974-76; assoc. Bayard, Handelman & Murdoch, P.A., Wilmington, 1976—; senate atty. Del. State Senate, Dover, 1974-77; pres., bd. dirs. Dur-Cel, Inc. 1984-86. treas. Lt. Gov. Campaign Fund, Dover, 1976-80; chmn. Ins. Dept. Transition Commn., Dover, 1985, Worker's Compensation Task Force, Del., Dover, 1984—. Mem. ABA, Del. Bar Assn., Va. Bar Assn., Kent County Bar Assn. Democrat. Presbyterian. Club: Del. Mobile Surf Fisherman. Legislative, Insurance, Workers' compensation. Home: Rd 2 Box 954 Smyrna DE 19977 Office: Bayard Handelman & Murdoch PA 200 Bank Delaware Bldg Suite 200 Dover DE 19901

HUDSON, HENRY E., lawyer. U.S. atty. ea. dist. State of Va., Alexandria. Office: 2d Floor 701 Prince St Alexandria VA 22314 *

HUDSON, JAMES PATRICK, lawyer; b. Georgetown, S.C., Feb. 4, 1955; s. Samuel Bosket and Sara Vermelle (Thompson) H.; m. Zina Audinet Ashton, Feb. 5, 1983. BA in Psychology, Davidson Coll., 1977; JD, U. S.C., 1980. Bar: S.C. 1980, U.S. Dist. Ct. S.C. 1980, U.S. Ct. Appeals (4th cir.) 1984, D.C. 1985. Mem. atty. gens. office State of S.C., Columbia, 1984-85; assoc. Johnson, Toal & Battiste, Columbia, S.C., 1985—. Served to capt. JAGC, U.S. Army, 1981-84. Mem. Assn. Trial Lawyers Am., S.C. Trial Lawyers Assn. (long range planning com. 1985—). Democrat. Baptist. State civil litigation, Personal injury, Criminal. Home: 2104 Sapling Dr Columbia SC 29210 Office: Johnson Toal & Battiste PA 1801 Gadsden St PO Box 1431 Columbia SC 29202

HUDSON, PAUL STEPHEN, lawyer, consultant; b. N.Y.C., June 25, 1947; s. William Burchill and Maybelle (Schleicher) H.; m. Eleanor J. Rossi, June 6, 1970; children: Stephen, Melina, Paul, David. BS, U. Mich., 1968; JD, Cleve. State U., 1974. Bar: Ohio 1974, N.Y. 1976. Systems analyst Chase Brass & Copper Co., Cleve., 1969-71; investigator Ohio Civil Rights Commn., Cleve., 1971-73; legal intern Cleve. Legal Aid Soc., 1973; staff atty. N.Y. Pub. Interest Research Group, Inc., Albany, 1974-77; legis. counsel Pub. Utility Law Project, Albany, 1977; counsel N.Y. State Crime Victims Bd., Albany and N.Y.C., 1977-87; cons. ABA, Washington, 1982-83, Nat. Inst. Justice, Hindelany Criminal Justice Ctr., 1987. Contbr. articles to profl. jours. Co-chmn., co-founder Ohio Pub. Interest Research Group, Cleve., 1974; exec. dir. N.Y. Student Voter Registration Drive, Albany and N.Y.C., 1976; mem. Ctr. Sq. Neighborhood Assn., Albany, 1976—; pres. Citizens Protecting the Environment, Schenectady, 1979-80. Mem. ABA (crime victims com. 1984—), Nat. Orgn. of Victims Assistance (chmn. litigation com. 1983-84). Democrat. Presbyterian. Administrative and regulatory, Legislative, Criminal. Office: 90 State St Suite 527 Albany NY 12207

HUDSPETH, CHALMERS MAC, lawyer, educator; b. Denton, Tex., Oct. 18, 1919; s. Junia Evans and Ethel (Burns) H.; m. Demaris Eleanor De Lange, Jan. 30, 1945; children: Albert James, Thomas Richard, Helen Demaris. B.A., Rice U., Houston, 1940; J.D., U. Tex., 1946. Bar: Tex. 1946. Practiced in Houston, 1947—; sr. mem. firm De Lange, Hudspeth, Pitman & Katz, 1968—; asst. prof. law U. Tex. at Austin, 1946-47; lectr. govt. Rice U., 1947—, bd. govs., 1980—, trustee, 1982—; vis. prof. law U. Houston, 1950-52; dir. Stewart Info. Services Corp., Stewart Title Guaranty Co. Author: Torts—A Baker's Dozen, 2d edit, 1976; Contbr. articles to profl. jours. Mem. bi-racial com. Houston Ind. Sch. Dist., 1955-56; trustee, v.p. Brown Found., 1983—. Served to lt. USNR, 1942-45. Fellow Am. Bar Found., Tex. Bar Found., Am. Coll. Probate Counsel; mem. ABA, Tex. Bar Assn., State Bar Tex. (dir. 1966-68, v.p. 1968-69), Houston Philos. Soc. (pres. 1964-65), Houston Com. on Fgn. Relations (chmn. 1973-74), Petroleum Club of Houston, Chancellors, Order of Coif, Phi Delta Phi. Federal civil litigation, Estate planning, Real property. Office: 2800 Summit Tower 11 Greenway Plaza Houston TX 77046

HUDSPETH, HARRY LEE, judge; b. Dallas, Dec. 28, 1935; s. Harry Ellis and Hattilee (Dudney) H.; m. Vicki Kathryn Round, Nov. 27, 1971; children—Melinda, Mary Kathryn. B.A., U. Tex., Austin, 1955, J.D., 1958. Bar: Tex. bar 1958. Trial atty. Dept. Justice, Washington, 1959-62; asst. U.S. atty. Western Dist. Tex., El Paso, 1962-69; mem. firm Peticolas, Luscombe & Stephens, El Paso, 1969-77; U.S. magistrate El Paso, 1977-79; U.S. dist. judge Western Dist. Tex., El Paso, 1979—. Bd. dirs. Sun Carnival Assn., 1976, Met. YMCA El Paso, 1980—. Mem. U. Tex. Ex-students Assn. (exec. council 1980-86), Am. Bar Assn., El Paso Bar Assn., Chancellors, Order Coif, Phi Beta Kappa. Democrat. Mem. Christian Ch. (Disciples of Christ.). Jurisprudence. Home: 9337 Turrentine St El Paso TX 79925 Office: 433 US Courthouse El Paso TX 79901

HUDSPETH, STEPHEN MASON, lawyer; b. Pitts., Jan. 22, 1947; s. Harold Mason and Edna Mary (Lawrenson) H.; m. Rebecca Anne Ellis, Apr. 3, 1971; children—David, Catherine. B.A., M.A. magna cum laude, Yale U., 1968, J.D., 1971. Bar: N.Y. 1973, Pa. 1973, U.S. Dist. Ct. (so. and ea. dists.) N.Y. 1973, Mass. 1974, U.S. Dist. Ct. (ea. dist.) Pa. 1975, U.S. Ct. Appeals (1st cir.) 1976, U.S. Ct. Appeals (2d cir.) 1973, U.S. Ct. Appeals (3d cir.) 1977, U.S. Supreme Ct. 1980, Maine 1987. Assoc., Lord, Day & Lord, N.Y.C., until 1979, ptnr., 1979-86, ptnr., Coudert Bros., 1986—, N.Y.C. adj. asst. prof. bus. law Wagner Coll., 1973-83. Contbr. articles to profl. jours. Vestryman St. Alban's Episcopal Ch., S.I., N.Y., 1979-85, warden, 1985-87; chmn. Stewardship Commn. Diocese of N.Y., 1987—; trustee S.I. Zool. Soc., 1982-87. Served from 2d lt. to capt. C.E., USAR, 1968-73. Mem. ABA, N.Y. State Bar Assn., Assn. Bar City N.Y., Phi Beta Kappa. Episcopalian. Antitrust, Federal civil litigation. Address: 25 Broadway New York NY 10004

HUEBNER, KURT BENOIT, lawyer; b. Hammond, Ind., Feb. 17, 1955; s. Paul B. and Carol A. (Lindholm) H. BA, Butler U., 1976; JD, Ind. U., 1979. Bar: Ind. 1979, U.S. Dist. Ct. (so. dist.) Ind. 1979, Calif. 1982, U.S. Dist. Ct. (cen., so., ea. and no. dists.) Ind. 1982, U.S. Ct. Appeals (9th cir.) 1982, U.S. Supreme Ct. 1983. Chief dep. court reporter Ind. Ct. of Appeals, Indpls., 1979-81; assoc. Severson, Werson, Berke & Melchior, Los Angeles, 1981-83, Parker, Milliken, Clark & O'Hara, Los Angeles, 1983-84, Wyman, Bautzer, Rothman, Kuchel & Silbert, Los Angeles, 1984-85, Pachter, Gold & Schaffer, Los Angeles, 1985-86; sole practice West Hollywood, Calif., 1986—. Mem. ABA, Calif. Bar Assn., Ind. Bar Assn., Los Angeles County Bar Assn., Assn. So. Calif. Def. Counsel, Phi Kappa Psi. Democrat. Presbyterian. Federal civil litigation, State civil litigation, Insurance. Home and Office: 1025 N Kings Rd #110 West Hollywood CA 90069

HUEBNER, TED RAYMOND, lawyer; b. Portage, Wis., Feb. 6, 1950; s. William Joseph and Agnes (Lytle) H.; m. Wendy Ann Lansing, May 20, 1979; children: Julie Kim, Katie Michelle, Michael Scott. BS, U. Minn., 1972; JD, UCLA, 1975. Bar: Calif. 1975. Assoc. Ansell & Ansell, Los Angeles, 1975-77, McLaughlin & Irvin, Los Angeles, 1977-79; ptnr. Lober, Clark & Huebner, Los Angeles, 1979-83, Huebner & Hirshfield, Los Angeles, 1983—. Mem. Los Angeles County Bar Assn., U. Minn. Alumni Assn., Beta Gamma Sigma, Delta Sigma Pi. Avocations: golf, flower gardening, creative writing. Labor. Office: Huebner & Hirshfield 6380 Wilshire Blvd #1115 Los Angeles CA 90048

HUEGEL, PETER ANDREW VINCENT, lawyer; b. South Bend, Ind., Apr. 4, 1951; s. Frank John and Berdine Katherine (Greenleaf) H.; m. Palmira Reyna, Nov. 28, 1975; children: Melina Rae, Kaitlin Brier. BA, U. Calif., Berkeley, 1973; MS, Troy State U., 1978; JD magna cum laude, U. Houston, 1981. Bar: Tex. 1982, Calif. 1983, U.S. Supreme Ct. 1985. Assoc. Kemp, Smith, Duncan & Hammond, El Paso, Tex., 1981-82, Pillsbury, Madison & Sutro, San Francisco, 1982-84; sr. counsel Am. Pres. Companies, Oakland, Calif., 1984—. Served to lt (j.g.) USNR, 1974-79. Mem. ABA, Order of Barons, Phi Beta Kappa. Republican. Avocations: mountaineering, rockclimbing. General corporate, Contracts commercial, Securities. Home: 2789 Canyon Creek Dr San Ramon CA 94583 Office: Am Pres Companies Ltd 1800 Harrison St Oakland CA 94612

HUETTNER, RICHARD ALFRED, lawyer; b. N.Y.C., Mar. 25, 1927; s. Alfred F. and Mary (Reilly) H.; children—Jennifer Mary, Barbara Bryan; m. 2d, Eunice Bizzell Dowd, Aug. 22, 1971. Marine Engrs. License, N.Y. State Maritime Acad., 1947; B.S., Yale U. Sch. Engring., 1949; J.D., U. Pa., 1952. Bar: D.C. 1952, N.Y. 1954, U.S. Ct. Mil. Appeals 1953, U.S. Ct. Claims 1961, U.S. Supreme Ct. 1969, U.S. Ct. Appeals (fed. cir.) 1982, also other fed. cts, registered to practice U.S. Patent and Trademark Office 1957, Canadian Patent Office 1968. Engr. Jones & Laughlin Steel Corp., 1954-55; assoc. atty. firm Kenyon & Kenyon, N.Y.C, 1955-61; mem. firm Kenyon & Kenyon, 1961—; specialist patent, trademark and copyright law. Trustee N.J. Shakespeare Festival, 1972-79, sec., 1977-79; trustee Overlook Hosp., Summit, N.J., 1978-84, 86—, vice chmn. bd. trustees, 1980-82, chmn. bd. trustees, 1982-84; trustee Overlook Found., 1981—, chmn. bd. trustees, 1986—; trustee Colonial Symphony Orch., Madison, N.J., 1972-82, v.p. bd. trustees 1974-76. pres. 1976-79; chmn. bd. overseers N.J. Consortium for Performing Arts, 1972-74; mem. Yale U. Council, 1978-81; bd. dirs. Yale Communications Bd., 1978-80; chmn. bd. trustees Center for Addictive Illnesses, Morristown, N.J., 1979-82; rep. Assn. Yale Alumni, 1975-80, chmn. com. undergrad. admissions, 1976-78, bd. govs., 1976-80, chmn. bd. govs., 1978-80; chmn. Yale Alumni Schs. Com. N.Y., 1972-78; assoc. fellow Silliman Coll., Yale U., 1976—; bd. dirs., exec. com. Yale U. Alumni Fund, 1978-81; mem. Yale Class of 1949 Council, 1980—; bd. dirs. Overlook Health Systems, 1984—. Served from midshipman to lt. USNR, 1945-47, 52-54; cert. JAGC 1953; Res. ret. Recipient Yale medal, 1983. Fellow N.Y. Bar Found.; mem. Am., N.Y. State bar assns., Assn. Bar City N.Y., N.Y. Patent-Trademark-Copyright Law Assn. (chmn. com. meetings 1961-64, chmn. com. econ. matters 1966-69, 72-74), AAAS, N.Y. Acad. Scis., N.Y. County Lawyers Assn., Am. Intellectual Property Law Assn., Internat. Patent and Trademark Assn., Am. Judicature Soc., Yale Sci. and Engring. Assn. (v.p. 1973-75, pres. 1975-78, exec. bd. 1972—), Fed. Bar Council. Clubs: Yale (N.Y.C.); Yale of Central N.J. (Summit) (trustee 1973—, pres. 1975-77), Morris County Golf (Convent, N.J.); The Graduates (New Haven). Patent, Trademark and copyright, Federal civil litigation. Home: 150 Green Ave Madison NJ 07940 Office: Kenyon & Kenyon One Broadway New York NY 10004

HUEY, DIANE MARIE, lawyer; b. Tacoma, Apr. 29, 1941; d. Robert A. and Frankie (Lytle) H. BA, U. Wash., 1963, MA in Teaching, 1971; JD, U. Puget Sound, Tacoma, 1978. Bar: Wash. 1978, U.S. Dist. Ct. (we. dist.) Wash. 1978. Tchr. Shoreline Sch. Dist., Seattle, 1963-75; sole practice Seattle, 1978—. Editor A Gourmet's Notebook mag., 1977—. Mem. Seattle Women Bus. Owners Assn. (pres. 1981), Women Plus Bus. (bd. dirs. 1983-85), Mortar Bd. Democrat. State civil litigation, General practice, Probate. Office: 226 Summit Ave E Seattle WA 98102

HUFF, R. ROBERT, lawyer; b. El Dorado Springs, Mo., Oct. 19, 1924; s. Roy M. and Rubena M. (Johnson) H.; m. Barbara Lemmon, Nov. 9, 1946; children: Harriet Huff Gooding, Beverly Huff Blair. Student U. Tulsa, 1942-43; BS, U. Okla., 1946, JD, 1949. Bar: Okla. 1949, U.S. Dist. Ct. (no. dist.) Okla. 1950, U.S. Dist. Ct. (ea. and we. dists.) Okla. 1953, U.S. Ct. Appeals (10th cir.) 1953, U.S. Ct. Appeals (5th cir.) 1969, U.S. Supreme Ct. 1979. Assoc. Kulp, Pinson, Lupardus & Kothe, Tulsa, 1949; ptnr. Kothe & Huff, Tulsa, 1950-57; sole practice, 1957-64; ptnr. Huff & Huff, Inc., 1964—; of counsel Doerner, Stuarrt, Saunders, Daniel & Anderson, 1985—; temporary instr. wills and estates U. Tulsa; dir. various corps. Chmn. bd. trustees Southwestern Art Assn.-Philbrook Art Center, Tulsa, 1974-75. Served with inf. U.S. Army, 1943-45. Decorated Bronze Star. Mem. Tulsa County Bar Assn., Okla. Bar Assn., ABA, Am. Coll. Probate Counsel, Tulsa Estate Planning Forum, Tulsa Mineral Law Assn. Author: Oklahoma Probate Law and Practice, 2d edit., 1982. General corporate, Oil and gas leasing, Probate. Office: 1000 Atlas Life Bldg Tulsa OK 74103

HUFFAKER, GREGORY DORIAN, JR., lawyer; b. Phila., Nov. 30, 1944; s. Gregory Dorian Sr. and Suzanne (Adams) H.; m. Katrina Morris, Aug. 28, 1976; 1 child, Gregory D. III. BA, Columbia U., 1973; JD, Harvard U., 1976. Bar: N.Mex. 1977; U.S. Dist. Ct. N.Mex. 1977; U.S. Ct. Appeals (10th cir.) 1978. Law clk. assoc. justice John Paul Stevens, U.S. Supreme Ct., Washington, 1976-77; dir. Poole, Tinnin & Martin, Albuquerque, 1977—. Author: (with others) Your New Lawyer, 1983. Bd. dirs. La Luz Landowners Assn., Albuquerque, 1982—; rep. Coalition Albuquerque Neighborhoods, 1984; active Albuquerque Com. Fgn. Relations, 1983—. Served to 1st lt. U.S. Army, 1967-69. Mem. ABA, Rocky Mountain Mineral Law Inst. Federal civil litigation, Environment, Civil rights. Home: 19 Tennis Ct NW Albuquerque NM 87120 Office: Poole Tinnin & Martin 219 Central NW Albuquerque NM 87102

HUFFMAN, GERALD JAMES, JR., lawyer; b. St. Louis, Aug. 5, 1955; s. Gerald James and Eithel Patricia (Caldwell) H.; m. Gwendolyn Gretchen Roesky, Feb. 15, 1985; 1 child, Gerald James III. BA, Rice U., 1976; JD, U. Houston, 1979. Bar: Tex. 1979, La. 1981. Assoc. Neel, Hooper & Kalmans, Houston, 1979-80, Milling, Benson, Woodward, Hillyer, Pierson & Miller, New Orleans, 1981—; sec., bd. dirs. Control Techs., Metairie, La. Mem. ABA (labor and employment law sect.), Fed. Bar Assn., La. Bar Assn. (labor law sect.), New Orleans Bar Assn., New Orleans and River Region East Bank Council C. of C., Metairie Jaycees. Republican. Avocations: computer, books, sports. Labor, Civil rights, Construction. Home: 4936 Purdue Dr Metairie LA 70003 Office: Milling Benson Woodward et al 1100 Whitney Bldg New Orleans LA 70130

HUFFMAN, GREGORY SCOTT COMBEST, lawyer; b. Austin, Tex., Dec. 19, 1946; s. Calvin Combest and Olive Agnes (Weaver) H.; m. Mary L. Murphy, Feb. 1, 1986. Student, Stanford U., France, 1966-67; BA in History with honors, Stanford U., 1969; postgrad., London Sch. of Econs., 1971-72; JD, Harvard U., 1973. Bar: Tex. 1973, U.S. Dist. Ct. Tex. 1974, U.S. Ct. Appeals (5th cir.) 1975, U.S. Supreme Ct. 1976. From assoc. to sr. ptnr. Thompson & Knight, Dallas, 1973—. Chief editor: Monograph Texas Free Enterprise and Antitrust Act, 1984. Pres. Northern Hills Neighborhood Assn., 1980; bd. dirs. Common Cause of Tex., 1979-81, Love Field Citizens Action Commn., 1980-83. Fellow Tex. Bar Found.; mem. ABA (antitrust and litigation sect.), Tex. Bar Assn. (antitrust and litigation sect., chmn. unlawful practice of law com. 1981-83, chmn. lawyer referral service com. 1982-83, bd. legal specialization 1974-77, bd. dirs. antitrust sect. 1983—), Dallas Bar Assn. (antitrust sect., sec.-treas. 1981, chmn. unauthorized practice of law com. 1979, chmn. lawyer referral service com. 1980-81, chmn. profl. services com. 1986—, bd. dirs. antitrust sect. 1981), Phi Beta Kappa, Sigma Alpha Epsilon. Club: Tower (Dallas). Antitrust, Federal civil litigation, State civil litigation. Home: 3610 Armstrong Ave Dallas TX 75205 Office: Thompson & Knight 3300 First City Ctr Dallas TX 75201

HUFFMAN, JAMES LLOYD, legal educator; b. Fort Benton, Mont., Mar. 25, 1945; s. Roy E. and Menga (Herzog) H.; m. Katherine A. Schultz, June 27, 1946; children—Kurt Andrew, Erica Leigh. Student Stanford U., 1963-64; B.S., Mont. State U., 1967; M.A.L.D., Fletcher Sch. Law and Diplomacy, 1967-68; J.D., U. Chgo., 1972. Asst. prof., then assoc. prof. Lewis and Clark Law Sch., Portland, Oreg., 1973-78, prof. law, 1978—, assoc. dean, 1978-80, dir. natural resources law inst.; vis. prof. Auckland U. (N.Z.), 1980-81; mem. com. socioecon. effects of earthquake prediction Nat. Acad. Scis., 1977-80. NSF grantee, 1976-77, 81-84; Office of Water Research Dept. Interior grantee, 1978-80; Raymond fellow, 1973. Mem. Am. Soc. Legal History, Rocky Mountain Mineral Law Found. (trustee). Author: The Allocation of Water to Instream Flows: A Comparative Study of Policy Making and Technical Information in the States of Colorado, Idaho, Montana and Washington, 1980; Government Liability and Disaster Mitigation: A Comparative Study, 1986; contbr. articles to profl. jours. Constitutional, Jurisprudence, Environment. Home: 3708 SW Canby Portland OR 97219 Office: Lewis & Clark Sch Law Portland OR 97219

HUFFMAN, ROBERT ALLEN, JR., lawyer; b. Tucson, Dec. 30, 1950; s. Robert Allen and Ruth Jane (Hicks) H.; m. Marjorie Kavanagh Rooney, Dec. 30, 1976; children—Katharine Kavanagh, Elizabeth Rooney, Robert Allen III. B.B.A., U. Okla., 1973, J.D., 1976. Bar: Okla. 1977, U.S. Dist. Ct. (no. dist.) Okla. 1977, U.S. Ct. Appeals (10th cir.) 1978, U.S. Supreme Ct.

1982. Assoc. Huffman, Arrington, Kihle, Gaberino & Dunn, Tulsa, 1977-81, ptnr. 1981—. Mem. ABA, Tulsa County Bar Assn., Fed. Energy Bar Assn. Republican. Roman Catholic. Clubs: Southern Hills Country (Tulsa), Tulsa Club. General corporate, Public utilities, Real property. Home: 5808 S Delaware Tulsa OK 74105 Office: Huffman Arrington Kihle Gaberino & Dunn 1000 ONEOK Plaza Tulsa OK 74103

HUFFMAN, ROBERT ALLEN, lawyer; b. Havelock Nebr., May 1, 1921; s. Orville Frank and Stella (Winkler) H.; m. Ruth Hicks, Dec. 30, 1946; children—Robert Allen, Margaret Jane, William Hicks, Elizabeth Kay. J.D., U. Ariz., 1952. Bar: Ariz. 1952, Okla. 1952. Assoc. Huffman Arrington Kihle Gaberino & Dunn and predecessors, Tulsa, 1952-54, ptnr., 1954-61, sr. ptnr., 1961—; mem. legal com. Interstate Oil Compact Commn., 1971—. Chmn. bd. dirs. Tulsa Charity Horse Show, 1977-80, pres., 1975-77, exec. v.p., 1974-75; mem. exec. com. Children's Med. Ctr., 1982—, pres. bd. of trustees, 1986—. Served to lt. col. AUS, Decorated Bronze Star, Purple Heart. Mem. Mid-Continent Oil & Gas Assn. (legal com. 1965—), Am. Gas Assn. (mem. legal sect. mng. com. 1978—), ABA, Ariz. Bar Assn., Okla. Bar Assn., Tulsa County Bar Assn. Clubs: Southern Hills Country, Summit, Tulsa (Tulsa); Garden of the Gods (Colorado Springs, Colo.). General corporate, Public utilities. Home: 7232 S Atlanta Pl Tulsa OK 74136 Office: 1000 ONEOK Plaza Tulsa OK 74103

HUFFMAN, WILLIAM HICKS, lawyer; b. Tulsa, June 21, 1955; s. Robert Allen and Ruth Jane (Hicks) H.; m. Julia Lynn Webb, Sept. 19, 1981 (div. May 1986); 1 child, William Hicks Jr. BBA, U. Okla., 1977; JD, U. Tulsa, 1982. Bar: Okla. 1982. Atty. State of Okla. Commn., Oklahoma City, 1982-84; assoc. Carson, Rayburn, Pierce & Mueller, Oklahoma City, 1984—; active Interstate Oil Commn., Oklahoma City, 1985—. Mem. ABA (natural resources sect.), Okla. Mineral Bar Assn., Oklahoma County Bar Assn. Republican. Presbyterian. Club: Southern Hills Country Club (Tulsa). Avocation: golf. Oil and gas leasing, Administrative and regulatory, State civil litigation. Home: 2517 NW 61st Oklahoma City OK 73112 Office: Carson Rayburn Pierce & Mueller 3727 NW 63d Oklahoma City OK 73116

HUFFORD, CARL BENSON, lawyer; b. Frankfort, Ind., Oct. 1, 1943; s. Carl Benson and Martha Katherine (Merchant) H.; m. Brea Ann Manetta, July 5, 1981; 1 son, Cameron Benson. B.A. cum laude, Coll. Wooster, 1965; J.D., Columbia U., 1968. Bar: Ohio 1968, U.S. Ct. Appeals (6th cir.) 1968, Ariz. 1971, U.S. Dist. Ct. Ariz. 1971, U.S. Ct. Appeals (9th cir.) 1979, U.S. Ct. Appeals (D.C. cir.) 1980. Assoc., Taft, Stettinius and Hollister, Cin., 1968-70; atty. in charge Tuba City (Ariz.) office DNA People's Legal Services, 1971-74; ptnr. Ward, Hufford and Blue, Flagstaff, 1974-79; sole shareholder, pres. C. Benson Hufford, P.C., Flagstaff, 1979-82; shareholder, pres. Hufford and Horstman, P.C., Flagstaff, 1982—. Mem. NSBA Council Sch. Attys.; bd. dirs., vice-pres. DNA People's Legal Services, 1980-84; bd. dirs. Hozhoni Found. for Handicapped, Inc., Big Bros. of Falstaff. Served with U.S. Army, 1968-69. Fellow Ariz. State Bar Found. (founding); mem. ABA, Nat. Orgn. Legal Problems of Edn., Am. Arbitration Assn. (panel of arbitrators), Ariz. Bar Assn., Ohio Bar Assn., Coconino County Bar Assn. (pres. 1982), Navajo Nation Bar Assn., Phi Alpha Delta. Democrat. Legal education. Office: PO Box B Flagstaff AZ 86002

HUFFSTETLER, NOAH HAYWOOD, III, lawyer; b. Charlotte, N.C., Mar. 26, 1951; s. Noah Haywood Jr. and Ruth (Bumgardner) H.; m. Dorothy Barnette Carnes, Aug. 10, 1974; 1 child, Noah Haywood IV. AB, U. N.C., 1973, JD, 1976. Bar: N.C. 1976, U.S. Dist. Ct. (ea. dist.) N.C. 1976, U.S. Ct. Appeals (4th cir.) 1981, U.S. Supreme Ct. 1983. Assoc. Moore & Van Allen (formerly Allen, Steed & Allen), Raleigh, N.C., 1976-79; ptnr. Moore, Van Allen, Allen & Thigpen (formerly Allen, Steed & Allen), Raleigh, N.C., 1979-87, Moore & Van Allen (formerly Moore, Van Allen, Allen & Thigpen), Raleigh, N.C., 1987—. Contbr. articles to profl. jours. Bd. advisors U. N.C. Sch. Pub. Health. Morehead scholar John Motley Morehead Found., Chapel Hill, N.C., 1969. Mem. ABA, Am. Arbitration Assn. (nat. panel of comml. arbitrators), N.C. Bar Assn. (health law sect.), N.C. Soc. Health Care Attys., Wake County Soc. for Prevention of Cruelty to Animals, Raleigh C. of C., Phi Beta Kappa. Baptist. Lodge: Civitan (parliamentarian Raleigh club). Health, Federal civil litigation, State civil litigation. Home: 2109 Fallen Oaks Ct Raleigh NC 27608 Office: Moore & Van Allen PO Box 26507 Raleigh NC 27611

HUG, PROCTER RALPH, JR., judge; b. Reno, Mar. 11, 1931; s. Procter Ralph and Margaret (Beverly) H.; m. Barbara Van Meter, Apr. 4, 1954; children—Cheryl Ann, Procter James, Elyse Marie. B.S., U. Nev., 1953; LL.B., J.D., Stanford U., 1958. Bar: Nev. 1958. With firm Woodburn, Wedge, Blakey, Folsom & Hug, Reno, 1963-77; U.S. judge 9th Circuit Ct. Appeals, Reno, 1977—; Chmn. Nev. State Bar Com. on Jury Inst.; dep. atty. gen., State of Nev.; v.p., dir. Nev. Tel. & Tel. Co., 1958-77. Vice pres. Young Democrats Nev., 1960-61; Chmn. bd. regents U. Nev.; bd. visitors Stanford Law Sch. Served to lt. USNR, 1953-55. Recipient Outstanding Alumnus award U. Nev., 1967, Disting. Nevadan citation, 1982. Mem. ABA (bd. govs. 1976-78), Nat. Assn. Coll. and Univ. Attys. (past mem. exec. bd.), U. Nev. Alumni Assn. (past pres.), Stanford Law Soc. Nev. (pres.). Office: 601 Liberty Center 350 S Center St Reno NV 89501

HUGE, HARRY, lawyer; b. Deshler, Nebr., Sept. 16, 1937; s. Arthur and Dorothy (Vor de Strasse) H.; m. Reba Kinne, July 2, 1960; 1 child, Theodore. A.B., Nebr. Wesleyan U., 1959; J.D., Georgetown U., 1963. Bar: Ill. 1963, D.C. 1965, S.C. 1985. Assoc. Chapman & Cutler, Chgo., 1963-65; assoc. Arnold & Porter, Washington, 1965-71, ptnr., 1971-76; sr. ptnr. Rogovin, Huge & Lenzner, Washington, 1976—; dir. DBA Systems, Inc., Melbourne, Fla., 1967-78, 81—, Huge Sales, Inc., Gatlinburg, Tenn., 1978—, Signal Apparel Co., Inc., Chattanooga, 1983—, Nat. Bank of Washington, 1986—; chmn. Am. Equity Investors, Inc., Washington, 1986—; chmn., trustee United Mine Workers Health and Retirement Funds, 1973-78. Contbr. articles to legal jours. Pres. Voter Edn. Project, Atlanta, 1974-78; mem. Pres.'s Gen. Adv. Com. Arms. Control, 1977-81; bd. trustees Nebr. Wesleyan U., 1978—; mem. task force local govt. Greater Washington Research Ctr., 1981-82. Served with U.S. Army, 1960; with USNG, 1960-65. Mem. ABA (co-chmn. legis. com. litigation sect. 1981), D.C. Bar Assn. (bd. profl. responsibility 1976-81). General corporate, General practice, Federal civil litigation. Home: 628 Boyle Ln McLean VA 22102 Office: Rogovin Huge & Lenzner 1730 Rhode Island Ave NW Washington DC 20036 also: Suite 311 Marriott Ctr Hilton Head Island SC 29938

HUGHES, ANDY KARL, lawyer; b. Mendenhall, Miss., June 6, 1958; s. William Nathan and Nellie Joyce (Kirkley) H.; m. Elizabeth Margett McGhee, Aug. 18, 1984. BA, Miss. Coll., 1978; JD, U. Miss., 1981. Bar: Miss. 1981, U.S. Dist. Ct. (no. and so. dists.) Miss. 1981, U.S. Ct. Appeals (5th cir.) 1981, U.S. Ct. Mil. Appeals 1984, U.S. Ct. Mil. Rev. 1984, U.S. Ct. Appeals (11th cir.) 1985, Ala. 1986, U.S. Dist. Ct. (mid. dist.) Ala. 1986. Sole practice Magee, Miss., 1981-84; commd. 1st lt. JAGC, U.S. Army, 1984, advanced through grades to capt., 1985; legal asst. officer JAGC, U.S. Army, Ft. Rucker, Ala., 1985, trial counsel, 1985-86, sr. defense counsel, 1986—. Mem. ABA, Am. Trial Lawyers Assn., Miss. Prosecuters Assn. (bd. dirs. 1982-83), Alpha Chi, Omicron Delta Kappa, Phi Alpha Delta. Southern Baptist. Lodges: Magee Lions (sec.-treas. 1981-84), Optimists (v.p. local chpt. 1983-84). Avocations: reading, electronics. Military, Criminal, General practice. Home: 806 Pine Ave Ozark AL 36360 Office: US Army Trial Defense Service Fort Rucker AL 36362-5355

HUGHES, BYRON WILLIAM, lawyer, oil exploration company executive; b. Clarksdale, Miss., Nov. 8, 1945; s. Byron B. and Francis C. (Turner) H.; m. Sarah Eileen Goodwin, June 23, 1973; children—Jennifer Eileen, Stephanie Ann. B.A., U. Miss., 1968; J.D., Jackson Sch. Law (now Miss. Coll. Law), 1971. Bar: Miss. 1971, U.S. Supreme Ct. 1975. Atty., abstractor Miss. Hwy. Dept., 1971-76; atty., ind. landman Byron Hughes Oil Exploration Co., Jackson, Miss., 1976—; tchr. high sch.; real estate broker. Mem. ABA, Miss. Bar Assn., Hinds County Bar Assn., Am. Judicature Soc., Am. Landmen Assn., Miss. Landmen Assn., Ala. Landmen Assn., Black Warrior Basin Petroleum Landmen Assn., Ole Miss. Alumni Assn., Miss. Coll. Alumni Assn. Methodist. Club: Miss. Art Assn. Oil and gas leasing, Real property. Home: 101 Spencer Cove Clinton MS 39056 Office: PO Box 1485 Jackson MS 39205

HUGHES, CARL DOUGLAS, lawyer; b. Sapulpa, Okla., Aug. 29, 1946; s. Kenneth Gordon and Louise (Coffield) H.; m. Alice M. Hughes, May 12, 1978; children—Sarah Elizabeth, Kenneth James. B.B.A., U. Okla., 1968, J.D., 1971. Bar: Okla. 1971, U.S. Sup. Ct. 1974. Assoc. Stipe, Gossett, Stipe & Harper, Oklahoma City, 1971-76; ptnr. Hughes & Nelson, and predecessors, Oklahoma City, 1976—. Legal counsel Okla. Democratic Party, 1978-83; gen. counsel Spl. Olympics, 1976—, chmn., 1981, 84, 85, 86, 87. Served to capt. U.S. Army Res., 1968-73. Mem. Okla. Trial Lawyers Assn. (dir. 1971-78, chmn. judiciary com. 1977-78, chmn. criminal law com. 1981), Okla. Bar Assn., Oklahoma County Bar Assn. Episcopalian. Mem. editorial bd., torts editor Advocate mag., 1975-78. Personal injury, Criminal, Federal civil litigation. Home: 5909 Oak Tree Rd Edmond OK 73034 Office: 5801 N Broadway Ext Suite 302 Oklahoma City OK 73118

HUGHES, DAVID EMERY, lawyer; b. Pitts., Aug. 24, 1947; s. William George and Margaret (Torok) H. BA, Am. U., 1968; JD, Georgetown U., 1971. Bar: D.C. 1971, U.S. Dist. Ct. D.C. 1971, U.S. Ct. Appeals (D.C. cir.) 1972, Maine 1975, U.S. Supreme Ct. 1975. Assoc. Steptoe & Johnson, Washington, 1971-75; asst. counsel Unum Life Ins. Co., Portland, Maine, 1975-76, 2d v.p. external affairs, 1976-84, v.p., gen. counsel, 1984, sr. v.p., gen. counsel, 1984—; bd. dirs. Union Mutual/NY, N.Y.C. bd. dirs. United Way Greater Portland, 1981-85, Budget Rev. Orgn. Maine; bd. dirs., exec. com. Maine Council Econ. Edn. Mem. Maine Bar Assn., D.C. Bar Assn., Am. Soc. CLU, Health Ins. Assn. Am. (chmn. govt. relations com. 1985—), Maine State C. of C. (bd. dirs.). Democrat. Unitarian. Club: Portland Yacht. Avocations: sailing, skiing, tennis. General corporate, Insurance, Legislative. Office: Unum Life Ins Co 2211 Congress St Portland ME 04122

HUGHES, DENNIS MICHAEL, lawyer; b. N.Y.C., Apr. 6, 1951; s. Richard Lawrence Sr. and Mary Lorraine (Carney) H.; m. Teresa Maria Lonczynski, Aug. 11, 1979; children: Erin Lindsey, Alison Marie. BS, St. John's U., N.Y.C., 1978; JD, Cath. U. Am., 1981. Bar: D.C. 1981, Md. 1982, U.S. Dist. Ct. D.C. 1982, U.S. Dist. Ct. Md. 1982, U.S. Ct. Appeals (4th and D.C. cirs.) 1982. Assoc. Plaia & Schaumberg, Washington, 1981-86, Howrey & Simon, Washington, 1986—. Editor Cath. U. Law Rev., 1980-81. Served with USN, 1972-76. Mem. ABA, Md. Bar Assn., D.C. Bar Assn., Montgomery Bar Assn., Assn. Trial Lawyers Am. Contracts commercial, Federal civil litigation, Trademark and copyright. Office: Howrey & Simon 1730 Pennsylvania Ave NW Washington DC 20006

HUGHES, JAMES DONALD, lawyer; b. Houston, June 5, 1951; s. D. E. and Ruby Christine (Wagstaff) H. BS, Stanford U., 1973; JD, U. Tex., 1976; LLM in Taxation, NYU, 1978. Bar: Tex. 1976, Ala. 1979, U.S. Dist. Ct. (so. dist.) Ala. Assoc. O.N. Baker Inc., Houston, 1977, Armbrecht, Jackson, Demovy, Crowe, Holmes & Reeves, Mobile, Ala., 1978—. Mem. ABA (taxation and real property probate and trust sects.). Avocations: photography, stained glass, sports. Pension, profit-sharing, and employee benefits, Probate, Corporate taxation. Office: Armbrecht Jackson Demovy et al PO Box 290 Mobile AL 36601

HUGHES, JOHN DAVID, lawyer, consultant; b. Lubbock, Tex., Apr. 24, 1935; s. John A. and Pauline (Goode) H.; m. Karin Lillian Lofgren, Apr. 17, 1965; children: John Erik, Stefan David. BBA, U. Tex., 1958; JD, Am. U., 1961. Bar: Tex. 1964, U.S. Dist. Ct. (no. dist.) Tex. 1964, U.S. Supreme Ct. 1973, U.S. Ct. Appeals (5th and D.C. cirs.) 1975, D.C. 1976. Asst. atty. Lubbock County, Tex., 1964; assoc. Evans, Pharr, Trout & Jones, Lubbock, 1964-73; asst. atty. gen. State of Tex., Austin, 1974-80; commr. FERC, Washington, 1980-84, cons. regulatory, natural gas, 1984-85; atty., spl. cons. ARTA, Inc., Washington, 1985-86; of counsel Ross, Marsh & Foster, Washington, 1986—; chief Pub. Utilities and Transp. Div., State of Tex., 1976-78, Energy Div., 1978-80. Contbr. articles to profl. jours. Recipient Disting. Service award Dept. of Energy, 1984; named Disting. Alumnus Am. U., 1984. Mem. Tex. Bar Assn. (chmn. pub. utility sect. 1979-80), Lubbock County Bar Assn. (bd. dirs. 1968-71), Gas Research Inst. (adv. bd. dirs. 1984—), D.C. Bar Assn. Episcopalian. Administrative and regulatory, FERC practice, Public utilities. Home: 904 Saint Stephens Rd Alexandria VA 22304 Office: Ross Marsh & Foster 888 16th St NW Washington DC 20006

HUGHES, JOHN NEWELL, lawyer; b. Rushville, Ind., Oct. 9, 1908; s. Thomas and Luta Belle (Kinney) H.; m. Helene J. Beerkircker, Feb. 20, 1946; children: Pamela Jo, Sarah Louise, Bonnie Belle, Julie Ann. AB, Butler U., 1930; LLB, Ind. U., 1933. Bar: Ind. 1933, U.S. Dist. Ct. (so. dist.) Ind. 1933, U.S. Supreme Ct. 1958. Ptnr. Hughes & Young, Rushville, 1946—. Served to 1st. lt. U.S. Army, 1942-46, ETO. Mem. Ind. Bar Assn., Rush County Bar Assn., Am. Legion, VFW, DAV. Republican. Methodist. Lodge: Masons. Probate. Home: 806 N Jackson Rushville IN 46173 Office: Hughes & Young 223 N Perkins PO Box 65 Rushville IN 46173

HUGHES, JOHN ROBERT, lawyer; b. Huron, S.D., Mar. 9, 1957; s. R. Frank and Angeline (Siciliani) H.; m. Beth Ellen Guthmiller, Aug. 8, 1978. BA cum laude, S.D. State U., Brookings, 1979; JD with distinction, U. Nebr., 1982. Bar: Nebr. 1982, U.S. Dist. Ct. Nebr. 1982, S.D. 1983, U.S. Dist. Ct. S.D. 1984, U.S. Ct. Appeals (8th cir.) 1986. Assoc. Baird, Holm, McEachen, Pedersen, Hamann & Strasheim, Omaha, 1982-84; ptnr. Fisher & Hughes, Sioux Falls, S.D., 1984. Editor Nebr. Law Rev., 1981-82. Arbitrator Better Bus. Bur., Omaha, 1984; bd. dirs. Performing Artists of Omaha Inc., 1984. Mem. ABA, S.D. Bar Assn., S.D. Trial Lawyers Assn., Nebr. Bar Assn., Order of Coif, Phi Kappa Phi. Club: Sioux Falls Cosmopolitan (bd. dirs.). Contracts commercial, State civil litigation, Federal civil litigation. Office: Fisher & Hughes 601 S Minnesota Ave Suite 101 Sioux Falls SD 57104

HUGHES, JOYCE A., law educator; b. 1940. B.A., Carleton U., 1961; J.D., U. Minn., 1965. Bar: Minn. 1965, Ill. 1976. Law clk. Earl R. Larson U.S. Dist. Judge Minn., 1965-67; assoc. Howard, LeFevere, Lefler, Mpls., 1967-71; assoc. prof. U. Minn., 1971-75; assoc. prof. Northwestern U., 1975-79, prof., 1979—; gen. counsel Chgo. Transit Authority, 1984—; dir. Fed. Home Loan Bank of Chgo.; mem. Ill. Sup. Ct. Com. on Evidence, 1971-77; mem. U.S. del. to Belgrade Conf. to Review Helsinki Accord, 1977-78. Mem. Chgo. Bd. Edn., 1980-82. Mem. Order of Coif, Phi Beta Kappa. Office: Northwestern University Law Sch 357 East Chicago Ave Chicago IL 60611 *

HUGHES, KAREN GRAY, lawyer; b. Marshall, Tex., Dec. 9, 1954; d. John W. and Wanda (Smith) Gray; m. Craig Thomas Hughes, Dec. 27, 1975. Student, Kilgore Jr. Coll., 1973; BA with honors, Stephen F. Austin U., 1976; JD, So. Meth. U., 1980. Bar: Tex. 1980, U.S. Dist. Ct. (no. and ea. dists.) Tex. 1981, U.S. Ct. Appeals (5th cir.) 1986. Loan clk. Preston State Bank, Dallas, 1976-78; assoc. Davis, Wardlaw, Hay & Wittenburg, San Angelo, Tex., 1980-86, Hardy & Atherton, Tyler, Tex., 1987—. Contbg. editor Gen. Practice Digest, 1983—. Bd. dirs. Concho Valley Home Girls, San Angelo, 1984-86, Planned Parenthood San Angelo, Inc., 1984-86; dist. chairperson Am. Cancer Soc., San Angelo 1985; vol. Ft. Concho, San Angelo, 1984-86, Fiesta Del Concho, San Angelo, 1985-86; mem. Concho Valley Estate Planning Council 1981-86, bd. dirs. 1984-85, pres. 1985-86. Mem. Tex. Bar Assn. (com. assistance to local bar assns. and law day), Tex. Young Lawyers Assn. (com. law focused edn. and juror edn. 1984-85, com. citizens legal edn. 1985-86), Tom Green County Bar Assn., Tom Green County Young Lawyers Assn. (sec., treas. 1984-85, pres. elect 1985-86). Episcopalian. Avocations: travel, reading, stained glass artwork, Tex. history. State civil litigation, Family and matrimonial, Insurance. Office: Hardy & Atherton 909 ESE Loop 323 Suite 300 Tyler TX 75707

HUGHES, KENNETH RUSSELL, lawyer; b. Newport, Ky., Feb. 3, 1925; s. Isaac Hugh and Martha (Becknell) H.; m. Ann B. Ollinger, June 18, 1949 (dec. 1986); children—Kenneth Russell, Sharon Ann, Mark Edward. B.B.A., U. Cin., 1949; J.D., Salmon P. Chase Law Sch., 1956. Bar: Ohio bar 1956; C.P.A., Ohio. Conferee appeals div. IRS, Cin., 1949-57; partner firm Freiberg, Katz & Hughes, Cin., 1957-65, Santen, Shaffer & Hughes, L.P.A., Cin., 1965—; instr. fed. taxation Salmon P. Chase Law Sch., 1962-68. Served with inf. U.S. Army, 1943-46. Mem. Am. Bar Assn., Ohio State Bar Assn., Cin. Bar Assn. Club: Bankers of of Cin. Corporate taxation, Estate taxation, Personal income taxation. Home: 383 Neville Penn Rd Neville OH 45156 Office: Santen Shaffer & Hughes LPA 105 E 4th St Suite 1800 Cincinnati OH 45202

HUGHES, LEO A., JR., lawyer; b. Balt., Apr. 6, 1936; s. Leo Aloysius and Mary Edna (O'Ryan) H.; m. Geraldine Fisher; children: Kelly Lynn, Kevin Leo. Student, Johns Hopkins U., 1953-55; LLB, Mt. Vernon Law Sch., 1959. Bar: Md. 1959, U.S. Dist. Ct. Md. 1961. Assoc. Rollins, Smalkin, Weston & Andrew, Balt., 1959-64; ptnr. Allen, Theiblot & Hughes, Balt., 1964-69; sole practice Balt., 1969-73, 86—; ptnr. Steen, Hughes & Seigel, Balt., 1973-85; of counsel Steen, Seigle, Tulley & Furrer, Balt., 1986—; asst. county solicitor Baltimore County, 1965-67; trial magistrate Baltimore County, 1967-69. Contbr. author: Maryland Pattern Jury Instructions, 1984. Fellow Am. Coll. Trial Lawyers; mem. Assn. Trial Lawyers Am. (bd. govs. 1979-82), Md. State Bar Assn. (chmn. litigation sect. 1983-84), Md. Trial Lawyers Assn. (pres. 1977-78), Bar Assn. Balt. City (pres. 1982-83). Avocations: golf, travel. Federal civil litigation, State civil litigation, Personal injury. Home: 309 Patleigh Rd Baltimore MD 21228 Office: 712 Park Ave Baltimore MD 21201

HUGHES, LINDA RENATE, trial lawyer, educator; b. Hanau, Germany, Oct. 25, 1947; came to U.S. 1950; d. J.A. and Ilga (Vankins) Eglite. B.A. magna cum laude, U. Minn., 1968; J.D. cum laude, Wayne State U., 1980. Bar: Mich. 1980, Ga. 1982, Fla. 1984. Human resource mgr. Browning Marine Co., St. Charles, Mich., 1973-76; law clk. to judge U.S. Dist. Ct. (ea. dist.) Mich., 1980-81; assoc. Miller, Cohen, Martens & Surgerman, Detroit, 1982, Thompson, Sizemore & Gonzalez, Tampa, 1984-85; asst. county atty. Hillsborough County, Fla., 1985—; instr. Valdosta State Coll. (Ga.), 1981; adj. prof. U. Detroit Law Sch., 1982; researcher comparative labor policy, Leigh Creek, Australia, 1983. Editor-in-chief Advocate, Wayne State U. Law Sch., 1979-80, also law rev. Vol. Community Mental Health Crisis Intervention, Saginaw, Mich., 1975-76, Ann Arbor, Mich., 1976-78, Clearwater Fla., 1984; dept. registrar Voter Registration Program, Pinellas County, Fla., 1983-84. Author: Employer's Price for Polygraph, 1986. Mem. State Bar Mich., Ga. State Bar, Fla. State Bar Assn. (exec. com. govt. lawyers sect. 1986-88), Hillsborough County Bar Assn. (appellate rules com. 1986-87) , Fla. Women Lawyers Assn. (officer, bd. dirs.), ABA, AAUW (Saginaw chpt. sec. 1974-75). Club: Tampa. Federal civil litigation, State civil litigation, Labor.

HUGHES, MARY KATHERINE, lawyer; b. Kodiak, Alaska, July 16, 1949; d. John Chamberlain and Marjorie (Anstey) H.; m. Andrew H. Eker, July 7, 1982. B.B.A. cum laude, U. Alaska, 1971; J.D., Willamette U., 1974; postgrad. Heriot-Watt U., Edinburgh, Scotland, 1971. Bar: Alaska 1975. Ptnr., Hughes, Thorsness et al, Anchorage, 1974—; trustee Alaska Bar Found., pres., 1984—; bd. visitors Willamette U. Coll. Law, Salem, Oreg., 1980—; mem. Willamette Law Fund Leadership Com., 1981-83; bd. dirs. Alaska Repertory Theatre, 1986—, pres.-elect, 1987—; mem. Coll. of Fellows U. Alaska Found., 1985—. Mem. Alaska Bar Assn. (bd. govs. 1981-84, pres. 1983-84), Anchorage Assn. Women Lawyers (pres. 1976-77), AAUW, Delta Theta Phi. Republican. Roman Catholic. Club: Soroptimists (v.p. 1981-83, pres. 1986-87). Administrative and regulatory, Local government, Condemnation. Home: 2240 Kissee Ct Anchorage AK 99517 Office: Hughes Thorsness Gantz Powell & Brundin 509 W 3d Ave Anchorage AK 99501

HUGHES, NANCY NUTTO, lawyer; b. Midland, Tex., May 26, 1957; s. William James and Betty (Bradley) Nutto; m. Donald Wayne Hughes, Mar. 3, 1984. BA, Trinity U., 1979; JD, Baylor U., 1982. Bar: Tex. 1982. Briefing atty. Ct. Appeals, Eastland, Tex., 1982-83, research atty., 1983-84, staff atty., 1984—. Tchr. sunday sch./youth group, Eastland, 1983—; leader Girl Scouts U.S., Eastland, 1985—, 1st v.p. bd. dirs.; bd. dirs. Eastland goodfellows United Fund; 1st v.p., bd. dirs. Girl Scouts U.S.; speaker various civic groups, Eastland, 1984—. Mem. ABA, Tex. Bar Assn., Tex. Young Lawyers Assn. Methodist. Avocations: camping, hunting, arts and crafts, fishing. State civil litigation, Criminal. Office: Ct Appeals Box 271 Eastland TX 76448

HUGHES, PATRICK PAUL, lawyer; b. Ft. Dix., N.J., Sept. 21, 1952; s. Paul Winfred and Marion Laraine (Brightbill) H.; m. Patricia Lynn Orr, Aug. 12, 1978 (div. Mar. 1984); m. Beth Mullins, Feb. 22, 1986; 1 child, Parker Garrett. BA, U. Ala., 1975, JD, 1978. Bar: Ala. 1978, U.S. Dist. Ct. (no. dist.) Ala. 1978, U.S. Ct. Appeals (11th cir.) 1981. Assoc. Lybrand, Sides & Hamner, Anniston, Ala., 1978-80, Bolt, Isom, Jackson & Bailey, Anniston, 1980-83; sole practice Anniston, 1983—. Bd. dirs. United Way, Calhoun County, Ala., 1980-84, United Cerebral Palsy, Calhoun County, 1982—, Boys Club of Anniston, 1984—. Mem. ABA (family law sect., litigation sect.), Ala. Bar Assn. (charter, family law sect.), Calhoun County Bar Assn. (sec. 1979-82), Assn. Trial Lawyers Am., Ala. Trial Lawyers Assn. (bd. of govs.). Democrat. Roman Catholic. State civil litigation, Family and matrimonial, Personal injury. Home: 625 E 6th St Anniston AL 36201 Office: PO Box 2627 Anniston AL 36202

HUGHES, ROY FREDERICKS, lawyer; b. Honolulu, Nov. 11, 1947; s. John Harold and Marcelle (Figueroa) H.; m. Heidi Catil Schroder, Aug. 18, 1973; children: Hallie, Nathan, Benjamen. BA, Ripon Coll., 1970; JD, Marquette U., 1976. Bar: Wis. 1976, Hawaii 1976, U.S. Dist. Ct. Hawaii 1976. Assoc. Libkuman, Ventura, Honolulu, 1976-82, ptnr., 1982—. Mem. Assn. Trial Lawyers Am., Def. Research Inst., Fedn. Ins. and Corp. Counsel, Hawaii Assn. Def. Attys. State civil litigation, Insurance, Personal injury.

HUGHES, STEVEN JAY, lawyer; b. Fayetteville, Ark., Nov. 7, 1948; s. Howard and Jimmie Louise (Williams) H.; m. Leora Donna Halfhill, July 22, 1972; children: Christopher Blake, Clayton Brent. BS in Edn., U. Ark., Fayetteville, 1970; JD, U. Ark., Little Rock, 1978. Bar: Ark. 1978, U.S. Dist. Ct. (ea. dist.) Ark. 1978, U.S. Ct. Appeals (8th cir.) 1978, U.S. Supreme Ct. 1981. Sole practice Jacksonville, Ark., 1978—. Alderman Jacksonville City Council, 1979-81; commr. Jacksonville Planning Commn., 1982-85; mem. U. Ark. Razorback Letterman's Club, Little Rock, 1985, Ark. Sports Hall of Fame, 1985; bd. dirs. Jacksonville Boys Club, 1979—, pres. 1982-83. Mem. Assn. Trial Lawyers Am., Ark. Bar Assn., Delta Theta Phi (lifetime, dist. chancellor 1983—). Baptist. Lodge: Kiwanis (pres. Jacksonville club 1983-84, Kiwanian of Yr. award 1979-80, Disting. Club Pres. award 1984). Avocation: sports. Family and matrimonial, General practice, Consumer commercial. Home: 5 Silver Fox Cove Jacksonville AR 72076 Office: 3000 N 1st St Jacksonville AR 72076

HUGHES, THOMAS MORGAN, III, lawyer; b. Racine, Wis., June 14, 1949; s. Thomas Morgan and Rosemary (Navratil) H.; m. Teresa Lee Cloud, Aug. 10, 1974; 1 child, Gwyneth Leigh. B.B.A., U. Wis.-Madison, 1971; J.D., St. Louis U., 1974. Bar: Ark. 1974, U.S. Dist. Ct. (ea. dist.) Ark. 1974. Sole practice, Beebe, Ark., 1974-78; ptnr., Hughes & Hughes, Beebe, 1978—; instr. Ark. State U., Beebe, 1975. City atty. City of Beebe, 1975-76; treas. Beebe Indsl. Devel. Corp., Beebe, 1983—; judge City Ct., Beebe, 1985-87, Beebe Mcpl. Ct., 1987—. Mem. Am. Trial Lawyers Assn. (charter mem.), White County Bar Assn., Beebe C. of C. (pres. 1984—). Democrat. Lodge: Kiwanis (pres. 1981-82, bd. dirs. 1979—). Banking, General practice, Personal injury. Home: 709 N Magnolia Beebe AR 72012 Office: Hughes & Hughes 1709 West Center Beebe AR 72012

HUGHES, WILLIAM AUGUSTUS, JR., judge; b. Decatur, Tex., June 29, 1920; s. William Augustus Sr. and Jessie Maria (Whitmore) H.; m. Martha Lou Thornton, May 27, 1945; children: Carter, Daniel. BS, No. Tex. State U., 1942; JD, Baylor U., 1948. Bar: Tex. 1948, U.S. Supreme Ct. 1980. Sole practice Decatur and Gainesville, Tex., 1948-57; dist. judge Tex. Dist. Ct. (43d and 235th dists.), Decatur, 1957-76; assoc. justice Tex. Ct. Civil Appeals (2d cir.), Ft. Worth, 1976-81, Tex. Ct. Appeals (2d cir.), Ft. Worth, 1981-85; sr. justice Tex. Ct. Appeals, 1985—; of counsel Wynn, Brown, Mack, Renfro & Thompson, Ft. Worth. Author: (column) Wise Quacks From a Lame Duck, 1984-85. Served to lt. USNR, 1942-46, PTO. Recipient Silver Beaver award Boy Scouts Am., 1968, Red Cross of Constantine medal St. Timothy Conclave, 1984. Mem. Tex. Bar Assn. (bd. dirs. jud. sect. 1965), Wise County Bar Assn. (poet laureate 1965—, poet's club), Tarrant County Bar Assn., Decatur C. of C., Am. Legion (comdr. Decatur post 1958). Democrat. Methodist. Club: Decatur Country. Lodges: Masons (33 degree), KP. Judicial administration. Office: Wynn Brown Mack Renfro & Thompson 1st City Bank Tower Fort Worth TX 76102

HUGHES, WILLIAM JEFFREY, lawyer; b. San Gabriel, Calif., Dec. 6, 1951; s. William Drennan and Rosetta Jane (Duff) H. B.A., Stanford U., 1973; J.D., Hastings Coll., 1977; M.L., London Sch. Econ., 1979. Bar: Calif., 1977, U.S. Dist. Ct. (no. dist.) Calif. 1977, U.S. Ct. Appeals (9th cir.) 1980, U.S. Supreme Ct. 1982. Assoc. Alexander Anolik, P.C., San Francisco, 1978-80; mem. Brooks & Hughes, San Leandro, Calif., 1980-83; inheritance tax referee State of Calif., Alameda County, 1981-83; gen. counsel Bicara, Ltd., Carson, Calif., 1983—; dir. Food Wholesalers Am., Carson, 1984—. Contbr. articles to profl. jours. Mem. Thomas Scotto Scholarship Fund Com., San Francisco, 1981-82. Mem. Alameda County Bar Assn., Los Angeles County Bar Assn. Democrat. Private international, Contracts commercial, General corporate. Home: 242 Linnie Canal Venice CA 90291 Office: Bicara Ltd 1065 E Walnut St Carson CA 90749

HUGHSTON, HAROLD VAUGHAN, JR., lawyer; b. Tuscumbia, Ala., Jan. 9, 1954; s. Harold Vaughan and Lucy Caroline (Allison) H.; m. Cynthia Ann Adams, Nov. 24, 1979; children: Harold V. III, Mary Louise, Ann Merideth Hughston. BA, U. Ala., 1976, JD, 1979. Bar: Ala. 1981, Fla. 1981. Ptnr. Hughston, Hughston & Hughston, Tuscumbia, 1981—; bd. dirs. New Southland Nat. Life Ins. Co., Tuscumbia, 1981—. Named one of Outstanding Young Men Am., 1979, 82. Mem. Ala. Bar Assn., Fla. Bar Assn., Ala. Trial Lawyers Assn. Democrat. Presbyterian. Lodge: Kiwanis (v.p., pres, lt. gov. div. Tuscumbia club 1983-86). General corporate, Probate, Real property. Home: 701 E 3d St Tuscumbia AL 35674 Office: Hughston Hughston & Hughston 103 E 3d St Tuscumbia AL 35674

HUGIN, ADOLPH CHARLES, lawyer, engineer, educator, inventor; b. Washington, Mar. 28, 1907; s. Charles and Eugenie Francoise (Vigny) H. BSEE, George Washington U., 1928; MSEE, MIT, 1930; cert. in patent law and practice, JD, Georgetown U., 1934; cert. radio communication Union Coll., 1944; cert. better bus. mgmt. Gen. Electric Co., 1946; LLM, Harvard U., 1947; SJD, Cath. U. Am., 1949; cert. in Christian Doctrine and Teaching Methods, Conf. of Christian Doctrine, 1960; cert. in social services and charity Ozanam Sch. Charity, 1972. Bar: D.C. 1933, U.S. Ct. Customs and Patent Appeals 1934, U.S. Supreme Ct. 1945, Mass. 1947, U.S. Ct. Claims, 1953, U.S. Ct. Appeals (fed. cir.) 1982; registered U.S. Patent and Trademark Office Atty. Bar, 1933; registered profl. elec. and mech. engr., D.C. Examiner U.S. Patent and Trademark Office, 1928; with Gen. Electric Co., 1928-46, engr. Instruments Research and Devel. Lab., West Lynn Works, Mass., 1928, engr.-in-charge Insulation Lab. River Works, Lynn, 1929, Engine-Electric Drive Devel. Lab., River Works, 1929-30, patent legal asst., Schenectady, 1930, patent investigator, Washington, 1930-33, patent lawyer, Washington, 1933-34, Schenectady, 1934-46; engr.-in-charge section aeros. and marine engring. div., Schenectady, 1942-45; organizer, instr. Gen. Electric patent practice course, 1945-46; sole practice law and cons. engring., Cambridge and Arlington, Mass., 1946-47; vis. prof. law Cath. U. Am., Washington, 1949-55; assoc. Holland, Armstrong, Bower & Carlson, N.Y.C., 1957; sole practice law and cons. engr. Washington and Springfield, Va., 1947—. Author: International Trade Regulatory Arrangements and the Antitrust Laws, 1949; editor-in-chief Bull. Am. Patent Law Assn., 1949-54; editor notes and decisions Georgetown U. Law Jour., 1933-34, staff, 1930-34; contbr. articles on patents, copyrights, antitrust, radio and air law to profl. jours.; inventor dynamoelectric machines, insulation calipers, ecology and pollution controls, musical instruments, dynamometers, viscosimeters, synchroscope, inherent constant voltage characteristic generators, water-cooled eddy-current clutches, brakes, and others. Mem. Schenectady N.Y. Com. Boy Scouts Am., 1940-42, North Springfield Civic Assn.; charter mem., 1st bd. mgrs. Schenectady Cath. Youth League, 1935-38, hon. mem., 1945; mem. adv. bd. St. Michael's Parish, Va., lector, commentator, 1969-80; bd. dirs. St. Margaret's Fed. Credit Union, 1963-67, 1st v.p., 1965-67; chmn. St. Margaret's Bldg. Fund, 1954; lector St. Margaret's Parish, 1966-69, retreat group capt., 1965-68; mem. legis. com. Schenectady C. of C., 1940-46. Recipient Dietzen Drawing prize, George Washington U., 1926, Georgetown U. Law Jour. Key award, 1934, Aviation Law prize Cath. U. Am., 1948, Radio Law prize Cath. U. Am., 1949, Charities Work award St. Margaret's Ch., 1982; elected to Gen. Electric Col. Elfun Soc. for Disting. Exec. Service, 1942. Mem. Am. Intellectual Property Law Assn. (life; cert. of Honor for 50 Yrs. Service), ABA (life), John Carroll Soc., NSPE, D.C. Soc. Profl. Engrs., St. Vincent de Paul Soc. (parish conf. v.p. 1949-65, pres. 1965—, pres. Prince Georges County, Md. council 1958-61, founding pres. Arlington, Va. Diocesan council 1975-77, nat. trustee 1975-77), Nocturnal Adoration Soc., St. Margaret's Parish Confraternity Christian Doctrine (pres., instr. 1960-61), Archdiocesan Council Cath. Men (pres. So. Prince County deanery 1956-58, 65-68), Holy Name Soc. (pres. parish 1950-52, Prince Georges County section 1953, Washington Archdiocesan Union 1953-55), Men's Retreat League (Wash. exec. bd. 1954-58), Delta Theta Phi (Georgetown U. Law Sch. Scholarship Key award 1934). Patent, Trademark and copyright, Antitrust. Address: 7602 Boulder St Springfield VA 22151

HUHN, RICHARD M., lawyer; b. Washington, Dec. 28, 1944; s. Lester S. and Myrtle G. (Trenk) H.; m. Marcia D. May, Dec. 20, 1969; 1 child, Kimberly Lynn. BA cum laude, Ohio U., 1966; JD, Ohio State U., 1969. Bar: Ohio 1969, U.S. Dist. Ct. (no. and so. dists.) Ohio, U.S. Ct. Appeals (6th cir.), U.S. Supreme Ct. Spl. agt. FBI, 1969-73; asst. atty. gen. State of Ohio, 1973-75; ptnr. Grieser, Schafer, Blumenstiel & Slane Co., L.P.A., Columbus, 1975—; adj. prof. criminal law Park Coll., 1974-75; officer (hon.) Ohio State Hwy. Patrol, 1975. Mem. ABA, Columbus Bar Assn., Assn. Trial Lawyers Am., Ohio Acad. Trial Lawyers, Franklin County Trial Lawyers Assn., Am. Arbitration Assn. (panel mem. 1976—). Club: Agonis (Columbus). Personal injury, Federal Employers' Liability Act (railroad). Home: 1225 Chatham Ridge Rd Westerville OH 43081 Office: Grieser Schafer Blumenstiel & Slane 261 W Johnstown Rd Columbus OH 43230

HULBERT, WILLIAM ROWSELL, JR., lawyer; b. N.Y.C., Apr. 8, 1916; s. William Rowsell and Olga Craven H.; m. Aline Davis, Mar. 13, 1948; children—David, William Truxton, Lucy. A.B., Brown U., 1937; J.D., Harvard U., 1940. Bar: Mass. 1940, U.S. Dist. Ct. Mass. 1946, U.S. Ct. Appeals (1st cir.) 1953, U.S. Ct. Appeals (Fed. cir.) 1982, Maine 1973, U.S. Dist. Ct. Maine 1974, U.S. Supreme Ct. 1956. Assoc. Fish, Richardson & Neave, Boston, 1940-53, ptnr., 1953-68; ptnr. Fish & Richardson, Boston, 1968—, Lincolnville, Maine, 1976—; spl. agt. FBI, 1941-45; legal attaché Am. embassy, Quito, Ecuador, 1943, Asunción, Paraguay, 1944. Dir. Camden, Maine, Area YMCA, 1984—. Mem. Boston Patent Law Assn. (past pres.), Am. Patent Law Assn. (past. dir.), ABA, Maine Bar Assn., Waldo County Bar Assn., Am. Coll. Trial Lawyers, Inter-Am. Bar Assn. Clubs: Harvard, Union (Boston); Harvard Faculty. Patent, Trademark and copyright. Office: Fish & Richardson PO Box 90 Lincolnville ME 04849 also: One Financial Ctr Boston MA 02111

HULL, DANIEL LOUIS, lawyer; b. Mpls., June 5, 1956; s. Louis Edward and Jane Ann (Bakken) H.; m. Nancy Renae Morton, June 14, 1980; children: Eric Daniel, Justin Thomas. BA, Concordia Coll., Moorhead, Minn., 1978; postgrad., Valparaiso U., 1978-79; JD, U. N.D., 1981. Bar: Minn. 1981, U.S. Dist. Ct. Minn. 1982, N.D. 1985, U.S. Dist. Ct. N.D. 1985. Assoc. Mundt & Hall, Duluth, Minn., 1981-84, Cahill & Maring P.A., Moorhead, 1984—. Mem. ABA, Minn. Bar Assn., N.D. Bar Assn., Clay County Bar Assn., Cass County Bar Assn., Minn. Trial Lawyers Assn. Avocations: racquetball, softball. State civil litigation, Insurance, Personal injury. Home: 1619 39th Ave S Fargo ND 58103 Office: Cahill & Maring PA 403 Center Ave Moorhead MN 56560

HULL, DANIEL TALMADGE, lawyer; b. Birmingham, Ala., Sept. 3, 1942; s. Daniel Talmadge and Kathleen (Wells) H.; m. Joan Parker, Aug. 13, 1965; 1 child, Daniel T. III. BSChemE, U. Ala., 1964; JD, Samford U., 1972. Bar: Ala. 1973, U.S. Dist. Ct. (no. dist.) 1974, U.S. Ct. Appeals (5th cir.) 1974, U.S. Ct. Appeals (11th cir.) 1983, registered profl. engr. Ala. Process engr. Monsanto, Decatur, Ala., 1964-65; sales engr. Goslin-Birmingham, 1965-67; staff, project engr. Rust Internat., Birmingham, 1967-72, staff atty., 1972-73, asst. gen. counsel, 1973-76; sole practice Birmingham, 1976—; lectr. on engrs. and the law U. Ala. Birmingham, 1982—. Chmn. troop com. Boy Scouts Am., Birmingham, 1984—. Recipient training award, wood badge Boy Scouts Am., 1985—. Mem. ABA (forum com. on constrn. industry), Ala. Bar Assn. (com. on legal services for elderly), Birmingham Bar Assn., Am. Arbitration Assn., Am. Inst. Chem. Engrs. Baptist. Clubs: Exchange (pres. 1983-84), Downtown (Birmingham). Avocations: hiking, fishing, gardening. Federal civil litigation, Construction, General practice. Office: 417 N 20th St 1020 1st Ala Bank Bldg Birmingham AL 35203

HULL, DAVID JOHN, lawyer; b. Daytona Beach, Fla., Oct. 31, 1948; s. Elmer J. and Lilly Mae (Darby) H.; m. Donna Jane Davis, June 1, 1971; children: Gina Leah, Holly Kristine, Elizabeth Ann. BS, Stetson U., 1970; MA, Ind. State U., 1972; JD, U. Fla., 1979, LLM, 1986. Bar: Fla. 1979. Assoc. Mahoney, Adams, Milam, Surface & Grimsley, Jacksonville, Fla., 1979; law clk. to presiding justice U.S. Ct. Appeals (5th cir.), Jacksonville, 1979-80; from assoc. to ptnr. Mahoney, Adams, Milam, Surface & Grimsley, Jacksonville, 1980—. Served to maj. U.S. Army, 1972-85. Mem. Fla. Estate Planning Council, Profl. Businessman's Assn., Order of Coif, Phi Kappa Phi, Kappa Mu Epsilon. Republican. Presbyterian. Club: Fla. Yacht (Jacksonville). Corporate taxation, Estate taxation, Personal income taxation. Home: 3521 Riverside Ave Jacksonville FL 32201 Office: Mahoney Adams Milam Surface & Grimsley 100 Laura St Jacksonville FL 32202

HULL, J(AMES) RICHARD, lawyer, business executive; b. Keokuk, Iowa, Dec. 5, 1933; s. James Robert and Alberta Margaret (Bouseman) H.; m. Patricia M. Kiesner, June 14, 1958; children—Elizabeth Ann Hull Whims, James Robert, David Glen. B.A., Ill. Wesleyan U., 1955; J.D., Northwestern U., 1958. Bar: Ill. 1958, Fla. 1978. V.p., sec., gen. counsel Honeggers & Co., Inc., Fairbury, Ill., 1959-65, also bd. dirs.; staff atty. Am. Hosp. Supply Corp., Evanston, Ill., 1965-68, chief atty., asst. sec., 1968-70, corp. sec., 1970-71, corp. sec., corp. gen. counsel, 1971-79, gen. counsel, 1979-84; sr. v.p., gen. counsel Household Internat., Northbrook, Ill., 1984—; mem. planning com. Northwestern U. Corp. Counsel Inst., 1982—. Bd. trustees, bd. of visitors Ill. Wesleyan U. Fellow Am. Bar Found.; mem. ABA, Ill. Bar Assn., Fla. Bar Assn., Chgo. Bar Assn. (chmn. corp. law dept.), Am. Soc. Corp. Secs., North Shore Gen. Counsels, Northwestern U. Sch. Law Alumni Assn. (treas.), Sigma Chi. Clubs: Legal, Executive (Chgo.); Skokie (Ill.) Country; Gator Creek Golf (Sarasota, Fla.); T.P.C. (Prestonica, Fla.). General corporate, Antitrust, Contracts commercial. Home: 2603 Oak Ave Northbrook IL 60062 Office: Household Internat Inc 2700 Sanders Rd Prospect Heights IL 60070

HULL, PHILIP GLASGOW, lawyer; b. St. Albans, Vt., Feb. 17, 1925; s. Charles Herman and Gladys Gertrude (Glasgow) H.; A.B., Middlebury Coll., 1949; LL.B. (Ellis fellow, Kent scholar, Stone scholar), Columbia U., 1952; m. Gretchen Elizabeth Gaebelein, Oct. 24, 1952; children—Jeffrey R., Sanford D., Meredyth Hull Smith. Admitted to N.Y. bar, 1952, Fla. bar, 1977; staff mem. sub-com. on adminstrn. internal revenue laws, com. on ways and means U.S. Ho. of Reps., Washington, 1951; assoc. firm Winthrop, Stimson, Putnam & Roberts, N.Y.C., 1952-63; ptnr., 1964—. Mem. Sch. Revenue Com., Cold Spring Harbor, N.Y., 1963-65; bd. dirs. Eagle Dock Found., Cold Spring Harbor, 1971-74, People's Symphony Concerts, N.Y.C., 1977—. L.I. Philharm, 1979-81; trustee Latin Am. Mission, Bogota, N.J., 1969-79; elder Central Presbyn. Ch., Huntington, N.Y., 1958-78; mem. nat. missions bd. United Presbyn. Ch. U.S.A., 1967-73; mem. Lloyd Harbor Conservation Adv. Council, 1973-77. Served with U.S. Army, 1943-46. Mem. N.Y. State Bar Assn., Assn. Bar City of N.Y., Fla. Bar Assn., Am. Coll. of Probate Counsel, Christian Legal Soc. (dir. 1984—), Fellowship Christians in Univs. and Schs. (trustee 1983—), Blue Key, Phi Beta Kappa. Clubs: Univ., Downtown Assn. (N.Y.C.); Cold Spring Harbor Beach. Estate planning, Probate, Estate taxation. Office: Winthrop Stimson Putnam & Roberts 40 Wall St New York NY 10005

HULL, THOMAS GRAY, judge; b. 1926; m. Joan Brandon; children: Leslie, Brandon, Amy. attended Tusculum Coll., J.D. U. Tenn., 1951. Ptnr. Easterly & Hull, Greeneville, Tenn., 1951-63; sole practice, Greenville, 1963-72; judge, State of Tenn. (20th jud. cir.), Greeneville, Morristown and Rogersville, 1972-79; legal counsel Tenn. Gov. Lamar Alexander, Nashville, 1979-81; ptnr. Hull, Weems, Greery & Terry, Greeneville, 1981-82; judge, U.S. Dist. Ct. (ea. dist.) Tenn., Greenville, 1983—. Served as cpl. U.S. Army, 1944-46. Mem. Tenn. Bar Assn. (chmn. East dist. com. 1969), Tenn. Jud. Conf. (del. 1972-79, vice chmn. 1974-75, com. to draft uniform charges for trial judges), Greeneville Bar Assn. (pres. 1969-71). Republican. Judicial administration. Office: US Courthouse 101 Summer St W Greenville TN 37743 *

HULL, THOMAS J., lawyer; b. Kingston, N.Y., Dec. 8, 1940; s. Martin Daniel and Beatrice Marie (O'Roarke) H.; m. Barbara Jane Gilbert, Sept. 10, 1966; children: Martin D., Patrick M., Cathleen M., Joseph T., Andrew J., Molly, Peter S. AB, U. Notre Dame, JD. Bar: N.Y. 1967, U.S. Supreme Ct. 1977, U.S. Dist. Ct. (no. dist.) N.Y. 1978. Assoc. Rappaport, Kaman & Hull, Binghamton, N.Y., 1966-75; ptnr. Kaman & Hull, Binghamton, 1976-84, assoc., 1984-85; ptnr. Grace, Hull and Vitanza, Binghamton, 1986—. Republican. Roman Catholic. Real property, General practice, Consumer commercial. Office: Grace Hull and Vitanza 29 Riverside Dr Binghamton NY 13902

HULLUM, BILLY DON, lawyer; b. Wills Point, Tex., Feb. 5, 1939; s. John Albert and Carrie Mae (Lea) H.; m. Teena Wilson, Feb. 16, 1970 (div. May 1985); children: Billy Albert, Nathaniel Wilson, Holly Lea; m. Dodie Sparks, Aug. 15, 1985. BBA, U. Tex., 1972; JD, Baylor U., 1976. Bar: Tex. 1977, U.S. Dist. Ct. (no. dist.) Tex. 1979, U.S. Dist. Ct. (ea. dist.)Tex. 1980, U.S. Ct. Appeals (5th cir.) 1983, U.S. Supreme Ct. 1984. Judge Van Zandt County, Canton, Tex., 1968-74; sole practice Wills Point, 1977-86, Granbury, Tex., 1985-86, Ft. Worth, Tex., 1986—. Democrat. General practice. Home: 4403 Alta Mesa Fort Worth TX 76133 Office: 5001 S Hulen Suite 103B Fort Worth TX 76132

HULLVERSON, JAMES EVERETT, JR., lawyer, educator; b. St. Louis, Sept. 20, 1953; s. James Everett and Shirley (Shaughnessey) H.; m. Laure Albers Bauer, Oct. 7, 1977; children—Everett James, Leigh Bauer. B.A., Yale U., 1975; J.D. cum laude, St. Louis U., 1978. Bar: Mo. 1978, U.S. Dist. Ct. (ea. dist.) Mo. 1978, Ill. 1979, U.S. Supreme Ct. 1981, U.S. Ct. Appeals (8th cir.) 1983; diplomate Am. Bd. Profl. Liability Attys.; cert. civil trial adv. Nat. Bd. Trial Advocacy. Ptnr. Hullverson, Hullverson & Frank, Inc., St. Louis, 1978—; adj. assoc. prof. law St. Louis U., 1983—; faculty Nat. Coll. Advocacy, 1983, 85; lectr. in field. Contbr. chpts. to books; author seminar program. Active Attys. Motivated for Mo. Mem. Assn. Trial Lawyers Am., Ill. Trial Lawyers Assn., Mo. Assn. Trial Attys., Mo. Bar Assn., Am. Soc. Law and Medicine. Roman Catholic. Clubs: Mo. Athletic, St. Louis Masters Swim, Yale (St. Louis). Personal injury, Federal civil litigation, State civil litigation. Home: 7937 Teasdale Ct University City MO 63130 Office: Hullverson Hullverson & Frank Inc 1010 Market St Suite 1550 Saint Louis MO 63101

HULSE, BRIAN DOUGLAS, lawyer; b. Seattle, Dec. 2, 1955; s. John E.B. and Barbara A. (Burns) H. BBA magna cum laude, U. Wash., 1978; JD, U. Calif., 1981. Bar: Wash. 1981. Assoc. Foster, Pepper & Riviera, Seattle, 1981—. Mem. ABA (bus. bankruptcy com., secured creditors subcom.), Wash. Bar Assn. (creditor debtor sect.), Seattle-King County Bar Assn. (bankruptcy sect.). Avocations: skiing, running, history, cooking. Bankruptcy, Contracts commercial, General corporate. Office: Foster Pepper & Riviera 1111 3d Ave 34th floor Seattle WA 98101

HULSE, MINARD EDWIN, JR., lawyer; b. Waukegan, Ill., Sept. 13, 1938; s. Minard Edwin and May Evelyn (Elliott) H.; m. Adrienne Mary Jean Rago, Apr. 29, 1967; children—Diane Evelyn, Scott Christopher. A.B., Grinnell Coll., 1960; J.D., Harvard U., 1963. Bar: Ill. 1964, U.S. Dist. Ct. (no. dist.) Ill. 1965. Assoc. Keck, Mahin & Cate, Chgo., 1964-72, ptnr., 1972—; mem. adv. com. Taxpayers' Fedn. Ill. Active United Way, Lake Forest, Ill. Served to lt. USNR, 1966-68. Mem. ABA, Ill. Bar Assn., Chgo. Bar Assn., Internat. Assn. Assessment Officers. Clubs: Legal, River (Chgo.). Real property, State and local taxation, State civil litigation. Office: Suite 8300 233 S Wacker Dr Chicago IL 60606

HULSE, WILLIAM FREDERICK, lawyer; b. Charlotte, N.C., Feb. 23, 1942; s. Ronald S. and Mildred (Barnecut) H. BS, U. N.C., 1964, JD, 1968. Bar: N.C. 1968, U.S. Dist. Ct. (we. dist.) N.C. 1968, U.S. Supreme Ct. 1972. Asst. dist. atty. State of N.C., Charlotte, 1968-72; sole practice Charlotte, 1972-83; ptnr. Myers, Hulse & Brown, Charlotte, 1983—. Served to capt. U.S. Army, 1968-74. Mem. ABA, Assn. Trial Lawyers Am., N.C. Bar Assn., Meclenburg Bar Assn. Republican. Episcopalian. Personal injury, Criminal, Family and matrimonial. Home: 6021 Creola Rd Charlotte NC 28226 Office: 122 N McDowell PO Box 36385 Charlotte NC 28236

HULSTON, JOHN KENTON, lawyer; b. Dade County, Mo., Mar. 29, 1915; s. John Fred and Myrtle Rosa (King) H.; m. Ruth Amis Luster, Dec. 18, 1944; 1 son, John Luster. A.B., Drury Coll., Springfield, Mo., 1936; J.D., U. Mo., Columbia, 1941. Bar: Mo. 1941, U.S. Supreme Ct. 1949. Tchr., coach Ash Grove (Mo.) High Sch., 1936-38; individual practice law Springfield, 1946—; ptnr. Hulston, Jones & Sullivan, 1984—; sec., dir., v.p. Ozark Air Lines Inc. (now TWA), St. Louis, 1971-86, Ozark Holdings Inc., St. Louis, 1984—; pres. Bank of Ash Grove, 1959—, Citizens Home Bank, Greenfield, Mo., 1966—, Bank of Springfield, 1968-69; co-founder, dir., v.p., sec. Pioneer Oil Co., Ft. Worth, Tex., 1954-79, Reed Oil Co., Big Spring, Tex., 1951-68; vice chmn., dir. Centerre Bank of Springfield, 1969—; operator Copperhead Hill farms (beef production), 1955—; instr. real estate law Drury Coll., 1948-64; vis. lectr. corp. law E.R. Breech Sch. Bus., 1953. Author: Daniel Boone's Sons in Missouri, 1947, West Point and Wilson's Creek-1861, 1955, An Ozark Boy's Story, 1971, An Ozark Lawyer's Story, 1976, Hulston on History, 1979-83, Col. John Trousdale Coffee, C.S.A., 1983, (with James W. Goodrich) History of Bank of Ash Grove, 1883-1983, 1983, A Look at Dade County, Missouri, 1905-85, 1985. Chmn. Wilson's Creek Nat. Battlefield Commn., 1969-79; vice chmn. Springfield Home Rule Charter Commn., 1953; chmn. Springfield City Charter Commn., 1977; pres. Greene County Estate Planning Council, 1952; trustee Springfield Pub. Library, 1955-69, Drury Coll., 1973—, State Hist. Soc. Mo., 1974—; trustee Lester E. Cox Med. Center, 1959—, pres., 1966, vice chmn., 1967—; chmn. Greene County Dems., 1947-48; introduced Pres. Harry S. Truman at 1st Whistle Stop Speech, Springfield, July 5, 1948; presdl. elector, 1948; mem. Mo. Civil War Centennial Commn., 1961-65; trustee U. Mo. Law Sch. Found., Columbia, 1981—, v.p., 1982-85, pres., 1985—; co-founder Civil War Round Table of the Ozarks, 1948, Wilson's Creek Battlefield Found., 1952, Greene County Hist. Soc., 1960, Mus. of the Ozarks, 1974; mem. devel. fund bd. U. Mo.-Columbia, 1986—. Served to maj. U.S. Army, 1941-46. Recipient Springfield Young Man of Year award, 1950, Disting. Alumni award Drury Coll., 1974, Springfieldian of Year award, 1978, Ozark Heritage award, 1979, Spl. commendation Nat. Park Service, 1981. Mem. Am. Judicature Soc., Am. Acad. Hosp. Attys., ABA (probate/trust reporter Mo. 1974—), Mo. Bar Assn. (chmn. legal aid 1952), Greene County Bar Assn. (pres. 1973), Springfield C. of C. (pres. 1950, 51, 54), Supreme Ct. of Mo. Hist. Soc. (co-founder, trustee 1984—), SAR, Order of Coif, Phi Delta Phi, Kappa Alpha Order. Democrat. Presbyterian. Clubs: Hickory Hills Country (Springfield); University of Mo. Jefferson (trustee 1976-82). Lodges: Masons (32 deg.), Shriners (potentate 1963), Jester. Home: 1300 E Catalpa St Springfield MO 65804 Office: 2060 E Sunshine St Springfield MO 65808

HULSTRAND, GEORGE EUGENE, lawyer; b. Cannon Falls, Minn., Aug. 3, 1918; s. John George and Alice Elizabeth (Holm) H.; m. Mabel Elizabeth Ericson, Sept. 7, 1946; children: George E. Jr., Brian Douglas, Darlene Lucette, Jeanne Louise. BA, Gustavus Adolphus Coll., 1943; JD, Yale U., 1946. Bar: Minn. 1947, U.S. Dist. Ct. Minn. 1951, U.S. Supreme Ct. 1977. Assoc. Roy A. Hendrickson, Willmar, Minn., 1947-53; ptnr. Hulstrand, Anderson & Larson and predecessor firm Hulstrand, Anderson, Larson & Boylan, Willmar, 1953—; asst. county atty. Kandiyohi County, Willmar, 1947-50. Contbr. articles to mags. Mem. Willmar City Council, 1953-56; chmn. Planning Commn., Willmar, 1956-57, 74-80, Kandiyohi County Dem. Farm Labor Party, Willmar, 1957-72; mem., bd. dirs. Willmar Community Coll. Found., 1965—. Mem. ABA, Minn. Bar Assn. (bd. govs. 1977-83), 12th Dist. Bar Assn., Am. Judicature Soc., Willmar Jaycees (Disting. Service award 1952, Outstanding Citizen award 1979). Lutheran. Lodges: Lions, Elks. Avocations: music, writing, golf, travel. General practice, Probate, Real property. Home: 325 N 7th St Willmar MN 56201 Office: Hulstrand Anderson & Larson 331 Profl Plaza PO Box 130 Willmar MN 56201

HULTQUIST, ROBERT CHARLES, lawyer; b. Chgo., July 31, 1931; s. Clarence C. Hultquist and Viola Helen (Ade) Sipes; m. Mary Louise Hahn, May 16, 1959; children: Robert C. Jr., Michael D., Lisa M., James T., Mary Lou, Christopher A. JD, Loyola U., 1957. Bar: Ill. 1957, U.S. Dist. Ct. (no. dist.) Ill. 1958, U.S. Ct. Appeals (7th cir.) 1958, U.S. Tax Ct. 1971. Assoc. William T. Kirby Law Offices, Chgo., 1957-59; sole practice Chgo., 1959-64; sr. ptnr. Hultquist & Hudzik P.C. and predecessor firms, Downers Grove, Ill., 1964—; assoc. prof. Loyola U., Chgo., 1960-61; sec., treas. Plastic Shipping Container Inst., Downers Grove, 1978—. Exec. com. Marquette U. Exec. Senate, Milw., 1980—; pres. Glen Ellyn Youth Ctr., Ill., 1982; chmn. Loyola Law Dean's Club, Chgo., 1976. Served to cpl. U.S. Army, 1953-55. Mem. Ill. Bar Assn., Chgo. Bar Assn. (matrimonial law com. 1978, fee com. 1981—, chmn. 1984, sport law com. 1985—, continuing legal edn. com. 1986—, trade assn. com. 1986), DuPage County Bar Assn., South Side Bar Assn. Chgo (exec. sec. 1961-70, pres. 1970-71), Ill. Trial Lawyers Assn., Trial Lawyers Club Chgo., Glenbriar Tennis Assn. (pres. 1978-79), Phi Alpha Delta (justice Webster chpt. 1957). Roman Catholic. Avocations: tennis, golf, photography, travel. State civil litigation, General corporate, Personal injury. Home: 473 Sunset Ct Glen Ellyn IL 60137 Office: Hultquist & Hudzik PC 1411 Opus Pl Suite 111 Downers Grove IL 60515

HULVEY, CRAIG WALLACE, lawyer; b. Pocatello, Idaho, Feb. 9, 1950; s. Henry James and Elizabeth (Wallace) H. B.A., George Washington U., 1972, J.D., 1975. Bar: Va. 1975, D.C. 1975. Ptnr. Grove Jaskiewicz Gilliam and Cobert, Washington, 1975—. Co-author chpt. in book. Mem. ABA (sects of adminstrv. law and natural resources law), Fed. Energy Bar Assn., Bar Assn. of D.C., Lutheran. Club: Pisces. Administrative and regulatory, FERC practice, Federal civil litigation. Home: 3553 Nelly Custis Dr Arlington VA 22207

HUME, JOHN, lawyer; b. Mexico City, May 11, 1944; s. Allan James Lea and Josephina Matilde (Gonzalez) H.; m. Barbara Jean Price; children—John David, Robert Bruce. B.A. in Polit. Sci., U. Fla., 1966, J.D., 1971. Bar: Fla. 1971. Mem. Graham, Hodge, Larson & Hume, P.A., Ft. Lauderdale, Fla., 1971-79; mem. Hume & Johnson, P.A., Coral Springs, 1979—. Bd. dirs. Legal Aid Services Broward County, Inc., 1985-86. Mem. Fla. Bar (exec. council econs. and mgmt. of law practice sect. 1979-82, bar counsel 1977, realtor-atty. joint com. 1983, editor Fla. Real Estate Manual, chmn. grievance com. 17-C, 1987), Broward County Bar Assn. (pres. young lawyers sect. 1974-75, Pres.'s award 1978, 86, chmn. real property, probate and trust law sect. 1976, exec. com. 1978-85), North Broward County Bar Assn. (pres. 1984-85). Real property, General corporate, Banking. Home: 5941 NE 15th Ave Fort Lauderdale FL 33334 Office: Hume & Johnson PA 1401 University Dr Suite 301 Coral Springs FL 33071-6039

HUMICK, THOMAS CHARLES CAMPBELL, lawyer; b. N.Y.C., Aug. 7, 1947; s. Anthony and Elizabeth Campbell (Meredith) H.; m. Nancy June Young, June 7, 1969; 1 dau., Nicole Elizabeth. B.A., Rutgers U., 1969; J.D., Suffolk U., 1972; postgrad. London Sch. Econs. and Polit. Sci., 1977-78. Bar: N.J. 1972, U.S. Ct. Appeals (3d cir.) 1976, U.S. Supreme Ct. 1977, N.Y. 1981. Law clk. Superior Ct. N.J., 1972-73; assoc. Riker, Danzig, Scherer & Debevoise, Newark and Morristown, N.J., 1973-77; ptnr. Francis & Berry, Morristown, 1978-84, Dillon, Bitar & Luther, Morristown, 1985—; arbitrator U.S. Dist. Ct. N.J., 1985—; del. to Jud. Conf. for Third Jud. Cir. U.S., 1975-79; counsel to Bd. Edn. of Borough of Middlesex (N.J.), 1977—; mem. dist. x ethics com. N.J. Supreme Ct., 1983—. Trustee, Richmond Fellowship of N.J., 1982—, pres., 1984. Mem. ABA, N.J. Bar Assn., Fed. Bar Assn., Morris County Bar Assn. Republican. Presbyterian. Clubs: Bay Head Yacht (N.J.), Roxiticus Golf. Editorial bd. Suffolk U. Law Rev., 1970-71; contbg. author: Valuation for Eminent Domain, 1973. General corporate, State civil litigation, Federal civil litigation. Home: Hardscrabble Rd Bernardsville NJ 07924 Office: Dillon Bitar & Luther 53 Maple Ave Morristown NJ 07960

HUMPERT, SAMUEL JAY, lawyer; b. Saginaw, Mich., Feb. 20, 1947; s. John Urban and Mollie (Fries) H.; m. Margi Hayes, July 7, 1984; children: Eliza, Sarah, Becky. BA, Nasson Coll., Springvale, Maine, 1973; JD, Franklin Pierce Law Ctr., Concord, N.H., 1981. Bar: Maine 1981, U.S. Dist. Ct. Maine 1981. Sole practice Waterville, Maine, 1981-86; assoc. Joly & Dubord, Waterville, 1986—. Ward chmn. City Dem. Com., Waterville, 1986. Served with U.S. Army, 1966-68, Vietnam. Democrat. Congregationalist. General practice, Real property, Bankruptcy. Office: Joly & Dubard 222 Main St PO Box 54 Waterville ME 04901

HUMPHREY, HUBERT HORATIO, III, Minnesota attorney general; b. Mpls., June 26, 1942; s. Hubert Horatio and Muriel (Buck) H.; m. Nancy Lee Humphrey, Aug. 14, 1963; children: Lorie, Pam, Hubert Horatio IV. B.A. in Polit. Sci., Am. U., Washington, 1965; J.D., U. Minn., 1969. Bar: Minn. Sole practice law 1970-82; mem. Minn. State Senate, 1972-82; atty. gen. State of Minn., St. Paul, 1983—. Bd. mgmt. Northwest br. YMCA. Mem. ABA, Minn. Bar Assn., Hennepin County Bar Assn. Mem. Democratic-Farmer-Labor Party. Home: 8116 40th Ave N New Hope MN 55427 Office: 102 State Capitol St. Paul MN 55155

HUMPHREY, JAMES WILLIAM, JR., lawyer; b. Kansas City, Mo., Apr. 13, 1930; s. James W. and Agnes (O'Keefe) H.; m. Charlotte R. Rogers, Sept. 7, 1957; children—Christine, James, John, Thomas, Elizabeth, Mary. B.S., Benedictine Coll., 1952; J.D., U Mo.-Kansas City, 1957. Bar: Mo. 1957, U.S. Dist. Ct. (we. dist.) Mo. 1957, U.S. Ct. Appeals (8th cir.) 1964, U.S. Supreme Ct. 1976. Ptnr. Kuraner, Schwegler, Humphrey, Lowe & Fishman, Kansas City, Mo., 1957—; speaker trial advocacy U. Mo.-Kansas City. Bd. dirs. Benedictine Coll., 1978—. Served with U.S. Army, 1952-54. Decorated Bronze Star. Mem. Nat. Bd. Trial Advocacy (diplomate). Roman Catholic. Contbr. writings to publs. Federal civil litigation, State civil litigation, Workers' compensation. Address: Room 500 922 Walnut Kansas City MO 64106

HUMPHREYS, NOEL DUTTON, lawyer; b. Marion County, Ind., Feb. 19, 1948; s. Sexson Eckles and Frances Reid (Dutton) H.; m. Sharon E.A. Hammill, Aug. 21, 1971; 1 child, Hayes O. BA, DePauw U., 1970; MS in Journalism, Columbia U., 1971, MA in Internat. Affairs, 1972; JS, Harvard U., 1979. Bar: N.Y. 1980, U.S. Dist. Ct. (so. and ea.) 1980. Reporter AP, N.Y.C., 1971-72; assoc. editor Parade Mag., N.Y.C., 1972-76; assoc. Dewey, Ballantine, Bushby, Palmer & Wood, N.Y.C., 1979-81, Morgan, Lewis & Bockius, N.Y.C., 1981-85, Eaton & Van Winkle, N.Y.C., 1985—. Mem. ABA, Assn. of Bar of City of N.Y. General corporate, Banking, Securities. Office: Eaton & Van Winkle 600 3d Ave New York NY 10016

HUMPHRIES, DERRICK ANTHONY, lawyer, lobbyist; b. Detroit, Apr. 3, 1947; s. Andrew John and Mary Jane (Leigh) H.; m. Linda Ann Smith, June 21, 1975 (div. Mar. 1981); 1 child, Taylor; m. Jonca Camille Bull, Oct. 20, 1984; children: Alexander, Auguste. BA, U. Mich., 1968; JD, Wayne State U., 1972. Bar: Mich. 1973, U.S. Dist. Ct. (ea. dist.) 1973, U.S. Ct. Appeals (D.C. cir.) 1974, U.S. Dist. Ct. D.C. 1977, U.S. Supreme Ct. 1977. Jud. clk. to presiding judge U.S. Dist. Ct. (ea. dist.) Mich., 1972; fellow Reginald Heber Smith Program, Washington, 1972-73; lawyer FCC, Washington, 1973-77; counsel, media dir. Congl. Black Caucus, Washington, 1977-79; sole practice Washington, 1979-82; ptnr. Brown & Finn, Washington, 1982-86, Humphries & Humphries, Washington, 1986—; spl. counsel small bus. com. U.S. Ho. of Reps., Washington, 1981-82, Detroit City Council, 1983, 84, 85, Bapt. Ministers Conf., Washington; asst. sec., spl. counsel elem. and secondary edn. U.S. Dept. Edn., 1979-81. Head usher Washington Nat. Cathedral, 1983—; pres. Detroit Renaissance Assn. of Washington, 1983—; Ark.-16th St. Neighborhood Assn., 1984—; trustee Protestant Episc. Found. of Washington, 1986—; bd. dirs. Mich. Human Services, Inc., Livonia, 1986—, Woodley House, Washington, 1986—. Served to capt. U.S. Army, 1968-76. Mem. ABA, Nat. Bar Assn., Mich. Bar Assn., D.C. Bar Assn., Wolverine Bar Assn., Nat. Cathedral Assn. (trustee 1986—), Kappa Alpha Psi. Democrat. Clubs: Detroit Renaissance (Washington) (chmn. 1986—), Assn. of Washington. Lodge: Masons. Avocations: cross-country running, bible studying, horse riding. Telecommunications, Legislative, Administrative and regulatory. Home: 4112 Arkansas Ave NW Washington DC 20011

HUMPHRIES, JAMES DONALD, III, lawyer; b. Newark, Ohio, Sept. 27, 1944; s. Howald Garland and Marjorie Louise (Bailey) H.; m. Patricia Lawver, Apr. 8, 1972; children: James Donald IV, P. Laing. BS, Washington and Lee U., 1966, JD cum laude, 1969. Bar: Ga. 1970. Assoc. Kilpatrick & Cody, Atlanta, 1969-73; ptnr. Harland, Cashin, Chambers & Parker, Atlanta, 1973-75, Morton, Humphries & Payne, Atlanta, 1976-79, Varner, Stephens, Wingfield, McIntyre & Humphries, Atlanta, 1979—; bd. dirs. various cos. Mem. Lawyers Club Atlanta (pres. 1982-83), Atlanta Lawyers Found. (trustee 1984—, chmn. 1986). Republican. Episcopalian. Clubs: Capital City, Old War Horse Lawyers. Construction, Labor. Home: 790 Kinloch St NW Atlanta GA 30327 Office: 1000 Grant Bldg Atlanta GA 30303

HUMPHRIES, JUDY LYNN, lawyer, nurse; b. Charleston, W.Va., Nov. 20, 1946; d. Robert Elmer and Arravelva Virginia (Davis) H.; m. Michael Allen Grant, Dec. 29, 1971; children: Susan Lindley, Christopher Allen, Elizabeth Davis. BSN, W.Va. U., 1968; MS, U. Md., 1970; JD, William & Mary Coll., 1977. Bar: Va. 1977, W.Va. 1978, D.C. 1980. Instr. in psychiatric nursing W.Va. U., Morgantown, 1970-72, asst. prof. upper div. nursing, 1977-78; psychiat. nurse Veterans Hosp., Clev., 1972-73; asst. prosecutor Monongalia County, Morgantown, 1978-81; sole practice Fairmont, W.Va., 1981—; instr. health law and med. ethics Fairmont State Coll., 1984—; cons. J.B. Lippincott Pubs., Phila., 1985; asst. prosecutor Marion County, W.Va., 1986—; bd. dirs. Hope, Inc. Bd. dirs. Monongalia county Youth Services Ctr., 1981-83. Mem. ABA, LWV. Democrat. Episcopalian. Health, Criminal, General practice. Home and Office: 1160 Avalon Rd Fairmont WV 26554

HUNDT, REED ERIC, lawyer; b. Ann Arbor, Mich., Mar. 3, 1948; s. Neal H. and Viola (Pullan) H.; m. Elizabeth Ann Katz, Oct. 26, 1980; children: Adam Elias, Nathaniel Pullan. BA, Yale U., 1969, JD, 1974. Bar: U.S. Dist. Ct. Md. 1974, U.S. Ct. Appeals (4th cir.) 1975, U.S. Dist. Ct. (cen. and no. dists.) Calif. 1976, U.S. Ct. Appeals (9th cir.) 1976, U.S. Supreme Ct. 1977, U.S. Tax. Ct. 1978, U.S. Ct. Appeals (3d cir.) 1979, U.S. Dist. Ct. D.C. 1980, U.S. Ct. Appeals (D.C. cir.) 1980. Law clk. to presiding justice U.S. Ct. Appeals (4th cir.), Balt., 1974-75; assoc. Latham & Watkins, Washington, 1975-81, ptnr., 1982—. Book rev. editor Yale U. Law Rev., 1974-75; author: (chpt. 9) Antitrust Adviser '85. Mem. Environ. Task Force of Dem. Policy Com., Washington, 1986. Mem. ABA. Environment, Federal civil litigation, State civil litigation. Home: 4811 Cumberland Ave Chevy Chase MD 20815 Office: Latham & Watkins 1333 New Hampshire Ave NW Suite 1200 Washington DC 20036

HUNGATE, WILLIAM LEONARD, judge, former congressman; b. Benton, Ill., Dec. 14, 1922; s. Leonard Wathen and Maude Irene (Williams) H.; m. Dorothy N. Wilson, Apr. 13, 1944; children—William David, Margie Kay (Mrs. Branson L. Wood III). A.B., U. Mo., 1943; LL.B., Harvard U., 1948; LL.D. (hon.), Culver-Stockton Coll., Canton, Mo., 1968; J.D. (hon.), Central Meth. Coll., Fayette, Mo., 1975. Bar: Mo. 1948, Ill. 1949, U.S. Supreme Ct 1960, D.C. 1967. Practiced law Troy, Mo., 1948-68, St. Louis, 1977-79; sr. partner firm Hungate and Grewach, 1956-68; partner firm Thompson and Mitchell, St. Louis, 1977-79; judge U.S. Dist. Ct. Eastern Dist. Mo., 1979—; pros. atty. Lincoln County, Mo., 1951-55; spl. asst. atty. gen. of Mo. 1958-64; research adminstrn. criminal justice in U.S. Am. Bar Found., 1956; mem. 88th-94th congresses, 9th Dist. Mo.; mem. judiciary com., chmn. subcom. criminal justice, select com. on small bus., chmn. subcom. on activities of regulatory agys.; vis. prof. polit. sci. U. Mo., St. Louis; also composer. Trustee William Woods Coll.; chmn. small bus. adv. com. Treasury Dept., 1977; chmn. Mo. Gov.'s Commn. on Campaign Reform and Ofcl. Conduct, 1978-79; mem. Adv. Com. on Criminal Rules, 1977—. Mem. Ill. Bar Assn., Fed. Bar Assn., ABA (nat. conf. of fed. trial judges exec. com. 1980—, chmn. 1985-86), Mo. Bar Assn., D.C. Bar Assn., Harvard Law Sch. Assn. Mo. (pres. 1962-64, 83-84, council mem.), ASCAP, Mo. Squires, Jud. Conf. U.S. (budget com.), 8th Cir. Dist. Judges Assn. (pres. 1984-86, mem. budget com. of Jud. Conf. U.S.). Mem. Christian Ch. (chmn. bd. 1964). Club: Kiwanian (Troy) (pres. 1951, lt. gov. 1959). Jurisprudence. Home: 26 Chapel Hill Estates Town and Country MO 63131 Office: U S Dist Ct 1114 Market St Saint Louis MO 63101 *

HUNJI, PREM LITTA, lawyer; b. Yuba City, Calif., May 25, 1954; d. Hardial Singh and Kushlia (Devi) H. Student, Calif. State U.; JD, Lincoln U., 1979. Bar: Calif. 1979, U.S. Dist. Ct. (ea. dist.) 1979. Legal asst. Sacramento County Legal Aid Soc., 1971-72; adminstrv. asst. to Senator Omer Rains Calif. State Senate, Sacramento, 1974; field investigator Sacramento County Pub. Defender, 1975-76; aide to gov.'s spl. asst. Office of Gov. Edmund G. Brown, Jr., Sacramento, 1976-77; dir. consumer edn. unit Calif. State Dept. Real Estate, Sacramento, 1977; coordinator spl. projects unit Calif. State Bur. Automotive Repair, Sacramento, 1978-80; assoc. Kahn, Soares & Conway, Sacramento, 1980—, sole practice. Contbr. articles ot profl. jours. Former mem. Gov.' Asian-Indian Adv. Council. Mem. ABA (corp., banking and bus. law sect., nat. resources law sect.), Sacramento County Bar Assn. (bd. dirs. young lawyers assn. 1981-82, treas. 1982), Calif. Trial Lawyers Assn., Calif. Women Lawyers Assn., Sacramento Women Lawyers Assn., Nat. Women's Polit. Caucus. Democrat. Club: Barristers of Sacramento (pres. 1985). Administrative and regulatory, General corporate, Legislative. Home: 12 Mast Ct Sacramento CA 95831 Office: Law Offices of Prem L Hunji 555 Capitol Mall Suite 1500 Sacramento CA 95814

HUNKER, GEORGE HENRY, JR., lawyer; b. Las Vegas, N.Mex., Sept. 1, 1914; s. George H. Sr. and Emma (Vasse) H.; m. Margaret H. Klett, Dec. 21, 1940; children: George Henry III, Margaret Katherine. LLB, U. Colo., 1939. Bar: Kans. 1939, N.Mex. 1939, U.S. Supreme Ct. 1944. Ptnr. Hunker-Fedric, Roswell, N.Mex., 1939—. Oil and gas leasing. Home: 1710 W 3d St Roswell NM 88201 Office: Hunker & Fedric PA 210 Hinkle Bldg PO Box 1837 Roswell NM 88201

HUNKINS, RAYMOND BREEDLOVE, lawyer; b. Culver City, Calif., Mar. 19, 1939; s. Charles F. and Louise (Breedlove) H.; m. Mary Deborah McBride, Dec. 12, 1968; children: Amanda, Blake, Ashley. BA, U. Wyo., 1966, JD, 1968. Bar: Wyo. 1968, U.S. Dist. Ct. Wyo. 1968, U.S. Ct. Appeals (10th cir.) 1969, U.S. Supreme Ct. 1971. Ptnr. Jones, Jones, Vines & Hunkins, Wheatland, Wyo., 1968—; chmn. bd. dirs. 1st State Bank of Wheatland; spl. counsel U. Wyo., Laramie, State of Wyo., Cheyenne. Chmn. Platte County Reps., Wheatland, 1972-74; commr Wyo. Aeronautics Commn., 1987—. Served to sgt. USMC, 1955-57. Mem. ABA (aviation com. 1980—, litigation sect., forum com. on constrn. industry), Wyo. Bar Assn. (chmn. grievance com. 1980—), Assn. Trial Lawyers Am., Wyo. Trial Lawyers Assn. (pres. 1980-81), U. Wyo. Alumni Assn. (past pres.). Lodges: Lions, Elks, Mosse. Federal civil litigation, State civil litigation, Construction. Office: Jones Jones Vines & Hunkins PO Drawer 189 Wheatland WY 82201

HUNSUCKER, PHILIP CARL, lawyer; b. San Diego, May 13, 1957; s. Harry Thomas and Lieselotte (Phillips) H.; m. Kristi Kay Helmecke, Mar. 22, 1978; 1 child, Joshua. AA, N.Mex. Mil. Inst., 1977; BA, BS, Howard Payne U., 1979; JD, So. Meth. U., 1982. Bar: Tex. 1982, U.S. Dist. Ct. (no. dist.) Tex. 1982, U.S. Dist. Ct. (so. dist.) Tex. 1983, U.S. Ct. Mil. Appeals 1984. Assoc. Robins, Zelle, Larson & Kaplan, Dallas, 1982-83, 87—. Served to capt. (JAGC) U.S. Army, 1983-87. Mem. ABA (litigation sect.), Assn. Trial Lawyers Am. Democrat. Methodist. Avocations: golf, running. Insurance, State civil litigation, Federal civil litigation. Home: 10960 Middle Knoll Dallas TX 75238 Office: Robins Zelle Larson & Kaplan 2700 Interfirst Plaza 901 Main St Dallas TX 75202

HUNT, DAVID WALLINGFORD, lawyer; b. Washington, Sept. 27, 1952; s. Donald Harvey and Dorothy Walter (Johnson) H.; m. Sylvia Fortney, Aug. 10, 1974. BA with high distinction, U. Va., 1974, JD, 1977. Bar: Ga. 1977, D.C. 1982, U.S. Ct. Appeals (5th cir.) 1981, U.S. Ct. Appeals (11th cir.) 1982. Law asst. Ga. Supreme Ct., Atlanta, 1977-78; atty. Troutman, Sanders, Lockerman & Ashmore, Atlanta, 1978-80; counsel Turner Broadcasting System, Inc., Atlanta, 1980-81; atty. O'Neill & Haase, Washington, 1981-84, ptnr., 1985-86; prin. Taubman, Hunt, Hodin & Costelloe, P.C., Washington, 1986—; gen. counsel Congl. Award Bd., Washington, 1986—. Mem. editorial bd. Va. Law Review, 1975-77. Pres. Wingdate of Arlington, Va., 1982-84. Dillard fellow U. Va., Charlottesville, 1976-77. Mem. ABA, Ga. Bar Assn., D.C. Bar Assn., Order of the Coif, Phi Beta Kappa. Episcopalian. Securities, General corporate, Banking. Home: 6308 Hardy Dr McLean VA 22101 Office: Taubman Hunt Hodin & Costelloe 1129 20th St NW Suite 500 Washington DC 20036

HUNT, GEORGE ANDREW, lawyer; b. Salina, Utah, Mar. 5, 1949; s. Loyd G. and Inez (Rinkerhoff) H.; m. Elizabeth Jean Brandise, July 28, 1973; children: Rachael, Rinaldo, Andrew, Geoffrey. BS in Internat. Relations cum laude, U. Utah, 1971, JD, 1974. Bar: Utah 1974, U.S. Dist. Ct. Utah 1974, U.S. Ct. Appeals (10th cir.) 1976, U.S. Supreme Ct. 1978, U.S. Ct. Appeals (9th cir.) 1984. Assoc. Snow, Christensen & Martineas, Salt Lake City, 1974-78, ptnr., 1978—. Pres. U. Utah Coll. of Law, Salt Lake City, 1974, mentor, 1986—; treas. Shearer for U.S. Congress, Salt Lake City, 1984. Mem. Utah Bar Assn. (bar examiner 1976-80, chmn. constrn. law sect. 1985—), Salt Lake County Bar Assn. (mem. exec. com. 1979—, treas. 1984, sec. 1985, v.p. 1986—). Republican. Roman Catholic. Clubs: Ft. Douglas Country. Avocations: flying, reading, music, gardening. Construction, Real property, Contracts commercial. Office: Snow Christensen & Martineau 10 Exchange Pl PO Box 45000 Salt Lake City UT 84145

HUNT, ISAAC COSBY, JR., college dean, lawyer; b. Danville, Va., Aug. 1937; s. Isaac Cosby and Evelyn Doris (Allen) H.; m. Elizabeth D. Ravenell, Aug. 16, 1966; 1 child, Isaac Cosby III. B.A., Fisk U., 1957; LL.B., U. Va., 1962. Bar: U.S. Dist. Ct. D.C. 1963, U.S. Ct. Appeals (D.C. cir.) 1963. Staff atty. SEC, Washington, 1962-67; field team leader Nat. Adv. Commn. on Civil Disorders (Kerner Commn.), 1967-68; exec. asst. to commr. EEOC, 1968; mem. research staff Rand Corp., 1968-71; asst. prof. Law Sch., Catholic U. Am., Washington, 1971-77; assoc. Jones, Day, Reavis & Pogue, 1977-79; prin. dep. gen. counsel Dept. Army, 1979-81; dean Antioch Sch. Law, Washington, 1981—; cons. Ford Found., 1971. Author: (with B. Cohen) Minority Recruitment in N.Y. City Police Dept. Co-chmn. D.C. Consumer Goods Repair Bd., 1975-76. Recipient Outstanding Civilian Service award Dept. Army, 1980. Mem. ABA, D.C. Bar Assn., Nat. Bar Assn., Soc. Am. Law Tchrs. (bd. govs. 1970). Democrat. Presbyterian. Club: Nat. Lawyers. Office: Antioch Sch of Law 1624 Crescent Pl, NW Washington DC 20009

HUNT, JOHN FLOYD, lawyer; b. Grand Rapids, Mich., Dec. 10, 1946; s. Manard Wenger and Kathryn Lorraine (Stein) H.; m. Janet Catherine Trainor, Aug. 30, 1969; 1 child, Angela Kay. B in Chem. Engring., Mich. State U., 1969; JD, St. Mary's U., San Antonio, 1977. Bar: Mich. 1978, U.S. Dist. Ct. (ea. dist.) Mich. 1978, U.S. Patent Office 1979. Assoc. Gifford et al, Birmingham, Mich., 1978-80, Ethyl Corp., Ferndale, Mich. and Baton Rouge, 1980-85; sr. patent atty. Exxon Chem. Co., Baytown, Tex., 1985—. Served to capt. USAF, 1970-75. Roman Catholic. Avocations: golf, tennis, fishing, hunting. Patent, Trademark and copyright, General corporate. Office: Exxon Chem Co PO Box 5200 Baytown TX 77520

HUNT, LAWRENCE BOYD, lawyer; b. Portland, Oreg., Jan. 30, 1950; s. Thomas Newton and Norma Lucile (Beer) H.; m. Jean Marie Larson, June 24, 1972; children: Damian B., Marion L., Abigail M., Lucile A. BA with honors, Northwestern U., 1971; JD, U. Oreg., 1975. Bar: Oreg. 1975, U.S. Dist. Ct. Oreg. 1976, U.S. Ct. Appeals (9th cir.) 1976, U.S. Tax Ct. 1976, Wash. 1986. Assoc. Becker & Sipprell, Portland, 1976-80; ptnr. Becker, Sipprell & Hunt, Portland, 1980-86, Becker and Hunt, Portland, 1986—. Mem. ABA (corp. banking and bus. law com., UCC subcom. gen. provisions, sales and trade fers and documents of title, litigation sect.), Oreg. State Bar Assn. (newsletter subcom., debtor/creditor sect. 1984-85). Contracts commercial, State civil litigation, Federal civil litigation. Office: Becker and Hunt 1 SW Main St Portland OR 97204

HUNT, LAWRENCE HALLEY, JR., lawyer; b. Chgo., July 15, 1943; s. Lawrence Halley Sr. and Mary Hamilton (Johnson) H.; m. Valerie C. Smith, Aug. 8, 1976; children: Caroline Smith, Laura Hamilton, Darwin Halley. AB, Dartmouth Coll., 1965; Cert. l'Institut d'Etudes Politiques, Paris, 1966; JD, U. of Chgo., 1969. Bar: N.Y. 1970, Ill. 1971, U.S. Ct. Appeals (9th cir.) 1980, U.S. Ct. Appeals (2nd cir.) 1981, U.S. Supreme Ct. 1981. Assoc. Davis Polk & Wardwell, N.Y.C., 1969-70; assoc. Sidley & Austin, Chgo., 1970, ptnr., 1975—; dir. Resource Fund Internat. Ltd. Advisor securities adv. com. Ill. Sec. of State, Springfield, 1977—; James B. Reynolds scholar Dartmouth Coll., 1965-66. Mem. ABA (com. on commodity regulation, past chmn. subcom. on futures commn. merchants, mem. exec. council). Republican. Congregationalist. Clubs: Racquet of Chgo., Mid-Day; Indian Hill (Winnetka, Ill.). Private international, Administrative and regulatory. Home: 825 Mount Pleasant St Winnetka IL 60093 Office: Sidley & Austin One First National Plaza Chicago IL 60603

HUNT, MERRILL ROBERTS, lawyer; b. Portland, Maine, Jan. 23, 1939; s. Merrill Dewey and Lillian Katherine (McIntosh) H.; m. Janet McLean, July 21, 1962; 1 dau., Virginia Elizabeth. B.A., Trinity Coll., 1962; J.D., U. Maine, 1969. Bar: Maine 1969. Assoc., Mahoney, Robinson, Mahoney & Norman (and predecessors), Portland, 1969-70, ptnr., 1971-75; ptnr. Robinson, Hunt & Kriger, Portland, 1976-78; ptnr. Hunt, Thompson & Bowie, Portland, 1979—. Chmn., Falmouth (Maine) Sewer Bd. Appeals, 1972-73; mem. Falmouth Bd. Zoning Appeals, 1974-78, chmn., 1976-78. Mem. ABA, Maine Bar Assn., Cumberland County Bar Assn., Am. Judicature Soc., Def. Research Inst. Federal civil litigation, State civil litigation, Personal injury. Office: 4 Canal Plaza Portland ME 04111

HUNT, PHILIP COURTNEY, lawyer; b. West Chester, Pa., Nov. 15, 1950; s. Mitchell J. and Marjorie Lou (Nelson) H.; m. Susan Jane Callaghan, June 17, 1972; children: Sarah Jane, Miles Clinton. BA, Lehigh U., 1972; JD, Harvard U., 1975. Bar: Maine 1975, U.S. Ct. Mil. Appeals 1976, U.S. Tax. Ct. 1980. Ptnr. Perkins, Thompson, Hinckley & Keddy, Portland, Maine, 1980—. Mem. Sch. Facilities and Enrollments Com., Cumberland, Maine, 1982—, Sch. Bldg. Com., Cumberland, 1984—, Bd. Appeals, Cumberland, 1984—; trustee Tuttle Rd. United Meth. Ch., 1986—. Served to maj. USAFR, 1972—. Mem. ABA, Maine Bar Assn., Cumberland Bar Assn. Estate planning, General corporate, Pension, profit-sharing, and employee benefits. Home: 250 Main St Cumberland ME 04021 Office: Perkins Thompson Hinckley & Keddy 1 Canal Plaza PO Box 426 Portland ME 04112-0426

HUNT, RICHARD MARTIN, lawyer; b. Dallas, Dec. 15, 1955; s. David Glenn and Princess Gloria (Martin) H.; m. Karen Lynne Zander, Sept. 5, 1981. BA, Rice U.; JD, U. Tex. Bar: Tex. 1981, U.S. Dist. Ct. (no., ea. and we. dists.) Tex. 1982, U.S. Ct. Appeals (5th cir.) 1982. Assoc. Durant & Mankott, Dallas, 1981-83, Glast, Miller & Allen, Dallas, 1983-86, Pettit & Martin, Dallas, 1986—. Mem. ABA (assoc. editor computer litigation com. newsletter 1985—), Tex. Bar Assn., Dallas Bar Assn., Order of Coif, Phi Beta Kappa. Democrat. Methodist. Federal civil litigation, State civil litigation, Bankruptcy. Office: Pettit & Martin 510 Tex Commerce Bank Tower Plaza Ams Dallas TX 75201

HUNT, RONALD FORREST, lawyer; b. Shelby, N.C., Apr. 18, 1943; s. Forrest Elmer and Bruna Magnolia (Brackett) H.; m. Judy Elaine Shultz, May 19, 1965; 1 child, Mary. A.B., U. N.C., 1966, J.D., 1968. Mem. staff SEC, Washington, 1968-69, legal asst. to chmn., 1970-71, sec. of commn., 1972-73; dep. gen. counsel, sec. Student Loan Marketing Assn., Washington, 1973-78, sr. v.p., gen. counsel, sec., 1979-83, exec. v.p., gen. counsel, 1983—; vice chmn., dir. 1st Capital Corp., Southern Pines, N.C., 1984—. Mem. Montgomery County Commn. Landlord and Tenant Affairs, Md., 1976-81, chmn., 1979-81; bd. dirs. D.C. chpt. ARC, 1976-83; trustee Arena Stage, Washington, 1984—. Mem. ABA, N.C. Bar Assn., D.C. Bar Assn., Fed. Bar Assn., Order of Coif. Republican. Presbyterian. Avocations: sailing; gardening. Office: Student Loan Marketing Assn 1050 Thomas Jefferson St NW Washington DC 20007

HUNT, THOMAS REED, JR., lawyer; b. Elkton, Md., Feb. 22, 1948; s. Thomas R. and Marian D. (Decker) H.; m. Nancy J. Hannigan, Oct. 23, 1971; children: Reed Thomas, Clifton Bowie. Ptnr. Morris, Nichols, Arsht & Tunnell, Wilmington, Del., 1972—.

HUNT, WILLIAM E., state supreme court justice. Justice Mont. Supreme Ct., Helena. Office: Mont Supreme Ct State Capitol Helena MT 59601 *

HUNT, WILLIAM JOHN, lawyer; b. N.Y.C., Jan. 31, 1951; s. William James and Martha Jeannette (Hultborg) H.; m. Alison Penney Ross, Jan. 8, 1977. BA cum laude, Dickinson Coll., 1973; JD, Suffolk U., 1976. Bar: Pa. 1976, Mass. 1978, N.J. 1982. Asst. staff counsel Southeastern Pa. Transp. Authority, Phila., 1977-78; vol. atty. U.S. Peace Corps., Saipan, Mariana Islands, 1978-79; dep. atty. gen. tort litigation unit Pa. Dept. of Justice, Phila., 1979-80; supr. litigation INA, Piscataway, N.J., 1981-83; assoc. Giordano, Halleran & Ciesla, Middletown, N.J., 1983-86; ptnr. Hayes, Clark & Embry, Cambridge, Mass., 1986—; instr. Nat. Inst. for Trial Adv., 1985—; vol. instr. trial adv. program Hofstra U., Hempstead, N.Y., 1986—. Bd. dirs., treas. Princeton (N.J.) Youth Baseball Assn., 1982-86. Mem. ABA, Soc. CPLU's, Assn. Trial Lawyers Am., Nat. Inst. Trial Adv. Republican. Avocations: scuba diving, tennis. Federal civil litigation, State civil litigation, Insurance. Home: 500 Colonial Dr #112 Ipswich MA 01938 Office: Hayes Clark & Embry 43 Thorndike St Cambridge MA 02141

HUNT, WILLIAM WALTER, III, lawyer; b. Murray, Ky., Jan. 3, 1951; s. William Walter Jr. and Isabelle (Waldrop) H.; m. Nikki Sothras, Dec. 22, 1972; 1 child, William Walter IV. BA, So. Meth. U., 1973; JD, U. Va., 1976. Bar: Tenn. 1976, U.S. Dist. Ct. (mid. dist.) Tenn. 1976, U.S. Ct. Appeals (6th cir.) 1976, U.S. Supreme Ct. 1981. Asst. atty. gen. State of Tenn., Nashville, 1976-81; disciplinary counsel Bd. of Profl. Responsibility, Nashville, 1981—. Contbr. articles to profl. jours. Chaplain U. Va. Hosp., Charlottesville, 1973-76; counsellor Tenn. Alive Hospice, Nashville, 1982—; chairperson Tenn. Common Cause, Nashville, 1983—; advisor Tenn. Japan Ctr., Murfreesboro, Tenn., 1985—. Mem. ABA, Tenn. Bar Assn. (ho. of dels. 1978-81), Nashville Bar Assn., Nat. Orgn. of Bar Counsel. Episcopalian. Lodge: Kiwanis. Jurisprudence, Civil rights, Computer. Home: 1409 Hampshire Pl Nashville TN 37221 Office: Bd of Profl Responsibility 1101 Kermit Dr Suite 405 Nashville TN 37217

HUNT, WILLIS, state judge. Judge Ga. Supreme Ct., Atlanta, 1985—. Office: 533 State Judicial Bldg Atlanta GA 30344 *

HUNTER, CHRISTOPHER BUCK, lawyer; b. Jacksonville, Ill., Jan. 28, 1953; s. James G. and Mary Ann (Grubb) H.; m. Ann G. Zaeske, May 21, 1977 (div.). B.A., MacMurray Coll., 1975; J.D., St. Louis U., 1978. Bars: Ill. 1978, U.S. Dist. Ct. (so. dist.) Ill. 1979, Mo. 1979, U.S. Dist. Ct. (ea. dist.) 1979, U.S. Ct. Appeals (7th cir.) 1980, U.S. Ct. Appeals (8th cir.) 1980, U.S. Tax Ct. 1985. Atty., Land of Lincoln Legal Assistance, Alton, Ill., 1977-81; assoc. Farrell & Long, P.C., Godfrey Ill., 1981—. Mem. Saukee Area council Boy Scouts Am. Recipient Order of Arrow, Boy Scouts Am., 1967. Mem. ABA, Ill. Bar Assn., Am. Trial Lawyers Assn., Madison County Bar Assn. (treas. 1986—), Alton-Wood River Bar Assn. (sec. 1981-82), Phi Alpha Delta (local treas. 1981—). Republican. Roman Catholic. Home: 11051 Mollerus Dr Apt 307 Saint Louis MO 63138 Office: Farrell & Long PC 1310 W Delmar St Godfrey IL 62035

HUNTER, DONALD FORREST, lawyer; b. Mpls., Jan. 30, 1934; s. Earl Harvey and Ruby Cecilia (Lagerston) H.; m. Marlys Ann Zilge; Jeffrey, Cheri, Kathryn. BA, U. Minn., 1962, JD, 1963. Bar: Minn. 1963, U.S. Dist. C. Minn. 1965, U.S. Ct. Appeals (8th cir.) 1965, Ill. 1977. Assoc. Gislason, Dosland, Hunter & Malecki, New Ulm, Minn., 1963-76; exec. v.p., sec., gen. counsel Wirtz Prodn. Ltd. Ice Follies/Holiday on Ice, Chgo., 1976-79; ptnr. Gislason, Dosland, Hunter & Malecki, Mpls—. Fellow Am. Coll. Trial Lawyers; mem. ABA, Minn. Bar Assn. (bd. of govs. 1973-76), 5th Dist. Bar Assn. (pres. 1971-72), Hennepin County Bar Assn., Minn. Def. Lawyers Assn. (bd. dirs. Minn.). Club: Decathlon Athletic (Bloomington, Minn.). Federal civil litigation, State civil litigation, Insurance. Office: Gislason Dosland Hunter & Malecki 10201 Wayzata Blvd Minnetonka MN 55343

HUNTER, EMMETT MARSHALL, lawyer, oil investments co. exec.; b. Denver, Aug. 18, 1913; s. Emmett Marshall and Pearl Joe (Hubby) H.; m. Marjorie Louise Roth, Nov. 21, 1941; children—Marsha Louise, Marjorie Maddin, Margaret Anne. LL.B., So. Meth. U., 1936, grad. U.S. Naval Mine Warfare Sch. Bar: Tex. 1936. Assoc. Vaughan & Work, Dallas, 1936, Thornton & Montgomery, 1937; sole practice, Dallas, Longview, Houston, 1937-42; with Humble Oil & Refining Co., and successor firm Exxon Co. USA, 1945-78; pres., gen. counsel Internat. Oil Investments, Tyler, Tex., 1978—. Bd. dirs. Tex. Rose Festival, Tyler; bd. mgrs. SAR Tex. state registrar, 1973-85, registrar emeritus, pres. Tyler chpt., 1973. Served with USN, 1942-45; PTO. Recipient Gold Good Citizenship medal SAR, 1979, Patriot's medal, Meritorious medal, 1984. Mem. Am. Petroleum Inst., State Bar Tex., U.S. Naval Inst., Pi Upsilon Nu, Lambda Chi Alpha. Author: Adventuring Abroad on a Bicycle, 1938; Marinas, A Boon to Yachting,

1948. Oil and gas leasing, Real property. Office: PO Box 7402 Tyler TX 75711

HUNTER, EUGENIA C., lawyer; b. Waterbury, Conn., Feb. 18, 1941; m. Robert Hunter, July 19, 1964. BA, So. Ill. U., 1963, MS, 1970, JD, 1976. Bar: Ill. 1977, U.S. Dist. Ct. (so. dist.) Ill. 1977, U.S. Ct. Appeals (7th cir.) 1986. Ptnr. Hunter & Schwartz, Carbondale, Ill., 1977-86; sole practice Carbondale, 1986-87; ptnr. Hunter and Murray, Carbondale, 1987—; asst. state's atty. Jackson County, Murphysboro, Ill., 1978. Pres. Humane Soc. So. Ill. Inc., Carbondale, 1968—, Found. for Justice Under Law Inc., Carbondale, 1970—, Mus./Art Gallery Assn., So. Ill. U., Carbondale, 1982. Recipient Annetta Dieckman award ACLU, 1973. Mem. Ill. Bar Assn., Jackson County Bar Assn. (treas. 1981-84, sec. 1984-85, v.p. 1985-86, pres. 1986-87), Assn. Trial Lawyers Am., Irish Wolfhound Club Am. (v.p. 1976-87, pres. 1987—). Avocations: animal welfare, antiquities, flowers. General practice, Family and matrimonial, Real property. Office: 905 W Cherry Carbondale IL 62901

HUNTER, FREDERICK DOUGLAS, lawyer; b. Pitts., Jan. 30, 1940; s. Charles and Elizabeth Virginia (Randolph) H.; m. Rosie Mae Kirkland, June 5, 1964; children: Frederick D. Jr., Deborah Rose. BS, U. Pitts., 1961, PhD, 1967; JD, U. Md., 1974. Bar: D.C. 1975, Del. 1976. Patent atty. E.I. du Pont de Nemours & Co., Wilmington, Del., 1975-81, sr. patent atty., 1981-83, supervisory atty., 1984-85, corp. counsel, 1985—. Mem. ABA, Am. Intellectual Property Law Assn. Democrat. Avocation: photography. Patent. Home: 18 Stone Brook Circle RD5 Hockessin DE 19707 Office: EI du Pont de Nemours & Co 1007 Market St Wilmington DE 19898

HUNTER, JACK DUVAL, insurance holding company executive, lawyer; b. Elkhart, Ind., Jan. 14, 1937; s. William Stanley and Marjorie Irene (Upson) H.; m. Marsha Ann Goodsell, Nov. 14, 1958; children: Jack, Jon, Justin. B.B.A., U. Mich., 1959, LL.B., 1961. Bar: Mich. 1961, Ind. 1962. Atty. Lincoln Nat. Life Ins. Co., Ft. Wayne, Ind., 1961-64, asst. counsel, 1964-68, v.p., gen. counsel, 1975-79, sr. v.p., gen. counsel, 1979-86, exec. v.p., gen. counsel, 1986—; asst. gen. counsel, asst. sec. Lincoln Nat. Corp., Ft. Wayne, 1968-71, gen. counsel, 1971-72, v.p., gen. counsel, 1972-79, sr. v.p., gen. counsel, 1979-86, exec. v.p., gen. counsel, 1986—. Mem. ABA, Mich. Bar Assn., Ind. Bar Assn., Allen County Bar Assn., Assn. Life Ins. Counsel., Am. Corp. Counsel Assn. General corporate. Office: 1300 S Clinton St PO Box 1110 Fort Wayne IN 46801

HUNTER, JAMES AUSTEN, JR., lawyer; b. Phoenix, June 19, 1941; s. James Austen and Elizabeth Aileen (Holt) H.; m. Donna Gabriele, Aug. 24, 1973; 1 child, James A. A.B., Cath. U. Am., 1963, LL.B., 1966. Bar: N.Y. 1967, Pa. 1975, U.S. Supreme Ct. 1974. Assoc. firm Sullivan & Cromwell, N.Y.C., 1967-74; assoc. firm Morgan, Lewis & Bockius, Phila., 1974-77; ptnr. Morgan, Lewis & Bockius, 1977—. Banking, General corporate. Home: 1001 Red Rose Ln Villanova PA 19085 Office: Morgan Lewis & Bockius One Logan Sq Philadelphia PA 19103

HUNTER, JAMES GALBRAITH, JR., lawyer; b. Phila., Jan. 6, 1942; s. James Galbraith and Emma Margaret (Jehl) H.; m. Pamela Ann Trott, July 18, 1969 (div.); children—James Nicholas, Catherine Selene. B.S. in Engring. Sci., Case Inst. Tech., 1965; J.D., U. Chgo., 1967. Bar: Ill. 1967, U.S. Dist. Ct. (no. dist.) Ill. 1967, U.S. Ct. Appeals (7th cir.) 1967, U.S. Ct. Claims, 1976, U.S. Ct. Appeals (4th and 9th cirs.) 1978, U.S. Supreme Ct. 1979, U.S. Dist. Ct. (cen. dist.) Ill. 1980, Calif. 1980, U.S. Dist. Ct. (cen. and so. dists.) Calif. 1980, U.S. Ct. Appeals (5th cir.) 1982, U.S. Ct. Appeals (fed. cir.) 1982. Assoc. Kirkland & Ellis, Chgo., 1967-68, 70-73, ptnr., 1973-76; ptnr. Hedlund, Hunter & Lynch, Chgo., 1976-82, Los Angeles, 1979-82; ptnr. Latham & Watkins, Hedlund, Hunter & Lynch, Chgo. and Los Angeles, 1982—. Served to lt. JAGC, USN, 1968-70. Mem. ABA, State Bar Calif., Los Angeles County Bar Assn., Chgo. Bar Assn. Clubs: Metropolitan (Chgo.), Chgo. Athletic Assn., Los Angeles Athletic. Exec. editor U. Chgo. Law Rev., 1966-67. Federal civil litigation, State civil litigation, Antitrust. Office: Suite 6900 Sears Tower Chicago IL 60606 also: 555 S Flower St Los Angeles CA 90071

HUNTER, KEITH ALAN, lawyer; b. Hershey, Pa., Nov. 25, 1957; s. Brook Leo and Nancy Louise (Bachman) H.; m. Ellen Nichole Grun, Mar. 26, 1985. BA, SUNY, Oswego, 1979; JD, Case Western Res. U., 1982. Bar: Pa. 1982. Chief counsel Saltax Cons., Inc., Hershey, 1983. Republican. Avocations: painting, model ship bldg., computers. State and local taxation, Administrative and regulatory, Personal injury. Office: Mahler & Shaffer Martz Tower 2d Floor 46 Public Sq Wilkes Barre PA 18701

HUNTER, LARRY DEAN, lawyer; b. Leon, Iowa, Apr. 10, 1950; s. Doyle J. and Dorothy B. (Grey) H.; m. Rita K. Barker, Jan. 24, 1971; children—Nathan, Allison. B.S. with high distinction, U. Iowa, 1971; A.M., U. Mich., 1974, J.D. magna cum laude, 1974, C.Phil. in Econs., 1975. Bar: Va. 1975, Mich. 1978, U.S. Ct. Appeals (4th cir.). Assoc. McGuire Woods & Battle, Richmond, Va., 1975-77; asst. counsel, internat. counsel Clark Equipment Co., Buchanan, Mich., 1977-80; ptnr. Honigman, Miller, Schwartz and Cohn, Detroit, 1980—; sec., gen. counsel Allied Supermarkets, Inc., Detroit, 1985—. Mem. Order of Coif. General corporate, Securities, Contracts commercial. Home: 10 Lake Ct Grosse Pointe MI 48230 Office: Honigman Miller Schwartz and Cohn 2290 First Nat Bldg Detroit MI 48226

HUNTER, MARTHA LOUISE, lawyer; b. Pitts., Nov. 23, 1948; s. Samuel Knox and Dorothy Louise (Newnham) H. BA, Wellesley Coll., 1970; JD, U. Pitts., 1973, M in Pub. Health, 1979. Bar: Pa. 1974, U.S. Dist. Ct. (we. dist.) Pa. 1974, Fla. 1981. Sole practice Pitts., 1974—; law clk. Pitts. Ct. Common Pleas., 1974-78; mgr. for artist Rachel McClelland Sutton, Pitts., 1973-81; asst. to president judge Allegheny County Ct. Common Pleas., Pitts., 1978—, cons. tax assessment, 1983-85. Mem. Jr. League Pitts., 1975-80; bd. dirs. Winchester Thurston Sch., Pitts., 1972-80, Planned Parenthood Pitts., 1981—. Mem. ABA, Pa. Bar Assn., Fla. Bar Assn., Allegheny County Bar Assn. (real property officer 1979—), Urban Regional Info. Systems Assn. Republican. Presbyterian. Clubs: Pitts. Wellesley (pres. 1984-86), Harvard Yale Princeton. Avocations: current affairs, cats, jogging, cooking, gardening. Computer, Real property, Voting rights and apportionment. Home: 5426 Plainfield St Pittsburgh PA 15217 Office: 618 City-County Bldg Pittsburgh PA 15219

HUNTER, PAMELA ANNE, lawyer; b. Durham, N.C., Mar. 5, 1954; d. Walter Allen Jr. and Madelynn Newana (Gill) H. BS, N.C. A&T State U.; JD, N.C. Cen. U. Bar: N.C. 1978, U.S. Dist. Ct. (we. dist.) N.C. 1978, U.S. Dist. Ct. (mid. dist.) N.C. 1986. Mng. atty. Legal Services So. Piedmont, Gastonia, N.C., 1980-84; ptnr. Hamrick, Hunter, Pickard & Finch, Charlotte and Gastonia, N.C., 1984-86, Hunter, Pickard & Cannon, Charlotte and Gastonia, 1986—, Hunter, Pickard, Cannon & Swann, Charlotte, 1987—. Reginald Heber Smith fellow, 1978-80. Mem. N.C. Bar Assn., N.C. A&T Alumni. Democrat. Episcopalian. Club: First Friday (Charlotte). Avocations: reading, walking, running. Pension, profit-sharing, and employee benefits, Workers' compensation, General practice. Home: 4918 Issac Dr Charlotte NC 28216 Office: Hunter Pickard & Cannon 129 W Trade St Suite 1116 Charlotte NC 28202

HUNTER, RICHARD SAMFORD, JR., lawyer; b. Montgomery, Ala., May 8, 1954; s. Richard Samford and Anne (Arendell) H.; m. Jane Messer, June 28, 1981; children: Richard Samford III, Benjamin Arendell. Student, Berklee Coll. of Music, 1974-75; BA, U. N.C., 1977; JD, Samford U., 1980. Bar: N.C. 1980, U.S. Dist. Ct. N.C. 1981. Assoc. Green & Mann, Raleigh, N.C., 1980-82, Smith, Debnam, Hibbert & Pahl, Raleigh, 1982-85; ptnr. Futrell & Hunter, Raleigh, 1985—; program chmn. media law U. N.C., Chapel Hill, 1983-84. Composer, performer (TV musical) The Tomorrow Show, 1975. Corp. fund raiser United Way, Wake County, N.C., 1984-85; mem. clergy's sermon evaluation com. Christ Episcopal Ch., Raleigh; bd. dirs., Raleigh Chamber Music Guild, 1986—. Mem. ABA (litigation sect.), N.C. Bar Assn. (litigation sect.), Wake County Bar Assn. (bd. dirs. 1987—), Assn. Trial Lawyers Am., N.C. Acad. Trial Lawyers (program chmn., speaker various seminars, chmn. speakers bur. 1984-85, bd. of govs. 1986—), Phi Alpha Delta. Democrat. Club: Sphinx. Lodge: Kiwanis. Avocations: sports, music, hunting, fishing. State civil litigation, Personal injury, Criminal. Home: 813 Graham St Raleigh NC 27605 Office: Futrell & Hunter 207B Fayetteville St Mall Raleigh NC 27602

HUNTER, ROBERT FREDERICK, lawyer; b. Ft. Worth, June 7, 1937; s. Homer Alexander and Pauline (Steely) H.; m. Elisabeth Loader, July 1, 1961 (div. Sept. 1982); children: Homer Alexander II, Robert Frederick Jr.; m. Barbara Bailey, June 7, 1984. BBA, BS in Civil Engring., Tex. A&M U., 1960; MS, M.I.T., 1964; JD, So. Meth. U., 1974. Bar: Tex. 1975, Mo. 1976. Pres., chief exec. officer Hydro-Air Engring., St. Louis, 1974-84; sole practice Dallas, 1985-86; ptnr. Ashley and Welch, Dallas, 1987—. Mem. ABA, ASCE, Tex. Bar Assn., Mo. Bar Assn., Phi Delta Phi. Republican. Lodge: Rotary (pres. 1970). Avocations: cameras, woodworking. General corporate, General practice, Private international. Home: 5319 Royal Crest Dr Dallas TX 75229

HUNTER, TODD AMES, lawyer; b. Bartlesville, Okla., Aug. 26, 1953; s. Richard A. and Patricia L. (Ames) H.; m. Alexis Taylor, May 24, 1981; 1 child, Todd A. Jr. BA, U. Kans., 1975; JD, So. Meth. U., 1978. Bar: Tex. 1978, U.S. Dist. Ct. (so. dist.) Tex., U.S. Ct. Appeals (5th cir.). Assoc. Meredith & Donnell, Corpus Christi, Tex., 1978-81; ptnr. Kleberg, Dyer, Redford & Weil, Corpus Christi, 1981—; bd. dirs. Security State Bank, Portland, Tex. Chmn. civil service bd. Civil Service Commn., Corpus Christi, 1982—, Leadership Corpus Christi, 1984, Charter Rev. Com., Corpus Christi, 1986—. Fellow Tex. Bar Found.; mem. Tex. Bar Assn., Nueces County Bar Assn. (pres. 1986—), Nueces County Young Lawyers Assn. (named outstanding young lawyer 1985), Phi Beta Kappa, Corpus Christi C. of C. (v.p. 1986—). Episcopalian. Lodge: Rotary. Avocations: tennis, traveling. Banking, Federal civil litigation, State civil litigation. Office: Kleberg Dyer Redford & Weil 1200 MBank Ctr N Corpus Christi TX 78471

HUNTER, WILLIAM CARLTON, lawyer; b. Wilmington, Del., Dec. 24, 1939; s. Carlton Estilow and Virginia Odell (Talbott) H.; m. Kathleen Donovan, Sept. 10, 1973; children—J. Craig, W. Douglas, Anne T., William D. B.S., U. Va., 1961, J.D., 1969; M.B.A. in Tax, Golden Gate U., 1972. Bar: Calif. 1970, U.S. Ct. Appeals (9th cir.) 1970. Assoc. Lillick, McHose, Wheat, Adams & Charles, San Francisco, 1970-71, Garret McEnerney II, San Francisco, 1971-74, McFarland, Kuchins & Jackson, 1974-75; ptnr. Hunter, Boyd & Murray, Santa Rosa, 1975-82; sole practice, Healdsburg, Calif., 1982—; assoc. prof. Grad. Bus. Sch. Golden Gate U., 1973-76; prof. Empire Law Sch., 1976-81. Bd. dirs. Boys and Girls Club, Healdsburg Found.; trustee Westside Union Sch. Dist. Served to capt. USMC, 1961-65. Mem. ABA, Calif. Bar Assn., Sonoma County Bar Assn., Calif. Trial Lawyers Assn., Redwood Empire Trial Lawyers Assn. (pres.), Healdsburg C. of C. (bd. dirs.). Estate planning, Probate, Estate taxation. Home: 7559 Mill Creek Rd Healdsburg CA 95448 Office: PO Box 328 Healdsburg CA 95448

HUNTLEY, DONALD WAYNE, lawyer; b. Chgo., Sept. 22, 1942; s. Joseph Edward and Emily Rose (Beran) H.; m. Margaret Helen Kopacek, Aug. 27, 1966; children: Richard A. II, Scott J., Mark B., C. Frederick M. BS, U. Ill., 1963, JD, 1966. Bar: D.C. 1967, Del. 1981, U.S. Supreme Ct. 1973. Patent counsel E. I. du Pont de Nemours & Co., Wilmington, Del., 1966-85, Remington Arms Co., 1985—; asst. pub. defender State of Del., Wilmington, 1972-78. Bd. dirs. Del. Symphony Assn., 1972-86, pres., 1976-79, chmn. music com., 1979-86; bd. dirs. Kalmar Nyckel Commemorative Com., 1983—, chmn. cultural com., 1983-86, mem. exec. com., 350th anniversary com., 1986—; counsel Ctr. for Creative Arts, Yorklyn, Del., 1983-84. Mem. ABA, Del. Bar Assn., Phi Delta Phi. Republican. Episcopalian. Patent. Home: RD 2 Box 392 Hockessin DE 19707 Office: E I du Pont de Nemours & Co Legal Dept Wilmington DE 19898

HUNTLEY, ROBERT CARSON, justice Idaho Supreme Court; b. Union City, Pa., Aug. 7, 1932; s. Robert Carson and Mildred (Kaltenmark) H.; m. Elfrieda Garvens, Feb. 11, 1955; children: Christopher F., Anthony R. B.S., U. Idaho, 1954, J.D., 1959. Bar: Idaho 1959. Ptnr. Racine, Huntley & Olson, Pocatello, Idaho, 1959-82; justice Idaho Supreme Ct., Boise, 1982—; mem. Idaho Jud. Council, 1967-81; bd. commrs. Idaho State Bar, 1982. Mem. Idaho Ho. of Reps., 1965-67; mem. Pocatello City Council, 1962-64, Gov.'s Blue Ribbon Tax Com., 1978-79, Com. to Promote Funding for Edn., 1980, Pocatello Fin. Resources Com., 1980; chmn. Idaho Energy Resources Policy Bd., 1980-82. Served to capt. USNR, 1954-79. Mem. ABA, Idaho Bar Assn., Am. Bar Found., Idaho Trial Lawyers Assn., Assn. Trial Lawyers Am. Democrat. Unitarian. Lodge: Elks. Home: 604 San Felipe Way Boise ID 83702 Office: Idaho Supreme Court 451 W State St Boise ID 83702 *

HUNTOON, HARRY KARL, lawyer; b. Davenport, Iowa, Dec. 19, 1949; s. Harry Kline and Margit (Anderson) H.; m. Andrea Dickgiesser, July 29, 1972; children: James K., Mark A. BS, U. Ill., 1972, JD, 1975. Bar: Ill. 1975, U.S. Dist. Ct. (cen. dist.) Ill. 1975. Ptnr. Churchill and Churchill, Moline, Ill., 1975—; vis. faculty mem. Augustana Coll., Rock Island, Ill., 1979-81; cons. personal computers, Moline, 1984—. Bd. dirs. Delta Upsilon Fraternity, Indpls., 1981-87. Mem. ABA, Rock Island County Bar Assn. (bd. dirs. 1985-86), Ill. State Bar Assn. Mem. United Ch. of Christ. Avocations: bicycle touring, photograpny. Real property, Probate, General practice. Home: 7607 36th Ave Moline IL 61265 Office: Churchill and Churchill 1610 Fifth Ave Moline IL 61265

HUNZIKER, FREDERICK JOHN, JR., lawyer, utility executive; b. Paterson, N.J., Apr. 13, 1928; s. Frederick John and Grace Allen (Bogert); m. Suzette Lovewell, Sept. 28, 1951 (dec. May 1979); children: Frederick John III, Robert Newton, Lynn Ann Hunziker Hunter; m. Patricia Kirkpatrick, Mar. 10, 1984. BS, Tufts U., 1949; postgrad., George Washington U., 1950, JD, 1956. Bar: Mass. 1956, N.Y. 1964. Sole practice Falmouth, Mass., 1956-58; tax atty. Joint Com. on Taxations, Washington, 1958-61, Texaco Inc., N.Y.C., 1961-65; tax dir., asst. treas. Continental Baking Co., Rye, N.Y., 1965-70; sr. tax atty. ITT, N.Y.C., 1970; gen. tax counsel Consol. Edison Co., N.Y.C., 1970—; chmn. tax com. Energy Assn., Albany, N.Y., 1975—, N.Y. Gas Group, N.Y.C., 1976—, Edison Electric Inst., Washington, 1980-81; tax analysis and research subcom. Edison Electric Inst., Washington, 1985—. Councilman City of Rye, 1970-81, mayor, 1982-85. Served to 1st lt. USAF, 1951-53. Mem. ABA, Tax Execs. Inst. (past v.p. N.Y. chpt.). Republican. Episcopalian. Avocations: boating, golf. Corporate taxation, State and local taxation, Public utilities. Home: 216 Purchase St Rye NY 10580 Office: Con Edison 4 Irving Pl New York NY 10003

HUNZIKER, ROBERT MCKEE, paper company executive; b. Paterson, N.J., Apr. 22, 1932; s. Walter Jacobus and Helen (McKee) H.; m. Joan DuBois, June 15, 1955; children—James D., William M., Hans B., Eric G. A.B. cum laude, Amherst Coll., 1954; LL.B., U. Mich., 1957. Bar: N.Y. State bar 1958, N.J. bar 1976. Asso. Shearman & Sterling, N.Y.C., 1957-64; gen. counsel, corporate sec. Riegel Paper Corp., N.Y.C., 1964-71; v.p. legal affairs Wheelabrator-Frye, Inc., N.Y.C., 1971-73; v.p. law, corporate sec. Union Camp Corp., Wayne, N.J., 1973-76; counsel White Papers Group, Internat. Paper Co., 1977-85, asst. gen. counsel, 1985—. Mem. Am., N.Y. State bar assns., Assn. Bar City N.Y., Delta Upsilon, Phi Delta Phi. General practice, Federal civil litigation, Environment. Office: Internat Paper Co 77 W 45th St New York NY 10036

HUPERT, JEFFREY DAVID, lawyer; b. St. Louis, Nov. 21, 1948; s. Edward and Susie (Bromberg) H.; m. Lillian Elizabeth Peters, May 23, 1970; 1 child, Deborah Rachel. BA with high honors, Mich. State U., 1970, MA, 1972; postgrad., U. Chgo., 1972-74; JD, DePaul U., 1978. Bar: Ill. 1978, U.S. Dist. Ct. (no. dist.) Ill. 1978, U.S. Ct. Appeals (7th cir.) 1980, Iowa 1983, U.S. Dist. Ct. (no. and so. dists.) Iowa 1983, U.S. Tax Ct. 1983, U.S. Ct. Appeals (8th cir.) 1983. Law clk. to presiding justice Ill. Appellate Ct. (2d cir.), Elgin, 1978-79; assoc. Arnstein, Gluck et al, Chgo., 1979-82, Bradley & Riley P.C., Cedar Rapids, Iowa, 1983-84; sole practice Chgo., 1984; assoc. Lynn & Levenstein Ltd., Chgo., 1985-86, ptnr., 1987—. Mem. ABA, Iowa Bar Assn., Chgo. Bar Assn., Decalogue Soc. Jewish. Avocations: reading, bridge. State civil litigation, Federal civil litigation. Home: 1220 W Albion Ave Chicago IL 60626 Office: Lynn & Levenstein Ltd 20 N Clark St Suite 500 Chicago IL 60626

HUPP, HARRY L., federal judge; b. 1929. AB, Stanford U., 1953, LLB, 1955. Judge, U.S. Dist. Ct. (cen. dist.) Calif., Los Angeles.; Sole practice Beardsley, Hufstedler and Kemble, Los Angeles, 1955-72; judge Superior Ct. of Los Angeles, 1972-84; appointed fed. dist. judge U.S. Dist. Ct. (cen. dist.), Los Angeles, 1984—. Served with U.S. Army, 1950-52. Mem. State Bar Assn. Calif., Los Angeles County Bar Assn. (Trial Judge of Yr. 1983). Judicial administration. Office: US Courthouse 312 N Spring St Los Angeles CA 90012 *

HUPPER, JOHN ROSCOE, lawyer; b. N.Y.C., June 16, 1925; s. Roscoe Henderson and Dorothy Wallace (Healy) H.; m. Joyce Shirley McCoy, June 14, 1952; children: John R. Jr., Gail J., Craig W. A.B., Bowdoin Coll., 1949; LL.B., Harvard U., 1952. Bar: N.Y. 1954, U.S. Supreme Ct. 1960. Assoc. Cravath, Swaine & Moore, N.Y.C., 1952-60, ptnr., 1961—. Overseer Bowdoin Coll., 1970-82, trustee, 1982—; trustee Allen-Stevenson Sch., 1968—; bd. dirs. Legal Aid Soc., N.Y.C., 1971-76, Travelers Aid Soc., N.Y., 1962-79. Served with U.S. Army, 1943-46. Fellow Am. Coll. Trial Lawyers; mem. Assn. Bar City N.Y., N.Y. County Lawyers Assn., N.Y. State Bar Assn., ABA. Republican. Clubs: Apawamis, Down Town, Univ, Union. Home: 105 E 67th St New York NY 10021 Office: Cravath Swaine & Moore 1 Chase Manhattan Plaza New York NY 10005

HUPY, MICHAEL FREDERICK, lawyer; b. Milw., Oct. 11, 1946; s. Wilfred Joseph and Phyllis Marie (Heintz) H.; 1 child, Lauren. BA, Marquette U., 1968, JD, 1972. Bar: Wis. 1972, U.S. Dist. Ct. (we. and ea. dists.) Wis. 1972, U.S. Ct. Appeals (7th cir.) 1976, U.S. Supreme Ct. 1976. Ptnr. Hupy & Glasschroeder, Milw., 1972-76, Hausmann, McNally & Hupy S.C., Milw., 1976—. Mem. ABA, Wis. Bar Assn., Milw. Bar Assn., Assn. Trial lawyers Am., Wis. Acad. Trial Lawyers, Nat. Assn. Criminal Def. Lawyers, Wis. Acad. Criminal Def. Lawyers. State civil litigation, Criminal. Home: 872 W Laramie Ln Milwaukee WI 53217 Office: Hausmann McNally & Hupy SC 633 W Wisconsin Ave Milwaukee WI 53203

HURABIELL, JOHN PHILIP, SR., lawyer, business executive; b. San Francisco, June 2, 1947; s. Emile John and Anna Beatrice (Blumenauer) H.; m. Judith Marie Hurabiell, June 7, 1969; children—Marie Louise, Michele, Heather, John Philip Jr. J.D., San Francisco Law Sch., 1976. Bar: Calif. 1977. Sole practice, San Francisco, 1977-86; ptnr. Huppert & Hurabiell, San Francisco, 1985—; pres. San Francisco S.A.F.E., Inc.; treas. Republican election coms.; Served with U.S. Navy, Vietnam. Decorated Navy Commendation Medal. Mem. ABA, Calif. Bar Assn., San Francisco Bar Assn., Assn. Trial Lawyers Am., Calif. Trial Lawyers Assn., San Francisco Trial Lawyers Assn., Lawyers Club San Francisco, St. Thomas More Soc., Sports Lawyers Assn., Hook and Ladder Soc. Roman Catholic. Clubs: Press of San Francisco, Ferrari Owners. Lodge: Masons. Editor, primary author: C.A.L.U. Business Practices Guidelines, rev. edit., 1980. Pension, profit-sharing, and employee benefits, Probate, Real property. Office: Huppert & Hurabiell 1355 Market St Suite 417 San Francisco CA 94103

HURD, CHARLES W., lawyer; b. Odessa, Tex., July 4, 1946. BA, Tex. Tech. U., 1969; JD, U. Tex., 1972. Bar: Tex. 1973. Ptnr. Fulbright & Jaworski, Houston. Office: Fulbright & Jaworski Bank Bldg 910 Travis St Houston TX 77002 *

HURD, PAUL GEMMILL, laywer; b. Salt Lake City, Nov. 23, 1946; s. Melvin Erskine and Marjorie (Gemmill) H. BS, Portland State U., 1968; JD, Lewis and Clark Coll., 1976. Bar: Oreg. 1976, Wash. 1984, U.S. Dist. Ct. Oreg. 1980, U.S. Ct. Appeals (9th cir.) 1981. Sr. dep. dist. atty. Multnomah County Dist. Atty., Portland, Oreg., 1976-80; trial counsel Burlington No. R.R., Portland, 1980-84; asst. gen. counsel Freightliner Corp., Portland, 1984—. Trustee Leukemia Assn. of Oreg., Portland, 1984—; sustaining mem. Rep. Nat. Com., Washington, 1985—. Mem. ABA, Oreg. Bar Assn., Wash. Bar Assn., Multnomah Bar assn., Am. Corp. Counsel Assn., Nat. Inst. for Trial Adv. (diplomate 1982). Republican. Presbyterian. Avocations: cross country skiing, history reading, running. Antitrust, Federal civil litigation, General corporate. Office: Freightliner Corp. Legal Dept. PO Box 3849 Portland OR 97208

HUREWITZ, DAVID LEWIS, lawyer; b. N.Y.C., May 4, 1942; s. Sidney and Anita (Haas) H.; m. Rodna Pass, June 19, 1966; children: Joel Brian, Barry Jason. AB, Union Coll., Schenectady, N.Y., 1964, BEE, 1964; LLB cum laude, Harvard U., 1967. Bar: U.S. Dist. Ct. D.C. 1968, U.S. Ct. Appeals (D.C. cir.) 1968, U.S. Patent Office, 1968, N.C. 1977, U.S. Dist. Ct. (mid. dist.) N.C. 1978. Patent atty. Bell Labs., Holmdel, N.J., 1967-74, Teletype, Skokie, Ill., 1974-76; atty. Western Electric, Greensboro, N.C., 1976-81, AT&T, Greensboro, 1982—. Mem. ABA. Patent, Intellectual property licensing. Home: 4502 Wild Oak Ln Greensboro NC 27406 Office: AT&T PO Box 25000 Greensboro NC 27420

HURLBERT, CLYDE OSBORNE, lawyer; b. Gulfport, Miss., Dec. 27, 1931; s. Henry Prentiss and Leona Mallison (Brady) H.; m. Paula Marie Maugel, Feb. 14, 1984. BBA, U. Miss., 1959, JD, 1960. Bar: Miss. 1960, U.S. Dist. Ct. (no. and so. dists.) Miss. 1960, U.S Ct. Appeals (5th cir.) 1965, U.S. Supreme Ct. 1971, U.S. Ct. Claims 1981, U.S. Ct. Appeals (11th cir.) 1982. Asst. dist. atty. 2d judl dist. State of Miss., 1960-67, bar examiner, 1979; sole practice Biloxi, Miss., 1960—; past mem. Miss. State Bd. Bar Examiners. Served with U.S. Army, 1953-55, Korea. Mem. Miss. Bar Assn. (criminal law com. 1966-67), Harrison County Bar Assn., Am. Radio Relay League (bd. dirs. 1982—), Miss. Deep Sea Fishing Rodeo. Democrat. Lodges: Masons, Elks (exalted ruler 1966-67). General practice. Office: PO Box 502 400 E Water St Biloxi MS 39533-0502

HURLBUTT, DANIEL CHATER, JR, judge; b. Evanston, Ill., Dec. 18, 1948; s. Daniel Chater and Elizabeth (Mitten) H.; m. Barbara Seff, Feb. 28, 1981; children: Bryan Jack, Julie Lucille. BA in Polit. Sci., Colo. Coll., 1971; JD, U. Denver, 1975. Bar: Ill. 1975, U.S. Dist. Ct. (no. dist.) Ill. 1976, Idaho 1979, U.S. Dist. Ct. Idaho, 1979, U.S. Ct. Appeals (7th cir.) 1979. Assoc. Chadwell, Kayser et al, Chgo., 1975-78; dep. pros. atty. Blaine County, Hailey, Idaho, 1979-80; magistrate judge State of Idaho, Shoshone, 1980-83; trial ct. adminstr. Idaho Dist Ct. (5th dist.), Twin Falls, 1982—; dist. judge. State of Idaho, Twin Falls, 1984—. Bus. editor Denver Jour. Internat. Law, 1974-75. Mem. Idaho Jud. Council, 1986—. Mem. ABA (antitrust sect., jud. adminstrn. sect.) Am. Judicature Soc. (bd. dirs. 1986—), Ill. Bar Assn., Idaho Bar Assn., Idaho Trial Lawyers Assn., Chgo. Bar Assn., Idaho Dist. Judges Assn. (pres. 1986—). Avocations: reading, bicycling, skiing, tennis. Judicial administration, State civil litigation, Antitrust. Office: 5th Dist Ct State of Idaho PO Box 1567 Twin Falls ID 83303

HURLEY, CORNELIUS KEEFE, JR., banker, lawyer; b. Boston, Oct. 16, 1945; s. Cornelius Keefe and Mildred G. (Anholt) H.; children—Emma, Eleanor, Cornelius. A.B., Holy Cross Coll., 1968; J.D., Georgetown U., 1974; postgrad., Harvard U., 1986. Bar: Mass. 1974, U.S. Supreme Ct. 1980, D.C. 1981. Law clk. McCarty & Noone, 1971-72; legis. aide Congressman Thomas O'Neill, 1973-74; bd. govs. Fed. Res., 1974-81, sr. atty.-counsel, 1977-80, asst. gen. counsel, 1981; sr. v.p., gen. counsel Shawmut Bank of Boston, 1981—; lectr. in field. Editor: International Banking: U.S. Laws and Regulations, 1984. Served to lt. USN JG, 1968-71. Mem. ABA, Mass. Bar Assn., Boston Bar Assn. (dir. Vol. Lawyers Project), Assn. Bank Holding Cos. (lawyers com. 1981—). Club: Harvard (Boston). Office: Shawmut Bank of Boston NA One Federal St Boston MA 02211

HURLEY, DANIEL GERARD, lawyer; b. Boston; s. Daniel J. and Mary (McAuley) H.; m. Sharon Lee Dolan, Aug. 9, 1969; children: Melissa, Sean. Grad., Northeastern U.; JD, New Eng. Sch. of Law. Bar: Mass., U.S. Supreme Ct. Budget dir. Middlesex County, Mass., 1976-80; exec. v.p., ptnr. Internat. Bus. Group, Inc., Boston, 1980—. Chmn. Dem. Com., Mass.; del. Dem. Nat. Conv., 1972, 76, 80; pres. St. Jude Children's Research Hosp., New Eng., 1981-85, Holy Name Soc., Mass., 1974-76; bd. dirs. Heart Assn., United Fund. Recipient Outstanding Leadership award City of Boston, 1980. Mem. ABA (immigration com.), Mass. Bar Assn., Middlesex County Bar Assn., Assn. Trial Lawyers Am. Immigration, naturalization, and customs, Criminal, General practice. Home: 170 Mystic St Ext Medford MA 02155 Office: 50 Milk St Suite 1902 Boston MA 02109

HURLEY, GEOFFREY KEVIN, lawyer; b. N.Y.C., Apr. 12, 1948; s. John J. and Evelyn M. (Hoffman) H.; m. C. Austin Fitts, May 19, 1979. B.A., Haverford Coll., 1970; J.D., Vanderbilt U., 1973. Bar: N.Y. 1974. Assoc., Brown, Wood, Ivey, Mitchell & Petty, N.Y.C., 1973-80; ptnr., 1981-84; ptnr. Skadden, Arps, Slate, Meagher & Flom, N.Y.C., 1984—. Articles editor Vanderbilt Law Rev., 1972-73. Mem. Assn. Bar City of N.Y., ABA, N.Y. State Bar Assn. Republican. Episcopalian. Securities. Home: 103 E 75th St New York NY 10021 Office: Skadden Arps Slate Meagher & Flom 919 3d Ave New York NY 10022

HURLEY, GRADY SCHELL, lawyer; b. New Orleans, Nov. 29, 1954; s. Daniel Patrick and Joycelyn Mary (Schell) H.; m. Elizabeth Lawrence, Jan. 4, 1980; children: Joshua Lawrence, Benjamin Patrick. BA, Tulane U., 1976, JD, 1979, LLM, 1981. Bar: La. 1979, U.S. Dist. Ct. (ea. and mid. dists.) La. 1979, U.S. Dist. Ct. (we. dist.) La. 1980, U.S. Ct. Appeals (5th and 11th cirs.) 1980, U.S. Supreme Ct. 1986.. Assoc. Jones, Walker et al, New Orleans, 1979-84, ptnr., 1984—. Editor: Damages Recoverable in Maritime Matters, 1984. Mem. Ports and Waterways Com., New Orleans, 1984—. Mem. ABA (subcom. on collision 1985), Fed. Bar Assn., La. Bar Assn., New Orleans Bar Assn. (membership com. 1985—), Maritime Law Assn., South East Admiralty Law Inst., Tulane Alumni Assn. (bd. dirs. 1986—). Democrat. Roman Catholic. Club: Mariners (pres. 1982). Avocations: sports, reading, painting, movies. Admiralty, Insurance, Personal injury. Home: #46 Bluebird New Orleans LA 70124 Office: Jones Walker Waechter et al 201 St Charles Ave New Orleans LA 70170

HURLEY, JAMES G., lawyer; b. Buffalo, Jan. 3, 1922; s. Jeremiah Joseph and Miriam Ulysses (Casey) H.; m. Joan Alice Cauley, Jan. 24, 1953; children—Mary Hurley Begley, Kathleen A., James G., Alice L. B.A., Princeton U., 1944; LL.B., Harvard U., 1948. Bar: N.Y. 1949, U.S. Supreme Ct. 1958. Assoc. Albrecht, Maguire, Heffern & Gregg, P.C., 1948-53, ptnr., 1954-76, v.p. and sec., 1971-83, pres., 1984-86; counsel, 1987—; dir. Arcade and Attica R.R. Corp., 1961—; trustee, chmn. bd. Messer Found., 1964—; trustee, sec. Vincent and Harriet Palisano Found., 1967—. Trustee Canisius Coll., 1977-83, chmn. planned gifts com. 1967—; mem. council D'Youville Coll., 1975-81; trustee Nichols Sch. of Buffalo, 1972-81; mem. adminstrv. bd. Bishop's Lay Council, 1975—, chmn., 1986—. Served with USAAF, 1944-46. Named Knight of Holy Sepulchre, Roman Catholic Ch., 1982. Mem. ABA, N.Y. State Bar Assn., Erie County Bar Assn., Harvard Law Sch. Assn. of Western N.Y. Republican. Clubs: Buffalo (dir., sec. 1982-83), Cherry Hill Country, Mid-Day, Princeton of Western N.Y., Harvard of Buffalo. General corporate, Estate planning, Estate taxation. Home: 2909 S Ocean Blvd Apt 2B Highland Beach FL 33431 Office: Albrecht Maguire Heffern & Gregg PC 2100 Main Pl Tower Buffalo NY 14202

HURLEY, LAWRENCE JOSEPH, lawyer; b. Plainfield, N.J., Nov. 17, 1946; s. Luke Michael and Gertrude Marie (Bremer) H.; m. Allyson J. Kingsley, May 28, 1977. B.S., U. Dayton, 1969; J.D., Cath. U. Am., 1974. Bar: N.J. 1974, U.S. Dist. Ct. N.J. 1974, D.C. 1976, N.Y. 1980, U.S. Ct. Appeals (3d cir.) 1980, U.S. Dist. Ct. (ea. and so. dists.) N.Y. 1981. U.S. Ct. Appeals (2d cir.) 1981, U.S. Ct. Appeals (D.C. cir.) 1982. Law clk. Superior Ct. N.J., New Brunswick, 1974-75; assoc. Lynch, Mannion, Lutz & Lewandowski, New Brunswick, 1975-76, Stryker, Tams & Dill, Newark, 1976-79; atty. AT&T Communications, Basking Ridge, N.J., 1979-85; asst. prosecutor in charge of econ. crimes and official corrpution Morris County Prosecutor's Office, Morristown, N.J., 1985—. Served with U.S. Army, 1969-71. Decorated Bronze Star, Army Commendation medal. Mem. ABA (litigation sect. 1976—, trial evidence com. 1980—, labor law sect. 1981-85, criminal law sect. 1985—), N.J. State Bar Assn., Nat. Dist. Attys. Assn. Clubs: Fish and Game, Jaycees (bd. dirs. 1982-83) (Chatham, N.J.). Criminal, Labor, Local government. Office: Morris County Prosecutors Office Hall of Records Morristown NJ 07960

HURLEY, PAUL EDWARD, lawyer; b. Arkansas City, Kans., Jan. 18, 1934; s. Paul Edward and Margaret Ellen (Ward) H.; m. Joy Lacour, Nov. 29, 1958; children—Shannon, Paul, Jeanne, Stephen, Gregory, Bridgette. B.S. in Engring., Notre Dame, 1956; J.D., Loyola U. of South, 1958; LL.M. in Taxation, Georgetown U., 1962. Bar: La. 1958. Prin. Hurley & Hoffman, 1965—; instr. taxation Loyola U. of South; arbitrator Am. Arbitration Assn.; dir., chmn. audit com. Bank of St. Charles. Served as lt. JAG, USNR, 1959-62. Mem. Am. Judicature Soc., ABA, New Orleans Bar Assn., New Orleans C. of C. (chmn. bus. task force on edn. 1985). Democrat. Roman Catholic. Clubs: Ormond Country (Destrehan, La.) (pres. 1982); Internat. House. Contbr. articles to profl. jours. Corporate taxation, Estate taxation, General corporate. Office: Hurley & Hoffmann 925 Common St Suite 825 New Orleans LA 70112

HURLEY, ROBERT JOSEPH, lawyer; b. Chgo., May 21, 1932; s. Michael James and Dorothy E. (Pries) H.; m. Emily Hurley Costello, Sept. 14, 1957; children: Brenda, Nancy, Robert, Christopher, Michael, Matthew. B.S., St. Benedict's Coll., 1953; J.D., Loyola U., Chgo., 1962. Acct., auditor Shell Oil Co., Chgo., 1957-64; atty. N.Y., 1965; atty Tulsa, 1966-69; atty. Chgo., 1969-72, Houston, 1972-77; sr. group counsel NL Industrial Inc., Houston, 1977-82; v.p., gen. counsel NL Industries Inc., Houston, 1982—. Mem. adv. bd. Southwestern Legal Found., Richardson, Tex., 1982-83. Mem. Am. Corp. Counsel Assn., ABA, Ill. Bar Assn., Tex. Bar Assn., Okla. Bar Assn. Home: 6202 Elmgrove St Spring TX 77379 Office: NL Industrial Inc 3000 N Belt E Houston TX 77032

HURLOCK, JAMES BICKFORD, lawyer; b. Chgo., Aug. 7, 1933; s. James Bickford and Elizabeth (Charls) H.; m. Margaret Lyn Holding, July 1, 1961; children: James Bickford, Burton Charls, Matthew Hunter. A.B., Princeton U., 1955; B.A., Oxford U., 1957, M.A., 1960; J.D., Harvard U., 1959. Bar: N.Y. 1960, U.S. Supreme Ct. 1967. Assoc. firm White & Case, N.Y.C., 1959-66, ptnr., 1967—; bd. dirs. Altex Resources Ltd., Calgary, Alta., Can. Trustee Columbia Presbyn. Hosp., Parker Sch. Internat. and Comparitive Law, Hofstra U., Western Rev. Acad. Rhodes scholar, 1955. Mem. ABA, Assn. Bar City N.Y., N.Y. Bar Assn., Am. Law Inst., Am. Assn. Internat. Law. Republican. Episcopalian. Clubs: Links, River, N.Y. Yacht. Home: 46 Byram Dr Greenwich CT 06830 Office: 1155 Ave of Americas New York NY 10036

HURNYAK, CHRISTINA KAISER, lawyer; b. Noblesville, Ind., Dec. 22, 1949; d. Albert Michael and Lois Angie (Gatton) Kaiser; m. Cyril Hurnyak, June 24, 1972. B.A. Wittenberg U., 1972; J.D., SUNY-Buffalo, 1979. Bar: N.Y. 1980. Mem. support staff McKinsey & Co., Inc., mgmt. cons., Chgo., 1972-75; law clk. Justice Norman J. Wolf, N.Y. Supreme Ct., Buffalo, 1980-81; assoc. Dempsey & Dempsey, Buffalo, 1979-80, 81—. Mem. ABA, N.Y. State Bar Assn., Erie County Bar Assn., N.Y. Women's Bar Assn. (legis. com.), Women Lawyers of Western N.Y. Democrat. Lutheran. Personal injury, Federal civil litigation, State civil litigation. Home: 25 Fairview Ct Grand Island NY 14072 Office: Dempsey & Dempsey 561 Franklin St Buffalo NY 14202

HURST, ERNEST CONNOR, lawyer; b. Lexington, Tex., Sept. 27, 1926; s. Ernest V. and Grace E. (King) H.; m. Barbara Ann Glaze, Oct. 19, 1951; 1 dau., Susan D. Hurst Hensley. Student Sam Houston State U., 1946-48; J.D. with honors, U. Tex.-Austin, 1950. Bar: Tex. 1950, U.S. Dist. Ct. (so. dist.) Tex. 1956, U.S. Ct. Appeals (5th cir.) 1969. Assoc. Liddell, Austin, Dawson & Huggins, Houston, 1951-57; sr. ptnr. Caldwell & Hurst, Houston, 1958—; corp. sec. Adams Resources & Energy, Inc., Houston, 1979-84, KSA Industries, Inc., Houston, 1979—; exec. pres., bd. dirs. Derrick Oil & Gas, Inc., Houston, 1977—; pres., bd. dirs. Bayoli Helicopter, Inc., Houston, 1985—. Served with USN, 1944-46. Mem. Houston Bar Assn., Tex. Bar Assn., Am. Judicature Soc., Internat. Platform Assn., Nat. Trust for Hist. Preservation, Phi Delta Phi. Republican. Methodist. Avocations: spectator sports, traveling, camping. Student editor Tex. Law Rev., 1950-51. State civil litigation, General corporate, Oil and gas leasing.

HURT, CHARLES E., lawyer; b. Charleston, W.Va., Aug. 3, 1930; s. John Franklin and Lillian Grace (McClain) H.; m. Carolyn Hanly, June 7, 1937; children—John Hanly, Sarah Jane. J.D., W.Va. U., 1957. Bar: W.Va. 1957, U.S. Dist. Ct. (so dist.) W.Va. 1957, U.S. Supreme Ct. 1959. Sr. ptnr. Hurt & Carrico, Charleston, 1957—; prof. Morris Harvey Coll., Charleston, 1961-67; v.p., dir. Elk Nat. Bank, Big Chimney, W.Va., 1977—. Served with USN, 1948-52; Korea. Mem. Internat. Platform Assn., Hon. Order Ky. Cols., Tenn. Squires, Am. Arbitration Assn., Phi Alpha Theta, Phi Alpha Delta, Tau Kappa Epsilon, Democrat. Lutheran. Lodge: Masons Insurance, State civil litigation, Federal civil litigation. Home: 1671 Woodvale Rd Charleston WV 25314 Office: PO Drawer 833 Charleston WV 25323

HURT, JOSEPH RICHARD, legal educator; b. Laurel, Miss., Nov. 17, 1953; s. James Albert Sr. and Wanda (Perreault) H.; m. Jan Marie Jones, Aug. 13, 1977; children: Rosanna Marie, Jan Elizabeth. BA, Miss. Coll., 1975; MA, Baylor U., 1978, JD, 1979; LLM, Yale U., 1986. Bar: Miss. 1980. Asst. prof Miss. Coll. Sch. Law, Jackson, 1980-82, asst. dean, asst. prof., 1982-83, asst. dean., assoc. prof., 1983-84, assoc. dean, assoc. prof., 1984—. Mem. Miss. State Bar Assn. (bd. dirs. Young Lawyers sect. 1981-84), Hinds County Bar Assn., Jackson Young Lawyers Assn. Baptist. Lodge: Lions. Avocations: antiques, furniture refinishing, photography, fishing. Office: Miss Coll Sch Law 151 E Griffith St Jackson MS 39201

HURT, MICHAEL CARTER, lawyer; b. Kokomo, Ind., Sept. 7, 1943; s. Eldon Carter and Jane Ann (McCool) H.; m. Susan Clay Lines, Jan. 18, 1964; children—Michael Carter II, Justin Patrick. J.D., U. Pacific, 1973. Bar: Wis. 1973, U.S. Dist. Ct. (ea. dist.) Wis. 1973, U.S. Ct. Appeals (7th cir.). Legal intern Sacramento County Pub. Defender, Sacramento, 1971-73; assoc. Laubenheimer, Patrick & Maegli, Menomonee Falls, Wis., 1973-74; ptnr. Patrick & Hurt, Menomonee Falls, 1974—; chmn. SE Wis. Corrections Adv. Com., Waukesha, 1978—; cir. ct. commr. Waukesha County Cir. Ct., 1983—; acting family ct. commr. Waukesha County Family Ct., 1983—. Bd. mgrs. Tri-County YMCA, Menomonee Falls, 1975—; panel mem. United Way of Waukesha County, 1981—; vol. XIII Winter Olympic Games, Lake Placid, N.Y., 1980. Served to sgt. USAF, 1966-70. Mem. Wis. State Bar, Waukesha County Bar, Menomonee Falls C. of C. (bd. dirs. 1976-82), Phi Alpha Delta (chpt. justice 1971-73, outstanding mem. 1973). Republican. Methodist. Lodge: Kiwanis. Family and matrimonial, Contracts commercial, General practice. Home: N87 W15611 Kenwood Blvd Menomone Falls WI 53051 Office: Patrick and Hurt N84 W15959 Appleton Ave Menomonee Falls WI 53051

HURTGEN, PETER JOSEPH, lawyer; b. Madison, Wis.; s. Peter Jospeh and Ethel Gertrude (Long) H.; m. June O'Brien, Aug. 12, 1967; children: Peter Jr., Matthew, William. BS, Georgetown U., 1963, LLB, 1966. Bar: Ill. 1966, D.C. 1973, U.S. Supreme Ct. 1974, Fla. 1977. Assoc. Seyfarth, Shaw & Fairweather, Chgo., 1966-72; ptnr. Seyfarth, Shaw & Fairweather, Washington, 1973-77, 82-83, Miami, Fla., 1977-82; ptnr. Morgan, lLewis & Bockius, Miami, 1983—. Republican. Roman Catholic. Avocations: sailing, running. Administrative and regulatory, Labor, Local government. Home: 15620 SW 74th Ave Miami FL 33157 Office: Morgan Lewis & Bockius 5300 SE Fin Ctr 200 Biscayne Blvd Miami FL 33131-2339

HURWICH, ROBERT ALLAN, natural resources company executive; b. South Bend, Ind., Nov. 1, 1941; s. Abe and Carolyne C. (Neisner) H.; m. Judith J. Jones, May 31, 1969; children—Katherine A., David A. A.B., Harvard U., 1963, LL.B., 1966. Bar: N.Y. 1967; U.S. Dist. Ct. (ea. dist.) N.Y. 1968, U.S. Dist. Ct. (so. dist.) N.Y. 1968. Law clk. U.S. Dist. Ct. (ea. dist.) N.Y., 1966-68; assoc. Cravath, Swaine & Moore, N.Y.C., 1968-75; gen. counsel, sec. Moore McCormack Resources, Inc., Stamford, Conn., 1975—, v.p., 1979—. General corporate, Securities. Office: Moore McCormack Resources Inc 1 Landmark Sq Stamford CT 06901

HUSKEY, DOW THOBERN, lawyer; b. Dothan, Ala., Sept. 23, 1946; s. Dow Thobern Huskey and Helen (Weathersbee) Morris; m. Julie Beth Courson, May 17, 1975; children—Dow, III, Whitney. B.S., Samford U., 1970; J.D., Cumberland Sch. Law, 1976. Bar: Ala. 1977, U.S. Dist. Ct. (mid. dist.) Ala. 1977, U.S. Ct. Appeals (5th cir.) 1977, U.S. Ct. Appeals (11th cir.) 1981, U.S. Supreme Ct. 1981. Ptnr. Huskey & Etheredge, Dothan, 1977-82, Johnson Huskey Hornsby & Etheredge, Dothan, 1982—. Author: Landlord and Tenant, The Law in Alabama, 1980; Damages, The Law in Alabama, 1985. Pres., Houston County chpt. Am. Cancer Soc., Dothan, 1979-81, Houston County chpt. Ala. Soc. Crippled Children and Adults, Dothan, 1982-83. Mem. Ala. Trial Lawyers Assn. (bd. govs. 1980-85), Nat. Assn. Coll. and Univ. Attys., Assn. Trial Lawyers Am., Ala. Def. Lawyers Assn. Republican. Episcopalian. Lodge: Rotary. Federal civil litigation, State civil litigation, General corporate. Home: 1108 Victoria Ave Dothan AL 36303 Office: Johnson Huskey Hornsby & Etheredge 131 N Oates St Dothan AL 36303

HUSNEY, ELLIOTT RONALD, lawyer, financier; b. Mpls., July 24, 1940; s. Edward and Betty (Malca) H.; m. Gloria Lynne Rudd, Dec. 15, 1962; children—Ronald Edward, Kenneth Logan, Evan James. A.A., U. Minn., 1960; BSBA, U. Denver, 1962, J.D., 1965. Bar: Colo. 1966. Staff examiner Nat. Assn. Security Dealers, Inc., 1965-66; trial atty. U.S. SEC, 1966-68; house counsel Denver Corp., 1968-69, Colo Corp., 1969-70; v.p. Petro Search Inc., Denver, 1970-71; pres. Denver Venture Capital, Inc., 1972-75; ptnr. Husney & Pansing, Denver, 1975-77; of counsel Pansing & Pansing; chmn. Elliott Enterprise Group, Denver, 1977—; ptnr. Walden Banking Ptnrs., Ltd., 1987—; pres. Am. Heliothermal Corp., 1977-79; chmn, U.S. Israel Investments, 1977-83; chmn. Vital Sci. Corp., div. Vital Sci., Ltd., 1985—, also dir.; dir. Pro Care Industries. Bd. dirs. Am. Jewish Com., 1982-85, Am.-Israel Friendship League, 1983-84; vice chmn. Com. for 18; Recipient Young Leadership award Allied Jewish Fedn. of Denver; named Man of Yr., Denver Jaycees, 1978. Mem. ABA, Denver Bar Assn., Colo. Bar Assn. Club: Inverness Country. General corporate, Securities. Office: 8460 E Prentice Ave Suite 625 Englewood CO 80111

HUSS, ALLAN MICHAEL, lawyer; b. Chgo., Sept. 29, 1949; s. Henry A. and Emily (Rosenheim) H.; m. Sandra Joyce Cohn, Aug. 16, 1970; children: Leah E., Samantha J. BS, Mich. State U., 1970; JD, U. Cin., 1973. Bar: Ohio 1973, Mich. 1982. Staff atty. U.S. Fed. Trade Commn., Cleve., 1973-81; sr. staff counsel Chrysler Corp., Detroit, 1982—; mem. fed. adv. com. FTC; bd. dirs. antitrust sect. State Bar Mich. Mem. ABA, Mich. Bar Assn., Greater Cleve. Bar Assn. Avocation: computer programming. Antitrust, Administrative and regulatory, General corporate. Home: 5049 Langlewood Dr West Bloomfield MI 48033 Office: Chrysler Corp 416-19-02 12000 Chrysler Dr Highland Park MI 48288

HUSTON, STEVEN CRAIG, lawyer; b. Morris, Ill., June 3, 1954; s. Raymond P. and Evelyn M. (Bass) H.; m. Jamie Anne Shaw, Sept. 21, 1985. BA, Ill. Coll., 1977; JD, John Marshall Law Sch., 1980; postgrad., Northwestern U., 1987—. Bar: Ill. 1980, U.S. Dist. Ct. (no. dist.) Ill. 1980, U.S. Ct. Appeals (7th cir.) 1980. Assoc. Siegel, Denberg et al, Chgo., 1980-83; staff atty. William Wrigley Jr. Co., Chgo., 1983-84, asst. sec. legal, 1984—. Mem. ABA, Chgo. Bar Assn. General corporate, Trademark and copyright, Securities. Office: William Wrigley Jr Co 410 N Michigan Chicago IL 60611

HUSZAGH, FREDRICK WICKETT, law educator, information management company executive, lawyer; b. Evanston, Ill., July 20, 1937; s. Rudolph LeRoy and Dorothea (Wickett) H.; m. Sandra McRae, Apr. 4, 1959; children—Floyd McRae, Fredrick Wickett II, Theodore Wickett II. B.A., Northwestern U., 1958; J.D., U. Chgo., 1962, LL.M., 1963, J.S.D., 1964. Bar: Ill. 1962, U.S. Dist. Ct. D.C. 1965, U.S. Supreme Ct. 1966. Market researcher Leo Burnett Co. Chgo., 1958-59; internat. atty. COMSAT, Washington, 1964-67; assoc. Debevoise & Liberman, Washington, 1967-68; asst. prof. law Am. U., Washington, 1968-71; program dir. NSF, Washington, 1971-73; assoc. prof. U. Mont., Missoula, 1973-76, U. Wis.-Madison, 1976-77; exec. dir. Dean Rusk Ctr., U. Ga., Athens, 1977-82; prof. U. Ga., 1982—; chmn. TWH Corp., Athens, 1982—; cons. Pres. Johnson's Telecommunications Task Force, Washington, 1967-68; co-chmn. Nat. Gov.'s Internat. Trade Staff Commn., Washington, 1979- 81. Author: International Decision-Making Process, 1964; Comparative Facts on Canada, Mexico and U.S., 1979; also articles. Editor Rusk Ctr. Briefings, 1981-82. Mem. Econ. Policy Council, N.Y.C., 1981—. NSF grantee, 1974-78. Republican. Presbyterian. Administrative and regulatory, Public international, Legislative. Home: 3890 Barnett Shoals Rd Athens GA 30605 Office: U Ga Law Sch Athens GA 30602

HUTCHINS, TERRY RICHARD, lawyer, educator; b. King, N.C., Feb. 15, 1938; s. Harry Spencer and Lida Alberta (Phillips) H.; m. Nora Nixon, Mar. 23, 1960 (div.); children—Terry Richard, Sheila Kim, Amber Star, Susan Kristina, Stephanie Lenora. Student High Point Coll., 1956-58; A.B., Pembroke (N.C.) State U., 1960; J.D., Wake Forest Sch. Law, 1965. Bar; N.C. 1965, U.S. Supreme Ct. 1970, U.S. Dist. Ct. (mid. dist.) N.C. 1982. Tchr. pub. schs. Hendry County, Clewiston, Fla., 1960-61, Live Oak, Fla., 1961; sole practice law, Pilot Mountain, N.C., 1965-66, Laurinburg, N.C., 1967—; dir. instl. research Pembroke (N.C.) State U., 1967-72, legal asst. to chancellor, 1972—, instr. bus. law, 1980; cons. Ind. Inst. Tech., Fort Wayne, 1972-77, Biscayne Coll., Miami, Fla., 1975. Pres. Stewartsville Vol. Fire Dept., Laurinburg, 1978—; area coordinator Knox for Gov., N.C., 1982-84. Fellow in acad. adminstrn Am. Council Edn., 1969; disting. guest scholar Woodrow Wilson Ctr. for Scholars of Smithsonian Instn., Washington, 1971. Mem. N.C. State Bar Assn., N.C. Assn. Campus Law Enforecment Admstrs., Nat. Assn. Coll. and Univ. Attys., Pembroke State U. Alumni Assn. (pres. 1969). Am. Council on Edn. Acad. Adminstrv. Intern Fellows Alumni. Democrat. Baptist. Club: Laura-Scott Quadrille (Laurinburg). Lodge: Masons. General practice, Legal education. Home: RD 3 Box 314 Laurinburg NC 28352 Office: Pembroke State Univ College St Pembroke NC 28372

HUTCHINSON, DENNIS JAMES, legal educator; b. Boulder, Colo., Dec. 28, 1946; s. Dudley Isom and Jane Wilcox (Sampson) H.; m. Diane Pamela Wood, Sept. 2, 1978; children—Kathryn Wood, David Edward, Jane Shattuck. A.B., Bowdoin Coll., 1969; LL.M., U. Tex.-Austin, 1974; M.A. (Rhodes scholar), Oxford U., 1977. Law clk. to judge U.S. Ct. Appeals 5th Cir., 1974-75, to Justice White, U.S. Supreme Ct., 1975, Justice Douglas, U.S. Supreme Ct., 1976; assoc. prof. law Georgetown U., 1977-81; Peter B. Ritzma assoc. prof. law, U. Chgo., 1981-82, assoc. prof. in the Univ., 1982—; faculty Cornell U. Law Sch., Ithaca, N.Y., 1985-86. Bd. overseers Bowdoin Coll., 1975—. Editor The Supreme Ct. Rev., 1981—. Mem. Selden Soc., Am. Soc. Legal History. Democrat. Legal education, Legal history, Constitutional. Office: U Chgo Law Sch 1111 E 60th St Chicago IL 60637

HUTCHINSON, EVERETT, lawyer; b. Hempstead, Tex., Jan. 2, 1915; s. Neely E. and Lida (Hosmer) H.; m. Elizabeth Stafford, Dec. 16, 1944; children: Stafford, Ann. B.B.A., U. Tex., 1939, LL.B., 1940. Bar: Tex. 1939, D.C. 1963. Practiced in Hempstead and Austin, Tex., 1940-55; asst. atty. gen. Tex., 1949-51; commr. ICC, Washington, 1955-65; chmn. commn. ICC, 1961; pres. Am. Bus. Assn., 1965-67; under-sec. transp. 1967-68; partner Fulbright & Jaworski, Washington, 1968-83, counsel, 1983—; mem. council Adminstrv. Conf. U.S., 1961-62. Mem. Tex. Ho. of Reps., 1941-45; orgn. dir. Young Democratic Clubs of Tex., 1939-40. Served from apprentice seaman to lt. USNR, 1942-45; capt. JAGC, USNR (Ret.). Mem. ABA, D.C. Bar Assn., Fed. Bar Assn., Nat. Def. Transp. Assn. (pres. 1975-77, chmn. bd. 1977-79), State Bar Tex., Friar Soc., Tex. Soc. Washington, Sigma Phi Epsilon. Episcopalian. Clubs: Metropolitan (Washington), Internat. (Washington); Houston Center (Houston); Pisces. Administrative and regulatory. Home: 5401 Albemarle St Bethesda MD 20816 Office: 1150 Connecticut Ave NW Suite 400 Washington DC 20036

HUTCHINSON, MARK RANDALL, lawyer; b. Christopher, Ill., Dec. 20, 1948; s. Mark James and Betty (Crain) H.; m. Marian Hutchinson, Aug. 14, 1974 (div. Aug. 1985); 1 child, Mark Bradley. BS, Murray State U., 1971; JD, U. Ky., 1974. Bar: Ky. 1974, U.S. Dist. Ct. (we. dist.) Ky. 1974. Ptnr. Lovett, Lamar & Hutchinson, Owensboro, Ky., 1974-83, Taylor, Meyer & Hutchinson, Owensboro, 1983—; instr. Grad. Realtors Inst., Lexington, Ky., 1976-85. Grad. Leadership Owensboro, 1985; bd. dirs. Owensboro Family YMCA, 1986. Mem. ABA, Ky. Bar Assn., Daviess County Bar Assn., Order of Coif. Republican. Methodist. Lodge: Optimists. Oil and gas leasing, Contracts commercial, Real property. Office: Taylor Meyer & Hutchinson 100 E 1st St Owensboro KY 42301

HUTCHINSON, WILLIAM DAVID, justice state supreme court; b. Minersville, Pa., June 20, 1932; s. Elmer E. and Elizabeth (Price) H.; m. Louise Meloney, 1957; children: Kathryn, William, Louise, Andrew. B.A. magna cum laude, Moravian Coll., 1954; J.D., Harvard U., 1957. Bar: Pa. Private practice law Pottsville, Pa., 1958-82; asst. dist. atty. Schuylkill County, Pa., 1963-69, solicitor, 1969-72; solicitor Blue Mountain Sch. Dist., Cressona, Pa., 1967-81; justice Pa. Supreme Ct., Harrisburg, 1982—; chmn. Joint State Govt. Commn. Pa. Gen. Assembly, 1981; mem. Pa. Jud. Council, 1980-82; mem. Pomeroy Commn. on Unified Jud. System, 1980-82. Mem. Pa. Ho. of Reps., 1973-81, chmn. ethics com., 1981; mem. Blue Mountain Sch. Bd., 1963-66. Recipient John Amos Comenius award Moravian Coll., 1982. Mem. ABA, Pa. Bar Assn., Assn. Trial Lawyers Am., Pa. Trial Lawyers Assn., Am. Judicature Soc., Schuylkill County Bar Assn. (com. continuing legal edn.). Republican. Methodist. Office: Pennsylvania Supreme Court PO Box 1172 Harrisburg PA 17108

HUTCHISON, ROBERT ALAN, lawyer; b. Prairie City, Iowa, Sept. 8, 1949; s. Raymond Lester and Edith Mae (McFadden) H.; m. Dawn Ellen Failey, June 12, 1971; children: Andrew Mark, Julie Joy. BA, Harvard U., 1971; JD, U. Iowa, 1974. Bar: Iowa 1974, U.S. Dist. Ct. (no. and so. dists.) Iowa 1974, U.S. Ct. Appeals (8th cir.) 1984. From assoc. to ptnr. Brown, Winick, Graves, Donnelly & Baskerville, Des Moines, 1974—. Mem. ABA, Iowa Bar Assn., Assn. Trial Lawyers Am., Iowa Trial Lawyers Am. Republican. Avocations: hunting, fishing, running, gardening. Federal civil litigation, State civil litigation, Administrative and regulatory. Home: 7980 Vandalia Rd Runnells IA 50237 Office: Brown Winick Graves et al 601 Locust St 2 Ruan Ctr Suite 1 Des Moines IA 50309

HUTCHISON, SAMUEL ROBERT, lawyer; b. Portsmouth, Ohio, Oct. 6, 1923; s. William G. and Ruth C. (Torner) H.; m. Sally Jane Brooder; children—Tammy Jane, Steven Robert, Leslie. Student The Citadel, 1943-44, Johns Hopkins U., 1944-45; B.A., Ohio State U., 1947, J.D., 1950. Bar: Ohio 1950, Colo. 1951, Wyo. 1959, Ariz. 1962, U.S. Supreme Ct. 1971, U.S. Ct. Appeals (8th cir.) 1972, U.S. Ct. Appeals (10th cir.) 1974. Assoc. Gallagher Co., Denver, 1950; regional counsel for Rocky Mountain Region, Standard Oil of Ind., Denver, 1952-55; gen. atty. for mktg. Husky Oil Co., Cody, Wyo., 1955-61; gen. counsel Western Am. Mortgage Co., Phoenix, 1961-63; ptnr. Botsford, Shumway & Hutchison, Scottsdale, Ariz., 1963-67; pres. Samuel Robert Hutchison, P.C., Phoenix, 1970—; dir. Cosanti Found., Scottsdale, various corps. Served with U.S. Army, 1943-46. Mem. ABA, Am. Judicature Soc. Republican. Clubs: Kiwanis, Elks. Probate, General corporate, Real property. Office: Suite 150C 4350 E Camelback Rd Phoenix AZ 85018

HUTFLESS, FRANK JAMES, lawyer, consultant; b. Omaha, Mar. 29, 1946; s. Frank Andrew and Bonnie May (Kirkpatrick) H.; m. Catherine Josephine Horine, Dec. 27, 1969 (div. 1985); children: Sarah Louise, Jessica Kimberly. BA, U. Calif., Berkeley, 1969; JD, Creighton U., 1974. Bar: Nebr. 1974, U.S. Dist. Ct. Nebr. 1974, U.S. Ct. Appeals (8th cir.) 1974; U.S. Supreme Ct. 1982. Assoc. judge Nebr. Dist. Ct. (16th dist.), 1976-81; asst. atty. gen. State of Nebr., 1981-83; v.p., gen. counsel Farm Credit Banks, Omaha, 1983—; counsel Nebr. Oil and Gas Com., Sidney, 1981-83, Nebr. State Lands Office, Lincoln, 1981-83, 8th Farm Credit Dist. Bd., Omaha, 1983—; lectr. Nebr. and Iowa CLE, 1981—. Author oil and gas, agrl. law and litigation ednl. materials. Served with USAF, 1969-70. Mem. ABA. Republican. Roman Catholic. Avocations: flying, golf, fishing. Banking, General corporate, Federal civil litigation. Office: Farm Credit Banks of Omaha 206 S 19th St Omaha NE 68102

HUTH, LESTER CHARLES, lawyer; b. Tiffin, Ohio, Nov. 21, 1924. J.D., U. Notre Dame, 1951. Bar: Ohio 1954. Sole practice, Fostoria, Ohio, 1954—; acting mcpl. judge, Fostoria, 1970, city solicitor, 1954-56, 60-64, police prosecutor, 1964-68; legal counsel to St. Wendelin Parish, Fostoria, 1972—; atty. Selective Service Bd. Appeals, 1956-75. Clk. city council, Fostoria, 1957-58; sec.-treas. Karrick Sch. Handicapped Children, 1966-77; Cub scoutmaster Boy Scouts Am., 1967-68; adviser to Fostoria Family and Child Service, 1977-83. Recipient certs. of appreciation Pres. Lyndon Johnson, 1966, SSS, 1975. Mem. Ohio Bar Assn., Senece County Bar Assn., C. of C. (dir. 1970-71), Fostoria Jaycees (founding pres. 1954). General practice. Home: 225 E High St Fostoria OH 44830 Office: 112 E North St Fostoria OH 44830

HUTSON, FRANK ALFRED, JR., lawyer, retired communications company executive; b. N.Y.C., Feb. 24, 1917; s. Frank Alfred and Irene (Rigby)

H.; m. Catherine Brent Halsey, Dec. 23, 1943; children: Catherine Wrenn (Mrs. John C. Boulton), William Halsey, Jean Rigby (Mrs. James C. Lister). B.A., Swarthmore Coll., 1937; LL.B., Yale U., 1940. Bar: N.Y. 1940, Mass. 1956. Atty. firm Winthrop, Stimson, Putnam & Roberts, N.Y.C., 1940-49; atty. Nat. Biscuit Co., N.Y.C., 1949-52; with AT&T, N.Y.C., 1952-56, 60-82; gen. atty. AT&T, 1966-72, sec., gen. atty., 1972-82; of counsel Kraft & Hughes, Newark, 1982-87; gen. solicitor New Eng. Tel. & Tel. Co., Boston, 1956-60; mem. industry adv. com. SEC, 1972—. Served to capt. AUS, 1941-45, ETO. Decorated Bronze Star; Croix de Guerre with palm and silver star, France. Mem. Am. Law Inst., ABA, Am. Soc. Corp. Secs. (chmn. 1978-79), Phi Beta Kappa, Phi Kappa Psi. Episcopalian. Clubs: Montclair (N.J.) Golf; Sakonnet Golf (Little Compton, R.I.); University (N.Y.C.). General corporate, Public utilities. Home: 56 Fellswood Dr Essex Fells NJ 07021

HUTSON, JEFFREY WOODWARD, lawyer; b. New London, Conn., July 19, 1941; s. John Jenkins and Kathryn Barbara (Himberg) H.; m. Susan Office, Nov. 25, 1967; children—Elizabeth Kathryn, Anne Louise. A.B., U. Mich., 1963, LL.B., 1966. Bar: Ohio 1966, Hawaii 1970. Assoc. Lane, Alton & Horst, Columbus, Ohio, 1966-74, ptnr., 1974—. Served to lt. comdr. USN, 1967-71. Fellow Am. Coll. Trial Lawyers; mem. ABA, Ohio Bar Assn. (past chmn. litigation sect.), Ohio Assn. Civil Trial Attys. (past pres.), Columbus Bar Assn., Internat. Assn. Ins. Counsel. Republican. Episcopalian. Clubs: Scioto Country, Athletic. Avocations: cycling; cross country skiing; reading; music. Federal civil litigation, State civil litigation, Construction. Office: Lane Alton & Horst 155 E Broad St Columbus OH 43215

HUTT, PETER BARTON, lawyer; b. Buffalo, Nov. 16, 1934; s. Lester Ralph and Louise Rich (Fraser) H.; m. Eleanor Jane Zurn, Aug. 29, 1959; children: Katherine Zurn, Peter Barton, Sarah Henderson, Everett Fraser. B.A. magna cum laude, Yale U., 1956; LL.B., Harvard U., 1959; LL.M., N.Y. U., 1960. Bar: N.Y. 1959, D.C. 1961, U.S. Supreme Ct. 1967. Assoc. firm Covington & Burling, Washington, 1960-68; partner Covington & Burling, 1968-71; chief counsel FDA, 1971-75; partner firm Covington & Burling, 1975—; dir. Am. Sterilizer Corp., Erie, Pa., 1975-84; mem. adv. com. to dir. NIH, 1976-81; mem. com. on research tng. Nat. Acad. Sci., 1976-80; counsel to Alcoholic Beverage Med. Research Found.; mem. adv. panel Scripps Clinic and Research Found., La Jolla, Calif., Ctr. for Study Drug Devel., Tufts U., Ctr. for Advanced Studies, U. Va., Inst. for Health Policy Analysis, Georgetown U., Food and Drug Law Inst., Washington; mem. various panels U.S. Congl. Office Tech. Assessment. Author: (with Patricia Wald) Dealing with Drug Abuse, 1972, (with Richard Merrill) Food and Drug Law, 1980; contbg. editor: Legal Times of Washington, 1978-86; mem. editorial bd. various jours. Bd. dirs. Sidwell Friends Sch., Washington, 1976-84, Legal Action Center, N.Y.C., Found. for Biomed. Research; mem. exec. com. Washington Lawyers Com. for Civil Rights Under Law; bd. dirs. Soc. Risk Analysis; mem. vis. com. Harvard Sch. Public Health, 1980-86. Recipient Disting. Service award HEW, 1974; Underwood-Prescott award Mass. Inst. Tech., 1977. Mem. Am. Bar Assn. (former chmn. life scis. com., sect. on sci. and tech.), Inst. Medicine, Nat. Acad. Scis.. Episcopalian. Club: Metropolitan (Washington). Administrative and regulatory, Environment. Home: 5325 Chamberlin Ave Chevy Chase MD 20815 Office: 1201 Pennsylvania Ave NW Washington DC 20004

HUTTER, ROBERT GRANT, lawyer, educator; b. Cleve., May 7, 1948; s. Russell G. and Tresa V. (Ireland) H.; m. Cheryl Felt. B.S.Ch.E., Va. Poly. Inst., 1969; J.D., U. Md., 1973; M.B.A., St. Bonaventure U., 1978. Bar: N.Y. 1980, U.S. Dist. Ct. N.Y. Chem. engr. Westinghouse, Balt., 1969-73; prof. law Alfred U., N.Y., 1974—; ptnr. Sootheran & Hutter, Andover, N.Y., 1981—. Contbr. numerous articles and book revs. to profl. publs. Mem. N.Y. State Bar Assn., Allegany County Bar Assn. (chmn. real estate law com. 1983—). Legal education, Probate, Real property. Home: RD 1 Box 81H Wellsville NY 14895 Office: Sootheran & Hutter Attys 15 Main St Andover NY 14806

HUTTON, ALBERT LEE, JR., lawyer; b. Boston, Jan. 29, 1925; s. Albert Lee Sr. and Josephine Margret (Lydon) H.; children—Susan Murray, Heidi Cross, Albert L. III, Jill. J.D., Suffolk U., 1955. Bar: Mass. 1956, U.S. Dist. Ct. Mass. 1957, U.S. Ct. Appeals (1st cir.) 1977, U.S. Supreme Ct. 1970. Counsel, Vol. Def. Com. Boston, 1957-59; 1st asst. counsel Mass. Def. Com., 1959-62; sole practice, Boston, 1962—. Served to pfc. USMC, 1942-45, PTO. Recipient Outstanding Alumnus award Suffolk Law Sch., 1983. Roman Catholic. Criminal, State civil litigation, Personal injury. Office: 6 Beacon St Boston MA 02108

HUTTON, JAMES LAWRENCE, lawyer; b. Marion, Va., June 29, 1932; s. Joseph Hugh and Creola (Hall) H.; m. Phyllis Meade, Sept. 19, 1958; children: Christopher Todd, Vicki Leigh. BA, Emory & Henry Coll., 1957; JD, U. Richmond, 1965. Bar: Va. 1965. Ptnr. Gilmer, Sadler, Ingram, Sutherland and Hutton, Blacksburg, Va., 1965—; judge Blacksburg Mcpl. Ct., 1968-73; assoc. judge Montgomery County Dist. Ct., Blacksburg, 1968-73; bd. dirs. First Nat. Bank, Christiansburg, Va. Chmn. 9th Dist. Young Dems. of Va., Marion, 1959-60; pres. Blacksburg Kiwanis Club, 1969-70, Marion Jaycees, 1962-63, Blacksburg C. of C., 1970. Served as cpl. U.S. Army, 1952-54. Democrat. Baptist. Home: 305 Hemlock Dr Blacksburg VA 24060 Office: Gilmer Sadler et al PO Box 908 Blacksburg VA 24060

HUTTON, SUSAN PAWLIAS, lawyer; b. Rochester, Minn., July 20, 1957; d. Kenneth Theodore and Shirley Jane (Mason) Pawlias; m. Noel Curtis Hutton, June 21, 1980. BA magna cum laude, Drake U., 1978, JD with honors, 1982. Bar: Iowa 1982, S.C. 1983, U.S. Tax Ct. 1983, U.S. Dist. Ct. S.C. 1986. Assoc. Dobson & Dobson PA, Greenville, S.C., 1982—. Troop leader Girl Scouts Am., Greenville, 1983—. Mem. ABA, Iowa Bar Assn., S.C. Bar Assn., Greenville County Bar Assn., Order of Coif, Phi Beta Kappa. Pension, profit-sharing, and employee benefits, Corporate taxation, Personal income taxation. Home: 4832 Coach Hill Dr Greenville SC 29615 Office: Dobson & Dobson PA 1306 S Church St PO Box 1923 Greenville SC 29602

HUYETT, DANIEL HENRY, 3RD, judge; b. Reading, Pa., May 2, 1921; s. Daniel Henry, Jr. and Emma Alice (Moyer) H.; m. Mary Jane Hallford, Mar. 23, 1946 (dec. Jan. 15, 1985); children: Cathy J. (Mrs. Tracy James Whitaker), Daniel B., Christina N. (Mrs. Harold G. Kelso III). A.B., U. Mich., 1942; J.D., U. Pa., 1948. Bar: Pa. 1949. Practiced in Berks County, 1949-70; city solicitor Reading, 1952-56; U.S. dist. judge Eastern Dist. Pa., Phila., 1970—; lectr. Fed. Jud. Ctr., Washington, 1977, 78, 79; instr. Atty. Gen. Advocacy Inst., 1978-87. Mem. Pa. Labor Relations Bd., 1966-68, Pa. Public Utility Commn., 1968-70. Served as 1st lt. USAAF, World War II; capt. USAF Res. Mem. Am., Pa., Berks County bar assns., Am. Judicature Soc., Supreme Ct. Hist. Soc., Am. Law Inst. Home: 403 Green Ln Greenfields Reading PA 19601 Office: 12614 N US Courthouse Philadelphia PA 19106

HWANG, ROLAND, lawyer; b. Detroit, May 17, 1949; s. David Nien-Tzu and Rose (Hsi) H.; m. Christina Grace Sieh, Aug. 19, 1983. BSME, U. Mich., 1971, MBA, 1976; JD, Wayne State U., 1980, LLM, 1984. Bar: Mich. 1981, U.S. Dist. Ct. (we. dist.) Mich. 1981. Substitute tchr. Livonia (Mich.) Pub. Schs., 1971-72; customer service rep. Manpower, Inc., Detroit, 1971; product engr. Ford Motor Co., Dearborn, Mich., 1972-81, staff atty., 1981—; mem. adv. com. Madonna Coll. Legal Assistance Tng. Program, Livonia, 1982-86. Contbr. articles, reports to profl. jours. Chmn. Gov.'s Adv. Commn. on Asian Am. Affairs, Lansing, Mich., 1986—. Fellow State Bar of Mich. Found.; mem. State Bar of Mich. (civil liberties com. 1986—), Am. Mgmt. Assns., Am. Citizens for Justice (treas. 1983, sec. 1985-86), Soc. Automotive Engrs., Assn. Chinese Americans of Detroit (pres. 1982), Asian Am. Bar Assn. Mich. (co-founder 1986, pres. 1986-87), Phi Alpha Delta. Methodist. Club: Economic (Detroit). Avocations: rafting, travel, aerobics, squash, reading. General corporate, Civil rights. Office: Ford Motor Co Office Gen Counsel 1 Parklane Blvd Suite 300 W Dearborn MI 48126

HYAMS, HAROLD, lawyer; b. Bklyn., May 19, 1943; s. Frank Charles and Celia (Silverstein) H.; m. Simone Elkeharrat, Nov. 18, 1973; children: Gabriel, Galite, Emilie, Jonathan. BA, U. Vt., 1965; MA in Latin Am. Studies, Georgetown U., 1966; JD, Syracuse U., 1970. Bar: N.Y. 1971, Ariz. 1974, U.S. Dist. Ct. Ariz. 1974, U.S. Ct. Appeals (9th cir.) 1974. Asst. to the gen. counsel Am. Express Co., N.Y.C., 1970-72; atty. Legal Aid Soc., Bklyn., 1973; ptnr. Harold Hyams and Assocs., Tucson, 1974—; mem. panel of arbitrators Am. Arbitration Assn., N.Y.C., 1971-73. Bd. dirs. Chafetz Chaim Congregation, Tucson, 1985-86, Tucson Hebrew Acad., 1985-86. Mem. Ariz. Trial Lawyers Assn., Pima County Bar Assn., Assn. Trial Lawyers Am. Avocation: travel. Federal civil litigation, Family and matrimonial, Personal injury. Home: 8148 E Galinda Dr Tucson AZ 85715 Office: 680 S Craycroft Tucson AZ 85711

HYATT, JOEL Z., lawyer, management services company executive; b. Cleve., May 6, 1950; s. David and Anna (B.) Zylberberg; m. Susan Metzenbaum, Aug. 24, 1975; children: Jared Z., Zachary Robert. B.A., Dartmouth Coll., 1972; J.D., Yale U., 1975. Founder, sr. ptnr. Hyatt Legal Services, Kansas City, Mo.; pres., chief exec. officer Block Mgmt. Co., Kansas City, Mo. Bd. fellows Brandeis U.; asst. treas. Democratic Nat. Com., 1981-83; bd. dirs. Ctr. for a New Democracy; founding mem. U.S. Senate Democratic Leadership Circle; mem. nat. young leadership cabinet United Jewish Appeal; mem. nat. exec. com. Am. Jewish Congress. Mem. Young Pres.'s Orgn. Office: Hyatt Legal Services 4410 Main St Kansas City MO 64111

HYATT, SUSAN METZENBAUM, lawyer; b. Cleve., Mar. 8, 1950; d. Howard M. and Shirley (Turoff) Metzenbaum; m. Joel Z. Hyatt, Aug. 24, 1975; 1 child, Jared. Student, U. Ariz., 1968-69; BS, U. Cin., 1972; JD, Case Western Res. U., 1981. Bar: Mo. 1981, U.S. Dist. Ct. (we. dist.) Mo. 1981. Dir. non-legal personnel Hyatt Legal Services, Cleve., 1977-80; sr. ptnr. Hyatt Legal Services, Kansas City, Mo., 1981—; dir. spl. projects Block Mgmt. Co., Kansas City. Chmn. Task Force on Developmentally Disabled Jewish Family Commn., Kansas City, 1986; bd. dirs. women's div. Jewish Fedn., Kansas City, 1986, Brandeis Woman's Div., Kansas City, 1985-86, Jewish Family Commn., Kansas City, 1984-86. Mem. Cen. Exchange. Democrat. Avocations: tennis, swimming, reading. Office: Hyatt Legal Services 4410 Main St Kansas City MO 64111

HYBL, WILLIAM JOSEPH, lawyer, investment company executive; b. Des Moines, July 16, 1942; B.A., Colo. Coll., 1964; J.D., U. Colo., 1967. Bar: Colo. 1967. Asst. dist. atty. 4th Jud. Dist., El Paso and Teller Counties, 1970-72; pres., dir. El Pomar Investment Co., 1973-86; exec. v.p., dir. Garden City Co., 1973—; dir. Broadmoor Mgmt. Co., 1975—, Broadmoor Hotel, Inc., 1973—, also vice-chmn., 1987—; bd. dirs. 1st Nat. Bank Colorado Springs, Affiliated Bankshares of Colo., 1986—; mem. Colo. Ho. Reps., 1972-73. Pres., dir. El Pomar Found., 1973—; trustee, vice chmn. Colo. Coll., 78—; trustee Am. Council Young Polit. Leaders, 1980—; pres., trustee Air Force Acad. Found.; bd. dirs. Vail Valley Found.; sec., trustee U.S. Olympic Found., 1984—; chmn. Colo. commn. on Bicentennial com. of U.S Constitution, 1986—; spl. White House counsel, 1981; civilian aide to sec. of army for State of Colo., 1986—. Mem. U.S. C. of C. (bd. dirs., pub. affairs com. chmn., 1985б—). Real property. Home: 2 Heather Circle Colorado Springs CO 80906 Office: 10 Lake Circle Colorado Springs CO 80906

HYDE, CLARENCE EDWIN, lawyer; b. Bryson City, N.C., Oct. 1, 1908; s. William A. and Rosa Lee (Grant) H.; m. Virginia Benton, Oct. 5, 1940; children: Rosalie, Peggy. AA, Mars Hill Coll., 1926; postgrad., Wake Forest U., 1932. Bar: N.C. 1932. Mayor Town of Andrews, N.C., 1933-34; mem. N.C. Ho. of Reps., Raleigh, 1935; justice Cherokee County, Murphy, N.C., 1954; ptnr. Hyde, Hoover & Lindsay, Murphy, 1954—. Chmn. Rep. Party, Cherokee County. Served to lt. comdr. USN, 1943-45, ETO. Mem. N.C. Bar Assn., Cherokee County Bar Assn. (pres.). Baptist. Avocation: golf. General practice, Real property. Home: 109 Moreland Ave Murphy NC 28906 Office: Hyde Hoover Lindsay & Nichols 212 Valley River Ave Murphy NC 28906

HYDE, DAVID ROWLEY, lawyer; b. Norwalk, Conn., Aug. 21, 1929; s. Thomas Arthur and Mary Julia (Sass) H.; m. Valerie Rosemary Worrall, Dec. 30, 1961; children: Meredith Ellen, Timothy Worrall. A.B., Yale U., 1951, LL.B., 1954. Bar: Conn. 1954, N.Y. 1956, U.S. Supreme Ct. 1969. Assoc. Cahill Gordon & Reindel, N.Y.C., 1954-59, 64-65, ptnr., 1966—; asst. U.S. atty. So. Dist. N.Y., 1959-63; chief civil div. U.S. Atty.'s Office, 1961-63. Federal civil litigation, State civil litigation. Home: 35 W 12th St New York NY 10011 Office: Cahill Gordon & Reindel 80 Pine St New York NY 10005

HYDE, PATRICK ALAN, lawyer; b. Hamilton, Ohio, Sept. 10, 1953; s. Clifton Joseph and Mary Ann (Streagle) H.; m. Marcia Lynn Meseck, June 2, 1979. AB magna cum laude, Brown U., 1978, AM, 1978; JD, U. Wis., Madison, 1980. Bar: Wis. 1981, U.S. Dist. Ct. (ea. dist.) Wis. 1981, D.C. 1986. Research assoc. U. Wis. Law Sch., Madison, 1980-81; lawyer Appalachian Research and Def. Fund Ky., Inc., Pikeville, 1982, Solicitor of Labor, Washington, 1982—; pres. Hyde Park Properties, Takoma Park, Md., 1984—. Contbr. articles to profl. jours. Commr. Landlord/Tenant Affairs City of Takoma Park, 1984, chmn., 1986—. Sustaining mem. Dem. Nat. Com. Recipient Nat. Hist. Soc. award Brown U., 1978; Lester Ward prize, 1978; spl. achievement award Solicitor of Labor, 1984. Mem. ABA (vice chmn. young lawyers div. alternative dispute resolution com.), Assn. Trial Lawyers Am. Presbyterian. Labor, Landlord-tenant, Pension, profit-sharing, and employee benefits. Home: 7307 Flower Ave Takoma Park MD 20912 Office: Div of Labor Mgmt Laws 200 Constitution Ave Washington DC 20210

HYLAND, WILLIAM FRANCIS, lawyer; b. Burlington, N.J., July 30, 1923; s. Theodore J. and Margaret M. (Gallagher) H.; m. Joan E. Sharp, Apr. 20, 1946; children: William Francis, Nancy E. Hyland Wiley, Stephen J., Emma L. Hyland McCormack, Margaret M. Hyland Frank, Thomas M. B.S. in Econs, U. Pa., 1944, LL.B., 1949; D.H.L., Hahnemann Med. Sch. and Hosp., 1976. Bar: N.J. 1949, U.S. Supreme Ct. 1960. Mem. Riker, Danzig, Scherer, Hyland and Perretti,, Morristown, N.J.; atty. gen. N.J., 1974-78; dir. Nat. Telephone Directory Corp., First Fidelity Bancorp., First Fidelity Bank, N.A., Am. Water Works Co., Wilmington, Del. Mem. N.J. Gen. Assembly from Camden County, 1954-61, speaker of house, 1958, acting gov., N.J., 1958; chmn. N.J. Sports and Expn. Authority, 1978-82, commr., 1982-84; pres. N.J. Bd. Pub. Utility Commrs., also mem. cabinet govs. Meyner, Hughes, Byrne, N.J., 1961-68, 74-78; chmn. N.J. Atomic Energy Council, 1968-69, N.J. Commn. Investigation, 1969-71; co-chmn. Reapportionment Commn.; Chmn. Brazilian Mission Com., 1962-65; permanent del. Fed. Jud. Conf. 3d Circuit.; Del.-at-large Dem. Nat. Conv., 1964, del., 1968; sec., bd. dirs. Waterloo Found. for Arts, Inc.; Assoc. trustee U. Pa., 1960-74. Served as officer USNR, 1943-46, ETO, PTO. Decorated knight Order of St. Gregory (Pope Paul VI), 1964; recipient Distinguished Service award Camden County Jaycees, 1954, Outstanding Young Man in Govt. N.J. award N.J. Jaycees, 1958, Myrtle Wreath award Camden County So. N.J. region Hadassah, 1977, Pub. Service award Anti-Defamation League of B'nai B'rith, 1982; named Outstanding Citizen of N.J. Advt. Club. N.J., 1979. Mem. Camden County Bar Assn. (pres. 1959), Nat. Assn. R.R. and Utilities Commrs. (exec. com. 1965-68), Nat. Assn. Attys. Gen. (exec. com. 1975-78, v.p. 1976, pres. elect 1977-78), Phi Kappa Psi., ABA (fellow N.J. chpt.), Essex County Bar Assn., Morris County Bar Assn. Administrative and regulatory, Public utilities. Home: 5 Ellyn Ct Convent Station NJ 07961 Office: Headquarters Plaza II One Speedwell Avenue Morristown NJ 07960

HYMAN, JERRY ALLAN, lawyer, bank officer; b. Bklyn., July 11, 1949; s. Seymour Magnus and Muriel Minerva (Cohen) H.; m. Karen Fern Stein, Aug. 28, 1983. BA, Rutgers U., 1971; M in Regional Planning, U. N.C., 1973; JD, U. Wis., 1979; LLM in Taxation, Temple U., 1984. Bar: U.S. Dist. Ct. D.C. 1981, U.S. Ct. Appeals (D.C. cir.) 1981, Del. 1984, U.S. Dist. Ct. Del. 1985. Planner Indpls. Dept. Met. Devel., 1974-75; planning analyst Wis. Dept. Adminstrn., Madison, 1975-76; law clk. Civil Aeronautics Bd., Washington, 1979-80; atty. FTC, Washington, 1980-83, Bayard, Handelman & Murdoch, Wilmington, Del., 1984-85; sr. trust tax officer Bank of Del., Wilmington, 1985—; adj. assoc. prof. U. Del., Newark, 1983. Rutgers U. scholar, New Brunswick, 1971. Mem. ABA, Del Bar Assn., D.C. Bar assn., Internat. Assn. Fin. Planning. Avocations: running, tennis. Personal income taxation, Estate taxation, Pension, profit-sharing, and employee benefits. Home: 4 Hayloft Circle Wilmington DE 19808 Office: Bank of Del 300 Delaware Ave Wilmington DE 19899

HYMAN, MONTAGUE ALLAN, lawyer; b. N.Y.C., Apr. 19, 1941; s. Allan Richard and Lilyan P. (Pollock) H.; m. Susann Podell, Jan. 25, 1965; children—Jeffrie-Anne, Erik. B.A., Syracuse U., 1962; J.D., St. Johns U., 1965. Bar: N.Y. 1965, U.S. Dist. Ct. (so. and ea. dists.) N.Y. 1967, U.S. Supreme Ct. 1973, U.S. Ct. Appeals (2d cir.) 1982. Assoc. Warburton, Hyman, Deeley & Connelly, Mineola, N.Y., 1965-67; ptnr. Hyman & Deeley, Mineola, 1967-69, Koeppel, Hyman, Sommer, Lesnick & Ross, Mineola, 1969-72, Hyman & Hyman, P.C., Garden City, N.Y., 1972-80, Costigan, Hyman, Hyman & Herman, P.C., Mineola, 1980—; lectr. Hofstra U., Adelphi U., Columbia Appraisal Soc., Practicing Law Inst. Mem. Nassau County Bar Assn., N.Y. State Bar Assn., Inst. Property Taxation. Contbr. articles to profl. jours. Real property, State and local taxation, Federal civil litigation. Office: Costigan Hyman Hyman & Herman PC 120 Mineola Blvd Mineola NY 11501

HYNES, JAMES PATRICK, lawyer; b. Chgo., Sept. 15, 1954; s. Francis Patrick and Elaine Marie (Drygalski) H.; m. Beth Williamson, Sept. 12, 1981. BA, Knox Coll., 1976; JD, John Marshall Sch. Law, 1981. Bar: Ill. 1981, U.S. Dist. Ct. (no. dist.) Ill. 1981. Assoc. Pollina & Phelan, Northbrook, Ill., 1981-84, Brodie & Reynolds, Chgo., 1984-86, Modesto, Reynolds & McDermott, Chgo., 1986—. Mem. ABA, Ill. Bar Assn., Chgo. Bar Assn., Northwest Suburban Bar Assn., Ill. Trial Lawyers Assn., Gavel Soc., Phi Delta Phi (v.p. 1980-81). Roman Catholic. Lodge: KC. Avocations: raquetball, weight lifting, boating, fishing. State civil litigation, Personal injury, Workers' compensation. Office: Modesto Reynolds & McDermott 111 W Washington Suite 1905 Chicago IL 60602

HYTKEN, FRANKLIN HARRIS, lawyer; b. Memphis, Dec. 25, 1948; s. Mac E. and Florence B. Hytken; m. Louise Grace Parks, Aug. 11, 1979; 1 child, Rachel Lee. Student, U. Louisville, 1965-66; BA cum laude, Northwestern U., 1969, JD, 1972. Bar: Tex. 1972, U.S. Dist. Ct. (no., ea. and we. dists.) Tex., U.S. Tax Ct., U.S. Ct. Appeals (5th and 11th cirs.), U.S. Supreme Ct. Assoc. Goins & Underkofler, Dallas, 1977-79; ptnr. Rhodus, Jones & Hytken, Dallas, 1979-83, Franklin, Harris & Hytken, P.C., Dallas, 1983—. Author: Pro-competitive Restraints of Trade, 1972. Chmn. Dem. Legis. Dist. Exec. Com., Dallas, 1984. Served to capt. (chief def. counsel 3d div. 1974, chief prosecutor Camp Zukeran 1975, mil. judge 1976-77) USMCR, 1972-77. Mem. ABA, Tex. Bar Assn., Dallas Bar Assn. (chmn. legal ethics com. 1983, fee disputes subcom. 1987—), North Dallas Bar Assn. (sec., treas. 1985—), Tex. Young Lawyers Assn. (chmn. fed. practice subcom. 1980—), North Dallas C. of C. (chmn. membership com., small bus. council 1984-85), Com. for a Qualified Judiciary (exec. com. 1986—). Democrat. Lodge: B'nai Brith (pres. couples unit 1980-81). Avocation: tennis. State civil litigation, Federal civil litigation, Bankruptcy. Home: 16515 Loch Maree Ln Dallas TX 75248 Office: 1710 One Galleria Tower Dallas TX 75240-6613

IALONGO, MICHAEL ANGELO, lawyer, investment company executive; b. Providence, Apr. 25, 1940; s. Michael Angelo and Frances (Saccoccia) I.; m. Karen Foley, Sept. 14, 1968; children—Michael S., Kerri Lee, Jason T. B.A., Providence Coll., 1962; J.D., Coll. William and Mary, 1965. Bar: R.I. 1966, U.S. Dist. Ct. R.I. 1969. Sole practice, Cranston, R.I., 1966-73; mem. firm Cappalli Greco & Ialongo, Cranston, 1974-83; Greco Ialongo & DiBona, Cranston, 1984—; treas. Colonial Deposit Co., Cranston, 1971-79; pres. CIBCO, Cranston, 1972-76; pres. Equity Mortgage Investment Corp., Cranston, 1982—; Mem. Cranston Indsl. Devel. Commn., 1980—. Served to cpl. U.S. Army, 1966-72. Mem. R.I. Bar Assn., Assn. Trial Lawyers Am., Phi Alpha Delta. Roman Catholic. Clubs: Alpine Country (tennis com.) (Cranston); Racquetime Tennis (Warwick, R.I.). Personal injury, Real property, General corporate. Home: 220 Olney Arnold Rd Cranston RI 02920 Office: 1700 Cranston St Cranston RI 02920

IAMELE, RICHARD THOMAS, law librarian; b. Newark, Jan. 29, 1942; s. Armando Anthony and Evelyn (Coladonato) I.; m. Marilyn Ann Berutto, Aug. 21, 1965; children—Thomas, Ann Marie. B.A., Loyola U., Los Angeles, 1963; M.S.L.S., U. So. Calif., 1967; J.D., Southwestern U., Los Angeles, 1976. Bar: Calif. 1977. Cataloger U. So. Calif., Los Angeles, 1967-71; asst. cataloger Los Angeles County Law Library, 1971-77, asst. reference librarian, 1977-78, asst. librarian, 1978-80, library dir., 1980—. Mem. ABA, Am. Assn. Law Libraries, Calif. Library Assn., So. Calif. Assn. Law Libraries. Librarianship. Office: Los Angeles County Law Library 301 W 1st St Los Angeles CA 90012

IANNARONE, ANTHONY JOSEPH, lawyer; b. Newark, Dec. 15, 1930; s. Anthony P.T. and Lena M. (Salerno) I.; m. Ruth Aitken, June 26, 1955; children: Lisa M. Iannarone Braner, Brian J., David B. BS, Rutgers U., 1952; JD, NYU, 1955, ML, 1966. Bar: N.J. 1956, U.S. Dist. Ct. N.J. 1956, U.S. Supreme Ct. 1963. Assoc. Toner, Crowley, Woelper & Vanderbilt, Newark, 1955-62; asst. gen. counsel Nopco Chem. Co., Newark, 1963-70; assoc. gen. counsel, asst. v.p., asst. sec., adminstrn. mgr. Hoffmann-La Roche Inc., Nutley, N.J., 1970—. Legal counsel Nutley (N.J.) Aux. Police, 1983—; trustee Mattia Award Com., Nutley, 1973—, Nutley Family Service Bur., 1980-86; pres. bd. of trustees Nutley Free Pub. Library, 1973—. Mem. ABA, N.J. Bar Assn., Essex County Bar Assn., Animal Health Inst. (chmn. law com. 1973-74), Phi Beta Kappa. Roman Catholic. General corporate, Food and drug, Law office administration. Home: 103 Rhoda Ave Nutley NJ 07110 Office: Hoffmann-La Roche Inc 340 Kingsland St Nutley NJ 07110

IANNUZZI, JOHN NICHOLAS, lawyer, author; b. N.Y.C., May 31, 1935; s. Nicholas Peter and Grace Margaret (Russo) I.; m. Carmen Marina Barrios, Aug. 1979; children: Dana Alejandra, Christina Maria, Nicholas Peter II; children from previous marriage: Andrea Marguerite, Maria Teresa. BS, Fordham U., 1956; JD, N.Y. Law Sch., 1962. Bar: N.Y., U.S. Dist. Ct. (so. and ea. dists.) N.Y. 1964, U.S. Dist. Ct. (no. and we. dists.) N.Y. 1965, U.S. Ct. Appeals (2d cir.) 1965, U.S. Supreme Ct. 1971, U.S. Dist. Ct. Conn. 1978, U.S. Tax Ct. 1978, U.S. Ct. Appeals (5th and 11th cirs.) 1982. Assoc. Law Offices of H.H. Lipsig, N.Y.C., 1962, Law Offices of Aaron J. Broder, N.Y.C., 1963; ptnr. Iannuzzi & Iannuzzi, N.Y.C., 1963—. Author: (novels) What's Happening, 1963, Part 35, 1970, Sicilian Defense, 1974, Courthouse, 1977, J.T., 1984; (non-fiction) Cross-Examination: The Mosaic Art, 1984. Mem. ABA, N.Y. County Bar Assn., N.Y. Criminal Bar Assn., Columbian Lawyers Assn. Roman Catholic. Criminal, Federal civil litigation, State civil litigation. Home: 118 Via Settembre, 9 Roma Italy Office: Iannuzzi & Iannuzzi 233 Broadway New York NY 10279

IATESTA, JOHN MICHAEL, lawyer; b. Orange, N.J., Dec. 29, 1944; s. Thomas Anthony and Marie Monica I.; m. Paulina Clare Pascuzzi, July 11, 1971. B.S. magna cum laude, Seton Hall U., 1967, J.D. cum laude, 1976, LL.M. in Corp. Law, NYU, 1986; M.S., Fordham U., 1968. Bar: N.J. 1976, U.S. Dist. Ct. N.J. 1976, U.S. Ct. Appeals (3d cir.) 1981, N.Y. 1982, U.S. Supreme Ct. 1985. Law sec. to presiding judge Appellate div. Superior Ct. N.J., Trenton, 1976-77; assoc. Wilentz, Goldman & Spitzer, Woodbridge, N.J., 1977-81, D'Alessandro, Sussman, Jacovino & Mahoney, Florham Park, N.J., 1981-83; corp. counsel Rhone-Poulenc Inc., Monmouth Junction, N.J., 1983—; mem. law com. Nat. Agrl. Chem. Assn., Washington, 1984—. Recipient Book prize, Tchrs. Coll. Columbia U., 1967. Mem. ABA, N.J. Bar Assn., Morris County Bar Assn. General corporate. Office: Rhone-Poulenc Inc Black Horse Ln Monmouth Junction NJ 08852

ICE, CLARENCE FREDERICK, lawyer; b. Clements, Kans., Oct. 30, 1901; s. Clement Valandingham and Jessie (Shaft) I.; m. Mildred Jane Branine, June 24, 1924; children—Winifred Ice Dewell, Theodore Branine. Student U. Calif.-Berkeley, 1920-21, Washburn U., 1921-22; LL.B., Kans. U., 1924. Bar: Kans. 1924, U.S. Dist. Ct. Kans. 1925, U.S. Supreme Ct. 1940. County atty. Marion County, Kans., 1929-33; city atty. City of Newton, Kans., 1933-39; county atty. Harvey County, Kans., 1940-42; mem. Ice, Turner & Ice, Newton, Kans., 1946—; dir. Kans. State Bank. Served to lt. col. U.S. Army, 1942-45. Decorated Bronze Star. Mem. ABA, Kans. Bar Assn., Newton C. of C. Republican. Presbyterian. Clubs: Masons, Lions, Elks. Oil and gas leasing, General practice, Probate.

ICE, NOEL CARLYSLE, lawyer; b. San Diego, Feb. 19, 1951; s. Noel Victor and Minnie Lee (Smith) I.; m. Catherine Kay Nash, Apr. 7, 1973; children: Rachel, Charlotte, Amanda. BA with honors, U. Tex., 1973; JD, U. Calif., Hastings Coll. Law, 1976. Bar: Tex. 1976, U.S. Dist. Ct. (no. dist.)

Tex. 1977, U.S. Tax Ct. 1980, U.S. Ct. Appeals (5th cir.) 1981. Assoc. Cantey, Hanger et al, Ft. Worth, 1973-79; ptnr. Watson, Ice & McGee, Ft. Worth, 1979-86, Cantey, Hanger, Gooch, Munn & Collins, Ft. Worth, 1986—. Contbr. articles to profl. jours. Mem. Tex. Bar Assn. (governing council mem. real estate, probate and trust law sect.), Tex. Bd. Legal Specialization (estate planning and probate law com.). Republican. Presbyterian. Club: Ft. Worth. Pension, profit-sharing, and employee benefits, Probate, Estate taxation. Office: Cantey Hanger Gooch Munn & Collins 2100 InterFirst Tower Fort Worth TX 76102

ICE, THEODORE BRANINE, lawyer; b. Newton, Kans., June 30, 1934; s. Clarence Frederick and Mildred Jane (Branine) I.; m. Rachel Sue Harper, Aug. 11, 1957; children: Laura Lynn, Nancy Ellen, Evan Harper. BA, U. Kans., 1956, JD, 1961. Bar: Kans. 1961, U.S. Dist. Ct. Kans. 1961, U.S. Supreme Ct. 1972. Ptnr. Ice, Turner & Ice, Newton, 1961—; bd. dirs. Bank IV Newton. Chmn. Harvey County Reps., Newton, 1966-81; alt. del. Nat. Rep. Conv., 1972; ordained elder Presbyn. Ch., 1965—; pres. United Way, Newton, 1979; pres. adv. bd. Bethel Coll., Newton, 1986-87; bd. dirs. Bethel Hosp., Newton, 1980—. Served to lt. USN, 1956-59. Mem. ABA, Kans. Bar Assn. (bd. editors jour. 1982—), Harvey County Bar Assn. (pres. 1975-76, 84-85), Newton C. of C. (pres. 1973-74). Lodge: Rotary (pres. 1975), Elks. Avocations: biking, swimming, golf. Contracts commercial, Probate, Real property. Office: Ice Turner & Ice 713 Main St Newton KS 67114

ICZKOVITZ, LESLIE KEITH, lawyer, computer consultant; b. Detroit, Oct. 8, 1952; parents: Hugo and Cecilie Iczkovitz. BS, U. Mich., 1974; JD, Wayne State U., 1978. Bar: Hawaii 1979, Calif. 1979, Mich. 1985. Assoc. Shigemura and Ching, Honolulu, 1979-83; sole practice Honolulu, 1983—; pres. More From Les, Inc., Honolulu, 1985—. Mem. ABA. Bankruptcy, Computer, Consumer commercial. Office: 1001 Bishop St Suite 7901 Honolulu HI 96813

IDEMAN, JAMES M., federal judge; b. 1931; m. Gertraud Erika Ideman. BA, The Citadel, 1953; JD, U. So. Calif., 1963. Dep. atty. gen. Los Angeles County, 1964-79; judge Los Angeles County Superior Ct., 1979-84; appointed judge U.S. Dist. Ct. (Cen. Dist.) Calif., Los Angeles, 1984—. Served to 1st lt. U.S. Army, 1953-56, lt. col. JAGC Res. Judicial administration. Office: US Courthouse 312 N Spring St Los Angeles CA 90012 *

IDEN, BRUCE FRANKLIN, lawyer; b. Detroit, Oct. 17, 1955; s. Jacob and Shirlee (Rose) I.; m. Lee Padnick, Sept. 24, 1983; 1 child, Daniel James. BA with honors, U. Mich., 1977; JD, George Washington U., 1981; LLM in Taxation, U. Miami, Fla., 1982. Bar: Fla. 1981, U.S. Dist. Ct. (so. dist.) Fla. 1981, U.S. Tax Ct. 1984, U.S. Ct. Appeals (9th and 11th cirs.) 1984. Adminstrv. asst. U.S. EPA, Washington, 1980; assoc. Milledge & Hermelee, Miami, 1982-85, ptnr., 1985; ptnr. Milledge, Iden & Snyder, Miami, 1985—. Mem. ABA, Fla. Bar Assn., Dade County Bar Assn. Democrat. Jewish. Avocations: pottery, scuba diving, sailing, photography. General practice, Contracts commercial, Real property. Home: 12984 SW 108 St Miami FL 33186 Office: Milledge Iden & Snyder 2100 Ponce De Leon Coral Gables FL 33134

IFSHIN, DAVID MICHAEL, lawyer, educator; b. Washington, Oct. 3, 1948; s. Harold and Shirley I.; m. Gail Grossman; Jan. 4, 1981. A.B. with honors in English, Syracuse U., 1970, J.D., Stanford U., 1977. Bar: Calif. 1978, D.C. 1978, U.S. Ct. Appeals (D.C. cir.), U.S. Supreme Ct. Assoc. Steptoe & Johnson, Washington, 1977-83; ptnr. Manatt, Phelps, Rothenberg & Evans, Washington, 1983—; gen. counsel Mondale for Pres. Com., 1982-84; vis. lectr. Yale U. Law Sch., 1978-81; cons. Harvard U. Study on Election Law; lectr. in field. Gen. counsel Ctr. for Nat. Policy, 1980-81. Mem. ABA (vice chmn. adminstrv. sect. com. on election law). Democrat. Jewish. Contbr. articles to legal jours. Federal civil litigation, Administrative and regulatory, Legislative. Office: 1200 New Hampshire Ave Suite 200 Washington DC 20036

IGO, LOUIS DANIEL, lawyer, legal educator; b. Boston, Sept. 21, 1939; s. L. Louis and Martha W. Igo; 1 child, John Daniel. B.S. in Econs. and Acctg., Mo. Valley Coll., 1963; postgrad. tax law U. Mo.-Kansas City, 1964-66; J.D., U. Tulsa, 1967; postgrad. Okla. Sch. Accountancy, 1967-68, U. So. Calif., 1979. Bar: Okla. 1968, U.S. Dist. Ct. (no. and so. dists.) Okla. 1968, U.S. Tax Ct. 1973, Calif. 1973, U.S. Dist. Ct. (cen. dist.) Calif. 1973, U.S. Ct. Mil. Appeals 1982, U.S. Ct. Appeals (9th cir.) 1982, U.S. Supreme Ct. 1973. Assoc., R.E. Harper, Lawndale, Calif., 1973—, M. Moustakas, Beverly Hills, Calif., 1973—; prof. law and acctg. Los Angeles Community Coll. Dist., 1973—; moderator, lectr. Instructional TV Show: Law for the Seventies, 1980; Mil. Magistrate, 1980-84; USNR Legal Assistance officer, 1976—. Served with U.S. Army, 1964-68; comdr. JAGC, USNR, 1968—. Cert. Scuba diver Nat. Assn. Underwater Instrs. Mem. Los Angeles County Bar Assn., Lawyers Club Los Angeles, Japanese Am. Bar Assn., Am. Arbitration Assn. (arbitrator), Naval Res. Assn., Res. Officers Assn., Alpha Phi Omega, Sigma Alpha Epsilon, Phi Alpha Delta. Episcopalian. Clubs: Skelton Congressional, Elks, Masons, Shriner, Navy Flying. Author scripts and syllabus for Law for the Seventies (Instructional TV award, 1976); revised The Time-Life Family Legal Guide, 1976; cons. editor Bus. Law West, 1984. State civil litigation, Estate planning, Military. Office: Law Offices of R E Harper 16216 Hawthorne Blvd Lawndale CA 90260 also: Los Angeles Community Coll 855 N Vermont Los Angeles CA 90029

IKARD, FRANK NEVILLE, lawyer; b. Henrietta, Tex., Jan. 30, 1913; s. Lewis and Ena (Neville) I.; m. Jean Hunter, Oct. 15, 1940 (dec. Apr. 1970); children—Frank Neville, William Forsyth; m. Jayne Brumley, July 22, 1972. A.B., U. Tex., 1936, LL.B., 1936. Bar: Tex. 1936. Mem. firm Bullington, Humphrey & Humphrey, Wichita Falls, 1937-47; judge 30th Jud. Dist. Ct., Wichita Falls, 1947-52; mem. 82d to 87th Congresses from 13th Tex. dist.; exec. v.p. Am. Petroleum Inst., 1961-63, pres., 1963-79; of counsel firm Finley, Kumble, Wagner, Heine, Underberg, Manley, Myerson & Casey, Washington, 1979—; dir. Sheller-Globe Corp., Toledo, First Am. Bank, N.A., Washington, Consol. Petroleum Industries, Inc., Ind. Refinery Group, Inc.; Mem. natural gas adv. council Fed. Power Commn., 1964-70; mem. adv. bd. Center for Strategic Studies, Washington, 1966-69; mem. Nat. Petroleum Council, 1964-83, Pres.'s Nat. Adv. Com. on Hwy. Beautification, 1966-68, Pres.'s Nat. Citizens Commn. on Internat. Cooperation, 1965-68, Pres.'s Industry-Govt. Spl. Task Force on Travel, 1966-68; mem. U.S. nat. conf. World Energy Congress, 1967-69, World Petroleum Congress, 1963-70. Sec., trustee John F. Kennedy Center for Performing Arts, Washington; chmn. Meridian House Internat.; vice chmn. bd. regents U. Tex. at Austin. Served with AUS, 1942-45. Mem. Am. Bar Assn., State Bar Tex., D.C. Bar, Ind. Petroleum Assn. Am., Japan-Am. Soc. Episcopalian. Clubs: Masons; Burning Tree (Chevy Chase, Md.); Carlton (Washington), City Tavern Assn. (Washington), Internat. (Washington), Met. (Washington); Hemisphere (N.Y.C.), Univ. (N.Y.C.). Home: 1801 Kalorama Sq NW Washington DC 20008 Office: 1120 Connecticut Ave NW Washington DC 20036

IKEJIRI, KRIS HAYATO, lawyer; b. Torrance, Calif., Dec. 30, 1955; s. Matsuo Mac and Gladys Shizuko (Kouno) I. BA in History, UCLA, 1977; JD, U. San Diego, 1980. Bar: Calif. 1980, D.C. 1981, U.S. Tax Ct. 1981, U.S. Dist. Ct. D.C. 1982, U.S. Ct. Appeals (D.C. cir.) 1982. Trial atty. USDA, Washington, 1980-86; assoc. Olsson, Frank & Weeda, Washington, 1986—. D.C. chpt. Pres. Japanese Am. Citizens League, Wash., 1983-85. Named One of Outstanding Young Men in Am., U.S. Jaycees, 1980. Mem. ABA, Asian Pacific Am. Bar Assn. (bd. dirs., community service award 1984). Democrat. Buddhist. Avocations: long distance swimming, tennis, golf. Administrative and regulatory. Home: 2560 B S Arlington Mill Dr Arlington VA 22206 Office: 1029 Vermont Ave NW Suite 400 Washington DC 20005

IMMERMAN, PAUL ALAN, associate counsel; b. Bklyn., Apr. 10, 1951; s. Louis and Clara (Lutwak) I. BBA, Baruch Coll., CUNY, 1972; JD, Bklyn. Law Sch., 1975. Bar: N.Y. 1976, U.S. Dist. Ct. (ea. and so. dist.) 1976, U.S. Ct. Appeals (2d cir.) 1976, U.S. Supreme Ct. 1979. Assoc. D'Amato and Lynch, N.Y.C., 1975-79; asst. counsel Frank B. Hall and Co., Inc., Briarcliff Manor, N.Y., 1979-81; sole practice N.Y.C., 1981-84; assoc. counsel US-LIFE Corp., N.Y.C., 1984—. Mem. ABA, (securities law com. Young Lawyers div. 1986—), Assn. Bar City N.Y., N.Y. County Lawyers Assn., Securities Industry Assn. (compliance and legal div.). Securities, Insurance, General corporate. Office: USLife Corp 125 Maiden Ln New York NY 10038

IMMKE, KEITH HENRY, lawyer; b. Peoria, Ill., Jan. 18, 1953; s. Francis William and Pearl Lenora (Kime) I. BA, U. Ill., 1975; JD, So. Ill. U., 1978. Bar: Ill. 1978, U.S. Dist. Ct. (so. and ea. dists.) Ill. 1979. Assoc. Lawrence E. Johnson & Assocs., P.C., Champaign, Ill., 1979—. Mem. ABA, Ill. State Bar Assn., U. Ill. Alumni Assn., Phi Kappa Phi, Pi Sigma Alpha, Phi Alpha Delta. General practice. Office: Lawrence E Johnson & Assocs PC 202 W Hill St Champaign IL 61820

IMMLER, MICHAEL EARL, lawyer; b. Roswell, N.Mex., Aug. 23, 1952; s. Thomas A. and Mary Nell (Lasater) I.; m. Karen Doss, Dec. 13, 1975; children: David Paul, Mark Gregory. BA, Auburn U., 1975; JD, Cumberland Law Sch., 1979. Bar: Ala. 1979, U.S. Ct. Mil. Appeals 1980. Chief civil law Dept. Air Force, Denver, 1984-86; asst. gen counsel Hdqrs. Army and Air Force Exchange Service, Dallas, 1986—. Served to capt. USAF, 1979-84. Mem. ABA, Fed. Bar Assn., Ala. Bar Assn. Republican. Methodist. Avocations: racquetball, snow skiing. General corporate, Federal civil litigation, Labor. Office: Hdqrs Army and Air Force Exchange PO Box 660202 GC-G Dallas TX 75266-0202

IMPERATI, SAMUEL J(OHN), lawyer; b. Detroit, Dec. 3, 1951; s. Samuel F. and Mary (Sullivan) I.; m. Kathryn Beaumont, Sept. 11, 1982; 1 child, Anthony Beaumont. BA in Humanities magna cum laude, U. Santa Clara, 1974; JD, U. Calif., Davis, 1979. Bar: Oreg. 1979, U.S. Dist. Ct. Oreg. 1979, U.S. Ct. Appeals (9th cir.) 1979, U.S. Ct. Appeals (D.C. cir.) 1983, U.S. Supreme Ct. 1983. Law clk. to presiding justice U.S. Ct. Appeals (9th cir.), Seattle, 1979; from assoc. to ptnr. Welch, Brunn and Green, Portland, Oreg., 1979-84; founding ptnr. Imperati, Barnett, Sherwood & Coon P.C., Portland, 1984—; mem. adv. bd. Portland Family Head Injury Support Group, 1985—. Contbr. articles to profl. jours. Mem. ABA, Oreg. State Bar Assn. (sec. workers compensation sect. 1984-85), Assn. Trial Lawyers Am., Oreg. Trial Lawyers Assn., Multnomah County Bar Assn. (head injury seminar coordinator 1986, lectr. wrongful termination 1986). Democrat. Roman Catholic. Avocations: soccer, softball, carpentry, travel. Personal injury, Workers' compensation, Labor. Office: Imperati et al 135 SW Ash Suite 600 Portland OR 97204-3540

INDEST, GEORGE FELIX, III, lawyer; b. New Orleans, Jan. 10, 1951; s. George F. Jr. and Clarice Edna (Johnson) I.; m. Angelyn Vickie Orr, Dec. 20, 1977; children: George F. IV, Alexander Lee. BA, Tulane U., 1973, JD, 1980; M in Pub. Adminstrn., U. West Fla., 1982; LLM, George Washington U., 1986. Bar: La. 1980, Fla. 1983, D.C. 1987. Commd. ensign USN, 1973, advanced through grades to lt. comdr., 1982, staff atty. JAGC, 1980—. Mem. Am. Soc. Internat. Law, Japan Internat. Law Soc., Am. Acad. Forensic Sci., Am. Soc. Pub. Adminstrn., Am. Judicature Soc., Aircraft Owners and Pilots Assn. Health, Public international, Admiralty. Office: Staff Judge Adv's Office Naval Hosp Portsmouth VA 23708

INES, VICTOR DOROTEO, lawyer, marketing executive; b. Vallejo, Calif., Aug. 14, 1945; s. D.B. and Irene J. Ines; m. Patricia E. Cox, Aug. 1, 1968 (div. 1976); children: Gregory Richard, Kimberly Deborah. AA, U. Fla., 1966, BS, 1968, JD, 1976. Bar: Fla. 1977. Staff atty. FCC, Washington, 1976-77; sr. account exec. J. Walter Thompson Co., St. Louis, 1977-79; dir. Paradyne Corp., Largo, Fla., 1979—; v.p., bd. dirs. Benson Solar Corp., Cocoa Beach, Fla., 1976—; bd. dirs. Evers Mktg. Group, Clearwater, Fla. Served to capt. USAF, 1968-73. Mem. ABA, Fla. Bar, Fla. Trial Lawyers Assn. Democrat. Avocations: tennis, photography, scuba diving, flying. Advertising Law, General corporate, State civil litigation. Office: Paradyne Corp 8550 Ulmerton Rd Largo FL 33541

INGBER, CLIFFORD JAY, security service executive, lawyer; b. N.Y.C., Apr. 1, 1950; s. Max and Nettie (Levine) I.; m. Victoria Gonzalez. BA, Hofstra U., JD, 1978. Bar: N.Y. 1978, U.S. Dist. Ct. (so. dist.) N.Y. 1978, U.S. Supreme Ct. 1978 . Gen. counsel Eaton Allen Corp., Bklyn., 1977-83; v.p. legal affairs Burns Internat. Security Services, Parsippany, N.J., 1983—. Office: Burns Internat Security Service 2 Campus Dr Parsippany NJ 07054

INGBER, JEROME BURTON, lawyer, educator; b. St. Paul, Sept. 28, 1943; s. Sam and Leah (Kejlis) I.; m. Judith Roslie Brin, June 21, 1971; children: Shai, Noah. BS, U. Minn., 1965; JD, William Mitchell Coll. Law, 1969. Bar: Minn. 1970, U.S. Dist. Ct. Minn. 1970, U.S. Supreme Ct. 1979. Asst. comml. attache Canadian Embassy, Tel Aviv, 1973-77; sole practice Mpls., 1977-81; sr. atty. Jerome B. Ingber & Assocs., Ltd., Mpls., 1981—; spl. referee conciliation ct. Hennepin County, 1971—; adj. prof. William Mitchell Coll. Law, St. Paul, 1981—. Mem. Israel Chamber Advs., 1975; pres. Jewish Community Ctr. Greater Mpls., 1986—. Mem. Minn. Bar Assn., Am. Immigration Lawyers Assn. (bd. govs. 1983—), Israel Chamber Advs. Democrat. Jewish. Lodge: B'nai B'rith (U. Minn. v.p. 1982-85). Immigration, naturalization, and customs. Office: Jerome B Ingber & Assocs Ltd 1221 Nicollet Mall Suite 225 Minneapolis MN 55043

INGERSOLL, WILLIAM BOLEY, lawyer, real estate developer; b. Washington, Sept. 21, 1938; s. William Brown and Loraine (Boley) I.; m. Carolyn Grace Potter, Sept. 8, 1963; children—William Brett, Courtney Lynn, Wayne Brandon, Dana Lee. B.S., Brigham Young U., 1964; J.D., Catholic U., 1968. Bar: Va. 1968, D.C. 1969. Atty., Office of Corp. Counsel D.C., 1967-69; atty. Office Gen. Counsel, HUD, 1969-70; ptnr. Fried, Klewans, Ingersoll & Bloch, Washington, 1970-72; pres. Ingersoll and Bloch Chartered, Washington, 1972—; gen. counsel Am. Resort and Residential Assn.; lectr. in field; Bd. dirs. Nat. Timesharing Council, 1981—; mem. Garrison Presdl. Commn., 1984. Mem. ABA, Fed. Bar Assn., D.C. Bar Assn., Va. Bar Assn., Va. Assn. Trial Lawyers, Land Devel. Inst. (vice chmn.), Brigham Young U. Alumni Assn. (dir. 1984—), Order of Coif. Coeditor-in-chief of Land Devel. Law Reporter, Land Trends, 1973—. Mormon. Club: Golf and Country (Springfield). Co-editor-in-chief Law Reporter and Land Trends, 1973—, Time Sharing Law Reporter, 1980—, The Digest of State Land Sales, 1976—, D.C. Real Estate Reporter, 1982—, Real Estate Opportunity Report, 1986. Contbr. in field. Mem. nat. adv. com. Inside Real Estate, 1985—. Real property, Administrative and regulatory, Legislative. Home: 6704 Emporia Ct Springfield VA 22152 Office: 1401 16th St NW Washington DC 20036

INGLE, JOHN D., lawyer; b. Indpls., Sept. 15, 1940; s. G. Clyde and Harriet (Neideffer) I.; m. Margaret Messer, Oct. 5, 1976. BS, Ind. U., 1963; JD, Mercer U., 1970; cert., Campbell Coll., 1971. Bar: U.S. Ct. Appeals (4th cir.) 1986. Corr. banking rep. Mcht.s Nat. Bank, Indpls., 1965-67; trust officer 1st Nat. Bank, Hickory, N.C., 1970-73; judge N.C. Dist. Ct., 1973-75; sole practice Hickory, N.C., 1975-80; ptnr. Lovekin & Ingle, Hickory, 1980—; fin. officer USA, BadKreuznach, Fed. Rep. of Germany, 1963-65; park ranger U.S. Park Service, Macon, Ga., 1968-70. Pres. Western Piedmont Humane Soc., Hickory, 1975. Served to capt. Fin. Corps., 1963-65. Mem. N.C. State Bar Assn., Acad. Trial Lawyers, Def. Research Inst. Republican. Presbyterian. Lodges: Masons, Shriners. Personal injury, Probate, Estate planning. Office: Lovekin & Ingle 27 1st Ave NE Hickory NC 28603

INGLIS, DAVID STUART, lawyer; b. Cleve., June 3, 1957. BA in Econs., Northwestern U., 1979; JD, U. Mich., 1982. Assoc. Benesch, Friedlander Coplan & Aronoff, Cleve., 1982—. Mem. ABA, Ohio Bar Assn., Cleve. Bar Assn. Democrat. Jewish. Securities, General corporate. Office: Benesch Friedlander Coplan & Aronoff 1100 Citizens Bldg Cleveland OH 44114

INGRAHAM, FRANK CALVIN, lawyer; b. Nashville, Mar. 26, 1929; s. Harold Edward and Sybil (Hawley) I.; m. Francis Rose Tomason, June 5, 1953; children—Harold Eric (dec.), Susan Rose, Marianna Ingraham Wilson. B.A. cum laude, Baylor U., 1951; J.D., Vanderbilt U., 1954. Bar: Tenn. 1954, U.S. Supreme Ct. 1971. Sr. ptnr. Ingraham, Corbett & Zinn, Nashville, 1954—. Served to capt. JAGC, USAF. Fellow Roscoe Pound Found.; mem. Tenn. Bar Assn., Nashville Bar Assn., Williamson County Bar Assn., Assn. Trial Lawyers Am., Tenn. Trial Lawyers Assn., Scribes, Phi Delta Phi. Clubs: Lions, Kiwanis. Editor Vandebilt Law Rev., 1952-54; contbr. articles on law to profl. jours. General corporate, Federal civil litigation, Personal injury. Office: 21st Floor Parkway Towers Nashville TN 37219

INGRAHAM, FREDERIC BEACH, lawyer, banker; b. Washington, Feb. 1, 1944; s. David and Laura Hall (Jennings) I.; m. Sarah McJilton Smoot, Mar. 30, 1974; children—David Smoot, Sarah Jennings. B.A., Boston U., 1966; J.D., Fordham U., 1969. Bar: N.Y. 1969. With Morgan Guaranty Trust Co., N.Y.C., 1969—, now v.p.; village justice Laurel Hollow Village Ct., N.Y., 1980—. Probate, Estate taxation, Estate planning. Home: 1654 Moore's Hill Rd Syosset NY 11791 Office: Morgan Guaranty Trust Co 9 W 57th St New York NY 10019

INGRAM, GEORGE CONLEY, lawyer; b. Dublin, Ga., Sept. 27, 1930; s. George Conley and Nancy Averett (Whitehurst) I.; m. Sylvia Williams, July 26, 1952; children: Sylvia Lark, Nancy Randolph, George Conley. A.B., Emory U., 1949, LL.B., 1951. Bar: Ga. 1952. City atty. Smyrna, Ga., 1958-64, Kennesaw, Ga., 1964; judge Cobb County Juvenile Ct., 1960-64, Superior Ct., Cobb Jud. Circuit, 1964-68; asso. justice Supreme Ct. Ga., 1973-77; partner firm Alston & Bird, Atlanta, 1977—. Trustee Agnes Scott Coll.; past bd. visitors Emory U.; chmn. council Emory U. Law Sch. Served with AUS, 1952-54. Recipient Distinguished Service award Kennesaw Mountain Jaycees, 1961, Distinguished Service award Ga. Jaycees, 1961; Distinguished Citizen award City of Marietta, Ga., 1973; Disting. Service award Emory Law Sch. Alumni Assn., 1985; Len Gilbert Leadership award Cobb County C. of C., 1985; hon. life mem. Ga. PTA. Fellow Am. Bar Found., Am. Coll. Trial Lawyers, Ga. Bar Found., Internat. Soc. Barristers; mem. ABA, Ga. Bar Assn., Lawyers Club Atlanta, Assn. Trial Lawyers Am., Old War Horse Lawyers Club, Am. Law Inst., Cobb County C. of C. (past pres., Pub. Service award 1970). Democrat. Methodist. Clubs: (Atlanta), Georgian (chmn. bd. dirs.), Piedmont Driving. Federal civil litigation, State civil litigation, General practice. Address: 540 Hickory Dr Marietta GA 30064

INGRAM, JEFFREY CHARLES, lawyer, educator; b. Santa Barbara, Calif., Apr. 8, 1953; s. John Samis and Jeanne Lorraine (McLaughlin) I.; m. Kathleen Brazis, Feb. 21, 1981; 1 child, Jeffrey C. II. Student, Miami U., Oxford, Ohio, 1971-72; BS, Suffolk U., 1974; JD cum laude, So. Calif. Inst. Law, 1979. Bar: Calif. 1979, U.S. Ct. Appeals 1979, U.S. Dist. Ct. (cen. dist) Calif. 1982. Assoc. McGahan & Engle, Ventura, Calif., 1979-82; prof. Oxnard (Calif.) Coll., 1981—; assoc. Henderson & Smith, Ventura, 1982—; prof. U. Calif., Santa Barbara, 1983—. Author: (photography book) Come and Get It, 1972; dir., producer of movie Come and Get It, 1972. Mem. ABA, Assn. Trial Lawyers Am., Barrister's Club (bd. dirs. 1981-83). Avocations: flying, golf. Insurance, Personal injury, Legal education. Home: 2630 Bellerive Ct Oxnard CA 93030 Office: Henderson & Smith 1893 Knoll Dr Ventura CA 93003

INGRAM, KEVIN RONEY, lawyer; b. Kansas City, Mo., Nov. 21, 1953; s. Edwin B. and Twyla L. (Roney) I. BBS, William Jewell Coll., 1976; postgrad., South Tex. Coll. Law, 1978-79; JD, U. Mo., Kansas City, 1980. Bar: Mo. 1981, U.S. Dist. Ct. (we. dist.) Mo. 1981; cert. fin. planner. Trust officer Boatman's 1st Nat. Bank, Kansas City, 1981-86; sr. trust officer Centerre Bank of Kansas City, 1986—. Named one of Outstanding Young Men in Am., 1978. Mem. ABA, Mo. Bar Assn., Kansas City Bar Assn., Assn. Trial Lawyers Am., Corp. Fiduciaries Assn., Delta Theta Phi, Pi Gamma Mu, Phi Gamma Delta. Probate. Home: 8330 Hillcrest Rd Apt D Kansas City MO 64138 Office: Centerre Bank 1130 Walnut Kansas City MO 64141

INGRAM, MICHAEL MAYHEW, lawyer; b. Tampa, Fla., Dec. 2, 1953. BA, Washington & Lee U., 1975; JD, Samford U., 1978. Bar: Fla. 1978. Assoc. Nelson, Hesse, Cyril, Weber, Smith & Widman, Sarasota, Fla., 1978—. Editor-in-chief: Am. Jour. Trail Advocacy, Samford U., 1977-78. Mem. ABA, Sarasota County Bar Assn., Assn. Trial Lawyers Am. Home: 3520B Cheshire Square Sarasota FL 33577 Office: Nelson Hesse Cyril et al 2070 Ringling Blvd Sarasota FL 33577

INGRAM, NIKI TERESA, lawyer; b. Wilmington, Del., May 1, 1954; d. Edward Kennard and Evonn (Ross) I.; m. Lawrence Unthank, Sept. 7, 1985. BA in Psychology, Smith Coll., 1976; JD, U. Pa., 1979. Bar: Pa. 1980, U.S. Dist. Ct. (ea. dist.) Pa. 1980. Staff atty. Juvenile Law Ctr., Phila., 1979-80; chief asst. city solicitor Phila. Law Dept., 1980-85; staff atty. PMA Ins. Co., Phila., 1985—. Mem. Nat. Bar Assn. (woman's div.), Phila. Bar Assn., Am. Fedn. Negro Affairs. Democrat. Christian Scientist. Club: Smith Coll. (Phila.) (jr. chairperson, 1982—). Personal injury, Workers' compensation, General practice. Home: 30 N Millick St Philadelphia PA 19139 Office: PMA Ins Co 925 Chestnut St Philadelphia PA 19107

INGRAM, ROBERT BRUCE, lawyer; b. Des Moines, July 19, 1940; s. Earl J. and Frances F. (Forquer) I.; m. Judith Jennings, Aug. 27; children—Stephanie, Ashley, Robert. Student U. Iowa, 1958-61; B.A., Drake U., 1962, postgrad., 1962-63; J.D., Coll. William and Mary, 1970. Bar: Calif. 1971, Hawaii 1982. With Law Offices of Melvin M. Belli, San Francisco, 1971-78; sole practice, San Rafael, Calif., 1978—; ptnr. Stearns & Ingram, Honolulu, 1982—; Superior Ct. jud. arbitrator, San Francisco and Marin County, 1980—; judge pro-tem Mcpl. Ct., County of Marin, 1984—; keynote speaker ann. meeting Ga. State Bar, 1979; lead counsel Pacific Mud Slide Litigation Class Action, 1985—. Served as capt. USAF, 1964-68. Mem. Assn. Trial Lawyers Am., Iowa Acad. Trial Lawyers (guest speaker seminar 1987), Calif. Trial Lawyers Assn., San Francisco Trial Lawyers Assn., ABA, Marin County Bar Assn. Presbyterian. Club: Rafael Racquet, Honolulu. Lodge: Elks. Contbr. articles to legal jours. Federal civil litigation, State civil litigation, Personal injury. Office: 4340 Redwood Hwy Suite 352 San Rafael CA 94903 Office: 733 Bishop St Suite 2300 Honolulu HI 96813

INGRAM, SAMUEL WILLIAM, JR., lawyer; b. Utica, N.Y., Mar. 20, 1933; s. Samuel William and Mary Elizabeth (Rosen) I.; m. Jane Austin Stokes, Sept. 30, 1961; children—Victoria, William. B.S., Vanderbilt U., 1954; LL.B., Columbia U., 1960. Bar: N.Y. 1960. Assoc. Sullivan & Cromwell, N.Y.C., 1960-67; assoc. Shea Gallop Climenko & Gould, N.Y.C., 1967-68; ptnr. Shea & Gould and predecessors, N.Y.C., 1968—. Bd. dirs. Legal Aid Soc., N.Y.C., 1974-86, sec., 1978-86; trustee Green Mountain Valley Sch., Waitsfield, Vt., 1984-87. Served to 1st lt. USMC, 1954-57. Mem. Assn. Bar City N.Y., ABA, N.Y. State Bar Assn. Avocations: athletic and outdoor activities. Real property. Home: Rural Route 1 Box 203 Long Ridge Rd Pound Ridge NY 10576 Office: Shea & Gould 330 Madison Ave New York NY 10017

INGRAM, TEMPLE BYRN, JR., lawyer; b. Gilmer, Tex., Mar. 12, 1949; s. Temple Byrn and Janet (Wofford) I.; m. Janet Marie Bandy, Mar. 11, 1979; children: Lon Cartwright, James Ross, Katherine Anne. BA, Harvard U., 1971; JD, So. Meth. U., 1979. Bar: Tex. 1979, N.M. 1982, U.S. Ct. Appeals (10th cir.) 1984, U.S. Supreme Ct. 1984. Consumer safety officer EPA, Boston, 1972-76; law clk. to presiding justice U.S. Dist. Ct. (we. dist.) Tex., San Antonio, 1979-81; assoc. Studdard, Melby, Schwartz, Crowson & Parrish, El Paso, Tex., 1981-83, ptnr., 1983-86; ptnr. Crowson & Ingram, El Paso, 1986—. Bd. dirs. El Paso Country Day Sch., 1985-86; del. Dem. state convention, El Paso, 1984. Mem. ABA, Tex. Bar Assn., N.Mex. Bar Assn., Am. Judicature Soc. Presbyterian. Avocations: photography, backpacking, canoeing. State civil litigation, Federal civil litigation, Contracts commercial. Home: 1407 Elm St El Paso TX 79930 Office: Crowson & Ingram 310 N Mesa Suite 706 El Paso TX 79901

INGRAM, WILLIAM AUSTIN, federal judge; b. Jeffersonville, Ind., July 6, 1924; s. William Austin and Marion (Lane) I.; m. Barbara Brown Lender, Sept. 18, 1947; children: Mary Ingram Mac Calla, Claudia, Betsy Ingram Friebel. Student, Stanford U., 1947; LL.B., U. Louisville, 1950. Assoc., Littler, Coakley, Lauritzen & Ferdon, San Francisco, 1951-55; dep. dist. atty. Santa Clara (Calif.) County, 1955-57; mem. firm Rankin, O'Neal, Luckhardt & Center, San Jose, Calif., 1955-69; judge Mcpl. Ct., Palo Alto-Mountain View, Calif., 1969-71, Calif. Superior Ct., 1971-76, U.S. Dist. Ct. No. Dist. Calif., San Jose, 1976—. Served with USMCR, 1943-46. Fellow Am. Coll. Trial Lawyers. Republican. Episcopalian. Jurisprudence. Home: 1211 College Ave Palo Alto CA 94306 Office: US Court House Dist Judge 280 S 1st St San Jose CA 95113 *

INKELLIS, BARBARA G., lawyer; b. Rockville Ctr., N.Y., Apr. 8, 1949; d. Adolph J. and Edith (Zackowitz) Greenberg; m. Steven Alan Inkellis, May 19, 1979; children: Elizabeth, David. AB, Dickinson Coll., 1971; MEd.,

George Washington U., 1973, JD, 1978. Bar: D.C. 1978, U.S. Dist. Ct. D.C. 1979. Assoc. Bracewell & Patterson, Washington, 1978-79, Fried, Frank, Harris, Shriver & Jacobson, Washington, 1979-81; gen. counsel Disclosure Information Group, Bethesda, Md., 1981—. Mem. ABA. Office: Disclosure Information Group 5161 River Rd Bethesda MD 20816

INMAN, ARTHUR JAMES, lawyer; b. Monroe, Wis., Apr. 21, 1942; s. Marshall O. and Thea Amanda (Buer) I.; m. Carolyn S. Putnam, July 31, 1971; children: Emily Sue, Erik James. BA in Polit. Sci., Ill. Wesleyan U., 1964; JD, U. Ill., 1967. Bar: Ill. 1968, U.S. Dist. Ct. (cen. dist.) Ill. 1975, U.S. Ct. Appeals (7th cir.) 1977, U.S. Supreme Ct. 1979. Asst. states atty. Vermillion County, Danville, Ill., 1967-68, Sangamon County, Springfield, Ill., 1968-72, Peoria (Ill.) County, 1972-75; sole practice Peoria, 1975—; instr. constl. law Bradley U., Peoria, 1985, polit. sci. Ill. Cen. Coll., East Peoria, 1975-79, Nat. Inst. Advocacy for State's Atty. Legal Tng., Springfield, 1979—. Served as cpl. USMCR, 1962-68. Mem. Ill. State Bar Assn. (chmn. criminal justice council sect. 1985-86, lobbyist for position concerning criminal justice 1984-86, sec. Criminal Justice sect. 1982-85), Comml. Law League of Am., Am. Assn. Criminal Def. Attys. Republican. Methodist. Lodge: Kiwanis (bd. dirs. Peoria club). Avocations: racquetball, bridge, chess. Criminal, Family and matrimonial, Consumer commercial. Office: 415 1st Nat Bank Peoria IL 61602

INMAN, MAURICE CUSHING, JR., lawyer; b. Portland, Oreg., Nov. 21, 1931; m. Mary Carol Roney, June 18, 1961; children: Michael Horrell, Peter Burke, Mary Elizabeth. JD, Harvard U., 1956. Assoc. Adams, Duque & Hazeltine, Los Angeles, 1956-60; co-founder, sr. ptnr. Alexander, Inman & Fine, Los Angeles, 1960-81; ptnr. Alexander, Inman, Tanzer & Wedemeyer, Los Angeles, 1981; gen. counsel Dept. Justice Immigration and Naturalization Service, Washington, 1981—. Immigration, naturalization, and customs. Home: 6100 Davenport Terr Bethesda MD 20817 Office: Dept Justice Immigration & Naturalization Service 425 Eye St NW CAB Bldg Washington DC 20536

INMAN, ROBERT DALE, lawyer; b. Mitchell, Ind., Feb. 6, 1920; s. Gideon Waldo Inman and Josie Frances Wible; m. Virginia Cook, Oct. 30, 1943 (dec. Sept. 1968); m. Betty J. Kontny, May 4, 1969; children: Michael, Tyler, Vincenne, Leesa, Debra, Greg. BA, U. Colo., 1941, LLB, 1947. Bar: Colo. 1947. Pub. trustee State of Colo., Boulder, 1951-53; asst. U.S. atty. State of Colo., Denver, 1953-56, asst. securities commn., 1956-58, asst. atty. gen., 1958-61; ptnr. Inman, Erickson & Flynn P.C., Denver, 1961—. Served to lt. col. U.S. Army, 1942-46, PTO. Mem. ABA, Colo. Bar Assn., Denver Bar Assn. Episcopalian. Lodge: Rotary. Avocation: choral music. Federal civil litigation, Bankruptcy, General practice. Office: Inman Erickson & Flynn 1660 Lincoln St #1700 Denver CO 80264

INSERRA, JOHN PHILLIP, lawyer; b. Omaha, Nebr., Oct. 3, 1950; s. Joseph Paul and Phyllis Marie (Smith) I.; m. Mary Beth Putnam; children: Jeffrey, Heather. BS, U. Nebr., 1972; JD, Creighton U., 1976. Bar: Nebr. 1976, U.S. Dist. Ct. Nebr. 1976, U.S. Ct. Appeals (8th cir.) 1983. Sole practice Omaha, 1976—. Mem. ABA, Nebr. Bar Assn., Assn. Trial Lawyers Am., NCLU. Democrat. Roman Catholic. Federal civil litigation, State civil litigation, Personal injury. Home: 5335 Izard St Omaha NE 68132 Office: 2580 S 90th St Omaha NE 68124

INTERDONATO, ANTHONY PAUL, lawyer; b. Washington, Jan. 8, 1949; s. Paul Frank and Amelia Theresa (Mirabile) I.; m. Kathleen Mary Gnau, May 11, 1985; 1 child, Paul Michael. AB in Econs., Xavier U., 1970; JD, Cath. U., 1973. Bar: Md. 1973, D.C. 1974, U.S. Dist. Ct. Md., U.S. Dist. Ct. D.C., U.S. Ct. Appeals (D.C. cir.), U.S. Supreme Ct. Law clk. to presiding judge Superior Ct. for D.C., Washington, 1973-74; asst. state's atty. State of Md., Upper Marlboro, 1974-78; ptnr. Interdonato & Ragione, Clinton, Md., 1978-80; sole practice Clinton, Md., 1981-82; ptnr. Interdonato, Reilly & Comstock and predecessor firm Interdonato, Lombard, Reilly & Comstock, Washington, 1982—. Mem. Consumer Protection Commn. Prince George's County, Upper Marlboro, 1978-79; bd. dirs. Lt. Joseph P. Kennedy Inst., Washington, 1982-84, Carroll Manor Nursing Home Inc., Hyattsville, Md., 1986—. Mem. ABA, Md. Bar Assn., D.C. Bar Assn., Prince George's County Bar Assn., Md. State's Atty's Assn. Roman Catholic. State civil litigation, General practice, Real property. Home: 808 Forest Dr S Oxon Hill MD 20745 Office: Interdonato Reilly & Comstock 4801 Massachusetts Ave NW Washington DC 20016

INZETTA, MARK STEPHEN, lawyer; b. N.Y.C., Apr. 14, 1956; s. James William and Rose Delores (Cirnigliaro) I.; m. Amy Marie Elbert, June 25, 1977; children: Michelle, Margot, Mallory. BBA summa cum laude, U. Cin., 1977; JD, U. Akron, 1980. Bar: Ohio 1980, U.S. Dist. Ct. (no. dist.) Ohio 1980. Legal intern City of Canton, Ohio, 1979-80; assoc. W.J. Ross Co. L.P.A., Canton, 1980-84; real estate counsel Wendy's Internat. Inc., Columbus, Ohio, 1984—; instr. real estate law Stark Tech. Coll., Canton, 1983. Case and comment editor: Akron Law Rev., 1979-80. Instr. religious edn. St. Peter's Cath. Ch.; bd. dirs. Brookside Village Civic Assn., 1985-87, treas., 1986-87; chmn. campaign Earle Wise Appellate Judge, North Canton, Ohio, 1982. Recipient Am. Jurisprudence award Lawyers Coop. Pub. Co., 1978; Dir. of Yr. award North Canton Jaycees, 1982, Presdl. award of honor, 1984; Dist. Dir. award of honor, Ohio Jaycees, 1984. Mem. ABA, Ohio Bar Assn., North Canton Jaycees (bd. dirs. 1981-82, v.p. 1982-83, pres. 1983-84), North Canton C. of C. (bd. dirs. 1983-84). Democrat. Roman Catholic. Real property, General corporate. Home: 1584 Sandy Side Dr Worthington OH 43085 Office: Wendy's Internat Inc 4288 W Dublin-Granville Rd Dublin OH 43017

IOVENKO, MICHAEL, lawyer; b. N.Y.C., Jan. 19, 1930; s. Michael James and Ludmila (Tenchova) I.; m. Sarah Montague Bingham, Dec. 3, 1965 (div. Nov. 1976); children—Christopher, William; 1 stepchild, Barry B. Ellsworth; m. Nancy R. Newhouse, Mar. 6, 1983. B.A., Dartmouth Coll., 1951; J.D., Columbia U., 1954. Asst. gen. sec. World Univ. Service, Geneva, 1955-58; assoc., then ptnr. Putney, Twombly, Hall & Hirson, N.Y.C., 1959-70; U.S. del. Gen. Assembly UN, N.Y.C., 1967; dep. supt., gen. counsel N.Y. State Banking Dept., N.Y.C., 1971-72; ptnr. LeBoeuf, Lamb, Leiby & MacRae, N.Y.C., 1972-85, Hughes Hubbard & Reed, N.Y.C., 1986—. Contbr. articles to profl. jours. Pres., bd. dirs. N.Y. State Council Family Child Care Agys., 1981-85; bd. dirs. Berkshire Farm Ctr. for Youth, Canaan, N.Y., Legal Aid, N.Y.C. Mem. ABA, N.Y. State Bar Assn. (ho. of dels. 1984—, chair banking law com. 1986—), Assn. Bar City of N.Y. Democrat. Club: Midday (N.Y.C.). Avocations: piano; gardening; singing. Banking, General corporate, Insurance. Home: 154 W 88th St New York NY 10024 Office: Hughes Hubbard & Reed One Wall St New York NY 10005

IRBY, HOLT, lawyer; b. Dodge City, Kans., July 4, 1937; s. Jerry M. and Virgie (Lorean) I.; m. LaVerne Smith, May 27, 1956; children—Joseph, Kathy, Kay, Karon, James. B.A., Tex. Tech U., 1959; J.D., U. Tex., 1962. Bar: Tex. 1962, U.S. Dist. Ct. (no. dist.) Tex. 1963. Asst city atty. City of Lubbock (Tex.), 1962-63; assoc. Hugh Anderson, Lubbock, 1963-66; gen. counsel, sec. Mercantile Fin. Corp. (Tex.), Dallas, 1966-69; gen. counsel, v.p. Ward Food Restaurants, Inc., Dallas, 1969-71; sole practice, Garland, Tex., 1971—. Mem. lawyer referal com. State Bar Tex., 1977, 78. Mem. bd. deacons First Baptist Ch., Garland, 1974-84, chmn., 1976-77; bd. dirs. Garland Assistance Program, 1980, Dallas Life Found., 1980—, Toler Children's Community, 1983-85, Garland Civic Theatre, 1986—. Named Outstanding Mem., Praetor Legal Frat., 1962. Mem. Garland Bar Assn. (bd. dirs. 1986—), Dallas Bar Assn., Tex. Bar Assn., Tex. Trial Lawyers Assn., Tex. Assn. Bank Counsel. Clubs: Lubbock Jaycees (dir. 1963-65); Kiwanis (dir. 1973-74) (Garland). General practice, State civil litigation, Contracts commercial. Office: Republic Bank Bldg Suite 410 Garland TX 75040

IRENAS, JOSEPH ERON, lawyer; b. Newark, July 13, 1940; s. Zachary and Bessie (Shain) I.; m. Nancy Harriet Jacknow, 1962; children—Amy Ruth, Edward Eron. A.B., Princeton U., 1962; J.D. cum laude, Harvard U., 1965; postgrad. NYU Sch. Law, 1967-70. Bar: N.J. 1965, N.Y. 1982. Law sec. to justice N.J. Supreme Ct., 1965-66; assoc. McCarter & English, Newark, 1966-71, ptnr., 1972—; trustee Hamilton Investment Trust, Elizabeth, N.J., 1980-83; mem. N.J. Supreme Ct. Dist. Ethics Com., 1984-86, vice chmn., 1986—; adj. prof. law Rutgers Sch. Law, Camden, 1985-86, N.J. Bd. Bar Examiners, 1986—; dir. T.A. & D.A. Troy Co., Inc., Fairfield, N.J. Contbr. articles to legal jours. Chmn. bd. trustees United Hosps. of Newark, 1982-83, trustee United Hosps. Found., 1985—. Fellow Royal Chartered Inst. Arbitrators (London); mem. ABA, Fed. Bar Assn., N.J. Bar Assn., Essex County Bar Assn., Comml. Law League Am., Assn. Trial Lawyers Am. Republican. Jewish. Clubs: Essex (Newark); Princeton (N.Y.C.). General corporate, Environment, Real property. Home: 196 Elm Rd Princeton NJ 08540 Office: McCarter & English 550 Broad St Newark NJ 07102

IRISH, MICHAEL WILLIAM, lawyer; b. Jackson, Mich., July 12, 1942; s. Forrest V. and Sadie B. (Blake) I.; m. Ann Lee Moore, Aug. 15, 1970; children: Jonathan Michael, Elizabeth Ann. BA with high honor, Mich. State U., 1970; JD cum laude, Wayne State U., 1973; MS in Taxation with distinction, F.E. Seidman Coll., 1984. Bar: Mich. 1973. From assoc. to ptnr. Landman, Latimer, Clink & Robb, Muskegon, Mich., 1973-86; ptnr. Culver, Lague & McNally, Muskegon, 1986—; adj. prof. in estate planning F.E. Seidman Coll., Allendale, Mich., 1984-85. Bd. dirs. Goodwill Industries, Muskegon County, 1976—, United Way, Muskegon County, 1983—. Served to Sgt. USMC, 1964-67, Vietnam. Fellow Am. Coll. Probate Counsel; mem. ABA, Mich. Bar Assn. (probate council). Clubs: Spring Lake Country, Muskegon Country. Avocations: golf, skiing. Estate planning, Probate, Estate taxation. Home: 17620 N Shore Estates Rd Spring Lake MI 49456 Office: Culver Lague McNally 500 Terrace Plaza Muskegon MI 49443

IRONS, WILLIAM LEE, lawyer; b. Birmingham, Ala., June 9, 1941; s. George Vernon and Velma (Wright) I.; m. Karen Phillips, Oct. 30, 1976. B.A., U.Va., 1963; J.D., Samford U., 1966. Bar: Ala. 1966, U.S. Dist Ct. (no. dist.) Ala. 1966, U.S. Ct. Appeals (5th cir.) 1966. Dir. mil. justice Maxwell AFB, Ala., 1963-69; law clk. Speir, Robertson & Jackson, Burmingham, 1964-65, assoc. James L. Shores, Jr., 1965-66; asst. judge adv. Whiteman AFB, Mo., 1966-67, Gunther AFB, 1967-68; ptnr. Speir, Robertson, Jackson & Irons, 1970-71, Speir & Irons, 1971-72, William L. Irons, 1972—. Candidate Ala. Ho. Reps. 1966. Served to capt. USAF. Mem. ABA, Birmingham Bar Assn., Assn. Trial Lawyers Am., Nat. Assn. Cert. Judge Advs., Fed. Bar Assn., Nat. Res. Officer Assn., Sigma Delta Kappa. Democrat. Baptist. Club: Nat. Lawyers. Real property, Probate, Bankruptcy. Home: 3855 Cove Dr Birmingham AL 35213 Office: 1227 City Fed Bldg Birmingham AL 35203

IRTZ, FREDERICK G., II, lawyer; b. Ft. Knox, Ky., Aug. 23, 1944; married; children: Kimberly, George III, Andrew. BS in Commerce, Eastern Ky. U., 1968; JD, U. Louisville, 1973. Bar: Ky. 1973, U.S. Dist. Ct. (we. dist.) Ky. 1974, U.S. Ct. Appeals (6th cir.) 1974, U.S. Tax Ct. 1975, U.S. Supreme Ct. 1977, U.S. Dist. Ct. (ea. dist.) Ky. 1979, Calif. 1981. Atty IRS, Louisville, 1974-78; sole practice Lexington, Ky., 1978—; speaker U. Ky. Estate Planning Seminar, 1978, 81, 82, 83, U. Ky. Agrl. Law Seminar, 1984, No. Ky. Soc. CPA's, Louisville Estate Planning Council, Lexington Soc. MBA's, Fayette County Bar Assn. Chmn. Dist. Internat. Youth Exchange, 1985, legal staff Oleika Temple legal staff, atty., chmn. budget com.; pres. Oleika Brass Band, 1982. Served with U.S. Army, 1968-70, to lt. col. USAR, 1970—. Decorated Bronze Star; named one of Outstanding Young Men Am., 1977. Mem. Bluegrass Estate Planning Council (pres. 1978, speaker 1978, 83), ABA taxation, real property, and probate sect.), Ky. Bar Assn. (taxation sect.), Fayette County Bar Assn. Lodge: Lions (pres. Bluegrass Breakfast club 1981-82, Lion of Yr. 1984). Probate, Estate taxation, Personal income taxation. Home: 501 Lakeshore Dr Lexington KY 40502 Office: PO Box 22777 Lexington KY 40522

IRVIN, CHARLES LESLIE, lawyer; b. Corpus Christi, Tex., Mar. 2, 1935; s. Joseph and Louise (Frelon) I.; m. Shirley Jean Smith, Feb. 8, 1964; children—Kimberley Antoinette, Jonathan Charles. B.A., Tex. So. U., 1961, LL.B., 1964. Bar: Tex. 1964, U.S. Dist. Ct. (so. dist.) Tex. 1973, U.S. Dist. Ct. (ea. dist.) Tex. 1973, U.S. Supreme Ct. 1971, U.S. Ct. Appeals (9th cir.) 1982. Atty. U.S. Dept. Labor, Kansas City, Mo., 1964-67, Chgo., 1964-73; atty. Texaco, Inc., Chgo., 1973-74, Houston, 1974-79, Harrison, N.Y., 1979-81, sr. atty., Houston, 1981—. Served as sgt. U.S. Army, 1955-58. Mem. Tex. Bar Assn., Tex. Bar Found., Houston Lawyers Assn. Congregationalist. Federal civil litigation, State civil litigation, Oil and gas leasing. Home: 16114 Kempton Park Dr Spring TX 77379

IRVIN, ROBERT JULIAN, lawyer; b. Balt., Oct. 1, 1948; s. Julian Rowe and Gloria Virginia (Johnson) I.; m. Norma Ann Walsh, May 9, 1981; children—Catharine Leigh. B.A., U. Fla., 1970; J.D., U. Va., 1974. Bar: Fla. 1974. Assoc. Mahoney Hadlow & Adams, Miami and Jacksonville, Fla., 1974-76; assoc. Steel Hector & Davis, Miami, 1976-80, ptnr., 1980-87, chief exec. officer Collier Fin. Holding Co., Miami and Naples, 1987—. Bd. dirs. Internat. Ctr. Fla., Miami, 1984-86, chmn. investment in Fla. com., 1983-86; mem. Fla. Atty. Gen.'s Study Commn. on Money Laundering, Miami, 1983-84. Mem. Am. Land Title Assn. (mem. lenders' counsel group 1984—), Fla. Bar (mem. exec. council real property, probate and trust law sect. 1980—, chmn. fgn. investment in real estate 1980-84, chmn. real estate investments by pension trusts 1984-87, real property sect. liaison to fgn. tax adv. com. tax sect. 1984). Republican. Episcopalian. Club: Coral Gables Country (Fla.). Home: 1706 Country Club Prado Coral Gables FL 33134 Office: Collier Fin Holding Co 4000 SE Fin Ctr Miami FL 33131

IRVIN, WILMOT BROWN, lawyer; b. Columbia, S.C., Oct. 10, 1950; s. Charles Warren and Josephine Brice (Brown) I.; m. Jeanne Marie Mitchell, May 27, 1978; children: Wilmot Brown Jr., Mary Brice, Ruth Foreman. BA, U. S.C., 1972, JD, 1977. Bar: S.C. 1977, U.S. Dist. Ct. S.C. 1978, U.S. Ct. Appeals (4th cir.) 1980. Assoc. Law Offices of Weston Adams, Columbia, 1977-79; law clk. to presiding justice S.C. Supreme Ct., Chester, 1979-80, U.S. Dist. Ct. S.C., Columbia, 1980-81; assoc. McNair Law Firm P.A. and predecessor firm McNair, Glenn, Konduros, Corley, Singletary, Porter & Dibble P.A., Columbia, 1981-84, ptnr., 1984—; Mem. bd. commrs. on grievance and discipline, S.C. Supreme Ct., 1985—, exec. com., 1986—. Mem. ABA (litigation sect.), Assn. Trial Lawyers Am., S.C. Def. Attys. Assn., S.C. Trial Lawyers Assn. Presbyterian. Clubs: Forest Lake, Palmetto (Columbia). Avocations: tennis, running, music. Federal civil litigation, State civil litigation, Personal injury. Home: 1823 W Buchanan Dr Columbia SC 29206 Office: McNair Law Firm PA PO Box 11390 Columbia SC 29211

IRVINE, THOMAS KENNETH, lawyer; b. Peoria, Ill., June 22, 1951; s. James D. Sr. and Mary (Colfer) I.; m. Jane Killion; Sept. 25, 1982; children: Mark, Matthew. AA, Phoenix Coll., 1971; BS, Ariz. State U., 1973, JD, 1980. Bar: Ariz. 1980, U.S. Dist. Ct. Ariz. 1980, U.S. Ct. Appeals (9th cir.) 1980, U.S. Supreme Ct. 1984. Assoc. Dushoff & Sacks, Phoenix, 1980-84; ptnr. Dushoff & McCall, Phoenix, 1984—; Mem. com. on capital improvements Ariz. Superior Ct., Phoenix, 1986—. Mem. editorial bd. Maricopa Lawyer, 1986—; contbr. articles to profl. jours. Chmn. Criminal Justice Service Comm., Phoenix, 1985-86; mem. Citizens Bond Oversight Com., 1986—; bd. dirs. Maricopa County Indsl. Devel. Authority, Phoenix, 1986—. Mem. ABA, Ariz. Bar Assn., Maricopa County Bar Assn. (jud. systems com.). Democrat. Episcopalian. Club: University (Phoenix). Avocation: pilot. Condemnation, Real property, Construction. Office: Dushoff & McCall 2025 N 3d St Suite 100 Phoenix AZ 85004

IRVING, J. LAWRENCE, federal judge; b. 1935. B.S., U. So. Calif., 1959, LL.B., 1963. Assoc. Higgs, Fletcher & Mack, San Diego, 1963-66, ptnr., 1966-69; ptnr. Jones & Irving, 1969-77, J. Lawrence Irving Inc., 1975-78, Irving & Butz Inc., 1978-82; judge U.S. Dist. Ct. (so. dist.) Calif., San Diego, 1982—. Judicial administration. Office: US Courthouse 940 Front St San Diego CA 92189 *

IRWIN, PHILIP DONNAN, lawyer; b. Madison, Wis., Sept. 6, 1933; s. Constant Louis and Isabel Dorothy (Elfving) I.; divorced; m. Sandra L. McMahon, Sept. 14, 1985; children: Jane Donnan, James Haycraft, Victoria Wisnom. B.A., U. Wyo., 1954; LL.B., Stanford U., 1957. Bar: Wyo. 1957, Calif. 1958. Assoc. O'Melveny & Myers, Los Angeles, 1957-65, ptnr., 1965—; mem. planning com. Inst. Fed. Taxation of U. So. Calif. Law Ctr., 1976—; speaker legal seminars. Contbr. articles legal jours. Trustee Mackenzie Found., Los Angeles, 1969—. Republican. Episcopalian. Club: California (Los Angeles). Corporate taxation. Office: O'Melveny & Myers 400 S Hope St Los Angeles CA 90071

IRWIN, R. ROBERT, lawyer; b. Denver, July 27, 1933; s. Royal Robert and Mildred Mary (Wilson) I.; m. Sue Ann Scott, Dec. 16, 1956; children—Lori, Stacy, Kristi, Amy. Student U. Colo., 1951-54, B.S.L., U. Denver, 1955, LL.B., 1957. Bar: Colo. 1957, Wyo. 1967. Asst. atty. gen. State of Colo., 1958-66; asst. div. atty. Mobil Oil Corp., Casper, Wyo. 1966-70; prin. atty. No. Natural Gas Co., Omaha 1970-72; sr. atty. Coastal Oil & Gas Corp., Denver 1972-83, asst. sec. 1972-83; ptnr. Baker & Hostetler, 1983—. Mem. ABA, Colo. Bar Assn., State Bar Wyo., Arapahoe County Bar Assn., Rocky Mountain Oil and Gas Assn. Republican. Clubs: Los Verdes Golf, Petroleum, Denver Law (Denver). General corporate, Oil and gas leasing, Real property. Home: 9960 E Chenango Ave Englewood CO 80111 Office: Baker & Hostetler 303 E 17th Ave Suite 1100 Denver CO 80203

IRWIN, RICHARD FRANK, lawyer; b. Rochester, N.Y., May 28, 1934; s. Albert Barrett and Agnes S. (Cizek) I.; m. Sonja M. Voyton, May 16, 1959; children—Elizabeth, Dean, Catherine, Robert. A.B., Wesleyan U., 1956; J.D., Columbia U., 1959. Bar: Va. 1960, U.S. Ct. Appeals (D.C. cir.) 1967, U.S. Supreme Ct. 1964. Atty., IRS, Washington, 1962-67; staff atty. ITT, N.Y.C., 1967-69, tax counsel ITTE Europe, 1970-74, dir. tax research and planning, 1975-81, assoc. gen. tax counsel, N.Y.C., 1981—. Pres. Town Club, Chappaqua, N.Y., 1981-83, gen. tax counsel, 1984—. Served with U.S. Army, 1959-62. Recipient IRS Spl. Service award, 1963. Mem. Electronic Industries Assn. (chmn. tax council), ABA. Corporate taxation, Private international, Immigration, naturalization, and customs. Home: 114 Deepwood Dr Chappaqua NY 10514 Office: 320 Park Ave New York NY 10022

ISAAC, TERESA ANN, lawyer, law educator; b. Lynch, Ky., July 3, 1955; d. Samuel Thomas Sr. and Barbara Ann (Thomas) I.; m. James Isaac Lowry IV, Dec. 30, 1978; children: Jacob, Alicyn. BA, Transylvania U., 1976; JD, U. Ky., 1979. Bar: Ky. 1979, U.S. Dist. Ct. (ea. dist.) Ky. 1979, U.S. Ct. Appeals (6th cir.) 1980, U.S. Supreme Ct. 1981, U.S. Ct. Appeals (D.C. cir.) 1984. Sole practice Lexington, Ky., 1979—; asst. atty. Fayette County Prosecutors Office, Lexington, 1986—; judge U. Ky. Trial Adv. Competition, Lexington, 1981; acting dir. Eastern Ky. U. Paralegal Program, Richmond, 1985; legal counsel Ky. Women's Heritage Mus., Inc., 1986—. Editor newsletter At Issue, Lexington Forum, 1983-85; pub. The Full Ct. Press, 1986—. Mem. Human Resources Adv. Bd., Lexington, 1982-85, Ky. Displaced Homemaker Adv. Bd., Lexington, 1982-84, NCAA Final Four Host Com., Lexington, 1985; chairperson legal panel ACLU, Lexington, 1983—; chmn. Ky. Women's Suffrage Day Celebration, 1986—; project dir. Sports Equity Program A Model for the South, Ky., 1986—; mem. Philharm. Guild, 1986—. Recipient Outstanding Service award Lexington Forum, 1985. Mem. ABA (exec. com. delivery of legal services to women, spl. com. on housing and urban devel. law, recipient Silver Key award 1979), Fed. Bar Assn., Ky. Bar Assn. (bd. of editors 1983-85), Ky. Acad. Trial Lawyers Assn., Am. Soc. for Pub. Adminstrn., Am. Assn. for Paralegal Edn., Nat. Assn. Women Lawyers (brief bank coordinator 1985—), ACLU (chairperson legal panel 1983—), League of Women Voters (voter service com. 1985—), Am. Assn. U. Women (sec. 1986), Phi Mi (legal advisor 1985—). Democrat. Roman Catholic. Avocation: running marathons. Civil rights, Criminal, Legal education. Home: 335 Garden Rd Lexington KY 40502 Office: Fayette County PO Box 22163 Lexington KY 40522

ISAACS, ALVIN, lawyer; b. Washington, Nov. 11, 1926; s. Joseph and Frances (Gusky) I.; m. Marta S. Lowy, June 24, 1973; children—(by previous marriage) Laurence F., Amy B. B.A. (settle scholar, acad. scholar), U. Richmond, 1947; J.D., Am. U., 1959. Bar: D.C. 1959, Mass. 1961, U.S. Ct. Cus. & Pat. Apls. 1959, U.S. Sup. Ct. 1982. Patent examiner U.S. Patent Office, 1955-59; with Polaroid Corp., Cambridge, Mass., 1959-85, now sr. patent atty., The Kendall Co., Boston, 1985—. prof. comparative patent law Franklin Pierce Law Inst., 1985—. Bd. dirs. Sci. Resource Found.; pres. Pop Welch Edn. Found. Served with C.E., U.S. Army, 1950-52. Mem. ABA, Am. Patent Law Assn., Boston Patent Law Assn., Pacific Indsl. Property Assn. Jewish. Patent, Trademark and copyright. Home: 995 Pleasant St Framingham Centre MA 01701 Office: One Federal St Boston MA 02110

ISAACS, LEONARD BERNARD, lawyer; b. Bklyn., Feb. 1, 1951; s. Louis Jack and Sadie (Groman) I.; m. Allison Meryl Grushack, Aug. 23, 1986. BA, Queens Coll., CUNY, 1973; JD, Hofstra U., 1976. Bar: N.Y. 1977, U.S. Dist. Ct. (ea. and so. dists.) N.Y. 1977, U.S. Ct. Appeals (2d cir.) 1978, U.S. Ct. Claims 1978, U.S. Tax Ct. 1978, U.S. Ct. Mil. Appeals 1978, U.S. Ct. Customs and Patent Appeals 1978, U.S. Ct. Internat. Trade 1980, U.S. Supreme Ct. 1980, U.S. Ct. Appeals (fed. cir.) 1982, U.S. Dist. Ct. (no. dist.) N.Y. 1983. Assoc. Jack B. Solerwitz Law Office, Mineola, N.Y., 1977-80; sole practice Valley Stream, N.Y., 1980—. Mem. N.Y. State Bar Assn., Nassau County Bar Assn., Queens County Bar Assn. Democrat. Jewish. Criminal, Personal injury, Family and matrimonial. Office: 108 S Franklin Ave Suite 16 Valley Stream NY 11580

ISAACS, MICHAEL BURTON, lawyer; b. Nashville, Mar. 22, 1947; s. Richard and Bertha (Levine) I.; m. Geri Spieler, Dec. 5, 1982; 1 child: Joshua Rotenberg. A.B., U. Rochester, 1969; J.D., Boston Coll., 1974. Bar: Mass. 1974, U.S. Dist. Ct. Mass. 1975, U.S. Ct. Appeals (D.C. cir.) 1975, D.C. 1979, U.S. Ct. Appeals (9th cir.) 1979. Staff atty. Mass. Cable TV Commn., Boston, 1974-75, gen. counsel, 1975-78; asst. gen. counsel Nat. Cable TV Assn., Washington, 1978-80; dir. planning and govt. affairs Colony Communications Inc., Providence, 1980-82; sole practice, Los Angeles, 1982-84; dir. corp. devel. Providence Jour. Co., Los Angeles, 1984-87, also dir. devel., regulatory and legal affairs, Providence (R.I.) Jour. Co., 1987—; panelist at numerous profl. convs. Mem. Temple Aliyah, Woodland Hills, Calif., Temple Aliyah Men's Club, 1984. Mem. ABA, Nat. Cable TV Assn. (utility relations, state-local coms. 1980-81), D.C. Bar Assn., City of Los Angeles Cable Operators Assn. (pres. 1986-87), Found. for Community Service Cable TV (bd. dirs.), Fed. Communications Bar Assn., New Eng. Cable TV Assn. (bd. dirs. 1981), Calif. Cable TV Assn. (bd. dirs. 1982-84), So. Calif. Cable TV Assn. (bd. dirs., v.p. 1986), City Los Angeles Cable Operators Assn. (pres. 1986-87). Democrat. Jewish. Communications, Administrative and regulatory. Office: Providence Jour Co 75 Fountain St Providence RI 02902

ISAACS, ROBERT CHARLES, lawyer; b. N.Y.C., July 16, 1919; s. David and Elsie (Weiss) I.; m. Doris Frances Shapiro, Nov. 20, 1943 (dec. 1982); 1 son, Leigh Richard; m. Mary Loe Anderson, Dec. 12, 1986. B.A. cum laude, NYU, 1941, J.D. (Maurice Goodman Meml. prize), 1943. Bar: N.Y. 1943. Asst. dep. atty. gen. N.Y. State Dept. Law, Albany, 1943, spl. asst. atty. gen., 1946; ptnr. Nordlinger Riegelman Benetar, N.Y.C., 1946-71, Aranow Brodsky Bohlinger Benetar & Einhorn, N.Y.C., 1972-79; ptnr. Benetar Isaacs Bernstein & Schair, N.Y.C., 1979—. Adj. prof. law St. John's U. Sch. Law, N.Y.C., 1961-72. Served to capt. U.S. Army, 1943-45, 51. Mem. ABA, N.Y. State Bar Assn., N.Y.C. Bar Assn. Club: N.Y.U. Alumni. Contbr. articles to profl. publs. Labor, Federal civil litigation. Home: 25 Sutton Pl S New York NY 10022 Office: 950 3d Ave New York NY 10022

ISAAK, GOTTHILF EUGENE, lawyer; b. Bismarck, N.D., Nov. 23, 1937; s. G. C. and Caroline (Jassman) I.; m. Elizabeth Baquet, Aug. 3, 1968; children: Jason E., Melissa E. BS, BA, U. N.D., 1959, JD, 1961; LLM, NYU, 1962. Bar: N.D. 1961, Ariz. 1963, U.S. Dist. Ct. Ariz. 1963, U.S. Ct. Appeals (9th cir.) 1965, U.S. Supreme Ct. 1965. Assoc. Dunseath, Stubbs & Burch, Tucson, 1962-73, Miller & Pitt, P.C., Tucson, 1973—; chmn. U. Ariz. Sch. Law Probate workshop, 1982. Asst. nat. legal officer CAP, 1976—. Fellow Am. Coll. Probate Counsel; mem. ABA, Ariz. Bar Assn. (probate and trust sect. com. 1985—), Pima County Bar Assn. Republican. Lutheran. Club: Am. Britany (nat. dir. 1982—). Estate planning, Estate taxation, Real property. Office: Miller & Pitt 111 S Church Ave Tucson AZ 85701

ISABELLA, MARY MARGARET, lawyer; b. Pitts., Oct. 16, 1947; d. Sebastian C. and Joanna C. (Ferris) I. BS in Biology, Duquesne U., 1969; cert. med. technologist, Mercy Hosp., Pitts., 1970; JD, Duquesne U., 1975. Bar: Pa. 1976, U.S. Dist Ct. (we. dist.) Pa. 1976, U.S. Supreme Ct., 1982. Sole practice Pitts., 1977—; instr. Wheeling (W.Va.) Coll., 1978-80. Mem. council Brentwood Whitehall Assn., Pitts., 1984—; bd. dirs. Dukes Ct., Duquesne U., Alcobar Fed. Credit Union. Mem. ABA, Pa. Bar Assn., Allegheny County Bar Assn., Brentwood-Whitehall C. of C. (bd. dirs.), Delta Theta Phi (past asst. dist. chancellor). Republican. Roman Catholic. Lodge: Italian Sons and Daughters of Am. (trustee local chpt.). Family and matrimonial, Probate. Office: 4101 Brownsville Rd Suite 200 Barone Bldg Pittsburgh PA 15227

ISBELL, DAVID BRADFORD, lawyer, educator; b. New Haven, Feb. 18, 1929; s. Percy Ernest and Dorothy Mae (Crabb) I.; m. Florence Bachrach, July 21, 1971; children—Christopher Pascal, Virginia Anne, Nicholas Bradford. B.A., Yale U., 1949, LL.B., 1956. Bar: Conn., 1956, D.C. 1957. Assoc. Covington & Burling, Washington, 1957-59, 61-65, ptnr., 1965—; asst. staff dir. U.S. Commn. on Civil Rights, Washington, 1959-61; lectr. U. Va. Sch. Law, 1962—. Bd. dirs. ACLU, 1964—, vice chmn., 1965-74, 79-80. Served to 2d lt. U.S. Army, 1951-53. Mem. ABA (ho. of dels. 1986—), D.C. Bar (gov. 1978-82, pres. 1983-84, ho. of dels. 1986—). Club: Federal City (Washington). Federal civil litigation, Libel, General corporate. Home: 3709 Bradley Ln Chevy Chase MD 20815 Office: Covington & Burling 1201 Pennsylvania Ave NW PO Box 7566 Washington DC 20044

ISELE, WILLIAM PAUL, lawyer; b. Plainfield, N.J., Sept. 8, 1949; s. Francis Joseph and Anna Mae (Hauser) I.; m. Linda Jean Bender, May 1, 1976; children—William Nicholas, Christopher Paul, David Francis. B.A. in Philosophy, Catholic U. Am., 1971, M.A. in Philosophy, 1972; J.D., Georgetown U., 1975. Bar: Va. 1975, Ill. 1976, U.S. Dist. Ct. (no. dist.) Ill. 1976, U.S. Dist. Ct. N.J. 1976; N.J. 1977, U.S. Supreme Ct. 1986. Asst. dir. health law div. AMA, Chgo., 1976-81; assoc. Gross & Novak, East Brunswick, N.J., 1981-84, ptnr., 1985—; instr. So. Ill. U. Regional Health Edn. Programs, Springfield, 1980-81; adj. prof. Seton Hall U. Law Sch., 1987—. Author: Confidentiality of Medical Records in N.J., 1983; The Hospital Medical Staff, 1984; contbr. articles to various jours. Mem. ABA, N.J. State Bar Assn., Nat. Health Lawyers Assn., Am. Acad. Hosp. Attys., N.J. Soc. Hosp. Attys., Middlesex County Bar Assn., Nat. Assn. Pastoral Musicians (treas. Metuchen chpt. N.J. 1981—). Roman Catholic. Health, Contracts commercial, Administrative and regulatory. Home: 313 Brook Dr Milltown NJ 08850 Office: Gross & Novak PO Box 188 East Brunswick NJ 08816

ISELIN, JOSEPHINE LEA, lawyer; b. Boston, Nov. 19, 1935; d. Charles Benjamin and Phoebe (Washburn) Barnes; m. John Jay Iselin, Sept. 8, 1956; children: William Jay, Benjamin Barnes, Josephine Lea, Fannie H., Alison J. Student, Smith Coll., 1953-56; BA, Am. U., 1964; JD, NYU, 1972. Bar: N.Y. 1972, U.S. Dist. Ct. (so. and ea. dists.) N.Y. 1972, U.S. Ct. Appeals (2d cir.) 1974. Assoc. Skadden, Arps, Slate, Meager & Flom, N.Y.C., 1972-77; assoc. Lankenau, Kovner & Bickford, N.Y.C., 1977-79, ptnr., 1980—; bd. advisors New Eng. Mut. Life Ins. Co., Boston, 1981-85. Mem. ABA, N.Y. State Bar Assn., Assn. of Bar of City of N.Y. Federal civil litigation, Probate, Trademark and copyright. Office: Lankenau Kovner & Bickford 30 Rockefeller Plaza New York NY 10112

ISEMAN, JOSEPH SEEMAN, lawyer; b. N.Y.C., May 29, 1916; s. Percy Reginald and Edith Helene (Seeman) I.; m. June Lorraine Bang, Dec. 10, 1966; children: Peter A., Frederick J., Ellen M.; stepchildren: Anne Hamilton Susan E. Hamilton, William C. Hamilton. B.A. magna cum laude, Harvard U., 1937; LL.B., Yale U., 1941. Bar: N.Y. State 1941, D.C. 1970. Investigator, clk. Comml. Factors Corp., 1937-38; atty. WPB, 1941-42; mng. dir. Iranian Airways Corp., 1946; assoc. Chadbourne, Wallace, Parke & Whiteside, N.Y.C., 1946-50, Paul, Weiss, Rifkind, Wharton & Garrison, N.Y.C., 1950-53; partner Paul, Weiss, Rifkind, Wharton & Garrison, 1954-86, European counsel, 1987—; counsel Charles F. Kettering Found.; dir. Gould Paper Corp. Author: A Perfect Sympathy, 1937; contbr. articles to profl. jours. Sec., bd. dirs. Acad. for Ednl. Devel., Wake Forest U.; bd. visitors Met. Assistance Corp.; trustee Bennington Coll., 1969-81, acting pres., 1976 Served to capt. USAAF, 1942-46. Woodrow Wilson vis. fellow Coll. William and Mary, 1977, Ripon Coll., 1979, Rollins Coll., 1980, De Pauw U., 1980, Fisk U., 1981, Albright Coll., 1982, Hood Coll., 1983, Southwestern U., 1984; named Conseil Juridique, France. Mem. Am., N.Y. State, N.Y.C. bar assns., Phi Beta Kappa. Democrat. Clubs: Century Assn. (N.Y.C.); Coveleigh (Rye, N.Y.); Cercle de L'Union Interallié e (Paris, France). General corporate, Private international, Probate. Home: 9 Place du Palais Bourbon, Paris 75007, France Office: 199 Blvd St Germain, Paris 75007, France also: 1285 Ave Americas New York NY 10019

ISENBERGH, JOSEPH, law educator; b. 1945. BA, Columbia U., 1966; AM, U. Rochester, 1967; JD, Yale U., 1970. Assoc. Caplin & Drysdale, Washington, 1976-80; asst. prof. U. Chgo., 1980-84, prof., 1984—. Office: Univ Chgo Law Sch 1111 E 60th St Chicago IL 60637 *

ISON, ROBERT ELWOOD, lawyer; b. Clark AFB, Philipines, Dec. 10, 1955; s. Ollie Elwood and Helen (Hightower) I.; m. Pamela Adams, July 11, 1977; 1 child, Robert Bradford. AB, U. Ga., 1977; JD, Samford U., 1981. Bar: Ala. 1981, Ky. 1983, U.S. Ct. Appeals (5th, 6th and 11th cirs.) 1983. Sole practice Birmingham, Ala., 1981-83; ptnr. Thomas & Ison, Hopkinsville, Ky., 1983—. Mem. ABA, Ala. Bar Assn., Ky. Bar Assn., Ky. Acad. Trial Attys. State civil litigation, Consumer commercial, Personal injury. Home: 120 Mooreland Dr Hopkinsville KY 42240 Office: Thomas & Ison PO Box 675 Hopkinsville KY 42240

ISQUITH, FRED TAYLOR, lawyer; b. N.Y.C., June 6, 1947; s. Santley and Rita (Hoskwith) I.; m. Susan Nora Goldberg, May 23, 1976: children: Fred, Rebecca. BA, Brooklyn Coll. of CUNY, 1968; JD, Columbia U., 1971. Bars: N.Y. 1972, U.S. Dist. Ct. (so. and ea. dists.) N.Y. 1975, U.S. Ct. Appeals (2d cir.) 1975, D.C. 1976, U.S. Supreme Ct. 1983, U.S. Ct. Appeals (8th cir.) 1985, U.S. Ct. Appeals (3d cir.) 1986. Assoc. Reavis & McGrath, N.Y.C., 1971-75, Kaye Scholer et al, N.Y.C., 1975-80; ptnr. Wolf Haldenstein Adler Freeman & Herz, N.Y.C., 1980—; bd. dirs. 103 East 84th St. Corp., N.Y.C., Sheinkopf Communications, Ltd. Mem. ABA, N.Y. State Bar Assn. (com. on legis.), D.C. Bar Assn., Assn. Bar of City of N.Y., Bklyn. Bar Assn. (civil process law and order com., legis. com. and fed. ct. coms.). Club: Columbia (N.Y.C.). Federal civil litigation, Securities, State civil litigation. Office: Wolf Haldenstein Adler et al 270 Madison Ave New York NY 10016

ISRAEL, NANCY DIANE, lawyer; b. Fall River, Mass., Apr. 20, 1955; d. David Joseph and Charlotte Millicent (Epstein) I. A.B. magna cum laude, Harvard U., 1976, J.D., 1979. Bar: Mass. 1979, N.Y. 1986. Mem. Hale & Dorr, Boston, 1980-83; atty. Harvard U., Cambridge, Mass., 1983-85, asst. gen. counsel for internat. div. Arthur Young and Co., N.Y.C. and Boston, 1985—; chmn. 21st, 22d ann. practical skills seminar, curriculum com., Mass. Continuing Legal Edn., Boston, 1985-86, Ctr. House, Inc., Boston, 1980-86. Bd. dirs., asst. clk. Center House, Inc., Boston, 1980—; mem. energy and environ. issues task force Dukakis gubernatorial campaign, Boston, 1982, southeastern Mass. coordinator, 1974; bd. dirs. nominating com. Mass. Council for Pub. Justice, Boston, 1971-76; mem. ad hoc com. Coalition for Better Judges, Boston, 1971-72. Mem. Mass. Bar Assn. (computer coll. steering com. 1984-86, del. bd. dels. 1984-87, chmn. elect young lawyers div. 1985-86, exec. com. 1985-86, commn. on professionalism 1985—) , Am. Corp. Counsel Assn. (chmn. nonprofit counsel com. 1983-85, chmn. elect young Lawyers com. 1986), ABA (exec. council young lawyers div., dist. rep. 1984-86, Mass. del. to ABA Ho. of Dels. 1987—, bd. dirs. continuing legal edn. young lawyers div. 1986—), Radcliffe Alumnae Assn., Mass. Bar Found. (trustee 1985—, Supreme Jud. Ct. IOLTA implementation com. 1985—), Boston Bar Assn. (bd. dirs. vol. lawyers project 1985—), Women's Bar Assn., Mass. Assn. Women Lawyers. Clubs: Harvard, Radcliffe, New Bedford Yacht. Public international, Private international.

ISRAEL, PERRY ELEMORE, lawyer; b. Denver, Jan. 29, 1952; s. Perry Elemore Israel Jr. and D.J. (Slater) Zerr; m. Anne Connolly, Aug. 11, 1979. AB, Princeton U., 1974; JD cum laude, Boston U., 1979, LLM, 1984. Bar: Mass. 1979, U.S. Dist. Ct. Mass. 1980, U.S. Tax Ct. 1980, U.S. Ct. Appeals (1st cir.) 1981, Calif. 1984, U.S. Dist. Ct. (no. dist.) Calif. 1984. Assoc. Palmer & Dodge, Boston, 1979-83, Orrick, Herrington & Sutcliffe, San Francisco, 1984—. Mem. ABA (tax sect.), Nat. Assn. Bond Lawyers. Municipal bonds, Corporate taxation, Personal income taxation. Office: Orrick Herrington & Sutcliffe 600 Montgomery San Francisco CA 94111

ISRAEL, SCOTT MICHAEL, lawyer; b. Milw., Oct. 22, 1955; s. Phillip David and Bella Dawn (Rubin) I.; m. Rachelle Laurie Zussman, Aug. 14, 1977; children: Benjamin, Eytan, Talia. BBA, U. Wis., 1977; JD, Marquette U., 1980. Bar: Wis. 1980, U.S. Dist. Ct. (ea. and we. dist.) Wis. 1980. Assoc. Rausch, Hamell, Ehrle & Sturm, Milw., 1980—. Mem. ABA, State Bar Wis., Phi Eta Sigma. Jewish. Consumer commercial, Bankruptcy, State civil litigation. Office: Rausch Hamell Ehrle Sturm SC 7500 W State St Milwaukee WI 53213

ISRAELS, MICHAEL JOZEF, lawyer; b. N.Y.C., Sept. 27, 1949; s. Carlos Lindner and Ruth Lucille (Goldstein) I.; m. Maija-Sarmite Jansons, Aug. 31, 1980; 1 child, Aleksandrs Lehman. A.B. magna cum laude, Amherst Coll., 1972; J.D., Harvard U., 1975. Bar: N.Y. 1976, U.S. Dist. Ct. (so. and ea. dists.) N.Y. 1976, D.C. 1977, N.J. 1980, U.S. Dist. Ct. N.J. 1980. Assoc. Shearman & Sterling, N.Y.C., 1975-79; sole practice, N.Y.C., 1979-81; ptnr. Courter, Kobert, Laufer & Pease, P.A., Hackettstown, N.J., 1981-83, Fitzpatrick & Israels, Bayonne, N.J., 1983—; gen. counsel Kearny (N.J.) Mcpl. Port Authority, 1985—, Jersey City Mcpl. Port Authority, 1986—; mem. N.J. Debt. Mgmt. Adv. Com., 1986—; cons. U.S./USSR Trade Council, N.Y.C., 1979, Council on Religion and Internat. Affairs, N.Y.C., 1980. Author: (with Moore, Thomson and Linsky) Report of the New England Conference on Conflicts Between Media and Law, 1977. Contbr. articles to legal jours. Bd. dirs. Community Tax Aid, Inc., N.Y.C., 1976-82, Am. Jewish Com., N.Y.C., 1980—, Anti-Defamation League N.J., Livingston, 1981—; mem. religious sch. com. Temple Emanu-El, N.Y.C., 1972-84. Mem. ABA (gov. Law Student div. 1974-75), Assn. Bar City N.Y., N.J. Bar Assn. Democrat. Clubs: Met. Opera, Harvard (N.Y.C.). General corporate, Estate taxation, Municipal bonds. Home: PO Box 22 Tranquility NJ 07879 Office: Fitzpatrick & Israels 90 W 40th St Bayonne NJ 07002

ISRAELSEN, NED ALMA, attorney; b. Logan, Utah, Dec. 6, 1954; s. Lyle E. and Marianna (Crookston) I.; m. Cynthia Kae Saunders, Jan. 13, 1977; children: Stanford, Lisa, Kurt. BS in Chemistry magna cum laude, Utah State U., 1978; JD with high honors, George Washington U., 1981. Bar: U.S. Patent Office 1979, Utah 1981, Va. 1981, Calif. 1984. Patent agt. Schwartz, Jeffery, Schwaab, Mack, Blumenthal & Koch P.C., Alexandria, Va., 1978-81; tech. asst. U.S. Ct. Customs and Patent Appeals, Washington, 1981-82; tech. law clk. U.S. Ct. Appeals Fed. Cir., Washington, 1982-83; patent atty., ptnr. Knobbe, Martens, Olson & Bear, Newport Beach, CA, 1983—; prof. law Loyola Law Sch., Los Angeles, 1986—. Mem. law rev. George Washington U., Washington, 1979-81. Scoutmaster Boy Scouts Am., Tustin, Calif., 1985—. Mem. ABA, Am. Chem. Soc., Am. Intellectual Property Law Assn., Deseret Bus. Assn., Assn. Former Ct. Customs and Patent Appeals Law Clks. and Tech. Assts. (bd. dirs. 1985—), Phi Kappa Phi. Mormon. Lodge: Order of Coif. Avocations: backpacking, scuba diving, photography. Patent, Trademark and copyright. Office: Knobbe Martens Olson & Bear 610 Newport Ctr Dr Suite 1600 Newport Beach CA 92660

ISSLER, HARRY, lawyer; b. Cologne, Germany, Nov. 14, 1935; s. Max and Fanny (Grunbaum) I.; m. Doris Helen Issler, June 1, 1958; children—Adriane P., M. Valerie, Stephanie L. B.S., U. Wis., 1955; J.D., Cornell U., 1958. Bar: N.Y. 1958, U.S. Supreme Ct. 1962, U.S. Ct. Mil. Appeals 1967, U.S. Dist. Ct. (so. and ea. dists.) N.Y. 1960, U.S. Customs Ct. 1964, U.S. Tax Ct. 1964; cert. specialist in civil trial advocacy Nat. Bo. Trial Advocacy. Assoc., Wing & Wing, N.Y.C., 1958-60, Fuchsberg & Fuchsberg, N.Y.C., 1960-62; ptnr. Issler & Fein, N.Y.C., 1963-68, Shaw, Issler & Rosenberg, N.Y.C., 1968-70; sole practice, N.Y.C., 1970-79; sr. ptnr. Issler & Schrage, P.C., N.Y.C., 1979-84; arbitrator Civil Ct., N.Y. County, 1979—; hearing officer N.Y. State Tax Appeals, 1975-77, Supreme Ct N.Y., N.Y. County Med. Malpractice Panel, 1980—. Served with U.S. Army, 1958-59, N.Y. Army N.G., 1963—. Ford Found. scholar, 1951-55. Mem. N.Y. State Bar Assn., Assn. of Bar of City N.Y., Am. Trial Lawyers Assn., N.Y. State Trial Lawyers Assn., Phi Alpha Delta. Club: 42d Infantry Division Officers (N.Y.C.); Officers (U.S. Mcht. Marine Acad.). State civil litigation, Family and matrimonial, Military. Home: 1365 York Ave New York NY 10021

ITKIN, PERRY STEVEN, lawyer; b. Bklyn., Dec. 25, 1944; m. Angela M. Monferrato, Nov. 9, 1978. B.A., Pa. State U., 1966; J.D., Dickinson Sch. Law, 1969. Bar: Fla. 1973, Pa. 1980, U.S. Dist. Ct. (so. dist.) Fla. 1974, U.S. Dist. Ct. (mid. dist.) Fla. 1984, U.S. Ct. Appeals (11th cir.) 1981, U.S. Supreme Ct. 1981. Spl. agt. FBI, 1969-73; assoc. Kirsch and Mills, P.A. Ft. Lauderdale, Fla., 1973-76; ptnr. Gibbs and Itkin, P.A., Ft. Lauderdale, 1976-80; sole practice, Ft. Lauderdale, 1980—; city prosecutor City of Margate (Fla.), 1973-74; mcpl. judge Sunrise Mcpl. Ct., 1976. Bd. dirs. Areawide Council on Aging of Broward County (Fla.), Inc., 1974-82, pres., 1981. Recipient Areawide Council on Aging award, 1982; Area Agy. on Aging Advocacy award, 1982. Mem. Am. Arbitration Assn. (panel of arbitrators), Broward County Bar Assn., Pa. Bar Assn., ABA, Fla. Bar, Acad. Fla. Trial Lawyers, Assn. Trial Lawyers Am., Broward County Trial Lawyers Assn., Soc. Former Spl. Agts. FBI. General corporate, Personal injury, State civil litigation. Office: 106 SE 9th St Fort Lauderdale FL 33316

ITTIG, GERARD W., lawyer; b. N.Y.C., June 21, 1945; s. Peter T. and Virginia P. (Breden) I.; m. Judith Bacorn, Aug. 17, 1968. BA in Math., SUNY, Buffalo, 1968, BS in Engring., 1971; JD, U. Tenn., 1975. Bar: Tenn. 1975, D.C. 1975, U.S. Dist. Ct. (ea. dist.) Tenn. 1975, Va. 1976, U.S. Dist. Ct. (ea. dist.) Va. 1976, U.S. Ct. Appeals (2d, 4th and 6th cirs.). Engr. Worthington Corp., Buffalo, 1969-71; sr. law clk. U.S. Dist. Ct. (ea. dist.), Chattanooga, 1975-76; assoc. Walstad, Wickwire et al, Vienna, Va., 1976-78; ptnr. Walstad, Kasimer, Tansey & Ittig, Washington, 1978-83, Kasimer & Ittig, Washington, 1983—. Author: International Contracting, 1985; comments editor Tenn. Law Rev., 1974-75; contbr. articles to profl. jours. m. ABA, IEEE (chmn. industry application soc. 1984-85), Am. Arbitration Assn. (nat. panel), Va. Bar Assn. (bd. govs. 1982—), D.C. Bar Assn., Tenn. Bar Assn., Associated Builders and Contractors Assn. Construction, Government contracts and claims, Surety law. Office: Kasimer & Ittig 1901 18th St NW Washington DC 20009

ITZKOFF, NORMAN JAY, lawyer; b. N.Y.C., Oct. 9, 1940; s. Louis and Rose Itzkoff; divorced; 1 child, Francesca Sandra. BS with honors, U. Buffalo, 1961; LLB cum laude, Columbia U., 1965. Bar: N.Y. 1965, U.S. Dist. Ct. (so. and ea. dists.) N.Y. 1967, U.S. Ct. Appeals (2d cir.) 1967, U.S. Supreme Ct. 1971. Law clk. to judge U.S. Dist. Ct. (so. dist.) N.Y., N.Y.C., 1965-66; assoc. Cravath, Swaine & Moore, N.Y.C., 1966-74; assoc. Rosenman, Colin, Freund, Lewis & Cohen, N.Y.C., 1974-76, ptnr., 1976-86; gen. counsel Assn. Internat. Photography Art Dealers Inc., N.Y.C., 1981—. Editor: Dealing with Damages, 1983, Columbia U. Law Rev., 1963-65. Mem. adv. bd. Catskill Ctr. for Photography, Woodstock, N.Y., 1982—. Harlan Fiske Stone scholar. Mem. ABA (jud. adminstrn. div. lawyers conf., com. on jud. qualification and selection), Fed. Bar Council, N.Y. State Bar Assn. (antitrust law sect., mcpl. law sect., trial lawyers sect., com. on fed. cts.), Assn. of Bar of City of N.Y. (adv bd. demonstration observation com., com. on nuclear tech. and law, liaison art law com., chmn. subcom. on state legislation 1983-84, Am. Arbitration Assn. (panel), Beta Gamma Sigma. Clubs: Columbia, Westchester Rugby (N.Y.C.). Avocations: fine art photography, running. Federal civil litigation, State civil litigation, Photographic art law. Home and Office: 1385 York Ave New York NY 10021

IVANICK, CAROL W. TRENCHER, lawyer; b. Springfield, Mass., Mar. 6, 1939; d. Joseph George and Daisy Wolf; m. Michael Ira Trencher, July 30, 1960 (div. Feb. 1984); children: Christopher, Daniel, Deborah; m. Peter Alan Ivanick. BA, Wellesley Coll., 1959; JD, Yale U., 1962. Bar: N.Y. 1963. Assoc. Cleary, Gottlieb et al, N.Y.C., 1962-67; ptnr. Dewey, Ballantine, Bushby, Palmer & Wood, N.Y.C., 1976—; chmn. adv. com. Pension Benefit Guaranty Corp., Washington, 1978-80; visiting lectr. Yale Law Sch., New Haven, Conn., 1978-79, 82-83. Club: India House (Hanover Sq., N.Y.), Yale (N.Y.C.). Avocations: ceramics, bowling, tennis. Pension, profit-sharing, and employee benefits. Home: 110 Riverside Dr New York NY 10024 Office: Dewey Ballantine Bushby Palmer & Wood 140 Broadway New York NY 10005

IVEY, SCOTT ELLSWORTH, lawyer; b. Cambridge, Mass., Apr. 14, 1948; s. Arthur Rodgers Ivey and Sherrill (Ellsworth) Lyon; m. Martha Mann, July 25, 1970 (div. Dec. 1983); children: Dana Ruth, Scott Ellsworth, Jennifer Barr. BA, Waynesburg Coll.; JD, U. Balt. Bar: Conn. 1974, U.S. Dist. Ct. Conn. 1977, U.S. Supreme Ct. 1984. V.p. Monumental Title Ins., Severna Park, Md., 1973-74; ptnr. Ivey, Barnum & O'Mara, Stamford, Conn., 1974-81; sole practice Darien, Conn., 1981-86; ptnr. Ivey & Schmidt, Darien, 1986—. Bd. dirs. Darien YMCA, 1977-1983. Mem. Fairfield County Young Lawyers Assn. (v.p. 1983, treas. 1984). Republican. Presbyterian. Club: Darien Toastmasters (pres. 1976-77), Darien Power Squadron (officer). Lodge: Rotary (pres. local chpt. 1980-81). State civil litigation, General corporate, Real property. Home: 34 Rowayron Woods Dr Norwalk CT 06854-3931 Office: Ivey & Schmidt 10 Corbin Dr PO Box 89 Darien CT 06820

IVORY, CECIL AUGUSTUS, lawyer, judge; b. Charlotte, N.C., June 28, 1947; s. Cecil Augustus and Emily (Richardson) I. BA, Lincoln U., Pa., 1969; JD, George Washington U., 1972. Bar: N.Y. 1974, U.S. Dist. Ct. (so. and ea. dists.) N.Y. 1974, U.S. Supreme Ct. 1983. Mem. staff Office of Dist. Atty., Queens, N.Y., 1972-74; asst. atty. gen. N.Y. Dept. Law, N.Y.C., 1974-85; judge N.Y. State Workers' Compensation Bd., 1985-86. Bd. dirs. Bowery Residence Com., N.Y.C., 1978-86; trustee A.L. Richardson Scholarship Fund, Charlotte, 1983-86; adviser Dem. Orgn., Bronx, 1984. Mem. Macon B. Allen Bar Assn., Third World Lawyers Caucus (corr. sec. 1983). Democrat. Presbyterian. Deceased Oct. 1986. Consumer commercial, Landlord-tenant.

IWAI, WILFRED KIYOSHI, lawyer; b. Honolulu, Aug. 21, 1941; s. Charles Kazuo and Michiko (Sakimoto) I.; m. Judy Tomiko Yoshimoto, Mar. 1, 1963; children: Kyle K., Tiffany Seiko. BS in Bus., U. Colo., 1963, JD, 1966. Bar: Hawaii 1966, Colo. 1966, U.S. Dist. Ct. Hawaii 1966, U.S. Ct. Appeals (9th cir.) 1966. Dep. corp. counsel State of Hawaii, Honolulu, 1966-71; assoc. Kashiwa & Kanazawa, Honolulu, 1971-75; ptnr. Kashiwa, Iwai, Motooka & Goto, Honolulu, 1975-82, also bd. dirs.; ptnr. Iwai, Motooka & Goto, Honolulu, 1982—, also bd. dirs. Mem. ABA, Hawaii Bar Assn., Assn. Trial Lawyers Am., Building Industry Assn. Club: Draftsmen's (Honolulu) (pres.). State civil litigation, Construction, Family and matrimonial. Office: Iwai Motooka & Goto 820 Mililani St #502 Honolulu HI 96813

IWAMOTO, RAYMOND SHIGEO, lawyer; b. Honolulu, Sept. 5, 1940; s. Masao and Eva Tomiko (Okubo) I.; m. Louise Lung, May 20, 1961; children: Stacey, Holly. BA, U. Hawaii, 1962, MSW, 1969; JD summa cum laude, U. Santa Clara, 1974. Bar: Hawaii 1974, U.S. Dist. Ct. Hawaii 1974. Assoc. Carlsmith, Wichman, Case, Mukai & Ichiki, Honolulu, 1974—; staff judge adv. Hawaii Army N.G., Honolulu, 1976-82. Bd. dirs. Hawaii Spl. Olympics, Honolulu, 1986. Served to capt. U.S. Army, 1963-67, Vietnam. Mem. Hawaii Bar Assn. (chmn. real property and fin. services sect.), Acad. Am. Hosp. Atty. Clubs: Honolulu, Pacific Island. Real property, Construction, Health. Home: 7535 Nakalele St Honolulu HI 96825 Office: Carlsmith Wichman Case Mukai Ichiki 1001 Bishop St Bishop Sq 2200 Pacific Tower Honolulu HI 96813

IZOR, DAVID E., lawyer; b. Dayton, Ohio, Feb. 24, 1947; s. Herbert E. and Mary C. (Boyer) I.; m. Maude G. Spencer, Dec. 7, 1970; children: Gillian M., Whitney K., Spencer K. BA, Miami U., Oxford, Ohio, 1969; JD, No. Ky. State U., 1974. Bar: Ohio 1974, U.S. Dist. Ct. (so. dist.) Ohio 1974, U.S. Supreme Ct. 1977. Sole practice Germantown, Ohio, 1974—. Trustee German Twp., Germantown, 1984; pres. bd. Germantown Pub. Library, 1979—. Mem. ABA, Ohio Bar Assn., Dayton Bar Assn., Colo. Outfitters Assn., Nat. Rifle Assn. Democrat. Club: N. American Hunting. Lodges: Rotary (pres. 1979), Odd Fellows (grand 1983), Masons (jr. deacon 1984). Avocations: hunting, fishing, golf. Probate, Real property. Office: 52 N Main St Germantown OH 45327

JABLONSKI, JAMES ARTHUR, lawyer; b. Sheboygan, Wis., Nov. 12, 1942; s. John Alfred and Dena (Kaat) J. BBA, U. Wis., 1965, JD, 1968. Bar: Wis. 1968, Calif. 1969, U.S. Supreme Ct. 1974, Colo. 1976, U.S. Ct. Appeals (7th cir) 1969, U.S. Ct. Appeals (8th and 10th cirs.) 1976. Assoc. Pillsbury, Madison & Sutro, San Francisco, 1969-72; asst. prof. law Washington U., St. Louis, 1972-76; ptnr. Gorsuch, Kirgis, Campbell, Walker & Grover, Denver, 1976—. Mem. ABA, Colo. Bar Assn., Denver Bar Assn., Indsl. Relations Research Assn. Democrat. Club: Pinehurst Country (Denver). Federal civil litigation, Construction, Labor. Home: 5253 S Golf Course Dr Morrison CO 80465 Office: Gorsuch Kirgis Campbell et al 1401 17th St Denver CO 80202

JACK, JAMES ERNEST, lawyer; b. Mercer County, Pa., July 15, 1901; s. William Lloyd and Maude (Gildersleeve) J.; m. Anne Irvine, Sept. 3, 1932; children—William I., Elizabeth Jack Bell. Grad. Slippery Rock State Normal Sch., 1921; B.S., Grove City (Pa.) Coll., 1926, LL.D. (hon.), 1970; LL.B., Duquesne U., 1931. Bar: Pa. 1932, U.S. Dist. Ct. (we. dist.) Pa. 1933, Tchr. Ellsworth (Pa.) Jr. High Sch., 1921-23, Etna (Pa.) High Sch., 1926-31, prin. 1931-32; sole practice, Titusville, Pa., 1932-60 ptnr. Jack, Kookogey & Felton, and predecessors Jack, Kookogey & Schug, Jack, Kookogey & Forssell, Jack & Kookogey, Titusville, Pa., 1961-77, sr. ptnr., 1977—. Mem. adv. bd. Titusville Salvation Army; mem. City of Titusville Sch. Bd., 1934-64; bd. dirs. Benson Meml. Library, 1935-47, 53-63; bd. dirs. Titusville YMCA. Recipient Cert. of Appreciation as atty. for registrants SSS, Pres. L. B. Johnson and Lewis B. Hershey; Citizenship award Titusville Area, C. of C., 1974. Mem. ABA, Pa. Bar Assn., Crawford County (Pa.) Bar Assn. (pres. 1968), Titusville Area C. of C. Republican. Clubs: Rotary, Masons. General practice, Probate, Real property. Office: Jack Kookogey Felton 144 W Spring St Titusville PA 16354

JACK, LARRY A., lawyer, title company executive; b. Oklahoma City, June 2, 1947; s. Clarence Albert and Dorothy Jo (Moore) J.; m. Diane Marie Jung, Dec. 21, 1968; children: Kira Christine, Stephen Christopher. BA, St. Mary's U., San Antonio, 1970, JD, 1973. Bar: Tex. 1973. Sole practice, San Antonio, 1973-81, 87—; closer, examiner Guaranty Abstract & Title Co., San Antonio, 1974-81; chief title officer Transam. Title Ins., San Antonio, 1981-83; v.p., sec., counsel Nat. Title Co., San Antonio, 1984—; instr. Acad. Real Estate, San Antonio, 1981-84. Mem. ABA, Tex. State Bar Assn., San Antonio Bar Assn., Phi Alpha Delta. Roman Catholic. Club: San Antonio Breakfast. Lodge: Lions. Estate planning, Family and matrimonial, State civil litigation. Home: 3407 Huntwick San Antonio TX 78230 Office: 7550 I H 10 W Suite 1050 San Antonio TX 78229

JACKLEY, MICHAEL DANO, lawyer; b. Balt., Oct. 1, 1942; s. Francis Dano and Jean Diantha (Dietz) J.; m. Mary Margaret Mixer, July 5, 1977 (div.); children—Megan, Dano Mixer, Jackley. B.A., U. Md., 1965, J.D., 1970; LL.M. with highest honors, George Washington U., 1977. Bar: D.C., Md., Pa. 1971, U.S. Tax Ct. 1973; Assoc., Williams, Brown, Eklund & Baldwin, Washington, 1971-74; assoc. Smith, Joseph, Greenwald & Laake and predecessor firms, Hyattsville, Md., 1974-77, ptnr., 1977—; mem. Select Com. to Redraft D.C. Corp. Statute, 1977—; tchr. Paralegal Inst., 1977-80. Adv. bd. Prince George's County Mental Health Assn., 1978—. Key Delta Theta Phi scholar, 1970. Mem. ABA, Md. State Bar Assn., Prince George's County Bar Assn. Democrat. Unitarian. General corporate, Corporate taxation. Address: 1345 University Blvd E Langley Park MD 20783

JACKMAN, ROBERT L., lawyer; b. N.Y.C., June 20, 1949; s. Edward F. and Molly B. Jackman; m. Susan L. Freedley, May 26, 1970; children: Katherine, Alexander. BA, Cornell U., 1973, JD, 1976. Bar: Conn. 1976. Atty. Gen. Electric Co., Fairfield, Conn., 1976-81, Holiday Corp., Memphis, 1981—. Mem. ABA. Private international, Antitrust, Labor. Home: 21 Townshend Rd, Richmond TW9 1XH Surrey, England Office: Holiday Inn Internat, Windmill House 80-82, Windmill Rd, Brentford TW8 0QH Middlesex, England

JACKSON, ANDREW DUDLEY, lawyer; b. Ft. Wayne, Ind., Nov. 19, 1943; s. Andrew D. and Helen (Namish) J. BA in History, Philosophy, St. Joseph's Coll., 1966; MA in History, Purdue U., 1971; JD, John Marshall Law Sch., 1981. Bar: Ill. 1981, U.S. Ct. Appeals (7th cir.) 1981, Ind. 1982, U.S. Dist. Ct. (no.and so. dists.) Ind. 1982, U.S. Supreme Ct. 1986. Baliff Whiting (Ind.) Mcpl. Ct., 1977; cons. Erewan Internat., Chgo., 1978-80; dep. coroner Lake County (Ind.) Coroner's Office, 1982; sole practice Whiting, Ind., 1982—. Served as specialist, U.S. Army Security Agy., 1971-74. Mem. Am. Security Council (nat. adv. bd. 1980—), ABA, Ind. State Bar Assn., Ill. State Bar Assn., Assn. Trial Lawyers Am., Art Inst. Chgo., Fraternal Order of Police. Avocations: marksmanship, defense, aviation. Antitrust, Federal civil litigation, General practice. Home and Office: 1526 Steiber St Whiting IN 46394

JACKSON, BLAINE ALBERT, lawyer; b. Alpena, Ark., Nov. 15, 1947; s. Clell C. and Erma Helen (Maples) J.; m. Helen Ruth Boevers, July 14, 1975; children: Blaine Alex, Aaron Scott. BEd, U. Ark., 1971, JD, 1979. Bar:

Ark. 1979, U.S. Dist. Ct. (we. dist.) Ark. 1979. Tchr. Bentonville (Ark.) Schs., 1971-76; assoc. Law Offices of Ernest G. Lawrence, Bentonville, 1979-85; sole practice Bella Vista, Ark., 1985—; Benton County Cir. and Probate Juvenile Master 1987—. Clk. City of Bentonville, 1983-86. Mem. ABA, Ark. Bar Assn., Benton County Bar Assn., Bentonville C. of C. Democrat. Methodist. Lodge: Kiwanis (local pres. 1985-86). Avocations: golf, reading. Estate planning, Probate, Real property. Office: 310A Town Center W Bella Vista AR 72714

JACKSON, BRUCE GEORGE, lawyer; b. Portland, Oreg., July 15, 1942; s. George William and Sally Marie (Dorner) J.; m. Jane Jackson, Sept. 8, 1972; children—Yvette, Scott. B.S. cum laude, U. Oreg., 1966; J.D., U. Calif.-Berkeley, 1970. Bar: Hawaii 1971, U.S. Dist. Ct. Hawaii 1971. Assoc. Case, Kay & Lynch, Honolulu, 1970-74; ptnr. Curtis W. Carlsmith, Honolulu, 1974-76; sole practice, Honolulu, 1977—; speaker on real property law, land trusts, estate planning, 1977—. Served with N.G., 1960-68. Mem. ABA, Hawaii Bar Assn., Sigma Phi Epsilon (life). Democrat. Clubs: Honolulu, Downtown Exchange (Honolulu). Student editor: Kragen & McNulty on Federal Income Taxation, 1970. Real property, Probate, General corporate. Office: Suite 1132 Pacific Tower 1001 Bishop St Honolulu HI 96813

JACKSON, CHARLES C., lawyer; b. Chgo., Apr. 4, 1952; s. Clark Edwin and Betty (Slowik) J.; m. Mary Dahlberg, June 4, 1977; children: Zachary, Caroline, Sarah. BA, Bethel Coll., 1974; JD, Northwestern U., 1977. Bar: Ill., U.S. Supreme Ct. Ptnr. Seyfarth, Shaw, Fairweather & Geraldson, Chgo., 1985—. Contbr. articles to law jours. Mem. Evang. Covenant Ch. Labor, Federal civil litigation, State civil litigation. Office: Seyfarth Shaw Fairweather & Geraldson 55 E Monroe Suite 4200 Chicago IL 60603

JACKSON, DAVID WILLIAM, lawyer; b. St. Louis, Aug. 14, 1956; s. Charles William and Marilyn (Connor) J.; m. Cynthia Smith, May 27, 1979; 1 child, Adam. BA in Bus., Washington State U., 1978; JD, Gonzaga U., 1982. Bar: Wash. 1982, U.S. Dist. Ct. (ea. dist.) Wash. Assoc. Winston-Cashatt, Spokane, Wash., 1982-84; sole practice Spokane, 1984—. Vice chmn. bd. dirs. East Wash. chpt. March of Dimes, Spokane, 1985-86, chmn. bd. dirs., 1986—. Mem. ABA, Wash. State Bar Assn., Spokane Bar Assn., Assn. Trial Lawyers Am., Wash. State Trial Lawyers Assn., Sigma Alpha Epsilon (bd. trustees 1984—). Repubican. Episcopalian. Club: Spokane. Personal injury. Home and Office: S 4112 Pittsburg Spokane WA 99203

JACKSON, DONALD H(ERBERT), JR., lawyer; b. Weymouth, Mass., Aug. 11, 1947; s. Donald H. and Marjorie W. (Chase) J.; m. Louise A. Balich, June 26, 1977; children: Donald H. III, Caroline L., Elizabeth G. AB, Clark U., 1969; JD, Duke U., 1973. Bar: Mass. 1973, U.S. Dist. Ct. Mass. 1974, U.S. Ct. Appeals (1st cir.) 1975, U.S. Tax Ct. 1983. Assoc. Holland, Johnson & Hays, Boston, 1972-74; ptnr. Steadman, Williams & Jackson, Boston, 1974-79, Williams & Jackson, Boston, 1979-85, Williams, Jackson & Spero, Boston, 1985—. Mem. Mass. Bar Assn., Am. Soc. Law and Medicine, Def. Research Inst., Mass. Acad. Trial Attys., New Eng. Hist. Geneal. Soc. Republican. Mem. Antiochian Orthodox Ch. Lodge: Masons (master 1980-81). Avocation: genealogy. State civil litigation, Personal injury, Probate. Home: 71 Hearthstone Way Hanover MA 02339 Office: Williams Jackson & Spero 50 Staniford St Boston MA 02114

JACKSON, FREDDIE NEWELL, lawyer, real estate broker; b. Helena, Ark., July 8, 1932; s. John Wesley and Ada Lee (Murphy) J.; m. Georgia Ann Morrow, Mar. 15, 1957 (div. Sept. 1963); children—Jacquelynn Jean, Freddie Newell, Darlene. B.S., U. Ark., 1955; cert. Renesselaer Poly. Inst., 1964; J.D., Tex. So. U., 1973. Bar: Tex. 1973. Tchr. sci. Eliza Miller High Sch., Helena, Ark., 1955; oceanographer U.S. Naval Oceanography Office, Suitland, Md., 1955-65; engring. writer/editor ITT, Houston, 1965-70; salesman Robinson Realty, Houston, 1970-73; asst. county atty. Harris County, Houston, 1973-74; sole practice, Houston, 1974—; broker Young Execs. Realty, Houston. Served with USN, 1951-52. Recipient commendation County Atty., Houston, 1974. Mem. Assn. Trial Lawyers Am., ABA, State Bar Tex., Houston Bar Assn., Phi Alpha Delta. Democrat. Baptist. Criminal, Jurisprudence, Real property. Home: 5258 Bungalow Ln Houston TX 77048 Office: 3001 Oakdale St Houston TX 77004

JACKSON, GARY DEAN, lawyer; b. Dallas, Sept. 13, 1935; s. Troy Byrl and Leslie Evelyn (Sitton) J.; m. Gloria Ann Galouye, Dec. 22, 1957; children—David MacArthur, Daniel Marshall. B.A. in Govt., So. Meth. U., 1957; J.D., Baylor U., 1961; grad. U.S. Army War Coll., 1979. Bar: Tex. 1961, U.S. Ct. Mil. Appeals 1968, U.S. Supreme Ct. 1968, U.S. Dist. Ct. (no., so., ea., we. dists.) Tex., U.S. Dist. Ct. (no. dist.) Ala., U.S. Ct. Claims, U.S. Ct. Appeals (1st, 3d, 4th, 5th, 7th, 8th, 9th, 10th ctrs.). Budget examiner Tex. Legis. Budget Bd., 1957-59; ptnr. Pace, Jarvis & Jackson, Tyler, Tex., 1961-66; mcpl. judge Arlington, Tex., 1966-69; spl. asst. Dept. Justice, Washington, 1969-74; ptnr. Colvin & Jackson, Dallas, 1974-78; ptnr. Jackson Jenkins & Rowton, Dallas, 1978-81, Jackson, Jackson & Loving, 1982-83, Jackson, Jackson, Loving & Gutman, 1984—; instr. in bus. law Tyler Jr. Coll., 1962-65, fraud seminars, 1972—. Pres. Smith County Republican Men's Club, 1965; counselor Baylor U. Law Sch., 1974. Recipient commendations Dir. FBI, 1971, 72, Atty. Gen. U.S., 1971, also others. Mem. ABA, Fed. Bar Assn., Dallas Bar Assn., So. Meth. U. Alumni Assn., Baylor U. Law Sch. Alumni Assn., Nat. Assn. Criminal Def. Lawyers, Tex. Criminal Def. Lawyers Assn., Mil. Order World Wars, Civil Affairs Assn., Army Res. Assn., Baylor Law Rev. Former Editors (pres. 1979), Delta Theta Phi. Republican. Baptist. Contbr. articles to legal jours. Home: 5534 Williamstown St Dallas TX 75230 Office: Suite 500 Murray Financial Ctr 5550 LBJ Freeway Dallas TX 75240

JACKSON, JAMES RONALD, lawyer; b. Dexter, Ky., Dec. 10, 1942; s. Legal and Jessie (Woodall) J.; m. Linda Kay Crouse, Feb. 1, 1964; children: Lisa Gail, Laura Kay, Steven James. BS, Murray (Ky.) State Coll., 1964; MBA, U. Ky., 1972, JD, 1975. Bar: Ky. 1975, U.S. Dist. Ct. (we. dist.) Ky. 1979, U.S. Tax Ct. 1981, U.S. Ct. Appeals (6th cir.) 1986. Field auditor Ky. Dept. of Revenue, Paducah, 1964-65; acct. Schuette & Taylor, CPAs, Paducah, 1965-69; asst. prof. acctg. Eastern Ky. U., Richmond, 1969-75; ptnr. Peck, Jackson & Jackson, Paducah, 1975—. Mem. ABA, Ky. Bar Assn., McCracken County Bar Assn., Ky. Soc. CPA's, Am. Assn. Atty.-CPA's, Am. Inst. CPAs, Am. Assn. Atty.-CPAs Inc. Democrat. Methodist. Lodge: Rotary. Probate, Pension, profit-sharing, and employee benefits, Estate taxation. Office: Peck Jackson & Jackson 2320 Broadway Suite 400 PO Box 7603 Paducah KY 42002-7603

JACKSON, JOE DAVID, lawyer; b. Lithonia, Ga., Dec. 17, 1953; s. Charles Ray and Roberta (Locke) J.; m. Margaret Susan McClung, July 1, 1978; children: Margaret Katherine, Charles Stephen, Laura Gentry. BBA, U. Ga., 1975; JD, Mercer U., 1980. Bar: Ga. 1980, U.S. Dist. Ct. (no. dist.) Ga. 1980, U.S. Supreme Ct. 1984, U.S. Ct. Appeals (11th cir.) 1985. Asst. gen. counsel State Bar Ga., Atlanta, 1980—. Bd. dirs. Met. Atlanta Recovery Residences, Atlanta, 1983. Named one of Outstanding Young Men in Am., 1985. Mem. ABA, Atlanta Bar Assn., Decatur-DeKalb Bar Assn., Nat. Orgn. Bar Counsel. Methodist. Lodge: Optimists (pres. 1982-83, bd. dirs. 1984-86, outstanding leadership award local club 1983). Avocations: softball, tennis, swimming. Jurisprudence. Home: 4576 Bob's Ct Stone Mountain GA 30083 Office: State Bar Ga 800 The Hurt Bldg 50 Hurt Plaza Atlanta GA 30303

JACKSON, JOHN HOLLIS, JR., lawyer; b. Montgomery, Ala., Aug. 21, 1941; s. John Hollis and Erma (Edgeworth) J.; m. Rebecca Mullins, May 27, 1967; 1 child, John Hollis III. A.B., U. Ala., 1963, J.D., 1966. Bar: Ala. 1966, U.S. Dist. Ct. (no. dist.) Ala. 1969. Sole practice, Clanton, Ala., 1967—; county atty. Chilton County Commn., Clanton, 1969—; mcpl. judge Clanton, 1971—, Jemison, Ala., 1984—; dir. First Nat. Bank, Clanton, 1974-83; mem. adv. bd. Colonial Bank, Clanton, 1983—. Bd. dirs. Chilton-Shelby Mental Health Bd., Calera, Ala., 1974-83, pres., 1974-79; mem. State Democratic Exec. Com., Birmingham, Ala., 1974—; del. Democratic Nat. Conv., N.Y.C., 1976; mem. County Democratic Exec. Com., Chilton County, 1982—. Served to 1st lt. U.S. Army, 1966-67. Mem. Ala. Young Lawyers Sect. (exec. com. 1969-70), Chilton County Bar Assn., (pres. 1969, 74), Ala. State Bar Assn. (bd. bar commrs. 1984—, chmn. adv. com. to bd. bar examiners 1986—, 19th cir. indigent def. commn. 1983—), Phi Alpha Delta. Democrat. Methodist. Lodge: Kiwanis. General practice. Home: Samaria Rd Clanton AL 35045 Office: PO Box 1818 500 2d Ave S Claton AL 35045

JACKSON, JOHN HOWARD, lawyer; b. Kansas City, Mo., Apr. 6, 1932; s. Howard Clifford and Lucile (Deischer) J.; m. Joan Leland, Dec. 16, 1962; children: Jeanette, Lee Ann, Michelle. AB, Princeton U., 1954; JD, U. Mich., 1959. Bar: Wis. 1959, Mo. 1959, Calif. 1964, Mich. 1970. Sole practice Milw., 1959-61; assoc. prof., prof. law U. Calif., 1961-66; prof. law U. Mich., 1966—; on leave gen. counsel U.S. Office Spl. Trade Rep., 1973-74, acting deputy spl. rep. for trade, 1974; vis. prof. U. Brussels, 1975-76; Hessel E. Yntema prof. law U. Mich., 1983—; disting. vis. prof. law Georgetown Law Ctr., Washington, 1986-87; Ford Found. cons. legal edn., vis. prof. U. Delhi, India, 1968-69; cons. U.S. Treasury Dept., U.S. Office Spl. Trade Reps, U.S. Senate Finance Com., 1978-79, UN Conf. Trade and Devel., 1980; vis. fellow Inst. Internat. Econs., Washington, 1983. Author: World Trade and the Law of GATT, 1969, Contract Law in Modern Society, 1973, 2d edit. (with Lee Bollinger), 1980, Legal Problems of International Economic Relations, 1977, 2d edit. (with William Davey), 1986, (with Jean-Victor Louis and Mitsuo Matsushita) Implementing the Tokyo Round, 1984; bd. editors: Jour. World Trade Law, Am. Jour. Internat. Law, Jour. Law and Policy in Internat. Bus., others; contbr. articles to profl. jours. Served with M.I. U.S. Army, 1954-56. Rockefeller Found. fellow for study European community law Brussels, 1975-76. Mem. ABA, Am. Soc. Internat. Law, Am. Law Inst., Council Fgn. Relations, Phi Beta Kappa, Order of Coif. Private international, Public international. Home: 1 Heatheridge Ann Arbor MI 48104 Office: Sch Law U Mich Ann Arbor MI 48109

JACKSON, LOUISE ANNE, lawyer; b. Bowling Green, Ohio, July 27, 1948; d. John Edward and Patricia Anne (Messmer) J.; BSBA, Bowling Green State U., 1970; MBA, U. Colo., 1971; JD, U. Toledo, 1976. Bar: Ohio 1977; CPA Ohio. Sr. staff acct. Arthur Young and Co., Toledo, 1972-75; ptnr. Marshall & Melhorn, Toledo, 1976-85; sole practice, Toledo, 1985—. Mem. ABA, Toledo Bar Assn., Ohio Soc. CPA's (sec. 1983-84, bd. dirs. 1982-83). Club: Zonta of Toledo II (treas. 1978-79, v.p. 1981-82, pres. 1982-83). Corporate taxation, Pension, profit-sharing, and employee benefits, General corporate.

JACKSON, MARK ANDREW, lawyer; b. Adrian, Mich., July 3, 1958; s. Richard Edgar and Margreet Lucille (Coleman) L.; m. Beth Carol Tuckerman, Aug. 14, 1981; children: Kyle Andrew, Kathryn Beth. Student, Mich. State U., 1976-77; BA, Adrian Coll., 1979; JD, U. Toledo, 1982. Bar: Mich. 1982, U.S. Dist. Ct. (ea. dist.) Mich. 1983. Assoc. Walker & Watts, Adrian, 1982-83; ptnr. Walker, Watts & Jackson, Adrian, 1983—; atty. Raisin Twp., 1984—, Adrian Twp., 1985—. Bd. dirs. Lenawee Humane Soc., Adrian, 1985—, Region II Substance Abuse Adv. Bd., Jackson, 1985—. Mem. Lenawee County Bar Assn., Mich. Trial Lawyers Assn., Lenawee County Twps. Assn. (lectr. 1985). Republican. Congregationalist. Avocations: camping, fishing, canoeing. Personal injury, General corporate, Estate planning. Office: Walker Watts & Jackson 160 N Winter St Adrian MI 49221

JACKSON, MICHEAL STEWART, lawyer; b. Montgomery, Ala., July 12, 1954; s. James J. and Mildred G. (McGuire) J.; children: Micheal Stewart Jr., James Francis. BA, Auburn U., 1976; JD, Samford U., 1979. Bar: Ala. 1979. Law clk. to presiding justice Ala. Supreme Ct., Montgomery, 1979-83, U.S. Dist. Ct. (no. dist.) Ala., Birmingham, 1980-81; assoc. Melton & Espy, P.C., Montgomery, 1981—. Mem. Assn. Trial Lawyers Am., Ala. Trial Lawyers Assn., Ala. Def. Lawyers Assn., Ala. Bar Assn., Montgomery County Bar Assn. Presbyterian. Avocations: tennis, racquetball. State civil litigation, Federal civil litigation, Insurance. Office: Melton & Espy PO Box 1267 Montgomery AL 36102

JACKSON, MICHELE CHICKERELLA, lawyer; b. Redwood City, Calif., Jan. 17, 1954; d. Joseph Anthony and Enessa (Mandy) Chickerella; m. Warren Bruce Jackson, Aug. 14, 1976. BA with honors, Stanford U., 1976; JD cum laude, U. San Francisco, 1979. Bar: Calif. 1979, U.S. Dist Ct. (no. dist.) Calif. 1979, U.S. Ct. Appeals (9th cir.) 1981, U.S. Dist Ct. (cen. dist.) Calif. 1985. Assoc. Furth, Fahrner, Bluemle and Mason, San Francisco, 1979—. Mem. ABA, San Francisco Bar Assn., San Francisco Barristers Club. Club: San Francisco Barrister's. Avocations: hiking, travel. Antitrust, Federal civil litigation, Unfair trade practices. Office: Furth Fahrner Bluemle and Mason 201 Sansome Suite 1000 San Francisco CA 94104

JACKSON, PAMELA CURULEWSKI, lawyer; b. Munich, Fed. Republic Germany, Dec. 15, 1952; came to U.S., 1953; d. Francis Thomas and Noreen Phyllis Curulewski. BS, Northwestern U., 1975; JD, Loyola U., 1979; LLM in Tax, McGeorge Sch. Law, 1981. Bar: Calif. 1979, U.S. Dist. Ct. (ea. dist.) Calif. 1979, U.S. Tax Ct. 1982, U.S. Dist. Ct. (no. dist.) Calif. 1983, U.S. Ct. Appeals (9th cir.) 1983. Staff cons. Auto Club of So. Calif., Los Angeles, 1975-79; assoc. Whitaker, de Bie & Jackson, Dixon, Calif., 1979-81; ptnr. Debevec, Jackson, Usnick & James Inc., Vacaville, Calif., 1981—. Bd. dirs. Upper Solano Assn. Retarded Citizens, 1986—. Recipient Outstanding Service award Loyola Law Sch. Alumni, 1979, Fundraising award Children's Network Solano County, Fairfield, Calif., 1985. Mem. Calif. Bar Assn., Solano County Bar Assn. (bd. dirs. 1985—), Solano County Women Lawyers (bd. dirs. 1985—). Avocations: showing dogs, bicycling, bridge. Bankruptcy, Real property, Probate. Home: 406 Corte Cadiz Vacaville CA 95688 Office: 479 Mason St Suite 325 Vacaville CA 95688

JACKSON, RANDALL CALVIN, lawyer; b. Baird, Tex., Mar. 21, 1919; s. J. Rupert and Anna C. (Faust) J.; m. Betty J. Jackson, June 18, 1955; 1 son, Randall Calvin. B.B.A., U. Tex., 1941, J.D. 1946. Bar: Tex. 1946. Sole practice, Baird, 1947-49; mem. firm Jackson & Jackson, Baird, 1949-62, Abilene, Tex., 1962-86. Past chmn. legal specialization bd., chmn. dist. trustees Meth. Ch. of Abilene. Fellow Am. Coll. Probate Counsel; mem. State Bar Tex. (bd. legal specialization), ABA, Taylor County Bar Assn. (pres. 1980), Tex. Bar Found. (charter), Am. Judicature Soc., Southwestern Legal Bar Found., Tex. Hereford Assn., (pres. 1982-83), West Tex. Hereford Assn. (pres. 1981-82). Clubs: Masons, Shriners. Estate planning, General practice, FERC practice. Office: 235 Market St Baird TX 79504

JACKSON, REGINALD SHERMAN, JR., lawyer; b. Toledo, Ohio, Oct. 8, 1946; s. Reginald Sherman and Frances (Holland) J.; m. Joanne Marie Warren, Aug. 31, 1968; children—Reginald Sherman III, Michael W., Adam H. BA, Ohio State U., 1968, JD, 1971. Bar: Ohio 1971, U.S. Supreme Ct. 1976. Mem. Fuller, Henry, Hodge & Snyder, Toledo, 1971-76; asst. U.S. atty. no. dist. Ohio, U.S. Dept. Justice, 1976-78; mem. Connelly, Soutar & Jackson, 1978—; adj. prof. trial practice U. Toledo Coll. Law, 1976—. Trustee Toledo Boy's Club, 1981—. Mem. ABA, Ohio Bar Assn., Toledo Bar Assn. (trustee 1978-86, v.p. 1986—). Club: Toledo Country (trustee 1981—). Lodge: Rotary. Federal civil litigation, State civil litigation. Home: 2907 River Rd Maumee OH 43537 Office: Connelly Soutar & Jackson 2100 Ohio Citizens Bank Bldg Toledo OH 43604

JACKSON, RICHARD BROOKE, lawyer; b. Bozeman, Mont., Mar. 5, 1947; s. William T. and Myra (McHugh) J.; m. Elizabeth Ciner, Sept. 19, 1971; children: Jeffrey, Brett, Jennifer. AB magna cum laude, Dartmouth Coll., 1969; JD cum laude, Harvard U., 1972. Bar: Colo. 1972, U.S. Dist. Ct. Colo. 1972, D.C. 1980, U.S. Dist. Ct. D.C. 1980,U.S. Ct. Appeals (10th cir.) 1972, U.S. Ct. Appeals (D.C. cir.) 1980, U.S. Supreme Ct. 1980. Assoc. Holland & Hart, Denver, 1972-78; ptnr. Holland & Hart, Denver and Washington, 1978—; instr. trial practice U. Colo. Law Sch., Boulder, 1984-85, 87, Nat. Inst. Trial Advocacy, 1986. Editor: A Better New Hampshire, 1968. Mem. ABA, Colo. Bar Assn., Denver Bar Assn. Democrat. Avocations: skiing, tennis, reading, travel, fgn. langs. Personal injury, State civil litigation, Federal civil litigation. Home: 5355 W Yellowstone Littleton CO 80123 Office: Holland & Hart 555 17th St Suite 2900 Denver CO 80202

JACKSON, ROBERT HOWARD, lawyer; b. Cleve., Dec. 12, 1936; s. Herman Herbert and Frances (Goldman) J.; m. Donna Lyons, Mar. 22, 1959; children—Karen, Douglas. A.B., U. Ill., 1958; J.D., Case Western Res. U., 1961. Bar: Ohio 1961. Sole practice Cleve., 1961—; fin. trial atty. SEC, Cleve., 1961-66; ptnr. Kohrman Jackson & Krantz, 1969—; lectr. law Case Western Res. Sch. Law, Cleve., 1967-69. Contbr. articles to legal and lit. jours. Mem. ABA (chmn. subcom. proxy solicitations, shareholders proposals, fed. securities com. 1970-73), Fed. Bar Assn. (chmn. Cleve. chpt. fed. securities com. 1972-73), Internat. Bar Assn., Cleve Bar Assn. Club: Rowfant. General corporate, Real property, Administrative and regulatory. Home: 10 Lyman Circle Shaker Heights OH 44122 Office: 20th Floor One Cleveland Ctr 1375 E 9th St Cleveland OH 44114

JACKSON, RONALD JAMES LEONARD, lawyer; b. Chester, Pa., Oct. 10, 1939; s. James Leonard and Emily Marie (Charlton) J.; m. Paulette Frances Grant, Sept. 22, 1978; 1 dau., Afiya Inez Grant Jackson. A.B., U. Pa.-Phila., 1962; J.D. with honors, Georgetown U., 1973. Bar: N.Y. 1974, U.S. Ct. Appeals (2d cir.) 1974, U.S. Dist. Ct. (so. and ea. dists.) N.Y. 1974. Dir. child devel. Delaware County, Chester, Pa., 1966-70; legal intern U.S. Atty.'s Office, U.S. Dist. Ct. (so. dist.) N.Y., N.Y.C., 1973-75; spl. counsel N.Y. Stock Exchange, N.Y.C., 1975-78; asst. gen. counsel C.I.T. Fin., N.Y.C., 1978-79; sole practice, N.Y.C., from 1979; now with Williams, Watts & Watts, Bklyn. Mem. legal redress com. NAACP, Bklyn., 1981—; campaign mgr. Assemblyman Clarence Norman, 1980; chairperson Crown Heights Neighborhood Improvement Assn. Inc., 1982-86. Served with AUS, 1963-65. Mem. N.Y. County Lawyers Assn., Met. Black Bar Assn. Inc. Democrat. Mem. Ecumenical Ch. Securities, Civil rights, Personal injury. Home: 207 Park Pl Apt 3W Brooklyn NY 11238 Office: Williams Watts & Watts 26 Court St Suite 2113 Brooklyn NY 11242

JACKSON, THOMAS GENE, lawyer; b. N.Y.C., Mar. 9, 1949; s. Alan Clark and Clare Seena (Werther) J.; m. Beatrice Lafrance Korab, June 11, 1972; children—Sarah Ann, Alan Edward. A.B. magna cum laude with highest distinction in English, Dartmouth Coll., 1971; J.D., U. Va., 1974. Bar: N.Y. 1975, U.S. Dist. Ct. (so. and ea. dists.) N.Y. 1975, U.S. Ct. Appeals (2d cir.) 1975, U.S. Ct. Appeals (5th cir.) 1978, U.S. Supreme Ct. 1978, U.S. Ct. Appeals (D.C. cir.) 1986. Editor, The Research Group, Charlottesville, Va., 1973-74; assoc. Phillips, Nizer, Benjamin, Krim & Ballon, N.Y.C., 1974-82, ptnr., 1982—. Mem. Village of Irvington Cable TV adv. com., N.Y., 1979—; sec. Village of Irvington Environ. Conservation Bd., 1983—; mem. Dartmouth Coll. Alumni Council, 1986—. Mem. ABA (premerger notification subcom. of Sect. 7, com. of sect. on antitrust 1982—), Assn. Bar City N.Y., Dartmouth Coll. Class Secs. Assn. (v.p. 1984-85, pres. 1985-86), Dartmouth Coll. Alumni Council. Democrat. Jewish. Club: Dartmouth of Westchester (sec. 1984-87, pres. 1987—). Federal civil litigation, Antitrust, Securities. Home: 32 Hamilton Rd Irvington NY 10533-2311 Office: Phillips Nizer Benjamin Krim & Ballon 40 W 57th St New York NY 10019

JACKSON, THOMAS HALLER, JR., lawyer; b. Shreveport, La., Jan. 7, 1924; s. Thomas Haller and Helen Marian (Hutchinson) J.; m. Hudlah Holladay Edens, Dec. 28, 1946 (dec. Mar. 1965); children: Louise R., Thomas Haller III, Robert H.; m. Ruth Grey Knighton, June 6, 1967 (dec. Apr. 1973); 1 child Thomas G.; m. Jeanne Gray, June 10, 1975. JD, Washington and Lee U., 1948; M in Civil Law, Tulane U., 1949. Bar: La. 1949, U.S. Ct. Appeals (5th cir.) 1949, U.S. Supreme Ct. 1960, U.S. Tax Ct. 1965. Sole practice Shreveport, 1949-52; ptnr. Tucker, Jeter & Jackson and predecessor firms, Shreveport, 1952—; council La. State Law Inst. 1950—, pres., 1982-84; bd. dirs. Home Fed. Savs. and Loan Assn. Bd. dirs. Caddo Parish Sch. 1960-72, pres. 1969-70; mem. Selective Service Bd. Appeals We. Dist. La. Served to capt. C.E. AUS, 1943-46. Decorated Bronze Star. Fellow ABA; mem. La. State Bar Assn. (chmn. jr. bar 1956), Shreveport Bar Assn. (pres. 1962). Methodist. Club: Shreveport. General practice. Office: Tucker Jeter & Jackson 905 Louisiana Tower 401 Edwards St Shreveport LA 71101

JACKSON, THOMAS HUMPHREY, legal educator; b. Kalamazoo, Mich., June 20, 1950; s. William Humphrey and Louise Longstreth (Cone) J.; m. Bonnie Eileen Gelb, Aug. 16, 1981. B.A., Williams Coll., Mass., 1972; J.D., Yale U., 1975. Bar: N.Y. 1976, Calif. 1979, U.S. Dist. Ct. (no. dist.) Calif. 1979, U.S. Supreme Ct. 1985. Law clk. Justice William Rehnquist, U.S. Supreme Ct., 1976-77; asst. prof. law Stanford U. Law Sch., Calif., 1977-79, prof., 1981-86; prof., Harvard University, Cambridge, MA. 1986—. assoc. Heller, Ehrman, White & McAuliffe, San Francisco, 1979-81. Co-author: (with Baird) Cases, Problems and Materials on Security Interests in Personal Property, 1984, Cases, Problems and Materials on Bankruptcy, 1985. Bankruptcy, Contracts commercial. Office: Harvard University Law School Cambridge MA 02138 *

JACKSON, THOMAS PENFIELD, judge; b. Washington, Jan. 10, 1937; s. Thomas Searing and May Elizabeth (Jacobs) J.; m. Jean FitzGerald, Sept. 12, 1959; children—Leila T., Sarah M.; m. Carolyn Gardiner, Feb. 6, 1982. A.B. in Govt., Dartmouth Coll., 1958; LL.B., Harvard U., 1964. Bar: D.C., Md., U.S. Supreme Ct. 1970. Assoc., ptnr. Jackson & Campbell, P.C., Washington, 1964-82; U.S. dist. judge U.S. Dist. Ct. D.C., Washington, 1982—. Vestryman All Saints' Episcopal Ch., Washington, 1969-75; trustee Gallaudet Univ., Washington. Served to lt. (j.g.) USN, 1958-61. Fellow Am. Coll. Trial Lawyers; mem. ABA, Bar Assn. D.C. (pres. 1982-83). Republican. Clubs: Chevy Chase, Metropolitan, Capitol Hill, Lawyers', Barristers. Lodge: Rotary. Home: 5 Cathedral St Annapolis MD 21401 Office: US Dist Ct 3d and Constitution Ave NW Washington DC 20001

JACKSON, WILLIAM ELDRED, lawyer; b. Jamestown, N.Y., July 19, 1919; s. Robert Houghwout and Irene Alice (Gerhart) J.; m. Nancy Dabney Roosevelt, Sept. 24, 1944; children—Miranda, Melissa, Melanie, Melinda, Marina. B.A., Yale U., 1941; LL.B., Harvard U., 1944. Bar: N.Y. bar 1944, U.S. Supreme Ct. bar 1952, D.C. bar 1960. Asso. firm Milbank, Tweed, Hadley & McCloy, N.Y.C., 1947-54; partner Milbank, Tweed, Hadley & McCloy, 1954—. Served to lt. (j.g.) USNR, 1944-46. Mem. Am. Coll. Trial Lawyers, Am. Soc. Internat. Law, Assn. Bar City N.Y. (sec. 1953-54), N.Y. State Bar Assn., Am. Bar Assn., Fed. Bar Council, Am. Judicature Soc., Council Fgn. Relations. Democrat. Episcopalian. Clubs: Century, Downtown, Pilgrims, River. On staff Nuremburg trial. Antitrust, Federal civil litigation, Private international. Home: 530 E 87th St New York NY 10128 Office: One Chase Manhattan Plaza New York NY 10005

JACKSON, WILLIAM PAUL, JR., lawyer; b. Bexar, Ala., July 7, 1938; s. William Paul and Evelyn Mabel (Goggans) J.; m. Barbara Anne Seignious, Sept. 30, 1966; children: Jennifer Anne, Susan Barrett, William Paul III. B.S. in Physics, U. Ala., 1960, J.D., 1963. Bar: Ala. 1963, D.C. 1969, Va. 1975; amateur radio operator. Law clk. to judge Ala. Ct. Appeals, Montgomery, 1965; assoc. Bishop and Carlton, Birmingham, Ala., 1965-68, Todd, Dillon and Sullivan, Washington, 1968-70; founding ptnr. Jackson & Jessup, Washington and Arlington, Va., 1970-76; pres., sr. atty. Jackson & Jessup, P.C., Washington and Arlington, Va., 1976—; advisor Oren Harris chair of transp. U. Ark., 1974—. Comments editor U. Ala. Law Rev., 1962, leading articles editor, 1963; conbtr. articles to legal jours. Vice pres. McLean Hunt Homeowners Assn., Va., 1974, pres., 1975-76; bd. dirs. McLean Citizens' Assn., 1976-78; pres. McLean Legal Action Fund, Inc., 1977-81; session mem. Lewinsville Presbyn. Ch., 1981-84. Served to 1st lt. Signal Corps U.S. Army, 1963-65. Recipient Pub. Service awards Am. Radio Relay League, 1958; recipient merit award Armed Forces Communications and Electronics Assn., 1963; Sigma Delta Kappa scholar, 1963. Mem. ABA, Arlington Bar Assn., Fed. Bar Assn., Fed. Communications Bar Assn., Ala. State Bar, Va. State Bar, D.C. Bar, Va. Bar Assn., Bar Assn. D.C., Transp. Lawyers Assn. (com. on govtl. relations), Assn. Transp. Practitioners (legis. com.), Am. Judicature Soc., So. Transp. League (exec. dir. 1970—), Eastern Indsl. Traffic League (exec. sec. 1978—), Bench and Bar. Presbyterian (elder). Administrative and regulatory, General corporate, Legislative. Home: 7807 Foxhound Rd McLean VA 22102 Office: Jackson & Jessup PC 3426 N Washington Blvd PO Box 1240 Arlington VA 22210

JACKSON-GILLISON, HELEN LUCILLE, lawyer; b. Colliers, W.Va., July 9, 1944; d. George William and Helen Loretta (Wells) Jackson; m. Edward Lee Gillison Sr.; 1 child, Edward Lee II. BS cum laude, West Liberty State Coll., 1977; JD, W.Va. U., 1981. Bar: W.Va. 1981, U.S. Dist. Ct. (so. and no. dists.) W.Va. 1981. Sole practice Weirton, W.Va., 1981—. Mem. adv. bd. Blot Out Litter Today, Inc. Clean Community System, Weirton; with office of sec. W.Va. Northern Community Coll., 1983—, adv. council friends of coll., 1983—, bd. dirs. 1983—; bd. dirs. W.Va. Civil Liberties Union, ARC, Weirton, Sheltered Workshop of W.Va., Hancock County, Housing Authority, Weirton, Ft. Steuben council Boy Scouts Am. Recipient Black Atty. Yr. award BALSA W.Va. Coll. Law, 1986. Mem.

ABA, Assn. Trial Lawyers Am., Mountain State Bar Assn., Nat. Bar Assn., Hancock Bar Assn., W.Va. Trial Lawyers Assn. (bd. govs. 1986—, pub. relations com.), W.Va. Bar Assn. (bd. govs. 1986—, various coms.), Weirton Bus. and Profl. Women's Club (chmn. polit. action com. 1982-83), Assn. Community Coll. Trustees (assoc.), NAACP (bd. dirs. Steubenville chpt. 1982-84), Million Dollar Club, Phi Alpha Delta. Democrat. Baptist. Avocations: reading, writing. Personal injury, Insurance, Family and matrimonial. Home: 264 Lakeview Dr Weirton WV 26062 Office: 3139 West St Weirton WV 26062

JACOB, BRUCE ROBERT, legal education administrator; b. Chgo., Mar. 26, 1935; s. Edward Carl and Elsie Berthe (Hartmann) J.; m. Ann Wear, Sept. 8, 1962; children—Bruce Ledley, Lee Ann, Brian Edward. B.A., Fla. State U., 1957; J.D., Stetson U., 1959; LL.M., Northwestern U., 1965; S.J.D., Harvard U., 1980. Bar: Fla. 1959, Ill. 1965, Mass. 1970, Ohio 1972. Asst. atty. gen. State of Fla., 1960-62; assoc. Holland, Bevis & Smith, Bartow, Fla., 1962-64; asst. to assoc. prof. Emory U. Sch. Law, 1965-69; research assoc. Ctr. for Criminal Justice, Harvard Law Sch., 1969-70; staff atty. Community Legal Assistance Office, Cambridge, Mass., 1970-71; assoc. prof. Coll. Law, Ohio State U., 1971-73, prof., dir. clin. programs, 1973-78; dean, prof. Mercer U. Law Sch., Macon, Ga., 1978-81; v.p., dean, prof. Stetson U. Coll. Law, St. Petersburg, Fla., 1981—. Contbr. articles to profl. jours. Mem. Fla. Bar. Democrat. Club: Rotary. Legal education, Criminal, Civil rights. Address: 1800 North Shore Dr Saint Petersburg FL 33704

JACOB, EDWIN J., lawyer; b. Detroit, Aug. 25, 1927; s. A. Aubrey and Estelle R. (Vesell) J.; m. Constance Dorfman, June 15, 1948; children—Louise B., Beth D., Ellen P. A.B. cum laude, Harvard U., 1948, J.D. cum laude, 1951. Bar: N.Y. 1951, U.S. Dist. Ct. (so. dist.) N.Y. 1953, U.S. Dist. Ct. (ea. dist.) N.Y. 1953, U.S. Ct. Appeals (2d cir.) 1954, U.S. Supreme Ct. 1963, U.S. Ct. Appeals (8th cir.) 1981, U.S. Ct. Appeals (10th cir.) 1987. Assoc. Davis Polk Wardwell, Sunderland & Kiendl, N.Y.C., 1951-62; ptnr. Cabell, Medinger, Forsyth & Decker, N.Y.C., 1962-69, Lauterstein & Lauterstein, N.Y.C., 1969-72, Jacob, Medinger, & Finnegan, N.Y.C., 1973—. Contbr. articles to profl. jours. Served with USN, 1945-46. Mem. Am. Law Inst., Am. Judicature Soc., Assn. Bar City N.Y. Club: Harvard of N.Y.C. Federal civil litigation, State civil litigation. Home: 1 W 72d St New York NY 10023 Office: Jacob Medinger & Finnegan 1270 Ave of Americas New York NY 10020

JACOB, MARK CRAIG, lawyer; b. Phila., June 5, 1951; s. Winston Jack and Carol Theresa (Riff) J.; m. Karen Joy Kesluk, May 20, 1972; children: Michael, Pamela, Marni. BA, Temple U., 1972, JD, 1976. Bar: Pa. 1976, U.S. Dist. Ct. (ea. dist.) Pa. 1977. Law clk. Temple U. Legal Aid, Phila., 1974-76; assoc. Monheit & Mammuth, Phila., 1977, David A. Silverstein, Phila., 1977-79, Arthur Wolk Assocs., Phila., 1979-81; ptnr. Wolk & Jacob, Phila., 1981-82; sole practice Phila., 1982—. Recipient Dinsting. Service award legal Aid Soc., 1976. Mem. ABA, Pa. Bar Assn., Pa. Trial Lawyers Assn., Phila. Bar Assn., Phila. Trial Lawyers Assn., Law Pac. Democrat. Jewish. General practice, State civil litigation, Federal civil litigation. Office: 1201 Chestnut St 2d Floor Philadelphia PA 19107

JACOBELLIS, MIKE, lawyer; b. Huntington Station, N.Y., Jan. 19, 1955; s. Nicholas Joseph and Phyllis (Evancie) J.; m. Amy Joanna Greer, June 10, 1978; children—Michael Greer, Joanna Marie, George Michael. B.A., Cornell U., 1977; J.D., St. John U., Jamaica, N.Y., 1980. Bar: N.Y. 1981, Tex. 1981, U.S. Dist. Ct. (ea. dist.) Tex. 1981, U.S. Ct. Appeals (5th cir.) 1984. Law clk. to judge U.S. Dist. Ct. (ea. dist.) Tex., Beaumont, 1980-82; ptnr. Tonahill, Hile, Leister & Jacobellis, Beaumont, 1982—. Editor, St. John's Law Rev. Mem. Assn. Trial Lawyers Am., Tex. Trial Lawyers Assn., Southeast Tex. Trial Lawyers Assn. (bd. dirs.), Jefferson County Bar Assn. Personal injury, Workers' compensation, Federal civil litigation. Home: 6090 Longwood Ln Beaumont TX 77707 Office: Tonahill Hile Leister & Jacobellis PO Box 9807 Beaumont TX 77704

JACOBO, PAULINA MORENO, lawyer; b. Mexico, Sept. 19, 1946; came to U.S., 1948; d. Simon Hilario and Cristina (Moreno) J.; m. Robin Morris Green, Jan. 7, 1983. B.A., Tex. Tech. U., 1968, M.A., 1975; J.D., U. Calif.-San Francisco, 1973. Bar: Tex. 1973, U.S. Dist. Ct. (no. and ea. dists.) Tex. 1974, U.S. Ct. Appeals (5th cir.) 1975. Asst. regional atty. HEW, Dallas, 1973-78; asst. dist. atty., Lubbock, Tex., 1979-80; asst. U.S. atty. Dept. Justice, Lubbock, 1980-85; assoc. Galey & Assocs., 1985—; task force mem. Lau v. Nichols, HEW, Dallas, Washington, 1974-75, Indian Task Force, Dallas, also Washington, 1974-78. Mem. Concerned Citizens Crime Com., 1979—, Women's Interface Network, 1980—; bd. dirs. Cath. Family Service, 1981—, Legal Aid of Lubbock, 1983—, United Way Lubbock, 1984—; bd. dirs., pres. bd. Lubbock Day Care Assn., 1981—; mem. steering com., task force Com. for Women, 1983—; mem. steering com. Leadership Lubbock, Lubbock C. of C., 1983—; mem. steering com., exec. com. Double T Connection, Tex. Tech. U., 1984—. Hiram Parks scholar Tex. Tech. U., 1965-68, Fulbright scholar U. Madrid, 1968-70, Tex. Tech. U. fellow, 1969-70, John Hay Whitney Found. scholar, 1970-71, Mexican-Am. Legal Def. and Ednl. Fund scholar, 1972-73. Mem. LWV, Hispanic Assn. Women, State Bar Tex., Lubbock County Bar Assn. Democrat. Roman Catholic. Administrative and regulatory, Federal civil litigation, Criminal. Office: PO Box 2691 Lubbock TX 79408

JACOBO, WINSTON WENDLE, lawyer, agricultural reorganization consultant; b. Honolulu, Apr. 4, 1945; s. Primo M. and Julia (Rodriguez) Thomas J.; m. Deloris Greene, Apr. 10, 1976; children—Nicole, Primo M. B.A. in English, Jacksonville U., 1971; J.D., U. Fla., 1973. Bar: Fla. 1973, U.S. Dist. Ct. (mid. and no. dists.) Fla. 1977, U.S. Dist. Ct. (mid. dist.) Ga. 1979, U.S. Ct. Appeals (5th and 11th cirs.) 1978, U.S. Supreme Ct. 1979; diplomate Ct. Practice Inst. Asst. Pub. defender 3d Jud. Circuit, Lake City, Fla., 1975-77; assoc. Airth, Sellers & Lewis, Live Oak, Fla., 1977-78; agrl. cons., Crystal River, Leesburg, Clearwater, Fla., 1978-84; sole practice, Fruitland Park, Fla., 1984—. Served with USAF, 1963-67. Mem. Acad. Fla. Trial Lawyers, Assn. Trial Lawyers Am., ABA. Democrat. Methodist. Agricultural reorganization consultant, Federal civil litigation, State civil litigation. Home: 409 S Dixie Ave Fruitland Park FL 32731

JACOBOWITZ, HAROLD SAUL, lawyer; b. N.Y.C., Aug. 26, 1950; s. William and Miriam (Spector) J.; m. Estrella B. Rivera, Oct. 26, 1972. BA, CUNY, 1972; JD, Rutgers U., 1977. Bar: N.Y. 1977, U.S. Dist. Ct. (so. dist.) N.Y. 1978, U.S. Dist. Ct. (ea. dist.) N.Y. 1978. Assoc. Goldman & Heffernan, N.Y.C., 1977-78, Zola & Zola, N.Y.C., 1978-79, Goldberg & Lysaght, N.Y.C., 1979-82; atty. of record Am. Internat. Group (Jacobowitz & Lysaght), N.Y.C., 1982—. Mem. ABA, N.Y. State Bar Assn., Assn. Bar City N.Y., N.Y. County Lawyers Assn., N.Y. State Trial Lawyers Assn. Personal injury, Insurance, State civil litigation. Office: Jacobowitz & Lysaght 80 Maiden Ln New York NY 10038

JACOBS, ALAN, lawyer; b. Balt., Jan. 7, 1947; s. Jerome and Mildred (Carlin) J.; m. Paula Ference Kaiser, May 16, 1979; children: Mark, Michelle, Jeremy. BS, U. Md., 1969; JD, U. Balt., 1975. Bar: Calif. 1977, D.C. 1978; CPA, Md., Calif. Sr. br. acct. SEC, Washington, 1972-76; mem. Zipser, Heller et al, Los Angeles, 1976-79; gen. counsel House of Fabrics, Inc., Van Nuys, Calif., 1979-80; v.p., sec., gen. counsel ICN Pharms., Inc., Covina, Calif., 1980-81; mem. Finley, Kumble et al, Los Angeles, 1981-83, Jones, Day, Reavis & Pogue, Los Angeles, 1983—; adj. prof. Southwestern U. Sch. of Law, 1985-86; dir. COMBANCORP. Vice chmn. fin. com. Yes on Proposition 15, Los Angeles, 1982. Served with USAR, 1969-75. Mem. ABA, Am. Inst. CPA's. Home: 29022 Garden Oaks Ct Agoura Hills CA 91301 Office: Jones Day Reavis & Pogue 355 S Grand Ave Suite 3000 Los Angeles CA 90071

JACOBS, ANDREW ROBERT, lawyer; b. Newark, Sept. 18, 1946; s. Seymour B. and Pearle (Flaschen) J.; m. Yardana Steinberg, July 10, 1976; 1 child, Suzanne Michal. BA with high honors, Rutgers U., 1968; JD, Columbia U., 1971. Bar: N.J. 1971, U.S. Dist. Ct. N.J. 1971, U.S. Ct. of Appeals (3rd cir.) 1974, U.S. Ct. Appeals (D.C. cir.) 1976, U.S. Supreme Ct. 1979, U.S. Dist. Ct. (ea. and so. Dists.) N.Y. 1980, N.Y. 1980, Pa. 1981, U.S. Ct. Appeals (2nd cir.) 1981, U.S. Claims Ct. 1986. Law clk. to chief judge U.S. Dist. Ct., Newark, 1971-72; asst. U.S. atty. U.S. Atty.'s Office, Newark, 1972-76; assoc. Cole Berman & Belsky, Rochelle Park, N.J., 1976; assoc. Lanigan O'Connell Jacobs & Chazin, Basking Ridge, N.J. and N.Y.C., 1977, ptnr., 1979-82; asst. U.S. atty., chief spl. pros., dep. chief criminal div. U.S. Atty.'s Office (ea. dist.), N.Y., 1983-85; ptnr. Horowitz & Jacobs, Hackensack, N.J. and N.Y.C., 1985—; faculty Practicing Law Inst., N.Y.C., 1980-82; legal writing instr. N.Y. Law Sch., 1981-82. Bd. dirs. N.J. YM-YWHA Camps, Fairfield, N.J. and Milford Pa., 1985; trustee Congregation Shomrei Emunah, Montclair, N.J., 1985—. Served to capt. U.S. Army, 1977. Harlan Fisher Stone scholar; recipient U.S. Dept. Justice Spl. commendation award, 1973,75. Mem. ABA, N.J. State Bar Assn., N.Y. County Lawyers Assn., Assn. Trial Lawyers Am., Assn. Criminal Def. Lawyers N.J., Bergen County Bar Assn., Essex County Bar Assn., Fed. Bar Council, Assn. the Fed. Bar N.J. Criminal, Federal civil litigation, State civil litigation. Home: 87 Lloyd Rd Montclair NJ 07042 Office: Horowitz & Jacobs 32 Mercer St Hackensack NJ 07601 also: 140 Cedar St Suite 2320 New York NY 10006

JACOBS, ANN ELIZABETH, lawyer; b. Lima, Ohio, July 28, 1950; d. Warren Charles and Virginia Elizabeth (Lewis) J. BA, George Washington U., 1972; JD, Cath. U., 1976. Bar: Ohio 1977, Calif. 1977, U.S. Ct. Appeals (D.C. cir.) 1980, U.S. Dist. Ct. (no. dist.) Ohio 1982. Asst. atty. gen. State of Ohio, Columbus, 1977-78; trial atty. EEOC of Ohio, Miami, Fla., 1978-80; sole practice Lima, 1980—. Chairperson, fundraiser for Lima Symphony Orch., 1985; v.p., bd. dirs. Ottawa Valley Ctr., Lima, 1986; bd. dirs. Allen County Mental Health Assn., Lima, 1987—. Recipient Recognition award US Naval Air Sta., Jacksonville, Fla., 1979. Mem. Ohio Bar Assn., Calif. Bar Assn., D.C. Bar Assn., Allen County Bar Assn., LWV, YWCA. Avocations: sailing, tennis, reading. Personal injury, Bankruptcy, Family and matrimonial. Home: Greentree Circle Apt 13 Cridersville OH 45806 Office: 558 W Spring St Lima OH 45801

JACOBS, ARNOLD STEPHEN, lawyer; b. N.Y.C., Feb. 26, 1940; s. Charles E. and Harriet (Flug) J.; m. Ellen Margaret Kheel, June 10, 1962; children: Beryl Kheel, Arnold Stephen Jr. BME, Cornell U., 1961, MBA, 1963, JD, 1964. Bar: N.Y. 1964. Assoc. Hughes, Hubbard & Reed, N.Y.C., 1964-65, 1967-71; ptnr. Shea & Gould, N.Y.C., 1971—; adj. prof. law N.Y. Law Sch.; bd. dirs. Signal Apparel Co., Chattanooga, Graphic Scanning Corp., Teaneck, N.J. Author: The Impact of Rule 10b-5 (3 vols.), 1974, Litigation and Practice Under Rule 10b-5 (5 vols.), 1986, Manual of Corporate Forms for Securities Practice (2 vols.), 1986, Opinion Letters In Securities Matters: Text-Clauses-Law (2 vols.), 1986, Manual of Corporate Forms for Securities Practice, 1987; contbr. articles to profl. jours. Served to capt. U.S. Army, 1965-67. Mem. ABA, N.Y. State Bar Assn., Assn. of Bar of City of N.Y. (chmn. securities regulation com. 1982-86). Club: Harmonie (N.Y.C.). General corporate, Securities. Home: 108 E 82d St Apt 7A New York NY 10028 Office: Shea & Gould 330 Madison Ave New York NY 10017

JACOBS, GREGORY ALEXANDER, lawyer; b. Bilwaskarma, Nicaragua, Mar. 10, 1952; came to U.S., 1952; s. Solomon Napoleon and Lynette Gwenelda (Henry) J.; m. Beverly Faye Canzater, Sept. 30, 1978; children: Charlotte, Stephanie. AB, Princeton U., 1974; JD, Columbia U., 1977. Bar: Ohio 1977, U.S. Dist. Ct. (no. dist.) Ohio 1977, U.S. Ct. Appeals (6th cir.) 1984. Assoc. Thompson, Hine and Flory, Cleve., 1977-85, ptnr., 1985—; sec., bd. dirs. Durrah Corp., Brooklyn Heights, Ohio, 1982—. Mem. allocations panel United Way, Cleve., 1985—; vestry Emmanuel Episc. Ch., Cleve., 1985—; trustee Shaker Youth Ctr., Shaker Heights, Ohio, Inst. for Creative Living, Cleveland Heights, Ohio. Mem. ABA, Fed. Bar Assn., Cleve. Bar Assn., Princeton Alumni Assn. (Cleveland v.p. 1982-86). Democrat. Episcopalian. Avocations: black history and literature, softball, volleyball, basketball. Labor. Home: 3330 Elsmere Rd Shaker Heights OH 44120 Office: Thompson Hine and Flory 1100 Nat City Bank Bldg Cleveland OH 44114

JACOBS, GREGORY R., lawyer; b. N.Y.C., Mar. 19, 1948; s. Morton Maurice and Adele (Engelson) J.; m. June Aziza Khani, Sept. 12, 1970 (div. Nov. 1981); m. Patrice Elaine Taylor, Dec. 28, 1981; children: Rochelle, Jessica Lynn. BS in Pharmacy, Bklyn. Coll. of Pharmacy, 1969; JD, Del. Law Sch., 1977. Bar: N.Y. 1978, Fla. 1978, N.J. 1979, U.S. Dist. Ct. N.J. 1979, Tex. 1980, U.S. Dist. Ct. (no. dist.) Tex. 1980. Supervising pharmacist Hampton Pharmacy, N.Y.C., 1970-77; staff counsel Block Drug Co., Jersey City, 1977-79; atty. Frito-Lay, Inc. subs. PepsiCo, Inc., Dallas, 1979-81; ptnr. Galloway & Jacobs, Dallas, 1981-84; assoc. G.A. Schmidt, P.C., Dallas, 1984-86; sole practice Dallas, 1986—. Assoc. editor Del. Jour. of Corp. Law, Wilmington, 1976. N.Y. State Conservative Party candidate U.S. Ho. of Reps., 1972, N.Y. State Sen., 1974; Rep. Party candidate for N.Y. State Sen., 1976. Served with USAR, 1969—. Republican. Jewish. Lodge: Pentagon Masons (32 degree) (chaplain 1983-85, jr. deacon 1982). Avocations: militaria, weaponry, target shooting. Real property, Public international, Entertainment. Office: 8222 Douglas Suite 800 Dallas TX 75225

JACOBS, JACK BERNARD, judge; b. Houston, July 23, 1942; s. Louis K. and Phoebe J.; m. Marion Antiles, Apr. 2, 1967; 1 son, Andrew Seth. A.B., U. Chgo., 1964; LL.B., Harvard U., 1967. Bar: Del. 1968, U.S. Dist. Ct. Del. 1968, U.S. Ct. Appeals (3d cir.) 1968, U.S. Supreme Ct. 1975. Law clk. Del. Chancery and Superior Cts., 1967-68; assoc. Young, Conaway, Stargatt & Taylor, Wilmington, Del., 1968-71, ptnr., 1971-85, vice chancellor, Ct. of Chancery State of Del., 1985— ; mem. faculty Continuing Legal Edn. Programs, ALI-ABA and Del. Law Sch., Widener U. Vice chmn. Nat. Jewish Community Relations Adv. Council, 1981-89; bd. dirs. Jewish Fedn. Del., Milton & Hattie Kutz Home. Mem. Del. Bar Assn. (corp. law com. 1973—, chmn. program com. 1980-81), ABA (litigation sect., bus., corp. and banking sect.), Phi Beta Kappa. Democrat. Jewish. . Contbr. articles to profl. jours. General corporate, Contracts commercial. Home: 28 Beethoven Dr Wilmington DE 19807 Office: Vice Chancellor Ct of Chancery 1000 King St Public Bldg Wilmington DE 19801

JACOBS, JAMES ETHAN, lawyer; b. Lima, Ohio, May 2, 1940; s. Oscar Raymond and Florine (Baransy) J.; m. Nancy Lee Lutman, June 29, 1963; children: Eric Raymond, Christine. AB, Harvard U., 1962; JD with honors, U. Mich., 1965; postgrad., Universitaet Tuebingen, Fed. Republic Germany, 1965-66. Bar: Ill. 1966, U.S. Dist. Ct. (no. dist.) Ill. 1967, U.S. Supreme Ct. 1972, Calif. 1973. Assoc. Kirkland & Ellis, Chgo., 1966-72; gen. counsel Sierra Pacific Industries Inc., Walnut Creek, Calif., 1972-74; v.p. law Fiat-Allis N.Am. Inc., Deerfield, Ill., 1974-82; counsel FMC Corp., Chgo., 1982-87, assoc. gen. counsel, 1987—. Mem. Calif. Bar Assn., North Suburban Bar Assn., Am. Corp. Counsel Assn. Clubs: Plaza, Harvard (Chgo.). Private international, Contracts commercial, General corporate. Home: 120 Church Rd Winnetka IL 60093 Office: FMC Corp 200 E Randolph Dr Chicago IL 60601

JACOBS, JOSEPH JAMES, lawyer, communications company executive; b. Toronto, Ont., Can., Mar. 18, 1925; came to U.S., 1925; s. Sidney and Hildred Veronica (Greenberg) J.; m. Carole Evelyn Bent, Jan. 22, 1946 (div. 1972); children—Carole Lynn Urgenson, Joseph James III; m. Edna Mae Meincke, Jan. 5, 1973. J.D., Tulane U., 1950. Bar: La. 1950, N.Y. 1951, U.S. Dist. Ct. (so. dist.) N.Y. 1953, U.S. Ct. Mil. Appeals 1953, U.S. Ct. Appeals (2d cir.) 1977, U.S. Ct. Appeals (D.C. cir.) 1980. Assoc. Proskauer, Rose, Goetz & Mendelsohn, N.Y.C., 1950-53; asst. gen. counsel, asst. to pres. Am. Broadcasting Co., N.Y.C., 1954-60; gen. atty. Metromedia, Inc., N.Y.C., 1960-61; dir. program and talent negotiations United Artists TV, Inc., 1961-66; atty. United Artists Corp., N.Y.C., 1966-69; v.p., counsel United Artists Broadcasting, Inc., N.Y.C., 1969-71; gen. atty. ITT World Communications Inc., N.Y.C., 1972-74; v.p., legal dir. ITT Communications Ops. and Info. Services Group (formerly U.S. Telephone & Telegraph Corp.), N.Y.C. and Secaucus, N.J., 1974-83, ITT Communications and Info. Services, Inc., Secaucus, 1983—; v.p., gen. counsel U.S. Transmission Systems, Inc., Secaucus, 1984—, ITT World Communications Inc., Secaucus, 1984—. Bd. editors Tulane Law Rev., 1949, asst. editor-in-chief, 1950. Served with parachute inf. U.S. Army, 1943-46, ETO, PTO, to maj. USAFR ret. Mem. Assn. Bar City of N.Y., Fed. Bar Assn., Order of Coif. Republican. Jewish. Administrative and regulatory, General corporate, Entertainment. Home: 572 Sanderling Ct Secaucus NJ 07094 Office: ITT Communications Services Inc 100 Plaza Dr Secaucus NJ 07094

JACOBS, JULIAN I., federal judge; b. Balt., Aug. 13, 1937; s. Sidney and Bernice (Kellman) J.; children—Richard S., Jennifer K. B.A., U. Md., 1958, J.D., 1960; LL.M., Georgetown U., 1965. Bar: Md., 1960. Atty. chief counsel's office IRS, Washington, 1961-65; trial atty. regional counsel's office IRS, Buffalo, 1965-67; assoc. Weinberg & Green, Balt., 1967-69, Hoffberger & Hollander, Balt., 1969-72; assoc. Gordon Feinblatt Rothman Hoffberger & Hollander, Balt., 1972-74, ptnr., 1974-84; judge U.S. Tax Ct., Washington, 1984—; chmn. Md. Tax Ct. Study Commn., 1978-79; mem. spl. study group Md. Gen. Assembly, 1980; mem. rules com. Md. Tax Ct., 1980; lectr. Mem. U. Md. Law Rev. Bd. dirs. Md. Med. Research Inst., Inc. Mem. Md. State Bar Assn. (past chmn. sect. taxation), Balt. City Bar Assn. (past chmn. tax legis. subcom.), ABA. Judicial administration, Jurisprudence. Office: US Tax Ct 400 2d St Washington DC 20217

JACOBS, LEEDIA GORDEEV, lawyer; b. Vienna, Austria, Jan. 22, 1944; came to U.S., 1951; d. Volodimir Gordeev and Nadia (Bobrova) Gordeev-Hyczar; m. Ralph Raymond Jacobs, June 5, 1966; children: Aleda Anne, Liana Lizabeth. BA in Hist., NYU, 1965; MA in Am. Hist., So. Conn. State Coll., 1977; JD, U. Santa Clara, 1980. Bar: Calif. 1980, U.S. Dist. Ct. (no. dist.) Calif. 1980. Asst. mgr. radio and TV Grey Advt., N.Y.C., 1965-66; mgr. talent dept. Kenyon & Ekhardt, N.Y.C., 1966-67; mem. pub. relations and project execution depts. New Haven (Conn.) Redevel. Agy., 1967-69; v.p., counsel Bank of Calif., San Francisco, 1981—; v.p., corp. sec. Bank of Calif. N.Y. Trust Co., N.Y.C., 1984-86. Articles editor U. Santa Clara Law Rev. Mem. ABA, Calif. Bar Assn., San Francisco Bar Assn., Am. Soc. Corp. Secs., Dealer Bank Assn. (lawyers com.), SCRIBES, League Women Voters (treas. 1970). Avocations: music, art. General corporate, Probate, Securities. Home: 47180 Zapotec Dr Fremont CA 94539 Office: Bank of Calif 400 California St San Francisco CA 94104

JACOBS, LESLIE WILLIAM, lawyer; b. Akron, Ohio, Dec. 5, 1944; s. Leslie Wilson and Louise Frances (Walker) J.; m. Laurie Hutchinson, July 12, 1962; children—Leslie James, Andrew Wilson, Walker Fulton. Student, Denison U., 1962-63; B.S., Northwestern U., 1965; J.D., Harvard U., 1968. Bar: Ohio 1968, D.C. 1980, U.S. Supreme Ct. 1971. Law clk. to Chief Justice Kingsley A. Taft Ohio Supreme Ct., 1968-69; assoc. Thompson, Hine and Flory, Cleve., 1969-76, ptnr., 1976—; lectr. Ohio Legal Ctr. Insts., Ohio State Bar Assn. Antitrust and Corp. Csl. Insts., Fed. Bar Assn., ABA. Contbr. articles to profl. jours. Pres. Juvenile Fund, 1978-80, 81-85; chmn. Citizens Adv. Bd. Cuyahoga County Juvenile Ct., 1978-81; trustee Citizens League Greater Cleve., 1972-78, Clev. Ctr. Econ. Edn., 1983—; mem. vis. com. Case Western Res. U. Sch. Law, 1985—, Ho. of Dels., 1986—. Served to lt. comdr. USNR, 1967-79. Fellow Am. Bar Found., Ohio State Bar Found. (trustee 1985-87); mem. ABA (ho. dels. 1986—, antitrust law sect., council 1985—), Ohio State Bar Assn. (pres. 1986-87), Bar Assn. Greater Cleve. (chmn. jud. selection com. 1982, trustee 1983-85), Am. Law Inst., Nat. Conf. Bar (pres. 1985—), Ohio State Legal Services Assn. (trustee 1985—). Republican. Presbyterian. Clubs: Internat. (Washington); Harvard (N.Y.C.); Chagrin Valley Hunt (Gates Mills, Ohio). Antitrust, Administrative and regulatory, Private international. Office: Thompson Hine and Flory 1100 National City Bank Bldg Cleveland OH 44114

JACOBS, PAUL ELLIOT, lawyer; b. Sioux City, Iowa, Feb. 11, 1946; s. Leonard D. and Ruth (Jelenk) J.; m. Renee M. Glennon, Mar. 4, 1972; children—Sarah, Andrew, Ian. B.A., Northwestern U., 1968; J.D., Santa Clara U., 1971. Bar: Calif. 1972. Dep. dist. atty. Santa Clara County Dist. Atty., San Jose, Calif., 1972-76; ptnr. Beauzay, Hammer, Ezgar, Bledsoe & Sprenkle, San Jose, 1976-85, ptnr. Hammer & Jacobs, 1985—; lectr. CEB, ABA, San Diego County Bar Assn., Santa Clara County Bar Assn., Calif. Family Law Reports. Contbr. articles on family law to profl. jours. Chmn. Santa Clara County Hist. Heritage Commn., 1977-80, San Jose Hist. Mus. Assn., 1977-80. Fellow Am. Acad. Matrimonial Lawyers (treas. No. Calif. chpt. 1983-85); mem. Santa Clara County Bar Assn. (chmn. family law com. 1981, 82) State Bar Calif. (lectr. family law sect., family law adv. commn. 1981-86, chmn., 1985-86). Family and matrimonial. Office: Hammer & Jacobs 1960 The Alameda San Jose CA 95126

JACOBS, RANDALL SCOTT DAVID, lawyer; b. N.Y.C., Sept. 6, 1944; s. Irving and Lea Sylvia (Kerner) J.; m. Jill Barbara Weiss, June 20, 1981; children—Evan, Todd. B.S. in B.A., NYU, 1967, LL.M. in Corp. Law, 1971; J.D., Temple U., 1970. Bar: N.Y. 1977, U.S. Dist. Ct. (ea. dist.) N.Y. 1979, U.S. Dist. Ct. (so. dist.) N.Y. 1979, U.S. Ct. Appeals (2d cir.) 1980, U.S. Supreme Ct. 1980. Assoc. Coudert Brothers, N.Y.C., 1968; with Comml. Coverage Corp., N.Y.C., 1971-78; assoc. Levy, Tandet, Sohn and Loft, N.Y.C., 1978-82; of counsel Harvis and Zeichner, N.Y.C., 1982-84, Rich, Lillienstein, Krinsly, Dorman & Hochhauser, P.C., N.Y.C., 1984—; sec. Pro Service Forwarding Co., Inc., Inglewood, Calif., 1982—. Staff mem. Temple Law Quarterly Law Rev., 1969-70. Mem. N.Y. State Bar Assn., N.Y.C. Bar Assn., ABA. Federal civil litigation, State civil litigation, Letters of credit. Office: Rich Lillienstein Krinsly Dorman and Hochhauser PC 99 Park Ave New York NY 10016

JACOBS, ROGER BRUCE, lawyer; b. Newark, Apr. 9, 1951; s. Seymour B. and Pearle (Flaschen) J.; m. Robin Hodes, July 2, 1978; 1 child, Joshua Seymour. BS, Cornell U., 1973; JD, NYU, 1976, LLM, 1979. Bar: N.J. 1977, D.C. 1978, N.Y. 1980. Asst. prosecutor Hudson County Prosecutor's Office, Jersey City, 1977-79; assoc. Guggenheimer & Untermyer, N.Y.C., 1979-82, Rosen, Gelman & Weiss, Newark, 1982-83; sole practice N.Y.C., 1983—; adj. prof. N.Y. Law Sch., Rutgers U. Inst. Mgmt. and Labor Relations. Contbr. articles to profl. jours. Bd. Trustees, exec. com. Garden State Polit. Action Com., N.J. Mem. ABA (labor and employment law sects., com. on equal opportunity law young lawyers div.), Assn. Bar City N.Y., D.C. Bar Assn., Essex County Bar Assn., N.J. State Bar Assn. (labor law and young lawyers sects.), N.Y. County Lawyers Assn. (com. on labor), N.Y. State Bar Assn. (labor law com.). Democrat. Jewish. Labor. Home: 31 Undercliff Terr West Orange NJ 07052 Office: 460 Park Ave ve New York NY 10022

JACOBS, RONALD HEDSTROM, lawyer; b. York, Pa., Oct. 23, 1945; s. Jerry S. and Ann E. (Hedestrom) J.; 1 dau., Heidi. A.B., Dickinson Coll., 1967; J.D., U. Denver, 1970. Bar: Colo. 1971. Regional counsel Transam Title Ins. Co., Denver, 1971-75; v.p., resident counsel Midland Fed. Savs. and Loan Assn., Denver, 1975-81; ptnr. Brownstein, Hyatt, Farber & Madden, Denver, 1981-84, Sherman & Howard, 1984—; mem. adv. bd. Arapahoe Community Coll., 1974-76; instr. in real estate law Emily Griffith Opportunity Sch., 1971-73, Inst. Fin. Edn., 1975-78; lectr. continuing legal edn., title ins. and real estate seminars. Mem. ABA (past mem. exec. council law, young lawyers sect.), Colo. Bar Assn. (forms com., chmn. legal asst. com. 1976-78, ad hoc com. Uniform Condominium Act 1977-80, chmn. young lawyers sect. 1981-82, chmn. by laws com. 1983—, mem. long range planning com. 1983—, convention com. 1985—), Denver Bar Assn. (past chmn. topical luncheon com.), Am. Arbitration Assn., U.S. Savs. and Loan League (attys. com.). Banking, Real property, Savings and Loan. Home: 315 Vine St Denver CO 80206 Office: 633 17th St Denver CO 80202

JACOBS, SETH ALAN, lawyer; b. Englewood, N.J., Aug. 1, 1956; s. Robert and Shirley Ann (Levine) J.; m. Julie Ann Stern, Aug. 12, 1979; 1 child, Jessica Lynn. BA, U. Rochester, 1978; JD, Case Western Res. U., 1981. Bar: Ohio 1981, U.S. Dist. Ct. (no. dist.) Ohio 1981, Mich. 1985. Assoc. Buckingham, Doolittle & Burroughs, Akron, Ohio, 1981-84, Dykema, Gossett, Spencer, Goodnow & Trigg, Detroit, 1984—. Rep. human studies com. Cleve. VA Hosp., 1981. Mem. ABA, Ohio Bar Assn., Mich. Bar Assn., Nat. Health Lawyers Assn., Am. Acad. Hosp. Attys., Soc. Ohio Hosp. Attys. Health. Office: Dykema Gossett Spencer Goodnow & Trigg 400 Renaissance Ctr 35th Floor Detroit MI 48243

JACOBS, SHERRY RAPHAEL, textile executive, lawyer; b. N.J., June 29, 1943; d. Leon L. and Fay (Silverstein) Raphael; m. Stephen Edward Jacobs, Jan. 4, 1976; children from previous marriage: Jeremiah Raphael and Deborah Feinsmith. BA, Fairleigh Dickinson U., 1967; JD, Loyola U., Chgo., 1970. Bar: Ill. 1970, N.Y. 1975. Assoc. Weil, Gotshal & Manges, N.Y.C., 1972-75, Wachtell, Lipton, & Rosen & Katz, N.Y.C., 1975-76; assoc. counsel Estee Lauder Inc., N.Y.C., 1976-77; v.p. legal R.H. Macy & Co., Inc., N.Y.C., 1977-79; v.p., gen. counsel Saks Fifth Ave., N.Y.C., 1979-83, v.p., gen. counsel, dir. loss prevention, 1983-84, v.p., gen. mgr., 1984-86; v.p. adminstrn., gen. counsel, Guilford Mills, Inc., 1986—, also bd. dirs. Bd. dirs. Manhattan Theater Club. Mem. ABA, N.Y. State Bar Assn., N.Y. County Bar Assn., Assn. of Bar City N.Y. General corporate, General practice, Labor. Office: Guilford Mills Inc 180 Madison Ave New York NY 10016

JACOBS, WENDELL EARLY, JR., lawyer; b. Detroit, Nov. 15, 1945; s. Wendell E. and Mildred P. (Horton) J.; m. Elaine M. Lott; children: Wendell E. III, Damon R. BFA, Denison U., 1969; JD, Wayne State U., 1972. Bar: Mich. 1972, U.S. Dist. Ct. (ea. dist.) Mich. 1973, Fla. 1974. Asst. prosecutor Jackson County, Mich., 1973-76; ptnr. Jacobs & Engle, Jackson, 1977—. Mem. Assn. Trial Lawyers Am., Nat. Assn. Criminal Def. Lawyers, Mich. Trial Lawyers Assn., Criminal Def. Attys. Mich., Jackson County Bar Assn. Republican. Club: Grotto (Jackson). Avocations: paddleball, motorcycling. Criminal, Family and matrimonial, General practice. Home: 9281 Greenwood Rd Grass Lake MI 49420 Office: Jacobs & Engle 755 W Michigan Jackson MI 49201

JACOBSEN, RAYMOND ALFRED, JR., lawyer; b. Wilmington, Del., Dec. 14, 1949; s. Raymond Alfred and Margaret (Walters) J.; m. Marilyn Perry, Aug. 4, 1973. BA, U. Del., 1971; JD, Georgetown U., 1975. Bar: D.C. 1975, U.S. Supreme Ct. 1982. Assoc. Howrey & Simon, Washington, 1975-82, ptnr., 1983—. Spl. projects editor Law & Policy in International Business, 1974-75. Served to capt. U.S. Army, 1975. Mem. ABA (antitrust law sect., adminstrv. law sect., corp. banking and bus. law sect., litigation sect.), D.C. Bar Assn., U.S. Supreme Ct. Bar Assn. Republican. Lutheran. Club: Army & Navy (Washington). Antitrust, Federal civil litigation, General corporate. Home: 4205 Maple Tree Ct Alexandria VA 22304 Office: Howrey & Simon 1730 Pennsylvania Ave NW Washington DC 20006

JACOBSON, ALLAN JEFFREY, lawyer; b. N.Y.C., Nov. 13, 1942; s. Joseph and Shirley Jacobson. BSEE, CUNY, 1965; MSEE, U. So. Calif., 1967; JD, U. of Pacific, 1976. Bar: Calif. 1977, Pa. 1979, N.J. 1979; registered agt. U.S. Patent Office. Patent atty. RCA Corp., Princeton, N.J., 1978-81; patent counsel Gen. Instrument, N.Y.C., 1981—. Mem. State Bar Pa., State Bar of N.J., State Bar Calif. Patent, Trademark and copyright. Home: 343 Milford Ct Newtown PA 18940 Office: Gen Instrument 767 Fifth Ave New York NY 10153

JACOBSON, BARRY STEPHEN, lawyer, administrative judge; b. Bklyn., Mar. 30, 1955; s. Morris and Sally (Ballaban) J. Cert. in drama, Sch. of Performing Arts, N.Y.C., 1973; BA, CUNY, 1977, MA, 1980; JD, Bklyn. Sch. Law, 1980. Bar: N.Y. 1981, U.S. Dist. Ct. (ea. and so. dists.) N.Y. 1981, U.S. Ct. Appeals (2d cir.) 1981, U.S. Supreme Ct. 1984, D.C. 1985, U.S. Ct. Claims 1985, U.S. Ct. Internat. Trade 1985, U.S. Ct. Mil. Appeals 1985. Sole practice Bklyn., 1981; asst. corp. counsel N.Y.C. Law Dept., Bklyn., 1981-84; asst. dist. atty. Borough of Queens, Kew Gardens, N.Y., 1984-85; judge adminstrv. law N.Y. Dept. Motor Vehicles, Bklyn., 1985-86, 87—; assoc. counsel N.Y. State Dept. Health, N.Y.C., 1986; arbitrator N.Y.C. Small Claims Ct., 1986—; gen. counsel Amersfort Flatlands Devel. Corp., Bklyn., 1981-82; arbitrator small claims div. N.Y.C. Civil Ct. Mem. Roosevelt Dem. Party, Bklyn., 1984—, Kings Hwy. Dem. Party, Bklyn., 1982—; King's County Dem. com., 1986—; gen. counsel, advisor Bklyn. Coll. Student Govts., 1980—. Named one of Outstanding Young Men Am., 1983, 85, 86. Mem. ABA, N.Y. State Bar Assn. (spl. com. juvenile justice), Bklyn. Bar Assn. (family ct. com.), N.Y. County Lawyers Assn. (family ct. com.), Am. Judicature Soc., Bklyn. Coll. Alumni Assn. (gen. counsel student govt. affiliate 1983—, bd. dirs. 1985—), Jaycees (named one of Outstanding Young Men of Am. 1983, 85). Jewish. Lodges: B'nai B'rith, Hillel (bd. dirs. 1983—). Avocations: drama, theatre, target shooting, flying. Criminal, Juvenile, Health. Home: 2912 Brighton 12th St Brooklyn NY 11235 Office: NY State Dept Motor Vehicles 350 Livingston St 4th Floor Brooklyn NY 11217

JACOBSON, DAVID EDWARD, lawyer; b. Port Chester, N.Y., May 17, 1949; s. Robert Herzel and Ruth Doris (Rosenzweig) J.; m. Debra Ann Denkensohn, Aug. 10, 1975; 1 child, Andrew. B.A. in Econs., U. Rochester, 1971; J.D., SUNY-Buffalo, 1974; LL.M. in Taxation, Georgetown U., 1977. Bar: N.Y. 1975, D.C. 1976, U.S. Tax Ct. 1982, U.S. Ct. Appeals (fed. cir.) 1983. Atty.-adviser Office of Chief Counsel, IRS, Washington, 1974-79; tax counsel com. on fin. U.S. Senate, Washington, 1979-81; assoc. firm Reid & Priest, Washington, 1981-86, ptnr., 1986—. Vol. Income Tax Assistance, Arlington, Va., 1977-81; treas. Overlook Townhouse Homeowners Assn., Arlington. Mem. ABA (mem. tax sect. 1982-84, mem. regulated utilities com.), N.Y. State Bar Assn. Corporate taxation, Public utilities, Personal income taxation. Office: Reid & Priest 1111 19th St NW Washington DC 20036

JACOBSON, GARY STEVEN, lawyer; b. Holyoke, Mass., Sept 4, 1951; s. Rudolph Milton and Frederika Helena (Vanderryn) J.; m. Sharon W. Turkish, June 16, 1974; children—Lowell Daniel, Lee Stuart. B.A. cum laude, Wesleyan U., Middletown, Conn., 1973; J.D., Northwestern U., 1976. Bar: Conn. 1976, N.Y. 1977, N.J. 1977, U.S. Ct. Appeals (3d cir.) 1981. Investigative atty. N.Y. State Commn. on Jud. Conduct, N.Y.C., 1976-77; spl. asst. atty. gen. Office Spl. State Prosecutor N.Y.C., 1977-79; assoc. Hofheimer, Gartlir, Gottlieb & Gross, N.Y.C., 1979-80; assoc. Kleinberg, Moroney, Masterson & Schachter, Millburn, N.J., 1980-85, ptnr., 1986—. Editor: Judicial Discipline Reporter, 1976. Republican. Jewish. Bankruptcy, Contracts commercial, Federal civil litigation. Home: 99 Susan Dr Chatham NJ 07928 Office: Kleinberg Moroney et al 225 Millburn Ave Suite 104 Millburn NJ 07041

JACOBSON, JEFFREY ELI, lawyer, consultant; b. N.Y.C., Aug. 19, 1956; s. Murray and Adele (Ebert) J.; m. Linda Moel, Aug. 11, 1984; 1 child, Justin Myles. BA, Fordham U., 1976; JD, N.Y. Law Sch., 1980. Bar: N.Y. 1982, D.C. 1982, U.S. Tax Ct. 1982, U.S. Ct. Internat. Trade 1982, U.S. Dist. Ct. (so. and ea. dists.) N.Y. 1982. Assoc. SESAC, Inc., N.Y.C., 1980-82; sole practice N.Y.C., 1982-85; sr. ptnr. Jacobson & Colfin, N.Y.C. and Washington, 1985—; asst. mgr. Embassy Theatre, N.Y.C., 1975, Criterion Theatre, N.Y.C., 1976; mgr., sec. Squirrels Prods., Ltd., N.Y.C., 1978-80; cons. Orange Records Ltd., N.Y.C., 1976—; counsel Box Office Media, N.Y.C., 1982—. Contbr. articles to profl. jours. Speaker Songwriter's Guild, N.Y.C, 1983—; entertainment arbitrator Am. Arbitration Assn., N.Y.C., 1984—; guest speaker Ctr. for Media Arts, N.Y.C., 1985. Recipient Eagle Scout Silver Palm, Boy Scouts Am., N.Y., 1972, Cert. of Merit Bronx House, N.Y., 1978, Plaque of Appreciation, Am. Arbitration Assn., N.Y.C., 1985. Mem. ABA (patent trademark, copyright law, forum com. on entertainment and sports law sects., chmn. subcom. on sattelites), Assn. Bar of City of N.Y., Copyright Soc. USA, Phi Delta Phi. Republican. Jewish. Clubs: Republican (v.p. Pelham Parkway 1983—), Candidate Assembly. Lodge: B'nai B'rith (editor 1982-85), Order of the Arrow Brotherhood. Avocations: music, photography, swimming, stereo equipment, traveling. Entertainment, Trademark and copyright, Federal civil litigation. Office: Jacobson & Colfin 150 Fifth Ave New York NY 10011

JACOBSON, JEROLD DENNIS, lawyer; b. N.Y.C., Oct. 12, 1940; s. Sidney and Lillian D. (Fink) J.; m. Nancy E. Barber, Aug. 22, 1965; children—Diana, Lisa, Pamela. B.A., U. Vt., 1962; J.D., Cornell U., 1965; LL.M. in Labor Law, NYU, 1966. Bar: N.Y. 1966, U.S. Dist. Ct. (so. and ea. dists.) N.Y. 1968, U.S. Dist. Ct. (no. dist.) N.Y. 1981, U.S. Ct. Appeals (2d cir.) 1979, U.S. Ct. Appeals (5th cir.) 1980, U.S. Ct. Appeals (11th cir.) 1981, U.S. Supreme Ct. 1982. Assoc. to gen. counsel ILGWU, AFL-CIO, N.Y.C., 1966-69; assoc. Rains, Pogrebin and Scher, N.Y.C. and Mineola, N.Y., 1969-70; assoc. Guggenheimer & Untermyer, N.Y.C., 1970-74, ptnr., 1975-85; ptnr. Summit, Rovins & Feldesman, N.Y.C., 1986—; lectr. in labor and employment relations law Practising Law Inst., N.Y. State Bar Assn., Am. Soc. Law and Medicine. Bd. dirs. Nassau County chpt. N.Y. State Civil Liberties Union. Mem. Legal Aid Soc., Am. Arbitration Assn., Am. Acad. Hosp. Attys., Nat. Health Lawyers Assn., N.Y. State Bar Assn., ABA. Contbr. articles to profl. jours. Labor, Administrative and regulatory, Health. Office: Summit Rovins & Feldesman 445 Park Ave New York NY 10022

JACOBSON, JONATHAN M., lawyer; b. N.Y.C., Feb. 14, 1952; s. David R. and Phyllis A. (Rosen) J.; m. Fran B. Abrams, Sept. 29, 1979. AB, Columbia Coll., 1973; JD magna cum laude, Bklyn. Sch. Law, 1976. Bar: N.Y. 1977, U.S. Dist. Ct. (ea. and so. dists.) N.Y. 1977, U.S. Ct. Appeals (D.C. cir.) 1978, U.S. Supreme Ct. 1980, U.S. Ct. Appeals (2d cir.) 1981. Assoc. Lord, Day & Lord, N.Y.C., 1976-85, ptnr., 1985-86; ptnr. Coudert Bros., N.Y.C., 1986—. Contbr. articles to profl. jours. Mem. ABA. Democrat. Antitrust, Federal civil litigation. Home: 218 Northwood Ct Jericho NY 11753 Office: Coudert Bros 200 Park Ave New York NY 10166

JACOBSON, KENNETH MARK, lawyer; b. Chgo., May 24, 1954; s. Stanford and Ceil (Glantz) J.; m. Bronwyn Brosk, Aug. 13, 1977. BA summa cum laude, U. Ill., 1976; JD, Stanford U., 1979. Bar: Ill. 1979. Assoc. Sidley & Austin, Chgo., 1979-83; assoc. Katten, Muchin, Zavis, Pearl, Greenberger & Galler, Chgo., 1983-86, ptnr., 1986—. Mem. ABA, Ill. Bar Assn., Chgo. Bar Assn., Chgo. Mortgage Attys. Assn. Avocations: running, photography. Real property. Office: Katten Muchin Zavis et al 525 W Monroe Chicago IL 60606-3693

JACOBSON, MARC, lawyer; b. Furth, Fed. Republic Germany, Nov. 9, 1952; came to U.S., 1952; s. Harold Grundfest Jacobson and Naomi (Weinstein) Warren; m. Jill Bonnie Zipern, June 16, 1974; 1 child, Carly Allison. BA, SUNY, Buffalo, 1974; postgrad., U. San Diego, 1974-75; JD, NYU, 1977. Bar: N.Y. 1978, Calif. 1978, U.S. Dist. Ct. (so. and ea. dists.) N.Y. 1978, U.S. Ct. Appeals (2d cir.) 1982, U.S. Supreme Ct. 1982, Fla. 1985. Assoc. Paskus, Gordon & Mandel, N.Y.C., 1977-79, Proskauer, Rose, Goetz & Mendelsohn, N.Y.C., 1979-80; sole practice N.Y.C., 1980; ptnr. Jacobson & Bailin, N.Y.C., 1980-86; counsel Berger & Steingut, N.Y.C., 1986—; mem. faculty The New Sch. Bd. editors Entertainment Law and Finance, 1986—. Mem. ABA (patent, trademark and copyright law sect., pictorial, graphic and sculptural works com., entertainment law forum com.), N.Y. State Bar Assn. (chmn. spl. com. entertainment law, spl. com. copyright law). Democrat. Jewish. Avocation: squash. Entertainment, General corporate, General practice. Office: Berger & Steingut 600 Madison Ave New York NY 10022

JACOBSON, MARIAN SLUTZ, lawyer; b. Chgo., Nov. 10, 1945; d. Leonard Doering and Emily Dana (Wells) Slutz; m. Fruman Jacobson, Sept. 21, 1975; 1 child, Lisa Wells. BA, Ohio Wesleyan U., 1967; JD, U. Chgo., 1972. Bar: Ill. 1972, U.S. Dist. Ct. (no. dist.) Ill. 1972, U.S. Ct. Appeals (7th cir.) 1973. Assoc. Sonnenschein, Carlin, Nath & Rosenthal, Chgo., 1972-79, ptnr., 1979—. Mem. ABA, Chgo. Council Lawyers. General corporate. Office: Sonnenschein Carlin Nath & Rosenthal 8000 Sears Tower Chicago IL 60606

JACOBSON, MICHAEL, lawyer; b. Atlantic City, Aug. 3, 1943; s. Howard and Anne J.; m. Sarah Lee Harris, Oct. 4, 1969; children—Jenessa Louise, Daniel Elliot, Laura Ruth, Julie Anna. B.S., Temple U., 1964, postgrad. Am. U. Grad. Sch. Govt.; J.D., Baylor U., 1969. Bar: Tex. 1969, N.J. 1971. Assoc. Abney & Burleson, Dallas, 1969-72; sole practice, Atlantic City, 1972-81; sr. ptnr. Jacobson & Winkelstein, 1981-86; solicitor Twp. of Egg Harbor, Midlantic Nat. Bank/South, N.J. Nat. BAnk, Trump Castle Hotel Casino, Atlantis Hotel Casino; lectr. law Atlantic Community Coll. Bd. dirs. Temple Emeth Shalom, Jewish Community Ctr. Atlantic County; trustee Stockton State Coll. Mem. Tex. Bar Assn., N.J. Bar Assn., Atlantic County Bar Assn., ABA, Comml. Law League Am. Clubs: Exchange (Atlantic City), Masons (master Justice Lodge Atlantic City). Contracts commercial, Local government, Real property. Office: 1125 Atlantic Ave Suite 208 West Wing Atlantic City NJ 08401

JACOBSON, MIRIAM NECHAMAH, lawyer; b. Westfield, Mass., Feb. 25, 1941; d. Bernard and Rose (Heller) J.; m. S. David Scher, Apr. 23, 1978. BA summa cum laude, CUNY, 1975; JD, Yale U., 1978. Bar: Pa. 1978, U.S. Dist. Ct. (ea. dist.) Pa. 1978. Assoc. Mesirov, Gelman, Phila., 1978-82, Cohen, Shapiro, Phila., 1983; v.p., assoc. counsel Fidelity Bank and predecessor firms, Phila., 1984—. Co-founder, treas. lawyers com. Reproductive Rights, Phila., 1978-85. Mem. ABA, Pa. Bar Assn. (real property and banking sects.), Phila. Bar Assn. (real property and banking sect.), Women Real Estate Attys. (organizer, coordinator 1979—), ACLU, Nat. Abortion Rights Action League, Nat. Orgn. for Women. Real property, Banking. Office: Fidelity Bank NA Legal Dept 123 S Broad St Philadelphia PA 19109

JACOBSON, RICHARD LEE, lawyer, educator; b. Los Angeles, Nov. 2, 1942; s. Joseph and Betty (Koenig) J.; m. Candice J. Nelson, June 30, 1973; children—David, Peter. S.B., U. Chgo., 1964; J.D., U. So. Calif., 1970. Bar: Calif. 1971, U.S. Ct. Appeals (9th cir.) 1971, D.C. 1980, U.S. Ct. Appeals (4th cir.) 1980, U.S. Ct. Appeals (D.C. cir.) 1980, U.S. Supreme Ct. 1980, U.S. Ct. Appeals (6th cir.) 1983. Law clk. U.S. Ct. Appeals for 9th Circuit, 1970-71; law clk. to Assoc. Justice William O. Douglas U.S. Supreme Ct., Washington, 1971-72; assoc. Irell & Manella, Los Angeles, 1973-76; mem. trial unit SEC, Washington, 1977-78, spl. counsel to chmn., 1978-79; ptnr. Mayer, Brown & Platt, Washington, 1980-85; spl. counsel Heller, Ehrman, White & McAuliffe, Palo Alto, 1986—; adj. prof. law Georgetown U., Washington, 1979—. Exec. editor So. Calif. Law Rev., 1969-70. Mem. ABA (chmn. subcom. uniformity of local discovery rules), Washington Council Lawyers (bd. dirs. 1982-86, pres. 1985-86, exec. com. Washington lawyers' com. for civil rights under law 1983-86), D.C. Bar Assn. (steering com. computer law div. 1985-86), Order of Coif. Democrat. Federal civil litigation, State civil litigation, Computer. Address: 328 Cowper St Palo Alto CA 94301

JACOBSON, SUSAN CURTIS, lawyer; b. Bklyn., Sept. 27, 1946; d. Edwin Arthur and Mathilde Anne (Nettels) Charles; m. W. James Tillett, June 13, 1969 (div. June 1975); m. Arvid Victor Jacobson, Feb. 28, 1976. BA, U. Kans., 1978, JD, 1980. Bar: Kans. 1980, U.S. Dist. Ct. Kans. 1980. Exec. editor Nat. Orgn. on Legal Problems in Edn., Topeka, Kans., 1974-78; assoc. Robertson & Jacobson, Junction City, Kans., 1980-82; ptnr. Jacobson & Jacobson, Junction City, 1982—. Editor: Contemporary Legal Problems in Education, 1974, New Directions in School Law, 1975, Nolpe Sch. Law Jour., 1974-77; mem. U. Kans. Law Rev., 1980; contbr. articles to legal jours. Bd. dirs. United Way of Junction City, 1984-85, ARC, Junction City, 1984-85, Armed Forces YMCA, Junction City, 1983-84, Crisis Ctr., Manhattan, Kans., 1980-84; bd. dirs. Geary County Council Social Agys., Junction City, 1981-84. Mem. Kans. Bar Assn., Geary County Bar Assn. (Law Day chmn. 1981, award of Merit 1981), Kans. Trial Lawyers Assn. (bd. govs. 1986—, bd. editors jour. 1987—), Assn. Trial Lawyers Am., Junction City C. of C. (young ambassadors 1981-84, old trooper regiment 1983-85, bd. dirs. 1985-86), Assn. U.S. Army. Republican. Episcopalian. Personal injury, Medical malpractice, Military. Home: 1012 Kingsbury St Junction City KS 66441 Office: Jacobson & Jacobson 526 W 6th St Junction City KS 66441

JACOBS-SCHWARTZ, LORETTA (BARBARA), lawyer; b. Buffalo, N.Y., June 6, 1952; d. John Joseph and Margaret Elizabeth (Toner) J.; m. Ira Schwartz, July 30, 1977. AA, Genesee Community Coll., 1972; BS summa cum laude, SUNY, Buffalo, 1974; JD, Bklyn. Law Sch., 1980. Bar: Mass. 1980, Ariz. 1981, U.S. Dist. Ct. Ariz. 1982. Assoc. Law Offices of Anthony DiFruscia, Lawrence, Mass., 1981, McKendree & Lubin, Phoenix, Ariz., 1981-83; gen. counsel Agrl. Employment Relations Bd., Phoenix, 1983-85; ptnr. Santaguida & Jacobs-Schwartz, Phoenix, 1984-86; sole practice Phoenix, 1986—. Big sister Valley Big Sisters, Phoenix, 1982—. Mem. ABA (labor and law employment sect., devel. of individual rights and responsibilities in the workplace com.) Ariz. Bar Assn. (sec. labor sect. 1983-84, treas. 1984-85, chmn. elect 1985-86), Law and Counselling Com. (lectr. labor sect. 1986—), Mass. Bar Assn. Avocations: reading, boating, traveling, skiing. Labor, Civil rights. Home: 1002 E Monte Cristo Phoenix AZ 85002 Office: 5110 N 40th St Suite 258 Phoenix AZ 85018

JACOBSTEIN, J(OSEPH) MYRON, educator, librarian; b. Detroit, Jan. 27, 1920; s. Benjamin and Etta (Roberts) J.; m. Belle Lottman, Sept. 29, 1949; children—Ellen R., Bennett M. B.A., Wayne State U., 1946; M.S., Columbia, 1950; J.D., Chgo.-Kent Coll. Law, 1953. Cataloger U. Chgo. Library, 1950-51; librarian Cowles Commn. for Research in Econs., 1951-53; asst. law librarian U. Ill., 1953-55, Columbia U., 1955-59; law librarian, prof. law U. Colo., Boulder, 1959-63, Stanford U., 1963—. Author: (with R.M. Mersky) Fundamentals of Legal Research, 1987; editor: (with M. Pimsleur) Law Books in Print, 4 vols, 1976. Served with USAAF, 1942-45. Mem. Am. Assn. Law Libraries (pres. 1978-79), Am. Soc. Info. Sci., Am. Soc. Internat. Law. Librarianship. Home: 19 Pearce Mitchell Pl Stanford CA 94305

JACOBUS, CHARLES JOSEPH, lawyer, title company executive, author; b. Ponca City, Okla., Aug. 21, 1947; s. David William and Louise Graham (Johnson) J.; m. Heather Jeanne Jones, June 6, 1970; children—Mary Helen, Charles J. B.S., U. Houston, 1970, J.D., 1973. Bar: Tex. 1973; cert. specialist in residential and comml. real estate law Tex. Bd. Legal Specialization. Sole practice, Houston, 1973-75; staff counsel Tenneco Realty, Inc., Houston, 1975-78; chief legal counsel Speedy Muffler King, Deerfield, Ill., 1978-79; v.p., gen. counsel Tenneco Realty, Inc., 1979-83; v.p. Commerce Title Co., Houston, 1983-85, sr. v.p., gen. counsel Charter Title Co., 1986—; dir. Park Tower Nat. Bank, Houston; adj. faculty Coll. Architecture and Environ. Design Tex. A&M U., 1986—; instr. advanced real estate law State Bar of Tex. Author: Texas Real Estate Law, 4th edit., 1985; Real Estate Law, 1986; co-author, Texas Real Estate, 4th edit., 1987; editor-in-chief Tex. Law Reporter. Chmn. Planning and Zoning Comm., Bellaire, Tex., 1976-77; bd. dirs. Tax Increment Fin. Dist., Bellaire, 1984—. Mem. ABA, Houston Bar Assn. (chmn. real estate sect. 1987—), Tex. Bar Assn. (faculty advanced real estate law courses), Houston Bd. Realtors, Am. Coll. Real Estate Lawyers, Houston Real Estate Lawyers Council, Real Estate Educator's Assn. (pres. 1987—), Tex. Land Title Assn., Am. Coll. Real Estate Lawyers, Nat. Assn. Corp. Real Estate Execs. (chpt. v.p.), Am. Land Devel. Assn. (bd. dirs.), Republican. Roman Catholic. Real property. Home: 5223 Pine St Bellaire TX 77401 Office: Charter Title Co 4265 San Felipe Suite 350 Houston TX 77027

JACOBY, JAMES JOSEPH, lawyer; b. N.Y.C., Feb. 19, 1932; s. Alexander and Adelaide (Auerbach) J.; m. Susan Goldberger, Apr. 7, 1971; children—Paul, Jonathan, Peter. B.A., Fordham U., 1953, LL.B., 1959. Bar: N.Y. 1960, U.S. Tax Ct. 1976. Assoc. H. Howard Babcock, N.Y.C., 1960-71; counsel Bush & Schlesinger, 1971-73; ptnr. Schlesinger & Jacoby, 1973-79, Sive Paget & Riesel, P.C., 1979—. Vice pres. Madison Sq. Boys Club Inc., 1971—, trustee, 1961—. Served to 1st lt. USAF, 1953-55. Mem. ABA, N.Y. Bar Assn., N.Y.C. Bar Assn. Club: New York Athletic. Probate, Estate taxation, Estate planning. Office: 460 Park Ave New York NY 10022

JACOVER, JEROLD ALAN, lawyer; b. Chgo., Mar. 20, 1945; s. David Louis and Beverly (Funk) J.; m. Judith Lee Greenwald, June 28, 1970; children—Aric Seth, Evan Michael, Brian Ethan. B.S.E.E., U. Wis., 1967; J.D., Georgetown U., 1972. Bar: Ohio 1972, Ill. 1973, U.S. Ct. Appeals (7th cir.) 1974, U.S. Ct. Appeals (Fed. cir.) 1983. Atty. Ralph Nader, Columbus, Ohio, 1972-73, Willian, Brinks & Olds, Chgo., 1973—; lectr. Mallinckrodt Coll., Wilmette, Ill., 1977-78. Mem. Evanston Environ. Control Bd., 1983-86; asst. pack leader Northeast Ill. Council Boy Scouts Am., 1982-84. Mem. Am. Patent Law Assn. (com. chmn. 1980-86, co-editor jour. 1980-81), ABA, Decalogue Soc. Lawyers, Patent Law Assn. Chgo. (treas. 1983-84). Jewish. Club: Nippersink Community (Genoa City, Wis.) (bd. dirs. 1978-86). Patent, Trademark and copyright, Federal civil litigation. Home: 1409 Lincoln St Evanston IL 60201 Office: Willian Brinks & Olds 1 IBM Plaza Suite 4100 Chicago IL 60611

JACQUES, RAOUL THOMAS, lawyer; b. Milw., Aug. 7, 1934; s. Arthur Francis and Maude (Mayotte) J.; m. Alice C. Jacques, June 15, 1957 (div. Oct. 1973); children: Marian, Stephen; m. Diana Lynn Hunt, Dec. 20, 1975 (div. Nov. 1983); children: Carina, Michelle, Emilie, Ashley. BS, Marquette U., 1957; LLB, U. Ariz., 1959. Bar: Ariz. 1959, U.S. Dist. Ct. Ariz. 1971. From trust officer to v.p. TransAm. Title (Ariz.), Tucson and Phoenix, 1959-65, 67—; ptnr. MacLean & Jacques, Phoenix, 1965-67; bd. dirs. Land Registrations Inc., Phoenix; del. E. Webb Home Realty, Inc. Republican. Roman Catholic. Real property, Construction. Home: 3447 E Ashurst Dr Phoenix AZ 85044 Office: MacLean & Jacques 40 E Virginia St Phoenix AZ 85004

JADD, ROBERT IRA, lawyer; b. Buffalo, Feb. 9, 1949; s. Henry W. and Sylvia J. (Stock) J.; m. Ellen Barron, June 14, 1981; children: Stephanie Diane, Philip Andrew. BA, SUNY, Buffalo, 1971; JD, New Eng. Law Sch., 1974. Bar: Fla. 1974, U.S. Dist. Ct. (so. dist.) Fla. 1974, N.Y. 1975, U.S. Dist. Ct. (we. dist.) N.Y. 1975, U.S. Ct. Appeals (11th cir.) 1975, U.S. Supreme Ct. 1978, Mass. 1985. Ptnr. Jadd & Jadd, Buffalo, 1974—. Mem. ABA, N.Y. State Bar Assn., Erie County Bar Assn. (chairperson practice and procedure in surrogates ct. 1985—), Marshall Club (pres. 1979-80). Republican. Jewish. Club: Midday (Buffalo) (sec. 1987—, bd. of trustees 1987—), Bridgewater Country (Ft. Erie, Ont., Can.). Avocations: skiing, golf, real estate investment. Probate, Real property, Estate taxation. Home: 32 Bradenham Pl Eggertsville NY 14226 Office: 1720 Liberty Bldg Buffalo NY 14202

JADWIN, TED RICHARD, lawyer; b. Phila., Oct. 10, 1948; s. David H. Jadwin and Lorraine (Weil) Weinzimmer; m. Margery Kaye, Nov. 24, 1979; children: David B., Kate M., Ari D. BA, U. Pa., 1971; JD cum laude, U. Chgo., 1974. Bar: Ill. 1974, U.S. Ct. Appeals (7th cir.) 1974, U.S. Dist. Ct. (no. dist.) Ill. 1975. Law clk. to presiding judge U.S. Dist. Ct. (no. dist.) Ill., Chgo., 1974-75; assoc. Sonnenschein, Carlin, Nathan & Rosenthal, Chgo., 1975-80; ptnr. Dardick & Jadwin, Chgo., 1980-84, D'Ancona & Pflaum, Chgo., 1984—. Assoc. editor U. Chgo. Law Rev., 1973-74. Sec. Express-Ways Childrens Mus., Chgo.; pres. Jewish Family Community Service, Chgo. Mem. ABA, Ill. Bar Assn., Order of Coif. General corporate, Contracts commercial, Real property. Office: D'Ancona & Pflaum 30 N LaSalle #3100 Chicago IL 60602

JAFFE, FROHM FILMORE, lawyer; b. Chgo., May 4, 1918; s. Jacob Isadore and Goldie (Rabinowitz) J.; m. Mary Main, Nov. 7, 1942; children: Jo Anne, Jay. Student, Southwestern U., 1936-39; J.D., Pacific Coast U., 1940. Bar: Calif. 1945, U.S. Supreme Ct. 1964. Practiced law Los Angeles, 1945—; ptnr. Bernard & Jaffe, Los Angeles, 1947-74; partner Jaffe & Jaffe, Los Angeles, 1975—; mem. Los Angeles Traffic Commn., 1947-48; arbitrator Am. Arbitration Assn., 1968—; chmn. pro bono com. Superior Ct. Calif., County of Los Angeles, 1980-85. Served to capt. inf. AUS, 1942-45. Decorated Purple Heart, Croix de Guerre with Silver Star, Bronze Star with oak leaf cluster; honored Human Rights Commn. Los Angeles, Los Angeles County Bd. Suprs.; recipient Pro Bono award State Bar Calif., commendation State Bar Calif., 1983. Mem. Los Angeles County Bar (honored by family law sect. 1983), ABA, Los Angeles Criminal Ct. Bar Assn. (charter mem.), Calif. Trial Lawyers Assn., U.S. Supreme Ct. Bar Assn. Club: Mason (Shriner). State civil litigation, Family and matrimonial, General practice. Office: 6420 Wilshire Blvd Los Angeles CA 90048

JAFFE, GARY, lawyer; b. Phila., Sept. 16, 1956; s. Edward I. and Dorothy (Kaplan) J.; m. Beverly Ann Pfifferling, Oct. 25, 1981; 1 child, Warren Lee. BA, Temple U., 1978; JD, Widener U., 1981. Bar: Pa., N.J. Asst. gen. counsel MEDIQ Inc., Pennsauken, N.J., 1981-85; ptnr. Wurman & Jaffe P.C., Wyndmoor, Pa., 1985-86, Nemeroff, Roberts, Jaffe & Nemeroff P.C., Wyndmoor, 1986—; bd. dirs. Newbold Group, Wyndmoor, Mackler Prodns., Phila., Sedgwick Printout Systems, Princeton. N.J. Mem. ABA, Pa. Bar Assn. Republican. Jewish. Contracts commercial, General corporate, Real property. Home: 780 Cotlar Ln Warminster PA 18974 Office: Nemeroff Roberts Jaffe & Nemeroff PC 8200 Flourtown Ave Suite 2 Wyndmoor PA 19118

JAFFE, JAY, lawyer; b. Indpls., Mar. 12, 1957; s. Jack and Pearl R. (Soloff) J. BA, Ind. U., 1979, JD, 1982. Bar: Ky. 1982, Ind. 1982, U.S. Dist. Ct. (ea. and we. dists.) Ky. 1982, U.S. Dist. Ct. (so. dist.) Ind. 1982, U.S. Ct. Claims 1984. Assoc. Wyatt, Tarrant & Combs, Louisville, 1982-85, Baker & Daniels, Indpls., 1985—; trustee chpt. 7 U.S. Bankruptcy Ct. (so. dist.) Ind., Indpls., 1986—. Mem. ABA, Ind. Bar Assn., Ky. Bar Assn., Indpls. Bar Assn. (chmn. program comml. law and bankruptcy sect.), Phi Beta Kappa. Bankruptcy, Consumer commercial. Office: Baker & Daniels 810 Fletcher Trust Bldg Indianapolis IN 46204

JAFFE, PAUL LAWRENCE, lawyer; b. Phila., June 24, 1928; s. Albert L. and Elsie (Pelser) J.; children: Marc David, Richard Alan, Peter Edward. B.A., Dickinson Coll., 1947; J.D., U. Pa., 1950. Bar: Pa. Sole practice Phila.; sr. ptnr. Mesirov, Gelman, Jaffe, Cramer and Jamieson (and predecessors), 1959—. Trustee Fedn. Jewish Agencies Phila.; trustee Moss Rehab. Hosp., pres., 1977-80, chmn. bd., 1980-84, hon. chmn. bd., 1984—; trustee, mem. exec. com. Union Am. Hebrew Congregations; chmn. United Law Network, 1987—. Mem. ABA, Pa. Bar Assn., Phila. Bar Assn. Jewish (pres. congregation 1974-77). Clubs: Locust, Union League, Lawyers (Phila.); Loveladies Tennis. Real property. Home: 1326 Spruce St Philadelphia PA 19107 Office: 123 S Broad St Philadelphia PA 19109

JAFFE, ROBERT A., lawyer; b. N.Y.C., Nov. 29, 1952; s. Martin and Gayle Jaffe; m. Deborah A. DeMasi, June 12, 1982. Diploma in Internat. Law, U. Vienna, Austria, 1973; AB, NYU, 1974; JD with high honors, U. N.C., 1978. Bar: N.Y. 1979, U.S. Supreme Ct. 1985, D.C. 1986. Assoc. Mudge, Rose, Guthrie, Alexander & Ferdon, N.Y.C., 1978-85; ptnr. Wolf, Arnold & Monroig, P.C., Washington, 1986—. Contbr. articles to profl. jours. Active various civic orgns. Mem. ABA, N.Y. State Bar Assn., D.C. Bar Assn. Avocations: community affairs, sports, traveling. Private international, Federal civil litigation, Administrative and regulatory. Office: Wolf Arnold & Monroig PC 1850 M St NW Washington DC 20036

JAFFE, SHELDON E., lawyer; b. Newark, July 13, 1946; s. Joseph L. and Claribel (Pinnas) J.; m. Mary Janis Clepper, Jan. 15, 1977; children: Mark Joseph, Cara Elizabeth, Lauren Ann. AB, Rutgers U., 1968; JD, U. Pa., 1971. Bar: N.J. 1971, U.S. Dist. Ct. N.J. 1971, Pa. 1972. Law clk. to presiding justice N.J. Superior Ct., Newark, 1971; assoc. Bendit, Weinstock & Sharbaugh, Newark, 1972-73; corp. counsel The March Cos., Inc., Willingboro, N.J., 1973-75; asst. corp. counsel Midlantic Mortgate Corp., Newark, 1975-78; assoc. Kraft & Hughes, Newark, 1979-83; ptnr. Wilentz, Goldman & Spitzer, Woodbridge, N.J., 1984—. Mem. ABA, N.J. Bar Assn. (chmn. EDA and mcpl. fin. subcom. of fin. transactions com. 1985—), Essex and Middlesex Bar Assn., Omicron Delta Epsilon. Avocations: skiing, backpacking, golf. Banking, Municipal bonds, Real property. Home: 31 East Dr Livingston NJ 07039 Office: Wilentz Goldman & Spitzer 900 Rt 9 PO Box 10 Woodbridge NJ 07095

JAFFE, STEPHEN R., lawyer; b. Detroit, May 21, 1945; s. Louis and Lillian (Hertz) J.; m. Colleen M. O'Grady; children—David, Matthew, Jordan. B.A., U. Mich., 1967; J.D., Wayne State U., 1970. Bar: Calif. 1971, Oreg. 1981, D.C. 1981, N.Y. 1984. Assoc. Cotton, Seligman & Ray, San Francisco, 1970-71, Gustlin, Gale & McCabe, Los Angeles, 1972-74; sole practice, Beverly Hills, Calif., 1974-81; ptnr. Hershner, Hunter, Miller, Moulton & Andrews, Eugene, Oreg., 1981-84; of counsel McQuaid, Bedford, & Brayton, San Francisco, 1986—; judge pro tem Los Angeles County mcpl. ct., 1977-81, Los Angeles County super. ct., 1978-81. Judge trial practice U. Oreg., 1981. Bd. dirs. Eugene Symphony Assn., 1981-84; coach Eugene Sports Program, 1981. Mem. ABA, State Bar Calif., State Bar Oreg., Bar of D.C., Am. Arbitration Assn. (nat. panel arbitrators 1977—). Republican. Antitrust, Federal civil litigation, State civil litigation. Office: 650 California St Suite 800 San Francisco CA 94108

JAFFEE, ARTHUR JOSEPH, lawyer; b. San Francisco, Aug. 12, 1923; s. Boris and Sarah (Margulius) J.; m. Mary Marguerite Weed, May 29, 1952; children: Valerie, Cynthia, Laurence, Bryan. AB with distinction, Stanford U., 1947, LLB, 1949. Bar: Calif. 1949, U.S. Dist. Ct. (no. and so. dists.) Calif. 1949, Nev. 1975. Asst. dist. atty. County of San Joaquin, Calif., 1950-57; dep. pub. defender County of Los Angeles, 1952-58; mng. ptnr. Jaffee, Mallery, Thompson, Talbott & Lemaster, Pomona, Calif., 1959-73; pres. Law Offices of Arthur J. Jaffee P.C., Pomona, 1973—; v.p. Medi-Legal Inst., Beverly Hills, 1981-83, pres., Sherman Oaks, Calif., 1983-85. Served to 1st lt. USAAF, 1943-45, ETO. Mem. Am. Trial Lawyers Assn., Calif. Trial Lawyers Assn. (pres. local chpt. 1982-84), Los Angeles County Bar Assn., Eastern Bar Assn. Democrat. Lodge: Masons. State civil litigation, Medical-Legal Matters, Products Liability Litigation. Office: 301 W Mission Blvd Pomona CA 91766

JAFFER, DAVID HUSSAIN, lawyer; b. Ellendale, N.D., Nov. 15, 1954; s. Majduddin Mohammed and Patricia Anne (Norton) J.; m. Johanna Pullman, Aug. 25, 1979. BA, Reed Coll., 1976; PhD, Cambridge (Eng.) U., 1979; JD, Stanford U., 1982. Bar: Colo. 1982, Calif. 1985, U.S. Dist. Ct. (no. dist.) Calif. 1985, U.S. Patent Office 1986, U.S. Ct. Appeals (fed. cir.) 1986, U.S. Ct. Appeals (6th and 9th cirs.) 1987. Assoc. Sherman & Howard, Denver, 1982-85, Rosenblum, Parish & Bacigalupi, San Jose, Calif., 1985—. NSF fellow, 1976-79. Mem. ABA, Calif. Bar Assn., Santa Clara County Bar Assn., Patent Office Soc., Am. Intellectual Property Law Assn., Phi Beta Kappa, Almaden Cycle Club. Democrat. Methodist. Avocations: bicycling, camping, racquet sports. Patent, Trademark and copyright, General corporate. Home: 355 Ryegate Ct San Jose CA 95133 Office: Rosenblum Parish & Bacigalupi 55 Almaden Blvd Suite 500 San Jose CA 95113

JAGER, MELVIN FRANCIS, lawyer; b. Joliet, Ill., Mar. 23, 1937; s. Melvin Van Zandt and Lucille Marie (Callahan) J.; m. Virginia Sue Maitland, Aug. 15, 1959; children: Lori, Jennifer, Scott, Christy. Diploma Joliet Jr. Coll., 1957; BSME, U. Ill.-Champaign-Urbana, 1962, JD, 1962. Bar: Ill. 1962, D.C. 1962. Assoc. Iron, Birch, Swindler & McKie, Washington, 1962-65; ptnr. Hume, Clement, Brinks, Willian & Olds Ltd., Chgo., 1965-80, Lee, Smith & Jager, Chgo., 1981-83, Niro, Jager & Scavone, Chgo., 1984-85, Willian Brinks Olds Hofer Gilson & Lione Ltd., 1985—; adj. prof. law No. Ill. U. Sch. Law, 1979-80. Author: Trade Secrets Law, 1984; editor U. Ill. Law Forum, 1961-62; contbg. author monograph: Sorting Out the Ownership Rights in Intellectual Property: A Guide to Practical Counseling and Legal Representation, 1980. Bd. edn. Glen Ellyn, Ill., 1974-80; chmn. Civic Betterment Party Nominating Com., Glen Ellyn, 1982; chmn. Glen Ellyn Enrivon. Protection Com., 1971—; chmn. budget rev. com. Glen Ellyn United Fund 1972, Glen Ellyn Ednl. Loan Fund Trust, 1973. Mem. ABA (chmn. litigation sect. intellectual properties and patents com.), Ill. State Bar Assn. (chmn. patent, trademark and copyright, council 1982-83, editor newsletter 1979-82), Chgo. Bar Assn. (chmn. intellectual properties litigation sect.), Am. Patent Law Assn., Chgo. Patent Law Assn., Lic. Execs. Soc. (U.S.A./Can.), Glen Ellyn Jaycees (life mem., pres. 1972), Phi Gamma Delta, Phi Delta Phi. Republican. Roman Catholic. Clubs: Chgo. Law, Union League (Chgo.); Delavan Yacht (Delavan, Wis.). Author: Trade Secrets Law Handbook, 1984; editor U. Ill. Law Forum, 1961-62; contbg. author monograph: Sorting Out the Ownership Rights in Intellectual Property: A Guide to Practical Counseling and Legal Representation, 1980. Patent, Trademark and copyright, Federal civil litigation. Home: 579 Forest Ave Glen Ellyn IL 60137 Office: One IBM Plaza Suite 4100 Chicago IL 60611

JAGGER, JAMES CLOYD, lawyer; b. Vancouver, Wash., May 8, 1945; s. Albert Cloyd and Virginia Gwen (Moon) J.; m. Alice Brown Janes, July 20, 1968 (div. May 1984); children: Justin James, Jennifer Gwen; m. Lauren Susan Holland, Aug. 17, 1984; 1 child, Dawn Ashley. B, Northwest Nazarene Coll., 1967; JD, Willamette Law Sch., 1970. Bar: Oreg. 1970, U.S. Supreme Ct. 1975, U.S. Dist. Ct. Oreg. 1976, U.S. Ct. Appeals (9th cir.) 1976. Dep. dist. atty Coos County, Coos Bay, Oreg., 1970-72; dep. dist. atty. Lane County, Eugene, Oreg., 1972-75; ptnr. Diment, Jagger & Billings, Eugene, 1975-80, Jagger & Holland, Eugene, 1980—. Republican. Avocations: sports, coaching, camping. Personal injury, Criminal, Family and matrimonial. Home: 5375 Donald St Eugene OR 97401 Office: Jagger & Holland 540 Oak St Suite C Eugene OR 97401

JAGIELLO, BARBARA ANNE, lawyer; b. Phila., Feb. 16, 1944; d. Lawrence and Barbara (Dunn) Sterk; m. Robert Jagiello, Oct. 3, 1971 (div. 1982); m. Robert K. Wilson, May 20, 1984. BA, Calif. State U., San Francisco, 1969, MA, 1971; M in Study/Law, Yale U., 1974; JD, U. So. Calif., Los Angeles, 1976. Bar: Calif. 1979, U.S. Dist. Ct. (no. dist.) Calif. 1979. Sole practice San Francisco, 1979-84; ptnr. Anderson, Anderson, & Jagiello, San Francisco, 1984-86; sole practice San Francisco, 1986—; chairperson Amicus Briefs/Queens Bench, 1986—. Mem. Am. Trial Lawyers Assn., Calif. Trial Lawyers Assn. Democrat. Roman Catholic. State civil litigation, Personal injury, Construction. Home: 101 Lombard St #406E San Francisco CA 94111 Office: One Market Plaza Spear St Tower Suite 2210 San Francisco CA 94105

JAGLOM, ANDRE RICHARD, lawyer; b. N.Y.C., Dec. 23, 1953; s. Jacob and Irene (Moore) J.; m. Janet R. Stampfl, Apr. 12, 1980; 1 child, Peter Stampfl Jaglom. BS in Physics and Mgmt., MIT, 1974; JD, Harvard U., 1977. Bar: N.Y. 1978, U.S. Dist. Ct. (so. and ea. dists.) N.Y. 1978, U.S. Supreme Ct. 1982. Assoc. Paul, Weiss, Rifkind, Wharton & Garrison, N.Y.C., 1977-84; mng. ptnr. Stecher, Jaglom & Prutzman, N.Y.C., 1984—. Computer mktg. and distbn. editor Computer Law Reporter, 1984—, faculty, 1983—, co-chmn., 1987—; contbr. articles to law jours. Mem. ABA, Bar Assn. City of N.Y. (computer law com.). Antitrust, Contracts commercial, Computer. Office: Stecher Jaglom & Prutzman 900 Third Ave New York NY 10022

JAGOW, CHARLES HERMAN, lawyer, finance consultant; b. Winona, Minn., Jan. 23, 1910; s. Walter Paul and Anna Marie (Thode) J.; m. Alice MacFarlane, Aug. 3, 1940 (dec. 1967); children—Paul M., Richard C. Student LaCrosse (Wis.) State Tchrs. Coll., 1928-30; A.B. cum laude, U. Wis., 1932, LL.B. cum laude, 1934; LL.M., Columbia U., 1936. Bar: N.Y. 1937. Assoc., Cravath, Swaine & Moore, N.Y.C., 1936-52; atty. Met. Life Ins. Co., N.Y.C., 1952-75, assoc. gen. counsel, 1957-75, v.p., 1967-75; dir. corp. debt financing project Am. Bar Found., Chgo., 1975-81; cons. in corp. fin., N.Y.C., 1975—; counsel Am. Assn. Gifted Children, 1975-85; project dir. Mortgage Bond Indenture Form, English text, 1981, Japanese text, 1982. Elder Presbyn. Ch. Mem. Assn. Life Ins. Counsel, ABA, Assn. Bar City N.Y., Order of Coif, Phi Kappa Phi, Delta Sigma Rho. General corporate, Insurance, Private international. Home: RD 3 Smalley Corners Rd Carmel NY 10512 Office: 510 E 23d St 1F New York NY 10010

JAHN, GREGORY DEAN, lawyer; b. Omaha, Aug. 30, 1949; s. Walter R. and Gloria Ann (Clapp) J.; m. Mary Frances Dodson, May 29, 1972; children: Madeline Ann, Julia Therese. BA summa cum laude, Creighton U., 1971; JD summa cum laude, U. Notre Dame, 1974. Bar: Nebr. Assoc. Fitzgerald and Brown, Omaha, 1974-79; ptnr. Hotz, Kizer and Jahn, Omaha, 1979-85, Fitzgerald and Brown, Omaha, 1985—. Pres., dir. Landmarks, Inc., Omaha, 1980—; officer, bd. dirs. Wellness Council of Midlands, Omaha, 1983—. Served to capt. USAR, 1971-79. Named Outstanding Young Omahan, 1984. Mem. ABA, Nebr. State Bar Assn., Omaha Bar Assn., Health Lawyers Assn. Am. Republican. Clubs: Omaha, Field (Omaha). General corporate, Health, Pension, profit-sharing, and employee benefits. Home: 4811 California Omaha NE 68132 Office: Fitzgerald and Brown 1000 Woodmen Tower Omaha NE 68102

JAIN, LALIT K., lawyer; b. Bhagalpur, Bihar, India, Aug. 10, 1944; came to U.S. 1971; s. Baij Nath and Janki Devi (Agrawal) J.; m. Abha Gupta, May 28, 1973; children; Monika, Konika. B in Commerce, Patna U., India, 1964, LLBwith distinction, 1967. Bar: India 1975, N.Y. 1978, U.S. Tax Ct. 1979, U.S. Supreme Ct. 1982, U.S. Dist. Ct. (so. and ea. dists.) N.Y. 1983. Pvt. practice tax and acctg. Patna, Bihar, India, 1967-71; sr. tax acct. Gen. Adjustment Bur., Inc., N.Y.C., 1972; sr. tax acct. St. Regis Corp., N.Y.C., 1973-76, legal asst., 1976-78, atty., 1978-80, gen. atty., 1981-83; mgr. tax research and planning Champion Internat. Corp., N.Y.C., 1983-85; sr. atty. corp. law dept. Merrill Lynch & Co., Inc., N.Y.C., 1985-86, v.p. corp. staff, counsel, 1986—; bd. dirs. Forest Industries Tele-Communications, Eugene, Oreg. Nat. Merit scholar Govt. of India, 1960, 64, 67. Fellow Inst. Chartered Accts. (S. Vadyanath Aiyar Meml. scholar 1966); mem. Chartered Inst. Secs. and Adminstrs., Inst. Co. Secs. India, Inst. Cost and Works Accts. India. Hindu. Avocations: tennis, swimming, bowling, billiards, table tennis. Pension, profit-sharing, and employee benefits, Corporate taxation, Personal income taxation. Home: 61-22 Booth St Rego Park NY 11374 Office: Merrill Lynch and Co Inc 1 Liberty Plaza 165 Broadway New York NY 10080

JAKES, PETER H., lawyer; b. N.Y.C., July 17, 1946; s. Walter and Liesel (Lilienfield) J.; m. Karen J. Sorkin, Aug. 23, 1970; children: Susan J., Aaron G. AB with honors, Brown U., 1968; JD, Yale U., 1971. Bar: N.Y. 1972, U.S. Dist. Ct. (so. dist.) N.Y. 1972. Assoc. Willkie, Farr & Gallagher, N.Y.C., 1971-79, ptnr., 1979—. Mem. ABA, Assn. of Bar of City of N.Y. Securities, General corporate. Home: 525 E 86th St New York NY 10028 Office: Willkie Farr & Gallagher 153 E 53d St New York NY 10022

JAKUBCZYK, JOHN JOSEPH, lawyer; b. New Britain, Conn., Dec. 21, 1953; s. Stanley Walter and Madeline Regina (Hinchliffe) J.; m. Petra Kunigunda Mead, Jan. 8, 1983; children: Kristan Marie, John Joseph II, Jamie Nicole. BA in Bus. Adminstrn. and Polit. Sci., U. San Diego, 1976; JD, U. Ariz., 1979. Bar: Ariz. 1979, U.S. Dist. Ct. Ariz. 1979. Sole practice, Phoenix, 1979—; speaker in field. Author pro-life articles; radio commentator and host. Bd. dirs., cons. Ariz. Youth for Life, Phoenix, 1979-82; chmn. polit. action com. Arizonans for Life, 1980-81; pres. Ariz. Right to Life, Phoenix, 1983-85, bd. dirs.; bd. dirs. Life Ednl. Corp., 1984—, sec.; founder, pres. Southwest Life and Law Ctr.; bd. advisers Free Speech Advs.; precinct committeeman Republican Party, Phoenix, 1982—. Recipient Pro-Life Action League Protector award, 1987. Mem. Assn. Trial Lawyers Am., Ariz. State Bar Assn. (arbitrator 1983—), Phi Delta Phi. Roman Catholic. Lodge: K.C. (pro-life chmn. 1982-83). Construction, Personal injury, Civil rights. Office: 4607 N 24th St #100 Phoenix AZ 85016

JAMAIL, JOSEPH DAHR, JR., lawyer; b. Houston, Oct. 19, 1925; s. Joseph Dahr and Marie (Anton) J.; m. Lillie Mae Hage, Aug. 28, 1949; children: Joseph Dahr III, Randall Hage, Robert Lee. B.A., U. Tex., 1950, J.D., 1953. Bar: Tex. 1952. Since practiced in Houston; asst. dist. atty. Harris County, Tex., 1954-55; prof. tort law U. Tex., 1981. Contbr. articles to profl. jours. Served to sgt. USMCR, 1943-46. Fellow Internat. Acad. Law and Sci., Internat. Soc. Barristers, Internat. Acad. Trial Lawyers, Am. Coll. Trial Lawyers, Inner Circle of Advocates; mem. Am., Houston bar assns., Houston Jr. Bar (dir. 1954-55, treas. 1955-56, v.p. 1956-57, pres. 1957-58), State Bar Tex. (chmn. grievance com. 1963, chmn. town hall task force 1973-74), Tex. Assn. Plaintiff Attys. (dir. 1961-63), Tex. Trial Lawyers Assn., Assn. Trial Lawyers Am., Am. Judicature Soc., Am. Bd. Trial Advocates, Lawyer-Pilot Bar Assn., Delta Theta Phi. Home: 5750 Indian Circle Houston TX 77057 Office: 3300 One Allen Center 500 Dallas Houston TX 77002

JAMAR, STEVEN DWIGHT, lawyer; b. Ishpeming, Mich., May 11, 1953; s. Dwight W. and Lorraine (Persgard) J.; m. Shelley June Von Hagen, May 19, 1979; children: Alexander S. Von Hagen, Eric D. Von Hagen. BA, Carleton Coll., 1975; JD, Hamline U., 1979. Bar: Minn. 1979, U.S. Dist. Ct. Minn. 1979, U.S. Ct. Appeals (8th cir.) 1986, U.S. Supreme Ct. 1985. Jud. clk. Minn. Supreme Ct., St. Paul, 1979-80; assoc. Meagher, Geer, Markham, Anderson, Adamson, Flaskamp & Brennan, Mpls., 1980-86; prof. William Mitchell Coll. of Law, Mpls., 1987—; sole practice Mpls., 1987—. Contbr. articles to profl. jours. Bd. dirs. Legal Advice Clinics, Hennepin County, Mpls., 1980-87, exec. com. 1986-87. Mem. ABA, Minn. Bar Assn. (computer law sect.), Hennepin County Bar Assn., Sierra Club. Club: Twin Cities Go (St. Paul) (sec. 1986—). Avocations: computers, canoe camping, cross country skiing, swimming. Computer, Construction, Federal civil litigation. Office: 1625 Park Ave S Minneapolis MN 55404

JAMBOIS, ROBERT JAMES, lawyer; b. Madison, Wis., Feb. 1, 1952; s. William Henry and Eleanor (Joyce) J.; m. Beverly Ann Norman, June 9, 1979; 1 child, Stacey Marie. BA, U. Wis., Parkside, 1978; JD, U. Wis., Madison, 1981. Bar: Wis. 1981, U.S. Dist. Ct. (ea. and we. dists.) Wis. 1981. Atty. City of Kenosha, Wis., 1981—. Mem. ABA, Wis. Bar Assn., Kenosha County Bar Assn. Democrat. Local government, Government contracts and claims. Office: City Atty's Office 625 52d St Kenosha WI 53140

JAMES, ANN NIXON, lawyer; b. Floyd, Va., Nov. 11, 1944; d. Pierce Nixon Weeks and Lorraine Ann Sutphin; m. Donald L. Holmquest, Oct. 24, 1972; 1 child, Hilary Catharine. BA cum laude, Radford Coll., 1965; PhD, Baylor Coll., 1975; JD, U. Houston, 1980. Bar: Tex. 1981, U.S. Dist. Ct. (so. dist.) Tex. 1982, U.S. Ct. Appeals (5th cir.) 1982. Scientist Teledyne Brown, Huntsville, Ala., 1961-71; instr. Baylor Coll. Medicine, Houston, 1971-80; assoc. Vinson & Elkins, Houston, 1980-82; ptnr. Wood, Lucksinger & Epstein, Houston, 1982—; adj. asst. prof. Dept. Rehab., Baylor Coll. Medicine, Houston, 1982-85; adj. prof. law, U. Houston, 1981—; instr. Dept. Engring., U. Ala., Huntsville, 1968-71; resident research assoc. cellular biology lab., Johnson Space Ctr., Houston, 1977-79; staff dir. congl. liasion Tex. Infant Mortality Task Force, Houston, 1979-82; counsel to pres. Inst. for Rehab. and Research, Houston, 1982-83; lectr. various orgns. Contbr. articles to profl. jours. Active Leadership Houston, 1984. Recipient Outstanding Alumnna award Radford U., 1981; NSF, fellow NIH, Nat. Research Council of Nat. Acad. Sci.; named Women on the Move honoree, 1986. Mem. ABA, AAAS (congl. sci. fellow 1979-80), DAR, Houston Bar Assn., Nat. Health Lawyers Assn., Am. Soc. Microbiology, Am. Women in Sci., Houston Scientific and Engring. Council (bd. dirs., chmn. com. on minority edn. 1979-80), Nat. Women's Polit. Caucus, Chi Beta Pi, Sigma Xi. Democrat. Methodist. Avocations: skiing, running. Health, Administrative and regulatory. Office: Wood Lucksinger & Epstein 1221 Lamar St Suite 1400 Houston TX 77010

JAMES, ERICH WILLIAM, lawyer; b. Memphis, Mar. 25, 1931; s. Jesse Arvin and Alma Louise (Meyer) J.; m. Edith Brooks Proctor, Jan. 16, 1965; children: Letitia Vance, Erich William Jr. BA, Vanderbilt U., 1953, JD, 1960. Ptnr. Lee, James & Hall, Memphis, 1960-63; assoc. Waring, Walker, Cox & Lewis, Memphis, 1963-65, ptnr., 1965-78; of counsel Waring, Cox, Memphis, 1978—. Assoc. editor Vanderbilt U. Law Rev., 1959-60. Served to maj. USMC, 1953-57, with Res. 1957-69. Mem. ABA, Tenn. Bar Assn., Tenn. Def. Lawyers Assn., Memphis Bar Assn., Shelby County Bar Assn., Nat. Rifle Assn. Republican. Episcopalian. Lodge: Masons. Avocations: hunting, fishing. State civil litigation, Insurance, Workers' compensation. Home: 5620 Barfield Rd Memphis TN 38119 Office: Waring Cox Law Firm 50 N Front St Memphis TN 38103

JAMES, GUS JOHN, II, lawyer; b. Koma Yiolou, Cyprus, Dec. 29, 1938; s. John and Salome J.; m. Helen Alexion, July 25, 1964; children: Mary Margaret, Nicole. BS in Bus., U. Richmond, 1962; JD, Coll. William and Mary, 1966, LLM in Taxation, 1967. Bar: Va. 1966. Assoc. Kaufman and Oberndorfer, Norfolk, Va., 1966-72, ptnr., 1972-76, mng. ptnr., 1976-81; mem. Kaufman & Canoles, Norfolk, 1982—, chmn. exec. com., 1982-84; lectr. in field. Editor-in-chief: William and Mary Law Rev., 1965-66. Bd. dirs. Annunciation Greek Orthodox Ch., Norfolk, 1972-80, 1981-84, pres. parish council, 1973-84, chmn. Neptune Festival com., 1977-84, chmn. Azalea Festival com., 1976-84; bd. dirs. Med. Ctr. Hosps., Norfolk Symphony, Va. Orch. Group, Old Dominion U. Intercollegiate Found., Old Dominion U. Ednl. Found.; chmn. Old Dominion U. Soccer Com. Served with USAR, 1963-68. Mem. ABA, Va. Bar Assn., Norfolk-Portsmouth Bar Assn., Va. Assn. Hosp. Attys. Club: Order Ahepa. Contracts commercial, General corporate, Corporate taxation. Home: 4137 Country Club Circle Virginia Beach VA 23455 Office: 2000 Sovran Ctr Norfolk VA 23510

JAMES, JIMMY ROBERT, lawyer; b. Chattanooga, Apr. 7, 1933; s. Fulton Mark and Alberta (Cooke) J.; m. Elizabeth Munn, Feb. 26, 1960; children—Scott, Mark, David (dec.). B.S., U. Houston, 1955; J.D., South Tex. U., 1973. Bar: Tex. 1959, U.S. Dist. Ct. (so. dist.) Tex., U.S. Ct. Appeals (5th cir.). Asst. dist. atty. Harris County Dist. Attys. Office, Houston, 1960-69; criminal def. lawyer James & Price, Houston, 1969-77; judge 248th Dist. Ct. Harris County, Houston, 1977-81; assoc. 14th Ct. Appeals Harris County, Houston, 1981-82; sole practice, Houston, 1983-87; vis. dist. judge, Houston, 1987—; spl. cons. Criminal Justice Counsel Tex., 1970-71. Mem. Tex. Bar Assn. Republican. Episcopalian. Criminal. Office: 301 San Jacinto Houston TX 77002

JAMES, JOYCE MARIE, lawyer; b. Cin., Oct. 23, 1951; d. James Andrew and June Eleanor (Catterall) C.; m. Daniel K. James; children: James Andrew, June Eleanor. Student, Shimer Coll., 1968-70; BA, U. Minn., 1974; JD cum laude, William Mitchell Coll. Law, 1979. Bar: Minn. 1979, U.S. Dist. Ct. Minn. 1979. Law clk. to presiding justice Minn. Dist. Ct., Stillwater, 1977-79; assoc. Dorsey & Whitney, Mpls., 1979-83, MacIntosh & Commers, Mpls., 1983-84; trust officer First Bank System, Mpls., 1984—. Chairperson legal advice clinics, Mpls., 1985-86. Mem. ABA, Minn. State Bar Assn. (probate and trust law sect., chmn. community relations com. 1984-87, pub. affairs task force 1987—), Hennepin County Bar Assn., Minn. Women Lawyers Assn. (pres. 1984-85), Young Women Christian Assn. (deferred giving com. 1986), Minn. Womens Fund (deferred giving com. 1985). Avocations: golf, piano, biking, reading and discussing scriptures. Probate, Estate planning, Estate taxation.

JAMES, KEITH ALAN, lawyer; b. Wichita, Kans., Sept. 29, 1957; s. Anthony Ray James and Patricia Ann Jones; Elaine Penelope Johnson, Aug. 14, 1982. BA, Harvard U., 1979, JD, 1982. Bar: Pa. 1982, U.S. Dist. Ct. (ea. dist.) Pa. 1982. Atty. Girard Bank, Phila., 1982-84; assoc. Wolf, Block, Schorr & Solis-Cohen, Phila., 1984—. bd. dirs. A Better Chance in Lower Merion, Ardmore, Pa., 1984—. Named one of Outstanding Young Men in Am., 1983. Democrat. Clubs: Harvard (Phila.); Fox (Cambridge, Mass.). Computer, General corporate, Bankruptcy. Office: Wolf Block Schorr & Solis-Cohen Packard Bldg 12th Floor Philadelphia PA 19102

JAMES, L. C., lawyer; b. Poplarville, Miss., Feb. 27, 1945; s. Charles Edwin and Lessie Mae (Baucum) J.; m. Sheila Gillis, Aug. 20, 1967; children—Rachel Diane, April Marian, David Edwin. B.A., U. So. Miss., 1967; J.D., U. Miss., 1973. Ptnr. Wilkins, Ellington & James, Jackson, Miss., 1973-83, James & Assoc., Jackson, 1984—. State chmn. Young Lawyer's Child Abuse Com., Jackson, 1980. Served with USAF, 1967-71. Mem. ABA, Assn. Trial Lawyers Am., Phi Delta Phi. Republican. Baptist. Club: Optimist. Family and matrimonial, Criminal, Personal injury. Office: PO Box 897 105 N State St Jackson MS 39205

JAMES, LARRY HOLLIDAY, lawyer; b. Elyria, Ohio, Dec. 26, 1950. BA in Polit. Sci., Wittenberg U., 1974; JD, Cleve. State U., 1977. Bar: Ohio 1977, U.S. Dist. Ct. (so. and no. dists.) Ohio 1977, U.S. Supreme Ct. 1983. From assoc. to ptnr. Crabbe, Brown, Jones, Potts & Schmidt, Columbus, Ohio, 1981—; asst. atty. City of Columbus, Ohio, 1978-81; adj. prof. Franklin U., Columbus, 1979-80; asst. commr., legal counsel div. of air pollution control City of Cleve., 1977-78. Mem. Mayor's Adv. Com., 1983—; atty. Century Found.; advisor to pres. of City Council, 1982—; bd. trustees Netcare, 1985—, Vets. Meml., 1985—. Mem. ABA, Ohio Bar Assn. (council of dels. 1983-85), Columbus Bar Assn. (long range planning com., noon luncheon com., vice chmn. ethics com. 1983, chmn. unauthorized practice of law com. 1981-83, co-chairperson law day 1981). Civil rights, State civil litigation, Legislative. Home: 369 Jackson St Columbus OH 43206 Office: Crabbe Brown Jones Potts & Schmidt 2500 One Nationwide Plaza Columbus OH 43215

JAMES, RICHARD ROBERT, lawyer, air force officer; b. Belleville, Ill., Apr. 25, 1946; s. Robert Huey and Alma Evelyn (Watts) J. B.A., U. Ga., 1968, J.D., 1970. Bar: Ga. 1970, U.S. Ct. Mil. Appeals 1971, U.S. Supreme Ct. 1974, U.S. Tax. Ct. 1981, U.S. Ct. Claims 1981, U.S. Ct. Appeals (D.C. and fed. cirs.) 1982, U.S. Army Ct. Mil Rev. 1982, D.C. 1983. Commd. capt. U.S. Air Force, 1970, advanced through grades to lt. col., 1982; asst. staff judge adv. Hill AFB, Ogden, Utah, 1970-73; cir. def. counsel Maxwell AFB, Montgomery, Ala., 1973-76; faculty Air Force JAG Sch., Montgomery, 1976-80; staff mem. Office of JAG, Washington, 1980-84; staff judge adv., Kunsan, Republic Korea, 1984-85, acting staff judge adv. First Air Force, Langley AFB, Va., 1985-86; dir. civil law Tactical Air Command, Langley AFB, 1986—. Co-draftsman: Manual for Courts-Martial, 1984. Mgr., editor FBA News and Jour., 1983. Mem. Fed. Bar Assn. (chpt. treas. 1981-82, v.p. 1982-83, pres. 1983-84), ABA, Assn. Trial Lawyers Am., D.C. Bar Assn., Judge Advs. Assn. (bd. dirs. 1984—), Air Force Assn., Mensa. Republican. Military, Criminal, Legislative. Home: RFD 3 Box 331 Amherst VA 24521 Office: HQ TAC/JAC Langley AFB VA 23665-5001

JAMESON, DAVID ALAN, lawyer; b. Galveston, Tex., Jan. 29, 1952; s. Henry Jameson. BA, U. Houston, Clear Lake City, 1977; JD, U. Tex., 1980. Sole practice Galveston, 1983-86; ptnr. Yarbrough, Jameson and Gray, Galveston, 1986—; mem. profl. staff Ho. Com. on Govt. Ops., Washington, 1980-83. Chmn. social action Temple B'nai Israel, Galveston, 1983; treas. Galveston County Dems., 1983. Named to Order of Barristers, U. Tex. Law Bd. Advocates, 1980. Mem. Galveston County Bar Assn. (bd. dirs. 1983), Galveston County Young Lawyers Assn. (treas. 1985-86, Outstanding Young Lawyer of Galveston County 1986). Criminal, Family and matrimonial. Office: 520 20th St Galveston TX 77550

JAMESON, GENE LANIER, lawyer; b. Dallas, Jan. 18, 1936; s. Joseph Andrew and Minnie (Kittrell) J.; m. Lois Marie Shanahan, July 19, 1958; children: Holly, Scott. BA in Econs., Tex. A&M, 1958; LLB, U. Tex., 1966. Bar: Tex. 1966, U.S. Supreme Ct. 1975, U.S. Ct. Appeals (5th and 11th cirs.) 1981. Assoc. Stubbeman, et al, Midland, Tex., 1966-69; staff atty. 1st Nat. Bank Dallas/1st Internat. Bankshares, 1969-77; assoc. Coke & Coke, Dallas, 1977-79, ptnr., 1979-84; ptnr. Jones, Day, Reavis & Pogue, Dallas, 1984—. Served to capt. U.S. Army, 1958-63. Banking, Contracts commercial. Home: 13650 Peyton Dr Dallas TX 75240 Office: Jones Day Reavis & Pogue 2001 Ross Ave 2300 LTV Ctr PO Box 660623 Dallas TX 75266-0623

JAMESON, PAULA ANN, lawyer; b. New Orleans, Feb. 19, 1945; d. Paul Henry and Virginia Lee (Powell) Bailey; 1 child, Paul Andrew. B.A., La. State U., 1966; J.D., U. Tex., 1969. Bar: Tex. 1969, D.C. 1970, Va., 1973, N.Y. 1978, U.S. Dist. Ct. D.C. 1970, U.S. Dist. Ct. (ea. dist.) Va. 1976, U.S. Ct. Appeals (D.C. cir.) 1972, U.S. Ct. Appeals (4th cir.) 1976, U.S. Ct. Appeals (5th cir.) 1978, U.S. Supreme Ct. 1973, U.S. Ct. Appeals (2d cir.) 1985. Asst. corp. counsel D.C. Corp. Counsel's Office, 1970-73; sr. asst. county atty. Fairfax County Atty.'s Office, Fairfax, Va., 1973-77; atty. Dow Jones & Co., Inc., Princeton, N.J., 1977-79; house counsel Dow Jones & Co., Inc., N.Y.C., 1979-81; asst. to chmn. bd., 1981-83, house counsel, dir. legal dept., 1983-86; sr. v.p., gen. counsel, PBS, Alexandria, Va., 1986—. Mem. ABA, Fed. Communications Bar Assn., D.C. Bar Assn., Assn. Bar City N.Y. Democrat. Roman Catholic. General corporate, Trademark and copyright, Communications. Office: PBS 1320 Braddock Place Alexandria VA 22314

JAMIESON, JAMES PHILLIPS, lawyer; b. Miami, Fla., Jan. 15, 1953; s. Joseph G. and Betty M. (Phillips) J.; m. Deborah R. Nelson, June 9, 1973; children: Matthew, Ian, Trevor. BA, Fla. Atlantic U., 1975; JD, U. Fla., 1977. Bar: Fla. 1977, U.S. Dist. Ct. (mid. dist.) Fla. 1978, U.S. Ct. Claims 1978, U.S. Tax Ct. 1978, U.S. Ct. Customs and Patent Appeals 1978, U.S. Ct. Appeals (5th cir.) 1980, U.S. Ct. Appeals (11th cir.) 1981. Atty. State of Fla., Sarasota, 1977-80; atty. law dept. State of Fla., Miami, 1980-81; ptnr. Barton, Davis, Fernandez & Jamieson, Gainesville, Fla., 1981-85; mng. ptnr. Krugman-Kadi & Jamieson, Gainesville, 1985-86; sole practice Gainesville, 1986—; supr. Fla. Parole & Probation Comm., Ft. Lauderdale, 1971-73. Mem. ABA, 8th Jud. Cir. Bar Assn., Assn. Trial Lawyers Am., Acad. Fla. Trial Lawyers (bd. dirs. 1980-81). Lodge: Elks. Personal injury, Criminal, State civil litigation. Home: 1521 NW 71st Gainesville FL 32601 Office: PO Box 2597 Gainesville FL 32601

JAMIESON, MICHAEL LAWRENCE, lawyer; b. Coral Gables, Fla., Mar. 2, 1940; s. Warren Thomas and Ruth Amelia (Gallman) J.; m. Margaret Wayne Bishop, Aug. 18, 1962; children—Ann Layton, Thomas Howard. B.A. in English, U. Fla., 1961, J.D. with honors, 1964. Bar: Fla. 1964, U.S. Dist. Ct. (mid. dist.) Fla. 1964. Teaching asst. U. Fla., 1964; law clk. U.S. Ct. Appeals (5th cir.), 1964-65; with Holland & Knight and predecessor firms, Tampa, Fla., 1965—; ptnr. Holland & Knight and predecessor firms, 1969—; trustee U. Fla. Law Ctr., chmn. bd., 1986—. Editor-in-chief U. Fla. Law Rev., 1963. Recipient Gertrude Brick Law Rev. award, 1963. Fellow Am. Bar Found.; mem. Am. Law Inst., ABA (com. on corp. laws, com. on fed. regulation of securities), Hillsborough County Bar Assn., Greater Tampa C. of C., Tampa Leadership Conf., Golden Triangle Civic Assn., Order of Coif, Phi Kappa Phi. Clubs: University, Palma Ceia Golf and Country, Tampa (bd. dirs. 1985—, pres. 1987—). General corporate, Securities, Contracts commercial. Office: PO Box 1288 Tampa FL 33601

JAMIN, NOAH NED, judge; b. N.Y.C., Jan. 10, 1924; s. Isaac Noah and Frances Jamin; m. Ilse Wallach, Aug. 27, 1949; children: Teri Susan Guzman Jamin, Judith Ilene. B in Social Sci., City Coll. N.Y., 1946; JD, Boston U., 1948. Bar: N.Y. 1950, Calif. 1963, U.S. Dist. Ct. (so. dist.) Calif. 1965, U.S. Dist. Ct. (no. dist.) Calif. 1966, U.S. Supreme Ct. 1971. Ptnr. Keller & Jamin, N.Y.C., 1955-61; sole practice Palm Springs, Calif., 1963-79; judge Calif. Mcpl. Ct., Palm Springs, 1979-82, Calif. Superior Ct., Palm Springs, 1982—. Chmn. Human Relations Commn. Community Services, Palm Springs, 1976-78; sec. United Way, Palm Springs, 1979-80. Mem. Queens County Bar Assn., Desert Bar Assn. (pres. 1976-77), Assn. Trial Lawyers Am., Calif. Trial Lawyers Assn., N.Y. County Lawyers Assn., Calif. Judges Assn. Lodge: Shriners (pres. Palm Springs 1973). Avocations: reading, travel. Judicial administration. Office: Courthouse Indio CA 92201

JAMISON, JAMEY WILLIAM, lawyer; b. Denver, Aug. 31, 1955; s. Francis Wesley and Joyce Lorraine (Axton) J.; m. Ann Marie Geldaker, Aug. 23, 1980; children: Natalie Michelle, Francis Wesley II, Olivia Joan. BA, U. Denver, 1977, JD, 1980. Bar: Colo. 1981, U.S. Dist. Ct. Colo. 1981. Staff asst. to presiding justice U.S. Dist. Ct. Colo., Golden, 1979-81; assoc. Stuart L. Boulter, P.C., Denver, 1981-84; ptnr. Boulter & Jamison, Denver, 1984—. Mem. Assn. Trial Lawyers Am., Colo. Bar Assn., Denver Bar Assn., 1st Jud. Dist. Bar Assn. Democrat. Club: F.I.S.A. Avocations: golf, tennis, softball, basketball. Personal injury, Insurance, State civil litigation. Home: 442 S Moore St Lakewood CO 80226 Office: Boulter and Jamison 1435 Stuart St Denver CO 80204

JAMISON, JOHN AMBLER, retired circuit judge; b. nr. Florence, S.C., May 14, 1916; s. John Wilson and Elizabeth Ambler (Fleming) J.; m. Mildred Holley, Sept. 22, 1945. LL.B. cum laude, Cumberland U., Lebanon, Tenn., 1941; postgrad., George Washington U., 1943-44, also Indsl. Coll. Armed Forces, 1961; J.D., Samford U., 1969, LL.D. (hon.), 1983. Bar: S.C. 1941, Va. 1942, U.S. Supreme Ct. 1945. Atty. Va. Div. Motor Vehicles, 1947-54; practiced law Fredericksburg, Va., 1954-72; assoc. judge Stafford and King George County Cts., also Fredericksburg Municipal Ct., 1956-72; judge 15th Jud. Circuit Va., 1972-87, chief judge, 1976-78, 84-86; Counsel, dir. Nat. Bank Fredericksburg, 1968-73. Mem. adv. bd. Va. Gov.'s Hwy. Safety Commn., 1956-62, Cumberland Sch. Law, 1980—; pres. Fredericksburg Rescue Squad, 1960-62, now hon. life mem.; chmn. bd. Fredericksburg Area Mental Hygiene Clinic, 1962-63; hon. chmn. Fredericksburg Area Bicentennial Commn., 1975-77; charter mem. Thomas Jefferson Inst. for Religious Freedom, 1975; bd. visitors Coker Coll., Hartsville, S.C.; bd. dirs. Rappahannock Area Devel. Commn., 1960-66. Served from ensign to comdr. USNR, 1941-46; comdg. officer Richmond Naval Res. Div. 1948-54; mem. Res. 1946-54; naval aide to govs. Va. 1954-72. Recipient award S.C. Confederate War Centennial Commn., 1965, Cross of Mil. Service UDC. Mem. ABA, Va. Bar Assn., S.C. Bar Assn., 15th Jud. Circuit Bar Assn. (pres. 1959-60, 69-70), Am. Judicature Soc., Am. Law Inst., Res. Officers Assn., Mil. Order World Wars, Naval Res. Assn., Nat. Soc. S.A.R., Am. Legion (post comdr. 1951-52), Cumberland Law Sch. Alumni Assn. (nat. pres. 1978-79, dean's council 1980—, Disting. Alumnus award 1986), Jud. Conf. Va., Cumberland Order Jurisprudence, Hon. Order Ky. Cols., Blue Key, Sigma Delta Kappa. Episcopalian (past vestryman, warden, lay reader). Lodges: Masons, Shriners, Jesters, Kiwanis. Jurisprudence. Home: 509 Hanover St Fredericksburg VA 22401 Office: PO Drawer 29 Fredericksburg VA 22404

JANICH, DANIEL NICHOLAS, lawyer; b. Chgo., Aug. 8, 1952; s. Nicholas and Antoinette (Colasurdo) J. BA with honors, Marian Coll., 1974; JD, John Marshall Law Sch., 1978; LLM in Taxation, DePaul U., 1986. Bar: Ill. 1978, U.S. Dist. Ct (no. dist.) Ill. 1978, U.S. Ct. Appeals (7th cir.) 1980, U.S.Tax Ct. 1986. Mem. legal dept. Liberty Mutual Ins. Co., Chgo., 1978-84; instr. law DePaul U., Chgo., 1984-85; assoc. O'Keefe, Ashenden, Lyons & Ward, Chgo., 1985-87, Nisen, Elliott & Meier, Chgo., 1987—. Mem. ABA, Chgo. Bar Assn., Am. Arbitration Assn., Delta Theta Phi. Roman Catholic. Corporate taxation, General corporate. Home: 8730 W 45th Pl Lyons IL 60534 Office: Nisen Elliott & Meier One N LaSalle St Suite 2300 Chicago IL 60602

JANIS, N. RICHARD, lawyer; b. Washington, Nov. 23, 1946; s. Mortimer Lewis and Mildred (Sacks) J.; m. Jan C. Campbell, July 23, 1972 (div. 1980); 1 child, Taylor Lael. BA, U. Wis., 1968; JD, Harvard U., 1972. Bar: D.C. 1973, U.S. Dist. Ct. D.C. 1973, U.S. Ct. Appeals (D.C. cir.) 1973, U.S. Supreme Ct. 1978, U.S. Dist. Ct. Md. 1985. Asst. U.S. atty. U.S. Dept. Justice, Washington, 1972-76; ptnr. Sharp, Randolph & Janis, Washington, 1976-79; sole practice Washington, 1979; ptnr. Janis, Schuelke & Wechsler, Washington, 1979—; lectr. George Washington U. Grad. Sch. Forensic Sciences, Washington, 1977-83. Mem. ABA, D.C. Bar Assn. (hearing examiner bd. on profl. responsibility 1985—), Assn. Trial Lawyers Am. Avocations: tennis, oriental rugs, antiques. Federal civil litigation, Criminal, Personal injury. Home: 5063 Overlook Rd NW Washington DC 20016 Office: Janis Schuelke & Wechsler 1728 Massachusetts Ave NW Washington DC 20036

JANIS, RICHARD ALAN, lawyer; b. N.Y.C., Sept. 21, 1951; s. J. William and Edna (Hirsch) J.; m. Carol Lee Johnson, May 29, 1982. BA in Econs., Northwestern U., 1973; JD, Gonzaga U., 1976; LLM in Taxation, NYU, 1977. Bar: Ill., Wash., U.S. Dist. Ct. (no. dist.) Ill. Sr. tax analyst United Airlines, Chgo., 1977-81, mgr. tax research and planning, 1985—; assoc. tax counsel Fluor Corp., Irvine, Calif., 1981-84; tax counsel Fluor Corp., Irvine, 1984-85. Mem. ABA (chmn. rates and credits taxation sect. 1980—), Wash. State Bar Assn. Corporate taxation, State and local taxation. Home: 2 Sheffield Ct Lincolnshire IL 60015 Office: United Airlines Inc PO Box 66100 Chicago IL 60666

JANKE, RONALD ROBERT, lawyer; b. Milw., Mar. 2, 1947; s. Robert Erwin and Elaine Patricia (Wilken) J.; m. Mary Ann Burg, July 3, 1971; children—Jennifer, William, Emily. B.A. cum laude, Wittenberg U., 1969; J.D. with distinction, Duke U., 1974. Bar: Ohio 1974. Assoc. Jones, Day, Reavis & Pogue, Cleve., 1974-83, ptnr., 1983—. Served with U.S. Army, 1970-71, Vietnam. Mem. ABA (chmn. environ. control com. 1980-83), Ohio Bar Assn., Greater Cleve. Bar Assn., Eastern Mineral Law Found. Environment. Office: Jones Day Reavis & Pogue 1700 Huntington Bldg Cleveland OH 44115

JANKLOW, DONALD EMANUEL, lawyer; b. East Saint Louis, Ill., Aug. 31, 1946; s. Bernard Milton and Helen (Silberman) J.; m. Lynn Dani Saslow, Aug. 16, 1981; children: Danielle Lynn, Erin Leah. AA, Foothill Coll., 1966; BBA, U. Denver, 1968, JD, 1972; spl. tng. Nat. Coll. Criminal Def., 1975, Nat. Inst. Trial Advocacy, 1976, Assn. Trial Lawyers Am. Advanced Advocacy Coll., 1977, 78. Bar: Colo. 1972, U.S. Dist. Ct. Colo. 1972. Atty., Student Legal Services, U. No. Colo., Greeley, 1972-85; sole practice Greeley, 1985—. Bd. dirs. Greeley Ctr. for Human Devel., 1977-79; Weld County Dem. precinct committeeman, Greeley, 1976-78, 82-84, 86—. Served with U.S. Army, 1969-70. Mem. Weld County Bar Assn., Colo. Trial Lawyers Assn., Colo. Bar Assn. (chmn. bill of rights com. 1978), Nat. Assn. Student Attys., Weld County Young Lawyers Assn. (pres. 1980), Nat. Legal Aid And Defender Assn. (chmn. student legal services sect. 1982-84, sec.-treas. 1981-82). Jewish. State civil litigation, Criminal, Personal injury. Office: Greeley Nat Plaza Suite 505 Greeley CO 80631

JANNEY, OLIVER JAMES, lawyer, diversified company officer; b. N.Y.C., Feb. 11, 1946; s. Walter Coggeshall and Helen Jennings (James) J.; m. Suzanne Elizabeth Lenz, June 21, 1969; children—Oliver Burr, Elizabeth Flower. B.A. cum laude, Yale Coll., 1967; J.D., Harvard U., 1970. Bar: Mass. 1970, N.Y. 1971. With Walston & Co., Inc., N.Y.C., 1970-73, asst. v.p., 1971-73; assoc. Cleary, Gottlieb, Steen & Hamilton, N.Y.C., 1973-76; with RKO Gen., Inc., N.Y.C., 1976—, asst. sec., 1977-85, asst. gen. atty., 1978-82, asst. gen. counsel, 1982-85, sec., gen. counsel, 1985—. Pres. River Rd. Assn., Scarborough, N.Y.; vestryman St. Mary's Episcopal Ch., Scarborough, 1977-82, treas., 1978-82. Served to 1st lt. USAR, 1969-77. Mem. ABA, N.Y. State Bar Assn., Assn. Bar City N.Y., Fed. Communications Bar Assn. Republican. Club: Sleepy Hollow Country (Scarborough). General corporate, Administrative and regulatory, Entertainment. Home: PO Box 326 Scarborough NY 10510 Office: RKO Gen Inc 1440 Broadway New York NY 10018

JANOS, JOSEPH JOHN, III, lawyer; b. Brownsville, Pa., Mar. 27, 1953; s. Joseph John Jr. and Helen S. (Mickalovich) J. BA, Calif. State U., 1975; MS, W.Va. U., 1976; JD, Temple U., 1981. Bar: Pa. 1982, U.S. Dist. Ct. (we. dist.) Pa. 1982, U.S. Dist. Ct. (ea. dist.) Pa. 1986, U.S. Supreme Ct. 1986. Personnel coordinator Standard Oil Co., Cleve., 1976-81; sole practice Pitts., 1982-84; ptnr. Janos & Gardner, Phila., 1984—; adj. prof. Calif. State U., 1982—; corp. counsel TPFD Corp., San Francisco, 1983-85; corp. counsel, sec. and bd. dirs. JANDEZ Pacific Holding Co., Phila., 1986—; pres., bd. dirs. Asian Pacific Securities Corp., Phila., 1986—, Penn Thai Corp., Phila., 1986—; bd. dirs. Janos Found., Phila., 1986—, Panda Internat., Walnut Creek, Calif., Pacific Basin Tng. Inst., Agana, Guam; of spl. counsel Casey and Co., Washington, Zurich, Switzerland. Coordinator United Way, Lima, Ohio, 1976-78; advisor Jr. Achievement, Lima, 1977; v.p. Pitts. Golden Panthers, 1984-85; chmn. campaign United Way, Beaver County, 1983. Mem. ABA, Pa. Bar Assn., Phil. Bar Assn., Allegheny Bar Assn., Am. Soc. of Personnel Adminstrs., Am. Philippine C. of C. (assoc.). Democrat. Presbyterian. Club: Soc. Hill (Phila.), Manila Polo. Immigration, naturalization, and customs, Labor, Private international. Home: 1420 Locust St Academy House Suite 14G Philadelphia PA 19102 Office: Janos & Gardner 1801 Market St Ten Penn Ctr Suite 1000 Philadelphia PA 19103

JANSEN, DONALD ORVILLE, lawyer; b. Odessa, Tex., Nov. 17, 1939; s. Orville Charles and Dolores Elizabeth (Olps) J.; children—Donald Orville, Lauren, Christine, David, Margaret. B.B.A. magna cum laude, Loyola U., New Orleans, 1961, J.D. cum laude, 1963; LL.M., Georgetown U., 1966. Bar: La. 1963, Tex. 1965. Ptnr. Fulbright and Jaworski, Houston, 1966—. Served to capt. JAGC, U.S. Army, 1963-66. Mem. ABA, Fed. Bar Assn. State Bar Tex., La. Bar Assn., Am. Coll. Probate Counsel. Roman Catholic. Estate planning, Probate, Estate taxation. Home: 806 Magdalene St Houston TX 77024

JAQUA, DAVID PALMER, lawyer; b. Meridian, Miss., July 24, 1951; s. Francis Palmer Jaqua and Thellis (Knight) Harvey; m. Joy Harvey, June 8, 1973; children: Allyn Elizabeth, Benjamin Hudson. BS, U.S. Naval Acad., 1973; JD, U. Miss., 1976. Bar: Miss. 1977, Tenn. 1977, U.S. Ct. Appeals (6th cir.) 1979. From assoc. to ptnr. Armstrong, Allen, Braden, Goodman, McBride & Prewitt, Memphis, 1977—. Served with USN, 1973-74. Mem. ABA, Tenn. Bar Assn., Miss. Bar Assn. Republican. Methodist. Avocations: amateur astronomy, running. Labor, Administrative and regulatory, Civil rights. Home: 2342 Massey Rd Memphis TN 38119 Office: Armstrong Allen Braden Goodman et al 1900 One Commerce Sq Memphis TN 38103

JAQUES, FRANK HESKETH, lawyer; b. Oklahoma City, Nov. 8, 1934; s. Robert Hesketh and Eula Hester (Shelton) J.; m. Frances Rebecca Ballard, Nov. 18, 1960; children—Robert H. II, John Fell. B.A. with distinction, U. Okla., 1956, LL.B., 1958. Bar: Okla. 1958, U.S. Dist. Ct. (ea. dist.) Okla., U.S. Dist. Ct. (we. dist.) Okla., U.S. Ct. Appeals (10th cir.), U.S. Supreme Ct. Mem. firm Lambert, Roberts & Jaques, Inc., and predecessor firms Kerr, Lambert, Conn & Roberts, Kerr, Lambert, Roberts, Lambert, Roberts & Lewis, Lambert, Roberts Jaques & Scrivner, Ada, Okla., 1961—; mem. bd. dirs. The Gloria Corp., Pre-Paid Legal Services, Inc., Profl. Motor Service Club, Okla. State Bank, Ada; judge Ct. of Appeals, Okla. Temporary Div. 23. Ex officio bd. dirs. Okla. Cardiovascular Inst.; past chmn. Heart Fund; former chmn. gifts com. Community Chest; active Okla. U. Assocs., pres. adv. council East Central U. Served to capt. USAF, 1958-61. Editor Okla. U. Law Rev. Mem. ABA, Okla. Bar Assn., Pontotoc County Bar Assn. (past pres.), Okla. Bd. Bar Examiners (past chmn.). Democrat. Presbyterian. Federal civil litigation, State civil litigation, General corporate. Home: 114 E Kings Rd Ada OK 74820 Office: Lambert Roberts & Jaques 201 W 14th PO Box 130 Ada OK 74820

JAQUES, LEONARD C., lawyer; b. Jefferson, Iowa, Oct. 8, 1927; s. Leonard Benjamin and Minnie Olive (Whitecotton) J.; m. Sybil June Smith, Oct. 8, 1965; 1 child, Alisa. BA, U. Calif., Berkeley, 1954; JD, Am. U., 1962. Bar: Iowa 1962, U.S. Dist. Ct. (so. dist.) Iowa 1962, Mich. 1964, U.S. Dist. Ct. (ea. dist.) Mich. 1964, U.S. Dist. Ct. (we. dist.) Tenn. 1967, U.S. Dist. Ct. (so. dist.) Ala. 1967, U.S. Dist. Ct. (no. dist.) Ohio 1967, U.S. Dist. Ct. (so. dist.) Ind. 1968, U.S. Ct. Appeals (6th cir.) 1968, U.S. Supreme Ct. 1970, U.S. Ct. Appeals (5th cir.) 1979, U.S. Dist. Ct. (ea. dist.) Tex. 1981, U.S. Dist. Ct. (we. dist.) La. 1981, U.S. Dist. Ct. (no. dist.) Miss. 1981, U.S. Dist. Ct. Md. 1981, U.S. Dist. Ct. (no. dist.) Calif. 1981, U.S. Dist. Ct. (no. dist.) Okla. 1981, U.S. Dist. Ct. Nebr. 1981, U.S. Dist. Ct. (we. dist.) Mich. 1981, U.S. Ct. Appeals (4th cir.) 1983. Sole practice Detroit, 1962—; bd. dirs. Detroit Econ. Growth Corp.; lectr. in field. Contbr. articles to profl. jours. Mem. Detroit Inst. of Arts, The Founders Soc., Heart and Lung Assn., The Cancer Soc.; trustee United Seamen Service, N.Y.C.; commr. Detroit Hist. Dept.; bd. dirs Detroit Hist. Commn., Grosse Pointe Symphony Orch., Detroit Symphony Orch. Served with USAF, 1952-55, Korea. Mem. Mich. Bar Assn., Detroit Bar Assn., Great Lakes Maritime Bar Assn., Fed. Bar Assn., Internat. Bar Assn., Maritime Law Assn. of U.S., Assn. Trial Lawyers Am., Asia-Pacific Lawyers Assn., Phi Alpha Delta. Presbyterian. Clubs: Detroit Golf; Grosse Pointe (Mich.) Yacht; Hotel and Beach (Boca Raton, Fla.), Bear Creek Golf (Hiltonhead, S.C.); Cleve. Athletic; Detroit Ren Cen;. Avocations: golf, tennis, race walking, swimming, hist. lit. enthusiast. Admiralty. Home: 936 Lakeshore Rd Grosse Pointe Shores MI 48236 Office: 1370 Penobscot Detroit MI 48226

JARBLUM, WILLIAM, lawyer; b. Havana, Cuba, Aug. 29, 1945; came to U.S., 1946; s. Richard S. and Dora F. (Nadel) J.; m. Susan P. Reich, May 24, 1970; children—Kimberly, Meredith. Student U. Va., 1962-64; B.A., C.W. Post Coll. of L.I.U., 1967; J.D., Georgetown U., 1970. Bar: N.Y. 1971, U.S. Dist. Ct. (so. and ea. dists.) N.Y. 1972. Assoc., Otterbourg, Steindler, Houston & Rosen, P.C., N.Y.C., 1970-71, Finley, Kumble, Underberg, Persky & Roth, P.C., N.Y.C., 1971-73; ptnr. Persky & Jarblum, P.C., N.Y.C., 1973-75, Fine, Tofel & Saxl, N.Y.C., 1975-77; sole practice, N.Y.C., 1977-79; ptnr. Jarblum Solomon & Fornari, P.C., N.Y.C., 1979—. Asst. regional dir. western states Citizens for Humphrey-Muskie, Washington, 1968. Mem. Assn. Bar City N.Y., N.Y. State Bar Assn., N.Y. County Bar Assn. (com. on securities and exchanges). General corporate, Real property, Securities. Home: 86 Heritage Ct Woodcliff Lake NJ 07675 Office: Jarblum Solomon & Fornari PC 650 Fifth Ave New York NY 10019

JARBOE, JOHN BRUCE, lawyer; b. Tulsa, Mar. 28, 1940; s. Joseph Ralph and Mildred Marie (Maguire) J.; m. Sally Lea Bauer, Aug. 1, 1969; children: J.B., Sarah, Susanne. BA, U. Okla., 1962; JD, U. Tulsa, 1965. Bar: Okla. 1965, La. 1967. Law clk. to presiding judge U.S. Dist. Ct. Okla., Tulsa, 1964-65; trial atty. U.S. Dept. Justice, Washington, 1965-66; sole practice Tulsa, 1968—; ptnr. Jarboe, Keefer & Swinson, Tulsa, 1984—; judge temp. div. Okla. Ct. Appeals, 1982. Editor in chief Tulsa Law Jour., 1964-65. Dem. nominee U.S. Congress 1st Dist., Okla., 1968; mem. bd. regents U. Okla. Coll. Arts and Scis., 1971-79, chmn. bd. regents, 1971-72; mem. Okla. Water Resources Bd., 1979-83. Served with U.S. Army, 1966-68. Mem. ABA, La. Bar Assn., Okla. Bar Assn. (chmn. bankruptcy and reorganization sect. 1983-84), Tulsa County Bar Assn. (v.p. 1985-86), Sigma Chi. Roman Catholic. Club: So. Country, Tulsa. Avocations: photography. Bankruptcy, Antitrust, General corporate. Home: 2186 S Owasso Tulsa OK 74114 Office: Jarboe Swinson & Stoermer 1810 Mid Continent Bldg Tulsa OK 74103

JARBOE, MARK ALAN, lawyer; b. Flint, Mich., Aug. 19, 1951; s. Lloyd Aloysius and Helen Elizabeth (Frey) J.; m. Patricia Kovel, Aug. 20, 1971; 1 child, Alexander. Student, No. Mich. U., 1968-69; AB with high distinction, U. Mich., 1972; JD magna cum laude, Harvard U., 1975. Bar: Minn. 1975, U.S. Dist. Ct. Minn. 1975, U.S. Ct. Appeals (8th cir.) 1975. Law clk. to presiding justice Minn. State Ct., St. Paul, 1975-76; from assoc. to ptnr. Dorsey & Whitney, Mpls., 1976—. Pres. parish council Ch. of Christ the King, Mpls., 1981-83. Mem. Phi Beta Kappa. Republican. Roman Catholic. Municipal bonds, Banking, Indian law. Home: 4816 W Lake Harriet Pkwy Minneapolis MN 55410 Office: Dorsey & Whitney 2200 1st Bank Pl East Minneapolis MN 55402

JARDINE, JOHN HAWLEY, lawyer; b. Rochester, N.Y., Sept. 10, 1922; s. Andrew Hawley and Irene (Smith) J.; widowed; 1 child, Merridy Jardine Hocking. BA in Econs., U. Rochester, 1948; LLB, U. Mont., 1951. Bar: Mont. 1951, U.S. Supreme Ct. 1959. Sr. ptnr. Jardine, McCarthy & Grauman, Whitehall, Mont., 1952—; pres. The Whitehall State Bank, 1966-70, chmn. bd. dirs., 1970-83, bd. dirs. Rep. Mont. State Legislature, Helena, 1959-60; mem. Mont. Bd. Welfare Appeals, Helena, 1970-71. Served to 1st lt. AC, USAF, 1940-45, ETO, 1951-52. Decorated D.F.C., Air medal with four bronze oak leaf clusters. Mem. Nat. SBA Adv. Council, Greenland Expedition Soc. (bd. dirs. 1984—). Democrat. Avocations: Cert. commercial and instrument flying, sailing and gliding instructor, skiing. Banking, State civil litigation, Probate. Office: Jardine McCarthy & Grauman PO Box 488 12 N Main Whitehall MT 59759

JARRETT, GLENN ALAN, lawyer; b. Bklyn., Mar. 28, 1949; s. Julian Everett and Melba (Gold) J.; m. Judith Barber, Sept. 5, 1982; 1 child, Benjamin Atwood. AB, Middlebury Coll., 1970; JD, Georgetown U., 1973. Bar: Vt. 1973, U.S. Dist. Ct. Vt. 1973, U.S. Ct. Appeals (2d cir.) 1975, U.S. Supreme Ct. 1980. Law clk. to presiding judge U.S. Dist. Ct. Vt., Burlington, 1973-74; assoc. Downs, Rachlin and Martin, St. Johnsbury, Vt., 1974-76; dep. defender gen. Office of Defender Gen., Montpelier, 1976-77; pub. defender Office of Pub. Defender, Burlington, 1977-78; asst. atty. gen. Office of Atty. Gen., Montpelier, 1978—. Mem. ABA, Vt. Bar Assn. (bd. mgrs. 1977-79). Antitrust, Federal civil litigation, Administrative and regulatory. Home: 105 Robinson Pkwy Burlington VT 05401 Office: Agy of Transp 133 State St Montpelier VT 05602

JARRETT, VALERIE BOWMAN, lawyer; b. Shiraz, Iran, Nov. 14, 1956; d. James Edward and Barbara (Taylor) B.; m. William Robert Jarrett, Sept. 3, 1983; 1 child, Laura Allison. BA, Stanford U., 1978; JD, U. Mich., 1981. Bar: Ill. 1981, U.S. Dist. Ct. (no. dist.) Ill. 1981. Assoc. Pope, Ballard, Shepard & Fowle Ltd., Chgo., 1981-84, Sonnenschein, Carlin, Nath & Rosenthal, Chgo., 1984—. Bd. dirs. Southeast Chgo. Commn., 1985—, Planned Parenthood Assn., Chgo. Leadership Greater Chgo. fellow, 1985-86. Mem. ABA, Ill. Bar Assn., Chgo. Bar Assn. Democrat. Avocations: opera, tennis, swimming. Real property, General corporate. Office: Sonnenschein Carlin Nath & Rosenthal 8000 Sears Tower Chicago IL 60606

JARVIS, JAMES HOWARD, judge; b. Knoxville, Tenn., Feb 28, 1937; s. Howard F. and Eleanor B. J.; m. Martha Stapleton, June 1957 (div. Feb. 1962); children—James Howard III, Leslie; m. Pamela K. Duncan, Aug. 23, 1964; children—Ann, Kathryn, Louise. B.A., U. Tenn., 1958, J.D., 1960. Bar: Tenn. 1961, U.S. Dist. Ct. (ea. dist.) Tenn. 1961, U.S. Ct. Appeals (6th cir.) 1965. Assoc. O'Neil, Jarvis, Parker & Williamson, Knoxville, Tenn., 1960-68, mem., 1968-70; mem. Meares, Dungan, Jarvis, Maryville, Tenn., 1970-72; judge Law and Equity Ct., Blount County, Tenn., 1972-77, 30th Jud. Cir. Ct., Blount County, 1977-84, U.S. Dist. Ct. (ea. dist.) Tenn., Knoxville, 1984—. Bd. dirs. Maryville (Tenn.) Coll., Met. Knoxville YMCA; past mem. and chmn. fin. com. St. Andrews Episcopal Ch.; past bd. dirs. Detoxification Rehab. Inst. of Knoxville. Mem. ABA (com. ethics and profl. responsibility), Tenn. Bar Assn. (bd. govs. 1983-84), Am. Judicature Soc., Tenn. Trial Judges Assn. (past mem. exec. com.), Tenn. Jud. Conf. (pres. 1983-84), Blount County Bar Assn., Knoxville Bar Assn., Phi Delta Phi, Sigma Chi. Republican. Judicial administration. Home: 406 Willard St Maryville TN 37801 Office: 224 US Post Office & Courthouse 501 Main Ave PO Box 2484 Knoxville TN 37902

JARVIS, KINGSLEY ALBRIGHT, lawyer, educator; b. Montreal, Can., Dec. 18, 1928; s. Kingsley and Esther Albright-Bennell (Langley) J.; m. Maureen Connolly, Dec. 31, 1960; children—Christopher Albright, Diana Albright. A.B., Dartmouth Coll., 1950; J.D., Harvard U., 1953. Bar: Pa. 1954, U.S. Ct. Appeals (3d cir.) 1969, U.S. Supreme Ct. 1970. Sole practice, Scranton, Pa., 1956-60, Norristown, Pa., 1960—; lectr. in law Temple U., 1962-65, Montgomery County Community Coll., 1966—. Chmn. bd. Central Montgomery Mental Health/Mental Retardation, 1980-84, Norristown Human Relations Commn., 1967-69. Served in U.S. Army, 1953-55. Mem. ABA, Pa. Bar Assn., Am. Trial Lawyers Assn. Club: Kiwanis (dir. 1980-83). Author: Pennsylvania Crimes Code and Criminal Law, 1974 and annual supplements; editor: Pennsylvania Guide to Criminal Practice and Procedure, Dunlop-Hanna Criminal Law Forms, 1978—. General practice, Personal injury, Criminal. Home: 1615 DeKalb St Norristown PA 19401 Office: One Montgomery Plaza Suite 707 Norristown PA 19401

JARZABEK, JOSEPH EDWARD, lawyer; b. Phoenix, Sept. 22, 1954; s. Edward John and Doris Jean (Weiss) J.; m. Janice L. Simeone, July 5, 1980; children: Edward, Timothy, Michael. BS, Northern Ariz. U., 1976; JD, U. Idaho, 1980. Bar: Idaho 1980, U.S. Dist. Ct. Idaho 1980. Ptnr. Grudem, Verdy, Elsaesser & Jarzabek, Sandpoint, Idaho, 1980—. Mem. ABA, Assn. Trial Lawyers Am., Idaho Trial Lawyers Assn. Democrat. Roman Catholic. Club: Sandpoint (Idaho) West Athletic. Avocations: travel, running, racquetball, baseball. State civil litigation, Workers' compensation, Personal injury. Office: Grudem Verby Elsaesser & Jarzabek PO Box 1049 Sandpoint ID 83864

JASEN, MATTHEW JOSEPH, state justice; b. Buffalo, Dec. 13, 1915; s. Joseph John and Celina (Perlinski) Jasinski; m. Anastasia Gawinski, Oct. 4, 1943 (dec. Aug. 1970); children: Peter M., Mark M., Christine (Mrs. David K. Mac Leod), Carol Ann, (Mrs. J. David Sampson); m. Gertrude O'Connor Travers, Mar. 25, 1972 (dec. Nov. 1972); m. Grace Yungbluth Frauenheim, Aug. 31, 1973. Student, Canisius Coll., 1936; LL.B., U. Buffalo, 1939; postgrad., Harvard U., 1944; LL.D. (hon.), Union U., 1980, N.Y. Law Sch., 1981. Bar: N.Y. 1940. Partner firm Beyer, Jasen & Boland, Buffalo, 1940-43; pres. U.S. Security Rev. Bd., Wurttemberg-Baden, Germany, 1945-46; judge U.S. Mil. Govt. Ct., Heidelberg, Germany, 1946-49; sr. partner firm

Jasen, Manz, Johnson & Bayger, Buffalo, 1949-57; Supreme Ct. justice State N.Y. 8th Jud. Dist., 1957-67; sr. assoc. judge N.Y. State Ct. Appeals, Albany, 1968—. Contbr. articles to profl. jours. Mem. council U. Buffalo, 1963-66; trustee Canisius Coll. Chair of Polish Culture, also, Nottingham Acad. Served to capt. AUS, 1943-46, ETO. Fellow Hilbert Coll.; recipient Distinguished Alumnus award State U. N.Y. at Buffalo Sch. Law, 1969, Distinguished Alumnus award also Alumni Assn., 1976, Distinguished Alumnus award Canisius Coll., 1978, Edwin F. Jaeckle award, 1982. Mem. Nat. Conf. Appellate Judges, State U. N.Y. at Buffalo Law Sch. Alumni Assn. (pres. 1964-65), Am., N.Y. State, Erie County bar assns., Am. Law Inst., Am. Judicature Soc., Lawyers Club Buffalo (pres. 1961-62), Nat. Advocates Club, Profl. Businessmen's Assn. Western N.Y. (pres. 1952), Phi Alpha Delta, DiGamma Soc. Roman Catholic (mem. Bishop's Bd. Govs., Buffalo diocese 1951—). Clubs: K.C. (4 deg.). Home: 26 Pine Terr Orchard Park NY 14127 Office: Court of Appeals Chambers Erie County Hall Buffalo NY 14202

JASINSKI, PAUL C., corporate lawyer. Gen. counsel Republic Airlines, Mpls. Office: Republic Airlines Inc 7500 Airline Dr Minneapolis MN 55450 *

JASKIEWICZ, LEONARD ALBERT, lawyer; b. Norwich, Conn., Aug. 25, 1927; s. Michael and Eleanor C. (Smigiel) J.; m. Ruth Evelyn Lalor, Jan. 31, 1953; children: Jon Michael, Barbara Joan, Virginia Ruth. BA, U. Conn., 1949; MA, Syracuse U., 1950; JD, George Washington U., 1954. Bar: D.C. 1954, U.S. Supreme Ct. 1961. Fiscal mgmt. ofcl. U.S. Dept. Navy, Washington, 1950-53; sole practice Washington, 1953—; from assoc. to ptnr. Dow, Lohnes and Albertson, 1954-64; ptnr. Grove, Jaskiewicz, Gilliam & Cobert, 1964—. Served with AUS, 1946-47, USAR, 1950-62. Mem. ABA, D.C. Bar Assn., Transportation Lawyers Assn. Lodges: Masons, Shriners. Administrative and regulatory, General corporate, Legislative. Office: Grove Jaskiewicz Gilliam & Cobert 1730 M St NW Suite 501 Washington DC 20036

JASPER, SEYMOUR, lawyer; b. N.Y.C., May 15, 1919; s. Louis and Gussie (Levitch) J.; m. Geulah Eidelsberg, Nov. 24, 1940 (dec.); children: Michael, Ronald, Jeffrey, Idylia; m. Barbara Gray, Feb. 11, 1975. BS, NYU, 1939; JD, Columbia U., 1956. Bar: N.Y. 1956. Assoc. Young, Kaplan & Edelstein, N.Y.C., 1956-59; ptnr. Jasper, Sandler & Lipsay, N.Y.C., 1959-62; sole practice N.Y.C., 1962—; dir. Hale Realty Corp., Loru Corp. Served with USN. Mem. ABA, Assn. of Bar of City of N.Y. (estate planning, probate and real property). Office: 18 E 48th St New York NY 10017

JASSY, EVERETT LEWIS, lawyer; b. N.Y.C., Feb. 4, 1937; s. David H. and Florence A. (Pollak) J.; m. Margery Ellen Rose; children: Katherine Ann, Andrew Ralph, Jonathan Scott. AB, Harvard U., 1957, JD, 1960. Assoc. Dewey, Ballantine, Bushby, Palmer & Wood, N.Y.C., 1960-68, ptnr., 1968—. Mem. ABA, N.Y. State Bar Assn., Assn. of Bar of City of N.Y., The Tax Forum, The Tax Club. Clubs: Harmonie (N.Y.C); Fairview Coutry (Greenwich, Conn.). Avocations: tennis, travel. Corporate taxation, Personal income taxation. Home: 20 Tompkins Rd Scarsdale NY 10583 Office: Dewey Ballantine Bushby Palmer & Wood 140 Broadway New York NY 10005

JAUVTIS, ROBERT LLOYD, lawyer; b. Bklyn., Oct. 19, 1946; s. Louis and Betty (Slomiansky) J. B.A., U. Rochester, 1968; J.D., Albany Law Sch., 1973; LL.M. in Labor Law, NYU, 1976. Bar: N.Y. 1974, U.S. Ct. Appeals (2d cir.) 1975, U.S. Supreme Ct. 1980. Assoc. Vladeck, Waldman, Elias & Engelhard, P.C., N.Y.C., 1974-78; assoc. Epstein Becker Borsody & Green, P.C., N.Y.C., 1978-82, ptnr., 1982—; moot ct. judge N.Y. Law Sch. Wagner Labor Law Competition, N.Y.C., 1980-82; lectr. Contbr. articles to legal jours. Served with USAR, 1969-70. Mem. ABA, N.Y. State Bar Assn., Assn. Bar City N.Y., Am. Soc. Personnel Adminstrn. (bd. dirs. met. N.Y. chpt. 1983-85), Def. Research Inst. Labor, Federal civil litigation, Civil rights. Office: Epstein Becker Borsody & Green PC 250 Park Ave New York NY 10177

JAWIN, PAUL GREGORY, lawyer; b. N.Y.C., Sept. 22, 1955; s. Edward Henry and Ann (Juliano) J.; m. Michele Rodin, Jan. 22, 1983; 1 child, Alixandra. BA in History, Ithaca Coll., 1977; JD, Syracuse U., 1979. Bar: N.Y. 1980, U.S. Dist. Ct. (so. dist.) N.Y. 1980, U.S. Ct. Appeals (2d cir.) 1980. Dep. asst. atty. gen. N.Y. State Dept. Law, N.Y.C., 1980-82; assoc. Burns, Summit, Rovins & Feldesman, N.Y.C., 1982-83; ptrn. Demov, Morris & Hammerling, N.Y.C., 1983—. Mem. N.Y. State Bar Assn., Audubon Soc. Democrat. Unitarian. Avocation: fishing. Securities, Real property, Syndications. Office: Demov Morris & Hammerling 40 W 57th St New York NY 10019

JAYSON, LESTER SAMUEL, lawyer, educator; b. N.Y.C., Oct. 25, 1915; s. Morris and Mary (Gardner) J.; m. Evelyn Sylvia Lederer, Feb. 6, 1943; children: Diane Frankie, Jill Karen Jayson Ladd. BSS with spl. honors in History and Govt., CCNY, 1936; JD (bd. student advisers), Harvard U., 1939. Bar: N.Y. bar 1940, also D.C. bar, U.S. Supreme Ct 1940. With firm Oseas and Pepper, N.Y.C., 1939-40, Marshall, Bratter & Seligson, N.Y.C., 1940-42; spl. asst. to atty. gen. U.S. 1942-50; trial atty. Dept. Justice, 1951-56, chief torts sect. civil div., 1957-60; sr. specialist Am. pub. law, chief Am. law div. Congl. Research Service, Library of Congress, 1960-62, dep. dir. service, 1962-66, dir., 1966-75; prof. law Potomac Sch. Law, 1975-81; Vice chmn. Interdeptl. Fed. Tort Claims Com., 1958-60; rep. Justice Dept. to legal div., air coordinating com. Internat. Civil Aviation Orgn., 1959-60; mem. com. exec. privilege Justice Dept., 1956-60; adv. statutory studies group Commn. Govt. Procurement, 1970-72; mem. adv. council Office Tech. Assessment, 1973-75; cons. govt. relations com. Nat. Assn. Theatre Owners, 1978-79. Author: Handling Federal Tort Claims: Judicial and Administrative Remedies, 1964-87; also articles; supervising editor: The Constitution of the United States of America-Analysis and Interpretation, 1964, 72. Mem. ABA, Fed. Bar Assn. (chmn., then vice chmn. fed. tort claims com. 1963-66, 70-74, chmn. 1967-68, mem. nat. council 1967-73), Am. Friends of Wilton Park, Assn. Trial Lawyers Am., Pi Sigma Alpha (hon.). Clubs: Cosmos (Washington), Harvard (Washington). Federal civil litigation, Government contracts and claims, Personal injury. Home: 7512 Newmarket Dr Bethesda MD 20817

JAYSON, MELINDA GAYLE, lawyer; b. Dallas, Sept. 29, 1956; d. Robert and Louise Adelle (Jacobs) J. BA, U. Tex., 1977, JD, 1980. Bar: Tex. 1980, U.S. Dist. Ct. (no. dist.) Tex. 1980, U.S. Ct. Appeals (5th and 11th cirs.) 1981. Assoc. Akin, Gump, Strauss, Hauer & Feld, Dallas, 1980-86, ptnr., 1987—. Mem. Am. Jewish Com., Dallas, 1982—. Named one of Outstanding Young Women Am., 1983. Mem. Tex. Bar Assn., Dallas Bar Assn. Federal civil litigation, State civil litigation. Office: Akin Gump Strauss Hauer & Feld 1700 Pacific Ave 4100 1st City Ctr Dallas TX 75201-4618

JEAVONS, NORMAN STONE, lawyer; b. Cleve., Apr. 18, 1930; s. William Norman and Mildred (Stone) J.; m. Kathleen Taze, Oct. 18, 1936; children: Kathleen Stone, Ann Lindsey. B.A., Dartmouth Coll., 1952; LL.B., Case Western Res. U., 1958. Bar: Ohio 1958. Atty. firm Baker & Hostetler, Cleve., 1958—, ptnr., 1968—. Trustee Laurel Sch., Shaker Hts., Ohio, 1980—; trustee Beech Brook, Cleve., 1972—. Served to lt. j.g. USCG, 1952-55. Mem. ABA, Ohio Bar Assn., Cleve. Bar Assn., Order of Coif. Republican. Clubs: Univ. (Cleveland); Cleveland Racquet (Pepper Pike). Home: 22550 Shelburne Rd Shaker Heights OH 44122 Office: 3200 National City Center Cleveland OH 44114

JEDEIKIN, JOSEPH, lawyer; b. Kobe, Japan, Jan. 4, 1927; s. Louis and Vera S. (Bitker) J.; m. Josephine Morris, Apr. 15, 1957 (div. Nov. 1972); children: Lorraine Sylvia, Jennifer Ann, Louis James; m. Judith Susan Stusser, Dec. 1, 1972; 1 child, Jonathan Carroll. AA, U. Calif., Berkeley, 1948; JD, U. Calif., San Francisco, 1951. Staff adjuster Ins. Co. of N.Am., San Francisco, 1953-54; ptnr. Jedeikin, Connor & Green, San Francisco, 1954—. Served with U.S. Army, 1952-53. Mem. ABA (vice chmn. self insurers and risk mgrs. com. 1982—), Am. Arbitration Assn. (arbitrator San Francisco Superior Ct. 1980—). Insurance, Landlord-tenant, Libel. Home: 23 Sienna Way San Rafael CA 94903 Office: Jedeikin Connor & Green 445 Washington St San Francisco CA 94111

JEDZINIAK, LEE PETER, lawyer, educator; b. Springfield, Mass., June 1, 1956; s. Leo Stanley and Helena (Ludwin) J. BA in Polit. Sci., The Citadel, 1978; JD, U. S.C., 1981. Bar: S.C. 1981, U.S. Dist. Ct. S.C. 1982, U.S. Ct. Appeals (4th cir.) 1982, U.S. Ct. Appeals (11th and D.C. cirs.) 1983, U.S. Ct. Appeals (3d, 5th and 10th cirs.) 1984, U.S. Tax Ct. 1985, U.S. Ct. Appeals (9th cir.) 1985, U.S. Supreme Ct. 1985. Law clk. to presiding justice 15th Jud. Cir. Ct., Conway, S.C., 1981-83; atty. consumer advs. office State of S.C., Columbia, 1983-85, staff counsel dept. ins., 1985—; legal instr. M. Pub. Adminstrn., MBA depts. Golden Gate U., Sumter, S.C., 1984—. Mem. Assn. Trial Lawyers Am., Fed. Bar Assn., S.C. Bar Assn., Citadel Alumni Assn., S.C. Trial Lawyers Assn. Roman Catholic. Club: Greater Columbia Citadel. Insurance, Administrative and regulatory, State civil litigation. Home: 2039 Fairlawn Circle Cayce SC 29033 Office: SC Dept Ins 1612 Marion St Columbia SC 29202-3105

JEFFER, HERMAN, lawyer; b. Hawthorne, N.J., June 6, 1925; s. Garrett and Petronella (Von Beek) J.; m. Marjorie Sisco, Sept. 6, 1952. A.B., Calvin Coll., Grand Rapids, Mich., 1950; postgrad. Duke U., 1950-51; J.D., N.Y. U., 1955. Bar: N.J. 1955, Fla. 1974. Sr. ptnr. Jeffer, Hopkinson & Vogel and predecessors, Hawthorne, N.J., 1955—; dir. various banks, bank holding co., others. Served with AUS, 1943-45. Mem. N.J. Bar Assn., ABA, Passaic County Bar Assn. Clubs: Ridgewood (N.J.) Country, Jupiter (Fla.) Hills Country, Joe Jefferson (Saddle River, N.J.). Banking, General corporate, Probate. Home: 501 Hartung Dr Wyckoff NJ 07481 Office: PO Box 507 Route 208 N Hawthorne NJ 07507

JEFFERIES, JACK P., lawyer; b. Radford, Va., Dec. 5, 1928; s. Raymond L. and Artelia P. Jefferies; m. Patricia Ann Carl, Sept. 8, 1962; m. Karen S. Sommarstrom, Oct. 14, 1972; 1 child, Elizabeth Karling. B.S. in Commerce, U. Va., 1949, J.D., 1951, LL.M., 1952; J.S.D., Yale U., 1954. Bar: Va. 1953, N.Y. 1959, U.S. Dist. Ct. (so. dist.) N.Y., U.S. Ct. Appeals (D.C. cir.), U.S. Supreme Ct. With Lord, Day & Lord, N.Y.C., 1958—, now ptnr.; legal cons. Office Gen. Counsel, Dept. Def., 1957; mem. White House Conf. on Equality to Fulfill These Rights, 1966; mem. U.S. Pres.'s Com. on Employment of Handicapped, 1981. Author: Understanding Hotel/Motel Law, 1983, Important New York State Laws for Hotels/Motels; primary editor for Dept. Army publs. on internat. law, 1956; editorial bd. Va. Law Rev., 1950-51; contbr. articles to legal jours. Pres. Policy Scis. Ctr.; exec. com., bd. dirs. Downtown Lower Manhattan Assn.; trustee Am. Waterways Wind Orch.; elder Presbyn. Ch., Palisades, N.Y. Served with JAGC, U.S. Army, 1954-57. Decorated Army Commendation ribbon with medal pendant. Mem. Assn. Bar City of N.Y., ABA, U. Va. Alumni Assn. N.Y. (exec. com.). Democrat. Clubs: Down Town Assn. (N.Y.C.); Masons. General corporate, Private international, Trademark and copyright. Home: Lawrence Ln Sneden's Landing Palisades NY 10964 Office: Lord Day & Lord 25 Broadway New York NY 10004

JEFFERIES, ROBERT AARON, JR., furniture co. exec.; b. Richmond, Ind., June 30, 1941; s. Robert Aaron and Roberta June (Hart) J.; m. Sylvia Mae Gilmore, Apr. 16, 1962; children—David E., Michael S., Stephen R. A.B. with honors in Govt, Earlham Coll., Richmond, 1963; J.D. with distinction (Herman C. Krannert scholar 1963-65), Ind. U., 1966. Bar: Ohio bar 1966, Ind. bar 1966, Ill. bar 1970, Mo. bar 1970. Asso. firm Shumaker, Loop & Kendrick, Toledo, 1966-69; asst. gen. counsel, asst. sec. May Dept. Stores Co., St. Louis, 1969-77; v.p., gen. counsel, sec. Leggett & Platt, Inc., Carthage, Mo., 1977—. Contbr. articles to legal jours.; bd. editors law jour., Ind. U., 1965-66. Mem. Am. Bar Assn., Ind. Bar Assn., Ohio Bar Assn., Ill. Bar Assn., Mo. Bar Assn., St. Louis Bar Assn., Order of Coif. Office: PO Box 757 Carthage MO 64836

JEFFERS, ALBERT BROWN, lawyer; b. Providence, R.I., July 23, 1928; s. Albert Brown Jeffers and Ruth Almira Nichols; m. Suzanne Lawton, Oct. 28, 1950 (div. July 1968); children: Christopher B. (dec.), Ann M., Charles H.L.; m. Victoria W. Wilkinson, Aug. 10, 1968; children: Albert B. III, James W. AB, Brown U., 1950; JD, Columbia U., 1955. Bar: N.J. 1955, U.S. Dist. Ct. N.J. 1955, U.S. Ct. Appeals (3d cir.) 1986, U.S. Tax Ct. Ptnr. Jeffers & Mountain, Morristown, N.J., 1955-66, Hoyt, Jeffers & Weiland, Morristown, 1966-75; sole practice Morristown, 1975—. Counsel, bd. mgrs. Family Service of Morris County, Morristown, 1958—; counsel, trustee St. John Bapt. Sch., Mendham, N.J., 1964—. Served to capt. USMC, 1950-52. Republican. Mem. Soc. of Friends. Club: Morristown. Federal civil litigation, General corporate, Real property. Home: 24 Franklin St Morristown NJ 07960 Office: 26 De Hart St PO Box 901OM Morristown NJ 07960

JEFFERS, ALBERT LAVERN, lawyer; b. Duff, Ind., Feb. 12, 1925; s. Daniel B. and Martha (Carson) J.; m. Mary Lea Miles, June 6, 1948; 1 child, Adele L. BSME, U. Evansville, 1949, BS in Indsl. Tech., 1949; JD, George Washington U., 1952. Bar: Ind., U.S. Ct. Appeals (D.C. cir.), U.S. Supreme Ct. Ptnr. Jeffers, Irish & Hoffman, Ft. Wayne, Ind., 1961—; bd. dirs. Lincoln Foodservice Products, Inc., Ft. Wayne, 1986—; trustee U. Evansville, Ind., 1964—. Mem. Ft. Wayne Bd. Zoning Appeals, 1975-80. Served with USN, 1943-46, PTO. Club: Olympia (Ft. Wayne) (pres. 1968-70). Patent, Trademark and copyright, Federal civil litigation. Home: 3112 Oakwood Dr Fort Wayne IN 46816 Office: Jeffers Irish & Hoffman Wayne Bank Bldg 1500 Anthony Fort Wayne IN 46802

JEFFERS, FRED HARDS, lawyer; b. Montrose, Pa., Apr. 19, 1899; s. James Murray and Emily (Hards) J.; m. Marian Rooksby, 1926 (div. 1945); 1 son, James Murray; m. Jean Joy Barber, Nov. 2, 1949; 1 dau., Patricia L. B.S. in Econs., U. Pa., 1922; J.D., Cornell U. Bar: N.Y. 1926. Mem. firm Mandeville, Waxman, Buck, Teeter & Harpending, Elmira, N.Y., 1935-39; sole practice law, Binghamton, N.Y., 1939-65, Windsor, N.Y., 1965—. Author: Jeffers Motion Practice, 1938; A Study in Old Poultry Books, 1945. Pres. Broome County Sch. Bd. Assn., Binghamton, 1947-48; chmn. Broome County Vets. Adv. Council, Binghamton, 1947-48, Delahanna Dist., Boy Scouts Am., 1949-50. Served with U.S. Army, 1918. Mem. Broome County Bar Assn. Republican. Methodist. Probate, Real property. Address: 1 Church St Windsor NY 13865

JEFFERS, RONALD THOMAS, lawyer; b. Kokomo, Ind., June 7, 1954; s. Warren Thomas and Lois Jane (Lynn) J. BBA, Ind. U., 1976, JD, 1981. Bar: Ind. 1982, Tex. 1982. Dept. mgr. Wm. H. Block Co., Indpls., 1976-78; mgr. unit claims Allstate Ins. Co., Indpls., 1978-81; tax atty. Touche Ross & Co., Houston, 1981-83; corp. counsel Woodward Energy Group Inc., Houston, 1983-86; pres. Jeffers & Ellis, P.C., Houston, 1986—. Mem. ABA, Ind. Bar Assn., Tex. Bar Assn., Houston Bar Assn., Tex. Young Lawyers Assn., Houston Young Lawyers Assn., Houston C. of C. (bd. dirs.), Houston Jaycees (pres., Key Man award 1984-86, Leadership Achievement award 1986), Ind. Alumni Houston (advisor), Beta Gamma Sigma. Avocations: computers, photography, antiques. Corporate taxation, Personal income taxation, General practice. Home: 2001 Bering Dr #12B Houston TX 77057 Office: Jeffers & Ellis PC 3013 Fountainview Suite 275 Houston TX 77057

JEFFERS, WILLIAM A., JR., lawyer; b. Washington, Apr. 18, 1943; s. William A. and Alice (Combs) J.; m. Billie Street, Nov. 1965; children—Virginia Gray, Aimé e Louise. B.A. with honors, U. Tex., 1964, J.D. with honors, 1968. Bar: Tex. 1968. Ptnr. Groce, Locke & Hebdon, San Antonio, 1968-86 ; officer Jeffers, Brook, Kreager & Gragg, Inc., 1986—; judge Mcpl. Ct., Terrell Hills, Tex., 1974-84. Mem. Fiesta Commn., San Antonio, 1980-82; councilman City Council, Terrell Hills, 1984—. Mem. ABA, Comml. Law League, Am. Bankruptcy Inst., State Bar of Tex. (fin. instns. com., comml. lending services com.), Nat. Cattlemen's Assn., Tex. Assn. Bank Counsel (founding dir., pres. 1976—), Tex. and Southwest Cattle Raisers Assn., Order of Coif, Phi Delta Phi, Sigma Alpha Epsilon. Republican. Episcopalian. Club: Order of Alamo (San Antonio) (pres. 1977-78). Banking, Bankruptcy, Real property. Office: Jeffers Brook Kreager & Gragg Inc 660 N Main Suite 300 San Antonio TX 78205

JEFFERSON, JANICE LEE ROEHLER, lawyer; b. Pitts., May 3, 1938; d. Otto Frederick and Lillian Lydia (Castrodale) Roehler; m. Charles Garland Shaw, June 23, 1957 (div. 1966); children: Christopher Graylan, Nathan Garland; m. James Floyd, Nov. 17, 1967. Student, Ball State U., 1956-58; BS in Bus. and Fin., U. Louisville, 1970, JD, 1978. Bar: Ky. 1979, U.S. Dist. Ct. (we. dist.) Ky. 1979. Sole practice Elizabethtown, Ky., 1979-85; ptnr. Jefferson & Shaw, Elizabethtown, 1985—; adminstr. Pub. Defender System, Elizabethtown, 1982-83, 86—, treas., 1983-84. Mem. Hardin County (Ky.) Rep. Women's Club; Lively Arts Com., Elizabethtown, 1970-74, Hardin Meml. Hosp. Bd., Elizabethtown; active gubernatorial campaign Hardin County Reps., 1979; chairperson campaign Reagan/Bush/McConnell, Hardin County, 1984; treas. Gloria Dei Luth. Ch., Elizabethtown, 1985-86. Mem. ABA, Ky. Bar Assn., Ky. Acad. Trial Lawyers, Hardin County Bar Assn. Avocations: reading, aerobics, gourmet cooking, traveling. Criminal, Workers' compensation, Family and matrimonial. Home: 109 Lakeview Dr Elizabethtown KY 42701 Office: Jefferson & Shaw 39 Pub Sq Elizabethtown KY 42701

JEFFRIES, MCCHESNEY HILL, JR., lawyer; b. Atlanta, Dec. 25, 1954; s. McChesney Hill Sr. and Alice Elizabeth (Mitchell) J.; m. Virginia Lee Hartley, Aug. 2, 1980; children: Virginia Hartley, McChesney Hill III. BA with high distinction, U. Va., 1977, JD, 1980. Bar: Ga. 1980, U.S. Dist. Ct. (no. dist.) Ga. 1980, U.S. Ct. Appeals (11th cir.) 1980. Assoc. Hurt, Richardson, Garner, Todd & Cadenhead, Atlanta, 1980-85; assoc. Long, Aldridge & Norman, Atlanta, 1985-87, ptnr., 1988—; vol. atty. Atlanta Vol. Lawyers Assn., 1980—. Contbr. articles to profl. jours. Mem. ABA, Am. Judicature Soc., Atlanta Bar Assn., Atlanta Lawyers Club. Presbyterian. Club: Piedmont Driving (Atlanta). Avocation: sports. Securities, Banking, General corporate. Home: 2631 Orchard Knob Dr Atlanta GA 30339 Office: Long Aldridge & Norman 1900 Rhodes-Haverty Bldg 134 Peachtree St Atlanta GA 30043-1863

JEGEN, LAWRENCE A., III, law educator; b. Chgo., Nov. 16, 1934; s. Lawrence A. and Katherine M. (Stibgen) J.; m. Janet M. Holmberg, Aug. 30, 1958; children: Christine M., David L. BA, Beloit Coll., 1956; JD, U. Mich., 1959, MBA, 1960, LLM, NYU, 1963. Bar: Ill. 1959, U.S. Dist. Ct. (no. dist.) Ill. 1959, U.S. Dist. Ct. (so. dist.) Ind. 1962; Ind. 1966, U.S. Tax Ct. 1966, U.S. Ct. Appeals (7th cir.) 1980, U.S. Supreme Ct. 1980. Tax cons. Coopers & Lybrand, N.Y.C., 1960-62; asst. prof. law Ind. U., Indpls., 1962-64, assoc. prof., 1964-66, prof., 1966—, Thomas F. Sheehan prof. tax law and policy, 1982—, vis. prof. Bloomington campus, 1965, 67; spl. counsel Ind. Dept. Revenue 1963-65, Gov.'s Commn. on Med. Edn., 1970-72; mem. commr.'s adv. com. IRS., 1981-82; mem. Ind. Corps. Survey Commn., 1965—; commr. Nat. Conf. Uniform State Laws, 1981—. Author: Indiana Will and Trust Manual, 1967—; Lifetime and Estate, Personal and Business Planning, 1987; Estate Planning and Administration in Indiana, 1979. Contbr. numerous articles to profl. jours., chpts. to books. Ford fellow, 1963; Recipient Spl. Alumni Teaching award Ind. U. Alumni Assn., 1970, 76, 80, 85, Most Outstanding Prof. award, Sch. Law, Ind. U., 1970, 80, 85; Tchr. of Significance award Ind. U., 1980; named hon. sec. of state State of Ind., 1967, 80, hon. dep. atty. gen., 1968; hon. state treas., 1969. Fellow Am. Bar Found. (life), Am. Coll. Probate Counsel, Am. Coll. Tax Counsel; mem. Mid-West Inst. Estate and Tax Planning (adv. bd.), ABA, Ind. Bar Assn. (chmn. taxation sect. 1969-70; presdl. citation 1971), Fed. Bar Assn., Indpls. Bar Assn., Ind. Trial Lawyers Assn. Corporate taxation, Estate taxation, State and local taxation. Office: Indiana Univ Sch Law 735 W New York St Indianapolis IN 46202-2888

JEHU, JOHN PAUL, lawyer; b. N.Y.C., Oct. 17, 1908; s. John Milton and Pauline (Burger) J.; m. Dorothy Elvira Kellog Ferris (dec.); children—Lynn Jehu Amadon, Susan Jehu Kessler; m. Virginia Linder Corones, 1974; 1 stepson, James P.; Student U. Munich, U. Leipzig, U. Erlangen, Germany, 1927-32; D. Roman and Canon Law, U. Erlangen, 1932; LL.B., Cornell U., 1937. Bar: N.Y. 1939; U.S. Dist. Ct. (no. dist.) N.Y. 1954, U.S. Dist. Ct. (so., ea. dists.) N.Y. 1963, U.S. Ct. Appeals (2d cir.) 1965, U.S. Supreme Ct. 1968, U.S. Dist. Ct. (we. dist.) N.Y. 1971. Assoc. firm Sherry and Picarello, 1937-39; with contract div. Mergenthaler Linotype Co., 1937-42; research counsel Temp. N.Y. State Commn. for Revision and Codification of Laws relating to Mcpl. Fin., Albany, 1942-43, asst., then assoc. counsel to Joint Legis. Com. on State Edn. System, 1945-47, sr. atty. law div. State Edn. Dept., 1947-50, dir. law div., 1950-67, assoc. counsel to Bd. Regents, 1967-76, assoc. counsel State Dept. Edn., 1967-76; sole practice, Albany, 1976—; legal cons. to state comptroller, comptroller's com. on Constl. Tax and Debt Limitations and City-Sch. Fiscal Relations, Temp. State Commn. on Ednl. Fin.; assoc. prof. ednl. adminstrn. SUNY-Albany, 1956-76; spl. counsel V.I. Bd. Edn., 1967-68, assoc. counsel, 1968-76; lectr. univs., colls. including NYU, Rochester, SUNY-Buffalo. Bd. dirs. Albany Symphony Orch., 1973—, mem. exec. com., chmn. nominating com.; elder Presbyterian Ch. Served with M.P., JAGC, AUS, 1943-45, ETO. Decorated 3 Battle Stars. Mem. N.Y. State Bar Assn., Albany County Bar Assn., Cornell Law Assn., St. David's Soc. (pres. Capital dist. 1976-84, hon. sec. 1980—, counsellor state orgn. 1977—), Am. Legion (Blanchard Post), Albany Inst. of History and Art, Nat. Welsh-Am. Found. (adv. council 1979—, counsel 1986—), English-Speaking Union. Clubs: Evergreen Country, University, Torch, Cornell, Capital Dist. Mineral (Albany); Powysland (Welshpool, Wales). School district law, Federal civil litigation, State civil litigation. Address: 49 Dove St Albany NY 12210

JEKEL, LOUIS G., lawyer; b. Denver, June 2, 1941; s. Louis G. and Margaret (Roark) J.; m. Linda Smallman, Aug. 4, 1964 (div. Mar. 1981); children: Kristen Kathleen, Holly Linda. AB, Occidental Coll., 1963; JD, U. Ariz., 1966. Bar: Ariz. 1966, U.S. Dist. Ct. Ariz. 1966, U.S. Ct. Appeals (9th cir.) 1968. Ptrn. Simon & Jekel, Scottsdale, Ariz., 1966-76; sole practice Scottsdale, 1976-80; ptnr. Jekel & Howard, Scottsdale, 1980—; bd. dirs., legal counsel Rural Metro Corp., Scottsdale, 1968—. Chmn., bd. dirs. adv. bd. Camelback Hosp. Mental Health, Scottsdale, 1970-76; bd. dirs. Scottsdale YMCA, 1970-76. Mem. ABA, Assn. Trial Lawyers Am., Scottsdale Bar Assn. (bd. dirs. 1972-78, pres. 1977-78), Scottsdale C. of C. (pres. 1980, outstanding contribution award 1980). Republican. Presbyterian. Club: Scottsdale Charro. Administrative and regulatory, Real property, General corporate. Home: 6313 N 75th St Scottsdale AZ 85253 Office: Jekel & Howard 4323 N Brown Ave Scottsdale AZ 85251

JELIN, BETH MALONEY, lawyer; b. Upper Darby, Pa., July 21, 1953; d. James Henry and Joan (Sweeney) Maloney; m. Frederick Theodore Jelin, Apr. 14, 1985. BA, Rutgers U., 1976; student, Boston U., 1972-74; JD, Rutgers U., 1981. Bar: Calif. 1981, Pa. 1981, N.J. 1981, Fla. 1981, U.S. Dist. Ct. N.J. 1981. Assoc. Spector, Cohen, Gadon & Rosen, Phila., 1981, Rifkind & Sterling, Beverly Hills, Calif., 1981-83; assoc. Bushkin, Gaims et al, Los Angeles, 1983-86, ptnr., 1987—. Contbr. articles to profl. jours. Mem. ABA, Calif. Bar Assn., Los Angeles County Bar Assn. (exec. com. intellectual property and unfair competition sect.). Entertainment, Securities, General corporate. Office: Bushkin Gaims et al 2121 Ave of Stars Los Angeles CA 90067

JELKIN, JOHN LAMOINE, lawyer; b. Hildreth, Nebr., Dec. 24, 1952; s. Lamoine George and Verna Mae (DeJonge) J.; m. Diane Louise Davis, June 10, 1978; children: Jessica Jean, Jaclyn Jade. BA, Kearney State U., 1975; JD, U. Nebr., 1978. Bar: Nebr. 1978, U.S. Dist. Ct. Nebr. 1978. Assoc. Duncan & Duncan, Franklin, Nebr., 1978-81; ptnr. Duncan, Duncan & Jelkin, Franklin, 1981—; sec., treas. Hildreth Area Bus. Devel. Corp., 1983—; dep. atty. Buffalo County, Kearney, Nebr., 1986—. Vol. fireman; chmn. Franklin County Dems., 1984—. Mem. ABA, Nebr. Bar Assn., Buffalo County Bar Assn., Nebr. Assn. Trial Attys., 10th Jud. Bar Assn. Democrat. Lutheran. Lodge: Lions (pres. Hildreth 1985-86, v.p. 1982-85, sec. 1981-82). Probate, Real property, Personal income taxation. Office: Duncan Duncan & Jelkin PO Box 340 Hildreth NE 68947

JELLINEK, MILES ANDREW, lawyer; b. Phila., Dec. 27, 1947; s. Alfred Marquis and Rena Elizabeth (Felberg) J.; m. Annabelle Francis O'Leary, Apr. 9, 1976; children—Beth Elise, Laura Anne. B.A., U. Pa., 1969, J.D., 1974. Bar: Pa. 1974. Law clk. Ct. Common Pleas, Phila., 1974-75; sr. mem. Cozen and O'Connor, Phila., 1975—. Democrat. Jewish. Club: Germantown Cricket (Phila.). Lodge: B'nai B'rith. Avocations: tennis; squash. State civil litigation, Federal civil litigation, Insurance. Office: Cozen & O'Connor 1900 Market St Philadelphia PA 19103

JENKINS, BRUCE STERLING, fed. judge; b. Salt Lake City, May 27, 1927; s. Joseph and Bessie Pearl (Iverson) J.; m. Margaret Watkins, Sept. 19, 1952; children—Judith Margaret, David Bruce, Michael Glen, Carol Alice. B.A. with high honors, U. Utah, 1949, LL.B., 1952, J.D., 1952. Bar: Utah bar 1952, U.S. Dist. Ct. bar 1952, U.S. Supreme Ct. bar 1962, U.S. Circuit Ct. Appeals bar 1962. Individual practice law Salt Lake City, 1952-

59; asso. firm George McMillan, 1959-65; asst. atty. gen. State of Utah, 1952; dep. county atty. Salt Lake County, 1954-58; bankruptcy judge U.S. Dist. Ct., Dist. of Utah, 1965-78, U.S. dist. judge, 1978—, chief judge, 1984—. Research, publs. in field; contbr. essays to Law jours.; bd. editors: Utah Law Rev, 1951-52. Mem. Utah Senate, 1959-65, minority leader, 1963, pres. senate, 1965, vice chmn. commn. on orgn. exec. br. of Utah Govt., 1965-66; Mem. adv. com. Utah Tech. Coll., 1967-72; mem. instl. council Utah State U., 1976. Served with USN, 1945-46. Mem. Utah State Bar Assn., Salt Lake County Bar Assn., Am. Bar Assn., Fed. Bar Assn., Order of Coif, Phi Beta Kappa, Phi Kappa Phi, Phi Eta Sigma, Phi Sigma Alpha, Tau Kappa Alpha. Democrat. Mormon. Office: Room 235 US Courthouse 350 S Main St Salt Lake City UT 84101

JENKINS, DONALD M., law educator, university dean; b. 1928. J.D., U. Akron, 1964; LL.M., Case Western Res. U., 1970. Bar: Ohio 1964, U.S. Dist. Ct. Ohio, U.S. Supreme Ct. Assoc. prof. bus. law Akron Coll. Bus. Adminstrn., Ohio, 1965-70; prof. law U. Akron, 1970—, dean Law Sch., 1981—. Served to capt. USAF, 1950-58; ret. maj. gen. USAFR. Office: University of Akron C Blake McDowell Law Ctr 302 E Buchetl Ave Akron OH 44325

JENKINS, DOUGLAS TUCKER, lawyer; b. Evanston, Ill., July 9, 1957; s. William Wesley and Elizabeth Ann (Tucker) J. BA in Econs., Middlebury (Vt.) Coll., 1979; JD, Coll. William and Mary, 1982. Bar: Va. 1982, U.S. Dist. Ct. (ea. dist.) Va. 1982. Assoc. Williams, Worrell, Kelly & Greer, PC, Norfolk, Va., 1982—. Mem. Norfolk City Rep. Com., 1985—, Tidewater Young Reps. Mem. ABA, Va. Bar Assn., Norfolk-Portsmouth Bar Assn., Jaycees (Norfolk newsletter com. 1985—). Episcopalian. Club: Harbor (Norfolk). Avocations: soccer, basketball, softball, reading, writing. State civil litigation, Federal civil litigation, Insurance. Home: 1106 Lexan Ave Norfolk VA 23508 Office: Williams Worrell Kelly & Greer 600 United Va Bank Bldg PO Box 3416 Norfolk VA 23510

JENKINS, JAMES M(ICHAEL), lawyer; b. St. Charles, Mo., Aug. 21, 1933; s. Joseph Marion and Rose Ann (Schroeder) J.; m. Jenanne Barber, Oct. 16, 1965; 1 child, Thomas Scott. BS, U. Mo., 1955, JD, 1959. Bar: Mo. 1959. Assoc. Barker Fallon Jones, Kansas City, Mo., 1959-61; ptnr. Fallon Guffey Jenkins, Kansas City, 1962-69, Popham Law Firm, Kansas City, 1970-79, Linde Thomson et al, Kansas City, 1980-82, Husch, Eppenberger, Donohue, Cornfeld & Jenkins, St. Louis and Kansas City, 1982—. Served to capt. USAR, 1959-66. Mem. ABA, Mo. Bar Assn. (exec. com., probate/trust com. 1978-81) Kansas City Bar Assn. (chmn. real estate com. 1985), Phi Delta Phi. Republican. Presbyterian. Clubs: Carriage, Kansas City. Avocation: tennis. Real property, Banking, General corporate. Home: 402 W 50th St Kansas City MO 64112 Office: Husch Eppenberger et al 1100 Main St Kansas City MO 64105

JENKINS, JON MARK, lawyer; b. Newark, May 22, 1956; s. Frederick F. and Mary Elizabeth (Compton) J.; m. Linda Claybourn, June 2, 1984. BA, Lafayette Coll., 1978; JD, Duke U., 1981. Bar: N.Y. 1982, U.S. Dist. Ct. (so. dist.) N.Y. 1982. Assoc. Donovan, Leisure, Newton & Irvine, N.Y.C., 1981—. Trustee Presbyterian Ch., Irvington, N.Y., 1984—. Republican. Avocation: sports. General corporate. Office: Donovan Leisure Newton & Irvine 30 Rockefeller Plaza New York NY 10112

JENKINS, MATTHEW RICHARD, lawyer; b. Dayton, Ohio, Dec. 5, 1956; s. William Russell and Jeanne Louise (Steinmann) J.; m. Cheryl Ann Wells; children: Jamielynne, Nicole Ann. BS, Ohio State U., 1979; JD, U. Dayton, 1982. Bar: Ohio, U.S. Dist. Ct. (so.dist.) Ohio. Assoc. Coopers & Lybrand, Columbus, Ohio, 1982-84; atty. Nat. Cash Register Corp., Dayton, 1984—. Mem. Ohio Bar Assn., Dayton Patent Law Assn., Fed. Bar Assn. Club: Nat. Cash Register Country. Computer, Patent, Trademark and copyright. Home: 158 Brookmont Rd Dayton OH 45429

JENKINS, NEIL EDMUND, lawyer; b. Nanticoke, Pa., Nov. 1, 1949; s. F. Edmund and Margaret (Hunter) J.; m. Jean Ann Collins, Aug. 15, 1981; children: Anne, Max. AB, Brown U., 1971; JD, Loyola U., Chgo., 1981. Bar: Ill. 1981, U.S. Dist. Ct. (no. dist.) Ill., U.S. Ct. Appeals (7th cir.) 1981. Dir. labor relations Bally Mfg. Corp., Chgo., 1975-81, assoc. gen. counsel, 1981-85, sec., gen. counsel, 1985-87, v.p., 1987—. Treas. Bally's PAC, 1982. Served with U.S. Army, 1971-74. Mem. ABA, Ill. Bar Assn., Am. Soc. Corp. Secs., Internat. Assn. Gaming Attys. General corporate. Office: Bally Mfg Corp 8700 W Bryn Mawr Chicago IL 60631

JENKINS, RICHARD COLEMAN, lawyer; b. Little Rock, Nov. 10, 1937; s. Clarence Richard and Virginia Coleman; m. Marian Jack, Oct. 7, 1961; 1 son, Jack Coleman; m. 2d, Roxanne Denardos, Feb. 19, 1974. Student U. Ark., 1955-58; A.B., So. Meth. U., 1959, LL.B., 1962. Bar: Tex. 1962, U.S. Dist. Ct. (no. dist.) Tex. 1963, U.S. Dist. Ct. (ea. dist.) Tex. 1982. Asst. city atty. Dallas, 1962-64; sole practice, Dallas, 1964-67, 1980—; assoc. Richard D. Haynes, 1967-69, Muse Currie & Kohen, 1971-74; ptnr. McClung & Jenkins, 1969-71, Jenkins and Ederer, 1974-76, Jackson, Jenkins & Rowton, Dallas, 1977-80. Mem. State Bar Tex. (cert. criminal law), Dallas Bar Assn., Dallas County Criminal Bar Assn. Republican. Methodist. Clubs: Dallas Rotary, Dallas Country. Criminal, Federal civil litigation, State civil litigation. Office: Manor House Suite 503 1222 Commerce Dallas TX 75202

JENKINS, ROBERT ROWE, lawyer; b. Norwalk, Ohio, Aug. 8, 1933; s. Robert Leslie and Millie Leona (Rowe) J.; m. Francis Jean Cline, June 12, 1955 (div. July 1972); children: Diane Elaine, Katherine Eileen; m. Jean Dingus, July 9, 1972. Student, Lebanon Valley Coll., 1951-55; BS in Chemistry, Eastern Coll. (now U. Balt.), 1967; JD, U. Balt., 1975. Bar: Md. 1976, U.S. Dist. Ct. Md. 1976, U.S. Ct. Appeals (4th cir.) 1979, U.S. Supreme Ct. 1979. Atty. Social Security Adminstrn., Balt., 1975-76; trial atty. Nelson R. Kandel, Balt., 1976-77; sole practice Balt., 1977-81; ptnr. Jenkins & Block, Balt., 1981—; faculty continuing profl. edn. of lawyers Md. Inst., Balt., 1986—. Ruling elder Faith Christian Fellowship Presbyterian Ch. Am., Balt., 1982—. Served with U.S. Coast Guard, 1955-59. Mem. ABA, Md. Bar Assn., Balt. City Bar Assn., Assn. Trial Lawyers Am., Md. Trial Lawyers Assn., Christian Legal Soc., Nat. Orgn. Social Security Claimant's Rep. (exec. com.). Republican. Avocations: fishing, boating. Administrative and regulatory, Pension, profit-sharing, and employee benefits, Personal injury. Home: 1910 Greenberry Rd Baltimore MD 21209 Office: Jenkins & Block 711 W 40th St Suite 218 Baltimore MD 21211

JENKINS, THOMAS A(LLAN), lawyer; b. Texas City, Tex., July 18, 1952; s. Lloyd T. and S. Wylodine (Reeves) J. BS, U. W. Fla., 1976; JD, Atlanta Law Sch., 1985. Bar: Ga. 1986, U.S. Dist. Ct. (no. dist.) Ga. 1986, U.S. Ct. Appeals (11th cir.) 1986. Ptnr. The Keenan Law Firm, Atlanta; lectr. People's Law Sch.; group leader Lawyer's New Beginning; research and devel. dir. Lawline TV programming. Mem. Fulton County Recreation Commn., Atlanta. Fellow Roscoe Pound Found; mem. Met. Area Lawyers Recreation Assn., ABA (litigation sect, tort and ins. sect.), Ga. Bar Assn. (ins. law sect., gen. practice and trial sect.), Assn. Trial Lawyers Am. (lectr., asst. regional dir., judge in student advocacy mock trial regional competition), Ga. Trial Lawyers Assn., Ga. Law Pac Gold Star Club, N.Y. State Trial Lawyers Assn., Atlanta Law Sch. Alumni Assn. Avocations: team sports, sailing, golf. Personal injury, Federal civil litigation, State civil litigation. Office: The Keenan Law Firm 148 Nassau St NW Atlanta GA 30303

JENKS, THOMAS EDWARD, lawyer; b. Dayton, Ohio, May 31, 1929; s. Wilbur L. and Anastasia A. (Ahern) J.; m. Marianna Fischer, Nov. 10, 1961; children—Pamela, William, David, Christine, Daniel, Douglas. Student, Miami U., Oxford, Ohio, 1947-50; J.D. cum laude, Ohio State U., 1953. Bar: Ohio 1953, U.S. Dist. Ct. (so. dist.) Ohio 1961, U.S. Supreme Ct. 1971, U.S. Ct. Appeals (6th cir.) 1984. Sole practice Dayton, 1955—; ptnr. Jenks, Surdyk & Cowdrey, Dayton; lectr. med. malpractice law. Served to 1st lt. USMC, 1953-55. Fellow Am. Coll. Trial Lawyers, Am. Bar Found., Ohio Bar Found.; mem. ABA (ho. of dels. 1985—), Dayton Bar Assn. (pres. 1978-79), Ohio Bar Assn., Internat. Assn. Def. Counsel, Ohio Assn. Civil Trial Attys., Nat. Conf. Bar Pres., Kettering C. of C. (past pres.), Kettering Holiday at Home (past pres.), Order of Coif, Phi Delta Phi, Sigma Chi. Republican. Roman Catholic. Clubs: Dayton Lawyers, Optimist (past pres. Oakwood chpt.). State civil litigation, Insurance, Personal injury. Office: Jenks Surdyk & Cowdrey 205 E 1st St Dayton OH 45402

JENNE, KIRK, lawyer; b. Balt., Jan. 3, 1945; s. William K. and Robina Laurie (Kirk) J.; m. Margaret Keats, Aug. 22, 1970; 1 child, Thomas. BA, U. Pa., 1967, JD, 1971. Bar: Pa. 1972, U.S. Dist. Ct. (we. dist.) Pa. 1972. Law clk. to Judge Theodore O. Rogers Commonwealth Ct. of Pa., Harrisburg, 1971-73; assoc. Kenney, Stevens, Clark & Semple, Pitts., 1973-75; atty. H.J. Heinz Co., Pitts., 1975-81, Cyclops Corp., Pitts., 1981—. Chmn. Avonworth Mcpl. Authority, Pitts., 1983-84. Mem. ABA, Pa. Bar Assn., Allegheny County Bar Assn. Republican. Presbyterian. Club: The Pa. Soc. General corporate, Private international. Office: Cyclops Corp 650 Washington Rd Pittsburgh PA 15202

JENNER, ALBERT ERNEST, JR., lawyer; b. Chgo., June 20, 1907; s. Albert E. and Elizabeth (Owens) J.; m. Nadine N., Mar. 19, 1932; 1 dau., Cynthia Lee. J.D., U. Ill., 1930, LL.D., 1979; LL.D., John Marshall Law Sch., 1961, Columbia Coll., 1974, U. Notre Dame, 1975, Northwestern U., 1975, William Mitchell Law Sch., 1976, U. Mich., 1976. Bar: Ill. 1930. Practiced in Chgo., 1930—; sr. partner firm Jenner & Block; counsel, dir. Gen. Dynamics Corp.; spl. asst. atty gen. Ill., 1956-68; counsel Ill. Budgetary Commn., 1956-57; prof. law Northwestern U., 1952-53; chmn. U.S. Supreme Ct. Adv. Com. on Fed. Rules of Evidence, 1965-75; Chmn. Ill. Commn. on Uniform State Laws, 1950-80; mem. Nat. Conf. Commrs. Uniform State Laws, 1952—, pres., 1969-71; mem. Adv. Com. Fed. Rules of Civil Procedure, U.S. Supreme Court, 1960-70, Nat. Conf. Bar Assn. Pres.'s U.S., 1950—, pres., 1952-53; mem. U.S. Loyalty Review Bd., 1952-53; mem. council U. Ill. Law Forum, 1948-51; sr. counsel Presdl. Commn. to Investigate the Assassination of President Kennedy (Warren Commn.), 1963-64; chief spl. counsel to minority Ho. of Reps. Judiciary Com. that conducted impeachment inquiry regarding Pres. Richard M. Nixon.; Law mem. Ill. Bd. Examiners Accountancy, 1948-51. Author and co-author: Illinois Civil Practice Act Annotated, 1933, Outline of Illinois Supreme Court and Appellate Court Procedure, 1935, Smith-Hurd Ill. Annotated Statutes, Volumes on Pleading, Evidence and Practice, 10 edits, 1933-87, also Vols. on Uniform Marriage and Dissolution of Marriage; Mem. permanent editorial bd.: Uniform Commercial Code, 1961—; Contbr. to law revs. and legal publs. on various phases of practice, pleading, evidence, procedure and other legal subjects. Mem. Pres. Lyndon B. Johnson's Nat. Commn. on Causes and Prevention of Violence in U.S., 1968-69; sec. U.S. Navy Meml. Found.; trustee Evanston-Glenbrook Hosp. Arthritis Found., Cerebral Palsey Found., Northwestern U. Library Bd.; mem. presdl. adv. bd. Mus. Sci. and Industry. Recipient Distinguished Service award for outstanding pub. service Chgo. and Ill. Jr. C. of C., 1939, U. Ill. Disting. Alumni award, 1962, Disting. Civic Achievement award Am. Jewish Com., 1973, N.Y. U. Distinguished Citizen's award, 1975; named Chicagoan of Year Chgo. Press Club, 1975; laureate Lincoln Acad. of Ill. Fellow Am. Coll. Trial Lawyers (bd. regents, pres. 1958-59), Internat. Acad. Trial Lawyers, Am. Bar Found.; mem. Ill. Soc. Trial Lawyers, Nat. Assn. Def. lawyers in Criminal Cases, Inter-Am. Bar Assn., Internat. Bar Assn., Am. Bar Assn. (ho. of dels. 1948—, fellow Young Lawyers Sect., state del. 1975-78, chmn. standing com. on fed. judiciary 1965-68, chmn. sect. individual rights and responsibilities 1973-74, mem. council sect. legal edn. 1967-75, bd. govs. 1977-80), Ill. Bar Assn. (pres. 1949-50), Chgo. Bar Assn. (bd. dirs. 1934-47, sec. 1947-49), Assn. Bar City N.Y., Am. Judicature Soc. (pres. 1958-60), Am. Inst. Jud. Adminstrn., Nat. Lawyers Com. for Civil Rights Under Law (dir., nat. co-chmn. 1975-77), Bar Assn. U.S. Ct. Appeals 7th Circuit (bd. govs. 1955-60, Robert Maynard Hutchins Distinguished Service award 1976), Am. Law Inst., Chgo. Council Lawyers, NAACP Legal Def. Fund, Center for Study Dem. Instns. (dir. 1975-79), Order of Coif, Alpha Chi Rho, Phi Delta Phi. Republican. Clubs: Tavern, Midday, Skokie Country, Law, Legal, Chicago. Office: One IBM Plaza Chicago IL 60611

JENNER, GREGORY FRANKLIN, lawyer; b. Portland, Oreg., Aug. 8, 1953; s. Edward and Val Jane (Southwell) J. BS, Portland State U., 1975; JD, NYU, 1979. Bar: Oreg. 1979, U.S. Dist. Ct. Oreg. 1979, U.S. Ct. Appeals (9th cir.) 1979, U.S. Tax Ct. 1980. Adminstrv. asst. state senator Mary Roberts, Salem, Oreg., 1973-75; assoc. Stoel, Rives, Boley, Fraser & Wyse, Portland, 1979-83, Weiss, Des Camp, Botteri & Huber, Portland, 1983-85; tax counsel fin. com. U.S. Senate, Washington, 1985—. Note and comment editor NYU Law Rev., 1978-79. Bd. dirs. United Cerebral Palsy of Oreg., 1983—. Mem. ABA (editor Tax Lawyer), Order of Coif. Avocations: racquetball, golf, softball, volleyball, trivia. Corporate taxation, Estate taxation, Personal income taxation. Home: 2415 N Madison St Arlington VA 22205 Office: US Senate Fin Com 205 Dirksen Senate Office Bldg Washington DC 20510

JENNINGS, ALSTON, lawyer; b. West Helena, Ark., Oct. 30, 1917; s. Earp Franklin and Irma (Alston) J.; m. Dorothy Buie Jones, June 12, 1943; children: Alston, Eugene Franklin, Ann Buie. A.B., Columbia U., 1938; J.D., Northwestern U., 1941. Bar: Ark. 1941. Practiced law Little Rock, 1947—; spl. agt. intelligence unit Treasury Dept., 1946; asso. Wright, Harrison, Lindsey & Upton, 1949-51, mem., 1951-60; mem. Wright, Lindsey, Jennings, Lester & Shults, 1960-65, Wright, Lindsey and Jennings, 1965—. Bd. dirs. Community Chest Greater Little Rock; mem. adv. bd. Salvation Army, Pulaski County. Served to lt. USNR, 1941-45. Fellow Am. Bar Found.; mem. ABA, Ark. Bar Assn., Pulaski County Bar Assn. (past pres.), Internat. Assn. Ins. Counsel (pres. 1972-73), Am. Coll. Trial Lawyers (regent 1975-79, treas. 1979-80, pres.-elect 1980-81, pres. 1981-82). Antitrust, Federal civil litigation, State civil litigation. Home: 5300 Sherwood Little Rock AR 72207 Office: 2200 Worthen Bank Bldg Little Rock AR 72201

JENNINGS, CHARLES THOMAS, lawyer; b. Jonesboro, Ark., Jan. 5, 1948; s. Frank Arnold Jennings and Beatrice (Prestidge) Antrim; m. Karen E. France, Mar. 9, 1969 (div. Jan. 1982); m. Susan J. Clevenger, Oct. 1, 1984; children: Kristin E., Lisa P. AB, Ind. U., 1969; JD summa cum laude, Ind. U., Indpls., 1978. Bar: Ind. 1978, U.S. Dist. Ct. (so. dist.) Ind. 1978, U.S. Dist. Ct. (no. dist.) Ind. 1983, U.S. Ct. Appeals (7th cir.) 1984; CPCU. Claims rep. Meridian Mut. Ins. Co., South Bend, Ind., 1970-72, Cin. Ins. Co., 1972-74, Aetna Ins. Co., Indpls., 1974-78; ptnr. Dutton, Kappes & Overman, Indpls., 1978-85, Jennings, Maas & Stickney, Indpls., 1985—; Chmn. Ins. Com. on Arbitration, Indpls., 1977. Mem. State Fire Marshal's Arson Com., Indpls., 1986. Recipient commendation Internat. Acad. Trial Lawyers. Mem. ABA, Ind. Bar Assn. (chmn. ins. law seminar 1985, 86), Indpls. Bar Assn., Def. Research Inst. Personal injury, Insurance, Federal civil litigation. Office: Jennings Maas & Stickney 8555 N River Rd Suite 470 Indianapolis IN 46240

JENNINGS, DAVID VINCENT, JR., judge; b. Milw., Feb. 10, 1921; s. David V. and Mary (Hanrahan) J.; divorced; m. Margaret R. Jennings, Sept. 26, 1985; children—Maureen, David, Kathleen, Sheila, Robert, Ellen, Therese, Steven, Colleen, Janet, Bridget; m. Margaret R. Horan, July 26, 1985. A.B., Holy Cross Coll., 1943; LL.B., Marquette U., 1948. Bar: Wis. 1948, U.S. Dist. Ct. (ea. dist.) Wis. 1948, U.S. Ct. Appeals (7th cir.) 1951, U.S. Supreme Ct. 1955. Sole practice, Milw., 1948-66; judge Cir. Ct., Milw., 1966—. Served as lt. USNR, 1942-46, PTO. Mem. ABA, Wis. Bar Assn., Ozaukee County Bar Assn., Milw. County Bar Assn. Roman Catholic. Clubs: Mill Creek Hunt (pres., chmn. bd.) (Lake Forest, Ill.); Milw. Hunt (dir., treas.), Wis. Real property, General practice, Landlord-tenant. Office: Milwaukee County Courthouse 901 N 9th St Room 208 Milwaukee WI 53233

JENNINGS, GEORGE MAHLON, lawyer; b. Grand Rapids, Mich., Nov. 15, 1947; s. Floyd Marlin and Kathryn (Tharalson) J.; m. Connie Carson, Dec. 27, 1982; 1 child, Randy. BA in Econs., U. Washington, Seattle, 1970; JD, Willamette Law Sch., 1975. Bar: Oreg. 1975, U.S. Dist. Ct. Oreg. 1976, U.S. Tax Ct. 1985. Account mgr. Foster & Kleiser, Seattle, 1970-72; researcher Mcpl. Research and Services Ctr., Seattle, 1972-75, Environ. Law Inst., Washington, 1975; ptnr. McArthur & Jennings, P.C., Monmouth, Oreg., 1975-82, Garrett, Seideman et al, P.C., Salem, Oreg., 1982—; bd. dirs. Western Found., Monmouth; mgr. Dun & Bradstreet, Seattle, 1970-72; spl. grader Oreg. Bar Examiners, Portland, 1986—; mem. Bd. Bar Examiners, Portland. Co-author Handbooks for 3d and 4th Class Cities, 1974. Pres. Edgar H. Smith Fine Arts, Western Oreg. State Coll., 1981; chmn. bd. dirs. Cen. Sch., Monmouth, 1984-86. Mem. Oreg. State Bar Assn., Monmouth C. of C. (pres. 1977, First Citizen award 1982). Lodge: Elks. Avocations: golf, tennis, skiing, jogging. Real property, General corporate, Contracts commercial. Office: Garrett Seideman et al PC 1011 Commercial Salem OR 97308

JENNINGS, JEFFREY HOWELLS, lawyer; b. Pitts., Feb. 16, 1919; s. Elroy Jeffrey and Bertha Marie (Howells) J.; m. Patricia Walmsley, Oct. 26, 1945; children—Randolph, Sharon, Thomas, Andrea, Alison. A.B., Columbia U., 1941, J.D., 1944. Bar: N.Y. 1944. Assoc. to counsel Columbia U., N.Y.C., 1944-55; asst. U.S. atty. Eastern Dist. N.Y., 1961-66; now sole practice, Smithtown, N.Y.; librarian Old Mill Sch., N.Y.C., 1973. Prin. clk. Smithtown Hwy Dept., 1961. Recipient Cross of Honor Order of DeMolay, 1972. Mem. Columbia U. Secondary Sch. Com., Friends Assn. for Higher Edn., Smithtown C. of C. (pres. 1959-60), Phi Delta Phi. Republican. Quaker. Clubs: Dramatists Guild (N.Y.C.). Works include: Battle of the Andes, The Classmate, 1934; Laws into Song, The Fossil, 1963; Manhattan 2, New Oberammergau Players, 1982. Computer. Home: 1348 Bridgewater Ct Wichita KS 67209 Office: 11 Rainbow Dr Hauppauge NY 11788

JENNINGS, KAREN LYNN, lawyer; b. Mt. Holly, N.J., Nov. 14, 1956; d. Duane Merville and Lois (Harrison) L. BA cum laude, Wells Coll., 1978; JD, U. N.Mex., 1982. Bar: N.Mex. 1982, U.S. Dist. Ct. N.Mex. 1983, Tex. 1986, U.S. Dist. Ct. (no. dis.) Tex. 1986. Asst. dist. atty. N.Mex. 10th Jud. Dist., Tucumcari, 1982-84; asst. dist. atty. felony div. N.Mex. 11th Jud. Dist., Farmington, 1984-86; assoc. Moeller & Burnham, Farmington, 1986; asst. pub. defender N.Mex. Pub. Defender Dept., Roswell, 1986; sole practice Amarillo, Tex., 1986—; substitute judge City of Farmington, 1986. Tutor Amarillo Adult Literacy Program; bd. dirs. Econ. Council Helping Others, Farmington, 1985. Mem. ABA, N.Mex. Bar Assn. (criminal law sect.), San Juan County Bar Assn. (program com. 1986-87), Amarillo Area Bar Assn., Quay County Bar Assn. (pres. 1984). United Methodist. Criminal, Family and matrimonial, Consumer commercial. Home: 1612 Stubbs Amarillo TX 79106 Office: 400 W 15th St PO Box 10171 Amarillo TX 79116

JENNINGS, MARIANNE MOODY, lawyer, educator; b. Johnstown, Pa., Sept. 11, 1953; d. James L. and Jennie (Ure) Moody; m. Terry H. Jennings, Nov. 5, 1976; children: Sarah Anne, Claire Elizabeth. B.S. in Fin., Brigham Young U., 1974, J.D., 1977. Bar: Ariz. 1977, U.S. Dist. Ct. Ariz. 1977. Law clk. Fed. Pub. Defender, Las Vegas, 1975; U.S. Atty., Las Vegas, 1976, Udall, Shumway, Bentley, Allen & Lyons, Mesa, Ariz., 1976; asst. prof. bus. law Ariz. State U., Tempe, Ariz., 1977-80, assoc. prof., 1980-83, prof., 1983—, acting assoc. dean, 1986-87 . Bd. dirs. Ariz. Girls Ranch, Inc.; gubernatorial appointee Ariz. Corp. Commn., 1984-85. Bd. dirs. Ariz. Pub. Service, Inc. Named Outstanding Undergrad. Bus. Prof., Ariz. State U., 1980, 85; recipient Provost Research Incentive Fund Ariz. State U., 1982, Burlington No. Teaching Excellence award, 1986, No. Found. Teaching Excellence award. Mem. Ariz. Bar Assn., Am. Bus. Law Assn., Pacific Southwest Bus. Law Assn., Faculty Women's Assn., Beta Gamma Sigma. Republican. Mormon. Author: (with Michael Litka) Business Law, 1983; Business Strategy for the Political Arena, 1984; Real Estate Law, 1985, Law for Business, 1985. Probate, Legal education, Consumer commercial. Office: Ariz State U Coll Business Tempe AZ 85287

JENNINGS, SUSAN JANE, lawyer; b. Providence, June 23, 1952; s. John Edward and Betty Jean (Frost) Stedman; m. James Albert Jennings, Jan. 2, 1982; children: Olivia Arden, Caroline Alexis. BA, Ind. U., 1973; JD, Tex. Tech U., 1978; LLM in Taxation, So. Meth. U., 1985. Bar: Tex. 1978, U.S. Dist. Ct. (no. dist.) Tex. 1979, U.S. Tax Ct. 1986. Advanced mktg. cons. Southwestern Life Ins., Dallas, 1978-81; asst. gen. counsel Res. Life Ins., Dallas, 1981-85; gen. counsel, v.p. Life Ins. Co. SW, Dallas, 1986—; of counsel Erhard, Ruebel and Jennings, Dallas, 1981—; editorial cons. R&R Newkirk Co., Indpls., 1981-83. Contbr. articles to profl. jours. Sponsor 500 Inc., Dallas, 1982—; mem. Innovators Symphony League, Dallas, 1982-85. Mem. ABA (chmn. career planning and placement com. 1984—, various other coms., leadership award 1978), Dallas Bar Assn. (bd. dirs. probate and trust sect. 1981-83), Dallas Estate Planning Council, Kappa Delta (pres. Dallas alumnae 1983-84), Phi Delta Phi. Republican. Presbyterian. Clubs: Lone Star Masters Swim Team (Dallas). Lodge: Daus. of Penelope. Avocations: swimming, cycling, cooking, music. General corporate, Insurance, Estate planning. Home: 3638 Granada Dallas TX 75205 Office: Life Ins Co SW 1300 W Mockingbird PO Box 47421 Dallas TX 75247

JENNINGS, WILLIAM HATHAWAY, II, lawyer; b. Kansas City, Mo., Nov. 18, 1948; s. William Hathaway and Evalynn (Baker) J. AB, St. Louis U., 1970, JD, 1974. Bar: Mo. 1974, U.S. Dist. Ct. (ea. dist.) Mo. 1975, U.S. Ct. Appeals (8th cir.) 1979, U.S. Supreme Ct. 1983. Assoc. Shaw, Howlett & Schwartz, Clayton, Mo., 1974-75; sole practice Clayton, 1975-77, 79—; staff atty. Mo. Ct. Appeals (ea. dist.), St. Louis, 1977; asst. city counselor City of St. Louis, 1978-79; staff atty. Lawyers Reference Service, St. Louis, 1983—. Atty. St. Louis Vol. Lawyers Assn., Clayton, 1984—; mem. The Cath. Commn. for the Handicapped, St. Louis, 1980—; treas. pro-life com. Archdiocese of St. Louis, 1981-83; mem. adv. bd. Pro-Life Commn., St. Louis, 1983—. Mem. ABA, Mo. Bar Assn. (handicapped, elderly and low income persons com.), Bar Assn. Met. St. Louis (handicapped com.), St. Louis County Bar Assn., Am. Blind Lawyers Assn. (bd. dirs. 1985—). Avocations: automobiles, music, reading. handicapped law, mental health law, Probate, General practice. Home: 722 S Central Clayton MO 63105 Office: 230 S Bemiston Ave Suite 1000 Clayton MO 63105

JENSEN, ALLEN REED, lawyer; b. Tremonton, Utah, Sept. 13, 1950; s. Reed C. and Pauline (Michaelis) J.; m. Carlyn L. Phinney, June 6, 1975; children: Ashley, Kirstin, Christopher. BS in Chemistry magna cum laude, Utah State U., 1974; JD with high honors, George Washington U., 1977. Bar: Utah 1977, U.S. Ct. Appeals (Fed. cir.) 1978, U.S. Patent and Trademark Office 1976, D.C. 1980. Patent agt. Morton, Berrard, Brown, Roberts & Sutherland, Washington, 1975-77; tech. advisor, law clk. U.S. Ct. Customs and Patent Appeals, Washington, 1977-79; assoc., patent atty. Fox, Edwards & Gardiner, Salt Lake City, 1979-82, patent atty., dir., 1982-84; patent atty. Workman, Nydegger & Jensen, Salt Lake City, 1984—, also bd. dirs., 1984—; adj. prof. J. Reuben Clark Law Sch. of Brigham Young U., Provo, Utah, 1985—; bd. dirs. Nat. Inventors Hall of Fame. Mem. Utah State Bar Assn. (chmn. patent trademark and copyright sec. 1981-82), Nat. Council Patent Law Assns. (editor newsletter 1977—, councilman for Utah 1981—), Am. Intellectual Property Law Assn. (com. chmn. 1984-86), Am. Chem. Soc. Patent, Trademark and copyright, Federal civil litigation. Office: Workman Nydegger & Jensen 57 West 200 South 3d floor Salt Lake City UT 84101

JENSEN, DALLIN W., lawyer; b. Afton, Wyo., June 2, 1932; s. Louis J. and Nellie B. Jensen; m. Barbara J. Bassett, Mar. 22, 1958; children—Brad L., Julie N. B.S., Brigham Young U., 1954; J.D., U. Utah, 1960. Bar: Utah 1960, U.S. Dist. Ct. Utah 1962, U.S. Ct. Appeals (10th cir.) 1974, U.S. Ct. Appeals D.C. 1980, U.S. Supreme Ct. 1971. Asst. atty. gen. Utah Atty. Gen., Salt Lake City, 1960-83, solicitor gen., 1983—; alt. commr. Upper Colo. River Commn., 1983—; mem. Colo. River Basin Salinity Adv. Council, 1975—; spl. legal cons. Nat. Water Commn., Washington, 1971-73; mem. energy law center adv. council U. Utah Coll. Law, 1976—. Edit. bd. Rocky Mountain Mineral Law Found., 1983-85. Author: (with Wells A. Hutchins) The Utah Law of Water Rights, 1965. Contbr. articles on water law and water resource mgmt. to profl. jours. Served with U.S. Army, 1955-57. Mem. Ch. Jesus Christ Latter-day Saints. Natural resources, Federal civil litigation, Administrative and regulatory. Home: 3565 S 2175 E Salt Lake City UT 84109 Office: Utah Atty Gen 1636 W N Temple #300 Salt Lake City UT 84116

JENSEN, DENNIS LOWELL, lawyer, legislative aide, political consultant; b. Erie, Pa., July 5, 1951; s. Lowell and Roberta (Umbaugh) J. Student Cornell Coll., 1969-70; B.A., Macalester Coll., 1973; J.D., U. Houston, 1977. Bar: Tex. 1977, U.S. Dist. Ct. (so. dist.) Tex. 1978, Calif. 1981. Sole practice, Houston, 1977-78; asst. housing coordinator Santa Ana Housing Authority, Calif., 1979; polit. cons., Huntington Beach, Calif., 1980-81; legis. analyst Tosco Corp., Los Angeles, 1981-82; polit. cons. Lynn Wessell Co., 1982-83, George Young & Assocs., 1983-84; legis. aide to Los Angeles City Councilman Ernani Bernardi, 1984-86, dep. atty. Los Angeles City Atty.'s Office, 1986—; lectr. in field. Contbr. articles to profl. jours. Campaign mgr. for Congressman Tom Kindness, Hamilton, Ohio, 1978, Initiative to Abolish Inheritance Tax, Bakersfield, Calif., 1980; alumni admissions rep. Macalester

Coll., 1984. Mem. Am. Assn. Polit. Cons., Order of Barons, Phi Delta Phi. Republican. Legislative, Local government, Election. Home: 18801 Gregory Ln Huntington Beach CA 92646 Office: Los Angeles City Attys Office 200 N Main St 1600 City Hall E Los Angeles CA 90012

JENSEN, DOUGLAS BLAINE, lawyer; b. Fresno, Calif., Feb. 10, 1943; s. Rodger Blaine and Margaret Mae J.; m. Lesley S. Smith, Sept. 4, 1967 (div.); children—Clayton B., Kelly E. A.B., Stanford U., 1964, J.D., 1967. Bar: Calif. 1967, U.S. Dist. Ct. (ea. dist.) Calif., U.S. Dist. Ct. (no. dist.) Calif., U.S. Ct. Appeals (9th cir.). Clk. to judge U.S. Ct. Appeals 9th Cir., Fresno and San Francisco, 1967-68; Internat. Legal Ctr. fellow, Santiago, Chile, 1968-70; assoc. Miller, Groezinger, Pettit, Evers & Martin, San Francisco, 1970-72, Baker, Manock & Wanger, Fresno, Calif., 1972-74; ptnr. Baker, Manock & Jensen, Fresno, 1974—; adj. prof. water law San Joaquin Coll. Law, 1980-83. Chmn. Valley Children's Hosp., 1976—. Mem. ABA, State Bar Calif., Fresno County Bar Assn. (pres. 1982-83). Club: Rotary. Contbr. article to legal publ. Real property, General corporate, Local government. Office: 5260 N Palm Ave 4th Floor Fresno CA 93704

JENSEN, FRODE, III, lawyer; b. Denver, Colo., May 30, 1950; s. Frode and Camille McLean (Anderson) J.; m. Catherine Spotswood Hall, Aug. 16, 1980; children—Christian McLean, Catherine Spotswood Hall. B.A., Williams Coll., 1972; J.D., Columbia U., 1976. Bar: N.Y. 1977, U.S. Dist. Ct. (so. and ea. dists.) N.Y. 1979, Conn. 1985. Law clk. U.S. Dist. Ct. Del., Wilmington, 1976-77; assoc. Davis Polk & Wardwell, N.Y.C., 1978-83; assoc. Cummings & Lockwood, Stamford, Conn., 1983-85, ptnr., 1985—. Mem. ABA, Bar Assn. City of N.Y., Conn. Bar Assn. General corporate, Banking, Securities. Office: Cummings & Lockwood PO Box 120 Stamford CT 06904

JENSEN, GAIL KATHLEEN, lawyer; b. Ponca City, Okla., Dec. 14, 1953; d. Warren L. and Norma J. (Zeleny) J. BA, Duke U., 1976; postgrad., U. de Grenoble, France, 1976-77; JD, American U., 1981. Bar: D.C. 1981, N.Mex. 1982. Assoc. Behles & Behles, Albuquerque, 1982, Martin & Behles, Albuquerque, 1983-84, Becker & Anderson, Albuquerque, 1984-85; atty. FDIC, Washington, 1985—. Mem. D.C. Bar Assn., N.Mex. Bar Assn. Avocations: cross-country skiing, fine arts. Bankruptcy, Consumer commercial, Banking.

JENSEN, J. CHRISTOPHER, lawyer, educator; b. Pocatello, Idaho, June 27, 1947; s. Malcolm Hodson and Norma Jean (Christofferson) J.; m. Gail S. Goldman, May 27, 1973; children: Heather, Meredith. BA, Columbia U., 1969; JD, NYU, 1973. Bar: N.Y. 1974, U.S Ct. Appeals (2d cir.) 1974, U.S. Dist. Ct. (so. dist.) N.Y. 1975, U.S. Supreme Ct. 1978, U.S. Dist. Ct. (ea. dist.) N.Y. 1980, U.S. Ct. Claims 1983. Assoc. counsel Suburban Action Inst., Tarrytown, N.Y., 1973-75; asst. U.S. atty. ea. dist. U.S. Atty's Office (ea. dist.) N.Y., Bklyn., 1975-80; assoc. Cowan, Liebowitz & Latman P.C., N.Y.C., 1980-82, ptnr., 1982—; adj. prof. Bklyn. Law Sch., 1978-79; adj. instr. NYU Sch. Law, 1978—. Mem. East Meadow Bd. Edn., 1980-83. Mem. ABA, Assn. of Bar of City of N.Y., N.Y. State Bar Assn., Fed. Bar Council. Democrat. Federal civil litigation, State civil litigation, Legal education. Office: Cowan Liebowitz & Latman PC 605 3d Ave New York NY 10158

JENSEN, JACK ALBERT, lawyer; b. Grand Rapids, Mich., Apr. 26, 1928; s. William Bertel and Williene (Sterkenberg) J.; m. Ruth Louise Parmenter, June 18, 1951; children: Philip Edward, Karl Gunnar, Julia Ann. AB, U. Mich., 1949, MA, 1951; JD, U. Miami, 1974. Bar: Fla. 1975. Plant mgr. Grand Rapids Container Co., 1958-60; dir. new products container div. The Mead Corp., Cin., 1960-65; mgr. mktg. devel. container div. Internat. Paper Co., N.Y.C., 1965-68; pres. Nat. Honeycomb Corp., Pompano Beach, Fla., 1968-71; sole practice Deerfield Beach, Fla., 1974—. Mem. Assn. Trial Lawyers Am., Deerfield Beach C. of C. (pres. 1984). Republican. Presbyterian. Lodge: Rotary (pres. Deerfield club 1983), Masons. Avocations: opera singing, snow skiing. General practice, Contracts commercial, State civil litigation. Home: 1537 E Hillsboro Blvd Deerfield Beach FL 33441 Office: 850 SE 7th St Deerfield Beach FL 33441

JENSEN, JOHN ROBERT, lawyer; b. Rapid City, S.D., Aug. 9, 1946; s. Edwin Robert and Roxina Althier (Hollinger) J.; m. Susan McClelland, Aug. 27, 1977; children—Margaret Marie, Jennifer Jo. B.A., Calif. State U.-Northridge, 1971; J.D., Baylor U., 1976. Bar: Tex. 1977, U.S. Dist. Ct. (no. dist.) Tex. 1977, U.S. Ct. Appeals (5th cir.) 1982. Asst. ins. dir. Groesbeck Fin., Los Angeles, 1971-73; v.p. Capital Cons., Dallas, 1973-74; assoc. McConnell & Assocs., Arlington, Tex., 1977; sole practice, Arlington, 1978-84; ptnr. Jensen & Jensen, Arlington, 1984—. Author: Checklist for Texas Lawyers, 1979, 81. Served with U.S. Army, 1966-68, Vietnam. Decorated Army Commendation medal. Mem. Assn. Trial Lawyers Am., Arlington Bar Assn., Baylor Order Barristers, Delta Theta Phi (treas. Baylor chpt. 1976). Democrat. Lutheran. State civil litigation, Criminal, Federal civil litigation.

JENSEN, PATRICIA ANN, lawyer; b. Osage City, Kans., Apr. 27, 1942; d. Warren G. and Velma Louise (Evans) Glenn; m. Richard Henry Passman, Sept. 2, 1961 (div. Feb. 1977); children: Ramona Jean, Richard Henry, John Patrick Passman; m. Carl Arthur Jensen, June 14, 1977. BA in Psychology, St. Catherine's U., 1974; JD, William Mitchell Coll. Law, 1978; postgrad., Dartmouth Coll., 1982. Bar: Minn. 1978, U.S. Dist. Ct. Minn. 1978. Researcher State Senate, St. Paul, Minn., 1976-78; ptnr. Jensen and Jensen, Sleepy Eye, Minn., 1978-79; spl. asst. Gov. of Minn., St. Paul, 1979-81; dir. govt. relations Pillsbury Co., Mpls., 1981-86; ptnr. Popham, Haik, Mpls., 1985—; bd. dirs. Pillsbury Polit. Action Com., Mpls., 1983-86; mem. Chem. Dependency Appeals Bd., St. Paul, 1983-85. Mem. YMCA Adv. Bd., St. Paul, 1983-84, Ramsey County Abuse Council, St. Paul, 1985-86, Nat. Adv. Bd. Am. Pvt. Edn., Washington, 1984-85; exec. dir. Nat. Adv. Council Womens Edn., Washington, 1984; mem. Citizens League, Mpls. Mem. ABA, Minn. Bar Assn., Ramsey County Bar Assn. Democrat. Roman Catholic. Clubs: Midland Hills (Arden Hills); Minnesota (St. Paul). Avocations: golf, canoeing, hiking. Legislative, Administrative and regulatory, Environment. Home: 3530 Ridgewood Rd Arden Hills MN 55112 Office: Popham Haik 4344 IDS Ctr Minneapolis MN 55402

JENSEN, ROBERT ARTHUR, lawyer; b. Cin., Mar. 24, 1934; s. Carroll Miller and Phyllis G. (Walters) J.; m. Helen Bishop, April 7, 1957 (div. Mar. 1973); children: Anne, Sara; m. Jacqueline M. Haimes, Dec. 7, 1973; children: Cynthia, Susan. BA, Oberlin Coll., 1956; JD, U. Chgo., 1962. Bar: Minn. 1962, Ariz. 1966. Assoc. Dorsey & Owen, Mpls., 1960-65; ptnr. Lewis & Roca, Phoenix, 1965-70, Murphy & Posner, Phoenix, 1970-78, Mitchell, Jensen & Timbanard, Phoenix, 1978-83, Jensen and Kjos, Phoenix, 1983—. Served to 1st lt. USAF, 1956-59. Mem. ABA, Ariz. Bar Assn. (lectr.), Maricopa County Bar Assn. (lectr.), Am. Trial Lawyers Assn. Democrat. Avocation: sailing. Family and matrimonial, Personal injury, State civil litigation. Office: Jensen and Kjos 3246 N 16th St Phoenix AZ 85016

JENSEN, SAM, lawyer; b. Blair, Nebr., Oct. 30, 1935; s. Soren K. and Frances (Beck) J.; m. Marilyn Heck, June 28, 1959; children—Soren R., Eric, Dana. B.A., U. Nebr., 1957, J.D., 1961. Bar: Nebr. 1961. Mem. firm Smith Bros., Lexington, Nebr., 1961-63, Swarr, May, Smith and Andersen, Omaha, 1963-83, Erickson & Sederstrom, P.C., Omaha, 1983—; v.p. bd. dirs. Omaha Public Power Dist., 1979-81; chmn. Nebr. Coordinating Commn. for Postsecondary Edn., 1976-78. Del. Nat. Republican Conv., 1960; mem. Nebr. Rep. Central Com., 1968-70, Regents Commn. Urban U., U. Nebr., Omaha; chmn. Task Force on Higher Edn. Recipient Disting. Service award U. Nebr., 1981. Mem. Omaha Bar Assn. (past exec. com.), Nebr. Bar Assn. (chmn. com. public relations 1973-76), Am. Bar Assn., U. Nebr. Alumni Assn. (pres. 1976-78), Beta Theta Pi, Phi Delta Phi. Clubs: Rotary, Omaha, Racquet. Labor, Trademark and copyright, Federal civil litigation. Office: One Merrill Lynch Plaza 10330 Regency Pkwy Dr Omaha NE 68114

JENSEN, SHERMAN HOLBROOK, lawyer; b. Pocatello, Idaho, Aug. 20, 1953; s. Jay Henry and Melva Mae (Bell) J.; m. Jane Holbrook, Mar. 20, 1981; children: Diane Holbrook, Ainsley Holbrook. AB, Stanford U., 1975; JD, U. Calif., Berkeley, 1982. Bar: Wash. 1982. Assoc. Garvey, Schubert & Barer, Seattle, 1982—. Mem. ABA, Wash. Bar Assn. (francise act rev. com. 1985-86, legis. com. young lawyers div. 1984—). Avocation: fly fishing. General corporate, Trademark and copyright, Computer. Office: Garvey Schubert & Barer 1011 Western 10th Floor Seattle WA 98104

JENSEN, WALTER EDWARD, JR., finance, insurance and law educator, lawyer; b. Chgo., Oct. 20, 1937. A.B., U. Colo., 1959; J.D., Ind. U., 1962, M.B.A., 1964; Ph.D. (Univ. fellow), Duke U., 1972. Bar: Ind. 1962, Ill. 1962, D.C. 1963, U.S. Tax Ct. 1982, U.S. Supreme Ct. 1967. Assoc. prof. Colo. State U., 1964-66; assoc. prof. Ill. State U., 1970-72; prof. bus. adminstrn. Va. Poly. Inst. and State U., beginning 1972, now prof. fin., ins. and law; with Inst. Advanced Legal Studies, U. London, 1983-84; prof. U.S. Air Force Grad. Mgmt. Program, Europe, 1977-78, 83-85; Duke U. legal research awardee, researcher, Guyana, Trinidad and Tobago, 1967; researcher U. London Inst. Advanced Legal Studies, London Sch. Econs. and Inst. Commonwealth Studies, summers, 1969, 71, 74, 76, winter 1972-73; Ford Found. research fellow Ind. U., 1963-64; faculty research fellow in econs. U. Tex., 1968; Bell Telephone fellow in econs. regulated pub. utilities U. Chgo., 1965. Recipient Teaching award Ind. U., 1964, Dissertation Travel award Duke U. Grad. sch., 1968; Ind. U. fellow, 1963, 74, scholar, 1963-64. Mem. D.C. Bar Assn., Ill. Bar Assn., Ind. bar Assn., ABA, Am. Polit. sci. Assn., Am. Soc. Internat. Law, Am. Judicature Soc., Am. Bus. Law Assn., Alpha Kappa Psi, Phi Alpha Delta, Pi Gamma Mu, Pi Kappa Alpha. Contbr. articles to profl. publs.; staff editor Am. Bus Law Jour., 1973—; vice chmn. assoc. editor for adminstrv. law sect. young lawyers Barrister (Law Notes), 1975-83; book rev. and manuscript editor Justice System Jour: A Mgmt. Rev., 1975—; staff editor Bus. Law Rev., 1975—. Legal education. Home: PO Box 250 Blacksburg VA 24060 Office: Va Poly Inst and State U Blacksburg VA 24060

JENSON, DENNIS DION, lawyer; b. Wickenburg, Ariz., Dec. 5, 1942; s. Elmo C. and Ernestine L. (Waller) J.; divorced; 1 child, Rebecca Lynn. BS, BA, U. Ariz., 1965, JD, 1968. Bar: Ariz. 1968, U.S. Dist. Ct. Ariz. 1969, U.S. Ct. Appeals (9th cir.) 1976. Staff atty. Pinal county Legal Aid, Florence, Ariz., 1968-70; ptnr. Wood, Platt & Jenson, Coolidge, Ariz., 1970-76, Platt & Jenson, Coolidge, 1976-78, 84—, Platt, Jenson & Johnson, Coolidge, 1978-84. Pres. Coolidge Rotary Club, 1977-78, Pinal County Bar Assn., Florence, 1973; city atty., Coolidge, 1978-86. Recipient Boss of Yr. award Pinal County chpt. Nat. Secs. Assn., Casa Grande, Ariz., 1977. Democrat. Lodge: Elks. State civil litigation, Family and matrimonial, Personal injury. Home: 880 Toltec Dr Coolidge AZ 85228 Office: Platt & Jenson PC 161 W Central Ave PO Box 279 Coolidge AZ 85228

JENTES, WILLIAM ROBERT, lawyer; b. Kalamazoo, Mich., Oct. 2, 1932; s. Tedrel Krantz and Gretchen Elizabeth (Hawk) J.; m. Janet Sue Oberg, Sept. 15, 1956; 1 dau., Justine Devereaux. A.B., U. Mich., 1953, J.D., 1956; postgrad., Universite de Grenoble, France, 1956-57. Bar: Ill. 1957. Assoc Kirkland & Ellis, Chgo., 1957-62, ptnr., 1962—, firm com., 1975—; lectr. U. Chgo. Law Sch., 1980—, numerous orgns. Trustee Orchestral Assn. Chgo., 1982—; trustee Latin Sch., Chgo., 1981-85 ; sec. Chgo. Opera Theater, 1980—; sustaining fellow Art Inst. Chgo., 1981—. Served with USN, 1953-55. Recipient Fulbright scholar Universite de Grenoble, 1956-57. Mem. ABA, Bar Assn. Seventh Cir., Econ. Club Chgo., Order of Coif, Phi Beta Kappa. Clubs: Saddle and Cycle, Mid-Am. Home: 1500 N Lake Shore Dr Apt 3-c Chicago Il 60610 Office: Kirkland & Ellis Suite 5800 200 E Randolph Chicago IL 60601

JENTZ, GAYLORD ADAIR, lawyer, educator; b. Beloit, Wis., Aug. 7, 1931; s. Merlyn Adair and Delva (Mullen) J.; m. JoAnn Mary Hornung, Aug. 6, 1955; children: Katherine Ann, Gary Adair, Loretta Ann, Rory Adair. B.A., U. Wis., 1953, J.D., 1957, M.B.A., 1958. Bar: Wis. 1957. Pvt. practice law Madison, 1957-58; from instr. to assoc. prof. bus. law U. Okla., 1958-65; vis. instr. to vis. prof. U. Wis. Law Sch., summers 1957-65; asso. prof. to prof. U. Tex., Austin, 1965-68; prof. U. Tex., 1968—, Herbert D. Kelleher prof. bus. law, 1982—, chmn. gen. bus. dept., 1968-74, 80-86. Author: (with others) Business Law Text and Cases, 2d edit, 1968, Tex. Uniform Comml. Code, 1967, rev. edit., 1975, Business Law; Text and Cases, 1978, West's Business Law, 6th edit., 1987, 2d edit., 1983, 3d edit., 1986, West's Business Law: Alternate UCC Comprehensive Edition, 3d edit., 1987, Tex. Family Law, 6th edit., 1987; contbr. articles to profl. jours.; dep. editor Social Sci. Quar., 1966-82, editorial bd., 1982—; editorial staff, dep. editor Am. Bus. Law Jour., 1967-69, editor in chief, 1969-74, adv. editor, 1974—. Served with AUS, 1953-55. Recipient Outstanding Tchr. award Tex. U. Coll. Bus., 1967, Jack G. Taylor Teaching Excellence award, 1971, Joe D. Beasley Grad. Teaching Excellence award, 1978, CBA Found. Adv. Council award, 1979, Grad. Bus. Council Outstanding Grad. Bus. Prof. award, 1980, James C. Scorboro Meml. award for outstanding Leadership in Banking Edn. Colo. Grad. Sch. Banking, 1983. Mem. Southwestern Fedn. Adminstrv. Disciplines (v.p. 1979-80, pres. 1980-81), Am. Arbitration Assn. (nat. panel 1966—), Am. Bus. Law Assn. (pres. 1971-72, Faculty award of excellence 1981), So. Bus. Law Assn. (pres. 1967), Tex. Assn. Coll. Tchrs. (pres. Austin chpt. 1967-68, exec. com. 1969-70, state pres. 1971-72), Wis. Bar Assn., Omicron Delta Kappa, Phi Kappa Phi. (pres. 1983-84). Legal education, Contracts commercial, Consumer commercial. Home: 4106 North Hills Dr Austin TX 78731 Office: U Texas Coll Bus Adminstrn CBA5-202 Austin TX 78712

JEPPSON, JOSEPH GADDIS, lawyer; b. Millville, Utah, Oct. 10, 1904; s. Joseph Rudolph and Christina Rossetti (Mayer) J.; m. Zorah Henrietta Horne, June 8, 1929; children: Joseph Horne, Mary Alice. BS, U. Utah, 1928, JD, 1930, postgrad., 1945; HHD (hon.), Weber State Coll., 1974. Bar: Utah 1932, U.S. Dist. Ct. Utah 1932, U.S. Supreme Ct. 1944. Judge Salt Lake City, 1940-45; dist. ct. judge State of Utah, Salt Lake City, 1945-74; sole practice Salt Lake City, 1974—; instr. acctg. U. Utah, 1946. Author: Prophetic Proof of Divinity of Christ. Commr. Boy Scouts Am., Los Angeles, 1924-25; participant Centennial Trek Nauvoo, Ill. to Salt Lake City. Recipient (with Zorah Jeppson) Merit Honor, U. Utah, 1975, Cert. Appreciation, Utah Supreme Ct., 1985. Mem. ABA (adviser 1945), Utah Bar Assn. (50 yr. cert. merit 1980), Am Judicature Soc., Am. Bar Jud. Adminstrn. (adviser 1945), Internat. Assn. Probate Judges, Dist. Judges Assn. (pres. 1972), Nat. Sons Utah Pioneers (v.p. 1959, judge adv.), Phi Kappa Phi, Delta Theta Phi. Club: Bonneville Knife and Fork (charter, pres. 1974-75) (Salt Lake City). Lodge: Sons Utah Pioneers (pres. Sugarhouse chpt. 1978-79). Probate, Estate taxation, Estate planning. Home and Office: 460 S 12th East St Salt Lake City UT 84102

JERNIGAN, ANNA MICHELLE, lawyer; b. Orlando, Fla., Feb. 15, 1957; d. Alex McGowin and Anna (Lewis) J. BS in Polit. Sci., Stetson U., 1979, JD, 1981. Bar: Fla. 1982, U.S. Dist. Ct. (mid. dist.) Fla. 1982. Asst. atty. State of Fla., Orlando, 1982-83; assoc. Broad & Cassel, Maitland, Fla., 1983-85, Law Offices of Stephen M. Stone, Orlando, 1985-86; ptnr. Woods Roberts & Jernigan, Orlando, 1987—; realtor, assoc. Mary Ann Baker, Inc., Winter Park, Fla., 1985—. Sec., bd. dirs. Big Bros./Big Sisters of Cen. Fla., Orlando, 1985—; youth conselor First Presbyn. Ch., Orlando, 1984-85, mem. various ch. coms. Named one of Outstanding Young Women of Am., 1984. Mem. ABA, Orange County Bar Assn. (news media and pub. relations com., chmn. law week prayer breakfast com.), Orlando Area Bd. Realtors. Republican. State civil litigation, Real property, Contracts commercial. Office: Woods Roberts & Jernigan 201 E Pine St Suite 310 Orlando FL 32801

JERSILD, THOMAS NIELSEN, lawyer; b. Chgo., Dec. 12, 1936; s. Gerhardt S. and Martha M. (Beck) J.; m. Colleen Gay Campbell, June 15, 1963; children: Karen, Paul. BA, U. Chgo., 1957, JD, 1961. Bar: Ill. 1961, U.S. Dist. Ct. (no. dist.) Ill. 1961. Ptnr. Mayer, Brown & Platt, Chgo., 1969—. Editor: U. Chgo. Law Rev., 1959-61. Mem. ABA, Fed. Energy Bar Assn. (former chmn. crude oil and natural gas liquids com. 1980-81), Chgo. Bar Assn. (corp. law com., former chmn. pub. utility law com.), Ill. Bar Assn. (corp. and securities law sect.), Eastern Mineral Law Inst. (coal com.), Legal Club Chgo. (sec., treas. 1976-77), Law Club Chgo. Club: Univ., Attic (Chgo.). Banking, General corporate, Oil and gas leasing. Office: Mayer Brown & Platt 190 S LaSalle St Chicago IL 60603

JERSIN, EDWARD ANTHONY, lawyer; b. Pueblo, Colo., Oct. 12, 1920; s. Anthony and Frances (Nolan) J.; m. Nikki C. Chier; children—K. Suzanne, Robert A., Anthony A., Mary F. B.A., U. Denver, 1942, J.D., 1946. Bar: Colo. 1946. Sole practice, Denver, 1946—. Commr., Jud. Selection of County Judges, Denver County, 1977-82; commr. Community Relations Commn., Denver County, 1962-83. Served as spl. agt. CIC, U.S. Army, 1943-45. Mem. Colo. Bar Assn. (bd. govs. 1971-74), Denver Bar Assn. (1st v.p. 1976-77), Colo. Bar Found., ABA. Democrat. Roman Catholic. Clubs: Denver Athletic, Petroleum. Lodges: KC, Rotary. Personal injury, Real property, Probate. Address: 1430 First Interstate Tower S 621 17th St Denver CO 80293

JESPERSON, JOHN EDWARD, lawyer; b. Summit, N.J., Mar. 29, 1956; s. Albert Peter and Patricia (Kennet) J.; m. Kim Marie Carneglia, Oct. 16, 1982. Student, U. Colo., 1974-75; BA in Adminstrv. Studies magna cum laude, Glassboro State Coll., 1978; JD, Rutgers U., 1981. Bar: N.J. 1981, U.S. Dist. Ct. N.J. 1981. Asst. prosecutor Cumberland County, Bridgeton, N.J., 1981-84, Cape May County, N.J., 1985-86; asst. dep. pub. defender Cumberland Region, Vineland, N.J., 1986—; Mem. ABA, Cumberland County Bar Assn. Avocations: karate, music. Criminal. Office: Office of Pub Defender 234 Landis Ave Vineland NJ 08360

JESSER, STEVEN H., lawyer; b. Chgo., Feb. 29, 1948. JD, Ill. Inst. Tech., 1974. Assoc. gen. counsel Northwestern Meml. Group, Chgo., 1981—. Mem. Am. Coll. Health Execs., Chgo. Bar Assn. (chmn. health com. 1982, 84). Health, General corporate, Insurance. Office: Northwestern Meml Group 750 N Lake Shore Dr #540 Chicago IL 60611

JESSUP, WARREN T., patent lawyer; b. Eureka, Calif., Aug. 1, 1916; s. Thurman W. and Amelia (Johnson) J.; m. Evelyn Via, Sept. 13, 1941; children: Thurman W., Paul H., Stephen T., Marilyn R. Jessup Huffman. B.S., U. So. Calif., 1937; J.D., George Washington U., 1942. Bar: D.C. 1941, Calif. 1947, U.S. Dist. Ct. (cen., so., no. dists.) Calif. 1947, U.S. Ct. Appeals (Fed. cir.) 1947, U.S. Supreme Ct. 1947. Engr. Gen. Electric Co., 1937-38, patent dept., 1938-42; mem. patent div. USN, 1944-46; patent counsel 11th Naval Dist., 1946-50; mem. Huebner, Beehler, Worrel & Herzig, 1950-56; ptnr. Herzig & Jessup, 1957-59; individual practice law 1959-68; mem. firm Jessup & Beecher, Sherman Oaks, also, Los Angeles, 1968-85, Jessup Beecher & Slehofer, Westlake Village, Calif., 1985—; instr. patent law, grad. div. Law Sch., U. So. Calif.; instr. bus. law U. Calif. at Los Angeles. Author: Patent Guide for Navy Inventors, 1950; Contbr. to: Ency. of Patent Practice and Invention Mgmt. Chmn. citizens adv. com. Point Mugu State Park, 1973; mem. Ventura County Mental Health Adv. Bd., 1977-82, chmn., 1979. Served from ensign to lt. comdr. USN, 1942-46; comdr. Res. Mem. Patent Law Assn. Los Angeles (pres. 1974-75), Nat. Soc. Profl. Engrs., Am. Intellectual Property Law Assn., Conejo Valley Bar Assn. (v.p. 1986), Conejo Valley Hist. Soc. (dir. 1971-83), Order of Coif, Tau Beta Pi, Eta Kappa Nu, Phi Kappa Phi, Phi Delta Phi. Baptist. Patent, Trademark and copyright. Office: Jessup Beecher & Slehofer 875 Westlake Blvd Suite 205 Westlake Village CA 91361

JETER, KATHERINE LESLIE BRASH, lawyer; b. Gulfport, Miss., July 24, 1921; d. Ralph Edward and Rosa Meta (Jacobs) Brash; m. Robert McLean Jeter, Jr., May 11, 1946. B.A., Newcomb Coll. of Tulane U., 1943; J.D., Tulane U., 1945. Bar: La. 1945 U.S. Dist. Ct. (we. dist.) La. 1948, U.S. Tax Ct. 1965, U.S. Supreme Ct. 1971, U.S. Dist. Ct. (ea. dist.) La. 1975, U.S. Ct. Appeals (5th cir.) 1981, U.S. Dist. Ct. (mid. dist.) La. 1982. Assoc. Montgomery, Fenner & Brown, New Orleans, 1945-46, Tucker, Martin, Holder, Jeter & Jackson, Shreveport, 1947-49; ptnr. Tucker, Jeter & Jackson and predecessors, Shreveport, 1980—; judge pro tem 1st Jud. Dist. Ct., Caddo Parish, La., 1982-83; mem. adv. com. to joint legis. subcom. on mgmt. of the community. Pres. YWCA of Shreveport, 1963; hon. consul of France; Shreveport; pres. Little Theatre of Shreveport, 1966-67; pres. Shreveport Art Guild, 1974-75; mem. task force crim justice La. Priorities for the Future, 1978; pres. LWV of Shreveport, 1950-51. Recipient Disting. Grad. award Tulane Law Sch., 1983. Mem. La. State Law Inst. (mem. council 1980—, adv. com. La. Civil Code 1973-77, temp. ad hoc. com. 1976-77), Public Affairs Research Council (bd. trustees 1976-81, exec. com. 1981—, area exec. committeeman Shreveport area 1982), ABA, La. Bar Assn., Shreveport Bar Assn. (pres. 1986), Nat. Assn. Women Lawyers, Shreveport Assn. for Women Attys., C. of C. Shreveport (bd. dirs. 1975-77), Order of Coif, Phi Beta Kappa. Baptist. Contbr. articles on law to profl. jours.; editor Tulane Law Rev., 1945. General corporate. Home: 3959 Maryland Ave Shreveport LA 71106 Office: 401 Edwards St Shreveport LA 71101

JETT, EDWARD STEPHEN, lawyer; b. Chattanooga, Tenn., Nov. 25, 1945; s. W. Harry and Mary Ellen (McCullough) J.; m. Wanda Hayes, Dec. 17, 1966; children: Christy Kay, Austin Hayes. BS, Tenn. Tech, 1967; MS, U. Tenn., 1969; JD, U. Tex., 1973. Bar: Tenn. 1974, U.S. Dist. Ct. (ea. dist.) Tenn. 1974. Assoc. Stophel, Caldwell & Heggie, Chattanooga, 1973-78, ptnr., 1978-86; ptnr. Stophel & Stophel, Chattanooga, 1986—. Bd. dirs. Boyd-Buchanan Sch., Chattanooga, 1976—, Chattanooga (Tenn.) Regional Transp. Authority, 1980—. Mem. ABA, Tenn. Bar Assn. (vice chmn. banking, comml. and bankruptcy law 1986—), Chattanooga Bar Assn. Mem. Ch. of Christ. Avocations: running, backpacking. Contracts commercial, General corporate, Pension, profit-sharing, and employee benefits. Home: 1725 Clayton Dr Chattanooga TN 37421 Office: Stophel & Stophel PC Maclellan Bldg 3d Floor Chattanooga TN 37402

JETT, JOSEPH CRAIG, lawyer; b. Nashville, Aug. 27, 1951; s. Joseph Taylor and Mickey (Rucker) J.; B.A. in Govt., U. Tex., 1973; J.D., So. Meth. U., 1977. Bar: Tex. 1977, U.S. Dist. Ct. (no. dist.) Tex. 1981, U.S. Ct. Appeals (5th cir.) 1984. Assoc., Willoughby Brown et al, Dallas, 1977-79; sole practice, Dallas, 1979—. Co-writer, co-dir., actor (video tape): Crime & Punishment, 1983 (numerous awards). Bd. dirs. Greenland Hills Neighborhood Assn., Dallas, 1983-84; mem. Mayor's Task Force on N. Central Expressway, Dallas, 1984. Mem. ABA, Dallas Bar Assn., Dallas Assn. Young Lawyers (bd. dirs. 1984, treas. 1985), Dallas Trial Lawyers Assn., Tex. Criminal Def. Lawyers Assn. Democrat. Criminal, Family and matrimonial, Federal civil litigation. Home: 5210 Monticello Dallas TX 75206 Office: Amberton Tower 4144 N Central Expressway Suite 580 Dallas TX 75204

JEWELL, FRANKLIN P., lawyer; b. Frankfort, Ky., Sept. 26, 1952; s. Wilbert Franklin and Lucille (Perry) J.; m. Rebecca Ann Wright, June 22, 1974; children—Brandon Neil, Amanda Wright. B.A., U. Ky., 1974; J.D., U. Louisville, 1977. Bar: Ky. 1977, U.S. Dist. Ct. (we. dist.) Ky. 1979. Interviewer, clk. Jefferson Dist. Pub. Defender, Louisville, 1975-77, staff atty., 1977-79, asst. chief juvenile div., 1979-82, chief trial atty. adult div., 1982—; speaker ednl. instns. and seminars. Mem. Kenwood Elem. PTA, Louisville, 1983-84, Parkland Elem. PTA, 1984-85. Recipient awards for advocacy in felony cases, juvenile cases, capital trials, Jefferson Dist. Pub. Defender, 1977—. Mem. Ky. Bar Assn. (continuing legal edn. award 1981), Louisville Bar Assn., Phi Alpha Delta. Democrat. Mem. Disciples of Christ Ch. Criminal, Juvenile. Office: Jefferson Dist Pub Defender 200 Civic Plaza 719 W Jefferson St Louisville KY 40202

JEWELL, GEORGE HIRAM, lawyer; b. Fort Worth, Jan. 9, 1922; s. George Hiram and Vera (Lee) J.; m. Betty Elizabeth Jefferis, July 21, 1944; children: Susan Jewell Cannon, Robert V., Nancy Jewell Wommack. B.A., U. Tex., 1942, LL.B., 1950. Bar: Tex. 1950. Geophysicist Gulf Research and Devel. Corp., Harmarville, Pa., 1946-47; assoc. Baker & Botts, Houston, 1950-60, ptnr., 1960-70, sr. ptnr., 1970—; dir. Schlumberger Ltd., N.Y., Paris; dir. Pogo Producing Co., Houston, MCorp, Dallas and Houston, MBank, Houston. Contbr. articles to profl. jours. Trustee Tex. Children's Hosp., Houston, 1977—, pres., 1982-83, chmn., 1984-86; bd. dirs. Schlumberger Found., N.Y.C., 1982—; mem. adv. council Coll. Natural Scis., U. Tex. Served to lt. USNR, 1943-46, 50-51. Fellow Am. Coll. Tax Counsel, Am. Bar Found.; mem. ABA, Order of Coif, Phi Beta Kappa, Phi Delta Phi. Clubs: Houston Country, Coronado (pres. 1976-77), Tejas, Old Baldy, Castle Pines Golf; Eldorado (Tex.) Country. Corporate taxation, Personal income taxation. Home: 6051 Crab Orchard Ln Houston TX 77057 Office: Baker & Botts 3000 One Shell Plaza Houston TX 77002

JEWELL, JOHN J., lawyer; b. Kokomo, Ind., Aug. 31, 1954; s. G.M. and Kathryn (Knepper) J. AB, Ind. U., 1975, JD, 1979, MBA, 1979. Bar: Ind. 1979, U.S. Dist. Ct. (so. dist.) Ind. 1979. Assoc. Trimble & Jewell, Evansville, Ind., 1979—. Mem. ABA, Ind. Bar Assn., Evansville Bar Assn., Ind. Jaycees (legal counsel 1983-84), Evansville Jaycees (pres. 1982-83). Episcopalian. Consumer commercial, General corporate, Real property. Home:

PO Box 291 Evansville IN 47702-0291 Office: Trimble & Jewell 700 Vine PO Box 1003 Evansville IN 47706-1003

JEWELL, ROBERT HART, lawyer; b. Portchester, N.Y., Apr. 29, 1931; s. Robert Hart Jewell and Hieberta (Garcia) Goldfinger; m. Joanne Gregory, July 4, 1952; children: Melissa Anne, Robert Kenneth. BA, Colgate U., 1953; LLB, Columbia U., 1956. Bar: N.Y. 1958, U.S. Dist. Ct. (ea. dist.) N.Y. 1979, U.S. Supreme Ct. 1986. Sole practice N.Y.C. and Garden City, N.Y., 1958-75, Mineola, N.Y., 1985-86; ptnr. Banno, Pajion, Jewell & Livoti, Mineola, 1975-79, A'Hearn & Jewell, Garden City, 1979-83; law sec. to presiding justice N.Y. Supreme Ct., Mineola, 1983-85; ptnr. Haber & Jewell, Williston Park, N.Y., 1987—; bd. dirs., gen. counsel Video Technics, Inc., N.Y.C., 1969-74. Active Freeport Rep. Club. Served to 1st lt. USMC, 1956-58. Nat. War Meml. scholar, 1949. Mem. N.Y. State Bar Assn., Bar Assn. Nassau County N.Y. Inc., N.Y. State Trial Lawyers Assn., Assn. Trial Lawyers Am., Nassau Suffolk Trial Lawyers Assn., Law Secs. Assn., Phi Delta Phi. Republican. Methodist. Avocations: golf, bowling, sailing. Family and matrimonial, Personal injury, State civil litigation. Home: 62 Kinsbury Rd Garden City NY 11530 Office: 181 Hillside Ave Williston Park NY 11596

JIANOS, JEAN TERESE, lawyer; b. Foxborough, Mass., June 30, 1957; d. Joseph Aristotle and Jean Terese (McLellan) J. BA, Regis Coll., 1979; JD, Georgetown U., 1982. Bar: Mass. 1982, D.C. 1982, U.S. Dist. Ct. D.C. 1983, U.S. Ct. Appeals (D.C. cir.) 1983. Assoc. Howard, Poe & Bastian, Washington, 1982-83, Howard & Law, Washington, 1983-85; asst. regional counsel The Travelers Cos., Alexandria, Va., 1985-86, assoc. regional counsel, 1986—. Mem. ABA, AAUW (state legis. chairperson 1984-85). Real property. Office: The Travelers Cos 201 N Union St Alexandria VA 22314

JIBILIAN, GERALD ARSEN, home products mfg. corp. exec., lawyer; b. Toledo, Mar. 30, 1938; s. Gary Sarkis and Rochelle M. (Rochlin) J.; m. Jary Sue, Dec. 26, 1965; 1 son, John Frederick. A.B., Duke U., 1960; J.D., U. Mich., 1963. Bar: Ohio 1963. Assoc. Cobourn, Yaser, Smith & Falvey, Toledo, 1963-65; chief prosecutor City of Toledo, 1965-69; gen. counsel and v.p. Ogden Foods, Inc., N.Y.C., 1969-71; counsel and exec. v.p. Schrafft's div. Pet Inc., N.Y.C., 1971-73; sr. atty. Am. Home Products, Corp., N.Y.C., 1973-85, asst. gen. counsel, 1985-86, assoc. gen. counsel, 1987—. Mem. ABA, Grocery Mfrs. Assn. (legal com. 1972—), Med. Device Assn. (legal com. 1972—). Republican. Clubs: University (N.Y.C.); Burning Tree Country (Greenwich, Conn.). General corporate, Administrative and regulatory, FERC practice. Home: 19 Spring House Rd Greenwich CT 06830 Office: Am Home Products Corp 685 3d Ave New York NY 10017

JIMMERSON, JAMES JOSEPH, lawyer; b. Las Vegas, Nev., Apr. 8, 1951; s. James L. and Lorene M. (Michael) J.; m. Carlene E. Jimmerson, June 19, 1982; children: James Mark, Chad Joseph. Student, Am. Coll., Paris, 1970; BA with distinction, George Washington U., 1973; JD, Columbia U., 1976. Bar: Nev. 1976, U.S. Dist. Ct. Nev. 1976, Calif. 1977, U.S. Ct. Appeals (9th cir.) 1978, U.S. Dist. Ct. (cen. dist.) Calif. 1981, U.S. Supreme Ct. 1982. Assoc. Galane & Jimmerson, Las Vegas, 1976-80, ptnr., 1980-83; ptnr. James J. Jimmerson & Assocs. P.C., Las Vegas, 1983-85, Jimmerson & Combs P.C., Las Vegas, 1985—. Mng. editor Columbia Human Rights Law Rev., 1975-76. Pres. Family Counseling Services, Las Vegas, 1983; assoc. U. Nev. Found., Las Vegas, 1985—. Mem. ABA (various coms.), Nev. Bar Assn. (adminstrv. com., bd. govs. 1983—), Calif. Bar Assn., Clark County Bar Assn., Assn. Trial Lawyers Am., Nev. Trial Lawyers Assn., Am. Judicature Soc., Columbia U. Alumni Assn. (Nev. chmn. 1985—), Nev. C. of C., Phi Beta Kappa, Phi Delta Phi. Democrat. Avocations: reading, golf, tennis, skiing. Federal civil litigation, State civil litigation, Bankruptcy. Office: Jimmerson & Combs PC 701 E Bridger Suite 600 Las Vegas NV 89101

JINKINS, MARK ALLEN, lawyer, accountant; b. Dodgeville, Wis., Apr. 9, 1954; s. Kenneth William and Charlotte Jane (Brun) J.; m. Ann M. Zwicky, Oct. 11, 1980; children: David, Michael. BBA in Acctg. and Mgmt., U. Wis., 1976, JD, 1979. Bar: Wis. 1979, U.S. Dist. Ct. (we. dist.) Wis. 1979, U.S. Dist. Ct. (ea. dist.) Wis. 1980. Sole practice Sturgeon Bay, Wis., 1980; assoc. Pinkert, Smith, Koehn & Weir, Sturgeon Bay, 1981-83; ptnr. Pinkert, Smith, Koehn, Weir & Jinkins, Sturgeon Bay, 1984-86, Pinkert, Smith, Weir & Jinkins, Sturgeon Bay, 1987—. Pres., bd. dirs. HELP of Door County Inc., Sturgeon Bay, 1980-84; bd. dirs. Door County Child Care Services Inc., Sturgeon Bay, 1983—, Door County unit Am. Cancer Soc., 1986—. Mem. ABA, Wis. Bar Assn., Door Kewaunee Bar Assn. (pres., sec.), Door County C. of C. (bd. dirs. 1984-85), U. Wis. Alumni Assn. (local pres., bd. dirs. 1982—). Mem. United Ch. Christ. Club: Sturgeon Bay Yacht (bd. dirs. 1986—). Lodge: Rotary. Avocations: golf, boating, reading. General corporate, General practice, Family and matrimonial. Home: 220 S Hudson St Sturgeon Bay WI 54235 Office: Pinkert Smith Weir & Jinkins PO Box 89 Sturgeon Bay WI 54235

JINNETT, ROBERT JEFFERSON, lawyer; b. Birmingham, Ala., May 9, 1949; s. Bryan Floyd Jr. and Elizabeth Coleman (Borders) J.; m. Doreen S. Ziff, Aug. 2, 1975; children: Brynn Leigh, Maren Alexandra. BA, Harvard U., 1971; JD, Cornell U., 1975. Bar: N.Y. 1976, U.S. Dist. Ct. (no. dist.) N.Y. 1976, U.S. Dist. Ct. (so. dist.) N.Y. 1978, U.S. Dist. Ct. (ea. dist.) N.Y. 1979. Law clk. N.Y. State Ct. Appeals, Albany, 1975-77; assoc. Rogers & Wells, N.Y.C., 1977-82; assoc. LeBoeuf, Lamb, Leiby & MacRae, N.Y.C., 1983-86, ptnr., 1986—. Contbg. author: High Tech Real Estate, 1985. DAAD fellow U. Heidelberg, Fed. Republic Germany, 1971-72; recipient 3d Nat. Prize, Nathan Burkan Meml. Comp. ASCAP, 1974. Mem. Assn. of Bar of City of N.Y. Episcopalian. Avocation: genealogy. General corporate, Real property, Private international. Office: LeBoeuf Lamb Leiby & MacRae 520 Madison Ave New York NY 10022

JOCK, PAUL F., II, lawyer; b. Indpls., Jan. 25, 1943; s. Paul F. and Alice (Sheehan) J.; m. Gail A. Webre, Sept. 16, 1967; children: Craig W., Nicole L. BBA, U. Notre Dame, 1965; JD, U. Chgo., 1970. Bar: Ill. 1970. Ptnr. Kirkland & Ellis, Chgo., 1970—; v.p. legal affairs Tribune Co., Chgo., 1981. Assoc. editor U. Chgo. Law Rev., 1969-70. Served to lt. USN, 1965-67. Mem. ABA, Chgo. Bar Assn. Securities, Banking, General corporate. Office: Kirkland & Ellis 200 E Randolph Dr Chicago IL 60601

JOEL, JACK BOWERS, lawyer, testing company executive; b. Crawfordsville, Ind., Mar. 1, 1925; s. Clarence J. and Iloe (Bowers) J.; m. Patricia Henchie, Mar. 2, 1957. A.B., Wabash Coll., 1947; J.D., Ind. U., 1951. Bar: Ind. 1954, U.S. Dist. Ct. (so. and no. dists.) Ind. 1954. With trust dept. Continental Ill. Nat. Bank, Chgo., 1951-53; field underwriter Home Life Ins. Co., Chgo., 1953-54; with legal and adminstrv. depts. Pure Oil Co. (now Union Oil Co.), Chgo., 1954-56; atty. Cities Service Oil Co., N.Y.C., 1956-62; asst. gen. counsel Kellogg div. ITT, 1962-63; gen. counsel, sr. v.p. U.S. Testing Co., Inc. and numerous subs. and affiliated cos., Hoboken, N.J., 1963—, also dir; dir. Nationwide Consumer Testing Inst., Inc., Supts. Pipeline Inspection Co., Ltd., Quali-test, Inc., U.S. Testing Co. (U.K.) Ltd.; lectr. in field. Served to lt. USN, 1943-46. Mem. ABA, Internat. Bar Assn. (chmn. com. products liability, advt., unfair competition and consumer affairs), Ind. Bar Assn., N.Y. Bar Assn., Am. Corp. Counsel Assn., ASTM, Am. Nat. Standards Inst., Am. Council Ind. Labs. (exec. com.). Clubs: Rotary, Elks. General corporate, Federal civil litigation, Product liability. Address: 1415 Park Ave Hoboken NJ 07030

JOFFE, ROBERT DAVID, lawyer; b. N.Y.C., May 26, 1943; s. Joseph and Bertha (Pashkovsky) J.; m. Selby Hickey, June 13, 1964 (div.); children—Katherine, David; m. Virginia Ryan, June 20, 1981; stepchildren—Elizabeth DeHaas, Ryan DeHaas. A.B., Harvard U., 1964, J.D., 1967. Bar: N.Y. 1970, U.S. Dist. Ct. (so. and ea. dists.) N.Y. 1971, U.S. Ct. Appeals (2d cir.) 1972, U.S. Supreme Ct. 1973. Ford Found. Africa Pub. Service fellow Republic of Malawi, 1967-69, state counsel, 1968-69; assoc. Cravath, Swaine & Moore, N.Y.C., 1969-75, ptnr., 1975—. Bd. dirs. Jericho Project. Mem. ABA, N.Y. Bar Assn., Assn. Bar City N.Y. (chmn. trade regulation com. 1980-83, bd. dirs. Jericho Project). Club: Wall Street (N.Y.C.). Antitrust, Federal civil litigation, State civil litigation. Home: 300 West End Ave Apt 13A New York NY 10023 Office: Cravath Swaine & Moore One Chase Manhattan Plaza New York NY 10005

JOHANSON, STANLEY MORRIS, legal educator; b. Seattle, July 12, 1933; s. Emil Bernhard and Martha Paulsen (Vik) J.; m. Geraldine Rae Cunningham, June 24, 1955; children—Susan, Barbara, Carolyn, David, Robert, John. B.S. in English, Yale U., 1955; LL.B., U. Wash., 1958; LL.M., Harvard U., 1963. Bar: Wash. 1958, Tex. 1973. Teaching fellow Harvard U. Law Sch., 1961-63; asst. prof. law U. Tex.-Austin, 1963, assoc. prof., 1963-66, prof., 1966—, holder Bryant Smith chair in law, 1982—; vis. prof. various univs.; mem. adv. bd. Bur. Nat. Affairs Estates, Gifts and Trusts Council; chmn. Southwestern Legal Found. Short Course on Estate Planning. Trustee Tarrytown United Methodist Ch., Austin. Served to capt. USAF, 1958-61. Recipient Teaching Excellence award U. Tex., 1968, 72, 73. Fellow Am. Coll. Probate Counsel (acad.); mem. Am. Law Inst., Law Sch. Admission Council, Am. Coll. Tax Counsel. Author: (with J. Dukeminier) Family Wealth Transactions: Wills, Trusts and Estates, 2d edit., 1978; contbr. numerous articles on estate planning and community property to law revs. Estate planning, Probate, Estate taxation. Office: 727 E 26th St Austin TX 78705

JOHANSON, SVEN LENNART, lawyer, insurance company executive; b. St. Paul, Nov. 21, 1931; s. Sven Nathaniel and Elsa Marie (Sandberg) J.; m. Karen Petersen Beidel, Mar. 20, 1983; children: Erik David, Kimberly D. B.S. in Bus, U. Colo., 1957; J.D., U. Denver, 1961. Bar: Colo. 1961, Ill. 1969. Atty. SEC, Washington, 1961-69; corp. sec., corp. counsel Kemper Group, Long Grove, Ill., 1969—. Mem. ABA, Chgo. Bar Assn., Am. Soc. Corp. Secs. Office: Kemper Center Long Grove IL 60049

JOHANSON, THOMAS JONATHAN, lawyer; b. Phila., Aug. 20, 1952; s. Louis Carl and Kathleen Ann (Rodden) J.; m. Susan Lynne Torbush, Oct. 25, 1980; 1 child, Kristen Marie. BA, St. Joseph U., Phila., 1974; JD, Widener U., 1978. Bar: Pa. 1979, U.S. Dist. Ct. (ea. dist.) Pa. 1979, N.J. 1985, U.S. Ct. Appeals (3d cir.) 1986. Asst. dist. atty. Phila., 1979-85; assoc. Krusen, Evans & Byrne, Phila., 1985—. Mem. ABA, Phila. Bar Assn., Def. Research Inst. Roman Catholic. Avocations: skiing, golf, bicycling. Federal civil litigation, State civil litigation. Office: Krusen Evans & Byrne 500 Public Ledger Philadelphia PA 19106-3473

JOHN, ROBERT MCCLINTOCK, lawyer; b. Phila., May 21, 1947; s. Lewis Timothy and Marie (McClintock) J.; m. Barbara Ann Weand, May 10, 1975; children: Jennifer, Ryan. BA, Villanova U., 1969, JD, 1972. Bar: Pa. 1972, U.S. Dist. Ct. (ea. dist.) Pa. 1973. Atty. Schneider, Nixon & John, Hatboro, Pa., 1972-74, ptnr., 1975—. Scoutmaster Boy Scouts Am., Hatboro, 1972—; mgr. Little League, Horsham, Pa., 1985—. Recipient Silver Beaver award Boy Scouts Am., 1981. Mem. ABA, Pa. Bar Assn., Montgomery County Bar Assn., Pa. Trial Lawyers Assn., Greater Hatboro C. of C. (pres. 1983, Honored Citizen Service to Youth award 1984). Republican. Roman Catholic. Club: U.S. Navy League (sec. southeastern Pa. council 1975—). Lodge: Rotary (pres. 1984). Avocations: scouting, baseball, swimming, cycling, backpacking. Family and matrimonial, General practice, Probate. Home: 83 Home Rd Hatboro PA 19040 Office: Schneider Nixon & John 76 Byberry Ave PO Box 698 Hatboro PA 19040

JOHN, SIDNEY CHARLES, lawyer; b. Montrose, Pa., July 8, 1939; s. Charles Alfred and Pauline Loomis (Grow) J.; m. Marta Lou Hoge, Aug. 17, 1963; children: Joel, Jason. Student, U. Ariz., 1957-58; BA, Ohio State U., 1962; JD, Ohio No. U., 1965. Bar: Ohio 1965, U.S. Dist. Ct. (no. dist.) Ohio 1969, U.S. Ct. Appeals (6th cir.) 1979. Assoc. E. Donald DeMuth, Toledo, 1965-70; ptnr. DeMuth & John, Toledo, 1970—; instr. real estate law Owens-Tech. Coll., Toledo, 1977; bd. dirs. Sports Arena, Toledo, State Home Svgs. Assn., Bowling Green, Ohio. Chmn. Civil Service Commn., Maumee, Ohio, 1969—. Mem. ABA, Ohio Bar Assn., Toledo Bar Assn. Republican. Presbyterian. Club: Laurel Hill Swim and Tennis (Toledo). Real property, Probate, Banking. Office: DeMuth & John 626 Madison Ave Toledo OH 43604

JOHNS, HAROLD MAC, lawyer; b. Russellville, Ky., Feb. 27, 1957; s. Harold R. and Susan (McReynolds) J.; m. Katherine Michelle Meadows, Sept. 3, 1983; 1 child, Alex Talbott. BA with honors, U. Ky., 1979; JD, U. Louisville, 1982. Bar: Ky. 1982, U.S. Dist. Ct. (we. dist.) Ky. 1983, U.S. Dist. Ct. (ea. dist.) Ky. 1986. Assoc. Kenneth Dillingham, Elkton, Ky., 1982; ptnr. Dillingham & Johns, Elkton, 1983—; asst. commonwealth atty. 7th Jud. Cir. Ky., Russellville, 1985—; asst. atty. Todd County, Elkton, 1983-85. Chmn. adminstrv. bd. Petrie Meml. United Meth. Ch., Elkton, 1986—. Mem. Ky. Bar Assn., Assn. Trail Lawyers Am., Ky. Acad. Trial Lawyers, Todd County Jaycees (pres. 1984-85). Democrat. Lodges: Rotary (sec. 1984-85, Elkton pres. 1985-86), Masons. General practice, Personal injury, Real property. Office: Dillingham & Johns PO Box 816 Elkton KY 42220

JOHNS, RICHARD WARREN, lawyer; b. Fullerton, Calif., Oct. 13, 1957; s. Warren L. Johns and Elaine C. Magnuson; m. Gaylene Melashenko, Dec. 23, 1979. Student, U. Md., 1976, Harvard U., 1977; BS, Pacific Union Coll., 1979; JD, USC, 1982. Bar: Calif. 1982, Md. 1983, D.C. 1984. Ptnr. Johns & Carson, Washington, 1982—; adj. prof. Columbia Union Coll., 1986—. Contbg. author: Hospital Contracts Manual, 1984; exec. editor J.D., 1984—. Bd. dirs. Calif. Achievement Ctrs. Inc., St. Helena, 1985—. Taft Law scholar, 1979. Mem. ABA, Calif. Soc. for Healthcare Attys., Am. Soc. Law and Medicine, Am. Acad. Hosp. Attys. Republican. Adventist. Avocations: diving, sailing, ballooning. General corporate, Health. Office: Johns & Carson 6840 Eastern Ave NW Washington DC 20012

JOHNS, WARREN LEROI, lawyer; b. Nevada, Iowa, June 9, 1929; s. Varner Jay and Ruby Charlene (Morrison) J.; m. Elaine C. Magneson, July 24, 1955 (div. June 1983); children: Richard Warren, Lynn Cherie Johns Pence; m. Ruth Page, Sept. 29, 1985. BA, Loma Linda U., 1950; MA, Andrews U., 1951; JD, U. So. Calif., 1958. Bar: Calif. 1959, U.S. Dist. Ct. (cen. dist.) Calif. 1959, Md. 1963, D.C. 1963, U.S. Supreme Ct. 1963, U.S. Dist. Ct. Md. 1976, U.S. Dist. Ct. D.C. 1976, U.S. Tax Ct. 1976, U.S. Ct. Appeals (4th cir.) 1976, U.S. Ct. Appeals (10th cir.) 1977, U.S. Ct. Customs and Patent Appeals 1979. Gen. counsel So. Calif. Conf. Seventh Day Adventists, Glendale, 1959-63, Pacific Union Conf. Seventh Day Adventists, Glendale and Sacramento, 1964-69; sole practice Sacramento, 1969-75; gen. counsel Gen. Conf. Seventh Day Adventists, Washington, 1975—, trustee; trustee Pacific Union Coll., Angwin, Calif., La Sierra Coll., Riverside, Calif.; spl. counsel Adventist Health Systems U.S., Arlington, Tex., 1978—. Author: Dateline Sunday USA, 1967; producer, editor: Man Alive, 1973, Tall in the Saddle, 1976, Vision Bold, 1977; founding editor JD, 1978—. Chmn. bd. dirs., pres. Sacramento Area Econ. Opportunity Council, 1974. Recipient Frank Yost award Ch. State Council, Glendale, 1972, Alumnus of Achievement award Andrews U., 1981. Mem. ABA, Am. Judicature Soc., Assn. Trial Lawyers Am., Nat. Health Lawyers Assn., Internat. Religion Liberty Assn. (trustee, v.p.),. Democrat. Avocations: sports, photography, book collecting. General corporate, General practice, Health. Office: Johns and Carson 6840 Eastern Ave NW Washington DC 20012

JOHNSEN, PETER HENRY, lawyer; b. Balt., Feb. 16, 1950; s. Henry E. and Marion E. (Kummen) J.; m. Margaret Ellen Irwin, Aug. 27, 1972; children: Henry Alexander, Thomas Christopher, Peter Carl. AB suma cum laude, Dartmouth Coll., 1972; MBA, JD, U. Va., 1976. Bar: Ind. 1976, Md. 1979. Assoc. Barnes, Hickam, Pantzer & Boyd, Indpls., 1976-79; assoc. counsel Potomac Electric Power Co., Washington, 1979-80; dep. gen. counsel Planning Research Corp., McLean, Va., 1980-86; gen. counsel Entre Computer Ctrs., Inc., Vienna, Va., 1986—. Bd. dirs. Hazardous Waste Action Coalition, 1986. Mem. ABA (forum com. on constrn. industry, steering com. div. design devel. and financing of constrn. 1985-86), Nat. Republic Lawyers Assn. (newsletter editor 1985-86), Washington Met. Area Corp. Counsel Assn. (bd. dirs. 1984—, sec. 1985—), Order of Coif, Phi Beta Kappa. General corporate. Home: 7954 Helmart Dr Laurel MD 20207

JOHNSON, ALLAN RICHARD, lawyer; b. New Haven, Mar. 25, 1933; s. Karl G. and Anna S. (Nelson) J.; m. Nancy C. Prins, June 23, 1955; children—Joshua W., Gilead G., Abigail A. B.A., Wesleyan U., 1955; J.D., U. Va., 1958. Bar: Conn. 1959, U.S. Dist. Ct. Conn. 1960, U.S. Ct. Appeals (2d cir.) 1966, U.S. Supreme Ct. 1981. Assoc. Willis & Willis, Bridgeport, Conn., 1959-71; ptnr. Tate, Capasse and Johnson, Westport, Conn., 1971—. Mem. Greater Bridgeport Regional Planning Agy., 1975—; mem. Sasquanaug Assn., Southport, Conn., past pres., v.p. and bd. dirs., 1961—; mem. Pequot Library, Southport, past v.p. and bd. dirs., 1961—; chmn. bd., pres. Southport Conservancy, 1982. Mem. Westport Bar Assn., Conn. Bar Assn. (med.-legal com., civil justice sect.), ABA (medicine and law com.), Am. Judicature Assn., Am. Arbitration Assn. Republican. Congregationalist. Club: Pequot Yacht (Southport). State civil litigation, Family and matrimonial, Personal injury. Home: 96 Taintor Dr Southport CT 06490 Office: 5 Imperial Ave Westport CT 06880

JOHNSON, BARBARA JEAN, lawyer, judge; b. Detroit, Apr. 9, 1932; d. Clifford Clarence and Orma Cecile (Boring) Barnhouse; m. Ronald Mayo Johnson, June 24, 1965; 1 dau., Belinda Etezad. B.S., U. So. Calif., 1953, J.D., 1970. Bar: Calif. 1971. Ptnr. Anglea, Burford, Johnson & Tookay, Pasadena, Calif., 1970-77; judge Los Angeles Mcpl. Ct., 1977-81; judge Los Angeles Superior Ct., 1981—; lectr. U. So. Calif. Law Sch. profl. program; adj. prof. Southwestern U. Law Sch. Recipient Ernestine Stahlhut award, 1981. Mem. Calif. Judges Assn., Nat. Assn. Women Judges, Calif. Women Lawyers Assn., Women Lawyers Assn. of Los Angeles. Juvenile, State civil litigation, Family and matrimonial. Office: Superior Ct 111 N Hill St Los Angeles CA 90012

JOHNSON, BRUCE CANNON, lawyer; b. Conway, N.C., Dec. 22, 1934; s. Russell Hagood and Mary Sue (Cannon) J.; m. Rosalyn Worell Railey, Dec. 24, 1961; children—Lynne, Amy, Jenny, Polly. A.B., U. N.C., 1957, LL.B., 1960. Bar: N.C. 1960, U.S. Ct. Mil. Appeals 1960, U.S. Supreme Ct. 1963. Ptnr. Johnson, Johnson & Johnson, Conway, 1963-83, Johnson & Jones, Conway, 1984—; solicitor Recorders Ct., Jackson, N.C., 1967-68; asst. solicitor Superior Ct., Jackson, 1967-68; dir. 1st Citizens Bank of Conway. Served to capt. U.S. Army, 1960-63. Mem. ABA, N.C. Bar Assn., Assn. Trial Lawyers Am., N.C. Acad. Trial Lawyers, Northampton Bar Assn. (pres. 1978-80, 84-86), 6th Jud. Bar Assn. (pres. 1978), Phi Beta Kappa. Democrat. Methodist. Club: Ruritan. Lodge: Masons. Criminal, State civil litigation, General practice. Home: Terrace Ln PO Box 27 Conway NC 27820 Office: Johnson & Jones PO Drawer 510 Conway NC 27820

JOHNSON, CLARK CUMINGS, lawyer, educator; b. Traverse City, Mich., Nov. 19, 1940; s. Harold Eugene and Mary Deilght (Cumings) J.; m. Mary Joanne Carney, Dec. 21, 1968; children: James, Christopher. BA, U. Mich., 1963; JD cum laude, Wayne State U., 1970, MS., 1985; postgrad., 1985—. Bar: Mich. 1970, U.S. Dist. Ct. (ea. dist.) Mich. 1970, U.S. Supreme Ct. 1974. Asst. atty gen. Mich., 1970-71; ptnr. Schmidt, Nahas, Coburn & Johnson, Mount Clemens, 1971-74; prof. law Detroit Coll. Law, 1974—, assoc. dean, 1984-85. Bankruptcy, Contracts commercial. Home: 128 Meadow Ln Grosse Pointe Farms MI 48236 Office: Detroit Coll Law 130 E Elizabeth Detroit MI 48201

JOHNSON, CRAIG ROBERT, lawyer; b. Milw., Aug. 17, 1951; s. Roynald Bastian and Doris Mamie (Hawkinson) J.; m. Lynn Ellen Dannenfelser, Sept. 6, 1975; children: Christopher, Leah. BBA with distinction, U. Wis., 1973; JD, Marquette U., 1978. Bar: Wis. 1978, U.S. Dist. Ct. (we. and ea. dists.) Wis. 1978, U.S. Tax Ct. 1986. Ptnr. Vance, Wilcox, Short, Johnson & Ristow S.C., Ft. Atkinson, Wis., 1979—. V.p. Ft. Fest Inc., Ft. Atkinson, 1982-83, pres. 1984, bd. dirs. 1985. Mem. ABA, Wis. Bar Assn., Jefferson County Bar Assn. (v.p. 1986—). Republican. Lutheran. Lodge: Optimists. Avocations: golf, skiing, racquetball. Consumer commercial, Real property, State and local taxation. Home: 120 E Main St PO Box 111 Cambridge WI 53523 Office: Vance Wilcox Short Johnson & Ristow SC 79 N Main St Fort Atkinson WI 53538

JOHNSON, D. THOMAS, lawyer; b. Danville, Ill., Jan. 22, 1939; s. Frank Dale and Gwendolyn Marie (Willhite) J.; m. Ruth Ellen Smith, Aug. 14, 1960; children—Michael Thomas, Melissa Anne, Tracey Dale, Jennifer Ellen. B.A., Ind. U., 1961; J.D., U. Tex., 1966; postgrad. Nat. Inst. Trial Advocacy, 1981. Bar: Tex. 1966, U.S. Dist. Ct. (no. dist.) Tex. 1966, U.S. Dist. Ct. (ea. and we. dists.) Tex. 1979, U.S. Dist. (so. dist.) Tex. 1981, U.S. Ct. Appeals (5th cir.) 1969, U.S. Ct. Appeals (11th cir.) 1981, U.S. Supreme Ct. 1970. Assoc. McWhorter, Cobb and Johnson, Lubbock, Tex., 1966-68, ptnr., 1968—; adj. prof. law, trial advocacy Tex. Tech. U. Sch. Law. Mem. Lubbock City-County Library Bd., 1973-79, chmn., 1977-79; pres. Coronado High Sch. PTA, 1980-81 bd. dirs. Lubbock Civic Ctrs. and Civic Lubbock, Inc., 1981; mem. Tex. Tech. U. Pres.'s Council, 1981-83; chmn. profl. div. United Way of Lubbock, 1982. Fellow Tex. Bar Found.; mem. Lubbock County Bar Assn. (pres. 1979-80), State Bar of Tex. (dir. 1984—), ABA, Fedn. Ins. Counsel, Nat. Assn. R.R. Trial Counsel, Tex. Bd. Legal Specialization, Adv. Commn. for Civil Trial Law, Tex. Assn. Def. Counsel, Tex. Assn. Cert. Civil Trial Lawyers, Tex. Assn. Sch. Bds. Council Sch. Attys., Nat. Sch. Bds. Assn. Served to capt. U.S. Army, 1961-63. Republican. Mem. Ch. of Christ. Club: S.W. Lubbock Rotary (dir. 1975-79, pres. 1977-78, dist. gov.'s rep. 1980-81). Contbr. articles to legal jours. Federal civil litigation, State civil litigation, Personal injury. Home: 4707 19th St Lubbock TX 79407 Office: 1722 Broadway Lubbock TX 79401

JOHNSON, DALE ELIOT, lawyer; b. Los Angeles, Apr. 12, 1946; s. Bert and Lilian Carolina (Kerston) J.; m. Elaine T. Sisemore, Nov. 27, 1976; children: Ashley, Matthew. BA, Colo. Coll., 1968; JD, U. Colo., 1971. Bar: Colo. 1971, U.S. Dist. Ct. Colo. 1971, U.S. Dist. Ct. (10th cir.) 1979. Sole practice Boulder, Colo., 1971—. Mem. Parks and Recreation Adv. Bd., City of Boulder, 1976-79, chmn. 1978-79; chmn. sub com. Colo. State Juvenile law com., 1985. Mem. Colo. Bar Assn., Boulder County Bar Assn. (head law day com. 1963-74), Assn. Trial Lawyers Am., Colo. Trial Lawyers Assn. State civil litigation, Family and matrimonial. Office: Canyonside Office Park 100 Arapahoe Suite 5 Boulder CO 80302

JOHNSON, DANIEL PATRICK, lawyer; b. Sioux Falls, S.D., Mar. 17, 1956; s. George O. and Clare A. (Murray) J.; m. Kim D. Kelly, Aug. 4, 1984; 1 child, Patrick. BS, U. S.D., 1978; JD, Harvard U., 1981. Bar: Ga. 1981, U.S. Dist. Ct. (no. dist.) Ga. 1983, U.S. Ct. Appeals (11th cir.) 1986. Law clk. to presiding chief justice U.S. Dist. Ct. (no. dist.) Ga., Atlanta, 1981-83; assoc. Lord, Bissell & Brook, Atlanta, 1983-87, Meals, Kirwan, Goger, Winter & Parks, P.C., Atlanta, 1987—. Vol. Am. Diabetes Assn., Atlanta, 1985, law div. United Way Campaign, Atlanta, 1984. Taft scholar, 1979, Presdl. scholar, 1974. Mem. ABA, Ga. Bar Assn., Atlanta Bar Assn., Assn. Trial Lawyers Am., Lawyers Club Atlanta, Phi Beta Kappa. Clubs: Ansley Golf (Atlanta), Harvard Ga. Avocations: golf, tennis, sailing. Federal civil litigation, Antitrust, Insurance. Office: Meals Kirwan Goger Winter & Parks 800 Candler Bldg 127 Peachtree St Atlanta GA 30303

JOHNSON, DARRELL BRUCE, legal educator; b. St. Cloud, Minn., Nov. 13, 1938; s. Abel Lawton and Georgia Adeline (Yockey) J.; m. Joanne Belle Christenson, Jan. 24, 1964; 1 dau., Kelli Joanne; m. 2d, Janet Kay Wiig, Dec. 29, 1972. B.A. with honors, St. Cloud State U., 1964; J.D., U. Chgo., 1968. Bar: Minn. 1968. Assoc. Fredrikson, Byron, Colborn, Bisbee & Hansen, P.A., Mpls., 1968-73, ptnr. 1973-76; assoc. prof. Southwestern U. Sch. Law, Los Angeles, 1976-79, prof. 1979—, dir. SCALE (Southwestern's Conceptual Approach to Legal Edn.), 1977-82, assoc. dean, 1979-80, 81-85; vis. prof. Boston Coll. Law Sch., 1984; vis. prof. U. Colo. Sch. Law, 1985. Mem. adv. com. Mpls. City Ctr., 1975. Served with USAF, 1956-60. Mem. ABA, Assn. Am. Law Schs. (chmn. sect. adminstrn. of law schs. 1983). Contbr. chpts. to books, articles to legal jours. Legal education, Contracts commercial, Real property. Office: 675 S Westmoreland Ave Los Angeles CA 90005

JOHNSON, DARRELL THOMAS, JR., lawyer; b. Columbia, S.C., Oct. 10, 1949; s. Darrell Thomas and Lorena Beckett (McDonald) J.; m. Wanda Jones, June 2, 1972; children: Darrell Thomas III, Warren Paul. BS, U. S.C., 1971, JD, 1974. Bar: S.C. 1975, U.S. Dist. Ct. S.C. 1976, U.S. Ct. Appeals (4th cir.) 1981. County atty., Jasper, S.C., 1984-85; town atty. Bluffton, S.C., 1982-83, Hardeeville, S.C., 1975-81. Author: (with others) Crime Law and Justice, 1974, Criminal Defence in S.C., 1973. Bd. dirs. Jasper Dept. Social Services, S.C., 1978-82; ; adv. mem. Coastal Council, Jasper, 1978—; treas. Dem. Party, 1978—; mem. election commn., Jasper, 1978—. Mem. ABA, Def. Trial Lawyer Assn., Assn. Trial Lawyers Am., S.C. Trial Lawyers Assn. Personal injury, Workers' compensation, General practice. Office: 7 Hwy 17 S Hardeeville SC 29927

JOHNSON, DAVID RAYMOND, lawyer; b. Bartlesville, OK, Sept. 12, 1946; s. Lloyd Theodore and Mary Pauline (Auten) J.; m. Marion Frances Monroe, May 14, 1977; children: Marc, Meredith. BA, Tulane U., 1968; JD, U. Va., 1971. Bar: Tex. 1971, D.C. 1977, U.S. Dist. Ct. D.C. 1979, U.S. Ct. Appeals (D.C. cir.) 1981, U.S. Supreme Ct. 1982, U.S. Claims Ct. 1984. Assoc. Fulbright & Jaworski, Houston, 1971-72; assoc. Fulbright & Jaworski, Washington, 1974-78, ptnr., 1978-87; atty.-advisor Office of Gen. Counsel of Air Force, Washington, 1972-74; ptnr. Gibson, Dunn & Crutcher, Washington, 1987—; bd. dirs. Martin-Baker Aircraft Inc., Falls Church, Va. Served to capt. USAF, 1972-74. Mem. ABA, D.C. Bar Assn., Tex. Bar Assn., Phi Beta Kappa, Raven Soc., Order of Coif. Democrat. Private international, Government contracts and claims, Administrative and regulatory. Office: Gibson Dunn & Crutcher 1050 Connecticut Ave NW Washington DC 20036

JOHNSON, DAVID STAFFORD, lawyer; b. Red Wing, Minn., Mar. 27, 1952; s. Melvin Carl and Ann (Curran) J.; m. Stephanie Radisi, Sept. 24, 1983. AB, Dartmouth Coll., 1974; MBA, Ariz. State U., 1976; JD, U. Ariz., 1979. Corp. counsel Duval Corp., Houston, 1979-81; gen. counsel, corp. sec. Amselco Minerals, Inc., Denver, 1981—. Mem. ABA, Colo. Bar Assn., Tex. Bar Assn., Ariz. Bar Assn., Denver Bar Assn., Dartmouth Lawyers Assn. (spl. mem., state bd. dirs. 1984—). Republican. Episcopalian. Administrative and regulatory, General corporate, Securities. Home: 811 Marion St Denver CO 80218 Office: Amselco Minerals Inc 999 18th St Suite 201 Denver CO 80202-2484

JOHNSON, DAVID WHITLEY, lawyer; b. Charleston, W.Va., Sept. 16, 1954; s. Alonzo and Mary Alice (Neale) J.; m. Julia Vail Smith, Aug. 25, 1979. AB, Marshall U., 1976; JD, Washington and Lee U., 1979. Bar: W.Va. 1980, U.S. Dist. Ct. (so. dist.) W.Va. 1980, U.S. Ct. Appeals (4th and 6th cirs.) 1985. Atty. tax dept. State of W.Va., Charleston, 1979-83; assoc. Hill & Wood, Charleston, 1983; ptnr. Wood, Segal, Davis & Johnson, Charleston, 1983-84; assoc. Law Offices of Sterl F. Shinaberry, Charleston, 1985-86; asst. atty. gen. appellate div. State of W.Va., Charleston, 1986—. Mem. ABA, Kanawha County Bar Assn., W.Va. Trial Lawyers Assn., Am. Coll. Trial Lawyers (Lewis F. Powell medal 1978), Phi Delta Phi, Pi Sigma Alpha. Republican. Avocations: painting, reading, skiing, hiking, white water rafting. Federal civil litigation, State civil litigation, Personal injury. Office: Office of Atty Gen State of WVa Room E-26 State Capitol Charleston WV 25305

JOHNSON, DAVID WILLIAM, lawyer; b. Albany, N.Y., Jan. 29, 1950; s. Melvin William and Betty Jane (Bagley) J.; m. Cynthia Marie Seidle, Jan. 6, 1973; children: Scott William, Gregory Edward. BA in Latin Am. Studies, U. Colo., 1972; JD, N.Y. Law Sch., 1976. Bar: Colo. 1976, U.S. Dist. Ct. Colo. 1976. Sole practice Boulder, Colo., 1976-78; ptnr. Gunning & Johnson, Boulder, 1978-80, princ., 1980-82; sole practice Boulder and Longmont, Colo., 1982—. Computer. Office: PO Box 2212 Longmont CO 80501

JOHNSON, DELOS ROZELUS, JR., lawyer; b. Franklinton, La., Dec. 23, 1924; s. Delos Rozelus and Pearl (Griffith) J.; m. Leah Ott, Jan. 31, 1930; children—John Keller, Jeffrey Adrian, Caroline Griffith Johnson McKowen. B.A., La. State U., 1950; J.D., Tulane U., 1952. Bar: La. 1952, U.S. Dist. Ct. (ea. dist.) La. 1953, U.S. Supreme Ct. 1966. Mem. Delos R. Johnson & Son, 1952-56, Johnson & James, 1957-65, Johnson & Johnson, 1966-74, Johnson & Kuhn, 1974-82. Served with USCG, 1943-46. Fellow Am. Coll. Probate Counsel; mem. Assn. Trial Lawyers Am., Am. Judicature Soc. Baptist. Club: Rotary. Probate, Banking, Real property. Office: PO Box 503 Franklinton LA 70438

JOHNSON, DENNIS ROBERT, lawyer; b. Mpls., Aug. 1, 1946; m. Barbara Jean Swain, Feb. 25, 1984. B.S. in Bus., U. Minn., 1972, J.D., 1975. Bar: Minn. 1975, U.S. Dist. Ct. Minn. 1975. Ptnr. Meshbesher, Singer & Spence, Ltd., Mpls., 1975—. Bd. dirs. Minn. Legal Advice Clinics, Mpls., 1978-82. Served to 1st lt. U.S. Army, 1966-69, Vietnam. Mem. Minn. Trial Lawyers Assn. (bd. dirs. 1979—, chmn. legis. com. 1980-84 , chmn. edn. com. 1984-86, exec. com. 1984, chmn. fin. com. 1986), Minn. State Bar Assn. (mem. med. legal com. 1982—), Assn. Trial Lawyers Am. Personal injury, Insurance, State civil litigation. Office: Meshbesher Singer & Spence Ltd 1616 Park Ave Minneapolis MN 55404

JOHNSON, DONALD (DON) WAYNE, lawyer; b. Memphis, Feb. 2, 1950; s. Hugh Don and Oline (Rowland) J.; m. Jan Marie Mullinax, May 12, 1972; 1 son, Scott Fitzgerald. Student Memphis State U., 1968, Lee Coll., 1968-72; JD, Woodrow Wilson Coll. Law, 1975. Bar: Ga. 1975, U.S. Dist. Ct. (no. dist.) Ga. 1975, U.S. Ct. Appeals (5th cir.) 1976, U.S. Tax Ct. 1978, U.S. Ct. Claims 1978, U.S. Supreme Ct. 1979, U.S. Ct. Appeals (11th, 9th, Fed., D.C. cirs.) 1984. Ptnr. Barnes & Johnson, Dalton, Ga., 1975-77, Johnson & Fain, Dalton, 1977-80; sole practice, Dalton, 1980-85, Atlanta, 1985—. Bd. dirs. Pathway Christian Sch., Dalton, 1978-85, Jr. Achievement of Dalton, 1978-84, bd. dirs. Dalton-Whitfield County Day Care Ctrs., Inc. Mem. Ga. Trial Lawyers Assn. (bd. govs. 1984), Assn. Trial Lawyers Am., Ga. Bar Assn., ABA, Christian Legal Soc. Mem. Ch. of God. General corporate, Personal injury, State and federal civil litigation. Office: 1900 The Exchange Suite 305 Atlanta GA 30339

JOHNSON, DONALD E., lawyer; b. Harrisburg, Pa., Sept. 25, 1946; s. Robert Gordon and Anne (O'Neill) J.; m. Margaret B., Nov. 22, 1969; children: Christopher, Philip, Meredith. BA, LaSalle Coll., 1968; JD, Villanova U., 1972. Bar: Pa. 1972, U.S. Ct. Appeals (3d cir.) 1979, Minn. 1985, U.S. Ct. Appeals (8th cir.) 1985. Prosecutor Dist. Atty.'s Office, City of Phila., 1972-73; prosecutor Delaware County, Media, Pa., 1973-78, spl. prosecutor, 1978-80; sr. trial atty. Atty. Gen.'s Office, State of Pa., 1980-82; chief counsel Pa. Crime Commn., 1982-85; assoc. gen. counsel Burlington No. R.R., St. Paul, 1985—; instr. Phila. Police Acad., 1972-73; mem. faculty Temple U., Phila., 1973-76; cons. Pa. State Police, 1973-84. Recipient Trial Advocacy award U. Chgo., 1981, cert. Rochester-influenced and Corrupt Orgns. div. Justice Dept., 1983; named Ky. col., 1983. Mem. ABA, Pa. Bar Assn., Minn. Bar Assn., Nat. Inst. Trial Advocacy (trial advocacy award 1985), Nat. R.R. Trial Lawyers Assn. Avocations: hunting, fishing, fly-tying, trap and skeet shooting. Federal civil litigation, State civil litigation, General corporate. Office: Burlington No RR Law Dept 176 E 5th St Saint Paul MN 55082

JOHNSON, DONALD EDWARD, JR., lawyer; b. Denver, Sept. 24, 1942; s. Donald Edward and Miriam Bispham (Chester) J.; m. Charlotte Marie Hassett, Aug. 15, 1964; children—Julie Anna, Jenny Marie. Student Lewis and Clark Coll., 1960-62; B.A. in History, U. Ariz., 1968; J.D., U. Wyo., 1971. Bar: Wyo. 1971, Colo. 1971, U.S. Dist. Ct. Colo. and Wyo., 1971, U.S. Supreme Ct. 1978. Assoc., Hammond and Chilson, Loveland, Colo., 1971-72; dep. dist. atty. 8th Jud. Dist., Loveland, and Ft. Collins, Colo., 1972-80, chief dep. dist. atty., 1977-80; assoc. Allen, Rogers, Metcalf and Vahrenwald, Ft. Collins, 1980-82; ptnr., 1982—; asst. city atty. City of Loveland, 1971-72; asst. mcpl. judge, Loveland, 1972; instr. bus. law Ames Coll., 1972-74; lectr. Regional Homocide Sch., 1977; mem. state tng. com. Colo. Dist. Atty's. Council, 1978-80. Chmn. 45th Republican House Dist., 1977-82; mem. Colo. Rep. Central Com., 1980-85, Larimer County Rep. Central Com., 1980—; mem. Loveland Open Space Adv. Bd., 1977-78; bd. dirs. Loveland United Way, 1977-84, allocations chmn., 1980, pres., 1981-83; bd. dirs. Larimer County Alcohol Services, 1972-78, pres., 1977-78; bd. dirs. Loveland Midget Athletic Assn., sec. 1974-78. Served to sgt. USMC, 1966-68. Mem. ABA (Gold Key award, 1970), Larimer County Bar Assn., Colo. Bar Assn., Wyo. Bar Assn., Nat. Dist. Attys. Assn., Colo. Trial Lawyers Assn. Episcopalian. Lodge: Elks (Fort Collins, Colo.). Author: Criminal Conspiracy—The Colorado District Attorney's Evidence Manual, 1976. State civil litigation, Criminal, General practice. Office: Citizens Comml & Savs Bank One Citizens Banking Center Flint MI 48502

JOHNSON, DONALD MILBY, lawyer; b. Portsmouth, Va., Oct. 14, 1944; s. Donald Milby and Harriett Eloise (Brown) J.; m. Lana Gene Kelly, June 10, 1966; children: Kelly Gene, Kara Christine. BA, U. Wyo., 1968, JD, 1971. Bar: Wyo. 1971, Alaska 1972, U.S. Dist. Ct. Alaska 1972. Asst. atty. City of Anchorage, 1971-75; asst. dist. atty. State of Alaska, Anchorage and Bethel, 1975-78; acting dist. atty. State of Alaska, Bethel, 1976; ptnr. Moderow, Walsh, Johnson & James, Anchorage, 1978-79; sole practice Anchorage, 1979-85; ptnr. Tobey & Johnson, Anchorage, 1985—. Chmn. Gov's. Com. Revision Title 28 Alaska Statutes, 1973-77. Mem. Alaska Bar Assn. (spl. counsel 1981), Am. Judicature Soc., Assn. Trial Lawyers Am., Order of Barristers. Methodist. Avocations: flying, boating, fishing, woodworking. Criminal, Family and matrimonial, Personal injury. Home: 3440 Korovin Bay Circle Anchorage AK 99515 Office: Tobey & Johnson 880 H St Suite 200 Anchorage AK 99501

JOHNSON, DONALD RAY, lawyer; b. La., Jan. 25, 1954; s. Lucille (Allen) Bindon Johnson. BS, Southern U., 1976; JD, La. State U., 1982. Bar: La. 1082, U.S. Dist. Ct. (mid. and ea. dists.) La. 1982, U.S. Ct. Appeals (5th cir.) 1982, U.S. Dist. Ct. (we. dist.) La. 1983. Staff asst. S.W. Bell Telephone, St. Louis, 1978-82; asst. dist. atty. East Baton Rouge, La., 1982-85; sole practice Baton Rouge, 1985—. Home and Office: 328 Government St Baton Rouge LA 70802

JOHNSON, DOUGLAS WELLS, lawyer; b. Denver, May 31, 1949; s. Robert Douglas and Mildred Irene (Fehr) J.; m. Kathryn Ann Hoberg, Oct. 18, 1980. B.A., U. Denver, 1971, J.D., 1974. Bar: Colo. 1974, U.S. Dist. Ct. Colo. 1974, U.S. Ct. Appeals (10th cir.) 1974; U.S. Supreme Ct. 1977, Ill. 1980, U.S. Dist. Ct. (no. dist.) Ill. 1980, U.S. Ct. Appeals (7th cir.) 1981, D.C. 1981, U.S. Ct. Internat. Trade 1981, U.S. Dist. Ct. (ea. dist.) Mich. 1983, U.S. Ct. Appeals (6th cir.) 1984, U.S. Ct. Appeals Fed. Cir. 1984, U.S. Dist. Ct. (no. dist.) Ind. 1986, U.S. Ct. Appeals (4th and 8th cirs.) 1986. Ptnr. Mellman, Mellman & Thorn, Denver, 1974-80; atty. Amoco Corp., Chgo., 1980—. U. Denver Alumni scholar, 1967-71. Mem. ABA, Ill. Bar Assn., D.C. Bar Assn., Chgo. Bar Assn., Kappa Delta Pi. Federal civil litigation, Contracts commercial, Antitrust. Home: 1002 Linden Ave Wilmette IL 60091 Office: Amoco Corp 200 E Randolph Chicago IL 60601

JOHNSON, DREW MARTIN, lawyer; b. Canton, S.D., Aug. 18, 1939; s. Andrew Martin nad Ardes Eileen (Brown) J.; m. Judith Kay Tiffany, Jan. 30, 1961 (div. Feb. 1985); children: Heather, Paige. BJ, U. Mo., 1961; JD, U. of Pacific, 1967. Bar: Calif. 1967, U.S. Dist. Ct. (no. dist.) Calif. 1967, U.S. Dist. Ct. (ea. dist.) 1968, U.S. Ct. Appeals (9th cir.) 1972. Assoc. Luther & Luther, Sacramento, 1967-69; ptnr. Luther, Luther, O'Connov & Johnson, Sacramento, 1969-71, Johnson, Nash & Vinson, Sacramento, 1971-80; sole practice Sacramento, 1980—; arbitrator Sacramento Superior Ct., 1982, Am. Arbitration Assn.; judge pro tem Placer Superior Ct., Auburn, Calif., 1986. Mem. ABA, Calif. Bar Assn. (vol. voluntary legal services program 1982—), Sacramento County Bar Assn. Republican. Presbyterian. Lodge: Rotary (past pres., Paul Harris fellow1982). Avocations: skiing, running, golf. Construction, General corporate, Real property. Office: 50 Fullerton Ct Suite 101 Sacramento CA 95825

JOHNSON, EDWARD MICHAEL, lawyer, investment banker; b. Waco, Tex., July 12, 1944; s. Edward James and Anne Margaret (Stuchly) J.; m. Yvonne Margaret Hill, May 7, 1977; children—Hilary Yvonne, Megan Joy. B.A. in Polit. Sci., Southwest Tex. State U., 1967; J.D., St. Mary's U. 1970. Bar: Tex. 1971, U.S. Dist. Ct. (we. dist.) Tex. 1972, U.S. Supreme Ct. 1972. Briefing atty. U.S. Dist. Judge John H. Wood Jr., San Antonio, Tex., 1971-72, asst. U.S. atty. Dept. Justice, San Antonio, 1972-76, sole practice, San Antonio, 1976—; sr. atty. Wiley, Garwood, Hornbuckle, Higdon & Johnson, San Antonio, 1980-81; pres. McCabe Petroleum Corp., San Antonio, 1981; chmn., pres. Harvest Investments Corp., San Antonio, 1984—; also dir.; chmn. bd., chief exec. officer Blue Chip Petroleum Corp., San Antonio, 1981—; gen. ptnr. Med. Mobility Ltd. IV, San Antonio, 1984—; mgr. Med. Mobility Joint Venture, San Antonio, 1984—; gen. ptnr. Harvest Venture Capital Ltd. I, San Antonio, 1986—; pres. Blue Chip Securities Corp., San Antonio, 1984—. Co-chmn. fund raising com. Am. Heart Assn., San Antonio, 1982-84; bd. dirs. Am. Cancer Soc., San Antonio, 1982-84; chmn. San Fernando Cathedral Endowment Fund, San Antonio, 1986—; mem. Gideons Internatl., San Antonio, 1982—; bd. dirs. Tex. Bible Inst., 1984—, Christian Businessmen's Com., San Antonio, 1981—; mem., speaker Full Gospel Businessmen's Fellowship, 1981—; scoutmaster Alamo area council Boy Scouts Am., San Antonio, 1973-74; founder, chmn. Christian Businessmen's Focus on the Family, San Antonio, 1984—. Recipient spl. commendation Dept. Transp. 1973, Dept. Air Force HQ, ATC, 1974, Dept. Treasury, 1974; named Outstanding Asst. U.S. Atty. Dept. Justice, 1974, 75, one of Outstanding Young Men Am., 1975, one of Outstanding Young Texans, 1976. Mem. Fed. Bar Assn. (pres. San Antonio chpt. 1975-76; v.p. 1973-74, sec. 1972-73, named outstanding chpt. pres. 1976), Tex. Bar Assn., San Antonio Bar Assn., Fed. Practice Licensing Com. Republican. Investment banking, Securities, General corporate. Office: Harvest Investments Corp Ashford Oaks Exec Tower 8122 Datapoint Dr Suite 830 San Antonio TX 78229

JOHNSON, ELIZABETH DIANE LONG, lawyer; b. Pasadena, Calif., Nov. 16, 1945; d. Volney Earl and Sylvia Irene (Drury) Long; m. Lynn Douglas Johnson, Oct. 22, 1966; 1 child, Barbara Annette. BA, U. of Houston, 1967; JD, Rutgers U., 1980. Bar: N.J. 1980, U.S. Dist. Ct. N.J. 1980, Pa. 1984, U.S. Supreme Ct. 1986. Sole practice Riverside, N.J., 1980—. Mem. Tenby Chase Civic Assn., Delran, N.J., 1972—, treas. 1976, v.p. 1974. Mem. ABA, N.J. Bar Assn., Pa. Bar Assn., Burlington County Bar Assn., Assn. Trial Lawyers Am., Tri-County Women Lawyers, Mensa, Phi Alpha Delta, Delta Gamma. Methodist. General practice. Office: 23 Scott St Suite C Riverside NJ 08075

JOHNSON, ELMER WILLIAM, automotive executive, lawyer; b. Denver, May 2, 1932; s. Elmer William and Lillian Marie (Nelson) J.; m. Constance Dorothy Mahon, June 18, 1955; children: Julianne Marie, Valerie Lynn, Garrett Douglas. B.A., Yale U., 1954; J.D., U. Chgo., 1957. Bar: Ill. 1957. Assoc. Kirkland & Ellis, Chgo., 1956-62, ptnr., 1962-71, mng. ptnr., 1971—; v.p., group exce. gen. counsel Gen. Motors Corp., Detroit, 1983—; gen. counsel Internat. Harvester, Chgo., 1982-83; spl. counsel to chmn. of regional holding co. for 5 midwestern Bell Telephone operating cos., Chgo., 1983; dir. Fed. Signal Corp., Oak Brook, Ill. Trustee U. Chgo., 1977—; vice chmn. Detroit Symphony Assn. Mem. ABA, Ill. State Bar Assn., Mich. Bar Assn. Republican. Presbyterian. Clubs: Bloomfield Hills Country, Birmingham Athletic. Home: 1710 Hillwood Dr Bloomfield Hills MI 48013 Office: Gen Motors Corp 14-154 Gen Motors Bldg Detroit MI 48202

JOHNSON, FRANK MINIS, JR., federal judge; b. Winston County, Ala., Oct. 30, 1918; s. Frank M. and Alabama (Long) J.; m. Ruth Jenkins, Jan. 16, 1938; 1 son, James Curtis (dec.). Grad., Gulf Coast Mil. Acad., Gulfport, Miss., 1935, Massey Bus. Coll., Birmingham, 1937; LLB, U. Ala., 1943, LLD (hon.), 1977; also LLD (hon.), Notre Dame U., 1973; LLD (hon.), Princeton U., 1974, Boston U., 1979, Yale U., 1980; J.D. (hon.), St. Michael's Coll., 1975. Bar: Ala. 1943. Ptnr. Curtis, Maddox & Johnson, 1946-53; U.S. atty. No. Dist. Ala., 1953-55; U.S. dist. judge Middle Dist. Ala., 1955-79; U.S. judge Ct. Appeals for 5th Circuit, 1979-81, Ct. Appeals for 11th Cir., Montgomery, Ala., 1981—; mem. Temporary Emergency Ct. Appeals of U.S., 1972-82; mem. rev. com. Jud. Conf., 1969-78, jud. ethics com., 1978-85, spl. com. on habeas corpus, 1971-78, chmn. adv. com. on civil rules, 1985-86. Served from pvt. to capt. inf. AUS, 1943-46. Decorated Purple Heart with oak leaf cluster, Bronze Star. Mem. Ala. Acad. Honor. Jurisprudence. Office: US Court Appeals PO Box 35 Montgomery AL 36101

JOHNSON, G. WELDON, lawyer; b. Orleans, Nebr., Oct. 3, 1930; s. Grant O.Q. and Mildred Helen (Baxley) J.; m. Juanita Jane Trotter, June 22, 1952; children: Jeffrey David, Kathy Lynn Johnson Much, Nancy Sue Johnson Heck. BS, Ind. U., 1952, JD, 1957. Bar: Ind. 1957, U.S. Dist. Ct. (so. dist.) Ind. 1957, U.S. Tax Ct., U.S. Supreme Ct. 1965, U.S. Ct. Appeals (7th cir.) 1970. Ptnr. Hilgedag, Johnson, Secrest & Murphy, Indpls., 1957-81; sole practice Indpls., 1981-83; ptnr. Johnson and Hall, Indpls., 1983-84; pres. Johnson, Hall & Lawhead, P.C., Indpls., 1984—. Past trustee Indpls. Mus. Art, N. United Meth. Ch., Indpls, past treas. capital . Served to 1st lt. USAF, 1952-54. Disting. charter fellow Indpls. Bar Found. (bd. dirs. 1983—); fellow Am. Coll. Probate Counsel; mem. ABA, Ind. Bar Assn., Indpls. Bar Assn. (pres 1982). Republican. Clubs: Meridian Hills Country, Skyline (Indpls.); Pointe Country (Bloomington, Ind.). Lodges: Kiwanis (pres. N. Side club 1964), Masons, Shriners. Probate, Estate taxation, Corporate taxation. Home: 7147 Huntington Rd Indianapolis IN 46240 Office: Johnson Hall Lawhead PC 8900 Keystone Crossing Suite 940 Indianapolis IN 46240

JOHNSON, GARY THOMAS, lawyer; b. Chgo., July 26, 1950; s. Thomas G. Jr. and Marcia (Lunde) J.; m. Susan Elizabeth Moore, May 28, 1978; children: Christopher Thomas, Timothy Henry. BA, Yale U., 1972; BA (hon.), Oxford U., 1974, MA, 1983. Bar: Ill. 1977, U.S. Dist. Ct. (no. dist.) Ill. 1977, U.S. Ct. Appeals (7th cir.) 1985, U.S. Supreme Ct. 1986. Assoc. Mayer, Brown & Platt, Chgo., 1977-84; ptnr. MAyer, Brown & Platt, Chgo., 1985—; mem. Com. on Cts. Justice, Chgo., 1981—, profl. adv. bd. Atty. Gen. Hartigan, Chgo., 1982—, Spl. Commn. on Adminstrn. of Justice Cook County, Chgo., 1984—. Rhodes scholar Oxford U., 1972-74. Fellow Am. Bar Found.; mem. ABA, Chgo. Bar Assn., Chgo. Council Lawyers (pres. 1981-83). Democrat. Presbyterian. Securities, General corporate, Civil rights. Office: Mayer Brown & Platt 190 S LaSalle St Chicago IL 60603

JOHNSON, GARY WILLIAM, lawyer; b. Lakewood, Ohio, June 18, 1954; s. Thomas C. and Mary A. (O'Malley) J.; m. Mary Elizabeth Schmitz, Sept. 22. 1979. BSBA, Georgetown U., 1976; JD, Toledo U., 1979. Bar: Ohio 1979, U.S. Dist. Ct. (no. dist.) Ohio 1979. Law clk. to presiding justice U.S. Ct. Appeals (8th cir.), Cleve., 1979-81; asst. prosecutor Cuyahoga County, Cleve., 1981-84; assoc. Weston, Hurd, Fallon, Paisley & Howley, Cleve., 1984—. Bd. dirs. Cath. Youth Orgn., Cleve., 1980—, Cath. Charities, Cleve., 1983; past pres. St. Ignatius Alumni Assn., Cleve., 1981-82; local pres. Georgetown U. Alumni Assn., Cleve., 1982—; tres. Lakewood (Ohio) Dems., 1983—. Roman Catholic. Insurance, Federal civil litigation, State civil litigation.

JOHNSON, GRANT LESTER, lawyer, mfg. co. exec.; b. Virginia, Minn., Aug. 16, 1929; s. Ernest and Anna Elizabeth (Nordstrom) J.; m. Esther Linnea Nystrom, June 16, 1956, (dec. July 1985); children—Karen Elisabeth, Elise Ann. A.B., Cornell U., 1951; LL.B., Harvard, 1957. Bar: Ohio bar 1958, Ill. bar 1972. Asso. Squire, Sanders & Dempsey, Cleve., 1957-58; atty. Pickands Mather & Co., Cleve., 1958-71; asso. gen. counsel Pickands Mather & Co., 1967, gen. counsel, 1968-71, sec., 1969-71; corporate counsel Interlake, Inc., Chgo., 1971-73; v.p. law Interlake, Inc., 1974-78, v.p. law and adminstrn., 1978-84, sr. v.p., gen. counsel, 1984-86; gen. counsel The InterLake, Corp., 1986—. Served to lt. (j.g.) USN, 1951-54. Mem. Am. Iron and Steel Inst. General corporate. Home: G-205 4 Oak Brook Club Dr Oak Brook IL 60521 Office: Commerce Plaza 2015 Spring Rd Oak Brook IL 60521

JOHNSON, H. ALLEN, lawyer; b. Lawton, Okla., Mar. 1, 1936; s. Herbert Allen and Virginia (Garrett) J.; m. Judy Kay Matthews, Feb. 4, 1961; 1 child, Blake Allen. BS, Okla. U., 1959; JD, Oklahoma City U., 1976. Bar: Okla., U.S. Dist. Ct. Okla. Owner LaSill Milk and Ice Cream, Lawton, 1959-73; assoc. Rhoads & Johnson, Lawton, 1977-79; ptnr. Johnson & Wright, Lawton, 1979-86; sole practice Lawton, 1986—. Mem. Okla. Bar Assn., Comanche County Bar Assn., Okla. Trial Lawyers Assn. Methodist. Bankruptcy, Family and matrimonial, General practice. Home: 4616 Meadowbrook Lawton OK 73505 Office: 816 W Gore Lawton OK 73501

JOHNSON, HAROLD GENE, lawyer; b. St. Louis, July 20, 1934; s. Edward Henry Johnson and Betty (Burton) Pallister; m. Sue Ann Giesecke, Oct. 10, 1953; children: H. Mark, Deborah S. Johnson Schnitzer, Michael R., Laura A. Johnson Schwent, Mitchell D. BBA, Washington U., St. Louis, 1961, LLB, 1962. Bar: Mo. 1962, U.S. Dist. Ct. (ea. dist.) Mo. 1964, U.S. Ct. Appeals (8th cir.) 1981. Assoc. Schomburg, Marshall & Craig, St. Louis, 1962-63, Green & Raymond, St. Louis, 1963-64; ptnr. Johnson & Hayes, St. Louis, 1964—. Judge mcpl. ct. City of Bridgeton, Mo., 1973-85. Served with U.S. Army 1954-56. Recipient Spl. Service award City of Bridgeton, 1985; Honored with ann. presentation of The Judge Harold Johnson award Pro-Life Direct Action League, 1985. Bar: Mo. Bar Assn., Met. Bar St. Louis, St. Louis County Bar Assn. Avocation: woodworking. State civil litigation, General practice, Personal injury. Office: Johnson & Hayes 500 Northwest Plaza Suite 715 Saint Louis MO 63074-2252

JOHNSON, J. RODNEY, law educator; b. Richmond, Va., July 9, 1939; m. Catherine White Dorman, Jan. 28, 1967; children: William Taylor, Abigail Elizabeth. BA in Jurisprudence, Coll. William and Mary, 1965, JD, 1967. Bar: Va. 1967. Instr. law Marshall-Wythe Sch. Law, Coll. William and Mary, Williamsburg, Va., 1967-68; asst. prof. Marshall-Wythe Sch. Law, Coll. William and Mary, Williamsburg, 1968-70; asst. prof. law T.C. Williams Sch. Law, U. Richmond (Va.), 1970-72, prof., 1972—; vis. adj. prof. law Marshall-Wythe Sch. Law Coll. William and Mary, 1977-78, U. Va., 1983. Contbr. articles to profl. jours. Mem. Estate Planning Council of Richmond. Acad. fellow Am. Coll. Probate Counsel; mem. ABA (real property, probate and trust law sect.), Va. Bar Assn. (com. on wills, trusts and estates, trusts and estates sect.), Nat. Coll. Probate Judges (life), Richmond Bar Assn. Home: 1200 Peachtree Blvd Richmond VA 23226 Office: Univ Richmond TS Williams Sch Law Richmond VA 23173

JOHNSON, JAMES MCDADE, lawyer; b. Shreveport, La., Dec. 5, 1939; s. Leslie N. and Nell (McDade) J.; m. Glenda Roth, Jan. 27, 1962; children—Danielle Johnson Soufi, Kimberly Dawn. B.A., La. State U., 1962, J.D., 1964. Bar: La. 1964. First asst. dist. atty. 26th Jud. Dist. La., Minden, 1975-83; ptnr. Campbell, Campbell & Johnson, Minden, 1964—; assoc. nat. legal counsel U.S. Jaycees, Tulsa, 1970-71, nat. legal counsel, 1971-72. Chmn. Minden Democratic Exec. Com., La., 1964-74. Named Outstanding Vice Pres. La. Jaycees, 1969. Mem. Assn. Trial Lawyers Am. Episcopalian. Personal injury. Office: Campbell Campbell & Johnson PO Box 834 Minden LA 71058

JOHNSON, JAMES WALKER, lawyer; b. Cleve., Aug. 17, 1953; s. John Everett and Jane (Walker) J.; m. Joan Essex, Oct. 24, 1982; 1 child, Robert Everett. BA, Cornell U., 1975; JD, U. Kans., 1978; LLM, Georgetown U., 1983. Bar: Kans. 1978, U.S. Ct. Claims 1979, U.S. Tax Ct. 1979, D.C. 1983. Trial atty. tax div. U.S. Justice Dept., Washington, 1978-84; assoc. Steptoe & Johnson, Washington, 1984—; adj. prof. law Georgetown U., 1987—. Contbr. articles to profl. jours. Mem. ABA (tax sect.). Corporate taxation, Personal income taxation. Home: 3312 Camalier Dr Chevy Chase MD 20815 Office: Steptoe & Johnson 1330 Connecticut Ave NW Washington DC 20036

JOHNSON, JOHN PAUL, lawyer, administrative law judge; b. Omaha, Dec. 4, 1944; s. John and Dorothy (Mullen) J.; m. Suzanne Alice Smiley, July 12, 1974; children—James Thomas, Jennifer Anne. B.A., Washburn U., Topeka, 1967; J.D., U. Nebr., 1971. Bar: Nebr. 1972. Claims examiner VA, St. Paul, 1972; staff atty. Bd. Vets. Appeals, Washington, 1973-79, sr. atty., 1979-81; adminstrv. law judge Office of Hearings and Appeals, Des Moines, Iowa, 1981—. Served with U.S. Army, 1968-70 (Vietnam). Decorated Bronze Star; recipient Exceptional Service award VA, 1974. Mem. Nebr. State Bar Assn., Fed. Adminstrv. Law Judge Conf., Kappa Sigma. Episcopalian. Administrative and regulatory, Personal injury, Federal civil litigation. Home: 228 39th St West Des Moines IA 50265 Office: Office Hearings and Appeals 950 Office Park Rd W Des Moines IA 50265

JOHNSON, JOHN RICHARD, lawyer, information group administrator; b. Oklahoma City, Nov. 22, 1951; s. Houston Gayle and Mary Jo (Estes) J.; m. Jo Ellen McDermott, Dec. 30, 1972; children: Simon, Carolyn. BA, U. Okla., 1974; JD, Georgetown U., 1978. Bar: D.C. 1979. Staff atty. Migrant Legal Action Program, Washington, 1978-80; mgr. tech. improvements Legal Services Corp., Washington, 1980-83; mgr. law sch. programs Mead Data Cen., Dayton, Ohio, 1983-85, mgr. edn. programs, 1985-86, mgr. membership groups, 1986—, also bd. dirs. small law firm market. Recipient Outstanding Achievement award Mead Data Cen., Inc., 1984. Mem. ABA, D.C. Bar Assn., Assn. Trial Lawyers Am., Am. Assn. Law Libraries, Phi Beta Kappa. Democrat. Unitarian. Avocations: bicycling, opera, reading. Librarianship, Computer. Home: 1933 Burbank Dr Dayton OH 45406 Office: Mead Data Cen Inc PO Box 933 Dayton OH 45401

JOHNSON, JOSEPH BERNARD, lawyer; b. Cambridge, Minn., July 6, 1919; s. Joseph B. and Ruth (Barker) J.; m. Kathryn M. Dabelstein, Feb. 20, 1943; children—Joseph Bernard III, Christine Ruth. Student, Carleton Coll., 1938-41; J.D., U. Mich., 1948. Bar: Minn. 1948, Fed. Dist. Ct., U.S. Ct. Appeals (8th cir.), U.S. Supreme Ct., U.S. Tax Ct. Assoc. Holmes, Mayall, Reavill & Neimeyer, Duluth, Minn., 1948-51; ptnr. Reavill, Neimeyer, Johnson, Fredin, Killen & Thibodeau and predecessor firms,

Duluth, 1951-74; chmn., sr. mem. Johnson, Killen, Thibodeau & Seiler, P.A., 1974—; Corp. officer, dir. W.P.&R.S. Mars. Co., Lindoln Stores, Inc., Daugherty Howe Inc., Polar Gas, Inc., Conveyor Belt Service, Inc., Duluth Photographics Inc., Arrowhead Energy Products Inc., Easy Housing Inc., Valley Homes Inc.; dir. Northwest Bank Duluth. Vice chmn. Minn. Bd. Law Examiners, 1956-59; chmn. budget com. Duluth Community Chest, 1952-63; chmn. Duluth Welfare Council, 1967-70; bd. dirs. Duluth YMCA, pres., 1977-79, chmn. bd. trustees, 1979—; mem. Nat. Council YMCA's; bd. dirs. St. Luke's Hosp., Duluth, 1970-76; trustee Hunt Scholarship Fund, 1957-69, chmn., 1967-69; bd. dirs., chmn. United Way of Duluth; v.p. St. Louis County Heritage and Arts Ctr., 1985—. Served to capt. AUS, 1941-45; now lt. col. Res. Decorated Bronze Star medal with two oak leaf clusters, Purple heart with two oak leaf clusters (U.S.), Croix de Guerre (France), Order of Holland (Netherlands). Fellow Am. Coll. Probate Counsel; mem. ABA (taxation sec., probate and trust law sect.), Minn. Bar Assn. (bd. govs. 1967-70, chmn. jud. selection com. 1969-73), 11th Dist. Bar Assn. (pres. 1966-67), Am. Judicature Soc., Duluth C. of C. (chmn. tax and tax laws com.), Duluth Jr. C. of C. (v.p. 1950-51). Republican. Lutheran. Clubs: Northland Country (pres. 1962-63), Kitchi Gammi. Lodge: Rotary (chmn. jud. com.). General practice, Probate, Estate taxation. Home: 3715 Greysolon Pl Duluth MN 55804 Office: Johnson Fredin Killen Thibodeau & Seiler 811 Norwest Ctr Duluth MN 55802

JOHNSON, JOSEPH CLAYTON, JR., lawyer; b. Vicksburg, Miss., Nov. 15, 1943; s. Joseph Clayton and Rose Butler (Levy) J.; m. Cherrian Frances Turpin, Oct. 24, 1970; children—Mary Clayton, Erik Cole. B.S., La. State U., 1965, J.D., 1969. Bar: La. 1969, U.S. Dist. Ct. (ea. dist.) La. 1969, U.S. Dist. Ct. (mid. dist.) La. 1969, U.S. Dist. Ct. (we. dist.) La. 1979, U.S. Ct. Appeals (5th cir.) 1982. Ptnr. Taylor, Porter, Brooks & Phillips, Baton Rouge, 1969-. Served with U.S. Army, 1969-75. Mem. ABA, La. Bar Assn. (mem. ho. of dels. 1979-87, council rep. mineral law sect. 1986-89), Baton Rouge Bar Assn. Republican. Methodist. Club: Kiwanis. Oil and gas leasing. Office: PO Box 2471 Baton Rouge LA 70821

JOHNSON, JOSEPH DAVIS, lawyer; b. Toccoa, Ga., Apr. 10, 1952; s. John Davis and Amelia Elizabeth (Woodall) J. AB, U. N.C., 1974, JD with honors, 1977. Bar: N.C. 1977. Research asst. N.C. Ct. of Appeals, Raleigh, 1977-78; assoc. Charles W. Hipps P.A., Waynesville, N.C., 1978-79; ptnr. Jones, Key, Melvin & Patton P.A., Franklin, N.C., 1979—; instr. So. Tech. Coll., Webster, N.C., 1979-80. Mem. ABA, N.C. Bar Assn. Democrat. Baptist. Avocations: boating, kayaking, skiing (water, cross country), backpacking. Real property, Probate, State civil litigation. Office: Jones Key Melvin & Patton PA 19 E Main St Franklin NC 28734

JOHNSON, JOSEPH H., JR., lawyer; b. Dothan, Ala., July 14, 1925. Student La. Poly. Inst.; LL.B., U. Va., 1949. Bar: Ala. 1949. Ptnr. Johnson & Thorington, Birmingham, Ala. Mem. Assn. Bar City N.Y., Birmingham Bar Assn. (chmn. com. on profl. ethics 1978-79), ABA (mem. council 1962-66, 1968-72, 1973-77, chmn. 1981-82 sec. of urban, state and local govt. law), Ala. State Bar, Nat. Assn. Bond Lawyers (bd. dirs. 1985—, sec. 1986—), Am. Soc. Hosp. Attys. Municipal bonds, Local government, Securities. Office: Johnson & Thorington 920 First Ala Bank Bldg Birmingham AL 35203

JOHNSON, JUDITH SUGG, lawyer; b. Washington, Aug. 30, 1948; d. Irvin Douglas and Bernice (Humphrey) Sugg; divorced; children: Carmen, Nichole. BSBA, Va. State U., 1966; postgrad in econs., Swarthmore Coll., 1967; JD, Cath. U., 1975. Bar: Va. 1975, U.S. Ct. Appeals (4th cir.) 1975. Corp. v.p. and gen. cousel Systems Mgmt. Am. Corp., Norfolk, 1985—; bd. dirs. The Travelers Health Network. Mem. editorial adv. bd. Met. Women mag. Bd. dirs. Va. Mus. Theatre, The Va. Water Project, Longwood Coll., The Cultural Alliance of Greater Hampton Roads, Downtown Norfolk Devel. Corp.; mem. adv. bd. Colonial Council Girl Scouts U.S.; mem. legis. com. Va. Perinatal Assn. Rockefeller Found. fellow; recipient Community Service award NAACP; named Va.'s Outstanding Woman Atty., Va. Woman of Achievement in Govt.; named one of Outstanding Young Women of Am.; White House intern. Mem. ABA, Va. Bar Assn., Old Dominion Bar Assn., Iota Phi Lambda (Outstanding Woman award). Avocations: politics, mcpl. bond financing, real estate devel. Office: 254 Monticello Ave Norfolk VA 23510

JOHNSON, KAREN LEE, lawyer; b. Houston, Feb. 29, 1948; d. Bailey Edward and Frances Bette (Pfefferle) J. B.S. in Edn., Tex. Tech. U., 1970, J.D., 1973. Bar: Tex. 1973. Research asst. office legal affairs Tex. Tech. U., Lubbock, 1972-73, staff asst., 1973; univ. legal counsel W. Tex. State U., Canyon, 1973-76; asst. gen. counsel Tex. Edn. Agy., Austin, 1976-78; gen. counsel Tex. State Tchrs.' Assn., Austin, 1978—; cons. on legal problems in edn. Tex. Jr. Coll. System, 1976-80. Council program chmn. Explorer Scouts, Amarillo, Tex., 1976; mem. Gov.'s Commn. on Juvenile Justice, San Marcus and Austin, 1983; mem. adv. council Windham Sch. Dist., Huntsville, Tex., 1984. Recipient Outstanding Service award Llano Estacado Explorer Scouts, 1976, Windham Sch. System, 1984. Mem. Tex. Bar Assn., Austin Young Lawyers, Nat. Assn. Tchr. Attys., Nat. Orgn. Legal Problems in Edn., Pi Beta Phi. Democrat. Presbyterian. General corporate, Labor, Civil rights. Office: Texas State Tchrs Assn 316 W 12th St Austin TX 78701

JOHNSON, KATHRYN GIBBONS, lawyer; b. Canton, Ohio, July 26, 1952; d. Harry DeRomana and Mary Lou (Wild) Gibbons; m. W. Bruce Johnson, Dec. 30, 1978; children: Christopher Charles, Matthew Henry, David William. BA, Wittenberg U., 1974; JD, Duke U., 1977. Bar: Ohio 1977, D.C. 1977, U.S. Dist. Ct. D.C. 1977, U.S. Ct. Appeals (5th cir.) 1977, U.S. Ct. Appeals (D.C. cir.) 1978, N.Y. 1979. Law clk. to presiding justice U.S. Ct. Appeals (5th cir.), New Orleans and Jacksonville, Fla., 1977-78; assoc. Ginsburg, Feldman & Bress, Washington, 1978-79, Fried, Frank, Harris, Shriver & Jacobson, N.Y.C., 1979-86. Mem. ABA. Republican. Avocation: politics. General corporate, Mergers and acquisitions. Home: 56 Valley Rd Bronxville NY 10708

JOHNSON, KEITH KARLETON, lawyer; b. Springfield, Ohio, Mar. 3, 1950; s. Charles Robert and Elsie Mae (Hupman) J.; m. Linda Marie Haubert, June 29, 1974; children: Amanda Louise, Brett Richard. BA, Bowling Green State U., 1971; JD, Ohio State U., 1977; MBA, U. Toledo, 1984. Assoc. Doyle, Lewis & Warner, Toledo, 1977-82; trust officer Ohio Citizens Bank, Toledo, 1982-85, First Nat. Bank Ohio, Akron, 1985-86; assoc. Roetzel & Andress, Akron, Ohio, 1986. Served to 2d lt. U.S. Army, 1972-74. Mem. ABA, Ohio State Bar Assn., Akron Bar Assn., Estate Planning Council. Republican. Lutheran. Club: Akron City. Avocations: tennis, wood refinishing. Probate, Estate taxation. Home: 2868 Bancroft Akron OH 44313 Office: Roetzel & Andress 75 E Market St Akron OH 44308

JOHNSON, KENNETH NOLAN, lawyer; b. Madison, Wis., Nov. 3, 1956; s. Nolan A. and Mary J. (Lembrich) J. BA, U. Wis., 1978; JD, U. N.D., 1982. Bar: Wis. 1982, U.S. Dist. Ct. (ea. and we. dists.) Wis. 1982. Asst. dist. atty. Dodge County, Juneau, Wis., 1982-86; spl. asst. U.S. atty. Ea. Dist. State of Wis., Milw., 1985, dist. atty., 1985—. Treas. Dodge County Rep. Party, 1985-86; dist. atty. Dodge County, 1987—. Named one of Outstanding Young Men of Am., 1984-86. Mem. ABA, Wis. Bar Assn. (young lawyers div., law reform, community edn. coms.), Wis. Dist. Attys. Assn., Dodge County Bar Assn. Lodge: Lions. Criminal. Home: 134 1/2 Walnut St Beaver Dam WI 53916

JOHNSON, KENNETH THEODORE, lawyer; b. Jamestown, N.Y., May 28, 1912; A.B., Allegheny Coll., 1934; J.D., U. Mich., 1937. Bar: N.Y. 1938, U.S. Supreme Ct. 1956, U.S. Tax Ct. 1961. Assoc. Lombardo & Pickard, Jamestown, N.Y., 1937-39; assoc. Clive L. Wright, Jamestown, 1939-40; sole practice, Jamestown, 1940-43, 46-52; ptnr. Johnson & Peterson, now Johnson, Peterson, Tener & Anderson, Jamestown, 1952-56, mng. ptnr., 1956—. Mem. ABA, Jamestown Bar Assn., N.Y. State Bar Assn., Motor Carrier Lawyers Assn., Assn. ICC Practitioners. General corporate, Probate. Home: Waldheim Jamestown NY 14701 Office: Key Bank Bldg Jamestown NY 14701

JOHNSON, KEVIN BLAINE, lawyer, educator; b. Wichita, Kans., Aug. 28, 1956; s. Howard Blaine and Ruth Signe (Hornlund) J.; m. Suzanne Kay Wright, Aug. 29, 1981. B.A., Wichita State U., 1978; J.D., Washburn U., 1981. Bar: Kans. 1982, U.S. Dist. Ct. Kans. 1982. Sole practice, Overland Park, Kans., 1981-82; asst. dist. atty. Wyandotte, County, Kans., 1982-84; assoc. Law Office of A. B. Fletcher, Wichita, Kans., 1984-86, Law Office of Stan R. Singleton, Derby, Kans., 1986—; prof. law Kans. Newman Coll., Wichita, 1984—. Author: The 11th Kansas Volunteer Cavalry, 1986. Mem. Wichita Citizen Participation Orgn. Council, 1985-86 . Contbr. articles to profl. jours. Drum instr. Sky Ryders Drum and Bugle Corps, Hutchinson, Kans., 1978-81; dir. High Plains Drum Corps, Inc., 1987—. Mem. Assn. Trial Lawyers Am., Wichita Bar Assn. Republican. Lutheran. Bankruptcy, Contracts commercial, Criminal. Home: 1612 Brendonwood Derby KS 67037 Office: PO Box 40 Derby KS 67037

JOHNSON, L. CHARLES, lawyer; b. Pocatello, Idaho, Feb. 8, 1927; s. Luvern Charles and Jace Esther (Palmer) J.; m. Marcene Sue Foreman, Aug. 18, 1930; children—Charles, Kaari Swope, Ethan Whitney, Eric Collins. J.D., Northwestern U., 1952. Bar: Ill. 1952, Idaho 1952, U.S. Dist. Ct. (no. dist.) Ill. 1953, U.S. Dist. Ct. Idaho 1954, U.S. Ct. Appeals (9th cir.) 1958, U.S. Ct. Appeals (7th, 10th, D.C. cirs.) 1976, U.S. Ct. Appeals (fed. cir.) 1982, U.S. Ct. Claims 1977, U.S. Tax Ct. 1957, U.S. Supreme Ct. 1968. Ptnr. Johnson Olson Robison, Chartered, Pocatello, 1957—. Pres. Idaho Easter Seal Soc., 1960-63, Eastern Idaho Lincoln Day Assn., 1959. Served with U.S. Army, 1945-47. Mem. Ill. Bar Assn., Idaho Bar Assn. (trustee Rocky Mountain Mineral Law Found.), Pocatello C. of C. (pres. 1960). Republican. Methodist. Clubs: Alta (Salt Lake City); Elks (exalted ruler 1962-63). Federal civil litigation, State civil litigation, General corporate. Office: PO Box 1725 Pocatello ID 83201

JOHNSON, LAEL FREDERIC, lawyer; b. Yakima, Wash., Jan. 22, 1938; s. Andrew Cabot and Gudney M. (Fredrickson) J.; m. Eugenie Rae Call, June 9, 1960; children: Eva Marie, Inga Margaret. A.B., Wheaton (Ill.) Coll., 1960; J.D., Northwestern U., 1963. V.p., gen. counsel Abbott Labs., Abbott Park, Ill., 1966—. Mem. ABA, Chgo. Bar Assn., Ill. State Bar Assn., Am. Corp. Counsel Assn. Office: Abbott Labs Rts 137 & 43 Abbott Park IL 60064

JOHNSON, LAURENCE FLEMING, lawyer; b. Dallas, Oct. 14, 1948; s. Milton G. and Miriam (Fleming) J.; m. Mary Louise Nichols, May 10, 1980; children: Andrew William, Margaret Elizabeth. BA, U. Md., 1970, JD, 1973. Bar: Md. 1974, D.C. 1978, U.S. Dist. Ct. Md. 1977, U.S. Dist. Ct. D.C. 1978, U.S. Ct. Appeals (4th cir.) 1977, U.S. Ct. Appeals (D.C. cir.) 1980, U.S. Supreme Ct. 1977. Staff atty. Md. Pub. Interest Research Group, College Park, 1974-76; sole practice, Silver Spring, Md., 1976-77; spl. asst. to commr. Pub. Service Commn. Md., Balt., 1977-78; asst. to U.S. Congressman, Silver Spring, 1979-80; sole practice, Wheaton, Md., 1980-82; pres. Laurence F. Johnson, P.C., Wheaton, 1982-87; mng. ptnr. Johnson & Freedman, 1987—; legis. agt. Greenbelt Consumer Services, Inc., Savage, Md., 1977-81; research asst. various state legislators, Annapolis, Md., 1976-77. Pres. Ayrlawn Citizens Assn., Bethesda, Md., 1984—. Recipient Outstanding Performance award Montgomery County Dem. Com., Kensington, Md., 1976, Citation of Appreciation, Greenbelt Consumer Services, 1978; named one of Outstanding Young Men Am., 1977. Mem. Am. Immigration Lawyers Assn. (softball chmn. 1983, 84, 86), ABA (chmn. subcom. nonimmigrant visas, gen. practice sect. 1984), Fed. Bar Assn., Md. State Bar Assn., Bar Assn. Montgomery County (co-chmn. immigration 1984, chmn. 1986), Nat. Eagle Scout Assn. Democrat. Roman Catholic. Immigration, naturalization, and customs. Home: 6004 Henning St Bethesda MD 20817 Office: 11141 Georgia Ave Suite 418 Wheaton MD 20902-4637

JOHNSON, LAWRENCE WILBUR, JR., lawyer; b. Columbia, S.C., Apr. 17, 1955; s. Lawrence Wilbur and Ruth (Cooper) J.; m. Cindy Ann Small, May 26, 1979. BS in Acctg., U. S.C., 1976, JD, 1979. Bar: S.C. 1979, U.S. Dist. Ct. S.C. 1979, U.S. Ct. Appeals (4th cir.) 1980. Jud. clk. 3d Jud. Cir. Ct., Bishopville, S.C., 1979-80; ptnr. Robinson, McFadden, Moore, Pope, Williams, Taylor & Brailsford, P.A., Columbia, 1980-87, Adams, Quackenbush, Herring & Stuart, P.A., Columbia, 1987—. Mem. S.C. House of Dels., Columbia, 1986—. Mem. S.C. Bar Assn., Richland County Bar Assn. (pres. bankruptcy law sect. 1982-85), S.C. Def. Trial Lawyers Assn., Greater Columbia C. of C. (chmn. leadership Columbia 1983-84, bd. dirs. 1984—), U. S.C. Alumni Assn. (bd. dirs. 1980-82), Omicron Delta Kappa. Republican. Baptist. Avocation: golf. Banking, Bankruptcy, Consumer commercial. Home: 6015 Gill Creek Rd Columbia SC 29206 Office: Adams Quackenbush Herring & Stuart PA 1400 Main St 6th Floor Palmetto Bldg PO Box 394 Columbia SC 29202 Mailing: PO Box 944 Columbia SC 29202

JOHNSON, LEONARD JAMES, lawyer; b. Belmond, Iowa, May 25, 1951. BA in Govt., St. Johns U., Collegeville, Minn., 1974; JD, U. Iowa, 1977. Bar: Mo. 1977, Kans. 1978, U.S. Dist. Ct. (we. dist.) Mo. 1977 , U.S. Dist. Ct. Kans. 1978, U.S. Ct. Appeals (10th cir.) 1985, U.S. Ct. Appeals (8th cir.) 1986 . Assoc. Morrison, Hecker, Curtis, Kuder & Parrish, Kansas City, Mo., 1977-82, ptnr., 1982—; mem. fed. practice com. Western Dist. Mo., Kansas City, 1986—. Mem. ABA, Mo. Bar Assn., Def. Research Inst. Federal civil litigation, Personal injury, Construction. Home: 5340 W 101 Terr Overland Park KS 66207 Office: 1700 Bryant Bldg 1102 Grand Kansas City MO 64106

JOHNSON, LESTER BENJAMIN, III, lawyer; b. Savannah, Ga., Dec. 4, 1953; s. Lester Benjamin Jr. and Constance Marquita (Mosely) J.; m. Salyon Dorret Harris, May 24, 1975; children: Ayesha Khalilah, Khalil Ahmadu, Faisal Bashir. AB in Polit. Sci., Coll. Holy Cross, 1975; JD, U. Miami, 1978. Bar: Ga. 1979. Atty. Ga. Legal Services, Brunswick, 1978-80; assoc. Martin, Thomas & Bass, Savannah, 1980-83; ptnr. Martin & Johnson, Savannah, 1983-86; sole practice Savannah, 1986—; asst. atty. City of Savannah, 1982—; judge pro tem Recorders Ct., Savannah, 1985—. Mem. Coastal Area Minority Bus Devel., Savannah, 1981, exec. com. Savannah Dems., 1982, Neighborhood Housing Services, Savannah, 1985, Parent and Child Devel., Savannah, 1986—. Named one of Outstanding Young Men Am., Jaycees, 1983; recipient Law award St. Mary's Ch., 1983, PTA award Hodge Elem. Sch., 1985. Mem. ABA, Nat. Bar Assn., Ga. Trial Lawyers Assn., Ga. Bar Assn., Plaintiffs Lawyers Assn., Port City Bar Assn. (pres. 1983), Savannah Bar Assn., Savannah C. of C. (leadership award 1982). Democrat. Muslim. Avocations: basketball, reading, jazz music, drums. Workers' compensation, Personal injury, Pension, profit-sharing, and employee benefits. Home: 1 Bridgeport Rd Savannah GA 31419 Office: 216 W Broughton St PO Box 8285 Savannah GA 31412

JOHNSON, MARGARET MARY JOYCE, lawyer; b. Detroit, Oct. 17, 1948; d. William G. and Bertha H. (Duey) Joyce; m. Steven M. Johnson, Aug. 11, 1972; children: Kirk, Erika. Student, Marygrove Coll., Freiburg, Fed. Republic of Germany, 1968-69, Wayne State U., 1969; BS, Siena Heights Coll., 1970; MA, U. Colo., 1973; postgrad., L'Inst. Internat. D'Etudes Francaises, Castelnaudary, France, Summer 1976; JD, U. Mont., 1980. Bar: Mont. 1980, U.S. Dist. Ct. Mont. 1980, U.S. Ct. Appeals (9th cir.) 1983, U.S. Supreme Ct. 1984. Assoc. Hughes, Bennett, Kellner & Sullivan, Helena, Mont., 1980-82; asst. atty. gen. State of Mont., Helena, 1983-84; assoc. Church, Harris, Johnson & Williams, Great Falls, Mont., 1985—; grader Mont. Bd. of Bar Examiners, 1983—. Bd. dirs. Mont. Christian Conciliation Service, Billings, Mont., 1983-85. Fulbright scholar, 1971-72. Mem. ABA (torts and ins. practice sect., bus. law sect., real property sect.), Mont. Bar Assn., Assn. Trial Lawyers Am., Mont. Trial Lawyers Assn., Mont. Assn. Def. Counsel, Christian Legal Soc., Order of Barristers, Phi Delta Phi. Avocations: travel, reading, hiking, backpacking, camping. Personal injury, Federal civil litigation, State civil litigation. Office: Church Harris Johnson & Williams Norwest Bank Bldg 3d Floor PO Box 1645 Great Falls MT 59403

JOHNSON, MARK EUGENE, lawyer; b. Independence, Mo., Jan. 8, 1951; s. Russell Eugene and Reatha (Nixon) J.; m. Vicki Ja Lane, June 11, 1983. AB with honors, U. Mo., 1973, JD, 1976. Bar: Mo. 1976, U.S. Dist. Ct. (we. dist.) Mo. 1976, U.S. Ct. Appeals (8th cir.) 1984. Ptnr. Morrison, Hecker, Curtis, Kuder & Parrish, Kansas City, Mo., 1976—. Editor: Mo. Law Rev., 1974-76. Pres. Lido Villas Assn., Inc., Mission, Kans., 1979-81. Mem. Kansas City Bar Assn., ABA, Mo. Bar Assn., Lawyers Assn. Kansas City, Def. Research Inst., Western Mo. Def. Lawyers Assn., Order of Coif, Phi Beta Kappa, Phi Eta Sigma, Phi Kappa Phi, Omicron Delta Kappa. Republican. Methodist. Clubs: Carriage, Kansas City. Federal civil litigation, State civil litigation. Home: 4905 Somerset Dr Prairie Village KS 66207 Office: Morrison Hecker Curtis et al 1102 Grand Ave Kansas City MO 64106

JOHNSON, MICHAEL ALMER, educator, lawyer, consultant; b. St. Paul, Minn., Apr. 17, 1944; s. Almer M. and Marvel C. (Heinen) J.; m. Carol J. Neumann, Nov. 5, 1966; children: Michael K., Jill L. BA in Counseling Psychology, U. Minn., 1966; JD, William Mitchell Coll. Law, 1974. Bar: Minn. 1975. Dir. mgmt. devel. Minn. Transp. Dept., St. Paul, 1968-74; sole practice St. Paul, 1975—; co-owner, sr. v.p. Performax Systems, Mpls., 1976-84; owner, pres. M. Johnson & Assocs., St. Paul, 1984—; prof. organizational mgmt. U. Minn. Sch. Dentistry, Mpls., 1975—; dental contract and bus. cons. to various U.S. dental orgns. and clinics; mgmt. devel. and profl. tng. cons. IBM, Apple Computer, U.S Army C.E., other orgns. Author: (with Randall Berning) Personalized Guide to Dental Legal Issues, 1985. Grantee Am. Dental Assn., Chgo., 1985-86; recipient cert. of appreciation for valuable sci. contbn. Minn. Dental Assn., 1986. Mem. ABA, Minn. Bar Assn., Oreg. Soc. Dentistry for Children (hon.). Roman Catholic. Avocations: golf, tennis. Health, Legal education, Dental Contract and Business Law. Home: 1152 Amble Dr Arden Hills MN 55112 Office: U Minn Sch Dentistry 515 Delaware St SE Moos Tower 15-117 Minneapolis MN 55455

JOHNSON, MORDECAI CHRISTOPHER, lawyer; b. Florence County, S.C., Oct. 29, 1931; s. Willie Adosious and Annie Mae (Palmer) J.; m. Navonia Allen, Dec. 29, 1958; children—Palmer, William, Odishi, Mordecai. Student Morris Coll., 1946-48; B.A., S.C. State Coll., 1951; J.D., Howard U., 1959; LL.M., George Washington U., 1961. Bar: S.C. 1960, U.S. Dist. Ct. S.C. 1960, D.C. 1960, U.S. Ct. Appeals (4th cir.) 1970. Tchr., S.C. Pub. Schs., 1951-52, 54-56; practice, Washington, 1961-62; atty.-advisor Office of Gen. Counsel, edn. br., HEW, Washington, 1962-66; atty.-advisor Office Gen. Counsel, U.S. Commn. on Civil Rights, Washington, 1966-67; project dir. TEAM, Greenville, S.C., 1967-68; sole practice, Florence, S.C., 1968—; lectr. various colls. and univs., 1985-86. Columnist Charlotte Observer newspaper, 1987—. Mem. City Council Florence, 1977-81, ho. of dels. 12th jud. cir. S.C., 1987—; sec. Carolina Regional Legal Services, Inc., 1979-84; past pres. S.C. Council on Human Relations; bd. dirs. So. Regional Council; trustee, choir dir., historian, tchr. Sunday Sch. Savannah Grove Ch., Florence. Mem. Nat. Bar Assn. (life), ABA, S.C. Bar, Florence County Bar Assn. Baptist. Club: Masons. Personal injury, General practice, State civil litigation. Office: PO Box 1804 Florence SC 29503

JOHNSON, NORMA HOLLOWAY, fed. judge; b. Lake Charles, La.. B.S., D.C. Tchrs. Coll., 1955; J.D., Georgetown U., 1962. Bar: D.C. bar 1962, U.S. Supreme Ct. bar 1967. Practiced in Washington, 1963; atty. Dept. Justice, Washington, 1963-67; asst. corp. counsel D.C. 1967-70; judge D.C. Superior Ct., 1970-80, U.S. Dist. Ct. for D.C., 1980—; Bd. dirs. Nat. Children's Center, Washington, National Street Law Inst. Mem. Am. Bar Assn., Nat. Bar Assn., D.C. Bar, Nat. Council Juvenile Ct. Judges, Am. Judicature Soc. (dir.), Nat. Assn. Women Judges (dir.). Jurisprudence. Office: US District Court US Courthouse 3d and Constitution Ave NW Washington DC 20001 *

JOHNSON, OLIVER THOMAS, JR., lawyer; b. San Antonio, July 3, 1946; s. Oliver Thomas and Joan Elizabeth (Edwards) J.; m. Susan Caroline Nelson, Nov. 6, 1976; children: Caroline Elizabeth, Thomas Christian. BA, Stanford U., 1968, JD, 1971. Bar: Calif. 1972, D.C. 1975, U.S. Tax Ct. 1982, U.S. Ct. Internat. Trade 1983. Atty. office of legal adviser U.S. Dept. State, Washington, 1971-73, spl. asst. to legal adviser, 1973-75; assoc. Covington & Burling, Washington, 1975-80, ptnr., 1980—. Contbg. author: The Registration of Foreign Agents in the United States, 1981; contbr. articles to profl. jours. Bd. dirs. Project Victory, Washington, 1985. Mem. ABA, Am. Soc. Internat. Law, Internat. Law Assn., Order of Coif. Private international, Public international. Home: 1406 Langley Pl McLean VA 22101 Office: Covington & Burling 1201 Pennsylvania Ave NW PO Box 7566 Washington DC 20044

JOHNSON, PATRICK, JR., lawyer; b. New Orleans, June 6, 1955; s. Patrick and Louise (Durand) J.; m. Gayle Marie Daniel, Feb. 24, 1979; children: Patrick III, Daniel Hartman. BS, U. New Orleans, 1977; JD magna cum laude, Tulane U., 1979; diploma with distinction, U. Stockholm, 1980. Bar: La. 1980, U.S. Dist. Ct. (ea. and mid. dists.) La. 1980, U.S. Ct. Appeals (5th and 11th cirs.) 1981, U.S. Supreme Ct. 1985, U.S. Dist. Ct. (we. dist.) La. 1986. Assoc. Lemle, Kelleher et al, New Orleans, 1980-85, ptnr., 1985—; mem. local bankruptcy rules drafting com. U.S. Dist. Ct. (ea.dist.) La., New Orleans, 1985—, exec. com. in charge of publicity 61st ann. Nat. Conf. Bankruptcy Judges, 1987. Articles editor Tulane U. Law Rev., 1978-79, mem. bd. student editors, 1977-78. Mem. ABA, La. Bar Assn., New Orleans Bar Assn. Club: World Trade Ctr. (New Orleans). Bankruptcy, Federal civil litigation, State civil litigation. Home: 315 Jefferson Heights Ave Jefferson Parish LA 70121 Office: Lemle Kelleher et al 601 Poydras Pan-Am Life Ctr 21st Floor New Orleans LA 70130

JOHNSON, PAUL BRYAN, lawyer; b. Tampa, Fla., June 25, 1926; s. Harry Paul and Pauline (Love) J.; m. Annamae Houx, June 21, 1975. JD, U. Fla., 1950. Bar: Fla. 1950, U.S. Dist. Ct. (so. dist.) Fla. 1950, U.S. Supreme Ct. 1964, U.S. Dist. Ct. (mid. dist.) Fla., U.S. Ct. Appeals (5th and 11th cirs.) 1981. Soliciter Hillsborough County, Tampa, 1953-60; state atty. 13th jud. cir. State of Fla., Tampa, 1960-64; ptnr. Johnson & Hayes, Tampa, 1965%. Served with USMC, 1943-45, PTO. Named one of Fla.'s 5 Outstanding Young Men, Fla. Jaycees, 1960. Mem. ABA (chmn. criminal justice sect. 1985-86), Fla. Bar Assn., Hillsborough County Bar Assn., Fla. Pros. Attys. Assn. (pres. 1962-64). Democrat. Mem. Christian Ch. Clubs: Exchange, Tampa Yacht. Federal civil litigation, Criminal, State civil litigation. Home: 75 Ladoga Tampa FL 33606 Office: Johnson & Hayes PO Box 3416 Tampa FL 33601

JOHNSON, PAUL OREN, chem. co. exec., lawyer; b. Mpls., Feb. 2, 1937; s. Andrew Richard and LaVerne Delores (Slater) J.; m. Georgene Howalt, July 1, 1961; children: Scott, Paula, Amy. BA, Carleton Coll., 1958; JD cum laude, U. Minn., 1961. Bar: Minn. 1961. Atty. Briggs & Morgan, St. Paul, 1961-62; atty. Green Giant Co., Le Sueur, Minn., 1961—, asst. sec., 1967-74, sec., 1975-79, v.p., gen. counsel, 1971-79, v.p. corporate relations, 1973-79, mem. mgmt. com., 1976-79; gen. counsel H.B. Fuller Co., St. Paul, 1979-84, sr. v.p., sec., 1980—, mem. mgmt. com., 1981—; bd. dirs. Sta. WCAL-PBS, Northfield, Minn. Council mem. at large Boy Scouts Am., chmn. Republican County Com., 1965; bd. dirs. Minn. State U., 1979-82 , v.p., 1980-82. Served with U.S. Air N.G., 1961. Named One of Outstanding Young Men of Am., Jaycees, 1965. Mem. ABA., Minn. Bar Assn., Ramsey County Bar Assn., Assn. Corp. Secs. Home: Rural Rt 1 Box 112 Nerstrand MN 55053 Office: H B Fuller Co 2400 Energy Pk Dr Saint Paul MN 55108

JOHNSON, PHILIP EDWARD, lawyer; b. Denver, Oct. 17, 1947; s. William Edward Johnson and Margarete Eileen (Brandon) Schmaltz; m. Lelia Kathleen Holden Carroll, May 2, 1970; children: Brooke, Brandon, Dara, Bryce. BA, U. Colo., 1969; JD, U. Denver, 1974. Bar: Colo. 1975, U.S. Dist. Ct. Colo. 1975, U.S. Ct. Appeals (10th cir.) 1981. Corp. counsel Tosco Corp., Denver and Los Angeles, 1975-76; assoc., ptnr. Mosley, Wells, Johnson & Ruttum P.C., Denver, 1976—; bd. dirs. Tech. Resources, Inc., Research Systems, Inc., J.M. Foster Co., Inc., CRL Inc., OEA, Inc. Vol. U.S. Peace Corps, Panama, 1969, 70. Club: YMCA. Avocations: athletics, sailing, traveling. Federal civil litigation, State civil litigation, Real property. Home: 4061 E 19th Ave Denver CO 80220 Office: Mosley Wells Johnson et al 303 E 17th Ave Denver CO 80203

JOHNSON, PHILIP MCBRIDE, lawyer; b. Springfield, Ohio, June 18, 1938. A.B. with honors, Ind. U., 1959; LL.B., Yale U., 1962. Bar: Ill. 1962, D.C. 1983, N.Y. 1984. Partner firm Kirkland & Ellis, Chgo., 1962-81; chmn. Commodity Futures Trading Commn., Washington, 1981-83; ptnr. Wiley, Johnson & Rein, Washington, 1983-84, Skadden, Arps, Slate, Meagher & Flom, Washington, 1984—; speaker, panelist on Commodity Exchange Act Fed. Bar Assn., others; past mem. adv. com. definition and regulation Commodity Futures Trading Commn., adv. com. state jurisdiction and responsibility. Author: Commodities Regulation, 2 vols., 1982; Mng. editor: Yale U. Law Jour, 1962, Agrl. Law Jour; contbr. articles to legal jours. Mem. ABA (chmn. com. on commodities regulation 1975-81, governing council sect. corp. banking and bus. law 1981-83), Internat. Bar Assn. (chmn. subcom. on commodities, futures and options 1986—), Futures

Industry Assn. (bd. dirs. 1980-81, 86—). Office: Skadden Arps Slate et al 919 3d Ave New York NY 10022

JOHNSON, PHILIP WAYNE, lawyer; b. Greenwood, Ark., Oct. 24, 1944; s. John Luther and Flora (Joyce) J.; m. Carla Jean Newsom, Nov. 6, 1970; children—Betsy, Carl, Jeff, Laura, Philip. B.A., Tex. Tech U., 1965, J.D., 1975. Bar: Tex. 1975, U.S. Dist. Ct. (no. and we. dists.) Tex. 1976, U.S. Ct. Appeals (5th cir.) 1984, U.S. Supreme Ct. 1984. Assoc. Crenshaw Dupree & Milam, Lubbock, Tex., 1975-80, ptnr., 1980—; dir. Indian Maiden Cosmetics, Lubbock; mem. pattern jury charge and adminstrn. of justice coms. State Bar Tex., 1985—. Bd. dirs., pres. Lubbock County Legal Aid Soc., Tex., 1977-79; bd. dirs., chmn. Trinity Christian Schs., Lubbock, 1978-83, 85—; bd. dirs., pres. S.W. Lighthouse for Blind, Lubbock, 1978—. Served to capt. USAF, 1965-72. Decorated Silver Star, D.F.C. (3); Cross of Gallantry (Vietnam). Mem. Def. Research Inst., ABA, Tex. Bar Assn., Tex. Assn. Def. Counsel (v.p. 1983-85), Lubbock County Bar Assn. (pres. 1984-85), Phi Delta Phi. Federal civil litigation, State civil litigation, Personal injury. Home: 2301 60th St Lubbock TX 79412 Office: Crenshaw Dupree & Milam 1500 Broadway Lubbock TX 79401

JOHNSON, PHILLIP E., law educator; b. 1940. AB, Harvard U., 1961; JD, U. Chgo., 1965. Law clk. to justice Roger Traynor U.S. Supreme Ct., Washington, 1965-66, law clk. to justice Earl Warren, 1966-67; acting prof. U. Calif., Berkeley, 1968-71, prof., 1971—. Office: U Calif Berkeley Sch of Law Berkeley CA 94720 *

JOHNSON, PHILLIP EDWARD, lawyer; b. Cleve., Mar. 19, 1950; s. Donald Marquis and Jeannette (Tetinek) Johnson; m. Priscilla Dwinnell, Sept. 12, 1981. B.A., Miami U., Oxford, Ohio, 1972; J.D., Case Western Res. U., Cleve., 1975. Bar: Ohio 1975, U.S. Dist. Ct. (no. dist.) Ohio 1975, Maine 1977, U.S. Dist. Ct. Maine 1977. Assoc. Arter & Hadden, Cleve., 1975-77; assoc. Pierce, Atwood, Scribner, Allen, Smith & Lancaster, Augusta and Portland, Maine, 1977-82, ptnr., 1983—. Mem. ABA, Maine State Bar Assn., Kennebec County Bar Assn. (pres. 1983-85), Lawyer-Pilots Bar Assn. Republican. State civil litigation, Federal civil litigation. Home: 18 Summer St PO Box 150 Hallowell ME 04347 Office: Pierce Atwood Scribner et al 77 Winthrop St Augusta ME 04330

JOHNSON, PRESTON KING, lawyer; b. Belleville, Ill., Apr. 23, 1915; s. Preston King and Celia Halsey (Alexander) J.; m. Ruth Helen Leunig, Nov. 2, 1940; 1 child, Preston King Jr. B.S., U. Ill., 1937, J.D., 1939. Bar: Ill. 1939, U.S. Dist. Ct. (so. dist.) Ill. 1939, U.S. Ct. Appeals (7th cir.). Mem. Johnson & Johnson, 1939-55, Johnson, Johnson & Ducey, 1955-65, Johnson Johnson Ducey & Dixon, 1965-70, Johnson Ducey & Fedn., 1970-73 (all Belleville); master in chancery Cir. Ct. 20th Jud. Cir. State of Ill., Belleville, 1949-51; city atty. City of Belleville, 1949-72; ptnr. Johnson & Johnson, Belleville, 1973—; dir. Gen. Bank, N.A., Belleville. Mem. St. Clair County Bd. Suprs., 1941-63; co-chmn. Belleville Bd. Fire and Police Commrs., 1978—. Served to lt. JAGC, AUS, 1943-45. Mem. Ill. Bar Assn. (bd. dirs. 1956-58), Phi Alpha Delta. Republican. Episcopalian. Club: St. Clair Country (Belleville). Lodges: Rotary (pres. 1950-51), Elks. General practice, Probate, Real property. Home: 401 Garden Blvd Belleville IL 62221 Office: Johnson & Johnson 27 N Illinois St PO Box 454 Belleville IL 62223

JOHNSON, RENA, lawyer; b. N.Y.C., Jan. 18, 1943; d. Roy and Wanda (Klusek) Udoh. BA, St. Lawrence U., 1964; MS, Columbia U., 1969; JD, Temple U., 1980. Bar: U.S. Dist. (ea. dist.) Pa. 1980. Sr. atty. Mellon Bank, Phila., 1980-85; asst. gen. counsel 1st Pa. Bank, Phila., 1985—. Atty. Support Ctr. for Child Advs., Phila., 1981—, Pa. Vol. Lawyers for Arts, Phila., 1981—; mem. Com. to Elect Women Judges, Phila., 1981—, Women's Rights Com., 1986—. Mem. ABA, Phila. Bar Assn. Banking, Consumer commercial. Office: 1st Pa Bank Centre Sq Philadelphia PA 19101

JOHNSON, RICHARD ARLO, lawyer; b. Vermillion, S.D., July 8, 1952; s. Arlo Goodwin and Edna Marie (Styles) J.; m. Diane Marie Zephier, Aug. 18, 1972 (div. Jan. 1979); m. Sheryl Lavonne Mader, June 5, 1981; 1 stepson, Chadwick O. Wagner; 1 child, Sarah N. B.A., U.S.D., 1974, J.D., 1976. Bar: S.D. 1977, U.S. Dist. Ct. S.D. 1977. Ptnr. Pruitt, Matthews & Muilenberg, Sioux Falls, S.D., 1977—. Mem. Pub. Defender Adv. Bd., Sioux Falls, 1983—. Mem. Assn. Trial Lawyers Am., S.D. Trial Lawyers Assn., ABA, S.D. Bar Assn., Am. Orthopsychiatric Assn., Phi Delta Phi (pres. 1976-77). Democrat. Lutheran. Lodges: Masons, Shriners. Family and matrimonial, Criminal, Consumer commercial. Home: 409 E Lotta Sioux City SD 57105 Office: 141 N Main Ave Suite 801 Sioux Falls SD 57102

JOHNSON, RICHARD BRUCE, lawyer; b. Leavenworth, Wash., Nov. 10, 1928; s. William E. and Frances (Cameron) J.; m. Ann Lohrman, Feb. 4, 1984. BA, Washington State U., 1950; JD, U. Wash., Seattle, 1959. Bar: Wash. 1959, U.S. Dist. Ct. (we. dist.) Wash. 1960. Sole practice Everett, Wash., 1959—. Mem. Wash. Bar Assn., Def. Research Inst., Wash. Assn. Def. Counsel (pres. 1983), Assn. Ins. Attys., Fed. Assn. Ins. Counsel. Republican. Lodge: Elks. Avocations: boating, golfing. State civil litigation, Personal injury, General practice. Office: 301 1st Nat Bank Bldg Everett WA 98201

JOHNSON, RICHARD FRED, lawyer; b. Chgo., July 12, 1944; s. Sylvester Hiram and Naomi Ruth (Jackson) J.; m. Sheila Conley, June 26, 1970; children—Brendon, Bridget, Timothy, Laura. B.S., Miami U., Oxford, Ohio, 1966; J.D. cum laude, Northwestern U., 1969. Bar: Ill. 1969, U.S. Dist. Ct. (no. dist.) Ill. 1969, U.S. Ct. Appeals (7th cir.) 1977, U.S. Supreme Ct. 1978, U.S. Ct. Appeals (2d cir.) 1980. Law clk. U.S. Dist. Ct. (no. dist.) Ill., Chgo., 1969-70; assoc. firm Lord, Bissell & Brook, Chgo., 1970-77, ptnr., 1977—; lectr. legal edn. Contbr. articles to profl. jours. Recipient Am. Jurisprudence award, 1968. Mem. Chgo. Bar Assn., Ill. State Bar Assn. Club: Union League (Chgo.). Insurance, Personal injury, Admiralty. Home: 521 W Roscoe St Chicago IL 60657 Office: Lord Bissell & Brook 115 S LaSalle St Chicago IL 60603

JOHNSON, RICHARD TENNEY, lawyer; b. Evanston, Ill., Mar. 24, 1930; s. Ernest Levin and Margaret Abbott (Higgins) J.; m. Marilyn Bliss Meuth, May 1, 1954; children: Ross Tenney, Lenore, Jocelyn. A.B. with high honors, U. Rochester, 1951; postgrad., Trinity Coll., Dublin, Ireland, 1954-55; LL.B., Harvard, 1958. Bar: D.C. 1959. Trainee Office Sec. Def., 1957-59; atty. Office Gen. Counsel. Dept. Def., 1959-63; dep. gen. counsel Dept. Army, 1963-67, Dept. Transp., 1967-70; gen. counsel CAB, 1970-73, NASA, 1973-75, ERDA, 1975-76; mem. CAB, 1976-77; chmn. organizational integration Dept. Energy Activation, Exec. Office of Pres., 1977; ptnr. firm Sullivan & Beauregard, 1978-81; gen. counsel Dept. Energy, 1981-83; ptnr. firm Zuckert, Scoutt, Rasenberger & Johnson, 1983—. Served to lt. USNR, 1951-54. Mem. ABA, Fed. Bar Assn., Phi Beta Kappa, Theta Delta Chi. Government contracts and claims, Administrative and regulatory, Aviation. Office: 888 17th St NW Washington DC 20006

JOHNSON, RICHARD WALTER, lawyer; b. Northfield, Minn., June 5, 1928; s. Emil August and Mary Ann (Forster) J.; m. Patricia Jo-Ann Meredith, Apr. 27, 1957; children: Brent Adams, Robyn Marie. JD, U. Minn., 1952. Bar: Minn. 1952, N.Y. 1954, U.S. Dist. Ct. Minn. 1956, U.S. Ct. Appeals (8th cir.) 1984. Assoc. Cahill, Gordon, N.Y.C., 1952-54, Schermer & Gensler, Mpls., 1956-58; assoc. counsel No. States Power, Mpls., 1954-56; ptnr. Pierro & Johnson, Mpls., 1958-75, Johnson & Utter, Mpls., 1982—; sole practice Mpls., 1975-82; prof. jurisprudence Northwestern Coll. Chiropractic, Mpls., 1967-75. Served with U.S. Army, 1946-48. Mem. Minn. Bar Assn., Assn. Trial Lawyers Am., Minn. Trial Lawyers Assn., Nat. Bd. Trial Advocacy (diplomate), Acad. Cert. Trial Lawyers Minn. (bd. dirs., gen. counsel). Republican. Roman Catholic. Avocations: woodworking, golf. Federal civil litigation, State civil litigation, Personal injury. Home: 6668 Rustic Rd SE Prior Lake MN 55372 Office: Johnson & Utter 5200 Wilson Rd #407 Minneapolis MN 55424

JOHNSON, RICHARD WESLEY, lawyer; b. Stockton, Calif., Aug. 15, 1933; s. Ralph Wesley and Elizabeth Louise (Pucci) J.; m. Suzanne Marie Waldron, Feb. 18, 1962 (div. 1979); children: Scott Wesley, Elizabeth Nancye, Alexis Marie. JS, U. Calif., San Francisco, 1961. Bar: Calif. Assoc. Pillsbury, Madison & Sutro, San Francisco, 1961-65; sole practice A&J Publs., Walnut Creek, 1963—, ptnr., 1985—. Author: Express Your Love, 1986; editor-in-chief: Hastings Law Rev. Founding trustee J.F.K. Univ., Orinda, Calif., 1963-66, sec., dean of law, 1964-66. Served as pvt. U.S. Army, 1953-55. Mem. Calif. Bar Assn. (com. mem. 1972), Calif. Bar Assn., Mt. Diablo Bar Assn. (bd. dirs. 1974), Nat. Ski Patrol (patrol leader). Republican. Roman Catholic. Avocations: photography, sailing, poetry, songwriting. Criminal, Personal injury, Trial attorney. Office: 2224 A Oak Grove Rd Walnut Creek CA 94598

JOHNSON, ROBERT HENRY, lawyer; b. Denver, Aug. 16, 1916; s. Henry and Samantha Ellen (Haines) J.; m. Helen Marie Hamm, July 11, 1949; children: Susan M., Glen R., Leslie E. BA, U. Wyo., 1938, JD, 1963. Bar: Wyo. 1963, U.S. Dist. Ct. Wyo. 1963, U.S. Ct. Appeals (10th cir.) 1977. Editor, mgr. McCraken Newspaper Group, Wyo., 1938-41, 46-61; assoc. Galicich & Hamm, Rock Springs, Wyo., 1963-65; sole practice Rock Springs, 1965—; city atty. Rock Springs, 1973-79; dist. ct. commr. Sweetwater County, Wyo., 1980—; bd. dirs. Big Horn Basin Newspapers Inc., Worland, Wyo. Contbr. articles to profl. jours. Mem. Wyo. Senate, 1967-78, minority leader, 1977-78; del. Dem. Nat. Conv., 1972; trustee, v.p. Western Wyo. Coll. Found., Rock Springs, 1968—; chmn. Sweetwater County Library Bd., 1970-71, Wyo. Water Devel. Commn., 1979-81; mem. Sweetwater County Dem. Cen. Com., 1984-83, chmn., 1979-83; mem. Wyo. State Dem. Commn., 1966-79. Served to capt. AC, U.S. Army, 1941-45, ETO. Decorated D.F.C., Air Medal with four oak leaf clusters; named Hon. Mayor, City of Rock Springs, 1979. Mem. ABA, Wyo. State Bar Assn., Sweetwater County Bar Assn. (pres. 1985—), Assn. Trial Lawyers Am., Wyo. Trial Lawyers Assn., Wyo. Press Assn. (pres. 1960), U. Wyo. Alumni Assn. (pres. 1959), Am. Legion. Lodge: Elks. State civil litigation, General practice, Personal injury. Home: 1515 Albany Circle Rock Springs WY 82901 Office: 514 Broadway Rock SPrings WY 82901

JOHNSON, ROBERT HOWARD, lawyer; b. Kansas City, Mo., Feb. 17, 1943; s. Robert Melbourne and Margaret Buchanan (Ripley) J.; m. Bonnie Lee MacKenzie, Apr. 15, 1967 (div. Oct. 1968); m. Ann Katherine Williamson, Dec. 12, 1970; children: Katherine Anne (dec.), Jennifer Anne, Todd Robert. BA with distinction, U. Redlands, 1964; JD, NYU, 1967. Bar: N.Y. 1967, U.S. Dist. Ct. (so. and ea. dists.) N.Y. 1969, U.S. Ct. Appeals (2d cir.) 1969, Calif. 1971, U.S. Dist. Ct. (ea. dist.) Calif. 1971, U.S. Supreme Ct. 1971, U.S. Dist. Ct. (no. dist.) Calif. 1980, U.S. Ct. Appeals (9th cir.) 1981. Assoc. Donovan, Leisure et al, N.Y.C., 1967-69; adminstrv. asst. to majority leader Calif. State Assembly, Sacramento, 1969-71; trial atty. civil rights U.S. Dept. Justice, Washington, 1971-73; asst. U.S. atty. Dept. Justice, Sacramento, 1973-74; assoc. Memering et al, Sacramento, 1974-77, ptnr., 1977-81; ptnr. Johnson & Hoffman, Sacramento, 1981—. Del. intelligence Rockefeller Presdl. campaign, N.Y.C., 1968, candidate Bush Presdl. campaign, Sacramento, 1980; mem. Citizens Commn. Investigate Stockton State Hosp., Sacramento, 1976. Recipient Spl. Recognition award Calif. Assn. State Hosp. Patient Assns., 1976. Mem. ABA, Sacramento County Bar Assn., No. Calif. Assn. Def. Counsel. Presbyterian. Avocations: cross country skiing, fishing, music, theatre. Insurance, Federal civil litigation, State civil litigation. Home: 6161 Colgate Ct Sacramento CA 95831

JOHNSON, ROBERT KEITH, lawyer; b. Toluca, N.C., Dec. 2, 1953; s. Richard Paul and Guy Ann (Hull) J.; m. Dale Huffstetler, June 20, 1976. AB cum laude, Davidson Coll., 1976; JD, U. N.C., 1979. Bar: N.C. 1979, U.S. Dist. Ct. (we. dist.) N.C. 1979, U.S. Ct. Appeals (4th cir.) 1982, U.S. Dist. Ct. (ea. dist.) N.C. 1984, U.S. Dist. Ct. (mid. dist.) N.C. 1986. Law clk. to presiding justice U.S. Bankruptcy Ct., Charlotte, N.C., 1979-81; ptnr. Badger & Johnson P.A., Charlotte, 1981—. Mem. ABA, Nat. Assn. of Bankruptcy Trustees, N.C. Bar Assn., N.C. Acad. Trial Lawyers. Democrat. Bankruptcy, Real property. Home: 321 Northwest Dr Davidson NC 28036 Office: Badger & Johnson 701 E Trade St Suite 7 Charlotte NC 28202

JOHNSON, ROBERT R., lawyer; b. Eldorado, Ill., June 15, 1948; s. Eugene and Ruth Marie (Hensley) J.; m. Nancy Kay Myran, June 12, 1982. BA, Eastern Ill. U., 1970; JD, U. Minn., 1973. Bar: Minn. 1974. Assoc. Gross & Von Holtum, Mpls., 1974-76; atty. State of Minn., St. Paul, 1976-78; ptnr. Robert R. Johnson & Assocs., Mpls., 1978—. Bd. dirs. Nat. Handicapped Housing Inst., Mpls., 1979-82. Mem. ABA, Minn. Bar Assn., Minn. Trial Lawyers Assn. (sec. 1983-84, v.p. 1984-85, pres. 1985-86, Mem. of Yr.). Democrat. Baptist. Club: Apollo (Mpls.)(bd. dirs.). Lodges: Masons, Shriners. Personal injury, Workers' compensation. Office: 710 Cargill Bldg Northstar Ctr 625 Marquette Ave Minneapolis MN 55402-2385

JOHNSON, ROBERT STEVEN, lawyer; b. Ottumwa, Iowa, Apr. 6, 1947; s. Robert S. and C. Kathryn (Sullivan) J.; m. Janet Lanita Herbold, July 20, 1968; children: R. Scott, Stephanie H., Julie A. BS, Colo. State U., 1965; JD cum laude, Drake U., 1974. Bar: Iowa 1974, U.S. Dist. Ct. (no. and so. dists.) Iowa 1974. Asst. personnel supr. Green Giant Co., Glencoe, Minn., 1969-71; assoc. Wasker, Sullivan & Ward, Des Moines, 1974-77; sr. ptnr. Matthias, Tyler, Nuzum, Johnson & Matthias, Newton, Iowa, 1978—; magistrate Iowa Jud. Ct., 1980—. Mem. Iowa Bar Assn. (bd. dirs. young lawyers sect. 1982), Jasper County Bar Assn. (pres. 1985—), Assn. Trial Lawyers Am., Iowa Assn. Trial Lawyers, Izaak Walton League. Lutheran. Lodge: Elks. Real property, Public utilities, State civil litigation. Home: 2201 N 2d Ave E Newton IA 50208 Office: Matthias Tyler Nuzum Johnson & Matthias 112 N 2d Ave E Newton IA 50208

JOHNSON, ROBERT VEILING, II, lawyer; b. Laconia, N.H., Apr. 29, 1939; s. Robert Veiling and Pauline Leora (Roberts) J.; m. Sigrid Maria Ericsson, June 6, 1964; children: Celia Annah, Jared Veiling. BA, Boston U., 1961; diploma, Internat. Grad. Sch., 1963; MS, U. Stockholm, 1964; JD, Boston U., 1967. Bar: N.H. 1967, U.S. Dist. Ct. N.H. 1968, U.S. Ct. Appeals (1st cir.) 1971, U.S. Supreme Ct. 1974. Instr. Wilbraham-Monson Acad., Wilbraham, Mass., 1961-62; assoc. Upton, Sanders & Smith, Concord, N.H., 1967-71; asst. atty. gen. Chief of Criminal Div., State of N.H., Concord, 1971-77; chmn. Bd. of Tax and Land Appeals, State of N.H., Concord, 1977-82; sr. ptnr. Law Offices of Robert V. Johnson II, Concord, 1977—; bd. dirs. George C. Stafford & Sons, Inc., Laconia, N.H., Stafford Oil Co., Inc., Laconia, Stokes Architect, Inc. Laconia. Author: European Economic Community Law, 1964. Chmn. Concord Conservation Commn., 1971-84; bd. dirs. N.H. Assn. Conservation Commns., Concord, 1977-78; legal counsel Exec. Council, State of N.H., Concord, 1974. Am.-Scandinavian Found. fellow, Sweden, 1962; recipient leadership award Rotary Internat., Laconia, N.H., 1955. Mem. ABA, N.H. Trial Lawyers Assn., Assn. Trial Lawyers Am., Internat. Assn. Assessing Ofcls., Boston U. Alumni Assn. Republican. Congregationalist. General practice, State civil litigation, Federal civil litigation. Home: Oak Hill Rd RFD 13 Box 404 Concord NH 03301 Office: 64 N State St Concord NH 03301

JOHNSON, RONALD ADAMS, lawyer; b. New Orleans, Jan. 6, 1945; s. C. Gordon and Leone (Adams) J.; m. Cheryl Fouche, Apr. 15, 1978; 1 child, Julienne Fouche. BA, Tulane U., 1966, JD, 1969. Bar: La. 1969, U.S. Dist. Ct. (ea. dist.) La. 1969, U.S. Dist. Ct. (we. and mid. dists.) La., U.S. Dist. Ct. (ea. dist.) Tex., U.S. Cir. Ct. (5th and 11th cirs.). Assoc. Phelps, Dunbar, Marks, Claverie & Sims, New Orleans, 1969-74, ptnr., 1974-76; prin. Johnson & McAlpine, New Orleans, 1977—. Republican. Episcopalian. Clubs: Pass Christian (Miss.) Yacht, Pickwick, Stratford (New Orleans). Avocations: sports, fishing. Admiralty, Insurance, Federal civil litigation. Office: Johnson & McAlpine 701 S Peters St Suite 300 New Orleans LA 70130

JOHNSON, RUTH BRAMMER, lawyer; b. Traverse City, Mich., Feb. 6, 1955; d. Robert Christian and June Florence (Stromberg) Brammer; m. Jeffrey Thomas Johnson, Aug. 18, 1979; children: Kristen, Brian. BA, Albion Coll., 1977; JD, U. Mich., 1979. Bar: Colo., U.S. Ct. Appeals (10th cir.). Assoc. Davis, Graham & Stubbs, Denver, 1980-83; atty. Sohio Petroleum Co., Denver, 1983-85, Amoco Prodn. Co., Denver, 1985—. Oil and gas exploration and production, Environment, Administrative and regulatory. Home: 5950 E 6th Ave Denver CO 80220 Office: Amoco Prodn Co PO Box 800 Denver CO 80201

JOHNSON, SAM D., judge; b. Hubbard, Tex., Nov. 17, 1920; s. Sam D. and Flora (Brown) J.; m. June Page, June 1, 1946; children: Page Johnson Harris, Janet Johnson Clements, Sam. J. B.B.A., Baylor U., 1946; LL.B., U. Tex., 1949. Bar: Tex. bar 1949. Sole practice Hillsboro, Tex., 1949-53; county atty. Hill County, Tex., 1953-55; dist. atty. and dist. judge 66th Jud. Dist. of Hill County, Tex., 1955-65; judge 14th Ct. Civil Appeals, Houston, 1967-72; assoc. justice Supreme Ct. Tex., Austin, 1973-79; now judge U.S. Ct. of Appeals for 5th Circuit, 1979—; Bd. dirs. Houston Legal Found. 1965-67. Served with AUS, 1942-45. Recipient Disting. Alumnus award Baylor U., 1978-79. Mem. ABA (chmn. appellate judges conf. 1976-77, bd. govs. 1979-82), Am. Bar Found., Am. Judicature Soc., Tex. Bar Assn., Houston Bar Assn., Baylor Ex-Students Assn. (pres. 1972-73). Democrat. Jurisprudence. Office: US Court Appeals 999 MBank Tower 221 W 6th St Austin TX 78701

JOHNSON, SCOTT WARREN, lawyer; b. Houston, May 1, 1953; s. James W. and Marjorie D. (Parker) J. BS, Sul Ross State U., 1975; JD, Tex. Tech U., 1980. Bar: Tex. 1980, U.S. Dist. Ct. (we. dist.) Tex. 1983, U.S. Ct. Appeals (5th cir.) 1984. Staff atty. Tex. Ct. Appeals (8th cir.), El Paso, Tex., 1980-81, Tex. Dist. Ct. (we. dist.) Tex., Midland, Tex., 1981-83; atty. City of Pecos, Tex., 1983—, Reeves County, Pecos, 1984—. Mem. ABA, Tex. Bar Assn. Democrat. Baptist. State civil litigation, Government contracts and claims, General practice. Home: PO Box 2245 Pecos TX 79772 Office: PO Box 749 Pecos TX 79772

JOHNSON, SHEILA MARY, lawyer, consultant; b. Bridgeport, Conn., Jan. 9, 1949; d. Frank Otto and Aurora Cecelia (Cueto) Miller. AS in Nursing, Belleville Area Coll., 1968; AB, U. Mich., 1977; JD, U. Detroit, 1980. Bar: Mich. 1980, U.S. Dist. Ct. (ea. dist.) Mich. 1980, U.S. Ct. Appeals (6th cir.) 1984. Assoc. Sommers, Schwartz, Silver & Schwartz P.C., Southfield, Mich., 1980-84, Suidara, Rentrop, Martin & Morrison, Bloomfield Hills, Mich., 1984-85; ptnr. Johnson & Feldstein, Birmingham, Mich., 1985—; lectr. Am. Assn. Hosp. Adminstrs., Wayne County Med. Soc., Detroit; bd. dirs., legal consultant The Med. Team, Southfield. Active campaign re-elect Judge Jessica Cooper, Southfield, 1984, 86. Mem. ABA, Oakland County Bar Assn., Nat. Assn. Women Bus. Owners, Am. Bus. Women's Assn. (writer publ. local chpt.), Mich. Women Lawyers Assn., Mich. Profl. Women Network (writer publ.), Mich. Bar Assn. Avocations: bicycle touring, scuba diving. Personal injury. Office: Johnson & Feldstein 1760 S Telegraph Rd Suite 300 Bloomfield Hills MI 48013

JOHNSON, SHELLI WRIGHT, lawyer; b. LaPorte, Ind., Apr. 1, 1953; d. Burdette Baxter and Doris Dunfee (Childs) Wright; m. James Alan Johnson, May 22, 1980; children: Andrew James, Scott Robert, Jenna Marie. BS, Ball State U., 1975; JD, Valparaiso U., 1979. Bar: Ind. 1979, U.S. Dist. Ct. (no. and so. dists.) Ind. 1979. Tchr. lang. arts Coffee County Schs., Douglas, Ga., 1975-76; assoc. Law Offices of Larry W. Rogers, Portage, Ind., 1979-83, Harper & Rogers, Valparaiso, Ind., 1983-85, Law Offices of James A. Johnson, Portage, 1985—; ednl. cons. Discovery Toys. Mem. ABA, Ind. Bar Assn. (family and juvenile law sect., bankruptcy anf creditors rights sect.), Porter County Bar Assn., Profl. Womens Network, Women Lawyers Assn. Lake and Porter Counties, The Attys. Group, Northwest Ind. Archeol. Assn., Delta Theta Phi. Republican. Methodist. Family and matrimonial, Bankruptcy, Personal injury. Home: 651 Lorraine Dr Valparaiso IN 46383 Office: Law Offices of James A Johnson 3437 Airport Rd Portage IN 46368

JOHNSON, TERRY TURNER, lawyer; b. N.Y.C., May 5, 1957; s. Rolland Dale and Leanne Kay (Atkinson) J.; m. Susan Elizabeth Hodge, Dec. 29, 1979; children: Bonnie Elizabeth, Deborah Anne. AB, Stanford U., 1978; JD, U. Calif., Berkeley, 1981. Bar: Colo. 1981, U.S. Dist. Ct. Colo. 1981, U.S. Ct. Appeals (9th and 10th cirs.) 1984, Calif. 1985, U.S. Dist. Ct. (no. dist.) Calif. 1985. Assoc. Holland & Hart, Denver, 1981-85, Wilson, Sonsini, Goodrich & Rosati, Palo Alto, Calif., 1985—. Mem. ABA, Calif. Bar Assn., Santa Clara County Bar Assn. Federal civil litigation, State civil litigation, Securities. Home: 10804 Alderbrook Ln Cupertino CA 95014 Office: Wilson Sonsini Goodrich & Rosati 2 Palo Alto Sq Suite 900 Palo Alto CA 94306

JOHNSON, THEODORE MARVIN, JR., lawyer; b. Tacoma, May 26, 1947; s. Theodore M. and Gere Johnson; Ann E. Johnson; children: Theodore M. III, Rodger M. BA, U. Puget Sound, 1969; JD, Lewis and Clark U., 1973. Bar: Wash. 1973. Assoc. Muscek, Adams & Baker, Tacoma, 1973-78; atty. Pierce County, Tacoma, 1978-79; gen. counsel Pacific 1st Fed. Saving Bank, Tacoma, 1979—. Bd. dirs. Pantages Ctr., Tacoma, 1985. Mem. Wash. State Bar Assn. (fin. insts. subsect.). Episcopalian. Club: Tacoma Country. Avocation: golf. Banking. Office: Pacific First Fed Savs Bank 1145 Broadway Suite 1200 Tacoma WA 98402

JOHNSON, THOMAS STUART, lawyer; b. Rockford, Ill., May 21, 1942; s. Frederick C. and Pauline (Ross) J. BA, Rockford Coll. 1964; JD, Harvard U., 1967. Bar: Ill. 1967. Ptnr. Williams & McCarthy, Rockford, 1967—; bd. dirs. John S. Barnes Corp., Rockford, Odin Corp., Rockford. Contbr. articles to profl. jours. Chmn. bd. trustees Rockford Coll., 1986—; chmn. bd. dirs. Ill. Inst. Continuing Legal Edn., Chgo., 1984-86, Swedish Covenant Hosp., Chgo., 1984—, Emanuel Med. Ctr., Trulock, Ala., 1984—; treas. Lawyers Trust Fund of Ill., Chgo., 1984-86, Svenson Charitable Found., 1985—; mem. bd. govs., mem. council Regent's Coll., London, 1985—; bd. benevolence dir. Covenant Ch. Am., Chgo., 1984—; vice chmn. Svenson Charitable Found., 1984—; Served U.S. Army, 1965-67. Fellow Am. Bar Found.; mem. ABA (ho. dels. 1982—, chmn. commn. on advt. 1984—), Ill. Bar Assn. (bd. govs. 1976-82), Am. Judicature Soc. (bd. dirs. 1986—). Republican. Clubs: Rockford Country, University City Club of Rockford (Rockford). Estate planning, General corporate, General practice. Home: 913 N Main St Rockford IL 61103

JOHNSON, VINCENT ROBERT, law educator; b. Latrobe, Pa., Oct. 10, 1953; s. Harry Paul and Anna Ruth (Gozlick) J. BA, St. Vincent Coll., 1975; JD, U. Notre Dame, 1978; LLM, Yale U., 1979. Bar: Pa. 1978, U.S. Ct. Appeals (7th cir.) 1981, Tex. 1985, U.S. Supreme Ct. 1986. Law clerk Hon. Bernard S. Meyer, N.Y.C., Albany, N.Y., 1979-80, Hon. Thomas E. Fairchild, Chgo., 1980-82; asst. prof. St. Mary's U., San Antonio, 1982-85, assoc. prof., 1985—; arbitrator United Steel Workers, Am. Can Co., Houston, 1984—; lectr. Tex. Mun. Ct. Tng. Ctr., Austin, 1985—. Coauthor: Personal Injury: Actions, Defenses, Damages, 1985, 86, 87. Mem. ABA, State Bar Tex. (lawyer advt. com. 1985-86), Assn. Am. Law Schs. (chmn. teaching methods sect. 1985—), Phi Delta Phi (Teaching Excellence award 1986), Phi Alpha Delta (Disting. Service award 1984). Democrat. Roman Catholic. Legal education, Personal injury, Libel. Home: 8415 Fredericksburg Rd #503 San Antonio TX 78229 Office: St Marys U Sch Law One Camino Santa Maria San Antonio TX 78229

JOHNSON, WALTER FRANK, JR., lawyer; s. Georgiana, Ala., Apr. 14, 1945; s. Walter F. and Marjorie Ellen (Carnathan) J.; m. Emily Waldrep, Nov. 23, 1969; children—Brian W., Stacey E. B.S. in Bus. Adminstrn., Auburn U., 1968; J.D., Samford U., 1973. Bar: Ala. 1973, Ga. 1974. Assoc. Hatcher, Meyerson, Oxford and Irvin, Atlanta, 1973-74, Thompson and Redmond, Columbus, Ga., 1974-78; sole practice, Columbus, Ga., 1978—; asst. pub. defender, Columbus, 1978; acct. Union Camp Corp., 1968-70. Mem. ABA, Ala. State Bar, State Bar of Ga., Columbus Lawyers Club, Am. Coll. Mortgage Attys. Methodist. Real property, Bankruptcy, Probate. Home: 3235 Flint Dr Columbus GA 31907 Office: 3006 Cody Rd PO Box 6507 Columbus GA 31907

JOHNSON, WAYNE THOMPSON, JR., judge; b. Dothan, Ala., Apr. 5, 1950; s. Wayne Thompson and Blanche (Herring) J; m. Kathy Camille Woodward, Sept. 15, 1973 (divorced); children: Thomas Wayne, Jennifer Katherine. BS in Mktg., Auburn U., 1973; JD, U. Ala., 1976. Bar: Ala. 1976, U.S. Ct. Appeals (11th cir.) 1976. Ptnr. Faulk & Johnson, Phenix City, Ala., 1976-78; judge 26th Jud. Cir., Phenix City, 1978—; Assoc. faculty mem. Ala. Jud. Coll., 1980—; mem. jud. time standards com. Unified Jud. System, 1985—. Pres. Russell County Cancer Crusade, Phenix City, 1978. Named one of Outstanding Young Men of Am. U.S. Jaycees, 1980. Mem. ABA, Am. Judicature Soc., Nat. Conf. State Trial Judges, Ala. Bar Assn. (procedure com. 1985—), Ala. Congress Parents and Teachers. Democrat. Methodist. Lodge: Lions (v.p., bd. dirs. Phenix City club 1984-85). Avocations: golf, reading, woodworking. Office: Russell County Courthouse PO Box 368 Phenix City AL 36868

JOHNSON, WILLIAM ASHTON, lawyer; b. St. Louis, June 26, 1933; s. William Stuart and Adele (Balmer) J.; m. Anne Chartrand, Nov. 11, 1961; children: Mark, Anthony, Jocelyn, Jennifer. BA, St. Louis U., 1955, JD,

1957; postdoctoral, Northwestern U., 1969. Bar: Mo. 1957. Asst. sec. Mercantile Bank NA, St. Louis, 1969-73, asst. trust officer, 1973-76, trust officer, 1976-78, asst. v.p., 1978-83, v.p., 1983—. Author St. Louis U. Law Rev., 1971. Served with U.S. Army, 1957-59. Mem. Alpha Sigma Nu. Democrat. Roman Catholic. Banking, Municipal bonds, Securities. Home: 4732 Prague Ave Saint Louis MO 63109 Office: Mercantile Bank NA One Mercantile Ctr Saint Louis MO 63101

JOHNSON, WILLIAM R., state judge. Judge N.H. Supreme Ct., Concord, 1986—. Office: Supreme Ct Bldg Concord NH 03301 *

JOHNSON, WILLIAM VINCENT, lawyer; b. Owensboro, Ky., Jan. 7, 1940; s. James J. and Martha E. (Kerrick) J.; m. Diane Donovan, 1963; children: Laura, Mark, Kristen, Matthew. BS, Marquette U., 1962; JD, Ill. Inst. Tech., 1966. Bar: Ill. 1966, U.S. Dist. Ct. (no. dist.) Ill. 1967. Assoc. Frank Glazer, Chgo., 1966-68, Pretzel & Stouffer, Chgo., 1968-69; ptnr. Udoni & Johnson, Chgo., 1970-75, Steinberg, Burtker & Johnson, Chgo., 1975, Johnson, Cusack & Bell, Chgo., 1975—. Fellow Am. Coll. Trial Lawyers; mem. ABA, Ill. Bar Assn., Chgo. Bar Assn., Soc. of Trial Lawyers (v.p.), Fedn. Ins. and Corp. Counsel, Trial Lawyers Club of Chgo. Democrat. Roman Catholic. Personal injury. Office: Johnson Cusack & Bell Ltd 211 W Wacker Dr Chicago IL 60606

JOHNSON-CHAMP, DEBRA SUE, legal librarian, educator; b. Emporia, Kans., Nov. 8, 1955; d. Bert John and S. Christine (Brigman) Johnson; m. Michael W. Champ, Nov. 23, 1979; children—Natalie, John. B.A., U. Denver, 1977; J.D., Pepperdine U., 1980; postgrad. in library sci. U. So. Calif., 1983—. Bar: Calif. 1981. Sole practice, Long Beach, Calif., 1981-82, Los Angeles, 1981—; legal reference librarian, instr. Southwestern U. Sch. Law, Los Angeles, 1982—. Editor-in-chief: Southern Calif. Assn. Law Libraries Newsletter, 1984-85. Contbr. articles to profl. journs. Mem. law rev. Pepperdine U., 1978-80. West Pub. Co. scholar, 1983; trustee United Meth. Ch., Tujunga, Calif., 1986—. Recipient H. Wayne Gillis Moot Ct. award, 1980, Vincent S. Dalsimer Best Brief award, 1979. Mem. ABA, So. Calif. Assn. Law Libraries, Am. Assn. Law Libraries, Calif. Bar Assn., Southwestern Affiliates, Friends of the Library Los Angeles. Democrat. Librarianship, Legal education, Personal injury. Home: 8258 Wentworth St Sunland CA 91040 Office: Southwestern Univ Sch of Law 675 S Westmoreland Ave Los Angeles CA 90005

JOHNSTON, A. SIDNEY, lawyer, physicist; b. Hinton, W.Va., Apr. 4, 1937; s. Duncan McNeer and Julia (Altizer) J.; m. Julia M. Toohill, Apr. 2, 1977; children: Laura, Caroline. BS in Physics, Va. Poly. Inst. and State U., 1959; MS in Physics, Carnegie Mellon U., 1961, PhD, 1965; postgrad., U. Calif., Davis, 1972-73; JD, Ill. Inst. Tech., 1978. Bar: Ill. 1978, U.S. Dist. Ct. (no. dist.) 1978, U.S. Supreme Ct. 1982, U.S. Ct. Appeals (fed. cir.) 1986. Sr. scientist Westinghouse Corp., Pitts., 1965-68; asst. prof. Pratt Inst., Bklyn., 1968-72; nuclear medicine staff mem. Michael Reese Hosp., Chgo., 1973-80; assoc. Keil and Witherspoon, Chgo., 1978-82; patent atty. Bell Telephone Labs., Holmdel, N.J., 1982-84, Square D Co., Palatine, Ill., 1984—; sole practice Palatine, 1978—; asst. prof. U. Chgo., 1974-80. Author: Physics Laboratory Manual, 1970; contbr. articles to profl. jours. Mem. Health Physics Soc., Patent Law Assn. Chgo., Chgo. Bar Assn., Am. Physics Soc. Patent, Personal injury, Trademark and copyright. Home: 951 N Stark Palatine IL 60067 Office: Square D Co Executive Plaza Palatine IL 60067

JOHNSTON, CHARLES MOTLEY, lawyer; b. Coral Gables, Fla., May 5, 1951; s. Charles Motley and Mary Virginia (DeTardo) J.; m. Barbara Christie, Sept. 2, 1978; 1 child, David Townshend. Student, Stetson U., 1969-71; BA, U. Fla., 1975, JD, 1978. Bar: Fla. 1978, U.S. Dist. Ct. (mid. dist.) Fla. 1982, U.S. Dist. Ct. (no. dist.) Fla. 1985, U.S. Ct. Appeals (11th cir.) 1984, U.S. Supreme Ct. 1985. Asst. pub. defender 4th Jud. Cir., Jacksonville, Fla., 1978-82; law clk. to presiding justice U.S. Dist. Ct. (mid. dist.) Fla., Jacksonville, 1982-83; assoc. Taylor, Day, & Rio, Jacksonville, 1983-86, ptnr., 1986—. Mem. ABA, Jacksonville Bar Assn., Fed. Bar Assn., Fla. Def. Lawyers Assn. Federal civil litigation, State civil litigation, Personal injury. Home: 1726 Challen Ave Jacksonville FL 32205 Office: Taylor Day Rio & Mercier 121 W Forsyth St 10th Floor Jacksonville FL 32202

JOHNSTON, DAVID FREDERICK, lawyer; b. Tiffin, Ohio, Sept. 9, 1943; s. Frederick Walter and Aleta Marguerite (Ruehle) J.; m. Ona Lee Graham, June 18, 1966; children—Matthew, Rebecca, Elisabeth, Benjamin. B.A. in Chemistry, Oreg. State U., 1965; J.D., Golden Gate U., 1971. Bar: Calif. 1972, Oreg. 1973, U.S. Ct. Mil. Appeals 1974, U.S. Supreme Ct. 1983. Commd. officer U.S. Coast Guard, 1965; sea duty U.S. Coast Guard Cutter Magnolia, 1966-67; staff atty. U.S. Coast Guard, 1971-79; dept. chief U.S. Coast Guard Marine Safety Office, Norfolk, Va., 1979-82; appeal decision supr. U.S. Coast Guard Hdqrs., Washington, 1982-85, sole practice, 1985—. Author: Suspension and Revocation of Mariner's Licenses, Certificates and Documents, 1984. Elder Presbyn. Ch., Green Acres Ch., Portsmouth, Va., 1979, Multnomah Ch., Portland, Oreg., 1986; com. chmn. Clermont Sch., Fairfax County, Va., 1983. Mem. Oreg. State Bar, Phi Kappa Phi, Phi Lamdba Upsilon. Presbyterian. Administrative and regulatory, Admiralty. Home and Office: 0550 SW Palatine Hill Rd Portland OR 97219

JOHNSTON, DAVID GRAHAM, accountant, lawyer; b. Pitts., Apr. 22, 1954; s. Allan Howard and Elaine (Graham) J.; m. Emily Kate Hightower, May 22, 1982; 1 child, Peter Worth. BS, Emory U., 1976, JD, 1979. Bar: Ga. 1979; CPA, N.C. Ptnr. Stephens & Johnston, Atlanta, 1979-80; tax specialist A.M. Pullen & Co., Atlanta, 1981-82, Greensboro, N.C., 1982-83; tax mgr. Seidman & Seidman, Greensboro, 1983-86, sr. tax mgr., 1986—. Mem. ABA, Ga. Bar Assn., Am. Inst. CPAs, N.C. Assn. CPAs. Methodist. Corporate taxation, Estate taxation, Personal income taxation. Home: 209 S Tremont Dr Greensboro NC 27403 Office: Seidman & Seidman 101 W Friendly Ave Suite 300 Greensboro NC 27401

JOHNSTON, DONALD ROBERT, lawyer; b. Duluth, Minn., Apr. 20, 1926. B.S., U. Minn., 1949, J.D., 1957. Bar: Minn. 1957, U.S. Dist. Ct. Minn. 1957, U.S. Supreme Ct. 1964. Corp. credit mgr. Honeywell Inc., Mpls., 1960-63; city atty. City of Two Harbors (Minn.), 1958-59; mem. Wagner, Johnston & Flaconer, Ltd., and predecessors, Mpls., 1963—; lectr. continuing legal edn. gen. extension div. U. Minn., 1968-71 , program chmn., 1976 ; guest lectr. Nat. Assn. Credit Mgmt., 1974, 79—. Mem. ABA, Minn. Bar. Assn., Comml. Law League Am. Bankruptcy, Contracts commercial, Consumer commercial. Office: 2650 IDS Center 80 S 8th St Minneapolis MN 55402

JOHNSTON, FABER LAINE, JR., lawyer; b. San Jose, Calif., June 25, 1927; s. Faber Laine Sr. and Ilma (Koch) J.; m. Dorynda Wine, June 23, 1956; children: Faber, Dorinda, Amy, Timothy, Jennifer, Elizabeth. JD, Santa Clara U., 1950. Bar: Calif. 1951, U.S. Dist. Ct. (no. dist.) Calif. 1951, U.S. Ct. Appeals (9th cir.) 1951. Assoc. Campbell, Hayes & Custer, San Jose, 1951-55; ptnr. Johnston & Johnston, San Jose, 1955-60; sr. ptnr. Johnston, Miller & Giannini, San Jose, 1960-; atty. City of Saratoga, Calif., 1956-82, City of Scotts Valley, Calif., 1965-82; lectr. continuing edn. of bar U. Calif., 1975-. Author: The Soviet Judicial System, 1983, The Judicial System on China, 1985. Served to lt. (j.g.) USN, 1944-46. Republican. Roman Catholic. State civil litigation, Local government, Real property. Office: Johnston Miller & Giannini 84 W Santa Clara #800 San Jose CA 95113

JOHNSTON, HARRY MELVILLE, III, lawyer; b. Houston, Jan. 22, 1945; s. Harry M. II and Lanetta (McDaniel) J.; m. Ruth D. Goldstein, Nov. 22, 1970. AB, Columbia U., 1965; JD, NYU, 1968, LLM, 1971. Bar: N.Y. 1969. Staff atty. United Welfare League OEO, N.Y.C., 1968-70; staff atty. Time Inc., N.Y.C., 1970—, gen. counsel, 1981—, gen. counsel mag. group, 1981—; adj. lectr. pub. law Pace U., N.Y.C., 1985—. Mem. editorial adv. bd. Media Law Reporter, 1978—. Chmn. Libel Def. Resource Ctr., 1981—. Mem. ABA, Assn. of Bar of City of N.Y., Mag. Pubs. Assn. (legal affairs com. 1981—), Assn. Am. Pubs. (freedom to read com. 1978—), Copyright Soc. of USA (trustee 1986—). Entertainment, Libel, Trademark and copyright. Home: 16 Hudson St New York NY 10013 Office: Time Inc 1271 Ave of the Americas New York NY 10020

JOHNSTON, HENRY RICHARD, III, lawyer; b. West Reading, Pa., Jan. 24, 1954; s. Henry Richard II and E. Jean (Fisher) J.; m. Frances Waugh Cook, Aug. 11, 1979; 1 child, Henry Richard IV. AB in Econs., Boston U., 1976; JD, U. Pitts., 1979. Bar: Pa. 1979, U.S. Dist. Ct. (we. dist.) Pa. 1979. Assoc. Costello & O'Toole, North Versailles, Pa., 1980-81; law clk. to presiding judge Superior Ct. Pa., Pitts., 1981-84; assoc. Anderson, Moreland & Bush, Pitts., 1984-85, Springer, Bush & Perry P.C., Pitts., 1985—. Bd. dirs. Nat. Youth Sports Coaches Assn. of Pa. Mem. Pa. Bar Assn., Allegheny County Bar Assn. Episcopalian. Personal income taxation, Pension, profit-sharing, and employee benefits, Probate. Home: 457 Salem Dr Pittsburgh PA 15243 Office: Springer Bush & Perry PC 2300 301 Fifth Ave Bldg Pittsburgh PA 15222

JOHNSTON, LORENE GAYLE, lawyer; b. Wellston, Ohio, Jan. 15, 1952; d. Joseph Lewis and Gladys Leona (Bocook) J. BS, Miami U., Oxford, Ohio, 1974; MA in Polit. Sci., Ohio U., 1978; JD, U. Dayton, 1982. Bar: Ohio 1982. Tchr. Gallia County Local Shs., Vinton, Ohio, 1974-79; sole practice Wellston, 1982—. Councilman City of Wellston, 1977; committeewomen 10th Dist. Rep. State Com., Columbus, Ohio, 1978-82. Mem. ABA, Ohio Bar Assn., Jackson County Bar Assn. (pres. 1986, v.p. 1985, sec. 1984, treas. 1982), Phi Alpha Delta. Roman Catholic. Lodge: Order Eastern Star. General practice, Consumer commercial, Banking. Home: 424 W Broadway Wellston OH 45692 Office: 111 S Ohio Ave Wellston OH 45692

JOHNSTON, RONALD ALLEN, lawyer; b. Vancouver, Wash., Oct. 23, 1950; s. Don E. and Marjorie J. (Blank) J.; m. Deborah M. Riolo, Aug. 3, 1973; 1 child, Christopher. BA in Polit. Sci. with honors, Pacific U., 1972; JD, Cath. U. Am., 1976. Bar: Oreg. 1976, U.S. Dist. Ct. Oreg. 1976, U.S. Ct. Appeals (9th cir.) 1976. Assoc. Shannon & Johnson, Portland, 1977-81, McCormick & Reynolds, Portland, 1981-84; ptnr. Reynolds & Johnston, Portland, 1984—. Legal advisor Father's PAC, Portland, 1985—. Mem. ABA (family law sect.), Oreg. Bar Assn. (family law sect.), Multnomah County Bar Assn. Avocations: boating, fishing. Family and matrimonial, State civil litigation, Consumer commercial. Office: Ronald Allen Johnston & Assocs 1500 SW 1st #630 Portland OR 97201

JOHNSTON, SHEPHERD DAVIS, lawyer; b. Miami, Fla., Sept. 17, 1947; s. Thomas McE. and Lorine (Davis) J.; m. Muriel Everton, Oct. 7, 1972 (div. 1982). BA, Davidson (N.C.) Coll., 1969; JD, U. Fla., 1972. Bar: Fla. 1972, U.S. Dist. Ct. (so. dist.) Fla. 1973, U.S. Ct. Appeals (5th cir.) 1974. Legis. aide Gov. Robert Graham, Fla., 1971; assoc. Smathers & Thompson, Miami, 1972-80; gen. counsel Pan Am. Banks, Miami, 1981-85; exec. v.p., chief operating officer Sunbelt Investment Holdings Inc, Delray Beach, Fla., 1986-87, pres., 1987—. Served to capt. USAR, 1969-75. Mem. ABA, Fla. Bar (exec. council, corp. banking and bus. law sect. 1982-86), Corp. Counsel Assn. So. Fla. (bd. dirs. 1983-86, v.p. 1985-86). Democrat. Presbyterian. Avocations: sailing, scuba, tennis. Real property, Banking, Contracts commercial. Home: 3160 Mary St Miami FL 33133 Office: Sunbelt Investment Holdings Inc 220 Congress Park Dr Delray Beach FL 33445

JOHNSTON, WILLIAM DAVID, lawyer; b. Aberdeen, Md., Jan. 31, 1957; s. David Irvine and Nancy (Smith) J.; m. Mary Teresa Miller, May 29, 1983; 1 child, Ellen Christine. AB, Colgate U., 1979; JD, Washington and Lee U., 1982. Bar: Del. 1982, U.S. Dist. Ct. Del. 1983. Judicial law clk. to chief justice Daniel L. Herrmann Del. Supreme Ct., Wilmington, 1982-83; assoc. Potter, Anderson and Corroon, Wilmington, 1983-85, Young, Conaway, Stargatt and Taylor, Wilmington, 1985—. Contbr. articles to profl. jours. Mem. choir, adminstrv. bd. Aldersgate United Meth. Ch., Wilmington, 1970—; com. chmn. Boy Scouts of U.S. troop 67, 1982-85. Best Brief Worldwide award Am. Soc. Internat. Law, Washington, 1980. Mem. ABA, Am. Trial Lawyers Assn., Am. Judicature Soc., Del. State Bar Assn., Del. Trial Lawyers Assn., Sigma Chi (pres. Colgate U. chpt. 1984—). Methodist. Clubs: Univ. and Whist, Rodney Square (Wilmington). Avocations: running, raquetball, reading, travel. General corporate, State civil litigation, Federal civil litigation. Office: Young Conaway Stargatt and Taylor Rodney Sq N PO Box 391 Wilmington DE 19899-0391

JOHNSTONE, DEBBI MERRIMAN, lawyer; b. Indpls., Jan. 26, 1956. BA in Polit. Sci., Northwestern U., 1977; JD, Ind. U., 1980. Bar: Ind. 1980, U.S. Dist. Ct. (so. dist.) Ind. 1980, Tex. 1982, U.S. Dist. Ct. (so. dist.) Tex. 1982. Law clk. to presiding justice Ind. Ct. Appeals, Indpls., 1980-81; assoc. Wood, Lucksinger & Epstein, Houston, 1982—. Contbr. articles to profl. jours. Mem. ABA, Houston Bar Assn., Houston Young Lawyers Assn., Nat. Health Lawyers Assn., Phi Alpha Delta. Health, Administrative and regulatory, General corporate. Office: Wood Lucksinger & Epstein 1221 Lamar Suite 1400 Houston TX 77010

JOHNSTONE, EDWARD H., judge; b. 1922. J.D., U. Ky., 1949. Bar: Ky. Ptnr. firm Johnstone, Edlred & Paxton, Princeton, Ky., 1949-76; judge 56th Circuit Ct. Ky, 1976-77, U.S. Dist. Ct. (we. dist.) Ky., 1977—. Mem. ABA, Ky. Bar Assn. Judicial administration. Office: US Courthouse 219 Federal Bldg Paducah KY 42001 *

JOHNSTONE, IRVINE BLAKELEY, III, lawyer; b. Newark, Dec. 21, 1948; s. Irvine Blakeley Jr. and Ruth (Morton) J.; m. Phyllis Nevins, Oct. 16, 1983. BA with honors, Lehigh U., 1972; JD, Duke U., 1975. Bar: N.J. 1975, U.S. Dist. Ct. N.J. 1975, U.S. Ct. Appeals (3d cir.) 1979, N.Y. 1981. Assoc. Riker, Danzig, Scherer & De bevoise, Newark, 1975-76, Shanley & Fisher, Newark, 1976-80; ptnr. Johnstone, Skok, Loughlin & Lane, Westfield, N.J., 1980—. Mem. bd. of govs. Blair Acad., 1978-84; atty. Rahway Lifers Group (N.J.) State Prison, 1980-85, Planning Bd., Clark, N.J., 1981-82, Bd. of Adjustment, Clark, 1982-84. Mem. ABA, N.J. Bar Assn., Union County Bar Assn., Def. Research Inst. Republican. Presbyterian. Club: Baltisrol (Springfield, N.J.). Avocations: flying, golf, sports. Personal injury, State civil litigation, Family and matrimonial. Home: 349 Bartles Rd Lebanon NJ 08833

JOHNSTONE, JEFFREY MARWILL, lawyer; b. N.Y.C., July 10, 1945; s. Douglas E. and Maxine L. (Krohn) J.; m. Martha A. Turner, June 17, 1967; children: David R., Martha A. AB, Colgate U., 1967; MA, Georgetown U., 1969; JD, Cornell U., 1974. Bar: N.Y. 1975, U.S. Dist. Ct. (no. dist.) N.Y. 1975, U.S. Tax Ct. 1980, Fla. 1982, U.S. Ct. Appeals (2d cir.) 1984. Assoc. Nixon, Hargrave, Devans & Doyle, Rochester, N.Y., 1974-79, Goldstein, Goldman, Kessler & Underberg, Rochester, 1979-82; sole practice Rochester, 1982-84; ptnr. Johnstone & Sheldon P.C., Rochester, 1984-86, Lane, Johnstone, Sheldon & Neild, P.C., Rochester, 1987—. Editor Cornell Law Rev. Mem. Brighton (N.Y.) Planning Bd., 1985—; dist. leader Brighton Rep. Town and Country Com., 1986—. Served to lt. USNR, 1970-71. Mem. ABA, N.Y. State Bar Assn. (tax sect.), Monroe County Bar Assn. (chmn. tax sect. 1984-86), Phi Beta Kappa. Republican. Presbyterian. Lodge: Rotary (bd. dirs. 1986—). Avocation: Russian. Corporate taxation, Personal income taxation, General corporate. Office: Lane Johnstone Sheldon & Neild PC 144 Exchange Blvd Rochester NY 14614

JOHNTZ, JOHN HOFFMAN, JR., lawyer; b. Alva, Okla., Apr. 26, 1937; s. John H. and Veenetia E. (Burchfiel) J.; m. Linda B. Dover, June 9, 1962; children—John H., Jason Dover. B.A., Harvard U., 1959; J.D., U. Kans., 1965. Bar: Kans. 1965, U.S. Supreme Ct. 1971. Ptnr. Payne & Jones, P.C., Overland Park, Kans., 1965—; mem. family law adv. com. Kans. Jud. Council; mem. Kans. Bd. Admission of Attys.; speaker domestic relations law. Pres. Kans. Arts Commn. Served to lt. (j.g.) USN, 1959-61. Fellow Am. Acad. Matrimonial Lawyers; mem. Johnson County Bar Assn., Kans. Bar Assn., ABA, Phi Delta Phi (grad. of year 1965), Phi Beta Kappa. Co-author: Tax Aspects of Litigation; contbr. articles to profl. jours.; bd. editors Kans. Bar Jour. Real property. Home: 4424 W 84th St Shawnee Mission KS 66207 Office: Commerce Terr Bldg C 11000 King PO Box 25625 Overland Park KS 66225-5625

JOIKE, TREVOR B., lawyer; b. Evergreen Park, Ill., Sept. 17, 1943; s. Fritz William and Barbara Ann (Dilts) J.; m. Rebecca Ann Upchurch, Feb. 13, 1965; children: Michele Kathleen, Trevor William. BSEE, U. Ill., 1966; JD, Am. U., 1970. Bar: Minn. 1970, U.S. Dist. Ct. Minn. 1970. Atty. Honeywell Inc., Mpls., 1970-85, asst. corp. patent counsel, 1985-87; chief patent counsel Sundstrand Corp., Rockford, Ill., 1987—. Commr. Burnsville Athletic Commn., Minn., 1983-85; mem. Ad Hoc Sch. Dist. Com., Burnsville, 1984. Mem. ABA, Am. Intellectual Property Law Assn., Minn. Intellectual Property Law Assn. Patent, Computer, Personal injury.

JOLLEY, WILLIAM A., lawyer; b. Springfield, Mo., June 11, 1939; s. Cecil B. and Veronica I. (Rotty) J.; m. Betty A. Whelan, Aug. 25, 1962; children: Diane, David, Mary Beth, Karen. BA, Cardinal Glennon Coll., 1960; LLB, St. Louis U., 1963. Bar: Mo. 1963, U.S. Dist. Ct. (ea. and we. dists.) Mo. 1963, U.S. Ct. Appeals (8th cir.) 1963, U.S. Supreme Ct. 1963. Assoc. Bond & Dominique, Jefferson City, Mo., 1963-64; atty. NLRB, Kansas City, 1964-68; ptnr. Jolley & Walsh and predecessor firms, Kansas City, 1968—; lectr. labor U. Extension, Mo., 1969-74; bd. dirs. World Market Perspective, 1985—. Recipient 1st Prize Essay award Ins. Inst. of Am., 1963. Mem. ABA (labor com.), Mo. Bar Assn. (past co-chmn. labor law sect.), Kansas City Bar Assn. (past co-chmn. labor com.). Democrat. Roman Catholic. Labor. Home: 101 W 115th St Kansas City MO 64106 Office: Jolley & Walsh 1125 Grand Kansas City MO 64106

JOLLY, CHARLES NELSON, pharmaceutical company executive, lawyer; b. New Brunswick, N.J., Aug. 14, 1942; s. Nelson Frederick and Marie Mercedes (Montemayor) J.; m. Katherine Bonita Phelan, June 4, 1966; children—T. Christopher, Susan Noel. B.S., Holy Cross Coll., 1964; LL.B., George Washington U., 1967. Bar: D.C. 1968, Tenn. 1984. Atty. Swift & Co., 1966-70; atty. Miles Labs., 1970-71, dir. legis. affairs, Washington, 1971-75, assoc. gen. counsel, Elkhart, Ind., 1975-77; bd. dirs., v.p. legal affairs Chattem Inc., Chattanooga. Mem. ABA, Tenn. and D.C. Bar Assn., Proprietary Assn. (dir.), Better Bus. Bur. of Chattanooga (vice chmn., bd. dirs.). Clubs: The Narrows (McConnelsburg, Pa.), Chattanooga Retriever (dir.). General corporate, Administrative and regulatory, Health. Office: 1715 W 38th St Chattanooga TN 37409

JOLLY, E. GRADY, federal judge. Judge U.S. Ct. Appeals (5th cir.). Judicial administration. Office: US Court Appeals PO Drawer 2368 Jackson MS 39205 *

JOLLY, RAYMOND A., JR., lawyer; b. Anderson, S.C., Feb. 23, 1936; s. Raymond Alonzo and Quinton Elizabeth (Lassiter) J.; m. Kimm Howard, Aug. 21, 1960; children: Carole Lynn, Christopher Howard, David Lassiter. BA in English, U. N.C., 1958, JD, 1961. Bar: N.C. 1961. Asst. staff judge adv. gen. USAF, Denver, 1961-64; assoc. Firm, Ruff, Perry, Bond, Cobb & Wade, Charlotte, N.C., 1964-67; ptnr. Firm, Ruff, Perry, Bond, Cobb & Wade, Charlotte, 1968-70, Hedrick, McKnight, Parham, Helms, Warley & Jolly, Charlotte, 1971-72; asst. gen. counsel Duke Power Co., Charlotte, 1972-74, assoc. gen. counsel, 1974—; p.t. instr. real estate law Cen. Piedmont Community Coll., Charlotte, 1970-72. Pres. Family and Children's Service, Charlotte, 1979. Served to capt. USAF, 1961-64. Mem. Mecklenburg County Bar Assn. (sec., treas. 1970-71). Episcopalian. Club: Olde Providence Racquet and Swim (Charlotte) (sec. 1983-84). Lodge: Civitan (pres. of council Charlotte chpt. 1969-70). Contracts commercial, Public utilities, Real property. Office: Duke Power Co 422 S Church St PO Box 33189 Charlotte NC 28242

JOLLY, THOMAS R., lawyer; b. Albany, N.Y., Aug. 29, 1943; s. Hubert George and Helen Mary (Dunham) J.; m. Beth Hardwick, Nov. 24, 1984. BA, U. Mich., 1968; JD, Georgetown U., 1972. Bar: Mich. 1972, D.C. 1975, U.S. Supreme Ct. 1976. Legis. asst. to congressman William D. Ford U.S. Ho. of Reps., Washington, 1970-73, counsel com. edn. and labor, 1973-78; ptnr. O'Connor & Hannan, Washington, 1978—; bd. dirs. Am. League Lobbyists, Washington. Served with USAF, 1961-65. Mem. ABA, Mich. Bar Assn., D.C. Bar Assn. Club: University (Washington). Legislative. Home: 7908 Burdette Rd Bethesda MD 20817 Office: O'Connor & Hannan 1919 Pennsylvania Ave #800 NW Washington DC 20006

JONES, AIDAN DREXEL, lawyer; b. Wilmington, Del., Dec. 17, 1945; s. Richard Leonard and Dorothy Drexel (Walsh) J.; m. Kathleen Dellert, Aug. 19, 1972; 4 children. BA, Wesleyan U., 1967; JD, Georgetown U., 1974. Bar: D.C. 1975, U.S. Supreme Ct. 1984. Law clk. U.S. Dist. Ct., Washington, 1974-75; assoc. Edward Greensfelder Jr. P.C., Washington, 1975-77, Haight, Gardner, Poor & Havens, Washington, 1977-83; ptnr. Finley, Kumble, Wagner, Heine, Underberg, Manley, Myerson & Casey, Washington, 1983—. Contbr. articles to profl. jours. Sch. com. Wesleyan U., Middletown, Conn., 1975—, 1967 class agent. 1985—. Served to lt. USN, 1968-71, Vietnam. Mem. ABA (vice chmn. aviation and space law com. 1985—). Federal civil litigation, Administrative and regulatory, Private international. Home: 4612 Brandywine St NW Washington DC 20016 Office: Finley Kumble Wagner et al 1120 Connecticut Ave NW Washington DC 20036

JONES, ALBERT PEARSON, lawyer, former educator; b. Dallas, July 19, 1907; s. Bush and Ethel (Hatton) J.; m. Annette Lewis, Oct. 3, 1936; children—Dan Pearson, Lewis Avery. B.A., U. Tex.-Austin, M.A., 1927, LL.B., 1930. Bar: Tex. 1930, U.S. Ct. Appeals (5th cir.) 1935, U.S. Supreme Ct. 1950. Assoc. Baker & Botts, Houston, 1930-43; ptnr. Helm & Jones, 1943-62; Joseph C. Hutcheson prof. law U. Tex.-Austin, 1962-77; adj. prof. law U. Houston, 1981; 1st asst. atty. gen. Tex., 1963. Editor-in-chief Tex. Law Rev., 1929-30; pres. Tex. Law Rev. Publs., 1971-74; co-author: Texas Trial and Appellate Procedure, 1974, The Judicial Process in Texas Prior to Trial, 2d edit., Cases and Materials on Employees' Rights, 1970; contbr. articles to profl. jours. Fellow Am. Coll. Trial Lawyers; mem. State Bar Tex. (pres. 1950-51), Houston Bar Assn., Am. Law Inst. (life), Am. Judicature Soc., Phi Beta Kappa, Order Coif, Phi Delta Phi. Democrat. Episcopalian. Clubs: Houston Country. Lodge: Masons. Legal education, Workers' compensation, Personal injury. Home: 3195 Del Monte St Houston TX 77019 Office: 2700 America Tower 2929 Allen Pkwy Houston TX 77019

JONES, ALEXANDER GRAY, lawyer; b. Princess Anne, Md., Mar. 25, 1927; s. Edgar Alexander and Sally Waterman (Gray) J.; m. Catherine Margaret McGoohan, July 1, 1952; children: Kathleen G., Peyton A., Patrick G., Karen F. BA, Washington Coll., 1951, LLD (hon.), 1986; JD, U. Md., 1955. Bar: Md. 1955, U.S. Dist. Ct. Md. 1957, U.S. Supreme Ct. 1966. Ptnr., pres. Jones & Jones, P.A. and predecessor firm Jones & Jones, Princess Anne, 1955-85, Jones & Bruce, P.A., Princess Anne, 1986—; gen. counsel Penisula Bank, Md., 1972—, bd. dirs.; mem. standing com. on rules of practice and procedure, Md. Ct. Appeals, 1969—. Bd. visitors and govs. Washington Coll., Chestertown, Md., 1967—; active various charitable and ednl. orgns., Md., 1956—. Served with U.S. Army, 1945-47. Fulbright scholar U. Sheffield, 1951-52. Fellow Am. Coll. Trial Lawyers, Md. Bar Found.; mem. ABA, Md. Bar Assn. (bd. govs. 1967-68, 74-75), Somerset County Bar Assn. Democrat. Avocations: family activities, salt water fishing. Probate, Real property. Home: Linden Ave PO Box 186 Princess Anne MD 21853-0186 Office: Jones & Bruce PA 311 S Somerset Ave Princess Anne MD 21853-0567

JONES, ANNA BELLE, lawyer; b. Mercer, Pa., Feb. 2, 1924; d. G. Wesley and Ethel Margaret (Anderson) Kelso; m. William N. Jones, Oct. 12, 1946; 1 child, James K. BS in Commerce, Grove City Coll. Assoc. Stranahan and Stranahan, Mercer, 1965-79; ptnr. Jones-McConnell, P.C., Mercer, 1979—. Mem. Pa. Bar Assn., Mercer County Bar Assn. General practice. Home: 237 W Market St Mercer PA 16137 Office: PO Box 579 Mercer PA 16137

JONES, BARRY KENT, lawyer; b. San Diego, Feb. 1, 1955; s. Kenneth Manton and Elizabeth C. (Blackmon) J.; m. S. Gale Graham, 1978 (div. 1984); 1 child, Graham Ellis. BS, U. So. Miss., 1975; JD, Emory U., 1978, LLM in Taxation, 1980. Bar: Ga. 1978, U.S. Dist. Ct. (no. dist.) Ga. 1978, U.S. Dist. Ct. (mid. dist.) Ga. 1980, U.S. Ct. Appeals (5th and 6th cirs.) 1980, Tenn. 1982, U.S. Tax Ct. 1982, U.S. Dist. Ct. (ea. dist.) Tenn. 1983, Miss. 1986. Law clk. office gen. counsel HEW, Atlanta, 1976-78; atty. office gen. counsel HHS, Atlanta, 1978-80; sr. tax acct. Joseph Decosimo & Co., CPA, Chattanooga, 1980-82; atty. tax div. Weill, Ellis, Weems & Copeland, Chattanooga, 1982-84; sr. tax cons. Ernst & Whinney, Chattanooga, 1984-86; atty. tax div. Dossett, Dossett & Goode, Jackson, Miss., 1986—; judge mock trial competition Miss. State Bar, Jackson, 1987—; bd. dirs. WCJU, Inc., Columbia, Miss., The Broadcasting Co., Columbia. Author: Post-Mortem Disclaimers: Less Can Be More, 1987. Mem. ABA, Ga. Bar Assn., Tenn. Bar Assn., Chatanooga Bar Assn., Chatanooga Tax Practitioners, Miss. Bar Assn., Phi Delta Phi, Lamda Iota Tau, Pi Gamma Mu, Phi Alpha

Theta, Sigma Nu. Republican. Episcopalian. Avocations: tennis, sailing. Estate planning, Estate taxation, Pension, profit-sharing, and employee benefits. Home: PO Box 405 Jackson MS 39205-0405 Office: Dossett Dossett & Goode 202 N Congress Suite 500 PO Box 2449 Jackson MS 39225-2449

JONES, BILLY RAY, lawyer; b. Amarillo, Tex., Apr. 29, 1954; s. Roy George and Marie (Bailey) J.; m. Lou Hedrick, Dec. 18, 1982. B.B.A., Baylor U., 1976, J.D., 1977. Bar: Tex. 1977, U.S. Dist. Ct. (no. dist.) Tex. 1980, U.S. Ct. Appeals (11th cir.) 1982, U.S. Ct. Appeals (5th cir.) 1983. Assoc. firm Crouch & McClain, Dallas, 1977-79, Shannon, Gracey, Ratliff & Miller, Ft. Worth, 1979-81; ptnr. Crouch & Jones, Dallas, 1981-83, Boyd, Veigel & Hance, Dallas, 1984—; dir. First Richardson Bancshares, Inc., First Nat. Bank Richardson Tex., First Nat. Bank, Richardson, Lincoln Nat. Bank. Mem. Dallas County Republican Assembly. Mem. ABA, State Bar Tex., Dallas Bar Assn., Tex. Assn. Bank Counsel, Am. Judicature Soc. Baptist. Clubs: Towne, University (Dallas); Ft. Worth. Banking. Home: 6215 LaVista Dallas TX 75214

JONES, BONNIE DEE DURHAM, lawyer, consultant; b. Ansted, W.Va., Oct. 5, 1935; d. Edmond Terrink and Fern Catherine (McCleary) Roetman; m. Edward Allen Durham, Oct. 1, 1960 (div. 1976); 1 child, Mark Allen Durham; m. Roger Rittenhouse Jones, Dec. 19, 1981. BS in Sociology and Criminal Justice, U. Nebr., 1973; JD, Creighton U., 1976. Bar: Nebr. 1976, N.C. 1983, U.S. Dist. Ct. Nebr. 1976, U.S. Dist. Ct. (mid. dist.) N.C. 1984, U.S. Supreme Ct. 1983. Law clk., probation officer 4th Jud. Dist. Probation Dept., Omaha, 1973-75; law clk., felony prosecutor Douglas County Atty. Hall of Justice, Omaha, 1975-76; law clk., bailiff 4th Jud. Dist. Ct. State of Nebr., 1976-77; asst. city prosecutor City of Omaha Legal Dept., 1977-82; sole practice Winston-Salem, N.C., 1983—; assoc. Womble, Carlyle, Sandridge & Rice, Winston-Salem, 1984—. Mem. ABA, N.C. Bar Assn. (practical tng. com.), Nebr. State Bar Assn., Forsyth County Bar Assn., Forsyth County Criminal Bar Assn. (past v.p.), N.C. Assn. Women Attys. (past legis. chmn.), Forsyth County Women Attys. Assn., Nat. Dist. Attys. Assn., Assn. Trial Lawyers Am., N.C. Acad. Trial Lawyers, Am. Assn. Univ. Women, N.C. Mothers in Prison Program, N.C. Vol. Lawyers Program (pro bono atty.), Alpha Phi Sigma. Republican. Lutheran. Criminal, General corporate, State civil litigation. Home: 7022 Brandemere Ln-H Winston-Salem NC 27106 Office: Womble Carlyle Sandridge & Rice 301 N Main St 2400 Wachovia Winston-Salem NC 27101

JONES, BRADLEY MITCHELL, lawyer; b. Mankato, Minn., Oct. 11, 1952; s. John Hayden and Charlotte Lorraine (Mitchell) J.; m. Cheryl Ann Dilly, Aug. 9, 1975; children: Suzanne Louise, Richard Hayden. BA, Mankato State U., 1974; JD, Seton Hall U., 1978. Bar: Minn. 1978, U.S. Ct. Appeals (8th cir.) 1979, N.D. 1984, Wis. 1985, U.S. Dist. Ct. Minn. 1978, U.S. Supreme Ct. 1982, U.S. Dist. Ct. N.D. 1984, U.S. Dist. Ct. (ea. and we. dist.) Wis. 1985, U.S. Ct. Appeals (7th cir.) 1985. Assoc. Meagher, Geer, Markham, Anderson, Adamson, Flaskamp & Brennan, Mpls., 1978-84, ptnr., 1984—. Mem. ABA (tort and Ins. section), Minn. State Bar Assn., N.D. State Bar Assn., Wis. State Bar Assn., Hennepin county Bar Assn. Insurance, Federal civil litigation, State civil litigation. Home: 9557 Xylon Ave S Bloomington MN 55438 Office: Meagher Geer et al 4200 Multifoods Tower 33 S 6th St Minneapolis MN 55402

JONES, BRADLEY TYLER, lawyer; b. Vermillion, S.D., June 24, 1917; s. Robert W. and Alice (Tyler) J.; m. Phyllis Howard, June 24, 1941; children: Carolyn, Tyler, Robert. BA, U. Wash., 1939, LLB, 1941. Bar: Wash. 1941, D.C. 1941, U.S. Ct. Appeals (9th cir.) 1946, U.S. Supreme Ct. 1968. Lawyer Falknor, Emory & Howe, Seattle, 1941, 45-48; officer Pictsweet Foods, Mt. Vernon, Wash., 1948-56; ptnr. Davis Wright & Jones, Seattle, 1956—; trustee U. Wash. Law Sch. Found., Seattle, 1979—; trustee Wash. State Bar Found. 1981-84. Served to maj. inf. U.S. Army, 1941-45, PTO. Fellow Am. Bar Found.; mem. Wash. State Bar Assn. (pres. 1980-81), Seattle-King City Bar Assn. (pres. 1970-71). Episcopalian. Club: Rainier (Seattle) (sec. 1983-84). Contracts commercial, Real property. Home: 25853 W Canyon Rd NW Poulsbo WA 98370 Office: Davis Wright & Jones 2600 Century Sq 1501 Fourth Ave Seattle WA 98101

JONES, BRADLEY WAYNE, lawyer; b. Endicott, N.Y., Feb. 9, 1955; s. Robert Lionel and Lilian Mary (Collacott) J.; m. Adele Catherine Barbagallo; children: Victoria Lilian, Brandon Michael. BA in Internat. Relations, Syracuse U., 1977, JD, 1979. Bar: N.Y. 1980, U.S. Dist. Ct. (no. dist.) N.Y. 1980, U.S. Ct. Appeals (D.C. cir.) 1982, Ga. 1985. Lectr. Ark. Sch. of Law, Fayetteville, 1979-80; staff atty. U.S. Nuclear Regulatory Commn., Washington, 1980-82; regional counsel region II U.S. Nuclear Regulatory Commn., Atlanta, 1982-87; legal asst. to the chmn. U.S. Nuclear Regulatory Commn., Washington, 1987—. Mgr. campaing com. to elect Rod Burak as County Legislator, Endicott, 1976. Mem. ABA, N.Y. State Bar Assn., Ga. Bar Assn. Democrat. Roman Catholic. Avocations: church activities, computers, porcelain collecting. Administrative and regulatory, Nuclear power, Public international. Home: 1111 Meurilee Ln Silver Spring MD 20901 Office: US Nuclear Regulatory Commn Washington DC 20555

JONES, C. PAUL, lawyer; b. Grand Forks, N.D., Jan. 7, 1927; s. Walter M. and Sophie J. (Thorton) J.; m. Helen M. Fredel, Sept. 7, 1957; children—Katherine, Sara H. B.B.A., U. Minn., 1950, J.D., 1950; LL.M., William Mitchell Coll. of Law, 1955. Assoc. Lewis, Hammer, Heaney, Weyl & Halverson, Duluth, Minn., 1950-51; asst., chief dep. Hennepin County Atty., Mpls., 1952-58; asst. U.S. atty. U.S. Atty's. Office, St. Paul, 1959-60; assoc. Maun & Hazel, St. Paul, 1960-61; ptnr. Dorfman, Rudquist, Jones, & Ramstead, Mpls., 1961-65; state pub. defender Minn. State Pub. Defender's Office, Mpls., 1966—; prof. law William Mitchell Coll. of Law, St. Paul, 1970—; adj. prof. U. Minn., Mpls., 1970—;. Author: Criminal Procedure from Police Detention to Final Disposition, 1981; Jones on Minnesota Criminal Procedure, 1955, 64, 70, 75; Minnesota Police Law Manual, 1955, 67, 70, 76. Mem. Minn. Gov.'s Crime Commn., St. Paul, 1970s, Minn. Fair Trial-Free Press Assn., Mpls., 1970s, Citizens League, Mpls., 1955—, Mpls. Aquatennial Assn., Mpls., 1955-60. Recipient Reginald Heber Smith award Nat. Legal Aid and Defender Assn., 1969. Fellow Am. Coll. Trial Lawyers; mem. Am. Bd. Trial Advs., ABA, Minn. State Bar Assn., Hennepin County Bar Assn., Ramsey County Bar Assn., Nat. Legal Aid & Defender Assn. Democrat. Lutheran. Clubs: Suburban Gyro of Mpls., Mpls. Athletic. Lodge: Rotary. Avocations: fishing; hunting; golfing; desert watching. Criminal. Home: 4617 Edina Blvd Edina MN 55424 Office: Minn State Pub Defender Univ Minn Law Sch Minneapolis MN 55455

JONES, CHARLES ROBERT, lawyer, army officer; b. Sculthorpe AFB, Frankenham, Eng., July 20, 1955; came to U.S., 1955; s. Robert Frank Jones and Margery Elizabeth (Gibson) Occhionero; m. Claudia Jean Donelson, May 8, 1976; children: Jonathan Charles, Jennifer Joy. Student, U. Miami, 1973-74, Case Western Res. U., 1975; BA, Cameron U., 1978; JD, Ohio State U., 1981. Bar: Ohio 1981. Commd. U.S. Army, 1975, advanced through grades to capt., 1981; trial counsel U.S. Army, Ft. Eustis, Va., 1982-83, chief of criminal law, 1983-84; def. counsel U.S. Army, Ft. Wainwright, Alaska, 1984—; instr. Tanana Valley Community Coll., Fairbanks, Alaska, 1985—. Republican. Avocations: camping, traveling. Military, Criminal. Home: 1027-5 Chestnut St Fort Wainwright AK 99703 Office: Trial Def Service Office of the Post Judge Advocate Fort Wainwright AK 99703

JONES, CLIFFORD AARON, lawyer, international businessman; b. Long Lane, Mo., Feb. 19, 1912; s. Burley Monroe and Arlie (Benton) J.; widowed, 1975; m. Christina Wagner, Dec. 24, 1978. LL.B., U. Mo., 1938, J.D., 1969. Bar: Nev. 1938, U.S. Dist. Ct. Nev. 1939, D.C. 1982, U.S. Ct. Appeals (9th and D.C. cirs.) 1983, U.S. Supreme Ct. 1983. Founder, sr. partner firm Jones, Jones, Close & Brown, Las Vegas, Nev., 1938—; majority leader Nev. Legislature, 1941-42; judge 8th Jud. Dist., Nev., 1945-46; lt. gov., State of Nev., 1947-54; owner, builder, chmn. bd. Thunderbird Hotel, Inc., Las Vegas, 1948-64; founder Valley Bank of Nev., 1953; founder, sec., dir. First Western Savs. and Loan Assn., 1954-66; pres., chmn. bd. Caribbean-Am. Investment Co., Inc., 1960-78; pres., dir. Income Investments, Inc., 1963-65; sr. v.p., dir. First Western Fin. Corp., 1963-66; dir., past pres. Baker & Hazard, 1966—; dir. Barrington Industries, Inc., 1966-70, Internat. Commodities Exchange, 1973—; chmn. bd., pres. Central African Land and Cattle Co., 1974-76. Mem. Clark County (Nev.) Democratic Central Com., 1940—, chmn., 1948; nat. committeeman from Nev. Dem. Party, 1954; mem. Nev. Dem. State Central Com., 1945-60; 4 time del. Dem. Nat. Conv. Served as lt. col. F.A. U.S. Army, 1942-46, ETO. Mem. ABA (past mem. tax sect.), Am. Coll. Probate Counsel, Nev. Bar Assn., D.C. Bar Assn., Am. Legion, V.F.W., Phi Delta Phi, Kappa Sigma. Clubs: United Nations Lions (Las Vegas), Elks (Las Vegas), Lions (Las Vegas) (past pres.). General corporate, Private international, Probate. Office: Jones Jones Close & Brown 300 S 4th St Valley Bank Plaza Suite 700 Las Vegas NV 89101

JONES, CRAIG WARD, lawyer; b. Pitts., June 14, 1947; s. Curtis Edison and Margaret (McFarland) J. BA, Carleton Coll., 1969; JD, U. Pitts., 1976. Bar: Pa. 1976, U.S. Dist. Ct. (we. dist.) Pa. 1976, U.S. Ct. Appeals (3d cir.) 1981. Ptnr. Reed, Smith, Shaw & McClay, Pitts., 1976—. Served to lt. USNR, 1969-73. Mem. Allegheny County Bar Assn. Presbyterian. Federal civil litigation, State civil litigation. Home: 201 Virginia Ave Pittsburgh PA 15215 Office: Reed Smith Shaw & McClay 435 6th Ave Pittsburgh PA 15219

JONES, DAVID ARTHUR, law and public administration educator, lawyer, author, consultant; b. Concord, N.H., Aug. 22, 1946; s. Arthur Leonard and Pearl (Tabor) J.; m. Catherine Mary Mita, Sept. 18, 1971; 4 children. A.B. in History, Clark U., 1968; J.D., Union U., Albany, N.Y., 1971; Ph.D. in Criminal Justice, SUNY-Albany, 1975. Bar: Mass. 1972, N.Y. 1972, D.C. 1976, Pa. 1979, U.S. Dist. Ct. (no. dist.) N.Y. 1972, U.S. Dist. Ct. (we. dist.) N.Y. 1973, U.S. Dist. Ct. Mass. 1975, U.S. Dist. Ct. D.C. 1976, U.S. Dist. Ct. (we. dist.) Pa. 1978, U.S. Ct. Claims 1976, U.S. Ct. Internat. Trade 1980, U.S. Tax Ct. 1976, U.S. Ct. Custom and Patent Appeals 1976, U.S. Ct. Mil. Appeals 1976, U.S. Ct. Appeals (1st and 2d cirs.) 1975, U.S. Ct. Appeals (D.C. cir.) 1976, U.S Ct. Appeals (5th, 8th and 9th cirs.) 1978, U.S. Ct. Appeals (4th, 7th, and 10th cirs.) 1979, U.S. Ct. Appeals (3d and 6th cirs.) 1980, U.S. Ct. Appeals (11th and fed. cirs.) 1982, U.S. Supreme Ct. 1975. Staff atty. N.H. Gov.'s Commn. on Crime and Delinquency, Concord, 1971; asst. prof. sociology U. Tenn., 1972-73; asst. prof. criminal justice SUNY-Buffalo, 1973-75; dep. dir. Inst. Criminal Law and Procedure, Georgetown U. Law Ctr., 1975-76; asst. prof. law and justice U. Pitts., 1977-79, assoc. prof., 1979-81, prof., 1981—, prof. sociology Faculty Arts and Scis., 1981—; sole practice, 1972-81; chmn. Crime, Inc.; adj. prof. criminal justice Am. U., 1975-76; cons. to nat. insts., city and state bodies; mem. comml. panel Am. Arbitration Assn., 1980—; host Talking Law, Sta-WTKN, Pitts., 1981; mem. Pa. Commn. on Sentencing, 1981-86. Served with Army ROTC, 1966. Recipient Eagle Scout with silver palm award Boy Scouts Am. 1960; N.Y. State Office Crime Control planning fellow, 1971-72; CHOICE Acad. Book of Year award, 1983. Mem. Am. Soc. Polit. and Legal Philosophy, Am. Soc. Legal History, Am. Soc. Criminology, Am. Mgmt. Assn., Boston Bar Assn., Internat. Soc. Criminology, Selden Soc., Assn. Trial Lawyers Am., Am. Judicature Soc., Nat. Rifle Assn. (life), AFTRA, Phi Kappa Phi, Delta Tau Kappa. Republican. Author books, the most recent being: Crime Without Punishment, 1979; The Law of Criminal Procedure: An Analysis and Critique, 1981; The Law of Marriage and Marital Alternatives, 1982, History of Criminology: A Philosophical Perspective, 1986. Legal education, Criminal, Family and matrimonial. Office: 435 Cathedral of Learning U Pitts Pittsburgh PA 15260

JONES, DAVID CHRISTOPHER, lawyer; b. Springfield, Mo., June 15, 1953; s. Ralph and Mary Elizabeth (Helton) J.; m. Ginger T. Wagner, Feb. 23, 1986. AB, Albright Coll., 1975; JD, Del. Law Sch., 1978. Bar: Pa. 1978, Mo. 1984, U.S. Dist. Ct. (mid. dist.) Pa. 1979, U.S. Dist. Ct. (we. dist.) Mo. 1982, U.S. Ct. Appeals (3d cir.) 1979, U.S. Ct. Appeals (8th cirs.) 1982. Asst. dist. atty. City of Phila., 1978-79; asst. U.S. atty. U.S. Dept. Justice, Lewisburg, Pa., 1979-81, Springfield, Mo., 1981—; legal adv. counsel Drury Coll. Springfield, 1983—. Avocations: photography, traveling. Criminal, Personal income taxation, Federal civil litigation. Home: Box 452 Springfield MO 65801 Office: US Attys Office US Courthouse Room 227 870 Boonville Springfield MO 65801

JONES, DAVID L., lawyer, educator; b. Elkton, Md., Sept. 19, 1947; s. Alvin and Amelia (Carr) J. Student, U.S. Mcht. Marine Acad., 1965-66, Lincoln U., 1968-70; B.A. cum laude, U. Evansville, 1972; J.D., Ind. U., 1976. Bar: Ind. 1976, U.S. Dist. Ct. (so. dist.) Ind. 1976, U.S. Ct. Appeals (7th cir.) 1983. Securities examiner Ind. Sec. State, Indpls., 1972-73; bail commr. Mcpl. Cts., Indpls., 1973-76; ct. commr. Vanderburgh Cir. Ct., Evansville, Ind., 1976-77; county council atty. Vanderburgh County, Ind., 1978-86 ; ptnr. Jones & Wallace, Evansville, 1986—; formerly ptnr. Frick & Powell, Evansville; formerly assoc. and ptnr. Bowers, Harrison, Kent & Miller, Evansville; atty. Venderburgh County, 1981-86; instr. Am. Inst. Banking, U. Evansville, 1979-85. Atty. Evansville-Vanderburgh Visitors and Conv. Commn., Evansville, 1978-80; Bd. dirs. Wish Upon a Star Inc., 1985-86; mem. Evansville YMCA. Served with USNR, 1965-66, USMC, 1966-68, Vietnam. Recipient Inter-faith Inter-race award B'nai Brith, 1970, Densmore award Ind. Fedn. for Blind, 1986; named one of Outstanding Young Men in Am., 1973, Boss of Yr. Evansville Legal Secretaries, 1986-87. Mem. ABA, Ind. Bar Assn., Evansville Bar Assn., Nat. Assn. R.R. Trial Counsel, Ind. Def. Lawyers Assn., Def. Research Inst., Barristers Soc., Nat. Fedn. for Blind. Democrat. Mem. United Ch. of Christ. Clubs: U. Evansville Tip-Off (bd. dirs. 1984-85), Long Distance Runners, Petroleum. Federal civil litigation, Insurance, State civil litigation. Home: 1873 Pueblo Pass Evansville IN 47715 Office: Jones & Wallace One Riverfront Pl Suite 202 PO Box 1065 Evansville IN 47706

JONES, DAVID MATTERN, lawyer; b. Altoona, Pa., May 22, 1934; s. Benjamin Charles and Kathleen (Stover) J.; m. Sondra Neuman, Sept. 11, 1983. AB, Princeton U., 1956; LLB, U. Pa., 1962. Bar: Pa. 1962, U.S. Supreme Ct. 1970, D.C. 1980. Assoc. MacCoy, Evans & Lewis, Phila., 1962-64, Clark, Ladner et al, Phila., 1964-72; ptnr. Pierson, Jones et al, Phila., 1972-81, Jones & Stepanuk, Phila., 1981—. Served to capt. USMC, 1954-68. Mem. ABA, Pa. Bar Assn., Phila. Bar Assn., Union League. Republican. Mem. Unitarian Ch. Club: Army/Navy (Washington); Princeton (N.Y.). Private international, Probate. Office: Jones & Stepanuk 1314 Chestnut St SUite 1000 Philadelphia PA 19107

JONES, DAVID STANLEY, lawyer; b. Columbus, Ohio, July 16, 1948; s. Herbert Morton and Gertrude Olivia (McKeon) J.; m. Mary Elizabeth Lyman, July 8, 1972; children—Colin David, Brian Christopher, Scott Lyman. B.B.A., U. Notre Dame, 1970; J.D., U. Houston, 1976. Bar: Tex. 1976, U.S. Dist. Ct. (no. dist.) Tex. 1979, (ea. and we. dists.) Tex. 1980, U.S. Ct. Appeals (5th and 11th cirs.) 1981, U.S. Supreme Ct. 1983. Assoc. counsel Campbell Taggart, Inc., Dallas, 1976-78; trial atty. U.S. Dept. Labor, Dallas, 1978-80, assoc. Gresham, Davis et al, San Antonio, 1980-83; ptnr. Baldwin, Gilliland & Jones, Dallas, 1984—. Editor U. Houston Law Rev., 1975. Mem. State Bar Assn. Tex. (labor law specialist Tex. Bd. Legal Specialization, 1981, author and editor Tex. Practice Guide 1983), ABA (contbr. labor law sect. ann. report 1981-82, 84-86), Fed. Bar Assn. Dallas (treas. 1985-86, v.p. 1986-87), Tex. Young Lawyers Assn., Dallas Bar Assn., Phi Delta Phi. Roman Catholic. Labor, Federal civil litigation, State civil litigation. Home: 3321 Norcross Ln Dallas TX 75229 Office: Baldwin Gilliland & Jones 750 Two Energy Sq 4849 Greenville Ave Dallas TX 75206

JONES, DONALD RICHARD, III, lawyer; b. Atlanta, Feb. 28, 1952; s. D. R. and Martha Jane (Davis) J.; m. Elizabeth W. Jones, July 30, 1983; 1 child, D. Richard IV. BA, U. Va., 1974; postgrad., U. Birmingham, Stratford, Eng., 1974; JD, Emory U., 1978. Ptnr. Jones & Jones, Atlanta, 1978—. Sec. Ga. Dressage and Combined Tng. Assn., Atlanta, 1982-85, sec., 1986; sec. Young Riders Team, Atlanta, 1983—, vol. Interfaith Vol. Lawyers, Atlanta, 1984-86. Mem. Sandy Springs Bar Assn. (sec.), Assn. Trial Lawyers Am., Ga. Trial Lawyers Assn., Lawyers Club Atlanta. Republican. Methodist. Avocation: horse showing. State civil litigation, Estate planning, Sales of business. Home: 735 Mabry Rd Atlanta GA 30328 Office: 180 Allen Rd Suite 205 S Bldg Atlanta GA 30328

JONES, DWAIN LEON, lawyer; b. Lincoln, Nebr., Jan. 4, 1927; s. Paul Jones and E. Fern (Pardee) Schroeder; m. Jacqueline True, Nov. 27, 1946; children: Annette, Nancy, Randal. BA, Wesleyan U., Lincoln, Nebr., 1950; JD, U. Nebr., 1958. Bar: Nebr. 1958, Ohio 1966, Ill. 1969. Atty. Bankers Life Ins. Co., Lincoln, 1958-60; asst. atty. gen. State of Nebr., Lincoln, 1960-62; gen. counsel Western Life Ins. Co., St. Paul, 1962-66; sr. counsel Western-Southern Life Ins. Co., Cin., 1966-69; sr. v.p., gen. counsel Benefit Trust Life Ins. Co., Chgo., 1969—, also bd. dirs.; v.p., bd. dirs. Real and Personal Holdings, Chgo., 1982—, Nat. Mktg. Service, Malvern, Pa., 1983—, Star Mktg. and Adminstrn. Co., Park Ridge, Ill., 1985—; sr. v.p., bd. dirs. Trustmark Life Ins. Co., Chgo., 1985—. Served with USNR, 1950-53. Mem. ABA, Ill. Bar Assn., Chgo. Bar Assn., Assn. Life Ins. Counsel. Republican. Episcopalian. Club: Waukegan (Ill.) Yacht (bd. dirs. 1983—). Avocations: boating, cabinetmaking. Insurance. Home: 38901 Gilbert Ave Zion IL 60099 Office: Benefit Trust Life Ins Co 1771 Howard St Chicago IL 60626

JONES, E. STEWART, JR., lawyer; b. Troy, N.Y., Dec. 4, 1941; s. E. Stewart and Louise (Farley) J.; m. Constance M., Dec. 28, 1968; children: Christopher, Brady, Erin. BA, Williams Coll., 1963; JD, Albany Law Sch., 1966. Bar: N.Y. 1966, U.S. Dist. Ct. (no. dist.) N.Y. 1966, U.S. Supreme Ct. 1970, U.S. Ct. Appeals (2d cir.) 1976, U.S. Dist. Ct. (we. dist.) N.Y. 1987; cert. specialist in civil and criminal trial advocacy. Asst. dist. atty. Rensselaer County (N.Y.), 1968-70, spl. prosecutor, 1974; ptnr. E. Stewart Jones, Troy, N.Y., 1974—; lectr. in field; mem. com. on profl. standards of 3d jud. dept. State of N.Y., 1977-80; mem. merit selection panel for selection and appointment of U.S. magistrate for No. Dist. N.Y., 1981; bd. dirs., trustee Troy Savs. Bank. Contbr. numerous articles to profl. jours. Served with USNG, 1966-72. Fellow Am. Bar Found., Am. Bd. Criminal Trial Lawyers Am. Coll. Trial Lawyers, Roscoe Pound Assn.; mem. N.Y. State Bar Assn. (Outstanding Practitioner award 1980, mem. continuing edn. com. 1977-78, mem. exec. com. of criminal justice sect. 1977—, mem. exec. com. trial lawyers sect. 1981—, mem. spl. com. med. malpractice, other coms.), N.Y. State Trial Lawyers Assn. (dir. 1982—, co-chmn. com. on med. jurisprudence 1973-74, vice chmn. com. criminal law and procedure 1974-76, co-chmn. criminal law sect. 1978), Capital Dist. Trial Lawyers Assn. (dir. 1973-76), ABA (numerous coms.) Calif. Attys. for Criminal Justice, Practising Law Inst., Am. Judicature Soc. (sustaining), Rensselaer County Bar Assn., Am. Soc. Law and Medicine, ACLU, N.Y. Civil Liberties Union, Lawyer to Lawyer Consultation (panel), Albany County Bar Assn., N.Y. State Defenders Assn., Nat. Orgn. for Reform of Marijuana Laws, Am. Arbitration Assn., Fed. Bar Council, Upstate Trial Attys. Assn., Inc. Clubs: Schuyler Meadows, Troy Country, Troy, Steuben Athletic, Fort Orange, Wychmere Harbor; Stone Horse Yacht (Harwich Port, Mass.); Equinox Country (Manchester, Vt.). Personal injury, Federal civil litigation, Criminal. Home: 46 Schuyler Rd Loudonville NY 12211 Office: 28 2d St Troy NY 12181

JONES, EDGAR ALLAN, JR., educator, arbitrator, lawyer; b. Bklyn., Jan. 8, 1921; s. Edgar Allan and Isabel (Morris) J.; m. Helen Callaghan, Sept. 15, 1945; children: Linda Marie, Anne Marie, Carol Marie, Edgar Allan III, Denis James, Robert Morris, David Llewellyn, Therese Marie, Catherine Marie, Nancy Marie, Daniel Anthony. BA, Wesleyan U., 1942; LLB, U. Va., 1950. Bar: Va. bar 1948. Faculty U. Calif. at Los Angeles Law Sch., 1951—, prof. law, 1958—, asst. dean, 1957-58; dir. Law-Sci. Research Center, 1963-66; labor dispute arbitrator, mediator, fact finder for pvt. and pub. employers and unions 1953—. Appeared as judge: network TV programs Accused, 1958-59, Traffic Ct, 1958-61, Day in Court, 1958-64; moderator: ednl. TV program Forum West, 1966; contbr. numerous labor law, arbitration and polygraph articles to law revs.; editor: Law and Electronics: The Challenge of a New Era, 1960; founding editor: Va. Law Weekly, 1948-50, NAA Chronicle, 1977-78. Pres. Creddalt Research, Inc., 1959—; dir. Deauville Restaurant, Inc. (Jimmy's); Pub. mem. Calif. Commn. Manpower Automation and Tech., 1963-67, Calif. Manpower Adv. Com., 1964-67; nat. enforcement commr. WSB, 1951; Sec. Californians for Kennedy, 1960. Served to 1st lt. USMCR, 1942-45. Mem. Nat. Acad. Arbitrators (pres. 1980-81), ABA, Va. State Bar, AFTRA. Legal education. Office: U Calif at Los Angeles Law Sch 405 Hilgard Ave Los Angeles CA 90024

JONES, EDGAR WAGSTAFF, lawyer; b. Bellevoe, Ky., Mar. 6, 1908; s. Harry Ross and Madeline (Pocock) J.; m. Christine Oby (dec. May 1981); 1 child, Edgar W. Jr. AB, Yale U., 1929; JD, Harvard U., 1932. Bar: Ohio 1933, U.S. Dist. Ct. (no. dist.) Ohio 1934, U.S. Supreme Ct. 1947, U.S. Ct. Claims 1950. Ptnr. Hart & McHenry, Canton, Ohio, 1933-40, Amerman & Mills, Canton, 1940-50, Amerman & McHenry, Canton, 1950-57; prin. Amerman, Burt & Jones Co., L.P.A., Canton, 1957—. Trustee Aultman Hosp., Canton, 1937-81. Served to lt. USN, 1943-46, ETO. Mem. ABA (50 yr. award 1986), Ohio Bar Assn., Am. Acad. Hosp. Attys. Republican. Episcopalian. Clubs: Canton (pres. 1952-53), Brookside Country (Canton). Health, Insurance, Probate. Home: 1603 S Main St Apt B North Canton OH 44709 Office: Amerman Burt & Jones Co LPA 624 N Market Ave Canton OH 44702

JONES, EDITH HOLLAN, judge; b. Phila., Apr. 7, 1949; d. O. Roger and Edith (Lingle) Hollan; m. Sherwood O. Jones, Dec. 27, 1973; children—Andrew and David. B.A., Cornell U., 1971; J.D. with honors, U. Tex., 1974. Bar: Tex. 1974, U.S. Supreme Ct. 1979, U.S. Ct. Appeals (5th and 11th cirs.), U.S. Dist. Ct. (so. and no. dists.) Tex. Assoc. Andrews & Kurth, Houston, 1974-82, ptnr., 1982—; judge U.S. Ct. Appeals (5th cir.),1985—. Gen. counsel Republican Party of Tex., 1981-83. Mem. ABA, State Bar Tex. Presbyterian. Bankruptcy, Federal civil litigation, State civil litigation. Office: US Court Appeals 8631 US Courthouse 515 Rusk Ave Houston TX 77002 *

JONES, EDWARD WHITE, II, lawyer; b. Phila., Jan. 21, 1921; s. Clifford Buckman and Alice Robinson (McKinly) J.; m. Martha Elizabeth Calhoun, Oct. 7, 1950; children: Clifford B. II, Elisabeth J. Baker. BA, Wesleyan U., Middletown, Conn., 1943; JD, U. Pa., 1949. Bar: Pa. 1950. Law clk. to presiding justice Orphan's Ct., Phila., 1949-50; assoc. Rawlet Henderson, Phila., 1950-52; trust officer Phila. Nat. Bank, Phila. and Montgomery, 1951-65; v.p. trust div. United Penn Bank, Wilkes-Barre, Pa., 1965-80; of counsel Griffith, Aponick & Musto, Wilkes-Barre, 1981—. Chmn. speakers com. Phila. Citizens for Eisenhower, 1952; bd. dirs. Wyo. Valley Alcohol and Drug Services, Inc., Kingston, Pa., 1975—. Served to staff sgt. U.S. Army, 1942-46. Mem. ABA, Pa. Bar Assn., Phila. Bar Assn., Luzerne County Bar Assn., Wyo. Valley Estate Planning Council, Legion of Honor. Republican. Avocations: reading, politics, sports. Probate, Estate taxation. Office: Griffith Aponcik & Musto 39 Pub Sq Suite 408 Wilkes Barre PA 18701

JONES, ERIKA ZIEBARTH, lawyer; b. Washington, June 10, 1955; d. Thomas Arthur and Ruth (Helm) Ziebarth; m. Gregory Monroe Jones, June 2, 1978; 1 child, Katherine Anne. AB, Georgetown U., 1976, JD, 1980. Bar: D.C. 1980, U.S. Ct. Appeals (D.C. cir.) 1987, U.S. Supreme Ct. 1987. Atty., regulatory analyst U.S. Office Mgmt. and Budget, Washington, 1980-81; spl. counsel Nat. Hwy. Traffic Safety Adminstrn., Washington, 1981-85, chief counsel, 1985—. Bd. dirs. Immaculata Coll. High Sch., Rockville, Md., 1985—. Mem. ABA (com. vice chmn. 1983—), Fed. Bar Assn. (com. chmn. 1985-86), Women's Bar Assn. D.C., D.C. Bar Assn., Phi Beta Kappa. Republican. Roman Catholic. Administrative and regulatory, Legislative. Home: 6612 31st Pl NW Washington DC 20015 Office: Nat Hwy Traffic Safety Adminstrn 400 7th St SW Washington DC 20590

JONES, FRANKLIN CHARLES, lawyer; b. Hanover, N.H., July 2, 1948; s. Laurence Harry and Dorothy Selma (Covey) J.; m. Jan Lynn Griggs, June 18, 1966; children—Gregory Allen, Matthew Scott, Benjamin Albert, Kathryn Covey. B.A., U. N.H., 1970; J.D., Boston U., 1973. Bar: N.H. 1973, U.S. Dist. Ct. N.H. 1978, U.S. Ct. Appeals (1st cir.) 1978, U.S. Supreme Ct. 1979. Atty. Michael & Wallace, Rochester, N.H., 1973-76; ptnr. Michael & Jones, Rochester, 1976-78, Michael Jones & Wensley, 1979-86, assoc. judge, Rochester Dist. Ct., 1986—; instr. Paralegal Studies Program, U. N.H., Durham, 1979-81, Tax Inst., 1981-85. Mem. Rochester Sch. Bd., 1978-84, chmn. bd., 1983-84; chmn. Rochester chpt. ARC, 1976-78; moderator City of Rochester, Ward 4, 1984-86; spl. justice Rochester Dist. Ct., 1986—. Mem. ABA, Nat. Assn. Criminal Def. Lawyers, Assn. Trial Lawyers Am., N.H. Bar Assn. (chmn. com. on econs. of practice law 1982-83, mem. clients indemnity fund com. 1984—). Republican. Roman Catholic. Lodge: Rotary (bd. dirs. Rochester). Real property, General corporate, Bankruptcy. Home: 50 Chesley Hill Rd Rochester NH 03867 Office: Rochester Dist Ct PO 1500 Rochester NH 03867

JONES, GLOWER WHITEHEAD, lawyer; b. Atlanta, May 4, 1936; s. Samuel L. and Alma (Powell) J.; m. Joanna Dayvault, Apr. 5, 1980; children: Mark, Jeff, Tom, Frank, Michael. Grad. Dartmouth Coll. 1958; JD, Emory U., 1963. Bar: Ga. 1962, U.S. Dist. Ct. Ga. 1963, U.S. Ct. Apls. (5th and

11th cirs.), U.S. Ct. Claims, U.S. Supreme Ct. Assoc. Smith, Swift, Currie, McGhee & Hancock, Atlanta, 1963-65; ptnr. Smith Currie & Hancock, Atlanta, 1967—. Mem. editorial bd. Ga. State Bar Jour. Mem. exec. bd. Met. Atlanta Boys' Clubs, Inc., asst. sec., 1973-80, sec., 1980-83; bd. dirs. Samuel L. Jones Boys' Club, Inc., So. region Boys Clubs Am.; trustee, past pres. Atlanta Florence Crittendon Services, Inc.; bd. dirs. Carrie Steele Pitts Home for Orphans; bd. dirs., asst. treas. Gate City Day Nursery Assn. Recipient Golden Boy award Met. Atlanta Boys' Club, 1971. Mem. ABA, Fed. Bar Assn., Internat. Bar Assn., Ga. Bar Assn., State Bar Ga., Atlanta Bar Assn. (chmn. prepaid legal services com., engr. lawyers relations com.), Lawyers Club Atlanta, Internat. Constrn. Contracts Commn., Am. Judicature Soc., Assn. Trial Attys. Am., Assn. Trial Lawyers Ga., Dartmouth Coll. Alumni Club, Baylor Alumni Club, Emory U. Alumni Club, Phi Delta Theta. Clubs: Atlanta Athletic, Ansley Park Golf, Dartmouth, World Trade. Construction, Government contracts and claims, Federal civil litigation. Home: 78 Peachtree Circle NE Atlanta GA 30309 Office: 2600 Harris Tower 233 Peachtree St NE Atlanta GA 30043

JONES, H(AROLD) GILBERT, JR., lawyer; b. Fargo, N.D., Nov. 2, 1927; s. Harold Gilbert and Charlotte Viola (Chambers) J.; m. Julie Squier, Feb. 15, 1964; children: Lenna Lettice Mills Jones Carroll, Thomas Squier, Christopher Lee. B.Eng., Yale U., 1947; postgrad., Mich. U., 1948-49; J.D., UCLA, 1956. Bar: Calif. 1957. Mem., ptnr. Overton, Lyman & Prince, Los Angeles, 1956-61; founding partner Bonne, Jones, Bridges, Mueller & O'Keefe, Los Angeles, 1961—. Bd. dirs. Wilshire YMCA, 1969-75. Served with U.S. Army, 1950-52. Fellow Am. Coll. Trial Lawyers, Internat. Acad. Trial Lawyers; mem. State Bar Calif., ABA, Los Angeles County Bar Assn. (past chmn. legal-med. relations com.), Orange County Bar Assn., Wilshire Bar Assn., Am. Bd. Trial Advs. (nat. bd. dirs.1977—, past pres. Los Angeles chpt.), Am. Acad. Forensic Scis., So. Calif. Assn. Def. Counsel. Clubs: Jonathan, Transpacific Yacht (judge adv.), Calif. Yacht, Los Angeles Yacht, Newport Harbor Yacht. Home: 7 Morning Glory Irvine CA 92715 Office: 1700 CNA Park Pl 600 S Commonwealth Ave Los Angeles CA 90005 also: 801 Civic Center Dr Suite 400 Santa Ana CA 92701

JONES, HARTWELL KELLEY, JR., lawyer, insurance company executive; b. Columbia, S.C., Mar. 4, 1941; s. Hartwell Kelley and Lora (Bussey) J.; B.A. in Journalism, U. S.C., 1963, M.A. in Internat. Studies, 1966, J.D., 1970. Bar: S.C. 1970, U.S. Ct. Appeals (4th cir.) 1974, U.S. Dist. Ct. S.C. 1975, U.S. Supreme Ct. 1976. Reporter Columbia Record, 1961-64; press sec. to S.C. Rep. A. W. Watson, 1964-67; reporter govt. affairs The State newspaper, Columbia, 1967-68, night city editor, 1968-70; legal asst., press sec. to Gov. of S.C., 1970-74; gen. counsel S.C. Ins. Dept. Columbia, 1974-78; sole practice, Cayce, S.C., 1978-83, West Columbia, S.C., 1983—; pres., gen. counsel Grange Mut. Fire Ins. Co. S.C., West Columbia, 1982—, also dir.; S.C. legis. counsel Carolinas Assn. Profl. Ins. Agts.; gen. counsel S.C. Optometric Assn.; legis. counsel S.C. Acad. Profl. Psychologists. Second v.p. Cayce Precinct 2 Democratic party; bd. dirs. S.C. Animal Protection League, Riverland Park Neighborhood Assn. Served with U.S. Army, 1964. Decorated Order of Palmetto, S.C. Mem. S.C. Bar, S.C. Law Enforcement Officers Assn., S.C. Game and Fish Assn. (charter mem.), Richland County Game and Fish Assn., S.C. Wildlife Fedn., Am. Striped Bass Soc. (charter), Striper, Stripers Unltd., Sigma Delta Chi. Baptist. Clubs: Master Palmetto Grange (West Columbia, S.C.); Midlands Striper; S.C. State Grange (Dalzell); Soc. of Stranders (gen. counsel) (Richmond, Va.). Monthly columnist Carolina Agt., 1978—; contbr. articles to fishing publs. Insurance, Personal injury. Home: 2609 Riverland Dr Cayce SC 29033 Office: PO Box 2561 West Columbia SC 29171

JONES, HENRY W., JR., lawyer; b. Raleigh, N.C., Oct. 13, 1952; s. Henry W. and Peggy (Siler) J.; m. Mary June Schmick, Aug. 4, 1979; 1 child, Henry W. III. BA, N.C. State U., 1974; JD, U. Richmond, 1978. Bar: N.C. 1978, U.S. Dist. Ct. (ea. dist.) N.C. 1978, U.S. Ct. Appeals (4th cir.) 1979, U.S. Supreme Ct. 1982. Assoc. Jordan, Brown, Price & Wall, Raleigh, 1978-85; ptnr. Jordan, Price, Wall, Gray & Jones, Raleigh, 1986—. Treas., chmn. fin. Wake County Dems., 1987-87, chmn., 1987—; pres. Spring Garden Homeowners Assn., Raleigh, 1983-86; chmn. Hayes Barton Counicl Ministries, Raleigh, 1984—; mem. Raleigh Planning Commn., 1986—. Recipient Outstanding Service award Am. Cancer Soc., 1982-83. Mem. N.C. Bar Assn., Wake County Bar Assn., N.C. Acad. Trial Lawyers. Methodist. Lodge: Rotary. Avocations: travel, reading, politics. Federal civil litigation, General corporate, Legislative. Home: 3302 Turnbridge Dr Raleigh NC 27609 Office: Jordan Price Wall Gray & Jones 225 Hillsborough St PO Box 709 Raleigh NC 27602

JONES, IDA MAE, lawyer, educator; b. Omaha, Aug. 18, 1953; d. Jonathan and Mary (Cooper) J.; m. Harry Edward Williams, Aug. 16, 1977 (div.); children—Kenneth Elliott, Kamali Allen, Jamilla Marie, John Eugene. B.A. in Sociology, Creighton U., 1974; J.D., NYU, 1977. Bar: N.Y. 1978, Nebr. 1980, U.S. Dist. Ct. (so. dist.) N.Y. 1978, U.S. Dist. Ct. Nebr. 1980. Law clk. HEW, N.Y.C., 1976-77; assoc. appellate counsel Legal Aid-Criminal Appeals, N.Y.C., 1977-79; staff atty. Legal Aid Soc., Omaha, 1979-81; sole practice, Omaha, 1981—; asst. prof. U. Nebr., Omaha, 1981-85, assoc. prof., 1986-87; prof. Calif. State U., Fresno, 1987—; bd. dirs. PILCO, Omaha, 1981-84. Mem. adv. bd. Child Saving Inst., Omaha, 1981-87, Ctr. Stage, 1985-86 ; bd. dirs. Gt. Plains Black Mus., 1984-85. Contbr. articles to profl. jours. Mem. adv. bd. NCCJ, 1985-87, care of candidates com. Mo. Valley Presbytery, 1986-87. Fellow ABA, Nebr. Bar Assn., Midlands Bar Assn., Am. Bus. Law Assn. Democrat. Contracts commercial, Bankruptcy, Family and matrimonial. Office: U Nebr Omaha Coll Bus 60th & Dodge Sts Omaha NE 68182

JONES, JAMES EDWARD, JR., law educator, university administrator; b. Little Rock, June 4, 1924. B.A., Lincoln U., Mo., 1950; M.A., U. Ill. Inst. Labor and Indsl. Relations, 1951; J.D., U. Wis., 1956. Bar: Wis., U.S. Supreme Ct. Indsl. relations analyst U.S. Wage Stabilization Bd., Region 7, 1951-53; legis. atty. Dept. Labor, Washington, 1956-63, counsel for labor relations, 1963-66, dir. office labor mgmt., policy devel., 1966-67, assoc. solicitor labor div. labor relations and civil rights, 1967-69; vis. prof. law and indsl. relations U. Wis.-Madison, 1969-70, prof., 1970—, Bascom prof. law, 1983—; dir. Inst. Relations, Research Inst., 1971-73, assoc. Inst. for Research on Poverty, 1970, dir. Ctr. for Equal Employment and Affirmative Action, Indsl. Relations Research Inst., 1974—; mem. research and edn. staff Pulp, Sulphite and Paper Mill Workers, AFL-CIO, 1958; mem. Fed. Service Impasses Panel, 1978-82; mem. pub. rev. bd. Internat. Union UAW, 1970—; mem. adv. com. NRC Nat. Acad. Scis., 1971-73; mem. Wis. Manpower Planning Council, 1971-76; mem. spl. com. on criminal justice, standards and goals Wis. Council Criminal Justice, 1975-76; bd. dirs. labor law sect. Wis. State Bar, 1976; mem. Fed. Mediation and Conciliation Arbitration Panel, 1975—; spl. arbitrator U.S. Steel and United Steel Workers, 1976—; mem. expert com. on family budget revision Dept. Labor Series, 1978-79; cons. in field. Mem. Madison Police and Fire Commn., 1973-77, pres., 1976-77. Recipient Sec. Labor Career Service award Dept. Labor, 1963; John Hay Whitney fellow, 1953, 54. Mem. Labor Law Group Trust (chmn. editorial policy com. 1978-82), Indsl. Relations Research Assn. (treas. Washington chpt. 1968-69, exec. bd. 1977-80), Fed. Bar Assn. (chmn. labor law com. 1967-69, dep. chmn. council on labor law and labor relations 1979-80), State Bar Wis., Nat. Bar Assn. (nat. adv. com. of equal employment clin. project 1970-79), Nat. Acad. Arbitrators, Order of Coif. Legal education, Labor, Civil rights. Office: U Wis Law Sch Madison WI 53706

JONES, JAMES LEONARD, lawyer; b. Helena, Mont., Sept. 25, 1945; s. Vernon Leonard and Mary Elizabeth (Conn) J.; m. Madilyn Charmaine Bell, June 17, 1967; children—Mathew James, Aaron Christopher, Steven Ryan. B.A., U. Mont., 1967, J.D., 1970. Bar: Mont. 1970, U.S. Dist. Ct. Mont. 1970, U.S. Ct. Appeals (9th cir.) 1973. Law clk. to chief judge U.S. Dist Ct. Mont., Missoula, 1970-71; asst. U.S. atty. U.S. Dept. Justice, Billings, Mont., 1971-74; prin. Anderson, Brown, Gerbase, Cebull & Jones, P.C., Billings, 1974-86, ptnr. Dorsey & Whitney, 1986—. Mem. Yellowstone County Republican Central Com. Served to capt. USAR, 1970. Mem. Mont. Bar Assn. (pres. young lawyers sect. 1974-75), ABA, Yellowstone County Bar Assn., Mont. Assn. Def. Counsel (pres. 1981-82), Def. Research Inst. (state dir. 1983-84), Internat. Assn. Ins. Counsel. Methodist. Federal civil litigation, Insurance, Personal injury. Home: 3016 Brentwood Billings MT 59102 Office: Anderson Brown Gerbase Cebull & Jones PC 315 N 24th St Billings MT 59103

JONES, JAMES THOMAS, state official, lawyer; b. Twin Falls, Idaho, May 13, 1942; s. Henry C. and Eunice Irene (Martens) J.; m. Nancy June Babson, Nov. 25, 1972; 1 dau., Katherine A. Student, Idaho State U., 1960-61; B.A., U. Oreg., 1964; J.D., Northwestern U., 1967. Bar: Idaho 1967. Legis. asst. to U.S. Senator, Washington, 1970-72; law practice Jerome, Idaho, 1973-82; atty. gen. State of Idaho, Boise, 1973—. Bd. dirs. Idaho Cancer Soc. Served to capt. U.S. Army, 1967-79, Vietnam. Decorated Bronze Star; decorated Air medal with 4 oak leaf clusters, Cross of Gallantry (Vietnam), Army Commendation medal. Mem. Idaho Bar Assn., Am. Legion, Idaho Farm Bur., VFW. Republican. Lutheran. Administrative and regulatory. Office: Office Atty Gen Statehouse Room 210 Boise ID 83720

JONES, JEFFREY RUSSELL, lawyer; b. Balt., Jan. 16, 1955; s. William Thomas Russell and Doris (Erb) J.; m. Elaine Elizabeth Schott, July 1, 1978. BA, Oberlin Coll., 1977; JD, U. Pa., 1980. Bar: N.Y. 1981, U.S. Dist. Ct. (we. dist.) N.Y. 1981. Assoc. Nixon, Hargrave, Devans & Doyle, Rochester, N.Y., 1980-84; asst. counsel Chase Lincoln First Bank, N.A., Rochester, 1984-87, sr. atty., 1987—. Active Monroe County Dem. Party, Rochester, 1982—. Mem. Monroe County Bar Assn. Banking, Securities, General corporate. Home: 117 Shoreham Dr Rochester NY 14618 Office: Chase Lincoln First Bank NA One Lincoln First Sq Rochester NY 14643

JONES, JOHN ARTHUR, lawyer; b. San Antonio, Fla., Oct. 9, 1921; s. Charles Garfield and Catherine Magdalene (Smith) J.; m. Margarette Lorraine Johnson, Nov. 19, 1949; children—Matthew, Lisa, Malcolm, Darby. J.D. with honors, U. Fla., 1949. Bar: Fla. 1949, U.S. Dist. Ct. (so. dist.) Fla. 1952, U.S. Ct. Appeals (11th cir.) 1982, U.S. Supreme Ct. 1978. Assoc., Holland and Knight and predecessors, Tampa, Fla., 1949-54; ptnr., 1954—; faculty Fla. Sch. of Banking. Served in U.S. Army, 1940-46; served to lt. col. USAR. Fellow Am. Coll. Probate Counsel, mem. ABA, Fla. Bar Assn. (cert. estate planning and probate, past chmn. real property probate & trust sect.), Hillsborough County (Fla.) Bar Assn., Internat. Acad. Estate and Trust Lawyers, Am. Coll. Real Estate Lawyers, Phi Delta Phi, Phi Kappa Phi. Clubs: Masons, Scottish Rite, Shrine. Editor, contbr.: How To Live and Die With Florida Probate, 1972. Banking, Contracts commercial, Probate. Home: 5027 San Miguel Tampa FL 33629 Office: PO Box 1288 Tampa FL 33601

JONES, JOHN EDWARD, lawyer; b. Bainbridge, Ga., Mar. 24, 1943; s. Percy Price and Hilda Eloise (Tarpley) J.; m. Carolyn Kenn Morris, Aug. 21, 1965; children—Randall Edward, Julianne, Andrew John. Student, Mercer U., 1961-62; B.A., Fla. State U., 1965; J.D., Stetson U., 1968. Bar: Fla. 1968, U.S. Dist. Ct. (mid. dist.) Fla. 1969, U.S. Supreme Ct. 1972. Law clk. U.S. Dist. Ct., Middle Dist. Fla., Tampa, 1968-69; ptnr. Carroll, Jones, Rooks & Owen, Casselberry, Fla., 1973-80; pres. John Edward Jones P.A., Casselberry, 1980—; dir. Seminole County Legal Referral Com., Altamonte Springs, Fla., 1976-78; dir., sec. Calvary Towers, Inc., 1983—. Contbr. articles to profl. jours; author: Reconciliation, 1983. Served to lt. comdr., USN, 1968-72, with Res., 1974—. Paul Harris fellow; Charles Dana Scholar, 1968; named to Fla. State U. Hall of Fame, 1965. Mem. Seminole County Bar Assn. (dir. 1978-79), Christian Legal Soc., Acad. Fla. Trial Lawyers (diplomate), Assn. Trial Lawyers Am. (sustaining), Omicron Delta Kappa. Lodges: Rotary, Eagle. Personal injury, Products liability, Criminal. Home: 450 Andrews Dr Longwood FL 32750 Office: PO Box 1985 5200 S US Hwy 17-92 Casselberry FL 32707

JONES, JOHN FRANK, lawyer, cons.; b. Carrington, N.D., Feb. 24, 1922; s. Dwight Frank and Veronica Esther (Sheehy) J.; m. Sally Oppegard; children—Janna Jones Bellwin, John M., Jeramy Ridder, Jill Jones Nester, Julie, Jeffrey, J. David. B.S., U. N.D., 1946; M.S. in Organic Chemistry, U. Wis., 1953; J.D., U. Akron, 1956. Bar: Ohio 1956, U.S. Patent Office, U.S. Ct. Appeals. Patent atty. B. F. Goodrich Co., Akron, Ohio, 1956-62; sr. patent atty. Standard Oil Co., Cleve., 1962-70, patent counsel, 1970-81, food and drug atty. Vistron Corp. subs. Standard Oil Co., Cleve., 1968-81, ret., 1981; cons. to Standard Oil Co., Cleve. and Ashland Chem. Co. (div. Ashland Oil Co.), Columbus, Ohio, 1981—. Served with USAAF, 1943-46. Decorated D.F.C., Air medal. Mem. Am. Chem. Soc., Ohio Bar Assn., ABA, Am. Patent Law Assn., Cleve. Patent Law Assn. Republican. Patentee in chem. and polymer fields; contbr. articles on polymer sci. to profl. jours. Patent, Trademark and copyright. Home and Office: 2724 Cedar Hill Rd Cuyahoga Falls OH 44223

JONES, JOHN GORNAL, lawyer; b. St. Louis, July 30, 1938; s. Walter F. and Dorothy C. (Schoenthaler) J.; m. Ruth B. Siler, June 28, 1968; children—Jason G., Walter W. J.D., Washington U., St. Louis, 1966. Bar: Mo. 1966. Counsel, Kellwood Co., St. Louis, 1966-72; ptnr. Willemin & Jones, St. Louis, 1972-74; v.p., gen. counsel, sec. Centex Corp., Dallas, 1974—. General corporate, Contracts commercial, Real property. Office: Centex Corp 3333 Lee Parkway Dallas TX 75219

JONES, JOHN THOMAS, JR., lawyer; b. Dayton, Ohio, Feb. 28, 1956; s. John Thomas Sr. and Jean (Phillips) J.; m. Imogene A. King, Oct. 29, 1983. BA in Sociology, U. Cin., 1978; JD, U. Tenn., 1981. Bar: Tenn. 1981, U.S. Dist. Ct. (ea. dist.) Tenn. 1981, U.S. Dist. Ct. (ea. dist.) Ky. 1982, U.S. Ct. Appeals (6th cir.) 1982. Jr. ptnr. Basista, Hatmaker & Hall, Jacksboro, Tenn., 1981-83; assoc. Bernstein, Susano & Stair, Knoxville, Tenn., 1983—. Mem. ABA, Tenn. Bar Assn. (bankrupcy subcom. 1986—), Knoxville Bar Assn. Avocations: golf, baseball. Bankruptcy, Federal civil litigation, State civil litigation. Home: 5705 Green Valley Rd Knoxville TN 37914 Office: Bernstein Susano & Stair 600 1st Tenn Bank Bldg Knoxville TN 37902

JONES, JOHNNIE ANDERSON, lawyer; b. Laurel Hill, La., Nov. 30, 1919; s. Henry Edward and Sarah Ann (Coats) J.; m. Sebell Elizabeth Chase, June 1, 1948; children—Johnnie, Adair Darnell, Adal Dalcho, Ann Sarah Bythelda. B.S. in Psychology, So. U., Baton Rouge, 1949; J.D., 1953. Bar: La. 1953, U.S. Dist. Ct. (ea. and mid. dists.) La. 1953, U.S. Ct. Appeals (5th cir.) 1982, U.S. Supreme Ct. 1961. Ins. agt. Universal Life Ins. Co., Baton Rouge, 1947-48; letter carrier U.S. Post Office, Baton Rouge, 1948-50; practice, Baton Rouge, 1953—; sr. lawyer Jones & Jones, Baton Rouge, 1975—; asst. parish atty. City-Parish Govt., Baton Rouge, 1969-72. Mem. La. Ho. of Reps., 1972-76; bd. dirs. La. Human Relations Council, Baton Rouge, 1984. Served with U.S. Army, 1942-46, ETO. Recipient Cert. of Appreciation, L.B. Johnson and H.H. Humphrey, Washington, 1964, Plaque, Alpha Kappa Alpha, 1972; named Most Outstanding Man of Yr., Mt. Zion First Bapt. Ch., Baton Rouge, 1970, Frontiersman of Yr., Frontiers Club Internat., Baton Rouge, 1962. Mem. Am. Judicature Soc., ABA, Nat. Bar Assn., Louis A. Marinet Legal Soc., Baton Rouge Bar Assn., Am. Legion, NAACP, Alpha Phi Alpha. Democrat. Baptist. Civil rights, Federal civil litigation, Labor. Office: Jones & Jones 251 Florida St Suite 215 Baton Rouge LA 70801

JONES, KEITH ALDEN, lawyer; b. Tulsa, July 11, 1941; s. Leonard Virgil and Bernadine (Hutchison) J.; m. Renata Skuta, June 15, 1974; 1 child, Emily Isobel. BA, Harvard U., 1963, LLB, 1966. Bar: Mass. 1966, D.C. 1978, U.S. Supreme Ct. 1972. Asst. prof. Boston U. Law Sch., 1966-67; lectr. Harvard U. Law Sch., 1967-68; assoc. Ropes & Gray, Boston, 1968-70; minority counsel U.S. Senate Select Com. on Small Bus., 1970-72; asst. to Solicitor Gen. of U.S., 1972-75; dep. solicitor gen. 1975-78; ptnr. Fulbright & Jaworski, Washington, 1978—; mem. D.C. Cir. Adv. Com. on Procedures. Mem. ABA (spl. com. on amicus curiae briefs), Am. Law Inst. Club: Univ. (Washington). Federal civil litigation, FERC practice. Office: Suite 400 1150 Connecticut Ave NW Washington DC 20008

JONES, KEITH DUNN, lawyer; b. Monroe, La., July 17, 1951; s. Arnott Lewis and Edwina Lorraine (Dunn) J.; m. Eilleen Kean, July 5, 1974; children—Christopher Keith, Kathleen Conley, Gordon Lewis. B.A., La. Tech. U., 1973; J.D., La. State U., 1976. Bar: La. 1976, U.S. Dist. Ct. (mid. dist.) La. 1977, U.S. Ct. Appeals (5th cir.) 1982, U.S. supreme Ct. 1982. Ptnr. firm McKernan & Jones, Baton Rouge, La., 1976-80, firm Gill, Bankston & Morgan, Baton Rouge, 1980-81; sole practice, Baton Rouge, 1981-85; ptnr. Jones & Coxe, 1985—; counsel La. Ins. Rating Commn., Baton Rouge, 1977-80. Pres. Oak Hills Civic Assn., Baton Rouge, 1981. Mem. La. State Bar Assn., ABA, Assn. Trial Lawyers Am., La. Trial Lawyers Assn. (bd. govs. 1980—), Kappa Sigma Alumni Assn. (pres. 1982). Club: Baton Rouge Country. Lodge: Cortana Kiwanis (Baton Rouge). Personal injury, Insurance, State civil litigation. Home: 1033 Woodstone Dr Baton Rouge LA 70808

JONES, KELSEY A., criminal justice educator, clergyman; b. Holly Springs, Miss., July 15, 1933; m. Virginia Bethel Ford; children—Kelsey A., Cheryl Darline Jones Campbell, Eric Andre, Claude Anthony. B.A. in English summa cum laude, Miss. Indsl. Coll., 1955, D.D., 1969; M.Div., Northwestern U., 1959; postgrad. U. Mich., 1960; cert. clin. pastoral care Wesley Med. Ctr., Wichita, Kans., 1967. Ordained to ministry Methodist Ch., 1956. Staff counselor State Prison So. Mich., Jackson, 1959-62; developing minister Lane Meml. Ch., Jackson, 1959-62; sr. minister Cleaves Temple, Omaha, 1962-65; chmn. Kans. Bd. Probation and Parole, 1965-70; minister St. Matthew Ch., Wichita, 1965-70; minister of celebration and human resources Israel Met. Ch., Washington, 1970-72; assoc. prof. social scis. U. D.C., Washington, 1972-77, assoc. prof. criminal justice, 1978-82, prof., 1982, chmn. dept. social/behavioral scis., 1977-78, chmn. dept. criminal justice, 1979—; spl. asst. to Pres. for environ. health, occupational safety and instl. security, Washington, 1984—. Bd. dirs. D.C. Corrections Found; trustee Washington Internat. Coll. Recipient Presdl. citation Nat. Assn. for Equal Opportunities in Higher Edn., 1979, Disting. Service award Howard U., Washington, 1980, Lorton Student Govt. Assn., U. D.C., 1980. Mem. Acad. Criminal Justice Scis., N. Atlantic Conf. Criminal Justice Educators, Am. Soc. Pub. Adminstrn., Assn. for Study in Higher Edn., Alpha Phi Alpha. Home: 5427 Kansas Ave NW Washington DC 20011 Office: Univ DC Dept Criminal Justice 4200 Connecticut Ave NW Washington DC 20008

JONES, KENNETH RAY, JR., lawyer; b. Memphis, June 3, 1954; s. Kenneth Ray Sr. and Joanne (Hope) J.; m. Bridget Ann Lacey, Sept. 11, 1976; 1 child, Alan Brandon. BA summa cum laude, Memphis State U., 1976; JD, Vanderbilt U., 1980. Bar: Tenn. 1980, U.S. Dist. Ct. (mid. dist.) Tenn. 1980, U.S. Ct. Appeals (6th cir.) 1982, U.S. tax Ct. 1983, U.S. Dist. Ct. (ea. dist.) Tenn. 1985. Assoc. Bass, Berry & Sims, Nashville, 1980-83; assoc. O'Hare, Sherrard & Roe, Nashville, 1983-85, ptnr., 1986—. Exec. editor Vanderbilt Law Rev., 1979-80. Bd. dirs. Project to End Abuse Through Counseling and Edn., Nashville, 1986—. Mem. ABA, Tenn. Bar Assn. (legis. com., gen. sessions ct. com), Nashville Bar Assn. Democrat. Club: Nashville City. Avocations: fishing, boating, golf. Federal civil litigation, State civil litigation, Administrative and regulatory. Home: 6728 Pennywell Dr Nashville TN 37205 Office: O'Hare Sherrard & Roe 500 Church St Nashville TN 37219

JONES, KENT LEONARD, lawyer; b. Tulsa, May 25, 1947; s. Leonard V. and Bernadine E. (Hutchison) J.; m. Janice J. Jacopian, Dec. 28, 1968; children: Kristen L., Kent W. BA, Amherst Coll., 1969; JD, Harvard U., 1975. Bar: D.C. 1976, Okla. 1980, U.S. Supreme Ct. 1981, U.S. Ct. Appeals (D.C. 1976), U.S. Ct. Appeals (5th, and 10th cirs.) 1982, U.S. Ct. Appeals (4th cir.) 1985. Law clk. to presiding judge U.S. Ct. Appeals (2d cir.), Brattleboro, Va., 1975-76; assoc. Shea & Gardner, Washington, 1976-78; asst. solicitor gen. U.S. Dept. Justice, Washington, 1978-80; ptnr. Hall, Estill, Tulsa, 1980—. Articles editor Harvard Law Rev., 1973-75. Served to lt. USN, 1969-72. Mem. ABA, Okla. Bar Assn., Tulsa Bar Assn., D.C. Bar Assn., Phi Beta Kappa. Club: Tulsa. Federal civil litigation, State civil litigation, Oil and gas leasing. Home: 3150 E 67th St Tulsa OK 74136 Office: Hall Estill 4100 Bank Okla Tower Tulsa OK 74172

JONES, LARRY ALAN, lawyer; b. Kansas City, Mo., Aug. 6, 1950; s. John Edward Jones and Donna LaRue (Redenbaugh) Malac; m. Nancy Anne Parks, July 28, 1972; children: Kaci DiAnne, Jonathan Edward, Jefferson Alan.. AA, Paris (Tex.) Jr. Coll., 1970; BA, East Tex. State U., 1971, MS in History, 1978; JD, Okla. City U., 1981. Bar: Okla. 1981. Asst. dist. atty. Oklahoma County, Oklahoma City, 1980—. Mem. ABA, Okla. Bar Assn. Avocations: writing, research in legal and religious fields. Criminal. Office: Oklahoma County Dist Atty 518 County Office Bldg Oklahoma City OK 73102

JONES, LAWRENCE RAY, JR., lawyer; b. Dallas, Feb. 16, 1943; s. Lawrence Ray and Bernice (Eastman) J.; m. Carol Ann Mitchell, July 17, 1971; children: Michelle Teresa, Julie Marie, Jill Ann. BBA, Tex. Christian U., 1965; JD, So. Meth. U., 1968; LLM in Taxation, Georgetown U., 1973. Bar: Tex. 1968. Trial atty. tax div. U.S. Dept. Justice, Dallas, 1969-77; assoc. Chamberlain, Hardlicka, White, Johnson & Williams, Houston, 1977-79; ptnr. Jones, Brutsché, Hider, Thoeming & Peele, Dallas, 1979—; adj. prof. So. Meth. U. Law Sch., Dallas, 1980—; pres. DFW Rand Group, 1982-85; pres., broker Brittany Realty Co., 1982—. Author: Criminal Tax Fraud and the CPA, 1986. Served with USAR, 1968-74. Republican. Methodist. Avocation: soccer. Corporate taxation, Personal income taxation. Office: Jones Brutsché Hider Thoeming & Peele 2902 Carlisle Suite 200 Dallas TX 75204

JONES, LAWRENCE TUNNICLIFFE, lawyer; b. Mineola, N.Y., Jan. 20, 1950; s. Carroll Hudson Tunnicliffe and Florence Virginia (Greene) J. BA, U. Va., 1972; JD, U. Richmond, 1975. Bar: Va. 1975, D.C. 1976, N.Y. 1976, U.S. Dist. Ct. (ea. and so. dist.) N.Y. 1976, U.S. Supreme Ct. 1986. Ptnr. Carroll Hudson Tunnicliffe Jones and Lawrence Tunnicliffe Jones Atty.-at-Law, Mineola, 1976—. Bd. dirs. Friends of Hist. St. George's Ch., Hempstead, N.Y., 1982—, St. Mary's Devel. Fund, Garden City, N.Y., 1983—; pres. counsel Cathedral Sch. St. Paul Alumni Fund, Inc., Garden City, 1984—; bd. govs. Cathedral Sch. St. Mary, Garden City, 1983—. Mem. ABA, Va. State Bar Assn., N.Y. State Bar Assn., Nassau County Bar Assn., Nassau County Tax and Estate Planning Council. Episcopalian. Clubs: University (N.Y.C. 1976—); University (L.I.) (pres. 1986—); Garden City Golf. Avocation: hist. building preservation. Probate, Real property, General practice. Home: 158 Cathedral Ave Hempstead NY 11550 Office: Jones & Jones 286 Old Country Rd Mineola NY 11501

JONES, LINDY DON, lawyer; b. Vernon, Tex., Aug. 20, 1949; s. Earl Irven Jones and Avis June (Koontz) McDowell; m. M. Kathryn Sanders, June 6, 1969; children—Brandi Kim, Megan Dawn, Ty Jeffrey. B.B.A. in Mgmt. with honors, U. Tex.-Arlington, 1971; J.D., So. Meth. U., 1974. Bar: Tex. 1974, U.S. Ct. Appeals (5th cir.) 1974, U.S. Dist. Ct. (no. dist.) Tex. 1975, U.S. Dist. Ct. (we. dist.) Tex. 1977, U.S. Dist. Ct. (ea. dist.) Tex. 1978, U.S. Dist. Ct. (so. dist.) Tex. 1979. Ptnr. Moseley, Enoch & Martin and predecessors Moseley, Jones & Enoch, and Moseley & Jones, Dallas, 1974-81; Moseley Jones Allen & Fuquay, Dallas, 1981-86, Jones, Allen & Fuquay, 1986—. Pres. Highland Park United Meth. Ch. Men's Club, Dallas, 1979; chmn. bd. dirs. Dickinson Pl. Charitable Corp., Dallas, 1984-86. Recipient hon. life membership Highland Park United Meth. Ch. Men's Club, 1980. Mem. Dallas Bar Assn. (com. mem. 1974—), State Bar Tex., ABA, Delta Theta Phi. Republican. Banking, Contracts commercial, State civil litigation. Home: 8068 Moss Meadow Dallas TX 75231 Office: Jones Allen & Fuquay 8828 Greenville Ave Dallas TX 75243-7143

JONES, LLOYD WESLEY, lawyer; b. Severy, Kans., Apr. 1, 1903; s. William Sherman and Nellie Salina (Banta) J.; m. Edith Makemson, May 3, 1924 (dec. 1963); children—Lloyd Wesley, Ann Nell; m. Doris Mae Embry, July 18, 1964. Student Oklahoma City U., 1934, Oklahoma Central Sch. Law, 1935. Bar: Okla. 1930, Kans. 1936, Tex. 1959. With Mo.-Kans.-Tex. R.R. Co., 1922-68, chief clk. Okla. Law Dept., Oklahoma City, 1938-43, claim agt., atty., Oklahoma City, 1943-46, gen. atty. for Kans., Parsons, 1946-57, gen. atty., Denison, Tex., 1957-64, Dallas, 1964-68; sole practice, Dallas, 1969-82, Parsons, Kans., 1982—. Mem. Okla. State Bar Assn. Kans. State Bar Assn., Tex. State Bar Assn., Labette County (Kans.) Bar Assn., Dallas Bar Assn. Republican. Methodist. Lodge: Rotary. General corporate, Probate. Address: 1321 30th Pl Parsons KS 67357

JONES, LUCIAN COX, lawyer; b. Kew Gardens, N.Y., Dec. 22, 1942; s. Richard Jeter and Ruth Virginia (Cox) J.; m. Ann Waters, Aug. 22, 1964; children—L. Rustin, Norman W., Warren R. A.B., Davidson Coll., 1964; J.D., Columbia U., 1967. Bar: N.Y. 1967. Assoc. Shearman & Sterling, N.Y.C., 1967-68, 70-76, ptnr., 1976—. Served to capt. U.S. Army, 1968-70. Mem. ABA, N.Y. State Bar Assn., Assn. Bar City N.Y. Banking, Antitrust, Contracts commercial. Office: Shearman & Sterling 153 E 53d St New York NY 10022

JONES, MARVIN COLEMAN, lawyer; b. Monroe, La., June 15, 1944; s. Warren Harding and Marjorie Anne (Coleman) J.; m. Diane Norwig, June 11, 1966; children: Christopher Coleman, Catherine Jess. BA in Polit. Sci., The Citadel, 1966; JD, U. S.C., 1973. Bar: S.C. 1973, U.S. Dist. Ct. S.C. 1973, U.S. Ct. Appeals (4th cir.) 1974, U.S. Supreme Ct. 1977. Asst. atty. gen. State of S.C., Columbia, 1973-78; assoc. Callison, Tighe, Nauful & Rush, Columbia, 1978-79; ptnr. Bogoslow & Jones, Walterboro, S.C., 1980—. Mem. Western Carolina Higher Edn. Commn., Allendale, S.C., 1984-86, S.C. Commn. on Higher Edn., Columbia, 1986—. Served to maj. USAF, 1966-69, Vietnam and CBI. Mem. ABA, S.C. Bar Assn., S.C. Def. Trial Attys. Assn., Walterboro -Colleton C. of C. (pres. 1986—). Episcopal. Lodge: Lions (pres. Walterboro chpt. 1985-86. State civil litigation, Insurance, Bankruptcy. Home: PO Box 982 Walterboro SC 29488 Office: Bogoslow & Jones PO Box 1515 Walterboro SC 29488

JONES, MICHAEL CHARLES, lawyer; b. Balt., Mar. 15, 1952; s. Charles Edgar and Alice Anna Mae (Franklin) J.; m. Randi Christine Rouhier, Aug. 14, 1976; children: Erin Christine, Sean Michael. BA cum laude, Captial U., 1974, JD, 1979. Bar: Ohio 1979, U.S. Dist. Ct. (no. dist.) Ohio 1981, U.S. Ct. Appeals (6th cir.) 1983. Research atty. Nat. Legal Research Group Inc., Charlottesville, Va., 1979-81; ptnr. Young & Jones, Paulding, Ohio, 1981—. Mem. council St. Paul Lutheran Ch., Paulding, 1983-86; v.p. Friends of Library, Paulding, 1986—; dist. chmn. Shawnee council Boy Scouts Am., 1986—; bd. dirs. Friend to Friend, Paulding, 1986. Mem. Ohio Bar Assn., Ohio Acad. Trial Lawyers, Paulding County Bar Assn., Northwest Ohio Bar Assn. Republican. Lodge: Kiwanis. Avocations: collecting baseball cards, photography, reading. Criminal, Family and matrimonial, State civil litigation. Home: 762 N Williams St Paulding OH 45879 Office: Young & Jones 106 E Jackson St Paulding OH 45879

JONES, MICHAEL EARL, lawyer; b. Easton, Md., Oct. 23, 1950; s. Lawrence F. and Marlen N. Jones. BA, Denison U., 1972; MBA, U. Pa., 1974; JD, U. Miami, 1978. Bar: N.H. 1978, U.S. Dist. Ct. N.H. 1978, U.S. Tax Ct. 1978, U.S. Supreme Ct. 1983, U.S. Ct. Internat. Trade 1985, U.S. Ct. Appeals (D.C. cir.) 1986, U.S. Ct. Appeals (1st cir.) 1986. Sole practice Pelham, N.H., 1978—; asst. prof. U. N.H., Durham, 1978-82; asst. prof. law U. Lowell, Mass., 1984—; mem. Ho. of Reps., Concord, N.H., 1982—; legal counsel New Eng. Swimming Inc., Boston, 1985—. Contbr. articles to profl. jours. Chmn. Pelham Cable TV Adv. Commn., N.H., 1981-85, Pelham Conservation Commn., 1982-83, Pelham Parks and Recreation Commn.; mem. Judiciary Com., 1982—. Named Outstanding Speaker Midwest Quality Control Soc., 1982. Mem. N.H. Bar Assn., Am. Bus. Law Assn., Water Polo Assn., Masters Swimming Assn., Phi Alpha Delta (clk. 1977-78), Omicron Delta Epsilon (pres. 1971-72), Internat. Law Assn. (officer 1984—). Avocations: water polo, swimming. Legal education, General practice. Home: PO Box 397 Pelham NH 03076 Office: U Lowell One University Ave Lowell MA 01853

JONES, MICHAEL FRANK, lawyer; b. Chgo., May 5, 1948; s. Martin F. and Joan M. (Harvey) J.; m. Susan C. Drozda. AB in Econs. Middlebury Coll., 1970, JD, 1973. Bar: Ill. 1973, Utah 1981. Assoc. Coles & Wise Ltd., Chgo., 1973-78; assoc. Rosenberg, Savner & Unikel, Chgo., 1978-80, ptnr., 1980-81; assoc. Fabian & Clendenin, Salt Lake City, 1981-82, mem., 1982-83; assoc. Hansen, Jones, Maycock & Leta, Salt Lake City, 1983-84; ptnr. Tibbals, Howell, Jones & Moxley, Salt Lake City, 1984—. Contbr. articles to profl. jours. Trustee Utah Heritage Found., Salt Lake City, 1984—. Mem. ABA, Ill. Bar Assn., Am. Coll. Real Estate Lawyers, Utah State Bar Assn. (chmn. real property sect. 1985-86). Clubs: Ft. Douglas-Hidden Valley Country (Salt Lake City). Real property, Contracts commercial, General corporate. Home: 1703 Yalecrest Ave Salt Lake City UT 84108 Office: Tibbals Howell Jones & Moxley 257 East 200 South Suite 850 Salt Lake City UT 84111-2048

JONES, MICHAEL MORRIE, lawyer; b. Bonne Terre, Mo., Nov. 22, 1953; s. Marshall Patrick and Doris Irene (Spry) J. BA, U. N.C., 1976, JD, 1979. Bar: U.S. Dist. Ct. (ea. dist.) N.C. 1980. Assoc. Dees, Smith, Powell, Jarrett & Dees, Goldsboro, N.C., 1979-80; ptnr. Dees, Smith, Powell, Jarrett Dees & Jones, Goldsboro, 1980—. Editor projects U. N.C. Law Rev., 1979. Mem. Wayne County Young Dems., Goldsboro, 1979—; bd. dirs. Am. Cancer Soc., Goldsboro, 1985—, Wayne County United Way, 1986—. Mem. ABA, N.C. Bar Assn., Wayne County Bar Assn. (sec., treas. 1980-81, chmn. law day 1981), Wayne County Young Lawyers Assn. (pres. 1981-82, chmn. U.S. constl. bi-centennial project 1986—), Assn. Trial Lawyers Am., N.C. Acad. Trial Lawyers, Phi Beta Kappa, Goldsboro Jaycees (pres. 1986—), Wayne County C. of C. Democrat. Presbyterian. Avocations: racquetball, tennis, water skiing. General practice, Personal injury, Criminal. Home: 1703 N Berkeley Blvd Goldsboro NC 27530 Office: Dees Smith Powell Jarrett Dees & Jones 100 N William St Goldsboro NC 27533-0008

JONES, NATHANIEL RAPHAEL, federal judge; b. Youngstown, Ohio, May 13, 1926; s. Nathaniel B. and Lillian J. (Rafe) J.; m. Lillian Graham, Mar. 22, 1974; 1 dau., Stephanie Joyce; stepchildren: William Hawthorne, Rickey Hawthorne, Marc Hawthorne, Pamela Haley. A.B., Youngstown State U., 1951, LL.B., 1955, LL.D. (hon.), 1969; LL.D. (hon.), Syracuse U., 1972. Editor Buckeye Rev. newspaper, 1956; exec. dir. FEPC, Youngstown, 1956-59; practiced law 1959-61; mem. firm Goldberg & Jones, 1968-69; asst. U.S. atty. 1961-67; asst. gen. counsel Nat. Adv. Commn. on Civil Disorders, 1967-68; gen. counsel NAACP, 1969-79; judge U.S. Ct. of Appeals, 6th Circuit, 1979—; dir. Buckeye Rev. Pub. Co.; chmn. Con. on Adequate Def. and Incentives in Mil.; mem. Task Force-Vets. Benefits. Served with USAAF, 1945-47. Mem. Ohio State Bar Assn., Mahoning County Bar Assn., Fed. Bar Assn., Nat. Bar Assn., Am. Arbitration Assn., Youngstown Area Devel. Corp., Urban League, Nat. Conf. Black Lawyers, ABA (co-chmn. com. constl. rights criminal sect. 1971-73), Kappa Alpha Psi. Baptist. Clubs: Houston Law (Youngstown); Elks. Office: 432 US Post Office Cincinnati OH 45202 *

JONES, PATRICK ALLEN, lawyer; b. Huntsville, Ala., Sept. 25, 1956; s. Allen H. and Gussie M. (Patterson) J. BS in Acctg., Auburn U., 1978; JD, Samford U., 1981. Bar: Ala. 1981, U.S. Dist. Ct. (no. dist.) Ala. 1981. Assoc. Knight & Griffith, Cullman, Ala., 1981-82; sole practice Huntsville, 1982-83, 86—; assoc. Berry, Ables et al, Huntsville, 1982-86; prof. Calhoun Community Coll., Decatur, Ala., 1983-84. Mem. ABA, Ala. Bar Assn., Assn. Trial Lawyers Am., Ala. Trial Lawyers Assn., Ala. Jaycees (legal counsel 1985—, region dir. 1985—), Huntsville Jaycees (v.p. 1985—). State civil litigation, Federal civil litigation, General corporate. Home: 146 Will Holt Rd Hazel Green AL 35758 Office: 112-F South Side Sq Huntsville AL 35801

JONES, PAUL LAWRENCE, lawyer; b. Snow Hill, N.C., Mar. 15, 1948; s. LeRoy and Esther Belle (Harper) J.; m. Asonia Lynette Battle, June 14, 1980; 1 child, Krystle Paulette. B.S., N.C. Agrl. and Tech. State U., 1971; J.D., N.C. Central U., 1974. Bar: N.C. 1975, D.C. 1976, U.S. Tax Ct. 1976, U.S. Ct. Mil. Appeals 1976, U.S. Ct. Claims 1976, U.S. Dist. Ct. (ea. dist.) N.C. 1979, U.S. Supreme Ct. 1982. Atty., asst. clk. U.S. Supreme Ct., Washington, 1974-76; assoc. firm Beech & Pollock, Kinston, N.C., 1979-80; mng. atty. Eastern Carolina Legal Services, Wilson, N.C., 1980-82; ptnr. firm Beech & Jones, Kinston, 1982—. Mem. N.C. State Banking Commn., Raleigh, 1983; treas. Lenoir County Democratic Com., Kinston, 1983. Served as capt. JAGC, U.S. Army, 1976-79. Mem. ABA, N.C. Bar Assn., Assn. Trial Lawyers Am., N.C. Acad. Trial Lawyers, Lenoir County Bar Assn. (pres. 1983), Lenoir County C. of C. (bd. dirs. 1983), Phi Alpha Delta. Mem. African Methodist Episcopal Ch. Lodges: Rotary, Masons, Shriners. State civil litigation, Criminal. Home: 205 Summit Ave Kinston NC 28501 Office: Beech & Jones 308 S Queen St Kinston NC 28501

JONES, RAYMOND EDWARD, JR., brewing executive; b. New Bern, N.C., Jan. 27, 1927; s. Raymond Edward and Ellen LaVerne (Mallard) J.; children: Leslie Anne, Raymond Edward III. B.S., U. Md., 1953; LL.B., U. Balt., 1962. Bar: Md. 1962. Office mgr. Hopkins Furniture Co., Annapolis, Md., 1953-55; sr. v.p. legal, sec. Nat. Brewing Co., Balt., 1956-75; (merged with Carling Brewing Co. 1975); sr. v.p. legal and indsl. relations, dir. Carling Nat. Breweries, Inc., 1975-78; sec., asso. gen. counsel Miller Brewing Co., 1978-84, v.p., gen. counsel, sec., 1984—; house counsel and/or officer Divex, Inc., Laco Products, Inc., Laco Corp., C.W. Abbott, Inc., Pompeian, Inc., Interhost Corp., Solarine Co., Balt. Baseball Club, Inc., 1967-75. Bd. dirs. Soc. Preservation Md. Antiquities, 1969-71. Served with USNR, 1942-45. Mem. ABA, Md. Bar Assn., Balt. Bar Assn., Sigma Chi, Sigma Delta Chi. Presbyterian. Home: 2543 W Hunt Club Circle Glendale WI 53209 Office: 3939 W Highland Blvd Milwaukee WI 53208

JONES, RICHARD CYRUS, lawyer; b. Oak Park, Ill., Oct. 20, 1928; s. Ethler E. and Margaret S. (Stoner) J.; m. Betty Jane Jones; children: Richard C., Carrie, William. Ph.B., DePaul U., 1960, J.D., 1963. Bar: Ill. 1963. Dept. mgr. Chgo. Title & Trust Co., 1947-64; mem. Sachnoff, Schrager, Jones, Weaver & Rubenstein Ltd. and predecessor firms, Chgo., 1964-81; of counsel Sachnoff, Weaver & Rubenstein, Chgo., 1981—; instr. Real Estate Inst., Chgo., 1970—. Trustee, sec. Income Properties/Equity Trust, 1974—; trustee and chmn. Ind. Dirs. of Wis. Real Estate Investment Trust, 1980—. Served with U.S. Army, 1951-52. Decorated Bronze Star. Mem. ABA, Ill. Bar Assn., Chgo. Bar Assn. (com. chmn. real property law 1970-72, 76—), Chgo. Council Lawyers, Delta Theta Phi. Lodge: Kiwanis. Real property, General corporate, Probate. Home: 1044 Forest Ave River Forest IL 60305 Office: 30 S Wacker Dr 29th Floor Chicago IL 60606

JONES, RICHARD L., justice Ala. Supreme Ct.; b. Carrollton, Ala., Mar. 3, 1923; m. Jean Leslie; children—Rick, Marilyn, Leslie. LL.B., U. Ala. Bar: Ala. bar. Practiced law Aliceville, Ala., Bessemer, Ala., Birmingham, Ala.; asso. justice Ala. Supreme Ct., Montgomery; mem. Uniform State Law Commn., Ala. Jud. Conf. and Code Revision Com. Elder, tchr. Shades Valley Presbyterian Ch. Served to col. USAR. Mem. Ala. Trial Lawyers Assn. (pres.). Office: Supreme Court 445 Dexter Ave PO Box 218 Montgomery AL 36130 *

JONES, ROBERT EDWARD, justice state supreme court; b. Portland, Oreg., July 5, 1927; s. Howard C. and Leita (Hendricks) J.; m. Pearl F. Jensen, May 29, 1948; children—Jeffrey Scott, Julie Lynn. B.A., U. Hawaii, 1949; J.D., Lewis and Clark Coll., 1953; LL.D. (hon.), City U., Seattle, 1984. Bar: Oreg. 1953. Trial atty. Portland, Oreg., 1953-63; judge Oreg. Circuit Ct., Portland, 1963-83; justice Oreg. Supreme Ct., Salem, 1983—; mem. faculty Nat. Jud. Coll., Am. Acad. Jud. Edn.; pres. Oreg. Circuit Judges Assn., 1967—, Oreg. Trial Lawyers Assn., 1959; former mem. Oreg. Evidence Revision Commn., Oreg. Ho. of Reps.; former chair Oreg. Commn. Prison Terms and Parole Standards; adj. prof. Northwestern Sch. Law, Lewis and Clark Coll. 1963—. Bd. overseers Lewis and Clark Coll. Served to capt. JAGC, USNR. Recipient merit award Multnomah Bar Assn., 1979; Citizen award NCCJ; Service to Mankind award Sertoma Club Oreg.; James Madison award Sigma Delta Chi; named Disting. Grad., Northwestern Sch. Law. Mem. State Bar Oreg. (former chmn. continuing legal edn. com.). Judicial administration. Office: Supreme Ct Oregon 1147 State St Salem OR 97310

JONES, ROBERT JAMES, lawyer; b. Washington, Aug. 1, 1949; s. James Henry and Margaret (Fowler) J.; m. Carol Compton, children: Matthew Fowler, Jennifer Noelle. BA, Va. Mil. Inst., 1971; JD, Cath. U., 1974. Bar: Va. 1974, D.C. 1975, U.S. Dist. Ct. (ea. dist.) Va., U.S. Dist. Ct. D.C., U.S. Ct. Appeals (4th and D.C. cirs.). Assoc. Siciliano, Ellis, Sheridan & Dyer, Arlington, Va., 1974-80; ptnr. Stern & Jones, Fairfax, Va., 1980-84; sole practice Fairfax, 1984—. Served to 2d lt. USAF, 1971-74. Mem. ABA, Va. Bar Assn., D.C. Bar Assn. Roman Catholic. Avocation: sports. Consumer commercial, State civil litigation, Real property. Office: 5532 G Hempstead Way Springfield VA 22310

JONES, RONALD LEE, lawyer, writer; b. Ames, Iowa, Apr. 11, 1942; s. L. Meyer and Mary Elizabeth (Homer) J.; m. Susan Ann Smith, July 29, 1977. B.A., Ill. Wesleyan U., 1965; cert. Naval Justice Sch., Camp Pendleton, Calif., 1968; J.D., Calif. Western Sch. Law, 1972. Bar: Nebr. 1973, U.S. Ct. Appeals (8th cir.) 1973, U.S. Supreme Ct. 1979. Corp. counsel Gene Fuller, Inc., San Diego, 1972-73; asst. gen. counsel Daniel Internat. Corp., Greenville, S.C., 1974-79; v.p., gen. counsel, sec. Royster Co., Norfolk, Va., 1979-83; writer, Virginia Beach, Va., 1983—; counsel Peter Kiewit Sons, Inc., Omaha, 1984—; chmn. lawyers coordinating com. Fla. Phosphate Council, Tampa, 1980. Author: Practice Preventive Corporation Law, 1985. Editor Corp. Counsel Reporter newsletter, 1985—. Served to capt. USMC, 1965-69. Mem. ABA (corp., banking and bus. law sect., constrn. law forum com.), Fertilizer Inst., Am. Mfrs. Assn. Preventive Corporate, Construction, General corporate. Home: PO Box 37915 Omaha NE 68137 Office: Peter Kiewit Sons Inc One Thousand Kiewit Plaza Omaha NE 68131

JONES, RONALD RICHARD, lawyer; b. Pitts., Dec. 24, 1948; s. Richard Joseph and Dorothy Rosemary (McSteen) J.; m. Rosenda Mejia, Nov. 13, 1980; 1 child, Marina Christine. BA, U. Pitts., 1970; MA magna cum laude, Pitts. Theol. Sem., 1973; JD cum laude, Duquesne U., 1977. Bar: Pa. 1977, U.S. Dist. Ct. (we. dist.) Pa. 1977, U.S. Ct. Mil. Appeals 1979, Guam 1980, U.S. Dist. Ct. (mid. dist.) Pa. 1985. Assoc. Reed, Smith, Shaw & McClay, Pitts., 1981-87. Served to lt. comdr. USN, 1977-80. Mem. ABA, Allegheny County Bar Assn., Guam Bar Assn., Res. Officers Assn. Avocation: music. Federal civil litigation, State civil litigation, Personal injury. Office: Willman and Arnold 700 McKnight Park Dr Pittsburgh PA 15237

JONES, RUSSELL C., lawyer; b. Houston, Aug. 30, 1949; s. W.J. and Frieda (Russell) J.; m. Thelma Holoway, June 5, 1971; children: Stephanie, Jennifer. BA, Johns Hopkins U., 1971, MA in Internat. Studies, 1972; JD, U. Houston, 1979. Bar: Tex. 1979, U.S. Ct. Appeals (5th cir.), U.S. Dist. Ct. (so. dist.) Tex. Internat. banking officer First City Nat. Bank, Houston, 1972-74; fin. analyst Arabian Am. Oil Co., Dhahran, Saudi Arabia, 1974-76; fin. adminstr. Aramco Services Co., Houston, 1976-82; sole practice Stafford, Tex., 1982—. Mayor pro-tem City Missouri City, Tex., 1980-86; bd. dirs. Ft. Bend Cen. appraisal Dist., Rosenburg, Tex., 1984-85. Mem. State Bar Tex. Assn., Houston Bar Assn. Republican. Methodist. Banking, Consumer commercial, Local government. Home: 2307 Oakview Missouri City TX 77459 Office: 12603 Southwest Freeway Suite 360 Stafford TX 77477

JONES, SCRANTON, lawyer; b. Ft. Worth, Tex., July 29, 1921; s. Harper and Elizabeth (Boulware) J.; m. Marjorie Lewis, Feb. 8, 1975; children—Allison Simonton, Julianne Armstrong. B.A., U. Tex.-Austin, 1942, J.D., 1947. Bar: Tex. 1947. Asst. dist. atty. Tarrant County, Tex., 1947-49; ptnr. Jones & Morris, Ft. Worth, 1950-67; asst. atty. gen. Tex., Austin, 1962-63; adj. prof. bus. law Tex. Christian U., 1968-76; sole practice, Ft. Worth, 1976—. Councilman, mayor pro-tem, Ft. Worth, 1963-67; chmn. Tarrant County Hist. Marker Commn., 1965-66; pres., dir. Tarrant County Council on Alcoholism, 1967-70. Served with USNR, 1942-46. Mem. Ft. Worth Bar Assn. (dir. 1961), Tarrant County Hist. Soc. (v.p., dir. 1963-67). Episcopalian. Club: Rotary Internat. (dist. gov. 1967-68). Author: The Legal Environment of Business, 1972. General practice, Probate. Home: 5817 El Campo Terrace Fort Worth TX 76107 Office: 3030 Sandage St Fort Worth TX 76109

JONES, STEPHEN, lawyer; b. Lafayette, La., July 1, 1940; s. Leslie William and Gladys A. (Williams) J.; m. Virginia Hadden (div.); 1 son, John Chapman; m. 2d, Sherrel Alice Stephens, Dec. 27, 1973; children—Stephen Mark, Leslie Rachael, Edward St. Andrew. Student U. Tex. 1960-63; LL.B., U. Okla. 1966. Sec. Rep. Minority Conf., Tex. Ho. of Reps., 1963; personal asst. to Richard M. Nixon, N.Y.C., 1964; adminstrv. asst. to Congressman Paul Findley, 1966-69; legal counsel to gov. of Okla., 1967; spl. asst. U.S. Senator Charles H. Percy and U.S. Rep. Donald Rumsfeld, 1968; mem. U.S. del. to North Atlantic Assembly, NATO, 1968; staff counsel cesure task force Ho. of Reps. Impeachment Inquiry, 1974; spl. U.S. atty. No. Dist. Okla., 1979; spl. prosecutor, spl. asst. dist. atty. State of Okla., 1977; judge Okla. Ct. Appeals, 1982; civil jury instrn. com. Okla. Supreme Ct., 1979-81; adv. com. ct. rules Okla. Ct. Criminal Appeals, 1980; now mng. ptnr. Jones and Jennings, Enid, Okla.; adj. prof. U. Okla., 1973-76; instr. Phillips U., 1982—. Author: Oklahoma and Politics in State and Nation, 1907-62. Acting chmn. Rep. State Com., Okla., 1982; mem. vestry, sr. warden St. Matthews Episc. Ch. Mem. ABA, Okla. Bar Assn., Garfield County Bar Assn. Clubs: Capitol Hill, Nat. Lawyers (Washington), Whitehall (Oklahoma City), Oakwood Country (Enid), Tulsa. Contbr. articles profl. jours. Criminal, Civil rights, Federal civil litigation. Address: PO Box 472 Enid OK 73702

JONES, THEODORE LAWRENCE, lawyer; b. Dallas, Nov. 29, 1920; s. Theodore Evan and Ernestine Lucy (Douthit) J.; m. Marion Elizabeth Thomas, Feb. 29, 1944; children: Suzanne Lynn, Scott Evan, Stephen Lawrence, Shannon Elizabeth. B.B.A., U. Tex., 1944, J.D., 1948; postgrad., So. Meth. U., 1950-52, Am. U., 1965-66. Bar: Tex. 1948, U.S. Supreme Ct. 1962. Asso. Carrington, Gowan, Johnson & Walker, Dallas, 1948-51; gen. counsel W. H. Cothrum & Co., Dallas, 1951-54; practice law Dallas, 1955-56; asst. atty. gen. Tex.; chief div. ins., banking and corp. 1957-60; partner Herring & Jones, Austin, Tex., 1960-61; gen. counsel Maritime Adminstrn., U.S. Dept. Commerce, 1961-63; dep. gen. counsel Dept. Commerce, 1963-64, dep. fed. hwy. adminstr., 1964-66; pres. Am. Ins. Assn., N.Y.C., 1967-86; counsel Hunton & Williams, Washington, 1986—; chmn. interdeptl. com. for bilateral agreements for acceptance of nuclear ship, Savannah, 1962-63; lectr. Fgn. Service Inst., 1962-64; alt. U.S. rep. 11th session Diplomatic Conf. on Maritime Law, Brussels, 1962; advisor U.S. del. 6th session Council, Intergovtl. Maritime Consultative Orgn., London, 1962; mem. maritime subsidy bd. U.S. Dept. Commerce, 1962-63; acting hwy. beautification coordinator, 1965-66; del. White House Conf. on Internat. Cooperation; mem. Property-Casualty Ins. Council, 1976-86, Internat. Ins. Adv. Council, 1980-87; mem. adv. com. Pension Benefit Guaranty Corp., 1977; mem. Time Newstour, Eastern Europe and Persian Gulf, 1981, Mexico and Panama, 1983, Pacific Rim, 1985; bd. dirs. Nat. Safety Council, 1967, Ins. Inst. for Hwy. Safety, 1967-86. Contbr. articles to legal, ins. and fin. jours. Served to lt. (j.g.) USNR, 1944-46. Mem. ABA, Fed. Bar Assn. (chmn. nat. speakers bur. 1964), Tex. Bar Assn., Friars, Phi Delta Phi, Beta Gamma Sigma, Phi Eta Sigma. Democrat. Presbyterian. Clubs: Met., Capitol Hill (Washington), Nat. Democratic (Washington), Great Oaks Country (Floyd, Va.), World Trade Ctr. (N.Y.C.). Insurance, Environment, Legislative. Home: 648 S Carolina Ave SE Washington DC 20003 also: Rt 3 Box 182-B Floyd VA 24091 Office: Hunton & Williams 2000 Pennsylvania Ave NW Suite 9000 Washington DC 20036

JONES, THOMAS MCREYNOLDS, lawyer; b. Pasadena, Calif., Sept. 3, 1941; s. Paul McReynolds and Dora (Dixon) J.; m. Rita Mae Jones, Aug. 29, 1970; children: Felicia Anne, Tyler Thomas. BS, U. Calif. Berkeley, 1962; JD, UCLA, 1965. Bar: Calif. 1966, U.S. Dist. Ct. (so. dist.) Calif. 1966. Sole practice Los Angeles and Orange counties, Calif., 1966-70; asst. appointments sec. Office Gov. Reagan, Sacramento, 1970-73; chief dep. commr. Calif. Dept. Corps., Los Angeles, 1974-75; asst. gen. counsel, asst. sec. Wynn's Internat. Inc., Fullerton, Calif., 1975-79; sr. v.p. Dominion Capital Corp., Newport Beach, Calif., 1980-82; sole practice, Newport Beach, Calif., 1983-86; ptnr. Reed & Jones, Costa Mesa, Calif., 1986—. Mem. Gold Medal com. U.S. Olympic Com., Orange County chpt.; bd. dirs. Saddleback Coll. Found., 1983-87; benefactors com. S. Coast Repertory Theatre; v.p. Irvine Children's Fund, bd. dirs.; bldg. and devel. com. Irvine Med. Ctr.; gen. counsel, bd. dirs. Exec. Council Orange County; bd. dirs. Protocol Found. Orange County. Served to lt. USNR, 1968-74. Mem. ABA (corp., bus., real estate, internat. law sects.), Calif. Bar Assn., State Bar Calif. (corp. com.), Irvine C. of C. (pres., bd. dirs. 1983—), Calif. Alumni Assn., Costa Mesa C. of C., (UCLA Law Alumni Assn. (bd. dirs. 1974-77). General corporate, Administrative and regulatory, Real property. Office: Finley Kumble Wagner 4400 MacArthur Blvd Suite 300 Newport Beach CA 92660

JONES, THOMAS ROBERT, lawyer; b. Milw., Apr. 14, 1949; s. Robert Daniel and Dorothy (Stanton) J.; m. Christine Faupl, Dec. 10, 1976; 1 child, Anthony Faupl. BA, U. Wis., 1973; JD, Golden Gate U., 1979. Bar: Calif. 1980, Wis. 1980, U.S. Dist. Ct. (ea. dist.) Wis. 1980, U.S. Ct. Appeals (7th cir.) 1981. Assoc. Jones & Feldner, Milw., 1980-85, Cartwright et al, San Francisco, 1985-86; ptnr. Mentkowski & Jones, Milw., 1986-87; sole practice Mill Valley, Calif., 1987—. Served with U.S. Army, 1967-69. Mem. Assn. Trial Lawyers Am., Calif. Trial Lawyers Assn., Wis. Assn. Trial Lawyers. State civil litigation, Personal injury. Office: 100 Shoreline Hwy Mill Valley CA 94941

JONES, WILLIAM F., lawyer; b. Newark, July 8, 1921; s. George Fred and Edna Irene (Davis) J.; m. Gwendolyn A. Glenwood, July 27, 1946; children: Jacqueline A., Mark W. AB, Union Coll., 1942; JD, Albany Law Sch., 1948. Bar: N.Y., Ohio. Claims atty. Aetna Life & Casualty, Albany, N.Y., 1948-50; atty. underwriting, govt. affairs and corp. planning Royal Ins., N.Y.C., 1950—; adj. prof. Coll. of Ins., N.Y.C. Avocations: art, music, sports. Home: 416 Briarpatch Ln Charlotte NC 28211 Office: Royal Ins 9300 Arrowpoint Blvd Charlotte NC 28211

JONES, WILLIAM REX, law educator, lawyer; b. Murphysboro, Ill., Oct. 20, 1922; s. Claude E. and Ivy P. (McCormick) J.; m. Miriam R. Lamy, Mar. 27, 1944; m. 2d Gerri L. Haun, June 30, 1972; children: Michael Kimber, Jeanne Reeves, Patricia Combs, Sally Hatch, Kevin. B.S., U. Louisville, 1950; J.D., U. Ky., 1968; LL.M., U. Mich., 1970. Bar: Ky. 1969, Fla. 1969, Ind. 1971. Exec. v.p. Paul Miller Ford, Inc., Lexington, Ky., 1951-64; pres. Bill's Seat Cover Ctr., Inc., Lexington, Ky., 1952-65, Bill Jones Real Estate, Inc., Lexington, Ky., 1965-70; asst. prof. law Ind. U., Indpls., 1970-73, assoc. prof., 1973-75, prof., 1975-80; dean Salmon P. Chase Coll. Law No. Ky. U., Highland Heights, 1980-85, prof., 1980—. Author: Kentucky Criminal Trial Practice, 1985. Served as 1st sgt. U.S. Army, 1940-44. Cook fellow U. Mich., 1969-70; W.G. Hart fellow Queen Mary Coll. U. London, 1985. Mem. ABA, Nat. Legal Aid and Defenders Assn., Nat. Dist. Attys. Assn., Order of Coif. Legal education, Criminal. Office: Nunn Hall Northern Ky U University Dr Highland Heights KY 41076

JONES, WILLIAM ROBY, lawyer; b. Shreveport, La., Jan. 15, 1948; s. Roby D. and Wilma (Tyler) J., m. Laurie Ann Turner, May 30, 1981; children: Kris, Adam. BS, La. State U., 1971, JD, 1973. Bar: La. 1973. Ptnr. Horton & Jones, Coushatta, La., 1973-85; atty. 39th Jud. Dist., Coushatta, 1980—; bd. dirs. Am. Bank and Trust Co., Coushatta. Exec. com. Northwest Devel. Ctr., Shreveport, 1976-80; chmn. Red River Dem. Exec. Com., Coushatta, 1976-85. Mem. ABA, La. Bar Assn., Red River Parish Bar Assn., La. Dist. Attys. Assn., U.S. Dist. Attys. Assn., Coushatta/Red River C. of C. (pres. 1984). Baptist. Criminal, General practice. Home: PO Box 598 Coushatta LA 71019 Office: Office of Dist Atty PO Box 606 Coushatta LA 71019

JONTZ, DENNIS EUGENE, lawyer; b. Kewanee, Ill., Feb. 25, 1948; s. Lowell Milton and Maxine Alice (Bitting) J.; m. Mary Ann DeBasio, Jan. 18, 1974; 1 child, Ashlee. BA in Econs., Drake U., 1970, JD, 1973, MBA, 1974. Bar: Iowa 1973, U.S. Ct. Mil. Appeals 1974, N.Mex. 1977, U.S. Dist. Ct. N.Mex. 1977, U.S. Ct. Appeals (10th cir.) 1979, U.S. Supreme Ct. 1979, U.S. Claims Ct. 1979. Asst. atty. gen. State of Iowa, Des Moines, 1973-74; ptnr. Civerolo, Hansen & Wolf, Albuquerque, 1978—. Served to maj. JAGC, USAF, 1974-78. Mem. N.Mex. State Bar Assn. (chmn. computer automation com.). Lutheran. Lodge: Rotary. Avocation: golf. Contracts commercial, Government contracts and claims, Real property. Office: Civerolo Hansen & Wolf PO Box 887 Albuquerque NM 87111

JOOR, WILLIAM EUGENE, III, lawyer; b. Elizabeth, N.J., Jan. 25, 1940; s. William Eugene Jr. and Ruth Emily (Houston) J.; m. Diana Huff Marshall, Aug. 15, 1965 (dov. Apr. 1983); 1 child, David Marshall; m. Rose Ann Medlin, Sept. 17, 1983. BA, U. Tex., 1961; LLB, Harvard U., 1966. Bar: Tex. 1966, U.S. Dist. Ct. (so. dist.) Tex. 1966. Assoc. Vinson & Elkins, Houston, 1966-74, ptnr., 1974—. Trustee Houston Ballet Found., 1974-80, Alley Theater, Houston, 1976. Served to lt. USNR, 1961-66. Mem. ABA, Tex. Bar Assn. Methodist. Clubs: Coronado, Sugar Creek Country (Houston). Avocations: golf, skiing, gardening. General corporate, Securities. Home: 610 Grecian Way Houston TX 77024 Office: Vinson & Elkins 3600 First City Tower 1001 Fannin Houston TX 77002-6760

JORANDBY, RICHARD LEROY, lawyer; b. Grafton, N.D., June 19, 1938; s. Alvin Peder and Helene (Schmidt) J.; m. Cheryl Lantie Krauch, June 2, 1967; children: Elizabeth, Abigail. BA, U. Minn., 1960; JD, Vanderbilt U., 1966. Bar: Fla. 1966, U.S. Dist. Ct. (so. dist.) Fla. 1966, U.S. Supreme Ct. 1974, U.S. Ct. Appeals (5th, D.C. and 11th cirs.) 1986, N.Y., 1986. Assoc. Jones, Adams, Paine & Foster, West Palm Beach, Fla., 1966-69; sole practice Palm Beach, 1969-72; pub. defender State of Fla., West Palm Beach, 1973—; mem. juvenile law and practice com. Fla. Continuing Legal Edn. Contbr. articles to legal jour. Bd. dirs. Urban League Palm Beach County, 1975—, Pride, Inc., 1973—, CARP Rehab. Ctr., 1975—; treas. Rep. exec. com. Palm Beach County, 1970-74. Served with USAR, 1961-67. Recipient Dr. Theodore Norley Community Service award Urban League Palm Beach County, 1980; named One of Outstanding Young Men Am., U.S. Jaycees,

1973. Mem. ABA, Fla. Bar Assn., Palm Beach County Bar Assn., Nat. Assn. Criminal Def. Lawyers, Nat. Legal Aid and Defenders Assn., Nat. Inst. Justice (pres. adv. bd. 1982), Fraternal Order Police Assn. (pres. 1986—). Lodge: Lions (West Palm Beach) (officer 1986). Avocations: reading, jogging, tennis, swimming, traveling. Criminal. Home: 5554 Old Bridge Rd West Palm Beach FL 33415 Office: Office Pub Defender 224 Datura St West Palm Beach FL 33401

JORDAN, ALEXANDER JOSEPH, JR., lawyer; b. New London, Conn., Oct. 11, 1938; s. Alexander Joseph and Alice Elizabeth (Mugovero) J.; m. Mary Carolyn Miller, Aug. 8, 1964; children—Jennifer, Michael, Stephanie. B.S., U.S. Naval Acad., 1960; LL.B., Harvard U., 1968. Ptnr., Gaston Snow & Ely Bartlett, Boston, 1968—. Served with USN, 1960-65, capt. USNR, 1965—. Mem. ABA, Boston Bar Assn., U.S. Naval Inst. General corporate, Real property, Securities. Office: Gaston Snow & Ely Bartlett 1 Federal St Boston MA 02110

JORDAN, BRUCE, lawyer; b. Miami, Fla., Nov. 6, 1953; s. Charles William and Edith Harriet (Seidman) J.; m. Judith Ann Luck, Aug. 8, 1978; children: Jonathan E., Michael R. BS in Bus. Edn., U. Fla., 1975; JD, South Tex. Coll. of Law, 1978. Bar: Tex. 1979. Staff atty. Atwood Oceanics, Inc., Houston, 1979-86, sr. staff atty., 1986—. Mem. ABA, Am. Corp. Counsel Assn., Internat. Assn. Drilling Contractors (offshore legal group). Avocations: bicycling, racquetball. General corporate, Private international, Insurance. Office: Atwood Oceanics Inc 15835 Park Ten Place Dr Houston TX 77084

JORDAN, CHARLES MILTON, lawyer; b. Houston, Apr. 3, 1949; s. Milton Reginald and Jean (Burris) J.; m. Jan Patricia Kilpatrick, Dec. 23, 1969; children: Nicole Catherine, John Milton. BBA, U. Tex., 1971, JD, 1975. Bar: Tex. 1975, U.S. Dist. Ct. (so. dist.) Tex. 1976, U.S. Supreme Ct. 1978, U.S. Ct. Appeals (5th cir.) 1979, U.S. Ct. Appeals (11th cir.) 1981, U.S. Dist. Ct. (no. dist.) Tex. 1982, U.S. Dist. Ct. (we. and ea. dists.) Tex. 1983. Assoc. Troutman, Earle & Hill, Austin, 1975-76, Simpson & Burwell, Texas City, 1976-78, Smith & Herz, Galveston, Tex., 1978-80; ptnr. Dibrell & Greer, Galveston, 1980-85, Barlow, Todd, Crews & Jordan P.C., Houston, 1986—. Active Galveston County Mental Helath Assn., 1979; Galveston Hist. Found., 1980; commr. Commn. Texas City/Galveston Ports, 1984. Served to 1st lt. USAF, 1971-77. Recipient Outstanding Young Man Am. award, U.S. Jaycees, 1980. Mem. ABA, Tex. Bar Assn., Galveston County Bar Assn. (pres. 1981-82, bd. dirs. 1985—), Tex. Young Lawyers Assn (bd. dirs. 1982-85, Outstanding Dir. award 1983-84), Galveston County Young Lawyers Assn. (pres. 1979-80, Outstanding Young Lawyer award 1981). Democrat. Methodist. Federal civil litigation, State civil litigation. Office: Barlow Todd Crews & Jordan PC 17225 El Camino Real #400 Houston TX 77058

JORDAN, DANIEL PATRICK, JR., law librarian; b. Bklyn., July 15, 1951; s. Daniel Patrick and Nan (Sinnott) J.; m. Louise Harmon, May 25, 1985. BA, Bklyn. Coll., 1975; JD, U. Pacific, 1980; MLS, Pratt Inst., 1982. Ref. librarian Touro Coll., Huntington, N.Y., 1982-83, head pub. services, 1983-86, law librarian, 1986—; part-time ref. librarian Bklyn. Law Sch. Mem. ABA, Calif. Bar Assn., L.I. Hist. Soc., N.Y. Irish Hist. Roundtable, Am. Assn. Law Libraries. Librarianship, Legal education, Legal history. Office: Touro Coll Jacob D Fuchsberg Law Ctr 300 Nassau Rd Huntington NY 11743

JORDAN, DAVID FRANCIS, JR., lawyer; b. N.Y.C., Apr. 18, 1928; s. David Francis Jordan and Frances Marion (J.) Edebohls; m. Bess Vukas, Aug. 4, 1956; children—Melissa Marie, David Francis III, Dennis Paul. A.B., Princeton U., 1950; J.D., NYU, 1953, LL.M. in Taxation, 1970; postgrad. U. Oxford, 1949; grad. Judge Adv. Gen.'s Sch., 1964, Indsl. Coll. Armed Forces, 1973, Command and Gen. Staff Coll., 1968. Bar: N.Y. 1953, U.S. Dist. Ct. D.C. 1953, U.S. Ct. Appeals (D.C. cir.) 1953, U.S. Ct. Mil. Appeals 1953. U.S. Supreme Ct. 1957, U.S. Dist. Ct. (no., so., ea. and we. dists.) N.Y. 1958, U.S. Ct. Appeals (2d cir.) 1958, U.S. Tax Ct. 1958. Law clk. U.S. Ct. Appeals (2d cir.), 1957-58, chief dep., clk., 1958-59; sole practice, Smithtown, N.Y., 1959-63; ptnr. O'Rourke & Jordan, Central Islip, N.Y., 1963-67; asst. dist. atty. Suffolk County, Riverhead, N.Y., 1969-74; law clk. Supreme Ct., Suffolk County, 1975; investigator N.Y. Supreme Ct. Appellate Div. 2d dept., Bklyn., 1976; corp. counsel City of Newburgh, N.Y., 1976-78; acting city mgr., 1978; U.S. magistrate Ea. Dist. N.Y., Bklyn., Uniondale and Hauppauge, N.Y., 1978—; prosecutor 4th JAG Detachment, N.Y.C., 1958-64; mil. judge U.S. Army Judiciary, Washington, 1969-80; lectr. fed. procedure Suffolk County N.Y. Bar Assn., JAGC, 1978—. Adult leader Suffolk County council Boy Scouts Am., St. James, N.Y., 1960s. Served with JAGC, U.S. Army, 1954-57, to col. USAR. Decorated Meritorious Service medal. Mem. ABA, N.Y. State Bar Assn. (mem. fed. constn. com., lectr. fed. procedure 1978—), Suffolk County Bar Assn. (mem. various coms.). Roman Catholic. Lodges: K.C., Elks. Federal civil litigation, Criminal. Office: US Courthouse 300 Rabro Dr Hauppauge NY 11788

JORDAN, DENVER CHRISTIAN, lawyer; b. Indpls., Oct. 14, 1953; s. Denver Cecil Rhodes and Emily Christine (Sorhage) J.; m. Marsha Ann Shaffer, Oct. 29, 1983. B.S. in Bus., Purdue U., 1976, B.A. in Am. History, 1976, M.S.I.A., Krannert Sch., 1977; J.D., Ind. U., 1980. Bar: Ind. 1980, U.S. Dist. Ct. (no. and so. dists.) Ind. 1980, U.S. Ct. Appeals (7th cir.) 1983. Adminstrv. asst. Ind. U., Bloomington, 1978-80; assoc. Raver & Assocs., Fort Wayne, Ind., 1980-84; ptnr. Raver, Jordan & Assocs., Fort Wayne, 1985—; TV show host; lectr. in field. Pres. Directors, Fort Wayne, 1980-84. Mem. ABA, Assn. Trial Lawyers Am., Allen County Bar Assn. (dir. Speaker's Bur.). Club: U.S. Power Squadron. Lodges: Lions (sec. 1982-84), Masons. Contracts commercial, Bankruptcy, Personal injury. Home: 2734 Westmore Dr Fort Wayne IN 46825 Office: Raver Jordan & Assocs 520 S Calhoun St Fort Wayne IN 46802

JORDAN, FRANK J., lawyer; b. New Canaan, Conn., June 13, 1929; s. Michael and Anna (Markva) J.; m. Sheila Filene, June 19, 1960. B.S., U.S. Mcht. Marine Acad., 1953; J.D., N.Y. Law Sch., 1961. Bar: N.Y. 1961, U.S. Patent and Trademark Office 1961, U.S. Dist. Ct. (so. and ea. dists.) N.Y. 1963, U.S. Supreme Ct. 1967, U.S. Ct. Appeals (fed. cir.) 1968. Atty., Am. Standard, N.Y.C., 1963-65; assoc. Brown and Seward, N.Y.C., 1965-66; atty. Am. Can Co., Greenwich Conn., 1966-68; sole practice, N.Y.C., 1969-79; ptnr. Jordan & Hamburg, N.Y.C., 1979—. Contbr. regular column on patent law to bi-monthly publ. Served to lt. USN, 1953-55, Korea. Mem. Assn. Bar City N.Y., Internat. Patent and Trademark Assn., N.Y. Patent Law Assn., N.Y. Law Sch. Alumni Assn., U.S. Mcht. Marine Acad. Alumni Assn. Club: East Hampton Yacht. Patent, Trademark and copyright. Home: 205 3d Ave New York NY 10003 Office: Jordan & Hamburg 122 E 42d St New York NY 10168

JORDAN, GLENN ERVAL, lawyer, consultant; b. Findlay, Ill., Mar. 14, 1921; s. Erval and Edna Merle (Tracy) J.; m. Labonne Willine Haisty, May 1, 1948; B.S., U. Detroit, 1951, J.D., 1953. Bar: Mich. 1953, U.S. Dist. Ct. (ea. dist.) Mich. 1953, U.S. Ct. Appeals (6th cir.) 1953. Engr. Packard Motor Co., Detroit, 1952-54; ptnr. Suffety & Jordan, Saginaw, Mich., 1954-58; judge Saginaw Probate Ct., 1958-66, chief judge, 1966-82; sole practice, Saginaw, 1983—. Co-founder Childrens Charter Mich., Kalamazoo, 1964, Youth Protection Services, Saginaw, 1965. Served with U.S. Army, 1942-46. Mem. Saginaw County Bar Assn., Mich. Bar Assn., Mich. Probate Judges Assn. (pres. 1968-69, presiding judge 1967-68), Nat. Coll. Probate Judges, Am. Judicature Soc., Mich. Bar (chmn. juvenile affairs com. 1970). Democrat. Clubs: Pioneer, Germania (Saginaw). Lodge: Shriners. Probate, Judicial administration, State civil litigation. Home: 1122 Passolt Saginaw MI 48602 Office: Probate Ct Govt Ctr Saginaw MI 48602

JORDAN, HAROLD NATHAN, lawyer; b. Beloit, Kans., Jan. 19, 1906; s. Amzie Ensign and Maggie May (McKee) J.; m. Alice Evangeline Wolford, June 24, 1931; children: Rosemary Pearl Jordan Simmons, Linda Mae Jordan Melton, Robert Harold. Student, Kansas City U., 1923-25; LLB, U. Kans., 1928. Bar: Kans. 1928, U.S. Dist. Ct. Kans. 1966. Atty. Home Owners Loan Corp., Topeka, 1933-39; sole practice Beloit, 1928-33, 1939—; atty. Mitchell County, Kans., 1931-32. Past del. to gen. conf. United Brethren in Christ Ch. Mem. ABA, Kans. Bar Assn. Democrat. Methodist. Avocation: tennis. General practice, Probate, Personal income taxation. Home: 516 N Poplar Beloit KS 67420

JORDAN, HILARY PETER, lawyer; b. Mineola, N.Y., July 30, 1952; s. Thomas Francis and Clorinda G. (Beltramo) J.; m. Judith Lynn Spencer, Sept. 7, 1984. BA, U. Ariz., 1974; JD, Harvard U., 1977. Bar: Ga. 1977, U.S. Dist. Ct. (no. dist.) Ga. 1977, U.S. Ct. Appeals (5th cir.) 1978. Assoc. Kilpatrick and Cody, Atlanta, 1977-84, ptnr., 1984—. Banking, Contracts commercial, Consumer commercial. Office: Kilpatrick and Cody 100 Peachtree St Suite 3100 Atlanta GA 30043

JORDAN, HORACE WILLIAM, lawyer; b. Chgo., Nov. 26, 1916; s. John Garfield and Natalie (Young) J.; m. Constance Felt Tippens, June 30, 1951; children—Robert Y., Constance F., David Clark, Horace W. A.B., Amherst Coll., 1937; J.D., Northwestern U., 1940. Bar: Ill. 1940, U.S. Supreme Ct. 1957, U.S. Ct. Appeals (7th cir.) 1947, U.S. Dist. Ct. (no. dist.) Ill. 1947. Mem. legal dept. Montgomery Ward Co., Chgo., 1940-42, 45-49; ptnr. Kelly & Jordan, Chgo., 1949-51; ptnr. Van Duzer Gershon, Jordan & Petersen, Chgo., 1951—, v.p., 1980—. Served to lt. U.S. Army, 1942-45. Mem. ABA, Ill. State Bar Assn., Chgo. Bar Assn., Ill. Trial Lawyers Assn., Ill. Def. Counsel. Clubs: University, Michigan Shores. General practice, Insurance, State civil litigation. Home: 1115 Chestnut Dr Wilmette IL 60091 Office: 222 W Adams St Chicago IL 60606

JORDAN, JAMES D(EE), lawyer; b. Chattanooga, Oct. 23, 1956; s. Francis L. and Helen Virginia (Slaughter) J.; m. Paula Walker, Nov. 17, 1984. BA, U. Tenn., Chattanooga, 1978; JD, Vanderbilt U., 1981. Bar: Tenn. 1981, U.S. Dist. Ct. (ea. and mid. dists.) Tenn. 1983, U.S. Supreme Ct. 1986. Assoc. Chambliss, Bahner et al, Chattanooga, 1981-83; ptnr. Guenther & Jordan, Nashville, 1983—. Mem. Nashville Estate Planning Council, Cumberland Presbyn. Ch. Mem. ABA, Tenn. Bar Assn., Nashville Bar Assn., Order of Coif. Avocations: tennis, racquetball, woodworking. Probate, Estate taxation, Real property. Home: PO Box 447 Ridgetop TN 37152 Office: 302 Dominion Bank Bldg Nashville TN 37201

JORDAN, JAMES FRANCIS, lawyer; b. Washington, Feb. 9, 1933; s. John Alexander and Margaret Ellen (Leahan) J.; m. Mary Alice Fleming, Feb. 1, 1964; 1 child, Kathleen Delaney. B.S., Georgetown U., 1955, LL.B., 1962. Bar: D.C. 1965. With Travelers Ins. Co., 1958-66; assoc. Carr, Bonner, et al, 1967-75; ptnr. Carr, Jordan, Coyne & Savits, 1975-84; sr. ptnr. Jordan, Coyne, Savits & Lopata, Washington, 1984—. Served to 1st lt. USMCR, 1955-57. Mem. ABA (ho. of dels. 1984-85), The Counsellors (pres. 1983-84), D.C. Def. Lawyers Assn., Bar Assn. D.C. (bd. dirs. 1978-79, 83, sec. 1979-80, pres. 1984-85). Roman Catholic. Federal civil litigation, State civil litigation, Workers' compensation. Office: 1030 15th St NW Washington DC 20005

JORDAN, JOSEPH PATRICK, JR., lawyer; b. Buffalo, June 21, 1937; s. Joseph Patrick, Sr. and Helen (Mahoney) J.; m. Sheila Mary O'Loughlin, Aug. 19, 1961; children—Jennifer, Julie, Jodi, Melissa, Michelle. B.S., Xavier U., 1959; J.D., Marquette U., 1962. Bar: Ohio, Wis., U.S. Dist. Ct. (no. dist.) Ohio, U.S. Dist. (ea. dist.) Wis., U.S. Ct. Appeals (6th cir.). Asst. law dir. City of Toledo, Ohio, 1965-81; assoc. Jordan, Warrick & Disalle, Toledo, 1972-82; pres. Gen. Box Co., Toledo, 1982-85; sole practice, Toledo, 1985—. Thomas Moore scholar Marquette U., 1959-62. Mem. ABA, Ohio Bar Assn., Toledo Bar Assn., Lucas County Bar Assn. Republican. Roman Catholic. Clubs: Sylvania Country (Ohio) (v.p.), Toledo. Avocation: athletics. Federal civil litigation, State civil litigation, Personal injury. Home: 5235 Carlingfort Dr Toledo OH 43623 Office: 1400 Nat Bank Bldg Toledo OH 43604

JORDAN, LAWRENCE WHITING, JR., lawyer; b. San Francisco, Sept. 18, 1924; s. Lawrence Whiting and Elvira Elise (Coburn) J.; m. Frances Grimes, Dec. 30, 1949; children—Lawrence, Martha, Andrew, Sarah. B.S., U. Calif.-Berkeley, 1948; J.D., U. Calif., Hastings Coll. Law, 1952. Bar: Calif. 1952, U.S. Dist. Ct. (no. dist.) Calif. 1952. Assoc. Rogers & Clark, San Francisco, 1954-62; ptnr. Rogers, Clark & Jordan, San Francisco, 1962-68, merged with Kelso, Cotton, Seligman & Ray, 1968-80, named changed to Jordan, Keeler & Seligman, San Francisco, 1980—; dir. Barclays Bank of Calif.; past lectr. San Francisco Community Coll. Former trustee and counsel Grace Cathedral, San Francisco; trustee Mechanics Inst., San Francisco. Served to 1st lt. USAAF, 1943-45. Decorated Air medal with 3 oak leaf clusters. Mem. ABA, State Bar of Calif., San Francisco Bar Assn. Republican. Episcopalian. Clubs: Commonwealth of Calif. (past gov., chmn. lit. awards jury), Pacific Union (San Francisco). Contbr. articles to legal jours. Banking, Federal civil litigation, State civil litigation. Office: 1 Maritime Plaza San Francisco CA 94111

JORDAN, MICHAEL JAY, lawyer; b. Saginaw, Mich., Jan. 1, 1954; s. William Thomas and Luella Jean (Wilson) J.; m. Linda Sue Meyer, Aug. 16, 1986. Student, Kalamazoo Coll., 1972-73; BA, Ohio Wesleyan U., 1976; JD, George Washington U., 1979. Bar: Ohio 1979, U.S. Dist. Ct. (no. dist.) Ohio 1979, Mich. 1980, U.S. Dist. Ct. (ea. dist.) Mich. 1980, U.S. Dist. Ct. (we. dist.) Mich. 1981, U.S. Ct. Appeals (6th cir.) 1981. Assoc. Ford, Whitney, Crump & Schultz, Cleve., 1979-80; assoc. Braun, Kendrick, Finkbeiner, Schafer & Murphy, Saginaw, 1980-86, ptnr., 1986—. Pres., treas. Saginaw County Rep. Club, Saginaw Twp., Mich., 1981—; co-chmn. profl. sect. United Way, Saginaw, 1986—; mem. 8th Dist. com. Reps., 1983-85, exec. com. Saginaw County Reps., 1984—; chmn. Saginaw County Rep. Party, 1987—; bd. dirs. Pit and Balcony Community Theatre, Saginaw, 1983-84, Lake Huron Area counsel Boy Scouts Am., Auburn, Mich., 1985—. Recipient James J. Hearn award Ohio Wesleyan U., 1979; Rotary fellow, 1981. Mem. ABA, Mich. Bar Assn., Saginaw County Bar Assn., Mensa, Phi Beta Kappa, Pi Sigma Alpha, Omicron Delta Kappa. Methodist. Lodge: Rotary (bd. dirs. Saginaw club 1986—, pres. 1988, Service award 1979). Avocations: sports, rugby, weightlifting, theatre, creative writing. Health, State civil litigation, Antitrust. Office: Braun Kendrick Finkbeiner et al 812 2d Nat Bank Bldg Saginaw MI 48607

JORDAN, MICHAEL LEE MCADAMS, lawyer; b. Tucson, Dec. 13, 1946; s. William M. and Elizabeth (Washburn) J.; m. Virginia Baird, July 19, 1969; children: Whitney Davis, Michele McAdams, Elizabeth Noble. BBA, Pa. State U., 1968; MBA, U. Detroit, 1970, JD magne cum laude, 1973. Bar: S.C. 1973, U.S. Tax Ct. 1973, U.S. Dist. Ct. S.C. 1976, U.S. Ct. Appeals (4th cir.) 1983, U.S. Supreme Ct. 1983; specialist taxation law, estate planning and probate law. Personnel adminstr. Ford Motor Co., Dearborn, Mich., 1968-71; ptnr. Bethea, Jordan & Griffin, P.A., Hilton Head Island, S.C., 1973—; atty. Town of Hilton Head Island, 1983-84; adj. prof. bus. law U. S.C., Hilton Head Island, 1985—; bd. dirs. Citizens Nat. Bank S.C., So. Nat. Bank S.C. Chmn. com. self govt. options Hilton Head Island, 1978-80, co-chmn. transition com. 1983; bd. dirs. Assn. Sea Pines Plantation Property Owners, Hilton Head Island, 1982-86; trustee Hilton Head Island Civic Assn., 1985—. Mem. ABA, S.C. Bar Assn., Beaufort County Bar Assn., Hilton Head Island Bar Assn. (pres. 1981-82), Hilton Head Island C. of C. (bd. dirs. 1977-83). Episcopalian. Avocations: scuba diving, sailing, photography. Probate, Pension, profit-sharing, and employee benefits, Estate taxation. Home: 20 Audubon Pond Rd Hilton Head Island SC 29928 Office: Bethea Jordan & Griffin PA PO Box 5666 Hilton Head Island SC 29938

JORDAN, PAUL S., lawyer; b. Severy, Kans., Mar. 31, 1903; s. Frank L. and Teresa (Smiley) J.; m. Aida Mei, Feb. 27, 1931; 1 dau., Pamela. A.B., U. Calif.-Berkeley, 1925, J.D., 1927; LL.D., Golden Gate U., 1973. Bar: Calif. 1927, U.S. Dist. Ct. (no. dist.) Calif. 1927, U.S. Ct. Appeals (9th cir.) 1927. Ptnr. Jordan, Lawrence, Dawson & Carbone, P.C., San Francisco, 1932-80, chmn. bd., 1980—; dean Golden Gate U. Sch. Law, 1944-59, trustee, 1960—. Fellow Am. Bar Found.; mem. ABA, State Bar Calif., Bar Assn. San Francisco (pres. 1960), Am. Judicature Soc. Republican. Episcopalian. Clubs: Kiwanis, Family (San Francisco). Probate, Real property. Office: 235 Montgomery St San Francisco CA 94104

JORDAN, RICHARD ALLEN, insurance company executive, lawyer; b. Portsmouth, Ohio, May 19, 1946; s. Clifford Leslie and Roberta Elizabeth (Meade) J.; m. Tracie Marie Stiveson, May 25, 1984; children—Rebecca Christine, Christopher Todd, Amy Elizabeth. B.A., Dartmouth Coll., 1968; J.D., Lincoln U., San Jose, Calif., 1978. Bar: Calif. 1978, U.S. Dist. Ct. (no. dist.) Calif. 1978. Claims supr. Fireman's Fund, San Jose, 1970-77, home office claims supr., San Francisco, 1977-78, dir. claims tng., 1979-81, asst. v.p., Novato, Calif., 1981-84; v.p. Allianz Ins. Co., Los Angeles, 1984-86; v.p. claims, Asbestos Claims Facility, Princeton, N.J, 1986—. Served to 1st lt. U.S. Army, 1968-70. Mem. ABA, Calif. Trial Lawyers Assn., Assn. Trial Lawyers Am., Def. Research Inst., Pacific Claims Exec. Assn. Republican. Congregationalist. Insurance, Personal injury, Workers' compensation. Home: 12 Washington Dr Cranbury NJ 08512 Office: Asbestos Claims Facility 500 College Rd E Princeton NJ 08540

JORDAN, ROBERT LEON, lawyer, educator; b. Reading, Pa., Feb. 27, 1928; s. Anthony and Carmela (Votto) J.; m. Evelyn Allen Willard, Feb. 15, 1958; children—John Willard, David Anthony. B.A., Pa. State U., 1948; LL.B., Harvard U., 1951. Bar: N.Y. 1952. Assoc. White & Case, N.Y.C., 1953-59; prof. law UCLA, 1959-70, 75—, assoc. dean Sch. Law, 1968-69; vis. prof. law Cornell U., Ithaca, N.Y., 1962-63; co-reporter Uniform Consumer Credit Code, 1964-70; Fulbright lectr. U. Pisa, Italy, 1967-68. Co-author: (with W.D. Warren) Commercial Law, 2d edit., 1987, Bankruptcy, 1985. Served to lt. USAF, 1951-53. Contracts commercial, Bankruptcy. Office: UCLA School of Law 405 Hilgard Ave Los Angeles CA 90024

JORDAN, STEVEN BEN, lawyer; b. Memphis, Nov. 8, 1956; s. Ben F. and Marie T. (Trawick) J.; m. Lucy Jackson; children: Genevieve Ellen, Emily Kathrine. BA, Hendrix Coll., 1978; JD with honors, U. Ark., 1980. Bar: Ark. 1981, U.S. Dist. Ct. (ea. and we. dists.) Ark. 1981, U.S. Tax Ct., U.S. Ct. Appeals (8th cir.) 1983. Assoc. Law Office Richard F. Hatfield, Searcy, Ark., 1980-82; ptnr. Hatfield & Jordan, Searcy, 1982-85, Hatfield, Hodges, Marshall & Jordan, Searcy and Little Rock, 1985, Hatfield, Robinson, Hodges, Marshall, Jordan & Shively, Searcy and Little Rock, 1985—. Bd. dirs. Legal Services Ark., Little Rock, 1985-86. Mem. ABA, Ark. Bar Assn. (legal aid com., young lawyers and comml. lawyers sects.), White County Bar Assn. (sec., treas.). Methodist. Lodge: Kiwanis. Contracts commercial, General corporate, Probate. Home: 36 Jamestown Dr Searcy AR 72143 Office: Hatfield Robinson Hodges Marshall Jordan & Shively 209 W Market St Searcy AR 72143-1170

JORDAN, V. THOMAS, lawyer; b. Raleigh, N.C., Feb. 11, 1948; s. V. Thomas Sr. and Pauline (Cooke) J.; m. Joyce P. Pope, Sept. 1, 1968; children: Christine Noel, Jonathan Thomas. BA, U. N.C., 1970; JD cum laude, N.C. Cen. U., 1980. Bar: N.C. 1980, U.S. Ct. Appeals (4th cir.) 1981, U.S. Dist. Ct. (ea. dist.) N.C. 1985. Ptnr. Josey, Josey, Hanudel & Jordan, Scotland Neck, N.C., 1980-83, Calder, Narron & Jordan, Wendell and Knightdale, N.C., 1984-86, Weeks, Tantum, Hamrick & Jordan, Knightdale, Wendell and Zebulon, 1987—. Editor in chief N.C. Cen. U. Law Jour., 1979-80. Mem. ABA, N.C. Bar Assn., Halifax County Bar Assn. (v.p. 1981, pres. 1982), N.C. Trial Lawyers Assn. Democrat. Baptist. Avocations: golf, camping. General practice, Real property, Personal injury. Home: 722 Whitley Way Wendell NC 27591 Office: Weeks Tantum Homrick & Jordan 3127-109 Hwy 64 E Park Knightdale NC 27545

JORDAN, VERNON EULION, JR., lawyer, former urban league official; b. Atlanta, Aug. 15, 1935; s. Vernon Eulion and Mary (Griggs) J.; m. Shirley M. Yarbrough, Dec. 13, 1958 (dec. Dec. 29, 1985); 1 child, Vickee; m. Ann Dibble Cook, Nov. 22, 1986. BA, DePauw U., 1957; JD, Howard U., 1960; hon. degrees, DePauw U., Howard U., Boston Coll., Brandeis U., CUNY, U. Ill. Chgo. Duke U., U. Mass., NYU, Princeton U., Tulane U., Rutgers U., Tuskegee Inst., Yale U., Notre Dame U., Harvard U., plus 30 other instns. higher edn. Bar: Ga. 1960, Ark. 1964. Practice law Atlanta, 1960-61, Pine Bluff, Ark., 1964-65; Ga. field dir. NAACP, 1961-63; dir. Voter Edn. Project So. Regional Council, 1964-68; atty. OEO, Atlanta, 1969; exec. dir. United Negro Coll. Fund, N.Y.C., 1970-71; pres. Nat. Urban League, 1972-81; ptnr. firm Akin, Gump, Strauss, Hauer & Feld, Washington; dir. Am. Express Co., Atlanta U. Ctr. Corp., Bankers Trust Co., Bankers Trust N.Y. Corp., Union Carbide Corp., J.C. Penney Co., Inc., R.J. Reynolds Industries, Inc., Xerox Corp., Corning Glass Works, Dow Jones Co. Inc.; frequent guest on major nat. TV programs including Meet the Press, Face the Nation. Author weekly columnappearing in over 300 newspapers throughout U.S.; commentator Westinghouse Broadcasting Network. Mem. Nat. Adv. Commn. on Selective Service, 1966-67, Am. Revolution Bi-Centennial Commn., 1972—, Presdl. Clemency Bd., 1974; adv. council Social Security, 1974; bd. dirs. Atlanta U. Center, Brookings Inst., Clark Coll., N.Y. Hosp., Taconic Found., United Way Am.; adv. commn. on So. Africa, Sec. of State, 1985. Fellow 2Met. Applied Research Center, 1968; Fellow Harvard Inst. Politics, 1969. Mem. ABA, Nat. Bar Assn., Nat. Conf. Black Lawyers, Council on Fgn. Relations, Century Assn.. Mem. A.M.E. Ch. Office: Akin Gump Strauss Hauer & Feld 1333 New Hampshire Ave NW Washington DC 20036

JORDAN, W. CARL, lawyer; b. Mobile, Ala., Apr. 7, 1949; s. William Cecil and Lois Elizabeth (Smith) J.; m. Lisa Anne Gagne, Aug. 17, 1974; children: Kimberly Gardner, Hillary Elizabeth, William Christopher. BA, Baylor U., 1971; JD, Harvard U., 1974. Bar: U.S. Dist. Ct. (so. and ea. dists.) Tex. 1975, U.S. Ct. Appeals (5th cir.) 1975, U.S. Ct. Appeals (9th cir.), Tex. 1984, U.S. Supreme Ct. 1984. Assoc. Vinson & Elkins, Houston, 1974-81, ptnr., 1981—; gen. counsel, adv. dir. Tex. Employment Law Council, Austin, 1984—. Author: Developing and Enforcing Drug and Alcohol Work Rules: A Primer for Tex. Employers, 1986; contbr. articles to profl. jours. Mem. ABA (labor and employment law sect., equal employment opportunity law com., subcom. chmn. 1983-86). Labor, Federal civil litigation, State civil litigation. Home: 3739 Farbar Houston TX 77005 Office: Vinson & Elkins 1001 Fannin 3300 1st City Tower Houston TX 77002-6760

JORDON, DEBORAH ELIZABETH, lawyer; b. Pitts., June 24, 1951; d. Joseph Mitchell and Marjorie Odessa (Glaude) J. BA, Brown U., 1972; JD, Yale U., 1975. Bar: Pa. 1975, N.Y. 1978, U.S. Dist. Ct. (ea. and we. dists.) N.Y., 1978. Law clk. to presiding justice U.S. Dist. Ct. (ea dist.) Pa., Phila., 1975-77; assoc. Paul, Weiss, Rifkind, Wharton & Garrison, N.Y.C., 1977-79; asst. to mayor City of N.Y., 1979-82; counsel to pres. CCNY, 1982-84; sr. atty. NBC, N.Y., 1984—; chmn. bd. dirs. Harlem Legal Services Inc., N.Y.C.; bd. dirs. Met. Assistance Corp., N.Y.C. Bd. dirs. Bennett Coll., Greensboro, N.C., 1985—, Lifelong Learning Program, N.Y. 1981-82, Marymount Manhattan Coll., N.Y.C., 1984—. Mem. Phi Beta Kappa. Roman Catholic. Avocations: sailing, writing, photography. Satellite and telecommunications law, Local government, General practice. Home: 200 W 79th St New York NY 10024 Office: NBC Inc 30 Rockefeller Plaza New York NY 10112

JORGENSEN, ERIK HOLGER, lawyer; b. Copenhagen, July 18, 1916; s. Holger and Karla (Andersen) J.; children—Jette Friis, Lone Olesen, John, Jean Ann. J.D., San Francisco Law Sch., 1960. Bar: Calif. 1961. Sole practice, 1961-70; ptnr. Hersh, Hadfield, Jorgensen & Fried, San Francisco, 1970-76, Hadfield & Jorgensen, San Francisco, 1976—. Pres. Aldersly, Danish Retirement Home, San Rafael, Calif., 1974-77, Rebuild Park Soc. Bay Area chpt., 1974-77. Fellow Scandinavian Am. Found. (hon.); mem. ABA, Assn. Trial Lawyers Am., San Francisco Lawyers Club, Bar Assn. of San Francisco, Calif. Assn. Realtors (hon. life bd. dirs.). Author: Master Forms Guide for Successful Real Estate Agreements, Successful Real Estate Sales Agreements, 1982; contbr. articles on law and real estate law to profl. jours. General practice, Real property, Probate. Office: 3 Embarcadero #1685 San Francisco CA 94111

JORGENSEN, RALPH GUBLER, lawyer, accountant; b. N.Y.C., Mar. 12, 1937; s. Thorvald W. and Florence (Gubler) J.; m. Patricia June Spivey, June 21, 1971; 1 child, Misty. A.B., George Washington U., 1960, LL.B., 1962. Bar: D.C. 1963, Md. 1963, U.S. Dist. Ct. D.C. 1963, U.S. Ct. Appeals (D.C. cir.) 1963, U.S. Dist. Ct. Md. 1964, U.S. Supreme Ct. 1971, N.C. 1972, U.S. Dist. Ct. (ea. dist.) N.C. 1972, U.S. Ct. Appeals (4th cir.) 1974, U.S. Tax Ct. 1976, U.S. Dist. Ct. (mid. dist.) N.C. 1977, U.S. Ct. Clms. 1979. Sole practice, Washington and Silver Spring, Md., 1963-71, Tabor City, N.C., 1971—. Bd. dirs. Columbus County ARC, N.C., 1974. C.P.A., Md., Nev., N.C. Mem. N.C. Bar Assn., N.C. Acad. Trial Lawyers, Am. Assn. Atty.-C.P.A.s, Assn. Trial Lawyers Am., Alpha Kappa Psi. Democrat. Baptist. Federal civil litigation, State civil litigation, Tax litigation. Home: 5 Pireway Rd Tabor City NC 28463 Office: 12 W 4th St PO Box 248 Tabor City NC 28463

JOSEPH, DANIEL MORDECAI, lawyer; b. Paterson, N.J., Aug. 20, 1941; m. Susan Fields, July 30, 1972; children: Nicholas, Charles. AB, Columbia U., 1963; LLB, Harvard U., 1966. Bar: N.J. 1967, U.S. Supreme Ct. 1970, D.C. 1974. Law clk. to judge U.S. Ct. Appeals (5th cir.), Dallas, 1966-67; atty. civil div. U.S. Dept. Justice, Washington, 1967-71; asst. gen. counsel U.S. EPA, Washington, 1971-72; spl. asst. environ. affairs gen. counsel U.S. Dept. Transp., Washington, 1972-74; ptnr. Akin, Gump, Strauss, Hauer & Feld, Washington, 1974—. Federal civil litigation, Environment. Office: Akin Gump Strauss Hauer & Feld 1333 New Hampshire Ave NW Washington DC 20036

JOSEPH, FREDRIC ROBERT, lawyer; b. N.Y.C., Feb. 7, 1943; s. Harry and Stephanie (Warshauer) J.; m. Holly Taggert, Sept. 9, 1973; children: Stephanie Louise, David Taggert. BA, Am. U., 1965, JD, 1968. Bar: Md. 1969, D.C. 1969, U.S. Supreme Ct. 1975. Sr. ptnr. Joseph, Greenwald & Laake P.A., Hyattsville, Md., 1969—. dir. legal affairs Prince George's County (Md.) ACLU, 1980—. Mem. ABA, Assn. Trial Lawyers Am., Nat. Assn. Criminal Def. Lawyers. Criminal, State civil litigation, Federal civil litigation. Office: Joseph Greenwald & Laake PA 1345 University Blvd E Hyattsville MD 20783

JOSEPH, GREGORY PAUL, lawyer; b. Mpls., Jan. 18, 1951; s. George Phillip and Josephine Sheha (Nofel) J.; m. Barbara Jean Manion, Jan. 19, 1979. B.A. summa cum laude, U. Minn., 1972, J.D. cum laude, 1975. Bar: Minn. 1975, N.Y. 1979, U.S. Dist. Ct. Minn. 1975, U.S. Dist. Ct. (so. and ea. dist.) N.Y. 1979, U.S. Ct. Appeals (8th cir.) 1976, U.S. Ct. Appeals (2d cir.) 1979, U.S. Ct. Appeals (D.C. cir.) 1980, U.S. Supreme Ct. 1983. sole practice, Mpls., 1975-79, Fried, Frank, Harris, Shriver & Jacobson, N.Y.C., 1979-82; asst. U.S. spl. prosecutor Investigation of Labor Sec. Donovan, N.Y.C., Washington, 1981-82; ptnr. Fried, Frank, Harris, Shriver & Jacobson, N.Y.C., 1982—. Author: Modern Visual Evidence, 1986; co-author: Evidence in America, 1987. Editor: Emerging Problems Under the Federal Rules of Evidence, 1986; co-editor Sanctions, 1986; Contbr. articles to profl. jours. Fellow Am. Bar Found.; mem. ABA (chmn. trial evidence com. 1985—), N.Y. State Bar Assn., Minn. State Bar Assn., Assn. Bar City, N.Y., New York County Lawyers Assn. Federal civil litigation, State civil litigation. Home: 400 E 56th St Apt 22-O New York NY 10022 Office: Fried Frank Harris Shriver & Jacobson 1 New York Plaza New York NY 10004

JOSEPH, JOHN JAMES, lawyer; b. Owen Sound, Ont., Can., July 10, 1953; came to U.S., 1961; s. Thomas Anthony and Freda (Salome) J.; m. Sandra Jean Carr, Jan. 29, 1973; children: Jamie, Jennifer, Justin. BE summa cum laude, Ohio State U., 1978, JD with honors, 1981. Bar: Ohio 1981, U.S. Dist. Ct. (so. dist.) Ohio 1982. V.p., asst. to pres. T.A. Joseph Ltd., Owen Sound, 1971—; assoc. Carlile, Patchen, Murphy & Allison, Columbus, Ohio, 1981-86, ptnr., 1987—; lectr. in field. Trustee Annehurst Village Civic Assn., Westerville, Ohio, 1984—. Mem. ABA (corp. bus. and banking, real property probate and tax law sects.), Ohio Bar Assn., Columbus Bar Assn. (real property and fin. inst. coms.), Cen. Ohio Soccer Assn. (pres., trustee 1984—), Phi Kappa Phi. Democrat. Avocations: jogging, soccer, tennis, photography, guitar. Real property, Contracts commercial, Landlord-tenant. Home: 948 Danvers Westerville OH 43081 Office: Carlile Patchen Murphy & Allison 366 E Broad St Columbus OH 43215

JOSEPH, LEONARD, lawyer; b. Phila., June 8, 1919; s. Harry L. and Mary (Pollock) J.; m. Norma Hamberg, 1942; children—Gilbert M., Stuart A., Janet H. B.A., U. Pa., 1941; LL.B., Harvard U., 1947. Bar: N.Y. bar 1949. Since practiced in N.Y.C.; partner firm Dewey, Ballantine, Bushby, Palmer & Wood, 1957—. Served with AUS, 1943-46. Fellow Am. Bar Found., Am. Coll. Trial Lawyers; mem. Am. Bar Assn., N.Y. State Bar Assn., Bar Assn. City of N.Y., Legal Aid Soc. of N.Y. (bd. dirs.). Clubs: Harvard (N.Y.C.), Wall St. (N.Y.C.). Federal civil litigation, Antitrust, Public utilities. Office: 140 Broadway New York NY 10005

JOSEPH, PAUL R., law educator; b. Los Angeles, Apr. 30, 1951; s. Lawrence H. Joseph and Barbara A. (Acoff) Brittin. BA, Goddard Coll., 1973; JD, U. Calif., Davis, 1977; LLM, Temple U., 1979. Bar: Calif. 1977, U.S. Supreme Ct. 1981, U.S. Ct. Appeals (9th cir.) 1982. Lectr. law, teaching fellow Temple U., Phila., 1977-79; asst. prof. Salmon Chase Coll. Law No. Ky. U., Highland Heights, 1979-82, assoc. prof., 1982-84; assoc. prof. Nova U., Ft. Lauderdale, Fla., 1984—. Contbr. articles to prof. jours.; mem. editorial bd. Human Rights mag., 1986—. Mem. Broward County Human Rights Bd., 1986—; trustee Goddard Coll., 1981—, vice-chmn. bd. dirs. 1985-86; chmn. Broward County ACLU, 1985-86, chmn. legal panel 1984-85, 86—; state bd. dirs. Fla. ACLU (chmn. legal programs com. 1986—). Mem. ABA, Am. Arbitration Assn., Acad. Criminal Justice Scis.. Democrat. Avocations: computers, Irish music. Legal education, Criminal, Personal injury. Office: Nova Univ Law Center 3100 SW 9th Ave Fort Lauderdale FL 33315

JOSEPH, RAYMOND, lawyer; b. Lansing, Mich., Jan. 21, 1924; s. John Gamel and Lena (Tobia) J.; divorced; children: Gina Marie, Mark Raymond. Student, Mich. State U., 1948; JD, Wayne State U., 1951. Law clk. to presiding justice Mich. Supreme Ct., 1953-54; sole practice Lansing, 1952—. Pres. Lansing Symphony Assn. 1967-69; past officer, dir. Opera Co. Mid-Mich., Kresge Art Mus., Lansing Art Gallery, Lansing Ballet Assn., Mich. Orchestral Assn. Served to lt. USAAF, 1943-45, ETO. Decorated 7 Air medals for combat flying; recipient presdl. citation for 35 combat missions, 1944. Mem. ABA, Mich. Bar Assn., Ingham County Bar Assn. (sec. 1954-56), Assn. Trial Lawyers Am., Mich. Trial Lawyers Assn., Am. Judicature Soc. Democrat. Mem. Christian Ch. Avocations: art and art history, classical music, reading, tennis. Federal civil litigation, State civil litigation, Personal injury. Home: 713 Applegate Ln East Lansing MI 48823 Office: 908 Mich Nat Tower Lansing MI 48933

JOSEPH, ROBERT GEORGE, business executive, consultant; b. Cleve., Dec. 1, 1948; s. Shaffie Charles and Mary Alice (Joseph) J.; m. Diane Selinger, June 8, 1974; children: Daniel Selinger, Edward Michael. Student, U. Md., 1967-69; BA, U. Tenn., 1972; JD, Ohio State U., 1975. Bar: Ohio 1975, D.C. 1976, U.S. Ct. Appeals (D.C. cir.) 1976. Law clk. to judge U.S. Ct. Appeals (D.C. cir), Washington, 1975-76; assoc. Howrey & Simon, Washington, 1976-84; officer, dir. Law Resources Inc., Washington, 1984—. Editor-in-Chief Ohio State U. Law Jour., 1974-75. Served as sgt. USAF, 1966-70. Mem. ABA, D.C. Bar Assn., Phi Beta Kappa. Republican. Roman Catholic. Law related services. Home: 6515 Deidre Terr McLean VA 22101 Office: Law Resources Inc 1747 Pennsylvania Ave NW Washington DC 20006

JOSEPH, STEPHANIE RUDMAN, lawyer; b. N.Y.C., Nov. 7, 1946; d. Jacob and Frances (Zimmerman) Rudman; m. William K. Joseph, June 20, 1970; 1 child, H. Maxwell. AB in Polit. Sci., U. Mich., 1968; JD, NYU, 1971. Bar: N.Y. 1971, U.S. Dist. Ct. (so. dist.) N.Y. 1973. Assoc. Shearman & Sterling, N.Y.C., 1971-78; assoc. counsel Am. Express Bank, N.Y.C., 1978-79; counsel TC fin. Am. Express TRS, N.Y.C., 1979-81, sr. counsel TRS, 1981-84; assoc. gen. counsel Am. Express Co., N.Y.C., 1984—. Vol. Am. Heart Assn., N.Y.C. Mem. Assn. Bar City of N.Y. Democrat. Jewish. Securities, General corporate. Office: Am Express Co Am Express Tower World Fin Ctr New York NY 10285

JOSEPHSON, WILLIAM HOWARD, lawyer; b. Newark, Mar. 22, 1934; s. Maurice and Gertrude (Brooks) J. A.B., U. Chgo., 1952; J.D., Columbia, 1955; commoner, St. Antony's Coll., Oxford (Eng.) U., 1958-59. Bar: N.Y. bar 1956, D.C. bar 1966, U.S. Supreme Ct. bar 1959. Asso. Paul, Weiss, Rifkind, Wharton & Garrison, N.Y.C., 1955-58, Joseph L. Rauh, Jr., Washington, 1959; Far East regional counsel ICA, 1959-61; spl. asst. to dir. Peace Corps, 1961-62, dep. gen. counsel, 1961-63, gen. counsel, 1963-66; asso. Fried, Frank, Harris, Shriver & Jacobson, N.Y.C., 1966-67; ptnr. Fried, Frank, Harris, Shriver & Jacobson, 1968—; Spl. counsel N.Y.C. Human Resources Adminstrn., 1966-67, City Community Constrn. Fund, 1967—, N.Y.C. Bd. Edn., 1968-71, N.Y.C. Employees' Retirement System, 1975-86; Nat. Democratic vice presdl. campaign coordinator, 1972; pres. Peace Corps Inst., 1980—. Bd. editors: Columbia Law Rev, 1953-55. Recipient William A. Jump award exemplary achievement pub. adminstrn., 1965; Disting. Service award and Valerie Kantor awards Mex. Am. Legal Def. and Edn. Fund, 1980, 81. Mem. Assn. Bar City N.Y. (spl. com. on Congl. ethics 1968-70), Council on Fgn. Relations. Jewish. General corporate, Local government, Legislative. Home: 58 S Oxford St Brooklyn NY 11217 Office: 1 New York Plaza New York NY 10004

JOSLIN, GARY JAMES, lawyer, political scientist; b. Glendale, Calif., Nov. 14, 1943; s. James C. and Elsie Victoria (White) J.; m. Connie Ruth Hanson, Sept. 5, 1970; children: Julie A., James Scott. AA, Glendale Coll., 1963; BA, UCLA, 1965; JD, U. So. Calif., 1969; MA in Pub. Affairs, U. Oreg., 1971. Bar: Utah 1972, U.S. Dist. Ct. Utah 1972, U.S. Ct. Appeals (10th cir.) 1975, U.S. Supreme Ct. 1975, U.S. Ct. Claims 1977, U.S. Tax Ct. 1977, U.S. Ct. Appeals (9th cir.) 1977, U.S. Dist. Ct. (so. dist.) Ind. 1978, U.S. Ct. Appeals (7th cir.) 1979, U.S. Ct. Internat. Trade 1982, U.S. Ct. Appeals (D.C. cir.) 1984, U.S. Dist. Ct. Okla. 1986. Criminal justice planner, region VII Utah Law Enforcement Agy., 1971; sole practice Sandy, Utah; Instr. criminal procedure Weber State Coll. Extension; instr. polit. sci. Utah State U. Extension; prof. legal tech. Am. Legal Services Inst.; adj. prof. taxation, dir. grad. tax program, dean Jefferson Coll. Law, 1986; dean Washington Coll. Law; dep. county atty. Duchesne County, Utah; city atty. City of Salem, Utah, City of Santaguin, Utah. Author: The Living Trust, 1978, Compendium of International Transactions, 1982. Scoutmaster Boy Scouts Am., Roosevelt, Utah, 1972; dist. commr. Varsity Scouting, Sandy, 1986; Founder Citizens for Good Govt., Roosevelt, 1972; Served to 2d lt. Calif. N.G. Republican. Mormon. Avocation: scouting. Personal income taxation, Private international, Probate. Office: 2268 E Newcastle Dr Sandy UT 84092-1743

JOSLYN, ROBERT BRUCE, lawyer; b. Detroit, Jan. 9, 1945; s. Lee Everett, Jr. and Juanita Constance (McGonegal) J.; m. Karen Sue Glenny, July 8, 1967; children: Gwendolyn Constance, Robert Bruce. B.A., Fla. State U., 1967; J.D., Emory U., 1970. Bar: Mich. 1970. Law clk. Gurney, Gurney & Handley, Orlando, Fla., summer 1969; asso. Joslyn & Keydel, Detroit, 1970-74; partner Joslyn, Keydel, Wallace & Joslyn, 1975—; Vis. instr. Oakland U., Rochester, Mich., 1974; faculty Inst. Continuing Legal Edn., Ann Arbor, Mich., 1975—. Co-author: Manual for Lawyers and Legal Assistants: Probate and Trust Administration, 1977, Manual for Lawyers and Legal Assistants: Taxation of Trusts and Estates, 1977, 3d edit., 1980. Mem. U.S. All Am. Prep. Sch. Swim Team, 1963. Mem. ABA, Detroit Bar Assns. (chmn. taxation com.), State Bar Mich. (mem. probate and estate planning sect.), Am. Coll. Probate Counsel, Fin. and Estate Planning Council Detroit, Founders Soc. Detroit Inst. Arts, Phi Delta Phi, Phi Kappa Psi. Republican. Methodist. Clubs: Detroit Athletic, Grosse Pointe. Probate, Estate taxation, Personal income taxation. Home: 286 Hillcrest Ave Grosse Pointe Farms MI 48236 Office: 2211 Comerica Bldg Detroit MI 48226

JOSS, W. BRUCE, lawyer; b. Colorado Springs, Colo., Sept. 9, 1949; s. William and Edna Rose (Kincaid) J.; m. Lisa E. Joss, Aug. 10, 1974. BS, U. Colo., 1971, JD, 1974. Bar: Colo. 1974, U.S. Dist. Ct. Colo. 1974. Ptnr. Rautenstraus & Joss, Louisville, Colo., 1974-84, Rautenstraus, Joss & Midgley, P.C., Louisville, 1984—; atty. City of Louisville, 1974, pros. atty. 1986—; bd. dirs. 1st Nat. Bank, Louisville. Contracts commercial, Family and matrimonial, Probate. Office: Rautenstraus Joss & Midgley PC 728 Main St Louisville CO 80027

JOST, RICHARD FREDERIC, III, lawyer; b. N.Y.C., Sept. 25, 1947; s. Richard Frederic Jr. and Gertrude (Holoch) J.; m. Sally Ann Galvin, July 29, 1972; children: Jennifer, Richard IV. BA, Dickinson Coll., 1969; JD, Syracuse U., 1975. Bar: N.Y. 1976, Nev. 1978, U.S. Dist. Ct. Nev. 1979, U.S. Supreme Ct. 1984. Dep. dist. atty. Elko (Nev.) County Dist. Atty.'s Office, 1976-80; dep. atty. gen. Nev. Atty. Gen.'s Office, Carson City, 1980-83; ptnr. Jones, Jones, Close & Brown, Las Vegas, Nev., 1983—. Trustee United Meth. Ch., Carson City, Nev., 1982-83; bd. dirs. Ormsby Assn. Retarded Citizens, Carson City, 1982-83. Served to lt. USNR, 1970-74. Mem. ABA (urban, state and local govt. law sect.), Clark County Bar Assn., Nat. Assn. Bond Lawyers. Democrat. Municipal bonds, Administrative and regulatory. Home: 404 Lindy Dr Las Vegas NV 89107 Office: Jones Jones Close & Brown 300 S 4th St Suite 700 Las Vegas NV 89101-6026

JOSTEN, ROY JOSEPH, lawyer; b. Milw., Jan. 31, 1940; s. George John and Adelle L. (Lang) J.; m. Mary Woodruff, June 7, 1969; children—Mark Michael, Theodore Anthony, Alicia Widmer. B.A. magna cum laude, Marquette U., 1963; J.D. cum laude, U. Mich., 1969. Bar: Wis. 1969. Assoc. Whyte & Hirschboeck, S.C., Milw., 1969-72; ptnr. Stewart, Peyton, Crawford & Josten, Racine, Wis., 1972-78; mem. Josten, DuRocher Murphy and Pierce, S.C., Racine, 1978—. Co-founder Civil Legal Services, Inc., Racine, 1975, bd. dirs. 1975-78, pres., 1975-77; mem. adv. bd. Cath. Social Services, Racine, 1974-80, pres., 1975-77; bd. dirs. Racine County Opportunity Ctr., Inc., 1980-84, sec. 1981-84; bd. dirs. Downtown Racine Devel. Corp., 1981-83, pres., 1982-83; bd. dirs. Neighborhood Housing Services Racine, Inc., 1976-78, Racine County Area Found., Inc., 1984—, Catholic Social Services Found., Inc., 1983-85; bd. dirs., pres. Preservation Racine, Inc., 1980-81; mem. adv. bd. Ctr. for Community Concerns, 1984-85. Served with U.S. Army, 1963-66. Mem. ABA, State Bar Wis. (bd. govs. 1983-87), Racine County Bar Assn. Roman Catholic. Club: KC. Assoc. editor Mich. Law Rev., 1968-69. General practice, Contracts commercial, Real property. Home: 5501 Valley Trail Racine WI 53402 Office: 927 Main St Racine WI 53403

JOURNEY, DREXEL DAHLKE, lawyer; b. Westfield, Wis., Feb. 23, 1926; s. Clarence Earl and Verna L. Gilmore (Dahlke) Journey Gilmore; m. Vergene Harriet Sandsmark, Oct. 24, 1952; 1 child, Ann Marie. BBA, U. Wis., 1950, LLB, 1952; LLM, George Washington U., 1957. Bar: Wis. 1952, U.S. Dist. Ct. (we. dist.) Wis. 1953, U.S. Supreme Ct. 1955, U.S. Ct. Appeals (4th cir.) 1960, U.S. Ct. Appeals (5th cir.) 1961, U.S. Ct. Appeals (D.C. cir.) 1965, U.S. Ct. Appeals (7th and 9th cirs.) 1967, U.S. Ct. Appeals (1st cir.) 1969, D.C. 1970, U.S. Dist. Ct. D.C. 1970, U.S. Ct. Appeals (2d, 3d, 6th, 8th and 10th cirs.) 1976, U.S. Ct. Appeals (11th cir.) 1981. Counsel FPC, Washington, 1952-66, asst. gen. counsel, 1966-70, dep. gen. counsel, 1970-74, gen. counsel, 1974-77; ptnr. Schiff, Hardin & Waite, Washington, 1977—. Author: Corporate Law and Practice, 1975; contbr. articles to profl. jours. Pres. Am. U. Park Citizens Assn., Washington, 1970-72; trustee Lincoln-Wesmoreland Housing Project, Washington, 1978-79. Served with Mcht. Marine Res. USNR, 1944-46. Knapp scholar U. Wis., 1952. Mem. ABA, Fed. Bar Assn., Fed. Energy Bar Assn., Nat. Lawyers Club, Phi Kappa Phi, Phi Eta Sigma, Theta Delta Chi. Republican. Congregationalist. Lodge: Masons. Administrative and regulatory, FERC practice, Municipal bonds. Home: 4540 Windom Pl NW Washington DC 20016 Office: Schiff Hardin & Waite 1101 Connecticut Ave NW Washington DC 20036

JOY, DANIEL FOSTER, lawyer; b. Providence, Apr. 8, 1943; s. Daniel Foster and Ruth (Grange) J.; m. Madeline Risica, June 19, 1965; children: Daniel F. IV, Douglas Andrew. Student, Rutgers U., 1961-63; BA, U. R.I., 1965; JD, Stetson U., 1969. Bar: Fla. 1969, U.S. Dist. Ct. (mid. dist.) Fla. 1977, U.S. Supreme Ct. 1979, U.S. Ct. Appeals (11th cir.) 1983. Legis. asst. U.S. House Reps., Washington, 1970-73; asst. dir. to Exec. Office of Pres. U.S. Office of Econ. Opportunity, Washington, 1973; chief counsel U.S. senator James L. Buckley, Washington, 1973-77; sole practice Sarasota, Fla., 1977—; lectr. Del. Law Coll., Wilmington, 1974-75. Mem. ABA, Comml. Law League of Am., Am. Conservative Union (bd. dirs. 1972-78). State civil litigation, Federal civil litigation, Contracts commercial. Home: 7566 Biltmore Dr Sarasota FL 33581 Office: 900 First Fla Bank Plaza 1800 2d St Sarasota FL 33577

JOYCE, DENNIS ROBERT, lawyer; b. Syracuse, N.Y., June 5, 1948; s. Robert Joseph and Ruth (Costello) J.; m. Nancy Fulmer Joyce; children: Patrick Brendan, Sean Timothy. BBA with honors, U. Ky., 1970; JD, U. N.C., 1972. Sole practice Wilkesboro, N.C., 1973-75, 1976—; prosecutor Wilkes County Prosecutor's Office, N.C., 1975. Mem. ABA, N.C. Bar Assn., N.C. State Bar Assn., Wilkes County Bar Assn. (pres. 1977-78), 23d. Jud. Dist. Bar Assn. (pres. 1981-82), Assn. Trial Lawyers Am., N.C. Acad. Trial Lawyers (bd. dirs. 1981-85). Personal injury, Criminal, Federal civil litigation. Home: 210 E Main St Wilkesboro NC 28697

JOYCE, JAMES DONALD, chemical engineer, lawyer; b. Appleton, Wis., July 1, 1936; s. Donald Matthew and Elizabeth Alice (Breitenstein) J.; m. Joan Elizabeth Matt, Sept. 12, 1959; 1 child, Kimberly Joan. BS in Chem. Engring., U. Wis., 1963; MS in Chem. Engring., N.J. Inst. of Tech., 1967; JD, John F. Kennedy U., 1980. Bar: Calif. 1980, U.S. Ct. Appeals (9th cir.) 1980. Researcher Shell Chem. Co., Plainfield, N.J., 1963-70; product devel. engr. Shell Oil Co., Stamford, Conn., 1970-73; regional safety and health engr. Shell Oil Co., Houston, 1973-77, environ. rep., 1977-80; engr., atty. Shell Oil Co., Carson, Calif., 1980—; bd. dirs. Bldg. Corp., El Monte, Calif.; co. rep. Western Oil and Gas Assn., Los Angeles (vice chmn. environ. com. 1980-82, chmn. 1982-84). Patentee Rapid Setting Epoxides, 1965. Active PTO, Walnut Walk, Calif., 1974-80; v.p. PTO, Laguna Hills, Calif., 1981-84, vol. Calif. Prob. Dept., Calif. Youth Authority, 1984—; dir. Ridgefield Conn. Little League, 1968-80; bd. dirs. Walnut Walk Homeowners Assn. Served with USAF, 1954-57. Mem. Am. Inst. Chem. Engrs. Republican. Roman Catholic. Avocations: tennis, swimming, weight lifting. Administrative and regulatory, Environment, Legislative. Office: Shell Oil Co PO Box 6249 Carson CA 90749

JOYCE, JAMES JOSEPH, JR., lawyer; b. Worcester, Mass., Apr. 10, 1947; s. James Joseph and Phyllis Mary (Crowley) J.; m. Susan Plummer, Apr. 22, 1972. A.B. summa cum laude, Coll. Holy Cross, 1969; JD, Harvard U., 1976. Bar: Mass. 1977, U.S. Dist. Ct. Mass. 1978, U.S. Ct. Appeals (1st cir.) 1978, U.S. Supreme Ct. 1980. Assoc. Burns & Levinson, Boston, 1976-82; counsel Norton Co., Worcester, Mass., 1982—. Served to lt. Supply Corps, USN, 1969-73. Mem. ABA, Omicron Delta Epsilon, Alpha Sigma Nu. Democrat. General corporate. Office: Norton Co 1 New Bond St Worcester MA 01606

JOYCE, JOSEPH BENEDICT, lawyer; b. Council Bluffs, Iowa, July 18, 1932; s. Edward John and Marie Elizabeth Joyce; m. Donna S. Joyce, July 6, 1957; children: Julie A., Jill M., Michael C. AB, U. Notre Dame, 1954, LLB, 1956. Bar: Iowa 1956, U.S. Dist. Ct. (so. dist.) Iowa 1958, U.S. Dist. Ct. (no. dist.) Iowa 1977. Ptnr. Stewart, Wimer, Brehnan & Joyce, Des Moines, 1960-74, Adler, Brennan, Joyce & Steger, Des Moines, 1974—; gen. counsel Assoc. Grocers of Iowa Coop., Inc., Ankeny, Iowa, 1974-85. Note editor Notre Dame Lawyer, 1955-56. Chmn. bd. dirs. Goodwill Industries of Des Moines, 1975, Cath. Council for Social Concern, 1978-80; mem. City of Des Moines Bd. Adjustment, 1976-80; trustee Civic Ctr. Des Moines, 1980-87; Rep. nominee for State Senate, 1966, 70. Served with USNG, 1957-70. Fellow Internat. Acad. Law and Sci.; mem. ABA (chmn. com. on ethical practice and procedures 1983-84, family law sect. 1983-84, chmn. com. on juvenile law 1986—), Polk County Bar Assn. (chmn. family law com. 1980-85), Assn. Trial Lawyers Am., Iowa Assn. Trial Lawyers, South Des Moines C. of C. (sec. 1980), Sierra (pres. Des Moines chpt. 1987—). Roman Catholic. Clubs: Des Moines, Cambio (pres. 1985-86), Bishop Boylan, Notre Dame of Des Moines (pres. 1964-65). Lodge: KC (4th degree). State civil litigation, General corporate, General practice. Home: 4610 Wakonda Pkwy Des Moines IA 50315 Office: Adler Brenna Joyce & Steger First Interstate Bank Bldg Des Moines IA 50309

JOYCE, STEPHEN MICHAEL, lawyer; b. Los Angeles, Mar. 19, 1945; s. John Rowland and Elizabeth Rose (Rahe) J.; m. Bernadette Anne Novey, Aug. 18, 1973; children: Natalie Elizabeth, Vanessa Anne. BS, Calif. State U., Los Angeles, 1970; JD, U. San Fernando, 1976. Bar: Calif. 1976, U.S. Dist. Ct. (cen. dist.) Calif. 1977, U.S. Ct. Claims 1981. Sole practice Beverly Hills, Calif., 1976-81, Beverly Hills, 1984—; ptnr. Gold & Joyce, Beverly Hills, 1984—; personal atty. to Stevie Wonder and various other celebrities, 1977—. Contbr. articles to profl. jours. Served to pvt. USAR, 1963-69. Mem. ABA, Calif. Bar Assn., Los Angeles County Bar Assn., Beverly Hills Bar Assn., Los Angeles Trial Lawyers Assn. Democrat. Roman Catholic. Club: Calabasas (Calif.) Athletic. Avocation: long distance running. State civil litigation, General practice, Entertainment. Home: 4724 Barcelona Ct Calabasas Park CA 91302 Office: 241 S Beverly Dr Beverly Hills CA 90212

JOYE, E. MICHAEL, lawyer; b. Charleston, S.C., Oct. 16, 1944; s. A. Stoll and Amy (Evans) J.; m. Lucille Veronica Sticco, Oct. 25, 1975; children: Evan Michael, Russell Pierce. AB, U. N.C., 1966; JD, Columbia U., 1973. Bar: N.Y. 1974, U.S. Dist. Ct. (so. dist.) N.Y., U.S. Dist. Ct. S.C. Assoc. LeBoeuf, Lamb, Leiby & Macrae, N.Y.C., 1973-77, 81-84, ptnr., 1985—; asst. prof. law U. S.C., Columbia, S.C., 1977-78; assoc. McKay, Sherrill et al, Columbia, 1978-79; lectr. Ahmadu Bello U., Zaria, Nigeria, 1979-81. Author: (textbook) Nigerian Constitution, 1982. Served to lt. USN, 1966-70. Democrat. Avocations: golf, softball. Insurance, Legislative, General corporate. Home: 38 Hudson Rd Bellerose Village NY 11001 Office: LeBoeuf Lamb Leiby & MacRay 520 Madison Ave New York NY 10022

JOYNER, ARTHENIA LEE, lawyer; b. Lakeland, Fla., Feb. 3, 1943; m. Delano S. Stewart, Oct. 15, 1979; 5 daughters. BS in Polit. Sci., Fla. A & M U., 1964, JD, 1968. Tchr. Hillsborough County Bd. of Pub. Instructions, Tampa, Fla., 1964; adminstrv. asst. to state rep. Joe Lang Kershaw Fla. Ho. of Reps., Tallahassee, 1969; sole practice Tampa, 1969—; bd. dirs. Travellers Aid Inc.; nat. legal advisor Delta Sigma Theta Sorority, Inc., 1985—. Bd dirs. Bay Area Legal Services, Inc., 1979-86, pres. 1983; bd. dirs. Helping Hand Day Nursery; pres. Charmettes Inc. Named one of Am.'s Top 100 Black Bus. and Profl. Women, Dollars and Sense mag., 1985, one of 100 Most Influential Black Ams., Ebony mag., 1985; recipient OUtstanding Achievement and Community Service award Eastgate Community Ch., 1985, Tampa br. NAACP Human Rights award, 1985. Mem. ABA (house of dels. 1981-82), Nat. Bar Assn. (pres. 1984-85), Fla. Bar Assn., Hillsborough County Bar Assn., Nat. Assn. Women Lawyers, Hillsborough County Assn. Women Lawyers, Am. Judicature Soc. Avocations: collecting gold coins, pub. speaking, reading. Probate, Personal injury. Office: 400 E Buffalo Ave Suite 106 Tampa FL 33603

JOYNER, GARY KELTON, lawyer; b. Rocky Mount, N.C., Apr. 22, 1957; s. George Andrew and Mary Marjorie (Bone) J. BA, U. N.C., 1979; JD, Wake Forest U., 1982. Bar: N.C. 1982, U.S. Dist. Ct. (ea. dist.) N.C. 1982, U.S. Ct. Appeals (4th cir.) 1983. Assoc. Bailey, Dixon, Wooten, McDonald, Fountain & Walker, Raleigh, N.C., 1982-86, ptnr., 1986; assoc. Petree, Stockton & Robinson, Raleigh, 1986—. Allocations panel United Way, Wake County, N.C., 1985—; lt. in membership YMCA, Raleigh, 1985-86; mem. N.C. Legis. Forum, 1986—; capt. Wake County Boy's Club Campership Drive, Raleigh, 1986-87; exec. bd, dirs, N.C. Mus. Natural Scis. Soc., Raleigh, 1985—. Mem. ABA, N.C. Bar Assn. (sec. young lawyers div. 1986-87, chmn. law day com. 1985-86, spl. projects com. 1986-87), Wake County Bar Assn. Democrat. Real property, State civil litigation, Contracts commercial. Home: 612 Sampson St Raleigh NC 27609 Office: Petree Stockton & Robinson 2626 Glenwood Ave Suite 450 Raleigh NC 27608

JOYNER, WALTON KITCHIN, lawyer; b. Raleigh, N.C., Apr. 1, 1933; s. William Thomas and Sue (Kitchin) J.; m. Lucy Holmes Graves, Sept. 23, 1955; children: Sue Carson Clark, Walton K. Jr., James Y. II. AB in Polit. Sci., U. N.C., 1955, JD with honors, 1960. Bar: N.C.; lic. comml. pilot. Ptnr. Joyner & Hawison, Raleigh, 1960-80, Hunton & Williams, Raleigh, 1980—; sec., treas. N.C. R.R. Co., Raleigh, 1966; bd. dirs. United Title Ins. Co., Raleigh; bd. mgrs. Wamovia Bank & Trust Co., N.C., 1969—; bd. govs. U.S. Power Squadrons, 1974-81. Assoc. editor U. N.C. Law Rev. Pres. Rehab. and Cerebral Palsy Ctr. Wake County, Raleigh, 1974. Mem. ABA, N.C. Bar Assn. (treas. probate sect. 1983), Wake County Bar Assn. (chmn., bd. dirs. 1977), Law Alumni Assn. U. N.C. (bd. dirs.), Order of Coif, Phi Beta Kappa. Episcopalian. Club: Carolina Country (Raleigh) (pres. 1983-84). Avocation: flying. General corporate, Probate. Home: 626 Marlowe Rd Raleigh NC 27609 Office: Hunton & Williams 1 Hannover Sq PO Box 109 Raleigh NC 27602

JOYNT, JOHN HOWARD, lawyer; b. Birmingham, Ala., Feb. 6, 1903; s. John Howard and Minnie Lee (Spencer) J.; m. May Aberdeen Lepley, Oct. 10, 1932; children—John Howard III, Martha Maria. B.S., Carnegie Inst. Tech., 1925; M.S., MIT, 1929; LL.B., George Washington U., 1931. Bar: D.C. 1931, U.S. Supreme Ct. 1943, Va. 1971. Assoc., Janney, Blair & Curtis, N.Y.C., 1931-32; sole practice, Washington, 1932-70, Alexandria, Va., 1970—; examiner U.S. Patent Office, Washington, 1928-31. Trustee Carnegie-Mellon U.; life sponsor Ducks Unltd.; trustee, past pres. Hist. Alexandria Found.; chmn. Alexandria Hist. Restoration and Preservation Commn.; trustee Carlyle House Found.; sponsor Lee-Jackson Meml. Found.; life mem. Nat. Trust Hist. Preservation. Mem. ABA, Am. Patent Law Assn., Am. Judicature Soc., Bar Assn. D.C., Tau Beta Pi, Eta Kappa Nu, Theta Xi. Clubs: City Tavern (Washington); Md. (Balt.). Contbr. articles to profl.

jours. Patent, Trademark and copyright. Home: 601 Duke St Alexandria VA 22314

JOYNTON, STANLEY FORREST, lawyer; b. Bethesda, Md., Sept. 12, 1951; s. Harry Dudley Jr. and Mary Ruth (Jordan) J.; m. Lynne Deana Olson, Nov. 21, 1981; 1 child, Carrie Alice. BA, Rice U., 1973; JD with honors, U. Tex., 1978. Bar: Tex. 1978, U.S. Dist. Ct. (no. dist.) Tex. 1982. Assoc. Hall and Lane, San Angelo, Tex., 1978-83, ptnr., 1984—. Bd. dirs., sec. Highland Range Estates Owners Assn., San Angelo, 1985-87; sec. Concho Valley Estate Planning Council, 1980-81. Mem. ABA, Tom Green County Bar Assn. (sec. 1979-80). Baptist. Lodge: Lions (sec. 1985-86). Avocations: music, carpentry, backpacking, running, bicycling. Probate, Estate taxation, Personal income taxation. Home: 108 Kilt San Angelo TX 76901 Office: Hall & Lane PO Box 5460 San Angelo TX 76902

JUCEAM, ROBERT E., lawyer; b. N.Y.C., June 16, 1940; s. Benjamin T. and Amelia B. (Spatz) J.; m. Eleanor Pam, May 24, 1970; children—Daniel, Jacquelyn, Gregory. A.B., Columbia U., 1961, J.D., 1964; LL.M., NYU, 1966. Bar: N.Y. 1965, U.S. Dist. Ct. (so. and ea. dists.) N.Y. 1966, U.S. Tax Ct. 1968, U.S. Ct. Appeals (2d cir.) 1967, U.S. Ct. Appeals (5th cir.) 1978, U.S. Ct. Appeals (D.C. cir.) 1980, U.S. Supreme Ct. 1971. Law clk. U.S. Dist. Ct., N.Y., 1964-66; assoc. Fried, Frank, Harris, Shriver & Jacobson, N.Y.C., 1966-73, ptnr., 1974—; dir. Nat. Network Def. of the Right to Counsel, 1986—. Contbr. articles to legal jours. Trustee Mexican-Am. Legal Def. and Edn. Fund, 1986—; dir. Nat. Network for Def. of Right to Counsel, Inc., 1986—. Fellow Am. Bar. Found.; mem. ABA (ho. of dels. 1983—, chmn. com. on immigration sect. litigation 1985—, mem. coordinating com. on immigration law 1984—, mem. com. environ. controls sect. corp. banking and security law, 1983-87), N.Y. State Bar Assn., Assn. Bar City N.Y. (com. on trademarks and unfair competition 1983-86, Am. Judicature Soc. (life), Am. Bar Endowment, Nat. Conf. Bar Presidents (assoc.), Am. Immigration Lawyers Assn. (pres. 1982-83, bd. govs. 1971—, chmn. N.Y. chpt. 1971-72, gen. counsel 1986—, recipient Edith Lowenstein Meml. award 1981), Am. Arbitration Assn. (comml. panel 1973—), N.Y. County Lawyers Assn. (dir. law com. for human rights 1986—), Fed. Bar Assn., Fed. Bar Council, N.Y. Criminal Bar Assn., Nat. Conf. Bar Pres.'s, N.Y. State Trial Lawyers Assn., Nat. Assn. Criminal Def. Lawyers, Alpha Epsilon Pi. Clubs: Columbia, Broad St. (N.Y.C.). Federal civil litigation, Administrative and regulatory, Immigration, naturalization, and customs. Home: 106 Hemlock Rd Manhasset NY 11030 Office: 1 New York Plaza New York NY 10004

JUCHATZ, WAYNE WARREN, lawyer; b. N.Y.C., June 25, 1946; s. Warren Carl and Margaret E. (Trafford) J.; m. Linda K. Wilson, June 21, 1969; children: Bradley T., Scott W. BA, Franklin & Marshall Coll., 1968; JD, U. Va., 1974. Bar: N.Y. 1975, N.C. 1985. Assoc. Cadwalader, Wickersham & Taft, N.Y.C., 1974-77; asst. counsel R.J. Reynolds Industries Inc., Winston-Salem, N.C., 1977-79, assoc. counsel, 1979-80, sr. assoc. counsel, 1980-81; asst. gen. counsel R.J. Reynolds Tobacco Co., Winston-Salem, 1981-84, dep. gen. counsel, 1984-85, v.p., sec., gen. counsel, 1986-87, sr. v.p., sec., gen. counsel, 1987—. Served with U.S. Army, 1969-71. Office: RJ Reynolds Tobacco Co Corp Headquarters Bldg Box 2959 Winston-Salem NC 27102

JUDD, DENNIS L., county attorney; b. Provo, Utah, June 27, 1954; s. Derrel Wesley and Leila (Lundquist) J.; m. Carol Lynne Childberg, May 6, 1977; children: Lynne Marie, Amy Jo, Tiffany Ann, Andrew, Jacquelyn Nicole. BA in Polit. Sci., Brigham Young U., 1978, JD summa cum laude, 1981. Bar: Utah 1981, U.S. Dist. Ct. Utah 1981. Assoc. Nielson & Senior, Salt Lake City and Vernal, Utah, 1981-83; dep. county atty. Uintah County, Vernal, 1982-84; ptnr. Bennett & Judd, Vernal, 1983—; county atty. Daggett County, Utah, 1985—. Chmn. bd. adjustment Zoning & Planning Bd., Naples, 1982—; mem. Naples City Council, 1982—; mayor pro-tem City of Naples, 1983—; mem. resolution com. Utah League Cities and Towns, 1985-86, small cities com., 1985-86. Hinkley scholar Brigham Young U., 1977. Mem. ABA, Utah Bar Assn., Uintah Basin Bar Assn., Statewide Assn. Prosecutors, Vernal C. of C. (govt. affairs com.). Republican. Mormon. Avocations: hunting, photography, lapidary. General practice, Local government, State civil litigation. Home: 402 E 1500 South Naples UT 84078 Office: Bennett & Judd 319 W 100 South Suite B Vernal UT 84078

JUDD, JOEL STANTON, lawyer; b. Denver, Sept. 10, 1951; s. E. James and Eleanore Fay (Parelman) J. BA, New Coll., 1973; JD, U. Denver, 1976. Bar: Colo. 1976, U.S. Dist. Ct. Colo. 1976, U.S. Ct. Appeals (10th cir.) 1976, U.S. Supreme Ct. 1980. Assoc. Feder & Morris, Denver, 1976-77, Reckseen & Lau, Northglenn, Colo., 1977-82; sole practice Denver, 1982—. Mem. ABA, Colo. Bar Assn., Denver Bar Assn., Colo. Trial Lawyers Assn., Allied Jewish Fedn. (chmn. 1984—). Democrat. Lodge: Optimists (pres. 1980-83). Avocations: skiing, river rafting. Federal civil litigation, State civil litigation, Personal injury. Home: 2904 W 24th Ave Denver CO 80211 Office: 190 E 9th Ave Suite 520 Denver CO 80203

JUDD, LINDA, lawyer; b. Morrison, Okla., Oct. 30, 1939; d. John Benton and Mabel Edna (Humphries) Roberson; m. Richard D. Palmer, June 23, 1957 (dec. 1958); m. 2d, James F. Judd, July 4, 1970; 1 son, Richard J. B.A., U. Idaho, 1968; J.D., 1970. Bar: Idaho 1970, U.S. Dist. Ct. Idaho 1970, U.S. Ct. Appeals (9th cir.) 1974, U.S. Supreme Ct. 1983. Ptnr. Judd & Judd, Post Falls, Idaho, 1970-81; prin. Judd & Judd, P.A., 1981-86, Judd Law Firm, P.A., 1987—. Commr. Uniform State Laws Commn. Idaho, 1978—. Mem. ABA, Idaho Trial Lawyers Assn. (bd. govs. 1978-79), Internat. Acad. Trial Lawyers (commendation for disting. achievement in art and sci. of advocacy 1970), Phi Beta Kappa, Phi Kappa Phi. State civil litigation, Probate, General practice. Home and Office: PO Box 999 Post Falls ID 83854

JUDD, RICHARD D(ONALD), lawyer; b. Sapulpa, Okla., July 1, 1940; s. Donald H. and Mabel M. (Green) J.; m. Jamy Crawford, June 13, 1962 (div. Mar. 1976); m. Janis Ball Newens, May 29, 1976. AB, Williams Coll., 1962; LLB, U. Colo., 1965. Bar: Colo. 1965, U.S. Dist. Ct. Colo. 1965, U.S. Ct. Appeals (10th cir.) 1965. Assoc. Dawson, Nagel, Sherman & Howard, Denver, 1965-66, Inman, Flynn & Coffee, Denver, 1966-69; ptnr. Reno & Judd, Denver, 1970-74; sole practice Denver, 1975-80; ptnr. Baker & Hostetler, Denver, 1980—. Mem. ABA, Colo. Bar Assn., Denver Bar Assn., Denver Law Club. Clubs: University (Denver); Boulder (Colo.) Country. Avocations: golf, music, reading, tennis. Real property, State civil litigation, Federal civil litigation. Office: Baker & Hostetler 303 E 17th Ave Suite 1100 Denver CO 80203

JUDELL, HAROLD BENN, lawyer; b. Milw., Mar. 9, 1915; s. Philip Fox and Lena Florence (Krause) J.; m. Maria Violeta van Ronzelen, May 5, 1951 (div.); m. Celeste Seymour Grulich, June 24, 1986. B.A., U. Wis., 1936, J.D., 1938; LL.B., Tulane U., 1950. Bar: Wis. 1938, La. 1950. Mem. firm Scheinfeld Collins Durant & Winter, Milw., 1938; spl. agent, adminstrv. asst. to dir. FBI, 1939-44; ptnr. Foley Judell Beck Bewley Martin & Hicks, New Orleans, 1950—; chmn. bd. Rockwood Nat. Trustee, East Group Properties, 1981—, Greater New Orleans YMCA, Internat. House, 1981—. Mem. ABA, La. Bar Assn., Am. Judicare Soc., Nat. Assn. Bond Lawyers (bd. dirs., pres. 1984-85). Clubs: New Orleans Country, Lawn Tennis, Met. (N.Y.C.); Nacional (Lima, Peru). Municipal bonds. Office: Foley Judell Beck Bewley Martin & Hicks 535 Gravier St 8th Floor New Orleans LA 70130

JUDICE, C(HARLES) RAYMOND, lawyer, state official; b. Lafayette, La., July 3, 1929; s. Rene J. and Letie Maria (Bertrand) J. B.B.A., U. Houston, 1956; J.D., South Tex. Coll., 1960. Bar: Tex. 1961, U.S. Supreme Ct. 1967. Sole practice, Houston, 1961-64; mcpl. judge, Houston, 1964-73; judge Ct. Domestic Relations, Houston, 1974; exec. dir. Tex. Jud. Council, Austin, 1974—; adminstrv. dir. Tex. Office Ct. Adminstrn., 1977—. Mem. Houston Bar Assn., Am. Judicature Soc. (dir. 1972-76), Am. Judges Assn. (Amicus Curiae award 1968, Outstanding Jud. Service award 1973, Am. Jud. award for jud. adminstrn. 1978, bd. govs. 1969-75), Nat. Conf. on Judiciary, South Tex. Coll. Law Alumni Assn. (pres.1966), Phi Alpha Delta (bd. govs. 1966-78, internat. pres. 1974-76). Judicial administration, Legislative, Administrative and regulatory. Home: 3711 Greenway St Austin TX 78705 Office: Tex Law Ctr 1414 Colorado St Austin TX 78701

JUDSON, PHILIP LIVINGSTON, lawyer; b. Palo Alto, Calif., Oct. 25, 1941; s. Philip MacGregor and Elizabeth Stuart (Peck) J.; m. Dorothy Louisa Lebohner, Sept. 6, 1963; children: Wendy Patricia, Philip Lebohner, Michael Lee. BA, Stanford U., 1963; JD, U. Calif., Hastings, 1969. Bar: Calif. 1970, U.S. Dist. Ct. (no. dist.) Calif. 1970, U.S. Ct. Appeals (9th cir.) 1970, U.S. Dist. Ct. (cen. dist.) Calif. 1984, U.S. Dist. Ct. (ea. dist.) Calif. 1985. Assoc. Pillsbury, Madison & Sutro, San Francisco, 1969-76, ptnr., 1977—; lectr. Practising Law Inst. Pres. St. Mark's Sch., San Rafael, 1983-85, founding mem. trustee 1980-86; trustee Marin Acad., San Rafael, 1985—. Served to 1st lt. U.S. Army, 1963-65. Mem. ABA (antitrust and litigation sects.), San Francisco Bar Assn., Order of Coif, Phi Delta Theta. Republican. Episcopal. Antitrust, Federal civil litigation, State civil litigation. Home: 23 Rosewood Ct San Rafael CA 94901 Office: Pillsbury Madison & Sutro 225 Bush St PO Box 7880 San Francisco CA 94120

JUDY, JOHN DAVID, III, lawyer; b. Winchester, Va., May 29, 1956; s. William Hayes Jr. and Ruth E. (Kessel) J.; m. Deborah Ann McCulloh, Sept. 29, 1984. BS in Agr., W.V. U., JD. Bar: W.Va. 1982, U.S. Dist. Ct. (no. dist.) W.Va. 1982, U.S. Dist. Ct. W.Va. 1985. Ptnr. Judy & Judy, Moorefield, W.Va., 1982—. Named one of Outstanding Young Men Am., 1983. Mem. W.Va. Bar Assn., Assn. Trial Lawyers Am. Lodges: Lions, Masons. General practice, Criminal, State civil litigation. Office: Judy & Judy PO Box 636 Moorefield WV 26836

JUERGENSMEYER, JOHN ELI, lawyer; b. Stewardson, Ill., May 14, 1934; s. Irvin Karl and Clara Augusta (Johannaber) J.; m. Elizabeth Ann Bogart, Sept. 10, 1963; children—Margaret Ann, Frances Elizabeth. B.A., U. Ill., 1955, J.D., 1963; M.A., Princeton U., 1957, Ph.D., 1960. Bar: Ill. 1963. Mem. faculty extension div. U. Ill., 1961-63, U. Hawaii, 1958-60; mem. firm Kirkland, Brady, McQueen, Martin & Schnell, Elgin, Ill., 1963-64; founder, sr. ptnr. Juergensmeyer, Zimmerman, Smith & Leady, Elgin, 1964-81, Juergensmeyer & Assocs., 1981—; mgr., owner Tollview Office Complex, 1976—; asst. pub. defender Kane County, 1964-67, asst. states atty., 1976-78; spl. asst. atty. gen. State of Ill., 1978-85; hearing officer Ill. Pollution Control Bd., 1971-74; commr. U.S. Nat. Commn. on Libraries and Info. Scis., 1982—; lectr. Inst. for Continuing Legal Edn., Ill Bar Assn., 1971-73; trustee ALA Endowment Fund, 1979-84; assoc. prof. Judson Coll., Elgin, 1963—. Chmn. Hiawatha Dist. Boy Scouts Am.; v.p. Elgin Family Service Assn., 1967-71; sec. Lloyd Morey Scholarship Fund, 1967-73; commr. Elgin Econ. Devel. Commn., 1971-75; chmn. Elgin Twp. Republican Central Com., 1978-80; adv. bd. Ill. Youth Commn., 1964-68; bd. dirs. Wesley Found. of U. Ill., 1971-75; pres. adv. bd. Elgin Salvation Army, 1973-75. Served to capt. Intelligence Service, USAF, 1958-60. Recipient Anti-Pollution Echo award Defenders of the Fox River, Inc., 1971, Cert. Merit, Heart Fund, 1971, Outstanding Young Man award Jr. C. of C., Elgin, 1967; Princeton U. fellow, 1955-56, Merrill Found. fellow, 1956-58. Mem. Assn. Trial Lawyers Am., ABA, Ill. Bar Assn. (chmn. local govt. com. 1974-75, editor local govt. law newsletter 1973-74), Chgo. Bar Assn. (chmn. local govt. com. 1975-76), Kane County Bar Assn., Am. Arbitration Assn. (arbitrator), Am. Polit. Sci. Assn., Izaak Walton League, Fed. Bar Assn., Phi Beta Kappa, Phi Alpha Delta, Alpha Kappa Lambda. Author: President, Foundations, and the People-to-People Program, 1965. Contbr. to publs. in field. Methodist. Club: Union League (Chgo.). Lodges: Masons, Shriners, Elks, Rotary (pres. 1977-78). Local government, Personal injury, General practice. Office: 707-A Davis Rd Elgin IL 60120

JUETTNER, PAUL GERARD, lawyer; b. Evanston, Ill., Nov. 16, 1954; s. Thomas Richard and Vivian Dorthy (Bajork) J.; m. Mary Rose Angeleri, Nov. 13, 1982; children: Thomas Joseph, Joseph Vincent. B.S.C.E., U. Ill., 1977; J.D. with high honors, Chgo. Kent. Coll. Law, 1981. Bars: Ill. 1981, U.S. Dist. Ct. (no. dist.) Ill. 1981, U.S. Ct. Appeals (7th cir.) 1981, U.S. Patent Office (agent 1981) 1982. Civil engr. Harza Engring. Co., Chgo., 1974-79; assoc. Gary, Juettner & Pyle, Chgo., 1979—. Mem. ABA, Chgo. Bar Assn., Patent Law Assn. Chgo. Roman Catholic. Patent, Trademark and copyright, Entertainment. Home: 5872 Leonard St Chicago IL 60646 Office: Gary Juettner & Pyle 33 N Dearborn St Chicago IL 60602

JUHL, LOREN EARL, lawyer; b. New Holland, Ill., Nov. 19, 1918; s. Albert H. and Margaret (Krusemark) J.; m. Harriet Hanson, Mar. 8, 1941 (dec.); children: Cynthia Juhl Carpenter, Gloria Juhl Raney, Roger C.; m. Elaine M. Morey, Oct. 8, 1970. B.S., U. Ill.-Urbana, 1940; LL.B., Harvard U., 1948. Bar: Ill. 1949. Assoc. Sidley & Austin, Chgo., 1948-56, ptnr., 1957—. Co-author: Drafting Wills and Trust Agreements in Illinois, 1987. Bd. dirs. Northwestern Meml. Found., Chgo.; bd. dirs. The Thresholds, Chgo. Maternity Ctr., mem. planned giving adv. com. Art Inst. Chgo. Served to maj. U.S. Army, 1941-45. Fellow Am. Coll. Probate Counsel; mem. Illini Club Chgo., ABA, Ill. State Bar Assn. (sec. 1971-72), Chgo. Bar Assn. Republican. Lutheran. Clubs: Westmoreland Country (Wilmette); Mid-Day (Chgo.). Estate planning, Probate, Estate taxation. Home: 2245 Sanders Rd Northbrook IL 60062 Office: Sidley & Austin 1 First Nat Plaza Chicago IL 60603

JULIAN, JIM LEE, lawyer; b. Osceola, Ark., Dec. 14, 1954; s. John Roland and Lucille Angela (Potts) J.; m. Patricia Lynn Roberts, Jan. 26, 1980. BA, Ark. State U., 1976; JD, U. Ark., 1979. Bar: Ark. 1979, U.S. Dist. Ct. (ea. and we. dists.) Ark. 1979. Assoc. Skillman & Durrett, West Memphis, Ark., 1979-82; staff atty. Ark. Power and Light Co., Little Rock, 1982-84; assoc. House, Wallace & Jewell, Little Rock, 1984-85, ptnr., 1986—; instr. bus. law Eastern Ark. Community Coll., West Memphis, 1981-82. Pres. Crittenden County (Ark.) Young Dems., 1980-82; mem. Ark. Children's Hosp. Com., 1985—. Mem. ABA, Ark. Bar Assn. (civil procedure com.), Pulaski County Bar Assn., Major Sports Assn. Methodist. Club: North Hills Country (Sherwood, Ark.). Lodge: Kiwanis. Avocation: golf. State civil litigation, Personal injury, Condemnation. Home: 1901 Hasbrook Ct North Little Rock AR 72116 Office: House Wallace Nelson et al 1500 Tower Bldg Little Rock AR 72201

JULIN, JOSEPH RICHARD, lawyer, educator; b. Chgo., July 5, 1926; s. George Allan and Jennie Elizabeth (Carlsten) J.; m. Dorothy Marie Julian, Oct. 18, 1952; children: Pamela, Thomas, Diane, Linda. Student, Deep Springs Coll., 1944, George Washington U., 1946-49; B.S.L., Northwestern U., 1950, J.D., 1952. Bar: Ill. 1952, Mich. 1960. Assoc. firm Schuyler, Stough & Morris, Chgo., 1952-57; ptnr. Schuyler, Stough & Morris, 1957-59; assoc. prof. law U. Mich., Ann Arbor, 1959-62; prof. law U. Mich., 1962-70, assoc. dean, 1968-70; dean, prof. law U. Fla. Coll. Law, Gainesville, 1971-80; dean emeritus and prof. law U. Fla. Coll. Law, 1980—, Chesterfield Smith prof. law, 1985—; spl. Master U.S. Dist. Ct. 1985—. Author: (with others) Basic Property Law, 1966, 72, 79. Trustee Ann Arbor Bd. Edn., 1966-69, pres., 1968-69. Served with U.S. Army, 1944-46. Fellow Am. Bar Found.; mem. Legal Club of Chgo., Mich. Bar Assn., Ill. Bar Assn., Chgo. Bar Assn., Am. Bar Assn. (chmn. sect. on legal edn. and admissions to the bar 1977-78), Assn. Am. Law Schs. (pres. 1984), Order of Coif., Phi Beta Kappa. Republican. Real property. Home: 1657 NW 19th Circle Gainesville FL 32605 Office: U Fla Coll Law Gainesville FL 32611

JUNELL, ROBERT ALAN, lawyer; b El Paso, Tex., Jan. 27, 1947; s. Robert Frank and Maxine (Simmons) J.; m. Beverly Ann Singley, Dec. 26, 1968; children: Ryan, Keith, Elizabeth, Clay. AA, N.Mex. Mil. Inst., 1967; BS, Tex. Tech U., 1969, JD, 1976; MA, U. Ark., 1974. Bar: Tex. 1977, U.S. Dist. Ct. (no. dist.) Tex. 1979, U.S. Dist. Ct. (we. dist.) Tex. 1984. Assoc. Scott, Hulse, Marshall & Feuille, El Paso, 1977-79, Webb, Stokes & Sparks, San Angelo, Tex., 1979—. Mem. Tex. Tech Found., Lubbock. Served to capt. U.S. Army, 1970-73. Mem. Tex. Bar Assn. (cert.), Tom Green County Bar Assn. (bd. dirs.), Tex. Trial Lawyers Assn. (assoc. bd. dirs.), Tex. Tech Law Sch. Alumni Assn. (bd. dirs.). Democrat. Avocations: steer roping, snow skiing. Personal injury, Workers' compensation, Products liability. Office: Webb Stokes Sparks Parker et al 314 W Harris San Angleo TX 76901

JUNG, PETER MICHAEL, lawyer; b. Ossining, N.Y., May 12, 1955; s. Peter Joseph and Paula June (Moyer) J.; m. Gretchen Lee Megowen, June 19, 1976. SB, MIT, 1975; JD, Harvard U., 1979. Bar: Tex. 1979, U.S. Dist. Ct. (no. dist.) Tex. 1979, U.S. Ct. Appeals (5th cir.) 1980, U.S. Dist. Ct. (ea. dist.) Tex. 1981, U.S. Ct. Appeals (10th cir.) 1984. Tech. staff C.S. Draper Lab., Cambridge, Mass., 1975-76; law clk. to presiding judge U.S. Dist. Ct. (no. dist.) Tex., Dallas, 1979-80; assoc. Strasburger & Price, Dallas, 1980-85, ptnr., 1986—; lectr. El Centro Community Coll., Dallas, 1980-82; instr. So. Meth. U., Dallas, 1984-86. Co-author: An Alternative Entry-Through-Landing Guidance Scheme for the Space Shuttle Orbital Flight Test, 1976, Introduction to the American Legal System, Texas Edition, 1982; contbg. editor Legal Asst. Today Mag., 1983—. Sec. bd. dirs. Dallas Homeowners League, 1984-86, 1st v.p. 1986—; pres. White Rock Neighborhood Assn., Dallas, 1984-85; mem. adv. com. Dallas Zoning Ordinance, 1984—, Leadership Dallas, 1985-86. Mem. ABA, Tex. Bar Assn., Dallas Bar Assn., Tex. Assn. Def. Counsel (com. vice chmn. 1985—), Dallas Assn. Young Lawyers. Republican. Lutheran. Avocations: theater, travel. State civil litigation, Federal civil litigation. Home: 7306 Dominique Dr Dallas TX 75214 Office: Strasburger & Price 901 Main St LB 175 4300 InterFirst Plaza Dallas TX 75202

JUNGHANS, PAULA MARIE, lawyer; b. Balt., Sept. 3, 1949; d. Edward William and Marie (Murray) J. BA cum laude, Coll. Notre Dame, Balt., 1971; JD, U. Md., 1976. Bar: Md. 1976, U.S. Dist. Ct. Md. 1976, U.S. Tax Ct., U.S. Ct. Appeals (4th cir.), U.S. Supreme Ct. Ptnr. Garbis & Schwait, Balt., 1976-85, Garbis, Marvel & Junghans, Balt., 1985-86, Melnicove, Kaufman, Weiner, Smouse & Garbis, Balt., 1986—; mem. inquiry panel Atty. Grievance Commn., 1983—. Author: Federal Tax Litigation, 1985. Mem. Trial Ct. Jud. Nominating Commn., Balt., 1984. Mem. ABA (tax sect.), Md. State Bar Assn. (bd. govs. 1984-86). Criminal, Personal income taxation, Federal civil litigation. Office: Melnicove Kaufman et al 36 S Charles St Baltimore MD 21201

JUNKERMAN, WILLIAM JOSEPH, lawyer; b. N.Y.C., May 5, 1904; s. Otto J. and Margaret Anne (McCarthy) J.; m. Helen Veronica Barrett, June 28, 1930. A.B., NYU, 1925; LL.B., Fordham U., 1928. Bar: N.Y. 1929, U.S. Dist. Ct. (so. and ea. dists.) N.Y. 1929, U.S. Ct. Appeals (1st, 2d and 3d cirs.), U.S. Supreme Ct. 1946. Asst. counsel L.I. State Park Commn., 1929-32; sole practice, N.Y.C., 1932-41; regional atty. CAA, 7th Region, Seattle, 1947-48; mem. Haight, Gardner, Poor & Havens, N.Y.C., 1948-50, gen. ptnr., 1950-80. Served with USN, 1941-46; to comdr. USNR. Fellow Am. Coll. Trial Lawyers; mem. Nat. Pilots Assn., Naval Order of U.S., Am. Legion (past comdr.). Clubs: Quiet Birdmen, Wings. General practice, Aviation. Address: 311 W 245th St Fieldston NY 10471

JUNKIN, TIMOTHY DEFOREST, lawyer; b. Washington, Apr. 21, 1951; s. George Jr. and Elizabeth (Henry) J.; m. Kristen Newell Curran, May 12, 1986; 1 child, Isabel Curran. Student, Washington and Lee U.; BA, U. Md.; JD, Georgetown U. Bar: D.C., Md., U.S. Dist. Ct. D.C., U.S. Dist. Ct. Md. Staff atty. Pub. Defender Service for Washington D.C., 1977-81; ptnr. Asbill, Junkin, Myers & Buffone Ltd., Washington, 1981—; adj. prof. Am. U., Washington, 1981-84. Advisor Community for Creative Nonviolence, Washington, 1986. Federal civil litigation, Criminal, Personal injury. Office: Asbill Junkin et al 1607 New Hampshire Ave Washington DC 20009

JURKOVIC, DANIEL JOHN, political science and criminal justice educator; b. Whiting, Ind., Apr. 28, 1934; s. Samuel Milo and Julia (Plavec) J.; m. Kathryn Jean Sandvold, Aug. 20, 1960; children: Dana Jean, Daniel Jon. B.A. in Lit. and Classical Langs., Concordia Coll., 1957; M.Div. in Theology, Luther Theol. Sem., St. Paul, 1961; M.A. in Polit. Sci. and Philosophy, U. Minn.-Mpls., 1965, Ph.D. in Polit. Sci. and Philosophy, 1972. Asst. prof. Carthage Coll., Kenosha, Wis., 1967-72, assoc. prof., 1972-78, prof. dept. polit. sci./criminal justice, 1978—, criminal justice dir., 1969-78, 1984-86, polit. sci. chmn., 1986—. Mem. World Community Task Force Wis./Upper Mich. Synod, Lutheran Ch. in Am., 1971-75, chmn. world concerns com., 1984—; treas. Kenosha/Racine chpt. Wis. Civil Liberties Union, 1983—. Recipient Law Day Recognition award Kenosha Bar Assn., 1982; Criminal Justice Conf. grantee Carthage Coll., 1974, fed. tuition grantee Carthage Coll., 1970-77. Mem. Am. Polit. Sci. Assn., AAUP (sec.-treas. Carthage chpt. 1967-70), Midwest Polit. Sci. Assn., Wis. Criminal Justice Edn. Assn. (pres. 1976-77), Wis. Polit. Sci. Assn. (treas. 1975-79). Civil rights, Jurisprudence. Home: 4527 Garden Dr Racine WI 53403 Office: Carthage Coll Kenosha WI 53140

JURSIK, PATRICIA DOLORES, lawyer; b. Milw., Sept. 13, 1947; d. Roy R. and Dolores J. (Bayer) Carney; m. Robert J. Jursik, Nov. 21, 1970; children: Kathryn J., Leigh A. BS, U. Wis., 1969, MS, 1974; JD, Marquette U., 1980. Bar: Wis. 1980, U.S. Dist. Ct. (ea. and we. dists.) Wis. 1980. Tchr. Milw. Pub. Sch., 1969-78; ptnr. Jursik & Jursik, Cudahy, Wis., 1980—. Articles editor Marquette U. Law Rev., 1984. Bd. dirs. Milw. Area Tech. Coll., 1980-85, chmn. bd. dirs., 1981-83; bd. dirs. Cath. Social Services, 1986—. Mem. ABA, Wis. Bar Assn., Assn. for Women Lawyers, Lawyers Alliance for Nuclear Arms. Control. Roman Catholic. Family and matrimonial, Real property, Probate. Home: 4535 S Sheridan Dr Cudahy WI 53110 Office: Jursik & Jursik 4711 S Packard Ave Cudahy WI 53110

JUSTER, KENNETH IAN, lawyer; b. N.Y.C., Nov. 24, 1954; s. Howard H. and Muriel (Uchitelle) J. AB, Harvard U., 1976, MS in Pub. Policy, 1980, JD, 1980. Bar: D.C. 1981, U.S. Dist. Ct. D.C. 1981, U.S. Ct. Internat. Trade 1981, U.S. Ct. Appeals (D.C. cir.) 1981, U.S. Supreme Ct. 1981, U.S. Ct. Appeals (fed. ct.) 1982. Law clk. to presiding justice U.S. Ct. Appeals (2nd cir.), Brattleboro, Vt., 1980-81; assoc. Arnold & Porter, Washington, 1981—; staff asst. Nat. Security Council, 1978. Editor Harvard U. Internat. Law Jour., 1979-80; contbr. articles to profl. jours. Mem. ABA (internat. law sect.), D.C. Bar Assn. (internat. law sect.), Am. Soc. Internat. Law, Council on Fgn. Relations, Phi Beta Kappa. Private international, Federal civil litigation, Administrative and regulatory. Home: 2500 Q St NW Apt 745 Washington DC 20007 Office: Arnold & Porter 1200 New Hampshire Ave NW Washington DC 20036

JUSTICE, ROBERT SCOTT, lawyer; b. Lognsport, Ind., Mar. 8, 1912; s. Robert Owen and Ethel (Scott) J.; m. Catherine Augusta Leirer, June 20, 1942; children: Robert L., T. Jonathan, Margaret E., Samuel C., Elizabeth A., Amy C. AB, DePauw U., 1933; AM, U. Mich., 1937; JD, Harvard U., 1943. Bar: Ind. 1943, U.S. Dist. Ct. (no. dist.) Ind. 1947, U.S. Supreme Ct. 1958. Sole practice Logansport, Ind.; chmn. bd. dirs. Logansport Savings & Loan Assn. Former mem. Ind. Ho. Reps., 1944-48, 50-52; former Ind. senator, 1956-60. Mem. Ind. Bar Assn., Cass County Bar Assn. (past pres.), Assn. Trial Lawyers Am., Harvard Law Sch. Assn. Republican. Presbyterian. Lodge: Masons. General practice, Probate, Personal injury. Home: Rural Rt 2 Box 205 Logansport IN 46947 Office: 7th and Market Sts Logansport IN 46947

JUSTICE, THOMAS HARDWICK, III, lawyer; b. Shirley, Mass., May 20, 1955; s. Thomas Hardwick Justice Jr. and Elaine Rita (Poirier) Whyte; m. Virginia Pulley, May 1, 1982; 1 child, Benjamin Gerald. BA, U. Va., 1977; JD, Washington & Lee U., 1980. Bar. Va. 1980, U.S. Dist. Ct. (ea. dist.) Va. 1981, D.C. 1982, Fla. 1983, U.S. Dist. Ct. D.C. 1983, U.S. Dist. Ct. (mid. dist.) Fla. 1984, U.S. Ct. Appeals (11th cir.) 1984. Law clk. to presiding judge Cir. Ct., Alexandria, Va., 1980-81; assoc. Braude, Margulies, Sacks & Rephan, Washington, 1981-83, Vandenberg, Gay, Burke, Wilson & Arkin, P.A., Orlando, Fla., 1983-84, Shutts & Bowen, Orlando, 1984—. Mem. Fin. Devel. Com. Arthritis Found. Cen. Fla., Orlando, 1986. Mem. ABA (pub. contract com., forum com. on constrn. industry), Orange County Bar Assn. Roman Catholic. Avocations: sailing, reading, flying. Private international, Federal civil litigation, Construction. Home: 3212 Chelsea St Orlando FL 32803 Office: Shutts & Bowen 20 N Orange Ave Orlando FL 32801

JUSTICE, WILLIAM WAYNE, judge; b. Athens, Tex., Feb. 25, 1920; s. William Davis and Jackie May (Hanson) J.; m. Sue Tom Ellen Rowan, Mar. 16, 1947; 1 dau., Ellen Rowan. LL.B., U. Tex., 1942. Bar: Tex. bar. Ptnr. firm Justice & Justice, Athens, 1946-61; city atty. Athens, 1948-50, 52-58; U.S. atty. Eastern Dist. Tex., 1961-68; U.S. dist. judge Eastern Dist. Tex., Tyler, 1968-80, chief judge, 1980—. Vice pres. Young Democrats Tex., 1948; adv. council Dem. Nat. Com., 1954; alternate del. Dem. Nat. Conv., 1956, presdl. elector., 1960. Served to 1st lt. F.A. AUS, 1942-46, CBI. Recipient Nat. award Outstanding Fed. Judge Assn. Trial Lawyers Am., 1982. Mem. ABA, Am. Judicature Soc., VFW (past post comdr.). Baptist. Lodges: Rotary (pres. Athens 1961), Masons, K.T. Office: PO Box 330 Tyler TX 75701

JUSTUS, JO LYNNE, lawyer; b. Manhattan, Kans., Jan. 26, 1950; d. William Wade and Gertrude Eunice (Wheeler) J.; m. Richard Lee Whitson,

Mar. 27, 1976; 1 child, Willam Lee Whitson. B.A., U. Kans., 1972, J.D., 1975; grad. Nat. Inst. Trial Advocacy, 1983. Bar: Kans. 1975, U.S. Dist. Ct. Kans. 1975, U.S. Ct. Claims 1985, U.S. Ct. Appeals (10th cir.) 1985. Legal researcher Chambers & Mallon, Kansas City, Kans., 1974-75; sole practice, Kansas City, Kans., 1975-78, Lawrence, Kans., 1978-82; mng. atty. Kans. Legal Services, Topeka, 1982-83, regional dir., 1983-84; ptnr. Metcalf and Justus, Topeka, 1984—. Active Douglas County chpt. ARC, Lawrence, 1980-82. Mem. Kans. Bar Assn. (family law com. 1977-79, 83-84, legal issues affecting the elderly com. 1984—), U. Kans. Alumni Assn. (life). Republican. Presbyterian. Clubs: Lawrence Bus. and Profl. Women's (v.p. 1981, pres.-elect 1982, Outstanding Young Woman 1980). Bankruptcy, Federal civil litigation, State civil litigation. Office: 801 Western Topeka KS 66606

JUTERBOCK, RICHARD EDWIN, corporate counsel; b. N.Y.C., Sept. 30, 1946; s. Edwin Emil and Muriel Elisabeth (Yockel) J.; m. Deborah Knutzen, Sept. 29, 1979; 1 child, Elisabeth. BA, Washington and Lee U., Lexington, Va., 1968; JD, Duke U., 1968-71. Bar: N.Y. 1972, U.S. Dist. Ct. (so. dist.) N.Y. 1973. Assoc. Shearman & Sterling, N.Y.C., 1971-75; v.p., asst. resident counsel Morgan Guaranty Trust Co. of N.Y., N.Y.C., 1975—; bd. dirs., sec. Morgan Guaranty Internat. Bank, Miami, Fla., 1984—. Mem. ABA., Am. Youth Hostel Assn. (life). Avocation: bicycling, gardening, travel. Banking. Office: Morgan Guaranty Trust Co 15 Broad St New York NY 10015

KAAPCKE, WALLACE LETCHER, lawyer; b. Chgo., Oct. 3, 1916; s. Ernest Herman and Ophelia Bohannon (Jones) K.; m. Ellen Adams, Apr. 4, 1942; children: Peter L., Brian E., Gretchen. B.S., U. Oreg., 1937, J.D., 1939; postgrad. (Sterling fellow), Yale U. Law Sch., 1939-40. Bar: Oreg. 1939, Calif. 1941. Assoc. firm Hughes, Hubbard & Ewing, N.Y.C., 1940-41, Pillsbury, Madison & Sutro, San Francisco, 1941-51; mem. firm Pillsbury, Madison & Sutro, 1951—, chmn., 1977-80; gen. counsel San Francisco Bay Area Rapid Transit, 1958-69; lectr. U. Calif., 1961, 73. Contbr. articles to legal jours. Bd. dirs. U. Oreg. Found.; bd. dirs., mem. exec. com., sec. San Francisco Opera Assn. Fellow Am. Bar Found.; mem. ABA, Calif. Bar Assn. Clubs: Stock Exchange (past pres.), Bohemian (San Francisco); Claremont (Berkeley). Home: 18 Roble Ct Berkeley CA 94705 Office: Pillsbury Madison & Sutro 225 Bush St 19th Floor San Francisco CA 94104

KABAK, BERNARD JOSHUA, lawyer, urban planner; b. Bronx, N.Y., Dec. 22, 1941; s. Samuel Louis and Jeanne (Sirotin) K.; m. Ilana Etta Stern, June 15, 1982. AB, Columbia U., 1963; LLB, Harvard U., 1966; M Urban Planning, Hunter Coll., 1968. Bar: N.Y. 1967, Israel 1975. Sr. atty. N.Y.C. Dept. City Planning, N.Y.C., 1968-73; spl. advisor Ministry of Justice, Jerusalem, Israel, 1974-75; counsel Office of Spl. Dep. State Comptroller for N.Y.C., 1976—; counsel Nat. Mcpl. League, Council Mcpl. Performance, 1985—. Contbr. in field. Bd. govs. Lincoln Square Synagogue, N.Y.C., 1986—; divisional chmn. United Jewish Appeal-Fedn. Jewish Philanthropies, N.Y.C., 1973; mem. exec. com. Coalition to Free Soviet Jews, N.Y.C., 1978—. Avocation: silversmith. Local government, Land use and planning, Municipal bonds. Home: 393 West End Ave New York NY 10024 Office: Office Spl Dep Comptroller NYC 270 Broadway New York NY 10007

KABAKER, RICHARD ZOHN, lawyer; b. Chgo., Feb. 22, 1935; s. Herman A. and Eve (Horwitz) K.; m. Patricia Lee Florsheim, Sept. 18, 1964; children—Douglas J., Nancy L. B.A., U. Mich., 1956, J.D., 1959. Bar: Ill. 1959, U.S. Dist. Ct. (no. dist.) Ill. 1960, Ohio 1969, Wis. 1973, U.S. Dist. Ct. (we. dist.) Wis. 1973, U.S. Tax Ct. 1978, U.S. Ct. Appeals (7th cir.) 1960, U.S. Supreme Ct. 1978. Assoc. McDermott, Will & Emery, Chgo., 1960-69, Jones, Day, Cockley & Reavis, Cleve., 1969-71; assoc. prof. law. U. Detroit, 1971-72; asst. prof. U. Wis., Madison, 1972-77; ptnr. Murphy & Desmond, Madison, 1977—; lectr. in field. Author: Wisconsin Estate Planning, 1984; also articles. Editor: Will and Trust Forms, 1981. Chmn. lawyers div. Dane county chpt. capital campaign ARC, Madison, 1984. Smongeski research fellow U. Wis., 1976. Fellow Am. Coll. Probate Counsel (bd. regents 1985—), U. Wis. Found.; mem. Internat. Acad. Estate and Trust Law (internat. exec. com. 1986—), State Bar Wis. (chmn. com. on estate tax apportionment 1983—), ABA (vice chmn. com. on tax regulations and legis.: joint tenancy 1981-84, chmn. com. on creditors rights in estates and trusts 1986—). Club: Madison. Lodge: Rotary. Probate, Estate taxation, Estate planning. Home: 5122 Raymond Rd Madison WI 53711 Office: Murphy & Desmond SC PO Box 2038 Madison WI 53701

KABALA, EDWARD JOHN, lawyer, corporation executive; b. Phila., Mar. 21, 1942; s. Stan and Margaret (Toner) K.; m. Gail L., Dec. 28, 1963; children: Courtenay, Paxson. BS, Pa. State U., 1964; JD, Duquesne U., 1970. Bar: Pa. 1970, U.S. Dist. Ct. (we. dist.) Pa. 1970, U.S. Tax Ct. 1970. Indsl. engr. Allegheny Ludlum Steel Co., 1964-67; sr. indsl. engr. Titanium Metals Corp. Am., 1967-68; patent engr. U.S. Steel Corp., 1969, atty., 1970; atty. Houston, Cooper, Speer and German, Pitts., 1970-73; pres. Kabala & Geeseman and predecessor firm, Pitts., 1973—; pres. Profl. Retirement Plan Services Corp., P.F.G. Leasing Co.; counsel Allegheny Med. Soc.; lectr. pensions, estate planning, taxation, fin. planning Pa. State U., 1978—, Chatham Coll., 1978—, profl. orgns. of physicians, attys., accts., dentists, 1976—. Mem. ABA (sect. of taxation com. on closely held corps. and com. on profl. service corps., sect. of bus. banking and corp. law com. on employee benefits), Pa. Bar Assn., Allegheny County Bar Assn., Am. Acad. Hosp. Attys. Pension, profit-sharing, and employee benefits, Estate planning, Probate. Home: 18 Forest Glen Pittsburgh PA 15228 Office: The Waterfront 200 First Ave Pittsburgh PA 15222

KACAL, GEORGE JEROME, JR., lawyer; b. Oakland, Calif., Mar. 24, 1945; s. George Jerome Sr. and Catherine I. (Morrissey) K.; m. Linda Marie (Russo) K., June 26, 1966; children: Kyle, Amy. BBA, Tex. A & M U., 1968; JS, U. Houston, 1971. Bd. dirs. Dunn, Kacal, Adams, Livingston & Pappas, Houston; bd. dirs. Kacal's Oil and Gas Co., Houston, So. Continental Mortgage Co., Houston. Pres. Green Tee Terr. Civic Club, Pearland, Tex., 1976-80. Served to capt. Q.M.'s, 1968-76. Mem. ABA, Tex. Bar Assn., Tex. Assn. Def. Counsel, Def. Research Inst. Club: Golfcrest Country Club (Pearland, Tex.). Federal civil litigation, State civil litigation, Insurance. Home: 2307 Green Tee Dr Pearland TX 77581 Office: Dunn Kacal Adams Livingston Pappas & Law 2929 Allen Pkwy Suite 2600 Houston TX 77019

KACHIGIAN, MARK GEORGE, lawyer; b. Kingston, N.Y., June 2, 1952; s. Mark Sonny and Theresa May (Asadorian) K., Lou Anne Walpole, Mar. 17, 1980; 1 child, Mark George Jr. BS in Commerce, Rider Coll., 1974; JD, U. Tulsa, 1978. Bar: Okla. 1978, N.Y. 1980, U.S. Dist. Ct. (no. and ea. dists.) Okla. 1985. Gen. counsel UPI, N.Y.C., 1978-80; assoc. Parker, Duryee, Zunino, Malone & Carter, N.Y.C., 1980-84, Law Offices of Ellis Freedman, N.Y.C., 1984-85; ptnr. Dorman & Kachigian, Tulsa, 1985—. Bar: ABA, Okla. Bar Assn. (inventor assistance com. patent and trademark sect. 1985—), Assn. of Bar of City of N.Y., Tulsa Songwriters Assn. (bd. dirs. 1986—). Trademark and copyright, General corporate, Libel. Office: 1146th E 64th St Tulsa OK 74136

KACIR, BARBARA BRATTIN, lawyer; b. Buffalo, July 19, 1941; d. William James and Jean (Harrington) Brattin; m. Charles Stephen Kacir, June 3, 1973 (div.). B.A., Wellesley Coll., 1963; J.D., U. Mich., 1967. Bar: Ohio 1967, D.C. 1980. Assoc. Arter & Hadden, Cleve., 1967-74, ptnr., 1974-79; ptnr. Jones, Day, Reavis & Pogue, Washington, 1980-83, Cleve., 1983—; instr. trial tactics Case-Western Res. U., 1976-79. Mem. nat. com. visitors, nat. fund raising com. U. Mich. Mem. ABA, Ohio Bar Assn., D.C. Bar Assn., Cleve. Bar Assn. (trustee 1973-76, treas. 1978-79), Assn. Trial Lawyers Am., Am. Law Inst., Def. Research Inst. Republican. Federal civil litigation, General corporate, Administrative and regulatory. Home: 13705 Shaker Blvd Cleveland OH 44120 Office: Jones Day Reavis & Pogue 1700 Huntington Bldg Cleveland OH 44115

KACOYANIS, DENNIS CHARLES, lawyer; b. Arlington, Mass., Sept. 3, 1953; s. Paul and Faye (Vaghida) K. BA in Polit. Sci. with honors, Northeastern U., 1976; JD, DePaul U., 1979. Bar: Mass. 1979, U.S. Dist. Ct. Mass. 1980, U.S. Ct. Appeals (D.C. cir.) 1980, Va. 1981, U.S. Ct. Appeals (4th cir.) 1981. Trial atty. EEOC, Washington, 1979-81, gen. atty., 1981—. Mem. Fairfax County (Va.) Young Reps., 1982—; pres. young adult league St. Katherine's Greek Orthodox Ch. of No. Va., Falls Church, 1981-82. Named one of Outstanding Young Men Am., 1986. Mem. ABA (labor and employment law com.), Fed. Bar Assn., Va. Bar Assn., Mass. Bar Assn., Am. Hellenic Lawyers Assn., Am. Hellenic Edn. Progeressive Assn. (dist. gov. 1986-87, dist. lt. gov. 1985-86, dist. sec. 1984-85, dist. treas. 1983-84, dist. adv. Sons of Perceles 1982-83, dist. athletic dir. 1981-82, chpt. adv. Sons of Perceles 1980-82, scholarship com. 1980-84), Mason Dist. Jaycees, Falls Church Jaycees. Greek Orthodox. Lodge: AHEPA (officer dist. club 1981—). Avocations: athletics, music. Labor. Home: 5424 Leeway Ct Fairfax VA 22032 Office: EEOC 5203 Leesburg Pike Suite 900 Falls Church VA 22041

KACZYNSKI, STEPHEN JOHN, lawyer; b. Bklyn., Dec. 27, 1954. BA, St. John's U., Jamaica, N.Y., 1976, JD, 1978; LLM, U. Va., 1984. Bar: N.Y. 1978, U.S. Ct. Mil. Appeals 1979, U.S. Supreme Ct. 1984, U.S. Dist. Ct.(no. dist.) 1985, U.S. Dist. Ct. Ohio 1985, Ohio 1986. Assoc. Jones, Day, Reavis & Pogue, Cleve., 1985—. Contbr.: Modern Legal Systems, 1985; contbr. articles to profl. jours. Served to capt. JAGC, U.S. Army, 1979-85. Mem. ABA, Bar Assn. of Greater Cleve. Personal injury, Military, Federal civil litigation.

KADELA, DAVID ANTHONY, lawyer; b. Detroit, Apr. 17, 1956; s. John Leo and Margaret Lois (Cottrell) K.; m. J. Lynn Nordstrom, Apr. 1, 1978; children: David, Stacey, Adam. AB with Distinction, U. Mich., 1978; JD magna cum laude, U. Detroit, 1981. Bar: Va. 1982, U.S. Dist. Ct. (ea. and we. dists.) Va. 1982, U.S. Ct. Appeals (4th cir.) 1982, Ohio 1986, U.S. Dist. Ct. (so. dist.) Ohio 1987, U.S. Ct. Appeals (6th cir.) 1987. Assoc. Hunton & Williams, Richmond, Va., 1981-86, Schottenstein, Zox & Dunn, Columbus, Ohio, 1986—. Mem. ABA (labor and employment sect., litigation sect.), Va. Bar Assn. Labor, Workers' compensation. Office: Schottenstein Zox & Dunn 41 S High St Columbus OH 43215

KADET, SAMUEL, lawyer; b. N.Y.C., Oct. 5, 1949; s. Leo and Ethel (Genicoff) K.; m. Elyse Coltun, Aug. 29, 1976. BA, Harper Coll., 1971; JD, St. John's U., Jamaica, N.Y., 1977. Bar: N.Y., U.S. Dist. Ct. (no., ea. and so. dists.) N.Y. Assoc. Skadden, Arps, Slate, Meagher & Flom, N.Y.C., 1977-85, ptnr., 1985—. Federal civil litigation, State civil litigation, Securities. Office: Skadden Arps Slate Meagher & Flom 919 Third Ave New York NY 10022

KADISH, LLOYD ALAN, lawyer; b. Chgo., Feb. 6, 1946; s. Alvin and Beverly (Mottlowitz) K.; 1 son, Benjamin Justin. B.S., U. Pa., 1968, J.D., Northwestern U., 1971, LL.M., Georgetown U., 1974. Bar: D.C. 1971, Ill. 1971. Adj. prof. Georgetown U. Law Center, Washington, 1973-74; asst. prof. U. Tenn. Sch. Law, Knoxville, 1974-75; atty. SEC, Washington, 1975-76; regional counsel Commodity Futures Trading Commn., Chgo., 1976-78; ptnr. Lloyd Kadish & Assocs., Ltd. and predecessors, Chgo., 1978—. E. Barrett Prettyman fellow, 1971-74. Mem. Chgo. Bar Assn. (chmn. commodities com.), ABA (commodities com.). Jewish. Commodities and Trading, Federal civil litigation, State civil litigation.

KADISH, MARK J., lawyer; b. Bklyn., Jan. 14, 1943; s. Leon and Thelma Kadish; m. Carol Kadish, Aug. 1963 (div. Mar. 1974); children: Wendy Morgan, Dana; m. Rosalyn Kadish, Mar. 23, 1974 (div. June 1986). BA, Lafayette U., 1964; LLB, NYU, 1967. Bar: N.Y. 1967, Mass. 1973, Ga. 1975. Assoc. Bailey, Alch & Gillis, Boston, 1971-74; mng. ptnr. Garland, Nuckolls & Kadish, Atlanta, 1974-80; pres. Kadish, Davis & Brojman, P.C., Atlanta, 1980-83, Kadish & Kadish P.C., Atlanta, 1983-87; sole practice Atlanta, 1987—. Author: Criminal Law Advocacy, Criminal Investigation and Preparation, 1982. Served to capt. U.S. Army, 1968-71. Mem. ABA (defense function com.), Atlanta Bar Assn. (bd. dirs. 1980-81), Assn. Trial Lawyers Am. (chmn. criminal sect. 1982-83), Ga. Assn. Criminal Def. Lawyers (bd. dirs. 1982—). Jewish. Criminal, Federal civil litigation, State civil litigation. Home: 891 Adair Ave NE Atlanta GA 20306 Office: 44 Broad St Suite 600 Atlanta GA 30303

KADISH, SANFORD HAROLD, law educator; b. N.Y.C., Sept. 7, 1921; s. Samuel J. and Frances R. (Klein) K.; m. June Kurtin, Sept. 29, 1942; children: Joshua, Peter. B.S.S., CCNY, 1942; LL.B., Columbia U., 1948; Dr. Jur. (hon.), U. Cologne, 1983; LL.D. (hon.), CUNY, 1985. Bar: N.Y. 1948, Utah 1954. Practice law N.Y.C., 1948-51; prof. law U. Utah, 1951-60, U. Mich., 1961-64, U. Calif.-Berkeley, 1964—; dean Law Sch. U. Calif. at Berkeley, 1975-82, Morrison prof., 1973—; Fulbright lectr. Melbourne (Australia) U., 1956; vis. prof. Harvard U., 1960-61, Freiburg U., 1967, Stanford U., 1970; lectr. Salzburg Seminar Am. Studies, 1965; Fulbright vis. lectr. Kyoto (Japan) U., 1975; vis. fellow Inst. Criminology, Cambridge (Eng.) U., winter 1968. Author: (with M.R. Kadish) Discretion to Disobey—A Study of Lawful Departures from Legal Rules, 1973, (with Schulhofer and Paulsen) Criminal Law and Its Processes, 4th edit., 1983, Blame and Punishment - Essays in the Criminal Law, 1987; also articles; editor-in-chief Ency. Crime and Justice, 1983. Reporter Calif. Legis. Penal Code Project, 1964-68; public mem. Wage Stblzn. Bd., region XII, 1951-53; cons. Pres.'s Commn. Adminstrn. of Justice, 1966; mem. Calif. Council Criminal Justice, 1968-69. Served to lt. USNR, 1943-46. Fellow Center Advanced Study Behavioral Scis., 1967-68; Guggenheim fellow Oxford U., 1974-75; vis. fellow All Souls Coll. Oxford U. Fellow Am. Acad. Arts and Sci. (v.p. 1984-86); mem. AAUP (nat. pres. 1970-72), Nat. Acad. Arbitrators, Am. Soc. Legal and Polit. Philosophy, Am. Assn. Law Schs. (exec. com. 1960, pres. 1982), Phi Beta Kappa, Order of Coif (exec. com. 1966-67, 74-75). Criminal, Jurisprudence. Home: 774 Hilldale Ave Berkeley CA 94708

KADRI, TARIQ RASHID, corporate executive, lawyer; b. Altadena, Calif., Nov. 17, 1949; s. Syed Sirajuddin and Frema Sara (Fenton) K. AB, U. Calif., Berkeley, 1972; JD, Georgetown U., 1976. Bar: Calif. 1976. Legal analyst, Am. Law div. Congl. Research, Washington, 1973-76; assoc. Shahin, Wawro & Lorimer, Los Angeles, 1976-78; sec. and gen. counsel Oasis Petroleum, Culver City, Calif., 1978-83; pres. Triad Am. Internat., Santa Barbara, Calif., 1983; dir. Triad Am. and Triad Energy Corps., Salt Lake City, 1983-86, Am. Barrick and Barrick Investments Ltd., Toronto, Can., 1986—; pres. Concrete Tech. Corp., Santa Barbara, 1985, bd. dirs. Mem. ABA, Calif. Bar Assn. General corporate, Administrative and regulatory. Office: Triad Am Internat 3916 State St Suite 300 Santa Barbara CA 93105 Office: Barrick Investments Ltd, PO Box N 8181, Nassau Bahamas

KAESER, CLIFFORD RICHARD, food service industry executive, lawyer; b. Boise, Idaho, Feb. 17, 1936; s. Clifford Morgan and Bertha Marie (Minton) K.; m. Marjorie Ann, Sept. 21, 1959; children: Richard L., Cynthia M., Kenneth R.; m. Carol L. Roach, May 11, 1979. BA, Coll. of Idaho, 1959; JD, Yale U., 1962. Bar: Calif. 1962, Tenn. Assoc. Lawler, Felix & Hall, Los Angeles, 1962-63; asst. div. counsel Lockheed Missiles & Space Co., Sunnyvale, Calif., 1963-64; group counsel Litton Industries, Beverly Hills, Calif., 1964-66, acquisition counsel, 1966-68; gen. counsel, v.p. Hitco, Los Angeles, 1968-70; pres. Chapparel Inc., Denver, 1970-72; gen. counsel, v.p. Conroy, Inc., San Antonio, 1972-80; gen. counsel, v.p. Dobbs Houses, Inc., Memphis, 1980-84; sr. v.p., gen. counsel Howard Johnson Co., North Quincy, Mass., 1984-86; v.p., gen. counsel Delaware North Cos., Inc., Buffalo, 1986—; chmn., exec. com., dir. Dobbs-Paschal Midfield Corp., Atlanta, 1981—. Served with USMCR, 1954-61. Mem. ABA, State Bar Calif., State Bar Tenn., Nat. Restaurant Assn., Multi Unit Food Industry Assn., Am. Mgmt. Assn. Republican. General corporate. Home: 30 Breezewood Common East Amherst NY 14051 Office: Delaware North Cos Inc 700 Delaware Ave Buffalo NY 14209

KAESTNER, RICHARD DARWIN, lawyer; b. Milw., Feb. 10, 1934; s. Henry B., and Sophia (Schley) K.; m. Shirley Sue Higgins, Sept. 16, 1961; children: Richard, Kurtis. BS, Marquette U., 1956, JD, 1961. Bar: Wis. 1961, U.S. Dist. Ct. (ea. dist.) Wis. 1961, U.S. Supreme Ct. 1971. Assoc. Wiernick & Zurlo, Milw., 1961-63, Beaudry & Kershek, Milw., 1963-67; sole practice, Milw., 1976-77; ptnr. Harris & Kaestner, Wauwatosa, Wis., 1977-80; sole practice, Elm Grove, Wis., 1980—; ct. commr. Circuit Ct., Milwaukee County, Wis., 1981—, Waukesha County, Wis., 1987—. Examiner, Milwaukee County Civil Service Commn., 1983—; officer, bd. dirs. Willaura West Homeowner's Assn., 1976-84. Served with AUS, 1956-58. Mem. ABA, State Bar of Wis. (bd. attys. profl. responsibility com. 1976-85), Wis. Bar Assn., Milw. Bar Assn., Waukesha Bar Assn., Am. Coll. Probate Counsel, Delta Theta Phi. Lutheran. Club: Pewaukee Yacht. Probate, Family and matrimonial. Home: N30 W28935 W Lakeside Dr Pewaukee WI 53072 Office: 15255 Watertown Plank Rd Elm Grove WI 53122

KAFANTARIS, GEORGE NICHOLAS, lawyer; b. Kardamyla, Chios, Greece, May 11, 1953; came to U.S., 1966; s. Nicholas George and Evangelia M. (Frangias) K.; m. Maria G. Gampieris, June 3, 1977; children: Nicholas, Theologos, Mark, Constantine-Evangelos. BS, Youngstown (Ohio) State U., 1976; JD, U. Toledo, 1979. Bar: Ohio, 1981, U.S. Dist. Ct. (no. dist.) Ohio 1982. Sole practice Warren, Ohio, 1981—. Sec. United Chios Soc., Agia Markela, Warren, 1984-85; bd. dirs. St. Demetrios Orthodox Ch., Warren, 1984-85; Trumbull County Rep. Precinct Committeeman, Warren, 1984-85. Mem. ABA, Ohio Bar Assn., Mahoning County Bar Assn., Trumbull County Bar Assn., Am. Trial Lawyers Assn., Ohio Acad. Trial Lawyers. Avocations: photography, computers, swimming. State civil litigation, Personal injury, Labor. Home: 190 Atlantic St NW Warren OH 44483 Office: 183 W Market St Warren OH 44481

KAFES, WILLIAM O., lawyer; b. Trenton, N.J., Dec. 23, 1935; s. William G. and Gina B. (Owen) K.; m. Mary J. Wells, Nov. 27, 1965; children: Mary E., Victoria G., William W. BA, Swarthmore Coll., 1957; LLB, Yale U., 1960. Bar: Conn. 1960, N.J. 1971, U.S. Supreme Ct. 1972. Asst. counsel Aetna Life and Casualty Co., Hartford, Conn., 1960-69; assoc. gen. counsel The Okonite Co., Ramsey, N.J., 1969-72; asst. gen counsel Marriott Corp., Bethesda, Md., 1972—, v.p., sec., 1984—. Mem. ABA (clk. young lawyers sect., 1965), N.J. Bar Assn., Conn. Bar Assn. Phi Beta Kappa. Democratic. Episcopalian. General corporate, Securities. Office: Marriott Corp 10400 Fernwood Rd Bethesda MD 20058

KAFKA, ANNE G., lawyer; b. Chgo., Oct. 25, 1920; d. Rudolf D. and Gertrude (Thomas) K. B.A., Oberlin Coll., 1941; LL.D., St. John's U., 1949. Bar: N.Y. 1949, U.S. Dist. Ct. (so. dist.) N.Y. 1950, U.S. Dist. Ct. (ea. dist.) N.Y. 1951, U.S. Ct. Appeals (2d cir.) 1953. Assoc. J.D. Edwards, N.Y.C., 1950-60, C.J. Jones, N.Y.C., 1960-65; ptnr. Jones & Kafka, Mineola, N.Y., 1965-73; sole practice, Patchogue, N.Y., 1973—. Active Suffolk County Democratic Women's Caucus, Hauppauge, N.Y., 1978-80. Recipient award for Excellence, Cleve. Bd. Edn., 1936. Mem. N.Y. State Trial Lawyers Assn., N.Y. County Lawyers Assn., Suffolk County Bar Assn., N.Y. Workers Compensation Bar Assn. (pres. 1976-78, bd. dirs. 1960-82). Democrat. Club: Young Dems., World Federalists. State civil litigation, Federal civil litigation, Workers' compensation.

KAGAN, EDWIN BRUCE, lawyer; b. N.Y.C., Jan. 21, 1952; s. Aaron and Marcia (Rosen) K.; m. Marilyn Ann Kagan. BS in Indsl. Relations, Cornell U., 1973; JD cum laude, U. Miami, 1976. Bar: Fla. 1976, D.C. 1979, U.S. Dist. Ct. D.C. 1980, U.S. Supreme Ct. 1980, U.S. Ct. Appeals (5th and 11th cirs.) 1981, U.S. Dist. Ct. (mid. dist.) Fla. 1987. Atty. U.S. SEC, Washington, 1976-82; ptnr. Robbins, Gaynor, Burton, Hampp, Burns, Bronstein & Shasteen P.A., Tampa, Fla., 1983-86, Smith, Stratton, Wise, Heher & Brennan, Tampa, 1986—; spl. asst. U.S. atty. Dept. of Justice, Newark, 1981-82. Mem. Am. Philatelic Soc., State Coll., Pa., 1985—, Tampa Jewish Fedn., 1985—, St. Petersburg Mus. of Fine Arts, 1986—; mem. Tampa Bay Investment Council, 1983—, bd. arbitrators NASD. Regents scholar N.Y. State, 1969. Mem. ABA (corp., bus. and banking law sect.), D.C. Bar Assn., Fla. Bar Assn., Hillborough County Bar Assn. Republican. Club: Tampa. Avocations: sports, stamp collecting, reading. Contracts commercial, General corporate, Securities. Office: Smith Stratton Wise Heher & Brennan 3030 N Rocky Point Rd W Tampa FL 33607

KAGAN, IRVING, specialty chemicals and building materials executive; b. N.Y.C., Mar. 14, 1936; s. Abraham and Yetta (Hochberg) K.; m. Shirley Anne Wolfe, May 29, 1956; children: Michael A., David M., Joshua A. B.S., N.Y. U., 1956, LL.B., 1958. Bar: N.Y. 1958, U.S. Supreme Ct. 1964. Practice law N.Y.C., 1958-60; with antitrust div. Dept. Justice, 1960-68, acting chief evaluation sect., 1965, acting asst. chief N.Y. Field Office, 1968; trade regulation counsel, then asst. gen. counsel Hertz Corp., N.Y.C., 1968-74; v.p., gen. counsel Hertz Corp., 1974-83, sr. v.p., gen. counsel, 1983-86; sr. v.p., gen. counsel and sec. GAF Corp., Wayne, N.J., 1986—. Asso. editor: N.Y. U. Law Rev, 1957-58. Mem. Am., N.Y. State, N.Y. County bar assns., N.Y.U. Law Rev. Alumni Assn. (gov.), Am.-Israel Chamber of Commerce and Industry (dir.), Internat. League Human Rights. Antitrust, General corporate, Private international. Office: 1361 Alps Rd Wayne NJ 07470

KAGAN, ROBERT ALEXANDER, lawyer; b. Boston, Oct. 23, 1924; s. Jonas R. and Miriam (Lestchinska) K.; m. Ilse Lore Echt, Aug. 26, 1951; children: Jonathan, Miriam. AB, Harvard U., 1946, JD, 1950. Bar: N.Y. 1951, U.S. Supreme Ct. 1954, U.S. Tax Ct. 1960, U.S. Ct. Claims 1976, U.S. Ct. Appeals (2nd cir.) 1978. Sole practice, N.Y.C., 1950-51; teaching fellow Harvard U. Law Sch., Cambridge, Mass., 1951-52; with office gen. counsel U.S. Treasury Dept., Washington, 1952-58; gen. counsel North Atlantic Marine Co., Inc., N.Y.C., 1959-60; asst. counsel Equitable Life Assurance Soc., N.Y.C., 1960-65; with ITT Corp., N.Y.C., 1965-84, gen. tax counsel, 1974-84; spl. counsel Kronish, Lieb, Weiner & Hellman, N.Y.C., 1984—. Mayor, Village of Gt. Neck Estates (N.Y.), 1973-75. Served with U.S. Army, 1943-46. Mem. N.Y. Bar Assn. Corporate taxation, Personal income taxation. Office: Kronish Lieb Weiner & Hellman 1345 Ave of the Americas New York NY 10105

KAGLER, ROBERT WAYNE, lawyer; b. Balt., Feb. 21, 1951; s. Francis Harry and Frances Catherine (Hall) K.; m. Joanne Baitup, June 7, 1980; children: Steven Patrick, Terrence Scott, Alex Jordan. BA, Wheeling Coll., 1975; JD, W.Va. U., 1980. Bar: W.Va. 1980, U.S. Dist. Ct. (so. and no. dists.) W.Va. 1980. Ftnr. White & Kagler, Moundsville, W.Va., 1980-81; sole practice Moundsville, 1981—; asst. pros. atty. Marshall County, Moundsville, 1980—. Mem. Assn. Trial Lawyers Am., W.Va. Young Lawyers Assn. (exec. com.), W.Va. Bar Assn., W.Va. Sch. Bd. Attys., W.Va. Pros. Attys. Assn., Phi Alpha Delta. Democrat. Roman Catholic. Lodges: Kiwanis (pres. Moundsville club 1984), K.C. Bankruptcy, Probate, Real property. Home: 1105 7th St Moundsville WV 26041 Office: 604 6th St Moundsville WV 26041

KAHANE, DENNIS SPENCER, lawyer; b. N.Y.C., Oct. 28, 1947; s. Aaron and Frances (Asheroff) K. BA, Tulane U., 1969; JD with honors, George Washington U., 1972. Bar: D.C. 1973, U.S. Supreme Ct. 1976, La. 1981, Calif. 1983, U.S. Dist. Ct. D.C., U.S. Dist. Ct. Md., U.S. Dist. Ct. (ea., cen. and we. dists.) La., U.S. Dist. Ct. (no. and ea. dists.) Calif., U.S. Ct. Appeals (D.C., 5th, 7th, 9th and 11th cirs.). From atty. to sr. atty. Fed. Communications Commn., Washington, 1973-81; assoc. Jones, Walker, Waechter, Carrere & Denegre, New Orleans, 1981-82; from assoc. to of counsel to ptnr. Pillsbury, Madison & Sutro, San Francisco, 1982—; mem. com. bar examiners State Bar of Calif., San Francisco, 1984—, chmn. moral character subcom., 1985-86, chmn. 1986—, mem. lawyer performance and edn. consortium, 1986—; gen. counsel Calif. Broadcasters Assn., 1982—. Served to capt. USAR, 1969-80. Republican. Communications, Trademark and copyright. Office: Pillsbury Madison & Sutro 225 Bush St San Francisco CA 94104

KAHLENBECK, HOWARD, JR., lawyer; b. Fort Wayne, Ind., Dec. 7, 1929; s. Howard and Clara Elizabeth (Wegman) K.; m. Sally A. Horrell, Aug. 14, 1954; children: Kathryn Sue, Douglas H. BS with distinction, Ind. U., 1952, LLB, U. Mich., 1957. Bar: Ind. 1957. Ptnr. Krieg, DeVault, Alexander & Capehart, Indpls., 1957—; sec., bd. dirs. Maul Tech. Corp. (formerly Buehler Corp.), Indpls., Am. Monitor Corp., Indpls., Am. Interstate Ins. Corp. Wis., Milw., Am. Interstate Ins. Co. Ga., Am. Underwriters Group, Inc., Indpls.; bd. dirs. Pafco Gen. Ins. Co. Served with USAF, 1952-54. Mem. ABA, Ind. Bar Assn., Indpls. Bar Assn., Alpha Kappa Psi, Delta Theta Phi, Beta Gamma Sigma, Delta Upsilon Internat. (sec., bd. dirs. 1971-83, chmn. 1983-86, trustee found. 1983—). Lutheran. General corporate, Contracts commercial, Securities. Home: 6320 Old Orchard Rd Indianapolis IN 46226 Office: 2800 Indiana National Bank Tower Indianapolis IN 46204

KAHN, ALAN EDWIN, lawyer; b. N.Y.C., Aug. 9, 1929; s. Joseph and Harriet Rose (Rubel) K.; m. Regina Wolf, Aug. 7, 1960 (div. Jan. 1978); 1 child, Jolie Galen; m. Patricia Ann Dugan, June 4, 1978. BBA, CCNY, 1950; LLB, Bklyn. Law Sch., 1956. Bar: N.Y. 1956, U.S. Dist. Ct. (so. and ea. dists.) N.Y. 1978, U.S. Tax Ct. 1978. Staff asst. Feinberg, Jacobs & Furman, N.Y.C., 1956-57; sole practice N.Y.C., 1957—; tax cons. to various nonprofit orgns., N.Y.C., 1977—. Cons. Vol. Lawyers for the Arts, N.Y.C., 1978—. Served to sgt. U.S. Army, 1951-52. Mem. N.Y. State Bar Assn.,

Assn. Trial Lawyers Am., N.Y. State Trial Lawyers Assn. (chmn. subcom. on legislation estate and trusts 1979), N.Y. County Lawyers Assn., Assn. Trial Lawyers of City of N.Y., Jewish Lawyers Guild, N.Y. State Soc. CPA's. Democrat. Lodge: Odd Fellows (grand adv. State of N.Y. 1979-80). Avocation: collecting prints, paintings and oriental ceramics. State civil litigation, Probate, Personal income taxation. Home: 370 1st Ave New York NY 10010 Office: 299 Broadway New York NY 10007

KAHN, CHARLES FREDERICK, JR., lawyer; b. Milw., Apr. 19, 1949; s. Charles Frederick and Louise Ann (Hartmann) K.; m. Elizabeth Martha Brauer, Dec. 28, 1975. B.A., George Washington U., 1971; J.D., U. Wis., 1974. Bar: Wis. 1975, U.S. Dist. Ct. (ea. and we. dists.) Wis. 1975, U.S. Supreme Ct. 1983. Staff atty. Wis. Indian Legal Services, Keshena, 1975-76; trial atty. misdemeanor and felony divs. Legal Aid Soc. Milw., 1976-78, chief staff atty. juvenile div., 1978; ptnr. Kahn & Levine, 1979-83; sr. atty. Charles Kahn & Assocs., Milw., 1983-86, ptnr., shareholder Kahn and Flynn, S.C., Attys. at Law, 1987—; spl. prosecutor pro tem Milw. County, 1981-82; counsel for Bd. of Attys. Profl. Responsibility, 1981—; cir. ct. commr., part-time 1983—; mng. v.p. Colby-Abbot Bldg. Co., 1980—; vis. lectr. dept. criminal justice U. Wis.-Milw., 1982-85; moderator, speaker, panelist profl. seminars and convs.; testimonial witness Wis. Senate and Assembly, 1981, 83. Contbr. writings to profl. publs. Bd. dirs. Parents Anonymous of Greater Milw., 1980-84; vice chmn. Milw. County North Shore Unit, Democratic Party of Wis., 1982-84; mem. Gov.'s Exec. Trade Delegation to Israel, 1985. Recipient Pro Bono award Posner Found., 1983; named Outstanding Young Lawyer 1980, Milw. Jaycees. Mem. ABA, Milw. Bar Assn., Wis. Acad. Trial Lawyers, Bar Assn. 7th Fed. Cir., ACLU, Am. Jewish Com., Bldg. Owners and Mgrs. Assn. (bd. dirs. polit. action com. 1983-84), Milw. Young Lawyers Assn. (chmn. criminal justice com. 1980-81), Met. Milw. Assn. Commerce, Nat. Audubon Soc., Wis. Environ. Decade. Club: Photo Club of Schlitz Audubon Ctr. Federal civil litigation, Computer, Criminal. Home: 3043 N Summit Ave Milwaukee WI 53211 Office: Kahn and Flynn SC 759 N Milwaukee St Suite 500 Milwaukee WI 53202

KAHN, DAVID MILLER, lawyer; b. Port Chester, N.Y., Apr. 21, 1925. B.A., U. Ky., 1947; LL.B. cum laude, N.Y. Law Sch., 1950. Bar: N.Y. 1951, U.S. Dist Ct. (ea. and so. dists.) N.Y. 1953, U.S. Supreme Ct. 1958. Sole practice, White Plains, N.Y., 1951-60; ptnr. Kahn & Rubin, White Plains, 1960-66, Kahn & Goldman, White Plains, 1967-80; sr. ptnr. Kahn & Landau, White Plains and N.Y.C., 1980—; lectr. N.Y. Law Sch., 1982—; spl. counsel Village Port Chester, N.Y., 1960-63; commr. appraisal Westchester County Supreme Ct., 1973-77. Chmn. Westchester County Citizens for Eisenhower, 1950-52; pres. Westchester County Young Republicans Clubs, 1958-60; Founder, chmn. bd. dirs. Port Chester-Rye Town Vol. Ambulance Corps., 1968-77. Served with USAF, 1942-46. Fellow Am. Acad. Matrimonial Lawyers (bd. govs. N.Y. chpt. 1976-79); mem. ABA, N.Y. State Bar Assn., Westchester County Bar Assn., White Plains Bar Assn., N.Y. Law Sch. Alumni Assn. (bd. dirs. 1970—. Family and matrimonial, General corporate, Real property. Home: 6 Mark Dr Rye Brook NY 10573 Office: 175 Main St White Plains NY 10601 also: 551 Fifth Ave New York NY 10176

KAHN, DENNIS ALAN, lawyer; b. Buffalo, Oct. 4, 1951; s. Melvin and Jerry (Beck) K.; m. Carrie Weinstein, Aug. 16, 1981. AB magna cum laude, SUNY, Amherst, 1973; JD, U. Akron, 1976. Assoc. Siegel, McGee, Kelleher, Hirschorn & Munley, Buffalo, 1976-80; ptnr. Siegel, Kelleher & Kahn, Buffalo, 1980—. Mem. ABA, N.Y. State Bar Assn., Assn. Trial Lawyers Am., Erie County Bar Assn., Phi Beta Kappa. Republican. Jewish. Office: Siegel Kelleher & Kahn 426 Franklin St Buffalo NY 14202

KAHN, DOUGLAS ALLEN, legal educator; b. Spartanburg, S.C., Nov. 7, 1934; s. Max Leonard and Julia (Rich) K.; m. Judith Bleich, Sept. 24, 1959; m. Mary Briscoe, June 12, 1970; children—Margery Ellen, Jeffrey Hodges. B.A., U. N.C., 1955; J.D. with disting., George Washington U., 1958. Bar: D.C. 1958, Mich. 1965, U.S. Ct. Appeals (D.C. cir.) 1958, U.S. Ct. Appeals (5th and 9th cirs.) 1959, U.S. Ct. Appeals (3d, 4th and 6th cirs.) 1960. Atty. Civil and Tax div. U.S. Dept. Justice, 1958-62; assoc. Sachs and Jacobs, Washington, 1962-64; prof. law U. Mich., Ann Arbor, 1964—; vis. prof. Fordham Law Sch., 1980-81. Author: (with Gann) Corporate Taxation and Taxation of Partnerships and Partners, 1979, 2d edit., 1985; Basic Corporate Taxation, 3d edit., 1981; (with Waggoner) Federal Taxation of Gifts, Trusts and Estates, 2d edit., 1982; comment editor George Washington U. Law Rev., 1956-58; contbr. articles to profl. jours. Recipient Emil Brown Found. prize, 1969. Mem. ABA, Order of Coif. Republican. Jewish. Corporate taxation, Personal income taxation, Estate taxation. Office: U Mich Law Sch Ann Arbor MI 48109

KAHN, EDWIN LEONARD, lawyer; b. N.Y.C., Aug. 1, 1918; s. Max L. and Julia (Rich) K.; m. Myra J. Green, Oct. 20, 1946; children: Martha Lynn, Deborah Jane. AB, U. N.C., 1937; LLB cum laude, Harvard U., 1940. Bar: N.C. 1940, D.C. 1949. Atty., asst. head legislation and regulations div. Office Chief Counsel IRS, 1940-52, dir. tech. planning div., 1952-55; ptnr. Arent, Fox, Kintner, Plotkin & Kahn, Washington, 1955-86, counsel, 1986—; Lectr. NYU Tax Inst., mem. adv. bd., 1959-70; lectr. tax insts. Coll. William and Mary, U. Chgo., U. Tex. Editor: Harvard Law Rev, 1939-40; editorial adv. bd. Tax Advisor of Am. Inst. CPA's, 1974-86. Bd. dirs. Jewish Community Ctr. Greater Washington, 1972-78. Served with AUS, 1943-46, ETO. Decorated Bronze Star. Fellow Am. Bar Found.; mem. ABA (council 1963-66, vice chmn. sect. taxation 1965-66), Fed. Bar Assn. (chmn. taxation com. 1967-68), D.C. Bar Assn., Nat. Tax Assn.-Tax Inst. Am. (adv. council 1967-69, bd. dirs. 1969-73), Am. Law Inst., Am. Coll. Tax Counsel, Phi Beta Kappa. Jewish. Corporate taxation, Personal income taxation, Estate taxation. Home: 4104 N 40th St Arlington VA 22207 Office: 1050 Connecticut Ave NW Washington DC 20036

KAHN, ELLIS IRVIN, lawyer; b. Charleston, S.C., Jan. 18, 1936; s. Robert and Estelle Harriet (Kaminski) K.; m. Janice Weinstein, Aug. 11, 1963; children—Justin Simon, David Israel, Cynthia Anne. A.B. in Polit. Sci., Citadel, 1958; J.D., U. S.C., 1961. Bar: S.C. 1961, U.S. Ct. Appeals (5th cir.) 1963, U.S. Ct. Appeals (4th cir.) 1964, U.S. Supreme Ct. 1970, D.C. 1978; diplomate Nat. Bd. Trial Advocacy, Am. Bd. Profl. Liability Attys. Law clk. U.S. Dist. Ct. S.C., 1964-66; ptnr. Solomon, Kahn, Smith & Baumil, Charleston, 1966—; adj. prof. med.-legal jurisprudence Med. U. S.C., 1978—. Served to capt. USAF, 1961-64. Fellow Internat. Soc. Barristers; mem. S.C. Bar, ABA, Assn. Trial Lawyers Am. (state committeeman 1970-74), S.C. Trial Lawyers Assn. (pres. 1976-77), 4th Cir. Jud. Conf. (permament mem.). Federal civil litigation, State civil litigation, Personal injury. Home: 316 Confederate Circle Charleston SC 29407 Office: PO Drawer P Charleston SC 29402

KAHN, LAWRENCE EDWIN, judge; b. Troy, N.Y., Dec. 8, 1937; s. Moe and Ann (Coplon) K.; m. Michele Kagan, Sept. 15, 1968; three children. AB, Union Coll., Schenectady, N.Y., 1959; JD, Harvard U., 1962; cert., Oxford U., Eng., 1963. Bar: N.Y. 1963, U.S. Dist. Ct. (no. dist.) N.Y. 1964. Asst. corp. counsel City of Albany, N.Y., 1963-69; surrogate Albany County, 1974-79; justice N.Y. Supreme Ct., Albany, 1979—. Author: Divorce Lawyer's Casebook, 1972, When Couples Part, 1982. Served with N.Y. N.G., 1955-65. Recipient Bailey Cup Union Coll., 1959; named one of 10 Outstanding Young Men N.Y., N.Y. State Jaycees, 1967. Mem. N.Y. State Trial Lawyers Assn. (outstanding jurist 1982). Republican. Office: Albany County Courthouse Supreme Ct Chambers Room 310 Albany NY 12207

KAHN, MITCHELL CHARLES, lawyer; b. Chgo., Aug. 5, 1953; s. Eric and Florence (Berk) K.; m. Susan Lynn Meyer, Aug. 4, 1974; 1 child, Andrew Schuyler. BA, U. Ill., 1975; JD, Ill. Inst. Tech., 1978. Bar: Ill. 1978, U.S. Dist. Ct. (no. dist.) Ill. 1978, U.S. Ct. Appeals (7th cir.) 1979. Advisor Office of Sec. State, Chgo., 1978-79; staff atty. Gen. Fin. Corp., Evanston, Ill., 1979-82, sr. atty., 1982-83, asst. gen. counsel, 1983; v.p. adminstrn. and law div. First Ill. Finance Co., Northbrook, Ill., 1983-87, sr. v.p., 1987—. Mem. Chgo. Bar Assn., Am. Fin. Services Assn. (law com.), Conf. Consumer Fin. Law, Ill. Fin. Services Assn. (bd. dirs. 1984—). Consumer commercial, Contracts commercial, General corporate. Office: 1st Ill Fin Co 40 Skokie Blvd Suite 200 Northbrook IL 60062

KAHN, RICHARD DREYFUS, lawyer; b. N.Y.C., Apr. 25, 1931; s. David Effrian and Lucille (Kahn) K.; m. Judith Raff, Sept. 10, 1961 (div. 1977); children—Jason, Adam, Alexander; m. Elaine H. Peterson, July 21, 1983. A.B., Harvard U., 1952, J.D., 1955. Bar: N.Y. 1955. Assoc. Debevoise & Plimpton, N.Y.C., 1955-62, ptnr., 1963—. Editor Harvard Law Rev., 1953-55. Trustee Am. Soc. Psychical Research, N.Y.C., 1966-73; bd. dirs. The Emerson Sch., N.Y.C., 1968-71, J. M. R. Barker Found., N.Y.C., 1968—, Found. Child Devel., N.Y.C., 1970—, C. G. Jung Found. Analytical Psychology, 1984—. Mem. Assn. Bar City N.Y. (chmn. com. atomic energy 1965-68), ABA, N.Y. State Bar Assn., Phi Beta Kappa. General corporate, Securities, Philanthropic organizations. Home: 340 Riverside Dr New York NY 10025 Office: Debevoise & Plimpton 875 3d Ave New York NY 10022

KAHN, RONALD HOWARD, lawyer; b. Santa Monica, Calif., May 4, 1937; s. Howard and Edna Louise (Jones) K.; m. Beverly Reed, May 7, 1961; children—Kevin H., Christopher W., Anna Karen. Student Menlo Coll., 1955-56; B.A., U. Calif., Berkeley, 1959; J.D., San Francisco Law Sch., 1965. Bar: Calif. 1966, U.S. Sup. Ct. 1974. Ptnr., Sullivan, Roche & Johnson, San Francisco, 1966-76; ptnr. Browne & Kahn, San Francisco, 1976—; mem. faculty San Francisco Law Sch., 1966—, U.Calif. Ext., Berkeley and Los Angeles, 1976—; arbitrator Am. Arbitration Assn.; dir., officer Broadcast Services for Blind, San Francisco; mem. adv. com. Bank San Francisco. Fellow Am. Bar Found.; mem. San Francisco C. of C., Kappa Sigma. Served with USCGR, 1960-61. Mem. Bar Assn. San Francisco, ABA. Republican. Clubs: The Family, San Francisco Comml. (San Francisco.) Construction, Federal civil litigation, State civil litigation.

KAHN LEVENBERG, CORINNE BETH, lawyer, insurance executive; b. N.Y.C., May 22, 1953; d. Joseph and Toby (Grubel) Kahn; m. Lee Levenberg, Oct. 9, 1975; children: Hal Aaron, Amy Shayne. BA, NYU, 1974; JD, Hofstra U., 1977; MBA, Rutgers U., 1978. Bar: N.J., 1978, U.S. Tax Ct., 1978. Sr. advanced underwriting specialist Prudential Ins. Co., Newark, 1979-82; asst. v.p. Occidental Life of N.C., Raleigh, 1982-85; v.p. John Alden Life Ins. Co. div. Jamark, Miami, Fla., 1985—. Fellow Life Mgmt. Assn., LIfe Ins. Mktg. and Research Assn.; mem. Inst. Am. Fin. Planners (bd. dirs. 1986—), FLMI Soc. Eastern N.C. (pres. 1982-84), Soc. CLU. Avocations: swimming, aerobics. Estate planning, Estate taxation, Personal income taxation. Office: 9840 NW 10 St Plantation FL 33322

KAHRL, ROBERT CONLEY, lawyer; b. Mt. Vernon, Ohio, June 2, 1946; s. K. Allin and Evelyn Sperry (Conley) K.; m. LaVonne E. Rutherford, July 12, 1969; children: Kurt Freeland, Eric Allin, Heidi Elizabeth. AB, Princeton U., 1968; MBA, JD, Ohio State U., 1975. Bar: Ohio 1975, U.S. Ct. Appeals (6th cir.) 1976, U.S. Dist. Ct. (no. dist.) Ohio 1977, U.S. Ct. Appeals (9th cir.) 1979, U.S. Ct. Appeals (fed. cir.) 1984, U.S. Ct. Appeals (D.C. cir.) 1986. Law clk. to presiding judge U.S. Ct. Appeals (6th cir.), Cleve., 1975-76; assoc. Jones, Day, Reavis & Pogue, Cleve., 1976-84, ptnr., 1985—. Chmn. vis. com. Coll. Arts and Scis. Cleve. State U., 1985—. Served to lt. USNR, 1968-72. Mem. ABA, Order of Coif, Am. Guild Organists. Republican. Presbyterian. Club: Cleve. Athletic. Patent, Antitrust, Computer. Home: 7624 Red Fox Trail Hudson OH 44236 Office: Jones Day Reavis & Pogue 901 Lakeside Ave Cleveland OH 44114

KAIL, KENNETH STONER, lawyer; b. N.Y.C., Oct. 14, 1955; s. Morton and Adrienne (Stoner) K.; m. Ivy Hwang, Apr. 18, 1986. BS, SUNY, Albany, 1977; JD, U. Pa., 1980. Bar: N.Y. 1981. Law clk. to presiding justice U.S. Ct. Appeals (fed. cir.), Washington, 1980-81; assoc. Simpson, Thacher & Bartlett, N.Y.C., 1981—. Mem. ABA, N.Y. State Bar Assn., Assn. of Bar of City of N.Y. Corporate taxation, Personal income taxation. Office: Simpson Thacher & Bartlett One Battery Park Plaza New York NY 10004

KAIMOWITZ, GABE HILLEL, civil rights lawyer; b. N.Y.C., May 5, 1935; s. Abraham and Esther (Bialogursky) K.; m. Benita Rosenblum, July 7, 1956; children: David, Beth. BS, U. Wis., 1955; postgrad., U. Ill., 1958-59; LLB, NYU, 1967. Bar: N.Y. 1969, MIch. 1971, Fla., 1987, U.S. Dist. Ct. (mid. dist.) Fla., 1987, U.S. Ct. Appeals (6th cir.) 1971, U.S. Ct. Appeals (3d cir.) 1982, U.S. Ct. Appeals (2d cir.) 1983. Atty. Ctr. Social Welfare, Politics and Law, N.Y.C., 1967-70; sr. atty. Mich. Legal Services, Detroit, 1971-79; assoc. P.R. Legal Def., N.Y.C., 1980-84; exec. dir. Greater Orlando (Fla.) A. Legal Services, 1985-86; lectr. law Fla. State U., 1969—; cons. in field; bd. dirs. P.L.O.W., Apopka, Fla.; lectr., adj. prof. numerous univs. Contbr. articles to profl. jours.; author poems. Served with U.S. Army, 1956-57, with Res. 1958-60. Smith fellow, 1970-71, Legal Services Corp. fellow, 1979-80. Mem. Mich. Bar Assn., N.Y. State Bar Assn., Fla. Bar Assn. Jewish. Avocations: writing and editing fiction. Civil rights, Federal civil litigation, Poverty law. Home: 3173A Whisper Lake Ln Winter Park FL 32972 Office: GOALS 1036 W Amelia Orlando FL 32805

KAIN, WILLIAM HENRY, lawyer; b. York, Pa., Sept. 23, 1912; s. George Hay and Cara (Watt) K.; m. Emily Allen, Aug. 1, 1936; children: Carol Kain Woodbury, William H. AB with high honors, Swarthmore Coll., 1933; JD, Harvard U., 1936. Bar: Pa. 1937, U.S. Supreme Ct. 1946. Mem. Kain, Kain & Kain, York, 1937-58, Kain, Brown & Roberts, York, 1966—, sr. ptnr., 1963—; bd. dirs. York Water Co., 1958—, pres., 1970-80, chmn. bd., 1980—; founder, bd. dirs., mem. exec. com. Consumers Fin. Group and Consumers Life Ins. Co., 1966—; bd. dirs. Farmers Fire Ins. Co., 1958—. Pres., former sec. bd. trustees York County Acad.; treas. Zion Luth. Ch., 1939-42; bd. dirs. Better York, Inc., 1979—. Served with USNR, 1943-45. Mem. ABA, York County Bar Assn. (pres. 1966), Pa. Bar Assn., Am. Judicature Soc., Am. Coll. Probate Counsel (fellow), Nat. Assn. Water Cos. Republican. Lutheran. Clubs: Country of York, York Twinning Assn., York County Agrl. Soc., Masons. Contbr. articles to profl. jours. Probate, Public utilities, General corporate. Office: 119 E Market St York PA 17401

KAIRYS, DAVID MARC, lawyer, educator; b. Balt., Apr. 16, 1943; s. Bernard and Julia (Lovett) K.; m. Antje Mattheus, Mar. 10, 1980; children: Marah, Hannah. BS in engring., econs., Cornell U., 1965; LLB, Columbia U., 1968; LLM, U. Pa., 1971. Bar: D.C. 1969, U.S. Ct. Appeals (3d and D.C. cirs.) 1969, Pa. 1971, U.S. Ct. Appeals (5th cir.) 1976, U.S. Supreme Ct. 1978. Ptnr. Kairys & Rudovsky, Phila., 1971—; lectr. U. Pa., Phila., 1973-86, adj. prof., 1986—; lectr. U. Calif., Santa Cruz, 1975. Editor and co-author: The Politics of Law, A Progressive Critique, 1982; editor-in-chief Columbia U. Human Rights Law Rev.; also articles. Co-chmn. bd. dirs. Crisis Intervention Network, Phila., 1984—; bd. dirs. Ams. for Dem. Action, Phila. Fellow U. Pa. Law Sch. 1968-71; grantee NSF. Civil rights, Federal civil litigation. Office: Kairys & Rudovsky 924 Cherry St Philadelphia PA 19107

KAISER, BRUCE ALLEN, lawyer; b. Sheridan, Wyo., Nov. 30, 1952; s. Gary and Marjorie Kaiser. AA in Humanities, Columbia Basin U., 1972; BA in Prelaw, Wash. State U., Pullman, 1976; JD, Gonzaga U., 1980. Bar: Wash. 1980, U.S. Dist. Ct. (ea. dist.) Wash. 1980. Assoc. John McLendon, Spokane, Wash., 1980-81, Hagen, Van Camp & McLendon, Spokane, 1981-82, McLenon & Kaiser, Spokane, 1982-86; ptnr. Kaiser, Douglass & Lewis, Spokane, 1986—. Avocations: snow skiing, water skiing, hunting, fishing, boating. Personal injury, State civil litigation, Insurance. Home: N 11314 Guinevere Spokane WA 99218 Office: Kaiser Douglass & Lewis W 1321 Broadway Spokane WA 99201

KAISER, ERIK MICHAEL, lawyer; b. Monroe, Mich., Mar. 2, 1940; s. Wesley Mark and June Vivienne (Roberts) K.; m. Patricia Ann Lydon, Sept. 2, 1961; children—Cheryl Lynn, Timothy Michael. B.S., San Francisco State Coll., 1963; J.D., Golden Gate Coll., 1968. Bar: Calif. 1969, U.S. Dist. Ct. (cen. dist.) Calif. 1969, U.S. Supreme Ct. 1978. Mem. Chase, Rotchford, Drukker & Bogust, San Bernardino, Calif., 1969-87, ptnr., Redwine & Sherrill, 1987—; instr. Glendale Coll. Law, 1970-71; adj. prof. law LaVerne Coll. Law, 1971-77. Bd. dirs. San Andreas Council Camp Fire, 1976—, pres., 1979, 1980. Mem. Calif. State Bar Assn., Los Angeles Bar Assn., San Bernardino County Bar Assn., Am. Bd. Trial Advocates (pres. Riverside chpt. 1987—), Assn. So. Calif. Def. Counsel, Def. Research Inst. State civil litigation, Insurance, Federal civil litigation. Office: 1950 Market St Riverside CA 92501

KAISER, JOHN ATWOOD, lawyer; b. Marshfield, Wis., Sept. 24, 1951; s. Gerald A. and Harrio (Atwood) K.; m. Marcia Rae Van Beek, Oct. 29, 1977; children: John, Margaret. BA, U. Wis., Eau Claire, 1973; JD, U. Wis., Madison, 1976. Bar: Wis. 1976, U.S. Dist. Ct. (we. dist.) Wis. 1976. Assoc. Betz, LeBarron & Poquette, Eau Claire, 1976-78; ptnr. Betz, LeBarron, Poquette & Kaiser, Eau Claire, 1978-80; assoc. Losby, Riley, Farr & Ward, Eau Claire, 1980-83; ptnr. Riley, Ward & Kaiser, S.C., Eau Claire, 1984—; lectr. U. Wis. Eau Claire, 1979-81, U. Wis. Law Sch., Madison, 1980, 82-84; asst. atty. City of Altoona, Wis., 1976-80; atty. City of Altoona, 1986—, City of Augusta, Wis., 1980-84. Mem. Assn. Trial Lawyers Am., Wis. Acad. Trial Lawyers, Wis. Inst. Govtl. Lawyers, Nat. Orgn. Social Security Claimant's Reps., U. Wis. Law Alumni Assn. (bd. dirs. 1981—). Democrat. Roman Catholic. Lodge: Kiwanis (bd. dirs. Eau Claire 1985—). Avocations: cooking, biking, swimming. Personal injury, Workers' compensation, Local government. Home: 406 Gilbert Ave Eau Claire WI 54701 Office: Riley Ward & Kaiser SC PO Box 358 Eau Claire WI 54702-0358

KALAHER, RICHARD ALAN, lawyer; b. Milw., Apr. 4, 1940; s. Willard Michael and May (Koch) K.; m. Ann Hoogland, Aug. 8, 1970; children: Richard Alan Jr., Kathleen Marie, Kimberly Ann, Alison Helen. AB, Union Coll., Schenectady, 1962; JD, Northwestern U., 1965. Bar: N.Y. 1966. Assoc. Shearman & Sterling, N.Y.C., 1965-66, 69-74; sr. atty. AMAX Inc., N.Y.C., 1974-75; assoc. gen. counsel AMAX Inc., Greenwich, Conn., 1977-85, also v.p., 1985—; v.p., gen. counsel AMAX Coal Co., Indpls., 1975-77. Chmn. Bd. Fin. Wilton, Conn., 1981—. Served to capt. USAF, 1966-69. Mem. ABA, Assn. Bar of City of N.Y., Westchester-Fairfield Corp. Counsel Assn. Republican. General corporate, Contracts commercial, Private international. Home: 280 Chestnut Hill Rd Wilton CT 06897 Office: AMAX Inc AMAX Ctr PO Box 1700 Greenwich CT 06836

KALB, ROBERT JOSEPH, lawyer; b. Rochester, N.Y., Nov. 26, 1951; s. Joseph William and Lucy (Antonelli) K.; m. Christine Elizabeth Burke, Oct. 11, 1980; 1 child, Adam Christopher. AB, Cornell U., 1973; JD, Syracuse U., 1976. Bar: N.Y. 1977, U.S. Dist. Ct. (we. dist.) N.Y. 1977. From assoc. to ptnr. Forsyth, Howe, O'Dwyer & Kiley P.C., Rochester, 1977—. Mem. com. Monroe County (N.Y.) Reps., 1984—; bd. dirs. Boys and Girls Club of Rochester, Inc., 1977—, William Warfield Scholarship Found., Rochester, 1986—. Mem. ABA, N.Y. State Bar Assn., Monroe County Bar Assn. Republican. Roman Catholic. Club: Cornell (Rochester) (bd. dirs. 1977-84). Avocations: travel, reading, shooting. Real property, Contracts commercial, Local government. Home: 24 Chesham Way Fairport NY 14450 Office: Forsyth Howe O'Dwyer & Kiley PC 1600 Midtown Tower Rochester NY 14604

KALEC, ROBERT MICHAEL, lawyer; b. Detroit, Nov. 27, 1954; s. Edward Linhart and Margarite Mae (Barber) K.; m. Ann Williamson, Sept. 11, 1976; children: William, Michael, Stephen. BA, Mich. State U., 1976; JD, U. Mich., 1980. Bar: D.C. 1980, U.S. Dist. Ct. D.C. 1981, U.S. Ct. Appeals (D.C. cir.) 1981, U.S. Supreme Ct. 1984, U.S. Dist. Ct. (ea. dist.) Mich. 1985, U.S. Ct. Appeals (6th cir.) 1985, Mich. 1986. Assoc. Fried, Frank, Harris, Shriver & Kampelman, Washington, 1980-82; trial atty. U.S. Dept. Justice, Washington, 1982-85; asst. U.S. atty. U.S. Dist. Ct. (ea. dist.) Mich., Detroit, 1985—. Mem. ABA, Fed. Bar Assn., Am. Trial Lawyers Assn., Pros. Attys. Assn. Mich. Avocations: ice hockey, softball. Federal civil litigation, Criminal. Office: US Attys Office 231 W Lafayette Detroit MI 48226

KALIS, PETER JOHN, lawyer; b. Detroit, Feb. 20, 1950; s. Michael P. and Helen (Karageorge) K.; m. Beverly A. Poling, Feb. 1, 1976. BA, W.Va. U., 1972; D in Philosophy, Oxford U., 1976; JD, Yale U., 1978. Bar: Pa. 1980, U.S. Dist. Ct. (we. dist.) Pa. 1980, U.S. Ct. Appeals (3d cir.) 1983, U.S. Supreme Ct. 1985. Law clk. to judge U.S. Ct. Appeals (D.C. cir.), Washington, 1978-79; law clk. to justice White U.S. Supreme Ct., Washington, 1979-80; assoc. Kirkpatrick & Lockhart, Pitts., 1980-85, ptnr., 1985—; adj. prof. law U. Pitts., 1981—. Editor-in-chief Yale Law Jour., 1978; contbr. articles to profl. jours. Rhodes scholar, Oxford, Eng., 1973. Mem. ABA, Pa. Bar Assn., Allegheny County Bar Assn. Club: Rivers (Pitts.). Avocations: theater, literature, sports. Federal civil litigation, State civil litigation, Legal education. Office: Kirkpatrick & Lockhart 1500 Oliver Bldg Pittsburgh PA 15222

KALISH, ARTHUR, lawyer; b. Bklyn., Mar. 6, 1930; s. Jack and Rebecca (Biniamofsky) K.; m. Janet J. Wiener, Mar. 7, 1953; children: Philip, Pamela. B.A., Cornell U., 1951; J.D., Columbia U., 1956. Bar: N.Y. 1956, D.C. 1970. Assoc. Paul, Weiss, Rifkind, Wharton & Garrison, N.Y.C., 1956-64, ptnr., 1965—; lectr. NYU Inst. Fed. Taxation, Hawaii Tax Inst., Law Jour. Seminars. Contbr. articles to legal jours. Assoc. trustee L.I. Jewish Med. Ctr., New Hyde Park, N.Y., 1978-82, trustee, 1982—; bd. dirs. Community Health Program of Queens Nassau Inc., New Hyde Park, 1978—; pres. Community Health Program of Queens Nassau Inc., 1981—. Fellow Am. Coll. Tax Counsel; mem. ABA, N.Y. State Bar Assn., Assn. Bar City N.Y. Corporate taxation, Personal income taxation. Home: 2 Bass Pond Dr Old Westbury NY 11568 Office: Paul Weiss Rifkind Wharton & Garrison 1285 Ave of Americas New York NY 10019

KALISH, KATHERINE MCAULAY, lawyer; b. Pinehurst, N.C., Aug. 6, 1945; d. Hugh Page and Exie Katherine (Beasley) McAulay; m. David Marcus Kalish, Jr., June 18, 1967; children—David Marcus, Page McAulay. B.A., Agnes Scott Coll., 1966; J.D., Mercer U., 1979. Bar: Ga. 1979, U.S. Dist. Ct. (mid. dist.) Ga. 1979, U.S. Ct. Appeals (5th cir.) 1981, U.S. Ct. Appeals (11th cir.) 1982. Elem. sch. tchr. Clayton County, Jonesboro, Ga., 1966-67; in office claims adjuster C.N.A., Atlanta, 1967-68; customer account auditor So. Ry., Atlanta, 1968-69; office mgr. David M. Kalish, DDS, Macon, Ga., 1971-73; asst. city atty. Macon, 1979-81; sole practice, Macon, 1981—. judge pro hac Mcpl. Ct. City of Macon, Ga., 1981-82. Mem. Career Women's Network of Macon, Temple Beth Israel Sisterhood, Macon; bd. dirs. Ctr. for Continuing Edn. Women, Macon, 1981—, Macon Fire and Police Pension Bd., 1983—. Mem. Macon Bar Assn., Ga. Bar Assn., ABA, YLS Coll. Placement and Forums Com., LWV. Democrat. State civil litigation, Labor, Family and matrimonial. Home: 4800 Mumford Rd Macon GA 31204 Office: 3110 Ridge Ave Macon GA 31204

KALISH, STEVEN JOSEPH, lawyer; b. Boston, June 10, 1946; s. Sidney Charles and Louise (Gouterman) K.; m. Anita Suzanne Bollt, Jan. 9, 1977; children: Lauren Bollt, Dana Bollt. BA, U. Mass., 1968; JD, U. Pa., 1973. Bar: Mass. 1974, D.C. 1977, U.S.Ct. Appeals (4th, 9th and D.C. cirs.) 1978, U.S. Ct. Appeals (5th cir.) 1980, U.S. Ct. Appeals (7th cir.) 1984. Staff atty. ICC, Washington, 1973-76; prin. McCarthy, Sweeney & Harkaway P.C., Washington, 1976—. Co-author: Transportation Deregulation, 1986. Chmn. Westmoreland Children's Ctr. Inc., Bethesda, Md., 1984-85. Served with U.S. Army, 1969-71. Mem. ABA, Mass. Bar Assn., Fed. Bar Assn. (chmn. motor carrier com. 1977-78). Republican. Jewish. Administrative and regulatory, FERC practice, Transportation. Home: 5320 Ridgefield Rd Bethesda MD 20816 Office: McCarthy Sweeney & Harkaway PC 1750 Pennsylvania Ave NW Washington DC 20006

KALLBERG, KENNETH J(OSEPH), lawyer; b. Cleve., Sept. 13, 1953; s. Hamlin L. and Mildred (DeSopa) K. AB, U. Notre Dame, 1975; JD, Ohio State U., 1978. Bar: Ohio 1978, U.S. Dist. Ct. (no. dist.) Ohio 1979, Calif. 1981, U.S. Dist. Ct. (no. and cen. dists.) Calif. 1982. Asst. prosecuting atty. Geauga County, Ohio, 1978-80; assoc. Schell & Delamer, Los Angeles, 1981-84, Rosen, Wachtell & Gilbert, Los Angeles, 1984—. Mem. ABA, Ohio State Bar Assn., Calif. Bar Assn., Century City Bar Assn., Los Angeles Trial Lawyers Assn., So. Calif. Def. Counsel, Phi Beta Kappa. Democrat. Roman Catholic. Federal civil litigation, State civil litigation. Home: 868 Radcliffe Pacific Palisades CA 90272 Office: Rosen Wachtell & Gilbert 1888 Century Park E Suite 2100 Los Angeles CA 90067-1725

KALLMANN, STANLEY WALTER, lawyer; b. Bklyn., June 6, 1943; s. Silve and Erna (Clesius) K.; m. Carolee A. McDonald, Aug. 23, 1969; children: Alexander, Andrew. BA, Rutgers U., New Brunswick, 1964; LLB, Rutgers U., Newark, 1967. Bar: N.J. 1967, U.S. Dist. Ct. N.J. 1967, N.Y. 1984. Law clk. to judge U.S. Dist. Ct. N.J., Newark, 1967-69; assoc. Stryker, Tams & Dill, Newark, 1969-71; asst. U.S. atty. U.S. Atty.'s Office, Newark, 1971-75; ptnr. Gennet & Kallmann, Roseland, N.J., 1975—. Mem. ABA, N.J. Bar Assn. State civil litigation, Federal civil litigation, Insurance.

Home: 5 Valley View Dr Mendham NJ 07945 Office: Gennet & Kallmann 65 Livingston Ave Roseland NJ 07068

KALLSTROM, JAMES DAVID, lawyer; b. Akron, Ohio, Sept. 20, 1950; s. David H. and Mary (Joshua) K.; m. Phebe Gay Zimmerman, Jan. 2, 1982; 1 child, Adam J. AB, Kenyon Coll., 1973; JD, Case Western Res. U., 1976. Bar: Ohio 1976, Okla. 1982. Gen. counsel Kallstrom Real Estate, Cleveland, 1976-81; ptnr. Kallstrom & Ming, Edmond, Okla., 1982-84, Reed, Kallstrom, Shadid & Pipes, Oklahoma City, 1984—; instr. real estate law Akron U., 1979-81, Cen. State U., Edmond, 1982-84; instr. bus. law Okla. Christian Coll., Edmond, 1984. Mem. ABA, Okla. Bar Assn., Okla. City Land Title Atty.'s Assn. Real property, Oil and gas leasing. Office: Reed Kallstrom Shadid & Pipes 4508 Classen Blvd Oklahoma City OK 73118

KALODNER, HOWARD ISAIAH, legal educator; b. Phila., Dec. 16, 1933. BA, Haverford Coll., 1954; LLB, Harvard U., 1957. Bar: Pa. 1958. Law clk. U.S. Supreme Ct. 1958-59; assoc. Schnader, Harrison, Segal & Lewis, Phila., 1960; legal adviser U.S. Dept. State, Washington, 1961-62; spl. asst. to solicitor U.S. Dept. Labor, Washington, 1962-64; prof. law NYU, 1964-77; dean Western New Eng. Coll. Law, Springfield, Mass., 1977—; bd. dirs. Inst. Jud. Adminstrn., 1976-78. Legal education. Home: 38 Pineywoods Ave Springfield MA 01108 Office: Western New Eng Sch Law 1215 Wilbraham Rd Springfield MA 01119

KALOGREDIS, VASILIOS J., lawyer, health care management consultant; b. New Bedford, Mass., Mar. 3, 1949; s. John V. and Rose (Simeonidis) K.; m. Stephanie Pahides, May 26, 1974; children: Maria, John. BS in Acctg., Providence Coll., 1971; JD, Villanova U., 1974. Bar: Pa. 1974. Assoc. Beck & Kalogredis, Bala Cynwyd, Pa., 1974-81; ptnr. Kalogredis & Wade Law Assocs., Wayne, Pa., 1981—; speaker in field. Contbg. author: The Physician's Practice, 1980. Contbr. articles to profl. jours. Pres. St. George Greek Orthodox Ch., Media, Pa., 1980, 86, chmn. bldg. com., 1984—. Dougherty fellow Villanova U., 1971-74. Mem. ABA, Pa. Bar Assn., Soc. Med.-Dental Cons., Soc. Profl. Bus. Cons., Nat. Health Lawyers Assn. Republican. Pension, profit-sharing, and employee benefits, General corporate, Health. Office: 997 Old Eagle School Rd Suite 202 Wayne PA 19087

KALOOSDIAN, ROBERT ARAM, lawyer; b. Watertown, Mass., Oct. 29, 1930; s. Paul and Grace (Mugrditchian) K.; m. Marianne Kaloosdian, June 30, 1957; children—Paul, Lori, Sonia. A.B., Clark U., 1952; J.D., Boston U., 1957, LL.M., 1962. Bar: Mass. 1957, U.S. Supreme Ct. 1962. Assoc. Miles, Curran & Malkasian, Boston, 1958-60; sole practice, Watertown, 1960-82; ptnr. Kaloosdian, Ciccarelli & Lerman, Watertown, 1982—; corporator Watertown Savs. Bank, 1972—, trustee, 1976—. Corporator Mt. Auburn Hosp., Cambridge, Mass., 1978—; bd. dirs. Armenian Assembly of Am., 1972—, co-chmn., 1974-83; assoc. dir. State Dept. AID Grant to Lebanon, 1978—; mem. Gov.'s Task Force on Ethnic Heritage, Boston, 1976. Served with U.S. Army, 1952-54. Recipient Prince of Cilicia award, Catholosate of Antelias, Beirut, 1980. Mem. Watertown Lawyers Assn., Middlesex Bar Assn., Mass. Bar Assn., Assn. Trial Lawyers Am., Delta Theta Phi. Democrat. Mem. Armenian Apostolic Ch. Club: Rotary (pres. 1975-76). Real property, Probate, General practice. Home: 25 Fletcher Rd Belmont MA 02172 Office: Kaloosdian Cicarelli & Lerman 43 Mount Auburn St Watertown MA 02172

KALOW, DAVID ARTHUR, lawyer; b. Queens, N.Y., May 6, 1953; s. Samuel Jay and Joan Elaine (Peirce) K.; m. Janet Lee Samuels, June 18, 1978; children: Margaret Emily, Jacob Richard. B.A., U. Chgo., 1974, J.D., 1976. Bar: N.Y. 1977, U.S. Dist. Ct. (so. and ea. dists.) N.Y. 1977, U.S. Ct. Appeals (5th cir.) 1983, U.S. Ct. Appeals (2d cir.) 1984, U.S. Ct. Appeals (fed. cir.) 1984. Assoc. Chadbourne, Parke, N.Y.C., 1976-79, Amster, Rothstein, N.Y.C., 1980-81, Lieberman, Rudolph & Nowak, N.Y.C., 1981-85, ptnr., 1986—. Mem. ABA (com. on sci. and tech., computer law). Trademark and copyright, Patent, Federal civil litigation. Office: Lieberman & Nowak 292 Madison Ave New York NY 10017

KALSI, SWADESH SINGH, lawyer; b. Nairobi, Kenya, Apr. 10, 1943; came to U.S., 1971; s. Ujagar Singh and Kailash Kalsi; m. Sarla S. Mirchandani, Aug. 27, 1977; children: Surekha, Sanjay, Sandeep. BS in Econs. cum laude, London Sch. Econs., 1965; Barrister-at-law, Lincoln's Inn, London, 1970; LLM, George Washington U., 1972. Bar: Ind. 1977, U.S. Dist. Ct. (so. dist.) Ind. 1977. Statistician East African Statis Dept. East African Community, Nairobi, 1965-70; barrister-at-law S. Gautama, Esq., Nairobi, 1970-71; sr. atty., office gen. counsel Cummins Engine Co., Inc., Columbus, Ind., 1973—; adj. prof. Ind. U. Law Sch., Indpls., 1984—; mem. steering com. on internat. trade law, legal com. Nat. Council U.S.-China Trade. Contbr. articles to profl. jours. Bd. dirs. BAIF, Columbus ProMusica, Inc., Columbus Inst. for Performing Arts, Retirement Found. Bartholomew County. Mem. ABA, Internat. Law Assn., Internat. Bar Assn., Am. Soc. Internat. Law, Inter-Am. Bar Assn., Ind. Bar Assn. (chmn. internat. law sect. 1982-84), Constrn. Industry Mfrs. (exec. com. lawyers council), Union Internat. Adv., Licensing Execs. Soc. General corporate, Government contracts and claims, Private international. Home: 4315 Washington St Columbus IN 47203 Office: Cummins Engine Co Inc Box 3005 Columbus IN 47202

KAMARCK, MARTIN ALEXANDER, lawyer; b. Rome, May 15, 1949; came to U.S., 1950; s. Andrew Martin and Margaret Ellen (Goldenweiser) K.; m. Elaine Frances Ciulla, June 17, 1972; children: Abraham Andrew, Benjamin Alexander, Chloe Margaret. BA, Haverford Coll., 1971; JD, Stanford U., 1975. Bar: Calif. 1975, U.S. Dist. Ct. (no. dist.) Calif. 1975, D.C. 1976. Assoc. Morrison & Foerster, San Francisco, 1975-76; assoc. Morrison & Foerster, Washington, 1980-81, ptnr., 1981-87; assoc. Fried, Frank, Harris, Shriver & Jacobson, Washington, 1976-80; 1st v.p., assoc. gen. counsel Fin. Guaranty Ins. Co., N.Y.C., 1987—. Mem. Transp. Commn., Arlington, Va., 1981-85, chmn. 1985-86. Mem. ABA (corp. banking and bus. law sect.), D.C. Bar Assn. (real estate and internat. divs.). Democrat. Unitarian. Banking, General corporate, Real property. Home: 441 6th St Brooklyn NY 11215 Office: Fin Guaranty Ins Co 175 Water St New York NY 10038

KAMEI, SUSAN HIROKO, lawyer; b. Los Angeles, Aug. 13, 1956; d. Hiroshi and Tami (Kurose) K.; m. W. Bing Leung, Apr. 30, 1983. BA, U. Calif., Irvine, 1978; JD, Georgetown U., 1981. Bar: Calif. 1982, U.S. Dist. Ct. (cen. dist.) Calif. 1982. Assoc. Paul, Hastings, Janofsky & Walker, Los Angeles, 1981-85; region counsel Mobil Land Devel. Corp., Ontario, Calif., 1985—. Co-chmn. legis. edn. com. PSWD Fundraiser, Los Angeles, 1985-86; bd. dirs. Japanese Am. Citizens League (Selanoco chpt.), 1981—; bd. dirs., sec. Justice Stephen K. Tamura Scholarship Found., 1985—. General corporate, Real property. Office: Mobil Land Devel Corp 1131 W Sixth St Suite 385 Ontario CA 91762

KAMEN, HARRY PAUL, life insurance company executive; b. Montreal, Que., Can., June 17, 1933; came to U.S., 1936, naturalized, 1945; s. Benjamin and Manya (Manishin) K.; m. Susan J. Klein, Feb. 1, 1958; children—Katherine, Abigail. A.B., U. Pa., 1954; LL.B., Harvard U., 1957; Postgrad. Sr. Exec. Program, MIT. Bar: Ohio bar 1957, N.Y. bar 1958. With Met. Life Ins. Co., N.Y.C., 1959—; v.p., sec., asso. gen. counsel Met. Life Ins. Co., 1979-83, sr. v.p., sec., 1983-85, sr. v.p., dep. gen. counsel, 1985-86, sr. v.p., gen. counsel, 1987—. Co-author: Comentaries on Debenture Indentures, 1971. Mem. N.Y.C. Community Bd. 5, 1978-83. Served with AUS, 1957. Mem. ABA (sec. com. corp. laws, sect. corp., banking and bus. law 1979-82, chmn. com. corp. counsel 1981-83), N.Y. County Lawyers Assn. (chmn. corp. law dept., 1986—), Assn. Life Ins. Counsel, Phi Beta Kappa. Clubs: Harvard (N.Y.C.); E. Hampton Tennis. General corporate. Office: 1 Madison Ave New York NY 10010

KAMENS, HAROLD, lawyer; b. Passaic, N.J., Apr. 28, 1917; s. Isadore and Esther (Reingold) K.; m. Bernice F., Jan. 11, 1949; children—Roberta Kamens Rabin, Edward A., Elizabeth. J.D., Rutgers U., 1940, B.S. in Acctg., 1945. Bar: N.J. 1941, N.Y. 1981, U.S. dist. ct. 1941, U.S. Ct. Appeals (3d cir.), U.S. Supreme Ct. 1970. Sole practice, Newark, 1946—; lectr. Seton Hall U., Fairleigh Dickinson U., Instn. Continuing Legal Edn. and numerous other profl., bus. groups; chmn. estate planning com. probate sect. N.J. State Bar. Mem. Fed. Bar Assn. (chmn. com. taxation 1976-77), N.J. Bar Assn. (chmn. com. fed. taxation 1967), Essex County Bar Assn. (chmn. 1974-65), Passaic County Bar Assn. (chmn. fed. taxation 1965-75), Assn. Fed. Bar N.J. (v.p. taxation 1977—). Contbr. articles to legal jours.; editor, chief 8 vols. on estate planning techniques; editor Fed. Tax Notes of N.J. Law Jour., 1947—; Probate, Corporate taxation, Personal income taxation. Office: 744 Broad St Newark NJ 07102

KAMENSHINE, ROBERT D., law educator; b. 1940. B.A., CCNY, 1961; J.D., Columbia U., 1964; LL.M., Harvard U., 1967. Bar: N.Y. 1965, Tenn. 1972. Assoc. firm Botein, Hays & Sklar, N.Y.C., 1964-66; asst. prof. law Vanderbilt U., Nashville, 1967-70, assoc. prof., 1970-73, prof., 1973—; cons. antitrust div. U.S. Dept. Justice, 1968; vis. prof. Duke U., 1980-81; vis. Lee disting. prof. Inst. Bill of Rights Law, Marshall-Wythe Sch. Law, Coll. William and Mary, 1984-85. Mem. Phi Beta Kappa. Office: Vanderbilt U Law Sch Nashville TN 37240

KAMENSKY, MARVIN, lawyer; b. Chgo., Aug. 16, 1939; s. Frank and Fannie (Kagan) K.; m. Judy N. Ellis, Oct. 7, 1961; children: Todd, Robert, Daniel. BS, U. Ill., 1961; JD, DePaul U., 1966. Bar: Ill. 1966, U.S. Dist. Ct. (no. dist.) Ill. 1966, U.S. Tax Ct. 1969; CPA, Ill. Assoc. Altman, Kurlanner & Weiss, Chgo., 1967-70; ptnr. Kamensky & Rubinstein and predecessor firms Kamensky & Landan and Carlins & Kamensky, Chgo., 1970—; mem. adv. bd. Small Bus. Council Am., Washington, 1980—, Pension Cons. Mag., N.J., 1982—; editorial cons. Med. Econs., Oradell, N.J., 1975—; speaker in field; bd. dirs. Louis Zahn Drug Co., Chgo. Contbr. articles to profl. jours. Treas. Northfield Twp. (Ill.) Rep. Orgn., 1981-82; bd. dirs. West Northfield Twp. Bd. Edn., Northbrook, Ill., 1976-80, 82-84, Parents Adv. Council Glenbrook Twp. High Sch., Northbrook, 1985, Congregation Beth Shalom, Northbrook, 1979-85. Mem. ABA (subcom. chmn.), Ill. Bar Assn. (council mem. employee benefits com.), Chgo. Bar Assn., Assn. Trial Lawyers Am. Avocation: handball. Pension, profit-sharing, and employee benefits, Health, Personal income taxation. Home: 2101 Valley Rd Northbrook IL 60062 Office: Kamensky & Rubinstein 7250 N Cicero Ave Lincolnwood IL 60646 also Office: 120 S LaSalle St Chicago IL 60603

KAMIN, DANIEL TUCKER, lawyer; b. Victoria, Tex., Sept. 18, 1947; s. Morris and Carolyn (Tucker) K. B.S. in Speech, Emerson Coll., 1970; J.D., St. Mary's U., San Antonio, 1974; postgrad. NYU Sch. Law, 1982, Oxford U., Eng. 1984. Bar: Tex. 1974, U.S. Dist. Ct. (so. dist.) Tex. 1977, U.S. Ct. Appeals (5th cir.) 1977, U.S. Ct. Appeals (11th cir.) 1981, U.S. Supreme Ct. 1982. Asst. dist. atty. Corpus Christi, Tex., 1975, 76; asst. U.S. atty. U.S. Dist. Ct. (so. dist.) Tex., Houston, 1977-82; immigration judge, Atlanta, 1981; sole practice, Houston, 1982—; spl. master 129th Dist. Ct., Harris County, 1986—; spl. counsel to Harris County Sheriff's Dept., 1985—. Producer, writer, dir. documentary film Well Founded Fears, 1981. Founder The Kamin Orgn. (polit. media) 1986; media advisor Tex. gubernatorial race, 1972, Harris County sheriff's campaign, Houston, 1984. Recipient state, nat. awards for photography, commendations for litigation HEW, FBI, Secret Service, 1978-82; John Marshall Trial Litigation award U.S. Dept. Justice, 1981. Mem. ABA (entertainment and sports law sect. 1983—), Tex. Assn. Trial Lawyers, Tex. Assn. Intellectual Property Law, Phi Delta Phi. Criminal, Federal civil litigation, Trademark and copyright.

KAMIN, KAY HODES, lawyer; b. Chgo., July 3, 1940; d. Barnet and Eleanor (Cramer) Hodes; m. Malcolm S. Kamin, June 12, 1963; children—Kim Alison, Kyle Barret. BA, Vassar Coll., 1961, MA, U. Chgo., 1962, PhD, 1970; JD cum laude, Northwestern U., 1981. Bars: Ill. 1981, U.S. Dist. Ct. (no. dist.) Ill. 1981. Cert. tchr., Ill. History tchr. Lincoln Park High Sch., Chgo., 1963-67; social studies coordinator U. Chgo., 1968-69; assoc. prof. edn. Rosary Coll., River Forest, Ill., 1970-76; jud. law clk. Ill. Appellate Ct., Chgo., 1981-83; assoc. Mayer, Brown & Platt, Chgo., 1983-85; v.p., gen. counsel Glencorp Inc., 1985—, also bd. dirs. Co-author: Contract Law, 1983. Contbr. articles to profl. jours. Pres., Chgo. Council for Social Studies, 1967-69; gov. life. mem. Chgo. Art Inst., 1974—, pres. soc. for contemporary art, 1974-76; pres. Sedoh Found., 1986—. Grad. fellow U. Chgo., 1967-70. Mem. Chgo. Bar Assn., Ill. Bar Assn., ABA, Chgo. Council Lawyers. Club: Arts. Avocations: golf, jogging, skiing, art collecting. Banking, Contracts commercial, General corporate. Office: Glencorp Inc 1496 Waukegan Rd Glenview IL 60025

KAMIN, LAWRENCE O., lawyer; b. Boston, Oct. 8, 1950; s. Sherwin Kamin and Sylvia (Salkow) Klersfeld; m. Jacquelyn Ann Murch, Nov. 20, 1986; children: Diana, John. BA, SUNY, Stoney Brook, 1973; JD, Columbia U., 1976. Bar: N.Y. 1977, U.S. Dist. Ct. (so. and ea. dists.) N.Y. 1977, U.S. Ct. Appeals (2d cir.) 1984. Assoc. Willkie, Farr & Gallagher, N.Y.C., 1976-84, ptnr., 1985—. Bd. dirs. Community Action for Legal Services, N.Y.C., 1986—. Federal civil litigation, State civil litigation. Office: Willkie Farr & Gallagher 153 E 53d St New York NY 10022

KAMINE, BERNARD SAMUEL, lawyer; b. Oklahoma City, Dec. 5, 1943; s. Martin and Mildred Esther K.; m. Marcia Phyllis Haber, Sept. 9, 1982; children: Jorge Hershel, Benjamin Haber, Tovy Haber. BA, U. Denver, 1965; JD, Harvard U., 1968. Bar: Calif. 1969, Colo. 1969, U.S. Supreme Ct. 1973. Dep. atty. gen. Calif. Dept. Justice, Los Angeles, 1969-72; asst. atty. gen. Colo. Dept. Law, Denver, 1972-74; ptnr. Kamine, Steiner & Unger (and Predecessor firms), Los Angeles, Calif., 1976—; instr. Glendale (Calif.) U. Coll. Law, 1971-72; judge pro tem Beverly Hills Mcpl. Ct., 1974-77, Los Angeles Mcpl. Ct., 1977—; panel of arbitrators Am. Arbitration Assn., 1976—; mem. adv. com. legal forms Calif. Jud. Council, 1978-82; lectr. Calif. Continuing Edn. of the Bar Programs, 1979—. Mem. Los Angeles County Dem. Cen. Com., 1982-85. Served to maj., inf. USAR, 1969—. Mem. ABA, Calif. State Bar Assn. (conf. dels. Calif. coordinating com. 1987—), Los Angeles County Bar Assn. (chmn. Superior Cts. com. 1977-79, del. to state bar conf. dels., 1978-87, chmn. constrn. law subsect. of real property sect. 1981-83) Engring. Contractors' Assn. (bd. dirs. 1985—), Res. Officers Assn. (pres. chpt. 1977-78), Assoc. Gen. Contractors (legal adv. com. 1982—) . Contbr. articles to profl. jours. State civil litigation, Government contracts and claims, Construction. Office: Kamine Steiner & Ungerer 350 S Figueroa St Suite 250 Los Angeles CA 90071

KAMINE, CHARLES STEPHEN, lawyer; b. Denver, Nov. 4, 1952; s. Martin and Mildred (Gansberg) K.; m. Darlene M. Green, Aug. 12, 1973; 1 child, Elida. BA cum laude, Brandeis U., 1973; JD, U. Denver, 1975. Bar: Ohio 1976, U.S. Dist. Ct. (so. dist.) Ohio 1976, U.S. Ct. Appeals (6th cir.) 1976, U.S. Supreme Ct. 1985. Assoc. Beckman, Lavercombe, Fox & Weil, Cin., 1976-77; sole practice Cin., 1978—; asst. atty gen. Ohio Atty Gen.'s Office, Cin., 1982—; prof. U. Cin., 1984—; comml. arbitrator Am. Arbitration Assn., Cin., 1981—. Editor U. Denver Law Rev., 1975; contbr. articles to profl. jours. Precinct exec. Hamilton County Dem. Party Cen. Com., Cin., 1980—; bd. dirs. Comprehensive Community Child Care, Ohio, 1981—, Community Chest Day Care Adv. Bd., Cin., 1982-84, Amberley Village Planning Commn., Ohio, 1984—. Named one of Outstanding Young Men in Am., VIP Awards Ltd., 1984. Mem. ABA, Ohio State Bar Assn., Cin. Bar Assn. (chmn. young lawyer sect. 1981-82) chmn. real property law com. 1982-85), Am. Judicature Soc. (bd. dirs. 1981-85), MENSA. Democrat. Probate, Family and matrimonial, General practice. Office: 309 Gwynne Bldg 602 Main St Cincinnati OH 45202

KAMINER, PETER H., lawyer; b. Berlin, May 4, 1915; s. S.G. and Lucy K.; m. Marie P. Scott, Dec. 13, 1947; 1 son, Stevenson Scott. Student, U. Berlin, 1932-34, U. Leipzig, 1934-35; Dr.Jur., Basle U., 1936; J.D., Yale U., 1939. Bar: N.Y. 1943, D.C. 1979. Assoc. Winthrop, Stimson, Putnam & Roberts, N.Y.C., 1940-42, 43-44, 45-48; partner Winthrop, Stimson, Putnam & Roberts, 1948—; law clk. Office of Price Adminstrn., Washington, 1942-43; assoc. Gen. Counsel's Office, Gen. Motors Corp., N.Y.C., 1944-45; vis. lectr. Yale U. Law Sch., New Haven, 1974-81; guest prof. U. Munich, 1986; mem. character and fitness com. Appellate Div., Supreme Ct. State of N.Y., 1st Dept., 1977—; presdl. appointee conciliator Internat. Centre for Settlement of Investment Disputes, 1980—. Editor: Yale Law Jour, 1939. Mem. Am. Law Inst. (adv. Restatement Conflict of Laws 1954-71), Council Fgn. Relations, Am. Coll. Trial Lawyers, Assn. Bar City N.Y. (exec. com. 1958-61, chmn. grievance com. 1961-64, v.p. 1966-68), Am. Bar Assn., Internat. Bar Assn., Internat. Law Assn., Union Internationale des Avocats. Clubs: Century Assn; Met. (Washington); Down Town Assn, Mory's Assn. Federal civil litigation, State civil litigation, Private international. Home: 830 Park Ave New York NY 10021 Office: Winthrop Stimson Putnam & Roberts 40 Wall St New York NY 10005

KAMINER, STEVENSON SCOTT, lawyer; b. N.Y.C., May 3, 1952; s. Peter H. and Marie (Scott) K. BA, Amherst Coll., 1974; postgrad., Cambridge U., 1974-76; JD, Yale U., 1979. Bar: N.Y. 1980, D.C. 1984. Assoc. White & Case, N.Y.C., 1979-82; atty., advisor U.S. Dept. of Justice, Washington, 1982-83; spl. asst., gen. counsel FCC, Washington, 1983-84, asst. gen. counsel, 1984-87, chief legal br., policy and rules div.,mass media bur., 1987—. Mem. ABA, Assn. of Bar of City of N.Y., Internat. Bar Assn., Fed. Bar Assn. (chmn. freedom of press com. 1984-86). Republican. Roman Catholic. Clubs: Union (N.Y.C.), Met. (Washington), N.Y. Athletic. Avocations: sailing, windsurfing, skiing. General corporate, Administrative and regulatory. Home: 2737 Devonshire Place NW Washington DC 20017 Office: FCC 1919 N St NW Room 622 Washington DC 20554

KAMINS, BARRY MICHAEL, lawyer; b. Bklyn., Oct. 3, 1943; s. Abe and Evelyn Bertha (Goffen) K.; m. Fern Louise Kamins, Mar. 30, 1968; 1 dau., Allyson. B.A., Columbia U., 1965; J.D., Rutgers U., 1968. Bar: N.Y. 1969, U.S. Dist. Ct. (ea. dist.) N.Y. 1973, (so. dist.) N.Y. 1973, U.S. Supreme Ct. 1974. Asst. dist. atty., 1969-73; dep. chief Criminal Ct. Bur., 1971-73; ptnr. Flamhaft, Levy Kamins & Hirsch; now ptnr. Flamhaft, Levy, Kamins, Hirsch & Booth. Mem. ABA, N.Y. State Bar Assn., Bklyn. Bar Assn. (bd. trustees), Kings County Criminal Bar Assn. (pres.), Nat. Dist. Attys. Assn. Author: The Social Studies Student Investigates the Criminal Justice System, 1978; numerous articles in criminal law. Criminal. Office: 16 Court St Brooklyn NY 11201

KAMINS, JOHN MARK, lawyer; b. Chgo., Feb. 7, 1947; s. David and Beulah (Block) K.; m. Judith Joan Sperling, May 5, 1968; children—Robert, Heather. A.B. with high honors and distinction, U. Mich., 1968, J.D., 1970. Bar: Mich. 1971. Assoc., Honigman Miller Schwartz and Cohn, Detroit, 1971-75, ptnr., 1976—; lectr. Inst. on Continuing Legal Edn., Mich.; Trustee Temple Beth El, Birmingham, Mich. Mem. Nat. Assn. Bond Lawyers (vice chmn. com. on opinions 1985-86), Am. Acad. Hosp. Attys., Nat. Health Lawyers Assn. (lectr.), Mich. Bar Assn. (exec. council, pub. corp. law sect.). Jewish. Club: Renaissance (Detroit). Municipal Bonds, Securities, General corporate. Home: 1315 Stuyvessant Birmingham MI 48010 Office: 2290 First Nat Bldg Detroit MI 48226

KAMINSKI, STANLEY RONALD, lawyer; b. Chgo., Oct. 3, 1955; s. Stanley L. and Veronica J. (Dymon) K.; m. Margaret A. Gilmore, Nov. 17, 1979. BS in Commerce with highest honors, DePaul U., 1977, JD, 1980. Bar: Ill. 1980, U.S. Dist. Ct. (no. dist.) Ill. 1980; CPA, Ill. Assoc. Robert G. Peterson & Assocs., Chgo., 1980-81; sr. atty. supr. dept. law City of Chgo., 1981—. Bd. dirs. Brighton Park Neighborhood Council, Chgo., 1985—. Mem. ABA, Ill. Bar Assn., Chgo. Bar Assn., Am. Inst. CPA's, Adv. Soc. Roman Catholic. State and local taxation, Local government, General practice. Office: City of Chgo Dept Law 511 City Hall Chicago IL 60602

KAMINSKY, ARTHUR CHARLES, lawyer; b. Bronx, N.Y., Dec. 29, 1946; s. Daniel and Claire (Sternberg) K.; m. Andrea Lynn Polin, Dec. 28, 1969; 1 child, Alexis Kate. B.A. cum laude with distinction, Cornell U., 1968; J.D., Yale U., 1971. Bar: N.Y. 1974, U.S. Dist. Ct. (so. dist.) N.Y. 1975, U.S. Tax Ct. 1977, U.S. Supreme Ct. 1984. Assoc. Paul Weiss Rifkind Wharton & Garrison, 1973-74; ptnr. Taft & Kaminsky, N.Y.C., 1974—; pres. A.C.K. Sports, Inc. (now Athletes and Artists, Inc.), Plandome, N.Y., 1977—, Profl. Sports Investors, Inc., N.Y.C., 1982—; mem. selection com. U.S. Olympic Hockey Team, Mpls., 1980. Co-author: One Goal; A Chronicle of the 1980 U.S. Olympic Hockey Team, 1984; weekly columnist N.Y. Times, 1973-77; intern for 3d congl. dist. N.Y. Adlai E. Stevenson Meml., 1967. Dep. campaign mgr. Lindsay for Pres., N.Y.C., 1972; del. credentials com. Democratic Nat. Conv., Miami, 1972; adminstrv. asst. Rep. Michael Harrington, Washington, 1972-73; pres. Plandome Civic Assn., 1981-82. Recipient Outstanding Sr. award Cornell U., 1968; finalist Thurman Arnold moot ct. competition, 1970. Mem. N.Y. State Bar Assn., Assn. of Bar of City of N.Y., Com. Entertainment and Sports, ABA, New Sch. Soc. Research (lectr.), Quill and Dagger, Phi Beta Kappa (hon.). Democrat. Jewish. Club: Friars. Entertainment, Sports. Home: 25 Middle Dr Plandome NY 11030 Office: Athletes and Artists Inc 421 Seventh Ave Suite 1410 New York NY 10001

KAMINSKY, IRA SAMUEL, lawyer; b. Johnstown, Pa., Feb. 3, 1936; s. Louis J. and Gertrude (Leff) K.; m. Barbara Handmaker, Feb. 11, 1954; children—Sherry, Louis, Jay, Phillip; m. 2d, Phyllis Levitt, June 24, 1971; 1 son, Glenn. B.A., U. Mich., 1957, J.D., 1960. Bar: Pa. 1960, U.S. Dist. Ct. (we. dist.) Pa. 1961. Assoc. Kaminsky & Kelly, Johnstown, Pa., 1960-67; ptnr. Kaminsky, Kelly, Wharton & Thomas, 1967—. Hearing examiner Commonwealth of Pa. Liquor Control Bd., 1970—; mem. regulatory task force U.S. SBA, 1980-85; mem. com. on fed. assistance for alternative fuels U.S. Dept. Energy, 1982-86. Mem. ABA, Pa. Bar Assn. (bd. of govs. 1986—). Club: Sunnehanna Country. Bankruptcy, Family and matrimonial, Contracts commercial. Office: 360 Stonycreek St Johnstown PA 15901

KAMINSKY, LARRY MICHAEL, lawyer, insurance executive; b. San Diego, Feb. 1, 1952; s. Abram and Shirley Edith (Lederman) K.; m. Barbara Sue Kassenick, July 5, 1981. BA, UCLA, 1974; JD, U. San Fernando Valley, 1977. Bar: Calif. 1977, U.S. Dist. Ct. (cen. dist.) Calif. 1978, (ea., no. and so. dists.) Calif. 1982, U.S. Ct. Appeals (9th cir.) 1979, U.S. Supreme Ct. 1983. Assoc. Law Office Abeles & Markowitz, Beverly Hills, Calif., 1977-78; ptnr. Go, Kaminsky & Misrahi, Canoga Park, Calif., 1978-81; assoc. counsel Safeco Title Ins. Co., Panorama City, Calif., 1981-84; v.p., asst. gen. counsel Fidelity Nat. Title Ins. Co., Scottsdale, Ariz., 1984—; gen. counsel Southern Title Ins. Co. subs. Fidelity Nat. Title Ins. Co., Knoxville, Tenn., 1987—; staff grader Harcourt, Brace Jovanovich Legal Publs., Los Angeles, 1978-82. Mem. leadership devel. program of community service com. Jewish Fedn. Greater Los Angeles, 1979-80. Mem. ABA, Los Angeles County Bar Assn., Am. Corp. Counsel Assn., Assn. Real Estate Attys., Am. Corp. Counsel Assn. Republican. Jewish. Real property, Insurance. Office: Fidelity National Title Ins Co 4141 N Scottsdale Rd Suite 316 Scottsdale AZ 85251

KAMINSKY, RICHARD ALAN, lawyer; b. Toledo, Nov. 15, 1951; s. Jack and Sally (Kale) K. B.A., Johns Hopkins U., 1973; J.D., U. Mich., 1975. Bar: Ill. 1976, U.S. Dist. Ct. (no. dist.) Ill. 1983. Assoc. Vedder, Price, Kaufman & Kammholz, Chgo., 1976-83; atty. Borg-Warner Corp., Chgo., 1983—. Contbg. chpt. to book. Mem. Chgo. Bar Assn., Ill. Bar Assn., ABA, Ill. State C. of C., Am. Corp. Counsel Assn., Chgo. Vol. Legal Services Found. (vol. atty.). Labor, Federal civil litigation, State civil litigation. Home: 550 Sheridan Sq Apt 3d Evanston IL 60202 Office: Borg-Warner Corp 200 S Michigan Ave Chicago IL 60604

KAMMEN, RICHARD, lawyer; b. Indpls., Oct. 23, 1946; s. Leo and Ruth (Stern) K.; m. Linda Beth Jones, June 3, 1970; children—Amanda Jean, Claire Elizabeth. B.A. cum laude, Ripon Coll., 1968; J.D., NYU, 1971. Bar: Ind. 1971, U.S. Dist. Ct. (so. dist.) Ind. 1971, U.S. Ct. Appeals (7th cir.) 1973, U.S. Supreme Ct. 1975. Ptnr., Martz, Bowman & Kammen, Indpls., 1971-75; pub. defender Marion County (Ind.) Criminal Cts., 1972-74, 77, 78; assoc. McClure & McClure, Indpls., 1975-77; ptnr., 1977—; lectr. and cons. Ind. Pub. Defender Council; mem. faculty Nat. Coll. Criminal Def., 1982-86; adj. prof. law Ind. U. Sch. of Law, Indpls., 1983-86. Served to 1st lt. USAR, 1969-74. Mem. ABA, Ind. State Bar Assn., Indpls. Bar Assn. (chmn. young lawyers sect. 1978, bd. mgrs. 1980-82, v.p. 1983), Nat. Assn. Criminal Def. Lawyers, First Amendment Lawyers. Republican. Jewish. Contbr. Ind. Continuing Legal Forum, 1982. Criminal. Home: 6215 Lawrence Dr Indianapolis IN 46226 Office: 235 N Delaware Indianapolis IN 46204

KAMMER, ROBERT ARTHUR, JR., lawyer; b. Boston, July 31, 1945; s. Robert Arthur and Lorraine B. (Edgar) K.; m. Elizabeth Britton Helmes, Aug. 3, 1968; children: Scott, Betsy. BA, Northwestern U., 1967; JD cum laude, Syracuse U., 1975. Bar: Ill. 1975, U.S. Supreme Ct. 1980, U.S. Dist. Ct. (no. dist.) Ill. 1975, Wis. 1983, U.S. Dist. Ct. (ea. and we. dists.) Wis. 1983. Atty. Lord Bissell & Brook, Chgo., 1975-83, Mulcahy & Wherry, Milw., 1983-86; dir. litigation Sentry Ins., Stevens Point, Wis., 1986—. Mem. Lake Bluff (Ill.) Sch. Bd., 1980-83. Mem. ABA, Wis. Bar Assn. Avocations. golf, tennis. Insurance, Personal injury, State civil litigation.

Home: 1110 7th St Stevens Point WI 54481 Office: Sentry Ins 1800 N Point Dr Stevens Point WI 54481

KAMMERER, KELLY CHRISTIAN, lawyer; b. N.Y.C., Nov. 29, 1941; s. William Henry and Edith (Langley) K. B.A., U. Notre Dame, 1963; LL.B., U. Va., 1968. Bar: Va. 1968, N.Y. 1969, D.C. 1969, Fla. 1969. Peace Corps vol., Colombia, 1963-65; Reginald Heber Smith, atty./fellow U. Pa., Washington, 1968-70; atty.-advisor, dep. gen. counsel Peace Corps, Washington, 1970-74; atty.-advisor AID, Dept. State, Washington, 1975-76, asst. gen. counsel, 1976-78, sr. dep. gen. counsel, 1978-82, counselor, 1981-82, dir. congl. relations, 1983—. Recipient Disting. Honor award AID, 1979, Equal Opportunity award, 1982; presdl. rank of Disting. Sr. Exec., 1984. Mem. Inter-Am. Bar Assn., Soc. Internat. Law. Public international. Address: 2838 27th St NW Washington DC 20008

KAMP, ARTHUR JOSEPH, JR., lawyer; b. Rochester, N.Y., July 22, 1945; s. Arthur Joseph and Irene Catherine (Ehrstein) K.; m. Barbara Hays, Aug. 24, 1968. B.A., SUNY, 1968, J.D., 1970. Bar: N.Y. 1971, U.S. Dist. Ct. (we. dist.) N.Y. 1971, Va. 1973, U.S. Dist. Ct. (ea. dist.) Va. 1973. Atty. Neighborhood Legal Services, Buffalo, 1971; assoc. Diamonstein & Drucker, Newport News, Va., 1972-77; ptnr. Diamonstein, Drucker & Kamp, Newport News, 1977-84, Kamp & Kamp, Newport News, 1984-87, Kaufman & Canoles, 1987— ; v.p., dir. Peninsula Legal Aid Ctr., Inc. Bd. dirs. Hidenwood Presbyn. Ch. PreSch. Served to lt. USAF, 1971-72. Mem. ABA, Newport News Bar Assn. (past bd. dirs., chmn. legal aid com.), Va. Bar Assn. Democrat. Club: Rotary (bd. dirs. Newport News chpt., pres. 1987-88). Real property, General corporate. Office: Kaufman & Canoles 739 Thimble Shoals Blvd Newport News VA 23606

KAMP, STEVEN MARK, lawyer; b. Dallas, Feb. 14, 1956; s. Arthur Joseph and Ethyl Mary (Romine) K. BA, UCLA, 1978; JD, Yale U., 1981. Bar: Fla. 1982, Calif. 1984, D.C. 1985, U.S. Ct. Appeals (11th cir.) 1982, U.S. Ct. Appeals (D.C. cir.) 1985, U.S. Supreme Ct. 1985, U.S. Dist. Cts. (so. and mid. dists.) Fla. 1983, U.S. Dist. Ct. (so. and ea. dists.) Calif. 1985. Assoc. Paul & Thomson, Miami, Fla., 1981-83, Paul & Burt, Miami, Fla., 1983-85, Hornsby & Whisenand, Miami, Fla., 1986—. Co-author: Florida Libel Law Summary, Libel Resource Ctr. 1982, 83, 84, 4th rev. edit., 1985-86, Access, Communications Law, Practising Law Inst., 1981, 82, 83, 84, 85, 4th rev. edit. 1985. Mem. ABA, Dade County Bar Assn. (appellate ct. com. 1986—), Broward County Bar Assn. Democrat. Roman Catholic. Avocations: politics, telecommunications, fishing, reading. Federal civil litigation, State civil litigation, Libel.

KAMPELMAN, MAX M., ambassador, lawyer; b. N.Y.C., Nov. 7, 1920; s. Joseph and Eva (Gottlieb) Kampelmacher; m. Marjorie Buetow, Aug. 21, 1948; children: Anne, Jeffrey, Julie, David, Sarah. AB, NYU, 1940, JD, 1945; MA, U. Minn., 1946, PhD, 1951; PhD (hon.), Hebrew U. of Jerusalem, 1982; LHD (hon.), Hebrew Union Coll., 1984, Georgetown U., 1984; LLD (hon.), Bates, 1986. Bar: N.Y. 1947, D.C. 1950, Md. 1956. Mem. research staff Internat. Ladies Garment Workers Union, N.Y.C., 1940-41; instr. polit. sci. U. Minn., 1946-48; legis. counsel to U.S. Senator Hubert H. Humphrey, Washington, 1949-55; ptnr. Fried, Frank, Harris, Shriver & Kampelman, Washington, 1956-85; sr. advisor U.S. Delegation to UN, 1966-67; ambassador, chmn. U.S. Delegation to Conf. on Security and Cooperation in Europe, Madrid, 1980-83; ambassador, head U.S. Delegation to Negotiations on Nuclear and Space Arms, 1985—; vice chmn. Mayor's Com. on Charter Reform, Mpls., 1947-48; faculty Sch. for Workers U. Wis., summers 1947-48; faculty polit. economy Bennington Coll., Vt., 1948-50; vis. professorial lectr. Dept. Govt. Howard U., 1954-56; vis. prof. polit. sci. Claremont Coll., Calif., summer 1963. Author: The Communist Party vs. The C.I.O.: A Study in Power Politics, 1957, (with Kirkpatrick) The Strategy of Deception, 1963, Three Years at the East-West Divide, 1983; co-author: (with Kirkpatrick) Congress Against the President, 1976; contbr. articles to profl. publs.; moderator Washington Week in Rev. program Eastern Ednl. Network, 1967-70. Pres. Friends of Nat. Zoo, 1958-60, now hon. pres.; hon. vice chmn. Anti-Defamation League B'nai B'rith, 1981—, vice chmn., 1977-81; pres. Am. Friends of Hebrew U., 1975-77, chmn. bd., 1977-80, now chmn. emeritus; co-chmn. U.S. Delegation to observe elections in El Salvador, 1984; chmn. Freedom House, N.Y.C., 1983-85; chmn. emeritus Greater Washington Telecommunications Assn. (WETA-TV); v.p. Helen Dwight Reid Ednl. Found., 1959-85, Jewish Publ. Soc., 1978-85; hon. gov. The Hebrew U. Jerusalem, gov., 1973-85, chmn. Truman Research Inst. for Advancement of Peace, 1983-85; mem. exec. com. Com. on Present Danger, 1976-85; vice chmn. Coalition for a Dem. Majority, 1977-85; overseer Coll. V.I., 1963-80; bd. govs. U. Haifa, 1984-85, Tel Aviv U., 1984-85; bd. advisors Kennedy Inst. Ethics, 1984-85; chmn. Woodrow Wilson Internat. Ctr. for Scholars, 1979-81, bd. trustees, 1979—; trustee Law Cen. Found. NYU, 1978-85; bd. dirs. Georgetown U., 1978-84, Mt. Vernon Coll., 1972-80, U.S. Inst. Peace, 1985-86, Hebrew Immigrant Aid Soc., 1981-85, Am. Peace Soc., 1973-85. Mem. ABA (standing com. on law and nat. security 1979-85), Fed. Bar Assn., Bar Assn. D.C., Am. Polit. Sci. Assn. (treas. 1956-58), D.C. Polit. Sci. Assn. (pres. 1955). Clubs: Cosmos, Federal City, National Press (Washington). Home: 3154 Highland Pl NW Washington DC 20008 Office: Dept State 2201 C St NW Room 1206 S/DEL Washington DC 20520

KAMPINSKI, CHARLES, lawyer; b. Neustadt Holstein, Germany, Apr. 2, 1947; came to U.S., 1949; s. Isak and Marian K.; m. Paula Robin Vincent, Sept. 9, 1971; children: David, Lisa. BA, Ohio State U., 1970, JD, 1974. Bar: Ohio 1974. Assoc. Gallagher Sharp, Fulton & Norman, Cleve., 1974-82; prin. Kampinski & White, Cleve., 1982-85; Charles Kampinski Co., L.P.A., Cleve., 1986—. Served with USN, 1964-68. Mem. Assn. Trial Lawyers Amsn., Ohio State Bar Assn., Cuyahoga County Bar Assn. Federal civil litigation, State civil litigation, Personal injury. Office: 1530 Standard Bldg Cleveland OH 44113

KANAGA, LAWRENCE WESLEY, lawyer; b. Chgo., Dec. 25, 1940; s. Lawrence W. and Virginia (Honold) K.; m. Kareen DiBlanda, Sept. 1, 1962 (div. June 1984); children—Kerry Ann, Matthew Lawrence. B.A., Williams Coll., 1962; LL.B., Harvard U., 1965. Bar: Conn. 1965, U.S. Dist. Ct. Conn. 1965, U.S. Ct. Appeals (2d cir.) 1968. Assoc. Goldstein & Peck, Bridgeport, Conn., 1965-71; mem. firm Zeldes Needle & Cooper, Bridgeport, 1971—; mem. grievance com. U.S. Dist. Ct. Conn., 1984—. Mem. Assn. Trial Lawyers Am., ABA, Conn. Bar Assn. (mem. judiciary com. 1980-83), Conn. Trial Lawyers Assn. Democrat. Federal civil litigation, State civil litigation. Home: 113 Hillside Ave Milford Ct 06460 Office: Zeldes Needle & Cooper 333 State St Bridgeport CT 06604

KANAK, JOSEPH ROBERT, lawyer; b. Dayton, Ohio, Feb. 14, 1947; s. Joseph Charles and Loretta Theresa (Wieland) K.; m. Sandra Lee Nuttall, Sept. 30, 1977; children—Christina Louise, Erin Loretta. B.A., U. Dayton, 1969; J.D., U. Cin., 1974. Bar admittee: Ohio 1974, U.S. Dist. Ct. (so. dist.) Ohio 1977. Asso., Jack E. Staley Law Offices, Dayton, 1974-76, Jack E. Staley Co. L.P.A., Dayton, 1977; ptnr. Staley, Kanak, Dunn & Co. L.P.A., Dayton, 1978, Staley, Kanak & Co. L.P.A., Dayton, 1979-83; sole practice, Dayton, 1983—. Contbr. article to profl. jour. Mem. Leadership Dayton, 1980; mem. Northeast Dayton Priority Bd., 1978—, chmn., 1984—; chmn. Neighborhood Devel. Council, 1978—; pres. Old North Dayton Civic Assn., 1981—; Our Lady of Rosary Parish Council, 1981-83; mem. Dayton City Mgr.'s Task Force on Use of Police Ammunition, 1980; mem. City of Dayton Block Grant Task Force; mem. Neighborhood Leadership Inst. Selection Com., 1985. Served with inf. U.S. Army; Vietnam. Mem. ABA, Ohio Bar Assn., Dayton Bar Assn. (legis. com. 1978-80, com. on liaison with Ohio Bar Assn. 1981-82), Dayton Area C. of C. Democrat. General practice, Probate, Family and matrimonial. Home: 1301 Lamar St Dayton OH 45404 Office: 105 Valley St Dayton OH 45404

KANCLER, EDWARD, lawyer; b. Cleve., June 19, 1939; s. Edward E. and Martha (Grechny) K.; m. Audrey Percy, July 10, 1966; children: David, Robert. AB, Ohio U., 1961; JD, Case Western Res. U., 1964. Bar: Ohio 1964, U.S. Dist. Ct. (no. dist.) Ohio 1964, U.S. Tax Ct. 1982. Assoc. Stotter & Elden, Cleve., 1964-69, Stotter, Familo & Cavitch, Cleve., 1969-77, Elden & Ford, Cleve., 1978-79, Benesch, Friedlander, Coplan & Aronoff, Cleve., 1980—. Mem. ABA, Cleve. Bar Assn., Phi Beta Kappa, Phi Kappa Phi. Republican. Avocation: coaching baseball. Zoning litigation, State civil litigation, Federal civil litigation. Home: 1964 Plymouth Oval Hinckley OH 44233 Office: Benesch Friedlander Coplan & Aronoff 1100 Citizens Bldg Cleveland OH 44114

KANDEL, NELSON ROBERT, lawyer; b. Balt., Sept. 15, 1929; m. Brigitte Kleemaier, Feb. 28, 1957; children—Katrin, Christopher, Peter. B.A., U. Md., 1951, LL.B., 1954. Bar: Md. 1954, D.C., U.S. Supreme Ct. Prin. law firm, Balt., 1957—; mem. legal panel ACLU. Trustee Richmond Fellowship Halfway House, Balt. Served with U.S. Army. Mem. ABA, Md. Bar Assn., Balt. Bar Assn. Democrat. Lutheran. General practice. Office: 415 One North Charles Baltimore MD 21201

KANDEL, WILLIAM LLOYD, lawyer, lecturer, author; b. N.Y.C., Apr. 25, 1939; s. Morton H. and Lottie S. (Smith) K.; m. Joyce Roland, Jan. 27, 1974; 1 son, Aron Daniel. A.B. cum laude, Dartmouth Coll., 1961; J.D., Yale U., 1964; LL.M. in Labor Law, NYU, 1967. Bar: N.Y. 1965, U.S. Dist. Ct. (ea. dist.) N.Y. 1978, U.S. Dist. Ct. (so. dist.) N.Y. 1980, U.S. Ct. Appeals (2d cir.) 1982. Assoc. Lorenz, Finn & Giardino, N.Y.C., 1964-66; labor atty. NAM, N.Y.C., 1966-68; with Singer Co., N.Y.C., 1968-79, asst. v.p. personnel dept., 1973-76, mng. counsel personnel office of gen. counsel, 1976-79; assoc. Skadden, Arps, Slate, Meagher & Flom, N.Y.C., 1979-85; ptnr. Finley, Kumble, Wagner, Heine, Underberg, Manley, Myerson & Casey, N.Y.C., 1985—; lectr. to Law and bus. groups, 1974—; adj. prof. employment law Fordham U., 1983—; lectr. Practising Law Inst.'s Ann. Inst. on Employment Law, 1980—. Vice pres., bd. dirs. Assn. for Integration Mgmt., 1979-85; bd. dirs. N.Y. chpt. Am. Jewish Com., 1980-82. Recipient award of Merit, Nat. Urban Coalition, 1979. Democrat. Jewish. Contbg. editor Employee Relations Law Jour., 1975—; mem. adv. bd. Employment Relations Today, 1976—; contbr. articles to profl. jours. Labor, Federal civil litigation, Administrative and regulatory. Office: Finley Kumble et al 425 Park Ave New York NY 10022

KANE, ALICE T., lawyer; b. N.Y.C., Jan. 16, 1948. AB, Manhattanville Coll., 1969; JD, NYU, 1972; grad., Harvard U. Sch. Bus. Program Mgmt. Devel., 1985. Bar: N.Y. 1973, U.S. Dist. Ct. (so. dist.) N.Y. 1974. Atty. N.Y. Life Ins. Co., N.Y.C., 1972-83, v.p., assoc. gen. counsel, 1983-85, v.p. dept. personnel, 1985, sr. v.p., gen. counsel, 1986—. Mem. ABA (chmn. employee benefits com., tort and ins. practice sect. 1984-85, mem. corp., banking and bus. law sects., tort and ins. practice sects.), Assn. of Life Ins. Counsel. General corporate. Office: NY Life Ins Co 51 Madison Ave New York NY 10010

KANE, DAVID SCHILLING, lawyer; b. Far Rockway, N.Y., Jan. 20, 1907; s. David and Bertha Dorothy (Schilling) K.; m. Mildred Irene Thompson, Sept. 23, 1931; children—David H., T. Sheila, Kathleen. Student, N.Y. U., 1924-26; LL.B., NYU, 1930. Bar: N.Y. State 1931. Asso. firm Duell, Dunn & Anderson, N.Y.C., 1931-34; partner firm Duell & Kane, 1934-52; sr. partner Kane, Dalsimer, Kane, Sullivan & Kurucz (and predecessors), N.Y.C., 1952—; pres. Camloc Fastener Corp., 1942-44; asst. sec., dir. Sci. Devel. Corp.; lectr. grad. div. N.Y. U. Sch. Law, 1946-59, adj. asso. prof. law, 1960-64, adj. prof., 1964—. Contbg. author: Ann. Survey Am. Law, 1945—. Mem. sch. bd., Port Washington, N.Y., 1948-50, mem. bd. appeals, Village of Sands Point (N.Y.), 1948-63, trustee, 1963-65, mayor, 1965-69; bd. dirs. Vanderbilt Assocs. of NYU Law Sch., 1968-80, Fairleigh Dickinson Labs.; trustee N.Y. U. Law Center Found., 1967—, C. F. Mueller Scholarship Found. Recipient Cert. Meritorious Service, 1950; Albert Gallatin fellow NYU, 1982. Mem. Nat. Council Patent Law Assn. (chmn. 1963-64), Am. Patent Law Assn. (pres. 1962-63), N.Y. Patent Law Assn. (pres. 1958-59), NYU Law Alumni Assn. (bd. dirs.), Am. Bar Assn., N.Y. State Bar Assn., N.Y.C. Bar Assn., N.Y. County Lawyers Assn., Am. Judicature Soc., Fed. Bar Council, Nat. Lawyers Club, Phi Delta Phi. Clubs: Union League, NYU (N.Y.C.) (founder mem.); Naples (Fla.) Yacht, Masons. Patent, Trademark and copyright, Antitrust. Home: Union League Club 38 E 37th St New York NY 10016 also: 140 2d Ave N Naples FL 33940 Office: Kane Dalsimer Kane Sullivan & Kurucz 420 Lexington Ave New York NY 10170-0071

KANE, HENRY SMITH, lawyer; b. N.Y.C., Dec.1, 1926; m. Dorothy Jeanne Denham, Aug. 4, 1950. B.S. in Journalism, U. Oreg., 1950, J.D., Northwestern Sch. of Law of Lewis and Clark Coll., 1961. Bar: Oreg. 1961, U.S. Supreme Ct. 1975. News editor The Dalles (Oreg.) Chronicle, 1951-55; research dir. Oreg. Republican State Central Com., 1955-56; reporter Oreg. Jour., Portland, 1957-59; exec. sec. Oreg. Legis. Interim Com. on Public Welfare, 1960, Oreg. Legis. Interim Com. on Small Bus., 1961-62; asst. atty. gen., Oreg., 1963-69; chief antitrust div. Oreg. Dept. Justice, 1965-69; sole practice Beaverton, Oreg., 1969—. Chmn. Beaverton Library Subcom.; mem. Beaverton Capitol Improvement Com., 1973-78; 1st chmn., mem. Washington County Library Bd., 1976-82; sec., bd. dirs. Oak Hills Home Owners Assn., 1965-73. Named Lawyer Advocate of Yr., U.S. Small Bus. Adminstrn. Oreg., 1981. Mem. Oreg. State Bar, Oreg. Trial Lawyers Assn., ABA, Multnomah and Washington County Bar Assn., Washington County Public Affairs Forum. Contbr. articles to legal jours. Administrative and regulatory, Antitrust, Health. Home: 12077 SW Camden Ln Beaverton OR 97005 Office: 12275 SW 2d St PO Box 518 Beaverton OR 97075

KANE, JOHN JOSEPH, lawyer; b. Phila., Sept. 12, 1952; s. Joseph Steven and Mary Elizabeth (Molony) K.; m. Mary Denise Subotich, May 19, 1979. BS magna cum laude, Drexel U., 1974; JD, Temple U., 1977. Bar: Pa. 1977, U.S. Dist. Ct. (ea. dist.) Pa. 1977, N.J. 1979, U.S. Dist. Ct.N.J. 1979, U.S. Ct. Appeals (3d cir.) 1981, U.S. Supreme Ct. 1986. Assoc. Freedman & Lorry P.C., Phila., 1977-83, ptnr., 1983—. Mem. Queen Village Civic Assn., Phila., 1975-79, Pennsport Civic Assn., Phila., 1979—. Mem. ABA, Pa. Bar Assn., Phila. Bar Assn., N.J. Bar Assn., Fed. Bar Assn., Assn. Trial Lawyers Am., Pa. Trial Lawyers Assn., Phila. Trial Lawyers Assn., Brehon Law Soc., Temple U. Alumni Assn. Democrat. Roman Catholic. Admiralty, Personal injury, Workers' compensation. Office: Freedman & Lorry PC 800 Lafayette Bldg Philadelphia PA 19106

KANE, JOHN LAWRENCE, JR., judge; b. Tucumcari, N.Mex., Feb. 14, 1937; s. John Lawrence and Dorothy Helen (Bottler) K.; m. George Ann Berger, Oct. 17, 1969; children: Molly Francis, Meghan, Sally, John Patterson. B.A., U. Colo., 1958; J.D., U. Denver, 1961. Bar: Colo. 1961. Dep. dist. atty. Adams County, Colo., 1961-62; assoc. firm Gaunt, Byrne & Dirrim, 1961-63; ptnr. firm Andrews and Kane, Denver, 1964; pub. defender Adams County, 1965-67; dep. dir. eastern region of India Peace Corps, 1967-69; with firm Holme Roberts & Owen, 1970-77, ptnr., 1972-77; U.S. dist. judge Denver, 1978—; adj. prof. law U. Denver. Contbr. articles to profl. jours. Trustee. Fellow, Internat. Acad. Trial Lawyers. Democrat. Roman Catholic. Office: US Dist Ct C-218 US Courthouse Denver CO 80294 *

KANE, JONATHAN A., lawyer; b. Montgomery, Ala., Aug. 9, 1945; s. Alan H. and Carolyn (Gottlob) K.; m. Elizabeth Keating Sands, June 5, 1976; 1 child, Letitia Tyler. BS in Econs., U. Pa., 1967; JD, U. Va., 1973. Bar: Pa. 1973, U.S. Dist. Ct. (ea. dist.) Pa. 1973, U.S. Ct. Appeals (3d cir.) 1973. From assoc. to ptnr. Drinker, Biddle & Reath, Phila., 1973—. Co-author: NLRB Remedies for Unfair Labor Practices, 1986. Vice chmn. Mayor's Drug and Alcohol Exec. Commn., Phila., 1979; chmn. Easttown Twp. Planning Commn., Chester County, Pa., 1986—; mem. White House Blue Ribbon Drug and Alcohol Com., Washington, 1982-83; bd. dirs. Eagleville Hosp., Pa., 1973—, chmn. 1981-83. Served to 1st lt. U.S. Army, 1969-72, Vietnam. Decorated Bronze Star. Mem. ABA (com. on practice and procedure before NLRB of labor law sect.). Labor. Home: 309 Church Rd Devon PA 19333 Office: Drinker Biddle & Reath 1100 PNB Bldg Broad & Chestnut Philadelphia PA 19107

KANE, MARGARET MCDONALD, lawyer; b. Long Beach, Calif.; d. James LaSalle and Nora Margaret (Foley) McDonald; m. Donald D. Hoytt, Oct. 28, 1967 (div. 1974); children: Lawrence Andrew, Elyse Caron ; m. John J. Kane, May 18, 1985. BA, U. So. Calif., 1967; JD, Southwestern U., 1980. Bar: Calif. 1980, U.S. Dist. Ct. (cen. dist.) Calif. 1981, U.S. Ct. Appeals (9th cir.) 1981. Prin. Silver & Freedman P.C., Los Angeles, 1981—. Mem. ABA, Los Angeles County Bar Assn., Century City Bar Assn. General corporate, Real property, Contracts commercial. Office: Silver & Freedman PC 1925 Century Park East Suite 2100 Los Angeles CA 90067

KANE, TERRY RICHARD, military lawyer; b. Brookings, S.D., Mar. 11, 1947; s. Douglas Terry and Florence Bennett (Ogilvy) K.; m. Mary Margaret McArtor, June 11, 1970. AB, Duke U., 1970, LLM, 1986; MA, Boston U., 1978; JD, Vanderbilt U., 1980. Bar: Tenn. 1980. Commd. USMC, 1970, advanced through grades to lt. col.; officer-in-charge, atty. Camp Hansen Legal Service Br., Okinawa, Japan, 1980-82; atty. recruit depot USMC, Parris Island, S.C., 1982-85; atty. 2d Force Service Support Group, Camp LeJeune, N.C., 1986—; adj. prof. U. S.C., Beaufort, 1984-85. Assoc. editor: Vanderbilt Jour. Transnational Law. Mem. ABA, Tenn. Bar Assn., Fed. Bar Assn., Assn. Trial Lawyers Am. Military, Public international, Administrative and regulatory. Home: 447 Hunter Ln Charlotte NC 28211 Office: Legal Service Support Office 2d Force Services Support Group Camp LeJeune NC 28542

KANESHIGE, MELVIN YOSHIO, lawyer; b. Honolulu, Oct. 4, 1948; s. Tokuo and Stella Yoshiko (Nakamura) K.; m. Nancy Eleanor Pace, Sept. 18, 1982. AB cum laude, Harvard U., 1970; M in City Planning, JD, U. Pa., 1975. Bar: Hawaii, 1975, U.S. Dist. Ct. Hawaii, 1975. Assoc. Chun, Kerr & Dodd, Honolulu, 1975-77, ptnr., 1978-85, managing ptnr., 1985—. Bd. dirs. Aloha United Way, Honolulu, 1977-84; mem. city and county planning commn., Honolulu, 1977-80; mem. city and county comprehensive zoning code revision com., Honolulu, 1984-85; trustee Palama Settlement, Honolulu, Honolulu Bible Ch. Mem. ABA, Hawaii Bar Assn. (dir. young lawyers sect., chmn. various coms.), Am. Planning Assn. Club: Plaza (Honolulu). Administrative and regulatory, Real property, General corporate. Office: Chun Kerr & Dodd 1408 AMFAC Bldg 700 Bishop St Honolulu HI 96813-4188

KANIN, DENNIS ROY, lawyer; b. Boston, Feb. 22, 1946; s. Irving Lynwood and Doris May (Small) K.; m. Carol Ann Licht, July 9, 1978; children: Zachary Joshua, Jonah Louis. AB, Harvard U., 1968, JD, 1971. Bar: Mass. 1971, D.C. 1978. Assoc. Mahoney Atwood & Goldings, Boston, 1971-73; legis. asst. to congressman Frank Evans U.S. Ho. Reps., Washington, 1973-74, adminstrn. asst. to congressman Paul Tsongas, 1975-78; adminstrv. asst. to senator Paul Tsongas U.S. Senate, Washington, 1979-84; ptnr. Foley, Hoag & Eliot, Boston, 1985—. Mgr. campaign Tsongas for U.S. Senate, Boston, 1978; mem. exec. com. Mass. Ams. for Dem. Action, Boston, 1985—; mem. Nat. Dem. Charter Commn., Washington, 1973-74, Nat. Commn. Dem. Platform Accountabilty, Washington, 1983-84. Jewish. Legislative, Real property, Administrative and regulatory. Home: 65 Stuart Rd Newton MA 02159 Office: Foley Hoag & Eliot One Post Office Sq Boston MA 02109

KANNE, MICHAEL STEPHEN, judge; b. Rensselaer, Ind., Dec. 21, 1938; s. Allen Raymond and Jane (Robinson) K.; m. Judith Ann Stevens, June 22, 1963; children—Anne, Katherine. Student, St. Joseph's Coll., Rensselaer, 1957-58; B.S., Ind. U., 1962, J.D., 1968; postgrad., Boston U., 1963, U. Birmingham, Eng., 1975. Bar: Ind. 1968. Assoc. Nesbitt and Fisher, Rensselaer, 1968-71; sole practice Rensselaer, 1971-72; city atty. City of Rensselaer, 1972; judge 30th Jud. Cir. of Ind., 1972-82, U.S. Dist. Ct. (no. dist.) Ind., Hammond, 1982—; lectr. law St. Joseph's Coll., 1975—; faculty Nat. Inst. for Trial Advocacy, South Bend, Ind., 1978—. Bd. dirs. Sagamore council Boy Scouts Am., 1979—; trustee St. Joseph's Coll., 1984—. Served to 1st lt. USAF, 1962-65. Recipient Disting. Service award St. Joseph's Coll., 1973. Mem. Fed. Judges Assn., Fed. Bar Assn., Am. Judicature Soc., Ind. State Bar Assn. (bd. dirs. 1977-79, Presdl. citation 1979), Jasper County Bar Assn. (pres. 1972-76), Law Alumni Assn. Ind. U. (pres. 1980). Roman Catholic. Club: Nat. Lawyers (Washington). Avocation: woodworking. Jurisprudence. Home: 605 Milroy Ave Rensselaer IN 47978 Office: US Dist Ct 205 Federal Bldg Hammond IN 46320

KANNER, ALLAN, lawyer; b. Vineland, N.J., May 3, 1955; s. Mayer and Ella (Kremnitzer) K. BA, U. Pa., 1975; postgrad., Harvard U., 1976, JD, 1979. Bar: D.C. 1980, Pa. 1981, N.J. 1982, Calif. 1983, U.S. Supreme Ct. 1985. Law clk. U.S. Ct. Appeals (5th cir.), Birmingham, Ala., 1979-80; assoc. Berger & Montague, Phila., 1980-81; ptnr. Allan Kanner & Assocs., Phila., 1981—; bd. dirs. Radiontech Inc., Phila., Internat. Peace Policy Research Inst., Phila., CHAMNP Inc., Phila. Author: Toxic Tort Litigation. Mem. Commn. on Prenatal and Child Health, Washington, 1984—; adv. bd. Environ. Task Force, Washington, 1985—. Mem. Assn. Trial Lawyers Am. (vice chmn. environ. and toxic tort litigation sect. 1984-86, chmn. environ. and toxic tort litigation sect. 1986-87, chmn. hazardous materials litigation group), Trial Lawyers for Pub. Justice (co-founder). Federal civil litigation, Environment, Personal injury. Office: Allan Kanner & Assocs 1616 Walnut St Philadelphia PA 19103

KANNER, STEVEN ALAN, lawyer; b. N.Y.C., Dec. 17, 1954; s. Henry and Milena (Erson) K. BA, Albright Coll., 1976; student, Hebrew U. of Jerusalem, 1974-75; JD, DePaul U., 1979. Bar: Ill. 1979, U.S. Dist. Ct. (no. dist.) Ill. 1979, U.S. Ct. Appeals (7th cir.) 1979. Assoc. Much, Shelist, Denenberg, Ament & Eiger P.C., Chgo., 1979—. V.p. Zionist Orgn. of Chgo., 1984—; bd. dirs. U.S. Com. Sports for Israel, Phila. Jewish Nat. Fund (chmn. young leadership sect. 1985—). Mem. ABA, Ill. Bar Assn., Chgo. Bar Assn., Assn. Trial Lawyers Am., Decalogue Soc. of Lawyers (contbg. editor law jour. 1980-81), Chgo. Region Maccabi Assn. (pres. 1985—). Club: B'nai B'rith Sports (nominee dir. 1986—). Avocations: triathlete, tennis, sailing. Antitrust, Securities, Federal civil litigation. Home: 2800 N Lake Shore Dr Chicago IL 60657 Office: Much Shelist Freed et al 200 N LaSalle Chicago IL 60601

KANOVSKY, HELEN RENEE, lawyer; b. Warren, Pa., Mar. 4, 1951; d. Hershel and Rose (Gernstat) K.; A.B. cum laude, Cornell U., 1973; J.D. cum laude, Harvard U., 1976; m. Marc Bernard Dorfman, Aug. 8, 1976; children: Jennifer Lee, Emily Beth. Dir. vols. Biden for Senate, Wilmington, Del., 1972; legis. aide to U.S. Senator Joseph R. Biden, Washington, 1973; admitted to D.C. Ct. Appeals bar, 1976, U.S. Dist. Ct. bar for D.C., 1977, U.S. Ct. Appeals bar for D.C., 1977; assoc. firm Dickstein, Shapiro and Morin, Washington, 1976-79; spl. asst. to sec. HUD, Washington, 1979; spl. asst. to sec. HEW, Washington, 1979-80, spl. asst. to the sec., assoc. exec. sec. to HHS and exec. asst. to undersec., Dept. Health and Human Services, 1980-81; assoc., then ptnr. Dickstein, Shapiro & Morin, Washington, 1981-84; ptnr. Leff & Mason, Washington, 1984-85; ptnr. Mason, Perrin & Kanovsky, Washington, 1986—; v.p., litigation counsel, Skyline Fin. Services Corp., Falls Church, Va., 1987—. Bd. dirs. Women's Legal Def. Fund, 1981-83. Recipient cert. spl. achievement Sec. HUD, 1979. Mem. Am. Bar Assn., D.C. Bar, Bar Assn. D.C. (chairperson ethics com. sect. young lawyers 1978-79), Phi Beta Kappa. Democrat. Jewish. Editor Harvard Civil Rights—Civil Liberties Law Rev., 1975-76. Administrative and regulatory, Banking, Federal civil litigation. Home: 7004 Winslow St Bethesda MD 20817 Office: 5111 Leesburg Pike Falls Church VA 22041

KANT, HAROLD SANFORD, lawyer, author, social science researcher, motion picture producer and writer; b. N.Y.C., July 29, 1931; s. Samuel David and Pearl (Zeisel) K.; m. Jesse Kant, Aug. 11, 1976; children—Garth David, Anthony MacLurg, Jonas Wingate. B.A. in Sociology, U. Wash., 1951; M.S. in Clin. Psychology, Pa. State U., 1953; J.D. with honors, Harvard U., 1958. Bar: Calif. 1971, U.S. Supreme Ct. 1971. Law clk. to judge U.S. Ct. Appeals for 9th Circuit, San Francisco, 1958-59; assoc. Schwab & Sears, Beverly Hills, Calif., 1959-60; ptnr. Schwab & Kant, Beverly Hills, 1961-63, Kant Gordon & Meyers, Beverly Hills, 1964-70; judge pro tem Beverly Hills Mcpl. Ct., 1968; sole practice Beverly Hills and Los Angeles, 1970-80; sr. ptnr. Kant & Starr, Santa Monica, Calif., 1980-86; gen. counsel, dir. Macrodata Corp., Woodland Hills, Calif., 1968-76; exec. dir. Legal and Behavioral Inst., Los Angeles, 1968-73; dir. Cinema Products Corp., 1975-79. Author: Pornography and Sexual Deviance, 1973; contbg. author: Crime in Society, 1978; contbr. articles to profl. jours. and Playboy, Forum and Psychology Today mags.; writer motion picture screenplays. Bd. dirs. Rex Found., San Rafael, Calif., 1984—, Squaw Valley Creative Arts Soc., Calif., 1985—; chmn. adv. bd. Children's Assistance Trust. Served with M.C., U.S. Army, 1953-55. Research grantee U.S. Commn. on Pornography and Obscenity, 1968-73, research grantee USAF, 1951-52. Mem. Am. Psychol. Assn., Western Psychol. Assn., Am. Law and Psychology Soc., Am. Sociology Assn., Soc. Sci. Study of Sex, AAAS, Authors Guild Am., Writers Guild Am. West, Calif. Bar Assn., Los Angeles County Bar Assn., Beverly Hills Bar Assn. Club: Riviera Country (Pacific Palisades, Calif.). Private international, Entertainment, Contracts commercial. Home and Office: PO Box 2830 Olympic Valley CA 95730

KANTER, ALAN MICHAEL, lawyer; b. Detroit, Apr. 24, 1954; s. Erwin Jack and Geraldine Ruth (Harvey) K.; m. Deborah Helen Avery, Dec. 11, 1983. BA with high distinction, Wayne State U., 1976, JD, 1979. Bar: Mich. 1979, U.S. Dist. Ct. (ea. dist.) Mich. 1979, U.S. Dist. Ct. (we. dist.) Mich. 1981, U.S. Ct. Appeals (6th cir.) 1982. Assoc. Robert F. Wick, P.C., Rochester, Mich., 1979-80, Shapack, Singer & McCullough, P.C., Bloomfield Hills, Mich., 1980-85; ptnr. Shapack, McCullough & Frank, P.C., Bloomfield Hills, 1986—. Mem. ABA, Mich. State Bar Assn., Oakland County Bar Assn. (chmn. pub. relations com. 1985-86), Assn. Trial Lawyers Am., Mich. Trial Lawyers Assn., Comml. Law League, Jaycees, Phi Beta Kappa. Jewish. Avocations: music, photography, sports. Contracts commercial, General corporate, Securities. Office: Shapack McCullough & Frank PC 525 N Woodward Ave Suite 1000 Bloomfield Hills MI 48013-7193

KANTER, BURTON WALLACE, lawyer; b. Jersey City, Aug. 12, 1930; s. Morris and Beatrice (Wilsker) K.; m. Naomi R. Krakow, June 17, 1927; children: Joel, Janis, Joshua. BA, U. Chgo., 1951, JD, 1952. Bar: Ill. 1952. Cons. U.S. Treasury Dept., 1959-61; atty.-advisor Tax Ct. U.S., 1954-56; mem. Law Offices of David Altman, Chgo., 1956-60; ptnr. Altman, Levenfeld & Kanter, Chgo., 1961-64, Levenfeld & Kanter, Chgo. and San Francisco, 1964-80, Kanter & Eisenberg, Chgo., 1980—; bd. dirs. Hyatt Internat., Inmed Corp., Ruti-Sweetwater; Portage Industries, Inc., Sci. Measurement Systems, Inc., Med. SafeTEC, Logic Devices, Inc.; mem. adv. bd. Solcoor Inc.; faculty U. Chgo. Law Sch. Bd. dirs. Chgo. Internat. Film Festival, Midwest Film Ctr. of Sch. Art Inst., U. Chgo. Div. Biol. Scis., Pritzker Sch. Medicine; mem. U. Chgo. Tax Policy Council; mem. vis. com. Law Sch., U. Chgo.; trustee Mus. Contemporary Art. Mem. ABA, Ill. Bar Assn., Chgo. Bar Assn., Urban Land Inst. Editor Jour. Taxation; mem. editorial adv. bd. Internat. Tax Jour.; contbr. articles to profl. jours. Corporate taxation, Estate taxation, Real property. Office: 3 First National Plaza Suite 2200 Chicago IL 60602

KANTER, CARL IRWIN, lawyer; b. Jersey City, Feb. 17, 1932; s. Morris and Beatrice (Wilson) K.; m. Gail Herman, Nov. 27, 1963; children—Deborah, David, Andrew, Aaron. A.B., Harvard U., 1953, LL.B., 1956. Bar: Calif. 1956, N.Y. 1959. Assoc. Stroock & Stroock & Lavan, N.Y.C., 1959-67, ptnr., 1967—; sec. Walnut Capital Corp. Served with U.S. Army, 1957-58. Banking, General corporate. Home: 19 Tompkins Rd Scarsdale NY 10583 Office: Stroock & Stroock & Lavan 7 Hanover Sq New York NY 10004

KANTER, SEYMOUR, lawyer; b. Phila., Feb. 4, 1931; s. William and Elizabeth (Huberman) K.; m. Rhoda Rosen, Aug. 19, 1956; children—Cynthia, Gregg, Lawrence, Brad. B.S., Temple U., 1953, LL.B., U. Pa., 1956. Bar: Pa. 1957, U.S. Dist. Ct. (ea. dist.) Pa. 1957, U.S. Supreme Ct. 1965. Ptnr. Halbert & Kanter, Phila., 1958-74; sr. ptnr. Kanter & Bernstein, Phila., 1974—. Contbr. articles to bar assn. newspaper. Bd. dirs. Melrose Park Improvement Assn., Pa., 1967-72, Greater Basketball Assn., Melrose, Pa., 1966-70. Mem. Phila. Bar Assn. (chmn. fee disputes com. 1984, 87—), Acad. of Advocacy (faculty mem. 1981, 84), Pa. Bar Assn. ABA, Phila. Trial Lawyers Assn., Pa. Trial Lawyers Assn., Assn. Trial Lawyers Am. Republican. Jewish. Club: Pine Tree Rifle (sec., treas. 1970-75). Personal injury. Home: 1011 Valley Rd Melrose Park PA 19126 Office: Kanter & Bernstein 800 One E Penn Sq Philadelphia PA 19107

KANTOR, DAVID, lawyer; b. Riverside, Calif., Aug. 10, 1952; s. Jerome Herbert and Otomie Marie K.; m. Sharon Marie Niemi, Sept. 21, 1985. BA, U. Mich., 1974, JD, 1980; MA, Stanford U., 1975. Bar: Minn. 1980, U.S. Dist. Ct. Minn. 1981. Assoc. O'Connor & Hannan, Mpls., 1980-85, ptnr., 1985—. Vol. Legal Advice Clinics, Mpls., 1980—. Mem. ABA, Minn. Bar Assn., Hennepin County Bar Assn. Real property, Banking, Consumer commercial. Office: O'Connor & Hannan 3800 IDS Tower Minneapolis MN 55402

KANTOR, LAWRENCE DORN, lawyer; b. Woodbridge, N.J., Dec. 9, 1940; s. Benjamin I. and Frances Kantor; m. Karen Bernard, Mar. 27, 1965; children: Jonathan, Evan. BA, Rutgers U., 1962, LLB, 1964. Bar: N.J. 1965. Assoc. Kantor & Burns, Keyport, N.J., 1965; ptnr. Kantor & Kantor, Keyport, 1965-85; sr. ptnr. Kantor, Kusic & Brumel, Keyport, 1985—; mem. arbitration fee commn. N.J. Supreme Ct., 1983—; chmn. Lawyer Referral Service, 1976-77. Pres.troop com., scout coordinator Monmouth County Boy Scouts Am., Oakhurst, N.J., 1980-82. Served to staff sgt. U.S. Army, 1966-72. Fellow Am. Acad. Matrimonial Lawyers; mem. N.J. Bar Assn. (family law com., del. gen. council 1980—), Monmouth County Bar Assn. (chmn. unauthorized practice law com. 1981-86, trustee 1982—, chmn. family law com. 1986—, chmn. matrimonial early settlement panel 1984-86). Club: Bayshore Exchange (Keyport) (pres. 1971-72). Personal injury, Probate, Family and matrimonial. Office: Kantor Kusic & Brumel 58 W Front St PO Box 42 Keyport NJ 07735

KANTOR, STEPHEN EDWARD, lawyer; b. Portland, Oreg., May 22, 1949; s. Albert George and Rita Lois (Constantine) K.; m. Elaine Beth Londer, June 25, 1972; children: Allison, Lindsay. BS, U. Oreg., 1971; JD, Lewis & Clark Coll., 1974. Bar: Oreg.; CPA, Oreg. Acct., atty. Arthur Young & Co., Portland, 1973-77; ptnr. Samuels, Samuels, Yoelin & Weiner, Portland, 1977—. Editor: Oregon Inheritance Tax, 1981. Mem. council U. Oreg. Found. Endowment, Eugene, 1984—; pres. Jewish Family Service, Portland, 1985—; treas., bd. dirs. Com. to Re-elect Judge Londer, Portland, 1984; exec. com., bd. dirs. Jewish Community Ctr., Portland, 1979-85. Recipient Leadership award Assn. Jewish Welfare Bds., Portland, 1983, Jewish Fedn. Portland, 1985. Mem. ABA, Oreg. Bar Assn. (chmn. title ins. com. 1979-80, estate planning continuing legal edn. seminar com. 1984—, author manual 1987), Multnomah Bar Assn., Am. Inst. CPA's, Oreg. Soc. CPA's (vice chmn. estate and gift tax com. 1982). Club: Multnomah Athletic. Probate, Estate planning, Estate taxation. Office: Samuels Samuels Yoelin & Weiner 4640 SW Macadam Ave Portland OR 97201

KANTOWITZ, JEFFREY LEON, lawyer; b. Paterson, N.J., Feb. 16, 1959; s. Sam and Hilda (Graubart) K. BA, Yeshiva U., 1979; JD, Harvard U., 1982. Bar: N.J. 1982, N.Y. 1983. Law clk. to presiding justice U.S. Supreme Ct., Trenton, N.J., 1982-83; assoc. Clapp & Eisenberg PC, Newark, 1984—. Mem. Mizrachi New Leadership Council, N.Y.C., 1985—; committeeman Bergen County (N.J.) Dem. Commn., 1985—; del. Fair Lawn (N.J.) Jewish Community Council, 1986—. Walter D. Head Found. fellow, Hebrew U. Jerusalem, 1983-84. Mem. ABA, N.J. State Bar Assn. (land use and local govt. law sects.). Land use and planning, State civil litigation, Environment. Home: 15-28 Chandler Dr Fair Lawn NJ 07410 Office: Clapp & Eisenberg PC 80 Park Plaza Newark NJ 07102

KANTROWITZ, SUSAN LEE, lawyer; b. Queens, N.Y., Jan. 15, 1955; d. Theodore and Dinah (Kotick) Kantrowitz. B.S. summa cum laude, Boston U., 1977; J.D., Boston Coll., 1980. Bar: Mass. 1982. Assoc. producer Sta. KOCE-TV, Huntington Beach, Calif., 1980-81; account exec. Bozell & Jacobs, Newport Beach, Calif., 1981; atty. WGBH Ednl. Found., Boston, 1981-84, dir. legal affairs, 1984-86, gen. counsel, dir. legal affairs, 1986—. Co-Author: Legal and Business Aspects of the Entertainment, Publishing and Sports Industries, 1984. Mem. ABA, Mass. Bar Assn. Entertainment.

KAPETAN, ALEX NICK, lawyer; b. North East, Pa., Mar. 24, 1931; s. Nick Peter and Eva (Shorall) K.; m. Claudia Anne Stroyd, May 28, 1971; children: Alexander Nicholas Jr., Gust Griffith. BA, U. Mich., 1952; JD, U. Wis., 1955. Bar: Wis. 1955, Pa. 1960, U.S. Dist. Ct. (we. dist.) Pa. 1960. Assoc. Berger & Berger, Pitts., 1964-71; ptnr. Berger & Kapetan, Pitts., 1971-79; v.p., ptnr. Berger, Kapetan, Malakoff & Meyers P.C., Pitts., 1979—. Mem. com. 14th ward Dems., Pitts., 1970-72. Served with U.S. Army, 1955-57. Mem. Pa. Bar Assn., Allegheny County Bar Assn., Am. Arbitration Assn., Assn. Trial Lawyers Am., Pa. Trial lawyers Assn., Phi Delta Phi. Club: Rivers (Pitts.). Avocations: travel, hiking, bridge, tennis. Personal injury, Insurance. Home: 639 Osage Rd Pittsburgh PA 15243 Office: Berger Kapetan Malakoff & Meyers PC 508 Law and Finance Bldg Pittsburgh PA 15219

KAPLAN, CHESTER B., lawyer; b. Kansas City, Mo., May 24, 1917; s. Jacob David and Anne (Wildstein) K.; m. Dorothy M. Medoff, June 15, 1941; children: Edith Anne Kaplan Neusner, James D. LLB, U. Mo., 1940. Bar: Mo. 1940. Ptnr. Kaplan, Shanberg, Bigus & Osman, Kansas City, 1940—; sec., bd. dirs. Promotional Headwear Internat., Inc., Kansas City, 1975—; bd. dirs. Mid-Am. Cinema, Kansas City. Mem. Jackson County Bd. Equalization, Kansas City, 1975-82, nat. governing council Am. Jewish Congress, N.Y.C., 1977—; trustee bd. law U. Mo., Kansas City, 1970. Served to capt. M.I., U.S. Army, 1942-45, ETO. Harry S. Truman Library Inst. hon. fellow, 1976. Mem. ABA, Assn. Trial Lawyers Am., Mo. Bar Assn., Kansas City Bar Assn. Democrat. Jewish. Club: Oakwood Country (Kansas City). Lodge: Masons. Personal injury, Family and matrimonial, Workers' compensation. Home: 1301 W 94th Ct Kansas City MO 64114 Office: Kaplan Shanberg Bigus & Osman 1402 Mercantile Tower 1101 Walnut Kansas City MO 64106

KAPLAN, DAVID RICHARD, lawyer; b. N.Y.C., June 18, 1944; s. Alex Seymour and Myrtle (Fisher) K.; m. Janet Marion Rifkin, Aug. 4, 1974; children: Alexander, Nicholas. BA, Hobart Coll., 1966; JD, Bklyn. Law Sch., 1972. Bar: N.Y. 1973, U.S. Dist. Ct. (so. dist.) N.Y. 1973, Mass. 1974, U.S. Dist. Ct. Mass. 1974. Staff atty. Legal Aid Soc. N.Y., N.Y.C., 1972-74; ptnr. Kaplan, Lesser & Newman, Northampton, Mass., 1975-79, Bowen, Seigel, Gervais & Kaplan, Northampton, 1980-81, Brownell, Gliserman, Washburn, Gervais & Kaplan, Northampton, 1981—. Mem. Landlord-tenant Relations Com., Amherst, Mass., 1978-80; trustee Common Sch., Amherst, 1984—; bd. dirs. Dept. Mental Health, Northampton area, 1982. Served with U.S. Army, 1966-67. Mem. ABA, Mass. Bar Assn., Hampshire County Bar Assn. (exec. com. 1985—), Assn. Trial Lawyers Am., Nat. Lawyers Guild. Democrat. Jewish. Avocations: traveling, wine collecting. State civil litigation, Family and matrimonial, Personal injury. Office: Brownell Gliserman Washburn et al 8 Crafts Ave Northampton MA 01060

KAPLAN, EDWARD ALAN, lawyer; b. Marshal, Tex., Sept. 10, 1941; s. Joseph Harold and Norma (Harris) K.; m. Lawlene Crystal Bowers, Nov. 23, 1967; children: Lisa, Caroline, Laura, Deborah, David, Michael. BS, La. State U., 1964, JD, 1969. Bar: La. 1969, U.S. Dist. Ct. (ea. and we. dists.) La. 1970, U.S. Ct. Appeals (5th cir.) 1970. Law clk. to presiding justice U.S. Dist. Ct. (we. dist.) La., Lafayette, 1968-69; sole practice Alexandria, La., 1969—; instr. successions and real estate Northwestern State U., Natchitoches, La., 1983-85. Mem. Renaissance adv. bd., 1970—, Salvation Army adv. bd., 1970-79, Rapides Parish Police Jury 1971-73. Mem. ABA, La. Bar Assn., La. Trial Lawyers Assn., Alexandria Bar Assn. Democrat. Jewish. Personal injury, Consumer commercial, General practice. Home: 500 Wycliff Way Alexandria LA 71303 Office: 1307 Texas Ave Alexandria LA 71301

KAPLAN, EUGENE NEAL, lawyer; b. N.Y.C., Jan. 29, 1950; s. Louis I. and Beatrice (Field) K.;. BA with honors, NYU, 1970; JD with distinction, Cornell U., 1973. Bar: N.Y., 1974, U.S. Dist. Ct. (so. and ea. dists.) N.Y., 1974, U.S. Ct. Appeals (2d cir.) 1974, U.S. Ct. Appeals (D.C. cir.) 1975, U.S. Supreme Ct. 1986. Law clk. to judge U.S. Dist. Ct. N.Y., N.Y.C., 1973-75; asst. U.S. atty., dep. chief criminal div., sr. litigation counsel U.S. Atty.'s Office So. Dist. N.Y., N.Y.C., 1975-85; ptnr. Kaplan, Thomashower & Landau, N.Y.C., 1985—; reporter extraditions Inst. Higher Studies in Criminal Scis., Noto, Sicily, 1983; reporter organized crime Italian Judges Congress, Palermo, Sicily, 1983. Mem. ABA, Fed. Bar Council, Assn. Bar of City of N.Y. (criminal law com. 1983-86), Order of Coif. Democrat. Jewish. Criminal, Federal civil litigation, State civil litigation. Office: Kaplan Thomashower & Landau 747 3rd Ave New York NY 10017

KAPLAN, HARVEY FREDERICK, lawyer; b. St. Paul, Dec. 2, 1939; s. Louis I. and Mildred (Tankenoff) K.; m. Suzanne Spicer, July 8, 1962; children: Beth Lynn, Daniel Anthony, David Hyman, Michael Christopher. BBA, U. Minn., 1961, LLB cum laude, 1964. Bar: Minn. 1964. Ptnr. Maslon, Kaplan, Edelman, Borman, Brand & McNulty, Mpls., 1967-80, Kaplan, Strangis and Kaplan, Mpls., 1980—. Mem. editorial bd. U. Minn. Law Rev., 1962-63, note editor, 1963-64. Mem. ABA, Minn. State Bar Assn., Hennepin County Bar Assn., Order of Coif, Beta Gamma Sigma, Beta Alpha Psi. Jewish. General corporate, Corporate taxation. Office: Kaplan Strangis & Kaplan 555 Pillsbury Ctr Minneapolis MN 55402

KAPLAN, HOWARD GORDON, lawyer; b. Chgo., June 1, 1941; s. David I. and Beverly Kaplan. BS, U. Ill., 1962; JD, John Marshall Law Sch., Chgo., 1967. Bar: Ill. 1967, D.C. 1980, N.Y. 1982, Wis. 1983, U.S. Supreme Ct. 1971; CPA, Ill. Acct., Chgo., 1962-67; sole practice, Chgo., 1967—; ptnr. Angell, Kaplan & Zaidman, 1975—; asst. prof. Chgo. City Colls., 1967-78. Author papers in field. Mem. ABA, Ill. Bar Assn., Chgo. Bar Assn., Bar Assn. 7th Circuit, Decalogue Soc., Am. Inst. CPA's, Ill. Soc. CPA's. Clubs: Chgo. Athletic Assn., Standard, Bryn Mawr Country (Chgo.); Friars (Los Angeles). Lodge: B'nai B'rith. Corporate taxation, Contracts commercial, Probate. Office: 180 N LaSalle St 28th Floor Chicago IL 60601

KAPLAN, HOWARD MARK, lawyer; b. Bklyn., Apr. 4, 1938; s. Isaac M. and Dorothy M. (Penn) K.; m. Carol Rose Silber, Aug. 11, 1963; children: Rachel Dale, Deborah Michelle, Sarah Beth. BA cum laude, U. Pa., 1960; JD, Yale U., 1963. Bar: N.J. 1963, U.S. Dist. Ct. N.J. 1963, U.S. Supreme Ct. 1980. Sole practice Teaneck, N.J., 1967—. Chmn. ann. Community Blood Dr., Teaneck, 1980—, Community Scholarship Fund, Teaneck, 1976-86. Named Teaneck Man of Yr., 1979. Mem. ABA, N.J. Bar Assn., Bergen County Bar Assn., Assn. Trial Lawyers Am., Med. Jurisprudence Soc. Democrat. Jewish. Lodge: B'nai B'rith (pres. Palisades council 1979, pres. Teaneck 1973-76). Contracts commercial, Family and matrimonial, Personal injury. Home: 370 Churchill Rd Teaneck NJ 07666 Office: 175 Cedar Ln PO Box 78 Teaneck NJ 07666

KAPLAN, JOEL STUART, lawyer; b. Bklyn., Feb. 1, 1937; s. Abraham Larry and Phayne (Moses) K.; m. Joan Ruth Katz, June 19, 1960; children—Andrea Beth, Pamela Jill. B.A., Bklyn. Coll., 1958; LL.B., N.Y.U., 1961. Bar: N.Y. 1962, U.S. Dist. Cts. (ea. and so. dists.) N.Y. 1964, U.S. Ct. Appeals (2d cir.) 1966, U.S. Supreme Ct. 1979, Fla. 1982, S.C. 1987. Asst. town atty. Town of Hempstead, N.Y.C., 1962-67; ptnr. Jaspan, Kaplan, Levin & Daniels and predecessors, Garden City, N.Y., 1970-83; sole practice, Garden City, 1983—. Chmn., Hempstead Town Public Employment Relations Bd., 1973-81; mem. L.I. Regional Bd. Anti-Defamation League, 1976—; pres. Dist. #1 B'nai B'rith, 1986-87; Rep. candidate N.Y. State Senate, 1974. Mem. ABA, N.Y. State Bar Assn., Nassau County Bar Assn. Contbr. articles on law to profl. jours. State civil litigation, Family and matrimonial, General corporate. Home: 973 East End Woodmere NY 11598 Office: 200 Garden City Plaza Suite 130 Garden City NY 11530

KAPLAN, JOHN, legal educator; b. N.Y.C., July 9, 1929; s. Edward I. and Dorothy (Saron) K.; m. Elizabeth Brown, Nov. 5, 1960; children: Carolyn, Jonathan, Jessica. A.B. in Physics, Harvard U., 1951, LL.B., 1954. Bar: N.Y., Calif., D.C. Law clerk to Supreme Ct. Justice Tom. C. Clark, 1954-55; spl. atty. Dept. Justice, 1957-58; asst. U.S. atty. No. Dist. Calif., 1958-61; assoc. prof. law Northwestern U. Law Sch., 1962-64; vis. assoc. prof. law U. Calif., Berkeley Law Sch., 1964-65; Jackson Eli Reynolds prof. law Stanford Law Sch., Calif., 1965—. Author: Marijuna-The New Prohibition, 1970, Criminal Justice: Introductory Cases and Materials, 1973; co-author: (with Jon R. Waltz) The Trial of Jack Ruby, 1965; author: (with David Louisell and Jon R. Waltz) Cases and Materials on Evidence, 1968, Principles of Evidence and Proof, 1968, (with William Cohen) The Bill of Rights, 1976, The Court-Martial of the Kaohsiung Defendants, 1981, The Hardest Drug: Heroin and Public Policy, 1983. Mem. nat. adv. com. on alcoholism and alcohol abuse HEW. Legal education. Office: Stanford U Sch of Law Crown Quad Stanford CA 94305

KAPLAN, JOSEPH CHARLES, lawyer; b. N.Y.C., Apr. 10, 1947; s. Simon and Gertrude (Gross) K.; m. Sharon Susan Penkower, Mar. 29, 1970; children: Micole Seanne, Daniele Melinda, Raquel Elizabeth. BA, Yeshiva Coll., 1968; JD, Columbia U., 1971. Bar: N.Y. 1972, U.S. Dist. Ct. (so. and ea. dists.) N.Y. 1973, U.S. Ct. Appeals (2d cir.) 1973, U.S. Ct. Claims 1974, U.S. Tax Ct. 1974, U.S. Ct. Customs and patent Appeals 1974, U.S. Supreme Ct. 1975. Assoc. Olwine, Connelly, Chase, O"Donnel & Weyher, N.Y.C., 1971-80; sr. atty. J.C. Penney Co. Inc., N.Y.C., 1981—. Contbr. articles to profl. jours. Mem. ABA, N.Y. State Bar Assn., Assn. of Bar of City of N.Y. Democrat. Federal civil litigation, State civil litigation. Home: 534 S Forest Dr Teaneck NJ 07666 Office: JC Penney Co Inc 1301 Ave of Americas New York NY 10019

KAPLAN, LEE LANDA, lawyer; b. Houston, Jan. 26, 1952; s. Charles Irving and Ara Celine (Seligman) K.; m. Diana Morton Hudson, Feb. 6, 1982. AB, Princeton U., 1973; JD, U. Tex., 1976. Bar: Tex., U.S. Dist. Ct. (no., we., ea. and so. dists.) Tex., U.S. Ct. Appeals (5th, 11th and Fed. cirs.), U.S Supreme Ct. Law clk. to sr. cir. judge U.S. Ct. Appeals (5th cir.), Houston, 1976-77; assoc. Baker & Botts, Houston, 1977-84, ptnr., 1985—. Mem. State Bar Tex., Houston Bar Assn., Am. Intellectual Property Law Assn., Houston Intellectual Property Law Assn., Tex. Young Lawyers Assn. Democrat. Jewish. Avocation: history. Federal civil litigation, State civil litigation, Patent. Office: Baker & Botts 3000 One Shell Plaza Houston TX 77002

KAPLAN, LEWIS A., lawyer; b. S.I., N.Y., Dec. 23, 1944; s. Alfred H. and Dorothy A. K.; m. Nancy Gelberg, Aug. 29, 1968; 1 child, Merrill. A.B., U. Rochester, 1966; J.D., Harvard U., 1969. Bar: N.Y. 1970, U.S. Ct. Appeals (1st and 2d cirs.) 1970, U.S. Dist. Ct. (so. and ea. dists.) N.Y. 1971, U.S. Ct. Appeals (3d cir.) 1973, U.S. Supreme Ct. 1973, U.S. Dist. Ct. (we. dist.) N.Y. 1975, U.S. Ct. Appeals (D.C. cir.) 1976, U.S. Ct. Appeals (4th and 5th cirs.) 1979, U.S. Dist. Ct. (no. dist.) Calif. 1980, U.S. Ct. Appeals (9th cir.) 1980, U.S. Dist. Ct. (ea. dist.) Mich. 1983, U.S. Ct. Appeals (6th cir.) 1983, D.C. 1985. Law clk. to presiding justice U.S. Ct. Appeals (1st cir.), 1969-70; assoc. Paul, Weiss, Rifkind, Wharton & Garrison, N.Y.C., 1970-77, ptnr., 1977—; spl. master Westway litigation U.S. Dist. Ct. (so. dist.) N.Y., 1982. Mem. trustees' council U. Rochester, 1982—; mem. trustees' vis. com. William E. Simon Grad. Sch. Bus. Adminstrn., 1986—. Mem. ABA, N.Y. State Bar Assn., Fed. Bar Council, Am. Law Inst. Federal civil litigation, Antitrust, State civil litigation. Office: Paul Weiss Rifkind Wharton & Garrison 1285 Avenue of the Americas New York NY 10019

KAPLAN, MARK NORMAN, lawyer; b. N.Y.C., Mar. 7, 1930; s. Louis and Ruth (Hertzberg) K.; m. Helene L. Finkelstein, Sept. 7, 1952; children: Marjorie Ellen, Sue Anne. A.B., Columbia, 1951; J.D., 1953. Bar: N.Y. 1953. Asso. firm Garey & Garey, N.Y.C., 1953; law clk. Judge William Bondy, U.S. Dist. Ct. for So. Dist. N.Y., 1953-54; asso. at law Columbia Law Sch., 1954-55; asso. Wickes, Riddell, Bloomer, Jacobi & McGuire, N.Y.C., 1955-59; asso., partner, sr. partner Marshall, Bratter, Greene, Allison & Tucker, N.Y.C., 1959-70; sr. partner Burnham & Co., N.Y.C., 1970-71; pres. Drexel Burnham Lambert Inc., N.Y.C., 1972-77; also chief exec. officer Drexel Burnham Lambert Inc., 1976-77; pres. Engelhard Minerals & Chem. Corp., N.Y.C., 1977-79; mem. firm Skadden, Arps, Slate, Meager & Flom, N.Y.C., 1979—; dir. Elgin Nat. Industries, Inc., Am. Biltrite, Grey Advt., Inc., The Shepaug Corp., REFAC Tech. Devel. Corp., Diagnostic/Retrival Systems, Inc., Polo Fashions, Inc., Essanelle Ltd., Great Pacific Industries Inc., Vancouver, B.C., Can.; vice chmn. Am. Stock Exchange, N.Y.C., 1974, gov., 1975, vice chmn., 1976-77. Bd. dirs. Am. Place Theatre, N.Y.C.; mem. adv. council Center for Nat. Policy Rev., Washington; trustee Bard Coll.; chmn. audit com. City of N.Y.; bd. dirs. New Alternatives for Children; governing council The Courant Inst. Math. Scis. Mem. Council Fgn. Relations, Econ. Club N.Y., Harmonie, Scis. Inst. for Pub. Info. (trustee). Club: City Athletic (N.Y.C.). General corporate, Securities. Home: 146 Central Park W New York NY 10023 Office: 919 3d Ave New York NY 10022

KAPLAN, NEIL ALAN, lawyer; b. St. Louis, Oct. 17, 1947; s. Sol and Louise Bernice (Esler) K.; m. Kitty Kayrl Link, Aug. 16, 1975; 1 child, David Asher. BS in Chem. Engring., W.Va. U., 1969; JD, Georgetown U., 1973. Bar: D.C. 1974, Utah 1983, U.S. Dist. Ct. D.C., U.S. Dist. Ct. Utah, U.S. Ct. Appeals (D.C. cir.), U.S. Supreme Ct. Asst. U.S. atty. U.S. Atty.'s Office, Washington, 1974-78; trial atty. fraud sect. U.S. Dept. Justice, Washington, 1979-81; ptnr. Clyde & Pratt, Salt Lake City, 1984—; adj. prof. law Georgetown U., Washington, 1981-82; faculty Nat. Inst. Trial Advocacy; judge pro-tem Small Claims Ct., Salt Lake City, 1983—. Editor Georgetown U. Law Rev.; co-editor: Parallel Grand Jury and Administrative Agency Investigations, 1981. Mem. ABA, Utah Bar Assn., D.C. Bar Assn. Democrat. Jewish. Avocations: skiing, running, tennis. Federal civil litigation, State civil litigation, Criminal. Office: Clyde & Pratt 77 W 2d S Suite 200 Salt Lake City UT 84101

KAPLAN, PHILIP THOMAS, lawyer; b. Hartford, Conn., Sept. 30, 1928; s. George Gershon and Eva Lee (Levin) K.; m. Sigrid Margot Dede, Sept. 4, 1971; 1 child, Alexander Thomas. A.B., Yale U., 1950; LL.B. cum laude, Harvard U., 1953. Bar: N.Y., Mass.; conseil juridique, France. Assoc. Dewey Ballantyne, Bushby, Palmer & Wood, N.Y.C., 1956-63; ptnr. Weil, Gorshal & Manges, N.Y.C., 1963—; former adj. assoc. prof. law NYU; mem. Tax Mgmt. Adv. Bd.; dir. Food and Wines of France. Contbr. articles on internat. taxation to publs. N.Am. and France. Served to lt. USCG, 1954-56. Mem. Internat. Fiscal Assn., ABA, Mass. Bar Assn., N.Y. Bar Assn. Home: 114 E 72nd St New York NY 10021 also: East Dr Sag Harbor NY 11963 Office: Weil Gotshal & Manges 767 Fifth Ave New York NY 10153

KAPLAN, RICHARD ALAN, government official, researcher; b. San Francisco, Mar. 20, 1951; s. Murray M. and Beatrice (Ray) K. A.A., Canada Coll., 1973; B.A., San Francisco State U., 1975, 76, M.A., 1981. Editor, Jour. Contemporary Rev., San Francisco, 1974-76, New Labor Rev., San Francisco, 1976-78; def. and law researcher, London, 1978-80; cons. def. and law research, Concord, Calif., 1980-83; def. specialist U.S. Govt., Washington, 1983—. Author: An Interdisciplinary Study of the International Law of Armed Conflict, 1981. Mem. adv. bd. dirs. U.S. Congress, Washington, 1982-85; nat. adv. bd. dirs. Am. Security Council, Washington, 1978-84. Served with U.S. Army, 1968. Recipient cert. appreciation U.S. Army, 1968, 5th Spl. Forces Group, 1983, Fed. Emergency Mgmt. Agy., 1983, cert. achievement Congl. Adv. Bd., 1982-83. Fellow Inter-Univ. Seminar on Armed Forces and Soc., Internat. Inst. for Air and Space Law; mem. Internat. Law Assn. (com. on internat. terrorism 1983—, com. on armed conflict 1983—), Internat. Inst. of Humanitarian Law, Am. Soc. Internat. Law, Internat. Inst. Strategic Studies, Royal Inst. Internat. Affairs, Royal United Services Instn. for Def. Studies. Democrat. Club: Army/Navy (Washington). Public international, Military. Home: 1100 6th St SW #608 Washington DC 20024-2606

KAPLAN, RONALD IRA, lawyer; b. Phila., June 7, 1957; s. Herbert H. Kaplan and Lorraine (Ehrlich) Lebovitz; m. Deborah Ann Curley, Sept. 12, 1981. BA, Biscayne Coll., 1978; JD, Temple U., 1981. Bar: Pa. 1981, U.S. Dist. Ct. (ea. dist.) Pa. 1981, N.J. 1986, U.S. Dist. Ct. N.J. 1986. Dep. chief house counsel Temple Mut. Ins. Co., Phila., 1981-83; asst. house counsel Gen. Accident Group, Phila., 1983; assoc. Law Offices of Bernard Sacks, P.C., Phila., 1984, Law Offices of Jerome Taylor, P.C., Phila., 1984-85; ptnr. Leib & Kaplan, Phila., 1985—; tchr. Am. Inst. Paralegal Studies, Phila., 1981-83. Editor: The Driftwood, 1975-78; asst. editor jour. The Jurist, 1978-81. Cons. Landlord Tenant Adv. Group, Media, Pa., 1981-84. Mem. ABA, N.J. Bar Assn., Pa. Bar Assn., Phila. Bar Assn., Delaware County Bar Assn., Tau Epsilon Rho. Democrat. Club: Master Class (Phila.). Federal civil litigation, State civil litigation, Criminal. Home: 218 Walnut Hill Ln Havertown PA 19083 Office: Leib & Kaplan 1001 Lewis Tower Bldg Philadelphia PA 19102

KAPLAN, SHELDON, lawyer; b. Mpls., Feb. 16, 1915; s. Max Julius and Harriet (Wolfson) K.; m. Helene Bamberger, Dec. 7, 1941; children—Jay Michael, Mary Jo, Jean Burton, Jeffrey Lee. B.A. summa cum laude, U. Minn., 1935; LL.B., Columbia U., 1939. Bar: N.Y. 1940, Minn. 1946. Practice in N.Y.C., 1940-42, Mpls., 1946—; mem. firm Lauterstein, Spiller, Bergerman & Dannett, N.Y.C., 1939-42; partner firm Maslon, Kaplan, Edelman, Borman, Brand & McNulty, Mpls., 1946-80; firm Kaplan, Strangis and Kaplan, Mpls., 1980—; dir. Lone Star Industries, Inc., N.Am. Life & Casualty Co., Minn. Vikings Football Club, Inc., Stewart Enterprises, Inc., Skoglund Communications, Inc., Creative Ventures, Inc. Served to capt. AUS, 1942-46. Mem. Minn. Bar Assn., Phi Beta Kappa. General corporate, General practice, Corporate taxation. Home: 2695 Kelly Ave Excelsior MN 55331 Office: Kaplan Strangis and Kaplan 555 Pillsbury Center Minneapolis MN 55402

KAPLAN, SHELDON ZACHARY, international lawyer; b. Boston, Nov. 15, 1911; s. Jacob and Lizzie (Strogoff) K.; m. Megan Vondersmith, May 8, 1947; children: Eldon, Deborah Kaplan Kovach, Daniel, Philip, Rebecca, Abigail Kaplan McKenna. A.B. with honors, Yale U., 1933; postgrad.,

Harvard U. Law Sch., 1933-34; B.A. in Jurisprudence, Brasenose Coll., Oxford (Eng.) U., 1937; M.A., Oxford (Eng.) U., 1945; Licence en Droit equivalence, U. Nancy, France, 1944; internat. law student, U. Paris and l'Ecole Libre des Sciences Politiques, 1945; Dr. honoris causa, Inca Garcilaso de la Vega U., Lima, Peru, 1970, U. San Martin de Porres, 1979. Bar: Mass. 1940, D.C. 1957, U.S. Supreme Court 1957, also Gray's Inn of London. Research assoc. Elder, Whitman and Weyburn, Boston, 1937-40; sole practice Boston, 1940-42; asst. to legal adviser Dept. State, Washington, 1947-49; staff cons. House Fgn. Affairs Com., 1949-57; legal counsel to Govt. Guatemala in U.S., 1960-62, 77-78; gen. counsel Latin Am. and Cen. Am. Sugar Council, 1963-65; counsel Cen. Bank Honduras, 1962-64, Martin & Burt, 1959-62, Wilkinson, Cragun & Barker, Washington, 1962-67, SAHSA, Honduras Airlines, 1963-77; spl. internat. counsel Morrison-Knudsen Co., 1971-74; ptnr. Bechhoefer, Sharlitt & Lyman, Washington, 1975-79; counsel Ward & Mendelsohn, Washington, 1985—; Mem. U.S. Spl. Mission to Costa Rica, 1949, El Salvador, 1950, Europe, 1951, 53, Pakistan, India, Thailand, Indochina, 1953, Latin Am., 1954, Uruguay, 1955, C. Am., 1955, Guatemala, 1957, Europe, 1957; congl. adviser, mem. U.S. del. 10th Gen. Assembly of UN, 1955; del. Govt. Nicaragua 18th and 19th sessions Internat. Sugar Council, London, 1964, 65; Bd. dirs. Glaydin Sch., Leesburg, Va., 1965-70; adv. bd. Campion Hall, Oxford U., 1974-82. Author govt. pub. documents, reports on fgn. affairs.; Contbr. legal and fgn. affairs jours.; Composer popular songs. Served to capt. AUS, 1942-46, E.T.O. Decorated mé daille de la Reconnaissance Française (France); Bronze Star medal U.S.; Orden Del Quetzal (Guatemala); Orden al Merito (Peru). Mem. Nat. Bar Assn. Peru (hon.), Am. Soc. Internat. Law, Brasenose Soc. (Oxford, Eng.), ASCAP, Brit. Sporting Art Trust. Jewish. Clubs: Nat. Steeplechase and Hunt Assn. (N.Y.C.), Mil. Order of Carabao, Oxford and Cambridge (London), Yale (N.Y.C.), Kildaire St. (Dublin), Cosmos, Capitol Hill, Army and Navy, Harvard (Washington). Private international, Public international, Legislative. Home: 7810 Moorland Ln Bethesda MD 20814-1113 Office: Ward & Mendelsohn 1100 17th St NW Suite 900 Washington DC 20036

KAPLAN, STEVEN MARC, lawyer; b. Detroit, May 8, 1953; s. Sidney and Pauline Beverly (Brecher) K.; m. Lisa Weingarden. BA, Oakland U., Rochester, Mich., 1975; JD cum laude, Detroit Coll. Law, 1981. Bar: Mich. 1981. Law clk. to presiding justice Oakland County Cir. Ct., Mich., 1978-82; research atty. Mich. Ct. Appeals, 1982-83; assoc. Williams, Schaefer, Ruby & Williams, Bloomfield Hills, Mich., 1983-85; staff atty. U.S. Dist. Ct. (ea. dist.) Mich., 1985-86; asst. prosecuting atty. Macomb County, Mich., 1986—; adj. asst. prof. Mercy Coll., 1984—; bd. dirs. Common Ground, Birmingham, Mich., Wayne County Neighborhood Legal Services, Detroit. Mem. Selective Service Bd. Mich., 1981—, Hist. Designation Bd., City of Southfield, Mich., 1985—, Oakland County Dem. Club; small claims mediator 46th Dist. Ct. Southfield, 1984—; vol. atty. legal clinic Southfield, 1985—; treas., trustee Oakland County Law Library Found., Pontiac, 1984—; trustee Southfield Dem. Club, 1986—; bd. dirs. Help Addicts Vol. End Narcotics (HAVEN), Pontiac, 1984—. Mem. ABA, Mich. Bar Assn., Oakland County Bar Assn. (chmn. appellate com. 1985—). Lodge: B'nai B'rith (v.p. 1986—). Avocations: reading, writing, chess, softball, tennis. Criminal, State civil litigation, Legal history. Home: 28638 N Lowell Ct Southfield MI 48076 Office: Macomb County Prosecutor's Office 40 N Gratiot Mount Clemens MI 48043

KAPLAN, STEVEN SAMUEL, lawyer; b. Paterson, N.J., May 20, 1944; s. Irving and Rose (Cohen) K.; m. Anita Rose Safran, Mar. 23, 1968; children: Staci Michelle, Jennifer Robyn. BA, N.Y.U., 1966; JD, Ind. U., 1969. Bar: N.J. 1970, U.S. Dist. Ct. N.J. 1970, N.Y. 1985. Asst. prosecutor Passaic County, N.J., 1970-73; contract atty. Passaic County Pub. Defender's Office, N.J., 1974-78; dir. legal services Local 464 Prepaid Legal Fund, Little Falls, N.J., 1976—; cons. on prepaid legal services, Wayne, N.J., 1975—; v.p., gen. counsel Interstate Technologies, Inc., 1986—. Chmn. bd. West Paterson (N.J.) Bd. of Adjustment, 1969-70. Mem. ABA, N.Y. Bar Assn., N.J. Bar Assn., Am. Prepaid Legal Services Inst. (membership com. 1985—). Republican. Jewish. Pension, profit-sharing, and employee benefits, Family and matrimonial, Group and prepaid legal services. Home: 44 Joseph Pl Wayne NJ 07470 Office: Local 464 Prepaid Legal Services 219 Paterson Ave Little Falls NJ 07424

KAPLAN, SUSAN ROBIN, lawyer; b. Providence, Aug. 7, 1954; d. Leonard and Beverly (Olswäng) K. BA in Urban Studies magna cum laude, Mount Holyoke Coll., 1976; Masters in City and Regional Planning, Rutgers U., 1979, JD, 1980. Bar: N.J. 1980, U.S. Dist. Ct. N.J. 1980. Litigation assoc. Hannoch Weisman, Roseland, N.J., 1980-84; assoc. counsel K. Hovnanian Co. of N.J., Inc., Red Bank, 1984-85; asst. corp. counsel Lanidex Corp., Parsippany, N.J., 1985—. Mem. ABA, N.J. State Bar Assn. (bd. dirs. land use law sect.). Avocation: ballet. Real property.

KAPLIN, GALE P. SONNENBERG, lawyer; b. Hollywood, Calif., Aug. 14, 1958; d. Bernard William and Jessica Florance (Abrahams) S.; m. Andrew Harris Kaplin. A.B. magna cum laude, U. So. Calif., 1979; J.D., UCLA, 1982; postgrad. in law Oxford U. (Eng.), 1980. Bar: Calif. 1982, U.S. Dist. Ct. (cen. dist.) Calif.) 1982, U.S. Dist. Ct. (so. dist.) Calif. 1982, U.S. Dist. Ct. (ea. dist.) Calif. 1982, U.S. Dist. Ct. (no. dist.) Calif. 1982, U.S. Ct. Appeals (9th cir.) 1982. Law clk. Calif. Ct. Appeals, San Diego, 1981; assoc. McLaughlin & Irvin, Los Angeles, 1981—. Mem. staff ABA Internat. Law Jour., 1981-82. Recipient U. So. Calif. Outstanding Sr. Recognition award 1979. Mem. Calif. Women Lawyers Assn., Women Lawyers Assn. of Los Angeles, Los Angeles County Bar Assn., Bar Assn. Barristers Club, ABA, U. So. Calif. Gen. Alumni Assn., Phi Alpha Delta (sec. chpt. 1981-82, sect. rep. 1979-80), Phi Beta Kappa, Phi Kappa Phi, Pi Sigma Alpha, Phi Alpha Theta, Alpha Lambda Delta. Labor, Federal civil litigation, State civil litigation. Home: 4947 Blackhorse Rd Rancho Palo Verdes CA 90274 Office: Rockwell Internat Corp 2230 E Imperial Hwy El Segundo CA 90245

KAPLIN, JULIAN M., lawyer; b. Chgo., July 10, 1953; s. Julian M. and Marjorie (Zaller) K. BA, New Coll., 1976; JD, Columbia U., 1981. Assoc. Stroock & Stroock & Lavan, N.Y.C., 1981-86, Richards, O'Neil & Allegaert, N.Y.C., 1986—. Mem. ABA, N.Y. State Bar Assn. Office: Richards O'Neil & Allegaert 53d at 3d 885 Third Ave New York NY 10022

KAPLOW, ROBERT DAVID, lawyer; b. Bklyn., Feb. 6, 1947; s. Herbert and Geraldine Rhoda K.; m. Lois Susan Silverman, May 22, 1971; children: Julie, Jeffrey. BS, Cornell U., 1968; JD, U. Mich., 1971; LLM, Wayne State U., 1978. Bar: Mich. 1972, U.S. Dist. Ct. (ea. dist.) Mich. 1972, U.S. Tax Ct. 1972. Assoc. Milton Y. Zussman, Birmingham, Mich., 1972-75, Rubenstein, Isaacs, Lax & Bordman, Southfield, Mich., 1975—. Mem. hearing panel Atty. Discipline Bd. Mem. ABA, Mich. Bar Assn., Oakland County Bar Assn. Personal income taxation, General corporate, Real property. Office: Rubenstein Isaacs Lax Bordman 17220 W 12 Mile Rd Southfield MI 48076

KAPNER, LEWIS, lawyer; b. West Palm Beach, Fla., May 21, 1937; s. Irving Michael and Mildred Leah (Pikelny) K.; m. Dawn Beth Grossman, Aug. 30, 1964; children—Steven, Kimberly, Michael, Allison. Student Harvard U., 1956; B.A., U. Fla., 1958; student George Washington U. Law Sch., 1961; J.D., Stetson U., 1962; postgrad. in history Fla. Atlantic U., 1969-73. Bar: Fla. 1962, U.S. Dist. Ct. (so. dist.) Fla. 1963, U.S. Supreme Ct. 1968. Asst. county solicitor, West Palm Beach, Fla., 1962-65; ptnr. Kapner & Kapner, West Palm Beach, 1965-67; gen. counsel Palm Beach County Legis. Del., Tallahassee, 1967; judge Juvenile and Domestic Relations Ct., West Palm Beach, 1967-73; judge Cir. Ct. West Palm Beach, 1973-84, chief judge, 1981-83; head marital and family law dept. Montgomery, Searcy & Denney and predecessor firm, West Palm Beach, 1984—, Montgomery, Searcy & Denney, P.A., 1985—; faculty Nat. Jud. Coll., Reno, Nev., 1980—; faculty Fla. Jud. Coll., Gainesville, 1979-83, dean, 1982-83; adj. prof. law Nova U., 1982-84 ; mem. Supreme Ct. Commn. on Matrimonial Law, 1982—. Contbr. articles to profl. jours. Pres., Internat. Found. Gifted Children, 1972-74. Served with USMC, 1959-60. Fellow Am. Acad. Matrimonial Lawyers (Fla. chpt. bd. dirs., v.p., Outstanding Fla. Judge in Matrimonial Law 1982), Fla. Bar Assn. (past chmn. family law sect.), Actors Equity. Republican. Jewish. Family and matrimonial, State civil litigation. Office: Montgomery Searcy & Denney 2139 Palm Beach Lakes Blvd West Palm Beach FL 33401

KAPNICK, RICHARD BRADSHAW, lawyer; b. Chgo., Aug. 21, 1955; s. Harvey E. and Jean (Bradshaw) K.; m. Claudia Norris, Dec. 30, 1978; Sarah Bancroft. BA with Distinction, Stanford U., 1977; PhM in Internat. Relations, U. Oxford, 1980; JD with honors, U. Chgo., 1982. Bar: Ill. 1982, U.S. Dist. Ct. (no. dist.) Ill. 1982. Law clk. to justice Ill. Supreme Ct., Chgo., 1982-84; law clk. to assoc. justice John Paul Stevens U.S. Supreme Ct., Washington, 1984-85; assoc. Sidley & Austin, Chgo., 1985—. Mng. editor U. Chgo. Law Rev., 1981-82. Pres. jr. governing bd. Chgo. Symphony Orch., 1986—, chmn. funding com., 1985-86. Mem. ABA, Ill. Bar Assn., Chgo. Bar Assn., Order of Coif., Phi Beta Kappa. Republican. Episcopalian. Club: University. Banking, Federal civil litigation, State civil litigation. Home: 570 Orchard Ln Winnetka IL 60093 Office: Sidley & Austin 1 First Nat Plaza Chicago IL 60603

KAPP, MICHAEL KEITH, lawyer; b. Winston-Salem, N.C., Nov. 28, 1953; s. William Henry and Betty Jean (Minton) K.; m. Mary Jo Chancy McLean, Aug. 13, 1977. AB with honors, U. N.C., 1976, JD with honors, 1979. Bar: N.C. 1979, U.S. Dist. Ct. (ea. dist.) N.C. 1980, U.S. Ct. Appeals (4th cir.) 1982, U.S. Dist. Ct. (mid. dist.) N.C. 1986. Law clk. to presiding justice N.C. Ct. Appeals, Raleigh, 1979-80, N.C. Supreme Ct., Raleigh, 1980-81; assoc. Maupin, Taylor & Ellis, Raleigh, 1981-85; ptnr. Maupin, Taylor, Ellis & Adams, P.A., Raleigh, 1985—. Research editor U. N.C. Jour. Internat. Law and Comml. Regulation, 1978-79. N.C. teen Dem. advisor, 1983-85; mem. exec. council N.C. Dem. Party, 1983-85; founding dir. N.C. Vol. Lawyers for Arts, Raleigh, 1982-85; trustee, counsel Moravian Music Found., Winston-Salem, 1985—; bd. dirs. Moravian Ch. Archives, Winston-Salem, 1984—, Soc. for Preservation of Historic Oakwood, Raleigh, 1981-83. Morehead scholar U. N.C., 1972. Mem. ABA, N.C. Bar Assn. (chmn. young lawyer div. membership 1984-86, bd. govs. 1983-86) N.C. State Bar (ethics com., com. on professionalism), Wake County Bar Assn., Phi Beta Kappa, Phi Delta Phi, Pi Lambda Phi. Lodge: Kiwanis. Avocation: historic preservation. Administrative and regulatory, State civil litigation, Federal civil litigation. Home: 527 N East St Raleigh NC 27604 Office: Maupin Taylor Ellis & Adams PA 3201 Glenwood Ave Suite 200 Raleigh NC 27619

KAPS, WARREN JOSEPH, lawyer; b. Bklyn., June 4, 1930; m. Sydelle Tanenbaum, June 29, 1958; children: Lowell, Andrew. AB in Math. and Econs., Rutgers U., 1952, LLB, 1954; LLM, Yale U., 1955. Bar: N.J. 1955, D.C. 1955, U.S. Dist. Ct. N.J. 1955, U.S. Ct. Mil. Appeals 1957, U.S. Tax Ct. 1962, U.S. Ct. Appeals 1962, N.Y. 1964, U.S. Dist. Ct. N.Y. 1965. Law clk. to presiding justice N.J. Supreme Ct., 1954; asst. prof. law U. Ark., 1955-56, U. Md., 1959-60; assoc. Stein & Rosen, N.Y.C., 1960-64; ptnr. Stein & Rosen, N.Y.C. and Ft. Lee, N.J., 1964-75; sole practice Hackensack, N.J., and N.Y.C., 1975—. Contbr. articles to profl. jours. Served to capt. JAGC, USAR, 1956-59. Recipient Nathan Burkan Copyright award, Fidelity Union Trust Co. Prize; Bacon scholar, N.J. State scholar; Sterling Grad. fellow. Mem. ABA, N.J. State Bar Assn. (cert. civil trial atty.), Bergen County Bar Assn., Assn. of Bar of City of New York, N.Y. State Bar Assn. State civil litigation, General corporate, Real property. Home: 34 Clover St Tenafly NJ 07670 Office: Warren J Kaps & Assocs 15 Warren St Hackensack NJ 07601

KAPUR, DAVID EDMUND, lawyer; b. Binghamton, N.Y., Nov. 25, 1953; s. Kishen N. and E. Marie (Petrick) K.; m. Susan O. Cassidy, Apr. 29, 1983; children: Jennifer, David R. BA, SUNY, Buffalo, 1975; JD, Calif. Western Sch. Law, 1978. Bar: Pa. 1979, N.Y. 1979, U.S. Dist. Ct. (no. dist.) N.Y. 1979, U.S. Supreme Ct. 1985. Ptnr. Petrick & Kapur, Endicott, N.Y., 1979—. Mem. ABA, Assn. Trial Lawyers Am., Am. Arbitration Assn., N.Y. State Bar (Family Law, Real Property Law sects.), N.Y. State Trial Lawye s Assn. (treas. so. tier affiliate), Pa. Bar Assn., Broome County Bar Assn., Phi Alpha Delta. Roman Catholic. Real property, Family and matrimonial, State civil litigation. Home: 140 Meeker Rd Vestal NY 13850 Office: Petrick & Kapur 2200 E Main St Endicott NY 13760

KARA, PAUL MARK, lawyer; b. Valparaiso, Ind., Mar. 7, 1954; s. Charles J. and June F. (Williams) K.; m. Elizabeth Louise Smith, Aug. 18, 1979; children: Adeline M., Emily L., Charles J., Phillip H. BA, Ind. U., 1977, JD, 1980. Bar: Mich. 1980, U.S. Dist. Ct. (we. dist.) Mich. 1980, U.S. Ct. Appeals (6th cir.) 1985. Assoc. Landman, Luyendyk, Latimer Clink & Robb, Muskegon, Mich., 1980-84, ptnr., 1984-86; ptnr. Varnum, Riddering, Schmidt & Howlett, Grand Rapids, Mich., 1986—. Pres., bd. dirs. Sr. Services of Muskegon, Inc., 1985—, Cath. Social Services of Muskegon, 1985—. Glenn Peters fellow, Ind. U., 1977-79, Louden Meml. fellow Ind. U., 1977-79. Mem. ABA (labor law sect., litigation sect., com. on rights of individual, subcom. on rights of handicapped), Mich. Bar Assn. (labor relations law sect. council 1985—), Muskegon County Bar Assn. (pres. 1985-86), Grand Rapids Bar Assn. Republican. Club: Century (Muskegon, Mich.). Avocation: cross-country skiing. Labor, Civil rights, Federal civil litigation. Home: 1219 Ransom St Muskegon MI 49442 Office: Varnum Riddering Schmidt & Howlett 171 Monroe Ave NW Suite 800 Grand Rapids MI 49503

KARABA, FRANK ANDREW, lawyer; b. Chgo., Jan. 23, 1927; s. Frank and Katherine (Danihel) K.; m. Alice June Olsen, June 2, 1951; children: Thomas Frank, Stephen Milton, Catherine Alice. B.S. with highest distinction, Northwestern U., 1949, J.D., 1951. Bar: Ill. 1951. Teaching asso. Northwestern U. Law Sch., 1951-52; law sec. Ill. Supreme Ct., 1952-53; asso. firm Crowley, Barrett & Karaba, Chgo., 1953-60; partner Crowley, Barrett & Karaba, 1960-75, mng. partner, 1975—; dir. Am. Nat. Bank of South Chicago Heights, Citizens Nat. Bank of Downers Grove, A&R Printers, Inc., Caron Internat., Inc., O'Brien Corp., D.L.M. Inc.; Asst. counsel Emergency Commn. on Crime, Chgo. City Council, 1952. Pres. 7th Av. P.T.A., 1964-66; Bd. dirs. La Grange Little League, 1964-67, pres., 1968. Served with USNR, 1945-46. Mem. ABA, Ill. Bar Assn., (dir. client's security fund), Chgo. Bar. Assn. (bd. mgrs. 1962-63), Order of Coif. Presbyn. (elder). Clubs: Legal, Law. General corporate, Banking, Federal civil litigation. Home: 812 S Stone Ave La Grange IL 60525 Office: 111 W Monroe St Chicago IL 60603

KARAN, BRADLEE, lawyer, educator; b. Greensburg, Pa., Aug. 26, 1938; s. Nicholas and Anna (Bonovich) K.; m. Audette Rheta Cushman, May 5, 1961; children: Nicholas, Bradlee B., Jeffery, Gregory. BA summa cum laude, Pa. State U., 1960; MA, U. Minn., 1965, PhD, 1967; JD, U. Akron, 1981. Bar: Ohio 1981, Minn. 1982, U.S. Dist. Ct. Minn. 1982. Assoc. prof. polit. sci. Mich. State U., East Lansing, 1965-69; prof. polit. sci. Coll. of Wooster, Ohio, 1969-81; assoc. Stuurmans & Kelly P.A., Mpls., 1982-83; ptnr. Stuurmans & Karan P.A., Mpls., 1983—. Nat. Def. Edn. Act fellow. Mem. ABA, Minn. Bar Assn., Hennepin County Bar Assn., Assn. Trial Lawyers Am. Democrat. Federal civil litigation, State civil litigation. Home: 312 Harold Dr Burnsville MN 55337 Office: Stuurmans & Karan PA 400 2d Ave S Suite 600 Minneapolis MN 55401

KARAZIN, EDWARD ROBERT, JR., lawyer; b. N.Y.C., Feb. 24, 1940; s. Edward R. and Ann L. (Kampe) K.; m. Irene M. Karazin, May 8, 1965; children—Edward, Deborah, Michael. B.A., Boston Coll., 1961; LL.B., Fordham U., 1964, LL.D., 1968. Bar: Conn. 1964, U.S. Supreme Ct. 1971. Ptnr., Senie, Stock, LaChance, Karazin & Thiemann, Westport, Conn., 1964-74; sole practice, Westport, 1974-75; ptnr. Schine, Julianelle, Karp & Bozelko, Westport, 1975—; asst. pros. atty. state of Conn., 1969-76; mem. criminal justice adv. bd. Conn., 1972, 73. Chmn. profl. div. United Fund, Westport, 1972; bd. govs. Westport chpt. ARC, 1977-79; mem. Westport Bd. Fin., 1983—; mem. governing bd. Levitt Pavilion, 1980—. Served to capt. U.S. Army, 1965-67. Decorated Bronze Star. Mem. Conn. Trial Lawyers Assn. (gov. 1976—), Conn. Bar Assn. (civil justice sect. exec. com.), Westport Bar Assn. (pres.). Republican. Roman Catholic. State civil litigation, Personal injury, Family and matrimonial. Home: 3 Wisteria Ln Westport CT 06880 Office: 830 Post Rd E Suite 100 Westport CT 06880

KARCH, GEORGE FREDERICK, JR, lawyer; b. Cleve., Apr. 24, 1933; s. George Frederick, Sr. and Mary (Sargent) K.; m. Carolyn Biggar, Aug. 26, 1958; children—Geoffrey, George III, Margaret Ruth. A.B. cum laude, Amherst Coll.; L.L.B., U. Mich. Ptnr. Thompson, Hine and Flory, Cleve., 1959—. Mem. bd. trustees Geauga County Met. Housing Authority, Chardon, Ohio, 1960-84, chmn., 1981-83. Mem. ABA (life), Sixth Circuit Judi. Conf. Republican. Presbyterian. Clubs: Kirtland Country (Willoughby); Tavern (Cleve.). Avocations: reading; golf. Antitrust, Patent, Federal civil litigation. Home: 12112 Kile Rd Chardon OH 44024 Office: Thompson Hine and Flory 1100 Nat City Bank Bldg Cleveland OH 44114

KAREKEN, FRANCIS A., lawyer; b. Buffalo, Mar. 30, 1930; s. Michael and Gertrude (Lang) K.; m. Margaret Holland, Sept. 10, 1958; children: Michael, Susan. B.A. magna cum laude, U. Buffalo, 1954; J.D. cum laude, U. Chgo., 1958. Bar: D.C. 1959, N.Y. 1961, Wash. 1968. Law clk. 2d U.S. Circuit Ct. Appeals, N.Y.C., 1958-59; atty. antitrust div. Dept. Justice, Washington, 1959-61; asso. firm Hughes, Hubbard & Reed, N.Y.C., 1961-68; gen. atty., then asst. gen. counsel Weyerhaeuser Co., Tacoma, 1968-75; v.p., gen. counsel Weyerhaeuser Co., 1975-80; sr. v.p., gen. counsel Penn Central Corp., N.Y.C., 1980—. Mem. Am., Wash. bar assns., Bar Assn. City of N.Y., Assn. Gen. Counsel, Order of Coif., Phi Beta Kappa. Office: Penn Central Corp 500 W Putnam Ave Greenwich CT 06836 *

KARELL, ALLAN L., lawyer; b. Billings, Mont., June 1, 1951; s. Leroy W. and Betty L. (Becker) K.; m. Carol R. Fox, Apr. 15, 1978; 1 child, Sarah. BA, St. Olaf Coll., 1973; JD, U. Mont., 1976. Bar: Mont. 1976, U.S. Dist. Ct. Mont. 1976. Law clk. to presiding justice U.S. Dist. Ct. Mont., Billings, 1976-77; ptnr. Crowley Haughey Hanson Toole & Dietrich, Billings, 1977—. Pres., bd. dirs. Friendship House, Billings, 1984—. Mem. ABA, Mont. Bar Assn., Yellowstone County Bar Assn., Billings C. of C. Lodge: Rotary. Real property, Contracts commercial. Home: 4224 Rimrock Rd Billings MT 59106 Office: Crowley Haughey Hanson Toole & Dietrich 490 N 31st St 500 Transwestern II Billings MT 59101

KARGER, ARTHUR, lawyer; b. N.Y.C., Apr. 17, 1914; m. Helen Bock, Dec. 17, 1938; 1 son, Jeffrey H. A.B., CCNY, 1932; J.D., Columbia, 1935. Bar: N.Y. 1935, U.S. Supreme Ct. 1960. Sole practice, N.Y.C., 1967—; law sec. to chief judge N.Y. Ct. Appeals, 1943-44; confidential law sec. N.Y. Ct. Appeals, 1944-48; adj. assoc. prof. law NYU, 1953-67; mem. N.Y. State Bd. Law Examiners, 1967—, chmn., 1969-86; chmn. N.Y. State Com. to Regularize Bar Admission Procedures, 1972—; chmn. Nat. Conf. Bar Examiners, 1976-77. Fellow Am. Bar Found.; mem. Am. Law Inst., N.Y. State Bar Assn., ABA (ho. of dels. 1977-79), Bronx County Bar Assn., N.Y. County Lawyers' Assn., Assn. Bar City of N.Y., Phi Beta Kappa. Author: (with Cohen) The Powers of the New York Court of Appeals, 1952; Titles of Actions and Special Proceedings, 1957; editor Columbia Law Rev., 1933-35. Federal civil litigation, State civil litigation. Home: 3530 Henry Hudson Pkwy New York NY 10463 Office: 415 Madison Ave New York NY 10017

KARGULA, MICHAEL R., corporate lawyer; b. 1947. JD, U. Detroit, 1978; LLM, Georgetown U., 1980. Spl. counsel, staff atty. SEC, Washington, 1978-82; staff atty. Shell Oil Co., Houston, 1982-83, Mich. Consol. Gas Co., 1983-84; asst. sec., staff atty. Primark Corp., McLean, Va., 1984, corp. sec., 1984-85, corp. sec., gen. counsel, 1985—. Office: Primark Corp 8251 Greensboro Dr McLean VA 22102 *

KARLIN, CALVIN JOSEPH, lawyer; b. Hutchinson, Kans., Oct. 31, 1952; s. Norman Joseph and Edith Lucille (Biggs) K.; m. Janice Miller, May 25, 1975. BA, U. Kans., 1974, JD, 1977. Bar: Kans. 1977, U.S. Dist. Ct. Kans. 1977. Ptnr. Barber, Emerson, Six, Springer & Zinn, Lawrence, Kans., 1977—. Note and comments editor U. Kans. Law Rev.; contbr. articles to profl. jours. bd. dirs. United Fund, Lawrence, 1983-85, Kaw Valley Dance Theatre, Lawrence, 1982-85, Visiting Nurses Assn., 1987—. Mem. Kans. Bar Assn. (exec. com. corp. bus. and banking law sect. 1985—), Douglas County Bar Assn. (sec. 1982-83, v.p. 1986-87, pres. 1987—), Lawrence C. of C. (chmn. various coms.), Swarthout Soc. (corp. and bus. com. 1983—), Order of Coif, Phi Beta Kappa. Democrat. Avocation: softball. Consumer commercial, Pension, profit-sharing, and employee benefits, Probate. Office: Barber Emerson Six Springer & Zinn Massachusetts at South Park Lawrence KS 66044

KARLS, JOHN SPENCER, oil company executive, lawyer; b. Saginaw, Mich., Feb. 26, 1942; s. Harold M. and Mary Ellen (Spencer) K.; m. Andrea Lisbeth Berens, Dec. 23, 1967; children: Michael Berens, Hilary Marie. BA in Econs., U. Mich., 1964; JD, Harvard U., 1967; LLM in Taxation, NYU, 1973; MS in Acctg., Northwestern U., 1971. Bar: N.Y. 1967, Conn. 1978. Acct. Arthur Young & Co., N.Y.C., 1969-74; sr. tax atty., dir. tax planning Texaco Inc., White Plains, N.Y., 1974—. dir. Long Ridge Sch., Inc., Stamford. Sr. deacon First Congregational Ch., Stamford, Conn.; trustee Long Ridge Sch. Served to lt. USN, 1967-69. Recipient Elijah Watt Sells Silver medal Am. Inst. CPA's, 1971. Mem. ABA (sec. fgn. tax com.), Tax Execs. Inst., Westchester-Fairfield County Corp. Counsel Assn., YMCA. Club: Twin Lakes Swim and Tennis (Stamford, Conn.). Editorial asst. Oil and Gas: Federal Income Taxation (Kenneth G. Miller), 1971-74. Corporate taxation. Home: 22 Briar Brae Rd Stamford CT 06903 Office: 2000 Westchester Ave White Plains NY 10650

KARLTON, LAWRENCE K., federal judge; b. Bklyn., May 28, 1935; s. Aaron Katz and Sylvia (Meltzer) K.; m. Mychelle Stiebel, Sept. 7, 1958. Student, Washington Sq. Coll.; LL.B., Columbia U., 1958. Bar: Fla. 1958, Calif. 1962. Acting legal officer Sacramento Army Depot, Dept. Army, Sacramento, 1959-60; civilian legal officer Sacramento Army Depot, Dept. Army, 1960-62; individual practice law Sacramento, 1962-64; mem. firm Abbott, Karlton & White, 1964, Karlton & Blease, until 1971, Karlton, Blease & Vanderlaan, 1971-76; judge Calif. Superior Ct. for Sacramento County, 1976-79; judge U.S. Dist. Ct., Sacramento, 1979—, now chief judge. Co-chmn. Central Calif. council B'nai B'rith Anit-Defamation League Commn., 1964-65; treas. Sacramento Jewish Community Relations Council, chmn., 1967-68. Mem. Am. Bar Assn., Sacramento County Bar Assn. Club: B'nai B'rith (past pres.). Jurisprudence. Office: 2012 US Courthouse 650 Capitol Mall Sacramento CA 95814 *

KAROTKIN, STEPHEN K., lawyer; b. Hartford, Conn., July 27, 1951; s. Leonard K.; m. Nancy Kessler, Aug. 25, 1974; children: Joshua, Samuel. BS, Union Coll., 1973; LLB, NYU, 1976. Bar: N.Y. 1977, U.S. Dist. Ct. (so. and ea. dist.) N.Y. Ptnr. Weil, Gotshal & Manges, N.Y.C., 1976—. Mem. ABA. Bankruptcy. Office: Weil Gotshal & Manges 767 Fifth Ave New York NY 10153

KARP, DAVID BARRY, lawyer; b. Milw., Dec. 12, 1955; s. Joseph and Sally P. (Nashinsky) K.; m. Donna L. Boorse, Apr. 8, 1984. BA, U. Wis., Milw., 1977; postgrad., Am. U., 1978; JD, Marquette U., 1982. Bar: Wis. 1982, U.S. Dist. Ct. (we. and ea. dists.) Wis. 1982, U.S. Cir. Ct. (7th cir.) 1982. Assoc. Wiernick & Karp, Milw., 1982—; assoc. Women Pro Se, Inc., Milw., 1986—. Mem. ABA. Avocations: photography, music, tennis, travel. Family and matrimonial, Personal injury, Probate. Office: 2401 N Mayfair Rd Milwaukee WI 53220

KARP, DONALD MATHEW, lawyer, banker; b. Newark, N.J., Jan. 15, 1937; s. Michael N. and Beatrice (Laufer) K.; m. Margery Paula Lesnik, June 28, 1962; children—Jonathan David, Kathryn Jill. B.A., U. Vt., 1958; J.D., Cornell U., 1961. Bar: N.J. 1961 N.Y. 1981. Gen. counsel Broad Nat. Bank and Broad Nat. Bancorp., Newark, N.J., chmn. bd., 1985—; regional counsel SBA, N.J., 1966; pres. Karp & Bertone, P.A., Newark; mem. faculty, lectr. Bank Lending Inst. Bd. dirs. Mental Health Assn. of Essex County, Cancer Soc. of Essex County. Served to 1st lt. M.P.C., 1962-64. Mem. ABA, N.J. Bar Assn., N.Y. State Bar Assn., Fed. Bar Assn., Assn. Bar City of N.Y., Essex County Bar Assn. Comml. Law League of Am. Club: Mountain Ridge Country (West Caldwell). Consumer commercial, Banking, Real property. Office: Broad Nat Bank 905 Broad St Newark NJ 07102

KARP, RONALD ALVIN, lawyer; b. Bklyn., Feb. 12, 1945. BA, U. Md., 1967; JD, Washington Coll. Law, 1971. Bar: D.C. 1972, Md. 1972, U.S. Dist. Ct. Md. 1972, U.S. Dist. Ct. D.C. 1972, U.S. Ct. Appeals (D.C. cir.) 1972, U.S. Supreme Ct. 1975. Ptnr. Chaikin & Karp, Washington, D.C.; faculty Nat. Coll. Advocacy, Georgetown U., Washington, 1983. Producer, moderator legal programs for NBC Radio, 1974-79, TV programs, 1986—. Bd. trustees McLean Sch. Md., 1985—. Mem. ABA (litigation sect.), D.C. Bar Assn., Md. Bar Assn., Montgomery County Bar Assn., Assn. Trial Lawyers Am. (del. D.C.), Trial Lawyers Assn. of Met. Washington D.C. (bd. govs 1980-82, pres. 1985), Am. Arbitration Assn. (panel). Federal civil litigation, State civil litigation, Personal injury. Office: Chaikin & Karp 1232 17th St NW Washington DC 20036

KARR, CHARLES, lawyer; b. Coal Hill, Ark., Aug. 3, 1941; s. William Joe and Doris Jane (Coats) K.; m. Suzanne Mary Stoner, Dec. 23, 1962; children—Stephanie, Jennifer, Jeffrey. B.A., U. Ark., 1965, LL.B., 1967. Bar: Ark. 1968, U.S. Dist. Ct. (we. dist.) Ark. 1979, U.S. Ct. Appeals (8th cir.) 1982, U.S. Supreme Ct. 1985. Law clk. to assoc. justice Ark. Supreme Ct., Little Rock, 1968; dep. pros. atty. Sebastian County, Fort Smith, Ark., 1969-72; pros. atty. 12th Jud. Cir., Fort Smith, 1973-78; ptnr. Martin, Vater & Karr, Fort Smith, 1979—. Mem. Criminal Detention Facilities Bd., Pine Bluff, Ark., 1976-78, Gov.'s Commn. on Prisons, Little Rock, 1977; bd. dirs. United Way Fort Smith, Inc., 1977-79, Bost Human Devel. Services, Inc., Fort Smith, 1983—. Mem. ABA, Ark. Bar Assn. (chmn. criminal law sect. 1976-77), Ark. Pros. Attys. Assn. (pres. 1977). Democrat. Mem. Ch. of Christ. General practice, State civil litigation, Criminal. Home: 7415 Westminster Fort Smith AR 72903 Office: Martin Vater & Karr 505 1st Nat Bank Bldg Fort Smith AR 72901

KARR, LLOYD, lawyer; b. Monticello, Iowa, May 19, 1912; s. Charles L. and Margaret E. (Houston) K.; m. Margaret E. Phelan, May 14, 1938; children—Janet A., Richard L. Bar: Iowa bar 1937. Since practiced in Webster City; mem. firm Karr, Karr & Karr (P.C.); county atty. Hamilton County, 1940-48; Pub. Webster City Daily Freeman Jour., 1952-55, Winter Park (Fla.) Sun-Herald, 1959-65; Mem. adv. council naval affairs 6th Naval Dist., 1959-62. Contbr. articles to profl. publs. Served with AUS, 1943-45. Recipient Award of Merit Iowa Bar Assn., 1968. Fellow Am. Coll. Probate Counsel; mem. Am., Iowa State Bar Assn. (bd. govs. 1959-61, pres. 1962-63), Iowa Acad. Trial Lawyers, DeMolay Legion of Honor, Sigma Delta Chi. Clubs: Mason, Elk. Bankruptcy, Federal civil litigation, State civil litigation. Home: 1420 Wilson Ave Webster City IA 50595 also: 711 2d St Webster City IA 50595

KARRH, JOHN MAXWELL, judge; b. Carbon Hill, Ala., Dec. 7, 1947; m. Janice Tingle; children: Jamie Allyson, John Maxwell Jr., Joseph Madison. BA, Samford U., 1966; MA, U. Ga., 1971; JD, Cumberland Sch. Law, 1974; grad., Nat. Coll. State Judiciary, 1978. Bar: D.C., U.S. Ct. Mil. Appeals. County judge Tuscaloosa (Ala.) County, 1976; judge U.S. Dist. Ct., Ala., 1977, presiding dist. judge, 1977; cir. judge U.S. Ct. Appeals, 1983; presiding cir. judge U.S. Ct. Appeals 6th jud. cir., Tuscaloosa, 1986—; instr. Ala. Christian Sch., Ala. Jud. Coll., Shelton State Coll., U. Ala, Brewer State U.; faculty adv. Nat. Jud. Coll.; exec. asst. to Gov., 1974-75. Past pres. Ala. Council on Alcholism; bd. dirs. Regional Alcoholism Council; mem. adv. council Shelton State Coll., Law Enforcement Acad.; pres. Football Ofcls. Ala., 1982; pres. W. Ala. Umpires Assn.; mem. Ala. High Sch. Athletic Ofcls. Assn., YMCA; served as local fireman; past chmn. deacons Calvery Bapt. Ch. Recipient Good Samaritan award, 1980, Father of the Yr. award Cowbelles, 1982. Mem. ABA (chmn. jud. liability com., exec. com. spl. ct. judges), Ala. Bar Assn., Tuscaloosa County Bar Assn., Am. Trial Lawyers Assn., Am. Judicature Soc., Ala. Council Juvenile Judges, Dist. Judges Assn. (pres. 1981), Nat. Legal Aid and Defenders Assn., Internat. Law Soc., Environ. Law Soc., Ala. Cattlemen's Assn., Ala. Farm Bur., Tuscaloosa Jaycees, Phi Alpha Delta (alumnus of yr. 1978). Baptist. Clubs: Exchange (pres. 1981), Quarterback (Tuscaloosa). Lodges: Masons, Shriners, Elks. Administrative and regulatory, State civil litigation, Criminal. Home: 4002 Windermere Dr Tuscaloosa AL 35405 Office: Tuscaloosa County Ct House 714 Greensboro Ave Tuscaloosa AL 35401

KARST, KENNETH LESLIE, legal educator; b. Los Angeles, June 26, 1929; s. Harry Everett and Sydnie Pauline (Bush) K.; m. Smiley Cook, Aug. 12, 1950; children—Kenneth Robert, Richard Eugene, Leslie Jeanne, Laura Smiley. A.B., UCLA, 1950; LL.B., Harvard U., 1953. Bar: Calif. 1954, U.S. Dist. Ct. (cen. dist.) Calif. 1954, U.S. Ct. Appeals (9th cir.) 1954, U.S. Supreme Ct. 1970. Assoc. Latham & Watkins, Los Angeles, 1954, 56-57; teaching fellow law Harvard U. Law Sch., 1957-58; asst. prof. Ohio State U. Coll. Law, Columbus, 1958-60, assoc. prof., 1960-62, prof., 1962-65; prof. law UCLA, 1965—. Author: (with Harold W. Horowitz) Law, Lawyers and Social Change, 1969; (with Keith S. Rosenn) Law and Development in Latin America, 1975; assoc. editor Ency. of Am. Constn., 1986; contbr. articles to profl. jours. Served to 1st lt. JAGC, USAF, 1954-56. Law faculty fellow Ford Found., 1962-63. Mem. State Bar Calif. Legal education. Office: UCLA Sch Law 405 Hilgard Ave Los Angeles CA 90024

KART, EUGENE, lawyer; b. Chgo., Dec. 4, 1911; s. Isaac and Sarah (Beym) K.; m. Ruth Becker, Apr. 29, 1937; children—Lawrence, Judith Kart Hazan. B.S. with distinction, Northwestern U., 1933, J.D., 1936. Bar: Ill. 1936, U.S. Dist. Ct. (no. dist.) Ill. 1937, U.S. Ct. Mil. Appeals 1963, U.S. Ct. Claims 1963, U.S. Supreme Ct. 1963. Assoc. Remer and Shapiro, Chgo., 1936-37; ptnr. Fisk and Kart, Ltd., Chgo., 1937-71, pres., 1971—. Chmn. lawyers div. Jewish United Fund Met. Chgo., 1977; v.p., bd. dirs. Schwab Rehab. Hosp.; bd. dirs. North Shore Congregation Israel, 1967-76. Served to lt. (s.g.) USNR, 1944-46. Recipient Service award Northwestern U., 1984. Mem. ABA, Ill. Bar Assn., Chgo. Bar Assn., Am. Judicature Soc., Decalogue Soc., Law Club Chgo., Phi Beta Kappa, Phi Beta Kappa Assocs., Tau Epsilon Rho (past nat. chancellor). Democrat. Clubs: Winnetka Golf, John Evans of Northwestern U. (chmn. membership 1985-87). Bd editors Northwestern U. Law Rev., 1935-36. State and local taxation. Office: Fisk and Kart Ltd 77 W Washington St Chicago IL 60602

KARTIGANER, JOSEPH, lawyer; b. Berlin, Germany, June 5, 1935; came to U.S., 1939; s. Harold and Lilly (Wolkowitz) K.; m. Cathleen Vaudine Noland, Apr. 20, 1968; children: Deborah Lynn, Alison Beth. A.B., CCNY, 1955; LL.B., Columbia U., 1958. Bar: N.Y. 1960, Fla. 1978, D.C. 1979. Assoc. White & Case, N.Y.C., 1960-69, ptnr., 1969—; lectr. law Columbia Law Sch., N.Y.C. Fellow Am. Coll. Probate Counsel (regent 1978-84), Am. Coll. Tax Counsel; mem. ABA (div. dir. real property, probate and trust law sect. 1983-85, chmn. 1986—), Am. Law Inst., Internat. Acad. Estate and Trust Law (academician), Internat. Acad. Estate and Law (exec. com. 1980-84). Clubs: Board Room (N.Y.C.); Scarsdale Golf (Hartsdale, N.Y.). Home: 1040 Park Ave New York NY 10028 Office: White & Case 1155 Ave of Americas New York NY 10036

KASACAVAGE, KENNETH STEPHEN, lawyer; b. Shenandoah Heights, Pa., Oct. 1, 1953; s. Vincent Joseph and Anna Mae (Bumbal) K.; m. Debra Ann Wiggins, July 24, 1977; children: Stefan Wiggins, Emily Anne. BA, U. Ky., 1976; JD, U. Louisville, 1980. Bar: Ky. 1980, U.S. Dist. Ct. (we. dist.) Ky. 1984. Assoc. Trimble & Lindsay, Henderson, Ky., 1980-81, Cubbage & Thomason, Henderson, 1981-85; sole practice Henderson, 1986—. Author: Kentucky Mineral Law Handbook, 1985. Panel mem. United Way of Ohio Valley, Henderson, 1985—. Mem. ABA, Ky. Bar Assn., Henderson County Bar Assn. (pres. 1984), Jaycees (v.p. 1981). Democrat. Lutheran. Oil and gas leasing, Real property, Consumer commercial. Home: 224 Washington Henderson KY 42420 Office: 101 1st St PO Box 1346 Henderson KY 42420

KASHIWA, SHIRO, judge; b. Kohala, Hawaii, Oct. 24, 1912; s. Ryuten and Yukiko (Matsubara) K.; m. Mildred Aiko, July 20, 1941; children: Gregg, Wendy. B.S., U. Mich., 1934, J.D., 1936. Bar: Hawaii 1937. Individual practice law Honolulu, 1937-69; atty. gen. State of Hawaii, 1959-63; asst. U.S. atty. gen., head land and natural resources div. Dept. Justice, Washington, 1969-72; judge U.S. Ct. Claims, Washington, 1972-82, U.S. Ct. Appeals (fed. cir.), Washington, 1982-86. Home: 700 New Hampshire NW Washington DC 20037

KASHKASHIAN, ARSEN, JR., lawyer; b. Bristol, Pa., July 23, 1938; s. Arsen and Katherine (Mangaracinia) K.; m. Ellen Paula Herrick, Jan. 28, 1964; children—Arsen III, Valerie, Juliet. B.S., Temple U., 1960, J.D., 1963. Bar: Pa. 1964. Ptnr. Kashkashian, Kellis & Pechter, Phila., 1965-70, Simons, Kashkashian & Kellis, 1970-76, Kashkashian, Kellis & Krant, 1976-81; sr. ptnr. Kashkashian & Assocs., Phila., 1982—. Served with USAR, 1963-69. Mem. ABA, Phila. Bar Assn. Democrat. Armenian Orthodox. State civil litigation, Real property, General corporate. Home: 55 Briarwood Dr Holland PA 18966 Office: Kashkashian & Assocs 9023 Frankford Ave Philadelphia PA 19114

KASOLD, BRUCE EDWARD, army officer, lawyer; b. N.Y.C., Apr. 26, 1951; s. Edward Frederick and Louise Catherine (Gebler) K.; m. Patricia Ann Gatz, June 16, 1973. B.S., U.S. Mil. Acad., 1973; J.D., U. Fla., 1979; LL.M., Georgetown U., 1982. Bar: Fla. 1979, U.S. Ct. Mil. Appeals 1979. Commd. 2d lt. U.S. Army, 1973; advanced through grades to maj., 1983; commd. JAGC, 1979; chief legal counsel, Ft. Belvoir, 1979-81, chief legal counsel for affirmative claims litigation Sec. Army, Washington, 1981-83; chief legal counsel VII Corps Arty. comdr., Augsburg, W.Ger., 1983—; spl. asst. U.S. atty., 1980-81; spl. instr. Army Claims Service, 1981-83, Judge Adv. Gen.'s Sch., 1982-83. Decorated Meritorious Service medal, Army Commendation with 2 oak leaf clusters. Mem. ABA, Fla. Bar Assn., Order of Coif. Roman Catholic. Editor, pub. Medical Care Recovery Newsletter, 1981-83; contbr. The Army Lawyer, 1982—; contbr. articles to legal jours. Federal civil litigation, Personal injury, Military. Office: SJA Office APO New York NY 09178

KASPER, HORST MANFRED, lawyer; b. Dusseldorf, Germany, June 3, 1939; s. Rudolf Ferdinand and Lilli Helene (Krieger) K. Diplom-Chemiker, U. Bonn., 1963, Dr. rer. nat., 1965; J.D., Seton Hall U., 1978. Bar admittee: N.J. 1978, U.S. Patent Office, 1977. Mem. staff Lincoln Lab., M.I.T., Lexington, 1967-69; mem. tech. staff Bell Telephone Labs., Murray Hill, N.J., 1970-76; asso. Kirschstein, Kirschstein, Ottinger & Frank, N.Y.C., 1976-77; patent atty. Allied Chem. Corp., Morristown, N.J., 1977-79; sole practice, Warren, N.J., 1980-83; with Kasper and Weick, Warren, 1983—. Mem. ABA, N.J. Bar Assn., Internat. Patent and Trademark Assn., Am. Patent Law Assn., N.J. Patent Law Assn., Am. Chem. Soc., Electrochem. Soc., Am. Phys. Soc., AAAS, N.Y. Acad. Scis. Contbr. numerous articles to profl. jours.; patentee semicondr. field. Patent, Trademark and copyright, Private international.

KASS, BENNY LEE, lawyer; b. Chgo., Aug. 20, 1936; s. Herman and Ethel (Lome) K.; m. Salme Lundstrom, Aug. 30, 1963; children: Gale, Brian. B.S., Northwestern U., 1957; LL.B., U. Mich., 1960; LL.M., George Washington U., 1967. Bar: D.C. 1960. Atty. Maritime Adminstrn., 1960-61; counsel House Info. Subcom., 1962-65; asst. counsel Senate Adminstrv. Practice Subcom., Washington, 1965-69; pvt. practice law Washington, 1969—; mem. firm Kass & Skalet, P.C.; prof. communication law Am. U.; pub. mem. Nat. Advt. Rev. Bd., 1971-74; commr. D.C. Conf. on Uniform State Laws. Columnist: Washington Post; contbr. articles to profl. jours. Chmn. consumer affairs subcom. Mayors Econ. Devel. Com., 1968-70; chmn. Ad Hoc Com. on Consumer Protection, 1965—. Served with USAF, 1961-62. Am. Polit. Sci. Assn. Congl. fellow, 1966. Mem. Am., Fed. bar assns., Am. Polit. Sci. Assn., Sigma Delta Chi. Real property, Consumer commercial, General practice. Office: Kass & Skalet 1050 17th St NW Suite 1100 Washington DC 20036

KASSEBAUM, JOHN PHILIP, lawyer; b. Kansas City, Mo., Oct. 24, 1932; s. Leonard Charles and Helen Nancy (Horn) K.; m. Nancy Josephine Landon, June 8, 1955; children—John Philip, Linda J., Richard L., William A.; m. 2d, Llewellyn Hood Sinkler, Aug. 4, 1979; stepchildren—Llewellyn H. Sinkler, G. Dana, J. Marshall, Huger II. A.B., U. Kans., 1953; J.D., U. Mich., 1956. Bar: Kans. 1956, N.Y. 1979, U.S. Ct. Appeals (2d, 4th, 10th, D.C. cirs.), U.S. Tax Ct., 1976, U.S. Supreme Ct., 1971. Ptnr. Kassebaum & Johnson, N.Y.C. and Wichita, 1970—; spl. asst. atty. gen. Kans., 1970. Chmn. Gov.'s Adv. Commn. Kans. Instl. Mgmt., 1961-69; bd. dirs., pres. Carolina Art Assn. and Gibbes Art Gallery, Charleston, S.C.; pres. Spoleto U.S.A., Charleston; treas. Am. Arts Alliance, Washington; curator of ceramics Spencer Mus. Art, U. Kans., 1960—. Mem. Assn. Bar City N.Y., ABA, Assn. Trial Lawyers Am., Kans. Trial Lawyers Assn., Kans. Assn. Def. Counsel, Fedn. Ins. Counsel. Republican. Episcopalian. Author: Kassebaum Collection, Vol. I, 1981. General corporate, Federal civil litigation, Art. Home: 59 Meeting St Charleston SC 24901 Office: 575 Madison Ave New York NY 10022 also: 125 N Market St Wichita KS 67202

KASSELMAN, STEVENS JAY, lawyer; b. Mahanoy City, Pa., Mar. 16, 1944; s. Marcus and Leah (Galant) K.; m. Diane Judith Kohn, Sept. 20, 1970; children: Lora, Tracy. BA, Pa. State U., 1965; MBA, NYU, 1979; JD, St. John's U., Jamaica, N.Y., 1980. Bar: N.Y. 1981, Fla. 1981, U.S. Dist. Ct. (ea. dist.) N.Y. 1982. Systems engr. IBM, Jericho, N.Y., 1967-83; sole practice Sands Point, N.Y., 1981—; prof. St. John's U. Sch. Law, 1985—; cons. legal industry IBM, Valhalla, N.Y., 1983—. Served to capt. U.S. Army, 1965-67. Computer, General corporate, Probate. Home: 120 Harbor Rd Sands Point NY 11050

KASSENOFF, MELVYN MARK, lawyer; b. Queens, N.Y., Aug. 15, 1942; s. Charles and Naomi (Perlman) K.; m. Joan Harriet Borowick, Mar. 19, 1967; children: Laura, Allan. BA in Chemistry, Columbia U., 1964; MS in Organic Chemistry, MIT, 1966; JD, George Washington U., 1970. Bar: Md. 1971, D.C. 1971, U.S. Ct. Appeals (D.C. cir.) 1972, U.S. Supreme Ct. 1976, U.S. Ct. Appeals (fed. cir.) 1982. Patent examiner U.S. Patent and Trademark Office, Washington, 1966-72; patent atty. Sandoz Corp., East Hanover, N.J., 1972-81, sr. patent atty., 1982-86, assoc. dir. patents and trademarks, 1987—. Bd. dirs. Congregation Ahavas Achim B'nai Jacob and David, West Orange, N.J., 1980—, v.p., 1986—. Mem. Am. Chem. Soc., N.J. Patent Law Assn. (chmn. legis. com., fin. com., liaison com.). Republican. Jewish. Patent. Home: 3 Shelley Terr West Orange NJ 07052 Office: Sandoz Corp 59 Rt 10 East Hanover NJ 07936

KASSMEIER, RANDOLF FRANK, lawyer, educator; b. Columbus, Nebr., Feb. 1, 1952; s. Robert Ferdinand and Frances Clare (Wisnieski) K. BA, Holy Cross Coll., Worcester, Mass., 1974; JD, Vanderbilt U., 1978. Bar: Nebr. 1978, U.S. Dist. Ct. Nebr. 1978, Ky. 1983. Assoc. Cassem, Tierney et al, Omaha, 1978-80; atty., asst. corp. sect. Farm Credit Banks, Omaha, 1980-83; sr. atty. Farm Credit Banks, Louisville, 1983-84; atty., officer FirsTier Bank, Omaha, 1984—; instr. Metro Tech Community Coll., Omaha, 1985—. Mem. Third Century, Louisville, 1983-84, Douglas County Hist. Soc., Omaha, 1984—, Landmarks, Inc., Omaha, 1984—. Mem. Ky. Bar Assn., Nebr. Bar Assn., Phi Alpha Delta. Republican. Roman Catholic. Club: Park Avenue (Omaha). Avocations: swimming, running, horseback riding, antique cars, flying. Consumer commercial, Contracts commercial, General corporate. Home: 3000 Farnam St #8G Omaha NE 68131 Office: FirsTier Bank NA 17th & Farnam Sts Omaha NE 68102

KASSOFF, MITCHELL JAY, lawyer, educator; b. N.Y.C., June 11, 1953; s. Justice Edwin and Phyllis (Brafman) K.; m. Gwendolyn Jones, Mar. 3, 1979; children—Sarah, Jonathan. B.S. in Pub. Acctg., SUNY-Albany, 1975; J.D., U. Va., 1978. Bar: N.Y. 1979, N.J. 1983, U.S. Supreme Ct. 1982, U.S. Ct. Appeals (D.C. cir.) 1979, U.S. Tax Ct. 1979, U.S. Ct. Internat. Trade 1981, U.S. Ct. Customs and Patent Appeals 1979, U.S. Dist. Ct. (so., ea., no. and we. dists.) N.Y. 1979, U.S. Dist. Ct. N.J. 1983. Atty. Herzfeld & Rubin, P.C., N.Y.C., 1978-82, Tannenbaum, Dubin & Robinson, N.Y.C., 1982; asst. prof. taxation Pace U., N.Y.C., 1979—; sole practice, N.Y., 1982, N.J., 1983—. Contbr. articles to profl. jours. Mem. ABA, N.Y. State Bar Assn., Queens County Bar Assn. General corporate, Franchising, Real property. Home: 2 Foster Ct South Orange NJ 07079

KASTELLEC, PHILIP RICHARD, lawyer; b. Cleve., July 6, 1952; s. Philip Rudolph and Emily Jean (Poklar) K.; m. Megan Tallmen, Aug. 21, 1976; children: Jonathan, Michael. BA, Miami U., Oxford, Ohio, 1974; JD, Cornell U., 1977. Bar: N.Y. 1977, U.S. Dist. Ct. (ea. and so. dists.) N.Y. 1977, U.S. Supreme Ct. 1981. Assoc. Wenner, Kennedy & French, N.Y.C., 1977-85; v.p., counsel, asst. sec. Bond Investors Guaranty, N.Y.C., 1985—. Mem. ABA (tort and ins. practice sect., excess surplus lines and reins. com., vice chmn. com., program chmn. 1985-86), N.Y. State Bar Assn., Assn. of Bar of City of N.Y., Assn. Fin. Guaranty Insurors (treas.). Insurance, Municipal bonds. Office: Bond Investors Guaranty 70 Pine St New York NY 10270

KASTEN, CARL E., lawyer; b. Carlinville, Ill., Feb. 8, 1944; s. Archie J. and Mary (Sutton) K.; m. Donna J. Gerber, Sept. 11, 1965; children: Heather Anne, Martin Aaron. BA cum laude, Ill. State U., 1966; JD, Northwestern U., 1969. Bar: Ill. 1969, U.S. Dist. Ct. (cen. dist.) Ill. 1970, U.S. Supreme Ct. 1975, U.S. Ct. Appeals (7th cir.) 1978. Ptnr. Phelps, Carmody, Kasten & Ruyle, Carlinville, 1969—. Mem. ABA, Ill. Bar Assn., Macoupin County Bar Assn., Assn. Trial Lawyers Am., Ill. Trial Lawyers Assn. (bd. mgrs. 1978—). Democrat. Personal injury, State civil litigation, Probate. Office: Phelps Carmody Kasten & Ruyle 130 E Main St Carlinville IL 62626

KASTRINER, LAWRENCE GEORGE, lawyer, educator; b. Dec. 26, 1930; s. Ernest and June (Newman) K.; m. Mary Tydor, Oct. 26, 1957; children: Marianne, Susan, Cathryn. BA in Chemistry, Columbia U., 1954, BS in Chem. Engring., 1955, MS in Chem. Engring., 1959; JD with honors, George Washington U., 1963. Bar: Va. 1963, N.Y. 1965, U.S. Patent Office 1965, U.S. Ct. Appeals (fed. cir.) 1982. Patent examiner U.S. Patent Office, Washington, 1959-62; law clk., tech. advisor U.S. Ct. Customs and Patent Appeals, Washington, 1962-63; group patent counsel Union Carbide Corp., Danbury, Conn., 1963—; adj. prof. patent law Pace U., White Plains, N.Y., 1979—. Mem. ABA, Assn. of Bar of City of N.Y. (sec. patents sect. 1980-83), N.Y. Patent, Trademark and Copyright Law Assn., Am.Intellectual Property Law Assn., Assn. Former CAFC Law Clks. (bd. dirs.1976-80). Patent. Office: Union Carbide Corp 39 Old Ridgebury Rd Danbury CT 06817

KASWELL, STUART JOEL, lawyer, government official; b. Brookline, Mass., Oct. 17, 1954; s. Ernest Ralph and Yolande Marilyn (Romsey) K.; m. Sherry L. Kinland, Nov. 9, 1985. AB in Polit. Sci. with honors, Vassar Coll., 1976; JD, Am. U., 1979. Bar: Va. 1979, D.C. 1980, U.S. Dist. Ct. D.C. 1981, Md. 1981, U.S. Dist. Ct. Md. 1981, U.S. Ct. Appeals (4th cir.) 1981, U.S. Ct. Appeals (D.C. cir.) 1981, U.S. Supreme Ct. 1983. Staff atty. SEC, Washington, 1979-83, spl. counsel, 1983-84, branch chief div. market regulation, 1984-86; assoc. minority counsel Com. on Energy and Commerce, U.S. Ho. of Reps., Washington, 1986—. Co-chmn. spl. gifts Vassar 10th Reunion Fund, Poughkeepsie, 1984-86; alumnus interviewer Vassar Coll., 1984—; mem. Vassar Club of Washington, 1976—. Mem. ABA, Va. Bar Assn., Md. Bar Assn. Securities, Administrative and regulatory, Legislative. Home: 1 Lily Pond Ct Rockville MD 20852 Office: US Ho of Reps House Annex #2 Room 564 2d and D Sts SW Washington DC 20515

KATAYAMA, ALYCE COYNE, lawyer; b. St. Louis, Mar. 31, 1950; d. William and Vinette (Yockey) Coyne; m. K. Paul Katayama, Apr. 29, 1970; children: Christopher, Ellen. BA, Goucher Coll., 1972; JD, U. Md., 1974. Bar: Md. 1974, Wis. 1975, Calif. 1975. Ptnr. Quarles & Brady, Milw., 1975—. Mem. Wis. Bar Assn. (pres. health law sect. 1984-85, bd. dirs. 1980-86), Nat. Health Lawyers Assn., Am. Soc. Law and Medicine, Am. Immigration Lawyers Assn. (sec. Wis. chpt. 1985—), Nat. Assn. Coll. and Univs. Attys., Order of Coif, Phi Beta Kappa. Republican. Roman Catholic. Health, Immigration, naturalization, and customs. Home: 1185 Gray Fox Dr Waukesha WI 53186 Office: Quarles & Brady 411 E Wisconsin Ave Milwaukee WI 53202

KATAYAMA, ROBERT NOBUICHI, lawyer; b. Honolulu, Oct. 11, 1924; s. Sanji and Yuki (Kiriu) K.; m. Sachie Uyeno, June 8, 1974; children: Alyce A. Katayama Jenkins, Robert Nobuichi, Kent J. BA, U. Hawaii, 1950; JD, Yale U., 1955; grad., Command and Gen. Staff Coll., 1964; LLM, George Washington U., 1967; grad., Indsl. Coll. Armed Forces, 1971. Bar: Calif. 1956, Ill. 1973. Gen. counsel Overseas Mdse. Inspection Co., San Francisco, 1956-58; commd. 1st lt. JAGC U.S. Army, 1958, advanced through grades to col., 1973, ret., 1973; gen. counsel Army Contract Adjustment Bd., Washington, 1964-70; prof. law JAG Sch. U.Va., 1968-70; assoc. Baker & McKenzie, Chgo., Tokyo and San Francisco, 1973-74, ptnr., 1974-85; ptnr. Seki & Jarvis, San Francisco and San Jose, 1985-86, Nutter, McClennen & Fish, San Francisco, 1986—; bd. dirs. SEH Am. Inc., Vancouver, Wash., SP Am., Inc., San Jose, Calif., Nikko Trading Corp., San Bruno, Calif., SES Am. Inc., Los Angeles, SETS Inc., Torrance, Calif.; legal officer Go For Broke, Inc. Named Real Dean U. Hawaii, Honolulu, 1950; Community Chest scholar Honolulu Community Chest, 1950. Mem. ABA, Japanese C. of C. of No. Calif. (bd. dirs. 1979), Japanese Am. Soc. Legal Studies, Ret. Officers Assn. Democrat. Buddhist. Private international, General corporate, Government contracts and claims. Office: Nutter McClennen & Fish 4 Embarcadero Ctr Suite 3660 San Francisco CA 94111

KATHREIN, REED RICHARD, lawyer; b. Cadillac, Mich., Aug. 14, 1954; s. John Anton and Jean Ann (Reeder) K.; m. Margaret Ann McClellan, Aug. 24, 1980; children—Jonathan, Michael. Student Universidad Nacional Autonomo de Mexico, Mexico City, 1971, 73; B.A., U. Miami, 1974, J.D., 1977. Bar: Ill. 1977, Fla. 1978, U.S. dist. Ct. (no. dist.) Ill. 1977, U.S. Dist. Ct. (so. dist.) Fla. 1982. Clk. Racal-Milgo Corp., Miami, Fla., 1976-77; assoc. W. Yale Matheson, Chgo., 1977-79; assoc. Arnstein, Gluck, Lehr & Milligan, Chgo., 1979-85, ptnr., 1985-87; ptnr. Lehr & Milligan, 1987—. Author newsletter Internat. Bus. Council Midamerica Internat. Update, 1981—. Editor-in-chief Lawyer of the Americas, 1976-77. Mem. ABA (sect. internat. law and practice, chmn. pvt. internat. law com. 1984—), Chgo. Bar Assn. (chmn. internat. and fgn. law com. 1983-84), Ill. Bar Assn. (council mem., internat. and immigration law sect.), Internat. Bus. Council MidAm. (vice-chmn. policy com. 1982-86 , bd. dirs. 1983—, sec. 1985-87, v.p. 1987—), Am. Arbitration Assn. (panel of comml. arbitrators 1985—), Phi Kappa Phi., Omicron Delta Kappa, Sigma Alpha Epsilon. Republican. Club: River (Chgo.). Private international, Federal civil litigation, State civil litigation. Home: 209 Oxford Rd Tower Lakes Barrington IL 60010

KATICH, NICK, lawyer; b. Salerno, Italy, Apr. 9, 1947; came to U.S., 1950; s. Bosko and Danka (Sormaz) K.; m. Janet I. Morgan, June 27, 1970; children: Alexandra, Philip. AB magna cum laude, Wabash Coll., Crawfordsville, Ind., 1969; JD, U. Chgo., 1972. Bar: Ind. 1972, U.S. Dist. Ct. (no. and so. dists.) Ind. 1972, U.S. Ct. Appeals (7th cir.) 1973. Assoc. Addison, Stiles, Greenwald & Kinney, Merrillville, Ind., 1972-75; ptnr. Addison, Stiles & Katich, Merrillville, 1975-77, Addison, Stoner, Stiles & Katich, Merrillville, 1977—. Bd. dirs. Lakes of the Four Seasons Property Owners Assn., Crown Point, Ind., 1975—; del. Rep. State Conv., Ind., 1984; pres. Serbian-Am. Rep. Club, Lake County, Ind., 1985; diocesan council member Serbian Orthodox Free Diocese U.S.A. and Can., Grayslake, Ill., 1985—; bd. dirs. Lake County Park and Recreation Bd., 1986. Mem. ABA, Ind. Bar Assn., Fed. Bar Assn., Am. Trial Lawyers Assn., Phi Beta Kappa. Eastern Orthodox. Lodge: Lions (local bd. dirs. 1978-85, 3d v.p. 1986). Personal injury, Federal civil litigation, General corporate. Office: Addison Stoner Stiles & Katich 8585 Broadway Suite 780 Merrillville IN 46410

KATONA, GABRIEL PAUL, lawyer; b. Budapest, Hungary, May 16, 1932; came to U.S., 1957, naturalized, 1963; s. Arthur Weiss and Margaret ((Gardonyi) K.; m. Gabrielle. M.Chem. Engring., Budapest Inst. Tech., 1955; JD, NYU, 1965. Bar: N.Y. 1966, U.S. Patent Office 1963, U.S. Supreme Ct. 1973, U.S. Ct. Appeals (2d cir.) 1975, U.S. Ct. Appeals (fed. cir.). Sole practice N.Y.C. Contbr. articles to in tech., legal fields to U.S., fgn. jours. Patent, Trademark and copyright, Federal civil litigation. Office: 400 E 85 St New York NY 10028

KATSH, M. ETHAN, legal educator; b. N.Y.C., Sept. 3, 1945; s. Abraham Isaac and Estelle (Wachtell) K.; m. Beverly, children—Rebecca, Gabriel. B.A., NYU, 1967; J.D., Yale U., 1970. Bar: N.Y. 1970. Asst. prof. legal studies U. Mass., Amherst, 1970-76, assoc. prof., 1977—, dir. legal studies program, 1975-77. Co-author: Before the Law, 3d edit., 1984. Editor: Taking Sides: Clashing Views on Controversial Legal Issues, 1982, 2d edit., 1986. Contbr. articles on law and media to profl. jours. and mags. Cofounder U. Mass. Mediation Project, 1980; faculty Humanities and the Professions Program, Brandeis U., 1983—. Fellow East-West Ctr., Honolulu, 1977, Modern Media Inst., St. Petersburg, Fla., 1981, faculty workshop Annenberg Washington Program, 1976. Mem. Am. Legal Studies Assn. (pres. 1978-80). Legal education, Communications, Computer. Office: Dept Legal Studies U Mass Amherst MA 01003

KATSKEE, MELVIN ROBERT, lawyer; b. Omaha, Nov. 19, 1945; s. David William and Mabel Masha (Slutzkin) K.; m. Pola Bucheister, Jan. 11, 1981. AB cum laude, Creighton U., 1967; postgrad., Northwestern U.,

1967-68; JD, U. Nebr., 1970. Bar: Nebr. 1970, U.S. Dist. Ct. Nebr. 1970, U.S. Ct. Appeals (8th cir.) 1970. Law clk. to presiding justice U.S. Dist. Ct. Nebr., Omaha, 1970-71; assoc. White, Lipp, Simon & Powers, Omaha, 1971-73, Law Office Malcolm D. Young, Omaha, 1973; v.p., gen. atty. Omaha Nat. Bank (now Firstier Bank, N.A.), 1974—; adj. prof. Creighton U. Sch. Law, Omaha, 1972-77. Contbr. articles to profl. jours. Mem. adv. council Coll. Arts and Scis., Creighton U., 1978—. Mem. ABA, Nebr. Bar Assn., Omaha Bar Assn. Democrat. Jewish. Avocations: literature, music. Banking, Contracts commercial, Consumer commercial. Home: 5617 Erskine St Omaha NE 68104 Office: Firstier Bank NA 17th & Farnham Sts Omaha NE 68102

KATSORIS, CONSTANTINE NICHOLAS, legal educator, consultant; b. Bklyn., Dec. 5, 1932; s. Nicholas C. and Nafsika (Klonis) K.; m. Ann Kanganis, Feb. 19; children—Nancy, Nicholas, Louis. B.S. in Acctg., Fordham U., 1953, J.D. cum laude, 1957; LL.M., NYU, 1963. Bar: N.Y. 1957, U.S. Dist. Ct. (so. dist.) N.Y. 1959, U.S. Dist. Ct. (ea. dist.) N.Y. 1959, U.S. Tax Ct. 1959, U.S. Ct. Appeals (2d cir.) 1959, U.S. Supreme Ct. 1961. Assoc. Cahill, Gordon, Reindel & Ohl, N.Y.C., 1958-64; asst. prof. Fordham U. Law Sch., N.Y.C., 1964-66, assoc. prof., 1966-69, prof., 1969—; cons. N.Y. State Temporary Commn. on Estates, 1964-67; arbitration panelist N.Y. Stock Exchange, 1971—, Nat. Assn. Securities Dealers, 1968—, 1st Jud. Dept., 1972—; pub. mem. Securities Industry Conf. on Arbitration, 1977—. Mem. sch. bd. Greek Orthodox Parochial Sch. of St. Spyridon, 1975—, chmn. sch. bd., 1983—. Served with U.S. Army, 1963. Recipient Chapin prize Fordham Law Sch., 1957; cert. of appreciation Nat. Assn. Securities Dealers, 1982. Mem. ABA (fed. estate and gift tax com. 1966—, continuing legal edn. and research com. 1966-68), N.Y. State Bar Assn. (sect. on trust and estates 1969—), Assn. Bar City N.Y. trusts, estates and surrogates' cts. com. 1968-70, legal assistance com. 1965-67), Fordham Law Alumni Assn. (bd. dirs. 1972—, Fordham Law Rev. Alumni Assn. (pres. 1963-64). Republican. Greek Orthodox. Contbr. articles to legal jours. Estate taxation, Probate, Personal income taxation. Office: 140 W 62nd St New York NY 10023

KATZ, ALFRED B., lawyer; b. Cin., Sept. 17, 1911; s. Charles and Mollie (Gross) K.; m. Adele Stillpass, June 8, 1941; children—Ellen Ruth, Ronna M., Louis H. B.A., U. Cin., 1932, J.D., 1935; Bar: Ohio. Assoc. Gilbert Bettman, 1935-39, McIntosh Moore & Katz, Cin., 1950-54; ptnr. Freiberg Katz & Greenberger, Cin., 1954—; asst. city solicitor City of Cin., 1939-41; dir. Standard Textile Co., Fibre Glass-Evercoat, Cal Crim Security, Inc., Laurens Bros., Fulflo Specialties, Inc. Pres., Dunham T.B. Hosp., 1964-70; nat. com. mem. Jewish Nat. Fund, 1979—. Served to lt. comdr., USNR, 1943-46. Mem. Cin. Bar Assn., Ohio Bar Assn., ABA, Am. Trial Lawyers Assn., U.S. Mil. Res., Officers Assn. So. Ohio (pres.). Republican. Jewish. Clubs: B'nai B'rith, Masons (Shriner). General corporate, Personal injury, Labor. Office: 105 E 4th St Suite 1400 Cincinnati OH 45202

KATZ, ALLAN JACK, lawyer; b. Apr. 30, 1947; m. Nancy Cohn; children: Ethan, Matthew. BA, U. Mo., 1969, postgrad., 1971-72; postgrad., U. Toledo, 1969-70; JD, Am. U., 1974. Bar: Mo. 1974, Fla. 1979, U.S. Dist. Ct. (no. dist.) Fla. 1979, U.S. Ct. Appeals (Fed. cir.). 1979. Legis. counsel congressman Bill Gunter, 1973-75; legis. dir. congressman David R. Obey, 1975-76; gen. counsel com. of adminstrn. rev. Ho. of Reps., Tallahassee, 1976-78; asst. treas., ins. commr., gen. counsel dept. of ins. State of Fla., Tallahassee, 1979-82; assoc., mng. ptnr. Swann & Haddock P.A., Tallahassee, 1983—. Mem. ABA, Fla. Bar Assn., Mo. Bar Assn. Democrat. Jewish. Administrative and regulatory, Insurance, Municipal bonds. Home: 2508 Betton Woods Dr Tallahassee FL 32312 Office: Swann & Haddock PA 315 S Calhoun St Barnett Bank Bldg Suite 800 Tallahassee FL 32301

KATZ, ASCHER, lawyer; b. N.Y.C., Apr. 16, 1927; s. Morris Joseph and Tessie (Appel) K.; m. Barbara Dorothy Novins, Aug. 17, 1957; children: Arlene Elizabeth, Beverly Ann Wertheim, Rochelle Bonnie. BEE, CCNY, 1948; JD, Harvard U., 1951. Bar: N.Y. 1952, U.S. Dist. Ct. (so. and ea. dists.) N.Y. 1954, U.S. Tax Ct. 1955, U.S. Ct. Claims 1956, U.S. Supreme Ct. 1956, U.S. Ct. Appeals (2d cir.) 1966. Staff atty. Civil Branch Legal Aid Soc., N.Y.C., 1952-54; law asst. labor law div. prevailing rates of wages Office of N.Y.C. Corp. Counsel, 1954-55; sole practice N.Y.C., 1955-58, 1973-79; ptnr. Bobrow, Handman & Katz, 1958-63, Abelson, Katz & Susswein, 1963-68, Abelson, Bromberg & Katz, 1968-73, Katz & Klein, White Plains, N.Y., 1979—; former lectr. law Bklyn. Coll., justice Town of Greenburgh, Westchester County, N.Y., 1976—. Columnist Legal Plain Talk, White Plains Reporter-Dispatch, 1971. Former pres. Bklyn. div. Nat. Governing Council Am. Jewish Cong.; former trustee, chmn. religious sch. bd., former chmn. adult edn. com. Temple Israel, White Plains; former mem. Colo. House Adv. Bd. Westchester Devel. Ctr., N.Y. State Dept. Mental Health. Served with USNR, 1945-46. Mem. ABA (com. on new lawyers, gen. practice sect.), N.Y. State Bar Assn. (past chmn. com. on dist. city village and town cts., jud. sect., trusts and estates sect., criminal justice sect., gen. practice sect., family law sect.), Assn. of Bar of City of N.Y. (panel legal referral service), Westchester County Bar Assn. (criminal justice sect., family law sect., mcpl. law sect., real property sect., trust and estate sect., panel legal referral service), Assn. Trial Lawyers Am., N.Y. State Magistrates Assn., Westchester County Magistrates Assn. (past bd. dirs.), County C. of C. (bd. dirs., gen. counsel), NAACP, Jewish War Vets. (former sr. vice comdr. White Plains post), Urban League, CCNY Alumni Assn. (lifetime), Harvard Law Sch. Assn. Lodges: B'nai B'rith, Rotary (membership com. White Plains club). Avocations: oil painting, swimming. State civil litigation, General practice, Personal injury. Home: 24 Primrose Ave W White Plains NY 10607 Office: Katz & Klein 200 Mamaroneck Ave White Plains NY 10601

KATZ, AVRUM SIDNEY, lawyer; b. Melrose Park, Ill., Oct. 10, 1939; s. Joseph George and Bessie Goldie (Ancel) K.; m. Sheela Cara Cooperman, Sept. 1, 1963; children—Julie Anne, Aaron Richard, Michele Sharon. B.S. in Elec. Engring., Ill. Inst. Tech., 1962; J.D., George Washington U., 1966. Bar: Ill. 1966, U.S. Dist. Ct. (no. dist.) Ill. 1967, U.S. Patent Office 1967, U.S. Supreme Ct. 1977, U.S. Ct. Appeals (7th cir.) 1978; examiner U.S. Patent Office. Assoc. Leonard G. Nierman, Chgo., 1966-67; assoc. Fitch, Even, Tabin, Flannery & Welsh, and predecessor firms, Chgo., 1967-70, ptnr., 1971-82; ptnr. Welsh & Katz, Chgo., 1983—; dir. The Lase Co., Chgo. Mem. ad hoc com. Lake Forest (Ill.) City Council, 1970. Recipient award of distinction Patent Resources Group, 1983. Mem. ABA, Ill. Bar Assn., Chgo. Bar Assn., Patent Law Assn. Chgo., IEEE, Delta Theta Phi, Tau Beta Pi, Eta Kappa Nu, Sigma Iota Epsilon. Patent, Trademark and copyright, Federal civil litigation. Home: 475 Turicim Rd Lake Forest IL 60045 Office: Welsh & Katz 135 S LaSalle St Room 1625 Chicago IL 60603

KATZ, BARRY EDWARD, lawyer; b. Los Angeles, June 29, 1942; s. Morris and Jean (Monchick) K.; m. Jane W. Wolff, May 27, 1973; children: Lisa, Julie, Joanna. BA in Music, UCLA, 1965; MusM, U. Oreg., 1968; JD, U. Md., 1975. Bar: Md. 1976, D.C. 1976, U.S. Supreme Ct. 1979. Sole practice Silver Spring, Md., 1976-81; ptnr. Katz & Herman, Silver Spring, 1982—; govt. adminstr. U.S. Dept. Edn., Washington, 1969-80, legal policy analyst, 1980—. Mem. exec. bd. Nat. Capital Area ACLU, Washington, 1976—; pres. Woodside Forest Civic Assn., Silver Spring, 1984-86; pub. adv. com. rep. Met. Council Govts., Montgomery County, Md., 1985—. Served with U.S. Army, 1965-67. California State Scholar, 1960. Mem. ABA, Md. Bar Assn., D.C. Bar Assn. Democrat. Jewish. Avocations: music, jogging, basketball. Administrative and regulatory, Personal income taxation, Personal injury. Home: 1206 Edgevale Rd Silver Spring MD 20910

KATZ, CHARLES R., lawyer; b. N.Y.C., June 30, 1912; s. Jacob and Mary (Kort) K.; m. Rivie Blacker, Sept. 22, 1933; children—Barbara Rosen, Jack Katz, Janet Greenspan; m. 2d, Edythe Kotler, Nov. 9, 1967. B.S., NYU, 1932, J.D., 1935. Bar: N.Y. 1936, U.S. Supreme Ct. 1943. Fed. Ct. N.Y. 1937. Sole practice Law Offices Charles R. Katz, N.Y.C., 1936-77; pres. Charles R. Katz, P.C., 1977—. Recipient Golden Torch of City of Hope, 1979; YMHA Koved Medal, 1935. Mem. ABA, N.Y. State Bar Assn., N.Y. County Lawyers Assn., Am. Judicature Soc., Internat. Congress of Jewish Lawyers and Jurists, Internat. Soc. Labor Law. Democrat. Jewish. Club: B'nai B'rith. Contbg. editor various law books and mags.; NLRB editor of mag. Union Labor, 1968-71. Labor, Pension, profit-sharing, and employee benefits. Office: 360 Lexington Ave New York NY 10017

KATZ, GARY M., lawyer; b. N.Y.C., May 10, 1941; s. Leon W. and Helen (Dier) K.; m. Marylyn Dintenfass, Aug. 26, 1963; children: Robert A., Marc A. BBA, CUNY, 1963; JD, N.Y. Law Sch., 1965. Bar: N.Y. 1967, U.S. Dist. Ct. (ea. and so. dists.) N.Y. Office mgr. Haft & Haft C.P.A., Jerusalem, 1965-66; assoc. product mgr. General Foods, White Plains, N.Y., 1966-69; v.p. fin. dept. Information, Inc., N.Y.C., 1969-72; v.p. Fabrics Round the World, N.Y.C., 1972-74; ptnr. Katz, Kleinbaum, Farber & Karson & predecessor firms, White Plains, 1974—. Trustee Young Israel of Scarsdale, N.Y., 1981-85. Mem. ABA, N.Y. State Bar Assn. (del. 9th jud. dist. real property law sect., chmn. com. legis. of landlord and tenant), Westchester County Bar Assn. Jewish. Real property, Landlord-tenant, General corporate. Home: 7 Plymouth Dr Scarsdale NY 10583 Office: Katz Kleinbaum Farber & Karson 200 E Post Rd White Plains NY 10601

KATZ, HADRIAN RONALD, lawyer; b. Cambridge, Mass., Aug. 12, 1949; s. Samuel and Alice (Greenstein) K.; m. Candace Kay Kaufman, Apr. 1, 1977; children: Gwendlyn Rebecca, Jonathan Harold. AB, Harvard U., 1969, JD, 1976; MA, U. Calif., Berkeley, 1973. Bar: D.C. 1977, Mass. 1977, U.S. Dist. Ct. D.C. 1977, U.S. Ct. Appeals (D.C. cir.) 1979, U.S. Supreme Ct. 1983, U.S. Ct. Appeals (6th cir.)1985. Ptnr. Arnold & Porter, Washington, 1976—. Mem. ABA, Am. Phys. Soc., Assn. for Computing Machinery. Democrat. Avocation: computer. Federal civil litigation, Administrative and regulatory, Antitrust. Home: 1324 Lancia Dr McLean VA 22102-2204 Office: Arnold & Porter 1200 New Hampshire Ave NW Washington DC 20036

KATZ, HAROLD AMBROSE, lawyer, former state legislator; b. Shelbyville, Tenn., Nov. 2, 1921; s. Maurice W. and Gertrude Evelyn (Cohen) K.; m. Ethel Mae Lewison, July 21, 1945; children: Alan, Barbara, Julia, Joel. A.B., Vanderbilt U., 1943; J.D., U. Chgo., 1948, M.A., 1958. Bar: Ill. 1948. Ptnr. Katz, Friedman, Schur & Eagle, Chgo., 1948—; spl. legal cons. to Gov. of Ill., 1961-63; master-in-chancery, circuit ct. Cook County, Ill., 1963-67; mem. Ill. Ho. of Reps., 1965-83, chmn. judiciary com., co-chmn. rules com.; lectr. U. Coll., U. Chgo., 1959-64; Chmn. Ill. Commn. on Orgn. of Gen. Assembly, 1966-82; del. nat. Democratic conv., 1972. Author: (with Charles O. Gregory) Labor Law: Cases, Materials and Comments, 1948, Labor and the Law, 1979; editor: Improving the State Legislature, 1967; Contbr. articles to mags. Mem. ABA, Ill. Bar Assn. (chmn. labor law sect. 1979-80), Internat. Soc. for Labor Law and Social Legislation (U.S. chmn. 1961-67), Am. Trial Lawyers Assn. (chmn. workmen's compensation sect. 1963-64). Jewish. Labor, Federal civil litigation, State civil litigation. Home: 1180 Terrace Ct Glencoe IL 60022 Office: Katz Friedman Schur & Eagle 7 S Dearborn St Chicago IL 60603

KATZ, JASON LAWRENCE, lawyer, insurance executive; b. Chgo., Sept. 28, 1947; s. Irving and Goldie (Medress) K.; m. Aug. 17, 1968, 2 children. B.A., Northeastern Ill. U., 1969; J.D., DePaul U., 1973. Bar: Calif. 1976, Ariz. 1973, U.S. Ct. Appeals (9th cir.) 1976. Sole practice, Scottsdale, Ariz., 1973-76; v.p., corp. counsel Mission Ins. Group, Inc., Los Angeles, 1976-84; v.p., gen. counsel corp. affairs Farmers Group, Inc., Los Angeles, 1984—, bd. dirs., 1986—; v.p., bd. dirs. Calif. Def. Counsel, 1986—. Mem. Conf. Ins. Counsel (v.p., pres. Los Angeles 1981-82), Los Angeles County Bar Assn. (mem. exec. bd. corp. law sect. 1976). Insurance, Administrative and regulatory, General corporate. Office: Farmers Group Inc 4680 Wilshire Blvd Los Angeles CA 90010

KATZ, JAY, physician, educator; b. Zwickau, Germany, Oct. 20, 1922; came to U.S., 1940, naturalized, 1945; s. Paul and Dora (Ungar) K.; m. Esta Mae Zorn, Sept. 13, 1952; children: Sally Jean, Daniel Franklin, Amy Susan. B.A., U. Vt., 1944; M.D., Harvard U., 1949. Intern Mt. Sinai Hosp., N.Y.C., 1949-50; resident Northport (N.Y.) VA Hosp., 1950-51, Yale U., 1953-55; instr. psychiatry Yale U., New Haven, 1955-57; asst. prof. Yale U., 1957-58, asst. prof. psychiatry and law, 1958-60, asso. prof. law, asso. clin. prof. psychiatry, 1960-67, adj. prof. law and psychiatry, 1967-79, prof., 1979-81, John A. Garver prof. law and psychoanalysis, 1981—; tng. and supervising psychiatrist Western New Eng. Inst. for Psychoanalysis, 1972—; cons. to asst. sec. health and sci. affairs HEW, 1972-73, mem. artificial heart assessment panel, 1972-73. Author: (with Joseph Goldstein) The Family and the Law, 1964, (with Joseph Goldstein and Alan M. Dershowitz) Psychoanalysis, Psychiatry and Law, 1967, Experimentation with Human Beings, 1972, (with Alexander M. Capron) Catastrophic Diseases—Who Decides What?, 1975; The Silent World of Doctor and Patient, 1984. Bd. dirs. Family Service of New Haven. Served to capt. M.C. USAF, 1951-53. John Simon Guggenheim Meml. Found. fellow, 1981. Fellow ACP (William C. Menninger award 1983), Am. Psychiat. Assn. (Isaac Ray award 1975), Am. Orthopsychiat. Assn., Am. Coll. Psychiatry, Center for Advanced Psychoanalytic Studies; mem Inst. Medicine, Nat. Acad. of Scis., Group for Advancement of Psychiatry, Am. Psychoanalytic Assn. Jewish. Family and matrimonial, Health, Jurisprudence. Home: 27 Inwood Rd Woodbridge CT 06525 Office: 127 Wall St. New Haven CT 06520

KATZ, JEFFREY HARVEY, lawyer; b. Newark, Apr. 16, 1947; s. Jack and Beatrice (Weinstock) K.; m. Sharon R. Davis, Nov. 7, 1971; children: Stacey, Justin. BEngring, Stevens Inst. Tech., 1970; JD, Seton Hall U., 1981. Bar: N.J. 1981, U.S. Dist. Ct. N.J. 1981, U.S. Ct. Appeals (3d cir.) 1984, U.S. Supreme Ct. 1985. Engr. RKO Gen., WOR AM-FM-TV, N.Y.C., 1967-70; mgr., engr. Pub. Service Electric and Gas Co., Newark, 1977, mgr. telecommunications systems, 1977—; prosecutor Township of Springfield, N.J., 1982-85; chmn. Mcpl. Cable TV Adv. Com., Springfield, 1974-76. Trustee Stevens Inst. Tech., Hoboken, N.J., 1971-74, mem. presdl. search and selection com. 1974-75; lt. Police Res., Springfield, 1968—; mem. Gov's. Com. on Mgmt. Improvement, Trenton, N.J., 1982-83, Bd. Health, Springfield, 1986; committeeman Township Com. Governing Body, Springfield, 1985—. Named One of Outstanding Young Men of Am., U.S. Jaycees, 1971-73, Citizen of Yr., Springfield B'nai B'rith, 1976, Citizen of Yr., Policeman's Benevolent Assn. Local 76, Springfield, 1985. Mem. ABA, IEEE, Soc. Cable TV Engrs., N.J. State Bar Assn., Union County Bar Assn. Republican. Jewish. Avocations: amateur radio, running, photography. General practice, Computer, Criminal. Office: 182 Meisel Ave Springfield NJ 07081

KATZ, MARTHA LESSMAN, lawyer; b. Chgo., Oct. 28, 1952; d. Julius Abraham and Ida (Oiring) Lessman; m. Richard M. Katz, June 27, 1976; 1 child, Julia Erin. AB, Washington U., St. Louis, 1974; JD, Loyola U., Chgo., 1977. Bar: Ill. 1977, U.S. Dist. Ct. (no. dist.) Ill. 1977, Calif. 1981, U.S. Dist. Ct. (so. dist.) Calif. 1981, U.S. Dist. Ct. (no. dist.) Calif. 1982. Assoc. Fein & Hanfling, Chgo., 1977-80, Rudick, Platt & Victor, San Diego, 1981-82, 84—; asst. sec., counsel Itel Corp., San Francisco, 1982-84. Mem. ABA (corp. banking and bus. law, taxation sects.), Ill. Bar Assn., San Diego County Bar Assn., Lawyers Club San Diego, Phi Beta Kappa. Jewish. General corporate, Real property, Contracts commercial. Office: Rudick Platt & Victor 1770 4th Ave San Diego CA 92101

KATZ, MARVIN, federal judge; b. 1930. B.A., U. Pa., 1951; LL.B., Yale U., 1954. Sole practice 1954-77; asst. commnr. IRS, 1977-81; assoc. Mesirov, Gelman, Jaffe, Cramer & Jamieson, Phila., 1981-83; judge U.S. Dist. Ct. (ea. dist.), Phila., 1983—. Office: 3810 US Courthouse Independence Mall West 601 Market St Philadelphia PA 19106 *

KATZ, MAURICE HARRY, lawyer; b. N.Y.C., Jan. 18, 1937; s. Milton and Florence (Davies) K.; m. Margery Rosenberg, May 5, 1962; children: Brian, Bradley, Andrew. AB, Columbia U., 1958; JD, Harvard U., 1961. Bar: N.Y. 1962, Calif. 1963. Assoc. Loeb & Loeb, Los Angeles, 1962-64, Freshman, Marantz et al., Beverly Hills, Calif., 1964-66; ptnr. Grobe, Reinstein & Katz, Los Angeles, 1966-78; sole practice Los Angeles, 1978—; prof. law U. San Fernando, Los Angeles, 1965-76, U. W. Los Angeles, 1978-80; judge pro tem Beverly Hills Mcpl. Ct., 1978-86, Los Angeles Mcpl. Ct., 1985-87; hearing officer Los Angeles CSC, 1976-79. Program chmn. Am. Art Council, Los Angeles County Mus. Art, 1983-86; chmn. acquisition fine arts com. Skirball Mus., Hebrew Union Coll., Los Angeles, 1985-86. Served with USMCR, 1961-62. Mem. Los Angeles County Bar Assn., Century City Bar Assn., Beverly Hills Bar Assn., Wine and Food Soc. Hollywood (chmn. 1984-85), Phi Beta Kappa. General corporate, Consumer commercial, Estate planning.

KATZ, MELVIN SEYMOUR, lawyer; b. Hartford, Conn., June 1, 1915; s. Louis H. and Lena (Alpert) K.; m. Ruth Dobkin, Aug. 22, 1941; children—Linda Katz Kiner, Jane, Margery. B.A., Yale U., 1937, LL.B., 1940. Bar: Conn. 1940, U.S. Dist. Ct. Conn. 1951, U.S. Ct. Appeals (2d cir.) 1961. Ptnr. Levine & Katz, Hartford, Conn., 1940-41, 46-76, Schatz & Schatz, Ribicoff & Kotkin, Hartford, 1976—. Served to capt. U.S. Army, 1941-46. Fellow Am. Coll. Trial Lawyers; mem. ABA, Am. Judicature Soc. (bd. govs.), Am. Bd. Trial Advocates, Conn. Bar Assn., Hartford County Bar Assn., Assn. Trial Lawyers Am. (bd. govs.), Conn. Trial Lawyers Assn. (pres., bd. govs.). Jewish. State civil litigation, Federal civil litigation. Home: 40 Wiltshire Ln West Hartford CT 06117

KATZ, MICHAEL ALBERT, lawyer; b. Bklyn., May 8, 1942; s. Emanuel and Miriam (Fassler) K.; m. Marcia A. Potter, Feb. 18, 1979; 1 son, Nathaniel P. B.S., Bklyn. Coll., 1963; LL.B., NYU, 1966; LL.M., George Washington U., 1973. Bar: N.Y. 1966, D.C. 1970, Ill. 1976, U.S. Supreme Ct. 1975. Asst. U.S. atty. D.C., 1971-75; trial atty. United Airlines, Chgo., 1975-78, div. counsel eastern div., N.Y.C., 1978-81; counsel indsl. relations Trans World Airlines, Inc., N.Y.C., 1981-86; asst. gen. counsel, 1986—. Served to capt. JAGC, U.S. Army, 1967-71, now lt. col. Res. Decorated Bronze Star, Army Commendation medal with oak leaf cluster. Mem. ABA, Fed. Bar Assn., Judge Advs. Assn. Federal civil litigation, Labor, Military. Home: 7 Possum Way Murray Hill NJ 07974 Office: 605 3d Ave 43d Floor New York NY 10158

KATZ, MICHAEL JEFFERY, lawyer; b. Detroit, May 11, 1950; s. Wilfred Lester and Bernice (Ackerman) K. BE with honors, U. Mich., 1972; JD, U. Colo., 1976; cert., U. Denver Grad. Sch. Bus. and Pub. Mgmt., 1985. Bar: Colo. 1978. Research atty. immigration specialist Colo. Rural Legal Services, Denver, 1976-77, supervising atty. migrant farm lab., 1977-78, ind. contractor Colo. Sch. Fin., 1978-79; sole practice Denver, 1978—; lectr. on incorporating small bus. and real estate purchase agreements Front Rarye Coll., 1986—, real estate and landlord/tenant law, various seminars, 1980—; of counsel Levine & Pitler, P.C., Englewood, Colo., 1985—. Mem. Denver Bar Assn. (law day com. 1985—, real estate com. 1980—, pro bono services 1984—), Assn. Trial Lawyers Am. Club: Dillon Yacht (Colo.). Avocations: sailing, bicycling, swimming, art collecting, reading. Real property, General corporate, Contracts commercial. Office: 2303 E Dartmouth Englewood CO 80110

KATZ, MORTON HOWARD, lawyer; b. New Orleans, Feb. 5, 1945; s. David and Belle (Estes) K.; m. Carole Rae Deutch, Dec. 22, 1966; children: Brian David, Andrew Blair, Jonathan Ryan. BA, U. So. Miss., 1966; JD, Loyola U., New Orleans, 1969. Bar: La. 1969, U.S. Dist. Ct. (ea. dist.) La., U.S. Ct. Appeals (5th and 11th cirs.). Assoc. Law Offices of Ivor Trapolin, New Orleans, 1969-71, Herman & Herman, New Orleans, 1971-72; ptnr. Herman, Herman, Katz & Cotlar, New Orleans, 1972—. Prof. Jr. Achievemnt bd. dirs. assembly ctr. U. New Orleans, 1982—, Jewish Community Ctr., New Orleans, 1983—, New Orleans Alcohol Beverage & Control Bd., 1986—. Served to 2d Lt. USNG, 1969-74. Mem. Assn. Trial Lawyers Am. Democrat. Club: Endymion (New Orleans). Avocations: jogging, woodworking. Home: 5346 Prytania St New Orleans LA 70115 Office: Herman Herman Katz & Cotlar 820 O'Keefe Ave New Orleans LA 70113

KATZ, RICHARD W., lawyer; b. N.Y.C., Aug. 9, 1954; s. Walter M. and Trudy (Wellisch) K.; m. Ruth D. Perlman, May 1, 1983; 1 child, Emily. BA in History magna cum laude, Columbia U., 1976, JD, 1979. Bar: N.Y. 1980, U.S. Dist. Ct. (so. and ea. dists.) N.Y. 1980. Assoc. Ullman, Miller & Wrubel, P.C., N.Y.C., 1979-81, Demov, Morris & Hammerling, N.Y.C., 1981-87. Mem. ABA, N.Y. State Bar Assn., Assn. of Bar of City of N.Y., N.Y. County Lawyers Assn., Phi Beta Kappa. Jewish. General corporate, Contracts commercial, Banking. Home: 30 Madison Ave Rochelle Park NJ 07662

KATZ, ROBERT JAMES, lawyer; b. N.Y.C., Nov. 24, 1947; s. Seymour Milton and Naomi Bernice (Norek) K.; m. Jane Nan Lisman, Aug, 12, 1970; children: James Nicholas, Emily Austen. BA, Cornell U., 1969; JD magna cum laude, Harvard U., 1972; postdoctoral, London Sch. Econs., 1972-73. Bar: N.Y. 1973, U.S. Dist. Ct. (ea. and so. dists.) N.Y. 1973, U.S. Ct. Appeals (2d cir.) 1973, U.S. Supreme Ct. 1981. Law clk. to presiding justice U.S. Ct. Appeals (2d cir.), N.Y.C., 1973; assoc. Sullivan & Cromwell, N.Y.C., 1974-80, ptnr., 1980—. Mem. Cornell U. Council, Ithaca, N.Y., 1981-84. Knox fellow Harvard U., 1972. Mem. ABA, N.Y. State Bar Assn., Assn. of Bar of City of N.Y., Fed. Bar Council. Clubs: Cornell, Downtown Assn. (N.Y.C.). Federal civil litigation, Securities, Antitrust. Office: Sullivan & Cromwell 125 Broad St New York NY 10004

KATZ, ROBERT NATHAN, lawyer, educator; b. St. Joseph, Mo., Aug. 30, 1931; s. Phillip and Fannie Mae (Ginsberg) K.; m. Estelle Stern, Sept. 18, 1960; children—Leslie Rachael, Gary Alan, Rebecca Lynn. B.A., U. Tex.-Austin, 1953, J.D., 1955; M.B.A., Harvard U., 1960. Bar: Tex. 1955, Va. 1960, D.C. 1960, U.S. Supreme Ct. 1959, U.S. Ct. Appeals (D.C. cir.) 1961, U.S. Ct. Appeals (2d and 9th cirs.) 1966. Assoc. counsel Atlantic Research Corp., Alexandria, Va., 1961-62; sole practice, Washington, 1962-66; solicitor Fed. Maritime Commn., Washington, 1966-68; faculty U. Calif.-Berkeley, 1969-78; sole practice, Robert N. Katz, P.C., Berkeley, 1978—; adj. prof. Hastings Coll. Law, 1980—; vis. prof. Stanford U.Bus. Sch., 1978. Bd. dirs. Berkeley Stage Co., pres., 1980-81; mem. adv. council Lawrence Hall of Sci., 1980—. Mem. com. on study of intermodel transp. NSF, pub. contracts arbitration panel State of Calif. Served to lt. USAAF, 1955-57; with USN, 1959-61; to lt. col. USAFR, 1955-81. Mem. Berkeley C. of C. (dir. 1984—, v.p. 1986—). Democrat. Jewish. Club: Rotary (Berkeley). Author: Business Decision Making and Government Policy, 1966; Protecting Consumer Interest, 1976; editor Calif. Mgmt. Rev., 1969-82. Contracts commercial, Administrative and regulatory, General corporate. Home: 145 Poplar Berkeley CA 94708 Office: 2150 Shattuck Ave Berkeley CA 94704

KATZ, STANLEY HERBERT, lawyer; b. Balt., Dec. 6, 1948; s. Morris Jacob and Frances (Homel) K. B.A., U. Md., 1971; J.D., U. Balt., 1974; cert. Hague Acad. Internat. Law, 1972. Bar: U.S. Ct. Claims 1980, U.S. Supreme Ct. 1983. Assoc. atty. Bass & Denick, Balt., 1976-78; sole practice, Balt., 1978-79; assoc. Steinberg, Schlachman, Potler, Belsky and Weiner, P.A., Balt., 1979-85; staff atty. Alexander & Alexander, Inc., 1985-86; assoc. atty. Joel L. Katz, P.A., Annapolis, Md., 1986—; pub. defender panel atty., 1976-79. Legal commentator Lawyers Row, weekly talk show KBL-TV Channel 10, Baltimore County, Md., 1983. Patentee coin tray. Served with U.S. Army, 1969. Mem. ABA, Assn. Trial Lawyers Am., Md. State Bar Assn., D.C. Bar Assn., Balt. Council on Fgn. Affairs. Democrat. Jewish. Consumer commercial, State civil litigation, Criminal. Home: 9 Silverwood Circle #5 Annapolis MD 21403 Office: Joel L Katz PA 2444 Solomons Island Rd Annapolis MD 21401

KATZ, STANLEY NIDER, history-law educator, association executive; b. Chgo., Apr. 23, 1934; s. William Stephen and Florence (Nider) K.; m. Adria Holmes, Jan. 16, 1960; children: Derek Holmes, Marion Holmes. AB, Harvard U., 1955, MA, 1959, PhD, 1961; LLD (hon.), Stockton State Coll., 1981. Asst. prof. history Harvard U., 1961-65, U. Wis., Madison, 1965-71; prof. legal history U. Chgo., 1971-78; Class of 1921 Bicentennial prof. history Am. law and liberty Princeton U., 1978-86; pres. Am. Council Learned Socs., 1986—; vis. prof. law U. Pa., 1978-86; mem. Oliver Wendell Holmes Devise, Washington, 1976—; bd. govs. Inst. European Studies, Chgo., 1976—; chmn. Council on Internat. Exchange Scholars, Washington, 1981-85; mem. N.J. Supreme Ct. Com. on Model Rules of Profl. Conduct, 1982-83; vice chmn. ABA Comm. on Undergrad. Edn. in Law and Humnaities, 1977-81. Author: Newcastle's New York, 1968; editor: The Case and Tryal of John Peter Zenger, 1963 (rev. edit. 1972), Oliver Wendell Holmes Devise History of U.S. Supreme Ct., 1977—; co-editor: Colonial America, 1971, 76, 83, Am. History: Promise and Progress, 1983. Mem. N.J. Com. for Humanities, 1978-84. Mem. Am. Soc. Legal History (pres. 1978-81), Inst. Early Am. History and Culture (council 1974-76), Orgn. Am. Historians (exec. com. 1976-79, pres. elect 1986-87, pres. 1987-88), Am. Antiquarian Soc., Fed. Dist. Ct. N.J. Hist. Soc. (trustee 1986—), Phi Beta Kappa. Democrat. Jewish. Clubs: Quadrangle (Chgo.); Princeton (N.Y.C.). Legal history, Legal education. Office: Am Council Learned Socs 228 E 45th St New York NY 10017

KATZ, STEVEN MARTIN, lawyer, accountant; b. Washington, Feb. 8, 1941; s. Joseph and Pauline (Weinberg) K.; m. Lauri Gail Berman, Aug. 23, 1964; children—Benjamin, Aaron, Rebecca, Joshua. BS, U. Md., College Park, 1962; JD, George Washington U., 1965. Bar: D.C. 1966, Md. 1971; CPA Md. Ptnr., Euzent, Katz & Katz, Washington, 1966-69; sole practice, Washington, 1969-72; sr. ptnr. Katz, Frome Slan & Bleecker, P.A., and predecessors, Kensington, Md., 1972—. Mem. Md. Bar Assn., Md. Assn. of CPA's, Montgomery County Bar Assn. Jewish. General corporate, Probate. Office: 10605 Concord St Suite 300 Kensington MD 20895

KATZ, STUART CHARLES, lawyer, concert jazz musician; b. Chgo., June 9, 1937; s. Jerome H. and Sylvia L. (Singer) K.; m. Penny Schatz, Jan. 23, 1959; children—Steven, Lauren. B.A., Roosevelt U., Chgo., 1959; J.D. with distinction John Marshall Law Sch., 1964. Bar: Ill. 1964, U.S. Dist. Ct. (no. dist.) Ill. 1965, U.S. Supreme Ct. 1967; lic. real estate broker, Ill., Minn., Pa., Ohio, Va., Ky., Wis. Assoc. Raymond I. Suekoff, Chgo., 1964-67; ptnr. Yacker & Katz, Chgo., 1967-70; spl. in-house counsel Salk, Ward & Salk, Inc., Chgo., 1970-72; exec. v.p., gen. counsel Heitman Fin. Services Ltd., Chgo., 1972—; lectr. Internat. Council Shopping Ctrs., U.S. Law Conf., World Trade Inst. seminars on Fgn. Investment in U.S. Real Estate; jazz pianist and vibraphonist, appeared in concerts with Benny Goodman, Gene Krupa, Bud Freeman. Adv. bd. dirs. Jazz Inst. Chgo., 1979—. Mem. ABA, Chgo. Bar Assn., Ill. Bar Assn. Jewish. Real property, Contracts commercial. Office: Suite 3600 180 N LaSalle St Chicago IL 60601

KATZ, SUSAN STANTON, lawyer, consultant; b. Oil City, Pa., July 14, 1951; d. Alfred Bernard and Dorothy (Fell) Stanton; m. William Katz, Mar. 27, 1977; 1 child, Curren Elizabeth. BSN, Youngstown State U., 1971, BS, 1975; JD, U. Akron, 1978. Bar: Ohio 1979, U.S. Dist. Ct. (no. dist.) Ohio 1979; RN, Ohio. Nurse intensive care Youngstown Hosp. Assn., Ohio, 1971-75; assoc. Andrews, Kurth, Campbell & Jones, Houston, 1978-79; assoc. Harrington, Huxley & Smith, Youngstown, 1979-85, ptnr., 1986—; mem. instl. rev. bd. Youngstown Hosp. Assn., 1979—; consultant health care law Western Res. Care System, Youngstown, 1979—, bio-ethics com., 1985—. Mem. Youngstown Jewish Community Ctr., Leadership Youngstown; bd. dirs. Western Res. Care System Women's Bd., Western Res. Ballet. Mem. ABA, Ohio Bar Assn., Mahoning County Bar Assn. (chmn. med.-legal com. 1985—), Trumbull County Bar Assn., Soc. Ohio Hosp. Attys., Def. Research Inst., Ohio Civil Trial Lawyers Assn., Am. Arbitration Assn., Nat. Council of Jewish Women, Youngstown C. of C. (investor), Youngstown Jr. League (bd. dirs. 1985—, adminstrv. v.p. 1986-87). Club: Youngstown. Avocations: horses, fox hunting. Health, Insurance. Office: Harrington Huxley & Smith 1200 Mahoning Bank Bldg Youngstown OH 44425

KATZEN, SALLY, lawyer, former government official; b. Pitts., Nov. 22, 1942; d. Nathan and Hilda (Schwartz) K.; m. Timothy B. Dyk, Oct. 31, 1981; 1 child, Abraham Benjamin. B.A. magna cum laude, Smith Coll., 1964; J.D. magna cum laude, U. Mich., 1967. Bar: D.C. 1968, U.S. Supreme Ct. 1971. Congl. intern Sente Subcom. on Constl. Rights, Washington, summer 1963; legal research asst. civil rights div. Dept. Justice, Washington, summer 1965; law clk. to judge U.S. Ct. Appeals (D.C. cir.), 1967-68; assoc. Wilmer, Cutler & Pickering, Washington, 1968-74, ptnr., 1975-79, 81—; gen. counsel Council on Wage and Price Stability, 1979-80, dep. dir., 1980-81; mem. Jud. Conf. for D.C. Circuit, 1972-81, 83-86. Editor-in-chief U. Mich. Law Rev., 1966-67. Mem. com. visitors U. Mich. Law Sch., 1972-87. Mem. ABA (ho. of dels. 1978-80, council adminstrv. law sect. 1979-82; governing com. forum com. communications law 1979-82), D.C. Bar Assn., FCC Bar Assn. (exec. com. 1984-87), Women's Legal Def. Fund (pres. 1977, v.p. 1978), Order of Coif. Administrative and regulatory, Communications. Home: 4638 30th St NW Washington DC 20008 Office: 2445 M St NW Washington DC 20037

KATZENSTEIN, CHARLES BERNARD, lawyer; b. Bklyn., Apr. 3, 1952; s. Leon and Ruth (Deutscher) K. BA, Queens Coll., 1974; JD, Bklyn. Law Sch., 1979. Bar: N.Y. 1980, U.S. Dist. Ct. (ea. and so. dists.) N.Y. 1980. Assoc. Thacher Proffitt & Wood, N.Y.C., 1979-81, Demov, Morris et al, N.Y.C., 1981-83, Kramer, Levin, Nessen, Kamin, Fraskel, N.Y.C., 1983—; lectr. NYU, N.Y.C., 1986—. Mem. ABA, N.Y. Bar Assn. Real property, Banking. Home: 95 W 95th St New York NY 10025 Office: Kramer Levin et al 919 Third Ave New York NY 10022

KATZENSTEIN, LAWRENCE P., lawyer; b. Salem, Ill., Nov. 18, 1947; s. Friedrich C. and Mary (Sweed) K. AB, Washington U., St. Louis, 1969; JD, Harvard U., 1972. Bar: Mo. 1972. From assoc. to ptnr. Husch, Eppenberger, Donohue, Cornfeld & Jenkins, St. Louis, 1972—. Mem. ABA (chmn. com. on income of estates and trusts tax sect.), ACLU (eastern Mo. affiliate, pres. 1985—). Jewish. Avocation: classical music, hiking. Estate taxation, Personal income taxation, Charitable and deferred giving. Home: 7101 Delmar Blvd Saint Louis MO 63130 Office: Husch Eppenberger Donohue et al 100 N Broadway Suite 1800 Saint Louis MO 63102

KATZMANN, GARY STEPHEN, lawyer; b. N.Y.C., Apr. 22, 1953; s. John and Sylvia (Butner) K. AB summa cum laude, Columbia U., 1973; MLitt, Oxford U., 1976; MPPM, JD, Yale U., 1979. Bar: Mass. 1982, U.S. Dist. Ct. Mass. 1983, U.S. Ct. Appeals (1st cir.) 1983, D.C. 1984, U.S. Ct. Appeals (2d cir.) 1987. Law clk. to judge U.S. Dist. Ct. (so. dist.) N.Y., N.Y.C., 1979-80, U.S. Ct. Appeals (1st cir.), 1980-81; research assoc. ctr. criminal justice Harvard U. Law Sch., Cambridge, Mass., 1981-83; chief appellate atty., asst. U.S. atty. U.S. Atty.'s Office, Mass., 1983—. Editor law jour. Yale U. Mem. ABA, Phi Beta Kappa. Criminal, Federal prosecution. Office: US Attys Office 1107 JW McCormack POCH Boston MA 02109

KATZMANN, ROBERT ALLEN, legal educator, political scientist; b. N.Y.C., Apr. 22, 1953; s. John and Sylvia Edith (Butner) K. AB summa cum laude, Columbia U., 1973; MA in Govt., Harvard U., 1975, PhD in Govt., 1978; JD, Yale U., 1980. Bar: Mass. 1982, U.S. Ct. Appeals (1st cir.) 1983, D.C. 1984, U.S. Dist. Ct. Mass. 1984. Law clk. to judge U.S. Ct. Appeals (1st cir.), Concord, N.H., 1980-81; research assoc. Brookings Instn., Washington, 1981-85, sr. fellow, 1985—; adj. prof. law, pub. policy Georgetown U., Washington, 1984—. Author: Regulatory Bureaucracy: The Federal Trade Commission and Antitrust Policy, 1980, Institutional Disability, 1986; article and book editor Yale U. Law Rev., 1979-80. Pres. Governance Inst., Washington, 1986—. Mem. ABA, Am. Polit. Sci. Assn., Assn. Pub. Policy Analysis and Mgmt., Phi Beta Kappa. Administrative and regulatory, Judicial administration, Legislative. Home: 1400 20th St Apt 717 NW Washington DC 20036 Office: Brookings Instn 1775 Massachusetts Ave NW Govtl Studies Program Washington DC 20036

KAUFFMAN, ALAN CHARLES, lawyer; b. Atlantic City, Aug. 12, 1939; s. Joseph Bernard and Lilyan (Abraham) K.; children—Julie Beth, Debra Amy, Stacy, Sloane; m. 2d, Ronnie Ellen Trout, May 27, 1979. A.B., Rutgers U., 1961; J.D., Villanova U., 1964. Bar: Pa. 1964, U.S. Ct. Appeals (3d cir.) 1965, U.S. Dist. Ct. (ea. dist.) Pa. 1965, U.S. Supreme Ct. 1968. Law clk. Ct. Common Pleas Phila., 1964-65; ptnr. Obermayer, Rebmann, Maxwell & Hippel, Phila., 1965-77, Dilworth, Paxson, Kalish & Kauffman, Phila., 1977-87, Ruden, Barnett, McClosky, Smith, Schuster & Russell, Boca Raton, Fla., 1987—. Trustee Phila. Bar Found.; co-counsel Palm Beach (Fla.) County Devel. Bd.; mem. exec. com. Fight for Sight Greater Phila., fund raising campaign dir.; mem. fund raising com. Children's Hosp.; bd. dirs. Mimi Barrett Found. for Brain Tumor Research, Boca Raton Symphonic Pops, Am. Diabetic Assn., Fla. Victory Com.; chmn. Tay Sachs Adv. Bd.; mem. adv. bd. Fla. Atlantic U.; mem. Police Pension Bd. Lower Merion Twp., Internat. Bd. Weizmann Inst. Friends of Phila. Mus. Art., Nat. Rep. Senatorial Inner Circle. Mem. ABA, Pa. Bar Assn., Phila. Bar Assn. (exec. com. Young Lawyers Sect., bd. govs.), Assn. Trial Lawyers Am., Pa. Trial Lawyers Assn., Fla. Bar Assn., Palm Beach County Bar Assn., Phila. Trial Lawyers Assn., Comml. Law League Am. (com. on bankruptcy). Jewish. Clubs: Locust (Phila.), Green Valley Country, St. Andrews Country, Boca Beach. Antitrust, Federal civil litigation, State civil litigation. Home: 17169 Whitehaven Rd Boca Raton FL 33432 Office: 5355 Town Ctr Rd Crocker Plaza Suite 1105 Boca Raton FL 33432

KAUFFMAN, BRUCE WILLIAM, state supreme ct. justice; b. Atlantic City, Dec. 1, 1934; s. Joseph Bernard and Lilyan (Abraham) K.; m. Rita Marie Wisneski, Dec. 31, 1971; children—Bradley Leonard, Marjorie Beth, Robert Andrew, Lauri Ann, Christine Lynne. B.A., U. Pa., 1956; LL.B., Yale, 1959. Bar: N.J. bar 1960, Pa. bar 1961, U.S. Supreme Ct. bar 1965. Law clk. to judge N.J. Superior Ct., Trenton, 1959-60; asso. firm Dilworth, Paxson, Kalish, Levy & Kauffman, Phila., 1960-65; partner Dilworth, Paxson, Kalish, Levy & Kauffman, 1966-80, chmn. litigation dept., 1975-80; justice Supreme Ct. of Pa., 1980—; mem. com. of censors U.S. Dist. Ct., Eastern Pa., 1976-80; del. Pa. Constl. Conv., 1967-68; chmn. Montgomery County Govt. Study Commn., 1973-74; mem. Civil Service Commn., Lower Merion Twp., 1978-80, 82—, chmn., 1985—; mem. adv. com. to U.S. Commn. on Civil Rights, 1985—; pres. Merion Park Civic Assn., 1966-68; vice chmn. Jud. Inquiry and Rev. Bd., 1984. Trustee Phil. Coll. Art; bd. dirs. Alzheimer's Disease and Related Disorders Assns., Inc. Fellow Am. Coll. Trial Lawyers, Am. Law Inst.; mem. Am., Pa., Phila. bar assns., Am. Judicature Soc., Juristic Soc., Lawyers' Club Phila., Yale Law Sch. Assn. (v.p. 1985), Pa. Soc., USCG Aux., Pi Sigma Alpha, Phi Gamma Mu, Phi Beta Kappa, Order of Coif. Clubs: Union League, Locust, Yale. Antitrust, Federal civil litigation, State civil litigation. Office: 2600 Fidelity Bldg Philadelphia PA 19109

KAUFMAN, ALBERT I., lawyer; b. N.Y.C., Oct. 2, 1936; s. Israel and Pauline (Pardes) K.; m. Ruth Feldman, Jan. 25, 1959; 1 son, Michael Paul. A.A., Los Angeles City Coll., 1957; B.A., U. San Fernando Valley, 1964, J.D., 1966. Bar: Calif. 1967, U.S. Ct. Appeals (9th cir.) 1968, U.S. Supreme Ct. 1971, U.S. Dist. Ct. (cen. dist.) Calif. 1967, U.S. Tax Ct. 1971, U.S. Ct. Internat. Trade 1981. Sole practice, Encino, Calif., 1967—; judge pro tem Los Angeles Mcpl. Ct., 1980—; family law mediator Los Angeles Superior Ct., 1980—. Mem. Pacific S.W. regional bd. Anti-Defamation league of B'nai B'rith. Served with USAF, 1959-65, to lt. col. CAP, 1956—. Recipient Disting. service award B'nai B'rith, 1969; Exceptional Service award CAP, 1977. Mem. ABA, Los Angeles County Bar Assn., San Fernando Valley Bar Assn., Calif. Trial Lawyers Assn., Los Angeles Trial Lawyers Assn. Republican. Clubs: Toastmasters, Westerners 1117 (pres. 1969), B'nai B'rith (pres. 1971-72). Personal injury, Family and matrimonial, Civil rights. Office: 17609 Ventura Blvd Suite 201 Encino CA 91316

KAUFMAN, ANDREW MICHAEL, lawyer; b. Boston, Feb. 19, 1949; s. Earle Bertram and Miriam (Halpern) K.; m. Michele Moselle, Aug. 24, 1975; children: Peter Moselle, Melissa Lanes, Caroline Raney. BA cum laude, Yale U., 1971; JD, Vanderbilt U., 1974. Bar: Tex. 1974, Ga. 1976, U.S. Ct. Appeals (5th and 11th cirs.) 1981. Assoc. Vinson & Elkins, Houston, 1974-76, ptnr., 1982-83; ptnr. Vinson & Elkins, Austin, 1983—; assoc. Sutherland, Asbill & Brennan, Atlanta, 1976-80, ptnr., 1980-81. Editor in chief Vanderbilt U. Law Rev., 1973-74. Fund raiser alumni fund Yale U., 1971—, alumni schs. com., 1986—; div. chmn. United Way, Austin, 1986, mem. allocations com. 1987—; bd. dirs. Austin chpt. Orton Dyslexia Soc., Austin, 1986—, Austin Ballet, 1987—. Mem. ABA (small bus. com. corps. banking and bus. law sect. 1978—, sec. 1981-85), Tex. Bar Assn., Yale U. Alumni Assn. (schs. com. 1986—), Austin C. of C. (county budget rev. com. 1985—), Order of Coif. Clubs: Headliners, University, Yale (Austin). Avocation: sailing. Banking, General corporate, Real property. Office: Vinson & Elkins First City Centre 816 Congress Ave Austin TX 78701-2496

KAUFMAN, BRUCE ERIC, judge; b. Anderson, Ind., Nov. 28, 1929; s. Arthur Dale and Ann M. (Hermanscn) K.; m. Hazel Gordon; children: Robert, Jaclyn. AB, DePauw U., 1951; JD, U. Chgo., 1956. Bar: Ill. 1957, N.Mex. 1972, U.S. Supreme Ct. 1973. Asst. atty. gen. State of Ill., Springfield, 1956-57; assoc. Dixon & Seidenfield, Waukegan, Ill., 1957-60; ptnr. Kaufman, Strouse, Wasneski & Yastrow, 1961-68; chief dep. dist. atty. State of N.Mex., Santa Fe, 1973-75, asst. atty. gen., 1975-77, dist. ct. judge, 1977—; past. chief legal advisor N.Mex. State Police; past instr. N.Mex. Law Enforcement Acad. Served to capt. USMC, 1948-62. Mem. ABA (past vice chmn. com. on implementation of justice standards and goals, past regional rep. criminal justice ethics com.), N.Mex. Bar Assn., 1st Dist. Bar Assn. Democrat. Methodist. Judicial administration. Home: PO Box 1555 Santa Fe NM 87504 Office: NMex Dist Ct PO Box 2268 Santa Fe NM 87504

KAUFMAN, DAVID J., lawyer; b. Harrisburg, Pa., Apr. 7, 1931; s. S. Herbert and Bessie (Claster) K.; m. Virginia Stern, Aug. 30, 1959; children: David J. Jr., James H. BS in Econs. cum laude, Franklin and Marshall Coll., 1952; JD cum laude, U. Pa., 1955. Bar: Pa. 1955. First assoc., then ptnr. Wolf, Block, Schorr & Solis-Cohen, Phila., 1957—. Bd. dirs. Abington (Pa.) Mem. Hosp., 1981—; pres. Congregation Rodeph Shalom, Phila., 1983-86. Served with U.S. Army, 1955-57. Fellow Am. Coll. Probate Counsel; mem. Pa. Bar Assn. (chmn. real property, probate & trust sect. 1986-87), Phila. Bar Assn. (chmn. probate sect. 1977). Republican. Club: Locust (Phila.). Estate planning, Probate, Estate taxation. Home: 2191 Paper Mill Rd Huntingdon Valley PA 19006 Office: Wolf Block Schorr & Solis-Cohen 1200 Packard Bldg Philadelphia PA 19102

KAUFMAN, FRANK ALBERT, U.S. district judge; b. Balt., Mar. 4, 1916; s. Nathan Hess and Hilda (Hecht) K.; m. Clementine Alice Lazaron, Apr. 22, 1945; children: Frank Albert, Peggy Ann (Mrs. Fred Wolf III). A.B. summa cum laude, Dartmouth Coll., 1937; LL.B. magna cum laude, Harvard U., 1940; LL.D. (hon.), U. Balt., 1984. Bar: Md. 1940. Atty. Offices Gen. Counsel Treasury, Lend Lease Adminstrn. and FEA, 1941-42, 45; lend lease rep. Turkey, 1942-43; bur. chief Psychol. Warfare Allied Forces Hdqrs. and SHAEF, 1943-45; assoc. firm Frank, Bernstein, Conaway, Kaufman & Goldman (and predecessor), Balt., 1945-47; ptnr. Frank, Bernstein, Conaway, Kaufman & Goldman (and predecessor), 1948-66; U.S. dist. judge Md., 1966—; lectr. U. Balt., 1948-62, U. Md., 1953-54. Mem. Gov. Md. Commns. Mgmt. and Labor Relations, 1960, Uniform Comml. Code, 1961, Health Problems, 1968; chmn. Gov. Md. Commn. Study Sentencing Criminal Cases, 1962-66; bd. dirs. Am. Jewish Com., 1960-70, Balt. chpt., 1948-70, Goucher Coll., 1957-85, Md. Inst. Coll. Art, 1956-81, Park Sch., Balt., 1956-66, Sinai Hosp. Balt., 1957-75, Balt. chpt. NCCJ, 1950's, Balt Hebrew Congregation, 1940's, 50's, Balt. Jewish Council, 1954-66, Jewish Family and Children's Service, Balt., 1946-54; Assoc. Jewish Charities and Welfare Fund, 1953-54, Jewish Welfare Bd., 1965-67, Md. Partners of Alliance, 1965-72, Good Samaritan Hosp., Balt., 1967-73, Johns Hopkins Hosp. Nat. Forum on Medicine, 1983—, Harvard Law Sch. Assn. and Fund, 1954-60's. Mem. ABA (gov. 1982-85), Fed., Md., Balt. bar assns., Am. Law Inst., Am. Judicature Soc. (bd. dirs. 1985—), Harvard Law Sch. Assn. Md., Order of Coif, Phi Beta Kappa. Jewish (dir. congregation 1947-48, 60-62). Clubs: Suburban (dir. 1941-42, 53-60, pres. 1956-60), Rule Day, Wranglers, Law Roundtable, Hamilton Street (Balt.). Jurisprudence. Office: US Court House Baltimore MD 21201

KAUFMAN, IRA GLADSTONE, judge; b. N.Y.C., Dec. 13, 1909; s. Joseph and Esther K.; m. Lillian Kaufman, June 25, 1939; children—Harvey David, Sylvia Kaufman Delin. BS, NYU, 1933, JD, 1936; BSc in Bus. Adminstrn. (hon.), Cleary Coll., Ypsilanti, Mich., 1976. Bar: Mich. 1939. Sole practice, Detroit, 1939-59; judge of probate Wayne County Probate Ct., Detroit, 1958—, presiding judge, 1962-63, 66-67, 72-73, 77-85; chief judge pro tem Wayne County Probate and Juvenile Ct., 1981-85; Moot Ct. judge U. Detroit, 1966-72; lectr. Life pres. Adat Shalom Synagogue; trustee Children's Hosp. of Detroit, chmn. devel., 1980-83, hon. chmn. ann. concert 1983, chmn. ad hoc com. alcoholism Detroit United Communities Services, 1967-68; chmn. Detroit Com. Fgn. Relations, 1974-76, Mental Health Com., 1960-70; trustee Mich. Cancer Found., 1973; trustee Detroit Inst. Tech., 1962, Park Community Com., 1979; pres. Inter-Agy. Council on Alcoholism, 1957; pres., chmn. bd. Met. Soc. for Blind, 1966-70, bd. dirs., 1960—; mem. Gov.'s Com. Mental Health Statute Rev. Commn., 1970-72, Mich. Soc. Mental Health, 1960—; hon. mem. Children's Charter Mich., 1965—; exec. bd. League Handicapped-Goodwill 1970—; bd. overseers Dropsie Coll., 1973-75; bd. dirs. Hebrew Free Loan Soc. Detroit, Jewish Nat. Fund Bd.; v.p. United Hebrew Schs. Detroit, 1947-58; founding sec. Midrasha Coll. Hebrew Studies, 1948-58; nominating com. Mich. Cancer Found. Mem. Mich. Probate and Juvenile Ct. Assn. (exec. bd. 1969-72, pres. 1970-71), Mich. Bar Assn., Detroit Bar Assn., Fed. Bar Assn., ABA, U.S. Air Force Assn. (ann. installing officer 1983-84). Clubs: B'nai B'rith (hon. pres. Tikvah Lodge 1974), Masons (33 deg.; sovereign prince), Shriners. Contbr. biog. sketches of Mich. judges to Jewish Hist. Soc. publ., 1983-84. Address: 7409 Locklin Rd Union Lake MI 48085

KAUFMAN, IRVING ROBERT, federal judge; b. N.Y.C., June 24, 1910; s. Herman and Rose (Spielberg) K.; m. Helen Ruth Rosenberg; children: James Michael, Richard Kenneth. LLB, Fordham U., 1931; LLD, Jewish Theol. Sem. Am., Fordham U., Oklahoma City U.; LittD (hon.), Dickinson Sch. Law; DCL (hon.), NYU. Bar: N.Y. 1932. Spl. asst. to U.S. Atty., So. Dist. N.Y.; asst. U.S. Atty.; spl. asst. to Atty. Gen. U.S. charge of lobbying investigation; established permanent lobbying unit for Dept. Justice; individual practice law N.Y.C.; partner firm Noonan, Kaufman and Eagan; U.S. dist. judge So. Dist. N.Y., 1949-61; circuit judge U.S. Ct. Appeals (2d. circuit), 1961—, chief judge, 1973-80; U.S. del. to 2d UN Congress Prevention Crime and Treatment Offenders, Conf. Anglo-Am. Legal Exchange, Ditchley, Eng., 1969, 77, 80; mem. exec. com. U.S. Jud. Conf., 1975-80, mem. com. standards jud. conduct, chmn. com. operation jury system, 1966-73, chmn. com. jud. branch, 1979-83; chmn. Pres.'s Commn. on Organized Crime, 1983-86. Contbr. articles to profl. jours. Trustee Mt. Sinai Med. Center, Mt. Sinai Med. Sch., Mt. Sinai Hosp.; trustee emeritus Riverdale Country Sch. Recipient Achievement in Law award Fordham Coll. Alumni Assn.; Encaenia award Fordham Coll.; Chief Justice Harlan Fiske Stone award Assn. Trial Lawyers City N.Y. Fellow Inst. Jud. Adminstrn. (Silver Anniversary Vanderbilt award, pres. 1969-71, chmn. exec. com., chmn. juvenile justice standards project); mem. ABA, Fed. bAr Assn., N.Y. Bar Assn., Assn. Bar City N.Y. (Cardozo lectr.), Am. Judicature Soc. (Herbert Harley award 1980), Am. Law Inst., Fordham Law Alumni Assn. (bd. dirs.), Tau Epsilon Phi (Man of Year citation), Phi Alpha Delta. Jurisprudence. Office: US Courthouse Foley Sq New York NY 10007

KAUFMAN, JAMES MARK, lawyer; b. Oklahoma City, Feb. 28, 1951; s. Milford James and Frances Aileen (Knight) K.; m. Vicki Jane Johnston, Aug. 18, 1973 (div. June 1985); m. Katheryn Ann Kidd, Nov. 29, 1985; children—Nathan Jay, Kaitlin Ann, Jordan Paige. B.B.A., U. Okla., 1973, J.D., 1976. Bar: Okla. Supreme Ct. 1976, U.S. Dist. Ct. (we. dist.) Okla. 1976, U.S. Ct. Appeals (10th cir.) 1977, U.S. Supreme Ct. 1983. Intern, assoc. Carson-Trattner, Oklahoma City, 1975-77; assoc. firm Cheek, Cheek & Cheek, Oklahoma City, 1977-81, McKinney, Stringer & Webster, Oklahoma City, 1981-84; mem. firm Kaufman & Cheek, Oklahoma City, 1984—. Mem. Okla. Bar Assn., Oklahoma County Bar Assn., ABA, Def. Research Inst., Sigma Chi. Insurance, Personal injury, State civil litigation. Home: 1000 Stonehenge Dr Edmond OK 73034 Office: Kaufman & Cheek 3030 Northwest Hwy Suite 1511 Oklahoma City OK 73112

KAUFMAN, JOSHUA JACOB, lawyer, editor; b. N.Y.C., Oct. 31, 1950; s. Jay Herbert and Aviva (Goodman) K.; m. Nan Ellin Kaufman, July 12, 1980; children: Jay Laurence, Aaron Michael. BA, U. Md., 1972; JD, George Washington U., 1975. Bar: Md. 1977, D.C. 1978, Fed. Dist. Ct. 1978, U.S. Tax Ct. 1981, U.S. Ct. Claims 1981, N.Y. 1983. Ptnr. Lowe, Bressler & Kaufman, Washington, 1978-83; ptnr. Kaufman & Biel, P.C., Washington, 1984-86, Goldfarb & Singer, Washington, 1986—; legal editor EDP News Service, Washington, 1981—; exec. dir. Vol. Lawyers for Arts, Washington, 1977—; nat. rep. Am. Guild Musical Artists, Washington, 1982—. Author: Art of Investing in Art, 1980; columnist Aura Mag., 1980, Washington Lawyer mag., 1986—; contbr. articles to profl. jours. Co-dir. City Council Task Force on Cable Regulation, 1974-75. Mem. Computer Law Forum, Computer Law Assn., ABA (young lawyers sect., forum on Entertainment and Sports Industries, subcom. on copyright, various other sects.). Democrat. Jewish. Entertainment, General practice, Computer. Office: Goldfarb & Singer 918 16th St NW #503 Washington DC 20006

KAUFMAN, LISA NADINE, lawyer; b. Jacksonville, Fla., Sept. 7, 1953; d. Fred Robert and Faye Leah (Morgenstern) K. BA with distinction, Ind. U., 1975; JD, U. Fla., 1978. Bar: Fla. 1978, D.C. 1981, Mo. 1985, U.S. Dist. Ct. (mid. dist.) Fla., U.S. Ct. Appeals (D.C. cir.). Assoc. U.S. Patent and Trademark Office, Washington, 1979-84, Ralston Purina Co., St. Louis, 1984—. Fin. sec. No. Va. Hadassah-Einsof Group, Arlington, 1982, 83. Mem. D.C. Bar Assn. (trademark com.), Bar Assn. Met. St. Louis, U.S. Trademark Assn., Nat. Council Jewish Women (program com. mem. bus. and profl. sect. 1985-86), Phi Beta Kappa. Avocations: dance (ballet, tap, jazz), traveling. Trademark and copyright. Home: 9116 Eager Rd Saint Louis MO 63144 Office: Ralston Purina Co Checkerboard Sq Saint Louis MO 63164

KAUFMAN, PHYLLIS CYNTHIA, lawyer, author, theatrical producer; b. Phila., Nov. 4, 1945; d. Harry and Gertrude (Friend) K. BA cum laude, Brandeis U., 1967; JD, Temple U., 1974. Bar: Pa. 1974, U.S. Dist. Ct. (ea. dist.) Pa. 1974. Sole practice entertainment law, Phila., 1977—; exec. producer Playhouse in the Park, Phila., 1979; dir. entertainment Caesar's Hotel-Casino, Atlantic City, N.J., 1980-81; v.p. entertainment Sands Hotel-Casino, Atlantic City, 1981-83; v.p. Kanadus Entertainment Inc., Toronto, 1982—. Co-author: No-Nonsense Financial, Real Estate and Legal Guides, 1985—; assoc. editor Temple Law Quarterly. Bd. dirs. Phila. Coll. Performing Arts, 1977-85, Creative Artists Network, 1986—. Ford Found. grantee, 1965-67. Mem. Phila. Bar Assn. Democrat. Entertainment. Office: 1500 Locust St Suite 3805 Philadelphia PA 19102

KAUFMAN, ROSALIND FUCHSBERG, lawyer; b. Bklyn., Feb. 1, 1939; d. Jacob D. and Shirley G. (Cohen) Fuchsberg; m. Richard H. Kaufman, June 15, 1958; children: Gale, Michael, Diana. AB, Brandeis U., 1959; JD, NYU, 1977. Bar: N.Y. 1978, U.S. Dist. Ct. (ea. and so. dists.) N.Y. 1978, U.S. Ct. Appeals (2d cir.) 1979. Assoc. Berlack, Israels & Liberman, N.Y.C., 1978-82, Debevoise & Liberman, N.Y.C., 1982-83; ptnr. The Jacob D. Fuchsberg Law Firm, N.Y.C., 1983—. Pres. Hadassah, New Rochelle, N.Y., 1967-69, Solomon Schechter Sch. of Westchester PTA, White Plains, N.Y., 1970-72. Mem. Assn. of Bar of City of N.Y. (products liability com.), N.Y. State Bar Assn. (legis. com.). Personal injury, State civil litigation, Federal civil litigation. Office: The Jacob D Fuchsberg Law Firm 500 Fifth Ave New York NY 10110

KAUFMAN, STEPHEN E., lawyer; b. N.Y.C., Feb. 16, 1932; s. Herbert and Gertrude Kaufman; m. Marina Pinto, June 22, 1967; children: Andrew H. and Douglas P. BA, Williams Coll., 1953; LLB, Columbia U., 1957. Bar: N.Y. 1958, U.S. Ct. Appeals (2d cir.) 1958, U.S. Dist. Ct. (so. and ea. dists.) N.Y. 1960, U.S. Supreme Ct. 1963. Asst. U.S. Atty. U.S. Attys. Office, So. Dist., N.Y., 1964-69, chief of criminal div., 1964-69; pres. Stephen E. Kaufman, P.C., N.Y.C., 1976—; bd. dirs. Mich. Energy Resources, Monroe, U.N.A. Corp., Boston, Shearson High Yield Fund Inc., Shearson Govt. and Agys. Inc., Shearson Daily Dividend Inc. and other Shearson funds. Bd. dirs. Trinity Sch., N.Y.C., Police Athletic League, N.Y.C. Mem. ABA, N.Y. State Bar Assn., Am. Coll. Trial Lawyers, Assn. of Bar of City of N.Y. Criminal, Federal civil litigation, State civil litigation. Office: 277 Park Ave New York NY 10172

KAUFMAN, STEVEN MICHAEL, lawyer; b. Spokane, Wash., July 2, 1951; s. Gordon Leonard and Terri (Thal) K.; m. Connie Hoopes, June 7, 1973; children—Kristopher, Shana. B.S. magna cum laude, U. Utah, 1973; J.D. cum laude, Gonzaga U., 1977. Bar: Utah 1977, U.S. Dist. Ct. Utah, 1977, U.S. Ct. Appeals (10th cir.) 1977, U.S. Supreme Ct. 1985. Ptnr., Farr, Kaufman & Hamilton, Ogden, Utah, 1979. Chmn. Commn. on Pub. Defenders, Ogden, 1984. Mem. Assn. Trial Lawyers Am., ABA, Utah State Bar, Weber County Bar Assn. (pres. 1981-82). Jewish. Personal injury, Family and matrimonial, Criminal. Home: 5516 South 100 East Ogden UT 84405 Office: Farr Kaufman & Hamilton 205 26th St Suite 34 Ogden UT 84401

KAUFMANN, JACK, lawyer; b. Davenport, Iowa, May 14, 1942; s. Ed Kaufmann Jr. and Jean Gilchrist (Ploehn) Wernentin; m. Elizabeth Amanda Phillips, Jan. 27, 1973; children: Suzanne Cathryn, John Frederick, Christine Elizabeth, Amanda Jean. AB, Dartmouth Coll., 1964; JD, Columbia U., 1971. Bar: N.Y. 1972. Assoc. Dewey, Ballantine, Bushby, Palmer & Wood, N.Y.C., 1971-79, ptnr., 1980—. atty. Village of Pelham Manor, N.Y., 1977-83, trustee, 1983-87, mayor 1987—. Served as lt. (j.g.) USNR, 1964-68. Mem. ABA, N.Y. State Bar Assn., Assn. of Bar of City of N.Y. Republican. Episcopalian. Clubs: Pelham Country, Downtown Assn. (N.Y.C.). Federal civil litigation, State civil litigation, Antitrust. Home: 649 Ely Ave Pelham NY 10803 Office: Dewey Ballantine Bushby et al 140 Broadway New York NY 10005

KAUFMANN, ROY LESLIE, lawyer; b. Sept. 8, 1953. Attestation, U. Neuchatel, Switzerland, 1974; BA with honors, SUNY, Albany, 1975; JD, George Washington U., 1978. Bar: U.S. Dist. Ct. D.C. 1979, U.S. Ct. Mil.

Appeals 1979, U.S. Ct. Appeals (D.C. cir.) 1979. With Bur. Alcohol, Tobacco and Firearms, Washington, 1978; ptnr. Kaufmann and Assocs., Washington, 1978—. Mem. ABA, D.C. Bar Assn., Am. Arbitration Assn. (arbitrator). Contracts commercial, General corporate, Real property.

KAUGER, YVONNE, state justice; b. Cordell, Okla., Aug. 3, 1937; d. John and Alice (Bottom) K.; m. Ned Bastow, May 8, 1982; 1 child, Jonna Sinclair. B.A. magna cum laude, Southwestern State U., Weatherford, Okla., 1958; cert. med. technologist, St. Anthony's Hosp., 1959; J.D., Oklahoma City U., 1969. Med. technologist Med. Arts Lab., 1959-68; assoc. Rogers, Travis & Jordan, 1970-72; jud. asst. Okla. Supreme Ct., Oklahoma City, 1972-84, justice, 1984—; mem. appellate div. Ct. on Judiciary; mem. State Capitol Preservation Commn., 1983-84; mem. dean's adv. com. Oklahoma City U. Sch. Law. Founder Gallery of Plains Indian, Colony, Okla.; active Jud. Day, Girl's State, 1976-80; keynote speaker Girl's State Hall of Fame Banquet, 1984; bd. dirs. Lyric Theatre, Inc., 1966—, pres. bd. dirs., 1981; past mem. bd. dirs. Civic Music Soc., Okla. Theatre Ctr., Canterbury Choral Soc. Named to Outstanding Young Women Am., U.S. Jaycees, 1967, Byliner Honoree, Women in Communications, 1984, Woman of Yr., Oklahoma City chpt. Bus. and Profl. Women's Club, 1984, Woman of Yr., High Noon, 1985; adopted by Cheyenne-Arapaho tribes, 1984; honored by Okla. Hospitality Club, Ladies in the News, 1985; recipient Dist. Alumni award Southwestern Okla. State U., 1986, Oklahoma City U., 1986. Mem. ABA (law sch. accreditation com.), Okla. Bar Assn. (law schs. com. 1977—), Washita County Bar Assn., Washita County Hist. Soc. (life), St. Paul's Music Soc., Iota Tau Tau, Delta Zeta. Episcopalian. State civil litigation, Jurisprudence, Judicial administration.

KAUP, DANIEL JOHN, lawyer; b. West Point, Nebr., Apr. 25, 1951; s. Hilbert John and Marian Elizabeth (Foy) K.; m. Cheryl Kay Dudden, Nov. 27, 1976; children—Amber Dawn, Bret James. B.A. magna cum laude, Colo. State U., 1973; J.D., U. Denver, 1976. Bar: Colo. 1977, U.S. Dist. Ct. Colo. 1977, U.S. Ct. Appeals (10th cir.) 1977. Assoc., Lee & Marturano P.C., Englewood, Colo., 1976-78; dep. dist. atty. 8th Jud. Dist. Colo., 1978—; county atty. Jackson County (Colo.), Walden, 1978—; sch. bd. atty. North Park Sch. Dist., 1979—; gen. practice, Walden, 1980—. Vice pres. N. Park Sch. Dist. Bd. Edn., 1981—. Mem. Colo. legis. tchr. Tenure Study Commn., 1986. Mem. Colo. Bar Assn. (mem. com. alternatives to dispute resolution 1982-84); ABA (com. mem. 1981-83), NW Colo. Bar Assn., Colo. Assn. Sch. Bds. (regional dir. 1985—), Colo. Cattlemen's Assn. Roman Catholic. Lodge: Lions. Oil and gas leasing, Probate, Real property. Home: 721 6th St Walden CO 80480 Office: 452 Main St Walden CO 80480

KAUS, OTTO MICHAEL, lawyer; b. Vienna, Austria, Jan. 7, 1920; came to U.S., 1939, naturalized, 1942; s. Otto F. and Gina (Wiener) K.; m. Peggy A. Huttenback, Jan. 12, 1943; children: Stephen D., Robert M. B.A., UCLA, 1942; LL.B., Loyola U., Los Angeles, 1949. Bar: Calif. 1949. Pvt. practice Los Angeles, 1949-61; judge Superior Ct. Calif., 1961-64; assoc. justice Calif. Ct. Appeal (2d appellate dist., div. 3), Los Angeles, 1965-66; presiding justice Calif. Ct. Appeal (div. 5), 1966-81; assoc. justice Supreme Ct. Calif., San Francisco, 1981-85; ptnr. Hufstedler, Miller, Carlson & Beardsley, Los Angeles, 1986—; mem. faculty Loyola U. Law Sch., 1950-75, U. So. Calif., 1974-76. Served with U.S. Army, 1942-45. Mem. Am. Law Inst., Phi Beta Kappa, Order of Coif. Office: 700 S Flower St 16th Floor Los Angeles CA 90017

KAUSER, JANSON ALLEN, lawyer, judge; b. Southport, N.C., Aug. 13, 1949; s. Robert W. and Betty (Oliver) Beadle; m. Mary Ratterree, May 29, 1976; 1 child, Lance Oliver. BA, Coll. Charleston, 1979; JD, Campbell U., 1982. Bar: S.C. 1982. Ptnr. Belden & Fogel, Charleston, S.C., 1982-85; sole practice Charleston, 1985—; mcpl. ct. judge, Goose Creek, S.C., 1983—; instr. criminal justice Trident Tech. Coll., Charleston, 1982-84. Mem. Rep. exec. steering com., Charleston, 1986. Recipient J.P. Strom award, S.C. Criminal Justice Acad., 1972. Mem. S.C. Bar Assn. Baptist. Lodge: Kiwanis (v.p. Mt. Pleasant 1985—). Avocations: hunting, fishing. Criminal, Family and matrimonial. Office: 1219 Wappoo Rd Charleston SC 29407

KAUTTER, DAVID JOHN, lawyer; b. Wilkes-Barre, Pa., Mar. 20, 1948; s. William George and Mary (Flanagan) K.; m. Kathy Jane Price, May 22, 1976; children: Hilary, David Jr. BBA, Notre Dame U., 1971; JD, Georgetown U., 1974. Bar: D.C. 1975, U.S. Dist. Ct. D.C. 1981, U.S. Tax Ct. 1981, U.S. Supreme Ct. 1981. Staff acct. Coopers & Lybrand, Washington, 1971-74; mgr. Arthur Young and Co., Washington, 1974-78, ptnr., 1982-86, dir. Wash. Nat. Tax Group, 1986—; legis. asst. Senator John Danforth, Washington, 1979-82. Mem. ABA, Fed. Bar Assn., Am. Inst. CPA's. Republican. Roman Catholic. Avocation: cabinet making. Corporate taxation, Personal income taxation, Legislative. Home: 2353 Swaps Ct Reston VA 22091 Office: Arthur Young and Co 3000 K St NW Washington DC 20007

KAUTZMANN, DWIGHT C(LARENCE) H(ARRY), lawyer, magistrate; B. Bismarck, N.D., Dec. 30, 1945; s. Harry A. and Avis C. (Claflin) K.; m. Karen Ann Clausen, Aug. 19, 1972; children—Dreux C.H., Don C.H., De Ann C.H. B.A., N.D. State U., 1968; J.D., U. N.D., 1971. Bar: N.D. 1971, U.S. Dist. Ct. N.D. 1971, U.S. Ct. Appeals (8th cir.) 1974, U.S. Supreme Ct. 1977. Assoc., Vogel, Bair & Brown, Mandan, N.D., 1971-73; assoc. Bair, Brown & Kautzmann and predecessor, Mandan, 1973-74, ptnr., 1974—; magistrate U.S. Dist. Ct. N.D., 1978—; judge Mcpl. Ct. Mandan, 1974-76. Mem. Mandan Pub. Schs. Bd., 1977-83, pres. bd., 1979-83. Named Outstanding Mandanite, Mandan Jaycees, 1981. Mem. Morton County Bar Assn. (pres. 1980—), N.D. Bar Assn. (sec. 1973, bd. govs. 1985-87), ABA, Nat. Assn. Criminal Def. Attys., N.D. Trial Lawyers Assn. (sec. 1985-86), Nat. Assn. Criminal Def. Lawyers. Roman Catholic. Clubs: Optimists, Elks, K.C., Eagles (Mandan). Criminal, Family and matrimonial, Labor. Office: PO Box 100 Mandan ND 58554

KAVALER, THOMAS J., lawyer; b. N.Y.C., Dec. 10, 1948. BA, CCNY, 1969; JD, Fordham U., 1972; LLM, NYU, 1975. Bar: N.Y. U.S. Dist. Ct. (so., ea., we. and no. dists.) N.Y., U.S. Ct. Appeals (2d, 4th, 6th and 10th cirs.), U.S. Supreme Ct. Law clk. to presiding justice U.S. Dist. Ct. N.Y., N.Y.C., 1972-74; assoc. Cravath, Swaine & Moore, N.Y.C., 1974-75, Cahill Gordon & Reindel, N.Y.C., 1975-80; ptnr. Cahill, Gordon & Reindel, N.Y.C., 1980—. Served to capt. USAR, 1969-77. Federal civil litigation, State civil litigation, Securities. Office: Cahill Gordon & Reindel 80 Pine St New York NY 10005

KAVANAUGH, JAMES FRANCIS, JR., lawyer; b. New Bedford, Mass., Feb. 20, 1949; s. James Francis and Catherine Mary (Loughlin) K.; m. Cynthia Louise Ward, July 4, 1968; 1 child, James F. III. BA, Coll. of the Holy Cross, 1970; JD magna cum laude, Boston Coll., 1977. Bar: Mass. 1977, U.S. Dist. Ct. Mass. 1978, U.S. Ct. Appeals (1st cir.) 1978. Law clk. to assoc. justice Mass. Supreme Jud. Ct., Boston, 1977-78; assoc. Burns & Levinson, Boston, 1978-82, ptnr., 1983—. Editor, contbr. Boston Coll. Law Rev., 1975-77. Mem. ABA, Mass. Bar Assn., Boston Bar Assn. Democrat. Roman Catholic. Club: Winchester Country. Avocations: golf, basketball, reading fiction and history. Federal civil litigation, State civil litigation. Home: 49 Brookside Ave Winchester MA 01890 Office: Burns & Levinson 50 Milk St Boston MA 02109

KAVASS, IGOR IVAR, law educator, law librarian, consultant; b. Riga, Latvia, July 31, 1932; s. Nicholas and Iraida (Kushnarer) K.; m. Carmen Boada: children—Sybilla, Ariane, Lara, Veronica, Nicholas. LL.B. with honors, U. Melbourne, Australia, 1955. Bar: High Ct. Australia, Supreme Ct. Victoria (Australia), Supreme Ct. South Australia. Practice law Melbourne, 1956-59; sr. lectr. law U. Adelaide, Australia, 1959-66, U. Melbourne, 1959-66; vis. prof. law U. Ala., 1966-67, prof. law, dir. Law Library, 1968-70; assoc. prof. law Monash U., Melbourne, 1967-68; prof., law librarian Northwestern U., Chgo., 1970-72, Duke U., Durham, N.C., 1972-75; prof., dir. Legal Info. Ctr. Vanderbilt U., Nashville, 1975—; vis. prof. Free U. Berlin, 1975; Fulbright lectr. U. Los Andes, 1986; editorial cons. William S. Hein & Co., Buffalo; cons. legal research and info. Author numerous books including (with Michael Blake and Howard Hood) United States Legislation on Foreign Relations and International Commerce, 1789-1979, 5 vols., 1977, 78, 84 (Am. Soc. Internat. Law cert. merit 1979), (with B.A. Christensen) A Guide to North Carolina Legal Research, 1973, (with Adolf Sprudzs) A Guide to the United States Treaties in Force, annually 1982—; contbr. articles to profl. publs.; editor books including: International Military Law and History Reprint Series, 1972—; editor pub. Internat. Assn. Law Libraries Newsletter, 1976-79. Mem. Am. Assn. Advancement Slavic Studies, Am. Assn. Law Libraries, Am. Soc. Internat. Law, Assn. Am. Law Schs., Brit. Inst. Internat. and Comparative Law, Internat. Assn. Law Libraries (pres. 1976-83), Soc. Pub. Tchrs. Law (U.K.), Order of Coif. Consumer commercial, Contracts commercial, Legal education. Office: Vanderbilt U Sch Law Nashville TN 37240

KAVENEY, FRANK JOHN, lawyer; b. Indpls., Oct. 11, 1943; s. Frank Eugene and Helen Loretta (Lahey) K.; m. Mary Catherine Kaveney, June 27, 1970; children: Kevin Francis, Brian Edward, Maura Catherine. BA, St. Louis U., 1965, JD, 1967. Bar: Mo. 1967, U.S. Ct. Dist. Ct. (ea. dist.) Mo. 1967, U.S. Ct. Appeals (8th cir.) 1967. Asst. pros. atty. St. Louis County, 1971-75; asoc. Greensfelder-Hemker, St. Louis, 1975-76; sole practice St. Louis, 1976-80; ptnr. Kaveney, Beach et al, St. Louis, 1980—. Chmn. Bd. of Equalization, St. Louis, 1976-79; v.p. Indsl. Devel. Authority, St. Louis County, 1981-85. Served to capt. USMC, 1967-71, Vietnam. Mem. Bar Assn. Met. St. Louis, Bar Assn. St. Louis County, Lawyers Assn., Assn. Trial Lawyers Am. Republican. Roman Catholic. Clubs: Racquet (St. Louis, Ladue, Mo.). Avocations: tennis, coaching baseball, model railroading. General corporate, Criminal, Personal injury. Home: 19 Ridgetop Dr Saint Louis MO 63117 Office: Kaveny Beach Russell Bond & Mittleman 222 S Central #900 Saint Louis MO 63105

KAWAGUCHI, MEREDITH FERGUSON, lawyer; b. Dallas, Feb. 5, 1940; d. Hugh William Ferguson and Ruth Virginia (Perdue) Drewery; m. Harry H. Kawaguchi, Apr. 22, 1977. B.A., U. Tex., 1962, M.A., 1968; J.D., So. Meth. U., 1977. Bar: Tex. 1977. Legal examiner gas utilities div. Tex. Railroad Commn., Austin, 1977-84, legal examiner oil and gas div., 1984—; cons. in law, lectr. to profl. confs. Author position paper Tex. Energy Natural Resources Adv. Council. Mem., Sorority Adv. Council, Austin, 1980—, Japanese-Am. Citizens League, Houston, 1981—, Exec. Women in Tex. Govt., Austin, 1984. Recipient Cert. of Recognition, Tex. Railroad Commn., 1982. Mem. ABA, Tex. Bar Assn., Travis County Bar Assn. (oil gas and mineral law sect.), Travis County Women Lawyers Assn., Internat. Platform Assn. Administrative and regulatory, Public utilities, Oil and gas leasing. Home: 5009 Westview Dr Austin TX 78731 Office: Tex Railroad Commn 1701 N Congress Austin TX 78711-2967

KAWITT, ALAN, lawyer; b. Chgo., 1937. J.D., Chgo.-Kent Coll. Law, 1965; postgrad. Lawyers Inst. John Marshall Law Sch., 1966-68. Bar: Ill. 1966, U.S. Dist. Ct. (no. dist.) Ill. 1967, U.S. Ct. Appeals (7th cir.) 1971, U.S. Supreme Ct., 1971. Sole practice, 1970—. Mem. Am. Arbitration Assn. (arbitrator), Trial Lawyers Assn., Ill. Bar Assn., Ill. Trial Lawyers Assn., Chgo. Bar Assn., Decalogue Assn. Lawyers (coms. bankruptcy and reorgn., tort law, admiralty and maritime law, civil practice, mil. law). Bankruptcy, Landlord-tenant, Personal injury. Office: 30 W Washington St Chicago IL 60602

KAY, HERMA HILL, legal educator; b. Orangeburg, S.C., Aug. 18, 1934; d. Charles Esdorn and Herma Lee (Crawford) Hill. B.A., So. Meth. U., 1956; J.D., U. Chgo., 1959. Bar: Calif. 1960. Law clk. to Justice Roger Traynor, Calif. Supreme Ct., 1959-60; asst. prof. law U. Calif., Berkeley, 1960-62; assoc. prof. U. Calif., 1962, prof., 1963—, dir. family law project, 1964-67; co-reporter uniform marriage and div. law Nat. Conf. Commrs. on Uniform State Laws, 1968-70; vis. prof. U. Manchester, Eng., 1972, Harvard U., 1976; mem. Gov.'s Commn. on Family, 1966. Contbr. articles to profl. jours; contbg. author: Law in Culture and Society, 1969; author: Text, Cases and Materials on Sex-Based Discrimination, 1981, Conflict of Laws; Cases, Comments, Questions, 3d edit, 1981. Trustee, Russell Sage Found., N.Y., chmn. bd., 1980-84; trustee Rosenberg Found., Calif.; bd. dirs. Equal Rights Advs. Calif., 1976—, chmn., 1976-83, pres. bd. dirs., 1987—. Fellow Center Advanced Study in Behavioral Scis., Palo Alto, Calif., 1963-64. Mem. Calif. Bar Assn., Bar U.S. Supreme Ct., Calif. Women Lawyers (bd. govs. 1975-77), Am. Law Inst. (mem. council 1985—), Assn. Am. Law Schs. (exec. com. 1986-88), Order Coif (nat. pres. 1983-85). Democrat. Family and matrimonial, Labor, Conflicts. Office: School of Law University of California Berkeley CA 94720

KAY, JOEL PHILLIP, lawyer; b. Corsicana, Tex., Aug. 27, 1936. B.S. in Econs., Wharton Sch., U. Pa., 1958; LL.B., U. Tex., 1961; LL.M., Georgetown U., 1967. Bar: Tex. 1961. Trial atty. tax div. Dept. Justice, 1963-67; asst. U.S. atty. So. Dist. Tex., 1967-69; ptnr. Sheinfeld, Maley & Kay, Houston, 1969—; mem. Tex. Bd. Pub. Accountancy, 1984-85. Served with AUS, 1961-63. Fellow Am. Bar Found.; mem. ABA, Tex. Bar Assn. (dir. 1979-81, chmn. bd. 1981-82), Houston Bar Assn., Tex. Bar Found. (trustee 1983-86). Pension, profit-sharing, and employee benefits, Federal civil litigation. Office: 3700 First City Tower Houston TX 77002

KAY, KENNETH ROBERT, lawyer; b. Queens, N.Y., Nov. 16, 1951; s. Henry H. and Eleanor H. (Buchdahl) K.; m. Karen Kay Christensen, Sept. 2, 1977; 1 stepson, Jeff Smithson; children: Braden, Bergen. BA, Oberlin Coll., 1973; JD, U. Denver, 1976. Bar: D.C. 1976. Legis. asst. Congressman Ed Koch, Washington, 1976-77; chief minority counsel Separation of Power subcommittee Senate Judiciary Com., Washington, 1981-82; legal counsel Sen. Max. Baucus, Washington, 1978-81, legis. dir., 1982-84; ptnr. Preston, Thorgrimson, Ellis & Holman, Washington, 1984—; exec. dir. Coalition for Advancement of Indsl. Tech., Washington, 1984-86, exec. dir. Council on Research and Tech., 1987—. Democrat. Jewish. Legislative, Technology, Insurance. Office: Preston Thorgrison Ellis & Holman 1735 New York Ave NW #500 Washington DC 20006

KAY, STANLEY LLOYD, lawyer; b. Bklyn., Oct. 15, 1942; s. Erwin and Blanche (Sussman) K.; m. Carol S. Atkin, Aug. 10, 1968; 2 sons, Daniel, Jonathan. BA., U. Pa., 1964; LL.B., Harvard U., 1967. Bar: N.Y. 1968. Assoc. Solinger & Gordon, 1969-75, ptnr. 1976-79; gen. counsel Batus Retail Group, N.Y.C., 1980—. Mem. Town of Greenburgh (N.Y.) Urban Renewal Commn., 1973-75. Served to sgt. USAR, 1967-72. Mem. ABA, N.Y. State Bar Assn., Assn. Bar City of N.Y. General corporate. Office: Batus Retail Group 1270 Ave of Americas New York NY 10020

KAY, STEPHEN WILLIAM, lawyer; b. Omaha, Dec. 27, 1953; s. Harold Wallace and Patricia Lou (Larson) K.; m. Jean Marie Lawse, Aug. 5, 1978; children: Melissa Marie, Stephen William II, Robert Andrew. BS, U. Nebr., 1975; JD, Creighton U., 1978. Bar: Nebr. 1978, U.S. Dist. Ct. Nebr. 1978, U.S. Ct. Appeals (8th cir.) 1978, U.S. Ct. Appeals (Fed. cir.) 1984, U.S. Supreme Ct. 1984. Assoc. Kay & Satterfield, North Platte, Nebr., 1978-80; ptnr. Kay & Kay, North Platte, 1980—. Mem. standing com. Episcopal Diocese of Nebr., 1985—; exec. bd. dirs. Tri Trails council Boy Scouts Am., North Platte, 1982—; chmn. Lincoln County Reps., North Platte, 1982-84; cen. committeeman Nebr. Reps., 1984—, asst. chmn., 1986, exec. com., 1986. Mem. ABA, Nebr. Bar Assn., Western Nebr. Bar Assn., Lincoln County Bar Assn. (pres. 1982), Am. Judicature Soc., Assn. Ins. Council, Internat. Assn. Ins. Council, Nat. Assn. R.R. Trial Council., Def. Research Inst., Nebr. Def. Council. Episcopalian. Insurance, Personal injury, Federal civil litigation. Home: 1111 Custer Ct North Platte NE 69101 Office: 227 Parkade Plaza PO Box 1009 North Platte NE 69103

KAY, WILLIAM RICHARD, JR., lawyer; b. Richmond, Va., Oct. 19, 1948; s. William Richard and Isabel (Plummer) K.; m. Robyn Ransone, May 24, 1980; children: Hallie, Albert, William. BA, Hampden-Sydney Coll., 1971; JD, T.C. Williams Sch. Law, 1974. Bar: Va. 1974, U.S. Dist. Ct. (ea. dist.) Va. 1985. Spl. asst. atty. gen. State of Va., Richmond, 1974-81; gen. counsel Citizens Savs. and Loan, Richmond, 1981-84; corp. counsel Suburban Savs. and Loan, Annandale, Va., 1984; assoc. corp. counsel Bank of Va., Richmond, 1984—. Chmn. bd. dirs. Southside Montessori Sch., Richmond, 1986-87. Mem. ABA, Va. Bar Assn., Richmond Bar Assn. Republican. Episcopalian. Banking, General corporate. Home: 2131 Carbon Hill Dr Midlothian VA 23113 Office: Bank of Va PO Box 25970 Richmond VA 23260

KAY, WILLIAM THOMAS, JR., lawyer; b. Waynesville, Mo., May 1, 1944; s. William Thomas and Frances (Maloney) K.; m. Patricia Ann Pelant, Nov. 24, 1973; children: Breean Andrea, Meagan Kathleen. BA, Seattle U., 1966; JD, U. San Diego, 1972. Bar: Calif., U.S. Dist. Ct. (no. dist.) Calif., U.S. Ct. Appeals (9th cir.). Staff counsel Wells Fargo Leasing, San Francisco, 1973-76; dep. dist. atty. Santa Clara County, San Jose, Calif., 1976-77; ptnr. McKittrick & Kay, Eureka, Calif., 1977-85, Harland & Gromala, Eureka, 1985—. Recipient Boss of Yr. award Humboldt County Legal Secs. Assn., Eureka, 1986. Bd. dirs. St. Joseph Hosp., Eureka, 1985—, Humboldt State U. Ctr. for Arts, Arcata, 1986, United Way of Humboldt, Eureka, 1984—. Served to 1st lt. U.S. Army, 1967-69. Mem. ABA, Calif. Bar Assn., Humboldt County Bar Assn. (v.p. 1985, pres. 1986). Republican. Roman Catholic. Clubs: Ingomar, Baywood Golf and Country (Eureka). Lodge: Rotary (bd. dirs. Eureka club 1985—). Avocations: golf, reading, writing, cooking, aerobics. State civil litigation, Personal injury, Criminal. Home: 3608 Glenwood Eureka CA 95501 Office: Harland & Gromala 622 H St Eureka CA 95501

KAYE, JOEL MICHAEL, lawyer; b. Mt. Vernon, N.Y., Dec. 12, 1953; s. Joseph Mitchell and Miriam Diana (Kniznick) K.; m. Kimberly F. McKeever, Sept. 4, 1977. BA, Am. U., 1974; JD, U. Conn., 1977. Bar: Conn. 1977, N.Y. 1983, U.S. Dist. Ct. 1977, U.S. Supreme Ct. 1980. Assoc. John. F. Merchant, Stamford, Conn., 1977; ptnr. Merchant, Rosenblum & Kaye, Stamford, Conn., 1977-79, Kaye & Effron, Greenwich, Conn., 1979-81; prin. Kaye & Effron, P.C., Greenwich, Conn., 1981—. Co-author: Connecticut Practice Book Annotated, 1979. Mem. Greenwich Dem. Town Com., 1976-78; rep. Greenwich Town Meeting, 1976-83. Mem. ABA, Conn. Bar Assn., Greenwich Bar Assn. Democrat. Jewish. Lodge: Kiwanis (Greenwich) (pres. 1984). Avocations: piano, lyrics, composing music. Real property, General corporate, Probate. Home: 40 Halsey Dr Old Greenwich CT 06870 Office: Kaye & Effron PC 165 W Putnam Ave Greenwich CT 06830

KAYE, JUDITH SMITH, judge; b. Monticello, N.Y., Aug. 4, 1938; d. Benjamin and Lena (Cohen) Smith; m. Stephen Rackow Kaye, Feb. 11, 1964; children—Luisa Marian, Jonathan Mackey, Gordon Bernard. B.A., Barnard Coll., 1958; LL.B. cum laude, NYU, 1962; LL.D. (hon.), St. Lawrence U., 1985, Albany Law Sch., 1985, Pace U., 1985. Assoc. Sullivan & Cromwell, N.Y.C., 1962-64; staff atty. IBM, Armonk, N.Y., 1964-65; asst. to dean NYU Sch. of Law, 1965-68; ptnr. Olwine Connelly Chase O'Donnell & Weyher, N.Y.C., 1969-83; judge N.Y. State Ct. Appeals, N.Y.C., 1983—; dir. Sterling Nat. Bank. Contbr. articles to profl. jours. Former bd. dirs. Legal Aid Soc. Recipient Vanderbilt medal NYU Sch. of Law, 1983. Fellow Am. Bar Found.; mem. Am. Law Inst., Am. Judicature Soc. (bd. dirs. 1980-83). Democrat. Home: 101 Central Park W New York NY 10023 Office: Ct of Appeals State of NY 20 Eagle St Albany NY 12207 *

KAYE, RICHARD PAUL, attorney; b. East Meadow, N.Y., June 11, 1953; s. Maurice and Sarah (Chanin) K.; m. Susan Ann Strickler, April 21, 1985. BA magna cum laude, Clark U., 1975; JD, George Washington U., 1978. Bar: N.Y. 1979, U.S. Dist. Ct. (so. dist.) 1979, (ea. dist) 1982. Asst. dist. atty. State of N.Y., N.Y.C., 1978-81; assoc. Burlingham Underwood & Lord, N.Y.C., 1981-83, Danziger Bangser Klipstein Goldsmith Greenwald & Weiss, N.Y.C., 1983-86, Carb, Luria, Glassner, Cook & Kufeld, N.Y.C., 1987—. arbitrator Civil Ct. of the City of N.Y.C., 1986. Mem. ABA, N.Y. St. Bar Assn., Assn. of the Bar of the City of N.Y., Phi Delta Phi (magister 1977-78), Phi Beta Kappa. State civil litigation, Federal civil litigation, Family and matrimonial. Home: 110 Albemarle Rd White Plains NY 10605 Office: Carb Luria Glassner Cook & Kufeld 529 Fifth Ave New York NY 10017

KAYLOR, OMER THOMAS, JR., lawyer; b. Hagerstown, Md., July 14, 1923; s. Omer Thomas and Mabel E. (Slagen) K.; m. Jean Haskin Johnston, Aug. 23, 1947; children—Omer Thomas, Laura, Owen, Mark, John. B., Washington and Lee U., 1945, J.D., 1949. Bar: Md. Ptnr. Kaylor & Wantz, and predecessors, Hagerstown, 1949—; sec., dir. Farmer & Mchts. Bank, Hagerstown, 1960—. Pres., Hagerstown United Fund, Hagerstown YMCA; v.p. Washington County Mus., 1984—; mem. Md. State Legislature, 1950-54. Mem. Washington County Bar Assn. (past pres.), Phi Beta Kappa, Omicron Delta Kappa. Republican. Mem. United Ch. of Christ. Clubs: Assembly (Hagerstown); Fountain Head Country. Real property, Probate, General corporate. Home: 940 The Terrace Hagerstown MD 21740 Office: Kaylor & Wantz 123 W Washington Hagerstown MD 21740

KAYSON, DAVID, lawyer; b. Washington, Sept. 4, 1921; LL.B., George Washington U., 1950. Bar: D.C. 1952, Md. 1970, U.S. Ct. Appeals (D.C. cir.) 1952, U.S. Dist. Ct. Md. 1972, U.S. Supreme Ct. 1973. Sole practice, Washington and Kensington, Md., 1952—, Law Offices David Kayson & Assocs., 1982—. Served with USAF, 1943-46. Mem. D.C. Bar, Bar. Assn. D.C., Md. State Bar Assn., Montgomery County Bar Assn., Assn. Trial Lawyers Am. (gov. 1974-77), Assn. Plaintiff's Trial Attys. Met. Washington (pres. 1973-74), Md. Trial Lawyers Assn. (v.p. Montgomery County 1972-73), Nat. Bd. Trial Advocacy (founding). Personal injury, Federal civil litigation, State civil litigation. Address: Law Offices David Kayson & Assocs 10400 Connecticut Ave Kensington MD 20895

KAZANJIAN, PHILLIP CARL, lawyer, business executive; b. Visalia, Calif., May 15, 1945; s. John Casey and Sat-ten Arlene K.; m. Wendy Coffelt, Feb. 5, 1972. B.A. with honors, U. So. Calif., 1967; J.D. with honors, Lincoln U., San Francisco, 1973. Bar: Calif. 1979, U.S. Dist. Ct. (cen. dist.) Calif. 1980, U.S. Tax Ct. 1980, U.S. Ct. Appeals (9th cir.) 1980, U.S. Mil. Ct. Appeals 1980, U.S. Supreme Ct. 1983. Ptnr. Brakefield & Kazanjian, Glendale, Calif., 1981—; instr. U.S. Naval Acad., 1981. Mem. Calif. Atty. Gen.'s Adv. Commn. on Community-Police Relations, 1973; bd. dirs. Los Angeles County Naval Meml. Found., Inc., 1981—; pres. bd. trustees Glendale Community Coll. Dist., 1981—, Los Angeles World Affairs Council, Town Hall Calif., Republican Assocs. (dir.), Rep. Lincoln Club; bd. of govs. Calif. Maritime Acad. Served to comdr. USNR, 1969—. Decorated Navy Commendation medal, Navy Achievement medal; recipient Patrick Henry medal Am. Legion, 1963, Congressional Record tribute U.S. Ho. of Reps., 1974, Centurion award Chief of Naval Ops., 1978, award Res. Officers Assn. U.S., 1981, commendatory resolutions Mayor of Los Angeles, Los Angeles City Council, Los Angeles County Bd. Suprs., Calif. State Assembly and Senate, and Govt. of Calif., 1982, Justice award Calif. Law Student Assn., 1973. Mem. ABA (Gold Key 1972), Calif. Bar Assn., Los Angeles County Bar Assn., Am. Judicature Soc., Assn. Trial Lawyers Am., Glendale C. of C. (bd. dirs.), Res. Officers Assn. (nat. judg adv., nat. adv. com.), Naval Res. Assn., U.S. Naval Inst., Explorers Club. Republican. Episcopalian. Club: Commonwealth of Calif. Author: The Circuit Governor, 1972; editor in chief Lincoln Law Rev., 1973. State civil litigation, Personal injury. Office: 225 W Broadway Suite 500 Glendale CA 91204

KAZDIN, MARGARET ELLEN, lawyer; b. Cleve., Oct. 25, 1954; s. James J. and Agatha E. (Byrne) Stanard; m. Gary A. Kazdin (div.); 1 child, Matthew A. Kazdin. BA, John Carroll U., 1976; JD, Cleve. Marshall Law Sch., 1981. Bar: Ohio 1981, U.S. Dist. Ct. (no. dist.) Ohio 1981. Sole practice Cleve., 1981-86; assoc. Reid, Johnson, Downes, Andrachik, & Webster, Cleve., 1986—. Mem. ABA, Ohio Bar Assn., Cuyahoga County Bar Assn. (bd. dirs. family law sect. 1984), Cleve. Bar Assn., Assn. Trial Lawyers Am., Ohio Trial Lawyers Assn. Democrat. Club: Women Historians (Cleve.). Avocations: hockey, ballet. Family and matrimonial, Personal injury, Probate. Home: 3301 E Monmouth Cleveland Heights OH 44118 Office: 1300 Illuminating Bldg Cleveland OH 44113

KAZE, JAMES MICHAEL, lawyer; b. Buffalo, Wyo., Sept. 12, 1948; s. Ralph Alfred and Phyllis Lucille (Still) K.; m. Linda Gail Lee, June 26, 1971; children: Danna Leigh, Tennille Rose. BSCE, Mont. State U., 1970; JD, U. Mont., 1974. Bar: Mont. 1974, U.S. Dist. Ct. Mont. 1974. Civil engr. County of Los Angeles, 1971; assoc. atty. Weber, Bosch & Kuhr, Havre, Mont., 1974-78; ptnr. Bosch, Kuhr et al, Havre, Mont. Mem. No. Mont. Coll. Exec. Bd., Havre, 1983-86, Mont. Dem. Party State Rules Com., Helena, 1984-86; commr. City Police Commn., Havre, 1984—; pres. Messiah Luth. Ch., Havre, 1985-86; appointed by gov. to Mont. Bd. of Regents of Higher Edn., 1986. Recipient Rocky Mountain Mineral Law Found. award, 1974. Mem. ABA, 12th Jud. Dist. Bar Assn., Am. Mgmt. Assn. Democrat. Lutheran. Lodge: Lion's (Havre) (bd. dirs. 1985—). Avocations: snow skiing, oil painting, computers. General practice, Public utilities, Probate. Office: Bosch Kuhr Dugdale et al PO Box 7152 Havre MT 59501

KAZEN, GEORGE PHILIP, federal judge; b. Laredo, Tex., Feb. 29, 1940; s. Emil James and Drusilla M. (Perkins) K.; m. Barbara Ann Sanders, Oct. 27, 1962; children—George, John, Elizabeth, Gregory. B.B.A., U. Tex., 1960, J.D. with honors, 1961. Bar: Tex., U.S. Supreme Ct., U.S. Ct. Claims, U.S. Ct. Appeals (5th cir.), U.S. Dist. Ct. (so. dist.) Tex. Briefing atty. Tex. Sup. Ct., 1961-62; assoc. Mann, Freed, Kazen & Hansen, 1965-79; judge U.S. Dist. Ct., Laredo, Tex., 1979—; founder, first pres. Laredo Legal Aid Soc., 1966-69. Pres. Laredo Civic Music Assn.; chmn. St. Augustine-Ursuline Consol. Sch. Bd.; bd. dirs. Boys' Clubs Laredo; trustee Laredo Jr. Coll., 1972-79; bd. dirs., v.p., pres. Econ. Opportunities Devel. Corp., 1968-70; past bd. dirs. D.D. Hachar Found. Served with USAF, 1962-65. Decorated Air Force Commendation medal; named Outstanding Young Lawyer, Larado Jaycees, 1970. Mem. ABA, Tex. Bar Found., Tex. Bar Assn., Tex. Criminal Def. Lawyers Assn., Tex. Assn. Bank Counsel, Tex. Assn. Def. Counsel, Laredo C. of C. (bd. dirs. 1975-76), Fifth Cir. Dist. Judges Assn. (v.p. 1984-85, pres. 1986—), U. Tex. Law Sch. Alumni Assn. (bd. dirs. 1976-77). Roman Catholic. Judicial administration. Office: PO Box 1060 Laredo TX 78040

KEANE, EDWARD WEBB, lawyer; b. Detroit, Sept. 18, 1930; s. Lee A. and Florette (Webb) K.; m. Mary Burdell, 1954; children: Edward Webb, Jennie K., Metthea K. A.B., Harvard U., 1952, J.D., 1957. Bar: D.C. 1957, N.Y. 1960, U.S. Supreme Ct. 1965. Law clk. to Justice William J. Brennan, Jr. U.S. Supreme Ct., 1957-58; assoc. Sullivan & Cromwell, N.Y.C., 1958-65, ptnr., 1966—. Mem. ABA, N.Y. State Bar Assn., Assn. Bar City N.Y., other legal orgns. Home: 1 Lexington Ave New York NY 10010 Office: Sullivan & Cromwell 125 Broad St New York NY 10004

KEARFOTT, JOSEPH CONRAD, lawyer; b. Martinsville, Va., Sept. 24, 1947; s. Clarence P. and Elizabeth (Kelly) K.; m. Mary Jo Veatch, Feb.10, 1969; children: Kelly, David. BA, Davidson Coll., 1969; JD, U. Va., 1972. Bar: Va. 1972, U.S. Dist. Ct. (ea. and we. dists.) Va. 1973, U.S. Ct. Appeals (4th cir.) 1973, U.S. Tax Ct. 1979, U.S. Ct. Appeals (1st cir.) 1981, U.S. Ct. Appeals (5th cir.) 1982. Law clk. to presiding justice U.S. Dist. Ct. (ea. dist.) Va., Richmond, 1972-73; assoc. Hunton & Williams, Richmond, 1973-80, ptnr., 1980—; lectr. Va. Com. on Continuing Legal Edn., 1984—; mem. 4th Cir. Jud. conf. Mem. Richmond Bd. Housing, 1977—, Richmond Dem. Com., 1978-82; pres. William Byrd Community House, Richmond, 1982-84; chmn. profl. div. United Way of Greater Richmond campaign, 1985; vice-chmn. and chmn. elect Human Services Planning div. United Way of Greater Richmond, 1987—; trustee Trinity Episc. High Sch., 1986—. Served to capt. U.S. Army, 1973. Mem. ABA, Va. Bar Assn., Richmond Bar Assn., Order of Coif. Club: Bull and Bear (Richmond). Avocations: tennis, canoeing. Federal civil litigation, State civil litigation. Home: 4436 Custis Rd Richmond VA 23225 Office: Hunton & Williams 707 E Main St PO Box 1535 Richmond VA 23212

KEARLEY, TIMOTHY G., law librarian, consultant; b. Oak Park, Ill., Nov. 12, 1949; s. Eugene John Kearley and Louise Ida (Bloyd) Burnett; m. Jamie Sue Pielstick, Aug. 28, 1971; 1 child, Evan. BA, U. Ill., 1971, JD, 1976; MLS, U. Wash., 1977. Bar: Ill. 1978. Reference librarian Cook County Law Library, Chgo., 1977-78; asst. law librarian, asst. prof. library adminstrn. U. Ill., Urbana, 1978-84, assoc. dir., assoc. prof. library adminstrn., assoc. prof. law, 1984—. Mem. Ill. Bar Assn., Am. Assn. Law Libraries, Internat. Assn. Law Libraries (sec. 1986—), ACLU (steering com.), Phi Beta Kappa. Mem. Unitarian Ch. Avocation: auto racing. Legal education, Legal history. Office: U Ill Coll Law Library 504 E Pennsylvania Ave Champaign IL 61820

KEARN, ORENE LEVENSON, lawyer; b. Los Angeles, June 14, 1956; d. Donald and Harriet Levenson; m. Robert L. Kearn, Jan. 5, 1986. BA summa cum laude, UCLA, 1977; JD, Hastings Coll. Law, 1981. Bar: Calif., 1981. Assoc. Lillick, McHose & Charles, San Francisco, 1981-84, Musick, Peeler & Garrett, Burlingame, Calif. and Los Angeles, 1984—. Past editor Hastings Law Jour. Bd. dirs., mem. women's auxiliary Am. Paralysis Assn., San Francisco. Mem. ABA, Los Angeles County Bar Assn., San Mateo County Bar Assn., Bar Assn. San Francisco, Order of Coif, Phi Beta Kappa. Estate planning, Probate, Estate taxation. Office: Musick Peeler & Garrett 577 Airport Blvd Suite 500 Burlingame CA 94010

KEARNS, JAMES CANNON, lawyer; b. Urbana, Ill., Nov. 8, 1944; s. John T. and Ruth (Cannon) K.; m. Anne Shapland, Feb. 12, 1983; 1 child, Sarah Rose. BA, U. Notre Dame, 1966; JD, U. Ill., 1975. Bar: Ill. 1975, U.S. Dist. Ct. (cen. dist.) Ill. 1975, U.S. Ct. Appeals (7th cir.) 1976. Ptnr. Heyl, Royster, Voilker & Allen, Peoria, Ill., 1975-81, Urbana, 1981—. Mem. ABA, Am. Assn. RR Trial Counsel, Am. Soc. Law and Medicine, Ill. Bar Assn., Champaign County Bar Assn. Roman Catholic. Avocations: reading, jogging. Personal injury, Insurance, State civil litigation. Office: Heyl Royster Voilker & Allen Busey Bank County Plaza #300 PO Box 129 Urbana IL 61801

KEARNS, JOHN W., lawyer; b. Chgo., Sept. 9, 1933; s. John W. and Frances R. (Forch) K.; m. Karen E. Swanson, May 3, 1960 (div. 1979); children—Jennifer F., John W., Charles S. B.A., Yale U., 1955; J.D., Harvard U., 1958. Bar: Ill. 1958, Fla. 1970, U.S. Dist. Ct. (no. dist.) Ill. 1958, U.S. Dist. Ct. (so. dist.) Fla. 1970, U.S. Ct. Appeals (7th, 5th, 3d and 11th cirs.), U.S. Supreme Ct. 1971. With Peterson, Ross, Rall, Barber & Seidel, Chgo., 1958-61, Kirkland & Ellis, Chgo., 1961-69, Paul & Thompson, Miami, Fla., 1969-73; sole practice, Miami, 1973—. Bd. dirs. Fla. Zool. Soc., 1974-79. Mem. ABA, Fla. Bar Assn., Dade County Bar Assn., Chgo. Bar Assn. Clubs: Chgo. Yacht; Coral Reef Yacht (Miami). General practice, State civil litigation, Antitrust. Office: 431 Gerona Ave Coral Gables FL 33146

KEARNS, WILLIAM JOHN, JR., lawyer; b. Wilson Boro, Pa., Oct. 31, 1940; s. William John and Dorothy Lillian (Fenstermacher) K.; m. Ellen Katherine Butler, June 5, 1965; 1 son, Michael Patrick. B.S., St. Peter's Coll., Jersey City, N.J. 1962; J.D., Rutgers Sch. Law, 1965. Bar: N.J. 1965, U.S. Tax Ct. 1969, U.S. Supreme Ct. 1969. Law clk. Super. Ct. Judge Walter L. Hetfield, Elizabeth, N.J., 1965-66; assoc. Sidney W. Bookbinder, Burlington, N.J., 1966-67; assoc. Leonard Etz, Trenton, N.J., 1967-70; sole practice, Willingboro, N.J., 1970-77; ptnr. Kearns & Vassallo, Willingboro, 1977-78; ptnr. Kearns, Vassallo & Kearns, Willingboro, 1978-80; ptnr. Kearns, Vassallo, Kearns & LeBon, Willingboro, 1980-82; ptnr. Kearns & Kearns, Willingboro, 1982—; dir. Provident Bank N.J., 1974-76; mem. Willingboro Regional Adv. Bd. 1st Peoples Bank N.J., 1977-82; lectr. N.J. Inst. Continuing Legal Edn.; atty. Willingboro Twp., 1980—; atty. Bordentown Twp. Zoning Bd., 1982—. Councilman Twp. of Willingboro, 1972-80, mayor, 1973, 78, dep. mayor, 1975; mem. Willingboro Planning Bd., 1972-73, 75-78; mem. Local Assistance Bd., Willingboro, 1972-74, 76-77; pres. United Way of Burlington County, 1981, mem. exec. com., 1977-82, v.p. agy. relations, 1982; bd. dirs. Family Service Burlington County, 1974-81, pres., 1975-81; pres. Willingboro Democratic Club, 1970-71; chmn. Willingboro Dem. Com., 1984—, Burlington County Dem. Exec. Com., 1985—; trustee N.J. Inst. Continuing Legal Edn., 1985—; bd. dirs. Burlington County chpt. Multiple Sclerosis Soc., 1973-74, Burlington County chpt. ARC, 1977-79; chmn. adv. bd. Willingboro LWV, 1968. Mem. ABA, N.J. State Bar Assn. (gen. council 1970—, dir. local govt. law sect. 1970—, chmn. 1976-78, chmn. women's rights sect. 1982-84), Burlington County Bar Assn. (treas. 1981-82, 2d v.p. 1982-83, pres. 1984-85, dir. 1978-81), Nat. Inst. Mcpl. Law Officers (chairperson state N.J. 1984-86, regional v.p. 1986—). Roman Catholic. Local government, Family and matrimonial, General practice. Home: 20 Crosswick Pl Willingboro NJ 08046 Office: 215 Sunset Rd Willingboro NJ 08046

KEARSE, AMALYA LYLE, judge; b. Vauxhall, N.J., June 11, 1937; d. Robert Freeman and Myra Lyle (Smith) K. B.A., Wellesley Coll., 1959; J.D. cum laude, U. Mich., 1962. Bar: N.Y. State 1963, U.S. Supreme Ct. 1967. Assc. firm Hughes Hubbard & Reed, N.Y.C., 1962-69; partner Hughes Hubbard & Reed, 1969-79; judge U.S. Ct. Appeals, 2d Circuit, 1979—; lectr. evidence N.Y. U. Law Sch., 1968-69. Author: Bridge Conventions Complete, 1975, 2d edit., 1984, Bridge at Your Fingertips, 1980; translator, editor: Bridge Analysis, 1979; editor: Ofcl. Ency. of Bridge, 3d edit, 1976; Mem., Charles Goren Editorial Bd., 1974—. Bd. dirs. NAACP Legal Def. and Endl. Fund, 1977-79; bd. dirs. Nat. Urban League, 1978-79; trustee N.Y.C. YWCA, 1976-79, Am. Contract Bridge League Nat. Laws Commn., 1975—; mem. Pres.'s Com. on Selection of Fed. Jud. Officers, 1977-78. Mem. Am. Law Inst., Assn. Bar City N.Y., ABA, Lawyers Com. for Civil Rights Under Law (mem. exec. com. 1970-79). Womens Pairs Bridge Champion, Nat., 1971, 72, World, 1986. Office: US Court of Appeals US Courthouse Foley Sq New York NY 10007

KEATE, KENNETH EARL, lawyer; b. Alameda, Calif., Aug. 4, 1951; s. J Raybould and Martha Alice Keate. BA, Macalester Coll., 1973; JD, U. Minn., 1976. Bar: Minn. 1976, U.S. Dist. Ct. Minn. 1977, U.S. Tax Ct. 1983, U.S. Dist. Ct. (we. dist.) Wis. 1986. Sole practice St. Paul, 1976—. Deacon Metro. Community Ch., Mpls., 1977-79, bd. dirs. 1979-82, treas. 1979-81; bd. dirs. Minn. Freedom Band, Mpls., 1984-86; All God's Children Met. Community Ch., Mpls., 1984—. Mem. ABA (various sects.), Minn. Bar Assn. (various sects.), Hennepin County Bar Assn., Ramsey County Bar Assn. Democrat. Personal income taxation, Bankruptcy, Real property. Office: 1102 Grand Ave Saint Paul MN 55105

KEATING, GERARD F., lawyer; b. Mineola, N.Y., Jan. 29, 1953; s. Arthur Keating and Martha (Regniault) Keating Cronin; m. Sue McCoy, Dec. 20, 1980; children: Sean Arthur, Jessica Michelle. BA, Columbia U., 1975; JD, Fla. State U., 1981. Bar: Fla. 1981, U.S. Dist. Ct. (mid. dist.) 1981. Assoc. Peter Keating P.A., Daytona Beach, Fla., 1981-84; sole practice Daytona Beach, 1984-85; assoc. Arthur Gehris P.A., Daytona Beash, 1985-86; ptnr. Gehris & Keating P.A., Daytona Beash, 1986—; adj. prof. Daytona Beach Community Coll., 1981—. Mem. Assn. Trial Lawyers Am., Attys. Title Ins. Fund. Republican. Roman Catholic. Club: Columbia (N.Y.C.); Halifax (Daytona Beach), Daytona Beach Rugby (founder). Avocation: rugby. State civil litigation, Criminal, Personal injury. Home: 2039 S Peninsula Dr Daytona Beach FL 32018 Office: 501 Silver Beach Ave Daytona Beach FL 32018

KEATING, ROBERT CLARK, lawyer; b. Wallace, Idaho, Apr. 13, 1915; s. Charles August and Frances F. (McDiarmid) K.; m. Neysa B. Dalby, Nov. 13, 1944 (div. 1973); children: Robert D., Michael C., James M., Susan N.; m. Wanita Ekholm, Feb. 2, 1974. BA, U. Wash., 1937, JD, 1939. Bar: Wash. 1939, U.S. Dist. Ct. (we. dist.) Wash. 1941, U.S. Ct. Appeals (9th cir.) 1959. Claims atty. Ohio Casualty Ins. Co., Seattle, 1946-52; exec. v.p., gen. counsel Western Pacific Ins. Co., Seattle, 1952-66; ptnr. Merrick, Burgess, Hofstedt & Keating, Seattle, 1966-70; sr. ptnr. Keating, Bucklin & McCormack, Seattle, 1970—. Bd. dirs. Boy Scouts Am., Seattle, 1959-65, March of Dimes, Seattle, 1962-67, Nat. Football Found. and Hall of Fame, Seattle, 1965—. Served to capt. U.S. Army, 1942-46, PTO. Mem. ABA, Seattle-King County Bar Assn., Fedn. Ins. Counsel (sect. chmn.), Def. Research Inst., Wash. Assn. Def. Counsel (pres. 1984-85), Pacific Claim Execs. Assn. (pres. 1965-66), Delta Theta Phi, Sigma Nu. Republican. Lutheran. Clubs: Broadmoor Golf (pres. 1980-81), Wash. Athletic (Seattle). Insurance, Personal injury. Home: 3414 81st Pl SE Mercer Island WA 98040 Office: Keating Bucklin & McCormack 4141 Seafirst 5th Ave Plaza Seattle WA 98104

KEATINGE, CORNELIA WYMA, lawyer, architectural consultant; b. Poughkeepsie, N.Y., July 22, 1952; d. Edwin R. and Josephine B. (Brazis) Wyma; m. Robert Reed Keatinge, Aug. 21, 1982; 1 child, Courtney Elizabeth. BArch, U. Ky., 1974; MA in History and Theory of Architecture, U. Essex, Colchester, Eng., 1976; JD, U. Denver, 1982. Bar: Colo. 1982. Archtl. historian Kans. State Hist. Soc., Topeka, 1975-77; hist. architect Nat. Park Service, Denver, 1977-79; assoc. Richard E. Young, Denver, 1982-84; hist. architect Colo. Hist.Soc., Denver, 1984-86; sole practice, cons. architecture Denver, 1986; hist. preservation specialist Adv. Council Hist. Preservation, Golden, Colo., 1986—. Vol. Denver Art Mus., 1980—, Jr. League Denver, 1983—. Rotary fellow, 1974-75; recipient Spl. Achievement award, Nat. Park Service, 1980. Mem. ABA, Colo. Bar Assn., Denver Bar Assn. Real property, Construction, Historic preservation law. Home: 460 S Marion Pkwy #1904 Denver CO 80209 Office: 730 Simms St #450 Golden CO 80401

KEATINGE, RICHARD HARTE, lawyer; b. San Francisco, Dec. 4, 1919; m. Betty West, Apr. 20, 1944; children: Richard West, Daniel Wilson, Nancy Elizabeth. A.B. with honors, U. Calif., Berkeley, 1939; M.A., Harvard U., 1941; J.D., Georgetown U., 1944. Bar: D.C. 1944, N.Y. 1945, Calif. 1947, U.S. Supreme Ct. 1964. Sr. economist, sr. indsl. specialist WPB, Washington, 1941-44; practice law N.Y.C., 1944-45, Washington, 1945-47, Los Angeles, 1947—; sr. ptnr. Keatinge, Pastor & Mintz (and predecessor firms), 1948-79, Reavis & McGrath, 1979—; spl. asst. atty. gen., State of Calif., 1964-68; public mem. Adminstrv. Conf. of U.S., 1968-74. Mem.: Georgetown Law Jour, 1943-44. Mem. Calif. Law Revision Commn., 1961-68, chmn., 1965-67; trustee Coro Found., 1965-73; bd. trustees, mem. exec. com. U. Calif. Berkeley Found., 1983-87, chmn. bd. trustees, 1983-85. Fellow (life) Am. Bar Found., Am. Coll. Tax Counsel; mem. ABA (bd. govs. 1978-79, mem. ho. of dels. 1974-82, 82—, mem. council 1961-64, 65-69, 74-78, 82—, chmn. adminstrv. law sect. 1967-68, mem. standing com. on resolutions 1973-74, chmn. com. on sales, exchanges and basis taxation sect. 1963-65, mem. council econs. of law practice sect. 1974-75, mem. commn. on law and economy 1976-78, vice chmn. 1977-78, mem. spl. com. on housing and urban devel. law 1968-73, vice chmn. adv. commn. on housing and urban growth 1974-77, nat. sec. Jr. Bar Conf. 1949-50), State Bar Calif. (del. conf. of dels. 1966-67, 77—, mem. exec. com. public law sect. 1976-78), Los Angeles County Bar Assn. (chmn. taxation sect. 1966-67, mem. fair jud. election practices com. 1978-79, mem. exec. com. law office mgmt. sect. 1977-85, mem. housing and urban devel. law com. 1971-80, mem. arbitration com. 1974—, mem. new quarters com. 1979-80), Am. Coll. Tax Counsel, Assn. Bus. Trial Lawyers (bd. govs. 1974-79, pres. 1978-79), Inter-Am. Bar Assn., Internat. Bar Assn., Am. Judicature Soc., Am. Law Inst., Am. Arbitration Assn. (nat. panel of arbitrators 1950—), Com. to Maintain Diversity Jurisdiction, Lawyers Club Los Angeles, Phi Beta Kappa. Home: 220 S San Rafael Ave Pasadena CA 91105 Office: 700 S Flower St 6th Fl Los Angeles CA 90017

KEATINGE, ROBERT REED, lawyer; b. Berkeley, Calif., Apr. 22, 1948; s. Gerald Robert and Elizabeth Jean (Benedict) K.; m. Katherine Lou Carr, Feb. 1, 1969 (div. Dec. 1981); 1 child, Michael Towne; m. Cornelia Elizabeth Wyma, Aug. 21, 1982; 1 child, Courtney Elizabeth. BA, U. Colo., 1970; JD, U. Denver, 1973, LLM, 1982. Bar: Colo. 1974, U.S. Dist. Ct. Colo. 1974, U.S. Ct. Appeals (10th cir.) 1977, U.S. Tax Ct. 1980. Ptnr. Kubie & Keatinge, Denver, 1974-76; sole practice Robert Keatinge, Denver, 1976; assoc. Richard Young, Denver, 1977-86; counsel Durham & Assoc., P.C., Denver, 1986—; lectr. law U. Denver, 1982-83, adj. prof. grad. tax program, U. Denver, 1983—. Contbr. articles to profl. law jours. Speaker Continuing Leagl Edn. in Colo., 1984-85. Recipient Law Week award U. Denver Bur. Nat. Affairs, 1974. Mem. ABA (com. on real estate tax problems 1986), Colo. Bar Assn., Denver Bar Assn., Denver Tax Group (pres.), Denver Tax Assn., Greater Denver Tax Counsel's Assn. Lodge: Kiwanis. Corporate taxation, Personal income taxation, Securities. Home: 460 S Marion Pkwy #1904 Denver CO 80209

KEAY, DAVID HOLM, lawyer; b. Minot, N.D., June 23, 1951; s. Luther B. and Christine M. (Holm) K.; m. Susan E. Trowbridge, July 14, 1973; children: Kathryn, Andrew. BA, Luther Coll., 1973; JD, No. Ill. U., 1980. Bar: U.S. Ct. Appeals (7th cir.) 1981, Ill. 1983, U.S. Supreme Ct. 1985, U.S. Dist. Ct. (no. dist.) Ill. 1980. Asst. mgr. Jewel Cos., Oak Brook, Ill., 1973-74; sales, mktg. Vanco/Adidas, Grand Rapids, Mich., 1974-76; sole practice Wheaton, Ill., 1981—; tchr. Am. Bankers Assn., Chgo., 1983-84. Bd. dirs. Christian Conciliation Service DuPage County, Wheaton, 1984—. Mem. ABA, Ill. Bar Assn., DuPage County Bar Assn. (reference person 1983—). Lutheran. Avocations: sports, Christian edn. Real property, Family and matrimonial, State civil litigation. Office: 430 W Roosevelt Rd Wheaton IL 60187

KEBER, KENNETH JAMES, lawyer; b. Omaha, May 3, 1954; s. Mark Richard and Marguerite Claire (Moran) K.; m. Marianne Schmidt, Sept. 8, 1979; children: Jennifer, Andrew. BS, U. Nebr., 1975; JD, U. Notre Dame, 1978. Bar: Nebr. 1978, Ill. 1979. Mgr. tax Arthur Andersen & Co., Chgo., 1978-85, Coopers & Lybrand, South Bend, Ind., 1985—. Recipient Burket award ASCAP, 1978. Mem. ABA, Ill. Bar Assn., Nebr. Bar Assn., Am. Inst. CPA's, Ind. Soc. CPA's. Corporate taxation, Personal income taxation, Estate taxation. Home: 16338 Baywood Ln Granger IN 46530 Office: Coopers & Lybrand PO Box 4157 South Bend IN 46634

KECK, ROBERT CLIFTON, lawyer; b. Sioux City, Iowa, May 20, 1914; s. Herbert Allen and Harriet (McCutchen) K.; m. Ruth P. Edwards, Nov. 2, 1940; children: Robert, Laura E. Simpson, Gloria E. Sauser. A.B., Ind. U., 1936; J.D., U. Mich., 1939; L.H.D., Nat. Coll. Edn., 1973. Bar: Ill. 1939. Since practiced in Chgo; mem. firm Keck, Mahin & Cate, 1939—, partner, 1946—; sec., dir. Methode Electronics, Inc. Chmn. bd. trustees Nat. Coll. Edn., 1955—; trustee Sears Roebuck Found., 1977-79. Served with USNR, 1943-45. Fellow Am. Coll. Trial Lawyers; mem. Am., Fed., Ill., Chgo. assns., Bar Assn. Seventh Fed. Circuit (past pres.), Phi Gamma Delta. Republican. Methodist. Clubs: Westmoreland Country (Wilmette); Economic, Chicago, Metropolitan; Biltmore Forest Golf (Asheville, N.C.); Glen View (Golf, Ill.). Lodge: Masons. Antitrust, General corporate. Office: Sears Tower 83rd Floor Chicago IL 60606

KEEFE, WILLIAM JOHN, lawyer; b. Greenwich, Conn., June 3, 1954; s. John Miles and Ann (O'Shea) K. AB, Dartmouth Coll., 1976; JD, U. Maine, 1979. Bar: Maine 1979, N.H. 1979, U.S. Dist. Ct. N.H. 1979. Ptnr. Keefe & Keefe P.A., Wilton, N.H., 1980—. Sec. N.H. Sch. Bldg. Authority, Concord, 1981-85; pres. Wilton Bus. Assn., 1983-85. General practice, State civil litigation, Real property. Office: Keefe & Keefe PA Main St Box 599 Wilton NH 03086

KEEGAN, JOHN ROBERT, lawyer, educator; b. Boston, Aug. 22, 1950; s. Francis Harold and Margaret (Huntley) K.; m. Karen Mary Finn, July 27, 1975; children: Kathleen Elizabeth, Margaret Mary. BBA cum laude, Suffolk U., 1972, JD cum laude, 1976; LLM in Taxation, Boston U., 1980; chtd. fin. cons., Am. Coll., 1985. Bar: Mass. 1977; CLU. Group pension adminstr. New Eng. Life Ins. Co., Boston, 1972-75, pension legal specialist, 1975-78, group pension atty., 1978-80, pension atty., 1980-81; asst. counsel Sun Life Assurance Co. of Can., Wellesley Hills, Mass., 1981-83, advanced underwriting officer, 1983-87; assoc. Flynn, Joyce and Sheridan, Boston, 1987—; instr. Bentley Coll., Waltham, Mass., 1981—, adv. bd. 1984—; Northeastern U., Boston, 1985—, Mass. Soc. CPA's, Boston, 1984—. Mem. ABA, Boston Bar Assn., Am. Soc. CLU's. Roman Catholic. Avocations: softball, tennis. Pension, profit-sharing, and employee benefits, Estate planning, Personal income taxation. Office: Flynn Joyce and Sheridan 400 Atlantic Ave Boston MA 02210

KEELER, JEAN MARIE, lawyer; b. Bethlehem, Pa., July 19, 1954; d. Charles Harry and Gloria (Iasiello) K.; m. David Joseph Salabsky, Jan. 7, 1978. BS, Allentown Coll. St. Francis de Sales, 1976; JD, Villanova U., 1981. Bar: Pa. 1981, U.S. Dist. Ct. (ea. dist.) Pa. 1981, N.J. 1982. Law clk. to presiding justice Bucks County Ct. Common Pleas, Doylestown, Pa., 1981-82; assoc. Grim & Grim, Perkasie, Pa., 1982—. Mem. women's steering com. Bucks County Dems., 1986—. Mem. Bucks County Bar Assn. (vice chairperson young lawyers div. 1985-86, chairperson 1986—, chairperson practicum com. 1985-86). Personal injury, Criminal, Health. Office: Grim & Grim 6th & Chestnut St Perkasie PA 18944

KEELEY, GEORGE WILLIAM, lawyer; b. Chgo., May 31, 1947; s. John L. and Mary (Schneider) K.; m. Susan Isabelle Rice, 1969; children: Brian R., William H. BA, U. Notre Dame, 1969; MBA, Northwestern U., 1973; JD, Loyola U., Chgo., 1976. Bar: Ill. U.S. Dist. Ct. (no. dist.) Ill. 1976, U.S. Ct. Appeals (7th cir.) 1981. Assoc. Halfpenny, Hahn & Roche, Chgo., 1976-82, ptnr., 1982—; lectr. Chgo. Soc. Assn. Execs., 1986. Mem. ABA, Ill. Bar Assn., Chgo. Bar Assn., Northwestern Mgmt. Club of Chgo. Roman Catholic. Clubs: Notre Dame Chgo., Beverly Country (Chgo.). General practice, State civil litigation, General corporate. Home: 8901 S Leavitt Chicago IL 60620 Office: Halfpenny Hahn & Roche 20 N Wacker Dr Chicago IL 60606

KEELY, GEORGE CLAYTON, lawyer; b. Denver, Feb. 28, 1926; s. Thomas and Margaret (Clayton) K.; m. Jane Elisabeth Coffey, Nov. 18, 1950; children: Margaret Clayton, George C. (dec.), Mary Anne, Jane Elisabeth, Edward Francis, Kendall Anne. B.S. in Bus, U. Colo., 1948; LLB., Columbia U., 1951. Bar: Colo. 1951. Partner firm Fairfield & Woods, Denver, 1951—; v.p., dir. Silver Corp., East Wash. Ry. Co., 1966-86; mem. exec. com. Timpte Industries, Inc., 1970-78, now dir.; dir. Hugh M. Woods Co., 1971-84. Mem. Colo. Commn. Promotion Uniform State Laws, 1967—; regional planning adv. com. Denver Regional Council Govts., 1972-74; bd. dirs. Bow Mar Water and Sanitation Dist., 1970-74; trustee Town of Bow Mar, 1972-74; trustee, v.p. Silver Found.; mem. exec. bd. Denver Area council Boy Scouts Am., v.p. legal services, 1986—; bd. dirs. Pub. Broadcasting of Colo., Inc., 1986—. Served with USAAF, 1944-47. Fellow Am. Bar Found., Colo. Bar Found.; mem. Am. Bar Assn. (ho. of dels. 1977-79), Denver Bar Assn. (award of merit 1979), Colo. Bar Assn., Nat. Conf. Commrs. Uniform State Laws (sec. 1971-75, exec. com. 1971—, chmn. exec. com. 1975-77, pres. 1977-79), Am. Law Inst., Cath. Lawyers Guild of Denver (dir. 1965-67), Phi Delta Phi, Beta Theta Pi, Beta Gamma Sigma. Clubs: U. Denver (dir. 1966-75, pres. 1973-74), Law of Denver (pres. 1966-67), Pinehurst Country. Lodge: Rotary. Corporate taxation, Estate taxation, Banking. Home: 5220 Longhorn St Littleton CO 80120 Office: Fairfield & Woods One United Bank Ctr 1700 Lincoln Suite 2400 Denver CO 80203

KEEN, ANDREW NICK, lawyer; b. Astoria, N.Y., Oct. 9, 1956; s. Constantine Andrew and Kalliope Mary (Carajikis) K.; m. Rebecca Constant, Sept. 19, 1982; 1 child, Christopher John. BS, NYU, 1978; JD, Fordham U., 1981. Bar: N.Y. 1982, U.S. Dist. Ct. (so. and ea. dists.) N.Y. 1982. Assoc. Acito & Klein, P.C., N.Y.C., 1981-82, Condon & Forsyth, N.Y.C., 1982—. Mem. ABA, N.Y. State Bar Assn., Assn. of Bar of City of N.Y. Democrat. Greek Orthodox. Avocations: golf, tennis, reading. Federal civil litigation, Product liability, Aviation litigation. Home: 75 Essex Ct Port Washington NY 11050 Office: Condon & Forsyth 1251 Ave of Americas New York NY 10020

KEEN, ROBERT THOMAS, JR., lawyer; b. Boston, Jan. 27, 1957; s. Robert Thomas and Mary (Francis) K.; m. Elizabeth Ann Taylor, Aug. 23, 1980. BA with honors, U. Notre Dame, 1979, JD, 1982. Bar: Ind. 1982, U.S. Dist. Ct. (no. and so. dists.) Ind. 1982, U.S. Ct. Appeals (7th cir.) 1985. Assoc. Livingston, Dildine, Haynie & Yoder, Ft. Wayne, Ind., 1982—. Sec., coach Foster Park Little League, Ft. Wayne, 1983—. Mem. ABA, Ind. Bar Assn., Allen County Bar Assn., Ind. Def. Lawyers Assn. Democrat. Roman Catholic. Federal civil litigation, State civil litigation, Personal injury. Home: 304 E Paulding Rd Fort Wayne IN 46816 Office: Livingston Dildine Haynie & Yoder 1400 One Summit Sq Fort Wayne IN 46802

KEENAN, C. ROBERT, III, lawyer; b. Pitts., July 21, 1954; s. C. Robert Jr. and Catherine (Conley) K.; m. Joann R. Fogle, June 9, 1979; children: Rachel, Rosemary. BA, Bucknell U., 1976; JD, U. Pitts., 1979. Bar: Pa. 1979, U.S. Dist. Ct. (we. dist.) Pa. 1979, U.S. Ct. Appeals (3d cir.) 1981, U.S. Supreme Ct. 1983. Assoc. Shire & Bergstein, Monessen, Pa., 1979-80; ptnr. Jones, Gregg, Creehan & Gerace, Pitts., 1980—. Editor Real News Jour., 1984—. Solicitor Castle Shannon (Pa.) Community Library, 1984—, trustee, 1982-84; mem. claims adjudication bd. SSS, Pitts., 1984—, chmn., 1987—. Mem. ABA, Pa. Bar Assn., Pa. Trial Lawyers Assn., Allegheny County Bar Assn. (bd. dirs. real property sect. 1986—), Pi Sigma Alpha, Omicron Delta Kappa. Republican. Presbyterian. Clubs: Dormont (Mt. Lebanon, Pa.); Sportsmen's (Pitts.). Lodge: Rotary (past pres., disting. service award 1985). Avocations: marksmanship, music, swimming. Real property, State civil litigation, Workers' compensation. Office: Jones Gregg Creehan & Gerace 1600 Grant Bldg Pittsburgh PA 15219

KEENAN, JAMES FRANCIS, lawyer, insurance executive; b. Portland, Maine, Apr. 6, 1939; s. Michael Francis and Ruth Mary (Niles) K.; m. Sandra Annis, July 2, 1976; children—Tina, Michael, Angela, Paige, James, Jr. B.A., Bates Coll., 1961; J.D., Boston U., 1964, LL.M., 1975. Bar: Maine 1964, U.S. Dist. Ct. Maine 1965. Atty. Unionmutual Life Ins. Co., Portland, 1964-68, assoc. counsel, 1968-75, v.p., 1975—; dir. Unionmutual Charitable Found., Portland, 1980-84. Author: (with Douglas Thornsjo) The Mutual Company, 1972. Trustee Bates Coll., Center Meml. Hosp., Standish, Maine, Sch. Adminstrv. Dist., Buxton, Maine. Fellow Am. Coll. Investment Coun-

sel; mem. Am. Land Title Assn., Assn. Life Ins. Counsel, ABA, Maine Bar Assn. General corporate. Home: Route 1 Box 8450 Sebago Lake ME 04075 Office: UNUM Life Ins Co Unionmutual Life Ins Co 2211 Congress St Portland ME 04122

KEENAN, JOHN FONTAINE, federal judge; b. N.Y.C., Nov. 23, 1929; s. John Joseph and Veronica (Fontaine) K.; m. Diane R. Nicholson, Oct. 6, 1956; 1 child, Marie Patricia. B.B.A., Manhattan Coll., N.Y., 1951; LL.B., Fordham U., 1954. Bar: N.Y. 1954, U.S. Dist. Ct. (so. dist.) N.Y. 1970. From asst. dist. atty. to chief asst. dist. atty. New York County Dist. Atty.'s Office, 1956-76; spl. prosecutor, dep. atty. gen. City of N.Y., 1976-79; chmn. bd., pres. N.Y.C. Off-Track Betting Corp., 1979-82; criminal justice coordinator City of N.Y., 1982-83; judge U.S. Dist. Ct. So. Dist. N.Y., N.Y.C., 1983—; chief asst. dist. atty. Queens County Dist. Atty.'s Office, N.Y., 1973; adj. prof. John Jay Coll. Criminal Justice, N.Y.C., 1979-83. Contbr. articles to law jours. Chmn. Daytop Village, Inc., N.Y.C., 1981-83. Served with U.S. Army, 1954-56. Recipient Frank S. Hogan award Citizens Com. Control of Crime in N.Y., 1975; cert. of recognition Patrolmen's Benevolent Assn., 1976; 1st Ann. Hogan-Morgenthau Assocs. award New York County Dist. Atty.'s Office, 1976; Excellence award N.Y. State Bar Assn., 1978; award N.Y. Criminal Bar Assn., 1979; Disting. Faculty award Nat. Coll. Dist. Attys., 1978; Louis J. Lefkowitz award Fordham Urban Law Jour., 1983. Mem. N.Y. State Bar Assn. (criminal justice exec. com. 1980—), Assn. Bar City of N.Y. (criminal justice council 1982—), Nat. Dist. Attys. Assn., N.Y. State Dist. Attys. Assn. Republican. Roman Catholic. Clubs: Amackassin (Yonkers, N.Y.); Skytop (Pa.); Merchants (N.Y.C.). Judicial administration. Office: US Dist Ct US Courthouse 40 Foley Sq Room 420 New York NY 10007

KEENAN, KEVIN PATRICK, lawyer; b. Mankato, Minn., Dec. 16, 1951; s. Jerry D. and Delilah M. (Tentis) K.; m. Nancy Mary Beerling, Aug. 17, 1974; children: Daniel, Brian, Elizabeth. BA, St. Mary's Coll., 1974; JD, U. Minn., 1977. Bar: Minn., 1977, D.C., 1978. Ptnr. Bassford, Heckt, Lockhart & Mullin P.A., Mpls., 1977—. Mem. ABA, Minn. Bar Assn., Hennepin County Bar Assn., Minn. Def. Lawyers Assn., Minn. Trial Lawyers Assn., Lawyers Soc. St. Thomas Moore (pres. 1984—). Republican. Roman Catholic. Club: Mpls. Athletic. Avocations: golf, baseball. Admiralty, State civil litigation, Insurance. Home: 1445 Arden Oaks Dr Arden Hills MN 55112 Office: Bassford Heckt Lockhart & Mullin PA 3550 Multifoods Tower Minneapolis MN 55402

KEENAN, RICHARD, lawyer; b. Balt., Oct. 19, 1952; s. Robert Richard and Nance Yvonne (Baughman) K.; m. Kathleen McNamara, May 15, 1982. BBA, U. Notre Dame, 1974; JD, Yale U., 1977. Bar: Calif. 1977, U.S. Dist. Ct. (no. dist.) 1977, U.S. Dist. Ct. (so. dist.) 1981, U.S. Dist. Ct. (ea. dist.) 1984, U.S. Dist. Ct. (cen. dist.) 1985, U.S. Dist. Ct. (no. dist.) Ill. 1985, U.S. Dist. Ct. Hawaii 1986, U.S. Ct. Appeals (9th cir.) 1987. Law clk. to presiding justice U.S. Dist. Ct. (no. dist.) Ill., 1977-78; assoc. Morrison & Foerster, San Francisco, 1979-81; assoc. Folger & Levin, San Francisco, 1981-84, ptnr., 1984—. Chmn. bd. dirs. Point Bonita YMCA, 1982-86; mem. Guardsmen, San Francisco, 1982—. Mem. ABA, Calif. Bar Assn., Notre Dame Bay Area Alumni Club (pres. 1984-85). Democrat. Roman Catholic. Federal civil litigation, State civil litigation, Antitrust. Home: 171 15th Ave San Francisco CA 94118 Office: Folger & Levin 100 Green St San Francisco CA 94111

KEENE, JOHN CLARK, lawyer, educator; b. Phila., Aug. 17, 1931; s. Floyd Elwood and Marthe (Bussiere) K.; m. Ana Maria Delgado, July 21, 1973; children: Lisa, John, Suzanna, Katharine, Peter; stepchildren: Carlos, Rene, Mario, Raul, Silvio, Carmen. BA, Yale U., 1953; JD, Harvard U., 1959; M City Planning, U. Pa., 1966. Bar: Pa. 1960, U.S. Supreme Ct. 1976. Assoc. Pepper, Hamilton & Scheetz, 1959-64; prof. city and regional planning U. Pa., Phila., 1968—, ombudsman, 1978-84; ptnr. Coughlin, Keene & Assocs., Phila., 1982—. Fulbright fellow, 1985. Trustee ex officio Phila. Mus. Art, 1978-80. Served to lt. USN, 1953-56. Mem. Am. Inst. Cert. Planners, ABA, Pa. Bar Assn., Phila. Bar Assn. Author: Untaxing Open Space, 1976; The Protection of Farmland, 1981. Real property. Home: 119 Bleddyn Rd Ardmore PA 19003

KEENEY, JOHN CHRISTOPHER, JR., lawyer; b. Washington, Aug. 29, 1951; s. John Christopher Sr. and Eugena M. (Brislin) K. AB summa cum laude, U. Notre Dame, 1973; JD cum laude, Harvard U., 1976. Bar: Md. 1976, D.C. 1977, U.S. Dist. Ct. D.C. 1978, U.S. Dist. Ct. Md. 1977, U.S. Ct. Appeals (4th cir.) 1977, U.S. Ct. Appeals (D.C. cir.) 1978, U.S. Ct. Appeals (7th cir.) 1984, U.S. Supreme Ct. 1980. Law clk. to presiding judge U.S. Dist. Ct. Md., Balt., 1976-78; assoc. Hogan & Hartson, Washington, 1978-84, ptnr., 1985—. Co-author: Civil and Criminal Remedies for Racially and Religiously Motivated Violence, 1983. Mem. area bus. com. Nat. Symphony Orchestra, Washington, 1980-83, tech. adv. com. Dem. Nat. Com. Fairness Commn., Washington, 1985-86; cons. Common Cause of Md., Annapolis, 1980-86. Mem. ABA, D.C. Bar Assn., Washington Council of Lawyers. Roman Catholic. Civil rights, Federal civil litigation, Election law. Home: 8715 First Ave #1220C Silver Spring MD 20910 Office: Hogan & Hartson 555 13th St Washington DC 20004

KEEP, JUDITH N., federal judge; b. 1944. B.A., Scripps Coll., 1966; J.D., U. San Diego, 1970. With Defenders Inc., 1971-73; sole practice 1973-76; asst. U.S. atty. Calif., 1976; judge Mcpl. Ct., San Diego, 1976-80, U.S. Dist. Ct. (so. dist.) Calif., San Diego, 1980—. Judicial administration. Office: US District Court 940 Front St San Diego CA 92189 *

KEESHIN, SCOTT AVERY, lawyer; b. Chgo., July 28, 1952; s. Sanford Jerome and Marcelle (Greenberg) K.; m. Margaret Elizabeth Swistock, Aug. 1, 1979; 1 child, Matthew Scott. Student, U. Colo., 1970-73; JD, Baylor U., 1976. Bar: Tex. 1976, U.S. Dist. Ct. (no. dist.) Tex. 1976, Pa. 1982, U.S. Supreme Ct. 1982. Asst. dist. atty. Tarrant County, Ft. Worth, 1976-78; pres. The Keeshin Firm, Grapevine, Tex., 1978—; gen. counsel Lisa Motor Lines, Ft. Worth, 1985—, also bd. dirs.; bd. dirs. Tidwell Enterprises, Inc., Tidwell Properties, Inc., Ft. Worth; gen. counsel Trinity Valley MHMR Authority, Ft. Worth, 1977-78. Mem. Pub. Responsibility Com., Ft. Worth, 1977-78; campaign coordinator Mike Moncrief for Tarrant County judge, 1982; candidate Grapevine City Council, 1983. Mem. ABA, Tex. Bar Assn., Tarrant County Bar Assn., Tarrant County Young Lawyers Assn. Jewish. Lodge: Rotary. Federal civil litigation, State civil litigation. Home: 2017 Casa Loma Ct Grapevine TX 76051 Office: The Keeshin Firm 1340 S Main Suite 200 Grapevine TX 76051

KEETON, ROBERT ERNEST, federal judge; b. Clarksville, Tex., Dec. 16, 1919; s. William Robert and Ernestine (Tuten) K.; m. Betty E. Baker, May 28, 1941; children: Katherine, William Robert. B.B.A., U. Tex., 1940, LL.B., 1941; S.J.D., Harvard U., 1956; LL.D. hon., William Mitchell Coll., 1983. Bar: Tex. 1941, Mass. 1955. Assoc. firm Baker, Botts, Andrews & Wharton (and successors), Houston, 1941-42, 45-51; assoc. prof. law So. Meth. U., 1951-54; Thayer teaching fellow Harvard U., 1953-54, asst. prof., 1954-56, prof. law, 1956-73, Langdell prof., 1973-79; assoc. dean Harvard, 1975-79; judge Fed. Dist. Ct., Boston, 1979—; Commr. on Uniform State Laws from Mass., 1971-79; trustee Flaschner Jud. Inst., 1979-86; bd. dirs. Nat. Inst. Trial Advocacy, 1973-76; ednl. cons., 1976-79; mem. com. on ct. adminstrn. U.S. Jud. Conf., 1985—. Author: Trial Tactics and Methods, 1954, 2d edit., 1973, Cases and Materials on the Law of Insurance, 1960, 2d edit., 1977, Legal Cause in the Law of Torts, 1963, Venturing To Do Justice, 1969, (with Jeffrey O'Connell) Basic Protection for the Traffic Victim—A Blueprint for Reforming Automobile Insurance, 1965, After Cars Crash—The Need for Legal and Insurance Reform, 1967, (with Page Keeton) Cases and Materials on the Law of Torts, 1971, 2d edit., 1977, Basic Text on Insurance Law, 1971, (with others) Tort and Accident Law, 1983, (with others) Prosser & Keeton, Torts, 5th edit., 1984; also articles. Served to lt. comdr. USNR, 1942-45. Recipient Wm. B. Jones award Nat. Inst. Trial Advocacy, 1980; recipient Leon Green award U. Tex. Law Rev., 1981, Francis Rawle award Am. Law Inst.-ABA, 1983, Samuel E. Gates litigation award Am. Coll. Trial Lawyers, 1984. Fellow Am. Bar Found., mem., Am. Acad. Arts and Scis., Am. Bar Assn., Mass. Bar Assn., State Bar Tex., Am. Law Inst., Am. Risk and Ins. Assn., Chancellors, Friars, Order of Coif, Beta Gamma Sigma, Beta Alpha Psi, Phi Delta Phi, Phi Eta Sigma. Federal civil litigation, State civil litigation, Insurance. Home: 26 Bailey Rd Watertown MA 02172 Office: US Dist Ct McCormack Post Office and Courthouse Bld Boston MA 02109

KEETON, ROBERT TAYLOR, JR., lawyer; b. Nashville, June 21, 1937; s. Robert and Hannah Theresa (Curlin) T.; m. Laura Agnes Peterson, June 27, 1959; children: Robert Taylor III, Laura Agnes. BS, Memphis State U., 1959; JD, U. Tenn., 1962. Bar: Tenn. 1962, U.S. Dist. Ct. (we. dist.) Tenn. 1964, U.S. Supreme Ct. 1971. Assoc. Taylor & Keeton, Huntingdon, Tenn., 1962-63; jr. ptnr. Taylor & Keeton, Huntingdon, 1963-65, ptnr., 1965—; atty. City of Bruceton, Tenn., 1962-82, City of Huntingdon, 1983—, Carroll County, Huntingdon, 1972—. Mem. ABA, Tenn. Bar Assn., Carroll County Bar Assn., Assn. Trial Lawyers Am., Tenn. Trial Lawyers Assn. (pres. 1981-82, bd. govs.). Democrat. Baptist. Lodges: Lions (pres. Bruceton club), Elks, Shriners. Avocations: hunting, camping, farming. Workers' compensation, State civil litigation, Personal injury. Home: 107 Highland St Bruceton TN 38317 Office: Taylor & Keeton 346 E Main St Huntingdon TN 38344

KEGAN, ESTHER OSWIANZA, lawyer; b. Chgo.; d. Abraham and Ida (Segal) Oswianza; m. Albert I. Kegan, Jan. 29, 1939 (dec. 1963); children: Judith Gardiner, Daniel, Franklin. BS, Northwestern U., 1933, JD, 1936, MS, 1953. Bar: Ill. 1936, U.S. Patent Office, U.S. Supreme Ct. 1943. Research asst. Chgo. Dept. Law, 1936-41; ptnr. Kegan & Kegan, Chgo., 1943-63; owner Kegan, Kegan & Berkman, Chgo., 1963-84; pres. Kegan & Kegan, Ltd., Chgo., 1984—. Contbr. legal articles to profl. jours. Mem. ABA, Ill. Bar Assn. (patent and trademark council 1982—), Patent Law Assn. Chgo., Women's Bar Assn. Ill., Internat. Assn. for Protection Indsl. Property, World Peace Through Law, Decalogue Soc. Lawyers (bd. dirs.), Northwestern U. Law Alumni (bd. dirs.), Order of Coif, Phi Beta Kappa. Jewish. Trademark and copyright, Patent, Food, Drug and Medical Devices.

KEHL, RANDALL HERMAN, lawyer, military officer; b. Furstenfeldbruck, Fed. Republic of Germany, May 18, 1954; came to U.S., 1955; s. Raymond Herman and Annabelle (Fair) K.; m. Catherine Elizabeth Marak, July 10, 1976; children: Lindsey Elizabeth, Jessica Anne. BS, USAF Acad., 1976; MBA, U. N.D., 1980; JD, Pepperdine U., 1983. Bar: N.D. 1983, U.S. Dist. Ct. Alaska 1983, U.S. Dist. Ct. N.Mex. 1986. Commd. 2d lt. USAF, 1976, advanced through grades to maj., 1986; chief civil law Alaska Air Command, Anchorage, 1983-84, chief criminal law, 1984-85, commdr., 1985, chief def. counsel, 1985-86; dep. base atty. Kirtland AFB, Albuquerque, 1986—; asst. U.S. atty. U.S. Dept. Justice, Albuquerque, 1986—; adj. prof. law U. Alaska, 1985-86; bd. dirs., counsel Kirtland Fed. Credit Union, Albuquerque; bd. dirs., sec. Triad Communications, Inc., Albuquerque. Asst. scoutmaster Boy Scouts Am., Minot, N.D., 1977-80; tchr. Officers Christian Fellowship, Minot, 1977-80; civic arbitrator, commdr. Mediation and Conciliation Service Alaska, Anchorage, 1983-86; mem. sch. bd. Anchorage, 1984-85. Fellow Assn. Trial Lawyers Am.; mem. ABA, The Judge Advs. Assn., Phi Delta Phi. Republican. Presbyterian. Avocations: swimming, skiing, scuba diving, sailing, equestrian pursuits. Government contracts and claims, Environment, Military. Office: Kirtland AFB 1606 ABW/JA Kirtland AFB NM 87117

KEHOE, DENNIS JOSEPH, lawyer; b. Culver City, Calif., Nov. 12, 1937; s. Ignatius Dennis and Anne Theresa (Conroy) K.; m. Jacqueline Mona De Quincy, Aug. 25, 1962; children—Theresa, Suzanne, Patrick, Michael, Kevin. B.S. in Commerce, U. Santa Clara, 1960; LL.B., U. Calif. Hastings Coll. Law, 1963. Bar: Calif. 1964, U.S. Dist. Ct. (no. dist.) Calif. 1964, U.S. Ct. Appeals (9th cir.) 1964, U.S. Supreme Ct. 1980. Asst. county counsel Santa Cruz County (Calif.), 1964-66; assoc. Adams, Levin, Kehoe, Bosso, Sachs & Bates and predecessor Adams & Levin, Santa Cruz, Calif., 1966-70, ptnr., 1970-87; sole practice, 1987—. Mem. Calif. State Bar Assn., ABA, Calif. Trial Lawyers Assn., Santa Cruz County Bar Assn. Republican. Roman Catholic. Condemnation, State civil litigation, Personal injury. Home: 607 Cliff Dr Aptos CA 95003 Office: 323 Church St Santa Cruz CA 95060

KEHOE, JAMES W., judge; b. 1925. A.A., U. Fla., 1947, LL.B., 1950. Bar: Fla. Assoc. firm Worley, Kehoe & Willard, 1952-55; asst. county solicitor Dade County, Fla., 1955-57; assoc. firm Miltor R. Wasman, 1957-61; judge Civil Record Ct., Miami, 1961-63, 11th Jud. Circuit Ct., Fla., 1963-77, 3d Dist. Ct. Appeals, 1977-79, U.S. Dist. Ct. (so. dist.) Fla., 1979—. Mem. ABA, Fla. Bar Assn. Judicial administration. Office: US District Court PO Box 013097 Flagler Station Miami FL 33101 *

KEIR, DUNCAN WRAY, lawyer; b. Balt., Mar. 27, 1946; s. Wilfred Grenfell and Blanche (Scott) K.; m. Lisa Stefanon, Dec. 22, 1968; children: Duncan Scott, Andrew Wray. BA, Gettysburg Coll., 1968; JD with honors, U. Md., 1975. Bar: Md. 1975, U.S. Dist. Ct. Md. 1976, U.S. Ct. Appeals (4th cir.) 1982. Assoc. Miles & Stockbridge, Balt., 1975-81, ptnr., 1981—; active Dist. of Md. U.S. Bankruptcy Ct. Rules Com. Served to lt. USN, 1968-72. Mem. ABA, Md. State Bar Assn., Balt. Bankruptcy Discussion Group. Republican. Avocations: sailing, model trains. Bankruptcy, Banking. Office: Miles & Stockbridge 10 Light St Baltimore MD 21202

KEISER, HENRY BRUCE, lawyer, publisher; b. N.Y.C., Oct. 26, 1927; s. Leo and Jessie (Liebeskind) K.; B.A. with honors in Econs., U. Mich., 1947; J.D. cum laude, Harvard U., 1950; m. Jessie E. Weeks, July 12, 1953; children—Betsy Cordelia Keiser Smith, Matthew Roderick. Admitted to N.Y. bar, 1950, D.C. bar, 1955, Fla. bar, 1956, U.S. Supreme Ct bar, 1954; trial atty. CAB, Washington, 1950-51; head counsel alcoholic beverages sect. OPS, 1951-52; legal asst. to Judge Eugene Black, Tax Ct. U.S., 1953-56; practice in Washington, 1956—; founder, chmn. bd., pres., Fed. Pubs., Inc., 1959-85; chmn. bd. Gene Galasso Assos., Inc., Washington, 1963—; founder, chmn. Crown Eagle Communications Ltd., London, 1978-84; chmn. bd. The Arkhon Corp., Cherry Hill, N.J., 1983—; chmn. Empire Carriages, London, 1984—; chmn. bd., pres. Keiser Enterprises, Inc., Washington, 1985—; chmn. Lion Internat., London, 1985—; chmn. bd. U.S. Telemktg., Inc., Atlanta, 1986—; chmn. bd. The Inst. for Paralegal Tng., Phila., 1986—; chmn., sec. adv. com. on Constrn. Contract Document Reform, HUD, 1983-85; dir. Nat. Bank of Commerce, Washington, 1983-84; mem. adv. cabinet Southeastern U.,1965-75; judge, bd. of contract appeals, AEC, 1965-75; profl. lectr. Dept. Agr., 1960-77, George Washington U., 1961-79, U. San Francisco, 1965-82, Coll. William and Mary, 1966-75, Calif. Inst. Tech., 1967-72, U. So. Calif., 1973-74, U. Denver, 1975-85, Air Force Inst. Tech., 1975-76, U. Santa Clara, 1975-81, Trustee Touro Coll., 1979—. Served to 1st lt. Judge Adv. Gen. Corps, USAF, 1952-53; maj. Res. (ret.). Fellow Nat. Contract Mgmt. Assn.; mem. Am. (council pub. contract law sect. 1972-75), N.Y., Fla., D.C. (dir. 1965-66, chmn. adminstrv. law sect. 1964-65) bar assns. Jewish. Clubs: Cosmos, Nat. Press, Army Navy, Harvard (Washington); Crockford's (London). Construction, Government contracts and claims, Administrative and regulatory. Home: 7200 Armat Dr Bethesda MD 20817 Office: 2828 Pennsylvania Ave Washington DC 20007

KEISER, J. ALAN, lawyer; b. Fostoria, Ohio, Sept. 26, 1949; s. George Edward and June Adele (Riesenberg) K. BS in Agr., Ohio State U., 1973; JD, Toledo U., 1977. Bar: Ohio 1978, U.S. Dist. Ct. (no. dist.) Ohio 1978, Mich. 1979. Law clk. to judge Common Pleas Ct., Wauson, Ohio, 1975-78; assoc. Beard & Kaper Co., L.P.A., Delta, Ohio, 1978-79; sole practice Swanton, Ohio, 1979—. Nat. Merit scholar Sun Oil Co., 1967. Mem. Mich. Bar Assn., Fulton County Bar Assn., Mich. Trial Lawyers Assn., Ohio Trial Lawyers Assn., Fulton County Law Library Assn. (trustee 1979—). Democrat. Roman Catholic. Lodge: Rotary (pres. Swanton chpt. 1982-83, trustee Swanton Found., Inc. 1983—). Avcocations: opera, reading, gardening. General practice. Home: 1179 County Rd F Swanton OH 43558 Office: 110 W Airport Hwy PO Box 154 Swanton OH 43558

KEITH, DAMON JEROME, judge; b. Detroit, July 4, 1922; s. Perry A. and Annie L. (Williams) K.; m. Rachel Boone, Oct. 18, 1953; children: Cecile Keith, Debbie, Gilda. S.B., W.Va. State Coll., 1943; LL.B., Howard U., 1949; LL.M., Wayne State U., 1956; hon. degrees, U. Mich., Howard U., Wayne State U., Mich. State U., N.Y. Law Sch., Detroit Coll. Law, W.Va. State Coll., U. Detroit, Atlanta U., Lincoln U. Bar: Mich. 1949. Atty. Office Friend of Ct., Detroit, 1952-56; sr. ptnr. firm Keith, Conyers Anderson, Brown & Wahls, Detroit, 1964-67; mem. Wayne County Bd. Suprs., 1958-63; chief U.S. judge Eastern Dist. Mich., 1967-77; judge U.S. Ct. Appeals for 6th Circuit, Detroit, 1977—; Mem. Wayne County (Mich.) Bd. Suprs., 1958-63; chmn. Mich. Civil Rights Commn., 1964-67; pres. Detroit Housing Commn., 1958-67; commnr. State Bar Mich., 1960-67; mem. Mich. Com. Manpower Devel. and Vocat. Tng., 1964, Detroit Mayor's Health Advisory Com., 1969. Contbr. to legal jours. Trustee Med. Corp. Detroit; trustee Interlochen Arts Acad., Cranbrook Sch.; mem. Citizen's Advisory Com. Equal Ednl. Opportunity Detroit Bd. Edn.; vice pres. United Negro Coll. Fund Detroit; 1st v.p. emeritus Detroit chpt. NAACP; mem. com. mgmt. Detroit YMCA, Detroit council Boy Scouts Am., Detroit Arts Commn. Served with AUS, World War II. Recipient Alumni citation Wayne State U., 1968, Citizen award Mich. State U., numerous others; Spingarn medalist, 1974; named 1 of 100 Most Influential Black Ams. Ebony Mag., 1971, 77. Mem. Am. (council sect. legal edn. and admission to bar), Nat., Mich., Detroit bar assns., Nat. Lawyers Guild, Am. Judicature Soc., Alpha Phi Alpha. Baptist (deacon). Club: Detroit Cotillion. Office: US Ct Appeals 240 Fed Bldg Detroit MI 48226

KEITH, JOHN RAY, lawyer; b. Hillsboro, Ill., June 24, 1948; s. Clarence Robinson and Audrey Lucille (Settle) K. BA, Eastern Ill. U., 1969, MA, 1974; JD, Baylor U., 1974. Bar: Ill. 1974, U.S. Dist. Ct. (cen. dist.) Ill., U.S. Ct. Appeals (7th cir.), U.S. Supreme Ct. From assoc. to ptnr. Giffin, Winning et al, Springfield, Ill., 1974-83; sole practice Springfield, 1983; ptnr. Holley, Keith & Mehlick, Springfield, 1983-87, Holley, Keith & Huntley, Springfield, 1987—; staff counsel Ill. Senate Pres., Springfield, 1974-75, State Treas., Springfield, 1976, Ill. Legis. Redistributing Commn., Springfield, 1981-82; spl. asst. Ill. Atty. Gen., Springfield, 1983-86. Rep. Ill. Gen. Assembly, Springfield, 1976-77; mem. Springfield Ballet. Mem. ABA, Ill. Bar Assn., Sangamon County Bar Assn. (bd. dirs. 1986, v.p. 1987), Ill. Trial Lawyers Assn. Democrat. Lodges: Moose, Elks. Family and matrimonial, Election law. Home: Box 14 Hillsboro IL 62049 Office: Holley Keith & Huntley Box 5036 Springfield IL 62705

KEITHLEY, BRADFORD GENE, lawyer; b. Macomb, Ill., Nov. 23, 1951; s. Sanderson Irish and Joan G. (Kenneday) K.; m. Sarah Jane Ruebush, May 24, 1975. BS, U. Tulsa, 1973; JD, U. Va., 1976. Bar: Va. 1976, Okla. 1978, D.C. 1979. Atty. Office of Gen. Counsel to Sec. USAF, Washington, 1976-78; ptnr. Hall, Estill, Hardwick, Gable, Collingsworth and Nelson, Tulsa, 1978-84; sr. v.p., gen. counsel Arkla, Inc., Shreveport, La., 1984—; bd. dirs. La. Assn. Bus. and Industry. Public utilities, FERC practice. Home: 9828 Neesonwood Dr Shreveport LA 71106 Office: Arkla Inc PO Box 21734 Shreveport LA 71151

KEITHLEY, ROGER LEE, lawyer; b. Macomb, Ill., July 19, 1946; s. Gilbert Lee and Mary Jane (Torrance) K.; m. Karen Sue Metzger, Apr. 1, 1973; children: Roger Livingston, Terrance Christopher, Katherine Suzzane. BS, U. Ill., 1968; JD, Harvard U., 1973. Bar: Colo. 1973, U.S. Dist. Ct. Colo. 1973, U.S. Ct. Appeals (10th cir.) 1976. Law clk. to justice Colo. Supreme Ct., Denver, 1973-74; trial atty. SEC, Denver, 1974-76; assoc. Morrato, Gueck & Colantuno, Denver, 1976-80; ptnr. Krys, Boyle, Golz & Keithley, Denver, 1980-86; ptnr. Law, Knous & Keithley, Denver, 1986—; prof. physics U. Asmara, Eritrea, Ethiopia, 1969-70. Served with U.S. Army, 1968-70. Mem. ABA (litigation sect., corp. banking and bus. sect, criminal justice sect., mem. and officer various coms.) Colo. Bar Assn., Denver Bar Assn., Colo. Trial Lawyers Assn. Securities, Federal civil litigation, General corporate. Home: 5239 E 17th Ave Denver CO 80220 Office: Law Knous & Keithley 1873 S Bellaire St Suite 1415 Denver CO 80222

KEKER, JOHN WATKINS, lawyer; b. Winston Salem, N.C., Jan. 4, 1944; s. Samuel J. and Lucy Hearn (Spinks) K.; m. Christina Snowden Day, Sept. 11, 1965; children: Adam, Nathan. AB cum laude, Princeton U., 1965; LLB, Yale U., 1970. Bar: Calif. 1971, U.S. Dist. Ct. (so., no., ea., cen. dists.) Calif. 1971, U.S. Ct. Appeals (9th cir.) 1971, U.S. Supreme Ct. 1974. Law clk. to ret. chief justice Earl Warren U.S. Supreme Ct., Washington, 1970-71; staff atty. Nat. Res. Def. Council, Washington, 1971, Office Fed. Pub. Defender, San Francisco, 1971-73; ptnr. Kipperman, Shawn & Keker, San Francisco, 1973-78, Keker & Brockett, San Francisco, 1978—. Co-author: Effective Direct and Cross Examination, 1986; contbr. articles to profl. jours. Chmn. bd. Bay Area Water Quality Control, Oakland, Calif., 1980-82; bd. dirs. exec. com. Yale U. Law Sch. Alumni Com., Pub. Advs., San Francico, 1983—, CACJ, 1974-77. Served to 1st lt. USMC, 1965-67, Vietnam. Mem. Calif. Attys. for Criminal Justice. Federal civil litigation, State civil litigation, Criminal. Office: Keker & Brockett 807 Montgomery San Francisco CA 94133

KELBERMAN, DALE PRESTON, lawyer; b. N.Y.C., July 22, 1949; s. Murray and Dina (Chineson) K.; m. Lois Coulter, Oct. 7, 1975; children: Dina, Joshua. BA, Gettysburg Coll., 1971; JD, U. Balt., 1974. Bar: Md. 1975, U.S. Dist. Ct. Md. 1977, U.S. Supreme Ct. 1980. Asst. states atty. City of Balt., 1975-79; dep. chief criminal investigation div. Md. Atty. Gens. Office, Balt., 1979—; Mem. ABA, Md. Bar Assn. Criminal. Home: 85 Roads End Ln Severna Park MD 21146 Office: Md Atty Gens Office 7 N Calvert St Baltimore MD 21202

KELESIS, GEORGE PETER, lawyer; b. Las Vegas, Nev., Apr. 2, 1955; s. Peter George and Dina (Tsouras) K.; m. Angela Michele Touhey, Nov. 7, 1982. BA, U. Nev., 1976; JD with distinction, U. Pacific, 1981; LLM, NYU, 1982. Bar: Nev. 1981, U.S. Dist. Ct. Nev. 1982, U.S. Tax Ct. 1982, U.S. Ct. Appeals (9th cir.) 1982, U.S. Supreme Ct. 1982. Assoc. Manos & Cherry, Las Vegas, 1982-85; sole practice Las Vegas, 1985—; instr. Continuing Legal Edn., Las Vegas, 1983—; instr., lectr. SBA, Las Vegas, 1983—; speaker tax law women's council Las Vegas Bd. Realtors, 1987. Author: (instrn. manual) Divorce in Taxation, 1983, Small Business Operation, 1984, Practical and Theoretical View of Form 706 and 709, 1985. Cons. tax. St. John's Greek Orthodox Ch., Las Vegas, 1982—, Am. Cancer Soc., Las Vegas, 1984—; mem. So. Nev. Homebuilders Assn., Las Vegas, 1983—, Allied Arts Council, Las Vegas, 1986—; fund raiser United Way, Las Vegas, 1986—. Named one of Outstanding Young Men of Am., 1983. Mem. ABA (white collar crime com. 1986—, tax, corp. and real estate sects.), Nev. Bar Assn., Clark County Bar Assn., Order of Coif. Republican. Club: Ahepa (Las Vegas). Avocations: photography, real estate devel. Contracts commercial, Personal income taxation, Federal civil litigation. Office: 302 E Carson Suite 702 Las Vegas NV 89101

KELL, VETTE EUGENE, lawyer; b. Marengo, Iowa, Oct. 17, 1915; s. Eugene S. and Florence (Vette) K.; m. Alice Eaton, Sept. 3, 1938; 1 son, Michael V. LLB, U. Iowa. Bar: Iowa 1940, Ill. 1948. Ptnr. Joslyn, Parker & Kell, Woodstock, Ill., 1948-67, Kell, Conerty & Poehlmann, Woodstock, 1967-84; sr. ptnr. Kell, Nuelle & Loizzo, 1985—; lectr. Ill. Continuing Edn. Inst.; bd. dirs. Marengo Fed. Savs. and Loan Co. Served to lt. USN, 1942-45, PTO. Mem. Ill. State Bar Assn., Soc. Trial Lawyers, Am. Coll. Trial Lawyers, Internat. Coll. Trial Lawyers. Episcopalian. State civil litigation, General practice, Personal injury. Office: 121 E Calhoun St Woodstock IL 60098

KELLEHER, THOMAS F., justice R.I. Supreme Ct.; b. Providence, Jan. 4, 1923; m. Mary Frances. Grad., Boston U. Sch. Law, 1948. Bar: R.I. bar. Practice law, probate judge, solicitor Smithfield, R.I.; now justice R.I. Supreme Ct.; Mem. Gov.'s Task Force Mental Health, 1963; chmn. Com. on Juvenile Delinquency, 1961. Mem. R.I. Ho. of Reps., 1955-66, dep. majority leader, 1965. Served with USN, 1942-46; capt. USAR ret. Mem. Res. Officers Assn. Home: 8 Devonshire Dr Barrington RI 02806 Office: State Supreme Court Providence RI 02903

KELLER, ALEX STEPHEN, lawyer; b. Vienna, Austria, Mar. 18, 1928; came to U.S., 1940, naturalized, 1945; s. Frederick O. and Fanny (Margo) K.; m. Gloria G. MacMillan, Aug. 5, 1949; children: Susan Lynn, Stephen Eric. B.A., U. Denver, 1948, LL.B., 1950. Bar: Colo. 1950. Since practiced Denver; mem. firm Carl Cline, 1950-54, Early & Keller, 1954-69, Keller & Dunievitz, 1969-76, Keller, Dunievitz & Johnson, 1976-79, Keller, Dunievitz, Johnson & Wahlberg, 1979—; mem. Colo. Supreme Ct. Grievance Com., 1979-84; chmn. uniform jury instructions Colo. Supreme Ct. Com. 1983-84. Contbr. articles to legal jours. Pres. Young Democrats Colo., 1953; alternate del. Dem. Nat. Conv., 1952. Served as spl. agt. CIC, 1945-47. Mem. ABA (ho. dels. 1986—), Am. Coll. Trial Lawyers (chmn. state com. Colo. 1987), Internat. Acad. Trial Lawyers, Colo. Bar Assn. (Award of Merit 1978, bd. govs. 1972-74, exec. council 1974, pres. 1984-85), Denver Bar Assn. (trustee 1978-81), Arapahoe County Bar Assn., Internat. Soc. Barristers (pres. 1978-79). Lutheran. Club: Sports Car Am. (chmn. bd. 1969-72, 74, 75). State

civil litigation, Criminal, Federal civil litigation. Home: 4357 S Yosemite Ct Englewood CO 80111 Office: 1050 17th St Suite 2480 Denver CO 80265

KELLER, BRADLEY SCOTT, lawyer; b. N.Y.C., Nov. 16, 1954; s. David and Norma (Fagin) K.; m. Brandith G. Irwin, June 3, 1984. BA cum laude, Beloit Coll., 1976; JD magna cum laude, Bklyn. Law Sch., 1979. Bar: Wash., U.S. Dist. Ct. (ea. and we. dists.) Wash., U.S. Dist. Ct. (no. dist.) Calif., U.S. Ct. Appeals (9th cir.). Assoc. Bogle & Gates, Seattle, 1979-84; ptnr. Byrnes & Keller, Seattle, 1984—. Mem. ABA, Wash. State Bar Assn., Seattle-King County Bar Assn. Federal civil litigation, State civil litigation. Office: Byrnes & Keller 1000 2d Ave 38th Floor Seattle WA 98104

KELLER, COBY NORMAN, lawyer; b. Las Vegas, Nev., Mar. 2, 1949; s. Norman M. and Dolores (Kettler) K.; m. JoAnn M. Brue, Aug. 31, 1973; 1 child, Jonathan Coby. BA in Polit. Sci., Chapman Coll., 1971; JD, Western State U., 1975. Bar: Calif. 1975, U.S. Dist. Ct. (cen. dist.) Calif. 1975, U.S. Ct. Appeals (9th cir.) 1981, U.S. Supreme Ct. 1982, U.S. Dist. Ct. (so. dist.) Calif. 1986. Ptnr. Keller & Weiss, Newport Beach, Calif., 1975-81, Keller, Weber & Dobrott, Irvine, Calif., 1983—; sole practice Costa Mesa, Calif., 1981-83; instr. Calif. Community Coll., 1975—; judge pro tem harbor jud. dist. Orange County Mcpl. Ct., Newport Beach, 1986. Committeeman Irvine Indsl. League Govt. Affairs, 1986. Mem. ABA, Calif. Bar Assn., Orange County Bar Assn. Avocations: sailing, snow skiing. State civil litigation, General practice, General corporate. Home: 1467 Regatia Rd La Guna Beach CA 92651 Office: Keller Weber & Dobrott 18300 Von Karman Ave Suite 910 Irvine CA 92715

KELLER, DAVID SCOTT, lawyer; b. Waynesboro, Pa., July 17, 1954; s. John William and Margaret Louise (Etchberger) K.; m. Dawn Fischetti, Dec. 30, 1977; 1 child, Katherine Anne. BA, Bucknell U., 1976; JD, Dickinson Sch. Law, 1979. Bar: Pa. 1979, U.S. Dist. Ct. (mid. dist.) Pa. 1979. Assoc. Myers, Myers, Flower & Johnson, Lemoyne, Pa., 1979-83; assoc. Patterson, Kaminski, Keller & Kiersz, Waynesboro, 1983-84, ptnr., 1984—; solicitor Franklin County Clerk, Chambersburg, Pa., 1986—; instr. paralegal course Pa. State U., Chambersburg, 1984. Asst. editor Antietam Rev., 1983—. Group leader Explorer Law Post, Lemoyne, Pa., 1980-81; vol. United Way campaign, YMCA Capital Dr., West Shore, Pa., and Waynesboro, 1981—. Mem. ABA, Pa. Bar Assn. (county rep. young lawyers div. 1980-83), Franklin County Bar Assn., Assn. Trial Lawyers Am., Pa. Trial Lawyers Assn., Nat. Assn. Criminal Def. Lawyers. Republican. Lutheran. Lodge: Lions. Avocations: weighlifting, running, hunting. Criminal, Personal injury, Federal civil litigation. Home: 15414 Orchard Ave Blue Ridge Summit PA 17214 Office: Patterson Kaminski Keller & Kiersz 239 E Main St Waynesboro PA 17268

KELLER, ELIZABETH ANN, lawyer; b. Davenport, Iowa, June 3, 1949; d. Walter Paul and Elizabeth Ann (Bonnell) K.; m. Edward D. Baker, July 11, 1978. BE, Northeast Mo. State U., 1972; MS in Pub. Health, U. Mo., 1976, JD, 1980. Bar: Mo. 1980, U.S. Dist. Ct. (ea. and we. dists.) Mo. 1981. Sole practice Moberly, Mo., 1981-83; assoc. Clifford A. Falzone P.C., Moberly, 1983—. Mem. Bus. and Profl. Womens Assn. (v.p. 1985). Family and matrimonial, Probate, Real property. Office: Clifford A Falzone 222 N Williams Moberly MO 65270

KELLER, GERALD DOUGLAS, lawyer; b. N.Y.C., Oct. 24, 1943; s. Robert Irwin and Ann (Mund) K.; m. Judith Ann Singer, Mar. 22, 1964; children: Kevin Geoffrey, Rhondi Beth. BS in Psychology, Eastern Mich. U., 1967; JD, Detroit Coll. Law, 1972. Bar: Mich. 1972, U.S. Dist Ct. (ea. dist.) Mich. 1972, D.C. 1981. Spl. investigator Mich. Dept. Social Services, Detroit, 1968-72; assoc. Kozlow, Jasmer & Woll P.C., Southfield, Mich., 1972-74; ptnr. Levant, Keller & Grossman, Southfield, 1974-76, Keller & Katkowsky P.C., Southfield, 1976—; counsel, bd. dirs. Entertainment Resources Internat., Inc., Royal Oak, Mich., 1976—, Raymarco, Ltd., Plymouth, Mich., 1980—, Lit-Pac, Inc., Detroit, 1980—. Mem. Mich. Bar Assn., Southfield Bar Assn., D.C. Bar Assn., Assn. Trial Lawyers Am., Mich. Trial Lawyers Assn. Republican. Jewish. Entertainment, Family and matrimonial, Personal injury. Office: Keller & Katkowsky PC 17117 W 9 Mile Rd #537 Southfield MI 48075

KELLER, JOHN WILLIAM, judge; b. Waynesboro, Pa., Mar. 15, 1927; s. Niemond Foorman and Eva Rebecca (Nicodemus) K.; m. Margaret Louise Etchberger, Aug. 13, 1949; children: John Niemond, David Scott. BA, Gettysburg Coll., 1948; JD, Dickinson Sch. Law, 1951. Bar: Pa. 1952, U.S. Dist. Ct. (mid. dist.) Pa., U.S. Supreme Ct. 1958. Ptnr. Keller & Keller, Waynesboro, 1951-68; judge ct. common pleas (39th jud. dist.) Commonwealth of Pa., Chambersburg, 1968—; atty. Borough of Waynesboro, 1953-68; solicitor Franklin County Commrs., Chambersburg, 1960-68, County Planning and Zoning Comm., Chambersburg, 1963-68, Borough Planning and Zoning Commn., Waynesboro, 1956-68. Del. Constl. Conv. Commonwealth Pa., Harrisburg, 1967-68; pres., bd. dirs. Waynesboro Sch. Authority, 1965-70, numerous community orgns., 1951-68. Republican. Lutheran. Judicial administration. Home: 221 E 3d St Waynesboro PA 17265 Office: Franklin County Courthouse Judges Chambers Chambersburg PA 17201

KELLER, MICHELINE HERSKOVIC, film company executive, lawyer; b. Brussels, Belgium, Dec. 19, 1948; came to U.S., 1957; d. William and Maria Herskovic; m. Max H. Keller, Oct. 31, 1971; children—Nicole, David. B.A. in Polit. Sci., UCLA, 1971; J.D., Southwestern U., 1974. Bar: Calif. 1974. Ptnr. Keller & Keller, Beverly Hills, Calif., 1974-76; pres. Inter Planetary Pictures, Inc., Sherman Oaks, 1976—, Inter Planetary Prodns. Corp., Sherman Oaks, 1978—. Producer films: Summer of Fear, 1978, Kent State, 1980 (Emmy award 1981, Gold medal N.Y. Film Festival 1981), Grambling's White Tiger, 1981 (Golden Halo award 1981, NAACP award 1981, Gold medal N.Y. Film Festival 1982), Deadly Blessing, 1981, Voyage of the Rock Aliens, 1984, A Summer to Remember, 1985 (Best Movie 1985 Calif. Govs. Media Access award), Betrayed by Innocence, 1986 (Chgo. Film Festival award), Dreams of Gold: The Mel Fisher Story, 1986 . Mem. Women in Film, Am. Film Inst. (2d decade council), Acad. of TV Arts and Scis., United Jewish Welfare, Southwestern Themis. Soc. Jewish. Office: Inter Planetary Prodns Corp 14225 Ventura Blvd Sherman Oaks CA 91423

KELLER, ROBIN ELIZABETH, lawyer; b. N.Y.C., Sept. 20, 1953; d. Morton and Phyllis (Daytz) K.; m. Brian Mark Cogan, July 31, 1983. BA cum laude, Harvard U., 1975; JD, Boston U., 1978. Bar: N.Y. 1979, U.S. Dist. Ct. (so. and ea. dists.) N.Y. 1979. Law clk. to presiding judge Fed. Dist. Ct., N.Y.C., 1979, U.S. Bankruptcy Ct., N.Y.C., 1980; assoc. Stroock & Stroock & Lavan, N.Y.C., 1980—. Mem. ABA, Am. Judicature Soc. Republican. Jewish. Bankruptcy, Contracts commercial. Home: 75 Livingston St #16D Brooklyn NY 11201 Office: Stroock & Stroock & Lavan 7 Hanover Sq New York NY 10004

KELLER, WILLIAM D., federal judge; b. 1934. BS, U. Calif., Berkeley, 1956; LLB, UCLA, 1960. Asst. atty. U.S. Dist. Ct. (so. dist.) Calif., 1961-64; assoc. Dryden, Harrington, Horgan & Swartz, Calif., 1964-72; atty. U.S. Dist. Ct. (cen. dist.) Calif., Los Angeles, 1972-77, judge, 1984—; ptnr. Rosenfeld, Meyer & Susman, Calif., 1977-78; sole practice Calif., 1978-81; ptnr. Hahn & Cazier, Calif., 1981-84. Office: US Dist Ct 312 N Spring St Los Angeles CA 90012 *

KELLERMAN, HARRY MILES, lawyer, consultant; b. Pitts., Feb. 5, 1926; s. Maurice Kellerman and Helen (Berglas) Brownstein; m. Irene S. Gordon, Nov. 19, 1944 (div. 1971); children: Michael, Kevin, Paul. BS in Engring., Calif. State U., Los Angeles, 1959; MBA, U. So. Calif., 1970; JD, Cabrillo Pacific U., 1977. Bar: Ind. 1980, U.S. Dist. Ct. (so. dist.) Ind. 1980. Engring., mgmt. several cos. in def. and comml. industry, Los Angeles and San Diego, 1945-79; cons. mgmt. San Diego, 1979-80, 84—; sole practice Indpls., 1980-84; of counsel Edward Kelly Law Office, Indpls., 1984—. Served with USAC, 1944-45. Mem. ABA, Ind. Bar Assn., Assn. Trial Lawyers Am. Family and matrimonial, Personal injury, General corporate.

KELLEY, BRUCE GUNN, lawyer; b. Phila., Mar. 17, 1954; s. Robb Beardsley and Winifred Elizabeth (Murray) K.; m. Susan Aldrich Barnes, oct. 1, 1983; children: Dashle Gunn, Barnes Gunn. AB, Dartmouth Coll., 1976; JD, U. Iowa, 1979. Bar: Iowa 1979. Assoc. Bradshaw, Fowler, Proctor & Fairgrave, Des Moines, 1979-84, ptnr., 1984-85; gen. counsel Employees Mut. Casualty Co., Des Moines, 1985—; mem. Polk County Jud. Magistrate Appointing Com., Des Moines, 1985—. Bd. dirs. Calvin Community, Des Moines, 1983—. Mem. ABA, Iowa Bar Assn., Polk County Bar Assn. Republican. Presbyterian. Club: Des Moines. Lodge: Rotary, Masons. General practice, General corporate, Insurance. Home: 14 Glenview Dr Des Moines IA 50312 Office: Employees Mutual Casualty Co PO Box 712 Des Moines IA 50303

KELLEY, CHRISTOPHER DONALD, lawyer; b. Manhasset, N.Y., Nov. 6, 1957; s. Donald Kelley and Audrey (Wuestmann) Raebeck; m. Nancy Nagle, June 27, 1981. BA in History with high honors, Coll. William and Mary, 1978; JD cum laude, N.Y. Law Sch. cum laude, 1981. Bar: N.Y. 1982, U.S. Dist. Ct. (ea. dist.) N.Y. 1984. Assoc. Twomey Latham & Shea, Riverhead, N.Y., 1981-85; ptnr. Twomey Latham Shea & Kelley, Riverhead, N.Y., 1985—. Chmn. East Hampton (N.Y.) Dem. Com., 1982-86, 87—, East Hampton Town Zoning Bd. appeals, 1986-87. Mem. N.Y. Bar Assn. (environ. law sect.), Suffolk County Bar Assn., N.Y. County Bar Assn., Am. Trial Lawyers Assn. Roman Catholic. General practice, Environment, State civil litigation. Home: Box 641 691 Accabonac Rd East Hampton NY 11937 Office: Twomey Latham Shea & Kelley 33 W Second St Riverhead NY 11901

KELLEY, DENNIS SCOTT CLARK, lawyer; b. Bend, Oreg., May 22, 1941; s. Wendell C. and Esther Elizabeth (Von Damm) K.; m. Julienne Lower, June 14, 1963; 1 dau., Katherine Clark; m. 2d, Carol Ann Jones, Sept. 29, 1972; children—Ian Scott, Brendan Stallard, Alexandra Raleigh. B.A., U. Pa., 1963; student U. Calif.-Berkeley Law Sch., 1963-64; J.D., Villanova U., 1966. Bar: Pa. 1967, U.S. Dist. Ct. (ea. dist.) Pa. 1972, U.S. Ct. Appeals (3d cir.) 1972. Ptnr., Edward Scott Lower, West Chester, Pa., 1966-69; assoc. Clarence E. Hall, Bryn Mawr, Pa., 1969-72; sole practice, Bryn Mawr, 1972-77, 77-81; assoc. T.F. Dixon Wainwright, Bryn Mawr, 1977-81. Past pres. Bryn Mawr Bus. Assn.; past bd. dirs. YMCA, Ardmore, Pa.; sustaining mem. Rep. Nat. Com., 1982—. Mem. ABA, Pa. Bar Assn., Montgomery County Bar Assn., Colonial Soc. Pa. (sec. 1985—), Soc. Colonial Wars in Commonwealth of Pa., S.R., Mensa. Presbyterian. General practice, Personal income taxation, Probate. Office: 21 Elliott Ave Bryn Mawr PA 19010

KELLEY, FRANK JOSEPH, state government official; b. Detroit, Dec. 31, 1924; s. Frank Edward and Grace Margaret (Spears) K.; m. Nancy Courtier; children: Karen Ann, Frank Edward II, Jane Francis. Pre-law certificate, U. Detroit, 1948, J.D., 1951. Bar: Mich. 1952. Gen. practice law Detroit, 1952-54, Alpena, 1954-61; atty. gen. Mich. Lansing, 1962—; Instr. econs. Alpena Community Coll., 1955-56; instr. pub. adminstrn., Alpena County, 1956; atty. city real estate law U. Mich. Extension, 1957-61. Mem. Alpena County Bd. Supers., 1958-61; pres. Alpena Community Services Council, 1956; chmn. Gt. Lakes Commn., 1971; Founding dir., 1st sec. Alpena United Fund, 1955; founding dir., 1st pres. Northeastern Mich. Child Guidance Clinic, 1958; pres., bd. dirs. Northeastern Mich. Cath. Family Service, 1959. Mem. ABA, 26th Jud. Circuit Bar Assn. (pres. 1956), State Bar Mich., Nat. Assn. Attys. Gen. (pres. 1967), Internat. Movement Atlantic Union, Alpha Kappa Psi., K.C. (4 deg., past legal adv.). Criminal. Office: 525 W Ottawa Law Bldg 7th Floor Lansing MI 48913 *

KELLEY, GEORGE LAWRENCE, JR., lawyer; b. N.Y.C., July 26, 1937; s. George L. and Gertrude (Berger) K.; m. Dana Ruth Murray, Dec. 19, 1970; children—Jessica Wynne, Todd Sterling. A.B., Dartmouth Coll., 1959; J.D., Harvard U., 1962. Bar: N.Y. 1963, Pa. 1976. Vice pres. Hayden Stone, Inc., N.Y.C., 1966-70; asst. gen. counsel INA Corp., Phila., 1970-80; mem. firm Erskine, Wolfson & Kelley, P.C., Phila., 1980-82; of counsel Gratz, Tate, Spiegel, Ervin & Ruthrauff, Phila., 1982—; panel mem. Am. Arbitration Assn., Phila., 1982—. Pres., Wynnewood Civic Assn., Pa., 1984-85; co-chmn., founder Concerned Citizens for Rail Transp., Phila., 1981-83. Mem. ABA, Pa. Bar Assn., Phila. Bar Assn. Republican. Unitarian. Clubs: Union League (Phila.); Merion Cricket (Haverford, Pa.). General corporate, Securities. Home: 207 Almur Ln Wynnewood PA 19096 Office: Gratz Tate Spiegel Ervin & Ruthrauff Two Mellon Bank Ctr Suite 2500 Philadelphia PA 19102

KELLEY, JEFFREY WENDELL, lawyer; b. Urbana, Ill., June 8, 1949; s. Wendell J. and Evelyn V. (Kimpel) K.; m. Marsha Lynn Adams, Aug. 21, 1971; children: Julie M., Anna E., Adam J., Grant W. BA, Lipscomb Coll., 1971; postgrad., Vanderbilt U., 1971-72; JD, U. Ill., 1975. Bar: Ga. 1975, U.S. Dist. Ct. (mid. and no. dists.) Ga. 1975, U.S. Ct. Appeals (11th cir.) 1982. Assoc. Powell, Goldstein, Frazer & Murphy, Atlanta, 1975-82, ptnr. litigation dept., 1982—; speaker in field. Notes and comments editor U. Ill. Law Rev., 1974-75. Mem. ABA, Ga. Bar Assn., Atlanta Bar Assn. (law day chmn. 1980), DeKalb and Cobb County C. of C. Republican. Mem. Ch. Christ. Clubs: Georgian, Snapfinger Woods Country (Atlanta). Lodge: Civitan. Avocations: reading, golf, tennis. Bankruptcy, Federal civil litigation, State civil litigation. Office: Powell Goldstein Frazer & Murphy 900 Circle 75 Pkwy Suite 800 Atlanta GA 30339

KELLEY, THOMAS JOSEPH, lawyer; b. Los Angeles, Dec. 9, 1936; s. Thomas Joseph and Pauline Mary (O'Dea) K.; m. Kaye Saxon Baker, June 25, 1966; children—Sean, Thomas Joseph III, Scott. B.S. in History, U. Santa Clara, 1958; J.D., Loyola U., Los Angeles, 1966. Bar: Calif. 1966, U.S. Dist. Ct. (so. dist.) Calif. 1966, U.S. Supreme Ct. 1970. Assoc. Schell and Delamer, Los Angeles, 1966-73; assoc. Musick, Peeler & Garrett, Los Angeles, 1973-76, ptnr., 1976-84; ptnr. Moneymaker & Kelley, 1984—; hearing officer state bar cts., 1976-82. Served to maj. USMCR, 1958-78. Mem. ABA, Los Angeles County Bar Assn., Assn. Bus. Trial Lawyers, So. Calif. Def. Counsel, Lawyer-Pilots Bar Assn., Santa Clara Alumni Assn. (pres. 1981-82). Republican. Roman Catholic. State civil litigation, Real property, Insurance. Home: 16650 Linda Terr Pacific Palisades CA 90272

KELLISON, JAMES BRUCE, lawyer; b. Richmond, Va., June 18, 1922; s. John Ray and Clara (Cato) K.; m. Audrey Cresswell, May 5, 1962; children: Bruce, Jr., Elizabeth, Julia. B.A., U. Richmond, 1943; J.D., George Washington U., 1948. Bar: D.C. 1948. Asso. partner Hogan & Hartson, Washington, 1954-73; partner Altmann Kellison & Siegler, Washington, 1973-83; Mem. adv. com. on rules of probate procedure Superior Ct., 1972—. Pres., bd. trustees Louise Home, 1971—; trustee, sec. Columbia Lighthouse for the Blind, 1969-76; trustee Audubon Naturalist Soc., 1968-71; chmn. bd. trustees Washington Found., 1978—. Served with USNR, 1943-46. Fellow Am. Coll. Probate Counsel; mem. Am., D.C. bar assns., Am. Judicature Soc., Nat. Grange, Omicron Delta Kappa, Lambda Chi Alpha, Phi Delta Phi. Republican. Clubs: Metropolitan (Washington), Barristers (Washington), St. Albans Tennis (Washington); Chevy Chase (Md.); Lawyers, Siasconset (Mass.) Casino. Estate planning, Probate, Estate taxation. Home: 4518 Klingle St NW Washington DC 20016 Office: 1616 H St NW Washington DC 20006

KELLNER, LEON B., lawyer; b. 1945. BA, SUNY, Albany; JD, Harvard U. U.S. atty. so. dist. State of Fla., Miami. Office: US Attys Office 155 S Miami Ave Miami FL 33130 *

KELLOGG, EDWARD HERBERT, JR., lawyer; b. Ocala, Fla., Aug. 13, 1945; s. Edward H. Sr. and Margaret Vivian (Sietsma) K.; m. Linda Rainey, Sept. 2, 1967; children: Jennifer, Jerrianne. BA, Emory U., 1967, JD, 1972; MBA, Ga. State U., 1969. Bar: Ga. 1973. Atty. Neely & Player, Atlanta, 1972-73; pres. E.H. Kellogg Jr., P.C., Atlanta, 1973-82; ptnr. Pope, Herman & Kellogg, Atlanta, 1982-84, Pope & Kellogg, Atlanta, 1984-85, Pope, Kellogg, McGlamry, Kilpatrick & Morrison, Atlanta, 1985—. Served with U.S. Army, 1968-74. Mem. Assn. Trial Lawyers Am., Ga. Trial Lawyers Assn. Personal injury. Home: 3159 Terramar Dr Atlanta GA 30341 Office: Pope Kellogg McGlamry Kilpatrick & Morrison 83 Walton St Atlanta GA 30303

KELLS, RICHARD B., lawyer; b. Providence, Sept. 10, 1953; s. Richard B. and Ann M. (Pate) K. BS, Cen. Conn. State U., 1975; JD, Oklahoma City U., 1977; LLM, NYU, 1979. Bar: Okla., 1978; CPA, Okla. Assoc. Speck Philbin Fleig Trudgeon & Lutz, Oklahoma City, 1979-82, Andrews Davis et al, Oklahoma City, 1982—; adj. instr. Oklahoma City U. Law Sch., 1980-85; instr. Okla. Soc. CPA's, 1980—, Okla. Bar Rev., 1982—. Contbr. articles to profl. jours. Republican. Lodge: KC. Estate taxation, Probate, Personal income taxation. Office: Andrews Davis et al 500 W Main Oklahoma City OK 73102

KELLY, ANASTASIA DONOVAN, lawyer; b. Boston, Oct. 9, 1949; d. Charles A. and Louise V. Donovan; m. Thomas C. Kelly, Aug. 23, 1980. BA, Trinity Coll, 1971; JD magna cum laude, George Washington U., 1981. Bar: D.C. 1982, Tex. 1982. Analyst Air Line Pilots Assn., 1971-74; dir. employee benefits Martin Marietta Corp., Bethesda, Md., 1974-81; assoc. Carrington, Coleman, Sloman & Blumenthal, Dallas, 1981-85, Wilmer, Cutler & Pickering, Washington, 1985—; gen. counsel Coupe St. Thomas Ltd., 1981-85; advisor William Kissinger Fin. Planners, Timonium. Md., 1985—. Named one of Outstanding Young Women of Am., 1980. Mem. ABA, Dallas Bar Assn., Order of Coif. Republican. Roman Catholic. Banking, General corporate. Home: 5727 Moreland St NW Washington DC 20015 Office: Wilmer Cutler Pickering 2445 M St NW Washington DC 20037

KELLY, DANIEL GRADY, JR., corporate executive, lawyer; b. Yonkers, N.Y., July 15, 1951; s. Daniel Grady and Helene (Coyne) K.; m. Annette Susan Wheeler, May 8, 1976; children—Elizabeth Anne, Brigid Claire. Grad., Choate Sch., Wallingford, Conn., 1969; B.A. magna cum laude, Yale U., 1973; J.D., Columbia U., 1976. Bar: N.Y. 1977, U.S. Dist. Ct. (so. and ea. dists.) N.Y. 1977, Calif. 1986, U.S. DIst. Ct. (cen. dist.) Calif. 1987. Assoc. Davis Polk & Wardwell, N.Y.C., 1977-83; sr. v.p. Shearson Lehman Bros., N.Y.C., 1983-85; sr. v.p., gen. counsel Kaufman & Broad, Inc., Los Angeles, 1985-87; ptnr. Manatt, Phelps, Rothenberg & Phillips, Los Angeles, 1987—. Notes and comments editor Columbia Law Rev., 1975-76. General corporate, Securities, Banking. Office: Manatt Phelps Rothenberg & Phillps 11355 W Olympic Blvd Los Angeles CA 90064

KELLY, DEE J., lawyer; b. Bonham, Tex., Mar. 7, 1929; s. Dee and Era K.; m. Janice LeBlanc; children—Cynthia L. Kelly Barnes, Dee J. Craig L. B.A., Tex. Christian U., 1950; LL.B., George Washington U., 1954. Bar: Tex. 1954. Founding and sr. ptnr. Kelly, Appleman, Hart & Hallman, Fort Worth; bd. dirs. A.M.R., Justin Industries, Inc.; chmn. bd. North Tex. Bancshares. Trustee Tex. Christian U., 1971—, chmn. devel. com., 1982—; bd. dirs. Tex. Turnpike Authority, 1967-76, chmn., 1969-76; bd. regents Tex. State U. System, 1969-75; bd. visitors U. Tex. Cancer Ctr.; trustee U. Tex. Law Sch. Found.; bd. dirs. Southwestern Legal Found. Served to 1st lt. USAF, 1954-55. Named Disting. Alumni, Tex. Christian U., 1982. Mem. Fort Worth Bar Assn., Tarrant County Bar Assn., State of Tex. Bar Assn., ABA. Clubs: Fort Worth, City, Petroleum, Rivercrest Country, Shady Oaks Country; Castle Pines Golf (Castle Rock, Colo.). Home: 1315 Hillcrest Fort Worth TX 76107 Office: Kelly Appleman Hart & Hallman 2500 First City Bank Tower 201 Main St Fort Worth TX 76102

KELLY, EDWIN FROST, lawyer; b. Kearney, Nebr., Jan. 3, 1946; s. Edwin F. and Eora Louise (Ludlum) K.; m. Mary J. Barker, May 30, 1979; children: Christopher, Summer, Matthew. BA, Wayne (Nebr.) State Coll., 1968; JD, U. Iowa, 1971. Bar: Iowa 1971, U.S. Dist. Ct. (so. dist.) Iowa 1972, U.S. Ct. Appeals (8th cir.) 1975, U.S. Supreme Ct. 1975, U.S. Dist. Ct. (no. dist.) Iowa 1980. Sole practice Fairfield, Iowa, 1971-73; ptnr. Kelly & Morrissey, Fairfield, 1974—; prosecutor Jefferson County, Fairfield, 1971-83. Author: Iowa Legal Forms; Creditors Remedies, 1983, 2d rev. edition, 1986. Chmn. Jefferson County Reps., Fairfield, 1983—. Methodist. Lodges: Rotary, Elks. Avocations: private pilot, golf, sailing. State civil litigation, Federal civil litigation. Home: 1207 Glenview Circle N Fairfield IA 52556 Office: Kelly & Morrissey 109 N Court St Profl Bldg Fairfield IA 52556

KELLY, ERIC DAMIAN, lawyer, city planner; b. Pueblo, Colo., Mar. 16, 1947; s. William Bret and Patricia Ruth (Ducy) K.; m. Viana Eileen Rockel, 1980; children: Damian Charles, Eliza Jane, Valissitie Christina Heeren, Douglas Ray Heeren. B.A., Williams Coll., 1969; J.D., U. Pa., 1975, M.City Planning, 1975. Bar: Colo. 1975, U.S. Dist. Ct. 1976, U.S. Tax Ct. 1976, U.S. Ct. Appeals (10th cir.) 1986. Chief citizens' participation unit EPA, Region III, Phila., 1971-72; project planner Beckett New Town, N.J., 1972-73; v.p., project mgr. Rahenkamp Sachs Wells & Assocs., Inc., Denver and Phila., 1973-76; sole practice law, Pueblo, 1976-83; pres. Kelly & Potter, P.C., Pueblo, Albuquerque and Santa Fe, 1983—; adj. asst. prof. U. Colo. Coll. Planning and Design, 1976—, land use seminars Fed. Publs., Inc., 1976-84; instr. grad. sch. bus. U. So. Colo., 1986—; spl. counsel City of Westminster, Colo., 1976—; pres. Color Radio, Ltd., 1979—; sec., dir. Lodging Service Corp., 1980—; dir. Mar Tec Broadcasting Corp., Pueblo Growth Corp., Wildflower, Inc.; cons. Colo. Land Use Commn., 1976-77, Wyo. Land Use Adminstrn., 1977-78, City of Santa Fe, 1981-83, City of Reno, 1984-86, City of Albuquerque, 1985-86. Author: Land Use Controls, 1976-80, 82; editor, prin. author: The Roadtripper, 1969. Contbr. articles to profl. planning and legal jours. Bd. dirs. Broadway Theatre League, Pueblo, 1976-77, Pueblo Beautiful Assn., 1978-82; trustee Sangre de Cristo Arts and Conf. Ctr., 1981—, chmn. 1986, Christ Congl. Ch., 1982-83. Served with U.S. Army, 1969-71. Named outstanding student Am. Inst. Planners, 1976. Mem. Am. Inst. Cert. Planners (charter), Am. Planning Assn., Urban Land Inst., ABA, Colo. Bar Assn., Denver Bar Assn., Pueblo County Bar Assn., Williams Coll. Alumni Assn. (class sec. 1969-74, regional sec. 1980-82, class agt. 1985—). Democrat. Club: Pueblo Country. Lodge: Rotary. General corporate, Local government, Real property. Office: 200 E Abriendo Ave Pueblo CO 81004

KELLY, FRANCIS THOMAS, lawyer; b. N.Y.C., Mar. 15, 1947; s. Francis Thomas and Josephine Margaret (Tobin) K.; m. Eileen V. Starrs, Apr. 3, 1976; children: Eileen A., Francis J., Kathleen M. BA, Fordham U., 1968; MBA, JD, NYU, 1974. Bar: N.Y. 1975. Assoc. Milbank, Tweed, Hadley & McCloy, N.Y.C., 1974-77, Rosenman, Colin, Freund, Lewis & Cohen, N.Y.C., 1977-81; sr. staff atty. Coastal Corp., Houston, 1981—. Securities, Banking, General corporate. Office: Coastal Corp 9 Greenway Plaza Houston TX 77046

KELLY, JAMES MCGIRR, federal judge. BS, Wharton Sch., 1951; JD, Temple U., 1957. Law clk. to presiding justice U.S. Ct. Common Pleas, Phila., 1957-58, master jury selection bd., 1962-65; asst. dist. atty. Phila. County, 1958-60; asst. atty. U.S. Dist. Ct. (ea. dist.) Pa., Phila., 1960-62, judge, 1983—; sole practice Phila., 1962-83; spl. asst. atty. gen. Commonwealth of Pa., 1965. Mem. Pa. Pub. Utility Commn., 1966-77. Served with USN, 1951-53. Office: 8614 US Courthouse Independence Mall West 601 Market St Philadelphia PA 19106 *

KELLY, JAMES PATRICK, lawyer; b. Twin Falls, Idaho, Mar. 25, 1946; s. James Patrick Sr. and Ynes Mary (Alastra) K.; m. Carol Louise White, June 6, 1968; children: Mary Louise, Christopher John. AB, Harvard U., 1968, JD, 1975. Bar: Ga., U.S. Dist. Ct. (no. dist.) Ga., U.S. Ct. Appeals (11th cir.) . Assoc. Kilpatrick & Cody, Atlanta, 1975-80; ptnr. Morris & Manning, Atlanta, 1980-83, Smith, Gambrell & Russell, Atlanta, 1983-85, Asbill, Porter & Churchill, Atlanta, 1985-86; sr. ptnr. James P. Kelly & Assocs., Atlanta, 1986—; bd. dirs. Med. Services Corp., Atlanta, 1986—. Bd. dirs. Sr. Citizen Services of Met. Atlanta, 1980-83. Served to capt. U.S. Army, 1968-72. Mem. ABA (corp. and banking law sect.), Ga. Bar Assn., Am. Acad. Hosp. Atty.'s, Ga. Acad. Hosp. Atty.'s (bd. dirs. 1987—), Nat. Health Lawyers Assn., Am. Soc. Law and Medicine, Lawyers Club of Atlanta, Harvard Alumni Assn. (bd. dirs. 1983-84). Democrat. Episcopalian. Clubs: Cochise, Harvard (pres. 1982-83), Georgian (Atlanta). Avocations: public speaking, travel, little league baseball coaching. Health, General corporate, General practice. Home: 3240 Lemons Ridge NW Atlanta GA 30339 Office: 200 Galleria Pkwy Suite 1880 Atlanta GA 30339

KELLY, JOHN JAMES, lawyer; b. Rockville Centre, N.Y., July 4, 1949; s. John James Sr. and Eleanor Grace (Vann) K.; m. Clara Sarah Gussin; 1 child, John James III. AB in Govt., Georgetown U., 1971, JD, 1975. Bar: Pa. 1976, D.C. 1979, U.S. Dist. Ct. D.C. 1980, U.S. Claims Ct. 1982, U.S. Ct. Appeals (D.C. cir.) 1980, U.S. Ct. Appeals (fed. cir.) 1982. Law clk. to judge U.S. Dist. Ct., Washington, 1975-77; assoc. Corcoran, Youngman & Rowe, Washington, 1977-80; assoc. Capell, Howard, Knabe & Cobbs, Washington, 1980-83; assoc. Loomis, Owen, Fellman & Howe, Washington, 1983-86; ptnr., 1986—; mem. Jud. Conf. D.C. Cir., Washington, 1983. Contbr. articles to legal publs. Mem. D.C. Bar, Pa. Bar Assn., ABA, Fed. Bar Assn. Democrat. Roman Catholic. Club: Metropolitan. Federal civil

litigation, Antitrust, General corporate. Office: Loomis Owen Fellman & Howe 2020 K St NW Washington DC 20006

KELLY, JOHN MARTIN, lawyer; b. Oshkosh, Wis., Dec. 13, 1948; s. Martin Paul and Ivy Cecile (James) K.; m. Teresa Jean Wendland, July 21, 1982. B.A., U. Wis.-Madison, 1971; J.D., Georgetown U., 1974; postgrad. Harvard U. Bus. Sch., 1976-77. Bar: Wis. 1974, D.C. 1975. Atty. Chief Counsel's Office, IRS, Washington, 1974-76; assoc. Dempsey Law Office, Oshkosh, Wis., 1977-82, ptnr., 1983—. Mem. Wis. Bar Assn., D.C. Bar, Winnebago County Bar Assn., ABA. General practice. Office: Dempsey Law Office PO Box 886 Oshkosh WI 54902

KELLY, JOHN MICHAEL, lawyer; b. Ithaca, N.Y., Aug. 13, 1939; s. John Hennesy and Althea (Tisdel) K.; m. Nancy Harwood, Apr. 13, 1980. B.A. in History, Ithaca Coll., 1963; J.D., U. Miami, 1968; postgrad. U. Pa. Sch. Law, 1969. Bar: Fla. 1968, Calif. 1969, Wash. 1977. Mem. staff Miami Legal Services, 1966-68; ptnr. Grivi & Kelly, 1969, Kelly, Knapp, Sanders & Cogan, 1977-78, Sklar, Stashower, Kelly & Knapp, Los Angeles, 1978—; city marshall, Ithaca, 1958-63; tchr. advanced family law and divorce U. So. Calif. Chmn. Los Angeles Hunger Project, 1978—; dir. spl. projects OEO Los Angeles County; gen. counsel Holiday Project, 1980—; bd. dirs. First Los Angeles World Hunger Event, 1979. Served with USMCR, 1959-64. Mem. Fla. Bar Assn., Wash. Bar Assn., Los Angeles County Bar Assn. (client relations com.), State Bar Calif. (custody visitation com., chmn. custody com.), Beverly Hills Bar Assn., Santa Monica Bar Assn. (co-chmn. family law sect.). Creator of positive divorce process. Family and matrimonial. Office: 2632 Lincoln Blvd Santa Monica CA 90405

KELLY, JOHN PATRICK, lawyer; b. Boston, May 9, 1952; s. Patrick and Elizabeth (Glennon) K.; m. Eileen Linda Obuchowski, May 28, 1983. AB, Coll. Holy Cross, 1974; JD, Vanderbilt U., 1978. Bar: Mass. 1978, Fla. 1979, U.S. Dist. Ct. (so. dist.) Fla. 1980, U.S. Supreme Ct. 1981. Law clk. to presiding justice Tenn. Supreme Ct., Nashville, 1978-79; assoc. Fleming, O'Bryan & Fleming, Ft. Lauderdale, Fla., 1979-84, ptnr., 1984—; reviewer Fla. torts Matthew Bender & Co., 1986-87. Mem. ABA (Racketeer Influenced and Corrupt Orgns. subcom. torts and ins. practice sect., chmn. commercial jury instruction com. torts and ins. practice sect. 1986-87), Fla. Bar Assn. (comml. litigation com.), Phi Beta Kappa. Roman Catholic. Clubs: Tower, Alpha (Ft. Lauderdale). Avocations: scuba diving, photography. Federal civil litigation, State civil litigation, Insurance. Home: 1831 NW 32d Ct Oakland Park FL 33309 Office: Fleming O'Bryan & Fleming 1415 E Sunrise Blvd Fort Lauderdale FL 33304

KELLY, JOSEPH PATRICK, lawyer; b. Pecos, Tex., Mar. 5, 1940; s. Joseph Edwin and Sara Taylor (Ross) K.; m. Abbie Rose Noll, May 29, 1965; children: Sara Helen, Joseph Martin, Erin Fitzgerald, Patrick Noll, Christopher Ross. BBA, U. Notre Dame, 1961; JD, U. Tex., 1963. Bar: Tex. 1963, U.S. Dist. Ct. (so. dist.) Tex. 1967, U.S. Ct. Appeals (5th cir.) 1967, U.S. Supreme Ct. 1966. Enlisted USMC, 1963, commd. 2d lt., 1964, advanced through grades to capt., resigned, 1972; assoc. Anderson, Smith & Null, Victoria, Tex., 1967-71; ptnr. Kelly, Stephenson & Marr and predecessor firms, Victoria, 1971—; bd. dirs. Guadelupe-Blanco River Authority, Seguin, Tex. Dem. chmn. Victoria County, Tex., 1984-85; pres. St. Joseph High Sch., Victoria, 1978-86, Nazareth Acad., Victoria, 1973-84. Fellow Tex. Bar Found.; mem. Tex. Assn. Defense Counsel, Defense Research Inst. Democrat. Roman Catholic. Lodge: K.C. Avocation: reading. Federal and State civil litigation, Personal injury, General practice. Office: Kelly Stephenson & Marr 200 1st Victoria Nat Bank PO Box 1848 Victoria TX 77902

KELLY, JOSEPH SYLVESTER, JR., lawyer; b. N.Y.C., Aug. 27, 1949; s. Joseph Sylvester and Rita L. (Hernon) K.; m. Penny L. Hicks, May 29, 1971; children: Joseph Sylvester III, Shannon Nell. BA, U. Iowa, 1971; JD with honors, Drake U., 1974. Bar: Iowa 1974, U.S. Dist. Ct. (so. dist.) Iowa 1975, Ariz. 1977, U.S. Dist. Ct. (no. dist.) Iowa 1977, U.S. Dist. Ct. Ariz. 1977, U.S. Ct. Appeals (8th cir.) 1977. Asst. atty. gen. Iowa Dept. Justice, Des Moines, Iowa, 1974-77; asst. gen. counsel U-haul Internat., Phoenix, 1977-79, gen. counsel product div., 1979-84; gen. counsel U-haul Internat. Inc., Amerco Corp., Phoenix and Las Vegas, Nev., 1984-86; assoc. Susemihl & Davis, P.C., Phoenix, 1986—; bd. dirs. Products Liability Adv. Council, Detroit. Scoutmaster Boy Scouts Am., Scottsdale, Ariz, 1985—; mem. Ariz. Arthritis Found. Recipient Community Service award Arthritis Found., Phoenix, 1983. Mem. ABA, Iowa Bar Assn., Ariz. Bar Assn. Republican. Roman Catholic. Avocations: backpacking, golf. Federal civil litigation, State civil litigation, Personal injury. Home: 7416 E Vista Dr Scottsdale AZ 85253

KELLY, KATHRYN, lawyer; b. Spencer, Iowa, Jan. 30, 1953; s. Joseph Richard and Noreen M. (Smith) K.; m. Frank Dominic Musica, Aug. 16, 1980; children: Kathryn, Claire. BA, Butler U., 1975; JD, U. Notre Dame, 1978. Bar: D.C. 1978, Md. 1984, U.S. Dist. Ct. D.C., U.S. Ct. Appeals (D.C. cir.). Assoc. Jones, Day, Reavis & Pogue, Washington, 1979; assoc. Crowell & Moring, Washington, 1979-85, ptnr., 1985—; lectr. continuing legal edn. D.C. Bar, 1982, Fed. Publs., Washington and San Francisco, 1986. Co-author: Guide to Multistate Litigation, 1985, Product Liability: Cases and Trends, 1986; contbr. articles to profl. jours. V.p. Burleith Citizens Assn., Washington, 1985-86, treas., 1986—. Mem. ABA (co-chmn. uniform state laws com.), Women's Bar Assn. (co-chmn. working mothers forum 1985—). Democrat. Roman Catholic. Personal injury, Health, State civil litigation. Home: 3709 Reservoir Rd NW Washington DC 20007 Office: Crowell & Moring 1001 Pennsylvania Ave Washington DC 20004

KELLY, LAWRENCE EDWARD, lawyer; b. Washington, Mar. 2, 1957; s. Edward Joseph and Joan (Warner) K. BA, U. Va., 1979; JD, Vermont Law Sch., 1982. Bar: Va. 1982, D.C. 1983, U.S. Dist. Ct. (we. dist.) Va. 1984. Sole practice Falls Church, Va., 1982-83; sr. staff atty. Legal Aid Soc. New River Valley, Christiansburg, Va., 1984—; asst. atty. Loudon Countym 1986—,. Mem. Legal Aid Soc., New River Valley, 1984—. Recipient Cert. of Appreciation Legal Services No. Va., 1981; named one of Outstanding Young Men of Am., 1985. Mem. ABA, U. Va. Alumni Assn., Vt. Law Sch. Alumni Assn. Roman Catholic. Club: Va. Tech. Disc (Blacksburg). Avocations: sports, music, theater, cooking, skiing. Environment, Land use and planning. Home: 404 Edwards Ferry Rd NE Leesburg VA 22075 Office: Loudoun County Atty's Office 18 N King Stt Leesburg VA 22075

KELLY, LEON FRED, JR., lawyer; b. Birmingham, Ala., Mar. 21, 1945; s. Leon Fred and Frieda Mae (McCarter) K.; m. Judy Ann Thompson, June 11, 1966; children: Mollie Lockett, Leon Fred III. BS, U. Ala., 1967; JD summa cum laude, Cumberland Sch. Law, 1977. Bar: Ala. 1977, U.S. Dist. Ct. (no., middle, so. dist.) Ala., U.S. Ct. Appeals (5th, 11th cir.), U.S. Supreme Ct. Assoc. Hardin, Smart & Moncus, Birmingham, 1977-79, Edward L. Hardin Jr. PC, Birmingham, 1979-81; asst. U.S. atty. Dept. Justice, Birmingham, 1981-83, first asst. U.S. atty., 1983—. Served with USAF, 1968. Recipient Service award Fraternal Order Police, 1981; Outstanding Performance citation U.S. Dept. Justice, 1982, 83, 84, 85. Mem. Birmingham Bar Assn., Birmingham Trial Lawyers Assn., Ala. Trial Lawyers Assn., ABA, Assn. Trial Lawyers Assn., Bankruptcy Trustees Assn. Methodist. Bankruptcy, Consumer commercial, Personal injury. Home: PO Box 1266 Columbiana AL 35051 Office: US Attys Office 200 Federal Court House Birmingham AL 35203

KELLY, MARK DANIEL, lawyer; b. Milw., Apr. 18, 1953; s. Francis D. and Jane (Keogh) K.; m. Carrie A. Rosenberger, Apr. 9, 1982; 1 child, Lucy Adele. B in Music, U. Wis., 1977; JD, Marquette U., 1981. Bar: Wis. 1981, U.S. Dist. Ct. (we. and ea. dists.) Wis. 1981. Assoc. Regez, Callahan & Voegeli, Monroe, Wis., 1982-85; counsel Deutz-Allis Credit Corp., Milw., 1985—. Mem. ABA, Wis. Bar Assn., Green County Bar Assn. (sec.-treas. 1985). Roman Catholic. Avocations: classical guitarist, vocalist. Consumer commercial, Contracts commercial, Bankruptcy. Home: 5401 N Shoreland Ave Whitefish Bay WI 53217 Office: Deutz-Allis Credit Corp PO Box 933 Milwaukee WI 53201

KELLY, MICHAEL THOMAS, lawyer; b. Buffalo, N.Y., July 4, 1943; s. Thomas Edward and Anne Catherine (Donahue) K.; m. Sonia Helen Gembalski, Oct. 5, 1968; children—Michael, Kevin, Sean. Degree, Canisius Coll., 1970; J.D., Albany Law Sch., 1973. Bar: N.Y. 1974, U.S. Dist. Ct. (we. dist.) N.Y. 1975. Trial prosecutor Erie County Dist. Atty. Office, Buffalo, 1973-78, chief trial prosecutor, 1978-81; spl. prosecutor-in-charge Medicaid fraud N.Y. State Dep. Atty. Gen., Buffalo, 1981—; lectr. Nat. Coll. Dist. Atty., U. Houston, 1978—. Fellow Am. Acad. Forensic Scis. (chmn. jurisprudence sect. 1986-87); mem. Judges and Police Exec. Conf., Erie County Bar Assn. (mem. criminal law com.), N.Y. State Bar Assn. (exec. com. criminal justice sect., co-chmn. com. on prosecution criminal justice sect. 1983—). Democrat. Roman Catholic. Criminal. Home: 31 Vernon Place Buffalo NY 14214 Office: NY State Dep Atty Gen 468 Ellicott Square Bldg Buffalo NY 14203

KELLY, PATRICK F., federal judge; b. Wichita, Kans., June 25, 1929; s. Arthur J. and Reed (Skinner) K.; m. Joan Y. Cain, Jan. 3, 1953; children: Deanna Kelly Riepe, Patrick F. B.A., Wichita U., 1951; LL.B., Washburn Law Sch., 1953. Bar: Kans. Individual practice law Dunn & Hamilton, 1955; from asso. to partner firm Kahrs & Nelson, 1955-59; partner firm Frank & Kelly, 1959-68, Render, Kamas & Kelly, 1968-76; individual practice law Patrick F. Kelly (P.A.), Wichita, 1976-80; judge U.S. Dist. Ct., Dist. of Kans., Wichita, 1980—. Trustee Wichita State U., 1969-74, chmn., 1972-74; chmn. Midway chpt. ARC, 1967. Served with JAGC USAF, 1953-55. Fellow Am. Coll. Trial Lawyers; mem. Am. Bar Assn., Kans. Bar Assn., Kans. Trial Lawyers Assn., Am. Arbitration Assn. (arbiter), Internat. Soc. Barristers, Am. Bd. Trial Advocates. Office: US Courthouse 232 Federal Bldg Wichita KS 67202

KELLY, PETER MCCLOREY, II, lawyer; b. Chgo., Mar. 23, 1948; s. John Stephen and Helen (Patterson) K.; m. Colleen Marie Haas, May 23, 1970; children—Peter, Eli, Eamon, Liam. A.B., U. Notre Dame, 1970; J.D. cum laude, Ind. U., 1973. Bar: Ill. 1973. Assoc. McDermott, Will & Emery, Chgo., 1973-78, ptnr., 1979-81; ptnr. Kirkland & Ellis, Chgo., 1981-84, Bell, Boyd & Lloyd, Chgo., 1984—; adj. prof. Sch. of Law, Loyola U., Chgo., 1976-84, Ind. U. Law Sch., Bloomington, 1985; speaker to various profl. groups and orgns. Mem. U.S. C. of C. (employee benfits council 1981—), ABA, Ill. Bar Assn., Chgo. Bar Assn. (sec. employee benefits com. 1982-83, vice chmn. employee benefits com. 1983-84, chmn. 1984-85), Midwest Pension Conf. (exec. bd. 1984—), Order of Coif. Pension, profit-sharing, and employee benefits. Home: 1316 Davis St Evanston IL 60202 Office: Bell Boyd & Lloyd 70 W Madison Chicago IL 60602

KELLY, RAYMOND ALOYSIUS, JR., lawyer, educator; b. Yuma, Ariz., July 6, 1944; s. Raymond A. and Josephine V. (Schulz) K.; m. Mary Jo Battaglia, Mar. 8, 1980; 1 child, Kyle Patrick. B.A., Providence Coll., 1966; J.D., Albany Law Sch., 1973. Bar: N.Y. 1974, U.S. Dist. Ct. (no. dist.) N.Y. 1974, U.S. Ct. Appeals (2d cir.) 1984. Asst. dist. atty. Albany County, Albany, N.Y., 1974-80; asst. pub. defender Albany County, Albany, 1980—; sole practice, Albany, 1980—; mem. adj. faculty Albany Law Sch., 1975—; mem. continuing legal edn. faculty N.Y. State Lawyers and Advs., Albany, 1981—. Mem. editorial bd. Albany Law Rev., 1972-73. Contbr. articles to N.Y. State Defender, 1983-84. Active Big Bros.-Big Sisters, Providence, 1962-66. Served to capt. U.S. Army, 1966-70; Vietnam. Decorated D.S.C., Bronze Star, Purple Heart with 3 oak leaf clusters. Mem. Nat. Inst. Trial advocacy, Assn. Trial Lawyers Am., Nat. Coll. Criminal Def., N.Y. State Trial Lawyers Assn., N.Y. State Bar Assn. Democrat. Roman Catholic. Clubs: Wolferts Roost Country, Steuben Athletic (Albany). Federal civil litigation, Criminal, Personal injury. Home: 293 Loudonville Rd Loudonville NY 12211 Office: 112 State St Suite 1005 Albany NY 12207

KELLY, ROBERT EDWARD, JR., lawyer; b. Pitts., Nov. 28, 1950; s. Robert E. Sr. and Adelaide Cecelia (Harris) K.; m. Noreen Theresa Quinn, Oct. 23, 1976; children: Robert E. III, Christopher Patrick, Andrew Clifford. BA, Siena Coll., 1972; JD, Georgetown U., 1975. Bar: Pa. 1975, U.S. Dist. Ct. (we. dist.) Pa. 1975, U.S. Dist. Ct. (ea. and mid. dists.) 1978, U.S. Ct. Appeals (3d cir.) 1979, U.S. Supreme Ct. 1980. Assoc. Houston, Harbaugh, Cohen & Lippard, Pitts., 1975-77; dep. atty. gen. Commonwealth of Pa., Harrisburg, 1977-80; assoc. Duane, Morris & Heckscher, Harrisburg, 1980-86, ptnr., 1986—. Mem. ABA, Pa. Bar Assn., Dauphin County Bar Assn. Republican. Roman Catholic. Club: West Shore Country (Camp Hill, Pa.). Administrative and regulatory, Federal civil litigation, State civil litigation. Home: 3610 Horsham Dr Mechanicsburg PA 17055 Office: Duane Morris & Heckscher 240 N 3d St PO Box 1003 Harrisburg PA 17108

KELLY, THOMAS PAINE, JR., lawyer; b. Tampa, Fla., Aug. 29, 1912; s. Thomas Paine and Beatrice (Gent) K.; m. Jean Baughman, July 25, 1940; children: Carla (Mrs. Henry Dee), Thomas Paine III, Margaret Jo. A.B., U. Fla., 1935, J.D., 1936. Bar: Fla. 1936, U.S. Dist. Ct. (no. dist.) Fla. 1936, U.S. Ct. Appeals (5th cir.) 1936, U.S. Dist. Ct. (mid. dist.) Fla. 1940, U.S. Dist. Ct. (so. dist.) Fla., U.S. Ct. Appeals (11th cir.) 1983. Since practiced in Tampa; assoc. McKay, Macfarlane, Jackson & Ferguson, 1939-40; ptnr. McKay, MacFarlane, Jackson & Ferguson, 1940-48; partner Macfarlane, Ferguson, Allison & Kelly, 1948—, sr. ptnr., 1983—. Chmn. Tampa Com. 100, 1960-61; pres. Tampa Citizens' Safety Council, 1961-62; Bd. dirs. Tampa chpt. ARC, 1955-62, pres., 1958-59; bd. dirs. Boys Clubs Tampa, 1956-67, pres., 1966-67. Served to col. F.A. AUS, 1940-45. Decorated Silver Star. Fellow Am. Coll. Trial Lawyers, Internat. Acad. Trial Lawyers; mem. Am. Bar Assn., Bar Assn. Hillsborough County, Fla. Bar (chmn. com. profl. ethics 1953-58, chmn. com. ins. and negligence law 1962-63, chmn. fed. rules com. 1969-70). Democrat. Episcopalian. Federal civil litigation, State civil litigation, Personal injury. Home: 5426 Lykes Ln Tampa FL 33611 Office: Allison & Kelly 215 Madison St Tampa FL 33602

KELLY, WALTER FRANCIS, lawyer; b. Boston, Aug. 3, 1943; s. Walter Francis and Alice Mary (Hatch) K.; m. Constance Lynch, Aug. 27, 1966 (div.1973); 1 child, Colin Michael; m. Sandra Jean Hays, Apr. 19, 1980; 1 child, Katharine Elizabeth Hays. A.B. in History with honors, Holy Cross Coll., Worcester, Mass., 1965; J.D., Boston Coll., 1968. Bar: Mass. 1968, Wis. 1970, Ariz. 1980. Law clk. U.S. Dist. Ct. R.I., Providence, 1968-70; assoc. Foley & Lardner, Milw., 1970-71; exec. dir. Wis. Council on Criminal Justice, Madison, 1971-73; ptnr. Previant Goldberg & Uelmen, Milw., 1973-79, Sutton & Kelly, Milw., 1980—; lectr. employment and civil rights. Contbr. to law review. Mem. Ctr. Pub. Rep. Named Nat. Moot Court Champion, 1967, Best Civil Rights Lawyer in Wis. Milw. mag., 1985; recipient Private Practitioner of Yr. Pub. Interest award, 1977. Mem. Wis. Bar Assn., Ariz. Bar Assn., Mass. Bar Assn., ACLU (Wis. chpt.), Order of Coif. Democrat. Labor, Civil rights, Personal injury. Home: 3370 N Gordon Pl Milwaukee WI 53212 Office: Sutton & Kelly 1409 E Capitol Dr Milwaukee WI 53211

KELLY, WILLIAM CHARLES, JR., lawyer; b. Mpls., June 9, 1946; s. William Charles and Marian Eileen (Moritz) K.; m. Cynthia Ann Churchill, June 28, 1969; children: Patrick, Brian. AB, Harvard U., 1968; JD, Yale U., 1971. Bar: Maine 1972, D.C. 1973, U.S. Supreme Ct. 1973. Law clk. to presiding judge U.S. Ct. Appeals (1st cir.), Portland, Maine, 1971-72; law clk. to Justice Powell U.S. Supreme Ct., Washington, 1972-73; exec. asst. to sec. HUD, Washington, 1975-77; ptnr. Latham & Watkins, Washington, 1978—. Treas. Nat. Low Income Housing Coalition, Washington, 1983—. Served to lt. USNR. 1973-75. Mem. ABA, D.C. Bar Assn. Real property, Contracts commercial, Legislative. Office: Latham & Watkins 1333 New Hampshire Ave NW Washington DC 20036

KELLY, WILLIAM FRANKLIN, JR., lawyer; b. Houston, Feb. 12, 1938; s. William Franklin and Sara (McAshan) K.; m. Ingrid Leach, Sept. 11, 1965; children: Kristin Adams, Sara McAshan. BA, Stanford U., 1960; LLB, U. Tex., 1963. Bar: Tex. 1965. Assoc. Vinson & Elkins, Houston, 1965-72, ptnr., 1972—. Served to 1st lt. U.S. Army, 1963-65. Fellow Houston Bar Found; mem. ABA, Tex. Bar Assn., Houston Bar Assn. Episcopalian. Club: Forest (Houston). Avocation: sport diving. Securities, General corporate. Home: 600 E Friar Tuck Houston TX 77024 Office: Vinson & Elkins 3300 First City Tower 1001 Fannin Houston TX 77002

KELLY, WILLIAM WRIGHT, lawyer; b. New Castle, Pa., Aug. 25, 1916; s. Newell Andrew and Emma Price (Shaffer) K.; m. Joy Miller, Jan. 27, 1945; children: William W., Douglas K., Jeffrey B., Richard C. AB, Amherst Coll., 1938; JD, Georgetown U., 1952; MBA, George Washington U., 1963. Bar: D.C. 1952, U.S. Ct. Appeals (D.C. cir.) 1952, U.S. Ct. Mil. Appeals 1952, N.Y. 1974. Commd. ensign U.S. Navy, 1941, advanced through ranks to capt., 1960, ret., 1967; v.p. ops. Mohawk Airlines, Utica, N.Y., 1967-71; pres. Saunders Aircraft Corp., Gimli, Man., Can., 1971-73; ptnr. Penberthy & Kelly, Utica, 1973-81; pres. Kelly & Walthall, P.C., Utica, 1981—; dir. Bank of Utica, 1979—. Mem. N.Y. State Bar Assn. (real property com.), Oneida County Bar Assn., Phi Delta Phi. Republican. Clubs: Sadaquada Golf (Whitestown, N.Y.) (pres. 1974-77); Fort Schuyler (Utica) (pres. 1983). Lodges: Masons, Shriners. Real property, General corporate, Banking. Office: Kelly & Walthall PC 400 Mayro Bldg 239 Genesee St Utica NY 13501

KELMACHTER, BARRY LEE, lawyer; b. Bklyn., Mar. 25, 1946; s. Zelick and Miriam (Benjamin) K.; m. Andrea Lynn Neveleff, June 19, 1971; children: Heather, Michael. BS in Aero. Engring., Syracuse U., 1968, MS in Aero. Engring., 1971; JD, Am. U., 1979. Bar: Va. 1979, U.S. Ct. Appeals (4th cir.) 1979. Primary patent examiner U.S. Patent and Trademark Office, Arlington, Va., 1972-80; assoc. patent counsel Olin Corp., New Haven, 1980-87; assoc. Bachman & LaPointe, P.C., New Haven, 1987—. Patentee laser sizing of optical fiber. Treas. Temple Beth David of Cheshire, Conn., 1983-86, v.p., 1986—. Mem. Am. Intellectual Property Law Assn. Patent, Trademark and copyright. Home: 75 Meadowbrook Pl Cheshire CT 06410 Office: Bachman & LaPointe PC 55 Church St New Haven CT 06510

KELMAN, MARK GREGORY, law educator; b. N.Y.C., Aug. 20, 1951; s. Kurt and Sylvia (Etman) K.; m. Ann Barbara Richman, Aug. 26, 1979; 1 son, Nicholas. J.D., Harvard U., 1976. Bar: N.Y. 1977. Dir. criminal justice projects City of N.Y., 1976-77; prof. Stanford U. Law Sch., Calif., 1977—. Author: (novel) What Followed Was Pure Lesley, 1973. Contbr. articles to profl. jours. Mem. Conf. on Critical Legal Studies. Office: Stanford U Law Sch Stanford CA 94305 *

KELNER, ROBERT STEVEN, lawyer; b. N.Y.C., Dec. 13, 1946; s. Joseph and Libbie K.; m. Gail Kelner, Dec. 21, 1974. BA, Franklin & Marshall Coll., 1968; JD, Columbia U., 1971. Bar: N.Y. 1972, U.S. Dist. Ct. (so. and ea. dists.) N.Y. 1973. Atty. Kelner & Kelner, N.Y.C., 1971—; lectr. N.Y. County Lawyers Orgn. and other bar assns., 1983—. Contbr. monthly column to N.Y. Law Jour., 1976—. Mem. Assn. Trial Lawyers of Am., N.Y. State Trial Lawyers Assn. Personal injury, State civil litigation, Federal civil litigation. Office: 225 Broadway New York NY 10007

KELSCH, WILLIAM CHARLES, lawyer; b. Bismarck, N.D., Sept. 2, 1932; Clemens Fredrick and Mary Margaret K.; m. Jan Esther Wise, Aug. 16, 1954; children—Steven, Thomas, Mary, Jean. B.A., St. John's U., 1953; J.D., U. N.D., 1956. Bar: N.D. 1956, U.S. Dist. Ct. N.D., U.S. Ct. Appeals (8th cir.). Ptnr. Kelsch, Scanlon & Kelsch, Mandan & Bismarck, N.C., 1956-59; state's atty. Morton County, N.D., 1959-67; ptnr. Kelsch Law Firm, Mandan and Bismarck, 1967-75, Kelsch, Kelsch & Tudor, Mandan and Bismarck, 1975-79, Kelsch, Kelsch, Bennett, Ruff & Austin, Mandan and Bismarck, 1979—, sr. ptnr. Mem. N.D. Ho. of Reps., 1967-71, chmn. judiciary com., 1969-71; chmn. N.D. Parole Bd., 1976-82; del. N.C. Constl. Conv., 1972. Mem. ABA, Am. Judicature Soc., N.D. Bar Assn., Morton County Bar Assn. Republican. Roman Catholic. Club: Elks, K.C. Banking, Probate, State civil litigation. Home: 529 Marilyn Dr Mandan ND 58554 Office: PO Box 785 Mandan ND 58554

KELSEN, PETER FOSTER, lawyer; b. Phila., Dec. 25, 1956; s. Henry and Hilde (Herbst) K.; m. Gari Revka Julius, June 29, 1980 (div. June 1986). BA, U. Pa., 1978; JD, Case Western Res. U., 1981. Bar: U.S. Dist. Ct. (ea. dist.) Pa. 1981. Asst. solicitor Phila. Dept. of Law City Solicitors Office, 1982-84; assoc. Law Offices of Carl K. Zucker, Phila., 1984-86, Blank, Rome, Comisky & McCauley, Phila., 1986—; counsel Bd. of Rev. Taxes, Phila., 1982-84, Zoning Bd. Adjustment, Phila., 1982-84. Mem. ABA, Pa. Bar Assn., Phila. Bar Assn. (chmn. zoning, land use and eminent domain subcoms. 1987—). Jewish. Avocations: squash, fishing, sailing. Land use and planning, Condemnation, Real property. Home: 117 N 15th St #1804 Philadelphia PA 19102 Office: Blank Rome Comisky & McCauley 4 Penn Ctr Plaza Philadelphia PA 19103

KELSKY, RICHARD BRIAN, lawyer; b. N.Y.C., Apr. 29, 1955; s. Milton and Mildred Kelsky; m. Madonna M. Malin, May 4, 1985. BCE, Polytech. Inst. N.Y., 1976; JD, N.Y. Law Sch., 1979. Bar: N.Y. 1980, U.S. Dist. Ct. (so. and ea. dists.) N.Y. 1980, U.S. Ct. Appeals (2d cir.) 1981. Assoc. Towney & Updike, N.Y.C., 1979-83, Tenzer, Greenblatt, Fallon & Kaplan, N.Y.C., 1983-84; v.p., gen. counsel, sec. Monroe Systems for Bus. Inc., Morris Plains, N.J., 1984—; sec. Monroe Systems for Bus. Ltd., Toronto, 1986—; v.p., sec. Monroe Systems for Bus. (Puerto Rico) Inc., 1985—; v.p., dir. CA Monroe Sistemas Empresiales, Venezuela, 1985—; v.p. Monroe Systems for Bus., A.G., Zurich, Switzerland, 1985—; v.p., dir. Monroe Systems for Bus. Ltd., Hong Kong, 1987—. Mem. ABA, N.Y. State Bar Assn., ASCE (assoc.), Chi Epsilon. General practice, General corporate, Federal civil litigation. Office: Monroe Systems for Bus Inc The American Rd Morris Plains NJ 07950

KELTNER, DAVID E., lawyer, judge; b. Ft. Worth, Jan. 16, 1950; s. Edgar H. and Laura (Evans) K. BA, Trinity U., San Antonio, 1972; JD, So. Meth. U., 1975. Bar: Tex. 1975, U.S. Dist. Ct. (no. and ea. dists.) Tex., U.S. Ct. Appeals (5th and 11th cirs.), U.S. Supreme Ct. Ptnr. Shannon, Gracey, Ratcliff & Miller, Ft. Worth, 1975-86; judge Tex. Ct. Appeals, Ft. Worth, 1987—; lectr. continuing legal edn. programs State Bar Tex.; chmn. bd. dirs. West Tex. Legal Services, Ft. Worth; bd. dirs. Ft. Worth Prodns., Western Nat. Bank. Contbr. articles to profl. jours. Group leader lawyers div. United Way, Ft. Worth. Served with U.S. Army, 1971. Recipient Pres.'s award Tex. Bar, 1984. Fellow Tex. Bar Found. (outstanding law rev. article award 1986); mem. ABA (exec. council young lawyers div. 1982-84, exec. council tort and ins. practice sect. 1985-87, vice chmn. comm. appellate advs. 1986—), Am. Bd. Trial Advs. (adv. 1983), Tex. Young Lawyers Assn. (bd. dirs. 1979-83, chmn. 1982-83), Ft. Worth-Tarrant County Young Lawyers Assn. (pres. 1978, named outstanding young lawyer 1983-84), Tex. Assn. Def. Counsel (v.p. 1985). Democrat. Mem. Christian Ch. (Disciples of Christ). Clubs: Ft. Worth, River Crest Country (Ft. Worth). Federal civil litigation, State civil litigation, Judicial administration. Home: 5452 Northcrest Rd Fort Worth TX 76107 Office: Shannon Gracey Ratcliff & Miller 2200 1st City Bank Tower Fort Worth TX 76102

KELTNER, ROBERT EARL, lawyer, leagal researcher, business executive; b. Parkersburg, W.Va., Apr. 11, 1940; s. Earl L. and Chloe H. (Hendershot) K.; 1 child, David B. B.A., Marietta Coll., 1959; J.D., W.Va. U., 1962; Ph.D., Thomas Edison Coll., 1965. Bar: W.Va. 1962, U.S. Supreme Ct. 1968. Assoc. Redmond, Campbell & Keltner, Parkersburg, 1962-64; sr. ptnr. Keltner & Yankiss, Parkersburg, 1964-80; U.S. Apeals agt., Parkersburg, 1966-75; cons. Pacific Test Labs., Los Angeles, 1970—; pres. United Innkeepers Am., Lake City, Fla., 1973—. Author: Our Crumbling Country, 1984. Mem. W.Va. State Bar Assn., Wood County Bar Assn., ABA, Am. Arbitration Assn., Lawyer Pilots Assn., Internat. Platform Assn. Methodist. Lodge: Kiwanis (pres. 1968). Personal injury, Criminal, General corporate. Office: Keltner & Yankiss PO Box 1045 Parkersburg WV 26101

KELTNER, THOMAS NETHERY, JR., lawyer; b. Oklahoma City, June 1, 1946; s. Thomas N. and Tully Jo (Rowntree) K.; m. Paula Schonwald, June 17, 1972; children: Katherine, Jane. AB cum laude, Harvard U., 1968; JD, Columbia U., 1974. Bar: N.Y. 1975. Law clk. to judge U.S. Ct. Appeals (10th cir.), Oklahoma City, 1974-75; ptnr. Wien, Malkin & Bettex, N.Y.C., 1978—. Pres. parish council St. Thomas More, N.Y.C., 1982-83, trustee Convent Sacred Heart, N.Y.C., 1986—. Served to lt. (j.g.) USNR, 1968-70. Mem. ABA, (real estate syndication com. 1985-87), N.Y. County Lawyers Assn. (chmn. real estate devel. com. 1985-86, exec. com. real property law sect. 1985-86). Republican. Roman Catholic. Clubs: Tuxedo (Tuxedo Park, N.Y.) Harvard (N.Y.C.). Real property, Securities, General corporate. Office: Wien Malkin & Bettex 60 E 42d St New York NY 10165

KELTON, JOHN TREMAIN, lawyer; b. Bay City, Mich., Mar. 12, 1909; s. Frank P. S. and Jessie Eleanor (Tremain) K.; m. Carol E. Copeland, July 9, 1935; children: Carol E.M., Joy T. Student, Culver (Ind.) Mil. Acad., 1925-28; B.S. in Chem. Engring, Mass. Inst. Tech., 1932; LL.B., Harvard U., 1935. Bar: N.Y. 1935. Practiced patent law as asso. and mem. Watson,

Bristol, Johnson & Leavenworth, N.Y.C., 1935-40, 46-49; mem. Watson, Johnson, Leavenworth & Blair, 1950-53, Watson, Leavenworth, Kelton & Taggart, 1954-81, Darby & Darby (P.C.), 1981—. Served from 2d lt. to lt. col. AUS, 1940-46. Mem. ABA, N.Y. State Bar Assn., Assn. Bar City N.Y., Am. Intellectual Property Law Assn. (bd. mgrs. 1964-67, pres. 1973), N.Y. Patent Trademark and Copyright Law Assn. (pres. 1967). Congregationalist. Clubs: Harvard (N.Y.C.), Union League (N.Y.C.). Patent, Federal civil litigation. Office: 405 Lexington Ave New York NY 10174

KELTY, THOMAS WALSH, lawyer; b. Springfield, Ill., Jan. 8, 1945; s. James Thomas and Marian Eudora (Walsh) K.; m. Joan Webster, Aug. 6, 1966; children—Thomas W. Jr., Travis J., Erin M. B.A. in Polit. Sci., Creighton U., 1967; J.D. U. Mo.-Kansas City, 1971. Bar: Ill. 1971. Prin. ptnr. Pfeifer and Kelty, Springfield, 1971; cons. Ill. Inst. Continuing Legal Edn. Active Sangamon State U. Found. (Pres. 1982-84). Mem. ABA (vice chairperson self-insurers and risk mgrs. com. of sect. of tort and ins. practice 1986—, TIPS task force to develop proposals for alternative funding mechanisms to substitute for joint and several liability), Ill. Bar Assn.; Sangamon County Bar Assn.; Nat. Assn. Bond Lawyers, Ill. Assn. Trial Lawyers; Am. Bus. Club (past treas.); Phi Alpha Delta. Roman Catholic. Clubs: Island Bay Yacht, Sangamo (Springfield); Illini Country. Contbr. articles to profl. jours. Local government, Public utilities, Insurance. Office: Suite 1 Pfeifer and Kelty PO Box 1858 1300 So 8th St Springfield IL 62705

KELVIN, JEFFREY BARNETT, lawyer, law educator; b. Phila., Dec. 3, 1948; s. Carl Barton and Phyllis Deborah (Shavitz) K.; m. Randy Sue Moonblatt, Sept. 28, 1974; children: Jennifer Hope, Scott Cory. BA, Temple U., 1970, JD, 1973, LLM in Taxation, 1980. Bar: Pa. 1973, U.S. Dist. Ct. (ea. dist.) Pa. 1986, U.S. Ct. Appeals (3d cir.) 1986; CLU. Law clk. to presiding justice Phila. County Ct. Common Pleas, Phila., 1973-76; sr. cons. sales advt. INA Life Ins. Co., Phila., 1976-78; assoc. dir. advt. underwriting Penn Mut. Life Ins. Co., Phila., 1978-85; assoc. prof. taxation The Am. Coll., Bryn Mawr, Pa., 1985—; practicing atty. The Fin. Planners Assistance Corp., Plymouth Meeting, Pa., 1973—, pres. 1983—. Author: The Financial Handbook to Regulation and Successful Practice, 1983, 85, 86, The Registered Investment Adviser's Guide to Surviving an SEC Audit, 1986. Mem. ABA (taxation sect.), Phila. Bar Assn., Am. Soc. CLU. Republican. Jewish. Estate taxation, Corporate taxation, Securities. Home: 4145 Buttercup Ln Plymouth Meeting PA 19462 Office: The Am Coll 270 Bryn Mawr Ave Bryn Mawr PA 19010

KEMNITZ, RALPH A., lawyer; b. Aberdeen, S.D., Sept. 2, 1942; s. Ralph L. and Delphia F. (Benscoter) K.; m. Julianne K. Ufen, Jan. 19, 1965; children: Ralph, Candice, Kimberly. BS, No. State, 1966; JD, U. S.D., 1969. Bar: S.D. 1969. Atty. S.D. Legal Services, Ft. Thompson, 1969-71; assoc. Kemnitz Law Office, Philip, S.D., 1971-82; ptnr. Kemnitz & Barnett, Philip, 1982—; states atty. Haakon County, Philip, 1971-85. Chmn. S.D. Racing Commn., Pierre, 1984—; chmn., state del. Haakon County Reps., Philip, 1974-76. Named one of Outstanding Young Men in Am. Jaycees, 1973. Mem. ABA, S.D. Bar Assn., S.D. Trial Lawyers Assn., Philip City C. of C. (pres. 1972). Republican. Methodist. General practice, Probate, Real property. Home: PO Box 245 Philip SD 57567 Office: Kemnitz & Barnett PO Box 489 Philip SD 57567

KEMP, ALSON REMINGTON, JR., lawyer, educator; b. Rossville, Ga., July 3, 1941; s. Alson R. Dorothy (Walters) K.; m. Martha Gudenrath, Aug. 7, 1967; children—Alson Remington, Colin T. B.S., U. Tenn., 1962; J.D., U. Cin., 1965. Bar: Tenn. 1965, Ohio 1965, Calif. 1970, U.S. Dist. Ct. (no. and cen. dists.) Calif. 1971, U.S. Ct. Appeals (9th cir.) 1971, U.S. Ct. Appeals (D.C. cir.) 1982. Asst. prof. Hancock Coll., Santa Maria, Calif., 1966-68; asst. prof. U. Tenn., Chattanooga, 1969; mem. Morgan & Garner, Chattanooga, 1968-70, Pillsbury, Madison & Sutro, San Francisco, 1970—; ptnr. Pillsbury, Madison & Sutro, 1975—. Served to capt. USAF, 1965-68. Benwood Found. grantee, 1962-65. Mem. ABA, Calif. Bar Assn., San Francisco Bar Assn. Republican. Club: Stock Exchange. Federal civil litigation, State civil litigation, Environment.

KEMP, BARRETT GEORGE, lawyer; b. Dayton, Ohio, Feb. 22, 1932; s. Barrett M. and Gladys M. (Linkhart) K.; children—Becky A., Barrett George II. B.S.C., Ohio U., 1954; J.D., Ohio No. U., 1959. Bar: Ohio 1959. With FBI, 1959-61; mem. B.G. Kemp Law Firm, St. Marys, Ohio, 1961—; law dir. City of St. Marys, 1964-80. Sec., treas. Community Improvement Corp., 1967-79. Recipient Outstanding Citizen award City of St. Marys, 1973. Mem. Ohio Bar Assn., Auglaize County Bar Assn. Clubs: Rotary (v.p. 1968, pres. 1969), Masons (St. Marys); Shriners, Scottish Rite (Dayton). General practice. Office: Soc Bank Bldg Suite 203 Saint Marys OH 45885

KEMP, K(ENNETH) LAWRENCE, lawyer; b. Los Angeles, July 25, 1949; s. Kenneth L. and Mildred A. (Miser) K.; m. Kathleen Nagy, May 30, 1970; children: Paul Gregory, Carolyn Elaine. BA, U. Pitts., 1971, JD, 1975. Bar: Pa. 1975, U.S. Dist. Ct. (we. dist.) Pa. 1975, U.S. Supreme Ct. 1980, U.S. Ct. Appeals (3d cir.) 1981. Sole practice New Kensington, Pa., 1975-81; ptnr. Kemp and Kemp, New Kensington, 1981—. Sec. Planning Commn., New Kensington, 1982—; mem. Westmoreland County (Pa.) Indsl. Devel. Authority, 1983—; asst. treas. New Kensington chpt. ARC, 1985—. Mem. Pa. Bar Assn., Westmoreland Bar Assn., U.S. Chess Fedn. Democrat. Club: East Suburban Chess (Churchill, Pa.). Avocations: chess, jazz, literature. Consumer commercial, Real property, Bankruptcy. Home: 612 Clyde St New Kensington PA 15068 Office: 953 5th Ave New Kensington PA 15068

KEMP, WILLIAM FRANKLIN, lawyer; b. Austin, Nov. 7, 1932; s. Willie and Fannie T. (Ireland) K.; m. Frances Suzon Spiller, June 5, 1944; children: Frances, Louise, Katherine, Elizabeth, Will. BBA with honors, U. TEx., 1954, JD, 1959. Bar: Tex. 1959, U.S. Supreme Ct. 1967, U.S. Tax Ct., U.S. Ct. Claims. Ptnr. Kemp & Prud'homme, Austin, 1960-74, Kemp & Spiller, Austin, 1974-81; sole practice Austin, 1981—; lectr. Austin Community Coll., 1972-74. Legal counsel Austin Symphony Orch., 1969—; mem. Knights of Symphony, Austin, 1965—, King Brio, 1979. Recipient Spl. Achievement award Austin Symphony Orch., 1973. Mem. Tex. Bar Assn., Austin Lawyer Referral Service, Beta Gamma Sigma. Clubs: Headliners, Met., Austin Country. Lodge: Rotary. General practice, Probate, Home health services. Home: 2909 Greenlee Dr Austin TX 78703 Office: 702 W 34th St Austin TX 78705

KEMPER, EDWARD CRAWFORD, lawyer; b. Seattle, Dec. 7, 1942; s. Edward C. and Sarah (Tolman) K.; m. Joleen Osterling, Sept. 5, 1964; children: Kevin, Kirsten. BA, George Washington U., 1965, JD with honors, 1968. Bar: Hawaii 1969, U.S. Dist. Ct. Hawaii 1969, U.S. Ct. Appeals (9th cir.) 1974, U.S. Supreme Ct. 1974. Assoc. Cades, Schutte, Fleming & Wright, Honolulu, 1968-71; ptnr. Mattoch, Kemper & Brown, Honolulu, 1971-77, Kemper & Watts, Honolulu, 1977—. Editor-in-chief Hawaii Bar Jour., 1972—; author articles. Pres. Kokua Kalihi Valley, Honolulu, 1983, Friends of Kailua (Hawaii) High Sch.,1985-87. Mem. Hawaii Bar Assn. (bd. dirs. 1974). Club: Honolulu. State civil litigation, Federal civil litigation, Bankruptcy. Home: 1307 Onaona Pl Kailua HI 96734 Office: Kemper & Watts Pioneer Plaza Suite 1200 Honolulu HI 96734

KEMPF, DONALD G., JR., lawyer; b. Chgo., July 4, 1937; s. Donald G. and Verginia (Jahnke) K.; m. Nancy Kempf, June 12, 1965; children: Donald G. III, Charles P., Stephen R. AB, Villanova U., 1959; LLB cum laude, Harvard U., 1965. Bar: Ill. 1965, N.Y. 1986, U.S. Supreme Ct. 1972, N.Y. 1986. Assoc. Kirkland & Ellis, Chgo., 1965-70, ptnr., 1971—. Bd. govs. Chgo. Zool. Soc., 1975—, Art Inst. Chgo., 1984—, Orch. Assn. Chgo., 1985—; bd. dirs. United Charities Chgo., 1985—. Served to capt. USMC, 1959-62. Fellow Am. Coll. Trial Lawyers; mem. Am. Econ. Assn., ABA. Roman Catholic. Clubs: Chgo., Econ., Univ., Mid-Am. Saddle and Cycle (Chgo.). Federal civil litigation, Antitrust. Home: 1148 Seneca St Wilmette IL 60091 Office: 200 E Randolph St Suite 5800 Chicago IL 60691

KEMPF, DOUGLAS PAUL, lawyer; b. Mpls., July 24, 1954; s. James Dean and Carol Lois (Dahl) K.; m. Cathy Diane Jacobs, Sept. 7, 1985. BA, St. Olaf Coll., 1976; JD, U. Minn., 1980. Bar: Minn. 1980, U.S. Dist. Ct. Minn. 1982, U.S. Ct. Appeals (8th cir.) 1984. Assoc. Kempf Law Office, Bloomington, Minn., 1981—. Mgr. various Rep. campaigns, Bloomington, 1982—; commr. Bloomington Planning Commn., 1983—; active Leadership Bloomington, 1984-85; co-chmn. Vinter Sprinten Ski Race, Bloomington, 1985—. Mem. Minn. Bar Assn., Hennepin County Bar Assn., Assn. Trial Lawyers Am., Minn. Trial Lawyers Assn., Am. Judicature Soc., Minn. Jaycees (legal counsel Charitable Found. 1984—, Presdl. Medallion 1984), Bloomington Jaycees (pres. 1983-84, Silver Key award 1985, Project Chmn. of Yr. 1986). State civil litigation, General practice, Real property. Home: 7607 W 111th St Bloomington MN 55438 Office: 9633 Lyndale Ave S Bloomington MN 55420

KEMPLER, CECELIA, lawyer; b. Paterson, N.J., Dec. 13, 1940; d. Herbert I. and Selma (Bodner) K. Student, Tufts U., 1958-61; BA, CUNY, 1975; JD cum laude, N.Y. Law Sch., 1979. Bar: N.Y. 1980, U.S. Dist. Ct. (so. and ea. dists.) N.Y. 1980, U.S. Ct. Appeals (2d cir.) 1982. Pres. Kempler Inc., Irvington, N.J., 1969-85; assoc. Leboeuf, Lamb, Leiby & MacRae, N.Y.C., 1979-86, ptnr., 1986—. Mem. ABA (tort and ins. practice sect.), Assn. of Bar of City of N.Y. (ins. com. 1985—). Insurance, Administrative and regulatory, Federal civil litigation. Office: LeBoeuf Lamb Leiby & MacRae 520 Madison Ave New York NY 10022

KEMPSON, KENNETH EARL, lawyer; b. Ft. Worth, July 18, 1951; s. Farrell W. and Katherine (Ogle) K.; m. Catherine Cooke Mackay-Smith, Sept. 10, 1983; children: Emily Sumner, Alexander Mackay-Smith. BS, MIT, 1972; JD, U. Va., 1981. Bar: D.C. 1981, Va. 1986, U.S. Dist. Ct. (D.C. cir.) 1982. Law clk. U.S. Ct. Appeals (D.C. cir.), Washington, 1981-82; assoc. Covington and Burling, Washington, 1982—. Served to lt. USNR, 1973-78. Recipient Shannon Valedictory award, Alumni Academic Excellence award, U. Va. Law Sch., 1981. Episcopalian. Avocation: ice hockey. Corporate taxation, General corporate. Office: Covington and Burling PO Box 7566 Washington DC 20044

KENCHELIAN, MARK LEVON, lawyer; b. San Mateo, Calif., July 26, 1953; s. Karnig Karney and Geraldine Elizabeth (Earp) K. AB in Journalism, History with high honors, U. Calif., Berkeley, 1975, JD, 1982; MA, Columbia U., 1978. Bar: Calif. 1982, U.S. Dist. Ct. (no. dist.) Calif. 1982. Reporter Fortune Mag., N.Y.C., 1978-79; assoc. Morrison & Foerster, San Francisco, 1982-86; atty. advisor Dept. of State, Washington, 1986—. Mem. ABA (sect. of internat. law), Phi Beta Kappa, Order of Coif. Avocations: opera, skiing, writing. Computer, Private international, Public international. Home: 3615 38th St NW #310 Washington DC 20016 Office: Office of Legal Advisor Dept of State Washington DC 20520

KENDALL, DAVID MATTHEW, lawyer; b. N.Y.C., May 11, 1923; s. David Matthew and Louise (Benjamin) K.; m. Beryl Alma Beaurepaire; children—Keith, John, Susan, Janice, Paul. B.A., Queens Coll., CCNY, 1948; LL.B., Yale U., 1951. Bar: Tex. 1952. Assoc. Thompson & Knight, Dallas, 1951-62; ptnr. Woodruff, Hill, Bader & Kendall, Dallas, 1962-73; 1st asst. Office of Atty. Gen. of Tex., Austin, 1973-78; of counsel Thompson & Knight, Austin, 1979—; part-time lectr. So. Meth. U. Sch. Law, 1971-72. Mem. at large Capital Area council Boy Scouts Am. Served to 1st lt. AUS, 1942-46. Decorated Silver Star. Recipient Benjamin Sharpe Prize Yale U., 1951. Fellow Am. Bar Found., Tex. Bar Found. (charter life); mem. ABA, State Bar of Tex., Travis County Bar Assn., Dallas County Bar Assn., Order of Coif. Methodist. Federal civil litigation, State civil litigation, Administrative and regulatory. Home: 5806 Back Court Dr Austin TX 78731 Office: 208 W 14th St Austin TX 78701

KENDALL, WILLIAM THEODORE, lawyer; b. Houston, June 25, 1915; s. William Earl and Maria Theodora (Kuker) K.; m. Loretta Mary DuBois, Oct. 22, 1945; children—Mary Joanne, William Earl, Margaret Catherine, Gerard Dudley, Robert DuBois. B.A., Rice U., 1939; LL.D., U. Tex., 1945. Bar: Tex. 1946, U.S. Dist. Ct. (so. dist.) Tex. 1947, U.S. Ct. Appeals (5th cir.) 1947, U.S. Supreme Ct. 1953. Assoc. Blades, Kennerly, Houston, 1946-56, Vinson & Elkins, Houston, 1956-66; v.p. Tex. Eastern Corp., Houston, 1966-81, cons., 1981—. Served to comdr. USNR, 1941-46, ATO, PTO. Mem. Internat. Bar Assn., Tex. Bar Assn. General corporate, Oil and gas leasing. Office: 1716 Tex Am Bank Bldg Houston TX 77010

KENDRICK, HERBERT SPENCER, JR., lawyer; b. Brownfield, Tex., Nov. 16, 1934; s. Herbert Spencer and Elsie Kathryn (Woosley) K.; divorced; children: Herbert Spencer III, Kathryn Gene. B.B.A., So. Methodist U., 1957, LL.B., 1960; LL.M., Harvard, 1961. Bar: Tex. 1960. Trial atty. tax div. Justice Dept., 1961-65; pvt. practice Dallas, 1965—; sr. partner firm Akin, Gump, Strauss, Hauer & Feld; dir. Capital Bank, Dallas; adj. prof. taxation So. Meth. U. Law Sch., 1966—. Co-author: Texas Transaction Guide, 14 vols, 1972, 73. Recipient Disting. Alumni award So. Meth. U., 1986. Mem. Am., Tex., Dallas bar assns., Sigma Alpha Epsilon, Phi Alpha Delta. Presbyterian. Clubs: Dallas, Salesmanship of Dallas, Masons, Shriners, Brook Hollow Golf. Probate, Corporate taxation, Estate taxation. Home: 3831 Turtle Creek Blvd Apt 9F Dallas TX 75219 Office: Akin Gump et al 4100 First City Ctr 1700 Pacific Ave Dallas TX 75201

KENDRICK, JOHN JESSE, JR., lawyer; b. Brownfield, Tex., Nov. 22, 1943; s. John Jessie and Irma Ione (Smith) K.; m. Leanne Johanson, Mar. 18, 1967; children: John Jesse, III, Kristin Lee. B.B.A., So. Methodist U., 1965, J.D., 1968. Bar: Calif. 1969, Tex. 1970. Auditor Peat, Marwick, Mitchell & Co., C.P.A.s, Dallas, 1965; assoc. Nossaman, Waters, Scott, Krueger & Riordan, Los Angeles, 1968-69; assoc. corp. fin. dept. Bache & Co. Inc., N.Y.C., 1969-70; ptnr. Kendrick & Kendrick, Dallas, 1970-76, Jenkens & Gilchrist, Dallas, 1976-78, Johnson & Swanson, Dallas, 1978-85, Akin, Gump, Strauss, Hauer & Feld, Dallas, 1985—; dir. Capital Bank, Dallas; lectr. in field. Editor: Texas Transaction Guide, 12 vols, 1972; case note editor Southwestern Law Jour, 1968; contbr. legal jours. Mem. Am., Dallas bar assns., Order of Coif. Episcopalian. Clubs: Dallas, Brook Hollow Golf, Calyx. Home: 4800 Drexel Dr Dallas TX 75205 Office: 4100 First City Ctr Dallas TX 75201

KENDRICKS, GEORGE THOMAS, lawyer; b. Manistique, Mich., May 18, 1918; s. Ralph L. and Harriett E. (Durocher) K.; m. E. Jane Jory, Mar. 18, 1943; children—Linda L. Kendricks Peterson, Janet, Thomas J. B.A., No. Mich. U., 1938, LL.B., U. Wis., 1947. Bar: Wis. 1947, Mich. 1948. Ptnr., Kendricks, Bordeau, Adamini, Keefe & Smith, P.C., Marquette and Gwinn, Mich., 1948—. Served to lt. USNR, 1942-45. Mem. ABA, Wis. Bar Assn., Mich. Bar Assn., Marquette County Bar Assn., Am. Judicature Soc. Clubs: Kiwanis, Mason. Probate, Real property, State civil litigation. Home: 442 E Ohio St Marquette MI 49855 Office: 128 W Spring St Marquette MI 49855

KENNEDY, ANTHONY M., judge; b. Sacramento, July 23, 1936. A.B., Stanford U., 1958; student, London Sch. Edons.; LL.B., Harvard U., 1961. Bar: Calif. bar 1962, U.S. Tax Ct. bar 1971. Former partner firm Evans, Jackson & Kennedy; prof. constl. law McGeorge Sch. Law, U. of Pacific, 1965—; now judge U.S. Ct. Appeals, 9th Circuit, Sacramento., 1976—; Mem. bd. student advisors Harvard Faculty, 1960-61. Mem. Am., Sacramento County bar assns., State Bar Calif., Phi Beta Kappa. Office: US Ct of Appeals Suite 1400 555 Capitol Mall Sacramento CA 95814 *

KENNEDY, CHARLES ALLEN, lawyer; b. Maysville, Ky., Dec. 11, 1940; s. Elmer Earl and Mary Frances Kennedy; m. Patricia Ann Louderback, Dec. 9, 1961; 1 child, Mimi Mignon. A.B., Morehead State Coll., 1965, M.A. in Edn., 1968; J.D., U. Akron, 1969; L.L.M., George Washington U., 1974. Bar: Ohio 1969. Asst. cashier Citizens Bank, Felicity, Ohio, 1961-63; tchr. Triway Local Sch. Dist., Wooster, Ohio, 1965-67; with office of gen. counsel Fgn. Agr. and Spl. Programs Div., U.S. Dept. Agr., Washington, 1969-71; ptnr. Kauffman, Eberhart, Cicconetti & Kennedy Co., Wooster, 1972-86, Kennedy and Cicconetti, Wooster, 1986—. Mem. ABA, Fed. Bar Assn., Assn. Trial Lawyers Am., Ohio State Bar Assn., Ohio Acad. Trial Lawyers, Wayne County Bar Assn., Phi Alpha Delta, Phi Delta Kappa. Republican. Club: Exchange (Wooster). Lodges: Lions, Elks. State civil litigation, Criminal, Family and matrimonial. Home: 1770 Burbank Rd Wooster OH 44691 Office: Kennedy and Cicconetti 558 N Market St Wooster OH 44691

KENNEDY, CORNELIA GROEFSEMA, judge; b. Detroit, Aug. 4, 1923; d. Elmer H. and Mary Blanche (Gibbons) Groefsema; m. Charles S. Kennedy, Jr.; 1 son, Charles S. III. B.A., U. Mich., 1945, J.D. with distinction, 1947; LL.D. (hon.), No. Mich. U., 1971, Eastern Mich. U., 1971, Western Mich. U., 1973, Detroit Coll. Law, 1980. Bar: Mich. bar 1947. Law clk. to Chief Judge Harold M. Stephens, U.S. Ct. of Appeals, Washington, 1947-48; asso. Elmer H. Groefsema, Detroit, 1948-52; partner Markle & Markle, Detroit, 1952-66; judge 3d Judicial Circuit Mich., 1967-70; dist. judge U.S. Dist. Ct., Eastern Dist. Mich., Detroit, 1970-79; chief judge U.S. Dist. Ct., Eastern Dist. Mich., 1977-79; circuit judge U.S. Ct. Appeals, 6th Circuit, 1979—. Mem. Commn. on the Bicentennial of the U.S. Constitution (presdl. appointment). Recipient Sesquicentennial award U. Mich. Fellow Am. Bar Found.; mem. ABA, Mich. Bar Assn. (past chmn. negligence law sect.), Detroit Bar Assn. (past dir.), Fed. Bar Assn., Am. Judicature Soc., Nat. Assn. Women Lawyers, Am. Trial Lawyers Assn., Nat. Conf. Fed. Trial Judges (past chmn.), Fed. Jud. Fellows Commn. (bd. dirs.), Fed. Jud. Ctr. (bd. dirs.), Phi Beta Kappa. Jurisprudence. Office: US Ct of Appeals (6th cir) 744 Fed Bldg US Courthouse 231 W Lafayette St Detroit MI 48226

KENNEDY, CORNELIUS BRYANT, lawyer; b. Evanston, Ill., Apr. 13, 1921; s. Millard Bryant and Myrna Estelle (Anderson) K.; m. Anne Martha Reynolds, June 20, 1959; children: Anne Talbot, Lauren Asher. A.B., Yale U., 1943; J.D., Harvard U., 1948. Bar: Ill. bar 1949, D.C. bar 1965. Asso. firm Mayer Meyer Austrian & Platt, Chgo., 1949-54, 55-59; asst. U.S. atty. Dept. Justice, Chgo., 1954-55; counsel to Minority Leader, U.S. Senate, 1959-65; sr. mem. firm Kennedy & Webster, Washington, 1965-82; of counsel Armstrong, Teasdale, Kramer, Vaughan & Schafly, Washington, 1983—; public mem. Adminstrv. Conf. U.S., 1972-82, sr. conf. fellow, 1982—, chmn. rulemaking com., 1973-82. Contbr. articles to law jours. Fin. chmn. Lyric Opera Co., Chgo., 1954; chmn. young adults group Chgo. Council Fgn. Relations, 1958-59; pres. English Speaking Union Jrs., Chgo., 1957-59; trustee St. John's Child Devel. Center, Washington, 1965-67, 75—, pres., 1983-85 ; exec. dir. Supreme Ct. Hist. Soc., 1984—. Served to 1st lt., AC U.S. Army, 1942-46. Fellow Am. Bar Found.; mem. Am. Law Inst., ABA (council sect. adminstrv. law 1967-70, chmn. sect. 1976-77), Fed. Bar Assn. (chmn. com. adminstrv. law 1963-64). Clubs: Legal Club Chgo., Explorers, N.Y. City, Capitol Hill, Metropolitan (Washington); Chevy Chase (Md.); Sailing of Chesapeake (Annapolis, Md.); Adventurer's (Chgo.). Administrative and regulatory, Antitrust, Federal civil litigation. Home: 7720 Old Georgetown Pike McLean VA 22102 Office: 888 17th St NW Washington DC 20006

KENNEDY, CRAIG ALLEN, lawyer; b. Huron, S.D., Sept. 28, 1951; s. John Woodward and Helen Jean (Devine) K.; m. Joann Marie Smith, June 10, 1972 (div. Aug. 1977); m. Gail Marie Anderson, June 13, 1979; children: Michael Craig, Patrick John. Student, Georgetown U., 1970; BA, U. S.D., 1973, JD, 1976. Bar: S.D. 1976, U.S. Dist. Ct. S.D. 1976, U.S. Ct. Appeals (8th cir.) 1982. Law clk. to presiding justice U.S. Dist. Ct. S.D., Sioux Falls, 1976-77; assoc. Doyle, Bierle & Porter, Yankton, S.D., 1977-80; ptnr. Doyle, Bierle, Porter & Kennedy, Yankton, 1981-85, Doyle & Kennedy, Yankton, 1985—; states atty. Yankton County, 1985—; bd. dirs. East River Legal Services, Sioux Falls. Editorial bd. U. S.D. Law Rev., 1975-76. Drive chmn. Yankton Area United Way, 1982, bd. dirs. 1983-85; state cen. committeeman S.D. Dems., Pierre, 1982—. Named one of Outstanding Young Men Am., 1983, 85; named Outstanding Young Citizen, Yankton Jaycees, 1985. Mem. S.D. Bar Assn. (commr. 1979-81, bd. dirs. young lawyers sect. 1977-81, pres. young lawyers sect. 1982-83), Assn. Trial Lawyers Am., Nat. Assn. Dist. Attys., Am. Judicature Soc., U. S.D. Law Sch. Found. (v.p. 1985—). Roman Catholic. Lodges: Rotary, Sertoma (bd. dirs. Yankton 1979-80), Elks. Criminal, General practice, State civil litigation. Office: Doyle & Kennedy 322 Walnut PO Box 37 Yankton SD 57078

KENNEDY, DAVID TINSLEY, lawyer, labor arbitrator; b. Richmond, Va., Mar. 6, 1919; s. David Tinsley and Lilian Brady (Butcher) K.; m. Jean Elizabeth Stephenson, Nov. 26, 1949; children—David T. III, Thomas D., Michael F. J.D., U. Va., 1948. Bar: Va. 1948, W.Va. 1949, U.S. Dist. Ct. (so. dist.) W.Va. 1949, U.S. Ct. Appeals (4th cir.) 1963. Atty., Dist. 29, United Mine Workers Am., Beckley, W.Va., 1949-61; ptnr. Thornhill, Kennedy & Vaughan, Beckley, 1962—; arbitrator Coal Arbitration Service, Washington, 1970—; dir. Raleigh County Nat. Bank, Beckley. Mem. Raleigh County Dem. exec. com., 1980-86, chmn. 1986. Served to lt. col. U.S. Army, 1942-46, PTO. Mem. W.Va. State Bar, Va. State Bar, Assn. Trial Lawyers Am., ABA. Roman Catholic. General practice, Arbitration. Home: 102 Mollohan Dr Beckley WV 25801 Office: Thornhill Kennedy & Vaughan PO Drawer 1008 Beckley WV 25802

KENNEDY, HAROLD EDWARD, lawyer, corporate executive; b. Pottstown, Pa., Oct. 18, 1927; s. Freeman S. and Alice (Brehm) K.; m. Margaret W. Kempton, July 1, 1950; children—Kathleen, Nancy, Harold, Robert, Ellen, Anne, Susan; m. Eleanor Henry, Jan. 9, 1960. Student, Colgate U., 1945-47; LL.B., Syracuse U., 1952. Bar: N.Y. 1952, U.S. Dist. Ct. (no. dist.) N.Y. 1954, U.S. Supreme Ct. 1956, U.S. Dist. Ct. (so. dist.) N.Y. 1962. Ptnr. Taylor & Kennedy, Amsterdam, N.Y., 1952-59; sr. assoc. Kissam & Halpin, N.Y.C., 1959-60; sr. v.p. Foster Wheeler Corp., Livingston, N.J., 1960—. Editor Syracuse Law Rev., 1952. Trustee First Presbyn. Ch., Orange, N.J., 1973-76, St. Barnabas Med. Ctr., 1986—. Served with USAAF, 1945-47. Mem. ABA, Machinery and Allied Products Inst., Nat. Constructors Assn. (chmn. 1978), N.Y. State Bar Assn., Order of Coif. Clubs: Seaview Country (Absecon, N.J.); Baltusrol Golf (Springfield, N.J.). General corporate, Contracts commercial, Private international. Office: Foster Wheeler Corp 110 S Orange Ave Livingston NJ 07039

KENNEDY, JACK LELAND, lawyer; b. Portland, Oreg., Jan. 30, 1924; s. Ernest E. and Lera M. (Talley) K.; m. Clara C. Hagans, June 5, 1948; children: James M., John C. Grad., Southwestern U., Los Angeles; J.D., Lewis and Clark Coll., 1951. Bar: Oreg. 1951. Since practiced in Portland; partner firm Kennedy, King & Zimmer, 1971—; trustee Northwestern Coll. Law, Portland; dir. Profl. Liability Fund, 1979-82. Contbr. articles to legal jours. Bd. overseers Lewis and Clark Coll. Served with USNR, 1942-46. Fellow Am. Coll. Trial Lawyers, Am. Bar Found., Oreg. Bar Found. (charter); mem. ABA (Ho. of Dels. 1984—), Oreg. State Bar (bd. govs. 1976-79, pres. 1978-79), Multnomah Bar Assn. Republican. Clubs: City (Portland); Columbia River Yacht. State civil litigation, Federal civil litigation, General practice. Home: 1281 SW Davenport St Portland OR 97201 Office: Kennedy King & Zimmer 1211 SW 5th Ave Portland OR 97204

KENNEDY, JAMES EDWARD, lawyer; b. N.Y.C., Mar. 10, 1949. BBA, U. Notre Dame, 1971; JD, U. Pitts., 1974. Bar: Pa. 1974, U.S. Dist. Ct. (we. dist.) Pa. 1982, U.S. Ct. Appeals (3d cir.) 1982. From asst. to dep. atty. gen. Pa. Dept. of Justice, Pitts., 1974-77; assoc. Weis & Weis, Pitts., 1977-79, William K. Herrington and Assocs., Pitts., 1979-80; ptnr. Reale, Fossee & Ferry P.C., Pitts., 1980—. Mem. Allegheny County Bar Assn. (chmn. unauthorized practice of law com. 1981-82). Personal injury, Insurance, Family and matrimonial. Office: Reale Fossee & Ferry PC 900 Manor Bldg Pittsburgh PA 15219

KENNEDY, JOE JACK, JR., lawyer; b. Abingdon, Va., June 11, 1956; s. J. Jack Sr. and Bobbie Lee (Porter) K.; m. Susan Maura Muir, June 30, 1979; children: J. Jack III, Jillian Susanne. BS, U. Va., 1977; Cert. in Internat. Study, U. London, 1977; MA In Polit. Sci., East Tenn. State U., 1982; Cert. in Italian Study, U. London, 1977; studies with Va. atty., 1978-82. Bar: Va. 1982, U.S. Dist. Ct. (we. dist.) Va. 1982, U.S. Ct. Appeals (4th cir.) 1982. Legis. asst. Va. State Senate, Richmond, 1977-78; assoc. Cline, McAfee & Adkins, P.C., Norton, Va., 1982—; adj. faculty Mountain Empire Coll., Big Stone Gap, Va., 1981-84; pres., bd. dirs. Turkey Gap Coal Co., Coeburn, Va., 1979—. Campaign mgr. U.S. Rep. Rick Boucher, Abingdon, Va., 1984; pres. Young Dems. of Va. Inc., 1984-85, legal counsel 1985—; sec. Young Dems. of Am., 1985; chmn. City of Norton Dem. com., 1982—, 9th congl. dist. Dem. com., 1985—; del. 1984 Dem. Nat. Conv., San Francisco; state chmn. Va. Assn. Local Dem. Chairs, 1986—; envoy to Carribean Islands of Grenada, Jamaica and Trinidad, U.S. Youth Council, 1985. Named one of Outstanding Young Men Am., 1985, 86, Outstanding Young Dem. Va., 1985. Mem. ABA, Va. Bar Assn., Wise County Bar Assn., Va. Trial Lawyers Assn., Va. C. of C. (v.p. econ. devel. Wise County chpt., exec. com.), Phi Sigma Kappa (pres. Wise chpt. 1982-85). Baptist. Lodges: Moose, Kiwanis (bd. dirs. Coeburn 1980-81). Avocations: astronomy, travel, reading. General practice, Personal injury, Family and matrimonial. Home: 699 Fox Run Rd SE Norton VA 24273 Office: Cline McAfee & Adkins PC 1022 Park Ave NW Norton VA 24273-0698

KENNEDY, JOHN EDWARD, lawyer; b. Mpls., Feb. 18, 1947; s. John Edward and Margaret (Greathouse) K.; m. Linda Bagwell, June 22, 1968; children: John Harlan, Linda Elizabeth. AB cum laude, Harvard U., 1968, JD magna cum laude, 1971. Bar: Tex. 1971, U.S. Dist. Ct. (so. dist.) Tex. 1972, U.S. Ct. Appeals (5th cir.) 1972, U.S. Supreme Ct. 1975, U.S. Ct. Appeals (D.C. cir.) 1984. Assoc. Vinson & Elkins, Houston, 1971-80, ptnr., 1980—. Served to 2d lt. USAR, 1972. Mem. ABA, Houston Bar Assn., Fed. Energy Bar Assn. Presbyterian. Club: Houston Ctr. FERC practice, Federal civil litigation, State civil litigation. Home: 2617 Pemberton Dr Houston TX 77005 Office: Vinson & Elkins 3300 First City Tower 1001 Fannin Houston TX 77002

KENNEDY, JOHN FORAN, lawyer; b. Toronto, Ont., Can., July 25, 1924; came to U.S., 1926, naturalized, 1944; s. Francis Regis and Ellen Susanna (Lunney) K.; m. Carmelita Margaret Stanka, June 20, 1964; 1 son, John Regis Joseph. A.B., Dartmouth Coll., 1949; LL.B., Cornell U., 1952; postgrad. U. Chgo., 1958-60. Bar: Ill. 1954. Mem. trust dept. First Nat. Bank, Chgo., 1952-58; trust officer First Nat. Bank, Lake Forest, Ill., 1959-65; ptnr. Snyder, Clarke, Dalziel, Holmquist & Johnson, Waukegan, Ill., 1966-75; ptnr. Kennedy & Clark, Lake Forest, 1976-82; ptnr. Holmstrom & Green, P.C., 1983—. Pres. Family Service of South Lake County, Ill.; bd. dirs. Lake Forest/Lake Bluff United Way. Served with U.S. Army, 1943-46. Mem. Chgo. Bar Assn., Lake County Bar Assn., Lake Forest C. of C. (pres.), Phi Alpha Delta. Roman Catholic. Probate, Real property, Estate taxation. Home: 435 Park Ln Lake Bluff IL 60044 Office: 950 N Western Ave PO Box 951 Lake Forest IL 60045

KENNEDY, KAEL BEHAN, lawyer; b. Chgo., Sept. 1, 1941; s. W. McNeil and Dot (Behan) K.; m. Pam Wilt, Aug. 29, 1964; 1 child, Mark Wilt. BS, Loyola U., 1963; JD, U. Iowa, 1966. Bar: Iowa 1966, Ill. 1967, U.S. Dist. Ct. (no. dist.) Ill. 1967, (we. dist.) Mo. 1971, (ea. dist.) Mo. 1975, (so. dist.) Tex. 1977, (so. dist.) N.Y. 1978, Dist. S.C. 1982, U.S. Ct. Apls. (7th cir.) 1967, (8th cir.) 1973, (5th cir.) 1980, Mich. 1987, U.S. Dist. Ct. (ea. and we. dists.) Mich. 1987, U.S. Ct. Appeals (6th cir.) 1986. Assoc. Pope, Ballard, Shepard & Fowle, Chgo., 1966-73; ptnr. Pope, Ballard, Shepard & Fowle, Chgo., 1973-79, Katten, Muchin, Zavis, Pearl & Galler, Chgo., 1979-85, Varnum, Riddering, Schmidt & Howlett, Grand Rapids, 1986—; lectr. in field; instr. Arthur Andersen & Co., St. Charles, Ill., 1983, Ill. Inst. Continuing Legal Edn., Chgo., 1983, 84, Nat. Inst. Trial Adv., Chgo., 1986, 87. Co-author: Antitrust Consent Decree Manual, 1978. Editorial staff CCH Corp. Law Guide, 1963, 64. Bd. dirs. Lawyers Com. for Civil Rights Under Law, Chgo., 1983, 84; committeeman Deerfield Twp. Rep. Com., Highland Park, Ill., 1982-84; cooperating counsel ACLU, Chgo., 1967-72. Mem. ABA, Ill. Bar Assn. (council Antitrust Law sect.), Mich. Bar Assn. (council antitrust law sect.), Chgo. Bar Assn., Am. Soc. of Assn. Execs., Mich. Soc. of Assn. Execs. Clubs: University, Legal, Nat. Lawyers, Chgo., Macatawa Bay Yacht. Antitrust, Federal civil litigation, Associations and cooperatives. Home: 2720 Darby Rd SE East Grand Rapids MI 49506 Office: Varnum Riddering Schmidt & Howlett 171 Monroe Ave NW #800 Grand Rapids MI 49503

KENNEDY, MARC J., lawyer; b. Newburgh, N.Y., Mar. 2, 1945; s. Warren G. K. and Frances F. (Levinson) K.; m. Carol Feldstein, May 9, 1968 (div. 1978); m. Mahvash Rezvan, June 10, 1980; m. Debra L. Shaw, Apr. 19, 1986. BA cum laude, Syracuse U., 1967; JD, U. Mich., 1970. Bar: N.Y. 1971. Assoc. Davies, Hardy, Ives & Lawther, N.Y.C., 1971-72, London, Buttenweiser & Chalif, N.Y.C., 1972-73, Silberfeld, Danziger & Bangser, N.Y.C., 1973; counsel Occidental Crude Sales, Inc., N.Y.C., 1974-75; v.p., gen. counsel Internat. Ore & Fertilizer Corp., N.Y.C., 1975-82; asst. gen. counsel Occidental Chem. Corp., Houston, 1982; v.p., gen. counsel Occidental Chem. Co., Tampa, Fla., 1982—; faculty mentor Columbia Pacific U., Mill Valley, Calif., 1981—. Trustee Bar Harbor Festival Corp., N.Y.C., 1974—; bd. dirs. Am. Opera Repertory Co., 1982-85; mem. com. planned giving N.Y. Foundling Hosp., 1977—; Explorer post advisor Boy Scouts Am., 1976-78. Mem. ABA (vice-chmn. com. internat. law, liaison young lawyers sect. 1974-75, chmn. sub-com. proposed trade barriers to the importation of products into U.S. 1985—), Internat. Bar Assn., Maritime Law Assn., N.Y. State Bar Assn., Assn. Bar City N.Y. (admiralty law com. 1982-83). Club: Clearwater Yacht. Admiralty, Contracts commercial, General corporate. Home: 690 Island Way #1101 Clearwater FL 33515 Office: PO Box 25597 Tampa FL 33622

KENNEDY, MICHAEL JOHN, lawyer; b. Spokane, Wash., Mar. 23, 1937; s. Thomas Dennis Kennedy and Evelyn Elizabeth (Forbes) Gordon; m. Pamalee Hamilton, June 14, 1959 (div. July 1968); children: Lisa Marie, Scott Hamilton; m. Eleanore Renee Baratelli, July 14, 1968; 1 child, Anna Rosario. AB in Econs., U. Calif., Berkeley, 1959; JD, U. Calif., San Francisco, 1962. Bar: Calif. 1963, N.Y. 1976, U.S. Ct. Appeals (9th cir. 1963), U.S. Supreme Ct. 1967, U.S. Ct. Appeals (5th cir.) 1975, U.S. Ct. Appeals 2d cir.) 1977, U.S. Ct. Appeals (1st 3d and 4th cirs.) 1979, U.S. Ct. Appeals (3d and D.C. cirs.) 1982. Assoc. Hoberg & Finger, San Francisco, 1962-67; staff counsel Emergency Civil Liberties, N.Y.C., 1967-69; ptnr. Kennedy & Rhine, San Francisco, 1969-76; sole practice N.Y.C., 1976—. Served to 1st lt. U.S. Army, 1963-65. Mem. ABA, N.Y. Criminal Bar Assn., Nat. Assn. Criminal Defenders. Democrat. Roman Catholic. Club: N.Y. Athletic. Criminal, Libel, Civil rights. Home: 6 E 76th St New York NY 10021 Office: 148 E 78th St New York NY 10021

KENNEDY, MICHAEL KEVIN, lawyer; b. Dayton, Ohio, June 3, 1950; s. Robert Curtis and Patricia Ann (Frederick) K.; children: Jennifer, Robert Charles; m. Dawn Kennedy, Mar. 13, 1987. BA, Duke U., 1972; JD, U. Va., 1975. Bar: Ariz. 1975, U.S. Dist. Ct. Ariz. 1975, U.S. Ct. Appeals (9th cir.) 1978, U.S. Supreme Ct. 1982. Assoc. Snell & Wilmer, Phoenix, 1975-78; ptnr. Gallagher & Kennedy, Phoenix, 1978—; judge pro tem Ariz. Superior Ct., Ariz. Ct. Appeals. Bd. dirs. Ariz. Ctr. for Law in Pub. Interest, Phoenix, 1985—. Named Phoenix Young Man of Yr. Phoenix Jaycees, 1985. Mem. ABA, Ariz Bar Assn. (bd. of govs. 1987—), Maricopa County Bar Assn. (bd. dirs. 1980—, pres. 1986-87), Phoenix Assn. Def. Counsel (pres. 1985-86, bd. dirs. 1980—), Def. Research Inst., Phoenix Thunderbirds. Republican. Methodist. Clubs: Phoenix Country; The Ranch (Carefree, Ariz.). State civil litigation, Federal civil litigation, Personal injury. Home: 2035 E Colter Phoenix AZ 85016 Office: Gallagher & Kennedy 360 E Coronado Rd Phoenix AZ 85004

KENNEDY, NOLAN MALCOM, lawyer; b. Birmingham, Ala., Oct. 26, 1943; s. Nolan Malcom Sr. and Ina Doris (Carlisle) K.; m. Donna Close, May 18, 1968; children: Ryan Sanford, Brennan Carlisle. BA, Baylor U., 1965; JD, U. Calif., San Francisco, 1973. Bar: Calif. 1973. Assoc. Hoge, Fenton, Jones & Appel, Inc., Monterey, Calif., 1973-79, ptnr., 1979—. Trustee Calif. Bapt. Coll., Riverside, 1984—, Sunday Sch. Bd. So. Bapt. Conv., Nashville, 1985—; officer, bd. dirs. Carmel (Calif.) Bach Festival, 1985—. Served to 1st lt. U.S. Army, 1967-70. Mem. ABA, Monterey County Bar Assn. Contracts commercial, Real property, Corporate taxation.

KENNEDY, PAUL JOHN, lawyer; b. Phila., May 3, 1949; s. John Paul and Eileen Theresa (Whitaker) K.; m. Pamela Dee Miller, July 15, 1972; children: Christin, Megan, Katherine. BA in Internat. Relations, Latin Am. Studies, St. Josephs U., Phila., 1971; JD, Georgetown U., 1976. Bar: N.Mex. 1976, U.S. Dist. Ct. N.Mex. 1976, U.S. Ct. Appeals (10th cir.) 1976, U.S. Supreme Ct. 1986. Sole practice Albuquerque, 1978—. Nominee atty. gen. N.Mex. Reps., 1982. Served to cpl. USMC, 1971-73. Mem. ABA, Assn. Trial Lawyers Am., N.Mex. Trial Lawyers Assn., Nat. Assn. Criminal Def. Lawyers. Roman Catholic. Criminal. Office: 423 6th NW Albuquerque NM 87102

KENNEDY, RICHARD CARL, lawyer; b. Wareham, Mass., Nov. 9, 1945; s. William Dempsey and Jean Eleanor (Young) K.; m. Susanne Hedges, Aug. 25, 1968; children: Richard Charles, William Bennett, Elizabeth Hedges. BA, Johns Hopkins U., 1967; JD, Georgetown U., 1974. Bar: Tenn. 1974, U.S. Dist. Ct. (ea. and mid. dists.) Tenn., U.S. Ct. Appeals (6th cir.). Assoc. Weill, Ellis, Weems & Copeland, Chattanooga, 1974-79, ptnr., 1979-84; ptnr. Weill, Weems & Kennedy, Chattanooga, 1984-85, Kennedy, Fulton & Koontz, Chattanooga, 1986—. V.p. bd. dirs. Girls Clubs Chattanooga, 1985—; treas., bd. dirs. Chattanooga Teen Ctr., 1986—; chmn. bd. dirs. Camp O'Coee YMCA, Chatanooga, 1986—. Served to sgt. USAF, 1969-73. Mem. ABA, Chattanooga Bar Assn. (chmn. lawyer referral com. 1978-79, chmn. unauthorized practice com. 1980-81, 85-86, chmn. fee arbitration com. 1984-85, 86—), Tenn. Bar Assn., Civitan. Republican. Avocations: backpacking, hiking, tennis, stamp collecting. Bankruptcy, Contracts commercial, General corporate. Home: 713 Oxford Rd Chatanooga TN 37405 Office: Kennedy Fulton & Koontz 320 N Holtzclaw Ave Chatanooga TN 37404

KENNEDY, RODERICK THOMAS, lawyer; b. Toledo, Oct. 25, 1955; s. Thomas J. and Harriett Louise (Bean) K. BA, Coll. of Wooster, 1977; JD, U. Toledo, 1980. Bar: N.Mex. 1981, U.S. Dist. Ct. N.Mex. 1981. Asst. dist. atty. 2d Jud. Dist., Albuquerque, 1981-83; sole practice Albuquerque, 1984—; prosecutor Village of Corrales, N.Mex., 1982—; cons. Corrales Police Dept., 1982—. Mem. N.Mex. Bar Assn., Assn. Trial Lawyers Am. Republican. Presbyterian. Avocations: music, art, sailing. Criminal, General corporate, Entertainment. Office: 122 10th St NW Albuquerque NM 87102

KENNEDY, SHEILA SUESS, lawyer; b. Indpls., Oct. 20, 1941; d. Joseph S. and Annette (Marcus) Simkin; m. Roberet E. Suess, June 27, 1964 (div. 1977); children: Michael, Stephen, David; m. Robert N. Kennedy, Mar. 2, 1980. AA, Stephens Coll., 1960; BS, Ind. U., 1964; JD, Ind. U., Indpls., 1975. Bar: Ind. 1975, U.S. Dist. Ct. (so. dist.) 1975, U.S. Ct. Appeals (7th cir.) 1977. Assoc. Baker & Daniels, Indpls., 1975-77; corp. counsel City of Indpls., 1977-80; of counsel Treacy, Cohen, Mears & Crawford, Indpls., 1981-83; ptnr. Mears, Crawford, Kennedy & Eichholtz, Indpls., 1983-87, Carley Devel. Services, 1987—; of counsel Mears & Crawford, Eichholtz, 1987—; instr. bus. law Ind. Cen. U., 1978; tchr. Eng. composition and lit. Ind. pub. schs. Mng. editor Ind. Law Rev.; contbr. articles to legal jours. Mem. sch. liberal arts adv. com. Ind. U.-Purdue U., Indpls.; vice-chmn. Taxpayers for Better Indpls.; Rep. candidate U.S. Ho. of Reps., 11th Dist. Ind., 1980; vice-chmn. Ind. Women for Reagan-Bush; Rep. precinct committeeman, 1982-84; active Ind. Women's Rep. Club, also Indpls. chpt., numerous local, state and nat. polit. campaigns; bd. dirs. Jewish Community Relations Council, Jewish Welfare Fedn. Mem. ABA, Ind. Bar Assn., Indpls. Bar Assn., Fed. Jud. Merit Selections Commn., Nat. Assn. Women in Constrn., Associated Gen. Contractors Ind., Nat. Inst. Mcpl. Law Officers, NCCJ, Am. Jewish Com. (past nat. bd. dirs., chmn. Indpls. chpt.), Nat. Council Jewish Women, Am. Israel Pub. Affairs Com., Hadassah, Women's Polit. Caucus., Network of Women in Bus., Indpls. Symphony Soc. (jr. group), Channel 20, Hooverwood Guild, Ind. U. Law Sch. Alumni Assn. Club: Columbia (Indpls.). Real property, Administrative and regulatory. Home: 628 Lockerbie St Indianapolis IN 46202 Office: Mears Crawford Kennedy & Eichholtz 120 Monument Circle Suite 301 Indianapolis IN 46204

KENNEDY, WALLACE WALTON, lawyer, real estate developer; b. Century, Fla., Nov. 22, 1934; s. James Fountain and Evie Dean (Bell) K.; m. Dorothy Miller, May 8, 1965; children—Kimberly Dee, Troy Walton. A.B., U. Fla., Gainesville, 1962, J.D., 1964. Bar: Fla., 1965. Assoc., Beggs & Lane, Pensacola, Fla., 1965-67, Patterson, Maloney & Frazier, Ft. Lauderdale, Fla., 1967-69; ptnr. Devitt, Friedrick, Blackwell & Kennedy, Ft. Lauderdale, 1969-71, Kennedy & Melvin P.A., Ft. Lauderdale, Fla., 1971-83, sole practice, 1983—; dir. Capital City Bank, St. Paul. Mem. ABA, Broward County Bar Assn., Fla. Bar Assn. Served to maj. USMCR, 1953-58. Mem. Diversified Businessmen's Assn. (pres. 1969). Republican. Mem. Ch. Religious Sci. Club: Coral Ridge Country, Tower. Real property. Office: 1451 W Cypress Creek Rd Fort Lauderdale FL 33309

KENNEDY, WALTER JEFF, JR., lawyer; b. Kansas City, Kans., May 18, 1928; s. Walter Joseph and Emily (Knecht) K.; m. Norma Jeanne Buie, June 4, 1949 (dec. Mar. 1984); children—Kathleen Kim, Nancy Jo.; m. Geraldine N. Rieke, May 30, 1986. A.A., Kansas City Jr. Coll., 1952; A.B., Kans. U., 1954, J.D., 1956. Bar: Mo. 1956, Kans. 1956, U.S. Ct. Appeals (8th and 10th cirs.), U.S. Ct. Claims, 1971, U.S. Tax Ct., 1959, U.S. Dist. Ct. (we. dist.) Mo. 1956, U.S. Dist. Ct. Kans. 1956, U.S. Supreme Ct. 1970. Assoc. Davis, Thompson, Fairchild & Van Dyke, Kansas City, Mo., 1956—; sole practice, El Dorado, Kans., 1957-61; mem. legal staff Farmland Industries, Kansas City, Mo., 1961-63; assoc. Hoskins, King, McGannon, Hahn & Hurwitz, Kansas City, Mo., 1963-68, ptnr., 1968—. Served with USN, 1945-50; PTO. Mem. ABA, Mo. Bar Assn., Mo. Bar Assn. Corp. (banking and bus. orgns. com. 1984-86), Kans. Bar Assn., Lawyers Assn. Kansas City, Kansas City Bar Assn. Club: Milburn Country (Overland Park, Kans.). Author articles. Federal civil litigation, State civil litigation, Labor. Office: Commerce Trust Bldg Suite 1100 Kansas City MO 64106

KENNEDY, WILLIAM IRL, lawyer, real estate development executive; b. Los Angeles, June 20, 1929; s. Charles Irl and Leta Faye (Dow) K.; m. Marilyn Elizabeth Hinsch, Sept. 1, 1951; children—Jane Kennedy Warren, Katherine Kennedy Thorpe. B.A., U. So. Calif., 1951, J.D., 1954. Bar: Calif. 1954, U.S. Dist. Ct. (so. dist.) Calif. 1954, U.S. Supreme Ct. 1980. Atty. Union Pacific Co., Los Angeles, 1957-64, gen. atty., 1964-68, gen. solicitor, 1968-77; v.p., gen. solicitor Union Pacific Land Resources Co., Los Angeles, 1977—, also dir.; v.p., gen. solicitor Upland Industries Corp., Los Angeles, 1977—. Adviser Calif. Dept. Commerce, 1984. Served to lt. USN, 1954-57. Mem. ABA, Calif. Bar Assn., Los Angeles County Bar Assn., Urban Land Inst., Lambda Alpha (bd. dirs. 1979—). Republican. Clubs: Sunset Yacht (commodore 1970) (Huntington Beach, Calif.); Jonathan (Los Angeles). Real property, General corporate. Home: 2824 Rosemary Dr West Covina CA 91791 Office: Upland Industries Corp 5480 Ferguson Dr Los Angeles CA 90022

KENNELLY, JOHN JEROME, lawyer; b. Chgo., Dec. 11, 1918; s. Joseph Michael and Anna (Flynn) K.; m. Mary Thompson, Mar. 21, 1949. Ph.B., Loyola U., Chgo., 1939, LL.B., 1941. Bar: Ill. 1941, U.S. Dist. Ct. (no. dist.) Ill. 1941, U.S. Ct. Appeals (7th cir.) 1946, U.S. Supreme Ct. 1956. Sole practice, Chgo., 1946—. Served with USN, 1941-46. Fellow Internat. Acad. Trial Lawyers (past chmn. aviation sect.); mem. Chgo. Bar Assn. (bd. mgrs. 1965-67), Ill. State Bar Assn., ABA (aviation com. chmn. 1981-82), Inter-Am. Bar Assn., Ill. Trial Lawyers Assn. (pres. 1968-69), AIAA, Assn. Trial Lawyers Am., Am. Judicature Soc., Law Sci. Acad. Am., World Assn. Lawyers, Am. Coll. Trial Lawyers, Internat. Acad. Law and Sci., Internat. Soc. Barristers, Am. Soc. Internat. Law, Am. Bar Found. Clubs: Butterfield Country (Hinsdale, Ill.); Beverly Country (Chgo.). Author: Litigation and Trial of Air Crash Cases, 1969; contbr. articles to profl. jours. Federal civil litigation, State civil litigation, Personal injury. Office: 111 W Washington St Suite 1449 Chicago IL 60602

KENNEMER, JOHN MACLIN, lawyer; b. Sheffield, Ala., Mar. 23, 1955; s. Maclin Sloss and Dorothy Cleere (Sockwell) K.; m. Lacey Kay Stephenson, Aug. 25, 1979. BA, U. Ala., 1977; JD, Samford U., 1980. Bar: Ala. 1980, U.S. Dist. Ct. (no. dist.) Ala. 1982. Asst. dist. atty. Colbert County, Tuscumbia, Ala., 1980-81; ptnr. McKelvey & Kennemer, Tuscumbia, 1981-85; sole practice Tuscumbia, 1985—. Bd. dirs. regional chpt. Am. Heart Assn., Tuscumbia, 1982, Tenn. Valley Art Assn., Tuscumbia, 1981—. Democrat. Mem. Ch. Christ. Lodge: Kiwanis (v.p. Tuscumbia club 1985—). Personal injury, Probate, Contracts commercial. Home: 1808 Maclin Dr Tuscumbia AL 35674 Office: 106 W 2d St Tuscumbia AL 35674

KENNETT, JOHN HOLLIDAY, JR., lawyer; b. Atlanta, June 28, 1929; s. John Holliday and Alice Bruyere (Work) K.; m. Barbara Miller, Aug. 13, 1965; children—Elizabeth B., Leigh H. B.S. in Acctg., Va. Poly. Inst., 1951; LL.B., U. Va., 1954. Bar: Va. 1953, U.S. Supreme Ct. 1960. With Kennett & Kennett, C.P.A.s, 1954; assoc. with Holman Willis, Jr., Roanoke, 1954-61; sole practice, Roanoke, 1961—; instr. comml. law Va. So. Coll., Roanoke, 1961-67; dir. various corps. Named Boss of Yr., Roanoke Valley Legal Secs. Assn., 1980. Mem. ABA, Va. Bar Assn., Roanoke Bar Assn., Roanoke Estate Planning Council (pres. 1961). Presbyterian. Club: Roanoke Country. Criminal, Real property. Home: 3751 Parliament Rd SW Roanoke VA 24014 Office: 133 Kirk Ave PO Box 255 Roanoke VA 24002

KENNEY, BRUCE ALLEN, lawyer; b. Oklahoma City, Apr. 13, 1950; s. Jack H. and Betty J. Kenney; m. Kathryn Sue Burke, July 19, 1975; children—B. Allen, John Burke, Jayne Allyson. B.B.A., U. Okla., 1972, J.D., 1975. Bar: Okla. 1975, Tex. 1975, U.S. Dist. Ct. (so. dist.) Tex. 1975. Sr. atty. Sun Co., Inc., Dallas, 1975-81; sole practice law, Tulsa, 1981—; asst. sec. Kaiser-Francis Oil Co., Tulsa, 1981—. Mem. ABA, Tulsa County Bar Assn., Okla. Bar Assn., State Bar Tex. Methodist. Oil and gas leasing, General corporate. Home: 2246 E 26th St Tulsa OK 74114 Office: PO Box 3272 Citicorp Bldg Tulsa OK 74101

KENNEY, JOHN ARTHUR, lawyer; b. Oklahoma City, Aug. 3, 1948; s. Jack H. and Betty Jo (Hill) K.; m. Jane Francis, Sept. 4, 1971; children: John Graham, Lauren Elizabeth. BS in Indsl. Engring. with distinction, U. Okla., 1971, JD, 1975. Bar: Tex. 1975, U.S. Dist. Ct. (so. dist.) Tex. 1976, U.S. Ct. Appeals (5th cir.) 1977, Okla. 1981, U.S. Dist. Ct. Okla. 1981, U.S. Ct. Claims 1982, U.S. Ct. Appeals (10th cir.) 1983. Assoc. Baker & Botts, Houston, 1975-81; mem. McAfee & Taft, Oklahoma City, 1982—. sec., treas., bd. advisors dept. indsl. engring. U. Okla., Norman; bd. trustees Westminster Presbyn. Ch., Oklahoma City. Mem. ABA, Okla. Bar Assn., Okla. County Bar Assn. Federal civil litigation, State civil litigation. Office: McAffee & Taft Two Leadership Sq 10th Floor Oklahoma City OK 73102

KENNEY, JOHN JOSEPH, lawyer; b. N.Y.C., July 13, 1943; s. Joseph Charles and Regina Elizabeth (Hulbert) K.; m. Charlotte O'Brien, May 23, 1971; 1 child, Alexander Hulbert. BA, St. Michael's Coll., 1966; JD, Fordham U., 1969. Bar: N.Y. 1970, U.S. Dist. Ct. (so. dist.) N.Y. 1973, U.S. Ct. Appeals (2d cir.) 1973, U.S. Dist. Ct. (ea. dist.) N.Y. 1980. Assoc. Dunnington, Bartholow & Miller, N.Y.C., 1969-71; asst. U.S. atty. U.S. Dist. Ct. (so. dist.) N.Y., N.Y.C., 1971-80; assoc. Simpson, Thacher & Bartlett, N.Y.C., 1980-81, ptnr., 1981—. Counsel Village of Bronxville, 1983-86, Planning Bd., 1981-83. Recipient John Marshall award U.S. Dept. Justice, 1980. Mem. ABA, Fed. Bar Council (trustee 1983—), Assn. of Bar of City of N.Y. Republican. Roman Catholic. Clubs: Univ., Down Town (N.Y.C.). Federal civil litigation, Securities, Criminal. Home: 8 The By Way Bronxville NY 10708 Office: Simpson Thacher & Bartlett One Battery Park Plaza New York NY 10004

KENNICOTT, JAMES W., lawyer, consultant; b. Latrobe, Pa., Feb. 14, 1945; s. W.L. and Alice (Hayes) K.; m. Lynne Dratler Finney, July 1, 1984. AB, Syracuse U., 1967; JD, U. Wyo., 1979. Bar: Utah 1979, U.S. Dist. Ct. (Utah dist.) 1983. Sole practice Park City, Utah, 1979—; prin. Ski Cons., Park City, 1969—; cons. Destination Sports Specialists, Park City, 1984—. Trustee Park City Hist. Soc., 1980, Park City Museum Bd., 1983; trustee, pres. Park City Library Bd., 1985. Mem. ABA (real property, probate and trust law sects.), Utah State Bar Assn. (real propert sect.), Utah Library Assn. Avocations: skiing, sailing, hiking, cycling. Real property, Contracts commercial, Probate. Home: PO Box 2339 Park City UT 84060 Office: 1647 Shortline Rd Park City UT 84060

KENNY, CHARLES D., corporate lawyer. AB, Fairfield (Conn.) U., 1967; JD, Cath. U. Am., 1970. Atty. First Interstate Bancorp, 1975-76, asst. corp. sec., 1976-78, v.p., 1978-80, asst. gen. counsel, 1980-81; gen. counsel, sec. Union Bank, Los Angeles, 1981—. Office: Union Bank 445 S Figueroa St Los Angeles CA 90071 *

KENNY, JAMES MICHAEL, lawyer; b. N.Y.C., Nov. 13, 1940; s. Michael J. and Mary (Hayes) K.; m. Helen M. Mathews, Sept. 7, 1968; children: Christina, Kathleen, Denise, Elizabeth, James Jr. AB, St. Peter's Coll., 1962; LLB, Fordham U., 1965. Bar: N.Y. 1966, U.S. Dist. Ct. (so. dist.) N.Y. 1967, U.S. Ct. Appeals (2d cir.) 1970, U.S. Supreme Ct. 1984. Assoc. Donovan, Donovan, N.Y.C., 1966-70; ptnr. McHugh, Leonard & O'Conor, N.Y.C., 1970-84, Leonard, Kenny & Stearns, N.Y.C., 1984—. Mem. N.Y. State Bar Assn., N.Y. County Lawyers Assn. (chmn. com. on admiralty law 1979-82), Maritime Law Assn. U.S. Admiralty, Federal civil litigation, State civil litigation. Office: Leonard Kenny & Stearns 26 Broadway New York NY 10004

KENNY, PHILIP WILLIAM, lawyer; b. Mt. Vernon, N.Y., Nov. 9, 1946; s. Paul James and Ethel Roma (Dooley) K.; m. Ellen Goldberg, Feb. 16, 1974 (div. Nov. 1980); m. Christine Madge Dockum, Nov. 29, 1980; children: Merideth, Jason, Matthew. BA, Fordham U., 1968; JD, N.Y. Law Sch., 1973. Bar: N.Y. 1974. Sole practice Star Lake, N.Y., 1975-80; atty. Nationwide Ins. Co., Syracuse, N.Y., 1980-83; assoc. Meiselman, Farber, Poughkeepsie, N.Y., 1983-84, Grogan & Botti, P.C., Goshen, N.Y., 1984-86; atty. Office of Ct. Adminstrn., Poughkeepsie, N.Y., 1986—. Served with U.S. Army, 1968-70. Roman Catholic. Judicial administration. Home: 505 Stanton Terr Poughkeepsie NY 12603 Office: Dutchess County Ct Market St Poughkeepsie NY 12601

KENNY, ROBERT EMMETT, JR., lawyer; b. Chgo., July 10, 1932; s. Robert E. and Lauretta (Carmody) K.; m. Mary W. Ward, Nov. 25, 1954; children—Robert, Karen, Colleen, Eileen, Michael, Brian, William, James, Sean, Maureen. B.S.C., Loyola U., Chgo., 1954; J.D., DePaul U., 1961. Bar: Ill. 1961, U.S. Dist. Ct. (no. dist.) Ill. 1982. Asst. states atty. Cook County, Ill., 1961-65; sole practice, pres. Robert E. Kenny, Jr., P.C., Oak Lawn, Ill., 1965—. Bd. dirs. Oak Lawn Community Chest, 1970-75. Served to capt. U.S. Army, 1954-58. Mem. ABA, Ill. Bar Assn., Chgo. Bar Assn., Southwest Bar Assn. (dir. 1977-83), West Suburban Bar Assn. (dir. 1975-78). Democrat. Roman Catholic. Clubs: Oak Lawn, Elks, K.C., Serra (pres. 1976). Criminal, Probate, Real property. Address: 5210 W 95th St Oak Lawn IL 60453

KENRICH, JOHN LEWIS, chemical executive, lawyer; b. Lima, Ohio, Oct. 17, 1929; s. Clarence E. and Rowena (Stroh) Katterheinrich; m. Betty Jane Roehll, May 26, 1951; children: John David, Mary Jane, Kathryn Ann, Thomas Roehll, Walter Clarence. B.S., Miami U., Oxford, Ohio, 1951; LL.B., U. Cin., 1953. Bar: Ohio 1953, Mass. 1969. Asst. counsel B.F. Goodrich Co., Akron, Ohio, 1956-65; asst. sec., counsel W.R. Grace & Co., Cin., 1965-68; corp. counsel, sec. Standex Internat. Corp., Andover, Mass., 1969-70; v.p. Splty. Products Group div. W.R. Grace & Co., Cin., 1970-71; v.p., sec. Chemed Corp., Cin., 1971-82; sr. v.p., gen. counsel Chemed Corp., 1982-86, exec. v.p., chief adminstrv. officer, 1986—; bd. dirs. Chemed Corp., Nat. Sanitary Supply Co., Roto-Rooter Inc., Omnicare, Inc., Arocom Group Inc., Hesselbart & Mitten Inc., Dubois Chemie GmbH, Germany, DuBois Mexicana, DuBois Chemicalien BV, Netherlands. Trustee Better Bus. Bur. Cin., 1981—; mem. bus. adv. council Miami U., 1986—; mem. City Planning Commn., Akron, 1961-62. Served to 1st lt. JAGC, AUS, 1954-56. Mem. Am., Ohio, N.Y. bar assns., Beta Theta Pi, Omicron Delta Kappa, Delta Sigma Pi, Phi Eta Sigma. Republican. Presbyterian. Clubs: Queen City (Cin.), Bankers (Cin.). General corporate. Home: 947 Edwards Rd Cincinnati OH 45208 Office: 1200 DuBois Tower Cincinnati OH 45202

KENRICK, CHARLES WILLIAM, lawyer; b. Chgo., June 16, 1946; s. Ralph Schwarting and Angela Augusta (Shostrom) K.; m. Patricia June Ogilvie, Dec. 27, 1969; children: Hugh, Alex, Graham, Charlotte, Blair. AB cum laude, Kenyon Coll., 1968; JD, Duquesne U., 1972. Bar: Pa. 1972, U.S. Dist. Ct. (we. dist.) Pa. 1972, U.S. Ct. Appeals (3d cir.) 1977, U.S. Supreme Ct. 1984. From assoc. to ptnr. Dickie, McCamey & Chilcote, Pitts., 1972—. Articles editor Duquesne U. Law Rev., 1971; editor Pitts. Legal Jour., 1980-84. Mem. ABA, Pa. Bar Assn. (ho. of dels. 1980—), Allegheny County Bar Assn. (bd. govs. 1984—, adminstrv. v.p. 1986—), Kenyon Coll. Alumni Assn. Pitts. (pres. 1983-84), Duquesne U. Law Alumni Assn. (pres. 1985-86). Democrat. Club: Rivers (Pitts.); Nemacolin (Bealsville, Pa.). Federal civil litigation, State civil litigation. Office: Dickie McCamey & Chilcote 2 PPG Pl Suite 400 Pittsburgh PA 15222

KENT, DALE R., lawyer; b. Salt Lake City, Dec. 15, 1949; s. James E. Kent and Elaine (Peterson) Osborne; m. Cynthia Wilson, June 8, 1972; children: Dale Ryan, Jared Wilson, Elizabeth Anne, James Brice, Emily Gene. BS, USAF Acad., 1972; JD, U. Utah, 1975; grad., U. Calif., San Francisco, 1979, Advanced Coll. Adv., Reno, 1981. Bar: Utah 1975, U.S. Dist. Ct. Utah 1975, U.S. Ct. Appeals (10th cir.) 1975, U.S. Supreme Ct. 1979. Sole practice Salt Lake City, 1975—; exec. dir. Murray (Utah) City Devel. Agy., 1971-81, Murray City Redevelopment Agy., 1979-81; asst. atty. City Attys. Office, Murray, 1978-81; judge pro tem Small Claims Ct., Salt Lake City, 1982—. Mem., soloist Salt Lake City Symphonic Choir, 1980-85; scoutmaster Boy Scouts Am., Salt Lake City, 1981—; mem. com. City Planning and Zoning Com., Salt Lake City, 1982-84; chmn. com. Commn. for Redrafting City Ordinances, Centerville, Utah, 1983. Recipient Don Quixote award Nat. Assn. Advancement of Developmentally Disabled, 1979, Dist. Service award 5th cir. Ct. Utah 1983, 84, 85. Mem. ABA, Utah Bar Assn., Assn. Trial Lawyers Am. Republican. Mormon. Lodge: Rotary (bd. dirs. 1984—). Avocations: skiing, squash, running, music, backpacking. State

civil litigation, Banking, Consumer commercial. Home: 1678 N 400 W Centerville UT 84014 Office: 660 S 200 E Suite 100 Salt Lake City UT 84111

KENT, DAVID CHARLES, lawyer; b. Shreveport, La., July 23, 1953; s. Keith C. and Louise (Goode) K.; m. Carol Elizabeth Hittson, July 3, 1976; children: John, Meredith, Robert. BA, Baylor U., 1975, JD, 1978. Bar: Tex. 1978, U.S. Dist. Ct. (no. dist.) Tex. 1980, U.S. Ct. Appeals (5th cir.) 1980, U.S. Dist. Ct. (so. and we. dists.) Tex. 1981, U.S. Ct. Appeals (11th cir.) 1981, U.S. Dist. Ct. (ea. dist.) Tex. 1982. Briefing atty. Supreme Ct. Tex., Austin, 1978-79; ptnr. Hughes & Luce, Dallas, 1979—. Editor: Managing Scarce World Resources, 1975, Crime and Justice in America, 1976, Medical Care and Health in America, 1977, Meeting America's Energy Needs, 1978; contbr. articles to profl. jours. Employee campaign coordinator United Way, Dallas, 1981—; coordinator teamwalk March of Dimes, Dallas, 1981—; nat. exploring com. Boy Scouts Am., Irving, Tex., 1982—. Named one of Outstanding Young Men Am., 1984; recipient Cert. Recognition United Way, 1983. Mem. ABA, Tex. Bar Assn., Dallas Bar Assn., Assn. Trial Lawyers Am., Baylor U. Alumni Assn. (scholorship com. 1980-81). Republican. Methodist. State civil litigation, Consumer commercial, Personal injury. Office: Hughes & Luce 1000 Dallas Bldg Dallas TX 75201

KENT, DON WAYNE, lawyer; b. Tyler, Tex., May 27, 1952; s. Luther A. and Christine (Starr) K.; m. Cynthia Ann Stevens, May 24, 1975; children: Andrew Stevens, Jarad Lee, Wayne Anthony. BA, Baylor U., 1974; JD, U. Houston, 1976. Bar: Tex. 1976, U.S. Dist. Ct. (so. dist.) Tex. 1977, U.S. Dist. Ct. (ea. dist.) Tex. 1978, U.S. Dist. Ct. (no. dist.) 1981, U.S. Ct. Appeals (5th cir.) 1982, U.S. Supreme Ct. 1983. Assoc. DeLange, Hudspeth et al, Houston, 1976-78, Potter, Guinn, et al, Tyler, 1978-82; ptnr. Barnett, Schofield & Kent, Tyler, 1982-83, Buchanan, Barnett, Schofield & Kent, Tyler, 1983—. Alt. del. Rep. County Conv., Tyler, 1984, del. 1986; bd. dirs. Country Place Community Assn., Tyler, 1985—. Mem. ABA, Def. Research Inst., Tex. Bar Assn., Tex. Assn. Def. Counsel, Smith County Bar Assn. (treas. 1983). Republican. Baptist. Lodge: Kiwanis (v.p. Tyler club 1979-80). Avocations: tennis, skeet shooting, hunting. Insurance, Personal injury, Federal civil litigation. Home: Rt 4 Box 1038 Tyler TX 75703 Office: One American Ctr Suite 280 909 ESE Loop 323 Tyler TX 75701

KENT, FREDERICK HEBER, lawyer; b. Fitzgerald, Ga., Apr. 26, 1905; s. Heber and Juanita (McDuffie) K.; m. Norma C. Futch, Apr. 25, 1929; children: Frederick Heber, Norma Futch K. Lockwood, John Bradford, James Cleveland. LLB, J.D., U. Ga., 1926. Bar: Ga. 1926, Fla. 1926. Since practiced in Jacksonville, Fla.; ptnr. Carlton, Fields, Ward, Emmanuel, Smith, Cutler & Kent, P.A. (and predecessor firms); chmn. bd. Kent Theatres, Inc.; pres. Kent Enterprises, Inc., Kent Amusements, Inc. Chmn. local ARC, 1934, 1950; pres. Jacksonville's 50 Years of Progress Assn., 1951; bd. dirs. YMCA, pres., 1946-50; bd. dirs. Jacksonville Community Chest-United Fund, 1955-59, pres., 1958-59; chmn. Fla. State Plant Bd., 1955-56; bd. control (regents) Fla. Instns. of Higher Learning, 1953-58, chmn., 1955-56; bd. dirs. Riverside Hosp. Assn., 1956-76, pres., 1964-65; chmn. State Jr. Coll. Council, 1962-72; mem. adv. com. Fla. Higher Edn. Facilities Act, 1963, 64; chmn. bd. trustees Fla. Jr. Coll., Jacksonville, 1965-71; mem. Select Council on Post High Sch. Edn. in Fla., 1967, Fla. Gov.'s Commn. for Quality Edn., 1967; trustee Bolles Sch., Jacksonville, 1954-65, Theatre Jacksonville, 1966-76; chmn. Fla. Quadricentennial Commn., 1962-65; mem. Jacksonville City Council, 1933-1937; mem. Fla. Democratic Exec. Com., 1938-40. Served as lt. USNR, 1942-45. Recipient Distinguished Service award U.S. Jr. C. of C., 1933, Ted Arnold award Jacksonville C. of C., 1961; Fred H. Kent campus Fla. Community Coll. at Jacksonville named in his honor, 1974. Mem. Internat. Bar Assn., ABA, Fla. Bar Assn., Jacksonville Bar Assn., Jacksonville C. of C., Am. Judicature Soc., Soc. Colonial Wars, Am. Legion, Sigma Alpha Epsilon, Delta Sigma Pi. Republican. Clubs: Rotary (pres. 1958-59), Timuquana Country, Florida Yacht, Seminole, Friars, Ye Mystic Revellers, Ponte Vedra, River, Sawgrass Country. General practice. Home: 2970 St Johns Ave Jacksonville FL 32205 Office: PO Box 4700 Jacksonville FL 32201

KENT, JAMES ALBERT, JR., lawyer, coal and construction executive; b. Akron, Ohio, Oct. 2, 1944; s. James Albert and Anita Claire (Barbe) K. BA, W.Va. U., 1966, postgrad., 1966-67, JD, 1974. Bar: W.Va. 1974, U.S. Dist. Ct. (no. and so. dists.) W.Va. 1974, U.S. Supreme Ct. 1978, U.S. Ct. Appeals (4th cir.) 1982. Mktg. rep. service bur. corp. IBM, Milw., 1968-69; sr. sales engr. Statis. Tabulating Corp., Milw., 1969-71; mgr. sales RCA Computer Systems, Milw., 1971; pres. Shadow Mountain Farms, Morgantown, W.Va., 1986—; sole practice Morgantown, 1974—; v.p. Pinnacle Mining Co., Morgantown, 1984-86. Mem. Monongalia County Bar Assn., Assn. Trial Lawyers Am., W.Va. Trial Lawyers Assn. (bd. govs. 1983-84), Order of Coif, Phi Alpha Delta. Republican. Roman Catholic. Lodge: Elks. Avocations: riding horses, sailing, auto racing. Federal civil litigation, Contracts commercial, General practice. Office: PO Box 1217 Morgantown WV 26505

KENT, JAMES EWART, lawyer; b. N.Y.C., May 15, 1925; s. James E. and Margaret F. K.; m. Emily B. Bryson, Nov. 25, 1952; children—Deborah, James E., III, Kevin, Donald, Maura. B.S., Fordham U., 1948, LL.B., 1953. Bar: N.Y. 1955, U.S. Dist. Ct. (ea. and so. dists.) N.Y. 1955. Assoc., Hill Rivkins, N.Y.C., 1953-57, Foley & Martin, N.Y.C., 1957-61; ptnr. Warner & Kent, Pearl River, N.Y., 1962-64; sr. atty. Office of Gen. Services, State of N.Y., Albany, 1964-66; adminstrv. law judge N.Y. State Dept. Motor Vehicles, Albany, 1966-67; 1st asst. counsel N.Y. State Thruway Authority, Albany, 1967—. Bd. dirs. Empire State Speech and Hearing Clinic, Sight Conservation Soc. Northeastern N.Y., Albany Girls Club. Served with USN, 1943-46. Mem. Albany County Bar Assn. Republican. Roman Catholic. Club: Lions Internat. (bd. dirs. 1981-83, Ambassador of Goodwill award 1983, Melvin Jones fellow 1982). Administrative and regulatory, Oil and gas leasing, Real property. Home: 40 Pinewood Rd Guilderland NY 12084 Office: NY State Thruway Authority PO Box 189 Albany NY 12201

KENT, M. ELIZABETH, lawyer; b. N.Y.C., Nov. 17, 1943; d. Francis J. and Hannah (Bergman) K. AB, Vassar Coll. magna cum laude, 1964; AM, Harvard U., 1965, PhD, 1974; JD, Georgetown U., 1978. Bar: D.C. 1978, U.S. Dist. Ct. D.C. 1978, U.S. Ct. Appeals (D.C. cir.) 1978, U.S. Supreme Ct. 1983, U.S. Dist. Ct. Md. 1985. From lectr. to asst. prof. history U. Ala., Birmingham, 1972-74; assoc. Santarelli and Gimer, Washington, 1978; sole practice Washington, 1978—. Mem. Ripon Soc., Cambridge and Washington, 1968—; research dir. Howard M. Miller for Congress, Boston, 1972; vol. campaigns John V. Lindsay for Mayor, 1969, John V. Lindsay for Pres. 1972, John B. Anderson for Pres., 1980. Woodrow Wilson fellow 1964-65; Harvard U. fellow 1968-69. Mem. ABA, D.C. Bar Assn., Women's Bar Assn., Women's Legal Def. Fund, Superior Ct. Trial Lawyers Assn., Nat. Women's Polit. Caucus, ACLU, Phi Beta Kappa. Republican. Avocations: history, politics. Criminal, Civil rights, General practice. Home: 35 E St NW Apt 810 Washington DC 20001 Office: 1730 Rhode Island Ave NW Suite 910 Washington DC 20036

KENT, ROBERT WARREN, lawyer; b. Oceanside, N.Y., July 8, 1935; s. Meredith L. and Ruth W. K.; m. Sally Anne Macnair, Aug. 24, 1957; children: Robert W., William M., Richard M., Deborah K. A.B., Princeton U., 1957; J.D., Harvard U., 1960; postgrad., Advanced Mgmt. Program. Asso. firm Breed, Abbott & Morgan, N.Y.C., 1960-67; asso. counsel Armco Inc., Middletown, Ohio, 1967-69; asst. counsel Armco Inc., 1969-73, counsel, 1973-78, asst. gen. counsel, 1978-81, corp. v.p. law, gen. counsel, sec., 1981—. Pres. Moundbuilders Area council Boy Scouts Am., 1980-81. Mem. Ohio Mfrs. Assn. (chmn. bd. dirs. 1983-85), Am. Bar Assn. Episcopalian. Office: Armco Inc 300 Interpace Pkwy Parsippany NJ 07054-0324

KENT, THOMAS DAY, lawyer; b. Summit N.J., Nov. 9, 1929; s. Stephen Girard and Philena (Marshall) K.; m. Ann Matthews, Feb. 10, 1933; children—Celia Marin, Thomas D., Robert H. B.A., Williams Coll., 1951; J.D., Columbia U., 1958; student Tuck Exec. Program, Dartmouth Coll., 1976. Bar: N.Y. 1958, U.S. Dist. Ct. (so. dist.) N.Y. Assoc. Cravath, Swaine & Moore, N.Y.C., 1957-64; litigation counsel Allied Chem. Corp., N.Y.C., 1964-67, asst. sec., 1967-70, corp. counsel, Morristown, N.J., 1971-73; assoc. counsel, 1973-76, asst. gen. counsel, 1976-79, assoc. gen. counsel Allied Corp., 1979-83, staff v.p., assoc. gen. counsel, 1983—; vis. lectr. Williams Coll., 1981, Harvard Bus. Sch., 1982; adj. faculty mem. N.J. Inst. Tech., 1983—; dir. Century Sports, Inc., J.A. Cissel Mfg. Co., Inc. Mem. Summit (N.J.) City Council, 1980-85, mem. Planning Bd., 1980-82, 84-85, mem., vice chmn. Substandard Housing Bd., 1973-79; pres. United Way Summit and New Providence, 1977-79; pres. bd. deacons Cen. Presbyn. Ch., Summit, 1969-72; pres. Lincoln Sch. PTO, 1969-70. Served to lt. USNR, 1951-55. Mem. ABA, Assn. Corp. Counsel N.J., Comml. Panel, Am. Arbitration Assn. Republican. Clubs: Beacon Hill (Summit); .); Seabrook (S.C.) Island, Chatham (N.J.) Squash and Racquet. Contbr. to numerous profl. jours. Environment, General corporate, Federal civil litigation. Address: 7 Murray Hill Sq Murray Hill NJ 07974

KENWORTHY, THOMAS BAUSMAN, lawyer; b. Coatesville, Pa., Oct. 12, 1948; s. Hugh and Mary Jane (Bausman) K.; m. Karen Armstrong, Aug. 29, 1970; children: Jesse Lloyd, James Andrew, John Bausman. AB, Dartmouth Coll., 1970; JD cum laude, Dickinson Sch. Law, 1973. Bar: Pa. 1973, U.S. Ct. Mil. Appeals, U.S. Ct. Appeals (3d, 4th and Fed. cirs.), U.S. Supreme Ct. Law clk. to presiding justice Phila., 1973-74; dep. gen. counsel Presidential Clemency Commn., Washington, 1975; assoc. Morgan, Lewis & Bockius, Phila., 1978-83, ptnr., 1983—. Coordinator state fin. George Bush for Pres., Phila., 1980; treas. Michael Marino for Congress, Phila., 1982; bd. dirs. Hist. Yellow Springs Inc., Chester Springs, Pa., 1982—. Served with JAGC, USMC, 1975-78. Mem. ABA (award for profl. merit 1975), Pa. Bar Assn., Phila. Bar Assn. Republican. Episcopalian. Federal civil litigation, State civil litigation, Military. Home: 405 Little Conestoga Rd Glenmoore PA 19343 Office: Morgan Lewis & Bockius 2000 One Logan Sq Philadelphia PA 19103

KENYON, ALLEN FRANCIS, lawyer; b. Eau Claire, Wis., Aug. 9, 1949; s. Karl Philip and Margaret Carol (Ash) K. BA, U. Wis., Eau Claire, 1971; JD, U. Wis., 1978. Bar: Wis. 1978, U.S. Dist. Ct. (we. dist.) Wis. 1978. Assoc. Moran Law Offices, Ladysmith, Wis., 1978-80; sole practice Ladysmith, 1980—; atty. City of Ladysmith, 1980—; bd. dirs. Ladysmith Indsl. Devel. Corp. Sec. Rusk County Reps., Ladysmith, 1980—. Served to maj. USAFR, 1971—. Mem. ABA, Res. Officers Assn. (life), Air Force Assn. (life). Republican. Lutheran. Lodge: Kiwanis (bd. dirs. 1980-82). Consumer commercial, Real property, Probate. Office: 109 Miner PO Box 391 Ladysmith WI 54848

KENYON, DAVID V., federal judge; b. 1930; m. Mary Cramer; children: George Cramer, John Clark. B.A., U. Calif.-Berkeley, 1952; J.D., U. So. Calif., 1957. Law clk. to presiding justice U.S. Dist. Ct. (ce. dist.) Calif., 1957-58; house counsel Metro-Goldwyn-Mayer, 1959-60, Nat. Theatres and TV Inc., 1960-61; sole practice law 1961-71; judge Mcpl. Ct. Los Angeles, 1971-72, Los Angeles Superior Ct., 1972-80, U.S. Dist. Ct. (cen. dist.) Calif., Los Angeles, 1980—. Judicial administration. Office: US Courthouse 312 N Spring St Los Angeles CA 90012 *

KENYON, EDWARD TIPTON, lawyer; b. Summit, N.J., Jan. 27, 1929; s. Theodore S. and Martha (Tipton) K.; m. Dolores Cetrule, July 11, 1953; children: David S., James N., Jonathan W., Theodore H. A.B., Harvard U., 1950; LL.B., Columbia U., 1953. Bar: N.Y. 1956, N.J. 1957. Asso. firm Thacher, Proffitt, Prizer, Crawley & Wood, N.Y.C., 1955-56; law clk. to U.S. Dist. Judge Reynier J. Wortendyke, Newark, 1956-57; asso. firm Jeffers, Mountain & Franklin, Morristown, N.J., 1957-59, Bourne, Noll and Kenyon (and predecessor), Summit, 1959-62; partner Bourne, Noll and Kenyon (and predecessor), 1962—. Trustee Summit Art Ctr., 1960-72, Trinity-Pawling Sch., Pawling, N.Y., 1977—, Pingry Sch., Hillside, N.J., 1970—; deacon Cen. Presbyn. Ch., Summit, 1960-65, trustee, 1965-72, pres., 1970-72; trustee Overlook Hosp., Summit, 1964-72, chmn., 1970-72; trustee Overlook Hosp. Found., 1975-84 , sec., 1977-80, v.p., 1980-81, pres., 1981-84; trustee Winston Sch., Summit, 1986—. Served with M.C. U.S. Army, 1953-55. Mem. Summit Bar Assn. (pres. 1983-84), Union County Bar Assn., N.J. Bar Assn., N.Y. State Bar Assn., ABA, N.J. Soc. Hosp. Attys., Am. Soc. Hosp. Attys., Am. Coll. Probate Counsel, Am. Law Inst. Republican. Clubs: Beacon Hill (trustee 1977-81, pres. 1979-81), Harvard of N.Y.C, Harvard of N.J. (trustee 1958-69, pres. 1968-69). Home: 80 Bellevue Ave Summit NJ 07901 Office: 382 Springfield Ave Summit NJ 07901

KEOUGH, JOSEPH ALOYSIOS, lawyer, judge; b. Providence, Apr. 8, 1941; s. Joseph A. and Mary (Crane) K.; m. Joanne Lee, Oct. 29, 1965; children—Joseph, Maureen, Kathleen, Colleen. B.A., Providence Coll., 1962; J.D., Suffolk U., 1970. Bar: R.I. 1970, U.S. Dist. Ct. R.I. 1971. Assoc. atty. McGee, Gifford, Farrelly & Keough, Providence, 1970-75; ptnr. Keough, Parker, Gearon & Viner, Pawtucket, R.I., 1975—; mcpl. ct. judge City of Pawtucket, 1974—; dir., sec. First Bank & Trust, Providence; dir. East Greenwich Dairy; pres. Ross Brooks Ent., Pawtucket, 1979—. Exec. sec. R.I. Democratic Com., 1976; chmn. bd. appeals City of Pawtucket, 1968-74; del. Dem. Nat. Conv., R.I., 1972. Burke scholar, R.I. Golf Assn., 1958. Mem. Am. Arbitration Assn. Democrat. Roman Catholic. Clubs: Pawtucket Country (v.p., sec., pres.), TK. Lodges: Elks, Irish Kings. General practice. Home: 72 Anawam Rd Pawtucket RI 02860 Office: Keough Parker Gearon & Viner 100 Armistice Blvd Pawtucket RI 02860

KEOUGH, PAUL GERARD, lawyer; b. Boston, July 21, 1952; s. William Alexander and Rita Frances (Minahan) K. BA, St. Anselm's Coll., 1973; MPA, JD, Suffolk U., 1977. Bar: Mass. 1977, U.S. Dist. Ct. Mass. 1978, U.S. Ct. Mil. Appeals 1978, U.S. Ct. Appeals (1st cir.) 1978, D.C. 1979, U.S. Ct. Appeals (D.C. cir.) 1979, U.S. Supreme Ct. 1986. Adminstrv. asst. to superintendant MCI-Concord, Mass., 1973-77; atty. USN, Washington, 1977-83; ptnr. Keough & Keough, Boston, 1983-85; sole practice West Roxbury, Mass., 1985—. Vice pres. adv. council to mayor of West Roxbury, 1973-77; bd. dirs. Boy Scout Am., Boston, 1970—. Served to lt. commdr. USN, 1977-83, PTO. Fellow: ABA; mem. Mass. Bar Assn., Boston Bar Assn., D.C. Bar Assn., Fed. Bar Assn., Assn. Trial Lawyers Am., Mass. Acad. Trial Attys., Judge Adv. Gen.'s Assn., Greater Boston Real Estate Bd., Rental Housing Assn., West Roxbury Bus. and Profl. Assn., Mass. Businessmen's Assn., YMCA, Order of Arrow. Democrat. Roman Catholic. Club: Century YMCA. Lodge: KC. General practice, State civil litigation, Personal injury. Home: 6 Wedgewood Rd West Roxbury MA 02131 Office: 2057 Centre St West Roxbury MA 02132

KEPHART, JAMES WILLIAM, lawyer, insurance broker, consultant; b. Phila., Sept. 25, 1955; s. Alvin Evans and Marie Elizabeth (Kenny) K. BA in Polit. Sci., U. Ariz., 1977; JD, Dickinson Sch. of Law, 1980; M in Tax Laws, Temple U., 1983. Bar: Pa. 1980, U.S. Dist. Ct. (ea. dist.) Pa. 1981, U.S. Tax Ct. 1982. Law clk. to presiding justice Pa. Superior Ct., Phila., 1980-82; of counsel Kephart & Kephart, 1980—; staff atty. Union Cen. Life, Phila., 1982-83; assoc. David Milne and Assocs., Phila., 1983—; broker, cons. Union Cen. Life, Phila., 1983—; pres. Bar N Tax Seminars, Phila. and Mont., 1985—; bd. dirs. Pan Am. Assn., Phila. Mem. exec. com. Phila. Reps., 1983—; vol. Lawyers for the Arts, Phila., 1982—; fund raiser Phila. Com. for Homeless, 1984—; chmn. jr. com. Friends of Scheie Eye Inst., Phila., 1985—; bd. dirs. Friends of Wistar Inst., Phila., 1984—. Mem. ABA, Pa. Bar Assn., Phila. Bar Assn. Episcopalian. Club: Union League (Phila.). Probate, Pension, profit-sharing, and employee benefits, Personal income taxation. Home: Rittenhouse Plaza Suite 19F Philadelphia PA 19103 Office: David Milne and Assocs 118 Church St Philadelphia PA 19106

KEPLINGER, (DONALD) BRUCE, lawyer; b. Kansas City, Kans., Feb. 4, 1952; s. Donald Lee and Janet Adelheit (Viets) K.; m. Mari Lisbeth Phillips, May 23, 1975; children: Mark William, Lisbeth Marie. BA with distinction, U. Kans., 1974; JD, So. Meth. U., 1977. Bar: Kans. 1977, U.S. Dist. Ct. Kans. 1977, Mo. 1980, U.S. Dist. Ct. (we. dist.) Mo. 1980, U.S. Ct. Appeals (10th cir.) 1985. Assoc. Clark, Mize & Linville, Salina, Kans., 1977-79, Blackwell, Sanders et al, Kansas City, Mo., 1979-82; ptnr. Payne & Jones, Overland Park, Kans., 1982—; active Kans. Ins. Com., 1984—. Contbr. articles to profl. jours. V.p. Friends of Library, Johnson County, Kans., 1980-85; deacon Village Presbyn. Ch., 1982-86. Mem. ABA, Kans. Bar Assn., Mo. Bar Assn., Kans. Assn. Def. Counsel, Def. Research Inst. Republican. Avocations: reading, golf. Federal civil litigation, State civil litigation, Personal injury. Office: Payne & Jones 11000 King Overland Park KS 66210

KEPLINGER, HELEN BUNTEN, lawyer; b. Charleston, W.Va., Apr. 7, 1942; d. Ralph Thorn Sr. and Helen (Bode) Bunten; m. Michael Scott Keplinger Sr., Dec. 27, 1963; children: M. Scott Jr., Gregory Thomas. BA, W.Va. Univ., 1964; JD, Cath. U., 1979. Bar: Md. 1980. Atty., advisor U.S. EPA, Washington, 1979—. Mem. ABA. Administrative and regulatory, Environment. Home: 5905 Wilmett Rd Bethesda MD 20817

KEPPEL, WILLIAM JAMES, lawyer; b. Sheboygan, Wis., Sept. 25, 1941; s. William Frederick and Anne Elizabeth (Cinealis) K.; m. Polly Holmberg, June 26, 1965; children—Anne, Timothy, Matthew. A.B., Marquette U., 1963; J.D., U. Wis.-Madison, 1970. Bar: Minn. 1970, U.S. Dist. Minn. 1970, U.S. Ct. Appeals (8th cir.) 1973, U.S. Dist. Ct. (we. dist.) Wis. 1979, U.S. Supreme Ct. 1979, U.S. Ct. Claims 1982. Assoc. Dorsey & Whitney, Mpls., 1970-76, ptnr., 1979—; assoc. prof. Hamline U. Sch. Law, 1976-79; instr. U. Minn. Law Sch.; adj. prof. William Mitchell Coll. Law, St. Paul; chmn., dir. Legal Advice Clinics, Ltd.; dir. Legal Assistance of Minn., Inc., Hennepin County Pub. Defender's Office for Misdemeanors. Served to lt. USN, 1963-67; Vietnam. Mem. ABA, Minn. Bar Assn., Hennepin County Bar Assn., Am. Soc. Hosp. Attys., ACLU. Roman Catholic. Author: (with Mc Farland) Minnesota Civil Practice (4 vols.), 1979; Minnesota Administrative Practice and Procedure, 1982; contbr. articles and monographs to legal jours. Administrative and regulatory, Federal civil litigation, Environment. Home: 10 Luverne Ave Minneapolis MN 55419 Office: 2200 First Bank Pl East Minneapolis MN 55402

KERESTER, CHARLES JOHN, lawyer; b. Youngstown, Ohio, Feb. 6, 1927; s. John J. and Mary K.; m. Eleanor H. Kerester, Mar. 29, 1952; children: Alison, Scott, Brian, Dale. B.S. summa cum laude, Ohio State U., 1949, J.D., 1952. Bar: Ohio, D.C. Assoc. Jones, Day, Reavis & Pogue, Cleve., 1952-57, 60-61, ptnr., 1961—; atty., staff. joint com. on internal revenue taxation U.S. Congress, Washington, 1958-60; mem. adv. bd. Tax Mgmt. Inc., div. Bur. Nat. Affairs, Washington, 1961—. Author: Tax Treatment of Recapture of Depreciation, 1964, Tax Treatment of Executive Compensation, 1972; portfolios in field. Mem. law rev. Ohio State U. Coll. Law, 1952. Mem. ABA, Internat. Fiscal Assn. (U.S. Br.), Ohio Bar Assn., Cleve. Bar Assn., Tax Club of Cleve. (pres. 1976-77), Order of Coif. Corporate taxation, Personal income taxation. Home: 2986 Falmouth Rd Shaker Heights OH 44122 Office: Jones Day Reavis & Pogue 1700 Huntington Bldg Cleveland OH 44115

KERLIN, GILBERT, lawyer; b. Camden, N.J., Oct. 10, 1909; s. Ward Dix Sr. and Jenny (Gilbert) K.; m. Sarah Morrison, Aug. 23, 1941; children: Sarah Kerlin Gray, Gilbert Nye, Jonathan Otis. BA, Harvard U., 1933, LLB, 1936. Bar: U.S. Ct. Appeals (2d cir.) 1937, U.S. Supreme Ct. 1945. Sr. ptnr. Shearman & Sterling, N.Y.C., 1936—; pres., bd. dirs. Doll Med. Research Inc.; v.p., bd. dirs. Goelet Corp.; chmn. bd. dirs. Exmin Corp., Guerlain Inc., North Cen. Oil Corp., Olla Industries Inc., Silver Resources Inc., Wave Hill Inc.; bd. dirs. Brunswick Mining and Smelting Corp. Ltd., Christiani and Neilsen Corp., Dodge Found., Doll Found., R.I. Corp., Kerr Addison Mining Ltd., Uddeholm Corp., Utility Power Corp. Served to lt. col. USAF, 1942-46. Democrat. Unitarian. Home: Dodgewood Rd Riverdale NY 10471 Office: Shearman & Sterling 153 E 53d St New York NY 10022

KERMAN, LEWIS H., academic administrator, lawyer; b. Plainfield, N.J., Sept. 1, 1952; s. Oscar R. and Lillian (Peretz) K. Certificate, de Freie Universität Hamburg, 1973; BA, Yale U., 1974; JD, Rutgers U., 1977, MBA, 1981. Bar: N.J. 1978, U.S. Dist. Ct. N.J. 1978, U.S. Dist. Ct. (ea. dist.) N.Y. 1981. Law clk. to presiding judge civil div. Essex County, Newark, 1977-78; spl. asst. to dean Rutgers Law Sch., Newark, 1978-80, dean of students, 1984—; asst. dean adminstrv. and student services Bklyn. (N.Y.) Law Sch., 1980-83; sole practice Jersey City, N.J., 1978—; lectr. law Rutgers Law Sch., 1979-80, 85; adjunct instr. Bklyn. Law Sch., 1981-83. Mem. ABA (legal admissions to bar sect.), Rutgers Law Sch. Alumni Assn. (exec. council 1977—), Yale Alumni Assn. Cen. N.J., Phi Alpha Delta, Phi Delta Phi (advisor 1980-83), Order of Barrister (hon.). Avocations: hiking, skiing, off-off Broadway theatre. Legal education, Probate, Real property. Home: 23 Neptune Ave Jersey City NJ 07305 Office: Rutgers Sch Law 15 Washington St Newark NJ 07102

KERN, GEORGE CALVIN, JR., lawyer; b. Balt., Apr. 19, 1926; s. George Calvin and Alice (Gaskins) K.; m. Joan Shorell, Dec. 22, 1962; 1 child, Heath. B.A., Princeton U., 1947; LL.B., Yale U., 1952. Bar: N.Y. 1952. Chief U.S. Info. Ctr., Mannheim, W.Ger., 1947-48; dep. dir. pub. info. Office U.S. Mil. Govt. for Germany, Berlin, Nurnberg, 1948-49; assoc. Sullivan & Cromwell, N.Y.C., 1952-60, ptnr., 1960—; bd. dirs. Allied Stores Corp., N.Y.C., Soltex Polymer Corp., Houston. Served to lt. USN, 1944-46. Clubs: India House; Sky (N.Y.C.). Home: 830 Park Ave New York NY 10021 Office: Sullivan & Cromwell 125 Broad St New York NY 10004

KERN, KEITH WILLIAM, lawyer; b. Cleve., Nov. 3, 1951; s. Richard William and Louella Louise (Lyon) K.; m. Susan Ann Linsley, May 21, 1977; children: Michelle T., Erin E., Heather R. BS, Mich. State U., 1972; JD, Ohio State U., 1975; postdoctoral, Cleve. State U., 1979-82. Bar: Ohio 1975, U.S. Dist. Ct. (no. dist.) Ohio 1977, U.S. Tax Ct. 1983. Ptnr. Conway, Barclay, Deyo & Kurant Co. P.A., Cleve., 1975—; bd. dirs. various client corps. Trustee, sec. Euclid (Ohio) Gateway Found., 1985—. Mem. ABA, Cleve. Bar Assn., Ohio Bar Assn., Fraternal Order of Police, Euclid C. of C. (chmn. by laws com. 1982-85). Methodist. Lodge: Masons. Avocations: stamp collecting, auto restoration, golfing, bowling. Corporate taxation, General corporate, Estate planning. Home: 6123 Magnolia Dr Mentor OH 44060 Office: Conway Barclay Deyo & Kurant Co PA 730 SOM Center Rd 100 Georgian Ctr Cleveland OH 44143-2313

KERN, RAYMOND LEX, judge; b. Bedford, Ind., Apr. 17, 1947; s. Paul Raymond and Edna Iola (Benefield) K.; m. Shelley Kay Kinder, June 8, 1974; children: Adam, Andrea, Amber. AB in Human Physiology, Ind. U., 1970, JD, 1980; postgrad. MBA program, Ariz. State U., 1972-74. Bar: Ind. 1980, U.S. Dist. Ct. (so. dist.) Ind. 1981. Dep. prosecutor Lawrence County, Bedford, 1978-80; sole practice Bedford, 1980-82; judge Lawrence County Ct., Bedford, 1982—; atty. Bd. Aviation, Bedford, 1980-82. bd. dirs. Bedford Housing Authority, 1980—, N. Lawrence Schs. Found., Bedford, 1980—, United Way, Bedford, 1982—. Served to capt. USAF, 1970-77. Mem. ABA, Nat. Flight Instrs. Assn., Air Force Assn., Res. Officer's Assn., Ind. Judges Assn., Bedford C. of C., Kappa Sigma. Republican. Methodist. Club: Exchange. Lodge: Elks. Judicial administration, Military. Home: 1786 Saddler Dr Bedford IN 47421 Office: Lawrence County Ct Courthouse Bedford IN 47421

KERNEN, WILL, lawyer; b. Boston, July 4, 1951; s. Judson and Olive (Bardsley) K.; m. Cindy M. Krueger, June 21, 1970; children: Kerry, Kurt, Kyle, Kasey. BA, Bridgewater State Coll., 1974; JD, Ohio State U., 1976. Bar: Ohio, U.S. Dist. Ct. (so. dist.) Ohio. Mem. Lappen, Lilley, Kernen & Co., L.P.A., Logan, Ohio, 1977—; law dir. City of Logan, 1978-79; law librarian Hocking County Law Library, 1980-83; acting judge Hocking County Mcpl. Ct., Logan, 1983—. Bd. mem. Logan-Hocking City Sch. Dist., 1979-83; counsel Hocking County Rep. Party, 1979—. Served with U.S. Army, 1968-71, Germany. Mem. ABA, Ohio Bar Assn., Hocking County Bar Assn. (v.p. 1978-79), Jaycees (pres. Logan 1983-84, dist. dir. Ohio 1984-85). General practice, Real property, State civil litigation. Home: 26816 Darl Rd Rockbridge OH 43149 Office: Lappen Lilley Kernen & Co LPA 9 E 2d St PO Box 588 Logan OH 43138

KERNOCHAN, JOHN MARSHALL, lawyer, educator; b. N.Y.C., Aug. 3, 1919; s. Marshall Rutgers and Caroline (Hatch) K. A.B., Harvard U., 1942; J.D., Columbia U., 1948. Bar: N.Y. 1949. Asst. dir. Legis. Drafting Research Fund Columbia U., N.Y.C., 1950-51; acting dir. Columbia U., 1951-52, dir., 1952-69; lectr. law Columbia U. Sch. Law, 1951-52, assoc. prof., 1952-55, prof., 1955-77, Nash prof. law, 1977—; exec. dir. Columbia U. Council for Atomic Age Studies, 1956-59, co-chmn., 1960-62; chmn. bd. Galaxy Music Corp.; cons. Temporary State Commn. to Study Organizational Structure of Govt. N.Y.C., 1953. Contbr. articles to profl. jours. and textbooks. Mem. civil and polit. rights com. Pres.'s Commn. on Status of Women, 1962-63; bd. dirs. Vol. Lawyers for the Arts, Am. Symphony Orch. League; mem. legal and legis. com. Internat. Confedn. Socs. Authors and Composers. Mem. Assn. Bar City N.Y., Internat. Lit. and Artistic Assn. (exec. com., pres. U.S.A.). Legal education, Legislative, Trademark and copyright. Home: 16 Highgate Rd Riverside CT 06878 Office: Columbia U Sch Law 435 W 116th St New York NY 10027

KERNS, DAVID VINCENT, lawyer; b. Salt Lake City, Jan. 29, 1917; s. Clinton Bowen and Ella Mae (Young) K.; m. Dorothea Boyd, Sept. 5, 1942; children—David V., Clinton Boyd. B.Ph., Emory U., 1937; J.D., U. Fla., 1939. Bar: Fla. 1939, U.S. Dist. Ct. (mid. dist.) Fla. 1939, U.S. Dist. Ct. (so. dist.) Fla. 1978, U.S. Dist. Ct. (no. dist.) Fla., U.S. Ct. Appeals (11th cir.) 1981. Assoc. Sutton & Reeves, Tampa, Fla., 1939-41, Fowler & White, Tampa, 1945-47; ptnr. Moran & Kerns, Tampa, 1948-49; resident atty. Fla. Road Dept., 1949-53; research asst. Supreme Ct. Fla., 1953-58; dir. Fla. Legis. Reference Bur., 1958-68, Fla. Legis. Service Bur., 1968-71, Fla. Legis. Library Services, 1971-73; gen. counsel Fla. Dept. Adminstrn., 1973-82; mem. Fla. Career Service Commn., 1983-86. Contbr. articles to profl. jours. Served with U.S. Army, 1941-45. Mem. Fla. Govt. Bar Assn. (pres. 1966, J. Ernest Webb Meml. award 1982), Fla. Bar (bd. govs. 1978-84), Tallahassee Bar Assn. Democrat. Methodist. Club: Capital City Country. Administrative and regulatory, Legislative, Patent. Home: 418 Vinnedge Ride Tallahassee FL 32303

KERR, ANN LOUGHRIDGE, lawyer; b. St. Petersburg, Fla., Mar. 24, 1940; d. Glenn Eldridge and Kathleen (Hughes) Loughridge; m. Bruce Kerr (div.). BA, Tulane U., 1962, JD, 1965. Assoc. Gibbons, Tucker, Smith, Coffer & Taub, Tampa, Fla., 1966-70; sole practice Tampa, 1970—; mem. family law sect. Fla. Supreme Ct. Commn., 1983—. Editor: Southeast Litigation, 1984. Bd. dirs. Family Services Assn., Tampa, 1975; dir. Upper Pinellas Assn. Mentally Retarded, Clearwater, Fla., 1977, Community Council on Child Abuse, Tampa, 1978; bd. trustees U. Psychiat. Ctr. Council, Tampa, 1984. Named Child Adv. Yr. Wendy's Internat. and Children's Home Soc., 1983. Mem. ABA (vice-chmn. family law sect. 1980), Fla. Bar Assn. (exec. bd., officer family law sect. 1972—), La. Bar Assn., Hillsborough County Bar Assn. (bd. dirs. 1978-82), Am. Acad. Matrimonial Lawyers (sec., treas. 1979—), Jr. League. Republican. Episcopalian. Clubs: Carlouel Yacht (Clearwater); Tower (Tampa). Home: 1070 El Dorado Ave Clearwater FL 33615 Office: 100 S Ashley Dr Suite 1250 Tampa FL 33602

KERR, THOMAS DRAPER, JR., lawyer; b. Anniston, Ala., Dec. 6, 1946; s. Thomas D. Sr. and Mary Elizabeth (Nixon) K.; m. Christina Love, Sept. 29, 1978. JD, U. Tenn., 1971. Bar: Tenn., U.S. Dist. Ct. (ea. dist.) Tenn. Assoc. Ayres, Parkey, Scaggs & Ware, Knoxville, Tenn., 1971; staff atty. State of Tenn., Nashville, 1971-72; assoc. Herron & Sherwood, Johnson City, Tenn., 1972-73, Kennerly, Montgomery, Howard & Finley, Knoxville, 1973-76; ptnr. Kerr, Rule & Ray, Knoxville, 1977-84, Foglesong, Cruze, Shope & Kerr, Knoxville, 1984—; pres., chmn. Tellico Harbor Inc. Served with USAR, 1967-73. Mem. Tenn. Bar Assn. Avocation: boating. Federal civil litigation, State civil litigation, Landlord-tenant. Office: Foglesong Cruze Shope & Kerr PO Box 56 Knoxville TN 37901

KERR, THOMAS ROBERT, lawyer; b. Covington, Ky., July 25, 1950; s. Thomas Hoover and Joann (Moffett) K.; m. Janice Duncan, May 26, 1973; children: Julie Ann, Jennifer Suzanne, Jill Mackenzie. BBA, U. Ky., 1972; JD, Chase Coll. Law, 1977. Bar: Ky. 1977, U.S. Dist. Ct. (ea. dist.) Ky. 1977. Sole practice Covington, 1977—; mem. pro-bono panel, Covington, 1980—; pub. defender Kenton County Pub. Defender's Office, Covington, 1977—. State rep. Ky. Gen. Assembly, Frankfort, 1985—; dir. Community Council on Religious Edn., Covington, 1983—; mem. Kenton County Exec. Com., Covington, 1985—; dir. Victims Assistance Network, Frankfort, 1985—, Calvary Christian Sch., Covington, 1981—; deacon Calvary Bapt. Ch., Latonia, Ky., 1982—. Served with Air N.G., 1971-77. Named One of Outstanding Young Men of Am., 1980, 83. Mem. ABA, Ky. Bar Assn., No. Ky. Bar Assn., Am. Trial Lawyers Assn., Ky. Acad. Trial Attys., Covington Christian Businessmans Assn. Democrat. Baptist. Club: Taylor Mill (Ky.) Swim (bd. dirs. 1983—). Avocations: tennis, reading, various sports. State civil litigation, General practice, Real property. Home: 748 Carol Dr Taylor Mill KY 41015 Office: 732 Scott St Covington KY 41011

KERRICK, DAVID ELLSWORTH, lawyer; b. Caldwell, Idaho, Jan. 15, 1951; s. Charles Ellsworth and Patria (Olesen) K.; m. Eleanor Beale, Aug. 17, 1974 (div. 1977); m. Juneal Casper, May 20, 1980; children: Peter Ellsworth, Beth Anne, George Ellis, Katherine Leigh. Student, Coll. of Idaho, 1969-71; BA, U. Wash., 1972; JD, U. Idaho, 1980. Bar: Idaho 1980, U.S. Dist. Ct. Idaho 1980, U.S. Ct. Appeals (9th cir.) 1981. Ptnr. Alexanderson, Davis, Rainey, Whitney & Kerrick, Caldwell, Idaho, 1980—. Mem. ABA, Assn. Trial Lawyers Am., Idaho Bar Assn. (3d dist. pres. 1985-86), Idaho Trial Lawyers Assn., Canyon County Lawyers Assn. (pres. 1985). Republican. Presbyterian. Lodge: Elks. Avocations: skiing, photography. Personal injury, Insurance, Real property. Office: PO Box 26 110 N Ninth Ave Caldwell ID 83605

KERRICK, THOMAS NEAL, lawyer; b. Elizabethtown, Ky., Aug. 2, 1955; s. Merritt A. and Thelma P. (Hunt) K.; m. Robin Ann Childers, May 18, 1974; children: Angela Lynn, Michael Thomas. BS in Acctg., U. Ky., 1977, JD, 1980. Bar: Ky. 1980, U.S. Dist. Ct. (we. dist.) Ky. 1980, U.S. Dist. Ct. (ea. dist.) Ky. 1986, U.S. Ct. Appeals (6th cir.) 1986. Assoc. Campbell & Crandall, Bowling Green, Ky., 1980-84, Campbell, Smith, Kerrick & Grise, Bowling Green, 1984-85; ptnr. Campbell, Kerrick & Grise, Bowling Green, 1985—. Named one of Outstanding Young Men in Am., 1985. Mem. ABA, Ky. Bar Assn., Ky. Def. Bar, Bowling Green-Warren County Bar Assn., Assn. Trial Lawyers Am., Ky. Acad. Trial Laywers, Bowling Green-Warren County C. of C. Democrat. Baptist. Lodge: Rotary. Federal civil litigation, Personal injury, Insurance. Home: 2733 Utah Dr Bowling Green KY 42101 Office: Campbell Kerrick & Grise 1025 State St PO Box 9547 Bowling Green KY 42101

KERRIGAN, PAUL BRENDAN, lawyer; b. Scranton, Pa., Oct. 30, 1952; s. Paul Thomas and Marie (Manno) K. AB in History summa cum laude, U. Scranton, 1974, MS in Counselor Edn., 1979; JD cum laude, Dickinson Sch. Law, 1981. Bar: Pa. 1981, U.S. Dist. Ct. (ea. dist.) Pa. 1982, U.S. Ct. Appeals (3d cir.) 1982. Assoc. Dilworth, Paxson, Kalish & Kauffman, Scranton, 1985, Pepper, Hamilton & Scheetz, Phila., 1981-85, 85—. Mem. ABA, Pa. Bar Assn. Democrat. Roman Catholic. Construction, Personal injury. Office: Pepper Hamilton & Scheetz 123 S Broad St Philadelphia PA 19109-1983

KERRIGAN, THOMAS SHERMAN, lawyer; b. Beverly Hills, Calif., Mar. 15, 1939; s. Thomas Simpson and Ione Valentine (Sherman) K.; m. Elsie Marie Patterson, Dec. 28, 1960; children—Sean Thomas, Leda Elsie, Katherine Ione; m. 2d, Victoria Elizabeth Thompson, Dec. 31, 1980; children—Hilary Teresa, Christopher Sherman, Elizabeth Caitlin. Student UCLA, 1959, U. Calif.-Berkeley, 1961; J.D., Loyola U., Los Angeles, 1964. Bar: Calif. 1965. Atty., Calif. Dept. Justice, Los Angeles, 1965-68, Litton Industries, Inc., Beverly Hills, Calif., 1969; assoc. McLaughlin and Irvin, Los Angeles, 1970-74, ptnr., 1974—. Served with USNR, 1961-65. Nat. Council Arts grantee, 1972. Mem. ABA, Los Angeles County Bar Assn., San Francisco Bar Assn. Republican. Author: New Writing, 1980. Federal civil litigation, State civil litigation, Labor. Office: 801 S Grand Ave Suite 300 Los Angeles CA 90017

KERRINE, THEODORE MICHAEL, lawyer; b. Bklyn., Feb. 19, 1950. BA, Harpur Coll., 1971; JD, Columbia U., 1974. Bar: Pa. 1975, D.C. 1984, Md. 1987. Assoc. gen. counsel AMTRAK, Washington, 1979—. Mem. ABA, Assn. Trial Lawyers Am., D.C. Bar Assn. Avocation: tennis. Labor, Federal civil litigation. Office: Nat Railroad Passenger Corp 400 N Capitol St NW Washington DC 20001

KERRY, HENRY EUGENE, lawyer; b. Longview, Tex., Nov. 5, 1932; s. Henry and Mary Louise (Findley) K.; m. Carolyn Weaver Kerry; children—Linda Louise, Elizabeth Anne, Michael Jason. B.B.A., U. Tex., 1953, J.D., 1957. Bar: Tex. 1957, U.S. Dist. Ct. (no. dist.) Tex. 1957, U.S. Dist. Ct. (so. dist.) Tex. 1968, U.S. Ct. Claims 1981, U.S. Supreme Ct. 1964. Ptnr. Brewster, Pannell, Dean & Kerry, Ft. Worth, 1957-61, Pannel Dean & Kerry, Ft. Worth, 1961-65, Hooper Steves & Kerry, Ft. Worth, 1965-67, Hooper Kerry Chappell, Ft. Worth, 1967-71, Hooper Kerry Chappell & Broiles, Ft. Worth, 1972-77; sole practice, Ft. Worth, 1977-82; ptnr. Kerry & Harrison, Ft. Worth, 1982—; U.S. ambassador to UNESCO, 1977-79. Bd. dirs. Ft. Worth Ballet, Ft. Worth Symphony, Ft. Worth Opera; co-mgr. Kennedy-Johnson Campaign, 1960; mgr. campaign Jim Wright, 1964—. Served to 1st lt. USAF, 1954-56. Fellow Young Lawyers Assn.; mem. Jr. Bar of Tex. (dir., chmn. bd., pres.), ABA (exec. council young lawyers sect.), Trial Lawyers Assn. (Tex.), Tarrant County Trial Lawyers Assn., Am. Judicature Soc. Democrat. Episcopalian. Clubs: Shady Oaks Country, Fort Worth. Contbr. numerous articles to legal jours. State civil litigation, Family and matrimonial, General corporate. Home: 74 Legend Rd Fort Worth TX 76132 Office: 1701 River Run Suite 900 Fort Worth TX 76107

KERSH, JOHN DANZEY, JR., tax lawyer; b. Gastonia, N.C., June 16, 1950; s. John D. Sr. and Edith (Morrow) K.; m. Gayle Battley, July 31, 1982. BBA, U. N.C., Charlotte, 1972; JD, Wake Forest U., 1978; LLM in Taxation, Emory U., 1979. Bar: N.C. 1978, U.S. Ct. Appeals (4th cir.) 1981, U.S. Tax Ct. 1982. Regional tax atty. Cherry, Bekaert & Holland CPA's, Charlotte, 1979; tax atty. Garland & Alala, Gastonia, 1979—; adj. prof. Belmont (N.C.) Abbey Coll., 1981—; instr. N.C. Assn. CPA's, 1981—, S.C. Assn. CPA's, 1983—. Bd. dirs. Gastonia YMCA, 1985-86; v.p. Western Piedmont Estate Planning Council, Gastonia, 1986—. Mem. N.C. Bar Assn. (tax, probate sects.). Lodge: Civitan. Avocations: golf, jogging. Probate, Corporate taxation, Pension, profit-sharing, and employee benefits. Office: Garland & Alala 192 South St PO Box 859 Gastonia NC 28053

KERSHNAR, HARRIS EDWIN, lawyer; b. Bklyn., Apr. 8, 1953; s. Morton and Sally (Schayer) K.; m. Rhona Debbie Kantor, July 16, 1978; children: Michael David, Mindy Jill. BA, Alfred U., 1975; JD, U. Calif., Berkeley, 1978. Bar: Calif. 1978, U.S. Dist. Ct. (cen. dist.) Calif. 1978, U.S. Dist. Ct. (so. dist.) Calif. 1980, U.S. Dist. Ct. (no. dist.) 1980, U.S. Dist. Ct. (ea. dist.) 1981, U.S. Ct. Appeals (9th cir.) 1979. Assoc. O'Melveny and Myers, Los Angeles, 1978-81, Graham and James, Newport Beach, Calif., 1981-85; spl. counsel Wallin, Roseman & Klarich, Tustin, Calif., 1985—; judge pro tem Small Claims Ct., Orange County, 1986. Regional bd. dirs. Anti-Defamation League, Orange County, Calif.; draft bd. mem. SSS, Orange County, 1982—. Mem. ABA (EEO com., labor law sect. 1981—), Orange County Bar Assn. (labor law sect. 1984). Jewish. Avocations: softball, tennis. Labor, Civil rights. Home: 9 Candela Irvine CA 92720 Office: Wallin Roseman Klarich 17291 Irvine Blvd Suite 159 Tustin CA 92680

KERSON, PAUL EUGENE, lawyer; b. N.Y.C., Feb. 18, 1951. BA, MA, Case Western Res. U., 1972; JD, Columbia U., 1975. Bar: N.Y. 1976, U.S. Dist. Ct. (ea. and so. dists.) N.Y. 1976, D.C. 1978, U.S. Ct. Appeals (2d cir.) 1978, U.S. Supreme Ct. 1979. Spl. asst. atty. gen. N.Y. State Dept. Law, N.Y.C., 1975-77; ptnr. Leavitt, Kerson & Leffler and predecessor firms, Kew Gardens, N.Y., 1977—. Contbr. articles to profl jours. Bd. dirs. YM-YWHA, Flushing, N.Y., 1985—. Mem. ABA, D.C. Bar Assn., N.Y. State Bar Assn., Assn. of Bar of City of N.Y., Queens County Bar Assn., Queens County Criminal Cts. Bar Assn. (v.p. 1985—), N.Y. County Lawyers Assn., Flushing Lawyers Club (pres. 1985—). Criminal, Personal injury, State civil litigation. Office: Leavitt Kerson & Leffler 125-20 Queens Blvd Kew Gardens NY 11415

KERSTEN, DONALD NORBERT, lawyer; b. Fort Dodge, Iowa, May 10, 1925; s. Paul Ernest and Anne Blessington (Hinzie) K. m. Evelyn Merope Mitchell, July 6, 1949; children—Anne, Mary, Stephen, Marjorie. B.A., U. Notre Dame, 1948; J.D., Drake U., 1955. Bar: Iowa 1955, U.S. Supreme Ct. 1960. Ptnr. Kersten, Opheim & Carlson, Ft. Dodge, Iowa; pres. Bd. of Counsellors Drake Law Sch., 1962-64. Served in USAF, 1948-52. Mem. ABA, Iowa State Bar Assn. (pres. 1985-86), Iowa Acad. Trial Lawyers, Fedn. Ins. Counsel, Lawyer-Pilots' Bar Assn., Law Science Acad., Iowa Def. Counsel (pres. 1978-79), Am. Coll Trial Lawyers, Order of Coif. Federal civil litigation, State civil litigation, General corporate. Office: Box 957 Fort Dodge IA 50501

KERSTETTER, WAYNE ARTHUR, criminal justice educator, lawyer; b. Chgo., Dec. 1, 1939; s. Arthur Edward and Lillian (Asplund) K.; B.A., U. Chgo., 1964, J.D., 1967. Bar: Ill. 1968. Asst. commr. N.Y. Police Dept., N.Y.C., 1972-73; supt. Ill. Bur. Investigation, Chgo., 1973-76; assoc. dir. Ctr. for Studies in Criminal Justice, U. Chgo., 1976-78; assoc. prof. criminal justice, dept. criminal justice U. Ill.-Chgo., 1978—; research atty. Am. Bar Found., Chgo., 1982—; cons. U.S. Civil Rights Commn., U. Chgo., ABT Assocs., Univ. Research Assocs., Police Found. Mem. transition team Mayor Washington, Chgo., 1983. Served with USNR, 1962-64. Research grantee Nat. Inst. Justice, 1976, Chgo. Bar Found., 1979-80, Am. Bar Found., 1983; fellow Ctr. for Studies in Criminal Justice, U. Chgo. Law Sch., 1978—. Mem. ABA. Criminal. Office: Am Bar Found 750 N Lake Shore Dr Chicago IL 60611

KERWIN, J(AMES) EUGENE, lawyer; b. Detroit, May 16, 1930; s. James L. and Faye M. (McClear) K.; m. Barbara Standley; children: Katherine, Sarah, Timothy, David, Maureen, Anne, Steven. JD, U. Detroit, 1954, MBA, 1963. Bar: Mich. 1954. Title examiner Lawyers Title Ins. Corp., Detroit, 1957-60; servicing atty. Advance Mortgage Corp., Detroit, 1960-62; staff counsel Chrysler Corp., Detroit, 1962—. Served with U.S. Army 1954-56. Mem. Mich. State Bar Assn., Mich. Basic Property Ins. Assn. (bd. govs. 1982—). Roman Catholic. Insurance, Contracts commercial. Home: 18420 Bretton Dr Detroit MI 48223 Office: PO Box 1919 Detroit MI 48288

KERYCZYNSKYJ, LEO IHOR, lawyer, county official, educator; b. Chgo., Aug. 8, 1948; s. William and Eva (Chicz) K.; m. Alexandra Irene Okruch, July 19, 1980. B.A., DePaul U., 1970, B.S., 1970, M.S. in Public Service, 1975; J.D., No. Ill. U., 1979; postgrad. U. Ill.-Chgo., 1980-82. Bar: Ill. 1981, U.S. Dist. Ct. (no. dist.) Ill. 1981, U.S. Ct. Appeals (7th cir.) 1981, U.S. Tax Ct. 1981, U.S. Ct. Claims, 1982, U.S. Ct. Mil. Appeals 1982, U.S. Ct. Internat. Trade 1982, U.S. Ct. Appeals (fed. cir.) 1983, U.S. Supreme Ct. 1984. Condemnation officer Cook County Treasurer's Office, Chgo., 1972-75, adminstrv. asst., 1975-77, dep. treas., 1977—; adj. prof. DePaul U., Chgo., 1979—; bd. dirs. First Security Fed. Savs. Bank Chgo.; Capt. Ukrainian Am. Democratic Orgn., Chgo., 1971. Recipient Outstanding Alumni award Phi Kappa Theta, 1971. Mem. ABA, Ill. State Bar Assn., Ill. Trial Law Assn., Chgo. Bar Assn., Theta Delta Phi. Ukrainian Catholic. Real property, Immigration, naturalization, and customs, General practice. Home: 2324 W Iowa St Apt 3R Chicago IL 60622 Office: Cook County Treas Office 118 N Clark St Rm 212 Chicago IL 60602

KESHIAN, RICHARD, lawyer; b. Arlington, Mass., Aug. 11, 1934; s. Hamayak and Takuhe (Malkesian) K.; m. Jacqueline C. Cannilla, June 3, 1937; children—Carolyn, Richard. B.S. in Bus. Adminstrn., Boston U., 1956, J.D., 1958. Bar: Mass. 1958. Sole practice, Arlington, Mass., 1964-71; ptnr. Keshian & Reynolds, P.C., Arlington, 1971—; instr. bus. law George Washington Sch. Gen. Studies, 1961-63; instr. real estate law Inst. Fin. Edn., 1976-80; dir. Arlington Coop. Bank, 1980-84; mem. adv. bd. Cooperative Bank of Concord, 1983-86; corporator Arlington Five Cents Savs. Bank, 1984—. Chmn. Arlington Zoning Bd. Appeals, 1972-76; pres. Arlington C. of C., 1976; v.p. Mass. Fedn. Planning Bds., 1978-85. Served with USMC, 1958-64; maj. Res. ret. Mem. ABA, Mass. Bar Assn., Mass. Conveyancers Assn., Mass. Assn. Bank Counsel, Middlesex Bar Assn. Congregationalist. Real property, Probate, Banking. Home: 93 Falmouth Rd W Arlington MA 02174 Office: 1040 Massachusetts Ave PO Box 440 Arlington MA 02174

KESSLER, ALAN, lawyer; b. Bklyn., June 4, 1947; s. David J. Kessler and Helen (Schneider) Diamond; m. Ileen Gail Dublin, July 5, 1970; children—Dana Michele, Abby Elizabeth. B.S., CCNY, 1969; J.D. Capital U., 1975. Bar: Ohio 1975, U.S. Dist. Ct. (so. dist.) Ohio 1976, U.S. Dist. Ct. (no. dist.) Ohio 1981. Economist, Columbia Gas System, Columbus, Ohio, 1969-72; mgmt. analyst Ohio State U., Columbus, 1973-74; adminstrv. law judge Pub. Utilities Commn. Ohio, Columbus, 1975-78; gen. atty. Ohio Power Co., Canton, 1978—. Bd. trustees Berwick Civic Assn., Columbus, 1977-78, Shaaray Torah Synagogue, Canton, 1984. Mem. Ohio State Bar Assn., Canton Bar Assn., ABA, Canton C. of C. Club: Arrowhead Country (Canton). Public utilities, General corporate, Legislative. Office: Ohio Power Co 301 Cleveland Ave SW Canton OH 44701

KESSLER, ALAN CRAIG, lawyer; b. Washington, Sept. 16, 1950; s. Alfred Milton and Josephine (Taub) K.; m. Gail Elaine Strauss, June 16, 1974; children: Stacy Ilana, Mark Jay. BA with honors, U. Del., 1972; JD with honors, U. Md., 1975. Bar: Pa. 1975, U.S. Dist. Ct. (ea. dist.) Pa. 1975, U.S. Ct. Appeals (3d and 6th cirs.) 1975. Assoc. Dilworth, Paxson, Kalish, Levy & Kauffman, Phila., 1975-77, Berger & Montague, P.C., Phila., 1977-81; ptnr. Mesirov, Gelman, Jaffe, Cramer & Jamieson, Phila., 1981—; instr. Inst. for Paralegal Tng., Phila., 1977—. Mem. fin. com. Dem. City Com. of Phila., 1981-84, dep. counsel, 1980-84; chmn. Bd. of Bldg. Standards City of Phila., 1983-84, Bd. of Licenses and Inspections Rev. City of Phila., 1984—; bd. dirs., pres. Randolph Ct. Assn., Phila., 1980-85; bd. dirs., v.p. South St. Neighbors Assn., Phila., 1983—, Park Towne Pl. Tenants Assn., 1977-79; bd. dirs. Support Ctr. for Child Advs., 1983—. Mem. ABA, Pa. Bar Assn., Phila. Bar Assn. (chmn. city policy com., exec. bd. dirs. young lawyers sect., legis. liaison com.). Democrat. Jewish. Clubs: Soc. Hill, Racquet (Phila.). Antitrust, Local government, Federal civil litigation. Home: 204 Daisy Ln Wynnewood PA 19096 Office: Mesirov Gelman Jaffe Cramer & Jamieson 123 Broad St 1500 Fidelity Bldg Philadelphia PA 19109-1088

KESSLER, JEFFREY L., lawyer; b. N.Y.C., Feb. 19, 1954; s. Milton M. and Edith H. Kessler; m. Regina T. Dessoff, May 21, 1977; children: Andrew Zalman, Leora Miriam. BA, JD summa cum laude, Columbia U., 1977. Bar: N.Y. 1978, U.S. Dist. Ct. (so. dist.) N.Y. 1978, U.S. Supreme Ct. 1985. Assoc. Weil, Gotshal & Manges, N.Y.C., 1977-85, ptnr., 1985—. Bd. editors Columbia U. Law Rev., 1976-77; contbr. numerous articles on antitrust law and policy to profl jours. Kent scholar, 1975-76, Stone scholar, 1976-77. Mem. ABA (antitrust law sect.), Am. Mgmt. Assn. (lectr. 1980—), Georgetown U. Study Pvt. Antitrust Litigation (founder, bd. advisors 1983-85), Phi Beta Kappa. Democrat. Jewish. Antitrust, Federal civil litigation, Private international. Office: Weil Gotshal & Manges 767 Fifth Ave New York NY 10153

KESSLER, KATHLEEN, lawyer; b. Miami, Fla., Mar. 17, 1947; d. Harold L. and Grace Elizabeth (Selvey) Parker; m. Richard P. Kessler Jr., June 17, 1973; 1 child, Grace Elizabeth. BA, Duke U., 1969; JD, Emory U., 1972. Bar: Ga. 1972, U.S. Dist. Ct. (no. dist.) Ga. 1972, U.S. Ct. Appeals (11th cir.) 1981, U.S. Supreme Ct. 1982. Ptnr. Head & Kessler, Atlanta, 1972-86, Carr & Kessler, Atlanta, 1986—; mem. faculty Ga. Inst. Trial Advocacy, Atlanta, 1985-87, Nat. Inst. Trial Advocacy, Atlanta, 1986; arbitrator Fulton County Superior Ct., Atlanta, 1986—. Mem. ABA, Atlanta Bar Assn. (chmn. family law sect. program 1974-75), Assn. Trial Lawyers Am., Ga. Assn. Women Lawyers, Ga. Trial Lawyers Assn. (life, chmn. long range planning com. 1984-86, editor newsletter 1986-87, several other offices, Recognition award 1985, 86, 87). Club: Lawyers (Atlanta)(chmn. rules and jud. com. 1985-86). Avocation: history. Federal civil litigation, Environment, Personal injury. Home: 4064 Chippewa Pl NE Atlanta GA 30319 Office: Carr & Kessler 3384 Peachtree Rd NE Suite 250 Atlanta GA 30326

KESSLER, LAWRENCE BERT, international communications and entertainment company executive, lawyer; b. Hackensack, N.J., July 10, 1946; s. Samuel L. and Lenore (Corn) K.; m. Susan Gail Zolkower, June 13, 1971. BA, U. Mich., 1968; JD, Harvard U., 1972; MBA, Columbia U., 1974. Bar: N.Y. 1973. Assoc. Dewey, Ballantine, Bushby, Palmer & Wood, N.Y.C., 1973-79; v.p., asst. gen. counsel Westinghouse Broadcasting/Group W Cable, N.Y.C., 1979-81; sr. v.p., gen. counsel, and sec. Beker Industries Corp., Greenwich, Conn., 1981-86, also dir.; v.p., gen. counsel and sec. News Am. Holdings Inc., N.Y.C., 1986—. Editor Harvard Jour. on Legis., 1972. Columbia Bus. Sch. Bronfman fellow, 1972; U. Mich. Angell Scholar, 1967. Mem. ABA, N.Y. State Bar Assn., Phi Beta Kappa. Entertainment, Libel, General corporate. Office: News Am 210 South St New York NY 10002

KESSLER, RICHARD PAUL, JR., lawyer; b. Latrobe, Pa., July 11, 1945; s. Richard Paul and Dorothy Henrietta (Comp) K.; m. Kathleen Jane Parker, June 17, 1973; 1 child, Grace Elizabeth. BA, Fairfield (Conn.) U., 1968; JD Emory U., 1971. Bar: Ga. 1971, U.S. Dist. Ct. (no. dist.) Ga. 1973, U.S. Ct. Appeals (5th cir.) 1974, U.S. Ct. Appeals (11th cir.) 1981. Law clk. U.S. Dist. Ct. (no. dist.) Ga., 1971-73; ptnr. Macey, Wilensky, Cohen, Wittner & Kessler, Atlanta, 1973—; lectr. Practising Law Inst., 1981, 83, Fin. Service Corp. Career Conf., Atlanta, 1986; panelist Credit Union Nat. Assn., Inc. League Attys. Conf., 1980-82. Author: What You Should Know About the New Bankruptcy Code, 1979, Guide To the Bankruptcy Laws: The Bankruptcy Reform Act of 1978, 1979, Guide to the Bankruptcy Laws: The Bankruptcy Reform Act of 1978 (Bankruptcy Code) as Amended by the Bankruptcy Amendments and Federal Judgeship Act of 1984, 1984; author column in field of law; contbr. articles to profl. jours. including Estate Planning. Banking, Bankruptcy, Consumer commercial. Office: Suite 900 Carnegie Bldg 133 Carnegie Way NW Atlanta GA 30303

KESSLER, STEPHEN, lawyer; b. Gardner, Kans., May 31, 1949; s. William Russel Kessler and Mary Annette (Rothwell) Guenther; m. Susan Ford, Jan. 21, 1970 (div. Oct. 1974); 1 child, Virginia. BS, U. Kans., JD. Bar: Kans. 1974, U.S. Dist. Ct. Kans. 1974, U.S. Ct. Appeals (10th cir.). Atty. Legal Services for Prisoners, Hutchinson, Kans., 1974-76; exec. dir. Legal Services for Prisoners, Topeka, 1976-80; ptnr. McCullough & Kessler, Topeka, 1980—; adj. prof. Washburn Law Sch., Topeka, 1976-80; lectr. Nat. Legal Services Conf., Huntsvill, Tex., 1984. Bd. dirs. Breakthrough House, Topeka, 1978—. Mem. Kans. Bar Assn. (ethics com. grievance sect. 1977-79), Ducks Unltd. (steering com.), Phi Alpha Delta. Democrat. Roman Catholic. Club: Jayhawker (Topeka) (pres. 1985—). Lodge: Lions (bd. dirs. 1986—). Avocations: hunting, fishing, woodworking. General practice, Criminal, Personal injury. Home: 901 SE 43d Terr Topeka KS 66609 Office: McCullough & Kessler Bank Tower IV Suite 930 Topeka KS 66603

KESSLER, STEVEN FISHER, lawyer; b. McKeesport, Pa., June 29, 1951; s. Robert and Rae (Alpern) K.; m. Susan Joyce Pearlstein, June 3, 1979; children: Matthew, Katie. B.A., U. Pitts., 1973, J.D., 1976. Bar: Pa. 1976, U.S. Dist. Ct. (we. dist.) Pa. 1976. Staff atty. Neighborhood Legal Services, McKeesport, Pa., 1976-79; solicitor City of McKeesport, 1980-82; sole practice, McKeesport, 1982—; solicitor McKeesport Housing Corp., 1985—; instr. community coll., West Mifflin, Pa., 1982—. Bd. dirs. YMCA, McKeesport, 1981—; chmn. bd. dirs. McKeesport Devel. Corp., 1984—. Mem. Am. Arbitration Assn. (panel arbitrators 1981—). Democrat. General practice, Probate, Personal injury. Home: 916 Jefferson St McKeesport PA 15132 Office: 332 5th Ave McKeesport PA 15132

KESTER, RANDALL BLAIR, lawyer; b. Vale, Oreg., Oct. 20, 1916; s. Bruce R. and Mabel M. (Judd) K.; m. Rachael L. Woodhouse, Oct. 20, 1940; children: Laura, Sylvia, Lynne. A.B., Willamette U., 1937; J.D., Columbia U., 1940. Bar: Oreg. 1940. Assoc., then partner firm Maguire, Shields, Morrison & Bailey, Portland, 1940-57; justice Oreg. Supreme Ct., 1957-58; partner Maguire, Shields, Morrison, Bailey & Kester, 1958-66, Maguire, Kester & Cosgrave, 1966-71, Cosgrave & Kester, Portland, 1972-78, Cosgrave, Kester, Crowe, Gidley & Lagesen, Portland, 1978—; instr. Northwestern Coll. Law, 1947-56; gen. solicitor northwestern dist. U.P. R.R., 1958-79; sr. counsel UPRR Co., 1979-81. Past v.p. Portland area council Boy Scouts of Am.; past pres. Mountain Rescue and Safety Council Oreg.; past trustee Willamette U.; past bd. dirs. Oreg. Symphony Soc., Oreg. Mus. Sci. and Industry. Recipient Silver Beaver award Boy Scouts Am. Mem. ABA, Multnomah Bar Assn. (past pres.), Oreg. State Bar, Am. Law Inst., Inst. Jud. Adminstrn., Nat. Ski Patrol, Mt. Hood Ski Patrol (past pres.), Mazamas (past pres., climbing chmn.), Wy'east Climbers, Portland C. of C. (pres. 1973, chmn. bd. 1974), U.S. Dist. Ct. Oreg. Hist. Soc. (past pres.), Phi Delta Phi, Beta Theta Pi, Tau Kappa Alpha. Clubs: Arlington (Portland), City (Portland) (v.p. 1978-80, pres. 1986-87), University (Portland), Multnomah Athletic (Portland). Federal civil litigation, State civil litigation, Insurance and Railroad and transportation law. Home: 10075 SW Hawthorne Ln Portland OR 97225 Office: Cosgrave Kester Crowe Gidley & Lagesen 901 The 1515 Bldg 1515 SW 5th Ave Portland OR 97201

KETCHAM, ROBERT CONRAD, lawyer; b. Kansas City, Mo., Dec. 5, 1937; s. R. Lloyd and Margaret M. (Hoover) K.; m. Caroline Tatnall; children—John H., Caroline G., Christopher T., Pennock M. B.A., Washington and Lee U., Va., 1959, J.D., 1962. Bar: D.C. Spl. counsel House Com. on Coms., Washington, 1973-74; staff dir. Subcom. on Fossil and Nuclear Energy, U.S. Ho. of Reps., Washington, 1975-80; counsel Com. on Sci. and Tech., U.S. Ho. of Reps., Washington, 1981, gen. counsel, 1982—. Served to capt. U.S. Army, 1963-67. Legislative.

KETTER, DAVID LEE, lawyer; b. Portsmouth, Ohio, Jan. 7, 1929; s. William Leslie and Dorothy Aileen (Weidner) K.; m. Beverly Jane Kinker, June 10, 1951; children—Michael David, Sandra Lee, Beth Ann, Richard Douglass. A.B., Ohio U., 1953; J.D., U. Cin., 1955. Bar: Ohio 1955, Pa. 1964. Trial lawyer Dept. Justice, Washington, 1955-56; trial lawyer Chief

Counsel's Office, IRS, Pitts., 1956-62; assoc. Kirkpatrick, Pomeroy, Lockhart & Johnson, Pitts., 1962-65; ptnr. Kirkpatrick & Lockhart, Pitts., 1965—; dir. Shenango Furnace Co., Pitts. Served as sgt. USMC, 1946-47, 50-52. Mem. Pitts. Tax Club (pres. 1985-86), Estate Planning Council (bd. dirs. 1975-77), FEd. Bar Assn. (tax sect.), ABA (tax sect.), Pa. Bar Assn. (tax sect.), Allegheny County Bar Assn. (chmn. tax sect. 1964-66), Order of Coif. Republican. Methodist. Clubs: Duquesne, Rivers, Allegheny, Valley Brook Country (McMurray, Pa.) (sec. 1977-78). Avocations: golf; tennis; shooting. Corporate taxation, Estate taxation, Personal income taxation. Home: 160 Canterbury Rd McMurray PA 15317 Office: Kirkpatrick & Lockhart 1500 Oliver Bldg Pittsburgh PA 15222

KEUP, ERWIN J., lawyer; b. Milw., Aug. 8, 1930; s. Erwin Otto and Ellen Grace (Sheehan) K.; m. Mary K. Skibba, Aug. 10, 1957; children: Christopher, Ellen, Craig, Kenneth, Maricay, Karen, Elaine, Peter. BS, Marquette U., 1953, JD, 1958. Assoc. Affledt & Lichtsen, Milw., 1958-60; asst. counsel Miller Brewing Co., Milw., 1960-66; div. atty. Glidden Co., Cleve., 1966-67; v.p., gen. counsel Snelling & Snelling Inc., Paola, Pa., 1967-70; v.p. Avco Personnel Services Inc., Newport Beach, Calif., 1970-72; ptnr. Noble, Campbell & Uhler, Los Angeles, 1972-75; sole practice Newport Beach, 1975—. Author: Franchising Your Own Business; To Do it or Not and How, 1980, How to Select a Franchise, 1982, Mail Order Legal Manuel - Federal State Laws That You Must Know, 1987. Served with U.S. Army, 1953-55. Mem. Calif. Bar Assn., Ohio Bar Assn., Wis. Bar Assn,. Republican. Roman Catholic. Avocation: franchise lecturing. Franchise law, Trademark and copyright, General corporate. Home: 3015 Country Club Dr Costa Mesa CA 92626 Office: 1201 Dove St Suite 600 Newport Beach CA 92660

KEUTHEN, CATHERINE J. NORMAN, lawyer; b. Salem, Mass., Sept. 1, 1955; d. William and Barbara H. (Polansky) Norman; m. Frederick W. Keuthen; 1 child, Emily B. Student, Bowdoin Coll., 1975-76; AB, Mt. Holyoke Coll., 1977; JD, Boston Coll., 1980. Bar: Mass. 1980, U.S. Dist. Ct. Mass. 1981, U.S. Ct. Appeals (1st cir.) 1981, U.S. Supreme Ct. 1985. Assoc. Withington, Cross, Park& Groden, Boston, 1980-81; sr. counsel Boston Edison Co., Boston, 1981—. Mem. Mass. Bar Assn., Boston Bar Assn., Mass. Assn. Women Lawyers. Administrative and regulatory, Public utilities, General corporate. Home: 33 Martin Rd Wellesley MA 02188 Office: Boston Edison Co 800 Boylston St Boston MA 02199

KEYES, LEONARD JOHN, lawyer; b. Mpls., June 4, 1922; s. Leonard A. and Cecilia A. (Rogan) K.; m. Donna Fritz, Apr. 15, 1950; children: Anita, Thomas, Theresa, Elizabeth, Constance, Regan. BA, U. Minn., 1942; JD, Harvard U., 1948. Bar: Minn. 1948, U.S. Dist. Ct. Minn. 1949, U.S. Ct. Appeals (8th cir.) 1970, U.S. Ct. Appeals (5th cir.) 1975, U.S. Supreme Ct. 1980. Assoc. Otis, Faricy & Burger, St. Paul, 1948-53; ptnr. Allen, Courtney & Keyes, St. Paul, 1953-57; judge St. Paul Mcpl. Ct., 1957-61, Minn. Dist. Ct., St. Paul, 1961-70; mem. Briggs & Morgan PA, St. Paul, 1970—. Served to lt. USNR, 1943-46, PTO. Mem. Minn. Bar Assn. (pres. 1985-86), Ramsey County Bar Assn. (pres. 1975-76), Phi Beta Kappa. State civil litigation, Federal civil litigation. Office: Briggs & Morgan PA 2200 1st National Bank Bldg Saint Paul MN 55101 Home: 1869 Eagle Ridge Dr #6 Saint Paul MN 55118

KEYKO, DAVID GEORGE, lawyer; b. Waterbury, Conn., Oct. 17, 1952; s. George John and Anne (Romanchuk) K. BA magna cum laude, Yale U., 1974; JD cum laude, NYU, 1977. Bar: N.Y., U.S. Dist. Ct. (so. and ea. dists.) N.Y., U.S. Ct. Appeals (2d cir.). Assoc. Winthrop, Stimson, Putnam & Roberts, N.Y.C., 1977—. Contbr. articles to profl. jours. Bd. dirs. St. Elmo's Soc. Yale U., New Haven, 1977—. Mem. Assn. of Bar City of N.Y. (ethics com.), ABA. Republican. Episcopalian. Avocations: running, skiing, sailing, drawing. Antitrust, Federal civil litigation, State civil litigation. Home: One Fifth Ave # 10A New York NY 10003 Office: Winthrop Stimson Putnam & Roberts 40 Wall St New York NY 10005

KEYS, JERRY MALCOM, lawyer; b. Childress, Tex., Dec. 5, 1947; s. Earl Milas and Mary Maud (Furr) K. B.S.E.E. with honors, U. Tex., 1970, J.D. with honors, 1975. Bar: Tex. 1975, U.S. Dist. Ct. (so. and we. dists.) Tex. 1980, U.S. Ct. Appeals (5th cir.) 1982, U.S. Patent and Trademark Office. Assoc., Pravel & Wilson, Houston, 1975-76; assoc. Brown, Maroney, Rose, Baker & Barber, Austin, Tex., 1975-81; ptnr. Brown, Maroney, Rose, Barber & Dye, Austin, 1981—; adj. asst. prof. U. Tex., 1979-85; mem. tech. adv. com. Supreme Ct. Tex. 1983-85. Author: Legal Protection of Computer Technology and Software, 1983. Mem. IEEE, Tex. Young Lawyers Assn. (chmn. new atty. orientation 1982), Tex. Bar Assn. (profl. efficiency and econ. research com., chmn. office automation subcom. 1982-86). Environment, Patent, Computer. Office: Brown Maroney Rose Barber & Dye 1300 One Republic Plaza Austin TX 78701

KEYSER, GEORGE HAROLD, lawyer; b. Johnstown, Pa., Feb. 13, 1917; s. George Henry and Flora (Joseph) K.; m. Barbara Cosgrove, July 15, 1943; children—Judith Merrill, George R., Stephen B., Philip H. A.B., Wittenberg U., 1939; postgrad. in law U. Mich., 1939-40; J.D., Case Western U., 1942. Bar: Ohio 1946. Sole practice, Mansfield, Ohio, 1946-48; ptnr. Weldon, Huston & Keyser, Mansfield, 1948—; dir. Mechanics Bldg. and Loan Co., 1950-72, pres., 1972-86; dir. Bank One of Mansfield, 1952-82, Tappan Co., Mansfield, 1969-71, Am. Elec. Products, Mansfield, 1970-73. Chmn. Mansfield Charter Commn., 1949-50; trustee Richland County Found., 1952-82; trustee, pres. Mansfield Meml. Homes, 1953-86. Served with Air Corps, USN, 1942-45. Mem. ABA, Ohio State Bar Assn., Richland County Bar Assn., Am. Judicature Soc., Mansfield Area Estate Planning Council (founder, 1st pres.). Republican. Presbyterian. Clubs: Westbrook Country, Rotary, University (Mansfield); Long Cove (Hilton Head, S.C.); Bent Tree Country (Sarasota, Fla.). Probate, General corporate, Real property. Home: 615 Forest Hill Rd Mansfield OH 44907 Office: 28 Park Ave W Mansfield OH 44902

KHARASCH, ROBERT NELSON, lawyer; b. Washington, Dec. 13, 1926; s. Morris S. and Ethel May (Nelson) K.; m. Shari B. Teele, Dec. 26, 1966 (div.); children: Mark Robert, Frank William. BS, U. Chgo., 1946, PhD, 1948, JD, 1951. Bar: D.C. 1952, U.S. Supreme Ct. 1965. Assoc. Becker, Maguire, Reich & Galland, Washington, 1951-54; ptnr. Galland, Kharasch, Calkins & Short, Washington, 1955-80; ptnr., pres. Galland, Kharasch, Morse & Garfinkle, P.C., Washington, 1981—; cons. Dept. Transp., Washington. Author: The Institutional Imperative, 1973; inventor teaching machine. Mem. ABA, Maritime Law Assn. (com. chmn. 1984—), Maritime Adminstrv. Bar Assn., Order of Coif, Phi Beta Kappa. Clubs: Georgetown, Pisces (Washington). Administrative and regulatory, Federal civil litigation, Private international. Home: 2914 Fessenden NW Washington DC 20008 Office: Galland Kharasch et al 1054 31st St NW Washington DC 20007

KHIM, DIANE, lawyer; b. Honolulu, Oct. 19, 1951; d. Ernest and Peggy Khim; m. Bradley L. Waite, Sept. 2, 1984. BS, U. Oreg., 1973; JD, U. Miami, 1979. Bar: D.C. 1980, N.Y. 1981, Calif. 1982. Staff atty. FTC, N.Y.C. and Washington, 1979-81; assoc. Weil Gotshal & Manges, N.Y.C., 1981-82, Pillsbury, Madison & Sutro, San Francisco, 1982-85, Gordon & Rees, San Francisco, 1986—. Contbr. articles to profl. jours. Mem. ABA (antitrust and litigation sects.), Bar Assn. of San Francisco (judiciary com. 1986—, co-chairperson litigations com. 1984-86, del. to conf. of dels. 1985), Asian Bar Assn. (co-chairperson legis. com. 1986). Club: Barristers (San Francisco). State civil litigation, Environment. Office: Gordon & Rees 601 Montgomery St 4th Floor San Francisco CA 94111

KIBLER, RHODA SMITH, lawyer; b. Gainesville, Fla., Mar. 10, 1947; d. Chesterfield and Vivian Lee (Parker) Smith; children—John Vincent Cannon, Parker Smith Cannon. B.A., Skidmore Coll., 1972; J.D. cum laude, Fla. State Univ., 1982. Bar: Fla. 1982. Research asst. to U.S. Senator, Washington, 1967-68; lobbyist Colo. Civil Rights Commn., Denver, 1974-75; intern Fla. Commn. on Human Relations, Tallahassee, 1981-82; atty. Office of Gen. Counsel Dept. Ins., Tallahassee, 1982-84, hosp. cost containment spl. counsel, 1984—; ptnr. Kibler & Renard, Tallahassee, 1984-86, Ervin, Varn, Jacobs, Odom & Kitchen, Tallahassee, 1986—; legis. counsel Fla. Assn. HMOs, 1986—, Fla. Council Internat. Bus. Devel.; vice chmn. U.S. Bicentennial Commn. Fla., HMO Rules Adv. Task Force, Health Policy Council; mem. Ins. Commr's. Task Force on Discrimination in Ins., Tallahassee, 1983—; mem. Task Force on Elimination of Discrimination in Statutes, Tallahassee, 1984—. Bd. dirs. Capital Women's Network, Tallahassee, 1983—; mem. exec. com. Statute of Liberty-Ellis Island Centennial Commn., Fla., 1983—; bd. dirs. Anti-Recidivism Ctr., Denver, 1973-75, United Way Tallahassee; mem. LeMoyne art Found., Tallahassee, 1984—; state chmn. Overseas Edn. Fund Women, Law, and Devel., 1984-85; mem. S.E. Regional Conf. on Constl. System; Mem. Am. Judicature Soc., Nat. Inst. Trial Adv., Fla. Bar Assn. (chair com. individual rights and responsibilities com. 1986, chair ins. com. 1986, legis. com. Young Lawyers, health law com., jud. evaluation com. 1984), ABA (mem. sect. administrv. law, individual rights and responsibilities, taxation, ins. coms. forum com. health law), Fla. Assn. Hosp. Attys., Fla. Hosp. Assn., LWV, Tallahassee Bar Assn., Tallahassee Assn. Women Lawyers, Tallahassee C. of C. (trustee's com. of 100, Leadership Tallahassee, legis. affairs), Leadership Fla. (del. leader Peoples Republic China), Fla. Women's Network (chair jud. appts. com. 1984—). Clubs: Capital Tiger, Bay, Governor's (Tallahassee). Contbr. articles to profl. jours. Health, Administrative and regulatory, Legislative. Home: 2918 Bayshore Dr Tallahassee FL 32308 Office: Ervin Varn Jacobs Odom & Kitchen PO Drawer 1170 Tallahassee FL 23202

KIDD, DARYL LESLIE, lawyer; b. Nicosia, Cyprus, Feb. 12, 1954; came to U.S., 1956; s. John S. and Lois A. (McKnight) K.; 1 child, Darlene A. BS, Troy State U., 1979; JD, U. Ga., 1982. Bar: Ga. 1982, U.S. Dist. Ct. (no. dist.) Ga. 1982. Sole practice Atlanta, 1982-83, 86—; assoc. Bryant, Davis & Cowden, P.C., Atlanta, 1983-86; counsel Ga. state chpt. U.S. Jaycees, 1986—. Served with U.S. Army, 1974-77. Mem. Gwinnett County Bar Assn., Northside Atlanta Jaycees (v.p. 1983-84, pres. 1984-85, state dir. 1985-86). Methodist. Avocations: karate, skiing. Family and matrimonial, State civil litigation, General practice. Home: 2087-L Powers Ferry Rd Marietta GA 30067 Office: 3537 Habersham at Northlake Tucker GA 30084

KIDD, DAVID THOMAS, lawyer, corporate officer; b. Laramie, Wyo., Feb. 1, 1934; s. David T. and Sarah Lucille (Love) K.; m. Sally Noble, Sept. 1, 1956; children—Lynden Louise, David Thomas II. Student, Dartmouth Coll., 1952-55; B.A., U. Wyo., 1957, J.D., 1960. Bar: Wyo. 1960, U.S. Dist. Ct. Wyo. 1960, U.S. Ct. Appeals (10th cir.) 1978, U.S. Supreme Ct. 1974. Assoc. Brown, Healy, Drew, Apostolos & Barton, Casper, Wyo., 1960-62; mem. firm McCrary, Schwartz, Bon & Kidd, Casper, 1962-74; western counsel for natural resources Union Pacific Corp., 1974—; counsel subs. Union Pacific Corp., Champlin Petroleum Co., Rocky Mountain Energy and Upland Industries. Bd. dirs. litigation Mountain States Legal Found., 1977—, vice chmn., 1984—; judge Municipal Ct., Casper, 1963-68; mem. Wyo. Ho. of Reps., 1963-67; mayor, Casper, 1971. Mem. State of Wyo. Commn. on Edn., 1983-84, chmn. educator subcom. Mem. ABA, Wyo. Bar Assn., Am. Judicature Soc., Rocky Mountain Mineral Law Found., Rocky Mountain Oil and Gas Assn. (chmn. legal com. 1982-86, v.p. Wyo. 1985-87, pres. Petroleum Assn. Wyo. subs. 1985-87), Wyo. Mining Assn., Dartmouth Lawyers Assn. Clubs: Casper Petroleum, Casper Country. Contbr. articles to profl. jours. Real property, Federal civil litigation, State civil litigation. Home: 2076 Willow Creek Rd Casper WY 82604 Office: Union Pacific Corp 104 S Wolcott Suite 600 Casper WY 82601

KIDD, JOHN EDWARD, lawyer, business executive; b. Syracuse, N.Y., Jan. 17, 1936; s. Edward F. and Mary (Feczko) K.; m. Elaine Mitchell, Feb. 23, 1963; children—John Mitchell, David Alan, Cynthia Lorraine. BS in Physics, LeMoyne Coll., 1957; LLB, Georgetown U., 1961. Bar: Va. 1961, U.S. Supreme Ct. 1966, U.S. Tax Ct. 1966, N.Y. 1968, U.S. Ct. Appeals (2d cir.) 1968, U.S. Ct. Appeals (4th cir.), 1968, U.S. Dist. Ct. (so. and ea. dists.) N.Y. 1969, U.S. Dist. Ct. (no. dist. Calif.) 1980, U.S. Ct. Appeals (3d, 5th, 9th, 11th cirs.) 1981. Patent examiner U.S. Patent Office, Washington, 1957-60; patent advisor U.S. Navy, Washington, 1960-62; trial atty. Dept. Justice, Washington, 1963-67; counsel to Copyright Office, Washington, 1966-67; spl. counsel Dept. Justice, 1967; assoc. Kenyon & Kenyon, N.Y.C., 1967-70; ptnr. Pennie & Edmonds, N.Y.C., 1971-86, Anderson, Russell, Kill & Olick, P.C., 1986—; referee 9th Jud. Dept. N.Y. Supreme Ct., 1968-69; exec., chmn. bd. E.M. Kidd, Ltd.; chmn. Symposium on Presdl. Patent Reform Commn., 1966; lectr. Practicing Law Inst., 1967, 84, 85, Fed. Bar Assn., 1963; mem. Bicentennial Commn. U.S. Claims Ct., 1987—. Active United Fund of Westchester, Community Fund of Bronxville, Georgetown U. Alumni Fund, N.Y. Westchester Council Boy Scouts Am. Mem. ABA (lectr. 1984-86), N.Y. State Bar Assn. (chmn. spl. com. on patents and trademarks 1982-86), Fed. Cir. Bar Assn., Assn. Trial Lawyers Am., Am. Patent Law Assn., U.S. Trademark Assn., Copyright Soc. Am., N.Y. Patent Law Assn., Assn. Bar of City of N.Y., N.Y. Patent, Trademark and Copyright Law Assn., Licensing Exec. Soc., Delta Theta Phi. Roman Catholic. Clubs: Westchester Country, Bronxville Field, Princeton N.Y. Contbr. writings to legal jour. Federal civil litigation, Patent, Trademark and copyright. Office: Anderson Russell Kill & Olick PC 666 3d Ave New York NY 10017

KIDD, WILLIAM MATTHEW, federal judge; b. Burnsville, W.Va., June 15, 1918; s. Robert H. and Henrietta (Hornor) K.; m. Madelyn Conrad, June 28, 1943; 1 child, Madelyn Sue Kidd Shipe. Student, Glenville State Coll., 1936-38; J.D., W.Va. U., 1950. Bar: W.Va. 1950. Tchr. elem. schs., 1938-41, 45-46; mem. W.Va. Ho. of Dels., 1950-52; practice law 1952-74; cir. judge 14th Jud. Cir., Bluefield, W.Va., 1974-79, chief judge, 1976-79; judge U.S. Dist. Ct. (no. dist.) W.Va., Bluefield, 1979—; pros. atty. Braxton County, W.Va., 1962-70. Served with USN, 1942-45. Mem. W.Va. Jud. Assn., Am. Judicature Soc., U.S. 4th Cir. Jud. Assn., Phi Alpha Delta. Office: US Dist Ct PO & Fed Bldg Clarksburg WV 26301 *

KIDDER, FRED DOCKSTATER, lawyer; b. Cleve., May 22, 1922; s. Howard Lorin and Virgina (Milligan) K.; m. Eleanor (Hap) Kidder; children—Fred D., Barbara Anne Donelson, Jeanne Kidder-Appleton. B.S. with distinction, U. Akron, 1948; J.D., Case Western Res. U., 1950. Bar: Ohio 1950, U.S. Dist. Ct. (no. dist.) Ohio 1950, Tex. 1985, U.S. Dist. Ct. (no. dist.) Tex. 1985. Mem. firm Arter & Hadden and predecessors, Cleve., 1950-79, ptnr., 1960-79; ptnr. Jones, Day, Reavis and Pogue, Cleve., 1980-85, regional mng. ptnr. Tex., 1987—. Contbr. articles to profl. jours. Mem. Cleve. Growth Assn., Shaker Heights Citizens Com.; past mem. Shaker Heights Recreation Bd.; mem. U. Akron Alumni Council, Dallas Citizens Council, Dallas Mus. Art (corp. council); bd. govs. Dallas Symphony Orch. Recipient Throckmorton award in constl. law Case Western Res. U., 1950. Mem. Cleve. Bar Assn., ABA, Ohio Bar Assn., Tex. Bar Assn., Estate Planning Council, Ct. of Nisi Prius, Phi Eta Sigma, Beta Delta Psi, Phi Sigma Alpha, Phi Delta Theta, Phi Delta Phi. Clubs: Tax of Cleve., Soc. Benchers, Blue Coats, State Troopers of Ohio (sec.), Tavern, Union, Pepper Pike Country (Cleve.), Cleve. Skating; Tower (Dallas). General corporate, Corporate taxation. Office: Jones Day Reavis & Pogue 1700 Huntington Bldg Cleveland OH 44115

KIDNER, EDWARD FRANKLIN, lawyer, CPA; b. Wheeling, W.Va., Oct. 1, 1955; s. Robert and Edith Adeline (Hoffman) K.; m. Kimberly Renee White, May 31, 1980; 1 child, Courtney Renee. BS, Wheeling Coll., 1977; JD, W.Va. U., 1980. Bar: W.Va. 1980, U.S. Dist. Ct. (so. dist.) W.Va. 1980, Pa. 1983, U.S. Tax Ct. 1982, U.S. Dist. Ct. (we. dist.) Pa. 1983, U.S. Dist. Ct. (no. dist.) W.Va. 1985. Tax specialist DeLoitte, Haskins & Sells, Pitts., 1980-82; tax atty. Mellon Bank, N.A., Pitts., 1982-85; ptnr. Riley & Riley, Wheeling, 1985—; bd. dirs. Minit Car Wash, Inc., Wheeling. Mem. ABA (tax sect.) W.Va. Bar Assn. (taxation com.), Pa. Bar Assn., Am. Inst. CPA's, W.Va. Soc. CPA's. Democrat. Clubs: Wheeling Country, Ft. Henry (Wheeling). Lodge: Civitan (sec., treas. Wheeling 1985, pres. elect. 1986). Avocations: golf, tennis, reading, photography. Personal income taxation, Pension, profit-sharing, and employee benefits, General corporate. Home: One Woodlawn Ln Wheeling WV 26003 Office: Riley & Riley 200 Riley Bldg Wheeling WV 26003

KIEF, PAUL ALLAN, lawyer; b. Montevideo, Minn., Mar. 22, 1934; s. Paul G. and Minna S. K. B.A., U. Minn., 1957, LL.B., 1957. Bar: Minn. 1957, U.S. Dist. Ct. Minn. 1964, U.S. Tax Ct. 1968, U.S. Supreme Ct. 1981. Gen. practice Bemidji, Minn., 1959-83; ptnr. Kief, Fuller, Baer, Wallner & Rodgers, Ltd., Bemidji, Minn., 1983—; pub. defender 9th Jud. Dist. Minn., 1968—. Vice chmn. Beltrami County Planning Commn., 1964-68; chmn. adv. com. Gov.'s Crime Commn., 1971-77; mem. Minn. Task Force on Standards and Goals in Criminal Justice, 1975-76. Served with USAR, USNG, 1958-64. Mem. ABA, Assn. Trial Lawyers Am., Minn. Bar Assn., Minn. Trial Lawyers Assn., 15th Dist. Bar Assn., Beltrami County Bar Assn., Lawyer-Pilots Bar Assn. Democrat. Congregationalist. Club: Toastmasters. Criminal, General practice. Home: PO Box 212 Bemidji MN 56601 Office: 514 America Ave NW Box 880 Bemidji MN 56601

KIEFER, J(AMES) RICHARD, lawyer, educator; b. Lafayette, Ind., Jan. 15, 1948; s. Donald Edward and Doris Marie (Martindale) K.; m. Bessanne Miller, Jan. 31, 1970 (div. May 1978); children: James Richard, Bridgette Marie; m. Carol Glass, Oct. 4, 1980; children: Kristin Elizabeth, David Jonathan. BA, Purdue U., 1970; JD, Ind. U., 1975. Bar: Ind. 1975, U.S. Dist. Ct. (so. dist.) Ind. 1977, U.S. Dist. Ct. (no. dist.) Ind. 1979, U.S. Ct. Appeals (7th cir.) 1979, U.S. Supreme Ct. 1983. Exec. dir. Indpls. Lawyers Commn., 1974-77; dep. prosecutor Marion County, Indpls., 1977; sole practice, Indpls., 1977—; adj. prof. Ind. U., Indpls., 1980-85; chmn. juvenile justice div. Ind. Jud. Study Commn., 1975-79; faculty Nat. Dist. Attys'. Assn., Houston, 1980-84. Author: Juvenile Delinquency, 1984. Chmn. Lawyers Assistance Strike Force; bd. dirs. Ind. Juvenile Justice Task Force, Indpls., 1975—, Legal Services Orgn. Ind., Indpls., 1976. Mem. Nat. Assn. Criminal Def. Lawyers, Ind. Assn. Criminal Def. Lawyers (bd. dirs.), Indpls. Bar Assn. (chmn. criminal justice sect. 1984-86, bd. mgrs. 1987—), ABA, Ind. Bar Assn. (council family law sect. 1984-86). Democrat. Methodist. Criminal. Office: 8900 Keystone Crossing Suite 1000 Indianapolis IN 46240

KIEFER, JOHN B., lawyer; b. New Orleans, June 2, 1936; s. Archie B. and Ann B. K.; m. Ann Harris, Dec. 27, 1958; children: Sheree, Scott, Shayna, Shawn. BS, Tulane U., LLB, LLD (hon.). Asst. atty. City of New Orleans, 1964-67; assoc. Louis B. Graham, 1960-69; ptnr. Graham, Kiefer & Arceneaux, and predecessor firm Graham & Kiefer, New Orleans, 1969-82; sole practice, Metairie, La., 1982—; pres. Charter Title Ltd., 1985—. Mem. La. State Bar Assn., New Orleans Bar Assn., Jefferson Bar Assn., Fed. Bar Assn., Am. Judicature Soc. Real property, State civil litigation, Family and matrimonial. Address: 1207 N Causeway Blvd PO Box 65 Metairie LA 70004

KIEFER, LOUIS, lawyer; b. Jackson Heights, N.Y., Sept. 13, 1936; s. Louis and Jean (King) K.; div.; children—Louis, Dale. B.A., U. Vt., 1958; J.D., Syracuse U., 1961. Bar: N.Y. 1961, Conn. 1964, U.S. Supreme Ct. 1965. Chief claims and litigation div. 1st U.S. Army, Governors Island, 1963; trial atty., litigation div. Office JAG, Washington, 1964; gen. counsel Resolute Ins. Co., Hartford, Conn., 1965-67; assoc. Kiefer & Holtman, Simsbury, Conn., 1967-70; sole practice, Simsbury, 1970-81, Hartford, 1982—. Mem. ABA (family law com.), Conn. Bar Assn. (exec. com. family law sect.), Hartford County Bar Assn., Am. Arbitration Assn. (panel). Author: How to Win Custody, 1982; contbr. articles to legal jours. Family and matrimonial. Home: 264 Mountain Rd Glastonbury CT 06033 Office: 60 Washington St Suite 1403 Hartford CT 06106

KIEFF, NELSON RICHARD, lawyer; b. Phila., Oct. 28, 1941; s. Irving N. and Florence (Prussell) K.; m. Patricia Anne Altenburger, May 3, 1985. BA in Polit. Sci., U. Nebr., 1971; JD, George Mason U., 1980. Bar: Va. 1980, U.S. Dist. Ct. (ea. dist.) Va. 1981, U.S. Ct. Appeals (4th cir.) 1982, U.S. Ct. Appeals (3d and 9th cirs.) 1983, U.S. Supreme Ct. 1984. Law clk. to presiding judge U.S. Dist. Ct. (ea. dist.) Wash., Spokane, 1980-81; trial atty. Nat. Right to Work, Springfield, Va., 1981-86; sole practice Springfield, 1986—; cons. Farley, Farley & Samuels, Fairfax, Va., 1983—, Mesirov, Gelman, Jaffee, Phila., 1984, Legal Services Corp., 1986—; asst. regional counsel AT&T Long Lines, Oakton, Va., 1982; of counsel Intertect Ltd., Phila., 1983—. Served to capt. U.S. Army, 1967-73, Vietnam. Mem. ABA (internat. law com.), Fed. Bar Assn. Avocations: tennis, piano, stamp and coin collecting. Federal civil litigation, Private international, Constitutional law. Home: PO Box 1604 Springfield VA 22151 Office: 9402 Pakcard Way Burke VA 22015-3105

KIEFNER, JOHN ROBERT, JR., lawyer, educator; b. Peoria, Ill., May 31, 1946; s. John Robert and Luna Merle (Froment) K.; m. Harriett E. Kidd, Aug. 3, 1968; 1 son, John William. B.A., Johns Hopkins U., 1968; J.D., Stetson U., 1971. Bar: Fla. 1971, U.S. Ct. Appeals (D.C. cir.) 1971, U.S. Ct. Appeals (11th cir.) 1981, U.S. Supreme Ct. 1979, U.S. Ct. Mil. Appeals 1971, U.S. Tax Ct. 1981, U.S. Dist. Ct. (no. dist.) Fla. 1971, U.S. Dist. Ct. (mid. dist.) Fla. 1981. Staff atty. SEC, Washington, 1971-74, br. chief, 1974-77, regional trial counsel, 1977-82; mem. Robbins, Gaynor, Burton, Hampp, Burns, Bronstein & Shasteen, St. Petersburg, Fla., 1982-86; ptnr. Riden, Watson & Goldstein, St. Petersburg, 1986—; adj. prof. law Stetson U., St. Petersburg, 1982—. Past chmn. Combined Fed. Campaign, 1976-77. Served to capt. U.S. Army, 1968-76. Recipient Cert. of Merit, SEC, 1982; Charles A. Dana scholar, 1970-71. Mem. Fla. Bar Assn., ABA, St. Petersburg Bar Assn., Fla. Acad. Trial Lawyers, Am. Trial Lawyers Assn., Pinella County Trial Lawyers Assn., Fed. Bar Assn., Nat. Assn. Colls. and Univs. (recruitment com.), St. Petersburg Area C. of C., Johns Hopkins U. Alumni Assn. Lutheran. Lodges: Masons, Shriners. Administrative and regulatory, Federal civil litigation, Securities. Home: 1153 42d Ave NE Saint Petersburg FL 33703 Office: Riden Watson & Goldstein PA 100 2d Ave S City Ctr North Tower Suite 400 Saint Petersburg FL 33701

KIEHNHOFF, THOMAS NAVE, lawyer; b. Sept. 13, 1949; s. Martin W. and A. Floriene (Nave) K.; m. Tamsen Kathleen Larkin, Aug. 17, 1974; children: John Martin, Daniel Thomas. BA, Washington U., St. Louis, 1971; JD, St. Louis U., 1975. Bar: Colo. 1975, U.S. Dist. Ct. Colo. 1978. Ptnr. McDermott, Kiehnhoff & Meconi (formerly McDermott, Kiehnhoff & Marshall), Canon City, Colo.; lectr. in field. Mem. Colo. Bar Assn. (com. on availability legal services 1982, sec. gen. and small firm sect. 1985-86, chmn. elect 1986—), Assn. Trial Lawyers Am., Colo. Trial Lawyers Assn. Lutheran. State civil litigation, Local government, Consumer commercial. Office: McDermott Kiehnhoff & Meconi 601 Greenwood Canon City CO 81212

KIEL, EDWARD ROWLAND, lawyer; b. Phila., Aug. 10, 1944; s. Victor and Helen Constance (Kripaitis) K.; m. Carole Ann Scavone, June 14, 1967; children: Darren E., Stephen R., Justin D. BA in English, U. Conn., 1966, JD cum laude, 1971. Bar: Conn. 1971, Vt. 1972, U.S. Dist. Ct. Vt. 1972, U.S. Supreme Ct. 1975, U.S. Ct. Appeals (2d cir.) 1980. Dep. states atty. Franklin County, St. Albans, Vt., 1971-72; assoc. Whitcomb, Clark, Moeser & Zug, Springfield, Vt., 1972-74; sole practice Springfield, 1974-75; sr. ptnr. Kiel & Boylan and predecessor firm Kiel, Freeman & Boylan, Springfield, 1975—. Bd. dirs. Windsor County Mental Health Assn., 1973-74. Served as 1st lt. U.S. Army, 1966-68. Mem. ABA, Vt. Bar Assn. (profl. responsibility com.), Windsor County Bar Assn. (pres. 1976-79), Assn. Trial Lawyers Am., Conn. River Valley Sierra Club (bd. dirs. 1974-75). Federal civil litigation, Personal injury, Insurance. Home: 323 Breezy Hill Rd Springfield VT 05156 Office: Kiel & Boylan PO Box 679 20 Park St Springfield VT 05156

KIEL, PAUL EDWARD, lawyer; b. Jersey City, Mar. 14, 1957; s. Frank Thomas and Theresa Barbara (Miros) K.; m. Audrey Ann Szotak, Oct. 12, 1985. BA, Rutgers U., 1979; JD, Dickinson Sch. Law, 1982. Bart: N.J. 1983, Pa. 1983, U.S. Dist. Ct. N.J. 1983, U.S. Dist. Ct. (ea. dist.) Pa. 1983. Law clk. to judge Superior Ct. N.J., Elizabeth, 1982-83; assoc. MacDonald, Ryan & Jackel, Ridgewood, N.J., 1983-84, Harwood Lloyd, Hackensack, N.J., 1984—; advisor Explorer Law Post, Hackensack, 1985—. Mem. ABA, N.J. Bar Assn., Pa. Bar Assn., Bergen County Bar Assn., Phi Beta Kappa, Phi Alpha Theta. Republican. Roman Catholic. State civil litigation, Insurance, Personal injury. Office: Harwood Lloyd 130 Main St Hackensack NJ 07601

KIENBAUM, KAREN SMITH, lawyer; b. Flint, Mich., Aug. 10, 1943; d. George Arnold and Ellen Janice (Wills) Smith; m. Thomas Gerd Kienbaum, June 24, 1966; 1 child, Ursula. BA in History and Edn., U. Mich., 1965; JD, U. Detroit, 1975. Bar: Mich. 1975. Tchr. Donoero High Sch., Royal Oak, Mich., 1966-72; dep. defender Legal Aid and Defender Assn., Detroit, 1975-77; assoc. Blue Cross Blue Shield, Detroit, 1977-78, asst. gen. counsel, 1981—; assoc. Clark, Hardy, Lewis et al, Birmingham, Mich., 1978-80. Mem. Fed. Bar Assn., Mich. Bar Assn. (appointee prepaid legal services 1978-85), Detroit Bar Assn. (chmn. corp. sect. 1985—, Chair person of Yr. labor sect. 1983), ACCA (bd. dirs. 1985—), DBA Found. (trustee 1987—), Am. Assn. Corp. Counsel. Clubs: Renaissance, Grosse Pointe Hunt (Detroit). Labor, General corporate, Federal civil litigation. Home: 894 Edgemont Park Grosse Pointe Park MI 48230 Office: Blue Cross Blue Shield 600 Lafayette E Detroit MI 48226

KIENER, JOHN LESLIE, sessions judge; b. Ft. Madison, Iowa, June 21, 1940; s. Cyril Joseph and Lucille Olive (Golden) K.; m. Carol Lynn Winston, June 4, 1966; children—Susan, Gretchen. B.A. cum laude, Loras Coll., 1962; J.D., Drake U., 1965. Bar: Iowa 1965, Tenn. 1972, U.S. Supreme Ct. 1974. Practice, Decorah, Iowa, 1965-68; asst. atty. gen. State of Iowa, 1968-72; ptnr. firm Cantor & Kiener, 1972-80; city judge Johnson City (Tenn.), 1975-80; gen. sessions judge, Johnson City, 1980—; continuing edn. tchr., bus. law East Tenn. State U., 1975—. Mem. ABA, Tenn. Bar Assn., Washington County Bar Assn. Republican. Lodges: Rotary, Elks. Contbr. articles to profl. jours. Criminal, Probate, Juvenile. Office: Gen Sessions Ct Ashe St Courthouse Johnson City TN 37601

KIENZ, GLENN CHARLES, lawyer; b. Jersey City, Feb. 10, 1953; s. Robert G. Phyllis M. (Love) K.; m. Donna Marie Corso, Aug. 21, 1976. BA, Lafayette Coll., 1975; MA in Regional Planning, Pa. State U., 1977; JD, Seton Hall Law Sch., 1981. Bar: N.J. 1981, U.S. Dist. Ct. N.J. 1981. Legal staff for office regulatory affairs N.J. Dept. Environ. Protection, Trenton, N.J., 1979-80; atty. for div. of state regional planning N.J. Dept. Community Affairs, Trenton, N.J., 1980-82; assoc. Richard H. Downes, Sparta, N.J., 1982-85; ptnr. Downes & Kienz, P.A., Sparta, N.J., 1985—; co-adj. faculty mem. Rutgers U., New Brunswick, N.J., 1982—; atty. for various N.J. zoning and planning bds. Author: Guide to Planning Boards., 1981; editor: New Jersey Municipal Land Use Law, 1983 (rev. yearly since 1983). Mem. N.J. Bar Assn. (dir. land use sect. 1983—), N.J. Fed. Planning Officials (assoc. dir. 1983—), Sussex County Bar Assn., League of Municipalities (sec. mcpl. land use law drafting com. 1981—),. Baptist. Land use and planning, General practice, Environment. Office: Downes & Kienz PA 283 Sparta Ave Sparta NJ 07871

KIERNAN, EDWIN A., JR., lawyer, corporation executive; b. N.Y.C., Aug. 2, 1926; s. Edwin A. and Helen M. (Clarke) K.; m. Ellen Mary Irving, Feb. 18, 1952; children: Robert Clarke, Katherine Waters. A.B., Columbia, 1947, J.D., 1950; LL.M., NYU, 1957. Bar: N.Y. 1950. Asso. Simpson Thacher & Bartlett, N.Y.C., 1950-52, 54-55, Wickes, Riddell, Bloomer, Jacobi & McGuire, N.Y.C., 1956-59; atty. Western Electric Co., Inc., 1959-60; atty. Interpublic Group of Cos., Inc., N.Y.C., 1960-64, mng. atty., 1964-68, asst. gen. counsel, 1968-79, from asst. sec. and asst. gen. counsel to sec. and gen. counsel, 1980—, v.p., 1973-81, sr. v.p., 1981—; sec. McCann-Erickson, Inc., N.Y.C., 1962-79. Served to lt. (j.g.) USNR, 1944-46, 52-54. Mem. Am. Bar Assn., Assn. Bar City N.Y., Phi Beta Kappa. General corporate. Home: 544 1st St Brooklyn NY 11215 Office: 1271 Ave of Americas New York NY 10020

KIES, DAVID M., lawyer; b. N.Y.C., Jan. 25, 1944; s. Saul and Lillian (Schultz) K.; m. Emily Bardack, July 6, 1966 (div. 1985); children: Laura, Adam, Abigail. AB, Haverford Coll., 1965; JD, NYU, 1968. Bar: N.Y. 1968, U.S. Dist. Ct. (so. dist.) N.Y. 1969, U.S. Ct. Appeals (2d cir.) 1969. Assoc. Sullivan & Cromwell, N.Y.C., 1968-76, ptnr., 1976—. Root Tilden fellow, NYU Law Sch., 1965. Mem. ABA, N.Y. State Bar Assn. Democrat. Jewish. Clubs: The Bd. Room, India House (N.Y.C.). Securities, Private international, Mergers and acquisitions. Home: 22 Chestnut Ave Larchmont Ave NY 10538 Office: Sullivan & Cromwell 250 Park Ave New York NY 10177

KIESSLING, WILLIAM EDWARD, lawyer, judge; b. Watertown, Wis., Oct. 7, 1932; s. William Edward and Abigail (Hooper) K.; children: William, Laura, Mark. BS, LLB, U. Wis. Bar: Wis., U.S. Dist. Ct. (we. dist.) Wis. Claims rep. State Farm Ins., Milw., 1959-60; specialist Northwestern Mutual Life Ins. Co., Milw., 1960-66; sole practice, Lake Mills, Wis., 1966-77; ptnr. Kiessling & Lesperance, 1977—. Legal counselor Badger Boys State, Ripon, Wis., 1961-62; scoutmaster Sinissippi council Boy Scouts Am., 1967. Served as 1st lt. U.S. Army, 1954, Korea. Mem. State Bar Wis., Jefferson County Bar Assn. (pres. 1984-85). Moravian. Lodges: Lions (pres. 1970), Masons. Probate, General practice, General corporate. Office: PO Box 6 Lake Mills WI 53551

KIEVE, LOREN, lawyer; b. New Haven, Mar. 15, 1948; s. Rudolph and Pauline (Flint) K.; m. Anne Hughes, Jan. 7, 1973; children: David, Andrew, Alexander, Katherine. Student, Stanford U., 1965-68; BA with honors, MA, Oxford U., Eng., 1971; JD, U. N.M., 1972. Bar: Calif. 1973, N.Mex. 1973, D.C. 1974. Law clk. to presiding justice U.S. Ct. Appeals (10th cir.), 1973-74, U.S. Ct. Appeals (9th cir.), 1974; assoc. Steptoe & Johnson, Washington, 1974-80, ptnr., 1980—. Mem. ABA. Episcopalian. Clubs: Windermere Island (The Bahamas); Oxford Union (Eng.). Federal civil litigation, Libel, General corporate. Office: Steptoe & Johnson 1330 Connecticut Ave NW Washington DC 20036

KIEVER, PAUL KENNETH, lawyer; b. New Brunswick, N.J., Oct. 10, 1946; s. Paul Peter and Ann (Demyan) K.; m. Darlene Lynn Hicks, Aug. 21, 1971; 1 child, Caroline. BA, U. Pitts., 1969; JD, Case Western Res. U., 1972. Bar: Ohio 1972, Pa. 1979. V.p., gen. counsel Crown Am. Corp., Johnstown, Pa., 1973—. Real property, Landlord-tenant, Contracts commercial. Office: Crown Am Corp 131 Market St Johnstown PA 15907

KIEVIT, ROBERT WARREN, lawyer; b. Passaic, N.J., May 28, 1932; s. Louis I. and Marion A. (Piaget) K.; m. Johnette Carson, June 24, 1967; children: Louise C., Kelly P. BBA, Lehigh U., 1953; JD, Duke U., 1975. Bar: Fla. 1975. Indsl. mgr. Armstrong World Industries, Inc., Lancaster, Pa., 1956-72; ptnr. Ray & Kievit, Pensacola, Pa., 1975—. Served as capt. USAF, 1953-56. Mem. Estate Planning Council Northwest Fla., Escambia/Santa Rosa Bar Assn., Phi Beta Kappa. Republican. Episcopalian. Avocations: fishing, flying. Real property, General corporate, Probate. Office: 15 West Main St Pensacola FL 32501

KIHLE, DONALD ARTHUR, lawyer; b. Noonan, N.D., Apr. 4, 1934; s. J. Arthur and Linnie W. (Ljunngren) K.; m. Judith Anne, Aug. 18, 1964; children—Kevin, Kirsten, Kathryn, Kurte. B.S. in Indsl. Engring., U. N.D., 1957; J.D., U. Okla., 1967. Bar: Okla. 1967, U.S. Dist. Cts. (we. and no. dists.) Okla. 1967, U.S. Ct. Appeals (10th cir.) 1967, U.S. Supreme Ct. 1971. Asso., Huffman, Arrington, Scheurich & Kincaid, Tulsa, 1967-71, ptnr., 1971-78; shareholder, dir., officer Huffman Arrington Kihle Gaberino & Dunn, Tulsa, 1978—. Asst. scoutmaster Boy Scouts Am., 1979-86, dist. chmn., 1983-85, cubmaster 1986—; mem. Statewide Law Day Com., 1982-86, chmn., 1983-85. Served to 1st lt. U.S. Army, 1957-59. Mem. ABA, Okla. Bar Assn. (chmn. constnl. bicentennial com. 1986—), Constitution 200 (exec. com. 1986—), Tulsa County Bar Assn., Sigma Tau, Phi Delta Phi, Order of Coif, Sigma Chi. Republican. Clubs: Tulsa (bd. dirs. 1987—), Southern Hills County (Tulsa). General corporate, Oil and gas leasing, Securities. Home: 4717 S Lewis Ct Tulsa OK 74105 Office: 1000 ONEOK Plaza Tulsa OK 74103

KILBANE, THOMAS MARTIN, JR., lawyer; b. Cleve., Mar. 1, 1953; s. Thomas M. and Kathleen (Cusack) K.; m. Helen Crowley, June 26, 1976; children: Catherine Ann, Patrick Thomas.. BA magna cum laude, Xavier U., 1974; postgrad., Miami U., Oxford, Ohio, 1975; JD with highest distinction, John Marshall Law Sch., 1978. Bar: Ill. 1978, Wash. 1980, U.S. Dist. Ct. (no. dist.) Ill. 1978, U.S. Dist. Ct. (we. dist.) Wash. 1980, U.S. Ct. Appeals (5th and 9th cirs.) 1981. Jud. extern U.S. Dist. Ct. Ill., Chgo., 1977; jud. clk. to presiding justice Ill. Appellate Ct., Chgo., 1978-80; assoc. Garvey, Schubert, Adams & Barer, Seattle, 1980-85; ptnr. Garvey, Schubert & Barer, Seattle, 1986—. Editor-in-Chief John Marshall Sch. Rev., 1977-78. Bd. trustees Queen Anne Community Council, Seattle, 1983-85; mem. Queen Anne Land Use Rev. Com., 1983-85. Chgo. Bar Found. grantee, 1978. Mem. ABA, Wash. State Bar Assn. (land use and taxation sects.), Seattle-King County Bar Assn., Alpha Sigma Nu. Administrative and regulatory, Admiralty, State and local taxation. Home: 157 Raye St Seattle WA 98109 Office: Garvey Schubert & Barer 1011 Western Ave 10th Floor Seattle WA 98104

KILBANE, THOMAS STANTON, lawyer; b. Cleve., Mar. 7, 1941; s. Thomas Joseph and Helen (Stanton) K.; m. Sarah Conway, June 4, 1966; children: Sarah, Thomas, Eamon, James, Carlin. B.A. magna cum laude, John Carroll U., 1963; J.D., Northwestern U., 1966. Bar: Ohio 1966, U.S. Dist. Ct. (no. dist.) Ohio 1967, U.S. Supreme Ct. 1975, U.S. Ct. Claims 1981, U.S. Ct. Appeals (6th cir.) 1982. Assoc. Squire, Sanders & Dempsey, Cleve., 1966-76, ptnr., 1976—, mgmt. com., 1981-83. Editorial bd. Northwestern U. Law Rev., 1965-66. Served as capt. U.S. Army, 1967-69. Decorated Bronze Star. Mem. ABA, Ohio Bar Assn., Greater Cleve. Bar Assn., Def. Research Inst., Northwestern U. Law Alumni Assn. (regional v.p.), Am. Coll. Trial Lawyers (nominated for fellowship), Northwestern U. Law Alumni Assn. (regional v.p.). Republican. Roman Catholic. Clubs: Union, Cleve. Athletic, Mid-Day. Federal civil litigation, State civil litigation, Contracts commercial. Office: Suite 1800 Huntington Bldg Cleveland OH 44115

KILBERG, WILLIAM JEFFREY, lawyer; b. Bklyn., June 12, 1946; s. Jack and Jeanette Constance (Beck) K.; m. Barbara D. Greene, Sept. 27, 1970. Student, Bklyn. Coll., 1963-64; B.S., Cornell U., 1966; J.D., Harvard U., 1969. Bar: N.Y. 1970, D.C. 1972. White House fellow, spl. asst. to sec. Labor, Washington, 1969-70; gen. counsel Fed. Mediation and Conciliation Service, 1970-71; asso. solicitor U.S. Dept. Labor, 1971-73, solicitor, 1973-77; dep. team leader Dept. Labor, Reagan-Bush transition, 1980-81; ptnr. Breed, Abbott and Morgan, 1977-80, Gibson, Dunn & Crutcher, 1980—; dir. Palmer Nat. Bank. Editor-in-chief Employee Relations Law Jour., 1985—; contbg. editor The Lessons of Victory, 1969, Instead of Revolution, 1971; Contbr. articles to profl. jours. Bd. dirs. D.C. chpt. Anti-Defamation League of B'nai B'rith, mem. nat. civil rights com., 1972—; mem. legal affairs adv. com. Republican Nat. Com., 1977-80; class rep. Harvard Law Sch. Fund, 1973-74. Recipient Man of Year award Lafayette High Sch., 1970; League United Latin Am. Citizens award for outstanding service to Spanish-speaking, 1973; Arthur S. Flemming award, 1975; Judge Groat award, 1977; Father William J. Kelly scholar, 1964-66; N.Y. State scholar, 1963-66. Mem. ABA, Fed., N.Y., D.C. bar assns., Cornell, Harvard Alumni Assns., White House Fellows Assn. (1st v.p. 1981-82, pres. 1982-83), Nat. Jewish Coalition (bd.dirs.). Jewish. Labor, Pension, profit-sharing, and employee benefits. Office: Gibson Dunn & Crutcher 1050 Connecticut Ave NW Washington DC 20036

KILBOURNE, GEORGE WILLIAM, lawyer; b. Berea, Ky., Mar. 29, 1924; s. John Buchanan and Maud (Parsons) K.; m. Helen Spooner, Dec. 25, 1945 (div. 1968); m. Carole Marko, June 12, 1970 (div. 1984); children: Stuart, Charles. Student, Berea Coll., 1941-42, Denison U., 1944; BS in Mech. Engring., U. Mich., 1946; JD, U. Calif., Berkeley, 1951. Bar: Calif. 1952, U.S. Dist. Ct. (no. dist.) Calif. 1952, Ind. 1957, U.S. Appeals (9th cir.). Sole practice Berkeley, 1952-57; ptnr. Hays & Hays, Sullivan, Ind., 1957-59, Boyle & Kilbourne, Sullivan, 1961-63, Bernal, Rigney & Kilbourne, Berkeley, 1963-68, Sherbourne & Kilbourne, Pleasant Hill, Calif., 1968-75; sole practice Pleasant Hill and Martinex, Calif., 1975—; lectr. Lincoln Law Sch., San Francisco, 1956-57, John F. Kennedy Law Sch., Orinda, Calif., 1977-78. Served to 2d lt. USMC, 1942-46, PTO. Episcopalian. Lodge: Elks. Avocations: tennis, bowling, outdoors. Toxic tort litigation. Office: 3755 Alhambra Ave Martinez CA 94553

KILCARR, ANDREW JOSEPH, lawyer; b. N.Y.C., Jan. 28, 1932; s. Patrick Joseph and Mary Catherine (Finan) K.; m. Barbara Ann Puhala, Aug. 21, 1954; children: Theresa, Patrick. B.S., Manhattan Coll., 1953; J.D., Georgetown U., 1959. Bar: D.C. 1960. Atty. antitrust div. U.S. Dept. Justice, Washington, 1959-64; atty. Donovan, Leisure, Newton & Irvine, Washington, 1964-86, Hogan & Hartson, Washington, 1986—. Served to 1st lt. USMCR, 1953-55. Fellow Am. Coll. Trial Lawyers; mem. ABA, D.C. Bar Assn. Clubs: International (Washington); Washington Golf and Country (Arlington, Va.). Antitrust, Federal civil litigation, FERC practice. Home: 7003 Duncraig Ct McLean VA 22101 Office: Hogan & Hartson Columbia Sq 555 13th St NW Washington DC 20004

KILCREASE, IRVIN HUGH, JR., judge; b. Nashville, Nov. 21, 1931; s. Irvin Hugh and Carrie (Dalton) K.; m. Kathleen Lacy, Aug. 20, 1961; 1 child, Irvin Hugh. Student Tenn. State U.; JD, Nashville YMCA Law Sch.; cert. Nat. Jud. Coll. Bar: Tenn. Adjudicator VA, Nashville, 1966-68; sole practice, Nashville, 1966-72; asst. pub. defender City of Nashville, 1969-72; asst. U.S. atty. U.S. Dist. Ct. (mid. dist.) Tenn., Nashville, 1972-80; judge Tenn. Chancery Ct., Nashville, 1980—; presiding judge Trial Ct. Tenn., 1984-85. Bd. dirs. Napier-Looby Assn., 1984—, Nashville chpt. Urban League, 1971-72; vice chmn. Tenn. Gov.'s Commn. on Status of Women, 1971-72. Served with U.S. Army, 1952-54. Mem. ABA, Fed. Bar Assn. (chpt. pres. 1975), Nashville Bar Assn. (bd. dirs. 1982-85), Napier-Looby Bar Assn. (bd. dirs. 1984-86), Am. Legion (dist. comdr. 1961-62), Phi Beta Sigma. Democrat. Baptist. Club: Frontiers (Nashville) (pres. 1979). Lodge: Masons (grand master Nashville chpt. 1974-75). Judicial administration, State civil litigation, General practice. Home: 945 Inverness Ave Nashville TN 37204 Office: 401 Metropolitan Courthouse Chancery Ct Nashville TN 37201

KILEY, EDWARD JOHN, lawyer; b. Jersey City, N.J., Sept. 9, 1948; s. Charles Francis and Billee Ruth (Gray) K.; children—Jennie Elizabeth, Leah Anne. B.A. in Polit. Sci., Villanova U., 1970; J.D. with honors, George Washington U., 1973. Bar: D.C. 1973, U.S. Supreme Ct. 1982, U.S. Ct. Appeals (D.C., 3d, 5th, 6th and 11th cirs.) 1982, U.S. Dist. Ct. D.C. 1973, U.S. Claims Ct. 1976. Assoc., Grove, Jaskiewicz, Gilliam and Cobert, Washington, 1973-78, ptnr., 1978—; chmn. Transp. Law Inst., U. Denver Law Sch., 1982—. Contbr. articles to profl. jours. Rep. Loudoun County (Va.) Washington Met. Council Govts., Water Resources Council, 1977-80; mem. Loudoun County Sch. Bd., 1986—. Mem. Transp. Lawyers Assn. (chmn. com. 1981—, Disting. Service award 1984), Assn. Transp. Practitioners, ABA. Administrative and regulatory, Antitrust, Labor. Office: Grove Jaskiewicz et al 1730 M St NW Suite 501 Washington DC 20036

KILGARLIN, WILLIAM WAYNE, state supreme court justice; b. Houston, Nov. 29, 1932; s. William and Juanita Lillian (Lawther) K.; m. Margaret Rose Kruppa, Dec. 28, 1963. B.S., U. Houston, 1954; LL.B., U. Tex., 1962. Bar: Tex. Sole practice Houston, 1962-78; mem. Tex. House of Reps., Houston, 1959-61; chmn. Harris County Democratic Party, Houston, 1962-66; judge 215th Dist. Ct. Tex., Houston, 1978-82; justice Supreme Ct. Tex., 1982—. Served to 1st lt. U.S. Army, 1955-57. Methodist. Office: Supreme Court Texas PO Box 12248 Capitol Station Austin TX 78711

KILGORE, GARY LYNN, lawyer; b. Chattanooga, July 17, 1953; s. James Velton Jr. and Frankie Jean (Eggert) K. BA, U. Va., 1975; JD, U. Tex., 1978. Bar: Tex. 1978, U.S. Dist. Ct. (no. dist.) Tex. 1979, U.S. Dist. Ct. (we. dist.) Tex. 1980, U.S. Ct. Appeals (5th cir.) 1979, U.S. Ct. Appeals (11th cir.) 1981, U.S. Dist. Ct. Hawaii 1984, U.S. Supreme Ct. 1985. Assoc. Garcia & Ganne, Austin, 1978-81; pres. Garcia & Kilgore, P.C., Austin, 1981-83, Garcia, Kilgore & Hickman, P.C., Austin, 1983—; pres. Am. Inst. Defensive Driving, Inc. 1981-84. Author, research editor Am. Jour. Criminal Law, 1977-78 (Merit award 1978). Del. Travis County Dem. Conv., Austin, 1980, 84, Tex. State Dem. Conv., Houston, 1984. Mem. ABA, Tex. State Bar Assn., Assn. Trial Lawyers Am. Lodge: Lions. Avocations: gardening, tennis. Personal injury, Workers' compensation, State civil litigation. Home: 1605A Southgate Circle Austin TX 78704 Office: Garcia Kilgore & Hickman PC 2044 S Lamar Blvd Austin TX 78704

KILKENNY, JOHN JUDE, lawyer; b. Rockville Centre, N.Y., Feb. 15, 1950; s. Joseph William and Eileen Mary (Nolan) K.; m. Susan Ann LaGraff, Oct. 2, 1976; children: Mary Elizabeth, Catherine Burke. AB in Polit. Sci., Coll. of the Holy Cross, 1972; JD, Bklyn. Law Sch., 1979. Bar: N.Y. 1980, U.S. Dist. Ct. (so. and ea. dist.) N.Y. 1981. With Fed. Res. Bank of N.Y., N.Y.C., 1973-80; assoc. Brown & Wood, N.Y.C., 1980-83; sr. atty. Merrill Lynch & Co., N.Y.C., 1983-84, 1986—; investment banker Mfrs. Hanover Bank, N.Y.C., 1984-86. Served with USAR, 1972-78. Roman Catholic. Lodge: KC. Avocations: long distance running, sailing, music. Securities, Municipal bonds, Contracts commercial. Office: Merrill Lynch & Co 1 Liberty Plaza New York NY 10080

KILLARNEY, JOHN PAUL, lawyer; b. N.Y.C., Dec. 8, 1926; s. Michael Augustus and Theresa Ann (Callahan) K.; m. Iracema Maria Mello, May 14, 1960; children—Elizabeth, John. B.A., Manhattan Coll., 1951; LL.B., Fordham U., 1959. Bar: N.Y. 1960, U.S. Dist. Ct. (so. and ea. dists.) 1962, U.S. Supreme Ct. 1962. Claims mgr. Nat. Union Ins. Co., N.Y.C., 1958-60; sole practice, N.Y.C., 1960-66; ptnr. Kroll Edelman Elser and Wilson, N.Y.C., 1966-79; ptnr. Kroll Killarney, Pomerantz and Cameron, N.Y.C., 1979-82; ptnr. Killarney, Fabiani and Brody, N.Y.C., 1982-87, Killarney, Reid Brody & FaBiani, N.Y.C., 1987—. Served to sgt. USAAF, 1944-46; ETO. Mem. ABA, N.Y. State Bar Assn., Assn. Trial Lawyers Am., N.Y. Claims Council. Republican. Roman Catholic. Club: Elks (N.Y.C.). Personal injury, Insurance, Libel. Office: 757 Third Ave New York NY 10017

KILLEEN, HENRY WALTER, lawyer; b. Buffalo, Aug. 25, 1946; s. Henry W. and Ruth (Dold) K. BA cum laude, Harvard Coll., 1968; postgrad., Stanford U., 1969-70; JD cum laude, SUNY, Buffalo, 1975. Bar: N.Y. 1975, U.S. Dist. Ct. (we. dist.) N.Y. 1975, U.S. Dist. Ct. (no. dist.) N.Y. 1983, U.S. Ct. Appeals (2d cir.) 1981. Assoc. Jaeckle, Fleischmann & Mugel, Buffalo, 1975-80; ptnr. Jaeckle, Fleischmann & Mugel, Buffalo and Washington, 1980—. Mem. ABA, N.Y. State Bar Assn., Erie County Bar Assn. (chmn. fed. practice com.). Federal civil litigation, Environment, Libel. Home: 283 Summer St Apt 1 Buffalo NY 14222 Office: Jaeckle Fleischmann & Mugel 12 Fountain Plaza Buffalo NY 14202

KILLIAN, JOHN DORAN, III, lawyer; b. Woodhaven, N.Y., Nov. 5, 1928; s. John Doran Jr. and Lily Esmarelda (Gulliksen) K.; m. Sally Gephart, July 23, 1955; children: David, Joan. AB, Hofstra U., 1950; JD, Cornell U., 1953, LLM, 1954. Bar: N.Y. 1954, Pa. 1958, U.S. Ct. Appeals (3d cir.) 1958, U.S. Supreme Ct. 1958. Dep. atty. gen. dept. justice State of Pa., Harrisburg, 1957-64; sr. ptnr. Killian & Gephart, Harrisburg, 1964—. Contbr. articles to profl. jours. Chmn. Pub. Sch. Employees Retirement Bd., Harrisburg, 1971-80. Served to cpl. U.S. Army, 1955-57. Recipient Ecumenical Leadership citation Pa. Council of Chs., 1970, Presbyn. Homes, Inc., 1972. Fellow Pa. Bar Found.; mem. ABA, Pa. Bar Assn. (Spl. Achievement award 1983), Dauphin County Bar Assn. Democrat. Presbyterian. Lodge: Masons. Administrative and regulatory, Contracts commercial, General practice. Home: 3737 Maple St Harrisburg PA 17109 Office: Killian & Gephart 218 Pine St Harrisburg PA 17101

KILLIAN, ROBERT KENNETH, JR., probate judge; b. Hartford, Conn., Jan. 29, 1947; s. Robert Kenneth Sr. and Evelyn (Farnan) K.; m. Candace Korper, Oct. 16, 1979; children: Virginia, Carolyn. BA, Union U., 1969; JD, Georgetown U., 1972. Bar: Conn. 1972, D.C. 1974, U.S. Ct. Appeals (2d cir.) 1973, U.S. Ct. Appeals (D.C.) 1974. Spl. asst. Senator Abe Ribicoff, Washington, 1972-73; atty. Gould, Killian, Wynne et al, Hartford, 1972-84; judge Conn. Probate Ct., Hartford, 1984—; atty. Killian & Hamilton, Hartford, 1985—; spl. counsel lt. Gov. Conn., Hartford, 1974-78. Bd. dirs. Conn. chpt. March of Dimes, 1972, Hartford Chamber Orch., 1979—. Mem. ABA, Conn. Bar Assn., Am. Trial Lawyers Assn., Conn. Trial lawyers Assn., Nat. Conf. Probate Judges, Internat. Brotherhood Magicians, Soc. Am. Magicians. Democrat. Roman Catholic. Administrative and regulatory, Local government, Real property. Home: 83 Bloomfield Ave Hartford CT 06105 Office: Killian & Hamilton 45 Wyllys St Hartford CT 06106

KILLIAN, WILLIAM CHARLES, lawyer; b. Jasper, Tenn., Feb. 14, 1949; s. Herman Brown and Inez (Richardson) K.; m. Rebecca McManus, Mar. 16, 1974; children: Lindsay, Andy. BS in Polit. Sci., U. Tenn., 1971, JD, 1974. Bar: Tenn. 1975, U.S. Dist. Ct. (ea. dist.) Tenn. Sole practice South Pitts, Tenn., 1975-76; asst. dist. atty. 18th Judicial Dist., Tenn., 1976-78; sole practice Jasper, Tenn., 1978—; bd. dirs. Legal Services Corp., Southeast Tenn. Legal Services. Coach Dixie Youth Baseball, South Pitts, 1985-86; chmn. Jim Sasser for U.S. Senate campaign, Marion County, Tenn., 1976; treas. Jim Lewis for Tenn. Senate campaign, 1982-86. Served with U.S. Army, 1971. Mem. Am. Trial Lawyers Assn. (sustaining), Marion County Bar Assn. (pres. 1986—), Tenn. Trial Lawyers Assn. (bd. govs. 1984-86), Tenn. Bar Assn., U. Tenn. Alumni Assn. (pres. Marion County chpt. 1982). Democrat. Episcopalian. Club: Marion County Track (Jasper) (race dir. 1984-85). Avocations: triathalons, baseball, basketball, track. Home: Rt 1 Box 399G South Pittsburg TN 37380 Office: Hill & Killian Law Offices W Main St and Oak Ave Jasper TN 37347

KILLORIN, EDWARD WYLLY, lawyer, tree farmer; b. Savannah, Ga., Oct. 16, 1928; s. Joseph Ignatius and Myrtle (Bell) K.; B.S., Spring Hill Coll., Mobile, 1952; LL.B. magna cum laude, U. Ga., 1957; m. Virginia Melson Ware, June 15, 1957; children—Robert Ware, Edward Wylly, Joseph Rigdon. Admitted to Ga. bar, 1956; practice in Atlanta, 1957—; ptnr. firm Gambrell, Russell, Killorin & Forbes, 1964-78; sr. ptnr. firm Killorin & Killorin, 1978—; lectr. Inst. Continuing Legal Edn. Ga., 1967—. Adj. prof. law Ga. State U., 1984—. Chmn., Gov.'s Adv. Com. on Coordination State and Local Govt., 1973, Gov.'s Legal Adv. Council for Workmen's Compensation, 1974-76; bd. regents Spring Hill Coll., 1975-82, trustee, 1981—. Served with AUS, 1946-47, 52-54. Mem. ABA, Internat., Ga. (chmn. jud. compensation com. 1976-77, chmn. legis. com. 1977-78), Atlanta (editor Atlanta Lawyer 1967-70, exec. com. 1971-74, chmn. legislation com. 1978-80) bar assns., Am. Judicature Soc., Lawyers Club Atlanta, Atlanta Legal Aid Soc. (adv. com. 1966-70, dir. 1971-74), Nat. Legal Aid and Defender Assn., Internat. Assn. Ins. Counsel (chmn. environ. law com. 1976-78), Atlanta Lawyers Found., Ga. Def. Lawyers Assn. (dir. 1972-80), Ga. C. of C. (chmn. govtl. dept. 1970-75, chmn. workmen's compensation com. 1979—), Def. Research Inst. (Ga. chmn. 1970-71), Spring Hill Coll. Alumni Assn. (nat. pres. 1972-74), U. Ga. Law Sch. Assn. (nat. pres. 1986-87) Ga. Forestry Assn. (life, bd. dirs. 1969—, pres. 1977-79, chmn. bd. 1979-81), Am. Forestry Assn., Demosthenian Lit. Soc. (pres. 1957), Sphinx, Blue Key, Gridiron, Phi Beta Kappa, Phi Beta Kappa Assos., Phi Kappa Phi, Phi Delta Phi, Phi Omega. Clubs: Capital City, Peachtree Golf, Commerce (Atlanta); Oglethorpe (Savannah). Roman Catholic. Contbr. articles to legal jours. Federal civil litigation, Insurance, General corporate. Home: 436 Blackland Rd NW Atlanta GA 30342 Office: Killorin & Killorin 11 Piedmont Ctr Atlanta GA 30305

KILLOUGH, HOWARD PATRICK, JR., educator, lawyer; b. Pampa, Tex., Aug. 16, 1945; s. Howard Patrick and Winefred Sarah Killough; m. Karen Lee, Aug. 27, 1966. B.S., Kans. State U., 1967, B.S. in Psychology, 1972; J.D., U. Mo.-Kansas City, 1973. Bar: Kans. 1973. Bus. law instr. Kans. State U., 1974-83; sole practice, Manhattan, Kans., 1974-75; tax. instr. Manhattan (Kans.) Vo-Tech.), 1974; instr. criminal law Wichita State U., 1978; lawyer and mgr. for Lee Killough, novelist, Manhattan, 1978-83; cons. in copyright, Manhattan, 1983—. Served with USAF, 1967-69; with USAR, 1969-73. Mem. ABA (PLC com. 307 1981-83), Sci. Fiction Writers Am. (affiliate). Legal education, Trademark and copyright. Home and Office: PO Box 1821 Manhattan KS 66502

KILROY, JOHN MUIR, lawyer; b. Kansas City, Mo., Apr. 12, 1918; s. James L. and Jane Alice (Scurry) K.; m. Lorraine K. Butler, Jan. 26, 1946; children: John Muir, William Terence. Student, Kansas City Jr. Coll., 1935-37; A.B., U. Kansas City, 1940; LL.B., U. Mo., 1942. Bar: Mo. 1942. Practice in Kansas City, 1946—; ptnr. Shughart, Thomson & Kilroy, 1946—, pres., 1977-86, chmn. bd. dirs.; instr. med. jurisprudence U. Health Scis., 1973—; Panelist numerous med.-legal groups A.C.S., Mo. Med. Assn., Kans. U. Med. Sch., S.W. Clin. Soc. Contbr. articles to profl. jours. Chmn. bd. dirs. Kansas City Heart Assn. Served to capt. AUS, 1942-46. Fellow Am. Coll. Trial Lawyers; mem. Internat. Assn. Barristers, Internat. Assn. Ins. Counsel, Am. Coll. Legal Medicine, Am. Bd. Profl. Liability Attys., Fedn. Ins. Counsel, Lawyers Assn. Kansas City (pres.), ABA, Mo. Bar Assn., Mo. Bar (chmn. med. legal com.), Kansas City C. of C. Clubs: Univ. (v.p. 1984, pres 1985). Federal civil litigation, State civil litigation, Personal injury. Home: 6860 Tomahawk Rd Shawnee Mission KS 66208 Office: Shughart Thomson & Kilroy 120 W 12th St Kansas City MO 64106

KIM, EDWARD Y.N., lawyer; b. Makaweli, Hawaii, Mar. 14, 1918; s. Chin Ho and Eunhi (Choy) K.; m. Carol Kyoung Hi Yue, Apr. 1, 1949; children: Bruce B., Carl F., Gay E., Claire D. BA, U. Hawaii, 1940; JD, U. Iowa, 1950. Bar: Hawaii 1951. Asst. atty. gen. Trust Ter. Pacific, Pearl Harbor, Hawaii, 1950-51; atty. Hawaiian Ho of Reps., Honolulu, 1958; sole practice Honolulu, 1953-78; ptnr. Kim & Kim, Honolulu, 1978—; pres. C.E. Inc., Honolulu, 1983—; bd. dirs. Bando Air Agy., Seoul, Republic of Korea. Mem. Honolulu Acad. Art, Honolulu, 1962—; pres. Kook Min Hur Community Assn., Honolulu, 1960-66. Served to 1st lt. USAAF, 1942-45, ETO; JAGC, 1950-53, Korea. Decorated D.F.C., Air medal with two oak leaf clusters. Mem. Hawaii Bar Assn. Clubs: Waialae Country, Plaza (Honolulu). Civil rights, Federal civil litigation, State civil litigation. Home: 2156 Lanihuli Dr Honolulu HI 96816 Office: Kim & Kim 737 Bishop St Suite 1570 Honolulu HI 96813

KIMBALL, FRANKLYN DAVIS, lawyer; b. San Diego, May 8, 1953; s. George William and Martha Washington (Davis) K. BA mgma cum laude, UCLA, 1974; JD, U. Mich., 1977. Bar: N.Y. 1979, U.S. Dist. Ct. (so. dist.) N.Y. 1979, U.S. Ct. Appeals (2d cir.) 1980, U.S. Dist. Ct. (no. dist.) Calif. 1984. Assoc. Shearman & Sterling, N.Y.C., 1977-86; ptnr. McDermott Will & Emory, Chgo., 1986—. Editor: U. Mich. Law Jour., 1976-77. Mem. ABA, Fed. Bar Assn., Phi Beta Kappa. Republican. Federal civil litigation, State civil litigation, Securities. Office: McDermott Will & Emery 111 W Monroe St Chicago IL 60603

KIMBALL, JESSE DUDLEY BALDWIN, lawyer; b. Morristown, N.J., Mar. 24, 1947; s. Dudley Baldwin and Mary Chalfont (Smedley) K.; m. Virginia Yvonne Lindloff, Sept. 25, 1977; children: Jesse Baldwin, Jeremy Martin. AB, Hamilton Coll., 1969; JD, NYU, 1974, LLM in Taxation, 1978. Bar: N.Y. 1975, U.S. Dist. Ct. (so. and ea. dists.) N.Y. 1975, U.S. Ct. Claims 1975, U.S. Tax Ct. 1975, U.S. Ct. Appeals (2d cir.) 1975. Assoc. Everett, Johnson & Breckinridge, N.Y.C., 1974-79, ptnr., 1980—. Mem. ABA (articles editor The Tax Lawyer 1984—, taxation sect.), N.Y. State Bar Assn., N.Y. County Lawyers Assn. (lectr. 1986), Soc. Ins. Accts. (lectr. 1984, 86-87). Republican. Mem. Soc. of Friends. Personal income taxation, Corporate taxation, Pension, profit-sharing, and employee benefits. Home: 257 Bellair Rd Ridgewood NJ 07450 Office: Everett Johnson & Breckinridge 20 Exchange Pl New York NY 10005

KIMBALL, JOHN DEVEREUX, lawyer; b. Orange, N.J., Mar. 18, 1949; s. Robert Maxwell and Audrey Josephine (Kerr) K.; m. Astri Jean Baillie; children: Astri Blakstad, Emily Devereux, Elizabeth, Andrew. BA, Duke U., 1971; JD, Georgetown U., 1975. Bar: N.Y. 1976. Assoc., Healy & Baillie, N.Y.C., 1975-80, ptnr., 1980—; adj. assoc. prof. law NYU, 1986—. Co-author: Time Charters, 1982. Bd. editors Jour. of Maritime Law and Commerce. Mem. ABA, Maritime Law Assn., Assn. Bar City of N.Y. Admiralty, Private international, Federal civil litigation. Home: 3 Olde Greenhouse Ln Madison NJ 07940 Office: Healy & Baillie 29 Broadway New York NY 10006

KIMBALL, SHERMAN PAUL, judge; b. Ogdensburg, N.Y., Jan. 15, 1928; s. Louis Charles and Ruth (Blustone) K.; m. Estelle Marilyn Meltzer, June 29, 1958; children—Ilissa, Jon, Louis. A.B., NYU, 1948, J.D., 1952, LL.M., 1956. Bar: N.Y. 1953, U.S. Dist. Ct. (so. and ea. dists.) N.Y. 1957, U.S. Supreme Ct. 1958, U.S. Ct. Appeals (2d cir.) 1962, U.S. Ct. Claims 1971, U.S. Ct. Appeals (fed. cir.) 1982. Assoc., London, Simpson & London, N.Y.C., 1952-57; assoc. Cities Service Oil Co., N.Y.C., 1957; sole practice, Middletown, N.Y., 1958-60; ptnr. Gilman, Gilman & Kimball, Middletown, 1960-63; spl. counsel urban devel. City of Middletown, 1962-63; atty. Dept. Interior Solicitor's Office Div. Mineral Resources and Gen. Legal Services, Washington, 1963-66; hearing officer Dept. Interior Bd. Contract Appeals, 1966-68; adminstrv. judge, 1968-75; adminstrv. law judge U.S. Labor Dept., Washington, 1975; adminstrv. law judge Fed. Energy Regulatory Commn., Washington, 1975-86; bd. contract appeals, U.S. Dept. of Energy, 1986—, vice chmn., 1987— ; lectr. seminars. Chmn., City of Middletown (N.Y.) Bd. Zoning Appeals, 1962-63; pres. Walter Johnson High Sch. Parent-Tchr.-Student Assn., Bethesda, Md., 1976-78. Recipient Superior Performance award Sec. of Interior, 1972, 74; Outstanding Service award Walter Johnson High Sch., 1981. Mem. ABA (jud. adminstrn. div. Nat. Conf. Adminstrv. Law Judges, pub. contract law sect., adminstrv. law sect.), N.Y. State Bar Assn., Bd. Contract Appeals Judges Assn. (gen. counsel). Contbr. article to Chicago Bar Record. FERC practice, Administrative and regulatory, Government contracts and claims. Home: 9803 Depaul Dr Bethesda MD 20817

KIMBALL, SPENCER LEVAN, lawyer, educator; b. Thatcher, Ariz., Aug. 26, 1918; s. Spencer Woolley and Camilla (Eyring) K.; B.S., U. Ariz., 1940; postgrad. U. Utah, 1946-47; B.C.L., Oxford (Eng.) U., 1949; S.J.D., U. Wis., 1958; m. Kathryn Ann Murphy, June 12, 1939; children—Barbara Jean (Mrs. Thomas Sherman), Judith Ann (Mrs. William Stillion), Kathleen Louise (Mrs. James Mueller), Spencer David, Kent Douglas, Timothy Jay. Bar: Utah 1950, Mich. 1965, Wis. 1968, U.S. Dist. Ct. (we. dist.) Wis. 1968, U.S. Supreme Ct. 1982, U.S. Ct. Appeals (9th cir.) 1986. Asso. prof. U. Utah, 1949-50, dean, 1950-54, prof., 1954-57; prof. U. Mich., 1957-68, dir. legal research Law Sch., 1962-67; staff dir. Wis. Ins. Law Revision Project, 1966-79; prof. law, dean U. Wis. Law Sch., 1968-72; exec. dir. Am. Bar Found., Chgo., 1972-82; prof. law U. Chgo., 1972—, Seymour Logan prof., 1978—. Pres., bd. dirs. Ann Arbor br. Am. Civil Liberties Union, 1959-63. Served to lt. USNR, 1943-46. Fellow Am. Bar Found.; mem. Am., Mich., Utah, Wis. bar assns., Internat. Assn. Ins. Lawyers (past pres. U.S. chpt., mem. presdl. council), AAUP, Phi Beta Kappa, Phi Kappa Phi. Author: Insurance and Public Policy (Elizur Wright award), 1960; Introduction to the Legal System, 1966; Essays in Insurance Regulation, 1966, (with Werner Pfennigstorf) The Regulation of Insurance Companies in the United States and the European Communities: A Comparative Study, 1981; Co-editor: Insurance, Government and Social Policy, 1969. Legal Service Plans, 1977. Contbr. articles to profl. jours. Insurance, Personal injury, Legal history. Home: 5825 S Dorchester Chicago IL 60637 Office: U Chgo Law Sch 1111 E 60th St Chicago IL 60637

KIMBER, BRIAN LEE, lawyer; b. Beverly, Mass., Jan. 13, 1952; s. Kenneth Joseph and Shirley Althea (Bennett) K.; m. Helene Myra Marsh, Aug. 1, 1974; 1 child, Bret Michael. BBA, U. Miami, 1973; JD, Southwestern U. Sch. of Law, 1976. Bar: Fla. 1976, U.S. Dist. Ct. (so. dist.) Fla. 1980, U.S. Ct. Appeals (11th cir.) 1982, U.S. Supreme Ct. 1983. Assoc. Allsworth, Doumar, Shuler, Padula & Laystrom, Ft. Lauderdale, Fla., 1977-80; sole practice Ft. Lauderdale, 1980—. Mem. ABA, Fla. Bar Assn., Broward County Bar Assn., Delta Theta Phi. State civil litigation, Family and matrimonial, Probate. Home: 4764 Fox Hunt Trail Boca Raton FL 33432 Office: 5130 N Federal Hwy Fort Lauderdale FL 33308

KIMBERLING, JOHN FARRELL, lawyer; b. Shelbyville, Ind., Nov. 15, 1926; s. James Farrell and Phyllis (Casady) K. Student, Purdue U., 1945-46; AB, Ind. U., 1947, JD, 1950. Bar: Ind. 1950, Calif. 1954. Sole practice Muncie, Ind., 1950-51, Los Angeles, 1953—; assoc. Bracken, Gray, DeFur & Voran, 1950-51; assoc. Lillick McHose & Charles, and predecessor firms, 1953-86, ptnr., 1963-86; ptnr. Dewey, Ballantine, Bushby, Palmer & Wood, Los Angeles, 1986—; Bd. dirs. Mfrs. Bank, Olson Industries Inc. Served from ensign to lt. (j.g.) USNR, 1951-53. Fellow Am. Coll. Trial Lawyers; mem. Am. Bar Assn., State Bar Calif., Los Angeles Bar Assn., Los Angeles Jr. C. of C. (past pres.), Beta Theta Pi, Phi Delta Phi. Republican. Clubs: California, Chancery. Federal civil litigation, State civil litigation. Home: 2127 Beech Knoll Rd Los Angeles CA 90046 Office: 333 S Hope St Los Angeles CA 90071

KIMBLE, WILLIAM EARL, lawyer; b. Denver, May 4, 1926; s. George Wilbur and Grace (Fick) K.; m. Jean M. Cayia, Dec. 27, 1950; children: Mark, Cary, Timothy, Stephen, Philip, Peter, Michael. LL.B., U. Ariz., 1951. Bar: Ariz. 1951. Spl. agt. FBI, 1951-52; practice in Bisbee, 1952-60, Tucson, 1962—; judge Superior Ct. Ariz., 1960-62; partner firm Kimble, Gothreau, Nelson & Cannon, 1962—; Commr. Ariz. Oil and Gas Commn., 1958-60; adj. prof. law U. Ariz. Coll. Law, 1962-86. Author: The Consumer Product Safety Act, 1973, Products Liability, 1977; Sr. editor: Consumer Products Alert newsletter, 1980-81. Rep. nominee Ariz. atty. gen., 1956; Rep. nominee Ariz. U.S. Congress, 1964. Served with USNR, 1944-46. Fellow Am. Coll. Trial Lawyers; mem. Sigma Chi, Phi Alpha Delta. Federal civil litigation, State civil litigation, Insurance. Home: 95 Camino Miramonte Tucson AZ 85716 Office: 5151 E Broadway Tucson AZ 85712

KIMBROUGH, ALLEN WAYNE, lawyer; b. Childress, Tex., Mar. 2, 1953; s. Wade Elvin and Brownie (Mitchell) K.; m. Meredythe Gail Ricker, July 31, 1976. Student, John Brown U., 1971-72; B.A. with honors, Hendrix Coll., 1975; J.D., So. Meth. U., 1978. Bar: Tex. 1978. Assoc. Turner, Hitchins, McInerney, Webb & Hartnett, Dallas, 1978-82; assoc. Winstead, McGuire, Sechrest & Minick, Dallas, 1982—. Mem. The 500, Inc., Dallas, 1979-84. Hatton W. Sumners scholar So. Meth. U., 1975-78. Mem. ABA (gov. 1984-87, found. fellow 1985), Dallas Bar Assn. Democrat. Episcopalian. Club: City, Towne (Dallas). Avocations: organ; piano; literature; travel. Home: 9811 Shoreview Rd Dallas TX 75238 Office: Winstead McGuire Sechrest & Minick 1700 Dallas Bldg Dallas TX 75201

KIMMEL, MORTON RICHARD, lawyer; b. N.Y.C., Nov. 10, 1940; s. Benjamin Bert and Sylvia (Alabaster) K.; m. Marcia Harriet LaPotin, Sept. 10, 1967; children: Wayne Douglas, Michelle Wendy, Karen Paige. BA, Temple U., 1962; JD, George Washington U., 1965. Bar: D.C. 1966, Del. 1965. Law clk. to judge Del. Superior Ct., Wilmington, 1965-66; assoc. Tybout & Redfearn, Wilmington, 1966-70; ptnr. Kimmel, Spiller & Weiss P.A., Wilmington, 1970—; supr. Del. Justice of the Peace, 1970-72; mem. long range planning cts. planning com. Supreme Ct. Del., 1985-86, trustee clients security trust fund, 1985-87. Author: You Can Do It, 1973, Emergency Medicine, 1982. Mem. Fedn. Ins. Counsel, Def. Research Inst. (chmn. Del. 1976-77). Democrat. Jewish. Avocations: sports, reading. State civil litigation, Insurance, Personal injury. Office: Kimmel Spiller & Weiss PA 901 Market St Wilmington DE 19801

KIMMELL, THOMAS J., lawyer; b. Cin., June 26, 1952; s. Leonard S. and Kay Kimmell; m. Diane Elayne Allwine, Aug. 13, 1983. AB magna cum laude, Harvard U., 1975; JD, Columbia U., 1978. Bar: Colo. 1978, U.S. Dist. Ct. Colo., U.S. Ct. Appeals (10th cir.). Law clk. to presiding justice Colo. Supreme Ct., Denver, 1978-79; assoc. Holland & Hart, Denver, 1980-83; ptnr. Cogswell & Wehrle, Denver, 1983—. Mem. Congress Park Neighborhood Assn., 1986—. Harlan Fisk Stone scholar, 1976-77. Mem. ABA, Colo. Bar Assn., Denver Bar Assn. Democrat. Avocations: skiing, tennis. Oil and gas leasing, State civil litigation, Bankruptcy. Home: 1131 St Paul St Denver CO 80206 Office: Cogswell & Wehrle 1700 Lincoln St Suite 3500 Denver CO 80203

KIMMITT, ROBERT MICHAEL, lawyer, government official; b. Logan, Utah, Dec. 19, 1947; s. Joseph Stanley and Eunice L. (Wegener) K.; m. Holly Jean Sutherland, May 19, 1979; children—Kathleen, Robert, William, Thomas, Margaret. B.S., U.S. Mil. Acad., 1969; J.D., Georgetown U., 1977. Bar: D.C. 1977. Commd. 2d lt. U.S. Army, 1969, advanced through grades to maj., 1978, served in Vietnam, 1970-71, resigned, 1982; law clk. U.S. Ct. Appeals, Washington, 1977-78; sr. staff mem. NSC, Washington, 1978-83, dep. asst. to Pres. for nat. security affairs and exec. sec. and gen. counsel, 1983-85; gen. counsel U.S. Dept. Treasury, Washington, 1985—. Served as lt. col., USAR, 1982—. Decorated Bronze Star (3), Purple Heart, Air medal; recipient Arthur Flemming award, 1987. Mem. ABA (standing com. law and nat. security), Assn. Grads. U.S. Mil. Acad. (trustee 1976-82), Council Fgn. Relations. Roman Catholic. Club: Metropolitan (Washington). Office: US Treasury Dept 1500 Pennsylvania Ave NW Washington DC 20220

KIMPORT, DAVID LLOYD, lawyer; b. Hot Springs, S.D., Nov. 28, 1945; s. Ralph E. and Ruth N. (Hutchinson) K.; m. Barbara H. Buggert, Apr. 2, 1976; children—Katrina Elizabeth, Rebecca Helen. A.B. summa cum laude, Bowdoin Coll., 1968; postgrad. Imperial Coll., U. London, 1970-71; J.D., Stanford U., 1975. Bar: Calif. 1975, U.S. Supreme Ct. 1978. Assoc. Baker & McKenzie, San Francisco, 1975-82, ptnr., 1982—. Active San Francisco Planning and Urban Research, 1978—, Commonwealth Club of Calif., 1984—. Served with U.S. Army, 1968-70. Decorated Bronze Star; Fulbright grantee, 1970. Mem. ABA, San Francisco Bar Assn., Phi Beta Kappa. Democrat. Episcopalian. Contracts commercial, Real property, Private international. Office: 580 California St San Francisco CA 94104

KIMSEY, DALE BOYD, lawyer; b. Athens, Ga., June 10, 1950; s. Melbourne and Alta Leona (Vance) K.;m. Patricia Ann Hubbard, Aug. 25, 1973; children: Marcus, Rachel, David, Lauren. BS in Pub. Adminstrn., Brigham Young U., 1975; JD, Pepperdine U., 1978. Bar: Calif. 1979, U.S. Dist. Ct. (cen. dist.) Calif. 1980, U.S. Ct. Appeals (9th cir.) 1980. Assoc. Garrett & Dimino, Tustin, Calif., 1979-80; ptnr. Caldwell & Kimsey, Santa Ana, Calif., 1980-84; sole practice Placentia, Calif., 1984—; lectr. seminars on estate planning, civil precedure and depositions, 1982—; bd. dirs. EVF Constrn., Inc., Master Car of So. Calif., Irvine Funding, Inc., Textured Design Furnishings, Inc., Am. Slurry Seal, Inc., Patch & Seal, Inc., Bowen Ltd., Nurse Midwifery Care Orange County; gen. counsel Resort Commuter Airlines, Inc., 1985—, Biz & Assocs., Inc., 1983—. Mem. Rep. Cen. Com., Santa Ana, Rep. presdl. task force 1980—; pack leader Boy Scouts Am., Santa Ana, 1985. Mem. ABA, Orange City Bar Assn., Orange County Barristers Assn. (se. 1985-86, bd. dirs. 1981—), Calif. Young Lawyers Assn., Econs. of Law Assn. Avocations: skiing, sailing, backpacking, flying. State civil litigation, General corporate, Real property. Office: 1414 N Kraemer Blvd Placentia CA 92670

KINCAID, ARTHUR ROY, lawyer; b. Gardner, Kans., Apr. 24, 1911; s. Roy Porter and Sadie (Arnold) K.; m. Marion King, May 23, 1942; 1 dau., Carol Ann. A.B., William Jewell Coll., 1932; LL.B., U. Kansas City, 1941. Bar: Mo. 1941. Ptnr. firm Hale, Kincaid, Waters, and Allen, P.C., Liberty, Mo., 1944—, sr. mem., 1976—, pres., 1979—; mem. Mo. Ho. of Reps., 1937-42; city atty., Liberty, 1944-50. Chmn. bd. Liberty Pub. Works, 1960-70. Served to pvt. U.S. Army, 1943. Mem. ABA, Mo. Bar Assn., Clay County Bar Assn. Democrat. Mem. Christian Ch. Club: Rotary (Liberty). Probate, Estate taxation, Personal income taxation. Home: 726 W Mississippi St Liberty MO 64068 Office: Hale Kincaid Waters Allen 17 W Kansas St Liberty MO 64068

KINCAID, EUGENE D., III, lawyer; b. Uvalde, Tex., Mar. 7, 1941; s. Eugene D. and Lochie M. (Mundine) K. B.A., Baylor U., 1962; J.D., U. Tex.-Austin, 1966. Bar: Tex. 1966. Briefing atty. Tex. Ct. Criminal Appeals, 1967-68; asst. city atty. San Antonio, 1969; atty. Tex. Water Rights Commn., Austin, 1970-71; sole practice, Uvalde, 1971—. exec. v.p. EDK Ranches Inc., AVR Ranch Co. Chmn. Uvalde Housing Authority, 1972-80; mem. Uvalde Arts Council. Mem. State Bar of Tex., Border Dist. Bar Assn., Uvalde County Bar Assn. (pres. 1972), Magna Charta Barons, San Antonio Mus. Assn., Pi Sigma Alpha, Sigma Delta Pi. Republican. Anglican. Clubs: Uvalde Country. General practice, Mining and minerals. Office: 243 N Getty PO Box 1769 Uvalde TX 78801

KINCAID, WILLIAM H(ATTON), lawyer; b. Abilene, Tex., Jan. 14, 1947; s. William Lee and Naomi (Hatton) K.; m. Audette Vaughn, Feb. 8, 1974; children—Cheryl Annette, Christina Michelle. B.A., Hardin Simmons U., 1969; J.D., Tex. Tech. U., 1976, M.A., 1979. Bar: Tex. 1976. Assoc. John R. Hollums, Floydada, Tex., 1976-80; city atty. City of Floydada, 1977-80; sole practice, Bowie, Tex., 1980—. Author: Disposition of Selected Violent and Nonviolent Crimes in Lubbock County, Texas, 1969-1970, 1979. Bd. dirs. Dist. Camp Fire Assn. Served to capt. U.S. Army, 1969-76. Mem. Coll. of State Bar Tex. (charter). Baptist. Lodges: Masons, Rotary (bd. dirs.). Consumer commercial, General practice, Probate. Home: 802 Gray Bowie TX 76230 Office: 112 E Tarrant PO Box 1591 Bowie TX 76230

KIND, KENNETH WAYNE, lawyer, real estate broker; b. Missoula, Mont., Apr. 1, 1948; s. Joseph Bruce and Elinor Joy (Smith) K.; m. Diane Lucille Jozaitis, Aug. 28, 1971. B.A., Calif. State U.-Northridge, 1973; J.D., Calif. Western U., 1976. Bar: Calif. 1976, U.S. Dist. Ct. (ea. dist.) Calif. 1976. Mem. celebrity security staff Brownstone Am., Beverly Hills, Calif., 1970-76; tchr. Army and Navy Acad., Carlsbad, Calif., 1975-76; real estate broker, Bakersfield, Calif., 1978—; sole practice, Bakersfield, 1976—; lectr. mechanic's lien laws, Calif., 1983—. Staff writer Calif. Western Law Jour., 1975. Served as sgt. U.S. Army, 1967-70. Mem. ABA, VFW, Nat. Order Barristers. Libertarian. Real property, Insurance, State civil litigation. Office: 1715 Chester Ave Suite 300 Bakersfield CA 93301

KINDREGAN, CHARLES PETER, law educator; b. Phila., June 18, 1935; s. Charles Peter and Catherine (Delaney) K.; m. Patricia Ann Patterson, Aug. 18, 1962; children—Chad, Helen, Tricia, Brian. B.A., LaSalle Coll., 1957, M.A., 1958; J.D., Chgo.-Kent Coll. Law, 1966; LL.M., Northwestern U., 1967. Bar: Ill. 1966, Mass. 1968, U.S. Dist. Ct. Mass. 1970. Instr. Va. Mil. Inst., 1960-62, Loyola U., Chgo., 1964-67; prof. law Suffolk U., Boston, 1967—. Author: The Quality of Life, 1969; Malpractice and the Lawyer, 1981; Massachusetts Family Law Actions, 1985. Co-author: Massachusetts Pleading and Practice, 1983-87; author: contbr. articles to law revs., jours. Mem. Hull Bd. Zoning Appeals, Mass., 1969; pres. Beacon Hill PTA, Boston, 1974-75. Mem. ABA, Mass. Bar Assn. (task force on model rules of profl. conduct), Nantasket Beach C. of C. (past v.p.), Suffolk Ctr. for Continuing Profl. Devel. (dir. 1982-87). Democrat. Roman Catholic. Legal education, Family and matrimonial, Personal injury. Home: 79 Joy St Beacon Hill Boston MA 02114 Office: Suffolk U Law Sch 41 Temple St Boston MA 02114

KINDT, JOHN WARREN, law educator, lawyer, legal and managerial consultant; b. Oak Park, Ill., May 24, 1950; s. Warren Frederick and Lois Jeannette (Woelffer) K.; m. Anne Marie Johnson, Apr. 17, 1982. AB, Coll. William and Mary, 1972; JD, U. Ga., 1976, MBA, 1977; LLM, U. Va., 1978, SJD, 1981. Bar: D.C. 1976, Ga. 1976, Va. 1977. Advisor to Gov. of Va., 1971-72; congl. asst. to Congressman M. Caldwell Butler, 1972-73; mem. White House staff, 1976-77; vis. lectr. U. Ga., 1977; asst. prof. law U. Ill., 1978-81, assoc. prof., 1981-85, prof., 1985—; cons. 3d UN Conf. on Law of the Sea; lectr. U. Ill. Exec. MBA Program. Author: Marine Pollution and the Law of the Sea, 4 vols., 1986; contbr. articles to profl. jours. Caucus chmn., del. White House Conf. on Youth, 1970; co-chmn. Va. Gov.'s Adv. Council on Youth, 1971; mem. Athens (Ga.) Legal Aid Soc., 1975-76. Rotary fellow, 1979-80; Smithsonian ABA/ELI scholar, 1981 sr. fellow London Sch. of Econs., 1985-86. Mem. Am. Soc. Internat. Law, Assn. Trial Lawyers Am., ABA, D.C. Bar Assn., Va. Bar Assn., Ga. Bar Assn., Environ. Law Soc. Episcopalian. Legal education, Public international, Environment. Home: 1709 Lyndhurst Rd Waynesboro VA 22980 Office: U Ill 1206 S 6th St 350 Commerce West Champaign IL 61820

KING, C. A., II, lawyer; b. Lake Charles, La., Nov. 20, 1936; s. Albion S. and Violet (Holman) K. B.A., La. State U., 1957, J.D., 1960; LL.M. in Taxation, NYU, 1962. Bar: La. 1960. Law clk. 3d Circuit Ct. Appeals, 1960-61; sole practice, Lake Charles, 1962—; pres. King Corp; bd. dirs. Am. Bank of Commerce. Mem. La. Bar Assn. (admissions com. 1972—). Probate, Corporate taxation, Estate taxation. Office: 120 Pujo St Lake Charles LA 70601

KING, C. GLYN, lawyer; b. Sulphur Springs, Tex., Nov. 25, 1956; s. O.B. and B.L. (Green) K.; m. Karen Elaine Bumpus, Oct. 3, 1981; 1 child, C. Ryan. BS, East Tex. State U., 1977; JD, U. Tex., 1979. Land rep. Texaco Inc., Midland, Tex., 1980-85, atty., 1985—. Mem. ABA, Tex. Bar Assn., Midland County Young Lawyers Assn., Phi Alpha Delta. Democrat. Oil and gas leasing, Administrative and regulatory. Home: 2704 Maranatha Midland TX 79707 Office: Texaco Inc 500 N Lorraine Midland TX 79701

KING, CLARENCE LEROY, JR., lawyer; b. Salina, Kans., Apr. 5, 1932; m. Doris I. Altman, Aug. 18, 1951; children: Jeffrey E., Joni D. AB, Kansas Wesleyan U., Salina, 1954; JD, Washburn U., 1957. Bar: Kans. 1957, U.S. Supreme Ct. 1972. Sole practice Salina, 1957-58; ptnr., pres. King, Adrian, King, & Brown Chartered and predecessor firms, Salina, 1958—; faculty Kans. Coll. Trial Advocacy, mem. Govs. Regional Com. on Criminal Adminstrn., 1969; regional chmn. White House Conf. on Children and Youth, Kans. del., mem. exec. com., 1970; Kans. Hwy. Commr. 1974-75. Active Univ. Meth. Ch.; active against juvenile delinquency; del. Dem. Nat. Conv., 1968; mem. state platform com., 1968, 70, 76; mem. adult chpt. Fellowship Christian Athletes; mem. Kans. Citizens for the Arts Com.; life mem. PTA; pres. local PTA 1966-67; sec. youth com. YMCA, 1972-73; trustee Kans. Wesleyan U.; organizer, hon. bd. dirs. Big Bros. and Big Sisters, Salina Youth Care Home Found., Inc.; bd. dirs. Children's Spl. Edn. Ctr.; chmn. bd. dirs. Cen. Kans. Mental Health Ctr., 1964-65. Named Outstanding Young Man of Salina, 1961, Outstanding Young Alumnus, Kans. Wesleyan U., 1965; recipient St. Francis Disting. Service to Youth award, 1971, Patriot of Today award NAACP, 1976. Mem. ABA, Am. Trial Lawyers Assn., Am. Bd. Trial Advs. (adv., nat. exec. com. 1985, 1987, chpt. pres. 1983-84), Kans. Bar Assn. (mem. various coms., chmn. litigation sect. 1983-85), Northwest Kans. Bar Assn., Kans. Trial Lawyers Assn., Salina County Bar Assn. (mem. various coms., pres. 1973), Kans. Young Lawyers (v.p. 1959, pres. 1964), Def. Research Inst., Kans. Def. Council (bd. dirs. 1978-83, pres. elect), Kans. Coll. Ofcls. Assn., Salina C. of C. (bd. dirs. 1977-79, mem. various coms.), Kans. Wesleyan U. Alumni Assn. (pres. 1959-60). Avocations: horses, antiques. Personal injury, Insurance, State civil litigation. Home: Rt 1 Smolan KS 67479 Office: King Adrian King & Brown Chartered 116 W Iron PO Box 2120 Salina KS 67402-2120

KING, DANIEL DWADE, lawyer; b. Tucson, Jan. 17, 1955; s. Dwade Robert and Barbara Jean (Elston) K.; m. Colleen Kelli Brown, May 5, 1976; children: Jennifer Leigh, Daniel Taylor. BS, Trinity U., San Antonio, 1977; JD, S. Tex. Coll. Law, 1982. Bar: Tex. 1982. Trial atty. Wyckoff, Russell, Dunn & Frazier, Houston, 1982-85; gen. counsel St. Luke's Episc. Hosp. and Tex. Heart Inst., Houston, 1985—; lectr. risk mgmt. and med. malpractice, numerous seminars and symposia, Houston, 1982-85; cons. risk mgr. Tex. Children's Hosp., Houston, 1985—; adj. assoc. prof. Tex. Women's U., 1986—. Vice chmn. Greater Houston Skating Council, 1985; co-chmn. Houston Figure Skating Invitational, 1985—; staff mem. U.S. Olympic Festival Com., 1986, test chmn. Houston Figure Skating Club, U.S. Figure Skating Assn., 1986. Fellow Tex. Bar Found.; mem. ABA (medicine and law com.), Nat. Health Lawyers Assn., State Bar Tex. (health litigation, med. malpractice com.), Houston Bar Assn. (law day com.), Am. Acad. Hosp. Attys. Avocations: athletics, pub. speaking. Health, Insurance, Personal injury. Home: 12614 Vitry Ln Houston TX 77071 Office: St Luke's Episc Hosp 6720 Bertner Ave Houston TX 77030

KING, DENNIS WILLIAM, lawyer; b. Rock Springs, Wyo., May 9, 1954; s. Edward C. and Elinor M. (Smith) K.; m. Jean L. Butler, Mar. 20, 1982; children: Kristin Marie, Stephen Butler. BA, Brigham Young U., 1978; JD, U. San Francisco, 1981; LLM in Taxation, U. Denver, 1982. Bar: Wyo. 1981, U.S. Dist. Ct. Wyo., U.S. Tax Ct. 1981, US.. Ct. Appeals (10th cir.) 1981, Colo. 1982, U.S. Dist. Ct. Colo. 1982. Sole practice Denver, 1981—. Bd. dirs., v.p. Colo. Humane Soc., Denver, 1984—; bd. dirs. Am. Soc. Genealogy and Family History, Aurora, Colo., 1985—. Mem. ABA (devel. editor 1984—, tax sect.), Colo. Bar Assn., Brigham Young Mgmt. Soc. Democrat. LSD. Estate taxation, Probate, General corporate. Home: 5386 S Salida Ct Aurora CO 80015 Office: 1888 Sherman SUite 770 Denver CO 80203

KING, DOMINIC BENSON, lawyer; b. Butte, Mont., Jan. 12, 1928; s. Don B. and Irene M. (McDonell) K.; m. Georgena M. Anderson, Mar. 29, 1949; children: Mary, Kathleen King Mathews, David, Marcia King Round. B.S., U. Mont., 1949, LL.B., 1952; S.J.D., U. Mich., 1958. Bar: Mont. 1952, U.S. Dist. Ct. Mont. 1952, U.S. Ct. Appeals (3d, 4th, 5th, 8th, and 9th cirs.) 1953, Pa. 1959, U.S. Dist Ct. (we. dist.) Pa. 1959, U.S. Supreme Ct., U.S. Ct. Internat. Trade, U.S. Ct. Appeals (fed. cir.), U.S. Dist. Ct. D.C., U.S. Dist. Ct. (so. dist.) Fla., U.S. Dist. Ct. (cen. and so. dists.) Calif., U.S. Dist. Ct. Minn. Law clk. Judge Walter Pope, U.S. Ct. Appeals (9th cir.), San Francisco, 1952-53; legis. analyst U. Mich., Ann Arbor, 1956-58; with USX Corp., Pitts., 1958—, asst. gen. counsel, 1976-83, assoc. gen. counsel, 1983-84, gen. counsel, 1984—. Served to lt. USAF, 1949-50, capt., 1953-56. Mem. ABA, Pa. Bar Assn., Allegheny County Bar Assn., Internat. Bar Assn. Roman Catholic. Clubs: Valley Brook Country, Duquesne, KC, Pitts. Athletic. Author: (with Lauer and Ziegler) Water Resources and the Law, 1958. Antitrust, Federal civil litigation, Private international. Office: US Steel Co 600 Grant St Room 6180 Pittsburgh PA 15230 *

KING, DONITA MCRAE, lawyer; b. Phila., Apr. 21, 1954; d. Franchot McRae and Geneva (Solis) Darden; m. Edward Alan King, July 29, 1978. BA in Econs., LaSalle U., 1975; JD, Villanova U., 1978. House counsel, staff atty. Gen. Accident Ins. Co., Phila., 1978-80, staff atty., 1980-83, assoc. counsel, 1983-86, sr. counsel, 1986—. Bd. dirs. Girl Scouts U.S. Greater Phila., 1986—. Ford Found. grantee, 1974. Mem. ABA, Pa. Bar Assn., Phila. Bar Assn., Phila. Area Corp. Ins. Counsel, Am. Corp. Counsel Assn., Ins. Fedn. Pa. (property caualty steering com. 1986). Democrat. Lutheran. Insurance, Labor, General corporate. Office: Gen Accident Ins 434 Walnut St Philadelphia PA 19105

KING, DOUGLAS BRUCE, lawyer. BA, Butler U., 1973; JD summa cum laude, Ind. U., 1976. Bar: Ind. 1976, U.S. Dist. Ct. (so. dist.) Ind. 1976, U.S. Ct. Appeals (7th cir.) 1983, U.S. Supreme Ct. 1983. Law clk. Ind. Ct. Appeals, Indpls., 1975-76; assoc. Wooden, McLaughlin & Sterner, Indpls., 1976-81, ptnr., 1982—. Assoc. editor Ind. Law Rev., 1975-76. Cub Scout den leader Boy Scouts Am., Noblesville, Ind., 1985-86, Cub Scout pack com. chmn. Crossroads Am. council, Noblesville, 1986—. Mem. ABA (torts and ins. practice sect.), Ind. Bar Assn., Indpls. Bar Assn., 7th Cir. Bar Assn., Phi Delta Theta. Methodist. Club: Columbia (Indpls.). Personal injury, Federal civil litigation, State civil litigation. Office: Wooden McLaughlin & Sterner 909 Merchants Plaza E Tower Indianapolis IN 46204

KING, FRANKLIN WEAVER, lawyer; b. Alexandria, La., Aug. 8, 1942; s. William F. and Helen Kathleen (Weaver) K. B.A., U. Ala., 1965; J.D., Duke U., 1972. Bar: Calif. 1974. Sole practice, San Francisco. Served to lt. col. JAGC, USAFR, 1975—. Mem. Am. Trial Lawyers Assn., Calif. Trial Lawyers Assn., ABA, Calif. Bar Assn., Pi Kappa Phi, Phi Delta Phi. Consumer commercial, General practice, Personal injury. Office: 899 Ellis St San Francisco CA 94109-7897

KING, GEORGE SAVAGE, JR., lawyer; b. Columbia, S.C., Jan. 14, 1941; s. George Savage and Harriet (Witte) K.; m. Geraldine McNeal Frampton, Nov. 14, 1964; children: George Savage III, Elizabeth Gregorie. BA, U. N.C., 1963, JD with honors, 1972. Bar: S.C. 1972, U.S. Dist. Ct. S.C. 1972, U.S. Ct. Appeals (4th cir.) 1977, U.S. Supreme Ct. 1977. Ptnr. Sinkler & Boyd, Columbia, 1972—. Served to capt. USAF, 1964-69. Mem. ABA, Nat. Assn. Bond Lawyers, S.C. Bar Assn. (sec. corps., banking and securities sect. 1986), Order of Coif. Banking, Securities, General corporate. Office: Sinkler & Boyd PO Box 11889 Columbia SC 29211

KING, GERALD LEE, lawyer; b. Bogata, Tex., July 11, 1931; s. Julius Lafayette and Cora Willie (Speir) K. B.B.A., Tex. Tech. U., 1965; J.D., U. Tex., 1968. Bar: U.S. Ct. Appeals (5th cir.) 1968, U.S. Dist. Ct. (no. and so. dists.) Tex. 1968, Tex. 1968, U.S. Ct. Claims 1969, U.S. Tax Ct. 1969, U.S. Ct. Mil. Appeals 1969, U.S. Supreme Ct. 1978. Tax mgr. Centex Corp., Dallas, 1968-69; pres. Gerald L. King & Assocs. Inc., Spring, Tex., 1970—. Election judge State of Tex., 1978-80; Dem. nominee for Ho. of Reps., 1982. Served with USMC, 1949-52, Korean War (1950-51). Mem. ABA, Am. Judicature Soc., Fed. Bar Assn., Houston Bar Assn., Houston Northwest Bar Assn., Montgomery County Bar Assn., Houston Trial Lawyers Assn., Tex. Trial Lawyers Assn., Delta Theta Phi. Democrat. Methodist. General practice, Personal injury, Probate. Office: Gerald L King & Assocs Inc PO Box 698 Spring TX 77383

KING, IRA THOMAS, lawyer; b. Florence, Ala., Oct. 15, 1949; s. Ira Puller and Ellen (Maynor) K.; m. Deborah Thomas, Nov. 19, 1974; 1 child, Clifford Thomas. AA, Alvin (Tex.) Jr. Coll., 1973; BA, cert. in Law Enforcement, Sam Houston State U., 1974; JD, U. Tex., 1977. Bar: Tex. 1978, U.S. Dist. Ct. (we. dist.) Tex. 1980, U.S. Dist. Ct. (so. dist.) Tex. 1983. Assoc. Long, Dugger, Burner & Cotten, Austin, Tex., 1978-81; sole practice Austin, 1981-83; assoc. Hearne, Knolle, Lewallen, Livingston & Holcomb, Austin, 1983-86; asst. atty. gen. Tex. Atty. Gen.'s Office, Austin, 1986—; lectr. bus. law Austin Community Coll., 1982, estate planning Waddell Reed Fin. Cons., Austin, 1983. Advisor Inmate Assistance Project, Austin, 1973-74, Police Action Project, Austin, 1974, observer. Served with U.S. Army, 1967-71. Named one of Outstanding Young Men in Am., 1983. Mem. Tex. Assn. Def. Counsel, Phi Theta Kappa, Alpha Chi. Republican. Methodist. Avocation: martial arts. State civil litigation, Insurance. Home: 901 E Austin Ave Round Rock TX 78664 Office: Tex Atty Gens Office PO Box 12548 Austin TX 78711-2548

KING, JACK A., lawyer; b. Lafayette, Ind., July 29, 1936; s. Noah C. and Mabel E. (Pierce) K.; m. Mary S. King, Dec. 10, 1960; children—Jeffrey A., Janice D., Julie D. B.S. in Fin., Ind. U., Bloomington, 1958, J.D., 1961. Bar: Ind. 1961. Ptnr. Ball, Eggleston, King & Bumbleburg, Lafayette, 1961-70; judge Superior Ct. 2 of Tippecanoe County (Ind.), 1970-78; assoc. gen. counsel Dairyland Ins. Co., 1978, v.p. and assoc. gen. counsel, 1979, v.p., gen. counsel and asst. sec., 1980-85; v.p. and counsel Sentry Ctr. West, 1981-85; asst. gen. counsel Sentry Corp., 1979-85; v.p., gen. counsel, and asst. sec. Gt. S.W. Fire Ins. Co., 1980-85, Gt. S.W. Surplus Lines Ins. Co., 1981-85; v.p. and gen. counsel Dairyland County Mut. Ins. Co. Tex., 1980-85; v.p.-legal and asst. sec. Scottsdale Ins. Co. and Nat. Casualty Co., 1985—; bd. dirs. Ariz. Joint Underwriting Plan, 1978-81, mem. exec. com., 1980-81; mem. Ariz. Property & Casualty Ins. Commn., 1985-86, vice chmn., 1986; mem. Ariz. Study Commn. on Ins., 1986-87. Bd. dirs. Scottsdale (Ariz.) Art Ctr. Assn., 1981-84. Mem. ABA, Ind. Bar Assn., Maricopa County Bar Assn. Cons.: The Law of Competitive Business Practices, 2d edit. General corporate, Insurance. Office: 8370 E Via de Ventura Scottsdale AZ 85258

KING, JAMES FORREST, JR., lawyer; b. Salina, Kans., Jan. 9, 1949; s. James Forrest Sr. and Carolyn (Prout) K.; m. Marylou A. Goodwin, May 18, 1985. BA, U. Md., 1970; JD with honors, George Washington U., 1974. Bar: D.C. 1975, U.S. Dist. Ct. D.C. 1976, U.S. Ct. Appeals (D.C. cir.) 1977, U.S. Supreme Ct. 1979, Md. 1982, U.S. Ct. Appeals (4th cir.) 1985. Atty. Law Offices of Washington, 1975-76; ptnr. Reuss, McConville & King, Washington, 1976-80, Reuss, Herndon, McConville & King, Washington, 1980-85; of counsel Herndon, McConville, Brown, Teller & Hessler, Washington, 1986—. Commr. D.C. Commn. Human Rights, 1984—. Mem. Am. Arbitration Assn. (panel mem.), ABA (econs. law practice sect.), D.C. Bar Assn. (co-chmn. div. 6, 1981-84, arbitration bd. 1981-83, employment discrimination panel, 1977-80). Labor, Civil rights, Federal civil litigation. Office: Herndon McConville Brown Teller 729 15th St NW 800 Washington DC 20005

KING, JAMES LAWRENCE, federal judge; b. Miami, Fla., Dec. 20, 1927; s. James Lawrence and Viola (Clodfelter) K.; m. Mary Frances Kapa, June 1, 1961; children—Lawrence Daniel, Kathryn Ann, Karen Ann, Mary Virginia. B.A. in Edn., U. Fla., 1949, J.D., 1953. Bar: Fla. 1953. Assoc. Sibley & Davis, Miami, Fla., 1953-57; ptnr. Sibley Giblin King & Levenson, Miami, 1957-64; judge 11th Jud. Circuit Dade County, Miami, 1964-70; temp. assoc. justice Supreme Ct. Fla., 1965; temp. assoc. judge 2d, 3d, 4th Dist. Ct. Appeals, 1965-68; judge U.S. Dist. Ct. (so. dist.) Fla., Miami, 1970—, now chief judge; temp. judge U.S. Ct. Appeals 5th Circuit, 1977, 78; mem. adv. commn. jud. activities Jud. Conf. U.S., 1973—, mem. joint commn. code of jud. conduct, 1974-76, mem. commn. to consider standards for admission to practice in fed. cts., 1976-79, mem. com. bankruptcy legis., 1977-78; pres. 5th circuit U.S. Dist. Judges Assn., 1977-78; chief judge U.S. Dist. Ct. C.Z., 1977-78. Mem. state exec. council U. Fla., 1956-59; mem. Bd. Control Fla. Governing State Univs. and Colls., 1964. Served to 1st lt. USAF, 1953-55. Recipient Outstanding Alumnus award U. Fla. Law Rev., 1980. Mem. Fla. Bar Assn. (pres. jr. bar 1963-64, bd. govs. 1958-63, Merit award young lawyer sect. 1967), ABA, Am. Law Inst., Inst. Jud. Adminstrn., Fla. Blue Key, Pi Kappa Tau, Phi Delta Phi. Democrat. Judicial administration. Home: 11950 SW 67th Ct Miami FL 33138 Office: US Courthouse PO Box 014942 Miami FL 33101 *

KING, JIMMY R., lawyer; b. Anderson, S.C., Apr. 30, 1952; s. S. Marshall and Frances (Welborn) K.; m. JoVanna M. Johnson. BA, U. Ga., 1974; JD, U. S.C., 1976. Ptnr. Chapman, King & Byrholdt, Anderson, 1977—. Chmn. Anderson County (S.C.) Election Commn., 1984. Mem. ABA, S.C. Bar Assn., Assn. Trial Lawyers Am., S.C. Trial Lawyers Assn. (sustaining). Baptist. Personal injury, State civil litigation, General practice. Home: PO Box 417 Rt 1 Anderson SC 29621 Office: Chapman King & Byrholdt PO Box 2584 Anderson SC 29622

KING, JOHN FRANCES, lawyer; b. Waynesboro, Pa., Apr. 23, 1925; s. Thomas Henry and Victoria Walker (Beaver) K.; m. Nancy Lee Packard, Aug. 14, 1954 (div. June 1974); children: John. F. Jr., Anne Lee, Margaret Packard; m. Linda Louden Meding, June 10, 1977. BA, Dickinson Coll., 1949; JD, Georgetown U., 1951. Bar: Md. 1952. Faculty Johns Hopkins U., Balt., 1955-70, Md. Inst. for Continuing Legal Edn., Balt., 1980-85; ptnr. Anderson, Coe & King, Balt., 1962—; visiting faculty Harvard U. Law Sch., Cambridge, Mass., 1982. Contbr. articles to profl. jours. Pres. Md. chpt. Arthritis Found., 1967-69; bd. dirs. Lawyer Com. for Civil Rights, Balt., 1963-70, Md. Conf. Social Welfare, Balt., 1970-75, Md. chpt. ACLU, Balt., 1971-80. Fellow Am. Coll. Trial Lawyers, Md. Bar Found.; mem. ABA, Md. Bar Assn., Balt. City Bar Assn. (treas. 1962-65, sec. 1965-66), Am. Judicature Soc., AMA, Wig & Pen Club, Wednesday Law Club. Personal injury, State civil litigation, Federal civil litigation. Office: Anderson Coe & King 800 Fidelity Bldg Baltimore MD 21201

KING, JOHN THOMAS, lawyer; b. Adamsville, Ala., Oct. 28, 1923; s. Alta Lamar and Donna Lou (COllins) K.; m. Norma Kathryn Tibbetts, July 23, 1947; children: J. Thomas Jr., Alan Lamar, David Richard. BS in Commerce and Bus. Adminstrn., U. Ala., 1948, LLB, 1951. Bar: Ala. 1951, U.S. Dist. Ct. (no. dist.) Ala. 1952, U.S. Supreme Ct. 1958. Asst. U.S. atty. No. Dist. Ala., 1953-54; adminstrv. asst. to George Huddleston Jr. U.S. Ho. of Reps., 1955-60; ptnr. King & King, Birmingham, Ala., 1960—; atty. City of Adamsville, Ala., 1962-84, City of Birmingham, 1974-80; panel arbitrators fed. mediation and conciliation service Dept. Labor, Washington, 1962—. Mem. Ala. State Senate, Jefferson County, 1970-74; mem. Dem. exec. com. Ala., 1966-70, edn, commn. Ala. Bapt. Conv., Montgomery, 1978—; pres. Jefferson County chpt. Muscular Distrophy Assns., Birmingham, 1964; vice chmn. bd. deacons 1st Bapt. Ch. Birmingham, 1985—; chmn. bd. deacons Huffman Bapt. Ch., Birmingham, 1969-70, 1st Bap. Ch. Birmingham, 1986-87, Northeast br. YMCA, Birmingham, 1969-70, 73. Served to tech. sgt. U.S. Army, 1943-46. Mem. ABA, Ala. Bar Assn., Birmingham Bar Assn., Assn. Trial Lawyers Am., Ala. Trial Lawyers Assn., Am. Judicature Soc., Am. Arbitration Assn. (mem. panel arbitrators), Birmingham Bar Assn., Farrah Law Soc., Birmingham Brotherhood Assn., Phi Delta Phi, Omicron Delta Kappa. Avocations: reading, sports. State civil litigation, Labor, Probate. Home: 818 Rose Dr Birmingham AL 35235 Office: King & King 713 S 27th St Birmingham AL 35233

KING, JOHN WINSTON, commissioner; b. Bklyn., Sept. 30, 1937; s. Ruby (Cummings) K.; m. Dolores Chambers; children: John W. Jr., Candace Taylor. BS, Howard U., 1964, JD, 1968. Bar: D.C. 1972, U.S. Ct. Appeals (D.C. cir.) 1972. Lectr. Howard U., Washington, 1970-72; atty., prof. Antioch Sch. of Law, Washington, 1972-73; sole practice Washington, 1973-82; commr. D.C. Superior Ct., Washington, 1982—; gen. counsel East of the River Health Assn., Washington, 1977-82. Served to pvt. 1st class U.S. Army, 1956-58. Mem. ABA, D.C. Bar Assn., Nat. Bar Assn., Nat. Assn. Adminstrv. Law Judges, Phi Alpha Delta. Democrat. Roman Catholic. Avocations: chess, golf, swimming. Criminal, Family and matrimonial, Personal injury. Office: Superior Ct DC 500 Indiana Ave NW Washington DC 20001

KING, J(OSEPH) MICHAEL, lawyer; b. Oak Hill, W.Va., Nov. 13, 1953; s. Arden E. and Phyllis Gregory; m. Carol Jean Holt, Aug. 29, 1981; children: Jennifer Lyn, William Skye, Gregory. BA, Ohio State U., 1975, MA, 1976; JD cum laude, U. Dayton, 1979. Bar: Ohio 1979, U.S. Dist. Ct. (so. dist.) Ohio 1980. Law clk. to presiding judge Newark, Ohio, 1977-79; ptnr. Jones, Norpell, List, Miller & Howarth, Newark, 1979—. CPR instr. Am. Heart Assn., Newark, 1982—, pres. Licking County; chmn. human relations com. City of Newark. Named Outstanding Young Man Am., 1982-84. Mem. ABA, Ohio Bar Assn. (criminal justice sec. 1986—), Licking County Bar Assn., Basketball Officials Assn., Assn. Trial Lawyers Am., Ohio Trial Lawyers Assn., Ohio Jaycees (Outstanding chpt. pres. 1983), Newark Area Jaycees (pres. 1982-83, Disting. service award). Democrat. Methodist. Avocations: boating, fishing, hunting. Criminal, Personal injury, Family and matrimonial. Home: 1344 Londondale Pkwy Newark OH 43055 Office: Jones Norpell et al 2 N 1st St Newark OH 43055

KING, KERNAN FRANCIS, insurance company executive, lawyer; b. Providence, Feb. 2, 1944; s. Francis Joseph and Margaret Mary (Burke) K.; m. Mary Christine King, Jan. 9, 1983; children—Kurt, Jason, Allyson. A.B., Providence Coll., 1965; J.D., Boston U., 1968, LL.M. in Taxation, 1971. Bar: R.I. 1968, Mass. 1969, U.S. Dist. Ct. Mass. 1979; C.L.U. Law clk. presiding justice R.I. Supreme Ct., 1968-69; atty. New Eng. Life, Boston, 1969-70, tax atty., 1970-71, asst. tax counsel, 1971-75, assoc. counsel, 1975-76, counsel and dir., 1976-77, counsel and asst. sec., 1977-79, v.p., counsel and sec., 1979-84, sr. v.p., sec., gen. counsel, 1984—; instr. Northeastern U., Boston; lectr. New Eng. Life and various local seminars; bd. dirs., officer Sargasso Mut. Ins. Co., Hamilton, Bermuda. Trustee, Aquinas Jr. Coll., Newton, Mass., 1983—. Mem. R. I. Bar Assn., Mass. Bar Assn., ABA, Boston Bar Assn., Bd. Bar Overseers, Boston Estate and Bus. Planning Council, Am. Council Life Ins. (chmn. subcom. on policyholder taxation 1983-85), Am. Life Ins. Counsel. Insurance. Office: New Eng Life 501 Boylston St Boston MA 02117

KING, LAWRENCE PHILIP, lawyer, educator; b. Schenectady, N.Y., Jan. 16, 1929; s. Louis D. and Sonia K.; children—David J. Kaufman, Deborah J. King. B.S.S., CCNY, 1950; LL.B., NYU, 1953; LL.M., U. Mich., 1957. Bar: N.Y. 1954, U.S. Supreme Ct. 1963. Atty. Paramount Pictures Corp., N.Y.C., 1955-56; asst. prof. law Wayne State U., 1957-59; asst. prof. NYU, 1959-61, assoc. prof., 1961-63, prof., 1963—, Charles Seligson prof. law, 1979—, assoc. dean Sch. Law, 1973-77; of counsel Wachtell, Lipton, Rosen & Katz, N.Y.C.; assoc. reporter adv. com. on bankruptcy rules U.S. Jud. Conf., 1968-76, reporter, 1979-83, mem. adv. com. bankruptcy rules, 1983—; vis. prof. faculty of law Hebrew U. Jerusalem, 1971, 87, Tel Aviv U., 1987. Author: (with R. Duesenberg) Sales and Bulk Transfers under the U.C.C., 1966, (with M. Cook) Creditors' Rights, Debtors' Protection and Bankruptcy, Cases and Materials, 1985; contbr. articles, books revs. to legal jours.; editor-in-chief: Collier On Bankruptcy, 1964, 15th edit., 1979—; co-editor-in-chief: Collier Bankruptcy Practice Guide, 1981—. Trustee Village of Saltaire (N.Y.), 1980-84, mayor, 1984-86. Recipient NYU Law Alumni Achievement award, 1976, NYU Law Alumni 25-Yr. Faculty Service award, 1984, award Bankruptcy Lawyers div. UJA-Fedn., 1984. Mem. ABA, N.Y. State Bar Assn., Nat. Bankruptcy Conf., Am. Law Inst., Assn. Bar City N.Y., Comml. Law League Am. (Man of Yr. award 2d Dist. 1969). Bankruptcy, Contracts commercial. Office: NY U Sch Law 40 Washington Square S New York NY 10012

KING, MARGARET GRAM, lawyer; b. Detroit, Jan. 3, 1943; d. Harris James and Margaret (Edwards) Gram; m. Raymond Adam Sokolov, Sept. 15, 1963 (div. 1978); children: Michael Adam, Joseph Gram; m. Henry Lawrence King, Feb. 14, 1981. BA, Radcliffe Coll., 1965; JD, NYU, 1976. Bar: N.Y. 1977, U.S. Dist. Ct. (ea. and so. dists.) N.Y. 1977, U.S. Ct. Appeals (2d cir.) 1983. Assoc. Davis Polk & Wardwell, N.Y.C., 1976-79, Hughes, Hubbard & Reed, N.Y.C., 1979-83; dep. asst. chief appeals div. Law Dept. N.Y.C., 1983—. Contbr. articles to NYU Law Rev., 1975-76. Mem. ABA, N.Y. State Bar Assn., Assn. Bar City N.Y. Federal civil litigation, State civil litigation. Home: 960 Park Ave New York NY 10028 Office: Law Dept 100 Church St New York NY 10007

KING, MICHAEL HOWARD, lawyer; b. Chgo., Mar. 10, 1943; s. Warren and Betty (Fine) K.; m. Candice M. King, Aug. 18, 1968; children—Andrew, Julie. B.S. Washington U., St. Louis 1967, J.D. 1970. Bar: Ill. 1970, U.S. Dist. Ct. (no. dist.) Ill. 1970, U.S. Dist. Ct. (ea. dist.) Wis. 1972, U.S. Ct. Appeals (7th cir.) 1974, U.S. Ct. Appeals (5th cir.) 1979, U.S. Supreme Ct. 1975, U.S. Ct. Appeals (3d cir.) 1983, U.S. Tax Ct. 1987, U.S. Ct. Appeals (10th cir.) 1987. Spl. atty. criminal div. U.S. Dept. Justice, Washington, 1970-73; asst. U.S. atty. No. Dist. Ill., Chgo., 1973-75; assoc. Antonow & Fink, Chgo., 1976, ptnr., 1977-79; ptnr. Ross & Hardies, Chgo., 1979—; part-time lectr. trial practice John Marshall Law Sch., Chgo. Bd. dirs. Chgo. Youth Ctrs., 1977—; trustee Cove Sch., 1984—. Mem. ABA (litigation sect., antitrust sect., criminal practice procedure com.), Ill. Bar Assn., Chgo. Bar Assn. (judiciary com., antitrust com.), Am. Judicature Soc., Fed. Bar Assn., Assn. Trial Lawyers Am., Phi Delta Phi, Alpha Epsilon Pi. Club: Mid-America (Chgo.). Antitrust, Federal civil litigation, Criminal. Home: 1700 Overland Trail Deerfield IL 60015 Office: 150 N Michigan Ave Chicago IL 60611

KING, MICHAEL JAMES, lawyer; b. Washington, Aug. 23, 1956; s. Edward Luther and Gloria Helen (White) K.; m. Karen Lynn Massey, Apr. 2, 1983. BA, Tex. Tech U., 1978; JD, O.W. Coburn Sch. Law, 1982. Bar: Okla. 1982, U.S. Dist. Ct. (no. dist.) Okla. 1982, U.S. Dist. Ct. (ea. and we. dists.) Okla. 1983, U.S. Ct. Appeals (10th cir.) 1983. Advt. sales rep. Houston Post, 1978-79; assoc. Garrison and Comstock, Tulsa, 1982-83, Garrison and King, Tulsa, 1983—. Mem. adv. bd. Salvation Army, Sand Springs, Okla., 1985-86. Recipient Disting. Service award, Tulsa Coalition for Older People, 1984. Democrat. Lodge: Rotary. Avocations: sports, fishing. Personal injury, Criminal, Construction. Office: Garrison and King 1509 S Victor Tulsa OK 74104

KING, MICHAEL PAUL, lawyer; b. Lowell, Mass., Feb. 8, 1954; s. James Robert and Marguerite T. (Tremblay) K.; m. Eleanor Frances Clark, Aug. 18, 1979; children: Bethany, Timothy. BA, U. N.H., 1975; JD, Suffolk U., 1981. Bar: N.H. 1982, Mass. 1982, U.S. Dist. Ct. N.H. 1982, U.S. Ct. Appeals (1st cir.) 1982. Sole practice Goffstown, N.H., 1982-84; ptnr. King & Ryan, Goffstown, 1984—. Mem. ABA, N.H. Bar Assn. Avocations: bridge, tennis, church activities. Family and matrimonial, Probate, Real property. Office: King & Ryan PO Box 370 Goffstown NH 03045

KING, NICHOLAS NEAL, lawyer; b. Bklyn., Feb. 28, 1945; s. Nicholas King and Helen (Hubbert) Rauth; m. Carol Ann Zurkuhlen, Oct. 14, 1968; children: Eric Paul, Byron Neal. BA, Fla. State U., 1966; MA, U. Okla., 1971; JD, U. Louisville, 1973. Bar: Ky. 1974, U.S. Dist. Ct. (we. and ea. dists.) Ky. 1974. Assoc. Leibson & Franklin P.C., Louisville, 1974-76; ptnr. Franklin & King P.C., Louisville, 1976-86; prin. Nicholas King & Assocs., Louisville, 1986—. Served with capt. USAF, 1966-70. Mem. Louisville Bar Assn. (vice chmn., chmn. profl. responsibility com. 1978-87) Ky. Bar Assn. (ho. of dels. 1980—), Assn. Trial Lawyers Am., Ky. Acad. Trial Lawyers. Democrat. Roman Catholic. Avocation: skeet shooting. Federal civil litigation, State civil litigation, Personal injury. Office: Nicholas King & Assocs 900 Cherokee Rd Louisville KY 40204

KING, PETER JOSEPH, lawyer; b. Stowe Township, Pa., June 15, 1938; s. Peter and Mary (Dugan) K.; m. Dolly J. Mauro, Apr. 23, 1960; children: Linda, Carole, Ronald. BA, Duquesne U., 1960, JD, 1963. Bar: Pa. 1963, U.S. Dist. Ct. (we. dist.) Pa. 1963, U.S. Supreme Ct. 1967. Ptnr. Tucker & Arensberg, Pitts., 1964-80; sole practice Pitts., 1980-85; ptnr. King & Kulik, Pitts., 1986—. Editor-in-chief Duquesne U. Law Rev., 1962. Solicitor Montour Sch. Dist., McKees Rocks, Pa., 1969—. Irishman of Yr. award Knights of Equity, 1980. Mem. Allegheny County Bar Assn. (various offices), Duquesne U. Law Alumni Assn. (officer 1968—, past pres.), Duquesne U. Alumni Assn. (bd. dirs. 1970-82). Democrat. Roman Catholic. Lodge: Italian Sons and Daus. Am. (past. pres. Morningside club). Family and matrimonial, State civil litigation, Criminal. Home: 1441 Duffield St Pittsburgh PA 15206 Office: King & Kulik 20 Chatham Sq Pittsburgh PA 15219

KING, ROBERT LEWIS, lawyer; b. Johnson City, Tenn., June 20, 1950; s. Herbert and Ruth Marie (Dulaney) K. BA, Earlham Coll., 1973; MS, Columbia U., 1974; JD, U. Tenn., 1985. Bar: Tenn. 1986. Fgn. corr. AP, Paris, 1971-72; reporter The Miami (Fla.) Herald, 1974-75; polit. editor The Courier-Post, Cherry Hill, N.J., 1975-78; prof. communications East Tenn. State U., Johnson City, 1978—; mem. Tenn. Legislature, Nashville, 1978-84; sole practice Johnson City, 1986—; chmn. criminal law subcom. Tenn. Ho. Reps., 1978-84. Sec. Washington County Rep. Exec. Com. Precinct, Tenn., 1986—. Recipient Scripps-Howard Pub. Service citation, 1977. Mem. ABA (Silver Gavel award 1976), Assn. Trial Lawyers Am., Nat. Assn. Criminal Def. Lawyers, Tenn. Trial Lawyers Assn., N.J. Soc. Profl. Journalists (Investigative Reporting award 1976). Baptist. Avocations: writing, internat. affars. Federal civil litigation, State civil litigation, Criminal. Home: 1302 Sunset Dr Johnson City TN 37604 Office: 1st Am Bank 208 Sunset Dr Suite 351 Johnson City TN 37604

KING, ROBERT LUCIEN, lawyer; b. Petaluma, Calif., Aug. 9, 1936; s. John Joseph and Ramona Margaret (Thorson) K.; m. Suzanne Nanette Parre, May 18, 1956 (div. 1973); children—Renee Michelle, Candyce Lynn, Danielle Louise, Benjamin Robert; m. Linda Diane Carey, Mar. 15, 1974 (div. 1981); 1 child, Debra Robin; m. J'an See, Oct. 27, 1984; 1 child, Jonathan Fielding. A.B. in Philosophy, Stanford U., 1958, J.D., 1960. Bar: Calif., N.Y. 1961. Asst. U.S. atty. U.S. Atty's. Office (so. dist.), N.Y.C., 1964-67; assoc. Debevoise & Plimpton, N.Y.C., 1960-64, 67-70, ptnr., 1970—; lectr. Practising Law Inst., N.Y.C., NYU Labor Forum, N.Y.C., 1983, NYU Sch. Continuing Edn., N.Y.C., 1970s. Dir. Nat. Scholarship Service and Fund for Negro Students, N.Y.C., 1983—. Fellow Am. Coll. Trial Lawyers; mem. ABA, Assn. Bar City N.Y., Calif. Bar Assn. Democrat. Avocation: poetry. State civil litigation, Federal civil litigation, Criminal. Home: 235 W 71st St Apt 81 New York NY 10023 Office: Debevoise & Plimpton 875 3d Ave New York NY 10022

KING, ROBERT WILSON, lawyer; b. Durant, Miss., Sept. 30, 1926; s. Norman Edwards and Ethel (Pearson) K.; m. Bobbie Haynie, Aug. 10, 1950; children: Robin, Lowrey, Christian, Kimberley. BA, Cumberland U., 1948, JD, 1950. Bar: Miss. 1950, U.S. Dist. Ct. (so. dist.) Miss. 1950, U.S. Ct. Appeals (5th cir.) 1969. Ptnr. King & Spencer, Jackson; pres. Miss. Bankruptcy Conf., 1982-83. pres. Jackson Library Bd. 1973-76; pres., trustee Bapt. Children's Village, Jackson; bd. dirs. Jackson Prep. Sch., 1972-79. Served to capt. USAFR, 1944-53. Named one of Best Lawyers in Am., Harvard Law '77, 1983. Mem. ABA, Miss. Bar Assn., Hinds County Bar Assn., Am. Judicature Soc., Blue Key. Republican. Club: Petroleum (Jackson). Lodge: Masons (32 degree). Avocations: hunting, fishing, cooking. State civil litigation, Contracts commercial, Bankruptcy. Home: 3671 Woodward Pl Jackson MS 39216 Office: King & Spencer 429 Tombigbee Jackson MS 39205

KING, RONALD BAKER, lawyer; b. San Antonio, Aug. 16, 1953; s. Donald Dick and Elaine (Baker) K.; m. Cynthia Sauer, June 7, 1975; children: Karen Elizabeth, Ronald Baker Jr. BA, So. Meth. U., 1974; JD, U. Tex., 1977. Bar: Tex. 1977, U.S. Dist. Ct. (we. dist.) Tex. 1980, U.S. Ct. Appeals (5th cir.) 1981, U.S. Tax Ct. 1985. Briefing atty. Supreme Ct. Tex., Austin, 1977-78; assoc. Foster, Lewis, Langley, Gardner & Banack Inc., San Antonio, 1978-82, ptnr., 1982—. Mem. ABA, Tex. Bar Assn., San Antonio Young Lawyers Assn. Republican. Presbyterian. Avocations: piano, basketball, tennis, water sports. State civil litigation, Bankruptcy, Federal civil litigation. Home: 1702 Hounds Rise San Antonio TX 78248 Office: Foster Lewis Langley Gardner & Banack Inc Frost Bank Tower 16th Floor San Antonio TX 78205

KING, RONNIE PATTERSON, lawyer; b. Henderson, N.C., Nov. 25, 1946; s. Gerston Daniel and Ola (Mustian) K.; m. Barbara Hawks, July 22, 1973; children—Wells Patterson, Paige Rose. B.S., N.C. State U., 1969; J.D., U. N.C., 1972. Bar: N.C. 1972, U.S. Dist. Ct. (mid. dist.) N.C. 1975. Asst. dist. atty. N.C. 9th Jud. Dist., 1972-73; ptnr. Burke & King, Roxboro, N.C., 1974; sole practice, Roxboro, 1975—. 1st v.p. N.C. chpt. Arthritis Found., Durham, 1984, pres. 1985, Named Nat. Vol., Arthritis Found., 1981, Kiwanian of Yr., Roxboro Kiwanis, 1974-75. Mem. ABA, N.C. Bar Assn., Person County Bar Assn. (pres. 1982), Assn. Trial Lawyers Am., N.C. Trial Lawyers Assn., Roxboro C. of C. (pres. 1984). Democrat. Methodist. Lodge: Kiwanis (pres. 1978, lt. gov. Carolina's dist. 1980-81). State civil litigation, Personal injury, Criminal. Office: PO Box 738 300 S Main St Roxboro NC 27573

KING, RUFUS, lawyer; b. Seattle, Mar. 25, 1917; s. Rufus Gunn and Marian (Towle) K.; m. Janice L. Chase, June 15, 1941 (div. June 1951); children: Rufus III, Agnes S.; m. Elvine R. Rankine, Nov. 23, 1973. A.B., Princeton U., 1938; postgrad., Stanford U., 1940-41; J.D., Yale U., 1943. Bar: N.Y. 1944, D.C. 1948, Md. 1953. Instr. Princeton, 1938-39; partner Rice & King, Washington, 1953-64; pvt. practice Washington, 1964-75; partner King & Newmyer, Washington, 1977-83; of counsel Berliner & Maloney, Washington, 1983—; counsel Senate Crime Com., 1951, also other congl. coms.; cons. Nat. Commn. Law Enforcement and Adminstrn. Justice.; Chmn. joint com. on narcotic drugs Am. Bar Assn. and AMA, 1956—. Author: Gambling and Organized Crime, 1968, The Drug Hangup, 1971; Contbr. articles to profl. and popular jours. Pres. Montgomery County Community Psychiat. Clinic. Mem. ABA (chmn. criminal law sect. 1957-60, sec. 1954-57, mem. ho. of dels. 1960-66, chmn. spl. com. atomic attack 1962—, del. sect. individual rights, mem. spl. com. on standards for adminstrn. criminal justice), N.Y. State Bar Assn., Md. Bar Assn., Bar Assn. D.C., Am. Law Inst. (life). Episcopalian. Clubs: Princeton (N.Y.C.); Metropolitan (Washington); American (Miami). Federal civil litigation, General practice. Home: 3524 Williamsburg Ln NW Washington DC 20008 Office: 1101 17th St Washington DC 20036

KING, RUFUS GUNN, III, judge; b. New Haven, June 16, 1942; s. Rufus Gunn and Janice Livingston (Chase) K.; m. Karen Diane Jenkins, July 22, 1976. A.B., Princeton U., 1966; J.D., Georgetown U., 1971. Bar: D.C. 1971, Md. 1984. Clk., Superior Ct. D.C., 1968-71; since practiced in Washington; assoc. Karr & Greensfelder, 1971-73; Rollinson, Stein & Halpert, 1973; assoc. Law Offices of Rufus King, 1973-75; ptnr. King & Newmyer and predecessor, 1975-83, Berliner and Maloney, 1983-84; now superior ct. judge, Washington. Mem. D.C. Bar (ct. system study com. 1980-82, fee arbitration bd. 1980-84, chmn. 1980-82, div. 18 1983-84), Bar Assn. D.C., ABA (jud. adminstrv. div.), Am. Arbitration Assn., Phi Alpha Delta. Clubs: Barristers, Nat. Press Club. Judicial administration. Office: Superior Court of DC Washington DC 20001

KING, STEVE MASON, lawyer; b. Graham, Tex., Dec. 17, 1951; s. Beverly W. and Chloe (Stalcup) K.; m. Julia Ellen Milford, Mar. 30, 1974; children: Cassandra, Mason. BA cum laude, U. Tex., 1974; JD, Baylor U., 1976. Bar: Tex. 1977, U.S. Dist. Ct. (no. dist.) Tex. 1978, U.S. Ct. Appeals (5th cir.) 1981, U.S. Supreme Ct. 1981, U.S. Tax Ct. 1984. Assoc. Byrom, Butcher & Moore, Ft. Worth, 1977-78, Garrett & Stahala, Ft. Worth, 1978-83; ptnr. Garrett, Stahala & King, Ft. Worth, 1983-86, Epstein, Becker, Borsody & Green, Ft. Worth, 1986—. Trustee Buckner Bapt. Benevolences, Dallas, 1981—, Shakespeare in the Park, Ft. Worth, 1984—. Mem. ABA, Tarrant County Bar Assn., Tarrant County Young Lawyers, Nat. Health Lawyers Assn., Am. Acad. Hosp. Attys., Phi Delta Phi. Democrat. Club: Ft. Worth. Avocations: woodworking, hunting, genealogy. General corporate, Health, Probate. Office: Epstein Becker Borsody & Green 201 Main St Suite 1900 Fort Worth TX 76102

KING, THAD DENTON, real estate developer, lawyer; b. Atlanta, Dec. 4, 1951; s. John Dudley and Bea (Church) K.; m. Suzanne Reynaud, Sept. 2, 1972; children: Hunter Stone, Virginia Favrot, Thad Denton Jr., Chase Stephens. AB, Dartmouth Coll., 1973; MBA, JD, Emory U., 1975-79, JD, 1979. Bar: Ga. 1979, U.S. Dist. Ct. (no. dist.) Ga. 1979, U.S. Ct. Appeals (5th and 11th cirs.) 1981. Project engr. Holder Constrn. Co., Atlanta, 1973-75, project supt., 1976; constrn. cons. Holder Mgmt., Atlanta, 1975; assoc. Smith, Currie & Hancock, Atlanta, 1979-83; v.p. The Spectrum Group, Inc., Atlanta, 1983—; arbitrator nat. constrn. panel Am. Arbitration Assn., Atlanta, 1982—. Mem. editorial bd. Dartmouth Alumni Mag., Hanover, N.H., 1985—. Pres. Dartmouth Club of Ga., Atlanta, 1981-82; council rep. Dartmouth Alumni Council, Hanover, 1982-85. Rufus Choat scholar Dartmouth Coll., 1973. Mem. Ga. Bar Assn., Dartmouth Soc. Engrs., Beta Gamma Sigma. Republican. Presbyterian. Club: Cherokee Town & Country (Atlanta); Old Marsh Golf (pres. 1986—) (Palm Beach Gardens, Fla.). Real property, Construction. Home: 3006 Margaret Mitchell Ct Atlanta GA 30327 Office: The Spectrum Group Inc 3333 Peachtree St 617 S Tower Atlanta GA 30326

KING, THOMAS GEORGE, lawyer; b. Battle Creek, Mich., May 7, 1956; s. Bill and Elena Marie (Presson) K.; m. Susan Kathryn Sylver, Sept. 5, 1981; 1 child, Andrew Thomas. BA, Western Mich. U., 1977; JD, Loyola U., Chgo., 1981. Bar: Ill. 1981, Mich. 1982, U.S. Dist. Ct. (we. dist.) Mich. 1982, U.S. Ct. Appeals (7th cir.) 1982, U.S. Supreme Ct. 1985. Law clk. to presiding judge 9th Cir. Ct. Mich., Kalamazoo, 1981-82; asst. atty. City of Kalamazoo, 1982—. Mem. ABA, Ill. Bar Assn., Mich. Bar Assn., Kalamazoo County Bar Assn. State civil litigation, Personal injury, Local government. Office: Kalamazoo City Atty's Office 241 W South St Kalamazoo MI 49007

KING, THOMAS WESLEY, lawyer; b. Roanoke Rapids, N.C., May 17, 1954; s. Wiley and Ursula Louisa (Mooring) K.; m. Debra Carol Futrell, May 28, 1977; children: David Alexander, Michael Anthony. BS in Math., U. N.C., 1976, JD, 1979. Bar: N.C. 1979, U.S. Dist. Ct. (ea. dist.) N.C. 1980. Assoc. Henson, Fuerst & Willey, Rocky Mount, N.C., 1979-82; ptnr. Smith & King, Rocky Mount, 1982-83; sole practice Rocky Mount, 1983—; instr. bus. law Nash Tech. Coll., Rocky Mount, 1981, 83-85; adj. prof. law N.C. Wesleyan Coll., Rocky Mount, 1982. County mgr. Carl Stewart for Lt. Gov., Nash County, N.C., 1984; treas. Ezzell for Senate Com., 10th Dist., N.C., 1984; chmn. adminstrv. bd. Englewood United Meth. Ch., Rocky Mount, 1981-82. James M. Johnson scholar, U. N.C., 1972-76. Mem. ABA, N.C. Bar Assn., 7th Jud. Dist. Bar Assn., Edgecombe-Nash Bar Assn., N.C. Acad. Trial Lawyers, Rocky Mount Jaycees (legal counsel 1980-81, 85-86, internal v.p. 1986-87, pres. 1987—), Phi Beta Kappa, Phi Eta Sigma. Democrat. Real property, Consumer commercial, General practice. Home: 4004 Gloucester Rd Rocky Mount NC 27801 Office: 163 S Winstead Ave PO Box 7805 Rocky Mount NC 27804-7805

KING, WILLIAM J., lawyer; b. Los Angeles, Mar. 8, 1947; s. Clarence William and Virginia (Johnson) K.; m. Linda Henderson, Aug. 1, 1981. BS, Calif. State U., Los Angeles, 1970; JD, Southwestern U., 1976. Bar: Calif. 1976, U.S. Dist. Ct. (cen. dist.) Calif. 1976. Chief of staff to state assemblyman Calif. Assembly, Sacramento, 1970-72; assoc. Morgan, Wenzel & McNicholas, Los Angeles, 1976-80; ptnr. Engstrom, Lipscomb & Lack, Los Angeles, 1980—; judge pro tem Los Angeles Mcpl. Ct., 1980—. Trustee Tom Bradley Scholarship Endowment Fund, Los Angeles, 1976—. Served to sgt. USAR, 1969-75. Named one of Outstanding Young Men Am., 1972. Mem. ABA (gov. 9th cir. 1975-76, Gold Key award 1976), Los Angeles County Bar Assn., Am. Arbitration Assn. (arbitrator), So. Calif. Def. Counsel (bd. dirs. 1976—). Republican. Clubs: Jonathan (Los Angeles), Sunset Aquatic Yacht (Huntington Beach, Calif.), Magic Castle. Avocations: long distance running, boating, art collecting. State civil litigation, Insurance, Personal injury. Home: 1755 Hillcrest Ave Glendale CA 91202 Office: Engstrom Lipscomb & Lack 3250 Wilshire Blvd #2100 Los Angeles CA 90010

KING, WILLIAM KIMBLE, JR., lawyer; b. Scranton, Pa., Apr. 11, 1946; s. William K. and Shirley Theresa (Tolan) K.; m. Pavinee Phasaphant, Nov. 22, 1974; 1 child, Joseph Kim-Lee. BS in Polit. Sci., U. Scranton, 1968; MS in Human Resource Mgmt., Gonzaga U., 1978, JD, 1981; LLM, U. London, 1983. Bar: Wash. 1981, U.S. Dist. Ct. (ea. and we. dists.) Wash. 1981, U.S. Ct. Appeals (9th cir.) 1985. Commd. USAF, 1968, advanced through grades to maj., 1983; law clk. to presiding justice Wash. State Supreme Ct., Olympia, 1981-82; assoc. Davis, Wright & Jones, Seattle, 1983-85; gen. mgr. Dept. Trade and Econ. Devel., Seattle, 1986—. Mem. ABA, Wash. State Bar Assn., Seattle-King County Bar Assn., U. London Convocation. Club: Royal Air Force (London). Private international, Public international, Immigration, naturalization, and customs. Office: Dept Trade and Econ Devel Domestic/Internat Trade Div 312 1st Ave N Seattle WA 98109

KING, WILLIAM ROBERT, II, lawyer; b. Kansas City, Kans., July 23, 1954; s. William Robert Sr. and Dorothy (Mae) K.; m. Mary Kathleen Taylor, June 9, 1978; children: Kathleen Suzanne, Kelly Robert. AA, Donnelly Coll., 1974; BA in Acctg., U. Kans., 1976; JD, Washburn U., 1979. Bar: Mo. 1979, U.S. Dist. Ct. (we. dist.) Mo. 1979, U.S. Ct. Appeals (8th cir.) 1980, U.S. Tax Ct. 1983. Ptnr. Morris, Larson, King & Stamper, Kansas City, 1979—, dir., 1984—. Mem. ABA, Mo. Bar Assn., Kansas City Bar Assn., Lawyers Assn. Kansas City, Assn. Trial Lawyers Am. Club: Hillcrest Country Club (Kansas City). Avocations: sports, travel. Personal injury, Insurance, State civil litigation. Office: Morris Larson King & Stamper 2 Crown Center 4th Floor Kansas City MO 64108

KINGDON, VICTOR SCOTT, lawyer; b. Indpls., Aug. 23, 1950; s. Victor Rauh Kingdon and Betty Jane (Higbee) Kingdon Cruickshank. B.A. in Polit. Sci., Ind. U., 1972; J.D., George Washington U., 1976. Bar: Ind. 1976, U.S. Dist. Ct. (so. dist.) Ind. 1976. Assoc. counsel Lincoln Nat. Life Ins. Co., Ft. Wayne, Ind., 1977-81, N.Am. Co. Life and Health, Chgo., 1981-84, Lincoln Nat. Corp., Ft. Wayne, 1984—. Contbr. articles to profl. jours. Legal advisor Fine Arts Found., Ft. Wayne, 1984; vol. atty. Lawyers for Creative Arts, Chgo., 1982-83; bd. dirs. Ind. Assn. Hearing-Impaired Children; active Democratic Luncheon Club, Ft. Wayne, 1984. Mem. ABA, Ind. Bar Assn., Allen County Bar Assn., Am. Corp. Counsel Assn. (sec. Chgo. chpt. 1983-84, sec. Ind. chpt. 1986—, edit. bd. Docket 1987—), Phi Beta Kappa. Unitarian. Insurance, General corporate, Arts and cultural affairs. Office: Lincoln Nat Corp 1300 S Clinton St Fort Wayne IN 46801

KINGHAM, RICHARD FRANK, lawyer; b. Lafayette, Ind., Aug. 2, 1946; s. James R. and Loretta C. (Hoenigke) K.; m. Justine Frances McClung, July 6, 1968. BA, George Washington U., 1968; JD, U. Va., 1973. Bar: D.C. 1973, U.S. Dist. Ct. D.C. 1974, U.S. Ct. Appeals (D.C. cir.) 1974, U.S. Ct. Appeals (8th cir.) 1977, U.S. Supreme Ct. 1977, U.S. Ct. Appeals (5th cir.) 1980. Editorial asst. Washington Star, 1964-68, 69-70; assoc. Covington & Burling, Washington, 1973-81, ptnr., 1981—; lectr. law U. Va., Charlottesville, 1977—; mem. com. on issues and priorities for new vaccine devel. Inst. Medicine Nat. Acad. Scis., 1983—. Articles editor U. Va. law rev., 1972-73; contbr. articles to profl. jours. Served with U.S. Army, 1968-69. Mem. ABA, Food and Drug Law Inst., Soc. Vertebrate Paleontology, Order of Coif. Republican. Episcopalian. Avocation: vertebrate paleontology. Administrative and regulatory, Health. Home: 2432 Tracy Pl NW Washington DC 20008 Office: Covington & Burling 1201 Pennsylvania Ave NW Washington DC 20044

KINGSBURY, DOROTHEA JANE, lawyer; b. Cleve., Sept. 17, 1952; d. George Rothwell and Doris (Endress) K. BA, Ursuline Coll., 1974; JD, Cleve. State, 1981. Bar: Ohio 1981, U.S. Dist. Ct. (no. dist.) Ohio 1981. Assoc. Ulmer, Berne, Laronge, Glickman & Curtis, Cleve., 1981-82; sole practice Cleve., 1982—. Sec. Ohio Scottish Games, Inc., Oberlin, 1983—, pres., 1984—. Mem. ABA, Ohio State Bar Assn., Cleve. Bar Assn. Republican. Episcopalian. General corporate, Trademark and copyright. Home and Office: 910 W Park Dr Mayfield OH 44143

KINGSTAD, TIMOTHY LORENS, lawyer, government official; b. Williston, N.D., Jan. 2, 1954; s. Lorens J. and Mabel A. (Nelson) K.; m. Linda M. Johnson, Apr. 12, 1985. AA, Golden Valley Luth. Coll., 1974; BA summa cum laude, Concordia Coll., Moorhead, Minn., 1976; JD magna cum laude, U. Minn., 1980. Bar: N.D. 1980, U.S. Ct. Appeals (9th cir.) 1981, U.S. Dist. Ct. N.D. 1985. Assoc. Bjella, Neff, Rafhort, Wahl & Eiken, Williston, 1980-83; sole practice Williston, 1983-85; land commr. State of N.D., Bismarck, 1985—; bd. dirs. Williston Coop. Credit Union. Chmn. dist. #1 Dems., Williston, 1984-85. Lutheran. Land use and planning, Oil and gas leasing, Real property. Home: 1032 Crescent Ln Bismarck ND 58501 Office: ND Land Dept State Capitol Bismarck ND 58505

KINNAN, DAVID E., lawyer; b. Columbus, Ohio, May 15, 1946. BA, Pa. State U., 1968; JD, U. Tex., 1970. Bar: Tex. 1971. Atty. Shell Oil Corp., Houston, 1977—. Served to capt. USAF, 1971-76. Oil and gas leasing, Federal civil litigation, General corporate. Office: PO Box 2463 Houston TX 77001

KINNEARY, JOSEPH PETER, U.S. judge; b. Cin., Sept. 19, 1905; s. Joseph and Anne (Mulvihill) K.; m. Byrnece Camille Rogers, June 26, 1950. B.A., U. Notre Dame, 1928; LL.B., U. Cin., 1935. Bar: Ohio 1935, U.S. Supreme Ct 1960. Pvt. practice in Cin. and Columbus, 1935-61; asst. atty. gen. Ohio, 1937-39; 1st asst. atty. gen. 1949-51, spl. counsel to atty. gen., 1959-61; U.S. atty. So Dist. Ohio, 1961-66; judge U.S. Dist. Ct., So. Dist. Ohio, 1966—, chief judge, 1973-75; lectr. law trusts Coll. Law, U. Cin., 1948. Delegate Democratic Nat. Conv., 1952. Served to capt. AUS, World War II. Decorated Army Commendation ribbon. Mem. Phi Delta Phi. Roman Catholic. Judicial administration. Home: 2440 Northwest Blvd Columbus OH 43221 Office: U S Dist Ct 319 US Courthouse 85 Marconi Blvd Columbus OH 43215 *

KINNEY, ALDON MONROE, JR., business executive, lawyer; b. Cin., May 19, 1921; s. Aldon Monroe and Elsie Marguerite (Griffin) K.; m. Marjorie Ann Aszman, June 13, 1942; children: Gael Maureen Kinney Coleman, Roxanne Kinney Wiley, Aldon Monroe, III. Student, Denison U., 1939-41; A.B., U. Cin., 1943, J.D., 1948, LL.M., 1953. Bar: Ohio bar 1949, U.S. Supreme Ct. bar 1952. Partner firm Jenings & Kinney, Cin., 1949-53; individual practice law Cin., 1953-70; counsel, adminstrv. asst. to chmn. A. M. Kinney, Inc., Cin., 1953-66; chmn. A. M. Kinney, Inc., 1966—, Design Art Corp., Cin., 1966—, Kinlab, Inc., Cin., 1966—, Kinvernon Corp., Cin., 1966—, A. M. Kinney Assos., Inc., Chgo., 1966—, Kintech Services, Inc., Cin., 1969—, Walter Kidde Constructors, Inc., N.Y.C., 1973—, Walter Kidde Engrs. Internat., Inc., N.Y.C., 1973—, Vulcan Cin., Inc., 1975—; solicitor, City of Madeira, Ohio, 1953-70; dir. Bank One, Milford, 1961—. Mem. Newtown (Ohio) Bd. Edn., 1955-57; bd. dirs. Contemporary Arts Center, Cin., 1971-76. Served to sgt. USAAF, 1943-46. Mem. Cin. Bar Assn., Lawyers Club, Engrng. Soc. Cin. Clubs: Queen City, Bankers. General corporate, Probate, Real property. Office: 2900 Vernon Pl Cincinnati OH 45219

KINNEY, GREGORY HOPPES, lawyer; b. Anderson, Ind., July 15, 1947; s. Dalton Roth and Effie Eleanor (Hoppes) K. B.A., Mich. State U., 1969, M.Labor Relations, 1971; J.D., U. Detroit, 1974. Bar: Mich. 1975, U.S. Dist. Ct. (ea. dist.) Mich. 1975, U.S. Ct. Appeals (D.C. cir.) 1975. Labor law editor Bur. Nat. Affairs, Washington, 1974; pension cons. Edward H. Friend & Co., Washington, 1975, The Wyatt Co., Detroit, 1976-84; sole practice, Detroit, 1984-86, Troy, Mich., 1986—. Mem. ABA, Detroit Bar Assn., D.C. Bar Assn. Club: Detroit Yacht. Pension, profit-sharing, and employee benefits, Estate taxation. Home and Office: 2725 Charter Blvd #212 Troy MI 48083

KINNEY, JAMES HOWARD, lawyer; b. Oklahoma City, Mar. 2, 1937; s. William Edgar and Chrissie (Ballingall) K.; m. June Lassick, Mar. 26, 1961; children: Karen Jill, Scott James. BS in Bus. Mgmt., Calif. State U., Long Beach, 1963; JD, UCLA, 1966. Bar: Calif. 1966, U.S. Dist. Ct. (so. dist.) Calif. 1966. Dep. dist. atty. Ventura (Calif.) County, 1966-68; ptnr. Collins, Gleason & Kinney, Torrance, Calif., 1968-85, O'Melveny & Myers, Los Angeles, 1985—; lectr. Harbor Coll., Los Angeles, 1971-72. Councilman City of Palos Verdes Estates, Calif., 1983—, Mayor, 1985-86. Served to sgt. USMC, 1955-58. Mem. Los Angeles County Bar Assn., Internat. Council Shopping Ctrs., Sigma Alpha Epsilon. Republican. Real property. Office: O'Melveny & Myers 1800 Century Park E Los Angeles CA 90067

KINNEY, RICHARD GORDON, lawyer, educator; b. Chgo., May 8, 1939; s. Michael James, Sr., and Blanche Marie (Gill) K.; m. Katherine Choffen, Dec. 26, 1969; 1 son, Richard Greg. B.S.E.E., U. Ill., 1961; J.D., U. Chgo., 1964. Bar: Ill. 1964, Ind. 1981, U.S. Ct. Customs and Patent Appeals, 1975, U.S. Ct. Appeals (7th cir.) 1976, U.S. Ct. Appeals (3d cir.) 1981, U.S. Ct. Appeals (9th cir.) 1979, U.S. Ct. Appeals (D.C. cir.) 1976, U.S. Supreme Ct. 1970, U.S. Ct. Appeals (fed. cir.) 1982, U.S. Dist. Ct. (no. dist.) Ind. 1983. With patent dept. Zenith Radio Corp., Chgo., 1963-64; with patent dept. Borg-Warner Corp., Chgo., 1968-73; div. patent counsel Baxter Travenol Labs., Inc., Deerfield, Ill., 1973-76; prin. Richard G. Kinney & Assocs., Chgo. and Merrillville, Ind., 1976—; adj. instr. Purdue Calumet U. Rep. candidate Ill. State Senate, 1976; chmn. 6th Congl. Dist. Citizens for Goldwater-Miller, 1964. Mem. ABA, Am. Patent Law Assn., Ind. Bar Assn., Chgo. Bar Assn., Patent Law Assn. Chgo., The Inventors and Entrepreneurs Soc. Roman Catholic. Club: Union League (Chgo.). Lodge: Lions. Patent, Trademark and copyright, Federal civil litigation. Home: 12 Shore Dr Box 911 Ogden Dunes IN 46368 Office: South Twin Towers Suite 425 Merrillville IN 46410

KINNEY, STEPHEN HOYT, JR., lawyer; b. Albuquerque, Feb. 27, 1948; s. Stephen Hoyt and Harriet May (Gadsden) K.; m. Leslie vanLiew, June 10, 1972; 1 child, Erin. B.S., MIT, 1970; J.D., Harvard U., 1973. Bar: N.Y. 1974, U.S. Dist. Ct. (so. dist.) N.Y. 1974, U.S. Dist. Ct. (ea. dist.) N.Y. 1974, U.S. Dist. Ct. (no. dist.) N.Y. 1978, U.S. Ct. Apls. (2d cir.) 1975, U.S. Supreme Ct. 1982. Programmer, analyst MIT, 1968-70; law clk. N.J. Organized Crime Unit, Trenton, 1972; assoc. Reid & Priest, N.Y.C., 1973-85, sr. atty., 1985-86, ptnr. 1986—; sec., dir. Delta Transnational Inc., N.Y.C., 1976—. Author, editor: Outline of Arbitration, 1984. Authored computer programs. Mem., officer U.S. Power Squadron, Port Washington, 1978. Mem. Assn. Bar City N.Y., ABA, N.Y. State Bar Assn., Sigma Xi. Club: Harvard (N.Y.C.); MB Yacht (Port Washington, N.Y.). Contracts commercial, Construction, Computer. Office: Reid & Priest 40 W 57th St New York NY 10019

KINS, TONYA, lawyer; b. Junction City, Kans., Oct. 5, 1953; d. John Plummer and Betty Ann (Schwartz) K.; m. Bradley James Walcher, June 12, 1982; 1 child, Lauren Kins Walcher. BA in Econs. with honors, U. Wis., 1975, JD, 1979. Bar: Wis. 1979, U.S. Dist. Ct. (we. dist.) Wis. 1979, Colo. 1979, U.S. Dist. Ct. Colo. 1979. Assoc. McMartin, Burke, Loser & Fitzgerald P.C., Englewood, Colo., 1979-84, Roath & Brega P.C., Denver, 1984-86; dir. Burke & Kins, P.C., Denver, 1987—; prosecutor City of Wheat Ridge, Colo., 1980-81, Cherry Hills Village, Colo., 1981-82; asst. counsel South Suburban Met. Recreation and Park Dist., Littleton, Colo., 1983-84. Mem. ABA, Colo. Bar Assn., Wis. Bar Assn., Denver Bar Assn., Alliance Profl. Women, Phi Kappa Phi, Sigma Epsilon Sigma. Avocations: skiing, tennis, camping, photography, scuba diving. Real property, Contracts commercial, General corporate. Office: Burke & Kins PC 1776 Lincoln St Suite 1010 Denver CO 80203

KINSEY, CARROL HUGHES, JR., lawyer; b. Suffolk, Va., Apr. 26, 1954; s. Carrol Hughes Sr. and Ann Beaman (Martin) K.; m. Lucy Ann Dee, July 7, 1979; children: Katherine Ann, Monica Dee. BA in Psychology with distinction, U. Va., 1976; JD, Coll. William and Mary, 1979. Bar: Va. 1979. Atty. office gen. counsel U.S. Office Personnel Mgmt., Washington, 1982-86, spl. asst. to gen. counsel, 1986—. Mem. Greater Newington Jaycees, Springfield, Va., 1981-84. Served to capt. JAGC, U.S. Army, 1979-82. Named one of Outstanding Young Men Am. U.S. Jaycees, 1984-85. Mem. ABA, Va. Bar Assn. Avocations: tennis, travel, music. Administrative and regulatory, Labor, Federal personnel law. Home: 8621 Woodward Ave Alexandria VA 22309 Office: US Office Personnel Mgmt 1900 E St NW Washington DC 20415

KINTNER, EARL WILSON, lawyer; b. Corydon, Ind., Nov. 6, 1912; s. Lee and Lillie Florence (Chanley) K.; m. Valerie Patricia Wildy, May 28, 1948; 1 child, Christopher Earl Mackelcan; children by previous marriage: Anna Victoria, Jonathan M., Rosemary Jane (dec.). A.B., De Pauw U., 1936, LL.D. (hon.), 1970; J.D., Ind. U., 1938. Bar: Ind. 1938, U.S. Supreme Ct. 1945, D.C. 1953. Practice law Princeton, Ind., 1938-44; city atty. Princeton 1939-42; pros. atty. 6th Ind. Jud. Circuit, 1943-48; dep. U.S. commr. UN War Crimes Commn., 1945-48; sr. trial atty. FTC, 1948-50, legal adviser, 1950-53, gen. counsel, 1953-59, chmn., 1959-61; adj. prof. NYU Sch. Law, 1958; del., chmn. com. hearing officers Pres.'s Conf. on Adminstrv. Procedure, 1953-54; mem. panel on invention and innovation U.S. Dept. Commerce, 1965-66; mem. U.S. Adminstrv. Conf., 1972-76, 78-82; mem. adv. com. on civil rules U.S. Jud. Conf., 1971-82. Author: An Antitrust Primer, 1964, 73, Robinson-Patman Primer, 1970, 79, A Primer on the Law of Deceptive Practices, 1971, 78, A Merger Primer, 1973; co-author: An Intellectual Property Primer, 1975, An International Anti-trust Primer, 1975, Anti-trust Legislation, 11 vols., 1986, An Anti-trust Treatise, Vols. 1-6, 1986; editor: The United Nations War Crimes Commission and Development of the Laws of War, 1948, The Hadamar Trial, 1948, FTC staff legal manual, 1952. Bd. dirs. D.C. Legal Aid Soc., 1963—, pres., 1973-76; bd. visitors Ind. U. Law Sch., 1964—, chmn., 1973. Served from ensign to lt. USNR, 1944-46. Recipient Disting. Service award Ind. U., 1960, Disting. Alumni award DePauw U., 1965, 75. Mem. Fed. Bar Assn. (pres. 1956-57, 58-59), ABA (chmn. adminstrv. law sect. 1959-60, council antitrust law sect. 1958-61), N.Y. Bar Assn. (exec. com antitrust sect.), Fed. Bar Found. (pres. 1959—), Fed. Bar Bldg. Corp. (pres. 1959—), Bar Assn. D.C. (dir. 1972-74), Am. Judicature Soc. (dir. 1961-64), Am. Legion, DAV, Sigma Delta Chi, Phi Delta Phi (pres. Province II 1962-67), Pi Sigma Alpha, Delta Sigma Rho, Lambda Chi Alpha. Republican. Episcopalian. Clubs: Cosmos (Washington), National Lawyers (Washington) (pres. 1959—), Capitol Hill (Washington); Union League (N.Y.); Coral Beach and Tennis (Bermuda); Masons (32 deg.), Shriners. Antitrust, Administrative and regulatory, Trademark and copyright. Home: 3220 Idaho Ave NW Washington DC 20016 Office: 1050 Connecticut Ave NW Washington DC 20036

KINZLER, THOMAS BENJAMIN, lawyer; b. N.Y.C., June 19, 1950; s. David and Rhoda Lenore (Wolgel) K.; m. Carol Ada Loebel, Aug. 24, 1975; children: Katherine Diane, David James. BA, Columbia Coll., 1971; JD, Boston U., 1975. Bar: N.Y. 1976, U.S. Dist. Ct. (so. and ea. dists.) N.Y. 1976, U.S. Ct. Appeals (2nd cir.) 1976. Assoc. Kreindler, Relkin & Goldberg, N.Y.C., 1975-77, Arthur, Dry & Kalish, N.Y.C., 1977-80; assoc. Kelley Drye & Warren, N.Y.C., 1980-85, ptnr., 1985—; bd. dirs. Surg. Aid to Children of the World, Rockville Centre, N.Y. Mem. ABA, Assn. of the Bar City of N.Y.C. (products liability com. 1983-86, com. on state legis. 1978-80). Avocations: house renovation, tennis. Federal civil litigation, State civil litigation. Office: Kelley Drye & Warren 101 Park Ave New York NY 10178

KINZLER, WILLIAM CHARLES, lawyer; b. Bay Shore, N.Y., Feb. 20, 1949; s. William Andrew and Constance (Walker) K. BA, Georgetown U., 1971; JD, U. San Francisco, 1975. Bar: Calif. 1978, U.S. Dist. Ct. (no. dist.) Calif. 1978. Sole practice San Francisco, 1978—. Pres. Californians for Fair Wine Prices, San Francisco, 1985-86. Mem. ABA (patent trademark, copyright, antitrust sects.), State Bar Assn. Calif. (intellectual property, bus law sects.), Bar Assn. San Francisco. Roman Catholic. Club: Barristers (San Francisco). Avocations: wine, travel. Legislative, Trademark and copyright, Contracts commercial. Home: 491 Frederick St #10 San Francisco CA 94117 Office: 414 Gough St Suite 3 San Francisco CA 94102-4425

KIPPERMAN, LAWRENCE I., lawyer; b. Chgo., Nov. 22, 1941; s. Solomon and Idelle (Goldman) K.; m. Carol A. Kipperman, Jan. 29, 1967 (div. Sept. 1985); children: Anna, Lynne. BA, U. Ill., 1963, JD, 1966; LLM, George Washington U., 1968. Bar: Ill. 1966, U.S. Dist. Ct. (no. dist.) Ill. 1966, U.S. Supreme Ct. 1968, Ohio 1970, U.S. Ct. Appeals (7th cir.) 1973, U.S. Ct. Appeals (8th cir.) 1986. Atty. NLRB, Washington, 1966-70; assoc. Burke, Haber & Berick, Cleve., 1970-71; assoc. Sidley & Austin, Chgo., 1971-73, ptnr., 1973—; lectr. Ill. Continuing Legal Edn., 1985. Mem. Chgo. Bar Assn., Am. Judicature Soc., Legal Club Chgo. Jewish. Club: Monroe (Chgo.). Avocations: Architectural history, baseball, basketball, jazz. Labor. Office: Sidley & Austin One First Nat Plaza Chicago IL 60603

KIRBY, JACK ARTHUR, lawyer; b. Willard, Ohio, Feb. 27, 1941; s. Arthur Norris and Kathryn Elizabeth (Bell) K.; m. Candace Huber, Mar. 1, 1969; 1 dau.; Victoria Huber. Student, Va. Mil. Inst., 1959-60; B.A., Denison U., 1963; J.D., Washington and Lee U., 1970. Bar: Pa. 1971. Mem. rev. counsel staff estate planning dept. Girard Bank, Phila., 1970-72; mem. examinations dept. estate planning and taxation Am. Coll. Life Underwriters, Bryn Mawr, Pa., 1975-79; assoc. Harvey, Pennington, Herting & Renneisen Ltd., Phila., 1979-86; sole practice, Ardmore, Pa., 1986—; adj. asst. prof. bus. law Drexel U., 1978; spl. counsel Am. Soc. Farm Mgrs. and Rural Appraisers, U.S. Ho. of Reps. Ways & Means Com., 1977. Served with USN, 1964-67, to lt. comdr. JAGC, USNR, 1973-75. Mem. Phila. Bar Assn., Pa. Bar Assn., ABA. Republican. Clubs: Overbrook Golf, Rittenhouse. Author: Estate Planner's Kit, 1978. Contbr. articles to profl. jours. Probate, General corporate, Estate taxation. Home: 1516 County Line Rd Rosemont PA 19010 Office: 103 Sibley Ave Ardmore PA 19003

KIRBY, JAMES LYNN, lawyer; b. Ripley, Tenn., Sept. 19, 1949; s. James C. and Margaret (Parham) K.; m. Judith Murchison, Feb. 5, 1971; children: Amie Margaret, James Matthew, Daniel Andrew. BS, Union U., 1971; JD, Memphis State U., 1976. Bar: Tenn. 1976, U.S. Dist. Ct. (we. dist.) Tenn. 1976. Assoc. Harris, Shelton, Dunlap & Cobb, Memphis, 1976-80, ptnr., 1981—. Served with Tenn. Army N.G., 1971-77. Mem. ABA, Tenn. Bar Assn., Memphis and Shelby County Bar Assn. Baptist. Lodge: Kiwanis. Avocations: coaching children's sports. State civil litigation, General corporate, Insurance. Home: 2800 E Battlecreek Cove Memphis TN 38134 Office: Harris Shelton Dunlap & Cobb One Commerce Sq Suite 1300 Memphis TN 38103

KIRBY, MARK CLAYTON, lawyer; b. Wilson, N.C., Apr. 4, 1956; s. Wallace Hines and Sally Ann (Broome) K.; m. Lisa Hodges Delaney, Oct. 17, 1981; children: Greyson Elizabeth, Stewart Anne. BA cum laude, Duke U., 1978; JD, U. N.C., 1981. Bar: N.C. 1981, U.S. Dist. Ct. (ea., we. and mid. dists.) 1981. Assoc. Poyner, Geraghty, Hartsfield & Townsend, Raleigh, N.C., 1981-84, Haythe & Curley, Raleigh and N.Y.C., 1984-86; ptnr. Wyrick, Robbins, Yates, Ponton & Kirby, Raleigh, 1986—. Columnist In re Bankruptcy, 1985—; contbr. articles to profl. jours. Adminstrv. bd. Edenton St. United Meth. Ch., Raleigh, 1981. Mem. N.C. Bar Assn. (bus. law and bankruptcy sects. 1981—), Am. Bankruptcy Inst., Comml. Law League Chgo., Capital Soc. Republican. Lodge: Rotary. Avocations: hiking, gardening, sports. Bankruptcy, Contracts commercial, Real property. Home: 2019 St Marys St Raleigh NC 27608 Office: Wyrick Robbins Yates Ponton & Kirby 4700 Homewood Ct Suite 340 Raleigh NC 27609-7803

KIRBY, PETER MANGAN, lawyer; b. Washington, June 30, 1945; s. John and Rose (Mangan) K.; m. Linda P. Kirby; children: Clarise, Patrick, Celia. BA in English, Fordham U., 1967; JD, Georgetown U., 1979. Bar: D.C. 1981, U.S. Dist. Ct. D.C. 1981. Legis. asst. Tex. rep. John Young, Washington, 1967-70; dir. pub. affairs Corn Refiners Assn., Washington, 1970-71; dir. fed. legislation Air Transport Assn., Washington, 1971-76; assoc. Dawson, Riddell, Fox, Holroyd & Wilson, Washington, 1979-80; ptnr. Kirby, Gillick, Schwartz & Tuohey, Washington, 1980-86, Ginsburg, Feldman & Bress, Washington, 1987—. Mem. ABA, D.C. Bar Assn. Legislative, Public utilities, Administrative and regulatory. Home: 6805

Tammy Ct Bethesda MD 20817 Office: Ginsburg Feldman & Bress 1250 Connecticut Ave Washington DC 20036

KIRCHER, JOHN JOSEPH, law educator; b. Milw., July 26, 1938; s. Joseph John and Martha Marie (Jach) K.; m. Marcia Susan Adamkiewicz, Aug. 26, 1961; children: Joseph John, Mary Kathryn. BA, Marquette U., 1960, JD, 1963. Bar: Wis. 1963, U.S. Dist. Ct. (ea. dist.) Wis. 1963. Sole practice, Port Washington, Wis., 1963-66; with Def. Research Inst., Milw., 1966-80, research dir., 1972-80; with Marquette U., 1970—, prof. law, 1980—; chmn. Wis. Jud. Council, 1981-83. Author: (with J.D. Ghiardi) Punitive Damages: Law and Practice, 1981; mem. editorial bd. Def. Law Jour.; contbr. articles to profl. jours. Recipient Teaching Excellence award Marquette U., 1986, Disting. Service award Def. Research Inst., 1980. Mem. ABA, Wis. Bar Assn., Wis. Supreme Ct. Bd. Atty.'s Profl. Competence, Wis. Commnr. Ins. Property and Casualty Adv. Council, Am. Judicature Soc., Assn. Internationale de Droit des Assurances. Roman Catholic. Lodge: Scribes. Legal education, Insurance, Personal injury. Address: 1103 W Wisconsin Ave Milwaukee WI 53233

KIRCHHEIMER, ARTHUR E(DWARD), lawyer, business executive; b. N.Y.C., June 26, 1931; s. Arthur and Lena K.; m. Esther A. Jordan, Sept. 11, 1965. B.A., Syracuse U., 1952, LL.B., 1954. Bar: N.Y. 1954, Calif. 1973. Ptnr. Block, Kirchheimer, Lemax & Failmezger, Syracuse, N.Y., 1954-70; corp. counsel Norwich Pharmacal Co., N.Y., 1970-72; sr. v.p., gen. counsel Wickes Cos., Inc., San Diego, 1972-84; prin. Arthur E. Kirchheimer, Inc., P.C., San Diego, 1984—; sec., dir. Corp. Fin. Council San Diego, 1975. Pres. Mental Health Assn. Onondaga County, 1970; chmn. Manilus (N.Y.) Planning Commn., 1969-72; mem. Alternatives to Litigation Spl. Panel, 1984—. Mem. ABA, Fed., Calif., N.Y., San Diego bar assns., Internat. Platform Assn. General corporate, Antitrust, Securities. Home: 2876 Palomino Circle La Jolla CA 92037 Office: 1670 Wells Fargo Bank Bldg San Diego CA 92101

KIRCHMAN, CHARLES VINCENT, lawyer; b. Washington, June 28, 1935; s. Floyd Vincent and Dorothy Johanna (Johnson) K.; m. Erika Ottilie Knoeppel, July 4, 1959; children: Mark C., Eric H., Charles E. BA, U. Md., 1959; JD, George Washington U., 1962. Bar: D.C. 1962, Md. 1970. Security specialist Adj. Gen.'s Office, U.S. Army, 1962-64; sole practice, Washington, 1964-70, Wheaton, Md., 1970-73; ptnr. Andrews & Schick, Waldorf, Md., 1973-77; sole practice, Wheaton, Md., 1977—. Mem. adv. bd. Immigration Reform Law Inst. Served with AUS, 1953-56. Mem. Am. Trial Lawyers Assn., D.C. Bar Assn., Md. Bar Assn., Charles County Bar Assn., Am. Arbitration Assn. (nat. panel), Md. Hist. Soc. Democrat. Club: Manor Country. State civil litigation, Probate. Home: 14801 Notley Rd Silver Spring MD 20904 Office: 11141 Georgia Ave Wheaton MD 20902

KIRCHNER, THEODORE HARRY, lawyer; b. Riverside, N.J., Nov. 26, 1947; s. Theodore Henry and Rose Mae (Born) K.; m. L. Diane Kinsey, July 10, 1971; 1 child, Jennifer Rose. BA, Rutgers U., 1969; JD, U. Maine, 1977. Bar: Maine 1977, U.S. Dist. Ct. Maine 1977, U.S. Ct. Appeals (1st cir.) 1986, U..S. Supreme Ct., 1987. Assoc. Law Offices of Clayton N. Howard, Damariscotta, Maine, 1977-79, Norman & Hanson, Portland, Maine, 1979—. Served with U.S. Army, 1969-72. Mem. ABA, Def. Research Inst., Maine Bar Assn., Maine Trial Lawyers Assn. Democrat. Avocation: outdoor recreation. Civil rights, Insurance, Personal injury. Home: 192 Caleb St Portland ME 04102 Office: Norman Hanson & DeTroy 415 Congress St Portland ME 04111

KIRK, ALAN GOODRICH, II, utilities executive; b. Rosemont, Pa., Dec. 15, 1926; s. William Thompson and Edith Graves (Ely) K.; m. Patricia Joan Carr, Apr. 20, 1953; children: Augustus, Jennifer, William, Alison. A.B., Princeton U., 1950; LL.B., U. Pa., 1956. Bar: Pa. 1956. Assoc. Dechert, Price & Rhoads, Phila., 1956-58; asst. dean U. Pa. Law Sch., 1958-62; gen. counsel, asst. sec. William H. Rorer Co., Ft. Washington, Pa., 1962-69; assoc. solicitor (water) Dept. Interior, Washington, 1969; asst. to sec. Dept. Interior, 1969-70, asst. to solicitor, 1970-71; dep. gen. counsel EPA, Washington, 1971-72; asst. adminstr. for enforcement, gen. counsel EPA, 1973-75; gen. counsel Potomac Electric Power Co., Washington, 1975; v.p., gen. counsel Potomac Electric Power Co., 1976-81, sr. v.p., gen. counsel, 1981-85, sr. v.p., gen counsel, sec., 1985—. Served with U.S. Mcht. Marine, 1944-46; Served with AUS, 1950-53. Mem. ABA, Fed., D.C. bar assns. Clubs: Ivy (Princeton, N.J.); Metropolitan, Burning Tree, Chevy Chase (Washington). Office: Potomac Electric Power Co 1900 Pennsylvania Ave NW Washington DC 20068

KIRK, DENNIS DEAN, lawyer; b. Pittsburg, Kans., Dec. 13, 1950; s. Homer Standley and Maida Corena (Rouse) K. A.A., Hutchinson Community Jr. Coll., 1970; B.S. with distinction, No. Ariz. U., 1972; J.D., Washburn U., 1975. Bar: Kans. 1975, U.S. Dist. Ct. Kans. 1975, D.C. 1977, U.S. Ct. Appeals (D.C. cir.) 1978, U.S. Supreme Ct. 1979, U.S. Ct. Appeals (5th cir.) 1981, U.S. Dist. Ct. Md. 1984, U.S. Tax Ct. 1984, U.S. Claims Ct. 1984, U.S. Ct. Appeals (fed. cir.) 1984, U.S. Ct. Mil. Appeals 1984. Trial atty. ICC, Washington, 1975-77; assoc. Goff, Sims, Cloud, Stroud & Walker, Washington, 1977-82; sole practice, Washington, 1982—; dir., v.p. law Collegiate Challenge, Inc., Vienna, Va., 1984; dir., pres., Law Facilities, Inc., Washington, 1982—. Vol. parole and probation officer Shawnee County, Kans., 1973-74; mem. Citizens' Adv. Task Force Group, Md. Nat. Park and Planning Commn., 1978-80; mem. citizens' task force on gen. plan amendments study Fairfax County Council, Va., 1981-82; mem. Seven Corners Task Force, Fairfax County, 1981-82, chmn. transp. and housing subcoms.; pres. Seven Springs Tenants' Assn., College Park, Md., 1976-80, Ravenwood Park Citizens' Assn., 1981-82; dir. Greenwood Homes, Ic., Fairfax County Dept. Housing and Community Devel., 1983—; mem. Gala Com. Spotlight the Kennedy Ctr., Pres.' Adv. Com. on the Arts, 1986-87; founding chmn., charter mem. Mason Dist. Jaycees, 1984-86; sec., gen. counsel, bd. dirs. U.S. Assocs. for the Cultural Triangle in Sri Lanka, 1983—; commr. Consumer Protection Commn., Fairfax County, 1982—; mem. Mason Dist. Rep. Com., 1981—; Ravenwood precinct chmn. Republican Orgn., Falls Church, Va., 1982—; active Fairfax County Young Reps. Named to Honorable Order Ky. Cols. Mem. ABA, Assn. Trial Lawyers Am., Specialized Carriers and Rigging Assn., Regional Distbn. Carriers Conf., Nat. Rifle Assn. (life), Am. Fed. Musicians, Phi Kappa Phi, Phi Alpha Delta. Methodist. Lodge: Masons. Avocation: music. Administrative and regulatory, Federal civil litigation, General practice. Home: 6315 Anneliese Dr Falls Church VA 22044 Office: Dennis Dean & Kirk National Pl N Suite 1213 1331 Pennsylvania Ave NW Washington DC 20004

KIRK, JOHN MACGREGOR, lawyer; b. Flint, Mich., Mar. 9, 1938; s. R. Dean and Berenice E. (MacGregor) K.; m. Carol Lasko, June 8, 1971; children—John M. Jr., Caroline Dwyer. B.A., Washington and Lee U., 1960, LL.B., 1962; LL.M. in Taxation, NYU, 1967. Bar: Mich. 1962, U.S. Supreme Ct. 1966, U.S. Ct. Mil. Appeals 1966, U.S. Tax Ct. 1969, U.S. Dist. Ct. (ea. dist.) Mich. 1982 U.S. Ct. Appeals (6th cir.) 1983. Trial atty. Tax Div. Dept. Justice, Washington, 1967-72; assoc. Boyer and Briggs, Bloomfield Hills, Mich., 1972-74; ptnr. Butzel, Gust, Klein and Van Zile, Detroit and Bloomfield Hills, 1975-78; ptnr. Meyer, Kirk, Snyder & Safford, Bloomfield Hills, 1978—. Mem., past pres. Friends of Baldwin Pub. Library. Served as lt. USNR, 1962-66. Mem. ABA, State Bar Mich., Detroit Bar Assn., Oakland County Bar Assn., Oakland County Tax Com. Republican. Presbyterian. Club: Rotary (Birmingham). Estate taxation, Corporate taxation, General corporate. Office: 100 W Long Lake Rd Bloomfield Hills MI 48013

KIRK, JOHN ROBERT, JR., patent lawyer; b. Stuart, Va., June 21, 1935; s. John Robert and Mary Elise (Mustaine) K.; m. Linda Louise Davis, Feb. 3, 1962; children—Karen Louise, Laura Elise, Rebecca Elizabeth. student Rice Inst., 1953-56; B.S. in Chem. Engring., U. Tex.-Austin, 1959; J.D., U. Houston, 1966. Bar: Tex. 1966, U.S. Patent Office 1967, U.S. Supreme Ct. 1973, U.S. Customs and Patent Appeals 1973, U.S. Dist. Ct. (so. dist.) Tex. 1974, U.S. Ct. Claims 1975, U.S. Dist. Ct. (no. dist.) Tex. 1977, U.S. Ct. Appeals (5th cir.) 1980, U.S. Ct. Appeals (11th cir.) 1981, U.S. Ct. Appeals (fed. cir.) 1983. Patent atty. Jefferson Chem. Co., Houston, 1966-69, mgr. patent div., 1969-72; mem. Pravel, Gambrell, Hewitt, Kirk & Kimball, P.C., Houston, 1972-84, stockholder, 1973-84; stockholder Baker & Kirk, P.C., 1984—; dir. Nat. Inventors Hall of Fame Found., Inc., 1979-82, treas., 1983-84, pres., 1986—. Served to lt. USMCR, 1958-60. Fellow Tex. Bar Found., Houston Bar Found; mem. ABA, Am. Intellectual Property Law Assn., State Bar Tex. (chmn. intellectual property law sect. 1977-78), Nat. Counsel Patent Law Assns. (vice chmn. 1986—), Houston Intellectual Property Law Assn., Houston Bar Assn., Licensing Execs. Soc. Republican. Baptist. Clubs: The Houstonian, Inns of Court (Houston). Patent, Trademark and copyright, Oil and gas leasing. Office: 1020 Holcombe Blvd Houston TX 77030

KIRK, PATRICK LAINE, lawyer; b. South Bend, Ind., May 12, 1948; s. Jerry W. and Vivian E. (Evans) K.; m. Cheryl A. Ensminger, Dec. 30, 1967; children: Kevin P., Travis S. BA, Valparaiso U., 1970, JD, 1973. Bar: N.Y. 1974, U.S. Dist. Ct. (no. dist.) N.Y. 1977, U.S. Supreme Ct. 1986. Ptnr. Grilli & Kirk, Herkimer, N.Y., 1974—; counsel Herkimer Cen. Sch., 1974-76; asst. counsel Village of Frankfort, Herkimer and Cold Brook, N.Y., 1981—; asst. dist. atty. Herkimer County, 1976-78, chief asst. dist. atty., 1978-86, dist. atty., 1986—; lectr. Police Tng. Sch., Utica, N.Y., 1979—, Arson Seminar, 1987; tchr. Herkimer County Community Coll., 1981. Advisor Law Explorer Post, Herkimer, 1974-76; bd. dirs. Martin Luther Home, Clinton, N.Y., 1980; chmn. sect. Mohawk Valley United Fund, Ilion, N.Y., 1985; mem. Arson Task Force, 1986—. Mem. ABA, N.Y. State Bar Assn., Herkimer County Bar Assn. (bd. dirs.), Nat. Dist. Attys. Assn., N.Y. Dist. Attys. Assn., Assn. Driving While Intoxicated (legis. com.). Republican. Lutheran. Club: Ambassadors (Ilion). Lodge: Elks. Criminal, General practice. Home: 840 W German St Herkimer NY 13350 Office: Law Offices of Grilli & Kirk 412 N Prospect St Herkimer NY 13350

KIRKELIE, GREGORY EVAN, lawyer; b. Santa Monica, Calif., Mar. 30, 1942; s. George Evan and Margaret Allen (Moody) K.; m. Beverly Anne Ward, Aug. 7, 1967; children—Carrie Ann, Daniel Evan. B.A. cum laude, Calif. State U.-Northridge, 1964; J.D., U. So. Calif., 1970. Bar: Calif. 1970, U.S. Dist Ct. (cen. dist.) Calif. 1970. Ptnr. Ervin, Cohen & Jessup, Beverly Hills, Calif., 1970-80; v.p. legal and gen. counsel Factors Etc., Inc., Bear, Del., 1978-80; prin. Kirkelie Bus. Parks, Chatsworth, Calif., 1981—. Bd. dirs. Los Angeles Bapt. City Mission Soc., 1972—, Eastern Coll., St. Davids, Pa., 1982—. Served to lt. (j.g.) USNR, 1964-67. Mem. ABA, Calif. Bar Assn., Los Angeles County Bar Assn., Order of Coif. Republican. Baptist. General corporate, Real property, Corporate taxation. Address: 10951 Oso Ave Chatsworth CA 91311

KIRKHAM, FRANCIS ROBISON, lawyer; b. Fillmore, Utah, Aug. 23, 1904; s. Francis W. and Alzina (Robison) K.; m. Ellis Musser, July 9, 1929; children: James F., Elizabeth (Mrs. James Stillman, Jr.), Katherine (Mrs. Geoffrey Hallam Movius), Eugene R. A.B., George Washington U., 1930, LL.B., 1931. Bar: D.C. 1931, Calif. 1936. Law clk. Chief Justice Charles E. Hughes, 1933-35; with firm Pillsbury, Madison & Sutro, San Francisco, 1936—; partner Pillsbury, Madison & Sutro, 1940—; gen. counsel Standard Oil Co., Calif., 1960-70; Mem. atty. gen.'s nat. com. to study antitrust laws, 1953-55, mem. commn. on Revision Fed. Ct. Appellate System, 1973. Author: (with Reynolds Robertson) Jurisdiction of the Supreme Court of the U.S. Drafted for Supreme Court Revision of General Orders in Bankruptcy, 1936, 39. Recipient Alumni Achievement award; George Washington U., 1970; Alumni Merit Honor award U. Utah, 1976. Fellow Am. Coll. Trial Lawyers, Am. Bar Found.; mem. ABA (chmn. anti-trust law sect. 1961), San Francisco Bar Assn., State Bar Calif., Am. Law Inst., Am. Judicature Soc., Am. Soc. Internat. Law, Order of Coif, Delta Theta Phi. Clubs: Pacific Union (San Francisco), Bohemian (San Francisco), San Francisco Golf (San Francisco), Stock Exchange (San Francisco). Home: 3245 Pacific Ave San Francisco CA 94118 Office: Standard Oil Bldg San Francisco CA 94104

KIRKHAM, JAMES FRANCIS, lawyer; b. Washington, May 14, 1933; s. Francis Robinson and Ellis (Musser) K.; m. Katherine Drury Dibblee, June 17, 1960; children: Lila Haliday, James Dibblee. B.A., Yale U., 1954; LL.B., U. Calif.-Berkeley, 1957. Bar: Calif. 1957, U.S. Supreme Ct. 1967. Assoc. Pillsbury, Madison & Sutro, San Francisco, 1960-65, ptnr., 1966—; mem. exec. com. Calif. Bar, 1982-85; rev. com. Calif. State Bar Ct., 1985—. Co-author: Assassination and Political Violence, 1970. Served with U.S. Army, 1957-59. Mem. ABA (antitrust sect., litigation sect.), State Bar Calif., Am. Coll. Trial Lawyers. Clubs: Bohemian; Pacific Union (San Francisco). Home: 2239 Green St San Francisco CA 94123 Office: Pillsbury Madison & Sutro 225 Bush St San Francisco CA 94104

KIRKLAND, JUNE ANN, lawyer; b. Chgo., Apr. 5, 1944; d. Herbert Emerson and Anne Lee (White) Butts; m. Gene Benjamin McClure, July 9, 1963 (div. June 1974); 1 child, Meredith Ann; m. Edward Franklin Kirkland, Mar. 19, 1976 (div. July 1986); children: Kerry Lee, Christina Audrey. Student, Emory U., 1961-63, U. Md., 1964-65; BA, Colo. State U., 1967; JD, Emory U., 1972. Bar: Ga. 1972. Assoc. Troutman, Sanders, Lockerman & Ashmore, Atlanta, 1973-82, ptnr., 1982—. Contbr. articles to profl. jours. Named one of Outstanding Young Women of Am., 1980. Mem. Ga. Bar Assn. (sec. 1981-82, chmn.-elect 1982-83, chmn. 1983-84, chmn. antitrust sect. 1982-83, 83-84), Fed. Bar Assn. (chmn. constn. and by laws com. 1982-83, chmn. antitrust programs and pubs. com. 1979-83, nat. council 1979—, various other coms., Dist. Service award 1981, 82, 83). Antitrust, Federal civil litigation, State civil litigation. Home: 5610 Whitner Dr NW Atlanta GA 30327 Office: 127 Peachtree St NE 1400 Candler Bldg Atlanta GA 30043

KIRKLAND, THOMAS LEE, JR., lawyer; b. Meridian, Miss., Jan. 8, 1953; s. Thomas Lee and Eloise (Walker) K.; m. Mary Gayle Blackledge, Aug. 13, 1977; 1 child, Thomas Lee III. AA with honors, Meridian Jr. Coll., 1973; BA with honors, Miss. State U., 1975; JD, U. Miss., 1978. Bar: Miss. 1978, U.S. Dist. Ct. (no. and so. dists.) Miss. 1978, U.S. Ct. Appeals (5th cir.) 1978. Ptnr. Satterfield & Allred, Jackson, Miss., 1978—. Named one of Outstanding Young Men Am., 1982; H.M. Ivy scholar. Mem. ABA, Miss. Bar Assn., Assn. Trial Lawyers Am., Mid-Continent Oil & Gas Lawyers Assn., Def. Research Inst., Phi Delta Phi. Baptist. Oil and gas leasing, Federal civil litigation, Insurance. Home: 2010 Petit Bois Jackson MS 39211 Office: Satterfield & Allred 1000 Peoples Bank Bldg 120 N Congress St Jackson MS 39157 also: PO Drawer 1120 Jackson MS 39215

KIRKMAN, REYMOND FAUCHE, III, lawyer; b. Chgo., Feb. 13, 1940; s. Reymond Fauche Jr. and Sara (Foorman) K. Student, Macalester Coll., 1958-59; BA, U. Minn., 1962, JD, 1966. Bar: Minn. 1966, U.S. Dist. Ct. Minn. 1966, U.S. Supreme Ct. 1969, Calif. 1978, U.S. Dist. Ct. (so. dist.) Calif. 1983. Project mgr. Knutson Co., Mpls., 1971-73; v.p. Atty.'s Title Fund, Mpls., 1973-76; investor San Diego, 1976-79; v.p. Am. Fed. Fin., San Diego, 1979-82; sole practice San Diego, 1982-83; chief counsel real estate Litton Industries, Beverly Hills, Calif., 1983—. Served as comdr. USNR, 1967—. Mem. Calif. Bar Assn., Los Angeles County Bar Assn. (real estate sect.). Methodist. Real property. Office: Litton Industries 360 N Crescent Dr Beverly Hills CA 90210

KIRKMAN, ROBERT AKERIDGE, JR., lawyer; b. San Diego, Jan. 24, 1954; s. Robert Akeridge Sr. and Mary (Archer) K. BA cum laude, UCLA, 1975; JD, U. of Pacific, 1981. Bar: Calif. 1981, Nev. 1982, U.S. Dist. Ct. Nev. 1982, U.S. Ct. Appeals (9th cir.) 1984. Staff atty. Nev. Supreme Ct., Carson City, Nev., 1982-84; dep. atty. gen. Nev. Atty. Gen., Carson City, 1984—. Contbr. Sta. KNPB, 1986. Mem. ABA. Republican. Avocations: golf, racquetball, skiing. Administrative and regulatory, State civil litigation. Home: 820 W 4th St Carson City NV 89701 Office: Nev Atty Gen Capitol Complex Carson City NV 89710

KIRKMAN, WILLIAM LOUIS, lawyer; b. Walla Walla, Wash., Dec. 10, 1951; s. Robert and Margorie (Pifer) K.; m. Susan Lee Morgan, Oct. 16, 1982; children: Katherine Scott, Leslie Ann. BA, Tex. Christian U., 1975; JD, Baylor U., 1978. Bar: Tex. 1978. Ptnr. Godfrey & Decker, Ft. Worth, Tex., 1978—. Mem. ABA, Tex. Bar Assn., Tex. Trial Lawyers Assn. Republican. Baptist. Insurance, Federal civil litigation, State civil litigation. Home: 12 Cliffside Dr Fort Worth TX 76134 Office: Godfrey & Decker 3200 Continential Plaza Bldg Fort Worth TX 76102-5304

KIRKPATRICK, JOHN EVERETT, lawyer; b. Meadville, Pa., Aug. 20, 1929; s. Francis Earl and Marjorie Eloise (Roudebush) K.; m. Patricia Ann Benkert, Aug. 9, 1952 (div. June 1963); children: Amy Eloise, John Scot, Ann; m. Phyllis Jean Daeuble, Aug. 31, 1963. AB, Amherst Coll., 1951; JD, Harvard U., 1954. Bar: Ohio 1955, Ill. 1962. Assoc. Squire, Sanders & Dempsey, Cleve., 1954-61, Kirkland, Ellis, Hodson, Chaffetz & Masters, Chgo., 1962-64; sr. ptnr. Kirkland & Ellis, Chgo., 1965—. Contbr. articles on tax and estate planning to profl. jours. Chmn. Cen. DuPage Hsop. Devel. Commn., Winfield, Ill.; ruling elder 1st PResbyn. Ch., Wheaton, Ill., 1983—. Mem. ABA, Ill. Bar Assn., Chgo. Bar Assn. Republican. Clubs: Chgo. Golf (Wheaton), Mid Am. (Chgo.). Avocation: golf. General corporate, Probate, Estate taxation. Office: Kirkland & Ellis 200 E Randolph Dr Chicago IL 60601

KIRKPATRICK, RICHARD CHARLES, lawyer, retired judge; b. Englewood, Colo., Apr. 10, 1930; s. George Sidney and Bernice Irene (Needles) K.; m. Marjorie Hoefler, 1947 (div. Mar. 1968); children—Richard Charles, Colleen Kirkpatrick Lea; m. Anne Marie Iacelli, Mar. 21, 1969; stepchildren—Laura Nicholas Porter, Diana Nicholas Boswell, Jordana Nicholas Harper. J.D., Southwestern U., Los Angeles, 1964. Bar: U.S. Dist. Ct. (so. and cen. dists.) Calif. 1964, U.S. Supreme Ct. 1983. Ptnr. Kirkpatrick & Biely, Santa Maria, Calif., 1967-68; judge Santa Maria Mcpl. Ct., 1969-74; judge San Luis Obispo County Superior Ct., 1974-82; sole practice, Santa Maria, 1964-67, San Luis Obispo, 1982—; instr. in bus. law Allan Hancock Coll., Santa Maria, 1964-75; prof. law Cen. Coast Law Sch., San Luis Obispo, 1975-80, Calif. State U.-Sacramento, 1980-83; faculty lectr. Calif. Judges Coll., Berkeley, 1977-81. Chpt. v.p. Calif. Rep. Assembly, Santa Maria, 1964, chpt. pres., 1965; chmn. Ronald Reagan Election Com., Santa Maria, 1966; mem. Calif. Rep. Central Com., 1966-69. Mem. Calif. Judges Assn. (chmn. juvenile com. 1977-78), San Luis Obispo County Bar Assn., Calif. Bar Assn., Assn. Trial Lawyers Am., Calif. Trial Lawyers Assn., ABA. Personal injury. Home: 6291 Monterey Ct Atascadero CA 93422 Office: RC Kirkpatrick PLC 1045 Mill St San Luis Obispo CA 93401

KIRKPATRICK, SCOTT LUCILLIOUS, lawyer; b. Memphis, May 15, 1946; s. J.W. and Julia (Twist) K.; m. Jeannie Buckner, Jan. 14, 1969 (div. July 1976); 1 child, Scott L.; m. Narda Mae Mason, Aug. 23, 1976; children: Frank, Holley. BA, Vanderbilt U., 1968, JD, 1971. Bar: Tenn. Assoc. Kirkpatrick & Lucus, Memphis, 1971-77, ptnr., 1977-82; ptnr. Kirkpatrick, Kirkpatrick & Efird, Memphis, 1982—. Chmn. Memphis Alcohol Commn., 1972-82; bd. dirs. YMCA, Memphis, 1985—; gen. counsel Parents Without Ptnrs., Memphis, 1985—. Mem. ABA, Tenn. Def. Lawyers Assn., Tenn. Bar Assn., Memphis and Shelby County Bar Assn. Republican. Methodist. Insurance, Personal injury, Family and matrimonial. Office: Kirkpatrick Kirkpatrick & Efird 100 N Main St Suite 2900 Memphis TN 38103

KIRKSEY, WILLIAM BOYD, lawyer; b. Indianola, Ms., Aug. 7, 1951; s. Arthur Franklin and Mable Inez (Smith) K.; m. Beverly Ann Windham, Jan. 19, 1980; children: Melissa Kaye, Brandon Niles. Student, Delta State U., 1969-72; JD, Miss. Coll., 1975. Bar: Miss. 1976, U.S. Dist. Ct. (no. dist.) Miss. 1976, U.S. Dist. Ct. (so. dist.) Miss. 1977, U.S. Ct. Appeals (5th cir.) 1978, U.S. Supreme Ct. 1979, U.S. Dist. Ct. (we. dist.) Tenn. 1984. Sole practice Batesville, Ms., 1976-77; ptnr. Binder, Kirksey & DeLaughter, Jackson, Ms., 1977-83, Kirksey & DeLaughter, Jackson, 1983—. Named one of Outstanding Young Men in Am., 1982. Mem. Ms. Bar Assn., Hinds County Bar Assn., Ms. Trial Laywers Assn., Hinds County Trial Lawyers Assn., Ms. Assn. Criminal Def. Lawyers, Nat. Assn. Criminal Def. Lawyers, Jackson Young Lawyers Assn. (chmn. domestic relations arbitration family law mediation sect.), Am. Judicature Soc., Sigma Delta Kappa. Republican. Baptist. Avocation: reading. Criminal, Family and matrimonial, Personal injury. Home: 107 Cumberland Rd Brandon MS 39042 Office: Kirksey & DeLaughter 401 E Capitol at Congress Jackson MS 39205

KIRLIN, ANNE MARGET, lawyer; b. Rochester, Minn., May 7, 1944; d. Miles Justin and Pauline Lillian (Silas) Gillickson; m. John J. Kirlin, Aug. 18, 1968; children: Kristin, Heather. BA in Polit. Sci., Wellesley Coll., 1966; MPA, UCLA, 1967; JD, U. So. Calif., 1976. Bar: Calif. 1977. Researcher Calif. Tort Reform Commn., 1976-77; asst. atty. City of Santa Monica, Calif., 1977-79; assoc. Dickenson, Peatman & Fogarty, Napa, Calif., 1979—. Co-author: Public-Private Bargaining for Calif. Growth, 1982. Pres. Napa Valley Unified Edn. Found., 1986-87. Mem. ABA, Napa County Bar Assn., Napa County Women Lawyers Assn. Local government, Real property, Environment. Home: 2456 3d Ave Napa CA 94558 Office: Dickenson Peatman & Fogarty 809 Coombs St Napa CA 94559

KIRSCH, LAURENCE STEPHEN, lawyer; b. Washington, July 20, 1957; s. Ben and Bertha (Gomberg) K.; m. Celia Goldman, Aug. 19, 1979. BAS, MS, U. Pa., 1979; JD, Harvard U., 1982. Bar: D.C. 1982, U.S. Ct. Appeals (3d cir.) 1983, U.S. Dist. Ct. D.C. 1985, U.S. Ct. Appeals (D.C. cir.) 1985, U.S. Supreme Ct. 1987. Law clk. to presiding judge Pa. Dist. Ct., Phila., 1982-83; vis. asst. prof. law U. Bridgeport (Conn.) Law Sch., 1983-84; assoc. Cadwalader, Wickersham & Taft, Washington, 1984—. Editor-in-chief Indoor Pollution Law Reporter, 1987—; contbr. articles to profl. jours. Mem. ABA, Fed. Bar Assn., AAAS, Air Pollution Control Assn. (indoor air quality com.), Environ. Law Inst., Nat. Inst. Bldg. Scis. (indoor air quality com.), Am. Soc. Testing and Measurement (indoor air quality com.), Phi Beta Kappa. Environment, Administrative and regulatory, Federal civil litigation. Home: 5911 Gloster Rd Bethesda MD 20816 Office: Cadwalader Wickersham & Taft 1333 New Hampshire Ave NW Washington DC 20036

KIRSCH, STEVEN JAY, lawyer; b. St. Louis, Aug. 31, 1951. BS, U. Mo., 1973; JD, Hamline U., 1976. Bar: Minn. 1976, U.S. Dist. Ct. Minn. 1976, U.S. Ct. Appeals (8th cir.) 1977. Ptnr. Murnane, Conlin, White, Brandt & Hoffman, St. Paul, 1976—; adj. prof. law Hamline U., St. Paul, 1979-83; mem. adv. bd. Advanced Legal Edn., 1982—. Avocations: reading, writing, books, sports. Insurance, Personal injury, Federal civil litigation. Home: 3991 Birch Knoll Dr White Bear MN 55110 Office: Murnane Law Firm One Capital Centre Plaza Saint Paul MN 55102

KIRSCHBAUM, MYRON, lawyer; b. Bklyn., Nov. 20, 1949; s. Jonas and Doris (Rose) K.; m. Esther Weiner, June 23, 1971; children: Rachel, Shoshana, Robert. BA, Yeshiva U., 1971; JD, Harvard U., 1974. Bar: N.Y. 1975, U.S. Dist. Ct. (so. dist.) N.Y. 1975, U.S. Ct. Appeals (2d cir.) 1975. Law clk. U.S. Ct. Appeals (2d cir.), N.Y.C., 1974-75; assoc. Kaye, Scholer, Fierman, Hays & Handler, N.Y.C., 1975-82, ptnr., 1983—. Editor Harvard Law Rev., 1972-73, case and comment editor, 1973-74. Mem. exec. com. Coalition to Free Soviet Jews, N.Y.C., 1985—. Mem. ABA. Federal civil litigation, State civil litigation, Nuclear power. Office: Kaye Scholer Fierman Hays & Handler 425 Park Ave New York NY 10022

KIRSCHNER, LEONARD, lawyer; b. Cin., Feb. 3, 1928; s. Saul and Dorothy Sylvia (Chodash) K.; m. Yolanda Dorothy Negin, Aug. 28, 1960; children—Mark, Steven, Tami, Mindy, Debra, Barry. B.A., U. Cin., 1948, J.D., 1949. Bar: Ohio 1950, U.S. Dist. Ct. (so. and no. dists.) Ohio, U.S. Ct. Appeals (6th cir.) 1950, U.S. Supreme Ct. 1953. Sole practice, Cin., 1950—; asst. pros. atty. Criminal div. Hamilton County, Ohio, 1951-66, chief asst. pros. atty. Appellate div., 1966—; spl. prosecuter Village of Evendale, Ohio, 1974—, solicitor, 1980—; lectr. in field. Mem. ABA, Ohio State Bar Assn., Cin. Bar Assn., Fed. Bar Assn., Am. Judicature Soc., Nat. Assn. Dist. Attys., Ohio Assn. Pros. Attys. (Outstanding Asst. Pros. Atty. award 1979-80). Republican. Jewish. Clubs: B'nai B'rith, Masons. Criminal, General practice. Office: 10 W 9th St Cincinnati OH 45202

KIRSCHNER, PAUL DAVID, lawyer; b. Seattle, Dec. 2, 1955; s. Manuel and Sally Sarah (Kolberg) K. BBA, U. Wash., 1978; JD, Southwestern U., 1981. Bar: Wash. 1981, U.S. Dist. Ct. (we. dist.) Wash. 1981. Sole practice Seattle, 1981—. Avocations: golf, soccer, snow and water skiing, basketball. Personal injury, Probate, General corporate.

KIRSCHNER, RICHARD, lawyer; b. Phila., Apr. 3, 1932; s. Walter and Rebekah (Muller) K.; m. Beverly Yanoff, June 7, 1953; children—Stefi Lynn, Lee Scott, Linda Sue, Jason Alan; m. M. Kay Gartrell, July 30, 1978; 1 dau., Meredith Anne. B.A., Pa. State U., 1954; J.D., U. Pa., 1957. Bar: Pa. 1958, D.C. 1982. Practice labor law, 1958—; sr. ptnr. Kirschner Weinberg & Dempsey, Washington, 1982—; adj. prof. labor law Temple U., Phila., 1976-82; lectr., speaker in field. Mem. ABA, Pa. Bar Assn., Phila. Bar Assn., D.C. Bar Assn. Author articles on labor law. Labor. Office: 1615 L St NW Washington DC 20036

KIRSHBAUM, HOWARD M., judge; b. Oberlin, Ohio, Sept. 19, 1938; s. Joseph and Gertrude (Morris) K.; m. Priscilla Joy Parmakian, Aug. 15, 1964;

children—Audra Lee, Andrew William. B.A., Yale U., 1960; A.B., Cambridge U., 1962, M.A., 1966; LL.B., Harvard U., 1965. Ptnr. Zarlengo and Kirshbaum, Denver, 1969-75; judge Denver Dist. Ct., Denver, 1975-80, Colo. Ct. Appeals, Denver, 1980-83; justice Colo. Supreme Ct., Denver, 1983—; adj. prof. law U. Denver, 1972—; dir. Colo. Jud. Inst., Denver, Am. Law Inst. Phila., Am. Judicature Soc., Chgo., 1983-85; pres. Colo. Legal Care Soc., Denver, 1974-75. Bd. dirs. Young Artists Orch., Denver, 1976-85; pres. Community Arts Symphony, Englewood, Colo., 1972-74; dir. Denver Opportunity, Inc., Denver, 1972-74; vice-chmn. Denver Council on Arts and Humanities, 1969. Mem. ABA, Denver Bar Assn. (trustee 1981-83), Colo. Bar Assn., Colo. Bar Found., Am. Judicature Soc. Avocations: music performance; tennis. Judicial administration. Office: Colo Supreme Ct Two E 14th Ave Denver CO 80203

KIRSHNER, ROBERT ALAN, lawyer; b. Phila., June 18, 1955; s. Howard Aaron and Harriet (Elias) K. BA, U. Pa., 1976, MA, 1976; JD, Am. U., 1979. Bar: D.C. 1980, U.S. Supreme Ct. 1984. Assoc. environ counsel Nat. Forest Products Assn., Washington, 1980-85, environ. counsel, gen. counsel, 1986—. Mem. ABA. Republican. Office: Nat Forest Products Assn. 1250 Connecticutt Ave NW Washington DC 20036

KIRSNER, KENNETH STEPHEN, lawyer; b. Bklyn., Dec. 6, 1943; s. Isaac and Helen (Dickman) K.; m. Isabelle Goldstein, May 28, 1967; children: Deborah Ruth, Kevin Brian, Eric Howard. BS in Fin., L.I. Univ., 1965; JD, SUNY, Buffalo, 1968; postgrad., NYU Sch. Law, 1969-72. Bar: N.Y. 1968, Ill. 1974. Counsel to corp. sec. Kraft, Inc., N.Y.C., 1969-72; counsel to corp. sec. Kraft, Inc., Glenview, Ill., 1972-74, asst. sec., 1974-81, sr. atty., 1979-81; assoc. counsel, asst. sec. Dart & Kraft, Inc., Northbrook, Ill., 1981-82; sr. security counsel, asst. sec. Dart & Kraft, Inc., Northbrook, 1982-86; sr. corp. counsel, asst. sec. Kraft Inc., Glenview, 1986—. Mem. ABA, Ill. Bar Assn., Am. Soc. Corp. Secs. General corporate, Securities. Home: 1760 Overland Ct Deerfield IL 60015 Office: Kraft Inc Kraft Ct Glenview IL 60025

KIRTLEY, JANE ELIZABETH, professional society administrator; b. Indpls., Nov. 7, 1953; d. William Raymond and Faye Marie (Price) K.; m. Stephen Jon Cribari, May 8, 1985. BS in Journalism, Northwestern U., 1975, MS in Journalism, 1976; JD, Vanderbilt U., 1979. Bar: N.Y. 1980, U.S. Dist. Ct. (we. dist.) N.Y. 1980, D.C. 1982, U.S. Dist. Ct. D.C. 1982, U.S. Ct. Appeals (4th cir.) 1982, U.S. Ct. Claims 1982, U.S. Ct. Appeals (D.C. cir.) 1985, U.S. Supreme Ct. 1985. Assoc. Nixon, Hargrave, Devans & Doyle, Rochester, N.Y., 1979-81, Washington, 1981-84; exec. dir. Reporters Com. for Freedom of Press, Washington, 1985—; mem. adv. com. Nat. Network for Right to Counsel, Boston, 1986. Exec. articles editor Vanderbilt Jour. Transnat. Law, 1978-79; editor The News Media and The Law, 1985—, The First Amendment Handbook, 1987; edit. bd. dirs. Govt. Info. Quar. Bd. dirs. First Amendent Congress, Boulder; mem. steering com. Libel Def. Resource Ctr., N.Y.C. Mem. ABA, N.Y. State Bar Assn., D.C. Bar Assn., Sigma Delta Chi. Libel, First Amendment-News Media Law. Home: 724 Franklin St Alexandria VA 22314 Office: Reporters Com Freedom of Press 800 18th St NW Suite 300 Washington DC 20006

KIRVEN, GERALD, lawyer; b. Augusta, Ga., Apr. 26, 1922; s. Ceil LaCoste and Miriam Creber (Gerald) K.; m. Cara Carter Fisken, Sept. 11, 1948; children: James F., Cara M. Kirven Cox, Christine Y., Alfred C., Mary Lea. AB, U. Va., 1944; LL.B. cum laude, U. Louisville, 1948. Bar: Ky. 1948, U.S. Dist. Ct. (we. dist.) Ky. 1949, Calif. 1953, U.S. Dist. Ct. (ea. dist.) Ky. 1954, U.S. Ct. Appeals (6th cir.) 1954, U.S. Supreme Ct. 1975. Assoc. Bullitt, Dawson & Tarrant, Louisville, 1948-50; law clk. U.S. Dist. Ct. (we. dist.) Ky., 1953; assoc. Middleton, Seelbach, Wolford, Willis & Cochran, Louisville, 1953-80, ptnr., 1958-80; sr. ptnr. Baird, Kirven, Westfall & Talbott, Louisville, 1980-85; of counsel Greenebaum Young Treitz & Maggiolo, 1985—; instr. law U. Louisville, 1959, 64, 85—. V.p., bd. dirs. Arthritis Found., 1960,; pres., v.p. dir. Mental Health Assn., Ky., 1970—, pres., 1980-81; v.p., vice-chmn., bd. dirs. Seven Counties Services, 1978-81. Served to lt. comdr. USNR, 1943-46, 50-53. Recipient Disting. Service award Arthritis Found., 1961. Mem. ABA, Fed. Bar Assn., Ky. Bar Assn., State Bar Calif., Louisville Bar Assn. (past mem. exec. com.) Jud. Conf. U.S. 6th Cir., Phi Beta Kappa, Omicron Delta Kappa. Republican. Episcopalian. Clubs: Louisville Boat, Tavern (Louisville). General practice. Office: Greenebaum Young et al 2700 First National Tower 101 S Fifth St Louisville KY 40202-3174

KIRWAN, ALLAN AUGUST, bar executive; b. Washington, July 28, 1945; s. Edward Emmett and Eleanor Godwin (West) K.; m. Diane Pearson, Sept. 23, 1968; children—Kevin John, Nathan Stuart. Student Gordon Mil. Coll., 1965; A.A., DeKalb Coll., 1966; B.A., Oglethorpe U., 1968; M.B.A., U. Ga., 1969. Mgmt. and budget analyst DeKalb County, Decatur, Ga., 1970-76; asst. exec. dir. State Bar Ga., Atlanta, 1976-81, exec. dir., 1981—. Founder, pres. Avondale Community Action, Avondale Estates, Ga., 1982—, editor monthly newsletter, 1982-85; chmn. Avondale Estates Planning and Zoning Bd., 1980-83; co-founder Avondale Estates Gentlemen's Sporting & Philosophical Soc., 1986—; mayor City of Avondale Estates; curriculum advisor Dekalb Coll.; mem. Avondale Devel. Authority. Recipient Outstanding Alumnus award DeKalb Community Coll., 1984, Merit award City of Avondale Estates, 1984. Mem. Nat. Assn. Bar Execs., Am. Soc. Assn. Execs. Baptist. Clubs: Avondale Community, Avondale Swim and Tennis (pres. 1980). Home: 9 Avondale Plaza Avondale Estates GA 30002 Office: 800 the Hurt Bldg 45 Edgewood Ave SE Atlanta GA 30303

KISER, JACKSON L., federal judge; b. June 24, 1929; m. Carole Gorman; children: Jackson, William, John Michael, Elizabeth Carol. B.A., Concord Coll., 1951; J.D., Washington and Lee U., 1952. Bar: Va. Asst. U.S. atty. Western Dist. Va., 1958-61; assoc., then ptnr. R.R. Young, Young, Kiser, Haskins, Mann, Gregory & Young P.C., Martinsville, Va., 1961; now judge U.S. Dist. Ct. (we. dist.) Va. Mem. Martinsville City Sch. Bd., 1971-77. Served with JAGC, U.S. Army, 1952-54; served to capt. USAR, 1955-61. Mem. ABA, Am. Coll. Trial Lawyers (state com.), Va. Bar Assn. (exec. com.), Va. State Bar, Va. Trial Lawyers Assn., 4th Cir. Jud. Conf. (permanent mem.), Martinsville-Henry County Bar Assn., Order of Coif. State civil litigation, Federal civil litigation. Office: US Dist Ct PO Box 3326 Danville VA 24543 *

KISSANE, THOMAS, criminologist, educator; b. Bronx, N.Y., Mar. 14, 1927; s. James M. and Elizabeth (Sheridan) K.; B.S., John Jay Coll., 1969; M.S. Ed., Iona Coll., 1979; postgrad. Fordham U.; m. Marion O'Shea, Nov. 18, 1950; 4 children. With N.Y.C. Police Dept., 1949-74, capt., 1965-74; dir. cargo theft program U. Louisville, 1975-76; asst. prof. Iona Coll., New Rochelle, N.Y., 1976—; dir. staff services dept. public safety City of White Plains (N.Y.), 1983-85; cons. on criminal receiving U.S. Senate Com. Mem. Bd. Police Commrs., Town of Eastchester, N.Y. Named Man of Yr., N.Y. State Motor Truck Assn., 1974, Nat. Assn. Former State Troopers, 1972. Mem. Capts. Endowment Assn., Nat. Assn. Former State Troopers, Ret. Detectives Assn., Am. Soc. Indsl. Security, N.Y. Police Dept. Honor Legion. Criminal, Legal education. Office: Iona College Dept Criminal Justice 715 North Ave New Rochelle NY 10801

KISSEL, PETER CHARLES, lawyer; b. Watertown, N.Y., Sept. 29, 1947; s. Laurence Haas and Catherine Cantwell (Weldon) K.; m. Sharon Darlene Murphy, June 14, 1970. A.B., Syracuse U., 1969; J.D., Am. U., 1972. Bar: D.C. 1974, U.S. Dist. Ct. D.C. 1979, U.S. Ct. Appeals (9th cir.) 1979, U.S. Ct. Appeals (D.C. cir.) 1983, U.S. Ct. Claims 1976, U.S. Supreme Ct. 1978, U.S. Ct. Appeals (3d cir.) 1986. Atty.-advisor Fed. Power Commn., Washington, 1972-74; atty. pub. utilities, 1974-77; assoc. O'Connor & Hannan, Washington, 1977-79, ptnr., 1979—; co-bus. mgr. Energy Law Jour., Washington, 1981, asst. editor, 1982—; contbr. articles to profl. jours. Mem. vestry St. Patrick's Episcopal Ch., Washington, 1975-78, 82-85, 86—. Recipient Spl. award Fed. Power Commn., 1973. Mem. Bar Assn. D.C., Fed. Energy Bar Assn. (vice chmn. com. on publs. 1984-85), Am. Pub. Power Assn., Natural Gas Roundtable., Phi Kappa Psi. Democrat. Episcopalian. FERC practice, Administrative and regulatory, Federal civil litigation. Home: 5604 Utah Ave NW Washington DC 20015 Office: O'Connor & Hannan 1919 Pennsylvania Ave NW Washington DC 20006

KISSELL, TONY FRED, lawyer; b. Bellows Falls, Vt., Aug. 15, 1923; s. Florian and Antonina (Swekla) K.; married, June 30, 1956; children: Paul A., Ann Marie, Mary Anne, Pamela J., Melissa J. BS, Bradley U., 1949; JD, Ind. U., 1954. Bar: Vt. 1955, U.S. Dist. Ct. Vt. 1955. Ptnr. Kissell & Kissell, Bellows Falls, 1955-72; judge Bellows Falls Mcpl. Ct., 1965-67; sr. ptnr. Kissell & Massucco, Bellows Falls, 1973—; incorporator Savs. Bank Walpole, N.H.; trustee Kenneth & Bessie Ladeau Trust 1970—, Alfred & Kenneth Boule Ednl. Trust, 1983—. Pres. Westminster (Vt.) Inst. Served with USAAF, 1943-46. Mem. Vt. Bar Assn., Windham County Bar Assn. (pres. 1975). Republican. Roman Catholic. Lodge: Elks. Avocations: nature. Probate, Real property, General practice. Office: Kissell & Massucco 90 Westminster St Bellows Falls VT 05101

KITAGAWA, AUDREY EMIKO, lawyer; b. Honolulu, Mar. 31, 1951; s. Yonoichi and Yoshiko (Nagaishi) K. B.A. cum laude, U. So. Calif., 1973; J.D., Boston Coll., 1976. Bar: Hawaii, 1977, U.S. Dist. Ct. Hawaii, 1977. Assoc., Rice, Lee & Wong, Honolulu, 1977-80; sole practice, Honolulu, 1980—. Exec. editor Internat. Law Jour., 1976. Mem. Historic Hawaii Found., 1984. Mem. Hawaii Bar Assn., ABA, Assn. Trial Lawyers Am., Japan-Hawaii Lawyers Assn. (v.p. 1982—), Law Office Mgmt. Discussion Group, Hawaii Lawyers Care, Phi Alpha Delta. Republican. Club: Honolulu. Family and matrimonial. Office: 820 Mililani St Suite 615 Honolulu HI 96813

KITCHEL, JAN KELLY, lawyer; b. Hood River, Oreg., Aug. 14, 1951; s. William Howard and Marguerite Mary (Kelly) K.; m. Christine Kosse, Oct. 17, 1982; children: Kelly Catherine, Molly Jane. BS, Oreg. State U., 1973; JD cum laude, Willamette U., 1978. Bar: Oreg. 1978, Washington 1983. Ptnr. Schwabe, Williamson, Wyatt, Moore & Roberts, Portland, Oreg., 1978—. Mem. ABA, Oreg. Bar Assn., Wash. State Bar Assn., Multnomah County Bar Assn., Clark County Bar Assn. Republican. Presbyterian. Club: Multnomah Athletic (Portland). Avocations: skiing, hiking. Personal injury, Insurance, State civil litigation. Office: Schwabe Williamson Wyatt Moore & Roberts 1211 SW 5th Ave Suite 1700 Portland OR 97204

KITCHEN, CHARLES WILLIAM, lawyer; b. Cleve., July 17, 1926; s. Karl K. and Lucille W. (Keynes) K.; m. Mary Applegate, July 22, 1950; children—Kenneth K., Guy R., Ann Kitchen Campbell. B.A., Western Res. U., 1948; J.D., 1950. Bar: Ohio 1950, U.S. Dist. Ct. Ohio 1952, U.S. Ct. Appeals (6th cir.) 1972, U.S. Supreme Ct. 1981. Ptnr., Kitchen, Messner & Deery and predecessor, Cleve., 1950—, mng. ptnr., 1972—. Mem. Citizens League, Greater Cleve. Growth Assn.; vice chmn. Regional Council on Alcoholism, 1981-85, chmn., 1985-86. Served with A.C., U.S. Army, 1944-45. Fellow Am. Coll. Trial Lawyers (life del. 8th Ohio Jud. Conf.); mem. Am. Arbitration Assn. (panelist 1961—), Cleve. Assn. Civil Trial Attys. (pres. 1971-72), Ohio Assn. Civil Trial Attys. (pres. 1975-76, Greater Cleve. Bar Assn. (chmn. med.-legal com. 1974-75, chmn. lawyers assistance program 1981-83, trustee 1984—), Ohio Bar Assn. (Ho. of Dels. 1977-80), ABA, Def. Research Inst., Internat. Assn. Def. Counsel (med. malpractice com. 1982—, def. counsel com. 1986—), Am. Judicature Soc., Am. Soc. Hosp. Attys. of Am. Hosp. Assn., Am. Legion, Order of Coif, Beta Theta Pi, Phi Delta Phi. Presbyterian. Club: Westwood Country (Rocky River, Ohio). Lodge: Masons. State civil litigation. Home: 28949 Turnbridge Rd Bay Village OH 44140 Office: Kitchen Messner & Deery 1100 Illuminating Bldg 55 Public Sq Cleveland OH 44113

KITCHEN, JAMES DENNY, lawyer; b. Ross County, Ohio, Nov. 12, 1939; s. Noland Dwight and Tella Gwendolyn Theoline (Denehue) K. BBA, Ohio U., 1967; JD, Ohio State U., 1970. Ptnr. Leist & Kitchen, Circleville, Ohio, 1970-85, Young, Tootle & Kitchen, Circleville, 1985—; tchr. adult edn. Pickaway-Ross Vocat. Sch., Ross County, Ohio, 1983-84. Mem. Circleville-Pickaway Community Improvement Corp., 1985—, community devel. adv. council Circleville Bible Coll.; trustee Ctr. Ind. Living, Columbus, Ohio, Ohio Twp. Assn., Circleville. Mem. ABA, Columbus Bar Assn., Pickaway County Bar Assn. (pres. 1981), Pickaway County Law Library Assn. (sec. 1973—), Ohio Farm Bur. Assn., Circleville C. of C. Democrat. Episcopalian. Lodges: Rotary, Masons (master 1967-68, dist. dep., grand master 1970-72). Avocations: studying folk art, Am. decorative arts. General practice, Probate. Home: PO Box 505 Adelphi OH 43101 Office: Young Tootle & Kitchen 180 W Franklin St PO Box 27 Circleville OH 43113

KITCHEN, JOHN SCOTT, lawyer; b. Indpls., July 28, 1947; s. John Milton and Jane (Rauch) K.; m. Janice Hinkle; children: John Milton III, Henry Thomas William. BA, Williams Coll., 1969; JD, Boston U., 1973. Bar: N.H. 1974, U.S. Dist. Ct. N.H. 1974, U.S. Ct. Appeals (1st cir.) 1977, U.S. Supreme Ct. 1977. Asst. atty. gen. N.H. Atty. Gen.'s Office, Concord, 1975-77; prin. Law Offices of John S. Kitchen, Laconia, N.H., 1980—; spl. justice Loudon (N.H.) Mcpl. Ct., 1978—. Mem. ABA, N.H. Bar Assn., Belknap County Bar Assn., N.H. Judges Assn. Probate, State civil litigation, Federal civil litigation. Office: 395 Main St Laconia NH 03246

KITCHEN, JONATHAN SAVILLE, lawyer; b. Lincoln, Eng., UK, June 7, 1948; s. Walter Lawrence Michael and Helen Margaret (Hastings) K.; m. Nina Hatvany; children: Natalie, Vanessa, Paul. Student, Strasbourg U., France, 1966-67; BA with honors, Durham U., 1970; LLM, Univ. Coll., 1971; MA, Cambridge U., Eng., 1974, PhD, 1976. Bar: UK 1977, Calif. 1978, U.S. Dist. Ct. (no. dist.) Calif. 1978, U.S. Ct. Appeals (9th cir.) 1979, U.S. Ct. Appeals (7th cir.) 1981, U.S. Supreme Ct. 1982. Assoc. McCutchen, Doyle, Brown & Enersen, San Francisco, 1977-81; assoc. Baker & McKenzie, San Francisco, 1981-85, ptnr., 1985—; prof. Internat. Sch. for Study of Comparative Labor Law, Trieste, Italy, 1972-73; mem. City Council, Cambridge, 1972-74. Contbr. numerous articles to profl. jours. Duke of Edinburgh scholar Inner Temple, 1970, Evan Lewis-Thomas scholar Sydney Sussex Coll., Cambridge, 1972-74, Fulbright scholar, 1975-76; Bodosakis fellow, Churchill Coll., 1974-77, faculty research fellow Churchill Coll., 1977. Mem. ABA, Calif. Bar Assn., Bar Assn. of San Francisco. Club: St. Francis Yacht (San Francisco). Avocations: sailing, skiing. Federal civil litigation, State civil litigation. Office: Baker & McKenzie 580 California St #500 San Francisco CA 94104

KITE, RICHARD LLOYD, lawyer, real estate development company executive; b. Chgo., Jan. 26, 1934; s. Leonard Robert and Idelle (Berss) K.; m. Iris Goldberg, Aug. 26, 1984; children—Lawrence, Daniel, Jill. B.S. with highest honors in Bus. Adminstrn. and Acctg., UCLA, 1955, J.D., 1958. Bar: Wis. 1964, Calif. 1959. Sole practice, Beverly Hills, Calif., 1959-64; pres. Marcus Theatres Corp., Milw., 1964-80; pres. Kite Devel. Corp., Milw., 1980—; pres. Kite Investment Corp.; sec.-treas., trustee Regency Investors, 1982-83; v.p., sec., dir., chief legal counsel Marcus Corp., 1964-81; dir. Mid-Continental Bancorp., Milw., Am. Hampton Bank, Milw., Guardian State Bank, Milw., Continental Bank and Trust, Milw., Mid-Am. Bank, Milw. Pres. Variety Club of Wis., 1978-79, bd. dirs., 1964—; sec., bd. dirs. Mt. Sinai Glendale Health Ctr., Milw.; hon. bd. dirs. Ballet Found. Milw., Inc.; bd. govs. Wis. Israel Bonds Com., Milw. Jewish Fedn.; pres., bd. dirs. Wis. chpt., trustee Am. Friends Hebrew U. Mem. Young Pres.'s Orgn., Internat. Council Shopping Ctrs., Order of Coif. Editor UCLA Law Rev., 1957-58. Real property, Personal income taxation, General corporate. Office: 324 E Wisconsin Ave Milwaukee WI 53202

KITE, STEVEN B., lawyer; b. Chgo., May 30, 1949; s. Ben and Dolores (Braver) K.; m. Catherine Lapinski, Jan. 13, 1980; children: David, Julia. BA, U. Ill., 1971; JD, Harvard U., 1974. Bar: Ga. 1974, U.S. Dist. Ct. Ga. 1974, U.S. Ct. Appeals (5th and 11th cirs.) 1981, Ill. 1985, Fla. 1986. Ptnr. Kutak, Rock & Campbell, Atlanta, 1974-84, Gardner, Carton & Douglas, Chgo., 1984—. Author, editor: Law For Elderly, 1978. Bd. dirs. Atlanta Legal Aid Soc., 1979-84; trustee Sr. Citizens Met. Atlanta, 1980-83. Mem. ABA, Ill. Bar Assn., State Bar Ga., Atlanta Bar Assn., Chgo. Bar Assn. Club: Atlanta City. Avocations: travel, sports, reading. Municipal bonds. Office: Gardner Carton & Douglas 1 First Nat Bank Plaza Suite 3300 Chicago IL 60603

KITTA, JOHN NOAH, lawyer; b. San Francisco, Aug. 26, 1951; s. John E. and Norma Jean (Noah) K. BS, U. Santa Clara, 1973, JD, 1976. Bar: Calif. 1976. Asst. mgr. Transamerica Title Co., Dublin, Calif., 1977-78; assoc. Rhodes, McKeehan & Bernard, Fremont, Calif., 1978-79; sole practice Fremont, 1979—. Commr. Calif. Crime Resistance Task Force, Sacramento; trustee Alameda County Bd. Edn.; del. Dem. Cen. Com., Alameda County, 1980-81, 83-84. Democrat. Real property, General corporate, Personal injury. Home: 2135 Ocaso Camino Fremont CA 94539 Office: 39261 Liberty St Fremont CA 94538

KITTLER, LESLIE HOWARD, lawyer, petroleum exploration executive; b. Chgo., Oct. 5, 1940; s. Leslie John and Olga Elaine (Johnson) K.; m. Karen Lynn Black, June 25, 1963; children—Kurt Douglas, Kimber Lee. B.A. in History and Econs., Coe Coll., 1963; J.D., U. Minn., 1966. Bar: Minn. 1966, Tex. 1984. Ptnr., Rice & Efron, Mpls., 1966-73; v.p., mng. dir. Efron & Kittler, Mpls., 1973-76, Henson & Efron, Mpls., 1976-82; v.p. ACC Exploration Co., Liberty, Tex., 1982-84; pres. North Star Exploration Co., Humble, Tex., 1984—; cons. atty. for various oil and gas ind. operators, Houston, 1982-84. Bd. dirs., v.p. Bay Lake Improvement Assn. Minn., 1976-83; v.p. Parents Assn., Sam Houston U., Huntsville, Tex., 1984; pres. Walden Homeowners Assn., Houston, 1985-87. Leo Novak scholar U. Minn. Law Sch., 1963-66. Mem. Minn. Bar Assn., Tex. Bar Assn. Republican. Lutheran. Oil and gas leasing. Home: 18607 Walden Forest Dr Humble TX 77346 Office: North Star Exploration Co PO Box 2316 Humble TX 77347

KITTLESON, HENRY MARSHALL, lawyer; b. Tampa, Fla., May 13, 1929; s. Edgar O. and Ardath (Ayers) K.; m. Barbara Clark, Mar. 20, 1954; 1 dau., Laura Helen. B.S. with high honors, U. Fla., 1951, J.D. with high honors, 1953. Bar: Fla. 1953. Partner Holland & Knight, Lakeland and Bartow, Fla., 1955—; mem. adv. bd. Fla. Fed. Savs. & Loan Assn., 1974-86; mem. Fla. Law Revision Commn., 1967-76, vice chmn., 1969-71; mem. Gov.'s Property Rights Study Commn., 1974-75, Nat. Conf. Commrs. Uniform State Laws, 1982—. Mem. council U. Fla. Law Center, 1974-77. Served to maj. USAF, 1953-55. Fellow Am. Bar Found.; mem. ABA (chmn. standing com. on ethic and profl. responsibility 1980-81), Am. Law Inst., Am. Coll. Real Estate Lawyers, Fla. Bar (chmn. standing com. profl. ethics 1965-66, tort litigation rev. commn. 1983-84), Blue Key, Sigma Phi Epsilon, Phi Delta Phi, Phi Kappa Phi, Beta Gamma Sigma. Democrat. Presbyterian. Clubs: Lakeland Yacht and Country, Tampa. Real property. Mailing Address: PO Drawer BW Lakeland FL 33802 Home: 5334 Woodhaven Ln Lakeland FL 33803 Office: 92 Lake Wire Dr Lakeland FL 33802

KITTS, DEAN CARSON, lawyer, mfg. co. exec.; b. Matheson, Ont., Can., Dec. 9, 1934; s. James and Evelyn (Carson) K.; m. Elizabeth Ann Brawley, May 24, 1958; children—Dean, Robert, Mary. B.Sc. in Chem. Engring, U. Toronto, 1958; LL.B., Osgoode Hall, 1963. Bar: Called to Ont. bar 1963, named Queen's counsel 1979. Asso. firm Cavanagh & Norman (patent agts.), Toronto, Ont., 1963-64; corp. counsel John Labatt Ltd., London, Ont., 1966-81; v.p. John Labatt Ltd., 1971-81, sec., 1971—, v.p. adminstrn., gen. counsel, 1981—. Mem. Assn. Profl. Engrs. Ont., Canadian, Am. bar assns., Patent and Trade Mark Inst. Can. Clubs: London, St. Thomas Golf and Country. Home: 8 Drake St, Saint Thomas, ON Canada N5R 2H5 Office: 451 Ridout St N, London, ON Canada N6A 5L3

KITZMILLER, WILLIAM MICHAEL, government official; b. Bryn Mawr, Pa., Mar. 29, 1931; s. Richard Dale Kitzmiller and Virginia Hanford (Jones) Hedges; m. Lynn Grey Fisher, Dec. 31, 1955; children—Virginia Grey, Elizabeth Curtiss, Katherine Dale. B.A., Yale U., 1954, postgrad., 1956-57. Account exec. Selvage & Lee, Inc., N.Y.C., 1959-65; legis. asst. Congressman Richard L. Ottinger, Washington, 1965-68; press asst. V.P. Hubert H. Humphrey, Washington, 1968; pub. affairs dir. Nat. Commn. on Product Safety, Washington, 1968; exec. dir. Grassroots, Inc., Washington, 1968-71; exec. sec. Rep. Ogden R. Reid, Washington, 1971-74; freelance writer 1974-75; communications dir. Westchester County, White Plains, N.Y., 1975-76; staff coordinator Com. on Energy and Commerce U.S. Ho. of Reps., Washington, 1976-84, staff dir. Com. on Energy and Commerce, 1984—. Author: What Every Woman Should Know About the Environment: A Guide to Global Housekeeping, 1970; Citizen Action: Vital Force for Change, 1971; United State Trade Relations with Japan and China, 1979, 2d edit., 1983; editor: Energy and Helium: A Crisis in Future Energy Technology, 1979, China's Economic Development and U.S. Trade Interests, 1985. Contbr. artices to profl. jours. Mem. Sea Space Symposium (Ruby award 1985). Democrat. Club: Elizabethan. Avocations: sailing; chess; diving. Home: 335 10th St NE Washington DC 20002 Office: Com on Energy & Commerce 2125 Rayburn House Office Bldg Washington DC 20515

KIVELSON, NANCY LYNN, lawyer; b. N.Y.C., June 11, 1951; d. Arnold Joseph and Clare Ruth (Frieman) K.; m. Thomas Franklin Angstadt, Jan. 3, 1980; 1 child, Jordan C. BA, Brandeis U., 1972; JD, Boston U., 1975; LLM in Taxation, NYU, 1978. Bar: N.Y.1976, Tex. 1980. Assoc. Bell, Wolkowitz, Beckman & Klee, N.Y.C., 1976-78, Finley, Kimble, Wagner, Heine & Underberg, N.Y.C., 1978-79, Meyers, Miller, Middleton, Weiner & Warren, Dallas, 1979-81; ptnr. Jones, Day, Reavis & Pogue, Dallas, 1981—. Trustee Dallas Ballet, 1983—; co-chmn. Dallas Ballet Alliance, 1984; mem. Mus. Assocs., Dallas, 1985. Avocations: tennis, travel, dance, lit., food and wine. Real property, Real property finance--conventional and equity, Tax exempt financing. Home: 4711 N Lindhurst Dallas TX 75229 Office: Jones Day Reavis & Pogue 2100 Ross Ave Suite 2300 Dallas TX 75201

KIZER, JOHN FUQUA, lawyer; b. Milan, Tenn., Dec. 22, 1916; s. John William and Janie (Fuqua) K.; m. Virginia Martin Meacham, June 6, 1943; children: John F. Jr., Walter Morris. LLB, U. Va., 1940. Bar: Va. 1939, Tenn. 1940. Ptnr. Drake & Kizer, Milan, 1947-51; commr. fin. and taxation State of Tenn., 1951-52, judge 13th jud. cir., 1952-63; sole practice Milan, 1963-82; ptnr. Kizer, Bonds, Boswell & Crocker, Milan, 1982—. Served to capt. JAGC, U.S. Army, 1942-46. Mem. ABA, Tenn. Bar Assn., Gibson County Bar Assn. Baptist. Banking, General practice, Personal injury. Home: 315 Park Ave Milan TN 38358 Office: Kizer Bonds Boswell & Crocker 100 College Milan TN 38358

KIZZIA, DON BRADLEY, lawyer; b. Mercedes, Tex., Sept. 23, 1954; s. Harold Lee Kizzia and Billie Janet (Gentry) Keyes. BA, Austin Coll., 1977; JD, So. Meth. U., 1981. Bar: U.S. Dist. Ct. (no. dist.) Tex. 1981, U.S. Dist. Ct. (so. dist.) Tex. 1986. Assoc. Strasburger & Price, Dallas, 1981—; mem. faculty El Centro Coll., Dallas, 1986. Mem. ABA, Tex. Bar Assn., Dallas Bar Assn., Tex. Assn. Young Lawyers, Dallas Assn. Young Lawyers. Democrat. Methodist. Federal civil litigation, State civil litigation, Personal injury. Home: 1605 Cemetery Hill Carrollton TX 75007 Office: Strasburger & Price 4300 Interfirst Plaza Dallas TX 75250

KJOS, VICTORIA ANN, lawyer; b. Fargo, N.D., Sept. 17, 1953; d. Orville I. and Annie J. (Tanberg) K. BA, Minot State Coll., 1974; JD, U. N.D., 1977. Bar: Ariz. 1978. Assoc. Jack E. Evans, Ltd., Phoenix, 1977-78, pension and ins. cons., 1978-79; dep. state treas. State of N.D., Bismarck, 1979-80; freelance cons. Phoenix, 1980-81, Anchorage, 1981-82; asst. v.p., v.p., mgr. trust dept. Great Western Bank, Phoenix, 1982-84; assoc. Robert A. Jensen P.C., Phoenix, 1984-86; ptnr. Jensen & Kjos, P.C., Phoenix, 1986—; lectr. in domestic relations. Author: Employee Stock Ownership Plans: A Unique Concept in Corporate Financing and Employee Benefits, 1976; contbr. articles to profl. jours. Mem. Ariz. Dem. Council, Western Pension Conf.; bd. dirs. Arthritis Found., Phoenix, 1986—. Mem. ABA, Ariz. Bar Assn., Maricopa Bar Assn., Assn. Trial Lawyers Am., Ariz. Trial Lawyers Assn., Ariz. Women's Lawyers Assn., NOW, Phi Delta Phi. Lutheran. Club: Phoenix City. Family and matrimonial, Personal injury. Office: Jensen & Kjos PC 3246 N 16th St Phoenix AZ 85016

KLADNEY, DAVID, lawyer; b. N.Y.C., Oct. 25, 1948; s. Rubin and Gloria Anita (Serotick) K.; m. Deborah Bayliss, Aug. 20, 1978; children: Mathew Blair, Blythe Nicole. BA in Journalism, U. Nev., 1972; JD, Calif. Western Sch. of Law, 1977. Bar: Nev. 1977, U.S. Dist. Ct. (no. dist.) Nev. 1977. Sole practice Reno, Nev., 1977—; gen. counsel State of Nev. Employees Assn., Carson City, 1977-81. Writer, producer documentary Nevada Connection, 1973. Legal counsel Make-A-Wish Found. of Nev., Reno, 1984—; chmn. of bd. dirs. Nev. Festival Ballet, Reno, 1984; bd. dirs. Washoe Legal Services, Reno, 1978-79. Served with USAR, 1966-72. Mem. ABA, Nev. Bar Assn., Washoe County Bar Assn., Assn. Trial Lawyers Am. (sustaining), Nev. Trial Lawyers Assn. (bd. dirs. 1979-85; Outstanding Service award 1985), Phi Delta Phi. Avocations: skiing, cycling. Labor, Personal injury, General corporate. Home: 905 Joy Lake Rd Reno NV 89511 Office: 321 S Arlington Ave PO Box 18100 Reno NV 89501

KLAFF, RAMSAY LAING, lawyer; b. N.Y.C., May 18, 1946; d. Philip B. Scheffler and Mary Laing; m. Gary F. Klaff, Apr. 11, 1969; children: Benjamin, Alexandra. BA cum laude, DePaul U., 1977; JD cum laude, U. Chgo., 1980. Bar: Ill. 1980, U.S. Dist. Ct. (no. dist.) Ill. 1981, U.S. Ct. Appeals (7th cir.) 1981. Law clk. to presiding justice U.S. Ct. Appeals (7th cir.), Chgo., 1980-81, chief staff counsel, 1983-85; assoc. Plotkin & Jacobs Ltd., Chgo., 1981-83, 85-86; dep. corp. counsel City of Chgo., 1986—. Mem. ABA, Order of Coif. Local government, Federal civil litigation. Home: 4804 S Woodlawn Ave Chicago IL 60615

KLAFTER, CARY IRA, lawyer; b. Chgo., Sept. 15, 1948; d. Herman Nicholas and Bernice Rose (Maremont) K.; m. Kathleen Ann Kerr, July 21, 1974; children: Anastasia, Benjamin, Eileen. BA, Mich. State U., 1968, MS, 1971; JD, U. Chgo., 1972. Bar: Calif. 1972. Assoc. Morrison & Foerster, San Francisco, 1972-79, ptnr., 1979—. Served to capt. USAR, 1972-78. Mem. Calif Bar Assn. (editor newsletter 1979—, exec. com. bus. law sect. 1986—), Titanic Hist. Soc. Securities, Banking, Municipal bonds. Office: Morrison & Foerster 345 California St 30th Floor San Francisco CA 94105

KLAHR, GARY PETER, lawyer; b. N.Y.C., July 9, 1942; s. Fred and Frieda (Garson) K. Student Ariz. State U., 1958-61; LL.B. with high honors, U. Ariz., 1964. Bar: Ariz. 1967, U.S. Dist. Ct. Ariz. 1967. Assoc., Brazlin & Greene, Phoenix, 1967-68; sr. ptnr. Gary Peter Klahr, P.C., Phoenix, 1968—. Mem. Phoenix City Council, 1974-76; mem. CODAMA, bd. dirs., 1975—, pres. 1980-81; bd. dirs. 7th Step Found., 1978-84, pres. 1980-82; bd. dirs. Tumbleweed Runaway Center, 1972-76; chmn. Citizens Criminal Justice Comn., 1977-78; co-chmn. delinquency subcom. Phoenix Forward Task Force; vol. Juvenile Ct. referee, 1969; vol. adult probation officer; vol. counselor for Dept. Corrections youth programs, Phoenix; ex-officio mem., spl. cons. Phoenix Youth Commn.; mem. citizen adv. council Phoenix Union High Sch. Dist., 1985—; review bd. Phoenix Police Dept., 1985—; bd. dirs. Metro Youth Ctr., 1986—, Service/Employment/Redevel. (SER) Jobs for Progress, Phoenix, 1985—, pres., 1986-87; v.p. local chpt. City of Hope, 1985-86; Justice of the Peace Pro Tem Maricopa County Cts., 1985—; juvenile hearing officer Maricopa County Juvenile Ct., 1985—; v.p., cofounder Community Leadership for Youth Devel. (CLYDE); co-chmn. Phoenix Union High Sch. Citizens Adv. Com., 1970-72; del. Phoenix Together Town Hall on Youth Crime, 1982. Named 1 of 3 Outstanding Young Men Phoenix Jr. C. of C., 1969; Disting. Citizen award Ariz. chapt. ACLU, 1976. Mem. ABA, Ariz. State Bar (past sec., bd. dirs. young lawyers sect., vice chmn. unauthorized practice com. 1984—, mem. other coms.), Maricopa County Bar Assn. (past sec. and bd. dirs. young lawyers sect.), Am. Judicature Soc., Jewish Children's and Family Service, Common Cause, NAACP, Ariz. Consumers Council, Phoenix Jaycees, Order of Coif, Phi Alpha Delta. Democrat. Jewish. Club: B'nai B'rith. Contbr. numerous articles to profl. jours.; asst. editor Ariz. Law Rev. 1963-64. Criminal, Juvenile, Personal injury. Address: 2304 N 15th Ave Phoenix AZ 85007

KLAMEN, MARVIN, lawyer; b. St. Louis, Mar. 12, 1931; s. Charles and Leah (Markovitz) K.; m. Miriam, Klausner, Jan. 2, 1976; children: Karin, Jeffrey; stepchildren: Michael, Richard, Anne. AA, Harris Tchrs. Coll., 1951; AB, Washington U., 1953; LLB, 1955. Bar: Mo. 1955, U.S. dist. ct. (ea. dist.) Mo. 1958, U.S. Tax Ct. 1962, U.S. Ct. Apls. (7th, 8th cirs.) 1971. Sole practice, St. Louis, 1958-79; sr. ptnr. Klamen & Danna, St. Louis, 1979—; mem. attys. com. Mo. Savs. and Loan League, 1960-82. Mem. corp., industry and founds. com. Gateway chpt. Leukemia Soc. Am., Inc.; bd. dirs. St. Louis County Law Library, Ronald McDonald House, Health Club Jewish Community Centers Assn., mem. Bd. Edn., University City, Mo.; mem. Planning and Zoning Commn., Richmond Heights, Mo. Served to capt. JAGC USAF, 1955-58. Recipient Citation, Ronald McDonald House, 1982. Mem. Supreme Ct. Hist. Soc., ABA, (past chmn. coms. gen. practice sect., mem. econs. of bar sect., real estate sect., alternate dispute resolution com.), Mo. Bar Assn. (chmn. spl. com. on info. retrieval), St. Louis County Bar Assn. (mem. law office mgmt. com. bus. law sect.), Bar Assn. Met. St. Louis, DuBourg Soc. St. Louis U. Banking, General practice, Real property. Home: 7 Ridgetop Richmond Heights MO 63117 Office: 7820 Maryland Ave Clayton MO 63105

KLANCNIK, JAMES MICHAEL, lawyer; b. Chgo., July 23, 1942; s. Louis Michael and Dorothy Lucille (Evans) K.; m. Elizabeth Glover Paddock, July 11, 1970; children: James Michael, Margaret E., Gordon P., William D. BA, Amherst Coll., 1964; JD, U. Mich., 1967. Bar: Ill. 1967, U.S. dist. ct. (no. dist.) Ill. 1967, U.S. Supreme Ct. 1974, Tex. 1983, U.S. Tax Ct. 1984. Assoc. Wilson & McIlvaine, Chgo., 1967-74, McDermott, Will & Emery, Chgo., 1975-82; sr. cons. Coopers & Lybrand, Dallas, 1982-84; sole practice, Dallas, 1984—; lectr. employee benefits. Author articles. Trustee, v.p., pres., chmn. Lawrence Hall Sch. for Boys, Chgo., 1974-82. Mem. ABA (com. on employee benefits sect. taxation 1976—, com. on employee benefits and exec. compensation sect. corp. banking and bus. law 1983—, com. on plan terminations, mergers, asset transfers, termination ins. sect. real property, probate and trust law 1984—), Chgo. Bar Assn. (com. on employee benefits 1972-82, chmn. 1978-79), Southwest Pension Conf. Episcopalian. Pension, profit-sharing, and employee benefits. Home: 4174 Glenwick Ln Dallas TX 75205 Office: 15770 Dallas Pkwy Suite 600 Dallas TX 75248

KLAPERMAN, JOEL SIMCHA, lawyer; b. N.Y.C., June 8, 1946; s. Gilbert and Libby (Mindlin) K.; m. Barbara Archer, June 27, 1976; 1 child, Jeremy. BA, Columbia U., 1967, MA, 1969; JD, Harvard U., 1971. Bar: D.C. 1972, N.Y. 1974. Atty. office telecommunications policy The White House, Washington, 1971-73; assoc. Debevoise & Plimpton, N.Y.C., 1973-78; assoc. Shearman & Sterling, N.Y.C., 1979-82, ptnr., 1983—. General corporate, Securities. Home: 200 E 82d St #28A New York NY 10028 Office: Shearman & Sterling 153 E 53d St New York NY 10020

KLAPINSKY, RAYMOND JOSEPH, lawyer; b. Beaver Meadows, Pa., Dec. 7, 1938; s. Michael and Sophia S. (Soroko) K.; m. Dorothy E. Kakavas, July 15, 1961; children: Jennifer, Christopher. BA, U. Del., 1960; JD, George Washington U., 1967. Bar: D.C. 1967, U.S. Ct. Appeals (D.C. cir.) 1967, Pa. 1970, U.S. Supreme Ct. 1976. Trial atty. SEC, Washington, 1967-69; assoc. counsel Wellington Mgmt. Co., Valley Forge, Pa., 1969-75; v.p. law, sec. The Vanguard Group Investment Cos., Valley Forge, 1975-86, sr. v.p. law, sec., 1986—. Served to capt. USMC, 1960-64. Mem. Pa. Bar Assn., D.C. Bar Assn. Republican. Roman Catholic. Avocations: sports, golf, fishing. Securities, General corporate. Home: 180 Woodhill Ln Media PA 19063 Office: The Vangard Group 1300 Morris Dr PO Box 876 Valley Forge PA 19482

KLASKO, HERBERT RONALD, lawyer, educator, writer; b. Phila., Nov. 26, 1949; s. Leon Louis and Estelle Lorraine (Baratz) K.; m. Marjorie Ann Becker, Aug. 27, 1977; children: Brett Andrew, Kelli Lynn. BA, Lehigh U., 1971; JD, U. Pa., 1974. Bar: Pa. 1974, U.S. Dist. Ct. (ea. dist.) Pa. 1974, U.S. Ct. Appeals (3d cir.) 1981. Assoc. Fox, Rothschild, O'Brien & Frankel, Phila., 1974-75; chmn. immigration dept. Abrahams & Loewenstein, Phila., 1975—; instr., mem. adv. bd. Inst. for Paralegal Tng., Phila., 1974-81; instr. Temple Law Sch. Grad. Legal Studies, Phila., 1984; adj. prof. Villanova U., Pa., 1985—. Co-author: (with Matthew Bender) Employer's Immigration Compliance Guide, 1987. Exec. committeeman, bd. dirs. Jewish Community Relations Council, Phila., 1977—, chmn. exec. com., com. on unprosecuted Nazi War Criminals Nat. Jewish Community Relations Adv. Council, N.Y.C., 1983—, v.p. Hebrew Immigrant Aid Soc., Phila., 1977—; pres. Council of Tenants Assn. Southeastern Pa., 1980-81, chmn. 1983—. Recipient Legion of Honor award Chapel of Four Chaplains, 1977. Mem. ABA, Phila. Bar Assn., Am. Immigration Lawyers Assn. (chmn. Phila. chpt. 1980-82, bd. govs. 1980-84, nat. sec. 1984-85, 2d v.p. 1985-86, 1st v.p. 1986-87, pres.-elect 1987—). Avocations: politics, sports, traveling, organizations. Immigration, naturalization, and customs. Office: Abrahams & Loewenstein United Engrs Bldg 30 S 17th St 14th Fl Philadelphia PA 19103

KLATELL, ROBERT EDWARD, lawyer, electronics company executive; b. Tampa, Fla., Dec. 11, 1945; s. Jack S. and Arla M. (Bragin) K.; m. Penelope E. Manegan, June 14, 1970; children—Christopher J., James M., Jeremy N. B.A., Williams Coll., 1968; J.D., NYU, 1971. Bar: N.Y. 1972. Asso. Kramer, Lowenstein, Nessen, Kamin & Soll, N.Y.C., 1970-76; gen. counsel Arrow Electronics, Inc., N.Y.C., 1976—; v.p. Arrow Electronics, Inc., 1979—. Mem. ABA, Assn. Bar City N.Y., Westchester-Fairfield County Corp. Counsels Assn. General corporate, Securities. Office: Arrow Electronics Inc 25 Hub Dr Melville NY 11747

KLAUS, CHARLES, lawyer; b. Freiburg, Baden, Fed. Republic Germany, Feb. 11, 1935; came to U.S., 1939; children: Charles, Kathryn, Richard. BA, Cornell U., 1956, MBA, JD with distinction, 1961; postdoctoral, Case Western Res. U., 1964, Lakeland Community Coll., 1976. Bar: Ohio 1961, U.S. Dist. Ct. (no. dist.) Ohio 1961. Assoc. Baker & Hostetler, Cleve., 1961-72, ptnr., 1972—. Hon. trustee Cleve. Music Sch. Settlement, past pres.; past trustee Cleve. Audubon Soc.; past trustee, sec. Cleve. Area Arts Council, Lake Erie Opera Theatre, Northeast Ohio chpt. Arthritis Found.; former mem. Group Service Council Welfare Fedn. Cleve.; bird walk leader Holden Arboretum, Kirtland, Ohio, 1980—. Recipient Award of Merit, Cleve. Audubon Soc., 1979. Mem. Order of Coif, Phi Kappa Phi. Clubs: Rowfant (past sec.), Kirtland Country (Willoughby, Ohio). General corporate, Environment, Contracts commercial. Office: Baker & Hostetler 3200 Nat City Ctr Cleveland OH 44114

KLAUS, ROGER DEAN, lawyer, editor; b. Belleville, Ill., Sept. 4, 1945; s. Clarence Edward Sr. and Katherine (Augustin) K.; m. Rhonda Fern Rubin, May 3, 1982; 1 child, Rachel. BA, U. Ill., 1967; JD, Ill. Inst. Tech., 1972. Bar: Ill. 1972, U.S. Dist. Ct. (no. dist) Ill. 1972. Sole practice Chgo., 1972-76; instr. Triton Coll., River Grove, Ill., 1975-76; editor Callaghan & Co., Wilmette, Ill., 1976-82, mng. editor, 1982-84, editor-in-chief, 1984—. Served with U.S. Army, 1969-71. Mem. ABA, Assn. Trial Lawyers Am., Am. Assn. Law Librarians, Cen. States Archeol. Assn. Avocations: musician, songwriting, American Indian artifacts, football, basketball. Legal and Tax Publishing. Office: Callaghan & Co 3201 Old Glenview Rd Wilmette IL 60091

KLAWITER, DONALD CASIMIR, lawyer; b. Phila., Feb. 26, 1950; s. Joseph C. and Frances J. (Koniecki) K.; m. Marie M. Gabuzda, Jan. 2, 1982. BA, MA, U. Pa., 1972, JD, 1975. Bar: Pa. 1975, U.S. Supreme Ct. 1979, D.C. 1987. Trial atty. antitrust div. U.S. Dept. Justice, Phila., 1975-78; spl. asst. operations antitrust div. U.S. Dept. Justice, Washington, 1978-80; chief antitrust U.S. Dept. Justice, Dallas, 1980-82; sr. trial atty. antitrust U.S. Dept. Justice, Washington, 1982-86; of counsel Morgan, Lewis & Bockius, Washington, 1986—. Mem. ABA (litigation and antitrust law sects.). Democrat. Roman Catholic. Antitrust, Federal civil litigation, Criminal. Home: 5930 Munson Ct Falls Church VA 22041 Office: Morgan Lewis & Bockius 1800 M St NW Washington DC 20036

KLAYMAN, BARRY MARTIN, lawyer; b. Montclair, N.J., Sept. 26, 1952; s. Max M. and Sylvia (Cohen) K.; m. Anna Kornbrot, June 8, 1975; 1 child, Alison Melissa. BA magna cum laude, Columbia U., 1974; JD cum laude, Harvard U., 1977. Bar: Pa. 1977, U.S. Dist. Ct. (ea. dist.) Pa. 1977, U.S. Ct. Appeals (3d cir.) 1978. From assoc. to ptnr. Wolf, Block, Schorr & Solis-Cohen, Phila., 1977—. Bd. dirs. Phila. region B'nai B'rith Youth Orgn., 1984—. Nat. merit scholar, 1970. Mem. ABA (litigation sect., torts and ins. practice sect.), Phila. Bar Assn., Pa. Bar Assn., Assn. Trial Lawyers Am. Federal civil litigation, State civil litigation, Environment. Office: Wolf Block Schorr & Solis-Cohen Packard Bldg 12th Floor Philadelphia PA 19102

KLAZMER, GARY MICHAEL, insurance company executive, consultant; b. Phila., Aug. 28, 1956; s. Bernard and Gay Phyllis (Pasternack) K. JD, Temple U., 1981; cert. fin. cons., Am. Coll., Bryn Mawr, Pa., 1986. Bar: Pa. 1981, Conn. 1981; CLU. Assoc. Schatz, Schatz, Ribicoff & Kotin, Hartford, Conn., 1981-83; broker Inmark Security Corp., Phila., 1983-84, N.Y. Life Ins. Co., Phila., 1984—. Mem. ACLU. Mem. Nat. Assn. Life Underwriters, Million Dollar Round Table, Beta Gamma Sigma, Phi Kappa Phi. Insurance. Home: 906 Valley Glen Rd Elkins Park PA 19117 Office: 3 Mellon Bank Center Suite 1500 Philadelphia PA 19102

KLECKNER, ROBERT GEORGE, JR., lawyer; b. Reading, Pa., Mar. 14, 1932; s. Robert George and Elizabeth (Endlich) K.; m. Carol Espie, June 15, 1955; children—Anthony Savage, Susan Duffield. B.A., Yale U., 1954; LL.B., U. Pa., 1959. Bar: Pa. 1960, N.Y. 1964. Sole practice, Reading, 1960-63; assoc. Sullivan & Cromwell, N.Y.C., 1963-70; house counsel Goldman, Sachs & Co., N.Y.C., 1970-78; cons., N.Y.C., 1978-80; house counsel Johnson & Higgins, N.Y.C., 1980—. Served to 1st lt. USAR, 1955-57; Korea. Mem. ABA, N.Y. State Bar Assn., N.Y. County Lawyers Assn., Assn. Bar City N.Y., Pa. State Bar Assn., Berks County (Pa.) Bar Assn., Phi Beta Kappa. Republican. Lutheran. Clubs: India House, University (N.Y.C.). General corporate. Home: 80 East End Ave New York NY 10028 Office: 125 Broad St New York NY 10004

KLEE, JOHN P., lawyer, real estate broker; b. Pitts., Apr. 26, 1941; s. Harry A. and Garnet (Coulson) K.; m. Cynthia E. Gaisford, Sept. 2, 1978; children—Collyer Elizabeth, Caroline Watson. B.A., Washington and Jefferson Coll., 1963; J.D., U. Pitts., 1967. Bar: Pa. 1968, U.S. Dist. Ct. (we. dist.) Pa. 1968. Mem. Baskin & Sears, Pitts., 1968-78; counsel Dravo Corp., Pitts., 1979-81, sr. counsel, 1982-84, asst. gen. counsel, sr. asst. sec., dir. real estate ops. 1984—. Lic. real estate broker, Pa. Mem. Allegheny County Bar Assn., Pa. Bar Assn., ABA.Lutheran. General corporate, Real property, Contracts commercial. Office: Dravo Corp One Oliver Plaza Pittsburgh PA 15222

KLEE, KENNETH NATHAN, lawyer; b. Los Angeles, Apr. 12, 1949; s. Kenneth Haskell and Allene (Simpkins) K.; m. Doreen May Rotman, July 11, 1971; children: Kenneth Maxwell, Nathan Scott. BA with great distinction, Stanford U., 1971; JD cum laude, Harvard U., 1974. Bar: Calif. 1975, D.C. 1975, U.S. Dist. Ct. D.C. 1975, U.S. Dist. Ct. (no., so., cen. and ea. dists.) Calif. 1977, U.S. Ct. Appeals (9th and D.C. dirs.) 1977. Assoc. counsel U.S. Ho. of Reps. Judiciary Com., Washington, 1974-77; assoc. Shutan & Trost, P.C., Los Angeles, 1977-80; ptnr. Stutman, Treister & Glatt, Los Angeles, 1980—; cons. U.S. Ho. Reps., 1977-80, U.S. Dept. Justice, Washington, 1980-84; vis. lectr. UCLA Law Sch., 1979—; exec. com. Nat. Bankruptcy Conf., 1985—. Recipient Ephebian award City of Los Angeles, 1967. Mem. ABA (bus.-bankruptcy com. 1985—, chmn. new and pending legis. 1985—), Los Angeles County Bar Assn., Fin. Lawyers Conf. (pres. 1986-87), Am. Jewish Com. Republican. Lodge: Masons. Avocations: soccer referee, wine, bridge. Office: Stutman Treister & Glatt PC 3699 Wilshire Blvd #900 Los Angeles CA 90010

KLEID, WALLACE, lawyer; b. Balt., June 25, 1946; s. Max E. and Bess (Hubberman) K.; m. Loryn Sari Lesser, July 1, 1979; 1 son, Micah Saul; 1 dau. by previous marriage, Kathy Jill. B.A., U. Md., 1967; J.D., U. Md.-Balt., 1971. Bar: Md. 1972, U.S. Ct. Mil. Appeals 1973, U.S. Dist. Ct. Md. 1972, U.S. Supreme Ct. 1975, U.S. Ct. Appeals (4th cir.) 1975, D.C. 1982. Law clk. State's Atty. Baltimore County, Md., 1970-72, asst. state's atty., 1972-77; sole practice, Balt. and Towson, Md., 1972—; mem. Rape Adv. Commn., Baltimore County, 1974-75; presenter testimony on rape Md. Gen. Assembly, 1975 cons. TV program Women and the Law, 1976-77; lectr. in field. Bd. dirs. Colonial Village Neighborhood Assn., Balt., 1969-75, Citizens Dem. Club, Balt., 1972-75; v.p. Cheswolde Neighborhood Assn., Balt., 1981-84, pres., 1984-86 . Served to sgt. U.S. Army Res., 1968-74. Recipient Civilian award Balt. County Police Dept., 1975. Mem. ABA, Assn. Trial Lawyers Am., Baltimore County Bar Assn. (lawyer referral com. 1976-78, chmn. ins. trust 1980-87), Balt. City Bar Assn. (workmens compensation com.), Fed. Bar Assn., Md. State Bar Assn. (chmn. spl. com. to establish gen. practice sect. 1984-85, chmn. gen. practice sect. 1985-87, atty. grievance commn. 1982—), Md. State Atty.'s Assn., Md. Trial Lawyers Assn., Nat. Dist. Attys. Assn., D.C. Bar Assn., Zeta Beta Tau. Democrat. Jewish. General practice, Family and matrimonial, State civil litigation. Home: 6228 Benhurst Rd Baltimore MD 21209 Office: 1118 N Calvert St Baltimore MD 21202

KLEIER, JAMES PATRICK, lawyer; b. Covington, Ky., Jan. 30, 1956; s. Paul James and Mary Jeanne (Seissiger) K.; m. Maureen Ann Cronan, Aug. 2, 1980; 1 child, James Jr. BA, Thomas More Coll., 1976; JD, U. Ky., 1979. Bar: Calif. 1979, U.S. Dist. Ct. (no. dist.) Calif. 1979, U.S. Tax Ct. 1980, U.S. Supreme Ct. 1981. From assoc. to ptnr. Morrison & Foerster, San Francisco, 1979—; instr. law Golden Gate U., San Francisco, 1986—. Mem. ABA (chmn. spl. task force adminstrv. practice com. 1985—, tax sect.), Calif. Bar Assn., San Francisco Bar Assn. (chmn. barristers tax sect. 1984—), Order of Coif. Democrat. Roman Catholic. Avocations: skiing, racquetball, horse racing. State and local taxation, Corporate taxation, Criminal. Home: 20 Oak Knoll Rd Kentfield CA 94904 Office: Morrison & Foerster 345 California St San Francisco CA 94104

KLEILER, JAMES ROBERT, lawyer; b. Washington, Dec. 2, 1949; s. Frank Munro and Frances Pauline (Brezon) K.; m. Cathleen F. Miller, Aug. 17, 1974; 1 child, Christine Frances. AB in History, Georgetown U., 1971; JD, George Washington U., 1974. Bar: Md. 1974, U.S. Supreme Ct. 1978, D.C. 1982. Atty.-advisor U.S. Dept. Interior Office of Hearings and Appeals, Arlington, Va., 1975—. Mem. ABA. Democrat. Roman Catholic. Administrative and regulatory, Oil and gas leasing, Natural resources law, public land law. Home: 5113 White Flint Dr Kensington MD 20895 Office: US Dept Interior Office Hearings and Appeals 4015 Wilson Blvd Arlington VA 22203

KLEIN, ALAN RICHARD, lawyer; b. Chgo., July 24, 1950; s. Clarence and Lois Beverly (Jacobson) K.; m. Susan Lynn Kaplan, June 10, 1973; children—Jonathan Robert, Kimberly Anne. B.S. in History, UCLA, 1972; J.D., U. San Fernando Valley, 1975. Bar: Calif. 1976, U.S. Dist. Ct. (cen. dist.) Calif. 1978, U.S. Ct. Appeals (9th cir.) 1978. Ptnr. Kaplan, Klein, Kaplan & Steinberg, Los Angeles, 1976—. Mem. State Bar Calif., Los Angeles County Bar Assn., Beverly Hills Bar Assn., Am. Immigration Lawyers Assn., Alpha Epsilon Pi. Republican. Jewish. Immigration, naturalization, and customs, Personal injury, Entertainment. Home: 3411 Colville Pl Encino CA 91436 Office: Kaplan Klein Kaplan & Steinberg 3600 Wilshire Blvd Suite 2230 Los Angeles CA 90010

KLEIN, ALFRED, lawyer; b. Stuttgart, Germany, Oct. 22, 1946; s. Gerson and Viola (Greenberger) K. B.A., U. Mich., 1968; J.D., U. Calif.-Berkeley, 1971. Bar: Calif. 1972, U.S. Dist. Ct. (cen. dist.) Calif., U.S. Ct. Appeals (9th cir.). Field atty. NLRB, Los Angeles and San Francisco, 1971-73; instr. Hastings Coll. of Law, U. Calif.-San Francisco, 1973-75; assoc. Musick, Paeler & Garrett, San Francisco, 1973-75; atty., employee relations Atlantic Richfield Co., 1975-79, sr. atty., employee relations ARCO Petroleum Products Co. div. Atlantic Richfield Co., Los Angeles, 1979-85; sole practice, 1985—; lectr. UCLA, Am. Arbitration Assn., Town Hall of Calif. (indsl. relations sect.), Orange County Indsl. Relations Research Assn., Bur. Nat. Affairs, Inc. Winner 1st place and hon. mention in color photograph Los Angeles Athletic Club All Clubs Art Show, 1981; NSF scholar, 1963. Mem. Los Angeles County Bar Assn. (mem. exec. com., symposium planning com. 1985), Calif. Bar Assn., ABA. Clubs: Los Angeles Athletic, Town Hall Calif. (lectr. indsl. relations sect.) (Los Angeles). Contbg. editor: The Developing Labor Law, 2d edit. Labor, Pension, profit-sharing, and employee benefits, Administrative and regulatory. Office: 624 S Grand Ave #2900 Los Angeles CA 90017

KLEIN, ARNOLD SPENCER, lawyer; b. N.Y.C., Mar. 10, 1951; s. Paul and Ethel (Cooper) K.; m. Arlene Sandra Feinberg, Aug. 14, 1977; children: Jeffrey Daniel, Rachel Pauli. BA, SUNY, Stony Brook, 1974; JD cum laude, N.Y. Law Sch., 1977. Bar: N.Y. 1978, Fla. 1984, U.S. Dist. Ct. (so. and ea. dists.) N.Y., U.S. Dist. Ct. (so. dist.) Fla., U.S. Ct. Appeals (2d cir.), U.S. Supreme Ct. Mem. Kelley, Drye & Warren, N.Y.C., 1977-85, ptnr., 1986—. Mem. ABA, N.Y. State Bar Assn., Assn. of Bar of City of N.Y. Federal civil litigation, State civil litigation. Office: Kelley Drye & Warren 101 Park Ave New York NY 10178

KLEIN, GERALD S., lawyer; b. Washington, Aug. 27, 1941; s. Herbert M. and Mary (Olschansky) K.; m. Ellen F. Klein, Sept. 10, 1967. LL.B., U. Balt., 1963; LL.M., U. Chgo., 1965. Bar: Md., Sup., U.S. Ct. Apls. (4th cir.), U.S. Dist. Ct. Md. Atty., Singer Co., N.Y.C., 1966-67; sole practice, Balt., 1967—; asst. solicitor City of Balt., 1967-75. Served with USNR. Mem. ABA, Md. Bar Assn., Balt. City Bar Assn. Democrat. Jewish. Contracts commercial, General corporate, State civil litigation. Home: 3515 Overbrook Rd Pikesville MD 21208 Office: 2110 Charles Center S 36 S Charles St Baltimore MD 21201

KLEIN, HENRY, lawyer; b. N.Y.C., Oct. 6, 1949; s. Leo Herman and Florence (Silver) K.; m. Ann Laura Hallasey, July 30, 1972; children—Lauren Jennifer, Benjamin Jason. B.A., SUNY-Albany, 1971; J.D., U. San Diego, 1975. Bar: Calif. 1975, U.S. Ct. Customs and Patent Appeals 1976. Trademark atty. U.S. Patent Office, Washington, 1975-77; ptnr. Ladas & Parry, Los Angeles, 1978—. Mem. San Diego Law Rev., 1974-75; editor-in-chief Trademark Soc. Newsletter, 1977. Mem. U. San Diego Civil Legal Clinic, 1974, Civil Rights Research Council, San Diego, 1974, Calif. Pub. Interest Research Group, San Diego, 1975. N.Y. State scholar, 1967-71; Tex. State legal scholar State of Tex., 1972; recipient Am. Jurisprudence award Bancroft-Whitney Co. and Lawyer Co-Op. Pub. Co., Lubbock, Tex., 1972; Patent Trademark Spl. Achievement awards U.S. Dept. Commerce, Washington, 1976, 77. Mem. U.S. Trademark Assn. (v.p. 1976, pres., chmn. 1977), Los Angeles Patent Law Assn., Phi Delta Phi. Republican. Jewish. Trademark and copyright, Patent. Home: 6134 Cabrillo Ct Alta Loma CA 91701

KLEIN, HERMAN FRED, lawyer, former educator; b. Akron, Ohio, May 13, 1913; s. Fred and Elsie (Hartman) K.; m. Connie Pearl Fort, Sept. 15, 1944; children—Cindy, Melody (dec.). B.S. in Edn., U. Akron, 1935, M.S. in Edn., 1940, J.D., 1947; postgrad. Harvard U., U. Calif., Ohio Wesleyan U., Ohio State U. Bar: Ohio 1953. High sch. tchr., Ohio, 1935-47; faculty Armstrong Coll., 1947-51; atty. examiner State of Ohio Dept. Hwys., 1960-63, Pub. Utilities Commn. Ohio and Bd. Tax Appeals Ohio, 1969-71; sole practice, Groveport, Ohio, 1953—; assoc. H. & R. Block Tax Agy., Venice, Fla. Pres. Young Republicans Contra Costs County, Calif., 1951-52; mem. Nat. Police Officers Assn., Fla. Sheriff's Assn., South Venice Civic Assn.; disaster personnel coordinator Sarasota County (Fla.) chpt. ARC. Mem. Ohio Bar Assn., Res. Officers Assn. U.S. Lodges: Masons, York Rite, K.T. (past comdr.) (Urbana, Ohio), Shrine (press corps Sahib Temple) (Sarasota, Fla.). Scottish Rite, Order Eastern Star (Columbus, Ohio). Personal income taxation. Home: 1283 Piedmont Rd South Venice FL 33595

KLEIN, JEFFREY S., lawyer; b. Los Angeles, Apr. 15, 1953; s. Norman and Shirlee Klein; m. Karyn Kitson, Sept. 29, 1984, 1 child, Kevyn Michelle. BA, Claremont Mens Coll., 1975; M in Journalism, Columbia U., 1978; JD, Stanford U., 1980. reporter UPI-Radio, Los Angeles, 1983-84; mem. communications bd. UCLA, 1984. Assoc. Kaplan, Livingston, Goodwin, Berkowitz & Selvin, Beverly Hills, Calif., 1980-81, Garey, Mason & Sloane, Santa Monica, Calif., 1981-83; sr. staff counsel Times Mirror, Los Angeles Times, 1983—. Author Legal View weekly column, Los Angeles Times, 1985—, various book revs. Advisor Gov. Bruce Babbitt, Phoenix, 1980. Mem. Calif. Bar Assn. Libel, Trademark and copyright, General corporate. Office: Los Angeles Times Times Mirror Sq Los Angeles CA 90053

KLEIN, JOEL AARON, lawyer; b. Red Bank, N.J., Feb. 15, 1949; s. David M. and Sybil (Schwartz) K.; m. Patricia Caliguiri, May 17, 1975; children: Cynthia, Victoria. BA, Duquesne U., 1973, JD, 1979. Bar: Pa. 1979, U.S. Dist. Ct. (we. dist.) Pa. 1979, U.S. Ct. Mil. Appeals 1980, U.S. Ct. Appeals (fed. cir.) 1983. Staff atty. USAF, Ellsworth AFB, S.D., 1979-82, Castle AFB, Calif., 1982-83; sr. ptnr. Klein & Rayl, Pitts., 1984-85; sole practice Pitts., 1985—; adj. prof. U. S.D., Rapid City, 1981. V.p. S. Side Local Devel. Co., Pitts., 1985-86; chmn. Main St. Adv. Bd., Pitts., 1985-86, S. Side Planning Task Force, 1985. Served to capt. USAF, 1979-83. Mem. Air Force Assn., Assn. Trial lawyers Am., Pa. Trial Lawyers Assn., Pa. Bar Assn., Allegheny County Bar Assn. Democrat. Jewish. State civil litigation, Criminal, Family and matrimonial. Office: 1931 E Carson St Pittsburgh PA 15203

KLEIN, JONATHAN JOSEPH, lawyer; b. Yonkers, N.Y., Oct. 11, 1955; s. Sidney Benjamin and Nancy Julie (Isaacs) K.; m. Lisa Rae Brenner, June 13, 1982; children: Jessica Johanna, Amanda Bethany, Zachary Alexander. BA, Yeshiva U., 1977; JD, Fordham U., 1980. Bar: N.Y. 1981, U.S. Dist. Ct. (so. dist.) Ga. 1981, U.S. Ct. Appeals (5th and 11th cirs.) 1981, U.S. Ct. Mil. Appeals 1981, U.S. Ct. Appeals (2d cir.) 1984, U.S. Dist. Ct. (so. and ea. dists.) N.Y. 1985, Conn. 1986, U.S. Dist. Ct. Conn. 1986, U.S. Supreme Ct. 1986, U.S. Army Ct. Mil. Review 1986. Assoc. Paul K. Rooney P.C., N.Y.C., 1980-81; sr. enforcement atty. N.Y. Stock Exchange Inc., N.Y.C.,

1984-85, spl. counsel, 1985-86, sr. spl. counsel, 1986-87; atty. Gladstone, Schwartz, Baroff & Blum, Bridgeport, Conn., 1987—. Mem. Am. Israel Pub. Affairs Com., Washington, 1983—, N. Park Assn., Bridgeport, Conn., 1985—. Served to capt. U.S. Army, 1981-84, with Res. 1984—. Mem. ABA, Assn. of Bar of City of N.Y. (com. on mil. justice and mil. affairs 1984-87), Assn. Trial Lawyers Am., Conn. Bar Assn., Assn. of U.S. Army. Republican. Jewish. General corporate, Criminal, Military. Office: Gladstone Schwartz Baroff & Blum 1087 Broad St Bridgeport CT 06604

KLEIN, JUDAH B., lawyer; b. Bklyn., Feb. 9, 1923; s. Kolman Karl and Gladys Ruth (Edelson) K.; m. Paula Berk, Nov. 8, 1953; 1 dau., Caryn Ann. B.S., U. Md., 1947; LL.B., Bklyn. Law Sch., 1950. Bar: N.Y. 1951, U.S. Dist. Ct. (so. and ea. dists.) N.Y. Ptnr. Klein & Klein, N.Y.C., 1952-58; gen. counsel Paragon Industries Inc., Mineola, N.Y., 1959-70; sole practice, 1970-71; asst. chief counsel, sr. v.p. The Title Guarantee Co., N.Y.C., 1972-79; v.p., gen. counsel LTIC Assoc., Inc., N.Y.C., 1979—. Served to 1st lt. U.S. Army, 1943-46, 51-52. Mem. ABA, Assn. Bar City of N.Y., Nassau County Bar Assn., Am. Coll. Real Estate Lawyers, N.Y. State Bar Assn. Jewish. Club: Masons. Real property, Title Insurance.

KLEIN, LARRY A., lawyer; b. Springfield, Ohio, Oct. 1, 1939; s. Samuel and Anne (Rosenzweig) K.; m. Lynn Elsa Blicher, Dec. 28, 1961; children: Laura, Marc, Karen. BA, U. Mich., 1962; JD, U. Fla., 1964. Bar: Fla. 1964, U.S. Ct. Appeals (4th, 5th and 11th cirs.), U.S. Supreme Ct. Research aide Fla. 2d Dist. Ct. Appeals, Lakeland, 1964-65; from assoc.to ptnr. Cone, Wagner, Nugent, West Palm Beach, Fla., 1965-75; sole practice West Palm Beach, 1975-84; ptnr. Klein & Beranek, P.A., West Palm Beach, 1984—. Fellow Am. Coll. Trial Lawyers; Palm Beach County Bar Assn. (pres. 1975-76). Appellate practice. Office: Klein & Beranek PA 501 S Flagler Dr Suite 503 West Palm Beach FL 33401

KLEIN, MARINA SHANK, lawyer; b. Tegucigalpa, Honduras, Apr. 30, 1950; came to U.S., 1964; d. Rafael Silvio and Maria Alicia (Carranza) Pena; m. Creigh Franklin Shank, June 17, 1972 (div. June 1978); m. Michael Alan Klein, Sept. 15, 1981. BA, U. Miami, 1973, JD, 1977. Bar: Fla. 1977. Trial atty. SEC, Miami, Fla., 1976-79; asst. counsel Landmak Bankin Corp., Fort Lauderdale, Fla., 1979-81; assoc. Cassel & Cassel P.A., Miami, 1981-83, Britton, Cohen, Cassel, Kaufman & Schantz P.A., Miami, 1984-85; sole practice Miami, 1985—; trustee LG Investment, Cin., 1981—. Mem. investment com. Fedn. Jewish Philanthropists, Miami, 1984—. Served to lt. (j.g.) USN, 1975-77. Mem. ABA, Fla. Assn. Women Lawyers, Miami Forum (treas. 1984-85). Avocations: orchids, gardening. General corporate, Securities, Banking. Home: 9047 SW 67th Ave Miami FL 33156

KLEIN, MICHAEL CLARENCE, lawyer; b. Kearney, Nebr., July 16, 1952; s. Milton N. and Mary E. (Moore) K.; m. Jacqueline A. McGuigan, Aug. 14, 1971; children—Andrew M., Benjamin P., Molly E., Katherine A. B.A., Kearney State Coll., 1974; J.D., U. Nebr., 1977. Bar: Nebr. 1977, U.S. Dist. Ct. Nebr. 1977. Ptnr., Anderson, Strasburger, Klein, Peterson & Swan, Holdrege, Nebr., 1977—; chmn. 10th Jud. Dist. Mental Health Board, Holdrege, 1981—. Editor Nebr. Law Rev., 1975-77. Bd. dirs. Child Saving Inst., Omaha, Phelps County Community Found., Holdrege, Nebr. Mem. ABA, Nebr. Bar Assn., 10th Jud. Dist. Bar Assn. (sec. 1981-82), Phelps County Bar Assn. (pres. 1981). Republican. Roman Catholic. Lodge: Elks. General practice, Personal injury, Workers' compensation. Home: 820 Hancock St Holdrege NE 68949 Office: Anderson Strasburger Klein Peterson & Swan 417 East Ave Holdrege NE 68949

KLEIN, PAUL E., insurance company executive, lawyer; b. N.Y.C., Apr. 26, 1934. A.B., Cornell U., 1956; J.D., Harvard U., 1960. Bar: Mich. 1960, Ill. 1965, N.Y. 1967, U.S. Supreme Ct. 1977, U.S. Ct. Appeals (2d cir.) 1980. Atty. Dow Chem. Co., Midland, Mich., 1960-65; assoc. Gunther & Choka, Chgo., 1965-66; atty. Esso Research & Engring. Co., Linden, N.J., 1966-67; sr. mng. editor Matthew Bender & Co., N.Y.C., 1967-72; assoc. gen. counsel N.Y. Life Ins. Co., N.Y.C., 1972-80; v.p., assoc. gen. counsel N.Y. Life Ins. Co., N.Y.C., 1980-84; v.p., counsel Huggins Fin. Services Inc. mem. Hay Group, N.Y.C., 1984-86, with tax dept. Ernst & Whinney, 1986—; adj. asst. prof. L.I. U., 1972-79, adj. assoc. prof., 1979-80. Mem. Assn. Life Ins. Counsel (sec.-treas. 1979-83, bd. govs. 1983-87), ABA, N.Y. State Bar Assn., Chgo. Bar Assn. Columnist Jour. Real Estate Taxation; writer; editor. Office: 153 E 53d St New York NY 10022

KLEIN, PAUL IRA, lawyer; b. Newark, Sept. 30, 1948; s. Alexander and Yolanda (Klein) K.; m. Susan R. Rosenberg, Aug. 8, 1971; 1 child, Joshua. A.B., Rutgers U., 1970; J.D., St. John's U., 1974. Bar: N.Y. 1975, U.S. Dist. Cts. (so. and ea. dists.) N.Y. 1976, U.S. Dist. Ct. (no. dist.) N.Y. 1983, N.J. 1986, U.S. Dist. Ct. N.J. 1986. Assoc. Alexander, Ash, Schwartz & Cohen, N.Y.C., 1975-76, Morris & Duffy, N.Y.C., 1976-85; ptnr. Belair, Klein, Groman & Evans, N.Y.C., 1985—. Mem. ABA, N.Y. State Bar Assn. (ins. negligence and compensation law sect.), N.J. Bar Assn. Jewish. Federal civil litigation, State civil litigation, Personal injury. Home: 658 Pascack Rd Paramus NJ 07652

KLEIN, PETER MARTIN, lawyer, transportation company executive; b. N.Y.C., June 2, 1934; s. Saul and Esther (Goldstein) K.; m. Ellen Judith Matlick, June 18, 1961; children: Amy Lynn, Steven Ezra. A.B., Columbia U., 1956, J.D., 1962. Bar: N.Y. 1962, D.C. 1964, U.S. Supreme Ct. bar 1966. Asst. proctor Columbia U., 1959-62; asst. counsel Mil. Sea Transp. Service, Office Gen. Counsel, Dept. Navy, Washington, 1962-65; trial atty. civil div. U.S. Dept. Justice, N.Y.C., 1966-69; gen. atty. Sea-Land Service, Inc., Menlo Park, N.J., 1969-76; v.p., gen. counsel, sec. Sea-Land Service, Inc., 1976-79, Sea-Land Industries, Inc., Menlo Park, 1979-84; asso. gen. counsel R.J. Reynolds Industries, Inc., Winston-Salem, N.C., 1978-84; sr. v.p., gen. counsel, sec. Sea-Land Corp., N.J., 1984—; dir. Sea-Land Industries Investments, Inc., 1981-84, Reynolds Leasing Corp., 1981-86; mem. adv. com. on pvt. internat. law Dept. State, 1974—; mem. U.S. delegation UN Conf. on Trade and Devel., UN Commn. on Internat. Trade Law, 1975-76, trade regulation adv. bd. Bur. Nat. Affairs, 1986—. Trustee Jewish Edn. Assn. Met. N.J., 1973-76; trustee Temple B'nai Abraham of Essex County, N.J., 1973—, v.p., 1976-81, pres., 1981-83; mem. Essex County Dems. Com., 1986—. Served with USN, 1956-59, Antarctica. Mem. Am. Maritime Assn. (dir., chmn. coms. on law and legis. 1974-78), Am. Polar Soc., ABA, Navy League U.S. (life mem.), Fed. Bar Assn., N.Y. State Bar Assn., D.C. Bar Assn., Internat. Bar Assn., Maritime Law Assn., U.S. Club, Nat. Press. Home: 22 Sandalwood Dr Livingston NJ 07039 Office: PO Box 800 Iselin NJ 08830

KLEIN, RICHARD L., lawyer; b. N.Y.C., Feb. 20, 1954; s. Erwin L. and Marlys (Frensdorff) K.; m. Nina B. Karlen, Aug. 1980; children: Andrew, Lauren. BA, U. Rochester, 1976; JD, Columbia U., 1979. Bar: N.Y. 1980, U.S. Dist. Ct. (so. and ea. dists.) N.Y. 1980, U.S. Ct. Appeals (D.C. cir.) 1982, U.S. Ct. Appeals (2d cir.) 1985. Law clk. to presiding judge U.S. Dist. Ct. (so. dist.) N.Y., N.Y.C., 1979-81; assoc. Willkie, Farr & Gallagher, N.Y.C., 1981—. Mem. ABA, Fed. Bar Council, N.Y. State Bar Assn., Assn. of Bar of City of N.Y., N.Y. County Lawyers Assn. Federal civil litigation, State civil litigation.

KLEIN, ROBERT ALLAN, lawyer; b. Newark, July 28, 1944; s. Benjamin N. and Bella (Peckler) K.; m. Joan Carol Silverman, Jan. 5, 1969; children—Wendy R., Melissa S., Randall J. B.A., Rutgers U., 1966; J.D., Georgetown U., 1969; LL.M. in Taxation, George Washington U., 1972. Bar: D.C. 1969, Md. 1969, U.S. Supreme Ct. 1975. Assoc. Foreman, Cutler and Diamond, Washington, 1969-70; assoc. Danzansky, Dickey, Tydings, Quint and Gordon, Washington, 1970-75, ptnr., 1975-81; ptnr. Finley, Kumble, Wagner, Heine, Underberg, Manley, Myerson & Casey, Washington, 1981—. Contbr. articles to profl. publs. Vice chmn. commerce and professions United Jewish Appeal Fedn.; mem. Washington regional bd. Anti-Defamation League of B'nai B'rith. Mem. ABA, Md. Bar Assn., D.C. Bar Assn. Real property, General corporate, Personal income taxation. Office: 1120 Connecticut Ave NW Suite 1010 Washington DC 20036

KLEIN, ROBERT DALE, lawyer; b. Balt., July 29, 1951; s. James Robert and Madeline Margaret (Horak) K.; m. Patricia Kay Purvis, May 6, 1978; children—Morgan Elizabeth, Patrick Jameson, Evan Robert. Student U. Durham, Eng., 1971-72; B.S., MIT, 1973; J.D., Columbia U., 1976. Bar: Md. 1976, U.S. Dist. Ct. Md. 1977, U.S. Ct. Appeals (4th cir.) 1978, U.S. Dist. Ct. D.C. 1983, D.C. 1983. Assoc., Piper & Marbury, Balt., 1976-84, ptnr., 1984—. Author: Maryland Civil Procedure Forms: Practice, 1984; editor Def. Line Jour., 1983-84; contbr. articles to profl. jours. Alfred P. Sloan Found. scholar, 1969-73. Mem. ABA, Md. State Bar Assn., Balt. Bar Assn. (chmn. com. on long range planning 1986—, chmn. spl. com. on video 1983-84, chmn. standing com. on pub. relations 1984-86), Md. Assn. Def. Trial Counsel (v.p. 1985-86, pres. 1986—), D.C. Bar Assn., Chi Phi (sec. Beta chpt.). Roman Catholic. Product Liability, Personal injury. Home: 1501 Near Thicket Ln Baltimore MD 21153 Office: Piper & Marbury 1100 Charles Ctr S 36 S Charles St Baltimore MD 21201

KLEIN, WILLIAM A., lawyer, educator; b. 1931. A.B., 1952; LL.B., Harvard U., 1957. Bar: D.C. 1958, Wis. 1968. With Dept. Justice, Washington, 1957-59; law clk. Hon. David L. Bazelon, 1959; teaching fellow Harvard U., 1959-60; practice Boston, 1960-61; asst. prof. U. Wis., 1961-64, assoc. prof., 1964-66, prof., 1966-71; staff asst. to chief counsel IRS, Washington, 1966-67; vis. prof. UCLA Sch. Law, 1969-70, prof., 1971—; vis. prof. U. Hawaii, fall 1976, Yale U., spring 1982. Author: Policy Analysis of the Federal Income Tax, 1976; Business Organization and Finance, 1980; (with Bittker and Stone) Federal Income Taxation, 6th edit., 1984. Past mem. editorial bd. Harvard Law Rev. Legal education. Office: UCLA Law Sch 405 Hilgard Ave Los Angeles CA 90024 *

KLEIN, WILLIAM DAVID, lawyer; b. St. Cloud, Minn., Oct. 30, 1954; s. Wilfred George and Rita Christina (Gottwalt) K.; m. Rebecca Lynn Ready, May 26, 1979; 1 child, Michaela Laine. BA summa cum laude, St. Olaf Coll., 1976; JD magna cum laude, U. Mich., 1979. Bar: Minn. 1979, U.S. Dist. Ct. Minn. 1979, U.S. Claims Ct. 1983, U.S. Tax Ct. 1985. Law clk. Minn. Supreme Ct., St. Paul, 1979-80; assoc. Gray, Plant, Mooty, Mooty, & Bennett P.A., Mpls., 1980-84, ptnr., 1985—. Mem. ABA, Minn. State Bar Assn., Hennepin County Bar Assn. Corporate taxation, Personal income taxation, General corporate. Office: Gray Plant Mooty Mooty & Bennett 33 S 6th St Suite 3400 Minneapolis MN 55402

KLEINBERG, JOEL WILLIAMS HARRIS, lawyer; b. Madison, Wis., Apr. 8, 1943; s. Maurice Selig and Ida Zoe (Tanenbaum) K.; m. Laurie Wax, July 7, 1968; children: Leslie, Seth. BA, Yale U., 1964, JD, 1967. Bar: D.C. 1968, Calif. 1968., U.S. Supreme Ct. 1975. Assoc. Rose, Klein & Marias, Los Angeles, 1968-70; sole practice Los Angeles, 1970—; prof. law U. La Verne (Calif.) Law Ctr., 1971-80. Mem. ABA, Assn. Trial Lawyers Am. (bd. dirs. 1985—, Calif. Trial Lawyers Orgn. (bd. dirs. 1981-82, 84-85). Democrat. Jewish. Club: Yale (Los Angeles) (pres. 1973-74). Avocation: collecting hand-blown glass vessels by Am. artists. Personal injury. Office: One Wilshire Blvd Los Angeles CA 90017

KLEINBERG, ROBERT SAMUEL, lawyer; b. Jersey City, July 5, 1934; s. Sydney Harold and Florence (Jacobs) K.; m. Doris Schatzman, July 4, 1960; children—Michael, Deborah, Linda. B.S. magna cum laude, Boston U., 1958; J.D., Rutgers U., 1961. Bar: N.J. 1961, N.Y. 1984, U.S. Supreme Ct. 1966. Assoc., Rosenberg, Schmidt & Greenhalgh, Hackensack, N.J., 1961-64; ptnr. Zisa, Jacobs & Kleinberg, Hackensack, 1965-66; dep. atty. gen. State N.J., 1966-68; sole practice, Park Ridge, N.J., 1968-74; ptnr. Kleinberg and Taylor, Park Ridge, 1975-82; sole practice, Park Ridge, 1982—; judge mcpl. ct., 1985—. Corp. counsel Borough of Park Ridge (N.J.), 1970-75. Trustee, Temple Beth Sholom of Pascack Valley, Park Ridge, 1962-80, chmn., 1965-66, 75-76, pres., 1969-70, 76-77; mcpl. chmn. Park Ridge Democratic Party, 1965-75, 81-85; committeeman Bergen County (N.J.) Dem. Party, 1966-75, 80-85; mem. Park Ridge Planning Bd., 1965-70, sec., 1969-70. Mem. ABA, N.J. Bar Assn., Bergen County Bar Assn., N.J. Inst. Mcpl. Attys., Pascack Valley C. of C. Clubs: Rotary (pres. 1980-81, dist. gov. dist. 749, 1987—), Elks (Park Ridge); Masons, Park Ridge Dem. Family and matrimonial, Local government, General practice. Home: 7 Sturms Pl Park Ridge NJ 07656 Office: 127 Kinderkamack Rd Park Ridge NJ 07656

KLEINE, RICHARD ALLEN, lawyer; b. Lancaster, Pa., May 29, 1946; s. William Francis and Josephine (Ludwikowski) K.; m. Debra Louise Ennis, Sept. 13, 1980. BCE, Ga. Inst. Tech., 1968; JD cum laude, Ohio State U., 1971. Bar: Ohio 1971, D.C. 1972, U.S. Ct. Appeals (D.C. cir.) 1972, U.S. Supreme Ct. 1975, U.S. Ct. Appeals (6th cir.) 1978, U.S. Ct. Appeals (3d cir.) 1983, Mo. 1984. Assoc. Howrey & Simon, Washington, 1971-77, ptnr., 1978-83; antitrust counsel Monsanto Co., St. Louis, 1983-86, asst. gen. counsel, 1986—; lectr. seminars on antitrust law, 1978—. Contbr. articles on antitrust law to profl. jours. Served to capt. U.S. Army, 1968-76. Mem. ABA, D.C. Bar Assn., Bar Assn. Met. St. Louis. Republican. Roman Catholic. Clubs: Annapolis Yacht, Forest Hills Country (Chesterfield, Mo.). Avocations: sailing, golf. Administrative and regulatory, Antitrust, Federal civil litigation. Home: 2 Peakmount Ln Chesterfield MO 63017 Office: Monsanto Co 800 N Lindbergh Blvd Saint Louis MO 63167

KLEINPETER, ROBERT LOREN, lawyer; b. Baton Rouge, Feb. 13, 1955; s. Robert L. and Rachel Beth (Williams) K.; m. Ashley Ann Ward, Mar. 31, 1979; children: Laura Clayton, Alden Leigh. BS, La. State U., 1976, JD, 1978. Bar: La. 1979, U.S. Dist. Ct. (mid. dist.) La. 1979, U.S. Dist. Ct. (ea. dist.) La. 1981, U.S. Ct. Appeals (5th cir.) 1981. Ptnr. Kleinpeter & Kleinpeter, Baton Rouge, 1979—. Mem. ABA, La. Bar Assn., Baton Rouge Bar Assn. Republican. Baptist. Club: Baton Rouge Country. Lodge: Masons (worshipful master 1985-86). General practice, State civil litigation, Insurance. Home: 3988 S Ramsey Dr Baton Rouge LA 70808 Office: PO Box 66443 Baton Rouge LA 70896

KLEMANN, GILBERT LACY, II, lawyer; b. New Rochelle, N.Y., July 26, 1950; s. N. Robert and Rosemary Virginia (Gerard) K.; m. Patricia Louise Hild, June 16, 1973; children: Tricia Rosemary, Gilbert Hild. AB, Coll. Holy Cross, 1972; JD, Fordham U., 1975. Bar: N.Y. 1976, U.S. Dist. Ct. (so. and ea. dists.) N.Y. 1976. Assoc. Chadbourne, Parke, Whiteside & Wolff, N.Y.C., 1975-83; ptnr. Chadbourne & Parke formerly Chadbourne, Parke, Whiteside & Wolff, N.Y.C., 1983—. Editor Fordham Law Rev., 1974-75. Mem. ABA. Republican. Roman Catholic. Club: Greenwich (Conn.) Country. Avocation: golf. General corporate, General practice. Home: 36 Horseshoe Rd Greenwich CT 06807 Office: Chadbourne & Parke 30 Rockefeller Plaza New York NY 10112

KLEMESRUD, NORMAND CHARLES, lawyer; b. Charles City, Iowa, Aug. 9, 1947; s. James R. and Helen M. (Hansen) K.; m. Linda Link, Feb. 17, 1968; children—Nathaniel, Jason, Kari. B.A., U. No. Iowa, 1973; J.D., Hamline U., 1976. Bar: Iowa 1976, U.S. Dist. Ct. (no. dist.) Iowa 1976. Sole practice, Charles City, 1976-82, 1984-86; ptnr. Klemesrud & Huegel, Charles City, 1982-84. County chmn. Dem. Orgn., Charles City, 1984-86. Served with USN, 1968-71. Mem. ABA, Iowa Bar Assn., Am. Acad. Hosp. Attys., Iowa Soc. Hosp. Attys. Lutheran. State civil litigation, Health, General practice. Office: 500 Kelly Charles City IA 50616

KLEVANSKY, SIMON, lawyer; b. Phila., June 23, 1945. BA, U. Pa., 1967; JD, Stanford U., 1977. Bar: Calif. 1978, Washington 1978, Hawaii 1982. Law clk. to presiding justice Wash. Supreme Ct., 1978-79; assoc. Gelber & Gelber, Honolulu, 1983—. Fellow Ctr. for Law in Pub. Interest, 1977-78. Mem. ABA, Wash. State Bar Assn., Calif. Bar Assn., Hawaii Bar Assn., Phi Beta Kappa. Home: 2827 Dow St Honolulu HI 96817 Office: Gelber & Gelber 745 Fort St #1400 Honolulu HI 96813

KLEVORICK, ALVIN K., law and economics educator; b. 1943. BA, Amherst Coll., 1963; MA, 1965; PhD, Princeton U., 1967. Lectr. econs. Princeton U., 1966-67; asst. prof. econs. Yale U., 1967-70, assoc. prof. econs., 1970-73, vis. lectr. law, 1972-73, assoc. prof. law and econs., 1973-75, prof. law and econs., 1975-86; John Thomas Smith prof. law, 1986—. Fellow Ctr. for Advanced Study in Behavioral Scis., 1975-76. Mem. Am. Econ. Assn., Econometric Soc. Legal education. Office: Cowles Found Research Econs 2125 Yale Sta New Haven CT 06520

KLEWANS, SAMUEL N., lawyer; b. Lock Haven, Pa., Mar. 2, 1941; s. Morris and Ruth N. K.; m. Linda J. Wright, Aug. 28, 1986; children—Richard Bennett, Ruth Elise, Paul Henry, Margo Ilene. A.B., U. Pa., 1963; J.D., Am. U., 1966. Bar: Va. 1966, U.S. Dist. Ct. (ea. dist.) Va. 1966, U.S. Dist. Ct. D.C. 1967, U.S. Ct. Appeals D.C. 1967, U.S. Ct. Appeals (4th cir.) 1967, U.S. Supreme Ct. 1971. Law clk., U.S. Dist. Ct. Ea. Dist. Va. 1966-67; ptnr. Fried, Fried & Klewans, Springfield, Va., 1970-86; prin. Klewans & Assocs., 1986—. Served to 1st lt. JAGC-USAR, 1966-72. Mem. ABA (ins. com. real property, probate and trust sect. 1977—, com. closely-held corps. 1982—, com. profl. service orgns. 1982—), Fairfax County Bar Assn. (ethics and grievance com. 1971-72, mem. 75-76, courts com. 1975-76; jud. selection com. 1979-82, chmn. 1981-82), Va. State Bar (mem. disciplinary bd. 1976-84, vice chmn. 1982-83, chmn. tax sect. 1983-84), Va. Bar Assn. (chmn. profl. responsibility, 1987—), Va. Trial Lawyers Assn., Assn. Trial Lawyers Am., U.S. Supreme Ct. Hist. Soc., Fairfax County C. of C. General corporate, Corporate taxation, Public international. Address: 8500 Leesburg Pike Suite 7100 Vienna VA 22180

KLIMON, ELLEN LOUISE, lawyer, educator, consultant; b. Harrisburg, Pa., Jan. 17, 1946; d. George Michael and Irene Catherine (Gregor) Schmeltzer; children: William Michael, Ian Christopher. A.B. in Psychology, Rosemont Coll., 1972; J.D., U. Cin., 1978. Bar: Ohio 1978, U.S. Dist. Ct. (so. dist.) Ohio 1979, Pa. 1985, U.S. Ct. Appeals (3d cir. 1985); C.P.C.U. Occupational analyst Commonwealth of Pa., Harrisburg, 1972-74; ins. adjuster Lloyd Deist, Inc., Cin., 1977-78; asst. editor FC&S Bulls., Nat. Underwriter Co., Cin., 1978-81; assoc. dir. risk mgmt. U. Cin., 1981-84, dir. risk mgmt., 1984-85, dir. risk mgmt. U. Pa., 1985-87; ptnr. Fischer, Klimon, Salman & Harpster, Cin., 1984-85, ptnr. Klimon, Salman, Greve & Harpster, Phila., 1985—; pres. Neumann Ins. Co., 1987—; corp. dir. risk mgmt. Franciscan Health System, Chadds Ford, Pa., 1987—; cons. Don Malecki & Assocs., Fort Thomas, Ky., 1983-85; asst. atty. gen. State of Ohio, Columbus, 1983-85; asst. prof. family medicine U. Cin., 1984-85; legal adviser Children's Internat. Summer Villages, Cin., 1984-85. Editor: Insuring the Lease Exposure, Part II, 1981; contbr. articles to profl jours. Mem. Our Lady of Rosary Sch. Bd., Greenhills, Ohio, 1974-81; v.p. Covered Bridge Civic Assn., Cin., 1979-81, area rep., 1979-82; pres. Nat. Underwriter Co. Fed. Credit Union, Cin., 1980-81. Pa. Higher Edn. Assistance Agy. scholar Rosemont Coll., Phila., 1971-72. Mem. ABA, Ohio Bar Assn., Cin. Bar Assn., Soc. C.P.C.U.s, Am. Soc. Law and Medicine, Nat. Health Lawyers Assn., Am. Soc. Hosp. Risk Mgrs., Univ. Risk Mgmt. and Ins. Assn., Risk and Ins. Mgmt. Soc. Republican. Roman Catholic. Insurance, Personal injury, Health. Office: Neumann Ins Co US Rts 1 and 202 Brandywine One Bldg Chadds Ford PA 19317

KLINE, ALLEN HABER, JR., lawyer; b. Houston, June 17, 1954; s. Allen H. Sr. and Maude Rose (Brown) K.; m. Barbara Ann Byrd, July 24, 1982; 1 child, Allison Ashley. BA, U. Denver, 1976; JD, U. Miami, 1979. Bar: Tex. 1980, U.S. Dist. Ct. (so. dist.) Tex. 1980, U.S. Ct. Appeals (5th cir.) 1980, U.S. Ct. Appeals (11th cir.) 1983, U.S. Supreme Ct. 1985. Sole practice Houston, 1980—. Mem. Assn. Trial Lawyers Am., Tex. Trail Lawyers Assn., Houston Bar Assn. Club: City Wide (Houston) (life). Avocations: tennis, water, snow skiing. Personal injury, State civil litigation, Admiralty. Office: 440 Louisiana Suite 2440 Houston TX 77002

KLINE, DAVID ADAM, lawyer; b. Keota, Okla., Sept. 27, 1923; s. David Adam and Lucy Leila (Wood) K.; m. Ruthela Deal, Aug. 25, 1947; children—Steven, Timothy, Ruthanna. Student Oklahoma City U., 1945-47; J.D., Okla. U., 1950. Bar: Okla. 1949. Law clk., spl. master U.S. Dist. Ct., Okla., 1952-61; 1st asst. U.S. atty. Western Dist. Okla., 1961-69; judge Western Dist. Okla., U.S. Bankruptcy Ct., Oklahoma City, 1969-82; mem. U.S. Magistrates Selection Panel Western Dist. Okla., 1981; Fed. Jud. Ctr. faculty mem., Washington; mem. Nat. Seminar Bankruptcy Judges, 1971-86; adj. prof. law Oklahoma City U., 1980-84. Served with USNR, 1942-45. Ranked top Oklahoma County trial judge in survey Oklahoma County Bar Assn., 1974. Mem. Nat. Conf. Bankruptcy Judges (pres. 1977-78), Order of Coif, Phi Delta Phi. Bd. editors Norton Bankruptcy Law and Practice, 1986; bd. advisers Ann. Survey Bankruptcy Law, 1979; contbg. author Cowans Bankruptcy Law and Practice, 1982. Bankruptcy, Federal civil litigation, Criminal. Office: Kline & Kline 720 NE 63d St Oklahoma City OK 73105

KLINE, GARY ALAN, lawyer; b. Toledo, Apr. 10, 1956; s. Russell W. and N. Jean (Nolte) K.; m. Debra Louise Frays, Sept. 22, 1984. AB, Miami U., Oxford, Ohio, 1978; JD, U. Toledo, 1981. Bar: Ohio 1981, Ind. 1982, U.S. Dist. Ct. (no. and so. dists.) Ind. 1982. Corp. atty. Coachmen Industries, Inc., Elkhart, Ind., 1981-86; assoc. legal counsel Uniden Corp. Am., Indpls., 1986—. General corporate. Home: 9228-C Dansk Ridge Ct. Indianapolis IN 46250

KLINE, JAMES EDWARD, lawyer; b. Fremont, Ohio, Aug. 3, 1941; s. Walter J. and Sophia Kline; m. Mary Ann Bruening, Aug. 29, 1964; children: Laura Anne, Matthew Thomas, Jennifer Sue. BS in Social Sci., John Carroll U., 1963; JD, Ohio State U., 1966. Bar: Ohio 1966. Assoc. Eastman & Smith, Toledo, 1966-70; ptnr. Eastman, Stichter, Smith & Bergman, 1970-84, Shumaker, Loop & Kendrick, 1984—; corp. sec., Sheller-Globe Corp. 1977-84; bd. dirs. Bostleman Corp., Diversified Material Handling, Inc., Security Funding, Inc., Essex Devel. Group. Trustee Kidney Found. of Northwestern Ohio, Inc., 1972-81, pres., 1979-80; bd. dirs. Crosby Gardens, Toledo, 1974-80, pres., 1977-79; trustee Toledo Symphony Orch., 1981—; bd. dirs. Toledo Zool. Soc., 1983—, Toledo Area Regional Transit Authority, 1984—, Home Away From Home, Inc. (Ronald McDonald House NW Ohio), 1983—. Fellow Ohio Bar Found.; mem. ABA, Ohio State Bar Assn. (corp. law com. sec. 1973-76, vice chmn. 1977-82, chmn. 1977-82, 83-86), Toledo Bar Assn., Toledo Area C. of C. Roman Catholic. Clubs: Inverness, Toledo. General corporate, Corporate taxation. Home: 5958 Swan Creek Dr Toledo OH 43614 Office: 1000 Jackson Blvd Toledo OH 43624

KLINE, SIDNEY DELONG, JR., lawyer; b. West Reading, Pa., Mar. 25, 1932; s. Sidney D. and Leona Clarice (Barkalow) K.; m. Barbara Phyllis James, Dec. 31, 1955; children—Allison S., Leslie S., Lisa P. A.B., Dickinson Sch. Coll., 1954, J.D. with honors, 1956. Bar: Pa. 1956, U.S. Dist. Ct. (ea. dist.) Pa. 1961, U.S. Supreme Ct. 1967. Assoc. Stevens & Lee, Reading, Pa., 1958—; bd. dirs. Meridian Bancorp, Inc., Reading, Am. Title Ins. Co., Miami, Horrigan Am., Inc., Reading. Pres., United Way of Berks County, Reading, 1972-74; bd. dirs., v.p. Reading Ctr. City Devel. Fund, 1976—; trustee Dickinson Sch. Law, 1978—, Dickinson Coll., 1979—. Served with U.S. Army, 1956-58. Recipient Doran award United Way Berks County, 1979. Fellow Am. Coll. Probate Counsel; mem. Pa. Bar Assn., Berks County Bar Assn. Republican. Lutheran. Clubs: Berkshire Country (Reading); Moselem Springs Golf (Fleetwood, Pa.). Banking, Probate, Real property. Office: Stevens & Lee 607 Washington St PO Box 679 Reading PA 19603

KLINE, STEPHEN HIBBARD, lawyer; b. Cheyenne, Wyo., Aug. 24, 1954; s. Duane M. Jr. and Joanna (Wagstaff) K. BA cum laude, Williams Coll., 1976; JD, U. Wyo., 1979. Bar: Wyo. 1979, U.S. Dist. Ct. Wyo. 1979, U.S. Ct. Appeals (10th cir.) 1984. Sole practice Cheyenne, 1981-83; ptnr. Kline & Buck, Cheyenne, 1983-85, Kline, Buck & Asay, Cheyenne, 1985—. Del. Wyo. Rep. Conv., Jackson and Riverton, 1984, 86; candidate Wyo. Legis., Cheyenne, 1984, 86. Mem. ABA, Wyo. Bar Assn., Assn. Trial Lawyers Am., Wyo. Trial Lawyers Assn. Episcopalian. Lodge: Rotary. Civil rights, Federal civil litigation, State civil litigation. Office: Kline Buck & Asay Equality State Bank Bldg Suite 200 19th & Pioneer Ave Cheyenne WY 82001

KLINE, TIMOTHY DEAL, lawyer; b. Oklahoma City, July 16, 1949; s. David Adam and Ruthela (Deal) K.; m. Alyssa Lipp Krysler, Aug. 29, 1985. BA, U. Okla., 1971, JD, 1976. Bar: Okla. 1976, U.S. Dist. Ct. (we. dist.) Okla. 1977, U.S. Ct. Appeals (10th cir.) 1977. Law clk. to presiding justice U.S. Dist. Ct. (we. dist.) Okla., Oklahoma City, 1976-80; assoc. Linn, Helms, Kirk & Burkett, Oklahoma City, 1980-83; ptnr. Kline & Kline, Oklahoma City, 1983—; adj. prof. law Oklahoma City U., 1980-85. Mem. Phi Delta Phi. Democrat. Bankruptcy. Office: Kline & Kline 720 NE 63d St Oklahoma City OK 73105

KLINEDINST, JOHN DAVID, lawyer; b. Washington, Jan. 20, 1950; s. David Moulson and Mary Stewart (Coxe) K.; m. Cynthia Lynn DuBain, Aug. 15, 1981. BA in History, Washington and Lee U., 1971, JD, 1978; MBA in Fin. and Investments, George Washington U., 1975. Bar: Calif. 1979, U.S. Dist. Ct. (so. dist.) Calif. 1979. With comml. lending dept. 1st Nat. Bank Md., Montgomery County, 1971-74; assoc. Ludecke, McGrath & Denton, San Diego, 1979-80; ptnr. Whitney & Klinedinst, San Diego, 1980-

81, Klinedinst & Meiser, San Diego, 1981-86, Klinedinst, Fliehman & Rescigno, San Diego, 1986—. Mem. ABA, Calif. Bar Assn., San Diego Bar Assn., Phi Kappa Psi, Washington and Lee U. Alumni Assn. (bd. dirs. 1986—), Washington and Lee U. Club (pres. San Diego chpt. 1980—). Republican. Episcopalian. Federal civil litigation, State civil litigation. Home: 2161 Caminito Del Barco Del Mar CA 92014 Office: Klinedinst Fliehman & Rescigno 444 W C St Suite 330 San Diego CA 92101

KLING, EDWARD LEWIS, lawyer; b. Cin., Nov. 5, 1947; s. Harold George and Shirlee Ann K.; m. Sarah Caroline Kemsley, Mar. 31, 1974. B.S., Babson Coll., 1968; B.A., Oxford U., 1971; B.A., 1973, M.A., 1974. Bar: Calif. 1974. Assoc. Buchalter, Nemer, Fields & Chrystie, Los Angeles, 1973-77; v.p., gen. counsel Itel Internat. Corp., 1977-80; ptnr. Dechert, Price & Rhoads, London, 1980—. Mem. ABA, Internat. Bar Assn., Am. Soc. Internat. Law. Clubs: United Oxford and Cambridge University, Roehampton (London). Private international.

KLINGENBERG, DONALD HERBERT, lawyer; b. Cleve., Aug. 7, 1945; s. Adolph William and Dorothy May (McGoun) K.; children: David, Kristy; m. Gail A. Albritton, Dec. 31, 1982. BA, Case Western REs. U., 1967, JD, 1973. Bar: Ohio 1973, U.S. Dist. Ct. (no. dist.) Ohio 1974, U.S. Supreme Ct. 1977. Law clk. to presiding justice 8th Dist. Ct. Appeals, Cleve., 1973-75; ptnr. Blakely, Dean, Wilson & Klingenberg, Painesville, Ohio, 1976—; referee Lake County Juvenile Ct., Painesville, 1980-82; acting judge City of Mentor, Ohio, 1984—. Assoc. editor Case Western Res. U. Law Rev., 1972-73. Mem. exec. com. Lake County Reps., Ohio, 1979-81, precinct committeeman, 1977-81; pres. Lake Met. Housing Authority, Painesville, 1983. Mem. ABA, Ohio Bar Assn., Lake County Bar Assn. (sec. 1983-84, treas. 1984-85, v.p. 1985-86, pres. 1986-87), Assn. Ohio Trial Lawyers, Order of Coif. Republican. Mem. United Ch. Christ. Club: Exchange (Painesville) (pres. 1984). Lodge: Elks. Avocations: racquetball, astronomy. General practice, Personal injury, Family and matrimonial. Home: 14-3 Meadowlawn Dr Mentor OH 44060 Office: Blakely Dean Wilson & Klingenberg 56 Liberty St Painesville OH 44077

KLINGER, ALAN MARK, lawyer; b. Bklyn., July 19, 1956; s. David and Gloria (Feldman) K.; m. Susan Debra Wagner, Aug. 29, 1982. AB, Princeton U., 1978; JD, NYU, 1981. Bar: N.Y. 1982, N.J. 1982, U.S. Dist. Ct. N.J., U.S. Dist. Ct. (so., ea. and we. dists.) N.Y. 1982, U.S. Ct. Appeals (2d cir.) 1985. Law clk. to judge N.J. Supreme Ct., Trenton, 1981-82; assoc. Stroock & Stroock & Lavan, N.Y.C., 1982—. Rep. United Jewish Appeal, N.Y.C., 1985. Mem. ABA, N.Y. State Bar Assn., Fed. Bar Council, Assn. of Bar of City of N.Y., ACLU. Avocations: chess, table-tennis, basketball. Federal civil litigation, State civil litigation, Libel. Office: Stroock & Stroock & Lavan 7 Hanover Sq New York NY 10004-2594

KLINGER, MARILYN SYDNEY, lawyer; b. N.Y.C., Aug. 14, 1953; d. Victor and Lillyan Judith (Hollinger) K. BS, U. Santa Clara, 1975; JD, U. Calif., Hastings, 1978. Bar: Calif. 1978. Assoc. Chickering & Gregory, San Francisco, 1978-81, Steefel, Levitt & Weiss, San Francisco, 1981-82, Sedgwick, Detert, Moran & Arnold, San Francisco, 1982—. Sec. Hastings Dems., San Francisco, 1975-78; vol. atty. Lawyers Commn. on Urban Affairs, San Francisco, 1978-80; atty. Sta. KQED Call-a-Lawyer, San Francisco, 1979—; bd. dirs. Paradise Cay Homeowners Assn., Tiburon, Calif., v.p., 1985-87. Mem. ABA (tort and ins. practice sects., surety and fidelity coms.), Surety Forum (lectr.), Northern Calif. Surety Underwriters Assn., Northern Calif. Surety Claims Assn. (lectr.). Democrat. Clubs: Tiburon Yacht (hospitality chmn. 1985-86). Avocations: sailing, reading, softball. State civil litigation, Insurance, Contracts commercial. Home: 213 Jamaica St Tiburon CA 94920 Office: Sedgwick Detert Moran & Arnold 1 Embarcadero Ctr 16th Floor San Francisco CA 94111

KLINGER, PHILLIP DENNIS, lawyer; b. Cedar Rapids, Iowa, Dec. 8, 1942; s. Clarence F. and Kathleen Joan (Daley) K.; m. Loree Smith, Feb. 26, 1967; 1 child, Shantel; m. 2d, Jeri Lee Schroeder, Nov. 6, 1976; children—Matthew, Bradley. B.B.A., U. Iowa, 1964, J.D., 1968. Bar: Iowa, 1968, U.S. Dist. Ct. (no. dist.) Iowa 1968, U.S. Dist. Ct. (so. dist.) Iowa 1969, U.S. Supreme Ct. 1971. Asst. Linn County atty., 1968-74; assoc. Faches Klinger & Gloe, Cedar Rapids, Iowa, 1968-78, Klinger, Heckel & Robinson, 1978-79; mem. Klinger, Robinson & McCuskey, P.C., Cedar Rapids, 1979—. Mem. Linn County Council on Aging, 1970-76, pres., 1976; chmn. Cedar Rapids Noise Ordinance Com., 1981—; mem. Linn County Airport Zoning Commn., 1976-79. Mem. Iowa Bar Assn., Linn County Bar Assn. Real property, General corporate, Probate. Home: 3012 Adirondack Dr NE Cedar Rapids IA 52402 Office: 401 Old Marion Rd NE Cedar Rapids IA 52402

KLINGHOFFER, STEVEN HAROLD, lawyer; b. Newark, Aug. 20, 1950; s. Melvin and Phyllis (Herberg) K.; m. Lori Karen Kreitchman, June 3, 1972; children—Lisa, Rachel. B.S. in B.A., Boston U., 1972, J.D., 1975. Bar: N.J. 1975, U.S. Dist. Ct. N.J. 1975, U.S. Tax Ct. 1978, U.S. Ct. Internat. Trade 1981. Law sec. Superior Ct. N.J., Newark, 1975-76; assoc. Yankowitz, Tessler & Yankowitz, East Orange, N.J., 1976-79; ptnr. Starrett & Klinghoffer, West Orange, N.J., 1979-86; dir. Vertex Corp., Springfield, N.J.; pres. WPI Communications, Inc. V.p. Jewish Family Service of MetroWest, Millburn, N.J., 1984; trustee Jewish Community Fedn. of MetroWest, East Orange, 1984. Mem. ABA, N.J. State Bar Assn., Essex County Bar Assn. Jewish. Landlord-tenant, Real property, General corporate. Office: Starrett & Klinghoffer PC 55 Morris Ave Springfield NJ 07081

KLINGSBERG, DAVID, lawyer; b. N.Y.C., Feb. 4, 1934; s. Samuel S. and Dorothy (Wecker) K.; m. Fran Sue Morganstern, Aug. 16, 1959; 3 children. LL.B., Yale U., 1957; B.S., NYU, 1954. Bar: N.Y. bar 1957. Law clk. to U.S. Dist. Judge, N.Y., 1957-58; atty. U.S. Dept. Justice, Office Dep. Atty. Gen., Washington, 1958-59; asst. U.S. atty. criminal div. So. Dist. N.Y., 1959-61; chief appellate atty. U.S. Atty. Office, N.Y., 1961-62; asso. firm Kaye, Scholer, Fierman, Hays and Handler, N.Y.C., 1962-65; partner Kaye, Scholer, Fierman, Hays and Handler, 1966—. Contbr. articles to legal jours.; mem. editorial bd. Yale Law Jour, 1956-57. Fellow Am. Coll. Trial Lawyers; mem. Am. Bar Assn., Assn. of Bar of N.Y.C. (chmn. anti-trust and trade regulation com. 1986—), N.Y. State Bar Assn., Fed. Bar Council. Federal civil litigation, State civil litigation. Office: 425 Park Ave New York NY 10022

KLIPSTEIN, ROBERT ALAN, lawyer; b. N.Y.C., Sept. 23, 1936; s. Harold David and Hyacinth (Levin) K. A.B., Columbia U., 1957, J.D., 1960; LL.M. in Taxation, NYU, 1965. Bar: N.Y. 1960, U.S. Supreme Ct. 1964. Practice law, N.Y.C., 1961—; assoc. Saxe Bacon & O'Shea, 1961, Rosenman, Colin, Kaye, Petschek & Freund, 1962-63; law sec. to justice N.Y. County Supreme Ct., 1963-64; assoc. Bernays & Eisner, 1965-70; ptnr. Eisner, Klipstein & Klipstein, 1971-77; ptnr. Danziger, Bangser, Klipstein, Goldsmith, Greenwald & Weiss, 1977—; arbitrator City of N.Y. Small Claims Ct., 1971—. Served with U.S. Army, 1960-62. Mem. ABA, N.Y. State Bar Assn., Assn. Bar City of N.Y., N.Y. County Lawyers Assn., Am. Immigration Lawyers Assn., Westchester County Bar Assn., Am. Judges Assn. Club: Univ. Glee (N.Y.C.). Probate, Estate taxation, Immigration, naturalization, and customs. Home: 401 E 74th St New York NY 10021 Office: 230 Park Ave New York NY 10169

KLOCK, JOHN HENRY, lawyer; b. Gouverneur, N.Y., Mar. 29, 1944; s. John F. and Patricia M. (Chateau) K.; m. Connie E. McLaughlin, May 31, 1969; children: Thomas, Jacqueline. BA, St. Bonaventure U., 1966; MA, NYU, 1970; JD, Rutgers U., 1976. Law clk. to presiding justice N.J. State Ct., Newark, 1976-77; assoc. Crummy, Del Deo, Dolan, Griffinger & Vecchione, Newark, 1977-83, ptnr., 1983—. Mem. Scotch Plains (N.J.) Hist. Soc., 1983. Mem. N.J. Trial Lawyers Assn. Avocation: gardening. Environment, Construction, State civil litigation. Office: Crummy Del Deo Dolan Griffinger & Vechione Gateway 1 Newark NJ 07102

KLODOWSKI, AMY MARTHA AUSLANDER, lawyer; b. N.Y.C., Oct. 13, 1952; d. Oscar and Beatrice (Feinberg) Auslander; m. Harry F. Klodowski, Jr., Nov. 12, 1983; 1 child, Deborah Bea. B.A., Kent State U., 1974; J.D., U. Pitts., 1978. Bar: Pa. 1978. Atty., Equitable Resources, Inc., Pitts., 1978—. Mem. ABA, Fed. Energy Bar Assn., Pa. Bar Assn., Allegheny County Bar Assn. Club: Rivers (Pitts.). FERC practice, Public utilities. Office: Equitable Resources Inc 420 Blvd of the Allies Pittsburgh PA 15219

KLOEPPEL, BYRON PETER, lawyer; b. Mpls., Nov. 17, 1941; s. Vernon B. and Ruth E. (Pederson) K.; m. Pamela K. Cuthrell, Aug. 29, 1964; Children: Byron P. Jr., Marvin C. BA, U. Va., 1964, JD, 1970. Bar: Va. 1970, U.S. Dist. Ct. (ea. dist.) Va. 1970, U.S. Ct. Appeals (4th cir.) 1970. Law clk. to presiding justice U.S. Dist. Ct. (ea. dist.), Norfolk, Va., 1970-71, 72-73; assoc. Kanter & Kanter, Norfolk, 1971-72, Cooper & Davis, Portsmouth, Va., 1973-85, Moody, Strople & Lawrence, Portsmouth, 1985—. Served to lt. j.g. USN, 1964-67. Mem. Va. Bar Assn., Norfolk Bar Assn., Portsmouth Bar Assn., Assn. Trial Lawyers Am., Va. Trial Lawyers Assn. Democrat. State civil litigation, Personal injury. Home: 1503 S Sea Breeze Trail Virginia Beach VA 23452 Office: Moody Strople & Lawrence Ltd County and Court Sts Portsmouth VA 23705

KLOESS, LAWRENCE H., JR., lawyer; b. Mamaroneck, N.Y., Jan. 30, 1927; s. Lawrence H. and Harriette Adelia (Holly) K.; m. Eugenia Ann Underwood, Nov. 10, 1931; children—Lawrence H., Price Mentzel, Branch Donelson, David Holly. A.B., U. Ala., 1954, J.D., 1956. Bar: Ala. 1956, U.S. Dist. Ct. (no. dist.) Ala. 1956, U.S. Ct. Appeals (5th cir.) 1957, U.S. Ct. Mil. Appeals 1971, U.S. Supreme Ct. 1971, U.S. Ct. Appeals (11th cir.) 1981. Sole practice, Birmingham, Ala., 1956-60; corp. counsel Bankers Fire and Marine Ins. Co., sole practice, Birmingham, 1962-66; dist. counsel for Ala. Office of Dist. Counsel U.S. VA, Montgomery, 1966—. Vice chmn. Salvation Army Adv. Bd., 1981, mem. bd., 1978-81; mem. nat. conf. bar pres.'s ABA, 1981—. Served to col. Judge Adv. Gen. USAFR, 1972-86, ret. Mem. ABA (award of merit, nat. conf. bar. presidents 1981—), Ala. State Bar Assn. (chmn. editorial adv. bd. Ala. Lawyer, 1975-79, editorial bd. 1970-82, character and fitness com., chmn. law day com. 1973, chmn. citizen edn. com. 1974, continuing legal edn. adv. com. 1983), Ala. Law Found. (trustee), Montgomery County Bar Assn. (chmn. law day com. 1972, chmn. state bar liaison com. 1975, chmn. bd. dirs. 1977, bd. dirs. 1979, chmn. and editor Montgomery County Bar Jour., ABA Merit award, 1979-81 v.p. 1980, pres. 1981), Fed. Bar Assn. (pres. Montgomery Fed. Bar Assn. 1973), Citizens Conf. on Ala. Ct. (exec. com., sponsor of new jud. article to state constn. 1973), Citizens Conf. on Criminal and Juvenile Justice (mem. staff 1974), Farrah Law Soc., Res. Officers Assn. of U.S. (chpt. pres. 1978, state pres. 1982). Republican. Episcopalian. Clubs: Montgomery Country, Rotary (pres. 1979, Paul Harris fellow), Maxwell-Gunter Officers (Montgomery). Contbr. articles on law to profl. jours. Real property, Federal civil litigation, Bankruptcy. Home: 3174 Highfield Dr Montgomery AL 36111 Office: 474 S Court St Suite 234 Montgomery AL 36104

KLONOFF, ROBERT HOWARD, lawyer; b. Portland, Oreg., Mar. 15, 1955; s. Bernard and Charlotte (Plosker) K. AB, U. Calif., Berkeley, 1976; JD, Yale U., 1979. Bar: D.C. 1980, U.S. Dist. Ct. D.C. 1980, U.S. Ct. Appeals (D.C. and 5th cirs.) 1980, U.S. Supreme Ct. 1986. Law clk. to presiding judge U.S. Ct. Appeals (5th cir.), Houston, 1979-80; assoc. Arnold & Porter, Washington, 1980-83; asst. U.S. atty. Dept. Justice, Washington, 1983-86; asst. to solicitor gen. U.S. Dept. Justice, Washington, 1986—. Contbr. articles to profl. jours. Mem. ABA, Phi Beta Kappa. Democrat. Jewish. Avocations: music, sports. Federal civil litigation, Criminal, Appellate litigation. Home: 1104 Parrish Dr Rockville MD 20851 Office: US Dept Justice Office Solicitor Gen 9th & Constitution Ave NW Washington DC 20537

KLOS, JEROME JOHN, lawyer; b. LaCrosse, Wis., Jan. 17, 1927; s. Charles and Edna S. (Wagner) K.; m. Mary M. Hamilton, July 26, 1958; children—Bryant H., Geoffrey W. B.S., U. Wis., 1948, J.D., 1950. Bar: Wis. 1950. Practice law LaCrosse, Wis., 1950—; pres. Steele, Klos and Flynn; dir. Home Savs. & Loan Assn., LaCrosse, Union State Bank, West Salem, Wis., La Crosse Indsl. Devel., Inc. Mem. LaCrosse County Bd., 1957-74, vice chmn., 1972-74; pub. adminstr. La Crosse County, 1962-73; bd. dirs. West Salem Area Growth, Inc., La Crosse Area Growth, Inc., LaCrosse Community Theatre; trustee Sander and McKinly Scholarship Funds of West Salem Sch. Dist. Fellow Am. Coll. Real Estate Lawyers, Am. Coll. Probate Counsel; mem. ABA, Wis. Bar Assn. Lodges: Elks, K.C. Probate, General corporate, Banking. Home: 346 N Leonard St West Salem WI 54669 Office: 800 Lynn Tower Bldg La Crosse WI 54601

KLOSK, IRA DAVID, lawyer; b. N.Y.C., Nov. 9, 1932; s. Isidore and Freda (Braunstein) K. B.A., CCNY, 1955; LL.B., Bklyn. Law Sch., 1957. Bar: N.Y. 1958. Sole practice, Bklyn., 1958-81; sr. ptnr. firm Klosk and Ray, Mineola, N.Y., 1981—. Pres. Herricks Citizens Com. Better Schs., N.Y., 1970; mem. Herricks Citizens Budget Adv. Com., 1970, Herricks Sch. Bd., 1971-74; v.p. Hometown Party Mineola, 1979. N.Y. State scholar CCNY, 1951; recipient Richard R. Bowker Meml. award CCNY, 1954, Kupferman-Helm award, 1955. Hon. life mem. N.Y. PTA. Consumer commercial, General corporate. Office: Klosk & Ray 224 Mineola Blvd Mineola NY 11501

KLOTSCHE, JOHN CHESTER, lawyer; b. Milw., June 18, 1942; s. Johannes Martin and Roberta (Roberts) K.; m. Christine Elizabeth Nelson, May 12, 1975; children: Karrisa Faith, Jason Martin, Jonathan William. BS, U. Ariz., 1964; JD, U. Wis., 1967. Bar: Wis. 1967, Ill. 1968, U.S. Dist. Ct. (no. dist.) Ill. 1968, U.S. Ct. Appeals (5th, 6th, and 7th cirs.), U.S. Supreme Ct. Law clk. to presiding justice Wis. Supreme Ct., Madison, 1967-68; assoc. Baker & McKenzie, Chgo., 1968-73, ptnr., 1973—; bd. dirs. Am. Fastener Corp., Chgo. Contbr. articles to profl. jours. Mem. ABA, Ill. Bar Assn., Wis. Bar Assn., Order of Coif, Phi Delta Phi. Corporate taxation, Private international. Office: Baker & McKenzie 2800 Prudential Plaza Chicago IL 60601

KLOTT, DAVID LEE, lawyer; b. Vicksburg, Miss., Dec. 10, 1941; s. Isadore and Dorothy (Lipson) K.; m. Maren J. Randrup, May 25, 1975. BBA summa cum laude, Northwestern U., 1963; JD cum laude, Harvard U., 1966. Bar: Calif. 1966, U.S. Ct. Claims. 1968, U.S. Supreme Ct. 1971, U.S. Tax Ct. 1973, U.S. Ct. Appeals (Fed. cir.) 1982. Ptnr. Pillsbury, Madison & Sutro, San Francisco, 1966—; mem. tax adv. group to subchpt. C J and K., Am. Law Inst.; tchr. Calif. Continuing Edn. of Bar, Practising Law Inst., U. Calif., San Francisco. Served with USAR, 1967. Mem. ABA (tax exempt financing com.), Calif. Bar Assn., Am.-Korean Taekwondo Friendship Assn. (1st dan-black belt), Beta Gamma Sigma, Beta Alpha Psi (pres. local chpt.). Clubs: Harvard (San Francisco), Northwestern (San Francisco), Stock Exchange, Olympic, Commonwealth San Francisco, Commentator, New Calif. Nonprofit corporate law, Corporate taxation. Office: Pillsbury Madison & Sutro 225 Bush St San Francisco CA 94104

KLUCSIK, JOHN FRANCIS, lawyer; b. Bethlehem, Pa., Aug. 3, 1952; s. Frank Charles and Margaret Susan (Popovich) K.; m. Jane Helen Sinnott, Apr. 6, 1974; children: John Paul, Stephen Louis. BA, Lehigh U., 1973, MBA, 1974; JD, Capital U., 1980. Bar: Pa. 1980, Md. 1982, D.C. 1981, U.S. Dist. Ct. D.C. 1981, U.S. Ct. Appeals (D.C. cir.) 1981, U.S. Supreme Ct. 1981. Reporter Bethlehem (Pa.) Globe Times, 1974-75; spl. asst. to chief counsel subcom. transp. and commerce U.S. Ho. of Reps., Washington, 1975-77; law clk. Ohio Atty. Gen.'s Office, Columbus, 1978; atty. U.S. Nuclear Regulatory Commn., Washington, 1980-84; counsel Roy F. Weston, Washington, 1984—; bd. dirs., rules chmn. Georgian Colonies Condo Council; chmn. bd. dirs. Community Services Assn., Silver Spring, Md., 1982-83. Contbr. articles to profl. jours. Named one of Outstanding Young Men in Am., U.S. Jaycees, 1981,83, 84. Mem. ABA, Pa. Bar Assn., Md. Bar Assn., D.C. Bar Assn. Republican. Roman Catholic. Avocations: photography, reading. Nuclear power, Environment. Home: 3818 Dunsinane Dr Silver Spring MD 20906 Office: Roy F Weston PC 955 L'Enfant Plaza 6th Floor Washington DC 20024

KLUS, CHARLES ROBERT, JR., lawyer; b. Muncie, Ind., Mar. 30, 1945; S. Charles Robert Sr. and Catherine Irene (Hannon) K.; m. Sue Carrole Smith, June 7, 1964; children: Nikki Jo, Kristopher Scot. BA, Ball State U., 1972; JD, U. Wyo., 1980. Bar: Wyo. 1980, U.S. Dist. Ct. Wyo. 1980. Assoc. Morgan & Brorby, Gillette, Wyo., 1980-82; sole practice Gillette, Wyo., 1982—. Mem. ABA, Wyo. Bar Assn., Assn. Trial Lawyers Am., Wyo. Trial Lawyers Assn., Campbell County C. of C. (bd. dirs. 1986—), Wyo. State Auto Racing Assn. (sec. 1986), NRA. Republican. Club: Gillette Stock Car. Lodges: Lions (pres. Gillette Sundowners club 1982-84), Rotary. Avocations: auto racing, shooting sports, model building. State civil litigation, Oil and gas leasing, Real property. Home: 1023 Teewinot Circle Gillette WY 82716 Office: First Interstate Bank Bldg 2201 S Douglas Hwy Suite 130 PO Box 1388 Gillette WY 82716

KLYMAN, ANDREW MICHAEL, lawyer; b. Boston, Mar. 2, 1953; s. Leo and Beth (Murstein) K.; m. Carol Anne Cioe, May 20, 1984. B.A., U. Mass., 1974; J.D., U. Miami, Coral Gables, Fla., 1977. Bar: Fla. 1977, U.S. Dist. Ct. (so. dist.) Fla. 1981, Mass. 1987. Assoc. Victor Eskenas, P.A., Miami, Fla., 1978; asst. pub. defender, West Palm Beach, Fla., 1978-84; assoc.Cohen, Scherer, Cohn & Silverman, P.A., North Palm Beach, Fla., 1984-86; staff atty. Com. for Pub. Counsel Services, Springfield, Mass., 1986—. Mem. ABA (litigation sect.), Nat. Assn. Criminal Def. Lawyers, Fla. Bar Assn. (criminal law sect.). Criminal, State civil litigation. Home: 17 Sumner Terr Springfield MA 01108 Office: Com for Pub Counsel Services 1145 Main St Springfield MA 01103

KNAB, KAREN MARKLE, lawyer; d. Joseph George and Mary (Kelly) Markle. B.A., St. Marys Coll., South Bend, Ind., 1970; J.D., U. Chgo., 1975. Bar: Ill. 1975, U.S. Dist. Ct. (no. dist.) Ill. 1981, U.S. Ct. Appeals (7th cir.) 1981. Dep. dir. state cts. Wis. Supreme Ct., Madison, 1977-80; dep. dir. Dept. Revenue, State of Ill., Chgo., 1980-81; dir. family div. D.C. Superior Ct., Washington, 1981-84; dir. adminstrn. Pepper, Hamilton & Scheetz, Washington, 1984-86, cir. exec. U.S. Ct. Appeals (D.C.) Cir., 1986—; pres., cons. Knab Assocs., Chgo., 1980-81. Author: Courts of Limited Jurisdiction, 1977; Alternatives to Litigation, 1978. Contbr. articles to profl. jours. Mem. Nat. Assn. Trial Ct. Adminstrs., Assn. Legal Adminstrs. Judicial administration, Family and matrimonial, Legislative. Office: US Ct Appeals 4826 US Courthouse Washington DC 20001

KNAPP, A. MICHAEL, lawyer; b. N.Y.C., May 8, 1945; s. Mark I. and Dorothy E. (Lipkin) K.; 1 son, Joshua Max; m. Roberta L. Weiss, July 5, 1982. Student Miami U., Oxford, Ohio, 1963-65; B.A. with honors, U. Md., 1967; J.D., Georgetown U., 1970. Bar: Ohio 1970, U.S. Dist. Ct. (so. dist.) Ohio 1970, U.S. Dist. Ct. (so. dist.) Ind. 1972, U.S. Supreme Ct. 1973, U.S. Ct. Appeals (fed. cir.) 1983. Ptnr. Porter, Wright, Morris & Arthur, Columbus, Ohio, 1970—; mem. Ohio Supreme Ct. Rules Adv. Com., 1979-82; lectr. Ohio Legal Center Inst. Continuing Legal Edn. Program. Bd. dirs. Columbus 500 St. Race. Mem. ABA, Ohio Bar Assn. (chmn. jud. adminstrn. and legal reform com. 1979-82, select com. rules of evidence 1981-84), Columbus Bar Assn. (profl. ethics com. 1976-79), Am. Arbitration Assn. (arbitrator), Am. Topical Assn. (claims dir.). Club: Sports Car Am. (nat. adminstr. race control 1984-87) (Englewood, Colo.). Author: Dictionary of International Biography, 1987. Federal civil litigation, State civil litigation. Office: 116 E Second St Wellston OH 45692

KNAPP, GEORGE ROBERT, lawyer; b. Bethlehem, Pa., Oct. 8, 1947; s. Donald Albert and Adelaide Marie (Shogren) K.; m. Cynthia Louise Kallgren, June 12, 1971; children: Katherine, Laura. BA, Colgate U., 1969; JD, Harvard U., 1972. Bar: Pa. 1973, U.S. Dist. Ct. (we. dist.) Pa. 1973. Assoc. Kirkpatrick & Lockhart, Pitts., 1972-78, ptnr., 1978—; bd. dirs. Gateway Publs., Monroeville, Pa., Denney & Co., Pitts., Salem (Ohio) China Co. Mem. Pitts. Tax Club. Republican. Presbyterian. Club: Rivers (Pitts.). Avocations: travel, music, athletics. Contracts commercial, General corporate, Corporate taxation. Office: Kirkpatrick & Lockhart 1500 Oliver Bldg Pittsburgh PA 15222

KNAPP, JOHN ANTHONY, lawyer; b. Mason City, Iowa, June 14, 1949; s. John Emmett and Lois Jane (Feeney) K.; m. Maureen Anne Jacobs, Dec. 30, 1972; children—Christopher John, Kevin Anthony, Elizabeth Lael. B.A., St. John's U., Collegeville, Minn., 1971; J.D., U. Iowa, 1974. Bar: Iowa 1974, Minn. 1974, U.S. Dist. Ct. Minn. 1975, D.C. 1982. Asst. revisor of statutes Minn. Legislature, St. Paul, 1974-76; v.p. Hessian, McKasy & Soderberg, Mpls., 1976-85; ptnr. Winthrop & Weinstine, St. Paul, 1985—; adj. asst. prof. St. Mary's Coll. Grad. Ctr., Mpls., 1985—. Contbr. articles to profl. jours. Mem. ABA, Iowa Bar Assn., Minn. Bar Assn., D.C. Bar Assn., Ramsey County Bar Assn., Minn. Govt. Relations Council, Citizens League, Mortgage Bankers Assn. Minn. (chmn. law com. 1984—). Mem. Democratic Farm Labor Party. Roman Catholic. Club: St. Paul Athletic. General corporate, Administrative and regulatory, Legislative. Home: 2193 Sargent Ave Saint Paul MN 55105 Office: Winthrop & Weinstine 1800 Conwed Tower 444 Cedar St Saint Paul MN 55101

KNAPP, WHITMAN, U.S. judge; b. N.Y.C., Feb. 24, 1909; s. Wallace Percy and Caroline Morgan (Miller) K.; m. Ann Fallert, May 17, 1962; 1 son, Gregory Wallace; children by previous marriage—Whitman Everett, Caroline (Mrs. Edward M. W. Hines), Marion Elizabeth. Grad., Choate Sch., 1927; B.A., Yale, 1931; LL.B., Harvard, 1934. Bar: N.Y. bar 1935. With firm Cadwalader, Wickersham & Taft, N.Y.C., 1935-37; dep. asst. dist. atty. N.Y.C., 1937-41; with firm Donovan, Leisure, Newton & Lumbard, N.Y.C., 1941; mem. staff dist. atty. N.Y.C., 1942-50; chief, appeal bur. 1944-50; partner firm Barrett Knapp Smith Schapiro & Simon (and predecessors), 1950-72; U.S. dist. judge So. Dist. N.Y., 1972—; spl. counsel N.Y. State Youth Commn., 1950-53; Waterfront Commn. N.Y. Harbor, 1953-54; Mem. temp. commn. revision N.Y. State penal law and criminal code, 1964-69; chmn. Knapp Commn. to Investigate Allegations of Police Corruption in N.Y.C., 1969-72; gen. counsel Urban League Greater N.Y., 1962-72. Editor: Harvard Law Rev, 1933-34. Sec. Community Council Greater N.Y., 1952-58; pres. Dalton Schs., N.Y.C., 1950-53, Youth House, 1967-68; Trustee Univ. Settlement, 1945-64, Moblzn. for Youth, 1965-70. Mem. Am. Law Inst., Am. Bar Assn., Am. Bar Found., Am. Coll. Trial Lawyers, Assn. Bar City N.Y. (sec. 1946-49, chmn. exec. com. 1971-72). Home: 134 Greene St New York NY 10012 Office: US Courthouse Foley Sq New York NY 10007

KNAPPENBERGER, DON J., lawyer; b. Kansas City, Kans., June 30, 1950; s. Joseph F. and Opal S. (Schlickau) K.; m. Karen L. Knappenberger. B.S. cum laude, Kans. State U., 1972; J.D., Washburn U., 1975. Bar: Kans. 1975, U.S. Dist. Ct. Kans. 1975. County atty. Stafford County, Kans., 1975-80; ptnr. Gates & Knappenberger, St. John, Kans., 1975-82; sole practice, St. John, 1982—. Sec. Stafford County Fair, 1977-78; instr. Outreach, Great Bend., Kans.; mem. Stafford County Republican Central Com., 1975—. Mem. Kans. Bar Assn., ABA, St. John Bus. Assn., St. John Jaycees, Stafford County Hist. Soc. Lutheran. Club: Stafford County Country. General practice, Probate, Real property. Home: 115 S Monroe Saint John KS 67576 Office: PO Box 245 Saint John KS 67576

KNAUER, LEON THOMAS, lawyer; b. N.Y.C., July 16, 1932; s. Lawrence R. and Loretta M. (Trainor) K.; m. Traude Kunz, Sept. 11, 1976; children—Robert A., Katrine M. B.S. in Math., Fordham U., 1954; J.D., Georgetown U., 1961. Bar: Conn. 1961, D.C. 1961, U.S. Supreme Ct. 1965. Law clk. U.S. Dist. Ct. (D.C.), 1960-61; assoc. Wilkinson, Cragun & Barker, Washington, 1961-68, ptnr., 1968-82; ptnr. Wilkinson, Barker, Knauer & Quinn, Washington, 1982—; instr. Georgetown U. Law Center, 1964-68. Pres., Catholic Apostolic Mass Media, 1974-76; Knights of Malta, 1979—. Served as capt. USMC, 1954-57. Recipient award for outstanding legal service in media area NAACP., 1973. Mem. Fed. Communications Bar Assn. (editor Communications Bar Jour. 1960-69, treas. 1980-82, mem. exec. com. 1982-84). Democrat. Roman Catholic. Clubs: Univ., Washington Golf and Country (Washington); Fordham U. Alumni of Washington (pres. 1982-85). Telecommunications, Federal civil litigation, International private. Office: 1735 New York Ave NW Washington DC 20006

KNAUSS, ROBERT LYNN, legal educator, university dean; b. Detroit, Mar. 24, 1931; s. Karl Ernst and Loise (Atkinson) K.; m. Angela Tirola Lawson, Feb. 21, 1973; children by previous marriage: Robert B., Charles H., Katherine E.; 1 stepson, Ian T. Lawson. A.B., Harvard U., 1952; J.D., U. Mich., 1957. Bar: Calif., Tenn., Tex. Assoc. Pillsbury, Madison & Sutro, San Francisco, 1958-60; prof. law U. Mich., 1960-72; v.p. U. Mich. (Office Student Services), 1970-72; dean, prof. law Vanderbilt U., Nashville, 1972-79; vis. prof. Vt. Law Sch., South Royalton, Amos Tuck Sch. Bus. Adminstrn., Dartmouth Coll., Hanover, N.H., 1979-81; disting. univ. prof. law U. Houston Law Center, 1981—, dean, 1981—; cons. spl. studies security markets SEC, 1962-63; rapporteur, panel on capital formation Am. Soc. Internat. Law, 1967-71; dir. Houston Natural Gas, 1975-85, Mexico Fund, 1985—; gen. ptnr. Equus Ltd., 1984—. Editor: Small Business Financing, 4 vols., 1966, Securities Regulation Sourcebook, 1970-71, (with others) Cases

and Materials on Enterprise Organizations, 1987; contbr. articles to profl. jours. Regent Nat. Coll. Dist. Attys., 1981—. Served to lt. (j.g.) USNR, 1952-55. Mem. ABA, Calif. Bar Assn., Tenn. Bar Assn., Tex. Bar Assn., Am. Law Inst., Order of Coif. Legal education. Home: 2004 Milford St Houston TX 77098 Office: U Houston Law Center Univ Park Houston TX 77004

KNECHT, JAMES HERBERT, lawyer; b. Los Angeles, Aug. 5, 1925; s. James Herbert and Gertrude Martha (Morris) K.; m. Margaret Paton Vreeland, Jan. 3, 1953; children—Susan, Thomas Paton, Carol. BS, UCLA, 1947; LLB, U. So. Calif., 1957. Bar: Calif. bar 1957, U.S. Supreme Ct. bar 1969. Mem. firm Forster, Gemmill & Farmer, Los Angeles, 1957-84; sole practice 1985—. Fellow Am. Bar Found.; mem. Am. Bar Assn., Los Angeles County Bar Assn., Legion Lex, Caltech Assos., Los Angeles Area C. of C. (dir. 1979-83), Town Hall of Calif., Beta Theta Pi. Club: Jonathan. Probate, Estate taxation, Corporate taxation. Home: PO Box 2280 Paso Robles CA 93447 Office: PO Box 2280 Paso Robles CA 93447

KNECHT, TIMOTHY HARRY, lawyer; b. Flint, Mich., Nov. 6, 1953; s. Wayne Warren and Nancy Jane (Post) K.; m. Linda Marie D'Appolonia, Aug. 14, 1976; children: Nicole Constance, Colleen Lin. BA in Econs., Duke U., 1975; JD, Detroit Coll. of Law, 1979. Ptnr. Cline, Cline & Griffin, Flint, 1979—. Chmn. bd. dirs. Flint Inst. Arts, 1985—, trustee, 1985—; bd. dirs. Friends of Modern Art, Flint, 1980—, Flint Environ. Action Team, 1985—, treas., 1985—; century mem. Boy Scouts Am. Mem. ABA, Def. Research Inst., Mich. Def. Trial Cousel, Genesee County Bar Assn., Mich. Bar Assn. Club: Flint Golf. Avocations: snow skiing, water sports, sailing, running. Insurance, Landlord-tenant, Personal injury. Home: 5112 Territorial Grand Blanc MI 48439 Office: Cline Cline & Griffin 1000 Mott Foundation Bldg Flint MI 48502

KNEIPPER, RICHARD KEITH, lawyer; b. Kenosha, Wis., June 18, 1943; s. Richard F. and Esther E. (Beaster) K.; m. Sherry Hayes, Dec. 16, 1977; children: Ryan Hayes, Lindsey Merrill. BS, Washington and Lee U., 1965; JD, Cornell U., 1968. Bar: Tex. 1982, U.S. Dist. Ct. (so. dist.) N.Y. 1968, U.S. Ct. Appeals (2d cir.) 1971. Atty. Chadbourne & Parke, N.Y.C., 1968-81, Jones, Day, Reavis & Pogue, Dallas, 1981—; mem. adv. council Banking Law Inst., N.Y.C., 1984—; mem. adminstrv. procedures task force U.S. League Savs. Instns., Washington, 1984—; mem. Dallas/Ft. Worth Metroplex Film Commn. Task Force. Contbr. articles to profl. jours.; mem. film and video bd. Dallas Morning News, 1984. Mem. Dallas Assn. for Corp. Growth, 1981-84; bd. dirs. U.S.A. Film Festival, Dallas. Mem. ABA, N.Y. Bar Assn., Tex. Bar Assn., N. Dallas C. of C. Roman Catholic. Securities, Banking, General corporate. Office: Jones Day Reavis & Pogue 2001 Ross Ave 2300 LTV Center Dallas TX 75201

KNEPPER, WILLIAM EDWARD, lawyer; b. Tiffin, Ohio, Oct. 25, 1909; s. Russell Monroe and Mamie (Corn) K.; children: Richard Scott, Bonne Lee Knepper Marks; m. Mary Morrill Lichtenberg, Mar. 30, 1964; adopted children: Mary L. (Mrs. Daum), James W. Lichtenberg, John M. Lichtenberg. A.B., Ohio State U., 1931; postgrad., Columbus Coll. Law, 1931-32. Bar: Ohio 1933. Ptnr. Knepper, White & Dempsey, Columbus, Ohio, 1933-54, Knepper, White, Richards & Miller, Columbus, 1954-77, Knepper, White, Arter & Hadden, Columbus, 1977-86, Arter & Hadden, Columbus, 1987—; adj. prof. Ohio State U. Coll. Law, 1972—; Mem. Ohio Bar Examining Com., 1945-50, chmn., 1950. Author: Liability of Corporate Officers and Directors, 3d edit, 1979, Ohio Civil Practice, 1970; co-author: The Ohio Manual of General Practice, 1956, Judicial Conveyances and Eminent Domain (Ohio), 1960, Ohio Eminent Domain Practice, 1977; editor: Insurance Counsel Jour, 1955-61; contbr. numerous articles to profl. jours. and law revs. Pres. Def. Research Inst., Inc., 1965-66; Chmn. Franklin County Court House Annex Bldg. Commn., 1946-54, State Underground Parking Commn., 1955-58, 61-69; pres. United Appeal Franklin County, 1969. Fellow Am. Coll. Trial Lawyers; mem. ABA, Ohio State Bar Assn. (exec. commn. 1951-54), Columbus Bar Assn. (pres. 1947-48), Internat. Assn. Ins. Counsel (pres. 1962- 63), Am. Judicature Soc., Columbus Area C. of C. (chmn. 1963-65), Ohio State U. Alumni Assn. (pres. 1967-69), Columbus Players Club (pres. 1943), Pi Kappa Alpha, Kappa Kappa Psi. Democrat. Episcopalian. Clubs: Mason (Columbus) (33 deg.), K.T. (Columbus), Shriner (Columbus), Athletic (Columbus), Faculty (Columbus). Federal civil litigation, State civil litigation, Insurance. Office: One Columbus 10 W Broad St Columbus OH 43215

KNIERIM, K. PHILLIP, lawyer; b. Tacoma, Nov. 18, 1945; s. Oscar Fitzpatrick and Dorothy Margaret (King) K.; m. Pamela Gail Waller. B.S. in Sociology, U. Wash., Seattle, 1968; J.D. (Harlan Fiske Stone scholar 1971-72, James Kent scholar 1972-74), Columbia U., 1974. Dir. human resources planning N.Y. Telephone Co., 1969-71; assoc. Pillsbury, Madison & Sutro, San Francisco, 1974-76, Fulop, Polston, Burns & McKittrick, Beverly Hills, Calif., 1976-81, Gordon, Weinberg & Zipser, Los Angeles, 1982-84, Wood, Lucksinger & Epstein, Los Angeles, 1984-85; sole practice Los Angeles, 1985—; judge pro tem Beverly Hills Mcpl. Ct., 1979—, Los Angeles Mcpl. Ct., 1985—; guest lectr. Pepperdine U. Law Sch., Los Angeles, 1981; mem. Los Angeles City Atty.'s Regulatory Reform Task Force, 1982—; mem. U.S. Army War Coll. Nat. Security Seminar, 1984. Chmn. pub. affairs Planned Parenthood N.Y.C., 1971-74; gen. counsel Los Angeles Ballet, 1979-80; chmn. bd. Bethune Ballet, 1981-82, pres., 1982-83. Served with RNSC, 1957-63; with USNR, 1969. Decorated Nat. Def. Service medal; Order Hosp. St. John Jerusalem. Mem. ABA (vice chmn. young lawyers div. com. jud. tenure, selection and performance 1980-81), Calif. State Bar (del. 1980—), Los Angeles County Bar Assn. (arbitrator 1979—), Beverly Hills Bar Assn. (chmn. environ. law com. 1979-82, vice chmn. resolutions com. 1983-85), Beverly Hills Barristers (gov. 1979-81), U.S. Combined Tng. Assn., English Speaking Union. Anglican. Clubs: West Hills Hunt; Brit. United Services. Administrative and regulatory, Real property, State civil litigation. Home: 11700 Iowa Ave Apt 304 Los Angeles CA 90025 Office: 1900 Ave of Stars Suite 2200 Los Angeles CA 90067

KNIGHT, BERNARD JOHN, JR., lawyer; b. Chgo., Jan. 5, 1957; s. Bernard John and Carol Marie (McCarthy) K. BBA, Drake U., 1979; JD, U. So. Calif., 1982. Bar: Tex. 1982, Ill. 1985, U.S. Tax Ct. 1982. Assoc. Vinson & Elkins, Houston, 1982-84, Hopkins & Sutter, Chgo., 1984—. Mem. ABA (corp. stockholder relationships com. of taxation sect.), Ill. State Bar Assn., Chgo. Bar Assn. Corporate taxation. Home: 211 E Ohio St Apt 1508 Chicago IL 60611 Office: Hopkins & Sutter 3 First Nat Plaza Chicago IL 60602

KNIGHT, DAVID WEBSTER, lawyer; b. Fergus Falls, Minn., Feb. 11, 1943; s. David Lloyd and Marian Alice (Wyman) K.; m. Helen Martin; children: Richard, Joe, Janis. BA, St. Olaf Coll., 1965; postgrad., San Jose State U., 1966, U. Tenn., 1970-71; JD, U. S.C., 1973. Bar: S.C. 1980. Asst. trust officer Tower Grove Bank, St. Louis, 1969-70; instr. bus. law Midlands Coll., Columbia, S.C., 1977-83; sole practice Columbia, 1980-83; assoc. Monteith & Monteith, Columbia, 1983—. Served to capt. USAF, 1965-69. Club: Lake Murray Sailing (Ballantine, S.C.)(vice-commodore 1986—). Avocations: sailing, running, painting. State civil litigation, Family and matrimonial, Personal injury. Home: 236 Columbia Ave Chapin SC 29036

KNIGHT, FREDERICK HAWLEY, lawyer, former bus. exec.; b. Brattleboro, Vt., Sept. 29, 1906; s. Fred Samuel and Susan (Hawley) K.; m. Mary Lake Cox, July 7, 1936. B.S., Worcester Poly. Inst., 1928; LL.B., George Washington U., 1933. Bar: D.C. bar 1933. Test engr. Gen. Electric Co., Schenectady, 1928-29; patent examiner U.S. Patent Office, Washington, 1929-37; patent atty. Corning Glass Works, N.Y., 1937-45; asst. sec. Corning Glass Works, 1945-53, sec., 1953-71, corp. counsel, 1961-71, v.p., 1969-71, cons., 1971—; sec., dir. Corning Glass Works of Can., Ltd., 1946-71; sec. Corning Mus. Glass, 1952-71; sec., dir. Corning Glass Internat. S.A., 1960-71; dir. Corning Internat. Corp. Sec. Corning Glass Works Found., 1953-71, trustee, 1971-76. Mem. Am. Bar Assn. Presbyterian. Clubs: Univ. (N.Y.C.); Corning Country. Home: 257 Delevan Ave Corning NY 14830 Office: Corning Glass Works Corning NY 14830

KNIGHT, HERMAN ELVIN, JR., lawyer; b. Owensboro, Ky., July 14, 1944; s. Herman E. and Sarah D. (Brown) K.; m. Judith Spicer, Jan. 6, 1945; children—Kristin, Lindsay. Student, Washington and Lee U., 1962-63; J.D., U. Ky., 1967; postgrad., LL.M., U. Mo., 1971. Bar: Mo. 1968, U.S. Dist. Ct. (we. dist.) Mo. 1968, U.S. Tax Ct. 1977. Mem. firm Hillix, Brewer, Hoffhaus & Whittaker, Kansas City, Mo., 1968-86, gen. ptnr., 1974-86; ptnr. Polsinelli, White & Vardeman, Kansas City, 1986—; chmn. bd. dirs. First Trust Mid Am.; lectr. for Mo. Bar Assn. Continuing Legal Edn. program; lectr. in field of taxation. Bd. dirs. Kansas City Ballet Assn., 1978-81. Served to capt., JAGC, USAR, 1968-78. Mem. ABA, Mo. C. of C., Kansas City Bar Assn. (chmn. sect. taxation 1975-76), Estate Planning Assn. (dir. 1981-82), Mo. Bar Assn., Lawyers Assn. Kansas City. Clubs: Country, Kansas City, 1212 (pres. 1981), Rotary of Kansas City (Mo.). Real property, Corporate taxation, Probate. Address: 4705 Central Kansas City MO 64112

KNIGHT, MARTHA KATHRYN, lawyer; b. Troy, Ala., May 10, 1958; d. Herald Jackson and Joanne (Phillips) K. BA, Samford U., 1979; JD, U. Ala., 1982. Bar: Ala. 1982, U.S. Dist. Ct. (no., mid. and so. dists.) 1982. Instr. legal research and writing U. Ala., Tuscaloosa, 1982; law clk. to presiding justice U.S. Dist. Ct. (no. dist.) Ga., Atlanta and Gainesville, 1982-83; assoc. Miller, Hamilton, Snider & Odom, Mobile, Ala., 1984—. Student works editor U. Ala. Law Rev. 1981-82. Mem. ABA, Ala. Bar Assn., Mobile Bar Assn. Presbyterian. Environment, Contracts commercial, Landlord-tenant. Office: Miller Hamilton Snider & Odom 254 State St Mobile AL 36601

KNIGHT, PETER CARTER, lawyer; b. Worcester, Mass., Jan. 13, 1948; s. Carleton and Mary (Burnett) K.; m. Deborah L. Sanford, Jan. 8, 1977; children: Carter, Lydia. BSBA, Boston U., 1970; JD, Suffolk U., 1974. Bar: Mass. 1975, U.S. Dist. Ct. Mass. 1975, U.S. Ct. Appeals 1979. Asst. dist. atty. Suffolk County, Boston, 1975-78; ptnr. Morrison, Mahoney & Miller, Boston, 1978—. Federal civil litigation, State civil litigation. Home: 74 Loring Rd Weston MA 02193 Office: Morrison Mahoney & Miller 250 Summer St Boston MA 02293

KNIGHT, ROBERT HUNTINGTON, lawyer; b. New Haven, Feb. 27, 1919; s. Earl Wall and Frances Pierpont (Whitney) K.; m. Rosemary C. Gibson, Apr. 19, 1975; children—Robert Huntington, Jessie Valle, Patricia Whitney, Alice Isabel, Eli Whitney. Grad., Phillips Acad., Andover, Mass., 1936; B.A., Yale, 1940; LL.B., U. Va., 1947. Bar: N.Y. bar 1950. With John Orr Young, Inc. (advt. agy.), 1940-41; asst. prof. U. Va. Law Sch., 1947-49; asso. firm Shearman & Sterling & Wright, N.Y.C., 1949-55; partner Shearman & Sterling & Wright, 1955-58; dep. asst. sec. def. for internat. security affairs Dept. Def., 1958-61; gen. counsel Treasury Dept., 1961-62; ptnr. firm Shearman & Sterling, N.Y.C., 1962-80, sr. ptnr., 1980-85; dep. chmn. Fed. Res. Bank N.Y., 1976-77, chmn., 1978-83; counsel to bd. United Technologies Corp., 1974-85; dir. Owens-Corning Fiberglas Corp., Trans-Can. Pipelines, Brit. Steel Corp., Inc.; chmn. Trans Canada Pipelines Mercator Co., Howmet Turbine Corp.; mem. Intelsat Arbitration Panel, 1971—. Bd. dirs. Internat. Vol. Services; chmn. bd. dirs. U. Va. Law Sch. Found.; bd. dirs. Asia Found. Served to lt. col. USAAF, 1941-45. Mem. ABA, Fed. Bar Assn., Internat. Bar Assn., Inter-Am. Bar Assn., Assn. of Bar of City of N.Y., N.Y. County Lawyers Assn., Internat. Law Assn., Washington Inst. Fgn. Affairs, Council Fgn. Relations. Clubs: Down Town Assn., Pilgrims, India House, Links, Citicorp, World Trade Ctr., River (N.Y.C.); Army and Navy, Metropolitan, City Tavern (Washington); Round Hill (Greenwich, Conn.); Ocean (Ocean Ridge, Fla.). Home: 12 Knollwood Dr Greenwich CT 06830 also: 570 Park Ave New York NY 10021 also: 6767 N Ocean Blvd Ocean Ridge FL 33435 Office: 53 Wall St New York NY 10005

KNIGHT, WILLIAM D., JR., lawyer; b. Rockford, Ill., May 18, 1925; s. William D. and Lela Mae (Clark) K. A.B., Dartmouth Coll., 1949; J.D., Northwestern U., 1952. Bar: Ill. 1953, U.S. Dist. Ct. (no. dist.) Ill. 1957, U.S. Ct. Appeals (7th cir.) 1959. Ptnr., Knight & Knight, Rockford, 1953—. Bd. dirs. Boys Club Assn. of Rockford, 1959-75. Served to 1st lt., inf., U.S. Army, 1943-46. Mem. Ill. Bar Assn., Winnebago County Bar Assn., Internat. Assn. Ins. Counsel, Fedn. Ins. Counsel, Assn. Ins. Attys., Def. Research Inst. Republican. Methodist. Club: Rockford Country. Federal civil litigation, State civil litigation, General corporate. Home: 1205 Lundvall Ave Rockford IL 61107 Home: 575 S Lake Shore Dr, Lake Geneva 53147 Office: Knight and Knight 1111 Talcott Bldg 321 W State St Rockford IL 61101

KNIGHT, WILLIAM THOMAS, cosmetics company executive, lawyer; b. Hackensack, N.J., Aug. 25, 1937; s. William Thomas and Virginia (Chapin) K.; m. Suellen Peterson, Oct. 21, 1961; children: Alexander, Peter, Jessica. A.B., Brown U., 1959; M.A., Vanderbilt U., 1961; LL.B., U. Va., Charlottesville, 1967. Bar: Pa. 1967, U.S. Dist. Ct. (we. dist.)Pa. 1968. Trust officer Pitts. Nat. Bank, 1967-69; assoc. gen. counsel T.J. Lipton, Inc., Englewood Cliffs, N.J., 1969-73; gen. counsel, v.p., sec. Tetley, Inc., N.Y.C., 1973-76; counsel, asst. gen. counsel, v.p. legal, v.p. law, group v.p., gen. counsel, sec. Avon Products Inc., N.Y.C., 1977—. Served to lt. (j.g.) USNR, 1960-64. Fellow Bar City N.Y., ABA, Pa. Bar Assn., N.Y. State Bar Assn. (exec. com., corp. counsel), Allegheny County Bar Assn. Clubs: Princeton, Edgartown Yacht. Home: 42 Glendale Rd Rye NY 10580 Office: Avon Products Inc 9 W 57th St New York NY 10019

KNIGHTON, ALTON LEFLEUR, JR., lawyer; b. Roanoke, Va., Sept. 15, 1945; s. Alton Lefleur and Beverly (Wilkinson) K.; m. Susan Gertrude Kephart, Jan. 7, 1978; children—Alton Lefleur III, Jefferson Campbell. B.A. with high distinction, U.Va., 1967, J.D., 1974. Bar: Va. 1974, U.S. Dist. Ct. (we. dist.) Va. 1974, U.S. Tax Ct. 1975. Assoc. Woods, Rogers & Hazlegrove and predecessors, Roanoke, 1974-80, ptnr., 1980—. Bd. dirs. Med. Found. of Roanoke Valley. Served to staff sgt. USAF, 1968-72. Mem. ABA, Va. State Bar, Va. Bar Assn., Roanoke Bar Assn., Nat. Assn. Bond Lawyers, Roanoke Valley Estate Planning Council, Ferrum Coll. Estate Planning Council (chmn. 1986-87), Phi Beta Kappa. Presbyterian. Pension, profit-sharing, and employee benefits, Estate planning, Municipal bonds. Home: 2815 S Jefferson St Roanoke VA 24014 Office: Woods Rogers & Hazlegrove 105 Franklin Rd SW Roanoke VA 24004

KNIGIN, KENNETH SHELDON, lawyer; b. Bedford Hills, N.Y., Feb. 13, 1929; s. Jacob and Miriam (Sheldon) K.; children from previous marriage: Marcia, Randy; m. Pia Linda Buggert, June 22, 1979; children—Johanna, Alexandra. B.S., N.Y.U., 1951; J.D., Bklyn. Law Sch., 1954. Bar: N.Y. 1955, U.S. Dist. Ct. (so. and ea. dists.) N.Y. 1977, U.S. Ct. Appeals (2d cir.) 1977. Sr. litigating mem. Ballon, Stoll & Itzler, N.Y.C., 1968-78; counsel Regan, Goldfarb, Heller, Wetzler & Quinn, N.Y.C., 1978-79; ptnr. Amen, Weisman, Butler & Pearlman, N.Y.C., 1979-80; sole practice, N.Y.C., 1980—; pres. Traffic Enforcement and Adjudication Methods, Inc., N.Y.C., 1977—, Sennet Group, Inc., Chgo., 1982-86; gen. counsel, dir. AGP, Inc., N.Y.C., 1986—. Councilman, N.Y.C., 1968-70; dep. dir. counsel N.Y.C. Parking Violations Bur., 1970-72. Recipient State of Israel Bonds award, 1960. Mem. Am. Bar Assn., Assn. Trial Lawyers Am., N.Y. State Trial Lawyers Assn., N.Y. State Bar Assn., Law Sch. Alumnae Assn. Family and matrimonial, State civil litigation, Administrative and regulatory. Office: 33 W Patent Rd Bedford Hills NY 10507

KNISELY, PAUL EMIL, lawyer; b. Charleston, S.C., Sept. 10, 1952; s. William Hagerman and Marguerite Marie (Labasse) K.; m. Anne Francoise Gerard, Dec. 31, 1973; children: Annick Marie, Jacqueline Michelle. BA in Govt., U. Tex., 1973; JD, 1977. Bar: Tex. 1977, U.S. Dist. Ct. (we. dist.) Tex. 1980, U.S. Ct. Appeals (5th cir.) 1980, U.S. Dist. Ct. (so. dist.) Tex. 1981, U.S. Ct. Appeals (11th cir.) 1981, U.S. Supreme Ct. 1981, U.S. Ct. Appeals (9th cir.) 1983. Law clk. to presiding justice U.S. Dist. Ct., Austin, Tex., 1977-78; temporary assoc. Coudert Freres, Paris, 1978; law clk. to presiding justice U.S. Dist. Ct., Austin, 1979-80; assoc. Spivey & Grigg, Austin, 1980-85; ptnr. Spivey, Grigg, Kelly & Knisely, Austin, 1985—; arbitrator Alcoa/United Steelworkers Union, Rockdale and Point Comfort, Tex., 1985—. Mem. Tex. Bar Assn., Travis County Bar Assn., Assn. Trial Lawyers Am., Tex. Trial Lawyers Assn., Tex. Young Lawyers Assn., Order of Coif. Democrat. Avocations: basketball, jogging, photography. Federal civil litigation, State civil litigation, Personal injury. Office: Spivey Grigg Kelly & Knisely PO Box 2011 Austin TX 78768

KNOBLAUCH, LEO N., lawyer; b. Reading, Pa., July 4, 1917; s. Philip and Rose (Falkowitz) K.; m. Ruth F. Jaslow, Mar. 17, 1946; children: Steve H., Kenneth B., Patti J. BS in Econs., U. Pa., 1938; LLB, Seton Hall U., 1941. Bar: N.J. 1942, U.S. Dist. Ct. N.J. 1942, U.S. Supreme Ct. 1955. Mem. Gen. Assembly, Hudson County, 1952-58; asst. prosecutor Prosecutor's Office, Hudson County, 1959-64; asst. county counsel Dept. Law, Hudson County, 1964-74; sole pracice Hudson County, 1942—. Served to staff sgt. USAF, 1942-46. Mem. N.J. Bar Assn. (trustee 1952), Hudson County Bar Assn. (2d v.p. 1986, 1st v.p. 1987). Avocations: tennis, swimming. Federal civil litigation, State civil litigation, Consumer commercial. Office: 921 Bergen Ave Jersey City NJ 07306

KNOLL, JEROLD EDWARD, lawyer; b. Simmesport, La., Dec. 12, 1941; s. Edmond and Myrtle (Humphries) K.; m. Jeannette Theriot, June 10, 1967; Children: Triston, Eddie, Edmond, Blake, Jonathan. BA, La. State U., 1963; JD, Loyola U., New Orleans, 1966. Bar: La. 1966, U.S. Dist. Ct. (ea., mid. and we. dists.) La. 1967, U.S. Supreme Ct. 1982. Ptnr. Knoll, Roy & Sprull, Marksville, La., 1966—; atty. 12th Jud. Dist., Marksville, 1966-72. Dist. chmn. Boy Scouts Am., Alexandria, La., 1972-78. Served to 1st lt. U.S. Army, 1966-72. Mem. La. Dist. Attys. Assn. (bd. dirs. 1985—), Avoyelles Bar Assn. (pres. 1970), Marksville Jaycees (pres. 1972). Democrat. Roman Catholic. Avocations: athletics, farming, hunting. General practice, Personal injury, Criminal. Home: 115 Tarleton Marksville LA 71351 Office: Knoll Roy & Sprull 403 S Main Marksville LA 71351

KNOPF, WILLIAM LEE, judge; b. Louisville, Nov. 22, 1954; s. John Louis Sr. and Jean (Harrison) K.; m. Linda Jo McNeil, Dec. 31, 1975; children: Lauren Lene, Natalie Rene. B in Bus. Adminstrn., Fin., Loyola U., New Orleans, 1976; JD, U. Louisville, 1978. Bar: Ky. 1979, U.S. Dist. Ct. (we. dist.) Ky. 1979, U.S. Ct. Appeals (6th cir.) 1980. Asst. atty/ Commonwealth of Ky., Louisville, 1979-81; sole practice Louisville, 1981-84; judge Jefferson Dist. Ct., Louisville, 1984—. Mem. ABA, Ky. Bar Assn., Louisville Bar Assn., Assn. Trial Lawyers Am., Dist. Judges Assn. Ky. Democrat. Roman Catholic. Judicial administration, Local government. Home: 445 Oxford Pl Louisville KY 40207 Office: Jefferson Dist Ct 600 W Jefferson St Louisville KY 40202

KNOREK, JOHN LEE, lawyer; b. Toledo, Dec. 19, 1954; s. Daniel F. and Mary Frances (Minarcin) K.; m. Kim Goodell, June 14, 1980; 1 child, John Kenneth. BA in Polit. Sci. and Philosophy, U. Cin., 1976, M in Pub. Adminstrn., 1978; JD, Georgetown U., 1981. Bar: Hawaii 1981, U.S. Dist. Ct. Hawaii 1981, U.S. Ct. Appeals (9th cir.) 1982. Legal, legis. asst. U.S. Senate, Washington, 1979-80; assoc. Torkildson, Katz, Jossem, Fonseca & Moore, Honolulu, 1981—. Precinct officer Hawaii Dems., Honolulu, 1984—; mem. Hawaii Ednl. Council, Honolulu, 1985—; bd. dirs. Nuvanu Punchbowl Neighborhood, Honolulu, 1984-85. Mem. ABA, Hawaii Bar Assn., Fed. Bar Assn., Am. Soc. Personnel Adminstrs. Roman Catholic. Lodge: Rotary (program chmn. Pearl Harbor 1985—). Avocations: American creative music, jazz. Labor, Pension, profit-sharing, and employee benefits. Home: 248 Aikahi Loop Kailua HI 96734 Office: Torkildson Katz Jossem Fonseca & Moore 700 Bishop St 15th Floor Honolulu HI 96713

KNOTEN, THOMAS PATRICK, lawyer; b. St. Louis, Jan. 7, 1945; s. Edward Wicht and Rosalie Ann (May) K.; m. Mary Christine Martin, July 18, 1970; children: Conrad, Amelia, Edward, Martin. BA, Maryknoll Sem., 1966; JD, Washington U., St. Louis, 1973. Bar: Mo. 1973, U.S. Dist. Ct. (ea. dist.) Mo. 1973, U.S. Ct. Appeals (8th cir.) 1974, U.S. Ct. Claims 1977, U.S. Supreme Ct. 1977. Assoc. David L. Pentland, St. Louis, 1973-75; trial atty. Juvenile Ct. (22d jud. cir.), St. Louis, 1975-76; sr. atty. Emerson Electric Co., St. Louis, 1976-80; asst. gen. counsel Seven-Up Co., St. Louis, 1980-87. Served to capt. USAF, 1966-70, Vietnam. Decorated Bronze Star. Mem. ABA, Bar Assn. Met. St. Louis. Avocation: elementary sch. baseball and soccer head coach. General corporate, Contracts commercial, Private international. Home: 6363 Pershing Ave Saint Louis MO 63130

KNOWLES, EMMITT CLIFTON, lawyer; b. Pensacola, Fla., Oct. 9, 1951; s. Lawrence Clifton and Emily (Josey) K.; m. Leigh Walton, Jan. 1, 1985. BA magna cum laude, Vanderbilt U., 1973; JD, U. Tenn., 1977. Bar: Tenn. 1978, U.S. Dist. Ct. (ea. dist.) Tenn. 1978, U.S. Ct. Appeals (6th cir.) 1979, U.S. Dist. Ct. (mid. dist.) Tenn. 1980. Law clk. to chief judge U.S. Ct. Appeals (6th cir.), Cin., 1978-79; from assoc. to ptnr. Bass, Berry & Sims, Nashville, 1979—. Editor-in-chief U. Tenn. Law Rev., 1977. Mem. ABA (appellate practice com.), Tenn. Bar Assn. (fed. practice com. 1985-86), Nashville Bar Assn. (bd. dirs. young lawyers div. 1985-86), Am. Judicature Soc., Tenn. Trial Lawyers Assn., Phi Beta Kappa, Order of Coif. Democrat. Lodge: Kiwanis. Personal injury, Federal civil litigation, State civil litigation. Office: Bass Berry & Sims 2700 1st Am Ctr Nashville TN 37238

KNOWLTON, ROBERT YATES, lawyer; b. Columbia, S.C., Apr. 5, 1957; s. Charles Wilson and Mildred Yates (Brown) K.; m. Nina Zeigler, Dec. 23, 1981; children: Anne Lide, Robert Yates Jr., Nina McClenaghan. BA, U. Va., 1979; JD, U. S.C., 1982. Bar: S.C. 1982. Law clk. to judge U.S. Ct. Appeals (4th cir.), Spartanburg, S.C., 1982-83; assoc. Boyd, Knowlton, Tate & Finlay P.A., and Sinkler & Boyd, P.A., Columbia, 1983—. Named one of Outstanding Young Men of Am., 1985. Mem. ABA, S.C. Bar Assn., Richland County Bar Assn. Lodge: Kiwanis. Federal civil litigation, State civil litigation, Administrative and regulatory. Home: PO Box 11889 Columbia SC 29211 Office: Boyd Knowlton Tate & Finlay PA 1426 Main St Suite 1200 Columbia SC 29201

KNOX, ALAN ANTHONY, lawyer; b. Orange, Calif., Dec. 27, 1940; s. Joseph Allen and Marjorie (Campbell) K.; m. Colleen Denise Hill, Dec. 19, 1970 (div. Sept. 1983); 1 child, Melanie. AB, U. Redlands, 1962; JD, Pepperdine U., 1970. Bar: Calif. 1972, U.S. Dist. Ct. (cen. dist.) Calif. 1973, U.S. Supreme Ct. 1984. Cons. 1st Am. Title Ins. Co., Santa Ana, Calif., 1964-70; mem. debenture div. Perpetual Trustee Co. Ltd., Sydney, Australia, 1971; assoc. Mitchell, Hart & Brisco, Santa Ana, 1972-74; sole practice Santa Ana, 1974-77, 85—; ptnr. Knox & Coombs P.C., Santa Ana, 1977-85; lectr. continuing edn. U. Calif., Berkeley, 1981—; bd. dirs. Knox Indsl. Supplies, Santa Ana. Contbr. articles to profl. jours. Vol. atty. Amicus Publico, Santa Ana, 1984—; bd. dirs. Am. Lung Assn. Orange County, Santa Ana, 1985, OCPT United Way, Orange, Calif., 1982—. Mem. Calif. Bar Assn. (pro bono services award 1982, 83), Orange County Bar Assn. (chmn. real estate sect. 1977), Calif. Trial Lawyers Assn., Calif. Trustees Assn., Calif. Land Title Assn. (affiliate), Am. Arbitration Assn. Republican. Episcopalian. Lodge: Elks. Avocation: sailing. Real property, State civil litigation, Insurance. Office: 888 N Main St Suite 905 Santa Ana CA 92701

KNOX, JAMES EDWIN, executive, lawyer; b. Evanston, Ill., July 2, 1937; s. James Edwin and Marjorie Eleanor (Williams) K.; m. Rita Lucille Torres, June 30, 1973; children—James Edwin III, Kirsten M., Katherine E., Miranda G. B.A. in Polit. Sci., State U. Iowa, 1959; J.D., Drake U., 1961. Bar: Iowa 1961, Ill. 1962, Tex. 1982. Law clk. to Justice Tom C. Clark, U.S. Supreme Ct., 1961-62; assoc., then ptnr. Isham, Lincoln & Beale, Chgo., 1962-70; v.p. law Northwest Industries, Inc., Chgo., 1970-80; exec. v.p., gen. counsel Lone Star Steel Co., Dallas, 1980-86, sr. v.p., gen. counsel Itel Corp., Chgo., 1986—; instr. contracts and labor law Chgo. Kent Coll. Law 1964-69; arbitrator Nat. Ry. Adjustment Bd., 1967-68. Mem. ABA, Tex. Bar Assn., Ill. Bar Assn., Iowa Bar Assn., Dallas Bar Assn., Chgo. Bar Assn., Phi Beta Kappa, Order of Coif, Phi Eta Sigma. General corporate. Office: Itel Corp 2 N Riverside Plaza Chicago IL 60606

KNOX, JOHN THERYLL, lawyer, former state legislator; b. Reno, Sept. 30, 1924; s. Ernest B. and Jean (Monat) K.; A.B., Occidental Coll., 1949; J.D., Hastings Coll. Law, 1952; m. Jean Henderson, Dec. 27, 1949; children—John Henderson, Charlotte, Mary. Admitted to Calif. bar, 1953, in pvt. practice at Richmond; mem. Calif. Assembly from Richmond, from 1960, speaker pro tem, from 1976, mem. Ways and Means com.; now ptnr. Nossaman, Guthner, Knox & Elliott, San Francisco. Mem. Contra Costa County Dem. central com., 1955-60; trustee Occidental Coll., Hastings Coll. Law. Served with USAAF, 1943-45. Mem. ABA, Contra Costa County Bar Assn., Sigma Alpha Epsilon, Phi Delta Phi. Moose, Lion. Home: 229 Bishop Ave Richmond CA 94801 Office: 100 The Embarcadero San Francisco CA 94105

KNOX, WYCKLIFFE AUSTIN, JR., lawyer; b. Augusta, Ga., Nov. 1, 1940; s. Wyckliffe Austin Knox Sr. and Byrnece (Purcell) Swanson; m. Shell Hardman, Apr. 15, 1967; children: Wyckliffe Austin III, Dorothy Shell, John Hardman, Davis Purcell. BBA, U. Ga., 1962, JD, 1964. Bar: Ga. 1964, U.S. Dist. Ct. (so. dist.) Ga. 1964, U.S. Ct. Appeals (5th cir.) 1966, U.S. Ct.

Claims 1973, U.S. Supreme Ct. 1973, U.S. Ct. Appeals (11th cir.) 1981, U.S. Ct. Appeals (4th cir.) 1983. Assoc. Hull, Towill & Norman, Augusta, 1964-67; ptnr. Hull, Towill, Norman, Barrett & Johnson, Augusta, 1967-76, Knox & Zacks, Augusta, 1976-77; pres. Knox & Zacks P.C., Augusta and Atlanta, 1977—; bd. dirs. Claussen Concrete Co., Inc., Augusta, Ga. R.R. Bank and Trust Co., Augusta; chmn. bd. dirs. Knox-Rivers Constrn. Co., Thomson, Ga. Mem. bd. visitors sch. law U. Ga., Athens, 1973-76, bd. dirs. athletic assn., 1975—; mem. jud. com. Bus. Council Ga., Atlanta, 1986—; pres. Ga. council Boy Scouts Am., Augusta, 1974-75; pres.Richmond/Columbia County unit Am. Cancer Soc., Augusta, 1985, chmn. bd. dirs. 1986—; trustee Richard B. Russell Found., Atlanta, 1971—; pres.-elect Georgians for Better Transp. Mem. Augusta Bar Assn. (pres. 1984), Ga. Bar Assn., Ga. Acad. Hosp. Attys. (bd. dirs. 1979-80), Am. Acad. Hosp. Attys., Ga. Def. Lawyers Assn. (bd. dirs. 1973-76), YPO. Methodist. Clubs: Augusta Country (bd. dirs. 1984—, v.p. 1987—), Pinnacle (Augusta); Belle Meade Country (Thomson). Lodge: Rotary (pres. local club 1979-80). Avocations: farming, fishing, skiing. Federal civil litigation, State civil litigation, Construction. Home: 468 Stevens Creek Rd Augusta GA 30907 Office: Knox & Zacks PC Ga RR Bank Bldg Suite 1212 Augusta GA 30901

KNUCHEL, KARL G., lawyer; b. Missoula, Mont., Sept. 10, 1951; s. Harry Charles and Gladys G. (Reeves) K. BA, U. Mont., 1976, JD, 1979. Bar: Mont. 1978, U.S. Dist. Ct. Mont. 1979. Sole practice Livingston, Mont., 1983—; dep. atty. Park County, Livingston, 1979-83. Bd. dirs. Community Ctr., Livingston, 1979-81, United Way, Livingston, 1984—. Mem. ABA, Park County-Sweet Grass Bar Assn., Mont. Trial Lawyers Assn. Lodge: Elks. Avocation: flying. Personal injury, Criminal, Workers' compensation. Office: Knuchel & McGregor 126 E Callender PO Box 953 Livingston MT 59047

KNUDSEN, CURTIS EDWIN, lawyer; b. Hankinson, N.D., Feb. 26, 1953; s. Ray Maurice and Mable Eleanor (Rennerfelt) K.; m. Barbara Sharp, May 31, 1980; 1 child, Steven. BS in Secondary Edn., No. State Coll., Aberdeen, S.D., 1975; JD, U. S.D., Vermillion, 1978. Bar: S.D. 1978, U.S. Dist. Ct. S.D. 1978, Colo. 1979, U.S. Dist. Ct. Colo. 1979. Law clk. to presiding justice S.D. Supreme Ct., Pierre, 1978-79, Colo. Ct. Appeals, Denver, 1979-80; assoc. Minor & Brown, Denver, 1980-84, Roath & Brega, P.C., Denver, 1984-86; asst. gen. counsel Bill Walters Cos., Denver, 1986—. Mem. ABA, S.D. Bar Assn., Colo. Bar Assn. Democrat. Club: Denver Athletic. Avocations: golf, travel, music, woodworking. Real property, Contracts commercial, Banking. Home: 11598 E Adriatic Pl Aurora CO 80014 Office: Bill Walters Cos 7951 E Maplewood Ave Englewood CO 80111

KNUDSON, SCOTT GREGORY, lawyer; b. Mpls., Aug. 10, 1953; s. Harold Arthur and Mavis Catherine (Morreim) K. BA, Harvard U., 1975; JD summa cum laude, U. Minn., 1982. Bar: Minn. 1982, U.S. Ct. Appeals D.C. 1983, D.C. 1985, U.S. Ct. Appeals (9th cir.) 1985. Law clk. to presiding justice U.S. Ct. Appeals (D.C. cir.), Washington, 1982-83; law clk. to assoc. justice William Rehnquist U.S. Supreme Ct., Washington, 1983-84; assoc. Latham, Watkins & Hills, Washington, 1985—. Mem. ABA, Order of Coif. Avocations: cross country skiing, woodworking, travel. Federal civil litigation, Corporate taxation. Office: Latham & Watkins 1333 New Hampshire Ave NW Washington DC 20036

KNUPP, ROBERT LOUIS, lawyer; b. Harrisburg, Pa., June 16, 1941; s. Robert Ewing and Charlotte (Kishbaugh) K.; m. Judith Ann Pettigrew, Jan. 30, 1965; children: Kristen Paula, Andrew Robert. BA, Dickinson Coll., 1963; JD, Dickinson Sch. of Law, 1966. Bar: Pa. 1966. U.S. Ct. Mil. Appeals. 1968, U.S. Dist. Ct. (mid. dist.) 1972, U.S. Ct. Appeals (3d cir.) 1979, U.S. Supreme Ct. 1983. Asst. dist. atty. Dauphin County, Harrisburg, 1970-72; ptnr. Knupp & Andrews, Harrisburg, 1972-78; pres. Graf, Knupp & Andrews P.C., Harrisburg, 1978—; asst. solicitor Dauphin County, 1967-85, solicitor, 1986—. counsel Cen. Pa. Conf. United Meth. Ch., Harrisburg, 1976—. Served to capt. JAGC, U.S. Army, 1967-70. Mem. ABA (bankruptcy com.), Comml. Law League Am. Republican. Lodge: Rotary. Bankruptcy, Local government, Probate. Home: 98 Shetland Dr Hummelstown PA 17036 Office: Graf Knupp & Andrews PC 407 N Front Harrisburg PA 17108

KNUTZEN, RAYMOND EDWARD, criminal justice educator, cons.; b. Burlington, Wash., July 9, 1941; s. Erwin Edward Knutzen and Lillian Irene (Davis) Mowat; m. Cynthia Louise Neufeldt, Feb. 1, 1969; children: Traci Ann, Michael Edward. AAS with high honors, Everett Community Coll., 1970; BA magna cum laude, Pacific Luth. U., 1971; MA, Wash. State U., 1972. Asst. prof. criminal justice Northeast La. U., Monroe, 1972—. Coordinator Ouchita Valley council Boy Scouts Am., Monroe, 1979. Served with USAF, 1962-66, maj. USAR. Law Enforcement Edn. Program Pacific Luth. U. grantee, 1970-71. Mem. Acad. Criminal Justice Sci., La. Justice Educators Assn., Blue Key Soc., Lambda Alpha Epsilon, Alpha Phi Sigma, Omicron Delta Kappa. Republican. Lutheran. Legal education, State civil litigation. Home: 3807 Forsythe Ave Monroe LA 71201 Office: Northeast La U 700 University Ave Monroe LA 71209

KOBAYASHI, JOHN M., lawyer; b. Denver, May 1, 1944; s. Thomas Kenichi and Haruko (Terasaki) K.; m. Cheryl Ann Kozdruy, Apr. 12, 1986. BA, Columbia Coll., 1968, JD, 1971. Bar: Colo., U.S. Dist. Ct. Colo., U.S. Ct. Appeals (10th cir.), U.S. SUpreme Ct. Law clk. to presiding judge U.S. Ct. Appeals (10th cir.), Denver; atty. Securities Exchange Commn., Denver, 1973-74; asst. U.S. atty. U.S. Atty.'s Office, Denver, 1974-76; ptnr. Holme, Roberts & Owen, Denver, 1976—; panel chmn. Fed. Cts. Conduct Com., 1983-86. Fellow Internat. Acad. Trial Lawyers, Internat. Soc. Barristers; mem. ABA, Colo. Bar Assn. (bd. govs. 1979-81, 83-85). Antitrust, Federal civil litigation, State civil litigation. Office: Holme Roberts & Owen 1700 Broadway #1800 Denver CO 80290

KOBDISH, GEORGE CHARLES, lawyer; b. Casper, Wyo., June 30, 1950; s. Richard Matthew and Jo Earl (Uttz) K.; m. Mary Ellen Griffith, Jan. 24, 1969; children—George Charles, Jr., Kelly Rebecca, Kimberlee Nelle. B.B.A. with honors, U. Tex., 1971, J.D., 1974. Bar: Tex. 1974, U.S. Dist. Ct. (no. dist.) Tex. 1975. Asst. atty. gen. State of Tex., Austin, 1974-76; assoc. McCall, Parkhurst & Horton, Dallas, 1976-80, ptnr., 1981—; mem. Tex. Treasurer's Asset Mgmt. Adv. Com., Austin, 1983—. Disting. Service award, 1983. Mem. Nat. Assn. Bond Lawyers, ABA, Dallas Bar Assn., U. Tex. Law Sch. Assn. (Dallas bd.). Clubs: Austin, 2001, Exchange. Municipal bonds. Home: 9206 Arbor Branch Dr Dallas TX 75243 Office: McCall Parkhurst & Horton 900 Diamond Shamrock Tower Dallas TX 75201

KOBLENZ, MICHAEL ROBERT, lawyer; b. Newark, Apr. 9, 1948; s. Herman and Esther (Weisman) K.; m. Bonnie Jane Berman, Dec. 22, 1973; children—Adam, Alexander. B.A., George Washington U., 1969, LL.M., 1974; J.D., Am. U., 1972. Bar: N.J. 1972, D.C. 1973, N.Y. 1980, U.S. Dist. Ct. N.J. 1972, U.S. Dist. Ct. D.C. 1973, U.S. Dist. Ct. (so. dist.) N.Y. 1980, U.S. Ct. Appeals (7th cir.) 1976, U.S. Ct. Claims 1973, U.S. Tax Ct. 1973, U.S. Mil. Ct. Appeals 1974. Atty., U.S. Dept. Justice, Washington, 1972-75; lectr. Am. U., 1975-78; spl. asst. U.S. atty. Office of U.S. Atty., Chgo., 1976-78; atty. Commodity Futures Trading Commn., Washington, 1975-77; spl. counsel, 1977, asst. dir., 1977-78; regional counsel, N.Y.C., 1978-80; assoc. Rein, Mound & Cotton, N.Y.C., 1980-82, ptnr., Mound, Cotton & Wollan (and predecessor firms), 1983—. Contbr. articles to legal jours. Mem. bd. appeals Village of Flower Hill, Manhasset, N.Y., 1983-84, trustee, 1984-86. Recipient Cert. of Appreciation for Outstanding Service U.S. Commodity Futures Trading Commn., 1977. Commodities, Securities, General corporate. Home: 20 Hemlock Dr East Hills Roslyn NY 11576 Office: Mound Cotton & Wollan 125 Maiden Ln New York NY 10038

KOBRIGER, RICHARD ROMAN, JR., lawyer; b. Milw., Aug. 23, 1954; s. Richard R. Sr. and June Marie (Feldner) K.; m. Michelle M. Wiberg, June 25, 1977; children: Alyssa, Adam. BBA, St. Norbert Coll., 1976; JD, Marquette U., 1980. Bar: Wis. 1980, U.S. Dist. Ct. (ea. and we. dists.) Wis. 1980. Assoc. Cramer, Multhauf & Curran, Waukesha, Wis., 1980-85, ptnr., 1986—. Mem. bd. rev. City of Waukesha, 1983, family alumni assn. Boy Scouts Am., Waukesha, 1985—. Mem. ABA (taxation sect.), Wis. Bar Assn., Waukesha County Bar Assn. Roman Catholic. Lodge: Rotary. Banking, General corporate, General practice. Home: 2036 Cobblestone Ct Waukesha WI 53188 Office: Cramer Multhauf & Curran 316 N Grand Ave PO Box 558 Waukesha WI 53187

KOBRIN, LAWRENCE ALAN, lawyer; b. N.Y.C., Sept. 14, 1933; s. Irving and Hortense (Freezer) K.; m. Ruth E. Freedman, Mar. 5, 1967; children—Jeffrey, Rebecca, Debra. A.B., Columbia U., 1954, J.D., 1957. Bar: N.Y. 1957, U.S. Dist. Ct. (so. dist.) N.Y. 1958, U.S. Dist. Ct. (ea. dist.) N.Y. 1959, U.S. Ct. Appeals (2d cir.) 1959, U.S. Supreme Ct. 1966. Assoc. Cahill, Gordon, Reindel & Ohl, N.Y.C., 1958-59, Arthur D. Emil, N.Y.C., 1959-63; ptnr. Emil & Kobrin, N.Y.C., 1963-79, Milgrim, Thomajan, Jacobs and Lee, N.Y.C. 1979-83, Cahill Gordon & Reindel, N.Y.C., 1984—; asst. sec. Wurzweiler Sch. of Social Work, 1985— ; dir. UMB Bank and Trust Co., N.Y.C. Notes editor Columbia U. Law Rev.; contbr. articles to law jours. Vice pres., assoc. treas. chmn. dist. com. Fedn. Jewish Philanthropies, N.Y.C., 1981-84; chmn. Ramaz Sch., N.Y.C., 1978-83; sec. to bd. Bar Ilan U., N.Y.C., 1972-80. Kent scholar, 1955. Mem. Am. Coll. Real Estate Lawyers, Coop. Housing Lawyers Group (exec. com. 1972-80), Assn. of Bar of City of N.Y. (com. philosophical orgns. 1974-79, edn. and law com.), N.Y. County Lawyers Assn. (real property law sect.), Nat. Assn. Coll. and Univ. Attys. (1971-79), Phi Beta Kappa. Real property, General corporate. Home: 15 W 81st St New York NY 10024 Office: Cahill Gordon & Reindel 80 Pine St New York NY 10005

KOCH, EDNA MAE, lawyer; b. Terre Haute, Ind., Oct. 12, 1951; d. Leo K. and Lucille E. (Smith) K. BS in Nursing, Ind. State U., 1977; JD, Ind. U., 1980. Bar: Ind. 1980, U.S. Dist. Ct. (so. dist.) Ind. 1980. Assoc. Dillon & Cohen, Indpls., 1980-85; ptnr. Tipton, Cohen & Koch, Indpls., 1986—; leader seminars for nurses Ball State U., Muncie, Ind., St. Vincent Hosp., Indpls., Deaconess Hosp., Evansville, Ind., others; lectr. on med. malpractice Cen. Ind. chpt. Am. Assn. Critical Care Nurses, Indpls. "500" Postgrad. Course in Emergency Medicine, Ind. Assn. Osteo. Physicians and Surgeons State Conv., numerous others. Mem. ABA, Ind. State Bar Assn., Indpls. Bar Assn., Ind. Trial Lawyers Assn., Am. Nurses Assn., Ind. State Nurses Assn. Republican. Personal injury, Insurance, State civil litigation. Office: Tipton Cohen & Koch 47 S Meridian St Suite 200 Indianapolis IN 46204

KOCH, EDWARD RICHARD, lawyer, bank executive; b. Teaneck, N.J., Mar. 25, 1953; s. Edward J. and Adelaide M. (Wunner) K. BS in Econs. magna cum laude, U. Pa., 1975; JD, U. Va., 1980; LLM in Taxation, NYU, 1986. Bar: N.J. 1980, U.S. Dist. Ct. N.J. 1980, U.S. Tax Ct. 1981, U.S. Ct. Claims 1981. Staff acct. Touche Ross & Co., Newark, 1975-77; assoc. Winne, Banta & Rizzi, Hackensack, N.J., 1980-82; tax atty. Allied Corp., Morristown, 1982-87; asst. v.p. Chem. Bank, N.Y.C., 1987—. Vice chmn. law and legis. com. Athletics Congress, Indpls., 1985—; pres. N.J. Athletics Congress, Red Bank, 1986—. Mem. ABA, N.J. State Bar Assn., Am. Inst. CPA's, N.J. Soc. CPA's, Am. Assn. Attys.-CPA's. Republican. Roman Catholic. Club: N.J. Striders Track (Maywood) (chmn. 1981-86). Avocation: running. State and local taxation, Corporate taxation, Personal income taxation. Home: 47 Brandywyne Dr Florham Park NJ 07932 Office: Chem Bank Tax Dept 380 Madison Ave 11th Fl New York NY 10017

KOCH, JAN PAUL, lawyer; b. Cin., Sept. 11, 1951; s. James Charles and Barbara (Bock) K.; m. M. Diane Koch, July 21, 1979; 1 child, Andrew Patrick LaPille. BGS, U. Cin., 1973; JD, No. Ky. U., 1978. Bar: Ky. 1978, Ohio 1979, U.S. Dist. Ct. (ea. dist.) Ky. 1979, U.S. Dist. Ct. (so. dist.) Ohio 1979, U.S. Ct. Appeals (6th cir.) 1979. Instr. law U. Ky., Highland Heights, 1979-81; atty. City of Newport, Ky., 1980-82; sole practice Cold Spring, Ky., 1982-86, Las Vegas, Nev., 1986—; atty. City of Cold Spring, 1982-86; moot court advisor Salmon P. Chase Law Sch., U. Ky., 1978-81. Recipient Constl. Law Book award Lawyers Coop. Publ., Rochester, 1976. Republican. Roman Catholic. Avocation: securities analysis. Personal injury, State civil litigation, Federal civil litigation. Office: 710 S 9th St Las Vegas NV 89119

KOCH, KENNETH HOBSON, lawyer; b. Midland, Tex., July 27, 1955; s. Harold Kenneth and Martha Louise (Miller) K.; m. Barbara Louise Watkins, Sept. 18, 1982. BA in Econs., U. Pa., 1976; JD with distinction, Ohio State U., 1979; postdoctoral, Duke U., 1985. Bar: Ohio 1979, U.S. Dist. Ct. (so. dist.) Ohio 1979. Assoc. Porter, Wright, Morris & Arthur, Columbus, Ohio, 1979-84; v.p., gen. counsel Plaskolite, Inc., Columbus, 1984—. Mem. ABA, Columbus Bar Assn., Am. Corp. Counsel Assn. (nominating com. 1986—). Republican. Club: Columbus Country. Avocations: golf, skiing, basketball. General corporate. Home: 3611 Calumet St Columbus OH 43214 Office: Plaskolite Inc 1770 Joyce Ave PO Box 1497 Columbus OH 43216

KOCH, KENNETH RICHARD, lawyer; b. Bayside, N.Y., Apr. 14, 1955; s. Arthur and Suzanne Lois (Paymer) K.; m. Wendy Debra Williams, May 30, 1982. BA, Oberlin Coll., 1977; JD, NYU, 1980. Bar: N.Y. 1981. Assoc. Shea & Gould, N.Y.C., 1980—; asst. sec. Nova Pharm. Corp., Balt., 1984—; sec. Total Health Systems Inc., Great Neck, N.Y., 1986—, Jennifer Convertibles, Inc., Paramus, N.J., 1986—. General corporate, Securities. Office: Shea & Gould 330 Madison Ave New York NY 10017

KOCH, KY MARSHALL, lawyer; b. Bath, Maine, Oct. 25, 1952; s. Robert M. and Catherine M. (Marshall) K.; m. Melissa A. Adam, Apr. 8, 1978; 1 child, Courtney Leigh. B in Polit. Sci., U. Fla., 1975; JD, Hamline U., 1977. Bar: Fla. 1978, U.S. Dist. Ct. (mid. dist.) Fla. 1978. Asst. state atty. State of Fla., Clearwater, 1978-81; ptnr. Bauer, Koch, Platte & Mariani, Clearwater, 1981—. Pres. Girls Clubs Pinellas County, Clearwater, 1984-85; bd. dirs. 1st Step Inc. Mem. Clearwater Bar Assn. (pres. elect 1987-88, sec., treas.), Acad. Fla. Trial Lawyers, Pinellas County Trial Lawyers Assn., Pinellas County Criminal Trial Lawyers. Republican. Presbyterian. Criminal, Family and matrimonial. Home: 809 Ponce de Leon Blvd Belleair FL 33516 Office: Bauer Koch Platte & Mariani 1550 S Highland Ave Clearwater FL 33516

KOCH, RON, lawyer; b. Wilmington, del., July 26, 1951; s. Robert and Gladys (Lorenzoni) K.; m. Kari Elizabeth Brandenburg; 1 child, Brandi Leigh. BA in Philosophy, Polit. Sci., N.Mex. State U., 1973; JD, U. N.Mex., 1978. Bar: N.Mex. Sole practice Albuquerque, 1977—. Editor: N.Mex. Trial Lawyers Jour., 1984—. Fellow Am. Bd. Criminal Lawyers; mem. Am. Trial Lawyers Assn.,, N.Mex. Trial Lawyers Assn. (bd. dirs. 1985—), N.Mex. Bar Assn. (dir. criminal law sect. 1985—). Democrat. Criminal. Office: Koch & Jones PA 503 Slate Ave NW Albuquerque NM 87102

KOCH, SCOTT JAMES, lawyer; b. Mpls., Jan. 20, 1958; s. James R. and Joanne A. (Christiansen) K.; m. Carolyn Jo Budnicki, June 6, 1982. BA, U. Minn., 1979; JD cum laude, William Mitchell Coll. of Law, 1982. Bar: Minn. 1982. Assoc. Robert W. Johnson P.A., St. Paul, 1982—. Mem. Minn. Bar Assn., Assn. Trial Lawyers Am., Minn. Trial Lawyers Assn. Republican. Lutheran. Family and matrimonial, Legislative, Real property. Home: 1450 Knoll Dr Shoreview MN 55126 Office: Robert W Johnson PA 1732 Grand Ave Saint Paul MN 55105

KOCHANSKI, DAVID MAJLECH, lawyer; b. Bergen Belsen, Fed. Republic Germany, Jan. 12, 1948; came to U.S., 1949; s. Leon Josef and Maria (Kemp) K.; m. Adrienne Janet Laskowitz, June 6, 1969; children: Michael, Lori. BA, U. Md., 1969, JD, 1973. Bar: Md. 1973, D.C. 1974, U.S. Dist. Ct. Md. 1974, U.S. Supreme Ct. 1977. From assoc. to ptnr. Shulman, Rogers, Gandal, Pordy & Ecker, Silver Spring, Md., 1973—; instr. Savings and Loan League, Fairfax, Va., 1984. Mem. Citizens Adv. Bd., Bethesda and Chevy Chase, Md., 1981; pres. Woodmoor Civic Assn., Silver Spring, 1979; fin. com. Hebrew Home, Rockville, 1985. Mem. ABA, Montgomery County Bar Assn., Md. Bar Assn. Democrat. Real property, Consumer commercial, Banking. Home: 13709 Hobart Dr Silver Spring MD 20904 Office: Shulman Rogers Gandal Pordy & Ecker 8630 Fenton St #430 Silver Spring MD 20910

KOCHEMS, ROBERT GREGORY, lawyer; b. Cleve., Aug. 6, 1951; s. Roy George and Virginia Mae (Budniak) K.; m. Kathleen Anna McWilliams, May 31, 1975; 1 child, Alane Carin. BA cum laude, John Carroll U., 1973; JD, St. Louis U., 1976. Bar: Pa. 1976, U.S. Dist. Ct. (we. dist.) 1978. Sole practice Mercer, Pa., 1976-81; ptnr. Bogaty, McEwen, Sparks, & Kochems, P.C., Mercer, 1981—; asst. pub. defender Mercer County , 1977—; sub-com. chairperson Mercer County Juvenile Ct. Adv. Com., 1986. Assoc. editor St. Louis U. Law Jour., 1975-76. Mem. ABA, Pa. Bar Assn., Mercer County Bar Assn. (sec. 1977-79, bench bar com. 1982, 84). Republican. Roman Catholic. Lodges: KC (advocate 1978—), Kiwanis. Juvenile, Criminal, Family and matrimonial. Home: RD #1 Box 143 Birchwood Dr Transfer PA 16154 Office: Bogaty McEwen Sparks Kochems PO Box 226 Mercer PA 16137

KOCHER, WALTER WILLIAM, lawyer, foods company executive; b. N.Y.C., Dec. 8, 1934; s. Walter A. and Rose S. Kocher; m. Vivian Roy, June 11, 1960; children: Gary John, William Mark. B.S. in Mgmt., Fordham U.; J.D., U. Mich.; LL.M., NYU. Bar: U.S. Dist. Ct. (ea. and so. dists.) N.Y., U.S. Ct. Appeals (2d cir.), U.S. Ct. Appeals (7th cir.), U.S. Supreme Ct., Ohio, N.Y. Atty. Stauffer Chem Co.; v.p., gen. counsel Borden, Inc., Columbus, Ohio. Bd. dirs. Westchester County and Tarrytown United Way; capt., bd. dirs. Tarrytown Ambulance Corp.; mem. parish council Transfiguration Roman Catholic Ch. Mem. Columbus Bar Assn., ABA, N.Y.C. Bar Assn., Am. Corp. Counsel Assn. Clubs: Brookside Country, Columbus Athletic, Upper Arlington Booster (dir., treas.). General corporate, Antitrust, Federal civil litigation. Office: Borden Inc 277 Park Ave New York NY 10172 *

KOCIUBES, JOSEPH LEIB, lawyer; b. Frankfurt, W.Ger., June 16, 1947; came to U.S., 1949; s. Max and Rachel (Ackerman) K.; m. Peggy Ann Roth, May 18, 1969; children: Lisa Roth, Adam Roth. BA, U. Pitts., 1969; JD, Harvard U., 1974. Bar: Mass. 1974, U.S. Dist. Ct. Mass. 1974, U.S. Ct. Apls. (1st cir.) 1975, U.S. Sup. Ct. 1979. Asst. to dean Coll. Arts and Sci., U. Pitts., 1969; dir. health and edn. programs North Shore Community Action Program, Beverly, Mass., 1969-71; asst. dir. Project RAP, Beverly, 1971; assoc. Bingham, Dana & Gould, Boston, 1974-81, ptnr., 1981—, mem. mgmt. com., 1984—; trial teaching advisor Harvard Law Sch., 1979—; mem. adv. council Gov.'s Urea-Formaldehyde Trust Fund, 1986—; bd. dirs. Vol. Lawyers Project, Boston, 1985—. Mem. ABA (litigation sect. task force on uniform securities act 1985), Mass. Bar Assn., Boston Bar Assn. Democrat. Jewish. Club: Harvard (Boston). Libel, Federal civil litigation, State civil litigation. Home: 187 Nehoiden Rd Newton MA 02168 Office: Bingham Dana & Gould 100 Federal St Boston MA 02110

KOCK, ARLENE DOROTHY, lawyer; b. Oakland, Calif., Sept. 6, 1951; d. Bruce Alvin and Thelma Harriet (Marinoni) K. BA in Sociology, San Francisco State U., 1974; JD, U. San Francisco, 1977. Bar: Calif. 1978. Researcher Ctr. for Judicial Edn., Berkeley, Calif., 1978; assoc. Alfred A. Affinito, Pitts., 1978-79; dist. mng. atty. Yanello & Flippen, Oakland, 1977-83; sole practice Hayward, Calif., 1983—. Mem. ABA, Calif. Trial Lawyers Assn., Women Lawyers Assn., Gen. Counsel, State Regent of Calif., DAR. Democrat. Episcopalian. Family and matrimonial, Criminal, State civil litigation. Office: 24301 Southland Dr 308 Hayward CA 94545

KOCORAS, CHARLES PETROS, federal judge; b. Chgo., Mar. 12, 1938; s. Petros K. and Constantina (Cordonis) K.; m. Grace L. Finlay, Sept. 22, 1968; children: Peter, John, Paul. Student, Wilson Jr. Coll., 1956-58; B.S., Coll. Commerce, DePaul U., 1961; J.D., DePaul U., 1969. Bar: Ill. 1969. Assoc. Bishop & Crawford, 1969-71; asst. atty. Office of U.S. Atty. No. Dist. Ill. U.S. Dept. Justice, 1971-77; judge U.S. Dist. Ct., Chgo., 1980—; chmn. Ill. Commerce Commn., Chgo., 1977-79; ptnr. Stone, McGuire, Benjamin and Kocoras, Chgo., 1979-80; instr. trial practice, evening div. John Marshall Law Sch., 1975—; various positions IRS, Chgo., 1962-69. Served with Army N.G., 1961-67. Mem. Chgo. Bar Assn., Fed. Criminal Jury Instruction Com. Seventh Circuit, Beta Alpha Psi. Greek Orthodox. Jurisprudence. Office: US Courthouse 219 S Dearborn St Chicago IL 60604 *

KOEGEL, WILLIAM FISHER, lawyer; b. Washington, Aug. 18, 1923; s. Otto Erwin and Rae (Fisher) K.; m. Barbara Bixler, Feb. 2, 1946 (dec. 1968); children: John Bixler, Robert Bartlett; m. Ruth Swan Boynton, June 21, 1969 (dec. 1983); m. Irene Lawrence, Aug. 4, 1984. B.A., Williams Coll., 1944; LL.B., U. Va., 1949. Bar: N.Y. 1950. From assoc. to ptnr. Roger & Wells (and predecessors), N.Y.C., 1949—; head litigation dept. Roger & Wells (and predecessors), 1977—. Chmn. Scarsdale (N.Y.) Republican Town Com., 1965-71; pres. trustees Hitchcock Presbyn. Ch., Scarsdale, 1970-73, 78-79, 82-83. Served with AUS, 1943-45, ETO. Fellow Am. Coll. Trial Lawyers; mem. ABA, N.Y. State Bar Assn., Bar Assn. City N.Y., Order of Coif. Clubs: Town (Scarsdale) (pres. 1976-77); Sky (N.Y.C.), Williams (N.Y.C.); Shenorock Shore, Fox Meadow Tennis. Federal civil litigation, State civil litigation. Home: 7 Chesterfield Rd Scarsdale NY 10583 Office: 200 Park Ave New York NY 10166

KOEGEN, ROY JEROME, lawyer; b. Spokane, Wash., Mar. 1, 1949; s. Frank J. and Jeanne (Bardsley) K.; m. Ann Martinelli, Aug. 28, 1970; children: Jennifer, Christopher. BA, Gonzaga U., 1971; JD, U. Calif., San Francisco, 1974. Bar: Calif. 1974, Wash. 1979, U.S. Supreme Ct. 1982. Assoc. Wilson, Jones, Morton & Lynch, San Mateo, Calif., 1974-78, Blair & Koegen, Spokane, 1978-80; ptnr. Preston, Thorgrimson, Ellis & Holman, Spokane, 1980—. Chmn. exec. com. Community Alcohol Ctr., Spokane, 1982-84, Century II Park Dist., Spokane, 1982-84. Mem. ABA, Wash. Bar Assn., Calif. Bar Assn., Nat. Assn. Bond Lawyers. Roman Catholic. Municipal bonds, Local government, Securities. Office: Preston Thorgrimson Ellis & Holman Seafirst Fin Ctr Suite 1480 Spokane WA 99201

KOEHN, WILLIAM JAMES, lawyer; b. Winterset, Iowa, Mar. 24, 1936; s. Cyril Otto and Ilene L. (Doop) K.; m. Francis C. Leeper, Sept. 6, 1958; children—Cynthia Rae, William Fredric, James Anthony. B.A., U. Iowa, 1958, J.D., 1963. Bar: Iowa 1963, U.S. Ct. Appeals (8th cir.) 1971, U.S. Ct. Appeals (10th cir.) 1972, U.S. Ct. Appeals (2d cir.) 1972, U.S. Ct. Appeals (5th cir.) 1977, U.S. Supreme Ct. 1971. Ptnr., Davis, Hockenberg, Wine, Brown and Koehn, Des Moines, 1963—. Bd. editors Iowa Law Rev., 1961-63. Co-founder Big Bros.-Sisters of Greater Des Moines, 1969, pres., 1976-77; chmn. Des Moines Friendship Commn., 1970-71; bd. dirs. Greater Des Moines YMCA, 1983—; co-chmn. Des Moines Bicentennial Commn., 1975-76. Served to lt. USNR, 1958-61. Named Best Lawyer in Am. Naiffh & Smith Bus. Litigation Sect., 1983-87. Mem. Iowa State Bar Assn. ABA (environ. litigation com.), Polk County Bar Assn., Def. Research Inst., Order of Coif. Republican. Federal civil litigation, State civil litigation, Construction. Home: 607 Country Club Blvd Des Moines IA 50312 Office: 2300 Financial Ctr Des Moines IA 50309

KOELLER, ROBERT MARION, lawyer; b. Quincy, Ill., Apr. 8, 1940; s. Marion Alfred and Ruth (Main) K.; m. Marlene Meyer, June 1962; children—Kristin, Katherine, Robert. A.B., MacMurray Coll., 1962; LL.B., Vanderbilt U., 1965. Bar: Ind. 1968. Asst. gen. csl. Nat. Homes Acceptance Corp., Lafayette, Ind., 1967-70; gen. csl., sec. Herff Jones Co., Indpls., 1970-74; ptnr. Warren, Snider, Koeller & Warren, Indpls., 1974-76; sole practice, Indpls., 1976-86; ptnr. Mears & Crawford, 1987—; dir. various cos. Mem. ABA, Ind. Bar Assn., Indpls. Bar Assn. Republican. Methodist. General corporate, Securities, Venture Capital.

KOELTL, JOHN GEORGE, lawyer; b. N.Y.C., Oct. 25, 1945; s. John J. and Elsie (Bender) K. A.B. summa cum laude, Georgetown U., 1967; J.D. magna cum laude, Harvard U., 1971. Bar: N.Y. 1972, U.S. Dist. Ct. (so. and ea. dists.) N.Y. 1975, U.S. Ct. Appeals (2d cir.) 1975, U.S. Supreme Ct. 1978, U.S. Ct. Appeals (5th and 11th cirs.) 1981, U.S. Ct. Appeals (4th cir.) 1982, U.S. Dist. Ct. (no. dist.) N.Y. 1982. Law clk. to judge U.S. Dist. Ct. (so. dist.) N.Y., N.Y.C., 1971-72; law clk. to Justice Potter Stewart U.S. Supreme Ct., Washington, 1972-73; asst. spl. prosecutor Watergate Spl. Prosecution Force Dept. Justice, Washington, 1973-74; assoc. Debevoise & Plimpton, N.Y.C., 1975-78, ptnr., 1979—. Mem. ABA (vice chmn. securities com. adminstrv. law sect. 1979-81, co-dir. div. pubs. litigation sect. 1982-84, council mem. litigation sect. 1984—), Assn. Bar N.Y.C. (mem. com. on fed. legislation 1976-78, sec. fed. cts. com. 1978-81, mem. com. profl. and jud. ethics 1981-84, fed. cts. com. 1984-86, chmn. 1986—), N.Y. State Bar Assn., N.Y. County Lawyers Assn. (mem. fed. cts. com. 1984-96, chmn. 1986—). Assoc. editor Litigation (quar. jour. litigation sect. ABA), 1975-78, exec. editor, 1978-80, editor-in-chief, 1980-82; contbr. articles in field to law jours. Federal civil litigation, Libel, Administrative and regulatory. Home: 342 E 67th St New York NY 10021 Office: Debevoise & Plimpton 875 3d Ave New York NY 10022

KOELZER, GEORGE JOSEPH, lawyer; b. Orange, N.J., Mar. 21, 1938; s. George Joseph and Albertina Florence (Graul) K.; m. Patricia Ann Kilian, Apr. 8, 1967; 1 son, James Patrick. A.B., Rutgers U., 1962, LL.B., 1964. Bar: N.J. 1964, D.C. 1978, N.Y. 1980. Assoc. Louis R. Lombardino, Liv-

ingston, N.J., 1964-66, Lum Biunno & Tompkins, Newark, 1971-73, Giordano, Halleran & McOmber, Middletown, N.J., 1973-74; asst. U.S. atty. for N.J., U.S. Dept. Justice, 1966-71; ptnr. Evans, Koelzer, Osborne & Kreizman, N.Y.C. and Red Bank, N.J., 1974-86; ptnr. Ober, Kaler, Grimes & Shriver, Inc., N.Y.C., 1986—; mem. lawyers adv. com. U.S. Ct. Appeals (3d cir.) 1985-87, vice chmn., 1986—, chmn., 1987; mem. lawyers adv. com. U.S. Dist. Ct. N.J., 1984—; permanent mem. Jud. Conf. of U.S. Ct. Appeals for 3d cir. Recipient Atty. Gen.'s award, 1970. Mem. ABA (sect. litigation, co-chmn. com. on admiralty and maritime litigation 1979-82, mem. council sect. litigation 1985-88, program chmn. 9th ann. meeting sect. litigation 1984, dir. div. IV procedural coms. 1982-85, mem. nominating com. 1982, 84, 87), Maritime Law Assn. U.S. (ABA relations com., mcht. marine com.), N.Y. State Bar Assn. (admiralty com.), Assn. Bar City N.Y., New York County Lawyers Assn. (admiralty com.), D.C. Bar Assn., N.J. Bar Assn.(chmn. admiralty com. 1985-87), Fed. Bar Assn., Fed. Bar Council, Def. Research Inst. (chmn. admiralty com. 1982-85), Maritime Assn. Port N.Y., Assn. Average Adjusters Gt. Britain, Assn. Average Adjusters U.S. Democrat. Roman Catholic. Clubs: Downtown Athletic, Whitehall, World Trade (N.Y.C.); Nat. Lawyers (Washington); Wig and Pen, Marine, Directors (London); Navesink Country (Middletown); Mid-Ocean (Bermuda). Admiralty, Federal civil litigation, Criminal. Home: 10 Sycamore Ln Rumson NJ 07760 Office: 55 Broadway One Exchange Plaza New York NY 10006 also: 505 Thornall St One Metroplaza Edison NJ 08837

KOENIG, KENNETH JOHN, lawyer; b. Hamilton, Ohio, May 6, 1952; s. Melvin Bernard and Margaret M. (Helfrey) K.; m. Lora Ellen Tripp, July 14, 1979. A.B., Georgetown U., 1974; J.D., Fordham U., 1977. Bar: Ohio 1977, U.S. Dist. Ct. (so. dist.) Ohio 1977, U.S. Ct. Appeals (6th cir.) 1978, D.C. 1980, U.S. Supreme Ct. 1982. Adminstrv. asst. Mayor James T. Luken, Cin., 1977; sole practice, Cin., 1977-78, 85—; assoc. Shaffer & Meurer, Cin., 1978-79; trial counsel Hamilton County Pub. Defender Office, Cin., 1979—; ptnr. Koenig & Flagg, Cin., 1981-85. lectr. Am. Inst. for Paralegal Studies, Cin., 1982—; named to Ohio State Employment Relations Bd., Panel of Neutrals, 1985. Mem. Cin. Bar Assn., Ohio State Bar Assn., D.C. Bar Assn., Ohio Acad. Trial Lawyers, Assn. Trial Lawyers Am., ABA. Democrat. Roman Catholic. State civil litigation, Criminal, Labor. Home: 5061 Eastwood Circle Cincinnati OH 45227 Office: 1500 American Bldg 30 E Central Pkwy Cincinnati OH 45202

KOENIG, PETER EDWARD, lawyer; b. Cin., July 19, 1956; s. Robert P. and Mary Theresa (Kelly) K.; m. Susan Hilmer, May 18, 1985. Cert., Goethe Inst., Munich, 1976; BA summa cum laude, Ohio U., 1978; JD, Case Western Res. U., 1981. Bar: Ohio 1981, U.S. Dist. Ct. (so. dist.) Ohio 1981, U.S. Dist. Ct. (ea. dist.) Ky. 1983, U.S. Ct. Appeals (6th cir.) 1983, U.S. Supreme Ct. 1986. Law clk. to presiding justice Hamilton County Common Pleas Ct., Cin., 1981-82; assoc. Simon & Namanworth, Cin., 1982-84, Brumleve, DeCamp, Wood & Barron, Cin., 1984-86, Strauss & Troy Co. L.P.A., Cin., 1986—. Mem. ABA, Ohio Bar Assn., Cin. Bar Assn., Fed. Bar Assn., Assn. Trial Lawyers Am., Downtown Council Cin. C. of C. (membership com. 1984-86), Order of Barristers, Cin. Squash Racquets Assn. (sec. 1985—), Barrister, Potter Stewart Am. Inn. of Conn., Phi Beta Kappa. Clubs: Cin. Country, University (Cin.). Avocations: squash, tennis, swimming, lit., jazz music. State civil litigation, Personal injury, Real property. Home: 2905 Ziegle Ave Cincinnati OH 45208 Office: Strauss & Troy Co LPA 2100 Central Trust Ctr 201 E 5th St Cincinnati OH 45202

KOENIG, RODNEY CURTIS, lawyer, rancher; b. Black Jack, Tex., Nov. 21, 1940; s. John Henry and Elva Marguerite (Oeding) K.; m. Rebecca Anne Todd, June 3, 1962; children—Erik Jason, Jon Todd. B.A., U. Tex., 1962, J.D. with honors, 1969; postgrad., Auburn U., 1965-67. Bar: Tex. 1969, U.S. Dist. Ct. (so. dist.) Tex. 1970, U.S. Ct. Appeals (5th cir.) 1970, U.S. Tax Ct. 1980, U.S. Ct. Mil. Appeals 1986. Ptnr. Fulbright & Jaworski, Houston, 1969—; lectr. State Bar Tex., various univs., local estate planning councils; asst. prof. Auburn U., 1965-67. Contbr. articles to profl. jours. Pres. Houston Navy League, 1979-81; commr. Battleship Texas Commn.; mem. exec. com. March of Dimes; chmn. singing Houston Saengerbund; bd. dirs. Southwest Jazz Ballet Co., Houston div. Am. Heart Assn. Served with USN, 1962-67; served to capt. JAGC, USNR, 1967-86. Mem. ABA, College State Bar of Tex. (charter), U.S. Navy League (nat. dir.), Tex. Judge Adv. Res. Officers Assn., Tex. German Soc. (founding dir.), Res. Officers Assn., Sons of Republic of Texas, Wednesday Tax Forum (past chmn.), Order of Coif, Phi Delta Phi, Omicron Delta Kappa. Lutheran. Clubs: Houstonian, Inns of Court, Houston Ctr. Estate planning, Probate, Estate taxation. Office: 51st Floor 1301 McKinney Houston TX 77010

KOENIG, SHERMAN, law librarian; b. Poughkeepsie, N.Y., Apr. 25, 1913; s. Samuel and Bertha (Fuchs) K.; m. Celia E. Koenig (dec. July 1980); 1 child, Ira Warren. LLB, Bklyn. Law Sch., 1938. Bar: N.Y. 1938, U.S. Dist. Ct. (so. dist.) N.Y. Trial atty. Weisman et al, N.Y.C., 1938-45; sec., treas. All-State Dist., Newark, 1945-68; pres. All-State N.J., Newark, 1968-71; law librarian Becker, Poliakoff & Streitfeld, Ft. Lauderdale, Fla., 1980—; v.p., dir. Roxbury State Bank, N.J., 1966-72. Mem. Am. Assn. Law Libraries, So. Fla. Assn. Law Libraries (co-chmn. constitution sect. 1984—). Democrat. Jewish. Lodge: B'nai B'rith (local pres. 1977-79). Avocations: swimming, golf. Personal injury, Librarianship. Office: Becker Poliakoff & Streitfeld 6520 N Andrews Ave PO Box 9057 Fort Lauderdale FL 33310

KOEP, RICHARD MICHAEL, lawyer; b. Mpls., Dec. 4, 1949; s. Clifford Michael and Mary Corrine (Narey) K.; children: Matthew, Theodore, John. JD, William Mitchell Coll. Law, 1980. Bar: Colo. 1980, U.S. Dist. Ct. Colo. 1980, Calif. 1981, U.S. Dist. Ct. (cen. dist.) Calif. 1982. Officer Hill, Genson, Even, Crandall & Wade, Los Angeles, 1982—. Served with USMC, 1968-70, Vietnam. Mem. ABA. Roman Catholic. Personal injury. Office: Hill Genson et al 505 Shatto Pl Los Angeles CA 90020

KOERNKE, THOMAS FREDERICK, lawyer; b. Cleve., May 13, 1948; s. Fred G. and Hazel Louella (Huntsman) K.; m. Holly Jill Solem, July 4, 1981; children: Daniel, Molly. BA, Mich. State U., 1970; JD, U. Mich., 1974. Bar: Mich. 1974, U.S. Dist. Ct. (we. dist.) Mich. 1976, U.S. Ct. Appeals (6th cir.) 1976. Law clk. to presiding judge U.S. Ct. Appeals, Cin., 1974-76; assoc. Warner, Norcross & Judd, Grand Rapids, Mich., 1976-81; ptnr. Tolley, Fisher & Verwys, P.C., Grand Rapids, 1981—. Author: Comparative Negligence in Michigan, 1981. Chmn. Kent County Rep. Com., Grand Rapids, 1982-84, fund devel. Mich. Trails council Girl Scouts U.S., Grand Rapids, 1985; del. Rep. Nat. Conv., Dallas, 1984. Named Vol. of Yr. Kent County Chpt. Am. Cancer Soc., 1981. Mem. Mich. Bar Assn. (legal edn. com.). Baptist. Avocations: baseball, golf. Federal civil litigation, State civil litigation, Contracts commercial. Office: Tolley Fisher & Verwys PC 5650 Foremost Dr SE Grand Rapids MI 49506-7081

KOEVARY, A. GEORGE, lawyer; b. Bratislava, Czechoslovakia, Sept. 15, 1947; came to U.S., 1951; s. Theodore and Lilla (Grunfeld) K.; m. Gail Hannah Rhodes, Jan. 25, 1969; children: Jonathan Todd, Daniel James. BA, CCNY, 1969, MS, 1971; JD, Fordham U., 1978. Bar: N.Y. 1979, U.S. Dist. Ct. (so. and ea. dists.) N.Y. 1979, U.S. Ct. Appeals (2d cir.) 1981. V.p., gen. counsel Electro Dispersion Corp., N.Y.C., 1978-81; sole practice N.Y.C., 1981-84; ptnr. Milman & Shwergold, N.Y.C., 1984-86, Parker & Duryee, N.Y.C., 1986—. Mem. ABA, N.Y. State Bar Assn., Westchester County Bar Assn., N.Y. State Trial Lawyers Assn., N.Y. County Lawyers Assn. Jewish. Federal civil litigation, State civil litigation. Home: 4 School Ln Scarsdale NY 10583 Office: Parker & Duryee 529 Fifth Ave New York NY 10017

KOFF, HOWARD MICHAEL, lawyer; b. Bklyn., July 25, 1941; s. Arthur and Blanche Koff; m. Linda Sue Bright, Sept. 10, 1966; 1 son, Michael Arthur Bright. B.S., NYU, 1962; J.D., Bklyn. Law Sch., 1965; LL.M. in Taxation, Georgetown U., 1968. Bar: N.Y. 1965, D.C. 1966, U.S. Supreme Ct. 1969, U.S. Ct. Appeals (2d, 3d, 4th, 5th, 7th, 9th and D.C. cirs.), U.S. Dist. Ct. (no. dist.) N.Y. 1981. Appellate atty. Tax Div., U.S. Dept. Justice, Washington, 1965-69; tax supr. Chrysler Corp., Detroit, 1969-70; chief tax counsel Conn. Gen. Life Ins. Co., Hartford, Conn., 1970-77; chief tax counsel Rohm & Haus Co., Phila., 1977-78; ptnr. Dibble, Koff, Lane, Stern and Stern, Rochester, N.Y., 1978-81; pres. Howard M. Koff, P.C., Albany, N.Y., 1981—; lectr. tax matters. Recipient Founders Day award NYU, 1962; Lawyers Coop. award for gen. excellence Lawyers Coop. Pub. Co., 1965. Mem. Fed. Bar Assn. (past pres. Hartford County chpt.), ABA (past chmn. subcom. com. on partnerships tax sect.), Albany County Bar Assn., Estate Planning Council Eastern N.Y., Albany Area C. of C. Republican. Jewish. Clubs: Rotary, Colonie Guilderland N.Y. Charter mem. editorial adv. bd. Jour. Real Estate Taxation; contbr. articles to legal jours. Corporate taxation, Estate taxation, Personal income taxation. Home: 205 Bentwood Ct W Albany NY 12203 Office: 600 Broadway St Albany NY 12207

KOFFEY, RICHARD STEPHAN, lawyer; b. Albany, N.Y., Oct. 18, 1944; s. Barnett and Edythe (Polansky) K.; m. Anne Drake, Sept. 27, 1970; children: Nicole, Quentin. BA, Cornell U., 1966; JD, Columbia U., 1969. Bar: N.Y. 1969, Pa. 1978, U.S. Tax Ct. 1978. Assoc. Dewey, Ballantine, Bushby, Palmer & Wood, N.Y.C., 1970-75; acting tax legis. counsel, dep. tax legis. counsel, legal advisor U.S. Treasury Dept., Washington, 1975-78; ptnr. Morgan, Lewis & Bockius, N.Y.C., 1978—; vis. lectr. law Yale U., New Haven, 1984—. Served as pvt. USAR, 1969-74. Mem. ABA, Phila. Bar Assn., N.Y. State Bar Assn. (exec. com. 1987—). Jewish. Clubs: Merion Cricket (Haverford, Pa.), Radnor Hunt (Newton Sq., Pa.). Avocations: cross country skiing, horseback riding, fly fishing. Corporate taxation. Office: Morgan Lewis & Bockius 101 Park Ave New York NY 10178

KOFFLER, WARREN WILLIAM, lawyer; b. N.Y.C., July 21, 1938; s. Jack and Rose (Conovich) K.; m. Barbara Rose Holz, June 11, 1959; m. 2d, Jayne Audri Goetzel, May 15, 1970; children—Kevin, Kenneth, Caroline. B.S., Boston U., 1959; J.D., U. Calif.-Berkeley, 1962. Bar: D.C. 1962, N.Y. 1963, U.S. Dist. Ct. D.C. 1963, Fla. 1980, Va. 1981, Pa. 1982. Atty. FAA, Washington, 1964; sole practice, Washington, 1964, 78—, Hollywood and Miami, Fla., 1978—; atty. Fed. Home Loan Bank Bd., Washington, 1964-66; ptnr. Koffler & Spivack, Washington, 1967-77. Mem. ABA, Inter-Am. Bar Assn., Fed. Bar Assn., D.C. Bar Assn., Fla. Bar Assn., Va. Bar Assn., Assn. Trial Lawyers Am., Brit. Inst. Internat. and Comparative Law. Clubs: University (Washington); Bankers (Miami, Fla.). Administrative and regulatory, Banking, Private international. Office: Suite 1200 1000 Connecticut Ave Washington DC 20006

KOFFMAN, ROBERT LAWRENCE, judge; b. Maryville, Mo., Dec. 24, 1953; s. John H. and Carolyn Jane (Canon) K.; m. Doris B. Fry, Sept. 12, 1981; children—John Charles, Kathryn Elizabeth. B.S. in Bus. Adminstrn., Central Mo. State U., 1977; J.D., St. Mary's U., 1980. Bar: Mo. 1980, U.S. Dist. Ct. (we. dist.) Mo. 1980. Assoc. Woolsey, Fischer, Whiteacre, McDonald, Springfield, Mo., 1980-81; assoc. circuit judge 18th Jud. Circuit, Sedalia, Mo., 1981—. Mem. ABA, Mo. Bar Assn., Pettis County Bar Assn. (v.p.) Mo. Assn. Trial Attys., Am. Trial Lawyers Assn., Mace and Torch. Republican. Methodist. Lodges: Masons, Rotary. Probate, Judicial administration, Family and matrimonial. Home: 1904 S Kentucky St Sedalia MO 65301 Office: Courthouse 415 S Ohio St Sedalia MO 65301

KOFFORD, CREE-L, lawyer; b. Santaquin, Utah, July 11, 1933; s. Cree C. and Melba (Nelson) K.; m. Ila Jean Macdonald, Sept. 11, 1953; children—Kim, Jane, Bradley, Quinn, Tracy. B.S., U. Utah, 1955; J.D., U. So. Calif., 1961. Bar: Calif. 1962. Ptnr. Munns & Kofford, San Marino, Calif., 1962-68, Munns, Kofford, Hoffman, Hunt & Throckmorton, Pasadena, Calif., 1969—. Mem. ABA, Calif. Bar Assn., Los Angeles County Bar Assn. Republican. Mormon. Club: Univ. (Pasadena). Business, General corporate. Home: 1330 Rodeo Rd Arcadia CA 91006 Office: Munns Kofford Hoffman Hunt & Throckmorton 225 S Lake Ave Penthouse Pasadena CA 91101

KOGAN, GERALD, judge; b. Bklyn., May 23, 1933; s. Morris and Yetta (Weinstein) K.; m. Irene Vulgan, Nov. 17, 1955; children—Robert, Debra, Karen. B.B.A., U. Miami, 1955, J.D., 1955. Bar: Fla. 1955. Sole practice, Miami, Fla., 1955-60, 67-80; asst. state's atty. Dade County (Fla.), Miami, 1960-67, chief prosecutor homicide and capital crimes sect.; judge criminal div. Fla. 11th Jud. Cir. Ct., Miami, 1980-87; justice Supreme Ct. Fla, Tallahassee, 1987—. Adj. prof. law Nova U. Law Sch., U. Miami Sch. Law; mem. faculty Am. Acad. Jud. Adminstrn. Served with CIC, AUS, 1955-57. Mem. ABA, Fla. Bar, Dade County Bar Assn. Lodge: Optimists (pres. S.W. Miami 1959-60, lt. gov. Fla. 1961-62). Criminal, Jurisprudence. Office: Supreme Ct Bldg Tallahassee FL 32301

KOGAN, STEPHEN JAY, lawyer; b. Bklyn., Nov. 24, 1939; s. Morris and Yetta Kogan; m. Anne Mary Corona, Aug. 13, 1978; 1 child, Ashley Lynn. B.B.A., U. Miami, 1961, J.D., 1964. Bar: Fla. 1964, U.S. Dist. Ct. (so. dist.) Fla. 1964, U.S. Tax Ct. 1973, U.S. Ct. Appeals (5th and 11th cirs.) 1977, U.S. Supreme Ct. 1977. Asst. state atty., Miami, Fla., 1965-70; sole practice, Miami, 1970—. State dist. v.p. Young Democrats, Fla., 1962. Served with USCG, 1964-70, Mem. Fla. Criminal Def. Atty.'s Assn., Nat. Dist. Atty.'s Assn., Fla. Bar Assn. (vice chmn. cert. com. criminal law sect. 1984). Jewish. Criminal. Office: 1110 Brickell Ave Suite 303 Miami FL 33131

KOGOVSEK, DANIEL CHARLES, lawyer; b. Pueblo, Colo., Aug. 4, 1951; s. Frank Louis and Mary Edith (Blatnick) K.; m. Patricia Elizabeth Connell, June 30, 1979; 1 child, Ryan Robert. B.A., U. Notre Dame, 1973; J.D., Columbia U., 1976. Bar: Colo. 1976, U.S. Dist. Ct. Colo. 1976, U.S. Ct. Appeals (10th cir.) 1978, U.S. Supreme Ct. 1983. Asst. atty. gen. Colo. Dept. Law, Denver, 1976-79; campaign mgr. Congressman Kogovsek, Pueblo, 1980, 82; dir. Office Consumer Services, Denver, 1981; mem. firm Fish & Kogovsek, Denver, 1983-84; sr. assoc. Petersen & Fonda, P.C., Denver, 1984—. Mem. ABA, Assn. Trial Lawyers Am., Colo. Bar Assn., Colo. Def. Lawyers Assn., Pueblo Bar Assn. Roman Catholic. Club: Pueblo Country. State civil litigation, Bankruptcy, Probate. Home: 9 Windflower Ct Denver CO 81001 Office: Petersen & Fonda PC 650 Thatcher Bldg Pueblo CO 81003

KOH, HAROLD HONGJU, law educator; b. Cambridge, Mass., Dec. 8, 1954; s. Kwang Lim and Hesung (Chun) K.; m. Mary-Christy Fisher, Feb. 19, 1984. BA, Harvard U., 1975, Oxford U., Eng., 1977; JD, Harvard U., 1980. Bar: N.Y. 1981, D.C. 1981, U.S. Dist. Ct. D.C. 1981, U.S. Ct. Appeals (D.C. cir.) 1981, U.S. Ct. Claims 1982, Conn. 1985, U.S. Supreme Ct. 1985, U.S. Dist. Ct. Conn. 1987. Law clk. to presiding judge U.S. Ct. Appeals (D.C. cir.), Washington, 1980-81; law clk. to justice Harry A. Blackmun U.S. Supreme Ct., Washington, 1981-82; assoc. Covington & Burling, Washington, 1982-83; atty.-advisor Office of Legal Counsel, Dept. Justice, Washington, 1983-85; assoc. prof. law Yale U., New Haven, 1985—; Bd. dirs. Initiative for Pub. Interest Law at Yale U., New Haven, 1986, East Rock Inst., New Haven, 1986. Contbr. articles to profl. jours. Marshall scholar Oxford U., 1977. Mem. Am. Soc. Internat. Law. Private international, Public international, Federal civil litigation. Office: Yale Law Sch 127 Wall St PO Box 401A Yale Sta New Haven CT 06520

KOHL, DONALD PHILLIP, lawyer; b. Springfield, Ohio, Sept. 11, 1933; s. Harry F. and Irene B. (Powell) K.; m. Shirley R. Kohl, Feb. 11, 1955 (div. May 1975); children: Mark, Pam, Patricia; m. Diane E. Elaine, June 21, 1975 (separated); children: Jeff, Jennifer. BA, Ohio State U., 1955; JD, George Washington U., 1957. Bar: Va. 1960, Fla. 1962. Sole practice West Palm Beach, Fla., 1963-67; judge small claims/magistrate ct. Palm Beach County, West Palm Beach, 1967-72; ptnr. Kohl, Springer, Springer, Mighdoll, Salnick & Krischer and predecessor firm Kohl, Springer & Springer, Palm Springs, Fla., 1973-86, Kohl & Mighdoll, West Palm Beach, 1986—. Mem. Palm Springs Village Council, 1963-65; bd. dirs. U.S. Jaycees, Tulsa, 1966-68, Fla. v.p., Lakeland, 1966-68. Mem. Palm Beach County Bar Assn., Assn. Trial Lawyers Am. (sustaining), Fla. Acad. Trial Lawyers, Palm Springs Jaycees (pres. 1965-66, disting. service award 1971). Republican. Presbyterian. Club: Exchange (West Palm Beach) (pres. 1969-70, cog of yr. award 1973). Administrative and regulatory, Personal injury, Criminal. Home: 260 Ohio Rd Lake Worth FL 33467 Office: Kohl & Mighdoll 2324 S Congress Ave West Palm Beach FL 33406

KOHL, GLEN ARLEN, lawyer; b. Fairlawn, N.J., Feb. 2, 1956; s. Leonard and Laurel (Paris) K.; m. Julie Abrahamson, July 8, 1984. BS summa cum laude, Tufts U., 1978; JD, Yale U., 1981; LLM in Taxation, NYU, 1983. Bar: Calif. 1981. Assoc. Irell & Manella, Los Angeles, 1981-82; acting asst. prof. NYU, 1983-84; assoc. Wilson, Sonsini, Goodrich & Rosati, Palo Alto, Calif., 1984—. Mem. Phi Beta Kappa. Corporate taxation. Office: Wilson Sonsini Goodrich & Rosati 2 Palo Alto Sq Palo Alto CA 94306

KOHLSTEDT, JAMES AUGUST, lawyer; b. Evanston, Ill., June 1, 1949; s. August Lewis and Deloris (Weichelt) K.; m. Patricia Ann Lang, Oct. 8, 1977; children: Katherine, Matthew, Lindsey. BA, Northwestern U., 1971; JD, MBA, Ind. U., 1976. Bar: U.S. Dist. Ct. (no. dist.) Ill. 1976, U.S. Tax Ct. 1978. Tax specialist Peat Marwick, Mitchell & Co., Chgo., 1976-77; assoc. Bishop & Crawford Ltd., Oak Brook, Ill., 1977-83, assoc., 1984-85, ptnr. Arnstein, Gluck, Lehr & Milligan, Oak Brook, 1985—; ptnr., seminar chmn. Burr Ridge Seminars, Hinsdale, Ill., 1983—; legis. aide State Rep. James Stange. Bd. dirs. Nat. Entrepreneurship Found., Bloomington, Ind., 1981—, Camp New Hope Devel. Bd., Oak Brook, 1983; mem. sch. bd. Lyons Twp. High Sch. Dist. 204, La Grange, Ill., 1985—; mem. Hinsdale (Ill.) Community House Council, mem. bus. adv. bd. Westside Holistic Ctr. Recipient Outstanding Young Citizen of Chgo. award, 1987. Mem. ABA, Ill. Bar Assn., Chgo. Bar Assn. DuPage Estate Planning Council, Oak Brook Jaycees (pres. 1984—, chmn. bd. 1985, trustee 1985-86), Beta Gamma Sigma. Republican. Lutheran. General corporate, Probate, Computer. Office: Arnstein Gluck et al 2021 Spring Rd Suite 718 Oak Brook IL 60521

KOHN, ALAN CHARLES, lawyer; b. St. Louis, Feb. 14, 1932; s. William Kohn and Rose Kohn (Steinberg) K.; m. Joanne J. Kohn, Aug. 29, 1954; children: Tom, Jim, John. AB, Washington U., 1953, LLB, 1955. Law clk. to assoc. justice Charles E. Whittaker U.S. Supreme Ct., 1957-58; assoc. William Kohn, St. Louis, 1958-59; assoc. Coburn, Croft & Kohn, St. Louis, 1959-62, ptnr., 1962-70; ptnr. Kohn, Shands, Elbert, Gianoulakis & Giljum, St. Louis, 1970—; advocate Am. Bd. Trial Advocates, 1984; mem. Mo. Bd. Law Examiners, 1969-79, pres., 1975-79; mem. U.S. Dist. Ct. (ea. dist.) Mo. Bd. Admissions, 1969-72, chmn., 1970-72; mem. fed. practice com. U.S. Dist. Ct. (ea. dist.) Mo., 1987—. Editor-in-chief Washington U. Law Quarterly, 1955; contbr. articles to profl. jours. Chmn. Mo. Housing Devel. Com., 1975-79; treas. University City (Mo.) Bd. Edn., 1970-71. Served to 1st lt. U.S. Army Security Agy., 1955-57. Mem. ABA, Mo. Bar Assn., St. Louis Bar Assn., Order of the Coif, Phi Beta Kappa, Omicron Delta Kappa, Phi Eta Sigma. Republican. Avocation: tennis. Federal civil litigation, State civil litigation. Home: 40 Upper Ladue Rd Saint Louis MO 63124 Office: Kohn Shands et al 411 N 7th St Saint Louis MO 63101

KOHN, HAROLD ELIAS, lawyer; b. Phila., Apr. 5, 1914; s. Joseph C. and Mayme (Rumm) K.; m. Edith Anderson, Dec. 30, 1946; children: Amy, Ellen, Joseph Carl. A.B., U. Pa., 1934, LL.B., 1937. Bar: Pa. 1938. Pres. Kohn, Savett, Klein & Graf, P.C., Phila.; spl. counsel transit matters City of Phila., 1952-53, 56-62; counsel to gov. State of Pa., 1972; mem. bd. Southeastern Pa. Transp. Authority, 1972-77; mem. Pa. Jud. Inquiry and Rev. Bd., 1973-77; bd. consultors Villanova U. Law Sch. Sec., treas., bd. dirs. Kohn Found.; pres., bd. dirs. Arronson Found., Lavine Found.; bd. dirs. Moss Rehab. Hosp., Phila. Geriatric Ctr.; trustee, mem. exec. com. Phila. Fedn. Jewish Agys.; trustee Temple U.; past mem. exec. com. United Jewish Appeal; past mem. bd. dirs. Phila. Psychiat. Ctr.; past v.p., bd. dirs. Phila. chpt. ACLU. Mem. ABA, Pa., Phila., D.C. bar assns., Internat. Acad. Trial Lawyers, Jud. Conf. 3d Circuit, Am. Law Inst., Order of Coif, Phi Beta Kappa. Federal civil litigation, Antitrust, Libel. Home: 1801 J F Kennedy Blvd Philadelphia PA 19103 Office: 1101 Market St Philadelphia PA 19107

KOHN, IMMANUEL, lawyer; b. Jerusalem, Dec. 6, 1926; came to U.S., 1934; s. Hans and Yetty (Wahl) K.; m. Vera Sharpe, July 22, 1950; children: Gail, Peter, Sheila, Robert. Grad., Deerfield Acad., 1944; B.A. summa cum laude, Harvard U., 1949; LL.B cum laude, Yale U., 1953. Bar: N.Y. 1955, U.S. Dist. Ct. (ea. dist.) N.Y. 1955, U.S. Dist. Ct. (so. dist.) N.Y. 1957, U.S. Ct. Appeals (2d cir.) 1966, U.S. Supreme Ct. 1972. Assoc. Cahill, Gordon & Reindel, N.Y.C., 1953-62, ptnr., 1962, mem. exec. com., 1972—. Editor, Yale U. Law Jour., 1951-53. Served as ensign U.S. Maritime Service, 1946. Sheldon travelling fellow, 1949-50. Mem. Order of Coif, Phi Beta Kappa. Clubs: India House (N.Y.C.), Bd. Room (N.Y.C.), Met. Opera (N.Y.C.), Sky (N.Y.C.); Bedens Brook (N.J.). Home: 34 Puritan Ct Princeton NJ 08540 Office: Cahill Gordon & Reindel 80 Pine St New York NY 10005

KOHN, MICHAEL ELLIOTT, lawyer, educator; b. St. Louis, June 8, 1953; s. Melvin and Hortense E. (Goodman) K.; m. Catherine Kriegshauser, June 14, 1980; children: Lauren Rachael, Catherine Elizabeth, Jessica Claire. AB magna cum laude, St. Louis U., 1975, MBA, JD, 1979; LLM in Taxation, NYU, 1980. Bar: Mo. 1979, U.S. Dist. Ct. (ea. dist.) Mo. 1979, U.S. Tax Ct. 1979, U.S. Ct. Appeals (8th cir.) 1979. Assoc. Millsap, Eyerman & Heitmann, Clayton, Mo., 1976-79; assoc. Bryan, Cave, McPheeters & McRoberts, St. Louis, 1979-86, sr. ptnr., 1987—; adj. asst. prof. bus. law and taxation St. Louis U., 1981—; trustee subdiv. of Davis Pl., St. Louis, 1985—; bd. dirs. Madesco Investment Corp., St. Petersburg Madesco Corp., The Place, Inc., Claybel Inn, Inc., CCI, Inc., Towers Hotel Corp. Editor in chief St. Louis U. Law Rev., 1977-78; grad. editor NYU Tax Law Rev., 1979-80. Bd. dirs. Congregation Temple Israel. Gerald Wallace fellow NYU, 1979-80. Mem. ABA, Mo. Bar Assn., Bar Assn. Met. St. Louis, Alpha Sigma Nu, Phi Alpha Theta. Jewish. Clubs: Mo. Athletic, Noonday (St. Louis). General corporate, Corporate taxation, Personal income taxation. Home: 840 S Meramec Clayton MO 63105 Office: Bryan Cave McPheeters & McRoberts 500 N Broadway Saint Louis MO 63102

KOHN, RICHARD FREDRICK, lawyer; b. Chgo., Dec. 28, 1933; married; 2 children. AB, U. Mich., 1955, JD, 1957. Bar: Mich. 1957, Ill. 1959. Gen. counsel, sales mgr. Shur-Gloss Mfg. Co., Inc., Chgo., 1959-73; enforcement atty. region V, EPA, Chgo., 1973-74; assoc. The Abacus Group, Chgo., 1974-78, sr. counsel, 1978-83, v.p. law div., 1984; assoc. gen. counsel Heller Fin., Inc., Chgo., 1985; assoc. Baker & McKenzie, Chgo., 1986-87; ptnr. Wilson & McIlvaine, Chgo., 1987—. Served with JAGC, USAF, 1957-58. Mem. ABA (various sects. and coms.), Ill. Bar Assn. (various sects.), Chgo. Bar Assn. (vice chmn. 1984-85, chmn. 1985— real property law com., chmn. real estate fin. subcom. 1982-84, long range planning com.), Chgo. Mortgage Attys. Assn. (exec. com.), Mortgage Bankers Assn. Am. (legis. com.), Internat. Council Shopping Ctrs., Am. Land Title Assn. Real property. Home: 681 Smoke Tree Rd Deerfield IL 60015 Office: Wilson & McIlvaine 135 S LaSalle St Chicago IL 60603

KOHN, SHALOM L., lawyer; b. N.Y.C., Nov. 18, 1949; s. Pincus and Helen (Roth) K.; m. Barbara Segal, June 30, 1974; children—David, Jeremy, Daniel. B.S. in Acctg. summa cum laude, CUNY, 1970; J.D. magna cum laude, Harvard U., 1974, M.B.A., 1974. Bar: Ill. 1975, U.S. Dist. Ct. (no. dist.) Ill. 1975, U.S. Ct. Appeals (7th cir.) 1976, U.S. Supreme Ct. 1980. Law clk. to chief judge U.S. Ct. Appeals (2d cir.), N.Y.C., 1974-75; assoc. Sidley & Austin, Chgo., 1975-80, ptnr., 1980—. Contbr. articles to profl. jours. Mem. exec. com. Adv. Council Religious Rights in Eastern Europe and Soviet Union, Washington, 1984-86; bd. dirs. Brisk Rabbinical Coll., Chgo., 1980—. Mem. Chgo. Bar Assn., Ill. Bar Assn., ABA. Bankruptcy, Federal civil litigation, Libel. Office: Sidley & Austin 1 First Nat Plaza Chicago IL 60603

KOIS, GEORGE STEPHEN, lawyer; b. Chgo., June 24, 1949; s. George A. and Stephanie C. (Harbut) K.; m. Barbara L. Pickerl, Jan. 26, 1979. B.A., DePaul U., 1971, J.D., 1976. Bar: Ill., U.S. Dist. Ct. (no. dist.) Ill., U.S. Supreme Ct. Assoc., Vedder, Price, Kaufman & Kammholz, Chgo., 1976-79; ptnr. Kois & McLaughlin, P.C., Chgo., 1979-84; v.p., sec., gen. counsel Telesphere Internat., Inc., Oak Brook, Ill., 1984—; dir. Consol. Packaging Corp.; speaker in field of corp. and computer law. Contbg. editor: Illinois Business Corporation Act, Annotated, 1981. Bd. dirs. Bus. Consortium for the Gifted and Talented. Mem. ABA, Am. Soc. Corp. Sec., Christian Legal Soc., Computer Law Assn., Ill. State Bar Assn., Chgo. Bar Assn., Blue Key, Pi Gamma Mu. Republican. Contracts commercial, General corporate, General practice. Office: Telesphere Internat Inc 2211 York Rd Oak Brook IL 60522 *

KOJIMA, ROBIN DALE, legal editor; b. Ancon, Republic of Panama, Oct. 8, 1955; d. Nanao and Teresa (Ichiyama) K. BA, Stanford U., 1977; JD, U. Calif., Davis, 1980. Bar: Calif. 1980. Legal writer Matthew Bender Co Inc., San Francisco, 1981-82, sr. legal writer, 1982-84; coordinating editor Matthew Bender Co Inc., Oakland, Calif., 1984—. Co-author: Calif. Forms of Pleading and Practice, Calif. Points and Authorities, Calif. Family Law: Practice and Procedure. Legal publishing. Office: Matthew Bender Co Inc 2101 Webster PO Box 2077 Oakland CA 94604

KOLANSKY, JEFFREY MARK, lawyer; b. Phila., Oct. 29, 1952; s. Harold and Elsa (Harwitz) K.; m. Margaret M. Kelleher, May 20, 1982; 1 child, Jessica A. Student, Pa. State U., 1970-71; BA, Villanova U., 1975; JD, Antioch Sch. Law, 1978. Bar: Pa. 1978, U.S. Dist. Ct. (ea. dist.) Pa. 1985. Asst. dist. atty. Phila. Dist. Atty.'s Office, 1978-85; trial atty. Griffith & Burr, Phila., 1985—; guest lectr. Temple U., Phila., 1980-83. Contbr. articles to profl. jours. Recipient Mayor's Law Enforcement award City of Phila., 1981. Mem. ABA, Phila. Bar Assn., Pa. Bar Assn., Pa. Dist. Atty.'s Assn. Clubs: Eagle Lodge Country (Lafayette Hills, Pa.), Vesper (Phila.). Avocations: golf, writing. State civil litigation, Health, Insurance. Home: 906 Lomond Ln Philadelphia PA 19128 Office: Griffith & Burr 1608 Walnut St Philadelphia PA 19103

KOLASKY, WILLIAM JOSEPH, JR., lawyer; b. Springfield, Vt., Mar. 26, 1946; s. William Joseph and Valentina Katherine (Stankiewicz) K.; m. Judith Caroline Parker, Aug. 17, 1968; children: Robert, Caroline. AB, Dartmouth Coll., 1968; JD, Harvard U., 1971. Bar: Mass. 1971, D.C. 1975, U.S. Dist. Ct. D.C. 1975, U.S. Ct. Appeals (D.C. cir.) 1976, U.S. Supreme Ct. 1976. Law clk. U.S. Ct. Appeals (1st cir.), Boston, 1971-72; assoc. Wilmer, Cutler & Pickering, Washington, 1975-78, ptnr., 1979—. Served to capt. JAGC, U.S. Army, 1972-75. Mem. ABA, D.C. Bar Assn (co-chmn. antitrust com.). Contbr. articles to legal jours. Antitrust, Administrative and regulatory, Federal civil litigation. Office: 1666 K St NW Washington DC 20006

KOLBER, DANIEL HACKNER, lawyer; b. Miami, Fla., Mar. 27, 1953; s. Stanley and Marcia (Hackner) K.; m. Lesley Renee Houseman, Aug. 13, 1978; children: Lee, Sarah, Mark. BA in Polit. Sci. magna cum laude, Boston U., 1975; JD, U. Va., 1978; LLM, NYU, 1981. Bar: Va., 1978, Fla., 1978, N.Y., 1979, U.S. Dist. Ct. (ea. dist.) N.Y. 1979, U.S. Dist. Ct. (so. dist.) Fla. 1979, U.S. Ct. Appeals (4th cir.) 1979, Ga., 1985, U.S. Dist. Ct. (mid. dist.) Ga. 1985, U.S. Dist. Ct. (so. dist.) Ga. 1986. Assoc. Weil, Gotshal & Manges, N.Y.C., 1978-81; assoc. gen. counsel Kenai Corp., N.Y.C., 1981-84; exec. v.p. Air Atlanta, Inc., Atlanta, 1984—; arbitrator, Am. Arbitration Assn., N.Y.C., 1981—; registered prin., SEC, Washington, 1980—. Co-author, editor: Starting and Organizing a Business: A Legal and Tax Guide, 1980, 3d rev. ed., 1984; author legal articles on venture capital. Mem. Pres.' Adv. Council on Small Bus., 1985—. Mem. ABA (chmn. subcom. small bus. 1980-83, editor Corp. Notes mag., 1980-82, Gold Key award 1978), N.Y. State Bar Assn., Fla. Bar Assn., Ga. Bar Assn., Va. Bar Assn. Securities, General corporate. Office: Air Atlanta Inc Atlanta Internat Airport 1000 Toffie Terr PO Box 20887 Atlanta GA 30320

KOLBRENER, PETER D., lawyer; b. Far Rockaway, N.Y., Apr. 4, 1933; s. Martin M. and Frances D. (Denker) K.; m. Sandra Kolbrener, May 15, 1934; children—Jonathan, Michael, Abby, Beth. B.A., Franklin and Marshall Coll., 1954; J.D., Bklyn. Law Sch., 1959. Bar: N.Y. 1960, U.S. Dist. Ct., (so. and ea. dists.) N.Y. 1960, U.S. Ct. Appeals (2d cir.) 1962. Ptnr. Kolbrener & Kolbrener, N.Y.C., 1960-65, Shayne, Dachs, Weiss, Kolbrener, Stanisci & Harwood, Mineola, N.Y., 1965-80; sole practice, Garden City, N.Y., 1980-85; ptnr. Barhett & Kolbrener, Garden City, N.Y., 1985—; adj. prof. law Hofstra Law Sch., 1978—; instr. Emory U. Law Sch., 1982—; mem. malpractice panel Supreme Cts. of Nassau County and Queens County; instr. Nat. Inst. Trial Advocacy. Trustee, Hewlett Woodmere Pub. Library, 1970-76, pres., 1977—; pres. Nassau Library System, 1975-76. Served with U.S. Army, 1954-56. Mem. Nassau County Bar Assn., N.Y. Bar Assn., ABA, N.Y. County Lawyers Assn., Queens County Lawyers Assn., N.Y. State Trial Lawyers Assn. (bd. dirs.), Assn. Trial Lawyers Am., Am. Arbitration Assn. (panel arbitrators). State civil litigation, Federal civil litigation, Personal injury. Office: Barnett & Kolbrener 1600 Stewart Ave Westburg NY 11590

KOLE, JANET STEPHANIE, lawyer, writer, photographer; b. Washington, Dec. 20, 1946; d. Martin J. and Ruth G. (Goldberg) K. A.B., Bryn Mawr Coll., 1968; M.A., NYU, 1970; J.D., Temple U., 1980. Bar: Pa. 1980. Assoc. editor trade books Simon & Schuster, N.Y.C., 1968-70; publicity dir. Am. Arbitration Assn., N.Y.C., 1970-73; freelance photojournalist, N.Y.C., 1973-76; law clk. Morgan Lewis & Bockius, Phila., 1977-80; assoc. Schnader, Harrison, Segal & Lewis, Phila., 1980-85, Cohen, Shapiro, Polisher, Shiekman & Cohen, Phila., 1985—; author books including: Post Mortem, 1974; contbr. numerous articles to gen. interest publs., profl. jours.; bd. editors New Am. Rev. Mem. Mayor's Task Force on Rape, N.Y.C., 1972-77; adv. Support Ctr. Child Advs., Phila., 1980—; mem. Phila. Vol. Lawyers for the Arts; steering com. Lawyers' Com. Reproductive Rights. Mem. Assn. Trial Lawyers Am., ABA (former editor Litigation News, now chmn. com. on monographs and unpublished papers, com. spl. pubs.). Democrat. Federal civil litigation, State civil litigation, Trademark and copyright. Office: Cohen Shapiro Polisher Shiekman & Cohen 12 S 12th St Philadelphia PA 19107

KOLIBASH, WILLIAM ANTHONY, U.S. attorney; b. Wheeling, W.Va., Feb. 12, 1944; s. Albert Joseph and Josephine (Dicola) K.; m. Rita Patricia Scanlon, July 6, 1968; children: Shariane M., William Anthony, Christopher P. A.B., Brown U., 1966; J.D., W.Va. U., 1969. Bar: W.Va. 1969, U.S. Dist. Ct. for no. dist. W.Va. 1973. Asst. U.S. atty. Dept. Justice, Wheeling, 1973-80, U.S. Atty., 1980—. Served to capt. JAGC AUS, 1969-73. Mem. W.Va. State Bar. Republican. Roman Catholic. Home: 380 Oakmont Rd Wheeling WV 26003 Office: US Attys Office 12th and Chapline Sts Wheeling WV 26003 *

KOLKER, RICHARD LEE, lawyer; b. LeMars, Iowa, Apr. 17, 1939; s. Lawrence Francis and Genevieve Josephine K.; m. Janet Kay Shabino, Aug. 29, 1964; children—Martin, Audra, Anthony. B.A. in Econs., St. Mary's Coll., Winona, Minn., 1961; J.D., U. S.D., Vermillion, 1964. Bar: S.D. 1964, U.S. Dist. Ct. S.D. 1965, U.S. Tax Ct. 1980. Sole practice, Groton, S.D., 1964; ptnr. Maloney, Kolker, Fritz, Hogan & Johnson, Groton, 1965—; dep. states atty. Brown County, S.D., 1967-71, state atty., 1971-72; mem. S.D. Ho. of Reps., 1973-74; appointed to State Council for Legal Services, 1980, Gov.'s Adv. Com. on Outdoor Recreation, 1986—; chairperson Blue Ribbon com. S.D. Supreme Ct., 1985. Republican. Roman Catholic. Estate taxation, Personal income taxation, Trademark and copyright. Home: 807 N First Groton SD 57445 Office: Maloney Kolker Fritz et al 101 N Main Groton SD 57445

KOLKEY, DANIEL MILES, lawyer; b. Chgo., Apr. 21, 1952; s. Eugene Louis and Gilda Penelope (Cowan) K.; m. Donna Lynn Christie, May 15, 1982; children: Eugene, William. B.A., Stanford U., 1974; J.D., Harvard U., 1977. Bar: Calif. 1977, U.S. Dist. Ct. (cen., no., ea. dists.) Calif., U.S. Ct. Appeals (9th cir.) 1979, U.S. Supreme Ct., 1983. Law clk. U.S. Dist. Ct. judge, N.Y.C., 1977-78; ptnr. Gibson Dunn & Crutcher, Los Angeles, 1978—. Contbr. articles to profl. publs. Vice chmn. and sec. internat. relations sect. Town Hall of Calif., Los Angeles, 1981—; chmn. internat. trade legis. subcom., internat. commerce steering com. Los Angeles Area C. of C., 1983—; mem. adv. council Asia Pacific Ctr. for Resolution of Internat. Bus. Disputes; bd. dirs., sec., treas. Los Angeles Ctr. for Internat. Comml. Arbitration, 1986—; assoc. mem. central com. Calif. Rep. Party, 1983—; mem. Los Angeles Com. on Fgn. Relations, 1983—; mem. Los Angeles World Affairs Council, Rep. Assocs. Mem. ABA, Internat. Bar Assn., Los Angeles County Bar Assn. Chartered Inst. Arbitrators, London (assoc.), Wilton Park Alumni of So. Calif. (chmn. exec. com.). Jewish. Private international, State civil litigation, Federal civil litigation. Office: Gibson Dunn & Crutcher 333 S Grand Ave Los Angeles CA 90071

KOLLER, BENEDICT JOSEPH, lawyer; b. San Francisco, Sept. 2, 1954; s. Gordon William and Charlotte Icinda (Smith) K. BA, Thomas Aquinas Coll., 1979; JD, Santa Clara U., 1982. Bar: Calif. 1982, U.S. Dist. Ct. (no. and ea. dists.) Calif. 1983, U.S. Ct. Appeals (9th cir.) 1984. Assoc. Law Offices Harry A. Robertson, San Jose, Calif., 1982-84; project dir. Am. Legis. Exchange Council, Washington, 1985-87; project dir. solicitor's office Dept. Interior, Washington, 1987—. Mem. Vols. in Parole, Santa Clara County, 1980-82; mem. Action 22, Santa Clara County, 1980—. Named one of Outstanding Young Men of Am., 1985. Mem. ABA, Santa Clara County Bar Assn. Republican. Roman Catholic. Juvenile, Criminal, Environment. Home: 1600 S Eads #712-S Arlington VA 22202 Office: Am Legis Exchange Council 214 Massachusetts Ave NE Washington DC 20002

KOLLIN, GARY, lawyer; b. Miami Beach, Fla., Aug. 30, 1953; s. Michael and Shirley (Topolsky) K. BA, Harvard U., 1975; JD, U. Miami, 1979. Bar: Fla. 1979, U.S. Dist. Ct. (so. dist.) Fla. 1981, U.S. Ct. Appeals (11th cir.) 1981, U.S. Supreme Ct. 1982. Computer programmer, analyst Peter Bent Brigham Hosp., Roxbury, Mass., 1975-76; programmer U.S. Dept. Agr., Washington, 1976; asst. pub. defender Broward County, Ft. Lauderdale, Fla., 1979-81; asst. state atty. Broward County, Ft. Lauderdale, 1981-85; field counsel Medicaid Fraud Unit, Miami, Fla., 1985—. Mem. Young Dems. Fla., 1980—, Young Dems. Broward County, Ft. Lauderdale, 1986—; bd. dirs. Family Service Agy. of United Way, 1985-87, Isles of Inverrary Condominium Assn., 1984, 85. Named one of Outstanding Young Men Am., 1982; Broward County Judicial nominee, Commn. for Cir. Ct. Judgeship nominee, 1986. Mem. ABA, Fla. Bar Assn. (sentencing com. 1985-86, com. on elderly 1986—), Nat. Dist. Attys. Assn., Nat. Assn. Criminal Def. Lawyers, Fla. Pub. Defenders Assn., Broward County Criminal Def. Attys. Assn., Fla. Council on Crime and Delinquency, MENSA. Jewish. Clubs: Harvard (Broward) (bd. dirs. 1983-86), Harvard (Miami). Lodge: B'nai B'rith. Criminal, Legislative, Government contracts and claims. Home: 6575 W Oakland Park Blvd #516 Lauderhill FL 33313 Office: Medicaid Fraud Control Unit 20535 NW 2nd Ave Suite 204 Miami FL 33169

KOLMIN, KENNETH GUY, lawyer; b. N.Y.C., Oct. 22, 1951; s. Frank William and Edith (Pisk) K.; m. Suzan L. Frumm, Sept. 3, 1978; 2 children—Stephen Todd, Jennifer Dana. B.S. summa cum laude, SUNY-Albany, 1973; M.S., Syracuse U., 1975, J.D., cum laude, 1975. Bar: Ill. 1976, U.S. Dist. Ct. (7th dist.) Ill. 1976. Tax cons. Arthur Young and Co., Chgo., 1976-79; atty. Shefsky Saitlin & Froelich, Chgo., 1979-81; ptnr. Rooks Pitts & Poust, Chgo., 1981-84; ptnr. Schwartz & Freeman, 1984—. Contbr. articles to profl. jours. Mem. ABA, Ill., Bar Assn., Am. Inst. C.P.A.s, Ill. Soc. C.P.A.s. Home: 975 Eastwood Glencoe IL 60022 Office: Schwartz & Freeman 401 N Michigan Ave Suite 3400 Chicago IL 60611

KOLODEY, FRED JAMES, lawyer; b. LaCoste, Tex., Mar. 5, 1936; s. Raymond and Mamie V. (Newman) K.; m. Sylvia Kay Solomon, Mar. 30, 1985; children by previous marriage—Trecia Anne, Michele Leigh. B.A., Tex. Christian U., 1962; LL.B., So. Methodist U., 1964. Bar: Tex. 1964. Since practiced in Dallas; partner firm Kolodey & Thomas, 1975-83, of counsel, 1983—; dir. Farah Mfg. Co.; pres. Dallas Jr. Bar Assn., 1969. Comments editor: Southwestern Law Jour, 1963-64. Mem. dist. hearing office panel Dallas Community Coll., 1974, Democratic precinct chmn., 1968-73. Mem. Tex., Dallas bar assns., Delta Theta Phi (pres. 1963, Nat. award 1964), Alpha Chi, Pi Sigma Alpha. General corporate, Contracts commercial, Real property. Home: 307 Russwood St Rockwall TX 75087 Office: Suite 2300 Thanksgiving Tower 1601 Elm Dallas TX 75201-4713

KOMAR, MYRON, lawyer; b. Amsterdam, N.Y., June 26, 1930; s. Stephen and Tessie (Bazar) Komaranski; m. Maria Hawryluk, May 16, 1964; children—Mark, Michael. B.A., Union Coll., Schenectady, 1952; LL.B., Albany Law Sch., 1955, LL.D., 1968. Bar: N.Y. 1955, U.S. Dist. Ct. (no. dist.) N.Y. 1962, U.S. Dist. Ct. (we. dist.) N.Y., 1968. Assoc. Donohue and Bohl, 1955-60, mem., 1960-64; mem. Donohue, Bohl, Clayton & Komar, 1964-80; mem. Bohl, Clayton, Komar & Della Rocca, P.C., Albany, N.Y., 1980—. Mem. Ukrainian Congress com. Ams. for Human Rights in the Ukraine. Mem. ABA, N.Y. State Bar Assn. (seminar speaker 1982), Ukrainian-Am. Bar Assn., Albany County Bar Assn., Montgomery County Bar Assn., Justinian Soc., Internat. Platform Assn., Phi Beta Kappa. Ukrainian Catholic. Editorial bd. Law Rev. Albany Law Sch., 1954. Personal injury, State civil litigation, Probate. Home: 2 Stafford St Loudonville NY 12211 Office: Bohl Clayton Komar et al One Columbia Pl Albany NY 12207

KOMIE, STEPHEN MARK, lawyer; b. Chgo., Jan. 22, 1949; s. Leonard D. and Miriam (Wineberg) K. BA, U. Ariz., 1970, MA in Russian History, 1973; JD, DePaul U., 1976. Bar: Ill. 1976, U.S. Dist. Ct. (no. dist.) Ill. 1976, U.S. Ct. Appeals (7th cir.) 1976, U.S. Ct. Appeals (8th cir.) 1982, U.S. Dist. Ct. (cen. dist.) Ill. 1985, U.S. Dist. Ct. (no. dist.) Ind. 1985. Pres. Komie & Assocs., Chgo., 1976—; prin. Buffalo Grove (Ill.) Law Offices Ltd., 1977-86; prin. Drunken Drivers Def. Lawyers of Ill. Ltd., Chgo., 1982—. Mem. Ill. Bar Assn. (criminal justice council 1985-86), Chgo. Bar Assn. (chmn. criminal law com., 1983-84, def. of prisoners com., 1986-87, cert. appreciation 1984), Nat. Assn. of Criminal Def. Lawyers (bd. dirs. 1983-86, pres's. commendation 1982-83). Criminal, Federal civil litigation, Family and matrimonial. Office: 11 S LaSalle Suite 700 Chicago IL 60603

KOMINOS, BILL, lawyer; b. Antwerp, Belgium, Apr. 1, 1938; came to U.S., 1948, naturalized, 1954; s. Theodore B. and Sophie (Delantonis) K. B.A., Auburn U., 1963; J.D., Cumberland Sch. Law, 1966. Bar: Ala. 1966, U.S. Dist. Ct. (no. dist.) Ala. 1966, U.S. Ct. Appeals (5th cir.) 1971, U.S. Dist. Ct. (mid. dist.) Ala. 1979, U.S. Ct. Appeals (11th cir.) 1982; U.S. Supreme Ct. 1983. Ptnr. Kominos & Sarris, Birmingham, until 1975, ptnr. firm Fuqua & Kominos, Ozark, Ala., 1981—. Mem. Birmingham Bar Assn., Dale County Bar Assn. (pres. 1985-86), Ala. Criminal Def. Lawyers Assn., Ala. State Bar Assn., Ala. Trial Lawyers Assn. Criminal, Personal injury, State civil litigation. Home: 10 Wilson Ave Ozark AL 36360 Office: Fuqua & Kominos 300 A Painter Ave Ozark AL 36360

KOMOROSKE, JOHN H., lawyer; b. Ancon, Panama, Feb. 4, 1949; s. Alexander Bernard and Mary Angela (Schierloh) K.; m. Janet Elaine Meade, Oct. 9, 1976; children: Susan Anne, John Alexander. BA, Union Coll., 1971; JD, Ind. U., 1974, MPA, 1975. Bar: Ind. 1974, U.S. Dist. Ct. (so. dist.) Ind. 1974, D.C. 1980, U.S. Dist. Ct. (ea. dist.) Va. 1981. Atty. Bloomington City Council, Ind., 1975-76; budget examiner Exec. Office of Pres., Washington, 1976-82; spl. counsel to exec. dir. SEC, Washington, 1982-85, spl. counsel to dir. div. investment mgmt., 1985—. Mem. child care task force, Alexandria (Va). City Govt., 1985. Mem. ABA, Assn. Legal Adminstrns. Securities. Home: 3106 Circle Hill Rd Alexandria VA 22305 Office: SEC 450 5th St NW Washington DC 20549

KONDRACKI, EDWARD ANTHONY, lawyer; b. Camden, N.J., Oct. 10, 1946; s. Edward S. and Helen J. (Roman) K.; m. Mary A. Russo, Aug. 3, 1974; children: Elysia A., Michelle A. BA, Rutgers U., 1968, JD, 1971. Bar: N.J. 1971, U.S. Dist. Ct. N.J. 1971, U.S. Supreme Ct. 1977, U.S. Ct. Appeals (3d cir.) 1980. Law clk. U.S. Dist. Ct., Camden, 1971-72; assoc. Davis & Reberkenny, P.C., Cherry Hill, N.J., 1972-75, mem., dir., 1975—; counsel City of Bordentown, Evesham Mcpl. Utilities Authority, Bordentown Sewerage Authority. Counsel Greater Seventy Group, Medford, N.J. Mem. Authorities Assn. N.J. (chmn. legal com. 1981—), Assn. Trial Lawyers Am., Trial Attys. of N.J.(trustee 1985—), ABA, N.J. State Bar Assn., Camden County Bar Assn., Burlington County Bar Assn. Roman Catholic. State civil litigation, Environment, Local government. Home: 68 Fawn Ct Medford NJ 08055

KONDRACKI, EDWARD JOHN, lawyer; b. Elizabeth, N.J., Sept. 27, 1932; s. John and Catherin Chudio (Saas) K.; m. Barbara Terese Caruso; children—Carol Ann, Maryanne, Christopher. B.S.E.E., N.J. Inst. Tech., 1959; J.D. with honors, George Washington U., 1963. Bar: Va. 1964, D.C. 1965, U.S. Ct. Claims 1976, U.S. Ct. Customs and Patent Appeals 1976, U.S. Ct. Appeals (Fed. cir.) 1983. Patent atty. Gen. Electric Co., Washington, 1959-63; dir. Kerkam, Stowell Kondracki & Clarke, P.C. and predecessor Cameron, Kerkam & Sutton, Arlington, Va., 1963-65, ptnr., 1965—; dir. Patmark Paralegals. Served with USN, 1951-55. Mem. ABA, Am. Intellectual Property Law Assn., Internat. Assn. Protection Indsl. Property, Va. Bar Assn., U.S. Trademark Assn., Washington Patent Lawyers Club, D.C. Bar Assn. (chmn. com. internat. affairs), Gt. Falls Hist. Soc., Marmota Farm Assn., Tau Beta Pi, Eta Kappa Nu, Omicron Delta Kappa. Club: KC (Fairfax, Va.). Author: Trademarks-Servicemarks, Use, Usage and Protection, 1981; Proper Use of Trademarks and Service Marks, 1982; Common Pitfalls Encountered in Patenting Inventions, 1983; Copyright Protection of Computer Software. Patent, Trademark and copyright, Private international. Office: 6404 R Seven Corners Pl Falls Church VA 22044-2010

KONDZER, THOMAS ALLEN, lawyer; b. Cleve., Apr. 13, 1950; s. Andrew Francis and Ann (Ziegler) K.; m. Maureen Veronica Walsh, June 2, 1973; 1 child, Joseph Thomas. BBA, John Carroll U., 1972; JD, Case Western Res. U., 1975. Bar: Ohio 1975, U.S. Dist. Ct. (no. dist.) Ohio 1977, U.S. Ct appeals (6th cir.) 1980. Law clk. to presiding justice Ohio Ct. Appeals (8th dist.), Cleve., 1975-77; assoc. Amsdell and Slivka, Cleve., 1977-81; sole practice Cleve., 1981-85; prosecutor Village of Northfield, Ohio, 1981—; ptnr. Kolick and Kondzer, Cleve., 1985—; lectr. Cleve. State U., 1981-82; coop. counsel Cath. League for Religious and Civil Liberties, Milw., 1981—. Mem. Westlake Civil Service Commn., 1986—. Mem. ABA, Ohio State Bar Assn., Greater Cleve. Bar Assn., North Olmsted C. of C., Order of Coif, Beta Gamma Sigma. Democrat. Roman Catholic. General practice, State civil litigation, Probate. Home: 25668 Melibee Westlake OH 44145 Office: Kolick and Kondzer 24500 Center Ridge Rd Suite 175 Westlake OH 44145

KONOPISOS, KONSTANTINE A., lawyer; b. Sunrise, Wyo., Apr. 4, 1919; m. Arlene M. Peck; children: Dean Andrew, Linda Annette. BA, Morningside Coll., 1957; JD, Northwestern U., 1948; MA, Boston U., 1963, LLM, 1979; LLM in Internat. Law, George Washington U. Bar: Iowa 1948, Ill. 1948, U.S. Dist. Ct. (no. dist.) Iowa 1948, Calif. 1956, U.S. Dist. Ct. (so. dist.) Calif. 1956, Va. 1977, U.S. Dist. Ct. (ea. dist.) Va. 1977, U.S. Ct. Appeals (D.C. cir.) 1977. Sole practice Missouri City, Tex. Served with USN, 1942-48, Vietnam. Decorated Legion of Merit. Mem. Iowa Bar Assn., Ill. Bar Assn., Calif. Bar Assn., Tex. Bar Assn., Va. Bar Assn., D.C. Bar Assn., Houston County Bar Assn., Ft. Bend County Bar Assn., Am. Soc. Internat. Law, Internat. Amigo Orgn. U.S., Navy League U.S., Ret. Officers Assn., Mystic Knights of Sea, Delta Theta Phi. Club: Sweetwater Country. Admiralty, General practice, State civil litigation. Address: PO Box 842 Missouri City TX 77459

KONOVE, RONALD L., lawyer; b. N.Y.C., Aug. 7, 1946; s. Robert and Paula L. (Markenson) K.; m. Kay Alice Ethier, Dec. 22, 1968; children: Elissa, Jonathan, Andrew. BA, U. Calif., Santa Barbara, 1968; JD, U. Calif., San Francisco, 1971. Bar: Calif. 1972, U.S. Ct. Dist. Ct. (no., cen. and ea. dists.) Calif. 1972, U.S. Ct. Appeals (9th cir.), N.Y. 1974, U.S. Dist. Ct. (so. and ea. dists.) N.Y. 1974, U.S. Ct. Appeals (2d cir.). Counsel Dept. Social Welfare State of Calif., Sacramento, 1971-72; assoc. Law Offices A. John Merlo, Sacramento, 1972-73; ptnr. Konove & Konove P.C., N.Y.C., 1973—. Trustee Briarcliff Manor Sch. Dist.; mem. Briarcliff Manor Fire Dept. Mem. Assn. Trial Lawyers Am., Am. Arbitrator Assn., N.Y. State Bar Assn., Calif. Bar Assn., Assn. of Bar of City of N.Y. Republican. Jewish. Avocations: softball, sailing, tennis. State civil litigation, Federal civil litigation, Real property. Home: 58 Elm Rd Briarcliff Manor NY 10510 Office: Konove & Konove PC 60 E 42d St New York NY 10165

KONRAD, ALAN KARL, lawyer; b. Grand Rapids, Mich., Feb. 6, 1950; s. Charles Alan Konrad and Avis Jeane Julian. B in Urban Studies magna cum laude, U. N.Mex., 1972; JD cum laude, Harvard U., 1976. Bar: N.Mex. 1976, U.S. Ct. Appeals (10th cir.) 1976, U.S. Supreme Ct. 1984. Assoc. Modrall Law Firm, Albuquerque, 1976-80, Miller Law Firm, Albuquerque, 1980—. Mem. Assn. Trial Lawyers Am. Federal civil litigation, State civil litigation. Office: Miller Stratvert et al 200 Lomas NW Suite 900 Albuquerque NM 87102

KONRAD, BRUCE JOSEPH, lawyer; b. Indpls., Apr. 25, 1942; s. Eugene Walter and Casimira (Sienicki) K.; m. Irene Mindy Gilbert, June 10, 1973; 1 child, Mark Joseph. BS, Mich. State U., 1969; JD, Ill. Inst. Tech., 1974. Bar: Ill. 1974, U.S. Dist. Ct. (no. dist.) Ill. 1974, Ohio 1982. Sr. counselor Youngstown Sheet & Tube, Hammond, Ind., 1969-75; staff counselor Eastern Air Lines, Miami, Fla., 1975-76; mgr. employee relations Nat. Steel, Terre Haute, Ind., 1976-77, 79-81; dir. indsl. relations Pullman-Standard, Hammond, 1977-79; mgr. human resources Standard Oil Co., Toledo, 1981—. Trustee Toledo Bus. Health Care Coalition, 1983—; bd. dirs. Northwest Ohio Hospice, 1986—. Served with USN, 1960-63. Mem. ABA, Ill. Bar Assn., Toledo Personnel Assn., No. Ohio Hospice Assn. (bd. dirs. 1986—). Republican. Labor, Health, Workers' compensation. Home: 1880 Lynbrook Toledo OH 43614 Office: Standard Oil Co Toledo Refinery PO Box 696 Toledo OH 43694

KOO, RICHARD, lawyer; b. N.Y.C., Nov. 21, 1952; s. Freeman and Edith (Tsai) K.; m. Karènne Ho; 1 child, Derrick. BA, Columbia U., JD. Bar: Mass. 1977, N.Y. 1981. Assoc. Hale & Dorr, Boston, 1977-81; assoc. Townley & Updike, N.Y.C., 1981-86, ptnr., 1986—. chmn. bd. dirs. Chinatown br. YMCA, N.Y.C., 1986—. Mem. ABA. Avocations: bicycling, basketball, history. General corporate, Securities, Mergers and acquisitions. Office: Townley & Updike 405 Lexington Ave New York NY 10174

KOOB, CHARLES EDWARD, lawyer; b. Kansas City, Mo., Aug. 31, 1944; s. Charles H. and Adeline (Meinert) K.; m. Pamela Ann Nabseth, June 26, 1971; children: Jason Wyeth, Peter Nabseth. BA, Rockhurst Coll., 1966; JD, Stanford U., 1969. Bar: Calif. 1970, N.Y. 1971, U.S. Dist. Ct. (so. and ea. dists.) N.Y., U.S. Ct. Appeals (2d cir.). Assoc. Simpson, Thacher & Bartlett, N.Y.C., 1970-76, ptnr., 1976—. Mem. ABA, N.Y. State Bar Assn., Calif. Bar Assn. Antitrust, Federal civil litigation, Personal injury. Office: Simpson Thacher & Bartlett 1 Battery Park Plaza New York NY 10004

KOOMEY, RICHARD ALAN, lawyer; b. N.Y.C., Sept. 20, 1932; s. Garo H. and Ruth (Mushekian) K.; m. Cynthia C. Chaffee, Feb. 18, 1961 (div. 1974); children: Jonathan G., Gregory C., Christopher D. AB, Columbia Coll., 1957, MS, 1958; LLB, NYU, 1962. Bar: N.Y. 1962, U.S. Ct. Appeals (3d cir.) 1968, N.C. 1982. Assoc. Chadbourne, Parke, Whiteside & Wolf, N.Y.C., 1966-69; asst. gen. counsel Sperry & Hutchinson Co., N.Y.C., 1969-80; gen. counsel Sperry & Hutchinson Furniture Inc., High Point, N.C., 1980-82; of counsel Robert E. Sheehan Assocs., High Point, 1982-83, Contino, Ross & Benedict, N.Y.C., 1983-84; asst. gen. counsel Pechiney Corp. and Howmet Turbine Components Corp., Greenwich, Conn., 1984—; adj. prof. law St. John's U. Sch. of Bus., Jamaica, N.Y., 1983-85; bd. dirs. Recoma Inc., Fairfield, N.J. Trustee Union Free Sch. Dist. 3, Huntington Station, N.Y., 1966-67. Served to capt. USAF, 1952-56. Mem. ABA, N.Y. Bar Assn., Assn. of Bar of City of N.Y., N.C. Bar Assn. General corporate, Labor, Pension, profit-sharing, and employee benefits. Office: Pechiney Corp 475 Steamboat Rd Greenwich CT 06830

KOONCE, NEIL WRIGHT, lawyer; b. Kinston, N.C., July 8, 1947; s. Harold Wright and Edna Earle (Regan) K.; m. Joan Alice Boudrow, June 7, 1969; 1 child, Channing Marie. A.B., U. N.C., 1969; J.D., Wake Forest U., 1974; postgrad. exec. program U. Va., 1983. Bar: N.C. 1973, U.S. Dist. Ct. (mid. dist.) N.C. 1975, U.S. Ct. Appeals (4th cir.) 1978, U.S. Supreme Ct. 1981. Atty., Cone Mills Corp., Greensboro, N.C., 1974-81, sr. atty., 1981-85, asst. gen. counsel, 1985—. Bd. dirs. Family and Children's Services, Greensboro, 1981—, S.C. Energy Users Com., Columbia, S.C., 1984—, Carolina Utility Customer's Assn., Raleigh, 1983—; bd. dirs. N.C. Found. for Research and Econ. Edn., 1986—. Served with AUS, 1970-71. Mem. Greensboro Bar Assn., N.C. Bar Assn., ABA. Democrat. Presbyterian. Lodge: Rotary (sec. 1983—, bd. dirs. 1985—). Administrative and regulatory, General corporate, Personal injury. Home: 4931 Hackamore Rd Greensboro NC 27410 Office: Cone Mills Corp 1201 Maple St Greensboro NC 27405

KOONS, WILLIAM CONRAD, lawyer; b. New Orleans, Oct. 11, 1931; s. John Marshall and Lillian (Price) K.; m. Ida Blewett, May 23, 1953; children: Danny, Kathy Koons Hargrove, Marilyn Koons Womack. BA in Bus., Pre-law, So. Meth. U., 1956, JD, 1958. Assoc. Geary, Brice, Barron & Stahl, Dallas, 1957-59, ptnr., 1959-78; ptnr., pres. Koons, Rasor, Fuller & McCurley, Dallas, 1978—; mem. grievance com. State Bar Tex., 1982-84, chmn. family law adv. commn. State Bar Tex., 1984—. Contbr. articles to profl. jours. bd. dirs. So. Meth. U., Dallas, 1973-79, bd. visitors, 1978-79. Served with USNR, 1951-55. Mem. Am. Acad. Matrimonial Lawyers (bd. govs. 1985—, pres. Tex chpt. 1985), Tex. Acad. Family Law Specialists, So. Meth. U. Alumni Assn. (pres. 1976), Order of Woolsack. Club: Exchange (Dallas) (pres. 1979). Avocations: hunting, fishing, flying airplanes. Family and matrimonial. Office: Koons Rasor Fuller & McCurley 2311 Cedar Springs Rd Suite 300 Dallas TX 75201

KOONTZ, GEORGE EDWARD, lawyer; b. Knoxville, Tenn., Oct. 17, 1953; s. George Manassus and Mary O'Dell (Erickson) K.; m. Leslie Armstrong, Oct. 3, 1979 (div. Nov. 1982); m. Carolyn Randle Paris, Mar. 3, 1984. Bar: Tenn. 1979, U.S. Dist. Ct. (ea. dist.) Tenn. 1979. Assoc. Weill, Ellis, Weems & Copeland, Chattanooga, 1979-83; ptnr. Weill, Weems & Kennedy, Chattanooga, 1984-86; founding ptnr. Kennedy, Fulton & Koontz,

Chattanooga, 1986—; adj. prof. polit. sci. U. Tenn., Chattanooga, 1985—. Campaign worker Dem. Party, Chattanooga, 1974. Mem. ABA, Tenn. Trial Lawyers Assn., Chattanooga Bar Assn., Pi Kappa Alpha, Phi Delta Phi. Democrat. Methodist. Avocations: running races, weight lifting, tennis. State civil litigation, Bankruptcy, Family and matrimonial. Home: 6808 Tyhi Dr Chattanooga TN 37405 Office: Kennedy Fulton & Kkoontz 320 N Holtzclaw Ave Chattanooga TN 37404

KOOP, CHARLES HUBERT, lawyer; b. Plymouth, Wis., Feb. 23, 1950; s. Chester S. and G. Windred (Smith) K.; m. Christine A. Blue, Aug. 7, 1971; children: Haley, Sally, Charles II. BA, Eastern Mich. U., 1973; JD, Detroit Coll. Law, 1976. Bar: Mich. 1977, U.S. Dist. Ct. (ea. dist.) Mich. 1977, U.S. Dist. Ct. (we. dist.) Mich. 1979, U.S. Ct. Appeals (6th cir.) 1985, U.S. Supreme Ct. 1986, U.S. Ct. Claims 1987. Atty. Eastern Mich. Legal Service, Flint, 1977; sole practice Traverse City, Mich., 1977-80; chief trial prosecutor, office pros. atty. Grand Traverse County, Traverse City, 1980-84; ptnr. Thompson, Zirnhelt, Bowron, Koop & Seaman, P.C. and predecessor firm Thompson, Zirnhelt, Bowron & Rosi, P.C., Traverse City, 1984—. Grantee Nat. Dist. Attys. Assn., 1973, Pros. Attys. Assn. Mich., 1973. Mem. Mich. Bar Assn., Grand Traverse, Leelanau & Antrim Bar Assn. (pres. 1984-85, v.p. 1983, sec., treas. 1982, bd. govs. 1986). Episcopalian. Club: Exchange (Traverse City). Lodge: Rotary. Criminal, Oil and gas leasing, State civil litigation. Home: Box 411 R Juniper Shores Dr Kewadin MI 49648 Office: Thompson Zirnhelt et al 160 E State St PO Box 1067 Traverse City MI 49685-1067

KOPACK, LAURA REYES, lawyer; b. Laredo, Tex., June 23, 1953; d. Jose Lino and Dora Guillermina (Moreno) Reyes; m. Alan Joseph Kopack, Aug. 11, 1973; 1 child, Samantha Terese. BA in Philosophy, Wayne State U., 1975; JD, U. Detroit, 1980. Bar: Mich. 1980, U.S. Dist. Ct. (ea. dist.) Mich. 1980. Corp. counsel City of Detroit, 1979-82; staff atty. Detroit Edison Co., 1982—; bd. dirs. Inner City Bus. Improvement Forum/S.E. Mich. Bus. Devel. Ctr., Detroit, Internat. Inst., Detroit; chmn. bd. dirs. Service Employment Redevel., Detroit. Contbr. tax articles to profl. jours. Mem. New Detroit Inc., Pvt. Industry Council, Detroit, United Found. social work allocation com., Detroit, Future of Mich., Detroit; trustee S.W. Detroit Hosp., Westland Med. Clinic. Recipient Most Polit. award Hispanic Leadership Devel. Program, Detroit, 1981. Mem. ABA, Mich. Bar Assn., Detroit Bar Assn., Latin Bar Assn., Mich. Trial Lawyers Assn., Detroit C. of C. (Leadership Detroit VIII). Republican. Roman Catholic. Clubs: Hispanic Econ. (pres.), Edison Athletic (Detroit). Avocations: reading, aerobics, running, politics, travel. General corporate, Real property, Environment. Home: 7907 Hillcrest Westland MI 48185 Office: Detroit Edison Co 2000 2d Ave 688 WCB Detroit MI 48226

KOPACZ, STANLEY WILLIAM, JR., lawyer, military officer; b. Ironwood, Mich., May 8, 1951; s. Stanley William Sr. and Mildred Lillian (Bergquist) K.; m. Rene C. Fassino, June 26, 1976 (div. Sept. 1977); m. Sun Ok Chon, Nov. 12, 1981; children: James A., Steven E., Eugene W. AA, Gogebic Community Coll., 1972; BS, U. Wis., Superior, 1974; postgrad., U. Minn., 1977; JD, William Mitchell Coll. of Law, 1978. Bar: Minn. 1978, U.S. Supreme Ct. 1981, Wis. 1983. Commd. 2d lt. USAF, 1974, advanced through grades to capt., 1978, judge adv., 1978-82; atty. Clark & Clark, Ashland, Wis., 1983-84; atty., advisor USAF, Minot AFB, N.D., 1985—. Democrat. Roman Catholic. Government contracts and claims, Environment. Home: 1940 Skyline Dr Minot ND 58701 Office: USAF 91CSG/JA Minot AFB ND 58705-5000

KOPELMAN, LEONARD, lawyer; b. Cambridge, Mass., Aug. 2, 1940; s. Irving and Frances Estelle (Robbins) K. B.A. cum laude, Harvard U., 1962, J.D., 1965. Bar: Mass. 1966. Asso. Warner & Stackpole, Boston, 1965-73; sr. ptnr. Kopelman & Paige, Boston, 1974—; lectr. exec. mgmt. program Harvard Bus. Sch., 1965—; permanent master Mass. Superior Ct., 1971—; hon. consul of, Finland, Mass., 1975—; U.S. del. Soc. for Internat. Devel.; Chmn. Mass. Jud. Selection Com. for the Fed. Judiciary, 1971—; chief counsel AAUP. Trustee Cathedral of the Pines, 1972; pres. Hillel Found. of Cambridge, Inc., 1973—; trustee Faulkner Hosp., 1974—, Parker Hill Med. Ctr., 1976—. NEH grantee, 1975. Mem. ABA (exec. council 1969—), Mass. Bar Assn. (chmn. mcpl. law sect.), Am. Judges Assn., Mass. State C. of C. (pres. 1974-77). Clubs: Harvard Faculty, Algonquin, Bay, Harvard Union, Hasty Pudding Inst. Home: 231 Marlborough St Boston MA 02116 Office: 77 Franklin St Boston MA 02110

KOPIT, ALAN STUART, lawyer; b. Cleve., Aug. 26, 1952; s. Irving and Claire (Smira) K.; m. Ivy Jan Stoller. BA, Tufts U., 1974; JD, U. Chgo., 1977. Bar: Ohio, U.S. Dist. Ct. (no. dist.) Ohio, U.S. Ct. Appeals (6th cir.). Ptnr. Hahn, Loeser, Freedham, Dean & Wellman (later Hahn, Loeser & Parks), Cleve., 1977—; staff atty. Sta. WKYC-TV3 NBC, Cleve., 1982—. Mem. Leadership Cleve. Growth Assn., 1985-86; bd. dirs. Adam Walsh Child Resource Ctr., Cleve., 1984—, Fairmount Theatre of Deaf, Cleve., 1984—, Am. Jewish Com., Cleve., 1985—. Named one of Cleve.'s Most Interesting People, Cleve. Mag., 1984. Mem. ABA (chairperson young lawyers div. 1986—), Am. Bar Endowment (bd. dirs. 1986—), Ohio Bar Assn. (council dels. 1985—), Cleve. Bar Assn. (merit service award 1978, 79, 81, bd. dirs. 1981-82). Bankruptcy, Contracts commercial, State civil litigation. Home: 23547 Duffield Rd Shaker Heights OH 44122 Office: Hahn Loeser & Parks 800 National City E 6th Bldg Cleveland OH 44114

KOPIT, JONATHAN THRONE, lawyer; b. N.Y.C., May 23, 1946; s. Alexander and Charlotte Louise (Throne) K.; m. Ina Cheryl Cohen, June 28, 1978. AB, Columbia Coll., 1968; JD, Columbia U., 1972. Bar: N.Y. 1972, Mich. 1974, U.S. Supreme Ct. 1981. Research atty. Mich. Ct. Appeals, Lansing, 1972-76; from assoc. to ptnr. Plunkett, Cooney, Rutt, Watters, Stanczyk & Pedersen, Detroit, 1976—. Contbr. articles to profl. jours. Mem. Nat. and Mich. Chpt. Multiple Sclerosis Soc., 1974. Harlan Fiske Stone scholar Columbia U. Sch. Law, 1972. Mem. ABA (tort ins. and litigation sects., appellate com. 1984—), Mich. Bar Assn. (workers compensation sect.), Assn. Trial Lawyers Am., Mich. Trial Lawyers Assn., Columbia Law Alumni Assn. Avocations: swimming, reading history and finance. Workers' compensation, State civil litigation. Home: 10464 Lincoln Huntington Woods MI 48070 Office: Plunkett Cooney Rutt Watters Stanczyk and Pedersen 1695 Woodward Suite 210 Bloomfield Hills MI 48013

KOPLIK, MARC STEPHEN, lawyer; b. N.Y.C., Aug. 28, 1946; s. Arnold and Lillian (Weiner) K.; m. Deirdre Lee Henderson, May 30, 1970; children: Christopher Henderson, Timothy Henderson. AB cum laude, Brown U., 1968; JD, Yale U., 1971. Bar: N.Y. 1973. Assoc. Debevoise & Plimpton, N.Y.C., 1971-76; founder, mng. ptnr. Henderson & Koplik, N.Y.C., 1982—. Editor Yale Law Jour., 1970-71. Coll. scholar, Frances Wayland scholar. Mem. Assn. Bar City N.Y., N.Y. State Bar Assn., Woodstock (N.Y.) C. of C. Episcopalian. Club: Yale (N.Y.C.). General corporate, Private international, Alternative energy. Home: 4 E 95th St New York NY 10128 Office: Henderson & Koplik 950 3d Ave New York NY 10022

KOPLIN, BERNICE JUDITH, lawyer; b. Lynn, Mass., Oct. 6, 1943; d. Harold and Rita (Cohen) Berzof; m. Joseph K. Koplin, June 4, 1972; children: Jonathan, Joshua. BA, Douglass Coll., 1965; MA, Brandeis U., 1970; MS, Simmons Coll., 1972; JD, Temple U., 1981, LLM in Taxation, 1984. Bar: Pa. 1981, U.S. Dist. Ct. (ea. dist.) Pa. 1982, U.S. Tax Ct. 1982, U.S. Ct. Appeals (3d cir.) 1982, U.S. Ct. Claims 1986, U.S. Supreme Ct. 1986. Assoc. Meltzer & Schiffrin, Phila., 1981-82; sole practice Phila., 1982-83, 86—; ptnr. Goldman, Koplin & Marshall, P.C., Phila., 1983-86; enrolled agt. IRS. Contbr. articles to profl. jours. Mem. Ctl. Women's Com., Phila. Orch., 1978—; bd. dirs. Settlement Music Sch., Phila., 1985—. Mem. ABA, Pa. Bar Assn., Phila. Bar Assn. Jewish. Club: Cosmopolitan (Phila.) (bd. govs. 1985—, chmn. fin. com. 1985—). Avocation: bird watching. Probate, General corporate, Personal income taxation. Home: 251 St Joseph's Way Philadelphia PA 19106 Office: 1600 Atlantic Bldg 260 S Broad St Philadelphia PA 19102

KOPP, FREDERICK PHILIP, lawyer; b. Muscatine, Iowa, Mar. 4, 1949; s. Philip Frederick and Erma Nadine (Dallner) K.; m. Sharon Catherine Huegerich, Aug. 24, 1974; children—Elaine Marie, Philip Frederick. B.A., U. Iowa, 1971, J.D., 1974. Bar: Iowa 1974, Ill. 1974, U.S. Dist. Ct. (cen. dist.) Ill. 1974, U.S. Ct. Appeals (7th cir.) 1976. Assoc. lawyer Spector, Taber & Tappa, Rock Island, Ill., 1974-77; ptnr. Spector, Tappa, Kopp & Nathan, Rock Island, 1977—. Chmn., commr. Greater Met. Area Housing Authority of Rock Island County, East Moline, Ill., 1977—. Mem. ABA, Ill. State Bar Assn., Iowa State Bar Assn., Phi Beta Kappa. Democrat. Roman Catholic. General corporate, General practice, Entertainment. Home: 2521 20th Ave Rock Island IL 61201 Office: Spector Tappa Kopp & Nathan 300 1st Nat Bank Bldg Rock Island IL 61201

KOPPENHEFFER, JULIE B., lawyer; b. Lexington, Ky., July 14, 1945; d. Arthur S. and Mae (Bronfeld) Adler; m. Thomas Lynn Koppenheffer, Dec. 22, 1967; children—Michael, Alex. A.B., Boston U., 1966, J.D., 1969. Bar: Mass. 1969, Tex. 1979, U.S. Dist. Ct. Mass. 1970, U.S. Supreme Ct. 1976. Sole practice, Williamstown, Mass., 1974-79; sr. corp. atty. LaQuinta Motor Inn, San Antonio, 1979-83, assoc. gen. counsel, 1983-84; v.p., gen. counsel Texian Inns, San Antonio, 1984—; adj. prof. North Adams State Coll., Mass., 1977-79. Bd. dirs. Encino Park Homeowners Assn., San Antonio, 1984. Mem. Tex. Bar Assn., ABA, San Antonio Bar Assn. (chmn. Corp. Com. 1984-86). General corporate, Real property, Construction. Home: 20015 Park Bluff San Antonio TX 78259 Office: The New Texian Co 8000 IH-10 W Suite 1500 San Antonio TX 78230

KORB, KENNETH A., lawyer; b. Boston, Oct. 11, 1932; s. Allan and Mynue (Herbert) K.; m. Jaclyn C. Patricof, June 30, 1962; 1 son, Jason B. BA magna cum laude, Harvard Coll., 1953, JD cum laude, 1956. Bar: Mass. 1956. Law clk. Supreme Jud. Ct. Mass., 1956-57; assoc. Hutchins & Wheeler, Boston, 1957-60; assoc. Kargman & Kargman, Boston, 1960-63; sr. ptnr. Brown, Rudnick, Freed & Gesmer, Boston, 1963—; lectr. Mass. Continuing Legal Edn.; sec., dir., gen. counsel Safety Ins.Co., 1980—; underwriting mem. Lloyd's of London, 1984—. Internat. pres. Soc. Israel Philatelists, 1974-76, bd. dirs. 1976-80. Served with USAR, 1956-62. Mem. ABA, Mass. Bar Assn., Boston Bar Assn. Democrat. Contbr. articles to profl. jours. Real property, General corporate, Insurance. Home: 24 Helene Rd Waban MA 02168 Office: One Financial Place Boston MA 02110

KORCHIN, JUDITH MIRIAM, lawyer; b. Kew Gardens, N.Y., Apr. 28, 1949; d. Arthur Walter and Mena (Levisohn) Goldstein; m. Paul Maury Korchin, June 10, 1972; 1 son, Brian Edward. B.A. with high honors, U. Fla., 1971; J.D. with honors, 1974. Law clk. to U.S. Dist. Judge, 1974-76; assoc., Steel, Hector & Davis, Miami, Fla., 1976-81; ptnr., 1981-86; ptnr. Finley, Kumble, Wagner, Heine, Underberg, Manley, Myerson & Casey, Miami, 1986—. Bd. dirs. Fla. Film & Recording Inst., 1982-84; mem. U. Fla. Law Ctr. Council, 1980-83; pres. alumni bd. U. Fla. Law Rev., 1983. Mem. Dade County Bar Assn. (treas. 1982, sec. 1983, 3d v.p. 1984, 2d v.p. 1985, pres.-elect 1986, bd. dirs. 1981-82), Fla. Bar (vice chmn. jud. nominating commn. com. 1982, mem. civil procedure rules com. 1984—), Order of Coif, Phi Beta Kappa, Phi Kappa Phi. Exec. editor, contbg. author U. Fla. Law Rev., 1973-74. Federal civil litigation, State civil litigation. Home: 85 Bay Heights Dr Miami FL 33133 Office: Finley Kumble Wagner Heine Underberg Manley Myerson & Casey 777 Brickwell Ave Suite 1000 Miami FL 33131

KORCHIN, PAUL MAURY, lawyer; b. Bklyn., Aug. 1, 1949; s. Leo and Esther (Goldstein) K.; m. Judith Miriam Goldstein, June 10, 1972; 1 child, Brian Edward. B.A. with high honors, U. Fla., 1971, J.D., 1975. Bar: Fla. 1975, U.S. Dist. Ct. (so. dist.) Fla. 1975, U.S. Ct. Appeals (5th and 11th cirs.) 1976. Asst. fed. pub. defender Fed. Pub. Defender Office, Miami, Fla., 1975-79; sole practice, Miami, 1979—. Mem. Am. Bar Assn. (crim. law sect.), Fla. Bar (crim. law sect.), Fla. Crim. Def. Lawyers Assn., Nat. Crim. Def. Lawyers Assn., Phi Beta Kappa. Criminal. Office: 4649 Ponce de Leon Blvd Suite 300 Coral Gables FL 33146

KORDA, PETER J., lawyer; b. White Plains, N.Y., July 3, 1954; s. Gerard Victor and Trudy K. AB, Brown U., 1976; JD, NYU, 1979. Bar: N.Y. 1980. Assoc. Mudge, Rose, Guthrie, Alexander & Ferdon, N.Y.C., 1979—. Mem. ABA (real property com.), Assn. of Bar of City of N.Y. Real property. Office: Demov Morris & Hammerling 40 W 57th St New York NY 10019

KORDONS, ULDIS, lawyer; b. Riga, Latvia, July 9, 1941; came to U.S., 1949; s. Evalds and Zenta Alide (Apenits) K.; m. Virginia Lee Knowles, Juny 16, 1966. AB, Princeton U., 1963; JD, Georgetown U., 1970. Bar: N.Y. 1970, Ohio 1977. Assoc. Whitman & Ransom, N.Y.C., 1970-77, Anderson, Mari & Rabinowitz, Tokyo, 1973-75; counsel Armco Inc., Whippany, N.J., 1977-84; v.p., gen. counsel, sec. Sybron Corp., Saddle Brook, N.J., 1984—; bd. dirs. Brinkman Instruments Inc., Westbury, N.Y. Mem. nat. com. Boy Scouts Am., 1982—. Served to lt. USN, 1963-67, Vietnam. Mem. N.Y. Bar Assn., Ohio Bar Assn. Republican. Home: 13 Timberline Dr Ho Ho Kus NJ 07423 Office: Sybron Corp Park 80 W Plaza I Saddle Brook NJ 07662

KOREN, EDWARD FRANZ, lawyer; b. Eustis, Fla., Aug. 6, 1946; s. Edward Franz Sr. and Frances (Boyd) K.; m. Louise Poole, June 19, 1970; children: Daniel Edward, Susan Louise. BSBA, U. Fla., 1971, JD, 1974. Bar: Fla. 1975, U.S. Dist. Ct. (mid. dist.) Fla. 1977, U.S. Supreme Ct. 1980, U. S. Ct. Appeals (11th cir.) 1981, U.S. Tax Ct. 1985, U.S. Ct. Claims 1986. Instr. tax U. Fla., Gainesville, 1974-75; assoc. Holland & Knight, Lakeland, Fla., 1975-79, ptnr., 1980—; chmn. continuing legal edn. com. Fla. Bar, 1982-84, vice chmn. bd. cert., designation and advt. 1983-86, dir. probate div. 1985—. Contbr. articles to profl. jours. Served to capt. U.S. Army, 1971-72. Fellow Am. Coll. Probate Council; mem. Fla. Bar Assn. (various sects. and coms.), Am. Assn. Attys. and CPA's, Fla. Inst. CPA's, Order of Coif. Republican. Presbyterian. Clubs: Tampa (Fla.), Lakeland Yacht and Country, Centre (Tampa). Probate, Estate planning, Estate taxation. Home: 3335 Imperial Ln Lakeland FL 33803 Office: Holland & Knight 92 Lake Wire Dr PO Drawer BW Lakeland FL 33802

KORFF, IRA A., lawyer, clergyman, business executive; b. Boston, Aug. 30, 1949; s. Nathan and Helen (Pfeffer) K.; m. Shari E. Redstone, May 25, 1980; children: Kimberlee A., Brandon J., Tyler J. B of Jewish Edn., Hebrew Coll., 1968; BA, Columbia U., 1969; DD, Rabbinical Acad., 1971; JD, Bklyn. Law Sch., 1972; MA in Internat. Relations, Tufts-Harvard U., 1973, MA in Law and Diplomacy, 1975, PhD in Internat. Law, 1976; postgrad., Harvard U. Div. Sch., 1975; LLM, Boston U., 1980. Bar: Mass. 1974, U.S. Dist. Ct. Mass. 1975, U.S. Tax Ct. 1976, U.S. Ct. Appeals (1st cir.) 1976, U.S. Supreme Ct. 1978, D.C. 1980. Spl. cons. to dist. atty. Norfolk County, Mass., 1975-85; spl. asst. atty. gen. Commonwealth of Mass., 1977-85; ptnr. Berman, Lewenberg, Redstone & Korff, Boston, 1974—; mem. Rabbinical Ct. Justice, Boston, 1975—. Mem. Boston Consumers Council, 1975-80; bd. dirs. Council on Religion and Law, Boston, 1978-84, Friends of Fletcher Sch. Law and Diplomacy, 1974—; v.p., Nat. Amusements, Inc., bd. dirs. Mem. Internat. Bar Assn., ABA, Mass. Bar Assn., Boston Bar Assn., Internat. Law Assn., Am. Soc. Internat. Law, Am. Arbitration Assn. (mem. panel 1978—). Club: Harvard (Boston, N.Y.C). Private international, Public international, Probate. Office: Berman Lewenberg Redstone & Korff 211 Congress St Boston MA 02110

KORIN, JOEL BENJAMIN, lawyer; b. Phila., Apr. 15, 1945; s. Leon Aaron and Charlotte Sylvia (Snyder) K.; m. Kallen P. Stillwell, Aug. 11, 1968; children—Saul, Steven, A.B., Dickinson Coll., 1971; J.D. with honors, Rutgers U., 1971. Bar: N.J. 1971, U.S. Ct. Appeals (3d cir.) 1978, U.S. Supreme Ct. 1978; cert. civil trial atty., N.J. Supreme Ct., 1982, criminal trial atty., 1982. Assoc. Stransky & Poplar, Camden, N.J., 1971-72, James J. Florio, Camden, 1972-73; asst. dep. pub. defender, Camden, 1973-74; assoc. Brown, Connery, Kulp, Wille, Purnell & Green, Camden, 1975-77, ptnr., 1977-82; ptnr. George & Korin, P.A., Woodbury, N.J., 1982—; lectr. Rutgers U. Sch. Law, Camden. Served with Air N.G., 1969-75. Ralph E. Donges scholar Camden County Bar Assn., 1970. Mem. Camden County Bar Assn., Gloucester County Bar Assn., N.J. State Bar Assn., N.J. Trial Attys., ABA. Democrat. Jewish. Author: Clinicolegal Corr. Course, 1983; contbr. articles to legal jours. Federal civil litigation, State civil litigation, Criminal. Home: 127 N Hinchman Ave Haddonfield NJ 08033 Office: 238 S Evergreen Ave PO Box 319 Woodbury NJ 08096

KORMAN, EDWARD R., judge; b. N.Y.C., Oct. 25, 1942; s. Julius and Miriam K.; m. Diane R. Eisner, Feb. 3, 1979; children: Miriam M., Benjamin E. B.A., Bklyn. Coll., 1963; LL.B., Bklyn. Law Sch., 1966; LL.M., NYU, 1971. Bar: N.Y. 1966, U.S. Supreme Ct. 1972. Law clk. to judge N.Y. Ct. Appeals, 1966-68; assoc. Paul, Weiss, Rifkind, Wharton and Garrison, 1968-70; asst. U.S. atty. Eastern Dist. N.Y., N.Y.C., 1970-72; asst. to solicitor gen. of U.S., 1972-74; chief asst. U.S. atty. Eastern Dist. N.Y., 1974-78, U.S. atty., 1978-82; ptnr. Stroock & Stroock & Lavan, N.Y.C., 1982-84; prof. Bklyn. Law Sch., 1984-85; U.S. dist. judge Eastern Dist. N.Y., 1985—. Chmn. Mayor's Com. on N.Y.C. Marshals, 1983-85; mem. Temporary Commn. of Investigation of State of N.Y., 1983-85. Jewish. Office: US Courthouse 225 Cadman Plaza E Brooklyn NY 11201

KORMAN, IRIS J., lawyer; b. N.Y.C., Feb. 14, 1954; s. Herbert and Miriam Sarah (Ammer) K.; m. Barry Nostradamus Sher, June 15, 1980. Student, Queens Coll., 1971-72, Jewish Theol. Sem., 1972-75; BA, CUNY, 1975; JD, Bklyn. Law Sch., 1978. Bar: N.Y. 1979, U.S. Supreme Ct. 1982, U.S. Dist. Ct. (ea. and so. dists.) N.Y. 1984. Atty. N.Y.C. Conciliation and Appeals Bd., 1979-80, supervising atty., 1980-82, atty. litigation, 1982-84; atty. litigation N.Y. State Div. Housing and Community Renewal, 1984-86, supervising atty., 1987—. Alt. del. to jud. nominating conv. N.Y. County Dems., N.Y.C., 1983; chmn. judiciary com. Community Free Dems., N.Y.C., 1983-84; trustee Congrregation Ansche Chesed, N.Y.C., 1983—, pres. 1986—. N.Y. State Regents scholar, 1971-75. Mem. N.Y. County Lawyers Assn., N.Y. State Womens Bar Assn. Administrative and regulatory, State civil litigation, Landlord-tenant. Office: NY State Div Housing and Community Renewal 1 Fordham Plaza 4th Floor Bronx NY 10458

KORMAN, JAMES WILLIAM, lawyer; b. Washington, Apr. 29, 1943; s. Milton D. and Bernice (Rosensweig) K.; m. Barbara Dale Lewis, June 11, 1967; 1 child, Katherine Bernice. AB, William and Mary Coll., 1965; JD, George Washington U., 1968. Bar: Va. 1968, D.C. 1970, U.S. Supreme Ct. 1972, U.S. Ct. Appeals (4th cir.) 1974, U.S. Dist. Ct. (ea. dist.) Va. 1975. Assoc. Kinney, Smith and Barham, Arlington, Va., 1968-73, ptnr., 1973-78; ptnr. Bean, Kinney, Korman, Hylton and Moore, Arlington, 1979—; mem. Va. Bar Council, 1983—, 10th dist. Grievence Com., 1978-81. Bd. dirs. No. Va. Jewish Community Ctr., 1983—; mem. adv. bd. Sch. for Contemporary Edn., Springfield, Va., 1984—. Served to capt. USAR, 1972-74. Recipient Adult Exploring award Boy Scouts Am., 1974. Mem. ABA, Arlington Bar Assn. (pres. 1981-82, bd. dirs. 1977-81), Va. Bar Assn. (council 1983—), Va. Trial Lawyers Assn., Assn. Trial Lawyers Am., Plaintiffs Bar Ltd., Falls Ch. Jaycees (pres. 1974-75). Federal civil litigation, Family and matrimonial, Personal injury. Home: 3852 N 26th St Arlington VA 22207 Office: Bean et al 2007 N 15th St Arlington VA 22201

KORMES, JOHN WINSTON, lawyer; b. N.Y.C., May 4, 1935; s. Mark and Joanna P. Kormes; m. Frances W. Kormes, Aug. 19, 1978; 1 child, Mark Vincent. B.A. in Econs., U. Mich., 1955, J.D., 1959. Bar: Pa. 1961, D.C. 1961, U.S. Sup. Ct. 1968. With License and Inspection Rev. Bd. Phila., 1972-73; asst. dist. atty. City of Phila., 1973-74, asst. city solicitor, 1974-80; sole practice, Phila., 1961—; moot ct. advisor. Mem. staff Re-Elect the Pres. Com., 1972, Rizzo for Mayor Com., 1971, 75, Phila. Flag Day Assn., 1965—. Served with USAF, 1956-57. Recipient N.Y. Intercoll. Legis. Assembly award, 1954; R.I. Model Congress award, 1954. Fellow Lawyers in Mensa (charter; mem. Phila. Bar Assn., Phila. Trial Lawyers Assn., N.Y. State Trial Lawyers Assn., Am. Arbitration Assn., Fed. Bar Assn., Pitts. Inst. Legal Medicine, Am. Trial Lawyers Assn., Intertel, Internat. Platform Assn., Internat. Soc. Philos. Enquiry (legal officer 1986—), Delta Sigma Rho. Republican. Clubs: Masons, Shriners, KP, Lions. Family and matrimonial, State civil litigation, Personal injury. Home: 1070 Edison Ave Philadelphia PA 19116 Office: 2820 PSFS Bldg 12 S 12th St Philadelphia PA 19107

KORN, GARY CLIFFORD, lawyer; b. Englewood, N.J., Aug. 29, 1955; s. S. Winton and Theresa (Gross) K.; m. Jane B. Silverman, Mar. 3, 1985. BS, Cornell U., 1977; JD, St. John's U., Jamaica, N.Y., 1982; LLM, Columbia U., 1984. Bar: N.Y. 1983, U.S. Ct. Appeals (10th cir.) 1983, U.S. Dist. Ct. (so. dist.) N.Y. 1984, Ariz. 1986, U.S. Dist. Ct. Ariz. 1986. Law clk. to presiding justice U.S. Ct. Appeals (10th cir.), Denver, 1983; assoc. Willkie, Farr & Gallagher, N.Y.C., 1984-86, DeConcini, McDonald, Brammer, Yetwin & Lacy, Tucson, 1986—. Contbr. articles to profl. jours. Asst. counsel 1st dept. Gov. Cuomo's Jud. Screening Com., N.Y.C., 1985-86. Mem. ABA. Avocations: photography, tennis, skiing. Computer, Federal civil litigation, State civil litigation. Home: 4275 E Coronado Dr Tucson AZ 85718 Office: DeConcini McDonald Brammer et al 240 N Stone Ave Tucson AZ 85701

KORN, HAROLD LEON, legal educator; b. Bronx, N.Y., June 25, 1929; s. Jacob and Nettie (Wurzel) K. A.B., Cornell U., 1951; J.D., Columbia U., 1954. Bar: N.Y. 1955. Law clk. to judge N.Y. State Ct. Appeals, 1954-56; dir. research Adv. Com. on Practice and Procedure of N.Y. State Temporary Commn. on the Cts., 1956-60; lectr. law Columbia U. Law Sch., N.Y.C., 1962-64; prof. law SUNY, Buffalo, 1965-68, N.Y. U., 1968-71, Columbia U. Law Sch., 1971—; cons. evidence code N.Y. State Law Revision Commn., 1976-80. Author: (with Jack B. Weinstein and Arthur R. Miller) New York Civil Practice, 1962, (with Albert J. Rosenthal and Stanley B. Lubman) Catastrophic Accidents in Government Programs, 1963, (with others) Elements of Civil Procedure, 4th edit, 1985. Bd. dirs. Mobilization for Youth, 1974-76; bd. dirs. Columbia Found. for Public Interest Law, 1979-82. Mem. N.Y. State Bar Assn., Assn. Bar City of N.Y. Democrat. Jewish. Legal education. Home: 160 E 65th St New York NY 10021 Office: Columbia Law Sch New York NY 10027

KORN, ROBERT A., lawyer; b. Phila., Jan. 27, 1939; s. Joseph K. and Ida (Levin) K.; m. Susan F. Maislen, Aug. 29, 1965; children—Jonathan, Nancy. B.S., Temple U., 1961, LL.B., 1964. Bar: Pa. 1965, U.S. Dist. Ct. (ea. dist.) Pa. 1966, U.S. Ct. Appeals (3d cir.) 1968; assoc. Scirica & McGrory, Norristown, Pa., 1965-66, Rosenfeld & Weinrott, Phila., 1966-67, Winokur & Kahn, Phila., 1967-72; ptnr. Kahn, Bushman, Rosenberg & Weisberg, Phila., 1972-75; prin. Korn, Kline & Kutner, P.C., Phila., 1975—; assoc. staff atty. Lawyer Reference Service, Phila., 1967-69; lectr. in field. Bd. dirs. Moss Rehab. Hosp., Phila., 1974—; pres. Lafayette Hill (Pa.) Civic Assn., 1972—; bd. dirs. Citizens' Council Lafayette Hill, 1975—. Mem. ABA (fidelity and surety com., constrn. litigation forum and constrn. law com.), Am. Arbitration Assn. (arbitrator), Surety Claims Inst., Pa. Bar Assn., Pa. Def. Counsel Assn., Pa. Trial Lawyers Assn., Montgomery County Bar Assn., Montgomery County Trial Lawyers Assn., Phila. Bar Assn. (appellate cts. com.; former chmn. constrn. law com., real property sect.). Real property, Construction. Home: 1845 Walnut St 21st Floor Hill PA 19103 Office: 1521 Locust St Suite 500 Philadelphia PA 19102

KORNBLUM, GUY ORVILLE, lawyer; b. Indpls., Oct. 29, 1939; s. Guy J. and Gilmette Gilberta (Damart) K.; m. Carol Kornblum (div.); m. M. Victoria Adams, Apr. 15, 1977; children: Anna Victoria, Guy Laurence. AB, Ind. U., 1961; JD, U. Calif., San Francisco, 1966. Assoc. Ice, Miller, Donadio & Ryan, Indpls., 1966-67, Bledsoe, Smith et al, San Francisco, 1967-70; asst. dean, prof. law U. Calif., San Francisco, 1970-72; ptnr. Pettit & Martin, San Francisco, 1972-79; sr. ptnr. Kornblum, Kelly & Herlihy, San Francisco, 1979—; assoc. prof. law U. Calif., San Francisco, 1972-79; lectr. Rutter Group, Encino, Calif., 1979—, Calif. Continuing Edn. of the Bar, 1979, ABA Nat. Insts., 1979; co-founder Hastings Ctr. Trial and Appellate Advocacy, San Francisco, 1970-80. Editor Def. Law Jour.; contbr. articles to profl. jours. Served to 1st lt. M.I., U.S. Army, 1960-61. Ford Found. fellow NYU, 1971. Fellow Am. Bar Found.; mem. ABA, Calif. Bar Assn., San Francisco Bar Assn., Ind. Bar Assn., Def. Research Inst. (lectr. 1979), Fedn. Ins. Counsel, Internat. Assn. Def. Counsel, Northern and Southern Calif. Assn. Def. Counsel, Order of Coif, Phi Eta Sigma. Republican. Episcopalian. Clubs: Olympic (San Francisco); San Francisco Yacht (Belvedere, Calif.). Avocations: jogging, yachting, tennis, photography. Insurance, Contracts commercial, Personal injury. Office: Kornblum Kelly & Herlihy 445 Bush St 6th Floor San Francisco CA 94108

KORNBLUT, ARTHUR T., lawyer; b. Bridgeport, Conn., June 30, 1941; s. Alfred and Dorothy W. Kornblut; m. Jane Slaughter, Feb. 19, 1971; children: Anne, Emily. BArch, Rensselaer Poly. Inst., 1963; JD, U. Akron, 1969. Bar: Ohio 1969, D.C. 1970, U.S. Supreme Ct. 1972, U.S. Claims Ct. 1982. Adminstrv. profl. practice AIA, Washington, 1969-73; ptnr. Farquhar & Kornblut, Washington, 1973-78, Ford, Farquhar et al, Washington, 1978-

82, Kornblut & Sokolove, Washington, 1982—. Columnist Archtl. Record mag. Served to lt. USNR, 1963-65. Mem. ABA (chmn. forum com. on constrn. industry 1985—), AIA, Am. Arbitration Assn., Ohio Bar Assn., D.C. Bar Assn., Constrn. Scis. Research Found. (bd. dirs.). Construction, Insurance, Personal injury. Office: Kornblut & Sokolove 5028 Wisconsin Ave NW Suite 101 Washington DC 20016

KORNICHUK, ELLEN S., lawyer; b. Cleve., Sept. 22, 1956; d. Arthur and Florence Ellen Kornichuk. BS in Sociology, No. Ill. U., 1978; JD, John Marshall Law Sch., 1982. Bar: Ill. 1982, U.S. Dist. Ct. (no. dist.) Ill. 1982, U.S. Ct. Appeals (7th cir.) 1984. Law clk. Burlington No. R.R. Co., Chgo., 1981-85; sole practice Clarendon Hills, Ill., 1982-86; assoc. Paddy Harris McNamara Ltd., Chgo., 1985-86, Law Offices Beverly Susler Parkhurst, Chgo., 1985-86, Bell, Boyd & Lloyd, Chgo., 1986—. Mem. ABA, Ill. Bar Assn., Chgo. Bar Assn., Women's Bar Assn. Ill. General corporate, Federal civil litigation, State civil litigation. Home: 880 Benedetti #201 Naperville IL 60540 Office: Bell Boyd & Lloyd 3 First Nat Plaza Suite 3200 Chicago IL 60602

KORNSTEIN, MICHAEL ALLEN, lawyer; b. Bklyn., Feb. 7, 1951; s. Samuel and Goldie (Starker) K.; m. Margaret Ann Tomlinson, Jan. 2, 1983; 1 child, Harris. BS, Union Coll., Schenectady, N.Y., 1973; JD, Union U., Albany, N.Y., 1977. Bar: N.Y. 1978, U.S. Dist. Ct. (no. dist.) N.Y. 1978, U.S. Dist. Ct. (so., ea. and we. dists.) N.Y. 1984, U.S. Supreme Ct. 1982. Assoc. Cooper, Erving, Savage, Whalen, Nolan & Neller, 1978-82, ptnr., 1983—. Mem. N.Y. State Bar Assn. Democrat. Jewish. Real property, Banking, General practice. Office: Cooper Erving Savage Whalen Nolan & Neller 39 N Pearl St Albany NY 12207

KOROSEC, KENNETH DAVID, lawyer; b. Cleve., Oct. 15, 1943; s. Frank A. and Marion (Dunn) K.; m. Constance E. Johnson, June 25, 1966; children—Jason A., Jill A. B.A. cum laude, Western Res. U., 1963; J.D. cum laude, Cleve. State U., 1967. Bar: Ohio 1967, U.S. Dist. Ct. (no. dist.) Ohio 1976, U.S. Supreme Ct. 1986. Legal counsel Cleve.-Seven County Transp.-Land Use Study, 1967-69, N.E. Ohio Area Wide Coordinating Agy., 1969-71; county adminstr. Geauga County (Ohio) County, dir. County Planning Commn., 1971-75; gen. practice, Chesterland, Ohio, 1967—; dir. Docusystems Inc., Hedlund Fence, Inc., Chardon Tool, Inc. Mem. fund raising com. Univ. Sch. Parents Assn.; chmn. fund raising com. Laurel Sch. Parents Assn.; exec. v.p. Geauga County Community Improvement Corp., 1971—. Mem. Ohio Bar Assn., ABA, Geauga Bar Assn., Am. Trial Lawyers Assn. Contbr. articles to profl. jours. General corporate, General practice, Probate. Home: 11919 Caves Rd Chesterland OH 44026 Office: Diplomat Bldg 12573 Chillicothe Rd Chesterland OH 44026

KORTENHOF, JOSEPH MICHAEL, lawyer, educator; b. Kimberly, Wis., Aug. 18, 1927; s. Joseph Arthur and Marie Agnes (Probst) K.; m. Althea Hunting, June 7, 1952; children: Elizabeth Ann, Michael, Amy Jo. BA cum laude, Lawrence U., 1950; JD, U. Mich., 1953. Bar: Mo. 1953, U.S. Ct. Appeals (8th cir.) 1953, U.S. Dist. Ct. (ea. dist.) Mo. 1953. Assoc. Coburn, Storckman & Croft, St. Louis, 1953-60; sr. ptnr. Kortenhof & Ely, St. Louis, 1960—; adj. prof. law Washington U., St. Louis, 1984—. Served with USAF, 1945-47. Fellow Am. Coll. Trial Lawyers, Am. Bd. Trial Advs.; mem. ABA, Mo. Bar Found. (trial lawyer award 1962), St. Louis Bar Assn., Assn. Civil Def. Counsel, Am. Maritime Law Assn., Sigma Phi Epsilon. Democrat. Episcopalian. Admiralty, Federal civil litigation, State civil litigation. Home: 5340 Kenrick Park Dr Saint Louis MO 63119 Office: Kortenhof & Ely 1015 Locust St Suite 300 Saint Louis MO 63101

KORTH, FRED, lawyer; b. Yorktown, Tex., Sept. 9, 1909; s. Fritz R. J. and Eleanor Marie (Stark) K.; m. Vera Connell, Sept. 12, 1934 (div. Mar. 1966); children: Nina Maria, Fritz-Alan, Vera Sansom (dec.); m. Charlotte Brooks, Aug. 23, 1980. A.B., U. Tex., 1932; LL.B., George Washington U., 1935, LL.D. (hon.), 1960. Bar: Tex., D.C. bars 1935. Sole practice Ft. Worth, 1935-62; ptnr. Wallace & Korth, 1948-51; sole practice Washington, 1964—; dep. counselor Dept. Army, 1951-52, asst. sec. army, 1952-53, cons. to sec. army, 1953-60; exec. v.p. Continental Nat. Bank, Ft. Worth, 1953-59, pres., 1959-61; sec. of navy, 1961-63; treas. Ft. Worth Air Terminal Corp., 1953-60; bd. dirs. Fischbach Corp., First Fin. Enterprises, Knickerbocker Life Ins. Co., First Fin. Savs. Bank, Panama Canal Co. Pres. United Fund, Ft. Worth, Tarrant County, 1957-58; bd. dirs. Southwestern Exposition and Fat Stock Show, Ft. Worth, 1953-63, treas., 1960-61; co-executor, co-trustee Marjorie Merriweather Post Estate; mem. nat. council Salk Inst.; trustee Meridian House Internat., Washington, Nat. Def. U. Found. Served as lt. col. Air Transp. Command AUS, 1942-46. Recipient Exceptional Civilian Service award Dept. Army, 1953. Mem. ABA, Tex. Bar Assn., D.C. Bar Assn., Am. Law Inst. (life), Order St. Lazarus, Tex. and Southwestern Cattle Raisers Assn. (treas. 1957-61), Phi Delta Phi, Sigma Phi Epsilon. Democrat. Clubs: Internat. (Washington), Georgetown (Washington), Army-Navy (Washington); Ridglea (Ft. Worth); Argyle (San Antonio). Home: 4200 Massachusetts Ave NW 101 Washington DC 20016 also: El Retiro PO Box 13 Ecleto TX 78111 also: 1054 Torrey Pines El Paso TX 79912 Office: 1700 K St NW Suite 501 Washington DC 20006

KORTH, JAMES WILLIAM, lawyer; b. Ashland, Oreg., Sept. 4, 1938; Donald Francis and Mildred Lucille (Martin) K.; m. Linda Lee McKay, Dec. 20, 1963; children: Kelly Lee, Kimberley Ann, Steven James. AB, Stanford U., 1964; JD summa cum laude, Willamette Coll., 1967. Bar: Oreg. 1967, U.S. Dist. Ct. Oreg. 1968. Assoc. Johnson & Harrang, Eugene, Oreg., 1967-70, ptnr., 1970-82; of counsel Atherly, Butler & Burgott, Eugene, 1983-84; sole practice Eugene, 1984—; gen. mgr. Kilburn Wood Products, Drain, Oreg., 1986—; mem. Oreg. State Bd. Bar Examiners, Portland, 1973-77, bd. rev., 1983-84. Editor in chief: Willamette Law Jour., 1967. Served to 1st lt. USAF, 1961-66. Mem. ABA, Oreg. State Bar Assn., McKenzie Flyfishers (pres. 1972-73), Fedn. of Flyfishers. Republican. Lodge: Elks. Probate, Real property, General corporate. Home: 2989 Eldridge Ave Eugene OR 97405 Office: 975 Oak Suite 620 Eugene OR 97401

KOSARIN, JONATHAN HENRY, lawyer, director; b. Bklyn., Aug. 13, 1951; s. Lester and Norma (Higger) K.; m. Gayle C. Skarupa, Nov. 27, 1982. BA in History magna cum laude, Syracuse U., 1973; JD, Bklyn. Law Sch., 1976; LLM in Govt. Contract Law, George Washington U., 1984. Bar: N.Y. 1977, D.C. 1978, U.S. Supreme Ct. 1980, U.S. Ct. Claims 1981, U.S. Ct. Appeals (Fed. cir.) 1982. Commd. 2d lt. U.S. Army, 1973, advanced through grades to maj., 1977; prosecutor trial counsel U.S. Army, Ft. McClellan, Ala., 1977-78; adminstrv. law officer U.S. Army, Ft. McClellan, 1978-79, instr. law, 1979-80; trial atty. contract appeals div. U.S. Army, Washington, 1980-84; contracts atty. U.S. Army Hdqrs., Heidelberg, Fed. Rep. Germany, 1985—; bd. dirs. procurement law div. Fed. Home Loan Bank Bd., Washington. Mem. ABA, D.C. Bar Assn., Assn. Trial Lawyers Am., Titantic Hist. Soc., Phi Alph Delta, Phi Beta Kappa, Phi Kappa Phi. Democrat. Home: 5597 Seminary Rd Apt 2410 S Falls Church VA 22041 Office: Office Gen Counsel Fed Home Loan Bank Bd 1700 G St NW Washington DC 20552

KOSELKA, HARVEY ANTHONY, lawyer; b. Dearborn, Mich., June 10, 1934; s. Frank J. and Anne A. (Boehmer) K.; married; children: Rita, Helen, Harvery Jr., John, Margaret. Student, U. Detroit, 1952-56, U. Detroit, 1956-57, U. Mich., 1958; JD, Marquette U., 1959. Bar: Wis. 1959, Mich. 1959, U.S. Dist. Ct. Wis. 1959, U.S. Dist. Ct. (ea. dist.) Mich. 1959, U.S. Ct. Appeals 1960, U.S. Suprmee Ct. 1970. Pros. atty. Lenawee County, Adrian, Mich., 1961-82; sole practice Adrian, 1982—. Mem. ABA, Mich. Bar Assn., Pros. Assn. of Mich. (pres. 1970-71, bd. dirs. 1979-83), Nat. Dist. Attys. Assn. (bd. dirs. 1976-83, v.p. 1979-81).

KOSKINEN, DAVID JOHN, lawyer; b. Hibbing, Minn., Mar. 28, 1927; s. John W. and Ida S. (Mattson) K.; m. Agnes Martha Hannula, June 14, 1952; children: John David, Jane Martha, Anne Elizabeth. BA, U. Minn., Duluth, 1953; JD, U. Minn., Mpls., 1963. Bar: Minn. 1963, U.S. Dist. Ct. Minn. 1963, U.S. Supreme Ct. 1985. Ops. supr. M.A. Hanna Mining Co., Hibbing, 1950-60; ptnr. McCabe, Van Evera, Mundt, Koskinen & Clure, Duluth, 1963-84; sole practice Duluth, 1984—; adj. prof. U. Minn., Duluth, 1965-75. Contbg. editor: (book) The Developing Labor Law, 1979—. Active Boy Scouts Am., Duluth, 1966-72; advisor Duluth Preservation Soc., 1974-80. Served with USNR, 1945-53, PTO. Mem. ABA, Minn. Bar Assn. (sec. labor and employment law sect. 1979-81, bd. dirs. 1979-82), Maritime Law Assn. Lutheran. Club: Kitchi Gammi. Lodges: Rotary, Masons. Avocations: carpentry, American history, golf, skiing, curling. Labor, Employment, Admiralty. Home: 2724 Greysolon Rd Duluth MN 55812 Office: 707 Torrey Bldg 314 W Superior St Duluth MN 55802

KOSKO, GEORGE CARTER, lawyer; b. Tampa, Fla., Apr. 14, 1944; s. George and Margaret Elizabeth (Rea) K.; m. Polly Spann, Dec. 7, 1974. B.S., Univ. S.C., 1966, J.D., 1971; postgrad. Nat. Inst. Trial Advocacy, 1972. Bar: S.C. 1971, U.S. Supreme Ct. 1976, D.C. 1981, U.S. Customs Ct. 1976, U.S. Ct. Internat. Trade 1981. Ptnr. Kosko, Coffas & Sipes, 1975-82, sr. ptnr., 1976—. Mem. ABA (state reporter aviation com. sect. litigation). S.C. Bar Assn. Clubs: Spring Valley Country, Sertoma (gov. Wade Hampton dist.), Quiet Birdmen (Columbia). Federal civil litigation. Home: 21 Lake View Circle Columbia SC 29206 Office: 4910 Trenholm Rd Columbia SC 29206

KOSSAR, RONALD STEVEN, lawyer; b. Ellenville, N.Y., May 30, 1948; s. Emanuel and Helen (Panken) K.; m. Sandra Perlman, Aug. 25, 1973. B.A. cum laude, Boston U., 1970; J.D., Am. U., 1973. Bar: N.Y. 1974, D.C. 1974, U.S. Dist. Ct. (no. dist.) N.Y. 1974, U.S. Tax Ct. 1974, U.S. Ct. Appeals D.C. 1974. Tax law specialist Office of Asst. Commr. (Tech.), IRS, Washington, 1973-75; sole practice, Middletown, N.Y., 1976—; dir. Newburgh (N.Y.) Realty Corp., Cornwall Realty Corp., Just-Irv Sales, Inc., Newburgh. Mem. ABA, N.Y. State Bar Assn., Orange County Bar Assn., Middletown Bar Assn., D.C. Bar. Jewish. General practice, General corporate, Real property. Office: 402 E Main St PO Box 548 Middletown NY 10940

KOSTANT, RALPH BENNETT, lawyer; b. Phoenix, Oct. 23, 1951; s. Eli David and Esther (Cohen) K.; m. Laura Jane Cannon, Sept. 12, 1976; children: Sara, Esther, Elise, Nathan. BA, Stanford U., 1972; JD, Ariz. State U., 1976. Bar: Calif. 1978, U.S. Dist. Ct. (cen. dist.) Calif. 1978. Assoc. O'Melveny & Myers, Los Angles, 1977-84; assoc. Finley, Kumble, Wagner, Heine, Underberg, Manley, Myerson & Casey, Los Angeles and Beverly Hills, Calif., 1984-86, ptnr., 1986—. Co-author: American Law of Mining, 2d. edit., 1985. Nat. gov. council, exec. com. Pacific S.W. region, ch. commn. Jewish life and culture Am. Jewish Congress, Los Angeles, 1983—. Mem. ABA, Calif. Bar Assn. (Commendation for Pro Bono legal services 1982), Los Angeles County Bar Assn. (real property sect., steering com. comml. property subsect. 1984—). Democrat. Avocation: torah study. Real property, Oil and gas leasing, Energy, geothermal. Office: Finley Kumble Wagner Heine et al 707 Wilshire Blvd 44th Floor Los Angeles CA 90017

KOSTELANETZ, BORIS, lawyer; b. Leningrad, Russia, June 16, 1911; came to U.S., 1920, naturalized, 1925; s. Nachman and Rosalia (Dimschetz) K.; m. Ethel Cory, Dec. 18, 1938; children: Richard Cory, Lucy Cory. B.C.S., N.Y. U., 1933, B.S., 1936; J.D. magna cum laude, St. John's U., 1936, LL.D. (hon.), 1981. Bar: N.Y. 1936; CPA, N.Y. With Price, Waterhouse & Co., C.P.A.'s, N.Y.C., 1934-37; asst. U.S. atty. So. Dist. N.Y.; also confidential asst. to U.S. atty, 1937-43; spl. asst. to atty. gen. U.S. 1943-46; chief war frauds sect. Dept. Justice, 1945-46; spl. counsel com. investigate crime in interstate commerce U.S. Senate, 1950-51; ptnr. Kostelanzetz & Ritholz, and predecessors, N.Y.C., 1946—; instr. acctg. N.Y. U., 1937-47, adj. prof. taxation, 1947-69; Mem. com. on character and fitness Appellate div. Supreme Ct. N.Y., 1st dept., 1974—, chmn., 1985—. Author: (with L. Bender) Criminal Aspects of Tax Fraud Cases, 1957, 2d edit., 1968, 3d edit., 1980; Contbr. articles to legal, accounting and tax jours. Chmn. Kefauver for Pres. Com. N.Y. State, 1952. Recipient Meritorious Service award NYU, 1954, John T. Madden Meml. award, 1969; Pietas medal St. John's U., 1961, medal of honor, 1983; Torch of Learning award Am. Friends of Hebrew U. Law Sch., 1979. Fellow Am. Coll. Trial Lawyers, Am. Coll. Tax Counsel, Am. Bar Found.; mem. Internat. Bar Assn., Fed. Bar Assn., ABA (council sect. taxation 1978-81, ho. of dels. 1984—), N.Y. State Bar Assn., N.Y. County Lawyers Assn. (v.p. 1966-69, pres. 1969-71, dir. 1958-64, 66-69, 71-74, chmn. com. judiciary 1965-69), Assn. Bar City N.Y., N.Y. State Soc. C.P.A.s, N.Y. U. Sch. Commerce Alumni Assn. (pres. 1951-52), St. John's U. Law Sch. Alumni Assn. (pres. 1955-57), N.Y. U. Finance Club (pres. 1953-54). Clubs: India House, New York Univ. (N.Y.C.); Nat. Lawyers (Washington). Criminal, State civil litigation. Home: 37 Washington Sq W New York NY 10011 Office: Kostelanetz & Ritholz 80 Pine St New York NY 10005

KOSTELNY, ALBERT JOSEPH, JR., lawyer; b. Phila., July 11, 1951; s. Albert Joseph and Margaret (Naile) K. B.A., U. Pa., 1973, M.A., 1974; J.D., Fordham U., 1979. Bar: N.Y. 1980, U.S. Dist. Ct. (so. dist.) N.Y. 1983, U.S. Ct. Claims 1983, U.S. Supreme Ct. 1983, U.S. Ct. Internat. Trade 1985, U.S. Ct. Appeals (2d cir.) 1985. Atty. N.Y. State Div. Human Rights, N.Y.C., 1980-81, sr. atty., 1981—. Mem. ABA, N.Y. State Bar Assn., N.Y. County Lawyers Assn., Assn. Trial Lawyers Am. Republican. Roman Catholic. Labor, Civil rights, Administrative and regulatory. Office: NY State Div Human Rights 55 W 125th St New York NY 10027

KOSTER, ERIC DAVID, lawyer; b. N.Y.C., Feb. 8, 1947; s. Carl and Rose (Lotkin) K.; m. Gloria Jean Bussel, July 11, 1971; children—Megan Amanda, Charles Ross. B.A., Williams Coll., 1970; J.D., Hofstra U., 1974. Bar: N.J. 1975, U.S. Dist. Ct. N.J. 1975, N.Y. 1976, U.S. Dist. Ct. (so. dist. and ea. dist.) N.Y. 1976, U.S. Dist. Ct. (we. dist.) N.Y. 1981, U.S. Ct. Appeals (2d cir.) 1980, U.S. Supreme Ct. 1980. Asst. county atty. Westchester County Dept. Law, White Plains, N.Y., 1974-80; sr. asst. county atty. Westchester County Dept. Law, White Plains, 1980-85; prin. Eric D. Koster, P.C., White Plains, 1985-86, ptnr. Hoffman, Silverberg, Wachtell & Koster, 1986—; propr. Seaquestor Co., Pound Ridge, N.Y., 1979—. Pres. Pound Ridge Ambulance Corps, N.Y., 1982-83, trustee, 1983—, chmn. bd. trustees, 1985, pres., 1986—; bd. dirs. Pound Ridge Assn., 1984—, v.p., 1985—, treas., 1986—. Mem. N.Y. State Bar Assn., ABA, Westchester County Bar Assn. Real property, Federal civil litigation, Government contracts and claims. Home: Rural Route 3 Box 192A Siscowit Rd Pound Ridge NY 10576 Office: 50 Main St Suite 1000 White Plains NY 10606

KOSTYO, JOHN FRANCIS, lawyer; b. Findlay, Ohio, Feb. 9, 1955; s. Albert Robert and Mary Agnes (Welsh) K.; m. Shirley Ann Allgyre, June 9, 1984. BA in Polit. Sci. and Philosophy magna cum laude, John Carroll U., 1978; JD, Case Western Res. U., 1981. Bar: Ohio 1981, U.S. Dist. Ct. (no. dist.) Ohio 1982. Assoc. Weasel & Brimley, Findlay, 1981—; lectr. contracts and negotiable instruments Findlay Coll., 1981-84, sr. lectr. 1984—. Mem. ABA (corp., banking and bus. law div.), Ohio Bar Assn., Findlay/Hancock County Bar Assn., Ducks Unltd. (co-chmn. Findlay chpt. 1983-86, chmn. 1986—), United Conservation and Outdoor Assn. (v.p. 1986—), Alpha Sigma Nu. Republican. Roman Catholic. Club: Rockwell Springs Trout. Lodge: Elks, K.C. Avocations: sports, comml. trans., books, theater, personal computers. State civil litigation, Contracts commercial, General practice. Home: 3321 Gleneagle Dr Findlay OH 45840 Office: Weasel & Brimley 320 S Main St Findlay OH 45840

KOSUT, KENNETH PAUL, lawyer, corporation executive; b. Houston, Nov. 6, 1949; s. John Marial and Mary Angel (Garcia) K.; m. Susan Marlene Cooper, Sept. 5, 1970 (div. 1977); m. Patricia Rose Coughlin, Jan. 17, 1980 (div. May 1985). B.B.A., U. Houston, 1972; J.D., So. Tex. U., 1976. Bar: Tex. 1977, U.S. Dist. Ct. (so. dist.) Tex. 1977, U.S. Supreme Ct. 1986. Contract rep. Aramco Services & Co., Houston, 1977-78; atty. Crest Engrng. Inc., Houston, 1978-80; v.p., gen. counsel Behring Internat. Inc., Houston, 1980-85, ptnr. Cruver & Evans, 1986—. Mem. ABA, Houston Bar Assn., Tex. Bar Assn., Internat. Bar Assn., Houston World Trade Assn. (mem. maritime com.), Republican. Roman Catholic. Clubs: Houstonian, University. Private international, General corporate, Contracts commercial. Home: 3600 Jeanetta No 1405 Houston TX 77063 Office: 3 Riverway Suite 1776 Houston TX 77056

KOTLARCHUK, IHOR O. E., lawyer; b. Ukraine, July 31, 1943; came to U.S., 1946, naturalized, 1957; s. Emil and Lidia N. (Maceluch) K. BS in Fin., Fordham U., 1965; JD, 1968; LLM, Georgetown U., 1974, MA in Govt., 1982. Bar: N.Y. 1969, D.C. 1972, U.S. Ct. Mil. Appeals, U.S. Tax Ct., U.S. Supreme Ct. Trial atty. criminal sect. tax div. U.S. Dept. Justice, Washington, 1973-78, civil sect. tax div., 1978-80, fraud sect. criminal div., 1980-84, internal security sect. criminal div., 1984—; mem. U.S. Dept. Justice's Fgn. Corrupt Practices Act Rev. Com., 1980-81. Served with JAG, U.S. Army, 1969-73, now lt. col. USAR. Decorated Bronze Star. Mem. N.Y. State Bar Assn., D.C. Bar Assn., ABA, Res. Officers Assn., Phi Alpha Delta. Ukrainian Catholic. Criminal, Federal civil litigation. Address: 205 S Lee St Alexandria VA 22314

KOTLER, HELEN ROSE, lawyer; b. Pitts., Nov. 10, 1941; d. Morris and Ruth (Levin) Zasloff; m. Richard G. Kotler, June 6, 1962; children: Deborah S., Laurel E., David A. BFA, Carnegie-Mellon U., 1963; MLS, U. Pitts., 1967, JD, 1976. Bar: Pa. 1976, U.S. Dist. Ct. (we. dist.) Pa. 1976, U.S. Ct. Appeals (3d cir.) 1984, U.S. Supreme Ct. 1984. Librarian Monroeville (Pa.) Pub. Library, 1968-74; atty. Neighborhood Legal Services, Pitts., 1976-77; sole practice Pitts., 1978—. Commr. Forest Hills (Pa.) Planning Commn., 1974—; bd. dirs. Family Mediation Council, Western Pa., 1983—. Mem. Allegheny County Bar Assn. (chairperson social security com. 1983-84, legal rights of women sect. 1980-82, elected mem. judiciary com., elected mem. family law council). Democrat. Family and matrimonial, Personal injury, Labor. Home: 10 Bevington Rd Pittsburgh PA 15221 Office: 1603 Law and Finance Bldg 4th Ave Pittsburgh PA 15221

KOTLER, RICHARD LEE, lawyer; b. Los Angeles, Apr. 13, 1952; s. Allen S. Kotler and Marcella (Fromberg) Swarttz; m. Nancy Ellen Korman, Aug. 1, 1982. BA, Sonoma State Coll., 1976; JD, Southwestern U., 1979. Bar: Calif. 1980, U.S. Dist. Ct. (cen. dist.) Cal. 1980. Sole practice Newhall, Calif., 1980-83; sr. ptnr. Kotler & Hann, Newhall, 1983—. Chmn. S.C.V. Battered Womens Assn., Newhall, 1983—; bd. dirs. S.C.V. Hotline, Newhall, 1981-83, Life Animal Fund, Tojunga, Calif., 1983—. Recipient Commendation award Los Angeles County, 1983. Mem. S.C.V. Bar Assn. (v.p. 1985—), Los Angeles Astronomy Soc., Newhall Astronomy Club. Lodge: Kiwanis (interclub chmn. S.C.V. club). Avocations: astronomy, classic cars, collecting stamps, precious metals. State civil litigation, Family and matrimonial, Entertainment. Office: Kotler & Hann 23942 Lyons Ave #202 Newhall CA 91321

KOTOK, LESTER, judge; b. Bridgeton, N.J., July 5, 1949; s. Jack Benson and Jean (Lazzaroff) K.; m. Pamela Jane Stenberg, Sept. 30, 1983; children—Kimberly Rose, Matthew Benson. AA, Monmouth Coll., 1971; BA, Ft. Lauderdale U., 1973; JD, Del. Law Sch., 1976. Bar: N.J. 1977, U.S. Dist. Ct. N.J. 1977. Ins. salesman Metro. Life Ins., Ft. Lauderdale, Fla., 1971-73; pvt. detective John Lang Detective Agy., Ft. Lauderdale, 1971-73; ptnr. Kotok & Moore, P.C. and predecessor firm Kotok & Kotok, Bridgeton, N.J., 1976—; judge Bridgeton Mcpl. Ct., 1983—; atty. Sect. 8 Housing, Bridgeton, 1980-84. Mem. Alumni Assn. Boy Scouts Am., Bridgeton, 1983; solicitor for Bridgeton Housing Devel. Corp., 1980—, Hopewell Twp. Planning Bd., 1981—. Mem. N.J. Bar Assn., Fed. Bar Assn., Assn. Trial Lawyers Am., ABA, Am. Judges Assn., Delta Sigma Phi. General practice, Personal injury, General practice. Office: Kotok & Moore PC 38 N Laurel St Bridgeton NJ 08302

KOTT, DAVID RUSSELL, lawyer; b. Trenton, N.J., Jan. 22, 1952; s. Maurice G. and Ruth (Shulman) K.; m. Lauren Handler, Aug. 24, 1980; children: Emily R., Adam J. BA, Am. U., 1973; JD, Rutgers U., 1977. Bar: N.J. 1977, U.S. Dist. Ct. N.J. 1977, U.S. Ct. Appeals (3d cir.) 1980, N.Y. 1984, U.S. Dist. Ct. (so. and ea. dists.) N.Y. 1985. Law clk. to presiding justice N.J. Supreme Ct., Morristown, 1977-78; from assoc. to ptnr. McCarter & English, Newark, 1978—. Mem. ABA, N.J. Bar Assn., Essex County Bar Assn., Assn. Trial Lawyers Am., Trial Lawyers N.J. Republican. Jewish. Club: Essex (Newark). Insurance, State civil litigation, Federal civil litigation. Office: McCarter & English 550 Broad St Newark NJ 07102

KOTTAS, LEO JOSEPH, SR., magistrate, lawyer; b. Tobias, Nebr., Sept. 11, 1907; s. William James and Phillipina (Stienacher) K.; m. Mayrene King, May 5, 1971; children—Leo Joseph, Wendy, Kim, Kevin, Scott, Paul. B.A. in Geology, U. Mont., 1928, LL.B. with honors, 1931. Bar: Mont. 1931, U.S. Dist. Ct. Mont. 1932, U.S. Ct. Appeals (9th) cir. 1965. Asst., U.S. Atty.'s Office, Dept. Justice, Helena, Mont., 1931-34; assoc. W. D. Rankin, Helena, 1931-34; dep. county atty. Lewis and Clark County (Mont.), 1934-36; sole practice, Helena, 1936—; U.S. commr., 1942-71; magistrate U.S. Dist. ct. Mont., 1971-84; cons., tchr. on workings of Magistrate Ct. to field personnel U.S. Forestry Service; farmer. Recipient cert. merit Assn. Trial Lawyers Am., 1965. Mem. N. Am. Judges Assn., Phi Delta Phi. Republican. Methodist. Clubs: Elks, Eagles, Masons, Shriners. Pub. decisions on mining and pub. lands.; inventor live bait container and cover. General practice, Probate, Real property. Home: 3740 E Shore Dr Canyon Ferry Magpie Bay Helena MT 59601 Office: Suite 14 Gold Block PO Box 1713 Helena MT 59601

KOTZ, RICHARD FREDERICK, lawyer; b. Cleve., Dec. 11, 1940; s. Arthur August and Selma Phyllis (Meyers) K.; m. Debora Sara Locke, Aug. 23, 1964; children—Andrew, Kenneth, David. B.S. in Econs., U. Pa., 1962, LL.B., 1965; M.B.A., Am. U., 1969. Bar: Ohio 1965, U.S. Supreme Ct. 1968, U.S. Ct. Mil. Appeals 1968, Ill. 1969, U.S. Dist. Ct. (no. dist.) Ill. 1969. Trial atty., br. chief SEC, Washington, 1965-69; assoc. Aaron, Aaron, Schimberg & Hess, Chgo., 1969-71, ptnr., 1972-75; asst. gen. counsel, asst. sec., sec. audit com. Internat. Minerals & Chem. Corp., 1975-79; asst. gen. counsel Sears, Roebuck and Co., Chgo., 1979-82, asst. corp. gen. counsel, 1982—, asst. sec., 1984—; speaker, panel mem. seminars and symposia. Trustee Village Bd. of Glencoe (Ill.), 1978-83, mem. golf, fin. and pub. bldgs. coms., 1978-83; mem. Glencoe Village Nominating Com., 1973-77, chmn., 1976-77; chmn. pub. welfare com., transp. com., 1978-81; mem. Glencoe Sch. Bd. Nominating Com., 1973-74, dir. Friends of Glencoe Parks, 1977-78; rec. sec. Glencoe Human Relations Com., 1977-78, dir., 1974-76, 77-78; mem. exec. bd. Chgo. chpt. Am. Jewish Com., 1971—, sec., 1973-76; bd. dirs. Free St. Theater, 1977-78, Mental Health Assn. Greater Chgo., 1984—, sec. 1985— ; founder, chmn. Chgo. Alumni Group of U. Pa. Law Sch., 1978—. Mem. Chgo. Bar Assn. (chmn. securities law com. 1978-79), ABA (bd. dirs. Chgo. chpt. 1983-85), Am. Soc. Corp. Secs. (treas. 1985-86, sec. 1986-87), Am. Corp. Counsel Assn. (treas. 1985-86, sec. 1986—), U. Pa. Law Sch. Alumni Soc. (dir. 1983-85). Clubs: Glencoe Golf (dir. 1978-83); Metropolitan. Contbr. articles profl. jours. General corporate, Securities, Antitrust. Address: 330 Skokie Ln N Glencoe IL 60022

KOUSZ, CAROLYN GERTRUDE, lawyer; b. N.Y.C., Apr. 29, 1957; s. Stephen and Gertrude Carolyn (Eberle) Kousz. BS in Chemistry, Baylor U., 1978, BA in Religion History, 1979, JD, 1982. Bar: Tex. 1982. Sole practice Waco, Tex., 1982—. Mem. ABA, Assn. Trial Lawyers Am., Tex. Bar Assn., Tex. Criminal Def. Lawyers Assn. General practice, Criminal, State civil litigation. Office: 197 S Robinson Dr Waco TX 76706

KOUTOULAKOS, LOUIS, lawyer; b. Saco, Maine, Aug. 2, 1919; s. James and Pota K.; children—Mary Lou Koutoulakos Stancil, James. A.A. in Bus. Adminstrn., George Washington U., 1947, B.A. in Bus. Adminstrn., 1949, J.D. with honors, 1950. Bar: Va. 1951, D.C. 1951, U.S. Supreme Ct. 1957, U.S. Ct. Appeals D.C. 1952, U.S. Ct. Appeals (4th cir.) 1959. Asst. commonwealth atty. Va., Arlington, 1952-55; ptnr. Varoutsos & Koutoulakos, Arlington, 1953—; lectr. criminal law. Served with USN and USAAF, World War II. Fellow Am. Coll. Trial Lawyers; mem. ABA, Va. State Bar (bd. govs. criminal law sect. 1966-70), Assn. Trial Lawyers Am., Nat. Assn. Criminal Def. Lawyers, Order of Coif. Criminal, Federal civil litigation, State civil litigation. Home: 2030 N Adams St Apt 509 Arlington VA 22201 Office: 2054 N 14th St Suite 200 Arlington VA 22201

KOVACEVICH, ROBERT EUGENE, lawyer; m. Yvonne R. Stokke; children—Tawni, Mark, Phillip, Ben. Grad. St. Marins Coll., 1955; J.D., Gonzaga U., 1959; LL.M. in Taxation, NYU, 1960. Bar: Wash. 1960, U.S. Dist. Ct. (ea. and we. dists.) Wash., U.S. Ct. Appeals (9th cir.), U.S. Supreme Ct. Sole practice, Spokane, Wash., 1963-72; ptnr. Kovacevich & Algeo, Spokane, 1972-80; prin. Robert E. Kovacevich, P.S., Spokane, 1980—; speaker in field; instr. fed. taxation Sch. Bus., Gonzaga U., Spokane, 1967-84, instr. M.S. in Bus. program, 1975-84; spl. cons. on IRS, David Brinkley Spl., NBC, 1975; expert witness U.S. Senate Com. on Appropriations, 1976. Author Federal Taxation of Non-Competent Indians on Income Generated from Alloted Lands, 1981; arbitrator Spokane County Superior Ct., 1985—; fee arbitrator, 1985. Mem. steering com. Deaconess Hosp. Found. Mem. ABA, Spokane County Bar Assn. (ct. arbitrator 1985—), Wash. State Bar Assn. (local adminstrv. com. 1980-81, fee arbitrator 1984—), Estate Planning Council Spokane (past pres.), St. Martin's Coll. of Olympia (trustee 1984—). Club: Spokane. Lodge: Elks (past exalted ruler). Corporate taxation, Per-

sonal income taxation, State and local taxation. Home: S 4603 Pittsburg Spokane WA 99203 Office: 530 Lincoln Bldg Spokane WA 99201

KOVACIC, GARY ANTON, lawyer; b. Pasadena, Calif., Nov. 15, 1951; s. Anton A. and Florence A. (Lowe) K.; m. Barbara E. Appel, Sept. 15, 1974; children: Kelly, Casey. BA, UCLA, 1973; JD, Southwestern U., 1976. Bar: Calif. 1976. From assoc. to ptnr. Thorpe, Sullivan, Workman & Thorpe, Los Angeles, 1976-84; ptnr. Sullivan, Workman & Dee, Los Angeles, 1985—; lectr. condemnation law U. La Verne, 1982—; speaker inverse condemnation Am. Planning Assn. Zoning Inst., 1985. Note and comment editor Southwestern U., 1975-76. Commr. Arcadia (Calif.) Planning Commn., 1984—. Mem. ABA, Los Angeles Bar Assn. (del. state bar conf. 1985-86), Am. Planning Assn., Sierra Club, Internat. Right of Way Assn. Club: Los Angeles Town Hall. Avocations: camping, sports. Condemnation, Zoning and land use regulation, Environment. Office: Sullivan Workman & Dee 800 S Figueroa St 12th Floor Los Angeles CA 90017

KOVACIC, WILLIAM EVAN, law educator; b. Poughkeepsie, N.Y., Oct. 1, 1952; s. Evan Carl and Frances Katherine (Crow) K.; m. Kathryn Marie Fenton, May 18, 1985. AB with honors, Princeton U., 1974; JD, Columbia U., 1978. Bar: N.Y. 1979. Law clk. to sr. dist. judge U.S. Dist. Ct. Md., Balt., 1978-79; atty. planning office bur. competition FTC, Washington, 1979-82, atty. advisor to commr., 1983; assoc. Bryan, Cave, McPheeters & McRoberts, Washington, 1983-86; asst. prof. George Mason U. Sch. Law, Arlington, Va., 1986—; cons. in field; mem. U.S. Senate Judiciary Subcom. on Antitrust and Monopoly, Washington, 1975-76. Contbr. legal articles to profl. jours. Assoc. Father Ford Found. Columbia U. Cath. Campus Ministry, N.Y.C. 1985—. Harlan Fiske Stone fellow Columbia U., 1976-78. Mem. ABA (antitrust law sect.). Roman Catholic. Avocations: hiking, camping, photography. Antitrust, Government contracts and claims, Real property. Home: 1336 Constitution Ave NE Washington DC 20002 Office: George Mason U Sch Law 3401 N Fairfax Dr Arlington VA 22201

KOVACS, WILLIAM LAWRENCE, lawyer; b. Scranton, Pa., June 29, 1947; s. William Lawrence and Jane Claire (Weiss) K.; m. Mary Katherine Maras, Dec. 2, 1979; children: Katherine Elizabeth, William Lawrence III. BS magna cum laude, U. Scranton, 1969; JD, Ohio State U., 1972. Bar: Pa. 1972, D.C. 1973, U.S. Ct. Appeals (D.C. cir.) 1974, U.S. Supreme Ct. 1976, Va. 1981. Legis. asst., staff atty. Congressman Fred B. Rooney, Washington, 1972-74; chief counsel U.S. Ho. of Reps. Subcom. on Transp. and Commerce, Washington, 1975-77; assoc. Liebert, Short, FitzPatrick & Lavin, Phila., 1977-78; environ., litigation atty. Nat. Chamber Litigation Ctr., Washington, 1979; ptnr. Abrams, Kovacs, Westermeier & Goldberg, Washington, 1980-84, Kovacs & Bury, Fairfax, Va., 1984-85, Jaeckle, Fleischmann & Mugel, Washington, 1986—. Contbr. articles to profl. jours. Mem. Hazardous Waste Facilities Siting Bd., Richmond, Va., 1984-86; vice chmn., 1984-85, chmn., 1985-86. Mem. ABA (vice chmn. energy resources law com. sect. on torts and ins. practice 1981-83, chmn. 1983-84), U.S. C. of C. (mem. environ. law adv. com. 1986—). Democrat. Roman Catholic. Environment, Federal civil litigation, State civil litigation. Home: 10703 Schindel Ct Great Falls VA 22066 Office: Jaeckle Fleischmann & Mugel 2000 Pennsylvania Ave NW Washington DC 20006

KOVAL, JOSEPH PATRICK, circuit judge; b. Mt. Olive, Ill., Mar. 16, 1929; s. Michael Stephen and Anna Gertrude (Kasalko) K.; m. Rosemary Sidener Vidot, Apr. 29, 1967; children—Terri, Linda, Keith, Rhonda, George A.A., Blackburn Coll., 1950; B.A., U. Ill., 1952, LL.B., 1954. Bar: Ill. 1955. Ptnr., Kelsey & Koval, Carlinville, Ill., 1958-65; sole practice, Carlinville, 1965-76; states atty. Macoupin County, Carlinville, 1972-76; cir. judge State of Ill., Carlinville, 1976—; hearings officer Dept. Aeros., Springfield, Ill., 1961-69. Mem. Am. Judicature Soc., Ill. Judges Assn., Macoupin County Bar Assn. Democrat. Roman Catholic. Lodge: K.C. State civil litigation, Criminal, Probate. Office: Macoupin County Courthouse PO Box 39 Carlinville IL 62626

KOVAR, STUART CHARLES, lawyer; b. N.Y.C., Jan. 17, 1952; s. Philip Saul and Edith (Zuckerman) K.; m. Ellen Jane Jacobs, May 7, 1978; children: Rachel, Julie. BA, SUNY, Binghamton, 1974; JD, New Eng. Sch. Law, 1982. Bar: Mass. 1982, U.S. Dist. Ct. Mass. 1983. Atty. Law Offices of Irving Fanger, Boston, 1982-84; atty. Sprague Electric Co., Lexington, Mass., 1984-85, asst. gen. counsel, 1985—. Mem. ABA, Mass. Bar Assn. Avocations: cycling, camping, racquetball. Environment, Pension, profit-sharing, and employee benefits, General corporate. Home: 12 Proctor Rd Chelmsford MA 01824 Office: Sprague Electric Co 92 Hayden Ave Lexington MA 02173

KOVICH, DON EDMOND, lawyer; b. Harrison Twp., Pa., Aug. 11, 1953; s. Edmond Peter and Sabina (Mieszkowski) K.; m. Letitia Ayn Gwathney, Sept. 13, 1980. BA cum laude, U. Dayton, 1975, JD, 1978. Bar: Ohio 1978, U.S. Dist. Ct. (so. dist.) Ohio 1978. Assoc. Lankford & Berger, Dayton, Ohio, 1978-81; ptnr. Lankford, Klipfer & Kovich, Dayton, 1981-82, Meily, Mues & Kovich, Dayton, 1982-86, Legler, Singer & Kovich, Dayton, 1986; bd. dirs. Montgomery County Citizens Rev. Bd. Mem. ABA (tort and ins. sect.), Ohio State Bar Assn. (bd. govs. litigation sect., mem. negligence law com.), Dayton Bar Assn. (chmn. civil trial practice com. 1986-87), Greene County Bar Assn., Tau Alpha Pi, Pi Sigma Alpha. Avocations: fishing, gardening, sports. State civil litigation, Personal injury. Home: 2250 Manton Dr Miamisburg OH 45342 Office: Legler Singer and Kovich 124 E Third St Suite 100 Dayton OH 45402

KOWALOFF, STEVEN DAVID, lawyer; b. Bklyn., May 31, 1950. AB, U. Mich., 1971; M in Urban Planning, Hunter Coll., 1975; JD, Bklyn. Law Sch., 1980. Bar: N.Y. 1980, U.S. Dist. Ct. (so. and ea. dists.) N.Y. 1980. Atty. office of cousel N.Y.C. Planning Commn., 1978-80, asst. counsel, 1980-84; sole practice N.Y.C., 1984—. Author zoning advice column Real Estate Weekly. Mem. ABA, N.Y. State Bar Assn., Bklyn. Bar Assn., Assn. of Bar of City of N.Y., N.Y. County Lawyers Assn. Real property, Land use and planning. Office: 250 W 57th St New York NY 10107

KOWITT, ARTHUR JAY, lawyer; b. Chgo., Jan. 17, 1933; s. Harry and Jean (Gelfand) K.; m. Leonie Goldberg, June 16, 1957; children: Holly, Harlan, Susan. B.B.A., U. Wis., 1954; J.D., Northwestern U., 1957. Bar: Ill. 1958. Assoc. Mayer, Brown & Platt, Chgo., 1958-66, ptnr., 1966—; labor law faculty advisor Chgo.-Kent Sch. Law, 1978—. Editor: Northwestern Law Rev., 1955-57; author legal articles. Bd. dirs. Mayer Kaplan Jewish Community Ctr., Skokie, Ill., 1976-79. Mem. ABA, Decalogue Soc., Order of Coif, Phi Beta Kappa, Beta Gamma Sigma, Beta Alpha Psi, Phi Kappa Phi, Pi Lambda Phi, Tau Epsilon Rho. Home: 9448 N Drake Ave Evanston IL 60203 Office: Mayer Brown & Platt 231 S LaSalle St Chicago IL 60604

KOZAK, JOHN W., lawyer; b. Chgo., July 25, 1943; s. Walter and Stella (Palka) K.; m. Elizabeth Mathias, Feb. 3, 1968; children—Jennifer, Mary Margaret, Suzanne. B.S.E.E., U. Notre Dame, 1965; J.D., Georgetown U., 1968. Bar: Ill. 1968, D.C. 1968. Patent advisor Office of Naval Research, Corona, Calif., 1968-69; assoc. Leydig, Voit & Mayer, Ltd. (and predecessor firms), Chgo., 1969-74, ptnr., 1974—, chmn. mgmt. com., 1982—. Mem. ABA, Am. Intellectual Property Assn., Licensing Execs. Soc., Chgo. Patent Law Assn. Republican. Roman Catholic. Clubs: Law (Chgo.); Meadow (Rolling Meadows, Ill.). Patent, Federal civil litigation, Licensing. Office: Leydig Voit & Mayer One IBM Plaza Chicago IL 60611

KOZINSKI, ALEX, federal judge; b. Bucharest, Romania, July 23, 1950; came to U.S., 1962; s. Moses and Sabine (Zapler) K.; m. Marcy J. Tiffany, July 9, 1977; 1 son, Yale Tiffany. A.B. cum laude in Econs., UCLA, 1972, J.D., 1975. Bar: Calif. 1975, U.S. Ct. Appeals (9th cir.) 1978, U.S. Ct. Customs and Patent Appeals 1978, U.S. Customs Ct. 1978, D.C. 1978, U.S. Dist. Ct. (cen. dist.) Calif. 1979, U.S. Supreme Ct. 1979, U.S. Ct. Appeals (D.C. cir.) 1980, U.S. Dist. Ct. D.C. 1980, U.S. Ct. Appeals (4th cir.) 1980, U.S. Ct. Appeals (2d cir.) 1980. Law clk. to presiding justice U.S. Ct. Appeals 9th Cir., 1975-76; law clk. Chief Justice Warren E. Burger, U.S. Supreme Ct., 1976-77; assoc. Forry Golbert Singer & Gelles, Los Angeles, 1977-79, Covington & Burling, Washington, 1979-81; dep. legal counsel Office of Pres.-elect Reagan, Washington, 1980-81; asst. counsel Office of Counsel to Pres., White House, Washington, 1981; spl. counsel Merit Systems Protection Bd., PAS Ex-IV, Washington, 1981-82; chief judge U.S. Claims Ct., Washington, 1982-85; judge U.S. Court of Appeals Ninth Circuit, San Francisco, 1985—. Contbr. articles to legal jours.; mng. editor: UCLA Law Rev., 1974-75, assoc. editor, 1973-74. Calif. State scholar, 1968-72; fellow State of Calif., 1972-75. Mem. ABA, Fed. Bar Assn., Bar Assn. D.C., D.C. Bar, State Bar Calif., Order of Coif. Club: Nat. Lawyers (Washington). Federal civil litigation, Contracts commercial, Condemnation. Office: US Circuit Court PO Box 547 San Francisco CA 94101 *

KOZYRA, BARRY ALAN, lawyer; b. Rahway, N.J., Apr. 18, 1953; s. Louis John and Hilda (Booth) K.; m. Cheryl Ann Peduto, Dec. 28, 1985. BA in History with honors, U. Chgo., 1975; JD, Rutgers U., 1978. Bar: N.J. 1978, U.S. Ct. Appeals (3d cir.) 1980, N.Y. 1985, U.S. Supreme Ct. 1985. Assoc. Walder, Sondak, Berkeley & Brogan, Roseland, N.J., 1978—. Chmn. Cedar Grove (N.J.) Tenants Assn., 1980-81. Mem. ABA, N.J. Bar Assn., Essex County Bar Assn. (cert. appreciation, 1985, 86). Roman Catholic. Family and matrimonial, Federal civil litigation, Criminal. Home: 102 Marion Dr West Orange NJ 07052

KRACHT, ERIC ALAN, lawyer; b. St. Louis, Feb. 10, 1953; s. Conrad Ralph Kracht and Betty Lou (Bloom) Johnson; m. Charlotte Jacquelyn Martina, June 1, 1974; children: Jennifer Jacquelyn, Eric Martin. JD, La. State U., 1977. Bar: La. 1977, U.S. Dist. Ct. (mid. dist.) La. 1981, U.S. Dist. Ct. (ea. dist.) La. 1982, U.S. Ct. Appeals (5th cir.) 1984, U.S. Dist. Ct. (we. dist.) La. 1985, U.S. Supreme Ct. 1985. Ptnr. Wray, Robinson & Kracht, Baton Rouge, 1977—. Mem. ABA, La. Bar Assn., Baton Rouge Bar Assn. Republican. Baptist. Construction, General corporate, Personal injury. Office: Wray Robinson & Kracht 5643 Corporate Blvd Baton Rouge LA 70898

KRACKE, ROBERT RUSSELL, lawyer; b. Decatur, Ga., Feb. 27, 1938; s. Roy Rachford and Virginia Carolyn (Minter) K.; student Birmingham So. Coll.; B.A., Samford U., 1962; J.D., Cumberland Sch. Law, 1965; m. Barbara Anne Pilgrim, Dec. 18, 1965; children—Shannon Ruth, Robert Russell, Rebecca Anne, Susan Lynn. Bar: Ala. 1965, U.S. Tax Ct. 1971, U.S. Supreme Ct. 1971; individual practice law Birmingham, Ala., 1965—; ptnr. firm Kracke, Thompson & Ellis, 1980—. Mem. Jefferson County Dem. exec. com., 1972—; deacon Ind. Presbyn. Ch., Birmingham, 1973-76, pres. adult choir, 1968—, Housing Agy. Retarded Citizens; pres.-elect Ala. chpt. Nat. Voluntary Health Agys.; 1st v.p., trustee, mem. exec. bd. Birmingham Civic Opera Assn.; bd. dirs. Jefferson County Assn. Retarded Citizens; bd. dirs., founding pres. Birmingham chpt. Juvenile Diabetes Found. Served with USNR, 1955-57. Mem. Birmingham (exec. com., chmn. law library, law day 1976), Ala., Am. (award merit law day 1976) bar assns., Am. Judicature Soc., Ala. Hist. Assn., Phi Alpha Delta (pres. chpt. 1964-65), Sigma Alpha Epsilon. Democrat. Clubs: Downtown, Relay House. Lodge: Rotary (pres.-elect Shades Valley club; Paul Harris fellow). Editor, Birmingham Bar Bull., 1974—; bd. editors Ala. Lawyer, 1980-86; Contbr. articles to profl. publs. General practice, State civil litigation, Insurance. Home: 4410 Briarglen Dr Birmingham AL 35243 Office: Kracke Thompson & Ellis Lakeview Sch Bldg 808 29th St S Birmingham AL 35205

KRAEMER, JAY R., lawyer; b. St. Louis, Sept. 7, 1948; s. Jerome and Miriam J. (Lewin) K.; m. Ruth Joanne Wallerstein, Aug. 8, 1971; children: Julia, Jennifer. BA, George Washington U., 1970, JD, 1973. Bar: Md. 1973, D.C. 1974, U.S. Ct. Appeals (4th cir.) 1974, U.S. Supreme Ct. 1981, U.S. Ct. Appeals (fed. cir.) 1982. Law clk. U.S. Dist. Ct. Md., Balt., 1973-74; assoc. Fried, Frank, Harris, Shriver & Jacobson, Washington, 1974-81, ptnr., 1981—. Mem. ABA, Md. Bar Assn., D.C. Bar Assn., Internat. Nuclear Law Assn. Nuclear power, Private international, Environment. Office: Fried Frank Harris Shriver & Jacobson 1001 Pennsylvania Ave NW Washington DC 20004

KRAEMER, SANDY FREDERICK, lawyer; b. Chgo., May 10, 1937; s. Robert O. and Ruth B. (Young) K.; m. Dorothy L. Delabar, June 14, 1964; children—Christina L., Ericka L., Tyler D. B.S., Stanford U., 1960; J.D., Colo. U., 1963. Bar: Colo. 1963. Sole practice Denver, 1964; ptnr Asher & Kraemer, Colorado Springs, Colo., 1964-76; ptnr., pres. Kraemer, Kendall & Bowman, P.C., Colorado Springs, 1977—; dep. atty County of El Paso, Colo., 1976. Author: Solar Law, 1978, supplements, 1980—; contbr. articles to profl. jours.; inventor and patentee games and toys. Mem. bd. regents U. Colo., 1976—, chmn., 1982-83; mem. White House Conf. on Children and Youth, 1970. NSF grantee, 1975, German Marshall Fund grantee, 1979; named Colo. Conservationist of Yr., 1967. Mem. ABA, Colo. Bar Assn., El Paso Bar Assn., World Law Assn., World Peace Through Law (chmn. energy com. Madrid 1979, Berlin 1985, Seoul, 1987). Republican. Lutheran. Estate planning, Probate, Real property. Home: 2402 Cenesa Ln Colorado Springs CO 80909 Office: Kraemer Kendall & Bowman PC 430 N Tejon St Colorado Springs CO 80903

KRAFT, C. WILLIAM, III, lawyer; b. Upper Darby, Pa., Apr. 10, 1943; s. C. William Jr. and Frances (Mc Devit) K.; m. Christa Schuster, May 28, 1966; children: William H., Laurie R. BA, U. Pa., 1965; JD, Villanova U., 1968. Bar: Pa. 1968, U.S. Ct. Appeals (3d cir.) 1969, Colo. 1982, U.S. Ct. Appeals (10th cir.) 1983, U.S. Supreme Ct. 1985. Law clk. to presiding justice U.S. Ct. Appeals (3d cir.), Phila., 1968-69; assoc. Beasley, Hewson, Casey, Kraft & Colleran, Phila., 1969-76; ptnr. Kraft & Beebe, Media, Pa., 1976-80; assoc. gen. counsel ConRail, Phila., 1980-82; gen. counsel Burlington No. R.R., Denver, 1982-86; ptnr. Kraft & Johnson, Denver, 1987—. Bd. of editors Villanova Law Rev., 1967-68. Supr. Edgmont Twp., Pa., 1977-82. Mem. Colo. Bar Assn., Nat. Assn. R.R. Trial Counsel, Def. Research Inst. Republican. Presbyterian. Club: Lone Tree Country. Avocations: flying, fishing, hunting. Federal civil litigation, State civil litigation, General corporate. Home: 13305 S Resort Dr Conifer CO 80433 Office: Kraft & Johnson Alamo Plaza Suite 510 1401 17th St Denver CO 80202

KRAFT, HENRY R., lawyer; b. Los Angeles, Apr. 27, 1946; s. Sylvester and Freda (Schochat) K.; m. Terry Kraft, July 21, 1968; children: Diana, Kevin. BA in History, San Fernando Valley State Coll., 1968; JD, U. So. Calif., 1971. Bar: Calif. 1972, U.S. Dist. Ct. (cen. dist.) Calif. 1972, U.S. Ct. Appeals (9th cir.) 1985. Dep. pub. defender San Bernardino (Calif.) County, 1972-78; sole practice Victorville, Calif., 1979—; city atty. Victorville, 1987—; atty. City of Barstow, Calif., 1980—; instr. Victor Valley Coll., Victorville, 1986—. Atty. Barstow Community Hosp., 1980—. Mem. San Bernardino Bar Assn. (fee dispute com., jud. evaluation com.), High Desert Bar Assn. (pres., v.p., sec. 1979-81), Calif. Soc. Health Care Attys. Democrat. Jewish. Avocations: bicycling, travel, wine enthusiast. General practice, Bankruptcy. Office: 16239 Victor St Victorville CA 92397

KRAFT, MELVIN D., lawyer; b. N.Y.C., Jan. 12, 1926; s. George Kraft.; m. Katherine J. Kane, Nov. 23, 1966; children: Kathleen F., David D. BBA, Ohio State U., 1948; JD, Harvard U., 1953. Bar: Conn. 1953, N.Y. 1956, U.S. Dist. Ct. (so. dist.) N.Y. 1958, U.S. Supreme Ct. 1961. Sole practice N.Y.C., 1965-84; counsel Summit, Rovins & Feldesman, N.Y.C., 1984—; faculty chmn. P.L.I., N.Y.C., 1968—. Editor, contbr. author Using Experts in Civil Cases 2d ed., 1982. Served as cpl. U.S. Army, 1943-45. Mem. ABA, N.Y. State Bar Assn., N.Y.C. Bar Assn., Am. Arbitrators Assn. (arbitrator), Chartered Inst. Arbitrators (arbitrator). Club: Harvard (N.Y.C.). Federal civil litigation, State civil litigation, Commercial and real estate arbitration, domestic and international. Home: 169 E 69 St New York NY 10021 Office: Summit Rovins & Feldesman 445 Park Ave New York NY 10022

KRAFT, WARREN P(AUL), lawyer; b. Appleton, Wis., Feb. 12, 1952; s. Harold Charles and Gloria Antonette (Cavil) K.; m. Elizabeth Ann Detmer, June 21, 1975; 1 child, Jessica Reed. BA in Polit. Sci., U. Wis., Eau Claire, 1974; JD, Marquette U., 1982. Bar: Wis. 1982, U.S. Dist. Ct. (we. and ea. dists.) Wis. 1982, U.S. Supreme Ct. 1986. News editor Waushara Argus, Wautoma, Wis., 1974-75; city editor Daily Citizen, Beaver Dam, Wis., 1975-79; assoc. Hartman Law Office, Juneau, Wis., 1982-84; asst. atty. City of Oshkosh, Wis., 1984—. Active publicity fund raiser United Way Beaver Dam, 1975-78; pres. Resolve of Northeastern Wis. Inc., Appleton, 1986—; ruling elder 1st Presbyn. Ch., Neenah, Wis., 1985—; bd. dirs. Big Bros./Big Sisters Dodge County, Beaver Dam, 1977-79. Mem. Wis. Bar Assn., Winnebago County Bar Assn., Dodge County Bar Assn. (treas. 1983-84). Local government. Home: 1625 Villa Park Dr Oshkosh WI 54904-8271 Office: City of Oshkosh 215 Church St PO Box 1130 Oshkosh WI 54902-0113

KRAHELSKI, MICHAEL ANTHONY, lawyer. AB, UCLA, 1978, JD, 1981. Bar: Calif. 1981, U.S. Dist. Ct. (cen. dist.) Calif. 1981, U.S. Dist. Ct. (so. and ea. dists.) Calif. 1982, U.S. Ct. Claims 1984. Assoc. Manning, Leaver, Bruder & Berberich, Los Angeles, 1981-85; counsel Nissan Motor Acceptance Corp., Carson, Calif., 1985—. Mem. ABA, Phi Beta Kappa. Republican. General corporate, Consumer commercial, Bankruptcy. Office: Nissan Motor Acceptance Corp 18701 S Figueroa St Carson CA 90248-4504

KRAININ, HAROLD L., lawyer; b. N.Y.C., June 23, 1927; s. Joseph and Hedda (Winkler) K.; m. Carol Louise Hillman, Aug. 27, 1950; children—Fred, Richard, David, Daniel. B.B.S., NYU, 1949; J.D., St. John's U., 1952. Bar: N.Y. 1953, U.S. Supreme Ct. 1960. Assoc. Sidney Sugerman, N.Y.C., 1953-55; ptnr. Krainin & Ginsberg, N.Y.C., 1956-60; assoc. Hershkopf & Graham, N.Y.C., 1960-62; sole practice, N.Y.C., 1962-72, 78—; ptnr. Weingold, Berman, Wohl, Krainin & Wohl, N.Y.C., 1973, Brucker & Krainin, N.Y.C., 1974-78. Served with USN, 1945-46. Mem. ABA, N.Y. State Bar Assn., Assn. Bar City N.Y., Nassau County Bar Assn., Consular Law Soc. Democrat. Jewish. Author: Operating your Business as a Corporation, 1967. Probate, General practice, Trade Association. Office: 1370 Avenue of the Americas New York NY 10019

KRALOVEC, CHARLES VOPICKA, lawyer; b. Chgo., July 25, 1921; s. Edward V. and Elsie (Vopika) K.; m. Rosemary L. White, Sept. 15, 1951; children: Mary Elizabeth, Lynne, Karen, Charles, Amy. BA, U. Notre Dame, 1942; JD, U. Chgo., 1949. Bar: U.S. Dist. Ct. (no. dist.) Ill. 1950, U.S. Ct. Appeals (7th cir.) 1953. Assoc. Heineke and Conklin, Chgo., 1950-51; asst. U.S. atty. State of Ill., Chgo., 1951-54; assoc. Ross & O'Keefe, Chgo., 1954-58, Law Offices of James A. Dooley, Chgo., 1958-59; ptnr. Ross & Kralovec, Chgo., 1959-61, Kralovec, Marquard, Doyle & Gibbons, Chgo., 1961—. Served to lt. USN, 1942-46, PTO. Decorated Bronze Star. Fellow Am. Coll. Trial Lawyers; mem. ABA, Fed. Bar Assn., Am. Bd. Trial Advs. (adv.), Ill. Bar Assn., Chgo. Bar Assn. Roman Catholic. Club: University. State civil litigation, Insurance, Personal injury. Office: Kralovec Marquard Doyle & Gibbons 39 S LaSalle St Chicago IL 60603

KRAM, PETER, lawyer; b. Chgo., Nov. 15, 1946; s. Paul Lauer and Nancy Ellen (Dineen) K.; m. Margaret Mary Cassidy, Oct. 22, 1983. B.A., St. Louis U., 1968; M.A., U. Nev., 1972; J.D., U. Puget Sound, 1976. Bar: Wash. 1977, U.S. Dist. Ct. (we. dist.) Wash. 1977, U.S. Ct. Appeals (9th cir.) 1977. Sole practice, Tacoma, Wash., 1977-78; ptnr. Lewis, Shillito et al, Tacoma, 1978; assoc. James F. Leggett, Tacoma, 1978-82; ptnr. Leggett & Kram, Tacoma, 1983—. Trustee North End Athletic Assn., Tacoma, 1981—; mem. Charter Rev. Commn., Tacoma, 1983—. Served to capt. USAF, 1968-72. Mem. ABA, Wash. State Bar (corrections com.). Roman Catholic. Clubs: Lakewood Racquet; Tacoma Lawn and Tennis (bd. dirs. 1981). Family and matrimonial, Criminal, Personal injury. Home: 414 Tacoma Ave N Tacoma WA 98403 Office: Leggett & Kram 1901 South I St Tacoma WA 98405

KRAM, SHIRLEY WOHL, federal judge; b. N.Y.C., 1922. Student, Hunter Coll., 1940-41, CUNY, 1940-47; LL.B., Bklyn. Law Sch., 1950. Atty. Legal Aid Soc. N.Y., 1951-53, atty., 1962-71; assoc. Simons & Hardy, 1954-55; sole practice 1955-60; judge Family Ct., N.Y.C., 1971-83, U.S. Dist. Ct. N.Y., N.Y.C., 1983—. Author: (with Neil A. Frank) The Law of Child Custody, Development of the Substantive Law. Office: US District Court US Courthouse Foley Square New York NY 10007 *

KRAMARIC, PETER STEFAN, lawyer; b. Ljubljana, Yugoslavia, Apr. 29, 1930; came to U.S., 1956; s. Stefan and Ana (Vidic) K.; m. Susan R. Little, Aug. 15, 1959; 1 dau., Karen Louise. Abs. Iur., Law Sch., U. Ljubljana, 1954; LL.B., Yale U., 1960. Bar: N.Y. 1962. Internat. atty. Union Carbide Corp., N.Y.C., 1961-70; gen. counsel internat. Gen. Foods Corp., White Plains, N.Y., 1970-73; dir. office of east-west trade devel. Dept. Commerce, Washington, 1973-74; asst. gen. counsel Am. Home Products Corp., N.Y.C., 1974—, also officer various subs. Mem. ABA, N.Y. State Bar Assn., Pharm. Mfrs. Assn. (legal com.). Republican. Club: Yale (N.Y.C.). Private international, General corporate. Home: 242 Branch Brook Rd Wilton CT 06897 Office: Am Home Products Corp 685 3d Ave 24th New York NY 10017

KRAMER, ANDREW MICHAEL, lawyer; b. N.Y.C., Nov. 2, 1944; s. Irving and Ida (Kaplan) K.; m. Cheryle Lynn Safran, June 21, 1966; children—Howard, Jennifer; m. 2d, Bambi Lynne Albert, Mar. 13, 1983. B.A. cum laude, Mich. State U., 1966; J.D. cum laude, Northwestern U., 1969. Bar: Ill. 1969, D.C. 1977, U.S. Ct. Appeals (4th cir.) 1977, U.S. Ct. Appeals (5th cir.) 1972, U.S. Ct. Appeals (6th cir.) 1972, U.S. Ct. Appeals (7th cir.) 1970, U.S. Ct. Appeals (11th cir.) 1982. Assoc. firm Seyfarth, Shaw, Fairweather & Geraldson, Chgo., 1969-73, ptnr., Washington, 1974-83; ptnr. Jones, Day, Reavis & Pogue, Washington, 1983—; exec. dir. Ill. Office Collective Bargaining, Springfield, 1973-74. Mem. ABA, Chgo. Bar Assn., D.C. Bar Assn. Clubs: Congressional Country (Md.), Standard, Northmoor (Chgo.). Contbr. articles to profl. jours. Labor, Civil rights, Federal civil litigation. Office: 655 15th St NW Washington DC 20005

KRAMER, BARRY, lawyer; b. N.Y.C., Feb. 21, 1939; s. Julius and Anna (Fisher) K.; m. Judith Susan Singer, Mar. 26, 1961; children: David, Marc. B.Chem. Engrng. cum laude, Rensselaer Poly. Inst., 1961; JD cum laude, NYU, 1965. Bar: N.Y. 1966, Conn. 1970, U.S. Patent Office 1966. Patent atty. Union Carbide Corp., N.Y.C., 1961-67; chief patent and licensing counsel Goodrich-Gulf Chems., Inc., Cleve., 1967-69; ptnr. Kramer, Brufsky & Cifelli, P.C., Southport, Conn., 1969—; guest lectr. Case Western Res. Law Sch., 1967-68; mem. Nat. Panel Patent Arbitrators, 1984. Trustee, Park Ave. Temple, Bridgeport, Conn., 1980-83. Recipient Am. Jurisprudence prize, 1964, 65; Founder's Day award NYU Law Sch., 1965. Mem. ABA, Conn. Bar Assn., Am. Patent Law Assn., Conn. Patent Law Assn., Tau Beta Pi, Phi Lambda Upsilon. Editor: Intellectual Property Law Review, 1984-87; author: (with others) Patent Law Practice Forms, 1985, Trademark Law Practice Forms, 1986. Patent, Trademark and copyright, Unfair Competition. Home: 79 Meremere Dr Fairfield CT 06430 Office: 181 Old Post Rd Southport CT 06490

KRAMER, EDWARD GEORGE, lawyer; b. Cleve., July 15, 1950; s. Archibald Charles and Katherine Faith (Porter) K.; m. Roberta Darwin, June 15, 1974. BS in Edn., Kent State U., 1972; JD, Case Western Res. U., 1975. Bar: Ohio 1975, U.S. Dist. Ct. (no. dist.) Ohio 1975, U.S. Ct. Appeals (6th cir.) 1980, U.S. Supreme Ct. 1980. Assoc. dir. The Cuyahoga Plan of Ohio, Cleve., 1975-76; exec. dir. The Housing Advs., Inc., Cleve., 1976—; sr. ptnr. Kramer & Tobocman, LPA, Cleve., 1981—; spl. counsel atty. gen. State of Ohio, Columbus, 1983—; alt. consumer rep. FTC, Washington, 1976-77; cons. HUD, Washington, 1978-80, joint select. com. sch. desegregation, Ohio Gen. Assembly, Columbus, 1979; mem. vis. com. Case Western Res. U. Sch. Law, Cleve., 1977-83. Author: (with others) A Guide to Regional Housing Opportunities, 1979, (with Buchanan) Mobile Home Living: A Guide to Consumers' Rights, 1979. Chmn. Ohio Protection and Advocacy System for develepmentally disabled, Columbus, 1978-80; trustee Muscle Disease Soc., Cleve., 1979-81; sec. Cuyahoga County Housing and Econ. Devel. com., Cleve., 1983—; mem. Cleve. Mayor's Com. on Employment of the Handicapped, 1978-79. Named Disting. Recent Grad. Case Western Reserve U. Law Alumni Assn., 1985. Mem. ABA, Cleve. Bar Assn., Fed. Bar Assn., Nat. Audubon Soc., Citizens League, Plantiffs Employment Lawyers Assn., Practicing Law Inst. (assoc.), Wilderness Soc. Democrat. Mem. United Ch. Christ. Club: Cleve. Athletic. Lodge: Masons. Avocations: softball, scuba diving, collecting coins and stamps, chess, reading. Civil rights, Landlord-tenant, Federal civil litigation. Office: Kramer & Tobocman 526 Superior 240 Leader Bldg Cleveland OH 44114

KRAMER, FRANKLIN DAVID, lawyer; b. Liberty, N.Y., Nov. 13, 1945; s. Solomon and Carolyn Bertha (Cohen) C.; m. Noël Anketell, May 30, 1970; children: Katherine Anketell, Christopher Anketell. BA, Yale U., 1967; JD, Harvard U., 1971. Bar: N.Y. 1972, D.C. 1972, Supreme 1976. Law clk. to presiding justice U.S. Ct. Appeals (2d cir.), N.Y.C., 1971-72; assoc. Shea & Gardner, Washington, 1972-77, ptnr., 1982—; spl. asst. to asst. sec. def. Dept. Def., Washington, 1977-79, prin. dep. asst. to asst. sec. def. for internat. security affairs, 1979-81. Contbr. articles to profl. jours. Mem. ABA (chmn. com. on arms control and disarmament 1984-86), Internat. Inst. Strategic Studies, Am. Arbitration Assn. (comml. arbitrator). Democrat. Jewish. Banking, General corporate, Private international. Home: 3049

Ordway St NW Washington DC 20008 Office: Shea & Gardner 1800 Massachusetts Ave NW Washington DC 20036

KRAMER, GILDA LEA, lawyer; b. N.Y.C., July 16, 1954; d. William W. and Sylvia (Steinberg) K. BA, Swarthmore Coll., 1976; JD, U. Va., 1979. Bar: D.C. 1979, U.S. Dist. Ct. (D.C. dist.) 1980, D.C. Circuit Ct. 1980; Pa. 1982, Pa. Circuit Ct. (3d cir.) 1982, U.S. Dist. Ct. (ea. dist.) Pa. 1982. Assoc. Pepper Hamilton & Scheetz, Washington, 1979-81; asst. city solicitor City of Phila., 1981-83, dep. city solicitor, 1983-84; assoc. Schnader, Harrison, Segal & Lewis, Phila., 1984—. Mem. ABA, Phila. Bar Assn. Democrat. Jewish. State civil litigation, Federal civil litigation, Local government. Home: 1520 Spruce St #308 Philadelphia PA 19102 Office: Schnader Harrison Segal & Lewis 1600 Market St Suite 3600 Philadelphia PA 19103

KRAMER, KENNETH SCOTT, lawyer; b. Troy, N.Y., Nov. 7, 1957; s. David W. (stepfather) and Judith (Fell) Bernstein. BA, U. Pa., 1979; JD, U. So. Calif., 1982. Bar: Calif. 1982, N.Y. 1984. Assoc. Finley, Kumble, Wagner et al, Beverly Hills and Newport Beach, Calif., 1982-86, Pettit & Martin, Los Angeles and Costa Mesa, 1986—; asst. sec. Pacific Basin Restaurant Concepts Inc., Los Angeles, 1985—; lectr. Continuing Edn. of Bar, Calif., 1986—. Campaign organizer Citizens Against Proposition F, Beverly Hills, 1984. Named one of Outstanding Young Men of Am., 1983. Mem. ABA. Real property, Landlord-tenant, Construction. Office: Pettit & Martin 3200 Park Ctr Suite 1110 Costa Mesa CA 92626 also: 355 S Grand Ave Los Angeles CA 90071

KRAMER, KENNETH STEPHEN, lawyer; b. Washington, Oct. 5, 1941; m. Audrey Carol Reich, June 13, 1965; children—Beth, Ellen, Aaron. B.S. with high honors, U. Wis.-Madison, 1963; J.D. cum laude, Harvard U., 1966; postgrad. in law George Washington U., 1967-68. Bar: D.C. 1967, U.S. Ct. Claims 1967, U.S. Ct. Appeals (D.C. cir.) 1967, U.S. Ct. Appeals (fed. cir.) 1982, U.S. Supreme Ct. 1976. Law clk. to chief judge U.S. Ct. Claims, Washington, 1966-67; assoc. Fried, Frank, Harris, Shriver & Jacobson, Washington, 1970-75, ptnr., 1975—; editorial cons. Fed. Contracts Report, Washington, 1968-74. Served as capt. JAGC, U.S. Army, 1967-70. Mem. ABA. Republican. Jewish. Government contracts and claims. Office: 1001 Pennsylvania Ave NW Suite 800 Washington DC 20004

KRAMER, LEROY, III, lawyer; b. Chgo., Apr. 10, 1948; s. LeRoy Jr. and Elizabeth (Gillespie) K.; m. Andrea Osgood, May 30, 1970; children: Nathaniel C., Adam O. Student, Am. U., 1968-69; BA, Olivet Coll., 1970; JD, U. Detroit, 1976. Bar: Mich. 1976, U.S. Dist. Ct. (ea. dist.) Mich. 1976, U.S. Dist. Ct. (we. dist.) Mich. 1977, U.S. Ct. Appeals (6th cir.) 1978. Staff atty. U. Detroit Sch. of Law, 1976-77, Mich. Mut. Ins. Co., Grand Rapids, 1977-79; ptnr. Post, McMullen & Kramer, Grand Rapids, 1979-83; assoc. Twohey, Maggini, Muldoon, Mudie & Sullivan, Grand Rapids, 1984—; pres. Mich. Environ. Protection Found., 1983—. Contbr. articles to profl. jours. Commr. Library Com., East Grand Rapids, 1984. Mem. Mich. Bar Assn., U.S. Maritime Law Assn., Grand Rapids Bar Assn., West Mich. Marine Assn. (v.p. 1985-86, pres. 1986—), U.S. Yacht Racing Union (legal com.), Sierra (bd. dirs. Mich. chpt. 1981-82). Club: Grand Rapids (Mich.) Yacht. Avocation: boating. Admiralty, Immigration, naturalization, and customs, Federal civil litigation. Office: Twohey Maggini Muldoon Mudie & Sullivan 211 K Waters Bldg Grand Rapids MI 49503

KRAMER, MARTIN, lawyer; b. N.Y.C., Mar. 29, 1932. BS in Econs., U. Pa., 1953; JD, Harvard U., 1956. Bar: N.Y. 1956, U.S. Dist. Ct. (so. and no. dists.) N.Y. 1959, U.S. Tax. Ct. 1974, Fla. 1980, U.S. Supreme Ct. 1982. Ptnr. Wallman & Kramer, N.Y.C.; adj. prof. law, lectr. estates and trusts and in contract law NYU, 1975—, Manhattanville Coll., 1976-77, Iona Grad. Sch. of Bus. Adminstrn., 1979—; lectr. fed. taxation NYU, 1980, Hartford Tax Inst., 1983. Author: Estate Planning for the Troubled Marriage: Estate Planning for Living Together, 1983. Mem. com. City of New Rochelle, 1969—; del. to jud. convention N.Y. County, 1966-68; candidate to Westchester County Legis., 1973; bd. dirs. Beth El Synagogue, New Rochelle, 1972-76; commr. bd. of assessment rev. City of New Rochelle, 1974-82, chmn., 1977--82; trustee Bleuler Psychotherapy Ctr., Jamaica, N.Y., 1976—; mem. taxation and estate planning adv. com. NYU, 1978-80; commr. Westchester County Traffic Safety Commn., 1981—. Fellow Am. Coll. Probate Counsel; mem. ABA (co-chmn. subcom. on the role, function and liabilities of the estate lawyer, real property, probate and trust law sect.), N.Y. State Bar Assn. (trust and estate sect.), Westchester County Bar Assn. (trust and estate sect.), Assn. of Bar of City of N.Y. (housing and urban devel. com. 1967-70, corp. law com. 1972-74), New Rochelle Bar Assn. (trustee 1978-84), N.Y. State Trial Lawyers Assn. Office: Wallman & Kramer 275 Madison Ave New York NY 10016

KRAMER, MORRIS JOSEPH, lawyer; b. Bklyn., Nov. 18, 1941; s. William J. and Sylvia (Hameroff) K.; m. Linda Garshman, Feb. 11, 1967 (div. 1976); 1 child, Jeremy; m. Nancy Goldstein, Feb. 28, 1978; 1 child, Oliver. A.B., Dartmouth Coll., 1963; LL.B. Harvard U., 1966. Bar: N.Y. 1966, U.S. Ct. Appeals (2d cir.) 1966, U.S. Dist Ct. (so. dist.) N.Y. 1966, U.S. Dist. Ct. (ea. dist.) N.Y. 1966. Asst. counsel Temporary State Commn. Constl. Conv., N.Y.C., 1966-67; assoc. Cahill, Gordon and Reindel, N.Y.C., 1966-72; assoc. Skadden Arps et al, N.Y.C., 1972-75, ptnr. 1975—. Securities, General corporate. Home: 47 E 88th St New York NY 10128 Office: Skadden Arps Slate Meagher and Flom 919 3d Ave New York NY 10022

KRAMER, NOËL ANKETELL, judge; b. Bay City, Mich., Nov. 22, 1945; d. Thomas Jackson and Ruth Genevieve (LeRoux) Anketell; m. Franklin D. Kramer, May 30, 1970; children: Katherine, Christopher. BA with honors, Vassar Coll., 1967; JD with honors, U. Mich., 1971. Bar: D.C. 1972, U.S. Supreme Ct. 1975. Assoc. Wilmer, Cutler & Pickering, Washington, 1971-76; asst. U.S. atty. U.S. Atty. Office, Washington, 1976-84; judge D.C. Superior Ct., Washington, 1984—. Mem. ABA., Nat. Assn. Women Judges, Women's Bar Assn. D.C., D.C. Bar (chair person cts., lawyers and adminstrn. justice div. 1982-84), U. Mich. Law Club Washington (pres. 1976-78). Federal civil litigation, State civil litigation. Office: Superior Ct Dist DC 500 Indiana Ave NW Washington DC 20001

KRAMER, PAUL R., lawyer; b. Balt., June 6, 1936; s. Phillip and Lee (Labovitz) K.; m. Janet Amitin, Sept. 1, 1957; children—Jayne, Susan, Nancy. B.A., Am. U., 1959, J.D., 1961. Bar: Md. 1961, D.C. 1962, U.S. Supreme Ct. 1965. Staff atty., dep. dir. Legal Aid Agy., D.C. Fed. Pub. Defender's Office, Washington, 1962-63; asst. U.S. Atty. Dist. Md., 1963-69; dep. U.S. atty. Md., Balt., 1969-83; exec. bd. Balt. Area council Boy Scouts Am., 1970-83, adv. counsel to exec. bd., 1983—; instr. U. Md. Sch. Law, 1975-80; assoc. prof. law Villa Julie Coll., 1976-80; assoc. professorial lectr. George Washington U., 1979; instr. Nat. Coll. Dist. Attys., 1979. Exec. bd. Balt. Area council Boy Scouts Am., 1975-82. Mem. ABA, Fed. Bar Assn. (permanent mem. 4th cir. fed. jud. conf., pres. Balt. chpt. 1973-74, nat. dep. sec. 1985—, nat. sec. 1982-83, nat. cir. v.p. 1973-81, chmn. nat. cir. v.p. 1978-80, 85—, mem. nat. council fed. bar 1973—, faculty Fed. Practice Inst. 1981—), Md. Bar Assn., Balt. Bar Assn., Md. Criminal Def. Attys. Assn., Nat. Assn. Criminal Trial Attys., Md. Trial Lawyers Assn. Republican. Jewish. Club: Masons (past master). Criminal, Federal civil litigation, State civil litigation. Home: 6804 Hunt Ct Baltimore MD 21209 Office: 231 St Paul Pl Baltimore MD 21202

KRAMER, RUSSELL ARNOLD, lawyer; b. Maryville, Tenn., Dec. 13, 1918; s. Russell Reed and Alice Gray (Arnold) K.; m. Sara Lee Hellums, Mar. 8, 1942; children: John Reed, Sara Lynne, Randall A. B.A., Maryville Coll., 1940; postgrad., U. Tex., 1941; J.D., U. Mich., 1946. Bar: Tenn. 1942, Pa. 1975. Ptnr. Kramer, Johnson, Rayson, McVeigh & Leake, Knoxville, Tenn., 1947-74; of counsel Kramer, Johnson, Rayson, McVeigh & Leke, Knoxville, Tenn., 1984—; exec. v.p., dir., gen. counsel Aluminum Co. Am., Pitts., 1974-83. Served to capt. USAAF, 1942-46. Mem. ABA, Pa. Bar Assn., Tenn. Bar Assn., Knoxville Bar Assn., Am. Judicature Soc. (chmn. 1983). Methodist. General corporate. Home: 2201 Woodmere DR Knoxville TN 37920 Office: United Plaza Knoxville TN 37901

KRAMER, STEVEN EMERT, lawyer; b. Ann Arbor, Mich., May 19, 1954; s. Roy Foster and Sara Jo (Emert) K.; m. Christine Marie Moeggenberg, June 10, 1978; children: Jacob, Mattie. BA, Miami U., 1976; MBA, U. Southwestern La., 1979; JD, U. Tenn., 1981. Bar: Tenn. 1982, U.S. Dist. Ct. (ea. dist.) Tenn. 1982, U.S. Ct. Appeals (6th cir.) 1982. Ptnr. Hunter, Smith & Davis, Kingsport, Tenn., 1981—; bd. dirs. Meals on Wheels, Kingsport, Kingsport Grocery Co. Mem. ABA, Tenn. Bar Assn., Tenn. Mfg. Assn. (labor law adv. council), Kingsport C. of C. Roman Catholic. Avocations: backpacking, fishing, skiing, recreational sports. Labor, Entertainment, General corporate. Home: 718 Yadkin St Kingsport TN 37660 Office: Hunter Smith & Davis 1212 N Eastman Rd Kingsport TN 37664

KRAMER, WILLIAM DAVID, lawyer; b. Anniston, Ala., Feb. 2, 1944; s. John Robert and Janice Marian (Dye) K.; m. Johanna Scalzi, Dec. 1, 1973; children: Elizabeth Annemarie, David MacLaren. Student, Case Western Res. U., 1959-60; AB in Govt. with honors magna cum laude, Oberlin Coll., 1965; JD, M in Pub. Adminstrn., Harvard U., 1969. Bar: Mass. 1969, D.C. 1973, U.S. Ct. Appeals (D.C. cir.) 1974, U.S. Dist. Ct. D.C. 1976, U.S. Ct. Appeals (10th cir.) 1978, U.S. Ct. Internat. Trade 1983, U.S. Ct. Appeals (fed. cir.) 1983. Assoc. dir. Gov.'s Com. on Law Enforcement and Adminstrn. Criminal Justice, Boston, 1969-71, dep. dir., 1971-73; assoc. Squire, Sanders & Dempsey, Washington, 1973-79, ptnr., 1979—; mem. internat. law sect. D.C. Bar. Mem. Phi Beta Kappa. Private international, Administrative and regulatory, Banking. Office: Squire Sanders & Dempsey 1201 Pennsylvania Ave NW Washington DC 20004

KRAMER, WILLIAM JOSEPH, lawyer; b. Rockville Centre, N.Y., Mar. 21, 1939; s. John Conrad and Margaret Ann (Kenny) K.; m. Mary Lynore Whitney, Jan. 21, 1961; children—Elizabeth W., Joanne M., Lynore M., William L., Matthew C. B.S., Fairfield U., 1960; LL.B., Fordham U., 1963. Bar: N.Y. 1963, D.C. 1976. Assoc. Mudge Rose Guthrie Alexander & Ferdon and predecessor firms, N.Y.C., 1963, 1966-68, 69-74; ptnr. Mudge Rose Guthrie & Alexander and predecessor firms, N.Y.C., 1974—; asst. gen. counsel Avis Rent-A-Car Systems, Garden City, N.Y., 1969; counsel Zoning Bd. Appeals, Village of Massapequa Park, N.Y., 1969-70. Mem. St. Joseph's Sch. Bd., Garden City, 1973-76; mem. pres.'s adv. com. Fairfield U., 1978-79, trustee, 1982—, vice chmn., bd. trustees, 1985—; exec. bd. Univ. Fellows, 1979-81; mem. Archtl. Bd. Rev., Garden City, 1980-87. Served with USMC, 1963-66. Mem. ABA, N.Y. State Bar Assn., D.C. Bar Assn. Republican. Roman Catholic. Clubs: Garden City Golf (bd. govs.), Cherry Valley Country, Down Town Assn., Lawrence Beach. Estate taxation, Estate planning, Probate. Home: 15 Kensington Rd Garden City NY 11530 Office: Mudge Rose Guthrie et al 180 Maiden Lane New York NY 10038

KRAMPF, JOHN EDWARD, lawyer; b. Glens Falls, N.Y., Sept. 11, 1947; s. Charles Edward and Judith Carolyn (Strempel) K.; 1 child, Alison Seelye; m. Christine Ellen Bancheri, May 2, 1981. BA, Duke U., 1969; JD, U. Pa., 1972. Bar: Pa. 1972, U.S. Dist. Ct. N.J., U.S. Dist. Ct. (ea., we. and mid. dists.) Pa., U.S. Dist. Ct. (mid. dist.) Tenn. Assoc. Morgan, Lewis & Bockius, Phila., 1972-79, ptnr., 1979—. Editor: Employer's Guide to Pennsylvania Labor Laws and Regulations, 1985, Employer's Guide to N.J. Labor Laws and Regulations, 1986. Bd. dirs. Gilpin Hall Residential Care Facility, Wilmington, Del., 1978—, Senior Employment and Edn. Service, Phila., 1985—. Mem. ABA, Pa. Bar Assn., Phila. Bar Assn., Mfrs. Assn. Del. Valley (legal counsel 1985—). Labor, Pension, profit-sharing, and employee benefits, Civil rights. Office: Morgan Lewis & Bockius 2000 One Logan Sq Philadelphia PA 19103

KRANE, STEVEN CHARLES, lawyer; b. Far Rockaway, N.Y., Jan. 20, 1957; s. Harry and Gloria (Christle) K.; m. Faryda Ondine Alibey, Oct. 1, 1983. BA, SUNY, Stony Brook, 1978; JD, NYU, 1981. Bar: N.Y. 1982, U.S. Dist. Ct. (so. and ea. dists.) N.Y. 1982, U.S. Ct. Appeals (2d cir.) 1987, U.S. Supreme Ct. 1987. Assoc. Proskauer Rose Goetz & Mendelsohn, N.Y.C., 1981-84, 85—; law clk. to assoc. judge N.Y. Ct. Appeals, N.Y.C. and Albany, 1984-85. Securities Inst. NYU fellow, 1980-81; recipient Vol. Counsel award Legal Aid Soc., 1984. Mem. N.Y. State Bar Assn. (com. on cts. of appellate jurisdiction), Assn. of Bar of City of N.Y. (sec. com. on profl. and jud. ethics, com. on profl. responsibility), Phi Beta Kappa, Pi Sigma Alpha. Republican. Avocations: opera, Boston Red Sox baseball, ice hockey, golden retrievers. Federal civil litigation, Securities, Antitrust. Office: Proskauer Rose Goetz & Mendelsohn 300 Park Ave New York NY 10022

KRANITZ, THEODORE MITCHELL, lawyer; b. St. Joseph, Mo., May 27, 1922; s. Louis and Miriam (Saferstein) K.; m. Elaine Shirley Kaufman, June 11, 1944; children—Hugh David, Karen Gail and Kathy Jane (twins). Student, St. Joseph Jr. Coll., 1940-41; B.S. in Fgn. Service, Georgetown U., 1948, J.D., 1950. Bar: Mo. 1950, U.S. Supreme Ct. 1955. Ptnr. Kranitz & Kranitz, PC, St. Joseph, 1950—. Author articles in field. Active Boy Scouts Am.; pres. St. Joseph Community Theatre, Inc., 1958-60; bd. dirs. United Jewish Fund of St. Joseph, 1957—, pres., 1958-63; sec. Boys' Baseball St. Joseph, 1964-68; trustee Temple Adath Joseph, 1970-74, 77-80; bd. dirs. B'nai Sholem Temple, 1976—, Lyric Opera Guild of Kansas City, 1980—. Served from pvt. to 1st lt. USAAF, 1942-46; capt. USAFR (ret.). Fellow Am. Acad. Matrimonial Lawyers; mem. ABA, St. Joseph Bar Assn. (pres. 1977-78), Mo. Bar, Assn. Trial Lawyers Am., Nat. Assn. Criminal Def. Lawyers, Am. Legion, Air Force Assn., Res. Officers Assn. Lodge: B'nai B'rith (dist. bd. govs. 1958-61). State civil litigation, General corporate, Family and matrimonial. Home: 2609 Gene Field Rd Saint Joseph MO 64506 Office: Kranitz & Kranitz PC Boder Bldg 107 S 4th St Saint Joseph MO 64501

KRASNEY, REGINALD ALAN, lawyer; b. Richmond, Va., Jan. 26, 1950; s. Harvey M. and Uleanor L. (Uson) K.; m. Helene Nora Saltzman, Mar. 26, 1972; children: Benjamin, Brian. BA, Yale U., 1972; JD, Villanova U., 1977. Bar: Pa. 1977, D.C. 1978. Assoc. Pepper, Hamilton & Scheets, Phila., 1977-81, Blank, Rome, Comisky & McCauley, Phila., 1981-85, Sherr, Moses & Zuckerman, P.C., Norristown, Pa., 1985-86; sole practice Wayne, Pa., 1986—. Mem. ABA, D.C. Bar Assn., Pa. Bar Assn., Phila. Bar Assn., Montgomery County Bar Assn. Jewish. Avocations: tennis, fishing, gardening. Corporate taxation, Probate, General corporate. Office: 150 E Swedesford Rd Suite 104 Wayne PA 19087

KRASNOO, JAMES B., lawyer, educator; b. Boston, June 6, 1940; s. Carl and Ethel Harriet (Bennett) K.; m. Joan Virginia Birnbaum, July 23, 1972; children: Ethan Michael, Paul Adam. AB, Harvard U., 1961; JD, U. Chgo., 1964; postdoctoral, San Francisco State U., 1964-65; MA, Northeastern U., 1966. Bar: Mass. 1964, U.S. Dist. Ct. Mass 1964, Calif. 1965, U.S. Dist. Ct. (no. dist.) Calif. 1965, U.S. Ct. Appeals (1st and 9th cirs.) 1965, U.S. Supreme Ct. 1968., U.S. Ct. Appeals (D.C. cir.) 1985. legal asst. Commonwealth of Mass.; from asst. atty. to atty. gen. Commonwealth of Mass., Boston, 1965-68; assoc. Lyne, Woodworth & Evarts, Boston, 1968-69; asst. U.S. atty. U.S. Atty.'s Office, Boston, 1969-73; assoc. Swartz & Swartz, Boston, 1973-74; ptnr. Norris, Kozodoy, Krasnoo & Fong, Boston, 1974—; lectr. law Boston U. 1972-83, Northeastern U., Boston, 1983—. Mem. ABA, Fed. Bar Assn. (pres. Boston chpt. 1981-82), Mass. Bar Assn., Mass. Trial Lawyers Assn. Lodge: B'nai B'rith (pres. Joseph Koffman Lodge 1985—). Federal civil litigation, State civil litigation, Criminal. Home: 14 Candlewood Dr Andover MA 01810 Office: Norris Kozodoy Krasnoo & Fong 66 Canal St Boston MA 02114

KRASNOW, ERWIN GILBERT, lawyer; b. Bklyn., Jan. 8, 1936; s. Charles and Etta (Simowitz) K.; m. E. Judith Levine, Sept. 6, 1960; children—Michael Andrew, Catherine Beth. A.B. summa cum laude, Boston U., 1958; J.D., Harvard U., 1961; LL.M., Georgetown U., 1965. Bar: Mass. 1961, D.C. 1963, U.S. Dist. Ct. Mass. 1961, U.S. Ct. Appeals (D.C. cir.) 1963, U.S. Ct. Appeals (4th cir.) 1978, U.S. Ct. Appeals (5th cir.) 1982, U.S. Ct. Appeals (11th cir.) 1982, U.S. Supreme Ct. 1965. Research asst. Law Sch. Harvard U., Cambridge, Mass., 1961; adminstrv. asst. to Congressman Torbert H. Macdonald, U.S. Ho. of Reps., Washington, 1962-64; ptnr. Kirkland and Ellis, Washington, 1964-76; sr. v.p. and gen. counsel Nat. Assn. Broadcasters, Washington, 1976-84; ptnr. Verner, Liipfert, Bernhard, McPherson & Hand, Washington, 1984—; vis. prof. Ohio State U., 1974; disting. vis. lectr. Temple U., 1976; adj. prof. Am. U., 1975, Law Ctr. Georgetown U., 1984; professorial lectr. Grad. Sch. Arts and Scis. George Washington U., 1982, 83, Sch. Law Cath. U. Am., 1982; bd. dirs. Broadcast Capital Fund, Inc. (formerly Minority Broadcast Investment Fund), 1978—, treas., 1979—; govt. industry adv. council Ctr. for Telecommunications Studies, George Washington U., 1980-84; adv. bd. Inst. for Communications Law, Sch. Law, Cath. U. Am., 1982—; bd. advisors Communications Media Ctr., N.Y. Law Sch., 1982—; adv. com. UCLA Communications Law Program, 1983—. Co-author: The Politics of Broadcast Regulation, 1973, 2d edit. 1978, 3d edit. 1982; co-author: A Candidate's Guide to the Law of Political Broadcasting, 1977, 2d edit. 1980, 3d edit. 1984; Buying and Building a Broadcast Station: Everything You Want—and Need to Know, But Didn't Know Who to Ask, 1982; Political Broadcasting Flipchart: A Legal Guide for Broadcasters, Candidates and Advertising Agencies, 1982, 2d edit. 1984; editor: National Association of Broadcasters Legal Guide to FCC Broadcast Rules, Regulations and Policies, 1977; contbr. articles, writings to publs. in field; bd. editors Fed. Communications Bar Jour., 1973-75; editorial adv. bd. Jour. of Broadcasting, 1972—, Telematics and Informatics, 1982—; adv. com. COMM/ENT Law Jour., 1983—. Mem. ABA (vice chmn. agy. adjudication com. 1974-77, chmn. communications law com. administrv. law sect. 1980-81), Fed. Bar Assn. (pres. Capitol Hill chpt. 1963-64, dep. co-chmn. communications law com. 1967-69, co-chmn., 1970-71), Fed. Communications Bar Assn. (exec. com. 1976-79, 84—, treas. 1984—), Capitol Hill Bar Assn. (past pres.), Boston U. Alumni Club Washington (pres. 1967-70), Boston U. Nat. Alumni Assn. (bd. dirs. 1966-68, regional v.p. 1971, 73), Phi Beta Kappa. Administrative and regulatory. Home: 5604 Surrey St Chevy Chase MD 20815 Office: Verner Liipfert Bernhard et al 1660 L St NW Washington DC 20036

KRASNOW, JEFFREY HARRY, lawyer; b. San Francisco, Oct. 7, 1946; s. Clement K. and Winifred (Spandorfer) K.; m. Rita Jane Moore, Mar. 23, 1969; children: Mark Samuel, Daniel Edward. BA, Old Dominion U., 1969; JD, U. Va., 1972. Bar: Va. 1972, U.S. Dist. Ct. (ea. and we. dists.) Va., U.S. Ct. Appeals (4th, 5th and 6th cirs.), U.S. Supreme Ct. Assoc. Frank N. Perkinson Jr. Esq., Roanoke, Va., 1972-74; ptnr. Perkinson, Krasnow and Perkinson, Roanoke, 1974-77; sole practice Roanoke, 1977-82; sr. ptnr. Jeffrey H. Krasnow Esq., Roanoke, 1982-86, Jeffrey H. Krasnow & Assocs., Roanoke, 1987—. Mem. ABA, Assn. Trial Lawyers Am., Va. Trial Lawyers Assn., Comml. Law League, Roanoke Bar Assn. Personal injury, Criminal, State civil litigation. Office: 301 W Campbell Ave Roanoke VA 24011

KRASNOW, ROBERT LOUIS, lawyer; b. N.Y.C., Sept. 27, 1945; s. Bernard S. Krasnow and Lee Esther (Wagner) Stein; m. Helen I. Rubin, June 22, 1968; children: Brian Michael, Barbara Suzanne. AB, U. Rochester, 1967; JD, Bklyn. Sch. Law, 1972. Bar: N.Y. 1973, U.S. Dist. Ct. (so. and ea. dists.) N.Y. 1973, U.S. Supreme Ct. 1978, U.S. Ct. Appeals (2d cir.) 1979. Assoc. Lippman and Susswein, N.Y.C., 1972-75; ptnr. Gold and Lippman, N.Y.C., 1975-78; v.p. Lippman and Krasnow PC, N.Y.C., 1979—. Mem. ABA, N.Y. State Bar Assn., Westchester Bar Assn., Real Estate Tax Rev. Bar Assn. Avocations: wine collecting, skiing, tennis, theater, dining. Real property taxes, assessment proceedings, abatements and exemptions, Real property, General corporate. Office: Lippman and Krasnow PC 475 5th Ave New York NY 10017

KRASNOW, WILLARD, lawyer; b. Boston, Nov. 10, 1945; s. Louis and Edna (Halpern) K.; m. Marcia Lee Kauffman, June 15, 1969. BA, Boston U., 1967, JD, 1970. Bar: Mass. 1970, U.S. Dist. Ct. Mass. 1971, U.S. Ct. Appeals (1st cir.) 1978. Law clk. to justice R.I. Supreme Ct., Providence, 1970-71; assoc. Barron & Stadfeld, Boston, 1971-72; atty. Raytheon Co., Lexington, Mass., 1972-74; asst. indsl. relations counsel Raytheon Co., Lexington, 1974—; instr. employment law Northeastern U., Boston, 1984—. Rep. Town Meeting, Norwood, Mass., 1973-76, 79—; assoc. mem. Zoning Bd. of Appeals, Norwood, 1984—. Mem. ABA (fed. labor standards legis. com., labor law publs.), Norwood Jaycees (pres. 1977-78), Order of Coif. Avocations: tennis, basketball, politics, religious studies. Labor. Home: PO Box 841 Norwood MA 02062 Office: Raytheon Co 141 Spring St Lexington MA 02173

KRASS, MARC STERN, lawyer; b. Detroit, June 23, 1949; s. Marvin David and Ruth B. (Stern) K.; m. Jan Weintraub, Jan. 30, 1971; children: Jonathan, Matthew. AB, Oberlin Coll., 1970; postgrad., U. Pitts., 1970-71; JD cum laude, Northwestern U., 1976. Bar: Ill. 1976, U.S. Dist. Ct. (no. dist.) Ill. 1976, U.S. Dist. Ct. (we. dist.) Tex. 1980, Ohio 1981, U.S. Dist. Ct. (so. dist.) Ohio 1982. Assoc. Seyfarth, Shaw, Fairweather & Geraldson, Chgo., 1976-80; sr. counsel Procter & Gamble Co., Cin., 1980—. Bd. dirs. United Home Care, Inc., Cin., 1983—. Mem. Cin. Bar Assn. Labor, Civil rights. Home: 4407 Chesswick Dr Cincinnati OH 45242 Office: Procter & Gamble Co One Procter & Gamble Plaza Cincinnati OH 45202

KRATHEN, DAVID HOWARD, lawyer; b. Phila., Nov. 17, 1946; s. Morris S. and Lillian E. K.; m. Francine Ellen, Oct. 21, 1973; children: Richard, Stefanie, Michael. BBA, U. Miami, Fla., 1969, JD, 1972. Bar: Fla. 1972, D.C. 1972, N.Y. 1984, U.S. Supreme Ct. 1976. Atty. advisor ICC, Washington, 1972-73; asst. pub. defender 17th Jud. Cir., Ft. Lauderdale, Fla., 1973-74; ptnr. Glass, Krathen, Rastatter, Stark & Tarlowe, Ft. Lauderdale, 1974-78, Krathen & Sperry, P.A., Ft. Lauderdale, 1978-84, David H. Krathen, P.A., 1984—; mem. Fla. Bar Grievance Com. 17 C, 1982-85, vice chmn., 1985; mem. Jud. Adminstrn., Selection and Tenure Com., 1982-85, 4th Dist. Ct. of Appeal Jud. Nominating Commn., 1983-87, chmn. 1986-87. Mem. Acad. Fla. Trial Lawyers (diplomate), Broward County Trial Lawyers Assn. (dir. 1983-84, sec. 1984-85, v.p. 1985-86, pres. 1987—), Assn. Trial Lawyers Am., Fla. Bar (bd. cert. civil trial lawyer 1984—), Nat. Bd. Trial Advocacy (bd. cert. civil trial advocate 1986—). Personal injury, State civil litigation. Office: 524 S Andrews Ave Suite 203 N Fort Lauderdale FL 33301

KRATZ, PAUL DAVID, lawyer; b. Lincoln, Nebr., Mar. 27, 1950; s. Kent P. and Betty Jane (Williams) K.; m. Diane Hope Knudtson, Jan. 7, 1974; children: Jeffrey Paul, Gregory David. BS, U. Nebr., 1972, JD, 1975. Bar: Nebr. 1975, U.S. Dist. Ct. Nebr. 1975, U.S. Supreme Ct. 1979, U.S. Ct. Appeals (8th cir.) 1981. Asst. gen. counsel Nebr. Pub. Service Commn., Lincoln, 1975-78; assoc. Stern & Becker, Omaha, 1978-80; gen. counsel Nebr. Dept. Labor, Lincoln, 1980-85; ptnr. Kratz & Kratz, Omaha, 1985—. Active fund raising Rep. candidates, Omaha; trustee Ch. of Cross, Omaha. Mem. ABA, Nebr. Bar Assn., Omaha Bar Assn., Delta Upsilon, Phi Delta Phi (magistrate 1974-75). Republican. Presbyterian. Labor, Administrative and regulatory, State civil litigation. Home: 14730 Jefferson Circle Omaha NE 68137 Office: Kratz & Kratz 7171 Mercy Rd Suite 220 Xerox Bldg Omaha NE 68106

KRAUS, JAMES ALAN, lawyer; b. Long Beach, Calif., Dec. 30, 1947; s. Morris Stanley and Kay Fanny (Penn) K. B.S. in Laws, Western State U., San Diego, 1975, J.D., 1976. Bar: Calif. 1977, U.S. Dist. Ct. (so. dist.) Calif. 1977, U.S. Ct. Appeals (9th cir.) 1977, U.S. Supreme Ct. 1981, U.S. Tax Ct. 1981, U.S. Claims Ct. 1983, U.S. Ct. Internat. Trade 1983. Intern, U.S. Dept. Justice, 1976, Sheela, Lightner, Hughes, Castro & Walsh, 1976; chief trial counsel Tolman, Lefebvre & Kraus, San Diego, 1977-80; sole practice Law Offices of James A. Kraus, 1980—; cons. legal Pata Enterprises, Placentia, Calif., 1985—, Dolphin Enterprises, San Diego, 1986—, RUDOKEV Aviation, Houston, 1986—, R&L Devel. Co., 1986—; judge pro tempore San Diego Mcpl. Ct., 1980—; counsel San Diego Police Officers Assn., Security Pacific Nat. Bank, Calif. First Bank, Aztec Fin. Corp., Calif. Real Estate Assn., Westland Title Co., Nat. Am. Title Ins. Co., Bara Farms. Contbr. articles to legal publs. Former v.p. B'nai B'rith; chmn. Anti-Defamation League Com. Mem. ABA, Calif. Bar Assn., San Diego County Bar Assn., Assn. Trial Lawyers Am., San Diego Trial Lawyers Assn., Arabian Horse Registry, Mensa. Club: San Diego Track. Democrat. Served with USN, 1967-71. Family and matrimonial, General practice, State civil litigation. Office: 160 Thorn St Suite 3 San Diego CA 92103

KRAUS, NANCY JANE, lawyer; b. Hutchinson, Kans., Sept. 18, 1953; d. Lee Onnie and Margaret Jane (Abernathy) K. Cert., Université de Paris à la Sorbonne, 1972; BA, Kans. State U., 1975; JD, Yale U., 1978. Bar: Tex. 1978. Assoc. Butler, Binion, Rice, Cook & Knapp, Houston, 1978-82, Mayor, Day & Caldwell, Houston, 1982-85, Goins, Underkofler, Crawford & Langdon, Dallas, 1985—; regional atty. Rep. party Ballot Security program, 1986. Vol. legal counsel Cultural Arts Council Houston, 1979-84; mem dir's. circle Houston Grand Opera, 1984-85; tutor Literacy Vols. Am., 1986—. Mem. ABA, Tex. Bar Assn., Dallas Bar Assn., Dallas Assn. Young Lawyers, Dallas Women Lawyers Assn. Avocation: golf. Real property, Local government. Office: Goins Underkofler Crawford & Langdon 3300 Thanksgiving Tower Dallas TX 75201

KRAUS, ROBERT H., lawyer; b. Teaneck, N.J., May 10, 1939; s. Henry and Alice R. (Ziegler) K.; m. Carol A. Gerry, June 10, 1961; children—William R., Karen B., Kathryn L. A.B., Rutgers Coll., 1961, J.D., 1964. Bar: N.J. 1965, D.C. 1965. Assoc., Lowenstein & Sandler, Newark, 1966-69, Johnstone & O'Dwyer, Westfield, N.J., 1969-70, Shear & Kraus, Scotch Plains, N.J., 1971, Leib, Kraus, Grispin & Roth (formerly Read, Leib, Shear & Kraus), Scotch Plains, 1972—; gen. ptnr. Grand Prix Assocs., Scotch Plains, 1975—, Penthouse Assocs., Scotch Plains, 1979—, Flemington Trade Ctr., L.P. Bd. dirs., trustee Fanwood Scotch Plains YMCA, 1976—; pres. Fanwood Republican Club (N.J.), 1977; trustee Scotch Plains-Fanwood Scholarship Found., 1982—. Served as capt. U.S. Army, 1965-66. Recipient William D. Mason Disting. Service award Fanwood-Scotch Plains Jaycees, 1977. Mem. ABA, N.J. Bar Assn., Union County Bar Assn. Club: Scotch Plains-Fanwood Soccer Assn. (gen. mgr., coach 1977-83). Family and matrimonial, Real property, Contracts commercial. Home: 96 Forest Rd Fanwood NJ 07023 Office: Leib Kraus Grispin & Roth 328 Park Ave Scotch Plains NJ 07076-0310

KRAUSE, ANDREW JAMES, lawyer; b. Flint, Mich., Oct. 19, 1954; s. Seymour S. and Melba Violet (Simons) K.; m. Susan Retta Pirret, Aug. 18, 1954; children: Sara, Andrew Jr. BS in Bus. Adminstrn., Cen. Mich. U., 1977; JD cum laude, Thomas M. Cooley Law Sch., 1980; LLM in Estate Planning, U. Miami, 1981. Bar: Fla. 1981, U.S. Tax Ct. 1983. Assoc. Carlos and Abbott, Miami, Fla., 1981-83, Catalano, Myers and Fisher, Naples, Fla., 1983-85; ptnr. Myers, Krause and Stevens, Naples, 1985—; lectr. advanced estate planning programs continuing legal edn. Fla. Bar, 1984, 87. Bd. dirs. Cedar Montessori Sch., Naples, 1986—; participating lawyer Collier County Lawyers Vol. Project, Naples, 1985; legacy chmn. Collier County Unit Am. Cancer Soc., Naples, 1983—. Mem. ABA, Fla. Bar Assn., Collier County Bar Assn. Avocation: golf. Probate, Estate planning, Estate taxation. Office: Myers Krause and Stevens 5811 Pelican Bay Blvd #600 Naples FL 33963

KRAUSE, CHARLES FREDERICK, lawyer; b. Chgo., Aug. 28, 1931; s. Edgar H. and Edna L. (Pflug) K.; m. Joan Ames, Oct. 30, 1968; children: Kent C., Paul E., Jennifer A. B.A., Valparaiso U., 1957; LL.B., Rutgers U., 1960. Bar: N.Y. 1961. Ptnr. Speiser, Krause & Madole, N.Y.C., Washington, Calif., Tex., 1961—; lectr. in field; bd. dirs. Columbian Mutual Life Ins. Co.; pres., chief exec. officer Tex. Nat. Telecommunications Inc. Coauthor: Aviation Tort Law, 3 vols., 1980, The American Law of Torts, 1983; mem. bd. editors: N.Y. State Bar Jour.; contbr. articles to profl. publs. Served to capt. USMCR, 1952-56. Mem. ABA, Am. Trial Lawyers Assn., Am. Coll. Trial Lawyers. Clubs: Wings, Union League, Sky (N.Y.C.). Federal civil litigation, State civil litigation, Personal injury. Office: 200 Park Ave New York NY 10166

KRAUSE, SARRAINE SIEGER, lawyer; b. San Diego, Sept. 5, 1942; d. James Joseph and Rose Elizabeth (Keating) Sieger; m. Anthony Paul Krause, June 16, 1962; children: Adele Antoinette, James Anthony. BA, U. Tex., 1974; JD, U. San Diego, 1977. Bar: Calif. 1977, Tex. 1979, U.S. Dist. Ct. (no. dist.) Tex. 1980. Atty. So. Calif. Legal Ctr., Long Beach, 1978-79; asst. atty. legal dept. City of Ft. Worth, 1979-80; asst. dist. atty. Tarrant County, Ft. Worth, 1981; ptnr. Krause & Wells, Ft. Worth, 1982—. Mem. ABA, Tex. Bar Assn., Calif. Bar Assn., Tarrant County Bar Assn., Women Lawyers Tarrant County. Democrat. Family and matrimonial. Home: 8725 Canyon Crest Rd Fort Worth TX 76101 Office: Krause & Wells 1240 Southridge Suite 103 Hurst TX 76053

KRAVARIK, MARTIN EDWARD, judge; b. Bronx, N.Y., Jan. 20, 1936; s. Martin and Anna (Petrucha) K.; m. Manuela Preda, Mar. 11, 1961; children—Martin Donald, Marisa, Mark Stephen. B.A., Rutgers U., 1958; J.D., Seton Hall U., 1968; student Nat. Jud. Coll., 1982. Bar: N.J. 1968, U.S. Dist. Ct. N.J. 1968, U.S. Sup. Ct. 1978, U.S. Dist. Ct. N.J. 1985. Assoc., Philip L. Strong, New Brunswick, N.J., 1968-69; ptnr. Selesky & Kravarik, New Brunswick, 1969, Selesky, Kolsky, Kravarik & Epstein, New Brunswick, 1969-72; gen. atty. N.J. Hwy. Authority, Woodbridge, 1972-80; judge Monroe Twp. Mcpl. Ct., 1972-80; atty. Helmetta Planning Bd., 1970-72, 81-83; judge Middlesex County (N.J.) Dist. Ct. 1980-84; atty. Madison Twp. Bd. Health, 1970-72; mem. N.J. Gen. Assembly, 1970-71; prosecutor East Brunswick Twp., 1969-70. Bd. dirs. Easter Seal Soc. Crippled Children and Adults, N.J., 1976-79; pres., bd. dirs. Raritan Valley Workshop; elder, trustee 1st Presbyterian Ch. of Metuchen; adv. bd., sec. St. Peter's Med. Ctr., 1976-79; bd. dirs. Middlesex County Coll. Found., 1977-80; pres. Metuchen Republican Club, 1969-70. Served to capt. USAF, 1958-63. Recipient Disting. Mil. grad. Rutgers U., 1958; Disting. Service award Metuchen Jaycees, 1971; Humanitarian award Easter Seal Soc. for Crippled Children and Adults of N.J., 1976; citation of merit Valley Forge Mil. Acad., 1980. Mem. Middlesex County Conf. Mcpl. Ct. Judges (pres. 1979-80), Am. Judges Assn. (pubs. com.), Nat. Conf. State Judges (sentencing and corrections com.), N.J. Supreme Ct. (model jury charges-criminal com.), Middlesex County Bar Assn. (trustee 1977-80). Jurisprudence. Address: 480 Wakefield Dr Metuchen NJ 08840

KRAVER, RICHARD MATTHEW, lawyer; b. Bklyn., Nov. 27, 1946; s. Barnett L. and Pearl (Aronson) K.; m. Harriet Shapiro, Sept. 7, 1970; children—Michael E., Barry S. B.S., NYU, 1968, J.D., Syracuse U., 1971. Bar: N.Y. 1972, Fla. 1975, U.S. Dist. Ct. (so. and ea. dist.) N.Y. 1973, U.S. Tax Ct. 1973, U.S. Ct. Appeals (2d cir.) 1973, U.S. Ct. Appeals (D.C. cir.) 1983, U.S. Supreme Ct. 1976, U.S. Dist. Ct. (no. dist.) N.Y. 1986, U.S. Ct. Appeals (3d cir.) 1986. Assoc. Feldshuh & Frank, N.Y.C., 1972-76; sole practice, N.Y.C., 1977-79; ptnr. Kraver & Martin, N.Y.C., 1979-85, Kraver & Parker, N.Y.C., 1985—. Mem. ABA, N.Y. State Bar Assn., Fla. Bar Assn. General corporate, Federal civil litigation, Contracts commercial. Home: 153 Albemarle Rd White Plains NY 10605 Office: Kraver & Parker 885 3d Ave New York NY 10022

KRAVETZ, DAVID HUBERT, lawyer, educator; b. Cambridge, Mass., Feb. 2, 1938; s. Philip and Sadie (Winokur) K.; m. Phyllis E. Gouse, Aug. 16, 1984; children—Joel, Peter, Andrew. B.B.A., U. Mass., 1959; J.D., Boston Coll., 1962. Bar: Mass. 1962, U.S. Dist. Ct. Mass. 1965, U.S. Supreme Ct. 1980. Staff atty. FTC, Washington, 1962-63, Boston Legal Aid, 1963-64; ptnr. Widett, Slater & Goldman, P.C., Boston, 1965-84, also dir.; sole practice, Boston, 1984—; sr. lectr. in law Northeastern U., Boston, 1965—; adj. asst. prof. bus. law Bentley Coll., Waltham, Mass., 1984—. Trustee Charles River Acad., Cambridge, 1968-85; chmn. Heart Fund, Lexington, Mass., 1970-72; mem. Lexington Housing Authority, 1984-85. Mem. Boston Bar Assn., ABA, Mass. Bar Assn., Assn. Trial Lawyers Am., Comml. Law League Am. (chmn. New Eng. region 1979-80). Jewish. Lodge: Masons. Consumer commercial, General practice, Legal education. Home: 3 Abernathy Rd Lexington MA 02173 Office: Manoff & Kravetz 185 Devonshire St Suite 500 Boston MA 02110

KRAVITCH, PHYLLIS A., judge; b. Savannah, Ga., Aug. 23, 1920; d. Aaron and Ella (Wiseman) K. B.A., Goucher Coll., 1941; LL.B., U. Pa., 1943; LL.D. (hon.), Goucher Coll., 1981. Bar: Ga. 1943, U.S. Dist. Ct. 1944, U.S. Supreme Ct. 1948, U.S. Circuit Ct. Appeals 1962. Practice law Savannah, 1944-76; judge Superior Ct., Eastern Jud. Circuit of Ga., 1977-79, U.S. Ct. Appeals (5th cir.), Atlanta, 1979-81, U.S. Ct. Appeals (11th cir.), 1981—; mem. law sch. council Emory U., 1986. Trustee Inst. Continuing Legal Edn. in Ga., 1979-82; mem. Bd. of Edn., Chatham County, Ga., 1949-55, Law Sch. Council Emory U. Sch. Law, Atlanta, 1986. Recipient Hannah G. Solomon award Nat. Council of Jewish Women, 1978. Fellow Am. Bar Found.; mem. Am. Bar Assn., Savannah Bar Assn. (pres. 1976), State Bar of Ga., Am. Judicature Soc., Am. Law Inst. Office: US Court Appeals PO Box 8085 Savannah GA 31412

KRAVITT, JASON HARRIS PAPERNO, lawyer; b. Chgo., Jan. 19, 1948; s. Jerome Julius and Shirley (Paperno) K.; m. Beverly Ray Niemeier, May 11, 1974; children: Nikola Wedding, Justin Taylor Paperno. AB, Johns Hopkins U., 1969; JD, Harvard U., 1972; diploma in comparative legal studies, Cambridge U., Eng., 1973. Bar: Ill., U.S. Dist. Ct. (no. dist.) Ill. Assoc. Mayer, Brown & Platt, Chgo., 1973-78, ptnr., 1979—. Editor Harvard U. Law Rev., 1972. Bd. dirs. Mus. Contemporary Art, Chgo., 1974-75. Mem. Chgo. Council Lawyers, Chgo. Bar Assn. Banking, Contracts commercial, Securities. Home: 321 Greenwood Glencoe IL 60022 Office: Mayer Brown & Platt 190 LaSalle St Chicago IL 60603

KRAVITZ, JEFFREY STEPHEN, lawyer; b. Newark, Aug. 3, 1950; s. Raymond and Sue Mary (Bergman) K.; m. Rochelle Rose, July 5, 1980; 1 child, Matthew Allan. BA cum laude, UCLA, 1972; JD, Loyola U., Los Angeles, 1975. Bar: Calif. 1975, U.S. Dist. Ct. (cen. dist.) Calif. 1976, U.S. Dist. Ct. (no. and ea. dists.) Calif. 1977, U.S. Ct. Appeals (9th cir.) 1977. Dep. atty. gen. Calif. Dept. Justice, 1975-79; assoc. Lord, Bissell & Brook, Los Angeles, 1979-84, ptnr., 1984—. Legal com. Anti Defamation League, Los Angeles, 1983-85. Mem. Los Angeles County Bar Assn. Democrat. Jewish. Avocations: politics, cooking. Federal civil litigation, State civil litigation, Insurance. Office: Lord Bissell & Brook 3250 Wilshire Blvd #1208 Los Angeles CA 90010

KRAVITZ, MARTIN JAY, lawyer; b. Phila., Oct. 3, 1950; s. Louis L. and Shirley (Best) K.; m. Donna Marie Fawcett, Nov. 26, 1978; children—Daniel Jay, Andrew Stephen. B.A., U. Denver, 1972; J.D., U. Pacific, 1977. Bar: Nev. 1977, U.S. Dist. Ct. Nev. 1977, U.S. Ct. Appeals (9th cir.) 1978, U.S. Supreme Ct. 1985. Law clk. to presiding justice Nev. Supreme Ct., Carson City, 1977-78; jr. ptnr., assoc. Goodman, Oshins, Brown & Singer, Las Vegas, 1978-82, Oshins, Brown, Singer & Wells, 1982-83; ptnr. Brown, Wells, Beller & Kravitz, Las Vegas, 1983-86, Brown, Wells, Beler & Kravitz, Las Vegas, 1983-86, Brown, Wells & Kravitz, Las Vegas, 1986—; assoc. prof. bus. law Clark County Community Coll., 1979-80. Chmn. lawyers div. United Jewish Appeal, Las Vegas, 1978—. Mem. ABA, Am. Trial Lawyers Assn., Clark County Bar Assn. Democrat. Jewish. Personal injury, State civil litigation, Contracts commercial. Office: Brown Wells Beller & Kravitz 520 S 4th St Las Vegas NV 89101

KRAVITZ, WILLIAM N., lawyer; b. N.Y.C., Sept. 26, 1946; s. Louis I. and Grace (Fox) K.; m. Marilyn H. Piller, Jan. 2, 1971; children: Eric G., Meredith D., Jordan T. AB, Boston U., 1967; JD, St. John's U., N.Y.C., 1971. Bar: N.Y. 1972, U.S. Dist. Ct. (so. dist.) 1975, U.S. Tax Ct. 1975, U.S. Ct. Appeals (2d cir.) 1975, U.S. Supreme Ct. 1975. Assoc. Fried, Frank, Harris, Shriver & Jacobson, N.Y.C., 1972-76; dep. gen. counsel Bowery Savings Bank, N.Y.C., 1976; assoc. Skadden, Arps, Slate, Meagher & Flom, N.Y.C., 1976-78, ptnr., 1978—. Editor: Employee Benefit Palns: Mergers and Aquisitions, 1983, Esops and Esop Transactions, 1985; edtorial adv. bd. Jour. Pension Planning and Compliance. Mem. ABA (employee benefits com.), N.Y. State Bar Assn. (employee benefits com.), Assn. of Bar of City of N.Y. Avocations: tennis, skiing, reading, music. Pension, profit-sharing, and employee benefits. Home: 22 Ursuline Ct Oyster Bay Cove NY 11771 Office: Skadden Arps Slate Meagher & Flom 919 3d Ave New York NY 10022

KRAW, GEORGE MARTIN, lawyer; b. Oakland, Calif., June 17, 1949; s. George and Pauline Dorothy (Herceg) K.; m. Sarah Lee Kenyon, Sept. 3, 1983. B.A., U. Calif.-Santa Cruz, 1971; postgrad., Lenin Inst., Moscow, 1971, M.A., U. Calif.-Berkeley, 1974, J.D., 1976. Bar: Calif. 1976, U.S. Dist. Ct. (no. dist.) Calif. 1976, U.S. Supreme Ct. 1980. Assoc. Bachan, Skillicorn, Watsonville, Calif., 1976-79, Trepel & Clark, San Jose, Calif., 1979-81; ptnr. Mount, Kraw & Stoelker, San Jose, 1981—; asst. sec. Sysgen, Inc., Fremont, Calif., 1982—. Mem. ABA, Inter-Am. Bar Assn. Clubs: Metropolitan, University (San Jose). Contracts commercial, Private international, General corporate. Office: Mount Kraw Stoelker 333 W San Carlos 10th Floor River Park Tower San Jose CA 95112

KRAWITZ, SIDNEY L., lawyer, banker; b. Hawley, Pa., June 21, 1911; s. Louis and Helen (Krakower) K.; m. Lydia May Koff, Feb. 20, 1938; children—Nancy Ellen Krawitz Sigal, Olive Krawitz Gallagher. B.S. in Acctg., Syracuse U., 1933; J.D. magna cum laude, Dickinson Sch. Law, 1936, LL.D., 1970. Bar: Pa. 1937, U.S. Supreme Ct. 1948. Asst. dist. atty. Wayne County (Pa.), 1937-40; ptnr. Krawitz & Ridley, P.C., Milford, Pa., 1937—; v.p., gen. counsel Security Bank & Trust Co., Stroudsburg, Pa., 1972-83; pub. defender Pike County (Pa.), 1967-68, county solicitor, 1953-55; lectr. Dickinson Sch. Law, 1950-70; mem. disciplinary bd. of Supreme Ct. of Pa., 1980-84. Bd. dirs., exec. bd. Mercy Community Hosp., Port Jervis, Pa.; bd. dirs. Econ. Devel. Council of Northeastern Pa.; pres., bd. dirs. Milford Cemetery Assn. Served to lt. USN, recipient Outstanding Achievement award Dickinson Sch. Law, 1978; Arents Pioneer Medal for Excellence in field of law Syracuse U., 1983. Fellow Am. Coll. Trial Lawyers, Am. Bar Found.; mem. ABA (del. 1979-81), Pa. Bar Assn. (past pres.), Am. Judicature Soc., World Assn. Lawyers, Nat. Assn. Def. Lawyers, Pa. Trial Lawyers Assn. Jewish. Clubs: Union League (Phila.); Pa. Soc. (N.Y.C.); Lodges: Masons, Shriners. Author: The Tax Atlas, 1950. Banking, State civil litigation, Condemnation. Office: 104 W High St Milford PA 18337

KRAY, FRED MARTIN, lawyer; b. Sea Isle City, N.J., May 25, 1952; s. Fred and Emily (Gray) K. BA, Pa. State U., 1974; JD, U. Nebr., 1977. Bar: Fla. 1977, U.S. Dist. Ct. (so. dist.) Fla. 1979, U.S. Ct. Appeals (5th and 11th cirs.) 1981. Assoc. Dennis Brod P.A., Miami, Fla., 1977-78, Carl Hoffman P.A., Miami, 1978-79; ptnr. Virgin & Kray, Miami, 1979-86, Bedford & Kray, Miami, 1986—. Mem. ABA, Fla. Bar Assn., Dade County Bar Assn., Am. Arbitration Assn., Assn. Trial Lawyers Am., Acad. Fla. Trial Lawyers. Avocation: writing. State civil litigation, Personal injury, Insurance. Office: Bedford & Kray 66 W Flagler Suite 300 Miami FL 33130

KREAM, DEBORAH, lawyer; b. Newark, Sept. 21, 1957; d. Arnold Eli and Winifred Zelda (Perlman) K. BA in History, Rutgers U., 1979; JD, New England Sch. Law, 1982. Bar: Mass. 1982, U.S. Dist. Ct. Mass. 1983, U.S. Ct. Appeals (1st cir.) 1983. Assoc. Cohen & Sheils, Boston, 1982-83, Hayt, Hayt & Landau, Lynnfield, Mass., 1983-84, Goodman & Garr, Boston, 1984-86; corp. atty. NEC Info. Systems, Inc., Boxborough, Mass., 1986—. Mem. ABA, Mass. Bar Assn., Boston Bar Assn., Assn. Trial Lawyers Am. Avocations: travel, tennis. State civil litigation, Contracts commercial, Consumer commercial. Home: 1622 Worcester Rd Apt 303B Framingham MA 01701 Office: NEC Info Systems Inc 1414 Massachusetts Ave Boxborough MA 01719

KREAMER, SCOTT HARRISON, lawyer; b. Lawrence, Kans., Aug. 9, 1951; s. Hugh Harrison Kreamer and Sara Jayne (Scott) Breyfogle. BA in English Lit. with distinction, U. Kans., 1973; JD, Washburn U., 1976. Bar: U.S. Dist. Ct. Kans. 1978, U.S. Dist. Ct. (we. dist.) Mo. 1981, U.S. Ct. Appeals (10th cir.) 1982, U.S. Supreme Ct. 1984. Ptnr. Gardner, Davis, Kreamer, Norton, Hubbard & Ruzicke, Olathe, Kans., 1977-84, Watson, Ess, Marshall & Enggas, Olathe and Kansas City, Mo., 1984—; chmn. Orient Express Ltd., Olathe, 1985—; chmn., chief exec. officer Kreamer-Love Corp., Olathe, 1981—; bd. dirs., past chmn. Europa Distributors Inc., Olathe. Contbg. editor: Modern Trials (Melvin Belli), 2d edition, 1981. Sustaining mem. Rep. Nat. Com., 1986; mem. Olathe Ch. com., 1984—, Kansas City, Kans. Ch. com., 1984—, Johnson County Rep. com., 1976—. Named one of Outstanding Young Men in Am., 1985. Mem. ABA, Kans. Bar Assn., Mo. Bar Assn., Kansas City (Mo.) Bar Assn., Johnson County Bar Assn., Assn. Trial Lawyers Am., Kans. Trial Lawyers Assn., Nat. Assn. Criminal Def. Lawyers. Republican. Club: Brookridge Country (Overland Park, Kans.). Avocations: race car driving, tennis. Family and matrimonial, Personal injury. Home: 2505 W 83d Terr Leawood KS 66206 Office: Watson Ess Marshall & Enggas 130 N Cherry Olathe KS 66061

KREBS, ARNO W., JR., lawyer; b. Dallas, July 7, 1942; s. Arno W. and Lynette (Linnstaedter) K.; m. Peggy Sharon Stagg, Dec. 17, 1966; 1 child, Kirsten; m. Barbara Lyn Craig, Dec. 28, 1973. B.A., Tex. A&M U., 1964; LL.B., U. Tex., 1967. Bar: Tex. 1967, U.S. Dist. Ct. (so. dist.) Tex. 1968, U.S. Ct. Appeals (5th cir.) 1971, U.S. Ct. Appeals (11th cir.) 1981, U.S. Dist. Ct. (we. and no. dists.) Tex. 1981, U.S. Supreme Ct. 1983, U.S. Dist. Ct. (ea. dist.) Tex. 1984. Assoc. Fulbright & Jaworski, Houston, 1967-75, ptnr., 1975—. Contbr. articles to profl. jours. Mem. Tex. Commn. on Bicentennial U.S. Constn. Mem. Tex. Assn. Def. Counsel, Houston Bar Assn., ABA, Tex. Aggie Bar Assn., Tex. Bar Found., Houston Bar Found. Lutheran. Clubs: Houston Ctr., Forum Houston. Insurance, Personal injury, State civil litigation. Office: 1301 McKinney 51st Floor Houston TX 77010

KREDER, JOSEPH CASIMIR, lawyer; b. Seltzer, Pa., Feb. 24, 1924; s. William and Veronica (Margalis) K.; m. Elizabeth A. Judge, June 12, 1954; children—Elizabeth Kreder McCoy, Joseph J., Mary Veronica, Anne Kreder Shelburne. B.S., NYU, 1947; J.D., Dickinson Law Sch., 1950. Bar: Pa. 1950, U.S. Dist. Ct. (mid. dist.) Pa. 1951, U.S. Ct. Appeals (3d cir.) 1951. Law clk. to chief judge U.S. Dist. Ct. (mid. dist.) Pa., 1951-53; U.S. atty., 1953; ptnr. Henkelman, Kreder, O'Connell & Brooks, Scranton, Pa., 1955—; dir. Northeastern Bank Pa., Bermuda Properties, Ltd., Geisinger Found. Vice pres. Scranton C. of C., 1964-65; vice pres. United Way Lackawanna County, 1966-68. Served as sgt. U.S. Army, 1943-46. Mem. ABA, Pa. Bar Assn., Lackawanna Bar Assn. (treas. 1970-77), Jud. Conf. for U.S. 3d Cir. Ct. of Appeals. Roman Catholic. Clubs: Rotary (pres. 1959-60), Scranton Country. Probate, General corporate, Estate taxation. Office: Henkelman Kreder O'Connell Brooks PO Box 956 Scranton PA 18501

KREEK, LOUIS FRANCIS, JR., lawyer; b. Washington, Aug. 24, 1928; s. Louis F. and Experance (Agee) K.; m. Gwendolyn Schoepfle, Sept. 12, 1970. S.B., MIT, 1948; J.D., George Washington U., 1952. Bar: D.C. 1952, U.S. Dist. Ct. D.C. 1952, U.S. Ct. Appeals (D.C. cir.) 1952, Ohio 1955, N.Y. 1964, U.S. Dist. Ct. (so. and ea. dists.) 1964, N.J. 1972. Patent examiner U.S. Patent Office, Washington, 1948-53; patent atty. Pitts. Plate Glass Co., 1953-54, Battelle Meml. Inst., Columbus, Ohio, 1954-56, Merck & Co., Inc., Rahway, N.J., 1956-60; div. patent counsel Air Reduction Co., Murray Hill, N.J., 1960-63; assoc. Kenyon & Kenyon, N.Y.C., 1963-66; patent atty. Johns-Manville Corp., Manville, N.J., 1967-68; sr. patent atty. Esso Research and Engring. Co., Linden, N.J., 1968-73, ICI Ams. Inc., Wilmington, Del., 1973-85; assoc. Oldham, Oldham & Weber Co., L.P.A., Akron, Ohio, 1985—. Mem. MIT Alumni Fund Bd., 1977-80; mem. MIT Alumni Officers' Conf. com., 1981-84, chmn., 1983. Mem. ABA, Am. Intellectual Property Law Assn., Phila. Patent Law Assn. (chmn. publ. awards com. 1978-85), N.Y. Patent Law Assn. (assoc.), Cleve. Patent Law Assn., Akron Bar Assn., MIT Alumni Assn. (bd. dirs. 1982-84). Club: MIT of Delaware Valley (pres. 1978-80), MIT of No. Ohio (pres. 1986—). Lodge: Kiwanis. Patent. Home: 2321 Stockbridge Rd Akron OH 44313

KREFMAN, STEPHEN DAVID, lawyer; b. Detroit, Mar. 11, 1954; s. William and Muriel Elaine (Weinstein) K.; m. Rebecca Lee Harris, Feb. 4, 1978; children: Lee Harris, Jessica Faith, Nathaniel Isaac, Rachael Anna. BS in Mech. Engring., Wayne State U., 1974; postgrad., U. Ky., 1975-76, JD, 1979; postdoctoral, U. Mich., 1982-83. Bar: U.S. Patent Office 1977, Mich. 1979, U.S. Ct. Appeals (6th cir.) 1979, Pa. 1986, U.S. Ct. Customs and Patent Appeals. Assoc. patent counsel Masco Corp., Taylor, Mich., 1979-82; assoc. Gifford, Van Ophem & Sprinkle, Troy, Mich., 1982-84; assoc. counsel SPS Technologies, Newtown, Pa., 1984—. Mem. ABA, Am. Corp. Counsel Assn., Delaware Valley Corp. Counsel Assn., Am. Intellectual Property Law Assn., Phila. Patent Law Assn, Tau Epsilon Rho. Democrat. Jewish. Avocation: geneology. Patent, Trademark and copyright, General corporate. Home: 1387 Knox Dr Yardley PA 19067 Office: SPS Technologies Inc Newtown PA 18940

KREIFELS, FRANK ANTHONY, lawyer, corporation executive; b. Omaha, Nov. 26, 1951; s. Robert Frank and Mary Ellen (Basan) K.; 1 child, Katherine Joy. BBA in Fin., Creighton U., 1974, MBA in Fin. and Acctg., 1975; J.D., Hamline U., 1977. Bar: Minn. 1978, U.S. Dist. Ct. Minn. 1978, Nebr. 1983. Staff atty. NCR-Comten Inc., St. Paul, 1978-80; gen. counsel, sec. Agriventure Corp., Foxley & Co., Foxley Cattle Co., Herd Co., Flavorland Industries (and all affiliates), Omaha, 1980-85; mem. Ellsworth Law Firm, Omaha, 1985-87, exec. v.p., gen. mgr. Dale Beggs Devel. Co. (and all affiliates), 1987—; cons. Small Bus. Adminstrn., Omaha, 1974; corp. lobbyist Foxley Cattle Co./Herd Co., Omaha, 1981-85; appointed Neb. state reporter Am. Agrl. Law Update, 1985—. Campaign coordinator Nebr. Republican Party, 1982, 84. Smith. Recipient Cert. of Merit, Small Bus. Adminstrn., 1974. Mem. ABA, Am. Corp. Counsel Assn., Am. Agrl. Law Assn., Nebr. State Bar Assn., Phi Alpha Delta. Roman Catholic. Clubs: Omaha Barrister's, Omaha Westroads. Contracts commercial, Real property, Securities. Home: 10206 Ohio Dr Omaha NE 68134 Office: Dale Beggs Devel Co 5332 S 138th St Suite 300 Omaha NE 68137

KREITMAN, LENORE ROBERTS, lawyer; b. N.Y.C., June 6, 1947; d. Solomon and Mildred R. (Roberts) K. BA, Queens Coll., 1967; MA, U. Pa., 1969, PhD, 1976; JD in Internat. Law with honors, Columbia U., 1976. Bar: N.Y. 1977, U.S. Dist. Ct. (so. and ea. dists.) N.Y. 1977, D.C. 1979, U.S. Ct. Appeals (D.C. cir.), 1979. Assoc. Cravath, Swaine & Moore, N.Y.C., 1976-80, Kaye, Scholer, Fierman, Hays & Handler, N.Y.C., 1980-82, Burrows & Poster, N.Y.C., 1982-84, Hess, Segall, Guterman, Pelz, Steiner & Barovick, N.Y.C., 1984-86, Loeb & Loeb & Hess, N.Y.C., 1987—; exchange lectr. Université de Lyon, France, 1970-71; adj. lectr. French CCNY, 1972-73. Editor Columbia Law Rev., 1974-76. AAUW Ednl. Found. fellow 1975-76; Harlan Fiske Stone scholar. Mem. Internat. Bar Assn., Union Internationale des Avocats, ABA, N.Y. State Bar Assn., D.C. Bar Assn., Assn. Bar of City N.Y., Am. Br. of Internat. Law Assn., Am. Soc. Internat. Law. General corporate, Private international, Securities. Home: 16 W 16th St New York NY 10011 Office: Loeb & Loeb & Hess 230 Park Ave New York NY 10169

KRELL, BRUCE EDWARD, lawyer, author; b. N.Y.C., Apr. 28, 1943; s. Philip I. and Blanche (Gershwind) K.; m. Pamela Grossman, Oct. 4, 1966; children—Rebekah, Margret. B.A., Fla. State U., 1965; postgrad. Ohio State U., 1967; J.D., John Marshall Law Sch., 1971. Bar: Iowa 1971, U.S. Dist. Ct. (no. dist.) Ill. 1971, Calif. 1972, U.S. Dist. Ct. (no. dist.) Calif. 1972. Social worker Ohio Penitentiary, Columbus, 1966-68; instr. Chgo. Career Coll., 1970-71, John Marshall Law Sch., Chgo., 1972; law clk. Ill. Appeals Ct., Chgo., 1971-72; assoc. Law Offices of Melvin Belli, San Francisco, 1972; owner Bruce E. Krell, Inc., San Francisco, 1972—; assoc. prof., advisor Lincoln Law Sch., San Francisco, 1973-78. Contbr. articles to profl. jours. Bd. dirs. ACLU No. Calif., 1973-78, Legal Aid No. Calif., 1974-79; vol. atty. San Francisco Jewish Community Ctr., 1978-81, San Francisco Legal Aid Ctr., No. Calif., 1972-79. Mem. Am. Arbitration Assn., Am. Trial Lawyers Assn., Calif. Trial Lawyers Assn., Calif. State Bar Assn., San Francisco Bar Assn., Lawyers Club, San Francisco Trial Lawyers Assn., Barrister's Club, Gavel Soc. Democrat. Jewish. Personal injury, State civil litigation, Legal education. Office: 345 Grove St San Francisco CA 94102

KREMBS, PETER JOSEPH, lawyer; b. Madison, Wis., Dec. 12, 1944; s. John G. and Mary M. (Felker) K.; m. Nancy Smythe June 8, 1974; children—Joshua, Marcus. B.S., U. Wis., Madison, 1968; J.D., Case Western Res. U., 1973. Bar: Ohio 1973, U.S. Dist. Ct. (no. dist.) Ohio 1974, U.S. Ct. Appeals (6th cir.) 1975. Assoc., Ford, Whitney, Cleve., 1973-77; corp. atty. Midland-Ross Corp., 1977-81; ptnr. Gruber, Moriarty, Fricke & Jaros, Cleve., 1981—; legal officer, dir. of several small bus. Diplomate Ct. Practice Inst. Mem. Am. Arbitration Assn. (arbitrator 1981—), Greater Cleve. Bar Assn., Ohio State Bar Assn., ABA, Am. Trial Lawyers Assn. Federal civil litigation, State civil litigation, General corporate. Office: Gruber Moriarty Fricke & Jaros 1500 Terminal Tower Cleveland OH 44113

KRENSKY, MICHAEL IAN, lawyer; b. Washington, Sept. 15, 1951; s. Maurice Chidel and Charlotte Jane (Davis) K. AA, Montgomery Coll., 1972; BA, Am. U., 1974; JD, George Mason U., 1977. Bar: D.C. 1978, U.S. Dist. Ct. D.C. 1979, Md. 1980, U.S. Dist. Ct. (mid. dist.) Md. 1981, U.S. Supreme Ct. 1984. Assoc. Francke & Friedman, Rockville, Md., 1978-79; sole practice Rockville, 1980—. Mem. ABA, Md. Bar Assn. Democrat. Jewish. General practice, Personal injury, Consumer commercial. Home: 4 Monroe St Apt #1107 Rockville MD 20850 Office: 966 Hungerford Dr 15B Rockville MD 20850

KRENZLER, ALVIN IRVING, judge; b. Chgo., Apr. 8, 1921. A.B., Case Western Res. U., 1946, LL.B., 1948; LL.M., Georgetown U., 1963. Bar: Ohio 1948. Practice law Cleve., 1948-68; judge Cuyahoga County Ct. Common Pleas, Ohio, 1968-70, Ohio Ct. Appeals, Cleve., 1970-81; Judge U.S. Dist. Ct. (no. dist.), Ohio, 1981—; counsel, dir. Ohio Narcotics Investigation, 1953-55; asst. atty. gen. State of Ohio, 1951-56; trial atty. office chief counsel IRS, Washington, 1960-63. Chmn. Cuyahoga County Bd. Mental Retardation, 1967-70; trustee Cleve. State U., 1967-70, Mt. Sinai Hosp., Cleve., 1973-82; chmn. Ohio Criminal Justice Supervisory Commn., 1975-83. Mem. ABA; MEM. Greater Cleve. Bar Assn.; mem. Cuyahoga County Bar Assn., Fed. Bar Assn. Office: U S Dist Ct 400 U S Courthouse 201 Superior Ave Cleveland OH 44114

KREPPEL, MILTON MARK, lawyer; b. N.Y.C., June 30, 1951; s. Irving I. and Eva (Gross) K.; m. Geraldine Rienzi, Nov. 23, 1974; children: Rebecca, Rachel, Robyn. BS, U. Bridgeport, 1973; JD, South Tex. Coll. Law, 1978; MS, Pace U., 1985. Bar: Tex. 1978, U.S. Ct. Appeals (5th cir.) 1978, U.S.

Dist. Ct. (so. dist.) Tex. 1978, U.S. Tax Ct. 1978, U.S. Ct. Claims 1978, Fla. 1978, U.S. Ct. Mil. Appeals 1978, U.S. Ct. Customs and Patent Appeals 1979, N.Y. 1979, U.S. Dist. Ct. (ea. and so. dists.) N.Y. 1979, Temp. Emergency Ct. Appeals U.S. 1980, U.S. Ct. Internat. Trade 1981, U.S. Supreme Ct. 1981, U.S. Dist. Ct. (middle dist.) Fla. 1981, U.S. Ct. Appeals (11th cir.) 1981, U.S. Ct. Appeals (fed. cir.) 1983. Assoc. Brown, Goodman & Kreppel, New Rochelle, N.Y., 1978—; adj. prof. Mercy Coll., Dobbs Ferry, N.Y., 1986—. Merit badge counselor Boy Scouts Am., White Plains, N.Y., 1985. Mem. ABA, Assn. Trial Lawyers Am., N.Y. State Bar Assn., Fla. Bar Assn., Tex. Bar Assn., New Rochelle Bar Assn. (bd. dirs. 1986—), Westchester County Bar Assn. Republican. Jewish. Avocations: water skiing, auto mechanics, reading. Personal injury, General practice, General corporate. Office: 271 North Ave New Rochelle NY 10801

KREPPS, ETHEL CONSTANCE, lawyer; b. Mountain View, Okla., Oct. 31, 1937; d. Howard Haswell and Pearl (Moore) Goomda; R.N., St. John's Med. Center, 1971; B.S., U. Tulsa, 1974, J.D., 1979; m. George Randolph Krepps, Apr. 10, 1954; children—George Randolph, Edward Howard Moore. Nurse, St. John's Med. Center, Tulsa, 1971-75; admitted to Okla. bar, 1979; individual practice law, Tulsa, 1979—; mem. Indian law alumni com. U. Tulsa COll. Law; atty., dir. Indian Child Welfare Program, 1981—; atty. Native Am. Coalition, Inc., Kiowa Tribe Okla., Tulsa Indian Youth Council. Chmn., Okla. Indian Child Welfare Orgn., 1981—; tribal sec. Kiowa Tribe Okla., 1979-81. Mem. ABA, Fed. Bar Assn., Tulsa Women Lawyers Assn., AM. Indian Bar Assn., Okla. Indian Bar Assn., Okla. Bar Assn., Tulsa County Bar Assn., Am. Indian Nurses Assn. (v.p.), Nat. Indian Social Workers Assn. (pres. 1984—), Assn. Trial Lawyers Am., Phi Alpha Delta, Nat. Native Am. C. of C. (sec. 1980—). Democrat. Baptist. Author: A Strong Medicine Wind, 1979; Oklahoma Memories, 1981. Juvenile, Family and matrimonial, Indian law. Home: 1227 N Independence Oklahoma City OK 73107 Office: 1740 W 41st St Tulsa OK 74107

KRESS, MARJORIE MAE, lawyer; b. Green Bay, Wis., Aug. 26, 1952; d. Frederick F. and Elizabeth J. (Hansen) K.; children: Andrew Kress Joanis, Marie Kress Joanis. BA with distinction, U. Wis., 1974; JD, U. Minn., 1977. Bar: Minn. 1977, U.S. Dist. Ct. Minn. 1979, Wis. 1986. Asst. counsel Northwestern Nat. Life Ins. Co., Mpls., 1977-80; corp. counsel Western Life Ins. Co., St. Paul, 1980—. Mem. ABA (communications com., tort and ins. practice sect., forum com. on health law, labor and employment law sect., assoc. editor law jour. 1986—), Internat. Claim Assn. (law com. 1985—), Nat. Health Lawyers Assn. Insurance, Health. Office: Western Life Ins Co PO Box 64271 Saint Paul MN 55164

KRESS, RALPH HERBERT, lawyer; b. N.Y.C., Jan. 27, 1933; s. John H. and Clara (Laufer) K.; children—Robert B., Cynthia C. B.A., N.Y. U., 1953, J.D., 1956, LL.M., 1957. Bar: N.Y. 1957, U.S. Dist Ct. (ea. and so. dists.) N.Y. 1958, U.S. Tax Ct. 1958, U.S. Customs Ct. 1958, U.S. Ct. Appeals (2d cir.) 1958, U.S. Supreme Ct. 1961. Legal asst., atty. advisor to solicitor Port of N.Y., 1956-57; sole practice, N.Y.C., 1957-85; sr. ptnr. Kress & Kress, 1986—; spl. counsel to U.S. Congressman, 1962-72; spl. adv. to pres. Borough Queens, 1972-86; mem. Tricentennial Commn. 1983; counsel to deputy minority leader N.Y. State Senate, 1983; panelist Am. Arbitration Assn.; referee, arbitrator Civil Ct., City of N.Y., 1975—; referee, spl. guardian, cons. Supreme Ct. State of N.Y., 1976—; field counsel Fed. Nat. Mortgage Assn., Govt. Nat. Mortgage Assn., 1969—; mem. adv. bd. CUNY Law Sch.; mem. grievance com. appellate div. 2d jud. dept. for 2d and 11th Jud. Dists. Pres. emeritus Queensboro Soc. Prevention of Cruelty to Children; nat. past v.p. Muscular Dystrophy Assn.; trustee, v.p. Queens Mus. Named Hon. Citizen Republic of Korea; recipient numerous certs. of appreciation. Mem. ABA, Am. Judicature Soc., N.Y. State Bar Assn., N.Y. State Trial Lawyers Assn., Assn. of Bar of City of N.Y., Queens County Bar Assn. (com. on judiciary) Long Island City Lawyers Club, Assn. Trial Lawyers Am., Inst. Jud. Adminstrn., Am. Judges Assn., NYU Alumni Assn. Clubs: N.Y. Athletic, Rolls Royce Owners, Rolls Royce Enthusiasts. Probate, Real property, General litigation. Office: 37-09 30th Ave Long Island City NY 11103

KRETSINGER, TOM BARK, JR., lawyer; b. Kansas City, Mo., Dec. 12, 1955; s. Tom Bark and Carolyn (Trimble) K.; m. Jo Annis Hetherington, May 22, 1982; children: Mary Jo, Tom III. B.A., William Jewell Coll., 1978; J.D., U. Mo., 1981. Bars: Mo. 1981, U.S. Dist. Ct. (we. dist.) Mo. 1981, U.S. Ct. Appeals (8th cir.) 1983. Ptnr. Kretsinger & Kretsinger, Liberty, Mo., assoc. prof. bus. law William Jewell Coll., evening div., Liberty, 1984—. Campaign Coordinator Missourians for Roy Blunt, Clay County, 1984; vice chmn. Clay County Rep. Cen. Com., 1986—; vice chmn. Liberty Hist. Dist. Rev. Commn., 1985—, Clay County Rep. Cen. Com., 1986—; Mem. ABA, Mo. Bar Assn., Kansas City Bar Assn., Clay County Bar Assn. (sec./treas. 1983), Assn. Trial Lawyers Am., Transp. Lawyers Assn. Espicopalian. Motor carrier law, General corporate, General practice. Home: 139 N Water St Liberty MO 64068 Office: Kretsinger & Kretsinger 20 E Franklin Liberty MO 64068

KREUTZER, FRANKLIN DAVID, lawyer; b. Miami, Fla., June 5, 1940; s. Ernst and Elsa (Meitner) K.; m. Judith Sue Jacobs, June 16, 1963; children—Renee Charlotte, Jay Ernst. B.B.A., U. Miami, 1960, J.D., 1964. Bar: Fla. 1964, U.S. Dist. Ct. (so. dist.) Fla. 1965, U.S. Ct. Appeals (5th cir.) 1971, U.S. Ct. Appeals (11th cir.) 1982, U.S. Supreme Ct. 1971. Assoc., Shevin, Goodman & Holtzman, 1964-65; ptnr. Wallace & Kreutzer, P.A., 1966-74; sole practice, Miami, 1974—; participant White House Seminar on Legal Interns, 1963; spl. asst. atty. gen. State of Fla., 1975-78; spl. counsel to comptroller State of Fla., 1975-78; gen. counsel Democratic Exec. Com. Dade County, 1968-70. Mem. City of Miami Pension and Retirement Bd., 1966-68; chmn. Miami Charter Rev. Bd., 1967-81; mem. Dade County Charter Rev. Commn., 1981-82; pres. Greater Miami Hebrew Fla. Loan Assn., 1974-77; regional pres. S.E. region United Synagogue Am., 1980-84, v.p., 1983-85, chmn. council regional presidents, 1983-85, internat. pres., 1985—; internat. v.p. World Council of Synagogues, 1985—; exec. com., bd. dirs. Mercaz Conservative Zionism, 1984—; bd. dirs. Jewish Theol. Sem. of Am., 1985—; exec. com. Synagogue Council of Am., 1985—; pres. Temple Zion, 1977-79; bd. dirs. Gen. Council World Zionist Orgn., 1985—; bd. dirs. South Fla. Leukemia Soc., 1968-77; pres. South Fla. chpt. Cystic Fibrosis Found., 1970-74; endowment com. U. Miami, 1974—. Recipient cert. of appreciation City of Miami, 1968; recipient Order Golden Donkey, Dem. Exec. Com. Dade County, 1970. Mem. ABA, Fla. Bar Assn., Fla. Trial Lawyers Assn., Dade County Trial Lawyers Assn., Dade County Bar Assn., Acad. Trial Lawyers Am. (exec. com. 1985—), Am. Israel Pub. Affairs Com. (exec. com. 1985—), Nat. Jewish Community Relations Adv. Council, Conf. of Pres. of Major Am. Jewish Orgns, Omicron Delta Kappa, Phi Delta Phi. Democrat. State civil litigation, Insurance, Administrative and regulatory. Home: 8615 SW 48th St Miami FL 33155 Office: 3041 NW 7th St Suite 100 Miami FL 33125

KREUTZER, S. STANLEY, lawyer; b. N.Y.C., Jan. 24, 1907; s. Philip and Fannie (Bleecker) K.; m. Corinne A. Kreutzer, Aug. 21, 1932; children—Phyllis Lynn, Cynthia Ellen. LL.B., St. John's U., N.Y.C., 1929. Bar: N.Y. 1929. Assoc. Fletcher, Brown & Twyeffort, N.Y.C., 1929-32; ptnr. Kreutzer, Heller, Selman & Galt, N.Y.C., 1933-72; sole practice, 1972-82; mem. Jacob D. Fuchsberg Law Firm, N.Y.C., 1983—; mem. N.Y. State-City Fiscal Relations Com., 1955-56; spl. asst. atty. gen. State of N.Y., 1956-57; chief counsel N.Y.C. Council, 1957-59, N.Y. State Legislature, 1958-60, counsel N.Y. State Assembly, 1961-63, N.Y. State Legis. Ethics Commn., 1964-65; spl. counsel to Bd. Suprs. Suffolk County (N.Y.), 1969, All Town Govts. Nassau County (N.Y.), 1970; counsel Town of Hempstead, Town of Oyster Bay, Town of North Hempostead; chief counsel N.Y.C. Bd. Ethics, 1960-78; chmn., commr. N.Y. State Temporary Commn. on Lobbying, 1978-85; hearing officer N.Y. State Comptroller, 1968; spl. referee Appellate Div. Supreme Ct. N.Y. State, 1969, 70, 81—; cons. in field. Chmn. Kings County City Fusion Party, 1934-37; pres. Nassau Suffolk Legis. Clearing House, 1962-69; bd. dirs. N.Y. Legis. Service, 1962-86, N.Y. State Tb and Health Assn., 1970-74, Urban Acad., N.Y.C., 1974-77, N.Y.C. Bicentennial Com., 1974-78, Nat. Inst. Voter Registration, 1982-83, Honest Ballot Assn., 1981[5; mem. N.Y. State Gov.'s Com. on Judiciary, 1976-77. Recipient Coronet award and medal St. Thomas Coll., 1967, Golden Jubilee medal St. John's U., 1981, Council Govtl. Ethics Laws award. Fellow Am. Bar Found.; mem. U.S. Supreme Ct. Hist. Soc., ABA, N.Y. State Bar Assn., N.Y. County Lawyers Assn., Am. Judicature Soc., Bklyn. Bar Assn., Archaeol. Inst. Am. Clubs: Merchants, Advt., Masons. Contbr. articles to profl. jours. General practice, Administrative and regulatory, Federal civil litigation. Office: 500 Fifth Ave New York NY 10110

KRIEG, MARC SHEA, lawyer, engineer; b. N.Y.C., Oct. 27, 1942; s. Joseph and Helen (Bennett) K.; m. Linda Sue Solarsh, July 4, 1965; children—Randi, Stephen. B.M.E., CCNY, 1965, M.M.E., 1967; J.D., N.Y. Law Sch., 1971. Bar: N.Y. 1972, U.S. Dist. Ct. (so. dist.) 1974, U.S. Dist. Ct. (ea. dist.) 1975. Lic. profl. engr., N.Y. Mech. engr. Grumman Co., Bethpage, N.Y., 1965-68, 69-70, Avien, Woodside, N.Y., 1968-69, City of N.Y., 1970-71; assoc. Cummingham & Kaming, P.C., N.Y.C., 1971-78; ptnr. Sweeney, Cunningham & Krieg, N.Y.C., 1978-81; sole practice, Huntington, N.Y., 1981—. Democratic committeeman, Huntington Twp., 1973—; mem., vice chmn. Zoning Bd. Appeals, Huntington, 1978—; mem. YMCA. Recipient Cornelius W. Wickersham Jr. award Fed. Bar Council; Nathaniel Goldstein award; Am. Jurisprudence award. Mem. Nassau County Bar Assn., Suffolk County Bar Assn., Bar Assn. City N.Y., N.Y. State Profl. Engrs. Democrat. Jewish. State civil litigation, Criminal, Labor. Home and Office: 5 Heather Ct Dix Hills NY 11746

KRIEGER, ANDREW S., lawyer; b. Poughkeepsie, N.Y., Jan. 8, 1950; s. Eugene Brewer and Barbara (Smith) K.; m. Jane R. Russell, May 10, 1980; 1 child, Andrew R. BA in English, Lafayette Coll., 1972; JD, St. Johns U., N.Y.C., 1976. Bar: N.Y. 1977, U.S. Dist. Ct. (so., ea. and no. dists.) N.Y. 1977. Assoc. Duggan & Crotty, New Windsor, N.Y., 1977-79; sole practice New Windsor, 1979-82, 85—; assoc. Finkelstein, Kaplan, Levine et al, Newburgh, N.Y., 1982-85. Justice Town of New Windsor, N.Y., 1985. Mem. N.Y. State Bar Assn., Newburgh Bar Assn., Orange County Bar Assn. Lodge: Lions. Avocations: golf, bridge, hunting, history study. State civil litigation, General practice, Real property. Home: 17 Clintonwood Dr New Windsor NY 12550 Office: 219 Quassaick Ave New Windsor NY 12550

KRIEGER, FREDERIC MICHAEL, lawyer; b. Wilmington, Del., Apr. 28, 1950; s. Arthur H. and Edythe (Ploener) K.; m. Alice T. Whittelsey, Oct. 28, 1979; children: Daniel Marsh, Anna Caroline. AB, U. Pa., 1972; J.D., Emory U., 1975; student U. Lancaster, Eng., 1970-71. Bar: Ga. 1975, D.C. 1976, Pa. 1978, Ill. 1984, U.S. Dist. Ct. (no. dist.) Ga. 1976, U.S. Dist. Ct. (ea. dist.) Pa. 1978, U.S. Dist. Ct. D.C. 1976, U.S. Ct. Appeals (3d cir.) 1979, U.S. Dist. Ct. (no. dist.) Ill. 1984. Trial atty. SEC, Washington, 1975-78; assoc. firm Morgan, Lewis & Bockius, Phila., 1978-82; ptnr. firm Miller Schreiber & Sloan, Phila., 1982-83; assoc. gen. counsel Chgo. Bd. Options Exchange, 1983—; adj. faculty Am. U. Law Sch., 1977-78, Cath. U. Law Sch., 1977-78, IIT/Chgo. Kent. Coll., 1986—; lectr. Inst. for Paralegal Tng., Phila., 1982 . Contbr. articles to law jours. Bd. dirs. Friends of Glencoe (Ill.) Pub. Library, 1984; bd. dirs. Glencoe Human Relations Com., 1986—; mem. New Trier Democratic Assn., 1984. Mem. ABA (mem. subcom. on securities markets and market structure, fed. regulation of securities com.). Club: Univ. of Chgo. Securities, Federal civil litigation. Home: 354 Madison Ave Glencoe IL 60022 Office: Chgo Bd Options Exchange 400 S LaSalle St Chicago IL 60605

KRIEGER, PAUL EDWARD, lawyer; b. Fairmont, W.Va., Mar. 30, 1942; s. Paul Julius Krieger and Martha Frances (Graham) Ralph; m. Elizabeth N. Krieger, July 2, 1965; children: Andrew, Thomas. BS in Mining Engring., U. Pitts., 1964; postgrad. Pa. State U., 1964-65; LLB, U. Md., 1968; LLM, George Washington U., 1971. Bar: Md. 1968, D.C. 1973, Tex. 1979, U.S. Patent and Trademark Office, 1970. Faculty research asst. U. Md., 1967-70; assoc. Brumbaugh, Graves, Donohue & Raymond, N.Y.C., 1970-71; ptnr. Lane, Aitken, Dunner & Ziems, Washington, 1971-78; sr. pat. atty. Dresser Industries Inc., Dallas, 1978-79; ptnr. Pravel, Gambrell, Hewitt, Kimball & Krieger, Houston, 1979—; adj. prof. U. Houston Law Ctr., 1985—. Mem. ABA, Am. Pat. Law Assn., State Bar Tex., Houston Pat. Law Assn., N.Y. Pat. Law Assn. Patent, Trademark and copyright, Federal civil litigation. Home: 12714 Old Oaks Houston TX 77024 Office: 1177 W Loop S Suite 1010 Houston TX 77027

KRIER, JAMES EDWARD, legal educator, author; b. Milw., Oct. 19, 1939; s. Ambrose Edward and Genevieve Ida (Behling) K.; m. Gayle Marian Grimsrud, Mar. 22, 1962; children—Jennifer, Amy; m. Wendy Louise Wilkes, Apr. 20, 1974; children—Andrew Wilkes-Krier, Patrick Wilkes-Krier. B.S., U. Wis., 1961, J.D., 1966. Bar: Wis. 1966, U.S. Ct. Claims 1968. Law clk. to chief justice Calif. Supreme Ct., San Francisco, 1966-67; assoc. Arnold & Porter, Washington, 1967-69; acting prof., then prof. law UCLA, 1969-78, 80-83; prof. law Stanford U., Calif., 1978-80, U. Mich. Law Sch., Ann Arbor, 1983—; cons. Calif. Inst. Tech., EPA; mem. Nat. Acad. Scis. Pesticides Panel, 1972-75, Com. on Energy and the Environment, 1975-77. Author: Environmental Law and Policy, 1971, (with Stewart) 2d edit., 1978; (with Ursin) Pollution and Policy, 1977; (with Dukeminier) Property, 1981; contbr. articles to profl. jours. Served to lt. U.S. Army, 1961-63. Mem. Wis. State Bar Assn., Artus, Order of Coif, Phi Kappa Phi. Real property, Environment, Legal education. Office: U Mich Law Sch Ann Arbor MI 48109

KRIESBERG, SIMEON M., lawyer; b. Washington, June 4, 1951; s. Martin and Harriet M. Kriesberg. AB, Harvard U., 1973; M in Pub. Affairs, Princeton U., 1977; JD, Yale U., 1977. Bar: D.C. 1977, U.S. Dist. Ct. D.C. 1978, U.S. Ct. Appeals (D.C. cir.) 1978, U.S. Ct. Internat. Trade 1979, U.S. Ct. Appeals (Fed. cir.) 1981, U.S. Supreme Ct. 1982. Assoc. Leva, Hawes, Symington, Martin & Oppenheimer, Washington, 1977-83; sr. counsel internat. trade Sears World Trade Inc., Washington, 1983-85, v.p., gen. counsel, 1985—. Article and book rev. editor Yale U. Law Rev. Jour., 1976-77. Mem. ABA, Am. Soc. Internat. Law, D.C. Bar Assn., Internat. Human Rights Law Group. Private international, General corporate, Public international. Office: Sears World Trade Inc 633 Pennsylvania Ave NW Washington DC 20004

KRIGER, BRIAN ELLIOTT, lawyer; b. Paterson, N.J., Dec. 31, 1954; s. Philip and Rhoda (Odsess) K.; m. Barbara Siegel, May 29, 1983; children: Adam Scott, Benjamin Marc. BS, Syracuse U., 1976; JD cum laude, Western New England Coll., 1979; LLM in Corp. Law, NYU, 1980. Bar: Conn. 1980, U.S. Dist. Ct. N.J. 1980, N.J. 1981, U.S. Dist. Ct. Conn. 1981, U.S. Dist. Ct. (so. dist.) N.Y. 1981, U.S. Dist. Ct. (ea. dist.) N.Y. 1982, N.Y. 1983. Law clk. to chief judge U.S. Bankruptcy Ct., N.Y.C., 1980-82; assoc. Shea & Gould, N.Y.C., 1982—. Mem. ABA, Comml. Law League Am., Bankruptcy Lawyer Bar Assn. Bankruptcy, Consumer commercial. Home: 200 Old Palisade Rd Apt 8B Fort Lee NJ 07024 Office: Shea & Gould 330 Madison Ave New York NY 10017

KRINSKY, ANDREW NEAL, lawyer; b. Boston, Apr. 17, 1951; s. Joseph and Corinne (Susman) K. BA, Brandeis U., 1973; JD, U. Pa., 1976. Bar: N.Y. 1977, Mass. 1977, U.S. Dist. Ct. (so. and ea. dists.) N.Y. 1977, U.S. Ct. Appeals (2d cir.) 1981. Assoc. Olnick, Boxer, Blumberg, Lane and Troy, N.Y.C., 1983-85, ptnr., 1986—; ptnr. Stroock & Stroock & Lavan, N.Y.C., 1987—. Mem. Assn. of Bar of City of N.Y., Phi Beta Kappa. Federal civil litigation, State civil litigation, Real property. Office: Stroock & Stroock & Lavan 7 Hanover Sq New York NY 10017

KRINZMAN, RICHARD NEIL, lawyer; b. Orange, N.J., July 18, 1947; s. Robert I. and Krinzman and Lynn (Barg) Beller; m. Michele Robin Lundy, May 11, 1968; children: Melissa Ellen, Michael David. BBA, U. Miami, 1969, JD, 1972. Bar: Fla. 1972, U.S. Dist. Ct. (so. dist.) Fla. 1972. Assoc. Frank, Strelkow & Gay, Miami Beach, Fla., 1972-73, Marx & Squitero, Miami, Fla., 1973-76, Krongold & Bass, Coral Gables, Fla., 1976-78; ptnr. Holtzman & Krinzman P.A., Miami, 1978—. Mem. Miami Youth Fair Com., 1983—. Mem. ABA, Fla. Bar Assn., South Miami-Kendall C. of C., Indsl. Assn. Dade County. Democrat. Jewish. Avocations: boating, water skiing, white water rafting. Banking, Real property, Consumer commercial. Home: 9800 SW 121st St Miami FL 33176 Office: 8585 Sunset Dr #190 Miami FL 33143

KRIPKE, KENNETH NORMAN, lawyer; b. Toledo, Feb. 16, 1920; s. Maurice and Celia (Vine) K.; m. Derril Kanter, Nov. 4, 1945; children: Teri Schwartz, Marcie K. Gaon. Student, Ohio State U., 1937-41; LL.B., U. Colo., 1948. Bar: Colo. 1949, U.S. Ct. Appeals (10th cir.) 1954, U.S. Ct. Appeals (5th cir.) 1965, U.S. Supreme Ct. 1967, U.S. Ct. Appeals (8th cir.) 1974. Mem. firm Kripke & McLean, 1953-58, Kripke, Hoffman & Carrigan (and successors), 1965-73; individual practice law Denver, 1973-80; partner Kripke, Epstein & Lawrence (P.C.), Denver, 1980—; mem. nominating com. 9th Jud. Cir., 1976-78, standing com. on rules civil procedure Colo. Supreme Ct., 1978—; guest speaker Internat. Congress Hosp. laws, Tel Aviv, 1985. Treas. Denver Allied Jewish Fedn., 1978-84; chmn. Denver civil rights com. Anti-Defamation League B'nai B'rith, 1976-82; mem. nat. law com. Anti-Defamation League, 1980—, mem. nat. civil rights com., 1979—. Served with USAAF, 1942-46. Fellow Internat. Soc. Barristers, Roscoe Pound-Am. Trial Lawyers Found.; mem. ABA (discovery subcom. of litigation sect. 1982—), Assn. Trial Lawyers Am. (past bd. govs., past exec. adv. com., chmn. conv. 1962, 69), Western Trial Lawyers Assn. (sec. 1971-72, v.p. 1973, pres. 1974-75), Colo. Trial Lawyers Assn. (pres. 1958, amicus curiae com. 1977—), Colo. Bar Assn. (interprofl. com. 1975—, litigation council 1982—, chmn. 1985—), Arapahoe County Bar Assn., Am. Judicature Soc., Am. Arbitration Assn. (panel arbitrators), Colo. Exec. Forum, Internat. Assn. Jewish Lawyers and Jurists. Home: 4930 E 1st Ave Denver CO 80220 Office: 4100 E Mississippi Suite 710 Denver CO 80222

KRIPNER, GEORGE MARTIN, lawyer; b. Munich, Bavaria, Fed. Republic of Germany, July 17, 1954; s. Josef and Olga (Wlasjeva) K.; m. Alison Jane Schwartz, May 10, 1975 (div. Mar. 1982). BA, Johns Hopkins U., 1975; JD, U. Balt., 1978. Bar: Pa. 1978. Ptnr. Taylor & Kripner, Jacksonville, N.C., 1983—. Bd. dirs. Am. Cancer Soc., Onslow County, N.C., 1986—. Served to capt. U.S. Army, 1978-82, Korea. Mem. ABA, Assn. Trial Lawyers Am. Democrat. Military, Administrative and regulatory, Criminal. Home: 611 Myrtlewood Circle Jacksonville NC 28540 Office: Taylor & Kripner 824 Gum Branch Rd Jacksonville NC 28540

KRISTOL, DANIEL MARVIN, lawyer; b. Wilmington, Del., July 7, 1936; s. Abraham Louis and Pearl Cecile (Oltman) K.; m. Katherine Fairfax Chinn, Nov. 4, 1968; children—Sarah Douglas, Susan Fairfax. B.A., U. Pa., 1958, LL.B., 1961. Bar: Del. 1961, U.S. Dist. Ct. Del. 1962. Assoc., ptnr. Killoran & VanBrunt, Wilmington, Del., 1961-76; dir. Prickett, Jones, Elliott, Kristol & Schnee, P.A. and ptnr. predecessor Prickett, Ward Burt & Sanders, Wilmington, 1976—; pub. defender Ct. Common Pleas, Wilmington, 1966-69; asst. solicitor City of Wilmington, 1970-73; spl. counsel Div. Housing State of Del., 1972—, gen. counsel Del. State Housing Authority, 1973—. Served with USAR, 1964-67. Mem. ABA, Del. State Bar Assn. (chmn. real and personal property com. 1974-78, chmn. world peace through law com. 1980-81), Am. Coll. Real Estate Lawyers. Republican. Jewish. Clubs: Wilmington; Greenville (Del.) Country. Contracts commercial, Landlord-tenant, Real property. Office: PO Box 1328 Wilmington DE 19899

KRITSELIS, WILLIAM NICHOLAS, lawyer; b. Sault Sainte Marie, Mich., Apr. 5, 1931; s. Nicholas William and Theodora G. (Gianacopoulos) K.; m. Elaine John Jennings, Sept. 1, 1963; 1 child, Nicholas William. BA, Mich. State U., 1959; JD, Ohio No. U., 1962. Bar: Mich. 1962, U.S. Dist. Ct. (we. dist.) Mich. 1963, U.S. Supreme Ct. 1966, U.S. Dist. Ct. (ea. dist.) Mich. 1968. Asst. prosecutor Ingham County, Lansing, Mich., 1963-64, chief criminal div., 1964-65; sole practice Lansing, 1965—. Pres. Holy Trinity Greek Orthodox Ch., Lansing, 1977; lifetime mem. NAACP, Lansing. Served with USN, 1951-55. Fellow State Bar Mich. Found; mem. ABA, Fed. Bar Assn., Mich. Bar Assn. (med.-legal com. 1978-81, negligence com. 1982-85), Assn. Trial Lawyers Am. (lectr. product liability), Mich. Trial Lawyers Assn. (lectr. on construction, R.R. and product liabilty, bd. govs. 1978—), Lansing Trial Lawyers Assn. (pres. 1966-70), Am. Judicature Soc., Lawyers for Pub. Justice, Am. Arbitration Assn., Mich. State Alumni Assn. Club: Mich. State U. Pres.'s (East Lansing). Personal injury, Insurance, Federal civil litigation. Office: Church Kritselis Wyble & Robinson 3939 Capital City Blvd Lansing MI 48906

KRIVIT, DANIEL HENRY, lawyer; b. Jersey City, N.J., Feb. 20, 1933; s. Maurice M. and Syd Ruth (Baron) K.; children—Diane, John, Kenneth; m. Sandra M. Stephenson, Jan. 4, 1986. B.A., Brown U., 1954; J.D., Boston U., 1957; postgrad. studies in labor law Cornell U., 1965-66. Bar: Mass. 1957, N.J. 1959, D.C. 1971, U.S. Supreme Ct. 1969. Ptnr. Krivit & Krivit, Jersey City, N.J., 1959-65; exec. asst. to Senator Harrison Williams, 1966-67; chief counsel select com. on edn. U.S. Ho. of Reps., 1967-69; chief counsel subcom. on manpower, compensation and health and safety U.S. Ho. of Reps., 1969-76; practice, Washington, 1976—. Founder Krivit & Krivit, P.C. Mem. ABA, Am. Judicature Soc., Mass. Bar Assn., N.J. Bar Assn., Hudson County (N.J.) Bar Assn., Bar Assn. D.C., D.C. Bar Assn., U.S. Supreme Ct. Bar, Am. Acad. Polit. and Social Sci., Soc. for Occupational and Environ. Health, Nat. Council Urban Econ. Devel., Pi Lambda Phi (past nat. sec. nat. council). Clubs: Nat. Democratic, Capitol Hill. Author fed. edn. and labor legislation. Administrative and regulatory, Labor, Government contracts and claims. Office: 50 E St SE Washington DC 20003

KRIVOSHA, NORMAN, chief justice state supreme court; b. Detroit, Aug. 3, 1934; s. David B. and Molly K.; m. Helene Miriam Sherman, July 31, 1955; children: Terri Lynn, Rhonda Ann. B.S., U. Nebr., 1956, J.D., 1958; LL.D., Central Mich. U., 1983, Creighton U., 1985. Bar: Nebr. Ptnr. firm Ginsburg, Rosenberg, Ginsburg & Krivosha, Lincoln, Nebr., 1958-78; chief justice Nebr. Supreme Ct., Lincoln, 1978—; city atty. City of Lincoln, 1969-70; gen. counsel Lincoln Electric System, 1969-78, Lincoln Gen. Hosp., 1969-78; mem. Uniform Law Commn., 1973—. Pres. Lincoln council Camp Fire Girls; pres. Congregation Tifereth Israel, Lincoln; pres. central states region United Synagogue Am., v.p., 1983—; bd. dirs. Lincoln YMCA; Nebr. chmn. Israel Bonds; chmn. fund drive Lincoln Jewish Welfare Fedn.; mem. Lincoln Charter Revision Commn.; bd. dirs. Ramah Commn., Camp Ramah, Wis. Recipient Outstanding Jewish Leader award State of Israel Bonds, 1978. Mem. ABA, Nebr. Bar Assn. (chmn. com. on procedure), Lincoln Bar Assn., Am. Trial Lawyers Assn., Nebr. Assn. Trial Attys. (sec. 1961-64, v.p. 1964-65), Am. Soc. Hosp. Attys., Am. Pub. Power Assn. (chmn. legal sect.), Lincoln C. of C. (bd. dirs.), Sigma Alpha Mu (nat. pres. 1980-83). Judicial administration. Home: 2835 O'Reilly Dr Lincoln NE 68502 Office: Nebr Supreme Ct Suite 2214 State Capitol Bldg Lincoln NE 68509

KROENER, WILLIAM FREDERICK, III, lawyer; b. N.Y.C., Aug. 27, 1945; s William Frederick Jr. and Barbara (Mitchell) K.; m. Evelyn Somerville Bibb, Sept. 3, 1966; children—William Frederick, Mary Elizabeth, Evangeline Alberta, James Mitchell. A.B., Yale Coll., 1967; M.B.A., Stanford U., 1971, J.D., 1971. Bar: Calif. 1972, N.Y. 1979, D.C. 1983. Assoc. Davis Polk & Wardwell, N.Y.C. and London, 1971-79, ptnr., N.Y.C., 1979-82, Washington and N.Y.C., 1982—; dir. Indosuez & Ptnrs. N.Am. III N.V. and Mitsubishi Bank Trust Co. of N.Y. Mng. editor Stanford Law Rev., 1970-71. Mem. bd. visitors Stanford U. Law Sch., 1983—. Mem. ABA, N.Y. State Bar Assn., Assn. Bar City N.Y., Fed. Bar Assn., N.Y. Law Inst. Republican. Episcopalian. Clubs: Yale, Wall St. (N.Y.C.); University (Washington); Kenwood Golf (Bethesda, Md.). Banking, General corporate, Private international. Home: 6412 Brookside Dr Chevy Chase MD 20815 also: 404 E 79th St Apt 28-E New York NY 10021 Office: Davis Polk & Wardwell 1575 Eye St NW Suite 400 Washington DC 20005 also: One Chase Manhattan Plaza New York NY 10005

KROGER, CATHARINE ELISABETH, lawyer; b. Eindhoven, The Netherlands, June 19, 1949; came to U.S., 1964; d. Ferdinand Anne and Elisabeth Johanna Kroger. BA, U. So. Calif., 1970; MA, San Diego State U., 1977; JD, Western State U., 1979. Bar: Calif. 1980. Assoc. Sharron Voorhees, San Diego, 1980-81; sole practice San Diego, 1981—. Mem. Calif. Bar Assn., Assn. Trial Lawyers Am., Calif. Trial Lawyers Assn., San Diego Trial Lawyers Assn. Personal injury, Insurance. Office: 3258 4th Ave San Diego CA 92103

KROHN, FRANK RONALD, lawyer; b. Washington, Sept. 22, 1943; s. Herbert F. and Lucy (Snyder) K. BA, Denison U., 1965; JD, U. Minn., 1968. Bar: Minn. 1968, U.S. Dist. Ct. Minn. 1972, Calif. 1973, U.S. Dist. Ct. (ea. dist.) Calif. 1973, U.S. Ct. Appeals (9th cir.) 1973, Ill. 1975. Sec., gen counsel N. Cen. Co., St. Paul, 1968-71; v.p., assoc. gen. counsel Pacific Standard Life, Davis, Calif., 1971-73; sole practice San Francisco, 1973-75; assoc. gen. counsel Waste Mgmt. Inc., Oak Brook, Ill., 1975-80, staff v.p., dep. gen. counsel, 1984—; v.p., gen. counsel Chem. Waste Mgmt., Oak Brook, 1981-84. Served with USAR, 1969-75. Mem. ABA, Calif. Bar Assn., Ill. Bar Assn., Minn. Bar Assn., Am. Corp. Counsel Assn. General

corporate. Office: Waste Mgmt Inc 3003 Butterfield Rd Oak Brook IL 60521

KROLL, ARTHUR HERBERT, lawyer, legal educator; b. N.Y.C., Dec. 2, 1939; s. Abraham and Sylvia Kroll; m. Lois Handmacher, June, 1964; children—Douglas, Pamela. B.A., Cornell U., 1961; LL.B., St. John's U., 1965; LL.M. in Taxation, NYU, 1969. Bar: N.Y. 1965, D.C. 1982. Assoc. Patterson, Belknap, Webb & Tyler, N.Y.C., 1965-72, ptnr., 1972—; adj. prof. U. Miami Sch. Law; adv. bd. BNA Tax Mgmt., Inc.; PLI Tax Adv. Bd.; mem. adv. com. NYU ann. Inst. on Fed. Taxation; adv. bd. U. Miami Inst. on Estate Planning. Mem. ABA (chmn. com. on adminstrn., investment and employee retirement income security act litigation of real property, probate, and trust law sect.), Am. Pension Conf. (steering com). Author monthly newsletter on exec. compensation; author series on compensation, 3 vols.; mem. bd. contbg. editors and advisers Rev. of Taxation of Individuals; lectr. profl. confs. Pension, profit-sharing, and employee benefits, Corporate taxation, Probate. Office: Patterson Belknap Webb & Tyler 30 Rockefeller Plaza New York NY 10112

KROLL, ELLIOTT MARK, lawyer; b. N.Y.C., Jan. 8, 1953; m. Marcy Hochman; 1 child, Matthew Jay. B.A. in Govt., Bard Coll., 1974; J.D., Hastings Coll. Law, San Francisco, 1977. Bar: Calif. 1977, N.Y. 1978, D.C. 1979. Ptnr. Kroll & Tract, N.Y.C. Mem. ABA, Assn. Bar City N.Y., Calif. Bar Assn., Bar Assn. D.C., N.Y. State Bar Assn. Contbr. articles to profl. jours. Office: 500 Fifth Ave New York NY 10110

KROLL, SOL, lawyer; b. Russia, Aug. 10, 1918; m. Ruth Saslow; children: Gerald, Judy, Elise, Elliott. LLB, St. John's U., 1942. Bar: N.Y. 1942, U.S. Supreme Ct. 1956. Ptnr. Kroll, Tract, Harnett, Pomerantz & Cameron (formerly Kroll, Pomerantz & Cameron); U.S. counsel to the Inst. of London Underwriters; mem. com. of interfraud task force N.Y. Ins. Dept.; mem. Industry Adv. Com. on Ins.; bd. govs. Internat. Ins. Seminar. Contbr. articles on Am. ins. law to L'Argus mag. Mem. ABA, Fed. Bar Assn., N.Y. State Bar Assn., Internat. Assn. Ins. Csl., N.Y. Trial Lawyers Assn. Insurance. Home: 32 Stonewall Ln Mamaroneck NY 10543 Office: 500 Fifth Ave New York NY 10110

KRONE, PAUL WILLIAM, lawyer; b. Cin., June 18, 1925; s. Adalbert and May R. (Feinthel) K.; m. Dorothy E. Gebhart, Aug. 6, 1946; children: Jay A., Bruce A., Roger A., Carol A. BBA, U. Cin., 1950; JD, Chase Law Sch., 1958. Bar: Ohio 1958, U.S. Dist. Ct. Ohio 1959, Ind. 1979. Assoc. Hoover, Beall & Eichel, Cin., 1959-70; ptnr. Eichel & Krone Co. L.P.A., Cin., 1971—; tchr. real estate law U. Cin.; arbitrator Better Bus. Bur., Hamilton County Common Pleas Ct., Cin., 1984—. Served to 2d lt. USAF, 1943-46. Mem. ABA, Ind. Bar Assn., Ohio Bar Assn., Cin. Bar Assn., Hamilton County Arbitration Assn. (arbitrator), Am. Arbitration Assn. (arbitrator). Republican. Avocations: fly fishing, carpentry. General corporate, Probate, Real property. Home: 3068 Victoria Ave Cincinnati OH 45208 Office: Eichel & Krone Co LPA 524 Walnut St Suite 508 Cincinnati OH 45202

KRONENBERG, DEBRA ANN, lawyer; b. N.Y.C., June 1, 1952; d. Bernard and Marian R. (Caine) K. Student, Yale U., 1973-74; BA, U. Rochester, 1974; MA, U. Mich., 1976; JD, Lewis & Clark Coll., 1980. Bar: Oreg. 1981, U.S. Dist. Ct. Oreg. 1981. Law clk. Met. Pub. Defender, Portland, Oreg., 1978-79, Dept. of Justice, Portland, 1979-80; ptnr. Kronenberg & Miller, Portland, 1981-82; sole practice Portland, 1982—; treas. Occupational Health Council, Portland, 1983-86. Mem. Spl. Needs Hiring Task Force, Portland, 1984-85; bd. dirs. Portland Saturday Market, Portland, 1981-82, Northwest Dist. Assn., Portland, 1983-85, Northwest Neighborhood Fed. Credit Union, Portland, 1983-85. Mem. ABA, Multnomah Bar Assn. (status women lawyers com.). Democrat. Jewish. Club: Oreg. Velo (Portland). Avocations: cycling, celtic harp, cross country skiing. Family and matrimonial, Workers' compensation, Social Security. Office: 2066 NW Irving Suite 2 Portland OR 97209

KRONMAN, ANTHONY TOWNSEND, law educator, lawyer; b. 1945; m. Nancy I. Greenberg, 1982. B.A., Williams Coll., 1968, Ph.D., 1972; J.D., Yale U., 1975. Bar: Minn. 1975, N.Y. 1983. Assoc. prof. U. Minn., 1975-76; asst. prof. U. Chgo., 1976-79; vis. assoc. prof. Yale U. Law Sch., New Haven, 1978-79, prof., 1979—, Edward J. Phelps prof. law, 1985—. Editor: (with R. Posner) The Economics of Contract Law, 1979, (with F. Kessler and G. Gilmore) Cases and Materials on Contracts, 1986; past mem. editorial bd. Yale Law Jour.; author: Max Weber, 1983. Danforth Found. fellow, 1968-72. Mem. Selden Soc. Legal education. Office: Yale U Law Sch Drawer 401A Yale Sta New Haven CT 06520

KRONMAN, CAROL JANE, lawyer; b. Passaic, N.J., Mar. 25, 1944; d. Robert M. and Helen K. (Harris) K.; m. William D. Lipkind, Aug. 15, 1965 (div. 1975); children: Audrey Jane, Heather Sue. AB, Cornell U., 1965; MA, Columbia U., 1966; JD, Yeshiva U., 1980. Bar: N.Y. 1981, N.J. 1981, Fla. 1981, U.S. Dist. Ct. N.J., U.S. Dist. Ct. (so. dist.) N.Y. Asst. prof. William Paterson Coll., Wayne, N.J., 1967-69; treas. Capital Theatre Inc., N.J., 1977-83; coordinator paralegal studies Montclair State Coll., N.J., 1982-83, prof., 1982-85; ptnr. Kronman & Kronman P.A., Totowa, N.J., 1981-85; ptnr. N.J. office Max E. Greenberg, Cantor & Reiss, South Hackensack, N.J., 1986—; pvt. investment advisor, N.J., 1977-84. Recipient Certs. of Appreciation, Rotary Club, Caldwell and Parsippany, N.J. Mem. ABA, N.J. Bar Assn., N.Y. Bar Assn., Fla. Bar Assn., Bergen County Bar Assn. Federal civil litigation, Probate, Construction. Home: 26 Spruce Rd North Caldwell NJ 07006 Office: Max E Greenberg Cantor & Reiss 3 Empire Blvd South Hackensack NJ 07606

KRONMILLER, BERT WILSON, lawyer; b. Mt. Erie, Ill., Jan. 6, 1904; s. Jacob Michael and Clara Olive (Riggs) K.; m. Josephine Mary Bednar, Sept. 21, 1929 (dec. Mar. 1984); children—Bert W., Marie Joan, Myrna Jane, Patrick William; m. Loretta Page Nelson, Sept. 7, 1986. B.A., Creighton U., 1929, J.D., 1931. Bar: Mont. 1931, Nebr. 1931, U.S. Supreme Ct. 1964. Sole practice, Hardin, Mont., 1931—; county atty. Big Horn County, Mont., 1938-52; spl. asst. atty. gen. Mont., 1942-46; tribal atty. Crow Tribes, 1951-68, No. Cheyenne Tribe, 1952-68; mem. legal-med. panel Mont. Trustee Rocky Mountain Coll., Billings, Mont.; active Mont. Republicans. Recipient Award of Merit Creighton U., 1969. Mem. United Ch. of Christ. Mem. ABA, Mont. Bar Assn., Am. Judicature Soc. Probate. Home: 618 W 2d St Hardin MT 59034 Office: 314 N Custer Kronmiller Bldg Hardin MT 59034

KROUSE, GWIN M., lawyer; b. N.Y.C., Dec. 14, 1952; d. William J. and Florence E. L. (Richards) K. BA, Franklin and Marshall Coll., 1975; JD, New England Sch. Law, 1978. Bar: Pa. 1978, U.S. Dist. Ct. (ea. dist.) Pa. 1979. Law clk. Pa. Superior Ct., Carlisle and Allentown, 1978-79, 80-82; atty. FinanceAmerica Corp., Allentown, 1980; assoc. McGee and Wiener, Allentown, 1982-85; ptnr. Brown Brown Solt & Krouse, Allentown, 1985—; mental health rev. officer County of Lehigh, Allentown, 1984—. Case editor: Lehigh Law Jour., 1984-86. Mem. Mayor's Adv. Bd. on Affirmative Action, Allentown, 1984—; treas. Lehigh County Young Dems., 1984-85; active Turning Point, Allentown, 1981—, pres., bd. dirs. 1983-85; active Lehigh County Task Force on Women, 1983, Housing Rev. Bd., Allentown, 1982—. Named one of Outstanding Young Women Am., 1981, 82; recipient Spirit award Allentown City Council, 1984. Mem. Lehigh County Bar Assn., Women Lawyers Lehigh Valley, Pa. Elected Women's Assn., Juvenile Justice Project, Franklin and Marshall Alumni Assn. (v.p. 1982—, Coll. Nat. Alumni Bd. 1986—). Unitarian. Club: Women's Dem. Lehigh County. Family and matrimonial, General practice. Home: 211 S 14th St Allentown PA 18102 Office: Brown Brown Solt & Krouse 513 Linden St Allentown PA 18101

KRUCHKO, JOHN GREGORY, lawyer; b. Iowa City, Iowa, Sept. 3, 1948; s. Demitro M. and Caroline (Maloney) K.; m. Susan Lynn Clendaniel, Sept. 15, 1968; 1 child, Jennifer Lynn. B.A., Xavier U., 1970; M.A. in History, U. Cin., 1971, M.A. in Labor Relations, 1972; J.D., Coll. William and Mary, 1975. Bar: Pa. 1975, Md. 1977, D.C. 1983, U.S. Dist. Ct. (ea. and mid. dists.) Pa. 1976, Md. 1978, U.S. Ct. Appeals (4th cir.) 1978, (3d cir.) 1979, U.S. Supreme Ct. 1983. Assoc. Morgan, Lewis & Bockius, Phila., 1975-77, Venable, Baetjer & Howard, Balt., 1977-79; founder, sr. ptnr. Kruchko & Fries, Balt., 1979—. Author: Birth of a Union Local, 1973; The Maryland Employer's Guide to Labor and Employment Law, 1984. Contbr. articles to profl. jours. Chmn. fin. com. Balt. County Victory '84 Reagan/Bush, 1984. Mem. ABA (sect. labor and employment law, subcom. co-chmn. 1980—), Am. Acad. Hosp. Attys., Md. Bar Assn., Pa. Bar Assn. Roman Catholic. Clubs: Center (Balt.); University (Towson, Md.). Labor. Home: 1200 Boyce Ave Towson MD 21204 Office: Kruchko & Fries 28 W Allegheny Ave Suite 606 Baltimore MD 21204

KRUCKS, WILLIAM NORMAN, lawyer; b. Chgo., Oct. 28, 1949; s. William and Lorraine (Rauland) K.; m. Amy Danly, July 10, 1981; children: Kathryn Leigh, Greta Anne. BA, Tulane U., 1972; JD, U. Miss., 1976. Bar: Ill. 1976, Miss. 1976, U.S. Dist. Ct. (no. dist.) Ill. 1976, U.S. Dist. Ct. (no. dist.) Miss. 1976, U.S. Dist. Ct. (cen. dist.) Ill. 1984, U.S. Ct. Appeals (5th and 7th cirs.) 1976, U.S. Supreme Ct. 1980. Assoc. Rooks, Pitts and Poust, Chgo., 1976-83; founding ptnr. Freeborn & Peters, Chgo., 1983—; bd. dirs. Rauland Borg Corp. Editor Miss. Law Jour., 1974-76; contbr. articles to law jours. Atty. Chgo. Vol. Legal Services, 1982—. Named Outstanding Young Man Am., U.S. Jaycees, 1976; recipient Dean Robert T. Farley award U. Miss., 1977. Mem. Ill. Self-Insured Assn., Chgo. Assn. Commerce and Industry, Nat. Council Self-Insured, Better Govt. Assn., Am. Jud. Soc., Tulane U. Alumni Assn., U. Miss. Alumni Assn., ABA, Ill. Bar Assn., Chgo. Bar Assn., Miss. Bar Assn., Workers Compensation Lawyers Assn., Legal Club of Chgo., Phi Delta Phi, Sigma Nu. Republican. Methodist. Clubs: Union League. Labor, Workers' compensation, State civil litigation. Home: 344 Locust Rd Winnetka IL 60093 Office: Freeborn & Peters 11 S LaSalle St Suite 1500 Chicago IL 60603

KRUEGER, HERBERT WILLIAM, lawyer; b. Milw., Apr. 20, 1948; s. Herbert William Sr. and Lily (Kuphall) K.; m. Judith Ann Wanserske, July 20, 1970; children—Kara, Dana, Andrew, Christopher. B.A., U. Wis.-Milw., 1970; J.D., U. Chgo., 1974. Bar: Fla. 1974, Ill. 1975, U.S. Dist. Ct. (no. dist.) Ill. 1975. Instr. in law U. Miami Sch. Law, Coral Gables, Fla., 1974-75; assoc. Mayer, Brown & Platt, Chgo., 1975-80, ptnr., 1981—, head compensation dept., 1984—. Contbg. author Continuing Legal Education pension practice and securities laws handbooks. Contbr. articles to profl. jours. State dir. Wis. Coll. Republicans, 1969-70; exec. dir. Com. to Reelect Pres., Wis. Young Voters Campaign, 1972; chmn. fiduciary standards com. Ill. Study Commn. on Pub. Pension Investment Policies, 1981-82. Mem. ABA. Pension, profit-sharing, and employee benefits. Office: Mayer Brown & Platt 190 S LaSalle St Chicago IL 60603

KRUEGER, JAMES, lawyer; b. N.Y.C., Oct. 27, 1938; s. Carl and Ida (Levey) K.; m. Merry Michael Hill, July 5, 1967; children—Melissa Carlton, James Michael. B.A., UCLA, 1960; LL.B., Loyola U., Los Angeles, 1965. Bar: Hawaii 1966, U.S. Dist. Ct. Hawaii 1966, U.S. Ct. Appeals (9th cir.) 1967, U.S. Tax Ct. 1974, U.S. Supreme Ct. 1982. Assoc. firm Padgett, Greeley, Marumoto & Akinaka, Honolulu, 1967-72; pres. James Krueger Law Corp., Wailuku, Maui, Hawaii, 1972—; speaker, lectr. profl. orgn. convs.; spl. counsel County of Maui, 1974; spl. agt. Internat. Police Congress, Washington. Contbr. articles to profl. jours. Fellow Internat. Soc. Barristers, Internat. Acad. Trial Lawyers; mem. Assn. Trial Lawyers Am. (gov. 1976-82, state committeeman 1975-76, constl. revisions com. 1977-78, nat. exec. com. 1981-82, amicus curiae com. 1979-80, fed. liaison com. 1980-81, nat. vice chmn. profl. research and devel. com. 1980-81, nat. vice-chmn. publs. dept. 1982-83, nat. vice chmn. edn. policy bd. 1983-84), Hawaii Bar Assn., Fed. Bar Assn., Maui County Bar Assn. (pres. 1975), Melvin M. Belli Soc., Hawaii Acad. Plaintiffs Attys., Am. Coll. Legal Medicine, Am. Soc. Hosp. Attys., Phi Alpha Delta. Democrat. Jewish. Clubs: Outrigger Canoe (Honolulu); Transpacific Yacht (Los Angeles); Maui Country. Avocations: swimming, running, cycling, skiing. Personal injury, Insurance. Office: 2065 Main St PO Box T Wailuku HI 96793

KRUEGER, JAMES A., lawyer; b. Detroit, Sept. 21, 1943; s. A.A. and Margaret E. (Hurley) K.; m. Therese Eileen Connors, Aug. 2, 1968; 1 child, Colleen. B.A. cum laude, Gonzaga U., 1965; J.D., Georgetown U., 1968; LL.M., NYU, 1972. Bar: Wash. 1969, U.S. Supreme Ct. 1972, U.S. Tax Ct. 1972, U.S. Dist. Ct. (we. dist.) Wash. 1980, U.S. Ct. Appeals (9th cir.) 1982. With staff U.S. senator from Wash., 1967-68; assoc. firm Kane, Vandeberg & Hartinger, Tacoma, 1972-76, ptnr. Kane, Vandeberg, Hartinger & Walker, 1976—; spl. dist. counsel Wash. State Bar Assn., 1984—; adj. prof. law, U. of Puget Sound, 1974-76. Chmn. bd. dirs. Cath. Community Services of Pierce and Kitsap Counties, 1983-84; bd. dirs. United Way of Pierce County, 1973-82. Served to capt. U.S. Army, 1968-72. Decorated Bronze star, Army Commendation medal. Mem. ABA, Wash. State Bar Assn. (spl. dist. counsel), Tacoma-Pierce County Bar Assn., Am. Legion. Roman Catholic. Lodge: Rotary. Contbr. chpt. to Representing the Close Corporation, 1979, Partnership Agreements, 1981, Planning for the Small Business Enterprise, 1982, The Partnership Handbook, 1984. General corporate, Probate, Corporate taxation. Office: First Interstate Plaza Suite 2000 Tacoma WA 98402

KRUEGER, JOHN WILLIAM, lawyer; b. Marinette, Wis., Feb. 7, 1930; s. Jesse A. and Beulah M. (Elwood) K.; m. Phyllis Evancheck, Mar. 31, 1957; children—Jess W., Eric J., Susan E. B.S., U. Wis., Madison, 1952, J.D., 1955. Bar: Wis. 1955, U.S. Dist. Ct. (ea. dist.) Wis., U.S. Dist. Ct. (we. dist.) Wis., U.S. Supreme Ct. Ptnr., Krueger & Krueger, Rhinelander, Wis., 1957—. Former chmn. Oneida County Republican Party; former co-chmn. 10th Congl. Dist. Rep. Party; former mem. statutory exec. com. Wis. Rep. Party; former city atty. City of Rhinelander. Mem. Oneida-Vilas-Forest County Bar Assn. (pres. 1966-67), Wis. Bar Assn. (chmn. litigation sect.), Assn. Trial Lawyers Am., Am. Judicature Soc., Wis. Acad. Trial Lawyers, Ins. Trial Counsel Wis. Lutheran. Club: Rhinelander Kiwanis. State civil litigation, Insurance, Personal injury. Office: Krueger & Krueger 142 N Brown St Rhinelander WI 54501

KRUEGER, LARRY EUGENE, lawyer, import-export trade executive; b. Pasco, Wash., Apr. 22, 1944; s. Albert H. and Mabel K. (Mosgaard) K.; m. Barbara Kay Strunk, Apr. 9, 1966; children—Kelli Kay, Eric Alan. A.A., Columbia Basin Coll., 1965; B.A. in Edn., Gonzaga U., 1966, J.D., 1971; M.S. in Counseling, Whitworth Coll., 1984. Bar: Wash. 1972, U.S. Dist. Ct. (ea. dist.) Wash. 1973. Sole practice, Deer Park, Wash., 1973-76, Spokane, Wash., 1978—; rep. west coast CMA, Inc., Honolulu; propr. L.E. Krueger & Assocs., Spokane, 1976-78. Legal dir. County Homes Kiwanis Club, Spokane; asst. cub master, 1982, 83; leader Webelos CubScouts Am., 1984; coordinator St. Luke Luth. Ch., Boy Scouts Am.; leader 5th dist. Republican Central Com., Spokane, 1973-76; bd. dirs. Family Counseling Service, Spokane, 1976, Antonian Sch. Spl. Children, Spokane, 1978—. Served to capt. U.S. Army, 1963-73. Pasco Kiwanis scholar, 1965, Gonzaga U. Law Sch. scholar, 1966-67; named to Outstanding Young Men of Am., U.S. Jaycees, 1979. Mem. Wash. State Bar Assn., Wash. State Trial Lawyers Assn., ABA, Am. Trial Lawyers Assn., Spokane County Bar Assn., Phi Alpha Delta, Kappa Delta Pi. Lodges: Eagles, Moose. General practice, Personal injury, General corporate. Home: N 10714 Nelson St Spokane WA 99218 Office: PO Box 18589 Rosewood Sta N 10714 Nelson St Spokane WA 99218

KRUEGER, ROBERT BLAIR, lawyer; b. Minot, N.D., Dec. 9, 1928; s. Paul Otto and Lila (Morse) K.; m. Virginia Ruth Carmichael, June 3, 1956; children: Lisa Carmichael, Paula Leah, Robert Blair. A.B., U. Kans., 1949; J.D., U. Mich., 1952; postgrad., U. So. Calif., 1960-65. Bar: Kans. 1952, Calif. 1955, D.C. 1978. Practiced in Los Angeles, 1955—; assoc. O'Melveny & Myers, 1955-59; ptnr. Nossaman, Krueger & Marsh and predecessor firms, 1961-83, Finley, Kumble, Wagner, Heine, Underberg, Manley, Myerson & Casey, 1983—; chmn. Nat. Practice Group on Energy and Natural Resources; adj. prof. natural resource law U. So. Calif. Law Ctr., 1973—; Mem. Gov.'s Adv. Commn. on Ocean Resources, 1966-68, Calif. Adv. Commn. on Marine and Coastal Resources, 1968-73, chmn., 1970-73; mem. adv. council Inst. on Marine Resources, U. Calif., 1966-74, Commn. on California, 1977—; mem. Nat. Security Council Adv. Com. on Law of Sea, 1972-82, chmn. internat. law and relations subcom., 1972-82; U.S. del. to UN Seabeds Com., 1973, 3d UN Law of Sea Conf., 1974-82; cons. petroleum policy to UN, fgn. govts. U.S. Centre on Transnat. Corps.; mem. exec. bd. Law of Sea Inst., U. Hawaii, 1977-83; mem. Nat. Adv. Com. on Oceans and Atmosphere, 1986—; fellow U. So. Calif. Inst. on Marine and Coastal Studies., 1977—. Author: Study of Outer Continental Shelf Lands of the United States, 1968, The United States and International Oil, 1975, World Petroleum Policies Report, 1981; also articles on energy and natural resources.; Asst. editor: Mich. Law Rev., 1951-52; editor: Los Angeles Bar Bull., 1961-63; bd. editors: Calif. Bar Jour., 1962-68. Mem. com. visitors U. Mich. Law Sch.; founder Mus. Contemporary Art. Served to 1st lt. USMCR, 1952-54. Fellow Am. Bar Found.; mem. ABA (chmn. spl. com. on energy law 1979-83, chmn. coordinating group on energy law 1983-86), Los Angeles County Bar Assn., Internat. Bar Assn., Am. Soc. Internat. Law., Fellows Contemporary Art, Barristers, Tau Kappa Epsilon, Phi Alpha Delta. Republican. Clubs: Calif, University, Chancery; Metropolitan (Washington); Valley Hunt (Pasadena); Princeton (N.Y.C.). Oil and gas leasing, Environment, Private international. Home: 9828 La Jolla Farms Rd La Jolla CA 92037 Office: Finley Kumble Wagner Heine et al 707 Wilshire Blvd 44th Floor Los Angeles CA 90017

KRUEGER, WILLIAM FREDERICK, lawyer; b. Gillett, Wis., Oct. 12, 1905; s. William Frederick and Augusta (Hintz) K.; m. Zenith Evella Eaton; children—William F., Marianne Krueger Knudson. Student Marquette U., 1924-26; J.D., U. Wis., 1929. Ptnr., Stone & Krueger, Reedsburg, Wis., 1929-30, Regner & Krueger, Wausau, Wis., 1936-38, Krueger & Loeffler, 1938-42, Krueger & Fulmer, 1946-65, Krueger & Thums, 1966-74; sr. ptnr. Krueger, Thums, Tlusty and Hittner, Schofield, Wis., 1974—; instr. U. Wis. Law Sch., 1974-75; vis. lectr. N. Central Tech. Inst., Wausau, Wis.; city atty. Wausau, 1950-55, Schofield, 1942—, Rothschild, Wis, 1957—. Alderman, City of Wausau, 1945-50; supr. Marathon County, 1945-50, pub. adminstr., 1939-62; bd. dirs. Community Chest, 1950-52. Mem. Wis. State Bar (service award 1962, bd. dirs. 1958-62, chmn. grievance-profl. responsibility com. 1965—), Marathon County Bar Assn., C. of C. (dir. 1948-50). Republican. Clubs: Timber Ridge Country (Minocqua, Wis.); Mason (Wausau and Eau Claire, Wis.); Shriners (Madison, Wis.). Author: Preservation of Inheritance Tax Evidence, 1961. Probate, Local government, Real property. Home: F 1525 Co F PO Box 176 Minocqua WI 54548 Office: 1155 Grand Ave PO Box 261 Schofield WI 54476

KRUG, HOWARD BARRY, lawyer; b. N.Y.C., Oct. 26, 1946; s. Samuel and Florence K.; m. Ruth Ann Levin, Dec. 27, 1969; children: Lauren R., Julie S., Wendy M. BS, Dickinson Coll., 1968; JD, Fordham U., 1971. Bar: N.Y. 1972, D.C. 1972, U.S. Dist. Ct. (mid. dist.) Pa. 1973, U.S. Ct. Appeals (3d cir.) 1973, U.S. Supreme Ct. 1983. Trial atty. U.S. Dept. Justice, Washington, 1971-72; spl. asst. to U.S. Atty. Washington, 1972; pvt. counsel Purcell and Nissley, Harrisburg, Pa., 1973-77; ptnr. Purcell, Nissley, Krug & Haller, Harrisburg, 1978—; hearing examiner Pub. Sch. Employees Retirement System, Harrisburg, 1978—, State Employees Retirement System, 1978—. Pres. Windsor Farms Civic Assn., Harrisburg, 1978—; bd. dirs. Humane Soc. Harrisburg, 1976-83; active Tri-County United Way, Harrisburg, 1978—. Mem. ABA, Pa. Bar Assn., Dauphin County Bar Assn., Am. Trial Lawyers Assn., Pa. Trial Lawyers Assn. Personal injury, Family and matrimonial, Probate. Office: Purcell Nissley Krug & Haller 1719 N Front St Harrisburg PA 17102

KRUG, ROB ALAN, lawyer, real estate broker; b. Munich, Fed. Republic of Germany, May 11, 1951; came to U.S., 1952; s. Robert A. Krug and Dolores D. (Deihm) Webb; m. Suzanne M. Heller, Nov. 6, 1976 (div. June 1985). BA, Gettysburg Coll., 1973; postgrad., John Marshall Law Sch., 1974-75; JD, U. Balt., 1976. Bar: Pa. 1977, U.S. Dist. Ct. (mid. dist.) Pa. 1977. Assoc. Wiley, Schrack & Benn, Dillsburg, Pa., 1977-79; sr. assoc. Wiley & Benn, Dillsburg, 1979-80; sole practice Dover, Pa., 1980—; pres. Bill Geltz Realty, York, Pa., 1986—. Coach Dillsburg Area Soccer Club, 1979—, York Youth Soccer League, 1987—; officer Luth. Brotherhood Br., York, 1983. Mem. ABA, Pa. Bar Assn., York County Bar Assn. Democrat. Avocations: soccer, photography, racquetball. Family and matrimonial, Real property, General practice. Office: 53 E Canal St Dover PA 17315

KRUGER, GILBERT NELSON, lawyer; b. N.Y.C., May 15, 1941; s. Louis and Irene (Lieberman) K.; m. Paula Mathias; Mikail, Leslie. BS in Acctg., CUNY, 1963; LLB, U. Calif., San Francisco, 1966. Bar: N.Y. 1967, Calif. 1980. Assoc. Kaye, Scholer, Fierman, Hays & Handler, N.Y.C., 1966-69; asst. gen. counsel ADP, Clifton, N.J., 1970-80; ptnr. Malcolm & Daly, Newport Beach, Calif., 1980-82, Wyman, Bautzer, Rothman, Kuchel & Silbert, Newport Beach, 1982—. Mem. ABA, Computer Law Assn. (bd. dirs. 1979-86), Am. Arbitration Assn. (arbitrator). Democrat. Jewish. Avocations: reading, travel. Computer, General corporate. Office: Wyman Bautzer Rothman Kuchel & Silbert 2600 Michelson Ave Irvine CA 92715

KRUGER, MARK HOWARD, lawyer; b. Kenosha, Wis., Oct. 31, 1948; s. Henry Irving and Pearl (Paskal) K.; m. Mary Deborah Benoit, Sept. 5, 1976. BA, U. Wis., 1970; JD, Washington U., St. Louis, 1973. Bar: Ill. 1973, U.S. Dist. Ct. (no. dist.) Ill. 1975, Mo. 1981, U.S. Dist. Ct. (so. dist.) Ill. 1981, U.S. Ct. Appeals (8th cir.) 1982, U.S. Supreme Ct. 1982. Sole practice Chgo. and St. Louis, 1973-80; ptnr. Chorlins, Vines, Kruger, Kraner & Benoit, Clayton, Mo., 1980-87, Biggs & Hensley, St. Louis, 1987—; prof. Laclede Sch. Law, St. Louis, 1976-81. Author: Family Law. Mem. Mo. Bar Assn., Bar Assn. Met. St. Louis, Nat. Orgn. Social Security Claimant's Reps. Family and matrimonial, General practice. Office: Biggs & Hensley 319 N 4th St Saint Louis MO 63102

KRUKIEL, CHARLES EDWARD, lawyer; b. Kearny, N.J., Sept. 25, 1946; s. Edward Charles and Helen Marjorie (Meister) K.; m. Barbara Jane Turner, May 31, 1969; children—John Charles, Matthew Owen, Kathryn Marie. B.S. in Mech. Engring., Vanderbilt U., 1968; J.D., South Tex. Coll. Law, 1973. Bar: Tex. 1974, U.S. Patent and Trademark Office 1974. Patent atty. E.I. DuPont Co., Wilmington, Del., 1974-83, Monsanto Co., St. Louis, 1983-84; patent dir. Monsanto Singapore, Co. Area Hdqrs., 1984-86; sr. patent atty., 1986—. Republican. Presbyterian. Patent, Trademark and copyright, Legislative. Home: 1820 Mason Rd Saint Louis MO 63131 Office: care Monsanto Company 800 N Lindbergh Blvd Saint Louis MO 63167

KRUKOWSKI, THOMAS PAUL, lawyer; b. Milw., Nov. 7, 1944; s. Leo J. and Catherine (Malinger) K.; m. Nina A. Radmer, Nov. 27, 1965; children—Deborah, Michael. B.S., Marquette U., 1967, J.D., 1970. Bar: Wis. 1970, U.S. dist. ct. (ea. and we. dists.) Wis. 1970, U.S. Ct. Appeals (7th cir.) 1975, U.S. Ct. Appeals D.C. 1980, U.S. Supreme Ct. 1982, U.S. Ct. Appeals (8th cir.) 1985. Mem. firm Goldberg, Previant & Uelmen, Milw., 1970-75, Brigden, Petajan, Lindner & Honzek, Milw., 1975-78, Brigden, Petajan & Krukowski, Milw., 1978-79; ptnr. Krukowski & Costello S.C., Milw., 1979—; lectr. Mem. Am. Soc. Personnel Adminstrn., Personnel and Indsl. Relations Assn. Wis., Indsl. Relations Research Assn., Ind. Bus. Assn. Wis., Am. Trucking Assn. (indsl. relations com.). Roman Catholic. Clubs: Kiwanis, Wisconsin. Labor, Workers' compensation, Civil rights. Home: 5235 S 49th St Greenfield WI 53220 Office: 7111 W Edgerton Ave Milwaukee WI 53220

KRULEWICH, HELEN D., lawyer; b. Paterson, N.J., Apr. 6, 1948; d. George and Kathrine P. (Vanderheide) Dworetzky; m. Leonard M. Krulewich, Sept. 2, 1972; children—Sara Heide, David Samuel. B.S., Syracuse U., 1970; J.D., Suffolk U., 1974. Bar: Mass. 1974, N.J., U.S. Supreme Ct. Clk. Nutter, McClennen & Fish, 1970-74; assoc. Rackemann, Sawyer & Brewster, Boston, 1974-75; sole practice, Boston, 1975-78, assoc. regional counsel real estate ops. Prudential Ins. Co. Am., Boston, 1978-85; counsel Karger Krulewich & Arnowitz, Boston, 1985—. Bd. dirs., chmn. edn. com. Govt. Ctr. Childcare Corp.; bd. dirs. Hist. Neighborhoods Found., Urban Land Inst.; mem. auction com. Big Sisters. Mem. Mus. Fine Arts, Condominium Assn., Beacon Hill Civic Assn., Opera Assn., Inst. Contemporary Art, Mus. Modern Art New Eng. Women in Real Estate, ABA, Mass. Bar Assn., Boston Bar Assn., Mass. Conveyancers Assn., Mass. Assn. Women Lawyers (scholarship found.), Women's Bar Assn., LWV, Friends Pub. Garden. Real property, General corporate. Office: Karger Krulewich & Arnowitz 18 Tremont St Boston MA 02108

KRULEWICH, LEONARD M., lawyer; b. N.Y.C., Jan. 10, 1947; s. Wallace and Maxine K.; m. Helen Dworetzky, Sept. 2, 1973; children: Sara Heide, David Samuel. BA, Hofstra U., 1969; JD, Suffolk U., 1972; LLM, Boston U., 1977. Bar: Mass. 1972, U.S. Dist. Ct. Mass. 1972, N.Y. 1973, U.S. Supreme Ct. 1979, U.S. Ct. Appeals (1st cir.) 1984. Assoc. Cohn, Riemer & Pollack, Boston, 1974-78; ptnr. Krulewich & Arnowitz, Boston, 1979-81, Karger, Krulewich & Arnowitz, Boston, 1981—. Mem. ABA, Mass. Bar Assn., Boston Bar Assn., Comml. Law League Am. (pres. N.E. region 1981-82). Avocations: tennis, cooking, running. Bankruptcy, State

civil litigation, Consumer commercial. Office: Karger Krulewich & Arnowitz 18 Tremont St Boston MA 02108

KRUMP, GARY JOSEPH, lawyer; b. Breckenridge, Minn., June 27, 1946; m. Mary Kay Chermak; children: Adam, Jonathon. BA, N.D. State U., 1968; JD, U. Minn., 1971, postdoctoral, 1972; cert. in health care, So. Ill. U., Edwardsville, 1978, grad. cert., 1980; MBA, George Washington U., 1981. Bar: Minn. 1971, U.S. Ct. Mil. Appeals 1972, U.S. Supreme Ct. 1975, D.C. 1977. Commd. 2d lt. U.S. Army, 1970, advanced through grades to capt., capt. with JAGC, 1972-74, chief internat. law-Japan, 1974-76; chief adminstrv. law Walter Reed Army Med. Ctr., 1976-77; sr. staff atty. office of gen. counsel VA, Washington, 1978-83, nat. coordinator med. care recovery program, 1979, dep. asst. gen. counsel, 1983—; faculty Cen. Mich. U., U. Va. Served to maj. JAGC, U.S. Army, 1983—. Mem. Fed. Bar Assn. (nat. chmn. tort law com., health and human services council chmn. 1980-81, chmn. Nat. Tort Conf. 1979, editor Tort Law Newsletter 1978-81, Superior Service awards 1979, 81), Am. Coll.-Legal Medicine (assoc.), Internat. Soc. Mil. Law and Law of War, Internat. Legal Soc., Internat. Platform Assn., Res. Officers Assn., Mid-Atlantic Token Kai, Beta Gamma Sigma, Tau Kappa Epsilon. Construction, Government contracts and claims, Health. Home: 13812 Town Line Rd Silver Spring MD 20906 Office: VA 810 Vermont Ave NW Washington DC 20420

KRUPANSKY, ROBERT BAZIL, U.S. judge; b. Cleve., Aug. 15, 1921; s. Frank A. and Anna (Lawrence) K.; m. Marjorie Blaser, Nov. 13, 1952. B.A., Western Res. U., 1946, LL.B., 1948; J.D., Case Western Res. U., 1968. Bar: Ohio bar 1948, also Supreme Ct. Ohio 1948, Supreme Ct. U.S 1948, U.S. Dist. Ct. No. Dist. Ohio 1948, U.S. Circuit Ct. Appeals 6th Circuit 1948, U.S. Ct. Customs and Patent Appeals 1948, U.S. Customs Ct 1948, ICC 1948. Pvt. practice Cleve., 1948-52; asst. atty. gen. State of Ohio, 1951-57; mem. Gov. of Ohio cabinet and dir. Ohio Dept. Liquor Control, 1957-58; judge Common Pleas Ct. of Cuyahoga County, 1958-60; sr. partner Metzenbaum, Gaines, Krupansky, Finley & Stern, 1960-69; U.S. atty. No. Dist. Ohio, Cleve., 1969-70; U.S. dist. judge No. Dist. Ohio, 1970-82; judge U.S. Ct. Appeals (6th cir.), Ohio, 1982—; spl. counsel Atty. Gen. Ohio, 1964-68; adj. prof. law Case Western Res. U. Sch. Law, 1969-70. Served to 2d lt. U.S. Army, 1942-46; col. USAF Res. ret. Mem. Am., Fed., Ohio, Cleve., Cuyahoga County bar assns., Am. Judicature Soc., Assn. Asst. Attys. Gen. State Ohio. Jurisprudence. Office: US District Court 250 US Court House Cleveland OH 44114 *

KRUPKA, ROBERT GEORGE, lawyer; b. Rochester, N.Y., Oct. 21, 1949; s. Joseph Anton and Marjorie Clara (Meteyer) K.; m. Paula Kelly Leist, Sept. 15, 1973; children: Kristin Nicole, Kerry Melissa. BS, Georgetown U., 1971; JD, U. Chgo., 1974. Bar: Ill. 1974, U.S. Dist. Ct. (no. dist.) Ill. 1974, U.S. Dist. Ct. (ea. dist.) Wis. 1974, U.S. Ct. Appeals (7th cir.) 1976, U.S. Supreme Ct. 1978, U.S. Dist. Ct. (cen. dist.) Ill. 1980, U.S. Dist. Ct. (no. dist.) Calif. 1980, U.S. Ct. Appeals (4th and fed. cirs.) 1982, U.S. Ct. Appeals (6th cir.) 1985. Assoc. Kirkland & Ellis, Chgo., 1974-79, ptnr., 1979—. Mem. ABA (chmn. sect. com. 1982—), Chgo. Athletic Assn. Roman Catholic. Club: Mid-Am., Chicago. Federal civil litigation, Trademark and copyright, Patent. Home: 643 Deming Chicago IL 60614 Office: Kirkland & Ellis 200 E Randolph Dr Chicago IL 60601

KRUSE, JOHN ALPHONSE, lawyer; b. Detroit, Sept. 11, 1926; s. Frank R. and Ann (Nestor) K.; m. Mary Louise Dalton, July 14, 1951; children: Gerard, Mary Louise, Terence, Kathleen, Joanne, Francis, John, Patrick. BS, U. Detroit, 1950, JD cum laude, 1952. Bar: Mich. bar 1952. Ptnr. Alexander, Buchanan & Conklin, Detroit, 1952-69, Harvey, Kruse & Westen, Detroit, 1969—; Guest lectr. U. Mich., U. Detroit, Inst. Continuing Legal Edn.; city atty. Allen Park, Mich., 1954-59; twp. atty., Van Buren Twp., Mich., 1959-61. Past pres. Palmer Woods Assn.; mem. pres.'s cabinet U. Detroit. Served with USNR, 1944-46. Named One of 5 Outstanding Young Men in Mich., 1959. Mem. ABA, Detroit Bar Assn., State Bar Mich. (past chmn. negligence sect.), Assn. Def. Trial Counsel (bd. dirs. 1966-67), Am. Judicature Soc., Internat. Assn. Def. Counsel. Roman Catholic. Club: Detroit Golf (past pres.). Insurance, State civil litigation, Personal injury. Home: 19386 Cumberland Way Detroit MI 48203 Office: First National Bldg Detroit MI 48226

KRUSE, SCOTT AUGUST, lawyer; b. N.Y.C., July 15, 1947; s. Norman W. and Sarah E. (Doyle) K.; m. Ruth H. Cohnen, Dec. 9, 1986; 1 child, Eric. AB, Princeton U., 1969; JD, Harvard U., 1972. Bar: Calif. 1972. Assoc. Gibson, Dunn & Crutcher, Los Angeles, 1972-77, ptnr., 1980—; gen. counsel Fed. Mediation and Conciliation Service, Washington, 1977-79. Contbr. articles on labor law to profl. jours. Served to capt. USAR, 1969-77. Mem. ABA (chmn. 1978-79), Calif. Bar Assn., Industrial Relations Research Assn. Democrat. Labor. Office: Gibson Dunn & Crutcher 2029 Century Park East Los Angeles CA 90067

KRUSOR, MARK WILLIAM, lawyer, educator; b. Topeka, Kans., Nov. 6, 1951; s. William Albert and Gladys Eleanor (Lyon) K.; m. Carolyn Kay Gish, May 19, 1973 (div. Aug. 1984); 1 dau., Bethany Ellen; m. Teresa D. Garcia, Aug. 1, 1986. BA, Washburn U., 1973, JD, 1976. Bar: Kans. 1976, U.S. Dist. Ct. Kans. 1976. Assoc. Christenson, Mathews & Taylor, Winfield, Kans., 1976-79; ptnr. Mathews, Taylor & Krusor, Winfield, 1979—; instr. Southwestern Coll., Winfield, 1978—, Cowley County Community Coll. and Winfield State Hosp. and Tng. Ctr., Winfield, 1981, 82, 84, 85, 86, St. John's Coll., Winfield, 1984; pres. adv. com. Kans. Dept. Corrections Winfield Prerelease Ctr., 1986. Chmn. bd. trustees Winfield Pub. Library, 1981, 82; pres. bd. dirs. Winfield Child Care Ctr., 1979; chmn. drive Winfield United Way, 1978; pres. Holy Name Parish Council, Winfield, 1981; county chmn. Allegrucci for Congress com., Winfield, 1978; treas. Citizens Com. for Merit Selection of Judges, Winfield, 1984; mem. resident rights com. Winfield State Hosp. and Tng. Ctr., 1980-82; mem. adv. com. Winfield State Hosp., 1982—, Kans. Dept. Corrections-Winfield Ctr., 1984—; pres. Winfield Pub. Sch. Found. Mem. Kans. Bar Assn., Kans. Trial Lawyers Assn. (bd. govs. 1983—), Assn. Trial Lawyers Am., Cowley County Bar Assn. (sec.-treas. 1978, v.p. 1979, pres. 1980), Washburn Law Sch. Assn., Kans. Hist. Soc., Cowley County Hist. Soc. Democrat. Roman Catholic. Lodges: Optimists (pres. 1980-81), Jaycees, Elks, K.C. State civil litigation, Criminal, Family and matrimonial. Home: 1208 E 19th St Winfield KS 67156 Office: Mathews Taylor & Krusor First Nat Bank Bldg Winfield KS 67156

KRUTCH, RICHARD FRANCIS, lawyer; b. Spokane, Wash., June 2, 1930; s. L. Ed and Serene B. K.; m. Noel Nelson, Feb. 16, 1956; children—William C., Robin. B.A., U. Wash., 1952, J.D., 1955. Bar: Wash. 1955, U.S. Dist. Ct. Wash. 1958, U.S. Ct. Appeals (9th cir.) 1958. Ptnr., Smith, Lindell, Krutch, Carr, 1957-65, Clodfelter, Lindell, Carr, 1965-70, Krutch, Lindell, Judkins, 1970-81, Krutch, Lindell, Judkins & Keller, Seattle, 1981—. Served with U.S. Army, 1955-57. Mem. Am. Coll. Trial Lawyers. Aviation. Office: Krutch Lindell Judkins & Keller 1200 5th Ave Seattle WA 98101

KRUTECK, LAURENCE R., lawyer, cons.; b. N.Y.C., Dec. 11, 1941; s. Alan R. and Sylvia (Stekler) K.; m. Laura Branigan, Dec. 10, 1980; children—Michael, Sally. B.A., Dartmouth Coll.; J.D., U. Va.; grad. U.S. Army Command and Gen. Staff Coll. Bar: Va. 1966, N.Y. 1967. Ptnr. Kruteck & Leaness, N.Y.C.; bus. mgr., atty. Laura Branigan, Adrienne West, Plus Models, Iran Barkley, Lonnie Liston Smith, Don Mattingly; formerly dir., v.p. and gen. counsel Shenandoah Corp., Washington Diplomats Soccer Team, SJR Communications, Inc. Served to col. USAR. Mem. ABA, N.Y. State Bar Assn., Assn. Bar N.Y.C., Va. Bar Assn., Judge Advs. Assn., Res. Officers Assn. Club: Princeton (N.Y.C.). General corporate, Military, Entertainment. Office: 509 Madison Ave New York NY 10022

KRUTTER, FORREST NATHAN, lawyer; b. Boston, Dec. 17, 1954; s. Irving and Shirley Krutter. BS in Econs., MS in Civil Engring., MIT, 1976; JD cum laude, Harvard U., 1978. Bar: Nebr. 1978, U.S. Supreme Ct. 1986. Antitrust counsel Union Pacific R.R., Omaha, 1978-86; gen. counsel large risk div. Berkshire Hathaway Ins. Group, Omaha, 1986—. Co-author: Impact of Railroad Abandonments, 1976, Railroad Development in the Third World, 1978; author: Judicial Enforcement of Competition in Regulated Industries, 12 Creighton Law Review 1041, 1979. Mem. ABA, Assn. Transp. Practitioners, Phi Beta Kappa, Sigma Xi. Administrative and regulatory, Antitrust, Insurance. Office: Berkshire Hathaway Ins Group 3024 Harney St Omaha NE 68131

KRUTTSCHNITT, HERBERT, III, lawyer; b. East Orange, N.J., June 6, 1954; s. Herbert Jr. and Delores C. (Cromidas) K.; m. Barbara McD. Sauerwein, July 28, 1974; children: Brittany Elizabeth, Brianne Alexandra. BS magna cum laude, Monmouth Coll, 1976; JD cum laude, Seton Hall U., 1979. Bar: N.J. 1979, U.S. Dist. Ct. N.J. 1979, U.S. Ct. Appeals (3d cir.) 1981. Assoc. Novins Farley, Grossman & York P.A., Toms River, N.J., 1980-83; ptnr. Grossman & Kruttschnitt P.A., Toms River, 1983—; bd. dirs. Reil Investment Group Ltd., Toms River, Applied Biomedical Cons. Inc., Toms River. Mem. ABA, Ocean County Bar Assn., Trial Attys. N.J. Republican. Clubs: Seaside Park (N.J.) Yacht; Toms River Country. Avocations: sailboat racing, tennis, golf. Personal injury, State civil litigation, Insurance. Office: Grossman & Kruttschnitt PA 509 Main St Toms River NJ 98753

KRZEMIEN, LOUIS JOHN, lawyer; b. Norristown, Pa., Jan. 8, 1952; s. Louis John Krzemein and Pearl S. (Vidinski) Stenz; m. Theresa J. Brown, May 31, 1975. BA magna cum laude, King's Coll., 1973; JD, Duquesne U., 1978. Bar: Pa. 1978, U.S. Dist. Ct. (we. dist.) Pa. 1978, U.S. Ct. Appeals (3d cir.) 1981, U.S. Ct. Appeals (4th cir.) 1987. Assoc. McVerry, Baxter, Cindrich & Mansmann, Pitts., 1978-81, Mansmann, Cindrich & Huber, Pitts., 1981-84; ptnr. Mansmann, Cindrich & Titus, Pitts., 1984—. Mem. Assn. Trial Lawyers Am., Pa. Trial Lawyers Assn., Pa. Bar Assn., Allegheny County Bar Assn. Roman Catholic. Avocations: camping, fishing. Labor, Personal injury, Civil rights. Home: 260 Twin Hills Dr Pittsburgh PA 15216 Office: Mansmann Cindrich & Titus 1510 Two Chatham Ctr Pittsburgh PA 15219

KRZYZANOWSKI, RICHARD LUCIEN, lawyer, corporate executive; b. Warsaw, Poland, Mar. 25, 1932; came to U.S., 1967, naturalized, 1972; s. Andrew K. and Mary (Krzyzanowski); children: Suzanne, Peter. B.A., U. Warsaw, 1956; M.Law, U. Pa., 1960; Ph.D., U. Paris, 1962. Bar: Pa. With Crown Cork & Seal Co., Inc., Phila., 1967—, now dir., v.p. gen. counsel. Public international, Private international, General corporate. Home and Office: 9300 Ashton Rd Philadelphia PA 19136

KTORIDES, STANLEY, lawyer; b. Springfield, Mass., July 1, 1949; s. John Stanley and Galatia (Mavroyianni) K.; m. Anne Marie Lalikos, Apr. 19, 1980; children: Melanie, Angela, John. BS in Chem. Engring., U. Mass., 1971; JD, West New Eng. Coll., 1978. Bar: Ct., 1978, U.S. Patent Office, 1979, U.S. Ct. Appeals (D.C. cir.), 1984. Chem. engr. United Techs. Corp., East Hartford, Conn., 1972-77; div. patent counsel Union Carbide Corp., Danbury, Conn., 1977—. V.p. Assumption Ch., Danbury, 1984—. Served with U.S. Army, 1971-77. Mem. ABA, Am. Intellectual Property Law Assn., Am. Corp. Counsel Assn. Democrat. Eastern Orthodox. Patent, Technology creation and transfer. Home: 7 Oak Tree Ln New Fairfield CT 06812 Office: Union Carbide Corp 39 Old Ridgebury Rd Danbury CT 06817

KUBACKI, STANLEY LOUIS, judge; b. Phila., Aug. 25, 1915; s. Stanley Ignatius and Stella (Kapcia) K.; m. Sophia Maciejewski, Dec. 26, 1940; children—Christine S., Michael S. B.A., U. Mich. 1936; J.D., Temple U., 1948. Bar: Pa. 1948, U.S. Dist. Ct. (ea. dist.) Pa. 1949, U.S. Ct. Appeals (3d cir.) 1949. Sole practice, Phila., 1948-51, 1955-71; asst. dist. atty., Phila., 1951-55; judge Ct. Common Pleas, Phila., 1971—. Mem. Phila. Bar Assn. Democrat. Roman Catholic. Club: Mich. of Phila. (treas. 1983—, pres. 1984). Criminal, Condemnation, Legal history. Office: 532 City Hall Philadelphia PA 19107

KUBES, EUGENE LEONARD, judge; b. St. Paul, Oct. 22, 1926; s. Joseph John and Marie Ann (Kovaricek) K.; m. Mary Catherine Jeske, Aug. 26, 1961; children—Joseph, Andrea, Margaret, Daniel, John, Stephen. B.B.A. in Acctg., U. Minn., 1948; J.D., Stetson U., 1962. Bar: Minn. 1962, Fla. 1962, U.S. Dist. Ct. (mid. dist.) Fla. 1965, U.S. Ct. Appeals (11th cir.) 1981. Exec. dir. Jr. Achievement, Canton, Ohio, 1952-56; chief cost acct. Honeywell, Inc., St. Petersburg, Fla. 1957-59, mng. planning and control, 1962-65; ptnr. Allison & Kubes, St. Petersburg, 1965-68; trust officer Norwest Bank, St. Paul, 1968-71; referee of family ct. 2d Dist. Ct., St. Paul, 1971—; chmn. adv. com. on rules of family ct. procedure Minn. Supreme Ct., 1985—; lectr. continuing legal edn. seminars, Minn., 1971—, William Mitchell Coll. Law, St. Paul, 1975-80, Hamline U., St. Paul, 1979-80, Minn. Jud. Edn., St. Paul, 1976, 84-87. Author: Annual Family Law Legislative and Case Law Update, 1980—, Minnesota Marital Settlement Agreement Handbook, 1983; contbr. articles to legal jours.; editor Ramsey Bar Barrister, 1979-80; mem. adv. bd. editors Minn. Family Law Jour., 1983—. Active Boy Scouts Am. Served to lt. AUS, 1944-48. Fellow Am. Acad. Matrimonial Lawyers (treas. 1981-83, v.p. 1983-84, pres. 1984-85, bd. of mgrs. 1981—); mem. Minn. Bar Assn. (exec. council family law sect. 1983—), Ramsey County Bar Assn. (exec. council 1975-78), Nat. Assn. Accts. (bd. dirs. 1957-59), Nat. Sales Execs. (sec. 1955-57), Delta Sigma Pi (v.p.), Delta Theta Phi (treas.). Family and matrimonial. Home: 92 Exeter Pl Saint Paul MN 55104 Office: Second Dist Ct 1700 Courthouse Saint Paul MN 55102

KUBIAK, JON STANLEY, lawyer, auto parts manufacturing company executive; b. South Bend, Ind., Feb. 10, 1935; s. Stanley Michael Kubiak and Sylvia J. Frankowski; m. Mary Ann Rys, May 4, 1963 (dec. 1974); children—Karen Michelle, Kristin Jill; m. Elaine Michaelis, Feb. 26, 1977; 1 son, Mark Stanley. B.S. in Acctg. cum laude, U. Notre Dame, 1957, J.D., 1960. Bar: Ill. 1960, U.S. dist. ct. (no. dist.) Ill. 1960, U.S. Ct. Appeals (7th cir.) 1961. Budget examiner Chgo. City Council, 1960; asst. corp. counsel City of Chgo., 1960-61; asst. atty. gen. Ill. State Tollway Commn., Oak Brook, 1961-66; asst. sec. and corp. atty. Maremont Corp., Chgo., 1966-72, sec. and asst. gen. counsel, 1972-78, sec. and gen. counsel, 1979-86, v.p., sec., gen. counsel Prestolite Electric Inc., Toledo; dir. Prestolite Electric Inc., Prestolite Electricals Ltd., U.K. Sec. 28th Ward Regular Democratic Orgn., Chgo., 1960-68; vice chmn. Young Dems. Cook County, 1963-67; chmn. 7th Congl. Dist. Young Dems. Ill., 1963-67. Mem. ABA, Ill. State Bar Assn., Am. Corp. Counsel Assn. Roman Catholic. Club: Notre Dame of Chgo. (bd. govs. 1977-80). General corporate, Antitrust, Securities. Home: 4567 Torquay Toledo OH 43615 Office: Prestolite Electric Inc 4 Seagate Toledo OH 43691-0904

KUCIREK, JOSEPH CHARLES, lawyer; b. Wausau, Wis., Aug. 17, 1932; s. Joseph T. and Florence C. (Schreier) K.; m. Mary Kathryn Gritzmacher, Aug. 18, 1956; children—Peggy, Joseph, John, Virginia, Mary. B.S. with honors, U. Wis., 1954, LL.B./J.D. with honors (Knapp law scholar), 1956. Bar: Wis. 1956. Sole practice, Wausau, 1959-70, 78—; judge Wis. Cir. Ct. Marathon County, 1970-78; asst. city atty. Wausau, 1960-62. Mem. Marathon County Traffic Safety Commn., Wausau Common Council, 1962-64, Marathon County Bd., 1962-64; chmn. Marathon County Republican Com., 1967-70; pres. Wausau Jaycees, 1961, Wis. Jaycees, 1964-65; pres., sec. Wausau Serra Club; chmn. March of Dimes, Family Counseling Service. Served to capt. USAF, 1956-59. Named Outstanding Young Man in Wausau, Moose Lodge, 1962, Wausau Jaycees, 1965; Outstanding Young Man in Wis., Wis. Jaycees, 1965. Mem. ABA, State Bar Wis., Marathon County Bar Assn. (pres.). Clubs: Wausau Country, Elks (Wausau). Exec. editor Wis. Law Rev., 1955-56; contbr. articles to legal jours. Criminal, Family and matrimonial, Personal injury. Office: 530 McClellan St Wausau WI 54401

KUCZWARA, THOMAS PAUL, postal inspector, lawyer; b. Chgo., Dec. 21, 1951; s. Stanley Leo and Eleanore (Pawelko) K.; m. Diana Lynn Rychtarczyk, Sept. 8, 1979. B.A., Loyola U., Chgo., 1973; J.D., U. S.C., 1976. Bar: Ill. 1976, U.S. Dist. Ct. (no. dist.) Ill. 1982. Assoc., Doria Law Offices, Chgo., 1977-78; asst. corp. counsel City of Chgo., 1978-80; asst. city atty. City of Aurora (Ill.), 1980-82; postal insp. U.S. Postal Inspection Service, Salt Lake City, 1982-85, regional inspector atty. cen. region, Chgo., 1985—. Mem. St. Bartholomew's Parish Council, Chgo., 1978; vol. atty. Lawyers for Creative Arts, 1978. Ill. State scholar, 1969. Mem. Ill. State Bar Assn., Sierra Club, Pi Sigma Alpha. Roman Catholic. Administrative and regulatory, Federal civil litigation, Criminal. Office: Office Regional Chief Inspector 433 W Van Buren Chicago IL 60607-5401

KUDER, ARMIN ULRICH, lawyer; b. Phila., Nov. 14, 1935; s. David Dennis and Ethel Rose (Strasburger) K.; m. Patricia A. Hipple, June 28, 1959 (div. Mar. 1968); children: Carlyn Elizabeth, Eric David, Keith Ulrich. AB, Lafayette Coll., 1956; LLB, Harvard U., 1959. Bar: D.C. 1959, U.S. Ct. Mil. Appeals 1962, U.S. Dist. Ct. Md. 1968. Assoc. Coles & Goertner, Washington, 1963-65, Mehler, Smollar et al, Washington, 1963-65; ptnr. Kuder, Sherman et al, Washington, 1965-78, Kuder, Temple Smollar & Heller P.C., Washington, 1978—; lectr. continuing legal edn., various locations. Chmn. Nat. Health Agencies, NCAC, 1977-78, Ctr. Environ. Edn., Washington, 1981-83, NIMH human subjects rev. panel, 1978—, Hyde Sch., Bath, Maine, 1984—; vice chmn. Arthritis Found., Atlanta, 1979-80, New Art Assn., Washington, 1986-87; sec. Combined Health Appeal, Washington, 1984. Served to lt. comdr. JAGC, USN, 1959-63. Mem. ABA, D.C. Bar Assn. (trustee client security fund 1984—, hearing com. chmn. bd. on profl. responsibility 1985—). State civil litigation, Family and matrimonial, Personal income taxation. Office: Kuder Temple Smollar & Heller PC 1015 20th St NW Washington DC 20036

KUEHN, ANGELIKA MARIA, lawyer; b. Berlin, Feb. 28, 1949; came to U.S., 1951,; d. Heinz Richard and Regina Maria (Nowak) K. BA summa cum laude, Rosary Coll., River Forest, Ill., 1970; postgrad., U. de Morelos, Cuernavaca, Mex., 1973, Jesuit Sch. Theology, 1979-81; JD cum laude, Northwestern U., 1975. Bar: Ill. 1975, U.S. Dist. Ct. (no. dist.) Ill. 1975, U.S. Ct. Appeals (7th cir.) 1983. Assoc. Law Offices Treumann, Chgo., 1974-77; assoc., then ptnr. Boodell, Sears, Giambalvo & Crowley, Chgo., 1977-84; ptnr. Keck, Mahin & Cate, Chgo., 1984—. Contbr. articles to book revs., profl. jours. Bd. dirs. Travelers and Immigrants Aid, Chgo., 1984—; mem. com. on fgn. affairs, Chgo. Council on Fgn. Relations, 1985—; judge Jessup Internat. Moot Ct. Competition, Ind. and Ill., 1985-86. Nat. Merit scholar, Ill. State scholar, 1969; young am. leadership fellow Robert Bosch Found., 1987—. Mem. ABA, Chgo. Bar Assn., Legal Club Chgo., German-Am. C. of C. Chgo. Roman Catholic. Club: Can. of Chgo. Avocations: Scrabble, gardening, learning fgn. langs. Private international, Real property, Local government. Home: 233 S Ridgeland Ave Oak Park IL 60302 Office: Keck Mahin & Cate 8300 Sears Tower 233 S Wacker Dr Chicago IL 60606

KUEHN, GEORGE E., lawyer, beer company executive; b. N.Y.C., June 19, 1946; m. Mary Kuehn; children: Kristin, Rob, Geoff. BBA, U. Mich., 1968, JD, 1973. Bar: Mich. 1974. Assoc. Hill, Lewis et al, Detroit, 1974-78; ptnr. Butzel, Long et al, Detroit, 1978-81; v.p., gen. counsel The Stroh Brewery Co., Detroit, 1981—. Served with U.S. Army, 1969-71. General corporate. Office: The Stroh Brewery Co 100 River Pl Detroit MI 48207

KUEHNE, BENEDICT P., lawyer; b. Merced, Calif., Mar. 24, 1954; s. Ben and Jean T. Kuehne; m. Lynne A. Auerbach, Nov. 17, 1984. B.A. cum laude, U. Miami, 1974, J.D. cum laude, 1977; postgrad. Fla. Atlantic U., 1979—. Bar: Fla. 1977, D.C. 1978, U.S. Ct. Appeals (5th cir.) 1977, U.S. Dist. Ct. (so. and mid. dists.) Fla. 1977, U.S. Ct. Appeals (4th cir.) 1980, U.S. Ct. Appeals (7th and 11th cirs.) 1981, U.S. Ct. Appeals (9th and D.C. cirs.) 1982, U.S. Supreme Ct. 1981, U.S. Dist. Ct. (so. dist.) Ala. 1983, U.S. Ct. Appeals (2d cir.) 1984. Asst. atty. gen. State of Fla., West Palm Beach, 1977-79, spl. asst. state atty. 15th Jud. Cir., 1978-80; sr. assoc. Bierman, Sonnett, Shohat & Sale, P.A., Miami and Ft. Lauderdale, Fla., 1980—, ptnr., Sonnett, Slae & Kuehne, P.A., 1987—; lectr. in field. Contbr. articles to profl. jours. bd. dirs. Dem. Forum, Fla. 1987—; gen. counsel Fla. Young Democrats, 1984-85, polit. v.p. 1983-84, pres., 1986-87; pres. Dade County Young Dems. Fla., 1982-83, bd. dirs., 1983-84. Named one of Outstanding Young Men of Am., 1980, 82. Mem. Fla. Bar Assn. (edn. com. criminal law sect.), Fla. Criminal Def. Attys. Assn. (chmn. brief bank com., Cert. of Merit 1984) Pub. Interest Law Bank (Award of Merit 1984), Dade County Bar Assn., Greater Miami Jewish Fedn. (atty.'s div.), Nat. Eagle Scout Orgn., U. Miami Law Alumni Assn. (v.p. 1987—), U. Miami Gen. Alumni Assn. (bd. dirs. 1987—), Coconut Grove Assn. (pres. 1986—). Criminal, Immigration, naturalization, and customs, Administrative and regulatory. Home: PO Box 013329 Miami FL 33101 Office: Sonnett Sale & Kuehne PA 200 SE First St #500 Miami FL 33131

KUELBS, JOHN THOMAS, lawyer; b. Springfield, Minn., Sept. 8, 1942; s. Alois Nicholas and Lucille Marie (Neudecker) K.; m. Mary Pat St. Marie, June 19, 1965; children: Susan, Thomas. BA, St. John's U., Collegeville, Minn., 1965; JD, Creighton U., 1973. Bar: Nebr. 1973, Calif. 1980. Sr. counsel Ford Aerospace, Newport Beach, Calif., 1976-78, div. counsel, 1978-81; group counsel Hughes Aircraft, El Segundo, Calif., 1981-86; staff v.p., asst. gen. counsel Hughes Aircraft, Los Angeles, 1986—. Served to lt. col. JAGC, U.S. Army, 1976-87. Mem. ABA (chmn. sub contracting com. 1984—, co-chmn. 1986), Calif. Bar Assn., Nebr. Bar Assn., Fed. Bar Assn., Delta Theta Phi. Government contracts and claims. Office: Hughes Aircraft Co 7200 Hughes Terr Los Angeles CA 90045-0066

KUELTHAU, PAUL STAUFFER, lawyer; b. West Bend, Wis., Mar. 31, 1912; s. George Herman and Marie Louise (Rix) K.; m. Laura Parish, Aug. 16, 1937; children: Karen Allan, Marline Holmes. AB, U. Wis., 1934, JD, 1936. Bar: Wis. 1936, U.S. Ct. Appeals (10th cir.) 1941, U.S. Ct. Appeals (7th cir.) 1947, Mo. 1953, U.S. Dist. Ct. (ea. dist.) Mo. 1954, U.S. Ct. Appeals (8th cir.) 1962, U.S. Dist. Ct. (so. dist.) Ill. 1964, U.S. Supreme Ct. 1973, U.S. Ct. Appeals (D.C. cir.) 1974. Regional atty. NLRB, various locations, 1939-46; chief counsel to chmn. NLRB, Washington, 1946-53; assoc. Lewis, Rice, Tucker, Allen & Chubb, St. Louis, 1953-62; ptnr. Moller, Talent, Kuelthau, & Welch, St. Louis, 1962—. Contbr. articles to profl. jours. Mem. ABA, Mo. Bar Assn., Bar Assn. St. Louis, Indsl. Relations Research Assn. Presbyterian. Lodge: Rotary. Labor. Home: 8 Sherwyn Ln Saint louis MO 63141 Office: Moller Talent Kuelthau & Welch 720 Olive St Saint Louis MO 63101

KUENZEL, STEVEN PAUL, lawyer; b. Washington, Mo., Sept. 11, 1952; s. Paul R. and Shirley Mae (Kampschroeder) K.; m. Susan P. Bowen, May 16, 1980; 1 child, Steven P. Jr. BBA, U. Mo., 1974, JD, 1976. Bar: Mo. 1976, U.S. Dist. Ct. (ea. and we. dists.) Mo. 1976. Ptnr. Politte, Thayer & Kuenzel, Washington, Mo., 1976-83, Eckelkamp, Eckelkamp, Wood & Kuenzel, Washington, 1983—; adj. prof. East Cen. Coll., Union, Mo., 1977—. Pres. Washington Jaycees, 1979-80; bd. dirs. Washington Park Com., 1981—. Recipient Disting. Service award Washington Jaycees, 1985. Mem. Assn. Trial Lawyers Am., Mo. Assn. Trial Attys., Washington C. of C. (pres. 1983-85). Roman Catholic. Lodges: Lions (pres. Washington club 1984-85), Elks. State civil litigation, General practice, Personal injury. Home: 1507 E Eighth St Washington MO 63090 Office: Bank of Washington Bldg Washington MO 63090

KUERSTEINER, JONATHAN DANIEL BOONE, lawyer; b. Tallahassee, Nov. 8, 1946; s. Karl Otto and Martha Lee (Boone) K.; m. Priscilla Landrum; children—Garrett Landrum, Sarah Britton. A.A., Wentworth Mil. Acad., 1966; B.S. in Pub. Adminstrn., U. Mo., 1969; J.D., Fla. State U., 1971. Bar: Fla. 1972, U.S. Dist. Ct. (no. and so. dists.) Fla. 1972, U.S. Ct. Appeals (11th cir.) 1972. Asst. atty. gen., Fla., 1972-73; asst. gen. counsel Fla. Dept. Environ. Regulation, 1974-77; ptnr. Henry, Buchanan, Mick, English & Kuersteiner, P.A., Tallahassee, 1978-79, Akerman, Senterfitt, & Edison, Tallahassee, 1980-86, Huey, Guilday, Kuersteiner & Tucker, Tallahassee, 1986—. Contbg. author Environ. Network mag. Patron Tallahassee Symphony Orch.; mem. Tallahassee Jr. Mus. Served to capt. USAR, 1969-80. Mem. Fla. Bar (environ. law sect., adminstrv. law sect., chmn. continuing legal edn. com. 1977-79, exec. counsel 1978—, sec. 1978-79, vice chmn. 1979-80, chmn. 1980-81), ABA (vice chmn. com. on profl., officers' and dirs. liability law 1979—), Tallahassee Bar Assn., Am. Air Pollution Control Assn., Phi Delta Phi, Sigma Alpha Epsilon. Episcopalian. Clubs: Rotary, Capitol City Country, Governors. Contbg. author and lectr. Environ. Law Update Seminar, 1982; Environ. Regulation and Litigation Florida Handbook, 1978, 79, 80, 81, 82; contbr. articles to legal jours. Environment, Administrative and regulatory. Office: PO Box 1794 Tallahassee FL 32302

KUH, RICHARD HENRY, lawyer; b. N.Y.C., Apr. 27, 1921; s. Joseph Hellmann and Fannie Mina (Rees) K.; m. Joyce Dattel, July 31, 1966; children—Michael Joseph, Jody Ellen. B.A., Columbia Coll., 1941; LL.B. magna cum laude, Harvard U., 1948. Bar: N.Y. 1948, U.S. Dist. Ct. (so. dist.) N.Y. 1948, U.S. Dist. Ct. (ea. dist.) N.Y. 1967, U.S. Supreme Ct. 1968. Assoc. firm Cahill, Gordon & Reindel, 1948-53; asst. dist. atty. N.Y. County Dist. Attys. Office, 1953-64, dist. atty., 1974; sole practice law N.Y.C., 1966-71; ptnr. firm Kuh, Goldman, Cooperman & Levitt, N.Y.C., 1971-73, Kuh, Shapiro, Goldman, Cooperman & Levitt, P.C., N.Y.C., 1975-78, Warshaw Burstein Cohen Schlesinger & Kuh, N.Y.C., 1978—; adj. prof. N.Y. Law Sch., NYU Law Sch. Author: Foolish Figleaves, 1967; mem. bd.

editors: Harvard Law Rev, 1947-48; mem. adv. bd.: Contemporary Drug Problems, 1975—, Criminal Law Bull, 1976—; contbr. articles to popular and profl. jours. Trustee Temple Israel, N.Y.C., 1975-84, Grace Ch. Sch., 1981-85. Served with U.S. Army, 1942-45, ETO. Walter E. Meyer Research and Writing grantee, 1964-65. Mem. Am. Law Inst., Am. Bar Found., ABA (chmn. criminal justice sect. 1983-84, chmn. spl. com. on evaluation jud. performance 1983—), Assn. Bar City of N.Y., Phi Beta Kappa. Democrat. Jewish. Club: Harvard (N.Y.C.). Federal civil litigation, State civil litigation, Criminal. Home: 14 Washington Pl New York NY 10003 Office: 555 Fifth Ave New York NY 10017

KUHL, PAUL BEACH, lawyer; b. Elizabeth, N.J., July 15, 1935; s. Paul Edmund and Charlotte (Hetche) K.; m. Janey Mae Stadheim, June 24, 1967; children: Alison Lyn, Todd Beach. BA, Cornell U., 1957; LLB, Stanford U., 1960. Atty. Law Offices of Walter C. Kohn, San Francisco, 1961-63, Sedgwick, Detert, Moran & Arnold, San Francisco, 1963—. Served to lt. USCG, 1961. Mem. Am. Bd. Trial Advisors, ABA, Def. Research Inst., No. Calif. Assn. Def., Tahoe Tavern Property Owners Assn. (sec. 1979-81, pres. 1981-83).), San Francisco Trial Lawyers Assn., Am. Arbitration Assn. (mem. arbitration panel). Club: Canon Tennis (Fairfax, Calif.). Avocations: tennis, reading. Personal injury, Insurance, State civil litigation. Home: PO Box 574 Ross CA 94957 Office: Sedgwick Detert Moran & Arnold One Embarcadero Ctr 16th Floor San Francisco CA 94111-3765

KUHLMANN, FRED MARK, corporate lawyer; b. St. Louis, Apr. 9, 1948; s. Frederick Louis and Mildred (Southworth) K.; m. Barbara Jane Nierman, Dec. 30, 1970; children: F. Matthew, Sarah Ann. AB summa cum laude, Washington U., St. Louis, 1970; JD cum laude, Harvard U., 1973. Bar: Mo. 1973. Assoc. atty. Stolar, Heitzmann & Eder, St. Louis, 1973-75; tax counsel McDonnell Douglas Corp., St. Louis, 1975-82, corp. asst. sec., 1977—, corp. counsel fin. matters, 1982-84, assoc. gen. counsel, 1984—, staff v.p., 1985—. Bd. dirs. Luth. Charities Assn., 1982—, sec. 1984-86, chmn. 1986—; elder Ch. of Resurrection, 1977-80; mem. Regents Council Concordia Sem., 1981-84; chmn. cub scout pack 459 Boy Scouts Am., 1984-86; trustee Luth. Assn. Higher Edn., 1978-84, chmn. alumni assn., 1981. Recipient Disting. Leadership award Luth. Assn. for Higher Edn., 1981. Mem. ABA, Bar Assn. Met. St. Louis, Phi Beta Kappa, Omicron Delta Kappa. Republican. Club: Bellerive Country (Mo.). Corporate taxation, Pension, profit-sharing, and employee benefits, Acquisitions, divestitures. Home: 742 Briar Fork Rd Des Peres MO 63131 Office: McDonnell Douglas Corp PO Box 516 Saint Louis MO 63166

KUHN, HAROLD FRED, JR., lawyer; b. Portsmouth, Va., Sept. 3, 1956; s. Harold Fred Sr. and Emma Jean (Bates) K.; m. Everette Floyd, Oct. 11, 1980. BS, U. S.C., 1977, JD, 1980. Bar: S.C. 1980, U.S. Ct. Appeals (4th cir.) 1981, U.S. Supreme Ct. 1982. Assoc. Moss, Bailey & Dore, Beaufort, S.C., 1980-85; ptnr. Moss, Bailey, Dore & Kuhn, Beaufort, 1986—. Chmn. cir. S.C. Alliance Legis. Edn., Beaufort, 1983-85. Mem. S.C. Bar Assn., Beaufort COunty Bar Assn., S.C. Trial Lawyers Assn. (chmn. state amicus curaie com. 1984-85). Democrat. Baptist. Personal injury, Workers' compensation, State civil litigation. Home: 43 Wildwood Ln Beaufort SC 29902 Office: Moss Bailey Dore & Kuhn 1501 North St Beaufort SC 29901

KUHN, JAMES E., lawyer; b. Hammond, La., Oct. 31, 1946; s. Eton Percy and Mildred Louise (McDaniel) K.; m. Cheryl Aucoin, Dec. 27, 1969; children: James M., Jennifer L. BA, Southeastern La. U., 1968; JD, Loyola U. of South, 1973. Bar: La. 1973. Asst. dist. atty. 21st Jud. Dist. La., 1979—. Mem. ABA, La. State Bar Assn., 21st Jud. Bar Assn., Livingston Parish Bar Assn., Assn. Trial Lawyers Am., La. Trial Lawyers Assn., La. Assn. Def. Counsel, Delta Theta Phi. Criminal, State civil litigation, Federal civil litigation. Home: 8178 Hermitage Dr Denham Springs LA 70726 Office: 519 Florida Blvd Denham Springs LA 70726

KUHN, PERLA M., lawyer; b. Cordoba, Argentina, July 21, 1940; came to U.S. 1960; d. Juan and Aida (Bortnick) Meirovich; m. Richard D. Kuhn, Oct. 24, 1964; children: Daniel, Jonathan, Eric. Grad., U. Cordoba Law Sch., 1959; LLM, Tulane U., 1961; LLCM, U. Pa., 1962; LLB, NYU, 1967. Atty. asst. chief counsel's office Dept. Treasury, N.Y.C., 1968-72; assoc. Busby, Rivkin, Sherman, Levy & Rehm, N.Y.C., 1972-75; assoc. gen. counsel Hartz Mountain Corp., Harrison, N.J., 1975-78; ptnr. Kuhn & Muller and predecessor firm Offner and Kuhn, N.Y.C, 1978—; mem. adv. com. N.Y. State Commn. on Cable TV. Mem. ABA, Customs and Internat. Trade Bar Assn., Copyright Soc. U.S., U.S. Trademark Assn., Argentine-Am. C. of C. (bd. dirs. 1986—), N.Y. State Bar Assn., N.Y. Patent, Trademark and Copyright Law Assn. Avocations: tennis, reading. Trademark and copyright, Private international, Foreign trade. Home: 50 Edstone Dr Staten Island NY 10301 Office: 1412 Broadway New York NY 10018

KUHNMUENCH, JOHN RICHARD, JR., lawyer; b. Milw., Nov. 26, 1944; s. John Richard and Elizabeth Jane (Kelley) K.; m. Jane m. Salvaty, June 15, 1979; children: John, Jeffrey, Kevin, Andrew. BS, Marquette U., 1966, JD, 1969. Bar: Wis. 1969, U.S. Dist. Ct. (ea. dist.) Wis. 1969, U.S. Ct. Appeals (7th cir.) 1977, U.S. Supreme Ct. 1977, U.S. Ct. Appeals (9th cir.) 1981. Assoc. Patrick T. Sheedy & Assocs., Milw., 1969-79, Levine & Epstein, Milw., 1979-81; asst. gen. counsel A.O. Smith Corp., Milw., 1981-85, dep. gen. counsel, asst. sec., 1985—, chmn. polit. action com.; instr. bus. law Milw. Area Tech. Coll., 1977—. Bd. dirs. Transitional Living Services, 1980-82. Recipient Woolsack Soc. Merit award Marquette U., 1969. Mem. ABA, Wis. Bar Assn., Bar Assn. 7th Fed. Cir., Milw. Bar Assn., Am. Corp. Counsel Assn. Office: AO Smith Corp PO Box 23973 Milwaukee WI 53223-0973

KUHRAU, EDWARD W., lawyer; b. Caney, Kans., Apr. 19, 1935; s. Edward E. and Dolores (Hardman) K.; m. Janiece Christal, Dec. 8, 1959; children: Quentin, Clayton; m. Eileen Engeness, Oct. 30, 1983; 1 child, Edward. BA, U. Tex., 1960; JD, U. So. Calif., 1965. Bar: Calif. 1966, Wash. 1968, Alaska 1977, U.S. Dist. Ct. (so. dist.) Calif. 1966, U.S. Dist. Ct. (we. dist.) Wash., U.S. Dist. Ct. Alaska 1968, U.S. Ct. Appeals (9th cir.) 1966. Assoc. Adams, Duque & Hazeltine, Los Angeles, 1965-66, Louis Lee Abbot, Los Angeles, 1966-67, Perkins, Coie, Stone, Olsen & Williams, Seattle, 1968-72; ptnr. Perkins, Coie, Stone, Olsen & Williams, Seattle, 1973—, ptnr. in charge Anchorage office, 1977-78, partner in charge and chmn. real estate dept., Seattle, 1971—. Editor-in-chief Wash. Real Property Deskbook, 1979, 81, 86; contbr. articles to profl. jours. Mem. Seattle Sch. Bd. Adv. Com., 1970-71. Served with USAF, 1955-58. Mem. ABA, Wash. Bar Assn. (chmn. real property, probate and trust sect.), Alaska Bar Assn., State Bar Calif., Seattle-King County Bar Assn., Am. Coll. Real Estate Lawyers, Internat. Council Shopping Centers, Order of Coif. Clubs: Wash. Athletic, Seattle Yacht, Columbia Tower. Real property, Banking, Environment. Address: Suite 1900 Washington Bldg Seattle WA 98101

KUKLIN, ANTHONY BENNETT, lawyer; b. N.Y.C., Oct. 9, 1929; s. Norman B. and Deane (Cable) K.; m. Vivienne May Hall, Apr. 4, 1964; children: Melissa, Amanda. AB, Harvard U., 1950; JD, Columbia U., 1953. Bar: N.Y. 1953, D.C. 1970. Assoc. Dwight, Royall, Harris, Koegel & Caskey, N.Y.C., 1955-61; assoc. Paul, Weiss, Rifkind, Wharton & Garrison, N.Y.C., 1961-68, ptnr., 1969—. Contbr. articles to legal jours. Mem. Internat. Bar Assn. (chmn. div. one), ABA (chmn. elect., sec. real property, probate and trust law), N.Y. State Bar Assn. (exec. com. real property sect., chmn. 1981-82), Assn. Bar City N.Y., Am. Coll. Real Estate Lawyers (pres. 1981-82), Anglo-Am. Real Property Inst. (gov. 1981—). Real property. Home: 22 Pryer Ln Larchmont NY 10538 Office: Paul Weiss Rifkind et al 1285 Ave of Americas New York NY 10019

KUKLIN, JEFFREY PETER, lawyer, talent agency executive; b. N.Y.C., Dec. 13, 1935; s. Norman Bennett and Deane (Cable) K.; m. Jensina Olson, Nov. 18, 1960; 1 son, Andrew Bennett; m. 2d, Ronia Levene, June 22, 1969; children—Adam Blake, Jensena Lynne, Jeremy Brett. A.B., Columbia U., 1957, J.D., 1960. Bar: N.Y. 1962, U.S. Supreme Ct. 1965, Calif. 1973. Atty., TV sales adminstrn. NBC-TV, N.Y.C., 1966-67; asst. to dir. bus. affairs CBS News, N.Y.C., 1967-69; atty., assoc. dir. contracts ABC-TV, N.Y.C. and Los Angeles, 1969-73; v.p. bus. affairs and law Tomorrow Entertainment, Inc., Los Angeles, 1973-75; v.p. legal and bus. affairs Billy Jack Enterprises, Inc., Los Angeles, 1975-76; atty., bus. affairs exec. William Morris Agy., Inc., Beverly Hills, Calif., 1976-79, head TV bus. affairs, 1979-81, v.p., head TV bus. affairs, 1981—. Mem. ABA, Acad. TV Arts and Scis., Los Angeles Copyright Soc. Entertainment. Address: 151 El Camino Dr Beverly Hills CA 90212

KULEWICZ, JOHN JOSEPH, lawyer; b. Indpls., Mar. 22, 1954; s. Stanley J. and Marian F. (Tuggle) K. BA, Ohio State U., 1976; JD, Yale U., 1979. Bar: Ohio 1981, U.S. Dist. Ct. (so. dist.) Ohio 1981, U.S. Ct. Appeals (6th cir.) 1981, U.S. Dist. Ct. (no. dist.) Ohio 1983. Law clk. to presiding judge U.S. Ct. Appeals (6th cir.), Cin., 1979-80; assoc. Vorys, Sater, Seymour & Pease, Columbus, Ohio, 1981-86, ptnr., 1987—. Term mem. Council on Fgn. Relations; vice chmn. Ohio delegation to 1984 Dem. Nat. Conv.; Ohio coordinator Gary Hart for Pres. Campaign, 1984; trustee Columbus Zoo, 1982—. Mem. ABA, Ohio Bar Assn., Columbus Bar Assn. Democrat. Roman Catholic. Federal civil litigation, State civil litigation. Home: 3008 Neil Ave #73B Columbus OH 43202 Office: Vorys Sater Seymour & Pease 52 E Gay St PO Box 1008 Columbus OH 43216

KULIK, JOSEPH MICHAEL, lawyer; b. Pitts., Sept. 17, 1957; s. Joseph John and Katherine Anne (Katshir) K.; m. Donna Marie Kosarich, Mar. 23, 1985; 1 child, Sarah Rose. BA summa cum laude, Duquesne U., 1978, JD, 1981. Bar: Pa. 1981, U.S. Dist. Ct. (we. dist.) Pa. 1981, U.S. Ct. Appeals (3d cir.) 1981, U.S. Tax Ct. 1984, U.S. Supreme Ct. 1985. Assoc. Law Offices of Peter J. King, Pitts., 1981-85; ptnr. King & Kulik, Pitts., 1986—. Dir. sch. Montour Sch. Dist., Allegheny County, Pa., 1977—, chief negotiator, 1984—; sec. Montour Sch. Bd., Allegheny County, 1983—; bd. dirs., Parkway West Area Vocat.-Tech. Sch., Oakdale, Pa., 1977-85, treas., 1981-85; solicitor Kennedy Twp. (Pa.) Mcpl. Authority, 1984—. Recipient Detroit Renaissance award, 1980; named one of Outstanding Young Men Am., 1982-84. Mem. ABA, Pa. Bar Assn., Allegheny County Bar Assn., Nat. Sch. Bds. Assn. Democrat. Roman Catholic. Lodge: Italian Sons and Daus. Am. Avocations: history, tennis. General practice, General corporate, Family and matrimonial. Home: 121 Lorish Rd McKees Rocks PA 15136 Office: King & Kulik 20 Chatham Sq Pittsburgh PA 15219

KULLBY, ROY SIGURD, lawyer; b. N.Y.C., Sept. 26, 1927; s. John Sigurd and Florence Astrid (Loven) K.; m. Jane Fitzpatrick, Dec. 30, 1954 (div. 1979); children—Keith Sigurd, Kenton Rowe, Kirk Walter, Kevin Stuart, Kristen Jonsson; m. Deborah Morris Ross, May 24, 1981. B.S. in Engring., Purdue U., 1952; LL.B., Ind. U., 1952. Bar: Ind., Ill., Colo. Trial atty. antitrust div. U.S. Dept. Justice, Washington, 1955-57; asst. U.S. Atty. No. Dist. Ill., Chgo., 1957-59; ptnr. firm Pope & Ballard, Chgo., 1960-71, Magill & Kullby, Steamboat Springs, Colo., 1972-73, Vedder, Price, Kaufmann & Kammholz, Chgo., 1974-85; sole practice Law Offices of Roy S. Kulby, Boulder, Colo., 1986—; of counsel Law Offices of John W. Gerstner, Chgo., 1986—; pres. Estey Printing Co., Boulder, Colo., 1987—. Editor: Trade Secrets and Employment Agreements, 1982; editor Ind. Law Jour., 1951-52. Mem. Routt County Republican Central Com., Colo., 1972-74; mem. fin. com. 10th Ill. Dist. Congl. Com., Ill., 1980-85. Served with USMC, 1946-47. Mem. ABA (chmn. comml., fin. and banking litigation com. 1983-86), 7th Circuit Bar Assn. (chmn. Ill. programs 1982—), Chgo. Bar Assn. (chmn. fed. civil procedure com. 1984-85), Swedish American Hist. Soc. Republican. Clubs: University, Law, Legal. Lodge: Optimists. Federal civil litigation, State civil litigation, Antitrust. Office: Estey Printing Co 2005 32d St Boulder CO 80301 Office: 1200 W Monroe St Chicago IL 60606

KULLEN, RICHARD CHARLES, JR., lawyer; b. Detroit, June 22, 1938; s. Richard Charles and Margaret Mary (DeConinck) K.; m. Barbara Elizabeth Catoggio, Nov. 7, 1970; children—Richard C., Michael V.S., B. Elizabeth, V. Anthony. A.B., (Nat. Merit scholar) Georgetown U., 1960; J.D. (Root-Tilden Scholar), N.Y.U., 1963. Bar: N.Y. 1967, U.S. Dist. Ct. (so. dist.) N.Y. 1972. Assoc., Townley & Updike, N.Y.C., 1964-73, ptnr., 1974—. Mem. Cath. Big Bros. of N.Y., 1964—, bd. dirs. 1970—, pres. 1979-81. Served with USMCR, 1963. Mem. ABA, N.Y. State Bar Assn., Assn. Bar City of N.Y. Republican. Roman Catholic. Clubs: Orienta Beach, Shoreham (N.Y.) Country. Contracts commercial, General corporate, Banking. Home: 61 Maple Hill Dr Larchmont NY 10538 Office: 405 Lexington Ave New York NY 10174

KULLER, JONATHAN MARK, lawyer; b. Paterson, N.J., Jan. 2, 1951; George and Muriel (Kaplan) K.; m. Mardi Risa Adelman, Oct. 7, 1977; children: Brett Louis, Devin Howard. BS, Livingston Coll., 1972; JD, Rutgers U., 1976. Bar: N.J. 1976, U.S. Dist. Ct. N.J. 1976, U.S. Supreme Ct. 1985. Law clk. to presiding judge N.J. Superior Ct., Hackensack, 1976-77; assoc. Miller & Platt, Paterson, 1977-78; ptnr. Markus, Kuller & Cohen, Parsippany, N.J., 1978-87, Blaustein & Wasserman, Woodbridge, N.J., 1987—. Mem. N.J. Bar Assn., Morris County Bar Assn., Comml. Law League Am. Democrat. Jewish. Avocation: tennis. Consumer commercial, Bankruptcy, Real property. Office: Blaustein & Wasserman Parkway Towers Rt 1 S PO Box 597 Woodbridge NJ 07095

KULP, DOLORES ROCCO, lawyer; b. Phila., Feb. 26, 1952; d. Ralph Joseph and Helen O'Connor Rocco; m. Timothy Austin Kulp, Dec. 1, 1984. BA, Temple U., 1974, JD, 1977. Bar: Pa. 1977, U.S. Dist. Ct. (ea. dist.) Pa. 1977, U.S. Ct. Appeals (3d cir.) 1984. Trial atty. Southeastern Pa. Transp. Authority, Phila., 1977-79, sr. trial atty., 1981-83; assoc. Margolis, Edelstein & Scherlis, Phila., 1979-80; asst. city solicitor City of Phila., 1980-81; gen. atty. Consolidated Rail Corp., Phila., 1983-86; sole practice Phila., 1986—. Mem. Acad. Advocacy, Phi Beta Kappa. Democrat. Roman Catholic. Avocations: swimming, cake decorating. Personal injury, Federal employer's liability. Home and Office: 3416 W Penn St Philadelphia PA 19103

KUMBLE, STEVEN JAY, lawyer; b. July 3, 1933; m. Barbara Kumble (div.); children: Charles Todd, Roger Glenn; m. Peggy Basten Vandervoort. BA, Yale U., 1954; JD, Harvard U., 1959. Bar: N.Y. 1960. Ptnr. Finley, Kumble, Wagner, Heine, Underberg, Manley & Casey, N.Y.C., 1968—; chmn. bd. dirs. Lincolnshire Assoc., N.Y.C. Vice chmn. bd. dirs. L.I. U., Greenvale, N.Y., 1984—; chmn. bd. dirs. Gov.'s Com. on Scholastic Achievement, N.Y.C., 1981—. Served to 1st lt. U.S. Army, 1955-57. Mem. Assn. of Bar of City of N.Y., Phi Beta Kappa. Club: Yale (N.Y.C.), Ardsley Country (N.Y.). Avocations: skiing, golf, tennis. General corporate, Real property. Home: 950 Fifth Ave New York NY 10021 Office: Finley Kumble Wagner Heine et al 425 Park Ave New York NY 10022

KUMLI, KARL FREDRICK, III, lawyer; b. Lawrence, Kans., Aug. 17, 1956; s. Karl Fredrick Jr. and Lee M. (DiMeo) K.; m. Frances E. Draper, Dec. 30, 1981. BA, Stanford U., 1978; JD, U. Pacific, 1981. Bar: Calif. 1981, Colo. 1982, U.S. Ct. Appeals (D.C. cir.) 1982, U.S. Dist. Ct. Colo. 1984, U.S. Ct. Appeals (10th cir.) 1984. Assoc. Moses & Wittemyer, Boulder, Colo., 1981-82; sole practice Boulder, 1983—; bd. dirs. Ecocycle, Inc., Boulder. Bd. dirs. Winding Trail Village Assn., Boulder, 1985-86. Recipient Outstanding Legal Service award Ecocycle, Inc., Boulder, 1985. Mem. ABA, Colo. Bar Assn. (water law and real estate law sects.), Calif. Bar Assn. Democrat. Roman Catholic. Club: Stanford (bd. dirs. Rocky Mountain chpt. 1984). Avocations: traditional Irish music, wine collecting, swimming, skiing. Real property. Office: 1911 11th St Suite 201 Boulder CO 80306

KUMP, KARY RONALD, lawyer; b. Provo, Utah, Apr. 27, 1952; s. Ronald and Ann (Thomas) K.; m. Terri Renee Farley, Sept. 24, 1980; children: Kasey Ronald, Kyle Thomas, Kristopher Lewis, Kolby Lawrence. AA, Rio Hondo Coll., 1972; BA, U. Calif., Fullerton, 1976; JD, Western State U., Fullerton, 1980; cert. trial advocacy, Hastings Law Sch., 1982. Bar: Calif. 1982, U.S. Dist. Ct. (cen., no. and so. dists.) Calif. 1982. Assoc. William G. Kellen & Assocs., Riverside, Calif., 1980-83, Kellen & Luchs, Riverside, 1983-84; ptnr. Luchs, Kump & Milelich, Riverside, 1984-85, Carter & Kump, Riverside, 1985-87; sole practice Riverside, 1987—; panel atty. Lawyer Referral Service, Riverside, 1982—, Coll. Legal Clinic, Riverside, 1984—, Montgomery Wards Legal Services Plan, Riverside, 1986—; judge pro tem Riverside Mcpl. Ct. Mem. ABA, State Bar Calif. (bd. govs. Service Contbn. award 1984), Riverside Bar Assn. (panel atty. 1982), Calif. Pub. Defenders Assn., Am. Trial Lawyers Assn., Calif. Trial Lawyers Assn. Republican. Mormon. Avocations: golf, tennis, fishing, camping. Personal injury, Bankruptcy, State civil litigation. Office: 3579 Arlington Ave Suite 201 Riverside CA 92506

KUNIHOLM, JOHN GARDNER, lawyer; b. Gardner, Mass., Jan. 21, 1928; s. Waino Gardner and Esther Wendla (Norton) K.; m. Margot Alice Herring, Sept. 18, 1954; children—Thomas G., Julie G., Nancy C., Wendy E. B.A. cum laude, Amherst Coll., 1950; J.D., Harvard U., 1953; LL.M., NYU, 1954. Bar: Mass. 1953, Del. 1958. Counsel, Hercules, Inc., Wilmington, Del., 1956-66, sr. counsel, 1966-78, asst. gen. counsel, 1978—. Contbr. articles to profl. jours. Mem. panel of arbitrators Am. Arbitration Assn., 1984—. Served with U.S. Army, 1954-56. Mem. ABA, Internat. Bar Assn., Del. Bar Assn., N.Y. Bar Assn. Republican. Episcopalian. Club: Wilmington Country. Administrative and regulatory, General corporate, Private international. Home: RD 1 Box 469A Chadds Ford PA 19317 Office: Hercules Inc 1313 Market St Wilmington DE 19894

KUNIYUKI, KEN TAKAHARU, lawyer; b. Honolulu, Nov. 30, 1947; s. Henry Seiya and Emi (Takami) K.; m. Noreen Kanai, Aug. 20, 1971. B.A., U. Hawaii, 1969, M.A., 1970; J.D., U. Calif.-Berkeley, 1973. Bar: Hawaii 1973, U.S. Dist. Ct. Hawaii 1973, U.S. Ct. Appeals (9th cir.) 1976. Assoc. David Schutter, Honolulu, 1973-74; ptnr. Turk & Kuniyuki, Honolulu, 1974-77, Kuniyuki & Pang, Honolulu, 1978-80; sole practice, Honolulu, 1980-81; ptnr. Kuniyuki & Chang, Honolulu, 1981—; arbitrator Hawaii Med. Claims Panel, Honolulu, 1979—. Bd. dirs. ACLU, Hawaii, 1978-80, chmn. litigation com., 1978-81. Mem. Am. Arbitration Assn. Club: Hawaii Chess Fedn. (pres. 1982-83). State civil litigation, Criminal, Personal injury. Office: Kuniyuki & Chang 900 Fort St Suite 310 Honolulu HI 96813

KUNSTADT, ROBERT M., lawyer; b. Boston, Jan. 24, 1951. BA, Yale U., 1972; JD, UCLA, 1975. Bar: Calif. 1976, N.Y. 1979. Assoc. Pennie & Edmonds, N.Y.C., 1979—. Author: The Protection of Personal and Commercial Reputation, 1980. Mem. ABA, Assn. Bar City N.Y., N.Y. Patent, Trademark and Copyright Law Assn. Trademark and copyright, Patent, Federal civil litigation. Office: Pennie & Edmonds 1155 Ave of Americas New York NY 10036

KUNTZ, CHARLES POWERS, lawyer; b. Los Angeles, May 7, 1944; s. Walter Nichols and Katherine (Powers) K.; m. June Emerson Moroney, Dec. 23, 1969; children: Michael Nicholas, Robinson Moroney. AB with honors, Stanford U., 1966, JD, 1969; LLM, NYU, 1971. Bar: Calif. 1970, N.Y. 1970, U.S. Dist. Ct. (no. dist.) Calif. 1970, U.S. Ct. Appeals (9th cir.) 1970, U.S. Supreme Ct. 1979. Staff atty. project for urban affairs OEO, N.Y.C., 1969-71; dep. pub. defender Contra Costa County Pub. Defender's Office, Martinez, Calif., 1971-75; assoc. Treuhaft, Walker & Brown, Oakland, Calif., 1976-78; ptnr. Hirsch & Kuntz, San Rafael, Calif., 1979-85; sole practice San Rafael, 1985—; Ct appointed arbitrator Superior Ct., County of Marin, Calif., 1980—. Mem. San Francisco Bar Assn., Marin County Bar Assn., Assn. Trial Lawyers Am., Calif. Trial Lawyers Assn. Club: Marin Rod and Gun. State civil litigation, Insurance, Personal injury. Home: 1188 Butterfield Rd San Anselmo CA 94960 Office: 185 N Redwood Dr Suite 130 San Rafael CA 94903

KUNTZ, JOEL DUBOIS, lawyer; b. Dennis, Mass., Feb. 5, 1946; s. Paul Grimley Kuntz and Harriette (Hunter) Ainsworth; m. Karan Judd, June 29, 1968; children: Matthew Christopher, Kristin Lara. BA, Haverford Coll., 1968; JD, Yale U., 1971; LLM in Taxation, NYU, 1980. Bar: Conn. 1972, Oreg. 1974. Ptnr. Stoel, Rives, Boley, Fraser & Wyse, Portland, Oreg., 1974—; editor-in-chief Jour. of Taxation of Investments, 1983—. Co-author: (with James S. Eustice) Federal Income Taxation of S Corporations, 1982, 2d edition, 1985, (with James S. Eustice, Charles S. Lewis III and Thomas P. Deering) Tax Reform Act of 1986: Analysis and Commentary, 1987. Served as capt. USMC, 1971-74. Democrat. Corporate taxation, Personal income taxation, State and local taxation. Home: 149 Iron Mountain Blvd Lake Oswego OR 97034 Office: Stoel Rives Boley Fraser & Wyse 900 SW 5th Ave Portland OR 97204

KUPPERMAN, LOUIS BRANDEIS, lawyer; b. Augusta, Ga., Dec. 16, 1946; s. Herbert Spencer and Mollie (Kleven) K; m. Nancy Ann Coll, Nov. 30, 1967; children—David Evan, Robert Dennis. B.S., Farleigh Dickinson U., 1972; J.D., Bklyn. Law Sch., 1975. Bar: Pa. 1975, U.S. Dist. Ct. (ea. dist.) Pa. 1978, U.S. Ct. Appeals (3d cir.) 1978, U.S. Supreme Ct. 1982. Jud. law clk. to presiding justice Ct. of Common Pleas of Phila. County, 1975-76, 76-77; corp. counsel Health Corp. Am., Wayne, Pa., 1977-78; ptnr. Dilworth, Paxson, Kalish & Kauffman, Phila., 1978-86; mem. firm, chmn. real estate dept. Baskin, Flaherty, Elliott & Mannino, P.C., Phila., 1986—. Chancellor's del. to Phila. Farleigh Dickinson U., 1983, 86. Recipient Disting. Alumnus award Fairleigh Dickinson U., 1983. Mem. ABA, Pa. Bar Assn., Phila. Bar Assn., (chmn. real estate litigation com. 1983-85), Hist. Soc. U.S. Dist. Ct. (ea. dist.) Pa. Club: Racquet of Phila. Author: Real Estate Tax Assessment Appeals, 1987. Real property, State civil litigation, State civil litigation. Home: 424 Charles Ln Wynnewood PA 19096 Office: Baskin Flaherty Elliott & Mannino PC 1800 Three Mellon Bank Ctr Philadelphia PA 19102

KUREK, JAMES DAVID, lawyer; b. Toledo, Nov. 2, 1955; s. James and Genevieve Kurek; m. Melody Ann Jerkins, June 2, 1979; 1 child Jena Marie. BBA, U. Toledo, 1978; JD, U. Mich., 1981. Bar: Ohio 1981, U.S. Dist. Ct. (no. dist.) Ohio 1982, U.S. Ct. Appeals (6th cir.) 1983, U.S. Supreme Ct. Assoc. Fuller & Henry, Toledo, 1978, Buckingham, Doolittle & Burroughs, Akron, Ohio, 1984—. Mem. ABA, Ohio Bar Assn., Akron Bar Assn. Club: Cascade. Labor, Civil rights. Office: Buckingham Doolittle & Burroughs 50 S Main St PO Box 1500 Akron OH 44309

KURLAND, PAUL C., lawyer, educator; b. Bklyn., May 28, 1946; s. Marvin and Beatrice (Marmer) K.; m. Phyllis Pfeffer, Sept. 1, 1968; children—Joshua Ethan, Abigail Sara. B.A., Bklyn. Coll., 1967; J.D., NYU, 1970. Bar. N.Y. 1971, U.S. Ct. Appeals (2d cir.) 1971, U.S. Dist. Ct. (so. and ea. dists.) N.Y. 1972, U.S. Supreme Ct. 1974. Assoc. Cahill, Gordon & Reindel, N.Y.C., 1970-73, Emil Kobrin, Klein & Garbus, N.Y.C., 1973-77; ptnr. Kurland and Scheiman, N.Y.C., 1977-79, Baer Marks & Upham, N.Y.C., 1979-85, Snow, Becker & Krauss, P.C., N.Y.C., 1986—; mem. faculty Nat. Inst. Trial Advocacy, 1980—, trial techniques course Hofstra Law Sch., 1980—, Emory Law Sch., 1982—, Cardozo Law Sch. Yeshiva U., 1986—; arbitrator U.S. Dist. Ct. (ea. dist.) N.Y., Am. Arbitration Assn. Pres. Manhassett (N.Y.) Democratic Club, mem. Nassau County Democratic Com.; pres., bd. dirs. Guitar Workshop, Roslyn, N.Y.; mem. Nassau County Dem. Exec. Com.; active Fund for New Priorities in Am., ACLU. Mem. ABA, Assn. Bar City N.Y. Federal civil litigation, State civil litigation, Legal education. Home: 142 Hemlock Rd Manhasset NY 11030 Office: Snow Becker & Krauss PC 605 3d Ave New York NY 10158

KURLAND, PHILIP B., lawyer, educator; b. N.Y.C., Oct. 22, 1921; s. Archibald H. and Estelle (Polstein) K.; m. Mary Jane Krensky, May 29, 1954; children: Julie Rebecca, Martha Jennifer, Ellen Sarah. A.B., U. Pa., 1942; LL.B., Harvard U., 1944; LL.D., U. Notre Dame, 1977, U. Detroit, 1982. Bar: N.Y. 1945, Ill. 1972, U.S. Supreme Ct 1972. Law clk. to Judge Jerome N. Frank, 1944-45, Supreme Ct. Justice Felix Frankfurter, 1945-46; atty. Dept. Justice, 1946-47; mem. firm Kurland & Wolfson, N.Y.C., 1947-50; asst. prof. law Northwestern U. Law Sch., 1950-53; mem. faculty U. Chgo., 1953—, prof. law, 1956—, William R. Kenan, Jr. prof., 1973-76, William R. Kenan, Jr. disting. service prof., 1976—; counsel firm Rothschild, Barry & Myers, Chgo., 1972—; cons. Econ. Stblzn. Agy., 1951-52; chief cons., subcom. on separation of powers U.S. Senate Judiciary Com., 1967-77; cons. U.S. Dept. Justice, 1976; mem. Oliver Wendell Holmes Devise Com., 1975-83. Author or editor: Jurisdiction of Supreme Court of U.S, 1950, Mr. Justice, 1964, Religion and the Law, 1962, Frankfurter: Of Law and Life, 1965, The Supreme Court and the Constitution, 1965, The Great Charter, 1965, Moore's Manual, 1964-70, Felix Frankfurter on the Supreme Court, 1970, Politics, The Constitution and the Warren Court, 1970, Mr. Justice Frankfurter and the Constitution, 1971, Landmark Briefs and Arguments of the Supreme Court of the United States, 121 vols., 1975-86, Watergate and the Constitution, 1978, Cablespeech, 1983, The Founders' Constitution, 5 vols., 1987; editor: Supreme Court Rev., 1960—. Guggenheim fellow, 1950-51, 54-55. Fellow Am. Acad. Arts and Scis.; mem. Am., Chgo. bar assns., Am. Law Inst., New Brougham Soc. Jewish. Club: Quadrangle (U. Chgo.). Legal education, Federal civil litigation, Legal history. Home: 4950 Chicago Beach Dr Chicago IL 60615

KURNIT, RICHARD ALAN, lawyer, educator; b. N.Y.C., Mar. 22, 1951; s. Shepard and Jean Kurnit; m. Diane R. Katzin, Sept. 9, 1979. AB magna cum laude, Columbia U., 1972; JD cum laude, Harvard U., 1975. Bar: N.Y. 1976, U.S. Dist. Ct. (so. dist.) N.Y. 1976, U.S. Ct. Appeals (D.C. cir.) 1977, U.S. Ct. Appeals (2d cir.) 1978, U.S. Supreme Ct. 1980, U.S. Dist. Ct. (ea. dist.) N.Y. 1981. Law clk. to presiding justice U.S. Dist. Ct. (so. dist.) N.Y., N.Y.C., 1975-76; assoc. Paul, Weiss, Rifkind, Wharton & Garrison, N.Y.C., 1976-81; ptnr. Frankfurt, Garbus, Klein & Selz, N.Y.C., 1981—; instr. advt. law New Sch., N.Y.C., 1981—. Editor Harvard U. Civil Rights-Civil Liberty Law Rev., 1975; contbr. articles to profl. jours. Recipient Citizens Communications Ctr. award, 1975. Mem. ABA. Assn. Bar City of N.Y. (advt. industry subcom.), Phi Beta Kappa. Advertising, Libel, Trademark and copyright. Home: 515 W End Ave New York NY 10024 Office: Frankfurt Garbus Klein & Selz 485 Madison Ave New York NY 10024

KUROWSKI, JOHN JOSEPH, lawyer; b. East St. Louis, Ill., July 18, 1953; s. John Stanley and Gloria Louise (Simich) K.; m. Constance Anne Hastings, Apr. 17, 1982; children: Angela Christine, Joseph Michael. BA, Loyola U., Chgo., 1975; JD, St. Louis U., 1978. Bar: Ill. 1978, U.S. Dist. Ct. (so. dist.) Ill. 1978, U.S. Ct. Appeals (7th cir.) 1981. Ptnr. Gomric & Kurowski, P.C., Belleville, Ill., 1979-83; sole practice Belleville, 1983—; asst. state's atty. St. Clair County, Belleville, 1983—; bd. dirs. Cygan Family Catering, Highland, Ill., 1981—. Mem. ABA, Ill. Bar Assn. (co-chmn. uniform marital property act com., chmn. adoption and parentage com. family law sect. council 1986—, assembly 1982-84), St. Clair County Bar Assn. (legis. com., pro bono program, cert. appreciation 1986). Democrat. Roman Catholic. Lodge: KC. Personal injury, Family and matrimonial, Real property. Home: 134 Hickory Lake Belleville IL 62223 Office: 315 N Illinois St Belleville IL 62220

KURRELMEYER, LOUIS HAYNER, lawyer; b. Troy, N.Y., July 26, 1928; s. Bernhard and Lucy Julia (Hayner) K.; m. Phyllis A. Damon, June 14, 1952 (div. 1973); children: Ellen Laura, Louis Hayner, Nancy Snow; m. Martina Sophia Kluis, June 14, 1975. AB, Columbia U., 1949, LLB, 1953; MA in Econs., U. N.Mex., 1950. Bar: N.Y. 1953, U.S. Dist. Ct. (so. dist.) N.Y. 1957, U.S. Ct. Appeals (2d cir.) 1957, U.S. Dist. Ct. (ea. dist.) N.Y. 1958, D.C. 1968, U.S. Dist. Ct. D.C. 1968, U.S. Ct. Appeals (D.C. cir.) 1968, U.S. Tax Ct. 1973, U.S. Ct. Claims 1973, U.S. Dist. Ct. Vt. 1983, U.S. Ct. Internat. Trade 1984, U.S. Ct. Appeals (Fed. cir.) 1986. Assoc. Debevoise, Plimpton, Lyons & Gates, N.Y.C., 1953-66; ptnr. Hale Russell & Gray, N.Y.C., 1967-75, counsel, 1976-85; counsel Winthrop, Stimson, Putnam & Roberts, Washington, 1985—. Author: The Potash Industry, 1951; contbr. to CPLR Forms and Guidance for Lawyers, 1963. Asst. transp. adminstr. City of N.Y., 1966-67; v.p. Emerson Sch., N.Y.C., 1960-64, chmn., 1964-69; mem. Prudential Co. Fire Dist. No. 1, Shelburne, Vt., 1977—, chmn., 1977-84. Decorated knight 1st class Royal Swedish Order of North Star. Mem. ABA, D.C. Bar Assn. Private international, Aviation, Federal civil litigation. Home: 45 Clearwater Rd Shelburne VT 05482 Office: Winthrop Stimson Putnam & Roberts 1155 Connecticut Ave Washington DC 20036

KURTZ, JAMES LOUIS, lawyer; b. Chgo., Dec. 18, 1933; s. Louis Frank and Constance Ann K.; m. Carol May Gleisten, June 25, 1938; children—Kerry Ann, Kristin Ann, Kevin James. B.S. in Mech. Engring., U. Ill., 1955; J.D., John Marshall Law Sch., 1959. Registered profl. engr., Ill.; bar: Ill. 1959, U.S. Ct. Appeals (7th cir.) 1962, D.C. 1963, U.S. Ct. Appeals D.C. Cir. 1964, U.S. Ct. Appeals (5th cir.) 1968, U.S. Ct. Appeals (3d cir.) 1969, U.S. Ct. Appeals (4th cir.) 1974, U.S. Ct. Appeals (9th and 11th cirs.) 1981, U.S. Supreme Ct. 1981, U.S. Ct. Appeals Fed. Cir. 1982. Engr., Gen. Motors Corp., LaGrange, Ill., 1955-60; assoc. Mann, Brown & McWilliams, Chgo., 1961-63, Mason, Fenwick, Lawrence, Washington, 1964-69, Pope, Ballard, Shepard & Fowle, Washington, 1970-72; sole practice, Washington, 1972-82; of counsel Dickinson Wright, Moon, Van Dusen & Freeman, Washington, 1982—. pres., chmn. bd. dirs. Aloha Pacific Cruises, Inc. Mem. Ill. State Bar Assn., Chgo. Bar Assn., ABA, Bar Assn. D.C., Fed. Bar Assn., Am. Intellectual Property Assn., U.S. Trademark Assn., ASME, Soc. Automotive Engrs., Delta Theta Phi. Republican. Roman Catholic. Trademark and copyright, Federal civil litigation, Antitrust. Office: 1901 L St NW Suite 801 Washington DC 20036

KURTZ, JAMES P., administrative law judge; b. Highland Park, Mich., Dec. 5, 1932; s. A.T. and Virginia C. (Riley) K.; m. Barbara A. Gonczy, Feb. 2, 1957; children—Mary T., Christina M., Ann V., J. Peter, Karen M., Eileen M. A.B., U. Detroit, 1955, J.D., 1958. Bar: Mich. 1958, U.S. Dist. Ct. (ea. dist.) Mich. 1958, U.S. Ct. Appeals (6th cir.) 1964. Supervisory atty. 7th region NLRB, Detroit, 1958-67; ptnr. firm Brennan & Kurtz, Detroit, 1967-69; adminstrv. law judge Employment relations commn. State of Mich. Dept. Labor, Detroit, 1969—; instr. labor and real estate Detroit Coll. Bus., Dearborn, 1968-73; adj. prof. adminstrv. law U. Detroit, 1969-72. Editor-in-chief U. Detroit Law Jour., 1957-58; editor procs. Nat. Acad. Arbitrators, 1971-75. Mem. Mich. Bar Assn. (Labor Law sect.). Democrat. Roman Catholic. Labor, Administrative and regulatory. Home: R1 Craig Beach, Harrow, ON Canada N0R 1G0 Office: Mich Employment Relations Commn 1200 6th St 14th Floor Detroit MI 48226-2480

KURTZ, JEROME, lawyer; b. Phila., May 19, 1931; s. Morris and Renee (Cooper) K.; m. Elaine Kahn, July 28, 1956; children: Madeleine, Anne Nettie. BS with honors, Temple U., 1952; LLB magna cum laude, Harvard U., 1955. Bar: Pa. 1956, N.Y. 1981, D.C. 1982; CPA, Pa. Assoc. Wolf, Block, Schorr & Solis-Cohen, Phila., 1955-56, 57-63; ptnr. Wolf, Block, Schorr & Solis-Cohen, 1963-66, 68-77; tax legis. counsel Dept. Treasury, Washington, 1966-68; commr. IRS, 1977-80; ptnr. Paul, Weiss, Rifkind, Wharton & Garrison, 1980—; instr. Villanova Law Sch., 1964-65, U. Pa., 1969-74; vis. prof. law Harvard U., 1975-76; mem. adv. group to commr. IRS, 1976. Editor: Harvard Law Rev, 1953-55; contbr. numerous articles to profl. jours. Pres. Ctr. Inter-Am. Tax Adminstrn., 1980; bd. dirs. Common Cause, chmn. fin. com., 1985-87. Served with U.S. Army, 1956-57. Recipient Exceptional Service award Dept. Treasury, 1968, Alexander Hamilton award, 1980. Mem. ABA (chmn. tax shelter com. 1982-84), N.Y. Bar Assn. (exec. com. tax sect. 1981-82), Pa. Bar Assn., Phila. Bar Assn. (chmn. tax sect. 1975-76), Am. Law Inst., Am. Coll. Tax Counsel, Beta Gamma Sigma. Corporate taxation, Estate taxation, Personal income taxation. Home: 1619 35th St NW Washington DC 20007 Office: 1615 L St NW Washington DC 20036

KURTZ, LOUIS LAIRD, lawyer; b. Des Moines, Dec. 7, 1947; s. Louis Francis and Elizabeth Isletta (Laird) K.; m. Susan Maurine Whisenand, Sept. 21, 1968 (div.); children—Louis James, Jennifer Dianne; m. Lori Joan Jordan, Mar. 19, 1983. B.B.A., Regis Coll., 1970; J.D. cum laude, Creighton U., 1974. Bar: Nebr. 1974, U.S. Dist. Ct. Nebr. 1974, Oreg. 1976, U.S. Dist. Ct. Oreg. 1976. Law clk. Nebr. Supreme Ct., Lincoln, 1974-76; dep. legis. counsel Oreg. Legislature, Salem, 1976-77; assoc. firm Owens & Loomis, Eugene, Oreg., 1977-79; ptnr. firm Loomis, Tomlinson & Kurtz, Eugene, 1980-84; assoc. firm Luvaas, Cobb, Richards & Fraser, Eugene, 1984-85, ptnr., 1985—. Mem. Nebr. State Bar Assn., Oreg. State Bar Assn., Oreg. Assn. Def. Counsel, Lane County Bar Assn. Democrat. Roman Catholic. State civil litigation, Insurance, Personal injury. Office: Luvaas Cobb Richards & Fraser PC PO Box 10747 Eugene OR 97440

KURY, BERNARD EDWARD, lawyer; b. Sunbury, Pa., Sept. 11, 1938; m. Valerie Ann Conover, Aug. 4, 1962; children: Sabrina, Susannah. AB, Princeton U., 1960; LLB, U. Pa., 1963. Bar: N.Y. 1964. Assoc. Dewey, Ballantine, Bushby, Palmer & Wood, N.Y.C., 1963-71, ptnr., 1971—. Contbr. articles to profl. jours. Club: Heights Casino (Bklyn.) (gov. 1979-85). General corporate. Home: 7 Willow St Brooklyn NY 11201 Office: Dewey Ballantine Bushby Palmer & Wood 140 Broadway New York NY 10005

KURY, FRANKLIN LEO, lawyer; b. Sunbury, Pa., Oct. 15, 1936; s. Barney and Helen (Witkowski) K.; m. Elizabeth Heazlett, Sept. 14, 1963; children: Steven, David, James. Bar: Pa. 1962. Atty. Pa. Dept. Justice, Harrisburg, 1961-62; ptnr. Kury & Kury, Sunburg, 1963-80, Tive, Hetrick & Pierce, Harrisburg, 1981-82, Reed, Smith, Shaw & McClay, Harrisburg, 1983—. Mem. Ho. of Reps., Harrisburg, 1967-72, Senate of Pa., Harrisburg, 1973-80; del. at large Dem. Nat. Conv., San Francisco, 1984. Served to 1st lt. U.S. Army, 1962-66, with Res. Mem. Pa. Bar Assn. (chmn. environ. sect. 1984), Polish Nat. Alliance. Democrat. Avocation: fishing. Environment, Administrative and regulatory, Real property. Office: Reed Smith Shaw & McClay 300 N 2d St PO Box 11844 Harrisburg PA 17108

KURYK, DAVID NEAL, lawyer; b. Balt., Aug. 24, 1947; s. Leon and Bernice G. (Fox) K.; m. Alice T. Lehman, July 8, 1971; children—Richard M., Robert M., Benjamin A. B.A., U. Md., 1969; J.D., U. Balt., 1972. Bar: Md. 1972, U.S. Dist. Ct. Md. 1973, U.S. Ct. Mil. Appeals 1973, D.C. 1974, U.S. Ct. Appeals (4th cir.) 1974, U.S. Supreme Ct. 1976, U.S. Ct. Appeals (Fed. cir.) 1982. Assoc. Harold Buchman, Esq., Balt., 1970-76; sole practice, Balt., 1976—. Chmn. publicity Progressive Sick Benefit and Relief Assn., 1974—. Served to sgt. USAF, 1967-73. Mem. ABA (products, gen. liability and consumer law com. 1976—, com. auto law 1977), Md. State Bar Assn., Bar Assn. Balt. City, Assn. Trial Lawyers Am., U. Balt. Alumni Assn., Zeta Beta Tau. Democrat. Jewish. Mem. bd. editors Md. Bar Jour., 1973-76. Personal injury, State civil litigation, Contracts commercial. Home: 11200 Five Spring Rd Lutherville MD 21093 Office: 5 Light St Suite 950 Baltimore MD 21202

KURZ, THOMAS PATRICK, lawyer; b. Stevens Point, Wis., Dec. 26, 1951; s. Edward Albert and Bertha Marie (Schmidt) K.; m. Debra Kay Gentz, Jan. 6, 1979; children—Natalie Jean, Thomas Patrick Jr. B.A., U. Wis.-Madison, 1974; J.D., Georgetown U., 1977. Bar: Wis. 1977, Ill. 1982, U.S. Dist. Ct. (ea. dist.) Wis. 1977. Assoc. Foley & Lardner, Milw. and Madison, 1977-82; atty. A.E. Staley Mfg. Co., Decatur, Ill., 1982-85; sr. atty. Staley Continental, Inc., Rolling Meadows, Ill, 1985—. Mem. Georgetown Law Jour., 1975-76, editor, 1976-77. Lector, St. Patrick Parish, Decatur, 1983-86; bd. dirs. Millikin-Decatur Symphony Guild, 1985-86. Recipient Eagle Scout award Samoset council Boy Scouts Am., 1967; Wis. honors scholar, 1970. Mem. ABA, Ill. Bar Assn., Wis. Bar Assn., Phi Beta Kappa. Roman Catholic. General corporate, Contracts commercial, Securities. Home: 3385 Portshire Ct Palatine IL 60067 Office: Staley Continental Inc 1 Continental Towers 1701 Golf Rd Rolling Meadows IL 60008

KURZMAN, ROBERT GRAHAM, lawyer, educator; b. N.Y.C., July 3, 1932; s. Benjamin E. and Betty Kurzman; m. Carol Ellis, Aug. 26, 1956; children—Marc, Nancy, Amy. B.A., Hofstra U., 1954; J.D., Cornell U., 1957. Bar: N.Y. 1959, U.S. Supreme Ct. 1964, U.S. Dist. Ct. (no., so., ea. and we. dists.) N.Y. 1964. Assoc., Wynn, Blattmachr & Campbell, N.Y.C., 1959-63; ptnr. Leaf, Kurzman, Deull & Drogin, N.Y.C., 1963-79, Goldschmidt, Fredericks, Kurzman & Oshatz, 1979-82, Kurzman, Midler & Corbin , White Plains, N.Y., 1982—; adj. prof. law NYU; dir. Stratton Industries, Inc.; acting city ct. judge City of New Rochelle (N.Y.), 1981. Adv. bd. So. Meth. U. Sch. Law, Estate Planning Inst.; coordinator estates and trusts paralegal program Manhattanville Coll., 1974-75; pres. West Putnam council Boy Scouts Am., 1981, recipient Silver Beaver award, Silver Antelope award; former pres. New Rochelle Lions Club; trustee Temple Israel; former chmn. New Rochelle Republican Com. Served to capt. USAR, 1957-59. Named Man of Yr., New Rochelle B'nai B'rith, 1977. Fellow Am. Coll. Probate Counsel; mem. ABA, N.Y. State Bar Assn., Assn. Bar City N.Y., Westchester Bar Assn. Clubs: Ridgeway Country (White Plains, N.Y.); Masons; Cornell of N.Y.C. (pres.). Author: (with Rita Gilbert) Paralegals and Successful Law Practice, 1981; contbr. articles profl. jours. Probate, Estate taxation, Family and matrimonial. Home: 166 Tewkesbury Rd Scarsdale NY 10583 Office: 1 N Broadway White Plains NY 10601

KURZWEIL, HARVEY, lawyer; b. Bklyn., Mar. 23, 1945; s. Martin Kurzweil and Muriel (Krause) Kanow; m. Barbara Kramer; children: David, Paul, Emily, Elizabeth. AB, Columbia U., 1966, JD, 1969. Bar: N.Y. 1970. Assoc. Dewey, Ballantine, Bushby, Palmer & Wood, N.Y.C., 1969-77, ptnr., 1977—. Mem. ABA, N.Y. State Bar Assn., D.C. Bar Assn., Assn. of Bar of City of N.Y. (trade regulation com. 1982-85). Jewish. Club: Downtown Athletic (N.Y.C.). Avocations: reading, gardening, sports. Federal civil litigation, State civil litigation. Office: Dewey Ballantine Bushby et al 140 Broadway New York NY 10005 Home: 56 Hopper Farm Rd Upper Saddle River NJ 07458

KUSHEL, GLENN ELLIOT, lawyer; b. Bklyn., May 5, 1945. BME, CUNY, 1968; MSME, Columbia U., 1970; JD, Seton Hall U., 1974; LLM, NYU, 1978; cert., Coll. Fin. Planning, 1987. Bar: N.J. 1974, N.Y. 1977, U.S. Supreme Ct. 1978. Mem. tech. staff Bell Telephone Labs., Whippany, N.J., 1968-71; cost engr. Exxon Resource and Engr. Co., Florham Park, N.J., 1971-72; dep. atty. gen. State of N.J., Trenton, 1974-76; assoc. Rosenman and Colin, N.Y.C., 1976-81; sole practice Bklyn., 1981—. assoc. mem. malpractice panel N.Y. State Supreme Ct., Kings County, 1986-87. Atomic Energy Commn. fellowship, 1968. Mem. ABA, Bklyn. Bar Assn., N.Y. State Trial Lawyers Assn., Pi Tau Sigma, Tau Beta Pi. Avocations: skiing, running, financial planning. State civil litigation, Insurance, Personal injury. Office: 32 Court St Brooklyn NY 11201

KUSMA, KYLLIKKI, lawyer; b. Tartu, Estonia, Dec. 8, 1943; came to U.S., 1951, naturalized, 1958; d. August and Helju (Traat) K.; B.F.A., Ohio U., 1966; M.A. (Vets. Rehab. Adminstrn. fellow), Ohio State U., 1967; J.D., Ohio No. U., 1976; M.L.T., Georgetown U., 1980. Bar: Ohio 1977, D.C. 1978. Speech and hearing therapist Lima (Ohio) Meml. Hosp., 1967-70, Tipp City (Ohio) Schs., 1970-74; atty.-adv. Office Chief Counsel, IRS, Washington, 1977-81; v.p., asso. tax counsel Security Pacific Nat. Bank, Los Angeles, 1981-83; ptnr. Brownstein Zeidman & Schomer, Washington, 1983—; instr. Wright State U., 1972-76. Vol. local civic, polit. activities. Mem. ABA, D.C. Bar Assn., Ohio Bar Assn., D.C. Women's Bar Assn., Phi Kappa Phi. Democrat. Corporate taxation, Personal income taxation, Pension, profit-sharing, and employee benefits. Office: Brownstein Zeidman & Schomer 1401 New York Ave #900 Washington DC 20005

KUSS, HERBERT PATRICK, city attorney; b. Zittau, E. Ger., Sept. 13, 1947; came to U.S., 1956; naturalized; s. Gerhard Jan and Elfriede (Schantin) K.; m. Judy Diane Housekeeper, July 31, 1977; children—Ryan, Jana. B.S., U. San Francisco, 1970; J.D., McGeorge U. of Pacific, Sacramento, 1974; M.B.A., U. Alaska, 1983. Bar: Calif. 1976, Alaska 1977, U.S. Dist. Ct. Alaska 1976, U.S. Dist. Ct. (no. and so. dists.) Calif. 1976, U.S. Ct. Appeals (9th cir.) 1978. Assoc. atty. Johnson, Christenson & Linkl Fairbanks, Alaska, 1976-77; dep. city atty. City of Fairbanks, 1977-80, city atty., 1980—. Served to sgt. USAF, 1970-75. Mem. ABA, Alaska Bar Assn., San Francisco Bar Assn., Tanana Valley Bar Assn., Calif. Bar Assn. Democrat. Roman Catholic. Lodge: Kiwanis. Local government.

KUSS, MARK DAVIS, lawyer; b. New Orleans, Oct. 4, 1956; s. Joseph Andrew and Elizabeth Swinney (Davis) K.; m. Wendy Marie Higgins, Nov. 25, 1981. BA magna cum laude, U. New Orleans, 1978; JD cum laude, Tulane U., 1982. Bar: La. 1982, U.S. Dist. Ct. (ea. dist.) La. 1982, U.S. Dist. Ct. (we. dist.) La. 1983, U.S. Ct. Appeals (5th cir.) 1986. Assoc. Bailey & Leininger, New Orleans, 1982-83, Law Office Joseph C. Bartels, New Orleans, 1983—. Recipient Goethe Inst. award Fed. Republic Germany, 1979. Mem. ABA (criminal justice sect. 1982—), La. Bar Assn. (civil law sect. 1984—), Phi Beta Kappa, Phi Kappa Phi. Democrat. Methodist. Avocations: baseball, documentary films, teaching. Family and matrimonial, Personal injury, Criminal. Home: #1 Tradewinds Ct New Orleans LA 70128

KUST, LEONARD EUGENE, lawyer; b. Luxemburg, Wis., Mar. 14, 1917; s. Joseph Andrew and Anna (Mleziva) K.; m. Henrietta Bryan Logan, Apr. 17, 1948; children: Alice Lyon Kust Harding, Andrea Logan Kust. Ph.B., U. Wis., Madison, 1939; J.D., Harvard U., 1942. Bar: N.Y. 1946, Pa. 1957. Assoc. Cravath, Swaine & Moore, N.Y.C., 1946-55; gen. tax counsel Westinghouse Electric Corp., Pitts., 1955-65; v.p., gen. tax counsel Westinghouse Electric Corp., Pitts., 1965-70; ptnr. Cadwalader, Wickersham & Taft, N.Y.C., 1970—; mem. adv. com. Commr. Internal Revenue, 1959-61; chmn. Pa. Gov's Com. on Tax Adminstrn., 1963-65; chmn. task forces Pa. Gov.'s Tax Rev. Com., 1967-68. Contbr. articles to profl. jours. Trustee Ch. of Heavenly Rest Day Sch., N.Y.C., 1968-71, 1978-82, warden, 1980-86; mem. vestry, Ch. of Heavenly Rest, N.Y.C., 1975-80; warden Calvary Protestant Episcopal Ch., Pitts., 1966-67. Served to lt. USNR, 1942-46. Mem. U.S. C of C. (dir. 1967-73), Tax Execs. Inst. (pres. 1961-62), ABA, N.Y. Bar Assn., Nat. Tax Assn. (pres. 1969-70). Clubs: Union, Down Town Assn, Harvard; The Church (N.Y.C.) (bd. of trustees 1981—, v.p. 1986—). Home: 1115 Fifth Ave New York NY 10128 Office: Cadwalader Wickersham & Taft 100 Maiden Ln New York NY 10038

KUSTER, LARRY DONALD, lawyer; b. Kewanee, Ill., July 27, 1947; s. Donald Carl and Rosemary Ann (Riggins) K.; m. Mary Catherine Whitmore, July 11, 1970; children—David, Ryan. B.A., Augustana Coll., 1969; J.D with honors, U. Iowa, 1973. Bar: Ill. 1973, U.S. Tax Ct. 1979, U.S. Dist. Ct. (cen. dist.) Ill. 1980, U.S. Ct. Appeals (7th cir.) 1982. Assoc. Rammelkamp, Bradney, Hall, Dahman & Kuster, Jacksonville, Ill., 1973-75, ptnr., 1976—; arbitrator Am. Arbitration Assn.; lectr. continuing med. edn. seminar sponsored by Springfield Clinic, St. John's Hosp., Springfield, 1986; moderator continuing legal edn. program Ill. Inst. Continuing Legal Edn., 1985, 86; bd. dirs. Sherwood Eddy Meml. YMCA, 1975-80, Jacksonville Area C. of C., 1981-84, Jacksonville Area Visitors and Tourism Bur., 1986—; mem. Am. Council on Germany, 1982—, City of Jacksonville Heritage Cultural Ctr. Bd., 1986—; pres. Ill. Assn. Hist. Preservation Commns. 1982; mem. Jacksonville Hist. Preservation Commn., 1979—, vice chmn., 1981-83, chmn., 1983-84; mem. West Central Ill. Council on World Affairs, pres., 1982-83. Mem. Morgan County Bar Assn. (pres. 1977-78), Ill. Bar Assn. (civil practice and procedure council 1976-77, sec. workers' compensation sect. 1982-83, vice chmn. 1983-84, chmn. 1984-85). Contbr. articles to profl. jours. Personal injury, Workers' compensation, State civil litigation. Home: 149 Caldwell St Jacksonville IL 62650 Office: Rammelkamp Bradney Hall Dahman & Kuster 232 W State Jacksonville IL 62650

KUSTURISS, DENNIS JOHN, lawyer; b. Camden, N.J., Aug. 5, 1950; s. John E. and Marion Elizabeth (Kouvatas) K.; m. Marybeth Garver, Aug. 26, 1973; children: Elizabeth Frances, Dennis J. BA, U. Pitts., 1972; JD, Widener U., 1978. Bar: Pa. 1978, U.S. Dist. Ct. (we. dist.) Pa. 1981, U.S. Ct. Appeals (3d cir.) 1983. Sole practice Bryn Mawr, Pa., 1978-79; assoc. Francis P. Pilleggi, Woodlyn, Pa., 1979-80, Lord & Mulligan, Media, Pa., 1980-81, Feczko & Seymour, Pitts., 1981-84, Vuono, Lavelle & Gray, Pitts., 1984—. Mem. Pa. Bar Assn., ABA. Republican. Greek Orthodox. Federal civil litigation, State civil litigation, General practice. Office: Vuono Lavelle & Gray 2310 Grant Bldg Pittsburgh PA 15219

KUTA, JEFFREY THEODORE, lawyer; b. Oak Park, Ill., Aug. 30, 1947; s. Stanley Joseph and Helen Mary (Terpin) K.; m. Diane LaVerne Jancovic, June 22, 1969; children: Jonathan Paul, Joseph Anthony. BA with honors, U. Chgo., 1969, JD, 1972. Bar: Ill. 1969, U.S. Dist. Ct. (no. dist.) Ill. 1969. Assoc. Hopkins & Sutter, Chgo., 1972-76; assoc. to ptnr. Newman, Stahl & Shadur, Chgo., 1976-79, 1979-1980; ptnr. Holleb & Coff, Chgo., 1981—; instr. Kent Coll Law, Chgo., 1978-79; sec., treas. Chgo. Equity Fund, Inc., 1985—; sec. Nat. Equity Fund, Inc., 1987—. Sec., treas. Chgo. Equity Fund, Inc., 1985—; sec. Nat. Equity Fund, Inc., 1987—. Mng. editor U. Chgo. Law Rev., 1971-72. Mem. ABA, Chgo. Bar Assn. (chmn. mag. 1982-83), Chgo. Council Lawyers, U. Chgo. Law Alumni Assn. (v.p. 1973-76, chmn. law jour. 1973-76), Lambda Alpha Internat. General practice, Real property. Home: 442 W Melrose St Chicago IL 60657 Office: Holleb & Coff 55 E Monroe St Chicago IL 60603

KUTNER, MARK DAVID, lawyer; b. Millville, N.J., Feb. 12, 1952; s. Al and Lois (Dichter) K.; m. Susan Nunberg, Aug. 18, 1974; children: Benjamin, Aaron. BA, Cornell U., 1974; JD cum laude, Harvard U., 1977. Bar: N.J. 1977, U.S. Dist. Ct. N.J. 1977, U.S. Tax Ct. 1981, U.S. Ct. Appeals (3d cir.) 1983. From assoc. to ptnr. Shapiro, Eisenstat & Garbage P.A., Vineland, N.J., 1977-84; ptnr. Capizola, Fineman & Kutner P.A., Vineland, 1984—; instr. legal edn. program Cumberland County Coll., 1983. Chmn. ann. show Boy Scout Am., Vineland, 1979, dist. explorer scouts, 1987—; pres. Beth Israel Synagogue Men's Club, Vineland, 1983-85; bd. dirs. Cumberland County Jewish Fedn. Found., Vineland, 1984—, Vineland chpt. ARC. Mem. ABA, N.J. Bar Assn., Cumberland Bar Assn. (chmn. legal edn. com. 1985—, health ins. com. 1981—). Avocation: classical record collecting. Contracts commercial, Real property, Probate. Home: 1329 Singer Ln Vineland NJ 08360 Office: Capizola Fineman & Kutner PA 100 N Main Rd Vineland NJ 08360

KUTNER, MAURICE JAY, lawyer; b. Far Rockaway, N.Y., May 19, 1940; s. Norman S. and Helen (Pivar) K.; m. Marisol Mesa, Aug. 21, 1976; children—David Seth, Lori Kim, Tyson Jed. B.B.A. (scholar), U. Miami, 1962, J.D., 1965. Bar: Fla. 1965, U.S. Ct. Mil. Appeals 1965, U.S. Dist. Ct. (so. dist.) Fla. 1968, U.S. Ct. Appeals (D.C. cir.) 1974, U.S. Ct. Appeals (5th cir.) 1981, U.S. Supreme Ct. 1981, U.S. Ct. Appeals (11th cir.) 1982. Asst. librarian Miami Beach (Fla.) br. Dade County Law Library, 1962-65; spl. asst. atty. gen. State of Fla., Tallahassee, 1965; chief prosecutor U.S. Army Infantry Tng. Ctr., Fort Benning, Ga., 1967-68; asst. pub. defender Dade County, Fla., 1968-70; sole practice, Miami, Fla., 1970—; lectr. U. Miami, 1986, Divorce Law Inst., Can., Colo., Fla., Ariz.; lectr in field; chmn. grievance com. Fla. Bar, 1981-82, mem. exec. council family law sect., 1982-86, sec., treas. family law sect., 1985, chmn., 1986-87, mem. grievance com. A, 1979-81, chmn., 1981-82, chmn. children's rights seminar, 1985, chmn. exec. council com. on proposed summary of dissolution of marriage procedure, 1982, chmn., coordinator continuing legal edn. program, 1983-84, vice chair long range planning com., publ. devel. bd., attendant seminars. Served to 2d lt. USAR, 1962-65; served to capt. JAG Corps, U.S. Army, 1965-67. Recipient Meritorious Service award Fla. Bar 1982. Fellow Am. Acad. Matrimonial Lawyers (bd. mgrs. Fla. chpt. 1986, chmn. Eighth Ann. Inst. 1986, attendant seminars); mem. ABA (family law sect., mem. com. on alimony, maintenance and support, mem. com. on alimony, maintenance and support 1981-82, exec. mem. econs. of practice com. 1982-83, mem. domestic violence com. 1982-83, chmn. econs. of law practice com. 1983-84, mem. marriage law com. 1983, nominating com. 1983-84, spl. task force on needs of children 1984, task force on children's rights, 1984-85, publs. devel. bd. 1984-87, sec. long range planning com. 1985-86, vice chmn. 1986-87, co-chmn. continuing legal edn. com. 1986-87, attendant seminars), Fla. Bar Assn. (chmn.-elect family law sect. 1986-87), Dade County Bar Assn. (chmn. family law com. 1983-84) Concerned Matrimonial Lawyers Dade County (rotating chmn. 1983, treas. 1985), Internat. Acad. Matrimonial Lawyers (charter), Acad. Fla. Trial Lawyers, Assn. Trial Lawyers Am., Bar and Gavel Soc., Phi Alpha Delta, Omicron Delta Kappa. Family and matrimonial. Office: 28 W Flagler St 12th Floor Miami FL 33130

KUTTEN, LAWRENCE JOSEPH, lawyer, high technology writer, consultant; b. St. Louis, May 10, 1953; s. Joseph and Carolyn Jane (Yalem) K.; m. Linda Gail Ishibashi, Oct. 20, 1979; 1 child, Carolyn. BA, Claremont McKenna Coll., 1974; JD, Washington U., St. Louis, 1977. Bar: Mo. 1977, Ill. 1978. Assoc., Mann & Poger, Clayton Mo., 1977-78; ptnr. Chartrand, Harvey, Kutten, St. Louis, 1978-81. Author: Computer Buyer's Protection Guide: How to Protect Your Rights in the Micro-computer Marketplace, 1984. Contbr. articles to mags. including: Bus. Computing, Computer Shopper, Computer World, EDN, Infoworld, Mini-Micro, Today, Videotex/Computer Mag. Computer.

KUTTNER, BERNARD A., lawyer, former judge; b. Berlin, Ger., Jan. 13, 1934; s. Frank B. and Vera (Knopfmacher); children: Karen M., Robert D., Stacey M. AB cum laude, Dartmouth Coll., 1955; postgrad. U. Va. Law Sch., 1956; JD, Seton Hall U., 1959; postgrad. NYU. Bar: N.J. 1960, N.Y. 1982, D.C. 1982, U.S. Supreme Ct. 1964, U.S. Ct. Mil. Appeals., 1967. Assoc. Toner, Crowley, Woelper & Vanderbilt, 1959-62; sole practice, 1962-75; corp. counsel, Irvington, N.J., 1963-66; ptnr. Kuttner, Toner, DiBenedetto & Dowd, Roseland, N.J.; judge N.J. State Div. Tax Apls., 1977-79; instr. civil litigation Montclair State Coll., 1979-82; del. Jud. Conf. N.J. Supreme Ct., 1974-81; vice chmn. Supreme Ct. N.J. Dist. Ethics Com., 1984-85, chmn., 1985-86. Contbr. articles to legal publs. Commr. Essex County (N.J.) Park Commn., 1973-79. Served to lt. comdr. USNR, 1964-74. Named Outstanding Young Man N.J., N.J. Jaycees 1967. Mem. ABA (coeditor trial techniques newsletter sect. on tort and ins. practice, chmn.-elect trial techniques com. 1987—, sect. on litigation), D.C. Bar Assn., Irvington Bar Assn. (pres. 1968-70), Essex County Bar Assn. (chmn. 1973-75, com. trial and appellate litigation, judiciary com. 1972-75, treas. 1975-79, pres. 1980-81, products liability com. 1981—), Assn. Trial Lawyers Am., Am. Counsel Assn. Democrat. Jewish. Club: Orange Lawn Tennis. Federal civil litigation, State civil litigation, Personal injury. Home: 61 Sagamore Rd Millburn NJ 07041 Office: Kuttner Toner & DiBenedetto 744 Broad St Newark NJ 07102

KUTZ, ROBERT H., lawyer; b. Brookville, Pa., Oct. 18, 1943; s. Charles M. and Virginia M. (McAuley) K.; children—David P., Robert S. B.A., Allegheny Coll., 1965; J.D., Duquesne U., 1973. Bar: Pa. 1973, U.S. Dist. Ct. (we. dist.) Pa. 1973; C.L.U. Asst. mgr. Conn. Gen. Life Ins. Co., Pitts., 1968-74; mgmt. employee Aetna Life Co., Pitts., 1975-76; sole practice, Greensburg, Pa., 1973-76, 81—; ptnr. Kutz & Kutz, Greensburg, 1976-80. Mem. Westmoreland Bar Assn., Pa. Bar Assn., ABA. Clubs: University (Pitts); Pike Run Country (Donegal, Pa.). Lodge: Elks. Estate planning, Corporate taxation, Pension, profit-sharing, and employee benefits. Office: 217 E Otterman St Greensburg PA 15601

KUYKENDALL, RONALD EDWARD, lawyer; b. Lincolnton, N.C., Dec. 24, 1952; s. Ellis Clingman Jr. and Dorothy Mae (Leatherman) K.; m. Julie Elizabeth Maconaughay, Mar. 28, 1981; children—Erin Elizabeth, Laura Anne. B.A. with distinction, U. Va., 1975; J.D., U. Richmond, 1978. Bar: Va. 1978, U.S. Dist. Ct. Va. 1978, U.S. Ct. Appeals (4th cir.) 1978, U.S. Supreme Ct. 1981. Law clk. to presiding justice Va. Supreme Ct., Richmond, 1978-79; assoc. Parker, Pillard & Brown, P.C., Richmond, 1979-82; assoc. Minor & Lemons, P.C., Richmond, 1982-83; ptnr., Minor & Kuykendall, P.C., Richmond, 1984-86, assoc. corp. counsel Signet Bank/Va., Richmond, 1987—. Mem. Law Rev., Moot Ct. Bd., U. Richmond. Mem. Assn. Trial Lawyers Am., Va. Trial Lawyers Assn., Richmond Trial Lawyers Assn., Va. Bar Assn., Henrico County Bar Assn., Richmond Bar Assn., ABA (litigation and gen. practice sects.), Christian Legal Soc., Baptist. General practice, Contracts commercial, Family and matrimonial. Office: Signet Bank 7 N 8th St PO Box 25970 Richmond VA 23260

KUZINEVICH, JOHN JACOB, lawyer; b. New Britain, Conn., Dec. 22, 1953; s. Harry Joseph and Jeanne (Parks) K.; m. Helen Cangiano. BA, Boston Coll., 1975, MA, 1977, JD, 1980. Bar: Fla. 1980, U.S. Dist. Ct. (mid. dist.) Fla. 1980, Mass. 1985, U.S. Dist. Ct. Mass. 1985. Assoc. Carlton, Fields, Ward, Emmanuel, Smith & Cutler, P.A., Tampa, Fla., 1980-84; atty. New England Power Service Co., Westborough, Mass., 1984—. Mem. Phi Beta Kappa. Federal civil litigation, State civil litigation, Public utilities. Home: 2 Pease Rd Upton MA 01568 Office: New England Power Service Co 25 Research Dr Westborough MA 01581

KVINTA, CHARLES J., lawyer; b. Hallettsville, Tex., Feb. 16, 1932; s. John F. and Emily (Strauss) K.; m. Margie N. Brenek, Oct. 9, 1954; children—Charles, Sherri, Kenneth, Christopher. BA in Govt., U. Tex., 1954, LLB, 1959. Bar: Tex. 1959. Atty. Tex. Hwy. Dept., Yoakum, Tex., 1959-61; ptnr. Gaus & Kvinta, Yoakum, 1962-67, Kvinta, Young & Frietsch, Yoakum, 1975—, Kvinta & Kvinta, attys., 1986—; exec. v.p. First State Bank, Yoakum, 1968-74, atty., 1975—; city atty. City of Yoakum, 1980—. Co-founder Bluebonnet Youth Ranch, Yoakum, 1968. Served to 1st lt. U.S. Army, 1954-56. Recipient Outstanding Community Service award Sons of Herman, 1984, Outstanding Service award Bluebonnet Youth Ranch, 1975, Outstanding Service award Yoakum Little League, 1982, Outstanding Service award Yoakum Lions, 1982, Paul Gustwick Outstanding Community Service award, 1986. Mem. Tex. Bar Assn., Am. Legion. Democrat. Roman Catholic. Family and matrimonial, Probate, Real property. Home: 713 Coke St Yoakum TX 77995 Office: Kvinta & Kvinta attys 403 W Grand Yoakum TX 77995

KWALWASSER, HAROLD JOSEPH, lawyer; b. N.Y.C., Jan. 1, 1947; s. Simon and Marie (Kane) K.; m. Marsha Hoffman, Dec. 20, 1970. BA, Swarthmore Coll., 1968; JD, Yale U., 1971. Bar: Calif. 1972, D.C. 1982. Law clk. to presiding justice U.S. Ct. Appeals (3d cir.), Phila., 1971-72; assoc. Tuttle & Taylor, Los Angeles, 1972-76, ptnr., 1976—. Pres. Pub. Counsel, Los Angeles, 1978-79; policy dir. Dem. Nat. Com., Washington, 1981; commr. Los Angeles Fire Commn., 1984—. Mem. ABA. Antitrust. Home: 7172 La Presa Dr Los Angeles CA 90068 Office: Tuttle & Taylor 355 S Grand Ave 40th Floor Los Angeles CA 90071-3101

KWASS, SIDNEY J., lawyer; b. Pocahontas, Va., Nov. 11, 1908; s. Joseph Israel and Gussie Louise (Aaron) K.; m. Edna DeLott, Aug. 12, 1933; children: Robert M., Karel Kwass Forrester, Kathy Kwass Taylor. JD, W.Va. U., 1931. Bar: W.Va. 1931. Sole practice Bluefield, W.Va., 1931-46; ptnr. Kwass, Stone, McGhee & Feuchtenberger, Bluefield, 1946-80; of counsel 1981-87; atty. City of Bluefield, 1933-37; commr. Mercer County (W.Va.) Cir. Ct., 1938-46; referee in bankruptcy U.S. Dist. Ct. (so. dist.) W.Va., 1942-46; mem. W.Va. Compensation Appeals Bd., 1959-69, chmn., 1961-69; adj. prof. cts. and jud. processes Bluefield State Coll., 1976. Founding mem., first sec. Bluefield Community Chest, 1936; bd. dirs., past pres. Bluefield Princeton Jewish Congregation. Mem. 4th U.S. Jud. Cir. Conf., W.Va. State Bar (gov. 1956-60), Mercer County Bar Assn. (past pres.). Probate, Real property, Family and matrimonial. Home: 1208 Hilltop Ln Bluefield WV 24701 also: 6300 NW 2d Ave Boca Raton FL 33431 Office: 305 L&C Bldg Bluefield WV 24701

KWIATKOWSKI, THOMAS EUGENE, lawyer; b. Milw., Jan. 15, 1954; s. Eugene and Camille (Krawiecki) K.; m. Beth Marie Stellberg, July 23, 1976; children: Abraham John, Benjamin Thomas. BA in Polit. Sci. cum laude, Marquette U., 1976, JD, 1979. Bar: Wis. 1979, U.S. Dist. Ct. (ea. and we. dists.) Wis. 1979. Atty. and employment relations specialist State of Wis. Dept. Employment Relations Div. Collective Bargaining, Madison, 1979-83, 1987—; atty. Green Bay (Wis.) Area Pub. Schs., 1983-87. Mem. steering com. Brown County Reps., Green Bay, 1985—. Thomas More scholar, Marquette U., 1977; Coll. William and Mary scholar, Exeter, Eng., 1978. Mem. ABA, Wis. Bar Assn., Wis. Pub. Employers Labor Relations Assn., Nat. Pub. Employers Labor Relations Assn., Wis. Sch. Attys. Assn., Nat. Sch. Bd. Assn., Council of Sch. Attys. Labor, Local government, School law. Home: 1624 Halsey St Allouez WI 54301 Office: Dept Employment Relations div Collective Bargaining 137 E Wilson St PO Box 7855 Madison WI 53707

KYHOS, THOMAS FLYNN, lawyer; b. Cheverly, Md., May 13, 1947. B.A. in Econs., DePauw U., 1969; J.D., Cath. U., 1973. Bar: Md. 1974, D.C. 1974, U.S. Tax Ct. 1974, U.S. Supreme Ct. 1978. sole practice, Washington, 1974—; pres. First Oxford Corp., Washington, 1976—. Mem. ABA, Md. Bar Assn., D.C. Bar Assn. Home: 5714 Massachusetts Ave Bethesda MD 20816 Office: 3528 K St NW Washington DC 20007

KYLE, PENELOPE W., lawyer; b. Hampton, Va., Aug. 6, 1947; d. Lanny Astor and Penelope (Ward) K.; m. Charles L. Menges, Oct. 10, 1981. BA, Guilford Coll., 1969; postgrad., So. Meth. U., 1969-71; JD, U. Va., 1979; postgrad., Coll. William & Mary, 1986-87, MBA, 1987. Bar: Va. 1979, U.S. Ct. Appeals (4th cir.) 1979. Prof. Thomas Nelson Community Coll., Hampton, 1970-76; assoc. McGuire, Woods & Battle, Richmond, Va., 1979-81; assoc. counsel CSX Realty, Inc., Richmond, 1981-83, asst. corp. sec., 1983—. Bd. visitors James Madison U., Harrisburg, Va., 1984—; commr. Port of Richmond Commn., 1985—; trustee His. Richmond Found., 1983—. Mem. ABA, Va. Bar Assn. (pres. young lawyers conf. 1984-85, council 1984-85), Richmond Bar Assn. Real property, General corporate. Home: 201 Oxford Circle W Richmond VA 23221 Office: CSX Corp PO Box C-32222 Richmond VA 23261

LABARRE, JEROME EDWARD, lawyer; b. Mpls., May 6, 1942; s. Roy George and Mary Ann (Kennefic) LaB.; m. Mary R. Connelly, Feb. 17, 1968; children: Paul, Catherine, Sarah. BS, U. Oreg., 1964; JD, Georgetown U., 1969. Bar: Oreg. 1969, D.C. 1969, U.S. Supreme Ct. 1972, U.S. Ct. Appeals (9th cir.). Dep. dist. atty. Multnomah County, Portland, 1969-72; assoc. Carey & Stoll, Portland, 1972-74; sole practice Portland, 1974-79; ptnr. Glasgow, LaBarre & Kelly, Portland, 1980-82, LaBarre & Assocs., Portland, 1982—; asst. prof. Lewis & Clark Northwestern Coll. Law, Portland; instr. Portland Community Coll. Founder Cath. Lawyers for Social Justice, 1983; mem. Multnomah County Bar Assn. Legal Aid Service, 1971-74. Mem. ABA, Multnomah Bar Assn. (treas. 1981, sec. 1982, 3d v.p. 1983, 2nd v.p. 1984, 1st v.p./pres.-elect 1985, pres. 1986, award of Merit 1976, Spl. award for Dedicated Service to Pub., Bench and Bar 1978, chmn. corrections com. 1974-77), Oreg. Trial Lawyers Assn., Assn. Trial Lawyers Am., Internat. Bar Assn., ACLU, Portland Am. Inn of Ct. (pres. 1987—). Democrat. Roman Catholic. Club: Portland City. Federal civil litigation, State civil litigation, Antitrust. Office: 900 SW Fifth Ave Suite 1212 Portland OR 97204-1268

LABAY, EUGENE BENEDICT, lawyer; b. El Campo, Tex., July 20, 1938; s. Ben F. and Cecelia M. (Orsak) L.; m. Katherine Sue Ermis, Dec. 29, 1962; children—Michael, Joan, John, Paul, David, Patrick, Steven. B.B.A., St. Mary's U., San Antonio, 1960, J.D., 1965. Bar: Tex. 1965, U.S. Dist. Ct. (we. dist.) Tex. 1968, U.S. Dist. Ct. (no. dist.) Tex. 1973, U.S. Ct. Appeals (5th cir.) 1968, U.S. Ct. Appeals (11th cir.) 1981, U.S. Supreme Ct. 1980, U.S. Dist. Ct. (ea. dist.) Tex. 1986. Briefing atty. Supreme Ct. Tex., Austin, 1965-66; assoc. Cox & Smith Inc., San Antonio, 1966-71, ptnr., 1972-83, v.p., 1972—. Served to 1st lt. U.S. Army, 1960-62. Mem. ABA, State Bar Tex. (chmn. sect. internat. law 1979-80), San Antonio Bar Assn., Fed. Bar Assn., Inter-Am. Bar Assn., Am. Judicature Soc., Catholic Lawyers Guild San Antonio, Phi Delta Phi, Roman Catholic. Clubs: Serra (San Antonio); KC (council grand knight 1982-83). Contbr. articles to legal jours. State civil litigation, Oil and gas leasing, Real property. Home: 31720 Post Oak Trail Boerne TX 78006 Office: 600 Nat Bank Commerce Bldg San Antonio TX 78205

LABDON, KENNETH CHARLES, lawyer; b. Syracuse, N.Y., Dec. 10, 1949; s. Kenneth Brown Jr. and Janet (Manley) L.; m. Diane Freeman, Dec. 28, 1974 (div. 1978); m. Catherine Conner, May 15, 1982; 1 child, Charles Atwood. B.S., St. Lawrence U., 1972; J.D., Ariz. State U., 1980. Bar: Ariz. 1980, U.S. Dist. Ct. Ariz. 1981, U.S. Ct. Appeals (9th cir.) 1983. Assoc. F. Creasy, Phoenix, 1980-81; ptnr. Tidwell & Labdon, Apache Junction, Ariz., 1981-82; sole practice, Scottsdale, Ariz., 1982-85; ptnr. Labdon & Morgan, P.A., 1986—; judge pro tem. Tempe Mcpl. Ct., 1986; contract pub. defender Scottsdale Mcpl. Ct., 1983—; mem. Scottsdale Criminal Justice Com., 1983-85; mem. misdemeanor subcom. com. on representation of indigents Ariz. Supreme Ct., 1985, mem. Auto Negligence Group, Ariz. State Bar CLE Mini Task force, 1985—. Mem. Assn. Trial Lawyers Am., Ariz. Trial Lawyers Assn., ABA, Ariz. Bar Assn., Scottsdale Bar Assn., Phi Delta Phi (v.p. 1979-80). Personal injury, Family and matrimonial, State civil litigation.

LABEREE, PETER WALTER, lawyer; b. Wilmington, Del., July 31, 1956; s. John A. and Mary C. (Donahue) L. BA, U. Pa., 1978, JD, 1982. Bar: Del. 1982, Pa. 1986. Assoc. Morris, Nichols, Arsht & Tunnell, Wilmington, 1982-85, Spector, Cohen, Gadon & Rosen, Phila., 1986—. Bd. dirs. Wilmington Regional Big Bros./ Big Sisters, 1983-85. Mem. ABA, Del. Bar Assn., Pa. Bar Assn., Phila. Bar Assn. Republican. Avocations: traveling, pre-Columbian studies. Banking, General corporate. Home: Benjamin Franklin House 9th & Chestnut St Apt 1232 Philadelphia PA 19107 Office: Spector Cohen Gadon & Rosen 1700 Market St 29th Floor Philadelphia PA 19103

LABODA, BARRY CHARLES, lawyer; b. Phila., Aug. 18, 1955. BA, Columbia U., 1976; JD, Boston U., 1979. Bar: Fla. 1979, U.S. Dist. ct. (mid. dist.) Fla. 1979, U.S. Ct. Appeals (11th cir.) 1981. Sole practice Orlando, Fla., 1984. Bd. dirs. Parent Resource Ctr., Orlando, 1985—. Mem. ABA, Fla. Bar Assn., Orange County Bar Assn. (staff atty. legal aid soc. 1980-84, vol. mediator citizen dispute settlement program 1982—). Administrative and regulatory, Criminal, Family and matrimonial. Home: 4876 Tangerine Ave Winter Park FL 32792 Office: 13 S Magnolia Ave Orlando FL 32801

LABRE, WILLIAM LUKE, lawyer; b. Escanaba, Mich., July 12, 1944; s. William Luke and Lucile Mae (Roberge) LaB.; m. Patricia Ann Ruthsatz, Mar. 22, 1975; children: Jennifer Ann, Robert William. BA, Holycross Seminary, 1966; MA, U. Detroit, 1970; JD, U. Notre Dame, 1977; M in Div., St. John's Provincial Seminary, Plymouth, Mich., 1982. Bar: Mich. 1977, Ind. 1977, U.S. Dist. Ct. (so. and no. dists.) Ind. 1977, U.S. Dist. Ct. (we. dist.) Mich. 1977, U.S. Tax Ct. 1977, U.S. Supreme Ct. 1980. Deacon Guardian Angels Ch., Crystal Falls, Mich., 1969-70; assoc. pastor St. Michael's Ch., Marquette, Mich., 1970-71; chaplain Newberry (Mich.) State Hosp., 1971-74; marriage counselor Mishawaka (Ind.) Marriage Counseling Office, 1974-77; sole practice Edwardsburg, Mich., 1977—; atty. contracts Cassopolis (Mich.) County Juvenile Ct., 1986—. Columnist (weekly) Your Mental Health, 1971-74, Marriage and the Family, 1975-76, LaBre on Law, 1985—. Vol. atty. Cass County Council on Aging, 1977—; prosecutor Ontwa Edwardsburg Police Dept., 1978—; bd. dirs. Cass County Community Mental Health Services, 1981-82, Southwestern Mich. Growth Alliance, 1986—. Cert. of Commendation, Cass County Community Health Services Bd., 1982. Mem. ABA, Mich. Bar Assn., Ind. Bar Assn., Cassopolis County Bar Assn. (pres. 1985—), Am. Assn. Marriage and Family Therapy (clin.), Nat. Mgmt. Assn. (bd. dirs. Cass County chpt. 1986—), Nat. Assn. Cath. Chaplains (pasotral assoc.), Edwardsburg Area C. of C. (pres. 1979-80, bd. dirs.), Am. Legion. Republican. Lodge: KC (grand knight 1977-78). Avocations: hunting, fishing, target shooting, reading. General practice, Jurisprudence. Office: 68897 S Cass St PO Drawer X Edwardsburg MI 49112

LA BRIE, LAWRENCE JAMES, lawyer; b. Balt., Sept. 16, 1934. BA, Wesleyan U., 1956; LLB, U. Mich., 1959; LLM, NYU, 1973. Bar: N.Y. 1960, Ky. 1977. Assoc. Hall McNicol, N.Y.C., 1960-65; atty. M.W. Kellogg Co., N.Y.C., 1965-69; sr. atty. Sperry Rand, N.Y.C., 1969-73; counsel Chem. Constrn. Corp., N.Y.C., 1973-75; sr. atty. Ashland Oil Co., Russell, Ky., 1975; assoc. div. counsel Ashland Petroleum Co., Russell, 1975-79, counsel synthetic oils, 1982-83; dir. law dept. Ashland Services Co., Russell, 1983-85; asst. gen. counsel Ashland Oil, Inc., Russell, 1985—. Mem. exec. bd. Tri-State Area council Boy Scouts Am., 1982-86, v.p. fin., 1982-83, v.p. adminstrn., 1983-84. Served with USAR, 1959-64. Mem. ABA, N.Y. State Bar Assn., Ky. Bar Assn., Boyd County Bar Assn., Assn. of Bar of City of N.Y. Mem. Nazarene Ch. General corporate. Home: 216 Bellefonte Circle Ashland KY 41101 Office: Ashland Oil Inc 1000 Ashland Dr Russell KY 41114

LABUDDE, ROY CHRISTIAN, lawyer; b. Milw., July 21, 1921; s. Roy Lewis and Thea (Otteson) LaB.; m. Anne P. Held, June 7, 1952; children—Jack, Peter, Michael, Susan, Sarah. A.B., Carleton Coll., 1943; J.D., Harvard U., 1949. Bar; Wis. 1949, U.S. Dist. Cts. (ea. and we. dists.) Wis. 1950, U.S. Ct. Appeals (7th cir.) 1950, U.S. Supreme Ct. 1957. Assoc., Michael, Best & Friedrich, Milw., 1949-57, ptnr., 1958—; dir. DEC-Inter, Inc., Milw. Western Bank, Western Bancshares, Inc., Superior Die Set Corp.; Chmn., bd. dirs. Milw. div. Am. Cancer Soc. Served to lt. j.g. USNR, 1943-46. Mem. Milw. Estate Planning Counsel (past pres.), Wis. Bar Assn., Wis. State Bar Attys. (chmn. tax sch., bd. dirs. taxation sect.). Republican. Episcopalian. Clubs: University, Milw., Milw. Country (Milw.); Mason, Shriners. General corporate, Estate planning, Personal income taxation. Home: 9000 N Bayside Dr Milwaukee WI 53217 Office: 250 E Wisconsin Ave Room 2000 Milwaukee WI 53202

LACASSE, JAMES PHILLIP, lawyer, tax counsel; b. Delta, Colo., Oct. 21, 1948; s. Kyndall and Elizabeth Ann (Harrington) L.; m. Lynda Diane Manly, June 17, 1978; 1 child, Laura Elizabeth. BS in Acctg. with distinction, Ariz. State U., 1970; JD, Coll. of William and Mary, 1973. Bar: Va. 1973. Tax staff Arthur Andersen & Co., Washington, 1973-75; corp. tax coordinator Continental Telecom Inc., Atlanta, 1975-78; internat. tax mgr. R.J. Reynolds Co., Winston-Salem, N.C., 1978-83, western hemisphere treas., 1983-84; sr. tax counsel Sea-Land Corp., Iselin, N.J., 1984-86; dir. taxes Am. Pres. Cos., Ltd., Oakland, Calif., 1986—. Mem. Downtown Crisis Ctr. Winston-Salem, 1983; chairperson social ministry com. St. John's Lutheran Ch., Summit, N.J., 1986. Named one of Outstanding Young Men of Am. U.S. Jaycees, 1983. Mem. ABA, Va. Bar Assn., Tax Execs. Inst. Avocations: golf, photography, travel. Corporate taxation. Home: 4 Cavanaugh Ct Piedmont CA 94610 Office: Am Pres Cos Ltd 1800 Harrison St Oakland CA 94612

LACEK, MICHAEL JOSEPH, lawyer; b. Dolgeville, N.Y., Aug. 6, 1955; s. Harold Richard and Annabelle Alice (Ortlieb) L.; m. Virginia Kelly, Aug. 21, 1982. BA, SUNY, Albany, 1977; JD, Columbia U., 1980. Bar: N.Y. 1981, U.S. Dist. Ct. (so. dist.) N.Y. 1982, U.S. Ct. Appeals (D.C. cir.) 1982, U.S. Ct. Appeals (1st cir.) 1983, Mass. 1984, U.S. Dist. Ct. Mass. 1984. Assoc. Cravath, Swaine & Moore, N.Y.C., 1980-83, Palmer & Dodge, Boston, 1983—. Mem. ABA, N.Y. State Bar Assn., Mass. State Bar Assn., Phi Delta Phi. Republican. Roman Catholic. Avocations: theatre, movies, reading, outdoor sports, hiking. State civil litigation, Federal civil litigation, Trademark and copyright. Office: Palmer & Dodge One Beacon St Boston MA 02108

LACEY, DAVID MORGAN, lawyer; b. Denison, Tex., Feb. 3, 1950; s. Leon C. and Oneita Mae (Morgan) L.; m. Joy Mae Womack, June 3, 1971; children—Justin Louis, Heather Mae. B.A. summa cum laude, Harding Coll., 1972; M.A., Duke U., 1974; J.D. with high honors, U. Tex.-Austin, 1976. Bar: Tex. 1976, U.S. Dist. Ct. (so. dist.) Tex. 1977, U.S. Ct. Appeals (5th cir.) 1977. Law clk. to U.S. dist judge, Austin, 1976-77; assoc. Baker & Botts, Houston, 1977-84; ptnr. Gilpin, Pohl & Bennett, Houston, 1984—. Mem. Tex. Law Rev., 1975-76. Pres., Christian Sch. of East Harris County, Houston, 1984-87. Mem. ABA, State Bar Tex., Houston Bar Assn., Order of Coif. Mem. Ch. of Christ. Federal civil litigation, State civil litigation, Bankruptcy. Home: 14931 Grassington Dr Channelview TX 77530 Office: Gilpin Pohl & Bennett 1300 Post Oak Blvd Houston TX 77056

LACEY, FREDERICK BERNARD, lawyer, former judge; b. Newark, Sept. 9, 1920; s. Frederick Robert and Mary Agnes (Armstrong) L.; m. Mary C. Stoneham, May 20, 1944; children—Frederick Bernard, James, Virginia, Robert, Mary, Kathleen, John. A.B., Rutgers U., 1941; J.D., Cornell U., 1948; LL.D. (hon.), Montclair State Coll., 1971, Seton Hall U., 1973. Bar: N.Y. State bar 1948, N.J. bar 1952. Asso. firm Whitman & Ransom, N.Y.C., 1948-53; asst. U.S. atty. for N.J., 1953-55; U.S. atty. 1969-71; practiced in Newark, 1955-69; partner firm Shanley & Fisher, Newark, 1955-69; U.S. dist. judge for N.J., 1971-86; sr. litigation ptnr. LeBouef, Lamb, Leiby & MacRae, N.Y.C. and Newark, 1986—. Served to lt. comdr. USNR, 1942-46. Mem. Order of Coif, Phi Beta Kappa. Jurisprudence. Office: LeBoeuf Lamb Leiby & MacRae Gateway 1 Suite 603 Newark NJ 07102

LACEY, PAMELA SUE, lawyer, law educator; b. Rock Island, Ill., Dec. 22, 1953; d. Darrell Lee and Shirley Mae (Allen) Edgar; m. Vincent A. Lacey, Sept. 9, 1972. BA, So. Ill. U., 1977, MA, 1979, JD, 1982. Bar: Ill. 1982, U.S. Dist. Ct. (so. dist.) Ill. 1984. Dir. corp. legal dept. Hosp. and Physician Cons. Services, Inc., Marion, Ill., 1982-84; instr. So. Ill. U., Carbondale, 1983—; law clk. U.S. Dist. Ct. So. Dist. Ill., Benton, 1984-86; assoc. Hart & Hart, Benton, Ill., 1986—. Contbr. articles to law jours. Mem. Ill. State Bar Assn., Williamson County Bar Assn., Bus. and Profl. Women. Home: Rt 3 Box 53A Crainville IL 62918 Office: Hart & Hart 602 W Public Sq PO Box 676 Benton IL 62812-0676

LACHANCE, JAMES MARTIN, lawyer; b. Gardner, Mass., Nov. 16, 1947; s. Luke Armand and Eva Jeanette (Archambeault) L. BA in English Lit., Middlebury Coll., 1969; JD, Boston Coll., 1972. Bar: Mass. 1972, Ga. 1981, Fla. 1981, U.S. Dist. Ct. (so. dist.) Ga. 1982, U.S. Dist. Ct. (no. dist.) Ga. 1986. Staff atty. VISTA, Boston, 1972-73, Cambridge and Somerville Legal Services Inc., Cambridge, Mass., 1973-78; sole practice Gardner, Mass., 1978-81; asst. dist. atty. Chatham County, Savannah, Ga., 1981-84; litigation atty. Finch, McCranie, Brown & Blank, Atlanta, 1984-85, A. Russell Blank, P.C., Atlanta, 1985—. Served to capt. USAR, 1969-75. Mem. Assn. Trial Lawyers Am., Ga. Trial Lawyers Assn., Ga. Bar Assn., Fla. Bar Assn., Mass. Bar Assn., Atlanta Bar Assn. Personal injury, Federal civil litigation, State civil litigation. Home: 2067 Black Fox Dr Atlanta GA 30345 Office: A Russell Blank PC 100 Peachtree St NW 1020 Atlanta GA 30303

LACHAPELLE, ARTHUR WILLIAM, lawyer, educator; b. St. Paul, Apr. 15, 1939; s. William Joseph and Dorothy Frances (Thelin) LaC.; m. Mary Rachel LaChapelle, Dec. 12, 1969; children—William Joseph, Rachelle Marie. B.A. summa cum laude, Macalester Coll., 1973; J.D., U. Minn., 1977. Bar: Minn. 1978, U.S. dist. ct. 1979. Tchr. Russian, German, Latin and earth space scis. North St. Paul Pub. Schs., 1973-76; researcher, writer Water Resources Research Ctr., U. Minn., 1975-77; asst. city atty. criminal div. City of St. Paul, 1978-79; sole practice, St. Paul, 1979—; adj. prof. Legal Asst. Program of U. Minn., 1980—; adj. prof. civil and mineral engring. U. Minn., 1979—; cons. environ. law; lectr. hazardous waste liabilities, 1980—; referee Conciliation Ct. Ramsey County, 1983—; hearing examiner St. Paul Human Rights Commn., 1985—; family ct. mediator, Ramsey County Dist. Ct., 1986—. Mem. Men in Violent Relationships, Inc., 1978-85, vice chmn. 1979-85; vice chmn. DAV, 1966—; coach, teen counselor Am. Youth Assn., W.Ger., 1964-66. Served with USAF, 1961-66. Mem. ABA, Minn. Bar Assn., Hennepin County Bar Assn., Ramsey County Bar Assn., Nat. Assn. Geology Tchrs., Am. Legion. Roman Catholic. Author: Codified and Uncodified State Laws and Agency Rules and Regulations Bearing on Water and Related Land Resources in Minnesota, 2 vols., 1978. State civil litigation, Criminal, Probate. Office: Energy Park Law Office 1489 Energy Park Dr Saint Paul MN 55108

LACHEEN, STEPHEN ROBERT, lawyer; b. Phila., June 15, 1934; s. Irving H. and Jeannette S. (Silverman) L.; m. Arlen Green, July 5, 1955 (div. Apr. 1977); children—Caroline, Amy; m. 2d, Helen Hetherington, Apr. 5, 1981; children—Arthur, Christopher, Alexandra. B.A., U. Pa., 1953; J.D., U. Miami, 1957; postgrad. Temple U., Am. U. Bar: Fla. 1957, Pa. 1958, U.S. dist. ct. (ea. dist.) Pa. 1957, U.S. Ct. Apls. (3d cir.) 1975, U.S. Ct. Apls. (4th cir.) 1978 (11th cir.) 1983, (9th cir.) 1983, U.S. Supreme Ct. 1977. Sole practice, Phila., 1957-72; ptnr. LaCheen, Doner & LaCheen, Phila., 1972-82; ptnr. LaCheen & Alva, Phila., 1982-86, LaCheen, Alva & Dixon, 1986—. Mem. Fed. Criminal Justice Act. Panel, Phila., 1979—, Lawyer Reference Service Panel, Phila., 1975—. Bd. dirs. GENESIS II, Phila., 1974—. Nat. Endowment for Humanities fellow Yale U., 1978. Mem. ABA, Phila. Bar Assn. (fee dispute com. 1979—, gov. 1982), Pa. Bar Assn., Fla. Bar Assn., Internat. Bar Assn., Am. Bd. Criminal Lawyers, Am. Soc. Criminology, Nat. Assn. Criminal Def. Lawyers. Jewish. Editor: The Shingle, 1975—; contbr. numerous articles to profl. publs., also writer short stories. Criminal. Home: 739 Germantown Pike Lafayette Hill PA 19444 Office: 3100 Lewis Tower Bldg Philadelphia PA 19102

LACK, ROBERT JOEL, lawyer; b. Glen Ridge, N.J., Mar. 7, 1955; s. Walter Abraham and Carolyn Frances (Hoffman) L.; m. Colleen Phyllis Kelly, June 9, 1979. AB, Princeton U., 1977, M in Pub. Affairs, 1978; JD, Harvard U., 1981. Bar: N.Y. 1982, U.S. Dist. Ct. (so. and ea. dist.) N.Y. 1982, U.S. Ct. Appeals (3d cir.) 1982, U.S. Ct. Appeals (1st cir.) 1984, U.S. Ct. Appeals (2d cir.) 1985, U.S. Supreme Ct. 1986. Law clk. to judge U.S. Ct. Appeals (3d cir.), Newark, 1981-82; assoc. Sullivan & Cromwell, N.Y.C., 1982—. Editor Harvard Law Rev. 1979-81. Recipient Whitney North Seymour medal Columbia U. Law Sch., 1981. Mem. ABA, N.Y. State Bar Assn. (mem. com. on civil rights 1984—), N.Y.C. Bar Assn. (sec. com. on lectures and continuing edn. 1984-86). Federal civil litigation, State civil litigation. Office: Sullivan & Cromwell 125 Broad St New York NY 10004

LACKERT, CLARK WILLIAM, lawyer; b. Rockville Centre, N.Y., May 8, 1952; s. William Christopher and Gertrude Lackert; m. Marie Juliette Doris, July 10, 1982; 1 child, Christopher Michael. AB cum laude, Cornell U., 1973; JD, SUNY, Buffalo, 1976; LLM in Trade Regulation, NYU, 1983. Bar: N.Y. 1978, U.S. Dist. Ct. (so. and ea. dists.) N.Y. 1979, U.S. Ct. Appeals (Fed. cir.) 1979. Assoc. Haseltine, Lake & Waters, N.Y.C., 1978-79, Offner & Kuhn, N.Y.C., 1979-81; ptnr. Nims, Howes, Collison & Isner, N.Y.C., 1981—. Treas. Haldale Civic Assn., Huntington, N.Y., 1985—. Mem. ABA (chmn. com. 1985—, del. to confs.), N.Y. Patent, Trademark and Copyright Law Assn. Trademark and copyright, Private international. Home: 10 Evans Ct Huntington Station NY 11746 Office: Nims Howes Collison & Isner 500 Fifth Ave New York NY 10110

LACKEY, HARRINGTON ASHTON, lawyer; b. Nashville, June 16, 1925; s. Vaden Major and Mildred Adele (Harrington) L.; m. Jane Carter, Sept. 12, 1959; 1 son, Harrington Ashton, Jr. B.S. in Engring., Princeton U., 1949; J.D., Vanderbilt U., 1951; postgrad. George Washington U. Law Sch., 1952-54. Bar: Tenn. 1951, U.S. Dist. Ct. D.C. 1952. Assoc., A. Yates Dowell, Washington, 1951-54, Lamont Johnston, Chattanooga, 1954-57; sole practice, Nashville, 1957—. Served to sgt. U.S. Army, 1943-46. Decorated Bronze Star medal. Mem. ABA, Am. Pat. Law Assn., Tenn. Bar Assn., Nashville Bar Assn. Methodist. Clubs: Belle Meade, Exchange (Nashville). Patent, Trademark and copyright. Home: 1142 Crater Hill Dr Nashville TN 37215 Office: 4235 Hillsboro Rd Suite 203 Nashville TN 37215

LACKI, RALPH STEPHEN, lawyer; b. Cleve., Aug. 12, 1949; s. Jerome John and Jeannette Josephine (Hentka) L.; m. Paule Kaye Foster, Nov. 24, 1979; 1 child, Jameson Jerome. BA, Kent State U., 1971; JD, U. Toledo, 1977. Bar: Ohio 1977, U.S. Dist. Ct. (no. dist.) Ohio 1984, U.S. Ct. Appeals (6th cir.) 1984. Asst. prosecutor Stark City Prosecutor's Office, Canton,

Ohio, 1977-85; sole practice Coury, Burns, Demchak, Slagle & Lacki, Canton, 1985—; instr. Paralegal Inst., Cleve. 1978-84. Dist. mem. Boy Scouts Am., Canton, 1980-84. Mem. ABA, Stark County Bar Assn., Assn. Trial Lawyers Am., Canton Jaycees (bd. dirs. 1978-81). Republican. Roman Catholic. Avocations: golf, collecting stamps, family trips. Criminal, Personal injury, General practice. Office: Coury Burns Demchak Slagle & Lacki Suite 717 Ameritrust Bldg Canton OH 44702

LACKLAND, THEODORE HOWARD, lawyer; b. Chgo., Dec. 4, 1943; s. Richard and Cora Lee (Sanders) L.; m. Dorothy Ann Gerald, Jan. 2, 1970; 1 child, Jennifer Noel. B.S., Loyola U., Chgo., 1965; M.A., Howard U., 1967; J.D., Columbia U., 1975. Bar: N.J. 1975, U.S. Dist. Ct. N.J. 1975, Ga. 1982, U.S. Tax Ct. 1983, U.S. Supreme Ct. 1979, U.S. Dist. Ct. (no. dist.) Ga. 1982, U.S. Dist. Ct. (mid. dist.) Ga. 1985. Assoc. Dewey, Ballantine, Bushby, Palmer & Wood, N.Y.C., 1975-78; asst. U.S. atty. Dist. N.J., Newark, 1978-81; ptnr. Arnall Golden & Gregory, Atlanta, 1981—. Contbr. articles to profl. jours. Adv. dir. Atlanta Bus. Devel. Ctr., Minority Bus. Devel. Council, Atlanta, 1983—, Leadership Atlanta, 1986—. Served with U.S. Army, 1967-71. Decorated Bronze Star (2), Purple Heart, Air Medal, Army Commendation medal; recipient Leadership Atlanta award, 1986. Mem. ABA, N.J. Bar Assn., Ga. Bar Assn., Fed. Bar Assn., Gate City Bar Assn. Democrat. Roman Catholic. Federal civil litigation, State civil litigation. Home: 4400 Oak Ln Marietta GA 30062 Office: Arnall Golden & Gregory 55 Park Pl Atlanta GA 30335

LACKMAN, JAMES STEPHEN, lawyer; b. Phila., Apr. 26, 1949; s. Joseph Donald and Dorothy Elizabeth (Logan) L.; m. Irene Clarke, May 26, 1979. AB in Govt., Georgetown U., 1971; JD, U. Pa., 1974. Bar: Pa. 1974, U.S. Dist. Ct. (ea. dist.) Pa. 1974, U.S. Supreme Ct. 1979. Counsel trial Pa. Mfr. Ins. Co., Phila., 1975-76; sole practice Media, Pa., 1976-77; assoc. gen. counsel Day & Zimmermann Inc., Phila., 1977—. Mem. ABA, Pa. Bar Assn., Phila. Bar Assn., Am. Corp. Counsel Assn., Phi Beta Kappa. Roman Catholic. Avocation: songwriting. Government contracts and claims, Construction, General corporate. Home: 118 Bodine Rd Berwyn PA 19312

LACKMANN, ERNEST ALBIN, lawyer; b. San Francisco, Nov. 12, 1902; s. Ernest August and Eugenie Emilie (Coursinoux) L.; m. Mary Morey, June 30, 1938 (dec. Aug. 1953); m. Caroline Diane Kos, Apr. 24, 1962 (dec. Dec. 1983). A.B., U. Calif.-Berkeley, 1923. Bar: Calif. 1926, U.S. Dist. Ct. (no. dist.) Calif. 1926, U.S. Dist. Ct. (cen. dist.) Calif. 1976. Sole practice law, Sacramento and Modesto, Calif., 1926-36; dep. labor commr. State of Calif., 1936-38, atty. for state labor commr., 1938-45, referee Indsl. Accident Commn. and Workers Compensation Appeals Bd., 1945-71, referee in charge, Los Angeles, 1970-71, presiding referee for So. Calif., 1971; pres. Conf. of Referees, 1965. Contbr. chpt. to book. Mem. Coordinating Council, San Diego, Calif., 1937-38. Mem. Calif. Bar Assn., Los Angeles Bar Assn. (chmn. exec. com. workers compensation sect. 1979-80), Phi Alpha Delta.

LACOVARA, PHILIP ALLEN, lawyer; b. N.Y.C., July 11, 1943; s. P. Philip and Elvira L.; m. Madeline E. Papio, Oct. 14, 1961; children: Philip, Michael, Christopher, Elizabeth, Karen, Daniel, Andrew. A.B. magna cum laude, Georgetown U., 1963; J.D. summa cum laude, Columbia U., 1966. Bar: N.Y. 1967, D.C. 1974, U.S. Supreme Ct. 1970. Law clk. to Judge Harold Leventhal, U.S. Ct. Appeals D.C. Circuit, 1966-67; asst. to solicitor gen. U.S. Washington, 1967-69; assoc. Hughes Hubbard & Reed, N.Y.C., 1969-71; ptnr. Hughes Hubbard & Reed, N.Y.C. and Washington, 1974—; spl. counsel to N.Y.C. Police Commr., 1971-72; dep. solicitor gen. U.S. Dept. Justice, Washington, 1972-73; counsel to spl. prosecutor Watergate Spl. Prosecution Force, 1973-74; lectr. law Columbia U.; adj. prof. Georgetown U. Law Center; vis. lectr. various colls., univs.; mem. legal ethics com. D.C. Bar, 1976-81, chmn. code subcom., 1977-81; mem. Jud. Conf. D.C. Circuit, 1973—; sec. commn. on admissions and grievances U.S. Ct. Appeals for D.C. Circuit, 1980—; spl. counsel U.S. Ho. of Reps. Com. on Standards Ofcl. Conduct, 1976-77; chmn. bd. trustees Public Defender Service for D.C., 1976-81; sec. exec. com. bd. visitors Columbia U. Sch. Law; bd. govs. D.C. Bar, 1981-84, gen. counsel, 1985—. Contbr. articles to profl. jours. Co-chair, Washington Lawyers Com. for Civil Rights Under Law, 1982-84; mem. D.C. Jud. Nomination Commn., 1981-86. Mem. ABA (ho. of dels. 1978—, vice-chmn. sect. individual rights and responsibilities, 1985—), Am. Law Inst. Roman Catholic. Club: 1925 F Street. Administrative and regulatory, Federal civil litigation, Legislative. Home: 4819 V St NW Washington DC 20007 Office: 1201 Pennsylvania Ave NW Washington DC 20004

LACROIX, THOMAS RUSSELL, lawyer; b. Sioux Falls, S.D., Feb. 25, 1948; s. Russell Jacob and Harriett (Lamberton) LaC.; m. Linda Wilmer, Mar. 29, 1980; children: Katie, Betsy. BS, U. Wyo., 1971, JD, 1974. Bar: Wyo. 1974, U.S. Dist. Ct. Wyo. 1974, Colo. 1977, U.S. Dist. Ct. Colo. 1977. Ptnr. Patrick & LaCroix, Powell, Wyo., 1974-76; head land dept. Mineral Service, Grand Junction, Colo., 1976-77; ptnr. LaCroix, Achziger & Croker, Grand Junction, 1977—; instr. Mesa Coll., Grand Junction, 1977-83. Chmn. bd. Community Hosp., Grand Junction, 1977—; bd. dirs. Am. Lung Assn., 1977—, United Way, Grand Junction, 1981-85, Meth. Ch., Grand Junction, 1981—. Served to lt. U.S. Army, 1966-72. Mem. ABA, Wyo. Bar Assn., Colo. Bar Assn., Mesa County Bar Assn. Republican. Lodges: Elks, Kiwanis (bd. dirs. 1977-81). Avocations: flying, boating. Family and matrimonial, Real property, General practice. Office: LaCroix Achziger & Croker 725 Rood Ave Grand Junction CO 81501

LACY, ALEXANDER SHELTON, lawyer; b. South Boston, Va., Aug. 18, 1921; s. Cecil Baker and Lura Elizabeth (Byram) L.; m. Carol Jemison, Aug. 8, 1952; children: John Blakeway, Joan Elizabeth, Alexander Shelton. B.S. in Chemistry, U. Ala., 1943; LL.B., U. Va., 1949. Bar: Ala. bar 1949. Assoc. Bradley, Arant, Rose & White, Birmingham, Ala., 1949-54; with Ala. Gas Corp., Birmingham, 1954-86; v.p., asst. sec., atty. Ala. Gas Corp., 1969-74, v.p., sec., atty., 1974-86; with Patrick and Lacy, Birmingham, 1986—. Pres., chmn. bd. Birmingham Symphony Assn., 1964-67; chmn. Birmingham-Jefferson Civic Center Authority, 1965-71. Served with USN, 1943-46. Mem. Am. Bar Assn., Ala. Bar Assn., Birmingham Bar Assn., Am. Gas Assn. (chmn. legal sect. 1983-85), So. Gas Assn., Phi Gamma Delta, Phi Delta Phi. Episcopalian. Clubs: Relay House, Downtown, The Club. General corporate, FERC practice, Public utilities. Home: 3730 Montrose Rd Birmingham AL 35213 Office: Patrick and Lacy 1201 Financial Ctr Birmingham AL 35203

LACY, JOHN FORD, lawyer; b. Dallas, Sept. 11, 1944; s. John Alexander and Glenda Arcenia (Ford) L.; m. Cece Marianne Smith, Apr. 22, 1978. B.A., Baylor U., 1965; J.D., Harvard U., 1968. Bar: Tex. 1968. Assoc. firm Akin, Gump, Strauss, Hauer & Feld, Dallas, 1968-72, ptnr., 1973—; dir. Coca-Cola Bottling Group (Southwest), Inc., Dallas; v.p., dir. Le Sportsac Dallas, Inc.; chmn. Normandy Capital Co., Dallas. co-founder, co-chmn. Pres.' Research Council Univ. Tex. Health Scis. Ctr. at Dallas, 1985—. Mem. Dallas Bar Assn., Southwestern Legal Found (research fellow), State Bar Tex., ABA. Clubs: Dallas; Harvard (N.Y.C.). General corporate, Patent, Trademark and copyright. Office: Akin Gump Strauss Hauer & Feld 4100 First City Ctr 1700 Pacific Ave Dallas TX 75201-4618

LACY, ROBINSON BURRELL, lawyer; b. Boston, May 7, 1952; s. Benjamin Hammett and Jane (Burrell) L.; m. Elizabeth Coutrakon, Oct. 20, 1984. AB, U. Calif., Berkeley, 1974; JD, Harvard U., 1977. Bar: N.Y. 1978, U.S. Dist. Ct. (so. and ea. dists.) N.Y. 1979, U.S. Ct. Appeals (2d cir.) 1983, U.S. Supreme Ct. 1986. Law clk. to judge U.S. Dist. Ct. (so. dist.) N.Y., N.Y.C., 1977-78; law clk. to chief justice Warren Burger U.S. Supreme Ct., Washington, 1978-79; assoc. Sullivan & Cromwell, N.Y.C., 1979-85, ptnr., 1985—. Mem. ABA, Assn. of Bar of City of N.Y. Federal civil litigation, State civil litigation, Bankruptcy. Office: Sullivan & Cromwell 125 Broad St New York NY 10004

LADAR, JERROLD MORTON, lawyer; b. San Francisco, Aug. 2, 1933. A.B., U. Wash., 1956; LL.B., U. Calif., Berkeley, 1960. Bar: Calif. 1961, U.S. Supreme Ct. 1967. Law clk. U.S. Dist. Ct. No. Dist. Calif., 1960-61; asst. U.S. atty. San Francisco, 1961-70; chief criminal div. 1968-70; mem. firm MacInnis & Donner, San Francisco, 1970-72; prof. criminal law and procedure San Francisco Law Sch., 1962-83; prin. firm Jerrold M. Ladar, San Francisco.; lectr. Hastings Law Coll. Trial Advocacy, 1984—; chairperson pvt. defender panel U.S. Dist. Ct. (no. dist.) Calif.; appointed Criminal Justice Act Com. U.S. Ct. Appeals (9th cir.). Trustee Tamalpais Union High Sch. Dist., 1968-77, chmn. bd., 1973-74; mem. adv. com. Nat. PTA Assn., 1972-78. Fellow Am. Bd. Criminal Lawyers; mem. Am. Bar Assn., San Francisco Bar Assn. (editor In Re 1974-76), State Bar Calif. (cert. specialist in criminal law; pro-tem disciplinary referee 1976-78, vice chmn. public interest and edn. com. criminal law sect., mem. exec. com. criminal law sect. 1980—, editor Criminal Law Sect. News 1981—, chmn. exec. com. 1983-84), 9th Cir. Ct. Appeals (criminal justice act. com. 1983—). Criminal, Federal civil litigation, State civil litigation. Office: Suite 310 507 Polk St San Francisco CA 94102

LADD, JEFFREY RAYMOND, lawyer; b. Mpls., Apr. 10, 1941; s. Jasper Raymond and Florence Marguerite (DeMarce) L.; m. Kathleen Anne Crosby, Aug. 24, 1963; children: Jeffrey Raymond, John Henry, Mark Jasper, Matthew Crosby. BA, Loras Coll.; JD, Ill. Inst. Tech. Bar: Ill. 1973, U.S. Dist. Ct. 1973. V.p. mktg. Ladd Enterprises, Des Plaines, Ill., 1963-66; v.p. mktg. and fin. Ladd Enterprises, Crystal Lake, Ill., 1966-70; assoc. Ross & Hardies, Chgo., 1973-78, ptnr., 1978-81; ptnr. Boodell, Sears, Giambalvo & Crowley, Chgo., 1981—; spl. asst. atty. gen. for condemnation State of Ill., 1977-82. Former campaign chmn. Crystal Lake United Fund; bd. govs. Ill. State Colls. and Univs.; mem. Ill. Bd. Higher Edn.; bd. dirs. Regional Transp. Authority, Chgo., 1983-84; chmn. Met. Rail Bd., Chgo., 1984—; del. 1970 Ill. Constl. Conv., 1976, Nat. Rep. Conv., Kansas City. Mem. ABA, Chgo. Bar Assn., Nat. Assn. Bond Lawyers, Ill. Assn. Hosp. Attys., Am. Acad. Hosp. Attys., Crystal Lake Jaycees (Disting. Service award), Crystal Lake C. of C. (past pres.), Ill. Inst. Tech./Chgo. Kent Alumni Assn. (v.p. programs). Roman Catholic. Clubs: Hundred Club Cook County, The Attic (Chgo.); Bull Valley Hunt, Woodstock Country. Avocations: golf, hunting, fishing, tennis, skiing. General corporate, Health, Municipal bonds. Office: Boodell Sears et al 69 W Washington Chicago IL 60602

LADD, THOMAS A., lawyer; b. Midland, Mich., Apr. 19, 1947; s. Raymond and Helen (Montag) L.; m. Mary E. Kast; children: Kathleen, Patricia, Mark. BS in Engring., U. Mich., 1970; JD, U. Detroit, 1973. Bar: Mich. 1974, U.S. Dist. Ct. (we. dist.) Mich. 1976, Wis. 1983. Project engr. Proctor & Gamble, Cin., 1970-71; ptnr. Doyle & Ladd, P.C., Menominee, Mich., 1974—; atty. City of Menominee, 1976-87. Trustee Menominee County-Lloyd Hosp., 1974-83. Mem. ABA, Assn. Trial Lawyers Am., Phi Delta Phi. Republican. Roman Catholic. Lodge: Kiwanis. General practice, Labor, Probate. Office: Doyle & Ladd PC 1st Nat Bank Bldg Menominee MI 49858

LADIKOS, COSTAS ANGELO, lawyer; b. Norfolk, Va., Feb. 28, 1953; s. Angelo John and Irene (Augerinos) L. BA, Va. Poly. Inst., 1975; JD, Western State U., Fullerton, Calif., 1979. Bar: Calif. 1980. Assoc. Donine & Donine, West Covina, Calif., 1980-82, Klein & Cutler, Santa Ana, Calif., 1982-84, Schwamb, Stavile & Des Jardins, Santa Ana, 1984-85; sole practice Brea, Calif., 1985—. Atty. ACLU, Santa Ana, 1980-81. Mem. ABA, Calif. Bar Assn., Delta Theta Phi. Republican. Greek Orthodox. State civil litigation, Criminal, Family and matrimonial. Home: 1130 S Evening Star Anaheim CA 92806 Office: 690 S Brea Blvd Brea CA 92621

LAESER, ABRAHAM, lawyer; b. Münchberg, Fed. Republic of Germany, Apr. 11, 1947; came to U.S., 1949; s. Harry and Ester (Cukier) L.; m. Lynn Susan Oberman, July 11, 1970; children: Jason Adam, Marisa Alyson. BA, Christian Brothers Coll., 1969; JD, U. Miami, 1973. Bar: Fla. 1973, U.S. Dist. Ct. (so. dist.) Fla. 1982. Asst. states atty. State of Fla., Miami, 1973-81, dep. chief asst. states atty., 1981-84, chief asst. states atty., 1984—; instr. Fla. Prosecutor-Pub. Defender Clinics, various locations, 1977—, Trial Techniques Seminar, Hempstead, N.Y., 1986—; chmn. criminal rules com. Fla. Supreme Ct., 1983-84. Exec. com., bd. dirs., Greater Miami Hebrew Acad., 1984—, bd. edn., 1982—; bd. dirs. Temple Menorah Miami Beach, 1986—. Mem. Fla. Bar Assn. (chmn. criminal law sect., 1986—; chmn. criminal rules com. Fla. Supreme Ct., 1983-84. Criminal. Office: Office of States Atty 11th cir 1351 NW 12th St Miami FL 33125

LAFAVE, LEANN LARSON, legal educator; b. Ramona, S.D., May 31, 1953; d. Floyd Burdette and Janice Anne (Quist) L.; m. Richard Curtis Finke, May 19, 1973 (div. Jan. 1978); 1 child, Timothy; m. Dwayne Jeffery LaFave, May 31, 1981; 1 child, Jeffrey. BS, U. S.D., 1974, JD with honors, 1977. Bar: S.D. 1977, U.S. Dist. Ct. S.D. 1977, U.S. Ct. Appeals (8th cir.) 1977, N.D. 1978, U.S. Dist. Ct. N.D. 1978. Asst. atty. gen. State of S.D., Pierre, 1977-78, 79-81; assoc. Bjella, Neff, Rathert & Wahl, Williston, N.D., 1978-79, Tobin Law Offices, P.C., Winner, S.D., 1981-83; assoc. dean, asst. prof. U. S.D. Sch. Law, Vermillion, 1983-86, assoc. prof., 1986—, dir. continuing legal edn., 1983—; cons. S.D. Coalition Against Domestic Violence, 1983-84, juvenile code revision S.D. Dept. Social Services, Pierre, 1985-86; cert. hearing officer S.D. Div. Elementary and Secondary Edn., Pierre, 1982—. Contbr. articles to profl. jours. Mem. planning council Nat. Identification Program for Advancement of Women in Higher Edn. Adminstrn., Am. Council on Edn., S.D., 1984—; bd. dirs. Mo. Shores Womens Resource Ctr., Pierre, 1980, W.H. Over Mus., Vermillion, 1986—. Named S.D. Woman Atty. of Yr. Women in Law U. S.D., 1985. Mem. ABA, S.D. Bar Assn. (bd. govs. young lawyers sect. 1983-84), Assn. Continuing Legal Edn. Adminstrs., Am. Arbitration Assn. (comml. arbitrator 1985—), Epsilon Sigma Alpha (S.D. council sec. 1985-86). Episcopalian. Avocations: family, sailing, camping, reading, needlework. Legal education, Family and matrimonial. Home: 119 Catalina Vermillion SD 57069 Office: U SD Sch Law 414 E Clark Vermillion SD 57069

LAFAVER, JON FETHEROLF, lawyer; b. Reading, Pa., June 9, 1935; s. James A. and Ida J. (Fetherolf) LaF.; m. Janeen S. LaFaver, July 1, 1961; children—Karen E., Mark J. A.B. cum laude, Muhlenberg Coll., 1957; J.D., N.Y. U., 1960. Bar: Pa. 1961, U.S. Dist. Ct. (mid. dist.) Pa., 1963, U.S. Sup. Ct. 1966. Assoc., Updegraff, Weidner, Stone & LaFaver, 1961-63; sole practice, New Cumberland, Pa., 1963—; solicitor Cumberland County Recorder of Deeds, Borough New Cumberland, New Cumberland Borough Authority, West Shore Council Govts. Mem. exec. com. Republican Party, Cumberland County, Pa. Served with U.S. Army, 1961. Recipient Rotary Internat. Service Above Self award 1978, Legion of Honor award DeMolay, 1985. Mem. ABA, Pa. Bar Assn., Cumberland County Bar Assn. Lutheran. Clubs: Union League Phila.; West Shore Country (Camp Hill, Pa.); Lehigh Valley (Allentown, Pa.), Masons; Rotary (internat. dist. gov. 1979-80). Probate, General corporate, Local government. Home: 120 Carol St New Cumberland PA 17070 Office: 317 3d St New Cumberland PA 17070

LAFER, FRED SEYMOUR, data processing company executive; b. Passaic, N.J., Mar. 17, 1929; s. Abraham David and Pauline (Braer) L.; m. Barbara Bernstein, Apr. 4, 1954; children: Deborah, Gordon, Diana. B.I.E., NYU, 1950, J.D., 1961. Bar: N.J. 1961. Sec. to Justice Hayden Proector, N.J. Supreme Ct., 1961-62; partner firm Hoffman Humphreys Lafer, Wayne, N.J., 1962-67; sec., gen. counsel Automatic Data Processing, Inc., Clifton, N.J., 1967—; v.p. Automatic Data Processing, Inc., 1968-81, sr. v.p., 1981—; pres. N.J. Nets Profl. Basketball Team, 1984. Chmn. United Jewish Appeal Fedn. North Jersey, 1973-74; pres. Jewish Fedn. North Jersey, 1976-77; v.p. N.J. Bd. Edn., 1967-68; bd. dirs. Chilton Meml. Hosp., Pompton Plains, N.J., 1970-72; trustee William Paterson Coll., 1974—, vice-chmn. bd., 1977, chmn. bd., 1978-80; pres. Am. Friends of Hebrew U., 1985—. Served to lt. USAF, 1951-52. Mem. Computer Law Assn. (pres. 1972-74), Assn. Data Processing Service Orgns. (chmn. 1983), ABA. Office: One ADP Blvd Roseland NJ 07068

LAFFITTE, HECTOR M., federal judge; b. 1934. B.A., Interamerican U., 1955; LL.B., U. P.R., 1958; LL.M., Georgetown U., 1960. Assoc. Hartzell, Fernandez & Novas, 1959-64; sole practice 1965-66; ptnr. Nachman, Feldstein, Laffitte, & Smith, 1966-69, Laffitte & Dominquez, 1970-83; judge U.S. Dist. Ct. P.R., 1983—. Office: PO Box 3671 Old San Juan Sta San Juan PR 00904

LAFLEUR, GARY JAMES, lawyer; b. La Crosse, Wis., Feb. 2, 1952; s. Irvine Joseph and Florence Catherine (Hemmersbach) LaF.; m. Diane J. LaFleur, Apr. 24, 1986. BS, U. Wis., 1975; JD, Hamline U., 1979. Bar: Minn. 1980, Ariz. 1980, U.S. Dist. Ct. Minn. 1981, U.S. Ct. Appeals (5th cir.) 1984, U.S. Dist. Ct. Ariz. 1985, Guam 1986, U.S. Dist. Ct. Guam 1986, U.S. Ct. Appeals (9th cir.) 1986, No. Mariana Islands 1987, U.S. Dist. Ct. (cen. dist.) Mariana Islands 1987. Asst. county atty. Blue Earth County Atty.'s Office, Minn., 1980-81; sole practice Bloomington and Mpls., Minn., 1981-84; litigation atty. Levin and Jarvi, Tempe, Ariz., 1984-86; ptnr. Gayle, Teker and LaFleur, Agana, Guam, 1986—; instr. law Mpls., 1984-85, Am. Inst., Phoenix, 1985-86, U. Guam, 1987. Advisor Com. Against Domestic Abuse, Mankato, 1981-83; counselor Chrysalis Ctr., Mpls., 1982-84. Recipient Cert. of Accomplishment Nat. Judicial Coll., Reno, 1981. Mem. ABA, Ariz. Bar Assn., Maricopa County Bar Assn., Guam Bar Assn., Assn. Trial Lawyers Am. Avocations: reading, sailing, water sports. Federal civil litigation, Health, Private international. Office: Gayle Teker and Lafleur 220 E Marine Dr Agana GU 96911

LAFOLLETTE, ERNEST CARLTON, lawyer; b. Buffalo, Aug. 12, 1934; s. John and Mary Esther (Schramm) LaF.; m. Marcy Eleanore Freeman, June 16, 1979; children: Andre Michael, David Steven; children from previous marriage—Karen Yvonne, Brian Clark, Ernest Claud, Leah Ann. B.A. cum laude, Alfred U., 1956; J.D. summa cum laude, Syracuse Law Sch., 1959; LLM in Taxation U. Bridgeport, 1987; Bar: N.Y. 1959, Pa. 1964, Conn. 1978, U.S. Ct. Appeals (2d cir.) 1984, U.S. Supreme Ct. 1985. Law clk. Chief Justice, N.Y. Supreme Ct., Rochester, 1959; div. atty. Gen. Electric Co., King of Prussia, Pa., Bridgeport, Conn., 1962-70; prof. law Albany Law Sch., 1970-73; supr. attys. NLRB, Washington, 1973-75; labor relations counsel Norlin Corp., N.Y.C., 1975-78; sole practice, Bridgeport, 1978—. Served to capt., U.S. Army. Mem. ABA, Conn. Bar Assn., Justinian Soc., Order of Coif. Editor-in-chief Syracuse Law Sch. Rev., 1959. Labor, Corporate taxation, State civil litigation. Office: 1432 Post Rd Fairfield CT 06430

LAFOND, RICHARD CHARLES, lawyer; b. Chgo., Nov. 7, 1944; s. Charles Joseph and Marie F. (Lane) LaF.; m. Lois Jordan, Feb. 28, 1970; children: Arisa, Liam. BS, U. Detroit, 1967; JD, U. Denver, 1973. Bar: Colo. 1974, U.S. Dist. Ct. Colo. 1975, U.S. Dist. Ct. (no. dist.) Tex. 1975, U.S. Dist. Ct. S.D. 1976, U.S. Ct. Appeals (10th cir.) 1980, U.S. Supreme Ct. 1980. Trial atty. regional litigation ctr. EEOC, Denver, 1975-79; ptnr. LaFond & Evangelisti, Denver, 1979—. Civil rights, Federal civil litigation, Labor. Home: 1204 Upland Boulder CO 80302 Office: LaFond & Evangelisti 1756 Gilpin St Denver CO 80218

LA FORGE, GLADYS CANDACE, lawyer; b. Middletown, N.Y., Aug. 21, 1956; d. Arthur David and Gladys Ruth (Hume) La F.; m. Christos George Lecakes, June 30, 1984. BA in History, James Madison U., 1977; JD, SUNY, Buffalo, 1980. Bar: N.Y. 1981, U.S. Dist. Ct. (so., ea. and no. dists.) N.Y. 1981, U.S. Ct. Appeals (2d cir.) 1981. Asst. dist. atty. Orange County, Goshen, N.Y., 1980-82, chief trial asst., 1982-84; assoc. Markovits & Markov, Middletown, N.Y., 1984-85; sole practice Middletown, 1985-86; ptnr. Neuman, La Forge & Tamsen, Newburgh, N.Y., 1986—. Mem. Rep. Com., Middletown, 1985—. Mem. N.Y. State Bar Assn., Orange County Bar Assn. (bd. dirs.), Women's Bar of Orange and Sullivan County (pres. 1986—), N.Y. State Trial Lawyers Assn., Jr. League. Roman Catholic. Avocation: tennis. Criminal, Family and matrimonial. Office: Neuman La Forge & Tamsen 400 Gidney Ave Newburgh NY 12530

LAFRANCE, ANN JULIETTE, lawyer; b. N. Kingstown, R.I., July 29, 1954; d. Norman Aurele and Joan (Doherty) LaF.; m. Paul M. Winick. BA summa cum laude, Middlebury Coll., 1976; MS in Fgn. Service with honors, JD, Georgetown U., 1980. Bar: D.C. 1980. Assoc. Squire, Sanders & Dempsey, Washington, 1980—. Mem. ABA, D.C. Bar Assn., Fed. Communications Bar Assn., Women's Bar Assn. D.C. Administrative and regulatory, Telecommunications, postal, Immigration, naturalization, and customs. Office: Squire Sanders & Dempsey PO Box 407 Washington DC 20044

LAGERMAN, SUSAN BORDEN, lawyer; b. St. Paul, Aug. 13, 1952; d. Joseph Thomas and Mary Ann (O'Rourke) Borden; m. Lars Olof Lagerman, Dec. 23, 1972. BA cum laude, Gustavus Adolphus Coll., 1973; postgrad., Stockholm U., 1973; JD with distinction, U. Ariz., 1978. Bar: Ariz. 1978, Calif. 1985. Atty. securities Ariz. Corp. Commn., Phoenix, 1979-81; asst. atty. gen. State of Ariz., Phoenix, 1982—. Commr. Phoenix Women's Commn., 1985—. Mem. ABA, Ariz. Bar Assn. (pres. young lawyers div. 1986—, exec. council young lawyers div. 1982-86), Calif. Bar Assn., Maricopa County Bar Assn., Nat. Audubon Soc. Lodge: Vasa Order Am. Avocations: golf, swimming, aerobics. State civil litigation, Real property, Securities. Office: Ariz Atty Gen's Office 1275 W Washington St Phoenix AZ 85007

LAGESON, ERNEST BENJAMIN, lawyer; b. Sharon, N.D., Dec. 19, 1932; s. Ernest Benjamin and Eunice Adele Martin (McLean) L.; m. Jeanne Marie Lettiere, Apr. 12, 1955; children—Kristine Jeanne, Ernest Benjamin III. A.B., U. Calif.-Berkeley, 1952, B.S. in Bus. Adminstrn., 1954, LL.B., 1959. Bar: Calif. 1960, U.S. Dist. Ct. (no. dist.) Calif. 1960, U.S. Ct. Appeals (9th cir.) 1960, U.S. Supreme Ct. 1970. Dep. dist. atty. Office Dist. Atty. Contra Costa County, Richmond, Calif., 1959-60; assoc. Bronson, Bronson & McKinnon, San Francisco, 1961-67, ptnr., 1967-86, sr. ptnr., 1975-86, Archer, McComas & Lageson, Walnut Creek, Calif., 1986—; lectr. Calif. Continuing Edn. of Bar. Served as lt. (j.g.) USNR, 1954-56. Fellow Am. Coll. Trial Lawyers; mem. ABA, Calif. Bar Assn., San Francisco Bar Assn., Contra Coast County Bar Assn., No. Calif. Assn. Def. Counsel (dir. 1974-76), Internat. Assn. Def. Counsel (vice chmn. aviation com. 1980-83), Def. Research Inst. (area chmn. No. Calif. 1976-77, regional v.p. 1978-80, dir. 1980-83, v.p. info. 1983-85, pres. elect 1985, pres. 1986, chmn. bs. dirs. 1987—, hon. chmn. bd. dirs. 1987, sr. adv. com. 1987, Outstanding State Chmn. award 1977), Am. Bd. Trial Advocates, Am. Coll. Trial Lawyers. Republican. Roman Catholic. Clubs: Commonwealth of Calif., San Francisco Commerical; Richmond (Calif.) Country. Contbr. articles to legal jours. Personal injury, State civil litigation, Federal civil litigation. Office: 34th Floor 555 California St San Francisco CA 94104

LAGLE, JOHN FRANKLIN, lawyer; b. Kansas City, Mo., Jan. 22, 1938; s. Ernest J. and Hilda B. L.; m. Nina E. Weston, Aug. 1, 1959; m. Diana G. Fogle, July 14, 1962; children—Robert, Gregory. BBA, UCLA, 1961, JD, 1967. Bar: Calif. 1967, U.S. Dist. Ct. (no. dist.) Calif. 1967. Assoc. Hindin, McKittrick & Marsh, Beverly Hills, Calif., 1967-70, Macco Corp., Newport Beach, Calif., 1970, Rifkind & Sterling, Beverly Hills, 1971; mem. Fulop & Hardee, and predecessor Fulop, Rolston, Burns & McKittrick, Beverly Hills, 1971-82; ptnr. Leff & Stephenson, Beverly Hills, 1983; sole practice, Los Angeles, 1984; ptnr. Wildman, Harrold, Allen, Dixon, Barash & Hill, Los Angeles, 1985—. Served with U.S. Army, 1961-63. Mem. ABA, Calif. Bar Assn., Los Angeles County Bar Assn. Republican. Contbr. to Practice Under the California Corporate Securities Law of 1978. Real property, Securities, General corporate. Office: 2029 Century Park E #2050 Los Angeles CA 90067-3006

LAGOS, GEORGE PETER, lawyer; b. Concord, N.H., Oct. 23, 1954; s. Peter and Mary G. (Ahern) L.; m. Kathy Jean Bieniek, Nov. 21, 1981; children: Peter John, Andrew George. BA and hist. and philosophy, Keene State Coll., 1976; JD, Franklin Pierce Law Sch., 1981. Bar: N.H. 1981, U.S. Dist. Ct. N.H, 1981, Mass. 1982. Counsel N.H. Ins. Group, Manchester, 1981-84, v.p., gen. counsel, 1984—; adj. prof. U. N.H., 1986—. Mem. ABA, N.H. Bar Assn., Manchester Bar Assn., Chartered Property Casualty Underwriters, N.H. Assn. Domestic Ins. Cos. (pres. 1985—), N.H. Guaranty Assn., N.H. Tennis Assn. (pres. 1985), Fedn. Ins. and Corp. Counsel. Insurance, General corporate, Legislative. Office: NH Ins Co 1750 Elm St Manchester NH 03107

LAGOS, JAMES HARRY, lawyer, small business advocate; b. Springfield, Ohio, Mar. 14, 1951; s. Harry Thomas and Eugenia (Papas) L.; m. Nike Daphne Pavlatos, July 3, 1976. BA cum laude, Wittenberg U., 1969; JD, Ohio State U., 1972. Bar: U.S. Supreme Ct. 1976, U.S. Ct. Appeals (6th cir.) 1979, U.S. Dist. Ct. (so. dist.) Ohio 1973, U.S. Tax Ct. 1975, Ohio Supreme Ct. 1973. Asst. pros. atty. Clark County, Ohio, 1972-75; ptnr. Lagos & Lagos, Springfield, 1975—; mem. Springfield Small Bus. Council, past chmn., 1977—; del. Ohio Small Bus. Council, 1980—, past chmn., vice chmn.; del. Ohio Nat. Small Bus. United, v.p. issues, 1982—; del. Small Bus. Nat. Issues Conf., 1984, Ohio Gov.'s Conf. Small Bus., 1984, resource person regulatory and licensing reform com., 1984. Bd. dirs., pres. Greek Orthodox Ch., 1974—; mem. council Greek Orthodox Diocese of Detroit, 1985—; past chmn. Clark County Child Protection Team, 1974-82; past mem. Clark

County Young Rep. Club, past pres., sec., treas., 1968-76, chmn. Ohio del. White House Conf. Small Bus., 1985-86. Served to staff sgt. with Ohio Air NG, 1970-76. Recipient Dr. Melvin Emanuel award West Central Ohio Hearing and Speech Assn., 1983; Disting. Service award Springfield-Clark County, 1977; named one of Outstanding Young Men of Am., 1978. Mem. Am. Hellenic Inst. (bd. dirs., pub. affairs com. 1979—), Am. Hellenic Ednl. Progressive Assn. (past treas), C. of C. (past bd. dirs.), Jaycees (past chmn. several coms. 1977—, Spoke award 1974), ABA, Ohio State Bar Assn., Springfield Bar and Law Library Assn. (past sec., exec. com. 1973—), West Cen. Ohio Hearing and Speech Assn. (bd. dirs., pres., v.p. 1973-84), Alpha Alpha Kappa, Phi Eta Sigma, Tau Pi Phi, Pi Sigma Alpha. Personal injury, Family and matrimonial, Criminal. Home: 2023 Audubon Park Dr Springfield OH 45504 Office: Lagos & Lagos 31 E High St Suite 500 Springfield OH 45502

LAGOW, JOHN CHRISTOPHER, lawyer; b. Richmond, Va., Jan. 26, 1950; s. Homer Virgil and Louise Clarke (Childrey) L.; m. Jane Flounders, Aug. 26, 1972 (div. Apr. 1980); m. Nancy Ward Glaser, Aug. 16, 1980; children: Elizabeth Childrey, Caroline Christopher. BA, U. Richmond, 1972; postgrad., Oxford U., Eng., 1976; JD, Loyola U., Los Angeles, 1978. Bar: Va. 1979, U.S. Dist. Ct. (ea. dist.) Va. 1982. Assoc. Coates & Comess, Richmond, 1979-81, Morchower, Luxton & Whaley, Richmond, 1981—. Mem. Westhampton Civic Assn., Richmond, 1983; active fund raising small law firm campaign United Way, Richmond, 1985. Mem. ABA, Va. Bar Assn., Richmond Bar Assn. Democrat. Presbyterian. Clubs: Engineer's (Richmond); Rappahanock River Yacht (Irvington, Va.). Avocations: hunting, saltwater fishing. Legislative, Administrative and regulatory, State civil litigation. Home: 222 Ross Rd Richmond VA 23229 Office: Morchower Luxton & Whaley 9 E Franklin St Richmond VA 23219

LAGRONE, WILLIAM TAYLOR, lawyer; b. Browndell, Tex., Jan. 19, 1914; s. William Taylor and Lena Enola (Westmorland) LaG.; m. Alta Mae Atteberry, Oct. 12, 1940; children—Linda Lee, Alta Eloise, Suzanne. B.A., U. Tex., 1936, LL.B., 1939. Bar: Tex. 1939. Practiced law, Houston, 1939-52, Dallas, 1952—; v.p., gen. counsel Jake L. Hamon, Oil and Gas Operator, Dallas, 1952-79; pres. CNR Resources, Inc., Dallas, 1979-81; chmn. bd., chief exec. officer LaGrone Exploration, Inc., Dallas, 1981—; atty. Dallas Crime Commn., 1953-56. Served to col. AUS, 1940-46. Mem. ABA, Tex. Bar Assn., Dallas Bar Assn., Tex. Mid-Continent Oil and Gas Assn., Dallas Petroleum Landmen Assn. (pres. 1955-56), Ind. Producers Assn. Am., Tex. Ind. Producers and Royalty Owners Assn., Am. Assn. Petroleum Landmen, Ind. Producers Assn. Am. Methodist. Clubs: Northwood, Petroleum (Dallas). Oil and gas leasing. Home: 6308 Woodstream Ct Dallas TX 75240 Office: Two Hillcrest Green 12700 Hillcrest Rd Suite 507 Dallas TX 75230

LAHEY, EDWARD VINCENT, JR., soft drink co. exec.; b. Boston, Mar. 11, 1939; s. Edward Vincent and Margery Tharsilla (Mehegan) L.; m. Joan M. McCafferty, Sept. 26, 1964; children—Sheila, Edward Vincent III, Matthew. A.B., Holy Cross Coll., 1960; J.D., Georgetown U., 1964; postgrad., Bus. Sch. Columbia, 1969-70. Bar: D.C. bar 1964, N.Y. bar 1966. Mem. firm Hester, Owen & Crowder, Washington, 1964-65; atty. PepsiCo, Inc., Purchase, N.Y., 1965-68, asst. gen. counsel, 1969-73, sec., 1970—, v.p., gen. counsel, 1973-86, sr. v.p., 1986—. Trustee Village of Tuckahoe, N.Y., 1970. Served to lt. USNR, 1960-62. Mem. Am., D.C. bar assns., Am. Soc. Corporate Secs. General corporate. Office: PepsiCo Inc Purchase NY 10577

LAHNERS, RONALD DEAN, U.S. attorney; b. Grand Island, Nebr., Dec. 18, 1933; s. George H. and Velma LaVerne (Burch) L.; m. Mary Jo Colleen Vanosdall, Jan. 3, 1956; children: Guy Kenneth, Kelly Lee, Jay Scott. BS, U. Nebr., 1955, JD, 1959. Bar: Nebr. 1959, U.S. Dist. Ct. 1959. Atty. Nelson, Hardie & Acklie, Lincoln, Nebr., 1959-60; city prosecutor City of Lincoln, 1960-61; dep. county atty. Lancaster County, Nebr., 1961-72, chief dept. county atty., 1972-75, county atty., 1975-81; U.S. atty. U.S. Dept. Justice, Omaha, 1981—; instr. U. Nebr., Lincoln, 1963—. Mem. Nebr. Coalition for Prevention of Drug Problems, Nebr. Coalition for Victims of Crime. Served to 1st lt. U.S. Army, 1955-57. Mem. Nat. Dist. Attys. Assn. (dir. 1977-81), Nebr. State Bar Assn. (criminal and juvenile law com. chmn. 1977-82, ethics com. 1983—), Omaha Bar Assn., Lincoln Bar Assn., Nebraska County Attys. Assn. (pres. 1973), Nat. Footprinters Assn. Republican. Presbyterian. Lodges: Masons; Shriners. Criminal, Personal injury, General practice. Home: 5310 S 67th St Lincoln NE 68501 Office: US Attys Office 215 N 17th St Omaha NE 68101

LAIKIN, GEORGE JOSEPH, lawyer; b. Milw., June 21, 1910; s. Isadore and Bella (Schoene) L.; m. Sylvia Goldberg, Jan. 20, 1935; children: Michael B., Barbara (Mrs. Dan L. Funkenstein). B.A., LL.B., U. Wis., 1933. Bar: Wis. 1933, D.C. 1944, Ill. 1945, Calif. 1972, N.Y. 1980; Cert taxation specialist, Calif. Pvt. practice law Milw., 1933-42; spl. asst. to U.S. Atty.-Gen., Tax Div., Dept. Justice, Washington, 1942-45; pvt. practice law Wis., 1945, Milw., Washington, Chgo., 1945—, Los Angeles, 1972—; pres. Laikin & Laikin, S.C., Milw., 1980—; gen. counsel Milw. Assn. Life Underwriters, 1953-85, Wis. Assn. Life Underwriters, 1955-85; gen. counsel, dir. Schwerman Trucking Co., Milw., 1959-84, Continental Bank and Trust Co., Milw., 1963-70; counsel, dir. Mirisch Motion Pictures, Hollywood, Calif., 1960—; gen. counsel, dir. Empire Gen. Life Ins. Co., Los Angeles, 1963-77; chmn. bd., gen. counsel Univ. Nat. Bank, Milw., 1971-76; gen. counsel, dir. U.S. Life Ins. Co., Hinsdale, Ill., 1971-76; gen. counsel Liberty Savs. and Loan Assn., Milw., 1979—; spl. atty. M & I Marshall & Ilsley Bank, Milw., 1973—; also writer, lectr. in field. Contbr. articles to profl. publs. Chmn. Spl. Gifts and Bequests Com., Marquette U., 1967-70; pres. Wis. Soc. Jewish Learning, 1967-71; mem. Milw. Estate Planning Council. Mem. ABA, Wis. Bar Assn., Ill. Bar Assn., Calif. Bar Assn., Bar Assn. D.C., Assn. Trial Lawyers of Am., Nat. Assn. Criminal Def. Lawyers. Clubs: Milw. Athletic, Milw. Yacht; Standard of Chgo.; Carmel Yacht of Haifa (Israel). General corporate, Probate, Corporate taxation. Home: 1610 N Prospect Ave Milwaukee WI 53202 Office: 825 N Jefferson St Milwaukee WI 53202

LAIN, CLYDE, II, lawyer; b. Winnsboro, La., Oct. 3, 1947; s. Clyde Sr. and Bertha (Otis) L.; m. Norma Boyance, June 13, 1970; children: Clyde III, Jewel Renee. BA, So. U., 1969, JD, 1972. Bar: La. 1973, U.S. Dist. Ct. (mid. dist.) La. 1973, U.S. Ct. Appeals (5th cir.) 1973, U.S. Dist. Ct. (we. dist.) La. 1974, U.S. Supreme Ct. 1979. Sole practice Monroe, La., 1972—. Treas. Sickle Cell Anemia, Monroe, 1975-78. Mem. Omega Psi Phi (basileus 1979-85). Democrat. Roman Catholic. Avocations: remote airplanes, horsebackriding, swimming, jogging. General practice. Home: 400 Baylor Dr Monroe LA 71202

LAIRD, MORRIS E., lawyer; b. Mason City, Iowa, Mar. 31, 1908; s. Joseph Tuttle and Mary Etta (Dildine) L.; m. Ellis Bracken, Aug. 6, 1933 (dec. Nov. 2, 1950); m. Elizabeth Martin, Nov. 3, 1951 (dec. Sept. 1981); m. Kayrl S. Shaffer, Dec. 19, 1981; children: Moreen Fielden, Ellis Ann Newman, Jo Laird. BS, U. Iowa, 1929, JD, 1931. Bar: Iowa 1931. Ptnr. Laird Burington Heiny, Mason City, 1931—. Republican. Baptist. Lodges: Masons (master 1945), Elks. Probate, Real property, General corporate. Home: Rural Rt #4 Box 350 Mason City IA 50401 Office: Laird Burington Heiny 10 1st St NW PO Box 1567 30 Am Fed Bldg Mason City IA 50401

LAITOS, JAN GORDON, legal educator, commissioner; b. Colorado Springs, Colo., May 6, 1946. BA, Yale U., 1968; JD, U. Colo., 1971; SJD, U. Wis., 1975. Bar: Colo. 1971, D.C. 1974. Law clk. to chief justice Colo. Supreme Ct., Denver, 1971-72; fellow law U. Wis., Madison, 1972-74; atty. office of legal counsel U.S. Dept. Justice, Washington, 1974-76; prof. law, acting dir. natural resources law program U. Denver, 1976—; trustee Rocky Mountain Mineral Law Found., 1982—; commr. Colo. Water Quality Control Commn., 1985—; tchr. natural resources, pub. law U. Denver Coll. Law. Author: A Legal-Economic History of Air Pollution Controls, 1980, Cases and Materials on Natural Resources Law, 1985; monographs, Regulated Utilities and Solar Energy, 1980; contbr. articles to profl. jours. Sr. legal specialist Solar Energy Research Inst., 1978-81; co-prin. investigator N.W. Colo. Wildlife Consortium, 1981-82; adviser Colo. Dept. Natural Resources, 1979-80, U.S. Dept. Energy, 1979-81. James B. McDermott scholar, Yale U., 1967. Office: U Denver Coll Law 1900 Olive St Denver CO 80220

LAKE, BARBARA RUTH, lawyer; b. Ogdensburg, N.Y., Apr. 18, 1947; d. Thomas D. and Ina V. (Nolan) Cree; m. Richard W. Lake; children: Kerri R., Danielle L., Whitney A., Lindsay A.G. AA, Mater Dei Coll., 1975; BS in Psychology, St. Lawrence U., Canton, N.Y., 1979; JD, Syracuse U., 1978. Bar: N.Y. 1979, U.S. Dist. Ct. (no. dist.) N.Y. 1979, U.S. Supreme Ct. 1986. Legal sec. Brown & Silver, Morristown, N.Y., 1965-76; sole practice Morristown, 1979—; asst. dist. atty. St. Lawrence County, Canton, 1982-84, chief asst. dist. atty., 1984—. Trustee, v.p. Morristown Found., 1983—. Mem. N.Y. State Bar Assn., St. Lawrence County Bar Assn. (grievance com.), Assn. Trial Lawyers Am. Avocation: family. Criminal, Family and matrimonial, Real property. Office: 400 Main St. PO Box 242 Morristown NY 13664

LAKE, ROBERT CAMPBELL, JR., lawyer, state senator; b. Whitmire, S.C., Dec. 27, 1925; s. Robert Campbell and Susan Gaston (Howze) L.; LL.B., U. S.C., 1949; LL.D., Newberry Coll., 1981; m. Carolyn Young Gray, July 5, 1955; children—Robert Campbell III, Samuel Young, Linda (dec.). Practice law, Whitmire; chmn. adv. bd. First Fed. Savs. & Loan Assn. of Newberry (S.C.); mem. S.C. Senate, 1969-85, chmn. ethics com., 1980-84. Bd. dirs. United Fund; elder, moderator Presbyn. Ch.; mem. Jr. Coll. Study Com., 1966-67; pres. County Devel. Bd., 1965-67, Jr. C. of C., 1953; chmn. bldg. com. Whitmire Presbyn. Ch., 1966; mem. So. Regional Edn. Bd., also mem. exec. com.; mem. trustee adv. bd. Limestone Coll., Gaffney, S.C., 1987; trustee Winthrop Coll., 1977, Med. U. S.C., 1986—. Served with U.S. Army, 1944-45. Mem. Farm Bur., Blue Key. Democrat. Club: Shriners (potentate 1972). Banking, Government contracts and claims, Criminal. Home: 215 N Main St Whitmire SC 29178 Office: 310 Main St PO Box 338 Whitmire SC 29178

LAKE, SIMEON TIMOTHY, III, lawyer; b. Chgo., July 4, 1944; s. Simeon T. Jr. and Helen (Hupka) L.; m. Carol Illig, Dec. 30, 1970; children: Simeon Timothy IV, Justin Carl. BA, Tex. A&M, 1966; JD, U. Tex., 1969. Bar: Tex. 1969, U.S. Dist. Ct. (so. dist.) Tex. 1969, U.S. Ct. Appeals (5th cir.) 1969, U.S. Supreme Ct. 1976, U.S. Ct. Appeals (3d cir.) 1981, U.S. Dist. Ct. (no. dist.) Tex. 1983. From assoc. to ptnr. Fulbright & Jawrowski, Houston, 1969—. Served to capt. U.S. Army. Fellow Tex. Bar Assn., Houston Bar Assn. Federal civil litigation, State civil litigation, Environment. Home: 7516 Briar Rose Houston TX 77063 Office: Fulbright & Jaworski 1301 McKinney St Houston TX 77010

LAKE-SMITH, NANCY JOYCE, publishing company executive; b. Chgo., Aug. 25, 1951; d. Donald Kent and Elaine Joyce (Newman) Gedman; m. C.J. Lake-Smith, Nov. 8, 1985. B.A. in Journalism, U. Minn., 1973, J.D., 1977. Asst. dir. U. Minn. Alumni Assn., St. Paul, 1973-74; admitted to Minn. bar, 1977; partner firm Margoles & Gedman, St. Paul, 1978-80; mgr. acquisitions and mktg. Mason Pub. Co., St. Paul, 1980-81; pres. Butterworth Legal Pubs. div. Butterworth (London-established 1818)-Reed Internat. P.L.C., Stoneham, Mass., 1981-85; pres. Butterworth Legal Pubs., St. Paul, 1985—. Office: Butterworth Legal Pubs 289 E Fifth St Saint Paul MN 55101

LALLA, THOMAS ROCCO, JR., lawyer; b. Bronxville, N.Y., July 23, 1950; s. Thomas R. and Vincie Catherine (Cremona) L. BA, Fordham U., 1972; JD, Temple U., 1975. Bar: N.Y. 1986, U.S. Dist. Ct. (so. dist.) N.Y. 1978. Asst. dist. atty. Office of Dist. Atty. Westchester County, White Plains, N.Y., 1975-81; assoc. Buchman Buchman & O'Brien, N.Y.C., 1981-85, ptnr., 1985—. Mem. ABA, N.Y. State Bar Assn. Republican. Roman Catholic. Avocations: running, swimming, cycling. General corporate, Contracts commercial. Office: Buchman Buchman & O'Brien 10 E 40th St 20th Fl New York NY 10016

LALLY-GREEN, MAUREEN ELLEN, legal educator; b. Sharpsville, Pa., July 5, 1949; d. Francis Leonard and Charlotte Marie (Frederick) Lally; m. Stephen Ross Green, Oct. 5, 1979; children: Katherine Lally, William Ross, Bridget Marie. BS, Duquesne U., 1971, JD, 1974. Bar: Pa. 1974, D.C., U.S. Dist. Ct. (we. dist.) Pa. 1974, U.S. Ct. Appeals (3d cir.) 1974, U.S. Supreme Ct. 1978. Atty. Houston Cooper, Pitts., 1974-75, Commodity Futures Trading Commn., Washington, 1975-78; counsel Westinghouse Electric Corp., Pitts., 1978-83; adj. prof. law Duquesne U., Pitts., 1983-86, prof. in criminal, employment discrimination, health and profl. responsibility law and legal writing, 1986—. Chairperson, mem. Cranberry Twp. Zoning Hearing Bd., Mars, Pa., 1983—; counsel Cranberry Community Chest, Mars, 1985—; active Elimination of World Hunger Project, 1977—; bd. dirs. Boys Clubs of Western Pa., Pitts., 1983—. Mem. Allegheny County Bar Assn. (med. legal, antitrust and ethics coms., commendation 1986), Duquesne U. Alumni Assn. (bd. dirs. 1980—). Republican. Roman Catholic. Avocations: reading, computers, sports. Legal education, Estate taxation, Probate. Office: Duquesne U Sch Law G-11 Pittsburgh PA 15219

LALOR, OWEN PATRICK, lawyer; b. Bridgeport, Conn., Sept. 26, 1952; s. Edward Thomas and Theresa E. (Moody) L.; m. Jean Elizabeth Maloney, Aug. 10, 1974; children: Owen Patrick Jr., Conor P., John R. BA, St. Louis U., 1974; MBA, Vanderbilt U., 1978, JD, 1978. Bar: Miss. 1978, U.S. Dist. Ct. (so. dist.) Miss. 1978. Ptnr. Watkins, Ludlam & Stennis, Jackson, Miss., 1978—; bd. dirs. Silk Screen Printers of Southern Miss., Incentives Plus, Inc., Jackson, Pepsi-Cola Bottling Co. of Southern Miss., Jackson. Del. from Miss. White Ho. Conf. on Small Bus., Washington, 1986; chmn. exhibition com. Miss. Mus. Art. Named one of Outstanding Young Men in Am., 1977-78. Mem. ABA, Miss. Bar Assn., Hinds County Bar Assn., Nat. Assn. Bond Lawyers, Jackson C. of C. Clubs: Univ., Jackson (Miss.) Yacht. Securities, Banking, General corporate. Home: 4126 Hawthorne Dr Jackson MS 39206 Office: Watkins Ludlam & Stennis 633 N State St Jackson MS 39202

LAM, ERIC WING-SUM, lawyer; b. Hong Kong, Oct. 21, 1956; came to U.S., 1976; s. David B. and Joyce (Leung) L.; m. Mary Louise Taylor. BA cum laude, Macalester Coll., 1979; JD with distinction, U. Iowa, 1982. Bar: Iowa 1982, U.S. Dist. Ct. (no. and so. dists.) Iowa 1982, U.S. Ct. Appeals (8th cir.) 1984. Law clk. to chief justice Iowa Supreme Ct., Des Moines, 1982-83; law clk. to presiding justice U.S. Bankrupcy Ct., Cedar Rapids, Iowa, 1983-84; assoc. Moyer & Bergman, Cedar Rapids, 1984—. Mem. ABA, Am. Bankruptcy Inst., Iowa Bar Assn. (Mason Ladd Writing Competition award 2d place winner). Methodist. Bankruptcy, Contracts commercial. Home: 3809 Tomahawk Trail SE Cedar Rapids IA 52403 Office: Moyer & Bergman 2720 1st Ave NE Cedar Rapids IA 52402

LAMANCUSO, JOHN LORY, lawyer; b. Jamestown, N.Y., Aug. 20, 1954; s. Ignatius Frank and Loretta Grace (Lodestro) LaM.; m. Kathleen Sue Kinnear, Aug. 27, 1983; 1 child, John Ignatius. AS, Jamestown Community Coll., 1974; student, Eastern Ky. U., 1975; BA, Miami U., Oxford, Ohio, 1976; JD, Ohio No. U., 1979. Bar: N.Y. 1981, Ohio 1981, U.S. Dist. Ct. (we. dist.) N.Y. 1982. Assoc. Lodestro & Bailey, Jamestown, 1981-85; ptnr. Lodestro, Duncanson, LaMancuso & Cala, Jamestown, 1985—; seminar-legal cons. Automatic Data Processing Inc., Buffalo, 1986. Mem. allocation com. United Way, Jamestown, 1982, Dem. com. Cityof Jamestown, 1982—; bd. dirs. Jamestown Sch. Bd., 1981-84, Chautauqua Blind Assn. Inc., 1982-85, corp. counsel, 1983—; regional atty. Civil Service Employees Assn. Inc., Chautauqua and Cattaraugus Counties, N.Y., 1981—; chief counsel Jamestown Profl. Firefighters Assn., 1984—, Fredonia Profl. Firefighters Assn., 1986—. Samuel and Martha Meyer scholar Ohio No. U., 1978, Margaret Schwartz Hodges Meml. scholar Ohio No. U., 1979; named one of Outstanding Young Men Am., 1983. Mem. ABA, N.Y. State Bar Assn., Jamestown Bar Assn., Assn. Trial Lawyers Am. Democrat. Roman Catholic. Club: MOrton (Jamestown). Lodge: Elks. Avocations: golf, running, historical collections. State civil litigation, Family and matrimonial, Labor. Office: Lodestro Duncanson LaMancuso & Cala 111 W 2d St Jamestown NY 14702-0830

LAMB, FREDERIC DAVIS, consumer products company executive, lawyer; b. Oak Park, Ill., Nov. 23, 1931; s. Frederic Horace and Alice Emily (Davis) L.; m. Barbara Ann Bullard, Apr. 6, 1954; children—Deborah Ann Lamb Dunn, Jeffrey Davis. B.A., Wabash Coll.; J.D., U. Mich. Bar: Ohio. Atty. Vick Chem. Co., N.Y.C. and Cin., 1956-63; v.p., counsel Merrell div. Richardson-Merrell Inc., Cin., 1964-80; asst. gen. counsel Richardson-Vicks Inc., Wilton, Conn., 1981-83, v.p., gen. counsel, sec., 1984—. Mayor, councilman City of Forest Park, Ohio, 1971-75; chmn. Forest Park Charter Commn., 1969-70. Mem. ABA, Ohio Bar Assn., Westchester-Fairfield Corp. Counsel Assn., Am. Soc. Corp. Secs. Republican. Club: Silver Spring Country. Avocations: golf; tennis; boating. General corporate, Personal injury. Home: 30 Keelers Ridge Rd Wilton CT 06897 Office: Richardson-Vicks Inc 10 Westport Rd Wilton CT 06897

LAMB, JONATHAN HOWARD, lawyer; b. New Haven, June 5, 1954; s. Harry Richard and Elizabeth Marie (Schwarz) L. BA in History, Columbia U., 1976; JD, U. Conn., 1979. Bar: Conn. 1979, Tex. 1980, U.S. Dist. Ct. (so. dist.) Tex. 1981, U.S. Ct. Appeals (5th cir.) 1984. Sr. landowner relations analyst Exxon Co., Houston, 1980-82; assoc. Mullins, Box & Parish, Houston, 1982-83; sole practice Houston, 1983—. Mem. ABA, State Bar Tex. Republican. Episcopalian. Immigration, naturalization, and customs, General practice, State civil litigation. Home: 6330 Windswept #107 Houston TX 77057 Office: 3100 Richmond Suite 310 Houston TX 77098

LAMB, KEVIN THOMAS, lawyer; b. Quincy, Mass., Nov. 14, 1956; s. John Phillip and Kathleen Elaine (O'Brien) L. BA, Washington and Lee U., 1978, JD, 1982. Bar: Va. 1982. Law clk. to presiding justice U.S. Bankruptcy Ct. (we. dist.) Va., Lynchburg, 1982-84; atty. U.S. Dept. Justice, Los Angeles, 1984-85; assoc. Jones, Day, Reavis & Pogue, Los Angeles, 1985-86, Ballard, Spahr, Andrews & Ingersoll, Washington, 1986—. Mem. ABA, Fed. Bar Assn., Am. Bankruptcy Inst. (com. on legis.), Comml. Law League Am., Am. Judicature Soc., Fin. Lawyers Conf. Federal civil litigation, Bankruptcy, Contracts commercial. Home: 3215 Pauline Dr Chevy Chase MD 20815 Office: Ballard Spahr Andrews & Ingersoll 555 13th St NW Suite 900 E Washington DC 20004

LAMB, WILLIAM H., lawyer. m. Patricia Kelly Lamb; children: Amanda, Joshua. BA with honors, Duke U.; JD with honors, U. Pa. Bar: Pa., U.S. Tax Ct., U.S. Ct. Appeals (3d cir.), U.S. Supreme Ct. Law clk. to presiding justice Pa. Supreme Ct., 1965-66; asst. dist. atty. Chester County, 1967-72, dist. atty., 1972-80; ptnr. Lamb, Windle & McErlane P.C., West Chester, Pa., 1980—; bd. dirs. Jefferson Bank, Downingtown, Pa. Solicitor Reps. of Chester County, campaign chmn. 1966; campaign mgr. congressman John H. Ware, 1968; chmn. Chester County Reps., 1983—; del. Rep. Nat. Convention, 1984; former chmn. Upper Main Line Young Reps.; former vice chmn. Chester County Fedn. Young Reps.; mem. Rep. Exec. Com. Chester County; pres. Little People's Nursery Sch., Paoli, Pa.; past bd. dirs. Chester Valley Little League, Upper Main Line Red Cross; bd. dirs. St. Davids Ch. Nursery Sch., Devon, Pa., lay server, St. David's Episcopal Ch., Devon; vice chmn., trustee bd. Alumni mgrs. Episc. Acad. Fellow Am. Coll. Trial Lawyers; mem. ABA, Pa. Bar Assn., Chester County Bar Assn., Pa. Bar Inst. (lectr.), Pa. Trial Lawyers Assn. (lectr.). Lodge: Lions. Home: Brettagne # 4 Arbordeau Devon PA 19333 Office: Lamb Windle & McErlane PC 26 E Market St PO Box 565 West Chester PA 19381-0565

LAMBERT, ARTHUR GORMAN, lawyer; b. Washington, Feb. 10, 1899; s. Wilton John and Elizabeth Ann (Gorman) L.; m. Mary Lemon Sipple, Sept. 4, 1926; children—William S., Arthur Gorman. A.B., Princeton U., 1922; J.B., Harvard U., 1925. Bar: D.C. 1926, Md. 1935, Va. 1939, U.S. Supreme Ct. 1939. Asst. U.S. atty. for D.C., 1930; asst. to spl. asst. to atty. gen. Dept. Justice, Washington, 1932-33; sr. ptnr. Lambert, Furlow, Adelman & Haldeman, Rockville, Md., from 1981, now of counsel; counsel Lambert & Griffin, Washington, 1981-84, Ross, Marsh & Foster, 1984—; gen. counsel Town of Chevy Chase (Md.), 1963—; gen. counsel Suburban Hosp., Bethesda, Md., 1965—; organizer, former sr. v.p. and dir. Madison Nat. Bank. Served with inf. U.S. Army, 1918-19. Mem. ABA, D.C. Bar Assn., Md. Bar Assn., Va. Bar Assn. Republican. Episcopalian. Clubs: Met., Lawyers (Washington) (pres. 1985-86); Hillsboro, Chevy Chase, Burning Tree, Wianno. Probate, Jurisprudence, General practice.

LAMBERT, DALE JOHN, lawyer; b. Lethbridge, Alberta, Can., Mar. 1, 1946; s. Theron M. and Verl (Johansen) L.; m. Janice Noreen Clitheroe, July 29, 1975; children: Kristin, Kimberly, Tamara. BS, Brigham Young U., 1970; JD, U. Utah, 1973. Bar: Utah 1973, U.S. Dist. Ct. Utah 1975, U.S. Ct. Appeals (10th cir.) 1976. Legis. asst. Congressman Gunn McKay, Washington, 1973-75; ptnr. Christensen, Jensen & Powell, Salt Lake City, 1975—. Contbr. articles to profl. jours. exec. com. instl. council Dixie State Coll., St. George, Utah, 1983—; state chmn. Utah State Dem. Party, 1979-81, chmn. platform com., 1982, chmn. state conv., 1983. Recipient Golden Key award Gov.'s Commn. on Employment, 1978; named one of Outstanding Young Men of Am., Jr. C. of C., 1979. Mem. ABA (litigation sect.), Utah State Bar Assn. (litigation sect.), Def. Research Inst. Mormon. Avocations: golf, teaching, traveling. Federal civil litigation, Libel, Personal injury. Home: 2563 E Maywood Dr Salt Lake City UT 84109 Office: Christensen Jensen & Powell 900 Kearns Bldg Salt Lake City UT 84101

LAMBERT, GEORGE ROBERT, insurance company executive; b. Muncie, Ind., Feb. 21, 1933; s. George Russell and Velma Lou (Jones) L.; m. Mary Virginia Alling, June 16, 1956; children—Robert Allen, Ann Holt, James William. B.S., Ind. U., Bloomington, 1955; J.D., Ill. Inst. Tech. Chgo-Kent Coll. Law, 1962. Bar: Ill. 1962, Iowa 1984, U.S. Dist. Ct. (no. dist.) Ill. vice pres., gen. counsel, sec. Washington Nat. Ins. Co., Evanston, Ill., 1958-82; v.p., gen. counsel Washington Nat. Corp., Evanston, 1979-82; sr. v.p., sec., gen. counsel Life Investors Inc., Cedar Rapids, Iowa, 1982—. Alderman, Evanston City Council, 1980-82. Served to lt. USAF, 1955-57. Mem. ABA, Ill. State Bar Assn., Iowa State Bar Assn. Life Ins. Counsel (past pres.) Republican. Roman Catholic. Clubs: Cedar Rapids Country, Kiwanis, Westfield Tennis (Cedar Rapids). Contbr. in field. General corporate, Insurance, Legislative. Office: 4333 Edgewood Rd NE Cedar Rapids IA 52499

LAMBERT, RICHARD JUSTIN, JR., lawyer; b. White Plains, N.Y., May 4, 1953; s. Richard Justin and Dorothy (Doyle) L.; m. Evalyn Feller, Aug. 20, 1978; 1 child, Emily. BA, Fordham U., 1973, JD, 1979. Bar: N.Y. 1980, N.J. 1980, U.S. Dist. Ct. N.J. 1980, U.S. Dist. Ct. (so. dist.) N.Y. 1982. Assoc. Arthur, Dry & Kalish, N.Y.C., 1979-82; from assoc. to ptnr. Gutkin, Miller, Shapiro, Selesner & Shoobe, Millburn, N.J., 1982—. Author bus. law columns to Commerce mag., 1986. Mem. ABA, N.Y. State Bar Assn., N.J. State Bar Assn., Commerce and Industry Assn. of N.J. Republican. General corporate, Contracts commercial, Antitrust. Home: 2 Aberdeen Pl Fair Lawn NJ 07410 Office: Gutkin Miller Shapiro et al 225 Millburn Ave Millburn NJ 07041

LAMBERT, ROBERT BRADLEY, lawyer; b. Flint, Mich., Dec. 1, 1953; s. Robert Wiltz and Ruby Joyce Lambert; Lee Ann. Motter, Jan. 30, 1976; children: Daniel Bradley, Jennifer Ann. BBA, Saginaw Valley State Coll., 1975; JD magna cum laude, Wayne State U., 1982. Bar: Mich. 1982, U.S. Dist. Ct. (ea. dist.) Mich. 1982. Salesman Burroughs Co., Saginaw, Mich., 1975-76; loan officer First Nat. Bank Fenton (Mich.), 1977-79; assoc. Simpson & Moran, Birmingham, Mich., 1981—. John P. Murphy scholar Wayne State U., 1981. Mem. Order of Coif. Lodge: Optimists (v.p. Rochester area club 1985-86, pres. 1986—). Avocations: skiing, golf, astronomy. Real property, General corporate, Landlord-tenant. Home: 776 Dressler Ln Rochester MI 48063 Office: Simpson & Moran 555 S Woodward 5th Floor Birmingham MI 48011

LAMBERT, SAMUEL WALDRON, III, lawyer, foundation executive; b. N.Y.C., Jan. 12, 1938; s. Samuel W. and Mary (Hamill) L.; m. Louisa Garnsey, Aug. 25, 1962; children—Louisa Kelly, Samuel William, Sarah Hamill. B.A., Yale U., 1960; LL.B., Harvard U., 1963. Bar: N.J. 1964, U.S. Tax Ct. 1975. Assoc. Albridge C. Smith III, Princeton, N.J., 1964-67; ptnr. Smith, Cook, Lambert & Miller, and predecessors, Princeton, 1967-80; officer, dir. Smith, Lambert, Hicks & Miller, P.C., Princeton, 1981, chmn. bd., 1982-83; pres. Smith, Lambert, Hicks & Miller, P.C., 1983—; dir., trustee Horizon Trust Co., N.A. Peterson's Guides, Inc.; pres. The Bunbury Co., Princeton. Chmn. bd. Princeton Day Sch.; bd. dirs. Windham Found., Curtis W. McGraw Found.; capt. Princeton Republican County Com., 1967-69. Served with USAR, 1963-69. Mem. Princeton Bar Assn. (pres. 1976-77), N.J. Bar Assn., ABA. Probate, Estate planning. also: 1 Palmer Sq Suite 520 Princeton NJ 08542

LAMBERTH, J. MICHAEL, lawyer; b. Portline, Tenn., Mar. 24, 1948; s. J.B. and Agnes (Potts) L.; m. Sandra Nall, Nov. 28, 1981. BE, Vanderbilt U., 1970; JD, Duke U., 1973. Bar: Ga. 1974, U.S. Dist. Ct. (no. dist.) Ga. 1974, U.S. Ct. Appeals (11th cir.), U.S. Supreme Ct. Clk. to chief judge U.S. Dist. Ct., Atlanta, 1973-74, 1974-75; assoc. Cotton, White & Palmer PA,

Atlanta, 1975-80, ptnr., 1980-85; ptnr. Palmer, Lamberth, Bonapfel & Cifelli, P.A., Atlanta, 1985—. Mem. ABA, Ga. State Bar Assn., Atlanta Bar Assn., Lawyers Club Atlanta. Republican. Presbyterian. Federal civil litigation, General corporate, Bankruptcy. Office: Lamberth Bonapfel & Cifelli PA 1430 W Peachtree St Suite 400 Atlanta GA 30357

LAMBERTUS, CHRISTINE LUNDT, lawyer; b. St. Louis, Mar. 15, 1947; d. Marvin Leroy and Alice Isabel (Burton) Lundt; m. Arthur William Lambertus, July 10, 1971. BA in History, Hood Coll., 1969; JD, Northwestern U., 1972. Bar: Fla. 1981, U.S. Dist. Ct. (so. dist.) Fla. 1981. Trust officer Southeast Banks Trust Co., Miami, Fla., 1972-75, v.p., 1975-79, sr. v.p., corp. sec., 1979-81; ptnr. Lambertus & Lambertus, Ft. Lauderdale, Fla., 1981—. Mem. Leadership Broward, Ft. Lauderdale, 1982-83; mem. adv. com. Fla. Atlantic U., Boca Raton, 1984—; mem. adv. bd. for opportunities in nontraditional careers Broward County Sch. Bd., Ft. Lauderdale, 1984—; treas., bd. dirs. LWV of Broward, 1983—; bd. dirs. Planned Giving Council, Broward County, 1984—, Early Childhood Devel. Assn., Ft. Lauderdale, 1981-86. Mem. Fla. Bar Assn., Broward County Bar Assn., Broward County Women Lawyers, Estate Planning Council. Republican. Lutheran. Club: Tower Forum (Ft. Lauderdale). Avocations: needlework, reading nonfiction, competitive and recreational swimming. Estate planning, Probate, Trust & guardianship administration. Home: 1725 NE 58th St Fort Lauderdale FL 33334 Office: Lambertus & Lambertus Barnett Bank Tower Suite 700 2929 E Commercial Blvd Fort Lauderdale FL 33308

LAMBIRD, MONA SALYER, lawyer; b. Oklahoma City, July 19, 1938; d. B.M., Jr. and Pauline A. Salyer; m. Perry A. Lambird, July 30, 1960; children: Allison Thayer, Jennifer Salyer, Elizabeth Gard, Susannah Johnson. B.A., Wellesley Coll., 1960; LL.B., U. Md., 1963. Bar: Okla. 1968, Md. Ct. Appeals 1963, U.S. Supreme Ct. 1967. Atty. civil div. Dept. Justice, Washington, 1963-65; sole practice law Balt. and Oklahoma City, 1965-71; mem. firm Andrews Davis Legg Bixler Milsten & Murrah, Inc. and predecessor firm, Oklahoma City, 1971—; cons. World Orgn. China Painters; legal adv. Oklahoma City Election Bd., 1983—; minority mem. Okla. Election Bd., 1984—; mem. profl. responsibility tribunal Okla. Supreme Ct., 1984—; Master of Bench, sec.-treas., Am. Inn of Ct. XXIII in Oklahoma City, 1986—. Editor: Briefcase, Oklahoma County Bar Assn., 1976. Profl. liaison com. City Oklahoma City, 1974-80; mem. Hist. Preservation of Oklahoma City, Inc., 1970—; del. Oklahoma County and Okla. State Republican Party Conv., 1971—; women's com. Okla. Symphony Orch., legal advisor, 1973—, bd. dirs., 1973—; incorporator, bd. dirs. R.S.V.P. of Oklahoma County, pres., 1982-83; bd. dirs. Congregate Housing for Elderly, 1978—, Vis. Nurses Assn., 1983, Oklahoma County Friends of Library, 1980—. Mem. ABA, Okla. Bar Assn., Oklahoma County Bar Assn. (bd. dirs. 1986—), Jr. League Oklahoma City (dir. 1973-76, legal adv.), Oklahoma County and State Med. Assn. Aux. (dir.). Methodist. Clubs: Seven Colls. (pres. 1972-76), Women's Econ. (steering com. 1981—). Labor, Federal civil litigation. Home: 419 NW 14th St Oklahoma City OK 73103 Office: 500 W Main Oklahoma City OK 73102

LAMBROS, THOMAS DEMETRIOS, U.S. judge; b. Ashtabula, Ohio, Feb. 4, 1930; s. Demetrios P. and Panagoula (Bellios) L.; m. Shirley R. Kresin, June 20, 1953; children: Lesley P., Todd T. Student, Fairmount (W.Va.) State Coll., 1948-49; LL.B., Cleveland-Marshall Law Sch., 1952. Bar: Ohio bar 1952. Partner firm Lambros and Lambros, Ashtabula, 1952-60; judge Ct. Common Pleas, Jefferson, Ohio, 1960-67, U.S. Dist. Ct., No. Dist. Ohio, Cleve., 1967—; mem. faculty Fed. Jud. Center. Contbr. articles legal publs. Mem. exec. bd. N.E. Ohio council Boy Scouts Am.; pres. Ashtabula county chpt. National Found. Served with U.S. Army, 1954-56. Recipient Disting. Service award Ashtabula Jr. C. of C., 1962; Outstanding Young Man of Ohio award Ohio Jaycees, 1963; Man of Yr. award Delta Theta Phi, 1969; Outstanding Alumnus award Cleveland Marshall Coll. of Law, 1974. Fellow Internat. Acad. Law and Sci.; mem. ABA, Ohio Bar Assn., Ashtabula County Bar Assn. (past pres.), Atty. Gen. Advocacy Inst. Innovator of summary jury trial. Jurisprudence. Office: US Dist Ct 106 US Courthouse Cleveland OH 44114 *

LAMIA, THOMAS ROGER, lawyer; b. Santa Monica, Calif., May 31, 1938; s. Vincent Robert, II, and Maureen (Green) L.; m. Susan Elena Brown, Jan. 10, 1969; children—Nicholas, Katja, Jenna, Tatiana, Carlyn, Mignon. Student U. So. Calif., 1956, B.S., 1961; student U. Miss., 1957-58; J.D., Harvard U., 1964. Bar: Calif. 1965, U.S. Dist Ct. (cen. dist.) Calif. 1965, D.C. 1980, U.S. Dist. Ct. D.C. 1980, U.S. Ct. Appeals (D.C. cir.) 1980, U.S. Tax Ct. 1982. Assoc. McCutchen, Black, Verleger & Shea, Los Angeles, 1964-66; lectr. in law U. Ife, Ile-Ife, Nigeria, 1966-67, U. Zambia, Lusaka, 1967-68; assoc. Paul Hastings, Janofsky & Walker, Los Angeles, 1968-72, ptnr., 1972-80, D.C., 1980—, mng. ptnr. D.C. office, 1980-83; bd. dirs. Acme Rents Inc.; bd. dirs., mem. exec. com. IHOP Corp.; mem. mgmt. com. McCall Pattern Co. Bd. dirs. Nat. Aquarium Soc. Mem. ABA (bus., banking, fed. regulation of securities com., sec. adminstrn. and budget subcom., internat. law com., African law and extraterritorial application of U.S. law subcoms.), Internat. Bar Assn. (product liability, false advt. and consumer protection coms.), Harvard Law Sch. Assn. General corporate, Administrative and regulatory, Private international. Office: Paul Hastings Janofsky Walker 1050 Connecticut Ave NW Washington DC 20036-5331

LAMM, CAROLYN BETH, lawyer; b. Buffalo, Aug. 22, 1948; d. Daniel John and Helen Barbara (Tatakis) L.; m. Peter Edward Halle, Aug. 12, 1972. B.S., SUNY Coll.-Buffalo, 1970; J.D., U. Miami (Fla.), 1973. Bar: Fla., 1973, D.C., 1976, N.Y. 1983. Trial atty. frauds sect. civil div. U.S. Dept. Justice, Washington, 1973-78, asst. chief comml. litigation sect. civil div., 1978, asst. dir., 1978-80; assoc. White & Case, Washington, 1980-84, ptnr., 1984—; mem. faculty Nat. Inst. Trial Advocacy. Fellow Am. Bar Found.; mem. ABA (chmn. young lawyers div., del. from D.C. Bar Assn. to ho. of dels., sec. litigation sect., nominating com., com. chmn. sect. corp. banking and bus. law), Fed. Bar Assn. (chmn. sect. on antitrust and trade regulation), Bar Assn. D.C. (bd. dirs., sec.), D.C. Bar (steering com. litigation sect.), Am. Law Inst., Women's Bar Assn. D.C., Am. Soc. Internat. Law, Internat. Bar Assn., Nat. Women's Forum. Democrat. Club: City Tavern (Washington). Contbr. articles to legal publs. Federal civil litigation, Administrative and regulatory, Private international. Home: 2101 Connecticut Ave NW Washington DC 20008 Office: 1747 Pennsylvania Ave NW Suite 500 Washington DC 20006

LAMON, HARRY VINCENT, JR., lawyer; b. Macon, Ga., Sept. 29, 1932; s. Harry Vincent and Helen (Bewley) L.; m. Ada Healey Morris, June 17, 1954; children: Hollis Morris, Helen Kathryn. B.S. cum laude, Davidson Coll., 1954; J.D. with distinction, Emory U., 1958. Bar: Ga. 1958, D.C. 1965. Practice in Atlanta, 1958—; mem. firm Hurt, Richardson, Garner, Todd & Cadenhead; dir. Sockwell Enterprises Inc., Atlanta, Vulture Petroleum Corp., Clark Memls., Inc., Macon, Ga.; adj. prof. law Emory U., 1960—. Contbr. articles to profl. jours. Mem. adv. bd. Salvation Army, 1963—, chmn., 1975-79, mem. nat. adv. bd., 1976—; mem. Adv. Council on Employee Welfare and Pension Benefit Plans, 1975-79; mem. Pension Reporter adv. bd. Bur. Nat. Affairs; bd. visitors Davidson Coll.; trustee, past pres. So. Fed. Tax Inst. Inc.; trustee Inst. Continuing Legal Edn. in Ga., 1976—. Served to 1st lt. AUS, 1954-56. Recipient Others award Salvation Army, 1979. Fellow Am. Coll. Probate Counsel, Am. Coll. Tax Counsel, Internat. Acad. Estate and Trust Law; mem. Am., Fed., Atlanta bar assns., Am. Law Inst., Am. Pension Conf., So. Pension Conf. (pres. 1972), State Bar Ga. (chmn. sect. taxation 1969-70, vice chmn. commn. on continuing lawyer competency 1982—), Am. Judicature Soc., Atlanta Tax Forum, Lawyers Club of Atlanta, Nat. Emory U. Law Sch. Alumni Assn. (pres. 1967), Practicing Law Inst., ALI-ABA Inst., C.L.U.s Inst., Phi Beta Kappa, Omicron Delta Kappa, Phi Delta Phi, Phi Delta Theta (chmn. community service day 1969-72, legal commr. 1973-76). Episcopalian (vestryman). Clubs: Kiwanis (Atlanta) (pres. 1973-74), Breakfast (Atlanta), Peachtree Racket (Atlanta) (pres. 1986-87), Capital City (Atlanta), Commerce (Atlanta); University (Washington). Corporate taxation, Pension, profit-sharing, and employee benefits, Probate. Home: 3375 Valley Rd NW Atlanta GA 30305 Office: 1100 Peachtree Center-Harris Tower 233 Peachtree St NE Atlanta GA 30043 also: 1730 K St NW Suite 1302 Washington DC 20036

LAMONICA, P(AUL) RAYMOND, law educator; b. Baton Rouge, June 10, 1944; s. Leonard and Olivia (Frank) L.; m. Dianne Davis, Aug. 23, 1971; children: Drew, Neal, Leigh. BA, La. State U., 1965, MA, 1966, JD, 1970. Bar, La. 1970. Law clk. to chief judge U.S. Dist. Ct. (we. dist.) La., 1970-71; assoc. Hebert, Moss & Graphia, Baton Rouge, 1971; judge pro tem 19th Jud. Dist. Ct., East Baton Rouge Parish, 1979; prof. law La. State U. Law Sch., Baton Rouge, 1971-79, 80—; exec. counsel to La. Gov., 1983-84; U.S. attorney for middle Louisiana, 1986—. Counsel La. Ho. of Reps., 1976-79, 80-83. Mem. ABA, La. Bar Assn. (bd. govs. 1979). Republican. Roman Catholic. Federal civil litigation, State civil litigation, Legal education. Office: US Attorney's Office 352 Florida St Baton Rouge LA 70801

LAMONT, ROBERT SHELDON, lawyer; b. Detroit, May 23, 1943; s. Junior William and Oma Agnes (Casey) L.; m. Paula Jo Tondee, July 24, 1966; children: Robert Sheldon Jr., Michael Schaenen. BBA, Stetson U., 1966; JD cum laude, Samford U., 1972; LLM in Taxation, Georgetown U., 1975. Bar: Fla. 1972, U.S. Tax Ct. 1972, U.S. Supreme Ct. 1976, U.S. Dist. Ct. (so. dist.) Fla. 1979, U.S. Ct. Claims 1987. Sr. trial atty. Office Chief Counsel IRS, Washington, 1972-76; ptnr. Greenberg, Reiseman & Lamont, Miami, Fla., 1976-81; sr. ptnr. Lamont & Neiman, Miami, 1981—; adj. prof. taxation Fla. Internat. U., Miami, 1976-80; comml. law faculty Am. Inst. Banking, Birmingham, Ala., 1970-72. Editor: Casenote, Recusement and Replacement of Supreme Court Justices, 1972. Alt. elected del. White House Conf. on Small Bus., Washington, 1986; active Informed Families of Dade County. Served to capt. U.S. Army, 1966-69. Recipient James E. Markham, Jr. Meml. Award IRS, 1976. Mem. ABA, Fla. Bar Assn., Dade County Bar Assn., South Fla. Tax Litigation Assn. (chartered), Greater Miami Tax Inst., Greater Miami C. of C., Phi Delta Phi. Avocation: bowling. Corporate taxation, Personal income taxation, General corporate. Home: 8241 SW 91st St Miami FL 33156 Office: 3050 Biscayne Blvd Suite 610 Miami FL 33137

LAMP, JOHN ERNEST, U.S. attorney; b. Spokane, Wash., Jan. 17, 1943; s. Raymond Holmes and Marie (Cunningham) L.; m. Louise Edwards, June 26, 1976; children—Amanda Catherine Marie, Victoria Louise. B.A., Wash. State U., 1965; J.D., Williamette U., 1968. Bar: Wash. 1968. Asst. atty. gen. State of Wash., Olympia, 1968-69; sr. asst. atty. gen. chief Spokane and Eastern Wash. br. Wash. State Atty. Gen.'s Office, 1971-81; U.S. Atty. Eastern Dist. Wash. State, 1981—. Mem. Atty. Gen.'s adv. com. U.S. Attys., 1983-86; mem. Wash. State Organized Crime Adv. Bd., bd. dirs. Morning Star Boys Ranch; advisor Wash. State Substance Abuse Coalition. Served to capt. U.S. Army, Vietnam, 1969-71. Recipient Alumni Achievement award Wash. State U., 1986. Mem. Wash. Bar Assn. Federal civil litigation, Criminal, Personal injury. Home: 841 US Courthouse West 920 Riverside Spokane WA 99210

LAMPARD, CATHERINE ANN, lawyer; b. New Orleans, Feb. 9, 1951; d. Robert E. and Catherine (Hand) L.; m. Bruce E. Naccari, Dec. 8, 1984; 1 child, Paolo Atilio. BA in Anthropology, Tulane U., 1971; JD, Loyola U., 1982. Bar: La., U.S. Dist. Ct. (ea. dist.) La., U.S. Ct. Appeals (5th cir.). Assoc. Hand & Lampard, New Orleans, 1982—; dir., staff atty. Ecumenical Immigration Services Inc., New Orleans, 1983—, also bd. dirs.; lectr. law and ethics Loyola U., New Orleans; supr. law clinic student practitioners Loyola U. and Tulane U.; trainer legislation Immigration Reform and Control Act of 1986. Organizer, mem. New Orleans Task Force on the Rights of Aliens, 1985—. Mem. ABA, La. Bar Assn., Fed. Bar Assn., Am. Immigration Lawyers Assn. Democrat. Roman Catholic. Avocations: reading, films. Immigration, naturalization, and customs, Constitutional law, Civil rights. Office: 3200 N Turnbull Dr Metairie LA 70002

LAMPEL, ARTHUR HARRY, lawyer; b. Santa Monica, Calif., Dec. 12, 1949; s. J. Murray and Rose (Maltun) L.; m. Jacquelin Siegel, Feb. 15, 1981. B.A. in Econs., UCLA, 1971; J.D., Whittier Coll., 1977. Bar: Calif. 1977, U.S. Dist. Ct. (cen. dist.) Calif. 1978, U.S. Supreme Ct. 1985; cert. specialist in family law. Atty. Law Offices L.M. Schulner, Camarillo, Calif., 1978-80, Law Offices of Ronald Talkov, West Covina, Calif., 1980-81, Jacoby & Meyers, Torrance, Calif., 1981-82; sole practice, Culver City, Calif., 1982—; judge pro tempore Los Angeles Mcpl. Ct. and Santa Monica Mcpl. Ct., 1985—. Whittier Coll. scholar, 1975. Mem. Calif. Bar, Los Angeles County Bar Assn. (family law sect.), Culver City Bar Assn., South Bay Bar Assn., Marina Bar Assn. Democrat. Family and matrimonial, State civil litigation, Personal injury. Office: 11949 Jefferson Blvd Suite 105 Culver City CA 90230

LAMPEN, RICHARD JAY, lawyer, investment banker; b. New Brunswick, N.J., Nov. 12, 1953; s. J. Oliver and Miriam (Walsh) L.; m. Susan Matson, June 8, 1975; 1 child, Katharine. BA, John Hopkins U., 1975; JD, Columbia U., 1978. Bar: Fla. 1978, U.S. Dist. Ct. (so. dist.) Fla. 1978. From assoc. to ptnr. Steel Hector & Davis, Miami, Fla., 1978-86; v.p. Salomon Bros. Inc., N.Y.C., 1986—. Mem. U. Miami Citizens Bd., 1986—. Mem. Fla. Bar Assn. (chmn. securities law com. 1985-86). Club: City (Miami, Fla.), Exchange (N.Y.C.). Securities, General corporate. Home: 500 E 77th St Apt 3324 New York NY 10021 Office: Salomon Bros Inc 1 New York Plaza New York NY 10004

LAMPL, SANFORD MARK, lawyer; b. Youngstown, Ohio, Aug. 22, 1926; s. Alex and Irene E. (Berkowitz) L.; m. Betty Lou Kaufman, Aug. 23, 1949; children—Kathy, David, Peggy Lampl Kaufman; m. 2d, Ruth Spindell, Oct. 12, 1978. B.A., U. Pitts., 1947, J.D., 1950. Bar: Pa. 1950, U.S. Dist. Ct. (we. dist.) Pa. 1950, U.S. Ct. Appeals (3d cir.) 1952. Sole practice, Pitts., 1950-75; sr. ptnr. Lampl, Sable & Makoroff, Pitts., 1975—; adj. prof. U. Pitts. Sch. Law, 1972-75. Served with USN, 1944-46. Mem. ABA, Allegheny Bar Assn., Tau Epsilon Rho. Club: Concordia (Pitts.). Bankruptcy, General corporate. Office: 710 5th Ave Pittsburgh PA 15219

LAMSON, DAVID HINKLEY, lawyer; b. Williamstown, Mass., Apr. 29, 1939; s. Roy and Margaret (Friedlander) L.; m. Betsey Webster Gerrity, July 14, 1979. A.B., Brown U., 1961; LL.B., Boston U., 1964. Bar: Mass. 1965, N.Y. 1966, U.S. Ct. Appeals (1st cir.) 1969, U.S. Supreme Ct. 1971. Asst. dist. atty. N.Y. Dist. Atty.'s Office, N.Y.C., 1965-68; ptnr. Homans Hamilton & Lamson, Boston, 1968-79; sole practice, Boston, 1979—; dir. Key Concepts, Inc., Boston. Served with USMC, 1959-65. Federal civil litigation, State civil litigation, General corporate. Office: 85 E India Row Boston MA 02110

LAMUTIS, DONALD FRANKLIN, lawyer; b. Geneva, N.Y., Oct. 25, 1949; s. Alexander Franklin and Josephine Helen(Balawander) L.; m. Marjorie Ann Flatow, Nov. 28, 1982; 1 child, Danielle Beth. AB, Syracuse U., 1971; JD, Widener U., 1975; postdoctoral, U. Pa., 1978-79. Bar: Pa. 1979, N.Y. 1979, U.S. Dist. Ct. (we. dist.) N.Y. 1979. Assoc. prof. law Widener U., Wilmington, Del., 1975-76; assoc. Dutcher, Witt & Siditi, Rochester, N.Y., 1979-80; jud. counsel N.Y. State Supreme Ct., Rochester, 1980—. Mem. Rochester Philharmonic Orch., 1980—, Rochester Hist. Soc., 1980—, Rochester Meml. Gallery, 1981—, Landmark Soc. Rochester, 1986—, Hist. Pittsford Soc., 1986—; chmn. Selective Service System, Rochester, 1981—. Mem. ABA, Pa. Bar Assn., N.Y. State Bar Assn., Phila. Bar Assn., Monroe County Bar Assn., Rochester Jaycees, Syracuse U. Alumni Assn., Cert. Football Officials (cert. Rochester chpt. 1981—), Phi Beta Kappa, Phi Kappa Phi. Democrat. Family and matrimonial, Personal injury, Judicial administration. Home: 12 Fenimore Dr Pittsford NY 14534 Office: NY Supreme Ct Exchange St Hall Justice Room 400 Rochester NY 14614

LANAUSSE, ZORAIDA, lawyer; b. Salinas, P.R., Aug. 27, 1951. B.B.A. in Econs., Catholic U., P.R., 1972; J.D. magna cum laude, Interam. U., P.R., 1978. Bar: P.R., 1978. Law clk. Junta de Apelaciones, Sistema de Administracion de Personal, Commonwealth of P.R., Santurce, 1977-78; atty. Dept. Social Services, San Juan, 1978-81; atty. civil litigation div. R.R. Dept. Justice, 1981—. Mem. Colegio de Abogados de P.R. Editorial staff Interam. U. Law Rev., 1976-77. Office: Dept Justice PO Box 192 San Juan PR 00902

LANCASTER, KENNETH G., lawyer; b. Stafford Springs, Conn., Dec. 6, 1949; s. Talbot Augustin and Helen Collier (McRae) L.; m. Margaret Jane Royer, Aug. 25, 1973; children—Kimberly Jane, John Talbot. B.A., U. Miami, 1971, J.D., 1974. Bar: Fla. 1974, U.S. Dist. Ct. (so. dist.) Fla. 1975, U.S. Dist. Ct. (mid. dist.) Fla. 1976. Adminstr. Met. Dade County, Miami, Fla., 1971-73; assoc. Robert A. Spiegel, Coral Gables, Fla., 1973-78; sole practice, South Miami, Fla., 1978-80; ptnr. Clark, Dick & Lancaster, South Miami, 1980—; cons. 1st City Bank Dade County, Miami, 1983-84; bd. dirs. U. Miami Bus. Sch. Bd. dirs. Hurricane Club, U. Miami, Coral Gables, 1984—, exec. com. U. Miami Hall Fame, Coral Gables, 1984—, mem. endowment com., 1982-84. Mem. ABA, Fla. Bar Assn., Dade County Bar Assn. (Disting. Service award 1984), South Miami Bar Assn., Assn. Trial Lawyers Am., Acad. Fla. Trial Lawyers. Family and matrimonial, Probate, Real property. Home: 14700 SW 127 Ct Miami FL 33186 Office: Clark Dick & Lancaster PA 7600 Red Rd #225 South Miami FL 33143

LANCASTER, MICHAEL JAMES, lawyer; b. Berkeley, Calif., Apr. 18, 1952; s. George Lewis and Edith (Richter) L.; Pamela Sue Gunderman, Nov. 2, 1978. AA, Sacramento City Coll., 1973; BS, Western State U., 1977, JD, 1979. Bar: Calif. 1980, U.S. Dist. Ct. (cen. dist.) Calif. 1980, U.S. Ct. Appeals (9th cir.) 1980, U.S. Supreme Ct. 1985. Assoc. Schell & DeLamer, Santa Ana, Calif., 1980—. Mem. ABA (litigation sect.), Orange County Bar Assn., Def. Research Inst. and Trial Lawyers Am. (real estate sect.), Orange County Trial Lawyers Assn. (real estate), Assn. So. Calif. Def. Counsel Christian. Avocations: golf, martial arts, music, sports. State civil litigation, Personal injury, Real property. Office: Schell & DeLamer 313-N Birch 2d Floor Santa Ana CA 92701

LANCASTER, WILLIAM ROBERT, lawyer; b. Memphis, July 1, 1957; s. Clarence Murray jr. and Nancy Clara (McConnahey) L.; m. Margaret Michelle Purvis, Aug. 9, 1980; children: William Purvis, Leigh Elizabeth. BA, Millsaps Coll., 1979; JD, U. Miss., 1982. Bar: Miss. 1972, U.S. Dist. Ct. (no. and so. dists.) Miss., 1972 U.S. Ct. Appeals (5th cir.), 1972. Assoc. Ramsey and Andrews, P.A., Vicksburg, Miss., 1982-83; assoc. Varner, Parker & Sessums, Vicksburg, 1984-86, ptnr., 1986—. Mem. ABA, Miss. State Bar, Miss. Def. Lawyers Assn., Bar Assn. of 5th Cir. Episcopalian. Personal injury, State civil litigation, Federal civil litigation. Office: Varner Parker & Sessions 1110 Jackson St Vicksburg MS 39180

LANCE, JAMES WINSLOW, financial corporation executive, lawyer; b. Little Rock, Ark., July 26, 1943; s. Lawrence Winslow and Kathryn Joyce (Haggard) L.; m. Frances Virginia Shepherd, June 11, 1966; 1 child, Paige Virginia. BSBA, U. Ark., Fayetteville, 1965, JD, U. Ark., Little Rock, 1972; postgrad. Mich. State U., 1976, U. So. Calif., 1978. Bar: Ark. 1973, U.S. Dist. Ct. (ea. dist.) Ark. 1973, U.S. Ct. Appeals (8th cir.) 1984, U.S. Supreme Ct. 1979. Sr. mgmt. analyst, dir. corp. planning First Pyramid Life Ins. Co., Little Rock, 1969-70; exec. dir. Little Rock Unltd. Progress, Inc., 1970-72, exec. com. bd., 1972-83; exec. v.p. Ark. Fin. Services, Inc., Little Rock, 1972-73, pres., chief exec. officer, 1973—, chmn. bd. dirs., pres., AFS Fin. Group, 1983—; chmn. bd. dirs., chief exec. officer Heritage Fed. Savs. and Loan Assn., Monticello, 1984-87. Served to 1st lt. U.S. Army, 1967-69. Mem. Nat. Savs. and Loan League (bd. dirs. 1978-83), U.S. League Savs. Assn. (chmn. multiple owned service corp. group 1977-78, service corp. com. 1979-81), Mortgage Bankers Assn. of Am. (mem. income property com. 1977-81), Savs. Instns. Mktg. Soc. (mem. research com. 1975—), ABA (mem. subcom. on fin. markets and instns. 1977—, mem. savs. and loan com. 1978—), Ark. Bar Assn. (chmn. savs. and loan sect. 1980-82), Ark. State C. of C. (bd. dirs. 1981—), Old State House Mus. Assocs. (treas., bd. dirs. 1986—). Administrative and regulatory, Banking. Home: 10 Heritage Park Circle North Little Rock AR 72116 Office: Three Hundred Spring Bldg Suite 800 Little Rock AR 72201

LANCE, MILES A., lawyer; b. North Tonawanda, N.Y., Sept. 27, 1934; s. Miles A. and Josephine Victoria (Gardner) L.; m. Barbara J. Weaver, Dec. 12, 1964; children—John M., Christopher S., Mark A., Michael S. B.B.A., U. Buffalo, 1956; LL.B., SUNY-Buffalo, 1962, J.D., 1968. Bar: N.Y. 1962, U.S. Dist. Ct. (we. dist.) N.Y. 1962, Fla. 1977, U.S. Supreme Ct. 1983, U.S. Dist. Ct. (mid. dist.) Fla., U.S. Ct. Appeals (2d cir.) 1986. Assoc. Chester S. Grove, Lockport, N.Y., 1962-64, Smith, Murphy & Schoepperle, Buffalo, 1964-66; sole practice, North Tonawanda, N.Y., 1966-86; staff atty. City of Clearwater, Fla., 1986—; cons. bus. Pres. Town Rep. Club, 1971-72; active St. Johnsburg Fire Co., 1971-74, Am. Mensa, Ltd., 1979—. Served with USN, 1956-58. Recipient Alden-Baldy award SUNY-Buffalo. Mem. ABA, Clearwater Bar Assn. Lutheran. Federal civil litigation, State civil litigation, Personal injury. Office: 112 S Osceola St PO Box 4748 Clearwater FL 33518

LANCHNER, BERTRAND MARTIN, lawyer, advertising agency executive; b. Boston, Oct. 3, 1929; s. Abraham Joseph and Mina (Grossman) L.; m. Nancy Nelson, Apr. 26, 1979; 1 son by previous marriage, David; 1 stepdau., Renate. B.A., Stanford U., 1951; postgrad., Columbia U. Grad. Sch. Bus., 1951-52, U. Vienna, Austria, summer 1955; J.D., Harvard U., 1955. Bar: N.Y. bar 1956. Asso. firm Sage, Gray, Todd & Sims, N.Y.C., 1955-57; atty. Warner Bros. Pictures, N.Y.C., 1957-59; asst. gen. counsel Dancer-Fitzgerald-Sample, N.Y.C., 1959-62; gen. counsel Lawrence C. Gumbinner Advt. Agy., N.Y.C., 1962-63; dir. bus. affairs and sports contract negotiations CBS-TV, N.Y.C., 1963-69; gen. counsel, exec. v.p. Videorecord Corp. Am., Westport, Conn., 1969-73; also dir.; sr. v.p., sec., gen. counsel N.W. Ayer, Inc., N.Y.C., 1973—; dir. 170 E. 79th St. Corp.; guest lectr. Yale U. Law Sch. Mem. adv. bd.: Communications and the Law. Mem. Am. Bar Assn., N.Y. State Bar Assn., Assn. Bar City N.Y., Copyright Soc. U.S., Am. Assn. Advt. Agys. (chmn. lawyers com.). Clubs: Harvard of N.Y.C, Bridgehampton Racquet and Surf, Tennisport, Uptown Racquet. Entertainment, Communications. Office: care NW Ayer Inc 1345 Ave of Americas New York NY 10105

LANCIONE, BERNARD GABE, lawyer; b. Bellaire, Ohio, Feb. 3, 1939; s. Americus Gabe and June (Morford) L.; m. Rosemary C., Nov. 27, 1976; children—Amy, Caitin, Gillian, Bernard Gabe, Elizabetta Marie. B.S., Ohio U., 1960; J.D., Capitol U., 1965. Bar: Ohio 1965, U.S. Supreme Ct. 1969, U.S. Ct. Appeals (6th cir.) 1970, U.S. Ct. Appeals (4th cir.) 1982. With Lancione Law Office, Co., L.P.A., Bellaire, Ohio, 1965—, now pres.; solicitor Bellaire City (Ohio), 1968-72; asst. prosecutor County of Belmont (Ohio), 1969-72; legal counsel Young Democrats Am., 1971-73. Mem. ABA, Ohio Bar Assn., Belmont County Bar Assn., Assn. Trial Lawyers Am., Ohio Acad. Trial Lawyers (award of merit 1972). Club: Sons of Italy (Bellaire). Workers' compensation, Probate, Real property. Home: 190 N Sugar St Saint Clairsville OH 43950 Office: 3800 Jefferson St Bellaire OH 43906

LANCIONE, NELSON, lawyer; b. Bellaire, Ohio, July 10, 1918; s. John B. and Elizabeth (Del Guzzo) L.; m. Tillie L. Lapitsky, Feb. 12, 1948; children: Nelson William, Robert Michael, David. BS, Ohio State U., 1941, JD, 1943. Bar: Ohio 1943, U.S. Dist. Ct. (so. dist.) Ohio 1951, U.S. Supreme Ct. 1963. Atty. U.S. Treasury Dept., Washington, 1943-49; rep. U.S. Treasury Dept., Manila, 1945-47; asst. atty. gen. State of Ohio, Columbus, 1949-50; sole practice Columbus, 1951-82; gen. counsel, sec. N.E. Equitable Life Ins. Co., Columbus, 1959-68; ptnr. Lancione Law Offices, Columbus, 1983—. V.p. Young Dems. Clubs Am., Washington, 1956-57, pres. 1957-58; del. Atlantic Congress, London, 1959, Dem. Nat. Conv., Columbus, 1982; mem. Ohio Electoral Coll., Columbus, 1976; chmn. Gov.'s Inaugural Com., Columbus, 1970-71, Franklin County Bd. Elections, Columbus, 1972-79;. Fellow Ohio Bar Found., Columbus Bar Found.; mem. ABA, Ohio Bar Assn., Columbus Bar Assn., Am. Judicature Soc., Ohio Acad. Trial Lawyers, Assn. Trial Lawyers Am., Lawyers Club. Club: Capital (Columbus). Lodge: Moose (life member). Federal civil litigation, State civil litigation, Personal injury. Office: 42 E Gay St Suite 1200 Columbus OH 43215-3159

LANCIONE, RICHARD LEE, lawyer; b. Bellaire, Ohio, Apr. 26, 1941; s. Americus Gabe and Phyliss June (Morford) L.; m. Joyce E. Gianangeli, June 8, 1963; children: Tracey, Brant. Student, Wittenburg U., 1959-60; BSBA, Ohio State U., 1963, JD, 1966. Bar: Ohio 1966, U.S. Dist. Ct. (so. dist.) Ohio 1967, U.S. Ct. Claims 1971, U.S. Supreme Ct. 1974. Assoc. Nelson Lancione Law Office, Columbus, Ohio, 1966-68; ptnr. Lancione Law Office Co. L.P.A., Bellaire, 1968—. Mem. Ohio U. Regional Council, Belmont County, 1978—; pres. Save Imperial Com., Belmont County, 1984—; trustee Bellaire Glass Mus., Belmont County, 1979—. Mem. Ohio Bar Assn., Belmont County Bar Assn. (pres. 1975-76), Assn. Trial Lawyers Am., Ohio Acad. Trial Lawyers (med. negligence com. 1986—), Am. Judicature Soc., Am. Arbitration Assn. (panelist 1981—), Italian Am. Fedn. Democrat. Episcopalian. Lodge: Kiwanis (pres. Bellaire 1984-85), Sons of Italy. Avocation: glass collecting. Personal injury, State civil litigation, Probate. Office: Lancione Law Office Co LPA 3800 Jefferson St Bellaire OH 43906

LANCIONE, ROBERT MICHAEL, lawyer; b. Columbus, Ohio, May 19, 1951; s. Nelson and Tillie (Lapitsky) L.; m. Teresa Gail Johnson, May 20, 1985; children: Robert Michael Jr., Cara Christine. BA cum laude, Ohio U., 1973; JD, Capital U., 1976. Bar: Ohio, U.S. Dist. Ct. (so. dist.) Ohio, U.S. Supreme Ct. Assoc. Law Offices of Nelson Lancione, Columbus, 1976-79; ptnr. Lancione Law Offices, Columbus, 1980—. Vol. pro bono work Legal Aide Soc., 1980—. Recipient Disting. Service award Legal Aide Soc., 1984. Mem. ABA, Ohio Bar Assn., Columbus Bar Assn., Ohio Bar Coll., Assn. Trial Lawyers Am., Franklin County Trial Lawyers Assn. Democrat. Avocations: boating, fishing, waterskiing. Personal injury, Workers' compensation, Insurance. Home: 999 Stoney Creek Rd Worthington OH 43085 Office: Lancione Law Offices 42 E Gay St Suite 1200 Columbus OH 43215

LAND, CHARLES EDWARDS, lawyer; b. Washington, Nov. 18, 1952; s. Henry Carter and Marjorie (Nesbitt) L.; m. Margaret Dalton, Feb. 21, 1981; children: Juliet McLure, Charles Edwards Jr. BA, U. Va., 1975, JD, 1978. Bar: Va. 1978, U.S. Dist. Ct. (ea. dist.) Va. 1978. Ptnr. Kaufman & Canoles, Norfolk, Va., 1978—. Mem. ABA, Va. State Bar Assn., Va. Bar Assn. Episcopalian. Real property. Home: 302 Raleigh Ave Norfolk VA 23507 Office: Kaufman & Canoles 1 Commercial Pl Suite 2000 Norfolk VA 23510

LAND, DAVID POTTS, lawyer; b. Lancaster, Pa., Mar. 29, 1944; s. William Ortlip and Jean (Potts) L.; m. Susan Delano, Aug. 20, 1966; children: Katherine, Stephen, Elizabeth. BA in Religion, Kenyon Coll., 1966; JD, Vanderbilt U., 1969. Bar: N.Y. 1970, U.S. Dist. Ct. (so. dist.) N.Y. 1972, U.S. Ct. Appeals (2d cir.) 1972. Assoc. Seward & Kissel, N.Y.C., 1969-71; asst. U.S. atty. State of N.Y., N.Y.C., 1971-75; assoc. Rosenman, Colin, Freund, Lewis & Cohen, N.Y.C., 1975-77; v.p., asst. gen. counsel Combustion Engring. Inc., Stamford, Conn., 1977-86; v.p., gen. counsel Brown Boveri Inc., White Plains, N.Y., 1986—; chief tax unit U.S. Attys. Office, N.Y.C., 1973-75. Pres. Saugatuck Shores Assn., Westport, Conn., 1982-85; mem. bd. deacons Saugatuck Congl. Ch., 1986—. Mem. ABA, Bklyn. Bar Assn. Federal civil litigation, State civil litigation, General corporate. Home: 21 Marine Ave Westport CT 06880 Office: Brown Boveri Inc 2 Gannett Dr White Plains NY 10604

LAND, STEPHEN BRITTON, lawyer; b. Norwalk, Conn., Nov. 26, 1954; s. Gay Vallee and Elizabeth Edna (Cooper) L.; m. Jane Elizabeth Drew, June 15, 1974; children: Sarah Britton, John Drew. AB, Harvard U., 1975, JD, 1979, MBA, 1979. Bar: N.Y. 1980, U.S. Dist. Ct (so. and ea. dists.) N.Y. 1980, U.S. Ct. Claims 1980, U.S. Tax Ct. 1980. Assoc. Sullivan & Cromwell, N.Y.C., 1979-87; ptnr. Howard, Darby & Levin, N.Y.C., 1987—. Bd. dirs. Oxfam Am., Boston, 1979-85. Mem. ABA, N.Y. State Bar Assn. Republican. Presbyterian (elder). Clubs: Larchmont (N.Y.) Yacht, India House (N.Y.C.). Corporate taxation. Home: 29 Mohegan Rd Larchmont NY 10538 Office: Howard Darby & Levin 10 E 53rd St New York NY 10022

LANDA, HOWARD MARTIN, health care products company executive; b. Bklyn., Oct. 12, 1943; s. George and Lilli (Skolnik) L.; m. Nori Neinstein, Mar. 14, 1971; children—Alyson, David. B.A. (N.Y. State Regents scholar), Bklyn. Coll., 1964; J.D. (tuition scholar), U. Chgo., 1967. Bar: N.Y. 1968. Individual practice law N.Y.C., 1968-69; asso. firm Garfield, Solomon & Mainzer, N.Y.C., 1969-70, Szold, Brandwen, Meyers & Altman, N.Y.C., 1970-74; v.p., sec., gen. counsel IPCO Corp., White Plains, N.Y., 1974—; also dir. IPCO Corp.; lectr. Dental Lab. Conf., 1977. Mem. Mayor N.Y.C. Panel to Study Dept. Gen. Services' Div. Mcpl. Supplies, 1978-79. Mem. Am. Soc. Corp. Secs., Am. Mgmt. Assn., Health Industry Mfrs. Assn., Am. Bar Assn., New York County Lawyers Assn., Westchester-Fairfield County Corp. Counsel Assn. General corporate, Administrative and regulatory, Contracts commercial. Office: 1025 Westchester Ave White Plains NY 10604

LANDAU, SYBIL HARRIET, lawyer, educator; b. N.Y.C., Nov. 26, 1937; d. Sidney and Janice (Katz) L. B.A. in History and Polit. Sci.; with honors, Hunter Coll., 1958; LL.B. (Harlan Fiske Stone scholar), Columbia U., 1961; B.C.L., Oxford (Eng.) U., 1963. Bar: N.Y. State 1965, U.S. Supreme Ct. 1969, U.K. Barrister-at-law, mem. Middle Temple 1965. Asst. lectr. in law U. Bristol, Eng., 1963-65; asst. dist. atty. N.Y. County, 1965-72; assoc. prof. law Hofstra U., 1972-74; vis. adj. assoc. prof. law Bklyn. Law Sch., 1975; assoc. prof. Benjamin N. Cardozo Sch. Law, 1975-80, asst. dean, 1975-77; hearing examiner N.Y. State Family Ct. at, N.Y. County, 1981-82; lectr. in field of rape, sexuality and the law; mem. Brookdale Faculty, Brookdale Center of Aging, Hunter Coll., 1977-78. Contbr. articles to profl. publs. Bd. dirs. FDR-Woodrow Wilson Dem. Club, 1967-68; mem. Mayor's Task Force on Rape, 1974-77; mem. adv. bd. to subcom. on juvenile delinquency N.Y. State Commn. on Child Welfare; mem. adv. bd. Gerontol. Inst., Yeshiva U., 1977-78. Named to Hunter Coll. Hall of Fame, 1974. Mem. Am. Law Inst., ABA, Women's Bar Assn., N.Y. State Bar Assn., Assn. of Bar of City of N.Y., N.Y. County Lawyers, Hon. Soc. of Middle Temple, Hunter Coll. Alumni Assn. (dir. 1976-79, 80-83, 85—), Met. Women's Law Tchrs. Assn. (v.p. 1976-78), Animal Legal Def. Fund. Jewish. Club: N.Y.C. Women's. State civil litigation, Family and matrimonial, Landlord-tenant. Home: 8 W 13th St New York NY 10011 Office: 401 Broadway New York NY 10013

LANDAU, WALTER LOEBER, lawyer; b. New Orleans, Sept. 9, 1931; s. Walter Loeber and Mae (Wilzin) L.; m. Barbara Jane Gordon, June 23, 1954; children—Donna Ellen, Blair Susan, Gordon Loeber. B.A., Princeton U., 1953; LL.B., Harvard U., 1956. Bar: N.Y. 1956, U.S. Dist. Ct. (so. dist.) N.Y. 1962, U.S. Supreme Ct. 1971. Assoc. firm Sullivan & Cromwell, N.Y.C., 1959-66; ptnr. Sullivan & Cromwell, 1966—; dir. U.S. Life Ins. Co., N.Y.C., Esselte Bus. Systems Inc. Corp. Trustee Reece Sch., N.Y.C. Served to capt. USAF, 1956-59. Fellow Am. Bar Found.; mem. ABA, N.Y. State Bar Assn., Assn. Bar City N.Y., Am. Law Inst., N.Y. Law Inst. (treas., exec. com.). Republican. Securities, General corporate, Private international. Office: 250 Park Ave New York NY 10177

LANDAY, ANDREW HERBERT, lawyer; b. N.Y.C., Mar. 8, 1920; s. Max and Ida Rose (Fox) L.; m. Carolyn Anne Greco, Aug. 22, 1962; children—Vincent, Mark, James, Roseanne. B.A., UCLA, 1946; B.A., Mt. Angel Sem., Oreg., 1950; M.S., Columbia U., 1953; J.D., Southwestern U., 1964. Bar: Calif. 1964, U.S. Dist. Ct. (cen. dist.) Calif. 1964, U.S. Tax Ct. 1965, U.S. Ct. Appeals (9th cir.) 1966, U.S. Supreme Ct. 1971. Sole practice, Los Angeles, 1964-68; ptnr. Rozner, Yorty, Landay, Gibbs, Hodges, Bernstein & Wagner, Los Angeles, 1968-73, Bernstein, Wagner, Hodges & Landay, Beverly Hills, Calif., 1974-78; of counsel H. Bradley Jones, Inc., Beverly Hills, Calif., 1978—; arbitrator Calif. Superior Ct., Los Angeles, 1979—; judge pro-tem, arbitrator Santa Monica (Calif.) Mcpl. Ct., 1971—, Los Angeles Mcpl. Ct., 1971—. Bd. dirs. Santa Monica Republican Club, 1983—. Served with AUS, 1942-46. Mem. ABA, Los Angeles County Bar Assn. (mcpl. cts. com. 1977-78), Santa Monica Dist. Bar Assn., Am. Judicature Soc., Los Angeles County Lawyers Club (chmn. profl. ethics and unauthorized practice com. 1968-70, 77-78), Phi Alpha Delta. Republican. Roman Catholic. Club: KC. Probate, Estate taxation. Office: 322 12th St Santa Monica CA 90402-2098 also: 9601 Wilshire Blvd Suite 744 Beverly Hills CA 90210-5295

LANDE, JAMES AVRA, lawyer, engineering and construction company executive; b. Chgo., Oct. 2, 1930; s. S. Theodore and Helen C. (Hamburger) L.; m. Ann Mari Gustavsson, Feb. 21, 1959; children—Rebecca Susanne, Sylvia D. B.A., Swarthmore Coll., 1952; J.D., Columbia U., 1955; Bar: N.Y. 1958, Calif. 1967. Assoc. Rein, Mound & Cotton, N.Y.C., 1957-59; atty. VA, Seattle, 1959-61, Weyerhaeuser Co., Tacoma, 1961-63, Lande Assoc., San Francisco, 1963-67; with NASA, Ames Research Center, Moffett Field, Calif., 1967-70; house counsel Syntex Corp., Palo Alto, Calif., 1970-73; dir. contracts dept. Electric Pwer Research Inst., Palo Alto, Calif., 1973-81; corp. atty., dir contracts Lurgi Corp., Belmont, Calif., 1981-82; contracts mgr. Bechtel Nat., Inc., San Francisco, 1982—; adj. prof. U. San Francisco Sch. Law, 1972-73; lectr. law U. Santa Clara Sch. Law, 1968—. Pres. Syntex Fed. Credit Union, 1971-72. Served with U.S. Army, 1955-57. Mem. Calif. Bar Assn., ABA. Clubs: Commonwealth of Calif., Lawyers of San Francisco. Government contracts and claims, General corporate, Private international.

LANDER, DAVID ALLAN, lawyer; b. St. Louis, Oct. 2, 1944; s. Louis and Edna (Schramm) L.; m. Carole Weissman Aug. 12, 1965; children—Brad, Rachel. B.A. cum laude, Bowdoin Coll., 1966; J.D., U. Chgo, 1969. Bar: Mo. 1969, U.S. Dist. Ct. (ea. dist.) Mo. 1969, U.S. Ct. Appeals (8th cir.) 1970. Atty., exec. dir. Legal Aid Soc St. Louis City-County, 1975-80; asst. prof. law, St. Louis U., 1973-75, instr., 1980—; ptnr. Husch, Eppenberger, Donohue, Elson & Cornfeld, St. Louis, 1981—; lectr. numerous programs on secured lending, bus. bankruptcy and workouts. Exec. com. mem. Consumer Counseling Credit Service, St. Louis Opportunity Clearinghouse; dir. Legal Services Eastern Mo.; chmn. Southwestern Bell Mo. Consumer Adv. Panel. Mem. ABA (chmn. com. on agrl. and agri-bus. fin.), Mo. Bar Assn., Bar Assn. Met. St. Louis. Mng. editor Bankruptcy Reporter for Eastern Dist. Mo.; contbr. articles to profl. jours. Bankruptcy, Contracts commercial, Real property. Address: 12372 Woodline Dr Saint Louis MO 63141

LANDER, GARY DAVID, lawyer; b. Hackensack, N.J., June 1, 1946; s. Isidore and Frances (Shoenig) L.; m. Mildred Berenice Lamport, Sept. 6, 1981. BA cum laude, Brandeis U., 1967; JD, Vanderbilt U., 1970. Bar: Tenn. 1971, U.S. Dist. Ct. (mid. dist.) Tenn. 1971, U.S. Dist. Ct. (ea. dist.) Tenn. 1972, U.S. Ct. Appeals (6th cir.) 1971, U.S. Supreme Ct. 1974. Law clk. to presiding justice U.S. Ct. Appeals (6th cir.), 1970-71; assoc. Neal & Harwell, Nashville, 1971-72; spl. counsel Office of City Atty., Chattanoga, 1972-84; ptnr. Chambliss, Bahner, Crutchfield, Gaston & Irvine, Chattanooga, 1984—. Bd. dirs. Jewish Welfare Fedn., Chattanooga, 1976-80, B'Nai Zion Congregation, Chattanooga, 1981-86, Chattanooga Symphony Opera, 1984—, Arts & Edn. Council, Chattanooga, 1980-82, 85—. Mem. ABA, Tenn. Bar. Assn., Chattanooga Bar Assn., Am. Trial Lawyers Assn. Jewish. Avocations: non-comml. film programming, music. Federal civil litigation, State civil litigation, Local government. Home: 4109 Dogwood Ln Chattanooga TN 37411 Office: Chambliss Bahner Crutchfield et al 1000 Tallan Bldg Chattanooga TN 37402

LANDERS, DIANN JEANETTE, lawyer; b. Chgo., Jan. 26, 1952; d. Robert B. and Shirley G. (Goldberg) L.; m. Douglas J. Dok Jr., Apr. 19, 1980. BA, No. Ill. U., 1973; JD, DePaul U., 1976. Bar: Ill. 1976, Mich. 1977, U.S. Dist. Ct. (we. dist.) Mich. 1980. Mng. atty. family law unit Legal Aid of Western Mich., Grand Rapids, 1976-81; atty. Zerrenner, Landers & Haynes, Grand Rapids, 1981—. Mem. adv. com. YMCA Domestic Crisis Ctr., Grand Rapids, 1976-80; workshop facilitator Grand Rapids Women's Resource Ctr., 1976—, bd. dirs., 1983—; coordinator com. Irons for Judge, 1982; co-chair Com. to Elect Bowler Judge, 1984; mem. com. Citizens for Janet Neff, 1986. Recipient Merit award Voluntary Action Ctr. of Vols. in Action, United Way of Mich., 1982, 86; Tribute of Appreciation award Grand Rapids Women's Ctr., 1982, 84; named one of Outstanding Young Women In Am., 1982. Mem. ABA, Mich. Bar Assn. (chair character fitness com., mem. family law sect.), Ill. Bar Assn., Grand Rapids Bar Assn. (pro bono com., cert. of commendation 1982-86), Mich. Women Lawyers Assn. (v.p. 1985-86), Mich. Trial Lawyers Assn. Club: University (Grand Rapids). Avocations: sailing, antiques, dog obedience. Family and matrimonial. Office: Zerrenner Landers & Haynes 72 Ransom NE Grand Rapids MI 49503

LANDERS, GARY CLINTON, lawyer; b. Abilene, Tex., Apr. 24, 1951; s. Melvin Clifford and Ola B. (Head) L.; m. Belinda Kay Elmers, Aug. 3, 1975; children: Alison, Jonathan, Lindsay. Student, Chapman Coll., 1970; BA, McMurry Coll., 1973; JD, U. Tex., 1977. Bar: Tex. 1977, U.S. Dist. Ct. (no. dist.) Tex. 1978, U.S. Ct. Appeals (5th cir.) 1978, U.S. Supreme Ct. 1980, U.S. Dist. Ct. (ea. dist.) Tex. 1985. Sole practice Austin, Tex., 1977-78; asst. atty. City of Abilene, 1978-80, 1st asst. atty., 1980-85; atty. City of Tyler, Tex., 1985—. Named one of Outstanding Young Men in Am., 1984. Mem. ABA, Am. Trial Lawyers Assn., Smith County Bar Assn., Abilene Young Lawyers Assn. Methodist. Lodge: Kiwanis. Avocations: racquetball, tropical fish, travel. Local government. Office: City Attys Office PO box 2039 Tyler TX 75710

LANDES, WILLIAM M., law educator; b. 1939. A.B., 1960; Ph.D. in Econs., Columbia U., 1966. Asst. prof. econs. Stanford U., 1965-66; asst. prof. U. Chgo., 1966-69; asst. prof. Columbia U., 1969-72; assoc. prof. Grad. Ctr., CUNY, 1972-73; now prof. U. Chgo. Law Sch.; mem. sr. research staff Nat. Bur. Econ. Research, 1968—; mem. bd. examiners GRE in Econs., ETS, 1967-74. Mem. Am. Econ. Assn., Mont Pelerin Soc. Editor: (with Gary Becker) Essays in the Economics of Crime and Punishment, 1974; editor Jour. Law and Econs., 1974—. Legal education. Office: U Chgo Sch Law 1111 E 60th St Chicago IL 60637 *

LANDFIELD, RICHARD, lawyer; b. Chgo. Jan. 16, 1941; s. Joseph D. and Donna (Mayberg) L.; m. Ilona Kiraldi, Aug. 6, 1965; children—Anne, Katharine, Sarah. B.A. Amherst Coll., 1962; LL.B. cum laude, Harvard U., 1965. Bar: N.Y. 1966, D.C. 1972. Assoc. Breed, Abbott & Morgan, N.Y.C., 1965-66, 1969-72, Washington, 1972-75; ptnr. Landfield, Becker & Green, Washington, 1979—; bd. dirs. Carlson Holdings Corp. Active numerous Amherst Coll. alumni groups, lawyers com. Washington Opera Soc.; mem. building and grounds com. Holton-Arms Sch., Bethesda, Md., 1985—, trustee, 1984-86, 87—, past pres. Parents' Assn., mem. bldgs. and grounds com. 1987—. Served as 1st lt. U.S. Army, 1966-69. Decorated Army Commendation medal; John W. Simpson Law fellow Amherst, 1963. Mem. ABA; N.Y. Bar Assn., D.C. Bar . Republican. Clubs: University (Washington); Kenwood Country (Bethesda, Md.). General corporate, Private international, Real property. Home: 5620 Grove St Chevy Chase MD 20815 Office: Landfield Becker and Green 1818 N St NW Washington DC 20036

LANDIN, DAVID CRAIG, lawyer; b. Jamestown, N.Y., Aug. 1, 1946; s. David Carl and Rita Mae (Felthaus) L.; m. Susan Ann Gregory, July 11, 1970; children: Mary Stuart, Alexander Craig, David Reed. BA, U. Va., 1968, JD, 1972. Bar: Va. 1972, U.S. Supreme Ct. 1979. Ptnr. McGuire, Woods & Battle, Richmond, Va., 1972—, mgr. of product liability and litigation mgmt. group, 1987—. Trustee Va. Law Found., 1981—, v.p. 1986-87; trustee St. Anne's Belfield Sch., Charlottesville, Va., 1984—, chmn. trusteeship com., 1985—, exec. com. 1985—. Served to specialist 5 USAR, 1968-74. Mem. Va. Bar Assn. (chmn. young lawyers sect. 1979-80, chmn. com. on Issues of State and Nat. Importance 1982—), Va. Assn. Def. Attys. (regional v.p. 1982-84, treas. 1984—, pres.-elect 1986), ABA (vice chmn. arbitration com., tort and ins. practice sect. 1980, co-chmn. affiliate outreach com. young lawyers div. 1981-82), Charlottesville-Albemarle Bar Assn. (sec., treas. 1975-77, chmn. young lawyers sect. 1975-78), Richmond Bar Assn., Def. Research Inst., Am. Soc. Hosp. Attys., Assn. Ins. Attys. Roman Catholic. Clubs: Farmington Country Club (Charlottesville, Va.); Commonwealth (Richmond, Va.); N.Y. Athletic. Avocations: squash, tennis. Federal civil litigation, Personal injury, Industry wide litigation. Home: 310 Oak Ln Richmond VA 23226 Office: McGuire Woods Battle & Boothe One James Ctr Richmond VA 23219

LANDIS, ROBERT M., lawyer; b. Fleetwood, Pa., 1920; s. Jacob B. and Bertha (Moyer) L.; m. Mary Elizabeth Hatton, Aug. 24, 1946; children: Christopher Hatton, Geoffrey Budd. A.B., Franklin and Marshall Coll., 1941; J.D., U. Pa., 1947. Bar: Pa. 1947. Assoc. firm Dechert, Price & Rhoads, Phila., 1947-54; partner Dechert, Price & Rhoads, 1954—; chmn. Fed. Res. Bank, Phila., 1983-86; 1st dep. city solicitor Phila., 1952-53; mem. Pa. Supreme Ct. Advisory Judicial Qualifications Commn., 1968; mem. life U.S. Jud. Conf. Third Circuit; dir., mem. exec. com. Houghton Mifflin Co.; dir. Fed. Res. Bank Phila.; Chmn. Pa. Gov.'s Bd. Ethics, 1973-78; chmn. Bi-State Commn. Legislation Delaware River Port Authority Pa.-N.J., 1976-77. Co-chmn. Greater Phila. Partnership, 1977-79; bd. dirs. Greater Phila. Movement; pres. Children's Aid Soc. Pa., 1960-68; bd. dirs. Child Welfare League Am., 1964-66; pres. Fellowship Commn. Phila., 1972-74; past chmn. Pa. Council of Nat. Council Crime and Delinquency; mem. advisory council Villanova Inst. Correctional Reform, 1972-79; steering com. NAACP Legal Def. Fund; assoc. trustee U. Pa., Franklin and Marshall Coll.; chmn. bd. trustees Theodore F. Jenkins Law Library, 1970-71; elder, trustee First Presbyn. Ch., Lower Merion, Gladwyne, Pa. Fellow Am. Coll. Trial Lawyers (bd. regents 1981—), Am. Bar Found.; mem. Phila. Bar Assn. (numerous com. assignments, chmn. bd. govs. 1964, chancellor 1970—), Am. Bar Assn. (pres. Nat. Conf. Bar Presidents 1975-76, del. 1969-70, 77-78, bd. of govs. 1982, standing com. on fed. judiciary, chmn. standing com. on jud. improvements 1983-86), Pa. Bar Assn. (pres. 1981-82, ho. of dels. 1968—), Nat. Assn. R.R. Trial Counsel (pres. 1966-67), Am. Law Inst. (life), Am. Judicature Soc. (dir. 1974-77). Clubs: Franklin Inn, Socialegal, Sunday Morning Breakfast, Racquet, Phila. Country. Home: 1401 Monk Rd Gladwyne PA 19035 Office: Dechert Price & Rhoads 3400 Centre Sq W 1500 Market St Philadelphia PA 19102

LANDMAN, ERIC CHRISTOPHER, lawyer; b. N.Y.C., Aug. 1, 1948; s. Louis and Joan (Neill) L.; 1 child, Ian Foster. B.A., George Washington U., 1970; J.D., Cath. U. Am., 1973. Bar: N.J. 1973, U.S. Dist. Ct. N.J. 1973, U.S. Supreme Ct. 1983. Assoc. Randall, Randall & McGuire, Westwood, N.J., 1973-74; sole practice, Tenafly, Englewood, N.J., 1974-76; assoc. Joseph T. Skelley, Fort Lee, N.J., 1976-79, Davies, Davies, Pojanowski, Mennen & Sandberg, Paterson, N.J., 1979-83, Heilbrunn, Finkelstein, Heilbrunn, Alfonso & Goldstein, Old Bridge, N.J., 1983—; mem. N.J. Supreme Ct. Com. on Model Civil Jury Charges. Bd. dirs. Big Bros./Sisters of Middlesex County, 1983—. Mem. Assn. Trial Lawyers Am., Middlesex County Trial Lawyers Assn., N.J. State Bar Assn., Middlesex County Bar Assn. State civil litigation, Personal injury, General practice. Office: Heilbrunn Finkelstein Heilbrunn Alfonso & Goldstein PC 201 Hwy 516 Old Bridge NJ 08857

LANDMEIER, ALLEN LEE, lawyer; b. Elmhurst, Ill., Nov. 24, 1942; s. Vernon O. and Eleanor Marie (Forke) L.; m. Charlotte Landmeier, July 8, 1978; children—Matthew, Mark, Michael. B.S. in Elec. Engring., Valparaiso U., 1964, J.D., 1967. Bar: Ill. 1967, U.S. Dist. Ct. (no. dist.) Ill., U.S. Supreme Ct. 1977. Assoc. Muller & Aichele, 1970-71; mem. Smith & Landmeier, P.C., Geneva, Ill., 1971—; city atty. St. Charles, Ill.; Delnor Community Healthcare System (bd. mem. 1986—). Served to lt. JAGC, USNR, 1967-70. Mem. Ill. Bar Assn. (state taxation sect. council 1977-86), ABA, Kane County Bar Assn. (gen. counsel 1986—). Lutheran. General practice, Local government, Real property. Office: 15 N 2d St PO Box 127 Geneva IL 60134

LANDRON, MICHEL J., lawyer; b. Santurce, P.R., June 15, 1946; s. Francis X. and Francisca (Carretero) Healy. B.A., Lehman Coll., 1968, postgrad., 1969-73; J.D., Fordham U., 1977. Bar: N.Y., U.S. Dist. Ct. (so. dist.) N.Y. 1978, U.S. Dist. Ct. (ea. dist.) N.Y. Asst. atty. gen. Office of Atty. Gen., N.Y. State Dept. Law, N.Y.C., 1978-80; enforcement atty. N.Y. Stock Exchange, N.Y.C., 1980-81; sole practice, Bklyn., 1981-82, 84—; mem. Leaf, Duell, Drogin P.C., N.Y.C., 1982-84; gen. counsel Rockcom, Inc., 1985-87, adminstr. law judge City of N.Y., 1987—; of counsel Berger and Paul, N.Y.C., adj. instr. N.Y. Law Sch., Ramapo Coll.; arbitrator U.S. Dist. Ct. (ea. dist.) N.Y.; guest lectr. Lehman Coll.; cons. in field; arbitrator Civil Ct. N.Y.C., No Fault Ins. Panel State of N.Y. Mem. med. malpractice panel appellate div., 2d dept. rev. prologue to Nuremburg; arbitrator Am. Arbitration Assn. Mem. ABA (forum com. on entertainment and sports law), Bklyn. Bar Assn. (past chmn. patents trademark and copyrights com.), N.Y. State Bar Assn., N.Y. State Trial Lawyers Assn., Assn. Arbitrators City of N.Y., Phi Alpha Delta (disting. service award 1977). Contbr. to legal jours. General practice, Trademark and copyright, State civil litigation. Home: 323 46th St Brooklyn NY 11220

LANDY, BURTON AARON, lawyer; b. Chgo., Aug. 16, 1929; s. Louis J. and Clara (Ernstein) L.; m. Eleanor M. Simmel, Aug. 4, 1957; children: Michael Simmel, Alisa Anne. Student, Nat. U. Mex., 1948; B.S., Northwestern U., 1950; postgrad. scholar, U. Havana, 1951; J.D., U. Miami, 1952; postgrad. fellow, Inter-Am. Acad. Comparative Law, Havana, Cuba, 1955-56. Bar: Fla. 1952. Practice law in internat. field Miami, 1955—; ptnr. firm Ammerman & Landy, 1957-63, Paul, Landy, Beiley & Harper, P.A. and predecessor firm, 1964—; lectr. Latin Am. bus. law U. Miami Sch. Law, 1972-75; also internat. law confs. in U.S. and abroad; mem. Nat. Conf. on Fgn. Aspects of U.S. Nat. Security, Washington, 1958; mem. organizing com. Miami regional conf. Com. for Internat. Econ. Growth, 1958; mem. U.S. Dept. Commerce Regional Export Expansion Council, 1969-74, mem. Dist. Export Council, 1978—; dir. Fla. Council Internat. Devel., 1977—, chmn. 1986-87; mem. U. Miami Citizens Bd., 1977—; chmn. Fla. del. S.E. U.S.-Japan Assn., 1980-82; mem. adv. com. 1st Miami Trade Fair of Ams., 1978; dir., v.p. Greater Miami Fgn. Trade Zone, Inc., 1978—; mem. organizing com., lectr. 4 Inter-Am. Aviation Law Confs.; bd. dirs. Inter-Am. Bar Legal Found.; participant Aquaculture Symposium Sci. and Man in the Ams., Mexico City, Fla. Gov's Econ. Mission to Japan and Hong Kong, 1978; mem. bd. exec. advisors Law and Econs. Ctr.; mem. vis. com. U. Miami Sch. Bus.; mem. internat. fin. council Office Comptroller of Fla.; founding chmn. Fla.-Korea Econ. Coop. Com., 1982—, Southeast U.S.-Korea Econ. Com., 1985—; chmn. Expo 500 Fla.-Columbus Soc., 1985-87; founding co-chmn. So. Fla. Roundtable-Georgetown U. Ctr. for Strategic and Internat. Studies, 1982—; chmn. Fla. Gov.'s Conf. on World Trade, 1984—; gen. counsel Fla. Internat. Bankers Assn.; dir., former gen. counsel Fla. Internat. Ins. and Reins. Assn. Contbg. editor Econs. Devel. Lawyers of the Ams., 1969-74; contbr. numerous articles to legal jours. in U.S. and fgn. countries. Chmn. City of Miami Internat. Trade and Devel. Com., 1984—; dir. and chmn. internat. task force Beacon Council of Dade County, Fla., 1985; bd. dirs. Internat. Comml. Dispute Resolution Ctr.; appointed by Gov. of Fla. to Internat. Currency and Barter Commn. & Fla. Columbus Hemispheric Trade Commn., 1986. Served with JAGC USAF, 1952-54, Korea; to maj. Res. Named Internat. Trader of Yr., Fla. Council Internat. Devel., 1980, Bus. Person of Yr., 1986; recipient Pan Am. Informatica Comunicaciones Expo award, 1983, Lawyer of Americas award U. Miami, 1984; named hon. consul gen. Republic of Korea, Miami, 1983—, recipient Heung-in medal (Order of Diplomatic Service), 1986. Mem. Inter-Am. Bar Assn. (asst. sec.-gen. 1957-59, treas. 11th conf. 1959, co-chmn. jr. bar sect. 1963-65, mem council 1969—, exec. com. 1975—, pres. 1982-84), ABA (chmn. com. arrangements internat. and comparative law sect. 1964-65, com. on inter-Am. affairs 1985-87), Spanish Am. Bar Assn., Fla. Bar Assn. (vice chmn. adminstrv. law com. 1965, vice chmn. internat. and comparative law com. 1967-68, chmn. aero. law com. 1968-69), Dade County Bar Assn. (chmn. fgn. laws and langs com. 1964-65), Internat. Ctr. Fla. (pres. 1981-82), World Peace Through Law Ctr., Miami Com. Fgn. Relations, Instituto Ibero Americano de Derecho Aeronautico, Am. Soc. Internat. Law, Council Internat. Visitors, Am. Fgn. Law Assn. (pres. Miami 1958), Bar of South Korea (hon. mem.), Greater Miami C. of C. (bd. govs. 1986—), Columbian-Am. C. of C. (bd. dirs. 1986—), Phi Alpha Delta. Private international, Banking, General corporate. Home: 6255 Old Cutler Rd Miami FL 33156 Office: Penthouse Atico Fin Ctr Miami FL 33131

LANDY, JAMES LEONARD, lawyer; b. N.Y.C., Oct. 4, 1948; s. Charles Samuel and Christa (Canaubeus) L. BA, CCNY, 1971; JD, Bklyn. Law Sch., 1976. Bar: Mass. 1977, N.Y. 1977, U.S. Dist. Ct. Mass. 1977. Atty. Legal Aid Soc., N.Y.C., 1976-66, Correctional Legal Services, Boston, 1977-79; sole practice Cambridge, Mass., 1979-80; instr. U.S. Dept. State, Quito, Ecuador, 1980-83; sole practice Lawrence, Mass., 1983—. Mem. ABA, Am. Immigration Lawyers Assn., Mass. Bar Assn., Mass. Acad. Trial Attys., Family Service Assn. (bd. dirs. 1984—), Internat. Inst. (bd. dirs. 1984—), Centro Panamericano (bd. dirs. 1986—). Avocations: gardening, silkscreening. Criminal, Immigration, naturalization, and customs, Personal injury. Office: 261 Common St Lawrence MA 01840

LANDZBERG, ALAN JEFFREY, lawyer; b. Queens, N.Y., Sept. 29, 1954; s. Morris and Beatrice Landzberg. BA, NYU, 1975, LLM, 1983; JD, Fordham U., 1978. Bar: N.Y. 1979, U.S. Dist. Ct. (so. and ea. dists.) N.Y. 1979, U.S. Tax Ct. 1979, U.S. Claims Ct. 1984, U.S. Ct. Internat. Trade 1984. Tax mgr. M.R. Weiser & Co., N.Y.C., 1978-81; assoc. Lefrak, Newman & Myerson, N.Y.C., 1982-83, Dreyer and Traub, N.Y.C., 1984—. Mem. Nat. Polit. Action Com., Washington, 1982. Mem. ABA (tax sect.), N.Y. Bar Assn. (tax sect.), Defenders of Wildlife, N.Y. Zool. Soc., World Wildlife Fund. Club: N.Y. Road Runners. Avocations: scuba diving, martial arts, guitar, wildlife preservation. Personal income taxation, Taxation, magazines, cable TV and other media, Taxation, patents, copyrights and other intellectual property. Home: 200 W 70th St 8L3 New York NY 10023 Office: Dreyer and Traub 101 Park Ave New York NY 10178

LANE, ARTHUR ALAN, lawyer; b. N.Y.C., Dec. 2, 1945; s. George and Delys Lane; m. Jane Ficocella, Dec. 30, 1972; 1 child, Eva B. BA, Yale U., 1967; JD, Columbia U., 1970, MBA, 1971. Bar: N.Y. 1971. Assoc. Webster, Sheffield, Fleischmann, Hitchcock & Brookfield, N.Y.C., 1971-72; asst. to div. counsel Liggett & Myers Inc., N.Y.C., 1973; assoc. Wickes, Riddell, Bloomer, Jacobi & McGuire, N.Y.C., 1974-78, Morgan, Lewis & Bockius, N.Y.C., 1979; ptnr. Eaton & Van Winkle, N.Y.C., 1980—. Mem. ABA, Bar Assn. City N.Y. Banking, General corporate, General practice. Home: 315 W 70th St New York NY 10023 Office: Eaton & Van Winkle 600 3d Ave New York NY 10016

LANE, BRUCE STUART, lawyer; b. New London, Conn., May 15, 1932; s. Stanley S. and Frances M. (Antis) L.; m. Ann Elizabeth Stienberg, Aug. 10, 1958; children: Sue Ellen, Charles M., Richard I. Student, Boston U., 1948-49; AB magna cum laude, Harvard U., 1952, JD, 1955. Bar: Ohio 1955, D.C. 1966, U.S. Ct. Claims 1960, U.S. Tax Ct. 1961, U.S. Supreme Ct. 1961. Assoc. Squire, Sanders & Dempsey, Cleve., 1955-59; sr. trial atty. tax div. Dept. Justice, Washington, 1959-61; tax atty. Dinsmore, Shohl, Barrett, Coates & Deupree, Cin., 1961-65; sec., asst. gen. counsel corp. and tax matters Communications Satellite Corp., Washington, 1965-69; v.p., gen. counsel Corp. Nat. Housing Partnerships, Washington, 1969-70; pres. Lane and Edson P.C., Washington, 1970—. Co-editor-in-chief Housing and Devel. Reporter; author publs. and articles on tax, partnership and real estate. Incorporator, bd. dirs., past pres. D.C. Inst. Mental Hygiene; past chmn. citizens Com. sect. 5 Chevy Chase, Md.; past mem. Montgomery County Hist. Preservation Commn., Md. Served to maj JAG, USAR, 1952-68. Mem. ABA, Am. Law Inst., Am. Coll. Real Estate Lawyers (pres. 1986-87), Anglo-Am. Real Property Inst., Phi Beta Kappa. Club: Internat. (Washington). Corporate taxation, Real property, Legislative. Home: 3711 Thornapple St Chevy Chase MD 20815 Office: Lane & Edson PC 2300 M St NW Washington DC 20037

LANE, CHARLES RAY, lawyer; b. Oklahoma City, Feb. 11, 1944; s. Benny and Ysleta Edith (Davis) L.; m. Jill Reber, Nov. 28, 1968; children—Mark Michael, Carrie Jill. B.A., Okla. U., 1966, J.D., 1972, M.B.A., 1978. Bar: Okla. 1972, La. 1982, U.S. Dist. Ct. (we. dist.) Okla. 1972, U.S. Ct. Appeals (10th cir.) 1972, U.S. Dist. Ct. (ea. dist.) Okla. 1973, U.S. Ct. Appeals (5th cir.) 1973, U.S. Supreme Ct. 1975, U.S. Ct. Appeals (11th cir.) 1982, La. 1982, U.S. Dist. Ct. (mid., we., ea. dists.) La. 1982. Asst. dist. atty. 24th Jud. Dist., Shawnee, Okla., 1972-73; sr. counsel Halliburton Services, New Orleans, La., 1973—. Served as 1st lt. USMC, 1967-71. Decorated Combat Action Ribbon, Vietnamese Cross of Gallantry, Navy Commendation medal with Combat V. Mem. ABA, Okla. Bar Assn., La. Bar Assn., Assn. Trial Lawyers Am., La. Assn. Trial Lawyers, Okla. Assn. Def. Counsel, La. Def. Counsel, Maritime Law Assn., Halliburton Services Polit. Action Group, Phi Gamma Delta, Phi Alpha Theta. Presbyterian. Clubs: Beau Chene Country, Masons. Admiralty, Personal injury, Workers' compensation. Office: Halliburton Services Suite 2600 Canal Place I New Orleans LA 70130

LANE, JAMES EDWARD, lawyer, consultant; b. Stockport, Ohio, Jan. 22, 1921; s. Jesse Benton and Martha Elizabeth (Horn) L.; m. Betty Jayne Bucy, July 28, 1939; children—Betty Jayne, Roberta Lee, James Benton. Student Ohio State U., 1938-43; LL.B., William McKinley Sch. Law, Canton, Ohio, 1951; assoc. in mgmt. Ins. Inst. Am., 1970; C.P.C.U., Am. Inst. Property and Liability Underwriters, 1976. Bar: Ohio 1951, U.S. Dist. Ct. (so. dist.) Ohio 1977. Adjuster Allstate Ins. Co., Akron, Ohio, 1958-59, examiner, Cin., 1959-61, dist. claim mgr., Dayton, Ohio, 1961-68; v.p. claims Grange Mut. Casualty Co., Columbus, Ohio, 1968-76, exec. v.p. Ohio and W.Va. Ins. Guaranty Assn., Columbus, 1976—; sole practice, cons., Columbus, 1976—; lectr. Wright State U., Dayton, 1966, 67; cons. Mut. Reins. Bur., Cherry Valley, Ill., 1981—; presenter seminars; mem. speakers bur. Ohio Ins. Inst., Columbus, 1973-76. Pres. Worthington (Ohio) PTA, 1969-70; mem. vestry St. John's Episcopal Ch., Worthington, 1972-77; troop leader Cen. Ohio Dist. council Boy Scouts Am., Worthington, 1972-78. Served to 2d lt. U.S. Army, 1944-46; PTO. Recipient Century award cen. Ohio sect., Boy Scouts Am., 1975-78. Mem. Columbus Bar Assn., Ohio Bar Assn., Ohio Assn. Civil Trial Attys. (legis. chmn. 1974-76; recipient plaque 1976), Def. Research Inst., Columbus Claim Club, Ohio State Claim Club, Nat. Com. Ins. Guaranty Funds (ops. subcom.), Delta Theta Phi (vice dean Canton chpt. 1950-51). Republican. Insurance, Personal injury, General practice. Home: 6170 Middlebury Dr West Worthington OH 43085 Office: Ohio Ins Guaranty Assn PO Box 14328 Columbus OH 43214

LANE, JOHN, administrative judge; b. N.Y.C., Sept. 8, 1940; s. John and Mary Keyes (McCloskey) L.; m. Penelope Jeanne Sichol, Sept. 18, 1965; children—Jennifer, Gregory, Sharon, David, Alexander. A.B., Coll. Holy Cross, 1961; LL.B., Fordham U., 1964. Bar: N.Y. 1964, D.C., 1967, U.S. Claims Ct. 1968, U.S. Ct. Appeals (D.C. cir.) 1968, U.S. Supreme Ct. 1968. Assoc. firm Sullivan & Cromwell, N.Y.C., 1964-65, Sellers, Conner & Cuneo, Washington, 1968-70, Reavis, Pogue, Neal & Rose, Washington, 1970-72; atty.-adviser office of gen. counsel Sec. of Air Force, Washington, 1965-68; adminstrv. judge Armed Services Bd. Contract Appeals, Alexandria, Va., 1972—; spl. adviser statutory studies group Commn. on Govt. Procurement, Washington, 1970-72. Editor-in-chief Fordham Law Rev., 1963-64; contbr. articles to profl. jours. Chmn. lawyers' com. D.C., United Givers Fund, 1972. Served to capt. USAF, 1965-68. Recipient Gibbons Meml. award United Givers Fund, Washington, 1972. Mem. ABA (chmn. com. on current fed. procurement statutes, regulations and forms, sec. pub. contract law, 1972-73, sr. editor Pub. Contract Law Jour. 1977-78), Nat. Contract Mgmt. Assn. (officer Washington chpt. 1970-72), Fed. Bar Assn., N.Y. State Bar Assn. Republican. Roman Catholic. Lodge: K.C. Government contracts and claims. Home: 913 Dalebrook Dr Alexandria VA 22308 Office: Armed Services Bd Contract Appeals 200 Stovall St Alexandria VA 22332

LANE, MARC JAY, lawyer; b. Chgo., Aug. 30, 1946; s. Sam and Evelyn (Light) L.; BA, U. Ill., 1967; JD, Northwestern U., 1971; m. Rochelle B. Nudelman, Dec. 12, 1971; children: Allison, Amanda, Jennifer. Admitted to Ill. bar, 1971, since practiced in Chgo.; pres. Law Offices of Marc J. Lane, P.C., Chgo., 1971—; pres. Medico-Legal Inst., Chgo., 1976—; vis. instr. Ill. Coll. Optometry, 1974—. Mem. ABA, Chgo. Council Lawyers (chmn. com.), Chgo. Bar Assn. (com. on taxation), Ill. State Bar Assn. (Lincoln award 1973, 77, author Tax Planning for Smaller Business, 1981). Author: The Doctor's Lawyer, 1974, Legal Handbook for Small Business, 1977, The Doctor's Law Guide, 1980, Legal Handbook for Nonprofit Organizations, 1980, Taxation for the Computer Industry, 1980, Taxation for Small Business, 1980, 2d edit., 1982, Taxation for Engineering and Technical Consultants, 1980, Taxation for Small Manufacturers, 1980, Amortization of Intangibles, 1983, Corporations-Preorganization Planning, 1984; (with others) Annual Federal Tax Course, 1978, Purchase and Sale of Small Businesses, 1985, Purchase and Sale of Small Businesses: Tax and Legal Aspects, 1985, The Impact of the '86 Tax Code on Closely Held Business, 1986, Representing Corporate Officers and Directors, 1987; contbr. articles to profl. jours. Personal income taxation, Corporate taxation, General corporate. Home: 6715 N Longmeadow Lincolnwood IL 60646 Office: 180 N LaSalle St Chicago IL 60601

LANE, MARYL A., lawyer; b. Pitts., Jan. 18, 1958; s. Clifford McCalmont and Mildred Louise (Richards) L. BA, Chatham Coll., 1979; JD, U. Pitts., 1982. Bar: Pa. 1982, U.S. Dist. Ct. (we. dist.) Pa. 1982, U.S. Tax Ct. 1982, U.S. Ct. Appeals (3d cir.) 1982, D.C. 1985, U.S. Supreme Ct. 1987. Assoc. Thorp, Reed & Armstrong, Pitts., 1982-83; sole practice Pitts., 1983-85; assoc. Klehr, Harrison, Harvey, Branzburg, Ellers & Weir, Phila., 1985-86, Drinker Biddle & Reath, Phila., 1986—. Mem. ABA (various coms.), Pa. Bar Assn. (various coms.), Phila. Bar Assn. (various coms.), D.C. Bar Assn., Mensa. Lodge: Order of Eastern Star. General corporate, Securities. Office: Drinker Biddle & Reath Broad and Chestnut Sts 1100 Phila Nat Bank Bldg Philadelphia PA 19107

LANE, MATTHEW JAY, lawyer; b. Cin., Mar. 6, 1955; s. Joseph Alan and Adele (Stacks) L. BA, Emory U., 1977; JD, Northwestern U., 1980. Bar: Ohio 1981, U.S. Dist. Ct. (so. dist.) Ohio 1981, U.S. Ct. Appeals (6th cir.) 1981, Fla. 1982. Law clk. to chief judge U.S. Dist. Ct. (so. dist.) Ohio, Cin., 1980-82; assoc. Walker, Chatfield & Doan, Cin., 1982—; legal counsel Mothers Against Drunk Driving, Cin., 1984—. Legal counsel Juvenile Diabetes Assn., Cin., 1984—; mem. fund raising com. Big Bros./Big Sisters, Cin., 1984—, Cin. Bicentennial Commn., 1985, Cin. Dem. Com., 1985, Dem. Cen. Com., 1986, bd. edn. Isaac M. Wise Temple, 1986—. Mem. ABA, Ohio Bar Assn., Cin. Bar Assn. (conf. with acad. medicine, negligence law com., lawyers referral service com.), Phi Beta Kappa. State civil litigation, Federal civil litigation, Personal injury. Home: 8601 Constitution Dr Cincinnati OH 45215 Office: Walker Chatfield & Doan 1900 Carew Tower Cincinnati OH 45202

LANE, ROBERT CASEY, corporate lawyer; b. 1932. JD, Loyola U., 1960. Atty. U.S. Dept. Justice, Washington, 1960-61; assoc. Lewis, Overbeck & Furman, 1962-69; atty. Weyerhaeuser Co., Tacoma, 1969-71, adminstrv. asst. to sr. v.p., 1971-77, asst. gen. counsel, 1977-80, v.p., gen. counsel, 1980—. Office: Weyerhaeuser Co Tacoma WA 98477 *

LANE, ROBERT K., lawyer; b. Cleve., Sept. 1, 1944; m. Reiko June 30, 1970; children: Nysa, Mari, Lindsay. AB in History, U. Calif.-Berkeley, 1966; JD Loyola U., 1969. Bar: Calif. 1970. Mortgage banker, the Rouse Co., Columbia, Md., 1970; pres., chief counsel R. Kingsbury Lane, 1972-78, 83—; ptnr. Brott and Lane Corps., 1978-82. Served as 1st lt., U.S. Army Intelligence. Mem. ABA, Calif. Bar Assn., Alameda Bar Assn. Real property, Family and matrimonial, State and federal civil litigation. Office: 20th Floor R Kingsbury Lane Inc The Clorox Bldg 1221 Broadway Oakland CA 94612

LANE, ROBERT PITT, lawyer; b. Langdale, Ala., Sept. 20, 1954; s. James Marshall and Laura Sue (Adams) L.; m. Connie Leah Alexander, July 28, 1979; children: Alexander Marshall, Abby Mae. BBA cum laude, Samford U., 1975, JD cum laude, 1978. Bar: Ala. 1978, U.S. Dist. Ct. (no. dist.) Ala. 1979, U.S. Dist. Ct. (mid. dist.) Ala. 1980, U.S. Ct. Appeals (11th cir.) 1981, U.S. Supreme Ct. 1984. Staff atty. Birmingham (Ala.) Legal Services Corp., 1979-80; assoc. Phillips & Funderburk, Phenix City, Ala., 1980-85; ptnr. Phillips & Funderburk, Phenix City, 1985—. County chmn. Reagan-Bush Com., Russell County, Ala., 1984; bd. atty. Downtown Redevel. Authority, Phenix City, 1985—. Mem. ABA, Ala. Bar Assn., Ala. Trial Lawyers Assn. Real property, General practice, Contracts commercial. Home: 4406 Linda Dr Phenix City AL 36867 Office: Phillips & Funderburk 1313 Broad St Phenix City AL 36867

LANE, ROBIN R., lawyer; b. Kerrville, Tex., Nov. 28 1947; d. Rowland and Gloria (Benson) Richards; m. Stanley Lane, Aug. 22, 1971 (div. 1979); m. 2d, Anthony W. Cunningham, Nov. 12, 1980; children: Joshua Lane, Alexandra. BA with honors in Econs., U. Fla., 1969; MA, George Washington U., 1971; JD, Stetson Coll. Law, 1978. Bar: Fla. 1979, U.S. Ct. Appeals (11th cir.) 1981, U.S. Supreme Ct. 1986. Mgmt. trainee internat. banking Gulf Western Industries, N.Y.C.; internat. research specialist Ryder Systems, Inc., Miami, Fla., 1973, project mgr., 1974; assoc. Wagner, Cunningham, Vaughan & McLaughlin, Tampa, Fla., 1979-85; sole practice, 1985—; guest lectr. med. jurisprudence Stetson Coll. Law, 1982-87. Contbr. articles to various revs. Recipient Am. Jurisprudence award-torts, Lawyers Co-op. Fla., 1979; Scottish Rite fellow, 1968-69. Mem. Acad. Fla. Trial Lawyers (mem. com. 1983-84), Assn. Trial Lawyers Am., Fla. Bar Assn., ABA, Fla. Women's Network, Omicron Delta Epsilon, Delta Delta Delta. Clubs: Palma Ceia Tampa; Tower. Personal injury, Labor. Home: 3301 Bayshore Blvd Tampa FL 33609 Office: Barnett Plaza 101 E Kennedy Suite 1480 Tampa FL 33602

LANE, STEVEN JAY, lawyer; b. Bklyn., Mar. 29, 1955; s. Lawrence Hugh and Ellen Jane (Feinberg) L.; m. Mary Jane Lawrence. BA, SUNY, Buffalo, 1977; JD, Loyola U., 1980. Bar: La. 1981, U.S. Dist. Ct. (ea. dist.) La. 1981, U.S. Ct. Appeals (5th. 11th cirs.) 1981, U.S. Supreme Ct. 1986. Ptnr. Herman, Herman, Katz & Cotlar, New Orleans, 1981—; lectr. Tulane U. Custody Seminar, New Orleans, 1984, La. Soc. CPA's, 1985. Contbr. articles to profl. jours. Mem. ABA (family lawy sect.), La. Bar Assn. (family law sect.), Assn. Trial Lawyers Am., La. Trial Lawyers Assn., Am. Judicature Soc., Phi Delta Phi, Sigma Lambda Rho. Democrat. Jewish. Avocations: baseball card collecting, art collecting, jogging, tennis. Family and matrimonial, State civil litigation, Personal injury. Office: Herman Herman Katz and Cotlar 820 O'Keefe Ave New Orleans LA 70118

LANE, WILFORD JONES, lawyer; b. Roanoke, Ala., Oct. 4, 1947; s. Ernest Jones and Frances Gertrude (Smith) L.; m. Amy Jo Robinson, Sept. 23, 1972; children: Joshua, John, Emily. BA, Jacksonville (Ala.) St. U., 1974; JD, Birmingham (Ala.) Sch. of Law, 1978. Bar: Ala. 1978, U.S. Dist. Ct. (no. dist.) Ala. 1978. Sole practice Anniston, Ala., 1978—. Contbr. short stories to Family Jour. Organizer, mem. Saks Youth Activities, Anniston-Saks, Ala., 1984. Served with USN, 1966-70, Vietnam. Mem. ABA, Ala. Bar Assn., Ala. Trial Lawyers Assn. (family law div.), Calhoun County Assn. (treas., bd. dirs. 1982-84), Am. Legion, Sigma Delta Kappa. Lodges: Optomists, Elks (investigating com. 1986). Avocations: history, reading, research, baseball. Personal injury, Criminal, Family and matrimonial. Home: 1609 Pomotaw Trail Anniston AL 36201 Office: 1330 Noble St Anniston AL 36201

LANE, WILLIAM EDWARD, lawyer, inventor; b. Chgo., Apr. 29, 1906; s. Edwin J. and Caroline (Eisendrath) Levi. Student, U. Ill., 1925-26, Northwestern U., 1931-32; LL.B., Chgo.-Kent Coll. Law, 1929, LL.M., 1930, J.D., 1969. Bar: Ill. 1929, U.S. Supreme Ct. 1935, U.S. Dist. Ct. (no. dist.) Ill. 1936, U.S. Dist. Ct. Hawaii 1964. Ptnr. Lane & Jacobson, Chgo., 1930-36; sole practice, Chgo., 1936-42; ptnr. Lane, Duffy & Connell, Chgo., 1946-58, Lane & Terry, Wilmette, Ill., 1962-83; mem. adv. bd. Atty.'s Title Guaranty Co., Chgo., 1983—; lect. Patentee solar energy. Bd. dirs. Wilmette Vis. Nurse Assn., 1962-64; bd. dirs. New Trier Twp. Family Service Ctr., 1962-65. Served with AUS, 1942-45. Mem. ABA, Ill. Bar Assn., Chgo. Bar Assn., Lake County Bar Assn., Wilmette C. of C. (past pres.). Lodge: Elks (chmn. bd. trustees 1960-64, exalted ruler 1958-59). State civil litigation, Federal civil litigation, Real property. Office: 1200 Central Ave Wilmette IL 60091

LANER, RICHARD WARREN, lawyer; b. Chgo., July 12, 1933; s. Jack E. and Esther G. (Cohon) L.; m. Barbara Lee Shless, Aug. 15, 1954; children—Lynn, Kenneth. Student, U. Ill., 1951-54; B.S., Northwestern U., 1955, LL.B., 1956. Bar: Ill. bar 1956. Assoc. Laner, Muchin, Dombrow & Becker Ltd. (and predecessors), Chgo., 1956-62; ptnr. Laner, Muchin, Dombrow & Becker Ltd. (and predecessors), 1962—. Editor: Northwestern Law Rev, 1954-56; Contbr. articles to profl. jours. Mem. Chgo. Bar Assn. (chmn. com. labor law 1972-73), Chgo. Assn. Commerce, Industry, Order of Coif. Labor. Home: 1300 Edgewood Ln Northbrook IL 60062 Office: Laner Muchin Dombrow & Becker Ltd 350 N Clark 4th Floor Chicago IL 60610

LANEY, DANIEL MILTON, lawyer; b. Fort Worth, Mar. 9, 1949; s. Samuel M. and Jewell (Hart) L.; m. Marilyn Elsa Wyss, Dec. 31, 1970; children—Neely, Allison. B.B.A. magna cum laude, North Tex. State U., 1970; J.D., U. Tex., 1974. C.P.A., Tex. Bar: Tex. 1974, U.S. Dist. Ct. (we. dist.) 1976, U.S. Tax Ct. 1978. Acct., Price Waterhouse, Fort Worth, 1974-76; assoc. Law Office of John Blazier, Austin, Tex., 1976-77; ptnr. Blazier & Laney, Austin, 1977-81, Rash, Laney, & Schreiber, Austin, 1981-85, Rash, Laney & Schreiber, 1985—; dir. InterFirst Bank Oak Hill. Bd. dirs. Young Men's Bus. League, Austin, 1977-78, v.p., 1978-79, pres. 1980-81. Recipient award for Acctg. Excellence, Haskin & Sells, 1970; named Outstanding Young Men of Am., 1981. Mem. Travis County Bar Assn., Travis County Young Lawyers Assn., S.W. Legal Found., Tex. Soc. of C.P.A.s, Am. Inst. C.P.A.s, Austin Soc. C.P.A.s Democrat. Roman Catholic. Personal income taxation, Probate, Real property. Home: 2302 Cypress Pt W Austin TX 78746 Office: Rash & Laney 609 W 9th Austin TX 78701

LANEY, WILLIAM R., lawyer; b. Skowhegan, Maine, June 13, 1953; s. Richard Paul and Marion (Rock) L. BA, Holy Cross Coll., 1975; JD, U. Maine, 1978. Bar: Maine 1978, U.S. Dist. Ct. Maine 1979. Assoc. Carl R. Wright, P.A., Skowhegan, 1978-82; ptnr. Laney & Susi, Skowhegan, 1982—. Mem. Skowhegan Econ. Devel., 1982—, Skowhegan Planning Bd., 1986—. Mem. Maine Bar Assn., Maine Trial Lawyers, Somerset County Bar Assn. (v.p. 1985). Democrat. Roman Catholic. Lodge: Elks. Avocation: tennis. Workers' compensation, Personal injury, Family and matrimonial. Home: 92 North Ave Skowhegan ME 04976 Office: Laney & Susi 159 Water St Skowhegan ME 04976

LANG, EDWARD GERALD, lawyer; b. Stamford, Conn., Jan. 3, 1948; s. Ira and Bernice (Gelb) L.; m. Pamela Lois Howard, Jan. 8, 1972; children—Samantha, Colin. B.S. in Econs., U. Pa., 1969; J.D., U. Conn., 1973. Bar: Conn. 1973. Ptnr., Lang and Thomas, Middlefield, Conn., 1973—; atty. Catholic Charities, Middletown, 1982—. Chmn. Middlefield Charter Revision Commn., 1984; bd. dirs. Hartford Ballet, 1982—. Mem. ABA, Conn. Bar Assn., Middlesex County Bar Assn. Lodge: Lions. Administrative and regulatory, Probate, Family and matrimonial. Home: 183 Cherry Hill Rd Middlefield CT 06455 Office: Box 462 Main St Middlefield CT 06455

LANG, FRANCIS HAROVER, lawyer; b. Manchester, Ohio, June 4, 1907; s. James Walter and Mary (Harover) L.; m. Rachel Boyce, Oct. 20, 1934; children: Mary Sue, Charles Boyce, James Richard. A.B., Ohio Wesleyan U., 1929; J.D., Ohio State U., 1932. Bar: Ohio 1932. Practice in East Liverpool, 1932-42, 45—; with War Dept., 1942-45; Chmn. bd. First Fed. Savs. & Loan Assn., East Liverpool, 1959-82; dir. First Na. Bank, Chester, W.Va.; former pres., dir. Walter Lang companies; dir. Sayre Electric companies. Past bd. dirs. YMCA, Mary Patterson Meml.; past pres. Columbiana council Boy Scouts Am. regional com., E. Central region; mem. at large Nat. council, 1968—; bd. dirs. Bd. Global Ministries of United Methodist Ch., 1968-76. Mem. E. Liverpool C. of C. (past pres.), Columbiana County Bar Assn. (past pres.), Ohio State Bar Assn. Methodist. Clubs: Rotarian (past dist. gov.), E. Liverpool Country, Masons (33d degree). Banking, Probate, Real property. Home: Highland Colony East Liverpool OH 43920 Office: Potters Savs and Loan Bldg East Liverpool OH 43920

LANG, JAMES EDWARD, lawyer; b. Omaha, June 26, 1949; s. James Edward and Nellie (Fitzgerald) L.; m. Joan F. Cavanaugh, July 9, 1977; children: Colleen, Cathy, Mary Jo. BS, U. Nebr., 1971; JD, Creighton U., 1974. Bar: Nebr. 1974, Iowa 1974, U.S. Dist. Ct. Nebr., U.S. Dist. Ct. (no dist.) Iowa. Assoc. Qualley & Nelson, Sioux City, Iowa, 1974-76; ptnr. Laughlin, Peterson & Lang and predecessor firms, Omaha, 1976—; instr. law Creighton U., Omaha, 1981-82. Served to 1st lt. U.S. Army, 1974. Mem. Nebr. Bar Assn., Iowa Bar Assn. Democrat. Roman Catholic. Avocation: tennis. Real property, Federal civil litigation, Contracts commercial. Home: 12235 Farnam St Omaha NE 68154 Office: Laughlin Peterson & Lang 11306 Davenport St Omaha NE 68154

LANG, JOE ALLEN, lawyer; b. Memphis, Oct. 7, 1944; s. Harry and Eula Fern (Deyoe) L.; m. Teresa Ann Richards, Mar. 23, 1985. BA, Sterling Coll., 1966; MA, Emporia State U., 1972; JD, Washburn U., 1977. Bar: Kans. 1977, U.S. Dist. Ct. Kans. 1977, U.S. Ct. Appeals (10th cir.) 1979. Tchr. Luray and Fairfield High Schs., Luray and Langdon, Kans., 1966-74; research atty. Kans. Supreme Ct., Topeka, 1977-79; asst. atty. City of Wichita, Kans., 1980—; com. chmn. Nat. Inst. Mcpl. Law Officers, Washington, 1985-86. Del. Kans. Rep. Conv., 1976, 84; deacon First Presbyn. Ch., Wichita, 1983-85; Rep. precinct commiteeman, 1986—. Served with U.S. Army, 1967-69, Vietnam. Mem. ABA, Kans. Bar Assn., Wichita Bar Assn., City Atty. Assn. Kans. (com. chmn.). Presbyterian. Avocations: photography, stamp collecting, skiing, ham radio. Local government, Administrative and regulatory. Home: 1836 N Reca Wichita KS 67212 Office: City of Wichita Law Dept 455 N Main 13th Floor Wichita KS 67202

LANG, JOSEPH HAGEDORN, lawyer; b. Cleve., Sept. 30, 1937; s. Carl Frederick and Martha Clotilda (Hagedorn) L.; m. Elsie A. O'Berry, Aug. 8, 1965; children: Joseph H. Jr., Robert Warren, James O'Berry. AA, St. Petersburg Jr. Coll., 1959; BA, Duke U., 1961; JD, U. Fla., 1963. Bar: Fla. 1964, U.S. Dist. Ct. (mid. dist.) Fla. 1965, U.S. Ct. Appeals (5th cir.) 1965, U.S. Supreme Ct. 1975. Assoc. Baynard McLeod & Overton, St. Petersburg, Fla., 1964-69; ptnr. Baynard McLeod & Lang, St. Petersburg, 1969-80; pres. Baynard McLeod & Lang, P.C., St. Petersburg, 1980—. Active Police Community Council, Community Alliance; chmn. bd. dirs. St. Petersburg Jr. Coll., Pinellas County, 1983—. Served with USNR. Named Sch. Adv. Com. Mem. of Yr. Mem. Fla. Bar Assn., St. Petersburg Bar Assn., St. Petersburg C. of C., Phi Theta Kappa (Disting. Alumni award). Democrat. Roman Catholic. Clubs: Suncoasters, Dragon. Real property, Probate. Office: Baynard McLeod & Lang 669 1st Ave N Saint Petersburg FL 33701

LANG, PAMELA ANN, lawyer; b. New Orleans, Mar. 26, 1953; d. Jacob P. and Hazel M. Lang. BA in Social Ecology, U. Calif., Irvine, 1974; JD, U. Santa Clara, 1977. Bar: Calif. 1977, Wash. 1978, U.S. Dist. Ct. (we. dist.) Wash. 1982, U.S. Ct. Appeals (9th cir.) 1982, U.S. Dist. Ct. (ea. dist.) Wash. 1985. Trial atty. King County Prosecuters Office, Seattle, 1978-82, Safeco Ins. Co., Seattle, 1982-85; assoc. Hallmark, Griffith & Keating, Seattle, 1985—. Mem. ABA, Wash. State Women Lawyers Assn. (v.p. Seattle 1983-84), Seattle King County Bar Assn. (young lawyers coms. 1982-84). State civil litigation, Insurance, Personal injury. Office: Hallmark Griffith & Keating 1615 Seattle Tower Seattle WA 98101

LANG, RICHARD ARNOLD, JR., lawyer; b. New Rochelle, N.Y., Dec. 18, 1938; s. Richard Arnold and Muriel Herold (Goetz) L.; m. Nancy Elizabeth Caravajal, Apr. 12, 1966; children—Richard A., III, Jessica B. B.A., Cornell U., 1960, LL.B., 1964. Bar: N.Y. 1965, U.S. Ct. Appeals (2d cir.) 1972, Vt. 1973, U.S. Dist. Ct. Vt. 1973, Fla. 1981. Law clk. to judge U.S. Ct. Appeals (2d cir.), N.Y.C., 1964-65; assoc. McCutchen, Doyle et al, San Francisco, 1965-67, Whitman, Ransom et al, N.Y.C., 1967-70, Appleton, Rice & Perrin, N.Y.C., 1970-72; ptnr. Samuelson, Portnow et al, Burlington, Vt., 1972-80; Hoff, Wilson, Powell & Lang, Burlington, 1980—. Trustee Fletcher Library, Burlington; mem. Chittenden County Transp. Authority, Burlington. Mem. ABA, Vt. Bar Assn., Chittenden County Bar Assn. Republican. Episcopalian. Banking, Real property, Federal civil litigation. Home: 805 S Prospect St Burlington VT 05401 Office: Hoff Wilson Powell & Lang PC 192 College St Burlington VT 05402

LANG, SCOTT WESLEY, lawyer; b. Oceanside, N.Y., Oct. 25, 1950; s. Richard Lang and Norah (McLean) Pober; m. Marguerite A. Sheehy, Sept. 29, 1973. AB in Polit. Sci., History, Marquette U., 1972; JD, Georgetown U., 1976. Bar: Mass. 1977, U.S. Dist. Ct. Mass. 1979, U.S. Ct. Appeals (1st cir.) 1979, D.C. 1983, U.S. Supreme Ct. 1985. Exec. dir. CRC Dem. Nat. Com., Washington, 1973-78; asst. dist. atty. Bristol County Dist. Attys. Office, New Bedford, Mass., 1978—. Mem. Winograd Commn. Dems., Washington, 1976-78, Dem. Jud. Council, Washington, 1977-81, Hunt Commn., Washington, 1980-81. Mem. ABA, Boston Bar Assn., New Bedford Bar Assn., D.C. Bar Assn., Bristol County Bar Assn. Labor, Entertainment, Personal injury. Office: Lang Straus Xifaras & Bullard 81 Hawthorn St New Bedford MA 02740

LANGAN, KEITH EDWARD, lawyer; b. Kentfield, Calif., July 20, 1955; s. James Robert and Mary E. (Lennon) L.; m. Janice G. Picchi, Feb. 23, 1980; 1 child, Michael. BS, U. San Francisco, 1978; JD, Golden Gate U., 1980. Bar: Calif. 1982, U.S. Dist. Ct. (no. dist.) Calif. 1982. Atty. Calif. Pacific Ins. Service, Petaluma, 1982-83; asst. counsel gen. counsel's office Fireman's Fund Ins. Co., Novato, Calif., 1983-85, assoc. counsel gen. counsel's office, 1985-87; counsel Gen. Counsel's Office, 1987—. Mem. Calif. Bar Assn., Phi Alpha Delta. Insurance. Office: Firemans Fund Ins Co Gen Counsels Office 777 San Marin Dr Novato CA 94998

LANGBEIN, JOHN HARRISS, law educator, lawyer; b. Washington, Nov. 17, 1941; s. I. L. and M. V. (Harriss) L.; m. Kirsti M. Hiekka, June 24, 1973; children: Christopher, Julia, Anne. AB, Columbia U., 1964; LLB, Harvard U., 1968, Cambridge U., 1969; PhD, Cambridge U., 1971. Bar: D.C. 1969, Fla. 1970; barrister-at-law Inner Temple, Eng., 1970. Asst. prof. law U. Chgo., 1971-73, assoc. prof. law, 1973-74, prof. law, 1974-80, Max Pam prof. Am. and fgn. law, 1980—; commr. Nat. Conf. Commrs. on Uniform State Laws. Author: Prosecuting Crime in the Renaissance, 1974, Torture and the Law of Proof: Europe and England in the Ancient Regime, 1977, Comparative Criminal Procedure: Germany, 1977; (with L. Waggoner) Selected Statutes on Trusts and Estates, 1987; contbr. numerous articles on law and legal history and profl. jours. Mem. Nat. Conf. Commrs. on Uniform State Laws. Mem. ABA, Am Coll. Probate Counsel, Am. Law Inst., Am. Soc. Legal History, Am. Hist. Assn., Selden Soc., Gesellschaft fuer Rechtsvergleichung. Republican. Episcopalian. Probate, Legal history, Employee benefits. Office: U Chgo Law Sch 1111 E 60th St Chicago IL 60637

LANGDON, HERSCHEL GARRETT, lawyer; b. Lowry City, Mo., Oct. 6, 1905; s. Isaac Garrett and Della (Park) L.; m. Ethel Virginia Waterson, May 26, 1931 (dec. Apr. 1979); children: Richard G., Ann Virginia (Mrs. Charles Eugene Willoughby Ward); m. Miriam Pickett, May 17, 1982. B.A., U. Iowa, 1930, J.D., 1931. Bar: Iowa 1931. Since practiced in Des Moines; mem. firm Herrick, Langdon & Langdon (and predecessors), 1935—; bd. dirs. Allied Mut. Ins. Co. Fellow Am. Coll. Trial Lawyers, Am. Bar Found.; mem. Am., Iowa, Polk County bar assns., Phi Beta Kappa, Delta Sigma Rho, Phi Delta Pi. Conglist. Club: Mason. Federal civil litigation, General practice, Insurance. Home: 678 49th St Des Moines IA 50312 Office: 1800 Financial Center 7th and Walnut Des Moines IA 50309

LANGDON, RICHARD GARRETT, lawyer; b. Des Moines, July 9, 1936; s. Herschel Garrett and Ethel Virginia (Waterson) L.; m. Julia Houser, Nov. 21, 1958; children—Sarah Ann, John Douglass. A.B., Harvard U., 1958, J.D., 1961. Bar: Iowa 1961, U.S. Dist. Ct. (so. and no. dists.) Iowa 1961, U.S. Ct. Appeals (8th cir.) 1961, U.S. Ct. Appeals (10th cir.) 1982, U.S. Tax Ct. 1972. Assoc. Herrick, Langdon, Sandblom & Belin, Des Moines, 1961-62, ptnr., 1962-66; ptnr. Herrick, Langdon, Belin & Harris, 1966-70, Herrick, Langdon, Belin, Harris, Langdon & Helmick, 1971-78, Herrick, Langdon & Langdon, 1978—; lectr. in field. Recipient Boylston prize Harvard U., 1957. Fellow Am. Coll. Trial Lawyers; mem. ABA, Iowa State Bar Assn., Polk County Bar Assn., Internat. Assn. Def. Counsel, Fedn. Ins. and Corp. Counsel, Iowa Acad. Trial Lawyers. Republican. Clubs: Des Moines, Wakonda, Embassy. Contbr. articles to profl. jours. State civil litigation, Federal civil litigation, Personal injury. Home: 612 Glenview Des Moines IA 50312 Office: 1300 Financial Ctr Des Moines IA 50309

LANGE, C. WILLIAM, lawyer; b. St. Louis, June 15, 1946; s. Carl W. and Marion M. (Guenther) L.; m. Catherine L. Janowiak, June 7, 1981; 1 child, Courtney Anne. BA, Westminster Coll., 1968; MBA, St. Louis U., 1972; JD, Oklahoma City U., 1974. Bar: Mo. 1975, U.S. Dist. Ct. Mo. 1975, U.S. Ct. Appeals (8th cir.) 1986. With claims dept. MFA Ins. Cos., Columbia, Mo., 1968-71; ptnr. Lange & Lange, Cuba, Mo., 1976-81; sole practice Cuba, 1981—; pros. atty. Crawford County (Mo.), 1979-80; city atty. City of Cuba, 1978-80, 82—; prof. mgmt. Maryville Coll., St. Louis, 1974—; instr. East Central Coll., Union, Mo., 1975. Mem. Crawford County Child Welfare Adv. Com., 1979—, pres. 1984—; mem. Crawford County Child Abuse and Neglect Team, 1981—. Served with Air N.G., 1967-74. Mem. ABA, Mo. Bar Assn., 42d Jud. Cir. Bar Assn., St. Louis Met. Bar Assn., Cuba C. of C. Republican. Episcopalian. Lodges: Optimists, Lions. General practice, Family and matrimonial, General corporate. Home: Route 2 Cuba MO 65453 Office: 330 N Franklin Blvd Cuba MO 65453

LANGE, DAVID, legal educator; b. Charleston, Ill., Dec. 7, 1938; s. Charles W.S. and Mary Helen Lange; m. Teresa Tetrick, July 30, 1972; children—David, Adam, Daniel, Jennifer, William. B.S., U. Ill., Urbana, 1960, LL.B., 1964. Bar: Ill. 1964. Pvt. practice Chgo., 1964-71; gen. counsel media task force Nat. Commn. on Violence, Washington, 1968-69; gen. ptnr. Mediamix Prodns., 1970-71; assoc. prof. law Duke U., Durham, N.C., 1971-74; prof. law Duke U., 1974—. Trademark and copyright, Libel. Office: Law Sch Duke U Durham NC 27706

LANGE, FREDERICK EMIL, retired lawyer; b. Washington, May 24, 1908; s. Emil F. and Jane (Austin) L.; A.B., U. Nebr., 1928; J.D., M.P.L., Washington Coll. Law, 1932; m. Leila M. Benedict, Sept. 11, 1930; children—Frederick Emil, David W., James A. Admitted to D.C. bar, 1932, Minn. bar, 1943; examiner U.S. Patent Office, 1929-35; patent lawyer Honeywell, Inc., 1935-63, mgr. Mpls. patent dept., 1954-63; partner firm Dorsey, Marquart, Windhorst, West & Halladay, Mpls., 1965-73; individual practice law, Mpls., 1973-78; ptnr. Kinney & Lange, P.A., Mpls., 1978-86; spl. lectr. patent law U. Minn., 1949-51, Minn. Continuing Legal Edn., 1976. Bd. trustees 1st Unitarian Soc., 1970-71; chmn. Minn. br. World Federalists, 1958-60, nat. exec. com., 1958-64; bd. dirs. Group Health Plan, Inc., 1967-84, 1st v.p., 1975-78; bd. dirs. St. Paul Civic Symphony Assn., 1976-81, Environ. Learning Center, 1977-79; mem. Hennepin Ho. of Dels., 1987—. Minn. Funeral and Meml. Soc. Recipient Distinguished Service award U. Nebr., 1968. Mem. ABA, Minn. Bar Assn. (ho. of dels. 1987—), D.C. Bar Assn., Hennepin County Bar Assn., Am. Patent Law Assn., Minn. Patent Law Assn. (pres. 1954-55), Am. Judicature Soc., Sigma Nu Phi (lord high chancellor 1984-87). Holder U.S. patents. Patent, Trademark and copyright, Federal civil litigation. Home: 1235 Yale Pl Apt 210 Minneapolis MN 55403 Office: 625 4th Ave Suite 1500 Minneapolis MN 55415

LANGE, PAUL KRUSE, lawyer; b. Glens Falls, N.Y., June 26, 1935; s. Gilbert Henry and Emilie Louise (Walker) L.; m. Patricia Dudson, July 9, 1961 (div. Aug. 1980); children: Kyla, Erika, Jason; m. Dora Louise Mancine, Dec. 30, 1982. AB, Brown U., 1957; JD, U. Mich., 1960. Bar: Calif. 1961, U.S. Dist. Ct. (no. dist.) Calif. 1961, N.Y. 1962, U.S. Dist. Ct. (we. dist.) N.Y. 1962. Ptnr. Winchell, connors & Corcoran, Rochester, N.Y., 1965-72, Faraci, Guadagnino, Lange & Johns, Rochester, 1975—; v.p., gen. counsel Pacific Indemnity, Los Angeles, 1972-74. Mem. N.Y. State Bar Assn., Calif. Bar Assn., Monroe County Bar Assn., Assn. Trial Lawyer Am. Democrat. Avocations: music, tennis, art history. Federal civil litigation, State civil litigation. Home: 36 Birch Crescent Rochester NY 14607 Office: Faraci Guadagnino Lange & Johns 45 Exchange St Suite 300 Rochester NY 14614

LANGE, WILLIAM MICHAEL, lawyer; b. Hammond, Ind., Oct. 9, 1946; s. William Frederick L.; 1 child, William Robert. BA, Ind. U., 1968; JD, George Washington U., 1974. Bar: D.C. 1975, Colo. 1977, U.S. Ct. Appeals (D.C. cir.) 1975, U.S. Ct. Appeals (10th cir.) 1977, U.S. Ct. Appeals (5th cir.) 1981, U.S. Ct. Appeals (8th cir.) 1984, U.S. Supreme Ct. 1982. Assoc., Wolf & Case, Washington, 1974-75, J.R. Wolf, Washington, 1975-76; atty. Colo. Interstate Gas Co., Colorado Springs, Colo., 1976-79, sr. atty., 1979-82, gen. atty., 1982-84, asst. gen. counsel, 1984-87; asst. gen. counsel The Coastal Corp., 1985-87; assoc. gen. counsel ANR Pipeline Co, 1986-87; pvt. practice, Washington, 1987—. Served to lt. (j.g.) USN, 1968-71; Vietnam. Democrat. Episcopalian. FERC practice, Federal civil litigation, General corporate. Office: 1050 17th St NW Washington DC 20036

LANGENTHAL, STEPHEN ROGER, lawyer; b. N.Y.C., July 7, 1934; s. Harry H. and Sylvia (Samose) L.; m. Alba Bevacqua, Dec. 12, 1969; 1 child, Carla. BA, NYU, 1956; JD, Columbia U., 1959. Bar: N.Y. 1961, U.S. Supreme Ct. 1972. Atty. N.Y. State Com., N.Y.C., 1960-61; assoc. Johnson & Tannenbaum, N.Y.C., 1961-64; atty. legal dept. Warner Bros.-Seven Arts Inc., N.Y.C., 1964-70; gen. counsel Avco Embassy Pictures, N.Y.C., 1970-75; v.p., east coast counsel Warner Bros. Inc., N.Y.C., 1975—. Served with USAR, 1959-65. Mem. ABA. Jewish. Avocations: photography, travel, book collecting. Entertainment. Office: Warner Bros Inc 75 Rockefeller Plaza New York NY 10019

LANGER, BRUCE ALDEN, lawyer; b. N.Y.C., Mar. 17, 1953; s. Samuel S. and Yvette (Swirsky) L.; m. Bobbi Ann Horowitz, June 11, 1983; 1 child, Andrew Chase. BA summa cum laude with distinction, Boston U., 1975; JD cum laude, Boston U. Sch. Law, 1978. Bar: N.Y. 1979, U.S. Dist. Ct. (so. and ea. dist.) N.Y. 1979, U.S. Tax Ct. 1979, U.S. Ct. Appeals (2d cir.) 1983., U.S. Supreme Ct. 1985. Law intern to presiding justice U.S. Bankruptcy Ct. (ea. dist.) N.Y., summers 1976-77; assoc. atty. Breed Abbott & Morgan, N.Y.C., 1978-81, White & Case, N.Y.C., 1981-84; Fishman Forman & Landau, N.Y.C., 1984-85; mem. Fishman Forman and Langer, 1985-86; mem. Paradise & Alberts, N.Y.C., 1986—. Editor Boston U. Law Rev., 1977-78. Contbg. author: Pensions and Investments, 1979. Harold C. Case Presdl. scholar, 1974-75. Mem. Assn. Bar City of N.Y., N.Y. State Bar Assn. (com. profl. ethics), ABA (sect. internat. law), Assn. Trial Lawyers of Am., Phi Beta Kappa, Phi Alpha Theta. Federal civil litigation, State civil litigation, General corporate. Office: Paradise and Alberts 630 Third Ave New York NY 10017

LANGER, ROBERT MARK, lawyer, educator; b. Norwalk, Conn., Oct. 4, 1948; s. Melvin and Claire (Schnable) L.; m. Shelley Tishler, Dec. 26, 1970; children—Joshua Adam, Jennifer Rebecca. A.B., Franklin and Marshall Coll., 1970; J.D., U. Conn.-West Hartford, 1973. Bar: Conn. 1973, U.S. Dist. Ct. Conn. 1973, U.S. Ct. Appeals (2d cir.) 1975, U.S. Supreme Ct. 1976, U.S. Ct. Appeals (3d cir.) 1984. Asst. atty. gen. in charge antitrust and consumer protection Conn. Atty. Gen.'s Office, Hartford, 1973—; adj. prof. U. Conn. Sch. Bus. Adminstrn. MBA Program, 1979—. Contbr. articles to legal jours., newspapers. Chairperson, Our Children's Ctr., West Hartford, 1983—. Mem. Conn. Bar Assn. (chairperson antitrust sect. 1979-80), Acad. Continuing Profl. Devel. Antitrust, Administrative and regulatory. Office: Conn Atty Gen's Office 30 Trinity St Hartford CT 06106

LANGER, SIMON HRIMES, lawyer; b. Tel Aviv, Mar. 16, 1952; came to U.S., 1958; AB in Polit. Sci., U. Calif., Berkeley, 1974; MA in Polit. Sci., U. So. Calif., 1975; JD, Calif. Western Sch. Law, 1978; LLM, Columbia U., 1981. Bar: D.C. 1979, Pa. 1980, U.S. Dist. Ct. (so., no., ea. and cen. dists.) Calif. 1981, Calif. 1982, U.S. Ct. Appeals (9th cir.) 1982, U.S. Tax Ct. 1986. Atty.-advisor U.S. Internat. Trade Commn., Washington, 1979-80; assoc. Kindel and Anderson, Los Angeles, 1981-82; sr. assoc. Frandzel and Share, Beverly Hills, Calif., 1982-85; ptnr. Arthur M. Wilkof, Los Angeles, 1985-86, Stone & Wolfe, Los Angeles, 1986—. Exec. editor Am. Soc. Internat. Law Jour., 1977, editor-in-chief, 1978; contbr. articles to profl. jours. Charles A. Dana Found. fellow, Am. Soc. Internat. Law, 1978-79. Mem. ABA, Pa. Bar Assn., D.C. Bar Assn., Los Angeles County Bar Assn. Private international, Federal civil litigation, State civil litigation. Home: 1815 Franklin Canyon Dr Beverly Hills CA 90210 Office: Stone & Wolfe 2121 Ave of the Stars Suite 1530 Los Angeles CA 90067

LANGEVOORT, DONALD CARL, law educator; b. Paterson, N.J., Feb. 20, 1951; s. Garrett William and Kathleen Marjorie (Schneider) L.; m. Joni Jackson, Aug. 10, 1985. BA, U. Va., 1973; JD, Harvard U., 1976. Bar: D.C. 1976, U.S. Supreme Ct. 1980. Assoc. Wilmer, Cutler & Pickering, Washington, 1976-78; spl. counsel SEC, Washington, 1978-81; assoc. prof. law, assoc. dean Vanderbilt U., Nashville, 1981—. Author: Insider Trading Handbook, 1986, 2d edit., 1987. Legal education, Securities, Banking. Home: 2012 Galbraith Dr Nashville TN 37215 Office: Vanderbilt U Sch Law Nashville TN 37240

LANGFORD, JAMES TAFFORD, lawyer; b. N.Y.C., June 1, 1943; s. James Tafford and Josephine (Dorr) L.: m. Karen Smith, Aug. 12, 1972; 1 child, Katherine Cecile. AB, Fordham U., 1967; JD, Emory U., 1974. Bar: Ga. 1974, U.S. Dist. Ct. (no. dist.) Ga. 1975, U.S. Dist. Ct. (mid. and so. dists.) Ga. 1978. Staff lawyer Ga. Nurses Assn., Atlanta, 1974; assoc. Jacobs & JacobsP.A., Atlanta, 1975-79; ptnr. Jacobs and Langford PA, Atlanta, 1979—; adj. instr. labor law Ga. State U., 1980-81, grad. sch. bus. , 1984. Pres. Westminster-Milmar Home Owners Assn., Atlanta, 1984—; mem. instl. rev. bd.sch. nursing Emory U., 1984—; committeeman Fulton County Dem. Party, Atlanta, 1984—. Mem. ABA, Ga. Bar Assn. (sec. labor law sect. 1985-86), Atlanta Bar Assn. (sec. labor law sect. 1978-79, v.p. 1979-80, pres. 1980-81). Roman Catholic. Labor, Pension, profit-sharing, and employee benefits. Home: 3028 Westminster Circle Atlanta GA 30327 Office: Jacobs and Langford PA 134 Peachtree St Suite 1000 Atlanta GA 30303

LANGLEY, DOROTHY ANN, lawyer; b. Brockton, Mass., July 8, 1953; d. John J. and Elinore Marie (Demski) L.; m. Bryan Stephen O'Neill, June 22, 1985. BA, Boston U., 1979; JD, Washington U., St. Louis, 1982. Bar: Mass. 1982, U.S. Dist. Ct. Mass. 1983, U.S. Tax Ct. 1984, U.S. Ct. Mil. Appeals 1984. Assoc. Law Offices of Albert E. Grady, Brockton, 1982; chief civil law judge adv. office USAF, Tyndall AFB, Fla., 1983-84, area def. counsel 2d cir., 1985—. Contbr. articles to profl. jours. Served to capt. USAF, 1983—. Boston U. Trustee scholar, 1977-79, Finkelnburg scholar Washington U., 1981. Mem. ABA, Panhandles Writers Guild. Democrat. Roman Catholic. Labor, Military. Home: Rt 3 Box 1366 Panama City FL 32405

LANGLEY, EARNEST LEE, lawyer; b. Sweetwater, Tex., July 14, 1920; s. E. Lee and Willie (Pipkin) L.; m. Helen E. Richter, Dec. 28, 1941; children: Suzanne Wall, Barbara Langley Dorff, Camille Sproule, Carolyn Darden. BA, Tex. Tech U., 1946; JD, U. Tex., 1951. Bar: Tex. 1950, U.S. Dist. Ct. (no. dist.) Tex. 1952, U.S. Ct. Appeals (5th cir.) 1954, U.S. Ct. Claims 1957, U.S. Supreme Ct. 1959, U.S. Dist. Ct. (we. dist.) Tex. 1965, U.S. Tax Ct. 1967, U.S. Ct. Appeals (10th cir.) 1979, U.S. Ct. Appeals (11th cir.) 1981. Ptnr. Witherspoon, Aikin & Langley, Hereford, Tex., 1952—; atty. City of Hereford, 1954—; bd. dirs. First Nat. Bank, Hereford, 1957—. Editor U. Tex. Law Rev., 1950. Served to capt. U.S. Army, 1942-46, ETO. Fellow Tex. Bar Found., Am. Coll. Probate Counsel; mem. ABA, Assn. Trial Lawyers Am., Am. Judicature Soc., Order of Coif, Phi Delta Phi. Methodist. Club: Hereford Country (Pres.). Lodge: Masons. Banking, Federal civil litigation, General practice. Home: 502 Star St Hereford TX 79045 Office: Box 1818 Hereford TX 79045

LANGLIE, ARTHUR SHERIDAN, lawyer; b. Seattle, June 28, 1930; s. Arthur Bernard and Evelyn Pansy (Baker) L.; m. Jane Frances LeCocq, June 15, 1953; children: Karin Evelyn (Langlie) Glass, Emily Frances, Arthur Kristian. AB, Princeton U., 1952; LLB, U. Wash., 1958. Bar: Wash. 1959, U.S. Supreme Ct. 1964. Assoc. McMicken, Rupp & Schweppe, Seattle, 1959-65; ptnr. Langlie & Praeger, Seattle, 1966—; gen. counsel Am. Plywood Assn., Tacoma, 1966—; exec. bd. dirs. Presbyn. Ministries, Inc., Seattle, 1981—. Chmn. Salvation Army Adv. Bd., Seattle, 1972-73; pres. The Lakeside Sch., Seattle, 1969-71; bd. dirs. Coast Guard Acad. Found., New London, Conn., 1980-86. Served to capt. USCG, 1952-82. Mem. Seattle-King County Bar Assn. (chmn. civil rights com. 1966-67), Am. Laminators Assn. (exec. bd. dirs. 1984—). Republican. Club: Washington Athletic. Avocations: skiing, jogging, piloting. Antitrust, General corporate, Probate. Home: 5718-64th Ave NE Seattle WA 98105 Office: 419 Norton Bldg Seattle WA 98104-1584

LANG-MIERS, ELIZABETH ANN, lawyer; b. Mpls., Nov. 26, 1950; s. Ervin J. Jr. and Jacqueline H. (Kratky) Lang; m. Jeb. S. Miers, July 29, 1978; 1 child, Ellen Lang Miers. BA, U. Mo., 1972, JD, 1975. Bar: Mo. 1975, Tex. 1977, U.S. Ct. Appeals (5th cir.), U.S. Supreme Ct. Law clk. to presiding justice Mo. Supreme Ct., Jefferson City, 1975-76; dir. Locke, Purnell, Boren, Laney & Neely, Dallas, 1976—. Mem. editorial bd. Mo. Law Review. Mem. Dallas County Med. Soc. Auxiliary. Recipient Am. Jurisprudence awards 1973, 74. Fellow Tex. Bar Found.; mem. ABA, Tex. Bar Assn., Dallas Bar Assn. (chmn. media relations com. 1985, sec.-treas., bd. dirs. 1987), Tex. Young Lawyers Assn. Episcopalian. Office: Locke Purnell et al Republic Nat Bank Tower Dallas TX 75201

LANGROCK, PETER FORBES, lawyer; b. N.Y.C., Feb. 2, 1938; s. Frank Langrock; m. Joann Murphy, July 4, 1960; children: Frank, Catherine, Eric. BA, U. Chgo., 1958, JD, 1960. Bar: Vt. 1960, U.S. Supreme Ct. 1966. State's atty. Addison County, Vt., 1960-65; sr. ptnr. Landrock, Sperry, Parker & Wool, Middlebury, Vt., 1965—; commr. Nat. Conf. Commrs. on Uniform State Laws. Chmn. Vt. Breeders Stake Bd., 1984—. Mem. ABA (chmn. individual rights and responsibilities sect. 1980-81, del. 1982-83, ho. of dels. 1984—), Am. Law Inst. Avocations: horse breeding and raising, fishing, hunting. Criminal, State civil litigation, General practice. Home: RD Lower Plains Rd Salisbury VT 05769 Office: PO Drawer 351 Middlebury VT 05753

LANGSLET, JOHN LORING, lawyer; b. Portland, Oreg., July 16, 1944; s. Otto Halvor and Lucile Marion (Hyde) L.; m. Tylene M. Evans, June 22, 1984; children—Katherine Ann, Laura Amy, Margaret Elizabeth, William Loring. B.S., Portland State U., 1966; J.D., U. Calif.-Berkeley, 1972. Bar: Oreg. 1972, U.S. Dist. Ct. Oreg. 1972, U.S. Ct. Appeals (9th cir.) 1973, U.S. Ct. Claims 1975, U.S Supreme Ct. 1984. Assoc. firm Martin, Bischoff, Templeton, Biggs & Ericsson, Portland, 1972-75, ptnr., 1975—. Served to 1st lt. USMC, 1966-69; Vietnam. Recipient Am. Jurisprudence awards, U. Calif., 1969-72. Mem. Oreg. State Bar Assn., Assn. Trial Lawyers Am., Lawyer Pilots Bar Assn., Multnomah County Mar Assn., Am. Judicature Soc., ABA, Classic Car Am., Packard Portland (pres. 1974-76), Order of Coif. Democrat. Roman Catholic. State civil litigation, Contracts commercial, Consumer commercial. Home: 13550 NW Pettygrove St Portland OR 97229 Office: Martin Bischoff Templeton Biggs Ericsson 2908 First Interstate Bank Tower Portland OR 97201

LANGSON, SETH HARRIS, lawyer; b. N.Y.C., Sept. 12, 1951; s. Jerome and Evelyn (Dichter) L. BA cum laude, Hobart Coll., 1973; JD, Boston Coll., 1976. Bar: Mass. 1977, N.C. 1981. Assoc. Springer & Langson, Boston, 1978-79, Harris, Bumgardner & Carpenter, Gastonia, N.C., 1980-83; sole practice Charlotte, N.C., 1983-85; ptnr. Karro, Sellers & Langson, Charlotte, 1985—; instr. Cen. Piedmont Community Coll., Charlotte, 1984—. Mem. Assn. Trial Lawyers' Am., Nat. Orgn. of Social Security Claimants Representation, N.C. Acad. Trial Lawyers (pub. service com. 1986, patron), N.C. State Bar Assn., Mass. Bar Assn. Democrat. Personal injury, State civil litigation, Insurance. Office: Karro Sellers & Langson 428 E 4th St Suite 101 Charlotte NC 28202

LANGSTAFF, JAMES POPE, lawyer; b. Albany, Ga., Apr. 28, 1956; s. Robert Burch and Calista Mary (Pope) L. AB, Duke U., 1978; student, U. Va. Law Sch., 1979-80; JD, Yale U., 1982. Bar: Ga. 1982, U.S. Dist. Ct. (no. dist.) Ga. 1983, N.Y. 1984, U.S. Dist. Ct. (so. dist.) N.Y. 1986. Assoc. King & Spalding, Atlanta, 1982-84, Cravath, Swaine & Moore, N.Y.C., 1984-86, Langstaff & Plowden, Albany, 1986—. Mem. ABA, Ga. State Bar, N.Y. State Bar Assn. Federal civil litigation, Antitrust, Public utilities. Office: Langstaff & Plowden Albany GA 31707

LANGSTON, HOMER ANTHONY, JR., lawyer; b. Coal Hil, Ark., July 15, 1937; s. Homer Anthony and Orilla (Reeves) L.; m. Anita Langston, July 22, 1964 (div. 1974); children: David Mark, Carol Michelle. BA, Coll. Ozarks, 1959; JD, U. Ark., 1962. Bar: Tex. 1965, Ark. 1962. Asst. atty. City of Dallas, 1965-66; asst. v.p. Zale Corp., Dallas, 1966-74; counsel Deal Devel. Co., Dallas, 1974-75; asst. gen. counsel Tex. Pacific Oil Co., Dallas, 1975-78; counsel Hunt-Stevens Investors, Dallas, 1978-81; asst. gen. counsel Southland Fin. Corp., Dallas, 1981—. Bd. dirs. Dallas Free Med. Clinic, 1973-74; bd. dirs., coach North Dallas C. of C. Soccer Assn., 1975-78; Dem. dist. del., Dallas, 1984, 86. Served with USNR, 1955-63. Mem. Ark. Bar Assn., Tex. Bar Assn. Baptist. Avocations: art, sketching. Real property, Oil and gas leasing, General corporate. Home: 9968 Mixon Dallas TX 75220 Office: Southland Fin Corp 5215 N O'Connor Blvd Suite 1400 Irving TX 75039

LANGUM, DAVID JOHN, law educator, historian; b. Oakland, Calif., Oct. 24, 1940; s. John Kenneth and Virginia Anne (deMattos) L.; m. Bernadette M. Williams, 1970 (div. 1978); m. JoAnne Marie Adams, Mar. 2, 1981; children—Virginia Eileen, John David. A.B., Dartmouth Coll., 1962; J.D., Stanford U., 1965; M.A. in History, San Jose State U., 1976; LL.M. in Legal History, U. Mich., 1981, S.J.D. in Legal History, 1985. Bar: Calif. 1966, Mich. 1981, U.S. Supreme Ct. 1972. Research clk. Calif. Ct. Appeals, San Francisco, 1965-66; assoc. Dunne, Phelps & Mills, San Francisco, 1966-68; ptnr. Christenson, Hedemark, Langum & O'Keefe, San Jose, Calif., 1968-78; adj. prof. Lincoln U. Sch. Law, 1968-78; prof. law Detroit Coll. Law, 1978-83; prof. Old Coll. Sch. Law, Reno, Nev., 1983-85, dean, 1983-84; prof Cumberland Sch. Law Samford U., Birmingham, 1985—. Author: Law in the West, 1985, Law and Community on the Mexican California Frontier, 1987. Mem. House of Flag, pro bono litigation, San Francisco, 1973-76; past pres. Victorian Preservation Assn., Santa Clara County, Calif. Mem. Am. Soc. for Legal History, Orgn. Am. Historians, Western History Assn. (Bolton award 1978). Contbr. articles on law and history to profl. jours. Legal history, Evidence. Office: Cumberland Sch Law 800 Lakeshore Dr Birmingham AL 35229

LANGWAY, RICHARD MERRITT, bank holding company executive; b. N.Y.C., May 31, 1939; s. Francis E. and Mary M. L.; m. Jean Olson, Mar. 21, 1964; children—Merritt, Peter. A.B., Lafayette Coll., Easton, Pa., 1961; LL.B., Columbia U., 1964. Bar: N.Y. 1966, N.J. 1970, Ga. 1978. Assoc. firm Ide & Haigney, N.Y.C., 1966-70; chief criminal div. Office U.S. Atty. Dist. N.J., 1970-73; gen. counsel Midlantic Banks Inc., Edison, N.J., 1973-78, First Atlanta Corp., Atlanta, 1978—; sec. First Wachovia Corp., 1985—. Served with USAR, 1964-66, Vietnam. Decorated Army Commendation medal; recipient Spl. Achievement award Dept. Justice, 1971. Mem. ABA, Ga. Bar Assn., Bar Assn. City N.Y. General corporate, Banking. Address: 2 Peachtree St Atlanta GA 30383

LANHAM, CHARLES WARREN, lawyer; b. Cumberland, Md., Jan. 18, 1922; s. Charles Warren and Mary Shaw (Rawlings) L.; m. Nora Olivia Sherertz, Dec. 6, 1944; children—Charles Lamar, Eleanor Kathryn Lanham Bartley, Ann Elizabeth Lanham Cardwell. B.S. in Mech. Engring., Duke U., 1943; J.D., Georgetown U., 1951. Bar: D.C. 1951, U.S. Dist. Ct. D.C. 1951, U.S. Ct. Appeals (D.C. cir.) 1951, U.S. Ct. Customs and Patent Appeals 1951. Patent examiner U.S. Patent Office, Washington, 1946-63, primary examiner, 1963-65, supervisory primary examiner, 1965-79. Scoutmaster Boy Scouts Am., Silver Spring, Md, 1951-61; lay leader Good Shepherd Methodist Ch., Silver Spring, 1951-54, Glenmont Meth. Ch., Wheaton, Md., 1963-71; del. Balt. Ann. Conf., Meth. Ch., 1977-79; active Fla. Guardian Ad Litem Program. Served to lt. USN, 1944-46; PTO. Recipient Bronze medal award U.S. Dept. Commerce, 1975. Mem. Patent Office Soc. (exec. com. 1965), Washington Patent Lawyers Club (treas. 1952). Republican. Patent. Home: 330 Cornell Dr Daytona Beach FL 32018

LANHAM, SAMUEL WILBUR, JR., lawyer; b. Alexandria, Va., Dec. 13, 1951; s. Samuel W. and Georgia Mae (Read) L.; m. Stephanie Taylor Laite, Aug. 11, 1979; children: Samuel III, Andrew. BA in Govt., Coll. William and Mary, 1975; JD, Wake Forest U., 1980. Bar: Maine 1980, U.S. Dist. Ct. Maine 1981. Law clk. to presiding justice Supreme Jud. Ct. Maine, Portland, 1980-81; assoc. Mitchell & Stearns, Bangor, Maine, 1981-84; ptnr. Cuddy & Lanham, Bangor, 1984—; bd. dirs. Wellspring Inc., Bangor. Vice chmn. Penobscot County Rep. Com.; mem. Bangor Rep. City Com., 1983—; chmn. Bangor Commn. Commemorate Bicentennial of U.S. Constn. Named one of Outstanding Young Men of Am. U.S. Jaycees, 1980. Mem. Assn. Trial Lawyers Am., Maine Trial Lawyers Assn., Christian Legal Soc. Episcopalian. Avocations: swimming, flying, music. Federal civil litigation, State civil litigation, Insurance. Home: 30 Blackstone St Bangor ME 04401 Office: Cuddy & Lanham 27 State St Bangor ME 04401

LANIER, A(LFRED) CHRISTIAN, III, lawyer; b. Nashville, Mar. 24, 1951; s. Alfred Christian Jr. and Mary Louise (Owens) L.; m. Pamela Grace Rocke, Aug. 15, 1981. BA, Vanderbilt U., 1973; JD, Memphis State U., 1976. Bar: Tenn. 1976. Assoc. Noone, Stringer & Assocs., Chattanooga, 1977-81; sole practice Chattanooga, 1981—. State chmn. Tenn. Fedn. Young Reps., 1985—, E. Tenn. vice-chmn., 1985. Recipient Individual Devel. for Chattanooga Jaycees award, U.S. Jaycees, 1980, Programming Area-Sweepstakes award, U.S. Jaycees, 1981. Mem. ABA (taxation, internat. law, labor and employment law and litigation sects.), Tenn. Bar Assn., Chattanooga Bar Assn., Assn. Trial Lawyers Am., Chattanooga Jaycees (pres. 1981-82). Methodist. Club: Toastmasters (v.p. Chattanooga 1986). Avocations: piano, photography. Home: 1816 Mountain Bay Dr Hixson TN 37343 Office: 615 Lindsay St Suite 150 Chattanooga TN 37402

LANIER, DAVID WILLIAM, judge, farmer; b. Newbern, Tenn., Nov. 16, 1934; s. James Parker and Robbye Azelle (Sullivan) L.; m. Mary Joan Mills, Dec. 2, 1962; children—Leigh Anne, Robbye Claire. LL.B., U. Tenn., 1958. Bar: Tenn. 1959, U.S. Dist. Ct. (we. dist.) Tenn. 1960. Sole practice, Dyersburg, Tenn., 1959-82; mayor City of Dyersburg, 1966-80; judge, circuit and chancery, law and equity cts., also juvenile and probate cts. State of Tenn., Dyersburg, 1982—. Del. Constl. Conv. Nashville, 1959; alderman City of Dyersburg, 1964-65; chmn. Dyer County Dem. Exec. Com., Dyersburg, 1968-72. Served with Air N.G., 1959-65. Mem. Dyer County Bar Assn. (pres., v.p., sec. treas. 1959-66), Tenn. Bar Assn. Mem. Ch. of Christ. Lodges: Rotary, Lions, Moose, Hess, Shriners. Home: 2117 Starlight Dr Dyersburg TN 38024 Office: Courthouse Room 107 Dyersburg TN 38024

LANIER, JAMES OLANDA, lawyer, banker, state legislator; b. Newbern, Tenn., Sept. 8, 1931; s. James P. and Robbye S. L.; m. Carolyn Holland, June 1, 1950; children: James E., Kay Lanier Berkley, Amy Lanier Whitnel. BS, Memphis State U., 1955, JD, 1969. Bar: Tenn. 1969, U.S. Ct. Appeals (6th cir.) 1969, U.S. Supreme Ct. 1975. Prin., James O. Lanier & Assocs., Dyersburg, Tenn., 1969—; pres. Freightmasters, Inc., Union City, Tenn., Dyer County atty., 1973-79, 83—; pres., chmn. bd. Dukedom Bank, Dukedom, Tenn., 1979-82; chmn., hearing officer Tenn. Malpractice Rev. Bd. Commr. Dyer County Levee and Drainage Dist., Dyersburg; chief referee Dyer County Juvenile Ct., 1984—; mem. Tenn. Ho. of Reps., 1959-63, 69-81, Ho. of Dels., 1983—; chmn. Com. on Legis., 1985—, Tenn. Tollway Authority, 1975-79; statewide campaign coordinator Gov. Lamar Alexander, 1978; chmn. 8th Congl. Dist. Dem. Convention, 1972; dir. Memphis State U. Nat. Alumni Assn., 1976-80. Mem. Dyer County Bar Assn., Tenn. Bar Assn. (del.), ABA, Am. Trial Lawyers Assn., Tenn. Trial Lawyers Assn., Dyer County C. of C., Sigma Delta Kappa, Kappa Sigma. Methodist. Clubs: Dyersburg Country, Moose. General practice, Legislative, Personal injury. Home: Route 4 Box 349 Dyersburg TN 38024 Office: 208 N Mill Ave PO Box 742 Dyersburg TN 38024

LANIER, ROBERT SIMMONS, JR., lawyer; b. Statesboro, Pa., May 2, 1952; s. Robert Simmons and Doris Mae (Holmes) L. BS, Ga. So. U., 1974; JD with honors, John Marshall Sch. of Law, 1979. Bar: Ga. 1979, U.S. Dist. Ct. (so. dist.) Ga., U.S. Ct. Appeals, U.S. Supreme Ct. Pub. defender Ogeechee Juvenile Ct., Statesboro, 1979-85; sole practice Statesboro, 1979—. Aide to Rep. Ronald (Bo) Ginn, Washington, 1977. Mem. ABA, Ogeechee

Bar Assn. (pres. 1979-81), Assn. Trial Lawyers Am., Ga. Assn. Criminal Def. Lawyers. Avocations: skiing, running, golf, tennis. Criminal, State civil litigation, Family and matrimonial. Office: 9 Oak St PO Box 195 Statesboro GA 30458

LANKENAU, JOHN CLAUSEN, lawyer; b. Germantown, N.Y., July 9, 1928; s. Walter Henry and Lillie Marvene (Jurges) L.; m. Alison Lanckton, Sept. 2, 1965; children: Catherine Alison, Amy Barbara-Lillie, Christine Rebecca. BEE with honors, Cornell U., 1952, JD, 1955; LLM in Taxation, NYU, 1976. Bar: N.Y. 1955, U.S. Ct. Appeals (2d cir.) 1958, U.S. Supreme Ct. 1960, U.S. Tax Ct. 1975. Asst. U.S. atty. for so. dist. N.Y., N.Y.C., 1955-60; assoc. Gilbert, Segal & Young, N.Y.C., 1960-65; ptnr. Lankenau Kovner & Bickford, and predecessor, N.Y.C., 1965—. Chmn. N.Y.C. Adv. Commn. for Cultural Affairs 1979-84; bd. dirs. Javits Conv. Ctr. Operating Corp. 1979—. Served with USN, 1946-48. Mem. N.Y. State Bar Assn., Assn. Bar. City of N.Y. Democrat. Episcopalian. Club: Rockefeller Ctr. Lunch (N.Y.C.). Trademark and copyright, Federal and state civil litigation, Publishing. Home: 20 W 86th St Apt 10A New York NY 10024 Office: 30 Rockefeller Plaza Suite 4320 New York NY 10112-0150

LANPHEAR, MARTHA JEAN, lawyer; b. Wichita Falls, Tex., Jan. 28, 1944; d. Clarence Ernest and Kathern Martha (Golden) Eldridge; m. Thomas Joseph Lanphear, Jan. 5, 1974; children—Kathern Eileen, Laura Patricia. A.B., U. Mich., 1965; J.D., George Washington U., 1977. Bar: Va. 1977. Personnel specialist CSC, Washington, 1966-72, appeals officer, 1972-79; appeals officer, atty. Merit Systems Protection Bd., 1979-80, acting regional dir., Washington, 1982, hearing officer, 1980-86, adminstv. judge, 1986—. Recipient Performance award Merit Systems Protection Bd., 1982, 84, 85. Personnel law, Labor, Administrative and regulatory. Office: Merit Systems Protection Bd 5203 Leesburg Pike Suite 1109 Falls Church VA 22041

LANS, DEBORAH EISNER, lawyer; b. N.Y.C., Oct. 26, 1949; d. Asher Bob and Barbara (Eisner) L. A.B. magna cum laude, Smith Coll., 1971; J.D. cum laude, Boston U., 1974. Bar: N.Y. 1975, U.S. Dist. Ct. (so. and ea. dists.) N.Y. 1975, U.S. Ct. Appeals (2d cir.) 1975, U.S. Supreme Ct. 1983. Assoc. Lans Feinberg & Cohen, N.Y.C., 1975-80, ptnr., 1980-84; ptnr. Morrison Cohen & Singer, N.Y.C., 1984—. Mem. Am. Arbitration Assn. (comml. panel arbitrators 1984—), Assn. Bar City N.Y. (chmn. young lawyers com. 1981-83, joint com. fee disputes, 1982, judiciary com. 1984-85, exec. com. 1985—), N.Y. State Bar Assn. (ho. of dels. 1984—), N.Y. Bar Found. Federal civil litigation, State civil litigation. Office: Morrison Cohen & Singer 110 E 59th St New York NY 10022

LANSCHE, JOHN ELMER, lawyer; b. Memphis, Apr. 4, 1944; s. Francis Elmer and Virginia (Andrews) L.; m. Barbara Nexsen, Dec. 30, 1972; children: John E., William N. AB, U. N.C., 1966, JD, 1969. Bar: N.C. 1969, U.S. Dist. Ct. (ea. dist.) N.C. 1973. Sole practice Adam, Lancaster et al, Raleigh, N.C., 1969-73; asst. U.S. atty. Dept. Justice, Raleigh, 1973-74; dep. sec. N.C. Dept. Revenue, Raleigh, 1974-76; asst. gen. counsel Duke Power Co., Charlotte, N.C., 1977-86, assoc. gen. counsel, 1987—. Mem. ABA, N.C. Bar Assn. Republican. Presbyterian. Avocations: swimming, music. Environment, FERC practice, Administrative and regulatory. Office: Duke Power Co 422 S Church St Charlotte NC 28242

LANTIER, JAMES DANIEL, lawyer; b. N.Y.C., Mar. 20, 1947; s. James David and Jane Veronica (O'Connor) L.; m. Mary Eileen Hayes, May 17, 1975; children: Gregory, Meghan. BA, Boston Coll., 1969; JD, Syracuse U., 1973. Bar: N.Y. 1974, U.S. Dist. Ct. (no. dist.) N.Y. 1975. Assoc. Coulter & Fraser, Syracuse, 1973-75; asst. dist. atty. Onondaga County, Syracuse, 1975-82; ptnr. Smith & Sovik, Syracuse, 1982—. Pres. Boston Coll. Club of N.Y., Syracuse, 1980-86. Mem. ABA, N.Y. State Bar Assn., Onondaga County Bar Assn. Avocation: amateur theater. State civil litigation. Home: 5170 Skyline Dr Syracuse NY 13207 Office: Smith & Sovik 472 S Salina St Syracuse NY 13202

LANTZ, CHARLES JEFFERY, lawyer, city government official; b. Detroit, June 24, 1947; s. James A. and Eileen W. L.; m. Jacqueline Lekisch, Dec. 28, 1972; children: Leslie, Jennifer, Andrea. BA, Kenyon Coll., 1969; JD, Am. U., 1972. Bar: N.Y. 1973, Va. 1973, Ohio 1975, U.S. Dist Ct. (so. dist.) Ohio 1975, U.S. Ct. Appeals (2d cir.) 1975, U.S. Supreme Ct. 1977. Legis. asst. to U.S. Congressman John Ashbrook, Washington, 1966-69; instr. Mt. Vernon Coll., Washington, 1970; dir. Drug Offenders Rights Commn., Washington, 1971-72; trial atty. Legal Aid Soc. N.Y.C. and Westchester County, N.Y.C., 1972-75; ptnr. Lantz, Lantz & Lipp, Lancaster, Ohio, 1975—; pres. Lancaster City Council, 1984—, councilman at large, 1977-84; mem. Bd. Commrs. Grievances of Supreme Ct. Ohio, 1981-86, chmn. 1986, chmn. complaint rev. bd. 1987; spl. counsel Atty. Gen. Ohio, Columbus, 1983—. Chmn. His. Lancaster Commn., 1977—; mem. Community Improvement Corp., Lancaster, 1986. Mem. Assn. Trial Lawyers Am., Ohio Acad. Trial Lawyers, Va. Bar Assn., Ohio Bar Assn. (bd. govs. realty sect. 1985—). Jewish. Criminal, Family and matrimonial, Jurisprudence. Office: Lantz Lantz & Lipp 123 S Broad St Lancaster OH 43130

LANTZ, WILLIAM CHARLES, lawyer; b. Rochester, Minn., July 3, 1946; s. Charles E. and Doris (Greenwood) L.; m. Vicki L. Erickson, May 17, 1972; children: Charles Eric, Andrew William. BA, Hamline U., 1968; JD, U. Minn., 1971. Bar: Minn. 1971. From assoc. to ptnr. Dorsey & Whitney, Rochester, 1975—. Served to lt. JAGC, USNR, 1971-75. Mem. Minn. Bar Assn., Olmsted Bar Assn. Methodist. Lodge: Kiwanis. Real property, Landlord-tenant, Contracts commercial. Home: 807 Sierra Ln NE Rochester MN 55904 Office: Dorsey & Whitney 340 First National Bank Bldg PO Box 848 Rochester MN 55903

LANZA, SHELLEY BROWN, lawyer; b. Toledo, July 19, 1956; d. Charles Leo and Rose (Milano) Brown; m. Gregg Lanza, July 26, 1980; 1 child, Angelina. BA in Acctg. summa cum laude, Adrian Coll., 1977; JD, U. Calif., Berkeley, 1982. Bar: Ohio 1982. Assoc. Vorys, Sater, Seymour & Pease, Columbus, Ohio, 1982-86; counsel, mgr. legal dept. Honda of Am. Mfg. Inc., Marysville, Ohio, 1986—. Bd. dirs. Delaware (Ohio) Humane Soc. (v.p. 1986), Marysville Day Care Ctr.; pres. Child Conservation League, Powell, Ohio, 1986. Mem. ABA, Ohio Bar Assn., Columbus Bar Assn., Alpha Chi. Republican. Roman Catholic. Avocations: racquetball, softball, teaching volleyball. General corporate, Real property, Construction. Home: 4530 Millwater Dr Powell OH 43065 Office: Honda of Am Mfg Inc 24000 US Rt 33 Marysville OH 43040-1008

LANZO, JAMES R., lawyer; b. Youngstown, Ohio, Dec. 23, 1944; s. Louis and Josephine Lanzo; m. Kristine Primavera, July 25, 1970; children: James E., Jason L., Gina Marie. BE, Youngstown U., 1966; JD, Akron U., 1971. Bar: Ohio 1972, U.S. Dist. Ct. (no. dist.) Ohio 1974. Sole practice Struthers, Ohio, 1973—; dir. law City of Struthers, 1976—; village solicitor, Lowellville, Ohio, 1975—. Mem. ABA, Ohio Bar Assn., Mahiming County Bar Assn., Ohio Acad. Trial Lawyers. Democrat. Roman Catholic. Office: 32 State St Suite 205 Struthers OH 44471

LAPAYOWKER, ANDREW, lawyer; b. Wilmington, Del., Sept. 19, 1954; s. Marc Spencer and Isabel Rose (Gordy) L.; m. Sarah McCafferty, Aug. 27, 1983; 1 child, Emily McCafferty. BA, Northwestern U., Evanston, Ill., 1975; JD, George Washington U., 1978. Bar: D.C. 1983, U.S. Dist. Ct. D.C. 1983, U.S. Ct. Appeals (D.C. cir.) 1983, Md. 1979, U.S. Dist. Ct. Md. 1979, U.S. Ct. Appeals (4th cir.) 1979. Law clk. to presiding judge U.S. Dist. Ct. Md, Balt., 1978-79; assoc. Semmes, Bowen & Semmes, Balt., 1979-85; staff atty. Crown Cen. Petroleum Corp., Balt., 1985—. Mng. editor George Washington U. Law Rev., 1977-78. Mem. ABA, Md. Bar Assn. (pub. service com.), Bar Assn. Balt. City, Def. Research Inst., Md. Assn. Def. Trial Attys., Am. Corp. Counsel Assn. Home: 318 Paddington Rd Baltimore MD 21212 Office: Crown Cen Petroleum Corp PO Box 1168 Baltimore MD 21203

LAPELLE, WILLIAM J., lawyer; b. Chgo., June 2, 1953; s. William Joseph and Anna May (Gast) L.; m. Diane McDonnell, June 19, 1976. BA, U. Notre Dame, 1975; JD, John Marshall Law Sch., 1979. Bar: U.S. Dist. Ct. (no. dist.) Ill. 1980. Assoc. Epton, Mullin & Druth, Ltd., Chgo., 1979-84, Robbins, Rubinstein, Salomon & Greenblatt, Chgo., 1985-86; gen. council Thomas F. Seay & Assoc., Chgo., 1986. Mem. Assocs. St. Joseph Hosp., Chgo., 1981—. Mem. ABA, Chgo. Bar Assn. Roman Catholic. Real property, General corporate, Banking. Home: 1115 S Plymouth Ct #412 Chicago IL 60605 Office: Thomas F Seay & Assoc 200 E Randolph Dr Chicago IL 60601

LAPHAM, MARK WILLIAM, lawyer; b. Blue Earth, Minn., July 23, 1955; s. William P. Lapham and Mary Lou (Lindsay) Cain; m. Barbara C. Borowski, July 23, 1983; 2 children. BA, U. Minn., 1977; JD, Drake U., 1981. Bar: Minn. 1981. Sole practice Mpls. and Lindstrom, Minn., 1981-85; house counsel Western Nat. Mut. Ins. Co., Mpls., 1985—. Mem. Fed. Bar Assn. Republican. Insurance. Office: Western Nat Mut Ins Co 5350 W 78th St Minneapolis MN 55435

LAPIDUS, STEVEN RICHARD, lawyer; b. N.Y.C., Jan. 14, 1945; s. Leopold and Hortense (Klemons) L.; m. Iris R. Lerner, Mar. 18, 1973; children—Jennifer Lauren, Adam Ross. A.B., NYU, 1966; J.D., Bklyn. Law Sch., 1969; cert. Nat. Coll. Dist. Attys., U. Houston, 1972. Bar: N.Y. 1970, U.S. Dist. Ct. (so. and ea. dists.) N.Y. 1971, U.S. Ct. Appeals (2d cir.) 1971, U.S. Supreme Ct. 1973. Asst. dist. atty. Office Dist. Atty. Nassau County, N.Y., 1970-73; asst. atty. gen. N.Y. State Dept. Law, N.Y.C., 1973-77; spl. asst. atty. gen. N.Y. State Dept. Law, N.Y.C., 1977-78; ptnr. Lerner Franquinha & Lapidus, N.Y.C., 1977-78; sr. ptnr. Abrams Lerner Kisseloff Kissin & Lapidus, P.C., N.Y.C., 1978—; adj. asst. prof. Real Estate Inst., NYU, N.Y.C., 1979—. Served with Army NG, 1969-71. Mem. N.Y. State Bar Assn., Coop. Housing Lawyers Group. Jewish. Club: NYU. Real property, Administrative and regulatory, State civil litigation.

LAPIN, ANDREW WILLIAM, lawyer; b. Chgo., Feb. 2, 1953; s. Robert Allan and Elaine (Muhlrad) L.; m. Debra Nan Goldberg, July 7, 1979; children: Lauren Elise, Marisa Anne. BA, Ind. U., 1975; JD, John Marshall Law Sch., 1978. Bar: Ill. 1978, U.S. Dist. Ct. (no. dist.) Ill. 1978. Sole practice, Chgo., 1978-79, 81—; assoc. Tash & Slavitt, Ltd., Chgo., 1979-81; bd. dirs. Am. Soc. for Technion. Mem. ABA, Chgo. Bar Assn. (real property com., real property fin. subcom.), Ill. Bar Assn., Am. Soc. Tech. (bd. dirs.), Israel Inst. Tech. Real property, Contracts commercial, General corporate. Office: 35 E Wacker Dr 34th Fl Chicago IL 60601

LAPIN, HARVEY I., lawyer; b. St. Louis, Nov. 23, 1937; s. Lazarus L. and Lillie L.; m. Cheryl A. Lapin; children: Jeffrey, Gregg. BS, Northwestern U., 1960, JD, 1963; LLB in Taxation, Georgetown U., 1967. Bar: Ill. 1963, Fla. 1980, Wis. 1985. Cert. tax lawyer, Fla. Bar. Atty., Office Chief Counsel, IRS, Washington, 1963-65; trial atty. Office Regional Csl., IRS, Washington, 1965-68; assoc., then ptnr. Fiffer & D'Angelo, Chgo., 1968-75; pres. Harvey I. Lapin, P.C., Chgo., 1975-83; mng. ptnr. Lapin, Hoff, Spangler & Greenberg, 1983—; instr. John Marshall Law Sch., 1969—; facility adv. lawyers asst. program Roosevelt U., Chgo.; mem. cemetery adv. bd. Ill. Comptroller, 1974—. C.P.A., Ill. Mem. Chgo. Bar Assn., Ill. Bar Assn., ABA. Jewish. Asst. editor Fed. Bar Jour., 1965-67; contbg. editor Cemetery Business and Legal Guide; contbr. articles to trade assn. jours. Corporate taxation, Cemetery law, General corporate. Office: Lapin Hoff Spangler & Greenberg 115 S LaSalle St Chicago IL 60603

LAPIN, JAMES B., lawyer; b. Denver, Sept. 8, 1946; s. William and Dorothy Sue (Seiglbaum) L.; m. Juli Elizabeth Krill, June 14, 1980; 1 child, William Blaine. BA, U. Colo., 1969; JD, U. Denver, 1972. Bar: Colo. 1972, U.S. Dist. Ct. Colo. 1972, U.S. Ct. Appeals (10th cir.), U.S. Supreme Ct. Assoc. Pacheco, Aver & Manzanares, Denver, 1972-73, Bailey & Belfor P.C., Lakewood, Colo., 1973-74; ptnr. Belfor, Demuth & Lapin, Lakewood, 1973-74; sole practice Denver, 1974—. Mem. Am. Arbitration Assn. (arbitrator), Colo. Bar Assn., Colo. Trial Lawyers Assn., Denver Bar Assn. Club: Denver Athletic. State civil litigation, Consumer commercial. Office: 2719 E 3d Ave Denver CO 80206

LAPINS, SCOTT MICHAEL, lawyer; b. Lawton, Okla., Sept. 20, 1955; s. Sorrell H. and Lona B. (Kalman) L. BS with highest honors, U. Ill., 1977; JD cum laude, Northwestern U., 1980. Bar: Ill. 1980, U.S. Dist. Ct. (no. dist.) 1980, U.S. Tax Ct. 1980; CPA, Ill. Assoc. Rosenthal & Schanfield, Chgo., 1980-82, Miller, Shakman, Nathan & Hamilton, Chgo., 1982—. Mem. editorial bd. Jour. of Criminal Law and Criminology, 1979-80. Mem. ABA, Ill. Bar Assn., Chgo. Bar Assn. (contbr. jour. young lawyers div.), Am. Inst. CPA's, Ill. Inst. CPA's. Club: East Bank (Chgo.). Avocations: golf, raquetball, jogging. Real property, Contracts commercial, Corporate taxation. Home: 900 Lake Shore Dr Chicago IL 60611 Office: Miller Shakman Nathan & Hamilton 208 S LaSalle Chicago IL 60604

LA PLATA, GEORGE, federal judge; b. 1924; m. Frances Hoyt; children: Anita J. La Plata Rard, Marshall. AB, Wayne State U., 1951; LLB, Detroit Coll. Law, 1956. Sole practice 1956-79; judge Oakland County (Mich.) Cir. Ct., Pontiac, 1979-85, U.S. Dist. Ct. (ea. dist.) Mich., Ann Arbor, 1985—; prof. Detroit Coll. Law, 1985-86. Trustee William Beaumont Hosp., 1979—, United Found., 1983—. Served to col. USMC, 1943-46, 52-54. Mem. ABA, Oakland County Bar Assn., Hispanic Bar Assn. Lodge: Optimists. Office: US Dist Ct 200 E Liberty Suite 400 Ann Arbor MI 48104 *

LAPORTE, GERALD JOSEPH SYLVESTRE, lawyer; b. Windsor, Ont., Can., Oct. 16, 1946; came to U.S., 1948, naturalized, 1954; s. Rosaire Joseph and Catherine Rose (Sylvestre) L. B.A., Sacred Heart Sem. Coll., 1968; S.T.B., St. Paul U., Ottawa, Ont., 1971; B.Th., U. Ottawa, 1971; M.A., Georgetown U., 1974; J.D., George Washington U., 1976. Bar: Mich. 1976, D.C. 1977. Legis. asst. to U.S. Congressman Wm. J. Randall, Washington, 1971-75; law clk. to U.S. Dist. Judge, Washington, 1976-77; assoc. Wilmer, Cutler & Pickering, Washington, 1977-82; sr. spl. counsel, Office Gen. Counsel, SEC, Washington, 1982-85; counsel to SEC Commr., 1985-87; assoc. Nutter, McClennen & Fish, Washington, 1987—. Mng. editor George Washington Law Rev., 1975-76. Bd. dirs. Hannah House, Inc., Washington, Cluster Housing, Inc., Washington. Mem. ABA (fed. regulation of securities com., sec. corp. banking and bus. law, subcom. SEC adminstrn., budget and legis.). Democrat. Roman Catholic. Club: Capitol Hill Squash (Washington).ington). Securities, General corporate, Legislative. Home: 233 Kentucky Ave SE Apt 1 Washington DC 20003 Office: Nutter McClennen & Fish 1819 H St NW Suite 1175 Washington DC 20006

LAPORTE, ROCLYNE EMILE, lawyer; b. Troy, N.H., Aug. 30, 1939; s. Emile William and Ida (Koski) LaP.; m. Dolores J. Dinyon; 1 son: Damon J. BA, U. N.H., 1963; JD, U. Chgo., 1966, MBA, 1973. Bar: Ill. 1967, Pa. 1984. Law clk. Ill. Appelate Ct., 1967; appeals atty. City of Chgo., 1968-70; asst. counsel Sears, Chgo., 1970-76; asst. counsel Franklin Mint. Corp., Franklin Center, Pa., 1976-84, sole practice, Phila., 1984—. Mem. ABA. General corporate, Federal civil litigation, State civil litigation. Home: 510 Painter Rd Media PA 19063 Office: 100 N 20th St Suite 309 Philadelphia PA 19103

LAPPEN, TIMOTHY, lawyer; b. Los Angeles, Dec. 26, 1947; s. Chester Irwin and Jon Tyroler (Irmas) L.; m. Nancy Sisson Lewis, June 13, 1971; children: Amy Elizabeth, Jay Robert, Tyler Lewis. AB, U. Calif., Berkeley, 1972; JD, UCLA, 1975. Bar: Calif. 1975, U.S. Dist. Ct. (no. dist.) Calif. 1975, U.S. Ct. Appeals (9th cir.) 1975. Assoc. Lillick, McHose & Charles, San Francisco, 1975-77; ptnr. Lappen & Lappen, Los Angeles, 1977-84; of counsel Jeffer, Mangels & Butler, Los Angeles, 1984-87; pres. Lappen Realty and Constrn. Co., Santa Monica, Calif., 1987—; sole practice Santa Monica, 1987—; bd. dirs., sec. Dee Constrn. Co., Los Angeles. Pres. Santa Monica Protective Assn., Calif., 1982—. Mem. ABA, Calif. Bar Assn., Los Angeles County Bar Assn., Century City Bar Assn., Assn. Real Estate Attys., Bldg. Industry Assn. Democrat. Jewish. Clubs: Sand and Sea (Santa Monica); Century West (Los Angeles). Real property, Construction, General corporate.

LAPPIN, ROBERT SIDNEY, lawyer; b. Boston, Oct. 6, 1928; s. Albert S. and Pearl (Cooper) L.; m. Anne M. Theroux (div. 1982); children: Jane E. Lappin Griffiths, Joshua C. BA, Norwich U., 1951; MBA, Boston U., 1955; LLB, Boston Coll., 1959. Bar: Mass. 1959, U.S. Supreme Ct. 1961, U.S. Tax Ct. 1962, U.S. Ct. Appeals (fed. cir.) 1974. Ptnr. Lappin, Rosen & Goldberg, Boston, 1959-70, sr. ptnr., 1970-82, mng. ptnr., 1982—. Trustee Norwich U., Northfield, Vt. Mem. ABA, Mass. Bar Assn., Boston Bar Assn. Club: New Seabury Country. Corporate taxation, Estate taxation, State and local taxation. Home: 180 Beacon St Boston MA 02116 Office: Lappin Rosen & Goldberg 1 Boston Pl Boston MA 02108

LAPUZZA, PAUL JAMES, lawyer; b. Omaha, May 30, 1948; s. Anton T. and Elaine M. (Fitzsenry) LaP.; m. Mary L., July 5, 1975; children: Mark James, Tracey Marie. BSBA, Creighton U., 1970, JD, 1972. Bar: Nebr. 1972, U.S. Dist. Ct. Nebr. 1972, U.S. Ct. Appeals (8th cir.) 1975, U.S. Supreme Ct. 1981, U.S. Claims Ct. 1982. Sole practice, Omaha, 1972-78; ptnr. Young, LaPuzza & Stoehr and predecessor, Omaha, 1978—. Co-author: (manual) Phi Kappa Psi, 1984. Served to capt. U.S. Army, 1972. Mem. Nebr. State Bar Assn., Phi Kappa Psi (dept. atty. gen. 1972-78, 82—, atty. gen. 1978-82), Delta Sigma Rho, Tau Kappa Alpha. Democrat. Roman Catholic. General practice, Real property, Contracts commercial. Home: 9807 Ascot Dr Omaha NE 68114 Office: Young LaPuzza & Stoehr 6910 Pacific Suite 320 Omaha NE 68106

LARGENT, JEFFREY WILLARD, lawyer; b. Cleve., July 20, 1946; s. Jesse Willard and Gertrude Ann (Molnar) L.; m. Anne Louise Eckert, Dec. 14, 1968; children: Elizabeth Anne, Daniel Jeffrey. BA, Baldwin-Wallace Coll., 1968; JD, Cleveland State U., 1973. Bar: Ohio 1973, U.S. Dist. Ct. (no. dist.) Ohio 1975, U.S. Ct. Appeals (6th cir.) 1975, U.S. Supreme Ct. 1977, U.S. Ct. Claims 1982. Law clk. to presiding justice U.S. Dist. Ct. (no. dist.) Ohio, Cleve., 1972-74; prosecutor City of Highland Heights, Ohio, 1977-80, City of Westlake, Ohio, 1977-82; dir. law City of Middleburg Heights, Ohio, 1980-81, City of Maple Heights, Ohio, 1982-84; sole practice Strongsville, Ohio, 1984—; instr. sociology Baldwin-Wallace Coll., Berea, Ohio, 1976-78. Legal advisor com. Voinovich for Mayor, Cleve., 1978, Busch for Mayor, Westlake, 1981, Starr for Mayor, Middleburg Heights, 1981—; troop sponsor Girl Scouts U.S., Strongsville, 1981-83; mem. panel Citizens League of Greater Cleve., 1982. Mem. Ohio Bar Assn., Assn. Trial Lawyers Am., Delta Theta Phi. Republican. Club: Diogenes (pres. 1981—). AVocation: youth soccer coaching. Personal injury, Local government, State civil litigation. Home: 9737 Brookstone Way Strongsville OH 44136 Office: 11925 Pearl Rd Suite 302 Strongsville OH 44136

LARIMORE, TOM L., lawyer; b. Fort Worth, Sept. 21, 1937; s. T.R. and Mildred Elizabeth (Angell) L.; m. Jane Anne Kroeger, Mar. 17, 1958; children—Thomas Lee, Robert Karl, Susan Lynne. B.A., Washington and Lee U., 1959; LL.B., So. Meth. U., 1962. Bar: Tex. 1962, U.S. Dist. Ct. (no. dist.) Tex. 1965, U.S. Dist. Ct. (so. dist.) Tex. 1975, U.S. Ct. Appeals (5th cir.) 1977. Assoc. Walker & Bishop, Fort Worth, 1962-66; ptnr. Walker, Bishop & Larimore, 1966-73, Bishop, Larimore, Lamsens & Brown, 1973-79; v.p., gen. counsel, sec. Western Co. of N.Am., Fort Worth, 1979-80, v.p. law and adminstrn., sec., 1980-86; ptnr. Gandy, Michner, Swindle, Whitaker & Pratt, Ft. Worth, 1986—. Pres., bd. dirs. YMCA (West), Fort Worth, 1966-68; sr. warden, vestryman All Saints Episcopal Ch., Fort Worth, 1973-74, named Churchman of Yr., 1969; pres., bd. dirs. Sr. Citizens Ctrs., Fort Worth, 1974-78. Fellow Tex. Bar Found.; mem. ABA, Tarrant County Bar Assn. (bd. dirs. 1978-80), Am. Corp. Counsel Assn., Fort Worth Bar Assn. (chmn. dist. admissions com. 1975-77); Fort Worth C. of C. (bd. dirs. 1985—, chmn. West area council 1985-86), Tex. Research League (bd. dirs. 1980—). Republican. Clubs: River Crest Country, Shady Oaks Country (Fort Worth). Lodge: Rotary (pres., bd. dirs. West Fort Worth 1974-75, Paul Harris fellow 1982). General corporate, Federal civil litigation, State civil litigation. Home: 1200 Montego St Fort Worth TX 76116 Office: Gandy Michner Swindle et al 2501 Parkview Dr Suite 600 Fort Worth TX 76102

LARIO, FRANK M., JR., lawyer, judge; b. Phila., July 1, 1937; s. Frank M. and Marie Ann (Mandarino) L.; m. Kathleen A. Cowan, July 1, 1961; children—Michael James, Kathleen Marie, Frank M. III. A.B. cum laude, Georgetown U., 1959; postgrad. Harvard U., 1959; J.D. cum laude, Rutgers U., 1962. Bar: N.J. 1962, U.S. dist. ct. N.J. 1963, U.S. Ct. Apls. (3d cir.) 1978, U.S. Sup. Ct. 1969. Law sec. to Assoc. Justice Vincent S. Haneman, N.J. Sup. ct. 1962-63; ptnr. Lario and Nardi, Haddonfield, N.J. 1973—; mcpl. judge Borough of Magnolia (N.J.), 1969—; mcpl. judge Borough of Audubon Park (N.J.), 1970—; mcpl. judge Borough of Woodlynne (N.J.), 1971-76; mcpl. judge Borough of Bellmawr (N.J.), 1976—. Instr. estate planning Inst. Continuing Legal Edn., 1962-69, instr. legal ethics, 1973-78; mem. com. on mcpl. cts. N.J. Supreme Ct., 1980—; mem. Supreme Ct. Com. on Character, 1983—. Mem. alumni senate Georgetown U., 1981—; bd. govs. Georgetown U., 1978-81. Mem. ABA, N.J. Bar Assn. (chmn. mcpl. cts. of N.J. com. 1978-81), Camden County Bar Assn. (bd. mgrs. 1973-76, chmn. immigration and naturalization com. 1974-83, long range planning com. 1976-78, sec. 1979-80, treas. 1980-81, v.p. 1982-83, pres. 1984-85), Camden County Mcpl. Judges Conf. (sec. 1975, pres. 1976-77), Rutgers U. Law Sch. Alumni Assn. (chmn. scholarship com. 1971-82), Rutgers U. Law Sch. Alumni Assn. South Jersey (chancellor 1968-69, bd. mgrs. 1970-82), Georgetown U. Alumni Assn. (gov. 1976—), Men of Malvern (assoc. capt. 1968—). Clubs: Vesper (Phila.); Tavistock Country (Haddonfield); Seaview Country (Absecon, N.J.); KC; Greate Bay Country (Somers Point, N.J.); Georgetown U. Alumni South Jersey (pres. 1970-72). Assoc. editor: Rutgers Law Rev., 1961-62. General practice, General corporate, Probate. Office: 200 Haddon Ave PO Box 87 Haddonfield NJ 08033

LARKE, GEORGE JOSEPH, JR., lawyer; b. Houma, La., Aug. 18, 1948; s. George Joseph Sr. and Margaret (Doiron) L.; m. Donna Sue Babin, May 4, 1974; children: George Joseph III, John William. BA, U. Southwestern La., 1971; JD, La State U., 1975. Bar: La. 1976, U.S. Dist. Ct. (ea. dist.) La. 1976, U.S. Ct. Appeals (5th and 11th cirs.) 1981, U.S. Supreme Ct. 1981. From assoc. to ptnr. Authement & Larke, Houma, 1976—. Bd. dirs. United Way, Houma, 1979-82. Served to specialist 5th class U.S. Army, 1971-73, ETO. Democrat. Roman Catholic. Banking, Consumer commercial, Family and matrimonial. Home: 206 Raywood Dr Houma LA 70360 Office: Authement & Larke 421 E Park Ave Houma LA 70361

LARKIN, DANIEL EMMETT, lawyer; b. Mpls., May 1, 1955; s. James Phillip and Barbara Ann (Schuler) L.; m. Christine Lee Aamodt, July 3, 1982; 1 child, Julia. AB, Harvard U., 1977; JD, U. Chgo., 1980. Bar: Ill. 1980. Assoc. Law Offices of Borge and Pitt, Chgo., 1980-82, Mayer, Borge & Platt, Chgo., 1982-84; atty., sec. Ameritech Mobile Commn., Chgo., 1984—. Mem. panel for interviewing adminstrv. law judge candidates U.S. Office Personnel Mgmt., Chgo., 1984—. Mem. ABA, Chgo. Bar Assn.

LARKIN, LEE MARSHALL, lawyer; b. Houston, July 25, 1956; s. Joe Marshall and Jimmy Jo (Coulter) L.; m. Rebecca Anne Cheek, Nov. 18, 1978; 1 child, Erin Leigh. BA, Baylor U., 1978, JD, 1981. Bar: Tex. 1981. Briefing atty. Tex. Ct. Appeals (14th cir.), Houston, 1981-82; assoc. Fouts & Moore, Houston, 1982—. Deacon 2d Bapt. Ch., Houston, 1984—. Mem. ABA, Tex. Bar Assn., Houston Bar Assn., Houston Young Lawyers Assn. (bd. dirs. 1983-84), Delta Theta Phi. Republican. Federal civil litigation, State civil litigation. Home: 9901 Briarwild Houston TX 77080 Office: Fouts & Moore 1800 Bering Suite 500 Houston TX 77080

LARKIN, LEO PAUL, JR., lawyer; b. Ithaca, N.Y., June 19, 1925; s. Leo Paul and Juanita (Wade) L. A.B., Cornell U., 1948, LL.B., 1950. Bar: N.Y. 1950, U.S. Dist. Ct. (so. dist.) N.Y. 1951, U.S. Supreme Ct. 1967. Assoc., then ptnr. Rogers & Wells and predecessor firms, N.Y.C., 1950—; dir. Indal, Ltd., Weston, Ont., Can., Sch. for Strings, Inc., N.Y.C. Served with U.S. Army, 1943-45. Mem. ABA, N.Y. State Bar Assn., Assn. Bar City N.Y., Fed. Bar Council, Union Internationale des Avocats, Delta Phi, Phi Beta Kappa, Phi Kappa Phi, Theta Delta Phi. Clubs: Univ. (N.Y.C.), Sky (N.Y.C.). Antitrust, Federal civil litigation, Libel. Home: 200 E 66th St New York NY 10021 Office: Rogers & Wells 200 Park Ave New York NY 10166

LARKY, SHELDON GLEN, lawyer; b. Detroit, Sept. 16, 1941; s. Irving and Lucille C. (Ziegler) L.; m. Barbara T., Apr. 25, 1965; children: Adam, Howard. BA, U. Mich., 1964; postgrad. Wayne State U., 1964-65; JD, U. Detroit, 1969. Bar: Mich. 1970, U.S. Dist. Ct. (ea. dist.) Mich. 1970, U.S. Ct. Apls. (6th cir.) 1972. Claims adjuster Liberty Mut. Ins. Co., Chgo., Detroit, 1962-64; personnel dir. ITT Continental Baking Co., Detroit, 1964-69; law clk. to presiding justice 6th Jud. Cir. Ct. Mich., Pontiac, 1969-70; ptnr. Leib & Leib, Southfield, Mich., 1970-76; v.p. Hiller, Larky, Hoekenga & Amberg, P.C., Southfield, 1976-87, sole practice, 1987—. Contbr. articles to profl. jours. Mem. ABA, Mich. Bar Assn. (chmn. com. on character and fitness

1980-82, com. on plain English 1981-83, sec. profl. liability ins. com. 1985—, profl. devel. task force com. 1985-87), Oakland County Bar Assn. (dir. 1974-84, pres. 1983-84, editor Laches 1974-82, chmn. law office mgmt. and econs. com. 1986-87), Nat. Conf. Bar Pres., Am. Judicature Soc. Family and matrimonial, Personal injury, General practice. Home: 14730 Talbot St Oak Park MI 48237 Office: 30600 Telegraph Rd Suite 2160 Birmingham MI 48010

LAROCCO, JOHN BERNARD, lawyer, educator; b. Chgo., Mar. 8, 1951; s. Joseph John and Jeanette Dohrs (Mader) LaR; m. Christine Ann Bologna, Aug. 3, 1985. BS in Econs., U. Ill., 1973; JD, U. San Diego, 1977; MS in Indsl. Relations, Loyola U., Chgo., 1980; LLM, Georgetown U., 1981. Bar: Calif. 1977, Ill. 1978, U.S. Dist. Ct. (no. and so. dists.) Calif. 1978, U.S. Dist. Ct. (no. dist.) Ill. 1978, U.S. Ct. Appeals (7th and 9th cirs.) 1978, U.S. Dist. Ct. (ea. dist.) Calif. 1979, U.S. Supreme Ct. 1981, D.C. 1982. Gen. mgr. Sweningson Cartage Co., Addison, Ill., 1973-74; sole practice Chgo., 1977—; adj. prof. Cal. State U., Sacramento, 1983—. Mem. ABA (sect. labor and employment law), Am. Arbitration Assn., Indsl. Relations Research Assn., Soc. Profls. in Dispute Resolution, Italian-Am. Attys. Assn. Superior Calif. (pres. 1982-83). Roman Catholic. Avocations: reading, swimming. Labor, Arbitration. Home and Office: 160 Gifford Way Sacramento CA 95864

LAROWE, MYRON EDWARD, lawyer; b. Indpls., Nov. 22, 1939; s. Daniel Dale and Edith Bernice (Parsons) LaR.; m. Rosemary Waeffler, Aug. 24, 1963; children: Mark, Matthew, Christopher, Melinda. BS, U. Wis., 1962, LLB, 1965. Bar: Wis. 1965, U.S. Supreme Ct. 1971, U.S. Tax Ct. 1979, U.S. Ct. Claims 1979, Ind. 1980, D.C. 1981. Ptnr. LaRowe, Gerlach, Chiquoine & Kahler S.C., Reedsburg, Wis., 1965—; gen. counsel Wis. Dairies Coop., Baraboo, 1981—, Tri-State Breeders Coop., Baraboo, 1983—; atty. City of Reedsburg, 1967-86; bd. dirs. Wis. Lawyers Mut. Ins. Co., 1987—. Sec., treas. Reedsburg Meml. Found., 1976-85, pres., 1984; gen. counsel Reedsburg Meml. Hosp., 1974—, bd. dirs., 1979—, pres. 1986—. Named one of Outstanding Men in Am., 1972. Fellow Am. Bar Found.; mem. ABA (ho. of dels. 1982—), Wis. Bar Assn. (ct. commr. 1968—, bd. of govs. 1975—, pres. 1981-82), Sauk County Bar Assn. (sec., treas. 1967-71, pres. 1986—). Lutheran. Club: Reedsburg (Wis.) Country (pres. 1972-73). Lodge: Lions (pres. Reedsburg chpt. 1970-71). Avocations: hunting, fishing, golf. General corporate, Local government, Health. Home: 134 S Oak Reedsburg WI 53959 Office: LaRowe Gerlach Chiquoine & Kahler SC 110 Main Reedsburg WI 53959

LARROCA, RAYMOND G., lawyer; b. San Juan, P.R., Jan. 5, 1930; s. Raymond Gil and Elsa Maria (Morales) L.; m. Barbara Jean Strand, June 21, 1952 (div. 1974); children—Denise Anne Sheehan, Gail Ellen, Raymond Gil, Mark Talbot, Jeffrey William. B.S.S., Georgetown U., 1952, J.D., 1957. Bar: D.C. 1957, U.S. Supreme Ct. 1960. Assoc., Kirkland, Fleming, Green, Martin & Ellis, Washington, 1957-64; ptnr. Kirkland, Ellis, Hodson, Chaffetz & Masters, Washington, 1964-67, Miller, Cassidy, Larroca & Lewin, Washington, 1967—. Served with arty. U.S. Army, 1948-49, to 1st lt., inf., 1952-54. Mem. ABA, D.C. Bar, Bar Assn. D.C., The Barristers. Republican. Roman Catholic. Clubs: Congl. Country (Potomac, Md.); University (Washington). Criminal, Federal civil litigation, Private international. Office: 2555 M St NW Suite 500 Washington DC 20037

LARSEN, DIRK HERBERT, lawyer, magistrate; b. Minot, N.D., Jan. 3, 1931; s. Norman Herbert and Inez Lockman (Leighton) L.; m. Connie Grace McIver, Nov. 21, 1959; children—Kim, Kyle, Kary. B.S., U. Mont., 1952, LL.B., 1956. Bar: Mont. 1956, U.S. Dist. Ct. Mont. 1959, U.S. Ct. Mil. Appeals 1961, U.S. Ct. Appeals (9th cir.) 1959, U.S. Supreme Ct. 1961. Practice, Great Falls, Mont., 1956—; mem. Larsen and Gliko, 1972-79, Larsen and Neill, 1979—; U.S. commr., 1961-71; magistrate U.S. Dist. Ct. Mont., 1971—; legal officer Mont. Air N.G., 1958-80. Served to lt. col. USAFR, 1952-80. Decorated Air Force Commendation medal. Mem. Cascade County Bar Assn. (pres. 1973-74), Mont. Bar Assn. Clubs: Optimists (pres. club 1968-70), Toastmasters (pres. 1960-61); Elks (Great Falls). Author: Montana Collection Law, 1982. Consumer commercial, General practice, Judicial administration. Office: 121 4th St N Suite 2J Great Falls MT 59405

LARSEN, KAREN MARIE, lawyer; b. Cheyenne Wells, Colo., July 14, 1954; d. Jack D. and Emma (Hermes) L. BA, U. Denver, 1976; JD, Hamline U., 1979. Bar: Colo. 1979, U.S. Dist. Ct. Colo. 1979. Assoc. Law Offices of Norman L. Arends, Cheyenne Wells, 1979-81; sole practice Cheyenne Wells, 1981-83; gen. counsel RPJ Energy Fund Mgmt., Mpls., 1983—, also bd. dirs. and sec.; bd. dirs. AEI Real Estate Funds, Mpls.; bd. dirs., v.p. Kenecreek, Inc., Cheyenne Wells, 1982—; gen. counsel Colo. A.S.A., Denver, 1979-85. Del. State Dem. Conv., Colo., 1982; pres. Sacred Heart Parish Council, Cheyenne Wells, 1980-83; treas., East Cheyenne Bus. Assn., Cheyenne Wells, 1979-83. Named Colo. Woman of the Yr., Colo. Jaycees, 1983. Mem. ABA, Colo. Bar Assn., Sigma Nu Phi. Democrat. Roman Catholic. Avocation: sports. General corporate, Real property, General practice. Home: 1892 Gold Trail Eagan MN 55122 Office: AEI Inc 101 W Burnsville Pkwy 200 Burnsville MN 55337

LARSEN, LYNN BECK, lawyer; b. Salt Lake City, Feb. 26, 1945. BA magna cum laude, U. Utah, 1969; MS, U. Wash., 1971; JD with honors, George Washington U., 1975. Bar: Va. 1975, U.S. Dist. Ct. (ea. dist.) Va. 1975, D.C. 1976, U.S. Dist. Ct. D.C. 1976, U.S. Ct. Appeals (4th and D.C. cirs.) 1976, U.S. Claim Ct. 1977, Calif. 1978, U.S. Dist. Ct. (cen. dist.) Calif. 1978, U.S. Dist. Ct. (so. dist.) Calif. 1979, U.S. Ct. Appeals (9th cir.) 1979, U.S. Dist. Ct. (no. and ea. dists.) Calif. 1981, Utah 1983, U.S. Dist. Ct. Utah 1983, U.S. Ct. Appeals (fed. cir.) 1983. Engr. Boeing Co., Seattle, 1969-70; engring analyst CIA, Washington, 1971-73, contracting officer, 1973-74; ptnr. Wickwire, Gavin & Gibbs, P.C., Salt Lake City, 1974-86, Larsen & Wilkins, Salt Lake City, 1986—; chmn. legal adv. com. Associated Gen. Contractors Calif. 1983, Associated Gen. Contractors Utah, Salt Lake City, 1985—. Contbr. articles to profl. jours. Mem. Phi Beta Kappa. Mormon. Construction, Government contracts and claims. Office: Larsen & Wilkins 10 E S Temple Suite 500 Salt Lake City UT 84133

LARSEN, ROLF, state Supreme Court justice; b. Pitts., Aug. 26, 1934; s. Thorbjorn Ruud and Mildred (Young) L. Ed., Pa. State U., U. Pitts., Duquesne U. Sch. Philosophy, U. Santa Clara; LL.B., Dickinson Sch. Law, 1960. Bar: Pa. 1960. Sole practice 1960-73; judge Allegheny County Ct. Common Pleas, 1974-77; justice Pa. Supreme Ct., 1978—; lectr. Duquesne U. Sch. Law. Served with U.S. Army, 1954-56. Recipient Humanitarian award, Outstanding Jurist award Pa. Dist. Attys. Assn., 1985, Jud. Excellence award Pa. State AFL-CIO, 1986, Ann. award Pa. Trial Lawyers Assn., 1986, Justice Michael A. Musmanno award Phila. Trial Lawyers Assn., 1986. Lodge: Masons. Office: Pa Supreme Ct 2800 Grant Bldg Pittsburgh PA 15219 *

LARSON, ALLEN ROBERT, lawyer; b. Rochester, N.Y., Aug. 21, 1949; s. Robert Paul and Jessie Evelyn (Poole) L. BA, Dartmouth Coll., 1971; JD, Union U., 1974; MBA, U. Minn., 1979. Bar: N.Y. 1975, U.S. Dist. Ct. (no. dist.) N.Y. 1975, Mass. 1984, U.S. Dist. Ct. Mass. 1984. Adj. prof. criminal law U. New Haven, 1974-77; assoc. prof. U. Minn., Mpls., 1977-79; atty. FTC, Washington, 1980-83; sole practice Hyannis, Mass., 1984—; asst. to dir. City of New Haven, 1976-77; cons. mgmt. info. systems U. Minn. Research Ctr., 1978-79; exec. dir. Cape Cod Community Coll. Ednl. Found., West Barnstable, Mass., 1983-85; chmn. Mid Cape Ice Arena, Inc., Dennis, Mass., 1985—; pres. Barnstable Conservation Found., Hyannis, 1985—. Mem. Yarmouth (Mass.) Growth Policy Adv. Council, 1985-86; asst. coach Dennis-Yarmouth Regional High Sch., 1985; chmn. Yarmouth Recreation Commn., 1984-86. Mem. ABA, Mass. Bar Assn., Barnstable County Bar Assn., Beta Gamma Sigma. Republican. Avocations: sports. Administrative and regulatory, Antitrust, Real property. Office: 297 North St Hyannis MA 02601

LARSON, ANDREW ROBERT, lawyer; b. Pine County, Minn., Feb. 25, 1930; s. Gustaf Adolf and Mary (Mach) L.; B.A., U. Minn., 1953, B.S. Law, St. Paul Coll. Law, 1956; LL.B., William Mitchell Coll. Law, 1958; m. Evelyn Joan Johnson, Sept. 12, 1953 (div. 1980); children—Linda Suzanne, Mark Andrew; m. Barbara Louise Drager Coen, May 4, 1987; stepchildren: Mark Anthony Coen, Mary Coen, Susan Coen, Peter Coen, Teresa Coen. Bar: Minn. 1958. With Armour & Co., 1953-56, Minn. Dept. Taxation, 1956-58; individual practice law, Duluth, Minn., 1958—; municipal judge Village of Proctor, part-time 1961-74; dir., sec. various bus., real estate corps.; pres. Larson, Huseby and Brodin, Ltd.; v.p., sec. Sea Jay Corp. Arbitrator Minn. Bur. Mediation Services. chmn. Duluth Fair Employment and Housing Commn., 1965-76; vice chmn. Mayor's Arena Auditorium Com., Duluth, 1964-65; active United Way; mem. State Bd. Human Rights, 1967-73; Midwest regional rep. nat. standing com. on legislation United Cerebral Palsy, 1967-71, bd. dirs. nat. assn., 1971-72; bd. dirs. United Day Activity Ctr., 1969-76, Am. Cancer Soc., 1973-75, Light House for Blind, 1975-79, 80—, Environ. Learning Ctr., 1978-81; mem. Greater Downtown Council. Recipient Humanitarian Service award United Cerebral Palsy, 1965, I Care award Republican party, 1964, Disting. Service award local chpt. Jaycees, 1965. Mem. Minn. Bar Assn., Minn. Jud. Council, Am. Arbitration Assn., Nat. Fedn. Ind. Businessmen, Nat. Assn. Accts., Fresh Water Soc., Blue Army, Count Nuno Soc. (sec.), U.S. C. of C., Minn. Arrowhead Assn., Western Lake Superior Recreation Assn., Boat Owners Assn. U.S., Nat. Wildlife Fedn., Minn. Pub. Radio, Beta Phi Kappa. Republican. Roman Catholic. Clubs: 242 Yacht, Duluth Keel. Lodge: Kiwanis. General practice, General corporate, Real property. Home: 3002 E Superior St Duluth MN 55812

LARSON, CHARLES W., lawyer. U.S. atty. no. dist. State of Iowa, Cedar Rapids. Office: Post Office Box 4710 Cedar Rapids IA 52407 *

LARSON, DAVID CHRISTOPHER, lawyer, judge; b. Spencer, Iowa, Sept. 4, 1955; s. Leonard and Margaret Roxanne (Proctor) L.; m. Carol Ann Kuntz, Sept. 17, 1983. BS in Constrn. Engring., Iowa State U., 1978; JD, Creighton U., 1981. Bar: Iowa 1981, U.S. Patent Office 1981, U.S. Dist. Ct. (no. dist.) Iowa 1981, U.S. Ct. Appeals (8th cir.) 1981. Law clk. Henderson & Sturm, Omaha, 1981; ptnr. Stoller & Larson, Spirit Lake, Iowa, 1981-84; sole practice, 1984—; alt. dist. assoc. judge Iowa Jud. Dist. 3A, 1983—. Mem. Iowa State Bar Assn. (com. on patents, trademarks and copyrights 1982—), Dist. 3A Bar Assn. (pres. 1983-84), Dickinson County Bar Assn. (chmn. Am. citizen com. 1982-83, pres. 1983-84), ABA, Iowa Patent Law Assn., Iowa Great Lakes C. of C. (ambassador 1982—). Republican. Methodist. Club: Okoboji Yacht (trophy chmn. 1984—). Lodges: Kiwanis (fin. com. chmn. 1983, bd. dirs. 1984, pres.-elect 1986, pres. 1987), Masons. General practice, Family and matrimonial, Personal injury. Home: Rural Rt 5520 Spirit Lake IA 51360 Office: PO Box 246 Spirit Lake IA 51360

LARSON, FREDERICK ALBIN, lawyer; b. Jamestown, N.Y., Nov. 25, 1951; s. Gordon Albin and Mary Larson; m. Wendy A. Jacobson, Mar. 21, 1981; 1 child, Eric Albin. AB, Princeton U., 1973; JD, Yale U., 1976. Bar: N.Y. 1977, U.S. Dist. Ct. (we. dist.) N.Y. 1978. Assoc. Jaeckle, Fleischmann & Mugel, Buffalo, 1976-77; ptnr. Alessi, Willson & Larson, Jamestown, 1977-80; sole practice Jamestown, 1980—; instr. Jamestown Community Coll., 1985—. City councilman Jamestown, 1979-81; legislator Chautauqua County, Mayville, N.Y., 1985—. Mem. ABA, N.Y. State Bar Assn., Jamestown Bar Assn. Democrat. Lutheran. Lodge: Masons. General corporate, Probate, Real property. Home: 641 Lakeview Ave Jamestown NY 14701 Office: Hotel Jamestown Bldg Jamestown NY 14701

LARSON, JERRY L., state supreme court justice; b. Harlan, Iowa, May 17, 1936; s. Gerald L. and Mary Eleanor (Patterson) L.; m. Linda R. Logan; children: Rebecca, Jeffrey, Susan, David. B.A., State U. Iowa, 1958, J.D., 1960. Bar: Iowa. Partner firm Larson & Larson, 1961-75; dist. judge 4th Jud. Dist. Ct. of Iowa, 1975-78; justice Iowa Supreme Ct., 1978—. Office: Office of the Iowa Supreme Ct Des Moines IA 50319

LARSON, JOHN FRANCIS, lawyer; b. Portland, Oreg., Dec. 14, 1944; s. Francis George and June Alice (Henry) L.; m. Lois Irene Winans, Mar. 2, 1968; children: Jeffrey, Eric, Lara. Cert. in Russian Lang., Ind. U., 1967-68; BA in Polit. Sci., Portland State U., 1971; JD, Lewis & Clark U., 1975. Bar: Oreg. 1975. Acctg. clk., rate analyst, sr. property transfer agt. Pacific Power and Light Co., Portland, 1964-77; mgr. pub. affairs, environ. compliance, compensation and benefits Nerco, Inc., Portland, 1977-85; mgr. legal and regulatory affairs Nerco- Pacific Generation Services, Portland, 1985—. Alt. chmn. Multonmah County Rep. Cen. Com., Portland, 1976-78. Served to staff sgt. USAF, 1967-70. Mem. ABA (vice chmn. mktg. and rate structure com. 1986—, Silver Key award 1975, 75). Club: Portland City, Great Oreg. Pie. Public utilities, Environment, FERC practice. Home: 2225 NE Alameda Portland OR 97212 Office: Nerco Pacific Generation Services 101 SW Main St Suite 1290 Portland OR 97204

LARSON, JOHN WILLIAM, lawyer; b. Detroit, June 24, 1935; s. William and Sara Eleanor (Yeatman) L.; m. Pamela Jane Wren, Sept. 16, 1959; 1 dau., Jennifer Wren. B.A. with distinction, honors in Economics, Stanford, 1957; LL.B., Stanford U., 1962. Bar: Calif. 1962. Asso. firm Brobeck, Phleger & Harrison, San Francisco, 1962-68; partner Brobeck, Phleger & Harrison, 1968-71, 73—; asst. sec. Dept. Interior, Washington, 1971-73; exec. dir. Natural Resources Com., Washington, 1973; counsellor to chmn. Cost of Living Council, Washington, 1973; faculty Practising Law Inst.; bd. dirs. Measurex Corp., Caremark, Inc. Mem. U.S.-USSR Joint Com. on Environment; mem. bd. visitors Stanford Law Sch., 1974-77, 85-87; pres. bd. trustees The Katharine Branson Sch., 1980-83. Served with AUS, 1957-59. Mem. Am., Calif. bar assns., Order of Coif. Clubs: Pacific Union, Burlingame, Bohemian (San Francisco); Chevy Chase (Washington). Home: PO Box 349 Ross CA 94957 Office: Brobeck Phleger & Harrison Spear St Tower 1 Market Plaza San Francisco CA 94105

LARSON, MARK EDWARD, JR., lawyer; b. Oak Park, Ill., Dec. 16, 1947; s. Mark Edward and Lois Vivian (Benson) L.; m. Patricia Jo Jekerle, Apr. 14, 1973; children—Adam Douglas, Peter Joseph. B.S. in Acctg., U. Ill., 1969; J.D., Northwestern U., 1972; LL.M. in Taxation, NYU, 1977. Bar: Ill. 1973, U.S. Dist. Ct. (no. dist.) Ill. 1973, N.Y. 1975, U.S. Dist. Ct. (so. dist.) N.Y. 1975, U.S. Ct. Appeals (2d cir.) 1975, D.C. 1976, U.S. Ct. Appeals (7th cir.) 1976, U.S. Tax Ct. 1976, U.S. Supreme Ct. 1976, U.S. Dist. Ct. D.C. 1977, U.S. Ct. Appeals (D.C. cir.) 1977, U.S. Dist. Ct. Minn. 1982, U.S. Ct. Appeals (8th cir.) 1982, Minn. 1982, Tex. 1984. Acct. Deloitte Haskins & Sells, N.Y.C., 1973-75, tax cons., Chgo., 1978-81; atty. Haight, Gardner Poor & Havens, N.Y.C., 1976-78; Lindquist & Vennum, Mpls., 1981-83; ptnr., spl. counsel Farnsworth, Martin & Gallagher, Houston, 1983-86; v.p., gen. counsel Unitex Fin. Group Inc., Austin, Tex., 1986—; adj. prof. U. Minn., Mpls., 1982-83. Contbr. articles to profl. pubs. Fin. chmn. Elk Grove Twp. Rep. Party, Ill., 1979-81. Mem. Am. Assn. Atty.-CPA's, ABA, Am. Inst. CPA's, Nat. Assn. Bond Lawyers, Houston World Trade Assn. Corporate taxation, Securities, Private international. Office: 816 Congress Suite 1400 Austin TX 78701

LARSON, MARK VINCENT, lawyer, accountant; b. Hallock, Minn., Jan. 17, 1954; s. Oliven Vincent and R. Helen (Witt) L.; m. Nancy Joanne Bjork, Aug. 11, 1979; children: Shelby Kristine, Annika Britt. BA, U. N.D., 1976, JD, 1979, M in Acctg., 1985. Bar: Minn. 1979, N.D. 1979, U.S. Dist. Ct. N.D. 1979. Assoc. Lloyd H. Noack, Grand Forks, N.D., 1979-80; dir. cen. legal research U. N.D. Sch. of Law, Grand Forks, 1980-85; tax specialist Eide Helmeke & Co., Minot, N.D., 1985-86; assoc. McGee, Hankla, Backes & Wheeler Ltd., Minot, 1986—; lectr. bus. law U. N.D., Grand Forks, 1979-82, legal writing U. N.D., 1982-84; bd. dirs., treas. University Fed. Credit Union, Bismarck, N.D., 1983-85. Asst. dist. commdr. Boy Scouts Am., Grand Forks, 1981-84; asst. treas. Norsk Hostfest, Minot, 1985. Recipient Service award Boy Scouts Am., 1985. Mem. ABA, N.D. Bar Assn., Am. Inst. CPA's, N.D. Soc. CPA's, Ward County Bar Assn., N.D. Pattern Jury Instruction, N.D. Continuing Legal Edn. Commn. Lutheran. Lodges: Kiwanis, Elks. Avocations: sailing, golfing, skiing. Corporate taxation, Estate taxation, Personal income taxation. Home: 2519 11th Ave NW Minot ND 58701 Office: McGee Hankla Backes & Wheeler Ltd PO Box 998 Minot ND 58701

LARSON, RONALD FREDERICK, lawyer; b. Rock Springs, Wyo., July 8, 1948; s. Robert L. and Josephine M. (Donahue) L.; m. Mary Lucynda Henson, Sept. 6, 1969; children: Cheston James, Christon Joseph, Erin Jennifer. BS with honors, U. Wyo., 1970; JD summa cum laude, Ariz. State U., 1973. Bar: Ariz. 1973, U.S. Ct. Mil. Appeals 1973, U.S. Tax Ct. 1977, U.S. Supreme Ct. 1977. Ptnr. Ireland, Lange & Larson, Prescott, Ariz., 1977-79; assoc. Ryley, Carlock & Ralston P.A., Phoenix, 1979-82; ptnr. Farrer & Larson P.C., Sun City, Ariz., 1982-87, Larson & Lange, Sun City, 1987—; legal advisor Prescott Frontier Days, Inc., 1977-79, The Phoenix Found., Inc., 1980—. Ariz. Corr. Fed. Voting Rights Assistance Project, Washington, 1982—; mem. vestry All Saints' Episc. Ch.; bd. dirs. Samuel Gompers Meml. Rehab. Ctr., Phoenix, 1981—. Served to maj. U.S. Army, 1973-77. Mem. ABA (real property, probate and trust law sect. family law sect.), Cen. Ariz. Estate Planning Council, Maricopa County Bar Assn., Ariz. Bar Assn., Sun City Estate Planners Breakfast, Res. Officers Assn. Republican. Lodge: Masons, Shriners. Avocations: tennis, running, track and field official, chess. Probate, Estate planning, Family and matrimonial. Home: 850 Village Circle Dr Phoenix AZ 85022 Office: Larson & Lange 17220 Boswell Blvd Suite 137 Sun City AZ 85372

LARUE, PAUL HUBERT, lawyer; b. Somerville, Mass., Nov. 16, 1922; s. Lucien H. and Germaine (Choquet) LaR.; m. Helen Finnegan, July 20, 1946; children—Paul Hubert, Patricia G., Mary LaRue Hogan. Ph.B., U. Wis., 1947, J.D., 1949. Bar: Ill., 1955, Wis. 1949. Instr. polit. sci. U. Wis., 1947-48; mem. staff Wis. Atty. Gen., 1949-50; trial atty., legal adviser to commr. FTC, 1950-55; pvt. practice, Chgo., 1955—; mem. Chadwell & Kayser, Ltd.; speaker profl. meetings. Mem. Com. Modern Cts. in Ill., 1964; mem. Ill. Com. Constl. Conv., 1968, Better Govt. Assn., 1966-70, Lawyers com. Met. Crusade of Mercy, 1967-68, lawyers' com. United Settlement Appeal, 1966-68; apptd. pub. mem. Ill. Conflict of Interest Laws Commn., 1965-67. Served with AUS, 1943-45; ETO; as capt JAGC, USAFR, 1950-55. Decorated Purple Heart. Fellow Ill. Bar Assn. (life); mem. ABA (mem. council sect. antitrust law 1980-83), Fed. Bar Assn., 7th Circuit Bar Assn., Chgo. Bar Assn. (chmn. antitrust com. 1970-71), Am Judicature Soc. Roman Catholic. Club: Metropolitan (Chgo.). Contbr. articles to profl. jours. Antitrust, Public international, Federal civil litigation. Home: 250 Cuttriss Pl Park Ridge IL 60068 Office: 8500 Sears Tower Chicago IL 60606

LASAINE, DORIAN BARNETT, lawyer; b. Chgo., May 9, 1946; s. Max and Bernice (Rueben) L. BS, So. Ill. U., 1972; JD, John Marshall Law Sch., 1977. Bar: Ill. 1977, N.Y. 1985. Prosecutor Peoria County States Atty., Ill., 1977-78; sole practice Peoria, 1978—. Served to sgt. U.S. Army, 1967-69, Vietnam. Mem. ABA, Ill. Bar Assn., Peoria County Bar Assn. Republican. Jewish. Criminal, Consumer commercial, Family and matrimonial. Home: 3623 N Sterling A 12 Peoria IL 61602 Office: 1010 Savings Ctr Peoria IL 61602

LASALLE, LOWELL LEROY, lawyer; b. Clay County, Ind., Jan. 12, 1920; s. Oscar and Beulah Mae (Bailey) LaS.; m. Addine Gunn, Apr. 26, 1963. Student San Angelo Jr. Coll., 1937-39; B.A., U. Tex., 1941, LL.B., 1947. Bar: Tex. 1947, U.S. Dist. Ct. (ea. dist.) Tex. 1958. Briefing atty. Supreme Ct. Tex., 1947-49; mem. legal dept. Atlantic Refining Co., Dallas, 1949-51; judge Panola County, Tex., 1964-70; ptnr. LaSalle & Baker, Attys., Carthage, Tex., 1970-75; ptnr. LaSalle & Underwood, Carthage, 1975-85, LaSalle, Davidson & Selman, 1986—; sec., treas. Shelby-Panola Fed. Savs. & Loan Assn., Carthage. Chmn. Better Hwys. Assn., Panola County, Tex. Served with USAAF, 1942-46. Mem. ABA, State Bar Tex., Am. Judicature Soc. Methodist. Club: Rotary (Carthage). General practice, Probate, Oil and gas leasing. Office: PO Box 578 Carthage TX 75633

LASATER, THOMAS JOHN, lawyer; b. Monte Vista, Colo., Mar. 9, 1957; s. John L. and Jean (Flinchpaugh) L. Student, U. Kans., Lawrence, 1975-76; BS, West Tex. State U., 1979; JD, George Washington U., 1982. Bar: Kans. 1982, U.S. Dist. Ct. Kans. 1982. Assoc. Fleeson, Gooing, Coulson & Kitch, Wichita, Kans., 1982—. Recipient Merit award U.S. Dept. Labor, 1980; named one of Outstanding Young Men of Am., 1986. Mem. ABA, Kans. Bar Assn., Wichita Bar Assn., Wichita Young Lawyers Assn. (v.p. 1985-86, pres. elect 1986-87). Republican. Presbyterian. Club: Wichita (Kans.) Barbarians Rugby (treas. 1984-86). State civil litigation, Banking, Contracts commercial. Home: 755 S Erie Wichita KS 67211 Office: Fleeson Gooing Coulson & Kitch 125 N Market Suite 1600 Wichita KS 67202

LASCHER, ALAN ALFRED, lawyer; b. N.Y.C., Dec. 8, 1941; s. Morris Julius and Sadie Lillian (Chassen) L.; m. C. Amy Weingarten, July 12, 1969; children: David, Lauren, Alexandra. BS, Union Coll., 1963; LLB, Bklyn. Law Sch., 1967. Bar: N.Y. 1967. Assoc. Kramer, Leven et al, N.Y.C., 1969-75; ptnr., head real estate dept. Weil, Gotshal & Manges, N.Y.C., 1975—; mem. law com. N.Y. Real Estate Bd., N.Y.C., 1981—. Served to sgt. USAF, 1968-69. Named Real Estate Lawyer of Yr. Am. Lawyer, 1982. Real property. Office: Weil Gotshal & Manges 767 Fifth Ave New York NY 10153

LASCHER, EDWARD LEONARD, lawyer; b. Evanston, Ill., Jan. 19, 1928; s. Edward and Chrissie E. (Calvert) L.; m. Wendy Jean Cole; children—Edward Leonard, Thomas Robert, Susan Barbara, William Calvert. B.A., DePauw U., 1951; J.D., U. Mich., 1953. Bar: Ind. 1953, Calif. 1955, U.S. Supreme Ct. 1971. Assoc. Slaymaker, Locke & Reynolds, Indpls., 1953-54; mem. law dept. NBC and RCA, Hollywood, 1954-57; sole practice, Los Angeles, 1958-70, Ventura, Calif., 1966—; mem. firm Lascher & Lascher, Ventura, 1977—; bd. govs. State Bar Calif., 1975-78. Mem., chmn. Calif. Jud. Nominees Evaluation Commn., 1978-79. Served with U.S. Army, 1945-47. Fellow Am. Bar Found.; mem. Calif. Acad. Appellate Lawyers (pres. 1974-75), ABA, Los Angeles Bar Assn., Ventura Bar Assn., Sigma Delta Chi. Club: University (Los Angeles). Contbr. articles to profl. pubs. Civil and criminal appeals, Federal civil litigation, State civil litigation. Address: 605 Poli St Ventura CA 93001 Mailing Address: PO Box AJ Ventura CA 93002

LASCHER, WENDY JEAN COLE, lawyer; b. Palo Alto, Calif., July 14, 1950; d. John Louis and Peggy Ann (Stern) Cole; m. Roger Wilner, Jan. 5, 1969 (div. Aug. 1979); children: Joseph B., John J.; m. Edward Leonard Lascher, Feb. 7, 1980; 1 son, William C. BA with distinction in Polit. Sci., Stanford U., 1970; JD, U. Mich., 1973. Bar: Calif. 1973, U.S. Ct. Appeals (9th cir.) 1974, U.S. Supreme Ct. 1976, U.S. Ct. Appeals (7th cir.) 1978. Assoc., Law Offices of Edward Lascher, Ventura, Calif., 1973-77; ptnr. Lascher & Lascher, Ventura, 1977—; mem. com. appellate cts. Calif. State Bar, 1976-80, chmn., 1979-80; lectr. Calif. Continuing Edn. of Bar, 1982-86, Hastings Coll. Advocacy, 1985. Instnl. rev. com. Ventura County Gen. Hosp., 1981—. Mem. Calif. Acad. Appellate Lawyers (pres. 1986-87), Los Angeles Bar Assn., Ventura County Bar Assn. (newsletter editor 1982-85, 87—), Calif. Women Lawyers, Ventura County Women Lawyers. Democrat. Federal civil litigation, State civil litigation, Criminal. Home: 362 Agnus Dr Ventura CA 93003 Office: Lascher & Lascher 605 Poli St PO Box AJ Ventura CA 93002

LASH, DOUGLAS STEVEN, lawyer; b. Council Bluffs, Iowa, July 15, 1948; s. Donald Robert and Frances (Marshall) L.; m. Susan Marie Thompson, July 23, 1983; children: Rebecca, Sarah, Laura. Student, Lawrence U., 1966-67, Dana Coll., 1967-70; JD, Creighton U., 1983. Bar: Iowa 1973, U.S. Dist. Ct. (so. dist.) Iowa 1973, U.S. Dist. Ct. Nebr. 1978, U.S. Ct. Claims 1979. Assoc. Porter, Heithoff, Pratt & Reilly, Council Bluffs, 1973-76; ptnr. Porter, Lash & Tauke, Council Bluffs, 1976-82; v.p., gen. counsel Knudson, Inc., Council Bluffs, 1982-85; sole practice Council Bluffs, 1985—, Omaha, 1987—; v.p. XLand, Inc., 1984—. Chmn., bd. dirs. Chem. Dependency Agy., Council Bluffs, 1975-78; chmn. City of Council Bluffs Hist. Commn., 1979-82; bd. dirs. County Hist. Soc., Council Bluffs, 1986—. Mem. ABA (forum com. on construction), Iowa Bar Assn. Avocations: golf, gardening, racquetball. Construction, General corporate, Real property. Office: 100 Jackson Pl 13th & Jackson Sts Omaha NE 68102

LASHBROOKE, ELVIN CARROLL, JR., legal educator, consultant; b. Dec. 14, 1939; s. Elvin Carroll Sr. and Lois Lenora (Weger) L.; m. Margaret Ann Jones, Dec. 19, 1964; children: Michelle Ann, David C. BA, U. Tex., 1967, MA, 1968, JD, 1972, LLM, 1977. Bar: Tex. 1972, Fla. 1973. Legis. counsel Tex. Legis. Council, Austin, 1972-75; sole practice Austin, 1975-77; asst. prof. DePaul Coll. of Law, Chgo., 1977-79, Stetson Coll. of Law, St. Petersburg, Fla., 1979-80; assoc. prof. Notre Dame (Ind.) Law Sch., 1981-85; prof., chmn. bus. law dept. Mich. State U., East Lansing, 1985—; pvt. practice cons. East Lansing, 1986—; instr. St. Edward's U., Austin, 1975-76. Author: Tax Exempt Organizations, 1985; contbr. articles to profl. jours. Mem. ABA, Tex. Bar Assn., Fla. Bar Assn., Internat. Studies Assn. Avocations: computers. Legal education, Corporate taxation, General corporate. Home: 5305 Breeze Wood Dr Mishawaka IN 46544 Office: Mich State U Dept Gen Bus Law East Lansing MI 48824-1047

LASHINGER, JOSEPH A., lawyer; b. Aug. 7, 1953; m. Maria R. Donofrio, Apr. 3, 1976; children: Joseph A., Kristen Rose. BA in Polit. Sci. with honors, MA in Am. Nat. Govt. with honors, U. Pa., 1976; JD, Widener U., 1981. Assoc. Fox, Differ, Callahan, Ulrich & O'Hara, Norristown, Pa., 1981—; mem. Pa. House Jud. Com.; mem. Pa. Ho. of Reps., 1978—; bd. dirs. Worlco Inc., King of Prussia, Pa. coordinator com. Reagan for Pres., 1980; former chmn. Greater Norristown Corp.; bd. dirs. Pathway Sch., Cen. Montgomery County Mental Health/Mental Retardation Ctr., Montgomery County Children's Aid Soc., Cen. Montgomery County YMCA; co-chairperson Am. Heart Fund Dr. Assn., 1979-80. Named Outstanding Citizen of Yr. Greater Valley Forge C. of C., 1983, Outstanding Young Man of Yr. Jaycees, 1978; recipient Pub. Service award Montgomery County Pomona, 1983; named to High Sch. Hall Fame. Mem. ABA (family law com.), Pa. Bar Assn. (family law com.), Montgomery County Bar Assn. (family law com.), Assn. Trial Lawyers Am., Pa. Trial Lawyers Assn., Screen Actors Guild, Valley Forge Hist. Soc., AMBUCS, Norristown Zool. Soc. Republican. Roman Catholic. Club: Cedarbrook Country. Lodges: Optimists (Lower Providence), Sons of Italy. Office: Fox Differ Callahan Ulrich & O'Hara 317 Swede St Norristown PA 19401

LASHLEY, CURTIS DALE, lawyer; b. Urbana, Ill., Nov. 3, 1956; s. Jack Dale and Janice Elaine (Holman) L.; m. Tamara Dawn Yahnig, June 14, 1986. BA, U. Mo., Kansas City, 1978, JD, 1981. Bar: Mo. 1981, U.S. Dist. Ct. (we. dist.) Mo. 1981, U.S. Tax Ct. 1982. Assoc. Melvin Heller, Inc., Creve Coeur, Mo., 1982; ptnr. Domjan & Lashley, Harrisonville, Mo., 1983-86; asst. gen. counsel Mo. Dept. Revenue, Independence, 1986—. V.p. Cass County Young Reps., Harrisonville, 1985. Mem. ABA, Assn. Trial Lawyers Am., Mo. Mcpl. Attys. Assn. Republican. Presbyterian. Lodge: Kiwanis (treas. 1985-86). State government, Local government. Office: Mo Dept Revenue 16647 E 23d St Independence MO 64055

LASHMAN, SHELLEY BORTIN, judge; b. Camden, N.J., Aug. 18, 1917; s. William Mitchell and Anna (Bortin) L.; m. Ruth Horn, Jan. 3, 1959; children—Karen E. Lashman Hall, Gail A., Mitchell A., Christopher R. B.S., William and Mary Coll., 1938; postgrad. Columbia U., 1938, 39; J.D., U. Mich., 1946. Bar: N.Y. 1947, N.J. 1968. Judge N.J. Workers Compensation, Atlantic City, 1981—. Served with USNR, 1940-70. Mem. Res. Officers Assn., Atlantic County Bar Assn., Naval Res. Assn., Atlantic County Hist. Soc., Am. Judicature Soc., Ret. Officers Assn., U.S. Navy League, Fleet Res. Assn., Internat. Platform Assn., Mil. Order World Wars. Republican. Club: Atlantic City Country. Lodge: Elks. Workers' compensation. Home: 188-C Old Zion Rd Linwood NJ 08221 Office: Atlantic County Civil Courthouse 1201 Bacharach Blvd Atlantic City NJ 08901

LASKI, FRANK JOSEPH, lawyer, banker; b. Bklyn., May 1, 1929; s. Frank A. and Catherine V. (Corcoran) L.; m. Catherine E. Augustine, Aug. 8, 1953; children—John, Ruth, William, Richard, Mary, James, Ann. B.S. in Econs, Coll. Holy Cross, 1951; LL.B., J.D., Buffalo Law Sch., 1954. Bar: N.Y. bar 1954. Partner firm Phillips, Lytle, Hitchcock, Blaine & Huber, Buffalo, 1957-73; gen. counsel, sec. Marine Midland Banks, Inc., Buffalo, 1973—, Marine Midland Bank, Buffalo, 1976—. Served to lt. (j.g.) USNR, 1955-57. Mem. Am., N.Y. State, Erie County bar assns., Am. Soc. Corporate Secs., Assn. Bank Holding Cos. Roman Catholic. Clubs: Buffalo (Buffalo), Park Country (Buffalo); Bd. Room (N.Y.C.). Office: 2400 Marine Midland Center Buffalo NY 14203

LASKI, JAMES EMIL, lawyer; b. Chgo., Oct. 6, 1950; s. Emil J. and Dorothy (Mazer) L. BA cum laude, Loyola U., 1972; JD, U. Ill., 1975. Bar: Ill. 1975. Assoc. Miller and Pomper, Chgo., 1977-78, Charles E. Lindell Ltd., Chgo., 1978—. Mem. ABA, Ill. State Bar Assn. Roman Catholic. Avocations: horseback riding, running. Personal injury, General practice, Workers' compensation. Home: 1726 Stony Island Ave Crete IL 60417 Office: 9204 S Commercial Chicago IL 60617

LASOTA, PETER DOUGLAS, lawyer; b. Sacramento, Oct. 23, 1957; s. Peter Eugene and Helen Jane (Beyers) LaS.; div.; 1 child, Christopher Douglas. B.S. summa cum laude, Our Lady of Lake U., 1977; Cert., Inst. on Comparative Polit. and Econ. Systems, Georgetown U., 1976; J.D., Ariz. State U., 1980. Bar: Ariz. 1980, U.S. Dist. Ct. Ariz. 1980, U.S. Ct. Appeals (9th cir.) 1980. Prosecutor intern Maricopa County, Phoenix, 1979; asst. city prosecutor City of Phoenix, 1980-81, pub. defender, 1981-82; assoc. Thomas A. Thinnes P.A., Phoenix, 1981-82; pub. defender City of Mesa, Ariz., 1982-83; dep. pub. defender Maricopa County, Phoenix, 1983-85; sr. ptnr. Rice & LaSota, Phoenix, 1985—; cons. horse law, Phoenix, 1980—. Sen. Barry M. Goldwater scholar, 1976. Mem. ABA, Ariz. Bar Assn., Ariz. Buckskin Horse Assn. (bd. dirs.), Appaloosa Horse Club, Am. Quarter Horse Assn. Republican. Roman Catholic. Criminal, Juvenile, Personal injury. Home: 5021 E Pershing St Scottsdale AZ 85254 Office: Rice & LaSota 5060 N 19th Ave #112 Phoenix AZ 85015

LASSEN, JOHN KAI, lawyer; b. Youngstown, Ohio, Mar. 28, 1942; s. Kai Kierulff and Helen Susanne (Elsaesser) L.; children: Christian K., Laura Wick. BA, Yale, 1964; LLB, U. Pa., 1967. Bar: Del. 1971, U.S. Dist. Ct. Del. 1972. Assoc. Lord, Day & Lord, N.Y.C., 1967; assoc. Morris, Nichols, Arsht & Tunnell, 1971-77, ptnr., 1977-83; ptnr. Lassen, Smith, Katzenstein & Furlow, 1984—. Served to lt. USNR, 1967-70. Fellow Am. Coll. Probate Counsel; mem. ABA, Del. Bar Assn., Nat. Assn. Bond Counsel, Del. Com. of 100, Soc. Mayflower Descendants, Del. C. of C. Republican. Presbyterian. Clubs: Wilmington, Wilmington Country, Lincoln. Lodge: Rotary. General corporate, Probate, Corporate taxation. Office: PO Box 410 Wilmington DE 19899

LASSER, MARK LAWRENCE, lawyer; b. Pitts., Apr. 29, 1951; s. Harold H. and Bernice (Danovitz) L. BA in Econs., U. Mich., 1972, JD, 1975. Bar: Pa. 1975, Fla. 1976. Assoc. Ruden, Barnett, McClosky, Schuster & Russell, Ft. Lauderdale, Fla., 1975-77; gen. counsel, chief exec. officer Penn Plastic Inc., Creighton, Pa., 1977-84; v.p. merger and acquisitions legal div. The Buckley Group, Boca Raton, Fla., 1986—. Mem. ABA, Fla. Bar Assn., Pa. Bar Assn., Phi Beta Kappa. Avocation: pvt. pilot. Corporate taxation, General corporate. Home: 1361 S Ocean Dr #608 Pompano Beach FL 33062

LASSMAN, MALCOLM, lawyer; b. Bklyn., June 9, 1938; M. Barbara Turley (div.); children: Scott, Robin, Amy; m. Vivienne McIntosh; 1 child, Justine. BA, Washington & Lee U., 1960, LLB cum laude, 1963. Ptnr. Akin, Gump, Strauss, Hauer & Feld, Washington. Jewish. Lodge: Masons. Legislative. Home: 2883 Audubon Terr NW Washington DC 20008 Office: Akin Gump Strauss Hauer & Feld 1333 New Hampshire Ave NW Suite 400 Washington DC 20036

LASZYNSKI, ROBERT STEVEN, lawyer; b. Dowagiac, Mich., Aug. 27, 1953; s. Steve and Margaret (Hampel) L.; m. Cheryl Ann Florjancic, Oct. 15, 1977; children: Michael Steven, Jennifer Ann. BS, U. Notre Dame, 1975; JD, Ind. U., 1978. Bar: ind. 1978, U.S. Dist. Ct. (no. dist.) Ind. 1980. Ptnr. Cooke, Bache, Moore, Laszynski & Yeager, Lafayette, Ind., 1978—; bd. dirs, pres. Legal Aid Corp., Lafayette. Bd. dirs. Tippecanoe Arts Fedn., Lafayette, 1985—. Mem. ABA, Ind. Bar Assn., Tippecanoe County Bar Assn. (sec. 1980-81). Roman Catholic. Lodge: Elks. Avocation: sports. General practice, Probate, Real property. Home: 3530 Pine Needle West Lafayette IN 47906 Office: Cooke Bache Moore Laszynski & Yeager 331 Columbia St Lafayette IN 47901

LATCHAM, FRANKLIN CHESTER, lawyer; b. Tacoma, Feb. 5, 1922; s. Frank Albert and Betty Mulholland (Cook) L.; m. Patricia Peabody, Sept. 15, 1945; children: Jonathan, Margaret, Andrew, Franklin. B.S.L., U. Wash., 1943, LL.B., 1944; J.S.D., Yale U., 1951. Bar: Wash. 1944, Calif. 1946. Law clk. U.S. Ct. Appeals (9th cir.), 1944-46; assoc. Hoge, Pelton & Gunther, San Francisco, 1946-47; asst. prof., then assoc. prof. law Case-Western Res U., Cleve., 1948-54; assoc. Morrison & Foerster, San Francisco, 1954-61, ptnr., 1961—; lectr. NYU, 1952, U. Ill., 1954, U. San Francisco, 1958. Author: (with others) Shareholder Democracy, 1954, Open Space and the Law, 1965, California Taxes, 1978, Major Tax Planning, 1977, NYU Conference on State and Local Taxes, 1982, 83, 84, 85. Pres. bd. trustees San Anselmo Sch. Dist., Calif., 1965-73. Recipient Carkeek award U. Wash. Law Sch., 1943-44. Fellow Am. Coll. Tax Counsel; mem. ABA. Democrat. Episcopalian. Clubs: Commonwealth (San Francisco), Bankers (San Francisco). Home: PO Box 28 Mount Aukum CA 95656 Office: Morrison & Foerster 345 California St San Francisco CA 94104-2105

LATHAM, B. MILLS, lawyer; b. Amarillo, Tex., May 9, 1942; s. Bill Mason and Jo (Mills) L.; m. Sandra Manley, Nov. 26, 1965; children—Keven, David, Blakely, Chase; m. 2d, Beverly Martin, Sept. 26, 1980. Student U. So. Calif., 1960-61; B.S., West Tex. State U., 1965; J.D., U. Tex., 1969. Bar: Tex. 1969, U.S. Dist. Ct. (so. dist.) Tex. 1969, U.S. Ct. Appeals Ct. (5th cir.) 1975. Assoc., ptnr. Dyer, Redford, Burnett, Wray & Woolsay, Corpus Christi, Tex., 1970-78; sole practice, Corpus Christi, 1978-83; ptnr. Latham & Moss, 1984—; adj. prof. Columbia Coll. Bus. Law Sch. Chmn. Citizens for Pub. Safety, 1982; bd. govs. South Tex. Art Found., 1974-78; bd. dirs. Johnny Rodriguez Life Enrichment Ctr., 1976; bd. dirs. Lawyers Involved for Tex. Mem. State Bar Tex. (grievance com.), ABA, Nueces County Bar Assn. (bd. dirs.), Tex. Trial Lawyers Assn. (bd. dirs.), Assn. Trial Lawyers Am. Democrat. Admiralty, Personal injury, Workers' compensation. Home: 315 Grant Corpus Christi TX 78411 Office: 1660 Texas Commerce Plaza Corpus Christi TX 78470

LATHAM, JOSEPH AL, JR., lawyer; b. Kinston, N.C., Sept. 16, 1951; s. Joseph Al and Margaret Lee (Tyson) L.; m. Janet M. Wagner, Aug. 8, 1968; m. Elaine Frances Kramer, Dec. 19, 1981. B.A., Yale U., 1973; J.D., Vanderbilt U., 1976. Bar: Calif. 1976, U.S. Dist. Ct. (cen. dist.) Calif. 1977, U.S. Ct. Appeals (9th cir.) 1977, U.S. Dist. Ct. (no. and so. dists.) Calif. 1978, Ga. 1980, U.S. Dist. Ct. (no. dist.) Ga. 1981, U.S. Ct. Appeals (5th and 11th cirs.) 1981, U.S. Dist. Ct. (mid. dist.) Ga. 1982, D.C. 1984. Assoc. Paul, Hastings, Janofsky & Walker, Los Angeles and Newport Beach, Calif., 1976-80, Atlanta, 1980-83; chief counsel to bd. mem. NLRB, Washington, 1983-85; staff director, U.S Commission on Civil Rights, Washington, 1985-86; ptnr., Paul, Hastings, Janofsky & Walker, Costa Mesa, Calif., 1987—. Editorial asst. Employment Discrimination Law, 2d edit., 1983; author articles in Litigation, Employee Relations Law Jour.; articles editor Vanderbilt Law Rev., 1975-76. Mem. ABA (labor and employment law sect.), Order of Coif. Republican. Episcopalian. Labor. Office: Paul Hastings Janofsky & Walker 695 Town Ctr Dr Costa Mesa CA 92626

LATHAM, OLIVER BRADLEY, lawyer; b. Malden, Mass., Oct. 4, 1940; s. Earle and H. Irene (Morrison) L.; m. Janet M. Wagner, Aug. 8, 1968; children: Christopher M., Joshua E., John B. BA, Tufts U., 1963; JD, Boston U., 1969. Bar: Mass. 1969, U.S. Supreme Ct. 1973. Atty. John Hancock Ins. Co., Boston, 1969-71; ptnr. Latham & Latham P.C., Reading, Mass., 1971—; bd. dirs. Baybank Middlesex, Burlington, Mass. Pres. E. Middlesex region ARC, Melrose, Mass., 1975-82; chmn. Middlesex junction Am. Cancer Soc., Lynn, Mass., 1984-85; bd. dirs. Am. Heart Assn., Andover, Mass., 1973-77, Easter Seal Soc., Boston, 1979—. Served to capt. USMC, 1963-66, Vietnam. Avocations: hunting, fishing. Real property, Administrative and regulatory. Office: Latham & Latham PC 643 Main St Reading MA 01867

LATHAM, WELDON HURD, lawyer; b. Bklyn., Jan. 2, 1947; s. Aubrey Geddes and Avril (Hurd) L.; m. Constantia Beecher, Aug. 8, 1948; children—Nicole Marie, Brett Weldon. B.A., Howard U., 1968; J.D., Georgetown U., 1971; postgrad. George Washington U., 1975-76 advanced coures Bar: D.C. 1972, U.S. Ct. Mil. Appeals 1974, U.S. Ct. Claims 1975, U.S. Ct. Appeals (D.C. cir.) 1972, U.S. Supreme Ct. 1975, Va. 1981. Mgmt. cons. Checchi & Co., Washington, 1968-71; atty. Covington & Burling, Washington, 1971-73; sr. atty. Fed. Energy Adminstrn., Washington, 1974; asst. gen. counsel Exec. Office Pres., Office Mgmt. and Budget, 1974-76; atty. Hogan & Hartson, Washington, 1976-79; gen. dep. asst. sec. U.S. Dept. of HUD, 1979-81; v.p., gen. counsel Sterling Systems, Inc. (subs. PRC), exec. asst. to chmn. and chief exec. officer, assoc. gen. counsel Planning Research Corp., McLean, Va., 1981-86; ptnr. Reed Smith Shaw & McClay, Washington and McLean, Va., 1986—; adj. prof. Howard U. Law Sch., Washington, 1972-82; guest prof. U. Va. Law Sch., Charlottesville, 1976—; mem. Va. Gov.'s Bus. and Industry Adv. Com. on Crime Prevention, 1983-85; mem. Va. Gov.'s Regulatory Reform Adv. Bd., 1982-84; legal counsel Md. Mondale for Pres. Campaign, 1984. Bd. dirs. U. D.C. Found, Inc., 1982—; mem. Washington Steering Com. NAACP Legal Def. Fund, 1975—; dir. Washington Council Lawyers, 1973; bd. of trustees Va. Commonwealth U., Richmond, 1986—; bd. dirs. Washington Urban League, 1986—. Served as capt. USAF, 1973-74. Recipient Effective Mgr. award HUD, 1980, Opportunity in Higher Edn. award Nat. Assn. for Equal Achievement, 1987. Mem. ABA, Fed. Bar Assn., Nat. Bar Assn., D.C. C. of C. (gen. counsel 1979), State Va. Bar Assn., Washington Bar Assn., Bar Assn. D.C., Nat. Lawyers Club Washington, Washington Met. Area Corp. Counsels Assn., Nat. Contract Mgmt. Assn. Mem. editorial adv. bd. Washington Bus. Jour., 1985—. General corporate, Administrative and regulatory, Government contracts and claims. Home: 7638 Royal Dominion Dr Bethesda MD 20817 Office: Reed Smith Shaw & McClay Suite 900 1150 Connecticut Ave NW Washington DC 20006 also: 8201 Greensboro Dr Suite 800 McLean VA 22102

LATHROP, MITCHELL LEE, lawyer; b. Los Angeles, Dec. 15, 1937; s. Alfred Lee and Barbara (Mitchell) L.; children—Christin Lorraine, Alexander Mitchell, Timothy Trewin Mitchell. B.Sc., U.S. Naval Acad., 1959; J.D., U. So. Calif., 1966. Bar: D.C., Calif. 1966, U.S. Supreme Ct. 1969, N.Y. 1981. Dep. counsel Los Angeles County, Calif., 1966-68; with firm Brill, Hunt, DeBuys and Burby, Los Angeles, 1968-71; ptnr. firm Macdonald, Halsted & Laybourne, Los Angeles and San Diego, 1971-80; sr. ptnr. Rogers & Wells, N.Y.C., San Diego, 1980-86, Adams, Duque & Hazeltine, Los Angeles, N.Y.C. and San Diego, 1986—; presiding referee Calif. Bar Ct., 1984-86, mem. exec. com., 1981—; lectr. law Advanced Mgmt. Research Inc., Practicing Law Inst. N.Y., Continuing Edn. of Bar, State Bar Calif., ABA. Western Regional chmn. Met. Opera Nat. Council, 1971-81, v.p. and mem. exec. com., 1971—, now chmn.; trustee Honnold Library at Claremont Colls., 1972-80; bd. dirs. Music Ctr. Opera Assn., Los Angeles, sec., 1974-80; bd. dirs. San Diego Opera Assn., 1980—, v.p., 1985—; bd. dirs. Met. Opera Assn., N.Y.C. Served to capt. JAGC, USNR. Mem. ABA, N.Y. Bar Assn., Fed. Bar Assn., Fed. Bar Council, Calif. Bar Assn., D.C. Bar Assn., San Diego County Bar Assn. (chmn. ethics com. 1980-82, bd. dirs. 1982-85, v.p. 1985), Assn. Bus. Trial Lawyers, Assn. So. Calif. Def. Counsel, Los Angeles Opera Assos. (pres. 1970-72), Soc. Colonial Wars in Calif. (gov. 1970-72), Order St. Lazarus of Jerusalem, Friends of Claremont Coll. (dir. 1975-81, pres. 1978-79), Friends of Huntington Library, Am. Bd. Trial Advocates, Judge Advocates Assn. (dir. Los Angeles chpt. 1974-80, pres. So. Calif. chpt. 1977-78), Internat. Assn. Def. Counsel, Brit. United Services Club (dir. Los Angeles 1973-75), Mensa Internat., Calif. Soc., S.R. (pres. 1977-79), Phi Delta Phi. Republican. Clubs: California (Los Angeles); Valley Hunt (Pasadena, Calif.); Metropolitan (N.Y.C.). Environment, Insurance, Federal civil litigation. Home: 706 Stafford Pl San Diego CA 92107 Office: 401 W A St 23d Floor San Diego CA 92101 Office: 440 Madison Ave 22d Floor New York NY 10022

LATHROP, ROGER ALAN, lawyer; b. Fairfield, Iowa, Aug. 24, 1951; s. Melvin G. and Naomi Rose (Liles) L.; m. Cynthia Lee Topping, Aug. 14, 1971; 1 son, Benjamin Alan. B.S., U. No. Iowa, 1972; J.D., U. Iowa, 1976. Bar: Iowa 1976, U.S. Dist. Ct. (no. and so. dists.) Iowa 1976. Constrn. laborer Stewart Constrn. Co., Fairfield and Iowa City, 1969-71; mgmt. trainee Osco Drug Co., Waterloo, Iowa, 1971-72; traffic mgr. Waterloo Industries, 1972; assoc. Betty, Neuman & McMahon, Davenport, Iowa, 1976-79, ptnr., 1979—; instr. bus. law Scott Community Coll., Bettendorf, Iowa, 1976, Blackhawk Community Coll. Moline, Ill., 1977. Mem. Iowa State Bar Assn., Scott County Bar Assn. (pres. 1987-88, exec. council 1978—), ABA, Iowa Def. Counsel Assn., Def. Research Inst. (product liability and ins. law coms.), Iowa Acad. Trial Lawyers, Iowa Assn. Trial Lawyers, Assn. Trial Lawyers Am., U. Iowa Alumni Assn. Club: Pentacrest Soc. (Iowa City). Methodist. Federal civil litigation, State civil litigation, Personal injury. Home: 2214 Warren St Davenport IA 52804 Office: Betty Neuman & McMahon 600 Union Arcade Bldg Davenport IA 52801

LATHROP, TRAYTON LEMOINE, lawyer; b. Boscobel, Wis., Nov. 14, 1923; s. Ralph Waldo and Dessa May (Brownlee) L.; m. Ruth Eleanor Reynolds, Aug. 19, 1944; children: Mary Blanche, Carol Ruth Lathrop White, David Trayton, Louise Ann Lathrop Hemstead. BA, U. Wis., 1943, LLB, 1948. Bar: Wis. 1948, U.S. Dist. Ct. (we. dist.) Wis. 1948, U.S. Patent Office, 1953, U.S. Supreme Ct. 1960, U.S. Dist. Ct. (ea. dist.) Wis. 1966, U.S. Ct. Appeals (7th cir.) 1966. Ptnr. Isaksen, Lathrop, Esch, Hart & Clark, Madison, Wis., 1954—; spl. counsel City of Madison, 1955-62, City of Beloit, Wis., 1966-70, Wis. Assembly, Madison, 1978, Wis. Dept. Adminstrn., 1981; lectr. law U. Wis., Madison, 1958, 72, 74, 78; arbitrator Am. Arbitration Assn., 1966—. Contbr. articles to profl. jours. Sec. zoning bd. appeals, Madison, 1953-55; chmn. bd. trustees Presbytery of Madison, 1963-66; candidate for justice Wis. Supreme Ct., 1977, 83. Served to lt. USNR, 1943-46. Mem. ABA, Fed. Bar Assn., State Bar Assn. Wis., Bar Assn. 7th Fed. Cir., Dane County Bar Assn., Wis. Intellectual Property Law Assn., Wis. Acad. Scis., Arts and Letters, Bibl. Archeol. Soc. Madison. Lodge: Rotary (Madison) (dist. gov. 1985-86). State civil litigation, Federal civil litigation, General practice. Home: 1310 Whenona Dr Madison WI 53711 Office: 122 W Washington Ave PO Box 1507 Madison WI 53701

LATIMER, ALLIE B., lawyer, government official; b. Coraopolis, Pa.; d. Lawnye S. and Bennie Latimer. BS, Hampton Inst., 1947; JD, Howard U., 1953; LLM, Catholic U., 1958; postgrad., Am. U., 1960-61. Bar: N.C. bar 1955, D.C. bar 1960. Vol. in projects Am. Friends Service Com., N.J. and, Europe, 1948-49; correctional officer Fed. Reformatory for Women, Alderson, W.Va., 1949-51; personnel clk. NIH, Bethesda, 1953-55; realty officer Mitchell AFB, N.Y., 1955-56; with Office Gen. Counsel, GSA, Washington, 1957—; chief counsel Office Gen. Counsel, GSA, after 1966, asst. gen. counsel, 1971-76, gen. counsel, 1977—; asst. gen. counsel NASA, 1976-77; past chmn. central office com. Fed. Women's Program, GSA; mem. membership and budget com. Health and Welfare Council, 1967-72. Bd. dirs. D.C. Mental Health Assn., pres., 1977-79; bd. dirs. Friendship House, Washington; elder Presbyn. Ch.; pres. Interacial Council, 1964-75; chmn. Presbyn. Econ. Devel. Corp., 1975-81; mem. governing bd. Nat. Council Chs. of Christ in U.S.A. Recipient GSA Sustained Superior Service award, 1959, Meritorious Service award, 1964, Commendable Service award, 1964, Pub. Service award, 1971, Outstanding Performance award, 1971, Presdl. Rank award, 1983, Disting. Service award, 1984. Mem. ABA, Nat. Bar Assn. (sec. 1966-74), Fed. Bar Assn., Washington Bar Assn., N.C. Bar Assn., Nat. Bar Found. (dir. 1970-71, pres. 1974-75), Hampton Alumni Assn. (pres. Washington chpt. 1970-71), Howard Law Alumni Assn. (v.p. 1962-63) alumni assns), Links (pres. Washington chpt. 1971-74, nat. v.p. 1976-80), Federally Employed Women (founder, 1st pres.). Government contracts and claims, Computer, General practice. Home: 1721 S St NW Washington DC 20009

LATINO, ANTHONY LEON, lawyer; b. Beaumont, Tex., Apr. 29, 1951; s. Leon and Helen (Whitaker) L. BA in Govt., Lamar U., 1974, BA in Sociology, 1977; JD, Southwestern U., Los Angeles, 1980. Bar: Tex. 1981, U.S. Dist. Ct. (ea. and so. dists.) Tex. 1981, U.S. Ct. Appeals (5th cir.) 1982, U.S. Supreme Ct. 1986; cert, secondary tchr., Tex. Briefing atty. 13th Ct. Appeals, Corpus Christi, Tex., 1981-83; chief trial div. Jefferson County Dist. Atty., Beaumont, 1983-86; asst. atty. gen. State of Tex., Austin, 1986—; lectr. Lamar U. Dept. Criminal Justice, Beaumont, 1985—. Mem. Young Men's Bus. League, 1986, Leadership Beaumont, 1984. Named one of Outstanding Young Men of Am., 1985. Mem. ABA, Tex. Bar Assn., Tex. Dist. and County Attys. Assn., Jefferson County Young Lawyers Assn. (bd. dirs. 1984-86, sec. 1986—), LAmar U. Alumni Assn., Leadership Beaumont Alumni Assn., Kappa Sigma (sec. 1972-73, asst. alumnus advisor 1984—), Bus. and Profl. Men's Club. Democrat. Roman Catholic. Clubs: Beaumont. Avocations: racquetball, tennis, golf. Federal civil litigation, State civil litigation, Criminal. Office: State of Tex Atty Gens Office PO Box 12548 Austin TX 78711

LATOVICK, PAULA R(AE), lawyer; b. Detroit, Feb. 17, 1954; d. Raymond and Marjorie Camille (Peters) L.; m. William P. Weiner, Aug. 17, 1985. BA in Personnel with high honor, Mich. State U., 1976; JD cum laude, U. Mich., 1980. Bar: Mich. 1980, U.S. Dist. Ct. (ea. dist.) Mich. 1980, U.S. Dist. Ct. (we. dist.) Mich. 1981, U.S. Ct. Appeals (6th cir.) 1985. Assoc. Fraser, Trebilcock, Davis & Foster P.C., Lansing, Mich., 1980-86, ptnr., 1986—; adj. prof. Thomas M. Cooley Law Sch., Lansing, 1984-86. Head advisor law explorers Boy Scouts Am., Lansing, 1982-84; mem. Capitol Area Women's Network, Lansing, 1984—. Named One of Outstanding Young Women of Am., 1985. Mem. Mich. Bar Assn. (young lawyers exec. council 1984-86), Women Lawyers Assn. Mich., Ingham County Young Lawyers Bar Assn. (chmn. hist. com. 1984—, young lawyers bd. 1981-84, pres. 1983), Thomas M. Cooley Legal Authors Soc., NOW, Indsl. Research Assn., U. Mich. Alumni Assn. (life), Mich. State U. Alumni Assn. Democrat. Roman Catholic. Club: Zonta (recording sec. 1985-86), YWCA (Lansing)(bd. dirs.). State civil litigation, Local government, Public utilities. Office: Fraser Trebilcock Davis & Foster PC 1000 Mich Nat Tower Lansing MI 48933

LATSHAW, K. MICHAEL, lawyer; b. Decatur, Ill., Oct. 14, 1946; s. Kenneth Herbert and Eunice Alberta (Wheeler) L.; m. Grace Lisbeth Heitman, Mar. 20, 1969 (div. Feb. 1981); 1 child, Jennifer Blake. BA cum laude, Millikin U., 1968; JD, U. Ill., 1975. Bar: Ill. 1975, U.S. Dist. Ct. (cen. dist.) Ill. 1978, U.S. Supreme Ct. 1986. Atty. Champaign (Ill.) County Pub. Defender, 1975; assoc. Bennett & Carpel, Decatur, 1976; ptnr. Bennett, Willoughby & Latshaw, Decatur, 1976-84, Willoughby & Latshaw, Decatur, 1984—; hearing officer Ill. Sec. of State, Springfield, 1980-81; adv. council Ill. Atty. Gen., Chgo., 1985—. del. Dem. Nat. Conv., 1984; mem. fin. com. Macon County Dems., 1986—. Served to lt. USNR, 1980—. Mem. Assn. Trial Lawyers Am., Ill. Trial Lawyers Assn., Ill. Bar Assn., Decatur Bar Assn., Phi Alpha Delta, Phi Kappa Phi. Lodge: Masons. Avocation: flying. State civil litigation, Federal civil litigation, Workers' compensation. Office: Willoughby & Latshaw PC 502 W Prairie Decatur IL 62522

LATTOF, MITCHELL GEORGE, JR., lawyer; b. Mobile, Ala., July 3, 1956; s. Mitchell George and Frankie Jean (Trent) L.; m. Mary Elizabeth Davis, Sept. 3, 1983; 1 child, Mitchell George III. BA, U. Ala., Tuscaloosa, 1976, JD, 1979. Bar: Ala. 1979, U.S. Dist. Ct. (so. dist.) Ala. 1979, U.S. Ct. Appeals (5th cir.) 1979, U.S. Dist. Ct. (so. dist.) Miss. 1980, U.S. Dist. Ct. (no. dist.) Fla. 1980, U.S. Ct. Appeals (11th and D.C. cirs.) 1982, U.S. Supreme Ct. 1986. Assoc. Diamond, Lattof, Gardner, Pate and Peters, Mobile, 1979-80; assoc. Diamond, Lattof, Gardner and Flynn, Mobile, 1980-81, ptnr., 1982-83; ptnr. Lattof and Gardner, P.C., Mobile, 1983—. Mem. Ala. Trial Lawyers Assn. (bd. govs. 1983—, exec. com. 1986—), Am. Trial Lawyers Assn., Mobile Bar Assn., Southeastern Admiralty Lawyers Assn. Episcopalian. Admiralty, Personal injury, Workers' compensation. Office: Lattof and Gardner PC PO Box 3066 Mobile AL 36652

LATZ, ROBERT, lawyer; b. Mpls., July 15, 1930; s. Rubin and Rose (Arnove) L.; m. Carolyn M. Spater, Aug. 6, 1961; children: Ronald, Martin, Michael, Shari. BS, U. Minn., 1952, JD, 1954. Bar: Minn. 1954, U.S. Dist. Ct. Minn. 1954, U.S. Ct. Appeals (8th cir.) 1982. Asst. atty. gen. State of Minn., 1955-58; ptnr. Sachs, Latz & Kirshbaum, Mpls., 1960-81; pres. Robert Latz, P.A., Mpls., 1981—. Regent U. Minn., 1975-81, vice-chmn. bd. dirs. 1979-81; mem. nat. panel arbitrators Am. Arbitration Assn., 1975; Democratic-Farmer-Labor Party candidate Minn. Atty. Gen., 1966; chmn. Jewish Community Relations Council Anti-Defamation League, Minn. and Dakotas, 1980-82; chmn. Mpls. Urban Coalition Action Council, 1970-72; atty. Minn. Children's Lobby, 1970-73; pres. Greater Mpls. Met. Housing Corp., 1977-78; chmn. bd. govs. U. Minn. Hosp., 1987—. Served with USNR, 1958-60. Recipient Minn. Found. for Better Hearing and Speech Profl. Service award, 1980. Mem. ABA, Am. Soc. Law and Medicine, Assn. Trial Lawyers Am., Minn. Trial Lawyers Assn., Minn. State Bar Assn., Hennepin County Bar Assn., Delta Sigma Rho. Democratic Farmer Labor. Jewish. Lodges: Mason, B'nai B'rith. Contbr. articles to profl. jours. Labor, Legislative. Home: 6850 Harold Ave Minneapolis MN 55427 Office: 5353 Wayzata Blvd Minneapolis MN 55416

LAU, JEFFREY DANIEL, lawyer; b. Honolulu, May 2, 1948; s. Daniel B.T. and Evelyn (Yee Quil) L.; m. Susan Tilden Lau, June 1, 1974; 1 child, Daniel Prescott Tilden. BSBA in Econs., Lehigh U., 1970; MBA in Fin., Temple U., 1973; JD, U. Calif., San Francisco, 1977. Bar: Hawaii, U.S. Dist. Ct. Hawaii, U.S. Ct. Appeals (9th cir.) 1978. Law clk. to presiding justice U.S. Dist. Ct. Hawaii, Honolulu, 1975, U.S. Ct. Appeals (9th cir.), Honolulu, 1976; assoc. Frank D. Padett, Honolulu, 1977-80; ptnr. Chung, Lau, MacLaren and Lau, Honolulu, 1980-81, Fong and Miho, Honolulu, 1981-84, Oliver, Lee, Cuskaden Ogawa & Lau, Honolulu, 1985—; bd. dirs., asst. corp. sec. Fin. Factors, Ltd., Honolulu, Fin. Realty, Ltd., Honolulu; corp. sec. Grand Pacific Life Ins. Co., Ltd., 1984—. Served to capt. U.S.

Army, 1972-74. Mem. ABA, Assn. Trial Lawyers Am., Hawaii State Bar Assn. Mem. United Ch. of Christ. Avocations: skiing, volleyball, softball, surfing. Banking, Bankruptcy, State civil litigation. Office: Oliver Lee Cuskaden Ogawa & Lau 222 Kalakaua Ave Suite 1200 Honolulu HI 96815

LAUB, GEORGE COOLEY, lawyer; b. Easton, Pa., Jan. 16, 1912; s. Herbert F. and Hannah A. (Cooley) L.; m. Elizabeth Traill Green, Jan. 19, 1939 (dec. 1986). A.B., Lafayette Coll., 1933, LL.D. (hon.), 1983; LL.B., U. Pa., 1936. Bar: Pa. 1936, since practiced in Easton; legal adviser, mem. men's adv. bd. Easton Home for Aged Women, 1940-80; past dir. City of Easton Authority, Easton Nat. Bank and Trust Co.; mem. Northampton County Bd. Benchers, 1970-72. Bd. dirs. Community Chest, 1943-45, 49-52, drive chmn., 1949, pres., 1951; life trustee Lafayette Coll., 1958—, chmn. wills and trusts program, 1963-76, sec. bd., 1959-82, counsel, 1965—. Served to 1st lt., Judge Adv. Gen.'s Dept., AUS, 1945-47. Mem. ABA, Pa. Bar Assn., (exec. com. 1952-54), Northampton County Bar Assn. (pres. 1954-55), SAR, Northampton County Hist. Soc., Am. Judicature Soc., Nat. Assn. Coll. and U. Attys., Trout Unltd., Nat. Skeet Shooting Assn., Phi Delta Theta. Presbyterian (pres. bd. trustees 1957-59). Clubs: Country Northampton County: Pomfret; Skytop (Pa.); Easton Anglers. Estate planning, College law, Legal education. Home: 117 W Wayne Ave Easton PA 18042 Office: Laub Seidel Cohen & Hof Easton Dollar Savs and Trust Co Bldg 8 Centre Sq Easton PA 18042

LAUCHENGCO, JOSE YUJUICO, JR., lawyer; b. Manila, Philippines, Dec. 6, 1936; came to U.S., 1962; s. José Celis Sr. Lauchengco and Angeles (Yujuico) Sapota; m. Elisabeth Schindler, Feb. 22, 1968; children: Birthe, Martina, Duane, Lance. AB, U. Philippines, Quezon City, 1959; MBA, U. So. Calif., 1964; JD, Loyola U., Los Angeles, 1971. Bar: Calif. 1972, U.S. Dist. Ct. (cen. dist.) Calif. 1972, U.S. Ct. Appeals (9th cir.) 1972, U.S. Supreme Ct. 1975. Banker First Western Bank/United Calif. Bank, Los Angeles, 1964-71; assoc. Demler, Perona, Langer & Bergkvist, Long Beach, Calif., 1972-73; ptnr. Demler, Perona, Langer, Bergkvist, Lauchengco & Manzella, Long Beach, 1973-77; sole practice Long Beach and Los Angeles, 1977-83; ptnr. Lauchengco & Mendoza, Los Angeles, 1983—; mem. commn. on jud. procedures County of Los Angeles, 1979; tchr. Confraternity of Christian Doctrine, 1972-79; counsel Philippine Presdl. Commn. on Good Govt., Los Angeles, 1986. Mem. So. Calif. Asian Dem. Caucus, Los Angeles, 1977; chmn. Filipino-Am. Bi-Partisan Polit. Action Group, Los Angeles, 1978. Recipient Degree of Distinction, Nat. Forensic League, 1955. Mem. Criminal Cts. Bar Assn., Calif. Attys. Criminal Justice, Los Angeles County Bar Assn., Assn. Trial Lawyers Am., Calif. Trial Lawyers Assn., Los Angeles County Trial Lawyers Assn., U. Philippines Vanguard Assn. (life), Beta Sigma. Roman Catholic. Lodge: K.C. Avocations: classical music, opera, romantic paintings and sculpture, camping, shooting. Federal civil litigation, Personal injury, Criminal. Office: Lauchengco & Mendoza 2503 W Beverly Blvd Suite 4 Los Angeles CA 90057

LAUDERDALE, KATHERINE SUE, lawyer; b. Dayton, Ohio, May 30, 1954; d. Azo and Helen Ceola (Davis) L. BA in Soviet Studies, Ohio State U., 1975; JD, NYU, 1978. Bar: Ill. 1978, U.S. Dist. Ct. (no. dist.) Ill. 1978. Assoc. Schiff, Hardin & Waite, Chgo., 1978-82; dir. bus. and legal affairs Sta. WTTW-TV, Chgo., 1982-83, gen. counsel, 1983—. Bd. dirs. Midwest Women's Ctr., Chgo., 1985—; active Chgo. Council Fgn. Relations, 1981—, mem. fgn. affairs com. 1986—. Mem. ABA, Chgo. Bar Assn. (bd. dirs. Television Prodns., Inc. 1986—), Lawyers for Creative Arts (bd. dirs. 1984—), NYU Law Alumni Assn. Midwest (mem. exec. bd. 1982—). Democrat. Entertainment, General corporate. Office: WTTW/Chgo 5400 N St Louis Ave Chicago IL 60625

LAUER, ELIOT, lawyer; b. N.Y.C., Aug. 17, 1949; s. George and Doris (Trenk) L.; m. Marilyn Steinberg, June 5, 1977; children: Tamar Rachel, Ilana Jennifer, Michael Jonathan. BA, Yeshiva U., 1971; JD, Fordham U., 1974. Bar: D.C. 1975, N.Y. 1975, U.S. Dist. Ct. (so. and ea. dists.) N.Y. 1975, U.S. Ct. Appeals (2d cir.) 1975, U.S. Supreme Ct. 1984. Assoc. Curtis, Mallet-Prevost, Colt & Mosle, N.Y.C., 1974-82, ptnr., 1982—. Counsel Keren-Or Inc., N.Y.C., 1985—; bd. dirs. Hebrew Acad. Long Beach, N.Y., 1985—, Young Israel Lawrence, Cedarhurst, N.Y., 1984—. Mem. ABA, N.Y. State Bar Assn., Assn. of Bar of City of N.Y., Fed. Bar Council, Am. Arbitration Assn. (arbitrator 1979—), Nat. Futures Assn. (arbitrator 1983—). Republican. Federal civil litigation, Criminal. Office: Curtis Mallet-Provost Colt & Mosle 101 Park Ave New York NY 10178

LAUER, JUDY ANNE, law librarian; b. Delaware, Ohio, Nov. 1, 1950; d. Walter William and Jean (Clement) L.; m. Patrick James Leary, Aug. 11, 1984. BA, Gettysburg Coll., 1972; MLS, Syracuse U., 1975. Librarian Hancock & Estabrook, Syracuse, N.Y., 1978-82; law librarian N.Y. State Supreme Ct. Library, Binghamton, N.Y., 1982—. Mem. Am. Assn. Law Libraries, Assn. Law Libraries Upstate N.Y. (treas. 1980-81, bd. dirs. 1985-86, sec. 1986—), N.Y. State Unified Ct. Law Library Assn. (sec. 1984-85, treas. 1984-86). Mem. Unitarian Ch. Avocations: reading, gardening, camping. Librarianship. Home: RD 2 Box 49 Marathon NY 13803 Office: NY State Supreme Ct Library Broome County Courthouse Room 107 Binghamton NY 13901

LAUFENBERG, LYNN RAYMOND, lawyer; b. Prairie Du Chien, Wis., Dec. 11, 1949; s. Lee Ambrose and Rosemary Cecilia (Valentine) L.; m. Rachael Anne Joyce, Oct. 19, 1968 (div. Dec. 1980); m. Mary Jane Sobczak Comp, July 5, 1982; children: Melissa Lea, Michael Lynn. BA in Criminal Justice with honors, U. Wis., Platteville, 1972; JD cum laude, Marquette U., 1975. Bar: Wis. 1975, U.S. Dist. Ct. (ea. and we. dists.) Wis. 1975, U.S. Ct. Appeals (7th cir.) 1978. Law examiner Wis. Supreme Ct., Madison, 1975-76; assoc. Frisch, Dudek and Slattery, Ltd., Milw., 1976-80, ptnr., 1981—. Athletic dir. St. Agnes Parish Sch., Butler, Wis., 1980-81, mem. bd. dirs., 1978-80. Def. Research Inst., scholar, Milw., 1974. Mem. Assn. Trial Lawyers Am., Wis. Acad. Trial Lawyers (asst. editor Verdict, 1985—), Wis. Bar Assn. (interest on lawyers trust accounts study com. 1984-86). Democrat. Roman Catholic. Avocations: reading, history, running, biking, tennis. State civil litigation, Personal injury, Workers' compensation. Home: 848 Edgerton Ave Greendale WI 53129 Office: Frisch Dudek and Slattery Ltd 825 N Jefferson St Milwaukee WI 53202

LAUGESEN, RICHARD W., lawyer; b. Crawford, Nebr., Feb. 28, 1934; s. Richard William Sr. and Ava Faith (Markley) L.; m. Elisabeth M. Kennedy, July 21, 1962; children: Karen E., Amy K., Kristen L. BA, Colo. State Coll., 1952-56; JD, U. Denver, 1962. Bar: Colo. 1962. Ptnr. Anderson, Campbell & Laugesen, P.C., Denver, 1962—; lectr. law U. Denver, 1982—; mem. Gov.'s Task Force Ins. and Tort Reform, 1985-86; speaker profl. seminars. Contbr. articles to profl. jours. Chmn. Supreme Ct. Civil Rules Com., Colo., 1982—; mem. Colo. Apellate Rules Com., 1985—. Served to capt. USAF, 1956-59. Mem. Am. Coll. Trial Lawyers, Am. Trial Lawyers Assn., Fedn. Ins. Counsel, Colo. Bar Assn. (litigation sect.), Colo. Jud. Inst., Def. Research Inst. Avocations: horses, wood working, music, wheeling. State civil litigation, Insurance, Personal injury. Home: 3030 S Falton Ct Denver CO 80231 Office: Anderson Campbell & Laugesen 3464 S Willow St Denver CO 80231

LAUGHLIN, JAMES HAROLD, JR., lawyer; b. Charleston, W.Va., July 18, 1941; s. James Harold and Pearl Ruby L.; m. Eleanor Blackford Watson, II Aug. 3, 1968; children—C. Michele, Jeanette C., Cheryl Adele. B.S. in Chem. Engring., W.Va. U., 1964; J.D., Am. U., 1968. Bar: D.C. 1968, Va. 1969. Atty., Am. Cyanamid Co., Wayne, N.J., 1968-70, Xerox Corp., Rochester, N.Y., 1971-76; ptnr. Benoit, Smith & Laughlin, Arlington, Va., 1977—; legal counsel YMCA, 1981—. Mem. ABA, Am. Intellectual Property Law Assn. (treas. 1982-85, bd. dirs. 1976-79), Va. State Bar, (chmn. PTC sect. 1982-83), Nat. Council Patent Law Assns. (Va. del. 1983—). Patent, Federal civil litigation, Legislative. Office: 2001 Jefferson Davis Hwy Suite 501 Arlington VA 22202

LAUGHLIN, JAMES PATRICK, lawyer; b. Denver, Aug. 24, 1951; s. John Robert and Marjorie Rose (Carey) L.; m. Dona Metcalf, Apr. 1, 1978; 1 child, Colin Hamilton. BA in Polit. Sci. and Theology summa cum laude, Boston Coll., 1974, JD cum laude, 1977. Bar: N.Y. 1978, U.S. Dist. Ct. (so. dist.) N.Y. 1979, U.S. Dist. Ct. (ea. dist.) N.Y. 1981, U.S. Ct. Appeals (2d cir.) 1982. Assoc. White & Case, N.Y.C., 1977—. Editor Boston Coll. Law Rev., 1976-77. Mem. Order of Coif. Federal civil litigation, Securities, Bankruptcy. Office: White & Case 1155 Ave of the Americas New York NY 10036

LAUGHTER, RON D., lawyer; b. Detroit, Oct. 4, 1948; s. Harry Brookshire and Patsy Ruth (Coles) L.; m. Barbara Jane Morrison, Aug. 1, 1969; children: Heather Elizabeth, Shannon Marie. BS, Mich. State U., 1970; JD cum laude, T.M. Cooley Law Sch., 1980. Bar: Mich. 1980. Registered rep. Conn. Gen. Ins. Corp., Grand Rapids, Mich., 1972-73; dir. planned giving Am. Cancer Soc., Lansing, Mich., 1973-80; exec. dir. Mich. State U. Found., East Lansing, 1980—. Author: Planned Giving Guidebook, 1980. Treas. Family and Child Services, Lansing, Mich., 1981—. Mem. ABA, Mich. Bar Assn., Ingham County Bar Assn. (real property law com.), Council for Advancement and Support of Edn., Mich. State U. Pres.'s Club. Club: University (Lansing). Avocations: golf, boating, woodworking, sport fishing. Estate planning, Real property, Personal income taxation. Home: 3805 Hemmingway Okemos MI 48864 Office: Mich State U Found 4700 S Hagadorn Rd East Lansing MI 48823

LAUNER, JEANNETTE MAUREEN, lawyer; b. Portland, Oreg., Dec. 27, 1950; d. James Edward and Julia Marie (Springer) L.; m. Richard Lance Caswell, Apr. 24, 1976. B.A., U. Oreg., 1972, J.D., 1975. Bar: Oreg. 1975, U.S. Dist. Ct. Oreg. 1975, U.S. Ct. Appeals (9th cir.) 1978. Asst. city atty. City of Salem, Oreg., 1975-84; gen. counsel Portland Devel. Commn., 1985—. Bd. dirs. United Way of Midwillamette Valley, Salem, 1982-84; mem. long range planning com. of United Way, Salem, 1984-85. Charles M. Stout scholar U. Oreg., Eugene, 1968-72. Mem. ABA, Am. Planning Assn. (planning and law div.), Oreg. State Bar (com. on future of legal profession 1982-85), Multnomah County Bar Assn. Democrat. Roman Catholic. Club: Zonta (Salem) (area dir. 1984-86). Local government, Labor, Real property. Office: Portland Devel Commn 1120 SW 5th Ave Suite 1102 Portland OR 97204

LAURETA, ALFRED, U.S. judge; b. Ewa, Oahu, Hawaii, May 21, 1924; s. Laureano and Victoriana (Pascua) L.; m. E. Evelyn Reantillo, Feb. 21, 1953; children: Michael, Gregory, Pamela Ann, Lisa Lani. B.Ed., U. Hawaii, 1947, teaching cert., 1948; LL.B., Fordham U., 1953. Bar: Hawaii. Partner firm Kobayashi, Kono, Laureta & Ariyoshi, Honolulu, 1954-59; adminstr. to U.S. Congressman Inouye, 1959-63; dir. Hawaii Dept. Labor and Indsl. Relations, 1963-67; judge 1st Circuit Ct., Honolulu, 1967-69, 5th Circuit Ct., Kauai, 1969-78, U.S. Dist. Ct. No. Mariana Islands, Saipan, 1978—. Mem. Nat. Council Juvenile Ct. Judges, Am. Judicature Soc., Hawaii Bar Assn., Kauai Bar Assn. Democrat. Jurisprudence. Office: PO Box 687 Saipan CM 96950

LAURITA, ALAN JOHN, oil and gas company executive, lawyer; b. Flushing, N.Y., Nov. 19, 1946; s. Joseph and Marion Christine (Hinck) L.; m. Frankie Candice Bader, June 12, 1972; 1 child, Karen Ann. B.S., SUNY-Buffalo, 1968, J.D., 1973. Bar: N.Y. 1974, U.S. Dist. Ct. (we. dist.) N.Y. 1974, Pa. 1982. Assoc. Williams, Williams, Volgeneau & Tisdall, Buffalo, 1973-74; ptnr. DeMambro, Donovan & Laurita, Mayville, N.Y., 1974-81; asst. county atty. Chautauqua County, Mayville, 1967-81; v.p. land Envirogas Inc., Mayville, 1982—. Served with U.S. Army, 1969-71. Mem. N.Y. Bar Assn., Bar Assn. No. Chautauqua, Pa. Bar Assn. Lutheran. Oil and gas leasing, Real property. Home: RD 1 Moon Rd Jamestown NY 14701 Office: Envirogas Inc 100 E Chautauqua St Mayville NY 14757

LAURITSEN, THOMAS CHRISTIAN, lawyer; b. Sioux City, Iowa, June 1, 1951; s. Howard Christian and Estella Mae (Millard) L.; m. Ricki Renee Sogge, Nov. 20, 1971; children: Traci Kae, Travis Christian, Tana Renee. BA, Dana Coll., 1972; JD, Creighton U., 1974. Bar: Nebr. 1975, U.S. Dist. Ct. Nebr. 1975, U.S. Ct. Appeals (8th cir.) 1985. Assoc. Swarr, May, Smith & Andersen, Omaha, 1978, ptnr., 1979-86; ptnr. Andersen, Berkshire, Lauritsen & Brower, Omaha, 1986—. Chmn. bldg. com. Lord of Love Luth. Ch., Omaha, 1985-86; bd. dirs. Keystone Little League, Omaha, 1986. Mem. ABA, Nebr. Bar Assn., Omaha Bar Assn. Republican. Avocations: baseball, basketball, golf, coaching youth baseball and basketball. Federal civil litigation, Construction, Labor. Home: 11741 Roanoke Rd Omaha NE 68164 Office: Andersen Berkshire Lauritsen & Brower 8805 Indian Hills Dr Suite 200 Omaha NE 68114

LAURITZEN, DAVID KAY, lawyer; b. East Los Angeles, Calif., Apr. 28, 1950; s. Orson W. and Shirley I. (Rhoades) L.; m. Martha F. Lauritzen, May 8, 1975; children: Rachael, Rebecca, David, Jonathan, Jacob, Sarah. BA, Brigham Young U., 1973, JD, 1977; LLM, Georgetown U., 1978. Bar: Utah 1977, Mont. 1978, U.S. Dist. Ct. Utah 1977, U.S. Dist. Ct. Mont. 1978, U.S. Tax Ct. 1978, Ariz. 1981. Ptnr. Richards, Brandt, Miller & Nelson, Salt Lake City, 1978—. Pension, profit-sharing, and employee benefits, Corporate taxation, General corporate. Office: Richards Brandt Miller & Nelson 50 S Main Suite 700 Salt Lake City UT 84110

LAUSE, CHRISTOPHER ALLEN, lawyer; b. Pitts., May 26, 1957; s. Charles Joseph and Patricia Ann (Kelly) L. BA, Duke U., 1979; JD, Washington U., St. Louis, 1982. Bar: Ill. 1982, U.S. Dist. Ct. (no. dist.) Ill. 1982. Assoc. Chadwell & Kayser Ltd., Chgo., 1982-85, Seyfarth, Shaw, Fairweather & Geraldson, Chgo., 1985—. Mem. ABA, Ill. Bar Assn., Chgo. Bar Assn. Democrat. Episcopalian. Avocations: cycling, golf, fishing. General corporate, Securities. Office: Seyfarth Shaw Fairweather & Geraldson 55 E Monroe St 42d Floor Chicago IL 60603

LAUX, RUSSELL FREDERICK, lawyer; b. West New York, N.J., Dec. 30, 1918; s. Frederick and Theresa A. (Noble) L.; m. Ann deFriedberg, Aug. 22, 1962 (dec.). Student Pace Inst., 1938-40, Fordham U., 1946-48; LLB summa cum laude, N.Y. Law Sch., 1950; postgrad. Pace Coll., 1951, Columbia U., 1955. Bar: N.Y. 1951, U.S. Dist. (so. dist.) N.Y. 1951, U.S. Ct. Appeals (2d cir.) 1951, U.S. Ct. Claims 1952, U.S. Tax Ct. 1952, U.S. Dist. Ct. (ea. dist.) N.Y. 1953, U.S. Ct. Customs and Patent Appeals 1963, U.S. Ct. Mil. Appeals 1963, U.S. Supreme Ct. 1963. Mem. staff N.Y. State Dept. Law, Richmond County Investigations, 1951-54, N.Y. State Exec. Dept. Office of Commr. of Investigations, 1954-57; comptroller-counsel Odyssey Productions, Inc., 1957-59; ptnr. Ryan, Murray & Laux, N.Y.C., 1951-61, Ryan & Laux, N.Y.C., 1961; sole practice, N.Y.C., 1961—. Active Met. Opera Guild. Served with AUS, 1940-46; capt. Judge Adv. Gen. Vet. Corps of Arty., State of N.Y., 1975—; now col. U.S. Militia. Recipient Eloy Alfaro Grand Cross Republic of Panama. Mem. Bronx County Bar Assn. (recipient Townsend Wandell Gold medal), Nat. Acad. TV Arts & Scis., Internat. Platform Assn., VFW, Order of Lafayette, Sons of Union Vets. of Civil War, Soc. Am. Wars, The Nat. Sojourners, Heroes of '76, Navy League, St. Andrews Soc. N.Y., St. George Soc. N.Y., Soc. Friendly Sons of St. Patrick, English Speaking Union, Asia Soc., China Inst. Am., Army and Navy Union U.S.A., Am. Legion, Mid Manhattan C. of C., Reserve Officers Assn. of U.S. (col.), Delta Theta Phi. Presbyterian. Clubs: Order of Eastern Star, Masons (past comdr. N.Y. Masonic war vets.), Shriners, Knight of Malta, Lambs, Knights Hospitaller of St. John of Jerusalem. Probate, Real property, Estate taxation. Office: 71 W 23d St Suite 1530 New York NY 10010

LAVA, LESLIE MICHELE, lawyer; b. LaGrange, Ill., Mar. 18, 1957; d. James Edward and Ruth Jane (Hadraba) L. BA with honors, Vanderbilt U., 1978; JD with honors, U. Fla., 1981. Bar: Ill. 1981, U.S. Dist. Ct. (no. dist.) Ill. 1981, Fla. 1982, Calif. 1985, U.S. Dist. Ct. (no. dist.) Calif. 1985. Assoc. Chapman and Cutler, Chgo., 1981-84, Brown & Wood, San Francisco, 1984—. Mem. Edgewood Children's Ctr., San Francisco, 1985—, Calif. Marine Mammal Ctr., San Francisco, 1985—. Mem. ABA, Fla. Bar Assn., Calif. Bar Assn., San Francisco Mcpl. Bond Forum, Order of Coif, Phi Beta Kappa, Phi Kappa Phi, Pi Sigma Alpha. Republican. Club: Telegraph Hill (San Francisco); Harbor Point Racquet and Beach (Mill Valey, Calif.). Avocations: swimming, diving, tennis, piano. Municipal bonds. Office: Brown & Wood 555 California St Suite 5060 San Francisco CA 94104

LAVALLEY, RICHARD GERARD, lawyer, accountant; b. Detroit, Feb. 15, 1929; s. Loyal E. and Lydia J. (Campbell) LaV.; m. Mary Ann Chytil, Aug. 19, 1950; children: Dianne, Antoinette, Debra, Richard, Daniel, Laurie, Elaine. BBA magna cum laude, U. Toledo, 1951, JD summa cum laude, 1953. Bar: Ohio 1953, U.S. Dist. Ct. (no. dist.) Ohio 1956, U.S. Tax Ct. 1959, U.S. Ct. Appeals (6th cir.) 1961. With trust tax dept. Toledo Trust Co., 1951-52; staff acct. Arthur Young & Co., Toledo, 1952-55; ptnr. Boxell Bebout Torbet & Potter, Toledo, 1955-67; ptnr. Arthur Young & Co., Toledo, 1967-71; ptnr. LaValley, Stockwell & Cooperman, Toledo, 1971-86; pres. LaValley & Lavalley Co., L.P.A., Toledo, 1986—; instr. U. Toledo Coll. Law, 1962-65. Trustee St. Francis De Sales High Sch., 1971-78; pres. U. Toledo Coll. Law Alumni Assn., 1976. Served with AUS, 1946-47. Mem. ABA, Ohio State Bar Assn., Toledo Bar Assn., Am. Inst. CPA's, Ohio Inst. CPA's, Toledo Inst. CPA's, Am. Judicature Soc., Phi Kappa Phi. Republican. Roman Catholic. Clubs: Toledo, Sylvania Country, Catawba Island (Toledo); Adios Golf, Royal Palm Yacht (Boca Raton, Fla.). Corporate taxation, Probate, General corporate. Office: LaValley & LaValley Co LPA 5800 Monroe St Bldg F PO Box 8726 Toledo OH 43623

LAVELLE, BRIAN FRANCIS DAVID, lawyer; b. Cleve., Aug. 16, 1941; s. Gerald John and Mary Josephine (O'Callagahan) L.; m. Sara Hill, Sept. 10, 1966; children: S. Elizabeth, B. Francis D., Catherine H. BA, U. Va., 1963; JD, Vanderbilt U., 1966; LLM in Taxation, N.Y.U., 1969. Bar: N.C. 1966, Ohio 1968. Assoc. VanWinkle Buck, Wall, Starnes & Davis, Asheville, N.C., 1968-74, ptnr., 1974—; lectr. continuing edn. N.C. Bar Found., Wake Forest U. Estate Planning Inst., Hartford Tax Inst., Duke U. Estate Planning Inst. Contbr. articles on law to profl. jours. Trustee Asheville Country Day Sch., 1981—, sec., 1982-85; vice chmn. Buncombe County Indsl. Facilities and Pollution Control Authority, 1976-82; bd. dirs. Western N.C. Community Found., 1986—; mem. Asheville Tax Study Group, 1981—, chmn., 1984; bd. advs. U.N.C. Annual Tax Inst., 1981—. Served as capt. Judge Adv. Gen. USAF, 1966-67. Mem. N.C. Bar Assn. (bd. govs. 1979-82, councillor tax sect. 1979-83, councillor estate planning law sect. 1982—), ABA, Am. Coll. Probate Counsel (state chmn. 1982-85, regent 1984—, lectr. continuing edn.), N.C. State Bar (splty. com. on estate planning and probate law 1984—). Episcopalian (clk. vestry All Souls Ch.). Clubs: Rotary of Asheville, Biltmore Forest Country. Probate, Estate planning. Home: 45 Brookside Rd Asheville NC 28803 Office: 11 N Market St PO Box 7376 Asheville NC 28807

LAVELLE, JOHN PHILIP, lawyer; b. Athens, Ohio, Dec. 24, 1956; s. William Ambrose and Marion Helen (Yanity) L.; m. Ann Romaine Ward, Aug. 1, 1981. BBA, Mid. Tenn. State U., 1979; JD, Samford U., 1983. Bar: Ohio 1982, U.S. Dist. Ct. (so. dist.) Ohio 1982, U.S. Ct. Appeals (6th cir.) 1983. Ptnr. Lavelle, Carson, Lavelle & Lavelle, Athens, 1982—; spl. counsel office atty. gen. Hocking Tech. Coll., Nelsonville, Ohio, 1984—. Mem. exec. com. Athens County Dems., 1984—. Sam Paschal scholar, 1977; named one of Outstanding Young Men Am., U.S. Jaycees, 1982. Mem. ABA, Ohio Bar Assn., Athens County Bar Assn., Assn. Trial Lawyers Am., Alpha Gamma Rho, Delta Theta Phi, Athens Jaycees (sec. 1983-84). Democrat. Roman Catholic. Lodges: Rotary, KC (adv. 1984-85), Elks. Avocations: horseback riding, bow hunting, photography. Criminal, State civil litigation, Personal injury. Home: 29 Sunset Ln The Plains OH 45780 Office: Lavelle Carson Lavelle & Lavelle 8 N Court PO Box 661 Athens OH 45701

LAVENDER, ROBERT EUGENE, justice state supreme court; b. Muskogee, Okla., July 19, 1926; s. Harold James and Vergene Irene (Martin) L.; m. Maxine Knight, Dec. 22, 1945; children—Linda (Mrs. Dean Courter), Robert K., Debra (Mrs. Thomas Merrill), William J. LL.B., U. Tulsa, 1953; grad., Appellate Judges Seminar, 1967, Nat. Coll. State Trial Judges, 1970. Bar: Okla. bar 1953. With Mass. Bonding & Ins. Co., Tulsa, 1951-53, U.S. Fidelity & Guaranty Co., Tulsa, 1953-54; asst. city atty. Tulsa, 1954-55, practice, 1955-60; practice Claremore, Okla., 1960-65; justice Okla. Supreme Ct., 1965—, chief justice, to 1981; guest lectr. Okla. U., Oklahoma City U., Tulsa U. law schs. Republican committeeman, Rogers County, 1961-62. Served with USNR, 1944-46. Mem. Am., Okla., Rogers County bar assns., Am. Judicature Soc., Okla. Jud. Conf., Phi Alpha Delta (hon.). Methodist (adminstrv. bd.). Club: Mason (32 deg.). Home: 2910 Kerry Ln Oklahoma City OK 73120 Office: Room 208 State Capitol Bldg Oklahoma City OK 73105

LAVENHAR, JEFFREY DREW, lawyer; b. Plainfield, N.J., Feb. 20, 1951; s. Arthur Josef and Gladys Edyth (Schwartz) L.; m. Laurie Harriet Katz, Oct. 7, 1979. BA, Alfred U., 1973; JD, St. Mary's U., San Antonio, Tex., 1976. Bar: N.J. 1976, U.S. Dist. Ct. N.J. 1976, Colo. 1982, U.S. Dist. Ct. Colo. 1982. Assoc. Crane & Vastola, Plainfield, 1976-78; ho. counsel Amoco Prodn. Co., Denver, 1979-81, Fulton Producing Co., Denver, 1981-82; sole practice Denver, 1983-84; ptnr. Lavenhar & Moritz, Denver, 1985—; bd. dirs. First Continental Properties Corp., Denver, Milnex Resources Corp., Denver, Orchard Hills Homeowners Assn., Englewood, Colo. Mem. Rep. Coalition, Denver, 1985-86. Mem. ABA, Denver Bar Assn., Colo. Bar Assn. Oil and gas leasing, Securities, Real property. Home: 8960 E Big Canon Place Greenwood Village CO 80111

LAVENSTEIN, TERRY STUART, lawyer; b. Balt., Oct. 26, 1954; s. Melvin L. and Mary B. (Basile) L. BA in Polit. Sci., U. Md.; JD, Calif. Western Sch. Law, 1981. Bar: Md. 1981, D.C. 1986, U.S. Dist. Ct. Md. 1981, U.S. Ct. Appeals (4th cir.) 1981. Asst. state's atty. City of Balt., 1981-83; assoc. Nathanson & Frank, P.A., Balt., 1983-84; sole practice Balt., 1984—. Mem. ABA, Am. Trial Lawyers Assn., Assn. Trial Lawyers Balt., Md. Criminal Defense Assn., Md. Trial Lawyers Assn., Criminal Def. Lawyers Assn. Democrat. Jewish. Criminal. Office: 1300 Court Sq Bldg Baltimore MD 21202

LAVERGNE, LUKE ALDON, lawyer, law educator, retired military officer; b. Lawtell, La., May 7, 1938; s. Adam and Ida (Nero) L.; m. Catherine Malveaux, Oct. 15, 1960; children: Lance A., Cynthia A. BS in Bus., U. Nebr., 1969; MS in Edn. and Psychology, So. Ill. U., Edwardsville, 1974; JD, La. State U., 1982. Bar: La. 1982, U.S. Dist. Ct. (mid., ea. and we. dists.) La. 1982, U.S. Ct. Appeals (5th cir.) 1982. Commd. 2d lt. USAF, 1969, advanced through grades to capt., 1972, ret., 1979; asst. prof. La. State U., Baton Rouge, 1975-79; asst. dist. atty. East Baton Rouge Parish, 1982-84; sr. ptnr. LaVergne & Johnson Law Firm, Baton Rouge, 1984—. Pres. PTA Baton Rouge High Sch., 1976-78, Gifted Students Program, Baton Rouge, 1977-80, Homeowners Assn., Baton Rouge, 1984—; bd. dirs. St. Aloysius Cath. Ch., Baton Rouge, 1978-80. Mem. Phi Beta Sigma (state dir. La. 1984—). Democrat. Roman Catholic. General practice. Home: 5956 Valley Forge Ave Baton Rouge LA 70808 Office: LaVergne & Johnson 328 Government St Baton Rouge LA 70802

LAVERS, RICHARD MARSHALL, lawyer; b. Oak Ridge, Tenn., Apr. 15, 1947; s. Willard Douglas and Vashti Athena (Compton) L.; m. Christine Anne Jandl, June 2, 1973; children: Christian Douglas, Ansley McKay, Ti-Patrice, Rickey Elizabeth. BA, U. Mich., 1968; postgrad., Columbia U., 1968-69; JD cum laude, U. Mich., 1972; postdoctoral, U. Wis., 1977-81. Bar: Colo. 1972, U.S. Dist. Ct. (Colo.) 1972, U.S. Ct. Appeals (10th cir.) 1975, Wis. 1978, U.S. Dist. Ct. (mid. dist.) La. 1983, U.S. Ct. Appeals (5th cir.) 1983, N.Y. 1986. Dep. dist. atty. 9th Jud. Dist., Glenwood Springs, Colo., 1972-73; assoc. Martin Dumont, Glenwood Springs, 1972-74, Rovira, Demuth & Eiberger, Denver, 1974-76; assoc. resident counsel Nat. Presto Industries, Eau Claire, Wis., 1976-82; asst. counsel Ethyl Corp., Baton Rouge, 1982-87; ptnr. Mulcahy and Wherry, S.C., Milw., 1987—; editorial bd. U.S. Trademark Assn., N.Y.C., 1980-82. Counsel U.S. Rep. Steve Gunderson campaign, Eau Claire, Wis., 1980. Served with USAR, 1969-73. Mem. ABA, N.Y. Bar Assn., Wis. Bar Assn., La. Bar Assn., Eau Claire Jaycees (bd. dirs. 1976-80). Republican. Congregationalist. Club: Meridian (Eau Claire Wis.) (pres. 1981). Contracts commercial, General corporate, Private international. Office: Mulcahy and Wherry SC 815 E Mason St #1600 Milwaukee WI 53202-4080

LAVEY, STEWART EVAN, lawyer; b. Newark, July 24, 1945. A.B., Syracuse U., 1967; J.D., Fordham U., 1970. Bar: N.Y. State 1971. Assoc. firm Kelley Drye & Warren, N.Y.C., 1970-71, Emil Kobrin Klein & Garbus, N.Y.C., 1971-72, Zimet Haines Moss & Goodkind, N.Y.C., 1972-75; asst. sec., asst. gen. counsel Norlin Corp., N.Y.C., 1975-78; sec., asst. gen. counsel Norlin Corp., 1978-85; of counsel firm Shanley & Fisher, P.C., Morristown, N.J., 1985—; adj. assoc. prof. law Fordham U., N.Y.C., 1976-79, adj. prof., 1980—. Mem.: Fordham Law Rev., 1968-70. Mem. Am. Bar Assn., N.Y. State Bar Assn., Assn. Bar City N.Y. Securities, General corporate, Banking. Office: Shanley & Fisher PC 131 Madison Ave Morristown NJ 07960

LAVIGNE, LAWRENCE NEIL, lawyer; b. Newark, June 30, 1957; s. Daniel S. and Alice M. (Melon) L.; m. Benjie Panesh, Oct. 12, 1980; 1 child, Gabriel A. BA, Franklin & Marshall Coll., 1979; JD, Seton Hall U., 1982. Bar: N.J. 1982, U.S. Dist. Ct. N.J. 1982, U.S. Ct. Appeals (3d cir.) 1986, U.S. Supreme Ct. 1986. Assoc. Shanley & Fisher, P.C., Newark, 1982-83; ptnr. Hanlon, McHeffey, Herzfeld & Rubin, Edison, N.J., 1983—; instr. Am. Inst. Paralegal Studies, Mahwah, N.J., 1985—. Mem. ABA (litigation sect.), N.J. Bar Assn., Morris County Bar Assn., Trial Attys. N.J. Republican. Jewish. Avocations: tennis, music. State civil litigation, Federal civil litigation, Personal injury. Office: Hanlon McHeffey Herzfeld & Rubin 10 Parsonage Rd Suite 300 Edison NJ 08837

LAVORATO, LOUIS A., state judge. Judge Iowa Supreme Ct., Des Moines, 1986—. Office: Office of the Supreme Court Des Moines IA 50319 *

LAVORGNA, GREGORY JOSEPH, lawyer; b. Phila., Apr. 30, 1950; s. Emanuel and Mafalda (Gentile) L.; m. Christine J. Scherf, July 15, 1978; children: Stephanie Noelle, Cynthia Faith. BEE, Drexel U., 1972, MEE, 1975; JD cum laude, Temple U., 1981. Bar: Pa. 1981, U.S. Dist. Ct. (ea. dist.) Pa. 1981, U.S. Patent Office 1981, U.S. Ct. Appeals (Fed. cir.) 1982, D.C. 1986. Electronics engr. RCA Corp., Camden, N.J., 1972-75, Gen. Electric Co., Phila., 1975-79; assoc. Seidel, Gonda, Goldhammer & Abbott, P.C., Phila., 1981—. Editor in chief Drexel U. Tech. Jour., 1971-72. Trustee 1st Bapt. Ch., Phila., 1978—. Mem. ABA, Pa. Bar Assn., Phila. Bar Assn., Am. Intellectual Property Law Assn., Justinian Soc. Patent, Trademark and copyright. Home: 200 N Ormond Ave Havertown PA 19083 Office: Seidel Gonda Goldhammer & Abbott PC 1800 Two Penn Ctr Plaza Phildelphia PA 19102

LAW, ALFRED JOHN, III, lawyer; b. Chattanooga, Tenn., Jan. 2, 1935; s. Alfred J. Jr. and Mary Emerson (Turner) L.; children: Mary Eliza, Anna K., Margaret T. AB in English, Princeton U., 1957; MA Am. History, Columbia U., 1963; JD, NYU, 1967. Bar: N.Y. 1967, D.C. 1982. From assoc. to ptnr. Skadden, Arps, Slate, Meagher & Flom, N.Y.C., 1967—; mng. ptnr. Skadden, Arps, Slate, Meagher & Flom, Washington, 1982—. Hon. chmn. Musica Sacra N.Y.C., 1978-86; bd. dirs. Waverly Consort, N.Y.C., 1984—, Washington Opera, D.C., 1985—, Washington Performing Arts, D.C., 1985—. Served with U.S. Army, 1958-60. Mem. ABA, D.C. Bar Assn., N.Y. State Bar Assn., Nat. Press Club. Republican. Clubs: City, International, Pisces (Washington), Larchmont (N.Y.) Yacht. General corporate. Home: 2230 California St NW Washington DC 20008 Office: Skadden Arps Slate Meagher & Flom 919 18th St NW Washington DC 20006

LAW, JOHN MANNING, lawyer; b. Chgo., Dec. 5, 1927; s. Fred Edward and Elisabeth (Emmons) L.; m. Carol Lufkin Ritter, May 14, 1955; children: John E., Lucy L., Frederick R., Beth K. Student, U. Chgo., 1944-45, St. Ambrose Coll., 1945; BA, Colo. Coll., 1948; JD, U. Colo., 1951. Bar: Colo. 1951, Ill. 1952, U.S. Dist. Ct. Colo. 1952, U.S. Ct. Appeals (10th cir.) 1954. Atty. trust dept. Harris Bank, Chgo., 1951-52; assoc. Hall & Evans, Denver, 1952-53, Dickerson, Morrissey, Zarlengo & Dwyer, Denver, 1953-58; ptnr. Law, Nagel & Clark, Denver, 1958-84, also bd. dirs.; ptnr. Law & Knous, Denver, 1984—; mem. law com. Colo. State Bd. Law Examiners, 1971-81, Colo. State Officials Compensation Commn., 1985—. Mem. Moffat Tunnel Commn., Denver, 1966—. Served to capt. USNR, 1945-77. Fellow Colo. Bar Found. (charter); mem. ABA (legal assistance to mil. person 1972-77), Colo. Bar Assn. (bd. govs. 1968-71), Denver Bar Assn. (trustee 1971-74), Internat. Soc. Barristers, Def. Research Inst., Law Club. Republican. Presbyterian. Club: University (Denver) (past chmn. admissions com.). Insurance, State civil litigation, Federal civil litigation. Home: 3333 E Florida Ave #35 Denver CO 80210 Office: Law Knous & Keithley 1873 S Bellaire #1415 Denver CO 80222

LAW, MICHAEL R., lawyer; b. Rochester, N.Y., Nov. 30, 1947; s. George Robert and Elizabeth (Stoddart) L. BS, St. John Fisher Coll., 1969; JD, U. Louisville, 1975. Bar: N.Y. 1976, U.S. Dist. Ct. (we. dist.) N.Y. 1976, U.S. Supreme Ct. 1982. Assoc., Wood, P.C., Rochester, 1976-77; sole practice, Rochester, 1977-78; assoc. Sullivan, Peters, et al, Rochester, 1978-80, ptnr., 1980-81; ptnr. Phillips, Lytle, Hitchcock, Blaine & Huber, Rochester, 1982—. Editor (newsletter) 1986 Trial Techniques. Counselor Camp Good Days and Spl. Times, Rochester, 1984; speaker Am. Cancer Soc., 1984. Served with U.S. Army, 1968-74. Mem. Monroe County Bar Assn. (judiciary com. 1981-87), N.Y. State Bar Assn. (trial sect., ins. negligence com.), ABA (trial law sect., vice chair trial techniques com.). Republican. Roman Catholic. Clubs: Postprandial, Toastmasters (awards 1980-82). Personal injury, State civil litigation, Federal civil litigation. Home: 1495 Highland Ave Rochester NY 14618 Office: Phillips Lytle Hitchcock et al 1400 First Federal Plaza Rochester NY 14614

LAW, THOMAS HART, lawyer; b. Austin, Tex., July 6, 1918; s. Robert Adger and Elizabeth (Manigault) L.; m. Terese Tarlton, June 11, 1943 (div. Apr. 1956); m. Jo Ann Nelson, Dec. 17, 1960; children: Thomas Hart Jr., Debra Ann. AB, U. Tex., 1939, JD, 1942. Bar: Tex. 1942, U.S. Supreme Ct. 1950. Assoc. White, Taylor & Chandler, Austin, 1942; assoc. Thompson, Walker, Smith & Shannon, Ft. Worth, 1946-50; ptnr. Tilley, Hyder & Law, Ft. Worth, 1950-67, Stone, Tilley, Parker, Snakard, Law & Brown, Ft. Worth, 1967-71; pres. Law, Snakard, Brown & Gambill, P.C., Ft. Worth, 1971-84, Law, Snakard & Gambill, P.C., Ft. Worth, 1984—; bd. dirs., gen. counsel Gearhart Industries, Inc., Ft. Worth; bd. dirs. LIN Broadcasting Corp., N.Y.C.; gen. counsel Tarrant County Jr. Coll. Dist. Chmn. Leadership Ft. Worth, 1974—; bd. regents U. Tex. System, 1975-81, vice chmn., 1979-81. Served to lt. USNR, 1942-46. Recipient Nat. Humanitarian award Nat. Jewish Hosp./Nat. Asthma Ctr., 1983; named Outstanding Young Man, City of Ft. Worth, 1950, Outstanding Alumnus, Coll. of Humanities, U. Tex., 1977, Outstanding Citizen, City of Ft. Worth, 1984. Fellow Am. Bar Found., Tex. Bar Found., Am. Coll. Probate Counsel; mem. Ft. Worth C. of C. (pres. 1972), Mortar Bd., Phi Beta Kappa, Omicron Delta Kappa, Pi Sigma Alpha, Delta Sigma Rho, Phi Eta Sigma. Democrat. Presbyterian. Clubs: Ft. Worth (bd. govs. 1984—), Century II (bd. govs. to 1985), River Crest Country, Exchange (pres. 1972), Steeplechase. Lodge: Rotary (local club pres. 1960). Avocation: numismatics. Home: 6741 Brants Ln Fort Worth TX 76116 Office: Law Snakard & Gambill 3200 Tex Am Bank Bldg 500 Throckmorton St Fort Worth TX 76102

LAWATSCH, FRANK EMIL, JR., banker, lawyer; b. Avenel, N.J., May 11, 1944; s. Frank Emil and Jessie Margaret L.; m. Deanna Conover, May 25, 1969; children: Amanda, Abigail, Frank. BA, Colgate U., 1966; JD, Cornell U., 1969. Bar: N.Y. 1969. Assoc. Shearman & Sterling, N.Y.C., 1969-78; sr. v.p., sec., gen. counsel Midlantic Corp., Edison, N.J., 1978—. Mem. ABA, N.J. Bar Assn., Bar Assn. City N.Y., Am. Soc. Corp. Secs. Episcopalian. General corporate, Securities, Banking. Home: 185 Park St Montclair NJ 07042 Office: PO Box 600 Edison NJ 08818

LAWLER, EDWARD JAMES, lawyer; b. Chgo., Sept. 15, 1908; s. Edward James and Sarah Ann (Gahan) L.; m. Elizabeth Falls Dunscomb, Dec. 16, 1939. Ph.B., U. Chgo., 1930; J.D., Harvard U., 1933. Bar: Ill. 1933, Tenn. 1941. Atty., auditor income tax sect. Office Collector of Internal Revenue, Chgo., 1933-34; spl. atty. Office of Gen. Counsel, IRS, 1935-36; sole practice, Chgo., 1937-38; atty. SEC, 1939-41; sole practice, Memphis, 1941-62; ptnr. Lawler, Humphreys, Dunlap & Wellford, 1962-80, of counsel, 1980-82; sole practice, Memphis, 1983—; adv. panel internat. law Dept. of State, 1967-76; dir. Chromasco, Ltd. (Toronto). Served to lt. comdr. USNR, 1942-45; ETO. Decorated Bronze Star. Fellow Am. Bar Found. (chmn. 1966-67); mem. ABA, Internat. Bar Assn., Tenn. Bar Assn., Memphis-Shelby County Bar Assn., Chgo. Bar Assn., Am. Soc. Internat. Law, Am. Law Inst., Am. Judicature Soc., Phi Beta Kappa. Roman Catholic. Clubs: Royal and Ancient Golf (St. Andrews, Scotland), Memphis Hunt and Polo, Memphis Country. Estate taxation, Probate, General corporate. Home: 644 S Belvedere Blvd Memphis TN 38104 Office: 1808 1st Tennessee Bldg Memphis TN 38103

LAWLER, THERESA ANNE, lawyer; b. Linz, Austria, Aug. 30, 1950; came to U.S., 1952; d. Anton and Theresia (Steigerwald) Zimmermann; m. George S. Lawler, June 12, 1971; children: Katherine Anne, Michael Sturgis. BA, Northwestern U., 1971; JD with honors, U. Md., 1977. Bar: Md. 1978, U.S. Ct. Appeals (4th cir.) 1978. Law clk. to presiding justice Cir. Ct. Balt., 1977-78; assoc. Gordon, Feinblatt, Rothman, Hoffberger & Hollander, Balt., 1978-80; trust officer Md. Nat. Bank, Balt., 1980-81; v.p., trust officer Merc. Safe Deposit & Trust Co., Balt., 1981—; evening faculty paralegal program Dundalk Community Coll., Balt., 1980-81, Villa Julie Coll., Balt. 1980-83; mem. editorial bd. Baltimore Fin., 1982-83. Chmn. pub. affairs com. Jr. League Balt., 1983-84; bd. govs. St. Thomas More Soc., 1983-85; mem. Balt. Estate Planning Council, 1983—. Sally Stevens scholar, 1970-71. Mem. ABA, Women's Bar Assn., Md. Bar Assn., Balt. Bar Assn. (law speaker's program 1982—), Women's Law Ctr., Alpha Phi. (found. award). Democrat. Roman Catholic. Avocations: theatre, swimming. Probate. Office: Merc Safe Deposit & Trust Co 2 Hopkins Plaza Baltimore MD 21201

LAWLESS, JOHN MARTIN, lawyer; b. Peoria, Ill., Feb. 9, 1926; s. Thomas M. and Irma J. (Bibo) L.; m. Carol L. Sluser, July 6, 1963; children—Robert, Suzanne. B.S., U. Ill., 1948, J.D., 1950. Bar: Ill. 1950, U.S. Dist. Ct. (cen. dist.) Ill. 1952, U.S. Ct. Appeals (7th cir.) 1974, U.S. Supreme Ct. 1973. Asst. atty. gen., Ill., 1950-53; assoc. Chester Anderson Law Firm, Peoria, 1953-60; ptnr. Vonachen, Cation, Lawless, Trager & Slevin, Peoria, 1960—. Past pres. Peoria County Legal Aid Soc.; del. Democratic Jud. Nominating Convs. Served with USAAF, 1944-45. Mem. ABA, Am. Judicature Soc., Ill. State Bar Assn. (chmn. unauthorized practice of law com. 1973-75), Peoria County Bar Assn. (pres. 1975-76). Democrat. Roman Catholic. Clubs: Creve Coeur (Peoria, Ill.); Willow Knolls County (pres. 1973-74). Personal income taxation, Probate, Real property. Office: 309 Security Savs Bldg Peoria IL 61602

LAWLESS, JOSEPH FRANCIS, JR., lawyer; b. Phila., Apr. 17, 1951; s. Joseph F., Sr. and Margaret Mary (Hickey) L. B.A., St. Joseph's Coll., Phila., 1973; J.D., Villanova U., 1976. Bar: Pa. 1976, U.S. Ct. Appeals (3d cir.) 1982, U.S. Dist. Ct. (ea. dist.) Pa. 1984, U.S. Supreme Ct. 1984. Asst. dist. atty. Chester County Dist. Attys. Office, West Chester, Pa., 1976-79; assoc. Petrikin, Wellman, Damico & Carney, Media, Pa., 1979-81, Sprague & Rubenstone, Phila., 1981-82; sole practice, Phila., 1982—. Author: Prosecutorial Misconduct, 1985; (with Johnson) New Techniques for Narcotics Cases, 1987, (with Jacobs) Criminal RICO: The Gangs all Here, 1986. Reimel Moot Ct. Competition, Villanova Law Sch., winner, 1975. Fellow Melvin M. Belli Soc., Am. Trial Lawyers Found. (life), Roscoe Pound Found.; mem. Assn. Trial Lawyers Am. (sec. criminal law sect. 1984-85, 1st vice chmn. 1985-86), Pa. Bar Assn., Phila. Bar Assn., ABA, Nat. Assn. Criminal Def. Lawyers, Alpha Sigma Nu, Phi Delta Phi. Democrat. Roman Catholic. Criminal, State civil litigation, Federal civil litigation. Home: 208 E Chelsea Circle Newton Square PA 19102 Office: 1411 Walnut St Suite 1127 Philadelphia PA 19102

LAWLESS, THOMAS WILLIAM, lawyer; b. West Palm Beach, Fla., Mar. 14, 1954; s. Joseph Francis and Ethel Joan (Sliney) L.; m. Elizabeth Ann Harper, May 15, 1976; children: S. Joseph, Erin E. BS, Middle Tenn. State U., 1976; JD, Nashville Night Law Sch., 1980. BAr: U.S. Ct. Internat. Trade 1981, U.S. Dist. Ct. (cen. dist.) Tenn. 1981, U.S. Ct. Appeals (D.C. cir.) 1982, U.S. Dist. Ct. (ea. and we. dist.) Tenn. 1984, U.S. Supreme Ct. 1985. Ptnr. Webb & Lawless, Nashville, 1981-83; v.p., counsel First Am. Corp., Nashville, 1983-85; ptnr., sec., treas. Combos & Lawless, P.C., Nashville, 1985—. Mem. Cheatham County Rep. Exec. Com., Ashland City, Tenn., 1979-80. Mem. ABA, Tenn. Bar Assn., Nashville Bar Assn., Knoxville Bar Assn., Tenn. Trial Lawyers Assn., Assn. Trial Lawyers Am. Roman Catholic. Consumer commercial, Federal civil litigation, State civil litigation. Home: 7101 River Park Ct Nashville TN 37221 Office: Combos & Lawless PC 14th Floor Am Trust Bldg Nashville TN 37201

LAWLESS, WILLIAM BURNS, university president, lawyer; b. Buffalo, June 3, 1922; s. William B. and Margaret H. (Welton) L.; children—Sharon, Barbara, William, Cathy, Gregory, Richard, Robert, Jeannie, Therese, John, Maria, Thomas. A.B., Notre Dame U., U. Buffalo, 1950; J.D., Notre Dame U., 1944; LL.M., Harvard U., 1950. Bar: N.Y. 1946, U.S. Dist. Ct. (we. dist.) N.Y. 1946, U.S. Tax Ct. 1947, U.S. Supreme Ct. 1956, D.C. 1972, Mass. 1976, U.S. Dist. Ct. (ea. and so. dists.) N.Y. 1972, U.S. Ct. Appeals (2d cir.) 1972, U.S. Ct. Appeals (7th cir.) 1979, U.S. Ct. Appeals (D.C. cir.) 1978. Assoc. Kenefick, Cooke, Mitchell, Bass & Letchworth, Buffalo, 1946-50; ptnr. Williams, Crane & Lawless, Buffalo, 1950-54, Lawless, Offermann, Fallon and Mahoney, Buffalo, 1956-60; justice N.Y. State Supreme Ct., 8th Jud. Dist., 1960-68; dean Notre Dame Law Sch., 1968-71; ptnr. Mudge Rose Guthrie & Alexander, N.Y.C., 1971-75, Hawkins, Delafield & Wood, N.Y.C., 1975-79; sole practice, N.Y.C., 1979-81; pres. Western State U., Fullerton, Calif., 1982—; mem. faculty U. Buffalo Law Sch., 1950-59, Notre Dame Law Sch., 1968-71, Fordham U. Law Sch., 1974-81; spl. counsel to Gov. N.Y. State, 1956-58; del., sec. to judiciary com. N.Y. State Constl. Conv., 1967; pub. mem. N.Y. State Joint Legis. Com. on Ct. Reorgn., 1973-82; mem. N.Y. State Temporary Commn. on Jud. Conduct, 1974-75; mem. N.Y. State Gov.'s Adv. Panel on Ethical Disclosure Standards, 1974-75; trustee Pace U.; bd. dirs. Western State U., Encino, Calif. Corp. counsel City of Buffalo, 1954-56. Pres. Buffalo City Council, 1956-59. Served to lt. s.g. USNR, World War II; PTO. Mem. ABA, N.Y. State Bar Assn., Mass. Bar Assn., D.C. Bar Assn., Am. Law Inst., Am. Coll. Trial Lawyers, Calif. Trial Lawyers Assn. Clubs: Harvard of N.Y.C., N.Y. Athletic. Co-author: New York Pattern Jury Instruction, vol. I, 1965, vol. II, 1968; contbr. articles to law revs.; editor-in-chief Notre Dame Lawyer, 1943-44. Federal civil litigation, State civil litigation, Legal education. Office: 1111 N State College Blvd Fullerton CA 92631

LAWN, JOHN C., federal government official; b. Bklyn., June 2, 1935. BA, St. Francis Coll., 1957; MA, St. John's U., 1964. Supr. hdqrs. FBI, Washington, 1973-77, sect. chief hdqrs., 1979-80; asst. spl. agt. FBI, Kansas City, Mo., 1977-79; spl. agt. FBI, San Antonio, 1980-82; dep. adminstr. Drug Enforcement Adminstrn., Washington, 1982-84, adminstr., 1985—. Office: Dept. of Justice Drug Enforcement Adminstrn 1405 Eye St. NW Washington, DC 20537 *

LAWRENCE, GLENN ROBERT, administrative judge; b. N.Y.C., Nov. 8, 1930; m. Nina M. Scapurro; children: David P., Eric A. LLB, Bklyn. Law Sch., 1954; BA, U. Louisville, 1968; MA, Cath. U., 1977; PhD, Am. U., 1980. Bar: N.Y. 1955, D.C. 1973, U.S. Supreme Ct. 1976. Atty. N.Y.C. Legal Aid, 1955-57; ptnr. Lawrence & Lawrence, N.Y.C., 1957-65; agt. N.Y. State, Babylon, N.Y., 1965-66; atty. U.S. Army Engrs., Washington, 1966-69; assoc. chief trial atty. U.S. Dept. Navy, Washington, 1969-78; judge adminstrv. law HEW, Camden, N.J., 1978-79, U.S. Dept. Labor, Washington, 1979—; adj. prof. law George Mason U., Fairfax, Va., 1980-83, Cen. Mich. U., Washington, 1980-83, Nat. Jud. Coll., Reno, 1984—. Author: Condemnation Law, 1969. Mem. ABA (chmn. nat. conf. adminstrv. law judges edn. com. 1985—, chmn. internat. conf. jud. edn. London 1985), Fed. Bar Assn. (chmn. adminstrv. judiciary com. 1984—), Adminstrv. Trial Lawyers Assocs. (pres. 1974), Fed. Adminstrv. Law Judges Conf. (pres. 1985-86). Judicial administration, Administrative and regulatory, Workers' compensation. Office: US Dept Labor 1111-20th St NW Washington DC 20036

LAWRENCE, JOHN SCHRUMPF, lawyer; b. Irvington, N.J., Dec. 12, 1944; s. John Lawrence and Ruth (Cunningham) Schrumpf; m. Susan Lynn Burrows, Nov. 1978; children: Hiilani, Kathryn, Scott, Kristina. BS, Rollins Coll., 1962-66; JD, Rutgers U., 1966-69. Bar: D.C. 1970, U.S. Dist. Ct. D.C. 1971, Va. Ct. 1980, U.S. Dist. Ct. (ea. dist.) Va. 1980. Legis. counsel U.S. Dept. Interior, Washington, 1969-71; sr. atty. AMA, Washington, 1971-80; ptnr. Lawrence & Smith, Fairfax, Va., 1980—; chmn. Fairfax Lawyer Referral Service, 1983-85. Liaison dir. St. Francis Boy's Home; youth fellowship dir. Ch. of the Good Shepherd, Burke, Va., 1985—; bd. dirs. George Mason Forest, Fairfax, 1983—; alumni bd. dirs. St. Andrew's Sch., Middletown, Del., 1985—. Mem. Assn. Trial Lawyers Am., Fairfax Bar Assn. Episcopalian. State civil litigation, Criminal, Personal injury. Home: 10181 Red Spruce Rd Fairfax VA 22032 Office: Lawrence & Smith 3900 University Dr Fairfax VA 22030

LAWRENCE, LINWOOD GRANT, III, lawyer; b. Norfolk, Va., Jan. 30, 1948; s. Linwood Grant Jr. and Selma Ross (Hart) L.; m. Cheryl Rene Schelb, Nov. 11, 1967; 1 child, L. Grant IV. BA, Yale U., 1969; MA, Columbia U., 1973; JD, U. Va., 1977. Bar: N.Y. 1978. Assoc. atty. Shearman & Sterling, N.Y.C., 1977-80; atty. Pepsico, Inc., Purchase, N.Y., 1980-81, sr. atty., 1981-83; counsel Pepsico, Inc., Purchase, 1983-85, sr. counsel, 1986—. General corporate, Securities. Office: Pepsico Inc 700 Anderson Hill Rd Purchase NY 10562

LAWRIMORE, EUGENE SALMON NAPIER, lawyer; b. Conway, S.C., May 26, 1947; s. Earl Wilson Lawrimore and Mildred Napier (Salmon) McDonald Schofield; m. Katrina van Buskirk Douglass Paris, June 5, 1976; children: Peyton Harrison Napier, Hunter laMastus Powell. BS in Bus. Adminstrn., U. S.C., 1969, JD, 1976. Bar: S.C. 1976, U.S. Dist. Ct. S.C. 1979, U.S. Supreme Ct. 1980. Legis. asst. Sen. Strom Thurmond, Washington, 1976-77; sole practice Georgetown, S.C., 1977—; instr. Horry-Georgetown Tech. Coll., Georgetown, 1977-79; v.p. Mayo/Lawrimore Inc., Georgetown and Myrtle Beach, S.C., 1985—, also bd. dirs. Author: Doctrine of Unseaworthiness in the Fourth Circuit, 1976. Mem. exec. com. S.C. Reps., 1980, State Appeals Bd. Selective Service System, 1983—; bd.dirs. Georgetown County Hist. Commn., 1985—, chmn. 1986—. Mem. ABA, S.C. Bar Assn., Georgetown County Bar Assn. (sec. 1982-83). Episcopalian. Club: Palmetto (Columbia, S.C.). Avocations: landscape architecture, genealogy. General corporate, Real property, Contracts commercial. Home: Wicklow Hall Plantation Georgetown SC 29440 Office: 731 Prince St PO Box 1486 Georgetown SC 29440

LAWS, JAMES TERRY, lawyer; b. Greenville, S.C., Mar. 14, 1952; s. James Talmadge and Alma Dell (Ledford) L.; m. Lynn Marie Watson, June 6, 1973; children: Courtney Marie, Jourdan Elizabeth. BA, U. S.C., 1974, JD, 1977. Bar: S.C. 1977, U.S. Dist. Ct. S.C. 1978, U.S. Ct. Appeals (4th cir.) 1979, U.S. Supreme Ct. 1984. Ptnr. Laws & Daniel, Greenville, 1977-81, Laws, Daniel & Stewart, Greenville, 1981, Riley, Riley, Laws & Stewart, Greenville, 1982-86, Nelson, Mullins, Riley & Scarborough, Greenville, 1987—; pres., chmn. Travelers Rest (S.C.) Devel. Corp., 1980—, Marietta Mgmt. and Holding, Greenville, 1985—. Bd. dirs. Stroud Mem. Hosp., Marietta, S.C., 1978—; dem. precinct pres., Marietta, 1978-82, 1986—, county v.p., Greenville, 1982—; county coordinator Epps for gov., Greenville, 1986; mem. 300 for Greenville, 1986—; traveling ambassador Hdqrs. for Recruitement, Greenville, 1986—, bd. dirs., 1987—; bd. dirs. Greenville County Recreation Commn., Meals on Wheels, Greenville; chmn. Travelers Rest Great Towns Com., 1980-82. Named Young Businessman of the Yr., N. Greenville Area Econ. Devel. Group., 1985. Mem. ABA, S.C. Bar Assn., Greenville County Bar Assn., Greenville C. of C., Travelers Rest Jaycees (pres. 1983, Jaycee of the Yr. award 1981). Lodges: Rotary, Lions (local pres. 1979), Masons. Avocations: alpine skiing, sailing. Federal civil litigation, State civil litigation, Real property. Home: Rt 7 46 S Warwick Rd Greenville SC 29609 Office: Nelson Mullins Riley & Scarborough 24th Floor Daniel Bldg PO Box 10084 Greenville SC 29603

LAWS, JEAN SADOWSKY, lawyer; b. Worcester, Mass., May 29, 1954; d. Samuel and Edith (Miller) Sadowsky; m. Victor H. Laws III, June 5, 1982; children: Michael Hastings, Jessica Miller. BA with high honors, U. Md., 1975, JD with honors, 1978. Bar: Md. 1979, U.S. Dist. Ct. Md. 1979, U.S. Bankruptcy Ct. 1982. Staff atty. Nat. Ctr. for State Cts., Williamsburg, Va., 1978-79, Legal Aid Bur., Salisbury, Md., 1979-81; assoc. Nolan, Plumhoff & Williams, Towson, Md., 1981-82; legal counsel Lower Shore Area Agy. on Aging, Salisbury, 1982—; ptnr., officer Laws & Laws P.A., Salisbury, 1984—; instr. Wor-Wic Tech. Community Coll., Salisbury, 1983-84; instr., lectr. Salisbury State Coll., 1985. Mem., bd. dirs. Lower Shore Commn. on Employment of the Handicapped, Salisbury, 1985—, Wicomico County Humane Soc., Salisbury, 1983—; mem. Wicomico County Mental Health Adv. Bd., Salisbury, 1984-86, chmn. 1986. Mem. ABA, Md. Bar Assn., Wicomico County Bar Assn. Democrat. Methodist. General practice, Legal rights of the elderly. Home: 610 Hunting Park Dr Salisbury MD 21801 Office: Law & Laws PA 107 N Baptist St Salisbury MD 21801

LAWS-COATS, LAURIE ANN, lawyer; b. Pasadena, Calif., Feb. 21, 1954; d. Jennings B. and Marjorie (Friend) Gatlyn; m. James M. Coats Jr., Dec. 4, 1982; 1 child, James Donovan. BA in Econs., U. Calif. San Diego, La Jolla, 1974; JD, Calif. Western Sch. Law, 1977. Bar: Calif. 1979, U.S. Dist. Ct. (no., cen., ea. and so. dists.) Calif. 1979, U.S. Ct. Appeals (9th cir.) 1979, Ariz. 1983, U.S. Dist. Ct. Ariz. 1983. Sr. legal counsel Western Growers Assn., Phoenix and Irvine, Calif., 1979-85; sole practice Phoenix, 1985—. Mem. ABA, Ariz. Bar Assn., Calif. Bar Assn., Maricopa County Bar Assn., Jr. League Phoenix. Republican. Avocations: tennis, aerobics, racquetball. Labor. Office: 3636 N Central Ave Suite 990 Phoenix AZ 85012

LAWSON, EDWARD ALBERT, lawyer; b. San Francisco, May 8, 1950; s. Albert Walter and Bernice (Chambers) L.; m. Julie Claire Caughlin, Sept. 11, 1971; children: Sean Christopher, Patricia Laura. BA, U. San Francisco, 1972; JD, U. Calif. Hastings Coll. Law, San Francisco, 1975. Bar: Calif. 1975, Idaho 1979, U.S. Dist. Ct. (no. dist.) Calif. 1975, U.S. Ct. Appeals (9th cir.) 1975, U.S. Dist. Ct. Idaho 1979, U.S. Supreme Ct. 1983. Assoc. Tobin & Tobin, San Francisco, 1975-79; ptnr. Lawson & Peebles, Ketchum, Idaho, 1979—; instr. U. Calif. Hastings Coll. Law, 1976. Editor. Hastings Constl. Law Quar., 1975; contbr. articles to profl. jours. Mem. Hastings Constl. Rights Found., San Francisco, 1975; bd. dirs. Urban Community Mental Health, San Francisco, 1979. Mem. ABA, Idaho State Bar (pub. relations com. 1986—), Assn. Trial Lawyers Am., Idaho Trial Lawyers Assn. Real property, State civil litigation. Office: Lawson & Peebles 319 Walnut Ave Ketchum ID 83340

LAWSON, GARY B., lawyer; b. N.Y.C., Oct. 5, 1945; s. Dave and Rose Helen (Shapiro) Levy; m. Marcia Krauss, June 19, 1981; 1 child, Seth David. AA, Queens Coll., 1966; JD, St. Johns U., 1970; LLM in Taxation, NYU, 1974. Bar: N.Y. 1971, Wis. 1973, Ill. 1976, Ga. 1983, Mass. 1983, Tex. 1984. Atty. Mut. Life Ins. Co., N.Y.C., 1970-72; assoc. Hoyt, Greene, Meissner and Walsh, Milw., 1972-74, Walsh & Simon, Milw., 1974-76; ptnr. Katten, Muchin, Zavis, Pearl & Galler, Chgo., 1976-81; of counsel Haas, Holland, Lipshutz, Levison & Gilbert, Atlanta, 1981-82; of counsel Mintz, Levin, Cohn, Ferris, Glovsky & Popeo, P.C., Boston, 1982-84, Jenkens & Gilchrist, Dallas, 1984-87; Maxwell Godwin & CArlton PC, 1987—; instr. U. Wis.-Milw., 1975. Bd. dirs. Parental Stress Services, Chgo., 1980-81. Mem. ABA (tax sect.) New Eng. Employee Benefits Council (bd. dirs. 1983-85), Southwest Pension Conf. (bd. dirs. 1986—), Boston Estate and Bus. Planning Council. Pension, profit-sharing, and employee benefits, Corporate taxation, Personal income taxation. Office: Maxwell Godwin & Carlton PC 3300 InterFirst Plaza 901 Main St Dallas TX 75202

LAWSON, MARGARET AVRIL, lawyer; b. Cin., May 12, 1957; d. John George and Charlotte Elizabeth (Craig) A.; m. Jonathan Allen Lawson, June 12, 1982. BA, Dartmouth Coll., 1979; JD, Harvard U., 1982. Bar: Ohio 1982, U.S. Dist. Ct. (so. dist.) Ohio 1982. Assoc. Taft, Stettinius & Hollister, Cin., 1982—. Active Vol. Lawyers for Poor, Cin., 1983—; vol. Cin. Regatta, Community Chest, Cin. Mem. Ohio Bar Assn., Cin. Bar Assn. General corporate, Securities. Office: Taft Stettinius & Hollister 1800 First Nat Bank Ctr Cincinnati OH 45202

LAWSON, ROBERT WILLIAM, JR., lawyer; b. South Boston, Va., Sept. 20, 1908; s. Robert William and Mary Easley (Craddock) L.; m. Virginia Peyton Broun, Nov. 18, 1938; children—Robert William III, Fontaine Broun, Lewis Peyton. B.A., Hampden-Sydney Coll., 1930; LL.B., U. Va., 1935. Bar: Va. 1934, W.Va. 1935, U.S. Ct. Appeals (4th cir.) 1950. Assoc. Steptoe & Johnson, Charleston, W.Va., 1935-41; ptnr. Steptoe & Johnson, Charleston, 1941-62, sr. ptnr., 1962-84, of counsel, 1984—; dir. Fed. Res. Bank Richmond, 1967-75, dep. chmn., 1968-71, chmn., 1972-75. Trustee Episcopal High Sch., 1951-54, Hampden-Sydney Coll., 1950-77; chancellor Protestant Episcopal Diocese W.Va., 1956-77. Served to lt. comdr. USNR, 1944-46. Fellow Am. Bar Found.; mem. ABA (state del. 1975-84, bd. govs. 1984-86), Am. Law Inst., Am. Judicature Soc. (bd. dirs. 1986), Supreme Ct. Hist. Soc., 4th Cir. Jud. Conf. (life). Democrat. Lodge: Rotary. Avocations: golf; reading. State civil litigation, Federal civil litigation, State and local taxation. Home: 10 Grosscup Rd Charleston WV 25326 Office: Steptoe & Johnson PO Box 1588 Charleston WV 25326

LAWSON, THOMAS SEAY, JR., lawyer; b. Montgomery, Ala., Oct. 30, 1935; s. Thomas Seay and Rose Darrington (Gunter) L.; m. Sarah Hunter Clayton, May 27, 1961; children—Rose Gunter, Gladys Robinson, Thomas Seay. A.B., U. Ala., 1957, LL.B., 1963. Bar: Ala. 1963, U.S. Supreme Ct.

1969. Law clk. to chief justice U.S. Dist. Ct. (no. dist.) Ala., 1963-64; assoc. Steiner, Crum & Baker, Montgomery, 1964-68; ptnr. Capell, Howard, Knabe & Cobbs P.A., Montgomery, 1968—, asst. dist. atty. 15th jud. cir. of Ala., 1969-70; mem. lawyers adv. com. U.S. Ct. Appeals (11th cir.). Pres. The Lighthouse, 1978-79. Served to lt. USNR, 1957-60. Mem. ABA, Fed. Bar Assn., Ala. State Bar (pres. young lawyers sect. 1970-71), Montgomery County Bar Assn. (pres. 1980), Am. Judicature Soc., Eleventh Cir. Hist. Soc. (v.p.), Soc. of Pioneers of Montgomery (pres. 1983), Farrah Law Soc. (pres. 1986—). Democrat. Episcopalian. Clubs: Montgomery Country, Capital City (Montgomery). State civil litigation, Federal civil litigation, Administrative and regulatory. Home: 1262 Glen Grattan Montgomery AL 36111 Office: Capell Howard Knabe & Cobbs PA 57 Adams Ave PO Box 2069 Montgomery AL 36197

LAWSON, WILLIAM HOMER, lawyer; b. Champaign, Ill., Jan. 15, 1953; s. Joel Smith and Grace Colgate (Rumbough) L.; m. Laurie Anne Millikan, Nov. 24, 1979; children: William Stanley, Amy Rochelle. B.A., Trinity Coll., Hartford, Conn., 1974; J.D., Stanford U., 1977. Bar: Hawaii, 1977. Assoc. Cades, Schutte, Honolulu, 1977-79; sole practice, Honolulu, 1979—. Mem. Assn. Trial Lawyers Am., ABA, Hawaii Bar Assn. Bankruptcy, Federal civil litigation, State civil litigation. Office: 1188 Bishop St Suite 2902 Honolulu HI 96813

LAWTER, J. MIKE, lawyer, state legislator; b. Oklahoma City, Dec. 9, 1947; s. Zeddie Hampton and Loucile Pauline (Grant) L.; m. Martha Alice Krueger, Aug. 10, 1969; 1 son, Michael Jay. B.S. in Edn., Central State U., 1971; J.D., Oklahoma City U., 1974. Bar: Okla., U.S. dist. ct. (we. dist.) Okla. Ptnr., Lawter & Pitts, Inc., Oklahoma City, 1983—. Mem. Okla. Ho. of Reps., 1976-86. Served to maj. Signal Corps., USNG, 1970—. Recipient Alumni Assn. award Oklahoma City U., 1974. Mem. Oklahoma County Bar Assn., Am. Judicature Soc., ABA, Okla. Bar Assn., Okla. Trial Lawyers Assn. Democrat. Methodist. Lodges: Shriners, Masons. Workers' compensation, Labor. Home: 8020 Golden Oaks St Oklahoma City OK 73127 Office: 1330 Classen Blvd G-2 Oklahoma City OK 73106

LAWTON, BETTINA MARY, lawyer; b. Albany, N.Y., Oct. 10, 1954; d. John J. and Elizabeth M. (Hammond) L.; m. Richard S. Belous, Oct. 18, 1981; 1 child, Joshua J. AA, Hudson Valley Community Coll., 1974; BBA, MCL, Siena Coll., 1976; JD, Georgetown U., 1980. Bar: D.C. 1980, U.S. Dist. Ct. D.C. 1980, N.Y. 1981, U.S. Ct. Appeals (D.C. cir.) 1986, U.S. Supreme Ct. 1986. Assoc. Rosenman Colin et al, Washington, 1980-82, 84-86; sr. atty. SEC, Washington, 1982-84; assoc. Dechert, Price & Rhoads, Washington, 1986—. Named one of Outstanding Young Women in Am., 1985. Mem. ABA (womens caucus, corp. banking and bus. law sect.), D.C. Bar Assn. (corp. banking and bus. law sect.), Women's Bar Assn. of D.C. (treas. 1983-85, pres. 1985—), Washington Bar Assn., Fed. Bar Assn. Banking, Securities, Federal civil litigation. Office: Dechert Price & Rhoads 1730 Pennsylvania Ave NW Washington DC 20006

LAWTON, ERIC, lawyer, photographer; b. N.Y.C., Apr. 9, 1947; s. Leo and Vira (Michaels) L. AB, UCLA, 1969; JD, Loyola U., Los Angeles, 1972. Bar: Calif. 1972, U.S. Dist. Ct. (cen. dist.) Calif. 1974, U.S. Ct. Appeals (9th cir.) 1973, U.S. Supreme Ct. 1976. Assoc. West & Girardi, Los Angeles, 1972-76; sole practice Los Angeles, 1976—; guest lectr. UCLA, 1986. Active XXIII Olympic Games organizing com. (citizens adv. commn., cultural and fine arts adv. commn.), Los Angeles, 1983-84. Mem. ABA, Los Angeles Trial Lawyers Assn., Los Angeles County Bar Assn., Santa Monica Bar Assn. Avocation: photography. State civil litigation, Personal injury, Contracts commercial. Office: 2001 Wilshire Blvd 600 Santa Monica CA 90403

LAWTON, JAMES PATRICK, lawyer; b. Yuma, Ariz., Feb. 28, 1948; s. James Howard and Patricia Ann (Johnson) L.; m. Debra Ann Burlingame, June 14, 1979; 1 child, Kathryn Ann. BS, U.S. Naval Acad., 1970; JD, U. Va., 1978. Bar: N.Y. Assoc. Davis, Polk & Wardwell, N.Y.C., 1978-85, ptnr., 1985—. Served to lt. USN, 1970-75. Pension, profit-sharing, and employee benefits, General corporate, Corporate taxation. Office: Davis Polk & Wardwell 1 Chase Manhattan Plaza New York NY 10005

LAWTON, JEFF, lawyer; b. Syracuse, N.Y., Sept. 24, 1956; s. Joseph John and Mary (Clarke) L.; m. Kathy Melen, Apr. 23, 1983. BA magna cum laude, U. Colo., 1977; MA in History, SUNY, Binghamton, 1978; JD, St. John's U., 1981. Bar: N.Y. 1982, U.S. Dist. Ct. (so. and ea. dists.) N.Y. 1982. Assoc. Barowka & Golumb, Mineola, N.Y., 1981-83, Martin, Clearwater & Bell, N.Y.C., 1983—. Mem. N.Y. State Bar Assn. Personal injury, Federal civil litigation, State civil litigation. Home: 207 Coachlight Sq Montrose NY 10548 Office: Martin Clearwater & Bell 220 E 42nd St New York NY 10017

LAWTON, KENNETH WAYNE, lawyer; b. Hartford, Conn., Oct. 15, 1953; s. Donald David and Ethel Pearl (Biermacher) Lawton; m. Bonnie Louise Gordon, May 26, 1975; children—Carl Joseph II, Matthew Robert, Michelle Renee. B.S. summa cum laude, U. New Haven, 1976; J.D. with honors, Drake U., 1979. Bar: Iowa 1980, Tex. 1985, U.S. Dist. Ct. (so. dist.) Iowa 1980, U.S. Dist. Ct. (no. dist.) Iowa 1981, U.S. Ct. Appeals (8th cir.) 1981, U.S. Supreme Ct. 1983, U.S. Dist. Ct. (no. dist.) Tex. 1984, U.S. Dist. Ct. (ea. and we. dists.) Tex. 1985, U.S. Ct. Appeals (5th cir.) 1985. Assoc. Whitfield, Musgrave, Selvy, Kelly, Eddy, Des Moines, 1980-84; dir., sec. Geary, Stahl & Spencer, P.C., Dallas, 1984—; lectr. Iowa Defense Counsel Assn. Annual Mtg., 1982, Des Moines Area Community Coll. Legal Asst. Program, 1981-82, Human Resources Forum, Am. Electronics Assn., Dallas, 1986; legal research asst. Iowa State Bar Assn. Com. on Study Fed. Rules Evidence, 1982; chmn. spl. com. on Friends of Moot Ct. Drake Law Sch. Bd. Counsellors, 1983-84. Contbg. author: Understanding Iowa Law, 1984; editor: Energy and Nat. Resources Guide for Iowa, 1979. Adv. U. New Haven Law Enforcement Explorers Post Boy Scouts Am., 1975; coach Johnston Sr. High Sch. Mock Trial Teams, Iowa, 1984; del. Polk County Republican Conv., Des Moines, 1980, Iowa Republican State Convention, 1980; deacon Canyon Creek Bapt. Ch., 1986—; chmn. scholarship and fin. aid com. Canyon Creek Christian Acad., 1985—. Recipient Academic Scholarship U. New Haven, 1973-76; semi-finalist Midwest Regional Moot Ct. Competition, 1979. Mem. ABA (subcom. on fraudulent and deceptive trade practices sect. tort and ins. practice 1985-86), Iowa State Bar Assn. (mem. Young Lawyer Sect. ethics com. 1981, law schs. panel com. 1982, law-related edn. com. 1983-84), Polk County Bar Assn., Def. Research Inst., Iowa Defense Counsel Assn., Am. Trial Lawyers Assn., Iowa Assn. Trial Lawyers (founding dir., chmn. Drake U. Law Sch. student bd. dirs., 1978-79, ex-officio mem. bd. dirs. 1978-79), Dallas Bar Assn. (mock trial com., law in changing soc. com. 1985, speech com. 1985-86), State Bar Tex., Dallas Assn. Young Lawyers (liaison with other profls., fed. opinions com. 1986), Order of Barristers, Fed. Bar Assn., Drake U. Law Sch. Alumni Assn. (regional v.p. for Tex. and Okla. 1986—), Alpha Chi (vice chmn. Conn. chpt. 1975-76). Federal civil litigation, State civil litigation, Personal injury. Home: 1100 Princeton Dr Richardson TX 75081 Office: Geary Stahl & Spencer PC 6400 Interfirst Plaza 901 Main St Dallas TX 75202

LAWYER, VERNE, lawyer; b. Indianola, Iowa, May 9, 1923; s. Merrill Guy and Zella (Mills) L.; m. Sally Hay, Oct. 5, 1946; 1 dau., Suzanne; m. Vivian Jury, Oct. 25, 1959; children: Michael Jury, Steven Verne. LL.B., Drake U., 1949. Bar: Iowa 1949, U.S. Dist. Ct. (no. and so. dists.) Iowa, U.S. Supreme Ct. 1957. Practice law Des Moines, 1949—. Author: Trial by Notebook, 1964; co-author: Art of Persuasion in Litigation, 1966, How to Defend a Criminal Case from Arrest to Verdict, 1967, The Complete Personal Injury Practice Manual, 1983. Mem. Iowa Aeros. Commn., 1973-75; trustee ATL Roscoe Pound Found., 1965-71, fellow, 1973—. Recipient Outstanding Law Alumni award Phi Alpha Delta, 1964. Fellow Internat. Acad. Trial Lawyers (chmn. aviation & space law com. 1970, ABA ad hoc com. to study court congestion 1973), Am. Coll. Trial Lawyers, Am. Bar Found., Am. Bd. Trial Advocates, Internat. Soc. Barristers; mem. ABA, Iowa Bar Assn. (uniform instrn. com. 1962, rules com. 1965, chmn. Iowa rules of civil procedure 1968-69, spl. commn. fed. practice 1971-78, spl. automobile reparations com. 1972—), Polk County Bar Assn., Am. Trial Lawyers Assn./before 1962 the Nat. Assn. Claimant's Compensation Attys. (v.p. Iowa chpt. 1956-57, nat. sec. 1963-64, 67-68, bd. govs. 1962-63, com. on internat. membership 1957, nat. conv. com. 1952, co-chmn. sect. tort 1962-63, nat. seminar chmn. 1964-65, 66-67, chmn. nat. speakers bur. 1964-65, govt. liability com. 1971, state chmn. membership com. of ins. negligence compensation law 1970, com. on trial techniques 1969-70, com. on aviation litigation 1983-84), Assn. Trial Lawyers Am. (Iowa Key Man legis. session 1969, rules com. of ins. negligence and compensation law 1970, guest statutes com. 1970, chmn. comml. tort litigation 1970, membership chmn. for Iowa 1972-74, aviation sect. 1971—, automobile accident reparations com. 1971—, trial advs. scholarship com. 1973—, nat. council pub. affairs), Iowa Acad. Trial Lawyers (sec.-treas. 1962—, editor Verdict Summary 1970—, editor Acad. Alert, editor Court Says 1978—), Assn. Trial Lawyers Iowa, Law Sci. Acad. Am., Lawyer-Pilots Bar Assn., Am. Judicature Soc., World Peace Through Law Ctr., Trial Lawyers Assn. Des Moines, N.Y. State Trial Lawyers Assn., Calif. Trial Lawyers Assn., Okla. Trial Lawyers Assn., Tex. Trial Lawyers Assn., Am. Bar Found., Phi Alpah Delta, Sigma Alpha Epsilon. Personal injury, Federal civil litigation, State civil litigation. Home: 5831 N Waterbury Rd Des Moines IA 50312 Office: 427 Fleming Bldg Des Moines IA 50309

LAWYER, VIVIAN JURY, lawyer; b. Farmington, Iowa, Jan. 7, 1932; d. Jewell Everett Jury and Ruby Mae (Schumaker) Brewer; m. Verne Lawyer, Oct. 25, 1959; children—Michael Jury, Steven Verne. Tchr.'s cert. U. No. Iowa, 1951; B.S. with honors, Iowa State U., 1953; J.D. with honors, Drake U., 1968. Bar: Iowa 1968, U.S. Supreme Ct. 1986. Home econs. tchr. Waukee High Sch. (Iowa), 1953-55; home econs. tchr. jr. high sch. and high sch., Des Moines Pub. Schs., 1955-61; sole practice law, Des Moines, 1972—; bd. dirs. Micah Corp.; chmn. juvenile code tng. sessions Iowa Crime Commn., Des Moines, 1978-79, coordinator workshops, 1980; assoc. Law Offices of Verne Lawyer, Des Moines, 1981—; co-founder, bd. dirs. Youth Law Center, Des Moines, 1977—; mem. com. rules of juvenile procedure Supreme Ct. Iowa, 1981—, adv. com. on costs of ct. appointed counsel Supreme Ct. Iowa, 1985—; trustee Polk County Legal Aid Services, Des Moines, 1980-82; mem. Iowa Dept. Human Services and Supreme Ct. Juvenile Justice County Base Joint Study Com., 1984—; mem. Iowa Task Force permanent families project Nat. Council Juvenile and Family Ct. Judges, 1984—; mem. substance abuse com. Commn. Children, Youth and Families, 1985—. Editor: Iowa Juvenile Code Manual, 1979, Iowa Juvenile Code Workshop Manual, 1980; author booklet in field, 1981. Mem. Polk County Citizens Commn. on Corrections, 1977. Iowa Dept. Social Services grantee, 1980. Mem. ABA, Iowa Bar Assn., Polk County Bar Assn., Polk County Women Attys. Assn., Assn. Trial Lawyers Am., Assn. Family Counseling in Juvenile and Family Cts., Purple Arrow, Phi Kappa Phi, Omicron Nu. Republican. Juvenile. Home: 5831 N Waterbury Rd Des Moines IA 50312 Office: 427 Fleming Bldg Des Moines IA 50309

LAX, MICHAEL H., lawyer; b. Miami, Fla., June 12, 1949; s. Irving and Ida Lax; m. Deborah Stein, Aug. 20, 1972; 1 child, Nicole Renee. BA, George Washington U., 1971; JD, Washington U., St. Louis, 1974; MBA, U. Miami, 1981. Bar: Fla. 1974, U.S. Dist. Ct. (so. dist.) Fla. 1974. Assoc. Pyszka, Kessler, Adams & Solomon, Miami, 1976-77; mng. atty. INA Orgn., Miami, 1978-83; sr. ptnr. Peters, Pickle, Flynn & Niemoeller, Miami, 1984—; hearing examiner Met. Dade County, Miami, 1985—. Bd. dirs. LEGAL/Dade County Sch. Bd., Miami, 1985—; speaker Dade County Sch. Bd., Miami, 1984—. Cert. of Appreciation Dade Ptnrs., 1985. Mem. ABA, Fla. Bar Assn., Dade County Bar Assn., Dade County Def. Bar Assn. (program dir., sec.), Am. Arbitration Assn. (arbitrator, mediator). State civil litigation, Entertainment, Insurance. Office: Peters Pickle Flynn & Niemoeller 25 SE Second Ave #628 Miami FL 33131

LAY, DONALD POMEROY, judge; b. Princeton, Ill., Aug. 24, 1926; s. Hardy W. and Ruth (Cushing) L.; m. Miriam Elaine Gustafson, Aug. 6, 1949; children: Stephen Pomeroy (dec.), Catherine Sue, Cynthia Lynn, Elizabeth Ann, Deborah Jean, Susan Elaine. Student, U.S. Naval Acad., 1945-46; BA, U. Iowa, 1948, JD, 1951; LLD (hon.), Mitchell Coll. Law, 1985. Bar: Nebr. 1951, Iowa 1951, Wis. 1953. Assoc. Kennedy, Holland, DeLacy & Svoboda, Omaha, 1951-53, Quarles, Spence & Quarles, Milw., 1953-54, Eisenstatt, Lay, Higgins & Miller, 1954-66; judge U.S. Ct. Appeals (8th cir.), 1966-80, chief judge, 1980—; faculty mem. on evidence Nat. Coll. Trial Judges, 1964-65; mem. U.S. Jud. Conf., 1980—. Mem. editorial bd.: Iowa Law Rev., 1950-51; contbr. articles to legal jours. Pres. Douglas County (Nebr.) Dystrophy Assn., 1964; bd. dirs. Hattie B. Monroe Home, Omaha, 1961-67. Served with USNR, 1944-46. Recipient Hancher-Finkbine medal U. Iowa, 1980. Fellow Internat. Acad. Trial Lawyers; mem. ABA, Nebr. Bar Assn., Iowa Bar Assn., Wis. Bar Assn., Am. Judicature Soc. (bd. dirs. 1976—, exec. bd. 1979—), Law Sci. Acad. (v.p. 1960), Assn. Trial Lawyers Am. (bd. govs. 1963-65, Jud. Achievement award), U. Iowa Alumni Assn. (pres. Omaha-Council Bluffs chpt. 1958), Order of Coif, Delta Sigma Rho (Significant Sig award 1986), Phi Delta Phi, Sigma Chi. Presbyterian. Office: PO Box 75908 Saint Paul MN 55175

LAY, PATTI JANE, lawyer; b. Knoxville, Tenn., Mar. 1, 1955; d. Frank Edwin and Agnes (Hufstedler) L.; m. John Thomas Baugh, Sept. 21, 1986. BA, Emory U., 1976; JD, U. Tenn., 1979. Bar: Tenn. 1979, U.S. Dist. Ct. (mid. and ea. dists.) Tenn. 1979, U.S. Ct. Appeals (6th cir.) 1981. Assoc. Poore, Cox, Baker, Ray & Byrne, Knoxville, 1979-82, Kennerly, Montgomery & Finley, Knoxville, 1982—. Chmn. exec. com. Teen Bd., Knoxville, 1984—; bd. dirs. Vol. Ctr., Knoxville, 1985—; mem. Jr. League Knoxville, 1985—. Mem. ABA, Tenn. Bar Assn., Tenn. Trial Lawyers Assn., Tenn. Def. Lawyers Assn., Knoxville Bar Assn. (credentials com. 1983—, legis. liaison com. 1984—), Knoxville Barristers. Republican. Methodist. Club: LeConte (bd. dirs. 1985—). Avocations: water skiing, snow skiing, gourmet cooking. Federal civil litigation, State civil litigation, Insurance. Office: Kennerly Montgomery & Finley 1701 Plaza Tower Knoxville TN 37929

LAYCOCK, HAROLD DOUGLAS, law educator; b. Alton, Ill., Apr. 15, 1948; s. Harold Francis and Claudia Anita (Garrette) L.; m. Teresa A. Sullivan, June 14, 1971; 1 child, Joseph Peter. BA, Mich. State U., 1970; JD, U. Chgo., 1973. Bar: Ill. 1973, U.S. Dist. Ct. (no. dist.) Ill. 1973, Tex. 1974, U.S. Ct. Appeals (7th cir.) 1973, U.S. Dist. Ct. (we. dist.) Tex. 1975, U.S. Ct. Appeals (5th and 11th cirs.) 1975, U.S. Supreme Ct. 1976. Law clk. to judge U.S. Ct. Appeals (7th cir.), Chgo., 1973-74; sole practice Austin, Tex., 1974-76; from asst. prof. to prof. law U. Chgo., 1976-81; prof. law U. Tex., Austin, 1981—; prof. Fulbright & Jaworski, 1984-87; assoc. dean for acad. affairs U. Tex., Austin, 1985-86; endowed professorships, 1983—; reporter com. on motion practice Ill. Jud. Conf., Chgo., 1977-78. Author: Modern American Remedies, 1985; contbr. articles to law revs., 1977—. Adv. bd. Consumer Services Orgn., Chgo., 1979-80; mem. exec. bd. Ctr. for Church/State Studies, Depaul U., 1982—, adv. com. on religious liberty Presbyn. Ch. USA, N.Y.C., 1983—. Mem. Am. Law Inst., Chgo. Council of Lawyers (v.p. 1977-78), Assn. Am. Law Schs. (chmn., sec. on remedies 1983), AAUP (com. on Status of Women in Academic Profession 1982-85). Legal education, Federal civil litigation, Civil rights. Home: 4203 Woodway Austin TX 78731 Office: U Tex Law Sch 727 E 26th St Austin TX 78705

LAYDEN, CHARLES MAX, lawyer; b. Lafayette, Ind., Nov. 10, 1941; s. Charles E. and Elnora M. (Parvis) L.; m. Lynn D. McVey, Jan. 28, 1967; children: David Charles, Kathleen Ann, John Michael, Daniel Joseph. BA in Indsl. Mgmt., Purdue U., 1964; JD, Ind. U., 1967. Bar: Ind. 1967, U.S. Dist. Ct. (no. and so. dists.) Ind. 1967, U.S. Ct. Appeals (7th cir.) 1970. U.S. Tax Ct. 1986. Assoc. Vaughan & Vaughan, Lafayette, 1967-70; ptnr. Vaughan, Vaughan & Layden, Lafayette, 1970-86, Layden & Layden, Lafayette, 1986—. Chmn. profl. div. United Way Lafayette, 1986. Mem. ABA, Ind. Bar Assn., Tippecanoe County Bar Assn., Am. Bd. Trial Advs. (charter mem. Ind. chpt. 1984—), Ind. Trial Lawyers Assn. (bd. dirs. 1983—). Republican. Roman Catholic. Club: Lafayette Country. Avocations: photography, classic cars, flying. Federal civil litigation, State civil litigation, Personal injury. Home: 2826 Ashland St West Lafayette IN 47906 Office: Layden & Layden 201 Main St Suite 712 PO Box 909 Lafayette IN 47902

LAYDEN, DONALD WILLIAM, JR., lawyer; b. Bklyn., Dec. 2, 1957; s. Donald William and Barbara (Tepper) L.; m. Mary Jo DeWalt, Aug. 8, 1981; children: Christopher, Jacob. BA in Econs., Marquette U., 1979, JD cum laude, 1982. Bar: Wis. 1982, U.S. Dist. Ct. (ea. dist.) Wis. 1982. Assoc. Quarles & Brady, Milw., 1981—; lectr. securities regulation Marquette U., Milw., 1983—. Chmn. exploring north sect., exec. bd. Boy Scouts Am., Milw., 1983—; chmn. fin. com. St. Sebastian Parish, Milw., 1984—; mem. securities merit rev. com. Wis. Commr.'s Office, Madison, 1986—. Recipient Award of Merit Boy Scouts Am., 1982, Bronze Big Horn award Boy Scouts Am., 1986. Mem. ABA, Wis. Bar Assn., Milw. Bar Assn., Phi Kappa Theta. Roman Catholic. Club: Milw. Athletic. Avocations: reading, photography, softball, backpacking. General corporate, Securities. Office: Quarles & Brady 411 E Wisconsin Ave Milwaukee WI 53202-4497

LAYMAN, DAVID MICHAEL, lawyer; b. Pensacola, Fla., July 28, 1955; s. James Hugh and Winifred (Smith) L. BA with high honors, U. Fla., 1977, JD with honors, 1979. Bar: Fla. 1980. Assoc. Gunster, Yoakley, Criser & Stewart, West Palm Beach, Fla., 1980-83; assoc. Wolf, Block, Schorr & Solis-Cohen, West Palm Beach, 1983-87, ptnr., 1987—; mem. Attys. Title Ins. Fund. Contbg. editor U. Fla. Law Rev.; contbr. articles to profl. jours. Del. Statewide Rep. Caucus, Orlando, Fla., 1986; mem. Blue Ribbon Zoning Rev. Com., West Palm Beach, 1986—; bd. dirs., sec. Palm Beach County Planning Congress, 1984—; trustee South Fla. Sci. Mus. Named one of Outstanding Young Men in Am., 1980. Mem. ABA, Fla. Bar Assn. (conv. com. young lawyers sect. 1982-84), Palm Beach County Bar Assn. (pres.-elect young lawyers sect. 1986—, sec./treas. young lawyers sect.), Blue Key, Omicron Delta Kappa, Sigma Chi, Phi Kappa Phi. Episcopalian. Clubs: Palm Beach County Gator (pres., bd. dirs.); Governors (West Palm Beach). Real property, Landlord-tenant. Home: 5601 Gun Club Rd West Palm Beach FL 33406 Office: Wolf Block Schorr & Solis-Cohen 777 S Flagler Dr Suite 900 West Palm Beach FL 33401

LAYMAN, EARL ROBERT, lawyer; b. Knoxville, Tenn., Aug. 5, 1932; s. William Earl and Marie Francis (Little) L.; m. Nancy Doris Shaver, Oct. 30, 1954 (div.); children: William Douglas, Marilyn Lee, Linda Ann, Sharon Gail. BS, U. Tenn., 1955, JD, 1962. Bar: Tenn. 1963, U.S. Dist. Ct. (ea. dist.) Tenn. 1964, U.S. Ct. Appeals (6th cir.) 1979, U.S. Supreme Ct. 1971. Acct. E. Tenn. Packing Co., Knoxville, 1957-59; assoc. Joyce & Wilson, Oak Ridge, Tenn., 1962-64; ptnr. Key, Lee, Layman, Child, O'Connor & Petty, Knoxville, 1964—; instr. U. Tenn., Knoxville, 1966-70. Mem. adv. bd. YWCA, Knoxville, 1966, Knox County Election Commn., 1969-72, exec. com. Tenn. Reps., Knoxville, 1972-78. Served to 1st lt. AUS, 1955-57. Mem. ABA, Tenn. Bar Assn., Knoxville Bar Assn., Tenn. Def. Lawyers Assn., Internat. Assn. Ins. Counsel, Assn. R.R. Trial Counsel. Methodist. Club: LeConte. Federal civil litigation, State civil litigation, Personal injury. Home: Rt 1 Lakefront Dr Knoxville TN 37922 Office: Key Lee Layman Child OConnor & Petty 3d Nat Bank Bldg 14th Floor Knoxville TN 37901

LAYTON, GARLAND MASON, lawyer; b. Boydton, Va., Aug. 20, 1925. LLB, Smith-Deal-Massey Coll. Law, 1952; LLD, Coll. of William and Mary, 1962. Bar: Va. 1951, U.S. Dist. Ct. (ea. dist.) Va. 1961, U.S. Supreme Ct. 1968. Sole practice Virginia Beach, Va., 1952—. Served with USMC, 1940-45, PTO. Mem. ABA, Fed. Bar Assn., Nat. Lawyers Club, Va. Beach Bar Assn. Democrat. Methodist. Real property, Administrative and regulatory, General corporate. Home: PO Box 5211 Bayside Station Virginia Beach VA 23455 Office: 4809 Baybridge Ln PO Box 5211 Virginia Beach VA 23455

LAZAR, RAYMOND MICHAEL, lawyer, educator; b. Mpls., July 16, 1939; s. Simon and Hessie (Teplin) L; m. Susan Leah Krantz, Dec. 27, 1966; children: Mark, Deborah. BBA, U. Minn., 1961, JD, 1964. Bar: Minn. 1964, U.S. Dist. Ct. Minn. 1964. Spl. asst. atty. gen. State of Minn., St. Paul, 1964-66; sole practice Mpls., 1966-72; ptnr. Lapp, Lazar, Laurie & Smith, Mpls., 1972-86; ptnr., officer Fredrikson & Byron P.A., Mpls., 1986—; lectr. various continuing edn. programs, 1972—; adj. prof. law U. Minn., Mpls., 1983—. Fellow Am. Acad. Matrimonial Lawyers; mem. ABA, Minn. Bar Assn., Hennepin County Bar Assn. Family and matrimonial, State civil litigation. Home: 1908 Humboldt Ave S Minneapolis MN 55403 Office: Fredrikson & Byron PA 1100 Internat Centre Minneapolis MN 55402

LAZARUS, ARTHUR, JR., lawyer; b. Bklyn., Aug. 30, 1926; s. Arthur and Frieda (Langer) L.; m. Gertrude Chiger, Jan. 8, 1956; children—Andrew Joseph, Edward Peter, Diana Ruth. B.A. with honors, Columbia U., 1946; J.D., Yale U., 1949. Bar: N.Y. 1951, D.C. 1952, U.S. Supreme Ct. 1954. Assoc. Fried, Frank, Harris, Shriver & Jacobson, Washington, 1950-57, ptnr., 1957—, mng. ptnr. Washington office, 1974-86; vis. instr. law Yale U., 1973-82. Federal civil litigation, Administrative and regulatory. Home: 3201 Fessenden St NW Washington DC 20008 Office: 1001 Pennsylvania Ave NW Suite 800 Washington DC 20004

LAZO, IGNACIO JESUS, lawyer; b. Havana, Cuba, Dec. 29, 1955; came to U.S., 1960; s. Javier Lazo and Concepcion Arechabala; m. Lauren Traynor Diehl, Aug. 26, 1984. AB Polit. Sci. with honor, Stanford U., 1980; JD, U. Calif., Berkeley, 1982. Bar: Calif. 1982, U.S. Dist. Ct.(no., ea., so., and cen. dists.) Calif. 1983, U.S. Ct. Appeals (9th cir.) 1985. Library asst. Latham & Watkins, Los Angeles, 1980; assoc. Gendel, Raskoff, Shapiro & Quittner, Los Angeles, 1981, 82—. Articles editor, bd. editors Ecology Law Quarterly, 1981-82. Mem. ABA (litigation sect.), Fin. Lawyers Conf., Assn. Bus. Trial Lawyers, Cuban Am. Bar Assn. (sec. 1986—), Los Angeles County Bar Assn. (comml. law and bankruptcy sect., litigation sect.). Democrat. Roman Catholic. Avocations: fishing, travel. Federal civil litigation, State civil litigation, Contracts commercial. Office: Gendel Raskoff et al 1801 Century Park E 6th Floor Los Angeles CA 90067

LAZZARO, ROBERT WAYNE, lawyer; b. Balt., June 20, 1952; s. Robert Vincent and Carolyn Ruth (Duncan) L.; m. Susan Carol Smith, Sept. 27, 1980. BA, Washington Coll., Chestertown, Md., 1974; JD, U. Balt., 1978. Bar: U.S. Dist. Ct. Md. 1978. Asst. states atty. Balt. County, 1978-85; assoc. Bregel, Kerr & Heisler, Towson, Md., 1985—; chief child abuse and sex offense unit states atty. office Balt. County, 1980-85, dir. continuing legal edn., 1983-85. Mem. com. Md. Task Force for Child Abuse Legis., Annapolis, 1984-85, com. to elect sitting judges of Balt. County, Towson, 1986, com. to elect Charles Ruppersberger to County Council, Towson, 1986, com. to elect Joseph Curran Atty. Gen., Md., 1986. Bar: ABA, Md. Bar Assn., Balt. County Bar Assn., Assn. Trial Lawyers Am., Md. Trial Lawyers Assn., Md. States Attys. Assn. (continuing legal edn. com. 1983-85), Md. Criminal Def. Attys. Assn. Republican. Roman Catholic. Lodge: Elks. Avocations: golf, softball, guitar. Criminal, Personal injury, Family and matrimonial. Home: 11 Stream Run Ct Timonium MD 21093 Office: Bregel Kerr & Heisler 409 Washington Ave Suite 400 Towson MD 21204

LEA, LOLA STENDIG, lawyer; b. N.Y.C., Sept. 20, 1934; d. Hershel and Sophie (Golub) Stendig; m. Robert M. Lea, Sept. 12, 1953 (div. Apr. 1976); 1 child, Jennie. B.A. cum laude, NYU, 1954; LL.B., Yale U., 1957. Bar: N.Y. 1958. Law clk. to U.S. dist. judge So. Dist. N.Y., 1957-59, asst. U.S. atty., 1959-61; assoc. C.C. Davis, N.Y.C., 1961-67; mem. firm Davis & Cox, N.Y.C., 1967-71, Lea, Goldberg & Spellun (P.C.), N.Y.C., 1971-77, Trubin, Sillcocks, Edelman & Knapp, N.Y.C., 1977-80; counsel Parker & Duryee, 1983-86, mem., 1987—; spl. counsel to N.Y. 1st dept. joint interprofl. com. Drs. and Lawyers, 1972-78; lectr. Practising Law Inst., N.Y.C., 1969-70, 74, 79; spl. mediator Med. Malpractice Mediation part Supreme Ct. N.Y., 1971-80; chmn. N.Y. State Commn. Investigation, 1981-83. Fellow Am. Bar Found., N.Y. Bar Found.; mem. ABA, N.Y. Bar Assn. (del. 1972-77, 87—, mem. exec. com. 1976-77), Assn. Bar City N.Y. (chmn. grievance com. 1978-80, chmn. medicine and law com. 1969-71, chmn. spl. com. on drug laws, mem. other coms.), N.Y. County Lawyers Assn. (dir. 1978-81). Home: 24 Garden Pl Brooklyn NY 11201 Office: 529 Fifth Ave New York NY 10017

LEACH, RUSSELL, lawyer; b. Columbus, Ohio, Aug. 1, 1922; s. Charles Albert and Hazel Kirk (Thatcher) L.; m. Helen M. Sharpe, Feb. 17, 1945; children—Susan Sharpe, Terry Donnell, Ann Dunham. B.A., Ohio State U., 1946, J.D., 1949. Bar: Ohio 1949. Clk. U.S. Geol. Survey, Columbus, 1948-49; reference and teaching asst. Coll. Law, Ohio State U., 1949-51; asst. city atty. City of Columbus, 1951-54, sr. asst. city atty., 1954-55, chief counsel, 1956, 1st asst. city atty., 1957, city atty., 1957-63, presiding judge mcpl. ct., 1964-66; ptnr. Bricker & Eckler, 1966—, chmn. bd. dirs. Commr., Columbus Met. Housing Authority, 1968-74; chmn. Franklin County Republican Com., 1974-78. Served with AUS, 1942-46, 51-53. Named One of 10 Outstanding Young Men of Columbus, Columbus Jaycees, 1956, 57. Mem. ABA, Ohio Bar Assn. (council of dels. 1970-75), Columbus Bar Assn. (pres. 1973-74), Delta Theta phi, Chi Phi. Methodist. General practice, Local government, State civil litigation. Home: 1232 Kenbrook Hills Dr

Columbus OH 43220 Office: Bricker & Eckler 100 S 3d St Columbus OH 43215

LEACH, SYDNEY MINTURN, lawyer; b. Tuscaloosa, Ala., Dec. 13, 1951; s. Randall Peck and Jean (Key) L.; m. Catherine Louise Aertker, Mar. 31, 1984 (div. July 1986). Cert., U. Ala., 1975, BEE, 1975; JD, U. Va., 1978. Bar: U.S. Patent Office 1978, Tex. 1979, U.S. Dist. Ct. (so. dist.) Tex. 1979, U.S. Ct. Appeals (4th cir.) 1980, U.S. Ct. Appeals (fed. cir.) 1985, U.S. Supreme Ct. 1986. Ptnr. Arnold, White & Durkee, Houston, 1978—. Author: How to Sue in Small Claims Court, 1984, Tenants Rights, 1985; editor Current Aspects of Licensing Technology, 1981, Your Case in Traffic Court, 1984. Mem. steering com. campaign Judge Sheila Jackson Lee, Houston, 1984, Judge Lamar McCorkle, Houston, 1986—. Named one of Outstanding Young Men of Am., 1980-82, 85-86. Fellow Houston Bar Found., Tex. Bar Found.; mem. ABA, Tex. Young Lawyers Assn. (treas. 1984-85, bd. dirs. 1983-85, 1986—), Houston Young Lawyers Assn. (bd. dirs. 1981-82, Outstanding Service award 1982, 83), Am. Intellectual Property Law Assn., U. Ala. Alumni Assn. (pres. Houston chpt. 1980, 83), Capstone Engring. Soc. (bd. dirs. 1982—). Republican. Baptist. Club: Houstonian, University (Houston). Lodge: Rotary. Patent, Trademark and copyright, Federal civil litigation. Office: Arnold White Durkee PO Box 4433 Houston TX 77210

LEACH, TERRY RAY, lawyer, judge; b. Ft. Worth, Apr. 6, 1949; s. Herbert W. and Catherine A. (Flanary) L.; m. Dixie Gail Day, Jan 8, 1972; children: Michelle Rene, David Richard, Jennifer Anne. BS in Indsl. Engring., Tex. Tech U., 1971, JD with honors, 1975. Bar: Tex. 1975, U.S. Dist. Ct. (no. dist.) Tex. Engr. Southwest Bell Telephone, San Antonio, 1970; assoc. Whitley, Boring & Morrison, Bedford, Tex., 1975-76; ptnr. Evans, Leach & Ames, Hurst, Tex., 1976-82; sr. ptnr. Leach & Ames P.C., Hurst, 1982—; mcpl. ct. judge City of Bedford, 1979—, City of Lakeside, Tex., 1984—; lectr. real estate law Tarrant County Jr. Coll., Hurst, 1980-81. Mem. Zoning Bd. Adjustment, Hurst, 1985—, Hurst Found. Com., 1986; deacon Harwood Terr. Bapt. Ch., Bedford, 1983. Named one of Outstanding Young Men Am., 1977-78. Mem. ABA, Tex. Bar Assn., Northeast Tarrant County Bar Assn. (pres. 1980-81), Assn. Trial Lawyers Am., Tex. Mcpl. Cts. Assn., Phi Delta Phi. Baptist. Probate, General corporate, Contracts commercial. Home: 224 Carolyn Dr Hurst TX 76054 Office: Leach & Ames PC 1241 Southridge Ct #104 Hurst TX 76053

LEADER, ROBERT JOHN, lawyer; b. Syracuse, N.Y., Oct. 14, 1933; s. Henry John and Dorothy Alberta (Schad) L.; m. Nancy Bruce, Sept. 23, 1960; children—Henry, William, Catherine, Thomas, Edward. A.B., Cornell U., 1956; J.D., Syracuse U., 1962. Bar: N.Y. 1963. Assoc. Ferris, Hughes, Dorrance & Groben, Utica, N.Y., 1962-64; ptnr. Cole Leader & Elmer, Gouverneur, N.Y., 1964-66; ptnr. Case & Leader, Gouverneur, 1966—; sec. North Country Hosps. Inc., 1972—; atty. Village of Hermon (N.Y.), 1968—, Town of Gouverneur, 1967—, Town of Pitcairn (N.Y.), 1974—, Village of Edwards, 1974—; corp. counsel Village of Gouverneur, 1973—; bd. dirs. Gouverneur Savs. and Loan. Trustee Edward John Noble Hosp., Gouverneur, 1972—, chmn. bd., 1979-81; trustee North Country Hosps., Inc., Gouverneur, 1972—, Gouverneur Library, 1973-83; trustee Gouverneur Nursing Home Co., Inc., 1972—, past pres. 1979-81; Republican chmn. Town and Village of Gouverneur, 1969-72; del. N.Y. State Jud. Conv., 1981—. Served to capt. USAF, 1956-59. Roman Catholic. Club: Rotary. State civil litigation, General practice, Construction. Home: 187 Rowley St Gouverneur NY 13642 Office: 107 E Main St Gouverneur NY 13642

LEAF, FREDERICK PETER, lawyer, educator; b. New Haven, Dec. 4, 1946; s. Milton John and Jane (Collins) L.; m. Kimmy Jin, June 1, 1973; children: Alicia Jin, Thomas Collins. BBA in Acctg., Niagara U., 1968; JD cum laude, Boston Coll., 1971. Bar: Conn. 1971, U.S. Dist. Conn. 1971, U.S. Ct. Mil. Appeals 1972. Assoc. Gitlitz, Ronai & Bercham P.C., Milford, Conn., 1976-79; ptnr. Altham & Leaf, New Haven, 1980-84; sole practice New Haven, 1984—; atty. City of New Haven, 1980-84; spl. asst. corp. counsel, New Haven, 1980-84; adj. prof. N.H. Coll., 1981—. Served to maj. JAGC, U.S. Army, 1972-76. Democrat. Roman Catholic. Family and matrimonial, Personal injury, Real property.

LEAF, MARTIN NORMAN, lawyer; b. N.Y.C., Feb. 19, 1932; s. Jack and Shirley L.; m. Louise Sarkin, Dec. 29, 1956; children—Marc, Jenifer, Clifton. B.A., Washington U., St. Louis, 1952; J.D., NYU, 1958. Bar: N.Y. 1958, U.S. Ct. Customs and Patent Appeals 1964, U.S. Ct. Mil. Appeals 1964, U.S. Ct. Claims 1964, U.S. Supreme Ct. 1964. Sr. assoc. Jacob D. Fuchsberg, N.Y.C., 1958-63; sr. ptnr. Leaf, Sternklar & Drogin, N.Y.C., 1963—; spl. master N.Y. State Supreme Ct. Arbitrator, Am. Arbitration Assn.; village atty. Hastings-on-Hudson (N.Y.), 1969-82; spl. asst. dist. atty. Westchester Country. Bd. dirs. Buckminster Fuller Inst., Echo Hills Mental Health Clinic, 1973-87 , Trailblazers, 1979—, Nat. Black Theatre, 1973—, Am. Arab Affairs Council, 1983—; mem. internat. adv. bd. World Sikh Centre, 1980—; Hunger Project del. NGO, UN; mem. N.Y. State Conf. Village Ofcls. Served to 1st lt. U.S. Army, 1955-57. Recipient Disting. Service award VFW, 1983. Mem. Fed. Bar Council, ABA, N.Y. State Bar Assn., New York County Lawyers Assn., N.Y. Trial Lawyers Assn., Union Internationale des Avocats. Clubs: Players, St. Anthony (N.Y.C.). Assoc. editor Am. Trial Lawyers Assn. Jour., 1963-73. Private international, State civil litigation, General corporate. Home: 104 Burnside Dr Hastings-on-Hudson NY 10706 Office: 440 Park Ave S New York NY 10016

LEAHY, DANIEL JAMES, lawyer; b. Evergreen Park, Ill., Apr. 20, 1933; s. John G. and Francis A. (Henshaw) L.; m. Mariann Bullen; children: Kathleen, Mary Claire, Megan, Patrice, Monica. BS, Villanova U., 1954; LLB, DePaul U., 1959. Bar: Ill. 1959, U.S. Supreme Ct. 1963, Wis. 1978. Ptnr. Leahy & Eisenberg Ltd., Chgo., 1959—; bd. dirs. Addison Farmers Ins. Co., Lombard, Ill. Served to cpl. U.S. Army. Roman Catholic. Avocations: golf, hunting. Federal civil litigation. Home: 408 Concord Ln North Barrington IL 60010 Office: Leahy & Eisenberg Ltd 29 S LaSalle St Chicago IL 60603

LEAMER, ROBERT ELDON, lawyer, legislative counsel; b. Chgo., Jan. 4, 1950; s. Laurence Eugene and Helen Mae (Burkey) L.; m. Johanna Mary Kocik, Aug. 26, 1978; children—Stephen, Christina. A.B., Colgate U., 1972; J.D., Albany U., 1976. Bar: N.Y. 1977, U.S. Dist. Ct. (no. dist.) N.Y. 1977. Asst. counsel N.Y. State Assembly, Albany, 1976-79; sole practice, Binghamton, N.Y., 1979—; counsel N.Y. State Assembly Com. on Health, Albany, 1979—; lectr. on patients' rights, rights of mentally ill, legis. process. Mem. Forum Expansion Com., Binghamton, 1980, N.Y.-Pa. Health Systems Agy., 1980—; bd. dirs. Broome Legal Assistance Corp., 1985—. Mem. Nat. Health Lawyers Assn., ABA, N.Y. State Bar Assn., Broome County Bar Assn. (chmn. legis. com.). Democrat. Episcopalian. Club: Binghamton. Health, General practice. Home: 1508 Carnegie Drive Binghamton NY 13903 Office: 502 Press Bldg 19 Chenango St Binghamton NY 13901

LEAMING-ELMER, JUDY, lawyer; b. Dayton, Ohio, Nov. 23, 1942; d. Vaughn F. and Letha R. (Robinson) Leaming; m. Don Leaming-Elmer, Dec. 27, 1965. BA, Westmar Coll., 1964; MS in Edn., No. Ill. U., 1967; JD, Antioch Sch. Law, 1980. Bar: Colo. 1981, U.S. Dist. Ct. Colo. 1981. Staff counsel Nat. Congress Am. Indians, Washington, 1980-81; sole practice Denver and Twin Lakes, Colo., 1981-84; assoc. EGD & Assocs., Denver and Twin Lakes, 1984-86; gen. counsel Ute Mountain Ute Tribe, Towaoc, Colo., 1987—. Author: (with Don Leaming-Elmer) Spoken American English for Koreans, 1969. Bd. dirs. Indian Child Welfare Project, Denver, project adv. group Indian Law Support Ctr., Boulder, Colo. Mem. ABA, Fed. Bar Assn., Colo. Women's Bar Assn., Am. Indian Bar Assn. (bd. dirs. 1985—, pres. Colo. chpt. 1986—). Avocations: swimming, cross-country skiing, Catawba pottery. Indian law. Home: 227 S Harrison #2 Cortez CO 81321 Office: Ute Mountain Ute Nation Dept Justice PO Box AA Towaoc CO 81334

LEARNED, JAMES ROY, lawyer, petroleum consultant, geologist; b. Kenosha, Wis., Aug. 25, 1920; s. John James and Rhoda Belle (Cameron) L.; m. Joan Alice Ticknor, Nov. 11, 1944; 1 dau., Jocelyn Jean. A.B. in Geology, U. Wyo., 1943, J.D., 1948. Bar: Wyo. 1949, U.S. Dist. Ct. Wyo. 1959, U.S. Ct. Appeals (10th cir.) 1967, U.S. Supreme Ct. 1984. Atty. Husky Oil Co., Cody, Wyo., 1949-51, div. atty., 1951-53, gen. atty., 1953-56, mgr. land and exploration, 1956-59; v.p. Argus Exploration Corp., Guatemala, Guatemala, 1956-59; sole practice, Cheyenne, Wyo., 1960—; cons. petroleum geologist. Served to 1st lt. Coast Arty. Corps, 1943-46. Mem. ABA, Wyo. Bar Assn., Laramie County Bar Assn., Am. Assn. Petroleum Geologists, Wyo. Geol. Assn., Rocky Mountain Assn. Geologists, Mont. Geol. Soc., Rocky Mountain Oil and Gas Assn. Republican. Presbyterian. Rev. author Title X Am. Law of Mining, 1970-75. Oil and gas leasing, Real property, Administrative and regulatory.

LEARY, NANCY MAY, lawyer; b. Iola, Wis., May 26, 1955; d. Clifford C. and Irmina M. (Krebsbach) L. BA, U. Wis., 1977; JD, UCLA, 1980. Bar: Wis. 1980, U.S. Dist. Ct. (we. dist.) Wis. 1980, U.S. Dist. Ct. (ea. dist.) Wis. 1982. Assoc. Michael, Best & Friedrich, Milw., 1980—. Mem. Hist. 3d Ward Devel. Assn. Mem. ABA, Wis. Bar Assn., Milw. Young Lawyers Assn. Real property, Contracts commercial. Office: Michael Best & Friedrich 250 E Wisconsin Ave Milwaukee WI 53202

LEARY, THOMAS BARRETT, lawyer; b. Orange, N.J., July 15, 1931; s. Daniel and Margaret (Barrett) L.; m. Kathleen Phelps, June 2, 1984; children by previous marriage: Thomas A., David A., Alison L.E. AB, Princeton U., 1952; JD, Harvard U., 1958. Bar: N.Y. 1959, Mich. 1972, D.C. 1983. Assoc. White & Case, N.Y.C., 1958-68, ptnr., 1968-71; atty.-in-charge antitrust Gen. Motors Corp., Detroit, 1971-77, asst. gen. counsel, 1977-82; ptnr. Hogan & Hartson, Washington, 1983—. Served to lt. USNR, 1952-55. Mem. ABA. Antitrust, Administrative and regulatory, Federal civil litigation. Home: 155 E St SE Washington DC 20003 Office: Hogan & Hartson Columbia Square 555 13th St NW Washington DC 20004-1109

LEAS, PHILIP JOSEPH, lawyer; b. Omaha, Mar. 19, 1949; s. Harry Dale and Bernadine Marie (Venteicher) L.; m. Sheila Diane Robertson, Dec. 30, 1972; children: Monica, David. AB, Georgetown U., 1971; JD, Stanford U., 1974. Bar: Hawaii 1974, U.S. Dist. Ct. Hawaii 1974, U.S. Ct. Appeals (9th cir.) 1976. Assoc. Cades Schutte Fleming & Wright, Honolulu, 1974-80; ptnr. Cades, Schutte, Fleming & Wright, Honolulu, 1980—. Mem. ABA, Hawaii Bar Assn. Republican. Roman Catholic. Real property, Condemnation, Banking. Office: Cades Schutte Fleming & Wright 1000 Bishop St Suite 1200 Honolulu HI 96813

LEATHERBURY, GREGORY LUCE, JR., lawyer; b. Mobile, Ala., Feb. 11, 1947; s. Gregory Luce and Florence Morton (Greaves) L.; m. Susan Glover Thames, June 13, 1969; children—Gregory Luce III, Clifton Thames. B.A., U. Ala., 1969, J.D., 1972; LL.M. in Taxation, NYU, 1973. Bar: Ala. 1973, U.S. Dist. Ct. (so. dist.) Ala. 1973, U.S. Tax Ct. 1973. Ptnr. Hand, Arendall, Bedsole, Greaves & Johnston, Mobile, 1973—; chmn. 37th U. Ala. Fed. Tax Clinic, 1983; dir. Capital Marine Corp., Orange, Tex., Pa. Shipbuilding Co., Phila. Bd. dirs. Gulf Coast Conservation Assn., Mobile County Wildlife and Conservation Assn., Mobile Big Game Fishing Club. Mem. ABA, Ala. State Bar (chmn. tax sect. 1982-83), Mobile Bar Assn., Delta Kappa Epsilon. Episcopalian. Clubs: Athelstan (Mobile) (bd. dirs. 1978-80), Mobile Country. Lodge: Rotary. Corporate taxation, Real property, Probate. Home: 370 Tuthill Ln Mobile AL 36608 Office: Hand Arendall Bedsole Greaves & Johnston AL 36601

LEATHERBURY, THOMAS SHAWN, lawyer; b. Ft. Worth, Dec. 7, 1955; s. John Raymond and Hester Louise (Hoffecker) L.; m. Patricia Villareal, Nov. 27, 1982; children: Sean, Colin. BA, Yale U., 1976, JD, 1979. Bar: Tex. 1979, U.S. Dist. Ct. (no. dist.) Tex. 1979, U.S. Ct. Appeals (5th cir.) 1982, U.S. Dist. Ct. (we. dist.) Tex. 1984. Law clk. to presiding justice U.S. Dist. Ct. (no. dist.) Tex., Dallas, 1979-80; assoc. Locke, Purnell, Boren, Laney & Neely P.C., Dallas, 1980-86, ptnr., 1986—. Mem. Tex. Bar Assn., Dallas Bar Assn., Dallas Assn. Young Lawyers. Libel, Antitrust, Federal civil litigation. Home: 5115 Tremont Dallas TX 75214 Office: Locke Purnell et al 3600 Republic Bank Tower Dallas TX 75201

LEATHERS, MARVIN LIONEL, lawyer; b. Jan. 21, 1954; s. Marvin Jr. and Annie Lucille (Flanagan) L.; m. Nancy Taylor, April 17, 1975; children: Marvin Lionel Jr., Murray Taylor. BS, U. North Ala., 1976; JD, Samford U., 1980. Bar: Ala., 1980. Ptnr. Hollis & Leathers, Winfield, Ala., 1980—. Mem. ABA, Ala. Bar Assn., Marion County Bar Assn., Fayette County Bar Assn., Ala. Trial Lawyers Assn. Baptist. Office: Hollis & Leathers 109 1st St SE Fayette AL 35555

LEAVERTON, MARK KANE, lawyer; b. Lubbock, Tex., Dec. 26, 1949; s. Herbert Walker and Patricia (Kane) L.; m. Vicki Browder, Dec. 21, 1974; children—David, Lindsey. B.B.A. in Bus., Tex. Tech U., 1972; J.D., U. Tex., 1974. Bar: Tex. 1974. Assoc., Stuart Johnston Jr., Dallas, 1975-77; assoc. Stubbeman, McRae, Sealy, Laughlin & Browder, Midland, 1977-80, ptnr., 1980-85; sole practice, Midland, 1985—; lectr. in law. Contbr. articles to profl. jours. Active, Christmas in April, Midland, 1979—; chmn. Admissions Com., United Way, Midland, 1982-83, chmn. planning div., 1983-85; co-teaching dir. Midland Men's Community Bible Study. Mem. ABA, Tex. Bar Assn., Midland County Bar Assn. Republican. Oil and gas leasing. Home: 11 Marchelle Ct Midland TX 79705 Office: One Marienfeld Pl Suite 380 Midland TX 79701

LEAVITT, JACK, lawyer; b. N.Y.C., Apr. 1, 1931; s. Ezekiel and Goldie Leavitt; m. Isabel Anna Osthoff, July 1959 (div. 1974); children—Nancy Jo, Susan Elizabeth; m. 2d, Marilyn Jane Willey, May 18, 1979; 1 dau., Catherine Sayre. B.A., Bklyn. Coll., 1951; LL.B., U. Ill., 1957, M.A., 1958; LL.M., U. Calif.-Berkeley, 1963. Bar: Ill. 1958, Calif. 1961, U.S. Ct. Appeals (9th cir.) 1964. Copyboy, N.Y. Jour.-American, N.Y.C., 1951; legal editor Bancroft-Whitney, San Francisco, 1958-60; legal editor Continuing Edn. of the Bar, 1960-62; practice law, Berkeley, and San Francisco, 1962-80; cons. Calif. Jud. Council, 1970; dep. dist. atty. Alameda County, Calif., 1980-87; instr. San Francisco Law Sch., John F. Kennedy Law Sch.; TV host Legal Topics, 1975-80. Served with USNR, 1951-54. Hon. mention Best Mystery Stories of the Year submitted to TV Emmy award for program Insanity and the Law, 1978. Mem. Mystery Writers Am., Calif. Dist. Attys. Assn. Syndicated columnist Opening Argument, 1979-81. Co-author: California Evidence, 1971-80; California Crimes, 1971-80; California Criminal Procedure, 1971-80; author short stories; contbr. articles to profl. jours. Criminal. Home: 1019 Merced St Berkeley CA 94707 Office: 1615 California St Berkeley CA 94703

LEAVITT, JEFFREY STUART, lawyer; b. Cleve., July 13, 1946; s. Sol and Esther (Dolinsky) L.; m. Ellen Fern Sugerman, Dec. 21, 1968; children—Matthew Adam, Joshua Aaron. A.B., Cornell U., 1968; J.D., Case Western Res. U., 1973. Bar: Ohio 1973. Assoc. Jones, Day, Reavis & Pogue, Cleve., 1973-80, ptnr., 1981—. Contbr. articles to profl. jours. Trustee Bur. Jewish Edn., Cleve., 1981—, v.p. 1985—, Fairmount Temple, Cleve., 1982—, v.p. 1985—, Citizens League Greater Cleve., 1982—; sec. Kulas Found., 1986—. Mem. ABA (employee benefits coms. 1976—), Midwest Pension Conf. Jewish. Pension, profit-sharing, and employee benefits, Personal income taxation. Home: 25961 Annesley Rd Beachwood OH 44122 Office: Jones Day Reavis & Pogue 901 Lakeside Ave North Point Cleveland OH 44114

LEAVITT, MARTIN JACK, lawyer; b. Detroit, Mar. 30, 1940; s. Benjamin and Annette (Cohen) L.; m. Janice C. Leavitt; children: Michael J., Paul J., David A. LLB, Wayne State U., 1964. Bar: Mich. 1965, Fla. 1967. Assoc. Robert A. Sullivan, Detroit, 1968-70; officer, bd. dirs. Law Offices Sullivan & Leavitt, Northville, Mich., 1970—, pres., 1979—; bd. dirs. Premiere Video, Inc., Tyrone Hills of Mich., others. Served to lt. comdr., USNR, 1965-68. Detroit Edison Upper Class scholar, 1958-64. Mem. ABA, Mich. Bar Assn., Fla. Bar Assn., Transp. Lawyers Assn., ICC Practitioners. Jewish. Clubs: Meadowbrook Country, Huron River Hunting & Fishing, Chgo. Traffic, Savoyard, Rolls Royce Owners. General corporate, Administrative and regulatory, Federal civil litigation. Home: 20114 Longridge Northville MI 48167 Office: 22375 Haggerty Rd PO Box 400 Northville MI 48167

LEB, ARTHUR S., lawyer; b. Cleve., June 26, 1930; s. Ernest A. and Bertha (Stern) L.; m. Lois Shafron, Oct. 21, 1932; children—Gerald P., Judith A., Robert B. A.B., Columbia Coll., 1952; J.D., Western Res. Law Sch., 1955. Bar: Ohio 1955, U.S. Supreme Ct., 1965. Ptnr. Leb & Halm, Canton, Ohio, 1961-84, Amerman, Burt & Jones, L.P.A., Canton, 1985—; founding mem., exec. com. Ohio Council Sch. Bd. Attys., 1976-84, pres. 1983. Served to 1st lt. JAGC, USAF, 1955-57. Recipient award of merit Ohio Legal Ctr. Inst., 1964. Mem. Stark County Bar Assn. (pres. 1985-86), ABA, Ohio Bar Assn. General practice, Education and schools, Labor. Office: 624 Mannet Ave North Canton OH 44702

LEBAMOFF, IVAN ARGIRE, lawyer; b. Ft. Wayne, Ind., July 20, 1932; s. Argire V. and Helen A. (Kachandov) L.; m. Katherine S. Lebamoff, June 9, 1963; children—Damian I., Jordan L., Justin A. A.B. in History, Ind. U., 1954, J.D., 1957. Bar: Ind. 1957, U.S. Ct. Dist. Ct. (no. and so. dists.) 1958, U.S. Supreme Ct. 1963. Sole practice Ft. Wayne, Ind., 1957-68; ptnr. Lebamoff, Ver Wiebe & Snow, Ft. Wayne, Ind., 1968-71; mayor City of Ft. Wayne, 1972-75; sole practice Lebamoff Law Offices, Ft. Wayne, 1975—; U.S. commr. No. Dist. Ind., 1957-62; fgn. service officer USIA Dept. Commerce, Bulgaria, 1963; vis. prof. dept. urban affairs Ind. U.-Purdue, Ft. Wayne, 1976-77. Chmn. Allen County Democratic Com., 1968-75, Ft. Wayne Dept. Parks and Recreation, 1984—; nat. pres. Macedonian Patriotic Orgn. of U.S. and Can., 1983—. Served with USAF, 1958-64. Mem. Allen County Bar Assn., Ind. Bar Assn., Am. Trial Lawyers Assn., Ind. Trial Lawyers Assn. Eastern Orthodox. Lodge: Kiwanis, Masons. Personal injury, General practice. Home: 205 E Packard Ave Fort Wayne IN 46806 Office: Lebamoff Law Offices 918 S Calhoun St Fort Wayne IN 46802

LEBARON, CHARLES FREDERICK, JR., lawyer; b. Grand Rapids, Mich., Oct. 8, 1949; s. Charles Frederick and Barbara Jean (Day) LeB.; m. Elizabeth Ann Zwickert, Aug. 12, 1978; children: Ann Saunders, Katherine Clark. AA, Grand Rapids Jr. Coll., 1969; AB, U. Mich., 1971, AMLS, 1973; JD summa cum laude, Ind. U., 1980. Bar: Ill. 1980, U.S. Dist. Ct. (no. dist.) Ill. 1980, U.S. Ct. Appeals (7th cir.) 1981. Dir. Georgetown Library, Jenison, Mich., 1974-77; law clk. to cir. judge U.S. Ct. Appeals (7th cir.), Chgo., 1980-82; assoc. Mayer, Brown & Platt, Chgo., 1982-84; atty. Centel Corp., Chgo., 1984-85, staff atty., 1985-86; corp. counsel Acco World Corp., Northbrook, Ill., 1986—. Trustee Clarendon Hills Pub. Library, Ill., 1985—. Recipient Dyer-Ives Found. award, 1972. Mem. ABA, Chgo. Bar Assn., Order of Coif, Legal Club Chgo. Republican. Episcopalian. Contracts commercial, General corporate. Home: 150 Juliet Ct Clarendon Hills IL 60514 Office: Acco World Corp 2215 Sanders Rd Northbrook IL 60065

LEBELL, ROBERT, lawyer; b. Oahu, Hawaii, Nov. 22, 1948; s. Arnold and Helen Cohen LeB. BA, Grinnell Coll., 1970; JD, U. Iowa, 1973. Bar: Wis., U.S. Dist. Ct. (ea. and we. dists.) Wis., U.S. Ct. Appeals (7th cir.). Atty. Legal Aid Soc. of Milw., 1974-78; ptnr. Carter, LeBell & Finn, Milw., 1978-80, Styler, Kostich, LeBell & Dobroski, Milw., 1980-86; sole practice Milw., 1986—. Bd. dirs. Frederick Douglas Ctr. Halfway House, Milw., 1984—. Served with USAF Res., 1970-80. Mem. Wis. Bar Assn. Democrat. Jewish. Avocations: running, raquetball. Criminal, Personal injury, State civil litigation. Home: 2287 N Lake Dr Milwaukee WI 53202

LEBEN, JEFFREY MICHAEL, lawyer, educator; b. N.Y.C., Dec. 13, 1948; s. Bernard Jay and Florence Maxine (Keselenko) L.; m. Arlene Marsha Frank, Aug. 30, 1970; 1 child, Joshua Scott. B.A., NYU, 1970; J.D., St. John's U., Jamaica, N.Y., 1973. Bar: N.Y. 1974, U.S. Dist. Ct. (so. and ea. dist.) N.Y. 1974, U.S. Supreme Ct. 1980, U.S. Tax Ct. 1984. Sr. atty. Appellate div. 2d dept. N.Y. State Sup. Ct., Bklyn., 1973-80; sole practice, Yorktown Heights, N.Y., 1980—; instr. N.Y. Med. Coll., Valhalla, 1978—; instr. law Mercy Coll., Dobbs Ferry, N.Y., 1981—. Mem. N.Y. State Urban Devel. Corp. Community Adv. Com., Spring Valley, N.Y., 1973; mem. Town of Yorktown Drug Abuse Council, Yorktown Heights, 1977-80; bd. dirs. Rockland County Soc. Prevention of Cruelty to Children, Haverstraw, N.Y., 1980—. Named hon. dep. sheriff Westchester County Sheriff's Dept., 1980. Mem. N.Y. State Bar Assn., Yorktown Bar Assn. (pres. 1985). Democrat. Jewish. Lodge: K.P. Family and matrimonial, Personal injury, Health. Home: 186 Juniper Dr Yorktown Heights NY 10598 Office: The Yorktown Commons 1830 Commerce St Yorktown Heights NY 10598

LEBLANC, RICHARD PHILIP, lawyer; b. Nashua, N.H., Aug. 5, 1946; s. Ronald Arthur and Jeanette G. (Chomard) LeB.; m. Doris Julie Lavoie, May 25, 1968; children: Justin D., Renée M., Anne-Marie. AB summa cum laude, Coll. of the Holy Cross, 1968; JD cum laude, Harvard U., 1972. Bar: Maine 1972, U.S. Dist. Ct. Maine 1972. Assoc. Bernstein, Shur, Sawyer & Nelson, Portland, Maine, 1972-75, ptnr., 1976—; mem. Probate Law Revision Commn., Augusta, Maine, 1975-80. Pres. United Way of Greater Portland, 1982-84; trustee Cleverus High Sch., Portland, 1982—; bd. dirs. Habitat for Humanity, Portland, 1984—. Fellow Am. Coll. Probate Counsel; mem. ABA, Maine Bar Assn., Maine Estate Planning Council. Democrat. Roman Catholic. Probate, Estate planning, Estate taxation. Home: 142 Longfellow St Portland ME 04103 Office: Bernstein Shur Sawyer & Nelson PO Box 9729 Portland ME 04104-5029

LEBLANC, ROBERT EDMOND, III, lawyer; b. New Orleans, Mar. 23, 1923; s. Robert Edmond and Vivian Catherine (Baumann) LeB.; m. Betty Margaret Picou, Apr. 2, 1945; children—Linda A., Judith L., Robert B., Michael P., Lee A. B.S. in Elec. Engring., Tulane U., 1944; J.D., Georgetown U., 1950. Bar: D.C. 1950, Md. 1961, Va. 1982, U.S. Ct. Appeals (2d cir.) 1964, U.S. Ct. Appeals (7th cir.) 1966, U.S. Ct. Appeals (8th cir.) 1966, U.S. Ct. Appeals (Fed. cir.) 1982, U.S. Supreme Ct. 1964. Assoc. Bacon & Thomas, Washington, 1951-53; ptnr. Strauch, Nolan & Diggins, Washington, 1953-55, Diggins & LeBlanc, Washington, 1955-62, LeBlanc & Shur, Washington, 1962-79, LeBlanc, Nolan, Shur & Nies, Arlington, Va., 1979-85, Lowe, Price, LeBlanc, Becker & Shur, Alexandria, Va., 1986—; adj. prof. Georgetown U. Law Ctr., Washington, 1962-74. Author: What the Business Man Should Know About Patents, 1960; Trademarks and Unfair Competition, 1967. Served to lt. USN, 1943-46; PTO. Mem. ABA, D.C. Bar Assn., Md. Bar Assn., Va. Bar Assn., Fed. Cir. Bar Assn., Am. Intellectual Property Assn. Club: Bethesda Country (Md.). Patent, Trademark and copyright, Federal civil litigation. Home: 9301 Burning Tree Rd Bethesda MD 20817 Office: Lowe Price LeBlanc Becker & Shur 427 N Lee St Alexandria VA 22314

LEBOW, EDWARD MICHAEL, lawyer; b. Boston, Mar. 2, 1948; s. Saul Lawrence and Estelle Irene (Lipson) L.; m. Stephanie Ann Wick, Mar. 14, 1981; 1 child, Samuel Lawrence. BA, Harvard U., 1970, JD, 1974. Bar: Mass. 1974, D.C. 1977, U.S. Dist. Ct. D.C. 1978, U.S. Ct. Appeals (D.C. cir.) 1978, U.S. Supreme Ct. 1978, U.S. Ct. Internat. Trade 1980. Assoc. Nutter, McClennen & Fish, Boston, 1974-76; atty. U.S. Internat. Trade Commn., Washington, 1976-81, asst. gen. counsel, 1981; assoc. Dow, Lohnes & Albertson, Washington, 1982-85; ptnr. Kelley, Drye & Warren, Washington, 1985—. Avocations: Japanese and French languages. Private international. Home: 5459 31st St NW Washington DC 20015 Office: Kelley Drye & Warren 1330 Connecticut Ave NW Washington DC 20036

LEBOW, MICHAEL JEFFREY, lawyer; b. Detroit, Apr. 4, 1956; s. David and Thelma (Shainack) L.; m. Deby Fay Muskovitz, Dec. 23, 1978. BA, Wayne State U., 1978; JD, Detroit Coll. Law, 1981. Bar: Mich. 1982, U.S. Dist. Ct. (ea. dist.) Mich. 1982, D.C. 1986. Litigation assoc. Kemp Klein Endelman & Beer, Birmingham, Mich., 1982-83; sole practice Southfield, Mich., 1983-85; ptnr. Lebow & Tobin, Birmingham, 1985-86, Gropman, Lebow & Tobin, Birmingham, 1986—. Bd. dirs. Mich. Com. Human Rights, Oak Park, 1976—. Mem. ABA (Excellence Nat. Appellate Advocacy award 1981), Mich. Bar Assn., Assn. Trial Lawyers Am., Assn. Trial Lawyers Mich., Moto Guzzi Nat. Owners Assn. Jewish. Club: Mich. Handball Assn. Avocations: handball, motorcycle collecting, 1950's jazz. Federal civil litigation, State civil litigation, Libel. Office: Gropman Lebow & Tobin 401 S Woodward 306 Birmingham MI 48011

LEBOWITZ, JACK RICHARD, lawyer; b. Glens Falls, N.Y., Oct. 3, 1949; s. Harold Louis Lebowitz and Lila Ruth (Gould) Lebowitz Paul; m. Kathleen Maryann Griffin, Feb. 29, 1980; children:Gavin, Anne. BA with honors, Wesleyan U., Middletown, Conn., 1971; JD, Boston U., 1975. Bar: N.Y. 1976, U.S. Dist. Ct. (no. dist.) N.Y. 1977, U.S. Ct. Appeals (2d cir.) 1977, U.S. Supreme Ct. 1980, N.J. 1986. Assoc. Robert J. Kafin Law Offices, Glens Falls, 1975-77; staff counsel N.Y. Pub. Service Commn., Albany, 1977-84, ITT Communications Services, Secaucus, N.J., 1984-86; prin. Law Offices of Jack R. Lebowitz, Glens Falls, N.Y., 1986-87; atty. Miller, Mannix, Lemery & Pratt, P.C., Glens Falls, 1987—. Mem. Competitive Telecommunications Assn. (state affairs com. 1984—), N.Y. State Bar Assn.,

ABA. Democrat. Jewish. Administrative and regulatory, Public utilities, Environment. Office: One Broad St Plaza PO Box 765 Glens Falls NY 12801

LE BRUN, MICHAEL DAVID, real estate investment banker; b. Balt., Mar. 25, 1956; s. Jacques Melvin and Margaret Elizabeth (Bethke) L.; m. Marsha Kay Altice, Oct. 10, 1981; 1 child, Alexandra Carole. BA in Polit. Sci. cum laude, U. Md., 1978; JD, U. Balt., 1981. Bar: Md. 1981, U.S. Dist. Ct. (Md.) 1981. Assoc. editor, atty. Lawyers Coop. Pub. Co., Rochester, N.Y., 1981-82; mortgage analyst & counsel Wye Mortgage Corp., Balt., 1983-84; v.p. real estate Fairfax Savs. Assn., Balt., 1984-85; v.p. Oxford Devel. Corp., Bethesda, Md., 1985-87, Alex Brown Realty Advisors, Inc., Balt., 1987—; counsel H. Altice Mktg. Inc., Hunt Valley, Md., 1983—. Contbr. 22 articles to profl. jours. Mem. ABA, Md. State Bar Assn., Phi Kappa Phi, Pi Sigma Alpha. Avocations: fishing, skiing, swimming, outdoor sports. Real property, Contracts commercial. Home: 13884 Grey Colt Dr Gaithersburg MD 20878 Office: Alex Brown Realty Advisors Inc 225 E Redwood St Baltimore MD 21202

LECHNER, ALFRED JAMES, JR., U.S. district judge; b. Elizabeth, N.J., Jan. 7, 1948; s. Alfred J. and Marie G. (McCormack) L.; m Gayle K. Peterson, Apr. 3, 1976; children—Brendan Patrick, Coleman Thomas, Mary Kathleen. B.S., Xavier U., Cin., 1969; J.D., U. Notre Dame, 1972. Bar: N.J. 1972, N.Y. 1973; U.S. Dist. Ct. N.J. 1972, U.S. Dist. Ct. (so. and ea. dists.) N.Y. 1974, U.S. Ct. Appeals (2d cir.) 1974, U.S. Ct. Appeals (3d cir.) 1980, U.S. Supreme Ct. 1975. Assoc. Cadwalader, Wickersham & Taft, N.Y.C., 1972-75, MacKenzie, Welt & Duane, Elizabeth, N.J., 1975-76; ptnr. MacKenzie, Welt, Duane & Lechner, Elizabeth, 1976-84; judge Superior Ct. State N.J., 1984-86; judge U.S. Dist. Ct. N.J., 1986—. Mem. Union County (N.J.) adv. bd. Catholic Community Services, 1981-83, chmn., 1982. Mem. ABA, Assn. Fed. Bar of State N.J. Democrat. Roman Catholic. Clubs: Friendly Sons of St. Patrick (pres. 1982), Union County. Note and comment editor Notre Dame Law Rev., 1972; contbr. articles to legal jours. Office: US Post Office and Ct House Newark NJ 07101

LECHTER, KENNETH ALAN, lawyer; b. Washington, Sept. 30, 1945; s. Max and Clara Adele (Yavitz) L.; m. Karen Barbara Joseph; 1 son: Jonathan David. B.A. in Econs., U. Md., 1967, J.D., 1971. Bar: Md. 1971, D.C. 1973, U.S. Dist. Ct. Md. 1973, U.S. Dist Ct. D.C. 1975, U.S. Ct. Appeals (D.C. cir.) 1975, U.S. Supreme Ct. 1980, U.S. Ct. Appeals (4th cir.) 1981. Assoc., Hoyert, Diemer, Yoho, Hooten & McBride, Lanham, Md., 1971; assoc. Fisher & Walcek, Marlow Heights, Md., 1972-74, ptnr. 1975—. Past mem. citizens adv. bd. Md. Sec. Agr.; mem., legal counsel Potomac Springs Civic Assn., 1982—; mem. vol. atty. ACLU, 1973—; mem. Md. State Health Claims Arbitration Panel, 1983—; mem. exec. bd. Rockville Little Theatre, 1986—; mem. Cultural Arts Commn., Rockville, 1986—. Served USCGR, 1968-73. Mem. ABA, Md. State Bar Assn., Md. Trial Lawyers Assn., Prince George's County (Md.) Assn. (exec. bd. 1984-87), Phi Alpha Delta, Phi Sigma Delta. Democrat. Jewish. State civil litigation, Personal injury, General practice. Office: 4465 Old Branch Ave Marlow Heights MD 20748

LECKRONE, JAMES DAVID, lawyer; b. Salem, Ill., Nov. 25, 1940; s. James E. and Lucile L. (Lucas) L.; m. Kathleen W. Whitelock, Mar. 16, 1963 (div.); children—Chris, Jim, Matthew. B.S. in Acctg., So. Ill. U., 1962; J.D. Vanderbilt U., 1969. Bar: Tenn. Ptnr. Farris, Evans, & Warfield, Nashville, 1972-76; sole practice, Nashville, 1976-77; ptnr. Leckrone & Holton, P.C., Nashville, 1977—. Served to lt. USN, 1963-66. Mem. Am. Inst. C.P.A.s, Tenn. Soc. C.P.A.s, ABA (tax acctg. com. tax sect.), Tenn. Bar Assn. (pres. taxation sect. 1979). Republican. Corporate taxation. Home: 3401 Hillmeade Ct Nashville TN 37221 Office: Leckrone & Holton 3d Nat Bank Bldg Nashville TN 37219

LE CLAIR, DOUGLAS MARVIN, lawyer; b. Montreal, Que., Can., Nov. 13, 1955; s. Lawrence M. and Joan B. Le Clair; m. Debra L. Garland, Oct. 12, 1985. BA, Loyola U., 1977; JD, Southwestern U., 1980. Bar: Ariz. 1982, U.S. Dist. Ct. Ariz. 1983, U.S. Ct. Appeals (9th cir.) 1983. Corp. counsel Great Western Trading Co., Los Angeles, 1982-83; sole practice Mesa, Ariz., 1983—; corp. counsel various corps., Ariz. Author: Le Clair/Morgan Income Tax Organizer, 1982-83; prodn. editor Computer Law Jour., 1979-80; producer TV Advt., 1983. Res. officer Mesa Police Dept., 1984—. Named One of Outstanding Young Men Of Am., 1979. Mem. ABA (taxation sect.), Ariz. Bar Assn., Southwestern Student Bar Assn. (exec. bd. 1978-79), Southwestern U. Tax Law Soc., Delta Theta Phi. Corporate taxation, General corporate, State and local taxation. Home: PO Box 223 Mesa AZ 85201 Office: 805 First Interstate Bank Bldg 20 E Main St Mesa AZ 85201

LECLERE, DAVID ANTHONY, lawyer; b. New Orleans, Sept. 5, 1954; s. Paul Richard and Rosalee (Cefalu) LeC.; married. BA, La. State U., 1978, JD, 1979. Bar: La. 1979, U.S. Dist. Ct. (mid. dist.) La. 1979, U.S. DIst. Ct. (ea. dist.) 1982, U.S. Dist Ct. (we. dist.) 1983, U.S. Ct. Appeals (5th cir.) 1984. Assoc. Perrault & Uter, Baton Rouge, 1979-81, jr. ptnr., 1981-83; full ptnr. Perrault, Uter & LeClere, Baton Rouge, 1983-87; assoc. Schwab & Walter, Baton Rouge, 1987—. Assoc. chmn. East Baton Rouge Parish Notary Pub. Exam. Com., 1982. Mem. ABA, La. State Bar Assn., Comml. Law League of Am., Baton Rouge Bar Assn. Republican. Roman Catholic. Avocations: hunting, hiking, camping, gardening, gourmet cooking. Contracts commercial, Public utilities, Real property. Home: 11027 N Oak Hills Parkway Baton Rouge LA 70810 Office: Schwab & Walter PO Box 80491 Baton Rouge LA 70898

LEDBETTER, THOMAS DALE, lawyer, former aeronautical engineer, infosystems specialist; b. Pryor, Okla., Oct. 6, 1937; s. Jack and Buna (Hudson) L.; m. Martha Ann Milum, Dec. 28, 1962; children—Paul Milum, David Thomas. Student U. Okla., 1956-61; B.A. in Math., U. Denver, 1964; J.D., U. Ark., 1967. Bar: Ark. 1967, U.S. Dist. Ct. (ea. and we. dists.) Ark. 1967, U.S. Supreme Ct. 1974. Aero. engr. trainee, electronics data processing operator Tinker AFB, Midwest City, Okla., 1959-61; aero. logistics engr., computer programmer Martin-Marietta Corp., Denver, 1961-64; law clk. U.S. Dist. Ct., Little Rock, 1966-67; sole practice, Harrison, Ark., 1967—; pres. Atty.'s Title Guaranty Fund Inc., (formerly Ozark Title & Guaranty Co.), Harrison, 1972—. Cubmaster Westark Council Boy Scouts Am., 1973-77, dist. vice. chmn., 1975-81, chmn. Cub Round Table, 1979-82, asst. scoutmaster, 1979-85, bd. dirs. West Ark. area council, 1980—; chmn. Ozark Dist. Boy Scouts Am., 1981-83, dist. Eagle Scout chmn. 1981—; asst. sgt.-at-arms Republican Nat. Conv., 1964; mem. campaign staff Rockefeller for Gov., 1966, and subsequent campaigns; vice chmn. Boone County (Ark.) Rep. Com., 1971-73; committeeman 3d Congressional Dist. Ark. Rep. Party, 1972-74; lay reader Episcopal Diocese Colo., 1961-64, tchr. ch. sch., 1962-64; mem. vestry Episc. Diocese Ark., 1968-71, 1978-80, lay reader, 1964—, mem. exec. council, 1977-79, sec. exec. council, 1979, mem. Constn. and Canons Com., 1981-83; pres. Episc. Churchmen of Ark., 1977-79; bd. dirs. United Fund Boone County, Inc., Arkansans for Rev. Constn. Recipient Outstanding Commr. award Boy Scouts Am., 1981, St. George's Dist. award of Merit Boy Scouts Am., 1981; Hon. Farmer award Harrison chpt. Future Farmers Am., 1973; numerous awards Harrison Jaycees, Ark. Jaycees. Mem. ABA (chmn. computer com. econ. sect.), Boone County Bar Assn., Ark. Bar Assn. (vice chmn. 1968-70, mem. ho. of dels. 1978-80, exec. council, 1979-82, chmn. bar related title com. 1979-83), Ark. Trial Lawyers Assn., Ark. Land Title Assn., Assn. Trial Lawyers Am., Am. Land Title Assn., Harrison C. of C., Delta Upsilon, Phi Delta Kappa, Phi Alpha Delta. Lodge: Lions. General practice, Civil Litigation, Real property. Office: Ledbetter & Assocs Ltd PO Box 637 Harrison AR 72601

LEDDY, JOHN HENRY, lawyer; b. Bklyn., Mar. 14, 1929; s. John Henry and Josephine (Kratky) L.; m. Helen Jean Keating, June 10, 1951 (div. Mar. 1969); m. Rose Marie Smith, June 6, 1969 (div. Jan. 1983); m. Jane Ruddell, May 22, 1983; children—Kevin John, Craig William, Bruce James, Matthew Richard. B.A., Kalamazoo Coll., 1951; J.D., U. Mich., 1954. Bar: Mich. 1954, Ohio 1958, Pa. 1969. Assoc. Porter, Stanley, Treffinger & Platt, Columbus, Ohio, 1958-60, ptnr., 1960-69; ptnr. Schnader, Harrison, Segal & Lewis, Phila., 1969—. Served as lt. (j.g.) USNR, 1955-58; ETO. Mem. ABA (lectr. Am. Law Inst.), Pa. Bar Assn., Phila. Bar Assn. Republican. Club: Union League of Phila. (sec. com. on membership 1983-85, bd. dirs. 1986—). Avocations: gardening; jogging; reading. Labor, Civil rights, Federal civil litigation. Office: Schnader Harrison Segal & Lewis Suite 3600 1600 Market St Philadelphia PA 19103

LEDDY, JOHN THOMAS, lawyer; b. Burlington, Vt., Nov. 29, 1949; s. Bernard Joseph and Johannah Mercedes (Mahoney) L.; m. Louise Anne Thabault, Aug. 25, 1979; 1 child, Michael Joseph. Student, St. Michael's Coll., Winooski Park, Vt., 1967-68; AB, U. Vt., 1972; JD, New Eng. Sch. Law, 1978. Bar: Fla. 1980, Vt. 1981, U.S. Dist. Ct. Vt. 1981. Ptnr. McNeil, Murray & Sorrell, Burlington, 1978—. County treas. Chittenden County (Vt.) Dem. Com., 1973-75; mem. Burlington Bd. Aldermen, 1973-75, Vt. Dem. State Com., 1985—. Mem. Vt. Bar Assn., Fla. Bar Assn., Chittenden County Bar Assn. Roman Catholic. General practice, State civil litigation. Home: 126 Caroline St Burlington VT 05401 Office: McNeil Murray & Sorrell Inc 271 S Union St Burlington VT 05401

LEDEBUR, LINAS VOCKROTH, JR., banker, lawyer; b. New Brighton, Pa., June 18, 1925; s. Linas Vockroth and Mae (McCabe) L.; m. Conne Ryan, July 3, 1969; children: Gary W., Sally, Nancy, Sandra. Student, Geneva Coll., Beaver Falls, Pa., 1943, 45-46, Muhlenberg Coll., Allentown, Pa., 1943-44; J.D., U. Pitts., 1949. Bar: Pa. 1950. Assoc., then ptnr. Ledebur, McClain & Ledebur, New Brighton, 1950-63; trust mktg. mgr. Valley Nat. Bank Ariz., Phoenix, 1963-72; ptnr. Ledebur & Ledebur, New Brighton, 1972-76; sr. v.p., mgr. state trust div. Fla. Nat. Banks Fla., Inc., Jacksonville, 1976-81; sr. v.p. Fla. Nat. Bank, Jacksonville, 1977-81; pres. Northeastern Trust Co. Fla., N.A., Vero Beach, 1982-86; exec. v.p. PNC Trust Co. Fla., N.A., 1986-87; sole practice Beaver, Pa., 1987—; instr. bus. law Geneva Coll., 1951-52; past pres. Central Ariz. Estate Planning Council. Chmn. Beaver County chpt. Nat. Found.-March of Dimes, Pa., 1950-63; chmn. com. corrections Pa. Citizens Assn., 1958-63; bd. dirs., counsel Beaver County Mental Health Assn., 1962-63; bd. dirs. Maricopa County chpt. ARC, Ariz. 1968-72. Served with USMC, 1943-45, 51-53. Mem. ABA, Pa. Bar Assn. Probate, Estate taxation. Home: 652 Bank St Beaver PA 15009 Office: 348 College Ave Beaver PA 15009

LEDERER, FREDRIC IRA, legal educator; b. San Diego, Oct. 18, 1946; s. Seymour Gerson and Blossom (Sussman) L.; m. Diane Lynn Dillenberg, June 11, 1972; children: Caryn Cecelia, Alyssa Mira. BS, Poly. Inst. N.Y., 1968; JD, Columbia U., 1971; LLM, U. Va., 1976. Bar: N.Y. 1972, U.S. Ct. Appeals (2d cir.) 1972, U.S. Supreme Ct. 1976. Law clk. to presiding justice U.S. Dist. Ct. (so. dist.) N.Y., N.Y.C., 1971-72; commd. U.S. Army, 1968, advanced through grades to maj., 1978; prosecutor U.S. Army, Ft. Gordon, Ga., 1972-73; assoc. prof. law Judge Adv. Gen.'s Sch. U.S. Army, Charlottesville, Va., 1973-78; mem. joint service com. mil. justice working group, Office Judge Adv. Gen. U.S. Army, Washington, 1978-80; resigned U.S. Army, 1980; assoc. prof. law Coll. William & Mary, Williamsburg, Va., 1980-84, prof. law, 1984—, assoc. dean, 1984-85; lectr. in law U. Va., Charlottesville, 1975-77; U.S. mil. judge, res., 1980—; mem. com. to draft proposed rules evidence for Va., 1984-86. Author: Analysis of the Military Criminal Legal System, 1975; co-author: Criminal Evidence, 1979, Military Rules of Evidence, 1980, Evidence Codifications, 1980, 85, Courtroom Criminal Evidence, 1987; contbr. articles to profl. jours. Pres. Williamsburg Area Assn. Gifted and Talented, 1985-86. Fulbright fellow, 1977-78. Mem. ABA (rules of criminal procedure and evidence subcom. criminal justice sect. 1980-82, 83—), Internat. Soc. for Mil. Law and Law War, Judge Advs. Assn. Legal education, Military, Criminal. Home: 121 Justice Grice Williamsburg VA 23185 Office: Coll William & Mary Marshall-Wythe Sch Law Williamsburg VA 23185

LEDERER, WILLIAM JOSEPH, lawyer; b. Chgo., July 13, 1906; s. Arthur L. and Helen H. (Kohn) L.; m. Maxine Rose Salinger, Apr. 9, 1932; children—Clare Lederer Ross, John W., William B. B.S., Northwestern U., 1929, J.D., 1931. Bar: Ill. 1931, U.S. Customs Ct. 1956, U.S. Dist. Ct. (7th dist.) 1958, U.S. Supreme Ct. 1971. Ptnr. David, Fainman, Abrahams & Chapman, Chgo., 1931-46; gen. counsel Nat. Tea Co., Chgo., 1946-62, v.p., gen. counsel, 1962-73; sole practice, Glenview, Ill., 1973—; trustee Chgo. Law Inst., 1940-46; planning com. corp. law inst. Northwestern U., 1967-73. Mem. council North Shore Sr. Ctr., Winnetka, Ill., 1983-86; election judge Cook County, Glenview, Ill., 1982—. Mem. Ill. Bar Assn. (sr. counselor), Chgo. Bar Assn., Corp. Law Inst. (program com. 1967-73), Decalogue Soc. of Lawyers, Tau Delta Phi, Nu Beta Epsilon. Republican. Jewish. General corporate, Real property, Personal injury. Home and Office: 315 Ferndale Rd Glenview IL 60025

LEDERMAN, LAWRENCE, lawyer, educator; b. N.Y.C., Sept. 8, 1935; s. Herman Jack and Lillian (Rosenfeld) L.; m. Sally Ann Rossi, Jan. 26, 1958; children—Leandra, Evin. B.A., Bklyn. Coll., 1957; LL.B., N.Y.U., 1966. Bar: N.Y. 1968; Law clk. chief justice Calif. Sup. Ct., 1966-67; assoc. Cravath, Swaine & Moore, N.Y.C., 1968-74; ptnr. Wachtell, Lipton, Rosen & Katz, N.Y.C., 1975—; adj. prof. law N.Y.U. Sch. Law; Chmn. bd. Phoenix House Devel. Corp., mem. Phoenix House Found.; bd. dirs. Am. Chess Found. Served with U.S. Army, 1957-59. Mem. ABA, N.Y. State Bar Assn., Order of the Coif. Contbr. articles to profl. jours. General corporate. Office: 299 Park Ave New York NY 10171

LEDINGHAM, THOMAS MAX, lawyer; b. Scottsbluff, Nebr., Mar. 10, 1931; s. Harold and Lucile Olive Ledingham; m. Claudia Ann Christian, Apr. 18, 1970; children—Tommy Max, Kathy Lyn; m. Kris Krumm, June 30, 1979. Student U. Nebr., 1949-51; B.B.A. with honors, U. Tex., 1953; LL.B., U. Colo., 1959. Bar: Colo. 1959, N.Y. 1974, N.Mex. 1977; C.P.A., Nebr., Colo. Acct., Arthur Anderson & Co., Denver, 1959-60; assoc. Akolt, Shepherd & Dick, Denver, 1960-67, ptnr., 1967-68; atty. Mountain Bell Telephone Co., Denver, 1968-71, gen. atty., 1971-73, Albuquerque, 1976-84, Denver, 1984—; gen. atty. AT&T, N.Y.C., 1973-76; mem. faculty U. Colo., 1957-59, 1965-66. Served to 1st lt. USAF, 1953-55. Recipient Gold award U. Nebr., 1950. Mem. Albuquerque Bar Assn., N.Mex. Bar Assn., ABA, Am. Inst. C.P.A.s, Order of Coif. Republican. Club: Four Hills Country (Albuquerque). General corporate, Public utilities, Administrative and regulatory. Office: US West 7800 E Orchard Rd Englewood CO 80111

LEDLIE, DOUGLAS EDWARD, lawyer; b. Houston, Jan. 9, 1954; s. Raymond Bowyer and Laura Marie (Ramsay) L.; m. Susan Rudd, Sept. 3, 1983. BBA in Acctg. with honors, U. Tex., 1976, JD with honors, 1981; LLM, NYU, 1984. Bar: Tex. 1982. Sr. acct. Peat, Marwick, Mitchell & Co., Houston, 1976-79; assoc. Graves, Dougherty, Hearton et al, Austin, Tex., 1981-86, Clark, Thomas, Winters & Newton, Austin, 1986—. Mem. ABA (real estate problems com. taxation sect.), Tex. Bar Assn. (co-chmn. state legis. devels. com. taxation sect. 1985, partnership and real estate tax problems com.). Presbyterian. Corporate taxation, Real property, Taxation, partnerships. Office: Clark Thomas Winters & Newton 700 Lacava St Austin TX 78701

LEDWITH, JOHN FRANCIS, lawyer; b. Phila., Oct. 3, 1938; s. Francis Joseph and Jane Agnes (White) L.; m. Mary Evans, Aug. 28, 1965; children—Deirdre A., John E. A.B., U. Pa., 1960, J.D., 1963. Bar: Pa. 1965, U.S. Dist. Ct. (ea. dist.) Pa. 1965, U.S. Ct. Appeals (3rd cir.) 1965, U.S. Supreme Ct. 1970. Assoc. Joseph R. Thompson, Phila., 1965-71; mem. Schubert, Mallon, Wallheim & deCindis, Phila., 1971-81, LaBrum & Doak, Phila., 1981—. Author: (with others) Philadelphia CP Trial Manual, 1982. Bd. dirs. Chestnut Hill Community Assn., Pa., 1975, 76. Served to E-6 USCG, 1963-64. Mem. ABA, Phila. Bar Assn., Pa. Bar Assn., Def. Research Inst., Assn. Trial Lawyers Am. Republican. Roman Catholic. Clubs: Racquet (Phila.), Phila. Cricket; Avalon Yacht (N.J.) (commodore 1982). Federal civil litigation, State civil litigation, Insurance. Office: LaBrum and Doak 1700 Market St 6th Floor Philadelphia PA 19103

LEE, BRIAN EDWARD, lawyer; b. Oceanside, N.Y., Feb. 29, 1952; s. Lewis H. Jr. and Jean Elinor (Andrews) L.; m. Eleanor L. Barker, June 5, 1982; children: Christopher Martin, Alison Ruth. AB, Colgate U., 1974; JD, Valparaiso U., 1976. Bar: N.Y. 1977, U.S. Dist. Ct. (so. and ea. dists.) N.Y. 1978. Assoc. Marshall, Bellofatto & Callahan, Lynbrook, N.Y., 1977-80, Morris, Duffy, Ivone & Jensen, N.Y.C., 1980-84; sr. assoc. Ivone, Devine & Jensen, Lake Success, N.Y., 1984-85; ptnr. Ivone, Devine & Tensen, Lake Success, N.Y., 1985—. Pres., trustee Trinity Christian Sch. of Montville Inc., N.J., 1985—. Mem. ABA, N.Y. State Bar Assn., Christian Legal Soc. Republican. Baptist. State civil litigation, Personal injury, Insurance. Home: 292 Jacksonville Rd Pompton Plains NJ 07444 Office: Ivone Devine & Jensen 2001 Marcus Ave Lake Success NY 11042

LEE, CARL DOUGLAS, lawyer; b. Greenville, N.C., Jan. 7, 1952; s. Luke Haze and Joyce Marie (Braxton) L.; m. Debra L. Hargett, June 1, 1974; children: Kimberly Dawne, Tracy Rebecca, Carl Douglas II, Benjamin Barrett, Erin Elizabeth. Student, East Carolina U., 1970-71, 74-75; BA, U. N.C., 1977; JD, Samford U., 1980. Bar: N.C. 1980, Ariz. 1982. Assoc. Henderson & Baxter, New Bern, N.C., 1980-82, Joel Sacks, Phoenix, 1982-83; sole practice Phoenix, 1983—. Mem. Ariz. Trial Lawyers Assn., Assn. Trial Lawyers Am., N.C. Bar Assn., Ariz. Bar Assn. Republican. Mormon. Lodge: Rotary (bd. dirs. Phoenix club 1985-86). Personal injury, State civil litigation. Office: 700 W Dunlap Ave Phoenix AZ 85021

LEE, CAROL ELIZABETH, lawyer; b. Atlanta, Feb. 19, 1956; d. Raymond William Jr. and Marianne (Hollingsworth) L. AB, Duke U., 1978; JD, U. Ga., 1981. Bar: Ga. 1981, U.S. Dist. Ct. (no. dist.) Ga. 1981, U.S. Ct. Appeals (11th cir.) 1981. Staff atty. Kerman & Assocs., Atlanta, 1982; staff atty. Hyatt Legal Services, Atlanta, 1982-84, mng. atty., 1984-86, regional ptnr., 1986—. Named one of Outstanding Young Women of Am., 1983. Mem. ABA, Ga. Bar Assn., Atlanta Bar Assn., Cobb County Bar Assn. Republican. Episcopalian. General practice, Family and matrimonial, Bankruptcy. Home: 175 Westover Ln Marietta GA 30064 Office: Hyatt Legal Services 175B Mount Vernon Hwy Atlanta GA 30328

LEE, CHRISTOPHER PETER, lawyer; b. Hong Kong, July 14, 1949; came to U.S., 1949; s. Tong Chee Lee and Wong (Suey) Wah; m. Christine R. Tymczyn, Aug. 2, 1986. BA, Fordham U., 1971, JD, 1979; postgrad., New Sch. for Social Research, 1971-73. Bar: Mass. 1980, N.Y. 1981, U.S. Dist. Ct. (so. and ea. dists.) N.Y. 1984. Supr. quality control Citibank, N.Y.C., 1971-73; authorizer benefits Social Security Adminstrn., Rego Park, N.Y., 1974-78; atty., advisor Social Security Adminstrn., Jamaica, N.Y., 1980-84; specialist equal opportunity Office Civil Rights, N.Y.C., 1978-79; specialist equal opportunity EEOC, N.Y.C., 1979-80, sr. trial atty., 1984—. Named Most Valuable Player chess tournament Bankers Athletic League, 1984. Mem. ABA, Mass. Bar Assn., N.Y. State Bar Assn., N.Y. County Lawyers Assn., Fed. Bar Assn., Fed. Bar Council, N.Y. State Trial Lawyers Assn., U.S. Chess Fedn. (lifetime), U.S. Tennis Assn. (lifetime). Avocations: chess, tennis. Labor, Federal civil litigation, Pension, profit-sharing, and employee benefits. Home: 7 W 14th St 9-A So New York NY 10011 Office: EEOC 90 Church St Room 1301 New York NY 10007

LEE, DAN MCKINNON, state supreme court justice; b. Petal, Miss., Apr. 19, 1926; s. Buford Aaron and Pherbia Ann (Camp) L.; m. Peggy Jo Daniel, Nov. 29, 1947 (dec. 1952); 1 dau., Sheron Diane Lee Anderson; m. 2d Mary Alice Gray, Sept. 30, 1956; 1 son, Dan M. Student, Miss. State U., 1946-47; J.D., Miss. Coll., 1949. Bar: Miss. 1948. Ptnr. Franklin & Lee, Jackson, Miss, 1948-54, Lee, Moore and Countiss, Jackson, Miss., 1954-71; county judge Hinds County, Jackson, 1971-77; circuit judge Hinds-Yazoo Counties, Jackson, 1977-82; assoc. justice Miss. Supreme Ct., Jackson, 1982—; mem. Miss. Oil & Gas Bd., Interstate Oil Compact Commn. Served with USN, 1944-46. Mem. ABA, Hinds County Bar Assn., Miss. State Bar Assn., Jackson C. of C., Aircraft Owners and Pilots Assn. Democrat. Baptist. Lodges: Masons, Odd Fellows. Office: Mississippi Supreme Ct Gartin Bldg 4th Floor Jackson MS 39201

LEE, DAVID HAROLD, lawyer; b. N.Y.C., May 27, 1947. AB cum laude, Tufts Coll., 1969; JD, Boston U., 1973. Bar: Mass. 1973, U.S. Dist. Ct. Mass. 1974, U.S. Ct. Appeals (1st cir.) 1974, U.S. Supreme Ct. 1977, U.S. Tax Ct. 1984. Assoc. Mahoney, Atwood & Goldings, Boston, 1973-75; ptnr. Atwood & Wright, Boston, 1975-84, Bowser & Lee, Boston, 1984—. Contbr. articles to profl. jours. Mem. ABA (family law sect.), Mass. Bar Assn. (family law sect. council, continuing legal edn. adv. com. 1979—, various continuing legal edn. coms.), Boston Bar Assn., Middlesex County Bar Assn., Norfolk County Bar Assn., Norfolk County Bench Bar Com. (chmn. 1985—), Mass. Acad. Trial Attys. (faculty 1979), Am. Acad. Matrimonial Lawyers (Mass. chpt. 1979—, bd. mgrs. 1981-84, treas. 1984—). Family and matrimonial, Probate, State civil litigation. Office: Bowser & Lee 399 Boylston St Boston MA 02116

LEE, DENNIS PATRICK, lawyer, administrative judge; b. Omaha, Feb. 12, 1955; s. Donald Warren and Betty Jean (O'Leary) L.; m. Rosemarie Bucchino, July 28, 1979; children—Patrick Michael, Katherine Marie. B.A., Creighton U., 1977, J.D., 1980. Bar: Nebr. 1980, U.S. Dist. Ct. Nebr. 1980, U.S. Ct. Appeals (8th cir.) 1980. Assoc. Thompson Crounse & Pieper, Omaha, 1977-84; ptnr. Lee Law Offices, Omaha, 1984—; atty. Nebr. State Racing Commn., Lincoln, 1984-85, adminstrv. law judge, State of Nebr., 1985—; lectr. Creighton U., Omaha, 1982—. Author: Law of Conservatorships, 1981; Legal Aspects of Equine Veterinary Practice, 1984; others. Trustee, Holy Name Cath. Ch., Omaha, 1980—; chmn. nat. enforcement officers com. Nat. Assn. State Racing Commrs., Lexington, Ky., 1984—. Mem. Nat. Assn. Trial Attys., Comml. Law League Am., ABA, Nebr. Bar Assn., Omaha Bar Assn. (chmn. conservatorship com. 1981—). Democrat. Roman Catholic. Club: Nebr.-Iowa Referees Assn. (v.p. 1981—). Administrative and regulatory, State civil litigation, Consumer commercial. Home: 5401 Blondo St Omaha NE 68104 Office: Lee Law Offices 10810 Farnam Dr Suite 414 Omaha NE 68154

LEE, EDWARD B., III, lawyer; b. Pitts., Sept. 19, 1941; s. Edward B. Jr. and Helen (Lindsay) L. BS in Civil Engring., N.Mex. State U., 1965; JD, U. Pitts., 1971. Bar: Pa. 1972, U.S. Ct. Appeals (3d cir.) 1972, U.S. Supreme Ct. 1976. Assoc. Lindsay, McGinnis, McLandless & McCabe, Pitts., 1971—. Served to capt. C.E., U.S. Army, 1965-71, PTO. Mem. ASCE, Allegheny County Bar Assn., Pitts. Nat. Orgns. Republican. Mem. Swedenborgian Ch. Probate, Construction, Patent. Home: 1015 Jefferson Heights Dr Pittsburgh PA 15235 Office: Lindsay McGinnis McCandless & McCabe 345 4th Ave Standard Life Bldg Suite 200 Pittsburgh PA 15222-2156

LEE, HENRY, lawyer; b. N.Y.C., Dec. 18, 1952; s. Tong Shong and Toy (Wong) L. BA, Bklyn. Coll., 1973; JD, U. Iowa, 1977. Bar: Calif. 1979, N.Y. 1980. Research atty. Calif. Ct. Appeal, San Bernardino, 1977-78; ptnr. Mendes & Mount, N.Y.C., 1980—. Insurance, Personal injury, Environment. Office: Mendes & Mount 3 Park Ave New York NY 10016

LEE, JAMES HON QUON, lawyer; b. Honolulu, Nov. 23, 1956; s. Kin Ball and Miu Lin (Louie) L.; m. Vickie T.W. Cheng, Aug. 6, 1982. BBA, U. Hawaii, 1978, JD, 1981. Bar: Hawaii 1981, U.S. Dist. Ct. Hawaii 1981, U.S. Tax Ct. 1981. Ptnr. Ikazaki, Devens, Lo, Youth & Nakano, Honolulu, 1981—; bd. dirs. K.B. Lee Corp., Honolulu, Hee Hing Corp., Honolulu. Mem. fin. com. Hawaii Visitors Bur., Honolulu, 1985. Mem. ABA, Hawaii Bar Assn., Hawaii Soc. CPA, Chinese C. of C., Leong Doo Soc. (treas. 1985). Republican. Corporate taxation, Estate taxation, General corporate. Office: Ikazaki Devens Lo Youth & Nakano 220 S King St Suite 1600 Honolulu HI 96613

LEE, JAMES ROGER, lawyer; b. Marion, Va., Jan. 30, 1947; s. James Roy and Ethel Virginia (Petty) L.; m. Barbara Ann Clark, Aug. 14, 1971; children: Alison Suzanne, Kathryn Michelle, Melissa Renee, James Michael. AB, Coll. William and Mary, 1970; JD, Tulane U., 1973. Bar: La. 1973, U.S. Dist. Ct. (ea. dist.) La. 1973, U.S. Ct. Appeals (5th cir.)1973, Ill. 1977, U.S. Dist. Ct. (no. dist.) Ill. 1980, U.S. Ct. Appeals (7th cir.) 1980, Mo. 1986. Atty. Chaffe, McCall, Phillips, Toler & Sarpy, New Orleans, 1974-77, Standard Oil Co., Chgo., 1977-83, Apex Oil Co., St. Louis, 1983—. Author: The Law of Maritime Deviation, 1972, Pier Based Injury of Longshoreman, 1972, Access to Divorce Courts for Indigents, 1972; editor Tulane U. Law Rev., 1971. Mem. Maritime Law Assn. U.S. (com. carriage of goods), ABA (com. admiralty and maritime law), Mo. Bar (com. on internat. law). Baptist. Private international, Admiralty, Contracts commercial. Home: 1864 Seven Pines Dr Saint Louis MO 63146 Office: Apex Oil Co 8182 Maryland Ave Saint Louis MO 63105

LEE, JEROME G., lawyer; b. Chgo., Feb. 23, 1924; m. Margo B. Lee, Dec. 23, 1947; children—James, Kenneth. B.S. Ch.E., U. Wis., 1947; J.D., NYU, 1950. Bar: N.Y. 1950, U.S. Supreme Ct. 1952. Assoc. firm Jeffery, Kimball, Eggleston, N.Y.C., 1950-52; assoc. firm Morgan, Finnegan, Durham & Pine, N.Y.C., 1952-59; ptnr. Morgan, Finnegan, Pine, Foley & Lee, N.Y.C., 1959-86; sr. ptnr. Morgan & Finnegan (and predecessor firms), N.Y.C., 1986—;

lectr. in field. Contbr. articles to legal jours. Served to sgt. U.S. Army, 1944-46. Mem. N.Y. Patent Law Assn. (pres. 1980-81), Am. Intellectual Property Law Assn. (dir. 1984—), ABA (chmn. commn. fed. practice), Assn. Bar City N.Y., N.Y. State Bar Assn., N.Y. County Bar Assn. Clubs: Marco Polo, Yale (N.Y.C.). Patent, Trademark and copyright, Federal civil litigation. Home: 1030 Nautilus Ln Mamaroneck NY 10543 Office: 345 Park Ave New York NY 10154

LEE, JOHN JIN, lawyer; b. Chgo., Oct. 20, 1948; s. Jim Soon and Fay Yown (Young) L.; m. Jamie Pearl Eng, Apr. 30, 1983. BA magna cum laude, Rice U., 1971; JD, Stanford U., 1975; MBA, 1975. Bar: Calif. 1976. Assoc. atty. Manatt Phelps & Rothenberg, Los Angeles, 1976-77; asst. counsel Wells Fargo Bank N.A., San Francisco, 1977-79, counsel, 1979-80, v.p., sr. counsel, 1980, v.p., mng. sr. counsel, 1981—. Bd. dirs. Asian Bus. League of San Francisco, 1981—, gen. counsel, 1981. Mem. ABA (chmn. subcom. on housing fin., com. on consumer fin. services, sect. of corp., banking and bus. law 1983—), Consumer Bankers Assn. (lawyers com.), Asian Am. Bar Assn. of Greater Bay Area, Soc. Physics Students. Democrat. Baptist. Real property, Consumer commercial. Office: Wells Fargo Bank NA Legal Dept 111 Sutter St San Francisco CA 94163

LEE, JOHN TERRY, lawyer; b. Siloam Springs, Ark., Feb. 7, 1948; s. Morris L. and Trucilla (Carpenter) L.; m. Lorraine M. Denaro, June 27, 1971; children: Kathleen D., John M. BA, U. Ark., 1971, JD, 1974. Bar: Ark. 1974, U.S. Dist. Ct. (we. dist.) Ark. 1975, U.S. Dist. Ct. (no. dist.) Okla. 1982, U.S. Dist. Ct. (ea. dist.) Okla. 1983. Sole practice Siloam Springs, 1974-76; ptnr. Elrod & Lee, Siloam Springs, 1976—; Trustee U.S. Bankruptcy Ct. (we. dist.) Ark., 1983—. Atty. City of Siloam Springs, 1974-76; dep. pros. atty. Benton County, Ark., 1975-77; bd. dirs. Our Farm, Inc., Rogers, Ark., 1982—. Mem. ABA, Ark. Bar Assn., Nat. Assn. Bankruptcy Trustees, Debtor-Creditor Bar Assn. Cen. Ark. Avocations: automobiles, golf, show dogs. Bankruptcy, Contracts commercial, Federal civil litigation. Home: 1011 N Dogwood Siloam Springs AR 72761 Office: Elrod & Lee PO Drawer 460 Siloam Springs AR 72761

LEE, LANSING BURROWS, JR., lawyer, corporate executive; b. Augusta, Ga., Dec. 27, 1919; s. Lansing Burrows and Bertha (Barrett) L.; m. Natalie Krug, July 4, 1943; children—Melinda Lee Clark Lansing Burrows III, Bothwell Graves, Richard Hancock. B.S., U. Va., 1939; postgrad U. Ga. Sch. Law, 1939-40; J.D., Harvard U., 1947. Corp. officer Ga.-Carolina Warehouse & Compress Co., Augusta, 1947-57, pres., 1957—; admitted to Ga. bar, 1947, since practiced in Augusta. Chmn. bd. trustees James Brice White Found., 1962—. Served to capt. USAAF, 1942-46. Mem. Harvard U. Law Sch. Assn. Ga. (pres. 1966-67), Augusta Bar Assn. (pres. 1966-67), Soc. Colonial Wars Ga., Ga. Bar Found., Ga. Bar Assn. (former chmn. fiduciary law sect.). Episcopalian (sr. warden, chancellor, lay reader). Clubs: Augusta Country, Pinnacle, Harvard of Atlanta. Home: 2918 Bransford Rd Augusta GA 30901 Office: 904 First Union Bank Bldg Augusta GA 30901

LEE, MARK RICHARD, lawyer, educator; b. St. Louis, Jan. 23, 1949; s. Bernard and Leatrice (Lapin) Lee; m. Elaine D. Edelman, June 7, 1980; children: Shira Miriam, Benard David. BA, Yale U., 1967; JD, U. Tex., 1971. Bar: Tex. 1974, U.S. Ct. Appeals (2d, 4th, and 7th cirs.) 1975, U.S. Ct. Appeals(D.C. cir.) 1976. Asst. atty. gen. State of Tex., Austin, 1974-75; atty. antitrust div. U.S. Dept. of Justice, Washington, 1975-76; instr. law U. Miami, 1976-77; prof. law So. Ill. U., Carbondale, 1977—; vis. lectr. U. Warwick, Coventry, Eng., 1984, also presented several pub. lectures, 1984-86; cons. Peoria (Ill.) Park Dist., 1978, to Atty. Gen., Springfield, Ill., 1985. Author: Antitrust Law and Local Government, 1985; contbr. articles to profl. jours. Mem. Gov.'s Task Force on Utility Regulation Reform, Springfield, 1982-84. Research scholar Max Planck Inst. for Fgn. and Internat. Pvt. Law, Hamburg, Fed. Republic of Germany, 1986. Mem. ABA, Order of the Coif, Phi Kappa Phi. Avocations: volleyball, tennis, bridge, science fiction. Antitrust, General corporate, Public utilities. Home: 1021 Glenview Carbondale IL 62901 Office: So Ill U Sch of Law Carbondale IL 62901

LEE, MICHAEL G.W., lawyer; b. Honolulu, Nov. 26, 1947; s. Wilson Wai and Hilda (Fong) L. BA, U. Calif., Berkeley, 1969, JD, 1970. Bar: Calif. 1972, Hawaii 1985, U.S. Dist. Ct. (no. dist.) Calif., 1972, U.S. Cir. Ct. (9th Cir.) 1972, U.S. Supreme Ct. 1977. Staff atty. Asian Law Caucus, Oakland, Calif., 1972-73, San Francisco Neighborhood Legal Assistance Fund, 1973-74; assoc. Hardesty and Lau, San Francisco, 1974-77; ptnr. Lau and Lee, San Francisco, 1977-79, Lee and Hui, San Francisco, 1979—; lectr. in law Golden Gate U., San Francisco, 1977-78; adjunct faculty Hastings Coll. Law, San Francisco, 1978; judge pro tem San Francisco Mcpl. Ct., 1983-86; commr. Commn. on Judicial Nominees Evaluation, 1981-82. Contbg. author: Immigration Law and Defense, 1979. Mem. Asian Pacific adv. council Coro Found., San Francisco, 1985—; Bd. dirs. Chinese Cultural Found., San Francisco, 1978-85. Mem. Bar Assn. of San Francisco (bd. dirs. 1980-81), Asian Am. Bar Assn. (pres. 1978), Am. Immigration Law Assn. (chpt. chair 1980-81). Democrat. Club: Commonwealth Club of Calif. (San Francisco) (bd. govs. 1986-89, quarterly chair 1984). Avocations: tennis, boating, reading, skiing. State civil litigation, Immigration, naturalization, and customs, General practice. Office: Lee and Hui 300 Montgomery St Suite 1000 San Francisco CA 94101-1987

LEE, PAULETTE WANG, lawyer; b. Washington, July 25, 1947; d. Paul and Margaret Wang; m. David B.N. Lee, June 17, 1972. B.A., UCLA, 1969, M.Ed., 1971; J.D., Southwestern U., Los Angeles, 1976. Bar: Calif. 1976. Asst. sec., asst. gen. counsel Host Internat., Inc., Santa Monica, Calif., 1976—. Mem. So. Calif. Chinese Lawyers Assn. Real property, General corporate. Office: Host Internat Inc 3402 Pico Blvd Santa Monica CA 90405

LEE, RICHARD H(ARLO), lawyer; b. Glen Falls, N.Y., June 5, 1947; s. Donald D. and Jeanne M. (Uthus) L.; m. Mary Ahearn, June 10, 1972; children: Christine Marie Ahearn Lee, Andrea Elizabeth Ahearn Lee. BS with honors, Mich. State U., 1972; JD magna cum laude, Ariz. State U., 1976. Bar: Ariz. 1977, U.S. Ct. Appeals (6th cir.) 1977, U.S. Dist. Ct. Ariz. 1978, U.S. Ct. Appeals (9th cir.) 1981. Law clk. to justice U.S. Ct. Appeals (6th cir.), Cin., 1976-77; assoc. Sparks & Siler, Scottsdale, Ariz., 1977-78; assoc. Murphy & Posner, Phoenix, 1979-82, ptnr., 1983-86; assoc. Storey & Ross, Phoenix, 1986—. Comment and notes editor Ariz. State U. Law Jour., 1975-76. Chmn. Ariz. Canal Diversion Channel Task Force City of Phoenix, 1985-86, aesthetics com., 1986—; state committeeman Ariz. Dems., Phoenix, 1983-84, 1975 Bond Com. City of Phoenix, 1975; vol. VISTA Crow Indian Tribe, Crow Agy., Mont., 1969-71. Mem. ABA (litigation, real property, gen. practice and bus. law sects.), Ariz. Bar Assn. (chmn. com. on continuing legal edn. bankruptcy sect. 1985-87, chmn. bankruptcy sect. 1987—), Maricopa County Bar Assn., Maricopa County Bankruptcy Law Assn., Ariz. State U. Coll. Law Alumni Assn. (pres. 1981, bd. dirs. 1981-82), Kappa Sigma. Bankruptcy, Real property. Home: 331 W Orangewood Phoenix AZ 85021 Office: Storey & Ross 4742 N 24th St Court 1 4th Floor Phoenix AZ 85016

LEE, ROBERT BARTLETT, lawyer; b. South Bend, Ind., Nov. 16, 1912; s. Clarence Eugnene and Mary Lillian (Jennings) L.; m. Ruth Elisabeth Wade, Sept. 27, 1941; children: Nancy Lee Shavill, Edward Bartlett, William Patton, Judith Ann Lee-Hockett. AB, DePauw U., 1935; LLB magna cum laude, U. Notre Dame, 1940. Bar: Ind. 1940, Colo. 1941. Ptnr. Simon, Lee & Shivers, Englewood, Colo., 1945-49, Lee, Shivers & Banta, Englewood, 1958-61; judge Colo. 18th Jud. Dist. Ct., 1960-69; assoc. justice Colo. Supreme Ct., 1969-83; of counsel Medsker & Lee, P.C., Englewood, 1983-87; dep. dist. atty. Arapahoe County, 1943-49; mem. adv. coms. to legis. council, 1963, 68, civil jury instructions com. Supreme Ct. Colo. 1969, commn. jud. qualifications, 1967-69, commn. Calif. Rural Legal Assistance Inc., 1971; vis. lectr. practice moot ct. program U. Colo. Law Sch. Recipient Alumni citation DePauw U., 1985. Mem. ABA, Colo. Bar Assn., 18th Jud. Dist. Bar Assn. (pres.), Am. Judicature Soc., Nat. Coll. State Trial Judges, Order of Coif, Blue Key, Phi Kappa Psi. Methodist. Home: 3144 S Wheeling Way #306 Aurora CO 80014

LEE, ROBERT EDWARD, JR., lawyer; b. Bklyn., Feb. 6, 1941; s. Robert E. and Edna C. (Koerber) L.; m. Janet A., July 12, 1975; children—Kristen, Robyn. B.A. summa cum laude, Niagara U., 1962; LL.B., St. John's U., 1967. Bar: N.Y. 1967, N.J. 1975. Asso. Cunningham & Lee, and predecessor firms, N.Y.C., 1967-72, jr. ptnr., 1972-78, sr. ptnr., 1978—; assoc. Snevily, Ely & Williams, Westfield, N.J.; instr. St. Francis Coll., 1975-76. Served to 1st lt. U.S. Army, 1963-65. Mem. ABA, N.J. State Bar Assn., Bklyn. Bar Assn., Cath. Lawyers Guild (pres.). Republican. Roman Catholic. Clubs: Lawyers of Bklyn. (past pres.); KC (Westfield, N.J.). Banking, Probate, Real property. Home: 957 Woodmere Dr Westfield NJ 07090 Office: Cunningham & Lee 40 Gold St New York NY 10038

LEE, RONALD BRUCE, lawyer; b. Canton, Ohio, Jan. 28, 1952; s. Clifford Martin and Delores Anita (Lones) L.; m. Denise Louise Sutton, Jan. 9, 1977 (div. June 1979). BS, U. Akron, 1974, JD, 1978. Bar: Ohio 1978, U.S. Dist. Ct. (no. dist.) Ohio, U.S. Ct. Appeals (6th cir.). Assoc. Roetzel & Andress, Akron, Ohio, 1978-85, ptnr., 1985—. Editor U. Akron Law Rev., 1978. Legal chmn. Akron GolfCharities, 1986-87. Mem. ABA, Ohio Bar Assn., Akron Bar Assn., Def. Research Inst., Ohio Civil Trial Lawyers Assn. Democrat. Methodist. Avocations: golf, basketball. State civil litigation, Insurance, Construction. Home: 2065 Stabler Akron OH 44313 Office: Roetzel & Andress 75 E Market St Akron OH 44308

LEE, ROY NOBLE, justice state supreme court; b. Madison County, Miss., Oct. 19, 1915; m. Sue Epting; 5 children. B.A. with distinction, Miss. Coll., 1938; LL.B. with distinction, Cumberland U., 1939. Bar: Miss. 1939. Spl. agt. FBI, 1942-44; dist. atty. 8th Circuit Ct. Dist., 1951-64; circuit judge 8th Ciruit Ct. Dist., 1964-75; justice Miss. Supreme Ct., Jackson, 1975—; now presiding justice Miss. Supreme Ct. Trustee Miss. Coll. Served to ensign USNR, 1944-46. Mem. Miss. Bar Assn., Am. Judicature Soc., Am. Legion (past post comdr.), VFW (past dist. comdr.), Soc. Former FBI Agents. Baptist. Lodges: Masons, Shriners, Woodmen of World. Judicial administration. Office: Mississippi Supreme Court Gartin Bldg Jackson MS 39201 *

LEE, SHARON GAIL, lawyer; b. Madisonville, Tenn., Dec. 8, 1953; d. Charles James and Judith Ann (Burris) L.; m. Peter Joseph Alliman, Aug. 12, 1978; children: Sarah, Laura Elizabeth. BS, U. Tenn., JD. Bar: Tenn. 1978. Assoc. J.D. Lee & Assocs., Madisonville, 1978-80; ptnr. Lee & Alliman Law Offices, Madisonville, 1980—; atty. Town of Madisonville, 1982-86. Mem. ABA, Tenn. Trial Lawyer Assn., Am. Trial Lawyers Assn. Democrat. Methodist. General practice, Workers' compensation, Personal injury. Home: Oak Grove Rd Madisonville TN 37354 Office: PO Box 425 Madisonville TN 37354

LEE, WILLIAM CHARLES, federal judge; b. Fort Wayne, Ind., Feb. 2, 1938; s. Russell and Catherine (Zwick) L.; m. Judith Anne Bash, Sept. 19, 1959; children—Catherine L., Mark R., Richard R. A.B., Yale U., 1959; J.D., U. Chgo., 1962. Bar: Ind. 1962. Ptnr., Parry, Krueckeberg & Lee, Fort Wayne, 1964-70; dep. pros. atty. Allen County, Fort Wayne, 1963-69, chief dep., 1967-69; U.S. atty. No. Dist. Ind., Fort Wayne, 1970-73; ptnr. Hunt, Suedhoff, Borror, Eilbacher & Lee, Fort Wayne, 1973-81; U.S. Dist. judge No. Dist. Ind., Fort Wayne, 1981—; instr. Nat. Inst. Trial Advocacy. Cochmn. Fort Wayne Fine Arts Operating Fund Drive, 1978; past bd. dirs., v.p. Fort Wayne Philharm. Orch., Fort Wayne Fine Arts Found., Hospice of Fort Wayne, Inc.; past bd. dirs. Fort Wayne Civic Theatre, Neighbors; past bd. dirs., pres. Legal Aid of Fort Wayne, Inc.; past mem. Trinity English Lutheran Ch. Council; trustee Fort Wayne Community Schs., 1978-81, pres., 1980-81; trustee Fort Wayne Mus. Art, 1984—. Griffin scholar, 1955-59; Weymouth Kirkland scholar, 1959-62. Fellow Am. Coll. Trial Lawyers, Ind. Bar Found.; mem. ABA, Allen County Bar Assn., Ind. State Bar Assn., Fed. Bar Assn., Seventh Cir. Bar Assn. Republican. Lutheran. Federal civil litigation, State civil litigation. Office: US Dist Ct 243 Fed Bldg 1300 S Harrison St Fort Wayne IN 46802

LEE, WILLIAM CLEMENT, III, corporate patent attorney; b. Atlanta, July 17, 1948; s. William Clement Jr. and Barbara Anne (Wilson) L.; m. Mary Reed Evans, Apr. 16, 1982. B.S., U. Ga., 1970, M.S., 1974; J.D., Emory U., 1977. Bar: Ga. 1977, U.S. Patent Office 1980, U.S. Dist. Ct. (no., mid., so. dists.) Ga., U.S. Ct. Appeals (5th, 11th, fed. cirs.), U.S. Claims Ct., U.S. Tax Ct., U.S. Supreme Ct. Sole practice, Bremen, Ga., 1978-80; asst. sec. U. Ga. Research Found., Inc., Athens, 1981-84; patent atty., asst. to v.p. research, U. Ga., Athens, 1980-84; patent staff counsel The Coca-Cola Co., Atlanta, 1984—. Served with U.S. Army Res., 1970-76. Mem. Atlanta Bar Assn., Ga. Bar Assn., ABA, Am. Intellectual Property Law Assn., Licensing Execs. Soc., Am. Corp. Counsel Assn., Am. Judicature Soc., Phi Delta Phi, Delta Tau Delta (Outstanding Alumnus award 1981). Patent, General corporate. Home: 2344 Woodward Way NW Atlanta GA 30305 Office: Coca Cola Co PO Drawer 1734 Atlanta GA 30301

LEE, WILLIAM JOHNSON, lawyer; b. Oneida, Tenn., Jan. 13, 1924; s. William J. and Ara (Anderson) L.; student Akron U., 1941-43, Denison U., 1943-44, Harvard U., 1944-45; J.D., Ohio State U., 1948. Bar: Ohio 1948, Fla. 1962. Research asst. Ohio State U. Law Sch., 1948-49; asst. dir. Ohio Dept. Liquor Control, chief purchases, 1956-57, atty. examiner, 1951-53, asst. state permit chief, 1953-55, state permit chief, 1955-56; asst. counsel, staff Hupp Corp., 1957-58; spl. counsel City Attys. Office Ft. Lauderdale (Fla.), 1963-65; asst. atty. gen. Office Atty. Gen., State of Ohio, 1966-70; adminstr. State Med. Bd. Ohio, Columbus, 1970-85, also mem. Federated State Bd.'s Nat. Commn. for Evaluation of Fgn. Med. Schs., 1981-83; Mem. Flex 1/Flex 2 Transitional Task Force, 1983-84; pvt. practice law, Ft. Lauderdale, 1965-66; acting municipal judge, Ravenna, Ohio, 1960; instr. Coll. Bus. Adminstrn., Kent State U., 1961-62. Mem. pastoral relations com. Epworth United Meth. Ch., 1976; chmn. legal aid com. Portage County, Ohio, 1960; troop awards chmn. Boy Scouts Am., 1965; mem. ch. bd. Melrose Park (Fla.) Meth. Ch., 1966. Mem. Am. Legion, Fla., Columbus, Akron, Broward County (Fla.) bar assns., Delta Theta Phi, Phi Kappa Tau, Pi Kappa Delta. Served with USAAF, 1943-46. Editorial bd. Ohio State Law Jour., 1947-48; also articles. Administrative and regulatory, General practice, Health. Home: 4893 Brittany Ct W Columbus OH 43229

LEE, WILLIAM MARSHALL, lawyer; b. N.Y.C., Feb. 23, 1922; s. Marshall McLean and Marguerite (Letts) L.; m. Lois Kathryn Plain, Oct. 10, 1942; children: Marsha (Mrs. Stephen Derynck), William Marshall Jr., Victoria C. (Mrs. Larry Nelson). Student, U. Wis., 1939-40; BS, Aero. U., Chgo., 1942; postgrad., UCLA, 1946-48, Loyola U. Law Sch., Los Angeles, 1948-49; JD, Loyola U., Chgo., 1952. Bar: Ill. 1952. Thermodynamicist Northrop Aircraft Co., Hawthorne, Calif., 1947-49; patent agt. Hill, Sherman, Meroni, Gross & Simpson, Chgo.; 1949-51 Borg-Warner Corp., Chgo., 1951-53; ptnr. Hume, Clement, Hume & Lee, Chgo., 1953-72; sole practice William Marshall Lee, Chgo., 1973-74; sr. ptnr. Lee, Smith & Zickert (and predecessor), Chgo., 1974—; v.p., bd. dirs. Power Packaging, Inc. Speaker and contbr. articles on legal topics. Pres. Glenview (Ill.) Citizens Sch. Com., 1953-57; v.p. Glenbrook High Sch. Bd., 1957-63. Served as lt. USNR, 1942-46, CBI. Recipient Pub. Service award Glenbrook High Sch. Bd., 1963. Mem. ABA (sec. sect. patent, trademark and copyright law 1977-80, governing council 1980-84, vice chmn. sect. patent, trademark and copyright law 1984-85, chmn. 1986—), Ill. Bar Assn., Chgo. Bar Assn., 7th Fed. Circuit Bar Assn., Internat. Patent Law Assn., Am. Patent Law Assn., Chgo. Patent Law Assn., Licensing Execs. Soc. (treas. 1977-80, pres. 1981-82, internat. del. 1980—), Phi Delta Theta, Phi Alpha Delta. Republican. Clubs: Law, University, Tower (Chgo.), Snow Chase of Chgo. (pres. 1963-64), Sky Soaring. Patent, Trademark, Antitrust. Home: 84 Otis Rd Barrington IL 60010 Office: 150 S Wacker Dr Chicago IL 60606

LEECH, MICHAEL JOHN, lawyer; b. Cumberland, Md., Dec. 3, 1951; s. John Graydon and Florence Ore (Davey) L.; m. Barbara Jane Anderson, Aug. 28, 1976. BA, U. Va., 1973, JD, 1976. Bar: Ill. 1976, U.S. Dist. Ct. (no. dist.) Ill. 1976. Assoc. Chapman & Cutler, Chgo., 1976-78; assoc. Hinshaw, Culbertson, Moelmann, Hoban & Fuller, Chgo., 1978-83, ptnr., 1983—. Co-author: (with William J. Holloway) Employment Termination: Rights and Remedies, 1985. Mem. ABA (individual rights and responsibilities in the workplace com. labor sect.), Ill. Bar Assn., Chgo. Bar Assn. Democrat. Methodist. Federal civil litigation, State civil litigation, Labor. Home: 566 Oakdale Ave Glencoe IL 60022 Office: Hinshaw Culbertson Moelmann Hoban & Fuller 69 W Washington Suite 2700 Chicago IL 60602

LEECH, NOYES ELWOOD, lawyer, educator; b. Ambler, Pa., Aug. 1, 1921; s. Charles S. and Margaret Owens (Reid) L.; m. Louise Ann Gallagher, Apr. 19, 1954; children: Katharine, Gwyneth. AB, U. Pa., 1943, JD, 1948. Bar: Pa. 1949. Assoc. Dechert, Price & Rhoads (and predecessors), Phila., 1948-49, 51-53; mem. faculty dept. law U. Pa., Phila., 1949-56; prof. U. Pa., 1957-78, Ferdinand Wakeman Hubbell prof. law, 1978-85, William A. Schnader prof. law, 1985-86, prof. emeritus, 1986—. Co-author: The International Legal System, 2d edit, 1981, Cases and Materials on Corporations, 1977; former gen. editor: Jour. Comparative Bus. and Capital Market Law. Mem. Am. Law Inst., AAUP, Am. Soc. Internat. Law, Order of Coif, Phi Beta Kappa. Legal education, General corporate, Public international. Office: U Pa Law Sch 3400 Chestnut St Philadelphia PA 19104

LEED, ROGER MELVIN, lawyer; b. Green Bay, Wis., July 15, 1939; s. Melvin John and Veronica Sarah (Flaherty) L.; m. Jean Ann Burg, Mar. 1967; children: Craig, Maren, Jennifer. AB, Harvard U., 1961; JD cum laude, U. Mich., 1967. Bar: Wash. 1967, U.S. Dist. Ct. (we. dist.) Wash. 1968, U.S. Ct. Appeals (9th cir.) 1969, U.S. Supreme Ct. 1973. Law clk. Wash. Supreme Ct., Olympia, 1967-68; assoc. Perkins, Coie et al, Seattle, 1968-70; ptnr. Schroeter, Goldmark et al, Seattle, 1970-77; sole practice Seattle, 1977—; adj. prof. law U. Puget Sound, Tacoma, 1974-77. Editor Shorelines Mgmt., the Wash. Experience, 1972. Pres. Cen. Seattle Community Council Fedn., 1972, Wash. Environ. Council, 1980-82; bd. dirs. Allied Arts, Seattle, 1971-72, Downtown Human Services Council, Seattle, 1985—. Mem. Wash. State Bar Assn., Seattle-King County Bar Assn., Assn. Trial Lawyers Am. Clubs: Met. Dem., Washington Athletic, Corinithian Yacht. Environment, State civil litigation, Federal civil litigation. Office: 1411 4th Ave Suite 520 Seattle WA 98101

LEEDS, MINDY ROBIN, lawyer; b. Detroit, Mar. 23, 1954; d. Henry G. and Rita M. (Friedman) L. BBA, Eastern Mich. U., 1976, BS, 1977; JD, U. Toledo, 1981; postdoctoral, NYU, 1987—. Bar: Mich. 1982, Ohio 1982, U.S. Dist. Ct. (ea. dist.) Mich. 1982, U.S. Tax Ct. 1983. Mgr. K-Mart, Plymouth, Mich., 1972-78, Gen. Electric Co., Decatur, Ind., 1978-79; tax assoc. Touche Ross & Co., Detroit, 1982-84; assoc. Rosenman Colin et al, N.Y.C., 1984-86; atty. The Equitable, 1986—. Mem. ABA, Oakland County Bar Assn. Pension, profit-sharing, and employee benefits, Personal income taxation, Estate taxation.

LEEDY, WILLIAM H., lawyer; b. Kansas City, Mo., May 18, 1928; s. Caleb A. and Agnes (Hudson) L.; m. Jean Koontz, Sept. 11, 1953; children: Mildred Hudson, Laura Anne. AB, Washington & Lee U., 1949; LLB, U. Mo., 1952; LLM in Taxation, NYU, 1957. Bar: Mo. 1952, D.C. 1981. From assoc. to ptnr. Lathrop, Koontz, Norquist, Washington, 1954-62, 1964—; gen. counsel, sec. Fed. Res. Bank Kansas City, 1962-64; mem. appellate jud. com. Mo., 1974-80. Served to capt. USAF, 1952-54. Mem. ABA, Mo. Bar Assn. (bd. govs. 1967-73), D.C. Bar Assn. Democrat. Episcopalian. Club: Kansas City Country (bd. dirs. 1973-76). Corporate taxation, Banking. Home: 2315 Tracy Pl NW Washington DC 20008 Office: Lathrop Koontz Norquist 1050 Connecticut Ave #300 NW Washington DC 20036

LEEFE, RICHARD K., lawyer, educator; b. New Orleans, Feb. 17, 1947; s. Guy L. Jr. and Marjorie (Kibbe) L.; m. Barat Pollingue, June 25, 1981; children: Katherine, Kibbe, Eric. BS in Engring. Sci., La. State U., 1969; JD, Loyola U., New Orleans, 1974. Bar: La. Ptnr. Partee, Leefe, Waldrip & Mott, New Orleans, 1975—; lectr. Loyola Law Sch., New Orleans, 1977—. Served to 1st lt. U.S. Army, 1969-71, Vietnam. Republican. Presbyterian. Contracts commercial, Bankruptcy, Admiralty. Home: 1309 Leontine St New Orleans LA 70115 Office: Partee Leefe Waldrip & Mott 344 Camp St New Orleans LA 70130

LEE HING, ANTHONY COURTNEY, lawyer; b. Kingston, Jamaica, Sept. 8, 1942; came to U.S. 1980; s. John Alfonso and Beulah (Bonitto) Lee H.; m. Barbara Eleanor Rogers, June 29, 1963; children—Nadine, Conrad, Shelley, Anthea, Catherine. Barrister, Hon. Soc. Lincoln's Inn, London, 1967; J.D., Woodrow Wilson Coll., 1982. Bar: Ga. 1982; notary public, Ga. Asst. clk. of cts. Resident Magistrate's Cts., Jamaica, 1961-69, clk. of cts., 1969—; sole practice, Kingston, 1969-73; ptnr. Daley, Walker & Lee Hing, Kingston, 1973—, Decatur, Ga., 1985—; justice of peace, Jamaica, 1980—. Mem. ABA, Decatur Bar Assn., Assn. Trial Lawyers Am., Jamaica Bar Assn. Roman Catholic. General practice. Office: Daley Walker & Lee Hing 1st National Bank Bldg Suite 210 Decatur GA 30030 also: 114-120 Tower St, Kingston Jamaica

LEEMAN, WILLIAM KELLY, lawyer; b. Noblesvicce, Jan. 8, 1949; s. Hugh and Carolyn (Kelly) L.; m. Martha Ellen Wean, Feb. 14, 1976; children: Tim Kelly, Mark Kelly, Hugh Richard. BS in Bus. Econ. and Pub. Policy, Ind. U., 1971, JD, 1974. Bar: Ind., U.S. Dist. Ct. (no. and so. dist.) Ind., U. S. Ct. Appeals (7th cir.). Judge Cass County Ct., Longsport, Ind., 1976; sole practice Longsport, 1976—; city atty. City of Logansport, 1976-81, 1984—; mem. Pub. Def. Council. Mem. Ind. State Bar Assn. (criminal law study commn. 1986), Assn. Trial Lawyers Am., Ind. Assn. Trial Lawyers. Democrat. Methodist. Lodge: Rotary. Federal civil litigation, State civil litigation, Criminal. Home: 8 Parkwood Dr Logansport IN 46947 Office: 1300 E Broadway Logansport IN 46947

LEEN, DAVID ARTHUR, lawyer; b. Bellingham, Wash., Sept. 28, 1945; s. Gordon William and Margaretta (Verner) L.; m. Karen Lee Harvey, July 7, 1977. BA, Beloit Coll., 1968; JD, U. Oreg., 1971. Bar: Wash. 1971, U.S. Dist. Ct. (we. dist.) Wash. 1972, U.S. Ct. Appeals (9th cir.) 1983, U.S. Ct. Claims 1984, U.S. Supreme Ct. 1984. Staff atty. Seattle Legal Services, 1971-76; regional atty. FTC, Seattle, 1976-77, Econ. Devel. Adminstrn., Dept. Commerce, Seattle, 1977-78, Legal Services Corp., Seattle, 1978-79; sr. ptnr. Leen & Moore, Seattle, 1979—; judge pro tem King County Superior Ct., Seattle, 1980—; lectr. Nat. Bus. Inst., Eau Claire, Wis., 1985—. Author: (with others) Foreclosures, 1986; also articles. Reginald Heber Smith fellow U.Pa., Harvard U., 1971-73. Democrat. Real property. Home: 409 Highland Dr Seattle WA 98109

LEEPSON, PETER LAWRENCE, lawyer; b. N.Y.C., July 2, 1941; s. Emil and Betty (Appleby) L.; m. Betty Jane Hoffman, June 29, 1963 (div. June 1976); children: Jonathan, David, Brian, Jennifer; m. Anne Biernbaum, Sept. 2, 1977; stepchildren: Michel Sosnowitz, Holly Sosnowitz. BA, Brandeis U., 1963; JD, Fordham U., 1966. Bar: N.Y. 1966, Conn. 1980. Assoc. DeForest, Elder & Mulreany, N.Y.C., 1966-68; atty. CBS, N.Y.C., 1968-69; ptnr. Leepson, Rubman & Ross, N.Y.C., 1969-80; counsel Wofsey, Rosen et al, Stamford, Conn., 1980-81; sr. ptnr. Leepson & Lackland, Westport, Conn., 1981—. Pres. men's club Jewish Home for Elderly Fairfield County, Fairfield, Conn., 1984—, bd. dirs., 1983—. Mem. N.Y. State Bar Assn., Conn. Bar Assn., Westport Bar Assn. Democrat. Clubs: Nat. Realty (N.Y.C.) (v.p., gov. 1976-80); Birchwood Country (Westport) (gov. 1982-84, 86—). Real property, Probate, General corporate. Home: 37 Green Acre Ln Westport CT 06880 Office: Leepson & Lackland 3 Sylvan Rd S Westport CT 06880

LEES, STEVEN THOMAS, trust officer, lawyer; b. Quakertown, Pa., Apr. 11, 1949; s. Harry Lawrence and Dorothy (Clark) L.; m. Kathy Coogan, Sept. 6, 1986; 1 child from previous marriage, Abigail Susan; 1 stepchild, Becca B. Coogan. BA, Temple U., 1972, JD, 1975. Bar: Pa. 1975, U.S. Supreme Ct. 1979. Law clk. to presiding justice Bucks County Ct. Common Pleas, Doylestown, Pa., 1975-77; ptnr. Lees & Lees, Quakertown, 1977-81; sole practice Quakertown, 1981-84; trust officer 1st Nat. Bank & Trust Co., Newtown, Pa., 1984—. Sec., bd. dirs. Bucks County Estate Planning Council, Doylestown, 1986-87. Mem. ABA (co-author newsletter Fiduciary Income Taxation of Social Security Benefits 1985, Fiduciary Income Taxation of Accumulated Trust Income 1986, com. on income of estates and trusts tax sect.), Pa. Bar Assn., Bucks County Bar Assn. Republican. Lodge: Masons (master Quakertown 1981). Avocations: instrumental music, scuba diving. Banking, Estate planning, Probate. Office: PO Box 158 State St & Centre Ave Newtown PA 18940

LEETE, JOHN BRUCE, lawyer; b. Olean, N.Y., Oct. 11, 1945; s. William I. and Inez L. (Impress) L.; m. Georginna L. Kingsley, Apr. 22, 1972; children—Anne Kingsley, Elizabeth Impress. B.A., U. Pitts., 1967, J.D., 1970. Bar: Pa. 1970, U.S. Dist. Ct. (we. dist.) Pa. 1970. Chief atty. police affairs div. Neighborhood Legal Services, Pitts., 1970-72; assoc. Kaufman & Harris, Pitts., 1972-74; dep. dir. Neighborhood Legal Services, Pitts., 1974-

76; sole practice, Coudersport, Pa., 1976-78; ptnr. Leete & Glassmire, P.C., Coudersport, 1978—; bd. dirs. Commonwealth Bank and Trust Co., N.A., Coudersport. Mem. pub. relations com. Charles Cole Meml. Hosp. Mem. ABA, Pa. Bar Assn., Assn. Trial Lawyers Am., Potter County Bar Assn. (pres. 1978-80), Potter County Hist. Soc., ACLU, Amnesty Internat. Republican. Lodge: Rotary (pres. 1984-85) (Coudersport). General practice, Local government, Personal injury. Home: RD 3 Box 194AA Coudersport PA 16915 Office: 5 E 3d St Coudersport PA 16915

LEFEBVRE, DAVID MARSHALL, lawyer, engineer; b. N.Y.C., Aug. 16, 1953; s. Gabriel Felicien and Doris Jeanette (Germain) L.; m. Judith Phelps Rice, June 19, 1976; children: Timothy Rice, Laura Ashley, Leslie Elizabeth. B in Chem. Engring., Ga. Inst. Tech., 1976; JD, Georgetown U., 1979. Bar: Kans. 1979, U.S. Dist. Ct. Kans. 1979. Supr. legal environ. group Black & Veatch Engrs./Architects, Kansas City, Mo., 1979—. Chmn. northeast convocation Epis. Diocese of Kans., Overland Park, 1985-86. Mem. ABA, NSPE. Republican. Avocations: racquetball, softball, golf, reading. Environment, Administrative and regulatory, FERC practice. Home: 7621 W 97th St Overland Park KS 66212 Office: Black Veatch Engrs/Architects 11401 Lamar Overland Park KS 66211

LEFEVRE, EUGENE DE DAUGHERTY, publishing company executive, lawyer; b. Tsingtao, China, Nov. 8, 1926; came to U.S., 1927; s. Rufus Harry and Mary Lucinda (Daugherty) LeF.; m. Barbara Joan Calkins, June 27, 1953; children—Susan M., Carol E. Avina, Stephen R. Student U. Buffalo, 1944-45; B.A., Drew U., 1948; J.D., Cornell U., 1951. Bar: N.Y. 1952. Lawyer-editor Lawyers Coop. Pub. Co., Rochester, N.Y., 1951-57, sales trainer, 1957-60, tng. and devel. mgr., 1960-63, asst. to sales mgr., 1963-65, product mgr. nat. pubs., 1966-70, mgr. product planning and devel., 1970-73, v.p. mktg., bd. dirs., 1984—; dir. sales Bancroft-Whitney Co., San Francisco, 1973-79, v.p. mktg., 1979-83, bd. dirs., 1973-84. Contbr. articles to profl. jours. Active Community Chest fund dr., Monroe County (N.Y.), 1955-65; mem. Democratic Com., Penfield, N.Y., 1971-73. Mem. ABA, Monroe County Bar Assn., C. of C., Phi Alpha Delta. Methodist. Lawbook publishing. Home: 45 Avonmore Way Penfield NY 14526 Office: Lawyers Coop Pub Co Aqueduct St Rochester NY 14694

LEFF, DAVID, lawyer; b. Bklyn., Dec. 19, 1933; s. Solomon and Anna (Hahn) L.; m. Barbara Kantrowitz, Dec. 23, 1954; children—Abbey, Jody. B.A. with honors, Rutgers U., 1955, LL.B., J.D., 1958. Bar: N.J., 1958. Assoc., Eichenbaum, Kantrowitz Leff & Gulko, Jersey City, and predecessors, 1958-62, ptnr., 1962—, sr. ptnr., 1966—; acting judge Mcpl. Ct. Jersey City, 1977-80; com. dist. ct. practice and procedure Supreme Ct. N.J. Bd. dirs. United Community Fund Hudson County, 1972, pres., 1973; bd. dirs. Consumer Credit Dept. Counseling Service N.J.; bd. dirs. Rutgers Law Alumni Council; v.p. Hudson-Hamilton council Boy Scouts Am., 1974, dir., 1970; v.p., exec. bd. Jersey City C. of C.; v.p. exec. bd., bd. dirs. Jewish Hosp., Jersey City and River Vale; bd. dirs. Goodwill Industries N.J., named Man of Yr.; bd. dirs. Temple Sholom, River Edge, N.J., 1975; adv. com. Bergen Pines County Hosp.; bd. trustees Jersey City Med. Ctr. Found., Walter Head Found.; exec. bd. Bergen County United Jewish Appeal; bd. dirs. United Jewish Community Bergen County; bd. dirs. Tri-State United Way, Jersey City State Coll. Devel. Fund. Cert. consumer credit exec. Internat. Consumer Credit Assn., 1964. Mem. ABA, N.J. Bar Assn., Hudson County Bar Assn. (trustee, pres. 1976), Am. Judicature Soc., Hudson County C. of C., (chmn. bd. 1983-84), Kappa Alpha Tau (nat. pres. 1951). Club: Edgewood Country of River Vale (dir., pres. 1982, 83). Lodge: Rotary (dir. pres. Jersey City club 1974). Consumer commercial. Home: 7002 Boulevard E Guttenberg NJ 07093 Office: Eichenbaum Kantrowitz Leff & Scheer 574 Summit Ave Jersey City NJ 07306

LEFF, IRWIN, lawyer; b. N.Y.C., Dec. 22, 1924; s. Bernard and Anna Hilda (Epstein) L.; m. Enid Isabel Young, June 6, 1951; children: David Jonathan, Penelope Ann, Robert Adam. SB, Harvard U., 1947, LLB, 1951. Bar: Calif. 1952, U.S. Dist. Ct. (no. dist.) Calif. 1952, U.S. Ct. Appeals (9th cir.) 1952, U.S. Supreme Ct. 1974. Assoc. Law Offices Jay Darwin, San Francisco, 1951; economist Nat. Labor Bur., Los Angeles, 1951-53; personnel mgr. Glacier Metal Co., London, 1953-60; ptnr. Darwin, Rosenthal & Leff, San Francisco, 1960-68, Rosenthal & Leff Inc., San Francisco, 1969—. Chmn. Mental Health Adv. Bd., San Francisco, 1971-73. Mem. ABA, Calif. Bar Assn., Bar Assn. San Francisco (vice chmn. labor sect. 1984—), Calif. Psychol. Assn. (honorary). Democrat. Avocations: wood carving, photography. Labor, Workers' compensation, Administrative and regulatory. Home: 178 27th Ave San Francisco CA 94121 Office: Rosenthal & Leff Inc 100 Bush St San Francisco CA 94104

LEFFEL, RUSSELL CALVIN, lawyer; b. Kansas City, Mar. 23, 1948; s. Paul C. and Thelma W. (Wells) L.; m. Cynthia D. O'Brien, July 2, 1978; children: Brad, Saralyn. BA in Econs., U. Kans., 1970, JD, 1973. Bar: Kans. 1973, U.S. Dist. Ct. Kans. 1973, U.S. Ct. Appeals (10th cir.) 1977, U.S. Ct. Appeals (Fed. cir.) 1986, U.S. Supreme Ct. 1986. Sole practice Shawnee Mission, Kans., 1973-75, 77—; ptnr. Wirt & Leffel P.A., Shawnee Mission, 1975-77; pres. Leffel Co., Inc., Kansas City, 1976-86, Rule Realty Corp., Kansas City, 1978-86. Treas. Kans. Reps., Topeka, 1980-82, mem. state com., 1980-86; chmn. Johnson County Reps., Leawood, Kans., 1982-84; candidate republican nomination for U.S. Congress, 3d dist. Kans., 1984. Mem. ABA, Kans. Bar Assn., Johnson County Bar Assn. (program chmn. 5 yrs.), Fed. Bar Assn., Phi Alpha Delta. Lodge: Lions. Avocations: water/snow skiing, jogging, music, art. General corporate, Real property. Home: 12007 Ballentine Overland Park KS 66213 Office: 7315 Frontage Rd Suite 111 Shawnee Mission KS 66204

LEFFLER, BRUCE STEVEN, lawyer; b. N.Y.C., Feb. 13, 1951; s. Marvin and Shirley Leffler; m. Jacqueline Joy, Oct. 2, 1983. BA, NYU, 1973, JD, 1979. Bar: N.Y. 1977. Ptnr. Goldfarb & Fleece, N.Y.C., 1977—. Mem. ABA, Assn. of Bar of City of N.Y. Real property. Office: Goldfarb & Fleece 345 Park Ave New York NY 10154

LEFFLER, RODNEY G., lawyer; b. Greenville, Pa., Aug. 20, 1951; s. Jacob Harrison and Delores Jean (Smeltz) L.; m. Jill Lynn Roseman, May 3, 1975; children—Stephanie Ann, Jennifer Lynn. B.S., Pa. State U., 1973; J.D., George Mason U., 1979. Bar: Va. 1979, U.S. Dist. Ct. (ea. dist.) Va. 1979; U.S. Ct. Appeals (4th cir.) 1979, Pa. 1985, U.S. Supreme Ct. 1985. Police officer Fairfax County Police, Va., 1973-79; prosecutor Commonwealth's Atty., Fairfax, 1979-81; ptnr. Odin, Feldman & Pittleman, P.C., Fairfax, 1981—; instr. No. Va. Criminal Justice Acad., Fairfax, 1977-83; substitute judge Gen. Dist. Ct. 19th Jud. Cir., 1984—. Mem. Fairfax County Bar Assn., (legis. and jud. selection com.), Va. Trial Lawyers Assn. Club: Fairfax Country. Criminal, State civil litigation, Personal injury. Home: 5029 Oakcrest Dr Fairfax VA 22030 Office: Odin Feldman & Pittleman PC 10505 Judicial Dr Fairfax VA 22030

LEFKOW, MICHAEL FRANCIS, lawyer; b. Chgo., Dec. 9, 1940; s. Frederick Lord and Marjorie Claiborne (Freeman) L.; m. Joan Marilyn Humphrey, June 21, 1975; children—Maria, Helena, Laura. B.A., N. Central Coll., Naperville, Ill., 1962; J.D., Northwestern U., 1966. Bar: Ill. 1966, U.S. Dist. Ct. (no. dist.) Ill. 1967, Colo. 1969, U.S. Ct. Appeals (7th cir.) 1971, U.S. Supreme Ct. 1971, Fla. 1982, U.S. Ct. Appeals (D.C. cir.) 1986. Gen. counsel Chgo. Welfare Rights Orgn., Chgo., 1969-72, Ill. Welfare Rights Orgn., Chgo., 1972-76, sole practice, Chgo., 1977-78; mng. atty. Prairie State Legal Services, Inc., Wheaton, Ill., 1978-79; supervisory trial atty. EEOC, Miami, Fla., 1979-82; asst. regional labor counsel U.S. Postal Service, Chgo., 1982-85; sole practice Chgo., 1985—; spl. commr. U.S. Dist. Ct. (no. dist.) Ill., 1985—. Chpt. v.p. League United Latin-Am. Citizens, Miami, 1979; mem. Social Concerns Com., Episcopal Diocese S. Fla., Miami, 1981. Mem. Chgo. Council Lawyers (dir. 1972-74), ABA, Chgo. Bar Assn., Nat. Clearinghouse for Legal Services (past dir.), DuPage County Bar Assn., Fed. Bar Assn. Democrat. Episcopalian. Labor, Federal civil litigation, Civil rights. Home: 5206 N Lakewood Ave Chicago IL 60640 Office: 53 W Jackson Blvd Suite 1250 Chicago IL 60604

LEFKOWITZ, IVAN MARTIN, lawyer; b. Winston-Salem, N.C., Jan. 4, 1952; s. Ernest W. and Matilda C. (Center) L.; m. Fern Deutsch, Apr. 14, 1972; children: Aaron M., Shira B. BBA, U. Cen. Fla., 1973; JD, U. Miami, 1979, LLM Estate Planning, 1980. Bar: Fla. 1979, U.S. Dist. Ct. (mid. dist.) 1980, U.S. Tax. Ct. 1980; CPA, Fla. Sr. acct. Alexander Grant & Co. CPA, Orlando, Fla., 1974-76; assoc. Gray, Harris & Robinson P.A., Orlando, 1980-82; sole practice Orlando, 1982—; adj. prof. Am. Coll., Denver, 1984—. Bd. dirs. U. Cen. Fla. Found., Orlando, 1981—; bd. dirs., v.p. Nat. Kidney Found. Cen. Fla., Orlando and Tampa, 1984—. Mem. Orange County Bar Assn., Internat. Assn. Jewish Lawyers and Jurists, Cen. Fla. Estate Planning Council, Employee Benefits Council. Democrat. Lodge: Kiwanis. Corporate taxation, Estate planning, Pension, profit-sharing, and employee benefits. Office: 430 N Mills Ave Orlando FL 32803

LEFLAR, ROBERT B, lawyer, educator; b. Little Rock, Jan. 23, 1951. AB, Harvard U., 1972, JD, 1977, MPH, 1982. Bar: Ark. 1978, D.C. 1978, U.S. Ct. Appeals (6th cir.) 1978, U.S. Ct. Appeals (D.C. cir.) 1980. Law clk. to judge U.S. Ct. Appeals (6th cir.), Cin., 1977-78; staff atty. Pub. Citizen Health Research Group, Washington, 1978-81; assoc. prof. U. Ark. Sch. of Law, Fayetteville, 1982—; consumer rep. immunology devices adv. com. U.S. FDA, Washington, 1982—. Co-author Cataracts: A Consumers Guide to Choosing the Best Treatment, 1981. Mem. Govs. adv. com. on Hazardous Wastes, 1985-86; legis. co-chmn. Ark. Pub. Health Assn., 1984-86; legal chmn. Ozark Headwaters Group, 1984-87; v.p. Fayetteville Open Channel, 1985-86. Rotary fellow, 1972-73, Yoneyama Meml. fellow, 1973-74. Mem. Ark. Bar Assn., Am. Pub. Health Assn., Sierra Club, Phi Beta Kappa. Democrat. Avocation: backpacking. Health, Administrative and regulatory, Contracts commercial. Home: 1495 Finger Rd Fayetteville AR 72701 Office: U of Ark Sch of Law Fayetteville AR 72701

LEFSTEIN, NORMAN, law educator, lawyer; b. Rock Island, Ill., July 16, 1937; s. George M. and Rose Lefstein; m. Leah M. Lefstein, Apr. 15, 1962; children—Lisa, Adam, Susan. Student, Augustana Coll., 1955-58; LL.B., U. Ill., 1961; LL.M., Georgetown U., 1964. Bar: Ill. 1961, D.C. 1963. Asst. U.S. atty. Washington, 1964-65; project dir. Nat. Council Juvenile Ct. Judges, Chgo., 1965-68; staff mem. Dept. Justice, Washington, 1968-69; dep. dir. Pub. Defender Service for D.C., 1969-72, dir., 1972-75; assoc. prof. law U. N.C., Chapel Hill, 1975-79, prof., 1979—; vis. prof. Duke U., 1976-77, fall 1978. Bd. editors U. Ill. Law Forum, 1959-61. Mem. ABA (council criminal justice sect. 1979—, chmn. 1986-87, reporter Project to Update ABA Criminal Justice Standards 1977-85), Nat. Legal Aid and Defender Assn. (bd. dirs., mem. exec. com. 1975-80), Order of Coif. Criminal, Legal education. Home: 411 Granville Rd Chapel Hill NC 27514 Office: U NC Sch Law Chapel Hill NC 27514

LEGASEY, JOHN SAMUEL, lawyer; b. Medford, Mass., Apr. 20, 1946; s. Leroy A. and Ruth M. (Galvin) L.; m. Elizabeth Goldstein, Nov. 22, 1974; children: Peter, Lauren. BA, U. Mass., Amherst, 1968; JD, Northeastern U., 1975. Bar: Mass. 1975, U.S. Dist. Ct. Mass. 1975, U.S. Ct. Appeals (1st cir.) 1980. Assoc. Glovsky and Glovsky, Beverly, Mass., 1976-79; assoc. Ardiff and Morse, Danvers, Mass., 1979-82, ptnr., 1982—. Vol. Peace Corps, Libya, 1968-69; chmn. Personnel Bd., Lynnfield, Mass, 1983-85. Mem. Salem Bar Assn. (pres. 1982-83), Essex Bar Assn. (exec. com. 1983—), Mass. Bar Assn., Assn. Trial Lawyers Am. State civil litigation, Federal civil litigation, Family and matrimonial. Home: 5 Keniston Rd Lynnfield MA 01940 Office: Ardiff and Morse 32 Maple St Danvers MA 01923

LEGENDRE, JOHN PETER, lawyer; b. St. Louis, Jan. 23, 1938; s. Elmer Louis an Esther Ann (Middendorf) L.; m. Donna Benita Minor, June 7, 1963 (div. Feb. 1985); children: James, Laura. BS, U. Ill., 1961; JD, U. Tex., 1967; LLM, So. Meth. U., 1974. Bar: Tex. 1967, U.S. Dist. Ct. (no. ist.) Tex. 1968, U.S. Supreme Ct. 1971, U.S. Ct. Appeals (5th cir.) 1975, U.S. Ct. Appeals (10th cir.) 1978, U.S. Ct. Appeals (8th cir.) 1979, U.S. Dist. Ct. (so. dist.) Tex. 1981, U.S. Dist. Ct. (we. dist.) Tex. 1982, U.S. Ct. Appeals (D.C. cir.) 1982. Assoc. Humphrey, Gibson & Darden, Wichita Falls, Tex., 1967-70; atty. Tex. and Pacific Railway Co., Dallas, 1970-76; gen. atty. Mo. Pacific R.R. Co., Dallas, 1976-86; sole practice Dallas, 1986—. Served to 1st lt. USAF, 1961-64. Eduardo De Asses scholar U. Tex. Sch. Law, Austin, 1965. Mem. ABA, State Bar of Tex. Assn., Dallas Bar Assn., Council of R.R. Freight, Loss and Damage Counsel, Phi Delta Phi, Delta Tau Delta (treas. 1958-59). Mem. Ind. Bible Ch. Club: Fourth Session (Dallas). Federal civil litigation, State civil litigation, Administrative and regulatory. Home and Office: 5831 Caladium Dr Dallas TX 75230

LEGER, WALTER JOHN, JR., lawyer; b. New Orleans, Nov. 11, 1951; s. Walter John Sr. and Mildred Veronica (Brown) L.; m. Catherine Ann Buras, Aug. 4, 1973; children: Walter John III, Rhett Michael, Elizabeth Catherine. BA, La. State U., 1973; JD, Tulane U., 1976. Bar: La. 1976, U.S. Dist. Ct. (ea. dist.) La. 1976, U.S. Dist. Ct. (we. dist.) La. 1978, U.S. Ct. Appeals (5th and 11th cirs.) 1981, U.S. Supreme Ct. 1981. Assoc. Phelps, Dunbar, Marks, Claverie & Smith, New Orleans, 1976-78; ptnr. George & George, New Orleans, 1978-79; sr. ptnr. Leger & Mestayer, New Orleans, 1979—; lectr. law Tulane U., 1983—; adv. bd. dirs. First City Bank, New Orleans; bd. dirs. Bergeron Industries, Inc., St. Bernard, La., Nautical Aviation, Inc., New Orleans, Ryan Marine, Inc., Pearlington, Miss. Chmn. March of Dimes, Met. New Orleans and Southeastern La., 1980-84; mem. adv. com. bd. commrs. Port of New Orleans; bd. dirs. St. Bernard Community Coll. Found., Chalmette, La., 1986—. Named one of People to Watch in 1982 New Orleans Mag., 1982. Mem. ABA, Fed. Bar Assn., Assn. Trial Lawyers Am., La. Trial Lawyers Assn. (pres.'s adv. council 1982), Miss. Trial Lawyers Assn., N.Y. State Trial Lawyers Assn., Maritime Law Assn., Southeastern Admiralty Law Inst., La. State U. Fedn. (pres. elect St. Bernard chpt. 1986—), New Orleans/River Region C. of C. (chmn., bd. dirs. 1986—), Omicron Delta Kappa. Democrat. Roman Catholic. Avocations: jogging, sailing, tennis. Admiralty, Personal injury, Federal civil litigation. Home: #20 Carolyn Ct Arabi LA 70032 Office: Leger & Mestayer 600 Carondelet St New Orleans LA 70130

LEGG, MICHAEL WILLIAM, lawyer, management systems executive; b. Detroit, Sept. 1, 1952; s. Howard Wesley and Mary Elizabeth (Lucas) L. AA, Oakland Community Coll., 1972; BS, Mercy Coll., 1975; JD, Detroit Coll. Law, 1979. Bar: Mich. 1980, U.S. Supreme Ct. 1986. Assoc. Berry, Hopson, Francis, Mack and Seifman, Detroit, 1980-82; corp. counsel Compuware Corp., Birmingham, Mich., 1982-85, product mgr. law systems div., 1985—. Rep. dist. chmn., Mich., 1983—, presdl. elector, 1985, nat. conv. del., 1984. Mem. ABA (dist. rep. Young Lawyers div. 1986—), Mich. Bar Assn. (commr. 1985—, chmn. Young Lawyers sect. 1985-86), Livonia Bar Assn. (pres. 1985-86). Methodist. Law firm management, Computer, General corporate. Home: 15501 Northville Forest Plymouth MI 48170 Office: Compuware Corp 32100 Telegraph Birmingham MI 48010

LEGG, REAGAN HOUSTON, lawyer; b. Kaufman, Tex., Nov. 18, 1924; s. Edward and Mary Alta (Coon) L.; m. Norma Jean Eden, July 16, 1949 (div. 1976); children—John, Ellen, Emily, Reagan Houston. B.B.A., U. Tex.-Austin, 1947, LL.B., 1948. Bar: Tex. 1948, U.S. Dist. Ct. (we. dist.) Tex. 1951, U.S. Dist. Ct. (no. dist.) Tex. 1957, U.S. Ct. Appeals (5th cir.) 1960, U.S. Supreme Ct. 1961. County atty. Midland County (Tex.), 1951-55; ptnr. Legg, Saxe & Baskin, Midland, Tex., 1955-79, Legg, Aldridge & Carr, Midland, 1980-84, sole practice, 1984—. Trustee Midland Coll., 1971-86 , pres. bd., 1972-75; bd. dirs. Permian Basin Regional Planning Commn., 1977-86 ; pres. Leadership Midland, 1978-80, Tex. Community Coll. Trustees and Adminstrs., 1980-81, Nat. Assn. Community Coll. Trustees, 1982-83. Served with USN, 1942-46. Named Boss of Yr., Midland Legal Secs. Assn., 1969; recipient M. Dale Ensign Leadership award Assn. Community Coll. Trustees, 1977. Fellow Tex. Bar Found.; mem. ABA, Tex. Bar Assn. (chmn. com. group legal services 1968-74), Midland C. of C. (dir. 1968-73, 78-81), Midland County Bar Assn. (pres. 1967-68). Democrat. Methodist. Clubs: Midland Country, Masons. Federal civil litigation, State civil litigation, General corporate. Office: PO Box 10506 Midland TX 79702

LEGG, WILLIAM JEFFERSON, lawyer; b. Enid, Okla., Aug. 20, 1925; s. Garl Paul and Mabel (Gensman) L.; m. Eva Imogene Hill, Dec. 16, 1950; children: Melissa Lou, Eva Diane, Janet Sue. Grad., Enid Bus. Coll., 1943; student, Pittsburg State U., 1944; B.B.A., U. Tex.-Austin, 1946; J.D., U. Tulsa, 1954. Bar: Okla. 1954, U.S. Supreme Ct., U.S. Ct. Appeals (10th cir.), U.S. Dist. Ct. (Western dist.) Okla. Atty. Marathon Oil Co., 1954-61; sole practice Oklahoma City, 1962—; mem. Andrews Davis Legg Bixler Milsten & Murrah, Inc. (and predecessor firm), 1962—, sec., 1972-82, pres., 1983-86; adj. prof. law Oklahoma City U., 1975-80; lectr. Okla. U. Law Sch., 1986; dir., v.p. internat. oil cos.; dir., gen. counsel N.J. Nat. Resources Co.; lectr. energy seminars. Contbr. articles to profl. jours. Ordained Reorganized Ch. of Jesus Christ of Latter Day Saints, 1964, dist. pres., 1975-80, br. pres., 1986—; mem. com. Okla. Energy Adv. Council, 1973, Okla. Blue Ribbon Com. on natural gas well allowables, 1983; Chmn. bd. trustees Am. Inst. Discussion, 1969-72, now trustee, counsel; trustee Jenkins Found. Research, sec., 1975-81; trustee Restoration Trails Found., 1975, Graceland Coll., Lamoni, Iowa, 1986—, Okla. County Library Found., 1986—. Served with USN, 1943-46. Mem. ABA, Internat. Bar Assn., Okla. Bar Assn. (past com. chmn.), Oklahoma County Bar Assn. (past com. chmn.), Internat. Assn. Energy Economists. Clubs: Economic, Men's Dinner, Beacon, Petroleum (Oklahoma City). Oil and gas leasing, FERC practice, Real property. Home: 3017 Brush Creek Rd Oklahoma City OK 73120 Office: 500 W Main Oklahoma City OK 73102

LEGGE, CHARLES ALEXANDER, judge; b. San Francisco, Aug. 24, 1930; s. Roy Alexander and Wilda (Rampton) L.; m. Janice Meredith Sleeper, June 27, 1952; children: Jeffrey, Nancy, Laura. AB with distinction, Stanford U., 1952, JD, 1954. Bar: Calif. 1955. Ptnr. Bronson, Bronson & McKinnin, San Francisco, 1956-84, chmn., 1978-84; judge U.S. Dist. Ct. (no. dist.) Calif., San Francisco, 1984—. Atty. Children's Hosp. Med. Ctr., Oakland, Calif. Served with U.S. Army, 1954-56. Fellow Am. Coll. Trial Lawyers; mem. Calif. Bar Assn. (past chmn. adminstrn. justice com.). Republican. Clubs: Bohemian, World Trade (San Francisco); Orinda (Calif.) Country. Office: US Dist Courthouse 450 Golden Gate Ave PO Box 36060 San Francisco CA 94102 *

LEGGETT, JAMES FRANCOIS, lawyer; b. Tacoma, Wash., June 17, 1945; s. Earl Benjamin and Ellen Alice (Charleson) L. BA, U. Puget Sound, 1967; MS, U. So. Calif., 1973, JD, U. Wash., 1975; grad. U.S. Air Force Command and Staff Coll., 1979. Bar: Wash. 1976, U.S. Dist. Ct. (we. dist.) Wash. 1976, U.S. Ct. Appeals (9th cir.) 1976, U.S. Patent and Trademark Office 1977, U.S. Supreme Ct. 1981. Assoc. Magana & Cathcart, Los Angeles, 1976-77; sole practice, Tacoma, Wash., 1977-84; sr. ptnr. Leggett & Kram, Attys.-at-Law, Tacoma, 1984—; admissions liaison officer U.S. Air Force Acad., Colorado Springs, Colo., 1973—; vis. lectr. U. So. Calif., Los Angeles, 1977—. Author: A History of Mount Rainier, 1967, Real Estate Law in Washington, 1980. Mem. Urban Fin. Com., City of Tacoma, 1978-81; bd. dirs. Pierce County Boys and Girls Club, Tacoma, 1983. Decorated D.F.C. with 4 oak leaf clusters, Air medal with 14 oak leaf clusters; named one of Outstanding Young Men in Am., Jaycees, 1979. Mem. ABA (sect. on aviation law 1977—), Red River Rats Fighter Pilot Assn., Mensa, Aerospace Med. Assn., Internat. Soc. Air Safety Investigators (pres. NW region 1978-80, co-chmn. conv. 1979), Phi Alpha Delta, Pi Gamma Mu, Theta Chi (alumni soc. chmn. 1977). Democrat. Roman Catholic. Club: Tacoma. Lodge: Elks (trustee 1979-82). Patent, Personal injury, Real property. Home: 1131 N 26th St Tacoma WA 98403 Office: Legget & Kram 818 S Yakima Tacoma WA 98403

LEHAN, JONATHAN MICHAEL, lawyer; b. Los Angeles, Apr. 25, 1947; s. Bert Leon and Frances (Shapiro) L.; m. Annett Jean Garrett, Aug. 1, 1970; children: Joshua Michael, Melanie Janine. BA, Calif. State U., Fullerton, 1968; JD, Calif. Western Sch. Law, 1971. Bar: Calif. 1972, U.S. Dist. Ct. (no. dist.) Calif. 1973, U.S. Supreme Ct. 1975. Law clk. to presiding and assoc. justice Calif. Dist. Ct. Appeals, San Bernardino, 1971-73; dep. dist. atty. Mendocino County, Ukiah, Calif., 1973-76; coast asst. dist. atty. Mendocino County, Fort Bragg, Calif., 1976-83; sole pratice Fort Bragg, 1983-84; ptnr. Lehan & Kronfeld, Fort Bragg, 1984—; instr. Barstow Community Coll., Calif., 1972, Mendocino Community Coll., Ukiah, 1974-75, Coll. Redwoods, Fort Bragg, 1981-82. Bd. dirs. Salmon Restoration Assn., Fort Bragg, Gloriana Opera Co., Mendocino, Mendocino Art Ctr. Editor Calif. Western Sch. Law Law Rev., 1971. Mem. ABA, Mendocino Bar Assn., Phi Delta Phi, Mendocino C. of C. (bd. dirs.). Democrat. Avocations: violinist, violist, Mendocino string quartet, fly fishing. Criminal, State civil litigation, General practice. Office: PO Box 1677 Fort Bragg CA 95437

LEHAT, STEVEN BRUCE, lawyer; b. Bklyn., Mar. 7, 1951; s. Irving and Sheila Natalie (Brownstein) L.; m. Brigitte Alzerra, Apr. 10, 1983; children: Sarah Kimberley, Yehiel Vivien. BBA, U. Cin., 1973; JD, Southwestern U., 1979. Bar: Calif. 1980, U.S. Dist. Ct. (cen. dist.) Calif. 1980, U.S. Ct. Internat. Trade 1980, U.S. Ct. Appeals (fed. cir.) 1982. Internat. steel trader Marubeni Am. Corp., N.Y.C., 1974-76; atty. customs Glad & Ferguson, Los Angeles, 1980—. Mem. ABA (internat. law sect.), Am. Arbitration Assn. (panel arbitrator), Los Angeles County Bar Assn. (customs law com.), Fgn. Trade Assn. So. Calif. (import and export com.). International trade. Office: Glad & Ferguson 606 S Olive St #1420 Los Angeles CA 90014

LEHMAN, EDWARD GEORGE, lawyer; b. Jersey City, Jan. 7, 1956; s. George Lewis and Janet (Gorman) L. BA, Rutgers U., 1978; cert., Inst. Internat. and Comparative Law Oxford U., Eng., 1980; JD, U. San Diego, 1982. Bar: Calif. 1982. Organizer Am. Fedn. State, County and Mcpl. Employees, San Diego, 1982-84; bus. rep. council 36 Am. Fedn. State, County and Mcpl. Employees Los Angeles, 1984—. Alt. mem. Los Angeles County Dems., 1985—; mem. 40th assembly Dist. Caucus, Los Angeles, 1985—; committeman Hudson County Dems., N.J., 1975-76, 77-79. Mem. ABA (labor and employment law sect.), Indsl. Relations Research Assn., Coalition of Labor Union Women, PEOPLE, Acad. of Polit. Sci., Phi Alpha Delta. Democrat. Avocations: politics, travel. Labor, Public international, Local government. Office: AFSCME Council 36 3932 Wilshire Blvd #108 Los Angeles CA 90010

LEHMAN, LEONARD, lawyer, consultant; b. Bklyn, July 5, 1927; s. Samuel and Marcy (Dolgenas) L.; m. Imogene McAuliffe, June 11, 1954; children—Jeffrey, Toby, Amy, Zachary. B.A., Cornell U., 1949; J.D., Yale U., 1952. Bar: N.Y. 1953, U.S. Supreme Ct. 1969, D.C. 1979, U.S. Ct. Internat. Trade 1981, U.S. Ct. Appeals (fed. cir.) 1982. Atty.-advisor U.S. Tax Ct., Washington, 1952-55; sole practice, N.Y.C., 1955-63; sr. counsel Office Tax Legis. Counsel, U.S. Dept. Treasury, Washington, 1963-65; asst. to chief counsel U.S. Customs Service, 1965-67, dep. chief counsel, 1968-71, asst. commr. 1971-79; ptnr. Barnes, Richardson and Colburn, N.Y.C., Washington and Chgo., 1979—; cons. U.S. C. of C. Bd. dirs. Westchester Assn. Retarded Citizens. Recipient U.S. Treasury Meritorious Service award, 1971, Exceptional Service award, 1979; U.S. Customs Honor award, 1977. Mem. ABA (standing com. on customs law 1974-80, chmn. 1980, customs and tariff com., adminstrv. law sect. 1971—, vice chmn. 1981-83, chmn. 1984—), Fed. Bar Assn., Phi Beta Kappa, Phi Kappa Phi. Contbr. articles to profl. jours. Private international, Immigration, naturalization, and customs, Administrative and regulatory. Home: 18 Rich Branch Ct Gaithersburg MD 20878 Office: 1819 H St NW Washington DC 20006

LEHMAN, ROBERT FRANK, lawyer; b. Nappanee, Ind., Nov. 20, 1942; s. Charles R. and Dorothy L. (Hollar) L.; m. Bernadette Barry, June 11, 1967; children—John Barry, Mary Katherine. A.B., Ind. U., 1966, J.D., 1970; postgrad. Free U. Berlin, 1965-66, MA U. Dayton. Bars: Ind. 1970, U.S. Dist. Ct. (Ind.). 1970. Exec. Dir. Ind. Jud. Study Commn., 1969-70, Ind. Civil Code Study Commn., 1967-70, Ind. Continuing Legal Edn. Forum, 1970-73; asst. dean, assoc. prof. Ind. U. Sch. Law, Indpls., 1970-73; v.p., gen. counsel, dir. research/devel. Charles F. Kettering Found., 1973—; sec., gen. counsel Domestic Policy Assn., Inst. for Devel. Ednl. Activities; bd. dirs. Ohio Council on Humanities, United Theol. Sem.; Trustee Ohio Donors Forum. Recipient Ind. U. Disting. Alumni Service award, 1972; Ind. Bar Assn. Disting. Service award, 1974. Mem. ABA, Ind. Bar Assn., Am. Soc. Legal History. Episcopalian. Contbr. articles to profl. jours. General corporate, Legislative, Legal history. Address: 1300 Sugarhill Ln Xenia OH 45385

LEHNER, EDWARD HARVEY, judge; b. N.Y.C., Mar. 6, 1933; s. Irving R. and Bertha G. (Gold) L.; m. Lois J. Naftulin, July 26, 1981; children: Brynne, Ivy. BBA, CCNY, 1954; LLB, NYU, 1957. Bar: N.Y. 1958, U.S. Dist. Ct. (so. and ea. dists.) N.Y. 1960. Assoc. Meyer, Fink, Weinberger & Levin, N.Y.C., 1957-62; with Towers Mart Internat. Inc., N.Y.C., 1962-64; assoc. Guzik & Boukstein, N.Y.C., 1964-66, Aranow, Brodsky, Bohlinger, Einhorn & Dann, N.Y.C., 1966-72; mem. N.Y. State Assembly, 1973-80; judge Civil Ct. N.Y.C., 1981—; lectr. N.Y. Law Jour. Fourm, 1978, 79; mem. Com. on State Legislation of Citizens Union, 1970-72, Com. on State Legislation of Assn. Bar City N.Y., 1971-72. Co-author several articles in

N.Y. Law Jour. Office: Civil Ct of City of NY 111 Centre St New York NY 10013

LEHOUILLIER, PATRIC JAYMES, lawyer; b. San Diego, Feb. 8, 1948; s. Leo Clarence and Barbara (Selacek) LeH.; m. Alice Honey, May 28, 1966 (div. May 1986); children: Frank Dean, Joel Patrick. Student, San Diego State Coll.; JD, Syracuse U., 1974. Bar: N.Y. 1975, U.S. Dist. Ct. (so. and ea. dists.) N.Y. 1975, U.S. Ct. Appeals (2d cir.) 1975, Colo. 1977, U.S. Dist. Ct. Colo. 1977, U.S. Ct. Appeals (10th cir.) 1977, U.S. Supreme Ct. 1985. Spl. asst. atty. gen. Office of State Prosecutor, N.Y.C., 1974-76; dep. dist. atty. 10th Jud. Dist., Pueblo, Colo., 1976-77; ptnr. Barash & LeHouillier, Colorado Springs, Colo., 1978—; bd. dirs. Pikes Peak Legal Service, Colorado Springs, 1981—. Contbr. articles to law jours. Bd. dirs. Urban League Pikes Peak Region, Colorado Springs, 1980—, Pikes Peak area campfire, Colorado Springs, 1984—; chmn. El Paso City Dem. Party, Colorado Springs, 1985—. Mem. ABA, Assn. Trial Lawyers Am., Colo. Bar Assn., Colo. Trial Lawyers Assn., Order of Coif. Democrat. Roman Catholic. Avocations: marathon running, bicycling. State civil litigation, Federal civil litigation, Personal injury. Home: 3840 Roxbury Ct Colorado Springs CO 80906 Office: Barash & LeHouillier 403 S Tejon Colorado Springs CO 80903

LEHR, SHARON RUTH, lawyer; b. Humphreys, Mo., Feb. 2, 1943; d. Grant and Eloise (Hamilton) Hill; m. James H. Lehr, June 29, 1963 (div. Feb. 1976); children: Elizabeth H., Jonathan H. BA magna cum laude et cum distinctione, Mt. Holyoke Coll., 1964; MA, U. Mo., 1966, JD, 1979. Bar: Mo. 1979. Assoc. Fallon & Jones, Kansas City, Mo., 1980, Lem T. Jones, Kansas City, 1981-82; counsel Bapt. Med. Ctr., Kansas City, 1984-85; ptnr. Jones & Lehr, Kansas City, 1982-84, 85—. Mem. Women's Polit. Caucus, Kansas City. Mem. ABA, Am. Acad. Hosp. Attys., Mo. Bar Assn. (chmn. health and hosp. law com. 1984—), Mo. Soc. Hosp. Attys. (bd. dirs. 1984—), Kansas City Bar Assn., Kansas City Area Soc. Hosp. Attys. Democrat. Methodist. Avocation: reading. Health. Home: 42 E 106th St Kansas City MO 64114 Office: Jones & Lehr PC 9233 Ward Parkway Suite 270 Kansas City MO 64114

LEHR, WILLIAM, JR., food company executive; b. St. Louis, June 12, 1940; s. William and Emily (Healy) L.; m. Beverlee Balch, Dec. 19, 1961; children: Audrey M., William, James A. B.B.A., U. Notre Dame, 1961; J.D., Georgetown U., 1964. Bar: D.C. 1964. With Hershey Foods Corp., Pa., 1967—, asst. to the sec., 1968-78, asst. to sec., assoc. counsel, 1976-81, sec., 1978—, treas., 1980-85, sr. assoc. counsel, 1981-82, assoc. gen. counsel for securities, 1982—; v.p. Hershey Foods Corp., 1985—. Mem. Keystone area council Boy Scouts Am. Served to capt. U.S. Army, 1965-67. Mem ABA, Am. Soc. Corp. Sec., Fin. Execs. Inst., Nat. Assn. Corp. Dirs., Pa. Economy League (bd. dirs.), The Keystone Area Council, Inc. of Boy Scouts Am. Lodge: Rotary. General corporate. Home: RD 2 Box 112 Palmyra PA 17078 Office: Hershey Foods Corp 100 Mansion Rd E Hershey PA 17033

LEHTO, NEIL JOHN, lawyer; b. Detroit, Dec. 1, 1950; s. Ernest E. and Marian E. (Jones) L.; m. Deborah J. Spry, June 30, 1972; children: Amber, Amanda, Amelia. BA, Wayne State U., 1974; JD, Detroit Coll. of Law, 1978. Bar: Mich. 1978, U.S. Dist. Ct. (ea. dist.) Mich. 1978. Assoc. O'Reilly, Rancilio, Nitz, Andrews & Turnbull P.C., Sterling Heights, Mich., 1978—; asst. atty. City of Sterling Heights, 1978—, Twp. of Shelby, Mich., 1982-83; bd. dirs. Econ. Devel. Corp., Rochester Hills, Mich. Vice chmn. 12th congl dist. Dem. Com., Rochester, 1978-80; pres. Rochester Dem. Club, 1980-83, Friends of Rochester Hills Pub. Library, 1982-84, Gateway Montessori Sch., Birmingham, Mich, 1985—. Served to 2d lt. USNG, 1970-76. Mem. ABA, Mich. Bar Assn., Macomb County Bar Assn., Rochester Jaycees (v.p. 1973-75). Local government, State civil litigation, Family and matrimonial. Home: 1130 Avon Manor Rochester Hills MI 48063 Office: O'Reilly Rancilio Nitz Andrews & Turnbull PC 38800 Van Dyke Ave Sterling Heights MI 48077

LEIB, JEFFREY M., lawyer; b. Detroit, Nov. 21, 1941; s. Samuel W. and Lois (Miller) L.; m. Bryna L. Linden, June 16, 1965; children: Lawrence Jay, Jayme Renee, Jodi Rachelle. BA, Mich. State U., 1964; JD, U. Detroit, 1967. Bar: Mich. 1968, U.S. Dist. Ct. (ea. dist.) Mich. 1968. Asst. prosecutor Oakland County, Pontiac, Mich., 1968-70; legal advisor Oakland Probate Ct., Pontiac, 1970-71; pres. Leib and Leib, P.C., 1971—; pros. atty. Orchard Lake City, Mich., 1975-78; gen. counsel Franks Nursery and Craft, Inc., Detroit, 1978-83, Beech Tool Co., Inc., Detroit. Author, co-chmn. campaign for constl. amendment Taxpayers United for Tax Limitation, 1978; planning commr. West Bloomfield Twp. (Mich.), 1971-83, trustee, councilman, 1984—; vice chmn. West Bloomfield Symphony Orch. 1976-80; bd. dirs. Temple Israel. Mem. Mich. Bar Assn., Oakland County Bar Assn. (chmn. young lawyers sect., chmn. spl. events com., bd. dirs. 1983—), Southfield Bar Assn. (pres. 1981-82) C. of C. (West Bloomfield chpt. pres. 1979-80, Businessman of Yr. award 1980). Jewish. Lodges: Optimist, B'nai B'rith. Personal injury, Probate, Real property. Home: 3205 Parkland Dr West Bloomfield MI 48033 Office: Leib & Leib PC 24800 Northwestern Hwy Southfield MI 48075

LEIB, PATRICIA SHANE, lawyer; b. Tampa, Fla., June 28, 1955; d. Lester and Harriet (Weinstein) L.; divorced: 1 child, Leighton. Student, Tulane U., 1970-71, U. N.C., 1971-72; BA, U. So. Fla., 1975; enrolled fgn. study program, Fla. State U., London, 1975; JD, Stetson U., 1978. Bar: Fla. 1978, U.S. Dist. Ct. (mid. dist.) Fla. 1979. Asst. state Atty. State of Fla., Clearwater, 1978; instr. law contracts, bus. ops. Hillsborough Community Coll., Tampa, 1979-82; assoc. Anderson & Orcutt and predecessor firm Anderson, Thorn, Smith & Orcutt, Tampa, 1982—; adj. prof. div. continuing edn. U. Fla., Gainesville, Fla., 1986—. Speaker condominium and coop. conf. Fla. Div. Land Sales, Condominiums and Mobile Homes, Tallahassee, 1985; organizer, bd. dirs. Mothers Against Drunk Drivers, Tampa, 1984; bd. dirs. DWI Counterattack, Inc., Tampa, 1984-85. Cert. of Appreciation DWI Counterattack, Inc., Hillsborough, Tampa, 1985; cert. of appreciation Mothers Against Drunk Drivers, Inc., Tampa, 1984-85. Mem. ABA, Fla. Bar Assn., Fla. Assn. Women Lawyers, Hillsborough County Assn. Women Lawyers, Hillsborough County Bar Assn. Democrat. Jewish. Avocations: tennis, writing. Condominium, Real property, Construction. Home: 1909 S Westshore Blvd Tampa FL 33629 Office: Anderson Thorn Smith & Orcutt 341 Plant Ave Tampa FL 33606

LEIBEL, SHELLEY JOY, lawyer; b. Bklyn., Jan. 24, 1957; d. Sol and Lee (Kornbluth) L.; m. Ben J. Szwalbenest, Nov. 8, 1981. BA summa cum laude, Queens Coll., Flushing, N.Y., 1978; JD, Temple U., 1981. Bar: Pa. 1981. Law clk. to presiding judge Pa. Ct. Common Pleas, Phila., 1980; assoc. Law offices of Elaine Smith, Phila., 1980-82; ptnr. Smith and Leibel, Phila., 1982—; instr. Inst. Paralegal Tng., Phila., 1986—. Vol., advisor United Way Southeastern Pa., 1985—. Mem. Pa. Bar Assn., Phila. Bar Assn., Phi Beta Kappa. Family and matrimonial. Home: 1107 Bryn Mawr Ave Bala Cynwyd PA 19004 Office: Smith & Leibel 1420 Locust St Suite 110 Acad House Philadelphia PA 19102

LEIBMAN, MORRIS IRWIN, lawyer; b. Chgo., Feb. 8, 1911; s. Isadore M. and Clara (Leibman) L.; m. Mary Wolf, Oct. 14, 1981. Ph.B., U. Chgo., 1931, J.D., 1933. Bar: Ill. bar 1933. Since practiced in Chgo.; partner firm Sidley & Austin; lectr. law schs. U. Chgo., U. Ill., DePaul U., Northwestern U. Chmn. Nat. Adv. Council Econ. Opportunity; mem. Sec. Def. Adv. Com. Non-Mil. Instn., President's Panel Cons. Internal Affairs and Nat. Security; bd. dirs. Nat. Strategy Information Center, U.S. Inst. Peace, 1986-87; mem. exec. bd. Ctr. for Strategic and Internat. Studies, 1964—; civilian aide emeritus to Sec. of Army for life; mem. adv. bd. Edn. for Freedom, Atlanta; exec. bd. Center Strategic Studies, Georgetown U.; Trustee Loyola U. Recipient Presdl. Medal of Freedom, 1981. Fellow Am. Bar Assn. (chmn. law and nat. security); mem. Def. Orientation Conf. Assn., Ill., Chgo., N.Y. bar assns., Assn. Bar City N.Y., Chgo. Law Inst., Am. Judicature Soc. Clubs: Law (Chgo.), MidDay (Chgo.), Standard (Chgo.), Carlton (Chgo.); Sky (N.Y.C.); Army and Navy (Washington). Home: 1550 Lake Shore Dr Chicago IL 60610 Office: 1 First Nat Plaza Chicago IL 60603

LEIBOLD, ARTHUR WILLIAM, JR., lawyer; b. Ottawa, Ill., June 13, 1931; s. Arthur William and Helen (Cull) L.; m. Nora Collins, Nov. 30, 1957; children: Arthur William III, Alison Aubry, Peter Collins. A.B., Haverford Coll., 1953; J.D., U. Pa., 1956. Bar: Pa. 1957. With firm Dechert, Price & Rhoads, Phila., 1956-69; partner Dechert, Price & Rhoads, 1965-69, Washington, 1972—; gen. counsel Fed. Home Loan Bank Bd. and Fed. Savs. & Loan Ins. Corp., Washington, 1969-72, Fed. Home Loan Mortgage Corp., 1970-72; lectr. English St. Joseph's Coll., Phila., 1957-59. Contbr. articles to profl. publs. Mem. Pres. Kennedy's Lawyers Com. Civil Rights, 1963, Adminstrv. Conf. U.S., 1969-72; bd. dirs. Marymount Coll. Va., 1974-75; Mem. Phila. Com. 70, 1965-74, Fellowship Commn. Mem. ABA (ho. dels. 1967-69, 79—, treas. 1979-83, fin. com., bd. govs. 1977-83), Fed. Bar Assn. (nat. council 1971-80), D.C. Bar Assn., Phila. Bar Assn., Am. Bar Found. (treas. 1979-83), Am. Bar Ret. Assn. (dir. 1978-83), Am. Bar Endowment (bd. dirs. 1984—), Internat. Bar Assn., Order of Coif, Phi Beta Kappa. Republican. Roman Catholic. Clubs: Phila. Country (Gladwyne, Pa.); Skating (Phila.), Orpheus (Phila.). Administrative and regulatory, Banking. Home: 3604 Prospect St NW Washington DC 20007 Office: 1730 Pennsylvania Ave NW Washington DC 20006

LEIBOLD, WILLIAM JOSEPH, lawyer; b. Dayton, Ohio, July 14, 1957; s. Richard Joseph and Anna Rose (Buerschen) L.; m. Faye Ann Amrhein, June 12, 1982. BAsumma cum laude, U. Dayton, 1979; JD summa cum laude, Ohio State U., 1982. Bar: Ohio 1982. Assoc. Smith & Schnacke, Dayton, 1982—. Mem. ABA (corp. law sect.), Ohio Bar Assn., Dayton Bar Assn., Order of Coif, Omicron Delta Epsilon, Phi Kappa Phi. Democrat. Roman Catholic. Lodge: KC. Avocations: golf, music, tennis, sports. General corporate, Securities, Public utilities. Home: 98 Patterson Rd Dayton OH 45419 Office: Smith & Schnacke PO Box 1817 Dayton OH 45401

LEIBOWITZ, MATTHEW LEON, lawyer; b. Bklyn., Nov. 12, 1950; s. Jerry and Henriette Ruth (Ginsberg) L. BS in Law and Pub. Policy cum laude, Syracuse U., 1972; JD, U. Miami, 1975. Bar: D.C. 1976, U.S. Dist. Ct. (so. dist.) Fla. 1979, U.S. Ct. Appeals (D.C. cir.) 1979, U.S. Supreme Ct. 1979, U.S. Ct. Appeals (5th and 11th cirs.) 1981. Of counsel Atkinson, Golden, Bacen & Diner, Miami, Fla., 1979-81; sole practice Miami, 1981; ptnr. Leibowitz & Rice, Miami, 1981-82; sr. ptnr. Leibowitz & Spencer, Miami, 1982—; trial, staff atty. FCC, Washington, 1976-79. Contbr. articles to profl. jours. Mem. ABA, Fla. Bar Assn., Nat. Assn. Broadcasters (assoc.), Fla. Assn. Broadcasters (assoc., Big Mike award South Fla. 1981). Avocations: sailing, racquetball. Communications, Administrative and regulatory. Office: Leibowitz & Spencer 3050 Biscayne Blvd Miami FL 33137

LEIBSON, CHARLES M., state supreme court justice; b. Louisville, June 30, 1929; m. Margaret Leibson. LLB cum laude, U. Louisville, 1952; LLM, U. Va., 1986. Bar: Ky. 1952. Sole practice Louisville, 1954-76; judge Ky. Cir. Ct., Louisville, 1976-82; justice Ky. Supreme Ct., Louisville, 1982—; lectr. courtroom law U. Louisville Sch. Law, 1969-82; pres. Ky. Assn. Trial Attys., 1965. Chmn. bd. trustees Jefferson County Pub. Law Library, 1978-81. Served to 1st lt. JAGC U.S. Army, 1952-54. Recipient Disting. Alumni award U. Louisville Sch. Law, 1984, Outstanding State Trial Judge award Assn. Trial Lawyers Am., 1980, Outstanding State Appellate Judge award, Assn. Trial Lawyers Am., 1985. Fellow Internat. Acad. Trial Lawyers; mem. Louisville Bar Assn. (Judge of Yr. award 1979), Internat. Acad. Trial Judges, Inner Circle of Advs. Office: Ky Supreme Ct Room 216 State Capitol Frankfort KY 40601 *

LEIBY, LARRY RAYMOND, lawyer; b. Phila., Nov. 3, 1947; s. Leo R. and Virginia (Danter) L.; m. Cheryll Wadsworth, Jan. 20, 1968; children—Connie Marie, Bradley Ward. Mus. B., U. Miami, 1969, J.D., 1973. Bar: Fla. 1973, U.S. Dist. Ct. (so. dist.) Fla. 1974, U.S. Dist. Ct. (mid. dist.) Fla. 1984, U.S. Ct. Claims 1981, U.S. Ct. Appeals (11th cir.) 1981, U.S. Supreme Ct. 1980. Assoc. Law Office Daniel A. Kavanaugh, Miami, Fla., 1973-74; sole practice, Ft. Lauderdale, Fla., 1974-75; ptnr. Kavanaugh & Leiby, Miami, 1975-81, Leiby & Elder, Miami and Tampa, Fla., 1981—. Author: Subcontractor's Guide to Florida Mechanics Lien Law, 1976; Florida Construction Law Manual, 1981. Mem. Comml. Law League Am. Acad. Trial Lawyers Am., Fla. Bar Assn. (constrn. law com. chmn. 1976-87), ABA (forum com. on constrn. industry). Democrat. Presbyterian. Construction, Government contracts and claims. Office: Leiby and Elder 17131 NE 6 Ave Miami FL 33162

LEIFEL, DANNY JOHN, lawyer; b. Rockford, Ill., June 12, 1944; s. Delbert John and Evelyn (Rohlin) L.; m. Paula Rae Esworthy, Aug. 15, 1971; 1 child, Elizabeth Anne. B.S., Ill. State U., 1962-66, M.S. in Polit. Sci., 1971; J.D., U. Ill.-Champaign, 1974. Bar: Ill. 1974. Asst. state's atty., McLean County, Bloomington, Ill., 1974-77; gen. atty. Ill. Agrl. Assn., Bloomington, Ill., 1977—; adj. instr. Ill. State U., Normal, 1977-81. Vice-chmn., McLean County Republican Com., 1980—; bd. dirs. A.I.D. Crimestoppers, Bloomington, 1977-80, O.D.C. of McLean County, 1981—; chmn. McLean County Regional Planning Commn., Bloomington, 1978-82; mem. Bd. of Edn., Bloomington. Served with AUS, 1966-69. Mem. McLean County Bar Assn., Ill. State Bar Assn., McLean County Farm Bur., D.A.V. Republican. Methodist. Club: Lincoln. Lodge: Masons. General corporate, Local government. Home: 207 Leland St Bloomington IL 61701 Office: Ill Agrl Assn 1701 Towanda Ave Bloomington IL 61701

LEIFER, MAX DAVID, lawyer; b. Munich, Fed. Republic Germany, Feb. 2, 1946; s. Saul and Betty (Milch) L.; m. Erika Chaban, Nov. 20, 1971; children—Danielle, Seth. B.S., NYU, 1968; J.D., Bklyn. Law Sch., 1971. Bar: N.Y. 1972, U.S. Dist. Ct. (ea. and so. dists.) N.Y. 1974, U.S. Ct. Appeals (2d cir.) 1974, U.S. Supreme Ct. 1975, N.J., 1976, U.S. Dist. Ct. N.J. 1984, U.S. Ct. Internat. Trade, U.S. Ct. Appeals (fed. cir.). Supt. bldg. Leisure Tech., Lakewood, N.J., 1969-71; trial atty. Aetna Ins. Co., N.Y.C., 1972-77; sole practice, Astoria, N.Y., 1977—; mem. arbitration panel N.Y. Civil Ct. Mem. N.Y. Social Security Bar Assn. (v.p. 1983-84), Nat. Orgn. Social Security Reps., Queens Bar Assn., Nassau Bar Assn., N.Y. County Bar Assn., Fed. Bar Assn., N.Y. State Bar Assn., N.Y. State Trial Lawyers Assn., N.J. Bar Assn., Bay Ridge Lawyers Assn., Am. Arbitration Assn., Am. Judges Assn., L.I. City Lawyers Assn., Internat. Platform Assn., Queens C. of C., Bklyn. Law Sch. Alumni Assn. Republican. Jewish. Lodge: Masons (32 degree), Shriners. Pension, profit-sharing, and employee benefits, Contracts commercial, Personal injury. Home: 5 Joan Ct Woodbury NY 11797 Office: 33-29 Crescent St Astoria NY 11106 Office: 1501 Lanes Mill Rd Lakewood NJ 08701

LEIGH, GARY DEAN, lawyer; b. Danville, Ill., Jan. 14, 1955; s. Donald Dean and Myra Elizabeth (Stipp) L. B.A., U. Miami, 1978; J.D., John Marshall Law Sch., 1981. Bar: Ill. 1981, Calif. 1981, U.S. Dist. Ct. (no. dist.) Ill. 1981, U.S. Dist. Ct. (no. dist.) Calif. 1982, U.S. Dist. Ct. (so. dist.) Calif. 1982, U.S. Ct. Appeals (7th cir.) 1981, U.S. Ct. Appeals (9th cir.) 1982. Ptnr. Fisher, Leigh & Assocs., 1984-86; assoc. Leonard M. Ring & Assocs., Chgo., 1981-83, Susan E. Loggans & Assocs., Chgo., 1983—, Loggans & Reiter, 1984—. Contbr. articles to profl. jours. Mem. Assn. Trial Lawyers Am. (advanced trial advocacy cert. 1983), Ill. Trial Lawyers Assn. (products liability com. 1981—), Calif. Trial Lawyers Assn., Chgo. Bar Assn. (trial techniques sect. 1981—), Ill. State Bar Assn., ABA (tort and ins. practice sect. 1981—). Personal injury. Home: 1247 N State Pkwy Chicago IL 60610 Office: Susan F Loggans & Assocs 615 N Wabash Ave Chicago IL 60611

LEIGHNINGER, SALLY HEINZ, lawyer; b. Carlinville, Ill., Sept. 23, 1950; d. William Henry and Margaret (Denby) Heinz; m. Richard Howard Leighninger, Mar. 3, 1972; children: Christopher Heinz, Emily Wright. Student, Milliken U., 1968-69; BA in English, Blackburn Coll., 1972; postgrad., Lake Forest Coll., 1973-74; JD, U. Minn., 1980. Bar: Minn. 1980, U.S. Dist. Ct. Minn. 1981. Asst. dir. admissions Lake Forest (Ill.) Coll., 1974-77; ptnr. Kane & Leighninger, Edina, Minn., 1980—; co-chmn. Women's Trade Fair, Mpls., 1985. Mem. ABA, Minn. Bar Assn., Hennepin County Bar Assn., Nat. Assn. Women Bus. Owners (bd. dirs. 1984—). Episcopalian. Family and matrimonial, Small business, Real property. Office: Kane & Leighninger 5200 Wilson Rd # 315 Minneapolis MN 55424

LEIGHTON, GEORGE NEVES, judge; b. New Bedford, Mass., Oct. 22, 1912; s. Antonio N. and Anna Sylvia (Garcia) Leitao; m. Virginia Berry Quivers, June 21, 1942; children: Virginia Anne, Barbara Elaine. A.B., Howard U., 1940; LL.B., Harvard U., 1946; LL.D., Elmhurst Coll., 1964, John Marshall Law Sch., 1973, Southeastern Mass. U., 1975, New Eng. U. Sch. Law, 1978. Bar: Mass. 1946, Ill. 1947, U.S. Supreme Ct. 1958. Partner Moore, Ming & Leighton, Chgo., 1951-59, McCoy, Ming & Leighton, Chgo., 1959-64; judge Circuit Ct. Cook County Ill., 1964-69, Appellate Ct. 1st Dist., 1969-76; U.S. dist. judge No. Dist. Ill., 1976-86; sr. dist. judge U.S. Dist. Ct., 1986—; Mem. council sect. legal edn. and admissions to bar ABA, chmn. council, 1976; adj. prof. John Marshall Law Sch., Chgo.; commr., mem. character and fitness com. for 1st Appellate Dist., Supreme Ct. Ill., 1955-63, chmn. character and fitness com., 1961-62; mem. joint com. for revision jud. article Ill. and Chgo. bar assns., 1959-62; joint com. for revision Ill. Criminal Code, 1959-63; chmn. Ill. adv. com. U.S. Commn. on Civil Rights, 1964; mem. pub. rev. bd. UAW, AFL-CIO, 1961-70; Asst. atty. gen. State of Ill., 1950-51; pres. 3d Ward Regular Democratic Orgn., Cook County, Ill., 1951-53; v.p. 21st Ward, 1964. Contbr. articles to legal jours. Bd. dirs. United Ch. Bd. for Homeland Ministries, United Ch. of Christ, Grant Hosp., Chgo.; trustee U. Notre Dame, 1979-83, trustee emeritus, 1983—; bd. overseers Harvard Coll., 1983—. Served to capt., inf. AUS, 1942-45. Decorated Bronze Star.; Recipient Civil Liberties award Ill. div. ACLU, 1961; named Chicagoan of Year in Law and Judiciary Jr. Assn. Commerce and Industry, 1964. Fellow Am. Bar Found.; mem. Howard U. Chgo. Alumni Club (chmn. bd. dirs.), John Howard Assn. (dir.), Chgo., Ill. bar assns., NAACP (chmn. legal redress com. Chgo. br.), Nat. Harvard Law Sch. Assn. (council), Phi Beta Kappa. Jurisprudence. Office: Dirksen Fed Bldg 219 S Dearborn Chicago IL 60604

LEIGHTTY, DAVID, lawyer; b. Ft. Knox, Ky., Aug. 22, 1951; s. Ralph Sherrick and Virginia (Lewis) L.; m. Freeda Jean Flynn, Dec. 23, 1974; children: April, Paul. BA, U. Ky., 1973; JD, U. Louisville, 1977. Bar: Ky., U.S. Dist. Ct. (we. dist.) Ky., U.S. Ct. Appeals (5th, 6th and 7th cirs.). Assoc. Segal, Isenberg, Sales, Stewart & Cutler, Louisville, 1977-82, Tilford, Dobbins, Alexander & Buckaway, Louisville, 1983—; atty. dept. law City of Louisville, 1982—. Pres. 1st Unitarian Ch., Louisville, 1984-85. Mem. Assn. Trial Lawyers Am., Ky. Bar Assn., Louisville Bar Assn., Nat. Assn. of Individual Retirement Account Investors (bd. dirs. 1984-86). Democrat. Civil rights, Labor, Local government. Home: 3147 Pamela Way Louisville KY 40220 Office: Tilford Dobbins Alexander & Buckaway 600 W Main St Louisville KY 40202

LEININGER, WILLIAM JOSEPH, lawyer; b. Bklyn., June 16, 1947; s. Charles M. and Anna Leininger; m. Patricia M. Adams, July 24, 1971; 1 child, Rachel. BA, St. Francis U., Bklyn., 1969; JD, Fordham U., 1974. Atty. N.Y.C. Corp. Counsel, 1974-76, Cullen & Dykman, Bklyn., 1976-78, Jaffe & Asher, N.Y.C., 1978-81; sole practice Staten Island, N.Y., 1981—. Sec., treas. Greater N.Y. chpt. Latin Liturgy Assn., N.Y.C., 1986. Republican. Roman Catholic. Family and matrimonial, Personal injury, State civil litigation. Office: 3074 Hylan Blvd Staten Island NY 10306

LEIPHAM, JAY EDWARD, lawyer; b. Wilbur, Wash., Dec. 24, 1946; s. Albert Ellsworth and Margaret Lucille (Thomson) L.; m. Arlene R. Fegles, July 31, 1976; children: Hunter, Celeste. BA in Polit. Sci. with high honors, Wash. State U., 1969; JD, U. Chgo., 1972. Bar: Wash. 1973, U.S. Dist. Ct. (we. dist.) Wash. 1973, U.S. Dist. Ct. (ea. dist.) Wash. 1979. Assoc. Hullin, Roberts, Mines, Fite & Riveland, Seattle, 1973-76, Skeel, McKelvy, Henke, Evenson & Betts, Seattle, 1976-79; assoc., v.p. Underwood, Campbell, Brock, & Cerutti P.S., Spokane, Wash., 1979-80, ptnr., 1980—. Mem. ABA, Wash. State Bar Assn., Spokane Bar Assn., Assn. Trial Lawyers Am., Wash. State Trial Lawyers Assn., Def. Research Inst., Wash. Def. Trial Lawyers, Phi Beta Kappa, Phi Kappa Phi. Republican. Presbyterian. Federal civil litigation, State civil litigation, Personal injury. Home: W 629 23d Spokane WA 99203 Office: Underwood Campbell Brock et al 820 Lincoln Bldg Spokane WA 99201

LEISER, BURTON MYRON, philosophy educator, lawyer; b. Denver, Dec. 12, 1930; s. Nathan and Eva Mae (Newman) L.; m. Janet A. Johnson, Aug. 12, 1983; children by previous marriage—Shoshana, Illana, Phillip; stepchildren—Ellen Tabor, David Tabor, Susan Tabor, Sheri Johnson. B.A., U. Chgo., 1951; M.H.L., Yeshiva U., 1956; Ph.D. (fellow), Brown U., 1968; J.D., Drake U., 1981. Bars: Iowa 1981, N.Y. 1985, U.S. Dist. Ct. (so. dist.) N.Y. 1986, U.S. Supreme Ct. 1986. Instr. philosophy Fort Lewis Coll., Durango, Colo., 1963-65; asst. prof. philosophy SUNY, Buffalo, 1965-68; assoc. prof. 1968-70; vis. assoc. prof. Judaic studies Sir George Williams U., Montreal, Que., Can., 1969-71; assoc. prof. philosophy Sir George Williams U., 1971-72; prof. Drake U., Des Moines, 1972-83; chmn. dept. Drake U., 1972-78; Edward J. Mortola prof. philosophy Pace U., 1983—; legal asst. Iowa Ct. Appeals, Des Moines, 1982-83; of counsel Nobile, Magarian & DiSalvo, Yonkers, N.Y., 1986—. Author: Custom, Law, and Morality, 1969, Liberty, Justice and Morals, 3d edit, 1986, Values in Conflict, 1981; contbr. articles to profl. jours. Bd. dirs. Bur. Jewish Edn., Des Moines, 1973-76, Polk County Mental Health Assn., 1974-76; bd. dirs. Hillel of Greater N.Y., 1985—. Recipient Am. Jurisprudence award (contracts), 1979; Danforth fellow, 1981; SUNY Research Found. grantee, 1967-68; Meml. Found. for Jewish Culture grantee, 1970-71; Exxon Found. grantee, 1973-74; Nat. Endowment Humanities grantee, 1978. Mem. AAUP, Authors Guild, Am. Philos. Assn., Internat. Soc. Legal and Social Philosophy, Am. Soc. Value Inquiry (pres.), Soc. Philos. and Public Affairs, Soc. Polit. and Legal Philosophy, Am. Profs. for Peace in Middle East (nat. exec. com., nat. sec.). Republican. Jewish. Avocations: photography, music. General practice, Family and matrimonial, Jurisprudence. Home: 11 Meadow Pl Briarcliff Manor NY 10510 Office: Pace U Pace Plaza New York NY 10038 also: Nobile Magarian & DiSalvo 20 S Broadway Yonkers NY 10701

LEISER, HARVEY WAYNE, lawyer; b. Denver, Mar. 4, 1950; s. Earl H. and Rosalee (Fried) L.; m. Jane B. Bronstien, June 1, 1975; children: Nicole Michelle, Jordan Harris, Wendy Elsa. BA, Stanford U., 1971; postgrad., George Washington U., 1972-73; JD, U. Denver, 1975. Bar: Colo. 1975, U.S. Dist. Ct. Colo. 1975, U.S. Ct. Appeals (10th cir.) 1975. Law clk., bailiff to judge Denver Dist. Ct., 1975-76; assoc. Montgomery, Little, Young, Campbell & McGrew P.C., Denver, 1976-81, ptnr., 1981-85; sole practice Denver, 1985-86; ptnr. Waldbaum, Corn, Koff, Berger & Leiser, P.C., Denver, 1987—. Mem. ABA, Colo. Bar Assn., Denver Bar Assn., Assn. Trial Lawyers Am., Colo. Trial Lawyers Assn. Federal civil litigation, State civil litigation, Personal injury. Office: 303 E 17th Ave #940 Denver CO 80203

LEISURE, PETER KEETON, lawyer; b. N.Y.C., Mar. 21, 1929; s. George S. and Lucille E. (Pelouze) L.; m. Kathleen Blair; Feb. 27, 1960; children: Mary Blair, Kathleen. B.A., Yale U., 1952; LL.B., U. Va., 1958. Bar: N.Y. 1959, U.S. Supreme Ct. 1966, D.C. 1979, U.S. Dist. Ct. Conn. 1981. Assoc. Breed, Abbott & Morgan, 1958-61; asst. U.S. atty. So. Dist. N.Y., 1962-66; partner firm Curtis, Mallet-Prevost, Colt & Mosle, 1967-78; ptnr. Whitman & Ransom, N.Y.C., 1978-84; judge U.S. District Court Southern New York, New York, NY, 1984—; lectr. Practising Law Inst., 1968-70. Contbr. articles to legal jours. Bd. dirs. Retarded Infants Services, 1968-78, pres., 1971-75; bd. dirs. Community Council of Greater N.Y., 1972-79, Youth Consultation Services, 1971-78; trustee Ch. Club of N.Y., 1973-81. Served as lt. USAR, 1953-55. Fellow Am. Bar Found., Am. Coll. Trial Lawyers; mem. Am. Law Inst., ABA, N.Y. State, City of N.Y. bar assns., Fed. Bar Council (trustee, v.p. 1973-78), Delta Kappa Epsilon, Phi Alpha Delta. Clubs: Madison (Conn.); Yale, Country (Fairfield); Squadron A (gov. 1981—), Pilgrims. Jurisprudence. Home: One East End Ave New York NY 10021 Office: US District Court Foley Square New York NY 10007 *

LEITNER, ANTHONY JOSEPH, lawyer; b. Bklyn., Dec. 16, 1943; s. Anthony J. and Doris (Burns) L.; m. Jennifer A., Aug. 10, 1968; children: Megan M., Wendy A., Helen E. BA, Columbia U., 1965; JD, Northwestern U., 1969. Bars: N.Y. 1970, U.S. Dist. Ct. (so. dist.) N.Y. 1971, U.S. Ct. Appeals (2d cir.) 1971. Assoc. Curtis Mallet-Prevost Colt & Mosle, N.Y.C., 1969-79; v.p., assoc. gen. counsel Goldman, Sachs & Co., N.Y.C., 1979—. Mem. Bd. Edn. South Orange Maplewood Sch. Dist., 1983-87. Mem. ABA (co-chmn. comml. uses of futures sub-com., co-chmn. futures regulationsub-com. of corp. banking and bus. law sect.), N.Y. State Bar Assn. (mem. commodity and futures regulation com.). Roman Catholic. Club: Downtown Athletic (N.Y.C.). Avocations: sailing, fishing. General corporate, Securities. Office: Goldman Sachs & Co 85 Broad St New York NY 10004

LEITNER, DAVID LARRY, lawyer; b. Bklyn., Feb. 20, 1956; s. Sol and Beatrice (Brodsky) L.; m. Jana L. Grady, Sept. 11, 1983; 1 child, Morgan Blaire. Student, SUNY, Brockport, 1974-75; BA, SUNY, Stony Brook, 1976; JD, U. Iowa, 1979. Bar: Iowa 1979, U.S. Dist. Ct. (no. and so. dists.) Iowa 1979, U.S. Ct. Appeals (2d, 7th and 8th cirs.) 1980, U.S. Tax Ct. 1981. Asst. atty. various counties, Iowa, 1979-81; assoc. Cooper, Sinnard & Cooper, Forest City, Iowa, 1981-83; sole practice Forest City, 1983; atty. Grinnell (Iowa) Mut. Reins. Co., 1983-86, Allied Group/AID Ins. Co., Des Moines, 1986—; referee judicial hospitalization Winnebago County, Ia., 1983. Contbr. articles to profl. jours. Mem. ABA (speaker, mem. tort and ins. practice sect., regional editor Excess/Surplus Lines, reins. com. newsletter,), Iowa Bar Assn. (bridge gap com., Mason Ladd award com.), Assn. Trial Lawyers Am., Iowa Def. Counsel Assn., Fedn. Ins. and Corp. Counsel. Jewish. Avocations: photography, furniture bldg. Federal civil litigation, Personal injury, Insurance. Home: 4954 NW Lovington Dr Des Moines IA 50310 Office: Allied Group/AID Ins Co Box 974 Des Moines IA 50304

LEITNER, GREGORY MARC, lawyer; b. Chattanooga, Apr. 19, 1957; s. Paul Revere and Suzanne Joy Leitner; m. Cathy Anne Cannon, July 31, 1982; children Gregory Marc, Jr. and Ashley Meredith. BA cum laude, Memphis State U., 1978; JD, U. Tenn., Knoxville, 1980. Bar: Tenn. 1981, U.S. Dist. Ct. (ea. dist.) 1981, U.S. Ct. Appeals (6th cir.) 1983. Ptnr. Leitner, Warner, Moffitt, Williams, Dooley, Carpenter & Napolitan, Chattanooga, 1986—. Mem. ABA, Tenn. Bar Assn., Pi Sigma Alpha, Phi Delta Phi. Republican. Methodist. Avocations: politics, international politics, history. Federal civil litigation, Insurance, Labor. Home: 951 Whippoorwill Signal Mountain TN 37377

LEITNER, PAUL R., lawyer; b. Winnsboro, S.C., Nov. 11, 1928; s. W. Walker and Irene (Lewis) L.; m. Jeannette C. Card, Mar. 16, 1985; children by previous marriage: David, Douglas Gregory, Reid, Cheryl. A.B., Duke U., 1950; LL.B., McKenzie Coll., 1954. Bar: Tenn. 1954. Pvt. practice law Chattanooga, 1954; assoc. firm Leitner, Warner, Moffitt, Williams, Dooley Carpenter & Napolitan and predecessor firms, 1952-57, ptnr., 1957—; Tenn. chmn. Def. Research Inst., Inc., 1978—. Bd. dirs. Family Service Agy., 1957-63, Chattanooga Symphony and Opera Assn., 1986—; mem. Chattanooga-Hamilton County Community Action Bd.; mem. Juvenile Ct. Commn., Hamilton Country, 1955-61, chmn., 1958-59; chmn. Citizens Com. for Better Schs.; mem. Met. Govt. Charter Commn. Served with U.S. Army, 1946-47. Named Young Man of Yr. Chattanooga Area, 1957. Fellow Am. Coll. Trial Lawyers, Tenn. Bar. Found; mem. Jr. C. of C. (pres. 1956-57), ABA, Chattanooga Bar Assn., Tenn. Bar Assn., Am. Judicature Soc., Fed. Ins. Counsel, Internat. Assn. Ins. Council, Am. Acad. Hosp. Attys., Trial Attys. Am., Tenn. Def. Lawyers Assn. (pres. 1975-76), Am. Bd. Trial Advs. Methodist. Federal civil litigation, State civil litigation, Personal injury. Home: Augusta Dr Lookout Mountain TN 37350

LEKSAN, THOMAS JOHN, lawyer; b. Cleve., May 23, 1952; s. John J. and Bertha (Mulec) L.; m. Cynthia Lahke, May 5, 1979. AA, U. Cin., 1972, BA, 1975; JD, No. Ky. U., 1982. Bar: Ohio 1982, U.S. Dist. Ct. (so. dist.) Ohio 1982, Ky. 1983. Assoc. Rendigs, Fry, Kiely & Dennis, Cin., 1982-87. Mem. ABA, Ohio Bar Assn., Cin. Bar Assn. Republican. Federal civil litigation, State civil litigation, Personal injury. Office: 1140 Bartlett Bldg 36 E 4th St Cincinnati OH 45202

LELEIKO, STEVEN HENRY, lawyer, educator, adminstr.; b. Bklyn., Oct. 28, 1942; s. Max and Sylvia (Nagler) L.; m. Jane Ellen Thieberger, June 2, 1978. B.A., Bklyn. Coll., 1963; J.D., N.Y.U., 1966. Bar: N.Y. 1967. VISTA vol. Camden (N.J.) Episcopal Community Ctr., 1966-68; coordinator Urban Affairs Lab., NYU Sch. Law, 1968-71, supervising atty. project on urban affairs and poverty law, 1968-70, dir. fieldwork, 1970-71, asst. to dean, 1971-75, asst. dean, 1975-80; clin. asst. prof., 1975-77, clin. assoc. prof., 1977-80; exec. dir. Washington Sq. Legal Services, Inc., N.Y.C., 1973-80; gen. counsel and chief adminstrv. officer South Bronx Devel. Orgn., Inc., N.Y.C., 1980-82; asst. to exec. dir. Practising Law Inst., 1983, assoc. dir. for mgmt. ops., 1984—; cons. Inst. Jud. Adminstrn., 1973, 1976-77; staff dir. Assn. Am. Law Schs.-ABA Com. on guidelines for clin. legal edn., 1977-79; cons. to Pres.'s Com. on Employment of Handicapped, 1979-80. Mem. profl. adv. bd. to D.C. 37 Mcpl. Employees Legal Services Plan, 1977-85; chmn. N.Y. State Coll. Young Democrats, 1964-65. Recipient Urban Work award OEO, 1967; commendation Pres.'s Com. on Employment of Handicapped, 1981. Mem. N.Y. State Bar Assn., Assn. Bar City N.Y., ABA, Assn. Continuing Legal Edn. Adminstrs. Author: Camden, New Jersey, 1967; State Rules Permitting the Student Practice of Law: Comparisons and Comments, 1973; (with F. Klein and J. Mavity) Bar Admission Rules and Student Practice Rules, 1978; (with others) The Law and Disabled People, 1980; contbr. articles on law to profl. jours. General practice, Labor, Non-Profit Organizations.

LEMANN, THOMAS BERTHELOT, lawyer; b. New Orleans, Jan. 3, 1926; s. Monte M. and Nettie E. (Hyman) L.; m. Barbara M. London, Apr. 14, 1951; children: Nicholas B., Nancy E. A.B. summa cum laude, Harvard U., 1949, LL.B., 1952; M.C.L., Tulane U., 1953. Bar: La. 1953. Since practiced in New Orleans; asso. Monroe & Lemann, 1953-58, partner, 1958—; dir. B. Lemann & Bro., Mermentau Mineral & Land Co., Lastarmco, Inc. Contbr. articles to profl. publs. Mem. council La. State Law Inst., sec. trust adv. com.; chmn. Mayor's Cultural Resources Com., 1970-75; pres. Arts Council Greater New Orleans, 1975-80; mem. vis. com. art museums Harvard U., 1974-80; trustee Metairie Park Country Day Sch., 1956-71, pres., 1967-70; trustee New Orleans Philharmonic Symphony Soc., 1956-78, Flint-Goodridge Hosp., 1960-70, La. Civil Service League, pres., 1974-76; bd. dirs. Longue Vue Found., Zemurray Found., New Orleans Mus. Art.Served with AUS, 1944-46, PTO. Mem. ABA, La. Bar Assn. (bd. govs. 1977-78), New Orleans Bar Assn., Assn. Bar City N.Y., Am. Law Inst., Soc. Bartolus, Phi Beta Kappa. Jewish. Clubs: New Orleans Country, Wyvern (New Orleans); Harvard (N.Y.C.). Home: 6020 Garfield St New Orleans LA 70118 Office: 201 Saint Charles Ave New Orleans LA 70170

LEMANSKI, DAVID ALAN, lawyer; b. Ames, Iowa, Feb. 4, 1951; s. Lawrence Leonard and Mary Jean (Smith) L.; m. Ellen Margaret Dresang, May 18, 1974; children: Alexander, Aniela. BA, U. WIs., 1973, MA, 1976; JD, Drake U., 1979. Bar: Iowa 1979, Colo. 1979, U.S. Dist. Ct. Colo. 1979, U.S. Dist. Ct. (no. dist.) Iowa 1981. Assoc. Myles J. Dolan, P.C., Arvada, Colo., 1979-81; atty. Dubuque (Iowa) County Atty.'s Office, 1981-85; sole practice Dubuque, 1981-85; assoc. Fuerste, Carew, Coyle, P.C., Dubuque, 1985—. Mem. Dubuque County Dem. Cen. Com., 1984—. Mem. ABA, Colo. Bar Assn., Iowa Bar Assn., Dubuque County Bar Assn. Roman Catholic. Avocations: woodworking, American history, swimming. State civil litigation, Workers' compensation. Office: Fuerste Carew et al 200 Security Bldg Dubuque IA 52001

LEMBERG, FREDERIC GARY, lawyer; b. Los Angeles, Sept. 25, 1944; s. Jack and Rose (Zuckerman) L.; m. Sharon Lee Probst; children: William Derek, Carren Lynn, Serena Melody. BS in Acctg., Ariz. State U., 1966, JD magna cum laude, 1971. Bar: Ariz. 1971, U.S. Dist. Ct. Ariz. 1971, U.S. Ct. Appeals (9th cir.) 1977. Ptnr. Pollock & Lemberg, Phoenix, 1971-73, Lemberg, Green, Lester & Walsh, Phoenix, 1973-76, Mallin & Lemberg, Phoenix, 1980-83, Fannin, Terry, Hay & Lemberg, P.A., Phoenix, 1983—. Mem. ABA, Ariz. Bar Assn., Maricopa County Bar Assn., Assn. Trial Lawyers Am., Ariz. Trial Lawyers Assn., Ariz. State U. Law Sch. Alumni Assn. (bd. dirs. 1971-72). Federal civil litigation, State civil litigation. Office: Fannin Terry Hay & Lemberg 100 W Washington St Phoenix AZ 85003

LEMCOOL, MICHAEL JAMES, lawyer; b. Traverse City, Mich., Nov. 20, 1955; s. Carl Anthony and Wilma Louise (Seeley) L. AA, Northwest Mich. Coll., Traverse City, 1975; AAS in Legal Assisting, Ferris State Coll., Big Rapids, Mich., 1977, BS in Bus., 1977; JD, Wayne State U., 1980. Bar: Mich. 1980, U.S. Dist. Ct. (we. dist.) Mich. 1981. Assoc. Clancey & Price, P.C., Traverse City, 1980-82; prin. Lemcool & Assoc., P.C., Traverse City, 1983—; asst. prosecutor Leelanau County, 1983—. Parade com. Nat. Cherry Festival, Traverse City, 1980—; pres. Boys and Girls, Inc., Traverse City, 1982-83. Mem. Grand Traverse, Leelanau, Antrim Bar Assn. (treas. young lawyers sect. 1985-87, pres. exchange club 1986—). Republican. Club: Exchange of Traverse City (v.p. 1985-86). Lodge: Elks. Avocations: piloting, scuba diving, water skiing, skiing, theatre. General practice, Family and matrimonial, Real property. Office: Lemcool & Assocs PC 106 Rose St Traverse City MI 49684

LEMIRE, JEROME ALBERT, lawyer, geologist; b. Cleve., June 4, 1947; s. George A. and Matilda (Simon) L.; m. Sandra Marsick, Oct. 1, 1976; children—Laura, Lesley, Thomas. B.S. in Geology, Ohio State U., 1969, M.S. in Geology, 1973, J.D., 1976. Bar: Ohio 1976; cert. fin. planner. Geologist United Petroleum Co., Columbus, Ohio, 1976-77; assoc. Brownfield, Bowen & Bally, Columbus, 1977-79; land mgr. POI Energy Inc., Cleve., 1979-81; cons., Jefferson, Ohio, 1981-83; v.p. Carey Resources Inc., Jefferson, 1984-86; pres. Lemire & Assocs. Inc., Jefferson, 1986—. cons., 1986—. Vice chmn. Tech. Adv. Council, Columbus, 1984—. Served to 1st lt. U.S. Army, 1970-72. Mem. ABA, Ohio Bar Assn., Am. Assn. Petroleum Geologists, Am. Assn. Petroleum Landman, Inst. Cert. Fin. Planners. Democrat. Roman Catholic. Oil and gas leasing, Environment, State civil litigation. Home: 838 State Route 46 N Jefferson OH 44047

LEMLY, THOMAS ADGER, lawyer; b. Dayton, Ohio, Jan. 31, 1943; s. Thomas Moore and Elizabeth (Adger) l.; m. Kathleen Brame, Nov. 24, 1984; children: Elizabeth Hayden, Joanna Marsden. BA, Duke U., 1970; JD, U. N.C., 1973. Bar: Wash. 1973, U.S. Dist. Ct. (we. dist.) Wash. 1973, U.S. Ct. Appeals (9th cir.) 1975, U.S. Supreme Ct. 1980. Assoc. Davis, Wright & Jones, Seattle, 1973-79, ptnr., 1979—. Contbg. editor: Employment Discrimination Law, 1984. Chmn. Pacific Coast Labor Conf., Seattle, 1983; trustee Plymouth Congregational Ch., Seattle, 1980-84. Served to 1st lt. U.S. Army 1966-69. Mem. ABA (labor employment law sect. 1975—, subcom. chmn. 1984—, liaison com. 1982—), Seattle-King County Bar Assn. (chmn. labor sect.), U. N.C. Bar Found. (bd. dirs. 1973-76), Duke Alumni ASsn. (pres. 1979-84). Republican. Congregationalist. Club: Wash. Athletic (Seattle). Lodge: Rotary. Labor. Home: 1614 7th Ave W Seattle WA 98119 Office: Davis Wright & Jones 1501 4th Ave 2600 Century Sq Seattle WA 98101-1688

LEMMON, HARRY THOMAS, state supreme court justice; b. Morgan City, La., Dec. 11, 1930; s. Earl and Gertrude (Blum) L.; m. Mary Ann Vial; children: Andrew, Laruen, Roslyn, Carla, Jake, Patrick. B.S., Southwestern La. Inst., 1952; LL.B. cum laude, Loyola U., New Orleans, 1963. Atty. firm Vial, Vial & Lemmon, Hahnville, La., 1963-70; judge Court Appeals 4th Cir., 1970-80; assoc. justice Supreme Ct. La., New Orleans, 1980—; guest lectr. Loyola U., New Orleans; vis. prof. law La. State U. Law Ctr. Served with U.S. Army. Jurisprudence. Office: Supreme Ct La 301 Loyola Ave New Orleans LA 70112 *

LEMMON, JOHN VINCENT, lawyer; b. Sacramento, Mar. 26, 1917; s. Dal Millington and May Alice (Dunn) L.; m. Patricia Isabel High, Sept. 5, 1953; children: John, Paul, Patricia, Melanie, Mark, Christianne, Peter. BA, Stanford U., 1939; JD, U. San Francisco, 1951. Bar: Calif. 1952, U.S. Dist. Ct. (no. dist.) Calif. 1952, U.S. Tax Ct. 1983. Atty. Johnson & Lemmon, Sacramento, 1952-55, Lambert, Lemmon & Winchell, Sacramento, 1956-72; sole practice, Sacramento, 1972-79; ptnr. Lemmon & Lemmon, Sacramento, 1979—; mem. unlawful practice com. Sacramento County Bar, 1972-74; mem. Calif. Bar Commn. on Corrections, 1982—. Dist. chmn. Golden Empire council Boy Scouts Am., 1961-63; pres. Hosp. Planning Council, Sacramento, 1968-70; bd. dirs. Am. River Coll. Found., 1978—, pres., 1980. Served to lt. col. USAF, 1942-47. Decorated Air medal with 3 oak leaf clusters, D.F.C.; Paul Harris fellow Rotary Internat., 1976. Mem. State Bar Calif., Sacramento County Bar Assn. Republican. Roman Catholic. Lodges: Rotary (pres. Sacramento chpt. 1959, dist. gov. internat. dist. 519, 1964), K.C. (grand knight 1954-55). General corporate, Estate planning, Government contracts and claims. Home: 4744 Winding Way Sacramento CA 95841 Office: Lemmon & Lemmon 705 Merchant St Sacramento CA 95814

LEMON, LESLIE GENE, transportation company executive, lawyer; b. Davenport, Iowa, June 14, 1940. B.S., U. Ill., 1962, LL.B., 1964. Bar: Ill. 1964, Ariz. 1972. Asst. gen. counsel Am. Farm Bur. Fedn., Chgo., 1964-69; sr. atty. Armour and Co., Chgo., 1969-71; with Greyhound Corp., Phoenix, 1971—, sr. asst. gen. counsel, 1975-77, gen. counsel, 1977—, v.p., 1979—. Vestryman, All Saints Episcopal Ch., Phoenix, 1975—; trustee Phoenix Art Mus., 1985—. Mem. ABA, Assn. Gen. Counsel, Maricopa County Bar Assn., State Bar Ariz. General corporate. Home: 1012 W Las Palmaritas Dr Phoenix AZ 85021 Office: Greyhound Corp Greyhound Tower Phoenix AZ 85077

LEMPERT, RICHARD A., airline company executive, lawyer; b. 1932; married. B.A., Columbia U., 1953, LL.B., 1955. Assoc. Haight, Gardner, Poor & Haven, 1958-63; atty. Am. Airlines Inc., 1963-69, asst. v.p., asst. gen. counsel, 1969-72, v.p., gen. counsel, Dallas, 1972-83, sr. v.p., gen. counsel, 1983—. Served to lt. USCGR, 1955-58. General corporate. Office: AMR Corp PO Box 619616 Dallas/Ft Worth Airport TX 75261 *

LEMPERT, RICHARD OWEN, lawyer, educator; b. Hartford, Conn., June 2, 1942; s. Philip Leonard and Mary (Steinberg) L.; m. Cynthia Ruth Willey, Sept. 10, 1967; 1 child, Leah Rose. A.B., Oberlin Coll., 1964; J.D., U. Mich., 1968, Ph.D. in Sociology, 1971. Bar: Mich. bar 1978. Asst. prof. law U. Mich., Ann Arbor, 1968-72; assoc. prof. U. Mich., 1972-74, prof. law, 1974—, prof. sociology, 1985—; Mason Ladd disting. vis. prof. U. Iowa Law Sch., 1981; vis. fellow Centre for Socio-Legal Research, Wolfson Coll., Oxford (Eng.) U., 1982; mem. adv. panel for law and social sci. div. NSF, 1976-79, mem. exec. com. of adv. com. for social sci., 1979; mem. com. law enforcement and adminstrn. of justice NRC, vice chmn., 1984-87. Author: (with Stephen Saltzburg) A Modern Approach to Evidence, 1977, 2d edit., 1983; (with Joseph Sanders) An Invitation to Law and Social Science, 1986; editorial bd.: Law and Soc. Rev, 1972-77, editor, 1982-85; editorial bd. Evaluation Rev, 1979-82 , Violence and Victims, 1985—, Jour. Law and Human Behavior, 1980-82 ; contbr. articles to profl. jours. Mem. Am. Sociol. Assn., Law and Soc. Assn. (trustee 1977-80, exec. com. 1979-80, 82-87), Soc. Am. Law Tchrs., Order of Coif, Phi Kappa Phi, Phi Beta Kappa. Legal education, Evidence, law and social science. Office: Hutchins Hall Univ Mich Law Sch Ann Arbor MI 48109-1215

LENHART, JAMES THOMAS, lawyer; b. Cambridge, Mass., Nov. 3, 1946; s. James Wills and Martha Agnes (Everly) L.; m. Lynn Dexter Stevens, June 21, 1969; children—Amanda Brooks, James Edward, Abigail Ames. Cert. in History, U. Edinburgh, Scotland, 1967; A.B., Columbia U., 1968, J.D., 1972. Bar: N.Y. 1973, D.C. 1974. Clk. to judge U.S. Dist. Ct. (so. dist.) N.Y., 1972-73; assoc. Shaw, Pittman, Potts & Trowbridge, Washington, 1973-79, ptnr., 1980—; instr. Washington Coll. Law of Am. U., Washington, 1976-78. Exec. com. Westmoreland Congregational Ch., Washington, 1984, bd. dirs. 1978-79, 83-84. Harlan Fiske Stone scholar Columbia U.; 1968-69, 71-72. Mem. D.C. Def. Lawyers Assn., ABA, D.C. Bar Assn. Democrat. Mem. United Ch. of Christ. Federal civil litigation, Securities, Personal injury. Office: Shaw Pittman Potts & Trowbridge 2300 N St NW Washington DC 20037

LENIHAN, ROBERT JOSEPH, II, lawyer; b. Detroit, Jan. 16, 1947; s. Robert J. and Rita M. (O'Rourke) L.; m. Ann Carolyn Kelly, July 3, 1971; children: Robert J. III, James K. BS, Xavier U., 1969; JD cum laude, Wayne State U., 1972. Bar: Mich. 1972, U.S. Dist. Ct. (ea. dist.) Mich. 1972, U.S. Dist. Ct. (we. dist.) Mich. 1974, U.S. Ct. Appeals (6th cir.) 1986. Ptnr. Lenihan & Plese, Birmingham, Mich., 1972-85; of counsel Colombo & Colombo, Birmingham, 1986—. Served to maj. USAR, 1973—. Mem. ABA, Mich. Bar Assn., Oakland County Bar Assn., Fed. Bar Assn., Order of Barristers. Clubs: Detroit Boat (pres. 1985-86), Recess. Avocations: golf, carpentry, reading, boating. General corporate, Real property, Federal civil litigation. Office: Colombo & Colombo 1500 N Woodward Birmingham MI 48011

LENIHAN, THOMAS PARKER, lawyer; b. Jan. 10, 1952; s. Harold Eugene and Ruth Irene (Nelson) L.; children—Ryan Thomas, Katherine Erin. B.B.A., U. Iowa, 1974; J.D., Drake U., 1977. Bar: Iowa 1977, U.S. Dist. Ct. (so. dist.) Iowa 1978, U.S. Dist. Ct. (no. dist.) Iowa 1979. Asst. county atty. Polk County, Des Moines, 1977-79; assoc. Marks, Marks & Marks Law Firm, Des Moines, 1979-83; ptnr. Reed & Lenihan, West Des Moines, Iowa, 1983—. Chmn. parish council Sacred Heart Roman Catholic Ch., West Des Moines, 1982, parish trustee, 1982; chmn. Des Moines Ann. St. Patrick's Day Parade, 1981-82. Mem. Friendly Sons St. Patrick (pres. Des Moines 1982-83, Irishman of Yr. award 1984, chmn., bd. of govs. 1986—). Democrat. Probate, Real property, Workers' compensation. Office: Reed & Lenihan Suite 2600 72d St Suite D Des Moines IA 50322

LENN, STEPHEN ANDREW, lawyer; b. Ft. Lauderdale, Fla., Jan. 6, 1946; s. Joseph Abraham and Ruth Leah (Kreis) L.; m. Ksenia Jankovich, May 17, 1985; 1 child, Daniel. BA, Tufts U., 1967; JD, Columbia U., 1970. Bar: N.Y. 1971, U.S. Dist. Ct. (ea. and so. dists.) N.Y. 1971, Ohio 1978, U.S. Dist. Ct. (no. dist.) Ohio 1978. Assoc. Kronish, Lieb, Shainswit, Weiner & Hellman, N.Y.C., 1970-72, Shereff, Friedman, Hoffman & Goodman, N.Y.C., 1972-75; exec. v.p. Union Commerce Corp. Union Commerce Bank, Cleve., 1975-83; adminstrv. ptnr. Cleve. office Porter, Wright, Morris & Arthur, 1983—. Trustee Jewish Community Ctr., Cleve., 1980—, Northcoast Devel. Corp., Cleve., 1985-86, Cleve. Modern Dance Assn., 1985-86; bd. of govs. Cleve. Israel Bond, 1983—. Mem. ABA (charter, investment services com.), Ohio Bar Assn., Assn. of Bar of City of N.Y. Clubs: Union, Oakwood Country Club (Cleve.). Banking, General corporate, Securities. Office: Porter Wright Morris & Arthur 925 Euclid Cleveland OH 44115

LENT, BERKELEY, state supreme court justice; b. Los Angeles, Sept. 22, 1921; s. Oscar Paul and Patricia Lucile (Berkeley) L.; m. Joan Kay Burnett, Dec. 27, 1968; children: Patricia Brandt, Deirdre, Eric, Terry Ling. Student, Reed Coll., 1941, 46-47, Occidental Coll., Los Angeles, 1944-45; J.D., Willamette U., 1950. Bar: Oreg. 1950. Asso. editor Bancroft-Whitney Law Pub. Co., San Francisco, 1950; with Office Gen. Counsel, Bonneville Power Adminstrn., Portland, Oreg., 1950-51, 52-53; individual practice law Coos Bay, Oreg., 1951-52; asso. firm Peterson & Pozzi, Portland, 1952-53; partner firm Lent, York, Paulson & Bullock (and predecessor firms), Portland, 1953-70; individual practice law Portland, 1970-71; judge Circuit Ct., Multnomah County, 1971-77; assoc. Oreg. Supreme Ct., Salem, 1977-82, 83—, chief justice, 1982-83. Mem. Oreg. Ho. of Reps., 1957-65, minority whip, 1965; mem. Oreg. Senate, 1967-71, majority leader, 1971. Served with USNR, 1942-45. Mem. VFW, Am. Legion. Democrat. Club: Elks. Jurisprudence. Office: Oreg Supreme Ct 1147 State St Salem OR 97310

LENTS, ANN, lawyer; b. Houston, Sept. 4, 1949; d. Max Richey and Mary Frances (Hunsicker) L.; m. James David Heaney II, Aug. 11, 1973; children: J. David, Mary Elizabeth. BA, Wellesley Coll., 1971; JD, U. Tex., 1974. Bar: Tex. 1974, U.S. Dist. Ct. (so. dist.) Tex. 1975, U.S. Ct. Appeals (5th, 10th and 11th cirs.) 1981, U.S. Supreme Ct. 1982. Assoc. Vinson & Elkins, Houston, 1974-81, ptnr., 1981—. Fellow Tex. Bar Found., Houston Bar Found.; mem. ABA, Tex. Bar Assn., Houston Bar Assn. (bd. dirs. antitrust sect. 1977-79), Ex-editors Assn. Tex. Law Rev., Houston Bus. Forum (bd. dirs. 1982), U. Tex. Law Sch. Assn. (bd. dirs. 1981-82). Presbyterian. Antitrust, Federal civil litigation. Office: Vinson & Elkins 1001 Fannin 3300 First City Tower Houston TX 77002

LENTS, DON GLAUDE, lawyer; b. Kansas City, Mo., Nov. 4, 1949; s. Donald Victor and Helen Maxine (Draper) L.; m. Peggy Lynn Iglauer, Aug. 27, 1972; children: Stacie Lee, Kelsey Lynn. BA magna cum laude, Harvard U., 1971, JD magna cum laude, 1974. Bar: Mo. 1974, U.S. Dist. Ct. (ea. dist.) Mo. 1975, U.S. Ct. Appeals (8th cir.) 1975. Jr. ptnr. Bryan, Cave, McPheeters & McRoberts, St. Louis, 1974-81, ptnr., 1982, 84—; ptnr. Bryan, Cave, McPheeters & McRoberts, London, 1982-84; lectr. law Washington U., 1979-80. Bd. dirs. Leadership St. Louis, Inc., 1978-81, 86—, Coro Found., St. Louis, 1986—. Sheldon fellow Harvard U., 1974-75. Mem. ABA, Mo. Bar Assn., Met. St. Louis Bar Assn. (bus. law sect.), Inst. of Dirs., Hasty Pudding Inst. of 1776. Clubs: Noonday, Mo. Athletic, Westwood Country, Harvard (St. Louis) (exec. com. 1978-82); Inst. Dirs. (London). General corporate, Private international, Securities. Office: Bryan Cave McPheeters & McRoberts 500 N Broadway Saint Louis MO 63102

LENTZ, EDWARD JAMES, lawyer; b. Northampton, Pa., Dec. 29, 1952; s. Julius Edward and Pauline (Herber) L.; m. Claudia Jean Shultz, Aug. 4, 1975; children: Christopher Edward, Michael James. BA in Polit. Sci. summa cum laude, Moravian Coll., 1974; JD cum laude, U. Pa., 1977. Bar: Pa. 1977, U.S. Dist. Ct. (ea. dist.) Pa. 1977. Assoc. Pepper, Hamilton & Scheetz, Phila., 1977-82; ptnr. Butz, Hudders, Tallman, Stevens & Johnson, Allentown, Pa., 1982—. Assoc. editor U. Pa. Law Rev., 1976, editor, 1977. Trustee Good Shepherd Workshop/Vocat. Services, Allentown, 1982—; mem. Ad Hoc Planning Com., Lower Saucon Twp., Pa., 1984; bd. dirs. Lehigh Valley Easter Seals Soc., Bethlehem, Pa., 1985—. Mem. ABA, Pa. Bar Assn., Lehigh County Bar Assn., Lehigh Valley Estate Planning Council (bd. dirs. 1985—), Order of Coif. Democrat. Mem. United Ch. Christ. Clubs: Livingston (Allentown) (bd. dirs. 1986—), Saucon Valley Country (Bethlehem). Probate, Estate taxation, Estate planning. Home: RD #7 Black River Rd Bethlehem PA 18015 Office: Butz Hudders Tallman Stevens & Johnson 740 Hamilton Allentown PA 18101

LENTZ, ROBERT HENRY, lawyer; b. Lake Huntington, N.Y., Dec. 9, 1924; s. Henry Bernard and Mary (Mahony) L.; m. Ruth Tyerman (dec. Oct. 1985); children—Joanne, Kevin, Robert. Student, U. Ky., 1943; B.E.E. magna cum laude, Poly. Inst. Bklyn., 1951; J.D., Loyola U. at Los Angeles, 1956. Bar: Calif. bar 1956. Sr. v.p., gen. counsel Litton Industries, Inc., Beverly Hills, Calif., 1954—; past dir. Redcor Corp.; past chmn. bd. Topaz Industries. Served with AUS, 1943-46. Fellow Poly. Inst. N.Y., 1983; Mem. Los Angeles Patent Law Assn. Mem. State Bar Calif. (panelist for continuing edn. of bar on corp. law 1973-75, mem. corp. law com. of corp. and bus. law sect. 1978—), Am. Arbitration Assn. (Los Angeles adv. council 1968—, dir. 1984—), ABA, Los Angeles Patent Law Assn., Licensing Execs. Soc., Eta Kappa Nu, Tau Beta Pi. General corporate. Home: 10450 Wilshire Blvd Los Angeles CA 90024 Office: Litton Industries Inc 360 N Crescent Dr Beverly Hills CA 90210

LENZ, LAURENCE HENRY, SR., lawyer, insurance exec.; b. Springfield, Ill., Mar. 14, 1923; s. Edward L. and Dorothea A. (Bogaske) L.; m. Dorothy Joann Neu, Oct. 6, 1951; children—Cathy Lenz Shackelford, Larry, John, Steven, Richard. B.S. in Acctg., U. Ill., 1948, J.D., 1968. Bar: Ill. 1950, N.Y. 1975, La. 1981; C.L.U., C.P.C.U. Sole practice, Springfield, 1950-57; asst. atty. gen. Ill., 1957-59; counsel Ill. Ins. Dept., 1959-60; counsel Continental Casualty & Continental Assurance Co., Chgo., 1961-65; asst. gen. counsel III, Agrl. Assn. and Affiliated Ins. Mut. Fund and other service cos., Bloomington, Ill., 1965-67; corp. counsel Marsh-McLennan Cos., Inc., 1967-79, sec., 1967-76, sec. subs., 1967-79; corp. counsel William M. Mercer Inc., Putnam Fund Group, sec. Marsh and McLennan Cos., 1968-75, sr. atty. for ins. affairs, 1979-81; mem. Levy, Oubre, Lenz & Rosenthal, New Orleans, 1981-83, pres. Key Life Ins. Co. of S.C., 1981-83, Lenz Securities, Inc., 1982—; v.p. Petromar Assurance, Ltd., 1983-85; practice law, New Orleans, 1985—. Served with U.S. Army, 1942-45. Decorated Bronze Star, 3 battle stars. Mem. Am. Soc. Corp. Secs., Inc., Nat. Assn. Securities Dealers (registered prin.). Club: Bards of Bohemia (New Orleans). General corporate, Insurance, Contracts commercial. Office: Richards Bldg Suite 610 837 Gravier St New Orleans LA 70112 *

LENZI, ALBERT JAMES, JR., lawyer; b. Chgo.; s. Albert J. Sr. and Helen (Katsuleas) L.; m. Erin Jennifer Crowley, Mar. 31, 1985; children: April Lynn Sorensen, Sean Patrick Sorensen. Student, U.S. Naval Acad., 1972-74; BA, Loyola U., Chgo., 1976; JD, U. Pacific, 1979. Bar: Calif. 1979, U.S. Dist. Ct. (ea. dist.) Calif. 1982. Asst. prof. law Willamette U., Salem, Oreg., 1979-80; assoc. Thompson, Mayhew & Michel, Sacramento, 1980-81, Goldstein, Barceloux & Goldstein, Chico, Calif., 1981-82, Brislain & Zink, Chico, 1982-84; ptnr. Brislain, Zink & Lenzi, Chico, 1984—. Assoc. legis. editor Pacific Law Jour., 1978-79; contbr. articles and revs. to bar jours. Mem. ABA, Calif. Bar Assn., Assn. Trial Lawyers Am., Calif. Trial Lawyers Assn. Democrat. Greek Orthodox. Personal injury, Insurance, State civil litigation. Home: 939 Arbutus Ave Chico CA 95926 Office: Brislain Zink & Lenzi 20 Independence Sq Philadelphia Circle Chico CA 95926

LEON, JACK PAUL, lawyer; b. Harlingen, Tex., Oct. 17, 1950; s. Fred George Leon and Barbara Dallal; m. Rosemary Urrutia, June 1, 1977; stepchildren: Elaine, Katherine, Joe III, Jon Christian, Maria Luz, Laurence; 1 child from a previous marriage, Jack Paul Jr. BBA, Tex. A&I U., 1956; JD, St. Mary's U., San Antonio, 1959. Bar: Tex. 1959, U.S. Dist. Ct. (we., so., ea. and no. dists.) 1964, U.S. Ct. Appeals (5th cir.) 1974, U.S. Supreme Ct. 1974. Asst. dist. atty. Bexar County Dist. Attys. Office, San Antonio, 1959-62; ptnr. Ferro & Leon, San Antonio, 1962-68, Lieck, Lieck & Leon,

San Antonio, 1968-71; assoc. Baskin, Casseb, Gilliland & Rogers, San Antonio, 1971-74; ptnr. Casseb, Leon, Rodgers, Strong & Pearl, San Antonio, 1971-74, Leon & Bayless, San Antonio, 1980—; lectr. white collar crime, San Antonio; instr. Tex. Assn. New Lawyers; moderator, lectr. Criminal Def. Insts., Tex. Active Dem. Party, rep. Bexar County (Tex.) Dem. Party in Fed. Ct. various occasions. Served to tech. sgt. USAF, 1948-53. Recipient Disting. Alumni award St. Mary's U. Sch. Law, San Antonio, 1985-86. Mem. ABA, Tex. Bar Assn., San Antonio Bar Assn., San Antonio Trial Lawyers Assn. (chmn. criminal law and procedure com. 1967-68), San Antonio Criminal Def. Lawyers Assn. (bd. dirs. 1978), Tex. Criminal Def. Lawyers Assn. (bd. dirs. 1982-83), St. Mary's U. Sch. Law Alumni Assn. (bd. dirs. 1978-82, pres. 1980-81), VFW. Roman Catholic. Clubs: The Argyle, St. Anthony (San Antonio). Criminal, Federal civil litigation, Family and matrimonial. Home: 150 Thelma San Antonio TX 78212 Office: 500 Lexington San Antonio TX 78215

LEON, RICHARD JOHN, lawyer; b. South Natick, Mass., Dec. 3, 1949; s. Silvano B. and Rita (O'Rorke) L.; m. M-Christine Costa. A.B., Holy Cross Coll., 1971; J.D. cum laude, Suffolk Law Sch., 1974; LL.M., Harvard U., 1981. Bar: U.S. Supreme Ct. 1984, R.I. 1975, U.S. Ct. Appeals (2d cir.) 1977, U.S. Dist. Ct. R.I. 1976. Law clk. to justices Superior Ct. Mass., 1974-75, to justice R.I. Supreme Ct., 1975-76; gen. atty. immigration and naturalization U.S. Dept. Justice, 1976-77; spl. asst. U.S. atty. U.S. Dist. Ct. (so. dist.) N.Y., 1977-78; asst. prof. law St. John's U. Law Sch., 1979-83; trial atty., criminal sect., tax div. U.S. Dept. Justice, Washington, 1983—. Contbr. articles to legal jours. Mem. ABA, Am. Portuguese Soc., Order of Barristers, R.I. Bar Assn., Fed. Bar Council, Suffolk Law Sch. Assn. Met. N.Y. (past pres.), Suffolk Law Sch. Assn. Met. Washington (v.p. 1984—). Clubs: Harvard of N.Y.C., Harvard of Boston, University (Washington). Criminal, Personal income taxation, Legal education. Office: US Dept Justice Tax Div Criminal Sect 9th and Pennsylvania Ave Washington DC 20530

LEONARD, ARTHUR ALAN, lawyer; b. New Orleans, Oct. 3, 1952; s. Alan Jerry and Elizabeth Ann (Adney) L.; m. Andrea Marcia Roger, May 15, 1977; 1 child, Aaron. BA, U. Calif., Santa Barbara, 1976; JD cum laude, Tulane U., 1981. Bar: La. 1981, U.S. Dist. Ct. (ea. dist.) La. 1981, Calif. 1983, U.S. Dist. ct. (cen., no. and so. dists.) Calif. 1984. Assoc. McGlinchey, Stafford, Mintz, Cellini & Lang, New Orleans, 1981-83, Wilner, Narwitz, Lewin & Klein, Beverly Hills, Calif., 1983—. Mem. Maritime Law Assn. U.S. (assoc., com. on stevedoring and terminal ops.). Republican. Jewish. Admiralty. Home: 4124 Del Mar Long Beach CA 90807 Office: Wilner Narwitz Lewin & Klein 9601 Wilshire Blvd # 700 Beverly Hills CA 90210

LEONARD, ARTHUR SHERMAN, legal educator; b. Bklyn., Jan. 17, 1952; s. Harold A. and Jean (Moverman) L. B.S. in Indsl. and Labor Relations, Cornell U., 1974; J.D. cum laude, Harvard U., 1977. Bar: N.Y. 1978, U.S. Dist. Ct. (so. and ea. dists.) N.Y. 1978, U.S. Ct. Appeals (7th cir.) 1981, U.S. Supreme Ct. 1986. Assoc. Kelley Drye & Warren, N.Y.C., 1977-78, Seyfarth, Shaw, Fairweather & Geraldson, N.Y.C., 1979-82; asst. prof. law N.Y. Law Sch., 1982-83, assoc. prof., 1983—. lectr. on legal issues of AIDS. Editor Lesbian/Gay Law Notes, 1978—. Mem. Nat. Gay Task Force; active N.Y. Civil Liberties Union, Citizens Union of N.Y.; bd. dirs., mem. legal com. Lambda Legal Def. and Edn. Fund; counsel Congregation Beth Simchat Torah, N.Y.C.; legal cons. World Congress of Gay/Lesbian Jewish Orgns.; adminstr. Ind. Democratic Jud. Screening Panel, New York County, 1983; class agt. Harvard U. Law Sch. Fund. Mem. ABA (com. rights of gay people), Assn. Bar City N.Y. (com. sex and law 1982-85, chair 1987—, com. labor and employment law 1985-87), Am. Assn. Law Schs. (chmn. sect. gay/lesbian legal issues 1986), ACLU, Bar Assn. Human Rights of Greater N.Y. (pres. 1984—). Contbr. articles to legal jours. Labor, Civil rights, Legal education. Address: NY Law School 57 Worth St New York NY 10013

LEONARD, BRIAN FRANCIS, lawyer; b. Rolla, N.D., Jan. 27, 1948; s. Howard F. and Millie Mae (Olson) L.; m. Martha E. Ziff, Dec. 28, 1974; children: Sarah, Emily, Brian. BA, U. N.D.; JD, U. Minn. Bar: Minn. 1973, U.S. Dist. Ct. Minn. 1973, U.S. Ct. Appeals (8th cir.) 1976, U.S. Supreme 1981. Assoc. O'Neill, Burke and O'Neill, Ltd., St. Paul, 1973-78; ptnr. O'Neill, Burke and O'Neill, Ltd, St. Paul, 1978—; bus. law instr. adult extension St. Paul TV I, 1978—. Mem. ABA, Minn. Bar Assn. (bankruptcy sect.), St. Paul Jaycees (bd. dirs. 1975-79). Republican. Roman Catholic. Lodges: Rotary (chmn. com. St. Paul club 1985). Bankruptcy, Consumer commercial, Banking. Home: 1532 Tamberwood Trail Woodbury MN 55125 Office: 800 Norwest Ctr 55 E Fifth Saint Paul MN 55101

LEONARD, CHARLES JEROME, JR., lawyer; b. N.Y.C., June 2, 1936; s. Charles Jerome Sr.; m. Sara Ruth Jarrett, July 1, 1960; children: Cathia, Charles Jerome III. AB in Econs., U. N.C., 1960, JD, 1966. Bar: N.C. 1966, U.S. Supreme Ct. 1971. Supr. claims Travelers Ins. Co., Charlotte, N.C., 1960-64, 66-67; sole practice Charlotte, 1967—. Bd. dirs., counsel Charlotte Treatment Ctr., 1980—. Served to staff sgt. N.C. Air Nat. Guard, 1958-64. Mem. N.C. Bar Assn., N.C. Trial Lawyers Assn., N.C. Soc. Hosp. Attys. Republican. Episcopalian. Avocations: jogging, investments. General practice. Home: 1640 Maryland Charlotte NC 28205 Office: Leonard McNeely MacMillan & Durham 2460 First Union Plaza Charlotte NC 28282

LEONARD, GEORGE ADAMS, lawyer, retail food and drug company executive; b. Clinton, Iowa, June 16, 1924; s. George Tod and Lola Frances (Follett) L.; m. Viola Converse, Nov. 5, 1948 (div. 1985); children—Carolyn C., George T., Craig C., Julie A.; m. Donna Snider, July 2, 1986. A.B., U. Mich., 1948, J.D., 1951. Bar: Mich. 1951, Ohio 1956, U.S. Dist. Ct. (ea. dist.) Mich. 1951, U.S. Ct. Appeals (6th cir.) 1957, U.S. Ct. Appeals (D.C. cir.) 1964. Assoc. Slyfield, Hartman, Reitz & Tait, Detroit, 1951-56; atty. Kroger Co., Cin., 1956-61, supervising atty., 1961-64, gen. atty., 1964-66, gen. counsel, 1967—, v.p. 1968—, sec., 1968-86; dir. Gleaner Life Ins. Soc. Chmn. Greater Cin. United Appeal, 1984; bd. dirs. Community Chest; chmn. Cin. chpt. ARC. Served with USAAF, 1942-45. Decorated Air medal with five oak leaf clusters, D.F.C. Mem. ABA, Ohio Bar Assn., Mich. Bar Assn., Cin. Bar Assn., Am. Soc. Corp. Secs. (chmn. Cin. chpt. 1986—), Am. Corp. Counsel Assn. (pres. Cin. chpt. 1984). Clubs: Queen City, Kenwood Country. General corporate. Office: The Kroger Co 1014 Vine St Cincinnati OH 45201

LEONARD, JERRIS, lawyer; b. Chgo., Jan. 17, 1931; s. Jerris G. and Jean Marie (Reville) L.; m. Mariellen C. Mathie, Aug. 22, 1953; children: Mary Leonard Ralston, Jerris G., John E., Kathleen Ann, Francis X., Daniel J. B.S., Marquette U., 1952, J.D., 1955. Bar: Wis. 1955, D.C. 1973. Practice in Milw., 1955-69; mem. firm Michael, Best & Friedrich, 1964-69; asst. atty. gen. civil rights div. Dept. Justice, Washington, 1969-71; adminstr. Law Enforcement Assistance Adminstrn., 1971-73; ptnr. Leonard & McGuan, P.C., Washington, 1973—; Mem. Wis. Assembly from Milwaukee County, 1957-61; mem. Wis. Senate, 1961-69, senate majority leader, 1967-69; pres. Wis. Agys. Bldg. Corp., 1963-69; chmn. Wis. Legislative Council, 1967-69; Republican candidate for U.S. Senate, 1968; sr. adv. presdl. transition team, 1980-81. Named 1 of 5 Outstanding Young Men Wis. Jaycees, 1965. Mem. Am., Wis., D.C., Fed. bar assns., Am. Judicature Soc., Alpha Sigma Nu, Delta Sigma Pi, Sigma Nu Phi. Elections, State civil litigation, Federal civil litigation. Home: 5109 Manning Pl NW Washington DC 20016 Office: Manatt Phelps et al 1200 New Hampshire Ave NW Suite 200 Washington DC 20036

LEONARD, PAUL HARALSON, lawyer; b. Houston, Mar. 4, 1925; s. Paul Haralson and Dovie Lore (Shuler) L.; m. Barbara Ann Underwood, Nov. 26, 1948; children: Leslie Ann, Scott Paul. BA, Rice U., 1948; JD, South Tex. Coll. of Law, 1957. Bar: Tex. 1957, U.S. Patent and Trademark Office 1960, U.S. Supreme Ct. 1965, U.S. Ct. Appeals (5th cir.) 1981. Acct. Highland Oil Co., Houston, 1948-50; statis. acct. Union Oil & Gas Corp. of La., Houston, 1953-59; assoc. Hayden & Pravel, Houston, 1959-61; patent atty. Halliburton CO., Duncan, Okla., 1961-69; div. patent atty. Ethyl Corp., Baton Rouge, 1969; v.p. Cen. Foods, Inc., Baton Rouge, 1979—, bd. dirs. V.p. Plato Dependent Sch. Dist., Duncan, Okla., 1966-67, pres., 1968. Served to lt. comdr., USNR, 1942-67. Mem. Tex. Bar Assn., Am. Intellectual Property Assn. Republican. Club: Duncan Country. Lodge: Elks, Shriners, Masons. Avocations: U.S. coins, stamp collecting. Patent, General corporate, Personal income taxation. Home: 10639 Rondo Ave Baton Rouge LA 70815 Office: Ethyl Corp 451 Florida Baton Rouge LA 70801

LEONARD, WILL ERNEST, JR., lawyer; b. Shreveport, La., Jan. 18, 1935; s. Will Ernest and Nellie (Kenner) L.; m. Maureen Laniak; children—Will Ernest III, Sherry Elizabeth, Robert Scott, Stephen Michael, Christopher Anthony, Colleen Mary, Leigh Alison. B.A., Tulane U., 1956, LL.B., 1958; LL.M., Harvard U., 1966. Bar: La. 1958, D.C. 1963, U.S. Supreme Ct. 1963. Announcer sta. WVUE-TV, New Orleans, 1958-60; legislative asst. to U.S. Senator Russell B. Long, 1960-65; profl. staff mem. com. finance U.S. Senate, 1966-68; mem. Internat. Trade Commn. (formerly U.S. Tariff Commn.), 1968-77, chmn., 1975-76; Congl. staff fellow Am. Polit. Sci. Assn., 1965-66. Private international, Public international. Home: 7324 Bradley Blvd Bethesda MD 20817 Office: 1330 Connecticut Ave NW Suite 200 Washington DC 20036

LEONE, JAMES RUSSELL, lawyer; b. Washington, Apr. 28, 1943; s. George Russell and Dora Mae (Hougan) L.; m. Joyce Lynne Narem, June 12, 1965 (div. Dec. 1985); children: Thomas George, Mark Russell; m. RoseMary Louise Ciannella, Dec. 29, 1985. BS in Fin., U. Va., 1965; JD with honors, George Washington U., 1973. Bar: U.S. Dist. Ct. D.C. 1978, U.S. Ct. Appeals (D.C. cir.) 1978, Va. 1979, Ill. 1981, U.S. Dist. Ct. (no. dist.) Ill. 1981, Fla. 1985, U.S. Dist. Ct. (mid. dist.) Fla. 1986. Fin. analyst, atty. advisor U.S. SEC, Washington, 1966-81; assoc. Quinn, Jacobs, Barry and Miller, Chgo., 1981-84, Gray, Harris and Robinson, P.A., Orlando, Fla., 1984-85; sole practice Orlando, 1985—; chmn. Real Property Syndications Inc., Longwood, 1985—. EEO counselor U.S. SEC, Washington, 1973-81; mem. SEC EEO Coordinating subcom., Washington, 1976-77; pres. SEC Am. Fedn. Govt. Employees, Washington, 1970. Mem. ABA, Seminole County Bar Assn., Orange County Bar Assn., Am. Judicature Soc., Chgo. Bar Assn. (securities law com. 1981-85). Avocations: canoeing, sailing, camping, jogging. Real property, General corporate, Securities. Home: 3015 Moss Valley Pl Winter Park FL 32792 Office: 235 S Maitland Ave Suite 114 Maitland FL 32751

LEONHARDT, FREDERICK WAYNE, lawyer; b. Daytona Beach, Fla., Oct. 26, 1949; s. Frederick Walter and Gaetane Laura (Wirtanen) L.; m. Victoria Ann Cook, Dec. 27, 1975; children: Ashley Victoria, Frederick Whitaker. B.A., U. Fla. 1971, J.D., 1974. Bar: Fla. 1974, U.S. Dist. Ct. (mid. and no. dists.) Fla. 1975, U.S. Ct. Appeals (11th cir.) 1976, U.S. Supreme Ct. 1976, N.C. 1984, D.C. 1985. Gen. counsel com. on growth and energy Fla. Ho. of Reps., 1974-75; ptnr. Cobb & Cole, P.A., Daytona Beach, Fla., 1975-79; pres. Leonhardt, Upchurch & Parsons, P.A., Daytona Beach, Fla., 1979-86, Leonhardt & Upchurch, P.A., 1986—; bd. dirs. 1st Fla. Bank. Commr., Halifax Hosp. Dist. Bd., 1979—, sec., 1981-85, vice chmn., 1985—; pres. Volusia County Young Democrats, 1978—; pres. Seabreeze United Ch. Men's Assn.; trustee Seabreeze United Ch.; bd. dirs. Daytona Beach Area Com. of 100, Econ. Devel. Council; mem. bd. counselors Bethune-Cookman Coll.; mem. cabinet Volusia County United Fund, chmn. lawyers div.; chmn. United Way Community Found., gen. capmaign chmn. Volusia County, 1987; pres. Centurion council Statewide Service Orgn.; active Checkered Flag Com., Civic League; bd. dirs. Community Outreach Services; vice chmn. Volusia County Council Halifax Area Sports Complex Study Com.; bd. dirs. Nat. Collegiate Sports Festival. Served to 1st lt. USAR, 1974-75. Mem. ABA, Fla. Bar Assn., Volusia County Bar Assn. (dir.), Volusia County Alumni Club U. Fla. (pres.), Fla. Nat. Alumni Assn. (v.p. nominating com.), Fla. Bar (gov. young lawyers sect. 1981-84, chmn. legis. com. sect. 1982-84, chmn. com. conveyancing, chmn. continuing legal edn. program real estate law), Chamber Daytona Beach and Halifax Area (bd. dirs.), Fla. C. of C. (bd. dirs.), Phi Alpha Delta, Delta Chi. Club: Halifax. Lodges: Masons (32 degree), Rotary, Shriners. Real property, Administrative and regulatory, Contracts commercial. Office: Leonhardt & Upchurch PA Po Box 2134 Daytona Beach FL 32015

LEOPOLD, MARK FREUDENTHAL, lawyer; b. Chgo., Jan. 23, 1950; s. Paul F. and Corinne (Shapira) L.; m. Jacqueline Rood, June 9, 1974; children—Jonathan, David. B.A., Am. U., Washington, 1972; J.D., Loyola U., Chgo., 1975. Bar: Ill. 1975, Fla. 1976, U.S. Dist. Ct. (no. dist.) Ill. 1975, U.S. Ct. Appeals (7th cir.) 1976, U.S. Ct. Appeals (8th cir.) 1979. Assoc. McConnell & Campbell, Chgo., 1975-79; atty. U.S. Gypsum Co., Chgo., 1979-82, sr. litigation atty., 1982-84; sr. litigation atty. USG Corp., 1985-87, corp. counsel, 1987—; legal writing instr. Loyola U. Sch. Law, Chgo., 1978-79. Commr., Lake County, Ill., Waukegan, 1982-84, Forest Preserve, Libertyville, Ill., 1982-84, Pub. Bldg. Commn., Waukegan, Ill., 1980-82; chmn. Deerfield Twp. Republican Central Com., Highland Park, Ill., 1984-86 ; vice-chmn. Lake County Rep. Central Com., Waukegan, 1982-84. Recipient Disting. Service award Jaycees, Highland Park, Ill., 1983. Mem. ABA (antitrust com. 1976—, litigation com. 1980—, corps. com. 1981—), Chgo. Bar Assn. (antitrust com. 1976—, corp. counsel com. 1984—), Pi Sigma Alpha, Omicron Delta Kappa. Republican. Antitrust, Federal civil litigation, General corporate. Office: USG Corp 101 S Wacker Dr Chicago IL 60606

LEOPOLD, ROBERT BRUCE, lawyer; b. Toledo, Ohio, June 25, 1949; s. James A. and Florence B. (Barnett) L.; m. Cathryn Lucy Hagler, Nov. 2, 1978; 1 child, Maureen Ann. A.B., in Polit. Sci., Ind. U., 1971; J.D., Valparaiso U., 1974. Bar: Ill., Ind. 1975. Dep. prosecutor Lake County, Ind., 1975-76; assoc. Cohen, Cohen & Bullard, East Chicago, Ind., 1977-78; sole practice law, Munster, Ind., 1978—. Pres., Westlake Unit of Northwest Ind. div. Am. Heart Assn., 1982-85. Mem. ABA, Ind. Bar Assn., Ill. Bar Assn., Assn. Trial Layers of Am., Delta Theta Phi. State civil litigation, Family and matrimonial, General corporate. Address: 9335 Calumet Ave Suite D Munster IN 46321

LEOPOLD, VALERIE ANN, lawyer; b. Chgo., Feb. 13, 1953; d. Henry F. and Dorothy (Neldon). BA, Iowa State U., 1974; JD summa cum laude, Harvard U., 1977. Bar: Ill. 1978, U.S. Dist. Ct. (no. dist.) Ill. 1978, U.S. Ct. Appeals (5th cir.) 1979, U.S. Ct. Appeals (7th cir.) 1980. Assoc. Kirkland & Ellis, Chgo., 1977-82; ptnr. Levy, Leopold and Assoc., P.C., Chgo., 1982—. Bd. dirs. Harvard U. Legal Aid, Cambridge, Mass., 1976-77, Legal Clinic for Disabled, Chgo., 1985—. Guest faculty Nat. Inst. Trial Adv., Ill. Continuing Legal Edn., DePaul Law Sch.; mem. Chgo. Bar Assn. (legis. com.), Assn. Trial Lawyers Am., League of Women Voters, Phi Beta Kappa. Personal injury, Federal civil litigation, State civil litigation. Office: Levy Leopold and Assocs PC 35 E Wacker Dr Suite 3800 Chicago IL 60601

LEPORE, ALPHONSE PAUL, lawyer; b. Ambridge, Pa., Oct. 7, 1951; s. Alphonse Paul and Anne Marie (Bassetti) L.; m. Suzanne Diane Baird, June 23, 1982. BA in Polit. Sci., Pa. State U., 1973; JD, Duquesne U., 1976. Bar: Pa. 1976, U.S. Dist. Ct. (we. dist.) Pa. 1976, U.S. Ct. Appeals (3d cir.) 1978. Law clk. to presiding justice Fayette County Ct., Uniontown, Pa., 1975-77; assoc. William J. Franks, Atty., Uniontown, 1977-78; asst. pub. defender Fayette County, Uniontown, 1978-82, chief pub. defender, 1982—; ptnr. Lepore & Cicconi, Uniontown, 1982—. Bd. dirs. Fayette County Drug and Alcohol Assn. Mem. Pa. Bar Assn., Fayette County Bar Assn. (bd. dirs. 1980-82). Democrat. Roman Catholic. Avocations: flying, reading, handcraft models. Criminal, Real property, Family and matrimonial. Home: 45 Ben Lomond St Uniontown PA 15401 Office: Lepore & Cicconi 70 N Mount Vernon Uniontown PA 15401

LEPORE, RALPH THOMAS, III, lawyer; b. Framingham, Mass., Oct. 11, 1954; s. Ralph Thomas Jr. and Barbara (Ablondi) L.; m. Marianne Moruzzi, June 20, 1986; 1 child, Cristina Marie. BA, U. Mass., 1976; JD, Boston Coll., 1979. Bar: Mass. 1979, U.S. Dist. Ct. Mass. 1980, U.S. Ct. Appeals D.C. 1985. Assoc. Sheridan, Garrahan & Lander, Framingham, 1979-81; assoc. Warner & Stackpole, Boston, 1981-86, ptnr., 1987—. Mem. ABA, Mass. Bar Assn., Assn. Trial Lawyers Am., Lawyer-Pilots Bar Assn., Justinian Law Soc. (bd. dirs. 1984—). Democrat. Roman Catholic. Avocation: golf. Aviation, Environment, Insurance. Home: 1 Fox Hill Rd Framingham MA 01701 Office: Warner & Stackpole 28 State St Boston MA 02109

LE PROHN, ROBERT, lawyer, adminstrv. law judge; b. Boise, Idaho, Nov. 22, 1920; s. William Charles and Bonnie (Smith) Le P.; m. Frances Morrison, July 4, 1953 (div. 1968); children—Michele Frances, Nicole Suzanne, Robert Morrison. A.B., U. Calif., Berkeley, 1941, J.D., 1951. Bar: Calif. 1952, U.S. Dist. Ct. (no. dist.) Calif. 1952, U.S. Ct. Appeals (9th cir.) 1952, U.S. Supreme Ct. 1966. Assoc., ptnr. Tobriner, Lazarus, Brundage & Neyhart, San Francisco, 1952-60; ptnr. Le Prohn and Le Prohn, San Francisco, 1960-75; labor arbitrator, San Francisco, 1978—; adminstrv. law judge Agrl. Labor Relations Act, Calif., San Francisco, 1977—. Served to sgt. U.S. Army, 1944-46. Mem. ABA, San Francisco Bar Assn. Democrat. Contbg. author: Developing Labor Law, 1971. Labor. Home: 318 Chestnut St San Francisco CA 94133 Office: ALRB 915 Capitol Mall 2d Floor Sacramento CA 95814

LERMAN, CATHY JACKSON, lawyer; b. Norfolk, Va., Apr. 12, 1956; d. Donald Eugene and Shirley Pauline (Tetterton) Jackson; m. Steven Howard Lerman, June 23, 1985. BA in English, Old Dominion U., 1978; JD, Nova U., 1981. Bar: Fla. 1982, U.S. Dist. Ct. (so. dist.) Fla. 1982, U.S. Ct. Appeals (11th cir.) 1982, U.S. Supreme Ct. 1986. Assoc. Nancy Little Hoffman, P.A., Ft. Lauderdale, Fla., 1982-84; ptnr. Hoffman & Burris, Ft. Lauderdale, 1984-85; sole practice Ft. Lauderdale, 1985—; adj. prof. Nova U. Law Ctr., Ft. Lauderdale, 1984-85. Bd. dirs. Fla. Consumer Fedn. Named Outstanding Young Women of Yr. Outstanding Young Women in Am., 1981. Mem. ABA (chmn. appellate advocacy com. 1986, editor appellate advocacy newsletter 1986, rules and procedure com.), Assn. Trial Lawyers Am., Acad. Fla. Trial Lawyers (chmn. family law sect. 1985—, chmn. amicus com. 1986—), Fla. Bar Assn. (health law com.), Broward County Trial Lawyers Assn. (bd. govs. 1984—, newsletter editor 1985—, legis. com.). Presbyterian. Federal civil litigation, State civil litigation, Personal injury.

LERMAN, EILEEN R., lawyer; b. N.Y.C., May 6, 1947; d. Alex and Beatrice (Kline) L.; B.A., Syracuse U., 1969; J.D., Rutgers U., 1972; M.B.A., U. Denver, 1983. Admitted to N.Y. State bar, 1973, Colo. bar, 1976; atty. FTC, N.Y.C., 1972-74; corp. atty. RCA, N.Y.C., 1974-76; corp. atty. Samsonite Corp. and consumer products div. Beatrice Foods Co., Denver, 1976-78, assoc. gen. counsel, 1978—, asst. sec., 1979-85; ptnr. Davis and Lerman, Denver, 1985—; dir. Legal Aid Soc. of Met. Denver, 1979-80. Bd. dirs., vice chmn. Colo. Postsecondary Ednl. Facilities Authority, 1981—, HMO Colo.; bd. dirs., treas. Am. Jewish Com., also v.p.; mem. Leadership Denver, 1983. Mem. Colo. Women's Bar Assn. (dir. 1980-81), ABA, Colo. Bar Assn., Denver Bar Assn., N.Y. State Bar Assn., Rutgers U. Alumni Assn. Club: Soroptimist. General corporate, Family and matrimonial, State civil litigation. Home: 1018 Fillmore St Denver CO 80206 Office: Davis and Lerman 50 S Steele St Suite 420 Denver CO 80209

LERMAN, HERBERT S., lawyer; b. Cambridge, Mass., Mar. 15, 1938; s. Isaac and Anna (Wilner) L.; m. Ellen, July 1, 1962; children—David, Jonathan, Jennifer. A.B., Brown U., 1959; LL.B., New Eng. Sch. Law, 1962. Bar: Mass. 1962, U.S. Dist. Ct. Mass. 1963, U.S. Tax Ct. 1972, U.S. Ct. Appeals (1st cir.) 1985, U.S. Supreme Ct. 1986. Assoc. Nathanson & Rudofsky, Boston, 1962-64, Stanley Barron, Boston, 1964-66; ptnr. Lerman & Mann, Brookline, Mass., 1966—; lectr. real estate assns. including Rental Housing Assn. and Boston Real Estate; spl. citation Sec. Commonwealth Mass., 1984 Bd. Dir. Congregation Mishkan Tefila, Newton, Mass., 1979—, dir. Brotherhood, 1966—, pres., 1972-73; mem. Brookline Ct. Centennial Com., 1982, Oak Hill Park Assn., Newton, 1963—; apptd. to Newton Ambulance Com., 1976; mem. Jewish Big Bros. Assn.; chmn. tenant law subcommitee; trustee Boston Children's Theatre, 1980—; v.p. B'nai B'rith Realty Lodge, 1985—. Recipient Am. Jurisprudence prize, 1962, Jack Wilson Meml. award, 1984, B'nai B'rith awards 1985, 87. FellowMass. Bar Assn. (trustee, property sect., condominium law subcom., 21st Century Club); mem. Rental Housing Assn., Norfolk County Bar, Greater Boston Real Estate Bd., Mass. Acad. Trial Attys., Am. Judicature Soc., Am. Arbitration Assn., Mens Aux. (life), Recuperative Ctr. Assn. Club: New Century. Author: Residential Landlord-Tenant Law: A Modern Massachusetts Guide, 1977; developer standard leasing form for Rental Housing Assn. Real property, Landlord-tenant, General corporate. Home: 16 Kerr Path Newton MA 02159 Office: 111 Washington St Brookline MA 02146

LERMAN, LISA GABRIELLE, lawyer; b. Denver, Apr. 4, 1955; d. Leonard Solomon and Claire (Lindegren) L.; m. Philip Gordon Schrag, Dec. 29, 1985. BA, Barnard Coll., 1976; JD, NYU, 1979; LLM, Georgetown U., 1984. Staff atty. Ctr. for Women Policy Studies, Washington, 1979-81; clin. fellow Antioch Law Sch., Washington, 1982; adv. fellow Georgetown U. Law Ctr., Washington, 1982-84; vis. asst. prof. W.Va. U. Coll. of Law, Morgantown, 1984-85; assoc. Lobel, Novins, Lamont & Flug, Washington, 1985-87; cons. U.S. Army Family Adv. Program, 1983, U.S. Dept. Justice, 1982, Assn. of Family and Conciliation Cts., 1980-81. Sr. articles editor NYU Rev. of Law and Social Change, N.Y.C., 1978-79; contbr. various articles to law revs. and jours. Bd. dirs. Pub. Interest Law Found., NYU, 1979-81. Mem. Womens Legal Def. Fund, D.C. Womens Bar Assn. Democrat. Federal civil litigation, Family and matrimonial, Administrative and regulatory. Office: 2727 29th Ave St NW Apt 538 Washington DC 20008

LERNER, ALAN JAY, lawyer; b. Scranton, Pa., July 29, 1949; s. Jack and Dorothy Rene (Golob) L.; m. Mary Alicia Kincaid, Nov. 9, 1979; children—Hailey, Joan; m. Estelle Fields, Dec. 21, 1970 (div. Apr. 1978); children—Sonia, Bernadette. B.A. in Polit. Sci. cum laude, San Fernando Valley Coll., 1971; J.D. magna cum laude, U. Toledo, 1974. Bar: Mont. 1974, U.S. Dist. Ct. Mont. 1975, U.S. Ct. Appeals (9th cir.) 1975, U.S. Supreme Ct. 1984. Assoc. Crowley Law Firm, Billings, Mont., 1974-75, Hartelius & Lewin, Great Falls, Mont., 1975-76; ptnr. Richter & Lerner, 1976-81; sole practice, Bigfork, Mont., 1981—. Author U. Toledo Law Rev., 1973, editor, 1974. Author: (novel) Spare Parts, 1980. Teaching fellow U. Toledo, 1973; Ohio State Bar scholar, 1972, PAD Nat. scholar, 1973. Mem. Assn. Trial Lawyers Am., Mont. Trial Lawyers Assn., Mont. Bar Assn., N.W. Mont. Bar Assn. Democrat. Jewish. Workers' compensation, Personal injury, State civil litigation. Home: E Lake Shore St Bigfork MT 59911 Office: 128 Village Ln Bigfork MT 59911

LERNER, DEBORAH MAE, lawyer; b. Phila., Nov. 26, 1952; d. Marvin Norris and Joyce Roslyn (Altman) Lerner. AB cum laude, Bryn Mawr Coll., 1973; JD, Villanova U., 1977, LLm, 1986. Bar: Pa. 1977, U.S. Dist. Ct. (ea. dist.) Pa. 1977. Asst. solicitor City of Phila., 1977-78; assoc. Abrahams & Loewenstein, Phila., 1978-82; v.p., gen. counsel Joymar Corp., Darby, Pa., 1982-86; assoc. Pepper, Hamilton & Scheetz, Phila., 1986—. Mem. ABA, Phila. Bar Assn., Am. Arbitration Assn. (panel mem. 1982—). Corporate taxation, Personal income taxation, Estate taxation.

LERNER, HARRY, lawyer, corporate and international law consultant; b. Easton, Pa., Jan. 24, 1939; s. Albert I. and Shirley (Kraus) L.; m. Sherryl Adrienne Blumin, Nov. 18, 1962; 1 child, Michelle Hope. B.A., Cornell U., 1960; J.D., N.Y. U., 1963. Bar: N.Y. State bar 1963, N.J. bar 1966. Asso. firm Otterbourg, Steindler, Houston & Rosen, N.Y.C., 1964-65; firm Robert Greenberg, West New York, N.J., 1965-67; asst. house counsel Ronson Corp., Bridgewater, N.J., 1967-71; asst. to gen. counsel Ronson Corp., 1971-75, sec., corp. counsel, 1975-82; corp. law cons. 1982—. Served with U.S. Army, 1963-64. Mem. N.J. Bar Assn., Zeta Beta Tau. General corporate, Contracts commercial. Office: One Ronson Rd Bridgewater NJ 08807

LERNER, JEFFREY MICHAEL, lawyer; b. Chgo., July 8, 1946; s. Louis S. and Tillie G. (Garfinkel) L.; m. Marianne G. Lerner. B.S., So. Ill. U., 1969, M.S., 1970; J.D. with high honors, Ill. Inst. Tech., 1974. Bar: Ill., 1974, U.S. Dist. Ct. Ill., 1975, U.S. Ct. Appeals 1977, U.S. Supreme Ct., 1978. Jr. law clk. U.S. Dist. Ct., Chgo., 1973-74; asst. public defender felony trial div. Cook County, Chgo., 1974-78; ptnr. Lerner, Bridge and Reiss Ltd., Chgo., 1978—. Mem. ABA, Ill. Bar Assn., Chgo. Bar Assn., Am. Trial Lawyers Assn., Ill. Trial Lawyers Assn., Decalogue Soc., Internat. Assn. Jewish Lawyers and Jurists, Bar and Gavel Soc., Delta Theta Phi. Editor: Chgo.-Kent Law Rev., 1973-74, 7th Circuit Law Rev., 1973-74. Criminal, Civil litigation, General practice. Office: 208 S LaSalle St Suite 1855 Chicago IL 60604

LERNER, LAWRENCE, lawyer, engineer; b. Bklyn., Mar. 23, 1947; s. Julius and Mary (Finkelstein) L.; m. Ronnie Kay Prager, Dec. 19, 1968; children: Bryan Craig, Douglas Harry, Joshua Ian. BSCE, CUNY, 1971; JD, Pepperdine U., 1980. Bar: Calif. 1980, Mo. 1981, U.S. Dist. Ct. (we. dist.) Mo. 1981; registered profl. engr. Colo. Engr. Peter Kiewit Sons' Co., N.Y., Neb., Colo., 1971-77; assoc. Margolin & Kirwan, Kansas City, Mo., 1980-85; ptnr. Sandler, Balkin, Hellman & Weinstein, Kansas City, 1985—. com. mem. Boy Scouts Am., Kansas City, Beth Shalom Synagogue, Kansas City. Mem. ABA (various coms. and sects.), Fed. Bar Assn., Calif. Bar

Assn., Mo. Bar Assn., Jackson County Bar Assn., Kansas City Met. Bar Assn., Volunteer Atty. Project and Lawyers Assn. of Kansas City, Am. Soc. of Civil Engrs., Nat. Soc. of Profl. Engrs., Eastern Chpt. Kans. Engring. Soc. (lectr.), Western Chpt. Mo. Soc. of Profl. Engrs. (lectr.), Chi Epsilon. Democrat. Construction, Government contracts and claims, Insurance. Office: Sandler Balkin Hellman & Weinstein PC 3130 Broadway Kansas City MO 64111-2444

LERNER, RICHARD DAVID, lawyer; b. Buffalo, Nov. 27, 1955; s. Marvin Gabriel and Esther (Torczyner) L.; m. Melinda J. Frederick, Mar. 26, 1983. BA, U. Mich., 1977; JD, U. N.C., 1981. Assoc. Reed, Smith, Shaw & McClay, Pitts., 1981-83, Pierson, Ball & Dowd, Washington, 1983—. Mem. ABA, ACLU. Democrat. Jewish. Federal civil litigation, Antitrust. Home: 2312 Seminary Rd Silver Spring MD 20910 Office: Pierson Ball & Dowd 1200 18th St NW Suite 1000 Washington DC 20036

LERNER, WILLIAM C., lawyer; b. Phila., July 17, 1933; s. Al and Tillie (Goodman) L.; B.A., Cornell U., 1955; LL.B., NYU, 1960; m. G. Billie Campbell, Aug. 15, 1957; children—Bonnie, Edwina. Bar: N.Y. 1961. Atty. SEC, 1960-64; asst. v.p. Am. Stock Exchange, 1965-68; sr. v.p., sec. Carter, Berlind & Weill, Inc. (predecessor to Shearson, Am. Express, Inc.), N.Y.C., 1968-71, Berg & Cornell, Buffalo, 1970-71, Kavinoky & Cook, Buffalo, 1971-72, Saperston & Day, Buffalo, 1973-78; with firm Robshaw & Lerner, P.C., Buffalo, 1978-80; sr. partner firm Nasca and Lerner, Buffalo, 1982-85; v.p. and gen. counsel The Geneva Cos., Costa Mesa, Calif., 1986—; dir. Helm Resources, Inc., Geneva Holdings, Inc., Seisnic Enterprises, Inc., Teletrak Computer, Inc. Chmn., Erie County Public Utilities Task Force, 1974-75; mem. Cornell Univ. Arts Coll. Council, 1977-85, N.Y. Gov.'s Hazardous Waste Facilities Task Force, 1983-85. Served to 1st lt. Q.M.C., U.S. Army, 1955-57. Mem. Am., N.Y. State (regulation of securities com. 1968-86) bar assns., Phi Alpha Delta. Club: Buffalo. Contbg. editor The Stock Market Handbook, 1969.or The Stock Market Handbook, 1969. General corporate, Environment, Securities. Home: 27 Lantern Bay Dana Point CA 92629 Office: 575 Anton Blvd Costa Mesa CA 92626

LERRIGO, FRANK C., lawyer; b. Topeka, May 23, 1906; s. Charles H. and Annabelle (Barry) L.; m. Margaret Adams, 1937 (dec. 1968); m. Margaret Marrs, Sept. 20, 1970; children: Thomas F., William C. AB, Stanford U., 1928, LLB, 1931. Bar: Calif. 1931, U.S. Dist. Ct. (ea. dist.) Calif. 1935, U.S. Ct. Appeals (9th cir.) 1945. Dep. commr. of corp. State of Calif., 1931-32; counsel Fed. Intermediate Credit Bank, 1933-34; ptnr. then assoc. Lerrigo, Snyder, Nibler, Moss and Berryman, Fresno, Calif.; counsel Fed. Intermediate Credit Bank; U.S. Commr., 1936-71; U.S. Magistrate, 1971-77; chmn. Bank Counsel Seminar Panel on Agrl. Fin., 1970. Mem. ABA, Calif. Bar Assn. (local adminstrv. com. 1944-54) Fresno County Bar Assn., Delta Theta Phi. Banking, General corporate, Probate. Office: Lerrigo Snyder Nibler Moss Berryman Security Bank Bldg 8th Floor Fresno CA 93721

LESAR, HIRAM HENRY, lawyer, educator; b. Thebes, Ill., May 8, 1912; s. Jacob L. and Missouri Mabel (Keith) L.; m. Rosalee Berry, July 11, 1937 (dec. Oct. 1985); children: James Hiram, Albert Keith, Byron Lee; m. Barbara Thomas, Feb. 12, 1987. A.B., U. Ill., 1934, J.D., 1936; J.S.D., Yale U., 1938. Bar: Ill. 1937, Mo. 1954, U.S. Supreme Ct 1960. Asst. prof. law U. Kans., 1937-40, asso. prof., 1940-42; sr., prin. atty. bd. legal examiners U.S. CSC, 1942-44; assoc. prof. law U. Mo., 1946-48, prof., 1948-57; prof. law Washington U., St. Louis, 1957-72, dean Sch. Law, 1960-72; dean, prof. law So. Ill. U., Carbondale, 1972-80, interim pres. univ., 1974, acting pres., 1979-80, disting. service prof., 1980-82, prof. emeritus, 1982—, vis. disting service prof., 1983—; disting. vis. prof. McGeorge Ch. Law, 1982-83; vis. prof. law U. Ill., summer 1947, Ind. U., summer 1952, U. So. Calif., summer 1959, U. N.C., summer 1961, NYU, summer 1965. Author: Landlord and Tenant, 1957; Contbr. to: Am. Law of Property, 1952, supplement, 1977, also, Dictionary Am. History, Ency. Brit. Bd. dirs. Legal Aid Soc., St. Louis and St. Louis County, 1960-72, pres., 1966-67; mem. Human Relations Commn., University City, Mo., 1966-71, chmn., 1966, 67; bd. dirs. Land of Lincoln Legal Assistance Found., 1972-82; mem. Fed. Mediation and Conciliation Service, other arbitration panels; bd. dirs. Bacone Coll., 1981—; trustee Lincoln Acad. Ill., 1987—. Served from lt. (j.g.) to lt. comdr. USNR, 1944-46. Named Laureate Lincoln Acad. of Ill., 1985. Fellow Am. Bar Found.; mem. Am. Arbitration Assn., Am. Law Inst., ABA, Fed. Bar Assn., Mo. Bar Assn., St. Louis Bar Assn., Am. Acad. Polit. and Social Sci., Am. Judicature Soc., AAUP, Phi Beta Kappa, Order of Coif, Phi Kappa Phi, Phi Delta Phi (hon.). Baptist. Clubs: University (St. Louis); Nat. Lawyers (Washington); Yale (Chgo.); Jackson Country. Lodges: Masons, K.T., Shriners. Probate, Real property, Personal income taxation. Home: 11 Hillcrest Dr Carbondale IL 62901

LESATZ, STEPHEN, JR., lawyer; b. Greeley, Colo., Aug. 5, 1937; s. Stephen J. and Rose (Scholz) LeS.; m. LaDonna M. Distel, June 10, 1961; 1 son, Eric S. B.S. in Bus. Adminstrn., U. Denver, 1959, LL.B., 1961. Bar: Colo. 1962, Minn. 1968, Mich. 1969. Assoc. Haskell, Helmick, Carpenter & Evans, Denver, 1962-68, Arthur E. Anderson, LeSueur, Minn., 1968-69; atty. Whirlpool Corp., Benton Harbor, Mich., 1969-74; assoc. gen. counsel Rocky Mountain Energy Co., Denver, 1974—. Mem. Denver Art Mus., Denver Mus. Natural History, U. Denver Chancellor's Soc. Mem. ABA, Colo. Bar Assn., Denver Bar Assn. Republican. Congregationalist. Oil and gas leasing, General corporate, Labor. Office: PO Box 2000 Broomfield CO 80020

LESHER, STEPHEN HARRISON, lawyer; b. Tucson, Dec. 31, 1953; s. Robert Overton and June Ruth (Huffer) L. BA, U. Vt., 1975; JD, U. Ariz., 1978. Bar: Ariz. 1978, U.S. Dist. Ct. Ariz. 1978. Assoc. Lesher & Kimble PC, Tucson, 1978-79; ptnr. Lesher, Clausen & Borodkin PC, Tucson, 1980-83, Lesher & Borodkin PC, Tucson, 1983—. Mem. ABA, Def. Research Inst. Republican. Clubs: Tucson Country, Old Pueblo. Avocation: tennis. Personal injury, Insurance, State civil litigation. Home: 8931 E Chauncy Tucson AZ 85715 Office: Lesher & Borodkin PC 3773 E Broadway Tucson AZ 85716

LESHIN, RICHARD LEE, accountant; b. Corpus Christi, Tex., Feb. 26, 1953; s. Marvin S. and Yetta (Levinson) L.; m. Pamela Roots, Jan. 24, 1981; children: Leigh Allison, Chase Roots. BBA, U. Tex., 1975, JD, 1978. Bar: Tex. 1978. Acct. Kleberg, Dyer, Redford & Weil, Corpus Christi. Active Leadership Corpus Christi, 1983; treas. Gulf Coast council Boy Scouts Am., 1985—; trustee South Tex. Art Mus., Corpus Christi, 1986—. Mem. Nueces County Bar Assn., Corpus Christi Bus. and Estate Planning Council, Corpus Christi Estate Planning Study Group, Nueces County Young Lawyers Assn. (pres. 1982-83), Corpus Christi Chpt. CPA's. Jewish. Estate planning, Probate. Home: 146 Amistad Corpus Christi TX 78404 Office: Kleberg Dyer Redford & Weil 1200 MBank Ctr N Corpus Christi TX 78471

LESHNER, STEPHEN I., lawyer; b. N.Y.C., Sept. 26, 1951; s. Leo and Gloria (Perlman) L.; m. Mary Ann Relles, Oct. 28, 1978; children: Samuel Joseph, Harry Jacob. BA, SUNY, 1973; JD, Northeastern U., 1976. Bar: Ariz. 1976, U.S. Dist. Ct. Ariz. 1977, U.S. Ct. Appeals (9th cir.) 1981, U.S. Supreme Ct. 1980. Assoc. Legal Clinic of Bates & O'Steen, Phoenix, 1977; ptnr. O'Steen Legal Clinic, Phoenix, 1977-80, Van O'Steen and Ptnrs., Phoenix, 1980—; criminal law specialist Ariz. Bd. Legal Specialization, 1982—. Mem. Assn. Trial Lawyers Am., Ariz. Trial Lawyers Assn., State Bar Ariz. (criminal justice sect., group and prepaid legal services com. 1978-82), Nat. Assn. Criminal Def. Lawyers. Personal injury, Criminal. Office: Van O'Steen and Ptnrs 3605 N 7th Ave Phoenix AZ 85013

LESK, ANN BERGER, lawyer; b. N.Y.C., Feb. 7, 1947; d. Alexander and Eleanor A. (Dickinson) Berger; m. Michael E. Lesk, June 30, 1968. AB cum laude, Radcliffe Coll., 1968; JD with high honors, Rutgers U., 1977. Bar: N.Y. 1979. Law clk. to justice N.J. Supreme Ct., Mountain, 1977-78; assoc. Fried, Frank, Harris, Shriver & Jacobson, N.Y.C., 1978-84, ptnr., 1984—. Editor-in-chief Rutgers Law Rev., 1976-77. Mem. ABA, N.Y. State Bar Assn. Real property. Office: Fried Frank Harris Shriver & Jacobson One New York Plaza New York NY 10004

LESLIE, JOHN EDWARD, lawyer; b. Manitowoc, Wis., Oct. 17, 1954; s. Edward Lawrence and Gertrude Margaret (Ullrich) L.; m. Jane Ellen McDonald, Aug. 4, 1979; 1 child, Jonathan. BA, Carroll Coll., 1976; MBA, JD, U. Notre Dame, 1980. Bar: Wis. 1980, Tex. 1983, U.S. Dist. Ct. (no. dist.) Tex. 1983, U.S. Dist. Ct. (we. dist.) Tex. 1984. Tax cons. Touche Ross & Co., Milw., 1980-82; assoc. Cotton, Bledsoe, Tiene & Dawson, Midland, Tex., 1982-85; ptnr. Shannon, Gracey, Ratliff & Miller, Ft. Worth, 1985—. Co-author: Texas Mortgage Foreclosures, 1985; contbr. articles to profl. jours. Mem. ABA, Wis. Bar Assn., Tex. Bar Assn. (bankruptcy com.), Am. Bankruptcy Inst. Bankruptcy. Office: Shannon Gracey Ratliff & Miller 201 Main St Fort Worth TX 76102-3191

LESLIE, ROBERT BRUCE, lawyer; b. Warren, Ark., Jan. 8, 1939; s. Ellis Berry and Mary Odesa (Summnall) L.; m. Rita Loree Jernigan, May 26, 1961; children: John Barry, Leah Elizabeth. BS in Indsl. Edn., U. Ark., Monticello, 1961; JD, U. Ark., 1969. From assoc. to ptnr. Patten, Brown & Leslie, Little Rock, 1969-82; sole practice Little Rock, 1984—; atty. City of Redfield, Ark., 1970-78; mcpl. judge, 1980-85; bd. dirs. Fed. Home Loan Bank, Dallas Dist. Candidate for congress 4th Congl. Dist. Ark, 1982; chmn. Ark. Reps., 1984;del. Nat. Rep. Conv. Mem. Ark. Bar Assn., Assn. Trial Lawyers Am., Ark. Trial Lawyers Assn., Citizens Am. (state co-chmn. 1985-86). Club: Civitan (state judge adv. gen.). Lodges: Masons, Shriners. Avocation: duck hunting. General practice, Personal injury, Real property. Office: 10310 W Markham Suite 206 Little Rock AR 72205

LESLIE, ROBERT LORNE, lawyer; b. Adak, Alaska, Feb. 24, 1947; s. J. Lornie and L. Jean (Conelly) L.; children—Lorna Jean, Elizabeth Allen. B.S., U.S. Mil. Acad., 1969; J.D., Hastings Coll. Law, U. Calif.-San Francisco, 1974. Bar: Calif. 1974, D.C. 1979, U.S. Dist. Ct. (no. dist.) Calif. 1974, U.S. Ct. Claims 1975, U.S. Tax Ct. 1975, U.S. Ct. Appeals (9th and D.C. cirs.), U.S. Ct. Mil. Appeals 1980, U.S. Supreme Ct. 1980. Commd. 2d lt. U.S. Army, 1969, advanced through grades to maj., 1980; govt. trial atty. West Coast Field Office, Contract Appeals, Litigation Div. and Regulatory Law Div., Office JAG, Dept. Army, San Francisco, 1974-77; sr. trial atty. and team chief Office of Chief Trial Atty., Dept. Army, Washington, 1977-80; ret., 1980; ptnr. McInerney & Dillon, Oakland, Calif., 1980—; lectr. on govt. contracts CSC, Continuing Legal Edn. Program; lectr. in govt. procurement U.S. Army Materiel Command. Decorated Silver Star, Purple Heart, Meritorious Service medal. Mem. ABA, Fed. Bar Assn. Club: Commonwealth (San Francisco). Government contracts and claims, Construction, Contracts commercial. Home: 4144 Greenwood Ave Oakland CA 94602 Office: Ordway Bldg Suite 1850 Oakland CA 94612

LESSER, WILLIAM MELVILLE, lawyer; b. N.Y.C., Jan. 26, 1927; s. Sydney Edward and Hattie (Wolf) L.; m. Laura Helen Schwartz, Oct. 3, 1953; children: Robin, Debra, Nancy. BS, NYU, 1949, JD, 1958. Bar: N.Y. 1959, U.S. Dist. Ct. (so. and ea. dists.) N.Y. 1969. Sr. ptnr. Lesser, Werter & Collins, N.Y.C., 1959—. Treas., bd. dirs. Assn. Help Retarded Children, N.Y.C. chpt., 1961-67; chmn. Environ. Control Commn., Town of New Castle, N.Y., 1969-81. Served with USN, 1945-46, PTO. Mem. ABA, Assn. Trial Lawyers Am., N.Y. State Trial Lawyers Assn., Assn. Trial Lawyers City of N.Y., Am. Soc. Law and Medicine. Jewish. Insurance, Personal injury, State civil litigation. Home: 70 Taconic Rd Millwood NY 10546 Office: Lesser Werter & Collins 1500 Broadway New York NY 10036

LESTELLE, ANDREA SUCHERMAN, lawyer; b. Chgo., Sept. 30, 1949; d. Sol and Rhoda (Lewis) Sucherman; m. Terrence J. Lestelle, Sept. 21, 1975; children: Evan Pays, Nicole Jessica. BS in Journalism, Ohio U., 1971; JD, Loyola U., New Orleans, 1980. Bar: La. 1981, U.S. Dist. Ct. (ea. dist.) La. 1981. Assoc. Law Offices of Terrence J. Lestelle, New Orleans, 1981-84; ptnr. Lestelle & Lestelle, New Orleans, 1984—. Mem. Assn. Trial Lawyers Am., La. Bar Assn., Nat. Council of Jewish Women. Personal injury, Admiralty, Federal civil litigation. Office: Lestelle & Lestelle 715 Girod St New Orleans LA 70130

LESTER, ANDREW WILLIAM, lawyer; b. Mpls., Feb. 17, 1956; s. Richard G. and M. Louise (Kurtz) L.; m. Barbara R. Schmitt, Nov. 22, 1978. BA, Duke U., 1977; MS in Fgn. Service, JD, Georgetown U., 1981. Bar: Okla. 1981, D.C. 1985. Cons. Dresser Industries, Washington, 1979-81; assoc. Conner & Winters, Tulsa, 1981-82; asst. atty. City of Enid, Okla., 1982-84; ptnr. Long, Ford & Lester, Enid, 1984—; lectr. in field. Contbr. articles to profl. jours. Intern office senator Bob Dole, Washington, 1977-78; mem. transition team EEOC Office Pres.-Elect Reagan, Washington, 1980-81. Mem. ABA, Okla. Bar Assn., Assn. Trial Lawyers Am. Baptist. Federal civil litigation, State civil litigation, Local government. Home: 1811 Country Club Dr Enid OK 73703 Office: Long Ford & Lester PO Box 3832 Enid OK 73702

LESTER, CHARLES THEODORE, JR., lawyer; b. Norfolk, Va., July 4, 1954; s. Charles Theodore and Margaret M. (Trambley) L.; m. Kathleen Roberta Rodger, Aug. 3, 1974; children: Frances, Charles. AB, Thomas More Coll., 1974; JD, No. Ky. U., 1980. Bar: Ky. 1980, Ohio, 1980, U.S. Dist. Ct. (ea. dist.) Ky. 1981, U.S. Ct. Appeals (6th cir.) 1986. Sole practice Ft. Thomas, KY., 1980—; atty. Garrett Computer Services, Cin., Ohio, 1980—. Mng. editor No. Ky. Law Jour., 1979-80. Mem. bd. mgrs. Boys and Girls Club of Greater Cin., Campbell County, 1986-87. Mem. ABA, Ky. Bar Assn., Ohio State Bar Assn., No. Ky. Bar Assn., Cin. Bar Assn., Campbell County Jaycees (legal counsel 1986-87, named Jaycee of Month 1985). Democrat. Roman Catholic. Computer, Juvenile, Probate. Office: PO Box 69 Fort Thomas KY 41075-0069

LESTER, CHARLES TURNER, JR., lawyer; b. Plainfield, N.J., Jan. 31, 1942; s. Charles Turner and Marlyn Elizabeth (Tate) L.; m. Nancy Hudon Simmons, Aug. 19, 1967; children—Susan Hopson, Mary Elizabeth. B.A., Emory U., 1964, J.D., 1967. Bar: Ga. 1966, U.S. Dist. Ct. (no. dist.) Ga. 1967, D.C. 1970, U.S. Ct. Appeals (5th cir.) 1967, U.S. Ct. Appeals (11th cir.) 1982, U.S. Ct. Appeals (10th cir.) 1984. Assoc. Sutherland, Asbill & Brennan, Atlanta, 1970-77, ptnr., 1977—. Mem. Leadership Atlanta, 1980-81; pres. Atlanta Legal Aid Soc., 1979-80. Served to lt. JAGC, USNR, 1967-70. Mem. Ga. State Bar (pres. young lawyers sect. 1977-78, bd. govs. 1980—), ABA, Atlanta Bar Assn., Am. Judicature Soc., Lawyers Club Atlanta (treas. 1982-83, exec. com. 1982—, 2d v.p. 1986—), D.C. Bar Assn. Democrat. Presbyterian. General practice, State civil litigation, Antitrust. Home: 1955 Musket Ct Stone Mountain GA 30087 Office: Sutherland Asbill & Brennan 1st Nat Bank Tower Atlanta GA 30303

LESTER, EDGEL CELSUS, lawyer; b. Middletown, Ohio, Aug. 2, 1950; s. Edgel C. and Norma M. (Elam) L.; m. Deborah Moore, Mar. 18, 1977; 1 child, Whitney Dawn. BA in Psychology, Vanderbilt U., 1972; MA in Psychology, Mid. Tenn. State U., 1975; JD, U. Ky., 1982. Bar: Fla. 1982, U.S. Dist. Ct. (mid. dist.) Fla. 1982, U.S Ct. Appeals (11th and fed. cirs.) 1982. Counsellor Cen. State Psychiat. Hosp., Nashville, 1972-74; psychologist, team leader Southeast Ky. Comprehensive Care Ctr., Corbin, Ky., 1974-76; dir. adminstrn. and devel. Northwest Ala. Mental Health Ctr., Jasper, 1976-79; assoc. Holland & Knight, Tampa, Fla., 1982-83, Glenn, Rasmussen, Fogarty & Merryday, Tampa, 1983-85, Reed & Black P.A., Tampa, 1985—. Editor-in-chief: Kentucky Law Journal, 1981-82. Mem. Adminstrv. Bd. Palma Ceia United Meth. Ch., Tampa, 1986—; asst. dist. commr. Boy Scouts Am., Jasper, 1978-79; chmn. Clay County Ky. Youth Adv. Bd., Manchester, 1974-75. Named one of Outstanding Young Men. Am., 1978-79, Ky. Col., Commonwealth of Ky., 1982. Mem. Fla. Bar Assn., Hillsborough County Bar Assn. Democrat. Methodist. Contracts commercial, Real property, Banking. Home: 406 Royal Poinciara Tampa FL 33609 Office: Reed & Black PA 101 E Kennedy Blvd Tampa FL 33602

LESTER, HOWARD, lawyer; b. N.Y.C., Jan. 21, 1927; s. Harry and Fay (Aaron) L.; m. Patricia Barbara Briger, Mar. 6, 1956; children—Peter Bruce, Pamela Robin, Prescott Evan, B.A., Bklyn. Coll., 1949; LL.B., Yale U., 1952. Bar: N.Y. 1953. Practice, N.Y.C., 1953—; former mem. Emile Z. Berman and A. Harold Frost; mem. Lester Schwab Katz & Dwyer, N.Y.C., now sr. ptnr.; lectr. Practicing Law Inst., 1962—, mem. adv. com., 1984—; chmn. Joint Conf. Com. on Calendar Congestion and Related Problems 1st and 2d Jud. Depts., 1971-75. Trustee Buckley Country Day Sch., East Hills, N.Y., 1971-75. Served with U.S. Army, 1945-47. Mem. ABA, N.Y. State Bar Assn. (lectr.; chmn. exec. com. trial lawyer sect. 1972-73), Nassau County Bar Assn., Assn. Bar City N.Y. (ins. com. 1963-66, civil ct. com. 1968-71), Fedn. Ins. Counsel (v.p. 1967-68, gov. 1968—, pres. 1972-73, chmn. bd. 1973-74, bd. dirs. found. 1985—), Bklyn.-Manhattan Trial Lawyers Assn. (pres. 1971), N.Y. County Lawyers Assn., Def. Research Inst. (bd. dirs. 1972-77), Def. Assn. City N.Y., Am. Arbitration Assn. (law com. 1977—), Internat. Assn. Ins. Counsel, U.S. C. of C. (steering com. product liability task force 1977—), Am. Bd. Trial Advs. (adv.). Clubs: Glen Oaks, Yale (N.Y.C.); Banyan, Governors (West Palm Beach, Fla.); High Ridge (Hypaluxo, Fla.); Sands Point Bath and Tennis (N.Y.); Corbey Ct. (New Haven.). Federal civil litigation, Environment, Libel. Home: 14 Shorewood Dr Sands Point NY 11050 Other: 2100 S Ocean Blvd Palm Beach FL 33480 Office: 120 Broadway New York NY 10271

LESTER, JAMES LEE, lawyer; b. Rapid City, S.D., June 17, 1957; s. George William and Virginia (Lee) L.; m. Margaret Mary McCaig, Aug. 8, 1981; 1 child, Katherine Anne. BCE, MIT, 1979; JD, Duke U., 1982. Bar: Va. 1982, U.S. Ct. Appeals (4th cir.) 1982, U.S. Dist. Ct. (ea. dist.) Va. 1982. Assoc. Watt, Tieder, Killian & Hoffar, Vienna, Va., 1982—. Mem. ABA, Computer Law Assn., Am. Soc. Civil Engrs., Am. Soc. for Macro Engring. Computer, Government contracts and claims, Construction. Home: 2315 Jackson Pkwy Vienna VA 22180 Office: Watt Tieder Killian & Hoffar 8401 Old Courthouse Rd Vienna VA 22180

LESTER, JAMES LUTHER, lawyer; b. Augusta, Ga., Jan. 12, 1932; s. William M. and Elizabeth (Miles) L.; m. Gwendolyn Gleason, Jan. 18, 1958; children: James L. Jr., Frank G. AB, The Citadel, 1952; JD, U. Ga., 1957. Bar: Ga. 1957, U.S. Ct. Appeals (11th cir.), U.S. Supreme Ct. Assoc. Lester, Lester & Flynt, Augusta, 1957-60, ptnr., 1960—; Mem. Ga. Senate, 1971-86; chmn. Ga. tax reform commn., 1978-81, chmn. banking and fin. com., 1978-86. Chmn. Richmond County dem. exec. com., 1966-70; mem. Govs. Adv. Council on Mental Health and Mental Retardation, 1977-85, adv. com. Ga.-Carolina dist. Boy Scouts Am.; bd. dirs. Met. YMCA. Served to capt. U.S. Army, 1952-58, Korea. Recipient Outstanding Service award Augusta Assn. for Retarded Children, 1973, Pub. Affairs award Mental Health Assn. Met. Atlanta, 1976, Outstanding Service award Richmond County Educators Assn., 1977, Disting. Service award Ga. Assn. for Mental Health, 1977, Outstanding Service award Mental Health Assn. for Greater Augusta, 1978, Citation for Legis. Service, Ga. Mcpl. Assn., 1979, 80, 83, Herman Haas award Ind. Ins. Agents Ga., 1981, Senator of Yr. award Ga. Assn. Mental Health, 1984. Mem. ABA, Ga. Bar Assn., Augusta Bar Assn., Assn. Trial Lawyers Am. Methodist. Lodge: Kiwanis. Avocations: fishing, hunting, golf. General practice, Real property, Banking. Home: 770 Camellia Rd Augusta GA 30909 Office: Lester Lester & Flynt 985 Broad St Augusta GA 30901-1297

LESTER, PAUL ARTHUR, lawyer; b. Newton, Mass., Jan. 19, 1950; s. David and Rosalie Vivienne (Freedman) L.; m. Lois Joy Gross, July 3, 1971; children: Erica Joanne, Shari Diane. BA, U. Rochester, 1971; JD, U. Pa., 1974. Bar: Pa. 1974, Fla. 1975, D.C. 1975, U.S. Dist. Ct. (so. dist.) Fla. 1982, U.S. Ct. Appeals (11th cir.) 1982. Atty. FTC, Washington, 1974-77; assoc. Greenberg, Traurig, Miami, Fla., 1977-81; assoc. Broad & Cassel, Miami, 1981-83, ptnr., 1983-84; ptnr. Shapiro, Lester & Abramson PA, Miami, 1984—. Contbr. articles to profl. jours. Mem. ABA, Fla. Bar Assn., Phi Beta Kappa, Alpha Epsilon Pi. Democrat. Avocations: bicycling, reading, music. Real property, FERC practice, Municipal bonds. Office: 3250 Mary St Suite 204 Miami FL 33133

LESTER, ROY DAVID, lawyer; b. Middletown, Ohio, Jan. 16, 1949; s. Edgel Celsus and Norma Marie (Elam) L.; 1 child, Justin David. BS, Western Ky. U., 1970; JD, U. Ky., 1975. Bar: Ky. 1975, U.S. Tax Ct. 1979, U.S. Dist. Ct. (ea. dist.) Ky. 1976, U.S. Supreme Ct. 1979. Agt. Mut. Benefit Life, Louisville, 1970-72; ptnr. Stoll, Keenon & Park, Lexington, 1975—; bd. dirs. Almahurst Farm, Lexington. Contbr. articles to profl. jours. Bd. dirs., past pres. Lakeview Estates Lake Assn., Lexington, 1982—. Served with USNG, 1970-76. Mem. Fayette County Bar Assn. (auditor 1984), Order of Coif. Republican. Roman Catholic. Club: YMCA (Lexington). General corporate, Contracts commercial, Probate. Home: 2060 Norborne Dr Lexington KY 40502 Office: Stoll Keenon & Park 1000 1st Security Plaza Lexington KY 40507

LETTOW, CHARLES FREDERICK, lawyer; b. Iowa Falls, Iowa, Feb. 10, 1941; s. Carl Frederick and Catherine (Reisinger) L.; m. Sue Lettow, Apr. 20, 1963; children: Renee, Carl II, John, Paul. BS in Chem. Engring., Iowa State U., 1962; LLB, Stanford U., 1968. Bar: Calif. 1969, Iowa 1969, D.C. 1972. Law clk. to Judge Ben C. Duniway U.S. Ct. Appeals (9th cir.), San Francisco, 1968-69; law clk. to Chief Justice Warren E. Burger U.S. Supreme Ct., Washington, 1969-70; counsel Council on Environ. Quality, Washington, 1970-73; assoc. Cleary, Gottlieb, Steen & Hamilton, Washington, 1973-76, ptnr., 1976—. Contbr. articles to profl. jours. Trustee Potomac Sch., McLean, Va., 1983—, chmn. bd. trustees., 1985—. Served to 1st lt. U.S. Army, 1963-65. Mem. ABA, D.C. Bar Assn., Iowa Bar Assn., Order of Coif. Republican. Lutheran. Club: International (Washington). Federal civil litigation, Environment. Office: Cleary Gottlieb Steen & Hamilton 1752 N St NW Washington DC 20036

LETWIN, JEFFREY WILLIAM, lawyer; b. Pitts., Nov. 26, 1953; s. Myron Harvey and Phyllis Harriet (Unatin) L.; m. Roberta Lee Rosenbloom, July 24, 1983; 1 child, S. Ari; stepchildren: Andrew B. Filipek, Amanda H. Filipek. BA in History and Lit., U. Pitts., 1975; JD, Am. U., 1979. Bar: Pa. 1980, D.C. 1980. Staff atty. Dept. Justice, Washington, 1979-80; assoc. Gilloti, Goldberg & Capristi, Pitts., 1980-83, Finkel, Lefkowitz & Ostrow, Pitts., 1983-85, Rosenberg & Kirshner, Pitts., 1986—; lectr. Pa. Bar Inst., 1983; mem. Pitts. High Tech. Council, 1985—, Enterprise Group, Pitts., 1985—. Bd. dirs. Holocaust Commn., Pitts., 1983—, Jewish Family and Children's Service, Pitts., 1983—; bd. dirs. United Jewish Fedn., Pitts., 1984—, chmn. young bus. and profl. div., 1985—; mem. Young Leadership Cabinet USA, 1984—;. Named one of Outstanding Young Men in Am., 1985. Mem. ABA, Pa. Bar Assn., D.C. Bar Assn., Allegheny County Bar Assn. (bus., banking, and comml. sect., continuing legal edn. com.). Democrat. Avocations: racquetball, tennis, films. Securities, General corporate, Real property. Office: Rosenburg Kirshner PA 1500 Grant Bldg Pittsburgh PA 15219

LETWIN, LEON, legal educator; b. Milw., Dec. 29, 1929; s. Lazar and Bessie (Rosenthal) L.; m. Alita Zurav, July 11, 1952; children—Michael, Daniel, David. Ph.B., U. Chgo., 1950; LL.B., U. Wis., 1952; LL.M., Harvard U., 1964. Bar: Wis. 1952, Calif. 1969. Teaching fellow Harvard Law Sch., Boston, 1963-64; faculty Law Sch. UCLA, 1964—, prof., 1968—. Contbr. articles to profl. jours. Active ACLU. Mem. Conf. Critical Legal Studies, Nat. Lawyers Guild, State Bar Calif. Legal education. Home: 2226 Manning Ave Los Angeles CA 90064 Office: UCLA Law Sch 405 Hilgard Ave Los Angeles CA 90024

LEUNG, FRANKIE FOOK-LUN, lawyer; b. Guangzhou, Fed. Republic of China, 1949; married; 1 child. BA in Psychology with honors, Hong Kong U., 1972; MS in Psychology, Birmingham U., Eng., 1974; BA, MA in Jurisprudence, Oxford U., Eng., 1976; JD, Coll. of Law, London, 1977. Bar: Calif. 1987. Barrister Eng. and Hong Kong, 1977—; lectr. Chinese law for businessmen Hong Kong U., 1984-85, 85-86; vis. scholar Harvard U. Law Sch., 1983; barrister, solicitor Supreme Ct. of Victoria, Australia, 1983—; cons. prof. Chinese Law Diploma Program, U. East Asia, 1986—. Contbr. numerous articles to profl. jours.; contbr. chpts. to books. Mem. European Assn. for Chinese Law (mem. exec. council 1986—, country corr. 1985—), Am. C. of C. (chmn. subcom. on Chinese intellectual property law 1985-86), Am. Soc. Internat. Law (judge moot ct. 1984-86), Hong Kong Bar Assn. (law drafting subcom. 1986—). Office: Lewis D'Amato Brisbois & Bisgaard 5 Park Suite 300 261 S Figueroa St Los Angeles CA 90012

LEVA, MARX, lawyer; b. Selma, Ala., Apr. 4, 1915; s. Leo and Fannie Rose (Gusdorf) L.; m. Shirley Pearlman, Oct. 31, 1942; children: Leo Marx, Lloyd Leva Plaine. B.S., U. Ala., 1937, LL.D., 1978; LL.B., Harvard U., 1940. Bar: Ala. 1940, U.S. Supreme Ct. 1946, D.C. 1950. Law clk. to Justice Hugo Black, U.S. Supreme Ct., 1940; sr. atty. O.P.A., 1941; acting regional atty. for Mich. and Ohio WPB, 1942; counsel to fiscal dir. of Navy 1946, spl. asst. to sec. of navy, 1947; spl. asst. and gen. counsel to Sec. Def., 1947-49; asst. sec of def. (legal and legis.) 1949-51; partner firm Fowler, Leva, Hawes & Symington, 1951-67, Leva, Hawes, Symington, Martin & Oppenheimer, 1967-85, Leva, Hawes, Mason & Martin, 1985—; Chmn. civilian-mil. review panel for spl. com. U.S. Senate, 1957; mem. Pres.'s Commn. to Rev. Fgn. Aid, 1958-59, Pres.'s Com. on Def. Establishment, 1960-61. Note editor: Harvard Law Rev, 1939; overseer, 1950-55. Served

with amphibious forces USNR, 1942-45, ETO. Selected Outstanding Young Man In Govt. Washington Jr. C. of C., 1949; decorated Bronze Star with combat distinguishing device. Government contracts and claims, General practice, Legislative. Home: 7115 Bradley Blvd Bethesda MD 20817 Office: 1220 19th St NW Washington DC 20036

LEVAL, PIERRE NELSON, judge; b. N.Y.C., Sept. 4, 1936; s. Fernand and Beatrice (Reiter) L.; m. Susana Torruella, July 26, 1973; 1 child, India Luisa. B.A. cum laude, Harvard U., 1959, J.D. magna cum laude, 1963. Bar: N.Y. 1964, U.S. Ct. Appeals 2d Circuit 1964, U.S. Dist. Ct. So. Dist. N.Y 1966. Law clk. to Hon. Henry J. Friendly, U.S. Ct. Appeals, 1963-64; asst. U.S. atty. So. Dist. N.Y., 1964-68, chief appellate atty., 1967-68; asso. firm Cleary, Gottlieb, Steen & Hamilton, N.Y.C., 1969-74; partner firm 1973-75; 1st asst. dist. atty. Office of Dist. Atty., N.Y. County, 1975-76; chief asst. dist. atty. Office of Dist. Atty., 1976-77; U.S. dist. judge So. Dist. N.Y., N.Y.C., 1977—. Served with U.S. Army, 1959. Mem. Am. Law Inst., Assn. Bar City N.Y., N.Y. County Lawyers Assn. Jurisprudence. Office: US Courthouse Foley Sq New York NY 10007 *

LEVANDER, BERNHARD WILHELM, lawyer; b. St. Paul, Mar. 9, 1916; s. Peter Magni and Laura Marie (Lovene) LeV.; m. Dagne E. Anderson, Oct. 14, 1939; children: Kirsten Dawson, Peter A. BA, Gustavus Adolphus Coll., 1937, DL (hon.), 1981; JD, U. Minn., 1939. Bar: Minn. 1939, U.S. Dist. Ct. Minn. 1955, U.S. Ct. Appeals (8th cir.) 1972, U.S. Supreme Ct. 1973. Assoc. S. Bernhard Wennerberg, Center City, Minn., 1939-40, Kelly, LeVander & Gillen, South St. Paul, Minn., 1950-52; sole practice Mpls., 1952-57; assoc. Nehls, Anderson, LeVander, Zimpfer & Munson, Mpls., 1957-64; ptnr. LeVander, Zimpfer & Tierney, Mpls., 1964-75, LeVander, Zimpfer & Zotaley, P.A., Mpls., 1975—. Past orgn. dir., chmn. Minn. Reps.; chmn. Midwest and Rocky Mountain Rep. Chmns. Assn., 1946-50; pres. Am. Swedish Inst., Mpls. Served to lt. (j.g.) Supply Corps, USNR, 1943-46. Recipient Disting. Service and Significant Attainment in Field of Law award Gustavus Alumni Assn., 1977, Royal Order VASA 1st Class, King of Sweden, 1975. Mem. ABA, Minn. Bar Assn., Hennepin County Bar Assn., Am. Soc. Hosp. Attys., Am. Legion. Lutheran. General corporate, Probate, Health. Home: 3550 Siems Ct Saint Paul MN 55112 Office: LeVander Zotaley et al 720 Northstar Ctr Minneapolis MN 55402

LEVANDOSKI, DENNIS, lawyer; b. Queens, N.Y., Aug. 24, 1951; s. James Edward and Evelyn M. (Kimball) L.; m. Susan Ann Gleason, May 30, 1981; children: George Peter, Andrew Gleason. BS in Biology cum laude, Bklyn. Coll., 1973; JD, U. Maine, Portland, 1979. Bar: Mass. 1979, Maine 1979, U.S. Dist. Ct. Maine 1979, U.S. Ct. Appeals (1st cir.) 1981. Ptnr., trial lawyer Kettle, Carter et al, Portland, Maine, 1980-83, 84—; staff atty. dept. fisheries and wildlife State of Maine, Augusta, 1983-84; instr. paralegal program U. So. Maine, Portland, 1984-87. Coop. atty. Maine Civil Liberties Union, Portland, 1980—; mem. Maine Dem. Com., Augusta, 1980-82. Mem. ABA (litigation sect.), Assn. Trial Lawyers Am., Maine Trial Lawyers Assn., Nat. Assn. Criminal Def. Lawyers. Personal injury, Criminal, Civil rights. Office: Kettle Carter et al 30 Milk St Portland ME 04101

LEVAVY, BARDIN, lawyer; b. Perth Amboy, N.J., July 18, 1943; s. Zvi and Berenice (Bardin) L.; m. Sue-Ellen Davison, Aug. 26, 1967; children—Raphael Zev, Sara Beth. B.A., Johns Hopkins U., 1964; J.D., Harvard U., 1967; M.A. in English, N.Y. U., 1968. Bar: N.Y. 1968, N.J. 1975. Assoc., Orenstein Arrow & Silverman, 1968-70, Blumenthal Barandes Moss Matson & Arnold, 1970-72, Graubard Moskovitz McGoldrick Dannett & Horowitz, N.Y.C., 1972-80; sole practice, Upper Montclair, N.J., 1981—; of counsel Rabner, Allcorn & Widmark. Mem. N.J. Bar Assn., Essex County Bar Assn., Assn. Bar City N.Y. Jewish. Club: Unity of Maplewood. Trademark and copyright, Probate, Contracts commercial. Home: 41 Essex Rd Maplewood NJ 07040 Office: 52 Upper Montclair Plaza Upper Montclair NJ 07043

LEVENSON, ALAN BRADLEY, lawyer; b. Long Beach, N.Y., Dec. 13, 1935; s. Cyrus O. and Jean (Kotler) L.; m. Joan Marlene Levenson, Aug. 19, 1956; children—Scott Keith, Julie Jo. A.B., Dartmouth Coll., 1956; B.A., Oxford U., Eng., 1958, M.A., 1962; LL.B., Yale U., 1961. Bar: N.Y. 1962, U.S. Dist. Ct. D.C. 1964, U.S. Ct. Appeals (D.C. cir.) 1965, U.S. Supreme Ct. 1965. Law clk., trainee div. corp. fin. SEC, Washington, 1961-62, gen. atty., 1962, trial atty., 1963, br. chief, 1963-65, asst. dir., 1965-68, exec. asst. dir., 1968, dir., 1970-76; v.p. Shareholders Mgmt. Co., Los Angeles, 1969, sr. v.p., 1969-70, exec. v.p., 1970; ptnr. Fulbright & Jaworski, Washington, 1976—; lectr. Cath. U. Am., 1964-68, Columbia U., 1973; adj. prof. Georgetown U., 1964, 77, 79-81, U.S. rep. working party OECD, Paris, 1974-75; adv. com. SEC, 1976-77; mem. adv. bd. Securities Regulation Inst., U. Calif.-San Diego, 1975—, vice chmn. exec. com., 1979-83, chmn., 1984—; mem. adv. council SEC Inst., U. So. Calif., Los Angeles, Sch. Acctg., 1981-85; mem. adv. com. Nat. Ctr. Fin. Services, U. Calif.-Berkeley, 1985—, U. Iowa. Mem. bd. editorial advisors U. Iowa Jour. Corp. Law, 1978—; Bur. Nat. Affairs adv. bd. Securities Regulation and Law Report, 1976—; bd. editors N.Y. Law Jour., 1976—; contbr. articles to profl. jours.; mem. adv. bd. Banking Expansion Reporter. Recipient Disting. Service award SEC, 1972; James B. Richardson fellow Oxford U., 1956. Mem. ABA, Fed. Bar Assn., Am. Judicature Soc., Am. Law Inst., Practicing Law Inst. (nat. adv. com. 1974), Am. Inst. CPA's (pub. dir., bd. dirs. 1983—, chmn. adv. council auditing standards bd. 1979-80, future issues com. 1982-85, fin. com. 1984-85), Nat. Assn. Securities Dealers (corp. fin. com. 1981—, arbitration com. 1983—, gov.-at-large, bd. govs. 1987, exec. com. 1986-87, long range planning com. 1987—). Securities, Banking. Home: 12512 Exchange Ct S Potomac MD 20854 Office: 1150 Connecticut Ave NW Washington DC 20036

LEVENSON, STANTON DON, lawyer; b. Pitts., Jan. 5, 1942; m. Linda Sue Berger, July 31, 1966; children: Amy Beth, Michael David. BA, U. Pitts., 1963, LLB, 1966. Bar: Pa. 1967, U.S. Dist. Ct. (we dist.) Pa. 1967, U.S. Ct. Appeals (3d cir.) 1968, U.S. Supreme Ct. 1971, U.S. Ct. Appeals (4th cir.) 1984. Sole practice Pitts., 1966—. Bd. dirs. Jewish Community Ctr., Pitts., 1986. Mem. ABA (grand jury com., subcom. chmn. ethical considerations in prosecution and def. of criminal cases com., others.), Nat. Assn. Criminal Def. Lawyers (lawyers'assistance com.), Pa. Bar Assn., PA. Trial Lawyers Assn., Allegheny County Bar Assn. (lectr. legal practice 1976, spl. fee determination com., others). Democrat. Avocations: running, white water rafting, golf. Criminal. Office: 905 Grant Bldg Pittsburgh PA 15219

LEVENSTEIN, RICHARD HARRY, lawyer; b. Bronx, N.Y., July 2, 1953; s. Louis S. and Claire F. (Halper) L.; m. Pamela C. Cummins, Aug. 10, 1975; 1 child, Lauren J. BA, Tulane U., 1974, JD, 1976. Bar: La. 1976, Fla. 1977. Assoc. Gertler & Gertler, New Orleans, 1976-77, Goodhart & Rosner, Miami, Fla., 1977-79, Schnur & Lipnack, Ft. Lauderdale, Fla., 1979-81; ptnr. Levenstein, Posess & Heimberg, Boca Raton, Fla., 1981-84, Smith & Levenstein, P.A., Boca Raton, 1984—; pub. defender City of New Orleans, 1976-77; instr. legal research Fla. Atlantic U., Boca Raton, 1980-83. Mem. ABA, Fla. Bar Assn., La. Bar Assn., Assn. Trial Lawyers Am., Comml. Law League Am. Federal civil litigation, State civil litigation, Contracts commercial. Office: Smith & Levenstein PA 1650 S Dixie Hwy Boca Raton FL 33432

LEVENTHAL, A. LINDA, lawyer; b. Albany, N.Y., June 10, 1943; d. David Henry and Shirley R. (Asofsky) L. BA, SUNY, Buffalo, 1965; JD, Union U., 1968. Bar: N.Y. 1968, U.S. dist. ct. (no. dist.) N.Y. 1968. Ptnr. Rosenblum & Leventhal, Albany, 1968-78; sole practice, Albany, 1978-84, Schenectady, 1978-84; ptnr. Leventhal & Kirsch, Albany, 1984—; ptnr. Taub & Leventhal, Schenectady 1982—; lectr. continuing legal edn., family law sect. seminars N.Y. State Bar Assn., 1981—; bd. dirs. Legal Aid Soc. Northeastern N.Y., Inc. Bd. mgrs., pres. Commons of East Greenbush Condominium. Mem. ABA, N.Y. State Bar Assn., N.Y. State Women's Bar Assn., Nat. Assn. Women Lawyers, Nat. Assn. Female Execs., Nat. Assn. Bus. and Profl. Women. Lodge: Zonta. Family and matrimonial, Real property, General practice. Home: 420 West Lawrence St Albany NY 12208 Home: 9707 E Mountainview Dr Scottsdale AZ 85258 Office: Pieter Schuyler Bldg 600 Broadway Albany NY 12207 also: 115 Clinton St Schenectady NY 12305

LEVENTHAL, FREDERIC DANIEL, lawyer; b. Oakland, Calif., Apr. 7, 1954; s. Leon and Gerda Alexandra (Ziemsen) L.; m. Joye Marie Sutton, May 21, 1983. AB summa cum laude, U. Calif., Berkeley, 1976, JD, 1981. Bar: Calif. 1981, U.S. Dist. Ct. (no. dist.) Calif. 1981, U.S. Ct. Appeals (9th cir.) 1982. With ops. Bank of Am., Oakland, 1976-78; assoc. Brobeck, Phleger & Harrison, San Francisco, 1981—. Mem. ABA, Calif. Bar Assn., Bar Assn. San Francisco, San Francisco British Am. C. of C., Order of the Coif, Phi Beta Kappa. Club: Commonwealth, San Franciso Barristers. Banking, Municipal bonds, Private international. Home: 51 Menlo Pl Berkeley CA 94707 Office: Brobeck Phleger & Harrison One Market Plaza San Francisco CA 94105

LEVENTHAL, HOWARD G., lawyer; b. N.Y.C., Aug. 15, 1946; s. Charles M. and Beatrice (Dworin) L.; m. Jacqueline L. Nankin, Sept. 5, 1970; children—David, Jennifer. B.A. cum laude, CCNY, 1968; J.D., NYU, 1971. Bar: N.Y. 1971, U.S. Ct. Appeals (2d cir.) 1972, U.S. Dist. Ct. (ea. and so. dists.) N.Y. 1973, U.S. Supreme Ct. 1975. Assoc. Cahill, Gordon & Reindel, N.Y.C., 1971-75, Arrow, Silverman & Parcher, N.Y.C., 1975-76; sr. law asst. Supreme Ct. State N.Y., N.Y.C., 1976-80, law sec. to Justice Hortense W. Gabel, 1981-87; bd. dirs., sec. Park Reservior Housing Corp., Bronx, 1974—; bd. dirs. Kingsbridge-Riverdale-Van Cortlandt Devel. Corp., Bronx, 1986—. Author: Charges to the Jury and Requests to Charge in a Criminal Case, 1983. Contbr. articles to profl. jours. Mem. Law Secs. and Law Assts. Assn. (treas.), Law Secs. Assn. (dir.), Sigma Alpha. Democrat. Jewish. State civil litigation, Criminal, Family and matrimonial.

LEVERETTE, SARAH ELIZABETH, lawyer; b. Iva, S.C., Dec. 28, 1919; d. Stephen Ernest and Allie E. (McGee) L. A.A., Anderson Coll., 1938; A.B., U. S.C. 1940, LL.B., 1943; postgrad. Columbia U., summer 1947. Bar: S.C. 1943. Legal research S.C. Labor Dept., Columbia, 1945-47; with Law Sch., U. S.C., Columbia, 1947-72, law librarian, 1947-72; commr. S.C. Indsl. Commn., 1972-78, chmn., 1976-77; legal cons., Columbia, 1978—; mem. Com. to Study Constn. S.C.; chmn. fund-raising drive U. S.C. Law Sch., 1983-85. Recipient Outstanding Alumni award Anderson Coll. Mem. Am. Assn. Law Librarians (life, Carolinas pres. 1948-50, chmn. scholarship com. 1959-71, coms. on membership, exchange and duplicates 1963-64, pres. Southeastern chpt. 1968-70), S.C. Bar Assn. (jud. modernization com., merit selection of judges subcom. 1983-85), S.C. Trial Lawyers Assn., Am. Judicature Soc., S.C. State Employees Assn. (bd. dirs. 1958-60), LWV (pres. Columbia 1958-61, past 2d v.p. S.C.), Columbia Library Assn. (pres. 1951-52, class chmn. Law Sch. Assn. Devel. Commn. 1984—), Phi Beta Kappa, Zeta Tau Alpha. Episcopalian. Club: Pilot (past pres.) (Columbia). Co-compiler: Checklist of S.C. Session Laws, 1963. Workers' compensation, Probate. Address: 1182 Quail Run Apts Columbia SC 29206

LEVERING, ROBERT BRUCE, lawyer; b. Greenville, Pa., Aug. 6, 1953; s. Emerald Perry and Jane Irene (Miller) L.; m. Janet Braund, May 14, 1983. BS in Psychology, Ohio State U., 1975; JD, Capital U., 1980. Bar: Ohio 1980, U.S. Dist. Ct. (so. dist.) Ohio 1983. Prosecutor City of Columbus, Ohio, 1981-83. Mem. ABA, Ohio Bar Assn., Franklin County Bar Assn. Republican. Methodist. Administrative and regulatory, Labor, Federal civil litigation. Office: Columbus City Atty 90 W Broad St City Hall Columbus OH 43215

LEVERTY, VERNON EUGENE, lawyer; b. Stockton, Calif., May 8, 1945; s. Patrick Archie and Sarah (Boughton) L.; m. Mary McCarty, Nov. 18, 1972 (div. May 1985); children: Courtney Erin, James Tyler, Patrick Ryan. BS, U. Ariz., 1967; JD, U. of Pacific, 1970. Bar: Calif. 1971, Nev. 1971, U.S. Dist. Ct. Nev. 1971, U.S. Dist. Ct. (ea. dist.) Calif. 1971, U.S. Supreme Ct. 1984. Adminstr.environ. protection agy. State of Nev., Carson City, 1970-71, chief dep. ins. commr., 1971-79; v.p. Miller & Daar, Los Angeles, Reno, San franciso and Seattle, 1979—. Served to pvt. USMC, 1968—. Mem. Nev. Bar Assn. (chmn. lawyer referral com., chmn. ins. com.), Calif. Bar Assn. Democrat. Roman Catholic. Insurance, Bankruptcy, General corporate. Office: Miller & Daar 832 Willow St Reno NV 89509

LEVETOWN, ROBERT ALEXANDER, lawyer; b. Bklyn., July 20, 1935; s. Alfred A. and Corinne L. (Cohen) L.; m. Roberta S. Slobodkin, Oct. 18, 1959. Student, U. Munich, Fed. Republic Germany, 1954-55; A.B., Princeton U., 1956; LL.B., Harvard U., 1959. Bar: D.C. 1960, N.Y. 1982, Va. 1984, Pa. 1985. Assoc. Pierson, Ball & Dowd, Washington, 1960-62; asst. U.S. atty. Washington, 1962-63; atty. Chesapeake & Potomac Telephone Cos., Washington, 1963-66, gen. atty., 1966-68, gen. solicitor, 1968-73, v.p., gen. counsel, 1975-83; exec. v.p., gen. counsel Bell Atlantic, Phila., 1983—. Mem. Washington Met. Corp. Counsels' Assn. (bd. dirs. 1981-83), Nat. Legal Ctr. (legal adv. council 1986—), ABA (vice chmn. communications com., pub. utility law sect. 1986—). Republican. Jewish. Office: Bell Atlantic Corp 1600 Market St Philadelphia PA 19103

LEVI, DAVID F., lawyer; b. 1951. BA, Harvard U.; JD, Stanford U. Bar: Calif. 1983. U.S. atty. ea. dist. State of Calif., Sacramento. Office: 3305 Federal Building 650 Capitol Mall Sacramento CA 95814 *

LEVI, EDWARD HIRSCH, former attorney general U.S., university president emeritus; b. Chgo., June 26, 1911; s. Gerson B. and Elsa B. (Hirsch) L.; m. Kate Sulzberger, June 4, 1946; children: John, David, Michael. Ph.B., U. Chgo., 1932, J.D., 1935; L.H.D.; J.S.D. (Sterling fellow 1935-36), Yale U., 1938; LL.D., U. Mich., 1959, U. Calif. at Santa Cruz, Jewish Theol. Sem. Am., U. Iowa, Brandeis U., Lake Forest Coll., U. Pa., Dropsie U., Columbia U., Yeshiva U., U. Rochester, U. Toronto, Yale U., U. Notre Dame, Denison U., U. Nebr., U. Miami, Boston Coll., Brigham Young U., Duke U., Ripon Coll., Georgetown U.; L.H.D., Hebrew Union Coll., DePaul U., Loyola U., Kenyon Coll., Bard Coll., Beloit Coll.; D.C.L., N.Y. U. Bar: Ill. U.S. Supreme Ct. 1945. Asst. prof. U. Chgo. Law Sch., 1936-40, prof. law, 1945-75, dean, 1950-62; provost univ. U. Chgo., 1962-68, univ. pres., 1968-75, pres. emeritus, 1975—; Karl Llewellyn Distinguished Service prof. (on leave) U. Chgo. Law Sch., from 1975, Glen A. Lloyd Disting. Service prof., 1977-85, Glen A. Lloyd Disting. Service prof. emeritus, 1985—; atty. gen. U.S., 1975-77; Thomas Guest prof. U. Colo., summer 1960; Herman Phleger vis. prof. Stanford Law Sch., 1978; lectr. Salzburg (Austria) Seminar in Am. Studies, 1980; spl. asst. to atty. gen. U.S., Washington, 1940-45; 1st asst. war div. Dept. Justice, 1943, 1st asst. antitrust div., 1944-45; chmn. interdeptl. com. on monopolies and cartels, 1944; counsel Fedn. Atomic Scientists with respect to Atomic Energy Act, 1946; counsel subcom. on monopoly power Judiciary Com., 81st Congress, 1950; trustee Aerospace Corp., 1978-80; Mem. research adv. bd. Com. Econ. Devel., 1951-54; bd. Social Sci. Research Council, 1959-62, Council Legal Edn. and Profl. Responsibility, 1968-74; mem. Citizens Commn. Grad. Med. Edn., 1963-66, Commn. Founds. and Pvt. Philanthropy, 1969-70, Pres.'s Task Force Priorities in Higher Edn., 1969-70, Sloan Commn. Cable Communications, 1970, Nat. Commn. on Productivity, 1970-75, Nat. Council on Humanities, 1974-75, dir. Continental Ill. Holding Corp. Author: Introduction to Legal Reasoning, 1949, Four Talks on Legal Education, 1952, Point of View, 1969; editor: (with J. W. Moore) Gilbert's Collier on Bankruptcy, 1936, Elements of the Law, (with R. S. Steffen), 1950. Hon. trustee U. Chgo.; trustee Internat. Legal Ctr., 1966-75, Woodrow Wilson Nat. Fellowship Found., 1972-75, 77-79, Inst. Psychoanalysis Chgo., 1961-75, Urban Inst., 1968-75, Mus. Sci. and Industry, 1971-75, Russell Sage Found., 1971-75, Aspen Inst. Humanistic Studies, 1970-75, 77-79, Inst. Internat. Edn. (hon.), 1969; public dir. Chgo. Bd. Trade, 1977-80; bd. overseers U. Pa., 1978-82; chmn. bd. Nat. Humanities Ctr., 1979-83, trustee, 1978—; bd. dirs. MacArthur Found., 1979-84, William Benton Found., 1980—, Martin Luther King Jr. Fed. Holiday Commn., 1986. Decorated Legion of Honor (France); recipient Learned Hand medal Fed. Bar Council, 2nd. cir., 1976, Fordham-Stein award Fordham U., 1977, Brandeis medal Brandeis U., 1978. Fellow Am. Acad. Arts and Scis. (nat. pres. 1986—), Am. Bar Found.; mem. Am. Philos. Soc., Fed. (hon. award 1975), Am., Ill. (award of honor 1983), Chgo. (Centennial award 1975) Bar Assns., Am. Law Inst. (council), Am. Judicature Soc., Supreme Ct. Hist. Soc., Phi Beta Kappa, Order of Coif. Clubs: Century (N.Y.C.); Chgo. Comml. Quadrangle Mid-Am. (Chgo.); Columbia Yacht. Antitrust, Jurisprudence. Office: U Chgo 1116 E 59th St Chicago IL 60637

LEVI, MARK DAVID, lawyer; b. N.Y.C., Jan. 19, 1951; s. Irving and Ingrid (Aronstein) L.; m. Judith Seiden, Dec. 28, 1975; children: Thomas Scott, Tracey Erin. BA, Case Western Res. U., 1973; JD, Western New Eng. Sch. of Law, 1976. Bar: N.Y. 1977, U.S. Dist. Ct. (so. and ea. dists.) N.Y. 1977. Law asst. N.Y. Family Ct., N.Y.C., 1977-78, N.Y. Supreme Ct., N.Y.C., 1978-79; asst. gen. counsel, unit chief-litigation N.Y.C. Transit Authority, 1979—. Commr. So. Riverdale (N.Y.) Baseball League, 1986. Mem. ABA. Democrat. Jewish. Avocations: skiing, tennis, golf. State civil litigation, Federal civil litigation, Personal injury. Home: 3333 Henry Hudson Pkwy Riverdale NY 10463 Office: NYC Transit Authority Gen Counsel's Office 370 Jay St Brooklyn NY 11201

LEVICK, MARSHA LYNN, lawyer; b. Phila., Mar. 3, 1951; d. Leonard Jordon and Myra (Friedman) L.; m. Ronald David Boschan, Sept. 24, 1983. Student Northwestern U., 1968-70; B.A. in History, U. Pa., 1971; J.D. cum laude, Temple U., 1976. Bar: Pa. 1976, U.S. Dist. Ct. (ea. dist.) Pa. 1976, U.S. Supreme Ct. 1985. Exec. dir., co-founder Juvenile Law Ctr., Phila., 1975-82, bd. dirs. 1983—; adj. faculty instr. criminal justice dept. Temple U., Phila., 1981-82; legal dir. NOW Legal Defense and Edn. Fund., N.Y.C., 1982-86, exec. dir., 1986—; mem. steering com. Feminist Legal Strategies Project, 1983—; mem. exec. com. Pa. Judicial Selection Project, Phila., 1981-82; editorial adv. bd. Prison Law Monitor, Washington, 1978-80; Juvenile Justice Standards Project, 1977-78. Contbr. articles to legal jours. Mem. Temple U. Law Quarterly, 1973-75. Civil rights, Criminal, Juvenile. Office: NOW Legal Defense and Edn Fund 99 Hudson St New York NY 10013

LEVIE, JOSEPH HENRY, lawyer; b. N.Y.C.; s. Mortimer Joseph and Pearl (Seelig) L.; m. Hallie Ratzkin, Jan. 26, 1963; children: Matthew Benjamin, Jessica Ruth. AB, Columbia U., 1949, LLB, 1951. Bar: N.Y. 1952, U.S. Ct. Mil. Appeals 1953, U.S. Supreme Ct. 1954, U.S. Ct. Claims 1964. Assoc. Laporte & Meyers, N.Y.C., 1955-59; assoc. gen. counsel Loew Theatres Inc., N.Y.C., 1959-63; from assoc. to ptnr. Rathheim, Kassell, Hoffman & Levie, N.Y.C., 1964-81; ptnr. Rogers & Wells, N.Y.C., 1982—; prof. continuing law edn. Fordham U., N.Y.C., 1986—; bd. dirs. Korea First Bank of N.Y. Contbr. articles to profl. jours. Served to 1st lt. JAGC, U.S. Army, 1952-55. Mem. Assn. of Bar of City of N.Y., N.Y. County Lawyers Assn., Assn. Comml. Fin. Attys., U.S. Korea Soc. Clubs: Netherland, Sky (N.Y.C.). Banking, Bankruptcy, Contracts commercial. Home: 131 Riverside Dr New York NY 10024 Office: Rogers & Wells Pan Am Building 200 Park Ave New York NY 10166

LEVIN, ARNOLD, lawyer; b. Phila., Mar. 23, 1939; s. Meyer and Sylvia (Orenberg) L.; Barbara Silver, May 2, 1965; children: Dawn, Rodney, Daniel, Rebecca. BS, Temple U., 1961, LLB, 1964. Bar: Pa. 1964, U.S. Dist. Ct. (ea. dist.) 1964, U.S. Ct. Appeals (3d cir.) 1971, U.S. Supreme Ct. 1972, U.S. Ct. Appeals (7th and 10th cirs.) 1977, U.S. Dist. Ct. (mid. dist.) 1981, U.S. Ct. Appeals (4th and 6th cirs.) 1981. Assoc. Freedman, Borrowsky & Lorry, Phila., 1964-69, ptnr., 1969-76; ptnr. Adler, Barish, Levin & Creskoff, Phila., 1976-81, Levin & Fishbein, Phila., 1981—; lectr. on class action litigation various seminars and assns. Served to capt. U.S. Army, 1961-67. Roscoe Pound Found. fellow, 1979—. Mem. ABA (maritime law sect. 1978), Pa. Bar Assn., Phila. Bar Assn., Assn. Trial Lawyers Am. (sec. comml. litigation sect. 1977, vice chmn. 1978, chmn. 1979, chmn. environ. law essay contest 1983), Pa. Trial Lawyers Assn. (co-chmn. antitrust sect. 1977—), Phila. Trial Lawyers Assn., Maritime Law Assn. Republican. Jewish. Lodge: B'nai B'rith. Antitrust, Federal civil litigation, Admiralty. Home: 162 Gramercy Rd Bala Cynwyd PA 19004 Office: Levin & Fishbein 320 Walnut St Suite 600 Philadelphia PA 19106

LEVIN, ARNOLD SAMPSON, lawyer; b. Lorain, Ohio, Dec. 10, 1909; s. Morris and Mina (Kaufman) L.; m. Harriet Jacobs, Jan. 21, 1977. JD, Ohio State U., 1934. Bar: Ohio 1934, U.S. Dist. Ct. (no. dist.) Ohio 1935, U.S. Ct. Appeals (6th cir.) 1950, U.S. Ct. Claims 1950, U.S. Supreme Ct. 1958. Ptnr. Levin & Levin, Lorain, 1934-42, 46-64, Levin & Durfee, Lorain, 1965-81; sole practice Lorain, 1981—; acting mcpl. judge, Lorain, 1948. Served to 1st lt. USAF, 1942-46. Mem. ABA, Ohio Bar Assn., Lorain County Bar Assn., Assn. Trial Lawyers Am., Ohio Acad. Trial Lawyers, VFW. Lodges: Masons, B'nai B'rith. Personal injury, Probate, Real property. Office: 216 7th St Lorain OH 44052

LEVIN, BETSY, lawyer, university dean; b. Balt., Dec. 25, 1935; d. M. Jastrow and Alexandra (Lee) L.). A.B., Bryn Mawr (Pa.) Coll., 1956; LL.B., Yale U., 1966. Bar: D.C. 1967, Colo., 1982. Dean U. Colo. Law Sch., 1981-87; exec. dir. Assn. Am. Law Schs., 1987—; dir. edn. studies Urban Inst., 1968-73; mem. faculty Duke U. Law Sch., 1973-81; Mem. Nat. Council Ednl. Research, 1978-79; mem. civil rights reviewing authority HEW, 1979-80; gen. counsel U.S. Dept. Edn., 1980-81;. Editor: Future Directions for School Finance Reform, 1975, The Courts, Social Science and School Desegregation, 1977, School Desegregation: Lessons of the First 25 Years, 1979. White House fellow, 1967-68. Mem. Am. Law Inst. (council), Soc. Am. Law Tchrs., ABA. Legal education, Civil rights, Education law. Home: 3537 1/2 Alton Pl NW Washington DC 20013 Office: Assn Am Law Schs 1 DuPont Circle NW Suite 370 Washington DC 20036

LEVIN, BRUCE ALAN, lawyer, real estate developer; b. Jersey City, Sept. 5, 1939; s. Julius and Toby (Sand) L.; m. Pamela Jo Dillow, Dec. 23, 1975; children: Sean, Brett, Annalee; 1 child from previous marriage: Peter. Student, Rutgers U., 1957-58; BS in Econs., U. Pa., 1961; JD, Harvard U., 1964. Bar: Calif. 1965, Oreg. 1978, Nev. 1980. Ptnr. Glaser and Levin and Levin, Saphier & Rein, Los Angeles, 1968-76; sole practice Bend, Oreg., 1978-79; v.p., gen. counsel Golden Nugget, Inc., Las Vegas, Nev., 1979—. Trustee and counsel to Meadows Sch., Las Vegas, 1984—. Office: Golden Nugget Inc 129 E Fremont St Las Vegas NV 89101

LEVIN, CHARLES LEONARD, state justice; b. Detroit, Apr. 28, 1926; s. Theodore and Rhoda (Katzin) L.; children—Arthur, Amy, Fredrick. B.A., U. Mich., 1946, LL.B., 1947; LL.D. (hon.), Detroit Coll. of Law, 1980. Bar: Mich. bar 1947, N.Y. bar 1949, U.S. Supreme Ct. bar 1953, D.C. bar 1954. Practiced in N.Y.C., 1948-50, Detroit, 1950-66; partner firm Levin, Levin, Garvett & Dill, Detroit, 1951-66; judge Mich. Ct. Appeals, Detroit, 1966-73; justice Mich. Supreme Ct., 1973—; mem. Mich. Law Revision Commn., 1966. Trustee Marygrove Coll., 1971-77, chmn., 1971-74; mem. vis. coms. to Law Schs., U. Mich., U. Chgo., 1977-80, Wayne State U. Mem. Am. Law Inst. Office: 1008 Travelers Tower Southfield MI 48076

LEVIN, CHARLES ROBERT, lawyer; b. Cambridge, Mass., Dec. 14, 1945; s. Maurice and Mary Frances (Phillips) L.; m. Jo Ellen Lederman, Aug 29, 1971; children: Jonathan, Michael. BA, Colby Coll., 1967; JD, Suffolk U., 1973. Bar: Mass. 1973, U.S. Dist. Ct. Mass. 1982. Asst. v.p. New Eng. Life, Boston, 1967-81; sole practice Boston, 1981-83; ptnr. Glanz & Levin, Brookline, Mass., 1983—. Bd. dirs., clerk B'nai B'rith Sr. Citizen Housing Corp., Boston, 1981—. Lodges: B'nai B'rith (pres. New Eng. realty lodge 1985-86), Masons. Real property, Contracts commercial, Probate. Home: 95 Tower Ave Needham MA 02194 Office: Glanz & Levin 111 Washington St Suite 302 Brookline MA 02146

LEVIN, DAVID HAROLD, lawyer; b. Pensacola, Fla., Nov. 19, 1928. A.B., Duke U., 1949; J.D., U. Fla., 1952. Bar: Fla. 1952. Asst. county solicitor Escambia County (Fla.), 1952; sr. ptnr. Levin, Warfield, Middlebrooks, Mabie, Thomas, Mayes & Mitchell, Pensacola; chmn. 1st Jud. Circuit Fla. Jud. Nominating Commn., 1976-78; chmn. Fla. Pollution Control Bd., 1971-74. Chmn., Escambia County Cancer Crusade, 1963-65; pres. Escambia County unit Am. Cancer Soc., 1964-65; bd. dirs. W. Fla. Heart Assn., 1966-69; chmn. United Jewish Appeal Escambia County, 1967-68; former mem. human rights commn. W. Fla. Hosp. Mem. Fla. Alumni Assn. (pres. chpt. 1960), U. Fla. Alumni Assn. (dist. v.p. 1961-62), Blue Key. Recipient Good Govt. award Pensacola Jaycees, 1972; Service award Fla. Council for Clear Air, 1974; Francis Marion Weston award Audubon Soc., 1974; commendation Gov. Fla., 1974. mem. Am. Acad. Matrimonial Lawyers (pres.-elect Fla. chpt.). Family and matrimonial, State civil litigation, Personal injury. Home: 3632 Menendez Dr Pensacola FL 32503 Office: 226 S Palafox St Pensacola FL 32501

LEVIN, DEBBE ANN, lawyer; b. Cin., Mar. 11, 1954; d. Abram Asher and Selma Ruth (Herlands) L. BA, Washington U., St. Louis, 1976; JD, U. Cin., 1979; LLM, NYU, 1983. Bar: Ohio 1979. Staff atty. U.S. Ct. Appeals 6th Circuit, Cin., 1979-82; assoc. Schwartz, Manes & Ruby Co., LPA, Cin., 1983—; lectr. tax conf. U. Cin., 1984-86, adj. prof. coll. of bus., 1987. Editor: U. Cin. Law Review, 1972-79. Recipient Judge Alfred Mack prize U. Cin., 1979. Mem. ABA, Ohio Bar Assn., Cin. Bar Assn., Cin. Bus. & Profl.

Women's Club, Order of Coif. Jewish. Pension, profit-sharing, and employee benefits, Corporate taxation, Estate taxation. Office: Schwartz Manes & Ruby Co LPA 2900 Carew Tower Cincinnati OH 45202

LEVIN, EDWARD M., JR., lawyer, govt. adminstr.; b. Chgo., Oct. 16, 1934; s. Edward M. and Anne Meriam (Fantl) L.; m. Joan Davis, Dec. 3, 1961; children—Daniel Andrew, John Davis. B.S., U. Ill., 1955; LL.B., Harvard U., 1958. Bar: Ill. 1958, U.S. Supreme Ct. 1968. Mem. firm Ancel, Stonesifer, Glink & Levin and predecessors, Chgo., 1958, 61-68; draftsman Ill. Legis. Reference Bur., Springfield, 1961; spl. asst. to regional adminstr. HUD, Chgo., 1968-71, asst. regional adminstr. community planning and mgmt., 1971-73; asst. dir. Ill. Dept. Local Govt. Affairs, Chgo., 1973-77; of counsel Holleb, Gerstein & Glass, Ltd., Chgo., 1977-79; chief counsel Econ. Devel. Adminstrn., U.S. Dept. Commerce, Washington, 1979-85; sr. fellow Nat. Gov's. Assn., 1985-86, sr. counsel U.S. Dept. of Commerce, 1987— ; lectr. U. Ill., 1972-73, adj. assoc. prof. urban scis., 1973-79; lectr. Loyola U., 1976-79. Mem. Ill. Nature Preserves Com., 1963-68, Northeastern Ill. Planning Commn., 1974-77, Ill.-Ind. Bi-State Commn., 1974-77; bd. dirs. Cook County Legal Assistance Found., 1978-79; mem. Ill. div. ACLU, 1965-68, 77-79, v.p., 1977-78. Served with AUS, 1958-60. Mem. Ill. Bar Assn. (Lincoln award 1977), Chgo. Council Lawyers, Washington Council Lawyers. Clubs: Arts (Chgo.); Fgn. Service (Washington). Contbr. articles to profl. jours. Administrative and regulatory, Government contracts and claims, Local government. Home: 3218 Davenport St NW Washington DC 20008 Office: Hall of the States Rm 250 444 N Capitol St Washington DC 20001

LEVIN, FREDERIC GERSON, lawyer; b. Pensacola, Fla., Mar. 29, 1937; s. Abraham I. and Rose (Lefkowitz) L.; m. Marilyn Kapner, June 14, 1959; children: Marci Levin Goodman, Debra, Martin, Kimberly. BSBA, U. Fla., 1958, JD, 1961. Bar: Fla. 1961, U.S. Dist. Ct. (no. dist.) Fla., U.S. Ct. Appeals (5th cir.). Assoc. Levin, Warfield, Middlebrooks, Mabie, Thomas, Mayes & Mitchell, P.A., Pensacola, 1961—; counsel Fla. Senate, 1981-82. Author: Effective Opening Statements, 1983; contbr. articles to profl. jours. Fellow Acad. Fla. Trial Lawyers (dir. 1977-84), mem. Inner Circle of Advocates, Ala. Trial Lawyers Assn., Tex. Trial Lawyers Assn., Pa. Trial Lawyers Assn. Democrat. Jewish. Personal injury. Home: 3600 Menendez Dr Pensacola FL 32503 Office: Levin Warfield Middlebrooks et al 226 S Palafox Pensacola FL 32501

LEVIN, HARVEY PHILLIP, lawyer; b. Chgo., Oct. 22, 1942; s. Julius L. and Gertrude (Cohen) L.; m. Madeleine J. Raskin, Sept. 22, 1970; children—Arianne, Nicole, David. B.B.A., U. Mich., 1964, M.B.A., 1968; J.D., DePaul U., 1969. Bar: Ill., 1969, Tex., 1979, U.S. Dist. Ct. (no. dist.) Ill. 1970, U.S. Ct. Appeals (5th cir.) 1981, U.S. Ct. Appeals (7th cir.) 1971, U.S. Supreme Ct. 1972. Assoc. Potts Randall & Horn, Chgo., 1969-70, Randall Horn & Pyes, Chgo., 1970-71; assoc., jr. ptnr. Mehlman, Ticho, Addis, Susman, Spitzer, Randall, Horn & Pyes, Chgo., 1971-75; sole practice, Chgo., 1975-78, Dallas, 1979—; dir. Leedal Inc., Chgo., Sidran Sportswear Inc., Dallas. Bd. dirs. Solomon Schecter Acad. of Dallas, 1979—, Congregation Shearith Israel, Dallas, 1981—, Am. Jewish Congress, Dallas, 1980-85. Mem. Chgo. Bar Assn., Ill. Bar Assn., Dallas Bar Assn., Tex. Bar Assn., ABA (vice chmn. workers compensation com.). General practice, Occupational disease consultant. Home: 6918 Blue Mesa Dallas TX 75252 Office: 5310 Harvest Hill Suite 169 Dallas TX 75230

LEVIN, JACK K., lawyer, editor; b. Hammond, Ind., Mar. 23, 1950; s. Joseph and Irene (Weil) L. Student, U. Chgo., 1969-71, JD, 1974. Bar: Ill. 1974, U.S. Dist. Ct. (no. dist.) Ill. 1974. Sole practice Chgo., 1974-76; legal editor Lawyers Coop. Pub. Co., Rochester, N.Y., 1977—. Mem. ABA. Legal publishing. Office: Lawyers Coop Pub Co Aqueduct Bldg Rochester NY 14694

LEVIN, JACK S., lawyer; b. Chgo., May 1, 1936; s. Frank J. and Judy G. (Skerball) L.; m. Sandra Sternberg, Aug. 24, 1958; children: Lisa, Laura, Leslie, Linda. B.S. summa cum laude, Northwestern U., 1958; LL.B. summa cum laude, Harvard U., 1961. Bar: Ill. 1961; C.P.A. (gold medalist), Ill., 1958. Law clk. to chief judge U.S. Ct. of Appeals 2d Circuit, N.Y.C., 1961-62; asst. for tax matters to Solicitor Gen. of U.S., Washington, 1965-67; assoc. law firm Kirkland & Ellis, Chgo., 1962-65; partner 1967—; frequent lectr. on legal aspects of venture capital transactions, mergers and acquisitions, fed. income, tax matters. Case editor Harvard Law Rev., 1959-61; contbr. numerous articles to legal jours.; contbr. chpts. to law books. Parliamentarian Winnetka (Ill.) Town Meetings 1974-83; chmn. nat. fund raising drive Harvard Law Sch., 1985-86. Mem. ABA (chmn. subcom. 1968-79), Fed. Bar Assn., Chgo. Bar Assn. (exec. com. 1985—), Am. Coll. Tax Counsel. Clubs: Chgo., Mid-Am. (Chgo.) (bd. dirs. 1985—); Birchwood (Highland Park) (pres. 1980-82). Corporate taxation, General corporate. Home: 1220 Sunset Rd Winnetka IL 60093 Office: Kirkland & Ellis 200 E Randolph Dr Chicago IL 60601

LEVIN, JEFFREY KENNETH, lawyer; b. N.Y.C., May 17, 1956; s. Robert D. and Gladys L. (Schoen) L.; m. Fern Barbara Siegelstein, Aug. 3, 1980; children: Judith, Michael. BA, Northwestern U., 1977; JD, Fordham U., 1980; MBA, N.Y.U., 1985. Bar: N.Y. 1981. Asst. counsel N.Y. State Mortgage Loan Corp., N.Y.C., 1980-83; assoc. Sage Gray Todd & Sims, N.Y.C., 1983—. Mem. ABA, N.Y. State Bar Assn., U.S. Chess Fedn. Jewish. Real property. Home: 515 W 59th St 32E New York NY 10019 Office: Sage Gray Todd & Sims Two World Trade Ctr 100th Floor New York NY 10048

LEVIN, LON CARL, lawyer; b. Bklyn., Mar. 7, 1955; s. Albert and Joan (Loew) L.; m. Melanie Beth Shore, June 22, 1985. BA, SUNY, Albany, 1976; M in Profl. Studies, JD, Syracuse U., 1980. Bar: N.Y. 1981, D.C. 1982. Atty. FCC, Washington, 1980-83; assoc. Mintz, Levin, Cohn, Ferris, Glovsky & Popeo, Washington, 1983-85, Gurman, Kurtis & Blask, Washington, 1985—. Sr. editor: International Telecommunications Handbook, 1986—. Bd. visitors Syracuse U. Coll. Law. Mem. ABA, Fed. Bar Assn., Soc. Satellite Profls., Fed. Communications Bar Assn. (chmn. internat. telecommunications com. 1985—). Club: Nat. Space (Washington). Administrative and regulatory, Space commercialization, Trademark and copyright. Office: Gurman Kurtis & Blask 1730 M St Suite 700 Washington DC 20036

LEVIN, MARSHALL ABBOTT, judge, educator; b. Balt., Nov. 22, 1920; s. Harry Oscar and Rose (DeLaviez) L.; m. Beverly Edelman, Aug. 6, 1948; children—Robert B., Susan R. Levin Lieman, Burton H. B.A., U. Va., 1941; J.D., Harvard U., 1947. Bar: Md. 1947, U.S. Dist. Ct. Md. 1947, U.S. Ct. Appeals (4th cir.) 1950, U.S. Supreme Ct. 1953. Bill drafter, legis. asst. Dept. Legis. Reference, Annapolis, Md., 1948-49; research asst. Workers Compensation Comm., City of Balt., 1951, police magistrate, 1951-55, magistrate housing ct., 1955-58; ptnr. Levin & Levin, Balt., 1947-66; sole practice, Balt., 1966-68; ptnr. Edelman, Levin, Levy & Rubenstein, Balt., 1968-71; judge Circuit Ct. for Balt. City, 1971—; chmn. Mayor's Com. on Housing Law Enforcement, Balt., 1963; lectr. nationally on sentencing, death penalty, immunities; lectr. Nat. Conf. on Child Abuse, 1976; dir. Legal Aid Soc., Balt., 1979-81; chmn. jud. bd. sentencing State of Md., 1979-83; chmn. Sentencing Guidelines Bd. State of Md., 1983—; instituted One Trial/One Day jury system, Balt., 1983; prof. grad. sch. U. Balt., 1979—; prof. Nat. Jud. Coll., U. Nev., 1980—. Contbr. articles to law revs. Served to lt. USNR, 1941-45, ETO. NEH fellow, 1976; recipient spl. award for service to jud. edn. Nat. Jud. Coll., U. Nev., 1984. Mem. Jud. Disabilities Commn., ABA, Md. State Bar Assn. (Leadership award 1984), Balt. City Bar Assn. (commendation 1982). Democrat. Jewish. Legal education, Legal history, Jurisprudence. Home: 6106 Ivydene Terr Baltimore MD 21209 Office: 536 Courthouse E Baltimore MD 21202

LEVIN, MARVIN EUGENE, lawyer; b. Antigo, Wis., June 20, 1924; s. Jacob and Lillian (Goldberg) L.; m. Ruth Ganzfried, June 10, 1948; children—Randal Mark, Gregary. B.S., U. So. Calif., 1948, J.D., 1951. Bar: Calif. 1952. Sole practice, Los Angeles and Santa Monica, Calif., 1952-68; sr. ptnr. Levin & Freedman, Santa Monica, 1968—; author, lectr. continuing edn. of bar. Bd. dirs., founder mem. NCCJ, Santa Monica, 1959—, chmn. 1965, So. Calif. regional bd., 1984—; mem. regional bd. Anti-Defamation League 1958—, mem. exec. com. 1960-81; mem. bd. Univ. Synagogue, West Los Angeles, Calif., 1970-74. Served to capt. USAAF 1943-46. Decorated Air medal with oak leaf cluster; recipient Brotherhood award Santa Monica Bay Area chpt. NCCJ 1968. Fellow Am. Coll. Probate Csl.; mem. ABA, State Bar Calif. (sects. real property, probate and trust law), Los Angeles County Bar Assn., Santa Monica Bay Dist. Bar Assn. (trustee 1971-74, pres. 1973-74, chmn. sect. real property law 1982-84), Am. Arbitration Assn. (panel of arbitrators 1968—), Santa Monica C. of C. Club: Marina City (Marina Del Rey, Calif.). Lodges: Rotary (com. chmn. Santa Monica chpt. 1985—), B'nai B'rith (Pacific Palisades 1981—, 1st v.p. Ketubah unit West Los Angeles 1981—). Contbr. to Advising California Business Enterprises, 1958. Real property, Probate, Estate taxation. Office: Levin & Freedman 501 Santa Monica Blvd Suite 601 Santa Monica CA 90401

LEVIN, MICHAEL DAVID, lawyer; b. Chgo., Oct. 11, 1942; s. Joseph F. and Libbie (Landman) L.; m. Jane Reinsberg, May 21, 1966; children: Victoria, David, Elizabeth. AB, U. Mich., JD. Assoc. Arnstein, Gluck, Weitzenfeld & Minow, Chgo., 1967-73, ptnr., 1973-81; ptnr. Latham & Watkins, Chgo., 1982—. Mem. ABA, Chgo. Bar Assn. (chmn. securities law 1982-83). Republican. Jewish. Clubs: Standerd, Metropolitan (Chgo.). General corporate, Securities. Office: Latham & Watkins Sears Tower Suite 6900 Chicago IL 60606

LEVIN, MORRIS JACOB, lawyer; b. St. Louis, Aug. 30, 1909; s. Barnett and Jeanette (Rosenblatt) L.; m. Lillian Richman, Aug. 15, 1934; 1 son, Roger B.; m. 2d, Betty M. O'Brien, Jan. 7, 1972. J.D., Washington U., St. Louis, 1930. Bar: Mo. 1931, U.S. Ct. Appeals (8th cir.) 1942, U.S. Supreme Ct. 1938. Assoc. Victor Packman, St. Louis, 1931-44; sole practice, St. Louis, 1944-59; ptnr. Levin & Weinhaus, St. Louis, 1959—. Mem. ABA, Mo. Bar Assn., St. Louis Bar Assn., Mo. Assn. Trial Lawyers. Labor, Real property, Workers' compensation. Home: 4508 Pershing Pl St Louis MO 63108 Office: 906 Olive St Suite 900 Louis MO 63101-1463

LEVIN, ROBERT DANIEL, lawyer; b. N.Y.C., Feb. 27, 1930; s. Moses H. and Esther (Walzer) L.; m. Gladys Schoen, Apr. 8, 1954; children—Jeffrey, Donna. A.B., Rutgers U., 1951; J.D., Columbia, 1954. Bar: N.Y. bar 1954. Since practiced in N.Y.C.; with firm Demov, Morris, Levin & Hammerling, 1954-85, sr. ptnr., 1963-85; sr. ptnr. Lowenthal, Landau, Fisher & Ziegler, P.C., 1985—. Co-editor: N.Y. Law Jour. Realty Law Digest. Mem. N.Y. State Bar Assn., Bar Assn. City N.Y. (state legislation and real property law com., com. civil ct.), Phi Beta Kappa, Phi Alpha Delta. Real property, State civil litigation, Federal civil litigation. Home: 12 Varian Ln Scarsdale NY 10583 Office: 250 Park Ave New York NY 10177

LEVIN, ROGER MICHAEL, lawyer; b. N.Y.C., Oct. 20, 1942; s. Harold F. and Blanche M. (Tarr) L. B.A. in Polit. Sci., U. Chgo., 1964; Fulbright scholar U. Sri Lanka, 1964-65; M.A. with distinction in Polit. Sci. (Woodrow Wilson fellow), U. Calif.-Berkeley, 1966; J.D., NYU, 1969. Bar: N.Y. 1970, D.C. 1982, U.S. Dist. Ct. (so. and ea. dists.) N.Y., 1971, U.S. Ct. Appeals (2d cir.) 1971, U.S. Ct. Appeals (D.C. cir.) 1979, U.S. Customs Ct. 1974, U.S. Tax Ct. 1981, U.S. Ct. Customs and Patent Appeals 1974, U.S. Supreme Ct. 1974. Personal asst. to U.S. rep. Dept. State, Quang Nam Province, South Vietnam, 1966; asst. to dir. Nr. East/South Asia Bur., Office Internat. Security Affairs, Office Sec. of Def., Washington, 1967; assoc. Wien, Lane & Malkin, N.Y.C., 1969-70; ptnr. Levin & Weissman, N.Y.C., 1975—, mng. ptnr., 1982—. Named Best Oralist, Jessup Internat. Law Moot Ct. Regional Competition NYU, 1969. Mem. ABA, N.Y. State Bar Assn. (com. pension, welfare and related plans and ERISA subcom. labor law sect. 1981—), Assn. Bar City N.Y., D.C. Bar, Am. Soc. Internat. Law. Research editor NYU Jour. Internat. Law and Politics. Federal civil litigation, General corporate, Labor. Office: 122 E 42d St New York NY 10017

LEVIN, SUSAN BASS, lawyer; b. Wilmington, Del., July 18, 1952; d. Max S. and Harriet C. (Rubin) Bass; m. Benjamin A. Levin, June 10, 1972; children: Lisa, Amy. BA, U. of Rochester, 1972; JD, George Washington U., 1975. Bar: D.C. 1975, U.S. Ct. Claims 1975, N.J. 1976, Pa. 1981, U.S. Ct. Appeals (3d cir.) 1983, U.S. Supreme Ct. 1984. Law clk. to assoc. justice U.S. Ct. Claims, Washington, 1975-76; assoc. Covington & Burling, Washington, 1976-79; sole practice Cherry Hill, N.J., 1979-83; ptnr. Levin & Levin, Cherry Hill and Phila., 1983—; ptnr. Berman & Levin, Cherry Hill, 1983-86. Mem. Camden County Planning Bd., N.J., 1985-86; pres. Cherry Hill (N.J.) Twp. Council, 1986—; trustee N.J. Coalition of Small Bus. Orgns., 1985—, Youth Coordinating Council of Cherry Hill, 1986—. Recipient Woman of Achievement award Camden County Girl Scouts, 1986. Mem. N.J. Bar Assn., Camden County Bar Assn., Tri County Women Lawyers (pres. 1984-85), N.J. Assn. Women Bus. Owners (state pres. 1984-85 named Woman of Yr. 1985). General practice, Probate, Real property. Office: Levin & Levin 1701 E Rt 70 PO Box 1302 Cherry Hill NJ 08003 Office: Levin & Levin 1919 Two Penn Center Philadelphia PA 19102

LEVINE, ALAN, lawyer; b. Middletown, N.Y., Jan. 17, 1948; s. Jacques and Florence (Tananbaum) L.; m. Nancy Shapiro, June 7, 1971; children—Emily Jane, Malcolm Andrew. B.S. in Econs., U. Pa., 1970; J.D., NYU, 1973. Bar: N.Y. 1974, U.S. Dist. Ct. (so. dist.) N.Y. 1974, U.S. Dist. Ct. (ea. dist.) N.Y. 1980, U.S. Tax Ct. 1980, U.S. Ct. Appeals (2d cir.) 1975. Law clk. U.S. Dist. Ct. (so. dist.) N.Y., N.Y.C., 1973-75; asst. U.S. atty, U.S. Attys. Office, so. dist. N.Y., Dept. Justice, N.Y.C., 1975-80; assoc. Kronish, Lieb, Weiner & Hellman, N.Y.C., 1980-82, mem., 1982—. Trustee, v.p. Park Ave. Synagogue, N.Y.C., 1984; mem. exec. com. lawyers div., Am. Friends of Hebrew U., N.Y.C., 1984; mem. pub. policy com. United Jewish Appeal Fedn. Jewish Philanthropies, N.Y.C., 1981-84. Recipient Atty. Gen. Dirs. award U.S. Dept. Justice, 1980. Fellow Am. Bar Found.; mem. ABA (ho. of dels. 1983-84, spl. com. youth edn. for citizenship), N.Y. State Bar Assn. (chmn. com. on citizenship edn. 1979-84, ho. of dels. 1982-84, award of achievement 1984). Republican. Jewish. Club: Sunningdale Country (Scarsdale, N.Y.); Mask and Wig (Phila.). Federal civil litigation, Criminal. Home: 1185 Park Ave New York NY 10128 Office: Kronish Lieb Weiner & Hellman 1345 Ave of Americas New York NY 10105

LEVINE, BERNARD BENTON, lawyer; b. New Haven, Aug. 27, 1927; s. Charles and Mildred (Schwartz) L.; m. Joan A. Rapoport, Sept. 7, 1952; children—Stefanie, Kalman, Shelley Levine Kraft. B.A., U. Conn., 1950; LL.B., Boston U., 1953; LL.M. in Taxation, NYU, 1954. Bar: Mass. 1953, Conn. 1954, Mo. 1955. Assoc. Stinson, Mag, Thomson, McEvers & Fizzell, Kansas City, Mo., 1954-55; ptnr. Warrick, Levine & Greene, Kansas City, 1958-68, Levine & Green, Kansas City, 1968-81; sole practice, Kansas City, 1981—; instr. real estate, econs. and comml. law; pres. William Jewel Coll., 1985-87. Contbr. articles to legal jour. Bd. govs., past v.p., past bd. dirs. Jewish Geriatric and Convalescent Ctr., Kansas City, Jewish Family and Children's Services, Kansas City; bd. govs., past dir. Hyman Brand Hebrew Acad., Overland Park, Kans.; bd. dirs. Jewish Community Ctr., Kansas City, Am. Jewish Com., Kansas City, William Jewell Fine Arts Guild, Liberty, Mo., pres.; bd. dirs., mem. campaign cabinet Jewish Fedn., Kansas City. Served with U.S. Army, 1946-48. Mem. ABA (property and internat. savs. and loan div.), U.S. Savs. and Loan League, Mo. Savs. and Loan League, Mo. Bar Assn., Kansas City Bar Assn., Lawyers Assn. Kansas City, Conn. Bar Assn., Mass. Bar Assn. Real property, Corporate taxation. Home: 7318 Mercier St Kansas City MO 64114 Office: 2302 Power and Light Bldg 106 W 14th St Kansas City MO 64105

LEVINE, BERYL JOYCE, state supreme court justice; b. Winnipeg, Man., Can., Nov. 9, 1935; came to U.S., 1955; d. Maurice Jacob and Bella (Gutnik) Choslovsky; m. Leonard Levine, June 7, 1955; children: Susan Brauna, Marc Joseph, Sari Ruth, William Noah, David Karl. B.A., U. Man., Winnipeg, 1965; J.D. with distinction, U. N.D., 1974. Assoc. Vogel, Brantner, Kelly, Knutson, Weir & Bye, Ltd., Fargo, N.D., 1974-85; justice N.D. Supreme Ct., Bismarck, 1985—, chmn. jud. planning com. Bd. dirs. Fargo Youth Commn., 1974-77, Hospice of Red River Valley, Fargo; chmn. Gov.'s Commn. on Children at Risk, 1985. Named Outstanding Woman in N.D. Law, U. N.D. Law Women's Caucus, 1985. Mem. Cass County Bar Assn. (pres. 1984-85), N.D. State Bar Assn., Burleigh County Bar Assn., Order of Coif. Office: ND Supreme Ct Bismarck ND 58505 *

LEVINE, CURTIS GILBERT, lawyer; b. New Britain, Conn., Nov. 21, 1947; s. Louis Leon and Bernice Elaine (Sweig) L.; m. Marjorie Beth Schwarz, Jan. 17, 1972; children: Jessica Rachel, Deborah Lynn. BA, Northeastern U., 1970; JD, Suffolk U., 1973. Bar: Fla. 1973, U.S. Dist. Ct. (so. dist.) Fla. 1974, U.S. Dist. Ct. (mid. dist.) Fla. 1981, U.S. Ct. Appeals (5th and 11th cirs.) 1981, U.S. Supreme Ct. 1986. Chief asst. pub. defender capital crimes div. Palm Beach County, West Palm Beach, Fla., 1973-76; ptnr. Baskin & Sears, Boca Raton, Fla., 1976-84; sole practice Boca Raton, 1985-86; gen. counsel Coastline Title Co., Boca Raton, 1986—. Chmn. Environ. Adv. Bd. City of Boca Raton, 1980-85. Mem. ABA, Assn. Trial Lawyers Am., Acad. Fla. Trial Lawyers. Lodge: B'nai B'rith (pres. Boca Raton 1981). Real property, State civil litigation, Construction. Home: 2804 Banyan Blvd Circle NW Boca Raton FL 33431 Office: Crocker Ctr 5200 Town Ctr Suite 301 Boca Raton FL 33432

LEVINE, DAVID ETHAN, lawyer; b. Niagara Falls, N.Y., Feb. 28, 1955; s. Morree Morell Levine and Marbud Juel (Gagen) Prozeller; m. Ann Lee Ruhlin, May 23, 1981. BS in Bus., Miami U., 1977; JD, Capital U., 1981. Bar: N.Y. 1982, U.S. Dist. Ct. (we. dist.) N.Y. 1982. Assoc. Grossman, Levine and Civiletto, Niagara Falls, 1981—. Mem. Old Ft. Niagara Assn., Youngstown, N.Y., 1986, Niagara Council of Arts, Niagara Falls, 1986. Mem. N.Y. State Bar Assn., Niagara Falls Bar Assn. Unitarian Universalist. Club: Niagara Falls Country (Lewiston, N.Y.). Avocations: skiing, photography, tennis, camping. Personal injury, Family and matrimonial, Real property. Home: 456 Fuller Pl Lewiston NY 14092 Office: 331 Buffalo Ave Niagara Falls NY 14303

LEVINE, DAVID ISRAEL, lawyer, educator; b. Wilmington, Del., Oct. 11, 1953; s. Murray and Adeline Frances (Gordon) L.; m. Susan L. Shackman, June 13, 1982 (dec. Mar. 1986). AB, U. Mich., 1974; postgrad., U. London, Eng., 1974-75; JD, U. Pa., 1978. Bar: Pa. 1978, U.S. Ct. Appeals (5th cir.) 1979, Calif. 1980, U.S. Dist. Ct. (no. dist.) Calif. 1980, U.S. Ct. Appeals (9th cir.) 1980. Law clk. to judge U.S. Ct. Appeals (5th cir.), New Orleans, 1978-79; assoc. Morrison & Foerster, San Francisco, 1979-82; prof. law U. Calif. Hastings Coll. Law, San Francisco, 1982—; analyst U.S. Dist. Ct. (no. dist.) Calif., San Francisco, 1985—. contbr. articles to profl. jours. Grantee Nat. Inst. Dispute Resolution, 1985-87. Mem. Pa. Bar Assn., Calif. Bar Assn. Democrat. Jewish. Federal civil litigation, Legal education, Personal injury. Home: 1366 El Centro Ave Oakland CA 94602 Office: U Calif Hastings Coll Law 200 McAllister St San Francisco CA 94102

LEVINE, GARY H., lawyer; b. Denver, Nov. 3, 1951; s. Irwin D. and Bernadine (Hellerstein) L.; m. Linda Dale Campbell, June 24, 1978; 1 child, David G. BSBA in Acctg., U. Colo., 1974, JD, 1977. Bar: Colo. 1977, U.S. Dist. Ct. Colo. 1977, U.S. Tax Ct. 1981; CPA, Colo. Assoc. Levine & Pitler, Denver, 1977-81, Robinson, Waters, O'Dorisio & Rapson, Denver, 1981-83, Grant, McHendrie, Haines & Crouse, Denver, 1984—; of counsel McMichael & Benedict, Denver, 1983-84, Grant, McHendrie, Haines & Crouse, Denver, 1984—; instr. Community Coll. of Denver, Redrocks, Colo., 1977-78. Bd. dirs. Sch. Dist. #12 Edn. Found., Northglenn, Colo., 1985. Mem. ABA, Colo. Bar Assn., Denver Bar Assn., Adams County Bar Assn., Met. North C. of C. (small bus. adv. cabinet leadership program 1985). Real property, Contracts commercial, Estate planning. Home: PO Box 33064 North Glenn CO 80233 Office: Grant McHendrie Haines & Crouse 11990 Grant St #414 Northglenn CO 80233

LEVINE, HAROLD, lawyer; b. Newark, Apr. 30, 1931; s. Rubin and Gussie (Lifshitz) L.; m. Harriet B. Levine; children—Brenda Sue, Linda Ellen Levine Gersen, Louise Abby, Jill Anne Levine Zuvanich, Charles A., Cristina Gussie, Harold Rubin II; m. Cristina Cervera, Aug. 29, 1980. B.S. in Engring., Purdue U., 1954; J.D. with distinction, George Washington U., 1958. Bar: D.C. 1958, Va., 1958, Mass. 1960, Tex. 1972, U.S. Patent Office, 1958. Naval architect, marine engr. U.S. Navy Dept., 1954-55; patent examiner U.S. Patent Office, 1955-58; with Tex. Instruments Inc., Attleboro, Mass., 1959-77, asst. sec., Dallas, 1969-72, asst. v.p. and gen. patent counsel, 1972-77; ptnr. Sigalos & Levine, Dallas, 1977—; chmn. bd. Vanguard Security, Inc., Houston, 1977—; chmn. Tex. Am. Realty, Dallas, 1977—; lectr. assns., socs.; del. Geneva and Lausanne (Switzerland) Intergovtl. Conf. on Revision, Paris Pat. Conv., 1975-76. Mem. U.S. State Dept. Adv. Panel on Internat. Tech. Transfer, 1977. Mem. ABA (chmn. com. 407 taxation pats. and trdmks. 1971-72), Am. Patent Law Assn., Dallas Bar Assn., Assn. Corp. Pat. Csl. (sec.-treas. 1971-73), Dallas-Fort Worth Patent Law Assn., Pacific Indsl. Property Assn. (pres. 1975-77), Electronic Industries Assn. (pres. pat. com. 1972), NAM, Southwestern Legal Inst. on Patent Law (planning com. 1971-74), U.S. C. of C., Dallas C. of C., Alpha Epsilon Pi, Phi Alpha Delta. Republican. Jewish. Club: Kiwanis. Contbr. chpt. to book, articles to profl. jours. Editor: George Washington U. Law Rev., 1956-57; mem. adv. bd. editors Bur. Nat. Affairs, Pat., Trdmk. and Copyright Jour., 1979-87. Patent, Trademark and copyright, Private international. Office: Sigalos & Levine 1300 Republic Bank Tower Dallas TX 75201

LEVINE, HENRY DAVID, lawyer; b. N.Y.C., June 7, 1951; s. Harold Abraham and Joan Sarah (Price) L.; m. Barbara Wolgel, Aug. 28, 1976; children: David, Rachel. AB, Yale U., 1972; JD, M in Pub. Policy, Harvard U., 1976. Bar: N.Y. 1977, D.C. 1978, U.S. Supreme Ct. 1980. Assoc. Wilmer, Cutler & Pickering, Washington, 1976-80; assoc. Morrison & Foerster, Washington, 1981-83, ptnr., 1983—; adj. prof. law George Washington U., 1981-84. Editor Telematics, 1984—. Mem. Nat. Research Council Com on High Tech. Bldgs., 1985—. Mem. ABA (chmn. telecommunications subcom. corp., banking and bus. law sect.), Fed. Communication Bar Assn. Administrative and regulatory, Federal civil litigation, Telecommunications. Home: 5208 Edgemoor Ln Bethesda MD 20814 Office: Morrison & Foerster 2000 Pennsylvania Ave NW #5500 Washington DC 20006

LEVINE, HERBERT, lawyer; b. N.Y.C., June 5, 1924; s. Barnet and Mollie (Morris) L.; m. Pearl H. Kahn, Mar. 30, 1946; children—Barbara, Susan, Deborah, Steven. B.B.A., U. Wis.-Madison, 1950, J.D., 1950. Bar: Wis. 1950, U.S. Dist. Ct. (ea. dist.) Wis. 1950. Sole practice, Milw., 1950-66; assoc. Bernstein, Wessel & Lewis, Milw., 1967-75, Stupar & Schuster, S.C., Milw., 1976—; instr. Am. Inst. Banking, Milw., 1964—; lectr. Marquette U., 1968-79, Milw. Bd. Realtors, 1961. Pres. Bayside PTA, Wis., 1965-66; active Indian Guides, Bayside, Wis., 1972-73. Served as sgt. USAAF, 1943-46. Mem. Wis. Bar Assn., Milw. Bar Assn. Contracts commercial, General corporate, Real property. Home: 9055 N King Rd Milwaukee WI 53217 Office: Stupar & Schuster SC 633 W Wisconsin Ave Milwaukee WI 53203

LEVINE, HOWARD MICHAEL, lawyer; b. N.Y.C., July 14, 1954; s. Bernard and Sydelle (Tietler) L.; m. Jan Elaine Salta, Sept. 6, 1986. BSBA, Monmouth Coll., 1976; JD, U. Toledo, 1979. Bar: Oreg. 1980, U.S. Dist. Ct. Oreg. 1980, U.S. Ct. Appeals (9th cir.) 1980. Law clk. to judge U.S. Bankruptcy Ct., Oreg., 1980-82; assoc. Sussman, Shank, Wapnick, Caplan & Stiles, Portland, Oreg., 1982-87, ptnr., 1987—. Mem. Oreg. Bar Assn. (debtor-creditor sect., author articles for newsletter). Bankruptcy, Contracts commercial. Home: 5033 SW Evelyn St Portland OR 97919 Office: Sussman Shank et al 1001 SW 5th Ave Suite 1111 Portland OR 97204-1111

LEVINE, JEROME LESTER, lawyer; b. Los Angeles, July 20, 1940. m. Maryanne Shields, Sept. 13, 1966; children: Aron Michael, Sara Michelle. Student U. So. Calif., 1957-61; B.A. in Music, San Francisco State U., 1962; J.D., U. Calif., 1965. Bar: Calif. 1966, U.S. Supremem Ct., 1986. Dir. operational services, assoc. dir. Western Ctr. on Law and Poverty, Los Angeles, 1968-72; assoc. Swerdlow, Glikbarg & Shimer, Beverly Hills, Calif., 1972-77; ptnr. Lans Feinberg & Cohen, Los Angeles, 1977-79, Albala & Levine, Los Angeles, 1980-83, Neiman Billet Albala & Levine, Los Angeles, 1983—; lectr. in law U. So. Calif. Law Ctr., Loyola U. Sch. Law. Mem. ABA, Los Angeles County Bar Assn., Beverly Hills Bar Assn., Assn. Bus. Trial Lawyers. Federal civil litigation, State civil litigation, Entertainment. Office: 10960 Wilshire Blvd Suite 1908 Los Angeles CA 90024

LEVINE, JUDITH DEE, lawyer; b. N.Y.C., Sept. 2, 1950; d. Joshua and Selene Beverly (Davidson) L. BA, Kirkland Coll., 1972; JD, U. Denver, 1975. Bar: Colo. 1975, U.S. Dist. Ct. Colo. 1975, Ohio 1979, U.S. Ct. Appeals (9th cir.) 1979, N.Y. 1982. Assoc. Brownstein Hyatt Farber & Madden, Denver, 1975-78, Krupman, Fromson, Bownas & Selcer, Columbus, Ohio, 1979-80; assoc. Guren, Merritt, Feibel, Sogg & Cohen, Columbus, 1980-82, ptnr., 1982-84; ptnr. Benesch, Friedlander, Coplan & Aronoff, Columbus, 1984—. Speaker, steering com. mem. The Entrepreneurship Inst. Columbus, 1984-85,; vol. Sta. WOSU Auction, Columbus, 1984—; acct. exec. Franklin County United Way, 1985. Mem. ABA (chmn. subcom. on mortgage loan lenders and borrowers 1985—), Colo. Bar Assn., Ohio Bar Assn., Columbus Bar Assn., Women Lawyers of

Franklin County, Order of St. Ives. Democrat. Club: Capital. Avocations: skiing, tennis, photography. Real property, General corporate. Office: Benesch Friendlander et al 88 E Broad St Columbus OH 43215

LEVINE, JULIUS BYRON, lawyer, legal educator; b. Waterville, Maine, Feb. 8, 1939; s. Lewis Lester and Celia G. (Gurewitz) L.; m. Diane Groner, Aug. 26, 1965 (div.); children—Rachel A., Sarah L.; m. 2d Susan M. Ginns, Sept. 7,. 1980; 1 child, James G. A.B. summa cum laude, Harvard U., 1960, J.D. cum laude, 1964; Ph.D., Oxford U., Eng., 1969. Bar: Maine 1963, Mass. 1964, U.S. Ct. Appeals (1st cir.) 1964. Law clk. U.S. Dist. Ct. Maine, Portland, 1964-65; ptnr., of counsel Levine, Brody & Levine, Boston and Waterville, 1963-80, of counsel Levine, Bishop & Levine, Boston and Waterville, 1980—; assoc. prof. law Boston U., 1969-72, prof. law, 1972—; master Superior Ct. Mass., Boston, 1972—, coordinator jud. intern program, 1979; asst. dist. atty. Norfolk County, Mass., 1976; lectr. New Eng. Law Inst.-Mass. Continuing Legal Edn., Boston, 1977—, Nat. Coll. Probate Judges, Williamsburg, Va., 1979-82. Author: Discovery: A Comparison between English and American Civil Discovery Law with Reform Proposals, 1982, Trial Advocacy, 1987; co-author; Supplements to Massachusetts Pleading and Practice, 1981. Faculty editor Probate Law Jour.; legal editor Nat. Coll. Probate Judges Newsletter, 1979-82. Contbr. to legal jours. and books. Chmn. Citizens for Better Urban Renewal Plan, Waterville, 1962-63; mem. No. Kennebec Valley Regional Planning Commn., 1966-68, Maine Com. to Select Rhodes Scholars, 1971—; co-chmn. Aspinwall Hill Neighborhood Assn., Brookline, Mass., 1974-76; v.p. Ellis (South End) Neighborhood Assn., Boston, 1980-82, 87—, bd. dirs., 1986—; chmn. Mass. Victims of Crime, Boston, 1983—; legal dir. Nat. Victims of Crime, Washington, 1983—. John Harvard scholar Harvard U., 1957-59; Rhodes scholar Oxford U., 1960. Mem. ABA (mem. adv. council real property, probate and trust sect. 1972-81, contbg. editor jour. of litigation sect. 1974-77), Phi Beta Kappa, Omicron Chi Epsilon. Club: Mt. Auburn Tennis (Watertown, Mass.). Lodge: Masons. Federal civil litigation, Criminal, Probate. Home: 19 Lawrence St Boston MA 02116 Office: Boston Univ Law Sch 765 Commonwealth Ave Boston MA 02215

LEVINE, KENT JAY, lawyer, educator. m. Cynthia Gail Chadderton; children: Chad, Michelle. BA, Western State Coll., 1970; JD, Drake U., 1973. Bar: Colo., 1973, D.C., 1973, U.S. Ct. Appeals (10th cir.) 1973. Sole practice Englewood, Colo.; instr. Red Rocks Community Coll., U. Colo., U. No. Colo., U. Denver, Arapahoe Community Coll., various profl. insts.; lectr. in field; mem. Levine Ltd. Realtors, Denver; co-chmn. spl. adv. com. Standard and Approved Forms Colo. Real Estate Commn. Author: Public Trustee Foreclosures, Uniform Consumer Credit Code and Real Estate, Truth in Lending and Real Estate, Real Estate Agensts Guide to Colorado Real Estate Commission New Forms and Colorado U.C.C.C.; co-author: Handbook of Real Estate Law, 2d. ed.; contbg. author: Realtors' Liability, Business and the Law, Review Manual for the Multi-State Uniform Exam, Real Estate Fundamentals; contbr. articles to profl. jours. Mem. Colo. Bar Assn. (liason interprofl. com., unauthorized pracitce of law com.), Colo. Real Estate Educators Assn. (pres. 1985—), Colo. Assn. Realtors (chmn. regulatory agencies legis. com., profl. standards com.), Denver Bd. Realtors (zoning com., past chmn. profl. standards com., realtor/lawyer com.), Real Estate Securities and Syndications Inst. (past chmn. profl. standards com.). Real property. Office: 2303 E Dartmouth Ave Englewood CO 80110

LEVINE, LAURENCE HARVEY, lawyer; b. Cleve., Aug. 23, 1946; s. Theodore and Celia (Chaikin) Levine; m. Mary M. Conway, May 13, 1978; children: Abigail, Adam, Sarah. BA cum laude, Case Western Res. U., 1968; JD, Northwestern U., 1971. Bar: Ill., U.S. Supreme Ct. 1971, U.S. Dist. Ct. (no. dist.) Ill. 1972, U.S. Ct. Appeals (6th, 7th, 10th and D.C. cirs.). Law clk. to presiding judge U.S. Ct. Appeals (6th cir.), Detroit, 1971-72; assoc. Kirkland & Ellis, Chgo., 1972-76; ptnr. Latham & Watkins, Chgo., 1976—. Bd. editors Northwestern Law Rev., 1968-71. Mem. ABA, Chgo. Bar Assn. Clubs: Mid-Am., Saddle & Cycle (Chgo.). Environment, Antitrust, Federal civil litigation. Office: Latham & Watkins 6900 Sears Tower Chicago IL 60606

LEVINE, MARILYN MARKOVICH, lawyer, arbitrator; b. Bklyn., Aug. 9, 1930; d. Harry P. and Fannie L. (Hymowitz) Markovich; m. Louis L. Levine. June 24, 1950; children: Steven R., Ronald J., Linda J. Morgenstern. BS summa cum laude, Columbia U., 1950; MA, Adelphi U., 1967; JD, Hofstra U., 1977. Bar: N.Y. 1978, U.S. Dist. Ct. (so. and ea. dists.) N.Y. 1978, D.C. 1979, U.S. Supreme Ct. 1982. Sole practice Valley Stream, N.Y., 1978—; contract arbitrator Bldg. Service Industry, N.Y.C., 1982—; panel arbitrator Retail Food Industry, N.Y.C., 1980—; arbitrator N.Y. Dist. Cts., Nassau County, 1981—. Panel arbitrator Suffolk County Pub. Employee Relations Bd., 1979—, Nassau County Pub. Employee Relations Bd., 1980—, Nat. Mediation Bd., 1986—, N.Y. State Pub. Employee Relations Bd., 1984—; mem. adv. council Ctr. Labor and Industrial Relations, Tech. N.Y. Inst. Tech., N.Y., 1985—; counsel Nassau Civic Club, 1978—. Mem. ABA, N.Y. State Bar Assn., D.C. Bar Assn., Nassau County Bar Assn., N.J. Bd. Mediation (panel arbitrator), Am. Arbitration Assn. (arbitrator 1979—), Fed. Mediation Bd. (arbitrator 1980—). Labor arbitration - mediation, Labor. Home and Office: 1057 Linden St Valley Stream NY 11580

LEVINE, MELVIN CHARLES, lawyer; b. Bklyn., Nov. 12, 1930; s. Barnet and Jennie (Iser) L. BCS, N.Y. U., 1952; LLB, Harvard U., 1955. Bar: N.Y. 1956, U.S. Supreme Ct. 1964. Assoc., Kriger & Haber, Bklyn., 1956-58, Black, Varian & Simons, N.Y.C., 1959; sole practice, N.Y.C., 1959—; devel. multiple dwelling housing. Mem. N.Y. County Lawyers Assn. (civil ct. com., housing ct. com., liaison to Assn. Bar City of N.Y. on selection of housing and civil ct. judge, task force on tort reform). Democrat. Jewish. Real property, Landlord-tenant, State civil litigation. Home: 146 Waverly Pl New York NY 10014 Office: Suite 1404 271 Madison Ave New York NY 10016

LEVINE, NORMAN EDWARD, lawyer; b. Wilmington, Del., June 2, 1943; s. Ralph and Ethel (Cohen) L.; m. Aleta Rendina, July 30, 1972; children: Payton, Evan. AB, U. Pa., 1965, LLB, 1968. Bar: Del. 1968, U.S. Dist. Ct. Del. 1968, U.S. Ct. Appeals (3d cir.) 1969. U.S. atty. Dist. Del., Wilmington, 1972-73; commr. of pub. safety City of Wilmington, 1973-77; assoc. Levin, Spiller & Twer, Wilmington, 1977-79; sole practice Wilmington, 1979-83; ptnr. Levine & Thompson, Wilmington, 1983—; asst. prof. West Chester (Pa.) State Coll., 1975; dep. adminstr. Justice of Peace Cts., Wilmington, 1977; pub. defender State of Del., Wilmington, 1980. Treas. Brandywine Hills Civic Assn., Wilmington, 1983-85. Mem. ABA, Fed. Bar Assn., Del. Bar Assn. (chmn. family law sect. 1985—), Am. Judicature Soc. Democrat. Jewish. Family and matrimonial, Personal injury, State civil litigation. Home: 4401 Washington Blvd Wilmington DE 19802 Office: Levine & Thompson 928 French St Wilmington DE 19801

LEVINE, RONALD JAY, lawyer; b. Bklyn., June 23, 1953; s. Louis Leon and Marilyn Priscilla (Markovich) L.; m. Cindy Beth Israel, Nov. 18, 1979; children: Merisa, Alisha. BA summa cum laude, Princeton U., 1974; JD cum laude, Harvard U., 1977. Bar: N.Y. 1978, U.S. Dist. Ct. (so. and ea. dists.) N.Y. 1978, D.C. 1980, U.S. Supreme Ct. 1982, U.S. Ct. Appeals (2d cir.) 1983. Assoc. Phillips, Nizer, Benjamin, Krim & Ballon, N.Y.C., 1977-80, Debevoise & Plimpton, N.Y.C., 1980-84; assoc. Herrick, Feinstein, N.Y.C., 1984-85, ptnr., 1985—; gen. counsel Greater N.Y. Safety Council, N.Y.C., 1979-81; arbitrator Small Claims Ct. of Civil Ct. of City of N.Y., 1983-85. Mem. Site Plan Rev. Adv. Bd., West Windsor, N.J., 1986, planning bd., 1987—. Mem. ABA (litigation sect.), N.Y. State Bar Assn. (com. on legal edn. and bar admission, 1982—), Assn. of Bar of City of N.Y. (com. on legal assistance, 1983-86), Phi Beta Kappa. Federal civil litigation, State civil litigation, General practice. Home: 6 Arnold Dr Princeton Junction NJ 08550 Office: Herrick Feinstein 2 Park Ave New York NY 10016

LEVINE, SAMUEL, lawyer, physician; b. Denver, Dec. 5, 1917; s. Herman Gershon and Yetta (Kowslowsky) L.; m. Rowena Mae Damme, Apr. 20, 1946 (dec. Aug. 1974); children: Michael Samuel, Sonya Michelle, Tama Lynne, Rinah Devora; m. Elaine Jeannine Cloud, June 9, 1979. BA, U. Colo., 1940, MD, 1943; JD, U. Denver, 1981. Bar: Colo. 1981, U.S. Dist. Ct. Colo. 1981. Gen. practice medicine specializing in gen. and thoracic surgery Lakewood, Colo., 1940—; sole practice Lakewood, 1981—. Contbr. articles to profl. jours. Served to capt. U.S. Army, 1944-46, PTO. Mem. Colo. Bar Assn., Denver Bar Assn., Clear Creek County Med. Soc., Colo. State Med. Soc. Jewish. Avocations: stamps, coins. Health.

LEVINE, SAMUEL MILTON, lawyer; b. Syracuse, N.Y., Feb. 24, 1929; s. Joseph and Sophie Levine; m. Leona Miller, Sept. 9, 1950; children—Judith, Donald, Gary. B.B.A., Syracuse U., 1950; J.D., Bklyn. Law Sch., 1953. Bar: N.Y. 1953, U.S. Supreme Ct. 1960, U.S. Dist. Ct. (ea. and so. dists.) N.Y. 1962. Assoc. Law Office of William S. Miller, Esq., N.Y.C., 1954-62; Law Office of Ferdinand I. Haber, Esq., Mineola, N.Y., 1958-62; sole practice Nassau County, N.Y., 1962-65; counsel English and Haber (later English, Cianciulli, Reisman & Peirez), 1962-65; supt. of real estate Nassau County 1965-84; practice law, Garden City, N.Y., 1984—; lobbyist for handicapped; lectr. on law and handicapped. Past chmn. Sch. Aid Council L.I., Citizens Com. for Elmont Schs., N.Y.; former counsel, trustee, Temple Bnai Israel, Elmont; bd. visitors Pilgrim State Hosp.; treas., counsel N.Y. State Council Orgns. for Handicapped; past pres. Nassau County Epilepsy Found.; del. White House Conf. on Children and Youth, 1960; candidate N.Y. State Senate, 1964 counsel Health Advocates, Voice for Handicapped, Fedn. Parents Orgns., League of Voters for Handicapped; Contbr. numerous articles to profl. jours. Served with U.S. Army, 1948. Recipient Advocate of Yr. award L.I. council Fedn. Parents Orgns., 1978. Mem. Nassau County Bar Assn. (legis. com.), N.Y. State Bar Assn., Syracuse U. Alumni Club. Lodges; Kiwanis, K.P., Bnai B'rith. General practice, Real property, Estate planning. Home: 3882 Carrel Blvd Oceanside NY 11572 Office: 1539 Franklin Ave Mineola NY 11501

LEVINE, SANFORD HAROLD, lawyer; b. Troy, N.Y., Mar. 13, 1938; s. Louis and Reba (Semegren) L.; m. Margaret R. Appelbaum, Oct. 29, 1967; children—Jessica Sara, Abby Miriam. A.B., Syracuse U., 1959, J.D., 1961. Bar: N.Y. 1961, U.S. Dist. Ct. (no. dist.) N.Y. 1961, U.S. Dist. Ct. (we. dist.) N.Y. 1979, U.S. Dist. Ct. (ea. and so. dists.) N.Y. 1980, U.S. Ct. Appeals (2d cir.) 1962, U.S. Supreme Ct. 1967. Law asst. to assoc. judge N.Y. Ct. Appeals, Albany and to justice N.Y. Supreme Ct., 1962-66; law asst. to assoc. judge N.Y. Ct. Appeals, Albany, 1964; asst. counsel N.Y. State Temporary Commn. on Constl. Conv., N.Y.C., 1966-67; assoc. counsel SUNY System, Albany, 1967-70, dep. univ. counsel, 1970-78, acting counsel, 1970-71, acting univ. counsel, 1978-79, univ. counsel and vice chancellor legal affairs, 1979—; mem. paralegal curriculum adv. com. Schenectady County Community Coll., 1975—. Mem. ABA, N.Y. State Bar Assn. (spl. com. copyright law), Albany County Bar Assn., Nat. Assn. Coll. and Univ. Attys. (exec. bd. 1979-82, pres. 1986-87), Am. Soc. Pub. Adminstrn., Am. Acad. Hosp. Attys., Nat. Health Lawyers Assn. Editorial bd. Syracuse U. Law Rev., 1960-61; editorial adv. bd. Jour. Coll. and Univ. Law, 1977-81. Education and schools. Home: 1106 Godfrey Ln Schenectady NY 12309 Office: State Univ Plaza Albany NY 12246

LEVINE, STEVEN JON, lawyer; b. N.Y.C., Sept. 27, 1942; s. Irving I. and Freda S. (Silverman) L.; m. Linda Jane Silberman, Apr. 23, 1967; 1 son, Lawrence Alan. B.S., Syracuse U., 1964; J.D., St. John's U., 1966; M.A., CCNY, 1973; LL.M., NYU, 1978. Bar: N.Y. 1967. Assoc. Augustin J. San Filippo & Steven Jon Levine, P.C. and predecessor, N.Y.C., 1968-78; mem. Vittoria & Parker, N.Y.C., 1978—; arbitrator N.Y. County Civil Ct. Panel, 1980—; asst. csl. N.Y. State Senate Judiciary Com., 1977. Committeeman, Bronx County, 1970-76; bd. dirs. Jewish Conciliation Bd. Am., 1973—, atty. mem. conciliation panel, 1973—. Mem. ABA, Internat. Bar Assn., N.Y. State Bar Assn., Westchester County Bar Assn., Assn. Bar City N.Y. (sect. vice chmn. matrimonial com. 1977-80), Am. Arbitration Assn. (no-fault, comml. panels 1975—). Family and matrimonial, Personal injury, General practice. Office: 235 Main St Penthouse White Plains NY 10601 also: Vittoria & Parker 630 Fifth Ave New York NY 10111

LEVING, JEFFERY MARK, matrimonial lawyer; b. Chgo., July 2, 1951; s. Al and Rebecca Leving; B.S., So. Ill. U., 1974; J.D., Chgo.-Kent Coll. Law, 1979. Bar: Ill. 1979, U.S. Dist. Ct. (no. dist.) Ill. 1979, U.S. Ct. Appeals (7th cir.) 1980. Fed. tax law editor Commerce Clearing House, Chgo., 1979-80; staff atty. Chgo. Vol. Legal Services, 1980-81; sole practice, Chgo., 1981—; contbr. to drafting of Ill. Joint Custody law; testified as proponent of Grandparent Visitation Bill (H.B.1574) in Ill. Ho. Reps. Judiciary com.; guest speaker various radio and TV programs. Mem. Advs. for Shared Custody; panelist Fatherhood Forum Conf. Mem. Chgo. Bar Assn. (matrimonial law com.), Ill. Bar Assn. (commendation and recognition 1983), Fathering Support Services, Decalogue Soc. Democrat. Jewish. Family and matrimonial. Office: 105 W Madison Suite 1008 Chicago IL 60603

LEVINGS, THERESA LAWRENCE, lawyer; b. Kansas City, Mo., Oct. 24, 1952; d. William Youngs and Dorothy (Neer) Frick; m. Darryl Wayne Levings, May 25, 1974; 1 child, Leslie Page. BJ, U. Mo., 1973; JD U. Mo., Kansas City, 1979. Bar: Mo. 1979, U.S. Dist. Ct. (we. dist.) Mo. 1979, U.S. Ct. Appeals (8th cir.) 1982, U.S. Ct. Appeals (10th cir.) 1986. Copy editor Kansas City Star, 1975-78; law clk. to presiding judge Mo. Supreme Ct., Jefferson City, 1979-80; from assoc. to ptnr. Morrison, Hecker, Curtis, Kuder & Parrish, Kansas City, 1980—; treas. young lawyers council Mo. Bar, 1985-86, sec. 1986-87. Leadership grad. Kansas City Tomorrow, 1986—; account exec. United Way, 1986—. Recipient Outstanding Service award young lawyers council Mo. Bar, 1985, 86. Mem. Mo. Assn. Women Lawyers (pres. 1986—), Assn. Women Lawyers Greater Kansas City (bd. dirs. young lawyers sect. 1982-83, treas. 1985-86, pres. 1986-87). Avocations: antiques, history, cooking. Insurance, Personal injury, Contracts commercial. Office: Morrison Hecker Curtis Kuder & Parrish 1102 Grand Ave Kansas City MO 64106

LEVINSON, DANIEL RONALD, lawyer; b. Bklyn., Mar. 24, 1949; s. Gerald Sam and Risha Rose (Waxer) L.; m. Luna Frances Lambert, Sept. 13, 1980; 1 child, Luna Claire. AB, U. So. Calif., 1971; JD, Georgetown U., 1974; LLM, George Washington U., 1977. Bar: N.Y. 1975, Calif. 1976, D.C. 1976, U.S. Supreme Ct. 1978. Law clk. appellate div. N.Y. Supreme Ct., Bklyn., 1974-76; assoc. McGuiness & Williams, Washington, 1977-81, ptnr., 1982-83; dep. gen. counsel U.S. Office Personnel Mgmt., Washington, 1983-85; gen. counsel U.S. Consumer Product Safety Commn., Washington, 1985-86; chmn. U.S. Merit Systems Protection Bd., Washington, 1986—; adj. lectr. Am. U., Washington, 1981-82, Cath. U. Am., Washington, 1982. Notes and comments editor Am. Criminal Law Rev., 1973-74. Mem. ABA, Fed. Bar Assn., Nat. Lawyers Club, Phi Beta Kappa. Republican. Jewish. Club: Univ. (Washington). Administrative and regulatory, Labor. Home: 3529 Woodbine St Chevy Chase MD 20815

LEVINSON, DAVID LAWRENCE, lawyer; b. Bklyn., Jan. 9, 1945; s. Herman and Bertha (Fuchs) L.; m. Marjorie Joan Friedman, June 18, 1967; children—Andrew, Joshua, Lauren. B.A., Bklyn. Coll., 1966; J.D., Bklyn. Law Sch., 1969. Bar: N.Y. 1969, U.S. Dist. Ct. (so. dist.) N.Y. 1971, U.S. Supreme Ct. 1976. Asst. dist. atty. N.Y. County Dist. Atty.'s Office, N.Y.C., 1969-73; ptnr. law firm Rider, Weiner & Loeb, P.C., Newburgh, N.Y., 1973-80; ptnr. Mc Guirk, Levinson, Zeccola, Seaman, Reineke & Ornstein, P.C. and predecessor firms, 1980—. Pres., Monroe (N.Y.) Temple of Liberal Judaism, 1981-83; justice Town of Woodbury, 1978—, mem. Zoning Bd. Appeals, 1977-78. Mem. Orange County Bar Assn. (mem. judiciary com. 1980—, mem. grievance com. 1983—), Am. Arbitration Assn. (arbitrator 1978—), N.Y. State Bar Assn., Newburgh Bar Assn. Clubs: Lions (publicity com. 1983-84), Woodbury Community Assn. State civil litigation, Family and matrimonial, Criminal. Home: 4 Jones Dr Highland Mills NY 10930 Office: Mc Guirk Levinson Zeccola Seaman Reineke & Ornstein PC Route 32 Central Valley NY 10917

LEVINSON, KENNETH LEE, lawyer; b. Denver, Jan. 18, 1953; s. Julian Charles and Dorothy (Milzer) L.; m. Shauna Titus McCaffery, Dec. 21, 1986. B.A. with distinction, U. Colo.-Boulder, 1974; J.D., U. Denver, 1978. Bar: Colo. 1978, U.S. Ct. Appeals (10th cir.) 1978. Assoc. atty. Balaban & Lutz, Denver, 1979-83; shareholder Balaban & Levinson, Denver, 1984—. Contbr. articles to profl. jours. Pres., Dahlia House Condominium Assn., 1983-85; intern Reporters Com. For Freedom of the Press, Washington, 1977. Recipient Am. Jurisprudence award Lawyers Co-op., 1977. Mem. ABA, Denver Bar Assn., Colo. Bar Assn., Am. Arbitration Assn. (arbitrator), Internat. Platform Assn. Clubs: Denver Law, Denver Athletic. General practice, State civil litigation, Real property.

LEVINSON, L(ESLIE) HAROLD, law educator, lawyer; b. Bournemouth, Eng., Oct. 17, 1929; s. Abraham and Ada (Bloomberg) L.; m. Joan Gluck, Mar. 28, 1965; children: Andrea, Lara. BBA, 1957; LLB, U. Miami, 1962; LLM, NYU, 1964; JSD, Columbia U., 1974. Bar: Fla. 1962, N.Y. 1964; CPA. Ptnr. acctg. firm Miami, Fla., 1958-62; instr. acctg. NYU, 1962-64; lectr. on devel. financing UN, N.Y.C. and Geneva, summers 1963-65; asst. to legal dir. ACLU, N.Y.C., summers 1964-65; asst. prof. U. Fla., 1966-67, assoc. prof., 1967-70, prof., 1970-73; vis. prof. Vanderbilt U. Sch. Law, Nashville, 1973-74, prof., 1974—; mem. Fla. Law Rev. Council, 1972-74; cons. Adminstrv. Conf. U.S., 1976-86; reporter 1981 Revision Model State Adminstrv. Proc. Act, Nat. Conf. Commrs. Uniform State Laws, 1978-81. Mem. ABA, Am. Law Inst., Am. Inst. CPA's, Fla. Inst. CPA's. Legal education. Office: Vanderbilt U Sch Law Nashville TN 37240

LEVINSON, LESLIE J., lawyer; b. N.Y.C., Apr. 21, 1955; m. Joan Schiffer, Apr. 4, 1981. BA with honors, U. Wis., 1977; JD, Case Western Res. U., 1980. Bar: N.Y. 1981. Ptnr. Bloch, Graff, Danzig & Jelline, N.Y.C., 1980—. Exec. notes editor Case Western Jour. Internat. Law, 1976-77; contbr. articles to profl. jours. Advisor Fanwood (N.J.) Recreation Commn. Mem. ABA (com. fed. regulation of securities) Assn. of the Bar of the City of N.Y., N.Y. State Bar Assn., Omicron Delta Epsilon. General corporate, Securities, Real property. Office: Bloch Graff Danzig & Jelline 350 5th Ave New York NY 10118

LEVINSON, PAUL HOWARD, lawyer; b. N.Y.C., Nov. 9, 1952; s. Saul and Gloria (Samson) L.; m. Susan Norine Morley, May 29, 1983; 1 child, Lauren Hope. BA in Sociology, Northwestern U., 1973; JD, Columbia U., 1977. Bar: N.Y. 1978, U.S. Dist. Ct. (so. and ea. dist.) N.Y. 1983, U.S. Ct. Appeals (2d cir.) 1986, U.S. Supreme Ct. 1986. Asst. dist. atty., supervising sr. trial atty. Kings County, Bklyn., 1977-84; assoc. Blodnick, Shcultz & Abramowitz P.C., Lake Success, N.Y., 1984-85, Leavey, Rosensweig & Hyman (and predecessor firms), N.Y.C., 1985—. Harlan Fiske Stone scholar. Mem. ABA, N.Y. State Bar Assn., Assn. of Bar of City of N.Y., Bklyn. Bar Assn. (continuing legal edn. com.), Nat. Assn. Criminal Def. Lawyers, Columbia U. Alumni Assn., Northwestern U. Alumni Assn., Sierra Club. Democrat. Jewish. Club: Northwestern U. Alumni of N.Y.C. Avocations: tennis, skiing. Federal civil litigation, State civil litigation, Criminal. Home: 1365 York Ave Apt 15D New York NY 19921 Office: Leavy Rosensweig & Hyman 11 E 44th St 10th Floor New York NY 10017

LEVINSON, PETER JOSEPH, lawyer; b. Washington, June 11, 1943; s. Bernard Hirsh and Carlyn Virginia (Krupp) L.; m. Nanette Susan Segal, Mar. 30, 1968; children—Sharman Risa, Justin David. A.B. in History cum laude, Brandeis U., Waltham, Mass., 1965; J.D., Harvard U., 1968. Bar: Hawaii 1971, U.S. Supreme Ct. 1975. Summer supr. Harvard Legal Aid Bur., Cambridge, Mass., 1968; research asst. Harvard Law Sch., 1968-69; teaching fellow Osgoode Hall Law Sch., York U. (Can.), 1969-70, research assoc., 1969-70, asst. prof., 1970-71; dep. atty. gen. State of Hawaii, 1971-75; vis. fellow Harvard U., 1976-77; ptnr. Levinson and Levinson, Honolulu, 1977-79; spl. asst. to dir. Office Program Support, Legal Services Corp., Washington, 1979; cons. Select Commn. on Immigration and Refugee Policy, Washington, 1980-81; minority counsel subcom. on immigration, refugees and internat. law com. on Judiciary, U.S. Ho. of Reps., Washington, 1981-85, Minority counsel subcom. Monopolies and Comml. law, 1985—. Trustee, Hawaii Jewish Welfare Fund, 1972-75, chmn. fund drive, 1972; trustee Temple Emanu-El, Honolulu, 1973-75; mem. alumni admissions council Brandeis U., 1978-82. Recipient award of merit United Jewish Appeal, 1974. Mem. Hawaii State Bar Assn. (chmn. standing com. on continuing legal edn. 1972, chmn. standing com. on jud. adminstrn. 1979), ABA, Am. Judicature Soc. Contbr. articles to profl. jours. Legislative. Office: B351C Rayburn House Office Bldg Washington DC 20515

LEVIT, JAY J(OSEPH), lawyer; b. Phila., Feb. 20, 1934; s. Albert and Mary Levit; m. Heloise Bertman, July 20, 1962; children: Richard Bertman, Robert Edward, Darcy Francine. AB, Case Western Res. U., 1955; JD, U. Richmond, 1958; LLM, Harvard U., 1959. Bar: Va. 1958, D.C. 1961, U.S. Supreme Ct. 1961. Trial atty. U.S. Dept. Justice, Washington, 1960-64; sr. atty. Gen. Dynamics Corp., Rochester, N.Y., 1965-67; ptnr. Stallard & Levit, Richmond, Va., 1968-72, Levit & Mann, Richmond, 1973—; lectr. U. Mich. Law Sch., Ann Arbor, 1964-65, U. Richmond Law Sch., 1970-76; adj. lectr. Va. Commonwealth U., Richmond, 1970—. Mem. ABA (labor com.), Va. Bar Assn. (labor com.). Avocations: jogging, swimming, travel. Federal civil litigation, State civil litigation, Labor. Home: 1608 Harborough Rd Richmond VA 23233 Office: Levit & Mann 419 N Boulevard Richmond VA 23220

LEVIT, VICTOR BERT, lawyer, foreign representative, civic worker; b. Singapore, Apr. 21, 1930; s. Bert W. and Thelma (Clumeck) L.; m. Sherry Lynn Chamove, Feb. 25, 1962; children: Carson, Victoria. A.B. in Polit. Sci. with great distinction, Stanford, 1950; LL.B., Stanford U., 1952. Bar: Calif. 1953. Assoc. Long & Levit, San Francisco and Los Angeles, 1953-55, ptnr., 1955-83, mng. ptnr., 1971-83; ptnr. Barger & Wolen, San Francisco, Los Angeles and San Diego, 1983—; assoc. and gen. legal counsel U.S. Jaycees, 1959-61; legal counsel for consul gen. Ethiopia for San Francisco, 1964-71; hon. consul for Ethiopia for San Francisco, Ethiopia, 1971-76; guest lectr. Stanford U. Law Sch., 1958—, Haile Selassie I Univ. Law Sch., 1972-76; mem. com. group ins. programs State Bar Calif., 1980—; Mem. Los Angeles Consular Corps, 1971-77; mem. San Francisco Consular Corps, 1971-77, vice dean, 1975-76; Grader Calif. Bar Exam., 1956-61; del. San Francisco Mcpl. Conf., 1955-63, vice chmn., 1960, chmn., 1961-63. Author: Legal Malpractice in California, 1974, Legal Malpractice, 1977, 2d edit., 1983; Note editor: Stanford Law Rev, 1952-53; legal editor: Underwriters' Report, 1963—; Contbr. articles to legal jours. Campaign chmn. San Francisco Aid Retarded Children, 1960; mem. nat. com. Stanford Law Sch. Fund, 1959—; mem. Mayor's Osaka-San Francisco Affiliation Com., 1959-65, Mayor's Com. for Mcpl. Mgmt., 1961-64; mem. San Francisco Rep. Country Cen. Com., 1956-63; assoc. mem. Calif. Rep. Cen. Com., 1956-63, 70-72; campaign chmn. San Francisco Assemblyman John Busterud, 1960; bd. dirs. San Francisco Comml. Club, 1967-70, San Francisco Planning and Urban Renewal Assn., 1959-60, San Francisco Planning and Urban Renewal Assn. Nat. Found. Infantile Paralysis, 1958, Red Shield Youth Assn., Salvation Army, San Francisco, 1960-70, bd. dirs. NCCJ, San Francisco, 1959—, chmn., No. Calif., 1962-64, 68-70; mem. nat. bd. dirs., 1964-75; bd. dirs. San Francisco Tb and Health Assn., 1962-70, treas., 1964, pres., 1965-67; bd. dirs. San Francisco Assn. Mental Health, 1964-73, pres., 1968-71; mem. com. Nat. Assn. Mental Health, 1969-71; trustee United Bay Area Crusade, 1966-74, Ins. Forum San Francisco; bd. visitors Stanford Law Sch., 1969-75; mem. adv. bd. Jr. League San Francisco, 1971-75. Named Outstanding Young Man San Francisco mng. editors San Francisco newspapers, 1960, One of Five Outstanding Young Men Calif., 1961. Fellow ABA (chmn. profl. liability com. for gen. practice sect. 1979-81, council gen. practice sect. 1982-86, sec.-treas. gen. practice sect. 1986-87); mem. San Francisco Bar Assn. (chmn. ins. com. 1962, 73, chmn. charter flight com. 1962-66), State Bar Calif. (com. on group ins. programs 1980—), Consular Law Soc., Am. Arbitration Assn., World Assn. Lawyers (chmn. parliamentary law com. 1976—), Am. Law Inst. (adviser restatement of law governing lawyers 1986—), Internat. Bar Assn., San Francisco Jr. C. of C. (dir. 1959, pres. 1958), U.S. Jaycees (exec. com. 1959-61), Jaycees Internat. (life, senator), Calif. Scholarship Fedn., U.S. C. of C. (labor com. 1974-76), San Francisco C. of C. (dir.), Phi Beta Kappa, Order of Coif, Pi Sigma Alpha. Clubs: Commercial (San Francisco) (dir.); Commonwealth (quar. chmn.), California Tennis, Tiburon Peninsula, Concordia. Insurance, Federal civil litigation, State civil litigation. Home: 45 Beach Rd Belvedere CA 94920 Office: 650 California St San Francisco CA 94108

LEVIT, WILLIAM HAROLD, lawyer; b. San Francisco, Jan. 11, 1908; s. Morris and Fannie (Jacobs) L.; m. Barbara Kaiser, June 9, 1933 (dec. Aug. 1986); children: Jacqueline Weisberg, William H. Jr. B.A., Stanford U., 1928, J.D., 1930. Bar: Calif. 1930, U.S. Dist. Ct. (no. and cen. dists.) Calif. 1930, U.S. Ct. Appeals (9th cir.) 1930, U.S. Supreme Ct. 1942. Ptnr. Long & Levit, San Francisco and Los Angeles, 1930-62, of counsel, Los Angeles, 1976-78; judge Superior Ct. Calif. for Los Angeles County, 1962-76; of counsel Stroock & Stroock & Lavan, Los Angeles, N.Y.C., Washington and Miami, Fla., 1978—; instr. jud. adminstrn. U. So. Calif. Law Ctr., 1968-71; co-founder, dean Calif. Jud. Coll., 1971; mem. faculty Nat. Jud. Coll., 1965-68, 73, Jud. Council of Calif., 1969-71; founding mem., governing bd. Calif. Ctr.

for Jud. Edn. and Research, 1973-76. Vice pres. Calif. Judges Assn., 1971-72. Served to lt. col. JAGC, U.S. Army, 1942-45. Decorated Bronze Star; recipient President's Cup, Calif. Judges Assn., 1983. Fellow Am. Coll. Trial Lawyers; mem. Inst. Jud. Adminstrn., Italian Bar (hon.). Author: Pretrial Conference Manual, 1966; Coordination of Civil Actions, 1976; California Judicial Retirement Handbook, 3d edit., 1986; contbg. author: Fire Insurance (Western edit.), 1954; contbr. articles to legal and other profl. publs. Federal civil litigation, State civil litigation. Office: Stroock & Stroock & Lavan 2029 Century Park E Suite 1800 Los Angeles CA 90067

LEVIT, WILLIAM HAROLD, JR., lawyer; b. San Francisco, Feb. 8, 1938; s. William Harold and Barbara Janis (Kaiser) L.; m. Mary Elizabeth Webster, Feb. 13, 1971; children: Alison Jones, Alexandra Bradley, Laura Elizabeth Fletcher, Amalia Elizabeth Webster, William Harold, III. B.A. magna cum laude, Yale U., 1960; postgrad. (Ford Found. fellow), U. Pa., 1961-62; M.A. (NDEA fellow), U. Calif., Berkeley, 1962; LL.B., Harvard U., 1967. Bar: N.Y. 1968, Calif. 1974, Wis. 1979. Fgn. service officer Dept. State, 1962-64; assoc. firm Davis Polk & Wardwell, N.Y.C., 1967-73; assoc., then ptnr. firm Hughes Hubbard & Reed, N.Y.C. and Los Angeles, 1973-79; sec., gen. counsel Rexnord Inc., Milw., 1979-83; ptnr. Godfrey & Kahn, Milw., 1983—; substitute arbitrator Iran-U.S. Claims Tribunal, The Hague, 1984—; lectr. Practicing Law Inst., ABA, Calif.; Continuing Edn. of Bar, Corp. Practice Inst. Contbr. to: Mergers and the Private Antitrust Suit: The Private Enforcement of Section 7 of the Clayton Act, 1977. Bd. dirs., pres. Wis. Humane Soc.; bd. dirs. Vis. Nurse Corp., Milw., 1980—, chmn., 1985-87; bd. dirs. Wis. Soc. To Prevent Blindness; rep. Assn. Yale Alumni, 1976-79, 81-84; pres., dir. Yale Club So. Calif., 1977-79. Mem. Am. Soc. Corp. Secs. (pres. Wis. chpt. 1982-83, dir. 1981—), Am. Arbitration Assn. (panel arbitrators 1977—), ABA (com. on corp. counsel litigation sect.), Assn. Bar City of N.Y., State Bar Calif. (com. on continuing edn. of bar 1977-79), Bar Assn. of the 7th cir., Los Angeles County Bar Assn. (ethics com. 1976-79), State Bar Wis. (dir. internat. bus. transactions sect. 1985—; dist. 2 bd. attys. prof. responsibility com. 1985—), Bar Assn. 7th Cir., Am. Soc. Internat. Law, Inst. Jud. Adminstrn., Phi Beta Kappa. Clubs: Univ., Town, Milw. Private international, Federal civil litigation, State civil litigation. Office: 780 N Water St Suite 1500 Milwaukee WI 53202

LEVITAN, DAVID M(AURICE), lawyer, educator; b. Tver, Lithuania, Dec. 25, 1915; (parents Am. citizens). B.S., Northwestern U., 1936, M.A., 1937; Ph.D., U. Chgo., 1940; J.D., Columbia U., 1948. Bar: N.Y. 1948, U.S. Supreme Ct. 1953. Individual practice N.Y.C., 1948-66; ptnr. Hahn & Hessen, N.Y.C., 1966-86, counsel, 1986—; adj. prof. public law Columbia U., 1946-63; adj. prof. John Jay Coll. Criminal Justice, CUNY, 1966-75; adj. prof. polit. sci. Post Coll., 1964-66; adj. prof. law Cardozo Sch. Law, 1978-82. Contbr. articles to legal jours. Mem. Nassau County (N.Y.) Welfare Bd., 1965-69. Fellow Am. Coll. Probate Counsel; mem. ABA, Am. Polit. Sci. Assn., Am. Soc. Internat. Law, Am. Law Inst., N.Y. State Bar Assn., Assn. Bar City N.Y. Probate, Estate taxation, Constitutional. Home: 250 Scudders Ln Roslyn Harbor NY 11576 Office: Hahn & Hessen 350 Fifth Ave New York NY 10118

LEVITAN, JAMES A., lawyer; b. N.Y.C., Mar. 24, 1925; s. Leo and Della (Brody) L.; m. Ruth Terry White, Jan. 30, 1951; children—Deborah A., Judith T., Susan J. B.S. in Chem. Engring, M.I.T., 1948; LL.B. (mem. bd. Law Rev. 1950-51), Columbia U., 1951. Bar: N.Y. bar 1951. Since practiced in N.Y.C.; partner firm Skadden, Arps, Slate, Meagher & Flom, 1965—; regional chmn. for N.Y.C. M.I.T. Edn. Council, 1974—; lectr. in tax field. Served with USNR, 1944-46. Stone scholar, 1948-51; Kent scholar, 1950. Mem. N.Y. State Bar Assn., Assn. Bar City N.Y., Tau Beta Pi. Corporate taxation, Estate taxation, Personal income taxation. Home: 26 Wake Robin Ln Stamford CT 06903 Office: 919 3d Ave New York NY 10022

LEVITAN, KATHERINE D., lawyer; b. Vienna, Austria, July 8, 1933; came to U.S. 1938, naturalized 1942; d. Otto and Hedweega (Saltzer) Lenz; m. Leonard Levitan, Sept. 12, 1952; children—Joel, Jeffrey, Debbie, Diane. B.A. cum laude, N.Y.U. 1952, J.D. cum laude, 1955, LL.M. in Criminal and Family Law, 1977. Bar: N.Y. 1956, U.S. Dist. Ct. (ea. dist.) N.Y. 1972, U.S. Supreme Ct. 1974. Tchr. bus. law N.Y. Inst. Tech., Old Westbury, 1968-69; assoc. Bennett Reiss, Great Neck, N.Y., 1969-70, Malone and Dorfman, Freeport, N.Y., 1970-71; sole practice, Jericho, N.Y., 1971-80; practice with assocs., Mineola, N.Y., 1980—; also lectr. Bd. dirs., legal counsel For Our Children and Us, Inc.; legal counsel Temple Emmanuel; vol. atty. VAST, 1980—; bd. dirs. FOCUS, 1980—, Nassau chpt. ACLU, 1975—; mem. Nassau County Democratic Com., 1969—, law guardian adv. panel 2d dept. Human Rights Adv. Commn. Nassau County; v.p. Nassau chpt. N.Y. Civil Liberties Union. Mem. Nassau Bar Assn. (grievance com.), Nassau/Suffolk Women's Bar Assn. (past pres.), Nassau Civil Liberties Union, L.I. Women's Network, 110 Center for Women, Acad. Matrimonial Lawyers, L.I. Ctr. for Women's Rights. Contbr. articles to profl. publs. Family and matrimonial, Civil rights, General practice. Home: 113 Olive Ln New Hyde Park NY 11040 Office: 146 Old Country Rd Mineola NY 11501

LEVITAN, ROGER STANLEY, lawyer; b. Washington, Jan. 31, 1933; s. Simon Wolfe and Bessie (Abramson) L.; m. Maria Anneli Stennius, May 27, 1975 (div. 1980); children—Kaarlo Eino, Mark Howard; m. 2d, Laurel Lynn Allen, July 9, 1982; 1 child, Brandon Wolfe. B.S. in Econs., U. Pa., 1954; J.D., Columbia U., 1957. Bar: D.C. 1957, U.S. Ct. Appeals (D.C. cir.) 1957, Ariz. 1976. Tax specialist, reorgn. br. IRS, Washington, 1957-62; atty. McClure & Trotter, Washington, 1962-65; assoc. ptnr. Main Lafrentz, Washington and N.Y.C., 1970-72; dir. taxes U.S. Industries, Inc., N.Y.C., 1972-73; asst. tax counsel Am. Home Products Co., N.Y.C., 1973-75; atty., stockholder Bilby & Shoenhair, P.C., Tucson, 1976—; lectr. Am. Law Inst., State Bar Ariz. Trustee, Tucson Community Found., 1981—. Mem. ABA (chmn. ann. report com. 1965-67, continuing legal edn. com. 1969-70), Ariz. Bar Found., State Bar Ariz. (chmn. sect. taxation), D.C. Bar Assn. Contbr. articles to profl. jours. General corporate, Probate, Contracts commercial. Office: PO Box 871 Tucson AZ 85702

LEVITSKY, ASHER SAMUEL, lawyer; b. Wilkes-Barre, Pa., Nov. 4, 1973; s. Boris H. and Lillian F. (Fisher) L.; m. Iris Wolfe, Feb. 4, 1973; children: Joshua, Lily. BA, Cornell U., 1965; JD cum laude, NYU, 1968. Bar: N.Y. 1968, U.S. Ct. Appeals (2d cir.) 1969, D.C. 1970. Assoc. Powers & McNiff, N.Y.C., 1968-70, Rivkin Sherman and Levy, N.Y.C., 1970-78; ptnr. Rivkin Sherman and Levy, 1978-83; sole practice N.Y.C., 1983-85; ptnr. Levitsky & Serota, N.Y.C., 1985-86, Levitsky, Cohen & McAleenan, N.Y.C., 1986—. Mem. Order of Coif. Securities, General corporate, Contracts commercial. Home: 353 E 83d St New York NY 10028 Office: Levitsky Cohen & McAleenan 6 E 43d St New York NY 10017

LEVITT, BONNIE K., lawyer; b. Bklyn., Dec. 2, 1947; d. Seymour and Estelle (Jeffrey) Kresch; m. Daniel Jon Levitt, July 26, 1969; children: Jesse Simon, Kate Rachel. BA, Rutgers U., 1969; MST, U. Chgo., 1975; JD, Cumberland Sch. Law, 1981. Bar: Ill. 1981, U.S. Ct. Dist. (no. dist.) Ill. 1981, N.Y. 1984, U.S. Dist. (no. dist.) N.Y. 1985. Tchr. Homewood (Ill.) Pub. Schs., 1970-75, Solomon Schechter Sch., Woodbridge, Conn., 1976-77, Vestavia Hills (Ala.) High Sch., Ala., 1978; assoc. Schiff, Hardin & Waite, Chgo., 1981-83, Levene, Gouldin & Thompson, Binghamton, N.Y., 1983—. Contbr. articles to law jours. Mem. panel Broome County United Way, Vestal, N.Y., 1986—; trustee Temple Concord, Binghamton, 1986—. Recipient Am. Jurisprudence award Lawyer's Coop. Pub. Co., 1979, 80, Hornbook award West Pub. Co. Mem. ABA, N.Y. Bar Assn., Broome County Bar Assn., Estate Planning Council of So. Tier, Broome County C. of C. (speaker 1985, 86), Phi Beta Kappa. Pension, profit-sharing, and employee benefits, Real property, General corporate. Office: Levene Gouldin & Thompson 19 Chenango St Binghamton NY 13902-0106

LEVITT, DANIEL PHILIP, lawyer; b. Pitts., Apr. 24, 1936; s. Samuel N. and Florence D. Levitt; m. Harriet Ruth Laby, Sept. 22, 1957; children—Lee, Mark, Jonina. B.A., U. Pitts., 1956; B.A., Oxford (Eng.) U., 1958; LL.B., Harvard U., 1964. Bar: D.C. 1968, N.Y. 1976, U.S. Supreme Ct. 1981. Law clk. to U.S. Dist. judge So. Dist. N.Y., 1964-65; law clk. to U.S. Supreme Ct. Justice Arthur J. Goldberg, 1965, Justice Abe Fortas, 1965-67; assoc. Arnold & Porter, Washington, 1967-69; assoc. Paul, Weiss, Rifkind, Wharton & Garrison, Washington, 1969-74; ptnr., N.Y.C., 1974-76; ptnr. Kramer, Levin, Nessen, Kamin & Frankel, N.Y.C., 1976—; adj. prof. Georgetown Law Ctr., 1970-74. Co-chmn. trial lawyers sect. N.Y. United Jewish Appeal Fedn., 1980—. Served to 1st lt. USAF, 1958-61. Recipient Bushell prize in modern history Corpus Christi Coll., Oxford U., 1958. Mem. ABA (chmn. com. on pleadings, motions and pretrial of litigation sect. 1982—). Jewish. Supreme Ct. and note editor Harvard Law Rev., 1963-64. Federal civil litigation, State civil litigation, Private international. Office: Kramer Levin et al 919 3d Ave New York NY 10022

LEVITT, PRESTON CURTIS, lawyer; b. Queens Village, N.Y., July 23, 1950; s. Leon and Meryl Barbara (Rosenstock) L.; m. Maddy Charlene Domenitz, July 1, 1973; children—Taryn Audra, Brandon Ross. B.S., Am. U., 1972; J.D., Bklyn. Law Sch., 1975; LL.M., NYU, 1980. Bar: N.Y. 1976, Fla. 1977, U.S. Dist. Ct. (ea. and so. dists.) N.Y. 1976, U.S. Dist. Ct. (so. dist.) Fla. 1980, U.S. Ct. Claims 1980, U.S. Tax Ct. 1976, U.S. Ct. Appeals (5th cir.) 1980. Sr. tax acct. Arthur Young & Co., N.Y.C., 1975-80; mem. firm E.T. Hunter, Hollywood, Fla., 1980-81; sr. ptnr. Brydger & Levitt, P.A., Ft. Lauderdale, Fla., 1981—; dir. Atlantic Services Group Inc., Ft. Lauderdale; adv. bd. dirs. Regent Bank. Bd. dirs. Vis. Nurses Assn., Fort Lauderdale, 1983—. Mem. Fla. Bar Assn., Broward County Bar Assn., Am. Inst. Banking (bd. dirs. 1981—), Fraternal Order Police, Tau Epsilon Phi. Jewish. General corporate, Probate, Personal income taxation. Office: Brydger & Levitt PA 7770 W Oakland Park Blvd Fort Lauderdale FL 33321

LEVITT, THOMAS CHARLES, lawyer; b. Sioux City, Iowa, Nov. 12, 1954; s. David Jacob Levitt and Nancy Elaine (Rich); m. Elise Ann Parnes, June 25, 1977; children: Dana Rose, Jacob Kenneth. BS in Chem. Engring, U. Calif., Davis, 1976; JD, U. Calif., San Francisco, 1979; postgrad., U. Calif., Davis, 1983-85. Bar: Wash. 1979. Assoc. Layman, Mullin & Etter, Spokane, Wash., 1979-83; atty. Totem Pacific, Spokane, Wash., 1983—; exec. v.p. Totem Pacific Corp., Spokane, 1985—; of counsel Totem Pacific Corp. Mem. Am. Chem. Soc., Wash. State Trial Lawyers Assn. Avocation: family orchards. Home: 2720 Feather Pl Davis CA 95616 Office: E 8518 Green Bluff Rd Colbert WA 99005

LEVITT (TOPOL), ROBIN APRIL, lawyer; b. N.Y.C.; d. Anatole Roy and Phyllis Patricia (Redman) L.; m. Clifford Miles Topol, Oct. 23, 1982. BA, Barnard Coll., 1976; JD, NYU, 1979. Bar: N.Y. 1980, Fla. 1981. Assoc. Dreyer and Traub, N.Y.C., 1980-85, Willkie, Farr & Gallagher, N.Y.C., 1985—. Mem. Am. Israel Pub. Affairs Com., N.Y.C., 1985-86; exec. com. UJA Real Estate Div., N.Y.C., 1985-86. Mem. ABA (vice chmn. real property sect. 1985—), Women's Bar Assn. (chmn. real property sect. 1985—), Fla. Bar Assn., N.Y. County Bar Assn., Assn. of Bar of City of N.Y. (real property com. 1986—). Avocations: tennis, running, reading, movies. Real property.

LEVITTAN, SHIRLEY R., judge; b. N.Y.C., Sept. 8, 1918; d. Nathan William and Winifred (Silverstein) L. BA, Barnard Coll., 1939; Lic. es Lettres, Sorbonne, Paris, 1939; MA, Syracuse U., 1940; LLB, N.Y. Law Sch., 1956. Bar: N.Y. 1956, U.S. Ct. Appeals (2d cir.) 1956, U.S. Dist. Ct. (so. and ea. dists.) N.Y. 1957. Judge Criminal Ct. of City of N.Y., 1969-73; acting justice Supreme Ct. of State of N.Y., N.Y.C., 1973—. Contbr. articles to profl. jours. Office: Supreme Ct of N Y 100 Centre St New York NY 10013

LEVITZ, DANA MARK, judge; b. Balt., Dec. 8, 1948. BA, U. Md., 1970; JD cum laude, U. Balt., 1973. Bar: Md. 1973. Asst. state's atty. Baltimore County, Towson, Md., 1975-84, dep. state's atty., 1984-85; ptnr. Tully & Levitz P.A., Balt., 1977-82; spl. asst. U.S. Attys. Office, Balt., 1983; assoc. judge Cir. Ct. Baltimore County, Towson, 1985—; adj. prof. law U. Balt., 1985—; cons. rules com., Ct. Appeals Md., 1982-83. Bd. dirs. Jewish Big Bros. and Big Sisters League, 1982—, v.p. 1985, Baltimore County Sexual Assault and Domestic Violence Ctr., 1980-82. Mem. ABA, Md. Bar Assn., Baltimore County Bar Assn., Assn. Trial Lawyers Am., Nat. Dist. Attys. Assn., Md. Dist. Attys. Assn. Judicial administration. Home: Keller Ave Stevenson MD 21153 Office: Cir Ct Baltimore County 401 Bosley Ave Towson MD 21204

LEVUN, CHARLES R(ALPH), lawyer; b. Asbury Park, N.J., Sept. 13, 1944; s. Henry David and Esther (Silverman) L.; m. Nancy Gail Berman, June 18, 1967; children—Kari E., Jami A. B.S., U. Ill.-Urbana, 1966; J.D., U. Chgo., 1970. Bar: Ill. 1970, U.S. Dist. Ct. (no. dist.) Ill. 1970, U.S. Ct. Claims, 1973, U.S. Tax Ct. 1971. C.P.A., Ill. Assoc. Aaron, Aaron, Schimberg & Hess, Chgo., 1970-75, ptnr., 1975-78; ptnr. Arvey, Hodes, Costello & Burman, Chgo., 1978—; adj. prof. grad. tax program IIT-Chgo. Kent Coll. Law, 1985—. Mem. fed. tax com. Chgo. Assn. Commerce and Industry; mem. profl. adv. com. Jewish Fedn. Met. Chgo. Served with USAR, 1968-74. Mem. Chgo. Bar Assn. (chmn. div. on partnerships, real estate and other sheltered investments, tax acctg. 1980-81, co-chmn. spl. projects 1981-83), Ill. Bar Assn. (council fed. taxation sect. 1979-86, chmn. council 1984-85, co-editor Fed. Taxation Newsletter 1981-85), ABA (chmn. subcom. spl. allocations of com. partnerships 1982-86, chmn. subcom. on legislation and regulations of com. on Ptnrships., 1986—). Corporate taxation, Personal income taxation, Estate taxation. Office: 180 N LaSalle Suite 3800 Chicago IL 60601

LEVY, ADOLPH J., lawyer; b. New Orleans, Feb. 3, 1936; s. Adolph and Dorothy (Kaufman) L.; m. Carolyn Wilenzick, Mar. 20, 1967; 1 child, Elizabeth. BS in Econs., U. Pa., 1957; JD, Tulane U., 1960. Bar: La. 1960, U.S. Dist. Ct. (ea. dist.) La. 1962, U.S. Ct. Appeals (5th cir.) 1962, U.S. Supreme Ct. 1965. Sole practice New Orleans, 1960—. Editor (newsletter) Levy's Quotes, 1985-86; contbr. articles to profl. jours. Mem. consumer advocacy bd. New Orleans, FTC, 1970-71; bd. dirs. ACLU, 1970-78. Mem. ABA, Fed. Bar Assn., La. Bar Assn., Assn. Trial Lawyers Am. (state committeeman 1969-71, consumer protection com. workmen's compensation sect. 1970-71, co-vice chmn. pro bono legal services com. 1971-72, sec. 1975-76 comml. law sect., vice chmn. 1976-77, chmn. 1977-78), La. Trial Lawyers Assn., Acad. New Orleans Trial Lawyers (sec. 1979), Nat. Coll. Advocacy, La. Soc. CPAs, Beta Alpha Psi. Avocations: online computer research, legal and non-legal databases. Personal injury, Federal civil litigation, Legal consulting, motion practice. Home: 1525 Joseph St New Orleans LA 70115 Office: 518 S Rampart New Orleans LA 70113

LEVY, ALAN C(HESTER), lawyer, educator; b. Bklyn., Aug. 12, 1927; s. Daniel and Kitty (Durst) Eisler L.; m. Judith Ann Goldman, Dec. 2, 1984; children—Amy A., Seth P. Student L.I. U., 1951; LL.B., Bklyn. Law Sch., 1953. Bar: N.Y. 1953, U.S. Dist. Ct. (ea. and so. dists.) N.Y. 1955, U.S. Ct. Claims 1961, U.S. Ct. Appeals (2d cir.) 1962, U.S. Ct. Appeals (9th cir.) 1981, U.S. Supreme Ct. 1961. Sole practice, N.Y.C., 1953-56; ptnr. Levy, Heller, Kessler & Walzer, N.Y.C., 1956-68; sole practice, Bklyn., 1968-74, Mineola, N.Y., 1974—; adj. asst. prof. law Nassau Coll., Garden City, N.Y., 1978—; arbitrator Am. Arbitration Assn., N.Y.C., Garden City, N.Y., 1964—, N.Y. State Ct. System, Nassau County, 1982—. Served with U.S. Mcht. Marine, 1945-48. Mem. Assn. Trial Lawyers Am., N.Y. State Bar Assn., N.Y. County Lawyers Assn., Nassau County Bar Assn., Bklyn. Bar Assn. Lodge: B'nai B'rith, K.P. State civil litigation, General practice, Family and matrimonial. Home: 75 East End Ave New York NY 10028 Office: 100 Herricks Rd Mineola NY 11501

LEVY, CHARLOTTE LOIS, law librarian, law educator, consultant, lawyer; b. Cin., Aug. 31, 1944; d. Samuel M. and Helen (Lowitz) L.; m. Herbert Regenstreif, Dec. 11, 1980; 1 dau., Cara Rachael Regenstreif. B.A., U. Ky., 1966; M.S., Columbia U., 1969; J.D., No. Ky. U., 1975. Bar: Colo. 1979. Law librarian No. Ky. U., 1971-75; law librarian, assoc. prof. law Pace U., 1975-77; mgr. Fred B. Rothman & Co., Littleton, Colo., 1977-79; law librarian, assoc. prof. Bklyn. Law Sch., 1979—; adj. prof. Pratt Inst. Grad. Sch. Library and Info. Sci., 1982—; cons. to various libraries, pubs. Mem. Am. Assn. Law Libraries (cert. law librarian), Law Library Assn. Greater N.Y., ABA, Bklyn. Bar Assn. Democrat. Jewish. Author: The Human Body and the Law (Am. Jurisprudence Book award in domestic relations 1974, in trusts 1975), 1974, 2d edit., 1983; Computer-Assisted Litigation Support, 1984; mem. editorial bd. No. Ky. U. Law Rev., 1974-75. Legal education, Jurisprudence, Librarianship. Home: 3147 High Ridge Dr Lexington KY 40502 Office: Cabinet for Human Resources Office of the Counsel 275 E Main St Frankfort KY 40621

LEVY, DAVID, lawyer, executive consultant; b. Bridgeport, Conn., Aug. 3, 1932; s. Aaron and Rachel (Goldman) L. BS in Econs., U. Pa., 1954; JD, Yale U., 1957. Bar: Conn. 1958, U.S. Supreme Ct. 1963, D.C. 1964, Mass. 1965, N.Y. 1971, Pa. 1972; CPA, Conn. Acct. Arthur Andersen & Co., N.Y.C., 1957-59; sole practice Bridgeport, 1959-60; specialist tax law IRS, Washington, 1960-64; counsel State Mut. Life Ins. Co., Worcester, Mass., 1964-70; assoc. gen. counsel taxation Penn Mut. Life Ins. Co., Phila., 1971-81; sole practice Washington, 1982-87; v.p., tax counsel Pacific Mut. Life Ins. Co., Newport Beach, Calif., 1987—. Author: (with others) Life Insurance Company Tax Series, Bureau National Affairs Tax Management Income Tax, 1970-71. Mem. adv. bd. tax conf. Wharton Sch. Bus. U. Pa., 1977-84, Tax Mgmt., Washington, 1975—; chmn. state tax com. Greater Phila. C. of C., 1972-80; bd. dirs. Citizens Plan E Orgn., Worcester, 1966-70. Served with U.S. Army, 1957. Mem. ABA (vice chmn. employee benefits com., 1980-86, ins. cos. com. 1984-86, torts and ins. practice sect.), Assn. Life Ins. Counsel, Am. Inst. CPA's, Am. Assn. Atty. CPA's, Beta Alpha Psi. Jewish. Corporate taxation, Insurance, Pension, profit-sharing, and employee benefits. Office: Pacific Mut Life Ins Co Law Dept 700 Newport Center Dr Newport Beach CA 92660

LEVY, GEORGE MICHAEL, lawyer; b. Oceanside, N.Y., Aug. 8, 1948; s. Joseph Raoul and Bertha S. (Stern) L.; m. Susan L. Kaufman, June 10, 1972; children: Allyson Sabina, Ross Matthew. BA, L.I. U., 1970; JD, N.Y. Law Sch., 1974. Bar: N.Y. 1976, U.S. Dist. Ct. (no. dist.) N.Y. 1978, U.S. Dist. Ct. (so. and ea. dists.) N.Y. 1984, U.S. Supreme Ct. 1986. Asst. atty. gen. dept. law N.Y. State, Syracuse, 1977-83; trial counsel Finkelstein, Kaplan, Levine, Gittelsohn & Tetenbaum, Newburgh, N.Y., 1983-86, ptnr., 1987—. V.p., exec. bd. dirs. Temple Beth Jacob, Newburgh, 1985. Mem. N.Y. State Bar Assn., Orange County Bar Assn., Newburgh Bar Assn., Assn. Trial Lawyers Am., N.Y. State Trial Lawyers Assn., Internat. Brotherhood Magicians. Republican. Jewish. Lodge: Rotary. Avocations: magic, music. State civil litigation, Federal civil litigation, Personal injury. Office: Finkelstein Kaplan Levine et al 436 Robinson Ave Newburgh NY 12550

LEVY, HERBERT MONTE, lawyer; b. N.Y.C., Jan. 14, 1923; s. Samuel M. and Hetty D. L.; m. Marilyn Wohl, Aug. 30, 1953; children—Harlan A., Matthew D., Alison Jill. A.B., Columbia U., 1943, LL.B., 1946. Bar: N.Y. 1946, U.S. Dist. Ct. (so. dist.) N.Y. 1946, U.S. Ct. Appeals (2d cir.) 1949, U.S. Dist. Ct. (ea. dist.) N.Y. 1949, U.S. Supreme Ct. 1951, U.S. Ct. Appeals (10th cir.) 1956, U.S. Tax Ct. 1973. Assoc. Rosenman, Goldmark, Colin & Kaye, 1946-47, Javits & Javits, 1947-48; staff counsel ACLU, 1949-56; sole practice, 1956-64; ptnr. Hoffman, Gartlir, Hoffheimer, Gottleib & Gross, 1965-69; sole practice, N.Y.C., 1969—; faculty N.Y. County Lawyers Assn.; former lectr. Practising Law Inst. Exec. com. on law and social action Am. Jewish Congress, 1961-66. Mem. Fed. Bar Council (past trustee), Bar Assn. City N.Y., N.Y. County Lawyers Assn., 1st Amendment Lawyers Assn. Democrat. Jewish. Club: Businessmen's (N.Y.C.). Author How to Handle an Appeal (Practising Law Inst.), 1968, rev. edit. 1982; also legal articles. Antitrust, Federal civil litigation, State civil litigation. Home: 285 Central Park W Apt 12W New York NY 10024 Office: 60 E 42d St Suite 4210 New York NY 10165

LEVY, JAMES LEWIS, lawyer; b. N.Y.C., Sept. 30, 1943; s. Walter and Gertrude (Finkelstein) L.; m. Ann Selgin, Mar. 27, 1966; children: Robyn E., Daniel A. BA cum laude, Columbia U., 1965, LLB, 1968. Bar: Vt. 1969, U.S. Dist. Ct. Vt. 1969, U.S. Ct. Appeals (2d cir.) 1975, U.S. Supreme Ct. 1976. Ptnr. Costes, Levy & DeVries, St. Albans, Vt., 1969-76; sole practice St. Albans, 1976—. Grand juror City of St. Albans, 1969-71; justice of the peace State of Vt., 1979-87; mem. Vt. Profl. Conduct Bd. Vt. Supreme Ct., 1976-83, Dist. Environ. Commn., Vt., 1970-73, chmn. 1972-73. Mem. ABA, Vt. Bar Assn., Am. Arbitration Assn. (arbitrator, panel mem. 1985—), Columbia Coll. Alumni Assn. (bd. dirs. 1979-85). Democrat. Jewish. Club: University (Montreal). Avocations: skiing, sailing. General practice, Personal injury, General corporate. Home: 82 High St Saint Albans VT 05478 Office: 79 N Main St Saint Albans VT 05478

LEVY, JOEL C., lawyer; b. South Bend, Ind., Oct. 22, 1937; s. Ira and Lillian (Cooper) L.; m. Judith A. Amdur, June 4, 1961; children: Janice Ruth, Julie Ann. BS in Bus., Ind. U., 1959, JD, 1962. Bar: Ind. 1962, U.S. Dist. Ct. (no. dist.) Ind. 1962, U.S. Ct. Appeals (7th cir.) 1969, U.S. Dist. Ct. (no. dist.) Ill. 1971. Diplomate Nat. Bd. Trial Advocacy. Ptnr. Singleton, Levy & Crist and predecessor firm, Lake County, Ind., 1962—; lectr. Valparaiso Sch. of Law, Purdue U.-Calumet; atty. Sch. City of Hammond, 1967-70. Bd. dirs. Legal Aid Soc. of Gary, Ind. Mem. ABA (litigation and labor law sects.), Ind. Bar Assn. (mem. council trial lawyers sect.), Ind. Bar Found., Lake County Bar Assn. (bd. mgrs.), Hammond Bar Assn. (treas.), Assn. Trial Lawyers Am., Am. Judicature Soc. Jewish. Federal civil litigation, State civil litigation, Labor. Office: 9013 Indianapolis Blvd Highland IN 46322

LEVY, JULIUS, lawyer; b. N.Y.C., Feb. 15, 1913; s. Samuel and Esther (Pashman) L.; m. Jane Frederick, Nov. 7, 1940; children: Frederick J., Douglas J. BA, U. Mo., 1934; LLB, Columbia U., 1936. Bar: N.Y., U.S. Dist. Ct. (so. and ea. dists.) N.Y., U.S. Ct. Appeals (2d, 8th and D.C. cirs.), U.S. Supreme Ct. 1946. Of counsel Pomerantz, Levy, Haudek, Block & Grossman, N.Y.C. Bd. dirs., v.p. Univ. Settlement House, N.Y.C. Served to lt. (j.g.) USNR, 1943-45. Mem. Assn. of Bar of City of N.Y., N.Y. County Lawyers Assn., Am. Arbitration Assn. (nat. panel). Jewish. Lodge: B'nai B'rith. Avocations: tennis, vol. work. Federal civil litigation, State civil litigation, Securities. Office: Pomerantz Levy Haudek Block & Grossman 295 Madison Ave New York NY 10017

LEVY, KATHERINE JUDITH, lawyer; b. Chgo., Feb. 14, 1948; d. Meyer and Annette (Kaplan) Yeslin; m. Bruce Neil Levy, Aug. 30, 1970. BS in Acctg. with honors, U. Ill., 1969; MS in Taxation, DePaul U., 1972, JD, 1980. Bar: Ill. 1980, U.S. Dist. Ct. (no. dist.) Ill. 1980, U.S. Tax Ct. 1980, U.S. Ct. Appeals (7th cir.) 1980. CPA Touche Ross & Co., Chgo., 1969-70; revenue agt. IRS, Chgo., 1970-80; ptnr. Hirschtritt, Hirschtritt & Gold, P.C., Chgo., 1980-85; assoc. DeHaan & Richter, P.C., Chgo., 1985—. Mem. ABA (fin. planning com. 1986—), Ill. Bar Assn., Chgo. Bar Assn. (chmn. law com. 1984—, fed. taxation com. 1985—), Women's Bar Assn., Ill. Soc. CPA's, Beta Alpha Psi, Sigma Iota Epsilon. Corporate taxation, Probate, Personal income taxation. Office: DeHaan & Richter PC 55 W Monroe Suite 1000 Chicago IL 60603

LEVY, LAWRENCE ALAN, lawyer, educator; b. Kankakee, Ill., Feb. 5, 1943; s. Lawrence and Marjorie (Hefter) L.; m. Barbara Lynn Goldberg, June 19, 1966; children—Laura Sue, Jonathan. B.A. cum laude, U. Mich., 1964; student U. St. Andrews, Scotland, 1962-63; LL.B., Stanford U., 1967. Bar: Ind. 1967, Fla. 1977, U.S. Ct. Appeals (7th cir.) 1976, U.S. Supreme Ct. 1974. Legal asst. to chief counsel U.S. Senate Jud. Subcom. on Constl. Amendments, 1965; legal intern Dept. Justice, San Francisco, 1966; ptnr. Livingston, Dildine, Haynie & Yoder, Ft. Wayne, Ind., 1967-78; pres. Lawrence A. Levy, P.C., Ft. Wayne, 1979—; instr. bus. law Ind. U.-Ft. Wayne, 1971-72, St. Francis Coll., 1969-70. Pres. Tamarack Civic Assn., 1972-73. Mem. ABA, Am. Trial Lawyers Assn., Ind. Bar Assn., Fla. Bar Assn., Ind. Trial Lawyers Assn., Allen County Bar Assn. Clubs: Kiwanis (pres. 1978-79, lt. gov. 1982-83), U. Mich. Ft. Wayne Alumni (pres. 1982-84). General practice, State civil litigation, Personal injury. Home: 4232 Tamarack Dr Fort Wayne IN 46815 Office: 5904 East State Blvd Fort Wayne IN 46815

LEVY, LEONARD WILLIAMS, history educator, author; b. Toronto, Ont., Can., Apr. 9, 1923; s. Albert and Rae (Williams) L.; m. Elyse Gitlow, Oct. 21, 1944; children: Wendy Ellen, Leslie Anne. B.S., Columbia U., 1947, M.A., 1948, Ph.D. (Univ. fellow), 1951. Research asst. Columbia U., 1950-51; instr., asst. prof., assoc. prof., prof. Brandeis U., Waltham, Mass., 1951-70, first incumbent Earl Warren chair constl. history, 1957-70, dean Grad. Sch. Arts and Scis., 1958-63, dean faculty arts and scis., 1963-66; Andrew W. Mellon prof. humanities, history, chmn. grad. faculty history Claremont (Calif.) Grad. Sch., 1970—; Reiser lectr. U. Chgo. Law Sch., 1964; Gaspar Bacon lectr. Boston U., 1972; Elliott lectr. U. So. Calif. Law Sch., 1972; Hugo Black lectr. U. Ala., 1976; Bicentennial lectr., City of St. Louis, 1976. Author: The Law of the Commonwealth and Chief Justice Shaw, 1957, Legacy of Suppression; Freedom of Speech and Press in Early American History, 1960, Jefferson and Civil Liberties; The Darker Side, 1963, Origins

of the Fifth Amendment, 1968 (Pulitzer Prize in history 1969), Judgments: Essays on American Constitutional History, 1972, Against The Law: The Nixon Court and Criminal Justice, 1974, Treason Against God: History of the Offense of Blasphemy, 1981, Emergence of a Free Press, 1985, Constitutional Opinions, 1986, The Establishment Clause, 1986; editor: Major Crises in American History, 1962, The American Political Process, 1963, The Presidency, 1964, The Congress, 1964, The Judiciary, 1964, Parties and Pressure Groups, 1964, Freedom of the Press from Zenger to Jefferson, 1966, American Constitutional Law, 1966, Judicial Review and the Supreme Court, 1967, Freedom and Reform, 1967, Essays on The Making of the Constitution, 1969, The Fourteenth Amendment and the Bill of Rights, 1970, The Supreme Court Under Earl Warren, 1972, Jim Crow in Boston, 1974, Essays on the Early Republic, 1974, Blasphemy in Massachusetts, 1974, The Framing and Ratification of the Constitution, 1987; gen. editor: Am. Heritage Series, 60 vols., Harper Documentary History of Western Civilization, 40 vols.; editor-in-chief Ency. Am. Constn., 4 vols., 1986; gen. editor: Bicentennial History of the American Revolution; adv. bd.: Revs. in Am. History; Contbr. articles to profl. jours. Mem. nat. bd. Commn. on Law and Social Action, Am. Jewish Congress; mem. U.S. Bicentennial Commn. Am. Revolution, 1966-68; mem. exec. council Inst. for Early Am. History and Culture; mem. nat. adv. council ACLU, Pulitzer prize juror, chmn. biog. jury, 1974, history jury, 1976; adv. bd. The John Marshall Papers. Served with AUS, 1943-46. Recipient Sigma Delta Chi prize for journalism history, 1961, 86; Frank Luther Mott prize Kappa Tau Alpha, 1961; Pulitzer prize for history, 1969; Commonwealth Club prize for non-fiction, 1975; Ablor Meml. Prize of Am. Library Assn. for Intellectual Freedom, 1986; Cert. Merit ABA, 1986; Henry L. Mencken award Free Press Assn., 1986; Dartmouth Gold Medal Am. Library Assn., 1987; Guggenheim fellow, 1957-58; Center For Study Liberty in Am. fellow Harvard, 1961-62; Am. Bar Found. sr. merit fellow, 1973-74; Am. Council Learned Socs. fellow, 1973; NEH sr. fellow, 1974. Mem. Am. Hist. Assn. (Littleton-Griswald com. legal history), Orgn. Am. Historians, Am. Soc. Legal History (dir.), Am. Antiquarian Soc., Soc. Am. Historians, Inst. Early Am. History and Culture (exec. council), Kappa Delta Pi. Democrat. Legal history, Civil rights, Criminal. Home: 1630 Tulane Rd Claremont CA 91711

LEVY, MARK ALLAN, lawyer; b. Cambridge, Mass., May 31, 1939; s. Robert A. and Muriel (Goldman) L.; m. Ellen Grob, Oct. 2, 1966; children: Abigail R., Eric V.R. AB, Harvard U., 1961; LLB, Columbia U., 1964, MBA, 1965. Bar: N.Y. 1964, Mass. 1965. Assoc. Parker, Chapin, Flattau & Klimpl, N.Y.C., 1965-68; sr. ptnr. Stroock & Stroock & Lavan, N.Y.C., 1968—. Contbr. articles to profl. jours. Mem. N.Y. State Bar Assn. Corporate taxation, Personal income taxation, Real property. Home: 60 High Ridge Rd Hartsdale NY 10530 Office: Stroock & Stroock & Lavan 7 Hanover Sq New York NY 10004

LEVY, PETER LUDWIG, lawyer; b. Berlin, June 22, 1928; came to U.S., 1934; s. Fritz and Nanny (Lazar) L.; m. Dorothy Levy, June 24, 1950; children: Joan, Barbara, Eric. AA, U. Calif., Berkeley, 1948, BA, 1950, JD, 1953. Sole practice San Francisco, 1953—. Author numerous short stories, plays. Personal injury. Office: 115 Sansome St Suite 1200 San Francisco CA 94104

LEVY, RICHARD, lawyer; b. N.Y.C., Mar. 25, 1942; m. Sandra S. Levy, June 12, 1966; children: David, Joshua, Elizabeth. BA, Cornell U., 1963; MA, U. Chgo., 1966; JD, Georgetown U., 1976. Bar: Va. 1976, U.S. Dist. Ct. (ea. dist.) Va. 1977, D.C. 1980, U.S. Ct. Claims 1982. Sole practice Alexandria, Va., 1976-79, 82—; ptnr. Bassman, Mitchell & Levy, Washington, 1979-82. Author: Facing the DOE Audit, 1976. Chmn. ad hoc com. Citizen's Utility Franchises, 1984—; legal counsel city com. Alexandria Reps., 1984-86, parliamentarian, 1986—. Earhart Found. fellow U. Chgo., 1963-65. Mem. ABA. Jewish. Contracts commercial, Administrative and regulatory, Antitrust. Office: 4600 Duke St Suite 305 Alexandria VA 22304

LEVY, RICHARD HERBERT, lawyer; b. Chgo., Sept. 15, 1943; s. Milton David and Sophie (Lippert) L.; m. Bonnie Avis Bernstein, Jan. 9, 1972; children: Joshua, Rachel. BS, So. Ill. U., 1966; JD, DePaul U., 1976. Bar: Ill. 1976. Ptnr. Felwell, Galper & Lasky, Chgo., 1976; ptnr. Rudnick & Wolfe, Chgo., 1983—, also mem. adminstrv. com.; vice chmn. Home Bulders Chgo. Legis. Com., Oak Brook, Ill., 1986—. Bd. dirs. Housing Roundtable. Mem. ABA, Chgo. Vol. Lawyers Soc. Real property. Home: 3117 Centennial Ln Highland Park IL 60035 Office: Rudnick & Wolfe 30 N LaSalle St Chicago IL 60602

LEVY, ROBERT S., lawyer; b. N.Y.C., May 27, 1932; s. Harry Victor and Betty Ruth (Kaufman) L.; m. Lorna Iris Klein, June 30, 1957; children—Jill Arden, Kenneth Arlan. B.S. cum laude, N.Y.U., 1954, LL.B. cum laude, 1955. Bar: N.Y. 1956, U.S. Dist. Ct. (so. and ea. dists.) N.Y. 1962, U.S. Supreme Ct. 1967, U.S. Ct. Appeals (2d cir.) 1973. Assoc., Nordlinger, Reigelman, Benetar & Charney, N.Y.C., 1955-59; sr. assoc. Reich, Spitzer & Feldman, N.Y.C., 1959-64; sole practice, N.Y.C., 1964—; mem. nat. panel arbitrators Am. Arbitration Assn., N.Y.C., 1961—. Author: Guide to Franchise Investigation and Contract Negotiation, 1967; Woman's Guide to Franchises, 1967; Directory of State and Federal Funds for Business, 1968. Mem. N.Y. State Bar Assn., Phi Beta Kappa. Jewish. Club: Tam O'Shanter (Brookville, N.Y.). General corporate, General practice, State civil litigation. Home: 2495 Aron Dr W Seaford NY 11783

LEVY, RON KARL, lawyer; b. Chgo., Aug. 12, 1953; s. Elbert Edward and Fay (Gelder) L.; m. Lisa Kay Shepherd, Mar. 10, 1979. BS, Duke U., 1975; JD cum laude, Campbell U., 1982; PhD, U. N.C., 1982. Bar: N.C. 1982, Ind. 1983, U.S. Dist. Ct. (so. and no. dists.) Ind. 1983, U.S. Patent Office 1984. Patent atty. Eli Lilly & Co., Indpls., 1982—. W.N. Reynolds scholar Duke U., 1971-75; grantee U. N.C., 1981. Mem. Ind. Bar Assn., N.C. Acad. Scis. Avocations: computers, music, travel. Patent, Private international. Office: Eli Lilly & Co Lilly Corp Ctr Indianapolis IN 46285

LEVY, STEVEN ABRAHAM, lawyer; b. Washington, May 11, 1951; s. Aaron and Lillian Rae (Berliner) L.; m. Schelly Jane Reid, Jan. 17, 1982. BA, Cornell U., 1971, MA, 1974, PhD, 1976; JD, U. Chgo., 1978. Bar: D.C., 1978, U.S. Dist. Ct. D.C., U.S. Ct. Appeals (D.C., 2d, 3d, 5th and 10th cirs.), U.S. Supreme Ct. Atty., cons. office of telecommunication policy Exec. Office Pres., Washington, 1976; atty. office of gen. counsel COMSAT Gen. Corp., Washington, 1977; assoc. Hogan & Hartson, Washington, 1978-85; counsel Arent, Fox, Kintner, Plotkin & Kahn, Washington, 1985—. Contbr. articles to profl. jours. Mem. U.S. del. world adminstrv. radio conf. Internat. Telecommunications, Geneva, 1985. Fellow Carnegie Inst. for Internat. Peace, 1968-74; grantee Ford Found., 1972-75. Mem. ABA, Fed. Communications Bar Assn. Republican. Jewish. Private international, Public utilities, Telecommunications. Home: 3002 Holly St Edgewater MD 21037 Office: Arent Fox Kintner Plotkin & Kahn 1050 Connecticut Ave NW Washington DC 20006-5339

LEVY, STEVEN R., lawyer; b. Lakewood, N.J., Apr. 13, 1953; s. Robert Maurice and Natalie (Martinoff) L.; m. Ingrid G. Abelite, Dec. 31, 1977 (div. June 1982). AA in Bus. cum laude, Ocean County Coll., 1978; BA in Social Ecology magna cum laude, U. Calif., Irvine, 1979; JD, U. Santa Clara, 1981. Bar: Calif. 1982, U.S. Dist. Ct. (no. dist.) Calif. 1982. Owner Classic Wins Inc., Lakewood, N.J., 1977—; assoc. Glaspy, Elliott, Creech, McMahon, Roth & Reed, Campbell, Calif., 1980-85, Moore, Levy & Allison, San Jose, Calif., 1985—; arbitrator Santa Clara County Jud. Arbitration Panel, San Jose, 1985—. Recipient Am. Jurisprudence award Bancroft Whitney Co., 1979. Mem. ABA, Calif. Bar Assn., Santa Clara County Bar Assn., Assn. Trial Lawyers Am., Calif. Trial Lawyers Assn., Order of Barristers. Avocations: golf, skiing, harmonica playing, horticulture. Personal injury, Workers' compensation, Insurance. Home: 1452 Capurso Way San Jose CA 95125 Office: Moore Levy & Allison 84 W Santa Clara St Suite 888 San Jose CA 95113

LEW, GINGER, lawyer; b. San Mateo, Calif., Nov. 3, 1948; d. Bing and Suey Bow (Ng) L.; m. Carl Lennart Ehn, Feb. 2, 1984; children: Melissa, Jeremy. BS, UCLA, 1970; JD, U. Calif.-Berkeley, 1974. Bar: Calif. 1974, D.C. 1980. Dep. city atty. City of Los Angeles, 1974-75; asst. regional counsel Dept. Energy, San Francisco, 1975-77, dep. regional counsel, 1977-78, chief counsel, 1978-80; dep. asst. sec. of state for East Asia, Dept. of State, Washington, 1980-81, spl. adviser, 1981-82; ptnr. Stovall, Spradlin, Armstrong & Israel, Washington, 1983-86, Arthur Young Co., Washington, 1986—. Recipient Outstanding Achievement award Dept. of State, 1980, Meritorious Service award, 1981. Mem. ABA, Asian Pacific Am. Bar Assn. (bd. dirs. 1981-83), Women's Bar Assn., Orgn. of Chinese-Americans, Pi Sigma Alpha. Clubs: Commonwealth (San Francisco); Nat. Lawyers. Administrative and regulatory, Public international, General corporate. Office: Stovall & Spradlin 2600 Virginia Ave NW Suite 820 Washington DC 20037

LEWELLYAN, RONALD LEE, judge; b. Columbia, La., May 1, 1946; s. Ezzie R. and Janie Marteal (Lee) L.; m. Janis Gregory, Feb. 2, 1965 (div. July 14, 1983); children: Greg, Jennifer, Colin. BA, Northeast La. U., 1970; JD, La. State U., 1971. Bar: La. 1972. Ptnr. Burns & Lewellyan, Columbia, 1972-76, McKeithan, Burns & Lewellyan, Columbia, 1976; judge La. Dist. Ct. (37th dist.), Columbia, 1978—; adminstrv. asst. dist. atty., La. Dist. Ct. (28th dist.), 1973-76; mem. cts. and community relations, creation of new judgeships, trial ct. statistics coms. La. Supreme Ct., New Orleans. Bd. dirs. Haven Found., Columbia. Mem. ABA, La. Bar Assn., 37th Dist. Bar Assn., Assn. Trial Lawyers Am., La. Trial Lawyers Assn., Phi Alpha Delta, Ducks Unltd. Clubs: Post Oak Hunting Lodge, Lost Creek Hunting. Lodge: Lions (past. pres.). Home: Wall St Sleepy Hollow #3 Columbia LA 71418 Office: 37th Jud Dist Ct Main St Courthouse PO Box 177 Columbia LA 71418

LEWELLYN, BRUCE, lawyer; b. Hutchinson, Kans., Dec. 15, 1938; s. Paul Haines and Virginia Delight (Curt) L.; m. Jean Braddon, July 27, 1963; children—Braddon Scott, Megan Elizabeth, Curt Bryant. B.S., U. Kans., 1960; LL.B., Stanford U., 1966. Bar: Calif., 1967, Conn., 1967. Assoc., Tyler, Cooper, Grant, Bowerman & Keefe, New Haven, 1966-71; ptnr. Tyler, Cooper & Alcorn, New Haven, 1971—. Bd. dirs. Christian Community Action Inc., pres., 1975-76; bd. dirs. Mary Wade Home Inc., mem. adv. bd. YWCA Greater New Haven; trustee Ch. Redeemer, New Haven, chmn. bd. trustees, 1983. Served to lt. (j.g.) USNR, 1960-63. Mem. ABA, Conn. Bar Assn., New Haven County Bar Assn., Phi Beta Kappa. Clubs: New Haven Lawn (bd. govs.), Quinnipiack (New Haven). Banking, Pension, profit-sharing, and employee benefits.

LEWIN, JEFF LEE, law educator; b. Pitts., Apr. 17, 1951; m. Alison Ruth Williams, Mar. 27, 1982. BA, U. Mich., 1972; JD, Harvard U., 1975. Bar: Pa. 1976, U.S. Dist. Ct. (we. dist.) Pa. 1976, U.S. Ct. Appeals (3d cir.) 1981. Law clk. to sr. dist. judge U.S. Dist. Ct. Del., Wilmington, 1975-76; assoc. Reed Smith Shaw & McClay, Pitts., 1977-78; asst. mgr. Akrata Beach Camping, Porrovitsa, Greece, 1978-80; assoc. Titus, Marcus & Shapira, Pitts., 1980-83; assoc. prof. W.Va. U., Morgantown, 1983—. Contbr. articles to profl. jours. Bd. dirs. Greater Pitts. ACLU, 1981-83; bd. dirs., v.p. W.Va. Civil Liberties Union, 1984-85, adv. com., 1985—. Mem. ABA, Soc. of Am. Law Tchrs. Federal civil litigation, Legal education, Law and economics. Home: 309 Maple Ave Morgantown WV 26505 Office: WVa U Coll of Law Law Center Morgantown WV 26506

LEWINTER, WILLIAM JACOB, labor relations arbitrator, lawyer; b. Pitts., July 13, 1929; s. Samuel M. and Julia (Grogin) LeW.; m. Janet P. Sadler, Aug. 11, 1952; children—Mark J., Susan LeWinter Brauner; m. Beverly P. Goodstein, Mar. 12, 1977. A.B., U. Pitts., 1951, J.D., 1954. Bar: D.C. 1954, Pa. 1955, U.S. Dist. Ct. (we. dist.) Pa. 1955, U.S. Supreme Ct. 1977. Sole practice, Pitts., 1955-60; assoc. Lipsitz, Nassau & LeWinter and predecessor Lipsitz & Nassau, Pitts., 1960-65, ptnr., 1965-66; ptnr. Krimsly & LeWinter, Pitts., 1966-74; ptnr. Neely Krimsly, Stockdale and LeWinter, Pitts., 1974-75; pvt. practice labor arbitration, Pitts., 1975—, Miami, Fla., 1983— ad hoc lectr. in labor law, trade union adminstrn., labor and govt. Pa. State U., Ga. State U. Mem. Nat. Acad. Arbitrators, ABA, Allegheny County Bar Assn., Am. Arbitration Assn. Democrat. Jewish. Contbr. numerous opinions to publs. Labor. Home and Office: 5001 Collins Ave Apt 14B Miami Beach FL 33140 Office: 428 Forbes Ave Suite 1100 Pittsburgh PA 15219

LEWIS, ADAM AIKEN, lawyer; b. N.Y.C., July 6, 1947; s. Benjamin and Esther (Eibel) L.; m. Phyllis Lorraine Dunn Pottish, July 20, 1980; children: David James, Natasha Helena. BA in Philosophy, U. Calif., Santa Barbara, 1968, MA, 1974; JD, U. Calif., Davis, 1979. Bar: Calif. 1979, U.S. Dist. Ct. (no. dist.) Calif. 1979, U.S. Dist. Ct. (ea., cen. and so. dists.) Calif. 1980. Adminstrv. asst. Kaiser Hosp., San Diego, Calif., 1972-76; assoc. Morrison & Foerster, San Francisco, 1979-85, ptnr., 1985—; Mem. debtor/creditor relations and bankruptcy com. Calif. State Bar. Chmn. Assn. Montessori Internat. USA, Houston, San Francisco, 1983—. Mem. ABA (bus. bankruptcy com. 1983—, chptr. 11 subcommittee 1983—), Calif. Bar Assn. (debtor/creditor relation and bankruptcy com. bus. law sect. 1986—), Am. Bankruptcy Inst., U. Calif. Davis Sch. Law Alumni Assn., Order of Coif. Club: Commonwealth (San Francisco). Avocations: reading, gardening, camping, traveling, music. Bankruptcy, Consumer commercial. Office: Morrison & Foerster 345 California St San Francisco CA 94104-2105

LEWIS, ALBERT MICHAEL, lawyer; b. Rahway, N.J., Sept. 28, 1952; s. Albert F. and Iris (Roberts) L.; m. Lyn Mary Applegate, Aug. 11, 1979. BS, Rutgers U., 1978; JD, Seton Hall U., 1982. Bar: N.J. 1982, U.S. Dist. Ct. N.J. 1982, U.S. Ct. Appeals (D.C. cir.) 1984, U.S. Supreme Ct. 1986. With patent dept. AT&T Bell Labs, Holmdel, N.J., 1970-77; salesman AT&T Long Lines, N.Y.C, 1977-79; with mktg. dept. AT&T Long Lines, Bedminster, N.J., 1979-81, with personnel dept., 1981-82; atty. AT&T Communications, Basking Ridge, N.J., 1982—; Congl. asst. space sci. and application subcom., Washington, 1986-87. Deacon Colts Neck (N.J.) Reformed Ch., 1984-86. Mem. ABA (vice-chmn. pub. utility law com. young lawyers div. 1986-87), N.J. Bar Assn. Club: Holland Orchards Golf (sec. Men's Assn. 1982-84) (Marlboro, N.J.). Public utilities, Administrative and regulatory, Public international. Home: 55 Irving Pl Red Bank NJ 07701 Office: AT&T 295 N Maple Ave Room 3250G3 Room 236 Basking Ridge NJ 07920

LEWIS, ALVIN BOWER, JR., lawyer; b. Pitts., Apr. 24, 1986; s. Alvin Bower Sr. and Ethel Weidman (Light) L.; m. Marilyn Snyder Ware; children: Alvin B. III, Judith W., Robert B. II. BA, Lehigh U., 1954; LLB, Dickinson Sch. Law, 1957. Bar: Pa. 1957, U.S. Dist. Ct. (mid. and ea. dists.) Pa. 1958, U.S. Ct. Appeals (3d cir.) 1958, D.C. 1979. Ptnr. Lewis & Lewis, Lebanon, Pa., 1957-66, Lewis, Brubaker, Whitman & Christianson, Lebanon, 1967-76; spl. counsel, acting chief counsel, dir. select com. on assassinations of M.L. King, and J.F. Kennedy U.S. Ho. of Reps., Washington, 1976-77; ptnr. Lewis & Kramer, Phila., 1977-78, Hartman, Underhill & Brubaker, Lancaster, Pa., 1979—; dist. atty. County of Lebanon, Pa., 1962-70; chmn. Gov.'s Justice Commn., Pa., 1969-74, Pa. Crime Commn., Pa., 1979-85. Fin. chmn., exec. com. Rep. County Com., Lebanon, 1959-76; bd. dirs., chmn. adv. com. Urban League Lancaster County, 1986—. Recipient Furtherance of Justice award Mercyhurst Coll., 1979, Dist. Service award Ho. of Reps. Pa., 1982, Award of Distinction Pa. Senate, 1982, Outstanding Service award Gov. and Atty. Gen. Pa., 1974. Mem. ABA, Pa. Bar Assn. Lancaster County Bar Assn., Preservation Fund Pa., Inc., Lebanon County Bar Assn. (pres. 1974-76), Nat. Dist. Attys. Assn. (bd. dirs. 1966-68), Pa. Dist. Attys. Assn. (officer, pres. 1964-68). Lutheran. Lodge: Masons. Avocations: pilot, small airplanes. State civil litigation, Federal civil litigation, General corporate. Home: 27 Conestoga Woods Rd Lancaster PA 17601 Office: Hartman Underhill & Brubaker 221 E Chestnut St Lancaster PA 17602

LEWIS, ANTHONY, newspaper columnist; b. N.Y.C., Mar. 27, 1927; s. Kassel and Sylvia (Surut) L.; m. Linda Rannells, July 8, 1951 (div.); children: Eliza, David, Mia; m. Margaret H. Marshall, Sept. 23, 1984. A.B., Harvard U., 1948. Deskman Sunday dept. N.Y. Times, 1948-52; staff Democratic Nat. Com., 1952; reporter Washington Daily News, 1952-55, Washington bur. N.Y. Times, 1955-64; chief London bur. N.Y. Times, 1965-72; editorial columnist 1969—; lectr. on law Harvard U., 1974—. Author: Gideon's Trumpet, 1964 (award as best fact-crime book Mystery Writers Am.), Portrait of a Decade: The Second American Revolution, 1964; Contbr. articles to profl. jours. Bd. dirs., Fund for Free Expression. Recipient Heywood Broun award, 1955, Pulitzer prize for nat. reporting, 1955, 63; Nieman fellow, 1956-57. Clubs: Garrick (London); Tavern (Boston). Libel. Office: NY Times 2 Faneuil Hall Marketplace Boston MA 02109

LEWIS, CHRISTINE WHITESELL, lawyer; b. Montgomery, Ala., Sept. 8, 1956; d. Calvin Mercer and Jean (McCann) Whitesell; m. Timothy Alan Lewis, Aug. 15, 1981; children: Andrew McCann and Laura Allison (twins). Student, Southwestern U., 1975; BA in English, U. Ala., 1978, JD, 1981. Bar: Ala. 1981, U.S. Dist. Ct. (mid. dist.) Ala. 1983, U.S. Dist. Ct. (so. dist.) Ala. 1984, U.S. Ct. Appeals (11th cir.) 1984. Atty. Legal Services Corp., Tuscaloosa, Ala., 1982-83; assoc. Whitesell, Morrow & Romine, P.C., Montgomery, 1983-84; asst. atty. gen. Ala. Medicaid Agy., Montgomery, 1984-87; assoc. Calvin Whitesell, P.C., Montgomery, 1987—. V.p. ACLU Bd., Ala., 1984. Mem. ABA, Ala. Bar Assn., Montgomery Bar Assn., Bench and Bar. Democrat. Episcopalian. Avocation: reading. Administrative and regulatory, General practice, Legislative. Office: Calvin Whitesell PC 403 Washington Ave Montgomery AL 36104

LEWIS, CHRISTOPHER ALAN, lawyer; b. Phila., Sept. 16, 1955; s. Charles Edward and Florence (Scott) L.; m. Sheilah Diane Vance, Oct. 18, 1986. BA magna cum laude, Harvard U., 1975; JD magna cum laude, U. Mich., 1978. Bar: Pa. 1979, U.S. Dist. Ct. (ea. dist.) Pa. 1979, U.S. Ct. Appeals (3d cir.) 1979. Law clk. to presiding justice U.S. Dist. Ct. (ea. dist) Pa., Phila., 1978-80; assoc. Dilworth, Paxson, Kalish & Kauffman, Phila., 1980-85, ptnr., 1986-87; exec. dep. gen. counsel Commonwealth of Pa., Harrisburg, 1987—. Mem. steering com. 21st Century Inst. for Polit. Action, 1985—, Com. of Seventy; bd. dirs. Pub. Interest Law Ctr. of Phila., 1984—, Crime Prevention Assn., 1986-87. Mem. ABA, Fed. Bar Assn., Phila. Bar Assn., Barristers' Assn. Phila., Kappa Alpha Psi (treas. alumni chapt. 1981-83). Democrat. Episcopalian. Avocations: tennis, sailing. Federal civil litigation, State civil litigation. Home: 6425 Wayne Ave Philadelphia PA 19119 Office: Dilworth Paxson Kalish & Kauffman 2600 The Fidelity Bldg Philadelphia PA 19109

LEWIS, CYRUS ROYS, lawyer; b. Tuskegee, Ala., Feb. 8, 1915; s. Oscar Scott and Eva (Sage) L.; m. Madeleine Bryant, Apr. 26, 1947; 1 child, sarah. AB, U. Ala., 1937, LLB, 1939. Bar: Ala. 1939, U.S. Dist. Ct. (mid. dist.) Ala. 1939, U.S. Ct. Appeals (5th cir.) 1946, U.S. Supreme Ct. 1967. Ptnr. Lewis, Brackin & Flowers (and predecessor firm Lewis & Brackin), Dothan, Ala., 1939—. Served to lt. col. USAF, 1941-46. Decorated Air medal with oak leaf clusters. Mem. Ala. Bar Assn., Houston County Bar Assn. (pres. 1952, 72), Assn. Trial Lawyers Am., Ala. Trial Lawyers Assn., Phi Beta Kappa, Omicron Delta Kappa. Democrat. Episcopalian. Avocations: fishing, golf, hunting. Personal injury, General practice, State civil litigation. Home: 1604 W Newton St Dothan AL 36303 Office: Lewis Brackin & Flowers 114 S Oates St Dothan AL 36301

LEWIS, DANIEL EDWIN, lawyer; b. Goshen, Ind., May 2, 1910; s. Daniel Arthur and Emma (Williams) L.; m. Annette Jean Fewell, July 28, 1934; children—Daniel E., Nancy Jean Haswell. A.B., Hanover (Ind.) Coll., 1932; M.S., Ind. U., 1939; J.D., Valparaiso U., 1949. Bar: Ind. 1949. Tchr. secondary schs., Ind., 1932-43; dir. indsl. relations Allis-Chalmers, LaPorte, Ind., 1943-55; ptnr. Newby, Lewis & Kaminski, LaPorte, after 1955, now of counsel. Treas., Health Care Fedn., 1982; pres. LaPorte Bd. Edn., 1952-55; vice chmn. Pottawatomie County Boy Scouts Am., 1963-69; pres. United Fund, 1957-65; chmn. LaPorte County ARC, 1948-49; pres. LaPorte YMCA, 1960-62; pres. LaPorte County Family Service, 1975-77; pres. LaPorte County Human Relations Bd., 1967-68. Recipient Alumni Achievement award Hanover Coll., 1965. Mem. ABA, Ind. State Bar Assn., LaPorte City and County Bar Assn., Soc. Profls. in Dispute Resolution. Presbyterian. Clubs: Kiwanis, Elks, Masons. Author: (fiction) At the Crossroads, 1980; So It Comes to Arbitration, 1982. General practice, Labor, Probate. Home: 207 Edgewood Ln LaPorte IN 46350 Office: 916 Lincoln Way LaPorte IN 46350

LEWIS, DAVID L., lawyer; b. N.Y.C., Aug. 11, 1954; s. Albert B. and Sara Anne (Beresniakoff) L.; m. Carol Hayward, Dec. 21, 1983; 1 child, Alexandra Hayward. B.A., NYU, 1976; J.D., Fordham U., 1979. Bar: N.Y. 1980, U.S. Dist. Ct. (ea. dist.) N.Y. 1980, (so. dist.) N.Y. 1980, U.S. Ct. Appeals (2d cir.) 1981, U.S. Supreme Ct. 1983. Counsel to speaker pro tempore N.Y. State Assembly, Albany, 1980-83; ptnr. firm Lewis & Fiore, N.Y.C., 1980—. Columnist Decor mag., 1980—. Mem. law com. Kings County Dem. Party, Bklyn., 1980—; pres. Bensonhurst Redevel. Corp., Bklyn., 1981-82. Mem. Assn. Trial Lawyers Am. (author text on plea bargaining and settlement), N.Y. State Bar Assn., Assn. Bar City N.Y., N.Y. County Lawyers Assn., Nat. Assn. Criminal Def. Lawyers. Jewish. Criminal, Federal civil litigation, Legislative. Office: Lewis & Fiore 225 Broadway Suite 3300 New York NY 10007-3001

LEWIS, GERALD JORGENSEN, judge; b. Perth Amboy, N.J., Sept. 9, 1933; s. Norman Francis and Blanche M. (Jorgensen) L.; m. Laura Susan McDonald, Dec. 15, 1973; children by previous marriage—Michael, Marc. A.B. magna cum laude, Tufts Coll., 1954; J.D., Harvard U., 1957. Bar: D.C. 1957, N.J. 1961, Calif. 1962, U.S. Supreme Ct. 1968. Atty. Gen. Atomic, LaJolla, Calif., 1961-63; ptnr. Haskins, Lewis, Nugent & Newnham, San Diego, 1963-77; judge Mcpl. Ct., El Cajon, Calif., 1977-79; judge Superior Ct., San Diego, 1979-84; assoc. justice, Calif. Ct. of Appeal, San Diego, 1984—; adj. prof. evidence Western State U. Sch. Law, San Diego, 1977—, exec. bd., 1977—; faculty San Diego Inn of Ct., 1979—, Am. Inn of Ct., 1984—. Cons. editor: California Civil Jury Instructions, 1984. City atty. Del Mar, Calif., 1963-74, Coronado, Calif., 1972-77; counsel Comprehensive Planning Orgn., San Diego, 1972-73; trustee San Diego Mus. Art., 1986—; bd. dirs. Air Pollution Control Dist., San Diego County, 1972-76; trustee San Diego Mus. Art, 1986—. Served to lt. comdr. USNR, 1957-61. Named Trial Judge of Yr., San Diego Trial Lawyers Assn., 1984. Mem. Am. Judicature Soc., Calif. Judges Assn., Soc. Inns of Ct. in Calif., Confrerie des Chevaliers du Tastevin, Friendly Sons of St. Patrick. Republican. Episcopalian. Clubs: LaJolla Country (dir. 1980-83); Honkers Hunting (Niland, Calif.); Prophets. Judicial administration, Legal education. Home: 6505 Caminito Blythfield LaJolla CA 92037 Office: Ct of Appeal 1350 Front St San Diego CA 92101

LEWIS, GORDON, lawyer; b. Essex County, Va., Jan. 27, 1911; s. James Meriwether and Ellen Harvie (Latane) L., m. Olive Kathleen Messer, June 12, 1941; children: Richard Gordon, James Meriwether, Ellen Lewis Bane, William Latane. JD, U. Va., 1934. Bar: Va. 1933, U.S. Supreme Ct. 1949, U.S. Ct. Appeals (4th cir.) 1977. Ptnr. Lewis & Lewis, Tappahannock, Va., 1934-39; sole practice Tappahannock, 1939-59; ptnr. Lewis & Spruill, Tappahannock, 1959—; pres. Southside Bank, Tappahannock, 1961-82, chmn. bd. dirs., 1982—. Co-author: Virginia Annotations Conflict of Law, 1940; mem. editorial bd. U. Va. Law Rev., 1932, assoc. editor, 1933. Mem. Va. Ho. Dels., 1938-42. Served to col. USAFR, 1942-71. Mem. ABA, Va. Bar Assn. Republican. Episcopalian. Lodge: Arlington, Ruritan. Avocations: golf, sports. Probate, Real property. Office: Lewis & Spruill 300 Duke St Tappahannock VA 22560

LEWIS, GRANT STEPHEN, lawyer; b. N.Y.C., Apr. 27, 1942; s. Arnold R. and Gladys F.; m. Shari J. Gruhn, Sept. 15, 1974; 1 dau., Carrie Ann. A.B., Bates Coll., 1962; J.D., Harvard U., 1965. Bar: N.Y. 1966, U.S. Supreme Ct. 1975, all fed. cir. cts., various fed. dist. cts. With firm LeBoeuf, Lamb, Leiby & MacRae, N.Y.C., 1966—, ptnr., 1973—. Mem. ABA, Assn. Bar City N.Y. Clubs: University, Harvard (N.Y.C.). Contbr. articles to profl. jours. Federal civil litigation, Antitrust, Securities. Office: LeBoeuf Lamb Leiby & MacRae 520 Madison Ave New York NY 10022

LEWIS, H(ENRY) WORTHINGTON, lawyer; b. Washington, Aug. 3, 1958; s. James C. Jr. and Carolyn Elaine (Rosser) Parker; m. Evelyn Denise Martin, Aug. 11, 1984. BS in Polit. Sci. with honors, Tuskegee Inst., 1979; JD cum laude, Mercer U., 1982. Bar; Ga. 1982, U.S. Dist. Ct. (no. dist.) Ga. 1982. Staff atty. Reginald Heber Smith fellow lawyer fellowship program Atlanta Legal Aid Soc., 1982-83; law clk. to assoc. justice Ga. Supreme Ct., Atlanta, 1983-85; assoc. Dodd, Connell & Hughes, Atlanta, 1985—. Named one of Outstanding Young Men Am., 1981. Mem. ABA, Gate City Bar Assn., Atlanta Bar Assn., Alpha Phi Omega (pres. 1976-79), Omega Psi Phi (parliamentarian 1983—). Avocations: land and water sports, creative writing, reading, polit. sci. Federal civil litigation, State civil litigation, Entertainment. Office: Dodd Connell & Hughes 100 Peachtree St Suite 2900 Atlanta GA 30303

LEWIS, JAMES BERTON, lawyer; b. Lenox, Tenn., Oct. 29, 1911; s. Oscar and Maude (Kirby) L.; m. Irene Fogt, Dec. 9, 1961; children: Edward K., Robert L. Student, Centralia (Wash.) Jr. Coll., 1929-31, Wash. State

Coll., 1931; LL.B., Columbus U., Washington, 1940. Bar: D.C. 1942, N.Y. 1954. With Treasury Dept., 1931-34, IRS, 1934-42, 45-48; atty. Office Tax Legis. Counsel, Treasury Dept., 1948-52; spl. asst. to chief counsel IRS, 1952-53; assoc. firm Paul, Weiss, Rifkind, Wharton & Garrison, N.Y.C., 1953-55; partner Paul, Weiss, Rifkind, Wharton & Garrison, 1955-82, of counsel, 1982—; adj. prof. NYU Law Sch., 1962-83; vis. prof. Benjamin N. Cardozo Sch. Law, 1983—; cons. Am. Law Inst. estate and gift tax, income tax projects; mem. adv. group to commr. IRS, 1977, 87. Author: The Estate Tax, 4th edit, 1979, The Marital Deduction, 1984. Served with USNR, 1942-45. Mem. ABA (vice chmn. publns., sect. taxation 1980-83, chmn. 1984-85), Am. Law Inst., N.Y. State Bar Assn., N.Y. County Lawyers Assn., Assn. Bar City N.Y., D.C. Bar Assn. Democrat. Presbyterian. Club: Masons. Corporate taxation, Estate taxation, Personal income taxation. Home: 320 E 72d St New York NY 10021 Office: 1285 Ave of Americas New York NY 10019

LEWIS, JAMES BROOKE, lawyer; b. Miles City, Mont., Feb. 14, 1944; s. Vern Edward and Mary (Brooke) L.; m. Ruth Meerk; 1 child, Matthew Murray. AB cum laude, Georgetown U., 1965; JD, U. Chgo., 1968. Bar: Ill. 1969, U.S. Dist. Ct. (cen. dist.) Ill. 1971, U.S. Ct. Appeals (7th cir.) 1973. Trial atty. Heyl, Royster, Voelker & Allen, Peoria, Ill., 1970-77; sole practice Peoria, 1978—; assoc. mem. com. jury instrns. Ill. Supreme Ct., 1974-75. Mem. ABA (litigation sect.), Ill. Bar Assn., Phi Beta Kappa. Unitarian. Avocations: reading, classical music, carpentry. Federal civil litigation, State civil litigation, Personal injury. Home: 5934 N Elm Ln Peoria IL 61614 Office: 1009 First National Bank Bldg Peoria IL 61602

LEWIS, JAMES WILLIAM, lawyer; b. Columbus, Ohio, Oct. 31, 1947; s. Wayne Linkous and Rosemary (Adams) L.; m. Barbara Gay Bolt, Sept. 20, 1969; children: Marc Christopher, Michael Cameron. Student, George Washington U., 1965; BA, Ohio State U., 1969; JD cum laude, Capital U. Law Sch., 1975. Bar: Ohio 1975, U.S. Dist. Ct. (so. dist.) Ohio 1978, U.S. Supreme Ct. 1979, U.S. Ct. Appeals (6th cir.) 1982. Asst. pros. atty. Franklin County, Columbus, 1975-77, sr. asst. pros. atty., 1977-79, dir. econ. crime unit, 1979-80; assoc. Brownfield, Bally & Goodman, Columbus, 1980-85; ptnr. Brownfield, Cramer & Lewis, Columbus, 1986, Lewis & Spencer, Columbus, 1987—; spl. counsel Franklin County Pros. Atty., Columbus, 1980, 83—; counsel investigative subcom. on Medicaid HMO's Ohio Senate, Columbus, 1986—. Notes editor, author Capital U. Law Rev., 1974-75. Mem. cen. com. Franklin County Reps., Columbus, 1981—. Served to 1st lt. U.S. Army, 1969-72, PTO. Mem. ABA, Ohio Bar Assn., Columbus Bar Assn., Ohio Assn. of Civil Trial Attys., Internat. and Ohio Assn. of Arson Investigators., Order of Coif. Roman Catholic. Arson and insurance fraud defense law, Insurance, State civil litigation. Office: Lewis & Spencer 17 S High St #795 Columbus OH 43215

LEWIS, JOHN BRUCE, lawyer; b. Poplar Bluff, Mo., Aug. 12, 1947; s. Evan Bruce and Hilda Kathryn (Kassebaum) L.; m. Diane F. Grossman, July 23, 1977; children: Samantha Brooking, Ashley Denning. BA, U. Mo., 1969, JD, 1972; LLM, Columbia U., 1978; diploma, Nat. Inst. Trial Advocacy, 1982. Bar: Mo. 1972, U.S. Dist. Ct. (ea. dist.) Mo. 1973, U.S. Ct. Appeals (8th cir.) 1973, U.S. Dist. Ct. (no. dist.) Ohio 1979, Ohio 1980, U.S. Ct. Appeals (6th cir.) 1982, U.S. Dist. Ct. (ea. dist.) Mich. 1983. Assoc. Millar, Schaefer & Ebling, St. Louis, 1972-77, Squire, Sanders & Dempsey, Cleve., 1979-85; ptnr. Arter & Hadden, Cleve., 1985—. Contbr. articles to legal jours. Mem. Cleve. Council on World Affairs; mem. Greater Cleve. Growth Assn.; vol. solicitor attys. div. United Way Services. Mem. ABA (labor and employment law sect., com. EEO law), Ohio Bar Assn. (labor and employment law sect.), Greater Cleve. Bar Assn. (labor law sect.), Indsl. Relations Research Assn., Selden Soc. Civil rights, Federal civil litigation, Labor. Office: Arter & Hadden 1100 Huntington Bldg Cleveland OH 44115

LEWIS, JOHN FURMAN, lawyer, oil company executive; b. Fort Worth, Apr. 24, 1934; s. Ben B. and Minnie W. (Field) L.; m. Beverly Ann George, Feb. 16, 1963; children—Joyce Ann, George Field, William Patrick. Student, Tex. Christian U., summer 1955; B.A. in Econs., Rice U., 1956; J.D. with honors, U. Tex., 1962; postgrad., Princeton U., 1965-66; M.B.A., Bowling Green State U., 1971. Bar: Tex. 1962, U.S. Dist. Ct. 1965, U.S. Supreme Ct. 1967, Ohio 1968, U.S. Ct. Mil. Appeals 1971, Okla. 1987. Atty. Atlantic Richfield Co., 1962-67; with Marathon Oil Co., Findlay, Ohio, 1967-86, gen. atty., 1978, sr. atty., 1978-81, assoc. gen. counsel, 1983-84, v.p., gen. counsel., sec., 1985-86; sr. v.p., gen. counsel The Williams Cos., Tulsa, 1986—; mem. adv. bd. Internat. and Comparative Law Ctr. of Southwestern Legal Found.; mem. adv. bd. Internat. Oil and Gas Ednl. Ctr. of Southwestern Legal Found. Contbr. articles to profl. jours. Mem. exec. com., trustee United Way of Hancock County, Findlay, Ohio, 1984-86; bd. dirs. NO-WE-OH council Camp Fire, Inc., Findlay, Ohio, 1974-86. Served to lt. (j.g.) USN, 1956-59. Mem. ABA (subcom. chmn. 1984-85), Tex. Bar Assn., Am. Petroleum Inst. (lawyer-adviser mktg. com. 1982-84, gen. law com. 1983—), Ohio Bar Assn., Okla. Bar Assn., Tulsa County Bar Assn. Republican. Avocations; jogging; tennis. General corporate, Oil and gas leasing, Antitrust. Office: The Williams Cos One Williams Ctr Tulsa OK 74172

LEWIS, KAY MICHIE, lawyer; b. Heber City, Utah, Mar. 11, 1936; s. Sterling Samuel and Fern Elena (Michie) L.; m. Sherlyn Hart, Mar. 18, 1960; children—Julie, Bradley Kay, Craig Hart, Laura, Shaylyn, Devin Joseph. B.A., Brigham Young U., 1960; J.D., U. Utah, 1964. Bar: Utah 1964, U.S. Dist. Ct. Utah, 1964, U.S. Tax Ct., 1973, U.S. Ct. Appeals (10th cir.), 1964. Sole practice, Salt Lake City, 1964—; atty. Salt Lake County, 1964-65; chief dep. dist. atty. 3d Jud. Dist., Salt Lake City, 1965-69; trustee U.S. Bankruptcy Ct., Utah, 1966-70. Scoutmaster, Great Salt Lake council Boy Scouts Am., 1971-75; coach Western Boys Baseball Assn., 1974-76. Mem. Assn. Trial Lawyers Am., ABA, Utah State Bar, Utah Trial Lawyers Assn., Salt Lake County Bar Assn., Nat. Rifle Assn., Brigham Young U. Cougar Club, Phi Delta Phi. Republican. Mormon. Banking, Consumer commercial, Real property. Home: 1110 Alton Way Salt Lake City UT 84108 Office: Jensen & Lewis PC 320 South 300 East Salt Lake City UT 84111

LEWIS, KENNETH WAYNE, lawyer; b. Orange, Tex., Sept. 28, 1948; s. Henry Hunter and Violet May (Johnson) L.; m. Karensa Higdon, Sept. 13, 1973 (div. July 1980); children: Kara Rebekah, Joshua Houston; m. Kathleen Cole, Dec. 28, 1980; 1 child, Valerie Sarah. BS with honors, Lamar U., 1971; MA, Case Western Res. U., 1973, postdoctoral, 1972-73; JD, U. Tex., 1977. Bar: Tex. 1977, U.S. Dist. Ct. (ea. dist.) Tex. 1977, U.S. Ct. Appeals (5th and 11th cirs.) 1979. Assoc. Law Offices of Jim Mehaffy, Jr., Beaumont, Tex., 1977-78; ptnr. Mehaffy, Lewis & Garcia, Beaumont, 1979-80, Cribbs & Lewis, Beaumont, 1981-84; sole practice Beaumont, 1984-85; ptnr. Townsley, Bush, Lewis & Ramsey, Beaumont, 1985—; instr. Lamar U. Paralegal Inst., Beaumont, 1978-80. Bd. dirs. East Tex. Legal Services, Beaumont, 1981-87q. Mem. ABA, Tex. Bar Assn., Jefferson County Bar Assn. (bd. dirs. 1979), Port Arthur Bar Assn., Assn. Trial Lawyers Am., Tex. Trial Lawyers Am., Tex. Young Lawyers Assn. (ethics com.), Tex. Bd. Legal Specialization (cert.), Nat. Bd. Trial Adv. (cert.), Jefferson County Young Lawyers Assn. (chmn. Liberty Bell award com. 1984, chmn. monthly meeting com. 1978, bd. dirs. 1978-80, pres. 1979), Personal Injury Lawyers Am. (chartered). Democrat. Methodist. Avocations: fishing, sports, reading. Personal injury, Workers' compensation, Admiralty. Office: Townsley Bush Lewis & Ramsey PC 3550 Fannin St Beaumont TX 77701

LEWIS, LEAH H., lawyer; b. N.Y.C., Dec. 16, 1944; d. Judah and Shirley (Blau) Broyde; divorced; children: Yaacov, Chani, Yitzchok, David. BA, UCLA, 1976; JD, U. Balt., 1980. Bar: Md. 1980. Assoc. Sauerwein, Boyd, Decker & Levin, Balt., 1981-82, Boyd, Benson & Hendrickson, Balt., 1983—; Sec. Commn. Law and Pub. Affairs, Balt., 1984—. Mem. PTA Talmudical Acad., Balt., 1977—. Named one of Outstanding Young Women Am., Balt., 1980, 81. Mem. ABA, Md. Bar Assn., Women's Bar Assn., Bar Assn. Balt. City (family law com. 1985—). Democrat. Avocations: reading, gardening, crafts. Family and matrimonial, Probate, General practice. Office: Boyd Benson & Hendrickson 300 Cathedral St Baltimore MD 21201

LEWIS, LEONARD J., lawyer; b. Rexburg, Idaho, Jan. 10, 1923; s. Jack and Hannah (Beesley) L.; m. Lois Ann Cannon, Sept. 3, 1947; children—Leslie Ann, L. Lohn, James C., Janet. B.S., U. Utah, 1947; J.D., Stanford U., 1950. Bar: Utah 1950. With firm Van Cott, Bagley, Cornwall & McCarthy, Salt Lake City, 1950—, now, chmn.; bd. dirs. Temple St. Investment Co., Am. Ins. & Investment Corp. Chmn., Salt Lake County Pub. Arts Adv. Com., 1982—, bd. visitors Stanford Law Sch., mem. instl. council U. Utah; past chmn. Utah State Bldg. Bd. Served with U.S. Army, 1941-43. Mem. ABA, Assn. Trial Lawyers Am., Salt Lake County Bar Assn., Internat. Bar Assn., Utah Bar Assn. (past chmn. ct. adminstrv. com., 1974-75), Beta Theta Pi. Clubs: Alta, University, Hamilton Racquet, Salt Lake Country, YMCA (Salt Lake City). General corporate, Oil and gas leasing, General practice. Home: 910 Donner Way Salt Lake City UT 84108 Office: Van Cott Bagley Cornwall McCarthy 50 S Main St Suite 1600 Salt Lake City UT 84144

LEWIS, MARK RUSSELL, lawyer; b. Cin., Oct. 21, 1946; s. John Russell and Lillian (Hilgeman) L.; m. Tana Tillotson, Dec. 14, 1968 (div. Mar. 1974); m. Sharon R. Sullivan; 1 child, Mark R. II. BS in Engring., U. Cin., 1969, JD, 1973. Bar: Ohio 1973, Fla. 1975. Law clk. to presiding justice U.S. Ct. Appeals (6th cir.), Cin., 1973-75; assoc. Harrison, Greene, Mann, Rowe, Stanton & Mastry, St. Petersburg, Fla., 1975-77; sole practice St. Petersburg, 1977—; tchr. continuing edn. St. Petersburg Jr. Coll., 1984-86; atty. City of So. Pasadena, Fla., 1977-79. Author: Legalese, 1984, Fundamentals of Buying and Selling Real Estate, 1987l. Atty. Pinellas County Child Protection Team, St. Petersburg, 1982—. Mem. ABA, Fla. Bar Assn. Republican. Avocation: tennis. Real property, Probate, General corporate. Office: 3000 66th St N Suite B Saint Petersburg FL 33710

LEWIS, MURRAY F., lawyer; b. Ithaca, N.Y., June 26, 1931; s. Morris I. and Sydelle (Fisher) L.; m. Carol Penn, Feb. 7, 1957; children—Andrea J., Sheryl L., Patricia B. M.B.A., Cornell U., 1952, J.D., 1955. Bar: N.Y. 1955, U.S. Dist. Ct. (no. dist.) N.Y. 1959. Assoc. Walter J. Wiggins, Ithaca, 1955-56; asst. county atty. Tompkins County, N.Y., 1956-58; sole practice, Ithaca, 1956—; sec., dir. Morris' Men's Wear, Inc., Ames of Ithaca, Inc. Trustee, Tompkins County Hosp. Corp., 1969-75, pres. bd., 1975. Served as lt. U.S. Navy, 1951-57. Mem. ABA, N.Y. State Bar Assn., Tompkins County Bar Assn., Am. Assn. Trial Lawyers, N.Y. State Trial Lawyers Assn., Am. Arbitration Assn. (panel of arbitrators). Republican. Jewish. Clubs: Elks, Masons. Past contbg. editor N.Y. State Trial Lawyers Quar. General practice, Personal injury, Probate. Office: 200 E Buffalo St Suite 101 Ithaca NY 14850

LEWIS, NEAL RANDOLPH, lawyer; b. Reading, Pa., Oct. 4, 1946; s. Meyer and Grace (Lieberman) L.; m. Claudia Beth Krieger, Sept. 3, 1972; children—Kameron Ann, Zachary Owen, Nina Scottie. B.A., Albright Coll., 1968; J.D., Suffolk U., 1973. Bar: Pa. 1973, Fla. 1978, U.S. Dist. Ct. (so. dist.) Fla. 1978, U.S. Ct. Appeals (5th cir.) 1978, U.S. Supreme Ct. 1979, U.S. Dist. Ct. (mid. dist.) Fla. 1981, U.S. Ct. Appeals (11th cir.) 1981, N.Y. 1982, U.S. Dist. Ct. (ea. dist.) Mich. 1984, U.S. Dist. Ct. (ea. dist.) Pa. 1986, U.S. Ct. Appeals (3d cir.) 1987. Assoc., Lieberman & Dimitriou, Reading, Pa., 1973-78; ptnr. Heiman Krieger, Freiden & Silber, Miami, 1978-79; ptnr. Albert J. Krieger, P.A., Miami, 1979-82; sole practice, Miami, 1982—; dir. South Star Communications, Inc., Fort Lauderdale. Served with AUS, 1968-70, Vietnam. Mem. Nat. Assn. Criminal Def. Lawyers, Pa. Bar Assn., Berks County Bar Assn., Fla. Bar Assn., ABA, N.Y. County Lawyers Assn. Democrat. Jewish. Criminal, Federal civil litigation, State civil litigation. Office: 1899 S Bayshore Dr Miami FL 33133

LEWIS, ORME, lawyer; b. Phoenix, Jan. 7, 1903; s. Ernest W. and Ethel (Orme) L.; m. Barbara C. Smith (dec.), 1 son, Orme. Ed., Stanford, 1920-21; LL.B., George Washington U., 1926. Bar: Ariz. 1926, Calif. 1931, U.S. Supreme Ct. 1955, D.C. 1969. Practiced in Phoenix 1926—; mem. Lewis and Roca, 1950—; asst. sec. Dept. Interior, 1953-55; mem. 9th Ariz. State Legislature; U.S. rep. GATT, 1955. Fellow ABA. Clubs: Phoenix; Metropolitan (Washington), Capitol Hill (Washington). Legislative, Real property. Home: 2201 N Central Ave Phoenix AZ 85004 Office: 100 W Washington Phoenix AZ 85003

LEWIS, PETER, lawyer; b. N.Y.C., Dec. 9, 1931; s. Maxwell and Amelia (Dietrich) L. BA, Columbia U., 1953, MBA, 1955; JD, U. Md., 1971. Bar: Md. 1972, U.S. Dist. Ct. Md. 1972, U.S. Supreme Ct. 1977, D.C. 1979. Atty. Legal Aid Bur., Balt., 1972; asst. state's atty. City of Baltimore, 1972-73; sr. ptnr. Lees & Lewis, Balt., 1973-74; sole practice Balt. and Ocean City, Md., 1974—. Served with USN, 1953-55. Mem. Md. Bar Assn., Balt. City Bar Assn., Assn. Trial Lawyers Am., Am. Judicature Soc. Democrat. Personal injury, Criminal, Family and matrimonial.

LEWIS, ROBERT LEE, lawyer; b. Oxford, Miss., Feb. 26, 1944; s. Ernest Elmo and Johnice Georgia (Thirkield) L.; married; children: William Lovell, Dion Terrell, Viron Lamar; m. Twilla LaJoria Parks, Sept. 7, 1969; children: Yolanda Sherice, Robert Lee Jr. BA, Ind. U., 1970, JD, 1973; M in Pub. Service, West Ky. U., 1980. Bar: Ind. 1973, Ky. 1979, U.S. Ct. Claims, U.S. Ct. Internat. Trade, U.S. Tax Ct., U.S. Ct. Mil. Appeals, U.S. Ct. Appeals (fed. cir.), U.S. Supreme Ct. Sole practice Evansville, Ind., 1973-75, Gary, Ind., 1980—; atty., army officer U.S. Army, Ft. Knox, Ky., 1975-78; appellate referee Ind. Employment Security Div., Indpls., 1978-80. Mem. adv. com. Vincennes (Ind.) U., 1983—; bd. dirs. Opportunities Industrialization Ctr., Evansville, 1973-75. Served to maj. (JAGC) U.S. Army, 1962-66, 1975—, Vietnam. Mem. ABA, Ind. Bar Assn., Ky. Bar Assn., Nat. Bar Assn., Assn. Ky. Cols., Ind. Bd. Realtors, Ind. U. Alumni Assn., Phi Alpha Delta. Methodist. Criminal, Family and matrimonial, Personal injury. Home: 4818 Jefferson St Gary IN 46408 Office: 2148 W 11th Ave Gary IN 46404

LEWIS, SANFORD JAY, lawyer; b. Plainfield, N.J., Sept. 2, 1955; s. Wallace Alan and Beverly Libby (Levy) L. BS, Rutgers U., 1977; JD, U. Mich., 1982. Bar: Mass. 1982, U.S. Dist. Ct. Mass. 1983. Coordinator pub. participation N.J. Dept. Environ. Protection, Trenton, 1977-79; intern Conn. Fund for Environment, New Haven, 1980; extern Nat. Wildlife Fedn., Washington, 1981; mem. environ. com. Mass. Pub. Interest Research Group, Boston, 1982-85; sole practice Bedford and Boston, 1985—; counsel Nat. Campaign Against Toxic Hazards, 1985—. Mem. ABA, Boston Bar Assn. Democrat. Jewish. Environment, Personal injury, Negotiation and alternative dispute resolution. Home: 375 North Rd Bedford MA 01730 Office: PO Box 522 Bedford MA 01730

LEWIS, WALTER LAUGHN, lawyer, former air force officer; b. Charlottesville, Va., Aug. 22, 1924; s. Chauncey DePew and Clarice Undine (Laughon) L.; m. Karen Irvine, Sept. 22, 1956; children—Karen Hotchkiss, Robin Laughn. B.A., U. Va., 1947, J.D., 1950; postgrad. Acad. Internat. Law, The Hague, Netherlands, 1964, George Washington U. Law Sch., 1967-69, LL.M., 1969. Bar: Va. 1949, U.S. Ct. Mil. Appeals 1953, U.S. Supreme Ct. 1953, N.C. 1983. Commd. officer USAF, 1950, advanced through grades to col.; with Judge Adv. Gen.'s dept. 1950-80; dep. dir. internat. law U.S. Air Forces in Europe, 1962-65; mem. Air Force Bd. Rev. (Ct. Mil. Rev.), 1965-67; staff judge adv. Air Force Missile Devel. Ctr., Holloman AFB, N.Mex., 1969-70; legal officer U.S. Embassy, Bangkok, Thailand, 1971-72; chief mil. justice div. Office of Judge Adv. Gen., Washington, 1972-77, dir. USAF Judiciary, 1977-79; vice comdr. Air Force Legal Services Ctr., Washington, 1979-80, ret., 1980; chmn. rules adv. com. U.S. Ct. Mil. Appeals, Washington, 1981—; assoc. Everett & Hancock, Durham, N.C., 1983-84. Served with USAAF, 1943-45. Decorated Legion of Merit with oak leaf cluster, Air Force Commendation medal with 3 oak leaf clusters, Air Medal with four oak leaf clusters. Mem. Inter-Am. Bar Assn., ABA (co-chmn. criminal justice and mil. com., criminal justice sect. 1984-85, standing com. on mil. law, 1986—), Va. Bar Assn., Fed. Bar Assn., Am. Judicature Soc., Mil. Law Inst. (pres. 1986—), Delta Theta Phi. Presbyterian. Clubs: Nat. Lawyers, Mason, Shriners. Military, Public international, Administrative and regulatory. Home: 2674 N Upshur St Arlington VA 22207

LEWIS, WILLIAM ADAMS, lawyer; b. Panama City, Fla., Feb. 21, 1951; s. Charles Preasley and Elsie Maddox (adams) L.; m. Lucy Rebecca Reames, July 9, 1977; children: Courtney Rebecca, Olivia Corinne. BS, Auburn U., 1973; JD, Stetson U., 1981. Bar: Fla. 1982, U.S. Dist. Ct. (no. dist.) Fla. 1984. Dep. sheriff investigator Bay County Sheriff's Dept., Panama City, 1973-79; asst. state atty. Fla. 14th Cir., Panama City, 1982-85; assoc. Sale, Brown & Smoak, Panama City, 1984-87, ptnr., 1987—; atty. City of Callaway, Fla., 1984—; asst. atty. City of Panama City Beach, 1984—. Mem. dist. com. Lake Sands Dist. Boy Scouts Am., co-chmn. membership, 1986, fin. chmn. 1987; team service rep. Explorer Scouts; trustee 1st Meth. Ch., 1982—, chmn. 1985—, active various coms. Mem. Fla. Bar Assn., Fed. Bar Assn., Fla. Mcpl. Attys. Assn., Bay County Bar Ass. (sec., treas. 1983-84, v.p. 1984-85, pres. 1985-86), Assn. Trial Lawyers Am., Phi Alpha Delta, Panama City Auburn Alumni Assn. (bd. dirs.), Bay County C. of C. (local concerns com., state concerns com.). Lodge: Rotary.St. Andrews Bay Yacht (Panama City). Avocations: fishing, water sports, gardening. State civil litigation, Local government, General practice. Home: 217 Bunkers Cove Rd Panama City FL 32401 Office: Sale Brown & Smoak 304 Magnolia Ave PO Box 1579 Panama City FL 32402

LEWIS, WILLIAM HENRY, JR., lawyer; b. Durham, N.C., Nov. 12, 1942; s. William Henry Sr. and Phyllis Lucille (Phillips) L.; m. Jo Ann Whitsett, Apr. 17, 1965 (div. Sept. 1982); 1 child, Kimberly N. Student, N.C. State U., 1960-63; AB in Polit. Sci., U. N.C., 1965, JD with honors, 1969. Bar: Calif., D.C., U.S. Dist. Ct. (cen. dist.) Calif., U.S. Ct. Appeals (5th cir.), U.S. Supreme Ct. Assoc. Latham & Watkins, Los Angeles, 1969-74; exec. officer Calif. Air Resources Bd., Los Angeles and Sacramento, Calif., 1975-78; dir. Nat. Com. on Air Quality, Washington, 1978-81; counsel Wilmer, Cutler & Pickering, Washington, 1981-84; ptnr. Morgan, Lewis & Bockius, Washington, 1984—; spl. advisor on environ. policy State of Calif., Los Angeles and Sacramento, 1975. Bd. dirs. For Love of Children Inc., Washington, 1985—, Advs. for Families, Washington, 1985—, Hillandale Homeowners Assn., Washington, 1986—. Mem. ABA. Environment, Federal civil litigation. Home: 3900 Georgetown Ct NW Washington DC 20007 Office: Morgan Lewis & Bockius 1800 M St NW Washington DC 20036

LEWIS, WILLIAM THEODORE, JR., lawyer; b. Little Rock, Apr. 15, 1935; s. William Theodore and Hazel (Davis) L.; children: Elizabeth Joy, William Theodore III, Stephen Meredith. AB, Harvard U., 1957; M in Urban and Regional Planning, MIT, 1962; LLB, U. Ark., 1964. Bar: Ark. 1964, Kans. 1964, Okla. 1966, Wis. 1969, Ill. 1975. Staff atty. Urban Renewal Agy., Kansas City, Kans., 1964-65; dir. planning Hudgins, Thompson, Ball & Assoc., Inc., Tulsa, 1965-68; chief counsel Wis. Dept. Transp., Madison, 1969-75; hearings officer Ill. Commerce Commn., Springfield, 1975-77; ptnr. Pree & Pree, Springfield, 1978-81; sole practice, Springfield, 1982—. Served with USAF, 1957-58. Mem. ABA, Ill. Bar Assn. (assembly del. 1980-84, 86—), Am. Planning Assn., Am. Inst. Cert. Planners, Harvard U. Alumni Assn. Club: Sertoma Internat. General practice, Personal injury, Pension, profit-sharing, and employee benefits. Office: 920 S Spring St Springfield IL 62704-2725

LEY, ANDREW JAMES, lawyer; b. Boston, May 18, 1945; s. Douglas Leo and Ruth Hadley (Schauweker) L.; m. Susan Belle Wilde, Sept. 1, 1968 (div. Jan. 1985); children: Morgan B., Brooke A., Whitney B., Haven D. AB, Dartmouth Coll., 1967; JD, Boston U., 1975. Bar: Mass. 1975, U.S. Dist. Ct. Mass. 1975. Assoc. Tyler, Reynolds & Craig, Boston, 1975-78, Goodwin, Procter & Hoar, Boston, 1978-85; ptnr. McDermott, Will & Emery, Boston, 1985—. Alumni interviewer Dartmouth Coll., Hanover, N.H., 1973—, alumni fund agent, 1975—; pres. Chi-Heorot Assn., Boston, 1978—; cub scout leader Boy Scouts Am., Wellesley, Mass., 1979-81. Served to lt. col. USMCR, 1967—. Mem. Mass. Bar Assn., Boston Bar Assn., Mass. Conveyancer's Assn., Marine Corps Hist. Found., Marine Corps Res. Officers Assn. Avocations: flying, fishing, squash, tennis, rugby. Real property, Landlord-tenant, Contracts commercial. Home: 686 Webster St Needham MA 02192 Office: McDermott Will & Emery One Post Office Square Boston MA 02109

LEYDIG, CARL FREDERICK, lawyer; b. Denver, Jan. 24, 1925; s. Carl F. and Mae V. (Crowley) L.; m. Patricia L. Schwefer, July 2, 1949; children—Gregory F., Deborah A., Gary W., Suzann M. B.S. in Chem. Engring., Ill. Inst. Tech., 1945; J.D. DePaul U., 1950. Bar: Ill. 1950. Atty., Standard Oil Co. (Ind.), Chgo., 1950-54; assoc., ptnr. Leydig, Voit & Mayer, Ltd. and predecessor firms, Chgo., 1954—. Chmn., Young Republicans of Ill., 1953-55; pres. United Fund of Arlington Heights (Ill.), 1964, 65. Served to lt. j.g. USN, 1943-46. Mem. Am. Patent Law Assn. (dir. 1979-81), ABA, Chgo. Bar Assn., Patent Law Assn. of Chgo. (pres. 1980), Am. Coll. Trial Lawyers. Roman Catholic. Clubs: Univ., Law (Chgo.); Meadow (Rolling Meadows, Ill.), Inverness Golf (Palatine, Ill.), Innisbrook Golf (Tarpon Springs, Fla.). Patent, Federal civil litigation, Trademark and copyright.

LEZAR, TEX, lawyer; b. Dallas, Sept. 30, 1948; s. Harold Joseph and Norma Josephine (Styers) L.; m. Merrie Marcia Spaeth, May 17, 1984. BA, Yale U., 1970; JD, U. Tex., 1976. Bar: Tex. 1977, U.S. Dist. Ct. (no. dist.) Tex. 1977, U.S. Ct. Appeals (5th cir.) 1977, U.S. Supreme Ct. 1982. Asst. to William F. Buckley Jr. Nat. Rev., N.Y.C., 1970-71; staff asst., speech writer to pres. The White House, Washington, 1971-74; gen. counsel to sec. of state State of Tex., Austin, 1979-80; spl. counsel to U.S. atty. gen. U.S. Dept. of Justice, Washington, 1981-83, counselor to U.S. atty. gen., 1983-84, counselor to U.S. atty. gen., asst. U.S. atty. gen., 1984-85; ptnr. Carrington, Coleman, Sloman & Blumenthal, Dallas, 1985—; U.S. del. Internat. Conf. on African Refugee Assistance II, Geneva, 1984; vice chmn. U.S. Atty. Gen.'s Commn. on Pornagraphy. Editor in chief U. Tex. Law Rev., 1976-77. Mem. adv. council on econ. policy Rep. Nat. Com., Washington, 1979-80, fed. jud. evaluation com. Senator Phil Gramm, 1985—, fed. issues subcom. Mayor's Criminal Justice Task Force, 1986—, ad hoc jail capacity com. The Greater Dallas Crime COmmn. Inc., 1986—; spl. counsel Honorable John B. Connally, Houston, 1978-79; bd. dirs. Dallas County Rep. Club, 1986—. Fellow Inst. Jud. Adminstrn.; mem. Am. Law Inst. Republican. Presbyterian. Federal civil litigation, State civil litigation, Antitrust. Office: Carrington Coleman Sloman & Blumenthal 200 Crescent Court Suite 1500 Dallas TX 75201

L'HEUREUX, ROBERT DOLOR, lawyer; b. Washington, Nov. 16, 1942; s. Robert Dolor and Marguerite (Gelinas) L'H.; m. Constance Paton, Feb. 7, 1967 (div. Aug., 1970); m. Mary Martha McNamara, Nov. 23, 1979; children: Martin, Robert. BA, St. Joseph's Coll., Rensselaer, Ind., 1964; JD, Georgetown U., 1982. Bar: D.C. 1982. Commd. officer USMC, 1964, advanced through grades to capt., 1967, Served in Vietnam, 1966-67, 69-70, resigned, 1973; spl. agt. Naval Investigative Service, various locations, 1973-79; spl. asst. Insp. Gen.-Small Bus. Adminstrn., Washington, 1979-82; assoc. spl. counsel Office of Spl. Counsel, Merit Systems Protection Bd., Washington, 1982—. Mem. ABA, Nat. Lawyers Club. Republican. Roman Catholic. Avocations: hunting, fishing, golf. Administrative and regulatory, Government contracts and claims, Criminal. Home: 901 Little St Alexandria VA 22301 Office: Office of Spl Counsel Merit Systems Protection Bd 1124 Vermont Ave NW Washington DC 20009

LI, WINIFRED I., lawyer; b. Boston, Dec. 19, 1950; married; 2 children. BA, Yale U., 1972; JD, U. Calif., Berkeley, 1976. Bar: Mass. 1977, U.S. Dist. Ct. Mass., 1977, U.S. Ct. Appeals (1st cir.) 1977. Ptnr. Hill & Barlow, Boston, 1976—. Mem. ABA, Mass. Bar Assn., Asian Am. Lawyers Assn. Mass., Boston Estate and Bus. Planning Council, Boston Bar Assn., Mass. Continuing Legal Edn. Inc. (estate planning and adminstrn. curriculum adv. com. 1986—). Estate planning, Probate, Estate taxation. Home: 12 Lockeland Rd Winchester MA 01890 Office: Hill & Barlow 100 Oliver St 1 Internat Pl Boston MA 02110

LIABO, MARK ELLIOT, lawyer; b. Cedar Rapids, Iowa, Nov. 27, 1952; s. Leslie Carl and Doris Jane (Elliot) L.; m. Corenne M. Hinman, Dec. 29, 1979; children: Jeremy A., Erica J. BA in History, U. Iowa, 1975, MA in History, 1976; JD with honors, Drake U., 1979. Bar: Iowa 1979, U.S. Dist. Ct. (no. and so. dists.) Iowa 1979. Assoc. Simmons, Perrine, Albright & Ellwood, Cedar Rapids, 1979-85, Tom Riley Law Firm P.C., Cedar Rapids, 1985—; lectr. various adult and ednl. groups. mem. ho. com. YMCA, Cedar Rapids, 1984—; diaconate council 1st Congl. Ch., Cedar Rapids, 1981—. Mem. Iowa Bar Assn. (young lawyers sect.), Linn County Bar Assn. (com. on continuing legal edn.), Assn. Trial Lawyers Iowa, Order of Barristers. Democrat. Congregationalist. Avocations: reading, swimming. Federal civil litigation, State civil litigation, Personal injury. Office: Tom Riley Law Firm PC 3401 Williams Blvd SW Cedar Rapids IA 52404

LIACOS, PAUL JULIAN, state Supreme Court justice; b. Peabody, Mass., Nov. 20, 1929; s. James A. and Pitsa K. (Karis) L.; m. Maureen G. McKean, Oct. 6, 1954; children: James P., Diana M., Mark C., Gregory A. A.B. magna cum laude, Boston U. Coll. Liberal Arts, 1950; LL.B. magna cum

laude, Boston U., 1952; LL.M., Harvard U., 1953; diploma, Air Command and Staff Sch., 1954; LL.D. (hon.), Suffolk U., 1984, New Eng. Sch. Law, 1985. Bar: Mass. 1952, U.S. Fed. Dist. Ct. for Dist. of Mass. 1954, U.S. Ct. Mil. Appeals 1955, U.S. Circuit Ct. Appeals 1971, U.S. Supreme Ct. 1980. Partner firm Liacos and Liacos, Peabody, Mass., 1952-76; prof. law Boston U., 1952-76, adj. prof. law, 1976—; Distinguished lectr. on law U.S. Mil. Acad., West Point, N.Y., 1972; lectr. Suffolk U. Sch. Law, 1978-79; cons. to atty. gen. Mass. on staffing and personnel 1974-75; lectr. on criminal evidence Boston Police Acad., 1963-64; reporter New Eng. Conf. on Def. of the Indigent, Harvard Law Sch., 1963; reader and cons. on legal manuscripts Little, Brown & Co., Boston, 1968-76; editorial cons. Warren, Gorham & Lamont, 1968-69; asso. justice Mass. Supreme Jud. Ct., 1976—; mem. steering com. Lawyers Com. for Civil Rights under Law, Boston, 1969-72. Author: Handbook of Massachusetts Evidence, 1981, supplement, 1985; contbr. articles in field to legal jours.; book rev. editor: Boston U. Law Rev, 1952. Trustee exec. com. Chamberlayne Sch. and Jr. Coll., Boston, 1972-74, Anatolia Coll., Salonika, Greece, 1980—, exec. com. 1986—; hon. trustee Deree-Pierce Colls., Athens, Greece, 1976—. Served with USAF, 1953-56. Named Man of Year Law Sch., 1952; recipient Man of Year award Alpha Omega, 1977; named mem. Colleguum Distinguished Alumni Boston U. Coll. Liberal Arts, 1974; recipient Disting. Public Service award Boston U. Alumni, 1980, Allied Profl. award Mass. Psychol. Assn., 1987. Mem. ABA, Mass. Bar Assn. (criminal law com. 1964-66), Essex County Bar Assn., Peabody Bar Assn., Assn. Trial Lawyers Am. (editor 1968-73 Outstanding State Appellate Judge 1982), Harvard Law Sch Assn., Boston U. Law Sch. Alumni Assn. (Silver Shingle award 1977), Phi Beta Kappa. Democrat. Mem. Greek Orthodox Ch. Jurisprudence. Office: 1300 New Courthouse Pemberton Sq Boston MA 02108

LIBBIN, ANNE E., lawyer; b. Phila., Aug. 25, 1950; d. Edwin M. and Marianne (Herz) L.; m. Christopher J. Cannon, July 20, 1985. A.B., Radcliffe Coll., 1971; J.D., Harvard U., 1975. Appellate atty. NLRB, Washington, 1975-78; assoc. Pillsbury, Madison & Sutro, San Francisco, 1978-83, mem., 1984—. Mem. ABA (labor and employment sect.), State Bar Calif. (labor law sect.), Bar Assn. San Francisco, Nat. Women's Health Network, No. Calif. Field Hockey Assn. Club: Radcliffe (San Francisco). Labor. Office: Pillsbury Madison & Sutro PO Box 7880 San Francisco CA 94120

LIBERT, DONALD JOSEPH, lawyer; b. Sioux Falls, S.D., Mar. 23, 1928; s. Bernard Joseph and Eleanor Monica (Sutton) L.; m. Jo Anne Murray, May 16, 1953; children: Cathleen, Thomas, Kevin, Richard, Stephanie. B.S. magna cum laude in Social Scis., Georgetown U., 1950, LL.B., 1956. Bar: Ohio, D.C. From assoc. to ptnr. Manchester, Bennett, Powers & Ullman, Youngstown, Ohio, 1956-65; various positions to v.p., gen. counsel and sec. Youngstown Sheet & Tube Co., 1965-78; assoc. group counsel LTV Corp., Youngstown and Pitts., 1979; v.p. and gen. counsel Anchor Hocking Corp., Lancaster, Ohio, 1979—. Served to lt. (j.g.) USN, 1951-54. Mem. ABA (mem. corp. law depts. com.), Ohio Bar Assn., Fairfield County Bar Assn., Am. Corp. Counsel Assn. (dir. Cen. Ohio chpt.), Lancaster C. of C. Republican. Roman Catholic. Club: Lancaster Country. Lodge: Rotary. Administrative and regulatory, Antitrust, General corporate. Office: Anchor Hocking Corp 109 N Broad St Lancaster OH 43132

LIBIN, JEROME B., lawyer; b. Chgo., Oct. 27, 1936; s. Mitchell and Charlotte Libin; m. June Austin, Apr. 12, 1965; 1 child, Nancy Crawford. B.S., Northwestern U., 1956; J.D., U. Mich., 1959. Bar: D.C. 1961, Ill. 1961. Law clk. U.S. Supreme Ct. Justice Charles E. Whittaker, 1959-60; assoc. Sutherland, Asbill & Brennan, Washington, 1961-66, ptnr., 1966—; professorial lectr. in law George Washington U., 1974-80; cons. Am. Law Inst. Internat. Tax Study Project. Contbr. articles to profl. jours. Mem. D.C. Tax Revision Commn., 1976-78; mem. Mayor's Revenue Policy Com., 1980-82; counsel Lawyers' Com. for Civil Rights Under Law, 1980—; mem. com. visitors U. Mich. Law Sch. Served with USAFR, 1960-66. Mem. ABA, Fed. Bar Assn., D.C. Bar (chmn. taxation div. 1975-77), Am. Law Inst., Internat. Fiscal Assn. (sec. U.S.A. br.). Corporate taxation, Personal income taxation. Home: 3022 P St NW Washington DC 20007 Office: Sutherland Asbill & Brennan 1275 Pennsylvania Ave NW Washington DC 20004

LIBOTT, ROBERT YALE, lawyer, dramatist; b. Los Angeles, Dec. 20, 1925; s. Nathan Holman and May (Steerman) L.; m. Sharon Ann Kosell, Dec. 31, 1976; children: Philip Ried, Christopher R., Michael A. B.A. with distinction, Stanford U., 1943; LL.B. summa cum laude, UCLA, 1966. Bar: Calif. 1967. Assoc. Keatinge and Sterling, Los Angeles, 1966-69; ptnr. Keatinge and Sterling, 1970, Keatinge, Libott, Bates & Loo, Los Angeles, 1971, Keatinge, Libott, Bates & Pastor, Los Angeles, 1974-75; sr. ptnr. Libott, Yaspan & Mundy, 1977-81, Libott & Assos., Los Angeles, 1980—; lectr. advanced profl. program U. So. Calif. Law Ctr., 1968, adj. prof., 1969-72; co-chmn. Corp. Land and Fin. Inst., U. So. Calif., 1972-73. Freelance film, radio and TV writer including: Playhouse 90, 1947-66; (Recipient Nathan Burkan Copyright award ASCAP 1966); Author: Broadway play Too Late the Phalarope, 1956; Contbr. numerous articles to various publs. Trustee Jr. Statesman Found., 1975-79. Served with AUS, 1944-46. Recipient Alumni award UCLA Law Sch., 1967. Mem. ABA (chmn. various copyright and anti-trust coms. 1971-83), Los Angeles County Bar Assn., Los Angeles Copyright Soc., Copyright Soc. U.S., Order of Coif, Phi Beta Kappa, Phi Alpha Delta. Trademark and copyright, Antitrust, Federal civil litigation. Home: 5826 Farralone Ave Woodland Hills CA 91364 Office: 18455 Burbank Blvd Suite 103 Tarzana CA 91356

LICATA, ARTHUR FRANK, lawyer; b. N.Y.C., June 16, 1947; s. Arthur A. and Anne (Onorio) L. BA in English, Le Moyne Coll., 1969; postgrad., SUNY, Binghampton, 1969-71; JD cum laude, Suffolk U., 1976. Bar: Mass. 1977, U.S. Ct. Appeals (1st cir.) 1977, N.Y. 1985. Assoc. Parker, Coulter, Daley & White, Boston, 1977-82; sole practice Boston, 1982—; cons. Mass. Continuing Legal Edn., Boston, 1982—; mem. working group on drinking and drunk driving Harvard Sch. of Pub. Health Ctr. for Health Communications, 1986; speaker convention Nat. Fedn. Paralegal Assns., Boston, 1987. Panel mem. sta. WBZ TV, Boston; contbr. articles to profl. jours. Cons. State Coordinating Com. Mothers Against Drunk Driving, Mass., 1984-86; mem. State Adv. Com. Medical Malpracitce, Boston, 1985, adv. bd. Mass. Epilepsy Found., 1986—. Recipient Outstanding Citizen award Mothers Against Drunk Driving, 1986. Mem. ABA, Mass. Bar Assn. (bd. dirs. young lawyers sect. 1979-80, 21st Century Club 1984), Assn. Trial Lawyers Am., Mass. Trial Lawyers Edn. Found. (officer 1985, pres. 1986—), Mass. Acad. Trial lawyers. Avocations: travel, basketball. Personal injury, Insurance, State civil litigation. Home: 20 Chapel St Brookline MA 02146 Office: 43 Kingston St Suite 200 Boston MA 02111

LICATA, STEVEN BARRY, lawyer; b. Bklyn., Nov. 14, 1954; s. Robert and June B. Licata; m. Sharon Collings, May 26, 1979; children: Andrea Lauren, Robert Thomas. BA cum laude, U. S.C., 1976, JD magna cum laude, 1979. Bar: S.C. 1979, Ga. 1979. Assoc. Powell, Goldstein, Frazer & Murphy, Atlanta, 1979-83, Lewis, Lewis, Bruce & Truslow, Columbia, S.C., 1983-85; ptnr. Finkel, Georgaklis, Goldberg, Sheftman & Korn, Columbia, 1986—; sole practice Columbia, 1985. Mem. ABA, S.C. Bar Assn., Ga. Bar Assn., Order of Wig & Robe. Federal civil litigation, State civil litigation, Bankruptcy. Office: Finkel Georgaklis Goldberg et al PO Box 1799 1331 Elmwood Ave Columbia SC 29202

LICCARDO, SALVADOR A., lawyer; b. San Francisco, Mar. 15, 1935; s. Samuel and Rosalie (Pizzo) L.; m. Laura Liccardo, Nov. 21, 1959; children—Laura, Kathleen, Paul, Rosalie, Sam. B.A., U. Santa Clara, 1956, J.D., 1961. Bar: Calif. 1962, U.S. Ct. Appeals (9th cir.) 1962, U.S. Supreme Ct. 1966. Sole practice law, San Jose, Calif., 1962-65; ptnr. Caputo & Liccardo, San Jose, 1965-76; pres. Caputo, Liccardo, Rossi & Sturges, P.C., San Jose, 1976-82; pres. Caputo, Liccardo, Rossi, Sturges & McNeil, San Jose, 1982—; mem. Santa Clara County Joint Com. of Bench and Bar on Ct. Reorgn.; lectr. in field. Editor-in-chief Jour. Calif. Trial Lawyers Assn., 1981. Contbr. articles to profl. jours. Founder, bd. dirs., officer Trial Lawyers for Pub. Justice, Washington, 1983—; pres. bd. regents Bellermine Prep. Coll., San Jose, 1982—; mem. bd. fellows U. Santa Clara. Served to 1st lt. U.S. Army, 1956-58. Recipient Cert. of Appreciation for Service as Judge Pro Tem Santa Clara County Superior Ct., 1982-84; Michael Shallo award in polit. sci. U. Santa Clara, 1956, Silver medal for outstanding student, 1956. Fellow Internat. Acad. Trial Lawyers; mem. Inner Circle of Advocates, Am. Bd. Trial Advocates, Assn. Trial Lawyers of Am., ABA, Calif. Trial Lawyers Assn. (bd. dirs. 1976-82, 87—), Am. Bd. Profl. Liability Attys. Democrat. Roman Catholic. Club: Civic. State civil litigation, Personal injury. Office: Caputo Liccardo Rossi Sturges & McNeil 1960 The Alameda 2d Floor San Jose CA 95126

LICCIONE, STEPHEN JOHN, lawyer; b. Milw., Jan. 6, 1955; s. John V. and Helen (Byrne) L. Student, Washington and Lee U., 1973-74; BA, Duke U., 1976; JD, Northwestern U., 1980. Bar: Wis. 1981, U.S. Dist. Ct. (ea. dist.) Wis. 1981, U.S. Ct. Appeals (7th cir.) 1984. Law clk. to chief judge U.S. Dist. Ct. (ea dist.) Va., Norfolk, 1980-81; assoc. Foley & Lardner, Milw., 1981-83; asst. atty. U.S. Dept. Justice, Milw., 1983—. Mem. ABA, Wis. Bar Assn., Milw. Bar Assn. Roman Catholic. Avocations: tennis, basketball, baseball. Criminal, Federal civil litigation, Government contracts and claims. Office: US Dept Justice 517 E Wisconsin Ave 330 Fed Bldg Milwaukee WI 53202

LICHT, FRANK, lawyer; b. Providence, Mar. 3, 1916; s. Jacob and Rose (Kassed) L.; m. Dorothy Shirley Krauss, June 16, 1946; children: Beth Ellen Licht Laramee, Carol Ann Licht Kanin, Judith Joan. AB, Brown U., 1938; LLB, Harvard U., 1941; LLD, St. Francis Coll., 1969, Yeshiva U., 1970, R.I. Coll., 1971, U. R.I., 1971; LHD, Hebrew Union Coll., 1971, Suffolk U., 1971; LLH, Our Lady of Providence Sem., 1973; LLD, Brown U., 1975. Bar: U.S. Supreme Ct. 1942, R.I. 1952. Law clk. to presiding justice U.S. Ct. Appeals (1st cir.), Boston, 1942-43; ptnr. Letts & Quinn, Providence, 1943-56, Letts, Quinn & Licht, Providence, 1973—; assoc. justice R.I. Superior Ct., 1956-68; mem. R.I. Senate from Providence, 1949-56; gov. R.I., 1969-73; lectr. Bryant Coll., Providence, 1958-64, Nat. Conf. Trial Ct. Judges Coll., Reno, 1967; teaching fellow Kennedy Inst. of Politics, 1972-73. Contbr. articles to profl. jours. Vice pres. bd. Gen. Jewish Com. Providence, 1960-66, Gen. Jewish Com. R.I., 1967-68; co-chmn. So. New Eng. Conf. Christians and Jews, 1959-68; chmn. Chapin Hosp. Commn., Providence, 1967; v.p. Temple Emanuel, 1968; pres., bd. dirs. R.I. council Community Services; trustee, bd. dirs. Butler Hosp., Providence, Jewish Home for Aged; bd. dirs. Providence Human Relations Commn.; exec. com. Nat. Govs. Conf., 1971; trustee Brown U., 1981—; pres. R.I. Philharmonic, 1981-84. Recipient Lehman award for R.I., 1965, Herbert H. Lehman Ethics award Jewish Theol. Sem. Am., 1969, Herbert H. Lehman citation Nat. Info. Bur. for Jewish Life, Inc., 1970; named Man of Yr. Providence Sunday Jour., 1969; hon fellow Hebrew U., Jerusalem, 1969; Ford found. grantee; naming of courthouse Frank Licht Jud. Complex Providence County, 1986. Mem. ABA, R.I. Bar Assn., Nat. Conf. Trial Ct. Judges (exec. com.), Phi Beta Kappa, Delta Sigma Rho. Jewish (v.p. temple). Home: 640 Elmgrove Ave Providence RI 02906 Office: Licht & Semonoff 1 Park Row Providence RI 02903

LICHTENBERG, J(OAN) CATHY, lawyer; b. Chgo., Mar. 18, 1943; d. Norman Jack and Esther Lois (Grobstein) Friedman; m. Jay Bernard Lichtenberg, June 29, 1968 (dec. Apr. 1981); 1 child, Ian Robert. BS, U. Wis., 1964; JD, Cath. U., 1977. Bar: U.S. Ct.Appeals (D.C. cir.) 1977, D.C. 1978, U.S. Ct. Appeals (7th cir.) 1979, U.S. Ct. Appeals (2d cir.) 1979, U.S. Supreme Ct. 1981, U.S. Ct. Appeals (3d cir.) 1984. Research librarian Library Congress, Washington, 1964-66; legislative research specialist Am. Pub. Power Assn., Washington, 1966-71; assoc. Duncan, Weinberg & Miller, Washington, 1977-83, ptnr., 1983—; spl. asst. atty. gen. State of N.D., 1979-86. Mem. ABA, D.C. Bar Assn., Bar Assn. D.C., Women's Bar Assn., Fed. Energy Bar Assn. (chmn. fed. power act parts I & II 1985-86). Democrat. Jewish. Avocations: oenophile, gourmet cooking. Antitrust, Federal civil litigation, FERC practice. Home: 9008 Quintana Dr Bethesda MD 20817 Office: Duncan Weinberg & Miller PC 1615 M St NW Suite 800 Washington DC 20036

LICHTENSTEIN, ELISSA CHARLENE, legal association executive; b. Trenton, N.J., Oct. 23, 1954; d. Mark and Rita (Field) L. AB cum laude, Smith Coll., Northampton, Mass., 1976; JD, George Washington U., 1979. Bar: D.C. 1980, U.S. Dist. Ct. (D.C. dist.) 1980, U.S. Ct. Appeals (D.C. cir.) 1980. Law clk. U.S. EPA, Washington, 1978-79; staff dir. ABA, Washington, 1979—, assoc. dir. pub. services div., 1981-85, dir., 1985—. Editor, contbr.: Common Boundary/Common Problems: The Environmental Consequences of Energy Production, 1982; editor Environ. Law, newsletter ABA; co-editor, contbr. The Environ. Network; editor: Exit Polls and Early Election Projections, 1984, The Global Environment: Challenges, Choices and Will, 1986. Mem. Nat. Trust for Hist. Preservation, WETA-TV Pub. Broadcasting. Named Outstanding Young Woman of Am., 1982. Mem. Women in Communications, Inc., Nat. Assn. Female Execs., Environ. Law Inst. (assoc.), Met. Washington Environ. Profls. (bd. dirs., pres.), D.C. Bar Assn. Democrat. Jewish. Environment. Office: ABA Standing Com Environ Law 1800 M St NW Washington DC 20036

LICHTENSTEIN, NATALIE G., lawyer; b. N.Y.C., Sept. 17, 1953; d. Abba G. and Cecile (Geffen) L.; m. Willard Ken Tom, June 10, 1979. AB summa cum laude, Radcliffe Coll., 1975; JD, Harvard U., 1978. Bar: D.C. 1978. Atty., advisor U.S. Dept. Treasury, Washington, 1978-80; counsel World Bank, Washington, 1980—; adj. prof. chinese law Georgetown U., Washington, 1982—. Contbr. articles on Chinese law to profl. jours. Public international.

LICHTENSTEIN, SARAH CAROL, lawyer; b. East Orange, N.J., May 25, 1953; d. Carl and Hilda Ruth (Warshaw) L. BA, Wellesley Coll., 1975; JD, Columbia U., 1978. Bar: N.Y. 1979, U.S. Dist. Ct. (ea. and so. dists.) N.Y. 1979, U.S. Ct. Appeals (2d cir.) 1981. Assoc. Milbank, Tweed, Hadley & McCloy, N.Y.C., 1978-84; assoc. Dreyer and Traub, N.Y.C., 1984-87, ptnr., 1987—. Contbr. articles to profl. jours. Wellesley scholar, 1975, Stone scholar Columbia U., 1977-78. Mem. ABA, N.Y. Bar Assn., Assn. of Bar of City of N.Y. (com. on sex and law, sec. 1981-85, com. on state legis. 1986—). Federal civil litigation, State civil litigation, Bankruptcy. Office: Dreyer and Traub 101 Park Ave New York NY 10178

LICHTER-HEATH, LAURIE JEAN, lawyer; b. Bklyn., Mar. 13, 1951; d. Irving and Beatrice (Gelber) Lichter; m. Donald Wayne Heath, Feb. 28, 1981; 1 son: Michele Samuel. B.S. with honors, U. Tenn.-Knoxville, 1972; J.D., John Marshall Law Sch., 1975; postgrad. NYU, 1978; LL.M., Georgetown U., 1979. Bar: Ill. 1975, D.C. 1977, N.Y. 1980, Nev. 1981. Law clk. D.C. Ct. Appeals, Washington, 1975-77; atty. enforcement div. SEC, Washington, 1977-78; lectr. N. Y. U. Sch. Continuing Edn. in Law and Taxation, 1980-81; atty. govt. relations asst. Met. Life Ins. Co., N.Y.C., 1978-81; assoc. atty. Miller & Daar, Reno, Nev. 1981; legal cons. Stockton, Calif., 1981-84; asst. prof. U. Pacific, Stockton, 1984—. Instr., YMCA, Knoxville, 1969-72; leader Concerned Parents, Stockton, Calif., 1984. Mem. Coalition to Stop Food Irradiation. U. Ill. fellow, 1972. Contbr. papers to Am. Bus. Law Jour. Mem. Nev. Bar Assn., N.Y. Bar Assn. D.C. Bar Assn., Ill. Bar Assn., ABA, AAUW, Western Bus. Law Assn. (exec. sec.), Sierra Club. Legal education, Environment, Legislative.

LICHTOR, DAVID T., lawyer; b. Ft. Campbell, Ky., Nov. 4, 1956; s. Joseph Meyer and Margery Ann (Orchard) L.; m. Mary Elizabeth Tainter, May 9, 1981. BS, U. Kans., 1976; MBA, U. Wis., Eau Claire, 1979; JD, Hamline U., 1980. Bar: Minn. 1981, U.S. Tax Ct. 1982, U.S. Dist. Ct. Minn. 1983, U.S. Ct. Appeals (8th cir.) 1983. Sole practice St. Paul, 1981-83; assoc. Stern & Gurstel, Mpls., 1983—. Mem. ABA, Minn. Bar Assn., Hennepin County Bar Assn., Aircraft Owners and Pilots Assn. Avocations: golf, flying. Insurance, Personal injury. Home: 4331 Heritage Dr Vadnais Heights MN 55127

LICKER, JEFFREY ALAN, lawyer; b. N.Y.C., Sept. 19, 1955; s. Harold and Shirley (Betheil) L. BA summa cum laude, Bklyn. Coll., 1976; JD, SUNY, Buffalo, 1979. Bar: N.Y. 1980, Tex. 1983, U.S. Dist. Ct. (no. dist.) Tex., U.S. Dist. Ct. (ea. and so. dists.) N.Y., U.S. Tax Ct. Assoc. Wilson, Elser, Edelman & Dicker, N.Y.C., 1979-81, Lipsig, Sullivan & Liapakis, N.Y.C., 1981-82, Jones, Hirsch, Freidman, Carney & Bull, N.Y.C., 1982; sr. atty. Granoff Law Offices, Dallas, 1982-83; ptnr. Jeffrey A. Licker & Assocs., Dallas, 1983-85; sole practice N.Y.C., 1985—; Bd. dirs. Varsity Cons., Dallas. bd. dirs., chmn. Capitol Closing Co., Dallas, 1983-85; chmn., pres. Great Southwestern Estate Planning, Dallas, 1983-85; pres. Intercity Catering Co., N.Y.C., 1985—. Author: Discretion in Jury Selection, 1975; contbr. articles to profl. jours. Mem. ABA, N.Y. State Bar Assn., Tex. Bar Assn., Trial Lawyers Assn. General corporate, Real property, Federal civil litigation. Home: PO Box 3452 Ridgewood NY 11386-3452 Office: 153-15 80th St Howard Beach NY 11414

LIDA, CARL HOWARD, lawyer; b. Bronx, N.Y., Sept. 28, 1950; s. Emanuel and Harriet Lida; m. Joyce Birken, June 2, 1973; children: Melissa, Stacy. BA, U. Fla., 1972; JD, U. Miami, 1975. Bar: Fla. 1975, U.S. Dist. Ct. (so. dist.) Fla. 1983. Asst. pub. defender Dade County, Miami, Fla., 1976; sole practice Miami, 1977—; mem. steering com. Fla. Bar, 1983, pres. adv. program, 1983-85. Mem. Fla. Bar Assn., Dade County Bar Assn., Nat. Criminal Lawyers Assn., Fla. Criminal Lawyers Assn. Democrat. Criminal. Office: 2000 S Dixie Hwy Suite 217 Miami FL 33133

LIDE, VINTON DEVANE, lawyer; b. Greenville, S.C., May 4, 1937; s. Theodore Ellis and Mary Elizabeth (DeVane) L.; m. Carol Jean Keisler, July 8, 1979; children—Jonathan Randolph, Jennifer DeVane. A.B., Davidson Coll., 1959; LL.B. (now J.D.), U. Va. 1962. Bar: Va. 1962, S.C. 1962, U.S. Ct. Appeals (4th cir.) 1974, U.S. Supreme Ct. 1980. Assoc., Shand & Wilmeth, Hartsville, S.C., 1962-64; ptnr. Shand & Lide, Hartsville, 1964-78; pub. defender Darlington County, S.C., 1969-76; exec. asst./legal advisor to gov. S.C., 1978-79; asst. atty. gen. State of S.C., 1978-79; gen. counsel S.C. Dept. Social Services, 1979-81; chief counsel, staff dir. Com. on the Judiciary, U.S. Senate, 1981-85; adminstrv. asst. to U.S. Senator Strom Thurmond, 1985—; mcpl. ct. judge Hartsville, 1963-69. Recipient Cert. of Appreciation, Drug Enforcement Adminstrn., U.S. Dept. Justice, 1980. Mem. ABA (ho. dels. 1978-82), S.C. Bar Assn., Va. Bar Assn. Republican. Methodist. Criminal, Federal civil litigation, General corporate. Office: US Atty 1100 Laurel St Washington DC 29201

LIDSTONE, HERRICK KENLEY, JR., lawyer; b. New Rochelle, N.Y., Sept. 10, 1949; s. Herrick Kenley and Marcia Edith (Drake) L.; m. Mary Lynne O'Toole, Aug. 5, 1978; children: Herrick Kevin, James Patrick, John Francis. AB, Cornell U., 1971; JD, U. Colo., 1978. Bar: Colo. 1978, U.S. Dist. Ct. Colo. 1978. Assoc. Roath & Brega, P.C., Denver, 1978-85, Brenman, Epstein, Raskin & Friedlob, P.C., Denver, 1985-86; ptnr. Brenman, Raskin, Friedlob & Tenenbaum, P.C., Denver, 1986—; adj. prof. U. Denver Coll. Law, 1985—; speaker in field various orgns. Editor U. Colo. Law Rev., 1977-78; contbr. articles to profl. jours. Served with USN, 1971-75, with USNR, 1975-81. Mem. ABA, Colo. Bar Assn., Denver Bar Assn. (legal fee arbitration com.), Denver Assn. Oil and Gas Title Lawyers. Fluent in Spanish. General corporate, Securities. Office: Brenman Raskin Friedlob & Tenenbaum 1400 Glenarm Pl Denver CO 80202

LIEB, ARTHUR HILARY, juvenile ct. official; b. Morton County, N.D., Aug. 4, 1920; s. Arthur L.F. and Hilda Amelia (Krause) L.; m. Louise Carolyn Iverson, June 25, 1954; 1 dau., Carolyn Louise. J.D., U. N.D., 1951; cert. Inst. Ct. Mgmt., 1976, 78; cert. Nat. Coll. Juvenile Justice, 1982. Bar: N.D. 1951. Juvenile commr. Counties of Cass, Grand Forks, Griggs, Nelson, Steele and Barnes, N.D., 1951-58; juvenile commr. Cass County, N.D., 1958-69, juvenile supr., 1969-73, chief juvenile supr., referee, 1973-79; chief juvenile supr., referee East Central Dist. N.D., Fargo, 1979-87; mem. accreditation team Nat. Council Juvenile and Family Ct. Judges, 1979; mem. N.D. Combined Law Enforcement Council, 1977-78, staffing standards subcom. State Ct., 1982, family case law referee subcom. State Ct., 1984, 85; mem. Juvenile Detention Task Force, 1979-80; lectr. in field. Chmn., founding bd. dirs. F M Family Service Assn., 1958-64; mem. Mayor's Com. for Employment of the Handicapped, 1959-63; pres. Cass County Mental Health Assn., 1961. Served with U.S. Army, 1945-46. Recipient N.D. Conf. Social Welfare 20 Yr. Pub. Service award 1980; N.D. Mental Health Assn. cert. appreciation 1963. Mem. State Bar Assn. N.D., Cass County Bar Assn., Internat. Platform Assn., N.D. Peace Officers Assn., N.D. Juvenile Correction Assn. (pres. 1976-78), N.D. Conf. Social Welfare, VFW. Republican. Lutheran. Clubs: Cosmopolitan, Elks (Fargo). Criminal. Home: 213 30th Ave N Fargo ND 58102 Office: 1015 3d Ave S Fargo ND 58108

LIEB, CHARLES HERMAN, lawyer; b. N.Y.C., July 21, 1907; s. Herman and Belle (Levy) L.; m. Maron Hatton, Nov. 29 1933. B.S., U. Pa., 1927; LL.B. cum laude, Fordham U., 1930. Bar: N.Y. 1931, Conn. 1959. Assoc. Paskus, Gordon & Hyman, N.Y.C., 1931-39, ptnr., 1940-52, sr. ptnr., 1952—; dir. John Wiley & Son, Inc., N.Y.C.; adv. com. on internat. intellectual property Dept. State. Served to 1st lt. ordinance corps AUS, 1942-45. Mem. ABA, N.Y. State Bar Assn., N.Y. County Bar Assn., Conn. Bar Assn., Copyright Soc. U.S.A. Clubs: Players, Harmonie (N.Y.C.); Aspetuck Valley Country (Weston, Conn.). Contbr. articles to profl. jours. Trademark and copyright, General corporate, General practice. Office: Paskus Gordon & Mandel 45 Rockfeller Plaza New York NY 10111

LIEB, JOHN STEVENS, lawyer; b. N.Y.C., Jan. 31, 1911; s. Hermann Johan and Evelyn Viola (Walls) L.; m. Helena Ann Warne, Sept. 18, 1942; children—Thomas (dec.), William. B.S. in Elec. Engring., NYU, 1936; J.D., Marquette U., 1948; B.A., U. Ariz., 1982; M.A., 1984. Bar: Wis. 1948; U.S. Dist. Ct. (ea. dist.) Wis. 1948, U.S. Ct. Customs and Patent Appeals 1953, U.S. Ct. Appeals (3d cir.) 1969, U.S. Ct. Appeals (Fed. cir.) 1982; registered patent agent U.S. Patent and Trademark Office, 1948; registered profl. engr., Wis. Patent atty. Allis-Chalmers, West Allis, Wis., 1948-57, corp. law atty., 1957-63, asst. gen. atty., 1963-64, gen. atty., asst. sec., 1964-71; examiner in chief Bd. Appeals, U.S. Patent Office, Washington, 1971-73; of patent counsel Richard R. Mybeck, Scottsdale, Ariz., 1983—; bd. dirs. Allis-Chalmers; lectr. patent law Marquette U. Law Sch., 1955; lectr. math. Pima Community Coll., Tucson, Ariz., 1985. Bd. dirs. Allis Chalmers Found., Milw., 1977-79. Author: (with Colleran and Jordan) Sketches of the Ordnance Research and Development Center in World War II, 1946; contbr. articles to profl. jours. Pres. Wauwatosa Bd. Edn., Wis., 1962-64; pres. Friends of Green Valley Library, Ariz., 1983; bd. dirs. Tucson Urban League, 1985. Served to maj. AUS, 1941-46; Mem. IEEE (sr.; life), ABA (life), Wis. Bar Assn., Am. Soc. Corp. Secs. (life sr.), N.Y. Acad. Scis., Am. Intellectual Property Law Assn., Patent Office Soc., Am. Hist. Assn., Hist. Sci. Soc., OAH, AAAS, Delta Upsilon, Phi Alpha Theta. Republican. Episcopalian. Antitrust, Patent, Trademark and copyright. Home: 226 Los Rincones Green Valley AZ 85614 Office: Richard R Mybeck 4251 N Brown Ave Suite A-1 Scottsdale AZ 85251

LIEB, L. ROBERT, lawyer, real estate developer; b. Jersey City, July 15, 1941; s. Nathan Philip and Elizabeth (Blum) L.; m. Sherry Young, Sept. 11, 1971; children—Elizabeth Ann, Nathan Young. B.A., U. Buffalo, 1962; LL.B., NYU, 1965. Bar: N.J. 1967, U.S. Dist. Ct. N.J. 1967, N.Y. 1970, U.S. Dist. Ct. (so. and ea. dists.) N.Y. 1970. Law clk. appellate div. Superior Ct. N.J., 1965-66; sr. ptnr. firm Kimmelman, Lieb, Wolf & Samson, West Orange, N.J., 1972-77, Lieb & Ford, West Orange, 1977-80, Lieb, Samnick & Lukashok, N.Y.C., 1980-83; counsel Lukashok & Liebman, N.Y.C., 1983-84; chmn. Mountain Devel Corp., West Orange, 1978—, Bretton Woods Corp., N.H., 1980-84; chmn. bd. dirs. NorCrown Bank of Roseland, 1984-87 . Mem. Republican Presdl. Task Force, Washington, 1982—. Served to 1st lt. JAGC, USAF, 1966-72. Harry Rudin scholar NYU, 1963-65. Mem. Essex County Bar Assn. Republican. Jewish. Club: Green Brook Country (North Caldwell, N.J.); Hamilton (Patterson, N.J.). Real property. Office: Mountain Devel Corp 5 Garret Mountain Plaza West Patterson NJ 07424

LIEB, ROSLYN CORENZWIT, lawyer; b. Phila., July 19, 1942; s. Samuel and Anne (Goldberg) Corenzwit; m. Michael J. Lieb, Aug. 18, 1963; children: Laurence, Mark. AB in History, Rutgers U., 1964; JD magna cum laude, DePaul U., 1976. Bar: Ill. 1976, U.S. Ct. Dist. Ct. (no. dist.) Ill. 1976, U.S. Ct. Appeals (7th cir.) 1976, U.S. Supreme Ct. 1983. Law. clk. to presiding justice U.S. Dist. Ct. (no. dist.), Chgo., 1976-77; law. clk. to presiding judge U.S. Ct. Appeals (7th cir.), Chgo., 1977-78; assoc. Coffield, Ungretti, Harris & Slavin, Chgo., 1978-79; vis. asst. prof. Northwestern U. Sch. of Law, Chgo., 1979-85; exec. dir. Chgo. Lawyers Com. for Civil Rights Under Law, Chgo., 1985—. Contbr. articles to profl. jours. Mem. ABA, Women's Bar Assn. of Ill., Chgo. Council of Lawyers (gov. 1985—). Civil rights, Labor. Office: Chgo Lawyers Com for Civil Rights Under Law 220 S State St Suite 300 Chicago IL 60604

LIEBBE, WILLIAM HOWARD, lawyer; b. San Antonio, Sept. 20, 1953; s. Robert Henry and Evelyn (Warner) L.; m. Donna Denise Inman, June 30, 1973; children: Jeremy Michael, Kelly Michelle. BA in Polit. Sci. with distinction, So. Meth. U., 1976, JD, 1980. Bar: Tex. 1980. Assoc. McKool &

Vassallo P.C., Dallas, 1980-86, Vassallo & Ashmore P.C., Dallas, 1986-87, Windle Turley, P.C., Dallas, 1987—; cons. Wholesale Distbr. Assn., Dallas, 1984—. Mem. ABA, Tex. Bar Assn., Assn. Trial Lawyers Am., Tex. Trial Lawyers Assn., Dallas Trial Lawyers Assn. Republican. Roman Catholic. Club: Diamond M (bd. dirs. 1983—). Avocations: water sports, skiing, softball, music. State civil litigation, Personal injury. Home: 1911 Forestwood Richardson TX 75081 Office: Windle Turley PC 1000 University Tower 6440 N Central Expressway Dallas TX 75200

LIEBER, JOHN HOWARD, lawyer; b. Ardmore, Okla., Nov. 19, 1953; s. James H. and Maxine Helen (Glotzbach) L.; m. Pamela Mary Romanello, Jan. 4, 1975; children: Katheryn, Bryan. BBA, U. Tulsa, 1975, JD, 1978. Bar: Okla. 1978, U.S. Dist. Ct. (no., ea. and we. dists.) Okla. 1978, U.S. Ct. Appeals (10th cir.) 1978. Ptnr. Knight, Wagner, Stuart, Wilkerson & Lieber, Tulsa, 1978—. Mem. ABA, Okla. Bar Assn., Tulsa County Bar Assn. Republican. Methodist. Insurance, Personal injury, Civil rights. Home: 2724 S Delaware Pl Tulsa OK 74114 Office: Knight Wagner Stuart et al PO Box 1560 Tulsa OK 74101-1560

LIEBERMAN, DENNIS ALAN, lawyer; b. South Bend, Ind., Nov. 2, 1952; s. David and Olive (Metzger) L. BS, Miami U., Oxford, Ohio; JD cum laude, U. Dayton. Bar: Ind. 1978, Ohio 1978, U.S. Dist. Ct. (so. dist.) Ind. 1978, U.S. Dist. Ct. (so. dist.) Ohio 1978, U.S. Ct. Appeals (6th cir.) 1980. Assoc. Smith & Schnacke, Dayton, Ohio, 1978-80; ptnr. Lieberman, Landon, Gehres & Smith, Dayton, 1980-84, Flanagan, Lieberman, Hoffman & Swain, Dayton, 1984—. Steering com. chmn. United Way of Dayton, 1978; founder Legal Assistance to Elderly, Dayton, 1977-79; mem. Council on Aging, Dayton, 1978. Mem. Assn. Trial Lawyers Am. (trustee 1982—), Ohio State Bar Assn. (chmn. criminal procedures com. 1978-86), Ind. State Bar Assn., Montgomery County Trial Lawyers Assn., Dayton Bar Assn. (ethics com.). Democrat. Avocations: sailing, scuba diving, skiing. Criminal, Federal civil litigation, State civil litigation. Home: 1715 Shafesbury Dayton OH 45406 Office: Flanagan Lieberman Hoffman & Swain 318 W Fourth Dayton OH 45402

LIEBERMAN, EUGENE, lawyer; b. Chgo., May 17, 1918; s. Harry and Eva (Goldman) L.; m. Pearl Naomi, Aug. 3, 1947; children—Mark, Robert, Steven. J.D., DePaul U., 1940. Bar: Ill. 1940, U.S. Supr. Ct. 1963. Mem. firm Jacobs and Lieberman, 1954-60; sr. ptnr. Jacobs, Lieberman and Aling, 1960-74; spl. hearing officer U.S. Dept. Justice, 1967-78; hearing officer Ill. Pollution Control Bd., 1973—; sole practice, Chgo. Served with U.S. Army, 1942-45; PTO. Recipient 1st in State award Moot Ct. Championship, 1940; Gold award Philatelic Exhbn., Taipei, 1981; Gold award World Philatelic Exhbn., Melbourne, 1984, others. Fellow Am. Acad. Matrimonial Lawyers; mem. Ill. State Bar Assn., Chgo. Bar Assn., Chgo. Philatelic Soc. (pres. 1964-68). Club: Ill. Athletic (Chgo.). Contbr. articles to legal publs. Federal civil litigation, State civil litigation, Environment. Home: 801 Leclaire Ave Wilmette IL 60091

LIEBERMAN, GEORGE ERIC, lawyer; b. N.Y.C., Sept. 1, 1942; s. David and Sarah (Chomsky) L.; m. Terry Sandra Feldman, Aug. 15, 1965; children—Susan April, Stacey Helen. B.A., CCNY, 1964; J.D., Northwestern U., 1967. Bar: Calif. 1968, Pa. 1969, U.S. Dist. Ct. (ea. dist.) Pa. 1969, U.S. Ct. Appeals (3d cir.) 1969. Ptnr. firm Morgan, Lewis & Bockius, Phila., 1977—; judge regional competition Nat. Mock Trial Competition; mem. Com. of 70 for Gen. and Primary Elections; speaker profl. meetings. Contbr. articles to profl. publs. Mem. ABA (chmn. com. r.r. law sect. torts and ins. practice, 3d cir. chmn. trial practice com. sect. litigation), Pa. Bar Assn., Phila. Bar Assn. (fed. cts. com.), Calif. Bar Assn., Nat. Assn. R.R. Trial Counsel (sec., program chmn.). Railroad, Federal civil litigation, State civil litigation. Home: 517 Hoyt Rd Huntingdon Valley PA 19006 Office: Morgan Lewis & Bockius 1 Logan Sq Philadelphia PA 19103

LIEBERMAN, JOSEPH I., attorney general; b. Stamford, Conn., Feb. 24, 1942; s. Henry and Marcia (Manger) L.; m. Hadassah Freilich, Mar. 20, 1983; children: Matthew, Rebecca, Ethan. B.A., Yale U., 1964, J.D., 1967. Bar: Conn. 1967. Mem. Conn. Senate, 1971-81, Senate majority leader, 1975-81; ptnr. Lieberman, Segaloff & Wolfson, New Haven, 1972-83; atty. gen. State of Conn., Hartford, 1983—. Author: The Power Broker, 1966, The Scorpion and the Tarantula, 1970, The Legacy, 1981, Child Support in America, 1986. Trustee Wadsworth Atheneum. Democrat. Jewish. Office: Office of Atty Gen 30 Trinity St Hartford CT 06106 *

LIEBERMAN, MARVIN SAMUEL, lawyer; b. N.Y.C., Apr. 26, 1935; s. Abe and Gertrude (Connelly) L.; m. Kathryn Fuhrer, Aug. 10, 1963; children—Kathryn, Willis. B.A., Lafayette Coll., 1955; J.D., Rutgers U. 1962. Bar: N.J. 1962, U.S. Ct. Appeals (3d cir.) 1965. Cert. civil trial atty., N.J. Assoc., Jacob, Alfred & Richardson Levinson, Perth Amboy, N.J., 1962-69; ptnr. Levinson, Conover, Lieberman & Fink, Perth Amboy, 1969-71; Lieberman & Ryan, Somerville, N.J., 1971-83, Lieberman, Ryan, Richardson, Welaj & Miller, Somerville, 1983—. Served with USAF, 1955-58. Mem. N.J. Bar Assn., Assn. Trial Lawyers Am., N.J. Trial Lawyers Assn., Middlesex County Trial Lawyers Assn., N.J. Lawyers Assn. Personal injury, Workers' compensation. Home: RD1 Riverview Terr Belle Mead NJ 08502 Office: Lieberman Ryan Richardson Welaj & Miller 21 N Bridge St Somerville NJ 08876 also: Rt 206 Hillsborough Township NJ 08876

LIEBERMAN, STEVEN PAUL, lawyer; b. N.Y.C., Apr. 6, 1945; s. Lawrence James and Alice (Levin) L.; m. Enid Marsha Gross, Dec. 24, 1968; children: Amy Greer, Jeffrey Lawrence. BA, George Washington U., 1966; JD, NYU, 1969. Bar: N.Y. 1970. Assoc. Goodstein, Zamore, Mehlman & Krones, N.Y.C., 1970-72; staff atty. Standard Oil Calif., Perth Amboy, N.J., 1972-77; sr. corp. atty. Perkin-Elmer Corp., Norwalk, Conn., 1977-79; corp. counsel Technicon Instruments Corp., Tarrytown, N.Y., 1979—. Mem. ABA, Am. Corp. Counsel Assn., Westchester-Fairfield Corp. Counsel Assn. (internat. law, SEC, antitrust and trade regulation coms.). Antitrust, Computer, General corporate. Home: 187 Winesap Rd Stamford CT 06903 Office: Technicon Instruments Corp 511 Benedict Ave Tarrytown NY 10591

LIEBERSBACH, RICHARD WILLIAM, lawyer; b. Glendale, Calif., Oct. 22, 1952; s. Francis Carl and Dorothy Lois (Jones) L.; m. Nancy Carol Eischeid, Apr. 22, 1978; children: Matthew Edward, Jennifer Anne. AA, Glendale Coll., 1972; BA, U. So. Calif., 1974; JD, Loyola U., Los Angeles, 1977. Bar: Calif. 1977, U.S. Dist. Ct. (cen. dist.) Calif. 1977. V.p., gen. counsel Gregg-Gandi Devel., Glendale, 1977-81, Lodestar Co., Mammoth Lakes, Calif., 1981-86; assoc. Law Offices of Paul Rudder, Mammoth Lakes, 1986—. Mem. Verdugo Hills Hosp. Assocs., La Canada, Calif., 1980; Mono County chmn. Antonovich for Senate Com., Mammoth Lakes, 1986—. Named one of Outstanding Young Men Am., 1980. Mem. ABA, Phi Beta Kappa. Republican. Methodist. Lodge: Rotary (bd. dirs. 1983—, pres. 1986—). Avocations: water skiing, snow skiing, fishing, bowling. Real property, Contracts commercial, Construction. Home: PO Box 8032 Mammoth Lakes CA 93546

LIEBLING, NORMAN ROBERT, lawyer; b. Chgo., Feb. 17, 1917; s. Louis and Frances (Geller) L.; m. Florence Levinson, Feb. 25, 1950; children: James, Fred. BA, U. Ill., 1937; JD, Harvard U., 1940. Ptnr. Freeman & Liebling, Chgo., 1948-54, Freeman, Liebling, Adelman & Watson, Chgo., 1955-67; sr. ptnr. Liebling, Adelman & Bernstein, Chgo., 1968-81, Liebling, Uriell & Hamman, Chgo., 1976-82, Liebling & Uriell, Chgo., 1982-83, Schuyler, Roche & Zwirner, Chgo., 1984—; bd. dirs. Mid-Am. Nat. Bank, Chgo., The United Equitable Corp., Lincolnwood, Ill. Spl. asst. to atty. gen. State of Ill., Chgo., 1958-61; bd. dirs. Rosenbaum Found., Chgo., 1982—. Served to capt. U.S. Army, 1942-46, CBI. Mem. ABA, Chgo. Bar Assn., Harvard Law Soc. Ill. (bd. dirs. 1986—). Clubs: Chgo. Athletic, The Plaza, International (Chgo.). Avocations: swimming, reading. Banking, General corporate, Insurance. Home: 970 Sunset Ave Winnetka IL 60093 Office: Schuyler Roche & Zwirner 3100 Prudential Plaza Chicago IL 60601

LIEBMAN, EMMANUEL, lawyer; b. Phila., Mar. 26, 1925; s. Morris and Pearl (Zucker) L.; m. Anita Forman, Dec. 24, 1953; children—Judith H. Winslow, Lawrence H. B.S. in Econs., U. Pa., 1950; J.D., Rutgers U., 1954. Bar: N.J. 1954, U.S. Tax Ct. 1955, U.S. Supreme Ct. 1960, D.C. 1972, U.S. Ct. Appeals (3d cir.) 1977. Sole practice, Camden, N.J., 1954-70; pres. Emmanuel Liebman, P.A., Cherry Hill, N.J., 1970-72, Liebman & Flaster, P.A., Cherry Hill, 1972-86, pres. Emmanuel Liebman, chartered, Cherryhill, 1986—. lectr., moderator Inst. Continuing Legal Edn., 1962—. Served with USNR, 1943-46, PTO. Mem. Camden County Bar Assn. (chmn. com. on fed. tax 1964, 68-70, chmn. retirement plan com. 1986—), N.J. State Bar Assn. (chmn. com. on bus. taxes 1967-69, 71-73, chmn. state capitol com. 1973-77, chmn. ad hoc com. on financing legal fees 1976-79, exec. council 1974—), ABA (taxation sect.), D.C. Bar Assn., N.J. State Bar Found. (trustee 1972—, pres. 1979-83), Am. Judicature Soc., Am. Arbitration Assn. (panelist 1964—), Camden County Bar Found. (trustee 1986—). Clubs: Haddon Field (Haddonfield, N.J.); Woodcrest Country (Cherry Hill). Lodge: B'nai B'rith. Corporate taxation, Personal income taxation, Probate. Home: 46 Dublin Ln Cherry Hill NJ 08003 Office: 409 E Marlton Pike Cherry Hill NJ 08034

LIEBMAN, LANCE MALCOLM, lawyer; b. Newark, Sept. 11, 1941; s. Roy and Barbara (Trilinsky) L.; m. Carol Bensinger, June 28, 1964; children: Jeffrey, Benjamin. B.A., Yale U., 1962; M.A., Cambridge U., 1964; LL.B., Harvard U., 1967. Bar: D.C. 1968, Mass. 1976. Asst. to Mayor Lindsay, N.Y.C., 1968-70; asst. prof. law Harvard U., 1970-76, prof., 1976—, assoc. dean, 1981-84. Successor trustee Yale Corp., 1971-83. Legal education. Office: Langdell Hall Harvard U Law Sch Cambridge MA 02138 *

LIEBMAN, RONALD STANLEY, lawyer; b. Balt., Oct. 11, 1943; s. Harry Martin and Martha (Altgenug) L.; m. Simma Liebman, Jan. 8, 1972; children: Shana, Margot. BA, Western Md. Coll., Westminster, 1966; JD, U. Md., 1969. Bar: Md. 1969, D.C. 1977, U.S. Dist. Ct. (ea. dist.) Va. 1970, U.S. Dist. Ct. Md. 1970, U.S. Dist. Ct. D.C. 1982, U.S. Ct. Appeals (4th cir.) 1972, U.S. Ct. Appeals (D.C. cir.) 1982, U.S. Ct. Appeals (5th cir.) 1985. Law clk. to chief judge U.S. Dist. Ct. Md., 1969-70; assoc. Melnicove, Kaufman & Weiner, Balt., 1970-72; asst. U.S. atty. Office of U.S. Atty., Dept. Justice, Balt., 1972-78; ptnr. Sachs, Greenebaum & Tayler, Washington, 1978-82, Patton, Boggs & Blow, Washington, 1982—. Author: Grand Jury, 1983; co-editor: Testimonial Privileges, 1983. Recipient spl. commendation award U.S. Dept. Justice, 1978. Mem. ABA, D.C. Bar Assn., Md. Bar Assn. Club: Sergeants Inn (Balt.). Criminal, Federal civil litigation, State civil litigation. Office: 2550 M St NW Washington DC 20037

LIEBMANN, HERBERT CHARLES, III, lawyer; b. Green Bay, Wis., May 22, 1942; s. Herbert C. and Marie V. Liebmann; m. Diane Valenti, June 17, 1967; children: Herbert IV, Matthew. AB in English cum laude, Regis Coll., 1964; JD, Harvard U., 1967. Bar: Wis. 1968, U.S. Dist. Ct. (ea. and we. dist.) Wis. 1968. Assoc. Cohen, Parins Cohen & Grant, Green Bay, 1968-76; ptnr. Liebmann, Conway, Olejniczak & Jerry S.C., Green Bay, 1976—. Active bd. edn. Green Bay Joint Sch. Dist., 1974-79, pres. 1976-77, Cerebral Palsy Inc., 1968—, pres. 1971-72; adv. council St. Vincent Hosp., 1976-82; mem. exec. com. Brown County Rep. 1970-74, Brown County Mental Health, Mental Retardation, Alcoholism, Drug Abuse, and Devel. Disabilities Bd., 1973-75; bd. dirs. Scholarships Inc., 1970-78, United Cerebral Palsy of Wis. Inc., 1971-83, Ecumenical Found., 1982—, Heritage Hill Found., 1986—, Com. for Campus Ministry U. Wis., Green Bay, 1972-86, pres. 1973-74, 81-83, Green Bay Community Theater Inc., 1970-81, pres. 1970-73; bd. dirs., sec. Brown County Day Care Services Bd., 1967-70. Mem. ABA (vice chmn. gen. practice sect. 1985—), Wis. Bar Assn. (chmn. gen. practice sect. 1984-85, bd. dirs. 1984—), Brown County Bar Assn. (program chmn. 1969-70, sec. 1970-72), Assn. Trial Lawyers Am., Wis. Trial Lawyers Assn., Green Bay area C. of C. (bd. dirs. 1986—). Probate, General practice, General corporate. Home: 512 Hilltop Green Bay WI 54301 Office: Liebmann Conway Olejniczak & Jerry S.C. 231 S Adams St Green Bay WI 54301

LIED, ERIK ROBERT, lawyer; b. Renton, Wash., Dec. 4, 1953; s. Alf Simon and Ruth (Devik) L. BS in Psychology, U. Wash., 1976; JD, UCLA, 1980. Bar: Wash. 1980, U.S. Dist. Ct. (we. dist.) Wash. 1980, U.S. Dist. Ct. (ea. dist.) Wash. 1984, U.S. Dist. Ct. (no. dist.) Calif. 1985. Assoc. Bogle & Gates, Seattle, 1980—; spl. dep. pros. atty. King County, Seattle, 1981—; guardian atty. King County Guardian Ad Litem Program, 1981—. Mem. ABA (products liability litigation com., bus. torts. com. litigation sect. 1980—), Wash. State Bar Assn., Seattle Bar Assn., King County Bar Assn., Phi Beta Kappa (trustee, pres. 1984-85). Club: Wash. Athletic (various coms. 1981—). Federal civil litigation, State civil litigation, General corporate. Office: Bogle & Gates Bank Calif Ctr Seattle WA 98164

LIEGL, JOSEPH LESLIE, lawyer; b. Fond du Lac, Wis., Jan. 20, 1948; s. Melvin Theodore and Verna Lavinia (Jagdfeld) L.; m. Janet L. Meyer, Feb. 1, 1969; children: Matthew, Jeremy. BA with distinction, U. Wis., 1970, JD cum laude, 1973. Bar: Wis. 1973, U.S. Supreme Ct. 1976, Ohio 1978, U.S. Dist. Ct. (no. dist.) Ohio 1978, U.S. Ct. Claims 1978, U.S. Tax Ct. 1978. Assoc. Muchin & Muchin S.C., Manitowoc, Wis., 1973-74; trial atty. U.S. Dept. Justice, Washington, 1974-78; assoc. Jones, Day, Reavis & Pogue, Cleve., 1978-83, ptnr., 1983—. Mem. ABA (chmn. subcom. tax. sect. 1985—), Cleve. Bar Assn. (vice chmn. tax sect. 1985—), Order of Coif, Phi Eta Sigma, Phi Kappa Phi. Avocation: music. Corporate taxation, Personal income taxation. Home: 16824 Holbrook Rd Shaker Heights OH 44120 Office: Jones Day Reavis & Pogue 1700 Huntington Bldg Cleveland OH 44115

LIFLAND, WILLIAM THOMAS, lawyer; b. Jersey City, Nov. 15, 1928; s. Charles and Carolyn (Francks) L.; m. Nancy Moffat, May 29, 1954; children—Carol M., Charles C., J. Kerin, David T. B.S., Yale U., 1949; J.D., Harvard U., 1952. Bar: D.C. 1954, N.Y. 1955, N.J. 1965. Law clk. to Justice John M. Harlan U.S. Supreme Ct., 1954-55; assoc. Cahill Gordon & Reindel, N.Y.C., 1955-58, Paris, 1958-60; ptnr. Cahill Gordon & Reindel, N.Y.C., 1965—; adj. prof. Fordham Law Sch., N.Y.C.; dir Commodities Corp., Princeton, N.J. Served as lt. USAF, 1952-54. Mem. ABA, N.Y. State Bar Assn., N.J. Bar Assn., D.C. Bar Assn., N.Y. County Lawyers Assn., Assn. Bar City N.Y. Democrat. Episcopalian. Club: India House (N.Y.C.). Antitrust, Administrative and regulatory, Federal civil litigation. Office: Cahill Gordon & Reindel 80 Pine St New York NY 10005

LIFSCHITZ, JUDAH, lawyer; b. N.Y.C., Nov. 28, 1952; s. Morris and Edna (Love) L.; m. Marilyn Feder, Dec. 8, 1974; children: Lisa, Ira, Tamar. BA magna cum laude, Yeshiva U., 1974; JD, George Washington U., 1977. Bar: Md. 1977, U.S. Dist. Ct. D.C. 1980, U.S. Claims Ct. 1980, U.S. Ct. Appeals (D.C. cir.) 1980, U.S. Ct. Appeals (4th cir.) 1982, U.S. Ct. Appeals (fed. cir.) 1985, U.S. Supreme Ct. 1985. Assoc. Hudson, Creyke, Koehler & Tacke, Washington, 1980, Epstein, Becker, Borsody & Green, Washington, 1980-83; ptnr., chmn. govt. contracts dept. Finley, Kumble, Wagner, Heine, Underberg, Manley & Casey, Washington, 1983—. Washington counsel Nat. Council Young Israel, N.Y.C., 1980—; pres. Yeshiva of Greater Washington, 1985—; bd. dirs. Jewish Community Council, Washington, 1980—, United Jewish Appeal Fedn., Washington, 1985. Recipient Schofar award Nat. Council Young Israel, 1980. Mem. ABA. Government contracts and claims, Construction. Office: Finley Kumble Wagner et al 1120 Connecticut Ave NW Washington DC 20036

LIFSCHULTZ, PHILLIP, financial and tax consultant; b. Oak Park, Ill., Mar. 5, 1927; s. Abraham Albert and Frances Rhoda (Seigel) L.; m. Edith Louise Leavitt, June 27, 1948; children: Gregory, Bonnie, Jodie. BS in Acctg., U. Ill., 1949; JD, John Marshall Law Sch., 1956. Bar: Ill. 1956. Tax mgr. Arthur Andersen & Co., Chgo., 1957-63; v.p. taxes Montgomery Ward & Co., Chgo., 1963-78; fin. v.p., controller Henry Crown & Co., Chgo., 1978-81; prin. Phillip Lifschultz & Assocs., Chgo., 1981—. Mem. adv. council Coll. Commerce and Bus. Adminstrn. U. Ill., Urbana-Champaign, 1977-78; chmn., Civic Fedn. Chgo., 1980-82; chmn. adv. bd. to Auditor Gen. of Ill., 1965-73; project dir. Exec. Service Corps of Chgo., Chgo. Bd. Edn. and State of Ill. projects, 1980—. Served with U.S. Army, 1945-46. Mem. Ill. Bar Assn., Chgo. Bar Assn., Am. Inst. CPA's, Ill. CPA Soc., Am. Arbitration Assn. (comml. panel 1983—), Nat. Retail Merchants Assn. (chmn. tax com. 1975-78), Am. Retail Fedn. (chmn. taxation com. 1971). Clubs: Standard, City (bd. govs.). Corporate taxation, Personal income taxation. Home: 976 Oak Dr Glencoe IL 60022 Office: 450 E Devon Itasca IL 60143

LIGELIS, GREGORY JOHN, lawyer; b. N.Y.C., Mar. 30, 1950; s. John and Roseanne (McCoy) L.; m. Calliope Stephanos Kalogeras, Jan. 19, 1980; 1 child, Gregory John, Jr. B.A. magna cum laude, Hofstra U., 1972; J.D., U. Pa., 1975; postgrad. NYU, 1982—. Bar: N.Y. 1976, U.S. Dist. (so. dist.) N.Y. 1976, U.S. Ct. Appeals (2d cir.). Ptnr. Poles, Tublin, N.Y.C., 1975—. Mem. Maritime Law Assn., ABA, N.Y. County Bar Assn. Club: N.Y. Athletic, India House (N.Y.C.). Admiralty, Private international. Home: PO Box 1454 West Churchill Rd Washington CT 06793 Office: Poles Tublin 46 Trinity Pl New York NY 10006

LIGGIO, CARL DONALD, lawyer; b. N.Y.C., Sept. 5, 1943. A.B., Georgetown U., 1963; J.D., N.Y. U., 1967. Bar: N.Y. 1967, D.C. 1967, Wis. 1983. Cons. firm Arent, Fox, Kintner, Plotkin & Kahn, Washington, 1968-69; asso. firm White & Case, N.Y.C., 1969-72; gen. counsel Arthur Young & Co., N.Y.C., 1972—. Contbr. articles to legal and bus. jours. Mem. Am., N.Y. State, D.C. bar assns., Assn. Bar City N.Y., Am. Corp. Counsel Assn. (chmn. bd. dirs. 1984, mem. exec. com. 1982—). General corporate, Federal civil litigation, Securities. Home: 11 E 86th St New York NY 10028 Office: 277 Park Ave New York NY 10172

LIGHT, ALFRED ROBERT, lawyer, political scientist; b. Atlanta, Dec. 14, 1949; s. Alfred M. Jr. and Margaret Francis (Asbury) L.; m. Mollie Sue Hall, May 28, 1977; children—Joseph Robert, Gregory Andrew. Student Ga. Inst. Tech., 1967-69; B.A. with highest honors, Johns Hopkins U., 1971; Ph.D., U. N.C., 1976; J.D. cum laude, Harvard U., 1981. Bar: D.C. 1981, Va. 1982. Tax clk. IRS, 1967; lab. technician Custom Farm Services Soils Testing Lab., 1968; warehouse asst. State of Ga. Mines, Mining and Geology, 1970; clk.-typist systems mgmt. div., def. contract adminstrv. services region Def. Supply Agy., Atlanta, 1971, research and teaching asst. dept. polit. sci. U. N.C., Chapel Hill, 1971-74; research asst. Inst. Research in Social Sci., 1975-77; program analyst Office of Sec. Def., 1974; asst. prof. polit. sci., research scientist Ctr. Energy Research, Tex. Tech U., Lubbock, 1977-78; research asst. grad. sch. edn., Harvard U., 1978-79; assoc. Butler, Binion, Rice, Cook & Knapp, Houston, summer 1980, Bracewell & Patterson, Washington, summer 1980, Hunton & Williams, Richmond, Va., 1981—. Active Cystic Fibrosis Found, First Bapt. Ch. Served to capt. USAR, 1971-85. Grantee NSF, Inst. Evaluation Research, U. Mass., Ctr. Energy Research, Tex. Tech U.; recipient William Anderson award Am. Polit. Sci. Assn.; Julius Turner award Johns Hopkins U. Mem. ABA, Am. Soc. Pub. Adminstrn., Am. Polit. Sci. Assn., Va. State Bar Assn., Richmond Bar Assn., So. Polit. Sci. Assn., Phi Beta Kappa, Phi Eta Sigma, Pi Sigma Alpha. Democrat. Baptist. Contbr. articles to profl. jours. Administrative and regulatory, Environment, Legislative. Home: 11406 Yeomans Dr Richmond VA 23233 Office: Hunton & Williams 707 E Main St Richmond VA 23212

LIGHT, KENNETH J., lawyer; b. Cleve., Feb. 3, 1951; s. Arthur and Dolores (Vinocur) L. BS in Bus. Adminstrn., Ohio State U., 1972; JD, U. San Fernando Valley (now LaVerne U.), 1976. Bar: Ind. 1981, U.S. Tax Ct. 1983, U.S. Ct. Appeals (7th cir.) 1985, U.S. Supreme Ct. 1985. Sole practice Indpls., 1981-83; ptnr. Garrison & Light, Muncie, Ind., 1983-85; sole practice Muncie, Ind. and Indpls., 1985—; bd. dirs., v.p. East Cen. Ind. Tax and Pacing Assn., Muncie, 1985—; lectr. conf. The Law and Children, 1984, Assn. Children with Learning Disabilities, 1985. Mem., atty. screening com. Ind. Civil Liberties Union, 1986—. Mem. ABA, Ind. Bar Assn. (bankruptcy and creditors rights com. 1985), Muncie Bar Assn., Comml. Law League. Consumer commercial, Computer, Real property. Home: 401 S Lombard Dr Muncie IN 47305 Office: Garrison & Light 119 E Charles St Suite 104 PO Box 1735 Muncie IN 47305

LIGHTNER, MERRIE TURNER, lawyer, real estate syndicator; b. Glendale, Calif., Feb. 19, 1956; d. John Craig and Joanne Constance (Schlarb) Turner; m. William Lightner Jr. BA, Pomona Coll., 1976; JD, U. Calif., Davis, 1980. Bar: Calif. 1981, U.S. Dist. Ct. (no. dist.) Calif. 1981, U.S. Ct. Appeals (9th cir.) 1981. Assoc. Littler, Mendelsohn, Farstiff & Tichy, San Francisco, 1981; assoc. broker Clarke & Cramer, San Francisco, 1982-84; ptnr. Lightner & Lightner, San Francisco, 1984—; co-founder Real Exchange, San Francisco, 1982. Mem. ABA, Calif. Bar Assn., San Francisco Bar Assn., Lawyers Club San Francisco. Republican. Real property. Office: Lightner & Lightner PO Box 27056 San Francisco CA 94127

LIGHTSEY, HARRY MCKINLEY, JR., university administrator, lawyer; b. Dec. 27, 1931. BS, Clemson U., 1952; DVM, U. Ga., 1956; JD, U. S.C., 1961. Bar: S.C. 1961. Legal counsel S.C. Senate, Columbia, 1961-64; gen. counsel S.C. Pub. Service Commn., Columbia, 1964-67; ptnr. Berry, Lightsey, Gibbes, & Bowers, Columbia, 1965-72, Barnes, Austin & Lightsey, Columbia, 1972-80; prof. U. S.C. Sch. Law, Columbia, 1977-80, dean, 1980-86; pres. Coll. of Charleston, S.C., 1986—. Author: A Study of S.C. Med. Orgns., 1970, S.C. Code Pleading, 1974; (with Flanagan) S.C. Civil Practice, 1985; editor S.C. Law Rev., 1961. Chmn. March of Dimes Campaign, Columbia, 1962, S.C. Dem. Party, Columbia, 1970; vestryman Trinity Episcopal Cathedral, Columbia, 1970-72. Served to lt. U.S. Army, 1952. Recipient Sapp Meml. award, 1961, Outstanding Prof. award U. S.C. Law Sch., 1973. Mem. ABA, U.S. Supreme Ct. Bar and Hist. Soc., S.C. Bar Assn. (bd. govs. 1980-86), S.C. Bar Found. Clubs: ATE Summit, Forest Lake (Columbia). Avocations: fly fishing, golf. Legal education. Home: 6 Glebe St Charleston SC 29401 Office: Coll of Charleston Charleston SC 29424

LIGHTSTONE, RONALD, lawyer; b. N.Y.C., Oct. 4, 1938; s. Charles and Pearl (Weisberg) L.; m. Nancy Lehrer, May 17, 1973; 1 dau., Dana. A.B., Columbia U., 1959; J.D., N.Y. U., 1962. Atty. CBS, N.Y.C., 1967-69; assoc. dir. bus. affairs CBS News, N.Y.C., 1969-70; atty. NBC, N.Y.C., 1970; asso. gen. counsel Viacom Internat. Inc., N.Y.C., 1970-75; v.p., gen. counsel, sec. Viacom Internat. Inc., 1976-80; v.p. bus. affairs Viacom Entertainment Group Viacom Internat., Inc., 1980-82, v.p. corp. affairs, 1982-84, sr. v.p. corp. and legal affairs, 1984—. Served to lt. USN, 1962-66. Mem. ABA, Assn. Bar City N.Y., Fed. Communications Bar Assn. General corporate, Entertainment. Office: Viacom Internat Inc 1211 Ave of Americas New York NY 10036

LIGORIO, MARIO EDUARD, lawyer; b. Dubrovnik, Yugoslavia, Sept. 2, 1946; came to U.S., 1949; s. Eduard Miho and Nada Olga (Mozzara) L. Student, Queens Coll. CUNY, 1966-67; JD, Belgrade U., Yugoslavia, 1969; LLM, Columbia U., 1970, JD, 1973. Bar: N.Y. 1977, U.S. Dist. Ct. (so. and ea. dists.) N.Y. 1977. Editor West Pub., N.Y.C., 1975-76, Prentice-Hall Inc., N.J., 1976-77; assoc. Lynton & Klein, N.Y.C., 1978-80; atty., corp. counsel C. Itoh & Co. (Am.) Inc., N.Y.C., 1980-86; assoc. Arthur I. Frankel P.C., N.Y.C., 1986—. Mem. ABA, Assn. of Bar of City of N.Y., Am. Corp. Counsel Assn. (dir. at large N.Y. chpt. 1985-86). Democrat. Roman Catholic. Avocations: tennis, basketball, softball. Contracts commercial, General corporate, Real property. Home: 77-11 35th Ave Apt #4L Jackson Heights NY 11372 Office: Arthur I Frankel PC 110 E 59th St New York NY 10022

LIHOTZ, MARIE ELAINE, lawyer; b. Chestnut Hill, Pa., Dec. 1, 1955; d. Francis A. and Gloria V. (Puya) L.; m. Louis J. Procacci, May 23, 1981; 1 child, Christina Marie. BA, U. Del., 1977; JD, Villanova U., 1980; LLM in Taxation, NYU, 1985. Bar: U.S. Dist. Ct. (ea. dist.) Pa. 1980, U.S. Dist. Ct. N.J. 1980, U.S. Ct. Appeals (3rd cir.) 1981, U.S. Supreme Ct. 1985. Legal intern to presiding justice U.S. Dist. Ct., Phila., 1978-79, 1979-80; assoc. Myers Matteo Rabil, Pluese & Norcross, Cherry Hill, N.J., 1980-86; ptnr. Myers Matteo Rabil, Pluese & Norcross, Cherry Hill, 1986—. Atty. Camden County Reg Legal Services Pro Bono Panel, N.J., 1983—. Mem. ABA, Burlington County Bar Assn. (family law com.), Tri County Women Lawyers (v.p. 1985—), N.J. Bar Assn. (family law, taxation com.), Pa. Bar Assn, Camden County Bar Assn. (lectr.), Moorestown Bus. Women's Assn. Republican. Roman Catholic. Avocation: woodworking. Estate taxation, Bankruptcy, Family and matrimonial. Home: 5 South Colonial Ridge Moorestown NJ 08057 Office: Myers Matteo Rabil Pluese & Norcross 1010 Kings Hwy S Suite 2C Cherry Hill NJ 08034

LILE, CHARLES ALAN, lawyer; b. Hopkinsville, Ky., Feb. 15, 1952; s. Raymond L. and Louise (Thomas) L.; m. Joyce Lee Prince, Aug. 18, 1973; 1 child, Samantha Lauren. BS in Acctg., U. Ky., 1974, JD, 1977. Bar: Ky. 1977. Asst. resident counsel East Ky. Power Coop. Inc., Winchester, 1977-80, corp. counsel, 1980-84, sr. corp. counsel, 1984—. Mem. ABA, Ky. Bar Assn., Am. Corp. Counsel Assn., Order of Coif. Republican. Baptist. Avocation: photography. General corporate, Labor, Public utilities. Home:

3440 Oakbrook Dr Lexington KY 40515 Office: East Ky Power Coop Inc PO Box 707 Winchester KY 40391

LILES, JOHN H(ENRY), JR., lawyer; b. Houston, Apr. 10, 1947; s. John H. and Eleanor (Pillot) L.; m. Mary Louise Liles, June 10, 1978. BS in Psychology, U. Houston, 1969; JD, South Tex. Coll. Law, 1976. Bar: Tex. 1976; cert. residential and comml. real estate law Tex. Bd. Legal Specialization. House counsel Horne Co., Houston, 1972-78; div. counsel Transam. Title Co., Houston, 1978-82; pres. Capitol City Title Co., Austin, Tex., 1983-84; sole practice Austin, 1984—; chmn. of bd. Kiwi, Inc., Austin; lectr. So. Title Guaranty. Mem. ABA, Tex. Bar Assn. (lectr.), Travis County Bar Assn., Harris County Bar Assn., Am. Land Title Assn., Tex. Land Title Assn. Republican. Roman Catholic. Avocations: photography, treasure hunting. Real property, Landlord-tenant, Contracts commercial. Home: 11610 Parkfield Dr Austin TX 78758 Office: 901 S Mopac Suite 370 Austin TX 78746

LILES, RUTLEDGE RICHARDSON, lawyer; b. Miami, Fla., Jan. 30, 1942; s. Rutledge Person and Kathryn (Richardson) L.; m. Noel Doepke, Dec. 28, 1963; children: Ashley Faye, Hillary Lynn, Stacey Noel. BA, Fla. State U., 1964; JD, U. Fla., 1966. Bar: Fla. 1966, U.S. Dist. Ct. (mid. dist.) Fla. 1967, U.S. Supreme Ct. 1972, U.S. Dist. Ct. (no. dist.) 1978. Pres. Howell, Liles, Braddock & Milton, Jacksonville, Fla., 1966—; bd. of govs. Fla. Bar, 1981—, pres.-elect 1987-88, pres. 1988-89. Mem. Jacksonville U. Council, 1966—; trustee Episcopal High Sch. of Jacksonville, 1986—, U. Fla. Coll. Law Ctr. Assn., 1981—. Recipient Pres.'s award Fla. Bar, 1986. Fellow ABA; mem. Jacksonville Bar Assn. (pres. 1976-77), Jacksonville C. of C., Fla. Blue Key. Democrat. Club: University (Jacksonville) (bd. govs. 1986—). Personal injury, Insurance, State civil litigation. Home: 1013 Maple Ln Jacksonville FL 32207 Office: Howell Liles Braddock & Milton 901 Blackstone Bldg Jacksonville FL 32202

LILIENSTERN, O. CLAYTON, lawyer; b. Houston, Nov. 13, 1943; s. Oscar C. and Suzanne (Haughton) L.; m. Helen A. Andronis, Jan. 14, 1979; children—Robert, Susan, Kelli. A.B., U. Ala., 1965; J.D., U. Houston, 1968; LL.M., George Washington U., 1972. Bar: Tex. 1968, U.S. Dist. Ct. (so. dist.) Tex. 1973, U.S. Tax Ct. 1975, U.S. Supreme Ct. 1976, U.S. Dist. Ct. (we. dist.) Tex. 1978, U.S. Dist. Ct. (ea. dist.) Tex. 1987, U.S. Ct. Appeals (5th, 9th and 11th cirs.); cert. civil trial law Tex. Bd. Legal Specialization; civil trial advocate Nat. Bd. Trial Advocacy. Assoc. Andrews & Kurth, Houston, 1972-79, ptnr., 1979—; adv. dir. 1st City Bank, Bellaire. Served to capt. JAGC, U.S. Army, 1968-72. Decorated Joint Service Commendation medal. Fellow Tex. Bar Found., Houston Bar Found.; mem. ABA, State Bar Tex., Houston Bar Assn., U. Houston Law Alumni Assn. (pres. 1982-83). Federal civil litigation, State civil litigation. Home: 4821 Maple St Bellaire TX 77401 Office: 4200 Tex Commerce Tower Houston TX 77002

LILJEQUIST, JON LEON, patent lawyer; b. Chgo., Apr. 24, 1936; s. Leon Rogner and Muriel Alice (Staples) L.; m. Bonnie Ann Barrow, Aug. 20, 1960; children: Lisa Jean, Laura Kirsten, Lars Christian. BSME, U. Ill., 1958; JD, Loyola U., Chgo., 1964. Bar: Ill. 1964, U.S. Dist. Ct. (no. dist.) Ill. 1964, U.S. Patent Office 1964, U.S. Ct. Appeals (D.C. cir.) 1980; registered profl. engr., Ill. Design engr. Outboard Marine Corp., Waukegan, Ill., 1958-60; instr. engring. U. Ill., Chgo., 1960-63, prof. in structural engring., undergrad. law, 1964—, patent cons., 1984—; assoc. Hofgren, Wegner, et al, Chgo., 1963-64, Darbo, Robertson et al, Arlington Heights, Ill., 1964-66; patent counsel Appleton Electric Co., Chgo., 1966—; owner, pres. Timark Co., Mt. Prospect, Ill., 1969-76; legal and engring. cons. Hannafan & Handler, Chgo., 1985—, Dressler, Goldsmith, Shore, Sutker & Milnamow, Chgo., U. South Fla., Tampa. Patentee in field. Recipient Silver Circle award U. Ill., Chgo., 1983, 86. Mem. Licensing Execs. Soc., Soc. Univ. Patent Adminstrs., Patent Law Assn. Chgo. Patent, Legal education, Trademark and copyright. Home: 5770 Pine Tree Dr Sanibel FL 33957 Office: U Ill 1737 W Polk St Chicago IL 60612

LILLARD, JOHN FRANKLIN, III, lawyer; b. Cheverly, Md., Aug. 2, 1947; s. John Franklin, Jr. and Madeline Virginia (Berg) L. B.A., Washington and Lee U., 1969, J.D., 1971. Bar: N.Y. 1972, D.C. 1974, U.S. Dist. Ct. (so. and ea. dists.) N.Y. 1974, U.S. Ct. Appeals (2d cir.) 1972, U.S. Ct. Appeals (D.C. cir.) 1974, U.S. Dist Ct. (D.C.) 1974, U.S. Ct. Claims 1976, U.S. Supreme Ct. 1975, U.S. Ct. Appeals (4th cir.) 1977, Md. 1978, U.S. Dist. Ct. Md. 1978. Assoc. Donovan, Leisure, Newton & Irvine, N.Y.C., 1971-74, Pierson, Ball & Dowd, Washington, 1974-76; trial atty. civil div. Dept. Justice, Washington, 1976-77; ptnr. Lillard & Lillard, Washington, 1977—. Vice chmn. Village Council of Friendship Heights, Chevy Chase, Md., 1975-77; candidate U.S. Congress from 5th dist. Md., 1981; bd. dirs. Am. Solar Energy Assn. Served to 1st lt. USAF Aux., 1973-77. Recipient Eastman award Am. Arbitration Assn., 1971. Mem. Bar Assn. D.C., Md. Bar Assn., Assn. Bar City N.Y., Prince George's County Bar Assn., Anne Arundel County Bar Assn. Republican. Episcopalian. Clubs: Metropolitan (Washington); Metropolitan (N.Y.C.); Tred Avon Yacht (Oxford, Md.); Marlborough Hunt (Upper Marlboro, Md.). Federal civil litigation, General practice. Office: Lillard & Lillard 910 17th St NW Washington DC 20006

LILLEHAUG, DAVID LEE, lawyer; b. Waverly, Iowa, May 22, 1954; s. Leland Arthur and Ardis Elsie (Scheel) L.; m. Winifred Sarah Smith, May 29, 1982. BA summa cum laude, Augustana Coll., Sioux Falls, S.D., 1976; JD cum laude, Harvard U., 1979. Bar: Minn. 1979, U.S. Dist. Ct. Minn. 1979, D.C. 1981, U.S. Ct. Appeals (8th cir.) 1981, U.S. Dist. Ct. D.C. 1982. Law clk. to presiding judge U.S. Dist. Ct. Minn., Mpls., 1979-81; assoc. Hogan & Hartson, Washington, 1981-83, 84-85; issues aide, exec. asst. to Walter Mondale, Washington, 1983-84; assoc. Leonard, Street & Deinard, Mpls., 1985—. Mem. ABA, Minn. Bar Assn. (governing council civil litigation sect.). Democrat. Lutheran. Avocations: fishing, racquetball. Construction, Insurance. Home: 5129 Logan Ave S Minneapolis MN 55419 Office: Leonard Street & Deinard 100 S 5th St Minneapolis MN 55402

LILLEY, ALBERT FREDERICK, III, lawyer; b. Harrisburg, Pa., Dec. 21, 1932; s. Frederick Anthony and Jane Sander (Ingham) L.; m. Judith Carter Pennock, Sept. 1, 1956; children: Kirk Anthony, Kristin Sander, James Alexander. A.B., Bowdoin Coll., 1954; LL.B., U. Va., 1959. Assoc. Milbank, Tweed, Hadley & McCloy, N.Y.C., 1959-67, ptnr., 1967—. Trustee No. Highlands Regional High Sch., Allendale, N.J., 1964-65; mem. Bd. Zoning Adjustment, Allendale, 1965-66; overseer Bowdoin Coll., 1976—; trustee Valley Hosp., Ridgewood, N.J., 1978—, vice chmn. bd. trustees, 1985—. Served to 1st lt. U.S. Army, 1954-56. Mem. Am. Law Inst., ABA, N.Y. State Bar Assn., Assn. Bar City N.Y. (securities regulation). General corporate, Securities, Public utilities. Home: 180 Lincoln Ave Ridgewood NJ 07450 Office: Milbank Tweed Hadley & McCloy 1 Chase Manhattan Plaza New York NY 10005

LILLEY, ROY STUART, lawyer; b. New Orleans, July 29, 1937; s. Roy and Margaret (McFarland) L.; m. Barbara Ann Ritter, Dec. 22, 1962 (div. Aug. 1981); 1 child, Paige Elizabeth; m. Sherry Ann Bigner, Mar. 27, 1982. BS, U. S.W. La., 1962; JD, Loyola U., New Orleans, 1973. Bar: La. 1973, U.S. Dist. Ct. (ea. dist.) La. 1974, U.S. Ct. Appeals (5th cir.) 1974, U.S. Ct. Appeals (11th cir.) 1981, U.S. Supreme Ct. 1977. Systems analyst Avondale (La.) Shipyards, 1969-73; ptnr. Lea & Lilley, Metairie, La., 1973-81; sole practice Metairie, 1981—; Ad hoc juvenile ct. judge Jefferson Parish, Gretna, La., 1981-82; legal advisor Am. Legion, Jefferson, La., 1978. Author: Offloading Amphibious Ships, 1968 (Commendation 1968). Served with USN 1962-69, comdr. Res. Mem. ABA, La. Trial Lawyers Assn., Naval Res. Assn. (legal advisor 1979-83). Democrat. Methodist. Banking, Real property, Probate. Home: 225 Shaunell Dr Mandeville LA 70448 Office: 3500 N Causeway Suite 1208 Metairie LA 70002

LILLIE, CHARISSE RANIELLE, lawyer, educator; b. Houston, Apr. 7, 1952; d. Richard Lysander and Vernell Audrey (Watson) L.; m. Thomas L. McGill, Jr., Dec. 4, 1982. B.A. cum laude, Conn. Wesleyan U., 1973; J.D., Temple U., 1976; LL.M., Yale U., 1982. Bar: Pa. 1976, U.S. Dist. Ct. (ea. dist.) Pa. 1977, U.S. Ct. Appeals (3d cir.) 1980. Law clk. U.S. Dist. Ct. (ea. dist.) Pa., Phila., 1976-78; trial atty., honors program, civil rights div. Dept. Justice, Washington, 1978-80; dep. dir. Community Legal Services, Phila., 1980-81; asst. prof. law Villanova U. Law Sch., Pa., 1982-83, assoc. prof., 1983-84, prof., 1984-85; asst. U.S. atty. U.S. Dist. Ct. (ea. dist.) Pa., 1985—; mem. 3d Cir. Lawyers Adv. Com., 1982-85, legal counsel Pa. Coalition of 100 Black Women, Phila., 1983—; bd. dirs. Juvenile Law Center, Phila., 1982—; trustee Women's Law Project, Phila., 1984—; mem. Mayor's Commn. on May 13 MOVE Incident, 1985—. Bd. dirs. Women's Way, Phila. Davenport fellow, 1973; Yale Law Sch. fellow, 1981. Mem. ABA, Nat. Bar Assn., Fed. Bar Assn. (1st v.p. Phila. chpt. 1982-84, pres. Phila. chpt.1984-86), Nat. Conf. Black Lawyers (pres. 1976-78, Outstanding Service award 1978), Phila. Bar Assn., Hist. Soc. U.S. Dist. Ct. (ea. dist.) Pa. (dir. 1983—). Civil rights, Federal civil litigation. Home: 6748 Emlen St Philadelphia PA 19119 Office: 3310 US Courthouse 601 Market St Philadelphia PA 19106

LILLY, NOLTE SCOTT AMENT, lawyer; b. Louisville, Aug. 10, 1951; s. Foster Dillard and Amber Helene (Ament) L.; m. Pamela Jane Clinard, Feb. 13, 1974; children: Andrea Nicole, Carson Clinard. BA in Telecommunications, U. Ky., 1973; JD, U. Louisville, 1977. Bar: Ky. 1977, U.S. Dist. Ct. (we. dist.) Ky. 1978, U.S. Ct. Appeals (6th cir.) 1979, U.S. Supreme Ct. 1984. Assoc. Carroll, Chauvin, Miller & Conliffe and predecessor firm, Louisville, 1977-82; asst. county atty. Jefferson County, Louisville, 1977-85, first asst. county atty., 1986—; ptnr. Conliffe, Sandmann, Gorman & Sullivan and predessor firm, Louisville, 1986—; lectr. civil rights seminar Salmon P. Chase Sch. Law, Covington, Ky., 1982; lectr. on county liability in state and fed. litigation Ky. Prosecutors Conf., Lexington, 1985. bd. dirs. Louisville Sch. Autistic Children, 1985-86, Ky. Ctr. for Spl. Children, Louisville, 1986. Claude Sullivan scholarship U. Ky. Com. of 101, 1969-73. Mem. ABA, Ky. Bar Assn. Democrat. Methodist. Avocations: golf, tennis, hunting. Local government, Civil rights. Office: Jefferson County Atty 1001 Fiscal Ct Bldg Louisville KY 40202

LILLY, TERENCE JOSEPH, lawyer; b. Lansing, Mich., Mar. 14, 1939; s. Charles Meredith and Florence Louise (Nash) L.; m. Carmen L. Lambert, July 29, 1961; children: Dorothy Gail, Joseph Paul. BA, U. Notre Dame, 1961; JD with distinction, U. Mich., 1964. Bar: Mich. 1964. Assoc. Troff, Lilly & Bonow, Kalamazoo, 1964-66, ptnr., 1966-70; pres. Lilly, Domeny, Durant, Byrne & Schanz, P.C., Kalamazoo, 1970—; mem. Mich. Supreme Ct. Com. on Standard Jury Instrns., Ann Arbor, Mich., 1971-78. Mem. ABA, Mich. State Bar Assn., Kalamazoo County Bar Assn. (sec.-treas. 1965-66), Internat. Assn. Ins. Counsel. Avocation: outdoor sports. Federal civil litigation, State civil litigation. Home: 3411 Willow Lake Dr Kalamazoo MI 49008 Office: Lilly Domeny Durant Byrne & Schanz PC 505 S Park St Kalamazoo MI 49007

LIMAN, ARTHUR L., lawyer; b. N.Y.C., Nov. 5, 1932; s. Harry K. and Celia L.; m. Ellen Fogelson, Sept. 20, 1959; children—Lewis, Emily, Douglas. A.B., Harvard U., 1954; LL.B., Yale U., 1957. Bar: N.Y. bar 1958. Asst. U.S. atty. So. Dist. N.Y., 1961-63, spl. asst. U.S. atty., 1965; with firm Paul, Weiss, Rifkind, Wharton & Garrison, N.Y.C., 1957-61, 63—; ptnr. Paul, Weiss, Rifkind, Wharton & Garrison, 1966—; chief counsel N.Y. State Spl. Commn. on Attica, 1972; chmn. Legal Action Center, N.Y.C., 1975; v.p. Legal Aid Soc., N.Y.C., 1973; pres. Legal Aid Soc., 1983-85; chmn. Gov. N.Y. Adv. Commn. Adminstrn. Justice in N.Y. State, 1981—; mem. N.Y. State Exec. Adv. Com. Sentencing, 1977; adv. com. civil rules U.S. Jud. Conf., 1980—; mem. commn. on reduction costs and delay U.S. 2d Circuit, 1976-80; bd. dirs. Continental Grain Co., Equitable Life Assurance Soc. U.S.; spl. counsel Sen. Select com. on Mil. Sales to Iran/Contra. Contbr. articles to legal jours.; Bd. editors: Nat. Law Jour, 1979—. Fellow Am. Coll. Trial Lawyers, Am. Bar Found.; mem. Am. Bar Assn., N.Y. State Bar Assn., Bar Assn. City N.Y. (exec. com.), Lawyers Com. Civil Rights Under Law. Home: 1060 Fifth Ave New York NY 10028 Office: Paul Weiss Rifkind Wharton & Garrison 1285 Ave of the Americas New York NY 10019

LIMANDRI, CHARLES SALVATORE, lawyer; b. San Diego, Aug. 19, 1955; s. Joseph John and Florence Ann (Dippolito) LiM.; m. Nancine Belfiore, Oct. 20, 1984. BA, U. San Diego, 1977; Diploma in Internat. Law, U. Wales, 1980; JD, Georgetown U., 1983. Bar: Calif. 1983, D.C. 1984. Tchr. St. Augustine High Sch., Washington, 1978-79; assoc. Adams, Duque, Los Angeles, 1983-85, Lillick, McHose & Charles, San Diego, 1985—. Rotary Internat. grad. fellow U. Wales at Aberystwyth, 1980; recipient Hattie M. Strong Found. award, Washington, 1983. Mem. ABA, Assn. Trial Lawyers Am., San Diego County Bar Assn., Italian-Am. Lawyers Assn., U. San Diego Alumni Assn. (bd. dirs.), Thomas More Soc. Am. (bd. dirs. 1982-84), Sons of Italy. Democrat. Roman Catholic. Lodge: Rotary. Avocations: running, weight lifting, skiing, scuba diving. Admiralty, Insurance, Personal injury. Home: 2755 Wyandotte Ave San Diego CA 92117 Office: Lillick McHose & Charles 101 W Broadway San Diego CA 92101

LIMBAUGH, STEPHEN NATHANIEL, judge; b. Cape Girardeau, Mo., Nov. 17, 1927; s. Rush Hudson and Bea (Seabaugh) L.; m. DeVaughn Anne Mesplay, Dec. 27, 1950; children—Stephen Nathaniel Jr., James Pennington, Andrew Thomas. B.A., S.E. Mo. State U., Cape Girardeau, 1950; J.D., U. Mo., Columbia, 1951. Bar: Mo. Prosecuting atty. Cape Girardeau County, Mo., 1954-58; judge U.S. Dist. Ct. for Eastern and Western Dists. of Mo., St. Louis, 1983—. Served with USN, 1945-46. Recipient Citation of Merit for Outstanding Achievement and Meritorious Service in Law, U. Mo., 1982. Fellow Am. Coll. Probate Counsel, Am. Bar Found.; mem. Mo. Bar (pres. 1982-83). Republican. Methodist. Office: US Dist Ct 1114 Market St Saint Louis MO 63101

LINCICOME, BRIAN LESLIE, lawyer; b. Manchester, Conn., July 16, 1957; s. Roy M. Lincicome and Gail A. (Gesner) Creed; m. Francine T. Lanni, Aug. 14, 1982. BA, U. Conn., 1979; JD, Villanova U., 1982. Bar: Pa. 1982, U.S. Dist. Ct. (ea. dist.) Pa. 1982. Assoc. White & Williams, Phila., 1982-85, 85—, Griffith & Burr P.C., Phila., 1985. Mem. ABA, Pa. Bar Assn., Phila. Bar Assn., Assn. Trial Lawyers Am., Pa. Def. Inst., Order of Coif. Avocations: literature, golf, racquetball. Personal injury, Federal civil litigation, State civil litigation. Office: White & Williams 1234 Market St Philadelphia PA 19107

LINCOLN, FRANKLIN BENJAMIN, JR., lawyer; b. Bklyn., Jan. 18, 1908; s. Franklin Benjamin and Anna (Ellensberg) L.; m. Helen C. Benz, Oct. 8, 1938; children: Carol Concors, Franklin Benjamin III. A.B., Colgate U., 1931, LL.D. (hon.), 1960; J.D., Columbia, 1934. Bar: N.Y. bar 1934, D.C. bar 1960, U.S. Supreme Ct. bar 1944. With Sullivan & Cromwell, N.Y.C., 1934-41, Lundgren, Lincoln & McDaniel, N.Y.C., 1941-59; prin. analyst Hdqrs. Army Service Forces, Washington, 1943; civilian counsel to fiscal dir. Dept. Navy, 1944-45; asst. sec. def. 1959-61; pres. Monroe Internat., Inc., 1961-64; v.p. Litton Industries, Inc., 1961-64; partner Seward & Kissel, 1964-66; sr. partner Mudge, Rose, Guthrie & Alexander, from 1966, now of counsel; v.p., dir. Cypress Communications Corp., 1965-69; dir., chmn. exec. com. Shelter Resources Corp., 1968-70; dir. Pacific Tin Consol. Corp., 1969—, Itel Corp., 1970-83, Barnes Engring. Co., 1958-59, 61-62; Advisory bd. Nat. Council for Gifted; Pres. Nixon's rep. in 1968-69 Transition; mem. Pres.' Fgn. Intelligence Advisory Bd., 1969-73. Author: Presidential Transition, 1968-1969. Trustee Colgate U., 1967-75, chmn. bd., 1975-79; bd. dirs. World Bd. of Trade, 1973-75; bd. dirs., chmn. Fed. Home Loan Bank Bd. N.Y., 1972-78. Served to lt. USNR, 1943-44. Recipient Disting. Pub. Service medal Def. Dept., 1961; Colgate U. Alumni award for disting. service, 1977. Mem. Phi Beta Kappa, Delta Upsilon, Delta Sigma Rho, Phi Delta Phi. Republican. Christian Scientist. General practice, Private international, Public international. Home: 22 Roland Dr Short Hills NJ 07078 Office: 180 Maiden Ln New York NY 10038

LINCOLN, J(AMES) ALDEN, lawyer; b. Bridgeport, Conn., Mar. 4, 1935; s. Alden A. and Katherine B. (Logan) L.; m. Elaine E. Fairman, Aug. 19, 1961; children—Stephen, Benjamin, Lista. B.A., Yale U., 1958; LL.B., U. Pa., 1963. Bar: Conn. 1964, Mass. 1970, U.S. Dist. Ct. Conn. 1965. Assoc. Marsh, Day & Calhoun, Bridgeport, Conn., 1963-67; atty. GTE Sylvania, Waltham, Mass., 1967-69, counsel, Danvers, Mass., 1969-73, sr. counsel, 1973-75; gen. counsel Precision Materials Group, GTE Products Corp., Danvers, 1975-80, v.p., gen. counsel, 1983-86; gen. counsel Lighting Products Group, Danvers, 1980-83; sole practice, Boxford, Mass., 1986—. Vice chmn. Boxford Planning Bd.; chmn. United Fund, Boxford; trustee Boxford Pub. Library. Served to lt. (j.g.) USNR, 1958-60. Mem. Boston Bar Assn. (chmn. com. corp. counsel 1981-83), ABA, Mass. Bar Assn. (lectr. preventive law). General corporate. Home and Office: Law Offices 5 Sprucewood Circle Boxford MA 01921 Office: GTE Products Corp One Stamford Forum Stamford CT 06904

LINCOLN, MICHAEL DAVID, lawyer, accountant; b. Attleboro, Mass., July 13, 1951; s. Wilfred H. and Marie Teresa (Chicoine) L.; m. Patricia Jay Beaulieu, June 27, 1971 (dec. June 1979); 1 child, Michael David Jr. BSBA, Bryant Coll., 1973; JD, Suffolk U., 1980. Bar: R.I. 1980, Mass. 1980, U.S. Dist. Ct. R.I. 1980. Cost and budget mgr. Nyman Mfg. Co., East Providence, R.I., 1973-76, customer service mgr., 1976-79; ptnr. Price Waterhouse, Providence, 1980—. Contbr. articles to profl. jours. Mem. Leadership R.I., 1985, program com., 1986; bd. dirs. Good News Housing, R.I., 1986; trustee R.I. Hist. Soc., 1987. Mem. R.I. Bar Assn. (legislation com. 1980-86), Mass. Bar Assn., R.I. Soc. CPA's (tax com. 1982-87, chair 1986-87, bd. dirs. 1987—). Avocations: white water rafting, golf, boating. Estate planning, Corporate taxation, Personal income taxation. Office: Price Waterhouse 50 Kennedy Plaza Providence RI 02903

LIND, DEBORAH CELIA, lawyer; b. N.Y.C., Nov. 15, 1956; d. Arthur and Mary Eveline (Dansereau) L. BA, Bryn Mawr Coll., 1979; JD, Syracuse U., 1982. Bar: Pa. 1982, U.S. Dist. Ct. (ea. dist.) Pa. 1982, U.S. Ct. Appeals (3d cir.) 1982. Assoc. Blank, Rome, Comisky & McCauley, Phila., 1982-84, Ballard, Spahr, Andrews & Ingersoll, Phila., 1984—. Mem. ABA, Pa. Bar Assn., Phila. Bar Assn. Pension, profit-sharing, and employee benefits. Office: Ballard Spahr Andrews & Ingersoll 30 S 17th St 20th Floor Philadelphia PA 19103

LIND, PETER EUGENE, lawyer; b. N.Y.C., Jan. 2, 1949; s. Sidney Edmund and Ilse (Dusoir) L.; m. Kathleen Vetter, June, 1971 (div. Oct. 1979); m. Judith Yankielun, July 14, 1984. BA, BE in Indsl. Engr., NYU, 1971, MBA, 1975; JD, Fordham U., 1976. Bar: N.Y. 1977, U.S. Dist. Ct. (so. and ea. dists.) N.Y. 1977, N.J. 1978, U.S. Dist. Ct. N.J. 1978, U.S. Supreme Ct. 1986. Mgr. contracts adminstrn. Dravo Constructors Inc., N.Y.C., 1972-82; assoc. Taub & Taub, Fairfield, N.J., 1983—; asst. gen. counsel Prime Motor Inns., Inc., Fairfield, 1983—. Mem. ABA, N.Y. State Bar Assn., N.J. Bar Assn., Delta Phi Alpha, Tau Beta Pi, Alpha Pi Mu. Club: Union County Hiking (N.J.). Avocations: classical music, skiing, softball, model railroads, reading. Construction, State civil litigation, General corporate. Office: Prime Motor Inns Inc 700 Rt 46 E Fairfield NJ 07007

LINDAUER, KENNETH ELLIOT, lawyer; b. N.Y.C., May 4, 1950; s. Walter and Margo (Wetzler) L.; m. Elaine B. Finbury, Sept. 7, 1980; 1 child, Margo Katherine. AB, Boston U., 1971; JD, Northeastern U., Boston, 1974; postdoctoral, U. Amsterdam, The Netherlands, 1975-76. Bar: Mass. 1974, U.S. Dist. Ct. Mass. 1976, U.S. Supreme Ct. 1977. Assoc. Israel & Goldenberg, Boston, 1974-75; sole practice Salem, Mass., 1977-87; ptnr. Finbury, Sullivan & Lindauer, Salem, 1987—. Office: Finbury Sullivan & Lindauer 14 Lynde St Salem MA 01970

LINDBERG, CHARLES DAVID, lawyer; b. Moline, Ill., Sept. 11, 1928; s. Victor Samuel and Alice Christine (Johnson) L.; m. Marian J. Wagner, June 14, 1953; children: Christine, Breta, John, Eric. A.B., Augustana Coll., Rock Island, Ill., 1950; LL.B., Yale U., 1953. Bar: Ohio 1953. Since practiced in Cin.; assoc. firm Taft, Stettinius & Hollister, 1953-61, partner, 1961—; dir. Cin. Reds Profl. Baseball Team, 1969-81, Cin. Bengals Profl. Football Team, Arga Co., Dayton-Walther Corp., Citation-Walther Corp.; corp. sec., dir. Taft Broadcasting Co.; sec. Hanna-Barbera Prodns., Inc. Bd. dirs.: Nat. Law Jour. Sec. Good Samaritan Hosp., Cin.; Bd. dirs. Augustana Coll., 1978—, sec., 1981-82, vice chmn., 1982—, chmn., 1983-86 ; pres. Cin. Bd. Edn., 1971, 74, Zion Lutheran Ch., Cin., 1966-69; chmn. policy com. Hamilton County Republican Party, 1981—; trustee Greater Cin. Center Econ. Edn., 1976—, pres. 1986— ; chmn. Better Neighborhood Sch. Com., Cin., 1975-82; chmn. law firm div. Cin. United Appeal, 1976; chmn. local govt. com. Cin. C. of C., 1977; trustee Pub. Library of Cin. and Hamilton County, 1982—. Mem. ABA, Ohio Bar Assn., Cin. Bar Assn., Greater Cin. C. of C. (trustee 1985—). Clubs: Queen City, Commonwealth, Cin. Country. Lodge: Optimists (pres. Queen City club 1987). General corporate. Office: 1800 First National Bank Ctr Cincinnati OH 45202

LINDBERG, MICHAEL CHARLES, lawyer; b. San Antonio, Oct. 5, 1951; s. Charles Loren and Phyllis Ardell (Grove) L.; m. Stephanie J. Bofferding, Oct. 28, 1978; 1 child, Peter. BA cum laude, Carleton Coll., 1973; JD cum laude, U. Minn., 1976. Bar: Minn. 1976. Assoc. Dean K. Johnson, Mpls., 1977-82; ptnr. Johnson & Lindberg P.A., Mpls., 1982—. Mem. Izaak Walton League, Bloomington, Minn. Mem. ABA, Minn. Bar Assn., Hennepin County Bar Assn., Minn. Def. Lawyers Assn. Lutheran. Insurance, State civil litigation, Federal civil litigation. Home: 8700 Lakeview Rd Bloomington MN 55438 Office: Johnson & Lindberg PA 1 Appletree Sq Suite 941 Minneapolis MN 55420-2054

LINDE, HANS ARTHUR, justice Oregon Supreme Court; b. Berlin, Germany, Apr. 15, 1924; came to U.S., 1939, naturalized, 1943; s. Bruno C. and Luise (Rosenhain) L.; m. Helen Tucker, Aug. 13, 1945; children: Lisa, David Tucker. B.A., Reed Coll., 1947; J.D., U. Calif., Berkeley, 1950. Bar: Oreg. 1951. Law clk. U.S. Supreme Ct. Justice William O. Douglas, 1950-51; atty. Office of Legal Adviser, Dept. State, 1951-53; individual practice law Portland, Oreg., 1953-54; legis. asst. U.S. Sen. Richard L. Neuberger, 1955-58; asso. prof., prof. U. Oreg. Law Sch., 1959-76; justice Oreg. Supreme Ct., Salem, 1977—; Fulbright lectr. Freiburg U., 1967-68, Hamburg U., 1975-76; cons. U.S. ACDA, Dept. Def., 1962-76; mem. Adminstrv. Conf. U.S., 1978-82. Author: (with George Bunn) Legislative and Administrative Processes, 1976. Mem. Oreg. Constl. Revision Commn., 1961-62. Served with U.S. Army, 1943-46. Fellow Acad. Arts and Scis.; mem. Am. Law Inst. (council), Order of Coif, Phi Beta Kappa. Jurisprudence. Office: Oreg Supreme Ct Salem OR 97310

LINDE, MAXINE HELEN, lawyer, corp. exec.; b. Chgo., Sept. 2, 1939; d. Jack and Lottie (Kroll) Stern; B.A. summa cum laude, UCLA, 1961; J.D., Stanford U., 1967; m. Ronald K. Linde, June 12, 1960. Applied mathematician, reseach engr. Jet Propulsion Lab., Pasadena, Calif., 1961-64; law clk. U.S. Dist. Ct. No. Calif., 1967-68; admitted to Calif. bar, 1968; mem. firm Long & Levit, San Francisco, 1968-69, Swerdlow, Glikbarg & Shimer, Beverly Hills, Calif., 1969-72; sec., gen. counsel Envirodyne Industries, Inc., Chgo., 1972—. Mem. Order of Coif, Phi Beta Kappa, Pi Mu Epsilon, Alpha Lambda Delta. General corporate. Office: Envirodyne Industries Inc 142 E Ontario St 10th Floor Chicago IL 60611

LINDEMER, LAWRENCE BOYD, lawyer, former utility executive, former state justice; b. Syracuse, N.Y., Aug. 21, 1921; s. George F. and Altamae (Reimers) L.; m. Rebecca Mead Gale, Dec. 31, 1940; children—Lawrence Boyd, David G. Student, Taft Sch., 1939, Hamilton Coll., 1939-41; A.B., U. Mich., 1943, LL.B., 1948. Bar: Mich. 1948. Asst. pros. atty. Ingham County, 1949-51; asst., commn. on orgn. Exec. Br. Govt., Hoover Comm., 1953-55; partner Foster, Lindemer, Swift & Collins (and predecessor firm), 1955-75; justice Mich. Supreme Ct., Lansing, 1975-76; sr. v.p., gen. counsel Consumers Power Co., 1977-86. Mem. Mich. Ho. of Reps., 1951-52; Republican state chmn., 1957-61; mem. Rep. Nat. Com., 1957-61; Rep. candidate atty. gen. Mich., 1966; bd. regents U. Mich., 1968-75; trustee Gerald R. Ford Found., 1985—. Served with USAAF, 1943-45. Mem. ABA, State Bar Mich. (commr. 1963-70), Mich. State Bd. Ethics, U. Mich. Alumni Assn. (pres. 1983-85), Auto Club Mich. (dir., chmn. bd.). Presbyterian (elder). General corporate, Public utilities. Home: 424 Morton St Stockbridge MI 49285 Office: Foster Swift Collins & Coey PC 313 S Washington Sq Lansing MI 48933

LINDEN, LOUIS FREDERICK, mariner, lawyer, writer, editor; b. Mpls., May 2, 1947; s. Morris and Virginia (Gaylord) L. A..B., Shimer Coll., 1969; J.D., U. Tex., Austin, 1976. Bar: Tex., 1976, U.S. Dist. Ct. (we. dist.) Tex. 1978, U.S. Ct. Appeals (5th cir.) 1980, U.S. Supreme Ct., 1981. Sole practice San Antonio, 1976-80; exec. dir. Nat. Assn. Criminal Def. Lawyers, Houston and Washington, 1980-86; now mariner, freelance writer and editor; mem. faculty Nat. Coll. Criminal Def., Houston, 1981-82. Editor The Champion mag., 1980-86. USCG ocean operator (auxiliary sail, 100 tons), 1986. Served with U.S. Army, 1969-71. Recipient Ammy award for civil rights Am. Lawyers Mag., 1981. Mem. Nat. Lawyers Guild, Nat. Maritime Hist. Soc.,

Tex. Criminal Def. Lawyers Assn., ACLU. Democrat. Jewish. Criminal, Civil rights. Home: 235 W 12th #7 New York NY 10014 Office: c/o H Bernard Esq 745 E Mulberry Suite 350 San Antonio TX 78212

LINDENBAUM, SAMUEL HARVEY, lawyer; b. N.Y.C., Mar. 29, 1935; s. Abraham M. and Belle (Axelrad) L.; m. Linda Marion Lewis, June 16, 1957; children—Erica Dale Lindenbaum Tishman, Laurie Ellen. B.A. cum laude Harvard U., 1956, J.D. cum laude, 1959; Fulbright fellow Oslo U., Norway, 1959-60. Bar: N.Y. 1960. Assoc. Fried, Frank, Harris, Schriver & Jacobson, N.Y.C., 1960-62; mem. Lindenbaum & Young, Bklyn., 1962-74; sr. mem. Rosenman & Colin, N.Y.C., 1974-83, of counsel, 1983—. Trustee Fedn. Jewish Philanthropies, N.Y.C., 1974—, mem. fin. com. 1980—; bd. dirs. Am. Friends of Israel Mus., exec. com., v.p.; bd. overseers Jewish Theol. Sem. Am., Albert Einstein Coll. Medicine; mem. N.Y. State Council on Arts. Mem. Bklyn. Bar Assn., Fulbright Alumni Assn. Clubs: Harmonie, Harvard (bd. mgrs.), Friars, Le Club (N.Y.C.). Home: 998 Fifth Ave New York NY 10028 Office: Rosenman & Colin 575 Madison Ave New York NY 10022

LINDENMUTH, NOEL CHARLES, lawyer; b. Chgo., Nov. 27, 1940; s. Charles Theodore and Bernice Dorothy (Chowanski) L.; m. Carol Jean Guercio, Nov. 28, 1963; children—Eric John, Steven Paul. J.D., Loyola U., Chgo., 1970. Bar: Ill. 1970, U.S. Dist. Ct. (no. dist.) Ill. 1970, U.S. Supreme Ct. 1977. Ptnr. Anesi, Ozmon, Lewin & Assocs., Ltd., Chgo. Served with U.S. Army, 1959-62. Mem. ABA, Ill. State Bar Assn., Chgo. Bar Assn., N.W. Suburban Bar Assn., Assn. Trial Lawyers Am., Ill. Trial Lawyers Assn., Chgo. Trial Lawyers Club, Am. Soc. Law and Medicine, Am. Arbitration Assn. (panel of arbitrators). Club: Park Ridge (Ill.) Country. State civil litigation, Personal injury, Workers' compensation. Office: 188 W Randolph St Chicago IL 60601

LINDER, HARVEY RONALD, lawyer, chemical processing executive; b. Pitts., July 23, 1949; s. Charles Joseph and Rose (Ruben) L.; m. Reva Rebecca Vestman, Aug. 14, 1971; children: Zalman F., Seth A. BA, Duquesne U., 1971, JD, 1975. Bar: Pa. 1975, U.S. Dist. Ct. (we. dist.) Pa. 1975, U.S. Supreme Ct. 1979. Legal intern Dist. Atty.'s Office, Pitts., 1974-75; asst. mgr. arbitration U.S. Steel, Pitts., 1975-80, mgr. labor relations, 1981-81; supt. employee relations U.S. Steel, Clairton, Pa., 1981-83; corp. dir. employee relations U.S. Steel Agri-Chemicals, Atlanta, 1984-86; corp. dir. law and human resources LaRoche Industries Inc., 1986—; v.p. A.C.I.R.A., 1985—. Contbr. poetry and photography to Duquesne Literary Mag., 1968-74. Exec. cons. Jr. Achievement, Pitts., 1978-83; head coach Atlanta Jewish Community Ctr., Dunwoody, Ga., 1984—; pres. Hunter's Woods Homeowners' Assn., Dunwoody, 1986—. Steel fellow Am. Iron and Steel Inst., 1977-85. Mem. ABA, Allegheny County Bar Assn., Indsl. Relations Research Assn., Duquesne U. Law Sch. Alumni Assn. (bd. dirs. 1980-84). Democrat. Lodge: B'nai B'rith (local v.p. 1975-80). Avocations: coaching, collecting books. Labor, Pension, profit-sharing, and employee benefits, Workers' compensation. Home: 235 Woodrill Way Dunwoody GA 30350 Office: LaRoche Industries Inc 1100 Johnson Ferry Rd Atlanta GA 30342

LINDER, REX KENNETH, lawyer; b. Chgo., Jan. 15, 1948; s. Kenneth Peter Linder and Pearl (Nord) Nefflen; 1 child, Mark. BS, Bradley U., 1969; JD, Washburn U., 1973. Bar: Ill. 1974, U.S. Dist. Ct. (cen. div.) Ill. 1974, U.S. Ct. Appeals (7th cir.) 1974, U.S. Supreme Ct. 1977. Ptnr. Heyl, ROyster, Voelker and Allen, Peoria, Ill., 1974—. Contbr. articles to profl. jours. Chmn. profl. div. Heart of Ill. United Way, 1984; mem. regional blood services com. ARC, 1985—, vice chmn., 1986-87; mem. Citizens Com. for the Civic Ctr., 1977; bd. dirs. Family House Inc., 1983—, chmn. bd. 1983-85; mem. adv. bd. Big Bros./Big Sisters of Peoria, 1981—; bd. dirs. Econ. Devel. Council for Peoria Area, 1982-84, counsel 1984—; bd. dirs., mem. exec. com. Peoria Econ. Devel. Assn., 1984; mem. Christian edn. com. 1st Federated Ch., 1975-76. Served to 2d lt. U.S. Army Res., 1970-75. Mem. ABA, Ill. State Bar Assn. (spl. Bankruptcy com., 1982-83), Peoria County Bar Assn. (chmn. young lawyers 1979-80, chmn. legis. 1983-84, chmn. cts. and civil procedure 1985-86, bd. dirs. 1985-86), Am. Judicature Soc., Internat. Assn. Def. Counsel (trial acad. faculty mem. 1987), Def. Research Inst., Peoria Area C. of C. (exec. com. 1980-86, bd. dirs., chmn. bd. 1982-84), Bradley U. Alumni Assn. (bd. dirs. 1983—, v.p. devel. 1984-85, pres. 1986—), Bradley U. Chiefs Club (bd. dirs. 1982—, v.p. 1986-87, pres. 1987—), Sigma Chi (bd. dirs. 1977—). Clubs: Country, Creve Coeur (Peoria) (sec., exec. com. 1984—, bd. govs. 1985—). Federal civil litigation, State civil litigation, Insurance. Office: Heyl Royster Voelkner & Allen 124 NE Adams Suite 600 Peoria IL 61602

LINDGREN, ARNE SIGFRID, lawyer; b. Huntington Park, Calif., Nov. 21, 1932; s. E. Roland and Sigrid Hulda (Eklof) L.; m. Marianne Ash, June 10, 1961 (div. Sept. 1976); children—Cynthia E., Sharon G.; m. Nancy Clark, Jan. 4, 1986. B.S., U. So. Calif., 1954, LL.B., 1960; Rotary Found. fellow, Cambridge U., Eng., 1955. Bar: Calif. 1961. Assoc. Latham & Watkins, Los Angeles, 1960-67, ptnr., 1967—; trustee, bd. dirs. John Tracy Clinic, Los Angeles, 1976—. Served to capt. USAF, 1955-57. Recipient Internat. Balfour award Sigma Chi, 1954; fellow Rotary Found., 1954-55. Fellow Internat. Acad. Estate and Trust Law (academician), Am. Coll. Probate Counsel; mem. ABA, Order of Coif. Republican. Lutheran. Avocations: fishing, horticulture. Probate, Estate planning. Home: 11301 Dona Isabel Dr Studio City CA 91604 Office: Latham & Watkins 555 S Flower St Los Angeles CA 90071

LINDGREN, D(ERBIN) KENNETH, JR., lawyer; b. Mpls., Aug. 25, 1932; s. Derbin Kenneth and Margaret (Anderson) L.; m. Patricia Ann Ransier, Dec. 17, 1955; children—Christian Kenneth, Carol Ann, Charles Derbin. B.S., U. Minn., 1954, J.D., 1958. Bar: Minn. 1958, U.S. Supreme Ct. 1968, U.S. Tax Ct. 1959, U.S. Ct. Appeals (D.C. cir.) 1981. Gen. practice law Mpls., 1958—; mem. Larkin, Hoffman, Daly & Lindgren, Ltd., Mpls., 1960—. Contbr. articles to profl. jours. Mem. Ind. Sch. Dist. 274 Bd. Edn., Hopkins, Minn., 1970-76, chmn., 1972-76; mem. Ind. Sch. Dist. 287 Bd. Edn. (Area Vocat. Tech. Schs.), 1979-83; trustee Mpls. Soc. Fine Arts, 1982—; bd. overseers Mpls. Coll. Art and Design, 1980-86, vice chmn., 1982-83, chmn., 1983-86; mem. Gov.'s Commn. on Reform of Govt., 1983. Served as lt. USAF, 1955-57. Fellow Am. Coll. Probate Counsel; mem. ABA, Minn. Bar Assn., Hennepin County Bar Assn., Alpha Delta Phi, Phi Delta Phi. Congregationalist. Clubs: Mpls. Athletic; Interlachen Country. Estate planning, Corporate taxation, General corporate. Home: 225 Hawthorne Rd Hopkins MN 55343 Office: 2000 Piper-Jaffray Tower 222 S 9th St Minneapolis MN 55402

LINDGREN, THOMAS BERNARD, lawyer; b. Chgo., Dec. 20, 1946; s. Ernst Frederick and Ruth Florence (Corwin) L.; m. Andrea Pavnick, June 5, 1981. BS with distinction, U. Ill., Chgo., 1969; MBA, Northwestern U., 1973; JD, U. Okla., 1977; MS in Taxation, DePauL U., 1980; LLM, John Marshall Law Sch., 1985. Bar: Okla. 1977, Ill. 1978, U.S. Dist. Ct. (no. dist.) Ill. 1978, U.S. Tax Ct. 1978, U.S. Ct. Appeals (7th cir.) 1978, U.S. Ct. Claims 1980, U.S. Supreme 1980, U.S. Ct. Internat. Trade 1981, U.S. Ct. Customs and Patent Appeals 1981. Patent atty. Motorola, Inc., Schaumburg, Ill., 1978-82; sr. atty. Hastle & Kirschner, Oklahoma City, 1983-85; patent atty. Thomas B. Lindgren & Assocs., Schaumburg, 1986—; adj. prof. Keller Grad. Sch. Bus., Chgo., 1981-82. Served with USAR 1970-77. Edmund J. James scholar U. Ill., 1969. Mem. Am. Inst. Indsl. Engrs., Am. Product and Inventory Control Soc., Am. Intellectual Property Law Assn., Patent Law Assn. of Chgo. Avocations: photography, canoeing, outdoors. Patent, Trademark and copyright, Corporate taxation. Home and Office: 905 Gregory Ln Schaumburg IL 60195

LINDLEY, DAVID MORRISON, lawyer; b. Montclair, N.J., June 17, 1949; s. Dwight Newton and Janie (Morrison) L.; m. Jane Cowan von der Heyde, June 12, 1971; children: Camilla von der Heyde, Carolyn Field. AB, Columbia Coll., 1971; JD, Harvard U., 1974. Bar: N.J. 1974, U.S. Dist. Ct. N.J. 1974, N.Y. 1976, U.S. Dist. Ct. (so. and ea. dists.) N.Y. 1977, U.S. Ct. Appeals (1st cir.) 1983. Assoc. McCarter & English, Newark, 1974-77; assoc. Hale Russell & Gray, N.Y.C., 1977-82, ptnr., 1983-85; ptnr. Winthrop Stimson Putnam & Roberts, N.Y.C., 1985—. Mem. ABA, Assn. of Bar of City of N.Y. Episcopalian. Federal civil litigation, State civil litigation, Antitrust. Home: 6 W 77th St New York NY 10024 Office: Winthrop Stimson Putnam & Roberts 40 Wall St New York NY 10005

LINDLEY, F(RANCIS) HAYNES, JR., lawyer; b. Los Angeles, Oct. 15, 1945; s. Francis Haynes and Grace Nelson (McCanne) L.; m. Hollinger McCloud, Apr. 1, 1977; 1 child, Anne Hollinger. BA, Claremont Men's Coll., 1967, MFA, 1972; JD, Southwestern U., 1976. Bar: Calif. 1976, U.S. Dist. Ct. (cen. dist.) Calif. 1977, U.S. Supreme Ct. 1980. Dep. pub. defender Los Angeles, 1977-79; atty. dept. trial counsel State Bar of Calif., Los Angeles, 1979-81; sole practice Santa Monica, Calif., 1981—. Trustee The John Randolph Haynes & Dora Haynes Found., Los Angeles, 1978—, pres. 1987—; bd. dirs. TreePeople, Los Angeles, 1985—, So. Calif. Assn. for Philanthropy, 1985, sec. 1987—; bd. fellows Calremont U. Ctr. and Grad. Sch., 1987—. Mem. ABA, Calif. Bar Assn., Los Angeles County Bar Assn. estate management. Home and Office: 644 E Channel Rd Santa Monica CA 90402

LINDLEY, MARK ROBERT, lawyer; b. Portland, Oreg., Apr. 2, 1957; s. Willard Eugene Lindley and Bonnae Jean (Helber) Hoofe. BS, Portland State U., 1979; JD, Lewis and Clark Coll., 1982. Bar: Oreg. 1982, U.S. Dist. Ct. Oreg. 1983. Ptnr. Buckley, Johnson, Bolen, Berg & Lindley, P.C., Lake Oswego, Oreg., 1982—. Bd. dirs. Miss Willamette Valley Scholarship Pageant, Portland, 1984—. Mem. ABA, Oreg. Bar Assn., Oreg. Trial Lawyers Assn., Multnomah County Bar Assn. Republican. Lutheran. Avocations: sports, music, outdoor activities. Contracts commercial, General corporate, Trademark and copyright. Home: 1850 Egan Way Lake Oswego OR 97034 Office: Buckley Johnson Bolen Berg & Lindley PC 3927 Lake Grove Ave PO Box 2189 Lake Oswego OR 97035

LINDSAY, DENNIS JOHN, lawyer; b. Winnipeg, Man., Can., Mar. 22, 1918; came to U.S., 1919; naturalized, 1941; s. Robert K. and Sadie (Gombriche) L.; m. Elizabeth D. Carpenter, Nov. 11, 1943; children: Betsy, Jimmy, Patsy, Susan. BA, Oberlin Coll., 1938; JD, U. Mich., 1941. Bar: Mich. 1941, N.Y. 1945, Oreg. 1948, U.S. Dist. Ct. D.C. 1981. Atty. Bituminous Coal Adminstrn., Washington, 1941-43; assoc. Cahill, Gordon & Reindel, N.Y.C., 1943-48; dep. dist. atty. Multnomah County, Oreg., 1948-50; ptnr. Krause, Evans & Lindsay and successors, Portland, Oreg., 1950-67; sr. ptnr. Lindsay, Hart, Neil & Weigler, Portland, 1967—; spl. counsel to sec. transp., Washington, 1979-80. Mem. ABA, Oreg. Bar Assn., Multnomah County Bar Assn., Maritime Law Assn., Am. Judicature Soc., Propeller Club U.S., Am. Assn. Average Adjusters. Democrat. Episcopalian. Clubs: Multnomah Athletic, Arlington, Portland Golf. Admiralty, Labor, Administrative and regulatory. Home: 4430 SW Carl Pl Portland OR 97201 Office: Lindsay Hart Neil & Weigler 222 SW Columbia Suite 1800 Portland OR 97201-6618

LINDSAY, GEORGE NELSON, lawyer; b. N.Y.C., Oct. 20, 1919. B.A., Yale U., 1941, LL.B., 1947. Bar: N.Y. 1947. Assoc. Debevoise, Plimpton, Lyons and Gates & sucessor firm Debevoise & Plimpton, N.Y.C., 1947-54; ptnr. Debevoise, Plimpton, Lyons and Gates & sucessor firm Debevoise & Plimpton, 1955—, presiding ptnr., 1980—; mem. adv. council of Africa, Dept. State, 1964-68; mem. exec. com. Lawyers Com. for Civil Rights Under Law, 1969—, co-chmn. 1969-71. Mem. Urban Design Council City of N.Y., 1969-75; bd. dirs. African-Am. Inst., 1969—, chmn. bd. dirs., 1981—; mem. council Yale U., 1974—, v.p., 1981-85; bd. dirs. Planned Parenthood-World Population, 1964-68, chmn., 1965-66; trustee Carnegie Endowment for Internat. Peace, 1981—, vice chmn., 1986—. Fellow Am. Bar Found.; mem. Am. Judicature Soc., ABA, N.Y. State Bar Assn., Assn. Bar City N.Y. (exec. com. 1973-77, chmn. exec. com. 1976-77, v.p. 1977), Am. Assn. Internat. Commn. Jurists (bd. dirs. 1969—, chmn. bd. dirs. 1983—). Home: 16 Sutton Pl New York NY 10022 Office: 875 3d Ave New York NY 10022

LINDSAY, STEPHEN PROUT, lawyer; b. Niagara Falls, N.Y., Oct. 3, 1944; s. Penn Reuben and Gertrude Mary (Prout) L.; m. Linda Gray, Sept. 2, 1967; children: Penn Gray, Stephen Prout Jr. BA, Yale U., 1966; JD, Mich. U., 1972. Bar: Mass. 1972. From assoc. to ptnr. Ropes & Gray, Boston, 1972—. Mem. adv. com. Town of Wellesley, Mass., 1983-86; bd. dirs. Wellesley Community Ctr., 1985—. Served to 1st lt. U.S. Army, 1966-69. Mem. ABA, Boston Bar Assn. (chmn. zoning and land use com.). Congregationalist. Clubs: Blue Hill (Maine) Country Club, Buck's Harbor Yacht (Brooksville, Maine). Avocations: sailing, golf, skiing, tennis. Real property. Home: 35 Clovelly Rd Wellesley Hills MA 02181 Office: Ropes & Gray 225 Franklin St Boston MA 02110

LINDSEY, ROGER LEIGHTON, lawyer; b. Jeffersonville, Ind., Nov. 7, 1952; s. Edward Mancel Lindsey and Genevieve Louise (Sillings) Lindsey Hochstetler; m. Julia Marie Maynard, June 9, 1984. Cert. mgmt. Ind. U., 1973, B.S., 1974; J.D., U. Louisville, 1976; cert. FBI Nat. Acad., 1978. Bar: Ind. 1977, U.S. Dist. Ct. (so. dist.) Ind. 1977. Sole practice, Jeffersonville, 1977—; legal adviser Clark County Police Dept., Jeffersonville, 1977-82; dep. prosecutor Clark County 4th Jud. Cir., 1982-84, chief dep. 1983; mem. adj. faculty dept. social services Ind. U., New Albany, spring 1979. Mem. ABA, Ind. Bar Assn., Clark County Bar Assn., Floyd County Bar Assn., Clark County C. of C., Delta Theta Phi (dean Henry Clary Senate 1976). Roman Catholic. Lodges: Masons, Shriners. Family and matrimonial, General practice, Personal injury. Office: 426 Watt St Jeffersonville IN 47131

LINDSEY, THOMAS LESLIE, JR., lawyer; b. Richmond, Va., June 18, 1953; s. Thomas Leslie and Mary Elizabeth (Carr) L. BSBA, U. Richmond, 1976, JD, 1980. Bar: Va. 1980, U.S. Ct. Appeals (4th cir.) 1980. Sole practice Richmond, 1980-81; asst. commonwealth atty. Petersburg, Va., 1981-85, Chesterfield County, Va., 1985—. Mem. Petersburg Bar Assn., Chesterfield Colonial Heights Bar Assn. Avocations: reading, jogging, tennis, bicycle riding. Criminal. Office: Commonwealth Attys Office PO Box 25 Chesterfield VA 23832

LINDSKOG, DAVID RICHARD, lawyer; b. New Haven, Aug. 4, 1936; s. Gustaf Elmer and Charlotte (Birely) L.; m. Elisabeth Lagg, Jan. 28, 1978; 1 child, Stefanie. B.A., Yale U., 1958; LL.B., U. Va., 1965. Bar: N.Y. 1966, conseil juridique France 1978. Assoc., Curtis, Mallet-Prevost, Colt & Mosle, N.Y.C., 1965-72, ptnr., 1973—. Served to lt. USNR, 1958-62. Mem. Internat. Bar Assn. Episcopalian. Club: Yale (N.Y.C.). Private international, Banking, Construction. Home: 22 Shore Acre Dr Old Greenwich CT 06870 Office: Curtis Mallet-Prevost Colt & Mosle 101 Park Ave New York NY 10178

LINDSLEY, BYRON FRANKLIN, judge, lawyer; b. Sarona, Wis., Apr. 28, 1915; s. Earl Franklin and Bertha (Zahn) L.; m. Estelle Rich, June 10, 1939 (Nov. 1976); children: Byron F. Jr., Philip P., Palmer E. (dec.); m. Faye Edmonds, Sept. 2, 1977. AB in Econs., San Diego State U., 1937; postgrad. in Pub. Adminstrn., Am. U., 1938; JD, Georgetown U., 1944. Bar: Calif. 1944, D.C. 1944, U.S. Dist. Ct. (so. dist.) Calif. 1944, U.S. Supreme Ct. 1959. Sole practice San Diego, 1947-51; ptnr. Crabtree & Lindsley, San Diego, 1951-60; judge Calif. Superior Ct., San Diego, 1960-80; of counsel Eigenhauser & Lindsley, San Diego, 1982-85; pvt. judging Alternatives to Litigation, San Diego, 1984—. Contbr. articles to profl. jours. Pres. San Diego Young Dems., 1947-48; chmn. Dem. Cen. Com., San Diego, 1948-49; pres. Urban League, San Diego, 1968-69, Dem. Profl. Club, San Diego, Council Dem. Clubs, San Diego; v.p. Friends of Library, San Diego State U.; bd. dirs. Legal Aid Soc., San Diego. Mem. Calif. Judges Assn., Calif. Trial Lawyers Assn. (named Calif. trial judge of yr. 1975), Assn. Family Conciliation Cts. (bd. dirs. 1965-80, pres. 1971-72). Avocation: horticulture. Home: 678 Dewane Dr El Cajon CA 92020 Office: 7380 Clairemont Mesa Blvd San Diego CA 92111

LINDSTEDT, NORMAN EDWARD, lawyer; b. Moline, Ill., Sept. 5, 1942; s. Paul Edward and Patricia A. (Stenzel) L.; m. Karole Jane Hartman, June 25, 1966; 1 son, David P. B.A., Valparaiso U., 1964, J.D., 1967. Bar: Ill. 1969, U.S. Dist. Ct. (no. dist.) Ill. 1972, U.S. Ct. Apls. (7th cir.) 1982. Labor relations Chrysler Corp., Belvidere, Ill., 1968-69; assoc. Maynard & Brassfield, Rockford, Ill., 1969-72, Yalden & Ridings, Rockford, 1972-74; ptnr. Ellis & Lindstedt, Rockford, 1974-77, Holmstrom & Green, Rockford, P.C., 1977—; instr. William Rainy Harper Coll.; spl. asst. atty. gen. State Ill., 1974-78. Bd. dirs., chmn. Rock River chpt. ARC, 1970-82; bd. dirs. Central Day Care Center, Rockford, 1975-77, Multiple Sclerosis, Rockford, 1974-75, Responsible Peer Programs The Mill, 1985—. Served with USAR, 1963-73. Mem. ABA, Ill. Bar Assn. (lectr. family law sect. 1984), Winnebago Bar Assn. (chmn. family law sect. 1973-84), Assn. Trial Lawyers Am. Lutheran. Clubs: Univ., City (Rockford). Family and matrimonial, State civil litigation, Federal civil litigation. Office: 800 N Church St Rockford IL 61103

LINE, JUDSON EDWARD, lawyer; b. Panhandle, Tex., Dec. 16, 1921; s. Henry Judson and Lucy Pamelia (Carter) L.; m. Elizabeth Ann Jordan, Oct. 6, 1950; children: Teresa Elizabeth Dillard, Lee Edward. BS, West Tex. State U., 1946; JD, U. Mich., 1949. Bar: Tex. 1949, U.S. Dist. Ct. (no. dist.) Tex. 1950. Assoc. Braly & Braly, Pampa, Tex., 1949-50; atty. Oldham County, Vega, Tex., 1951-53, Deaf Smith County, Hereford, Tex., 1953-65; ptnr. Cowsert, Bybeed & Line, Hereford, 1965-83, Cowsert, Line, Easterwood & Langelennig, Hereford, 1983—. Served to lt. USN, 1942-45, PTO. Mem. Deaf Smith County C. of C. (treas., bd. dirs. 1967-70). Baptist. Lodges: Masons, Lions. Avocations: golf, tennis. Probate, Real property, General practice. Home: 310 Sunset Hereford TX 79045 Office: Cowsert Line Easterwood & Langehennig 320 Schley Hereford TX 76045

LINE, WILLIAM GUNDERSON, lawyer; b. Loup City, Nebr., July 19, 1927; s. William Harrison and Lulu Mae (Gunderson) L.; children—Nancy Line Jacobs, Lindsey Line Natvig, Katherine Line Rasmussen, Julie Ann. Student Nebr. State Tchrs. Coll., 1943-44, U. Chgo., 1944-45; B.S.L., U. Nebr., 1948, J.D., 1950. Bar: Nebr. 1950, U.S. Dist. Ct. Nebr. 1950, U.S. Supreme Ct. 1965. County atty. Dodge County, Nebr., 1955-59; ptnr. Kerrigan, Line & Martin, Fremont, Nebr., 1962—; lectr. Nebr. State Patrol Tng. Camp, Ashland, 1959. Bd. dirs. Nebr. Civil Liberties Union, 1971-75. Mem. ABA (ins. sect., criminal law sect.), Nebr. Bar Assn., Dodge County Bar Assn. (pres. 1967), Phi Alpha Delta. Republican. Presbyterian. General practice, Family and matrimonial, Criminal. Home: 1930 N Nye Ave Fremont NE 68025 Office: 312 Equitable Fed Bldg Fremont NE 68025

LINEBERGER, JOHN RALPH, judge; b. Avinger, Tex., Aug. 8, 1937; s. Dale D. and Mamie E. (Johnson) L.; m. Barbara J. Fox, Mar. 7, 1954; children—Debra Lineberger Miller, Rocky. B.S.B.A., U. Ark., 1967, J.D., 1968. Bar: Ark. 1968, U.S. Dist. Ct. (ea. dist.) Ark. 1968, U.S. Dist. Ct. (we. dist.) Ark. 1968, U.S. Dist. Ct. (ea. dist.) Okla. 1971, U.S. Ct. Appeals (8th cir.) 1970, U.S. Ct. Appeals (10th cir.) 1972, U.S. Supreme Ct. 1976. Assoc. Ball & Gallman, Fayetteville, Ark., 1968-70; ptnr. Wommack, Lineberger & Davis, Fayetteville, 1970-75; pub. defender 4th Jud. Dist. Ark., 1970-75, cir. judge, 1975-76; chancellor, probate judge 4th Chancery Dist. Ark., Fayetteville, 1977—; lectr. in law U. Ark.; mem. faculty Nat. Jud. Coll.; dir. U. Ark. Criminal Proceudre Inst.; mem. Fayetteville Planning Commn. Mem. Washington County (Ark.) Bar Assn., Ark. Bar Assn., Ark. Jud. Council, Am. Judges Assn., Fayetteville C. of C., Phi Alpha Delta. Baptist. Author: (with J. Gallman) Law Enforcement Officers Criminal Procedure Manual, 1970; editor-in-chief Ark. Law Rev., 1967-68. Family and matrimonial, Probate. Office: PO Drawer BB Fayetteville AR 72702

LINEK, ERNEST VINCENT, lawyer; b. Seattle, July 10, 1953; s. Edwin Vincent and Alice Ruth (Solberg) L.; m. Martha Ann Finnegan, May 11, 1985. BS, SUNY-Fredonia, 1975; MS, U. N.H., 1977; JD, Seton Hall U., 1982. Bar: U.S. Patent Office 1980, N.J. 1982, U.S. Dist. Ct. N.J. 1982, U.S. Ct. Appeals (fed. cir.) 1983, Mass. 1985. Staff chemist Merck & Co., Inc., Rahway, N.J., 1977-79, patent searcher, 1979-80, patent agt., 1980-82, patent atty., 1982-84; assoc. Dike, Bronstein, Roberts, Cushman & Pfund, Boston, 1984-86; ptnr., 1987—. Contbr. articles to profl. jours. Recipient Am. Jurisprudence Equity award Lawyers Coop. Pub. Co., 1982; Class of 1963 Equity award Seton Hall U., 1982. Mem. ABA, Am. Intellectual Property Law Assn., N.Y. Acad. Sci., Am. Chem. Soc., Boston Patent Law Assn. Democrat. Roman Catholic. Patent, Trademark and copyright, Federal civil litigation. Home: 11 Sprague St N Billerica MA 01862 Office: Dike Bronstein Roberts Cushman & Pfund 130 Water St Boston MA 02109

LINETT, DAVID, lawyer, former county prosecutor; b. Perth Amboy, N.J., Apr. 9, 1934; s. Jack K. and Anne L.; children—Jon, Peter, Maren. B.A., Yale U., 1956; J.D., Harvard U., 1959. Bar: D.C. 1959, N.J. 1960. Law sec. to assignment judge Superior Ct. N.J., 1959-60; assoc. Gross, Weissberger & Linett, New Brunswick, N.J., 1960-62, ptnr., 1962-77; prosecutor Somerset County, N.J., 1977-82; of counsel Lowenstein, Sandler, Brochin, Kohl, Fisher, Boylan & Meanor, and predecessor, Roseland and Somerville, N.J., 1982-85; sole practice, 1985—; ptnr. Gindin & Linett, Bridgewater, N.J., 1985—; chmn. N.J. State Bar Com. on Programs for Law Enforcement Personnel, 1978-80; mem. com. on county dist. cts. N.J. Supreme Ct., 1980-82, mem. Post-Indictment Delay Task Force, 1980, dist. XIII ethics com., 1986—. Mem. N.J. Dem. State Com., 1973-77; counsel, trustee Franklin Arts Council, 1970-77; bd. dirs. Somerset County Resource Ctr. for Women and Their Families, 1982-83; chmn. bd. trustees Assn. for Advancement of Mentally Handicapped, 1987—; mem. Ct. House study com. Somerset County Bd. Freeholders, 1979-82. Mem. Nat. Dist. Attys. Assn. (nat. treas., exec. com. 1981-82, Pres.'s award for outstanding service as chmn. fin. com. 1982), New Brunswick Bar Assn. (pres. 1974), ABA (corp., real property law sect.), N.J. Bar Assn. (land use sect., real property sect.), Somerset County Bar Assn. (co-chmn. courthouse study com.), Somerset County C. of C. (bd. dirs. 1984—). Lodge: Rotary (pres. 1986-87). Real property, General corporate, Banking. Office: PO Box 6135 1170 Rt 22 Bridgewater NJ 08807

LINFIELD, JAMES CLARK TAYLOR, lawyer; b. Bozeman, Mont., Aug. 17, 1955; s. James Clark Taylor and Mary Joy (Grigg) Linfield; M. Patience Ratiff, Aug. 19, 1980. AB magna cum laude, Harvard U., 1977, JD magna cum laude, 1980. Bar: Colo. 1980. Assoc. Davis, Graham & Stubbs, Denver, 1980-85, ptnr., 1986—. Exec. com. MIT Enterprise Forum Colo, Denver. Mem. ABA, Colo. Bar Assn., Denver Bar Assn. Republican. Episcopalian. Clubs: Harvard (N.Y.C. and Denver) (pres. Denver 1985—), Denver Athletic. General corporate, Securities, Computer. Office: Davis Graham & Stubbs 370 17th St Denver CO 80201

LINGELBACH, ALBERT LANE, lawyer; b. N.Y.C., July 19, 1940; s. Robert Lane and Sarah (Lewis) L.; m. Ann Norton, July 31, 1965; children—Albert Lane, Charity Ann. B.S., U. Pa., 1962, LL.B., 1965. Bar: N.Y. 1967, U.S. Tax Ct. 1984. Assoc., Jackson & Nash, N.Y.C., 1965-72, ptnr., 1972—. Co-chmn. Port Washington (N.Y.) Community Chest Fund Drive, 1972-73, bd. dirs. 1973-74, sec. 1974-75, v.p. 1975-76, exec. v.p. 1976-78, pres. 1978-80. Mem. Assn. Bar of City of N.Y. (mem. com. on trusts estates and surrogates cts. 1980-83), ABA (com. on significant new devels. in probate and trust law practice 1983—), N.Y. State Bar Assn., Am. Coll. Probate Counsel, Estate Planning Council N.Y.C. Presbyterian (elder). Clubs: University (N.Y.C.); Southport (Maine) Yacht. Estate planning, Probate, Estate taxation. Home: Ketch Lady Ann PO Box 472 Port Washington NY 11050 Office: Jackson & Nash 330 Madison Ave New York NY 10017

LINGL, JAMES PETER, lawyer; b. Appleton, Wis., Dec. 19, 1946; s. Peter Lawrence and Barbara (Verstegen) L.; m. Lisa Ann Cordova, May 22, 1981; children: Jason, Julie, Jameson. Student, Loyola U., Rome, 1967-68; BA, Rockhurst Coll., 1969; JD, U. Wis., 1975. Bar: Wis. 1975, U.S. Dist. Ct. (we. dist.) Wis. 1975, Calif. 1977, U.S. Dist. Ct. (cen. dist.) Calif. 1977. Ptnr. Bowman & Lingl, Depere, Wis., 1975-77, Taylor, Churchman & Lingl, Camarillo, Calif., 1977-83; sole practice Camarillo, 1983—. Bd. dirs. Boys and Girls Club, Camarillo, 1977—, pres. 1986; bd. dirs. Camarillo Arts Council, 1984—, Make-a-Wish, Ventura, Calif., 1985—. Recipient Am. Jurisprudence award Bancroft-Whitney, 1975. Mem. ABA, Calif. Trial Lawyers Assn., Ventura County Trial Lawyers Assn. (bd. dirs. 1983-84), Community Assns. Inst., Ventura County Bar Assn. (various offices 1981-86). Democrat. Roman Catholic. Lodge: Rotary (bd. dirs. Camarillo 1982-83). Avocations: sailing, golf. Office: 400 Rosewood Suite 202 Camarillo CA 93010

LINK, ANTONY COLE, lawyer; b. Chickasha, Okla., Aug. 29, 1947; s. A.C. and Henrietta Pauline (Corn) L.; m. Carolyn Gay Darnold, Feb. 14, 1969; children: Anthony Cole, Brandon Todd, Carmen Renee, Melissa Rachelle. BA, Okla. U., 1969, JD, 1973. Bar: Okla. 1973, U.S. Dist. Ct. (we. dist.) Okla. 1973. Assoc. Bennett & Rodgers, Duncan, Okla., 1969-74; ptnr. Rodgers & Link, Duncan, 1974—. Chmn. United Fund, Duncan, 1975; mem., bd. dirs. continuing legal edn. com. Okla. Workers Compensation, 1985—. Served with USNG, 1970-72. Mem. Okla. Bar Assn. (workers' compensation com. 1982-85), Stephens County Bar Assn., Assn. Trial Lawyers Am. Democrat. Methodist. Lodges: Kiwanis (bd. dirs. Duncan 1975-76), Elks. Avocations: softball, tennis. Workers' compensation. Office: Rodgers & Link Inc 1212 Willow Duncan OK 73533

LINK, GEORGE HAMILTON, lawyer; b. Sacramento, Calif., Mar. 26, 1939; s. Hoyle and Corrie Elizabeth (Evans) L.; m. Betsy Leland, May 10, 1968; children—Thomas Hamilton, Christopher Leland. A.B., U. Calif., Berkeley, 1961; LL.B., Harvard U., 1964. Bar: Calif. 1962, U.S. Ct. Appeals (9th cir.) 1962, U.S. Dist. Ct. (no., cent. and so. dists.) Calif. Assoc. Brobeck, Phleger & Harrison, San Francisco, 1964-69, ptnr., 1970—; mng. ptnr. Brobeck, Phleger & Harrison, Los Angeles, 1976—. Bd. regents U. Calif., 1971-74; trustee Berkeley Found., 1970-74; bd. govs. United Way, 1979-81; trustee Jr. Statesmen Am.; chmn. Adv. Bd. to Gov. on Selection of Regents, 1975-76. Fellow Am. Bar Found.; mem. ABA, Calif. Bar Assn., Los Angeles Bar Assn., San Francisco Bar Assn. Republican. Methodist. Clubs: Calif., Bohemian, Jonathan. Banking, Federal civil litigation, State civil litigation. Home: 315 N Carmelina Ave Los Angeles CA 90049 Office: 444 S Flower St Los Angeles CA 90017

LINK, ROBERT JAMES, lawyer, educator; b. Washington, May 25, 1950; s. Robert Wendell and Barbara Ann (Bullock) L.; m. Cheryl Ann Brillante, Apr. 22, 1979; 1 child, Robert Edward. BA, U. Miami, 1972, JD, 1975. Bar: Fla. 1975, U.S. Dist. Ct. (mid. dist.) Fla. 1980, U.S. Ct. Appeals (5th cir.) 1980, U.S. Ct. Appeals (11th cir.) 1981, U.S. Supreme Ct. 1984. Asst. pub. defender City of Miami, Fla., 1975-78, City of Jacksonville, Fla., 1978-82; ptnr. Greenspan, Goodstein & Link, Jacksonville, 1982-84, Goodstein & Link, Jacksonville, 1984-85; sole practice Jacksonville, 1985—; instr. U. Miami, 1976, U. Fla., 1979—, Stetson Law Sch., 1984, Jacksonville U., 1987. Atty. legal panel ACLU, Jacksonville, 1982—. Mem. ABA (criminal law sect.), Fla. Bar Assn. (chmn. com. for representation of indigents criminal law sect. 1980), Jacksonville Bar Assn. (criminal law sect.), Nat. Assn. Criminal Def. Lawyers, Fla. Pub. Defender Assn. (death penalty steering com. 1980-82, instr. 1979-84). Democrat. Methodist. Avocations: sailing, fishing, diving, softball. Criminal. Home: 3535 Carlyon Dr Jacksonville FL 32207 Office: 353 E Forsyth St Jacksonville FL 32202

LINKER, RAYMOND OTHO, JR., lawyer; b. Charlotte, N.C., Jan. 18, 1946; s. Raymond Otho Sr. and Frances (Baucom) L.; m. Nola Grady Jenning, June 24, 1969; 1 child, John Raymond. BS in Chem. Engring., N.C. State U., 1968; JD, Georgetown U., 1972. Bar: N.C. 1972, U.S. Dist. Ct. (we. dist.) N.C. 1972, U.S. Patent Trademark Office 1972. From assoc. to ptnr. Bell, Seltzer, Park & Gibson, Charlotte, 1972—. Mem. N.C. Bar Assn., Am. Intellectual Property Assn. Presbyterian. Patent, Trademark and copyright, Computer. Home: 2511 Sherwood Ave Charlotte NC 28207 Office: Bell Seltzer Park & Gibson 1211 E Morehead St Charlotte NC 28204

LINKLATER, WILLIAM JOSEPH, lawyer; b. Chgo., June 3, 1942; s. William John and Jean (Connell) L.; m. Dorothea D. Ash, Apr. 4, 1986; children—Erin, Emily. B.A., U. Notre Dame, 1964; J.D., Loyola U., 1968. Bar: Ill. 1968, U.S. Dist. Ct. (no. dist.) Ill. 1968, (no. dist.) Calif., U.S. Ct. Appeals (7th cir.) 1971, U.S. Supreme Ct. 1971, U.S. Ct. Appeals Washington 1978, Calif. 1981, U.S. Dist. Ct. (cen. dist.) Calif. 1981, U.S. Tax Ct. 1982, U.S. Dist. Ct. (no. dist.) Calif. 1983. Atty. Fed. Defender Project, Chgo., 1966-68; assoc. Baker & McKenzie, Chgo., 1968-75, ptnr., 1975—; adj. prof. Northwestern U. Law Sch. Contbr. articles to profl. jours. Mem. ABA (criminal law com. antitrust sect.), Ill. Bar Assn., Seventh Cir. Bar Assn., Fed. Bar Assn., Chgo. Bar Assn., (v.p. judicial candidates evaluation com.), Calif. Bar Assn., Am. Coll. Trial Lawyers, Nat. Assn. Criminal Def. Lawyers, Alpha Sigma Nu. Criminal, Antitrust, Federal civil litigation. Office: 2700 Prudential Plaza Chicago IL 60601

LINN, MICHAEL CHARLES, exploration company executive; b. Pitts., Feb. 19, 1952; s. Earl and Patricia (Gardill) L.; m. M. Catharine Downey, Sept. 1977; children: Sarah, Matthew, Patrick. BA in Polit. Sci., Villanova U., 1974; JD, U. Balt., 1977. Bar: Pa. 1977, U.S. Dist. Ct. (we. dist.) Pa. 1977, U.S. Supreme Ct. 1981. Atty., Ecker, Ecker, Ecker, Zoffer and Rome, Pitts., 1977-80; gen. counsel Meridian Exploration Corp., Pitts., 1980-83, v.p., 1983-86; sr. v.p., 1986—; chmn. Appalachian Energy Group, 1984—. Editor Meridian Market Letter Quar. report, 1984-85. Mem., chmn. Mt. Lebanon Parking Authority, 1983—; mem. citizen's adv. council Dept. Environ. Resources, 1983-88; trustee Appalachian Polit. Action Commn. Mem. ABA, Allegheny Bar Assn., Pa. Bar Assn., Pa. Nat. Gas Assn. (pres.), Ind. Petroleum Assn. of Am. (bd. dirs., gas com.), Ind. Oil and Gas Assn. N.Y. (bd. dirs.), N.Y. State Oil Producers Assn., Am. Assn. Petroleum Landmen, Ind. Oil and Gas Assn. W. Va., Ohio Oil and Gas Assn. FERC practice, General corporate, Oil and gas leasing. Office: Meridian Exploration Corp 3514 Fifth Ave Pittsburgh PA 15213

LINNEHAN, JOSEPH ARTHUR, JR., lawyer; b. Lowell, Mass., Aug. 16, 1953; s. Joseph Arthur Sr. and Dorothy Marie (Mullen) L.; m. Linda Stewart, Nov. 3, 1979; children: Courtney Elizabeth, Katharine McLean. Bar: Mass. 1978, Fla. 1979, U.S. Ct. Appeals (11th cir.) 1981. Asst. atty. gen. State of Fla., Tallahassee, 1979-84; assoc. Fowler, White, Gillen, Boggs, Villareal & Banker P.A., Ft. Myers, Fla., 1984—. Mem. ABA, Lee County Bar Assn. Democrat. Roman Catholic. Club: Royal Palm Yacht (Ft. Myers). Avocations: tennis, automobiles, reading. Insurance, State civil litigation.

LINNEMEIER, PHILIP, lawyer; b. Bloomington, Ind., Feb. 18, 1953; s. Robert William and Mary Jane (Armstrong) L.; m. Paula Jean Cartmell, May 24, 1986. BA with honors, Ind. U., 1976; JD with highest honors, Valparaiso U., 1979. Bar: Ind. 1979, Ill. 1981. Teaching fellow Valparaiso (Ind.) U. Sch. Law, 1978-79; assoc. Stults, Custer, Kutansky and McClean, Gary, Ind., 1979-85, Kightlinger and Gray, Indpls., 1985—. Mem. ABA, Ill. State Bar Assn., Ind. State Bar Assn., Indpls. Bar Assn., Ind. Def. Lawyers Assn. Federal civil litigation, State civil litigation, Insurance. Office: Kightlinger and Gray 660 Market Sq Ctr Indianapolis IN 46204

LINNERT, TERRENCE GREGORY, lawyer; b. Cleve., Oct. 16, 1946; s. Ralph Marshall and Mary Gertrude (Gessner) L.; m. Susan Kay Chesnes, Jan 25, 1969; children: Michael, Patrick, Terrence, Timothy. BSEE, U. Notre Dame, 1968; JD, Cleve. State U., 1975. Bar: Ohio 1975. Engr. Cleve. Electric Illuminating, 1968-77, corp. counsel, 1977-84, sr. corp. counsel, 1984-86; sr. corp. counsel Centerior Service Co., Independence, Ohio, 1986—. Mem. Citizens' League, Cleve; pres. St. Gabriel's Parents' Assn., Concord, Ohio, 1984-85, v.p. parish council, 1986-87. Roman Catholic. Securities, General corporate, Pension, profit-sharing, and employee benefits. Home: 7260 Winchester Pl Concord OH 44077 Office: Centerior Service Co 6200 Oak Tree Blvd Independence OH 44131

LINSHAW, JACK G., lawyer; b. Phila., Feb. 19, 1937; s. Charles V. and Emily (Goetz) L.; m. Karin T. Leduc, July 23, 1978; children: Kara, Kimberly, Michael, Rosalyn. AB, Franklin & Marshall Coll., 1959; JD, Villanova U., 1962. Bar: Pa. 1964, U.S. Dist. Ct. (mid. and ea. dists.) Pa. 1964; cert. trial adv., Pa. Asst. in trusts U.S. Comptroller of Currency, Phila., 1964; asst. atty. gen. Pa. Dept. Transp., Harrisburg, 1967-69; ptnr. Gumble, Thomson & Linshaw, Milford, Pa., 1969-77; sole practice Milford, 1977—; staff atty. Community Legal Services, Phila., 1966-77; sheriff Pike County; chief pub. defender Pike County, 1982-84. Pres. Pike County Devel. Ctr., Milford, 1974-78; treas. Pike County Rep. Com., Milford, 1976-80; bd. dirs. Sunnyside Hosp., Port Jervis, N.Y., 1979-81; solicitor Milford and Matamoras Boroughs, Dingman and Palmyra (Wayne County) Twps. Zoning Bds. Mem. Pa. Bar Assn., Pike County Bar Assn. (pres. 1984-85), Assn. Trial Lawyers Am. (sustaining), Pa. Trial Lawyers Assn., Pike County C. of C. (bd. dirs. 1972-78). Republican. Lodges: Elks, Masons. General practice, State civil litigation, Real property. Home: 208 E High St Milford PA 18337 Office: 509 Broad St Milford PA 18337

LINT, LOUIS RAYMOND, lawyer; b. Grand Rapids, Mich., July 9, 1946; s. Angus R. and Maudie May (Shurlow) L.; m. Mary Jane Achterhoff, Aug. 14, 1981; 1 child, Joshua L. BS, Cen. Mich. U., 1969; JD, New Eng. Sch. Law, 1974. Bar: Mich. 1975. Sole practice Muskegon, Mich., 1975—. Mem. ABA, Mich. Bar Assn., Muskegon County Bar Assn. Republican. Clubs: Century (Muskegon); Press (Grand Rapids). Bankruptcy, Real property, Family and matrimonial. Office: Muskegon Bankruptcy Clinic 1065 4th St Suite A PO Box 747 Muskegon MI 49443-0747

LINXWILER, JAMES DAVID, lawyer; b. Fresno, Calif., Apr. 9, 1949; s. George Edwin and Stella Ruth (Schmidt) L.; m. Robyn Kenning, July 12, 1986. BA, U. Calif.-Berkeley, 1971; JD, UCLA, 1974. Bar: D.C. 1976, Alaska 1977, U.S. Ct. Appeals (9th and D.C. cirs.), U.S. Dist. Ct. Alaska. Lawyer, Dept. Interior, Washington, 1974-76; gen. counsel Cook Inlet Region Inc., Anchorage, 1976-78; lawyer Sohio Petroleum Co., Anchorage, 1978-81; ptnr. Guess & Rudd, Anchorage, 1981—. Contbr. chpts. to book, articles to profl. jours. Chmn. Alaska Coalition Am. Energy Security, 1986-87, Alliance ANWR Com., 1986-87; mem. Commonwealth N. Energy com., 1985, 86, 87. Mem. ABA, Alaska Bar Assn. (rules and bylaws com. 1982—), Fed. Bar Assn., D.C. Bar Assn.Democrat. Oil and gas leasing, Environment, Administrative and regulatory. Home: 2407 Loussar Dr Anchorage AK 99517 Office: Guess & Rudd 510 L St Anchorage AK 99516

LIONBERGER, RICHARD LEE, lawyer; b. Terre Haute, Ind., June 20, 1950; s. Paul Henry and Lois Pauline (Wells) L.; m. Margaret Lamond Chance, Dec. 20, 1975; children: Janet, Sarah, Douglas. BS in Petroleum Engring., Tex. A&M U., 1972; JD, U. Tex., 1979. Bar: Tex. 1980. Petroleum engr. Pennzoil Co., Houston, 1972-75; drilling engr. Continental Oil Co., Houston, 1975-77; v.p. legal div. Diamond M Co., Houston, 1980-84; atty. Kaneb Services Inc., Houston, 1984-85; sole practice Houston, 1985—; bd. dirs. Internat. Assn. Drilling Contractors. Bd. dirs. FT. Bend chpt. Am. Heart Assn., Sugar Land, Tex., 1985, Ft. Bend Office of Early Childhood Devel., Richmond, Tex., 1985—;. Mem. ABA, Tex. State Bar Assn., Houston Bar Assn., Soc. Petroleum Engrs. Republican. Methodist. General corporate, Private international, Oil and gas leasing. Office: One Sugar Creek Ctr Suite 340 Sugar Land TX 77478

LIPCON, CHARLES R., lawyer; b. N.Y.C., Mar. 20, 1946; s. Harry H. and Rose Lipcon; m. Irmgard Adels, Dec. 1, 1974; children—Lauren, Claudia. B.A., U. Miami, 1968, J.D., 1971. Bar: Fla. 1971, U.S. Dist. Ct. (so. dist.) Fla. 1971, U.S. Ct. Appeals (5th cir.) 1972, U.S. Supreme Ct. 1976, U.S. Ct. Appeals (D.C. cir.) 1980, U.S. Dist. Ct. (so. dist.) Tex. 1982. Sole practice, Miami, Fla., 1971—; lectr. U. Miami Sch. Law. Author: Help for the Auto Accident Victim. Named Commodore of High Seas, Internat. Seaman's Union. Mem. Fla. Bar Assn., Am. Trial Lawyers Assn., ABA, Fla. Trial Lawyers, Dade County Bar Assn., Dade County Trial Lawyers. Club. Rotary (Key Biscayne). Contbr. articles to profl. jours. Admiralty, Personal injury, Federal civil litigation. Office: 2 S Biscayne Blvd Suite 2480 Miami FL 33131

LIPKIN, GARY DENNIS, lawyer; b. Phila., Nov. 24, 1952; s. Clifford Stanley and Lenore Toby (Fogel) L.; m. Gail Linda Pavorsky, June 30, 1979. BA in Polit. Sci. cum laude with honors, Am. U., 1974; postgrad., Austro-Am. Inst. Edn., Vienna, Austria, 1972-73; JD, George Washington U., 1977. Bar: Pa. 1977, U.S. Dist. Ct. (ea. dist.) Pa. 1977, U.S. Ct. Appeals (fed. cir.) 1977, D.C. 1978, U.S. Dist. Ct. D.C. 1978, U.S. Tax Ct. 1978, U.S. Ct. Mil. Appeals 1978, U.S. Ct. Appeals (D.C. cir.) 1978, U.S. Supreme Ct. 1985. Atty., advisor U.S. Customs Service, Washington, 1977; atty. enforcement Fed. Election Commn., Washington, 1977-79; asst. gen. counsel Nat. Assn. Mfrs., Washington, 1979-83, sr. asst. gen. counsel, 1983—. Author: The Law of Corporate Political Activity, 1986; contbr. articles to profl. jours. Chmn. local bd. Selective Service System, Fairfax County, Va., 1981—. Recipient Cert. Appreciation So. Md. Assn. Realtors, 1980. Mem. ABA, Fed. Bar Assn. (chmn. election law conf. 1981), D.C. Bar Assn. (vice chmn. ethics com. 1985-86). Jewish. Avocations: cinema, video, racquetball, piano. General corporate, Labor, Election, campaign and political finance law. Home: 8010 Sleepy View Ln Springfield VA 22153 Office: Nat Assn Mfrs 1331 Pennsylvania Ave NW Suite 1500 N Washington DC 20004-1703

LIPMAN, HOWARD STEWART, lawyer; b. Troy, N.Y., Aug. 31, 1955; s. Marshall S. and Sondra (Aison) L.; m. Ivy E. Cutler, May 20, 1979; children: Jennifer, Jeffrey. BS, SUNY, Buffalo, 1977, JD, 1980. Bar: N.Y. 1981, U.S. Dist. Ct. (we. dist.) N.Y. 1981. Assoc. Sheldon M. Markel & Assocs. P.C., Buffalo, 1980—. Committeeman Amherst Dem. Com., Buffalo, 1983. Mem. N.Y. State Bar Assn., Erie County Bar Assn. Democrat. Jewish. Lodge: Masons. Personal injury, Family and matrimonial, General practice. Home: 1429 Eggert Rd Amherst NY 14226 Office: Sheldon M Markel & Assocs 888 Statler Towers Buffalo NY 14202

LIPMAN, STEPHEN I., lawyer; b. Boston, May 17, 1941; s. Jack H. and Dora M. (Solov) L.; m. Marguerite Theresa Jordan, Apr. 26, 1969; children—Roger Adlai, Jake Allegra, Andrew Charles, Katherine Fitzgerald. B.A., U. Mass., 1963; J.D., Boston U., 1966. Bar: Mass. 1966, U.S. Dist. Ct. Mass. 1967, U.S. Ct. Appeals (1st cir.) 1969, U.S. Supreme Ct. 1971, N.Y. 1983; diplomate Nat. Bd. Trial Advocacy; cert. civil trial advocate. Pvt. practice, Boston, after 1966; now ptnr. Wylie, Lipman & Frieze; legal counsel Joint Com. on Judiciary, Mass. Legislature, 1965-77; pub. adminstr. Norfolk County (Mass.), 1976—; lectr in field. Mem. Concord (Mass.) Democratic Town Com., 1970-73, Brookline (Mass.) Dem. Town Com., 1973—, Brookline Town Meeting, 1975-81, Brookline Hist. Commn., 1980—; pres. Precinct Six Neighborhood Assn., Boston, 1981—, Corner-Coop. Nursery Sch., Boston, 1983—. Fellow Mass. Bar Found., Mass. Trial Edn. Found.; mem. ABA, Assn. Trial Lawyers Am., Mass. Bar Assn. (council civil litigation sect. 1979—, chmn. arbitration com. 1979-80, chmn. edn. com. 1980-82, sect. chmn. 1982—, editor Mass. Law Rev. 1984—, med.-legal liaison com. 1984, others), Mass. Acad. Trial Attys. (amicus curiae brief com.1984—), Middlesex County Bar Assn., Norfolk County Bar Assn., Boston Bar Assn. (mem. family law com. 1983—, fee disputes com. 1983—, tort com. litigation sect. 1984—, steering com. litigation sect. 1984—), World Assn. Lawyers of World Peace Through Law Center. Democrat. Club: Univ. of Boston. Editor U. Mass. Law Rev., 1984; contbr. articles to profl. publs. Family and matrimonial, General practice, Personal injury. Home: 432 Washington St Brookline MA 02106 Office: 31 Milk St Boston MA 02109

LIPNACK, MARTIN I., lawyer; b. Bklyn., Apr. 6, 1936. BA, Bklyn. Coll., 1957, JD, 1960. Bar: N.Y. 1961, U.S. Supreme Ct. 1970, Fla. 1973. Ptnr. Applebaum & Eisenberg, Liberty, N.Y., 1968-73; asst. counsel Am. Title Ins. Co., Miami, Fla., 1973-74; ptnr. Schnur & Lipnack, Ft. Lauderdale, Fla., 1974-85; sole practice Ft. Lauderdale, 1985—. V.p., dist. chmn. Hudson Del. council Boy Scouts Am., Middletown, N.Y.; pres. Temple Beth Israel, Ft. Lauderdale; bd. dirs. Humanitarian Found. Ft. Lauderdale, Jewish Community Ctr. Ft. Lauderdale. Mem. ABA, Fla. Bar Assn., N.Y. State Bar Assn., Broward County Bar Assn., Acad. Fla. Trial Lawyers, Am. Israel Pub. Affairs Com. (bd. dirs.), Jewish Fedn. Ft. Lauderdale (bd. dirs.). Home: 7421 SW 20th St Plantation FL 33317 Office: 7880 W Oakland Park Blvd Fort Lauderdale FL 33321

LIPP, LOUIS ELLIS, lawyer; b. Omaha, May 23, 1907; s. Myer M. and Lena Adelaide (Heller) L.; m. Dorothy M. Kropman, Aug. 23, 1934; children—Susan Kay Lipp Kentoff, Myra Joan Lipp Sanderman. Ph.B., Creighton U., 1928, J.D., 1930. Bar: Nebr. 1930, U.S. dist. ct. Nebr. 1930. Assoc., Leon & White, Omaha, 1930-39; ptnr. Leon, White & Lipp, Omaha, 1939-43, White & Lipp, 1943-51, White, Lipp & Simon, 1951-58, White, Lipp, Simon and Powers, 1958-84; of counsel Erickson & Sederstrom, 1984—. Treas. United Way of Midlands, 1974-76, trustee, 1967-81, mem., 1966—, named Man of Yr., 1972, recipient disting. services award, 1968. Recipient Boss of Yr. award Legal Secs. Assn. of Omaha, 1967. Mem. Omaha Bar Assn., Nebr. State Bar Assn., ABA; fellow Nebr. State Bar Found. Republican. Jewish. Clubs: Highland Country, B'nai B'rith (Omaha). General corporate, Probate, Labor. Home: 663 Fairwood Ln Omaha NE 68132 Office: c/o Erickson & Sederstrom PC 10330 Regency Pkwy Dr Omaha NE 68114

LIPPE, EMIL, JR., lawyer; b. Waco, Tex., Nov. 4, 1948; s. Johann August Emil and Agnes Natalie (Fenske) L.; m. Dale Holle, June 18, 1983. B.A., Northwestern U., 1970, J.D. cum laude, 1973. Bar: Tex. 1973, U.S. Dist. Ct. (no. dist.) Tex. 1974, U.S. Ct. Appeals (5th cir.) 1974, U.S. Dist. Ct. (ea. dist.) Tex. 1976, U.S. Dist. Ct. (so. and we. dists.) Tex. 1977, U.S. Supreme Ct. 1977, U.S. Ct. Appeals (11th cir.) 1981. Practice law, Dallas, 1973—; assoc. Carrington, Coleman, Sloman & Blumenthal, 1973-76; assoc. Akin, Gump, Strauss, Hauer & Feld, 1976-80, ptnr., 1980-83; mem. Barlow & Lippe, 1983-84, Lippe & Lay, 1984-85, Lippe & Assocs., 1985—; lectr. dept. communications arts Loyola U., Chgo., 1972-73. Bd. dirs. Save Open Space Orgn., 1974-75. Recipient Outstanding Dir. award Tex. Young Lawyers Assn., 1980-81; Outstanding Young Lawyer in Dallas, 1983. Mem. ABA, Tex. Bar Assn., Dallas Bar Assn., Tex. Young Lawyers Assn., Order of Coif. Democrat. Lutheran. Contbr. articles to profl. jours. Federal civil litigation, State civil litigation, Antitrust. Home: 6828 Gaston Ave Dallas TX 75214-4030 Office: Lippe & Assocs 2800 Lincoln Plaza Dallas TX 75201

LIPPE, MELVIN KARL, lawyer; b. Chgo., Oct. 21, 1933; s. Melvin M. and Myrtle (Karlsberg) L.; children: Suzanne, Michael S., Deanna; m. Sandra M. Bauer, Jan. 5, 1974. B.S., Northwestern U., 1955, J.D., 1958; grad. cert., Grad. Sch. Banking, U. Wis., 1965; cert., Sr. Bank Officers Seminar, Harvard U., 1966. Bar: Ill. 1958; C.P.A. Asso. D'Ancona, Pflaum, Wyatt & Riskind, Chgo., 1958-61; asst. to chmn. bd. Exchange Nat. Bank of Chgo., 1961-62, asst. v.p., 1962-64, v.p., 1964-66, sr. v.p., sec. to bd. dirs., 1966-69, exec. v.p., dir., 1969-74, vice chmn. bd., 1974-76, also dir.; dir. Am.-Israel Bank, Ltd., 1974-76; partner firm Antonow & Fink, Chgo., 1977—; instr. Ill. Inst. Tech., 1960-63. Bd. dirs. Chgo. chpt. Am. Jewish Com., 1974-78; bd. dirs. Jewish Community Centers Chgo., 1972—, pres., 1980-82; bd. dirs. (for life) Young Men's Jewish Council, Chgo., pres., 1971. Served with Ill. N.G., 1959. Mem. Am., Ill., Chgo. bar assns., Am. Jewish Com., Phi Epsilon Pi, Tau Epsilon Rho, Beta Gamma Sigma. Jewish. Club: Standard (Chgo.). Contracts commercial, General corporate, Real property. Office: 111 E Wacker Dr Chicago IL 60601

LIPPE, RICHARD ALLEN, lawyer; b. Bklyn., July 24, 1938; s. Al A. and Thelma (Spaeth) L.; m. Gail C. Lippe, June 20, 1965; children—Wendy, David. B.A., Tufts U., 1960; LL.B., U. Pa., 1964. Bar: N.Y. 1965, U.S. Dist. Ct. (ea. and so. dists. N.Y.) 1965, U.S. Supreme Ct. 1975. Dept. county atty. Nassau County, N.Y., 1965-68; ptnr. Lippe, Ruskin, Schlissel & Moscou, Nassau County, 1968-79; ptnr. Meltzer, Lippe & Goldstein, Mineola, N.Y., 1979—; dir. corp. fin. Woolcott & Co.; village atty. Inc. Village of Great Neck Plaza, N.Y., 1972—; gen. counsel The Wainrite Group, Inc., 1981—; gen. counsel, dir. New Generation Foods, Inc., MicroGeneSys, Inc., Coinmach Industries Co., 1983—; bd. dirs. L.I. Venture Capital Group, Entrepreneurship L.I.; counsel Manhasset-Great Neck Econ. Opportunity Council, 1965-68; gen. ptnr. Contemporary Art Consortium; pres. Contemporary Art Pub. Consortium. Sec., Nassau Law Services Com., Inc., 1966—; dir. Nassau County Legal Aid Soc., 1978-81; bd. dirs. Waldemar Med. Research Found., 1966-68. Mem. ABA, N.Y. Bar Assn., Nassau County Bar Assn., Fed. Bar Council. Jewish. Contbr. articles to profl. jours. Federal civil litigation, General corporate, Local government. Home: 7 Amherst Rd Great Neck NY 11021 Office: 190 Willis Ave Mineola NY 11501

LIPPES, RICHARD JAMES, lawyer; b. Buffalo, Mar. 18, 1944; s. Thomas and Ruth (Landsman) L.; m. Sharon Richmond, June 4, 1972; children: Amity, Joshua, Kevin. BA, U. Mich., 1966; JD cum laude, SUNY-Buffalo, 1970. Bar: N.Y. 1970, U.S. Dist. Ct. Md. 1970, U.S. Ct. Appeals (4th cir.) 1970, U.S. Ct. Appeals (2d cir.) 1971, U.S. Dist. Ct. (we. dist.) N.Y. 1971. Clk. to presiding judge U.S. Ct. Appeals, Balt., 1970; exec. dir. Center for Justice Through Law, Buffalo, 1971; sole practice, Buffalo, 1971-77; ptnr. Moriarity, Allen, Lippes & Hoffman, Buffalo, 1977-79, Allen, Lippes & Shonn, Buffalo, 1979—; lectr. SUNY-Buffalo, 1978, 79. Chmn. Atlantic chpt. Sierra Club, 1980-83; chmn. Buffalo chpt. Am. Jewish Com., 1981, 83-84; bd. dirs. Empire State Ballet. Recipient Am. Jurisprudence award, 1968. Mem. ABA, N.Y. State Bar Assn., Erie County Bar Assn. (chmn. pub. interest law com., chmn. prepaid legal services com.), N.Y. Civil Liberties Union (bd. dirs., chmn. 1976-78). Democrat. Environment, Personal injury.

LIPPMAN, KYLE DAVID, lawyer; b. Radway, Alta., Can., Oct. 13, 1954; s. Glenn Edward and Barbara Joyce (Laughlin) L.; m. Valerie Alexis Lebeaux, Jan. 23, 1982. BS, So. Meth. U.; JD, U. Tex. Bar: Tex. 1980. Assoc. Wood, Campbell, Moody & Gibbs, Houston, 1980-83; ptnr. Wood & Lippman, Houston, 1984-85, Park Cen. Investment, Houston, 1985-86, Winstead, McGuire, Sechrest & Minick, Houston, 1987—. Mem. ABA, Houston Bar Assn. Republican. Roman Catholic. Club: Lakeside Country. Avocation: golf. Real property, Landlord-tenant, Banking. Home: 6146 Bordley Houston TX 77057 Office: Winstead McGuire Sechrest & Minick 910 Travis Suite 1938 Houston TX 77002

LIPPMAN, PETER IRA, lawyer; b. Chgo., Apr. 17, 1939; s. Morris and Rochel Lillian (Stone) L.; m. Ethel Lynn Danchik, Jan. 28, 1966 (div. Jan. 1978); 1 child, Leonard S.M. BS, Calif. Inst. Tech.; JD magna cum laude, Southwestern U. Bar: U.S. Patent Office 1964, Calif. 1982. Scientist, tech. publs. and patent mgr. Cary Instruments, Monrovia, Calif., 1961-70; patent agt. Pasadena, Calif., 1970-82; patent atty. Romney, Golant, Martin, Seldon & Ashen, Los Angeles, 1982—; adj. prof. UCLA Sch. Law, 1985-86. Editor San Gabriel Valley Alternative newspaper, 1969-70, Calif. Water Pollution Control Assn. Bull., 1971-78. Mem. Monrovia City Planning Commn., 1975-76. Mem. ASME (sec. San Fernando Valley chpt. 1984-85, treas. 1985-86, vice chmn. 1986—), Soc. Applied Spectroscopy, Los Angeles Patent Law Assn., Beverly Hills Bar Assn., ACLU, Sierra Club. Democrat. Club: Lawyers of Los Angeles County. Avocations: jogging, hiking, motorcycle touring, cross-country skiing, photography. Patent, Trademark and copyright. Home: 4385 Ocean View Blvd Montrose CA 91020 Office: Romney Golant Martin Seldon & Ashen 10920 Wilshire Blvd Suite 1000 Los Angeles CA 90024

LIPPO, TOM A., lawyer; b. Greensburg, Pa., Oct. 6, 1955; s. Veikko A. and Reeta S. Lippo; m. Eija Pynnönen. BA summa cum laude with distinction, Yale U., 1978; MA summa cum laude, U. Jyväskylä, Finland, 1979; JD, Stanford U., 1982. Bar: D.C. 1982, U.S. Dist. Ct. D.C. 1983, U.S. Ct. Appeals (D.C. cir.) 1983. Assoc. Landis, Cohen, Rauh and Zelenko, Washington, 1982-87; of counsel Marshall, Tenzer, Greenblatt, Fallon & Kaplan, Washington, 1987—; gen. counsel Finnish Am. Corp. Team, Inc., Washington and Helsinki, Finland, 1985—. Recipient Internat. Edn. award Rotary Found., 1976-77; Fulbright Scholar, 1978-79. Mem. Assn. Trial Lawyers Am., Finnish Am. C. of C., Phi Beta Kappa, Psi Chi. Federal civil litigation, Private international, Trademark and copyright. Office: Landis Cohen Rauh & Zelenko 4801 Massachusetts Ave NW Suite 400 Washington DC 20016

LIPSEY, HOWARD IRWIN, lawyer; b. Providence, Jan. 24, 1936; s. Harry David and Anna (Gershman) L.; children—Lewis Robert, Bruce Stephen. A.B., Providence Coll., 1957; J.D., Georgetown U., 1960. Bar: R.I. 1960, U.S. Dist. Ct. R.I. 1961, U.S. Supreme Ct. 1972. Assoc. Edward I. Friedman, 1963-67, Kirshenbaum & Kirshenbaum, 1967-82; ptnr. Abedon, Michaelson, Stanzler, Biener, Skolnik & Lipsey, 1982-83; ptnr. Lipsey & Skolnik, Esquires, Ltd., Providence, 1983—; lectr. trial tactics Nat. Coll. Adv., 1986, U. Bridgeport Law Sch., Yale U. Served to capt. JAGC, USAR, 1960-71. Fellow Am. Coll. Trial Lawyers, Am. Acad. Matrimonial Lawyers; mem. ABA, R.I. Bar Assn., Assn. Trial Lawyers Am. Clubs: B'nai B'rith (Anti-Defamation League). Contbg. author: Valuation and Distribution of Marital Property, 1984. Personal injury, Family and matrimonial, Workers' compensation. Office: Lipsey & Skolnik 369 S Main St Providence RI 02903

LIPSICH, JEROME K., lawyer; b. Cin., June 29, 1952; s. Harry and Gertrude (Nides) L.; m. Dianne Hiestand, Jan. 21, 1984. BA, SUNY, Binghamton, 1974; JD, Tulane U., 1980. Bar: La. 1980, U.S. Tax Ct. 1981. Assoc. Simon, Peragine, New Orleans, 1980-81, Sessions, Fishman, New Orleans, 1981-85; ptnr. Sessions, Fishman, 1986—. Mem. ABA, La. Bar Assn. Antitrust, Computer, Construction. Office: Sessions & Fishman 201 Saint Charles Floor 35 New Orleans LA 70170

LIPSIG, ETHAN, lawyer; b. N.Y.C., Dec. 11, 1948; s. Daniel Allen and Haddassah (Adler) L. BA, Pomona Coll., 1969; postgrad., Oxford U., 1969-70; JD, UCLA, 1974. Bar: U.S. Dist. Ct. (cen. dist.) Calif. 1974, U.S. Ct. Appeals (9th cir.) 1974, U.S Tax Ct. 1978. Author: (book) Individual Retirement Arrangements, 1980. Mem. ABA (tax and labor relations sect.), Western Pension Conf., Order of Coif. Avocations: travel, horticulture, wine. Pension, profit-sharing, and employee benefits. Home: 1290 Avocado Terr Pasadena CA 91403 Office: Paul Hastings Janofsky & Walker 555 S Flower St Los Angeles CA 90071

LIPSIG, HARRY HAVON, lawyer; b. Warsaw, Poland, Dec. 26, 1902; s. David and Rose Lipsig; m. Mildred Slonim, Nov. 14, 1923. LLB, Bklyn. Law Sch., 1924. Bar: U.S. Ct. Appeals (2d cir.) 1926. Sr. ptnr. Lipsig, Sullivan & Liapakis, P.C., N.Y.C.; adj. prof. N.Y. Law Sch. Chmn. exec. com. Crime Victims Rights Orgns., 1978; pres. Pub. Awareness Soc. Mem.

N.Y. State Bar Assn., N.Y. State Trial Lawyers Assn., N.Y. Claims Assn., Scribes, Am. Soc. Writers on Legal Subjects. Home: 860 United Nations Plaza New York NY 10017 Office: Lipsig Sullivan & Liapakis 100 Church St New York NY 10007

LIPSITZ, RANDY, lawyer; b. Balt., July 19, 1955; s. Harry and Bobbe (Seltzer) L.; m. Margaret Longo, Aug. 21, 1977; children: Lindsay, Diana. BA with distinction, Boston U., 1977; JD, Bklyn. Law Sch., 1980. Bar: N.Y. 1981, U.S. Ct. Appeals (2d and Fed. cirs.) 1982. Ptnr. Blum Kaplan (and predecessor firms), N.Y.C., 1978—. Mem. Phi Beta Kappa, Sigma Xi. Patent, Trademark and copyright, Federal civil litigation. Office: Blum Kaplan 1120 Ave of Americas New York NY 10036

LIPSITZ, ROBERT JOEL, lawyer, corporate executive; b. Pitts., June 30, 1949; s. Herman and Helen Virginia (Nobel) L.; m. Susan Dale Schechter, July 5, 1970; 1 child, Samantha Beth. B.B.A., U. Miami, 1971; J.D., U. Balt., 1975. Bar: Pa. 1975, U.S. Dist. Ct. (we. dist.) Pa., U.S. Ct. Appeals (3rd cir.), U.S. Supreme Ct. 1985. Ptnr. Lipsitz, Nassau & Schwartz, Pitts., 1975—; corp. counsel B. Lipsitz Co., Pitts., 1976—; conusel various other corps.; trustee several pension plans. Mem. Upper St. Clair Cable Commn., Pa., 1983, chmn., 1984-86; mem. Upper St. Clair Planning Commn., 1985—, sec. 1986. Mem. ABA, Allegheny County Bar Assn., Assn. Trial Lawyers Am. Lodges: Masons, Shriners. Labor, Real property, General corporate. Office: Lipsitz Nassau & Schwartz 1100 5th Ave Pittsburgh PA 15219

LIPSKY, BURTON G., lawyer; b. Syracuse, N.Y., May 29, 1937; s. Abraham and Pauline (Leichtner); m. Elaine B. Mannheimer, July 27, 1967; 1 dau., Erika S., m. 2d, Carol S. Samberg, Feb. 4, 1973; 1 son, Andrew H. B.B.A., U. Mich., 1959; J.D. summa cum laude, Syracuse U., 1962. Bar: N.Y. 1962, U.S. Ct. Claims 1969, U.S. Tax Ct. 1967, U.S. Sup. Ct. 1967. Trial atty. tax div. U.S. Dept. Justice, Washington, 1962-67; assoc. Kaye, Scholer, Fierman, Hays & Handler, N.Y.C., 1967-72; ptnr. Delson & Gordon, 1972—. Treas. Westchester Reform Temple, 1983—. Mem. ABA, N.Y. Bar Assn., Order of Coif, Justinian Soc. Corporate taxation, Estate taxation, Personal income taxation. Office: Delson & Gordon 605 3d Ave New York NY 10158

LIPSMAN, RICHARD MARC, lawyer, educator; b. Bklyn., Aug. 17, 1946; s. Abraham W. and Ruth (Weinstein) L.; m. Ellen J. Friedman, Nov. 22, 1969 (div. 1978); m. Geri A. Russo, June 20, 1980; children: Dara Briana, Eric. BBA, City Coll. of City of N.Y., 1968; JD, St. John's Univ., Jamaica, N.Y., 1972; LLM in Taxation, Boston U., 1976. Bar: N.Y. 1973, Mass. 1975, U.S. Dist. Ct. (ea. and so. dists.) N.Y. 1977, U.S. Supreme Ct. 1978, U.S. Tax Ct. 1979; CPA, N.Y., Mass. Tax atty. Arthur Young & Co., N.Y.C., 1972-74; assoc. Gilman, McLaughlin & Hanrahan, Boston, 1974-76, Lefrak, Fischer & Meyerson, N.Y.C., 1976-77; ptnr. Tarnow, Landsman & Lipsman, N.Y.C., 1978; sole practice N.Y.C., 1979—; faculty Baruch Coll. CUNY, 1984-86, curriculum specialist Research Found. CUNY, 1977-78; faculty Pratt Inst., Bklyn., 1974, Queensboro Coll., Bayside, N.Y., 1978-80. Author, producer book/cassette program, Learning Income Taxes, 1978. Mem. ABA, N.Y. State Bar Assn., Am. Inst. CPA's, N.Y. State Soc. CPA's. Jewish. Construction, General corporate, State civil litigation. Office: 275 Madison Ave New York NY 10016

LIPSON, ANN LOUISE, lawyer; b. Sheffield, Yorkshire, Eng., Nov. 6, 1948; came to U.S., 1964; d. Maurice and Rita (Cowan) Roseby; m. Edward H. Lipson, May 29, 1969; children: Paul, Gabrielle and Heather (triplets). BA, U. Mich., 1969; MS, Syracuse U., 1970, U. Wis., 1974; JD, U. Wis., 1980. Bar: Wis. 1980, Ariz. 1982, U.S. Dist. Ct. Ariz. 1982. Law clk. U.S. Dist. Ct. (we. dist.) Wis., Madison, 1980-81; assoc. Wentworth & Lundin, Phoenix, 1981-83; sole practice Phoenix, 1983-85; assoc. Sacks, Tierney & Kasen, Phoenix, 1985-86, Daughton, Hawkins & Bacon, Phoenix, 1986—. Atty., panel mem. Planned Parenthood, Phoenix, 1984—; coordinator children's health ctr. St. Joseph's Hosp., Phoenix, 1986—. Mem. Maricopa County Bar Assn., Am. Immigration Lawyers Assn. Jewish. Avocations: reading, travel, ballet, writing, fgn. langs. Immigration, naturalization, and customs, Public international, Juvenile. Home: 5363 E Sahuaro Dr Scottsdale AZ 85254 Office: Daughton Hawkins & Bacon 3636 N Central Ave Phoenix AZ 85012

LIPSON, BARRY J., lawyer, columnist; b. N.Y.C., May 30, 1938; s. Sidney J. and Irene (Abrams) L.; m. Lois J., June 7, 1975; children—Steven J., David J. B.S. in Econs., Wharton Sch., U. Pa., 1959; J.D., Columbia U., 1962; LL.M. in Trade Regulation, NYU, 1968; postgrad. in law Oxford U., 1982, Harvard U., 1984. Bar: N.Y. 1962, Pa. 1970, U.S. Supreme Ct. 1967. Dep. asst. atty. gen. State N.Y., 1963-64, asst. atty. gen., 1964-67; assoc. counsel, asst. sec. Block Drug Co., Inc. and Reed & Carnick, 1968-69; asst. sec., counsel trade regulation counsel Koppers Co., Inc., Pitts., 1969-81; dir. U.S Chem. Corp., 1971-81; v.p., gen. counsel, sec. Elkem Metals Co., Pitts., 1982-85; head of Corp. div. Weisman Bowen, Pitts., 1985— ; arbitrator, master Pa. Ct. Common Pleas, Allegheny County, 1970—; columnist Pitts. Bus. Times, 1986—; arbitrator Am. Arbitration Assn., 1978—, Better Bus. Bur., 1986— ; guest lectr. George Washington U., 1979-83; ; mem. Bus. Roundtable Lawyers Adv. Com., 1978-82; mem. Pa. C. of C. Antitrust Adv. Com., 1978—; nat., internat. lectr. on antitrust, trade regulations and legal compliance at legal and bus. seminars; mem. indsl. functional adv. com. on internat. standards U.S. Dept. Commerce and Office of U.S. Trade Rep., 1980—. Vice chmn. Pitts. chpt. ACLU, 1977-78, bd. dirs., 1972—, chmn. legal com., 1975-77; bd. dirs. Pa. ACLU, 1977-84. Served to lt. comdr. JAGC, USNR, 1965-75. Mem. ABA (chmn. monopolization taskforce 1976-79, chmn., lectr. monopolization program 1978, chmn. monopolization subcom. 1979-82; vice chmn. Sherman Act com. 1979, chmn. antitrust compliance counseling taskforce, 1979-82, mem. faculty Nat. Inst. 1980), Allegheny County Bar Assn. (founding; vice chmn. antitrust and class action com. 1979, chmn. 1980-82, vice chmn. hdqrs. com. 1983-85), Am. Corp. Counsel Assn. (founding mem. we. Pa. chpt., dir., sec. 1984-86), VFW. Lodges: Kiwanis, Masons, Elks. Contbr. to profl. publs.; founding editor Sherman's Summations, 1979. General corporate, Antitrust, Private international. Home: 102 Christler Ct Coraopolis PA 15108 Office: 520 Grant Bldg Pittsburgh PA 15219

LIPSON, GARY DAVID, lawyer; b. Buffalo, July 6, 1952; s. Avrome and Ethel (Tuchman) L. BA, U. Mich., 1974; JD, Cornell U., 1977. Bar: Fla. 1977, U.S. Dist. Ct. (so. dist.) Fla. 1977, U.S. Ct. Appeals (5th cir.) 1977, U.S. Ct. Appeals (11th cir.). Ptnr. Greenberg, Traurig, Askew, Hoffman, Lipoff, Rosen & Quentel P.A., Miami, Fla., 1977-85, Fine, Jacobson, Schwartz, Nash, Block & England P.A., Miami, 1985—. Mem. devel. com. Ctr. for Miami Fine Arts. 1982—; trustee Fla. Internat. U., Miami, 1986—. Mem. Fla. Bar Assn. (chmn. securities com. corp., banking and bus. law sect. 1986—), Entrepreneural Soc. So. Fla. (bd. dirs.), Phi Beta Kappa, Phi Delta Phi. Securities, General corporate, Contracts commercial. Office: Fine Jacobson Schwartz Nash Block & England PA One Centrust Financial Center Miami FL 33131

LIPSON, LEON, law educator, lawyer; b. 1921. A.B., Harvard U., 1941, M.A., 1943, LL.B., 1950. Bar: N.Y. 1951, D.C. 1951. Assoc. Cleary, Gottlieb et al., Washington, 1950-56; assoc. prof. Yale U. Law Sch., 1957-60, prof. 1960-79, Henry R. Luce prof., 1979—, assoc. provost, 1965-68; advisor U.S. del. UN Mission, 1959; cons. RAND Corp., 1956-70; bd. dirs. Social Sci. Research Council, 1969—, chmn., 1974-76, chmn. exec. com., 1976-78; bd. dirs. Internat. Research and Exchanges Bd., 1973-75; mem. acad. adv. bd. RAND Grad. Inst., 1977—. Am. Council Learned Socs. exchange scholar Acad. Sci. USSR, 1963; fellow Ctr. Advanced Study in Behavioral Scis., 1968-69; Rockefeller Found. scholar, Bellagio, Italy, 1978. Mem. Am. Assn. Advancement Slavic Studies (v.p. 1967-70, 81-82, pres. 1982-83). Author: (with N. Katzenbach) Report on the Law of Outer Space, 1961; editor: (with V. N. Chalidze) Papers on Soviet Law, vol. 1, 1977, vol. 2, 1979; past note editor Harvard Law Rev. Legal education. Office: Yale U Law Sch Drawer 401A Yale Sta New Haven CT 06520 *

LIPSTEIN, ROBERT A., lawyer; b. Wilmington, Del., Dec. 6, 1954; s. Eugene Joseph and Leona (Feld) L.; m. Cheryl A. Artibee-Wedlake, July 30, 1978; children: Rebecca Lynn, Matthew Wedlake. BA in Econs., Stanford U., 1975, JD, 1978. Bar: D.C. 1978, U.S. Dist. Ct. D.C. 1981, U.S. Ct. Appeals (D.C. cir.) 1981, U.S. Ct. Internatl. Trade 1984. Assoc. Morgan, Lewis & Bockius, Washington, 1978-84, Coudert Bros., Washington, 1984-86; ptnr. Coudert Bros., 1987—. Mem. ABA (antitrust sect.), D.C. Bar Assn., Phi Beta Kappa. Avocations: golf, wood working. Antitrust, Private international, Trademark and copyright. Home: 8004 Barron St Takoma Park MD 20912 Office: Coudert Bros 1 Farragut Sq S Washington DC 20006

LIPTON, ALVIN E(LLIOT), lawyer; b. Hackensack, N.J., Jan. 5, 1945; s. Irving and Goldie (Blickstein) L. BA, U. Rochester, 1966; JD, Boston U., 1969; LLM in Taxation, NYU, 1970. Bar: N.Y. 1972, U.S. Tax Ct. 1972, Conn. 1973, U.S. Ct. Claims 1977, U.S. Supreme Ct. 1977, Calif. 1983. Internat. tax analyst Price, Waterhouse & Co., N.Y.C., 1969-70; tax analyst Arthur Young & Co., N.Y.C., 1970; tax assoc. Weiss, Bronston, Rosenthal, Heller & Schwartzman, N.Y.C., 1971; tax atty, Conn. Gen. Life Ins. Co., Hartford, 1971-76; tax counsel Owens-Corning Fiberglas Corp., Toledo, 1976-80, Crown Zellerbach Corp., San Francisco, 1981—. Bd. dirs. San Francisco Choral, Instrumental & Theatrical for Youth, 1985—; bd. dirs. San Francisco Chanticleer, vice chmn. 1987—; citizens ambassador to People's Republic of China, 1987. Mem. ABA (tax sect. 1972—), Tax Execs. Inst., Calif. Bar Assn., San Francisco Bar Assn. (tax sect. 1982—). Avocations: reading, hiking, snorkling, choral and solo singing. Corporate taxation, Personal income taxation, International taxation. Home: 1800 Franklin St San Francisco CA 94109 Office: Crown Zellerbach Corp One Bush St San Francisco CA 94104

LIPTON, ANDREW S., lawyer; b. N.Y.C., Apr. 22, 1952; s. Milton Lipton and Elaine (Grossman) Stein; m. Beverly Ann Vanden Eynden, July 19, 1980; 1 child, Adam Seth. BA, Colby Coll., 1974; JD, Boston Coll., 1978. Bar: Mass. 1978, N.Y. 1979, Ohio 1984, U.S. Supreme Ct. 1984. Assoc. Norman J. Landau, N.Y.C., 1978-80; staff atty. Hamilton County Ct. Appeals, Cin., 1980-81; v.p. Manley, Burke & Fischer, Cin., 1981—, also bd. dirs. Mem. ABA, Ohio Bar Assn., Cin. Bar Assn., Assn. Trial Lawyers Am. Democrat. Jewish. Civil rights, Local government, Personal injury. Home: 1628 Elkton Pl Cincinnati OH 45224 Office: Manley Burke & Fischer 4100 Carew Tower Cincinnati OH 45202

LIPTON, FREDERICK STEVEN, lawyer; b. Harrisburg, Pa., Oct. 30, 1946; s. Ira Lipton and Rachel (Yarowsky) Ratowsky; m. Lillian B. Gaskin, Oct. 17, 1976; children: Alissa, Eric. BA, U. Pa., 1968; JD, U. Balt., 1974. Bar: Pa. 1974, D.C. 1975. Assoc. Perito, Duerk & Carlson, Washington, 1974-75; staff atty. office of gen. counsel Nat. Credit Union Adminstrn., Washington, 1975-82; sole practice Washington, 1982—. Mem. ABA, D.C. Bar Assn. Jewish. Administrative and regulatory, Banking, General corporate. Home and Office: 1325 18th St NW #408 Washington DC 20036

LIPTON, MARK DANIEL, lawyer; b. Chgo., Feb. 25, 1947; s. Samuel David and Annetta (Feld) L.; m. Delores Cole, Sept. 13, 1970; 1 child, Joshua Cole. BA, Knox Coll., 1968; JD, Northwestern U., 1975. Bar: Ill. 1975, U.S. Dist. Ct. (cen. dist.) Ill. 76, U.S. Ct. Appeals (7th cir.) 1979. Asst. state's atty. Champaign County State's Attys. Office, Urbana, Ill., 1975-82; from assoc. to ptnr. Meyer, Capel, Hirschfeld, Muncy, Jahn & Aldeen, P.C., Champaign, Ill., 1982—. Served with U.S. Army 1968-71, Vietnam. Mem. Ill. Bar Assn., Champaign County Bar Assn., Assn. Trial Lawyers Am., Ill. Trial Lawyers Assn. Lodge: Kiwanis (sec. Champaign 1983—). Avocations: hiking, canoeing, bowling. State civil litigation, Personal injury, Federal civil litigation. Home: 712 W University Ave Champaign IL 61820 Office: Meyer Capel Hirschfeld Muncy Jahn & Aldeen PC 306 W Church St Champaign IL 61820-0577

LIPTON, MARTIN, lawyer; b. N.J., June 22, 1931; s. Samuel D. and Fannie L.; m. Susan Lytle, Feb. 17, 1982; children: James, Margaret, Katherine, Samantha. B.S. in Econs., U. Pa., 1952; LL.B., NYU, 1955. Bar: N.Y. 1956. Ptnr. Wachtell Lipton Rosen & Katz, N.Y.C., 1965—. Office: Wachtell Lipton Rosen & Katz 299 Park Ave New York NY 10171

LIPTON, ROBERT S., lawyer; b. Malone, N.Y., Apr. 19, 1942; s. Robert Irwin and Marcia Naomi (Buff) L.; m. Gail Beth Lipton, Jan. 10, 1965; children: Jason H., Danna Marci. BS in Aero. and Astro. Engring., U. Mich., 1964; postgrad., U. Wash., 1965-66; JD, Temple U., 1972. Bar: U.S. Patent & Trademark Office 1970, Pa. 1972, U.S. Dist. Ct. (ea. dist.) Pa. 1973, U.S. Ct. Appeals (fed. cir.) 1982. Wind tunnel test engr. The Boeing Co., Seattle, 1965-67; patent adminstr. The Boeing Co., Phila., 1967-70, patent agt., 1970-72, patent atty., 1972-75; sole practice Media, Pa., 1975-84, Lipton & Famiglio, Media, 1984—; bd. dirs. Am. Heritage Fund Inc., Cupertino, Calif., Industry Fund Am., Cupertino, Basic Growth Fund Inc., Great Neck, N.Y., Transwestern Mut., Cupertino, Investment Indicators, Cupertino. Trustee, v.p. Temple Shalom, Broomall, Pa., 1973; trustee Workman's Circle Home, Media, 1984. Mem. ABA, Pa. Bar Assn., Del. County Bar Assn., Phila. Patent Laws Assn., Am. Intellectual Property Law Assn., Am. Helicopter Soc. Republican. Jewish. Club: Rose Valley Folk. Avocation: flying light airplanes. Patent, Contracts commercial, Computer. Home: 37 Shady Hill Rd Moylan PA 19065 Office: Lipton & Famiglio 201 N Jackson St Media PA 19063-0546

LIPTON, ROBERT STEVEN, lawyer; b. N.Y.C., May 12, 1946; s. Max and Mildred (Goodman) L.; m. Stephanie F. Kass, Aug. 8, 1971. BA, NYU, 1967, JD, 1971. Bar: N.Y. 1972, U.S. Ct. Appeals (2d cir.) 1972, U.S. Dist. Ct. (so. dist.) N.Y. 1973, U.S. Supreme Ct. 1975. Assoc. Curtis, Mallet-Prevost, Colt & Mosle, N.Y.C., 1971-80, ptnr., 1980—. Editor NYU Law Rev., 1969-71. Mem. ABA, Fed. Bar Council, N.Y. State Bar Assn., Assn. of Bar of City of N.Y., Phi Beta Kappa. Club: India House (N.Y.C.). Federal civil litigation, State civil litigation, Bankruptcy. Office: Curtis Mallet-Prevost Colt & Mosle 101 Park Ave New York NY 10178

LIRA, DAVID M., lawyer; b. Flushing, N.Y., Aug. 26, 1954; s. Jesus David and Teresa (Astorga) L. BA, CUNY, Flushing, 1977; JD, Cath. U., 1981. Bar: N.Y. 1982, D.C. 1982. Staff atty. FTC, Washington, 1981-85; sole practice Garden City, N.Y., 1985—. Mem. ABA, Nassau County Bar Assn., Hispanic Nat. Bar Assn. Democrat. Antitrust, General practice. Office: 1001 Franklin Ave Suite 305 Garden City NY 11530

LIRETTE, DANNY JOSEPH, lawyer; b. Houma, La., Sept. 21, 1948; s. Alexander Jean and Ouida (Pellegrin) L.; m. Carolyn Roe, Dec. 12, 1981; children—Dana L., Lauren E., Aimee C. B.S. in Polit. Sci., La. State U., 1970, J.D., 1974. Bar: La. 1974, U.S. Dist. Ct. (ea. dist.) La. 1974, U.S. Ct. Appeals (5th cir.) 1974. Ptnr. St. Martin & Lirette, Houma, 1974-79; sole practice, Houma, 1979-83; ptnr. St. Martin, Lirette & Gaubert, Houma, 1983—. Mem. La. Trial Lawyers Assn. (gov. 1979-80, 84-85), ABA, La. Bar Assn., Order of Coif, Phi Kappa Phi. Democrat. Roman Catholic. Admiralty, Personal injury. Home: 301 Hollygrove Blvd Houma LA 70360 Office: St Martin Lirette & Gaubert 3373 Little Bayou Black Rd Houma LA 70360

LISCH, HOWARD, accountant, tax lawyer; b. N.Y.C., Dec. 30, 1950; s. Simon and Edith (Secks) L.; m. Audrey Robin Ginsberg, 1973; children—Sari Victoria, Melissa Dawn, Jeremy Harold. B.S., NYU, 1972; J.D., Bklyn. Law Sch., 1975. CPA, Conn., N.J., N.Y. Tax acct. Arthur Andersen & Co., N.Y.C., 1975-77; tax supr. Coopers & Lybrand, Stamford, Conn., 1977-79; internat. tax mgr. Pitney Bowes, Stamford, 1979-80; tax mgr. Deloitte, Haskins & Sells, N.Y.C., 1980-82; chief fin. officer Campus Entertainment Network, N.Y.C., 1982-83, Black Tie Network, N.Y.C., 1982-83; tax mgr. Schachter & Co., White Plains, N.Y., dir. tax services Sobel & Co., Roseland, N.J., 1983-85; tax mgr. Rosenberg, Leffler & Zach, N.Y.C., 1985-86; pvt. practice acctg., N.Y.C., 1986—. Active Freehold Twp. Transp. Bd. Mem. Am. Arbitration Assn. (arbitrator), ABA, Am. Inst. CPA's, N.J. Soc. CPA's, N.Y. Soc. CPA's. Republican. Jewish. Corporate taxation, Personal income taxation, State and local taxation. Office: 299 Broadway New York NY 10007 Address: 225 W 34th St Suite 806 New York NY 10001

LISHER, JAMES RICHARD, lawyer; b. Aug. 28, 1947; s. Leonard B. and Mary Jane (Rafferty) L.; m. Martha Gettelfinger, June 16, 1973; children—Jennifer, James Richard II. A.B., Ind. U., 1969, J.D., 1975. Bar: Ind. 1975, U.S. Dist. Ct. (so. dist.) Ind. 1975. Assoc. Rafferty & Wood, Shelbyville, Ind., 1976, Rafferty & Lisher, Shelbyville, 1976-77; dep. prosecutor Shelby County Prosecutor's Office, Shelbyville, 1976-78; ptnr. Yeager & Lisher, Shelbyville, 1977—; pros. atty. Shelby County, Shelbyville, 1983—. Speaker, faculty advisor Ind. Pros. Sch., 1986. Editor: (seminar manual) Traffic Case Defenses, 1982. Bd. dirs. Girls Club of Shelbyville, 1979-84, Bears of Blue River Festival, Shelbyville, 1982—. Recipient Citation of Merit, Young Lawyers Assn. Mem. State Bar Assn. (bd. dirs.), Ind. State Bar Assn. (bd. dirs. young lawyer sect 1979-83), Shelby County Bar Assn. (sec./treas. 1986, v.p. 1987), Ind. Pros. Attys. Assn. (bd. dirs. 1985-86, sec./treas. 1987). Democrat. Lodges: Masons, Elks, Lions. General practice, Probate, Criminal. Home: 48 W Mechanic St Shelbyville IN 46176 Office: Yeager & Lisher Law Firm 406 S Harrison St Shelbyville IN 46176

LISHER, JOHN LEONARD, lawyer; b. Indpls., Sept. 19, 1950; s. Leonard Boyd and Mary Jane (Rafferty) L.; m. Mary Katherine Sturmon, Aug. 17, 1974. B.A. with honors in History, Ind. U., 1975, J.D., 1975. Bar: Ind. 1975. Dep. atty. gen. State of Ind., Indpls., 1975-78; asst. corp. counsel City of Indpls., 1978-81; assoc. Osborn & Hiner, Indpls., 1981-86; ptnr. Osborn, Hiner & Lisher, 1986—. Vol. Mayflower Clasic, Indpls., 1981—; asst. vol. coordinator Marion County Rep. Com., Indpls., 1979-80; vol. com. to reelect Theodore Sendak, Indpls., 1976—, Don Bogard for Atty. Gen., Indpls., 1980, Steve Goldsmith for Prosecutor, Indpls., 1979, 83, Sheila Suess for Congress, Indpls., 1980. Recipient Outstanding Young Man of Am. award Jaycees, 1979, 85, Indpls. Jaycees, 1980. Mem. ABA, Ind. Bar Assn., Indpls. Bar Assn. (membership com.), Assn. Trial Lawyers Am., Ind. U. Alumni Assn., Hoosier Alumni Assn. (charter, founder, pres.), Ind. Trial Lawyers Assn., Ind. Def. Lawyers Assn., Ind. U. Coll. Arts and Scis. (bd. dirs. 1983—, pres. 1986-87), Wabash Valley Alumni Assn. (charter), Founders Club, Presidents Club, Phi Beta Kappa, Eta Sigma Phi, Phi Eta Sigma, Delta Xi Alumni Assn. (charter, v.p., sec., Delta Xi chpt. Outstanding Alumnus award 1975, 76, 79, 83), Delta Xi Housing Corp. (pres.), Pi Kappa Alpha (midwest regional pres. 1977-86, parliamentarian nat. conv. 1982, del. convs. 1978-80, 82, 84, 86, trustee Meml. Found. 1986—). Presbyterian. Avocations: reading; golf; jogging; Roman coin collecting. State civil litigation, Insurance, Personal injury. Home: 7919 Buckskin Dr Indianapolis IN 46250 Office: Osborn Hiner & Lisher 8330 Woodfield Crossing Blvd Suite 380 Indianapolis IN 46240

LISKO, ROY KENNETH, lawyer; b. McKees Rocks, Pa., Sept. 27, 1950; s. Adam and Stephanie (Mycka) L.; m. Mary Louise Monaghan, July 21, 1984. BA, Pa. State U., 1972; JD, Capital U., 1978. Bar: Ohio 1978, U.S. Dist. Ct. (no and so. dists.) Ohio 1978, Pa. 1979, U.S. Dist. Ct. (ea. dist.) Pa. 1979, U.S. Ct. Appeals (3d cir.) 1979, U.S. Dist. Ct. (mid. dist.) Pa. 1986. Police officer State (Pa.) Coll. Police, 1973-75; asst. atty. gen. Ohio Atty. Gen.'s Office, Columbus, 1978-79; asst. dist. atty. Centre County, Bellefonte, Pa., 1979-81; assoc. Corneal, Mason & Lucas, State Coll., Pa., 1981-82; ptnr. Delafield, Lisko & McGee, State Coll., 1982—; instr. Pa. State U., Univ. Park, 1982—. Chmn. Centre County Reps., 1984-86. Mem. Pa. Bar Assn., Centre County Bar Assn., Assn. Trial Lawyers Am., Pa. Trial Lawyers Assn. Republican. Avocation: sports. Criminal, Personal injury, State civil litigation. Office: Delafield Lisko & McGee 204 Calder Way Suite 301 State College PA 16801

LISMAN, BERNARD, lawyer; b. N.Y.C., July 21, 1918; s. Samuel and Sarah (Cohen) L.; m. Natalie Kling, June 7, 1942. PhB, U. Vt., 1939; LLB, Harvard U., 1942. Bar: Vt. 1942, U.S. Dist. Ct. Vt. 1948, U.S. Ct. Appeals (2d cir.) 1955, U.S. Supreme Ct. 1964. Ptnr. Lisman & Lisman, Burlington, Vt., 1946—; trustee Vt. Law Sch., 1976—; judge Chittenden (Vt.) Mcpl. Ct., 1949-51; mem. Bd. Aldermen, City of Burlington, 1956-58; mem. Vt. Rep. State Com., 1956-60. Served to 1st lt. U.S. Army, 1942-46. Recipient Disting. Service award U. Vt., Burlington, 1984; winner Ames Moot Ct. Competition, Harvard Law Sch., 1942. Fellow Internat. Acad. Trial Lawyers (bd. dirs. 1985—); mem. ABA, Vt Bar Assn., Am. Trial Lawyers Assn., Am. Judicature Soc., Phi Beta Kappa. Jewish. Clubs: Ethan Allen, Burlington Country. Lodges: Elks, Masons, Shriners. State civil litigation, Personal injury, Probate. Home: 205 Summit St Burlington VT 05401 Office: PO Box 728 Burlington VT 05402

LISS, JEFFREY GLENN, lawyer; b. Chgo., Apr. 30, 1943; s. Ben and Clara Liss; m. Patricia E. Allison, June 12, 1971; children: Barbara, Debra. AB, Brown U., 1965; JD, Harvard U., 1968; LLM in Taxation, DePaul U., 1981. Bar: Ill. 1968, U.S. Supreme Ct. 1978, U.S. Tax Ct. 1984. Sole practice Chgo., 1968—. Contbr. articles to profl. jours. Mem. ABA, Ill. Bar Assn. (assembly 1978-84, 85—, resolutions and drafting com. 1981-84, council real estate sect. 1980-85, chmn. 1985-86), Chgo. Bar Assn. (real property law com. 1973—, fed. tax com. 1981—, devel. of law com. 1981—, vice chmn. 1986—), Brown U. Alumni Assn. (bd. dirs. 1977-79), Harvard U. Law Sch. Soc. Ill. Clubs: Brown U. (schs. chmn. 1970-84, pres. 1973-75), Harvard, Standard (civic affairs com. 1978-80) (Chgo.). General corporate, Real property, Estate planning. Office: 115 S LaSalle St Suite 2780 Chicago IL 60603

LIST, DAVID PATTON, lawyer; b. Belvidere, Ill., Feb. 4, 1920; s. Raymond Ford and Marguerite (Patton) L.; m. Patricia Porter, Jan. 7, 1949 (dec. 1978); children—John, Victoria, David Patton; m. Annette Kahlmorgan, 1979. A.B., Dartmouth Coll., 1942; LL.B., Harvard U., 1948. Bar: Ill. 1948. Since practiced in Chgo.; partner firm Sidley & Austin (and predecessors), 1955-85, of counsel, 1985—. Served with USAAF, 1942-45. Fellow Am. Coll. Trial Lawyers; mem. Am. Bar Assn., Ill. Bar Assn., Chgo. Bar Assn., Legal Club Chgo., Law Club Chgo. Republican. Episcopalian. Clubs: Westmoreland Country, U. Chgo. Federal civil litigation, State civil litigation. Address: 1 First Nat Plaza Chicago IL 60603

LISTER, CHARLES, lawyer; b. Columbus, Ind., June 18, 1938; s. Edward B. and Elvera A. (Hulse) L.; m. Sara E. Ball, June 23, 1961; children: Penelope, Jennifer. AB, Harvard U., 1960; MA, Oxford U., Eng., 1962, B in Civil Law, 1963; M in Civil Law, George Washington U., 1965. Bar: D.C. 1965, U.S. Ct. Appeals (2d, 3d, 6th, 8th and D.C. cirs.), U.S. Supreme Ct. Law clk. to justice John M. Harlan U.S. Supreme Ct., Washington, 1966-68; assoc. prof. law Yale U., New Haven, Conn., 1968-70; ptnr. Covington & Burling, Washington, 1970—; vis. lectr. U. Va., Charlottesville; cons. to state and fed. agys., 1969-78. Contbr. articles on constl. law and privacy to profl. jours. Served to capt. USAF, 1960-68. Rhodes scholar, 1960; recipient J.K. Lasser Prize, 1965. Mem. Lawyers Com. Human Rights (del. to rev. adminstrn. of justice in Pakistan 1985, 87). Federal civil litigation, State civil litigation, Administrative and regulatory. Office: Covington & Burling 1201 Pennsylvania Ave NW Washington DC 20044 Home: 3215 Newark St NW Washington DC 20008

LISTON, PAUL SPERRY, lawyer; b. N.Y.C., Nov. 13, 1939; s. Edward Paul and Emily (Sperry) L.; m. Linda Hamel, Feb. 24, 1962; 1 child, Jolie Lucia. BS, U. Fla., 1963; JD, Emory U., 1967. Bar: Ga. 1967. Asst. legis. counsel State of Ga., 1967-70; gen. counsel Ga. Senate Judiciary, 1971-72; ptnr. Liston & Schiller, Altanta, 1972—. Avocation: race horse and polo pony breeding. Federal civil litigation, Family and matrimonial, General practice. Home: 215 Valley Wood Rd Tyrone GA 30290 Office: Liston & Schiller 555 Candler Bldg Atlanta GA 30303-1810

LITMAN, JACK THEODORE, lawyer; b. N.Y.C., July 26, 1943; s. Charles Louis and Sarah G. (Hornblas) L.; m. Helena Dunica, Aug. 25, 1968; children: Sacha F., Benjamin S. BA, Cornell U., 1964; LLB, Harvard U., 1967; diplômé, Inst. of Criminology, Paris, 1968. Bar: N.Y. 1968, U.S. Dist. Ct. (so. and ea. dists.) N.Y. 1973, U.S. Ct. Appeals (2d cir.) 1973, U.S. Supreme Ct. 1975. Asst. dist. atty. N.Y. County, N.Y.C., 1968-74; sr. ptnr. Litman, Asche, Lupkin & Gioiella, N.Y.C., 1974—; adj. prof. law NYU, N.Y.C., 1970—. Editor: Criminal Trial Advocacy, 1975; contbr. articles to profl. jours. Fulbright scholar, 1967-68. Mem. N.Y. State Bar Assn. (mem. exec. com. criminal justice sect. 1980—, named Outstanding Practitioner of Yr. 1986), Assn. of Bar of City of N.Y., N.Y. Criminal Bar Assn. (pres. 1986—), Nat. Assn. Criminal Def. Lawyers. Democrat. Jewish. Avocations: chess, movies, sports, number theory. Criminal, Federal civil litigation, State civil litigation. Office: Litman Asche Lupkin & Gioiella 45 Broadway 2d fl New York NY 10006

LITMAN, ROSLYN MARGOLIS, lawyer, educator; b. N.Y.C., Sept. 30, 1928; d. Harry and Dorothy (Perlow) Margolis; m. S. David Litman, Nov. 22, 1950; children: Jessica, Hannah, Harry. B.A., U. Pitts., 1949, J.D., 1952. Bar: Pa. 1952. Practiced in Pitts. 1952—; partner firm Litman, Litman

Harris Brown & Watzman, P.A., 1952—; adj. prof. U. Pitts. Law Sch., 1958—; permanent del. Conf. U.S. Circuit Ct. Appeals for 3d Circuit; mem. Allegheny County Judiciary Com. Chmn., Pitts. Pub. Parking Authority, 1970-74; mem. curriculum com Pa. Bar Inst., 1986—; bd. dirs. Pa. Bar Inst. 1972-82. Mem. ABA (del., litigation sect., anti-trust health care com.), ACLU (nat. bd. dirs.), Pa. Bar Assn. (bd. govs. 1976-79), Allegheny County Bar Assn. (bd. govs. 1972-74, pres. 1975), Allegheny County Acad. Trial Lawyers (charter), ACLU of Western Pa. (former counsel, bd. dirs.). General practice, Federal civil litigation, State civil litigation. Home: 1047 Negley Ave S Pittsburgh PA 15217 Office: 1701 Grant Bldg Pittsburgh PA 15219

LITMANS, MURRAY IAN, lawyer; b. Pitts., May 21, 1937; s. Lazar M. and Brenda (Goldenhaar) L.; m. Rigmor Berglund, July 8, 1967; children—Ian Gregory, Brian Alexander. B.A., Amherst Coll., 1959; J.D., U. Mich., 1962; cert. Hague (Netherlands) Acad. Internat. Law, 1961; cert. Faculte de droit, U. Paris, 1963. Bar: Mich. 1962, N.Y. 1965, U.S. Ct. Appeals (D.C. cir.) 1968, U.S. Supreme Ct. 1968, Pa. 1970. Assoc. firm Nixon, Mudge, Rose, Guthrie & Alexander, N.Y.C., 1964-65; internat. legal advisor U.S. Dept. Def., Washington, 1965-69; sole practice, Pitts., 1970-72, 81-86; ptnr. Campbell, Thomas & Burke, Pitts., 1973-79, Eckert, Seamans, Cherin & Mellott, Pitts., 1986—; spl. ptnr. Grogan, Graffan, McGinley & Solomon, Pitts., 1979-80; dir. various corps. Bd. Animal Rescue League of Western Pa., 1970—. Fulbright scholar 1962. Mem. Assn. Bar City of N.Y., Am. Soc. Internat. Law, ABA, Allegheny County Bar Assn., Internat. Bar Assn. Republican. Clubs: University (Pitts.), Fox Chapel Racquet. Author: The International Lump-Sum Settlements of the United States, 1962. General corporate, Private international, Securities. Office: Eckert Seamans Cherin & Mellott US Steel Bldg 42d Floor Pittsburgh PA 15219

LITTEN, DONALD DOUGLAS, lawyer; b. New Market, Va., Mar. 24, 1930; s. Raye Zirkle and Georgia Grace (Swartz) L.; m. Frances Ann Minor, Dec. 23, 1949; children—Ann Litten Menefee, Donald D., Jonathan J. Ed. James Madison U. Bar: Va. 1957, U.S. Dist. Ct. (we. dist.) Va. 1958, Va. Supreme Ct. 1958. Assoc., George D. Conrad, Harrisonburg, Va., 1957-61; jr. ptnr. Conrad and Litten, Harrisonburg, 1961-68; ptnr. Conrad, Litten and Sipe, Harrisonburg, 1968-80; mng. ptnr. Litten, Sipe and Miller, Harrisonburg, 1980—; dir. Rockingham Mut. Ins. Co., Valley Nat. Bank, Rockingham Meml. Hosp., 1972-84, Hokeli Ltd. Active Massanutten Property Owners Assn. Inc.; bd. visitors James Madison U., 1980-83. Served with USN, 1947-49. Recipient Disting. Service award Va. Jaycees, 1962. Mem. ABA, Assn. Trial Lawyers, Nat. Inst. Mcpl. Law Officers. General corporate, Local government, Federal civil litigation. Home: 101 McGuffin Pl Bridgewater VA 22812 Office: PO Box 712 Harrisonburg VA 22801

LITTENEKER, EDWIN LEE, lawyer; b. Palo Alto, Calif., Dec. 1, 1951; s. Paul Edwin and Ada (Guinn) L.; m. Cindy Rae Dillehay, Mar. 21, 1980; children: Rachel Guinn, Edwin Joseph. BA in Polit. Sci., U. Idaho, 1974, JD, 1978. Bar: Idaho 1979, U.S. Dist. Ct. Idaho 1979. Ptnr. Roos & Litteneker, Boise, Idaho, 1979-80; atty. Idaho St. Home Builders, Boise, 1980-81, exec. dir., 1981-82; asst. atty. City of Lewiston, Idaho, 1982-83, atty., 1983—; adj. faculty Lewis Clark State Coll., Lewiston, 1984—; pres. Idaho Arbitration Services Inc., Lewiston, 1986—. Named one of Outstanding Young Men Am., 1984. Avocations: gardening, civil war history. Local government. Home: 1302 14th Ave Lewiston ID 83501 Office: City of Lewiston 1111 F St Lewiston ID 83501

LITTLE, F. A., JR., U.S. district judge; b. 1936; m. Gail Little; children—Sophie, Sabrina. B.A., Tulane, 1958, LL.B., 1961. Assoc. Chaffe, McCall, Phillips, Toler & Sarpy, New Orleans, 1961-65; assoc. Gold, Little, Simon, Weems & Bruser, Alexandria, La., 1965-69; ptnr. Gold, Little, Simon, Weems & Bruser, 1968-84; judge U.S. Dist. Ct. for Western La., Alexandria, 1984—. Office: Box 1031 Alexandria LA 71309

LITTLE, HAMPTON STENNIS, JR., lawyer; b. Meridian, Miss., Apr. 24, 1934; s. Hampton Stennis and Kathryn (Dale) L.; m. Susan Pilger July 23, 1965 (div.); children: Kathryn Ann, Michael Stennis. BS, Miss. State U., 1956; JD, U. Miss., 1964; LLM in Taxation, Georgetown U., 1967. Bar: Miss. 1964, Tenn. 1968, U.S. Supreme Ct. 1968, U.S. Tax Ct. 1968. Trial atty. tax div. U.S. Dept. Justice, Washington, 1964-68; assoc. Boult, Hunt, Cummings, & Conners, Nashville, 1968-70; pvt. practice, Nashville, 1970-80; ptnr. King, Ballow & Little, Nashville, 1980-84, of counsel, 1984-86; pres. Stennis Little, P.C., Nashville, 1986—; lectr. Vanderbilt U. Sch. Law, 1970-83. Served to lt. comdr. USNR, 1956-59. Mem. ABA, Miss. State Bar Assn., Nashville Bar Assn. Presbyterian. Contbr. numerous articles to profl. jours. Corporate taxation, Estate taxation, Pension, profit-sharing, and employee benefits. Office: 1900 First American Ctr Box 80 Nashville TN 37238

LITTLE, JAN NIELSEN, lawyer; b. Oakland, Calif., Jan. 20, 1958; d. Jack Harry and Patricia Ann (Holzknecht) N.; m. Rory K. Little (Mar. 19, 1983). AB, U. Calif., Berkeley, 1978; JD, Yale U., 1981. Bar: Calif. 1981, D.C. 1984. Law clk. to judge U.S. Dist. Ct. (no. dist.) Calif., San Francisco, 1981-82; trial atty. Dept. Justice, Washington, 1982-86; assoc. Keker & Brockett, San Francisco, 1986—. Recipient Spl. Commendation award Dept. Justice, Washington, 1984. Mem. ABA, Calif. Bar Assn. D.C. Bar Assn. Criminal. Home: 3853 22d St San Francisco CA 94114 Office: Keker & Brockett 807 Montgomery St San Francisco CA 94133

LITTLE, JOE HOLLIS, JR., lawyer; b. Mobile, Ala., Jan. 19, 1943; s. Joe Hollis Sr. and Dorothy (Adams) L.; m. Lynn Meighan, June 7, 1968; children: Joe H. III, John M. BS, Washington and Lee U., 1966; JD, U. Ala., 1968. Bar: Ala. 1968. Assoc., then ptnr. Gaillard, Little, Hume & Sullivan and predecessor firms, Mobile, 1968-85; sole practice Mobile, 1986—; gen. counsel Bd. Water and Sewer Commrs. City of Mobile, Jr. League Mobile; pres. McGowin Investment Co., Ala. Realty Co., Inc., L. C. Oil & Gas Corp. Bd. dirs. Met. YMCA of Mobile; chmn., trustee United Meth. Children's Home; bd. dirs., mem. fin. com. Dauphin Way United Meth. Ch., Mobile. Served with USAR, 1968-74. Mem. ABA, Mobile Bar Assn., Ala. Def. Lawyers Assn., Mobile Area C. of C., Mobile County Wildlife and Conservation Assn., South Ala. Field Trial Assn., Phi Delta Phi. Clubs: Athelstan, Mobile Touchdown, Mobile Country. Lodge: Kiwanis. Avocations: fishing, handball, skiing, tennis, scuba diving. Condemnation, General corporate, Estate planning. Home: 1802 S Indian Creek Dr Mobile AL 36607 Office: PO Box 421 Mobile AL 36601

LITTLE, MICHAEL FREDERICK, lawyer; b. New Orleans, Oct. 3, 1943; s. John Pat and Claire (Dolph) L.; m. Elizabeth J. Sherman; children: Michael F. Jr., Graham P. BA in History, Tulane U., 1966, JD, 1968. Bar: La. 1968. Assoc. Guste, Barnett & Little, New Orleans, 1968-70; from assoc. to ptnr. Little, Schwartz & Dussom, New Orleans, 1970-76; ptnr. Baldwin & Haspel, New Orleans, 1976-82, Hanemann & Little, New Orleans, 1982-83; sole practice New Orleans, 1983—; officer, bd. dirs. World Trade Ctr. New Orleans. Bd. dirs. Cancer Assn. Greater New Orleans, Internat. House New Orleans. Mem. ABA, La. Bar Assn., Fed. Bar Assn., New Orleans Bar Assn., Order of Coif. General corporate, Federal civil litigation. Home: #1 Honeysuckle Ln Covington LA 70433 Office: 3421 N Causeway Blvd Suite 900 Metairie LA 70002

LITTLE, WILLIAM SCOTT, lawyer; b. Balt., July 7, 1941; s. Walter Scott and Florence Eunice (Wise) L.; m. Betsy Muehlenweg, Apr. 5, 1986; children: Scott, Kathleen, Robert, Stephen, James. BS, Loyola U., 1963; JD, U. Md., 1966. Bar: Md. 1966, U.S. Dist. Ct. Md. 1969, U.S. Ct. Appelas (4th cir.) 1969, U.S. Supreme Ct. 1970. Assoc. Stark & Little, Balt., 1971-73, ptnr., 1973—; bd. dirs. Mid-Atlantic Credit Corp., Balt. Served to lt. col. USAR, 1967—. Clark Meml. scholar U. Md., 1965. Mem. ABA, Fed. Bar Assn., Md. Bar Assn. (alternate means of settling disputes com.), Balt. Bar Assn. (atty. grievance com., fee arbitration com.), Am. Arbitration Assn., Civil Affairs Assn., Res. Officers Assn. Federal civil litigation, State civil litigation, Consumer commercial. Home: 1285 William St Baltimore MD 21230

LITTLEFIELD, ROY EVERETT, III, assn. exec., legal educator; b. Nashua, N.H., Dec. 6, 1952; s. Roy Everett and Mary Ann (Prestipino) L.; m. Sharon Lynn Mahoney, Aug. 17, 1974; 1 dau., Leah Marie. B.A., Dickinson Coll., 1975; M.A., Catholic U. Am., 1976, Ph.D., 1979. Aide, U.S. Senator Thomas McIntyre, Democrat, N.H., 1975-78, Nordy Hoffman, U.S. Senate Sergeant-at-arms, 1979; dir. govt. relations Nat. Tire Dealers and Retreaders Assn., Washington, 1979-84; exec. dir. Service Sta. and Automotive Repair Assn., 1984—; cons. Am. Retreaders Assn., 1984—; mem. faculty Catholic U. Am., Washington, 1979—. Mem. Nat. Democratic Club, 1978—. Mem. Am. Soc. Legal History, Am. Retail Fedn., Small Bus. Legis. Council, Hwy. Users Fedn. (v.p.), Md. Soc. Assn. Execs. (bd. dirs.), N.H. Hist. Soc., C. of C., Phi Alpha Theta. Roman Catholic. Club: KC (Milford, N.H.). Author: William Randolph Hearst: His Role in American Progressivism, 1980; The Economic Recovery Act, 1982; The Surface Transportation Assistance Act; 1984; contbr. numerous articles to legal jours. Administrative and regulatory, Legal history, Legislative. Home: 15900 Pinecroft Ln Bowie MD 20716 Office: 1250 Eye St Suite 400 Washington DC 20005

LITTLETON, ARTHUR RICHARD, lawyer; b. Phila., May 29, 1926; s. Arthur and Jean Russell (Newbourg) L.; m. Mary E. Minster, June 19, 1948; children: Lucinda E., David G., Susan H. Student, Swarthmore Coll., 1944-45; B.A., U. Pa., 1948, LL.B., 1951. Bar: Pa. 1952. Asst. U.S. atty. Phila., 1955-57; ptnr. Morgan Lewis & Bockius, Phila., 1961-85, Hoyle Morris & Kerr, 1985—. Chmn. client's security fund Pa. Supreme Ct., 1982—; chmn. govt. study commn. Tredyffrin Twp., Chester County, Pa., 1972; elections judge Paoli-Easttown Sch. Authority, 1977—; bd. dirs. Haverford Sch., Pa., 1962-75. Served to lt. comdr. USNR, 1944-47, 52-54, Korea. Mem. ABA (legal asst. com. 1981—), Pa. Bar Assn., Phila. Bar Assn. (bd. govs. 1982-85), Motor Carrier Lawyers Assn. (chair ethics com. 1965-78 Spl. Achievement award). Republican. Presbyterian. Clubs: Union League (Phila.) (dir. 1982-86, v.p. 1987); Merion Cricket (Haverford). Office: Hoyle Morris & Kerr 1424 Chestnut St Philadelphia PA 19102

LITTMAN, DAVID BERNARD, lawyer; b. Plainfield, N.J., Oct. 16, 1949; s. Alexander and Muriel Roslyn (Block) L.; m. Deborah Joy Fields, Nov. 9, 1980; 1 child, Alexandra Ellen Pauline. AB, Lafayette Coll., 1970; JD, Rutgers U., 1973. Bar: N.J. 1974, U.S. Dist. Ct. N.J. 1974, U.S. Supreme Ct. 1983. Assoc. Winetsky & Winetsky, Linden, N.J., 1973-76; sole practice Linden, 1976—. Mem. ABA, N.J. Bar Assn., Union County Bar Assn., Linden Bar Assn. (pres. 1977-80), N.J. Trial Lawyers. Democrat. Jewish. Lodge: Masons (sec. Highland Park 1979—, treas. 1987—). General practice, Criminal, Family and matrimonial. Home: 1557 Ashbrook Dr Scotch Plains NJ 07076 Office: 129 N Wood Ave Linden NJ 07036

LITVIN, DAVID ANTHONY, lawyer, lobbyist; b. Balt., Nov. 7, 1946; s. Gilbert and Jeanne (Sullivan) L.; m. Diann Kay Rives, Jan. 13, 1979. BMetE, Drexel U., 1969; JD, George Washington U., 1973. Bar: D.C. 1976, Md. 1974, U.S. Supreme Ct. 1981. Atty. EPA, Washington, 1972-74; policy analyst U.S. Dept. Energy, Washington, 1974-79; lobbyist Kennecott Corp., Washington, 1979-81, Standard Oil Co., Washington, 1981—; asst. dir. fed. govt. affairs Standard Oil Co., Washington, 1985—. Mem. ABA, Sigma Alpha Mu, Phi Beta Kappa, Alpha Sigma Mu. Avocation: antiques. Legislative, Oil and gas, Environment. Office: Standard Oil Co 1001 22d St NW #600 Washington DC 20037

LITWIN, BURTON LAWRENCE, lawyer, theatrical producer; b. N.Y.C., Jan. 1, 1931; s. Samuel G. and Eleanor (Kos) L.; m. Dorothy Beth Lefkowitz, Nov. 18, 1956; children—Richard Seth, Robert Aron, Kenneth David. B.A., Washington and Lee U., 1951; LL.B., NYU, 1953. Bar: N.Y. 1954, U.S. Dist. Ct. (so. dist.) N.Y. 1958, U.S. Ct. Appeals (2d cir.). Assoc. Wilzin and Halperin, N.Y.C., 1956-64; ptnr. DaSilva and Litwin, N.Y.C., 1965; sole practice, N.Y.C., 1965-67; dir. bus. affairs Belwin-Mills Pub. Co., N.Y.C., 1967-74, v.p. and counsel, 1975-87; bd. dirs. Nat. Teaching Aids, Inc., Garden City Park, N.Y.; theatre producer Sophisticated Ladies, N.Y.C., 1981—, Poppy, London, 1982—, Stardust, N.Y.C., 1986—; pres., chief exec. officer Newcal Music Co., Newcal Properties and Prodns., Ltd., N.Y.C., 1986— . Pres., Temple Beth Abraham, Tarrytown, N.Y., 1982-83; bd. dirs. Creative Arts Rehab. Ctr., N.Y.C., 1983-84; mem. ASCAP Bd. Appeals, 1981-83, adv. com., 1985—. Served with U.S. Army, 1953-55. Recipient Tony award nomination League of N.Y. Theatres, 1982; annu. Image award NAACP, 1982. Mem. N.Y. State Bar Assn., ABA, Friars Club. Lodge: B'nai B'rith. Entertainment, Trademark and copyright. Home: 12 Crescent Lane Dobbs Ferry NY 10522

LIUZZO, ANTHONY L., economic educator; b. N.Y.C., June 17, 1947; s. Anthony S. and Anne M. (Caione) L.; m. Trudy Kule, June 12, 1971. BS, Fordham U., 1969; JD, St. John's U., Queens, N.Y., 1975; MBA, NYU, 1977, PhD, 1981. Bar: N.Y. 1976. Asst. prof. econs. and fin. Manhattan Coll., Bronx, N.Y., 1978—; expert witness, 1978—. Editor Scholarly Jour. Bus., 1983—; contbr. articles to profl. jours. Fellow Joseph Taggart, 1978-80. Mem. ABA, N.Y. State Bar Assn., Bronx County Bar Assn., Am. Econ. Assn. Avocations: music, electronics, sports, reading. Legal education, Law and economics. Home: 11 Whitfield Terr New Rochelle NY 10801 Office: Manhattan Coll Riverdale NY 10471

LIVAUDAIS, MARCEL, JR., federal judge; b. New Orleans, Mar. 3, 1925; m. Carol Black; children—Julie, Marc, Durel. B.A., Tulane U., 1945, J.D., 1949. Bar: La. Assoc. Boswell & Loeb, New Orleans, 1949-50, 52-56; ptnr. Boswell Loeb & Livaudais, New Orleans, 1956-60, Loeb & Livaudais, 1960-67, 71-77, Loeb Dillon & Livaudais, 1967-71; U.S. magistrate 1977-84; judge U.S. Dist. Ct. Eastern Dist. La., New Orleans, 1984—. Mem. Am. Judicature Soc. Office: US Courthouse 500 Camp St Room C-313 New Orleans LA 70130 *

LIVELY, PIERCE, federal judge; b. Louisville, Aug. 17, 1921; s. Henry Thad and Ruby Durrett (Keating) L.; m. Amelia Harrington, May 25, 1946; children: Susan, Katherine, Thad. A.B., Centre Coll., Ky., 1943; LL.B., U. Va., 1948. Bar: Ky. 1948. Individual practice law Danville, Ky., 1949-57; mem. firm Lively and Rodes, Danville, 1957-72; judge U.S. Ct. Appeals (6th cir.), Cin., 1972—, chief judge, 1983—; Mem. Ky. Commn. on Economy and Efficiency in Govt., 1963-65, Ky. Jud. Advisory Com., 1972. Trustee Centre Coll. Served with USNR, 1943-46. Mem. Am. Bar Assn., Am. Judicature Soc., Order of Coif, Raven Soc., Phi Beta Kappa, Omicron Delta Kappa. Presbyterian. Jurisprudence. Office: US Ct of Appeals PO Box 1226 Danville KY 40422 also: Room 626 US Courthouse Cincinnati OH 45202

LIVINGSTON, ANN CHAMBLISS, lawyer; b. Mpls., July 25, 1952; d. Johnston Redmond and Patricia A. L.; m. Leif M. Clark, Feb. 20, 1982. BA, Trinity U., San Antonio, 1974; JD, St. Mary's U., San Antonio, 1979. Bar: Tex. 1979, U.S. Ct. Appeals (5th cir.) 1981, U.S. Dist. Ct. (we. dist.) Tex. 1982. Briefing atty. Supreme Ct. of Tex., Austin, 1979-80; assoc. Groce, Locke & Hebdon, San Antonio, 1980-85, Gunn, Lee & Jackson, San Antonio, 1985—. Exec. editor St. Mary's U. Law Jour., 1978-79. Patent, Trademark and copyright. Home: 123 Montclair St San Antonio TX 78209 Office: Gunn Lee & Jackson 1650 Interfirst Plaza 300 Convent San Antonio TX 78205

LIVINGSTON, BRADFORD LEE, lawyer; b. Detroit, Apr. 15, 1954; s. L. Clayton and Helen Barbara (Grudzien) L.; m. Kathleen Ann Holuj, Mar. 9, 1980; 1 child, Clayton Thomas. BA, U. Mich., 1976, JD, 1979. Bar: Ill. 1979, U.S. Dist. Ct. (no. dist.) Ill. 1980, U.S. Dist. Ct. (ea. dist.) Wis. 1980, U.S. Ct. Appeals (7th cir.) 1983. Assoc. Seyfarth, Shaw, Fairweather & Geraldson, Chgo., 1979—. Mem. ABA (litigation and labor employment law sect.), Chgo. Bar Assn., Phi Delta Phi. Roman Catholic. Labor, Federal civil litigation, State civil litigation. Home: 9037 S Oakley Chicago IL 60620 Office: Seyfarth Shaw Fairweather Et Al 55 E Monroe Suite 4200 Chicago IL 60603

LIVINGSTON, EDWARD MICHAEL, lawyer; b. Gardner, Mass., Aug. 31, 1948; s. Elmer Harris and Pearl Alice (Gonyeo) L.; m. Dianne Mary Collette, Feb. 6, 1971; children: Erica Linda, Gregory Edward. BS in Mech. and Aerospace Engring., U. Mass., 1970; MBA, U. Wyo., 1974; JD, U. Miami, 1978. Bar: Fla. 1978, U.S. Dist. Ct. (mid. dist.) Fla. 1978, U.S. Ct. Appeals 1978. Assoc. Levine & Cohen, Orlando, Fla., 1979-80; ptnr. Livingston, Blau & Rutter, Orlando, 1980-81, Stamley, Lovett, Livingston & Whitmere, Orlando, 1981-86, Livingston & Whitmere, Winter Park, Fla., 1986—; probation counselor, Cheyenne, Wyo., 1972-75. V.p. Homeowners Assn., Orlando, 1979-81; coach Little League Baseball, Orlando, 1981. Served to maj. USAF, 1970—. Mem. ABA, Am. Intellectual Property Law Assn., Winter Park Jaycees, Beta Gamma Sigma, Omicron Delta Kappa. Democrat. Roman Catholic. Avocations: flying, all sports, golf. Patent, Trademark and copyright, General corporate. Office: Livingston & Whitmere 1455 W Fairbanks Ave Winter Park FL 32789

LIVINGSTON, JOHN L., lawyer; b. St. Mary's, Pa., Apr. 12, 1948; s. John and Helen Livingston; m. Carol A. Checinski; children: Christopher, Matthew. Student, St. Bonaventure U., 1966-68; BA, Duquesne U., 1970, JD, 1973. Bar: Pa., Colo., U.S. Dist. Ct. Colo., U.S. Dist. Ct. Pa. Dist. atty. State of Colo., Golden, 1976-78; assoc. Tinsley, Frantz, Fleming & Livingston, Lakewood, Colo., 1978-82; ptnr. Livingston & Norton, Lakewood, 1982—. Asst. editor Duquesne U. Law Rev., 1972. Den leader Boy Scouts Am., Lakewood, 1985, 86. Mem. Colo. Bar Assn. (chmn. subcom.), 1st Jud. Bar Assn. (chmn. continuing legal edn. 1985-86), Assn. Trial Lawyers Am., Colo. Trial Lawyers Assn. Avocations: golf, fishing, skiing. Personal injury, Family and matrimonial. Office: Livingston & Norton 143 Union Blvd #710 Lakewood CO 80228

LIVINGSTON, RICHARD B., lawyer; b. Newark, Feb. 22, 1946; s. Elias and Vivienne (Tractenberg) L.; m. Enid M., Dec. 5, 1975; children—Melissa, Michael, Robert. B.A., Upsala Coll., East Orange, N.J., 1967; J.D., So. Meth. U., 1970; M.B.A., Columbia U., 1972. Bar: Tex. 1970, N.J. 1971, N.Y. 1972, U.S. Supreme Ct. 1976. Sole practice, Livingston, N.J. Mem. Democratic County Com., 1978—. Served to 2d lt. C.E., AUS, 1970-72. Mem. ABA, N.J. Bar Assn., Am. Trial Lawyers Assn., Def. Research Inst. State civil litigation, General practice, Personal injury. Home: 30 Byron Rd Short Hills NJ 07078 Office: 155 S Livingston Ave Livingston NJ 07039

LIVSEY, ROBERT CALLISTER, lawyer; b. Salt Lake City, Aug. 7, 1936; s. Robert Frances and Rosezella Ann (Callister) L.; m. Renate Karla Guertler, Sept. 10, 1962; children: Scott, Rachel, Daniel, Benjamin. BS, U. Utah, 1962, JD, 1965; LLM, NYU, 1967. Bar: Utah 1965, Calif. 1967. Prof. Haile Selassie U., Addis Ababa, Ethiopia, 1965-66; spl. asst. to chief counsel IRS, Washington, 1977-79; assoc., then ptnr. Brobeck, Phleger & Harrison, San Francisco, 1967—; adj. prof. U. San Francisco Law Sch., 1970-77; mem. adv. com. IRS Dist. Dirs., 1986—. Research editor U. Utah Law Rev., 1964-65; editor Tax Law Rev., 1966-67; contbr. articles to profl. jours. Dist. bd. dirs. adv. com. IRS; pres. tax litigation San Francisco Club, 1986-87. Mem. State Bar Calif. (chmn. taxation sect. 1984-85), ABA (chmn. subcom. real estate syndications, 1981-84), San Francisco Bar Assn. (chmn. taxation sect. 1982), Am. Law Inst., Tax Litigation Club (pres. 1986—), Order of Coif, Beta Gamma Sigma. Democrat. Mem. Evangelical Covenant Ch. Club: Commonwealth (San Francisco). Personal income taxation, Corporate taxation. Home: 128 LaSalle Ave Piedmont CA 94610 Office: Brobeck Phleger & Harrison Spear St Tower San Francisco CA 94105

LLOYD, DAVID LIVINGSTONE, JR., lawyer; b. Butler, Pa., Aug. 28, 1952; s. David Livingstone and Jean Marie (Basher) L.; m. Dana L. Kadison, June 26, 1983; 1 child, John Gabriel. BS, AB, U. Pa., 1974, JD, 1977. Bar: N.Y. Assoc. Dewey, Ballantine, Bushby, Palmer & Wood, N.Y.C., 1977-85, ptnr., 1986—. General corporate, Securities, Municipal bonds. Office: Dewey Ballantine Bushby et al 140 Broadway New York NY 10005

LLOYD, JAMES HENDRIE, III, lawyer; b. Phila., Oct. 20, 1943; s. James Hendrie and Margaret Katherine (Koons) L.; m. Blakeslee Ann Benjamin, June 17, 1967; children—Meredith, William. A.B., Princeton U., 1965; M.B.A., U. Pa., 1967; J.D., U. Conn., 1973. Bar: Conn. 1973, U.S. Dist. Ct. Conn. 1973. Planner Capitol Region Planning Agy., Hartford, Conn., 1969-70; ptnr. Updike, Kelly & Spellacy, P.C., Hartford, 1973—. Editor-in-chief Conn. Law Rev., 1972-73. Mem. Democratic Town Com., Glastonbury, Conn., 1977—; chmn. Glastonbury Planning and Zoning Commn., 1985—. Served to 1st lt. U.S. Army, 1967-69, Vietnam. Decorated Bronze Star. Mem. Hartford County Bar Assn., Conn. Bar Assn., ABA, Am. Planning Assn. Congregationalist. Real property, General corporate, Municipal bonds. Home: 105 Farmcliff Dr Glastonbury CT 06033 Office: Updike Kelly & Spellacy PC One State St Hartford CT 06103

LLOYD, JAMES ROBERT (JIM), lawyer; b. Oklahoma City, Nov. 23, 1949; s. E. Leon and Juanita Fern (McGuire) L.; m. Nancy Louise Cofer, May 24, 1971; children—James R. (Buddy), Jamie Allison. B.S., Okla. State U., 1972; J.D., Tulsa U., 1975. Bar: Okla. 1975, U.S. Dist. Cts. (no. and ea. dists.) Tex. 1976. Contract atty. Texaco, Houston, 1975-76; corp. counsel, dir. LCS, Inc., Midland, Tex., 1979—. Author: The Third Trial, 1986. Active Tulsa Jaycees, 1977. Mem. Tulsa County Bar Assn. (chmn. speakers bur. 1978-80, fair booth com. 1978-80), Okla. Bar Assn. (named Outstanding Young Lawyer of State 1979), Tex. Bar Assn., Acad. Fla. Trial Lawyers, Tex. Trial Lawyers Assn., Calif. Trial Lawyers Assn., Colo. Trial Lawyers Assn., Kans. Trial Lawyers Assn., Wyo. Trial Lawyers Assn., Ct. Practice Inst. (diplomate), Assn. Trial Lawyers Am., Okla. Trial Lawyers Assn., Am. Acad. Forensic Scis. Democrat. Methodist. Personal injury, Federal civil litigation, State civil litigation. Home: 7305 E 83d Pl Tulsa OK 74133 Office: 23 W 4th St Skelly Bldg Room 707 Tulsa OK 74103

LLOYD, JOHN STODDARD, lawyer; b. Ebensburg, Pa., Aug. 25, 1914; s. Lewis and Bessie Alice (Stoddard) L.; m. Margaret Squatrito, Jan. 4, 1941. B.B.A. cum laude, U. Miami, 1950, J.D. magna cum laude, 1954. Bar: Fla. 1954. Asst. atty. gen. Fla., 1954, asst. state atty., 1955-56; mem. Boardman, Bolles, Davant & Lloyd, Miami, Fla., 1956-59; spl. counsel City of Miami, 1959-60, asst. city atty., 1960-73, city atty., 1973-76; of counsel Dubbin, Berkman, Garber, Bloom & Moriber, Miami, 1976—; lectr., panel mem. Nat. Inst. Mcpl. Law Officers Conv., 1972; cons. in field. Mem. Council Internat. Visitors, 1968-74. Served with USAAF, 1942-45; served to lt. col. USAFR, 1947-74. Decorated Air Medal, Bronze Arrowhead. Named Mobilization Augmentee of Year and Outstanding Reservist, USAFR, 1972; recipient resolutions of commendation, City of Miami, 1973, 74. Mem. ABA, Fla. Bar, Dade County Bar Assn., Res. Officers Assn. (pres. Coral Gables-Miami chpt. 1968-69), Am. Legion, VFW. Democrat. Roman Catholic. Clubs: KC. State civil litigation, Local government, Condemnation. Home and Office: 6880 Cartee Rd Miami FL 33158

LLOYD, LEONA LORETTA, lawyer; b. Detroit, Aug. 6, 1949; d. Leon Thomas and Naomi Mattie (Chisolm) L. BS, Wayne State U., 1971, JD, 1979. Bar: Mich. 1982. Speech, English tchr. Detroit Bd. Edn., 1971-75; instr. criminal justice Wayne State U., Detroit, 1981; sr. ptnr. Lloyd and Lloyd, Detroit, 1982—. Wayne State U. scholar, 1970, 75; recipient Kizzy Image award, 1985, Nat. Coalition of 100 Black Women Achievement award, 1986, Community Service award Wayne County exec. William Lucas, 1986, cert. merit U. Detroit Black Law Students Assn., 1986, Minority Bus. of Yr. award Wayne State U. Assn. Black Bus. Students, 1986, Fred Hampton Image award, 1984; named to Black Women Hall of Fame. Mem. ABA, Wolverine Bar Assn., Mary McLeod Bethune Assn. Entertainment, Probate, Juvenile. Office: Lloyd & Lloyd 600 Renaissance Ctr Suite 1400 Detroit MI 48243

LLOYD, ROBERT BLACKWELL, JR., lawyer; b. York, Pa., July 20, 1926; s. Robert Blackwell and Grace Irene (Dunkelberger) L.; m. Mary Ruth Hall, May 29, 1951; children—Lisa, Robert Bradford. A.B., Harvard Coll., 1947; LL.B., Duke U., 1950, J.D., 1971. Bar: N.C. 1950. Assoc. Norman Block, Greensboro, N.C., 1950-52; ptnr. Block, Meyland & Lloyd, Greensboro, 1952-80; sec. treas. Block, Meyland & Lloyd, P.A., Greensboro, 1981—. Bd. dirs. Eastern Music Festival, Greensboro, 1976—; bd. dirs. N.C. Symphony Soc., 1974-76; dist. chmn. Gen. Greene council Boy Scouts Am., 1962-65; deacon, elder, chmn. bd. deacons, clk. session Starmount Presbyterian Ch. Served with USNR, 1944-61. Fellow Am. Coll. Probate Counsel (N.C. state chmn. 1985—); mem. ABA, N.C. Bar Assn. (chmn. sect. probate and fiduciary law 1980-81), Greensboro Bar Assn., N.C. State Bar (vice chmn. splty. com. on estate planning and fiduciary law of bd. of specialization 1984—), 4th Fed. Circuit Jud. Conf. Democrat. Clubs: Lions, Greensboro City, Starmount Forest Country. Probate, General corporate, Personal income taxation. Office: PO Box 3365 Greensboro NC 27402

LLOYD, WILLIAM EMMONS, JR., lawyer; b. Richmond, Va., June 13, 1944; s. William Emmons and Alice Roberta (Hannah) L.; B. Chem. Engring. U. Va., 1967; J.D., Am. Univ., 1971; children—Jennifer Anne, Josena-June Clemens, Jason Damion, Jeannine Claudine, Danielle Ashley. Bar: U.S.

Patent Office 1968, Va. 1971, U.S. Ct. Customs and Patent Appeals 1973, U.S. Ct. Appeals (9th cir.) 1979, U.S. Supreme Ct. 1977, Calif. 1980. Assoc. Kelly & Cogan, Santa Monica, Calif., 1983-86; sole practice, Los Angeles, 1986—. Served with USNR, 1964-67. Scholar Calif. State, 1962, U. Va., 1962-64. Mem. Alexandria, Va. Jaycees (dir. 1977-79), Calif. Bar Assn., Los Angeles Trial Lawyers Assn. (chmn. def. doctors bank 1981), Calif. Trial Lawyers Assn. (co-chmn. toxics subcom. of legis. liason com. 1986—), Assn. Trial Lawyers Am., Va. Bar Assn., Delta Theta Phi. Democrat. Episcopalian. Personal injury, State civil litigation, Federal civil litigation. Office: 11601 Wilshire Blvd Suite 1830 Los Angeles CA 90025

LLOYD, WILLIAM NELSON, lawyer; b. Lewisburg, Tenn., July 24, 1920; s. William Houston and Rhoda Agnes (Hastings) L.; m. LaDelle Estes, Sept. 15, 1949; children—William Hastings, Robert Estes. Student, Cumberland U., 1939-40; U. South, Sewanee, 1942-46; LL.B., Vanderbilt U., 1948. Bar: Tenn. 1948, U.S. Dist. Ct. (mid. dist.) Tenn. 1949. Judge, Marshall County (Tenn.) Ct. Gen. Sessions, 1950-58; sole practice, Lewisburg, Tenn., 1958—; atty. Marshall County, 1966-82; mem. Tenn. Constl. Conv., 1965-70; chmn. Marshall County Democratic Party, 1981. Served USNR, Naval Aviation, 1942-46. Decorated Silver Star, D.F.C. with two gold stars. Mem. ABA, Tenn. Bar Assn., Marshall County Bar Assn., Assn. Trial Lawyers Am. (mem. com. nat. awards, 1973-74), Tenn. Trial Lawyers Assn. (bd. dirs. 1965-76), Am. Judicature Soc. Presbyterian. Clubs: Rotary, Mason, Elks. State civil litigation, Criminal, General practice. Office: William N Lloyd Law Firm PO Box 209 Lewisburg TN 37091

LOBEL, DOUGLAS ARTHUR, lawyer; b. N.Y.C., Sept. 28, 1946; s. Irving and Selma (Agar) L.; m. Nancy Ellen Bothamley, May 19, 1984. BS in Econs., U. Pa., 1968, MBA, 1970; JD, Georgetown U., 1973. Bar: N.Y. 1974, U.S. Dist. Ct. (so. dist.) N.Y. 1974, U.S. Ct. Appeals (2d cir.) 1975, U.S. Supreme Ct. 1986. Counsel, corp. sec. Seatrain Lines, Inc., N.Y.C., 1973-76; assoc. Morgan, Lewis & Backus, N.Y.C., 1976-79; gen. counsel Fame Fabrics, Inc., N.Y.C., 1980-81; assoc. Robinson, Perlman & Kirschner, N.Y.C., 1981-82; sr. ptnr. Douglas A. Lobel, Inc., N.Y.C., 1982—. Bd. dirs. The Bridge Inc., N.Y.C., 1975—, The Epilepsy Inst., Inc., N.Y.C., 1980—. Mem. ABA, N.Y. State Bar Assn., Assn. Bar of City of N.Y., Assn. Trial Lawyers Am., N.Y. State Trial Lawyers Assn., N.Y. County Lawyers Assn. Democrat. Avocations: fishing, tennis. General corporate, Contracts commercial, Real property. Home: 152 E 94th St New York NY 10128 Office: 19 W 44th St New York NY 10036

LOBEL, MARTIN, lawyer; b. Cambridge, Mass., June 19, 1941; s. I. Alan and Dorothy W. Lobel; m. Geralyn Krupp, Mar. 15, 1981; children: Devra Sarah, Rachel Melissa, Hannah Krupp. AB, Boston U., 1962, JD, 1965; LLM, Harvard U., 1966. Bar: Mass. 1965, D.C. 1968, U.S. Supreme Ct. 1968. Ptnr. Lobel & Lobel, Boston, 1965-66; asst. prof. law U. Okla., Norman, 1967; Congressional fellow, Washington, 1968; legis. asst. to Senator William Proxmire, 1968-72; ptnr. Lobel, Novins, Lamont & Flug, Washington, 1972—; lectr. Law Sch. Am. U., Washington, 1972—. Chmn. tax notes/tax analysts, sec. Ctr. Urban Environ. Studies. Mem. ABA (chmn. subcom. improving land records), Mass. Bar Assn., D.C. Bar Assn. (chmn. consumer affairs com. 1976-77, chmn. steering com. on antitrust and consumer affairs sect.), Order of Coif. Contbr. articles to legal jours. Administrative and regulatory, FERC practice, Legislative. Home: 4525 31st St NW Washington DC 20008 Office: Lobel Novins Lamont & Flug 1275 K St NW #770 Washington DC 20005

LOBENHERZ, WILLIAM ERNEST, legislative counsel, academic administrator; b. Muskegon, Mich., June 22, 1949; s. Ernest Pomeroy and Emajean (Krautheim) L.; m. Janet Ann McConnell, July 12, 1975; children: Jessica Anne, Rebecca Jean, Christopher William. BBA, U. Mich., 1971; JD cum laude, Wayne State U., 1974. Bar: Mich. 1974. Legal counsel Mich. Legis. Services Bur., Lansing, Mich., 1974-77; legal legis. cons. Mich. Assn. of Sch. Bds., Lansing, 1977, asst. exec. dir. for legal legis. affairs, 1977-79; asst. v.p. state and congl. relations Wayne State U., Detroit, 1979-81, assoc. v.p. state relations, 1981-82, v.p. govtl. affairs, 1982—; guest lectr. in govtl. affairs, Wayne State U., U. Mich., U. Detroit. Contbr. chpt. Mich. Handbook for School Business Officials, 1979, 2d ed. 1980, articles to profl. jours. and mags. Mem. govtl. affairs com. New Detroit Inc., 1984—, chmn. state subcom. of govtl. affairs com., 1986-87; chmn. ind. schs. campaign Greater Metro Detroit United Fund. Torch Drive, 1979, chmn. Colls. and Univs. campaign, 1980. Recipient Book award Lawyer's Cooperative Pub. Co., 1973; Silver scholar key Wayne State U. Law Sch., 1974. Mem. ABA, Mich. Bar Assn., NAACP, Council for Advancement and Support of Edn (Mindpower citation 1982), Mich. Delta Found. (bd. dirs. 1977—, sec. 1981-84), Greater Metro Detroit C. of C. (contact interviewer bus. attraction and expansion council 1984-86). Clubs: Economic (Detroit); City (Lansing). Legislative, Administrative and regulatory, Government contracts and claims. Home: 15425 Portis Plymouth MI 48170 Office: Wayne State U Detroit MI 48202

LOBENHOFER, LOUIS FRED, legal educator; b. Denver, Mar. 24, 1950; s. Frederick C. and Betty Lobenhofer; m. Carol E. Clarkson, June 16, 1973; children—Kristina M., Lauren E. A.B., Coll. William and Mary, 1972; J.D., U. Colo., 1975; LL.M., U. Denver, 1979. Bar: Colo. 1975, Tax Ct. 1982. Assoc. law firm Charles H. Booth, Denver, 1975-78; asst. prof. law Ohio No. U., 1979-82, assoc. prof., 1982-85, prof., 1985—. Denver Tax Inst. scholar, 1979. Mem. ABA, Soc. Am. Law Tchrs., Phi Beta Kappa, Omicron Delta Kappa, Delta Theta Phi. Republican. Roman Catholic. Legal education, Corporate taxation, Estate planning. Office: Ohio No U Coll Law Ada OH 45810

LOBERT, JAMES EDWARD, lawyer; b. Ft. Wayne, Ind., Feb. 10, 1951; s. Edward Eugene and Geraldine Lucille (Miller) L.; m. Kathryn Lynn Houseman, Aug. 12, 1972; children: Peter James, Daniel Houseman. BA in Polit. Sci., Ind. U., 1973; JD, So. Meth. U., 1977. Bar: Tex. 1977, U.S. Dist. Ct. (no. dist.) Tex. 1981. Assoc. Harris, Harris & Lobert, Arlington, Tex., 1977-78; ptnr. Rohne, Hoodenpyle, Lobert & Myers, Arlington, 1979—; adv. dir. First City Bank Cen. Arlington, Tex. Adv. dir. Arlington Meml. Hosp., 1985-86; chmn. bd. dirs. Pantego Christian Acad., Arlington, 1985—; adv. bd. dirs. Adoptive Learning Ctr. Mem. ABA, Tex. Bar Assn., Tex. Assn. Bank Counsel, Comml. Law League of Am., Tarrant County Bankruptcy Bar Assn. Lodges: Optimists (bd. dirs. Arlington 1979-83; pres. Arlington 1985-86). Banking, Bankruptcy, Consumer commercial. Office: Rohne Hoodenpyle Lobert & Myers 1323 W Pioneer Pkwy Arlington TX 76013

LOBL, HERBERT MAX, lawyer; b. Vienna, Austria, Jan. 10, 1932; s. Walter Leo and Minnie (Neumann) L.; m. Dorothy Fullerton Hubbard, Sept. 12, 1960; children—Peter Walter, Michelle Alexandra. A.B. magna cum laude, Harvard U., 1953, LL.B., 1959; Fulbright scholar U. Bonn., Germany, 1954. Bar: N.Y. 1960, U.S. Tax Ct. 1963, French Conseil Juridique 1973. Assoc. Davis, Polk & Wardwell, N.Y.C., 1959-60; assoc. counsel to Gov. Nelson Rockefeller, Albany, N.Y., 1960-62; assoc. Davis, Polk & Wardwell, New York and Paris, 1963-69, ptnr., Paris, 1969—; dir. CII-Honeywell Bull, Paris, 1976-81, Alcatel USA Corp., 1985-87; supervisory bd. mem. CII-HB Internationale, Amsterdam, Holland, 1977-82. Gov. Am. Hosp. Paris, 1981-83; trustee Am. Library, Paris, 1969-81. Served to 1st lt. USAF, 1954-56, Berlin. Mem. Internat. Fiscal Assn., Internat. Assn. Lawyers, Am. Soc. Internat. Law, N.Y. State Bar Assn., Assn. Bar City of N.Y. Club: Travellers (Paris); University, Harvard (N.Y.). Private international, Corporate taxation. Home: 242 Rue de Rivoli, Paris France Office: Davis Polk & Wardwell, 4 Place de la Concorde, Paris France American Address: Davis Polk & Wardwell 1 Chase Manhattan Plaza New York NY 10005

LOBNER, KNEELAND HARKNESS, lawyer; b. Sacramento, Feb. 2, 1919; s. Leo Kneeland and Laura (Roberts) L.; m. Adele Frances Ohe, Dec. 20, 1941; children—Breton K., Robert K., Susan. A. Lobner Schroeder. A.A., Sacramento City Coll., 1939; J.D., Hastings Coll. Law, 1944. Bar: Calif. 1946, U.S. Supreme Ct. 1960. City atty. of Auburn, Calif., 1946-47; asso. firm K.D. Robinson, Auburn, 1946-47; dep. dist. atty. Sacramento County, 1947-49; atty. Calif. Automobile Assn., Sacramento, 1949-52; ptnr. Lobner and Bull, Sacramento, 1958—; advocate Am. Bd. Trial Advocates, 1972, pres. Sacramento chpt., 1985; bd. dirs. Hastings Coll. Law, 1986. Councilman, City of Sacramento, 1957-62, vice mayor, 1962; mem. Sacramento Met. Adv. Com., 1957-59; mem. Sacramento Redevel. Agy., 1964-73, chmn., 1970-72; mem. Sacramento Estate Planning Council, 1960—, Sacramento County Republican Central Com., 1955-57, Calif. Rep. Central Com., 1962-68; bd. dirs. Am. Cancer Soc., Sacramento, 1956-64, pres., 1963-64; bd. dirs. Calif. Mus. Assn., 1968-73, pres., 1969-71; bd. dirs. Am. Heart Assn., Sacramento, 1958-68; bd. govs. Hastings Law Coll., 1960—, pres., 1966, bd. dirs. 1986—; pres. Hastings 1066 Found., 1976; bd. dirs. Sacramento Symphony Found.; bd. dirs., pres. Crystal Shores West Assn. Nev. Served with AUS, 1944-46. Recipient Outstanding Alumnus award Hastings Coll. Law, 1976. Fellow Am. Coll. Probate Counsel; mem. Am. Bd. Trial Advocates (advocate), ABA, Sacramento County Bar Assn. (pres. 1973), State Bar Calif., Am. Judicature Soc., Better Bus. Bur. Sacramento (pres. 1967), Sacramento Zool. Soc. (pres. 1965), Am. Legion, Sacramento County Bar Council. Clubs: Del Paso Country, Elks. Federal civil litigation, State civil litigation, General Corporate and Construction. Office: 717 20th St Sacramento CA 95814

LOCHER, RALPH S., justice Ohio Supreme Ct.; b. Moreni, Romania, July 24, 1915; s. Ephraim and Natalie (Voigt) L.; m. Eleanor Worthington, June 18, 1939; 1 dau., Virginia Lynn. B.A. with honors, Bluffton Coll., 1936; LL.B., Case Western Res. U., 1939. Bar: Ohio bar 1939. Former sec. to Gov. Ohio; former law dir. City of Cleve.; former mayor Cleve.; judge Ohio Ct. Common Pleas Cuyahoga County, 1969-72, Cuyahoga County Ct. Probate Div., 1973-77; justice Supreme Ct. Ohio, 1977—. Mem. Am. Bar Assn., Bar Assn. Greater Cleve., Cuyahoga County Bar Assn. Democrat. Office: State Office Tower 30 E Broad St Columbus OH 43215

LOCHHEAD, ROBERT BRUCE, lawyer; b. St. Louis, June 20, 1952; s. Angus Tulloch and Matilda Evangeline (Thurman) L.; m. KLynn Walker, June 21, 1974; children: Bruce, Richard, Cynthia, Melinda, Rebekah, Elizabeth. BA, Brigham Young U., 1975; JD, Columbia U., 1978. Bar: D.C. 1979, Utah 1980, U.S. Dist. Ct. Utah 1980, U.S. Ct. Appeals (10th cir.) 1980, U.S. Supreme Ct. 1986. Law clk. to presiding judge U.S. Ct. Appeals (10th cir.), Salt Lake City, 1978-79; assoc. Hogan & Hartson, Washington, 1979-80, Larsen, Kimball, Parr & Crockett, Salt Lake City, 1980-82; ptnr. Kimball, Parr, Crockett & Waddoups and predecessor firm Larsen, Kimball, Parr & Crockett, Salt Lake City, 1982—; judge pro tem Small Claims Ct., Salt Lake City, 1985—. Harlan Fiske Stone scholar, 1976-78. Mem. ABA, Am. Bankruptcy Inst. Mormon. Bankruptcy, Federal civil litigation, Contracts commercial. Home: 561 S 300 E Centerville UT 84014 Office: Kimball Parr Crockett & Waddoups 185 S State St #1300 Salt Lake City UT 84111

LOCKABY, ROBERT LEE, JR., lawyer; b. Chattanooga, Sept. 12, 1953; s. Robert Lee and Joan Carol (Gray) L.; m. Rebecca Lynn Tolley, June 26, 1976; 1 child, Matthew. BA, Furman U., 1975; JD, U. Tenn., 1978. Bar: Tenn. 1978, U.S. Ct. Mil. Appeals 1979, U.S. Dist. Ct. (ea. dist.) Tenn. 1982, Ga. 1984, U.S. Dist. Ct. (no. dist.) Ga. 1984, U.S. Ct. Appeals (5th cir.) 1984. Prosecutor 3d Inf. div. U.S. Army, Kitzingen, Fed. Republic Germany, 1979, def. counsel, 1979-80; sr. def. counsel 3d Inf. div. U.S. Army, Wuerzburg, Fed. Republic Germany, 1980-81; legal assistance officer U.S. Army, Ft. Gordon, 1982; assoc. Gearhiser, Peters & Horton, Chattanooga, 1982-86, ptnr., 1986—. Mem. ABA, Fed. Bar Assn., Tenn. Bar Assn., Chattanooga Bar Assn., Order of Coif, Phi Delta Phi. Republican. Methodist. Avocations: photography, travel, snow and water skiing, boating. Federal civil litigation, State civil litigation, General practice. Home: 7514 Island Manor Dr Harrison TN 37341 Office: Gearhiser Peters & Horton 801 Chestnut St Chattanooga TN 37402

LOCKE, JOHN HOWARD, lawyer; b. Berryville, Va., Sept. 4, 1920; s. James Howard and Mary Elizabeth (Hart) L.; m. Frances Rebecca Cook, Feb. 23, 1946; children—Anne Locke Carter, Nancy Locke Curlee, Rebecca Locke Leonard. B.S., U. Richmond, 1941; LL.B., U. Va., 1948. Bar: Va. 1948. Ptnr., Gentry, Locke, Rakes & Moore, Roanoke, Va. Founder, pres. Big Bros., Roanoke, 1960. Served with USN, 1942-46. Fellow Am. Coll. Trial Lawyers, Internat. Soc. Barristers (pres. 1970); mem. ABA, Va. Bar Assn., Roanoke City Bar Assn. (pres. 1970-71), Internat. Assn. Ins. Counsel, 4th Cir. Jud. Conf., Omicron Delta Kappa, Raven Soc. Presbyterian. Clubs: Shenadoah, Roanoke Country (Roanoke, Va.). Personal injury, Federal civil litigation, State civil litigation.

LOCKE, RONALD JACKSON, lawyer; b. Huntingdon, Pa., Feb. 6, 1947; s. William Jackson and Janet Ruth (Locke) L.; m. Linda Kay Snyder, Dec. 31, 1969; 1 child, Melissa Ann. BA, Shippensburg U., 1969; JD, George Mason U., 1980. Bar: Pa. 1981, U.S. Dist. Ct. (mid. dist.) 1982. Assoc. Law Offices of Gary Deane, P.C., McConnellsburg and Everett, Pa., 1981-82; sole practice Huntingdon, Pa., 1982—. Served with U.S. Army, 1969-75. Mem. ABA, Pa. Bar Assn., Huntingdon County Bar Assn. Republican. Mem. Brethren Ch. Lodge: Kiwanis (v.p. Huntingdon club 1985—). Avocations: golf, hunting, swimming, tennis, boating. General practice. Home: 1120 Warm Springs Ave Huntingdon PA 16652 Office: 1009 Mifflin St Huntingdon PA 16652-1819

LOCKETT, GEORGE HOUSTON, lawyer; b. Oliver Springs, Tenn., Dec. 29, 1921; s. Robert Pryor and Sallie Myrtle (Jones) L.; m. Mary D. Wright, Oct. 25, 1958; children—Karen, Mary Jane, Lisa. J.D., U. Tenn., 1950. Bar: Tenn. 1951, U.S. Dist. Ct. (ea. dist.) Tenn. U.S. Supreme Ct. 1976. Atty., TVA, 1951-55, U.S. Army C.E., 1955; sole practice, Harriman, Tenn., 1955—; city atty., Harriman, 1959-67, 83—; former tchr. Roane State Coll. Trustee, Carson-Newman Coll.; former chmn. exec. com. Tenn. Bapt. Found.; former chmn. exec. com. Republican Party; former chmn. Primary Bd., Roane County. Served with USAAF, 1943-46; PTO. Recipient 1st place award Hamilton Bank of Knoxville; Preston award U. Tenn. Coll. Law, 1950. Mem. Am. Bar Assn., Tenn. Bar Assn., Roane County Bar Assn., Am. Legion, Phi Delta Phi. Republican. Baptist (deacon). Clubs: Rotary, Masons (Harriman, Tenn.); Scottish Rite, Shriners (Knoxville). General practice, State civil litigation, Real property. Home: 553 Margrave St Harriman TN 37748 Office: 315 Devonia St PO Box 436 Harriman TN 37748

LOCKETT, TYLER C., state supreme court justice; b. Corpus Christi, Tex., Dec. 7, 1932; s. Tyler Coleman and Evelyn (Lemond) L.; m. Sue W. Lockett, Nov. 3, 1961; children—Charles, Patrick. A.B., Washburn U., 1955, J.D., 1962. Bar: Kans. Sole practice law Wichita, 1962—; judge Ct. Common Pleas, 1971-77, Kans. Dist. Ct. 18th Dist., 1977-83; justice Supreme Court Kans., Topeka, 1983—. Judicial administration. Office: Kans Supreme Ct Judicial Ctr 301 W 10th St Topeka KS 66612 *

LOCKETT, WILLIAM ALEXANDER, lawyer; b. Knoxville, Tenn., Mar. 28, 1949; s. William Lones and Wilma (Waller) L.; m. Janet Glidewell, June 14, 1980; 1 child, Julia Anne. Student, Rollins Coll., 1967-68; BS, U. Tenn., 1971, JD, 1973. Bar: Tenn. 1974, U.S. Dist. Ct. (ea. dist.) Tenn. 1979, U.S. Ct. Appeals (6th cir.) 1984. Assoc. Walter, Gilbertson & Clayborn, Knoxville, Tenn., 1973-76, Walter, Gilbertson & Assocs., Knoxville, 1976-79, Luther, Anderson, Cleary & Cooper, Chattanooga, 1979-81, Anderson, Cleary & Ruth, Chattanooga, 1981-82; assoc. Luther, Anderson, Cleary & Ruth, Chattanooga, 1982-83, ptnr., 1983—. Mem. ABA, Tenn. Bar Assn., Chattanooga Bar Assn. (chmn. membership com. 1986-87). Republican. Presbyterian. Avocations: photography, golf, travel. Personal injury, Workers' compensation, Civil rights. Office: Luther Anderson Cleary & Ruth 99 Walnut St Chattanooga TN 37403

LOCKHART, ROBERT EARL, lawyer; b. Fitchburg, Mass., Dec. 16, 1937; s. Earl Perry and Florence (Wuth) L.; m. Barbara Heusner, June 19, 1965; children—Robert, Jr., Andrew. B.B.A., Clark U., 1959; LL.B., Duke U., 1962. Bar: D.C. 1962. Atty., U.S. GAO, Washington, 1963-71; gen. counsel Com. on Post Office and Civil Service, U.S. Ho. of Reps., Washington, 1971—. Legislative. Office: Com on Post Office and Civil Service US Ho of Reps Washington DC 20515

LOCKNEY, THOMAS MICHAEL, educator, judge; b. Waukesha, Wis., Apr. 14, 1945; s. John Henry and Elizabeth (Stenz) L.; divorced; children: Marie Elizabeth, Amy Loden, Thomas Michael. BA, U. Wis., 1967; JD, U. Tex., 1970; LLM, Harvard U., 1974. Bar: Tex. 1970, N.D. 1972, U.S. Dist. Ct. N.D., U.S. Ct. Appeals (8th cir.). Atty. U.S. Dept. Justice, Washington, 1970-71; prof. law U. N.D., Grand Forks, 1971—; mcpl. judge Larimore, N.D., 1977—, Emerado, N.D., 1983—, Northwood, N.D., 1983—; dir. Ctl. Legal Research U. N.D. Sch. Law. Mem. Red River Bluegrass Assn. Criminal, Civil rights, Jurisprudence. Home: 1014 N 39th St F23 Grand Forks ND 58201 Office: U ND Sch Law Grand Forks ND 58202

LOCKWOOD, GARY LEE, lawyer; b. Woodstock, Ill., Dec. 3, 1946; s. Howard and Luella Mae (Behrens) L.; m. Cheryl Lynn Wittrock, Jan. 5, 1977; children: Jennifer, Lee, Cynthia. BA magna cum laude, Iowa Wesleyan Coll., 1968; student, Albert Ludwig U., Freiburg in Breisgau, Fed. Republic Germany, 1968-69; JD, Northwestern U., 1976. Bar: Ill. 1976, U.S. Dist. Ct. (no. dist.) Ill. 1976. Assoc. Lord, Bissell & Brook, Chgo., 1976-85, ptnr., 1985—. Bd. dirs. McHenry Sch. Dist. 15, Ill., 1974-85, pres., 1979-80. Served to sgt. U.S. Army, 1970-72. Mem. ABA (bus. and ins. com. 1985—), Ill. Bar Assn., Chgo. Bar Assn. Methodist. Avocations: sports, flying. Environment, Insurance. Home: 1319 Hillside Ln McHenry IL 60050 Office: Lord Bissel & Brook 115 S LaSalle St Chicago IL 60603

LOCKWOOD, JOHN ALLEN, lawyer; b. Wilmington, Del., Apr. 10, 1942; s. William Howard and Elizabeth Caswell (Allen) L.; m. Diana Allison Walsh, June 12, 1965; children—Andrew Allison, Carol Elizabeth. A.B., Colby Coll., 1964; J.D., Duke U., 1967. Bar: D.C. 1968, Hawaii 1972, U.S. Dist. Ct. Hawaii 1972. Assoc., Ashford & Wriston, Honolulu, 1974-78, ptnr., 1978—. Bd. dirs. Child and Family Service, Honolulu, 1972-77, pres., 1974-76; chmn. Windward Coalition Chs., 1973-74; bd. dirs. Windward Senior Day Care Ctr., 1975-81; trustee Seabury Hall, 1975-80; chancellor, Episcopal Diocese Hawaii, 1976—, chancellor province of Pacific (episcopal), 1983—; trustee Hawaii Loa Coll., 1979-85 , chmn., 1981-84. Served to maj. USMC, 1968-73. Decorated Nat. Def. Service medal. Fellow Am. Coll. Probate Counsel; mem. ABA, Hawaii State Bar Assn., Panel of Arbitrators first jud. cir., Hawaii, 1986. Clubs: Honolulu Rotary. Probate, Real property, Landlord-tenant. Office: Ashford & Wriston PO Box 131 Honolulu HI 96810

LOE, BRIAN ROBERT, lawyer; b. Denver, Dec. 28, 1954; s. Robert and Adah (Sahr) L.; m. Deborah Dedman, May 20, 1978. BA, U. Calif., San Diego, 1977; JD, Am. U., 1981. Bar: D.C. 1981, Va. 1982, U.S. Dist. Ct. (ea. dist.) Va. 1982, U.S. Dist. Ct. D.C. 1982, U.S. Ct. Appeals (4th cir.) 1982, U.S. Supreme Ct., 1986. Assoc. Holst & Hartshorn, Falls Church, Va., 1982-85; sole practice Falls Church, 1986—. Mem. ABA, Fairfax County Bar Assn. Republican. Criminal, Real property, State civil litigation. Office: 6400 Arlington Blvd 142 Falls Church VA 22042

LOEB, BEN FOHL, JR., lawyer, educator; b. Nashville, May 15, 1932; s. Ben Fohl and Frances (Paysinger) L.; m. Anne Nelson, Sept. 23, 1961 (div. 1982); children: Charles Nelson, William Nelson. BA, Vanderbilt U., 1955, JD, 1960. Bar: Tenn. 1960, U.S. Supreme Ct. 1966, N.C. 1975. Assoc. Crownover, Branstetter & Folk, Nashville, 1960-64; asst. dir. Inst. Govt. U. N.C., Chapel Hill, 1964—, prof. pub. law and govt. Inst. Govt., 1972—; counsel to N.C. legis. coms. on motor vehicle law and transp., Raleigh, 1973—. Author: Traffic Law and Highway Safety, 1970, Motor Vehicle Law, 1975, Legal Aspects of Dental Practice, 1977, Eminent Domain Procedure, 1984; assoc. editor Vanderbilt Law Rev., 1959-60. Served to lt. U.S. Army, 1955-57. Mem. ABA, Phi Beta Kappa, Phi Delta Phi, Pi Kappa Alpha (chpt. pres. 1954-55). Democrat. Baptist. Club: U. N.C. Faculty. Administrative and regulatory, Legal education. Home: 17 Bluff Trail Chapel Hill NC 27514 Office: U NC Knapp Bldg 059A Chapel Hill NC 27514

LOEB, DOROTHY PEARL, lawyer; b. N.Y.C., Mar. 2, 1935; d. Victor Joseph and Jean (Albert) Caesar; m. Frank David Loeb, June 26, 1955 (div. Oct. 1972); children: Matthew Stuart, Eric Victor. Student, Bates Coll., 1952-55; BA, Boston U., 1956; JD, Columbia U., 1971. Bar: N.Y. 1972, U.S. Dist. Ct. (ea. and so. dists.) N.Y. 1975, U.S. Supreme Ct. 1976. Asst. dist. atty. Rockland County, New City, N.Y., 1972-75; counsel to commr. dept. social services Rockland County, West Nyack, N.Y., 1975-77; asst. counsel litigation dept. social services N.Y. State, Albany, 1977-78, asst. dir. child support enforcement dept. social services, 1978-80. Counsel 1st Unitarian Ch. Rockland County, Pomona, N.Y., 1973-75; legal advisor, bd. dirs. Nyack (N.Y.) Child Care Ctr.; chmn. ad hoc com. on legal affairs The Rotanda Condominium, McLean, Va., 1985—. Mem. ABA, Fed. Bar Assn., N.Y. State Bar Assn., Assn. Trial Lawyers Am., Nat. Dist. Attys. Assn., Am. Judicature Soc., League of Women Voters (pres. Rockland, Md. br. 1965-67, membership chairperson, Fairfax, Va. dinner unit 1986—), Am. Assn. Univ. Women (sec. McLean, Va. br. 1986—). Real property, Condemnation, Environment. Office: USAF Office of Gen Counsel Pentagon Washington DC 20330

LOEB, LEONARD L., lawyer. BBA, U. Wis., 1950, JD, 1952. Bar: Wis. 1952, U.S. Supreme Ct. 1960. Sole practice Milw., 1952—; faculty family mediation inst. Harvard Law Sch.; lectr. family law Marquette U., U. Wis., Madison; cons. revisions Wis. Family Code Wis. Legislature; mem. com. for review of initiatives in child support State of Wis. Author: Systems Book for Family Law; contbr. articles to profl. jours. Served to col. JAGC, USAF, 1952-53. Fellow Am. Bar Found., Am. Acad. Matrimonial Lawyers (past v.p., past charter pres. Wis. chpt., editor in chief jour., editor newsletter); mem. ABA (past chmn. family law sect., del. to ho. of dels.), Wis. Bar Assn. (past chmn. family law sect.), Wis. Bar Found. (bd. dirs.), Milw. Bar Assn. (past chmn. family law sect.), Concordia Coll. (Wis.) Paralegal Adv. Bd. Family and matrimonial. Office: 111 E Wisconsin Ave Milwaukee WI 53202

LOEFFLER, JAMES JOSEPH, lawyer; b. Evanston, Ill., Mar. 7, 1931; s. Charles Adolph and Margaret Bowe L.; m. Margo M. Loeffler, May 26, 1962; children—Charlotte Bowe, James J. B.S., Loyola U.; J.D., Northwestern U. Bar: Ill. 1956, Tex. 1956. Assoc. Fulbright & Jaworski, Houston, 1956-69, ptnr., 1969—, sr. ptnr., 1986; sr. ptnr. Chamberlain, Hrdlicka, White, Johnson & Williams, Houston, 1986—. Mem. ABA, Ill. Bar Assn., Tex. Bar Assn., Houston Bar Assn. Club: Houston Country. Management labor law, Labor. Office: 1400 Citicorp Ctr 1200 Smith St Houston TX 77002

LOEFFLER, ROBERT HUGH, lawyer; b. Chgo., May 27, 1943; s. Julius and Faye (Fink) L.; m. Jane Canter, Sept. 6, 1970; children: James Benjamin, Charles Edward. AB magna cum laude, Harvard Coll., 1965; JD cum laude, Columbia U., 1968. Bar: N.Y. 1969, U.S. Ct. Appeals (2d cir.) 1969, D.C. 1970, U.S. Ct. Appeals (D.C. cir.) 1972, U.S. Ct. Appeals (9th cir.) 1981. Law clk. 1968-69; assoc. Covington & Burling, Washington, 1969-76; assoc., ptnr. Isham, Lincoln & Beale, Washington, 1976-79; ptnr. Morrison & Foerster, Washington, 1979—. Chmn. consumer com. Muskie presdl. campaign, 1972. Mem. ABA (vice chmn. energy law com. adminstrv. law sect.). Jewish. Clubs: University (Washington); Standard (Chgo.); Harvard (N.Y.C.). Administrative and regulatory, FERC practice, Federal civil litigation. Home: 2607 36th Place NW Washington DC 20007 Office: 2000 Pennsylvania Ave NW Suite 5500 Washington DC 20036

LOEHR, GERALD EDWARD, lawyer; b. Yonkers, N.Y., May 19, 1943; s. John F. and Gertrude A. (Sweetman) L.; children—Peter, Janine, Melissa, Gerald, Cariana. B.B.A., Manhattan Coll, Riverdale, N.Y., 1965; J.D., Fordham U., 1969. Bar: N.Y. 1969, U.S. Dist. Ct. (so. dist.) N.Y. 1973, U.S. Ct. Appeals (2d cir.) 1973, U.S. Supreme Ct. 1984; diplomate in trial advocacy Ct. Practice Inst., Chgo. Clk. City Ct. Yonkers, N.Y., 1968-69; asst. dist. atty. N.Y. County, 1969-73; assoc. Nobile & Magarian, Yonkers, 1973-76; sole practice Yonkers, 1976-83; ptnr. Ecker, Lochr & Ecker, 1983—. Councilman, City of Yonkers, 1976-79, mayor, 1980-81. Mem. ABA, N.Y. State Bar Assn., Assn. Trial Lawyers Am., N.Y. Dist. Attys. Assn., Westchester County Bar Assn., Yonkers Lawyers Assn. Democrat. Personal injury, General practice, State civil litigation. Office: 20 S Broadway Suite 1111 Yonkers NY 10701

LOEVINGER, LEE, lawyer; b. St. Paul, Apr. 24, 1913; s. Gustavus and Millie (Strouse) L.; m. Ruth Howe, Mar. 4, 1950; children: Barbara L., Eric H., Peter H. B.A. summa cum laude, U. Minn., 1933, J.D., 1936. Bar: Minn. 1936, Mo. 1937, D.C. 1966, U.S. Supreme Ct., 1941. Assoc. Watson, Ess, Groner, Barnett & Whittaker, Kansas City, Mo., 1936-37; atty., regional atty. NLRB, 1937-41; with antitrust div. Dept. Justice, 1941-46; ptnr. Larson, Loevinger, Lindquist & Fraser, Mpls., 1946-60; assoc. justice Minn. Supreme Ct., 1960-61; asst. U.S. atty. gen. charge antitrust div. Dept. Justice, 1961-63; commr. FCC, 1963-68; ptnr. Hogan & Hartson, Washington, 1968-85; of counsel Hogan & Hartson, 1986—; v.p., dir. Craig-Hallum Corp.,

Mpls., 1968-73; dir. Petrolite Corp., St. Louis., 1978-83; U.S. rep. com. on restrictive bus. practices Orgn. for Econ. Cooperation and Devel., 1961-64; spl. asst. to U.S. atty. gen., 1963-64; spl. counsel com. small bus. U.S. Senate, 1951-52; lectr. U. Minn., 1953-60; vis. prof. jurisprudence U. Minn. (Law Sch.), 1961; professorial lectr. Am. U., 1968-70; chmn. Minn. Atomic Devel. Problems Com., 1957-59; mem. Adminstrv. Conf. U.S., 1972-74; del. White House Conf. on Inflation, 1974; U.S. del. UNESCO Conf. on Mass Media, 1975, Internat. Telecommunications Conf. on Radio Frequencies, 1964, 66. Author: The Law of Free Enterprise, 1949, An Introduction to Legal Logic, 1952, Defending Antitrust Lawsuits, 1977; author first article to use term-Jurimetrics, 1949; contbr. articles to profl. jours.; editor, contbr.: Basic Data on Atomic Devel. Problems in Minnesota, 1958; adv. bd. Antitrust Bulletin, Jurimetrics Jour. Served to lt. comdr. USNR, 1942-45. Recipient Outstanding Achievement award U. Minn., 1968; Freedoms Found. award, 1977, 84. Mem. ABA (del. of sci. and tech. sect. to Ho. of Dels. 1974-80, del. to joint conf. with AAAS 1974-76, liaison 1984-87, chmn. sci. and tech. sect. 1982-83, council 1986—, standing com. on nat. conf. groups), Minn. Bar Assn., Hennepin County Bar Assn., D.C. Bar Assn., FCC Bar Assn., AAAS, Broadcast Pioneers, U.S. C. of C. (antitrust council), Phi Beta Kappa, Sigma Xi, Delta Sigma Rho, Sigma Delta Chi, Phi Delta Gamma, Tau Kappa Alpha, Alpha Epsilon Rho. Clubs: Cosmos, Internat. of Washington (D.C.), City Club (Washington). Antitrust, Administrative and regulatory. Home: 5669 Bent Branch Rd Bethesda MD 20816 Office: Hogan and Hartson 815 Connecticut Ave Washington DC 20006

LOEWENSTEIN, BENJAMIN STEINBERG, lawyer; b. Atlantic City, Aug. 22, 1912; s. Sidney and Cecilia (Steinberg) L.; m. Eleanor Lax Schieren, June 14, 1966; children-Sally L. (Mrs. David S. Well, Jr.), P. Edward; stepchildren-Susan (Mrs. Stanton A. Moss), Julie (Mrs. Robert Dreidink). A.B., Haverford Coll., 1934; J.D., U. Pa., 1937. Bar: Pa. 1937. Practiced in Phila., 1937—; sr. partner Abrahams & Loewenstein, 1937—; Sec., gen. counsel Oxford First Corp.; sec., dir. Rojess Corp., Gen. Syndicate Corp., Jonns Inc., Engelside Realty Corp., Sherill Corp., Oak Blvd. Inc., Kahn's Inc., Oxford Finance Cos., Inc., Atlas Rug Cleaners, Inc.; Counsel Diamond Council Am., Philadelphia County Dental Soc.; Del. White House Conf. on Aging, 1961; chmn. Task Force on Aging, Pa. Comprehensive Health Plan, 1966, Regional Comprehensive Health Planning Delaware Valley, Pa., 1968; mem. Pa. Human Relations Commn., 1974—. Hon. chmn. bd. Jewish Occupational Council, 1971—; pres. Jewish Employment and Vocat. Service, 1954-59, Health and Welfare Council Phila., 1969-71, So. Home for Children, 1968-69; hon. pres. Jewish Community Relations Council Phila., 1974—; bd. govs. Am. Jewish Com., 1968—, hon. chmn. Phila. chpt.; trustee Community Services Pa., 1968—; Bd. mgrs. Haverford Coll., 1970—; bd. dirs. Vocat. Research Inst., 1960—, United Way of Phila., Fedn. Jewish Agys., Phila., 1969—, Pa. Law and Justice Inst., 1971—, Fellowship Commn. Phila., 1972—, Phila. Anti-Poverty Action Commn., 1976—, Nat. Inst. on the Holocaust, 1977—; treas. Interfaith Council on the Holocaust, 1986—; v.p. Quadrangle-Haverford Coll., retirement community, 1977—; treas. Martins Run, retirement community, 1981—. Recipient Community Service award Allied Jewish Appeal Phila., 1956, certificate of appreciation Phila. County Med. Soc., 1961, certificate appreciation Fedn. Jewish Agys., 1972, Phila. Commn. Human Relations award, 1974; certificate Merit Am. Cancer Soc., 1974; Samuel Greenberg Meml. award Nat. Assn. Jewish Vocat. Services, 1980; Human Relations award Am. Jewish Com., 1981. Mem. Am., Pa., Phila. bar assns., Lawyers Club Phila., Socialegal Club Phila., Haverford Coll. Alumni Assn. (pres. 1956-57), Am. Arbitration Assn. (nat. panel arbitrators). General corporate, Family and matrimonial, Probate. Home: 2804 Kennedy House 1981 Kennedy Blvd Philadelphia PA 19103 Office: Abrahams and Loewenstein 1430 Land Title Bldg Philadelphia PA 19110

LOEWENTHAL, MARC SHELDON, lawyer; b. Newark, Feb. 15, 1949; s. Sydney Ira and Lenore Marion (Kestenbaum) L.; m. Nancy Joy Sokol, Mar. 19, 1977; children: Carrie, Emily. AB, Franklin & Marshall Coll., 1971; JD, Case Western Res. U., 1974. Asst. counsel Ameritrust Co., Cleve., 1974-78; ptnr. Kadish & Krantz, Cleve., 1978-84, Millet, Klein, Loewenthal & Sprague, Beachwood, Ohio, 1985—; of counsel Arter & Hadden, Cleve., 1984-85. Co-chmn. Shaker Heights (Ohio) Two Family Task Force, 1985—; trustee Am. Jewish Com., Cleve., 1976—. Mem. ABA, Cleve. Bar Assn., Cuyahoga County Bar Assn. General corporate, Real property, Contracts commercial. Office: Millet Klein Loewenthal & Sprague 23200 Chagrin Blvd 4 Commcerce Park Sq Suite 805 Beachwood OH 44122

LOEWI, ANDREW WILLIAM, lawyer; b. N.Y.C., May 15, 1950; s. Roger W. and Ruth C. (Chill) L.; m. Patricia Fotheringham Knous, Oct. 13, 1984; 1 child, Kimberly Ann. BA, Grinnell Coll., 1971; JD, Harvard U., 1982. Bar: Colo. 1982, U.S. Dist. Ct. Colo. 1982, U.S. Ct. Appeals (10th cir.) 1982. Assoc. Sherman & Howard, Denver, 1982-83; dep. dist. atty. Denver Dist. Atty.'s Office, 1983-86; assoc. Brownstein, Hyatt, Farber & Madden, Denver, 1986—; counsel spl. com. on ethics U.S. Senate, Washington, 1977. Pres. student govt. Grinnell (Iowa) Coll., 1970-71, bd. of trustees, 1985—; vice chmn. Colo. Common Cause, Denver, 1984—; mem. nat. governing bd. Common Cause, Washington, 1985—. Mem. Colo. Bar Assn. (council mem. criminal law sect. 1985—, availability of legal services com.), Denver Bar Assn. (co-chmn. criminal justice com. 1984-85, jud. selection and benefits com.), Denver C. of C. (Leadership Denver award 1985). Democrat. Jewish. Administrative and regulatory, Legislative, Land use and planning. Home: 1001 Pontiac St Denver CO 80220 Office: Brownstein Hyatt Farber & Madden 410 17th St 22d Floor Denver CO 80202

LOEWINGER, KENNETH JEFFERY, lawyer; b. Washington, Sept. 22, 1945; s. Myron Arthur and Lenore (Kopf) L.; m. Margaret Irene Krol, May 5, 1978. BA, Georgetown U., 1967, JD, 1971. Bar: U.S. Dist. Ct. D.C. 1971, U.S. Ct. Mil. Appeals 1972, U.S. Ct. Appeals (D.C. cir.) 1972, U.S. Supreme Ct. 1979. Law clk. to presiding judge U.S. Superior Ct., Washington, 1971-72; law clk. to presiding justice U.S. Ct. Appeals (D.C. cir.), Washington, 1972-74; sr. ptnr. Loewinger, Brand & Kappstatter, Washington, 1975—; com. mem. D.C. Superior Ct., 1976—; mem. adv. com. U.S. Bankruptcy Ct., 1985-86. Author: Loewinger on Landlord and Tenant, 1986. Commr. Housing Prodn. Com., D.C., 1986-87. Mem. ABA, D.C. Bar Assn., Supreme Ct. Hist. Soc. Landlord-tenant, Real property, Bankruptcy. Office: Loewinger Brand & Kappstatter 471 H St NW Washington DC 20001

LOEWINSOHN, ALAN STEWART, lawyer; b. Atlanta, Apr. 1, 1954; s. Ben David Loewinsohn and Toby (Lewis) Horn. BS, Northwestern U., 1976; JD, U. Va., 1979. Bar: Tex. 1979, U.S. Dist. Ct. (no. and so. dists.) Tex. 1979, U.S. Ct. Appeals (5th cir.) 1979. Assoc. Johnson & Swanson, Dallas, 1979-85, Law Offices of Frank Branson, Dallas, 1985-86; founding ptnr. Figari & Davenport, Dallas, 1986—; prof. jurisprudence Sch. Dentistry Baylor U., Dallas, 1981—. Mem. ABA, Tex. Bar Assn., Dallas Bar Assn., Dallas Trial Lawyers Assn., Tex. Trial Lawyers Assn., Assn. Trial Lawyers Am. Democrat. Jewish. Avocations: photography, tennis, sailing. Personal injury, Federal civil litigation, State civil litigation. Home: 3706 Mediterranean Dr Rockwall TX 75087 Office: Figari & Davenport 4800 Inter First Plaza Dallas TX 75202

LOEWY, IRA N., lawyer; b. Kew Gardens, N.Y., June 3, 1950; s. Henry H. and Madeline F. (Schack) L.; m. Jacklyn S. Silver, Mar. 18, 1972; children: Bradford, David. BA, Lafayette Coll., 1972; JD, NYU, 1975. Bar: Fla. 1975, U.S. Dist. Ct. (so. dist.) Fla. 1975, U.S. Ct. Appeals (1st, 3d, 4th, 5th, 6th, 7th, 8th, 9th, 10th, 11th and D.C. cirs.), U.S. Supreme Ct. 1980. Asst. atty. gen. Fla. Dept. Legal Affairs, Miami, 1975-78; asst. states atty. Dade County States Atty., Miami, Fla., 1978-82, deputy chief asst. states atty., 1982-84; assoc. Rierman, Sonnett, Shohat & Sale, Miami, 1984—. Mem. ABA, Dade County Bar Assn., Nat. Criminal Def. Lawyers Assn. Democrat. Jewish. Criminal. Home: 15401 SW 85th Ave Miami FL 33157 Office: Rierman Sonnett Shohat & Sale 200 SE 1st St Miami FL 33131

LOEWY, PETER HENRY, lawyer; b. N.Y.C., Oct. 2, 1955; s. Herbert and Ruth (Berger) L. B.A. summa cum laude, CCNY, 1976; J.D., Rutgers U., 1979. Bar: N.J. 1979, U.S. Ct. Appeals (3rd cir.) N.J. 1980, U.S. Dist. Ct. (ea. and so. dists.) N.Y. 1980, U.S. Ct. Appeals (2d cir.) N.Y. 1980, Fla. 1981, U.S. Dist. Ct. (so. dist.) Fla. 1981, U.S. Ct. Appeals (5th cir.) 1981, Calif. 1983, U.S. Dist. Ct. (cen. dist.) Calif. 1985, U.S. Ct. Appeals (9th cir.) 1985. Assoc. Fragomen Del Rey & Bernsen, N.Y.C., 1978-82, mng. ptnr. West Coast, Los Angeles, 1982-83, ptnr., 1984-85; mng. ptnr. Fragomen Del Rey Bersen & Inman, San Francisco and Los Angeles, 1985—. Contbg. editor Immigration Law Reports, 1983—. Vice chmn. Community Planning Bd., N.Y.C., 1979-81. Mem. N.Y. State Bar Assn. (immigration com.), N.Y. County Bar Assn. (immigration com.), Internat. Law Soc. (immigration com. 1980—), Assn. Immigration and Nationality Lawyers, Los Angeles County Bar Assn. (immigration com. 1983—), Century City Bar Assn. (immigration and nationality law com. 1985, bd. govs., bd. dirs. 1985—, chmn. immigration and naturalization com. 1985—), Phi Beta Kappa, Phi Alpha Theta. Clubs: 5th Ave. Squash (chmn. bd., dirs. 1982); So. Calif. Squash Racquets Assn. (pres. 1984). Immigration, naturalization, and customs. Office: Fragomen Del Rey et al 12011 San Vicente Blvd Suite #350 Los Angeles CA 90049

LOEWY, STEVEN A., lawyer; b. N.Y.C., Dec. 21, 1952; s. Samuel Alexander and Irene Dorothy (Aber) L.; m. Dina Rosenberg, Apr. 2, 1978; children: Tamar, David. BA, Washington U., St. Louis, 1974; JD, Yeshiva U., 1979. Bar: Md. 1980, U.S. Supreme Ct. 1983. Assoc. Gordon, Feinblatt, Rothman, Hoffberger & Hollander, Balt., 1980-81, Constable, Alexander, Daneker & Skeen, Balt., 1981-85, Weinberg & Green, Balt., 1985—; lectr. in law U. Balt., 1982-85; active edn. appeal bd. U.S. Dept. Edn., Washington, 1985—. Columnist Balt. Bus. Jour., 1985—. Vice chmn., counsel Friends of the Balt. Symphony, 1981-86. Research grantee U.S. Dept. Housing and Devel., 1979. Mem. ABA (real property sect.), Md. Bar Assn. (real property sect.), Balt. City Bar Assn. Republican. Jewish. Real property, Landlord-tenant, Banking. Home: 6715 Western Run Dr Baltimore MD 21215 Office: Weinberg and Green 100 S Charles St Baltimore MD 21201

LOFFMAN, LESLIE HOWARD, lawyer, writer, educator; b. N.Y.C., June 18, 1950; s. Murray Jay and Roslyn (Handleman) L.; m. Sharon Fern Shurack, Aug. 26, 1973; children: Steven Mathew, Amy Rachel. BS, Bklyn. Coll., 1972; MBA with distinction, Pace U., 1975; JD cum laude, Vt. U., 1978. Assoc. Barrett, Smith, Schapiro, Simon & Armstrong, N.Y.C., 1978-81; ptnr. Carro, Spanbock, Fass, Geller, Kaster & Cuiffo, N.Y.C., 1981-86, Finley, Kumble, Wagner, Heine, Underberg, Marley, Myerson & Casey, N.Y.C., 1986—; adj. assoc. prof. NYU Real Estate Inst., N.Y.C, 1983—. Author: (with others) Real Estate Syndication Handbook, 1985, Tax Sheltered Investments Handbook Special Update on Tax Reform Act of 1986, 1986, Real Estate Syndication Tax Handbook, 1986; contbr. articles to profl. jours. Mem. ABA (partnerships com. 1984—), N.Y. State Bar Assn. (partnerships com. 1984—), Delta Mu Delta. Corporate taxation, Personal income taxation, Legal education. Home: 45 Birchwood Park Dr Syosset NY 11791 Office: Finley Kumble Wagner Heine et al 425 Park Ave New York NY 10022

LOFFREDO, PASCO FRANK, lawyer; b. Providence, Apr. 22, 1950; s. Pasco and Adeline (Pitocchi) L.; m. Susan Elizabeth Hall, Aug. 7, 1977; children: Bethany, Amy. BA, Bethany Coll., 1972; JD, New Eng. Sch. of Law, 1976. Bar: R.I. 1976, U.S. Dist. Ct. R.I. 1977, Mass. 1979, U.S. Dist. Ct. Mass. 1979. Sole practice Cranston, R.I., 1976-79, Providence, 1986—; ptnr. Chaika & Loffredo, Cranston, 1979-85. Mem. adv. bd. Providence (R.I.) Foster Grandparents Program, 1983—; bd. dirs. R.I. Div. Mediation Council, Providence, 1984—. Mem. ABA, R.I. Bar Assn., R.I. Trial Lawyers Assn. (com. on state and fed. legis.). Democrat. Roman Catholic. Avocations: farming, politics, reading. Real property, Personal injury, Family and matrimonial. Office: 76 Dorrance St Suite 200 Providence RI 02903

LOFGREN, NORMAN ARTHUR, lawyer; b. Bridgeport, Conn., Apr. 24, 1947; s. Richard Joseph and Laura (Kelt) L.; m. Lynne Ames Murray, June 7, 1969; children: Richard, Christopher, Robert. AB, U. Mo., 1969; JD with honors, Okla. City U., 1977; LLM in Taxation, So. Meth. U., 1981. Bar: D.C. 1978, Tex. 1978, U.S. Dist. Ct. (no. dist.) Tex. 1978, U.S. Tax Ct. 1978. Tax and trial atty. Chief Counsel's Office, IRS, Dallas, 1977-82; assoc. tax counsel Sun Exploration & Prodn. Co., Dallas, 1982—. Advancements chmn. Boy Scouts Am., Richardson, Tex., 1983—; vestry mem. Epiphany Episcopal Ch., Richardson, 1986—. Served to lt. USN, 1969-75, to comdr. Res. Mem. ABA, Am. Corp. Counsels Assn., U.S. Naval Inst. Republican. Avocation: jogging. Corporate taxation, Taxation of Natural Resources. Office: Sun Exploration & Prodn Co PO Box 2880 Dallas TX 75221-2880

LOFTIN, MELINDA JAYNE, lawyer; b. Detroit, Jan. 25, 1956; d. Iverson L. and Patricia Diane (Haley) L. BA, Adrian Coll., 1977; JD, Detroit Coll. of Law, 1981. Bar: Mich. 1981, U.S. Dist. Ct. (ea. and so. dists.) Mich. 1981. Law clk. tank automotive command U.S. Army, Warren, Mich., 1980-81, atty., advisor tank automotive command, 1981-86; gen. atty., research devel. engring. ctr. U.S. Army, Natick, Mass., 1986—; bd. dirs. Adrian (Mich.) Coll., 1984—. Mem. ABA, Mich. Bar Assn., Sigma Sigma Sigma. Republican. Methodist. Avocations: travel, football. Military, Labor, Government contracts and claims. Office: US Army Research Devel and Engring Ctr STRNC-L Natick MA 01760-5000

LOFTIS, NANCY LYNN, lawyer; b. Ft. Hood, Tex., Dec. 30, 1956; d. Alan George and Francis Mae (Jurica) L. BA, U. Nebr., 1979, JD, 1982. Bar: Nebr. 1982. Assoc. Pierson, Ackerman et al, Lincoln, Nebr., 1982-84, ptnr., 1985—. Mem. ABA, Nebr. Bar Assn., Lincoln Bar Assn., Assn. Trial Lawyers Am., Nebr. Assn. Trial Lawyers. Republican. Bankruptcy, Contracts commercial, Real property. Home: 1720 C St Apt A Lincoln NE 68502 Office: Pierson, Ackerman et al 530 S 13th St Suite B Lincoln NE 68509

LOFTISS, THOMAS JEFFERSON, II, judge, lawyer; b. Augusta, Ga.; m. Debbie Hall; children: Allison, Emily. BA in Polit. Sci. and Psychology, Emory U., 1969; JD, U. Ga., 1973; postdoctoral, U. Nev., 1980. Ptnr. Altman, McGraw & Loftiss, Thomasville, Ga., 1973-77, Loftiss, Van Heiningen & Ward, Thomasville, 1977—; judge juvenile ct. Thomas County, Ga. Adult sunday sch. tchr., mem. nominations and personnel com. First United Meth. Ch.; past mem. Thomas County Mental Health Adv. Council, City Thomasville Recreation Bd., Thomas Area Recreation Bd.; mem. adv. council Southwestern State Hosp., Mayor's Council on Spl. Olympics, adv. bd. Camp Arrow, Inc., steering com. Thomas County Alliance for Children; bd. dirs., past pres. Thomas County Humane Soc., Thomasville. Mem. Assn. Trial Lawyers Am., Nat. Council Juvenile and Family Ct. Judges (lead judge State of Ga., permanent families for children project), Ga. Trial Lawyers Assn., Ga. Council Juvenile Ct. Judges (v.p., chmn. permanency planning com., legis. com., uniform rules com.). Lodge: Kiwanis (disting. past pres. Thomasville club). Office: Loftiss Van Heiningen & Ward PO Box 1935 Thomasville GA 31799

LOFTMAN, GUY RICKARD, lawyer; b. Cleve., Aug. 23, 1945; s. Rickard Nicholas and Ermin (Rack) L.; m. Connie Keisling, Mar. 19, 1967; children—Eve, Eric. A.B., Ind. U., 1967, J.D. cum laude, 1974. Bar: Ind. 1974, U.S. Dist Ct. (so. dist.) Ind. 1974, U.S. Ct. Appeals (7th cir.) 1974, U.S. Sup. Ct. 1977, U.S. Dist. Ct. (cen. dist.) Ill. 1982. Bd. dirs. Hospice of Bloomington, 1979-85; mem. bd. Unitarian Universalist Ch. Bloomington, 1982-85, pres., 1983, pres. Midwest Summer Assembly, 1985—; bd. dirs. Harmony Sch. Bd., 1976—. Conscientious objector, served alt. duty, 1968-70. Mem. Ind. Bar Assn., Monroe County Bar Assn. Democrat. Club: Bloomington Olde Time Music & Dance. General practice, Federal civil litigation, State civil litigation. Home: 4835 S Victor Pike Bloomington IN 47401 Office: 532 N Walnut St Bloomington IN 47401

LOFTUS, CARROLL MICHAEL, lawyer; b. Cheverly, Md., Oct. 9, 1946; s. Joseph P. and Margaret M. (Boland) L.; m. Claire E. Barbour, Oct. 12, 1968; children: Kevin M., Christopher D., James B., Elizabeth A. BS in Acctg., Wheeling (W.Va.) Coll., 1968; JD, Cath. U., 1973. Bar: Md. 1973, D.C. 1975, U.S. Dist. Ct. Md. 1974, U.S. Supreme Ct. 1978, U.S. Dist. Ct. D.C. 1984. Law clk. to presiding judge U.S. Dist. Ct. Md., Balt., 1973-74; assoc. Venable, Baetjer & Howard, Balt., 1974-75; from assoc. to ptnr. Slover & Loftus, Washington, 1975—; exec. dir. Eastern Coal Transp. Conf., Washington, 1981—. Contbr. articles to profl. jours. Mem. ABA, Md. Bar Assn., D.C. Bar Assn. Republican. Roman Catholic. Avocations: skiing, boating, fishing, hiking. Administrative and regulatory, Federal civil litigation, Energy, coal. Home: 13301 Beall Creek Ct Potomac MD 20854 Office: Slover & Loftus 1224 17th St NW Washington DC 20036

LOFTUS, THOMAS DANIEL, lawyer; b. Seattle, Nov. 8, 1930; s. Glendon Francis and Martha Helen (Wall) L. B.A., U. Wash., 1952, J.D., 1957. Bar: Wash. 1958, U.S. Ct. Appeals (9th cir.) 1958, U.S. Dist. Ct. Wash. 1958, U.S. Ct. Mil. Appeals, U.S. Supreme Ct. Trial atty. Northwestern Mut. Ins. Co., Seattle, 1958-62; sr. trial atty. Unigard Security Ins. Co., Seattle, 1962-68, asst. gen. counsel, 1969-83, govt. relations counsel, 1983—; mem. Wash. Commn. on Jud. Conduct (formerly Jud. Qualifications Commn.), 1982—, vice-chmn., 1987—; judge pro tem Seattle Mcpl. Ct., 1973-81. Sec., treas. Seattle Opera Assn., 1980—; pres., bd. dirs. Vis. Nurse Services, 1979—; pres., v.p. Salvation Army Adult Rehab. Ctr., 1979—; vice chmn. Young Republican Nat. Fedn., 1963-65; pres. Young Reps. King County, 1962-63; bd. dirs. Seattle Seafair, Inc., 1975; bd. dirs., gen. counsel Wash. Ins. Council, 1984-86, sec., 1986—; bd. dirs. Arson Alarm Found. Served to 1st lt. U.S. Army, 1952-54, to col. Res., 1954-83. Fellow Am. Bar Found.; mem. Am. Arbitration Assn. (nat. panel arbitrators 1965—), Wash. Bar Assn. (gov. 1981-84), Seattle King County Bar Assn. (sec., trustee 1977-82), ABA (ho. of dels. 1984—), Internat. Assn. Ins. Counsel, Def. Research Inst., Am. Judicature Soc., Res. Officers Assn., Wash. Ins. Council (v.p., sec., gen. counsel, bd. dirs. 1984—), U. Wash. Alumni Assn., Phi Delta Phi, Theta Delta Chi. Republican. Presbyterian. Clubs: Coll. of Seattle, Wash. Athletic. Insurance, Personal injury, General corporate. Home: 3515 Magnolia Blvd West Seattle WA 98199 Office: 1215 4th Ave 18th Floor Seattle WA 98161

LOGAN, CARL M., lawyer; b. Quenemo, Kans., Mar. 20, 1942; s. John L. and Maurine E. (Price) L.; m. Heidi E. Pfaff, June 19, 1965; children: Heather E., Holly M., Jane K., William K. BA, U. Kans., 1964; JD, Harvard U., 1967. Bar: Kans. 1967, U.S. Dist. Ct. Kans. 1967, U.S. Tax Ct. 1970, U.S. Supreme Ct. 1975. Assoc. Payne & Jones, Olathe, Kans., 1967-68, ptnr., 1968-80; ptnr. Logan and Martin, Olathe and Overland Park, Kans., 1980-86; of counsel Shook, Hardy and Bacon, Overland Park, 1986, ptnr., 1987—; bd. dirs. Olathe State Bank, WH of KC, Inc. Bd. dirs. Olathe Community Hosp., Olathe Community Health Devel. Corp. Mem. ABA, Kans. Bar Assn. (chmn. licensure com. 1984-86, Outstanding Service award 1985), Johnson County Bar Assn. (treas. 1971), Olathe Community Hosp. Assn. (bd. dirs.), The Group. Democrat. Methodist. Avocation: flyfishing. General corporate, Corporate taxation, Banking. Home: 1086 Wyckford Rd Olathe KS 66061 Office: Shook Hardy and Bacon PO Box 25128 Overland Park KS 66225

LOGAN, FRANCIS DUMMER, lawyer; b. Evanston, Ill., May 23, 1931; s. Simon Rae and Frances (Dummer) L.; m. Claude Riviere, Apr. 13, 1957; children: Carolyn Gisele, Francis Dummer. B.A., U. Chgo., 1950; B.A. Juris, Oxford U., 1954; LL.B., Harvard U., 1955. Bar: N.Y. 1956. Assoc. Milbank, Tweed, Hadley & McCloy, N.Y.C., 1955-64; ptnr. Milbank, Tweed, Hadley & McCloy, 1965—; dir. Chase Manhattan Overseas Banking Corp. Mem. ABA, N.Y. State Bar Assn., Assn. Bar City N.Y., Council on Fgn. Relations. Home: 1170 Fifth Ave New York NY 10029 Office: Milbank Tweed Hadley & McCloy 1 Chase Manhattan Plaza New York NY 10005

LOGAN, JAMES ASHLIN, lawyer; b. Wilmore, Ky., Jan. 29, 1905; s. Sanford McBrayer and Adele (Saufley) L.; m. Mary Ella Bedlinger, Oct. 1, 1949. A.B., Centre Coll., Danville, Ky.; J.D., Case Western Res. U.; post-grad. U. Cin., Oxford (Eng.) U. Bar: Ky. 1930. Sole practice, 1930-35; atty. Fed. Land Bank of Louisville, Home Owners Loan Assn.; conciliation commr. Farm Debtors, 1935-37; ptnr. Jouett and Logan, Winchester, Ky., 1937-43; spl. asst. U.S. Atty. Gen., 1943-46; authorization officer VA, 1946-49; atty. Employees Compensation Appeals Bd., Washington, 1949-51; atty. Inter-Ocean Ins. Co., 1951-65; sole practice, Walton, Ky., 1965—; del. 9th Conf. on Law of World, Madrid, 1979. Elder Richwood Presbyn. Ch., Boone County, Ky. Recipient numerous awards including Selective Service medal U.S. Congress, 1968, Keys to City of Louisville, 1968. Mem. Fed. Bar Assn., Ky. Bar Assn. (sr. counselor 1980—), Am. Legion, No. Ky. Heritage League, Ky. Hist. Soc., SAR (past pres. Ky. soc., Patriot's medal 1968), Cin. Council World Affairs, Phi Delta Phi, Omicron Delta Kappa, Pi Kappa Delta. Club: Filson of Louisville. Probate, Estate taxation. Office: 1154 Richwood Rd Walton KY 41094

LOGAN, JAMES FRANKLIN, JR., lawyer; b. Cleveland, Tenn., May 17, 1946; s. James Franklin and Lillie Mae (Cannon) L.; m. Jill Davis, Dec. 18, 1965; children—James Paul, Merri Lynn, m. 2d, Cindy Almond, Nov. 29, 1980. B.S., Tenn. Wesleyan Coll., 1968; J.D., U. Tenn.-Knoxville, 1970. Bar: Tenn. 1971, U.S. Dist. Ct. Tenn. 1971, U.S. Ct. Appeals (6th cir.) 1975. Assoc. Finnell, Thompson & Scott, Cleveland, 1971-74; ptnr. Finnell, Thompson, Logan & Rogers, Cleveland, 1974-80; sr. ptnr. Logan, Bates & Bass, Cleveland, 1980-85, ptnr., James F. Logan, Jr. and Assocs., 1985—. Active Tri-County Sportsman League, Cherokee chpt. Am. Kidney Fund., Cleveland State Community Coll.; chmn. March of Dimes; past chmn. Bradley County Dem. party. Mem. ABA, Tenn. Criminal Def. Lawyers Assn., Tenn. Bar Assn., Tenn. Trial Lawyers Assn., Nat. Assn. Criminal Def. Lawyers, Am. Judicature Soc., Bradley County Bar Assn., Chattanooga Trial Lawyers Assn., C. of C. Democrat. Baptist. Clubs: Lions, Tri-County Sportsman League; Cougar; Ducks Unlimited. Criminal, Personal injury. Address: #30 2d St NE PO Box 191 Cleveland TN 37364-0191

LOGAN, JAMES KENNETH, judge; b. Quenemo, Kans., Aug. 21, 1929; s. John Lysle and Esther Maurine (Price) L.; m. Beverly Jo Jennings, June 8, 1952; children: Daniel Jennings, Amy Katherine, Sarah Jane, Samuel Price. A.B., U. Kans., 1952; LL.B. magna cum laude, Harvard, 1955. Bar: Kans. 1955, Calif. 1956. Law clk. U.S. Circuit Judge Huxman, 1955-56; with firm Gibson, Dunn & Crutcher, Los Angeles, 1956-57; asst. prof. law U. Kans., 1957-61; prof., dean U. Kans. (Law Sch.), 1961-68; partner Payne and Jones, Olathe, Kans., 1968-77; judge U.S. Circuit Ct., 10th Circuit, 1977—; Ezra Ripley Thayer teaching fellow Harvard Law Sch., 1961- 62; vis. prof. U. Tex. Law Sch., 1964, Stanford, 1969, U. Mich., 1976; commr. U.S. Dist. Ct., 1964-67. Author: (with W.B. Leach) Future Interests and Estate Planning, 1961, Kansas Estate Administration, 5th edit., 1986, (with A.R. Martin) Kansas Corporate Law and Practice, 2d edit., 1979; also articles. Candidate for U.S. Senate, 1968. Served with AUS, 1947-48. Rhodes scholar, 1952; recipient Disting. Service citation U. Kans., 1986. Mem. Am., Kans. bar assns., Phi Beta Kappa, Order of Coif, Beta Gamma Sigma, Omicron Delta Kappa, Pi Sigma Alpha, Alpha Kappa Psi, Phi Delta Phi. Democrat. Presbyterian. Home: 1082 Wyckford Rd Olathe KS 66061 Office: Box 790 1 Patrons Plaza Olathe KS 66061

LOGAN, LEONARD GILMORE, JR., lawyer; b. Phila., May 16, 1937; s. Leonard Gilmore and Virginia (Shaw) L.; m. Sylvia Anne Fountain, Nov. 14, 1964 (div. Oct. 1986); children: Sylvia Katherine DeVries, Richard C., Leonard G. III, Letitia F., Eric; m. Elizabeth Pruitt Carbone, Dec. 21, 1986. AB, Duke U., 1959, JD, 1962. Bar: Iowa 1962, U.S. Mil. Appeals 1963, D.C. 1964, N.C. 1973, U.S. Dist. Ct. (ea. dist.) N.C. 1973, U.S. Supreme Ct. 1979. Commdr. lt. (j.g.) U.S. Navy, 1963, advanced through grades to lt. comdr. 1969; served with judge adv. gen. corps; Mil. judge 5th Naval Dist., Norfolk, Va., 1969-71, ret., 1971; project counsel Nat. Assn. Attys.'s Gen., 1971; govs.'s atty. for state govt. reorng., State of N.C., 1971-72; sr. ptnr. Leonard G. Logan, Jr., P.A., Kitty Hawk, N.C., 1972—; clin. adj. prof. law Wake Forest U. Sch. Law, 1982-83; instr. Coll. of Albemarle, 1983, 84; legal cons. to EPA, Office of Air Programs, 1971-72; com. counsel and spl. counsel to N.C. Gen. Assembly, 1973-74; guest panelist Nat. Environ. Conf., Arlie House, Warrenton, Va., sponsored by EPA, 1971, Ann. Meeting of Mid-Western Assn. Attys. Gen., Wis., 1971. Chmn. County Am. Cancer Soc., 1974-75; lay speaker United Meth. Ch., 1978-86; pres. Circus Tent Interdenominational Ministries, 1979; bd. dirs. Creative Puppet Ministries, Inc.; producer of TV show The Rainbow Factory, 1980-86; bd. dirs. Northeastern Pub. Co., Inc., 1981-85. Recipient Am. Jurisprudence Prize award, 1962. Mem. Dare County Bar Assn., 1st Jud. Dist. Bar Assn., N.C. State Bar, N.C. Bar Assn., Assn. Trial Lawyers Am., ABA, Christian Legal Soc., N.C. Coll. Adv., Internat. Legal Soc., Fed. Bar Assn., Dare County Legal Secs. Assn. (Boss of Yr. 1984), Outer Banks C. of C. (legis. affairs com.). Democrat. Club: Duck Woods (Southern Shores, N.C.). Lodges: Masons, Rotary, Shriners. Author: Environmental Control, 1972. General practice, Real property, State civil litigation. Office: PO Box 464 Kitty Hawk NC 27949

LOGAN, MICHAEL JAMES, lawyer; b. West Frankfort, Ill., Apr. 9, 1943; s. James A. and Helen M. (Malinosky) L.; m. Jennifer Ann James, June 24,

1967; children: James, Stephen, Daniel. BA, MacMurray Coll., 1965; JD, John Marshall Sch. Law, 1971. Bar: Ill. 1972, U.S. Dist. Ct. (cen. dist.) Ill. 1973. Asst. credit Carson, Pirie, Scott & Co., Chgo., 1967-69; law draftsman Legis. Reference, Springfield, Ill., 1971-73; ptnr. Calandrino, Logan and Lamarca, Springfield, 1973—. Mem. ABA, Ill. Bar Assn., Sangamon County Bar Assn., Soc. Preservation Barbershop Quartet Singing in Am. Baptist. Personal injury, General practice, State civil litigation. Home: 2909 Clifton Springfield IL 62704 Office: Calandrino Logan & Lamarca 837 2 4th St Springfield IL 62703

LOGAN, ROBERT L., lawyer; b. Peoria, Ill., July 2, 1931; s. Robert L. and Elizabeth (Schenck) L.; m. Barbara L. Doering, June 8, 1957; children—Barbara, Anne, James. A.B., Princeton U., 1953; J.D., U. Mich., 1958. Bar: Ohio, Pa. Atty. Frost & Jacobs, Cin., 1958-62; sr. counsel, asst. sec. Owens-Corning Fiberglas Corp., Toledo, 1962-77; v.p., gen. counsel and sec. H.H. Robertson Co., Pitts., 1977—. Served to capt. USMC, 1953-65. Home: 838 Valleyview Rd Pittsburgh PA 15243 Office: H H Robertson Co 2 Gateway Center Pittsburgh PA 15222

LOGAN, THOMAS JOSEPH, lawyer; b. Washington, Iowa, Aug. 13, 1951; s. John A. and Rhea (Buck) L.; m. Jean E. Wolf, Aug. 11, 1973; 1 child, Abigail E. BA, Drake U., 1973, JD, 1976. Bar: Iowa 1976, U.S. Dist. Ct. (no. and so. dists.) Iowa 1976. Assoc. Hopkins & Heubner, Des Moines, 1976-78; ptnr., dir. Hopkins & Heubner P.C., Des Moines, 1979—. Mem. ABA, Def. Research and Trial Lawyers, Iowa Bar Assn. (exec. council 1979—), Polk County Bar Assn. (pres. jr. bar assn. 1984-85). Democrat. Presbyterian. Club: Des Moines Golf. Federal civil litigation, State civil litigation, Personal injury. Office: Hopkins & Heubner PC 2700 Grand Ave Suite 111 Des Moines IA 50312

LOGAN, VALENTINE WEIR, lawyer; b. Sterling, Colo., June 29, 1916; s. William John and Beatrice (Weir) L.; m. Martha McGarity, Aug. 7, 1944; children: Marsha Campbell, Michael M. BA in Chemistry, U. Colo., 1941, JD, 1948. Bar: Colo. 1948, U.S. Dist. Ct. Colo. 1948, U.S. Ct. Appeals (10th cir.) 1950. Sole practice Denver, 1948—. Served to 1st lt. paratroop U.S. Army, 1942-46, PTO. Mem. Denver Bar Assn. Democrat. Methodist. Clubs: University, Law (Denver); Vail (Colo.) Racquet. Avocations: tennis, golf, swimming, reading, travel. State civil litigation, Personal injury, Probate. Home: 350 Bellaire Denver CO 80220 Office: 718 17th St Suite 707 Denver CO 80202

LOGAR, RONALD JOHN, lawyer; b. Erie, Colo., Aug. 15, 1935; s. Frank and Ann (Vinovich) L.; m. Nancy Charlene Hewins, Aug. 4, 1956 (div. 1974); children—Debra Lynn Logar Secary, John Richard, Linda Lee; m. Mary Jane Canonic, May 15, 1976. B.S., U. Nev.-Reno, 1958; LL.B., U. Ariz., 1961. Bar: Ariz. 1961, Nev. 1962, U.S. Dist. Ct. (no. dist.) Nev. 1964, U.S. Ct. Appeals (9th cir.) 1976. Law clk. Nev. Supreme Ct., Carson City, 1961-62; assoc. Springer, McKissick & Hug, Reno, 1962; ptnr. Bissett & Logar, Reno, 1962-79; sole practice, Reno, 1979—. Editor, Nev. Family Law Report. Former mem. Nev. State Bd. Edn.; active various polit. campaigns. Fellow Am. Acad. Matrimonial Lawyers; mem. Washoe County Bar, Nev. Bar Assn., Nev. State Bar (founder, 1st chmn. family law sect., chmn. ethics com., editor Nev. Family Law Report), Ariz. Bar Assn. (family law sect.), Ducks Unlimited. Republican. Lodges: Masons, Shrine, Elks. Family and matrimonial, General corporate, Probate. Office: Law Office of Ronald J Logar PC 243 S Sierra Reno NV 89501

LOGGANS, SUSAN ELIZABETH, lawyer; b. Clinton, Ill., Dec. 31, 1949; d. Rex and Cleta M. (Glenn) L.; m. Ronald H. Galowich, Sept. 18, 1977. A.B., U. Ill., 1971; J.D., DePaul U., 1974. Bar: Ill. 1974. Assoc. Philip H. Corboy & Assoc., Chgo., 1974-77; prin. Susan E. Loggans & Assocs., Chgo., 1977—; lectr. to univs., med. assns., legal orgns., others. Contbr. articles to profl. jours. Phi Alpha Delta scholar, 1974; recipient Spirit of Love Honoree award Little City Found., 1986. Mem. Am. Bar Found., Nat. Bd. Trial Advocacy (cert. civil trial adv.), ABA (vice chmn. com. on aviation and space law sect. tort and ins. practice 1979—, standing and adv. com. aero. law, 1980—), Ill. Bar Assn. (mem. assembly 1st jud. dist. 1979-81, civil practice and procedure sect. council 1978-80, tort law sect. council 1978-80, gov. 1980-82), Chgo. Bar Assn (chmn. aviation law sect. 1979-80, chmn. Tort Law sect., 1986-87), Fla. Bar Assn., Assn. Trial Lawyers Am. (sec. aviation law sect. 1978-80, vice chmn. 1980-82, chmn. 1982—, vice chmn. research and legal dept. 1982—, vice chmn. tort law sect. 1985-87, chmn. 1986—), Ill. Trial Lawyers Assn. (chmn. spl. com. on orgn. 1978, bd. govs. 1976-80, bd. mgrs. 1977-82), Am. Judicature Soc., Fla. Assn. Women Lawyers, Lawyers-Pilots Bar Assn. Personal injury. Home: 1248 N Astor St Chicago IL 60610 Office: 615 N Wabash Ave Chicago IL 60611

LOGIE, JOHN HOULT, lawyer; b. Ann Arbor, Mich., Aug. 11, 1939; s. James W. and Elizabeth H. (Hoult) L.; m. Susan G. Duerr, Aug. 15, 1964; children—John Hoult, Susannah, Margaret Elizabeth. Student Williams Coll., 1957-59; B.A., U. Mich., 1961, J.D., 1968; M.S., George Washington U., 1966. Bar: Mich. 1969. Ptnr., Warner, Norcross & Judd, Grand Rapids, Mich., 1969—; program coordinator Inst. Continuing Legal Edn., 1980—, conf. chmn., 1980—; guest lectr. Grand Rapids Jr. Coll., Grand Valley State Coll. Pres., Grand Rapids PTA Council, 1971-73, Heritage Hill Assn., 1976; chmn. Grand Rapids Urban Homesteading Commn., 1975-80, Target Area Leadership Conf., Grand Rapids, 1976-80, City/County Sesquicentennial Com., 1986, Grand Rapids Hist. Commn., 1987—; v.p. bd. dirs. Goodwill Industries, Grand Rapids, 1973-79, Am. Cancer Soc., Grand Rapids, 1970-81; sec., trustee Hist. Soc. Mich., 1984—; vice chmn. Grand Rapids Hist. Commn., 1985—. Served to lt. USN, 1961-66. Mem. ABA (forum com. on health law 1980—), Mich. Bar Assn. (chmn. condemnation sect. 1985—), Grand Rapids Bar Assn., Am. Acad. Hosp. Attys., Mich. Soc. Hosp. Attys. (pres. 1976-77), Am. Soc. Law and Medicine, Nat. Health Lawyers Assn. Clubs: Univ. (dir. 1979-82, pres. 1980-82), Peninsular, Athletic (Grand Rapids). Health, Condemnation, General corporate. Home: 601 Cherry St SE Grand Rapids MI 49503 Office: 900 Old Kent Bldg Grand Rapids MI 49503

LOGIGIAN, JOHN DOUGLAS, lawyer; b. Mahopac, N.Y., May 15, 1952; s. Edward Alfred and Enid Barbara (Green) L.; m. Marilyn A. Marlek, Aug. 7, 1977; children: Douglas Tate, Brandon Rhys. BA cum laude, Oberlin Coll., 1974; JD, Georgetown U., 1977. Bar: N.Y. 1978. Assoc. Gifford, Woody, Palmer & Serles, N.Y.C., 1977-79; atty. Columbia Pictures Industries, Inc., N.Y.C., 1979-81, United Artists Corp., N.Y.C., 1981-83; dir. bus. affairs and v.p. Orion Classics div., Orion Pictures Corp., N.Y.C., 1983—. Entertainment. Office: Orion Pictures Corp 711 5th Ave New York NY 10022

LOGLI, PAUL ALBERT, lawyer; b. Rockford, Ill., Nov. 20, 1949; s. Albert Joseph and Margaret (Salamone) L.; m. Jodean L. Miller, Oct. 26, 1985. BA cum laude, Loras Coll., 1971; JD, U. Ill., 1974. Bar: Ill. 1974, U.S. Dist. Ct. (no. dist.) Ill. 1975. Asst. state's atty. Winnebago County, Rockford, Ill., 1974-76; ptnr. North, Ohlson, Logli, Condon & Boyd, Rockford, 1976-81; assoc. judge 17th Jud. Cir., Winnebago and Boone counties, Rockford, 1981-86; state's atty. Winnebago County, 1986—; chmn. domestic relations com. Ill. Jud. Conf., 1983-84; mem. U.S. Dept. of Justice Law Enforcement Coordinating Com. (no. dist.) Ill. Bd. dirs. Rockford Symphony Orch., 1983-87, Rosecrance Meml. Homes for Children, Rockford, 1983—, Rockford Area Conv. and Visitors Bur., 1984—, Discovery Ctr. Children's Mus., 1986—; mem. adv. bd. St. Anthony Hosp. Med. Ctr., Rockford, 1983—; pres. Blackhawk Area council Boy Scouts Am., 1984-87; chmn. bldg. com. St. Peter's Cathedral. Recipient service award Northwest Ill. Chiefs of Police Assn., 1981, New Am. Theater, 1981; Disting. Service award Jaycees, 1982. Mem. Ill. State Bar Assn., Winnebago County Bar Assn., Ill. State's Attys. Assn., Nat. Dist. Attys. Assn. Republican. Roman Catholic. Lodge: Rotary (bd. dirs. 1984-85). Local government, Criminal. Office: Winnebago County Courthouse 400 W State St Suite 619 Rockford IL 61101

LOH, ROBERT DANIEL, JR., lawyer; b. New Rochelle, N.Y., Feb. 23, 1951; s. Robert Daniel Sr. and Julanne (Sullivan) L.; m. Patricia Freeman, Aug. 27, 1978; children: Robert Daniel III, Katherine Michelle, Timothy Francis. BA in Econs. cum laude, U. Vt., 1973; JD, U. Conn., 1976. Bar: Conn. 1976, N.Y. 1984. Securities specialist AMAX Inc., Greenwich, Conn., 1977-80, mgr. stock exchnge matters, 1980-84, mgr. shareholder and stock exchange relations, 1984-85, mgr. investor relations and stock exchange matters, 1985—. Mem. ABA, Conn. Bar Assn., N.Y. State Bar Assn., Nat. Investor Relations Inst. (bd. dirs. N.Y. chpt. 1984—). Corporate secretary, investor relations. Office: AMAX Inc PO Box 1700 Greenwich CT 06836-1700

LOHMAN, RICHARD VERNE, lawyer; b. Colorado Springs, Colo., July 19, 1951; s. Edward Verne and Pauline Elizabeth (Hook) L.; m. Barbara Jo Eichhorn, Nov. 3, 1973; children: Kristen Elizabeth, Brett Edward. BA in Polit. Sci. with honors, Colo. State U., 1973; JD with distinction, Washburn U., 1976. Bar: Colo. 1976, U.S. Dist. Ct. Colo. 1976, Kans. 1977, U.S. Dist. Ct. Kans. 1977. Assoc. Murphy, Morris & Susemihl, Colorado Springs, 1976-78; spl. county atty. El Paso County Colorado Springs, 1977; ptnr. Murphy, Morris & Susemihl, Colorado Springs, 1978-80, Morris, Susemihl, Lohman & Kent, Colorado Springs, 1980-83, Susemihl, Lohman, Kent, Carlson & McDermott, Colorado Springs, 1983—; mediator Colo. Council Mediation, Denver, 1983—; dir. Pikes Peak Legal Services, Colorado Springs. Author: Handbook for Caseworkers, 1978, Trial Strategy and Preparation in Divorce Cases, 1985, Marital Agreements and the Colorado Marital Agreement Act, 1986. Mem. Juvenile Justice Task Force, Colorado Springs, 1978; pres. Pikes Peak Children's Advocates, Colorado Springs, 1979; mem. Pikes Peak Range Riders, Colorado Springs, 1982—. Recipient Cert. of Appreciation, Kans. Bar Assn., 1978, Outstanding Guardian ad litem award Pikes Peak Children's Advocates, 1979, Spl. Recognition award Pikes Peak Children's Advocates, 1981. Fellow Am. Acad. Matrimonial Lawyers; mem. Nat. Assn. Counsel for Children (pres. 1979-80), ABA, Assn. Trial Lawyers Am., Colo. Bar Assn., El Paso County Bar Assn. (cert. appreciation 1983, chmn. mental health com. 1980-81, chairperson family com. 1985-86), Am. Arbitration Assn. (arbitrator), Aircraft Owners and Pilots Assn. Clubs: Country of Colo., Winter Nights, Plaza (Colorado Springs). Family and matrimonial, Juvenile. Home: 24 3d St Colorado Springs CO 80906 Office: Susemihl Lohman Kent et al 660 S Pointe Ct Colorado Springs CO 80906

LOHOFF, RANDY KEITH, lawyer; b. Tell City, Ind., July 25, 1952; s. Lewis Clark and Jerie (John) L.; m. Jean Bishop Gutting, Dec. 28, 1974; children: Bryan, Drew. BA, DePauw U., 1974; JD, U. Louisville, 1977. Bar: Ky. 1977. Atty. Ashland (ky.) Oil Co., 1977-82, sr. atty., 1983—. Co-founder, treas. Ashland Area Labor Mgmt. Council, Inc., 1984—. Mem. ABA (labor law sect., litigation sect.), Ky. Bar Assn., Boyd County Bar Assn., Brandeis Soc., Phi Kappa Phi, Omicron Delta Epsilon. Republican. Methodist. Labor. Office: Ashland Oil Co Inc Box 391 Ashland KY 41114

LOHR, GEORGE E., state supreme court justice; b. 1931. B.S., S.D. State U.; J.D., U. Mich. Bar: Colo. 1958, Calif. 1969. Former judge Colo. 9th Dist. Ct., Aspen; assoc. justice Colo. Supreme Ct., Denver, 1979—. Office: Colo Supreme Ct State Judicial Bldg 2 E 14th Ave Denver CO 80203 *

LOHSE, WILLIAM KURT, lawyer; b. Reno, May 15, 1942; s. George and Alice (Sauer) L.; m. Catherine Patrick, Aug. 17, 1963 (div. Dec. 1979); children: Kristen G., Stephen G.; m. Diana Christina Szabo, Feb. 14, 1985. BA, U. Nev., 1963; JD, U. Calif., San Francisco, 1966. Bar: Nev. 1966, U.S. Dist. Ct. Nev. 1966, U.S. Ct. Appeals (9th cir.) 1966, U.S. Supreme Ct. 1973, U.S. Tax Ct. 1981. Ptnr. Lohse & Lohse, Reno, 1969-76; sole practice Reno, 1976-81, 83—; atty. Accident Attys. Assocs., Reno, 1981-83. Mem. Friends UNR Med. Sch. Served to capt. U.S. Army, 1967-69. Mem. Washoe County Bar Assn., Internat. Bar Assn., Assn. Trial Lawyers Am., Nev. Trial Lawyers Assn., Nat. Maritime Hist. Soc., Cousteau Soc., Nat. Geographic Soc., Phi Alpha Delta. Republican. Roman Catholic. Club: Tahoe (Calif.) Yacht. Avocations: sailing, running, cycling, literature, travel. Personal injury. Office: 403 Flint St Reno NV 98501

LOIGMAN, LARRY SCOTT, lawyer; b. Neptune, N.J., Sept. 3, 1954; s. Bernard and Doris (Meyer) L.; m. Tracy Cohen, June 2, 1985. BA, Johns Hopkins U., 1974; JD, George Washington U., 1977. Bar: N.J. 1977, U.S. Dist. Ct. N.J. 1977, D.C. 1979, U.S. Supreme Ct. 1981, U.S. Ct. Appeals (D.C. cir.) 1983, U.S. Ct. Appeals (3d cir.) 1984. Sole practice Middletown, N.J., 1979—; legal advisor Middletown Twp. Police, 1977—. Chmn. Middletown Safety Council, 1980—. Mem. ABA (regional dir. disaster legal services 1985—), Nat. Fire Protection Assn., Internat. Assn. Chiefs of Police. Jewish. Local government, General practice, Law enforcement matters. Office: PO Box 97 Middletown NJ 07748

LOKER, F(RANK) FORD, JR., lawyer; b. Balt., Nov. 15, 1947; s. F. Ford and Catherine (Kenny) L.; m. Mary Guidera, Sept. 17, 1971. A.B., Coll. Holy Cross, 1969; postgrad. U. Va., 1969-70; J.D. with honors, U. Md., 1973. Bar: Md. 1973, U.S. Dist. Ct. Md. 1978, U.S. Ct. Appeals (4th cir.) 1977, U.S. Supreme Ct. 1980. Asst. state's atty. Office of State's Atty. Balt., 1973-76; asst. atty. gen. Office Atty. Gen. Md., Balt., 1976-81; assoc. Niles, Barton & Wilmer, Balt., 1981-83, ptnr., 1984-86; ptnr. Whiteford, Taylor & Preston, 1987—; asst. state reporter Adminstrv. Office Cts. Md.-State Reporter, Annapolis, 1983. Mem. exec. bd. Tuscany-Canterbury Assn., Balt., 1982-83, pres., 1984-85. Mem. ABA, Def. Research Inst., Md. State Bar Assn., Md. Assn. Def. Trial Counsel (exec. bd. mem. 1985—, editor The Defense Line, 1985—), Bar Assn. Balt. City (exec. bd. young lawyers sect. 1984-85), mem. exec. bd., chair continuing legal edn. com. 1984-86). Democrat. Roman Catholic. Federal civil litigation, State civil litigation, Personal injury. Office: Whiteford Taylor & Preston 7 St Paul St Baltimore MD 21201

LOKEY, HAMILTON, lawyer; b. Atlanta, Aug. 30, 1910; s. Hugh Montgomery and Rebecca Crawford (Hamilton) L.; m. Muriel Ann Mattson, July 18, 1944; children—Hamilton, William Mattson, Fletcher, Ann Montgomery, Rebecca Hazel. A.B., U. Ga., 1931, LL.B., 1933. Bar: Ga. bar 1933, U.S. Supreme Ct. bar 1938. Asso. firm Harold Hirsch & Marion Smith, Atlanta., 1933-37; individual practice law Atlanta, 1937-39; partner firm Lokey & Bowden, Atlanta, 1939—; mem. Ga. Gen. Assembly, 1953-56; practising lawyer in residence U. Ga. Law Sch., 1977; chmn. Ga. State Bd. Bar Examiners, 1974-78. Served with USN, 1942-45, 50-52. Mem. Am., Ga., Atlanta bar assns., Lawyers Club Atlanta, Internat. Assn. Ins. Counsel, Am. Coll. Trial Lawyers, Internat. Acad. Trial Lawyers, Am. Judicature Soc., World Assn. Lawyers, Phi Beta Kappa, Phi Kappa Phi. Democrat. Episcopalian. Club: Piedmont Driving. Federal civil litigation, State civil litigation, Personal injury. Home: 737 Woodward Way NW Atlanta GA 30327 Office: 2500 Tower Pl Atlanta GA 30026

LOLLI, DON R(AY), lawyer; b. Macon, Mo., Aug. 9, 1949; s. Tony and Erma Naomi (Gerlich) L.; m. Deborah Jo Mrosek, May 29, 1976; children: Christina Terese, Joanna Elyse. BA in Econs., U. Mo., 1971, JD, 1974. Bar: Mo. 1974, U.S. Dist. Ct. (we. dist.) Mo. 1974, U.S. Ct. Appeals (8th cir.) 1976, U.S. Ct. Appeals (10th cir.) 1979, U.S. Supreme Ct. 1979, U.S. Tax Ct. 1981. Assoc. Beckett & Steinkamp, Kansas City, Mo., 1974-79, ptnr., 1980—; lectr. continuing legal edn. seminar U. Mo. Sch. Law, Kansas City, 1984. Mem. ABA, Mo. Bar Assn., Kansas City Bar Assn., Lawyers Assn. Kansas City, U. Mo. Alumni Assn., Beta Theta Pi Alumni, Phi Delta Phi (pres. Tiedman Inn 1973-74, Merit cert. 1974). Democrat. Roman Catholic. Club: Kansas City (Mo.). Federal civil litigation, State civil litigation, Commodities. Home: 633 W 62d St Kansas City MO 64113 Office: Beckett & Steinkamp PO Box 13425 Kansas City MO 64199

LOMBARD, BENJAMIN (KIP), JR., lawyer; b. Seattle, Sept. 2, 1940; s. Ben Tongue and Jessie Craig (Smith) L.; m. Bernadette Ann Verschingel, Apr. 11, 1970; children—Christopher Hawkins, Ian Craig, Russell Benjamin. B.A. in Econs., U. Oreg., 1962; LL.B., U. Mich., 1965. Bar: Oreg. 1965, U.S. Dist. Ct. Oreg. 1967, U.S. Ct. Appeals (9th cir.) 1967. Assoc. Mautz, Souther, Spaulding, Kinsey & Williamson, Portland, Oreg., 1967-72; ptnr. Ben. Lombard, Jr., Ashland, Oreg., 1972—; mem. Oreg. Ho. of Reps., 1977-85. Bd. dirs. Jackson County Edn. Service Dist., 1973-78, chmn., 1976-78. Mem. ABA, Oreg. State Bar Assn., Jackson County Bar Assn., So. Oreg. Estate Planning Council, Western States Water Council, Ashland C. of C. (dir.), Oreg. Shakespearean Festival Assn. (dir.). Republican. Roman Catholic. Lodge: Kiwanis. General practice, Legislative, Probate. Office: PO Box 1090 Ashland OR 97520

LOMBARD, HERBERT WILLIAM, JR., lawyer; b. Eugene, Oreg., June 26, 1930; s. Herbert W. and Verna D. (Skade) L.; m. Rita Guard, July 10, 1980; children: Kurtis, Karen, Kristi, Erin, Tina. B.S. in Econs., U. Oreg., 1952, LL.B., 1957. Bar: Oreg. 1957, U.S. Dist. Ct. Oreg. 1957, U.S. Supreme Ct. 1975. Ptnr. Lombard, Lombard, Williams & Ackley, Cottage Grove, Oreg., 1957-69; gen. counsel Bohemia, Inc., Eugene, 1969-73; ptnr. Sahlstrom & Lombard, Eugene, 1973-77; ptnr. Lombard, Gardner, Honsowetz, Brewer & Schons, Eugene, 1977—. Served to 1st lt. USAF, 1952-54. Mem. ABA, Lane County Bar Assn. (past pres.), Oreg. State Bar (bd. govs., 1970-73), Oreg. Trial Lawyers Assn., Assn. Trial Lawyers Am., Oreg. Law Sch. Alumni Assn. (past pres.), Cottage Grove C. of C. (past dir., v.p.), Eugene Area C. of C. (past dir.). Republican. Clubs: Rotary Internat., Lions, Elks, Masons. State civil litigation, Personal injury, Family and matrimonial. Address: 1612 Russet Dr Eugene OR 97440 Office: Lombard Gardner Honsowetz Brewer & Schons 725 Country Club Rd PO Box 10332 Eugene OR 97440

LOMBARD, MICHAEL ALBERT, lawyer; b. New Orleans; s. Albert E. and Elsie (Trepagnier) L.; m. Susan M. Robin, June 10, 1978; children: Christine, Melissa, Trep, Casey. BA, U. New Orleans, 1972; JD, Loyola U., New Orleans, 1976. Bar: La. 1976, U.S. Dist. Ct. (ea., we. and mid. dists.) La. 1976, U.S. Ct. Appeals (5th cir.) 1981, U.S. Supreme Ct. 1985. Assoc. Burke & Ballard, New Orleans, 1975-77; sole practice Covington, La., 1977-82; assoc. Buckley & Ward, New Orleans, 1982-83, Bailey & Leininger, Metairie, La., 1983-85; sr. ptnr. Lombard & Silbert, Metairie, 1985—. Mem. ABA, New Orleans Bar Assn., La. Trial Lawyers Assn., La. Assn. Def. Counsel. Democrat. Episcopalian. Avocations: fishing, golf. Admiralty, Personal injury, Insurance. Home: 70 Magnolia Ct Covington LA 70433 Office: Lombard & Silbert 3636 N Causeway Blvd Suite 200 Metairie LA 70002

LOMBARDI, DAVID ENNIS, JR., lawyer, lectr.; b. San Francisco, Mar. 5, 1940; s. David E. and Ruth Harriet (Harrison) L.; m. Suzanne C. Woodbury, June 20, 1970; children—Sara Ennis, Eric David. B.A., U. Calif.-Berkeley, 1962; postgrad. U. Florence (Italy), 1964; J.D., Yale U., 1966. Bar: Calif. 1966. John Woodman Ayer fellow at law U. Calif.-Berkeley, 1963; assoc. Brobeck, Phleger & Harrison, San Francisco, 1967-73; adj. prof. bus. law U. Md., NATO Hdqrs., Belgium and Italy, 1974-75; sr. atty. Crown Zellerbach Corp., San Francisco, 1975-76; sr. ptnr. Lombardi & Lombardi, San Francisco, 1976-83; sr. ptnr. Steinhart & Falconer, San Francisco, 1983—; lectr. bus. litigation Golden Gate U. Sch. Law 1979; dir. various bus. corps., mem. chancellor's com. for univ. affairs U. Calif. 1962-63; mem. alumni adv. com. U. Calif., 1968-69; trustee, Head Royce Sch., 1983-86, San Dominco Sch., 1986—; trustee Kentfield Schs. Found., 1985—. Mem. ABA, Calif. Bar Assn. (prin. referee Calif. State Bar Ct. 1977-86), San Francisco Bar Assn., Am. Soc. Internat. Law, Yale U. Law Sch. Alumni Assn. (v.p. No. Calif. 1982-84). Clubs: Pacific-Union (San Francisco), Olympic (San Francisco), Priory (Kentfield, Calif.). General corporate, Federal civil litigation, Contracts commercial. Home: 30 Hanken Dr Kentfield CA 94904 Office: 333 Market St 32d Floor San Francisco CA 94105

LOMBARDI, JOSEPH EDWARD, court administrator, lawyer; b. Lyndhurst, N.J., Aug. 21, 1932. s. Joseph Edward and Helen Lucille (Carpentier) L.; children: Catherine, Peter, Joseph. BA, Fairleigh Dickinson U., 1958; JD, Columbia U., 1961. Bar: N.Y. 1961, U.S. Dist. Ct. (so. dist.) N.Y. 1964, N.Y. Ct. Appeals (2d cir.) 1964, U.S. Customs Ct. 1961, U.S. Ct. Internat. Trade 1980. Law asst. U.S. Customs Ct., N.Y.C., 1961-62; assoc. Ehrich, Stock, N.Y.C., 1962-66; reporter of decisions U.S. Customs Ct., 1966-68; clk. of ct. U.S. Ct. Internat. Trade, N.Y.C., 1968—; mem. adv. council U.S. Ct. Appeals (fed. cir.); lectr. Practising Law Inst., N.Y.C., 1970, N.Y. County Lawyers Assn., 1977, Law and Bus., N.Y.C., 1981. Author: U.S. Customs Court-Originiand Evolution, 1976. Pres. Bd. Edn., Irvington, N.Y., 1975; prosecutor Village of Irvington, 1967; bd. dirs. Echo Hills Mental Health Ctr., Dobbs Ferry, N.Y., 1983, County Symphony Assn., Westchester, N.Y., 1974. Served with USAF, 1952-56. Mem. ABA, N.Y. State Bar Assn., N.Y. County Lawyers Assn., Fed. Bar Council, Am. Judicature Soc., Phi Zeta Kappa. Judicial administration, Public international, Federal civil litigation. Office: US Ct Internat Trade 1 Federal Plaza New York NY 10007

LOMBARDI, VALENTINO DENNIS, lawyer; b. Providence, Feb. 5, 1943; s. Joseph and Angelina (DiDonato) L.; m. Linda Ann Dardeen, Sept. 5, 1966; children: Valerie Lynn, Nicole Maria, Joseph Thomas. AB, Providence Coll., 1966; JD, Suffolk U., 1971. Bar: R.I. 1971, U.S. Dist. Ct. R.I. 1971. Sole practice Providence, 1971—; legal counsel dept. employment security, State of R.I., 1978—, dept. social and rehabilitative services, 1972-73, dept. corrections, 1973-76, chief legal counsel, 1976-78; assoc. judge mcpl. ct. Town of North Providence, R.I., 1986—. Chmn. businessman's athletic club YMCA, Providence, 1976-80; bd. dirs. and sec. Ianetti Scholarship Fund. Mem. Providence Coll. Alumni Assn. (class agt. 1981—). Democrat. Roman Catholic. Lodge: Sons of Italy (treas. 1985-87). Avocations: handball, running, sports spectating. Real property, Family and matrimonial, Medicare Part B and OCHAMPUS Hearing Officer. Home: 11 Stephanie Dr North Providence RI 02904 Office: 127 Dorrence St Providence RI 02903

LOMBARDO, MICHAEL JOHN, lawyer, state assistant attorney general, educator; b. Willimantic, Conn., Mar. 25, 1927; s. Frank Paul and Mary Margaret (Longo) L.; children: Nancy C., Claire M. BS, U. Conn., 1951, MS, 1961, JD, 1973.Bar: Conn. 1974, U.S. Dist. Ct. Conn. 1975, U.S. Supreme Ct. 1979, U.S. Ct. Appeals (2d cir.) 1980. Div. controller Jones & Laughlin Steel Corp., Willimantic, 1956-67; adminstrv. officer health ctr. U. Conn., Hartford, 1968-69; dir. adminstrv. services South Central Community Coll., New Haven, 1969-70; asst. dir. adminstrn. Norwich (Conn.) Hosp., 1970-77; asst. atty. gen. State of Conn., Hartford, 1977—; adj. asst. prof. U. Hartford, 1961-70; adj. prof. bus. Old Dominion U., 1973-81; adj. lectr. in law and bus. Ea. Conn. State U., 1973—. Vol. Windham Ctr. (Conn.) Fire Dept. Served to sgt. U.S. Army, 1945-46, to 1st lt. USAF, 1951-53, ret. 1987, to col. USAFR 1953-87. Mem. Conn. Bar Assn., Windham County Bar Assn., Mensa Internat., Am. Legion, VFW. Lodge: Lions (bd. dirs. Willimantic chpt. 1960-64). Administrative and regulatory, Federal civil litigation, State civil litigation. Home: 35 Oakwood Dr Windham CT 06280 Office: 30 Trinity St Hartford CT 06106

LONARDO, CHARLES HENRY, lawyer; b. Providence, June 23, 1955; s. Pasco and Viola (Tomasso) L.; 1 child, Matthew David. BS in Broadcast Journalism cum laude, Syracuse U., 1977, JD, 1981. Bar: R.I. 1981, Mass. 1981, U.S. Dist. Ct. R.I. 1982, Mo. 1984, U.S. Dist. Ct. (we. dist.) Mo. 1985. Assoc. Connors & Kilguss, Providence, 1981-84; gen. counsel Monkem Co. Inc., Joplin, Mo., 1984; sole practice Joplin, 1984—; coordinator R.I. course SMH Bar Rev., Boston, 1981-84; bd. dirs. Legal Aid Western Mo., Kansas City. Mem. ABA, R.I. Bar Assn., Mo. Bar Assn. (com. family law), Phi Delta Phi, Order of Barristers. Republican. Roman Catholic. Lodge: Kiwanis. Avocations: officiating basketball, running, cross country skiing, cribbage. Family and matrimonial, Consumer commercial, Criminal. Home: 1322 Pennsylvania Joplin MO 64801-4691 Office: 610 Pearl Suite C Joplin MO 64801-2545

LONDON, BARRY JOSEPH, lawyer; b. Hartford, Conn., Nov. 3, 1946; s. Irving Walter and Lillian (Gottlieb) L.; divorced. B.S. cum laude, U. Pa., 1968, J.D. summa cum laude, 1971. Bar: D.C. 1971, Fla. 1972, U.S. Tax Ct. 1973, Calif. 1982. Assoc. firm Cohen & Uretz, Washington, 1971-77; ptnr. Cohen & Uretz, 1978-82, Lillick, McHose & Charles, San Francisco, 1982—; lectr. Nat. Law Ctr., George Washington U., 1977-81; adj. prof. law Georgetown U. Law Ctr., 1981. Co-author: Tax Return Preparer's Liability, 1985. Contbr. articles to legal publs. Recipient Peter McCall prize 1971, Bernard A. Chertcoff prize, 1971, Oscar Milton Davis prize, 1971; Carrye G. Barenkopf scholar, 1970-71. Mem. ABA, D.C. Bar, Fla. Bar, Calif. Bar, Order of Coif, Beta Gamma Sigma. Democrat. Club: Commonwealth. Corporate taxation, Estate taxation, Personal income taxation. Office: Lillick McHose & Charles 2 Embarcadero Ctr San Francisco CA 94111

LONDON, JACK EDWARD, lawyer; b. Hartford, Conn., Feb. 3, 1949; s. Irving Walter and Lillian (Gottlieb) L.; m. Trina June Fiedler, July 3, 1983; children: Sarah, Marissa. BBA, U. Miami, 1971, JD cum laude, 1974. Ptnr. Mills, Hodin & London P.A., Miami, Fla., 1979-81, Mills & London P.A., Miami, 1981-83; sole practice Hollywood, Fla., 1983-87; ptnr. London & Gamberg, Hollywood, 1987—. Atty., mem. bus. adv. council Meed Project,

Miami, 1986—; bd. dirs. Vietnam Vets. Leadership Program, Fla., 1983—. Mem. ABA, Fla. Bar Assn., Assn. Trial Lawyers Am., Acad. Fla. Trial Lawyers, Broward County Trial Lawyers Assn., South Broward Bar Assn., Vietnam Vets of Fla. (1st v.p. 1984), Vietnam Vets. of Am. (bd. dirs., atty. 1982-84, 1st v.p. Broward chpt.), Phi Kappa Phi. Avocations: tennis, golf, racquetball. State civil litigation, Consumer commercial, Personal injury. Office: 4601 Sheridan St 5th Floor Hollywood FL 33021

LONDON, LESLIE ANN, lawyer; b. Santa Fe, Aug. 8, 1944; d. Milton H. and Evelyn M. London; m. Leon London; children: Justin, Joanna. BS in Architechture and Design, U. Mich.; JD, U. Detroit, 1977. Bar: Mich. 1978. Atty. Mfrs. Nat. Bank Detroit, 1978—. Avocations: real estate, travel, art. Contracts commercial, Real property, Corporate taxation. Office: Mfrs Nat Bank Detroit 100 Rennaissance Ctr 9th Floor Detroit MI 48243

LONG, CHARLES THOMAS, lawyer; b. Denver, Dec. 19, 1942; s. Charles Joseph and Jessie Elizabeth (Squire) L.; m. Susan Rae Kircheis, Aug. 9, 1967; children: Brian Christopher, Lara Elizabeth, Kevin Charles. BA, Dartmouth Coll., 1965; JD cum laude, Harvard U., 1970. Bar: Calif. 1971, U.S. Dist. Ct. (cen. dist.) Calif. 1971, U.S. Ct. Appeals (9th cir.) 1975, D.C. 1980, U.S. Dist. Ct. D.C. 1981. Assoc. Gibson, Dunn & Crutcher, Los Angeles, 1970-77, ptnr., 1977-79; ptnr. Gibson, Dunn & Crutcher, Washington, 1979-83; dep. gen. counsel Fed. Home Loan Bank Bd., Washington, 1984-85; ptnr. Jones, Day, Reavis & Pogue, Washington, 1985—; speaker on savings and loan issues. Contbr. articles to profl. jours. Pres. Leigh Mill Meadows Assn., Great Falls, Va., 1980. Served to lt. USNR, 1965-67. Mem. ABA, Calif. Bar Assn., D.C. Bar Assn., U.S. League Savings Insts. (lawyers com.). Republican. Methodist. Club: Westwood Country (Vienna, Va.). Avocations: sailing, photography. Banking, Securities, General corporate. Office: Jones Day Reavis & Pogue Metropolitan Square 655 15th St NW Washington DC 20005-5701

LONG, CHRISTINE MATHEWS, lawyer; b. Lakewood, Ohio, Nov. 27, 1953; d. Laurence E. and Mary Louise (Davis) Mathews; m. C. David M. Long, Aug. 13, 1977; children: David M., Anne Elizabeth, Mary Colleen, Kelly Christine. BA in Polit. Sci., U. Dayton, 1974; JD, U. Pitts., 1977. Bar: Pa. 1977, U.S. Dist. Ct. (we. dist.) Pa. 1977, Ohio 1978, U.S. Ct. Appeals (3d dir.) 1983. With May & Long, P.C., Pitts., 1977—. Mem. ABA, Pa. Bar Assn., Allegheny County Bar Assn. (cert. commendation 1986). Roman Catholic. Family and matrimonial, Personal income taxation, Probate. Office: May & Long PC 600 Grant St Suite 670 Pittsburgh PA 15219

LONG, CHRISTOPHER FRANCIS, lawyer; b. Fall River, Mass., Nov. 27, 1955; s. William F. Jr. and Catherine (Kapitan) L.; m. Jane S. Gallone, Oct. 12, 1981; children: Megan E., Sarah C. BSCE, U. Vt., 1977; JD, New England Sch. of Law, 1980; LLM, Boston U., 1981. Bar: Mass. 1980, R.I. 1981, U.S. Dist. Ct. Mass. 1981, U.S. Dist. Ct. R.I. 1981, U.S. Tax Ct. 1981, U.S. Ct. Appeals (1st cir.) 1981, U.S. Ct. Claims 1982, U.S. Ct. Internat. Trade 1982, U.S. Ct. Mil. Appeals 1982, U.S. Supreme Ct. 1984. Ptnr. Long & Silvia, Fall River, 1981—; legal intern Office Mass. atty. Gen., 1979-80; adj. prof. law So. New England Sch. of Law, New Bedford, 1983—, Avins Law Sch., Fall River; asst. sec. Bristol County Estate Planning Council, 1983-84, 1st v.p. 1984-85, pres. 1985-86. Presdl. campaign aide Senator Edward M. Kennedy, 1980-81; v.p. Community Health Care Services, Inc. 1984-86, pres., 1986-87; bd. dirs. Dist. Nursing Assn. of Fall River, Inc., 1985-86, Home Health Mgmt., Inc., 1985-86; notary pub. 1981—. Mem. ABA, Mass. Bar Assn. (chmn. young lawyers div. elderly affairs com. 1982-86, sec. 1981-84, 85-86, bd. dirs. 1981—), R.I. Bar Assn. (banks and trusts com.), Boston Bar Assn., Bristol County Bar Assn. (sec. 1986-87, treas. 1987—, bd. dirs. 1985—), Fall River Bar Assn., Assn. Trial Lawyers Am., Mass. Trial Lawyers Assn., R.I. Trial Lawyers Assn., Am. Judicature Soc., Bristol County Bar Advs. Program. Democrat. Roman Catholic. Lodge: Lions. Avocations: skiing, squash, travel. State civil litigation, Criminal, Estate taxation. Home: 90 Randall Shea Dr Swansea MA 02777 Office: Long & Silvia 373 N Main St Fall River MA 02720

LONG, CLARENCE DICKINSON, III, lawyer; b. Princeton, N.J., Feb. 7, 1943; s. Clarence Dickinson and Susanna Eckings (Larter) L.; m. Clothilde Camille Jacxsens, June 24, 1972; children—Clarence IV, Andrew, Amanda, Victoria, Stephen. B.A., Johns Hopkins U., 1965; J.D., U. Md., 1971; postgrad. Judge Advocate Gen.'s Sch., 1979-80. Bar: U.S. Ct. Appeals Md. 1972, U.S. Dist. Ct. D.C. 1972, U.S. Ct. Mil. Appeals 1975, U.S. Supreme Ct. 1976, N.C. 1978, U.S. Ct. Claims 1982. Asst. state's atty., Balt., 1973-74; trial atty., trial team chief Office Chief Trial Atty. Contract Appeals div., U.S. Army, Washington, 1980-84; chief atty. Def. Supply Service, Washington, 1984—. Served to lt. col. U.S. Army. Decorated Silver Star, Bronze Star, Purple Heart (2), Meritorious Service medal, Army Commendation medal, Vietnamese Cross of Gallantry with gold star, Combat Infantry badge. Mem. Md. Bar Assn., D.C. Bar Assn., N.C. Bar Assn. Republican. Government contracts and claims, Criminal, Military. Home: 119 N Fairfax St Falls Church VA 22046 Office: Chief Atty Defense Supply Service Washington DC 20310

LONG, DOUGLAS PAUL, lawyer; b. Bloomington, Ind., Sept. 27, 1954; s. John Douglas and Hazel Elinor (Schnyder) L.; m. Lynette Royal, May 3, 1980; children: Andrew Douglas, Charles John. BS, Ind. U., 1976; JD, Harvard U., 1979. Bar: Ind. 1979, Ill. 1980, U.S. Dist. Ct. (so. dists.) Ind. 1979, U.S. Dist. Ct. (no. dist.) Ind. 1980, U.S. Ct. Appeals (7th cir.) 1980. Assoc. Barnes and Thornburg, Indpls., 1980-86, Sommer and Barnard, Indpls., 1986—. Mem. ABA (tax sect.) Ind. Bar Assn., Ill. State Bar Assn., Indpls. Bar Assn., Bar Assn. of 7th Fed. Cir., Ind. CPA Soc. (assoc.), Christian Legal Soc. Republican. General corporate, Corporate taxation, Probate. Home: 7211 Aldgate Ln Indianapolis IN 46250 Office: Sommer and Barnard 54 Monument Cir Indianapolis IN 46204

LONG, J. RICHARD, judge, lawyer, educator; b. Beardstown, Ill., Mar. 22, 1919; s. Joseph Lord and Nell (Baujan) L.; m. Barbara Holmes, Apr. 19, 1941; children: Joseph R. II, James P., Robert C. Assoc. in Applied Sci., Blackburn Coll., 1939; JD, U. Wis., 1949. Bar: Wis. 1949, U.S. Dist. Ct. (we. dist.) Wis. 1958, U.S. Dist. Ct. (no. dist.) Ill. 1967, U.S. Ct. Appeals (7th cir.) 1974, U.S. Supreme Ct. Ptnr. Woolsey, Blakely & Long, Beloit, Wis., 1949-52, Blakely & Long, Beloit, 1952-56, 66-74, Blakely, Long, Grutzner & Jaeckle, Beloit, 1956-66; sole practice Beloit, 1974-79; judge cir. ct. Rock County, Beloit, 1980—; lectr. U. Wis. Law Sch., Madison, 1973-75, dir. trial adv. seminars continuing legal edn., 1974-79, co-dir. gen. practice course, 1975-79. Contbr. articles to profl. jours. Dir. Beloit United Giver's Fund, 1954-57; vice chmn. Govs. Commn. Human Rights, Madison, 1960-67; pres., bd. dirs. Ctr. Pub. Representation, Madison, 1974-79; trustee Blackburn Coll., Carlinville, Ill., 1981. Served to capt. U.S. Army, 1940-46. Fellow Am. Bar Found.; mem. ABA, Assn. Trial Lawyers Am., Wis. Bar Assn. (gov. 1971-73), Wis. Acad. Trial Lawyers (bd. dirs. 1974-79), Order of Coif, Phi Kappa Phi, Phi Alpha Delta (hon.). Presbyterian. Judicial administration, State civil litigation, Criminal. Home: 2537 Hawthorne Dr Beloit WI 53511 Office: Rock County Cir Ct Br 5 250 Garden Ln Beloit WI 53511

LONG, LAWRENCE ALEXANDER, lawyer consultant; b. Lynchburg, Va., Apr. 6, 1908; s. Horace A. and Deborah (Taggart) L.; m. Elizabeth Lee Long, May 24, 1939; children: Lawrence Alexander Jr., Frederick W., Elizabeth Lee, Thomas M., Virginia Harrison. AB, U. Ala., 1932, LLB, 1935; postdoctoral, U. Denver. Bar: Fla. 1935, Colo. 1946, U.S. Dist. Ct. Colo. 1946, U.S. Ct. Appeals (10th cir.) 1951, U.S. Supreme Ct. 1953, U.S. Dist. Ct. Colo. 1970. From assoc. to ptnr. Milam, McIlvaine, Milam, Jacksonville, Fla., 1935-42; ptnr. Lawrence A. Long Assocs., Denver, 1946-50, Long & Jaudon, P.C., Denver, 1950—. Pres., cofounder, life mem. Denver Botanic Gardens Found., 1957-67; pres., life bd. dirs. Mt. Airy Hosp. Found., Denver, 1958-85, bd. dirs. 1985—; pres. English Speaking Union, Denver, 1982-84, bd. dirs. 1984—; various civic coms. Served to lt. col. U.S. Army, 1942-46, ETO. Fellow Internat. Soc. Barristers; mem. ABA, Am. Arbitration Assn., Colo. Bar Assn. (bd. govs. 1950-54, chmn. unauthorized practice com. 1953-56, chmn. negligence com. 1956-58), Denver Bar Assn., Denver Law Club, Internat. Assn. Ins. Counsel, Phi Delta Phi, Alpha Tau Omega (nat. pres. 1956-58). Republican. Episcopalian. Clubs: Denver Country, Denver Law, University, Mile High, Executive (Denver); Farmington Country (Charlottesville, Va.). Lodge: Masons. General corporate, Insurance, Probate. Home: 1510 E 10th Ave Denver CO 80218 Office: Long & Jaudon PC 1600 Ogden St Denver CO 80218-1414

LONG, MICHAEL EVANS, lawyer; b. St. Louis, June 4, 1938; s. La Cari and Mabel (Evans) L.; m. Mary Alice Pieske, June 11, 1961; children: Brian D., Christine A. AB, Wash. U., St. Louis, 1960, JD, 1962; MBA, St. Louis U., 1971. Bar: Mo. 1962, U.S. Dist. Ct. (ea. dist.) Mo. 1962, U.S. Ct. Appeals (8th cir.) 1962. Atty. Ralston Purina Co., St. Louis, 1962-71; corp. counsel Sundstrand Co., Rockford, Ill., 1972-76; sr. counsel May Dept. Stores Co., St. Louis, 1976-85; v.p., gen. counsel Drury Industries, Inc., St. Louis, 1985—; bd. dirs. Legal Assistance Ministry, St. Louis, 1983—. Chmn. Wash. U. Campus YMCA and YWCA, 1981-87; bd. dirs. St. Louis Met. YMCA, 1981-87; mem. com. Ill. Synod Luth. Ch. in Am., leadership com. St. Louis. Mem. ABA, Mo. Bar Assn., St. Louis Met. Bar Assn. (corp. counsel com.). Real property, General corporate, Landlord-tenant. Home: 617 Golfview Dr Ballwin MO 63011 Office: Drury Industries Inc 10801 Pear Tree Ln Saint Louis MO 63074

LONG, MICHAEL SIDNEY, lawyer; b. Tupelo, Miss., Dec. 26, 1942; s. George Winfred Long and Addie Louise Harris; m. Roseramey Spruill, July 17, 1979; 1 child, Ramey Michelle. BBA, Memphis State U., 1966, JD, 1971. Bar: Tenn. 1971. Atty. IRS, Raleigh, N.C., 1971, City of Memphis, 1972-74, Shelby County Atty. Gen. Office, Memphis, 1974-76; ptnr. Long, Umsted & Jones, Memphis, 1976—. Mem. Assn. Trial Lawyers Am., Tenn. Trial Lawyers Assn., Memphis Trial Lawyers Assn. Personal injury. Office: Long Umsted & Jones 314 Poplar Ave Memphis TN 38103

LONG, ROBERT JEFFREY, lawyer; b. Waukegan, Ill., July 25, 1954; s. John George and Virginia Marguerite (Kierland) L.; m. Marcia Ann Korducki, Aug. 16, 1980. BA, U. Ill., 1976; JD, DePaul U., 1981. Bar: Ill. 1981, U.S. Dist. Ct. (no. dist.) Ill. 1981, U.S. Dist. Ct. (ea. and we. dists.) Wis. 1984. Assoc. Law Offices A. Denison Weaver Ltd., Chgo., 1981-84, Law Offices Howard M. Lang, Libertyville, Ill., 1984-86, ptnr. Lang, Korducki, Steffens & Long, Libertyville, 1986; sole practice, Antioch, Ill., 1986—; classical guitarist. Recipient Am. Jurisprudence award in Torts, Lawyers Coop. Pub., 1978. Mem. Ill. State Bar Assn., Assn. Trial Lawyers Am., Ill. Trial Lawyers Assn., Cook County Bar Assn., Lake County Bar Assn. Presbyterian. State civil litigation, Personal injury, Local government. Office: 986 Main St Antioch IL 60002

LONG, STEPHEN MICHAEL, lawyer; b. Kittery, Maine, Apr. 30, 1954; s. Samuel Marsh and Nell (Chumley) L.; m. Cathy Ann Ferrara, May 20, 1984. B.A., Duke U., 1976; J.D., Temple U., 1980; postgrad. Nat. Coll. Dist. Attys., U. Houston, 1981. Bar: Pa. 1980, U.S. Dist. Ct. (ea. dist.) Pa. 1980, U.S. Dist. Ct. (ea. and so. dists.) N.Y. 1984. Assoc. Caine & Dipasquale, P.C., Media, Pa., 1980; asst. dist. atty. Chester County, West Chester, Pa., 1980-84; ptnr. Tupitza and Long, West Chester, 1983—; solicitor Chester County Constables, West Chester, 1982—. Election day chmn. Chester County Republicans, West Chester, 1980; vice chmn. Chester County Young Reps., West Chester, 1984. Recipient cert. of merit Dist. Atty. West Chester, 1984. Mem. Pa. Bar Assn., Chester County Bar Assn., Assn Trial Lawyers Am., Pa. Trial Lawyer Assn. Baptist. Club: Optomist (charter pres. 1981). Personal injury, Criminal, Federal civil litigation. Home: 205 Lionville Rd Downingtown PA 19335 Office: 212 W Gay St West Chester PA 19380

LONG, THEODORE JAMES, lawyer; b. Colgate, Wis., July 29, 1935; s. Harlowe W. and Helen L. (King) L.; m. Betty L. Mielke, Sept. 8, 1962; children—Kristine, Theodore James. B.S. in Mech. Engring., U. Wis., 1958, LL.B., 1961. Bar: Wis. 1961, U.S. Dist. Ct. (we. dist.) Wis. 1962, U.S. Dist. Ct. (ea. dist.) Wis. 1974, U.S. Ct. Appeals (7th cir.) 1981, U.S. Ct. Appeals (fed. cir.) 1982. Ptnr. Isaksen, Lathrop, Esch, Hart, Clark, and predecessors, Madison, Wis., 1961—. Chmn. bd. dirs. Meth. Hosp., 1982-86; pres. United Madison Community Found., 1981-83, United Way Dane County, 1973. Served to lt. C.E., U.S. Army, 1958. Mem. ABA, Am. Intellectual Property Law Assn., Wis. Bar Assn., Wis. Intellectual Property Law Assn. Congregationalist. Club: Rotary. Patent, Trademark and copyright, Environment. Office: PO Box 1507 Madison WI 53701

LONG, THOMAS LESLIE, lawyer; b. Mansfield, Ohio, May 30, 1951; s. Ralph Waldo and Rose Ann (Cloud) L.; m. Peggy L. Bryant, Apr. 24, 1982. AB in Govt., U. Notre Dame, 1973; JD, Ohio State U., 1976. Bar: Ohio 1976, U.S. Dist. Ct. (so. dist.) Ohio 1976, U.S. Dist. Ct. (no. dist.) Ohio 1977, U.S. Ct. Appeals (6th cir.) 1978. Assoc. Alexander, Ebinger, Fisher, McAlister & Lawrence, Columbus, Ohio, 1976-82, ptnr., 1982-85; ptnr. Baker & Hostetler, Columbus, 1985—. Mem. ABA, Ohio Bar Assn., Columbus Bar Assn., Fed. Bar Assn., Assn. Trial Lawyer Am. Democrat. Roman Catholic. Club: Capitol (Columbus). Federal civil litigation, State civil litigation, Legislative. Home: 1271 W 1st Ave Columbus OH 43212 Office: Baker & Hostetler 65 E State St Columbus OH 43215

LONGACRE, KENNETH WYATT, lawyer; b. Stephenville, Tex., Nov. 4, 1939; s. Clarence Elvin and Nedra Mae (Wyatt) L.; m. Susan Ann Burton, Aug. 29, 1964; children—Melissa Michelle, Christina Louise, B.A., U. Tex., 1963, J.D., 1967. Bar: Tex. 1968, U.S. Dist. Ct. (so. dist.) Tex. 1981. Sole practice, Houston, 1968—; commdr. Bayou City Squadron CAP. Vice chmn. profl. div. United Fund of Houston, 1970; maj. CAP, 1982—. Mem. Houston Bar Assn., Lawyer-Pilot Bar Assn., State Bar Tex. (com. on profl. ethics 1973-79, com agrl. law 1981-84). Real property. Home: 11721 Joan of Arc Hedwig Village TX 77024 Office: PO Box 19220 Houston TX 77224

LONGACRE, ROY LEE, lawyer; b. Anchorage, May 21, 1957; s. John Jackson and Constance Marie (Yarbrough) L. BS in Geology, Oreg. State U., 1979; JD, Williamette U., 1982. Bar: Alaksa 1982, U.S. Dist. Ct. Alaska 1982. Assoc. Law Office Arthur Hauver, Anchorage, 1982-84; ptnr. Hauver, Fenerty & Longacre, Anchorage, 1984-85, Hauver & Longacre, Anchorage, 1986—. Dist. commr. explorer div. Boy Scouts Am., Anchorage, 1985—, explorer com. chmn.. Mem. ABA, Alaska Bar Assn., Achorage Bar Assn. (young lawyers div.). Republican. Lodge: Rotary. Avocations: hiking, snow skiing, water skiing. Contracts commercial, General corporate, Consumer commercial. Home: 3410 Corona Circle Anchorage AK 99517 Office: Hauver & Longacre 550 W 7th Ave Suite 840 Anchorage AK 99501

LONGER, WILLIAM JOHN, lawyer; b. Vinton, Iowa, Oct. 20, 1951; s. Hal Owen and Patricia Diane (Milroy) L.; m. Deborah Ann Dagenais, Aug. 7, 1976; 1 child, Kathryn Johanna. BA, Valparaiso U., 1974, JD, 1977. Bar: U.S. Dist. Ct. (no. dist.) Ind. 1978. Assoc. John D. Breclaw & Assocs., Griffith, Ind., 1977-79; sole practice Hobart, Ind., 1979—; dep. pros. atty., Lake County, Ind., 1982—; asst. city atty., Hobart, Ind., 1986—; instr. bus. law Calumet Coll., Hammond, Ind., 1978-79. Assoc. mem. Fraternal Order of Police, Hobart and Lake Sta., Ind., 1984—; v.p. Hobart Family YMCA, 1985-86, pres. 1987-88. Mem. ABA, Ind. Bar Assn., Lake County Bar Assn., Hobart Bar Assn. (pres. 1985, sec. 1983-84), Hobart C. of C. (pres. 1986). Methodist. Lodge: Rotary. General practice, Probate, Real property. Home: 1046 State St Hobart IN 46342 Office: 306 Main St PO Box 69 Hobart IN 46342

LONGHOFER, RONALD STEPHEN, lawyer; b. Junction City, Kans., Aug. 30, 1946; s. Oscar William and Anna Mathilda (Krause) L.; m. Martha Ellen Dennis, July 9, 1981; children: Adam, Nathan, Stefanie. B.Music, U. Mich., 1968; J.D., 1975. Bar: Mich. 1975, U.S. Dist. Ct. (ea. dist.) Mich., U.S. Ct. Appeals (6th cir.), U.S. Supreme Ct. Law clk. to judge U.S. Dist. Ct. (ea. dist.) Mich., Detroit, 1975-76; ptnr. firm Honigman, Miller, Schwartz & Cohn, Detroit, 1976—. Editor Mich. Law Rev., 1974-75. Served with U.S. Army, 1968-72. Mem. ABA, Detroit Bar Assn., Fed. Bar Assn., Order of Coif, Phi Beta Kappa, Phi Kappa Phi, Pi Kappa Lambda. Clubs: Detroit Econ., U. Mich. Pres's. State civil litigation, Federal civil litigation. Home: 3901 Six Mile Rd S Lyon MI 48178 Office: Honigman Miller Schwartz & Cohn 2290 1st Nat Bldg Detroit MI 48226

LONGMIRE, GEORGE, lawyer, former state senator; b. La Follette, Tenn., Aug. 2, 1915; s. Lewis and Julia Ann (Jones) L.; m. Gloria Bergan, Aug. 2, 1947; children: Linda Ann, George William Jr. BA, Lincoln Meml. U., 1938; postgrad., George Washington U., Washington, 1939-41; JD, U. N.D., 1947. Bar: N.D. 1947, U.S. Dist. Ct. N.D. 1947. Spl. agt. FBI, various cities, 1942-45; sole practice Grand Forks, N.D., 1947—; mem. N.D. Senate, Bismarck, 1957-77; atty. Grand Forks County, N.D., 1948-50; mem. N.D. Constitutional Conv., Bismarck, 1972; past public defender Grand Forks County. Contbr. articles to profl. jours. Chmn. N.D. Rep. Party, 1952-58. Named Outstanding Young Man, Grand Forks C. of C., 1959; recipient Sioux award U. N.D., 1967. Mem. ABA, N.D. Bar Assn., Grand Forks County Bar Assn. (past pres.), Order of Coif. Baptist. Lodges: Lions (pres. Grand Forks 1967), Elks, Masons (32 degree), Odd Fellows. Home: 412 25th Ave S Grand Forks ND 58201 Office: 401 Metropolitan Bldg 600 DeMers Ave PO Box 1651 Grand Forks ND 58206-1651

LONGSTRETH, BEVIS, lawyer; b. N.Y.C., Jan. 29, 1934; s. Alfred Bevis and Mary Agnes (Shiras) L.; m. Clara St. John, Aug. 10, 1963; children: Katherine Shiras, Thomas Day, Benjamin Hoyt. B.S. cum laude, Princeton U., 1956; LL.M., Harvard U., 1961. Bar: N.Y. 1962. Assoc. Debevoise & Plimpton, N.Y.C., 1962-70, ptnr., 1970-81; commr. SEC, Washington, 1981-84; ptnr. Debevoise & Plimpton, 1984—; lectr. Columbia U. Sch. Law, N.Y.C., 1975-81; cons. Ford Found., 1971-72; cons. to Comptroller Gen. of U.S. Author books, numerous articles on investment, securities and law. Bd. dirs. Symphony Space Inc.; mem. fin. com. Rockefeller Family Fund, 1972-81, 84—; chmn. fin. com. Social Sci. Research Council, 1986—. Served to lt. USMC, 1956-58. Mem. Am. Law Inst., ABA, Assn. Bar City N.Y., Adminstrv. Conf. of U.S. Democrat. Home: 322 Central Park W New York NY 10025 Office: Debevoise & Plimpton 875 3rd Avenue New York NY 10022

LONGSTRETH, ROBERT CHRISTY, lawyer; b. Phoenix, Oct. 11, 1956. BA, Haverford Coll., 1978; JD, Yale U., 1981. Bar: N.Y. 1982, U.S. Ct. Appeals (3d cir.) 1982, U.S. Ct. Appeals (9th and 10th cirs.) 1985, U.S. Ct. Appeals (2d and 11th cirs.) 1986. Trial atty. U.S. Dept. Justice, Washington, 1983-87; assoc. Wilmer, Cutler & Pickering, Washington, 1987—. Mem. ABA, Amnesty Internat., Phi Beta Kappa. Democrat. Episcopalian. Federal civil litigation, Personal injury, Government contracts and claims. Home: 644 Massachusetts Ave NE 502 Washington DC 20002 Office: Wilmer Cutler & Pickering 2445 M St NW Washington DC 20037

LOO, JOHN, lawyer; b. Toledo, Apr. 28, 1944; s. Harry and Gan Park Loo;. BSEE, U. Toledo, 1966; MBA, U. Pitts., 1967; JD, Loyola U., Los Angeles, 1976. Bar: Calif. 1976, U.S. Dist. Ct. (cen. dist.) Calif. 1977. Assoc. Gibson, Dunn & Crutcher, Los Angeles, 1976-81, Rogers & Wells, Los Angeles, 1981-82; ptnr. Cruikshank, Antin & Grebow, Los Angeles, 1982-83, Fowler, Weagant & Loo, Los Angeles, 1983—. Mem. Town Hall of Calif. Mem. ABA, Calif. Bar Assn., Blue Key, Tau Beta Pi. Contracts commercial, General corporate, Securities. Office: Fowler Weagant & Loo 1900 Ave of the Stars Suite 1908 Los Angeles CA 90067

LOOMIS, DONALD ALVIN, lawyer; b. Roseburg, Oreg., Mar. 22, 1941; s. George and Vera Marguerite (Colson) L.; children—Scott D., Janelle C. B.S. in Pharmacy, Oreg. State U., 1965; J.D., Willamette U., 1968. Bar: Oreg. 1969, U.S. dist. ct. Oreg. 1973. Assoc., Jaqua, Wheatley & Gardner, Eugene, Oreg., 1970-73, ptnr. 1973-74; ptnr. Owens & Loomis, Eugene, 1975-78; ptnr. Loomis, Tomlinson & Kurtz, Eugene, 1978-84, Loomis & Tomlinson, Eugene, 1984—. Mem. ABA, Oreg. Bar Assn., Lane County Bar Assn., Assn. Trial Lawyers Am., Oreg. Trial Lawyers Assn., Oreg. Assn. Def. Csl., Def. Research Inst., Am. Soc. Law and Medicine, Am. Soc. Pharmacy Law, Nat. Health Lawyers Assn. Republican. Episcopalian. Clubs: Downtown Athletic; Beaver (dir.) (Oreg. State U.). Lodge: Elks. Federal civil litigation, State civil litigation, Personal injury. Home: 3783 Pine Canyon Dr Eugene OR 97405 Office: 299 E 11th Ave Suite 210 Eugene OR 97401

LOOMIS, JOHN ELMER, lawyer; b. Mauston, Wis., Apr. 25, 1924; s. Orland Steen and Florence Marie (Ely) L.; m. Sue Isaacson, June 15, 1947; children: John A., Laurie Marie. AB, Stanford U., 1947, JD, 1949. Bar: Calif. 1980. Dep. dist. atty. Fresno (Calif.) County, 1950-52, asst. counsel, 1952-55; ptnr. Staniford, Harris & Loomis, Fresno, 1955—; adj. prof. San Joaquin Coll. Law, Fresno, 1970-80, asst. dean. 1970-77, dean 1977-80, trustee 1970—. Served with U.S. Army, 1943-45, ETO. Mem. ABA, Calif. Bar Assn., Fresno County Bar Assn. Republican. Congregationalist. Club: Fresno Downtown (bd. dirs. 1970-73). Lodge: Kiwanis (pres. Fresno 1961). Probate, General practice, Real property. Home: 3865 N Wilson Fresno CA 93704 Office: Staniford Harris & Loomis 1221 Van Ness #310 Fresno CA 93704

LOOMIS, MICHAEL EUGENE, lawyer; b. Chgo., June 16, 1948; s. Robert E. and Joyce M. (Wood) L.; m. Gwen E. Freitag, July 27, 1974; children: Jennifer J., Joshua E., Elizabeth A. BA, Lehigh U., 1970; JD, Creighton U., 1974. Bar: Nebr. 1974, Pa. 1980. Assoc. Morsman, Fike, Davis & Polack, Omaha, 1974-79, Pepper, Hamilton & Sheetz, Phila., 1979-83; atty. The Great Atlantic & Pacific Tea Co., Montvale, N.J., 1983-84; assoc. Butz, Hudders, Tallman, Stevens & Johnson, Allentown, Pa., 1984—. Served to 1st lt. USAF, 1970-72. Mem. ABA, Lehigh County Bar Assn. Real property, Contracts commercial. Home: 4344 Country Ln Allentown PA 18104 Office: Butz Hudders Tallman Stevens & Johnson 740 Hamilton Mall Allentown PA 18101

LOOMIS, RICHARD FOSTER, lawyer; b. Dallas, June 27, 1918; s. Richard Foster and Wilhemina (McKay) L.; 1 child, Eris E. A.B., B.S., So. Meth. U., 1938; M.A., Columbia U., 1939; J.D., Baylor U., 1940; postgrad. U. Notre Dame, Northwestern U., Harvard U. Bar: Tex. 1940, U.S. Dist. Ct. (no. dist.) Tex. 1945, U.S. Ct. Appeals (5th cir.) 1945, U.S. Supreme Ct. 1950, U.S. Mil. Ct. Appeals 1955. Asst. dist. atty., Dallas, 1945-46; asst. atty. gen. State of Tex., Dallas, 1946-47; sole practice, Dallas, 1947—; law prof. So. Meth. U., Baylor U., and U. Calif. Active Heart Fund and United Way, Dallas; founder, bd. dirs. Dallas Civic Opera, Dallas Symphony; bd. dirs. State Fair and Southwest Expn. Served to capt. USN, 1942-45. Mem. Phi Alpha Delta, Sigma Delta Chi, Phi Delta Theta. Episcopalian. Clubs: Brook Hollow Golf, N.Y. Athletic. Lodges: Masons (33 deg.), Shriners. General practice. Office: PO Box 222234 Dallas TX 75222

LOONEY, JAKE WAYNE, college dean; b. Mena, Ark., June 29, 1944; s. Lee and Eunice (Cooper) L.; m. Era Brown Furr, Jan. 31, 1965; 1 child, Jason. BSA, U. Ark., 1966; MS, U. Mo., 1968; JD, U. Mo.-Kansas City, 1971, MS, U. Mo. 1976. Bar: Ark., 1972, Mo., 1972, Va., 1977. Sole practice, Mena, 1973-75; asst. prof. Va. Tech. U., Blacksburg, 1975-78, Kans. State U., Manhattan, 1979-80; dir. agrl. law program U. Ark., Fayetteville, 1980-82, dean law, 1982—. Author: Estate Planning for Farmers, 1977; Estate Planning for Business Owners, 1979; Business Management for Farmers, 1983; (with others) Agricultural Law: Principles and Cases, 1981. Mem. Am. Agrl. Law Assn. (pres. 1983-84), ABA, Ark. Bar Assn. (Golden Gavel award 1982), Democrat. Methodist. Lodge: Rotary. Avocations: travel, reading. Legal education, Real property, Estate planning. Home: 924 Eva Ave Fayetteville AR 72701 Office: U Ark Law Sch Fayetteville AR 72701

LOONEY, JAMES HOLLAND, lawyer; b. Dallas, May 11, 1944; s. Billy Albert and Helen Dorothy (Holland) L.; m. Kathleen Mitchell, Feb. 11, 1979; children by previous marriage—James Holland, Brenda Anne, Stephen B.; stepchildren—Mary Ann King, Margaret Ann King. B.A., Tex. Christian U., 1967, M.Div., 1970, postgrad., 1970-71; postgrad. New Orleans Bapt. Theol. Sem., 1970-71; J.D., Loyola U., 1978. Bar: La. 1978, U.S. Dist. Ct. (ea. dist.) La. 1978, U.S. Ct. Appeals (5th cir.) 1978, U.S. Supreme Ct. 1982. Assoc. Murray, Murray, Ellis, Braden & Landry, New Orleans, 1977-78, Gertler & Gertler, New Orleans, 1978-79; pres. James H. Looney, New Orleans, 1979—; arbitrator small claims div. First City Ct. for City of New Orleans, 1986—; notary pub. Orleans Parish, 1978—; mem. Criminal Justice Panel, Eastern Dist. La., 1982—; asst. pub. defender St. Tammany and Washington Parishes, 1987—. Chmn., Interfaith Com., United Way Greater New Orleans, 1972-74; mem. Links com. Tex. Christian U., 1980—; cubmaster Boy Scouts Am., New Orleans, 1975-77; bd. dirs. Christian Ch. La., 1974-77, Citizens for Quality Nursing Care, 1986—; mem. La. Interch. Conf., 1972-77, LINKS com. Tex. Christian U., 1981—; v.p. Greater New Orleans Fedn. Chs., 1971-77; active Children's Ctr., Inc., 1972-77. Mem. ABA, La. Bar Assn., Assn. Trial Lawyers Am., New Orleans Bar Referral Service, Theta Phi. Democrat. Christian Ch. Contbr. Articles to profl. jours. Federal civil litigation, State civil litigation, Criminal. Office: PO Box 337 Covington LA 70434-0337

LOONEY, ROBERT DUDLEY, lawyer; b. Tishomingo, Okla., Mar. 25, 1919; s. M.A. and Helen (Dudley) L.; m. Caroline Ambrister, Dec. 19, 1941; children—Caroline H. Hill, Robert D., John A. B.A., Okla. U., 1941, LL.B., 1943. Bar: Okla. 1942, U.S. dist. ct. Okla., 19, U.S. ct. apls. (10th Cir.) Okla., 1946. Sr. ptnr. Looney Nichols et al, Oklahoma City, 1942—; prof. law Oklahoma City U. Sch. Law, 1971-73; lectr. U. Okla. Sch. Law; dir. Mid-Continent Casualty Co., Quaker Life Ins. Co., both Tulsa. Fellow Am. Coll. Trial Lawyers, Internat. Coll. Trial Lawyers; mem. Oklahoma County Bar Assn. (dir.), ABA, Okla. Bar Assn. Mem. exec. bd. Wesleyan Youth Inc., 1958—. Served with USCGR, 1942-45. Presbyterian. Clubs: Oklahoma City Rotary (pres. 1961-62, dist. gov. internat. 1964-65), Masons. State civil litigation. Address: 1243 Westchester St Oklahoma City OK 73114 Office: 528 NW 12th St Oklahoma City OK 73103

LOONEY, WILLIAM FRANCIS, JR., lawyer; b. Boston, Sept. 20, 1931; s. William Francis Sr. and Ursula Mary (Ryan) L.; m. Constance Mary O'Callaghan, Dec. 28, 1957; children: Willam F. III, Thomas M., Karen D., Martha A. AB, Harvard U., JD. Bar: Mass. 1958, D.C. 1972, U.S. Supreme Ct. 1972, U.S. Dist. Ct. (ea. dist.) Mich. 1986. Law clk. to presiding justice Mass. Supreme Jud. Ct., 1958-59; assoc. Goodwin, Procter & Hoar, Boston, 1959-63; chief civil div. U.S. Attys. Office, 1964-65; ptnr. Looney & Grossman, Boston, 1965—; asst. U.S. atty. U.S. Dist. Ct. Mass., 1962-65; spl. hearing officer U.S. Dept. of Justice, 1965-68. Mem. Zoning Bd. of Appeals, Dedham, Mass., 1971-74; bd. dirs. Boston Latin Sch. Found., 1981-85, pres. 1981-84, chmn. bd. dirs. 1984-86). Served to capt. U.S. Army, 1953-55. Fellow Am. Coll. Trial Lawyers; mem. ABA (Ho. of Dels.), Mass. Bar Assn., Boston Bar Assn. (chmn. litigation sect. 1980-82, v.p. 1982-84, pres. 1984-85, council mem. 1985—), Nat. Assn. Bar Pres.'s, Boston Latin Sch. Assn. (v.p. 1978-80, pres. 1980-82, life trustee 1982—; Man of Yr. 1985). Democrat. Roman Catholic. Clubs: Harvard, Union (Boston), Boston Racquet. Federal civil litigation, State civil litigation, Criminal. Home: 43 Coronation Dr Dedham MA 02026 Office: 50 Congress St Suite 910 Boston MA 02109

LOOPER, DONALD RAY, lawyer; b. Ft. Worth, Sept. 4, 1952; s. Rudolph Winnard and Margie Lee (Nix) L.; m. Marcia Lynn Graves, May 8, 1976; children: Scott Aaron, Cory Michael, Jonathan Reed. BBA with honors, U. Tex., Austin, 1974, M in Profl. Acctg., 1976; JD cum laude, U. Houston, 1979. Bar: Colo. 1979, Tex. 1981. Assoc. Cohen, Brame, Smith & Krendl, Denver, 1979-81; dir. Reynolds, Allen & Cook, Houston, 1981-85, head tax sect., 1984-85; assoc., dir. Looper, Reed, Ewing & McGraw, Houston, 1985—; lectr. Houston Soc. CPA's, 1984. Coach Women's Softball Team 1st Bapt. Ch., Houston, 1981—. Named one of Outstanding Young Men Am., 1980, 84. Mem. ABA, Tex. Bar Assn. (speaker seminars 1983-85, divorce tax com. 1985-86, lectr. tax sect. 1983-86), Houston Bar Assn. (tax sect. council 1985—), Phi Delta Phi (Internat. Grad. of Yr. 1979, province pres. 1984-86), Am. Softball Assn. (winner Nat. Championship 1981). Republican. Baptist. Avocations: tennis, softball, backpacking, coaching. Corporate taxation, Private international, General corporate. Home: 4315 Silverwood Houston TX 77035 Office: Looper Reed Ewing & McGraw 9 Greenway Plaza 1717 Houston TX 77046

LOPACKI, EDWARD JOSEPH, JR., lawyer; b. Bklyn., June 4, 1947; s. Edward Joseph and Lillian Jane (Wallace) L.; m. Crystal May Miller, June 21, 1969; children: Edward Joseph III, Elizabeth Jane. BA in Sociology, Villanova U., 1971; JD, Vermont Law Sch., 1980. Bar: Fla. 1981. Mgmt. trainee Bankers Trust Co., N.Y.C., 1968-72; counselor N.J. State Employment Services, Red Bank, 1972-77; sole practice Bradenton, Fla., 1981—. Sec. DeSoto Boy's Club, Bradenton, 1986; bd. dirs. Manatee Council on Aging, 1986—, Boys' Clubs of Manatee County, Bradenton, 1986—; liaison Manatee County Sch. Bd. Mem. ABA, Fla. Bar Assn. (disability law com. 1985—, liason with real estate brokers commn.), Manatee County Bar Assn., Nat. Orgn. Social Security Claimant's Reps. Democrat. Roman Catholic. Lodges: Elks, KC, Lions (pres. local chpt. 1985-86). Avocations: golf, running, photography. Administrative and regulatory, Probate, Real property. Home: 6612 27th Avenue Dr W Bradenton FL 33529 Office: 3300 26th St W Bradenton FL 33505

LOPATIN, ALAN G., lawyer; b. New Haven, Conn., May 25, 1956; s. Paul and Ruth (Rosen) L.; m. Debra Jo Engler, May 17, 1981; children: Jonah Adam, Asa Louis. BA, Yale U., 1978; JD, Am. U., 1981. Bar: D.C. 1981, U.S. Supreme Ct. 1985. Law clk. Fed. Maritime Commn., Washington, 1980-81; counsel com. on post office and civil service U.S. Ho. of Reps., Washington, 1981-82, counsel com. on budget, 1982-86, dep. chief counsel, 1986—; counsel Temporary Joint Com. on Deficit Reduction, Washington, 1986. Mem. ABA, D.C. Bar Assn. Democratic. Jewish. Club: Yale (Washington). Lodge: B'nai B'rith. Legislative. Home: 4958 Butterworth Pl NW Washington DC 20016 Office: Com on the Budget 215 House Annex 1 Washington DC 20515

LOPATIN, ALBERT, lawyer; b. Windsor, Ont., Can., Oct. 29, 1929; came to U.S. 1951, naturalized, 1954; s. Israel and Yetta (Bluestone) L.; m. Beverly Lopatin; 2 children. Student Highland Park Coll., 1948-50; J.D., Detroit Coll., 1953. Bar: Mich. 1955, Fla. 1971. Sr. ptnr. Lopatin, Miller, Freedman, Bluestone, Erlich, Rosen & Bartnick, Detroit 1969—; lectr. in field. Served with U.S. Army 1953-55. Mem. Am. Trial Lawyers Assn., Mich. Trial Lawyers Assn., Detroit Bar Assn., Fla. Bar, Colo. Bar Assn. Federal civil litigation, State civil litigation, Personal injury. Office: 547 E Jefferson Ave Detroit MI 48226

LOPER, STEWART COLLINS, lawyer; b. Mpls., Mar. 29, 1948; s. John Yerxa and Marjorie (Collins) L.; m. Nancy Johnson, July 19, 1975; 1 child, Thomas. BA, Macalester Coll., 1970; JD, William Mitchell Coll. of Law, 1974. Bar: Minn. 1974, U.S. Dist. Ct. Minn. 1975, U.S. Ct. Appeals (8th cir.) 1976, U.S. Supreme Ct. 1983. Ptnr. Cochrane & Bresnahan PA, St. Paul, Minn., 1975—. Bd. dirs. St. Patrick's Assn., Inc., St. Paul, 1977—, pres., 1984-86. Mem. William Mitchell Coll. of Law Alumni Assn. (bd. dirs. 1974, pres. 1985-86). Admiralty, Antitrust, General practice. Office: Cochrane & Bresnahan PA 24 E Fourth St Saint Paul MN 55101-1099

LOPEZ, CHESTER HENRY, JR., lawyer; b. Yarmouth, Maine, Aug. 2, 1936; s. Chester Henry and Betty (Kinney) L.; m. Mary Lillian Jordan, Sept. 6, 1958; children—Steven Greg, Gary Allen, Susan Ellen. B.A., Colby Coll., 1958; J.D., U. Chgo., 1961. Bar: N.H. 1961, U.S. Dist. Ct. N.H. 1965, U.S. Ct. Appeals (1st cir.) 1970. Atty., mng. dir. Hamblett & Kerrigan, Nashua, N.H., 1961—, also dir. Trustee Nashua Hosp. Assn., 1981—, pres., 1984-86; trustee Andover Newton Theol. Sch., 1984-85. Mem. ABA, N.H. Bar Assn. (chmn. sect. on corps.), Nashua Bar Assn. (pres. 1984), Nashua C. of C. (bd. dirs. 1975-77). Republican. Baptist. Club: Nashua Country (bd. govs., v.p. 1985-86, pres. 1986-87), Rotary (pres. 1980-81) (Nashua, N.H.). General corporate, Estate planning. Home: 2 Rockland St Nashua NH 03060 Office: One Indian Head Plaza Nashua NH 03060

LOPEZ, GERALD P., law educator; b. 1948. BA, U. So. Calif., 1970; JD, Harvard U., 1974. Law clk. to presiding justice U.S. Dist. Ct. Calif., San Diego, 1974-75; sole practice San Diego, 1975-79; asst. prof. U. Calif., 1976-78; vis. prof. UCLA, 1978-79, acting prof., 1979-83, prof., 1983—. Office: UCLA Sch Law 405 Hilgard Ave Los Angeles CA 90024 *

LOPEZ, MARTIN, III, lawyer; b. Las Cruces, N.Mex., June 20, 1954; s. Abenicio Rafael and Angelina Cordelia (Griego) L.; m. Elizabeth Crawford, Aug. 5, 1978; 1 dau., Alisa Angelina Maria. B.A., U. N.Mex., 1976, M.A.P.A., 1982, postgrad., 1983—; J.D., George Washington U., 1979. Bar: N.Mex. 1979, U.S. Dist. Ct. N.Mex. 1980, U.S. Ct. Appeals (10th cir.) 1981, U.S. Supreme Ct. 1982, U.S. Ct. Claims 1983, U.S. Tax Ct. 1984, D.C. 1985. Legal intern State of N.Mex. Property Tax Dept., Santa Fe, 1977, Pub. Defender Service, Washington, 1977-78, EEOC, Washington, 1978-79; asst. pub. defender State of N.Mex., Albuquerque, 1979-82, asst. atty. gen., 1982-84; ptnr., dir. firm Lopez & Lopez, P.C., Albuquerque, 1984-86; pres. Lopez, Lopez & Jaffe, P.C., 1986—. Pres. Alternative House, Inc. Recipient Alumni award U. N.Mex., 1972. Mem. ABA, N.Mex. State Bar Assn., Albuquerque Bar Assn., D.C. Bar Assn., N.Mex. Trial Lawyers Assn., Assn. Trial Lawyers Am., Albuquerque Hispano C. of C., Greater Albuquerque C. of C., Albuquerque Jaycees, Socorro County C. of C., Phi Alpha Theta, Pi Alpha Alpha, Phi Alpha Delta. Democrat. Roman Catholic. General corporate, State civil litigation, Contracts commercial. Home: 1037 Riverview Dr NW Albuquerque NM 87105 Office: Lopez Lopez & Jaffe PC 908 Lomas Blvd NW Albuquerque NM 87102

LOPEZ, OWEN MICHAEL, lawyer; b. Albuquerque, Feb. 23, 1941; s. J. Joseph and Eleanor F. (Marron) L.; m. Vicki Spicer, Apr. 12, 1969; children—Christopher, Todd, Elizabeth. B.A., Stanford U., 1963; J.D., U. Notre Dame, 1968. Bar: N.Mex., 1968. Law clk. to judge 10th Circuit Ct. Appeals, 1968-69; with Montgomery & Andrews, P.A., Santa Fe N.Mex., 1970-82, Hinkle, Cox, Eaton, Coffield & Hensley, Santa Fe, 1982—. Bd. dirs. Santa Fe Festival Theatre, 1979-86, pres., 1983-84; bd. dirs. Santa Fe Chamber Music Festival, 1975-82, pres., 1981-82; mem. bd. regents N.Mex. Inst. Mining and Tech., 1976-82, pres., 1979; bd. dirs. Internat. Folk Art Found., 1975—; mem. bd. visitors, gov. St. John's Coll., Annapolis, Md. and Santa Fe. Mem. ABA, N.Mex. Bar Assn. Democrat. Club: Kiva (Santa Fe). Contbr. articles to profl. jours. Nuclear power, Oil and gas leasing, Real property. Office: PO Box 2068 Santa Fe NM 87501

LOPEZ-ROMO, DANIEL FRANCISCO, United States attourney; b. San Juan, P.R., Jan. 28, 1945; s. Daniel Earl and Amalia (Romo) Lopez-R.; m. Maria F. Lopez, Dec. 31, 1966; children: Daniel R., Francisco M., Maria A. B.A., U. P.R., 1966; J.D., Inter Am. U., 1969. Trial atty. Legal Aid Soc., San Juan, P.R., 1970; judge advocate USAF Offutt AFB (SAC), Omaha, 1970-74; asst. dist. atty. P.R. Dept. Justice, San Juan, 1974-76, asst. U.S. atty., 1976-80; sr. ptnr. Lopez Romo-Del Toro, San Juan, 1980-82; U.S. atty. U.S. Dept. Justice, Hato Rey, 1982—; staff judge advocate, lt. col. PRANG Hdqrs. P.R. Air Nat. Guard, San Juan, 1978-85. Mem. Govs. Commn. Employment of Handicapped, San Juan, 1982; mem. Republican Presdl. Task Force, Washington, 1982. Served to capt. USAF, 1970-74. Recipient Meritorious Service award Pres.'s Com. Employment of Handicapped, 1982, Fed. Exec. of Yr. award, 1985. Mem. Fed. Bar Assn. (bd. dirs. 1978-81, 86—), Mil. Order World Wars, Nat. Guard Assn., Nat. Guard Fund, Inc., Phi Sigma Alpha. Republican. Roman Catholic. Clubs: Rio Piedras Tennis (v.p. 1981-82); Nat. Guard Shooting (San Juan). Lodges: Elks; K.T. (32 deg.); Shriners. Criminal. Office: United States Attys Office US Dept Justice Fed Office Bldg Rm 101 Hato Rey PR 00918 *

LORD, G(EOFFREY) CRAIG, lawyer; b. Boston, Apr. 12, 1946; s. Charles A. and Shirley (Ellice) L.; m. Rosemary Crumlish, May 29, 1970; children: Patrick C., Frances C., Irene R. BA magna cum laude, Gettysburg Coll., 1968; JD magna cum laude, U. Pa., 1971. Bar: Pa. 1972, Fla. 1977. Law clk. to presiding justice Supreme Ct. Pa., 1971-72; assoc., then ptnr. Blank, Rome, Comisky & McCauley, Phila., 1972-86; gen. counsel Core Group, Phila., 1986—. Mem. Phila. City Planning Commn., 1983. Served to capt. USNR, 1972. Mem. ABA, Pa. Bar Assn., Phila. Bar Assn., U. Pa. Law Sch. Alumni Assn. (treas. 1977-79), Order of Coif, Phi Beta Kappa. Club: Clover (Phila.). Real property. Office: Core Group 8 Penn Ctr Plaza 18th Floor Philadelphia PA 19103

LORDI, KATHERINE M., lawyer; b. Jersey City, Mar. 24, 1949; d. Peter G. and Hilde E. (Illy) L. A.B., Trinity Coll., Washington, 1971; J.D., Fordham U., 1975. Bar: N.J. 1975, U.S. Supreme Ct. 1983. Law clk. Friedman & D'Alessandro, East Orange, N.J., 1974-75, assoc., 1975-76; sole practice, Bloomfield, N.J., 1976—; adj. instr. Coll. St. Elizabeth, Convent Station, N.J., 1978—; legal adviser Mcpl. Ct. Clks. Assn., 1977-84. Trustee, Cath. Family and Community Services, 1980—; adv. bd. Acad. St. Elizabeth, Convent Station, N.J., 1980-84; vice chmn. Essex County Adv. Bd. Status of Women, 1983-85, chmn., 1985-87. Mem. ABA, N.J. Bar Assn., Essex County Bar Assn., Bloomfield Lawyers Club (pres. 1983-84), Bloomfield C. of C. (bd. dirs.). Roman Catholic. Club: N.J. Profl. Women. General practice.

LORE, MARTIN MAXWELL, lawyer; b. Milw., June 13, 1914; s. Michael and Jean (Dinerstein) L.; m. Doris Silver, Mar. 19, 1944; children—Amy L. Kovner, Cathy Jo. B.A., U. Wis., 1934, LL.B., 1936; LL.M., Harvard, 1937; B.C.S., Strayer Coll. Accountancy, 1939. Bar: Wis. 1936, U.S. Supreme Ct. 1939, N.Y. 1946, D.C. 1947, Fla. 1977; C.P.A., D.C. Part-time employee Melnik & Karan, Milw., 1933-36; asso. Rubin, Zabel & Ruppa, Milw., 1936-37; with Office Undersec. Treasury, 1937-38; spl. atty. office chief counsel, bur. Internal Revenue, 1938-40; trial counsel Internal Revenue (New Eng. div. tech. staff), 1940-42, Internal Revenue (N.Y. div.), 1945-47; tax counsel Newark, 1947-48; pvt. law practice N.Y.C., 1948-72; mem. firm Zissu Lore Halper & Robson, N.Y.C., 1972-76; counsel Zissu Lore Halper & Robson, 1976-80; sr. ptnr. Lore & Levy, N.Y.C., 1981—; Pres. bd. Fed. Tax Forum, Inc.; lectr. Tax Workshop, 1953-55, Law Sch., St. John's U., 1954, Fairleigh Dickinson U., 1955-56; specialist fed. tax matters, lectr. taxation N.Y. U., 1946-50, 65, Practising Law Inst., 1947-48, Tax Inst., 1948, Pa. State Coll., 1949-50, U. W.Va., U. San Francisco, 1951, SUNY, Stony Brook, 1978-79; tax cons. Med. Econs.; pres., dir. Estate Planning Council N.Y.C. Author: The Administration of The Federal Income Tax Through the United States Board of Tax Appeals, 1937, How to Win a Tax Case, 1955, Thin Capitalization, 1958; Co-editor: Jour. of Taxation; chmn. bd. editors: How To Work with the Internal Revenue Code of, 1954; Contbr. articles to legal and accounting jours. Served to lt. comdr., Office Gen. Counsel U.S.N., 1942-44. Mem. Am. Inst. Accountants (sec. Fed. Tax Lawyers Com.), Am. Bar Assn. (com. income taxation estates and trusts), N.Y. State Bar Assn., Assn. Bar City N.Y. (taxation com.), Fed. Bar Assn. (chmn. com. fed. taxation), County Lawyers Assn. (taxation com.). Clubs: Seawane (bd. govs.); Lawyers (N.Y.C.), Harvard (N.Y.C.); Barristers Lodge (Washington). Corporate taxation, Estate taxation, Probate. Home: 46 Broome Ave Atlantic Beach NY 11509 Office: Lore & Levy 205 Lexington Ave New York NY 10016

LORE, STEPHEN MELVIN, lawyer; b. Smithfield, N.C., Nov. 11, 1956; s. Edwin Payne and Miriam Angelea (Lassiter) L.; m. Katharine Sewell, July 27, 1985. BA, Wake Forest U., 1979; JD, U. N.C., 1982. Bar: Ga 1982, U.S. Ct. Appeals (11th cir.) 1982. Assoc. Freeman & Hawkins, Atlanta, 1982—. Mem. ABA, State Bar Ga., Atlanta Bar Assn., Phi Beta Kappa, Omicron Delta Epsilon. Republican. Presbyterian. Avocations: golf, tennis, gardening. Federal civil litigation, State civil litigation, Personal injury. Office: Freeman & Hawkins 2800 First Atlanta Tower Atlanta GA 30383

LORENTZEN, JOHN CAROL, lawyer; b. Ft. Carson, Colo., Mar. 6, 1955; s. Carol Edward and Marilyn Martha (Jens) L.; m. Penney Louise Fillmer, March 14, 1981; Katherine Penney, Emily Jeanne. BBA, BA, Drake U., 1977; JD, U. Chgo., 1980. Bar: Ill. 1980, U.S. Dist. Ct. (no. dist.) 1980, U.S. Tax Ct. 1981. Atty. Winston & Strawn, Chgo., 1980—. Contbr. articles to profl. jours.; creator The Law Sch. Game. Mem. ABA, Chgo. Bar Assn. Avocations: splitting wood, bicycling, canoeing. Corporate taxation, State and local taxation, Private international. Office: Winston & Strawn One First Nat Plaza Suite 5000 Chicago IL 60603

LORENZ, DANIEL CHRISTOPHER, lawyer; b. Portland, Oreg., Dec. 13, 1954; s. Donald W. and Evelyn M. (Abel) L.; m. Judy Ann Hilgendorf, June 19, 1976; children: Katherine, Christopher. BA, Stanford U., 1975; JD, Lewis and Clark U., 1978. Bar: Oreg. 1978, U.S. Dist. Ct. Oreg. 1978, U.S. Ct Appeals (9th cir.) 1981, U.S. Supreme Ct. 1982, Wash. 1984, U.S. Dist. Ct. (we. dist.) Wash. 1984, Calif. 1985. Mem. Des Connall & Dan Lorenz, P.C., Portland, 1978—. Personal injury, Workers' compensation, Criminal. Office: Des Connall & Dan Lorenz PC 1501 SW Harrison Portland OR 97201

LORENZ, HUGO ALBERT, life ins. co. exec.; b. Elmhurst, Ill., July 5, 1926; s. Hugo E. and Linda T. (Trampel) L. B.S., Northwestern U., 1949; LL.B., Harvard U., 1952. Bar: Ill. 1954. Mem. patent staff Bell Telephone Labs., Murray Hill, N.J., 1952-53; atty. First Nat. Bank Chgo., 1954-58; gen. counsel N.Am. Life Ins. Co. of Chgo., 1958-73; dir., v.p., gen. counsel, sec. Globe Life Ins. Co., Chgo., 1973—; sec. Gt. Equity Life Ins. Co., Chgo., 1977-80, Pat Ryan & Assos. Inc., Va. Surety Co., Chgo., 1977—. Bd. dirs. Sr. Centers Met. Chgo., 1977—, pres., 1983-85; trustee Hull House Assn., 1983—. Served with USNR, 1944-46. Mem. Am. Bar Assn., Assn. Life Ins. Counsel, Connoisseurs Internat. (pres.), Internat. Wine and Food Soc. Chgo. (gov. and cellarer 1980—). Unitarian. Insurance, General corporate. Home: 950 N Michigan Ave Apt 3603 Chicago IL 60611 Office: Ryan Ins Group 123 N Wacker Dr Chicago IL 60606

LORENZ, JACK CHAPIN, lawyer; b. Minneapolis, Kans., Nov. 24, 1929; s. Ira V. and Anna (Chapin) L.; m. Margrit M. Hug, Oct. 7, 1955; 1 dau., Rebecca Lorenz. B.S., Kans. State U., 1952; J.D., Washburn U., 1959. Bar: Kans. 1959, Mo. 1966, U.S. Dist. Ct. (ea. and we. dists.) N.Y. 1968. Ptnr. Brown & Lorenz, Council Grove, Kans., 1959-61; county atty. Morris County (Kans.), Council Grove, 1960-61; atty. Southwestern Bell Telephone Co., Topeka, 1961-65, St. Louis, 1965-67, gen. atty., Kansas City, Mo., 1969-75, gen. solicitor Mo., 1975-83; atty. AT&T, N.Y.C., 1967-69; v.p., gen. counsel, sec. Southwestern Bell Publs., Inc., St. Louis, 1984-86, v.p. gen. counsel, sec. Southwestern Bell Yellow Pages, Inc., 1987— ; instr. comml. law, banking, 1960-61; mem. Kansas City Fair Employment Com., 1973-75; dir. Southwestern Bell Yellow Pages, Inc., Ad/Vent Grafx, Inc., Ad/Vent Info. Services, Inc. Bd. dirs. Robinwood West Improvement Assn., St. Louis, 1966-67. Served to 1st lt. USAF, 1952-54. Mem. ABA, Mo. Bar Assn. (chmn. ann. meetings, mem. various coms.), Morris County Bar Assn. (sec., treas. 1959-61), Kansas County Atty. Assn., Kans. State U. Alumni Assn., Washburn U. Alumni Assn., Kans. Jr. C. of C. (v.p. Council Grove 1960-61), Kans. C. of C., Kansas City Bar Assn., St. Louis Met. Bar Found. (dir. 1981—), St. Louis County Bar Assn., Assn. Trial Lawyers Am., Am. Judicature Soc. Republican. Presbyterian. Clubs: Paincourt, Creve Coeur Racquet, Forest Hills Country, Pioneers, Masons, Kiwanis (v.p. 1962) (Council Grove). Administrative and regulatory, General corporate, State civil litigation. Office: Southwestern Bell Publs Inc 12800 Publications Dr PO Box 31907 Saint Louis MO 63131

LORENZO, NICHOLAS FRANCIS, JR., lawyer; b. Norfolk, Va., Nov. 22, 1942; s. Nicholas 1982-84), Jean W. Lorenzo; m. Patricia C. Connare, Sept. 7, 1968; children—Nicholas Michael, Matthew Christopher. B.A., St. Francis Coll., 1964; J.D., Duquesne U., 1968. Bar: Pa. 1968, U.S. Dist. Ct. (we. dist.) Pa. 1969, U.S. Supreme Ct. 1976, U.S. Dist. Ct. (mid. dist.) Pa. 1977, U.S. Ct. Appeals (3d cir.) 1983. Assoc. R. Edward Ferrero, Punxsutawney, Pa., 1968-70; sole practice, Punxsutawney, 1970-79; pres. Nicholas F. Lorenzo, Jr. P.C., Punxsutawney, 1981—; pres. Lorenzo and Lundy, P.C., Punxsutawney, 1979-81; instr. Sch. Continuing Edn., Pa. State U., 1969-73. Bd. dirs. Punxsutawney Area Hosp., 1972-74; mem. parish council S.S.C.D. Roman Catholic Ch., 1978-84, pres., 1979-84; bd. dirs. dist. Council Boy Scouts Am., 1982-84. Mem. ABA, Jefferson County Bar Assn. (v.p. 1980-82, pres. 1982-84), Pa. Bar Assn., Pa. Trial Lawyers Assn., West Pa. Trial Lawyers Assn., Assn. Trial Lawyers Am., Am. Hosp. Attys., Nat. Bd. Trial Advocacy (civil cert.). Republican. Clubs: Punxsutawney Country, K.C., Elks, Eagles Pat Rotary (pres. Punxsutawney 1973). Personal injury, State civil litigation, Workers' compensation. Home: RD 4 Box 455 Punxsutawney PA 15767 Office: 410 W Mahoning St Punxsutawney PA 15767

LORIA, MARTIN ALAN, lawyer; b. N.Y.C., Apr. 11, 1951; s. Daniel Bernard and Estelle Miriam (Barasch) L.; m. Carol Berkowitz, June 3, 1973; children: Alyson, Marissa. BA, SUNY, Albany, 1972; JD, Suffolk U., 1975. Bar: Mass. 1975, U.S. Dist. Ct. Mass. 1976, U.S. Supreme Ct. 1979. Atty. New Eng. states counsel Lawyers Title Ins. Corp., Boston, 1979-82; ptnr. Adelson, Golden & Loria, P.C., Boston, 1983—. Mem. ABA, Mass. Bar Assn., Boston Bar Assn., Mass. Conveyancers Assn. (chmn. title standards com. 1986—). Real property, Banking. Office: Adelson Golden & Loria Sears Crescent Bldg City Hall Plaza Boston MA 02108

LORING, ARTHUR, lawyer, financial services company executive; b. N.Y.C., Oct. 13, 1947; s. Murray and Mildred (Rogers) L.; m. Vicki Hootstein, June 4, 1978. B.S. in Commerce, Washington and Lee U., 1969; J.D. cum laude, Boston U., 1972. Bar: Mass. 1972. Atty. Fidelity Mgmt. & Research Co., Boston, 1972; sr. legal counsel Fidelity Mgmt. & Research Co., 1980-82, v.p., gen. counsel, 1984—; v.p.-legal FMR Corp., Boston, 1982—; sec., clk. Fidelity Group of Funds, Boston, 1983—. Mem. ABA (securities regulation com.), Boston Bar Assn., Am. Corp. Counsel Assn. Republican. Jewish. Clubs: Cavendish (dir. 1981-84), Boston Chess (pres. 1981-83) (Brookline, Mass.). Avocations: bridge; backgammon; exercise. Securities. Home: 37 Brimmer St Boston MA 02108 Office: Fidelity Mgmt & Research Co 82 Devonshire St Boston MA 02109

LORING, DAVID CHARLES, lawyer; b. Los Angeles, Mar. 29, 1942; s. Charles A. and Ruth Elaine (Jenkins) L. BA, Pomona Coll., 1964; JD, Stanford U., 1967. Bar: Calif. 1968, N.Y. 1972, U.S. Ct. Appeals (2d cir.) 1972. Vis. prof. U. Costa Rica, San Jose, 1967-69; law clk. to presiding justice Calif. Supreme Ct., San Francisco, 1970; atty. Gen. Motors Corp., N.Y.C., 1971-79; internat. counsel Avon Products, N.Y.C., 1979; sr. internat. atty. Atlantic Richfield Co., Los Angeles, 1980—. Mem. exec. com. bd. of visitors Stanford U. Law Sch., 1983-86. Mem. ABA (vice chmn. internat. resources com.), Assn. of Bar of City of N.Y. (inter-american affairs com.). Republican. Episcopalian. Clubs: The Beach (Los Angeles), Los Angeles Racquet . Avocations: tennis, sailing, skiing. Private international, Oil and gas leasing, General corporate. Office: Arco Internat Oil and Gas Co 444 S Flower St #3397 Los Angeles CA 90017

LOSAVIO, PETER JOSEPH, lawyer; b. Baton Rouge, Mar. 14, 1949; s. Peter Joseph Sr. and Lena (Sarullo) L.; m. Sarah Renee Crifasi, May 5, 1972; 1 child, Kathryn A. BS, Tulane U., 1970, MS, 1973; JD, La. Sch. Law, 1975; LLM in Taxation, U. Fla., 1976. Assoc. Law Office Ernest R. Eldred, Baton Rouge, 1976-77; acct. Seidman & Seidman, Houston, 1977-78; ptnr. Sklar, Nachman, Schmidt & Bowsher, Baton Rouge, 1978-80, Losavio & Weinstein, Baton Rouge, 1980—. Contbr. articles on acctg. to profl. jours. Mem. ABA, La. Bar Assn. (tax sect.), Soc. La. CPAs, Internat. Assn. Fin. Planners, Nat. Assn. Accts. (Baton Rouge chpt.). Roman Catholic. Probate, Securities, Corporate taxation. Office: Losavio & Weinstein 8414 Bluebonnet Suite 100 Baton Rouge LA 70810-2823

LOSCALZO, ANTHONY JOSEPH, lawyer; b. Bklyn., May 13, 1946; s. Frank Anthony and Frances (Puliatti) L.; m. Kathryn Mary Pica, Aug. 4, 1973. BBA, St. John's U., 1967, JD, 1969. Bar: N.Y. 1969, Fla. 1971, U.S. Dist. Ct. (so. and ea. dists.) N.Y. 1973, U.S. Ct. Appeals (2d cir.) 1975, U.S. Supreme Ct. 1975. Ptnr. Longhi & Loscalzo, P.C., N.Y.C., 1981—. Mem. ABA, Assn. Trial Lawyers Am., Fla. Bar Assn., N.Y. State Trial Lawyers Assn., N.Y. State Bar Assn. State civil litigation, Personal injury, Workers' compensation. Office: Longhi & Loscalzo PC 14 E 4th St New York NY 10012

LOSEE, ARTHUR JARRELL, lawyer; b. Oklahoma City, Jan. 18, 1925; s. Arthur O. and Alma Berniece (Jarrell) L.; m. Dorothy Inglis, Sept. 3, 1946; children—Helen Elizabeth, Ann Ransome. LL.B., U. Okla., Norman, 1948. Bar: Okla. 1948, N.Mex. 1949. Sole practice, Artesia, N.Mex., 1949-55; from assoc. to ptnr. Losee & Carson and predecessors, 1956—; mem. Disciplinary Bd., Supreme Ct. N.Mex., 1976-81, chmn., 1978-81. Dir. local chpt. Nat. Found. Infantile Paralysis; chmn. Artesia Pub. Library; chmn. El Paso br. Fed. Res. Bank Dallas; active United Fund, Artesia Mcpl. Hosp. Served with USN, 1943-45. Mem. ABA, N.Mex. Bar Assn., Okla. Bar Assn. Democrat. Episcopalian. Oil and gas leasing, General corporate, Probate. Office: 300 Am Home Bldg Artesia NM 88210

LOSEY, RALPH COLBY, lawyer; b. Daytona Beach, Fla., May 26, 1951; s. George Spar and Alix (Colby) L.; m. Molly Isa Friedman, July 7, 1973; children: Eva Merlinda, Adam Colby. Student, Inst. European Studies, Vienna, Austria, 1971; BA, Vanderbilt U., 1973; JD cum laude, U. Fla., 1979. Bar: Fla. 1980, U.S. Dist. Ct. (mid. dist.) Fla. 1980. Assoc. Subin, Shams, Rosenbluth & Moran, Orlando, Fla., 1980-84, ptnr., 1984—. Mem. ABA, Fla. Bar Assn., Orange County Bar Assn. Democrat. Club: Criterion (Winter Park, Fla.) (bd. dirs. 1974—). Avocations: computers, golf, philosophy, reading. State civil litigation, Computer, Real property. Home: 7037 Edgeworth Orlando FL 32819 Office: Subin Shams Rosenbluth & Moran PO Box 285 Orlando FL 32801

LOTKIN, RALPH LOUIS, lawyer; b. Phila., Dec. 15, 1946; s. Mark Max and Edythe (Kitchner) L.; m. Pauline Emily Barton, June 9, 1968; children: Adam, Elisabeth. BA, So. Ill. U., 1968; JD, U. Tenn., 1971. Bar: U.S. Dist. Ct. Colo. 1971, U.S. Supreme Ct. 1974, U.S. Ct. Appeals (D.C. cir.). Sr. atty. Gen. Acctg. Office, Washington, 1971-85; chief counsel com. on standards of official conduct U.S. Ho. of Reps., Washington, 1985—. Mem. D.C. Bar Assn., Phe Delta Phi. Legislative, Jurisprudence, Legal history. Home: 7245 Meadow Wood Way Clarksville MD 21029 Office: Standards of Official Conduct HT-2 The Capitol Washington DC 20515

LOTMAN, ARLINE JOLLES, lawyer, writer; b. Phila., Feb. 5, 1937; d. Samuel and Sarah (Schiffrin) Jolles; m. Maurice Lotman, Sept. 27, 1959 (dec.); 1 child, Maurice. B.A., Temple U., 1960, J.D. with honors, 1977, M.A. in Communications, 1984. Bar: Pa. 1977, D.C. 1980. Pres., Gen. Models, Bala Cynwyd, Pa., 1969-74; exec. dir. Pa. Gov.'s Commn. on Status of Women, Harrisburg, 1972-74; policy expert HEW, Washington, 1976-78; sole practice law, Phila., 1977—; lectr. in law Temple U., Phila., 1983, Villanova Law Sch., 1985. Author Jewish Nostalgia column Jewish Exponent, 1971-74; author articles in field. Bd. dirs. Americans for Democratic Action, 1977-80, state com. mem. Pa. Dem. State Com. 1986—; exec. bd. Com. of 70, 1969—; mem. Am. Jewish Congress, 1980—; bd. dirs. Jewish Community Relations Council, 1979—, Nat. Inst. on the Holocaust, 1982—; mem. Com. to Elect Women Judges, 1983—; chairperson Jewish Law Day, 1986-87; chmn. Montgomery County Democratic Com., 1977-78. Recipient Legion of Honor award Chapel of the Four Chaplains, 1980; Outstanding Service award N. Atlantic region Soroptimist Internat., 1975; Louise Waterman Wise award Am. Jewish Congress, Phila., 1974; co-recipient award Pa. LWV, 1973; named Outstanding Young Woman of Pa., 1972; 1st hon. mem. NOW, Phila.; editorial citations Phila. Inquirer, Main Line Times. Mem. ABA, Pa. Bar Assn., Phila. Bar Assn. (bd. govs. 1983-84, jud. selection and retention commn. 1983, chmn. pub. sch. edn. com. 1982, assoc. editor The Shingle 1978-79, chmn. com. jud. appointments 1979-81, qualified judges hon. trustee 1986—), Assn. Trial Lawyers Am., Assn. Bond Lawyers, Lawyers Against Apartheid, Women in Communications, Temple U. Law Alumni Assn. (exec. com. 1979—), Gen. Alumni Assn. Temple U. (dir. 1983—). Municipal bonds, Contracts commercial, Legislative. Office: 1608 Walnut St Philadelphia PA 19103

LOTWIN, STANFORD GERALD, lawyer; b. N.Y.C., June 23, 1930; s. Herman and Rita (Saltzman) L.; m. Rosemarie Giboleau, Aug. 23, 1973; children: Lori Hope, David, Sean. BS, Bklyn. Coll., 1951, LLB, 1954, LLM, 1957. Bar: N.Y. 1954, U.S. Supreme Ct. 1961, Pa. 1986. Ptnr. Lotwin, Goldman, Rosen & Greene, N.Y.C., 1970-83; of counsel Frankfurt, Garbus, Klein & Selz, N.Y.C., 1983—. Served with U.S. Army, 1954-56. Fellow Am. Acad. Matrimonial Lawyers (bd. of mgrs. 1984—); mem. N.Y. State Bar Assn. (family law sect.), N.Y. County Trial Lawyers (lectr. 1980—). Family and matrimonial. Office: 485 Madison Ave New York NY 10022

LOUBE, IRVING, lawyer, corporation executive; b. Winnepeg, Can., Dec. 19, 1918; s. Samuel and Alice (Chasin) L.; m. Shirley P. lombardero, Feb. 22, 1922; children—Garrett David, Suzanne Adrienne. A.B., U. Calif.-Berkeley, 1941, J.D., 1951. Bar: Calif. 1951, U.S. Dist. Ct. (no. dist.) Calif., U.S. Ct. Apls. (9th cir.). Assoc., Harold Strom, 1952-53; ptnr. Loube & Rounseville, 1954-60, Loube & Lewis, 1961-66, Loube, Lewis & Blum, 1967-72, Loube, Lewis, Lowen & Albers, 1973-80, Loube, Lewis, Lowen, Albers & Klein, 1981-82; sr. ptnr. Loube, Lewis, Lowen, Klein & Lando, 1983—; chmn. First Security Savs. Bank; dir. Diversified Health Services, Van Nuys Psychiat. Hosp., Founders Title Co. Bd. dirs. Oakland Symphony. Mem. Calif. Bar Assn., County Alameda Bar Assn. Republican. Jewish. Clubs: Commonwealth, St. Francis Yacht, Waikiki Yacht, Lahaina Yacht, The Family, Richmond Yacht. Real property, General corporate, State civil litigation. Address: 410 Hampton Rd Piedmont CA 94611

LOUDON, TIMOTHY DALE, lawyer; b. Lincoln, Nebr., Jan. 4, 1953; s. Roy Virgil Jr. and Elizabeth Louise (Willie) L.; m. Stephanie Carol Brady, Nov. 19, 1976; children: Megan Brady, Timothy Paul, Catherine Ann. BA, U. Nebr., 1975, JD, 1981. Bar: Nebr. 1981, U.S. Dist. Ct. Nebr. 1981. Field rep. Nebr. Equal Opportunity Commn., Lincoln, 1981-85; assoc. Tate & Alden Law Firm, P.C., Lincoln, 1985—. Mem. ABA (labor and employment law sect.), Nebr. Bar. Assn. (young lawyers sect. and elder law sect., legal services/lawyer referral program, Cert. of Commendation, 1986), Lincoln Bar Assn. Democrat. Roman Catholic. Avocations: bicycling, camping, hiking, canoeing, basketball. Labor, Civil rights. Home: 3601 Pawnee St Lincoln NE 68506 Office: Tate & Alden Law Firm PC PO Box 81727 2546 S 48th St Lincoln NE 68501

LOUGEE, DAVID LOUIS, lawyer; b. Worcester, Mass., Mar. 20, 1940; s. Laurence H. and Erma Virginia (MacAllister) L.; m. Mary Anne Strebb, July 15, 1979; children—Adam, Sara, Barbara, Laurence. A.B., Bates Coll., 1962; LL.B., Duke U., 1965. Bar: Mass. 1965. Ptnr. Mirick, O'Connell, DeMallie & Lougee, Worcester, 1965—; dir. Vitronics Corp., Diversified Hospitality Group Inc., Brady & Sun, Inc. Sustaining mem. Republican Nat. Com.; charter mem. Rep. Presdl. Task Force; mem. Adv. Task Force on Mass. Securities Regulations. Incorporator Worcester Hahnemann Hosp., Worcester Craft Ctr. Mem. ABA (bus. law com.), Worcester County Bar Assn. (tax com., unauthorized practice of law com., fin. and budget com.), Mass. Bar Assn. (securities law com., legis. drafting subcom., small bus. subcom.), Smaller Bus. Assn. New Eng. (edn. and legislation coms., bd. dirs.). Congregationalist. Clubs: University (pres. 1971), Tatnuck Country (sec. 1972-75), Worcester County Hort. Soc., Worcester Area C. of C. (transp. com.), Phi Delta Phi. Club: Worcester Econ. General corporate, Securities, Corporate taxation. Home: Ridge Rd Hardwick MA 01037 Office: 1700 Mechanics Bank Tower Worcester MA 01608

LOUGHLIN, MARTIN FRANCIS, federal judge; b. Manchester, N.H., Mar. 11, 1923; m. Margaret M. Gallagher; children—Helen, Margaret, Shane, Mary, Sheila, Martina, Caitlin. A.B., St. Anselm's Coll., 1947; LL.B., Suffolk U., 1951. Bar: N.H. 1952. Assoc. Conrad Danaid, Esq., Manchester, 1935-58; firm Broderick & Loughlin, Manchester, 1958-63; judge N.H. Superior Ct., Manchester, 1963-79, chief justice, 1978-79; judge U.S. Dist. Ct., Concord, N.H., 1979—; instr. St. Anselm's Coll., Franklin Pierce Law Sch. Contbr. articles to legal jours. Mem. ABA, N.H. Bar. Jurisprudence. Office: US Dist Ct 55 Pleasant St PO Box 1454 Concord NH 03301 *

LOUGHRIDGE, JOHN HALSTED, JR., lawyer; b. Chestnut Hill, Pa., Oct. 30, 1945; s. John H. and Martha Margaret (Boyd) L.; m. Amy Claire Booe, Aug. 3, 1980; 1 dau., Emily Halsted. A.B., Davidson Coll., 1967; J.D., Wake Forest U., 1970. Bar: N.C. 1970. Div. head, v.p., counsel Wachovia Mortgage Co., Winston-Salem, N.C., 1971-79; v.p., counsel The Wachovia Corp., Winston-Salem, 1980—, also The Wachovia Bank & Trust Co. Served to maj. JAGC, USAR, 1970—. Mem. ABA, N.C. Bar Assn., N.C. State Bar, N.C. Coll. of Adv., Forsyth County Bar Assn., Phi Delta Phi, Phi Delta Theta. Republican. Presbyterian. Club: Union League (Phila.). General corporate, Banking, Real property. Home: 615 Arbor Rd Winston-Salem NC 27104 Office: 301 N Main St Winston-Salem NC 27150

LOUIE, DAVID MARK, lawyer; b. Oakland, Calif., Oct. 8, 1951; s. Paul and Emma (Woo) L.; m. Johanna C. Chuan, Sept. 6, 1986. AB cum laude, Occidental Coll., 1973; JD, U. Calif., Berkeley, 1977. Bar: Calif. 1977, U.S. Dist. Ct. (no. Dist.) Calif. 1977, U.S. Ct. Appeals (9th cir.) 1977, Hawaii 1978, U.S. Dist. Ct. Hawaii 1978. Ptnr. Case & Lynch, Honolulu, 1977—. Contbg. author: Going Back, 1972. Bd. dirs. Jr. Achievement Hawaii, Honoulu, 1986—. Mem. ABA, Hawaii Bar Assn., Calif. Bar Assn., Def. Lawyers Assn., Assn. Trial Lawyers Am. State civil litigation, Insurance, Personal injury. Home: 3665 Kawelolani Pl Honolulu HI 96816 Office: Case & Lynch 737 Bishop St Suite 2500 Honolulu HI 96813

LOUIS, ROBERT HENRY, lawyer; b. Dover, N.J., Oct. 6, 1947; s. Henry Albert and Priscilla Ruth (Schantz) L.; m. Carol Sites, June 28, 1969; children: Caroline Emily, Alexandra Mary. BS in Econs. summa cum laude, U. Pa., 1969; JD cum laude, Harvard U., 1972; LLM in Taxation, Temple U., 1976. Bar: Pa. 1972, U.S. Dist. Ct. (ea. dist.) Pa. 1972, U.S. Tax Ct. 1974, U.S. Ct. Claims 1978, U.S. Supreme Ct. 1980, U.S. Ct. Appeals (3d cir.) 1981, U.S. Ct. Appeals (fed. cir.) 1983. Ptnr. Fox, Rothschild, O'Brien & Frankel (formerly Meltzer & Schiffrin), Phila., 1982—. Bd. dirs. Abington (Pa.) Pub. Library, 1981—, pres. 1985—, sec. 1983-85. Mem. ABA, Pa. Bar Assn. Phila. Bar Assn., Selden Soc. Republican. Episcopalian. Club: Harvard (Phila.). Pension, profit-sharing, and employee benefits, Corporate taxation, Probate. Home: 236 Woodlyn Ave Glenside PA 19038 Office: Fox Rothschild O'Brien & Frankel 2000 Market St Philadelphia PA 19103

LOUNSBERRY, HAROLD CLAIRE, lawyer; b. Marshalltown, Iowa, May 19, 1923; s. Harold Claire and Nellie Eudora (Stewart) L.; m. Ruth Mary Newtson, May 21, 1955; children—Elizabeth Claire, Sheila Eudora. B.A. in Econs., U. Iowa, 1947; J.D., Harvard U., 1949; postgrad. Northwestern U., 1952-54. Bar: Iowa 1949, Ill. 1950, U.S. Dist. Ct. (so. dist.) Iowa 1957, U.S. Dist. Ct. (so. dist.) Ill. 1959, U.S. Supreme Ct. 1960. Supr., Am. Farmers Ins. Co., Chgo., 1949; atty. examiner FTC, Chgo., 1950-54; sole practice, Davenport, Iowa, 1954—. Adv. bd. mem. Salvation Army, Davenport. Served to lt. U.S. Army, 1943-46, lt. col. USAR ret. Mem. Res. Officers Assn., Am. Legion, Scott County Bar Assn., Iowa Bar Assn., Rock Island County Bar Assn., Ill. Bar Assn., Assn. Trial Lawyers Iowa. Republican. Methodist. Club: Toastmasters Internat. (dist. gov. 1960) (Rock Island, Ill.). Lodges: Masons, Kiwanis, Elks, Moose. State civil litigation, Probate, Real property. Home: 3 Oak Park Dr Bettendorf IA 52722 Office: 702 Putnam Bldg 215 Main St Davenport IA 52801

LOUSBERG, PETER HERMAN, lawyer; b. Des Moines, Aug. 19, 1931; s. Peter J. and Otillia M. (Vogel) L.; m. JoAnn Beimer, Jan. 20, 1962; children: Macara Lynn, Mark, Stephen. AB, Yale U., 1953; JD cum laude, U. Notre Dame, 1956. Bar: Ill. 1956, Fla. 1972, Iowa 1985. Law clk. to presiding justice Ill. Appellate Ct., 1956-57; asst. states atty. Rock Island County, Ill., 1959-60; ptnr. Lousberg and McClean, Rock Island, Ill, 1960—; opinion commentator Sta. WHBF, 1973-74; lectr., chmn. Ill. Inst. Continuing Edn.; lectr. Ill. Trial Lawyers seminars; chmn. crime and juvenile delinquency Rock Island Model Cities Task Force, 1969; chmn. Rock Island Youth Guidance Council, 1964-69; mem. adv. bd. Ill. Dept. Corrections Juvenile Div., 1976; Ill. commr. Nat. Conf. Commrs. Uniform State Laws, 1976-78; treas. Greater Quad City Close-up Program, 1976-80. Contbr. articles to profl. jours. Bd. dirs. Rock Island Indsl.-Comml. Devel. Corp., 1977-80; bd. govs. Rock Island Community Found., 1977-82. Served to 1st lt. USMC, 1957-59. Fellow Am. Bar Found., Ill. Bar Found. (bd. dirs., 1986—, vice chmn. 1986-87); mem. ABA, Ill. Bar Assn. (gov. 1969-74, chmn. spl. survey com. 1974-75, chmn. com. on mentally disabled 1979-80, chmn. spl. com. on professionalism 1986—), Chgo. Bar Assn., Rock Island Bar Assn., Rock Island C. of C. (treas. 1975, pres. 1978), Am. Trial Lawyers Assn., Ill. Trial Lawyers Assn. (bd. mgrs. 1974-78), Am. Judicature Soc., Nat. Legal Aid and Defenders Assn. (chmn. membership campaigns for Ill. 1969-71, for Midwest dist 2 1974-75), Quad Cities Council of C.'s of C. (1st chmn. 1979-80), Ill. Inst. Continuing Legal Edn. (bd. dirs. 1980-83, chmn. 1981-82), Lawyers Trust Fund Ill. (bd. dirs. 1984—), Fla. Bar Assn. (chmn. out-of-state practitioners com. 1985-86), U.S. Power Squadron. Roman Catholic. Clubs: Notre Dame, Quad Cities (Rock Island). Lodge: Rotary (bd. dirs. Quad Cities). Federal civil litigation, State civil litigation, Family and matrimonial. Home: 2704 27th St Rock Island IL 61201 Office: PO Box 1088 Rock Island IL 61201

LOVALLO, TIMOTHY ROBIN, lawyer; b. Buffalo, Jan. 25, 1953; s. Leonard C. and Arliss E. (Leonard) L.; m. Susan A. Williams, May 14, 1983. BA, SUNY, Binghamton, 1975; JD, U. Buffalo, 1978. Bar: N.Y. 1979, U.S. Dist. Ct. (we. dist.) N.Y. 1979, Md. 1986, U.S. Tax Ct. 1987. Assoc. Lovallo, Matusick & Spadafora, Buffalo, 1978-82; ptnr. Lovallo, Williams & Lovallo, Buffalo, 1982—. Active Citizen's Alliance, Buffalo, 1979, Frontier Dem. Club, Buffalo, 1982—; bd. dirs. Western N.Y. Com. Better Cts., Buffalo, 1984—. Mem. N.Y. State Bar Assn., N.Y. State Defenders Assn., Erie County Bar Assn. Avocations: forestry, philatelics, hist. renovation. General practice, Administrative and regulatory, Probate. Home: 1721 Main St Buffalo NY 14209 Office: Lovallo Williams & Lovallo 392 Ellicott Sq Bldg Buffalo NY 14203

LOVE, MARK STEVEN, lawyer; b. Phila., July 20, 1950; s. Allen and Florence (Botkiss) L.; m. Joyce Elaine Greer, Mar. 24, 1973; children: Stephanie, Valerie. BS in Biochemistry, Pa. State U., 1972; JD, Temple U., 1976. Bar: Pa. 1976, U.S. Dist. Ct. (mid. dist.) Pa. 1977, U.S. Supreme Ct. 1980. Law clk. to presiding justice Northampton County Ct. of Common Pleas, Easton, Pa., 1976-77; assoc. Mervine, Brown, Newman, Williams & Mishkin, Stroudsburg, Pa., 1977-85; ptnr. Miller & Love, Mt. Pocono, Pa., 1986—. Solicitor Polk Twp. Suprs., Monroe County, Pa., 1981—, Tunkhannock Twp. Suprs., Monroe County, 1981—, Borough of Mt. Pocono, 1986—. Named one of Outstanding Young Men Am., 1985. Mem. ABA, Pa. Bar Asn., Northampton County Bar Assn., Monroe County Bar Assn., Assn. Trial Lawyers Am., Pa. Trial Lawyers Assn. Democrat. Jewish. Personal injury, Criminal, Local government. Home: PO Box 106 Bartonsville PA 18321 Office: Miller & Love PO Box 186 Mount Pocono PA 18344

LOVE, WALTER BENNETT, JR., lawyer; b. Monroe, N.C., Nov. 14, 1921; s. Walter B. and Pearl (Hamilton) L.; m. Elizabeth Cannon, Dec. 28, 1951; children: Elizabeth Sheldon Love Sturges, Walter Bennett III, Linda Louise. BS in Commerce, U. N.C., 1942, JD, 1949; Indsl. Coll. Armed Services, 1972. Bar: N.C. 1949, Fed. bar 1949. Ptnr. Love and Love, Monroe, N.C., 1949-52; sr. ptnr. Love and Milliken, attys. for City of Monroe, 1958—; dir. and counsel Heritage Fed. Sav. and Loan Assn. of Monroe, N.C. Bd. dirs. Nat. Bd. Am. Cancer Soc., 1969-82, pres. N.C. div., 1984, chmn. bd., 1985; chmn. bd. trustees Cen. United Meth. Ch., 1977-86, lay leader, 1986—; past sec. bd. trustees, Ellen Fitzgerald Hosp. and Union Mem. Hosp. Served to col. USAF and USAFR, WWII and Korea. Decorated with Disting. Unit citation, Victory Medal. Mem. ABA, N.C. Bar Assn., 29th Jud. Dist. Bar Assn. (past pres.), Union County Bar Assn. (past pres.). Democrat. Methodist. Clubs: Rolling Hills Country, Lions (past pres. and zone chmn. Monroe). Probate, Real property, General practice. Home: 217 Ridgewood Dr Monroe NC 28110 Office: 108 E Jefferson St Monroe NC 28110

LOVEALL, GEORGE MICHAEL, lawyer; b. Brazil, Ind., Dec. 3, 1946; s. James Jackson and Jacquelyn (Kerr) L.; m. Brenda Tawnette Olson, Feb. 9, 1980. B.A., Franklin Coll., 1968; J.D., U. Cin., 1971. Bar: Ind. 1971, U.S. Dist. Ct. (so. dist.) Ind. 1971, U.S. Ct. Appeals (7th cir.) 1980. Ptnr., Jones & Loveall, Franklin, Ind., 1971—. Mem. ABA, Ind. Bar Assn., Indpls. Bar Assn., Johnson County Bar Assn., Ind. Trial Lawyers Assn. Republican. Club: Hillview Country. Lodges: Elks, Masons. Family and matrimonial, Criminal, Personal injury. Home: Rural Route 1 Morgantown IN 46160 Office: Jones & Loveall 150 N Main St Franklin IN 46131

LOVEJOY, ALLEN FRASER, lawyer; b. Janesville, Wis., Oct. 9, 1919; s. Henry Stow and Mary Fraser (Beaton) L.; m. Betty Foote, Dec. 20, 1944; children—Jennifer Lovejoy Craddock, Charles F., Allen P. B.A., Yale U., 1941, LL.B., 1948. Bar: N.Y. 1949, U.S. Ct. Appeals (2d cir.) 1975. Assoc. Breed, Abbott & Morgan, N.Y.C., 1948-58, ptnr., 1958—. Served with U.S. Army, 1941-46; ETO. Decorated Purple Heart with oak leaf cluster; recipient Frank M. Patterson award Yale U., 1941. Fellow Am. Numis Soc.; mem. ABA, N.Y. State Bar Assn., Assn. Bar N.Y.C., Am. Numis. Assn. Republican. Episcopalian. Clubs: Citicorp Ctr., Pilgrims (N.Y.C.); Mid Ocean (Bermuda); Royal Overseas League (London); Stanwich (Greenwich, Conn.); Riverside (Conn.) Yacht. Author: La Follette and the Establishment of the Direct Primary in Wisconsin, 1890-1904, 1941; co-author: Early United States Dimes, 1796-1837, 1984; contbr. articles to numismatic publs. General corporate, Banking, Private international. Office: Breed Abbott & Morgan 153 E 53d St New York NY 10022

LOVELL, CELIA COGHLAN, lawyer; b. N.Y.C., July 9, 1945; d. John Philip and Barbara (Blyth) Coghlan; m. Malcolm R. Lovell Jr., Nov. 18, 1978. BA, Stanford U., 1966; JD, Georgetown U., 1977. Bar: D.C. 1977, U.S. Dist. Ct. D.C. 1979, U.S. Ct. Appeals (D.C. cir.) 1979. Atty. So. Ry. Co., Washington, 1977-81, solicitor, 1981-84; asst. gen. solicitor Norfolk So. Corp., Washington, 1984-86, gen. atty., 1986—; mem. Bd. of Appeals and Rev., Washington, 1979-83. Mem. ABA, D.C. Bar Assn., Nat. Assn. R.R. Trial Counsel. Republican. Roman Catholic. Home: 3126 O Street NW Washington DC 20007 Office: Norfolk So Corp 1050 Connecticut Ave NW Suite 740 Washington DC 20016

LOVELL, CHARLES C., federal judge; b. 1929; m. Ariliah Carter. BS, U. Mont., 1952, JD, 1959. Assoc. Church, Harris, Johnson & Williams, Helena, Mont., 1959-85; judge U.S. Dist. Ct. Mont., Helena, 1985—; chief counsel Mont. Atty Gen.'s Office, Helena, 1969-72. Served to capt. USAF, 1952-54. Mem. ABA, Am. Judicature Soc., Assn. Trial Lawyers Am. Office: US Dist Ct PO Box 10112 301 South Park Helena MT 59626 *

LOVERCHECK, CHARLES LESTER, lawyer; b. Beaufort, Mo., July 5, 1914; s. Charles Lester and Mayme Susan (Adams) L.; m. Leila Asenith Miller, Aug. 22, 1942; children: Wayne Loren, Dale Robert, Mary Lee Stewart. BS in Mech. Engring., Iowa State U., 1942; LLB, JD, Georgetown U., 1951, LLM, 1952. Bar: Va. 1952, D.C. 1952, Pa. 1953, U.S. Patent Office 1953; lic. aircraft pilot. Student engr. Gen. Electric Co., Fort Wayne, Ind., 1942-43, engr., Schenectady, 1943-48; examiner U.S. Patent Office, Washington, 1948-51; head patent search U.S. Navy, Naval Research, Washington, 1951-52; mem. Lovercheck and Lovercheck, Erie, Pa., 1953—; adv. Council Gannon Coll. Sch. Engring., 1956-61. Mem. ASME, Am. Patent Law Assn., Nat. Soc. Profl. Engrs., ABA, Pa. Bar Assn., Erie County Bar Assn. (sec. 1954-55), Aircraft Owners and Pilots Assn., SAR, Delta Theta Phi. Republican. Presbyterian (elder). Club: Erie Philharmonic Soc. (pres. 1960), Saga. Lodges: Shriners, Rotary, Elks, Masons (32 degree), Y Mens (pres. 1964-65). Patent, Trademark and copyright. Office: Lovercheck and Lovercheck 931 State St Erie PA 16501

LOVINS, NELSON PRESTON, lawyer; b. Malden, Mass., Mar. 3, 1944; s. Max and Sophie Goldie (Singer) L.; m. Lois Sheinhait, Nov. 19, 1967; children—Kimberly Beth, Brett David. A.B., Tufts U., 1965; J.D., Suffolk U., 1968; postgrad. Nat. Coll. Criminal Def. Lawyers and Pub. Defenders, 1975. Bar: Mass. 1968, U.S. Dist. Ct. Mass. 1970, U.S. Ct. Claims 1977, U.S. Ct. Appeals (1st cir.) 1980. Assoc., Zamparelli & White, Medford, Mass., 1968-71; ptnr. Lovins, Frazer & Lewin, Boston, 1971-77, Lappin, Rosen, Goldberg, Boston, 1977-82, Lovins & Diller, Boston, 1982—; instr. paralegal program Northeastern U., 1982. Atty., advisor Winchester (Mass.) Citizens for a Cleaner Environ.; coach Winchester Soccer Club, 1982-83; mem. Temple Isaiah, Lexington, Mass., YMCA, Cambridge, Mass., Winchester Jewish Community Club. Mem. ABA (mem. coms.), Mass. Bar Assn. (21st Century Club 1981, lectr. 1981-82), Assn. Trial Lawyers Am. Editorial staff, contbr. articles Suffolk U. Law Sch. Law Review, 1967-68; author: Causes of Action Related to Intellectual Property, 1982. Federal civil litigation, State civil litigation, General corporate. Office: 1 McKinley Sq Boston MA 02109

LOVITKY, JEFFREY AERYAE, lawyer; b. Flint, Mich., Sept. 22, 1954; s. Bernard Lawrence and Lorraine (Hourvitz) L. BA, U. Mich., 1976; JD, Thomas M. Cooley Law Sch., 1980. Bar: Mich. 1980, Conn. 1982, Fla. 1982, D.C. 1986. Atty. U.S. Dept. Justice, Washington, 1984—. Contbr. articles to profl. jours. Served to capt. JAGC, U.S. Army, 1980-84. Mem. ABA (vice chmn. bid protest com. 1986—, contract related regulations com. 1984-86), Res. Officers Assn. Club: Army and Navy (Washington). Avocations: tennis, squash, backgammon. Government contracts and claims. Office: US Dept Justice 10th and Constitution Ave Washington DC 20530

LOW, JOHN T.C., lawyer; b. N.Y.C., Nov. 20, 1918; s. James and Charlotte (Manning) L.; m. Virginia Ball Kull; 1 dau., Virginia Nichols. A.B., Colgate U.; J.D., Columbia. Bar: Miss., N.Y., Ky. With firm Davis, Polk & Wardwell, N.Y.C., 1942-45; law asst. to Gov. T. Dewey, Albany, N.Y., 1945-47; with firm Dewey Ballantine, N.Y.C., 1947-57; ptnr. Low & Furby, Jackson, Miss., 1957—; lectr. law Pace Coll., N.Y.C. Contbr. articles on taxation to profl. jours. Mem. Nat. Assn. Bond Lawyers, Am., Miss., Hinds County bar assns. Clubs: Jackson Country, University. General corporate, Securities, Probate. Home: 133 Olympia Fields Dr Jackson MS 39211 Office: Low & Furby 1530 Capital Towers Jackson MS 39201

LOW, SUSAN A., lawyer; b. Wilmington, Del., Jan. 2, 1946; d. Allan Winthrop Low and Elizabeth Winthrop (Hersey) Tincher; m. C. Carleton Frederici, Oct. 1, 1983; 1 child, Charles Winthrop. Bar: D.C. 1972, U.S. Dist. Ct. (D.C.) 1972, U.S. Ct. Appeals (D.C. cir.) 1972, Va. 1978, U.S. Supreme Ct. 1980, Iowa 1984, U.S. Dist. Ct. (so. dist.) Iowa 1985. Law clk. to presiding justice Washington, 1971-72, asst. corp. counsel, 1972-74; atty. Washington Gas Light Co., 1974-81; sole practice Washington, 1981-84, Des Moines, 1984—. Mem. ABA, Fed. Energy Bar Assn., Nat. Found. for Women's Bar Assn. (bd. dirs. 1986—), D.C. Bar Assn., Women's Bar Assn. D.C. (v.p. 1980-81, pres. 1981-82), Iowa State Bar Assn., Iowa Assn. Women Attys., Polk County State Bar Assn., Polk County Women Attys. Assn. FERC practice, Administrative and regulatory. Home: 311 42d St Des Moines IA 50312

LOWE, BRYAN A., lawyer; b. San Bernardino, Calif., July 1, 1943; s. Kenneth A. and Marguerite (Bryan) L.; m. Tauna Lee Turley, Dec. 16, 1969; children: Krista, Alexander, Andrew, Aaron, Patrick. BA, Brigham Young U., 1967, MBA, 1969; JD, U. of Pacific, 1981, LLM in Bus. and Taxation, 1982. Bar: Nev. 1981, Ariz. 1982, Calif. 1982, U.S. Dist. Ct. Nev. 1981, U.S. Ct. Claims 1981, U.S. Tax Ct. 1981, U.S. Ct. Appeals (9th cir.) 1981, U.S. Supreme Ct. 1984; CLU. Mktg. rep. Gen. Electric Co., Pittsfield, Mass., 1970-74; agt. ins. Lincoln Nat. Life Ins. Co., San Francisco, 1974-75; ptnr. ins. group Richards. Lowe, Bindrup & Co., Las Vegas, Nev., 1975-82; ptnr. Jones, Holt, Cory, & Lowe, Las Vegas, 1982-84, Burr & Lowe, Las Vegas, 1984-85; sole practice Las Vegas, 1985—; bd. dirs. Info. Mgmt. Inc., Las Vegas. Gen. counsel Housing Authority Clark County, Las Vegas, 1983—. Mem. ABA (tax sect.), Am. Soc. CLU. Republican. Mormon. Club: Spanish Trail Country. Lodge: Rotary. General corporate, Estate planning, Probate. Home: 4370 Flowerdale Ct Las Vegas NV 89103 Office: 1900 E Flamingo Rd Suite 282 Las Vegas NV 89119

LOWE, JAMES ALLISON, lawyer, educator; b. Cleve., July 15, 1945; s. Allison S. and Betty B. (Bernstein) L.; m. Jacalyn S. Scholss, June 24, 1967; children: David, Joseph, Jeremiah. BA, U. Pa., 1967; JD cum laude, Cleve. State U., 1972. Bar: Ohio 1972, U.S. Dist. Ct. (no. dist.) Ohio 1973, U.S. Ct. Appeals (6th cir.) 1981, U.S. Supreme Ct. 1979. Assoc. Berkman, Gordon & Kancelbaum, Cleve., 1972-74; sole practice Cleve., 1974-76; ptnr. Sindell, Lowe & Guidubaldi Co., L.P.A., Cleve., 1976—; instr. law Cleve. State U., 1974-77, Case Western Res. U., 1979—. Active Jewish Community Fedn. Mem. ABA, Assn. Trial Lawyers Am., Ohio Acad. Trial Attys., Ohio Bar Assn., Greater Cleve. Bar Assn. Personal injury, Federal civil litigation. Office: Sindell Lowe & Guidubaldi Co LPA 910 Leader Bldg Cleveland OH 44114

LOWE, JOHN ANTHONY, lawyer; b. Paterson, N.J., Oct. 3, 1942; s. John William and Jane (Kelly) L.; m. Rose A. Farrell, Jan. 2, 1977; children—Theresa Anne, Katherine. AB, Holy Cross Coll., 1963; JD, Cornell U., 1968. Bar: N.Y. 1968, U.S. Dist. Ct. (no. dist.) N.Y. 1968, U.S. Dist. Ct. (so. dist.) N.Y. 1971, U.S. Dist. Ct. (ea. dist.) N.Y. 1982, U.S. Ct. Appeals (9th cir.) 1982. Assoc. Reavis & McGrath. N.Y.C., 1968-71, ptnr., 1979—; asst. U.S. atty. So. Dist. N.Y., N.Y.C., 1971-78; faculty Practicing Law Inst., 1977-78; lectr. U.S. Atty. Gen.'s Advocacy Inst., Washington, 1977; arbitrator Civil Ct. of the City of N.Y., 1978—, Nat. Assn. Security Dealers, 1984—. Contbr. articles to mags. Served to lt. (j.g.) USNR, 1963-65. Named Leading Cons. in High Tech. J. Dick & Co., 1983. Mem. Bklyn. Bar Assn., Order of Coif, Friendly Sons St. Patrick, Phi Alpha Delta (treas. 1964-65). Democrat. Clubs: N.Y. Athletic, Westhampton Country, La Ronde Beach. Federal civil litigation, Securities, Criminal. Home: 200 East End Ave New York NY 10128 Office: Reavis & McGrath 345 Park Ave New York NY 10154

LOWE, JON KENT, lawyer; b. Topeka, Aug. 6, 1947; s. John August and Philomine Marie (Brull) L. BA, U. Kans., 1969, JD, 1972. Bar: Kans. 1980, U.S. Ct. Appeals (10th cir.) 1980. Sole practice Ottawa and Kansas City, Kans., 1980—. Author (mag.) Feet Beat, 1982. Judge Walter Huxman scholar U. Kans., 1970-72. Mem. Franklin County Bar Assn. (treas. 1985—). Republican. Clubs: Kansas City Track, Piccolos Jazz (Kansas City) (pres. 1985—); Lawrence Track (bd. dirs. 1982—), Trailridge Athletic (Lawrence) (bd. dirs. 1985-86); Mid-Am. Masters. Avocations: running, bodybuilding, music. Criminal, Bankruptcy, Family and matrimonial. Home: 1519 W 27th St Lawrence KS 66046

LOWE, KATHLENE WINN, lawyer; b. San Diego, Dec. 1, 1949; d. Ralph and Grace (Rodes) Winn; m. Russell Howells Lowe, Oct. 7, 1977; 1 child, Taylor Rhodes. BA in English magna cum laude, U. Utah, 1971, MA in English, 1973, JD, 1976. Bar: Utah 1976, U.S. Dist. Ct. Utah 1976, U.S. Ct. Appeals (10th cir.) 1978. Assoc. Parsons, Behle & Latimer, Salt Lake City, 1976-80, ptnr., 1980-84; v.p. law Skaggs Alpha Beta Inc., Salt Lake City, 1984—. Contbg. editor Utah Law Rev., 1975-76. Mem. ABA, Utah Bar Assn., Salt Lake City Bar Assn., Phi Kappa Phi. Avocations: fly fishing, reading, skiing, golfing, traveling. Labor, General corporate, Contracts commercial. Office: Skaggs Alpha Beta Inc 5201 Amelia Earhart Dr Salt Lake City UT 84116

LOWE, LOUIS ROBERT, JR., lawyer; b. Indpls., May 30, 1937. BSCE, Purdue U., 1959; LLD, Ind. U., 1967. Bar: U.S. Dist. Ct. (so. dist.) Ind. 1967, U.S. Tax Ct. 1977. Engr. Clyde Williams and Assocs., Indpls., 1960-64, L.I. Couch and Assocs., Indpls., 1964-66, Ind. Hwy Needs Study, Indpls., 1966-67; ptnr. Lowe, Gray, Steele & Hoffman, Indpls., 1967—; bd. dirs. Indpls. Econ. Devel. Commn., Inc., Mineweld Co. of Ind., Inc. Author: Architect and Engineer Liability, 1981. Sec. English Speaking Union, Indpls., 1967—. Fellow Indpls. Bar Found.; mem. Ind. Bar Assn., Purdue Alumni Assn. (bd. dirs. 1984—). Republican. Presbyterian. Clubs: Gyro (bd. dirs. 1982-85), Indpls. Purdue Assn. (pres. 1968-69), Contemporary (pres. 1986—). Securities, Construction, Probate. Home: 535 Pine Dr Indianapolis IN 46260 Office: Lowe Gray Steele & Hoffman 1 Indiana Sq Suite 3130 Indianapolis IN 46204

LOWE, MARY JOHNSON, federal judge; b. N.Y.C., June 10, 1924; children by previous marriage: Edward H., Leslie H.; m. Ivan A. Michael, Nov. 4, 1961; 1 child, Bess J. Michael. B.A., Hunter Coll., 1952; J.D., Bklyn. Law Sch., 1954; LL.M., Columbia U., 1955. Bar: N.Y. State 1955. Practiced law N.Y.C., 1955-71; judge N.Y.C. Criminal Ct., 1971-73; acting justice N.Y. State Supreme Ct., 1973-74; judge Bronx County Supreme Ct., 1975-76; justice N.Y. State Supreme Ct., 1977-78, 1st Jud. Dist., 1978; judge U.S. Dist. Ct. for So. Dist. N.Y., 1978—. Recipient award for outstanding service to criminal justice system Bronx County Criminal Cts. Bar Assn., 1974, award for work on narcotics cases Asst. Dist. Attys., 1974. Mem. Women in Criminal Justice, Harlem Lawyers Assn., Bronx Criminal Lawyers Assn., N.Y. County Lawyers Assn., Bronx County Bar Assn., N.Y. State Bar Assn. (award for outstanding jud. contbn. to criminal justice Sect. Criminal Justice 1978), NAACP, Nat. Urban League, Nat. Council Negro Women, NOW. Jurisprudence. Office: US District Ct US Courthouse Foley Square New York NY 10007 *

LOWE, ROBERT CHARLES, lawyer, banker; b. Seattle, Jan. 15, 1927; s. Martin M. and Helen (Yaster) L.; m. Hope Lucille Sperstad, Mar. 21, 1952; children: Karen, Karlton, Nelson, Inez. B.A., U. Wash., 1953; LL.B., U. Denver, 1959. Bar: Alaska 1961. Accountant Haskins & Sells (C.P.A.s), Los Angeles, 1953-54; agt. Internal Revenue Service, 1954-57; atty. State Alaska, 1960; mem. firm Hughes, Thorsness, Lowe, Gantz & Clark, Anchorage, 1960-75; pres. Safeco Title Agy., Inc., Anchorage, 1975-79; chmn. bd. Peoples Bank & Trust Co., Anchorage. Served with USNR, 1944-46. Mem. Am., Alaska, Anchorage bar assns., Anchorage Estate Planning Council (pres. 1970). Club: Lion. Estate taxation, Probate. Home: 5705 Kingsway Anacortes WA 98221 Office: 807 G St Anchorage AK 99503

LOWE, ROBERT STANLEY, lawyer; b. Herman, Nebr., Apr. 23, 1923; s. Stanley Robert and Ann Marguerite (Feese) L.; m. Anne Kirtland Selden, Dec. 19, 1959; children—Robert James, Margaret Anne. A.B., U. Nebr., Lincoln, 1947, J.D., 1949. Bar: Wyo. bar 1949. Partner firm McAvoy & Lowe, Newcastle, 1949-51, Hickey & Lowe, Rawlins, 1951-55; county and pros. atty. Rawlins, 1955-59, individual practice law, 1959-67; asst. dir. Am. Judicature Soc., Chgo., 1967-68; assoc. dir., dir. programs and services Am. Judicature Soc., 1968-74; counsel True Oil and affiliated cos., Casper, Wyo., 1974—; bd. dirs. Mountain Plaza Nat. Bank, Hilltop Nat. Bank, Casper.; mem. Rawlins Police Civil Service Commn., 1952-54, Nat. Ski Patrol System div. legal adv., 1975— (Yellow merit award 1982, 85); pres., bd. dirs. Snowy Range Ski Corp., 1963-66; city atty., Rawlins, 1963-65. Co-editor: Selected Readings on the Adminstration of Justice and its Improvement, 1969, 71, 73, Current Issues on the Judiciary, 1971, Judicial Disability and Removal Commissions, Courts and Procedures, 1969, 70, 72, 73, others; Contbr. articles to legal jours. mem. Wyo. Ho. of Reps., 1952-54; del. Democratic Nat. Conv., 1952, alt. del., 1956; mem. exec. com. Wyo. Dem. Central Com., 1953-55; bd. dirs. Newcastle Zoning Com., 1950-51, Vols. in Probation, 1969—. Served to lt. (j.g.) U.S. Maritime Service, 1943-46. Recipient Dedicated Community Worker award Rawlins Jr. C. of C., 1967. Fellow Am. Bar Found.; mem. Am. Judicature Soc. (dir. 1961-67, 85—, bd. editors 1975-77, Herbert Harley award 1974), ABA (sec. jud. adminstrn. div. Lawyers Conf. 1975-76, chmn. 1977-78, council jud. adminstrn. div. 1977-78, past chmn., mem. exec. com. 1978-81, mem. com. to implement Jud. Adminstrn. Standards 1978-82, Ho. of Dels. 1978-80, 86—, Assembly del. 1980-83), Wyo. State Bar (chmn. com. on cts. 1961-67, 77—), Nebr. State Bar Assn., Ill. State Bar Assn., D.C. Bar, Inter-Am. Bar Assn., Inst. Jud. Adminstrn., Rocky Mountain Oil and Gas Assn. (legal com. 1976—, chmn. 1979-82), Rocky Mountain Mineral Law Found. (trustee 1980—), Am. Law Inst., Order of Coif, Delta Theta Phi (dist. chancellor 1982-83, chief justice 1983—; Percy J. Power Meml. award 1983). Christian Scientist. Club: Casper Country. Lodges: Masons, Shriners, Elks, Odd Fellows, Rotary (club pres. 1985-86, dist. 544 exec. commr. 1987—). Banking, General corporate, Oil and gas. Home: 97 Primrose Casper WY 82604 Office: 895 W River Cross Rd Casper WY 82601

LOWE, ROY GOINS, lawyer; b. Lake Worth, Fla., Apr. 8, 1926; s. Roy Sereno and May (Goins) L.; A.B., U. Kans., 1948, LL.B., 1951. Admitted to Kans. bar, 1951; gen. practice, Olathe, 1951—; mem. firm Lowe, Farmer, Bacon & Roe and predecessor, 1951—. Served with USNR, 1944-46. Mem. Bar Assn. State Kans., Johnson County Bar Assn., Am. Legion, Phi Alpha Delta, Sigma Nu. Republican. Presbyn. Probate, Oil and gas leasing, Real property. Home: 701 W Park Olathe KS 66061 Office: Colonial Bldg Olathe KS 66061

LOWELL, CYM HAWKSWORTH, lawyer; b. Missoula, Mont., June 2, 1946; s. Wayne R. and Mildred M. (Hawksworth) L.; m. Nancy Brown, June 10, 1967; children: Whitney S., Thomas W., Susannah M. BS, Ind. U., 1969; JD, Duke U., 1972. Bar: Ind. 1972, Ga. 1976. Assoc. Dutton, Kappes & Overman, Indpls., 1972-74; asst. prof. law U. Ga., Athens, 1974-76; assoc. Sutherland, Asbill and Brennan, Atlanta, 1976-81; ptnr. Barnes and Thornburg, Indpls., 1981—; cons. Pres.' Commn. on Olympic Sports, Washington, 1975-76; bd. dirs. Dawn Food Products, Inc., Jackson, Mich. Author: The Law of Sports, 1979; editorial bds. various tax publs.; contbr. articles to profl. jours. Mem. endowment com. Indpls. Mus. Art, 1984—. Served wtih USN, 1964-66, Vietnam. Fellow Ind. Bar Endowment; mem. ABA, Ind. Bar Assn., Sports Lawyers Assn., Orde r of Coif. Corporate taxation, Estate taxation, General corporate. Home: 7770 N Pennsylvania St Indianapolis IN 46240 Office: Barnes and Thornburg 11 S Meridian St Suite 1313 Indianapolis IN 46204

LOWENBERG, MICHAEL, lawyer; b. Bklyn., Mar. 6, 1943; s. Leo and Edna (Hanft) L.; m. Julie Goldberg, June 13, 1965; children: Daniel, Frances, Anthony. BA, Bklyn. Coll.; LLB, Harvard U. Bar: Tex. 1966, U.S. Dist. Ct. (no. dist.) Tex. 1966, U.S. Ct. Appeals (5th cir.) 1967. Assoc. Akin, Gump, Strauss, Hauer & Feld, Dallas, 1966-71, ptnr., 1972—. Pres. Dallas Legal Services Found., 1972; chmn. Dallas chpt. Am. Jewish com., 1973-74. Mem. ABA, Tex. Bar Assn., Dallas Bar Assn., Nat. Legal Aid and Defenders Assn., Def. Research Inst. Democrat. Club: Columbian Country (Dallas). Federal civil litigation, State civil litigation, Contracts commercial. Home: 5551 Montrose Dr Dallas TX 75209 Office: Akin Gump Strauss Hauer & Feld 4100 First city Ctr 7100 Pacific Ave Dallas TX 75201-4618

LOWENHAUPT, CHARLES ABRAHAM, lawyer; b. St. Louis, May 19, 1947; s. Henry Cronbach and Cecile (Koven) L.; m. Rosalyn Lee Sussman, Dec. 28, 1969; children: Elizabeth Anne, Rebecca Jane. BA cum laude, Harvard U., 1969; JD magna cum laude, U. Mich., 1973. Bar: Mo. 1973, U.S. Dist. Ct. (ea. dist.) Mo. 1975, U.S. Tax Ct. 1975, U.S. Ct. Claims 1975, U.S. Ct. Appeals (8th cir.) 1975. Law clk. to presiding justice U.S. Tax Ct., Washington, 1973-75; ptnr. Lowenhaupt, Chasnoff, Armstrong & Mellitz, St. Louis, 1975—; speaker Nat. Assn. Indsl. Sch., 1985; adv. bd. dirs. Cottonwood Gulch Found., Thoreau, N.Mex., Textile Mus., Washington; bd. dirs. Cen. West End Assn., St. Louis. Mem. adv. com. Washington U. Bus. Sch., St. Louis, 1981—; bd. dirs., v.p. Community Sch., St. Louis, 1982—; bd. dirs., pres. St. Louis U. Library Assts., St. Louis, 1982-83; bd. dirs. Temple Emanuel, St. Louis, 1982-85, Craft Alliance of St. Louis, 1987. Mem. ABA (tax sect., estate and gift sect., real property sect., probate and trust law, task force legal fin. planning), Mo. Bar Assn. (tax sect.), St. Louis Bar Assn. (tax sect.), St. Louis Estate Planning Council, Washinton U. Club. Club: Mo. Athletic. Estate taxation, Corporate taxation, Personal income taxation. Home: 58 Kingsbury Place Saint Louis MO 63112 Office: Lowenhaupt Chasnoff et al 408 Olive St Saint Louis MO 63102

LOWENSTEIN, LOUIS, legal educator; b. N.Y.C., June 13, 1925; s. Louis and Ralphina (Steinhardt) L.; m. Helen Libby Udell, Feb. 12, 1953; children: Roger Spector, Jane Ruth, Barbara Ann. B.S., Columbia, 1947, LL.B., 1953; M.F.S., U. Md., 1951. Bar: N.Y. 1953. Practice in N.Y.C., 1954-78; also dir.; law sec. Assoc. Judge Stanley H. Fuld, N.Y. Ct. Appeals, 1953-54; assoc., then partner Hays, Sklar & Herzberg, 1954-68; partner Nickerson, Kramer, Lowenstein, Nessen, Kamin & Soll, 1968-78; lectr. Columbia Law Sch., 1976-80, prof., 1980—; pres. Supermarkets Gen. Corp., Woodbridge, N.J., 1978-79; dir. Mathematica, Inc. Editor-in-chief: Columbia Law Rev, 1951-53. Vice pres., mem. exec. com. Fedn. Jewish Philanthropies N.Y.; pres. Jewish Bd. Family and Children's Services N.Y., 1974-78; trustee Beth Israel Med. Center, N.Y.C., 1975-81. Served to lt. (j.g.) USNR, 1943-46. Mem. Am., N.Y. bar assns., Assn. Bar City N.Y., Am. Law Inst., Phi Delta Phi. Home: 1 Fountain Sq Larchmont NY 10538 Office: Columbia Law Sch New York NY 10027 *

LOWENSTEIN, MARSHALL LEIGH, lawyer; b. Richmond, Va., May 12, 1928; s. Harry and Yetta (Brown) L.; married, Aug. 26, 1956; children: Terry, Nancy, Neil, Karen. AB, U. Chgo., 1947, JD, 1951. Assoc. Dervishian, Spinella & Dervishian, Richmond, 1954-58; ptnr. Dervishian, Hutzler & Lowenstein, Richmond, 1958-65, Cabell, Paris, Lowenstein & Baretord, Richmond, 1965-86; bd. dirs. Sands, Anderson, Marks & Miller, Richmond; bd. dirs. Cen. Coca-Cola Bottling Co., Richmond; gen. counsel Women's Bank, Richmond, 1983-85; commr. in chancery City Richmond Circuit Ct., 1980—. Mem. Va. adv. bd. Anti-Defamation League, Richmond, 1970—; bd. dirs. Jewish Community Ctr., Richmond, 1975-76; pres. Congregation Beth Ahabah, Richmond, 1984-85. Served to lt. U.S. Army, 1951-53, Korea. Mem. ABA, Richmond Bar Assn. Club: Jefferson-Lakeside (pres. 1980-81). Probate, Real property, General corporate. Office: Sands Anderson Marks & Miller Ross Bldg PO Box 1998 Richmond VA 23216-1998

LOWENTHAL, PHILIP HENRY, lawyer, educator; b. Cin., June 1, 1944; s. Charles P. and Phebe Jane (Segal) L.; m. Caroline Marie Remedios, Jan. 17, 1981; children: Alexander, Christopher, Benjamin, Jacob. BA, U. Calif., Berkeley, 1966, JD, 1969. Bar: Hawaii 1970, Calif. 1970, U.S. Dist. Ct. (no. dist.) Calif. 1970, U.S. Dist. Ct. (no. dist.) Hawaii 1970, U.S. Supreme Ct. 1978, U.S. Ct. Appeals (9th cir.) 1982. Supervising pub. defender Maui County, Wailuku, Hawaii, 1970-79; ptnr. Lowenthal, August & Graham and predecessor firms, Wailuku, 1980—; lectr. evidence and criminal law Maui (Hawaii) Community Coll., 1975—, Peoples Law Sch., Wailuku, 1986—. Pres. Maui Symphony, 1983; bd. dirs. Legal Aid Soc. Hawaii, 1982-85. Fellow Am. Bd. Criminal Lawyers (v.p. 1986—); mem. Hawaii Bar Assn. (jud. adminstrn. com., instr. trial advocacy 1984—), Hawaii Jud. Conf., Nat. Assn. Criminal Def. Lawyers, Assn. Trial Lawyers Am. Avocation: squash. Criminal, Personal injury. Office: Lowenthal August & Graham 2261 Aupuni St Wailuku HI 96793

LOWER, ROBERT CASSEL, lawyer, educator; b. Oak Park, Ill., Jan. 8, 1947; s. Paul Elton and Doris Thatcher (Heaton) L.; m. Jean Louise Lower, Aug. 24, 1968 (dec. Aug. 1985); children—David Elton, Andrew Bennett, James Philip Thatcher; m. Cheryl Bray, July 26, 1986. A.B. magna cum laude with highest honors, Harvard U., 1969, J.D., 1972. Bar: Ga. 1972. Assoc., Alston, Miller & Gaines (now Alston & Bird), Atlanta, 1972-78, ptnr., 1978—; adj. prof. Emory U., 1978—. Co-founder, pres. Ga. Vol. Lawyers for the Arts, Inc., 1975-79; chmn. Fulton County (Ga.) Arts Council, 1979—. Mem. ABA, Ga. Bar Assn., Atlanta Bar Assn., Phi Beta Kappa. Presbyterian. Club: Harvard (Atlanta). Contbr. articles to law jours. Commodities, Banking, Real property. Home: 935 Plymouth Rd NE Atlanta GA 30306 Office: Alston & Bird 35 Broad St 1200 C&S Nat Bank Bldg Atlanta GA 30335

LOWERY, WILLIAM HERBERT, lawyer; b. Toledo, June 8, 1925; s. Kenneth Alden and Drusilla (Pfanner) L.; m. Carolyn Broadwell, June 27, 1947; children: Kenneth Latham, Marcia Mitchell. Ph.B., U. Chgo., 1947; J.D., U. Mich., 1950. Bar: Pa. 1951, U.S. Supreme Ct. 1955. Assoc. Dechert Price & Rhoads, Phila., 1950-58, ptnr., 1958—, mng. ptnr., 1970-72; policy com. counsel S.S. Huebner Found. Ins. Edn., Phila., 1970—. Author: Insurance Litigation Problems, 1972, Insurance Litigation Disputes, 1977. Pres. Stafford Civic Assn., 1958; chmn. Tredyffrin Twp. Zoning Bd., Chester County, Pa., 1959-75; bd. dirs., pres. Paoli Meml. Hosp., Pa., 1964—. Served to 2d lt. USAF, 1943-46. Mem. ABA (chmn. life ins. com. 1984-85, chmn. Nat. Conf. Lawyers and Life Ins. Cos. 1984—), Jud. Conf. 3d Cir. Ct. Appeals. Clubs: Waynesborough Country (Paoli); Urban (Phila.); Naples Bath and Tennis (Fla.). Insurance, Federal civil litigation, Health. Home: 5 Etienne Arbordeau Devon PA 19333 Office: Dechert Price & Rhoads 3400 Centre Sq W Philadelphia PA 19102

LOWES, ALBERT CHARLES, lawyer; b. Oak Ridge, Mo., Dec. 1, 1932; s. Guy Everett and Lillian Bertina (Tuschhoff) L.; m. Peggy Rae Watson, Aug. 27, 1960; children: Danita Rae, Albert Charles II, Kurt Brandon. Student, Cape State Coll., 1954-56; JD, U. Mo., 1959. Bar: Mo. 1959, U.S. Dist. Ct. (ea. dist.) Mo. 1959, U.S. Ct. Appeals (8th cir.) 1971. With Buerkle, Lowes, Beeson & Ludwig, Jackson, Mo., 1959-84; sole practice Cape Girardeau, Mo., 1984-86; ptnr. Lowes & Drusch, Cape Girardeau, 1986—; atty. City of Jackson, Mo., 1960-62; judge adv. dept. of Mo. VFW, Jefferson City, 1962-64. Served to staff sgt. USMC, 1950-54, Korea. Mem. ABA, Mo. Bar Assn., Internat. Assn. Ins. Counsel. Democrat. Lutheran. Lodges: Elks, Masons, Shriners. Avocations: reading, history, legal fields. Insurance, Personal injury, Criminal. Office: Lowes & Drusch 2913 Independence Cape Girardeau MO 63701

LOWINGER, ALEXANDER I, lawyer; b. Chgo., June 29, 1917; s. Morris and Alwine (Alexander) L.; m. Muriel Rosencranz, Oct. 10, 1942; children: Margaret L. Needelman, Lloyd M., Frederick C. AB, U. Chgo., 1939, JD, 1941. Bar: Ill. 1941, U.S. Dist. Ct. (no. dist.) Ill. 1950. Assoc. Leo F. Tierney, Balt., 1941-42; spl. atty. U.S. Dept. Justice Antitrust Div., Washington, 1942; assoc. Rosenthal, King and Robin, Chgo., 1945-51; ptnr. King, Robin, Gale and Pillinger, Chgo., 1941-72; Tenney and Bentley, Chgo., 1972—; adj. prof. John Marshall Law Sch., Chgo., 1955-61. Pres. Friends of the Mentally Ill, Chgo., 1953-54; mem. bd. edn., pres. Highland Park-Deerfield High Sch. Dist. 113, Highland Park, Ill., 1967-73; mem. City of Highland Park Plan Commn., 1969-71. Served with U.S. Army, 1942-45, PTO. Mem. Chgo. Bar Assn., Ill. State Bar Assn., Law Club of Chgo., Chgo. Lit. Club. Club: City (Chgo.) (v.p. bd. govs. 1962-63). General corporate, Corporate taxation, Labor. Home: 522 Church St Evanston IL 60201 Office: Tenney and Bentley 111 W Washington St Chicago IL 60602

LOWINGER, LAZAR, lawyer; b. Antwerp, Berchem, Belgium, Nov. 7, 1934; came to U.S., 1954; s. Julius and Maria (Gilburd) L.; m. Audrey Schwelling, Aug. 15, 1965; children—Jeffrey Paul, Brian Marc. Student Boston U., 1956-57, Sir Geo. Williams Coll., 1957-59; J.D., New England Sch. Law, 1962. Bar: Mass. 1964, U.S. Dist. Ct. Mass. 1965. Sole practice, Brookline, Mass., 1964—. Sec. Republican Nat. Hispanic Assembly, Boston, 1984—; schedule chmn. New England Lawn Tennis Assn., Needham, Mass., 1983. Served with U.S. Army, 1954-56. Recipient Mem. of Honour award Cuban Bar in Exile, Miami, Fla., 1971. Mem. Mass. Bar Assn. (chmn.), Assn. Trial Lawyers Am., Mass. Acad. Trial Attys. Jewish. Clubs: Hazel Hotchkiss Wightman Tennis Ctr. (Weston, Mass.), Badminton and Tennis (Boston). General practice, Criminal, Personal injury. Home: 305 Woodcliff Rd Newton MA 02161 Office: Hearthstone Plaza 111 Washington St PO Box 749 Suite 201 Brookline MA 02147

LOWN, CAROLYN ANN, lawyer; b. Batavia, N.Y., May 16, 1953; d. Henry Kingsley and Patricia Ann (Pape) L. BA, Denison U., 1975; JD, U. Va., 1978. Bar: Ill. 1978, U.S. Dist. Ct. (no. dist.) Ill. 1978, U.S. Ct. Appeals (7th cir.) 1979. Assoc. Schiff, Hardin & Waite, Chgo., 1978-84, ptnr., 1984-85; environ. counsel Chem. Waste Mgmt., Oakbrook, Ill., 1985; assoc. gen. counsel Waste Mgmt. N.Am., Inc., Oakbrook, 1986—; atty. Manville Corp., Denver, 1982. Mem. ABA (natural resources law sect.), Chgo. Bar Assn. (environ. law com.), Phi Beta Kappa. Democrat. Episcopalian. Environment. Office: Waste Mgmt N Am Inc 3003 Butterfield Rd Oakbrook IL 60521

LOWNDES, JOHN FOY, lawyer; b. Medford, Mass., Jan. 1, 1931; s. Charles L. B. and Dorothy (Foy) L.; m. Rita Davies, Aug. 18, 1983; children: Elizabeth Anne, Amy Scott, John Patrick, Joseph Edward. B.A., Duke U., 1953, LL.B., 1958. Bar: Fla. 1958. Practice, Daytona Beach, Fla., 1958; practice, Orlando, Fla., 1959-69; sr. ptnr., chmn. bd. dirs. Lowndes, Drosdick, Doster, Kantor & Reed, P.A., Orlando, 1969—; mem. adv. bd. Atlantic Nat. Bank Fla., 1982-86; bd. dirs. First Union Nat. Bank Fla.; pres., trustee Orlando Mus. Art, 1986—; trustee Loch Haven Art Ctr.; bd. visitors Duke U.; mem. adv. bd. Coll. Bus. Adminstrs. U. Central Fla. Served to capt. USMC, 1953-55. Mem. So. Fed. Tax Inst. (founding trustee). Republican. Roman Catholic. Clubs: Orlando Country, Citrus, University (Orlando, Fla.). Real property, General corporate. Office: Lowndes Drosdick et al Box 2809 Orlando FL 32802

LOWRY, EDWARD FRANCIS, JR., lawyer; b. Los Angeles, Aug. 13, 1930; s. Edward Francis and Mary Anita (Woodcock) L.; m. Patricia Ann Palmer, Feb. 16, 1963; children—Edward Palmer, Rachael Louise. Student, Ohio State U., 1948-50; A.B., Stanford, 1952, J.D., 1954. Bar: Ariz. bar 1955, U.S. Supreme Ct. bar 1969, D.C. bar 1970. Camp dir. Quarter Circle V Bar Ranch, 1954; tchr. Orme Sch., Mayer, Ariz., 1954-56; trust rep. Valley Nat. Bank Ariz., 1958-60; practice in Phoenix, 1960—; assoc. atty. Cunningham, Carson & Messinger, 1960-64; partner Carson, Messinger, Elliott, Laughlin & Ragan, 1964-69, 70-80, Gray, Plant, Mooty, Mooty & Bennett, 1981-84, Eaton, Lazarus, Dodge & Lowry Ltd., 1985-86; gen. counsel Bus. Realty Ariz., 1986—; asst. legislative counsel Dept. Interior, Washington, 1969-70; Mem. Ariz. Commn. Uniform Laws, 1972—, chmn., 1976—; judge pro tem Ariz. State Ct. Appeals, 1986. Chmn. Council of Stanford Law Socs., 1968; vice chmn. bd. trustees Orme Sch., 1972-74, treas., 1981-83; bd. trustees Heard Mus., 1965—, pres., 1974-75, now mem. men's council; bd. visitors Stanford Sch. Law; magistrate Town of Paradise Valley, Ariz., 1976-83; juvenile ct. referee Maricopa County, 1978-83. Served to capt. USAF, 1956-58. Fellow Ariz. Bar Found. (founder); mem. ABA, Maricopa County, D.C. bar assns., State Bar Ariz. (chmn. com. on uniform laws 1979—), Stanford Law Soc. Ariz. (past pres.), Ariz. State U. Law Soc. (dir.), Nat. Conf. Commrs. Uniform State Laws, Delta Sigma Rho, Alpha Tau Omega, Phi Delta Phi. General corporate, Real property, Probate. Home: 6900 E Camelback Rd Suite 1040 Scottsdale AZ 85251 Office: 6900 E Camelback Rd Suite 1040 Scottsdale AZ 85251

LOWRY, HOUSTON PUTNAM, lawyer; b. N.Y.C., Apr. 1, 1955; s. Thomas Clinton Falls and Jean Allen (Day) L. BA, Pitzer Coll., 1976; MBA, U. Conn., 1980; JD cum laude, Gonzaga U., 1980; LLB in Internat. Law, U. Cambridge, Eng., 1981. Bar: Conn. 1980, U.S. Dist. Ct. Conn. 1981, U.S. Tax Ct. 1982, U.S. Ct. Mil. Appeals 1982, U.S. Ct. Appeals (1st, 2d, 5th and 11th cirs.) 1982, U.S. Ct. Claims 1984, D.C. 1985, U.S. Ct. Appeals (4th, 6th, 7th, 9th, fed., and D.C. cirs.) 1985, U.S. Ct. Appeals (8th and 10th cirs.) 1986, U.S. Supreme Ct. 1986. Law clk. to judge U.S. Dist. Ct., Birmingham, Ala., 1982-83; assoc. Tarlow, Levy, Mandell & Kostin, P.C., Farmington, Conn., 1983—. Mem. ABA (various coms.), Conn. Bar Assn. (various coms.), Hartford County Bar Assn., Am. Arbitration Assn., Am. Fgn. Law Assn., Am. Judicature Soc., Am. Soc. Internat. Law, Computer Law Assn., Inter-Am. Bar Assn. (various coms.), Internat. Law Assn., Internat. Law Inst. Clubs: United Oxford and Cambridge Univ., Hartford, Dauntless. Contracts commercial, Computer, Federal civil litigation. Office: Tarlow Levy Mandell & Kostin PC 10 Talcott Notch Rd PO Box 877 Farmington CT 06034

LOWRY, ROBERT DUDLEY, lawyer; b. Washington, D.C., Apr. 12, 1949; s. Robert Newton and Mary (Dudley) L.; m. Becky Jo Kangas, Aug. 3, 1974; children: Samuel Robert, Joseph Houston. BA, U. Oreg., 1971, postgrad. in Biology, 1971-73, JD, 1980. Bar: Oreg. 1980, U.S. Dist. Ct. Oreg. 1980. Law clk. Oreg. Supreme Ct., Salem, 1980-81; ptnr. Jaqua, Wheatley, Gallagher & Holland, P.C., Eugene, 1981—. Cubmaster Boy Scouts Am. Eugene, 1984—. Mem. ABA, Oreg. Bar Assn., Lane County Bar Assn. (chmn. fed. ct. com., 1985—, med. legal com. 1986—). Democrat. Episcopalian. Avocations: sailing, skiing, piano. Insurance, Health, Federal civil litigation. Home: 2085 Medina St Eugene OR 97401 Office: Jaqua Wheatley et al 825 E Park St Eugene OR 97401

LOWY, STEVEN ROBERT, lawyer; b. Los Angeles, Feb. 14, 1951; s. Mortimer J. and Sunny (Drobinsky) L.; m. Victoria Anne Cooper, Apr. 17, 1981. BS, UCLA, 1973; JD, Southwestern U., Los Angeles, 1976. Bar: Calif., U.S. Ct. Appeals (9th cir.). Law clk., dir. criminal pre-trial sect. Atty's. Office, Los Angeles, 1975-77; sole practice Los Angeles, 1977-80, 85—; ptnr. Lowy & Feldman, 1980-82, Medow & Lowy, 1982-84; bd. dirs. Bravura Records Ltd., London, 1985—, Strawberry Creek Music Festival, Los Angeles, 1986—. Editor: Ladies Above Suspicion, 1986. Mem. ABA (forum com. entertainment law and sports, copyright trademark and patent subcom.), Los Angeles County Bar Assn. (atty. client relations com., arbitrator), Calif. Copyright Conf., ACLU, Sierra Club. Avocations: fencing, fishing, gardening. Entertainment, Trademark and copyright. Office: 8444 Wilshire Blvd Beverly Hills CA 90211

LUBBEN, CRAIG HENRY, lawyer; b. Fort Lee, Va., Aug. 10, 1956; s. George and Dorothy Marion (Vree) L.; m. Lois Beth Zylstra, June 9, 1979; children—Christina Anne, Brian Craig. B.A., Calvin Coll., 1978; J.D. cum laude, Northwestern U., 1981. Bar: Mich. 1981, U.S. Dist. Ct. (we. dist.) Mich. 1981, U.S. Ct. Appeals (6th cir.) 1984. Assoc. Miller, Johnson, Snell & Commiskey, Grand Rapids, Mich., 1981-86, Kalamazoo, Mich., 1986—. Pres., Alternative Directions, Grand Rapids, 1985; trustee Grand Rapids Pub. Mus. Assn., 1984-86. Mem. Order of Coif. Mem. Christian Reformed Church. Federal civil litigation, State civil litigation, Contracts commercial. Office: Miller Johnson Snell & Commiskey 425 W Michigan Ave Kalamazoo MI 49007

LUBCKE, KIP CHARLES, lawyer; b. LaCrosse, Wis., Mar. 26, 1946. BA in Econs. and Math., Ripon Coll., 1968; MA in Econs., U. Va., 1970; JD, U. Wis., 1972. Bar: Wis. 1972, Mich. 1974, N.J. 1977. Assoc. Kostner, Ward & Koslo, Arcadia, Wis., 1972-73; atty. Dow Chem. Co., Midland, Mich., 1973-76, Hoechst Celanese Corp., Somerville, N.J., 1976—. Mem. ABA, Wis. Bar Assn., Mich. Bar Assn., N.J. Bar Assn., Am. Bus. Law Assn., Phi Beta Kappa. Contracts commercial, Computer, Environment. Home: 277-4C Gemini Dr Somerville NJ 08876 Office: Hoechst Celanese Corp Rt 202-206 N Somerville NJ 08876

LUBET, MARC LESLIE, lawyer; b. Atlanta, Sept. 13, 1946; s. Louis Lubet and Sylvia (Hirsch) Hoppes; m. Arlene Walsh, June 11, 1976 (div. Apr. 1982); m. Celinda G. Vestal, Nov. 17, 1984. BS in Journalism, U. Fla., 1969; JD, U. Miss., 1974. Bar: Miss. 1974, Fla. 1974, U.S. Dist. Ct. (no. dist.) Fla. 1974, U.S. Ct. Appeals (5th cir.) 1974, U.S. Supreme Ct. 1977, U.S. Ct. Appeals (11th cir.) 1981. Assoc. Pitts & Eubanks Law Firm, Orlando, Fla., 1974-75, Levine & Cohen, Orlando, 1975-76; sr. ptnr. Lubet & Woodard, Orlando, 1977—; mediator Citizens Dispute, Orlando, 1980—. Active Margarita Soc., Orlando, 1983—. Fellow Am. Bd. Criminal Lawyers; mem. Orange County Bar (mem. speakers bur. 1980-82, crim. law commn. 1983—), ABA, Fla. Bar Assn., Miss. Bar Assn., Nat. Assn. Criminal Def. Lawyers. Democrat. Jewish. Avocations: racquetball, fishing. Criminal. Office: Marc L Lubet Esq 209 E Ridgewood St Orlando FL 32801

LUBET, STEVEN, law educator; b. 1949. JD, U. Calif., Berkeley, 1973. Staff atty. Legal Asst. Fedn., Chgo., 1973-75; prof. Northwestern U., Evanston, Ill., 1975—; lectr. DePaul U., Chgo., 1974-75. Office: Northwestern U Sch Law 357 E Chgo Ave Chicago IL 60611 *

LUBIC, ROBERT BENNETT, legal educator, arbitrator; b. Pitts., Mar. 9, 1929; s. H. Murray and Rose M. (Schwartz) L.; m. Benita Joan Alk, May 31, 1959; children—Wendy, Bret, Robin. AB, U. Pitts., 1950, JD, 1953; M in Patent Law, Georgetown U., 1959. Bar: Pa. 1953, U.S. Supreme Ct. 1958, U.S. Ct. Appeals (D.C. cir.) 1958, U.S. Patent Office, 1959, U.S. Dist. Ct. D.C. 1964. Atty. adviser FCC, Washington, 1957-59; sole practice, Pitts., 1959-63; asst. prof. law Duquesne U. Law Sch., Pitts., 1963-65; prof. law Am. U. Law Sch., Washington, 1965—, assoc. dean, 1970-71; permanent panel arbitrator U.S. Postal System, Washington, 1978—, U.S. Dept. Labor, Washington, 1982-87; arbitrator Pub. Employee Relations Bd. D.C., Washington, 1984—, Pub. Employee Relations Bd. V.I., 1982—; dir. Labor Disputes Resolution Seminar, Hamilton, Bermuda, 1982, 83, Nassau, Bahamas, 1983, labor cons. Govt. of Bermuda, 1985—; creator, dir. Eastern European Summer Law Program, Moscow and Warsaw, 1979-81, Chinese Am.

Summer Law Program, Peking, Shanghai and Hong Kong, 1984-86; co-dir. Middle East Summer Law Program, Jerusalem, 1976, 78. Recipient Outstanding Tchr. award Am. U. Student Bar Assn., 1981. Mem. Internat. Soc. for Labor Law and Social Security, Soc. of Profls. in Disputes Resolution, Fed. Communications Bar Assn., D.C. Bar Assn., Am. Arbitration Assn. Democrat. Jewish. Contracts commercial, Private international, Labor. Home: 2813 McKinley Pl NW Washington DC 20015 Office: American U Law Sch 4400 Massachusetts Ave NW Washington DC 20016

LUBIN, DAVID S., lawyer; b. Lakewood, N.J., Aug. 24, 1956; s. Ernest G. and Ruth (Lobe) L.; m. Robin J. Gaizer, Oct. 7, 1984. BA, Brandeis U., 1978; JD, Georgetown U., 1981; LLM in Taxation, Temple U., 1986. Bar: Pa. 1981, N.J. 1981, U.S. Dist. Ct. (ea. dist.) N.J. 1981, U.S. Supreme Ct. 1986. Legis. intern ABA, Washington, 1979-81; assoc. Abramson, Freedman and Blackman, Phila., 1981-82; jud. clk. Phila. County Ct. Common Pleas, 1982-86; assoc. Narin and Chait, Phila., 1986-87; trial asst. Anapol, Schwartz, Weiss & Schwartz, Phila., 1987—. Assoc. editor The Tax Lawyer; contbr. articles to profl. jours. Mem. ABA, N.J. State Bar Assn., Pa. Bar Assn., Phila. Bar Assn. State civil litigation, Personal injury, General practice. Home: 1125 Rodman St Philadelphia PA 19147 Office: Anapol Schwartz Weiss & Schwartz 1900 Delancey Pl Philadelphia PA 19103 also: 200 Windward Ave Beachwood NJ 08722

LUBITZ, HOWARD ARNOLD, lawyer; b. N.Y.C., Apr. 7, 1928; s. Daniel and Ray (Felt) L.; m. JoAnn Boatner, Oct. 22, 1955; children: Pamela Dawn, Dana Beth. BA, NYU, 1948, JD, 1951, LLM, 1956. Bar: N.Y. 1952, U.S. Ct. Mil. Appeals 1954. Assoc. Nathan B. Kogan, N.Y.C., 1956-57; ptnr. Epstein, Newman and Lubitz, N.Y.C., 1958—; lectr. USNR, Freeport, L.I., 1956, Rockland County Bar Assn., N.Y.C., 1973, N.Y. State Trial Lawyers Assn., 1974; arbitrator Am. Arbitration Assn., N.Y.C., 1971—, Bronx County (N.Y.) Arbitration Panel, 1971—. Served to lt. USN, 1951-55. Recipient certs. of appreciation Rockland County Bar Assn., 1973, Kiwanis Internat., Bronx, 1972. Mem. Am. Trial Lawyers Assn., N.Y. State Trial Lawyers Assn. (bd. dirs. 1969—, lectr. 1974-76), N.Y. State Bar Assn., Bronx County Bar Assn. Jewish. Avocations: creative landscaping, rock gardening. Personal injury, Criminal, General practice. Home: 14 Keltz St Spring Valley NY 10977 Office: Epstein Newman & Lubitz 178 E 161st St Bronx NY 10451 also: 30 Irving Pl New York NY 10003

LUBLIN, MARK AARON, lawyer; b. Phila., Oct. 10, 1942; s. P. Paul and Sara (Raynes) L.; children—Adam, Robert. B.S., Temple U., 1964; J.D., Villanova U., 1967. Bar: Pa. 1967, U.S. Supreme Ct. 1977. Assoc., Klinger, Heller & Simone, 1967-72; jud. law clk. to adminstrv. judge Common Pleas Ct., Philadelphia County, Pa., 1972-81; ptnr. Gottlieb, Tolan & Lublin, Phila., 1972-73; sole practice, Phila., 1973-81; spl. counsel to Saul, Ewing, Remick & Saul, Phila., 1981-85; ptnr. Obermayer, Rebmann, Maxwell & Hippel, Phila., 1986—. Mem. ABA, Pa. Bar Assn., Phila. Bar Assn., Assn. Trial Lawyers Am., Tau Epsilon Rho. Democrat. Jewish. Family and matrimonial, Personal injury, Criminal. Home: Unit 405 Latches Lane Condo Merion PA 19066 Office: Obermayer Rebmann Maxwell Hippel Packard Bldg 14th Floor Philadelphia PA 19102

LUBLINSKI, MICHAEL, lawyer; b. Eskilstuna, Sweden, Sept. 11, 1951; came to U.S., 1956; s. Walter and Dora L. BA magna cum laude, CCNY, 1972; JD, Georgetown U., 1975. Bar: N.Y. 1976, Calif. 1980, Ct. Internat. Trade 1981, U.S. Dist. Ct. (cen. dist.) Calif. 1981, U.S. Dist. Ct. (so. dist.) N.Y. 1981, U.S. Ct. Appeals (D.C. cir.) 1982. Atty. U.S. Customs Service, Washington, 1975-79, U.S. Dept. Commerce, Washington, 1980; assoc. Mori & Ota, Los Angeles, 1980-84; assoc. Kelley Drye & Warren, Los Angeles, 1984-85, ptnr., 1986—. Panel moderator Calif. continuing edn. of bar Competitive Bus. Practices Inst., Los Angeles and San Francisco, 1984. Mem. ABA, Calif. Bar Assn., Los Angeles County Bar Assn. (arbitrator 1981-82, chmn. customs law sect. 1986). Avocations: travel, photography, movies. Immigration, naturalization, and customs, Trademark and copyright. Home: 2609 Creston Dr Los Angeles CA 90068 Office: Kelley Drye & Warren 624 S Grand Ave Los Angeles CA 90017

LUBY, THOMAS STEWART, lawyer; b. Meriden, Conn., Jan. 12, 1952; s. Robert M. and Ruth (McGee) L.; m. Paula P. Falcigno, July 19, 1985; 1 child, Elizabeth. BA, Yale U., 1974; JD, U. Conn., 1977. Bar: Conn., U.S. Dist. Ct. Conn., U.S. Ct. Appeals (2d cir). Law clk. to presiding judge U.S. Dist. Ct., Bridgeport, Conn., 1977-78; asst. U.S. atty. New Haven, Conn., 1978-81; ptnr. Luby, Olson, Mango & Gaffney, Meriden, 1981—; mem. grievance com. U.S. Dist. Ct. Conn., 1985—; bd. dirs. Home Bank & Trust Co., Meriden. State Rep. Conn. Gen. Assembly, 1987—; mem. Dem. Town Com., Meriden; bd. dirs. Meriden Boys Club. Recipient Spl. Achievement award U.S. Dept. Justice, 1980, Outstanding Pub. Service award United Way, 1986. Mem. Conn. Bar Assn. Democrat. Roman Catholic. Federal civil litigation, State civil litigation, Criminal. Home: 32 Westfield Rd Meriden CT 06450

LUCAS, CAMPBELL MACGREGOR, justice; b. La Jolla, Calif., Jan. 8, 1925; s. Robert and Georgina Macgregor (Campbell) L.; m. Elizabeth Helene Buse, Dec. 17, 1960; children—Scott Campbell, Stephen Edward, Lisanne Elizabeth. Student, Ark. State Coll., Jonesboro, 1943, Calif. Inst. Tech., 1946-47; B.A., UCLA, 1949; J.D., U. So. Calif., 1952. Bar: Calif. 1953. Ptnr. Lucas, Pino & Lucas, Long Beach, Calif., 1954-62, Lucas, Pino, Lucas & Deukmejian, Long Beach, 1962-65, Lucas, Lucas & Deukmejian, Long Beach, 1965-67, Lucas & Deukmejian, Long Beach, 1967-70; judge Superior Ct. County of Los Angeles, 1970-84; justice Ct. Appeal, 1984—; guest lectr. U. So. Calif. Law Ctr.; mem. Calif. State Bd. Registration for Profl. Engrs., 1967-70. Pres. Long Beach Area council Boy Scouts Am., 1980-81, mem. exec. bd., 1959—; bd. dirs. Community Welfare Fedn. Long Beach, 1969—. Served with Inf., AUS, 1943-45. Decorated Purple Heart with oak leaf cluster. Mem. ABA, Los Angeles County Bar Assn., Calif. Judges Assn. (chmn. jud. ethics com. 1980; chmn. civil law and procedure com. 1985), Am. Judicature Soc., U. So. Calif. Law Alumni Assn. (pres. 1979-80). Republican. Congregationalist. State civil litigation, Appellate judiciary. Office: 3580 Wilshire Blvd Suite 424 Los Angeles CA 90010

LUCAS, JO DESHA, legal educator, editor; b. Richamond, Va., Nov. 7, 1921; s. Robert Desha and Hill Miller (Carter) L.; m. Johanna Westley, June 17, 1950; children: Robin Desha, John Carter. A.B., Syracuse U., 1947, M.P.A., 1951; LL.B., U. Va., 1951; LL.M., Columbia U., 1952. Bar: Va. 1952. Asst. prof. law U. Chgo., 1953-57, assoc. prof., 1957-61, prof., 1961—, Arnold I. Shure prof. law, 1982—; chmn. Ill. Supreme Ct. Rules Com., 1974—; reporter Fed. Adv. Com. on Appellate Rules, 1976-78. Author cases on admiralty; co-author: Moore's Federal Practice, 1970—; contbr. articles to legal revs., 1970—. Served with USAAF, 1943-46. Mem. Va. Bar, Chgo. Bar Assn., Order of Coif, Phi Beta Kappa. Legal education. Home: 5504 S Harper Ave Chicago IL 60637 Office: Law Sch U Chgo 1111 E 60th St Chicago IL 60637 *

LUCAS, JOHN KENNETH, lawyer; b. Chgo., July 9, 1946; s. John and Catherine (Sykes) L.; m. Mary Ellen McElligott, Oct. 14, 1972; 1 child, John Patrick. BSEE with distinction, Ill. Inst. Tech., 1968; JD, DePaul U., 1972. Bar: Ill. 1972. Elec. engr. Commonwealth Edison Co., Chgo., 1968-72; assoc. Horton, Davis, McCaleb & Lucas, Chgo., 1972-74; ptnr. McCaleb, Lucas, & Brugman and predecessor firms, Chgo., 1975-84; counsel Willian, Brinks, Olds, Hofer, Gilson & Lione Ltd., Chgo., 1984-85, ptnr., 1986—; hearing officer Ill. Pollution Control Bd., 1981—; adj. prof. De Paul U. Coll. of Law, 1986—. Mem. ABA, Ill. Bar Assn., Chgo. Bar Assn., Bar Assn. of 7th Fed. Cir., Am. Intellectual Property Law Assn., Patent Law Assn. Chgo., Lic. Execs. Soc., Internat. Assn. Protection Indsl. Property, Legal Club of Chgo., Phi Alpha Delta, Tau Beta Pi, Eta Kappa Nu. Patent, Trademark and copyright, Federal civil litigation. Office: Willian Brinks Olds Hofer Gilson & Lione Ltd One IBM Plaza Suite 4100 Chicago IL 60611

LUCAS, JOHN MICHAEL, lawyer; b. Covington, Ky., Feb. 15, 1951; s. Chester Marion and Mary Evelyn (Lovelace) L.; m. Bonnie Sue Nezi, June 14, 1975; children—Tyler Franklin, Philip Orlando, Lauren Elizabeth. B.S., No. Ky. U., 1973; M.A., Xavier U., 1976; J.D., Chase Law Sch., Ky., 1976. Bar: Ky. 1979, U.S. Dist. Ct. (ea. dist.) Ky. 1980. Law clk. Smith & Wolenzak, Covington, 1977-79; corp. atty. ATE Mgmt. & Service Co., Cin., 1981—; trustee ATE Enterprise Liquidations Trust. Mem. Young Trial Lawyers Assn. (pres. 1978-79). Democrat. Episcopalian. General corporate, Transportation. Home: 741 Mill Valley Dr Taylor Mill KY 41015 Office: ATE Mgmt Inc 617 Vine St Cincinnati OH 45202

LUCAS, MALCOLM MILLAR, chief state justice; b. Berkeley, Calif., Apr. 19, 1927; s. Robert and Georgina (Campbell) L.; m. Joan Fisher, June 23, 1956; children: Gregory, Lisa Georgina. B.A., U. So. Calif., 1950, LL.B., 1953. Bar: Calif. 1954. Partner firm Lucas, Deukmejian and Lucas, Long Beach, Calif., 1955-67; judge Superior Ct., Los Angeles, 1967-71, U.S. Dist. Ct., Central Dist., Calif., 1971-84; assoc. justice Calif. Supreme Ct., 1984-87, chief justice, 1987—. Office: Calif Supreme Ct 350 McAllister St San Francisco CA 94102 also: Calif Supreme Ct Sacramento CA 95814

LUCAS, PATRICK HEWELL, lawyer; b. Chattanooga, Sept. 30, 1955; s. Earl Anderson and Helen (Hewell) L. BA, Vanderbilt U., 1978, JD, 1981; LLM in Taxation, U. Fla., 1982. Bar: Ala. 1982. Assoc. Balch & Bingham, Birmingham, Ala., 1982—. Mem. ABA (tax, corp. and real property sects.), Phi Beta Kappa, Phi Eta Sigma. Democrat. Presbyterian. Avocations: tennis, basketball. Corporate taxation, State and local taxation, Personal income taxation. Home: 203 D Foxhall Rd Birmingham AL 35213 Office: Baclch & Bingham 505 N 20th St Birmingham AL 35203

LUCAS, STEVEN MITCHELL, lawyer; b. Ada, Okla., Jan. 19, 1948; s. John Dalton and Cherrye (Smith) L. BA, Yale U., 1970; JD, Vanderbilt U., 1973. Bar: D.C. 1973, U.S. Ct. Mil. Appeals 1974, U.S. Dist. Ct. D.C. 1979, U.S. Ct. Appeals (D.C.) 1979, U.S. Supreme Ct. 1979. Assoc. Shaw, Pittman, Potts & Trowbridge, Washington, 1978-82, ptnr., 1983—; cons. on internat. relations, Rockefeller Found., N.Y.C., 1978, mem. negotiating team Panama Canal Treaty, Washington, 1975-77, legal adviser negotiations working group. Editor in chief Vanderbilt U. Jour. Transnational Law, 1972-73. Served to capt. JAGC, U.S. Army, 1974-77. Mem. ABA, Fed. Bar Assn. (chmn. internat. law com. 1978-80, Outstanding Com. Chmn. award 1979), Inter-Am. Bar Assn., Am. Soc. Internat. Law. Republican. Episcopalian. Clubs: Army-Navy Country (Arlington, Va.); Yale N.Y.C. Banking, Private international, Securities. Home: 1696 Dunstable Green Annapolis MD 21401 Office: Shaw Pittman Potts & Trowbridge 2300 N St NW Washington DC 20037

LUCCHESI, LIONEL LOUIS, patent lawyer; b. St. Louis, Sept. 17, 1939; s. Lionel Louis and Theresa L.; m. Mary Ann Wheeler, July 30, 1966; children—Lionel Louis III, Marisa Pilar. B.S.E.E., Ill. Inst. Tech., 1961; J.D., St. Louis U., 1969. Bar: Mo. 1969. With Emerson Electric Co., 1965-69; assoc. Polster, Polster & Lucchesi, St. Louis, 1969-74, ptnr., 1974—; city atty. City of Ballwin (Mo.), 1979-85 . Alderman City of Ballwin, 1977-79, mem. Zoning Commn., 1971-77. Served to lt. USNR, 1961-65. NROTC scholar, 1957-61; recipient Am. Jurisprudence award St. Louis U., 1968-69. Mem. ABA, Am. Patent Law Assn., Assn. Trial Lawyers Am., St. Louis Met. Bar Assn. (exec. com., pres.-elect 1984, pres. 1985-86), Newcomen Soc. N.Am. Republican. Roman Catholic. Clubs: Forest Hills, Rotary (St. Louis). Patent, Trademark and copyright, Federal civil litigation. Office: 763 S New Ballas Rd Saint Louis MO 63141

LUCE, CHARLES F., JR., lawyer; b. Walla Walla, Wash., Jan. 22, 1956; s. Charles F. Sr. and Helen (Oden) L.; m. Jean Hopler, July 28, 1984. BA with distinction, U. Colo., 1978; JD, U. Oreg., 1981. Bar: Colo. 1981, U.S. Dist. Ct. Colo. 1981, U.S. Ct. Appeals (10th cir.) 1981, U.S. Supreme Ct. 1987. Assoc. Moye, Giles, O'Keefe, Vermeire & Gorrell, Denver, 1981—; lectr. in law U. Denver, 1985—. Mem. ABA, Colo. Bar Assn. (ethics com. 1985—), Denver Bar Assn., Denver Law Club, Order of Coif, Phi Beta Kappa, Phi Kappa Tau. Avocations: musical composition, performance, production and recording. Federal civil litigation, State civil litigation, Trademark and copyright. Office: Moye Giles O'Keefe Vermeire & Gorrell 730 17th St Suite 600 Denver CO 80202

LUCE, KENYON ELDRIDGE, lawyer, municipal judge; b. Forest Hills, Mass., May 24, 1939. BA, Cen. Wash. U., 1964; JD, Willamette U., 1967. Staff atty. legal aid OEO, Tacoma, 1967-69; pros. atty. City of Fife, Wash., 1969-80, mcpl. judge, 1980—; sole practice Tacoma, 1967—. Trustee Annie Wright Sch., Tacoma, 1980—. Served with USNR, 1957-63. Mem. ABA (probate, real property and law office econs. sect.), Wash. State Bar Assn., Pierce County Bar Assn., Assn. Trial Lawyers Am., Wash. State Trial Lawyers Assn. Republican. Methodist. Club: Tacoma Yacht. Lodges: Rotary, Masons, Shriners. Avocation: computers. State civil litigation, Probate, Judicial administration. Office: 1409 54th Ave EA Tacoma WA 98424

LUCEY, JOHN DAVID, JR., lawyer; b. Phila., May 4, 1930; s. John David and Eleanor (Gallagher) L.; m. Carol Ann Henderson, Oct. 29, 1955; children—John David, Michael Dakin, Timothy Gallagher, Carol Anne. A.B., U. Pa., 1953, LL.B., 1956. Bar: Pa. 1957. Mem. firm LaBrum and Doak, Phila., 1957—; instr. estate counselling Temple U. Sch. Law, 1977-86; course planner, author, lectr. Pa. Bar Inst., 1967—. Mem. Phila. Bar Assn. (chmn. sect. probate and trust law 1976), Pa. Bar Assn., ABA, Am. Coll. Probate Counsel. Republican. Roman Catholic. Club: Union League of Phila. Probate, Estate taxation. Home: 1237 Hagy's Ford Rd Narberth PA 19072 Office: LaBrum and Doak 700 IVB Bldg 1700 Market St Philadelphia PA 19103

LUCHAK, FRANK ALEXANDER, lawyer; b. Alberta, Can., Feb. 19, 1950; came to U.S., 1956; s. George and Elizabeth (Szilagyi) L. AB in Econs., Princeton U., 1972; JD, SUNY, Buffalo, 1978. Bar: Pa. 1978, N.J. 1979, U.S. Dist. Ct. N.J. 1979, U.S. Dist. Ct. (ea. dist.) Pa. 1980, U.S. Supreme Ct. 1986. Assoc. Harvey, Pennington et al, Phila., 1977-81; assoc. Duane, Morris & Heckscher, Phila., 1981-86, ptnr., 1986—. Mem. ABA, Pa. Bar Assn., Phila. Bar Assn. (civil and jud. procedures rules com.), Pa. Assn. Def. Counsel, Phila. Assn. Def. Counsel, Def. Research Inst. Federal civil litigation, State civil litigation. Home: 303 Catharine St Philadelphia PA 19147 Office: Duane Morris & Heckscher 1400 One Franklin Plaza Philadelphia PA 19102

LUCHSINGER, JOHN FRANCIS, JR., lawyer; b. Pensacola, Fla., Mar. 3, 1944; s. John and Marion (Bex) L.; A.B., Syracuse U., 1966; J.D., Bklyn. Law Sch. 1971; m. Pamela I. Baumgartner, Aug. 19, 1967; children—Heather Leigh, Todd James, James Bradley. Law clk. N.Y. State Supreme Ct., Mineola, 1969; law intern Nassau County Dist. Atty.'s Office, Mineola, 1970; admitted to N.Y. bar, 1971; assoc. firm Pelletreau & Pelletreau, Patchogue, NY., 1971-73; trial atty. Hiscock, Lee, Rogers, Henley & Barclay, Syracuse, N.Y., 1973-79; gen. counsel v.p., Farmers and Traders Life Ins. Co., Syracuse, 1979—; guest lectr. Syracuse U. Sch. Law; Vice-pres., Jamesville-Dewitt Bd. Edn., 1977-82; pres. Canal Center, Inc., 1976-77, Dewitt Community Library, 1977—; pres. Am. Heart Assn. Upstate N.Y., 1984-85; referee N.Y. State Commn. Jud. Conduct. Served to 2d lt., Armored Corps, U.S. Army, 1967-70. Mem. Syracuse Def. Trial Lawyers Assn. (pres. 1980-81), Am. Bar Assn., N.Y. State Bar Assn., Onondaga County Bar Assn. (chmn. corp. sect. 1985-86), Assn. Life Ins. Counsel, Assn. Life Ins. Cos. N.Y., Jaycees (Jaycee of Yr. 1971-72). Republican. Clubs: Rotary (pres. 1978-79; dist. gov. 1983—), Onondaga Golf and Country, Century (bd. govs. 1986-89), Limestone Tennis, Willowbank Yacht. Insurance. Home: 45 Lyndon Rd Fayetteville NY 13066 Office: 960 James St Syracuse NY 13201

LUCHTEL, KEITH EDWARD, lawyer; b. Milford, Iowa, Sept. 7, 1941; s. Leroy Phillip and Gertrude (Marley) L.; m. Patricia Ann Moss, June 4, 1966; children: Kathleen, Kristina. BS, USAF Acad., 1964; JD, Drake U., 1973. Bar: Iowa 1973, U.S. Dist. Ct. (no. and so. dists.) Iowa 1973. Commd. 2d lt. USAF, 1964, advanced through grades to capt., 1968, resigned, 1970; assoc. Nyemaster Law Firm, Des Moines, 1973-76, ptnr., 1976—; atty. City of Clive, Iowa, 1978-86. Mem. Order of Coif. Republican. Roman Catholic. Avocations: electronics, golf, tennis, reading. Legislative, Administrative and regulatory, Local government. Home: 10521 Sunset Terr Clive IA 50322 Office: Nyemaster Goode McLaughlin et al 1900 Hub Tower Des Moines IA 50309

LUCK, BRADLEY JAMES, lawyer; b. Cleve., Sept. 7, 1952; s. Chester Albert and Bernice (Hrella) L.; m. Carla Ann Swanson; children: Amy Elizabeth, Jenna Marie, Angela Sara. Student, Seminole Jr. Coll., 1970-71, U.S. Naval Acad., 1971-73; BA with honors, U. Mont., 1974, JD with honors, 1977. Bar: Mont. 1977, U.S. Dist. Ct. Mont. 1977, U.S. Ct. Appeals (9th cir.) 1985, U.S. Supreme Ct. 1986. Assoc. Skelton & Knight, Missoula, Mont., 1977-79; ptnr. Garlington, Lohn & Robinson, Missoula, 1979—; active Gov.'s Council on Workers Compensation, Mont., 1985—. Mem. ABA, Mont. Def. Council Assn. (bd. dirs. 1984—). Roman Catholic. Workers' compensation, Personal injury. Home: 4415 Fox Farm Rd Missoula MT 59802 Office: Garlington Lohn & Robinson 199 W Pine Missoula MT 59807

LUCOW, MILTON, lawyer; b. Detroit, Oct. 4, 1924; s. Louis and Dora (Schupps) L.; m. Audrey B. Kline, Mar. 30, 1947; children: Celia (Mrs. James Stegman), Michael B. LL.D., Wayne State U., 1948. Bar: Mich. bar 1948. Since practiced in Detroit; partner, treas. firm Garan, Lucow, Miller, Seward & Cooper (P.C.), Detroit, 1948—; lectr. in field; mediator Wayne Circuit Ct. Mich., 1973—. Pres. Detroit Service Group, 1983—; bd. dirs. Jewish Welfare Fedn. Detroit; pres. Temple Emanu-El, 1960-62; chmn. Midrasha Coll. Jewish Learning, 1977-80. Served with AUS, 1943-45. Decorated Purple Heart, Metz medal, Bronze Star. Arbitrator Am. Arbitration Assn.; Mem. ABA, Detroit Bar Assn., Mich. Bar Assn. (mem. del. assembly 1979-80). Jewish religion (pres. United Hebrew Schs. Detroit 1974-77). Club: Tam-O-Shanter (pres. 1970-72). Personal injury, Insurance, Federal civil litigation. Home: 3159 Bloomfield Shore Dr Orchard Lake MI 48033 Office: 1000 Woodbridge St Detroit MI 48207

LUDLAM, WARREN VANGILDER, JR., lawyer; b. Meridian, Miss., Aug. 29, 1919; s. Warren VanGilder and Bessie (Hanley) L.; m. Helen Harvey McGee, Apr. 28, 1948; children—Helen Ludlam Dalehite, Warren McGee, Steven Hanley. A.B. cum laude, Davidson Coll., 1940; LL.B., Harvard U., 1943. Bar: Tex. 1944, Miss. 1944, D.C. 1975, U.S. Dist. Ct. (so. dist.) Miss., U.S. Ct. Claims, U.S. Tax Ct., U.S. Supreme Ct. Assoc. Baker, Botts, Andrew & Wharton, Houston, 1943-44; assoc. Watkins, Ludlam & Stennis, Jackson, Miss., 1944-50, ptnr. from 1950, mng. ptnr., 1967-68; mem. nat. adv. council Practising Law Inst., 1963-75, mem. council exec. com., 1969-75, lectr., 1965; commr. Miss. State Bar from 7th Jud. Dist., chmn. policy com. Joint Miss. State Bar-U. Miss. Continuing Legal Edn. Com., mem. bar taxation com., chmn. com.; officer, dir., ptnr. various local bus. corps. and partnerships; lectr. in field. Trustee Jackson Ballet (now Ballet Miss.), 1979—, chmn. ballet, 1980-81, vice chmn., 1981-83; mem. exec. com., bd. dirs. Miss. Ballet Internat., Inc. and II, III and IV USA Internat. Ballet Competition, Jackson, vice chmn. III, 1986, chmn. IV; chmn. Ballet Miss. (consol. of Jackson Ballet and Miss. Ballet Theatre), 1983—; mem. ofcl. bd. Galloway Meml. United Methodist Ch., Jackson, 1983—; bd. advs. Meth. Children's Home, Jackson. Fellow Miss. State Bar Found. (life); mem. ABA (council sect. taxation 1977-81, past chmn. assoc. and adv. com. to spl. com. on retirement benefits), Miss. State Bar Assn., Hinds County Bar Assn. (past mem. exec. com., past chmn. grievance com.), D.C. Bar Assn., Am. Coll. Tax Counsel, Scribes (dir. 1964-68, v.p. 1966-67, pres. 1967-68), Miss. Law Inst. (co-founder), Estate Planning Council Miss. (past pres.), English Speaking Union, Phi Beta Kappa, Omicron Delta Kappa, Phi Delta Theta (past dir. Jackson Alumni chpt.). Clubs: Country of Jackson, Univ., Exchange (dir. 1967-68, v.p. 1968-69, pres. 1969-70) (Jackson); Harvard of Miss. Author: (with others) Federal Taxation of Agriculture, 1980; contbr. articles to profl. jours.; probate and tax editor Law Notes, 1967-69; assoc. editor Tax Lawyer, 1973. Corporate taxation, Estate taxation, State and local taxation. Office: Suite 2000 Deposit Guaranty Plaza Jackson MS 39201

LUDOLPH, MARLA ROSE, lawyer; b. Portland, Oreg., May 5, 1955; d. Carl H. and Laura M. (Andrus) L. AA, Clark Community Coll., 1974; BA, George Fox Coll., 1976; JD, Willamette U., 1979. Bar: Wash. 1979, U.S. Dist. Ct. (we. dist.) Wash. 1979. Asst. dean George Fox Coll., Newberg, Oreg., 1979; from assoc. to ptnr. Landerholm, Memovich, Lansverk & Whitesides, Vancouver, Wash., 1980—. Chmn. Clark County (Wash.) Civil Service Commn.; mem. Evang. Ch. Trust Orgn., Vancouver; trustee George Fox Coll., 1983—; bd. dirs. Southwest Wash. Hosp., Vancouver, 1983—, sec. 1986—. Mem. Wash. State Bar Assn., Clark County Bar Assn. (trustee 1984, treas. 1985), Assn. Trial Lawyers Am., Wash. State Trial Lawyers Assn., Am. Assn. Univ. Women, Women in Action. Democrat. Avocations: tennis, cooking, gardening, music. Workers' compensation, Personal injury, Social security disability. Office: Landerholm Memovich et al 915 Broadway Vancouver WA 98660

LUDOLPH, ROBERT CHARLES, lawyer; b. Chgo., Oct. 28, 1948; s. Robert Charles and Wynne Mae (Nicolson) L.; m. Pamela Sears, Aug. 19, 1972. AB, Dartmouth Coll., 1970; MEd, U. Mass., 1972; JD, Wayne State U., 1980; PhD, U. Mich., 1982. Bar: Mich. 1981, U.S. Dist. Ct. (ea. dist.) Mich. 1981, U.S. Ct. Appeals (6th cir.) 1982, Ohio 1985, U.S. Dist. Ct. (no. dist.) Ohio 1985. Dir. spl. services Springfield (Mass.) Tech. Co., 1974-76; dir. acad. services Detroit Inst. Tech., 1977-80; assoc. Dykema, Gossett, Spencer, Goodnow & Trigg, Detroit, 1981-84, Pepper, Hamilton & Scheetz, Detroit, 1984—. Mem. ABA, Fed. Bar Assn., Detroit Bar Assn., Nat. Assn. Coll. and Univ. Attys. Labor, Civil rights, Health. Office: Pepper Hamilton & Scheetz 100 Renaissance Ctr 36th Floor Detroit MI 48243

LUDWIG, CHARLES FINE, lawyer; b. Phila., Sept. 29, 1931. AB with honors and distinction, U. Pa., 1953, LLB, 1956, postgrad., 1956-57. Bar: Pa. 1957. Assoc. Gordon and Gordon, Phila., 1956, Edward Davis, Phila., 1957-58; asst. gen. counsel Penn Mut. Life Ins. Co., Phila., 1963-70; vp., gen. counsel Union Fidelity Corp., Phila., 1970-72; assoc. Montgomery, McCracken, Walker and Rhoads, Phila., 1972-75; ptnr. Lovitz and Ludwig, Phila., 1975-78, Charles F. Ludwig and Assocs., Phila., 1978-85; v.p., gen. counsel Am. Integrity Corp., Phila., 1985—; supr. litigation, regulation of life ins., health ins., credit ins. cos.; lectr. in field. Co-founder Logan Sq. Neighborhood Assn., 1963, pres., 1966-69; gen. counsel, bd. dirs. Am. Found. Negro Affairs and Nat. Edn. and Research Fund; pres. Organized Classes, U. Pa., 1967-70, bd. dirs., 1960—, pres. Soc. of the Coll., 1965-68, bd. mgrs., 1960—, pres. Class of 1953, 1958-63, sec., 1968—, life dir. gen. alumni bd. Gen. Alumni Soc., 1967—, censor emeritus Philomathean Soc.; pres. Associated Alumni Cen. High Sch., Phila., 1968-72, bd. mgrs., 1950—; pres. Temple Beth Zion-Beth Israel, Phila., 1983—, chmn., co-founder library, 1965—; v.p. United Synagogue Bd. Jewish Edn., Phila., 1969-79; chmn. Center City Religious Sch. Bd., Phila., 1967-83; mem. exec. com., v.p. Solmon Schechter Day Sch., Phila., 1971—; bd. dirs. Gratz Coll., 1960-67, mem. library com., 1965—; co-founder, sec. Phila. Chamber Orch. Soc., 1960-70; chmn. bd. Phila. Musical Acad., 1964-65; sec., dir. bd. Musical Fund Soc. Phila., 1964-86; pres. Musical Fund Soc. Found., Phila., 1986—. Mem. Athenaeum of Phila., Phila. Soc. Preservation Landmarks Colonial Phila. Hist. Soc. (founding), Phila. Mus. Art, Phila. Bar Assn., Fed. Bar Assn., Ins. Fedn. Pa., Zionist Orgn. Am., Pi Gamma Mu, Pi Sigma Alpha (charter Pa. chpt.). Clubs: Peale, Lawyers (Phila.). Lodge: B'nai B'rith. General corporate, Insurance. Office: Am Integrity Corp Two Penn Ctr Plaza 2d Floor Philadelphia PA 19102

LUDWIG, EDMUND V., judge; b. Phila., May 20, 1928; s. Henry and Ruth (Viner) L.; m. Sara Marie Webster, Nov. 1, 1982; children from previous marriage: Edmund Jr., John, Sarah, David. AB, Harvard U., 1949, LLB, 1952. Law clk. to presiding justice Common Pleas Ct., Phila., 1952-53; assoc. Duane, Morris & Hecksher, Phila., 1956-59; ptnr. Barnes, Biester & Ludwig, Doylestown, Pa., 1959-68; judge Common Pleas Ct., Bucks County, Pa., 1968-85, U.S. Dist. Ct. (ea. dist.), Phila., 1985—; mem. faculty Pa. Coll. of the Judiciary, 1974-85; presenter Villanova (Pa.) U. Law Sch., 1975-85, lectr., 1984—; vis. lectr. Temple Law Sch., 1977-80; clin. assoc. prof. Hahnemann U., Phila., 1977-85; mem. Pa. Juvenile Ct. Judge's Commn., 1978-85; chmn. Pa. Chief Justice's Ednl. Com., 1984-85; pres. Pa. Conf. State Trial Judges, 1981-82. Chmn. Children and Youth Adv. Com., Bucks County, 1978-83; mem. Pa. Adv. Com. on Mental Health and Mental Retardation, 1980-85; founder, bd. dirs. Today, Inc., Newtown, Pa., 1971-85, Probation Vols., Bucks County, 1971-81; mem. Pa. Joint Council on Criminal Justice, Inc., 1979-80; mem. Joint Family Law Council Pa., 1979-85; vice chmn. Human Services Council Bucks County, 1979-81; mem. Com. to Study Unified Jud. System Pa., 1980-82. Recipient Disting. Service award Bucks County Corrections Assn., 1978, Spl. Service award Big Bros., 1979, Humanitarian award United Way Bucks County, 1980, Founder's award Vol. Services, 1982, Spl. award Bucks County Juvenile Ct., 1985. Mem. ABA, Pa. Bar Assn., Fed. Bar Assn. (hon.). Republican. Club: Harvard

(N.Y.C. and Phila.) (v.p. 1974-80). Jurisprudence, Family and matrimonial, Juvenile. Office: 5613 US Courthouse Independence Mall 601 Market St Philadelphia PA 19106

LUDWIG, R. ARTHUR, lawyer; b. Milw., Apr. 25, 1929; s. Arthur and Marie (Habein) L.; m. Evelyn L. Ludwig. B.B.A., U. Wis., 1955, LL.B., 1955, J.D.S., 1966. Bar: Wis. 1955, U.S. Dist. Ct. (ea. dist.) Wis. 1955, U.S. Ct. Appeals (7th cir.) 1963, U.S. Supreme Ct. 1977. Mem. firm Ludwig & Shlimovitz S.C., Milw. Mem. ABA, Milw. Bar Assn. (editor bankruptcy sect. newsletter), Wis. Bar Assn. (sect. bankruptcy, insolvency and creditors rights sect., dir. 1971-72, chmn. 1981-83, reporter 1979—), 7th Cir. Bar Assn., Beta Alpha Psi, Phi Beta Alpha, Delta Theta Phi. Roman Catholic. Club: Milw. Athletic. Bankruptcy, Probate, General corporate. Home: 5524 N 13th St Milwaukee WI 53209 Office: 1568 N Farwell St Milwaukee WI 53202

LUDWIG, RONALD L., lawyer, educator; b. Cleve., June 25, 1943; s. Julius and Helen (Saltzman) L.; m. Carrie Glaser, Dec. 28, 1968. AB, Duke U., 1965; JD, U. Mich., 1968. Bar: Ohio 1968, D.C. 1971, Calif. 1974. Tax law specialist IRS, Washington, 1968-69; sole practice Washington, 1969-73; ptnr. Kelso, Hunt & Ludwig, San Francisco, 1973-77, Ludwig & Curtis, San Francisco, 1977—; spl. counsel Employee Stock Ownership Plan Assn., Washington, 1978—; adj. prof. Georgetown U., Washington, 1971-73; lectr. Golden Gate U., San Francisco, 1980-82. Co-author Tax Mgmt. Portfolio, Employee Stock Ownership Plan, 1985. Mem. Gen. Acctg. Office, Washington, 1984-86; adv. com. Study of Employee Stock Ownership Plans. Mem. Western Pension Conf., ABA (sect. on taxation, employee benefits com.). Pension, profit-sharing, and employee benefits, Corporate Finance. Home: 640 Davis St San Francisco CA 94111 Office: 50 California St San Francisco CA 94111

LUIS, JUANITA BOLLAND, lawyer, insurance company executive; b. Wadena, Minn., July 17, 1950; d. Arnold Herman and Eva Louise (Steinke) Bolland; m. Richard Charles Luis Aug. 20, 1977. B.A. magna cum laude, U. Minn., 1972, J.D. cum laude, 1977. Bar: Minn. 1977. C.P.C.U. Atty. St. Paul Fire & Marine Ins. Co., 1978-79, asst. counsel, 1979-81, assoc. counsel, 1981-82, corp. sec., 1982—, asst. gen. counsel, 1985—, also dir. co. and several subs. Mem. ABA, Minn. Bar Assn., C.P.C.U. Soc., Nat. Assn. Ins. Women. Insurance, General corporate, Administrative and regulatory. Home: 175 E County Rd B-2 Saint Paul MN 55117 Office: St Paul Fire & Marine Ins Co 385 Washington St Saint Paul MN 55102

LUKER, LYNN MICHAEL, lawyer; b. Idaho Falls, Idaho, Aug. 30, 1953; s. Nephi Michael Luker and Betty Ruth (Schild) L.; m. Helen Marie Dahlquist, June 19, 1976; children: Daniel Jacob, Jean Marie, Rebecca Jane, David Alexander, Eric Carlyle. AB, U. Calif., Berkeley; JD, U. Idaho. Bar: Idaho 1980, U.S. Dist. Ct. Idaho 1981, U.S. Ct. Appeals (9th cir.) 1984, U.S. Supreme Ct. 1985. Law clk. to presiding justice Idaho Supreme Ct., Boise, 1980-82; sole practice Boise, 1982-83; assoc. Goioechea Law Office, Boise, 1983-85, ptnr., 1985—. Editor-in-chief U. Idaho Law Rev., 1979-80. Calif. State scholar, 1974-77, Warren scholar 1979-80. Mem. ABA, Assn. Trial Lawyers Am., Idaho Trial Lawyers Assn., Am. Travelors Assn., Idaho Travelors Assn. Republican. Mormon. Avocations: family, gardening, photography, German lang. Workers' compensation, Personal injury. Office: Goicoechea Law Office 701 W Franklin St Boise ID 83701

LUKEY, PAUL EMERAN, lawyer; b. Cin., Jan. 11, 1947; s. Frank Emeran and Anne Louise (Gutting) L.; m. Carol Marie Stoner, June 4, 1972 (div. Jan. 1978); m. Kimberly Sue Albright, June 10, 1978; children: Sarah Beth, Paul Adam. BS, St. Joseph's Coll., Rensselaer, Ind., 1969; MBA, U. Dayton, 1970; JD, Chase Law Sch., 1975. Bar: Ohio 1975, U.S. Dist. Ct. (so. dist.) Ohio 1975, U.S. Tax Ct. 1976, U.S. Supreme Ct. 1978, U.S. Dist. Ct. (ea. dist.) Ky. 1979, U.S. Ct. Appeals (6th cir.) 1979. Filed adjuster Ohio Civil Rights Commn., Cin., 1973-77; sole practice Cin., 1977—; lectr. U. Cin., 1976—. Mem. ABA, Ohio Bar Assn., Cin. Bar Assn., Butler County Bar Assn. Republican. Roman Catholic. Avocations: sports, legal history, study of names. Bankruptcy, Family and matrimonial. Home: 5728 Lake Meade Ave Fairfield OH 45014

LULIE, EDWARD, III, lawyer; b. Balt., Apr. 30, 1951; s. Edward and Lillian (Roheletter) L.; m. Harriet Elizabeth Lulie, Oct. 7, 1972. JD, U. Balt., 1977. Bar: Md., U.S. Dist. Ct. Md. Sole practice Frederick, Md., 1979—; asst. states atty. Frederick County, 1986—. Pres. alumni assn. U. Balt., Frederick. Mem. Assn. Trial Lawyers Am., Frederick County Bar Assn., Aircraft Owners and Pilots Assn. (panel atty. 1980-84). Avocation: umpiring U.S. Naval war games. Criminal, Federal civil litigation. Office: 34 S Market St Frederick MD 21701

LUM, HERMAN TSUI FAI, chief justice Hawaii Supreme Court; b. Honolulu, Nov. 5, 1926; s. K.P. and Helen (Tom) L.; m. Almira Ahn, June 17, 1949; children: Forrest K.K., Jonathan K.K. Student, U. Hawaii, 1945-46; LL.B., U. Mo., 1950. Bar: Hawaii 1950. Asst. public prosecutor City and County Honolulu, 1950-52; chief atty. Hawaii Ho. of Reps., 1955, chief clk., 1956-61; partner Suyenaga, Sakamoto & Lum, Honolulu, from 1956; U.S. atty. Dist. Hawaii, 1961-67; judge Circuit Ct. Honolulu, 1967-76, sr. judge Family Ct., 1977-80; assoc. justice Supreme Ct. Hawaii, 1980-83, chief justice, 1983—; Pres. Jr. Bar Assn. Hawaii, 1957. Mem. ABA, Bar Assn. Hawaii, Fed. Bar Assn. Hawaii (pres. 1963), Phi Delta Phi, Lambda Chi Alpha. Home: 2508 Makiki Heights Dr Honolulu HI 96822 Office: Supreme Ct of Hawaii PO Box 2560 Honolulu HI 96804 *

LUMBARD, ELIOT HOWLAND, lawyer, educator; b. Fairhaven, Mass., May 6, 1925; s. Ralph E. and Constance Y. L.; m. Jean Ashmore, June 21, 1947; m. Kirsten Dehner, June 28, 1981; children: Susan, John, Ann, Joshua Abel, Marah Abel. BS in Marine Transp., U.S. Merchant Marine Acad., 1945; BS in Econs., U. Pa., 1949; JD, Columbia U., 1952. Bar: N.Y. 1953, U.S. Supreme Ct. 1959, Pa. 1983. Assoc., Breed, Abbott and Morgan, N.Y.C., 1952-53; asst. U.S. atty. So. Dist. N.Y., 1953-56; assoc. Chadbourne, Parke, Whiteside & Wolff, N.Y.C., 1956-58; ptnr. Townsend & Lewis, N.Y.C., 1961-70; ptnr. Spear and Hill, N.Y.C., 1970-75; ptnr. Lumbard and Phelan, P.C., N.Y.C., 1977-82, Saul, Ewing, Remick & Saul, N.Y.C., 1982-84; sole practice, N.Y.C., 1984-86; ptnr. Haight, Gardner, Poor & Havens, N.Y.C., 1986—; chief counsel N.Y. State Commn. Investigation, 1958-61; spl. asst. counsel for law enforcement to Gov. N.Y., 1961-67; criminal justice cons. to Gov. Fla., 1967; chief criminal justice cons. to N.J. Legis., 1968-69; chmn. com. on organized crime N.Y.C. Criminal Justice Coordinating Council, 1971-74; mem. departmental disciplinary com. First Dept., N.Y. Supreme Ct., 1982—; trustee, bankruptcy, Universal Money Order Co., Inc., 1977-82; chmn. Palisades Life Ins. Co. (former Equity Funding subs. 1974-75); dir. RMC Industries Corp., 1983—; lectr. trial practice NYU, 1963-65; mem. vis. com. Sch. Criminal Justice, SUNY-Albany, 1968—; adj. prof. law and criminal justice John Jay Coll. Criminal Justice, CUNY, 1975-86; arbitrator Am. Arbitration Assn. and N.Y. Civil Ct.-Small Claims Part, N.Y. County; mem. Vol. Master Program U.S. Dist. Ct. (so. dist.) N.Y. Bd. dirs. Citizens Crime Commn. N.Y.C., Inc.; Big Bros. Movement, Citizens Union; trustee Trinity Sch, 1964-78, N.Y.C. Police Found., Inc., 1971—, chmn., 1971-74; bd. dirs. Ocean Liner Museum, N.Y.C., Big Bros. Served to lt. j.g. USNR, 1945-52. Recipient First Disting. Service award Sch. Criminal Justice, SUNY-Albany, 1976. Mem. Assn. Bar City N.Y., N.Y. County Lawyers Assn., ABA, N.Y. State Bar Assn., Maritime Law Assn. Republican. Clubs: Down Town Assn., Merchants (N.Y.C.). Contbr. articles to law jours. State civil litigation, Bankruptcy, Federal civil litigation. Home: 300 Central Park W Apt 5J New York NY 10024 Office: 1 State St Plaza New York NY 10004

LUMKES, DEBORAH LEE, lawyer; b. San Mateo, Calif., Jan. 3, 1951; d. Maynard and Dorothy-Jo (Mathers) L. BA, U. Nev., 1972; JD, U. Pacific, 1980. Bar: Nev. 1981, U.S. Dist. Ct. Nev. 1981, U.S. Ct. Appeals (9th cir.) 1981, Calif. 1983, U.S. Supreme Ct. 1986. Atty. City of Reno, 1981, Washoe County Dist. Atty.'s Office, Reno, 1981-85; sole practice Reno, 1985—; tchr. Washoe County Sch. Dist., Reno, 1984—, Nat. Coll. Juvenile Judges, Reno, 1985, also lectr. Chmn. Com. to Elect C. Mcgee Dist. Ct. Judge, Reno, 1984; Mem. Com. to Elect Mills Lane Dist. Atty., Reno, 1982, Com. to Elect Debra Agosti Justice of Peace, Reno, 1982, Com. to Elect Bert George Mcpl. Judge, Reno, 1984; judge pro tem mcpl. ct. Reno; bd. dirs. Parents United, Reno, 1983—, past pres., bd. dirs. YWCA. Named one of Outstanding Young Women in Am., 1984. Mem. Washoe County Bar Assn., Assn. Trial Lawyers Am., Nat. Dist. Attys. Assn., Nevada Women Lawyers Assn., U. Nev. Alumni Assn. (chmn. 1985). Criminal, Family and matrimonial. Office: 556 California Reno NV 89509

LUND, JAMES LOUIS, lawyer, business executive; b. Long Beach, Calif., Oct. 4, 1926; s. G. Louis and Hazel Eunice (Cochran) L.; m. Jo Alvarez, Aug. 5, 1950; 1 son, Eric James. Student Stanford U., 1943; B.A. in Math., U. So. Calif., 1946; postgrad. Grad. Sch. Annapolis, 1949; J.D., Southwestern U., 1955; postgrad. Sch. Law., U. So. Calif., 1956. Bar: Calif. 1955, U.S. Dist. Ct. (cen. dist.) Calif. 1955, U.S. Ct. Apls. (9th cir.) 1955, U.S. Tax Ct. 1955, U.S. Supreme Ct. Spl. agt., U.S. Govt., 1950-52; gen. mgr. Pacific ops., gen. counsel Holmes & Narver, Inc., Los Angeles, 1952-66; exec. v.p. Calif. Fabricators, Oakland and Honolulu, 1966-67; sr. ptnr. James Lund Law Firm, Beverly Hills, Tehran, London and Tokyo, 1967—; chmn. bd. Fortress-Icas-Continental Assocs., Tehran, Amsterdam, Beverly Hills, 1976—; pres., founder Fortres Mgmt. Co.; pres., dir. Overseas Craftsman's Assn.; ptnr. Lund & Lund, 1983—. Served to lt. comdr. USNR, 1943-46, 48-50. Mem. ABA, Los Angeles County Bar Assn., Internat. Bar Assn., Inter-Am. Bar Assn., Asia Pacific Lawyers Assn. Club: Les Ambassadeurs (London). Private international, Contracts commercial, General corporate. Office: 9th Floor 9595 Wilshire Blvd Beverly Hills CA 90212

LUND, JOHN RICHARD, lawyer; b. Joliet, Ill., Aug. 9, 1944; s. August Joel and Florence Christine (Seaborg) L.; m. Dorothy Armstrong, Sept. 3, 1966; children: August Joel, Dorothy Jane. B.A., Greenville Coll., 1966; J.D., U. Ill., 1969; Pvt. Int. Law, U. Cambridge, 1968. Bar: Wis. 1972, Ill. 1969. Atty., Continental Ill. Bank & Trust Co., Chgo., 1969-72; ptnr. Dobrinski & Lund, Minocqua, Wis., 1972-74; pres. Lund, Harrold, Cook & Danner, Minocqua, Wis., 1974-87, Lund, Cook & LaChance, S.C., 1987—; dir. Valley Nat. Bank of Minocqua. Bd. dirs. Howard Young Med. Ctr., 1976-83, Howard Young Found. mem. Wis. Com. on Unauthorized Practice of Law, 1982—. Mem. ABA (state del. 1980-83, chmn. com. on unauthorized practice of law 1983-84, chmn. com. on lawyer's responsibility for client protection 1984—), Wis. Bar Assn. Swedish Covenant Ch. Clubs: U. Chgo., Dairymen's Country. Probate, Real property, Health. Office: 8759 Hwy 51 Minocqua WI 54548

LUNDE, ASBJORN RUDOLPH, lawyer; b. S.I., N.Y., July 17, 1927; s. Karl and Elisa (Andenes) L.; A.B., Columbia U., 1947, LL.B., 1949. Admitted to N.Y. bar, 1949, since practiced in N.Y.C.; with firm Kramer, Marx, Greenlee & Backus, and predecessors, 1950-68, mem., 1958-68; individual practice law, 1968—; dir. numerous cos. Bd. dirs., v.p. Orchestra da Camera, Inc., 1964—; bd. dirs. Sara Roby Found., 1971—, The Drawing Soc., 1977—. Mem. Am., N.Y. State bar assns., Assn. Bar City N.Y., Met. Opera Club. Contracts commercial, General corporate, Private international. Home: 1120 Park Ave New York NY 10128 Office: La Branche Rd RD 1 Hillsdale NY 12529

LUNDIN, DAVID ERIK, lawyer; b. Middletown, Conn., May 8, 1949; s. Irving Erik and Majorie (Walker) L.; m. Gayle Williams, June 25, 1977; 1 child, Erik Stewart. BA, U. Redlands, 1971; JD, UCLA, 1974. Bar: Calif. 1974. Assoc. Haight, Dickson, Brown & Bonesteel, Los Angeles, 1974-76; atty. advisor FTC, Washington, 1976-77; ptnr. Fredman, Silverberg & Lewis, San Diego, 1977-85, Sternberg, Eggers, Kidder & Fox, San Diego, 1985—. Mem. bd. fellows U. Redlands, Calif., 1984—; trustee San Diego Art Ctr., 1984—. Mem. ABA (litigation and antitrust sects., pvt. antitrust litigation and antitrust exemptions com.), Western Behavioral Sci. Inst. (counsel 1981—). Republican. Mem. United Ch. Christ. Club: Cotillion (sec. 1984-85). Avocation: raising and riding horses. Office: Sternberg Egger Kidder & Fox 225 Broadway 19th Floor San Diego CA 92020

LUNDIN, JOHN W., lawyer, urban planner; b. Seattle, Mar. 16, 1943; s. John W. and Margaret (Odell) L.; m. Jane Echols, Mar. 28, 1970; children: J. Ingrid, Jason E. BA, U. Wash., 1965, JD, 1968; M in Urban and Regional Planning, George Washington U., 1975. Bar: Wash. 1968, D.C. 1972, U.S. Dist. Ct. (we. dist.) Wash. 1972, U.S. Dist. Ct. D.C. 1972; U.S. Ct. Appeals (9th cir.) 1973, U.S. Supreme Ct. 1976, U.S. Dist. Ct. (ea. dist.) Wash. 1985. Atty. FAA, Washington, 1968-70; asst. to asst. sec. U.S. Dept. Transp., Washington, 1970-72; asst. U.S. atty. U.S. Dept. Justice, Seattle, 1972-74; sole practice Seattle, 1976—. Contbr. articles to law jours. Mem. ABA, Wash. Bar Assn. (chmn. land use and environ. law sect., bd. dirs.), Nat. Assn. Criminal Def. Lawyers, Fed. Bar Assn. Criminal, Real property, Contracts commercial. Home: 2344 Delmar Dr E Seattle WA 98102 Office: 999 3d Ave Suite 3210 Seattle WA 98104

LUNDQUIST, WEYMAN I., lawyer; b. Worcester, Mass., July 27, 1930; s. Hilding Ivan and Florence Cecilia (Westerholm) L.; m. Joan Durrell, Sept. 15, 1956 (div. July 1977); children—Weyman, Erica, Jettora, Kirk; m. Kathryn E. Taylor, Dec. 28, 1978; 1 child, Derek. B.A., Dartmouth Coll., 1952; LL.B., Harvard U., 1955. Bar: Mass 1955, Alaska 1961, Calif. 1963. Assoc. Bowditch & Dewey, Worcester, 1957-60; atty. U.S. Attys. Office, Mass. and Alaska, 1960-62; assoc. Heller, Ehrman, White & McAuliffe, San Francisco, 1963-65, ptnr., 1967—; counsel, v.p. State Mut. Life Ins. Co., Worcester, 1965-67. Author: (fiction) The Promised Land, 1987; contbr. articles to profl. jours.; patentee ski rack. Trustee, Natural Resources Def. Council, Hastings Coll. Advocacy; bd. dirs. Calif. Tomorrow, League to Save Lake Tahoe. Fellow ABA (chmn. Soviet Bar Assn. liaison com., chmn. litigation sect. 1978-79, co-chmn. spl. com. for study discovery abuse 1976-83, spl. com. on tort liability system 1981-84, superfund 301e study group advisor to U.S. Congress, 1983); mem. Am. Coll. Trial Lawyers, Lawyers Alliance for Nuclear Arms Control (co-founder), Am. Antiquarian Soc., Fgn. Relations Council, Am. Coll. Trial Lawyers, Assn. Life Ins. Council, U.S. Supreme Ct. Hist. Soc., No. Dist. Hist. Soc., Sierra Club, Friends of the Earth, Sequoia, Dartmouth Lawyers Assn. Clubs: Bohemian, Olympic (San Francisco). Avocations: squash; soccer; skiing; running; writing. Federal civil litigation, State civil litigation, Environment. Home: 3725 Broderick San Francisco CA 94108 Office: Heller Ehrman White & McAuliffe 333 Bush Suite 3320 San Francisco CA 94104

LUNDY, AUDIE LEE, JR., lawyer; b. Columbus, Ga., Mar. 10, 1943; s. Audie Lee and Mary Blanche (Snipes) L.; m. Ann Porter, June 11, 1966; children: Travis Stuart, Katherine Porter. B.A., Yale U., 1965; LL.B. magna cum laude, Columbia U., 1968. Bar: N.Y. 1968, D.C. 1976. Assoc. firm White & Case, N.Y.C., 1968-71, 74-75, London, 1971-74, Washington, 1975-78; asst. gen. counsel Campbell Soup Co., Camden, N.J., 1978, gen. counsel, 1979—. Bd. mgrs. St. Christopher's Hosp. for Children, Phila., 1980—; trustee Food and Drug Law Inst., Washington, 1982—. Mem. ABA, Am. Soc. Internat. Law, Assn. Gen. Counsel. Republican. Presbyterian. Clubs: Merion Cricket, Phila. Skating. General corporate, Private international. Home: 810 Waverly Rd Bryn Mawr PA 19010 Office: Campbell Soup Co Campbell Pl Camden NJ 08101

LUNDY, DANIEL FRANCIS, communications company executive; b. N.Y.C., Nov. 29, 1930; s. Daniel M. and Josephine Elizabeth (Corcoran) L.; m. Janet M. Taylor, Dec. 27, 1952; children: Daniel Thomas, Joanne, Mary Elizabeth, Susan Teresa. B.S., Fordham U., 1952; J.D., St. John's U., N.Y.C., 1958. Bar: N.Y. 1959, D.C. 1970, N.J. 1971; C.P.A. Corp. tax dir. Merck & Co., Inc., 1964-70; tax atty. Shanley & Fisher (Esqs.), Newark, 1970-72; partner Coopers & Lybrand (C.P.A.s), N.Y.C., 1973-76; sr. v.p., dir. taxes ITT, N.Y.C., 1976—. Contbr. to profl. jours. Served with AUS, 1952-54. Mem. Am. Inst. C.P.A.s, Internat. Fiscal Assn. Legislative, Corporate taxation. Home: 121 E Sailboat Ave Peahala Park NJ 08008 Office: ITT Corp 320 Park Ave New York NY 10022

LUNEY, PERCY ROBERT, JR., law educator, lawyer, consultant; b. Hopkinsville, Ky., Jan. 13, 1949; s. Percy Robert and Alice Charline (Woodson) L.; m. Gwynn Teresa Swinson, Feb. 18, 1979; children: Jamille, Robyn. AB, Hamilton Coll., 1970; JD, Harvard U., 1974. Bar: D.C. 1975, Tenn. 1977, U.S. Supreme Ct. 1979, U.S. Dist. Ct. Tenn., U.S. Dist. Ct. D.C., U.S. Ct. Claims, U.S. Ct. Appeals (6th, 9th and D.C. cirs.). Asst. prof. econ., geology Cornell U., Ithaca, N.Y., 1974-75; atty., advisor office of solicitor U.S. Dept. of Interior, Washington, 1975-77; legal counsel, spl. asst. to pres. Fisk U., Nashville, 1977-79; assoc. Birch, Horton, Bittner, Monroe, Pestinger & Anderson, Washington, 1979-80; asst. dean, asst. prof. N.C. Cen. U., Durham, 1980-85, assoc. prof. law, 1985—; sr. lectr. Duke U. Sch. Law, 1985-87, vis. prof. law, 1987—. Producer, dir., editor: (videotape) Practicing Law in N.C., 1985; contbr. articles to profl. jours. Mem. adv. panel Z. Smith Reynolds Found., Winston-Salem, N.C., 1983-86; bd. dirs. Research Triangle Park (N.C.) Internat. Visitors Ctr., 1983—, N.C. Coastal Fedn., Raleigh, 1983-85. Thomas J. Watson research fellow, 1971-72; vis. research scholar U. Tokyo, 1983; Fulbright research scholar U. Tokyo, 1986; Martha Price research fellow Duke U. Sch. Law, 1985-87. Mem. ABA, Fed. Bar Assn., N.C. Bar Assn., Tenn. Bar Assn., D.C. Bar Assn., Delta Upsilon. Club: Harvard (N.C.). Legal education, Public international, Natural resources law. Home: 1311 Arnette Ave Durham NC 27707 Office: NC Cen U Law Sch Durham NC 27707

LUNGREN, JOHN HOWARD, law educator, oil and gas consultant, author; b. Chgo., Feb. 11, 1925; s. Charles Howard and Edna Hughes (Edwards) L.; m. Phyllis Joan Jolidon, Dec. 12, 1953 (div.); 1 son, John Eric; m. Susan Jeanette Whitfield, Sept. 22, 1984. B.A., Beloit Coll., 1948; J.D., Marquette U., 1952; M.A., U. Wis.-Milw., 1974. Bar: Wis. 1952, Ill. 1975, Kans. 1980. Assoc. gen. counsel A. O. Smith Corp., 1964-74; gen. atty. Clark Oil & Refining Corp., 1954-64; prof. law Lewis U., Glen Ellyn, Ill., 1975-80; assoc. prof. law Washburn U. Sch. Law, Topeka, 1980-85; practice, Chgo., from 1977; with Turner & Boisseau Ltd., Wichita, Kans., 1985-87; ptnr. Lungren and Whitfield-Lungren, Wichita, 1987—; cons. oil and gas; Kans. rep. legal com. Interstate Oil Compact. Chmn., Milwaukee County Republican Party, 1966-70; justice of peace, Wauwatosa, Wis., 1964-68. Served with USN, 1943-46. Mem. ABA, Ill. Bar Assn., Wis. Bar Assn., Kans. Bar Assn., Wichita Bar Assn. Oil and gas leasing, General corporate, Legal education.

LUNNEY, J. ROBERT, lawyer; b. N.Y.C., Dec. 15, 1927; s. Thomas John and Jessie May (Butcher) L.; m. Joan M. Guinan, July 10, 1976; 1 son, Alexander G. B.A., Alfred U., 1950; J.D., Cornell U., 1954. Bar: N.Y. 1955, U.S. Ct. Mil. Appeals 1973, U.S. Supreme Ct. 1962, D.C. 1983. Asst. U.S. atty. So. Dist. N.Y., 1955-59; assoc. law firm Shearman & Sterling, N.Y.C., 1959-68; partner Lunney & Crocco, N.Y.C., 1968—. Bd. trustees Lavelle Sch. for Blind, Bronx, 1973—. Served with USN, 1945-46, U.S. Merchant Marine, 1950-51, capt. JAGC, USNR. Mem. N.Y. State Bar Assn., SR (1st v.p. N.Y. State). Republican. Roman Catholic. Club: Univ. Federal civil litigation, State civil litigation, Criminal. Home: 3 Locust Ln Bronxville NY 10708 Office: 641 Lexington Ave New York NY 10022

LUNSFORD, DAVID H., lawyer, trust company executive; b. Huntington, W.Va., Nov. 9, 1956; s. Harold D. and Dorothy J. Lunsford; m. Dianne B. Lunsford, July 31, 1982. BS, W.Va. U., 1979, JD, 1982; postgrad., Northwestern U., 1985. Bar: W.Va. 1982, U.S. Dist. Ct. (so. dist.) W.Va., 1982. Trust asst. 1st Huntington Nat. Bank, 1982-83, asst. trust officer, 1983-84, trust officer, 1984-86, sr. trust officer, 1986—. Mem. ABA, Cabell County Bar Assn., W.Va. Bankers Assn. (sec. trust div. 1985-86, v.p. 1986-87, pres. 1987-88), Estate Planning Council of Huntington (v.p. 1985-86, pres. 1986-87), Colonial Investment Club (pres. 1985—). Avocations: golf, tennis, pub. speaking. Probate. Home: 11 Meacham Dr Barboursville WV 25504

LUPERT, LESLIE ALLAN, lawyer; b. Syracuse, N.Y., May 24, 1946; s. Reuben and Miriam (Kaufman) L.; m. Roberta Gail Fellner, May 19, 1968; children: Jocelyn, Rachel, Susannah. BA, U. Buffalo, 1967, JD, Columbia U., 1971. Bar: N.Y. 1971. Ptnr. Orans Elsen & Lupert, N.Y.C., 1971—. Contbr. articles to profl. jours. Mem. ABA, N.Y. State Bar Assn., N.Y.C. Bar Assn. (com. fed. legislation 1977-80, profl. and jud. ethics com. 1983-86, com. on fed. cts. 1986—), Phi Beta Kappa. Club: Columbia Univ. (N.Y.C.). Federal civil litigation, Criminal, State civil litigation. Office: Orans Elsen & Lupert 1 Rockefeller Plaza New York NY 10020

LUPICA, JOSEPH RICHARD, lawyer; b. Rome, N.Y., Mar. 27, 1955; s. Charles Anthony and Laura Marie (Nardozza) L.; m. Anne Elizabeth Hinkley, June 2, 1979; 1 child, Charles Michael. AB, Cornell U., 1976, JD, 1979. Bar: Conn. 1979, U.S. Dist. Ct. Conn. 1980. Assoc. Reid & Riege, Hartford, Conn., 1979-83; White House fellow Washington, 1983-84; ptnr. Pepe & Hazard, Hartford, Conn., 1985—; spl. asst. to sec. U.S. Dept. HUD, Washington, 1983-84; staff sec. fed. adv. com. Constn. Document Reform, Washington, 1983-84; mem. procurement rev. com. HUD, Washington, 1984. Commr. West Hartford (Conn.) Econ. Devel. Commn., 1985—, West Hartford (Conn.) Housing Authority, 1981-83; vice chmn. bd. dirs. Hartford (Conn.) YMCA, 1985—. Mem. Conn. Bar Assn. (mem. exec. com. 1983—, comml. law sect.) , Fed. Bar Assn., Hartford County Bar Assn., Conn. Trial Lawyers Assn. Republican. Roman Catholic. Bankruptcy, Federal civil litigation, Entertainment. Office: Pepe & Hazard One Corporate Center Hartford CT 06103

LUPPI, MICHAEL DENNIS, lawyer; b. Medford, Mass., Aug. 12, 1946; s. Armand Lazarus and Violet (Queques) L. B.A., UCLA, 1968, J.D., 1972. Bar: Calif. 1973, U.S. Dist. Ct. (cen. dist.) Calif. 1973, U.S. Ct. Appeals (9th cir.) 1978, U.S. Supreme Ct. 1976. Sole practice, Los Angeles, 1973-75; assoc. Myers and D'Angelo, Los Angeles, 1975-78; assoc. Pilot & Spar, Los Angeles, 1979-81; sole practice, Glendale, Calif., 1981—. Mem. Los Angeles County Bar Assn., ABA, Glendale Bar Assn. Democrat. Roman Catholic. Club: Los Angeles Turf (Arcadia, Calif.). State civil litigation, Bankruptcy, General practice. Address: 352 Amherst Dr Burbank CA 91506

LURIA, REMY, lawyer; b. N.Y.C., July 18, 1953; s. Buck and Leah Luria. BA, New Coll., 1974; JD, Cornell U., 1978. Bar: N.Y. Sole practice N.Y.C., 1979—. Mem. ABA (vice chmn. internat. law com. young lawyers div. 1986—), N.Y. State Bar Assn., Assn. of Bar of City of N.Y. Private international, Public international, General practice. Office: 440 E 23d St New York NY 10010

LURIE, ALVIN DAVID, lawyer; b. N.Y.C., Apr. 16, 1923; s. Samuel and Rose L.; m. Marian Weinberg, Aug. 21, 1944; children: James, Jeanne, Margery, Jonathan. A.B., Cornell U., 1943, LL.B., 1944. Bar: N.Y. 1944, D.C. 1978. Ptnr. various N.Y.C. law firms, 1944-74, including Lurie & Rubin, 1961-68, Aranow, Brodsky, Bohlinger & Einhorn, 1968-74; asst. commr. for employee plans and exempt orgns. IRS, Washington, 1974-78; partner firm Chadbourne, Parke, Whiteside & Wolff, N.Y.C., 1978-80; counsel Chadbourne, Parke, Whiteside & Wolff, 1980-84; ptnr. Meyers, Tersign, Lurie, Feldman & Gray, N.Y.C., 1984—. Author: Lurie's Commentaries on Pension Design, 1980, Lurie's Guide to VEBAs, 1983, Collected Commentaries on Pensions, 1984, ESOPs Made Easy, 1985. Contbr. articles to law revs., tax jours. Mem. Am. Bar Assn., Fed. Bar Assn., N.Y. State Bar Assn. (chmn. spl. com. pesion simplification 1986—), Assn. Bar City N.Y., Am. Coll. Tax Counsel, Am. Law Inst., N.Y. Bar Found. Office: Meyers Tersigni Lurie Feldman & Gray 630 3d Ave New York NY 10017

LURIE, DONNA ELLEN, lawyer; b. Fair Lawn, N.J., June 18, 1955; d. Stanley Jay and Shirley June (Levy) L.; m. Wesley Neal Sprague, Aug. 22, 1982. B.A. in Labor Studies summa cum laude, Pa. State U., 1977; J.D., U. Wis., 1980. Bar: Wis. 1980, U.S. Dist. Ct. (eastern and western dists.) Wis. 1980, Wash. 1983, U.S. Dist. Ct. (western dist.) Wash. 1983, U.S. Ct. Appeals (7th cir.) 1982. Law clk. Office of Atty. Gen., Madison, Wis., 1978; clk. firm Podell, Ugent & Cross, Milw., 1978-79; student intern Wis. Employment Relations Commn., Madison, 1979-80; project asst. U. Wis. Law Sch., Madison, 1980; atty. Shneidman Law Firm, Milw., 1980-82; assoc. exec. dir. Seattle Tchrs. Assn., 1982—; N.Y. dir. Frontlash, N.Y.C., 1977; labor edn. instr. Sch. for Workers, Milw., 1980-82. Author column: Grieve, Don't Gripe!, author research study: Facing Union Busters, 1982. Mem. Woodinville Design Rev. Com. Mem. ABA, Wash. Bar Assn., Seattle-King County Bar Assn., Wash. Women Lawyers, Nat. Audubon Soc., NOW. Phi Beta Kappa, Phi Kappa Phi. Democrat. Clubs: Downtown Athletic (racquetball awards 1980-82) (Milw.); Comparable Worth Project (Calif.). Labor. Office: Seattle Tchrs Assn 720 Nob Hill Ave N Seattle WA 98109

LURIE, JEANNE FLORA, lawyer, manufacturing company executive; b. N.Y.C., Aug. 20, 1946; d. Ralph A. and Irene (Chartier) LaFlamme; m. Robert M. Lurie, July 7, 1973; 1 child, Jane Margaret. B.A., Radcliffe Coll., 1968; J.D., Boston U., 1974. Bar: Mass. 1974, Fla. 1976. Assoc. firm Mahoney, Adams, Milam, Surface & Grimsley, Jacksonville, Fla., 1976-82, ptnr., 1982-84; corp. counsel, head legal dept., sec. Clow Corp., Jacksonville, 1984—; bd. dirs. Jacksonville Area Legal Services, 1979. Mem. program com. Leadership Jacksonville. Mem. Mass. Bar Assn., Fla. Bar Assn. (legal

aid com.), ABA (credit union com.), Jacksonville Women's Network (bd. dirs., chmn. membership com. 1980-82). Club: Harvard of Jacksonville (v.p., chmn. recruiting). Administrative and regulatory, General corporate. Home: 3507 Riverside Ave Jacksonville FL 32205

LURVEY, IRA HAROLD, lawyer; b. Chgo., Apr. 6, 1935; s. Louis and Faye (Grey) L.; m. Barbara Ann Sirvint, June 24, 1962; children: Nathana, Lawrence, Jennifer, Jonathan, David, Robert. BS, U. Ill., 1956; MS, Northwestern U., 1961; JD, U. Calif., Berkeley, 1965. Bar: Calif. 1965, Nev. 1966, U.S. Dist. Ct. (cen. dist.) Calif. 1966, U.S. Tax Ct. 1966, U.S. Ct. Appeals (9th cir.) 1966, U.S. Supreme Ct. 1975. Law clk. to presiding justice Nev. Supreme Ct., Carson City, 1965-66; from assoc. to ptnr. Shea & Gould and predecessor firm Pacht, Ross, Warne, Bernhard & Sears, Inc., Los Angeles, 1966-84; founding ptnr. Lurvey & Shapiro, Los Angeles, 1984—; lectr. legal edn. programs; mem. Chief Justice's Commns. on Ct. Reform. Editor Community Property Jour., 1979—; contbr. articles to profl. jours. Former chmn. Los Angeles Jr. Arts Ctr.; past pres. Cheviot Hills Homeowners Assn.; exec. v.p., counsel gen. studies com. Hillel Acad. Sch., Beverly Hills, Calif., 1977—. Served with U.S. Army, 1957-58. Fellow Am. Acad. Matrimonial Lawyers, Internat. Acad. Matrimonial Lawyers; mem. ABA (governing council 1986—, chmn. support com., chmn. continuing legal edn. family law sect., vice chmn. com. arbitration and mediation, bd. editors mag.), Calif. Bar Assn. (editor jour. 1982-85, chmn. family law sect. 1986-87, specialization adv. bd. family law), Los Angeles County Bar Assn. (chmn. family law sect.), Beverly Hills Bar Assn. (chmn. family law sect. 1982-83). Family and matrimonial, State civil litigation, Entertainment. Home: 2729 Motor Ave Los Angeles CA 90064 Office: Lurvey & Shapiro 2121 Avenue of the Stars Suite 1550 Los Angeles CA 90067

LUSHIS, JOHN FRANCIS, JR., lawyer; b. Easton, Pa., Aug. 2, 1955; s. John Francis Sr. and Dora Katherine (DeMonte) L.; m. Ann Corinne C. Sabatella, Sept. 29, 1984. BS in Mech. Engrng. cum laude, U. Notre Dame, 1977; JD, Dickinson Sch. Law, 1980. Bar: Pa. 1980, D.C. 1985, U.S. Patent Office 1985, U.S. Ct. Appeals (fed. cir.) 1985, U.S. Supreme Ct. 1985. Atty. Bethlehem (Pa.) Steel Corp., 1980-86, dir. bus. devel., 1986—. Pres. Boy's Club Easton, 1983-84; vol. Cath. Charities Appeal, Easton, Bethlehem, 1981—, Northampton County (Pa.) Prison, 1983-84; mem. Lehigh Valley Community Council, Bethlehem, Pa., 1983-84; campaign coordinator Reagan-Bush '84, Northampton County; mem. exec. com. Northhampton County Rep. Com., 1984, solicitor 1986—; mem. adv. council community leaders Pa. Ho. Reps. Rep. Caucus, 1986; mem. allocations com. United Way of Northampton and Warren Counties, 1987—; v.p. St. Vincent DePaul Soc. S.S. Simon & Jude Ch., 1987. Named Outstanding Young Man of Am., 1981, 83, 84; recipient U.S. Jaycees Disting. Service award 1984. Mem. ABA, Northampton County Bar Assn., Dickinson Sch. Law Alumni Assn. (exec. com. 1983-85), Pa. Bar Assn., Inst. Indsl. Engrs., Easton Area Jaycees (John. H. Armbruster Keyman award 1984-85). Lodge: KC. Avocations: bicycling, basketball. Real property, Patent, Landlord-tenant. Home: 604 2d Ave Bethlehem PA 18018 Office: Bethlehem Steel Corp Fin Dept Bethlehem PA 18016

LUSKIN, JOSEPH, criminal justice educator, researcher; b. N.Y.C., May 30, 1923; s. Harry and Anna (Sklar) L.; m. Mollie Winkler, July 11, 1944; children—Richard Terrence, Elizabeth Karen. Student Bklyn. Law Sch., 1961-62; B.B.A., CUNY, 1962; M.S. in Criminal Justice, Auburn U., 1979; M.A., Columbia U., 1971, Ed.D., 1976. Officer Port Authority Police Dept., N.Y.C., 1946-71; state project dir. Am. Justice Inst., Newark, 1971-73; project dir. Police Tng. Commn., Newark, 1973-74; asst. prof. Paterson State Coll., N.J., 1974-75; prof., dir. dept. criminal justice Ala. State U., Montgomery, 1975—. Pres. Ala. Vols. in Corrections, Montgomery, 1981-83, bd. dirs., 1978-84; bd. dirs. Ala. Office Vol. Citizen Participation, Montgomery, 1980—. Served with U.S. Army, 1942-46, PTO. Mem. Internat. Assn. Chiefs Police, Am. Soc. Criminology, Am. Criminal Justice Assn. (chpt. adviser 1978—), Ala. Consortium Criminal Justice Educators (pres. 1978). Lodges: Masons (32 deg.), Shriners. Criminal, Legal education. Office: Ala State U Dept Criminal Justice Montgomery AL 36195

LUSKIN, PAUL BANSECH, lawyer, business exec.; b. Balt., June 19, 1948; s. Joseph and Mildred Luskin; children: Shana, Diana. B.A., U. Miami; J.D., U. Balt., 1975. Bar: Fla. 1975, U.S. Dist. Ct. Fla. 1979. Sole practice, Hollywood, Fla., 1975—; pres. Luskin's Inc., Hollywood, 1976—, also gen. counsel; dir. Sight and Sound Inc.; anti-trust cons. to various firms. Bd. dirs. Broward County chpt. ARC; mem. U.S. Presdl. Task Force. Recipient Golden award, 1978, 79, 80, Hollywood Benevolent award, 1981; A.O.C. Achievement award U.S. Ho. of Reps. Adv. Com.; named Retailer of Yr., 1980, Dealer of Yr., 1981, 82. Mem. Browardand Dade County Attys., SAE Dealer Inventor Circle, Assn. Trial Lawyers Am., Fla. Pres.'s Counsel, Tau Kappa Epsilon, Phi Delta Pi. Republican. Designer audio receiver. Antitrust, General corporate, Family and matrimonial. Home: 4150 N 28 Terr Hollywood FL 33022 Office: 4150 N 28th Terr Hollywood FL 33022

LUSKY, LOUIS, legal educator; b. Columbus, Ohio, May 15, 1915; s. Leonard Morris and Amy (Kleeman) L.; m. Ruth Agnes Anderson, Aug. 31, 1946; children: Mary Hibbard Friedman, John Anderson; 1 child by previous marriage, Peter Joris. BA, U. Louisville, 1935; LLB, Columbia, 1937. Bar: N.Y. 1938, Ky. 1947. Law clk. to Supreme Ct. Justice Harlan F. Stone, 1937-38; assoc. Root, Clark, Buckner & Ballantine, N.Y.C., 1938-42, 44-45; civilian mem. ops. analysis sect. 8th Air Force, 1943-44; with legal div. U.S. Mil. Govt., Germany, 1945-46; ptnr. Wyatt & Grafton, Louisville, 1947-51; sole practice Louisville, 1952-63; prof. law Columbia Law Sch., 1963-85, Betts prof. law, 1979-85, prof. emeritus, 1985—. Author: (with others) Southern Justice, 1965, By What Right?, 1975. Mem. ABA, ACLU (nat. com. 1963-67, nat. bd. 1967-70), Am. Law Inst. Constitutional law, Probate. Home: 623 Eastbrook Rd Ridgewood NJ 07450 Office: 435 W 116th St New York NY 10027

LUSTBADER, PHILIP LAWRENCE, lawyer; b. Balt., May 14, 1949; s. I. William and Evelyn (Kandel) L.; m. Randy R. Tatarka, June 28, 1970; children—Michael Howard, Jamie Robyn. B.S., Wharton Sch., U. Pa., 1970; J.D. cum laude, Temple U., 1973. Bar: Pa. 1973, N.J. 1974, U.S. Dist. Ct. (ea. dist.) Pa. 1974, U.S. Dist. Ct. N.J. 1974, U.S. Ct. Appeals (3d cir.) 1975. Assoc. Wolf, Block, Schorr & Solis-Cohen, Phila., 1973-78; counsel Subaru of Am., Inc., Pennsauken, N.J., 1978-80, asst. v.p., corp. counsel, 1980-83, v.p., gen. counsel, 1983-86, group v.p., gen. counsel and sec., 1987—. Exec. editor Temple Law Quar., 1972-73. Mem. ABA, Phila. Bar Assn. General corporate, Contracts commercial, Franchising. Office: Subaru of America Inc Subaru Plaza PO Box 6000 Cherry Hill NJ 08034-6000

LUSTGARTEN, IRA HOWARD, lawyer; b. N.Y.C., July 31, 1929; s. Louis and Florine Josephine (Van Mindeno) L.; m. Rhoda Manne, Oct. 24, 1954; children—Lise Anne, Nancy Ellen. A.B., NY, 1950; LL.B., Columbia U., 1958. Bar: N.Y. 1958, Fla. 1978, U.S. Dist. Ct. (so. dist.) N.Y. 1959, U.S. Ct. Claims 1985, U.S. Ct. Appeals (fed. cir.) 1986. Assoc. Proskauer Rose Goetz Mendelsohn, N.Y.C., 1958-68, ptnr., 1968-79; ptnr. Willkie Farr & Gallagher, N.Y.C., 1979—; lectr. law Columbia U. Served to lt. USNR, 1951-55. Mem. Am. Law Inst., Am. Coll. Probate Counsel, ABA, N.Y. Bar Assn., Assn. Bar City N.Y., Fla. Bar Assn., Columbia Law Sch. Alumni Assn. (dir.). Probate, Estate taxation, Family and matrimonial. Office: One Citicorp Center 153 E 53d St New York NY 10022

LUSTIG, DAVID CARL, III, lawyer; b. Walden, N.Y., July 6, 1954; s. David Carl, Jr. and Violet (Rosenblum) L.; m. Debra Silver, Aug. 13, 1977; 1 child, David. BS, Syracuse U., 1975; JD, Hofstra U., 1978. Bar: N.Y. 1979, U.S. Dist. Ct. (so. dist.) N.Y. 1979, U.S. Dist. Ct. (ea. dist.) N.Y. 1979, U.S. Ct. Appeals (2d cir.) 1986. Assoc. Esau J. Mishkin, Garden City, N.Y., 1978-79, Arye & Kors, P.C., N.Y.C., 1979-84; ptnr. Arye, Kors & Lustig, N.Y.C., 1984—. Mem. Assn. Trial Lawyers Am., N.Y. State Trial Lawyers Assn., N.Y. County Lawyers Assn. Personal injury, State civil litigation, Federal civil litigation. Office: Arye Kors & Lustig 20 Vesey St New York NY 10007

LUTHER, CHARLES WILLIAM, lawyer, law educator; b. Bethany, Okla., Nov. 25, 1933; s. C.W. and Cordia Luther; m. Florence J., June 1961. AA, Am. River Coll., 1954; JD, U. Calif., San Francisco, 1958. Bar: Calif. 1959, U.S. Dist. Ct. (no. dist.) Calif. 1959, U.S. Ct. Appeals (9th cir.) 1959. Sole practice Sacramento, 1959-63; ptnr. Luther, Luther, O'Connor & Johnson, Sacramento, 1963-73; prof. law U. Pacific, Sacramento, 1965—, from asst. to assoc. dean, 1967-70; ptnr. Luther & Luther, Sacramento, 1973—; bd. advisers Ct. Practice Inst., Chgo., 1971-78. Author: Survey on Criminal Law, 1984, Survey on Torts, 1984, (with others) Materials on Community Property, 1985; decisions editor Community Property Jour., N.Y.C., 1974—; contbr. articles to profl. jours. Judge pro tem Sacramento Superior Ct., 1970; v.p. Nat. Orgn. for Animal Humaneness, Inc., Fair Oaks, Calif., 1983—, bd dirs. 1983—; bd. dirs. Legal Aid Soc. of Sacramento, 1969-70. Mem. ABA, Calif. State Bar Assn., Sacramento County Bar Assn., Assn. Trial Lawyers Am., Calif. Trial Lawyers Assn. Democrat. Real property, General corporate, State civil litigation. Home: PO Box 1030 Fair Oaks CA 95628 Office: Luther & Luther PC 11101 Fair Oaks Blvd Fair Oaks CA 95628

LUTHEY, GRAYDON DEAN, JR., lawyer, educator; b. Topeka, Sept. 18, 1955; s. Graydon Dean Sr. and S. Anne (Murphy) L.; m. Deborah Denise McCullough, May 26, 1979; children: Sarah Elizabeth, Katherine Alexandra. BA in Letters with high honors, U. Okla., 1976, JD, 1979; Diploma in Theology, Oxford (Eng.) U., 1976. Bar: Okla. 1979, U.S. Ct. Appeals (10th cir.) 1979, U.S. Dist. Ct. (no., we. and ea. dists.) Okla. 1980, U.S. Supreme Ct. 1982. Assoc. Jones, Givens, Gotcher, Bogan & Hilborne, Tulsa, 1979-84, ptnr., 1984—, also bd. dirs.; adj. assoc. prof. U. Tulsa, 1985—. Chancellor Diocese of Okla., 1985—. Nat. Merit scholar U. Okla., 1973; vis. research fellow Keble Coll., 1975. Mem. ABA, Okla. Bar Assn. (continuing legal edn. com.), Tulsa County Bar Assn. (bd. dirs. 1983—), Phi Beta Kappa, Omicron Delta Kappa. Clubs: Tulsa, Oaks Country (Tulsa). Federal civil litigation, State civil litigation, Securities. Office: Jones Givens Gotcher Bogan & Hilborne 3800 First Nat Tower Tulsa OK 74103

LUTHMAN, DAVID ANDREW, lawyer; b. Franklin, N.J., June 14, 1952; s. Carl A. and Susan C. (Gahs) L.; m. Lynn Ann Hoch, July 20, 1974 (div. Apr. 1985); children: Alison Rose, Paul Michael; m. Cynthia Holmes, Nov. 23, 1985. BA, Rutgers U., 1974, JD, 1977. Bar: N.J. 1977, U.S. Dist. Ct. N.J. 1977, U.S. Ct. Appeals (3d cir.) 1982, U.S. Supreme Ct. 1983. Assoc. Toll, Pinsky & Sullivan, Cherry Hill, N.J., 1978-80; ptnr. Toll, Pinsky, Sullivan & Luthman, Cherry Hill, 1980-82, Toll, Forkin, Sullivan & Luthman, Cherry Hill, 1982-84, Toll, Sullivan & Luthman, Cherry Hill, 1984—. Committeeman Camden County Dems., Pennsauken, N.J., 1986; dist. co-leader Pennsauken Dems., 1981—. Mem. Camden County Bar Assn., Assn. Trial Lawyers Am., Pennsauken Dem. Club. Presbyterian. Avocations: golf, politics, sports. State civil litigation, Personal injury, Local government. Home: 3644 Connecticut Ave Pennsauken NJ 08109 Office: Toll Sullivan & Luthman 905 N Kings Hwy Cherry Hill NJ 08034

LUTZ, JOHN SHAFROTH, lawyer, investment company general counsel; b. San Francisco, Sept. 10, 1943; s. Frederick Henry and Helena Morrison (Shafroth) L.; m. Elizabeth Boschen, Dec. 14, 1968; children—John Shafroth, Victoria. B.A., Brown U., 1965; J.D., U. Denver, 1971. Bar: Colo. 1971, U.S. Dist. Ct. Colo. 1971, U.S. Ct. Appeals (2d cir.) 1975, D.C. 1976, U.S. Supreme Ct. 1976, U.S. Dist. Ct. (so. dist.) N.Y. 1977, U.S. Tax Ct. 1977, U.S. Ct. Appeals (10th cir.) 1979, N.Y. 1984. Trial atty. Denver regional office U.S. SEC, 1971-74; spl. atty. organized crime, racketeering sect. U.S. Dept. Justice, So. Dist. N.Y., 1974-77; atty. Kelly Stansfield and O'Donnell, Denver, 1977-78; gen. counsel Boettcher & Co., Denver, 1978—; allied mem. N.Y. Stock Exchange, 1978—. Bd. dirs. Cherry Creek Improvement Assn., 1980-84, Spalding Rehab. Hosp., 1986—. Served to lt. jg, USN, 1965-67. Mem. ABA, Colo. Bar Assn., Denver Bar Assn., Am. Law Inst., Securities Industry Assn. (state regulations com. 1982-86), Nat. Assn. Securites Dealers, Inc. (arbitration com.). Republican. Episcopalian. Clubs: Denver Law, Denver Country, Denver Tennis, Denver Athletic, Rocky Mountain Brown (founder, past pres.); Racquet and Tennis (N.Y.C.). General corporate, Federal civil litigation, Criminal. Home: 144 Race St Denver CO 80206 Office: Boettcher & Co 828 17th St Denver CO 80202

LUTZ, KARL EVAN, lawyer; b. Dearborn, Mich., Dec. 18, 1949; s. Wallace G. and Marquerite E. (Smith) L.; m. Jeanne Daniel, June 30, 1973; children: Daniel Karl, Charles Littlefield, Kelsey Eldridge. BA, Yale U., 1972; JD, U. Mich., 1975. Assoc. Kirkland & Ellis, Chgo., 1975-81, ptnr., 1981—; bd. dirs. BRIntec Corp., Willimantic, Conn., Memtec N.Am., Inc., Chgo. General corporate. Office: Kirkland & Ellis 200 E Randolph Dr Chicago IL 60601

LUTZ, WILLIAM LAN, lawyer; b. Chgo., May 18, 1944; s. Raymond Price and Sibyl (McCright) L.; m. Jeanne M. McAlister, Dec. 27, 1969; children: William Lan, David Price. B.S., U. Tex., 1965, J.D., 1969. Bar: Tex. 1969, N.Mex. 1970. Assoc. Martin, Lutz, Cresswell & Hubert and predecessor firms, Las Cruces, N.Mex., 1969-82; U.S. atty. dist. N. Mex. U.S. Dept. Justice, Albuquerque, 1982—. Mem. ABA, N.Mex. Bar Assn. Mehodist. Criminal. Office: US Atty PO Box 607 Albuquerque NM 87103 *

LUTZKER, ARNOLD PAUL, lawyer; b. N.Y.C., June 30, 1947; s. Bernard and Pearl A. (Maloff) L.; m. Susan Jane, Aug. 9, 1970; children—Erica Rae, Robert Jeremy, Joanna Kate. B.A. magna cum laude, CCNY, 1968; J.D. cum laude, Harvard U., 1971. Bar: D.C. 1971, U.S. Supreme Ct. 1974. Legis. asst. to Congressman Jonathan B. Bingham, 1971-72; ptnr. Dow, Lohnes & Albertson, Washington, 1972—. Mem. ABA (subcom. the cable compulsory licensing 1985-86, subcom. on broadcasting and performance rights 1986—), D.C. Bar, Fed. Communications Bar Assn., Phi Beta Kappa. Democrat. Jewish. Author: (with D.W. Toohey, R.D. Marks) Legal Problems in Broadcasting, 1974; also articles. Administrative and regulatory, Trademark and copyright, Legislative. Office: 1255 23d St NW Suite 500 Washington DC 20037

LUTZKER, ELLIOT HOWARD, lawyer; b. Flushing, N.Y., Feb. 22, 1953; s. Stanley Lawrence and Mildred (Goldberg) L.; m. Jill Leslie Simon, Aug. 24, 1975; children: Stacey, Amanda. BA, SUNY, Stony Brook, 1974; JD, N.Y. Law Sch., 1978. Bar: N.Y. 1979, Fla. 1979, U.S. Dist. Ct. (so. and ea. dists.) N.Y. 1979. Atty. SEC, N.Y.C., 1978-81; assoc. Bachner, Tally, Polevoy, Misher & Brinberg, N.Y.C., 1981-85; ptnr. Snow, Becker, Krauss P.C., N.Y.C., 1985—. Mem. ABA (corp., banking law div.). Democrat. Jewish. Avocations: reading, stamps. Securities, General corporate. Home: 7 Maple Run Dr Jericho NY 11753 Office: Snow Becker Krauss PC 605 3d Ave New York NY 10158

LUX, ARTHUR EDWARD, lawyer; b. Detroit, June 9, 1944; s. G. Louis and Rose Marie (Helprin) L.; m. Donna Marie Beck, Nov. 20, 1970; children: Nicole, Kelly. BA, Eastern Mich. U., 1966; JD, Detroit Coll. of Law, 1970. Bar: Mich. 1970, U.S. Dist. Ct. (ea. dist.) Mich. 1970, U.S. Ct. Appeals (6th cir.) 1970, U.S. Supreme Ct. 1972. Asst. prosecutor Washtenaw County, Ann Arbor, Mich., 1971-73; chief exec. officer Allied Industries, Clawson, Mich., 1975—. Mem. Mich. Bar Assn., Assn. Trial Lawyers Am., Mich. Trial Lawyers Assn. Avocations: sailing, art collecting.

LUZZATTO, EDGAR, lawyer; b. Milan, Italy, Nov. 25, 1914; s. Enrico and Maria (Norsa) L.; m. Mirella Del Monte, Apr. 4, 1948; children—Diana, Ariel, Kfir, Marco, Rossana. Dr. Chem. Engrng., Polytechnic, Milan, 1935; Dr.Law, U. Milan, 1957. Patent agt. David Moscovitz, Atty., N.Y.C., 1946-48; sole practice, Milan, 1949-75, Ashkelon, Israel, 1976-81; sr. ptnr. Luzzatto & Luzzatto, Beer-Sheva, Israel, 1982—; lectr. Polytechnic, Milan, 1958-62; mem. Italian delegation to Lisbon Conf. for revision of Paris Conv., 1958. Author: Il Consulente Tecnico, 1954; Teoria e Tecnica Brevetti, 1960; The Industrial Property Factor in Industrial Research, 1978. Contbr. articles to profl. jours. Served with U.S. Army, 1941-46. Mem. Internat. Assn. for Protection Indsl. Property, Internat. Fedn. Indsl. Property Attys. Patent, Trademark and copyright. Office: Luzzatto & Luzzatto, Mercaz Ha'Negev Bldg Suite 27, Metzada Rd PO Box 5352, Beer-Sheva 84 548 Israel

LYDDANE, JOHN LAWRENCE ASHTON, lawyer; b. Balt., Aug. 22, 1947; s. Russell Hancock and Lucy Barnes (Ashton) L.; m. Virginia Ciurleo, Jan. 14, 1983; children: Ashley Elizabeth, Alexandra Marie. A.B., U. Rochester, 1969; J.D., Syracuse U., 1972. Bar: N.Y. 1973, U.S. Dist. Ct. (no. dist.) N.Y. 1973, U.S. Dist. Ct. (so. and ea. dists.) N.Y. 1975, U.S. Ct. Appeals (2nd cir.) 1975, U.S. Supreme Ct. 1976. Asst. atty. gen. N.Y. State, Albany, 1972-73; assoc. Harry H. Lipsig, N.Y.C., 1973-75; assoc. Martin, Clearwater & Bell, N.Y.C., 1975-78, ptnr. 1978—; claims counsel Richmond Meml. Hosp., N.Y.C., 1979—. Panelist, Supreme Ct. Malpractice Panel, Bronx, N.Y., 1979—. Mem. N.Y. Acad. Scis., ABA (2nd cir. rep. profl. liability com. 1980—, litigation sect. 1977—), N.Y. State Bar Assn., U. Rochester Assocs. Democrat. Episcopalian. Clubs: University (N.Y.C.), Belle Haven (Greenwich, Conn.). State civil litigation, Personal injury, Insurance. Home: 29 Meadow Wood Dr Greenwich CT 06830 Office: Martin Clearwater & Bell 220 E 42d St New York NY 10017

LYDON, THOMAS J., federal judge; b. Portland, Maine, June 3, 1927. B.A., U. Maine, 1952; LL.B., Georgetown U., 1955, LL.M., 1957. Bars: Maine, D.C. Trial atty. civil div. Dept. Justice, Washington, 1955-67, chief Ct. Claims sect. civil div., 1967-72; trial commr. US Ct. Clms., Washington, 1972—. Judicial administration. Office: US Claims Ct 717 Madison Pl NW Washington DC 20005 *

LYFORD, F. RICHARD, lawyer; b. N.Y.C., July 24, 1944; s. Fred Russell and Chloe Portlock (Adkisson) L.; m. Barbara J. Sorg, June 14, 1966; children: Frederick Raphael, Michael Edward. BA, U. Chgo., 1966; JD, U. Iowa, 1972. Bar: Iowa 1972, U.S. Dist. Ct. (no. and so. dists.) Iowa, 1972, U.S. Ct. Appeals (8th cir.) 1973, U.S. Supreme Ct. 1976. Admissions officer U. Chgo., 1966-67, Cornell Co., Mt. Vernon, Iowa, 1967-69; ptnr. Dickinson, Throckmorton, Mannheimer & Assocs., Des Moines, 1972—; pres. Iowa State Bar Rev. Sch., 1975; vol. referee juvenile ct. Dist. Ct., Des Moines, 1986; bd. dirs. Youth Law Ctr., Des Moines, 1983—, Family Counseling Ctr., Des Moines, 1983—. Served with U.S. Army, 1967-69, Vietnam. Mem. ABA, Iowa State Bar Assn., Polk County Bar Assn., Assn Trial Lawyers Am. Republican. Federal civil litigation, State civil litigation, Administrative and regulatory. Home: PO Box 219-51 Des Moines IA 50312 Office: Dickinson Law Firm 1600 Hub Tower Des Moines IA 50309

LYLES, HARRY ARTHUR, lawyer; b. Cheverly, Md., Aug. 16, 1950; s. Harry Arthur and Kathleen Mary (Durkin) L.; m. Brenda Harrison, Aug. 17, 1985. BS, Auburn U., Montgomery, Ala., 1974; JD, Faulkner U., 1978. Bar: Ala. 1979, U.S. Dist. Ct. (so. dist.) 1980, U.S. Ct. Appeals (5th and 11th cirs.) 1981, U.S. Dist. Ct. (no. and mid. dists.) 1982. Asst. gen. counsel dept. Indls. Relations State of Ala., Montgomery, 1978-83, gen. counsel dept. Corrections, 1983—. Mem. ABA, Ala. Bar Assn., Assn. Trial Lawyers Am. Democrat. Civil rights, Federal civil litigation, Labor. Home: 1324 Hillman Montgomery AL 36109 Office: Ala Dept Corrections 101 S Union St Montgomery AL 36130

LYMAN, CURTIS LEE, JR., lawyer; b. Albion, N.Y., Dec. 8, 1952; s. Curtis Lee and Evelyn M. (Lake) L.; m. Vicki D. Bongiovanni, Oct. 21, 1978. B.A., Hiram Coll., 1974; J.D., Case Western Res. U., 1977. Bar: N.Y. 1979. Ptnr. Lyman & Lyman, Albion, N.Y., 1979-85; 1st asst. dist. atty. Orleans County, 1979-85; town atty. Albion, 1980-85; county counsel Orleans Indsl. Devel. Agy., 1981-85; gen. counsel Albion Central Sch. Dist., 1983-85; assoc. Merrill, Lynch, Pierce Fenner & Smith, Palm Beach, Fla., 1985—; dir. Lyman Leasing, Ltd. Advisor, Albion Teen Club, 1982, Central Orleans Vol. Ambulance, 1979-85, Albion Fire Dept., 1979-85; exec. adv. council Palm Beach Deaf Service Ctr.; mem. giving com. Hanley-Hagelton Ctr., Palm Beach. Mem. ABA, N.Y. State Bar Assn., Orleans County Bar Assn. (pres. 1982), Lawyers-Pilots Bar Assn., Aircraft Owners and Pilots Assn., Albion Area C. of C. (pres. 1979-80). Republican. Presbyterian. Clubs: Albion Town (sec. 1978-79), Buffalo Ski, Masons, Kiwanis. General practice. Home: 1203 12th Terr Palm Beach FL 33418 Office: 401 S County Rd Palm Beach FL 33048

LYMAN, NATHAN M., lawyer; b. Albion, N.Y., Oct. 18, 1955; s. Curtis Lee Sr. and Evelyn Myra (Lake) L.; m. Gail Therese Boehm, June 25, 1983; 1 child, Laura Therese. BA cum laude, Hiram Coll., 1977; JD cum laude, Syracuse U., 1980. Bar: N.Y. 1981, U.S. Dist. Ct. (we. dist.) N.Y. 1981, U.S. Dist. Ct. (no. and ea. dists.) N.Y. 1985, U.S. Ct. Appeals (D.C. cir.) 1985. Ptnr. Lyman & Lyman, Albion, 1981—; ptnr. Softstar Computer, Albion, 1983—; asst. dist. atty. County of Orleans, Albion, 1983-85, dist. atty., 1985; v.p. Interstate Pay Phone, Albion, 1985—. Fireman Albion Fire Dept., 1981-85; trustee Village of Albion, 1982-85; mem. Nat. Ski Patrol, Buffalo, N.Y., 1984—; atty. Town of Albion, 1985-86; del. jud. nominating com. Buffalo Reps., 1985. Mem. ABA, N.Y. State Bar Assn., Orleans County Bar Assn., Pi Gamma Mu. Republican. Presbyterian. Lodge: Rotary. Avocations: tennis, skiing, computers. Contracts commercial, Computer, Criminal. Home: 19 W State St Albion NY 14411 Office: Lyman & Lyman 51 N Main St Albion NY 14411

LYMAN, PAUL D., lawyer; b. Oakland, Calif., Apr. 28, 1953; s. Dilworth N. and Faun P. Lyman; m. Dixie Lyman; six children. BS in Econs., Brigham Young U., 1976; JD, U. Chgo., 1979. Bar: Colo. 1979, U.S. Ct. Mil. Appeals 1980, Utah 1985. Assoc. Davis, Graham & Stubbs, Denver, 1979-80; sole practice Richfield, Utah, 1985—. Served to capt. USAF, 1980-85. Mem. ABA, Colo. Bar Assn., Utah Bar Assn. Personal injury, State civil litigation, Family and matrimonial. Office: 250 N Main Richfield UT 84701

LYNCH, CAROLE YARD, lawyer; b. Knoxville, Tenn., Aug. 29, 1951; d. Charles R. and Alma (Allred) Yard; m. Carter J. Lynch, III, Aug. 6, 1977; 1 child, Allison Kathleen. B.A., U. Tenn., 1972, J.D., 1977. Bar: Tenn. 1977, Ga. 1982. Assoc. Thomas, Leitner, Mann, Warner & Owens, Chattanooga, 1977-78, Thomas, Mann & Gossett, Chattanooga, 1978-80; assoc. Thomas, Mann & Gossett, P.C., Chattanooga, 1980-81, ptnr., v.p., 1981-86; ptnr. Grant, Konvalinka, & Grubbs, P.C., 1987—. Asst. editor Tenn. Law Rev., 1976-77. Vice chmn. allocations United Way of Chattanooga, mem. allocations steering com., 1985, vice chmn. pilot campaign, 1986; active Jr. League of Chattanooga, 1981—; mem. alumnae adv. council U. Tenn. Coll. Law, 1983—; bd. dirs. Mental Health Assn. Chattanooga Inc., 1986—. Mem. Chattanooga Bar Assn. (bd. govs. 1982-84, sec.-treas. 1985-86, pres.-elect, 1986-87, pres. 1987—), Tenn. Bar Assn., ABA, Ga. Bar Assn., Phi Alpha Delta. Episcopalian. General corporate, Probate, Securities. Home: 116 Green Gorge Signal Mountain TN 37377 Office: Grant Konvalinka & Grubbs PC 600 Tallan Bldg Chattanooga TN 37402

LYNCH, EUGENE F., federal judge; b. 1931. B.S., U. Santa Clara, 1953; LL.B., U. Calif., 1958. Assoc. O'Connor, Moran, Cohn & Lynch, San Francisco, 1959-64, ptnr., 1964-71; judge Mcpl. Ct., San Francisco, 1971-74; justice Superior Ct. City and County San Francisco, 1974-82; judge U.S. Dist. Ct. (no. dist.) Calif., San Francisco, 1982—. Judicial administration. Office: US Courthouse 450 Golden Gate Ave San Francisco CA 94102 *

LYNCH, JAMES DANIEL, lawyer; b. Chgo., Oct. 30, 1949; s. Jeremiah James and Genevieve (Paluch) L.; 1 child, Jessica Susan. AA, Coll. DuPage, 1969; BA, Rosary Coll., 1971; JD, U. Ill., 1976. Bar: Ill. 1976, Wis. 1980, U.S. Dist. Ct. (we. dist.) Wis. 1981, U.S. Dist. Ct. (no. dist.) Ill., 1982, U.S. Ct. Appeals (7th cir.) 1983, U.S. Supreme Ct. 1983, U.S. Dist. Ct. (so. and cen. dists.) 1984. Sole practice Chgo., 1976-77, 1983-84; adminstrv. law judge Wis. Employment Relations Commn., Madison, 1977-81; gen. counsel United Mine Workers Am., Dist. 12, Springfield, Ill., 1984-86; sole practice Springfield, 1986—. Contbr. articles to profl. jours. Mem. ABA (labor and employment sect., chmn. fed. preemption state labor laws subcom., 1980-83), Ill. Bar Assn. (apptd. to governing labor law sect. council 1984-86), Wis. Bar Assn., Assn. Trial Lawyers Am. Federal civil litigation, Labor, Pension, profit-sharing, and employee benefits. Office: 3695 S 6th St Springfield IL 62703

LYNCH, JAMES EDWARD, lawyer; b. Tampa, Fla., Aug. 5, 1951; s. John Thomas and Dorothy Bridget (Crosson) L.; m. Eileen Marie Baumgardner, Jan. 11, 1975; children: James Edward, Jr., Carolyn Marie. B.A., LaSalle Coll., 1973; J.D., Del. Law Sch., 1978. Bar: Pa. 1978, U.S. Dist. Ct. (ea. dist.) Pa. 1983, U.S. Supreme Ct. 1984, U.S. Ct. Appeals (3d cir.) 1984, U.S. Tax Ct. 1986. Ter. mgr. Clairol, Inc., N.Y.C., 1973-75; assoc. Ettinger, Silverman, Balka & Levy, Phila., 1978-80; ptnr. Lynch & Lynch, Bensalem, Pa., 1980-82, Kardos & Lynch, Newtown, Pa., 1982—. Mem. Lower Bucks C. of C., Langhorne, Pa., 1982. Mem. ABA, Pa. Bar Assn., Bucks County Bar Assn., Phila. County Bar Assn., Phi Alpha Delta. Republican. Roman Catholic. Club: Gradu-Eights (Phila.). Lodge: Lions. General corporate, General practice, Pension, profit-sharing, and employee benefits. Home: 115

Overlook Ave Washington Crossing PA 18977 Office: Kardos & Lynch 638 Newton-Yardley Rd Suite 1-E Newton Commons W Newtown PA 18940

LYNCH, JAMES JOSEPH, JR., lawyer; b. San Francisco, Aug. 12, 1939; s. James Joseph Sr. and Francis (Erskin) L.; m. Fidela Toribio Lazaro, June 14, 1969; children: Joy Frances, James Joseph III, Justin George. AA, Am. River Community Coll., 1971; BBA, Calif. State U., Sacramento, 1974; JD, U. Pacific, 1978. Bar: Calif. 1979, U.S. Dist. Ct. (ea. dist.) Calif. 1979, U.S. Ct. Appeals (9th cir.) 1980, U.S. Supreme Ct. 1982, U.S. Dist. Ct. (no. dist.) Calif. 1986.fi. Commd. ensign USAF, 1959, advanced through grades to sgt., 1962, resigned, 1969; sole practice Sacramento, 1979—. Contbr. articles to profl. jours. Mem. Sacramento County Dem. Cen. com., 1978; parliamentarian Filipino Family Fraternity, Sacramento, 1984—, mem., 1971—. Decorated Bronze Star. Mem. Assn. Trial Lawyers Am., Calif. Pub. Defenders Assn., Supreme Ct. Hist. Soc. Roman Catholic. Avocations: reading, photography, camping, hiking, family. Civil rights, Criminal, Constitutional law. Office: 1812 J St Suite 3 Sacramento CA 95814

LYNCH, JEFFREY SCOTT, lawyer; b. Dixon, Ill., Oct. 7, 1950; s. Walter Francis and Jacqueline (Olson) L.; m. Nancy Skeen Patterson, Dec. 28, 1971; children—Scott P., Kate O., Elizabeth A. B.B.A., So. Meth. U., 1971, J.D., 1975. Bar: Tex. 1975, U.S. Dist. Ct. (no. dist.) Tex. 1975, U.S. Dist. Cts. (so. and ea. dists.) Tex. 1977, U.S. Dist. Ct. (we. dist.) Tex. 1978, U.S. Dist. Ct. (ea. and we. dists.) Ark. 1980, U.S. Tax Ct. 1975, U.S. Ct. Claims 1975, U.S. Ct. Appeals (5th cir.) 1975, (11th cir.) 1983, U.S. Supreme Ct. 1978. Assoc. Maloney, Milner & McDowell, Dallas, 1975; assoc., ptnr. Vial, Hamilton, Koch & Knox, Dallas, 1975—; mem. legal asst. adv. com. El Centro Community Coll., Dallas; instr. So. Meth. U. Law Sch., Dallas, 1975-77, 87. Contbr. chpt. to book. Chmn. bd. deacons Casa Linda Presbyterian Ch., Dallas, 1984; election insp. Gen. Election, Tex., Dallas, 1982. Named one of Outstanding Young Men Am., 1979. Fellow Tex. Bar Found.; mem. Dallas Assn. Young Lawyers (bd. dirs. 1981, treas. 1982, grievance com. 1982—), Am. Bd. Trial Advocates (assoc.), Tex. Bd. Legal Specialization (cert. personal injury and civil trial law). Federal civil litigation, State civil litigation, Personal injury. Office: Vial Hamilton Koch & Knox 1500 Republic Bank Tower Dallas TX 75201

LYNCH, JOHN GREGORY, JR., lawyer; b. Boston, Dec. 29, 1943; s. John Gregory and Elizabeth Orient (Clancy) L. AB, Boston U., 1966; postgrad., U. Va., 1970; JD, Harvard U., 1973; cert. droit privée, Hague Acad., 1975. Bar: N.Y. 1974, U.S. Dist. Ct. (so. and ea. dists.) N.Y. 1974, Mass. 1984, U.S. Dist. Ct. Mass. 1984, U.S. Ct. Appeals (1st cir.) 1984. Assoc. Whitman & Ransom, N.Y.C., 1973-75; legal officer gen. legis. div. UN, N.Y.C., 1975-79, asst. under sec. gen. mgmt., 1979-83, head ins. and risk mgr., 1985—; ptnr. Lynch & Lynch, Boston, 1984-85; sole practice Boston, 1985—. Vol. U.S. Peace Corps. Chile, 1966-68; founder UN Child Care Centre, N.Y.C., 1984. Thomas Jefferson fellow, 1970, NATO fellow, 1972. Mem. ABA (probate com., real property com., internat. law sect.), Mass. Bar Assn. (probate law com.), Assn. of Student Internat. Law Socs. (v.p. 1971-72, pres. 1972-73), Am. Fgn. Law Assn. (v.p. 1983-86, bd. dirs. 1986—), Internat. Movement Cath. Jurists (bd. dirs. 1985—), Risk and Ins. Mgrs. Soc. (delegate 1985—), Am. Soc. Internat. Law (bd. dirs. 1972-75), Soc. for Preservation of New Eng. Antiquities, Soc. St. Dymphna (Phila v.p.). Club: Harvard (Boston). Avocations: photography, hist. preservation, squash. Private international, Pension, profit-sharing, and employee benefits, Probate. Home: 245 E 11th St New York NY 10003 Office: 20 Park Plaza Boston MA 02116

LYNCH, JOHN PETER, lawyer; b. Chgo., June 5, 1942; s. Charles Joseph and Anne Mae (Loughlin) L.; m. Judy Godvin, Sept. 21, 1968; children—Patrick, Julie, Jennifer. A.B., Marquette U., 1964; J.D., Northwestern U., 1967. Bar: Ill. 1967, U.S. Ct. Appeals (7th cir.) 1979, U.S. Ct. Appeals (5th cir.) 1976, U.S. Supreme Ct. 1979. Ptnr. Kirkland & Ellis, Chgo., 1973-76, Hedlund, Hunter & Lynch, Chgo., 1976-82, Latham, Watkins, Hedlund, Hunter & Lynch, Chgo., 1982-85, Latham & Watkins, Chgo., 1985—. Chmn. vis. com. Northwestern U. Law Sch. Served as lt. USN, 1968-71. Mem. ABA, Ill. Bar Assn., Assn. Trial Lawyers Am., Order of Coif. Clubs: City, Metropolitan (Chgo.); North Shore Country (Glenview, Ill.). Notes and Comments editor Northwestern U. Law Rev., 1967. Antitrust, Public international, Federal civil litigation. Home: 2007 Spruce St Glenview IL 60606 Office: Suite 6900 Sears Tower 233 S Wacker Dr Chicago IL 60606

LYNCH, JOHN TIMOTHY, lawyer; b. Rochester, N.Y., Feb. 7, 1950; s. Lawrence Thomas and Marion Rita (Schwab) L.; m. Karen Lee Seib, May 8, 1976; children—Kelly Lee, Kristy Lauren, Katie Lynn. B.S., SUNY, 1972; J.D., Albany Law Sch., 1975. Bar: N.Y. 1976, S.C. 1981, U.S. Dist. Ct. (no. dist.) N.Y. 1977, U.S. Dist. Ct. S.C. 1983, U.S. Ct. Appeals (4th cir.); CLU; chartered fin. cons. Asst. gen counsel Security Mutual Life Ins. Co., Binghamton, N.Y., 1975-79; counsel, v.p. Liberty Life Ins. Co., Greenville, S.C., 1979—. Chmn. Greenville Pvt. Industry Council, 1980-81; tchr. St. Mary's Sch. Ch. Edn., Greenville, 1982—; pres. St. Mary's Sch. Home Sch. Assn. Mem. ABA, Assn. Life Ins. Counsel, Greenville Estate Planning Council, N.Y. Bar Assn., S.C. Bar Assn., Greenville Bar Assn. Roman Catholic. Clubs: Commerce, Greenville City. Insurance, Pension, profit-sharing, and employee benefits, Estate planning. Office: 2000 Wade Hampton Blvd PO Box 789 Greenville SC 29602

LYNCH, JOSEPH MARTIN, legal educator; b. Jersey City, Aug. 28, 1924; s. Joseph Michael and Elizabeth Teresa (Coughlin) L.; m. Irene Mary O'Neil, July 26, 1952; children—Anne, Peter, Teresa, Mark, Patricia. A.B., St. Peter's Coll., Jersey City, 1948; LL.B., Harvard U., 1951. Bar: N.J. 1952. Law clk. Appellate div. N.J. Superior Ct., 1952-53; assoc. Charles A. Rooney, Jersey City, 1953-55, Guy W. Calissi, Hackensack, N.J., 1955-57, J. Seymour Montgomery, Princeton, N.J., 1957-60; mem. faculty Law Sch., Seton Hall U., Newark, 1961—, prof. law, assoc. dean, 1976-77. Trustee Stanley J. Seeger Hellenic Found. of Princeton U. Served with U.S. Army, 1942-45. Roman Catholic. Contbr. articles to profl. jours. Legal education. Home: 166 Jefferson Rd Princeton NJ 08540 Office: 1111 Raymond Blvd Newark NJ 07102

LYNCH, MARGARET COMARD, lawyer; b. Albany, N.Y., Dec. 2, 1956; d. Frank J. and Margaret M. (Mooney) Comard; m. Michael C. Lynch, July 2, 1983. BA, Coll. Holy Cross, 1978; JD, Union U., 1982. Bar: N.Y. 1983, U.S. Dist. Ct. (no. dist.) N.Y. 1983, U.S. Ct. Appeals (2d cir.) 1985. Assoc. Ainsworth, Sullivan, Tracy, Knauf, Warner & Ruslander, Albany, N.Y., 1982—. Bd. dirs. St. Catherines Ctr. for Children, Albany, 1983—. Mem. Def. Research Inst., N.Y. State Bar Assn. (toxic wastes and hazardous substances com.), Albany County Bar Assn., Am. Judicature Soc. State civil litigation, Insurance, Personal injury. Office: Ainsworth Sullivan PO Box 1579 75 State St Albany NY 12201-1579

LYNCH, NEIL L(AWRENCE), state supreme court justice; b. Holyoke, Mass., June 26, 1930. A.B. sum laude, Harvard U., 1952, LL.B., 1957. Bar: Mass. 1952. Assoc. firm. Hale, Sanderson, Byrnes & Morton, Boston, 1957-65; gen. counsel Mass. Port Authority, 1965-76; assoc. Herilhy and O'Brien, Boston, 1976-79; chief legal counsel to gov. State of Mass., 1979-81; assoc. justice Supreme Jud. Ct. Mass., 1981—; mem. Airport Operators Council Internat., 1965-76, chmn., 1974-75; adj. prof. law, legal writing and environ. law New Eng. Law Sch., 1968-74, assoc. prof. corp. law and evidence, 1974-76. Served to 1st lt. USAF, 1952-54. Mem. ABA (pub. contracts com. pub. contract law sect. 1975-76), Boston Bar Assn., Mass. Bar Assn. Judicial administration. Office: Supreme Judicial Court 1300 New Courthouse Boston MA 02108 *

LYNCH, PATRICK, lawyer; b. Pitts., Nov. 11, 1941; s. Thomas Patrick and Helen Mary (Grimes) L.; m. M. Linda Maturo, June 20, 1964; children: Megan, Kevin, Colin, Brendan, Erin, Brian, Liam, Eamonn, Kilian, Caitlin. BA in Philosophy, Loyola U., Los Angeles, 1964, LLB, 1966. Bar: Calif. 1967, U.S. Dist. Ct. (cen., so., no. and ea. dists.) Calif., U.S. Ct. Appeals, U.S. Supreme Ct. Ptnr. O'Melveny & Myers, Los Angeles, 1966—; adj. prof. antitrust/civil procedure Loyola U., Los Angeles, 1970-80; panelist Lyle L. Jones Antitrust Conf., 1982, advanced computer law invitational, Ariz. Law and Tech. Inst. and Ariz. State U., 1983. Mem. ABA (panelist banking law sect., antitrust sect., chmn. antitrust com. litigation sect. 1980-83), Los Angeles County Bar Assn., Tex. Bar Assn. (panelist conv. seminar), Competitive Bus. Practice Inst. (panelist), Fed. Practice Inst. (panelist Calif. continuing edn.), Practising Law Inst. (panelist). Office: O'Melveny & Myers 400 S Hope St Los Angeles CA 90071

LYNCH, ROBERT BERGER, lawyer; b. LaCrosse, Wis., June 10, 1931; s. Jan P. and Eve (Berger) L.; B.S., U.S. Merchant Marine Acad., 1955; J.D., U. of the Pacific, 1967; m. Ann Godfrey, May 30, 1980; 1 son, Jan Fredrick. Sr. engr. Aerojet Gen. Corp., Sacramento, Calif., 1955-61, proposal mgr., 1961-63, asst. contract adminstrn. mgr., 1963-66, contract adminstrn. mgr., 1967-70; admitted to Calif. bar, 1969, U.S. Supreme Ct. bar, 1972; individual practice law. Rancho Cordova, Calif., 1969—; instr. bus. law Solano Community Coll., 1977-79, San Joaquin Delta Coll., 1978-79. Monthly columnist Mil. History Rev. Active various charity fund-raising campaigns in Sacramento Calif., 1966-68; mem. mission com. St. Clements Episcopal Ch., Rancho Cordova, Calif., 1967-68; trustee Los Rios Community Coll. Dist., Calif., 1971-79. Served with USCG, 1949-51. Fellow Brit. Interplanetary Soc.; mem. Am. Bar Assn., Assn. of Trial Lawyers of Am., Calif. Trial Lawyers Assn., IEEE, Calif. Wildlife Fedn., Internat. Turtle Club, Marines Meml. Assn., Am. Legion, Mensa. Family and matrimonial, Probate, General practice. Home and Office: 10615 Coloma Rd Rancho Cordova CA 95670

LYNCH, ROBERT MARTIN, lawyer, educator; b. St. Louis, Mar. 28, 1950; s. Raymond Burns and Nancy Winn (Roeder) L.; m. Cynthia Kay Allmeyer, June 7, 1974; children: Christopher, Kelly, Stephanie. AB, St. Louis U., 1972, JD, 1975. Bar: Mo. 1975, D.C. 1985. Law clk. to presiding justice Mo. Ct. Appeals, St. Louis, 1975-76; atty. Southwestern Bell Telephone Corp., St. Louis, 1976-79, atty. network, 1979-83, gen. atty., 1983—; instr. paralegal studies St. Louis Community Coll., 1977—. Mem. ABA, Mo. Bar Assn. (adminstrv. law com. council), St. Louis Bar Assn. (chmn. adminstrv. law com. 1981-82). Republican. Avocations: racquetball, writing. General corporate, Corporate taxation, Securities. Office: Southwestern Bell Corp One Bell Ctr 40-Z-01 Saint Louis MO 63101-3099

LYNCH, ROBERT THOMAS, lawyer; b. San Francisco, May 4, 1938; s. Daniel J. and Anna Dorothy (Dunne) L.; children—Christine, Daniel, Gregory, Brian; m. Janice Marie Bailey, June 10, 1971. B.S., U. San Francisco, 1960, J.D., 1963. Bar: Calif. 1963, U.S. Dist. Ct. (no. dist.) Calif. 1963. Staff atty. Liberty Mut. Ins. Co., 1964-69; assoc. atty. Ericksen Kincaid Bridgman, 1969-70; ptnr. Ericksen Lynch, Mackenroth, 1970-78; sr. ptnr. Lynch, Loofbourrow, Helmenstine, Gilardi & Grummer, San Francisco, 1978—; lectr. in field. Mem. devel. bd. Mercy High Sch., San Francisco. Mem. ABA, Assn. Ins. Attys. (pres. 1983-84), Am. Bd. Trial Advocates, Def. Research Inst., Internat. Acad. Law and Scis., Fedn. Ins. Counsel, Am. Judicature Soc. Democrat. Roman Catholic. Club: Olympic. State civil litigation, Personal injury, Insurance. Address: 505 Beach St San Francisco CA 94133

LYNCH, THOMAS HALPIN, lawyer; b. N.Y.C., July 17, 1938; s. Thomas Henry and Bernadette (Faulhaber) L.; m. Carol Ann McLoughlin, May 4, 1963; children: Jeanne, Catherine. BS, SUNY Maritime Coll., Ft. Schuyler, 1961; JD, Fordham U., 1969; MBA, Columbia U., 1978. Bar: N.Y. 1969, U.S. Dist. Ct. (so. dist.) N.Y. 1969. Assoc. Haight, Garner, Poor & Havens, N.Y.C., 1968-72, Miller & Summit, N.Y.C., 1972-73; law sec. Appellate Div., N.Y.C., 1973-75; spl. asst. to gov. Albany, N.Y., 1975-76; commr. N.Y. State Tax Commn., Albany, 1976-81; sr. v.p., gen. counsel Ayco Corp., Albany, 1981—; spl. counsel legis. commn. on modernization and simplification of tax adminstrn. and the tax law, Albany, 1982-85. Vol. Fireman Tri-Village Fire Co., Old Chatham, N.Y., 1976—. Served with USCG, 1961-65. Mem. ABA, N.Y. State Bar Assn. Democrat. Roman Catholic. Avocations: gardening, raising and eventing horses. Personal income taxation, General corporate, Federal civil litigation. Home: Bachus Rd Malden Bridge NY 12136 Office: The Ayco Corp One Wall St Albany NY 12205

LYNCH, THOMAS WIMP, lawyer; b. Monmouth, Ill., Mar. 5, 1930; s. William Brennan and Mildred Maurine (Wimp) L.; m. Elizabeth J. McDonald, July 30, 1952; children: Deborah, Michael, Maureen, Karen, Kathleen. BS in Geology, U. Ill., 1955, MS in Geology, 1958, JD, 1959. Bar: Ill. 1960, Okla. 1960, U.S. Supreme Ct. 1971, Tex. 1978. Staff atty. Amerada Hess Corp., Tulsa, 1959-72, asst. gen. counsel, 1972-75; ptnr. Hall, Estill, Hardwick, Gable, Collingsworth & Nelson, Tulsa, 1975; v.p., gen. counsel Tex. Pacific Oil Co., Inc., Dallas, 1975-80; v.p., chief counsel Sun Exploration & Prodn Co., Dallas, 1980—; adj. prof. law U. Tulsa, 1974. Served with USN, 1948-49, U.S. Army, 1951-53. Mem. ABA, Southwestern Legal Found. (chmn., lectr. ann. oil and gas short course 1976—, chmn. Oil and Gas Edn. Ctr.), Am. Petroleum Inst. (past chmn. task group on unit ops.), Interstate Oil Compact Commn. (mem. legal com.), Tex. State Bar Assn., Dallas County Bar Assn. Roman Catholic. Club: Dallas Petroleum. Oil and gas leasing. Office: Sun Exploration & Prodn Co 5656 Blackwell Dallas TX 75231

LYNCH, VICTOR K., lawyer; b. Latrobe, Pa., Sept. 9, 1929; s. Victor E. and Helen (Kamerer) L.; m. Jane Louise Sutherland, June 11, 1951 (div. 1970); children: G. Michael, Janet L. Mutschler, Steven J., David J., Thomas S., Victoria A. BS in Sanitary Engring., Pa. State U., 1951; LLD (hon.), Duquesne U., 1958. Bar: Pa. 1959. Design engr., constrn. insp. The Chester Engrs., Pitts., 1953-54, project engr., 1954-58; assoc. Burgwin, Ruffin, Perry & Pohl, Pitts., 1958-62; ptnr. Ruffin, Perry, Springer, Hazlett & Lynch, Pitts., 1962-70; assoc. Litman, Litman, Harris & Specter, P.A., Pitts., 1971-74, Lynch, Lynch, Carr & Kabala, Pitts., 1974-78; ptnr. Lynch and Lynch, Pitts., 1978—. Recipient Bedell award Water Pollution Control Fedn., 1973. Mem. Water Pollution Control Assn. of Pa. (Sludge Shoveler's award 1970, Johnny Clearwater award 1971), Pa. Soc. Profl. Engrs. Municipal bonds. Home: 1000 Grandview Ave Pittsburgh PA 15211 Office: 316 Fourth Ave 903 Commonwealth Bldg Pittsburgh PA 15222

LYNG, REGINALD WILLIAM, lawyer; b. Cocoa Beach, Fla., July 20, 1952; s. Reginald William Jr. and Dora Frances (Dewey) L.; m. Janet Dierks Gallagher, Mar. 21, 1971 (div. Feb. 1978). Student, U. Fla., 1970-71; BA summa cum laude, Wright State U., 1973; JD, U. Toledo, 1976. Bar: Fla. 1977. Legal advisor Orlando (Fla.) Police Dept., 1976-78; sole practice Kissimmee, Fla., 1978—; instr. JC Stone Meml. Police Acad., Orlando, 1977-78. Coach Osceola YMCA Boy's Club, Kissimmee, 1981, Osceola Youth Soccer, Kissimmee, 1982-84, Kissimmee Little League, 1982; mem. Orange County Criminal Justice Council, Orlando, 1977-78; mediator Orange County Citizen Dispute Program, Orlando, 1978; trustee Osceola County Law Library, Kissimmee, 1984-86. Recipient Disting. Service award United Way Osceola County, 1980. Mem. ABA, Fla. Bar Assn., Osceola County Bar Assn., Fla. Legal Advisor's Assn., Phi Alpha Delta. Democrat. Episcopalian. State civil litigation, Family and matrimonial, Criminal. Home: 2909 Clay St Kissimmee FL 32741 Office: 122 Broadway Suite #2 Kissimmee FL 32741

LYNHAM, JOHN MARMADUKE, lawyer; b. Washington, Feb. 19, 1908; s. Edgar Hardwick and Mera Elsie (Marmaduke) L.; m. Adele Randolph Pugh, May 22, 1947; children: Adele Lynham Brey, John M. Jr., Mary Lynham Anderson, Gale Lynham Davis. B.S. in Govt., Am. U., 1935; J.D., George Washington U., 1931, LL.M., 1932. Bar: D.C. 1931, U.S. Supreme Ct. 1936, Md. 1953. Ptnr. Minor, Gatley & Drury, Washington, 1939-51; ptnr. Drury, Lynham & Powell, Washington, 1951-69; v.p., trust officer NS&T Bank, Washington, 1969-81, cons., 1981—; of counsel Ross, Marsh & Foster, Washington, 1981—. Author: The Chevy Chase Club, A History, 1958. Bd. mgrs. Chevy Chase Village, 1963-73, vice chmn., 1965-73; trustee Nat. Ballet Soc., 1969-72, Nat. U., 1947-54, TRS Landon Sch., 1966-74, chmn. bd. dirs., 1967-74; bd. dirs. Gunston Hall Sch., 1941-46. Served to comdr. USNR, 1941-45. Fellow Am. Bar Found.; mem. ABA, Am. Judicature Soc., Inst. Jud. Adminstrn., Bar Assn. D.C., D.C. Bar Assn., Md. Bar Assn. Episcopalian. Clubs: Chevy Chase (gov. 1949-55, 59-65, pres. 1955); Metropolitan (gov. 1968-73, pres. 1973), Lawyers (pres. 1981), Barristers (pres. 1960) (Washington). Construction, Estate planning, Insurance. Home: 14 Oxford St Chevy Chase Village MD 20815 Office: 888 16th St NW Washington DC 20006

LYNN, ARTHUR DELLERT, JR., educator, economist; b. Portsmouth, Ohio, Nov. 12, 1921; s. Arthur Dellert and Helen B. (Willis) L.; m. Pauline Judith Wardlow, Dec. 29, 1943; children: Pamela Wardlow (Mrs. Jon Benson), Constance Karen, Deborah Joanne, Patricia Diane. Student, Va. Mil. Inst., 1938-39, U.S. Naval Acad., 1939; BA, Ohio State U., 1941, MA in Econs., 1943, JD, 1948, PhD in Econs., 1951; postgrad. in law, U. Mich., 1968-70. Bar: Ohio 1948, U.S. Supreme Ct 1966. Mem. faculty Ohio State U., Columbus, 1941-86, prof. econs., 1961-86, asst. dean, 1959-62, assoc. dean Coll. Commerce and Adminstrn., 1962-65, assoc. dean faculties, assoc. provost, 1965-70, assoc. dean Coll. Adminstrv. Sci., 1984-86, assoc. dean emeritus Coll. Bus., 1986—, lectr. Coll. Law, 1961-67, adj. prof. law, 1967-86, prof. pub. adminstrn., 1969-86, prof. emeritus, 1986—, lectr. exec. devel. program, 1958-71, acting dir. div. pub. adminstrn., summers 1973, 74, acting dir. Sch. Pub. Adminstrn., summer 1975, 84-86; ptnr. Lynn & Lynn, Portsmouth, 1949-50; vis. prof. econs. Ohio Wesleyan U., 1958-59, U. Calif.-Berkeley, summer, 1972; mem. Gov. Ohio Econ. Research Council, 1966-70. Editor: The Property Tax and Its Administration, 1970, Property Taxation, Land Use and Public Policy, 1976, Land Value Taxation, 1982; editorial adv. bd.: Tax Bramble Bush, 1959-70; asso. editor: Nat. Tax Jour., 1971—; bd. editors: Am. Jour. Econs. and Sociology, 1981—. Trustee Griffith Meml. Found. Inst. Edn.; chmn. external econs. adv. com. Marietta Coll., 1975-79; inst. assoc. Nat. Regulatory Researh Inst., 1980—. Served to 1st lt. F.A. AUS, 1942-46. Mem. ABA (chmn. com. state and local taxes sect. taxation 1961-63), Ohio Bar Assn., Columbus Bar Assn., Am. Econ. Assn., Midwest Econ. Assn., Royal Econ. Assn., AAUP, ACLU, Nat. Tax Assn. (chmn. com. model property tax assessment and equalization methods and procedures 1961-65, mem. exec. com. 1965-73, v.p., pres. 1969-70), Tax Inst. (adv. council 1960-63), Nat. Tax Assn.-Tax Inst. Am. (sec. 1975-84, treas. 1984—, bd. dirs. 1975—), Am. Arbitration Assn. (nat. panel), AAAS, Acad. Mgmt., Ohio Council Econ. Edn. (bd. dirs. 1964-74), Com. on Taxation, Resources, and Econ. Devel. (chmn. 1979-86, co-chmn. 1986—), Internat. Fiscal Assn., Inst. Internat. des Finances Publiques, Internat. Assn. Assessing Officers (edn. adv. com.), Omicron Delta Epsilon, Beta Theta Pi, Phi Delta Phi, Beta Gamma Sigma, Pi Sigma Alpha, Pi Alpha Alpha. Republican. Episcopalian. Clubs: Rotary, Faculty, Torch (Columbus). Legal education, Personal income taxation, Probate. Home: 2679 Wexford Rd Columbus OH 43221 Office: 1775 S College Rd Columbus OH 43210

LYNN, JAMES BRUCE, lawyer, banker; b. Washington, Feb. 2, 1932; s. Kenneth Schuyler and Mary Catherine (Reese) L.; m. Jane Suzanne Kelly, Apr. 7, 1958; children—James B., William J., Mary C., Kathleen K., Patrick J., Elizabeth A. B.S.B.A., Georgetown U., 1958, J.D., 1961. Bar: U.S. Dist. Ct. D.C. 1962, U.S. Ct. Appeals (D.C. cir.) 1962, U.S. Supreme Ct. 1966, U.S. Tax Ct. 1967, U.S. Claims Ct. 1968, U.S. Mil. Ct. Appeals 1968, D.C. 1972, D.C. Ct. Appeals 1972. Clk., U.S. Atty.'s Office, Washington, 1959-61; law clk. presiding judge U.S. Dist. Ct., Washington, 1961-63; dep. auditor master U.S. Dist. Ct. D.C., Washington, 1963-72, Superior Ct. of D.C., Washington, 1972-80; v.p., trust officer The Riggs Nat. Bank, Washington, 1980—; v.p., pres., bd. dirs. The Unity Railways Co., Pitts., 1980—; mem. Greater Washington Bd. of Trade. Mem., Judicial Conf. U.S. Ct. Appeals, D.C. Ct. of Appeals, 1979—; trustee Client's Security Fund of the D.C. Ct. of Appeals, 1983—; pres. The Counsellor's, Washington, 1984. Served to cpl. USMC, 1952-55. Mem. ABA (ho. of dels. 1981—), John Carroll Soc., Bar Assn. D.C. (pres. Research Found. 1981, pres. Bar Assn. 1982-84), Nat. Lawyers Club of Washington. Republican. Roman Catholic. Clubs: Am. Legion (past comdr.), University, Rotary, Friendly Sons of St. Patrick (Washington). Banking, Probate, Municipal bonds. Address: 808 17th St NW Suite 1200 Washington DC 20006

LYNN, RICHARD C., lawyer, consultant; b. Chgo., May 29, 1943; s. Casimir Vincent and Lillian Constance (Habrelewicz) Cwiklinski; m. Karen Ann Parker, Nov. 28, 1970; children: Allison, Brian. BA, Northwestern U., 1965; JD, DePaul U., 1968. Bar: Ill. 1968. Atty. City Products Corp., Des Plaines, Ill., 1969-72; atty. Cotter & Co., Chgo., 1972-75, v.p., gen counsel, 1978—; sole practice Chgo., 1975—. Bd. dirs. YMCA, Chgo., 1984—, Jesse Owens Found., Chgo., 1986—. Club: Northwestern U. N. (pres. 1986—, award 1978). Avocations: world history, polit. sci., tennis, golf, running. Labor, General practice, Legislative. Home: 1540 Tulip Tree Ct Glenview IL 60025 Office: Cotter & Co 2740 Clybourn Ave Chicago IL 60614

LYNN, ROBERT JOHN, lawyer; b. New Haven, Aug. 26, 1949; s. Elaine Lynn; m. Valerie Lynn Poulton, Aug. 2, 1969; children: Jessica, Jamie, Kacey. BS, U. New Haven, 1971; JD, U. Conn., 1975. Bar: Pa. 1975, Conn. 1976, N.H. 1979, U.S. Dist. Ct. N.H. 1979, U.S. Ct. Appeals (1st cir.) 1979. Law clk. to presiding justice U.S. Dist. Ct. (ea. dist.) Pa., Phila., 1975-77; spl. atty. organized crime strike force U.S. Dept. Justice, Bklyn., 1977-78; asst. U.S. atty. Dist. N.H., Concord, 1978-82, 1st asst. U.S. atty., 1982-84; ptnr. Cleveland, Waters & Bass, Concord, 1984-86, McSwiney, Jones, Semple & Douglas, Concord, 1986—. Exec. editor U. Conn. Law Rev., 1974-75. Mem. Bow (N.H.) Sch. Bd., 1982—. Mem. ABA, N.H. Bar Assn. (com. on rules of criminal procedure 1985—), Nat. Rifle Assn. Republican. Roman Catholic. Lodge: Rotary. Avocation: rifle marksmanship. Criminal, Federal civil litigation, Personal injury. Home: RFD #3 Box 257 B Bow NH 03301 Office: McSwiney Jones Semple & Douglas 8 Centre St Concord CT 03301

LYNN, ROBERT PATRICK, JR., lawyer; b. N.Y.C., Nov. 17, 1943; s. Robert P. and Marie (Madeo) L.; m. Maria T. Zeccola, Nov. 18, 1967; children—Robert P. III, Stephanie M., Kerry Elizabeth. B.A., Villanova U., 1965; J.D., St. John's U., Bklyn., 1968. Bar: N.Y. 1969, U.S. Dist. Ct. (ea. dist.) N.Y. 1975, U.S. Ct. Appeals (1st cir.) 1978, U.S. Ct. Appeals (2d cir.) 1975, U.S. Supreme Ct. 1978. Clk., then assoc. Leboeuf, Lamb & Leiby, N.Y.C., 1966-69; dep. town atty. Town of North Hempstead, Manhasset, N.Y., 1969-71; assoc. Sprague Dwyer Aspland & Tobin, Mineola, N.Y., 1971-75, ptnr., 1975-76; ptnr. Lynn, Ledwith, Quinlan & White, Garden City, N.Y., 1976—; spl. prosecutor Inc. Village of Bayville, 1975-76; dir. Island Swimming Sales, Inc., N.Y. and Tex.; sec. Wild Heerbrugg Instruments, Inc., N.Y. and Switzerland. Bd. dirs. Cath. Charities, 1971—, chmn., 1982; vice chmn. Diocese of Rockville Centre Family Life Ctr., 1978-82. Mem. Nassau County Bar Assn., Suffolk County Bar Assn., N.Y. State Bar Assn. Roman Catholic. Clubs: Wheatley Hills Golf (East Williston, N.Y.); Lloyd Neck Bath (Lloyd Harbor, N.Y.). Federal civil litigation, State civil litigation, Antitrust. Home: Seaforth Ln Lloyd Harbor NY 11743 Office: Lynn Ledwith Quinlan & White 200 Garden City Plaza Garden City NY 11530

LYON, BRUCE ARNOLD, lawyer, educator; b. Sacramento, Sept. 24, 1951; s. Arnold E. and Arlene R. (Cox) L.; m. Patricia J. Gibson, Dec. 14, 1974; children—Barrett, Andrew. A.B. with honors, U. Pacific, 1974; J.D., U. Calif.-Hastings Coll. Law, 1977. Bar: Calif. 1977, U.S. Dist. Ct. (ea. and no. dists.) Calif. 1977. Ptnr. Ingoglia, Marskey, Kearney & Lyon, Sacramento, 1977-84; sole practice, Auburn, Calif., 1984—; instr. in law Sierra Coll., Rocklin, Calif., 1983—. Mng. editor Comment, A Jour. of Communications and Entertainment Law, 1974. Contbr. articles to trade publs. Campaign aide Democratic Party, Sacramento, 1972. Mem. State Bar Calif., ABA (liaison student div. 1974), Calif. Trial Lawyers Assn., Sacramento County Bar Assn., Placer County Bar Assn., Thurston Soc., Order of Coif. Club: Gourmet (Rocklin). Lodge: Lions. General practice, Real property, State civil litigation. Office: One California St Auburn CA 95603

LYON, CARL FRANCIS, JR., lawyer; b. Sumter, S.C., May 9, 1943; s. Carl Francis and Sophie (Goldstrum) L.; m. Maryann Mercier; children—Barbara Ruth, Sarah Frances, Carl Francis, III. A.B., Duke U., 1965, J.D. with honors, 1968. Bar: N.Y. 1969, D.C. 1977. Assoc., then ptnr. Mudge Rose Guthrie Alexander & Ferdon, N.Y.C., 1968—, mem. exec. com., 1986—. Contbr. articles to profl. publs. Mem. N.Y. State Bar Assn., D.C. Bar Assn., Am. Pub. Power Assn., Order of Coif, Phi Alpha Delta. General corporate, Local government, Public utilities. Office: Mudge Rose Guthrie Alexander & Ferdon 180 Maiden Ln New York NY 10038

LYON, EDWIN LEON, lawyer; b. Wichita, Kans., Apr. 14, 1947; s. Edwin W. Lyon and Norma Elaine (Hinkley) Hinshaw. BS cum laude, Southwest Mo. State U., 1969; JD, Washington U., St. Louis, 1972. Bar: Mo. 1972, D.C. 1975, U.S. Ct. Appeals (D.C. cir.) 1975. Atty. SEC, Washington, 1972-75; chief counsel Commodity Futures Trading Commn., Washington, 1975-77; assoc. Cadwalader, Wickersham & Taft, Washington, 1977-82, ptnr., 1982—. Mem. ABA (chmn. subcom. futures regulation com. 1982—), Mo. Bar Assn., D.C. Bar Assn., Futures Industry Assn. (arbitrator 1984—, compliance task force 1982). Democrat. Avocations: tennis, hiking. Commodities, Securities, General corporate. Office: Cadwalader Wickersham & Taft 1333 New Hampshire Ave NW Washington DC 20036

LYON, JAMES BURROUGHS, lawyer; b. N.Y.C., May 11, 1930; s. Francis Murray and Edith May (Strong) L. BA, Amherst Coll., 1952; LLB, Yale U., 1955. Bar: Conn. 1955, U.S. Tax Ct. 1970. Asst. football coach Yale U., 1953-55; assoc. Murtha, Cullina, Richter and Pinney (and predecessor), Hartford, Conn., 1956-61, ptnr., 1961—; mem. adv. com., lectr. and session leader NYU Inst. on Fed. Taxation, 1973-86. Chmn. 13th Conf. Charitable Orgns. NYU on Fed. Taxation, 1982, adv. com. Hartford Downtown Council, 1986—; trustee Kingswood-Oxford Sch., West Hartford, Conn., 1961—, chmn. bd. trustees, 1975-78; trustee Old Sturbridge Village, Mass., 1974—, Ella Burr McManus Trust, Hartford, 1980—, Hartford YMCA, 1985—, Conn. River Mus. at Steamboat Dock, Essex, 1985—, chmn., 1986—; trustee Wadsworth Atheneum, Hartford, 1968—, pres., 1981-84; corporator Inst. of Living, 1981—, Mt. Sinai Hosp., Hartford, 1972—, Hartford Hosp., 1975—, St. Francis Hosp., Hartford, 1976, Hartford Art Sch., 1979—, Hartford Pub. Library, 1979—. Recipient Eminent Service medal Amherst Coll., 1967, Nathan Hale award Yale Club Hartford, 1983, Disting. Am. award No. Conn. chpt. Nat. Football Found. Hall of Fame, 1983. Fellow Am. Coll. Tax Counsel, Am. Bar Found.; mem. ABA (tax sect. exempt orgn. com., chmn. com. mus.'s and other cultural instns. 1987—), Conn. Bar Assn. (lectr. continuing legal edn. programs 1963—), Hartford County Bar Assn., Assn. Bar City N.Y., Conn. Bar Found. (bd. dirs. 1975-86), Phi Beta Kappa. Republican. Roman Catholic. Clubs: Hartford, Hartford Golf, Univ. (pres. 1976-78), Tennis (Hartford); Yale, Union (N.Y.C.); Limestone Trout (East Canaan, Conn.); Univ. (Washington); Dauntless (Essex, Conn.). Corporate taxation, Personal income taxation, State and local taxation. Office: 185 Asylum St City Pl Hartford CT 06103

LYON, JIM ALLEN, lawyer; b. Searcy, Ark., Feb. 13, 1947; s. Rue Arvis and Martha (Klug) L.; m. Carolyn Ann McDonald, Dec. 23, 1972. BS in Econs., West Tex. State U., 1972, BS in Polit. Sci., 1977; JD, Oklahoma City U., 1981. Bar: Okla. 1982, U.S. Dist. Ct. (we. dist.) Okla. 1983, U.S. Ct. Appeals (10th cir.) 1985, Tex. 1987. Sole practice Oklahoma City, 1982—. Gov's. Task Force Okla. Energy Coalition, 1985—. Mem. ABA (natural law sect.), Tex. Bar Assn., Okla. City Title Lawyers Assn., Exam. Standards Com., Okla. City Assn. Petroleum Lease and Title Analysts, Interstate Oil Compact Commn. (standing com. mem. 1982—), Okla. Ind. Petroleum Assn., Oklahoma City Internat. Trade Assn., Oklahoma City C. of C., Internat. Visitors Assn., People to People, Phi Alpha Delta. Democrat. Presbyterian. Avocations: art, travel, reading, languages. Oil and gas leasing, General corporate, Consumer commercial. Office: 2212 NW 50th St Suite 241 Oklahoma City OK 73112

LYON, PHILIP KIRKLAND, lawyer; b. Warren, Ark., Jan. 19, 1944; s. Leroy and Maxine (Campbell) L.; m. Jayne Carol Jack, Aug. 12, 1982; children by previous marriage—Bradford F., Lucinda H., Suzette Phillips, John P., Martin K., Meredith Phillips. J.D. with honors, U. Ark., 1967. Bar: Ark. 1967, U.S. Supreme Ct. 1970. Sr. ptnr., dir. ops. House, Wallace, Nelson & Jewell, P.A., Little Rock, 1967-86; pres. Jack, Lyon & Jones, P.A. Little Rock, 1986—. Instr. bus. law, labor law, govt. bus. and collective bargaining U. Ark., Little Rock, 1979-80, lectr. practice skills and labor law, 1979-80. Co-author: Schlei and Grossman Employment Discrimination Law, 2d edit., 1982. Bd. dirs. Ark. Law Rev., 1978—, Southwestern Legal Found., 1978—. Mem. Greater Little Rock C. of C. (chmn. community affairs com. 1982-84, minority bus. affairs 1985—), Ark. State C. of C. (bd. dirs. 1984—), Greater LIttle Rock C. of C. (chmn. community affairs com. 1982-84, minority bus. affairs 1985), ABA (select com. for liason with office of fed. contract compliance programs 1982—, select com. liason with EEOC 1984—), Ark. Bar Assn. (chmn. labor law com. 1977-78, labor law sect. 1979-80, Golden Gavel award 1978), Pulaski County Bar Assn., Assn. Trial Lawyers Am., Ark. Trial Lawyers Assn., Am. Soc. Personnel Adminstrn. Clubs: Little Rock Racquet, Capitol. Labor, Civil rights. Home: 311 McAdoo Little Rock AR 72205 Office: Jack Lyon & Jones PA 3400 Capitol Tower Capitol at Broadway Little Rock AR 72201

LYON, R. DOUGLAS, lawyer; b. Los Angeles, Nov. 21, 1923; s. Leonard S. and Agnes I. (Adams) L.; m. Nancy Knight, Oct. 1, 1954; children—Patricia, Katherine Lyon Link, Robert Douglas, Thomas. B.A., U.S. Naval Acad., 1945; LL.B., Stanford U., 1949. Bar: Calif. 1950. Assoc. Lyon & Lyon, Los Angeles, 1949-54, ptnr., 1955—. Served as ensign U.S. Navy, 1945. Mem. ABA, Calif. Bar Assn., Los Angeles Bar Assn., Am. Pat. Assn., Los Angeles Pat. Assn. Clubs: Calif., Los Angeles Country, Beach (Los Angeles). Patent, Trademark and copyright, Federal civil litigation. Home: 250 S Rimpau Blvd Los Angeles CA 90004 Office: 611 W 6th St Los Angeles CA 90004

LYON, REXFORD LOWELL, lawyer; b. Binghamton, N.Y., Aug. 25, 1942; s. Walter Jefferson and Marian Ethel (Blass) L.; m. Lois Isobel Duncan, Jan. 19, 1967; 1 dau., Susan Elise. B.A., U. Ariz., 1964; J.D. with honors, Rutgers U., 1967. Bar: N.J. 1967, U.S. Dist. Ct. N.J. 1967. Assoc., Stryker, Tams & Dill, Newark, 1967-72; prin. Sobel & Lyon, P.C., East Hanover, N.J., 1972—, pres. 1980—. Mem. ABA, N.J. Bar Assn., Morris County Bar Assn. Club: Rotary of Florham Park (sec. 1982-83, pres. 1984-85). General corporate, Probate, Real property. Office: 188 Route 10 East Hanover NJ 07936

LYON, RICHARD KIRSHBAUM, lawyer; b. Washington, Apr. 24, 1912; s. Simon and Minnie Rose (Kirshbaum) L.; m. Marjorie Hausman, Aug. 26, 1948 (dec. Aug. 1955); children: Simon M., Richard H.; m. Dorothy Weisberg, Feb. 7, 1960; 1 child, Jon W. AB, Dartmouth Coll., 1933; JD, Georgetown U., 1936. Bar: D.C. 1936, U.S. Supreme Ct. 1939. Assoc. Lyon & Lyon, Washington, 1936-41; sole practice Washington, 1946—; commr. D.C. Jud. Disabilities and Tenure Commn., Washington, 1975—; gen. counsel Better Bus. Bur. Met. Washington, 1954—. Vice chmn. D.C. Dem. com., 1966; gen. counsel, legis. chmn. Johnson-Humphrey Inaugural com., Washington, 1965. Served to comdr. USNR, 1941-46. Mem. D.C. Bar Assn. (past v.p. and bd. dirs.), D.C. Organized Bar Assn., Nat. Lawyers Club. Jewish. Probate, Personal injury, General practice. Home and Office: 3107 Garfield St NW Washington DC 20008

LYONS, DAVID BARRY, philosophy educator; b. N.Y.C., Feb. 6, 1935; s. Joseph and Betty (Janower) L.; m. Sandra Yetta Nemiroff, Dec. 18, 1955; children—Matthew, Emily, Jeremy. Student, Cooper Union, 1952-54, 56-57; B.A., Bklyn. Coll., 1960; M.A. (Gen. Electric Found. fellow), Harvard U., 1963, PH.D. (Woodrow Wilson dissertation fellow), 1963; postgrad., Oxford (Eng.) U., 1963-64. Asst. prof. philosophy Cornell U., Ithaca, N.Y., 1964-67; asso. prof. Cornell U., 1967-71, prof. philosophy, 1971—, chmn. dept. philosophy, 1978-84, prof. law, 1979—. Author: Forms and Limits of Utilitarianism, 1965, In the Interest of the Governed, 1973, Ethics and the Rule of Law, 1984; editor: Philos. Rev, 1968-70, 73-75. Recipient Clark award Cornell U., 1976; Woodrow Wilson hon. fellow, 1960-61; Knox traveling fellow, 1963-64; Guggenheim fellow, 1970-71; Soc. for Humanities fellow, 1972-73; Nat. Endowment for Humanities fellow, 1977-78, 84-85. Mem. Am. Philos. Assn., Am. Soc. Polit. and Legal Philosophy, Soc. Philosophy and Public Affairs, Aristotelian Soc. Jurisprudence. Home: 309 Mitchell St Ithaca NY 14850 Office: Cornell University Dept Philosophy Ithaca NY 14853

LYONS, GEORGE SAGE, lawyer, oil jobber, former state legislator; b. Mobile, Ala., Oct. 1, 1936; s. Mark, Jr. and Ruth (Kelly) L.; m. Elsie Crain, Feb. 5, 1960; children-George Sage, Amelia C. B.A. in Econs, Washington and Lee U., Lexington, Va., 1958; LL.B., U. Ala., 1960. Bar: Ala. bar 1960. Practice in Mobile, 1962—; partner Lyons, Pipes & Cook, 1962—; mem. Ala. Ho. of Reps., 1969-75, speaker ho., 1971-75; pres., treas. dir. Crain Oil Co., Inc., Guntersville, Ala.; dir. First Bancgroup Ala., Inc., Jordan Industries, Inc., 1st Nat. Bank Mobile, Ala. State Docks; mem. exec. com. Ala. Petroleum Council; mem. Tenn-Tombigbee Waterway Devel. Authority, 1966-70; chmn. Ala. Commn. on Higher Edn., 1971-78. Served to capt., JAGC U.S. Army, 1960-62. Decorated Army Commendation medal. Mem. Am., Ala., Mobile County bar assns., Mid-Continent Oil and Gas Assn. (dir. Ala.-Miss. div.), Maritime Law Assn. U.S., Omicron Delta Kappa, Phi Delta Phi. Episcopalian. Oil and gas leasing, General practice, Federal civil litigation. Home: 107 Carmel Dr E Mobile AL 36608 Office: 2 N Royal St Mobile AL 36601

LYONS, KEVIN W., lawyer; b. Peoria, Ill., Sept. 16, 1956; s. William C. and Mary Belle (Harrison) L. BA, Judson Coll., 1977; JD, Drake U., 1981. Bar: Ill. 1981, U.S. Dist. Ct. (cen. dist.) Ill. 1984, U.S. Ct. Appeals (7th cir.) 1984. Law clk. Iowa Atty. Gen.'s Office, Des Moines, 1979-80; law clk. to chief judge 10th cir. Ill. Trial Ct., Peoria, 1980; sole practice Peoria, 1981—; asst. pub. defender County of Peoria, 1981—. Bd. trustees Village of Hanna City, Ill., 1981-82; sec. Farmington East (Ill.) Bd. of Edn. Dist. #324, 1981—; trustee Judson Coll., Elgin, Ill., 1986—, Village of Hanna City; pres. Farmington Dist. Bd. of Edn., 1987—. Mem. ABA, Ill. Bar Assn., Peoria County Bar Assn., Christian Legal Soc. Baptist. Avocations: golfing, writing. Criminal, Personal injury, General practice. Home: 110 Lakeshore Dr Hanna City IL 61536 Office: 619 First National Bank Bldg Peoria IL 61602

LYONS, KIRK MATTHEW, lawyer; b. Brockton, Mass., Jan. 27, 1954; m. Ann. C. Warren, Aug. 22, 1981. BS in Marine Transp., Mass. Maritime Acad., 1977; JD, New Eng. Sch. Law, 1981. Bar: Mass. 1981, Pa. 1981, U.S. Ct. Appeals (3d cir.) 1982, N.Y. 1985, U.S. Dist. Ct. (so. and ea. dists.) N.Y. 1985, U.S. Dist. Ct. Conn. 1985. Assoc. Palmer, Biezup & Henderson, Phila., 1981-84, Walker & Corsa, N.Y.C., 1984—. Mem. Maritime Law Assn. U.S. Avocations: running, golf. Admiralty. Office: Walker & Corsa 40 Wall St New York NY 10005

LYONS, LAURIE WILKINSON, lawyer; b. Shreveport, La., Apr. 25, 1954; d. Charlton Havard and Susybelle (Wilkinson) L.; m. Henry Clay Walker, May 25, 1985; stepchildren: Marian Grey Walker, Henry Clay Walker V.; 1 child, Alston Lyons Walker. BA with distinction, Rhodes Coll., 1976; JD, U. San Francisco, 1981. Bar: U.S. Dist. Ct. (we. dist.) La. 1982, U.S. Dist. Ct. (ea. dist.) Tex. 1983, U.S. Ct. Appeals (5th cir.) 1983. Assoc. Walker, Feazel & Tooke, Shreveport, 1982-83, Walker, Feazel, Tooke, Grubb & Perlman, Shreveport, 1983-84; assoc. Walker, Tooke, Grubb, Perlman & Lyons, Shreveport, 1984-85, ptnr., 1985—. Chairperson La. Choice, Shreveport, 1986—; bd. dirs. North La. Women's Polit. Fund, Shreveport, 1986—, ACLU, Shreveport, 1987—. Mem. ABA, La. Bar Assn., Assn. Trial Lawyers Am., La. Trial Lawyers Assn., Shreveport Assn. Women Attys. (pres. 1984-85), La. Assn. Women Attys. Democrat. Mem. Unitarian Ch. Avocations: swimming, tennis, skiing, scuba diving, reading. Civil rights, Federal civil litigation, Personal injury. Office: Walker Tooke Perlman & Lyons 1700 Irving Pl Shreveport LA 71106

LYONS, M. ARNOLD, lawyer, educator; b. Mpls., June 3, 1911; S. Simon Harry and Sarah (Schoenberger) Labovitz; m. Vera Nissenson Dec. 22, 1935; children: David, Barbara, Lisa. BA, U. Minn., 1932, JD, 1934. Bar: Minn. 1934, U.S. Dist. Ct. Minn. 1935, U.S. Ct. Appeals (8th cir.) 1938, U.S. Tax Ct. 1941, U.S. Supreme Ct. 1948. Ptnr. Robins, Zelle, Larson & Kaplan and predecessor firm Robins, Davis & Lyons, Mpls., 1938—; prof. law U. Minn., Mpls., 1974-76, Hamline U., St. Paul, 1975-85. Co-author: Stein on Probate, 1986. Mem. ABA, Minn. Bar Assn., Hennepin County Bar Assn, Am. Judicature Soc., Am. Arbitration Assn. (nat. panel). Lodges: Masons, Shriners. Avocations: fishing, biking, boating, gardening. Probate, Personal injury, General corporate. Home: 1235 Yale Pl #709 Minneapolis MN 55403 Office: Robins Zelle Larson & Kaplan 900 2d Ave S 1800 Internat Centre Minneapolis MN 55402

LYONS, NANCE, lawyer; b. Boston, Mar. 8, 1943; d. Dr. Timothy F.P. and Ann (Doherty) Lyons. BA, Boston Coll., 1964; JD cum laude, Suffolk U., 1977. Bar: Mass. 1977, U.S. Dist. Ct. Mass. 1977. Legis. and adminstrv. asst. to Sen. Edward M. Kennedy Washington, 1967-70; sole practice Boston, 1977-86; atty. Comras & Jackman, Boston, 1986—. asst. commr. Addiction Services Agy., N.Y.C., 1972-73, spl. corp. counsel City of Boston, 1977-82. Mem. ABA (legis. subcom. 1985—), Mass. Bar Assn. (legis. subcom., civil litigation sect.), Boston Bar Assn., Mass. Assn. Women Lawyers (bd. dirs. 1984—, chmn. legis. com. 1985—), Assn. Trial Lawyers Am., Mass. Acad. Trial Attys. (gov. 1987—). Democrat. Contracts commercial, Employment disputes, Administrative and regulatory. Office: Comras & Jackman 28 State St Boston MA 02109

LYONS, WILLIAM DREWRY, lawyer; b. Cresco, Iowa, Oct. 10, 1927; s. Gerald Edward and Florence (Drewry) L.; m. Elizabeth K. Kane, July 18, 1953; children—Catherine L., William Drewry Jane L., Judd H., Mary C. B.S.L., U. Minn., 1950, J.D., 1952, C.P.C.U., 1962. Bar: Minn. 1952, Iowa 1952, Nebr. 1974. Sole practice, Cresco, Iowa, 1952-56; asst. supt. claims Nat. Indemnity Co., Omaha, 1956-58; br. claim mgr. Nat. Indemnity Co., St. Paul, 1958-71, v.p., claim mgr., gen. counsel, Omaha, 1971—; v.p. Nat. Fire & Marine Ins. Co., Columbia Ins. Co.; dir. Gateway Underwriters Agy., Inc., Home and Automobile Ins. Co., Nat. Indemnity Co., Nat. Fire & Marine Ins. Co., Excess and Surplus Lines Claim Assn. Served with USN, 1945-46. Mem. Nebr. Bar Assn., Omaha Bar Assn., Internat. Assn. Ins. Counsel, Central Claims Assn., Excess and Surplus Lines Assn., Nebr. Claims Assn., ABA. Democrat. Roman Catholic. Insurance, General corporate. Home: 6405 Country Squire Ln Omaha NE 68152 Office: 4016 Farnam St Omaha NE 68131

LYONS, WILLIAM HARRY, legal educator; b. Fitchburg, Mass., Mar. 5, 1947; s. William Earl and Jeanette Underwood (Weed) L.; m. Karen Virginia Knapp, June 27, 1970; children: Virginia Lynne, Kevin Michael. BA, Colby Coll., Waterville, Maine, 1969; JD, Boston Coll., 1973. Bar: Maine 1973, Mass. 1973, U.S. Dist. Ct. Maine 1974, Nebr. 1985, U.S. Dist. Ct. Nebr. 1986, U.S. Tax Ct. 1986. Assoc. firm Vafiades, Brountas & Kominsky, Bangor, Maine, 1973-80, ptnr., 1980-81; prof. law U. Nebr., Lincoln, 1981—; mem. planning com. Gt. Plains Fed. Tax Inst., Lincoln, 1982—; mem. adv. com. Gt. Plains Studies, Lincoln, 1983—; prof. in residence IRS, 1987-88. Articles editor The Tax Lawyer, 1982-85; contbr. articles to law rev. Tax adviser Lincoln Nonprofit Devel. Corp., Lincoln, 1983—. Recipient Disting. Teaching award Nebr. U. Found., Lincoln, 1984, Student Bar Assn. U. Nebr.-Lincoln Coll. Law, 1984, 85. Mem. ABA (group editor taxation newsletter sect. 1986—), Mass. Bar Assn, Maine State Bar Assn., Nebr. State Bar Assn., Am. Judicature Soc., Delta Theta Phi. Democrat. Corporate taxation, Personal income taxation, General corporate. Home: 6208 Skylark Ln Lincoln NE 68516 Office: Univ Nebr Coll Law 40th and Holdrege Sts Lincoln NE 68583-0902

LYSAGHT, JAMES IGNATIUS, lawyer, judge; b. N.Y.C., Oct. 2, 1924; s. James Joseph and Mary (Quigley) L.; m. Helen Agnes, Nov. 28, 1946; 1 son, James John, LL.B., St. John's U., 1950. Bar: N.Y. 1950. With staff loan closing dept. Nat. City Bank, N.Y.C., 1950-52; assoc. Alexander & Keenan, N.Y.C., 1952-54; mem. Hartsell, Harrington, Jacobs & Lysaght, N.Y.C., 1954-60; trial atty., head legal dept. New Amsterdam & U.S. Casualty Ins. Co., N.Y.C., 1960-63; sole practice, N.Y.C., 1963-80; ptnr. Lysaght, Lysaght & Kramer, Mineola, N.Y., 1980—; village judge Valley Stream (N.Y.). Served with AUS, 1943-46. Mem. N.Y. State Bar Assn., N.Y. County Lawyers Assn., Nassau County Bar Assn., N.Y. State Magistrates Assn. Republican. Roman Catholic. Club: Elks (Valley Stream). Personal injury. Home: 17 Derby St Valley Stream NY 11581 Office: 1565 Franklin Ave Mineola NY 11501

LYSAUGHT, PATRICK, lawyer; b. Kansas City, Kans., Sept. 12, 1949; s. Mathew Aloysius and Loretta Rose (Storen) L.; m. Patricia Caspar, June 27, 1970; children: Geoffrey James, Kevin Michael. BA, Creighton U., 1971, postgrad. Law Sch., 1971; JD with distinction, U. Mo., 1974. Bar: Mo. 1975, U.S. Dist. Ct. (we. dist.) Mo. 1975, U.S. Ct. Appeals (8th cir.) 1975. Law clk. to chief judge U.S. Dist. Ct. (we. dist.) Mo., Kansas City, 1975-76; assoc., then shareholder firm Jackson & Sherman, P.C., Kansas City, Mo., 1976-83; v.p., bd. dirs. Sherman, Wickens, Lysaught & Speck, P.C., Kansas City, Mo., 1983—; bd. dirs. Western Mo. Def. Lawyers, 1985—. Author: Techniques in the Use and Management of Demonstrative Evidence, 1984. Mem. ABA (antitrust-civil practice com.), Kansas City Bar Assn. (fed. practice com.), Mo. Orgn. Def. Lawyers (charter), Internat. Assn. Def. Counsel (govtl. and civil rights com., products liability com.), Am. Bd. Trial Advocates, Mo. Orgn. Def. Lawyers, Inter. Assn. Def. Counsel (products liability com., civil rights com.), Def. Research Inst. (products liability and profl. liability coms.), Leawood Country Manor Homes Assn. (bd. dirs., v.p.), Phi Kappa Psi. Roman Catholic. Antitrust, Federal civil litigation, State civil litigation. Office: Sherman Wickens Lysaught & Speck PC 12th and Baltimore PO Box 26530 Top of City Ctr Sq Kansas City MO 64196

LYTHCOTT, STEPHEN XAVIER, lawyer; b. Boston, Aug. 2, 1950; s. George Ignatius and Ruth Louise (Andrade) L. B.A., Antioch Coll., Yellow Springs, Ohio, 1973; J.D., U. Wis., 1978. Bar: Wis. 1978, Ill. 1978, U.S. Dist. Ct. (no. dist.) Ill. 1978. Personnel specialist Fed. Govt., Washington, 1973-75; intern So. Regional Council, Atlanta, 1976; legal research asst. Wis. Legis. Council, Madison, 1976-78; staff atty. Legal Assistance Found. Chgo., 1978-82; adminstrv. law judge Ill. Human Rights Commn., Chgo., 1982-86; hearing officer Ill. Local Relations Labor Bd., Chgo., 1986; assoc. Watt & Thompson, Chgo., 1986—. Del., Nat. Black Polit. Conv., Gary, Ind., 1972. Recipient Minority Alumni of Yr. award U. Wis. Law Sch., Madison, 1983; fellow Joint Ctr. Polit. Studies, Washington, 1971. Mem. Ill. Jud. Council, Am. Judicature Soc., ABA, Chgo. Bar Assn., Cook County Bar Assn. Democrat. Labor, Administrative and regulatory. Home: 840 W Belle Plaine Chicago IL 60613 Office: Watt & Thompson 400 S Dearborn Suite 500 Chicago IL 60605

MAAS, JOHN EDWARD, lawyer; b. St. Louis, July 9, 1950; s. John Edward Sr. and Elizabeth Jean (Dangerfield) M. BA, U. Colo., 1976, JD, 1980. Bar: Colo. 1980, U.S. Dist. Ct. Colo. 1980, U.S. Ct. Appeals (10th cir.) 1980. Dep. dist. atty. Boulder County, Colo., 1980-81; assoc. Miller & Gray, Boulder, Colo., 1981-82; asst. U.S. atty. Dept. of Justice, Washington, 1982-83; assoc. Roath & Brega, Denver, 1984-86, dir., 1986—. Mem. ABA, Colo. Bar Assn., Denver Bar Assn. Bankruptcy, Contracts commercial, Banking. Office: Roath & Brega 1700 Lincoln Suite 2222 Denver CO 80203

MABE, HUGH PRESCOTT, III, lawyer; b. San Antonio, Sept. 28, 1945; s. Hugh Prescott and Maxine (Edwards) M.; m. Suzanne Marie White, Dec. 18, 1982. B.B.A., U. Okla., 1967; J.D., U. Tex., 1970. Trial atty. Dept. Justice, Washington, 1971-78; asst. U.S. atty. Office U.S. Atty. Dept. Justice, St. Thomas, V.I., 1978-82, U.S. atty., 1982-83, asst. U.S. atty., 1983—. Served to 1st lt. U.S. Army, 1970. Recipient Spl. Achievement award Atty. Gen., 1982. Mem. Tex. Bar Assn., V.I. Bar Assn. Episcopalian.

MABEY, RALPH RAMPTON, lawyer, educator; b. Salt Lake City, May 20, 1944; s. Rendell N. and Rachel (Wilson) M.; m. Sylvia States, June 5, 1968; children: Rachel, Elizabeth, Emily, Sara. BA, U. Utah, 1968; JD, Columbia U., 1972; student U. Basle (Switzerland), winter 1966. Bar: Utah 1972, N.Y. 1985, U.S. Dist. Ct. Utah 1972, U.S. Ct. Appeals (10th cir.) 1976. Law clk. to atty. gen. Utah, 1970; summer assoc. Willkie, Farr & Gallager, N.Y.C., 1971; law clk. to judge U.S. Dist. Ct. Utah, 1972-73; ptnr. Irvine, Smith & Mabey, Salt Lake City, 1973-79; judge U.S. Bankruptcy Ct. Dist. Utah, 1979-83; ptnr. LeBoeuf, Lamb, Leiby & MacRae, Salt Lake City, 1983—; asst. prof. mgmt. and bus. law Coll. and Grad. Sch. Bus., U. Utah, 1976-79, adj. asst. prof., 1979-84, adj. prof. law, 1984—; adj. prof. law Brigham Young U., 1984—. Mng. editor Norton's Bankruptcy Law Adviser, 1983-85; contbg. author: Collier on Bankruptcy. Served with USAR, 1968-74. Mem. Nat. Bankruptcy Conf. Bankruptcy, Federal civil litigation, Contracts commercial. Office: 1000 Kearns Bldg 136 S Main St Salt Lake City UT 84101

MACARTHUR, JOHN P., lawyer; b. Buffalo, Aug. 24, 1929; s. Charles P. and Katheryn (Carpenter) MacA.; m. Katharine Buckland, Mar. 23, 1957; children: Linda, James, William, Robert. AB, Yale U., 1952; LLB, U. Buffalo, 1956. Bar: N.Y. 1956, U.S. Dist. Ct. (we. dist.) N.Y. 1957, U.S. Dist. Ct. (so. and ea. dists.) N.Y. 1964, U.S. Ct. Appeals (2d cir.) 1958, U.S. Supreme Ct. 1974, U.S. Dist. Ct. (no. dist.) N.Y. 1975. Sole practice Buffalo, 1956-58; asst. U.S. atty. We. Dist. N.Y., Buffalo, 1958-60; asst. counsel N.Y. State Thruway Authority, Albany, 1960-61; asst. atty. gen. State of N.Y., Albany, 1961-62; sole practice Albany, 1962—. Mem. N.Y. State Bar Assn. Office: 284 State St Albany NY 12210

MACCALLUM, JAMES JUDSON, lawyer; b. Charleston, W.Va., Apr. 14, 1945; s. Oldrick Daniel and Arlene Olive (Barnette) MacC.; m. Sandra Suzanne Whitehouse, June 7, 1969; children—Katherine Jordan, Judson Campbell. A.B., Marshall U., 1968, M.A. in Polit. Sci., 1973; J.D., W.Va. U., 1977. Bar: W.Va. 1977, U.S. Dist. Ct. (so. dist.) W.Va. 1977, U.S. Dist. Ct. (no. dist.) W.Va. 1982. Assoc. Shaffer, Theibert, Ikner & Schlaegel, Madison, W.Va., 1977-79; ptnr. Shaffer & Shaffer, Madison, 1979—; bd. govs. W.Va. State Bar, Charleston, 1984—; pres. Boone County Bar, Madison, 1980-83. Mem. Boone County Parks and Recreation Commn., Madison, 1983-84; pres. Appalachian Community Theater, Madison, 1980-84; mem. Boone County Bd. Edn., Madison, 1984—, pres., 1986—; bd. dirs. Boone County United Way, 1987—. Served with USN, 1968-72. Mem. Internat. Assn. Arson Investigators (bd. dirs. W.Va. chpt. 1983—), Def. Research Inst., W.Va. Bar Assn., ABA. Democrat. Methodist. Lodge: Rotary. Federal civil litigation, Insurance, Personal injury. Office: PO Box 38 330 State St Madison WV 25130

MACCARINI, ANTHONY GEORGE, lawyer; b. Mt. Kisco, N.Y., May 5, 1948; s. Dominic Joseph and Clara M. (Jurdy) M. BS, Boston Coll., 1970; JD, St. John's, 1974. Bar: N.Y. 1975, U.S. Supreme Ct. 1978. Law clk. to presiding justice Putnam County Family Surrogate Ct., Carmel, N.Y., 1975-77; dep. atty. County of Putnam, Carmel, 1978-79, atty., 1979-81; assoc. counsel N.Y. State Assembly, Albany, 1981—; ptnr. Maccarini & Lusardi, Carmel, 1982—. Chmn. Putnam County United Way, Brewster, N.Y. 1985—; bd. dirs. Putnam Arts Council, Mahopac, N.Y., 1979—, Putnam Home Care Council, Carmel, 1983-86. Mem. N.Y. State Bar Assn., Putnam County Bar Assn. (sec., treas. 1975-77). Democrat. Lodge: Rotary (pres. Carmel 1982-83). Avocations: travel, gardening, cooking. Real property, Probate, Contracts commercial. Home: Kelley Rd Carmel NY 10512 Office: Maccarini & Lusardi Rt 52 Carmel NY 10512

MACCARTHY, TERENCE (F.), lawyer, defender; b. Chgo., Feb. 5, 1934; s. Frank E. and Catherine (McIntyre) MacC.; m. Marian Fulton, Nov. 25, 1961; children—Daniel Fulton, Sean Patrick, Terence Fulton, Megan Catherine. B.A. in Philosophy, St. Joseph's Coll., 1955; J.D., DePaul U., 1960. Bar: Ill. 1960, U.S. Dist. Ct. (no. dist.) Ill. 1961, U.S. Ct. Appeals (7th cir.) 1961, U.S. Supreme Ct. 1966. Assoc. prof. law Chase Coll. Law, Cin., 1960-61; law clk. to chief judge U.S. Dist. Ct., 1961-66; spl. asst. atty. gen. Ill., 1965-67; exec. dir. Fed. Defender Program, U.S. Dist. Ct. (no. dist.) Ill., Chgo., 1966—; mem. nat. adv. com. on criminal rules; 7th cir. criminal jury instrn. com.; chmn. Nat. Defender Com.; chmn. bd. regents Nat. Coll. Criminal Def.; faculty Fed. Jud. Ctr., Nat. Coll. Criminal Def., Nat. Inst. Trial Advocacy, U. Va. Trial Advocacy Inst., We. Trial Advocacy Inst., Northwestern U., U. Ill. Defender Trial Advocacy course, Loyola U. Trial Advocacy Program; lectr. in field. Contbr. articles on criminal law to profl. jours. Bd. dirs. U.S.O. Served as 1st lt. USMC, 1955-57. Named one of Ten Outstanding Young Men Chgo. Jr. Assn. Commerce, 1969, Outstanding Young Men of Am., 1970; NIADA & ABA Reginald Heber Smith award 1986; recipient St. Joseph Coll. Alumni Merit award, 1970; U.S.O. Cert. of Distinction, 1977. Fellow Am. Bar Found.; mem. ABA (standing com. on standards for criminal justice, vice chmn. council criminal justice sect.), Ill. Bar Assn., Chgo. Bar Assn., 7th Cir. Bar Assn., Nat. Assn. Criminal Def. Attys. (dir.), Nat. Legal Air and Defender Assn. (Reginald Heber Smith 1986). Democrat. Roman Catholic. Club: Union League of Chgo. (pres.). Criminal. Office: US Dist Ct Fed Defender Program 219 S Dearborn St Suite 1142 Chicago IL 60604

MACCHIA, VINCENT MICHAEL, lawyer; b. Bklyn., Dec. 30, 1933; s. Vincent and Lina Rose (Celli) M.; m. Irene Janet Audino, Feb. 27, 1965; children—Lauren, Michele, Michael. B.S., Fordham U., 1955, LL.B., 1958; LL.M., NYU, 1967. Bar: N.Y. 1958. Assoc., Bernard Remsen Millham & Bowdish, N.Y.C., 1959-60; atty. Equity Corp., N.Y.C., 1961-63, Pfizer Inc., N.Y.C., 1964, Trans World Airlines, Inc., N.Y.C., 1964-66; mem. Gifford, Woody, Palmer & Serles, N.Y.C., 1966-85, Townley & Updike, N.Y.C., 1985—; dir. Hudson Rev., Inc. Served with USAR, 1958-64. Mem. ABA, N.Y. State Bar Assn. Republican. Roman Catholic. Club: Shenorock Shore (Rye, N.Y.). Mem. editorial staff Fordham Law Rev., 1956-58. Corporate taxation, Estate taxation, Personal income taxation. Home: 4 Greentree Dr Scarsdale NY 10583 Office: 405 Lexington Ave New York NY 10174

MACCORD, HOWARD ARTHUR, JR., lawyer; b. Dayton, Ky., Aug. 10, 1950; s. Howard Arthur Sr. and Elsie Mae (Brunner) MacC.; m. Alison Blake, Jan. 8, 1983. BA with distinction, U. Va., 1972; JD, George Washington U., 1978. Bar: D.C. 1978. Assoc. Beveridge, DeGrandi & Kline, Washington, 1978-84; asst. patent counsel Burlington Industries Inc.,

Greensboro, N.C., 1984—. Pres. Glencourse Cluster Assn., Reston, Va., 1980-84. Mem. ABA, N.C. Bar Assn., Carolina Patent, Trademark & Copyright Law Assn., Nat. Council Patent Law Assn., Am. Intellectual Property Law Assn. Patent, Trademark and copyright. Home: 4 Hobbs Pl Greensboro NC 27403 Office: Burlington Industries Inc PO Box 21207 Greensboro NC 27420

MACCRATE, ROBERT, lawyer; b. Bklyn., July 18, 1921; s. John and Flora (MacNicholl) MacC.; m. Constance Trapp, May 4, 1946; children: Christopher Robert, Barbara Constance MacCrate Gatti, Thomas John. B.A., Haverford Coll., 1943, LLD (hon.), 1987; LL.B., Harvard U., 1948; LL.D. (hon.), Union U., 1986, Haverford Coll., 1987. Bar: N.Y. 1949, U.S. Supreme Ct. 1955, D.C. bar 1965. Asso. firm Sullivan & Cromwell, N.Y.C., 1948-51, 51-55; partner Sullivan & Cromwell, 1956-59, 62—; law sec. to N.Y.Appelate Div. Presding Justice David W. Peck, 1951; counsel to N.Y. Gov. Nelson A. Rockefeller, 1959-62; spl. counsel to U.S. Army for Investigation Mylai incident, 1969-70; counsel N.Y. State Ct. on Judiciary, 1971; mem. jud. selection com. for fed. judgeships Senator Jacob K. Javits, 1972-80; mem. jud. nominating com. N.Y. 2d Jud. Dept., 1975-82; trustee Lawyers Com. for Civil Rights Under Law, 1976—; chmn. emeritus Fund for Modern Cts., 1978—. Co-author Appellate Justice in New York, 1982; Contbr. articles to profl. jours. Bd. mgrs. Haverford Coll., 1971-85, emeritus 1986—. Served to lt. USNR, 1943-46. Fellow Am. Bar Found. (chmn. N.Y. state 1973-80); mem. Am. Bar Assn. (pres. 1987—, del. 1972-78, N.Y. State del. 1979-81, bd. govs. 1981-84, 2d circuit mem. standing com. on fed. judiciary 1984-86), N.Y. State Bar Assn. (pres. 1972-73, del. 1972—), Assn. Bar City N.Y. (v.p. 1969-71, chmn. exec. com. 1968-69, chmn. library com. 1977-80), N.Y. County Lawyers Assn., D.C. Bar Assn., Am. Coll. Trial Lawyers, Am. Soc. Internat. Law (exec. council 1975-80), Union Internationale des Avocats, Acad. Polit. Sci. (dir. 1975—), Am. Judicature Soc. (pres. 1979-81, dir. and mem. exec. com. 1974-83), Practising Law Inst. (trustee and mem. exec. com. 1972—), Am. Law Inst. (exec. com. council 1975—), N.Y. Bar Found. (pres. 1976—), Phi Beta Kappa. Federal civil litigation, Antitrust, State civil litigation. Home: 40 The Terrace Plandome NY 11030 Office: 125 Broad St New York NY 10004 also: 1775 Pennsylvania Ave Washington DC 20006 also: American Bar Ctr 750 N Lake Shore Dr Chicago IL 60611

MACCRINDLE, ROBERT ALEXANDER, lawyer; b. Glasgow, UK, Jan. 27, 1928; s. Fergus Robertson and Jean (Hull) MacC.; m. Pauline Dilys, Aug. 18, 1959; children: Guy Stephen, Claire. LLB, U. London, 1948; LLM, U. Cambridge, 1952. Bar: Eng. and Whales 1952, Hong Kong 1965. Barrister City of London, 1952-76; ptnr. Shearman & Sterling, N.Y.C., 1976—; Queen's counsel City of London, 1963; consiel juridique Frace, 1978—; internat. arbitrator, 1963—. Served to flight lt. RAF, 1948-50. Fellow Am. Coll. Trial Lawyers. Club: University (N.Y.C.). Avocation: golf. Contracts commercial, Insurance, Arbitration. Home: 88 Ave de Breteuil, Paris 75015, France Office: Shearman & Sterling, 21 Ave George V, Paris 75008, France

MAC DONALD, ALAN DOUGLAS, lawyer; b. Springfield, Mass., Oct. 23, 1939; s. Alexander Stuart and Josephine Ann (Czaja) MacD.; m. Jill Nickerson, May 20, 1978. B.S.S., Fairfield U., 1961; M.B.A., U. Mass., 1963; B.C.L., Coll. William and Mary, 1966. Bar: Va. 1966, N.Y. 1967, Ill. 1974. Asso. firm Carter, Ledyard & Milburn, N.Y.C., 1966-71; v.p. law dept., sr. staff counsel Motorola, Inc., Schaumburg, Ill., 1972-80; v.p., gen. counsel, sec. Ex-Cell-O Corp., Troy, Mich., 1980—. Mem. Am. Bar Assn. Machinery and Allied Products Inst. Office: Ex-Cell-O Corp 2855 Coolidge Rd Troy MI 48084

MACDONALD, JOSEPH J., lawyer. m. Catherine Alexander; children: Joseph Anthony, Diane Alexa. LLB, Fordham U., 1956. Bar: N.Y. 1957, N.J. 1958. Sr. ptnr. MacDonald, Jaekel, Seavers & Ford, Ridgewood, N.J., 1980—. Served to 1st lt. U.S. Army, 1950-53, Korea. Mem. ABA, N.Y. County Lawyers Assn. Trademark and copyright, Computer, Libel. Office: MacDonald Jaekel Seavers & Ford 113 Prospect St Box 683 Ridgewood NJ 07451

MACDONALD, RICHARD BARRY, lawyer; b. Hartford, Conn., Aug. 15, 1950; s. Robert James and Margie Juanita (Backes) MacD.; m. Barbara Arlene Breighner, Dec. 15, 1979; children: Miles Trevor, Morgan Michele. AA, Manchester (Conn.) Community Coll., 1974; BA, Colo. Coll., 1976; JD, Willamette U., 1979. Bar: Oreg. 1979, Pa. 1980, U.S. Dist. Ct. (ea. and cen. dists.) Pa. 1983, U.S. Supreme Ct. Assoc. Krank, Gross & Casper, Lancaster, Pa., 1981-84; sole practice Lancaster, 1984—. Bd. dirs. Boy Scout Law and Politics Explorers, Lancaster, 1984-85. Served to sgt. USAF, 1968-71, Vietnam. Mem. Lancaster County Bar Assn. (fin. com., law office econ. com., del. young lawyers div. 1983-86), Phi Delta Phi. Republican. Methodist. Avocations: sports, chess, reading, travel, cultural activities. State civil litigation, Family and matrimonial, General practice. Home and Office: 312 W Orange St Lancaster PA 17603

MACDONALD, THOMAS COOK, JR., lawyer; b. Atlanta, Oct. 11, 1929; s. Thomas Cook and Mary (Morgan) MacD.; m. Gay Anne Everiss, June 30, 1956; children: Margaret Anne, Thomas William. B.S. with high honors, U. Fla., 1951, LL.B. with high honors, 1953. Bar: Fla. 1953. Practice law Tampa, 1953—; mem. firm Shackleford, Farrior, Stallings & Evans, 1953—; dir. Jim Walter Corp.; legis. counsel Gov. of Fla., 1963; del. 5th Circuit Jud. Conf., 1970-81. Mem. Fla. Student Scholarship and Loan Commn., 1963-67, Fla. Jud. Qualifications Commn., 1983—, vice chmn., 1987—; bd. dirs. Univ. Community Hosp. Tampa, 1968-78; Mem. Hillsborough County Pub. Edn. Study Commn., 1965; lic. lay reader Episcopal Ch., 1961—, participant Cursillo and Kairos movements; bd. dirs. U. Fla. Found., 1978-86, Shands Teaching Hosp., U. Fla., 1981—; pres. U. Fla. Nat. Alumni Assn., 1973. Served to 1st lt., JAGD USAF, 1953-55. Recipient Disting. Alumnus award U. Fla., 1976. Fellow Am. Coll. Trial Lawyers, Am. Bar Found.; mem. ABA (com. on ethics and profl. responsibility 1970-76), Am. Law Inst., Fla. Bar (chmn. com. profl. ethics 1966-70, bd. govs. 1970-74, bar mem. Supreme Ct. com. on standards conduct governing judges 1976), 11th Circuit Hist. Soc. (trustee 1982—), Phi Kappa Phi, Phi Delta Phi, Fla. Blue Key, Kappa Alpha. Episcopalian. Federal civil litigation, State civil litigation. Home: 1904 Holly Ln Tampa FL 33629 Office: PO Box 3324 Tampa FL 33601

MACDOUGALL, WILLIAM RODERICK, lawyer, county official; b. Nevada City, Calif., May 14, 1914; s. William Stewart and Ethel Martha (Hutchison) McDougall; m. Carol Bernie Keane, May 1, 1937; children—Marcia MacDougall Williams, James Stewart. A.A., Sacramento City Coll., 1930-32; student U. Calif.-Berkeley, 1933-34; J.D., U. of Pacific, 1941. Bar: Calif. 1941, U.S. Dist. Ct. (no. dist.) Calif. 1941, U.S. Supreme Ct. 1950. Library page Calif. State Library, Sacramento, 1932-33; sr. auditor Office of Controller, State of Calif., Sacramento, 1934-37; chief bur. of collections Calif. Social Welfare Dept., Sacramento, 1937-42; gen. counsel County Suprs. Assn. Calif., Sacramento, 1946-70; exec. dir. U.S. Intergovt. Relations Commn., Washington, 1970-75; planning commr. County of Orange, Santa Ana, Calif., 1976-84; chief counsel Calif. Alcoholic Beverage Control Appeals Bd., 1984—; exec. dir. Calif. County Govt. Edn. Found., 1965-69; chmn. home rule com. Nat. Assn. Counties, 1963-67. Mem. Fed. Public Assistance Adv. Council, 1959-60, Gov.'s Commn. on Met. Problems, Calif., 1960; pres. Laguna Beach Sch. of Art (Calif.), 1983-84. Mem. Am. Planning Assn., Nat. Assn. County and Pros. Attys. (hon.), Calif. County Planning Commrs. Assn. (dir. 1981-84). Republican. Presbyterian. Local government, Environment. Office: 1001 6th St #401 Sacramento CA 95814-3324

MACFARLANE, ROBERT BRUCE, lawyer; b. Portsmouth, Eng., Jan. 29, 1896; s. Charles Stuart and Caroline (Capsey) M.; m. Rebecca Williams Fitzhugh, May 1, 1934; children—Mary Parke, Robert Bruce. J.D., U. Richmond, 1934. Bar: Va. 1932. Engrng. cons. Macfarlane & Sadler, Richmond, Va., 1938-60; sole practice law, Richmond, 1960-80; examiner U.S. Patent Office, Richmond, 1943-45. Mem. zoning appeals City Richmond, 1950-62, planning commn., 1954-62. Mem. Va. Bar Assn., Richmond Bar Assn. Club: Masons. General practice. Address: 406 Maple Ave Richmond VA 23226

MAC GOWAN, MARY EUGENIA, lawyer; b. Turlock, Calif., Aug. 4, 1928; d. William Ray and Mary Bolling (Gilbert) Kern; m. Gordon Scott Millar, Jan. 2, 1970; 1 dau., Heather Mary. A.B., U. Calif., Berkeley, 1950; J.D., U. Calif., San Francisco, 1953. Bar: Calif. bar. Research atty. Supreme Ct. Calif., 1954, Calif. Ct. Appeals, 1955; partner firm MacGowan & MacGowan, Calif., 1956-68; individual practice law San Francisco, 1968—. Bd. dirs. San Francisco Speech and Hearing Center, San Francisco Legal Aid Soc., J.A.C.K.I.E. Mem. Am., Calif., San Francisco bar assns., Queen's Bench. Clubs: San Francisco Lawyers, Forest Hill Garden. Family and matrimonial, Juvenile. Office: The Monadnock Suite 400 685 Market St San Francisco CA 94105

MACGREGOR, DAVID BRUCE, lawyer; b. Miami Beach, Fla., Feb. 21, 1953; s. Bruce Herbert and Mary Don (Doty) MacG.; m. Carol Louise Edler, Aug. 21, 1976; children: Meredith Elder, Christine Elder. BA magna cum laude, Bucknell U., 1975; JD magna cum laude, Georgetown U., 1978. Bar: Pa. 1978, U.S. Dist. Ct. (ea. dist.) Pa., U.S. Ct. Appeals (4th cir.). Law clk. to presiding justice U.S. Ct. Appeals (4th cir.), Richmond, Va., 1978-79; assoc. Morgan, Lewis & Bockius, Phila., 1979-85, ptnr., 1985—. Mem. ABA, Pa. Bar Assn., Phila. Bar Assn. Republican. Presbyterian. Avocation: golf. Public utilities, Environment, Health. Home: 620 Pembroke Rd Bryn Mawr PA 19010 Office: Morgan Lewis & Bockius 2000 One Logan Sq Philadelphia PA 19103

MACH, JOSEPH DAVID, lawyer; b. Bronx, N.Y., Nov. 3, 1944; s. Moses A. and Fanny (Schwartz) M.; m. Joan Maria Blassberg, June 16, 1968; children: Jeffrey Peter, Louis Wilson. BS in Econs., U. Pa., 1965, MS in Acctg., 1966; JD, Harvard U., 1969; LLM in Taxation, NYU, 1974. Bar: N.Y. 1970, U.S. Dist. Ct. (so. and ea. dists.) N.Y. 1971, U.S. Tax Ct. 1972. Assoc. Hellerstein, Rosier & Rembar, N.Y.C., 1969-71, Spear and Hill, N.Y.C., 1971; tax mgr. Richards, Ganly, Fries & Preusch, N.Y.C., 1971-74, Main Lafrentz & Co. (now Peat Marwick Main), N.Y.C., 1974-80; dir. tax planning, asst. tax treas. Becton Dickinson and Co., Franklin Lakes, N.J., 1980—. Contbg. editor (mag.) The Practical Accountant mag., 1976—; contbr. articles to profl. jours. Mem. Forum Sch. Parent's Assn., Waldwick, N.J. Mem. Am. Inst. CPA's, Tax Execs. Inst., N.Y. State CPA Soc. (pension com. 1975-80), N.J. State Soc. CPA's. Democrat. Jewish. Avocations: opera, family. Corporate taxation, Pension, profit-sharing, and employee benefits. Office: Becton Dickinson and Co One Becton Dr Franklin Lakes NJ 07417

MACHAN, MITCHELL ALAN, lawyer; b. Canton, Ohio, Dec. 3, 1955; s. Larry W. and Joyce A. (Ritzman) M. BA, Wittenberg U., 1978; JD, Akron U., 1981. Bar: Ohio 1981, U.S. Dist. Ct. (no. dist.) Ohio, 1984. Assoc. Day, Ketterer et al, Canton, Ohio, 1981-84, Amerman, Burt & Jones Co LPA, Canton, 1985—. Mem. ABA, Ohio Bar Assn., Stark County Bar assn., Canton Jaycees (cert. of merit 1985, 86). Republican. Avocations: golf, tennis. Family and matrimonial, Probate, Personal injury. Home: 263 Woodlawn NW Canton OH 44708 Office: Amerman Burt & Jones Co LPA 3848 Tuscarawas W Canton OH 44708

MACHLIN, MARC DAVID, lawyer; b. St. Louis, Apr. 8, 1957; s. Lawrence J. and Ruth (Beerman) M. AB magna cum laude, Brown U., 1978; JD cum laude, Harvard U., 1981. Bar: D.C. 1981, U.S. Dist. Ct. D.C. 1982, U.S. Ct. Appeals (3d and D.C. cirs.) 1982, U.S. Ct. Appeals (7th and 9th cirs.) 1984, U.S. Ct. Appeals (8th cir.) 1987. Assoc. Pepper, Hamilton & Scheetz, Washington, 1981—. Bd. editors Harvard U. Environ. Law Rev., 1980. Mem. Phi Beta Kappa. Avocations: tennis, squash. Administrative and regulatory, Public utilities, Environment. Home: 4604 Chestnut St Bethesda MD 20814 Office: Pepper Hamilton & Scheetz 1777 F St NW Washington DC 20006

MACHLOWITZ, DAVID STEVEN, lawyer; b. Phila., Jan. 23, 1954; s. Roy Alan and Eleanore (Levin) M.; m. Sheryl Lynn Steinberg, June 30, 1985. BA, U. Pa., 1974; JD, Yale U., 1977. Bar: Pa. 1977, U.S. Dist. Ct. (ea. dist.) Pa. 1977, N.Y. 1981, U.S. Dist. Ct. (so. and ea. dists.) N.Y. 1981, U.S. Ct. Appeals (2d cir.) 1981. Assoc. Ballard, Spahr, Andrews & Ingersoll, Phila., 1977-80, Christy & Viener, N.Y.C., 1981-85, Morrison, Cohen & Singer, N.Y.C., 1985-87; sr. atty. Gen. Instrument Corp., N.Y.C., 1987—. Mem. Assn. of Bar of City of N.Y. (fed. legis. com., author jour. 1981-85). Avocations: history, film, books, basketball. Federal civil litigation, Antitrust, Pension, profit-sharing, and employee benefits. Home: 301 E 87th St New York NY 10128 Office: Gen Instrument Corp 767 5th Ave New York NY 12121

MACIEL, RONALD JOHN, lawyer; b. Hanford, Calif., Nov. 25, 1943; s. John J. and Ludrie (Mendes) M.; m. Shirley Lucchesi, July 8, 1967; children: Virginia, Jennifer, Rosemarie. BS, UCLA, 1966; JD, Loyola U., Los Angeles, 1973. Bar: Calif. 1974, U.S. Tax Ct. 1980, U.S. Supreme Ct. 1981, U.S. Ct. Appeals (9th cir.) 1982. Agt., IRS, Los Angeles, 1966-76; sole practice law, Hanford, 1976—; pres. RJM Electronics, Inc. Mem. Kings County Cabillo Civic Club, Hanford; trustee Kings County Law Library. Mem. AAAS, N.Y. Acad. Scis., ABA, Fed. Bar Assn., Kings County Bar Assn., Am. Assn. Atty.-CPA's, Christian Legal Soc., Am. Film Inst. Tax planning or individual taxation, Corporate taxation, Probate. Office: 104 E 7th St Hanford CA 93230

MACIOCE, FRANK MICHAEL, JR., lawyer, financial services company executive; b. N.Y.C., Oct. 3, 1945; s. Frank Michael and Sylvia Maria (Morea) M.; children—Michael Peter, Lauren Decker. B.S., Purdue U., 1967; J.D., Vanderbilt U., 1972. Bar: N.Y. 1973, U.S. Dist. Ct. (so. dist.) N.Y. 1973, U.S. Ct. Appeals (2d cir.) 1975, U.S. Supreme Ct. 1976. Mem. law dept. Merrill Lynch, Pierce, Fenner & Smith Inc., N.Y.C., 1972-80, v.p., 1978—; mgr. corp. law dept. Merrill Lynch & Co., Inc., N.Y.C., 1980, asst. gen. counsel, 1982—, sec. of audit, compensation and nominating coms. bd. dirs., 1978-83, sec. exec. comm., 1981-83; mng. dir. Merrill Lynch Overseas Capital, N.V., Netherlands Antilles, 1980-85; sec., dir. Merrill Lynch Employees Fed. Credit Union, N.Y.C., 1978-82; dir. Merrill Lynch Pvt. Capital Inc., N.Y.C., 1981—. Served with U.S. Army, 1969-70. Mem. ABA, N.Y. State Bar Assn., Assn. Bar City N.Y., Chatham Fish and Game Protective Assn. General corporate, Securities. Home: 135 Pine Grove Ave Summit NJ 07901 Office: Merrill Lynch & Co Inc One Liberty Plaza 165 Broadway New York NY 10080

MACK, DENNIS WAYNE, lawyer, textile company executive; b. Chgo., Sept. 11, 1943; s. Walter Andrew and Betty Jane (Klimek) M. B.A., Yale U., 1965; J.D., Harvard U., 1969. Bar: N.Y. 1970. Assoc. firm Curtis Mallet-Prevost Colt & Mosle, N.Y.C. and Paris, 1969-78; sec., gen. counsel Dominion Textile (USA) Inc., N.Y.C., 1978—, v.p., 1986—. Mem. dept. fin. Presbytery N.Y., 1978-83. Mem. ABA, Textile Lawyers Assn., N.Y. State Bar Assn., Bar Assn. City N.Y. General corporate, Private international, Corporate taxation. Home: 180 Riverside Dr New York NY 10024 Office: 1040 Ave of the Americas New York NY 10018

MACK, JOHN OSCAR, lawyer; b. Columbus, Ohio, May 10, 1932; s. Eugene Henry and Eunice A. (Genthner) M.; m. Cristina Ann Iannone, Nov. 19, 1967; children—John Whitney, Elizabeth Ann, Andrew Laughlin. B.S. in Econs., U. Pa., 1954, LL.B. cum laude, 1961. Bar: Calif. 1962, U.S. Dist. Ct. (no. dist.) Calif. 1962, U.S. Supreme Ct. 1979, U.S. Ct. Appeals (9th cir.) 1981. Assoc. firm Pillsbury, Madison & Sutro, San Francisco, 1961-63; asst. v.p., sec. Bank of Calif. (N.A.), San Francisco, 1963-75, v.p., sec., 1972-75, BanCal Tri State Corp., 1972-75; practice law, San Francisco, 1976—; sr. mng. ptnr. firm Mack, Hazlewood, Franecke & Tinney, San Francisco, 1978—; gen. ptnr. Red Hills Investment Co., 1979—. Bd. dirs. Lone Mountain Children's Ctr., 1978-86, pres., 1973—. Served to lt. USNR, 1954-58. Republican. General corporate, Contracts commercial, Real property. Home: 2963 23d Ave San Francisco CA 94132 Office: Mack Hazlewood Franecke & Tinney 221 Pine St Suite 600 San Francisco CA 94104

MACK, THEODORE, lawyer; b. Fort Worth, Mar. 5, 1936; s. Henry and Norma (Harris) M.; m. Ellen F. Feinknopf, June 19, 1960; children—Katherine Norma, Elizabeth Ellen, Alexandra. A.B. cum laude, Harvard U., 1958, J.D., 1961. Bar: Tex. 1961, U.S. Sup. Ct. 1971, U.S. Ct. Apls. (5th cir.) 1967, U.S. Ct. Apls. (11th cir.) 1981, U.S. Dist. Ct. (no. dist.) Tex. 1961, U.S. Dist. Ct. (we. dist.) Tex. 1968, U.S. Dist. Ct. (so. dist.) Tex. 1968. Assoc., Mack & Mack, Ft. Worth, 1961-62, ptnr., 1963-70; ptnr. Wynn, Brown, Mack, Renfro & Thompson and predecessors, Ft. Worth, 1970—. Trustee Ft. Worth Country Day Sch., 1976-82; bd. dirs. Beth-El Congregation, 1964-73, 75-78, pres., 1975-77; bd. dirs. Jewish Fedn. Ft. Worth, 1965-72; mem. Leadership Ft. Worth, 1973-74; bd. dirs. Sr. Citizens Ctrs., Inc., 1969-81, Family and Individual Services, 1981-84 ; pres. Harvard Law Sch. Assn. Tex., 1976-77. Fellow Tex. Bar Found. (life); mem. Tex. Bar Assn., ABA, Ft. Worth-Tarrant County Bar Assn., Bar Assn. 5th Cir. Ct. Democrat. Jewish. Clubs: Colonial Country, Ft. Worth, City, Harvard (N.Y.C.). Bankruptcy, Antitrust, Federal civil litigation. Home: 2817 Harlanwood Dr Fort Worth TX 76109 Office: 1800 First City Bank Tower 201 Main St Fort Worth TX 76102-3186

MACKALL, HENRY CLINTON, lawyer; b. Ft. Lauderdale, Fla., Apr. 6, 1927; s. Douglass Sorrel and Mildred (Parker) M.; m. Mary Margaret Sullivan, June 21, 1952; children—Caroline Clark, Nancy Sorrel, Lucy Parker. B.A., U. Va., 1950, LL.B. 1952. Bar: Va. 1951. Ptnr. Mackall, Mackall, Walker & Silver, P.C. and predecessors, Fairfax, Va., 1952—; asst. commr. accounts Fairfax County (Va.); spl. commr. in chancery for audit functions for Cir. Ct. Fairfax County, 1976—; substitute judge Fairfax County Ct., Juvenile and Domestic Relations Ct. Fairfax County, 1964-69. Trustee, Fairfax Hosp. Assn., 1966-75; bd. dirs. Fairfax chpt. ARC. Served with AUS, 1945-46. Mem. ABA, Va. Bar Assn. (regional v.p. 1963-64), Va. State Bar Client Security Fund Bd. (chmn. 1977-78), Fairfax County Bar Assn. (pres. 1966-67), Am. Coll. Probate Counsel, Am. Coll. Real Estate Lawyers, Hist. Soc. Fairfax County (pres. 1970-72). Democrat. Episcopalian. Clubs: River Bend Country (pres. 1967-68) (Gt. Falls, Va.); Georgetown Assembly (Washington). Probate, Real property. Home: 1032 Towlston Rd McLean VA 22102 Office: 4031 Chain Bridge Rd Fairfax VA 22030

MAC KAY, DONALD M., lawyer; b. Cleve., Nov. 26, 1935; s. Ralph M. and Christine I. (Ingalls) M.; children: James, William. AB, Miami U., 1957; LLB, Ohio State U., 1961. Bar: Ohio 1962, Ill. 1963, U.S. Patent Office 1966, Pa. 1980. Patent atty. Successively Stauffer Chem. Co., Ferro Corp., PPG Industries, Inc., Xerox Corp., Gen. Electric Co., Koppers Co., Inc., Pitts.; sole practice Pitts. Mem. ABA, Pa. Bar Assn., Allegheny County Bar Assn., Am. Patent Lawyers Assn., Mensa. Office: Koppers Bldg Suite 1450 Pittsburgh PA 15219

MACKAY, JOHN NORMAN, lawyer; b. Rome, N.Y., Nov. 23, 1946; s. John Nye and Jeanne Maude (Sprangenburg) MacK.;. m. Linda Sue Sheldon, Aug. 30, 1968 (div. Sept. 1985); children: David Matthew, Mark Stanley. BA, U. Okla., 1968; JD summa cum laude, Ohio State U., 1975. Bar: Ohio 1975, U.S. Dist. Ct. (no. dist.) Ohio 1976. Assoc. Shumaker, Loop & Kendrick, Toledo, 1975-80, ptnr., 1980—. Served with USN, 1968-74. Mem. ABA, Ohio Bar Assn., Ohio Land Title Assn., Toledo Bar Assn. Presbyterian. Clubs: Toledo, Jolly Roger Sailing (Toledo); North Cape Yacht (LaSalle, Mich.). Contracts commercial, Consumer commercial, Real property. Office: Shumaker Loop & Kendrick 1000 Jackson Toledo OH 43624

MACKENZIE, RODERICK JOHN, JR., lawyer; b. Bridgeport, Conn., Oct. 12, 1946; s. Roderick John and Margaret (Lee) MacK.; B.B.A., Roanoke Coll., 1968; J.D., U. Miami (Fla.), 1971; m. Susan Lougheed, May 27, 1972; children—Meghan, Kate Shannon. Admitted to Fla. bar, 1972, Conn. bar, 1976, U.S. Dist. Ct. Conn. 1977; atty. VISTA, New Britain, Conn., 1971-73; legis. legal adv. Conn. Gen. Assembly, Hartford, 1973-75; employee relations mgr. Town of Greenwich (Conn.), 1976; assoc. Cutsumpas, Collins & Hannafin, Danbury, Conn., 1977-78; partner firm Nahoum and MacKenzie, Newtown, Conn., 1978-85; sole practice, Newtown, 1985—; dir. David H. MacKenzie, Inc.; vice chmn. bd. dirs. Children's Adventure Center, Inc., 1981-82. Parliamentarian exec. bd. Conn. Fedn. Young Republicans, 1972, atty., 1977-81; cons. New Britain (Conn.) Urban Renewal and Redevel. Projects, 1973; parliamentarian Town of Woodbury (Conn.) Town Meetings, 1974; chmn. Newtown Young Reps. Club, 1976-83; mem. Newtown Rep. Town Com., 1977-82, 84—, vice chmn., 1984—, parliamentarian, legal adv., 1978-82; mem. Newtown Legis. Council, 1978-84, minority leader, 1980-81, chmn., 1982-84; chmn. liturgy commn. St. Anthony's Ch., Danbury, Conn., 1985—. Mem. Am. Bar Assn. (Silver Key award, 1971, chmn. com. constitutionality of ordinance and adminstrv. regulations), Fla. Bar, Newtown Bar Assn., Assn. Trial Lawyers Am., Conn. Trial Lawyers Assn., Italian Club Am., Inc. (hon.). Roman Catholic. Lodges: Rotary (dir. 1979—, sec. 1981-84, 2d v.p. 1984-85, pres. 1985-86), Knights of Malta. Author articles. Personal injury, Family and matrimonial, Local government. Home: 6 Fox Run Ln Newtown CT 06470 Office: 87 S Main St Newtown CT 06470

MACKEY, BENJAMIN FRANKLIN, JR., lawyer, consultant; b. Little Rock, Jan. 26, 1931; s. Benjamin Franklin and Maxie (Walker) M.; m. Diane Stoakes, June 24, 1958; children: Benjamin Franklin III, Stuart Stoakes, Sarah Dryden. Student, Auburn U., 1948-50, U. Ark., Little Rock, 1955; JD, U. Ark., Little Rock, 1975; BA, Northwestern U., 1957. Bar: Ark. 1975, U.S. Dist. Ct. (ea. and we. dists.) Ark. 1975, U.S. Ct. Appeals (8th cir.) 1975. Personnel asst. brand mgmt. Proctor & Gamble, Cin., 1957-64; cons. Booz, Allen & Hamilton, Chgo., 1964; exec. asst. Ark. Power & Light, Little Rock, 1965-72; assoc. Spitzberg, Mitchell & Hays, Little Rock, 1975-77; sole practice Little Rock, 1977—. Bd. dirs., sec. Ingledwood Found., Little Rock, 1971—; mem. Little Rock Dist. Sch. bd., 1983-86, ct. of rev., Episc. Ch. Province VIII for the states of Ark., Kans., Mo., Okla., Tex., 1984—; pres. bd. dirs. U. Ark. for Med. Scis. Found., 1985—; pres. Ark. Community Found., Little Rock, 1985-86. Mem. ABA (various sects.), Ark. Bar Assn. (ho. of dels. 1981, ethics and grievances com. 1980-83, Meritorious Service award 1981), Pulaski County Bar Assn. (bd. dirs. 1982, Outstanding Contbn. award 1980). Democrat. Clubs: Little Rock Country, Little Rock. Avocations: travel, gardening, driving. Estate planning, General practice, Foundation law. Home: 5213 Grandview Rd Little Rock AR 72207 Office: 1030 Union Nat Plaza Little Rock AR 72201

MACKEY, RANDALL AUBREY, lawyer, educator; b. Salt Lake City, Dec. 1, 1945; s. Donald Aubrey and Marjorie (Warshaw) M.; m. Margaret Weilenman, Aug. 27, 1974; children: Marie, Katherine, Matthew, Sarah, Elizabeth, John, Marjorie. BS, U. Utah, 1968; MBA, Harvard U., 1970; JD, Columbia U., 1975; BCL, Oxford U., Eng., 1977. Bar: D.C. 1978. Legis. asst. to Congressman U.S. Ho. of Reps., Washington, 1970-71; mgmt. analyst HEW, Washington, 1971-72; assoc. Hogan & Hartson, Washington, 1978-79, Fabian & Clendenin, Salt Lake City, 1979-82; ptnr. Fabian & Clendein, Salt Lake City, 1982—; adj. prof. constl. law, internat. law U. Utah, Salt Lake City, 1981—; bd. dirs. Horn Silver Mines, Inc., Salt Lake City, Mansion Hotel Corp., Las Vegas, Nev. Mem. Utah Gov.'s Commn., Salt Lake City, 1984; chmn. issues and policy com. Utah Reps., Salt Lake City, 1985—, chmn. platform com., 1985—; bd. dirs. Utah Opera Co., Salt Lake City, 1981—; trustee dialogue A Jour. of Mormon Thought, Salt Lake City, 1982—. Mem. ABA, Utah Bar Assn., D.C. Bar Assn., Phi Beta Kappa, Oxford Soc. Republican. Mormon. Club: Alta (Salt Lake City). Avocations: reading, classical music, opera, basketball, tennis. General corporate, Securities, Banking. Home: 1474 Harvard Ave Salt Lake City UT 84105 Office: Fabian & Clendenin 215 S State St 12th Floor Salt Lake City UT 84111

MACKIEWICZ, EDWARD ROBERT, lawyer; b. Jersey City, July 2, 1951; s. Edward John and Irene Helen (Rakowicz) H. BA, Yale U., 1973; JD, Columbia U., 1976. Bar: N.J. 1976, U.S. Dist. Ct. N.J. 1976, N.Y. 1977, U.S. Dist. Ct. (so. and ea. dist.) N.Y. 1977, D.C. 1978, U.S. Dist. Ct. D.C. 1978, U.S. Ct. Appeals (D.C. cir.) 1978, U.S. Ct. Appeals (3d cir.) 1980, U.S. Supreme Ct. 1980, Md. 1984, U.S. Ct. Claims 1984, U.S. Ct. Appeals (4th cir.) 1986. Assoc. Carter, Ledyard & Milburn, N.Y.C., 1976-77, Covington & Burling, Washington, 1977-82; counsel for civil rights litigation solicitor's office U.S. Dept. Labor, Washington, 1982-83; sr. assoc. Jones, Day, Reavis & Pogue, Washington, 1983-85; gen. counsel Pension Benefit Guaranty Corp., Washington, 1985-87; of counsel Pierson, Ball & Dowd, Washington, 1987—. Mem. Am. Council Young Polit. Leaders (del. to Australia 1985). Clubs: Univ. (Washington), Yale (N.Y.C.). Pension, profit-sharing, and employee benefits, Labor, Bankruptcy. Home: 3001 Veazey Terr NW #1032 Washington DC 20008 Office: Pierson Ball & Dowd 1200 18th St NW Washington DC 20036

MACKINLAY, EDGAR HAROLD, lawyer; b. Everett, Pa., Sept. 16, 1936; s. Edgar Harold and Helene (Brown) MacK.; m. Julie Lawson Whitehurst, Aug. 1, 1964; children: Phoebe Virginia, Vanessa Juliet, Alexandra Lee,

Charlotte Campbell. BS, Washington and Lee U., 1958, LLB magna cum laude, 1964. Bar: N.Y. 1965, U.S. Dist. Ct. (so. dist.) N.Y. 1966, U.S. Ct. Appeals (2d cir.) 1966, Ohio 1971, Va. 1974, U.S. Dist. Ct. (ea. dist.) Va. 1975, U.S. Ct. Appeals (4th cir.) 1984. Assoc. Shearman & Sterling, N.Y.C., 1965-70; asst. counsel internat. Firestone Tire and Rubber Co., Akron, Ohio, 1970-71; ptnr. Buckingham, Doolittle & Burroughs, Akron, 1972-74; sole practice Norfolk, Va., 1974-81; ptnr. Hunton & Williams, Norfolk, 1981, Seawell, Dalton, Hughes & Timms, Norfolk, 1982-83; mem., pres. MacKinlay & Talbert, Norfolk, 1983—; bd. dirs. Am. GFM Corp., Williams Corp. Va. Editor in chief Washington and Lee Law Rev., 1964. Served to lt. USNR, 1958-62. Mem. ABA, Assn. Bar of City of N.Y., Va. Beach Bar Assn., Va. Bar Assn., Norfolk Portsmouth Bar Assn., Union Internat. Des Avocats, Order of Coif, Omicron Delta Kappa. Presbyterian. Clubs: Princess Ann Country (Va. Beach); Harbor, Virginia (Norfolk). Lodge: Masons. Private international, General corporate. Home: 1127 Crystal Lake Dr Virginia Beach VA 23451 Office: MacKinlay & Talbert 120 Atlantic St PO Box 3909 Norfolk VA 23514

MACKLES, GLENN FREDERICK, lawyer; b. Dover, N.H., Dec. 7, 1948; s. Louis Joseph and Charlotte Vita (Woolfson) M.; m. Randeen Meryl Rosen, Aug. 21, 1971. BA, George Washington U., 1971; JD, New Eng. Sch. Law, 1975. Bar: Mass. 1975. Tax law specialist IRS, Washington, 1977-81; ptnr. Touche Ross & Co., Washington, 1982-87; tech. advisor, assoc. chief counsel IRS, Washington, 1987—. Mem. ABA, Mass. Bar Assn., Computer Dealers and Lessors Assn. (cons. 1985—). Corporate taxation, Personal income taxation, Computer. Home: 10152 Sutherland Rd Silver Spring MD 20901 Office: IRS 1111 Constitution Ave NW Washington DC 20224

MACKLIN, CROFFORD JOHNSON, JR., lawyer; b. Columbus, Ohio, Sept. 10, 1947; s. Crofford Johnson, Sr. and Dorothy Ann (Stevens) M.; m. Mary Carole Ward, July 5, 1969; children—Carrie E., David J. B.A., Ohio State U., 1969; B.A. summa cum laude, U. West Fla., 1974; J.D. cum laude, Ohio State U., 1976. Bar: Ohio 1977, U.S. Tax Ct. 1978. Acct., Touche Ross, Columbus, 1976-77; assoc. Smith & Schnacke, Dayton, 1977-81; ptnr. Porter, Wright, Morris & Arthur, Dayton, 1983—; sole practice, Dayton, 1981-82; adj. faculty Franklin U., 1977; adj. prof. U. Dayton Law Sch., 1981. Contbr. articles to profl. jours. Bd. dirs. Easter Seals, 1984—. Served to capt. USMCR, 1969-74. Mem. Dayton Bar Assn. (chmn. probate com. 1981-83), Dayton Trust & Estate Planning (pres. 1983-84), Ohio Bar Assn., ABA. Presbyterian. Home: 7333 Timbernoll Dr West Chester OH 45069 Office: Porter Wright Morris & Arthur 2100 1st Nat Bank Bldg PO Box 1805 Dayton OH 45402

MACLAUGHLIN, HARRY HUNTER, judge; b. Breckenridge, Minn., Aug. 9, 1927; s. Harry Hunter and Grace (Swank) MacL.; m. Mary Jean Shaffer, June 25, 1958; children—David, Douglas. B.B.A. with distinction, U. Minn., 1949, LL.B., J.D., 1956. Bar: Minn. bar 1956. Law clk. to justice Minn. Supreme Ct.; ptnr. MacLaughlin & Mondale, MacLaughlin & Harstad, Mpls., 1956-72; asso. justice Minn. Supreme Ct., 1972-77; U.S. dist. judge Dist. of Minn., Mpls., 1977—; part-time instr. William Mitchell Coll. Law, St. Paul, 1958-63; lectr. U. Minn. Law Sch., 1973—; mem. 8th Cir. Jud. Conf., 1981-83. Bd. editors: Minn. Law Rev, 1954-55. Mem. Mpls. Charter Commn., 1967-72, Minn. State Coll. Bd., 1971-72, Minn. Jud. Council, 1972; mem. nat. adv. council Small Bus. Adminstrn., 1967-69. Served with USNR, 1945-46. Mem. Am., Minn., Hennepin County bar assns., Beta Gamma Sigma, Phi Delta Phi. Methodist. Jurisprudence. Office: 684 US Courthouse 110 S 4th St Minneapolis MN 55401

MACLAURY, RICHARD JOYCE, lawyer; b. Westbury L.I., N.Y., Apr. 6, 1918; s. Robert and Cassie Hatfield (Eastman) MacL.; m. Margaret Bodil Christensen, Apr. 24, 1942 (div.); children: Robert Ethan, Margerie Ruth, Richard Eastman, Joyce Anne; m. Susan Elizabeth Phister, Sept. 22, 1972. A.B., Yale U., 1940; J.D., Columbia U., 1948. Assoc. Pillsbury, Madison & Sutro, San Francisco, 1948-56; ptnr. Pillsbury, Madison & Sutro, 1956—. Contbr. articles to profl. jours. Bd. dirs. Ind. Colls. No. Calif., Inc., San Francisco, 1974-78; bd. dirs. Inst. Contemporary Studies; mem. Calif. Dem. Council. Served with USMCR, 1941-46. Fellow Am. Coll. Trial Lawyers (chmn. complex litigation com. 1981); mem. State Bar Calif., San Francisco Bar Assn., San Francisco Lawyer's Com. Urban Affairs, Fellows of Am. Bar Found., Am. Judicature Soc., U.S. Dist. Ct. Hist. Soc., Phi Delta Phi. Clubs: Pacific Union, San Francisco Fly Casting, St. Francis Yacht, Stock Exchange. Office: Pillsbury Madison & Sutro 225 Bush St San Francisco CA 94104

MACLEAN, BABCOCK, lawyer; b. N.Y.C., Jan. 26, 1946; s. Charles Chalmers and Lee Selden (Howe) MacL.; m. Cynthia Gannon, Feb. 15, 1983. B.A., Yale U., 1967; M.A., Columbia U., 1970; J.D., Case Western Res. U., 1975. Bar: Ohio 1975, N.Y. 1983. Assoc. Hadley, Mills & Matia, Cleve., 1976-77, mem., 1977-83; tax editor Research Inst. Am., N.Y.C., 1983-85; assoc. Javits, Robinson, Brog, Leinwand & Reich, 1985—; adj. asst. prof. taxation Pace U., N.Y.C., 1983-84. Mem. ABA (sect. taxation com. on closely-held corps.). Republican. Episcopalian. Clubs: Yale, St. Anthony (N.Y.C.). Corporate taxation, Personal income taxation. Home: 5555 Netherland Ave Riverdale NY 10471 Office: Javits Robinson Brog Leinwand & Reich 1345 Ave of the Americas New York NY 10105

MACLEAY, DONALD, lawyer; b. Tacoma, Dec. 27, 1908; s. Lachlan and Mabel (Nye) M.; m. Elizabeth Hall Fesser, Jan. 27, 1934; children: Donald, Linda Dewell, Murdo Lachlan. Student, Hill Mil. Acad., Portland, Oreg., 1922-24, Phillips Acad., Andover, Mass., 1924-25; J.D., U. Colo., 1931. Bar: Colo., Ill., D.C. 1931-33. Com. prevention, punishment of crime Chgo. Assn. Commerce, 1931-32; gen. practice of law 1933—; with Esch, Kerr, Woolley, Taylor & Shipe (and successor firm Kerr, Shipe & Macleay).; ptnr., now counsel Macleay & Lynch (and predecessor firms), Washington, 1946—. Served to lt. USNR, 1943-45. Mem. Am., D.C., Maritime Adminstrv. bar assns., Am. Judicature Soc., Assn. Transp. Practitioners, Maritime Law Assn. U.S., Clan Stewart Soc. in Am. (pres. 1980-85), Phi Delta Phi, Chi Psi. Episcopalian. Clubs: University, St. Andrews Soc. (pres. 1986) (Washington); Stephney Farm Gun (Chesterton, Md.); Belle Haven Country (Alexandria, Va.); Fairfax Rod and Gun (Manassas, Va.). Administrative and regulatory, Admiralty, Transportation. Home: 4800 Fillmore Ave Alexandria VA 22311 Office: 1625 I St NW Washington DC 20006

MACLEOD, ANTHONY MICHAEL, diversified utility company executive; b. Manila, Dec. 30, 1947; s. Anthony Macaulay and Dorothy (Amend) M.; m. Carol Jeanne Silvani, Aug. 5, 1972; children: Ryan Elissa, Anthony Matthew, Colin Macaulay. A.B. magna cum laude, U. Notre Dame, 1969; J.D., U. Va., 1972. Law clk. Supreme Ct. Conn., Hartford, 1972-73; assoc. atty. Hirschberg, Pettengill, Strong & Nagle (now Whitman & Ransom), Greenwich, Conn., 1973-76; div. counsel The Flintkote Co., Stamford, Conn., 1977-80, sec., chief counsel, 1980-82, v.p., sec., chief counsel, 1982-84; v.p., gen. counsel The Hydraulic Co., Bridgeport, Conn., 1984-86; sr. v.p. law and adminstrn. The Hydraulic Co., 1986—; dir. Stamford Water Co.; team dir. Mgmt. Decision Lab. NYU Grad. Sch. Bus. Adminstrn., Purchase, NY, 1983-84; law program chmn Conn. Career Opportunities Program, Greenwich, 1975-76. Chmn. exploring com. Greenwich council Boy Scouts Am., 1975-79, mem. exec. bd., 1975-81; mem. S.W. Area Commerce and Industry Assn. Conn., 1982-84, Greenwich Flood and Erosion Control Bd., 1987—; rep. Greenwich Town Meeting, 1984-85; bd. dirs. Youth Shelter, 1984-86; bd. regents Fairfield Coll. Prep. Sch., 1985—; bd. trustees Whitby Sch., 1986—. Mem ABA, Conn. Bar Assn. (exec. com. young lawyers sect. 1974-75), Conn. Supreme Ct. Law Clks. Assn., Am. Corp. Counsel Assn., Westchester Fairfield Corp Counsel Assn. Clubs: Notre Dame Alumni (Fairfield County, Conn.) (dir. 1982—); Greenwich Country. General corporate, Real property, Administrative and regulatory. Home: 124 Old Stone Bridge Rd Cos Cob CT 06807 Office: The Hydraulic Co 835 Main St Bridgeport CT 06601

MACLEOD, JOHN AMEND, lawyer; b. Manila, June 5, 1942; s. Anthony Macaulay and Dorothy Lillian (Amend) M.; children—Kerry, Jack. B.B.A., U. Notre Dame, 1963, J.D., 1969. Bar: D.C. 1969, U.S. Supreme Ct. 1980. Assoc., Jones, Day, Reavis & Pogue, D.C., 1969-73; ptnr., 1974-79; ptnr. Crowell & Moring, Washington, 1979—, mem. mgmt. com., 1979-82, 83-86, chmn., 1984-85. Trustee, mem. exec. com. Eastern Mineral Law Found.; bd. dirs. St. Francis Ctr. Served to lt. U.S. Army, 1963-65. Mem. ABA, D.C. Bar Assn., Notre Dame Law Assn. (dir., exec. bd.). Club: Metropolitan (Washington). Editor-in-chief Notre Dame Law Rev., 1968-69. Contbr. articles to profl. jours. Administrative and regulatory, Federal civil litigation, Environment. Home: 1733 Que St NW Washington DC 20009 Office: 1001 Pennsylvania Ave NW Washington DC 20004

MACLIN, ALAN HALL, lawyer; b. DuQuoin, Ill., Dec. 22, 1949; s. John E. and Nora (Hall) M.; m. Joan Davidson (div. Dec. 1981); children: Molly, Tess; m. Jeanne Sittlow, Nov. 17, 1984. B.A. magna cum laude, Vanderbilt U., 1971; J.D., U. Chgo., 1974. Bar: Minn. 1974, U.S. Dist. Ct. Minn. 1974, U.S. Ct. Appeals (8th cir.) 1974, U.S. Ct. Appeals (5th cir.) 1975, U.S. Supreme Ct. 1978. Asst. atty. gen. Minn. Atty. Gen., St. Paul, 1974-80; chief anti-trust div. Briggs & Morgan, St. Paul, 1980—. Mem. Minn. State Bar Assn. (treas. anti-trust sect. 1978-80), Ramsey County Bar Assn. (sec. jud. com. 1980—), Phi Beta Kappa. Unitarian. Antitrust, Federal civil litigation, Insurance. Office: Briggs & Morgan 2200 First National Bank Bldg Saint Paul MN 55101

MACMURRAY, WORTH DANIELS, lawyer, consultant; b. Washington, Mar. 15, 1954; s. Frank Goodnow and Rose (Chatfield-Taylor) MacM. AB, Princeton U., 1977; JD, Georgetown U., 1980. Bar: Oreg. 1981, Republic of Palau/Pacific Islands Trust Territory 1983. Assoc. Miller, Nash et al, Portland, Oreg., 1980-82; asst. legal counsel State Govt., Koror, Palau, 1982-83; v.p., gen. counsel LAN Systems Inc., N.Y.C., 1983-85; asst. to pres. Chantilly Devel. Corp., McClean, Va., 1986—; arbitrator computer systems Am. Arbitration Assn., N.Y.C., 1984—; bd. dirs. LAN Systems Inc., N.Y.C., Internet Solutions CO., Gaithersburg, Md. Mem. ABA, Oreg. Bar Assn., D.C. Computer Law Forum, Computer Law Assn. Computer, General corporate. Home: 4607 Davenport St NW Washington DC 20016 Office: 1505 Planning Research Dr McLean VA 22102

MACNAUGHTON, WILLIAM ALEXANDER, lawyer, consultant; b. Winchester, Ky., Jan. 18, 1922; s. Archibald J.F. and Anne Bart (Epperson) MacN.; m. Anne C. O'Hair, Aug. 23, 1943; children—Anne Lynn MacAnughton Douthit, Virginia Sue MacNaughton Jamison, William A., James Robert, Charles Thomas. B.B.A., U. Tex., 1943, J.D., 1948. Bar: Tex. 1948, U.S. Dist. Cts. (no. and so. dists.) Tex. 1948, U.S. Ct. Appeals (10th cir.) 1980. Ptnr. MacNaughton and Leveridge, Houston, 1948-51; assoc. Townes and Townes, Houston, 1951-55; city judge City of Bellaire, Tex., 1950-56; gen. atty. Ginther Warren & Ginther Oil Co., Houston, 1955-64; mng. ptnr. MacNaughton Brody and Marlatt, Houston, 1964-72, Nelson & Harding, Houston, 1973-76; gen. counsel Davis Oil Co., Denver, 1977-82; sole practice, Houston and Austin, Tex., 1983—; dir. Tex. Investment Bank, 1979-84. Mem. exec. com. Harris County Democratic Com., 1951-56. Served to 1st lt. USAAF, 1943-46, PTO. Democrat. Presbyterian. Clubs: Houston, Austin Country. Lodges: Mason, Shriners. Oil and gas leasing, Bankruptcy, Federal civil litigation. Home: 3203 El Toro Cove Austin TX 78746 Office: 6014 Winsome Suite 101 Houston TX 77057 also: 333 W Loop North Suite 13 Houston TX 77024

MACNEIL, IAN RODERICK, legal educator; b. N.Y.C., June 20, 1929. BA magna cum laude, U. Vt., 1950; LLB magna cum laude, Harvard U., 1955. Bar: N.H. 1956. Assoc. Sulloway Hollis Godfrey & Soden, Concord, N.H., 1956-59; asst. prof. law Cornell U., 1959-62, assoc. prof., 1962-63, prof., 1963-72, 74-76, Ingersoll prof., 1976-80; John Henry Wigmore prof. law Northwestern U., Chgo., 1980—; vis. prof. law U. East Africa, Dar es Salaam, Tanzania, 1965-67, Duke U., 1971-72; prof. law mem. Ctr. for Advanced Studies, U. Va., Charlottesville, 1972-74; vis. fellow Ctr. Sociolegal Studies, Wolfson Coll., Oxford U., 1979;. Author: Contracts, Exchange Transactions and Relations, 1971, Contracts, Exchange Transactions and Relations, 2d edit,, 1978, Bankruptcy Law in East Africa, 1966, (with Schlesinger et al) Formation of Contracts, a Study of the Common Core of Legal Systems, 1968, Morison Students and Decision Making, 1970. Hon. fellow faculty law Edinburgh U., 1979, 87; Guggenheim fellow, 1978-79. Mem. ABA, Am. Law Inst., Can. Law Tchrs. Assn., Soc. Pub. Tchrs. Law, N.H. Bar Assn., Phi Beta Kappa. Contracts commercial, Legal history, Arbitration. Office: Sch of Law Northwestern U 357 E Chicago Ave Chicago IL 60611

MACNISH, JAMES MARTIN, JR., judge; b. Richmond Heights, Mo., Sept. 3, 1935; s. James Martin and Virginia May (Kleissle) M.; m. Harriette Anne Rost, Aug. 29, 1964; children: Eleanore Miles, Margaret Calhoun. AB, Washington U., St. Louis, 1958, JD, 1964. Bar: Mo. 1964, U.S. Dist. Ct. (ea. dist.) Mo. 1964, Kans. 1967, U.S. Dist. Ct. Kans. 1967, U.S. Ct. Appeals (10th cir.) 1969, U.S. Supreme Ct. 1971. Assoc. Stein & Seigel, St. Louis, 1964-67; sole practice, Topeka, Kans., 1967-77; judge City of Topeka Mcpl. Ct., 1973-77; dist. judge 3d Jud. Dist. Ct. Kans., 1977—; assigned judge Kans. Ct. Appeals, 1986—. Bd. regents Washburn U., Topeka, 1971-85, chmn., 1974-75, vice chmn., 1981-82. Served to capt. USMC, 1958-61. Mem. ABA, Kans. Bar Assn., Mo. Bar Assn., Topeka Bar Assn., St. Louis Bar Assn., Am. Judicature Soc., Washburn U. Law Sch. Assn. (hon. life), Phi Delta Phi, Sigma Chi. Republican. Jurisprudence. Office: Shawnee County Courthouse Topeka KS 66603

MACPHAIL, DOUGLAS FRANCIS, lawyer; b. Englewood, N.J., Nov. 24, 1940; s. Wilbur and Francis Evelyn (Cobler) MacP.; m. Gertrude Juliet St. Marie, June 10, 1967; children—Douglas Dana, Matthew Allen. B.A. in Philosophy, Dartmouth Coll., 1962; J.D., Duke U., 1965; M.Bus. Adminstrn. with honors, Boston U. Sch. Mgmt., 1972. Bar: N.J. 1965, Ind. 1973, Ill. 1975, U.S. Dist. Ct. N.J. 1965, U.S. Ct. Mil. Appeals 1966. Assoc. Harrison, Hartman and MacDonald, Ridgewood, N.J., 1969-70; mem. corp. legal staff Eli Lilly and Co., Indpls., 1972-74; counsel FMC Corp., Chgo., 1974-77; assoc. gen. atty. Motorola, Inc., Schaumburg, Ill., 1977—; mem. adj. faculty M.A. program Webster U.; mem. faculty mgmt. program Elmhurst (Ill.) Coll. Mem. B. R. Ryall Masters Swim Team, Glen Ellyn, 1976, pres. B. R. Ryall Swim Team, 1978-79, publicity chmn.; pres., organizer Concerned Citizens of South End of Fall River, Mass., group organized to protest large liquified natural gas facility. Served to comdr. JAGC, USN, 1965-68, Res. 1968—. Mem. ABA (vice chmn. corp. counsel gen. practice sect.), N.J. Bar Assn., Ind. Bar Assn. Mem. editorial bd., assoc. editor ABA Law Notes. Contracts commercial, General corporate, Legal education. Home: 164 N Milton Ave Glen Ellyn IL 60137

MACRAE, CAMERON FARQUHAR, III, lawyer; b. N.Y.C., Mar. 21, 1942; s. Cameron F. and Jane B. (Miller) MacR.; m. Ann Wooster Bedell, Nov. 30, 1974; children—Catherine Fairfax, Ann Cameron. A.B., Princeton U., 1963; LL.B., Yale U., 1966. Bar: N.Y. 1966, D.C. 1967, U.S. Supreme Ct. 1971, U.S. Dist. Ct. (so. dist.) N.Y. 1975. Atty.-advisor Office of Gen. Counsel to Sec. Air Force, Washington, 1966-69; assoc. Davis, Polk & Wardwell, N.Y.C., 1970-72; dep. supt. and counsel N.Y. State Banking Dept., N.Y.C., 1972-74; ptnr. LeBoeuf, Lamb, Leiby & MacRae, N.Y.C., 1975—. Trustee St. Andrew's Dune Ch., 1982—; chmn. trustee Clear Pool Camp, 1978—, 1st v.p., 1986—. Served to capt. USAF, 1966-69. Mem. ABA, N.Y.C. Bar Assn., D.C. Bar Assn. Republican. Episcopalian. Clubs: Links, Racquet and Tennis (N.Y.C.); Meadow (sec., bd. govs.), Bathing Corp., Shinnecock Hills Golf (Southampton). Note and comment editor Yale Law Jour., 1965-66. Banking, Contracts commercial, Private international. Office: LeBoeuf Lamb Leiby & MacRae 520 Madison Ave New York NY 10022

MACRAE, HOWARD TAFT, JR., lawyer, securities executive; b. N.Y.C., Oct. 10, 1952; s. Howard Taft Sr. and Phyllis Lillian (Phin) M.; m. Linda M. Kramer, June 28, 1986. BA, U. Va., 1973; JD, U. Richmond, 1976; LLM in Taxation, William & Mary Coll. of Law, 1985. Bar: Va. 1976, U.S. Dist. Ct. (ea. and we. dists.) Va. 1976, U.S. Ct. Appeals (4t cir.) 1976. Atty. Richmond (Va.) Corp., 1976-77; counsel Continental Fin. Services Corp., Richmond, 1977-81; asst. gen. counsel Wheat First Securities, Inc., Richmond, 1981-82, v.p., asst. gen. counsel, 1982—; sec. Atlantic Venture Co., Inc., Richmond, 1981—, Wheat Ins. Services, Richmond, 1983—, WFS Real Estate Investment Corp., Richmond, 1984—; WFS Realty Corp, Richmond, 1982—; v.p., asst. gen. counsel WFS Fin. Corp., Richmond, 1984—. Mem. com. City of Richmond Reps., 1975-76, Chesterfield County Rep. Com., 1979-83; sec. Henrico County Rep. Com., 1977-79. Mem. ABA, Va. Bar Assn., Richmond Bar Assn. (corp. counsel sect. 1976—), Bar Assn. of City of Richmond. Clubs: Downtown (Richmond); Brandermill Country (Midlothian, Va.). Corporate taxation, Securities, Insurance. Office: Wheat First Securities Inc 707 E Main St Richmond VA 23219

MACRITCHIE, BRIAN JOHN, lawyer; b. Hillsdale, Mich., Oct. 26, 1952; s. William and Norma (Braga) MacR.; m. Sheree M. Quimby, Aug. 14, 1977; children: Travis, Shannon. Student, Western Mich. U., 1970-73; BS in Wildlife Biology, Mich. State U., 1975; JD, Willamette U., 1979. Bar: Oreg. 1979, Wash. 1980, U.S. Dist. Ct. Oreg. 1981, U.S. Ct. Appeals (9th cir.) 1985. Law clk. Wash. State Supreme Ct., Olympia, 1979-81; assoc. Gray, Fancher, Holmes & Hurley, Bend, Oreg., 1981-85; ptnr. MacRitchie & Lewis, Bend, 1985-86, MacRitchie, Petersen & Stiegler, Bend, 1987—. Mem. ABA, Oreg. Bar Assn., Cen. Oreg. Bar Assn., Nat. Ski Patrol. Avocations: skiing, hiking, parenting. State civil litigation, Contracts commercial, Real property. Home: 21636 Paloma Dr Bend OR 97701 Office: MacRitchie Petersen & Stiegler 709 NW Wall St Bend OR 97701

MACWHORTER, ROBERT BRUCE, lawyer; b. Phila., July 12, 1930; s. George Merritt and Marion (Ritchie) MacW.; m. Althea Lucille Davis, June 23, 1956; children: Susan Elizabeth, Nancy Jeanne (Mrs. Matthew Oja), Marjorie Anne. A.B., Oberlin Coll., 1953; LL.B., U. Va., 1956. Bar: Va. 1956, N.Y. 1957. Assoc. Shearman & Sterling, N.Y.C., 1956-65, ptnr., 1965—. Mem. ABA, Va. Bar Assn., Order of Coif. Club: Broad St. (N.Y.C.). Antitrust. Home: 85 Jefferson Ave Maplewood NJ 07040 Office: Shearman & Sterling 53 Wall St New York NY 10005

MACY, RICHARD, state judge. Judge Wyo. Supreme Ct., Cheyenne, 1986—. Office: Wyoming Supreme Court PO Box 1006 Cheyenne WY 82003 *

MADAN, ANIL, lawyer; b. Nairobi, Kenya, Mar. 13, 1947; s. Chunilal and Satya (Khanna) M.; m. Rosann Cacace, June 8, 1973; 1 child, Anjolie Elizabeth. AB, Cornell U., 1968; JD, Harvard U., 1971. Bar: Mass. 1973, U.S. Dist. Ct. Mass. 1973, U.S. Ct. Appeals (1st cir.) 1973. Assoc. Ficksman & Conley, Boston, 1973-75; mng. ptnr. Madan and Madan, Boston, 1975—. Mem. ABA, Mass. Bar Assn., Fed. Bar Assn. Federal civil litigation, State civil litigation, Insurance. Home: 113 Marlborough St Boston MA 02116 Office: Madan and Madan One Post Office Sq Boston MA 02109

MADDEN, DONALD PAUL, lawyer; b. Winthrop, Mass., Dec. 26, 1933; s. Francis Patrick and Mary Josephine (Doherty) M.; m. Sarah Anne Donovan, Aug. 12, 1966; children—Matthew James, Andrew Peter, Peter Thomas. A.B., Princeton U., 1955; J.D., Harvard U., 1961. Bar: N.Y. 1962, U.S. Dist. Ct. (so. dist.) N.Y. 1962. Assoc. White & Case, N.Y.C., 1961-69, ptnr., 1969—; resident ptnr. Paris office, 1971-76. Served to lt. USMC, 1955-58. Mem. ABA, Assn. Bar City N.Y. Club: Links (N.Y.C.). General corporate. Office: White & Case 1155 Ave of Americas New York NY 10036

MADDEN, JEROME ANTHONY, lawyer; b. Memphis, Aug. 24, 1948; s. Bernard Clark and Virginia Ann (Golas) M. BA, U. Steubenville, Ohio, 1971; JD summa cum laude, U. Dayton, 1978. Bar: Ohio 1978, D.C. 1979, U.S. Dist Ct. (D.C. dist.) 1979, U.S. Ct. Appeals (D.C. cir.) 1980, U.S. Ct. Claims 1984, U.S. Ct. Appeals (Fed. cir.) 1984, U.S. Supreme Ct. 1984. Law clk. to chief justices O'Neill and Leach Ohio Supreme Ct., Columbus, 1978-79; assoc. Cadwalader, Wickersham & Taft, Washington, 1979-85; trial atty. U.S. Dept. Justice, Washington, 1985—. Editor-in-chief U. Dayton Law Rev., 1977-78. Served with USMCR, 1970-76. Mem. ABA, D.C. Bar Assn. Roman Catholic. Avocations: jogging, golf, tennis. Federal civil litigation, Personal injury, Banking. Home: 2844 C South Wakefield St Arlington VA 22206 Office: Trial Atty Tort Br Civil div US Dept Justice PO Box 888 Benjamin Franklin Sta Washington DC 20044

MADDEN, JOHN JOSEPH, lawyer; b. N.Y.C., May 27, 1946; s. John L. and Bertha M. (Antonades) M.; m. Mary A. O'Neill, June 17, 1976; children: Elisabeth, Samuel. BA, U. Pa., 1968; JD, Fordham U., 1975. Bar: N.Y. 1976, U.S. Dist. Ct. (s. dist.) N.Y. 1976. Assoc. Shearman & Sterling, N.Y.C., 1975-83, ptnr., 1984—. Trustee St. David's Sch., N.Y.C., 1981—. Served to 1st lt. U.S. Army, 1969-71, Vietnam. Mem. ABA, N.Y. Bar Assn. Club: Down Town Assn. (N.Y.C.). General corporate, Securities. Office: Shearman & Sterling 53 Wall St New York NY 10005

MADDEN, MURDAUGH STUART, JR., lawyer; b. Washington, Dec. 1, 1948; s. Murdaugh Stuart and Louise (Mann) M. B.A., U. Pa., 1971; M.A., London Sch. Econs., 1972; J.D., Georgetown U., 1976. Bar: D.C. 1976, U.S. Ct. Appeals (D.C. cir.) 1977, U.S. Ct. Internat. Trade 1982, U.S. Cts. Appeals (5th and 11th cirs.) 1982. Assoc. Reed, Smith, Shaw & McClay, Washington, 1976-78, Weil, Gotshal & Manges, Washington, 1978-80, Santarelli & Gimer, Washington, 1980-83; ptnr. Santarelli & Bond, Washington, 1983-85; assoc. prof. Pace U. Sch. Law, White Plains, N.Y., 1986—; vis. prof. William Mitchell Coll. Law, St. Paul, 1985. Assoc. editor Georgetn Law Jour., 1975-76, Jour. Products Liability, 1984—. Contbr. articles to legal jours. Mem. legal concerns com. Nat. Capitol YMCA, Washington, 1978-85. Mem. ABA, Assn. Trial Lawyers Am., Phi Delta Phi. Episcopalian. Evidence, Products liability, Torts. Home: 47 Davis Ave White Plains NY 10605 Office: Pace U Sch Law 78 N Broadway White Plains NY 10603

MADDEN, STEPHAN DUPONT, lawyer; b. Oakland, Calif., June 12, 1954; s. Philip Stephan and Joan Marie (DuPont) M.; m. Christine Helen Severt, Sept. 10, 1983. AB in Botany, Miami U., Oxford, Ohio, 1976; JD, No. Ky. U., 1980. Bar: Ohio 1980, U.S. Dist. Ct. (so. dist.) Ohio 1980. Asst. pros. atty. City of Cin., 1980-81, asst. solicitor, 1981-83; assoc. Lindhorst & Dreidame, Co. L.P.A., Cin., 1983—. Chmn. ward Gradison campaign, Cin., 1982-83; mem. Cin. Hist. Soc., 1986—. Mem. ABA, Ohio Bar Assn., Cin. Bar Assn. (young lawyers sect.). Republican. Roman Catholic. Avocation: sports. Criminal, Personal injury, State civil litigation. Home: 4850 Sheffield Ave Cincinnati OH 45226 Office: Lindhorst & Dreidame Co LPA 1700 Central Trust Ctr Cincinnati OH 45202

MADDOX, ALVA HUGH, state justice; b. Andalusia, Ala., Apr. 17, 1930; s. Christopher Columbus and Audie Lodella (Freeman) M.; m. Virginia Ann Roberts, June 14, 1958; children: Robert Hugh, Patricia Jane. A.B. in Journalism, U. Ala., 1952; LL.B., U. Ala., 1957. Bar: Ala. bar 1957. With Florala News, 1947; cashier Treas.'s Office, U. Ala., 1948-52, 54-56; law clk. Ct. of Appeals of Ala. Montgomery, 1957, atty., field examiner VA, 1958; law clk. U.S. Dist. Ct., Montgomery, 1959-60; practice law Montgomery, 1961-64; asst. dist. atty. 15th Jud. Circuit, Montgomery; legal adviser Gov. George Wallace, 1965-67, Lurleen B. Wallace, 1967-68, Gov. Albert P. Brewer, 1968-69; circuit judge 15th Jud. Circuit, Montgomery, 1963; assoc. justice Supreme Ct. Ala., Montgomery, 1969—; adj. prof. Troy State U., 1976-82, 87—, Auburn U., Montgomery, 1981-82, 87—; prof. law Jones Law Inst., Montgomery, 1961-62, 76. Author: Billy Boll Weevil—A Pest Becomes a Hero, 1976. Mem. Jud. Planning Commn. Ala.; mem. Permanent Study Commn. Ala. Judiciary.; mem. Jud. Conf.; pres. youth legislature YMCA, 1978-79; bd. dirs. YMCA, Baptist Med. Center, 1970-80, Montgomery Baptist Hosp. Found., 1970-80. Served with USAF, 1952-54; col. Res. (ret.). Mem. ABA, Ala. Bar Assn., Am. Judicature Soc., Farrah Law Soc., Inst. Jud. Adminstrn., Ala. Law Inst., Arnold Air Soc., Pershing Rifles, Omicron Delta Kappa, Phi Alpha Delta, Sigma Delta Chi. Democrat. Baptist (deacon 1966—). Club: Maxwell AFB Officers Open Mess (Montgomery). Lodge: Kiwanis (bd. dirs.). Jurisprudence. Home: 3137 Hathaway Pl Montgomery AL 36111 Office: PO Box 218 Montgomery AL 36101

MADDOX, CHARLES J., JR., lawyer; b. Cameron, Tex., Oct. 8, 1949; s. Charles J. and Mary Jo (Fikes) M.; m. Sandra Peppin, Apr. 29, 1984; 1 child, Elizabeth Ashleigh. Student Tex. A&M U., 1968-70; B.B.A., U. Tex., 1972, J.D., 1976. Bar: Tex. 1977, U.S. Dist. Ct. (no., so., ea. and we. dists.) Tex. 1980, U.S. Ct. Appeal (5th and 11th cirs.) 1981, U.S. Supreme Ct. 1982. Staff auditor Walgreen Co., Chgo. and Houston, 1973; asst. atty. gen. State of Tex., Austin, 1977-80; sr. and mng. ptnr. firm Maddox, Perrin & Kirkendall, Houston, 1981—. Sponsor Rep. fund, Washington, 1983—; sustaining mem. Rep. Nat. Com., Washington, 1984—. NSF scholar 1965, Newhause scholar 1968. Mem. Tex. Bar Assn., Tex. Young Lawyers Assn., Houston Bar Assn., Houston Young Lawyers Assn., Sigma Iota Epsilon, Alpha Kappa Psi (life mem., treas. 1971-72). Republican. Presbyterian.

Clubs: Quail Valley Country (Missouri City, Tex.). State civil litigation, Federal civil litigation, Bankruptcy. Office: Maddox Perrin & Kirkendall 5100 Republic Bank Ctr Houston TX 77002

MADDOX, WILLIAM A., lawyer. U.S. atty. State of Nev., Las Vegas. Office: US Attys Office PO Box 16030 Las Vegas NV 89101 *

MADDUX, PARKER AHRENS, lawyer; b. San Francisco, May 23, 1939; s. Jackson Walker and Jeanette Ahrens M.; m. Mathilde G.M. Landman, Mar. 20, 1966; 1 child, Jackson Wilhelmus Quentin. A.B., U. Calif., 1961; J.D., Harvard U., 1964. Bar: Calif. 1965, U.S. Dist. Ct. (no. and ea. dist.) Calif. 1965, U.S. Ct. Apls. (9th cir.) 1972, U.S. Ct. Clms., 1974, N.Y. 1981, U.S. Supreme Ct. 1982, Assoc., Pillsbury, Madison & Sutro, San Francisco, 1965-72, ptnr., 1973—; lectr. in field. Bd. dirs. Friends of Recreation and Parks, San Francisco; trustee Coll. Preparatory Sch., Oakland, Calif. Fulbright fellow, 1964-65. Mem. ABA (chmn. antitrust legis. subcom. of litigation subcom.), Calif. Bar Assn., San Francisco Bar Assn. Republican. Unitarian. Clubs: St. Francis Yacht (San Francisco); Harvard (N.Y.C.). Contbr. articles to profl. jours. Antitrust, Federal civil litigation, State civil litigation. Office: Pillsbury Madison & Sutro 225 Bush St San Francisco CA 94104

MADEIRA, DAVID BECKMAN, lawyer, educational administrator; b. Waterville, Maine, Jan. 24, 1950; s. David Lehman and Anna-Lisa (Beckman) M.; m. Shelley Schaap, Nov. 23, 1972; children—Mary Anne, David Ward. B.A. in Sociology, Wheaton Coll., 1972; M.S. in Edn., Ind. U., 1975, J.D. cum laude, 1981. Bar: Pa. 1981. Dir. wilderness tours Westwind Tours, Nyack, N.Y., summers 1972-80; dir. student life Messiah Coll., Grantham, Pa., 1975-78, v.p. for coll. advancement and coll. counsel, 1981—; ptnr. Madeira & Morrison, Grantham; lobbyist to Gen. Assembly, Ind. U., Bloomington, 1980-81. Mem. ABA (del. to ho. of dels. 1979-81), Christian Legal Soc., Dauphin County Bar Assn., Council for Advancement and Support of Edn., Phi Alpha Delta, Phi Delta Kappa. Republican. Baptist. Clubs: Tuesday, Execs. (Harrisburg, Pa.). Estate planning, Legal education, General corporate. Office: Messiah Coll Grantham PA 17027

MADIGAN, KATHRYN GRANT, lawyer; b. Paterson, N.J., May 4, 1953; d. William Joseph and Patricia (McCaffrey) Grant; m. Robert James Madigan Jr., Oct. 28, 1978; children: R. James III, Grant Daniel. BA, U. Colo., 1975; JD, Union U., Albany, N.Y., 1978. Bar: N.Y. 1979, U.S. Dist. Ct. (no. dist.) N.Y. 1979. Asst. gen. counsel Security Mut. Life Ins. Co. N.Y., Binghamton, 1978-85; law asst. trial part Broome County Surrogate's Ct., Binghamton, 1985-86; ptnr. Madigan & Madigan, Binghamton, 1986—. V.p. Southern Tier Zool. Soc., Binghamton, 1980-82; co. chmn. Broome County United Way, Binghamton, 1980, 82, acct. exec., Network for Children, Binghamton, 1986. Mem. N.Y. State Bar Assn. (chmn. subcom. on law student membership 1979-82, del. 1983-86, exec. com. corp. counsel sect. 1982, award of merit 1985, 86, named outstanding young lawyer award young lawyers sect. 1987), Broome County Bar Assn. (2d v.p. 1986—, bd. dirs. 1981-85, chmn. continuing edn. com. 1984—), Phi Beta Kappa. Democrat. Roman Catholic. Clubs: Ms. Demeanors Rugby (Albany) (founder, pres. 1976-78), Binghamton Women's Rugby (founder, pres. 1978-82). Avocations: hiking, music, literature. Probate, General practice. Home: 7 West End Ave Binghamton NY 13905 Office: Madigan & Madigan 84 Court St Suite 201 Binghamton NY 13901

MADISON, JAMES ROBINSON, lawyer; b. Shreveport, La., Jan. 5, 1946; s. John Meek Madison and Ruth (Robinson) Marshall; m. Marilyn Newton, Aug. 30, 1980; children: James Robinson Jr. BA in Polit. Sci., Washington & Lee U., 1968; JD, La. State U., 1974. Bar: La. 1974, U.S. Dist. Ct. (we. dist.) La. 1974. Law clk. to presiding justice U.S. Dist. Ct. (we. dist.) La., Shreveport, 1974-75; assoc. Wiener, Weiss & Madison, Shreveport, 1975-78; ptnr. Wiener, Weiss, Madison & Howell, Shreveport, 1979-85; prin. Wiener, Weiss, Madison & Howell P.C., Shreveport, 1986—. Pres. Creative Craft Alliance Inc., Shreveport, 1983; chmn. bd. YMCA-Cen. Br., Shreveport, 1985; deacon First Presbyn. Ch., Shreveport, 1986—. Named Vol. of Yr., YMCA-Cen. Br., Shreveport, 1985. Mem. ABA, La. Bar Assn. Shreveport Bar Assn. Republican. Presbyterian. Clubs: Cambridge, Pierremont Oaks Tennis (Shreveport). Real property, Contracts commercial, Federal civil litigation. Office: Wiener Weiss Madison & Howell 505 Travis St Shreveport LA 71101

MADISON, VIVIAN L., lawyer; b. Lake Charles, La., Mar. 6, 1956; d. Harold Lee and Ruth Vivian (Mertzweiller) M.; m. Glenn Henry Brock, Dec. 18, 1976 (div. Aug. 1983). BA cum laude, Loyola U., New Orleans, 1978, JD, 1981. Bar: La. 1981, U.S. Dist. Ct. (ea. dist.) La. 1982, U.S. Ct. Appeals (5th cir.) 1982, U.S. Supreme Ct. 1985, U.S. Dist. Ct. (we. dist.) La. 1985, U.S. Dist. Ct. (mid. dist.) La. 1986. Law clk. to presiding justice La. Supreme Ct., New Orleans, 1981-82; assoc. Lemle, Kelleher, Kohlmeyer & Matthews, New Orleans, 1982; law clk. to presiding justice U.S. Dist. Ct. (ea. dist.) La., New Orleans, 1983; assoc. Jones, Walker, Waechter, Poitevent, Carrere & Denegre, New Orleans, 1983—. Pres. Pier 8 Condominium Assn., New Orleans, 1985-87. Recipient La. Trial Lawyers award for Appellate Adv., Loyola Law Sch. Faculty, New Orleans, 1979, Dr. Milton Sheen Community Service award Loyola Law Sch. Faculty, New Orleans, 1981. Mem. ABA, Fed. Bar Assn., La. Bar Assn., New Orleans Bar Assn., Assn. for Women Attys., Def. Research Inst., New Orleans Assn. of Def. Counsel. Democrat. Products liability, Federal civil litigation, Workers' compensation. Office: Jones Walker Waechter et al 201 St Charles Ave New Orleans LA 70170

MADOLE, DONALD WILSON, lawyer; b. Elkhart, Kans., July 14, 1932; m. Juanita M. Weisbach, July 12, 1975. Student Kans. State Tchrs. Coll., 1950-51; B.S., U. Denver, 1959, J.D., 1959. Bar: Colo. 1960, U.S. Dist. Ct. Colo. 1960, U.S. Ct. Appeals (10th cir.) 1960, D.C. 1971, U.S. Supreme Ct. 1972, U.S. Ct. Appeals (1st cir.) 1976, U.S. Ct. Appeals (5th cir.) 1977, U.S. Ct. Appeals (6th cir.) 1982, U.S. Ct. Appeals (7th and 9th cirs.) 1975, U.S. Ct. Appeals (11th cir.) 1981. Vice pres. Mountain Aviation Corp., Denver, 1958-59; trial atty. FAA, Washington, 1960-62; sr. warranty adminstr. Am. Airlines, Tulsa, 1962-63; chief hearing and reports div., atty. adviser CAB, Washington, 1963-66; ptnr. Speiser, Krause & Madole, Washington, 1966—; pres. Aerial Application Corp., Burlingame, Calif., 1968-69; v.p., dir. Environ. Power Ltd., Pitts., 1972—; dir. Unitrade Ltd., Washington, Bus. Ins. Mgmt. Inc., Bethesda, Md., Entertainment Capitol Corp., N.Y.C.; gen. counsel Nat. Aviation Club, 1978-80, Internat. Soc. Air Safety Investigators, 1977; mem. blue ribbon panel on airworthiness Nat. Acad. Sci., 1980; adviser U.S. Govt. del. Internat. Civil Aviation Orgn., 1965; U.S. Govt. rep. Aircraft Inquiry, Montreal, P.Q., Can., 1964. Author: Textbook of Aviation Statutes and Regulations, 1963; International Aspects of Aircraft Accidents, 1963; CAB, Aircraft Accident Investigation, 1964. Mem. chancellor's soc. U. Denver, 1982—. Served to comdr. USNR, 1953-57. Recipient Outstanding Performance award FAA, 1961; Meritorious Achievement award Am. Airlines, 1962; Outstanding Performance awards CAB, 1963-65; Fed. Govt. Outstanding Pub. Service award Jump-Meml. Found., 1966. Fellow Internat. Trial Lawyers; mem. ABA, Colo. Bar Assn., Fed. Bar Assn., D.C. Bar Assn., Assn. Trial Lawyers Am., Lawyer-Pilots Assn., Phi Delta Phi, Phi Mu Alpha. Clubs: Congl. Country, Nat. Aviation, Nat. Press. Federal civil litigation, Aviation. Home: 2800 Jenifer St NW Washington DC 20015 Office: 1216 16th St NW Washington DC 20036

MADORIN, A. RAYMOND, JR., lawyer; b. Hartford, Conn., Mar. 21, 1946; s. A. Raymond and Catherine Joan (O'Loughlin) M.; m. Lora Lissitchuk, Aug. 8. 1970; 1 child, Catherine. BA, Trinity Coll., Hartford, 1968; JD, U. Conn., 1971. Bar: Conn. 1971, U.S. Dist. Ct. Conn. 1972. Assoc. Law Office of Z. Rozbicki, Torrington, Conn., 1971-74, Law Office of G. Friedle, New Britain, Conn., 1974-76; ptnr. Friedle & Madorin, New Britain, 1976—. Served to capt. USAR. Mem. Hartford County Bar Assn. (treas. 1986—, chmn. ethics com. 1979—). Democrat. Episcopalian. Real property, Contracts commercial, General practice. Home: 7 Wyndwood Rd West Hartford CT 06107 Office: Friedle Madorin & Ustach 1 Prospect St New Britain CT 06050

MADORY, RICHARD EUGENE, lawyer; b. Kenton, Ohio, May 14, 1931; s. Harold Richard and Hilda (Strictland) M.; m. Barbara Jean Madory, Sept. 25, 1955; children—Richard Eugene, Terry Dean, Michael Wesly. B.S. in Edn., Ohio State U., 1952; J.D., Southwestern U., 1961. Bar: Calif., 1961, U.S. Ct. Mil. Appeals, U.S. Supreme Ct., U.S. Dist. Ct. (cen. dist.) Calif. With firm Madory, Booth, Zell & Pleiss, Santa Ana, Calif., 1962—, now pres., v.p., sec.-treas. lectr. Continuing Edn. of Bar State of Calif. Served to col. USMC. Fellow Am. Coll. Trial Lawyers; mem. ABA, Orange County Bar Assn., Los Angeles County Bar Assn., So. Calif. Def. Counsel Assn., Am. Bd. Trial Advs., Nat. Bd. Trial Advocacy. Personal injury, State civil litigation, Insurance. Office: 17822 E 17th St Suite 205 Tustin CA 92680

MADRID, PATRICIA ANN, district judge; b. Las Cruces, N.Mex., Sept. 25, 1946; d. Charles and Virginia (Fitch) M.; m. L. Michael Messina, May 2, 1975; 1 child, Giancarlo Anthony. B.A. in English and Philosophy, U. N.Mex., 1969; J.D., 1973; cert. Nat. Jud. Coll., U. Nev., 1978. Bar: N.Mex. 1973. Teaching asst. U. N.Mex., Albuquerque, 1969-70, Am. Indian Law Ctr., Albuquerque, 1971; law clk. to N.Mex. atty. gen., Santa Fe., 1972; atty. N.Mex. Legislature, Santa Fe, 1974; assoc. Kool, Bloomfield, & Eaves, P.A., Albuquerque, 1974-78; dist. judge 2nd Jud. Dist. State of N.Mex., Albuquerque, 1978—; presiding judge, 1984; ptnr. Messina, Madrid & Maynez, P.A., Albuquerque, 1984—. Editor N.Mex. Law Rev., 1972-73. Mem. State rules com. State Democratic Party, N.Mex., 1980, jud. council and credentials com. 1982-83; co-chmn. N.Mex. Carter for Pres. Com., 1980; bd. dirs. Am. Council Young Polit. Leaders, del. to Japan, 1982, Fechin Art Inst., Taos, N.Mex. Recipient Respect for Law Commendation, Mayor of Albuquerque, 1979, Hon. Commdr. award U.S. Air Force, 1979, Award of yr., Albuquerque Bus. and Profl. Women; named Outstanding Young Women of Am., 1980-81. Mem. N.Mex. Jud. Council (exec. com. 1982-83), N.Mex. Bar Assn., N.Mex. Judges Assn., Nat. Assn. Women Judges, U. N.Mex. Alumni Assn. (bd. dirs.), N.Mex. Assn. Women in Govt., N.Mex. Automobile Assn. (bd. dirs.).Democrat. Roman Catholic. Federal civil litigation, Real property. Home: 2219 Vista Larga NE Albuquerque NM 87106 Office: Messina Madrid & Maynez 501 Tijeras Suite 101 Albuquerque NM 87102

MADSEN, H(ENRY) STEPHEN, lawyer; b. Momence, Ill., Feb. 5, 1924; s. Frederick and Christine (Landgren) M.; m. Carol Ruth Olmstead, Dec. 30, 1967; children: Stephen Stewart, Christie Morgan, Kelly Ann. M.B.A., U. Chgo., 1948; LL.B., Yale U., 1951. Bar: Wash. 1951, Ohio 1953, U.S. Supreme Ct. 1975. Research asst. Wash. Water Power Co., Spokane, 1951; assoc. firm Baker, Hostetler & Paterson, Cleve., 1952-59; partner Baker, Hostetler & Paterson, 1960—; chmn. bd. trustees Blue Cross Northeastern, Ohio, 1972-81; Danish consul for Ohio, 1973—. Served with AC U.S. Army, 1943-46. Decorated Knight Queen of Denmark, 1982. Fellow ABA; mem. Am. Coll. Trial Lawyers (life), Am. Law Inst., Am. Judicature Soc., Ohio Bar Assn., Cleve. Bar Assn. Clubs: Union of Cleve.; Yale of N.Y.C. Federal civil litigation, State civil litigation. Office: 3200 Nat City Bank Center Cleveland OH 44114

MADSEN, ROGER BRYAN, lawyer; b. Logan, Utah, Dec. 1, 1947; s. Louis Linden and Edith Louise (Gundersen) M.; m. Leslie Sheryl Roberts, 1972; children: Rebecca, Deborah, Bryan, Benjamin, Melanie. B.A. in Polit. Sci. and French with distinction, Wash. State U., 1971; M.A. in Polit. Sci., Brigham Young U., 1972, J.D., 1976; M. Internat. Mgmt., Am. Grad. Sch. Internat. Mgmt., 1973. Bar: Idaho 1976, U.S. Dist. Ct. Idaho 1976. Jud. intern U.S. Supreme Ct., Washington, 1974; legal intern JAG's Sch., U. Va. Law Sch., Charlottesville, 1974, Wash. State Atty. Gen.'s Office, Pullman, 1975; asst. atty. gen. Idaho Atty. Gen.'s Office, Boise, 1976-80; dist. mgr. Gibbens Co., Inc., Boise, 1980-83; sole practice, Boise, 1983—. Contbr. numerous articles on employment law to profl. jours. Vice chmn. Idaho del. to White Ho. Conf. on Families, Los Angeles, 1980; mem. planning com., bus. lobbyist, mgmt. cons. Idaho Celebration of Bicentennial of U.S. Constn., 1986; chmn. Idaho Gov.'s Task Force on Unemployment Ins., 1983-84, Mayor-County Commn. Task Force on Pub. Housing Authority Investigation, 1986; mem. Gov.'s Workers Compensation Adv. Council, 1986—; polit. activist, fund-raiser; bd. dirs. Idaho Allied Civic Forces, Boise, 1981—; alumni ednl. counselor Am. Grad. Sch. Internat. Mgmt., Glendale, Ariz., 1974—; Mormon missionary in France and Belgium, 1986—, high council Ch. of Jesus Christ of Latter-day Saints, exec. sec. stake; gen. counsel Idaho Assn. Counties. Mem. Wash. State U. Alumni Assn. (bd. dirs., com. chmn.), J. Reuben Clark Law Soc. (charter), Idaho Bar Assn., Idaho Assn. Commerce and Industry. Republican. Administrative and regulatory, Civil rights, Labor. Home: 7842 Desert Ave Boise ID 83709 Office: 3775 Cassia St Boise ID 83705

MADSEN, STEPHEN STEWART, lawyer; b. Spokane, Wash., Oct. 13, 1951; s. H. Stephen Madsen and Sarah Pope (Stewart) Ruth; m. Rebecca Wetherill Howard, July 28, 1984. BA, Harvard U., 1973; JD, Columbia U., 1980. Bar: N.Y. 1981, U.S. Dist. Ct. (so. dist.) N.Y. 1981, U.S. Ct. Appeals (6th cir.) 1983, U.S. Ct. Appeals (8th cir.) 1985. Law clk. to presiding justice U.S. Ct. Appeals (2d cir.), N.Y.C., 1980-81; assoc. Cravath, Swaine & Moore, N.Y.C., 1981—. Mem. ABA, N.Y. State Bar Assn. Federal civil litigation. Office: Cravath Swaine & Moore One Chase Manhattan Plaza New York NY 10128

MADSON, CRAIG JAMES, lawyer; b. Payson, Utah, Oct. 29, 1951; s. James Elbert and Phyllis Rose (Milner) M.; m. Mary Karen Taylor, Mar. 17, 1972; children: Margaret Ann, Amber Karen, Zachary Craig, James Elbert II. BS, U. Utah, 1973, JD, 1978. Bar: U.S. Dist. Ct. (no. dist.) Ill. 1978, U.S. Patent Office 1979, U.S. Ct. Appeals (7th cir.) 1981, U.S. Dist. Ct. Utah 1982. Assoc. Neuman, Williams, Anderson & Olson, Chgo., 1978-81, Fox, Edwards & Gardiner, Salt Lake City, 1981-84, Workman, Nydegger & Jensen, Salt Lake City, 1984—. Contbr. articles to profl. jours. Mem. ABA (forum com. on franchising 1980—), Utah Bar Assn. (pres.-elect franchise sect. 1985-86), Am. Intellectual Property Law Assn., Centerville Jaycees (pres. 1985-86), Phi Beta Kappa, Pi Mu Epsilon. Avocations: sports, music. Trademark and copyright, Franchise law, Patent. Home: 1883 N 150 E Centerville UT 84014 Office: Workman Nydegger & Jensen 57 W 200 S 3d Floor Salt Lake City UT 84101

MADVA, STEPHEN ALAN, lawyer; b. Pitts., July 27, 1948; s. Joseph Edward and Mary (Zulick) M.; m. Deborah Zateeny, Feb. 14, 1979; children: Alexander, Elizabeth. BA cum laude, Yale U., 1970; JD, U. Pa., 1973. Bar: Pa. 1973, U.S. Dist. Ct. (ea. dist.) Pa. 1975, U.S. Ct. Appeals (3d cir.) 1976, U.S. Supreme Ct. 1985. Asst. defender Defender Assn. Phila., 1973-75, fed. defender, 1975-77, also bd. dirs., 1985—; assoc. Montgomery, McCracken, Walker & Rhoads, Phila., 1977-81, ptnr., 1981—; mem. Fed. Criminal Justice Act Panel. Mem. ABA, Phila. Bar Assn. (fed. cts. com.), Pa. Bar Assn., Am. Judicature Soc., Def. Research Inst., Hist. Soc. Pa., Yale Alumni Assn. (schs. com.). Democrat. Roman Catholic. Avocations: tennis, distance running, reading junk fiction. Federal civil litigation, Environment, Criminal. Home: 416 Chichester Ln Wynnewood PA 19096 Office: Montgomery McCracken Walker & Rhoads 3 Parkway 20th Floor Philadelphia PA 19102

MAEDER, GARY WILLIAM, lawyer; b. Los Angeles, Dec. 21, 1949; s. Clarence Wilbur and Norma Jean (Buckbee) M.; m. Stephen Gregory, Charlene Michelle. BA, UCLA, 1971, JD, 1975; student, Fuller Seminary, 1971-72. Bar: Calif. 1975. Assoc. Kindel & Anderson, Los Angeles, 1975-82, ptnr., 1982—. Author: The Christian Life: Issues and Answers, 1976. Elder adult edn. St. John's Presbyn. Ch., Los Angeles, 1981—; mem. adv. bd. Christian Legal Soc. Los Angeles, 1975—; bd. dirs. Christian Conciliation Service of Los Angeles, 1983—. Mem. ABA, Los Angeles County Bar Assn., Order of Coif, Phi Beta Kappa. Democrat. Corporate taxation, Personal income taxation, State and local taxation. Office: Kindel & Anderson 555 South Flower St Suite 2600 Los Angeles CA 90071

MAFFEI, ROCCO JOHN, lawyer; b. Portland, Maine, Nov. 23, 1949; s. Rocco and Grace Marie (Bartlett) M; m. Susan Marie Farrell, June 23, 1973; children: Rocco Francis, Christopher Matthew. BA in History, Trinity Coll., 1972; JD, U. Maine, 1975. Bar: Maine 1975, Mass. 1975, U.S. Dist. Ct. Maine 1975, Ohio 1977, Minn. 1981, U.S. Dist. Ct. Minn. 1981, U.S. Ct. Claims 1980, U.S. Supreme Ct. 1980. Ptnr. Briggs & Morgan Law Firm, St. Paul, 1980-83, Hart & Bruner Law Firm, Mpls., 1983-85; counsel Control Data Corp., Mpls., 1985—; adj. prof. law William Mitchell Sch. of Law, St. Paul, 1981—. Contbr. articles to profl. jours. Served to capt. USAF, 1975-80. Mem. ABA (com. chmn. pub. contract law sect. 1984-86), Fed. Bar Assn., Minn. Bar Assn., Nat. Contract Mgmt. Assn. (pres. Twin Cities chpt. 1985-86), Huber Heights Jaycees (Jaycee of Yr. 1978). Republican. Roman Catholic. Avocation: long distance running. Government contracts and claims, Construction, General corporate. Home: 5609 22d Ave S Minneapolis MN 55417 Office: Control Data Corp 8100 34th Ave S PO Box O Minneapolis MN 55440

MAFFITT, JAMES STRAWBRIDGE, lawyer; b. Raleigh, N.C., Oct. 29, 1942; s. James Strawbridge III and Lois (Handy) M.; m. Mildred Roxanne Heffner, Mar. 14, 1964 (div. Oct. 1978); children: Amy Elizabeth, Margaret Montgomery; m. Frances Holton, Aug. 15, 1981. BA, Washington and Lee U., 1964, LLB, 1966. Bar: Va. 1966, Md. 1969. Assoc. Apostolou, Place & Thomas, Roanoke, Va., 1966-67; trust officer Mercantile-Safe Deposit & Trust Co., Balt., 1967-71; from assoc. to ptnr. Cable, McDaniel, Bowie & Bond, Balt., 1971-82; ptnr. Maffit & Rothschild, Balt., 1982-85, Anderson, Coe & King, Balt., 1986—. Fellow Md. Bar Found.; mem. ABA (ho. dels. 1986—), Md. Bar Assn., Va. Bar Assn., Balt. City Bar Assn. (pres. 1985-86), Wednesday Law Club. Democrat. Presbyterian. Club: Ctr. (Balt.). Avocations: waterfowl hunting, handball. General corporate, Real property, Contracts commercial. Home: 119 E Montgomery St Baltimore MD 21230 Office: Anderson Coe & King 201 N Charles St Baltimore MD 21201

MAGANZINI, PAUL JOHN, lawyer; b. Bklyn., Aug. 29, 1948; s. Ercole and Ines (Mase) M.; m. Teresa C. Aversa, May 22, 1976. B.A. Summa Cum Laude, St. Mary's Coll., Minn., 1970; J.D., U. Notre Dame, 1973. Bar: Ill. 1973, U.S. Dist. Ct. (no. dist.) Ill. 1974, U.S. Ct. Apls. (7th cir.) 1982. Assoc., Frank P. Kays and Frank J. Smith, 1974-77; sole practice, Chgo., 1977-81; ptnr. Maganzini, McMahon & McNicholas, Chgo., 1982—. Served to capt. USAR, 1972-78. Mem. ABA, Ill. Bar Assn., Chgo. Bar Assn., Du Page County Bar Assn. Roman Catholic. General practice. Office: 1 N LaSalle St Chicago IL 60602 Office: 315 W St Charles Rd Lombard IL 60148

MAGANZINI, TERESA AVERSA, lawyer; b. Phila., Dec. 8, 1951; d. Mario Salvatore and Teresa Elena (Sava) Aversa; m. Paul John Maganzini, May 22, 1976. BA, Notre Dame U., 1973; JD, Villanova U., 1976. Assoc. Law Office of Paul Maganzini, Chgo., 1976; asst. state's atty. State's Atty. Office of Cook County, Chgo., 1977—. Mem. ABA, Ill. State Bar Assn., Chgo. Bar Assn. (v.p., bd. dirs. 1984—), Nat. Dist. Attys. Assn. Roman Catholic. Avocation: conducting tours of Frank Lloyd Wright homes. Juvenile, Criminal. Home: 1146 N Kenilworth Oak Park IL 60302 Office: States Atty Office Cook County 1100 S Hamilton Chicago IL 60612

MAGEE, WILLIAM EUGENE, tax lawyer; b. Tylertown, Miss., Feb. 12, 1952; s. William Otis and Mary Ruth (Pierce) M.; m. LuAnn Fortenberry, May 26, 1973; children: Kimberly Alaine, Claiborne Holmes. Student, La. State U., 1970-71; BA, U. Miss., 1973; postgrad., Miss. Coll., 1974-75, U. So. Miss., 1975-76; JD with honors, U. Miss., 1978; LLM in Taxation, NYU, 1978-79. Bar: Miss. 1978, U.S. Dist. Ct. (no. dist.) Miss. 1978, U.S. Tax Ct. 1981, U.S. Ct. Appeals (5th cir.) 1982; CPA. Acct. dairy div. Pet Inc., Jackson, Miss., 1973-75; tax atty. Butler, Snow, O'Mara, Stevens & Cannada, Jackson, 1979—; adj. prof. corp. law Miss. Coll., Jackson, 1981-82. Grad. editor NYU Tax Law Rev., 1978-79. Mem. legacies and planned giving com. Hinds-Madison-Rankin chpt. Am. Cancer Soc., Jackson, 1985—, bd. dirs. 1986—, com. co-chmn. 1986—; vol. for grant applications and tax advice Christian Conciliation Service of Cen. Miss. Inc., Jackson, 1985—. Named one of Outstanding Young Men of Am., U.S. Jaycees, 1983. Mem. ABA, Miss. Bar Assn. (taxation com. 1984-85), Miss. Soc. of CPA's (taxation com. cen. chpt. 1984—, sec. com., 1985-86), Jackson Tax Forum (sec. 1982-83, v.p. 1983-84, pres. 1984-85), Omicron Delta Kappa, Phi Kappa Phi, Acacia. Baptist. Avocations: cycling, history. General, federal, state and local taxation, Probate, General corporate. Home: 319 Longmeadow Dr Ridgeland MS 39157 Office: Butler Snow O'Mara Stevens & Cannada 210 E Capitol St 17th Floor Deposit Guaranty Plaza Jackson MS 39201

MAGGARD, SARAH ELIZABETH, educator, lawyer; b. Whittier, Calif., Nov. 17, 1948; d. William Alexander and Laura (Redford) M. B.A., Whittier Coll., 1970, M.A. in Ed., 1971; J.D., Western State U., Fullerton, Calif., 1981. Bar: Calif. 1982. Tchr., Rowland Unified Sch. Dist., Rowland Heights, Calif., 1971—, also sole practice, Whittier, 1982—. Recipient Am. Jurisprudence awards Bancroft-Whitney Co., 1979, 80. Mem. State Bar Calif., ABA, Los Angeles County Bar Assn., Lawyers Club Los Angeles. Republican. Presbyterian. Assoc. editor Western State U. Law Rev., 1980. Estate planning, Probate. Home: 10319 Tigrina Ave Whittier CA 90603 Office: Rowland Unified Sch Dist 1830 Nogales St Rowland Heights CA 91748

MAGINNESS, CRAIG RICHARD, lawyer, consultant; b. Glen Ridge, N.J., Oct. 4, 1954; s. George Pershing and Elizabeth (Ball) M.; m. Ellen Watkins Reath, Sept. 17, 1983. BA, Dartmouth Coll., 1976; JD, Syracuse U., 1979; postdoctoral in Econs., U. Colo., 1982—. Bar: Colo., U.S. Dist. Ct. Colo., U.S. Ct. Appeals (10th cir.) 1979. Assoc. Sherman & Howard, Denver, 1979-85, ptnr., 1985—; cons. econs. and law, Denver, 1984—; lectr. micro econs. U. Colo., Denver, 1984. Contbr. articles to profl. jours. Mem. com. Housing and Community Devel., Boulder, Colo., 1980-81; head class agt. alumni fund Dartmouth Coll., Rocky Mountain region, 1982—. Mem. ABA, Colo. Bar Assn., Denver Bar Assn., Am. Econs. Assn., Colo. Trial Lawyers Assn. (lectr. antitrust), Order of Coif. Republican. Avocations: piano, skiing. Antitrust, Federal civil litigation, State civil litigation. Office: Sherman & Howard 633 17th St #2900 Denver CO 80202

MAGLARAS, CHRIS, JR., lawyer; b. Somerville, N.J., Mar. 1, 1956; s. Chris and Phyllis (Lorenzo) M.; m. Alice Colleen Ward, Aug. 12, 1978; children: Kathleen, Christopher III, Lauren, Courtney. BA, U. San Diego, 1977, JD, 1980. Bar: Nev. 1980, U.S. Dist. Ct. Nev. 1981, U.S. Ct. Appeals (9th cir.) 1982, U.S. Supreme Ct. 1983. Assoc. George Graziadei Law Office, Las Vegas, Nev., 1980-82; ptnr. Ward & Maglaras, Las Vegas, 1982—. Arbitrator Govt. Employee Relations Bd., Las Vegas, Fee Dispute Com. State bar, Las Vegas , 1985—; mem. Clark County Pro Bono Program, Las Vegas, 1985—,. Mem. ABA, Assn. Trial Lawyers Am., Nev. Trial Lawyers Assn. Republican. Roman Catholic. State civil litigation, Personal injury, General corporate. Office: Ward & Maglaras 725 S 6th St Las Vegas NV 89101

MAGLARAS, NICHOLAS GEORGE, lawyer; b. N.Y.C., Apr. 21, 1951; s. George Nicholas and Angelica (Alexander) M. BA in Econs. cum laude, CUNY, Queens, 1973; JD, Fordham U., 1976. Bar: N.Y. 1977, U.S. Dist. Ct. (so. and ea. dists.) N.Y. 1977, U.S. Ct. Appeals (4th and 5th cirs.) 1983, U.S. Supreme Ct. 1985. Sr. assoc. Lambos, Flynn, Nyland & Giardino, N.Y.C., 1976—. Co-author: The Needs of the Growing Greek-American Community in the City of New York, 1973. Active Am. Hellenic Ednl. Progressive Assn., Washington, 1969—. Mem. ABA, N.Y. State Bar Assn., N.Y. County Bar Lawyers Assn. Democrat. Greek Orthodox. Avocations: dancing, skiing, softball, meteorology. Labor, Federal civil litigation, Pension, profit-sharing, and employee benefits. Home: 21-18 23d Dr Astoria NY 11105

MAGNESS, MICHAEL KENNETH, lawyer, management consultant; b. Tarentum, Pa., July 19, 1948; s. Kenneth Wilcox and Carolyn Frances (Harding) M.; m. Carolyn Marie Wehmann, Oct. 24, 1981; children: Sarah Elisabeth, Andrew Alexander. AB in History, Case Western Res. U., 1970, JD, 1973. Bar: Ohio 1973. Asst. dean Case Western Res. Law Sch., Cleve., 1973-76; dir. placement services NYU Sch. Law, N.Y.C., 1976-82; exec. dir. Martindale Services Inc., N.Y.C., 1982-84; v.p. Human Resource Services, Inc., N.Y.C., 1984-86; ptnr. Magness & Wehmann, N.Y.C., 1986—. Producer: (videotape) Brief Encounters, 1980, cons. (videotape) Beyond the Resume, 1980; contbr. articles on lawyer recruitment to profl. jours. Pres. Hudson Street Owners Corp., N.Y.C., 1984—, mem. vis. com. Case Western Res. Law Sch., 1984—. Fellow Am. Bar Found.; mem. ABA (sec. on legal edn., gen. practice sect., chmn. profl. competence com., chmn. career planning com. young lawyers div.), Nat. Assn. for Law Placement (pres. 1980-81), Phi Delta Phi, Phi Gamma Delta. Episcopalian. Avocations: travel, hiking, bicycling. Management consultant to legal profession.

MAGNUSON, PAUL A., federal judge; b. Carthage, S.D., Feb. 9, 1937; s. Arthur and Emma Elleda (Paulson) M.; m. Sharon Schultz, Dec. 21, 1959; children—Marlene, Margaret, Kevin, Kara. B.A., Gustavus Adolphus Coll, 1959; J.D., William Mitchell Coll., 1963. Ptnr. LeVander, Gillen, MIller & Magnuson, South St. Paul, Minn., 1963-81; judge U.S. Dist. Ct., St. Paul,

1981—. Mem. Met. Health Bd., St. Paul, 1970-72; legal counsel Ind. Republican Party Minn., St. Paul, 1979-81. Recipient Disting. Alumnus award Gustavus Adolphus Coll., 1982. Mem. ABA, 1st Dist. Bar Assn. (pres. 1974-75), Dakota County Bar Assn., Am. Judicature Soc. Presbyterian. Home: 3047 Klondike Ave N Lake Elmo MN 55042 Office: US Dist Ct 316 N Robert St Saint Paul MN 55101

MAGNUSON, ROGER JAMES, lawyer; b. St. Paul, Jan. 25, 1945; s. Roy Gustaf and Ruth Lily (Edlund) M.; m. Elizabeth Cunningham Shaw, Sept. 11, 1982; children—James Roger, Peter Cunningham, Mary Kerstin. B.A., Stanford U., 1967; J.D., Harvard U., 1971; B.C.L., Oxford U., 1972. Bar: Minn. 1973, U.S. Dist. Ct. Minn. 1973, U.S. Ct. Appeals (8th, 9th, 10th cirs.) 1974, U.S. Supreme Ct. 1978. Chief pub. defender Hennepin County Pub. Defender's Office, Mpls., 1973; ptnr. Dorsey & Whitney, Mpls., 1972—. Author: Shareholder Litigation, 1981, Are Gay Rights Right. Contbr. articles to profl. jours. Elder, Straitgate Ch., Mpls., 1980—. Mem. ABA, Christian Legal Soc. Republican. Federal civil litigation, Libel, Criminal. Home: 625 Park AVe Mahtomedi MN 55115 Office: Dorsey & Whitney Suite 2200 1st Bank Pl E Minneapolis MN 55402

MAGOON, BRIAN A(LAN), lawyer; b. Lawrence, Mass., June 28, 1949; s. Robert Arnold Magoon and Josephine (Grant) Midgett; m. Deborah Kay Harris, Sept. 13, 1980. BA with distinction, U. Va., 1971; JD, U. Denver, 1978. Bar: Colo. 1978, U.S. Dist. Ct. Colo. 1978, U.S. Ct. Appeals (10th cir.) 1986, U.S. Ct. Claims 1986. Assoc. Grant, McHendrie et al, Denver, 1978-83; of counsel McMartin, Burke et al, Englewood, Colo., 1983-84, ptnr., 1984-85; ptnr. Loser, Fitzgerald, Magoon and Davies, Englewood, 1985-86, Loser, Davies, Magoon & Fitzgerald, Denver, 1986—. Alt. mem. Lakewood (Colo.) Planning Commn., 1983-86. Served to 1st lt. USAF, 1971-75. Mem. ABA, Colo. Bar Assn. (vice chmn. grievance policy com. 1986—), Am. Trial Lawyers Assn., Colo. Trial Lawyers Assn., Am. Judicature Soc. Federal civil litigation, State civil litigation. Home: 1660 S Chase St Lakewood CO 80226 Office: Loser Davies Magoon & Fitzgerald 1512 Larimer St Suite 600 Denver CO 80202

MAGUIRE, MARGARET LOUISE, lawyer; b. Bklyn., Oct. 31, 1944; d. William L. and Elizabeth L. (Steinbugler) M.; 1 child, William Egginton. BA, Marymont Coll., 1965; MA, Colgate U., 1969; JD, U. Louisville, 1977. Bar: Ky. 1977. Counsel 1st Ky. Nat. Corp., Louisville, 1977-79; atty. Fed. Res. Bd., Washington, 1979-80; dep. to chmn. FDIC, Washington, 1980-85; atty. The Secura Group, Washington, 1985—. Co-author: Bank Holding Companies: A Practical Guide to Bank Acquisitions and Mergers, 1978-79. Mem. Fed. Bar Assn. (exec. council banking law com.), Women in Housing and Fin. Banking. Office: The Secura Group 1200 New Hampshire Ave NW Washington DC 20036

MAHAFFEY, GEORGE H., law educator; b. Eldorado, Ill., Feb. 22, 1928; s. Henry M. and Susie (Bowers) M.; m. Norma J. Sullivan, May 6, 1950; children—Carla, Deborah, Gaila. B.S.E., So. Ill. U., 1965, M.S.E., 1968, Ph.D., 1972. Tchr., prin. pub. schs., Ill., 1958-66, 69-71; dir. elem. edn. Eldorado Dist. 4, 1968-69; from asst. to assoc. prof. sch. law Central Mo. State U., Warrensburg, 1971-83, prof., 1983— ; cons. pub. sch. dists., Mo., 1972-84, Mo. State Dept. Edn., Jefferson City, 1981-84. Bd. dirs. Johnson County Mental Health Com., Warrensburg, 1982. Served with USN, 1944-46. Fulbright-Hayes fellow U.S. Dept. Edn, India, 1978. Mem. Mo. Profs. of Ednl. Adminstrn. (pres. 1984), Central Dist. Sch. Adminstrs. Assn., Central Dist. Elem. Prins. Assn., Phi Delta Kappa (treas. campus chpt. 1975-76, pres. 1977). Baptist. Lodge: Masons. Legal education, Libel. Home: 1108 Tyler St Warrensburg MO 64093 Office: Central Mo State U Lovinger 400 Warrensburg MO 64093

MAHAN, JOHN ERNEST, lawyer; b. Knoxville, Tenn., Feb. 18, 1950; s. Douglas M. and Imogene (Underwood) M.; m. Sharon Lynn Morris, Aug. 13, 1971; children: Sarah Katherine, John Ryan. BS, U. Tenn., 1972; JD, Atlanta U., 1980. Bar: Ga. 1982, U.S. Dist. Ct. (no. dist.) Ga. 1982. Sole practice Lilburn, Ga., 1982—. Mem. ABA, Ga. State Bar Assn., Atlanta Bar Assn., Gwinnett C. of C. Republican. Baptist. Lodge: Kiwanis (pres. 1984-85). Avocations: basketball, golf. Personal injury, Family and matrimonial, Real property. Home: 2978 Kelly Ct Lawrenceville GA 30245 Office: 455 Beaver Ruin Rd Lilburn GA 30247

MAHAR, THOMAS DANIEL, JR., lawyer; b. Poughkeepsie, N.Y., July 23, 1938; s. Thomas Daniel and Mary M. (Hoey) M.; m. Nancy Louise Daniels, Aug. 1, 1964; children—Thomas Daniel III, Mary Ellen, Kathleen Anne. B.A., Siena Coll., 1960; LL.B., Villanova U., 1963. Bar: N.Y. 1964, U.S. Mil. Ct. Appeals 1964, Ariz. 1967, U.S. Dist. Ct. (ea. and so. dists.) N.Y. 1968. Assoc., E.J. Mack, Attys. at Law, Poughkeepsie, 1967-69, Pagones & Cross, Attys. at Law, Beacon, N.Y., 1969-73; regional atty. N.Y. State Civil Service Employees Assn., 1973—; ptnr. Mangold & Mahar, Attys. at Law, Poughkeepsie, 1974—. Author: Legal Assistance Handbook, 1967. State committeeman N.Y. State Democratic Com., Poughkeepsie, 1968-70; coach Catholic Youth Orgn. basketball St. Mary's Ch., Wappingers Falls, N.Y., 1978-79. Served to capt. JAGC, U.S. Army, 1964-67. Named Outstanding Young Man of Am., U.S. Jr. C. of C., 1967; Soldier of Month, U.S. Army, 1967. Mem. ABA, N.Y. State Bar Assn., Dutchess County Bar Assn. (treas. 1967-71, judiciary com. 1983-84). Democrat. Roman Catholic. Clubs: Ketcham Boosters (pres. 1983-84), Poughkeepsie Soccer (rep. 1980-84). Labor, Probate, General practice. Home: 12 Malmros Terr Poughkeepsie NY 12601 Office: Mangold & Mahar 322 Mill St Poughkeepsie NY 12601

MAHER, DANIEL FRANCIS, JR., lawyer; b. Jersey City, June 5, 1956; s. Daniel Francis and Anna R. (Naughton) M.; m. Ann McLaughlin, Sept 11, 1982. BA in Polit. Sci. and Journalism, Rutgers U., 1978; JD, Calif. Western Law Sch., 1981. Bar: N.J. 1981, N.Y. 1982, U.S. Dist. Ct. N.J., U.S. Dist. Ct. (so. dist.) N.Y. Assoc. Greenhill, Speyer & Thurm, N.Y.C., 1981-82; gen. counsel DMT Fin. Group Inc., N.Y.C., 1982—; of counsel Kennedy & Daniels, Sea Gert, N.J., 1986—. Mem. Nat. Rep. Congl. Com. Mem. ABA, N.Y. County Lawyers Assn. Roman Catholic. Avocation: sports. Insurance, Real property, General corporate. Home: 264 Beach 134th St Belle Harbor NY 11694 Office: DMT Fin Group Inc 55 John St New York NY 10038

MAHER, DAVID WILLARD, lawyer; b. Chgo., Aug. 14, 1934; s. Chauncey Carter and Martha (Peppers) M.; A.B., Harvard, 1955, LL.B., 1959; m. Jill Waid Armagnac, Dec. 20, 1954; children—Philip Armagnac, Julia Armagnac. Admitted to N.Y. bar, 1960, Ill. bar, 1961; practiced in Chgo., 1961—; assoc. Kirkland & Ellis, and predecessor firm, 1960-65, ptnr., 1966-78; ptnr. Reuben & Proctor, 1978-86 , Isham, Lincoln & Beale, 1986—; Bd. dirs. Better Bus. Bur. Chgo. and No. Ill. Served to 2d lt. USAF, 1955-56. Mem. Am., Ill., Chgo. bar assns. Roman Catholic. Clubs: Bull Valley Hunt, Chicago Literary, Union League, Tavern. Trademark and copyright, Entertainment, Administrative and regulatory. Home: 311 Belden Ave Chicago IL 60614 Office: 19 S LaSalle St Chicago IL 60603

MAHER, EDWARD JOSEPH, lawyer; b. Cleve., Sept. 18, 1939; s. Richard Leo and Lucile (Thompson) M.; m. Marilyn K. Maher, Oct. 8, 1966; children—Richard A., David C., Michael E, Colleen Therese. B.S., Georgetown U., 1961, LL.B., 1964; student U. Fribourg, Switzerland, 1959-61. Bar: Ohio 1964, U.S. dist. ct. (no. dist.) Ohio 1964. Assoc., Sweeney, Maher & Vlad, Cleve., 1964-71; sole practice, Cleve., 1971—. Pres. parish council St. Raphael's Ch., Bay Village, Ohio, 1983-84; former adv. bd. Catholic Family and Children's Services; adv. bd. Cath. Youth Orgn., 1973-79, pres., 1975-76; chmn. Elyria Cursillo Ctr., 1974-75; lay del. to Ohio Cath. Conf., Diocese of Cleve., 1973-75; chmn. adv. bd. Cath. Social Services of Cuyahoga County, 1978-79; trustee Cath. Charities Corp., 1977—, treas., 1979, sec., 1981, 1st v.p., 1983, gen. chmn. campaign, 1983, 84, pres., 1985-86; pres. Diocesan adv. bd. Cath. Youth Orgn., 1980-82; team capt. United Way Services Agy. Team Group, 1981, nominating com., 1983. Mem. ABA, Ohio Bar Assn., Cuyahoga County Bar Assn., Cleve. Bar Assn., Cath. Lawyers Guild Cleve. (pres. 1970). Club: Irish Good Fellowship (pres.). Personal injury, Probate, Insurance. Office: 1548 Standard Bldg Cleveland OH 44113

MAHER, JOHN A., lawyer, educator; b. Bklyn., Dec. 3, 1930; s. John A. and Helen D. (Stack) M.; m. Joan Dawley, July 31, 1954; children: Jeanne M., John A. III, James A., Helen D., Joan T. AB, U. Notre Dame, 1951; LLB, NYU, 1956, LLM in Trade Regulation, 1957; cert. bus. adminstrn., U. Va., 1969; cert. fgn. and comparative law, Columbia U., 1974. Bar: N.Y. 1957, D.C. 1960, Pa. 1986. Assoc. Healy & Baillie, N.Y.C., 1957-59; staff atty. Swift & Co., N.Y.C, 1959-62; asst. gen. counsel Celanese Corp., N.Y.C., 1962-70; v.p. law Blount, Inc., Montgomery, Ala., 1970-73; prof. The Dickinson Sch. of Law, Carlisle, Pa., 1973—; bd. dirs., vice chmn. Atlantic Liberty Savs., Bklyn., 1960—, vice chmn. 1984—; counsel Eaton & Van Winkle, N.Y.C., 1974—; trustee Food & Drug Law Inst., Washington, 1984—. Author: Survey of Robinson-Patman Act, 1969; co-author: Export Opportunities and The Export Trading Act of 1982, 1984; contbr. articles to profl. jours. Mem. Pres.'s Adv. Com. on Textile Info., Washington, 1967-68. Served with USNR, 1951-55, retired lt. comdr. 1974. Food Law Inst. fellow NYU Law Ctr., 1956-57. Fellow Pa. Bar Found. (life); mem. Pa. Bar Assn. (chmn. corp. banking and bus. sect. 1987—). Roman Catholic. Club: Bklyn. Avocations: photography, reading, travel. Antitrust, Admiralty, Securities.

MAHER, MARY FRANCES, lawyer; b. Detroit, Apr. 27, 1955; s. Francis Joseph and Mary Lillian (McCarthy) M. BS in Speech, Northwestern U., MA in Speech; JD, Loyola U., Chgo. Bar: Ill. 1980, U.S. Dist. Ct. (no. dist.) Ill. 1981, Tex. 1985. Atty. office legal affairs Northwestern U., Evanston, Ill., 1981-82, SFN Cos. Inc., Glenview, Ill., 1983-84; assoc. Brown, Maroney, Rose, Barber & Dye, Austin, 1984—. Bd. dirs. Austin Lawyers and Accts. for the Arts, 1985—, sec. 1986—. Mem. ABA, Ill. Bar Assn. (chmn. copyright com. 1982-84), Tex. Bar Assn. (chmn. copyright com. 1986—), Chgo. Bar Assn., Travis County Bar Assn., Austin Young Lawyers Assn., Assn. Trial Lawyers Am., Speech Communications Assn., Internat. Communications Assn., Cen. States Speech Assn., Am. Forensics Assn. Roman Catholic. Avocations: swimming, reading. Trademark and copyright, Computer, General corporate. Office: Brown Maroney Rose Barber & Dye 1300 One Republic Plaza 333 Guadalupe Austin TX 78701

MAHER, O. KENT, lawyer; b. Winnemucca, Nev., Dec. 15, 1949; s. Robert N. Maher and M. Louise (Sheppard) Dennis; m. Dana Ceresola, July 22, 1972 (div. July 1984); children: Guy Russell, Colin Kent. BS, U. Nev., 1971, MS, 1976; JD, U. Pacific, 1982. Bar: Nev. 1982, U.S. Dist. Ct. Nev. 1982. Law clk. to presiding justice 6th Jud. Dist. Ct., Winnemucca, 1982-83; dep. dist. atty. Humboldt County, Winnemucca, 1983-85; ptnr. Callahan & Maher, Winnemucca, 1985—. Mem. Assn. Trial Lawyers Am., Nev. Trial Lawyers Assn., Alpha Zeta, Gamma Sigma Delta. Democrat. Lodge: DeMolay. Avocations: hunting, fishing, outdoors. Estate planning, General practice, Probate. Office: Callahan & Maher PO Box 351 Winnemucca NV 89445

MAHON, ARTHUR J., lawyer; b. N.Y.C., Jan. 13, 1934; s. Arthur Logan and Mary Agnes (Crane) M.; m. Myra E. Murphy, Aug. 10, 1957; children—Maura, Madonna, Arthur, Nancy. B.A., Manhattan Coll., 1955; LL.B., NYU, 1958. Bar: N.Y., Fla., D.C. Adj. prof. law NYU Sch. of Law, N.Y.C., 1964-78; ptnr. Mudge Rose Guthrie Alexander & Ferdon, N.Y.C., 1970—. Trustee Elizabeth Seton Coll., Westchester, N.Y., 1972—, Adrian and Jesse Archbold Charitable Trust, N.Y.C., 1976—; mem. adv. bd. N.Y. Hosp.-Cornell Med. Ctr., N.Y.C., 1982—; mem. com. on trust and estate gift plans Rockefeller U., N.Y.C., 1984—; mem. planned giving com. United Way of N.Y.C., 1983—; chmn. planned giving com. of lawyers, bankers and accts. Archdiocese of N.Y., N.Y.C., 1985—; bd. overseers Cornell Med. Coll., N.Y.C., 1986—. Served to capt. USAF, 1958-60. Mem. N.Y. State Bar Assn., Bar Assn. City of N.Y., Fla Bar Assn., D.C. Bar Assn., Royal Soc. Medicine Found. (bd. dirs. 1977—, pres. 1979—). Club: India House (Hanover Sq., N.Y.). Estate planning, Family and matrimonial, Probate. Home: 201 Hamilton Rd Chappaqua NY 10514 Office: Mudge Rose Guthrie Alexander & Ferdon 180 Maiden Ln New York NY 10038

MAHON, ELDON BROOKS, federal judge; b. Loraine, Tex., Apr. 9, 1918; s. John Bryan and Nola May (Muns) M.; m. Nova Lee Groom, June 1, 1941; children: Jana, Martha, Brad. B.A., McMurry Coll., 1939; LL.B., U. Tex., 1942. Bar: Tex. 1942. Law clk. Tex. Supreme Ct., 1945-46; county atty. Mitchell County, Tex., 1947; dist. atty. 32d Jud. Dist. Tex., 1948-60, dist. judge, 1960-63; v.p. Tex. Electric Service Co., Ft. Worth, 1963-64; mem. firm Mahon Pope & Gladden, Abilene, Tex., 1964-68; U.S. atty. No. Dist. Tex., Ft. Worth, 1968-72; judge U.S. Dist. Ct. for No. Tex., Ft. Worth, 1972—. Pres. W. Tex. council Girl Scouts U.S.A., 1966-68; Trustee McMurry Coll. Served with USAAF, 1942-45. Named an outstanding Tex. prosecutor Tex. Law Enforcement Found., 1957. Mem. Am., Fed., Ft.-Worth-Tarrant County bar assns., Am. Judicature Soc., State Bar Tex. Methodist (past del. confs.). Office: US Dist Court 403 US Courthouse Fort Worth TX 76102 *

MAHONEY, DAVID JOHN, lawyer; b. Buffalo, Dec. 16, 1928; s. David J. and Aileen L. (Leppelmann) M.; m. Heidi L. Lyon, Nov. 14, 1955; children: David, Neal J., John F. Grad. Canisius Coll., 1949; LLB, U. Buffalo, 1952. Bar: N.Y. 1953, Fla. 1977, U.S. Dist. Ct. (we. dist.) N.Y. 1953, U.S. Ct. Appeals (2d cir.) 1979, U.S. Dist. Ct. (no. dist.) Ohio 1975, U.S. Supreme Ct. 1958. Sole practice, Buffalo, 1953-59; ptnr. Offermann, Mahoney, Cassano, Pigott & Greco and predecessor firm Offermann, Fallon, Mahoney & Cassano, Buffalo, 1959—; pres. bd. dirs. Buffalo and Erie County (N.Y.) Legal Services Corp. Mem. ABA, N.Y. Bar Assn. (chmn. civil rights com., bd. dirs. Erie County), Erie County Bar Assn., N.Y. Trial Lawyers Assn., Am. Trial Lawyers Assn. Civil rights, General corporate, Family and matrimonial. Office: Offermann Mahoney Cassano Pigott & Greco Statler Towers Suite 1776 Buffalo NY 14202

MAHONEY, GEORGE LEFEVRE, lawyer; b. Washington, Mar. 28, 1952; s. George Francis Xavier and Elaine (LeFevre) M. BA, U. Va., 1974, JD, 1978. Bar: N.Y. 1979, U.S. Dist. Ct. (so. and ea. dists.) N.Y. 1979, U.S. Ct. Appeals (5th cir.) 1980, U.S. Ct. Appeals (2d cir.) 1981. Assoc. Satterlee & Stephens, N.Y., 1978-82; atty. Dow Jones & Co., Inc., N.Y.C. and Princeton, N.J., 1982—. General corporate, Real property, Trademark and copyright. Office: Dow Jones & Co Inc PO Box 300 Princeton NJ 08540

MAHONEY, PHILIP CHARLES, lawyer; b. Souix Falls, S.D., Jan. 21, 1934; s. Philip Eugene James and Hannah May (Cronn) M.; m. Gwendolyn Evans, June 1972 (div. 1975); children: Padraic, Siobhan. BA, U. Wash., 1960. Bar: Wash. 1968, U.S. Dist. Ct. (we. dist.) 1968, U.S. Ct. Appeals (9th cir.) 1969, U.S. Supreme Ct. 1970. Bailiff King County Superior Ct., Seattle, 1967-68; assoc. Office of Bill Lanning, Seattle, 1968-78; sole practice Seattle, 1978—. Pres. King County Young Dems., 1964, 32d Dist. Dem. Club, Seattle, 1966; Mcpl. League City ops. Com., Seattle, 1966; bd. dirs. Wing Luke Meml. Found. Served with USAR, 1957-63. Mem. Washington State Bar Assn., Seattle-King County Bar Assn. Avocations: reading, writing, hiking, attending concerts. Criminal, Personal injury, State civil litigation. Office: 550 Arctic Bldg Seattle WA 98104

MAHONEY, TIMOTHY WILLIAM, lawyer; b. Pasco, Wash., Oct. 1, 1946; s. Daniel F. and Geraldine F. (Shaughnessy) M.; m. Marcia L. Pelela, Mar. 3, 1981. AA, Columbia Basin Coll., Pasco, 1967; BA, Wash. State U., 1971; JD, Gonzaga U., 1975; LLM in Taxation, Georgetown U., 1977. Bar: Wash. 1975, U.S. Dist. Ct. (ea. dist.) Wash. 1976, U.S. Tax Ct. 1979, U.S. Ct. Appeals (9th cir.) 1980. Hotel mgr. Hyatt Corp., Seattle, 1971-72; assoc. Gladstone & Stancik, Richland, Wash., 1975-76; atty. Sullivan & Mahoney, Richland, Wash., 1977-79; partnership Kennewick, Wash., 1979-82, sole practice, 1982—. Personal injury, General practice, Personal income taxation. Office: 2632 W Bruneau Pl Kennewick WA 99336

MAICHEL, JOSEPH RAYMOND, lawyer, business executive; b. Stanton, N.D., Nov. 24, 1934; s. John and Sarfina (Hoffman) M.; m. Hilda Deichert, Jan. 7, 1961; children: Mary, Mark, Scott. B.S. in Acctg., U. N.D., 1957, J.D. with distinction, 1959. Bar: N.D. 1959. Spl. asst. atty. gen. State of N.D., 1959-71; atty. Mont.-Dakota Utilities Co., N.D., 1971-76; gen. counsel, sec. Mont.-Dakota Utilities Co., 1976-82, v.p., 1979-82, pres., 1985—; gen. counsel Knife River Coal Mining Co., Bismarck, 1979-82; also dir.; pres. Grassland, Inc., Bismarck, 1978-84; sec., dir. Fidelity Oil Co., 1980-83, Welch Coal Co., 1980-83, Wibaux Gas Co., 1980-83; dir. First Fed. Savs. & Loan, Bismarck, Mont. Dakota Utilities; tchr. bus. law, 1968—. Contbr. articles to legal jours. Mem. ABA, Am. Soc. Corp. Secs., North Central Electric Assn., Midwest Gas Assn., Edison Electric Inst., N.D. Bar Assn., Burleigh County Bar Assn. Public utilities, General corporate. Office: Mont-Dakota Utilities Co 400 N 4th St Bismarck ND 58501

MAIDMAN, RICHARD HARVEY MORTIMER, lawyer; b. N.Y.C., Nov. 17, 1933; s. William and Ada (Seegle) M.; m. Lynne Rochelle Lateiner, Apr. 3, 1960; children—Patrick, Mitchel, Dagny. B.A., Williams Coll., 1955; J.D., Yale U., 1959; postgrad. N.Y. U. Grad. Sch. Bus., 1957, Grad. Sch. Law, 1960, 77. Bar: N.Y. 1961, Fla. bar, 1961, U.S. Dist. Ct. 1962, 79, U.S. Ct. Appeals 1966, U.S. Supreme Ct., 1978. Assoc. Saxe, Bacon & O'Shea, N.Y.C., 1962-64; ptnr. Weiner, Maidman & Goldman, N.Y.C., 1964-67; sole practice, N.Y.C., and Fla., 1968—; dir. Microbiol. Scis., Inc.; Nat. Over-the-Counter List, Providence, 1971—, sec., 1971—; pres. MBS Equities, Inc., Fashion Wear Realty Co., Inc., N.Y.C., 1975—; mng. gen. ptnr. Richard and David Maidman, N.Y.C., 1972—, Barcelona Hotel Ltd., Miami Beach, Fla., 1975-84; legis. counsel Theodore R. Kupferman, 17th Congl. Dist. N.Y., 1966-68; of counsel Shwal, Thompson & Bloch, N.Y.C. and Geneva, 1976—; receiver Halloren House Hotel, N.Y.C., 1981. Mem. ABA, N.Y. State Bar Assn., Fla. Bar Assn., Assn. Bar City N.Y., Bankruptcy Lawyers Assn. N.Y.C. General corporate, Real property. Home: Steamboat Landing Sands Point NY 11050 Home and Office: 432 E 87th St New York NY 10128 Office: 1726 M St Washington DC 20036

MAIDMAN, STEPHEN PAUL, lawyer; b. Hartford, Conn., Feb. 8, 1954; s. Harry and Roslyn (Mandell) M. AB summa cum laude, Bowdoin Coll., 1976; MBA, U. Pa., 1979, JD, 1980. Bar: Pa. 1980, U.S. Dist. Ct. (ea. dist.) Pa. 1980, U.S. Ct. Appeals (3d cir.) 1980. Assoc. Drinker, Biddle & Reath, Phila., 1980-81; atty. IBM Corp., Boca Raton, Fla., 1981-84; staff atty. IBM Corp., N.Y.C., 1984—. Mem. ABA, Pa. Bar Assn., Phila. Bar Assn., Am. Corp. Counsel Assn., Phi Beta Kappa. Avocation: running. Computer, Antitrust, Labor. Home: 55 Mill Plain Rd #23-6 Danbury CT 06811 Office: IBM Corp 590 Madison Ave New York NY 10022

MAIER, HAROLD GEISTWEIT, legal educator, lawyer; b. Cin., Mar. 25, 1937; s. Alfred F. and Alberta (Wilmes) M.; m. Janice Marlene Mattie, Aug. 9, 1963; children—Marc L., Kurt S. B.A. in English Lit., U. Cin., 1959, J.D., 1963; postgrad. Free U. Berlin, 1959-60; LL.M., U. Mich., 1964; potgrad. U. Munich, 1964-65. Bar: Ohio 1963. Mem faculty of law Vanderbilt U., Nashville, 1965—, prof., 1970—, dir. Transnat. Legal Studies Program, 1973—; faculty San Diego Internat. & Comparative Law Inst. King's Coll. U. London, 1986; vis. prof. law U. Pa., 1985; cons. Office of Sec. Army, Panama Canal Treaty Negotiations, 1976, Office of Legal Adviser U.S. Dept. of State; guest scholar Brookings Instn., Washington, 1976-77; dir. PDS Patrons, Inc. (Univ. Sch. of Nashville), 1975—, pres., 1978-79; counselor on internat. law Office of Legal Adviser, U.S. Dept. State, 1983-84. Recipient Luftbrucke Dankstipendium, Free U. Berlin, 1959-60; Ford internat. studies fellow U. Mich., 1964-65; Vanderbilt U. faculty fellow, 1976-77. Mem. Am. Soc. Internat. Law (exec. council 1974-78, 84—), Am. Soc. for Comparative Study of Law (bd. dirs. 1984—), Am. Law Inst., Order of Coif, Omicron Delta Kappa, Phi Alpha Delta, Tau Kappa Alpha, Pi Delta Epsilon. Bd. editors Am. Jour. Internat. Law, 1984—; author: (with T. Buergenthal) Public International Law in A Nutshell, 1985; contbr. numerous articles in field to profl. jours. Public international, Private international, Federal civil litigation. Office: Vanderbilt U Sch Law Nashville TN 37240

MAIER, PETER KLAUS, law educator investment adviser; b. Wurzburg, Germany, Nov. 20, 1928; came to U.S., 1939, naturalized, 1945; s. Bernard and Joan (Sonder) M.; m. Melanie L. Stoff, Dec. 15, 1963; children—Michele Margaret, Diana Lynn. B.A. cum laude, Claremont McKenna Coll., 1949; J.D. cum laude, U. Calif. at Berkeley, 1952; LL.M. in Taxation, N.Y. U., 1953. Bar: Calif. 1953, U.S. Supreme Ct. 1957; cert. specialist in taxation law, Calif. Atty. tax div. U.S. Dept Justice, Washington, 1956-59; mem. firm Bacigalupi, Elkus, Salinger & Rosenberg, San Francisco, 1959-69, Brookes & Maier, San Francisco, 1970-73, Winokur, Maier & Zang, San Francisco, 1974-81; of counsel Crosby, Heafy, Roach & May, Oakland, Calif., 1986—; prof. law Hastings Coll. Law, U. Calif., San Francisco, 1967—; pres. Maier & Siebel, Inc., 1981—; sr. v.p. Siebel Capital Mgmt. Inc., Larkspur, Calif. Author books on taxation. Chmn. Property Resources Inc., San Jose, Calif., 1968-77. Served to capt. USAF, 1953-56. Mem. San Francisco Bar Assn. (chmn. sect. taxation 1970-71). Home: PO Box 391 Belvedere CA 94920 Office: 80 E Sir Francis Drake Blvd Larkspur CA 94939

MAIER, THOMAS ANDREW, lawyer; b. Chgo., Mar. 23, 1955; s. William E. and Helen Maier. BA, So. Ill. U., 1976; JD, U. Calif., Berkeley, 1979; LLM in Taxation, NYU, 1980. Bar: Calif. 1979, U.S. Tax Ct. 1981, U.S. Dist. Ct. (cen. dist.) Calif. 1986. Assoc. Heller, Ehrman, White & McAuliffe, San Francisco, 1980-84, McKenna, Conner & Cuneo, San Francisco, 1984-86, Horwich & Warner, San Francisco, 1987—. Corporate taxation, Personal income taxation, State and local taxation. Office: Horwich & Warner 353 Sacramento 19th Floor San Francisco CA 94111

MAILLIAN, LEANNE ELIZABETH, lawyer; b. Tacoma, July 10, 1952; d. Joseph Albert and Elizabeth (Lukins) M. BA magna cum laude, U. Calif., Santa Barbara, 1973; JD, Loyola U., Los Angeles, 1977. Bar: Calif. 1978, U.S. Ct. Appeals (9th cir.) 1978. Assoc. Nichols & Rose, Beverly Hills, Calif., 1978-80; sole practice Beverly Hills, 1980—; judge pro tem Los Angeles Mcpl. Ct., 1984—; counsel Nat. Assn. Women Bus. Owners, Los Angeles, 1984-85. Mem. ABA, Calif. Bar Assn. (chmn. law practice mgmt. sect. 1985-86, interim council sect. chmns. organizer 1985-86, chmn. council of sect. chmns. 1986—), Los Angeles County Bar Assn. (chmn. client relations com. 1985—, conf. of dels., errors and omissions prevention com., arbitrator atty. fee disputes). State civil litigation, Probate, General corporate. Office: 9454 Wilshire Blvd Penthouse Beverly Hills CA 90212

MAILMAN, STANLEY, lawyer; b. N.Y.C., Mar. 9, 1930; s. Nathan and Helen (Rubel) M.; m. Mary Ann Banks, Aug. 9, 1963; children: Joshua, Alexander. BA, Cornell U., 1950, LLB, 1952; LLM in Internat. Law, NYU, 1956. Bar: N.Y. 1953, U.S. Dist. Ct. (so. dist.) N.Y. 1957, U.S. Ct. Appeals (2d cir.) 1960. Assoc. Office of Elmer Fried, N.Y.C., 1955-58; ptnr. Fried & Mailman, N.Y.C., 1959-65; sole practices N.Y.C., 1965-73; ptnr. Mailman & Volin, N.Y.C., 1973-77, Mailman & Ruthizer, N.Y.C., 1978-87, Mailman & Schultz, N.Y.C., 1987—; adj. prof. St. John's U. Law Sch., N.Y.C., 1986—. Contbr. articles to profl. jours. Bd. dirs. Internat. Rescue Com., N.Y.C., 1976-80, Lawyers Com. for Human Rights, N.Y.C., 1982—. Served with U.S. Army, 1953-55. Mem. Am. Immigration Lawyers Assn. (pres. 1975-76), Consular Law Soc. (pres. 1985-86). Office: Mailman & Schultz 342 Madison Ave New York NY 10173

MAINE, MICHAEL ROLAND, lawyer; b. Anderson, Ind., Feb. 22, 1940; s. Roland Dwight and Vivian Louise (Browning) M.; m. Suzanne Bauman, Aug. 25, 1962; children: Christopher Michael, Melinda Louise. AB with high distinction, DePauw U.; JD with distinction, U. Mich. Bar: Ind., U.S. Dist. Ct. (so. dist.) Ind., U.S. Ct. Appeals (7th cir.), U.S. Supreme Ct. Assoc. Baker & Daniels, Indpls., 1964-71, ptnr., 1972—. Contbr. articles to profl. jours. Pres. Mental Health Assn. Ind., Indpls., 1985; bd. dirs. Ind. Repertory Theatre, Indpls., 1986—. Served to capt. USAF, 1965-68. Named Sagamore of Wabash, Gov. Ind., 1986. Fellow Ind. Bar Found., Indpls. Bar Found.; mem. Ind. Bar Assn. (chmn. fed. judiciary com. 1986—), Indpls. Bar Assn. (sec. 1983, pres. 1985, extraordinary service award 1985), Order of Coif, Phi Beta Kappa. Lodges: Kiwanis (lt. gov. Ind. club 1972, pres. Indpls. club 1969), Masons. Avocations: tennis, sailing. Labor, General corporate. Home: 7001 Central Indianapolis IN 46220 Office: 810 Fletcher Trust Bldg Indianapolis IN 45204

MAINES, JAMES ALLEN, lawyer; b. Tipton, Ind., Oct. 4, 1951; s. Lloyd Leon and Ruth Margaret (James) M. B.A. in Econs., Taylor U., 1973; J.D., U. Fla.-Gainesville, 1976. Bar: Fla. 1976, Ga. 1976, U.S. Dist. Ct. (no. dist.) Ga. 1976, U.S. Ct. Appeals (5th cir.) 1976, U.S. Ct. Appeals (11th cir.) 1981. Assoc. Hansell, Post, Brandon & Dorsey, Atlanta, 1976-84; ptnr. Hansell & Post, Atlanta, 1984—; mem. faculty Hastings Coll. Trial Advocacy, U. Calif., San Francisco, 1983—; lectr. Nat. Inst. Trial Advocacy, San Francisco, 1983; chief judge Emory U. Moot Ct., Atlanta, 1982. Pres. 26th St Community Assn., Atlanta, 1980-81; sustaining mem. Atlanta Arts Alliance, 1978—. Mem. ABA (litigation sect. 1976—), Fla. Bar, State Bar Ga., Atlanta Bar Assn. Republican. Methodist. Clubs: Lenox Athletic, Ski (Atlanta). Federal civil litigation, Contracts commercial, Computer. Office: Hansell & Post 3300 First Atlanta Tower Atlanta GA 30383

MAINZ, EDWARD CHARLES, JR., lawyer; b. San Antonio, June 27, 1938; s. Edward Charles Sr. and Bonita (Mears) M.; m. Patricia Ann Rolls, Feb. 22, 1964; children: Parke Edward, Susan Lynn, Jennifer Ann, Kevin Gerard, Christopher David. BA cum laude, St. Mary's U., San Antonio, 1960, JD magna cum laude, 1963. Bar: Tex. 1965, U.S. Dist. Ct. (so. dist.) Tex. 1967, U.S. Dist. Ct. (no. dist.) 1970, U.S. Dist. Ct. (ea. dist.) 1972, U.S. Ct. Appeals (5th cir.) 1974, U.S. Supreme Ct. 1975, U.S. Ct. Appeals (11th cir.) 1981, U.S. Dist. Ct. (we. dist.) Tex. 1982. Asst. atty. City of San Antonio, 1965; assoc. Atlas, Schwarz, Gurwitz & Bland, McAllen, Tex., 1965-69, Palmer, Palmer & Burke, Dallas, 1969-71, Green, Gilmore, Crutcher, Rothpletz & Burke, Dallas, 1971-72; ptnr. Stalcup, Johnson, Meyers & Miller, Dallas, 1972-78, Oppenheimer, Rosenberg, Kelleher & Wheatley, Inc., San Antonio, 1978-80; sole practice San Antonio, 1981—. Trustee North East Ind. Sch. Dist., 1985—, v.p., 1986—. Served to 1st lt. U.S. Army, 1963-65. Mem. ABA (assoc. editor Litigation News, 1977-78), Am. Judicature Soc., Tex. Bar Assn., Tex. Jr. Bar Assn. (dir. dist. 15 1968-69), Hidalgo County Bar Assn. (sec. treas. 1967-68), San Antonio Bar Assn., Dallas Bar Assn. Roman Catholic. Federal civil litigation, State civil litigation, Real property. Office: El Hidalgo Bldg 110 Sprucewood San Antonio TX 78216

MAIO, CARL ANTHONY, lawyer; b. Lancaster, Apr. 15, 1948; s. Anthony Raymond and Norma Theresa (Pietrobono) M.; m. Sheryl Rice Maio, Sept. 20, 1975. BA, Loyola U., Balt., 1970; JD, U. Balt., 1973; LLM, Acad. Internat. Law, Hague, The Netherlands, 1972. Bar: Md. 1973, Pa. 1974, D.C. 1978, U.S. Ct. Appeals (4th cir.) 1978, U.S. Supreme Ct. 1978, U.S. Ct. Appeals (3d cir.) 1980. Assoc. Steinberg, Schlachman, Potlar, Belsky & Weiner, Balt., 1973-80; asst. v.p., dir. litigation Harleysville (Pa.) Mutual Ins. Co., 1980—; lectr. Coll. Notre Dame Md., Balt., 1972-79; asst. pub. defender Balt. Office of Pub. Defender, 1973-79. Mem. nat. adv. council Ctr. for Study of Presidency, N.Y.C., 1973—. Mem. Am. Legion. Avocation: automobile restoration. Insurance, General corporate, Private international. Office: Harleysville Mutual Ins Co 355 Maple Ave Harleysville PA 19438

MAISSEL, RAINA EVE, lawyer; b. London, Apr. 12, 1931; came to U.S., 1956; d. Louis and Golde Pearl (Crowne) Corren; m. Leon Israel Maissel, Jan. 22, 1956; children—Simon Joseph, Gerda Sharon, Joseph Saul. LL.B., Univ. Coll. London, 1952. Barrister-at-law Eng. 1953; bar: N.Y. 1977, U.S. Dist. Ct. (so. dist.) N.Y. 1979, U.S. Dist. Ct. (ea. dist.) N.Y. 1979, U.S. Supreme Ct. 1982. Pupil to Hon. S.C. Silkin, London, 1953-54; sole practice, Bournemough, Eng., 1954-56; research assoc. Ballard, Spahr et al, Phila., 1956-58; counsel Moran, Spiegel, et al, Poughkeepsie, N.Y., 1977-80; sole practice, Wappingers Falls, N.Y., 1980-86; assoc. Gellert & Cutler P.C., Poughkeepsie, 1986—. Vice pres. Dutchess County Players, Poughkeepsie, 1962-64; pres. Merrywood Civic Assn., 1972-74; mem. 1st ward com. Democratic party, Poughkeepsie, 1973-74; mem. Poughkeepsie Zoning Bd. Appeals, 1982-83. Mem. ABA, N.Y. State Bar Assn., N.Y. State Bar (com. on mental and phys. disabilities), Dutchess County Bar (exec. com. 1984—). Jewish. General practice, Family and matrimonial. Home: 16 Smoke Rise Ln Wappingers Falls NY 12590 Office: Gellert & Cutler PC 54 Market St Poughkeepsie NY 12601

MAITLAND, GUY EDISON CLAY, lawyer; b. London, Dec. 28, 1942; mother Am. citizen; s. Paul and Virginia Francesca (Carver) M. B.A., Columbia U., 1964; J.D., N.Y. Law Sch., 1968. Bar: N.Y. 1969, U.S. Dist. Ct. (so. and ea. dists.) N.Y. 1969, U.S. Ct. Appeals (2d, D.C. cirs.) 1969. Assoc., Burlingham, Underwood & Lord, N.Y.C., 1969-74; admiralty counsel Union Carbide Corp., N.Y.C., 1974-76; exec. v.p., gen. counsel, dir. Liberian Services, Inc., N.Y.C. and Reston, Va., 1976—; del. UN Conf. on Trade and Devel., Manila, 1979, Belgrade, 1983; participant London Conf. on Limitation of Maritime Liability, 1976; mem. legal com. Internat. Maritime Orgn. (UN), London, 1980—; del. UN Conf. on Law of the Sea, 1976-82, London UN Maritime Law Conf., 1984. Author articles on maritime law, U.S. shipping policy. Sec. N.Y. Rep. County Com., 1976—; co-chmn. Citizens for Reagan, N.Y. State, 1979-80; mem. N.Y.C. Mayor's Port Devel. Council, 1983—. Named Outstanding Young Man of Am., U.S. Jaycees, 1975; hon. del Rep. Nat. Convention, Dallas, 1984. Mem. Assn. Bar City N.Y. (chmn. admiralty com. 1982-85), Maritime Law Assn. U.S., Maritime Assn. Port of N.Y. (dir. 1984—), ABA, D.C. Bar Assn., Phi Delta Phi. Republican. Episcopalian. Clubs: Capitol Hill, University (Washington). Admiralty. Office: Office of Gen Counsel Liberian Services Inc 548 Fifth Ave New York NY 10036

MAIWURM, JAMES JOHN, lawyer; b. Wooster, Ohio, Dec. 5, 1948; s. James Frederick and Virginia Anne (Jones) M.; m. Wendy S. Leeper, July 31, 1974; children: James G., Michelle K. BA, Coll. Wooster, 1971; JD, U. Mich., 1974. Bar: Ohio 1974, D.C. 1986. Assoc. Squire, Sanders & Dempsey, Cleve., 1974-82, ptnr., 1982-85; ptnr. Squire, Sanders & Dempsey, Washington, 1986—. Contbr. articles to profl. jours. Mem. ABA, D.C. Bar Assn., Ohio Bar Assn. (chmn. bd. govs. corp. counsel sect. 1986—). General corporate, Securities, Banking. Home: 9419 Brian Jac Ln Great Falls VA 22066 Office: Squire Sanders & Dempsey 1201 Pennsylvania Ave NW Washington DC 20004

MAJERUS, MICHAEL GERARD, lawyer; b. Billings, Mont., Jan. 24, 1956; s. Bernard Joseph and Marjorie Elizabeth (Funk) M.; m. Stephanie Ann Hurd, Jan., 2, 1982; 1 child, Ryan Michael. BA, Seattle U., 1977; JD, Georgetown U., 1980. Bar: D.C. 1980, Mont. 1982, U.S. Dist. Ct. Mont. 1982. Assoc. Tucker, Flyer, Sanger & Lewis, Washington, 1978-81, Moulton, Bellingham, et. al., Billings, 1982-83; sole practice Billings, 1983—. Yellowstone County coordinator U.S. senator Max Baucus Re-Election Campaign, Billings, 1983-84; pres. Yellowstone County Dem. Club, Billings, 1985-86. Mem. ABA, D.C. Bar Assn., Mont. Bar Assn. Roman Catholic. Avocation: politics. General practice, Personal injury, Contracts commercial. Home: 615 S 22nd St W Billings MT 59102 Office: 490 N 31st St #300 Billings MT 59101

MAJOR, RONALD DAVID, lawyer; b. Cin., Mar. 7, 1947; s. William Robert and Ruth Marion (Faust) M.; m. Karen Sue Keller, June 26, 1970; children—Michelle Christine, Lauren Nicole. B.A., U. Ky., 1969; J.D., Salmon P. Chase Law Sch., 1974. Bar: Ohio 1974, U.S. Dist. Ct. (so. dist.) Ohio 1974, Ky. 1978, U.S. Dist. Ct. (ea. dist.) Ky. 1979, U.S. Ct. Appeals (6th cir.) 1974, U.S. Supreme Ct. 1979. Legal editor Anderson Pub. Co., Cin., 1972-74, 75-76; assoc. Waite, Schneider, Bayless & Chesley, Cin., 1974-75; assoc. Beall, Hermanies & Bortz, Cin., 1976-83; ptnr. Beall, Hermanies, Bortz & Major, Cin., 1983—. Mem. Assn. Trial Lawyers Am., Ohio Acad. Trial Lawyers, Ohio State Bar Assn., Ky. Bar Assn., Cin. Bar Assn. Roman Catholic. Personal injury, State civil litigation, Workers' compensation. Home: 3572 Epworth Ave Cincinnati OH 45211 Office: Beall Hermanies Bortz & Major 30 Garfield Pl Suite 740 Cincinnati OH 45202

MAKEIG, THOMAS HOWARD, lawyer; b. Evanston, Ill., May 14, 1953; s. Daniel Clare Makeig and Kathryn Louisa (Howard) Leadbeater. BA with first class honors, U. Kent at Canterbury, Eng., 1975; JD, NYU, 1981. Assoc. Rosenman, Colin, Freund, Lewis & Cohen, N.Y.C., 1981-82, Jay B. Marcus, P.C., Fairfield, Iowa, 1982-84; sole practice Fairfield, 1985-86; gen. counsel, v.p. corp. planning Magna Motive Industries, Inc., Fairfield, 1986—. Editor: Annual Survey of Am. Law, 1980. Trustee Fairfield Mus. Soc., 1983—, Fairfield Cultural Soc., 1984—; bd. dirs. Jefferson County Arts Council, Fairfield, 1986—; mem. devel. adv. council Maharish Internat. Univ., Fairfield, 1985—. Mem. ABA. General corporate. Home and Office: PO Box 931 Fairfield IA 52556

MAKI, SUSAN KAY, lawyer; b. Virginia, Minn., Nov. 29, 1947; d. Edward John and Sophie Catherine (Lapinoja) M. BS, U. Minn., 1970; JD, William Mitchell Coll. of Law, 1979. Bar: Minn. 1979, U.S. Dist. Ct. Minn. 1979. Staff atty. State Pub. Defender's Office, Mpls., 1979—; clin. supr. criminal appeals clinic William Mitchell Coll. of Law, St. Paul, 1981—; coordinator 1st annual pub. Defense Tng. Seminar, Bloomington, Minn., 1985. Alt. Minn. Juvenile Code Recodification Task Force, St. Paul, 1984-85; mem. Minn. Interagency Task Force on Child Sexual Abuse, St. Paul, 1985—. Mem. ABA, Pub. Defenders Assn. (sec. Minn. chpt. 1986—). Democrat. Lutheran. Avocations: aerobic dance, cross country skiing, biking. Criminal, Juvenile. Office: State Pub Defenders Office U Minn 95 Law Ctr Minneapolis MN 55455

MAKOWSKI, RAYMOND EDMUND, lawyer; b. East Chicago, Ind., Nov. 26, 1944; s. Edmund F. and Victoria Eva (Mysliwiec) M.; m. Anastasia P. Rush; children: Andrew R., Brett R. AB, Ind. U., 1966; JD, Georgetown U., 1969. Bar: U.S. Ct. Appeals (D.C. cir.) 1970, Fla. 1974, Va. 1969, U.S. Dist. Ct. (mid. dist.) Fla. 1974, U.S. Ct. Appeals (5th cir.) 1974, U.S. Dist. Ct. (no. dist.) Fla. 1980, U.S. Ct. Appeals (11th cir.) 1982. Atty. adv. citizenship sect. U.S. State Dept., Washington, 1969-70; trial atty. Organized Crime & Racketeering Sect., U.S. Dept. Justice, Washington and Phila., 1970-74; sole practice, Jacksonville, Fla., 1974-76, 1980—; ptnr. Makowski & Davis, Jacksonville, 1976-80; lectr. Legal Assistance Program, Fla. Jr. Coll., Jacksonville, 1975-77. Pres. Pickwick Park Civic Assn., 1979-80. Recipient Nelson Poynter Civil Liberties award, Am. Civil Liberties Found. Fla., 1982. Mem. Fla. Bar, Va. Bar Assn., Nat. Assn. Criminal Def. Lawyers, Acad. Fla. Trial Laywers, Assn. Trial Lawyers Am. Roman Catholic. Clubs: Fla. Tackle and Gun, Toastmasters Internat. (Jacksonville). Contbr. articles to profl. jours. Federal civil litigation, State civil litigation, Criminal. Office: One San Jose Pl Suite 11 Jacksonville FL 32217

MAKOWSKI, THOMAS ANTHONY, lawyer; b. Wilkes-Barre, Pa., Nov. 1, 1952; s. Bruno B. and Evelyn M. (Decker) M. AB in History, King's Coll., 1974; JD, Georgetown U., 1979. Bar: D.C. 1979, U.S. Dist. Ct. D.C. 1980, U.S. Ct. Claims 1980, U.S. Ct. Appeals (D.C. cir.) 1980, Pa. 1982, U.S. Dist. Ct. (mid. dist.) Pa. 1983, U.S. Ct. Appeals (3d cir.) 1983, U.S. Ct. Mil. Appeals 1985, U.S. Supreme Ct. 1986. Legis. asst. U.S. Ho. of Reps., Washington, 1975-80; atty. Nat. Assn. Govt. Employees, Washington, 1980-82; sole practice Wilkes-Barre, 1982—; master Luzerne County Ct. of Common Pleas, Wilkes-Barre, 1983-84; atty. Pocono (Pa.) Order Police Lodge 70, 1986—; atty. Borough Plymouth, Pa., 1987—. Editor Georgetown U. Internat. Law Jour., 1977-79. Mem. numerous Democratic campaign coms., Luzerne County, Pa., 1982—; candidate 11th congl. dist. U.S. Ho. of Reps., Wilkes-Barre, 1982; legal advisor Young Dems. of Luzerne County, 1986—. Mem. ABA, Pa. Bar Assn. (legal ethics and profl. responsibility com.), Wilkes-Barre Law and Library Assn., Fraternal Order of Police. Democrat. Roman Catholic. Club: Wyoming Valley Country (Wilkes-Barre, Pa.). Lodge: Elks. Avocations: golf, hunting, waterskiing, politics. General practice, Probate, Real property. Office: 65 W Union St Wilkes-Barre PA 18701

MAKY, WALTER, lawyer; b. Cleve., June 4, 1916; s. Viktor and Saimi (Pahkala) M.; m. Helen Marian Rancken, Dec. 3, 1938; children: Pamela (Mrs. Ronald Boyarsky), Bonita. B.S., Cleve. State U., 1940, J.D., 1947. Bar: Ohio 1947. Spot welder Gray Wire Splty. Co., 1934-37; trouble shooter Ohio Bell Telephone Co., 1937-38; patent agt. Parker-Hannifin Corp., 1938-45; assoc. Oberlin & Limbach, 1945-57; mem. firm Maky, Renner, Otto & Boiselle (and predecessor firms), Cleve., 1957-85; of counsel Renner, Otto, Boisselle & Lyon, Cleve., 1985—. Consul of Finland State of Ohio, 1951—. Mem. Am., Greater Cleve. Bar Assn., Nat. Council Patent Law Assns. (councilman 1972-73), Cleve. Patent Law Assn. (pres. 1971-72), Am. Intellectual Property Law Assn. Club: Ashtabula (Ohio) Country. Patent, Trademark and copyright. Home: 33320 Cromwell Dr Solon OH 44139 Office: 1 Public Sq 12th Floor Cleveland OH 44113

MALACARNE, C. JOHN, insurance company executive, lawyer; b. St. Louis, Dec. 26, 1941; s. Claude John and Virginia E. (Miller) M.; m. Kathleen M. Morris, Aug. 27, 1966; children: Tracy, Kristen, Lisa. AA, Harris-Stowe State Coll., 1962; BS in Pub. Adminstrn., U. Mo., 1964, JD, 1967. Bar: Mo. 1967, U.S. Dist. Ct. (we. dist.) Mo. Asst. counsel Kansas City (Mo.) Life, 1967-71, assoc. counsel, 1971-74, asst. gen. counsel, 1974-76, assoc. gen. counsel, 1976-80, gen. counsel, 1980-81, v.p., gen. counsel, 1981—; bd. dirs. Nat. Res. Ins. Co., Sioux Falls, S.D., Kansas City Variable Life Co. Sec., bd. dirs. Mid-Continent Council of Girl Scouts, Inc., Kansas City, 1986—; v.p., bd. dirs. Kansas City Eye Bank, 1986—; pres., bd. dirs. Shepherd's Ctr., Kansas City, 1982-84. Mem. ABA, Kansas City Met. Bar Assn. (vice chmn. corp. counsel com. 1986—), Lawyers Assn. Kansas City (bd. dirs. 1976), Internat. Assn. Ins. Counsel (chmn. accident, health, life sects. 1982-84, ins. examining nominating com. 1986), Jr. C. of C. (bd. dirs. 1972). Lodge: Kiwanis (pres. Kansas City 1975-76). General corporate, Insurance. Home: 604 Tam-O-Shanter Dr Kansas City MO 64145 Office: Kansas City Life Ins Co PO Box 139 Kansas City MO 64141

MALACH, HERBERT JOHN, lawyer; b. N.Y.C., Aug. 3, 1922; s. James J. and Therese (Lederer) M.; A.B., Iona Coll., 1951; J.D., Columbia U., 1955; m. Patricia Sweeny, Sept. 12, 1953 (dec. 1972); children—Therese, Herbert John, Helen. Bar: N.Y. 1957, D.C. 1958, U.S. Dist. Ct. (so. and ea. dists.) N.Y. 1958, U.S. Ct. Appeals (2d cir.) 1960, U.S. Supreme Ct. 1961. Practiced in N.Y.C., 1957-72, New Rochelle, N.Y., 1960—; lectr. bus. law Iona Coll., New Rochelle, 1957-59, asst. to pres. for community services, 1959-62. Vice chmn., exec. dir. Iona Coll. Westchester County Law Enforcement Inst.; spl. counsel N.Y. State Temporary Commn. on Child Welfare; mem. Westchester County Youth Adv. Council, 1969-73; mem. Law Enforcement Planning. Agy., New Rochelle, 1968-69; adv. counsel Westchester Police Youth Officers Assn.; mem. Westchester County Child Abuse Task Force; mem. New Rochelle Narcotics Guidance Council, 1972-75; adv. council New Rochelle Salvation Army, 1976-79; legal adviser East-End Civic Assn.; law guardian Westchester County Family Ct.; referee New Rochelle City Ct.; arbitrator Civil Ct., Bronx; arbitrator Supreme and County Ct., Westchester. Bd. dirs. Art Inst., Iona Coll., mem. adv. bd. radio activities, adv. bd. criminal justice Iona Coll., bd. dirs. Westchester County Youth Shelter. Served with AUS, 1942-46. Recipient Patrick B. Doyle award for outstanding service, 1969, William B. Cornelia Founders award, 1976 (both Iona Coll.). Hon. dep. sheriff Westchester County. Mem. Am. (com. rights of family), N.Y. State (com. family law, com. family ct.), Bronx County (com. family law), Westchester County, New Rochelle Bar assns., Am. Judicature Soc., N.Y. County Lawyers Assn. (family ct. com.), Criminal Cts. Bar Assn. Westchester County, Am. Fedn. Police, Internat. Narcotic Enforcement Officers Assn., Internat. Acad. Criminology, Am. Acad. Polit. and Social Sci., Law Guardians Assn. Westchester County (pres.), Am. Psychology-Law Soc., Internat., N.Y. State, Bergen County chiefs of police, Nat. Assn. Council for Children, Nat. Sheriffs Assn., Am. Soc. Internat. Law, Iona Coll. Alumni Assn., Inc. (pres., chmn. bd. dirs. 1958-60, 62-64, 72-74, 74-76, dir. 1954-58, 68-72, 76-86, v.p. 1966-68). Family and matrimonial, Juvenile, Child Custody. Address: 105 Harding Dr New Rochelle NY 10801

MALADY, EUGENE JOSEPH, lawyer; b. Neptune, N.J., Feb. 1, 1947; s. Eugene Joseph and Mable (Sharpe) M. BA, Seton Hall U., 1971; JD, Widener U., 1976. Bar: Pa. 1977, U.S. Dist. Ct. (ea. dist.) Pa. 1978, U.S. Supreme Ct. 1986. Sole practice Upper Darby, Pa., 1977-82; ptnr. Malady & Donato, Media, Pa., 1982—. Mem. ABA, Pa. Bar Assn., Delaware County Bar Assn., Assn. Trial Lawyers Am., Pa. Trial Lawyers Assn. Roman Catholic. Bankruptcy, Personal injury, Family and matrimonial. Office: Malady & Donato 211 N Olive St Media PA 19063

MALAPERO, RAYMOND JOSEPH, JR., lawyer; b. Bklyn., Dec. 22, 1955; s. Raymond J. Sr. and Marion (Vaccaro) M.; m. Marianne Gioia, Dec. 22, 1979; 1 child, Raymond Joseph III. BA, Fordham U., 1977, JD, 1980. Bar: N.Y. 1981, U.S. Dist. Ct. (so. and ea. dists.) N.Y. 1981, N.J. 1982,. Ptnr. Lian, Geringer & Dolan, N.Y.C., 1980—. Mem. ABA, N.Y. State Trial Lawyers Assn., Bklyn. Bar Assn., Phi Delta Phi. Democrat. Roman Catholic. State civil litigation, Personal injury, General practice. Home: 2 Sharon Ln Holmdel NJ 07733 Office: Lian Geringer & Dolan 230 Park Ave New York NY 10169

MALAWSKY, DONALD N., lawyer; b. Milw., Dec. 5, 1935; s. Joseph and Anna (Brill) M.; m. Beryl York, Aug. 23, 1960; 1 child, Douglas. BS, U. Wis., 1959, JD, 1961. Bar: Wis. 1961, U.S. Supreme Ct. 1969, N.Y. 1974, U.S. Dist. Ct. (so. and ea. dists.) N.Y. 1974, U.S. Dist. Ct. D.C. 1974. Staff atty. SEC, Denver, 1962-67; various pos. SEC, N.Y.C., 1968-81, regional adminstr., 1981-84; sr. v.p. N.Y. Stock Exchange, 1984—; adj. prof. law N.Y. Law Sch., 1981—. Served to 1st lt. U.S. Army, 1961-62. Mem. ABA, Wis. Bar Assn., Fed. Bar Assn., D.C. Bar Assn. Democrat. Jewish. Administrative and regulatory, Securities. Home: 24 Norwood Ave Upper Montclair NJ 07043 Office: NY Stock Exchange 20 Broad St New York NY 10005

MALESKI, CYNTHIA MARIA, lawyer; b. Natrona Heights, Pa., July 4, 1951; d. Richard Anthony and Helen Elizabeth (Palovcak) M.; m. Andrzej Gabriel Groch, Aug. 7, 1982; 1 child, Elizabeth Maria. B.A. summa cum laude, U. Pitts., 1973; student U. Rouen (France), 1970; J.D., Duquesne U., 1976. Bar: Pa. 1976, U.S. dist. ct. (we. dist.) Pa. 1976, U.S. Supreme Ct. 1980, U.S. Ct. Appeals (3d cir.) 1984. Indsl. relations adminstr. Allegheny Ludlum Industries, Inc., Brackenridge, Pa., 1972-74; law clk. Conte, Courtney, Tarasi & Price, Pitts., 1974, Paul Hammer, Pitts., 1974-76; sole practice Natrona Heights, Pa., 1978—; gen. counsel Mercy Hosp., Pitts., 1976—; bd. dirs. legal adv. bd. Catholic Health Assn., 1980-82; gen. counsel, vice chmn. nat. assembly of reps. Nat. Confedn. Am. Ethnic Groups, 1980—; health law cons. and lectr.; task force on Pa. Med. Malpractice Reform, Hosp. Assn. Pa. Co-author: The Legal Dimensions of Nursing Practice (Nurses' Book of Month Club award 1982), 1982; contbr. articles to publs. Corp. sec., legal counsel Tamburitzan Nat. Folk Arts Ctr., Pitts., 1979—; mem. Council Self-Insured Hosps. of Pa.; vice chmn. Czechoslovak room com. Nationality Rooms Program, U. Pitts., 1983; elected mem. Allegheny County Dem. Com., 1986—; candidate for del. Democratic Nat. Conv. 20th Pa. Congl. Dist., 1984; chmn. Com. to Re-elect U.S. Congressman Doug Walgren, 1982; Ethnic Com. for Pa. Atty. Gen., 1980, Ethnic Com. for Judge Peter Paul Olszewski, 1983; U.S. del 4th Slovak World Congress, 1981; mem. adv. bd. Children's and Youth Services, Allegheny County, 1984—; soloist, speaker various groups, Pitts. Slovakians. Scholar U. Rouen, 1970; Allegheny Ludlum Industries scholar, 1969-73; Andrew Mellon scholar, 1969; tuition scholar U. Pitts., 1969-73; tuition remission grantee Duquesne U., 1975, 76; recipient acad. excellence award Duquesne U., 1976; Mem. ABA (forum com. on health law, tort and ins. sect.), Am. Soc. Hosp. Attys., Nat. Health Lawyers Assn., Soc. Hosp. Attys. of Hosp. Assn. Pa. (v.p.), Soc. Hosp. Attys. Western Pa., Pa. Bar Assn. (med.-legal com., long range planning com.), Allegheny County Bar Assn. (chmn. med.-legal com., council civil litigation sect., chmn. interprofl. code com. Allegheny County Bar Assn.-Allegheny County Med. Soc.), Slavic Edn. Assn. (nat. treas. 1981—), St. Thomas More Soc. (bd. govs. 1980—), First Cath. Slovak Union, 1st Cath. Slovak Women's Assn., Civic Club Allegheny Valley, Bus. and Profl. Women Allegheny Valley, Phi Beta Kappa. Roman Catholic. Health, State civil litigation, General practice. Home: 2413 Freeport Rd Natrona Heights PA 15065 Office: Mercy Hosp of Pitts 1400 Locust St Pittsburgh PA 15219

MALINA, MICHAEL, lawyer; b. Bklyn., Mar. 20, 1936; s. William and Jean (Kutlowitz) M.; m. Anita May Oppenheim, June 22, 1958; children: Rachel Lynn, Stuart Charles, Joel Martin. AB, Harvard U., 1957, LLB, 1960. Bar: N.Y. 1961, U.S. Dist. Ct. (so. and ea. dists.) N.Y. 1962, U.S. Ct. Appeals (2d, 4th, 9th, and D.C. cirs.) 1965, U.S. Supreme Ct. 1965. Assoc. Kaye, Scholer, Fierman, Hays & Handler, N.Y.C., 1960-69, ptnr., 1969—. Contbr. articles to profl. jours. Mem. ABA (antitrust sect.), N.Y. State Bar Assn. (chmn. antitrust sect. 1975-82, Robinson-Patman Act com.), Assn. of Bar of City of N.Y. (profl. ethics com. 1985—). Democrat. Jewish. Antitrust, Federal civil litigation. Home: 12 Innes Rd Scarsdale NY 10583 Office: Kaye Scholer Fierman Hays & Handler 425 Park Ave New York NY 10022

MALKIN, CARY JAY, lawyer; b. Chgo., Oct. 6, 1949; s. Arthur D. and Perle (Slavin) M.; m. Lisa Klimley, Oct. 27, 1976; 1 dau., Dorothy R. B.A., George Washington U., 1971; J.D., Northwestern U., 1974. Bar: Ill. 1974, U.S. Dist. Ct. (no. dist.) Ill. 1974. Assoc., Mayer, Brown & Platt, Chgo., 1974-80, ptnr., 1981—; speaker Banking Law Inst., Ill. Inst. for Continuing Legal Edn., 1985. Author: Acquisitions and Dispositions of Leasing Companies., 1986. Chmn. spl. events com. Mental Health Assn., 1984-85. Mem. Chgo. Council Lawyers, Order of the Coif, Phi Beta Kappa. Clubs: Saddle and Cycle, Standard, Chicago. Banking, General corporate, Leasing. Home: 233 E Walton Pl Chicago IL 60611 Office: Mayer Brown & Platt 190 S LaSalle St Chicago IL 60603

MALKUS, JAMES ALAN, judge; b. Chgo., May 5, 1937; s. Bernard L. and Gertrude S. (Yanovsky) M.; m. Marian Kurtz, Sept. 5, 1959; children—Heather, Matthew, Todd. A.B., U. Chgo., 1958, J.D., 1961. Bar: Ill. 1961, Calif. 1966, U.S. Supreme Ct., U.S. Dist. Ct. (so. dist.) Calif., U.S. Ct. Mil. Appeals. Assoc. firm Fredman, Silverberg & Shenas, San Diego, 1966-68; ptnr. firm Borovitz & Malkus, San Diego, 1968-77, Borovitz, Malkus, McDevitt & Hocket, San Diego, 1977-79; superior ct. judge State of Calif., San Diego, 1979—; lectr., panelist legal and civic orgns.; mem. faculty Nat. U. Law Sch. Co-editor Calif. Evidence Law Reporter, 1983—. Bd. dirs. San Diego Jewish Family Service, 1968-72, 84—, San Diego Ctr. for Children, 1970-78, New Entra Casa Halfway House, San Diego, 1980—. Served to lt. JAGC, USN, 1961-66. Named Trial Judge of Yr. San Diego Trial Lawyers Assn., 1986. Mem. San Diego County Bar Assn. (v.p. 1979, chmn. legis. com. 1977-79), Fed. Bar Assn. (pres. 1972), Calif. Trial Lawyers Assn., State Bar Calif. (chmn. pub. affairs com. 1980-81, commn. on corrections), Internat. Assn. Family Conciliation Cts., San Diego County Judges Assn., Am. Judicature soc., Calif Judges Assn. State civil litigation, Criminal, Judicial administration. Office: San Diego Superior Ct 220 W Broadway San Diego CA 92101

MALL, LOREN L(EE), lawyer; b. Clay Center, Kans., Nov. 21, 1938; s. Henry and Ellen (Eversmeyer) M.; m. Margaret Roberts, Feb. 25, 1978. B.S., Kans. State U., 1961; J.D., U. Denver, 1967. Bar: Colo. 1968. Mem. firm Hindry & Meyer, Denver, 1968-74, Roath & Brega, 1975—; instr. mining law U. Denver, 1979-82, 87—. Served to 1st lt. USAF, 1962-65. Mem. ABA, Colo. Bar Assn., Denver Bar Assn. Republican. Methodist. Author: Public Land and Mining Law, 3d edit., 1981; textbook Am. Law of Mining, 2d edit., 1985. General corporate, Real property, Natural resources. Office: Roath & Brega 1873 S Bellaire St 17th Floor Denver CO 80222

MALLERS, GEORGE PETER, lawyer; b. Lima, Ohio, Apr. 28, 1928; s. Peter G. and Helen (Daskalakis) M.; m. Rubie Loomis, Feb. 2, 1950; children—Peter G. II, William G., Elaine. B.S., Ind. U., 1951; J.D., Valparaiso U., 1955. Bar: Ind. 1955, U.S. Dist. Ct. (so. and no. dists.) Ind., U.S. Ct. Appeals (7th cir.). Practice law Ft. Wayne, Ind., 1955—; co-mng. ptnr. Beers, Mallers, Backs, Salin & Laramore and predecessor firms, 1955—; county atty., Allen County, Ind., 1964-73; pres. Mallers Theatres, Ft. Wayne, 1949—, Holiday Theatres, Inc., Mallers Mgmt., 1964—, Mallers & Spirou Enterprises, Inc., 1971—, Georgetown Sq. Theatres I & II, 1971—, Stage Door, Inc., 1972—, M-S Amusement Corp., 1972—, Georgetown Lounge & Restaurant, Inc., 1972—, Mallers-Spirou Mgmt. Corp., 1973—, Georgetown Bowl, Inc., 1976—. Mem. Allen County Police Merit Bd., 1967-77; pres. Allen County Young Republican Club, 1956-58; asst. to Rep. county chmn. Allen County, 1958—; chmn. City-County Bd. Health, 1980—. Fellow Ind. Bar Found.; mem. ABA, Ind. Bar Assn., Allen County Bar Assn. (sec., dir. 1961-63), Am. Judicature Soc., Valparaiso U. Law Sch. Alumni Assn. (nat. pres. 1978-80), Phi Alpha Delta. General corporate, Probate. Office: Ft Wayne Nat Bank Bldg Fort Wayne IN 46802

MALLEY, ROBERT JOHN, holding company executive, lawyer; b. Buffalo, Dec. 23, 1944; s. Chester John and Mary (Kinmartin) M.; m. Susan Jane Burdick, June 28, 1973; 1 child, Cullen Burdick. B.A. cum laude, Colgate U., 1966; J.D., Columbia U., 1969. Bar: N.Y. 1970. Assoc. Wickes, Riddell, Bloomer, Jacobi & McGuire, N.Y.C., 1969-72; assoc. London, Buttenwieser & Chalif, N.Y.C., 1972-74; v.p., counsel Citibank N.A., N.Y.C., 1975-81; sr. v.p., gen. counsel, sec. State Street Boston Corp., 1981—. Contbr. articles to William and Mary Law Rev. and profl. jours. Served with USAR, 1969-74. Mem. ABA (sect. on corp., banking and bus. law, corp. counsel), Phi Beta Kappa. Club: University (N.Y.C.). Banking, General corporate, Securities. Office: State Street Boston Corp 225 Franklin St Boston MA 02101

MALLIN, ROBERT HAROLD, lawyer; b. Bklyn., Apr. 20, 1945; S. Benjamin and Bella (Birman) M.; m. Marcia Lynne Levine, June 21, 1970; Elias, Jacob, Benjamin. BA, Bklyn. Coll., 1965; JD, Bklyn. Law Sch., 1973. Bar: N.Y. 1974, U.S. Dist. Ct. (ea. and so. dists.) N.Y. 1975, U.S. Ct. Appeals (2d cir.) 1975, Ariz. 1978, U.S. Dist. Ct. Ariz. 1978, U.S. Ct. Appeals (9th cir.) 1978. Asst. dist. atty. Kings County, Bklyn., 1974-77; assoc. Sternberg, Sternberg & Rubin, Phoenix, 1978-79; ptnr. Mallin, Lemberg, Brody & Brown, Phoenix, 1980-83, Mallin & Brown, Phoenix, 1983—. V.p. Beth El Congregation, Phoenix, 1982-83. Mem. ABA, N.Y. Bar Assn., Ariz. Bar Assn., Maricopa County Bar Assn. (family law com. 1984—). Family and matrimonial, Personal injury, General practice. Office: Mallin & Brown 201 W Coolidge St Phoenix AZ 85013

MALLORY, ARTHUR EUGENE, III, lawyer; b. LaGrange, Ga., Apr. 21, 1947; s. Arthur Eugene Jr. and Midlred (Avery) M.; children: Nina Markette, Arthur Eugene IV, Judson Dulin. BA in History, U. of the South, 1969; JD, U. Ga., 1972. Bar: Ga., U.S. Dist. Ct. (no. dist.) Ga., U.S. Ct. Appeals (5th cir.). Law clk. to presiding justice U.S. Ct. Appeals (5th cir.), Newnan, Ga., 1973-74; from assoc. to ptnr. Duncan & Thomasson, LaGrange, Ga., 1974-80; dist. atty. Coweta Jud. Cir., LaGrange, 1981—; judge LaGrange Recorders Ct., 1975-80; vice chmn., bd. dirs. Bank of Troup County, LaGrange, 1984—. Mem. Troup County Dem. Com., Ga., 1976; del. Dem. Constl. Convention, 1976; sec. LaGrange Downtown Devel. Corp., 1974-81; pres. Troup County Hist. Soc., LaGrange, 1984—. Served to 2d lt. U.S. Army, 1972-73; capt. Ga. N.G. Mem. ABA, Ga. Bar Assn. (co-chmn. appellate practice rules rev. com. 1975-76), Coweta Cir. Bar Assn. (v.p. 1980-81), Assn. Trial Lawyers Am., Am. Judicature Soc., Nat. Dist. Attys. Assn., LaGrange Area C. of C. (exec. com.), LaGrange Jaycees, Order of Barristers. Democrat. Episcopalian. Lodge: Rotary. Criminal. Home: 502 Sylvan Dr LaGrange GA 30240 Office: Coweta Jud Cir Troup Courthouse Annex LaGrange GA 30241

MALLORY, CHARLES KING, III, lawyer; b. Norfolk, Va., Nov. 16, 1936; s. Charles King Mallory Jr. and Dorothy Pratt (Williams) Swanke; m. Florence Beale Marshall; children: King, Raburn, Anne, Richard. BA, Yale U., 1958; JD, Tulane U., 1961. Bar: La. 1961, Calif. 1965, D.C. 1972. Ptnr. Monroe & Lemann, New Orleans, 1965-72; acting exec. dir. SEC, Washington, 1972; dep. asst. sec. U.S. Dept. Interior, Washington, 1973, acting asst. sec., 1974; v.p., gen. counsel Middle South Services, Inc., New Orleans, 1975-79; ptnr. Hunton & Williams, Washington, 1979—. Mem. Pres. elect Reagans' Transition Team, Washington, 1980-81, Grace Commn. on Pvt. Sector Survey Cost in the Fed. Govt., Washington, 1983-84. Served to lt. USNR, 1961-65. Mem. ABA, La. Bar Assn., Calif. Bar Assn., D.C. Bar Assn., Fed. Energy Bar Assn., Nat. Assn. Bond Lawyers. Republican. Episcopalian. Public utilities, Antitrust, Legislative. Office: Hunton & Williams 2000 Pennsylvania Ave NW PO Box 19230 Washington DC 20036

MALLORY, FRANK LINUS, lawyer; b. Calgary, Alberta, Can., May 5, 1920; s. Frank Louis and Anna Amy (Allstrum) M.; m. Jean Ellen Lindsey, Jan. 29, 1944; children: Susan Mallory Remund, Ann, Bruce R. AB with distinction, Stanford U., 1941, LLB, 1947. Bar: Calif. 1948. Assoc. Gibson, Dunn & Crutcher, Los Angeles, 1947-54; ptnr. Gibson, Dunn & Crutcher, Los Angeles and Newport Beach, Calif., 1955—; cert. specialist taxation law Calif. Bd. Legal Specialization, 1973—. Pres. Town Hall of Calif., Los Angeles, 1970, Boys Republic, Chino, Calif., 1962-64; bd. dirs. Braille Inst. Am., Los Angeles, 1983—. Served to lt. j.g., USNR, 1942-46. Mem. ABA, Calif. Bar Assn., Los Angeles County Bar Assn., Orange County Bar Assn., Internat. Acad. Estate and Trust Law (academican). Republican. Clubs: California (Los Angeles); Newport Harbor Yacht, Big Canyon Country (Newport Beach), Transpacific Yacht (rear commodore). Probate, Private international. Home: 32 Linda Isle Newport Beach CA 92660 Office: Gibson Dunn & Crutcher 333 S Grand Ave Los Angeles CA 90071 also: 800 Newport Center Dr #700 Newport Beach CA 92660

MALLORY, HAROLD DARLINGTON, lawyer; b. Tampa, Fla., Dec. 4, 1952; s. Harold Isham and Patricia Ann (Skelton) M.; m. Kathryn Elizabeth Campbell, May 27, 1977. A.B. magna cum laude, Dartmouth Coll., 1974; J.D., So. Meth. U., 1977. Bar: Tex. 1978, U.S. Dist. Ct. (no. dist.) Tex. 1978. Assoc. Henry D. Akin, Jr., Dallas, 1978-80, Norman A. Zable, P.C., Dallas, 1980-86, v.p., dir., 1986—. Mem. ABA, Dallas Bar Assn., Dallas Young Lawyers Assn. Club: University (Dallas). General practice, Probate. Address: 5340 Alpha Rd Dallas TX 75240

MALLOY, JOHN CYRIL, lawyer, educator; b. Jackson, Tenn., June 7, 1930; s. John Cyril and Jennie May (Mathis) M.; children—Angela May, Jennie Sue, John Cyril, Caroll Anne. Student Ill. Inst. Tech., 1950-53; B.S., Roosevelt U., 1953; J.D., Northwestern U., 1958. Bar: Fla. 1958, Ill. 1958, D.C. 1958, U.S. Patent Office 1958, U.S. Supreme Ct. 1963. Sole practice, Miami, Fla., 1959—; prof. patent, trademark law U. Miami Sch. Law, 1978—. State rep. Fla. Legislature, 1972-74, 76-82; mem. Nat. Hwy. Safety Adv. Com., 1976-79. Served to 1st lt. AUS, 1953-55. Recipient Outstanding Service award So. Fla. chpt. Fed. Bar Assn., 1972-73, Met. Dade County Appreciation for Legis. Service award, 1980, City of Miami Legis. Service commendation, 1980. Mem. ABA, Fed. Bar Assn. (pres. So. Fla. chpt. 1973-74), Am. Patent Law Assn., ASME. Patent, Trademark and copyright. Office: Consolidated Bank Bldg 168 SE First St Miami FL 33131

MALLOY, KATHLEEN SHARON, lawyer; b. Evergreen Park, Ill., Apr. 7, 1948, d. Clarence Edmund and Ruth Elizabeth (Petrini) M.; m. Randall Kleinman, Aug. 5, 1978; children: Brighid Malloy, Ellena Malloy. BA in Psychology, St. Louis U., 1970; JD, Loyola U., Chgo., 1976. Bar: Ill. 1976, Calif. 1977. Account exec. Complete Equity Mkts., Wheeling, Ill., 1970-76, corp. counsel, 1976-80, v.p., gen. counsel, 1980-83, exec. v.p., gen. counsel, 1983, chief operating officer, gen. counsel, 1984-85, vice chmn. bd., gen. counsel, 1986—; founding ptnr. firm Malloy & Kleinman, P.C., Des Plaines, Ill., 1985— Vol. atty. legal aid orgns., Calif., 1976-79. Mem. ABA, Calif. State Bar Assn., Nat. Legal Aid and Defender Assn. (ex-officio mem. ins. com. 1986—). General corporate, Insurance. Office: Malloy & Kleinman PC 640 Pearson St Suite 206 Des Plaines IL 60016

MALLOY, MICHAEL JOSEPH, lawyer; b. Phila., Dec. 31, 1950; s. Martin Joseph and Mary Rita (Hannigan) M.; m. Rosemary Elizabeth Dilworth, Aug. 30, 1975; children: Brian Patrick, Caroline Rose, Michael David. B.S., Villanova U., 1972; J.D., Widener Coll., 1976. Bar: Pa. 1976, U.S. Ct. Appeals (3d cir.) 1982, U.S. Supreme Ct. 1986. Sole practice, Media, Pa., 1976—; minor trial atty. Office of Pub. Defender, Media, 1976-79, maj. trial atty., 1979-81, chief maj. trial unit, 1981—; lectr. law Del. County Community Coll., 1977-80. Mem. Pa. Bar Assn., Phila. Bar Assn., Delaware County Bar Assn., Assn. Trial Lawyers Am., Nat. Legal Aid and Defender Assn., Brehon Irish Law Soc. Republican. Roman Catholic. Criminal, Personal injury, Workers' compensation. Home: 813 Garden Ave Havertown PA 19083 Office: 10 Veterans Sq Media PA 19063

MALLOY, MICHAEL PATRICK, lawyer, educator, consultant; b. Haddon Heights, N.J., Sept. 23, 1951; s. Francis Edward and Marie Grace (Nardi) M.; m. Mary McGinty, May 11, 1972; 1 child, Elizabeth McGinty. B.A. magna cum laude (scholar), Georgetown U., 1973, Ph.D., 1983; J.D. (scholar), U. Pa., 1976. Bar: N.J. 1976. Research asso. Inst. Internat. Law and Econ. Devel., Washington, 1976-77; atty.-advisor Office Fgn. Assets Control, Dept. Treasury, Washington, 1977-80, Office of Comptroller of Currency, Washington, 1981; spl. counsel SEC, Washington, 1981-82; asst. prof. N.Y. Law Sch., N.Y.C., 1982-83; spl. asst. Office of Gen. Counsel, U.S. Dept. Treasury, Washington, 1985; assoc. prof. Seton Hall U. Sch. Law, Newark, 1983-86, prof., assoc. dean, 1986-87; prof. law Fordham U., N.Y.C., 1987—; law lectr. Morin Ctr. Banking Law Studies Boston U. Sch. Law, 1986—; cons. banking and pvt. internat. law matters. Recipient Spl. Achievement award Dept. Treasury, 1982. Mem. Am. Soc. Internat. Law (exec. council), Hegel Soc. Am., L'Association des Auditeurs et Anciens Auditeurs de l'Academie de Droit International de la Haye, Phi Beta Kappa. Author: Corporate Law of Banks (3 vols.), 1987; contbr. articles, revs. and comments to profl. publs. Banking, Private international, Public international. Office: Fordham U Sch Law 140 W 62d St New York NY 10023

MALM, ERIC S., lawyer; b. Bklyn., Jan. 5, 1927; s. E. Sigfrid and Allin (Carlson) M.; m. Nancy Scarborough, June 28, 1960; children: Scott C., Karen G. BA, Colgate U., 1950; LLB, Columbia U., 1953. Bar: N.Y. 1954. Assoc. Mendes & Mount, N.Y.C., 1954-56; ptnr. Ferris, Bange, Davis, Trafford & Syz, N.Y.C., 1956-61, 1961-85; ptnr. Humes, Andrews, Botzow & Wagner, N.Y.C., 1985—. Past pres., bd. dirs. Bklyn. Kindergarden Soc., 1961—; trustee, sec. Brookgreen Gardens, Murrells Inlet, S.C., 1973—. Episcopalian. Probate. Office: Humes Andrews Botzow & Wagner 67 Broad St New York NY 10004

MALM, RICHARD ALLAN, lawyer; b. Pensacola, Fla., Aug. 6, 1949; s. Frank Stuart and Darlene Mae (Nelson) M.; m. Robbie Jean Gatchel, Sept. 4, 1971; children: Jonathan, Kathryn, Margaret. BSEE, Iowa State U., 1971; JD with honors, Drake U., 1974. Bar: Iowa 1974, U.S. Dist. Ct. (no. and so. dists.) Iowa 1974, U.S. Ct. Appeals (8th and 7th cirs.) 1978, U.S. Supreme Ct. 1985. Assoc. Dickinson, Throckmorton, Parker, Mannheimer & Raife, Des Moines, 1974-78, ptnr., 1978—. Mem. ABA, Iowa Bar Assn., Iowa Trial Lawyers Assn., Des Moines C. of C., Order of Coif, Tau Beta Pi, Eta Kappa Nu. Democrat. Federal civil litigation, State civil litigation, Contracts commercial. Home: 5812 N Waterbury Des Moines IA 50312 Office: Dickinson Throckmorton Parker Mannheimer & Raife 1600 Hub Tower Des Moines IA 50309

MALMGREN, JAMES H(OWARD), lawyer; b. Canton, Ill., Dec. 28, 1946; s. William H. and Gladys (Stansbury) M.; m. Valerina M. Quintana, 1971 (div. 1975); m. Karen E. Larsen, July 11, 1981; children: Owen Zachariah, Matthew James, Erik Christopher. BA in English, Lake Forest Coll., 1969; JD, John Marshall Law Sch., 1978. Bar: Ill. 1978, U.S. Dist. Ct. (cen. dist.) Ill. 1979. Sole practice Canton, 1978—; city atty. City of Canton, 1981—; chmn. West Cen. Ill. Water Commn., Canton, 1985—. Mem. Parlin-Ingersoll Library Bd., Canton, 1985—. Served as sgt. USAF, 1970-74, Vietnam. Mem. ABA, Assn. Trial Lawyers Am., Ill. State Bar Assn., Fulton County Bar Assn. Lutheran. Avocations: reading, camping, canoeing, hunting. General practice, Local government, Real property. Office: Malmgren Law Offices 369 N Main St Canton IL 61520

MALONE, DANIEL PATRICK, lawyer; b. Albany, N.Y., Jan. 25, 1953; s. Paul Timothy and Miriam Rose (Connolly) M.; m. Claudia Ann Hebel, June 3, 1978; 1 child, Danny Jr. AB, Cornell U., 1975; JD, U. Detroit, 1978. Bar: Mich. 1978. Law clk. to presiding judge U.S. Dist. Ct. (ea. dist.) Mich., Detroit, 1978-79; ptnr. Butzel, Long, Gust, Klein & Van Zile, Detroit, 1979—; faculty midwest region Nat. Inst. Trial Advocacy; instr. research, writing Detroit Coll. Law, 1979—, adj. prof. trial advocacy, 1984—; speaker Mich. Inst. Continuing Edn., 1986—. Bd. dirs. Boysville Mich.; advisor Hmong Community Greater Detroit; frequent donor program ARC. Mem. ABA, Mich. Bar Assn. (negligence sect., entertainment sect.), Detroit Bar Assn. Avocations: music, athletics. Federal civil litigation, Personal injury, Entertainment. Home: 372 Westwood Birmingham MI 48009 Office: Butzel Long et al 1650 First National Bldg Detroit MI 48226

MALONE, DAVID ROY, university dean, state senator; b. Beebe, Ark., Nov. 4, 1943; s. James Roy and Ila Mae (Griffin) M.; m. Judith Kaye Huff, June 20, 1965; 1 child, Michael David. BSBA, U. Ark., 1965, JD, 1969, MBA, 1982. Bar: Ark. 1969, U.S. Dist. Ct. (we. dist.) Ark. 1969, U.S. Tax Ct. 1972, U.S. Ct. Appeals (8th cir.) 1972, U.S. Supreme Ct. 1972. Sole practice Fayetteville, Ark., 1969-72; city atty. City of Fayetteville, 1969-72; asst. prof. law U. Ark., Fayetteville, 1972-76, asst. dean, 1976—. Contbr. articles to profl. jours. Mayor City of Fayetteville, 1979-80; state rep. State of Ark. Dist. 15, 1980-84, state senator Dist. 6, 1984-86. Recipient Service award Ark. Mcpl. League, 1980, Service award Fayetteville C. of C., 1982, Award of Merit Ark. Bar Found., 1983. Mem. ABA, Ark. Bar Assn. (ho. dels. 1977-81), Wash. County Bar Assn., Ark. Inst. of Continuing Legal Edn. (bd. dirs. 1979—). Democrat. Mem. Christian Ch. Legal education, Legislative. Home: 1928 Austin Dr Fayetteville AR 72703 Office: PO Box 1048 Fayetteville AR 72701

MALONE, ERNEST ROLAND, JR., lawyer; b. New Orleans, Nov. 26, 1947; s. Ernest Roland and Geraldine (Stack) M.; m. Mary Harper, June 26, 1971; children—Meredith Harper, Eric Gallatin, R. Chandler. B.S., La. State U., 1970; J.D., Tulane U., 1975. Bar: La. 1975, U.S. Supreme Ct. 1978, U.S. Dist. Ct. (ea. dist.) La. 1975, U.S. Ct. Appeals (5th cir.) 1975, U.S. Dist. Ct. (we. dist.) La. 1976, U.S. Ct. Appeals (6th cir.) 1980, U.S. Ct. Appeals (11th cir.) 1983. Ptnr., Kullman, Inman, Bee & Downing, New Orleans, 1975—. Contbg. editor: The Developing Labor Law, 1980—. Mem. Preservation Resource Ctr., New Orleans 1980—, People Assoc. With Children's Hosp., New Orleans, 1982—, Met. Area Com., New Orleans, 1983—. Served to 1st lt. U.S. Army, 1970-72; Vietnam. Decorated Bronze Star. Mem. La. State Bar Assn. (labor law sect. 1980—), ABA (labor and employment law sect. 1976-86, litigation sect.), Fed. Bar Assn. (1976-85), New Orleans Bar Assn. Labor, Pension, profit-sharing, and employee benefits, Workers' compensation. Home: 1024 Nashville Ave New Orleans LA 70115 Office: Kullman Inman Bee & Downing 615 Howard Ave PO Box 60118 New Orleans LA 70160

MALONE, GEORGIA JOAN, lawyer; b. Bklyn., May 3, 1953; d. Joseph F. and Emma (Guistra) Abbate; m. Peter Dechar, Dec. 21, 1985. BS with honors, Boston U., 1975; JD, New Eng. Law Sch., 1978. Bar: N.Y. 1979. Counsel Arlen Realty Devel. Corp., N.Y.C., 1979-80; assoc. Finkelstein, Borah, Schwartz, Altschuler & Goldstein, P.C., N.Y.C., 1980-83, ptnr., 1986—; counsel Rent Stabilization Assn., N.Y.C., 1983-85; adj. prof. NYU, 1984—. Author: Rent Stabilization Digest, 1983, Rent Registration, Tenant Challenges, 1985. Mem. ABA, N.Y. State Bar Assn. (landlord and tenant com.). Landlord-tenant, Real property. Office: Finkelstein Borah Schwartz et al 377 Broadway New York NY 10013

MALONE, JAMES LAURENCE, III, lawyer; b. Brighton, Mass., Aug. 5, 1947; s. James Laurence and Mary (Roberts) M.; m. Alice Reno, Nov. 30, 1974; 1 child, Virginia. AB cum laude, Boston Coll., 1969; JD, U. Va., 1972; LLM in Taxation, Georgetown U., 1978. Law clk. to presiding justice U.S. Ct. Claims, Washington, 1972-74; trial atty. U.S. Justice Dept., Washington, 1974-79, sr. trial atty., 1979-82; assoc. McDermott, Will & Emerson, Chgo., 1982, income ptnr., 1983-85, sr. ptnr., 1986—. Gen. counsel, bd. dirs. Northeast Ill. council Boy Scouts Am., Highland Park; pres., bd. dirs. Country Club of Reston, Va., 1978-80. Mem. ABA (adminstrv. practice subcom. tax sect.), Fed. Cir. Bar Assn. (tax appeals com.). Clubs: Union League (fin. com.) (Chgo.), Exmoor Country (Highland Park), Sankaty Head Golf (Nantucket, Mass.). Corporate taxation, Corporate taxation, Federal civil litigation. Home: 644 Spruce St Winnetka IL 60603 Office: McDermott Will & Emery 111 W Monroe St Chicago IL 60603

MALONE, SUE URWYLER, bar association executive; b. Portland, Oreg., Feb. 26, 1940; d. Fred and Frieda (Wyttenberg) U.; m. John S. Malone (div.); 1 child, Margaret Elizabeth. B.S., Portland State U., 1962. Asst. exec. sec. Bar Assn. San Francisco, 1963-68, exec. sec. 1968-73; exec. dir. Calif. Judges Assn., San Francisco, 1975-83; exec. dir. Boston Bar Assn., 1983—. Pres. Scott Valley Homeowners Assn., Mill Valley, Calif., 1981-83. Mem. Nat. Assn. Bar Execs. (exec. com. 1984-86, chair govtl. relations sect. 1982-84), Am. Soc. Assn. Execs. (mem. western council 1981-83), ABA, Internat. Assn. Bus. Communicators, New Eng. Soc. Assn. Execs. Club: Union (Boston). Office: Boston Bar Assn 16 Beacon St Boston MA 02108

MALONE, THOMAS PAUL, lawyer; b. Saginaw, Mich., May 4, 1945; s. John D. and Margaret (Baker) M.; m. Janet E. Petteys, Nov. 25, 1976; children: Katherine, John. AB, U. Notre Dame, 1967; JD, U. Mich., 1973. Bar: Colo. 1974, U.S. Dist. Ct. Colo. 1974, U.S. Ct. Appeals (10th cir.) 1974. Sole practice Denver, 1974-81; ptnr. McGuane & Malone, Denver, 1981—; lectr. in field. Author: Krendl's Colorado Practice Adoption and Name Change, 1982. Mem. ABA (family law sect.), Colo. Bar Assn. (vice chmn. law edn. com. family law sect. 1986—), Denver Bar Assn. (chmn. community edn. com. 1974-77), Interdisciplinary Com. on Child Custody (pres. 1981-82), Phi Alpha Delta. Family and matrimonial, Juvenile. Office: McGuane & Malone 3773 Cherry Creek North Dr Suite 725 Ptarmigan Place Denver CO 80209

MALONE, THOMAS WILLIAM, lawyer; b. Seattle, Sept. 16, 1946; s. James Edward and Marie Cecilia (Anderson) M.; m. Drexel Cox., June 19, 1978; children—Jason, Cary. B.A., U. Wash., 1968, J.D., 1972; M.B.A., Golden Gate U., 1981. Bar: Wash. 1972, U.S. Ct. Appeals (9th cir.) 1972, U.S. Tax Ct. 1980, U.S. Ct. Claims 1981, U.S. Supreme Ct. 1980. Prin. Treece, Richdale, Malone & Corning, Inc., P.S., Seattle, 1973—. Pres., Seattle Marine Bus. Coalition, 1983—; bd. dirs. Ballard Community Hosp., 1982—; chmn. bd. dirs. Ballard Community Hosp., 1986-87. Mem. ABA, Wash. Bar Assn., Seattle-King County Bar Assn., Ballard C. of C. (pres. 1981-84). General corporate, Estate planning, Corporate taxation. Home: 2116 NW 93d St Seattle WA 98107

MALONE, THOMAS WILLIAM, lawyer; b. Albany, Ga., Nov. 2, 1942; s. Rosser Admas and Sara Petrona (Underwood) M.; m. Tommye Joan Beall, June 5, 1965 (div. Aug. 1973); children: Thomas William Jr., Rosser Adams. BA, U. Ga., 1963; LLB, Mercer U., 1966. Bar: Ga. 1965. Ptnr. Malone, Drake & Malone, Albany, 1966-73; sr. ptnr. Thomas William Malone & Assocs. P.C., Albany, 1973-75, Malone, Woodall & Percilla P.C., Albany, 1975-78, Malone & Percilla P.C., Atlanta, 1978—; adj. asst. prof. sch. pharmacy U. Miami, Fla. Contbr. articles to profl. jours. Fellow Internat. Acad. Trial Lawyers; mem. ABA (trial techniques com.), Assn. Trial Lawyers Am. (bd. govs. 1981-83), Ga. Trial Lawyers Assn. (pres. 1980, life), The Belli Soc. (v.p. 1985—, editorial bd. jour.). Democrat. Presbyterian. Avocations: flying, deep sea fishing, scuba diving, racquetball. Personal injury, State civil litigation, Federal civil litigation. Office: Malone & Percilla PC PO Box 49406 Atlanta GA 30359

MALONE, WILLIAM GRADY, lawyer; b. Minden, La., Feb. 19, 1915; s. William Gordon and Minnie Lucie (Hortman) M.; m. Marion Rowe Whitfield, Sept. 26, 1943; children—William Grady, Gordon Whitfield, Marion Elizabeth, Helen Ann, Margaret Catherine. B.S., La. State U., 1941; J.D., George Washington U., 1952. Bar: Va. 1952, U.S. Supreme Ct 1971. Statis. analyst Dept. Agr., Baton Rouge, 1941; investigator VA, Washington, 1946-59; legal officer, dep., gen. counsel, asst. gen. counsel 1959-79; individual practice law Arlington, Va., 1979—. Editor: Fed. Bar News, 1972-73. Pres. Aurora Hills Civic Assn., 1948-49; spl. asst. to treas. Com. of 100, 1979-81, chmn., 1982-83; pres. Children's Theater, 1968-69; trustee St. George's Episcopal Ch., 1979—; chmn. Arlington County Fair Assn., 1979-83. Served to lt. col. AUS, 1941-46, ETO. Decorated Legion of Merit; recipient Disting. Service award, 1979, 3 Superior Performance awards, 1952-72, Outstanding Alumni award George Washington Law Sch., 1978. Mem. Fed. Bar Assn. (pres. D.C. chpt. 1970-71, nat. pres. 1978-79), Va. Bar Assn., Arlington County Bar Assn., Nat. Lawyers Club (dir.). Clubs: Arlington Host Lions, Ft. Myer Officers. Family and matrimonial, Personal injury, Probate. Home: 224 N Jackson St Arlington VA 22201 Office: 2060 N 14th St Suite 310 Arlington VA 22201

MALONEY, ANDREW J., lawyer; b. 1939. BS, U.S. Mil. Acad.; LLB, Fordham U. Bar: N.Y. 1961. U.S. atty. ea. dist. State of N.Y., Bklyn. Office: U S Courthouse 225 Cadman Plaza East Brooklyn NY 11201 *

MALONEY, BARRY CHARLES, lawyer; b. Waterbury, Conn., June 26, 1942; s. Randolph B. and Alice (Loban) M.; m. Marjorie Ann McAuliffe, Sept. 9, 1967; children: Jennifer, Brian, Kevin. BSBA, Georgetown U., 1964; JD, George Washington U., 1967. Bar: D.C. 1968; CPA, Md. Sr. atty. SEC, Washington, 1967-71; spl. counsel U.S. Econ. Stabilization Program, Washington, 1971-72; sr. ptnr. Berliner & Maloney, Washington, 1972—; bd. dirs. Ski America Corp., York, Pa.; pres. Robert Case Bennett Corp., Lake Placid, N.Y. Author: Avoiding Delays in the Processing of Registration Statements, Under the Securities Act of 1933, 1969. Coach Cath. Youth Orgn., Bethesda, Md., 1979—; pres. Team Washington Ice Hockey Orgn., Bethesda, 1984—. Mem. ABA, D.C. Bar Assn., Delta Theta Phi (named Outstanding Law Student in Nation 1967). Club: Kenwood Country (Bethesda). Avocations: skiing, ice hockey, sailing. General corporate, Securities, Franchise law. Office: Berliner & Maloney 1101 17th St NW #1004 Washington DC 20036

MALONEY, FRANK, lawyer; b. Worcester, Mass., Nov. 20, 1927; s. Francis James and Dora Marie (Berthiaume) M.; children—Catharine Frances, Edward James. B.A., U. Tex., 1953, LL.B., 1956. Bar: Tex. 1956 . Asst. dist. atty. Travis County, Austin, Tex., 1956-60; chief law enforcement div. Office of Tex. Atty. Gen., Austin, 1960-61; ptnr. firm Stayton, Maloney, Hearne & Babb, Austin, 1961-79; prin. Frank Maloney & Assocs., P.C., Austin, 1979-85, ptnr. Maloney, Gotcher & Yeager, P.C., 1985—. Author: (with Stumberg) Criminal Law and Administration. Served to capt. U.S. Army, 1946-51. Fellow Tex. Bar Found.; mem. Boston Bar Assn., Travis County Bar Assn., Tex. Bar Assn., Mass. Bar Assn., ABA, Tex. Trial Lawyers Assn., Am. Bd. Trial Advocates, Nat. Assn. Criminal Def. Lawyers (bd. dirs. 1972-83, 2d v.p. 1984-85, 1st v.p. 1985-86, pres. elect 1986-87), Tex. Criminal Def. Lawyers Assn. (pres. 1971-72), Am. Bd. Criminal Lawyers. Club: Town and Gown (Austin). Criminal. Home: 1414 Wathen Austin TX 78703 Office: Maloney Gotcher & Yeager PC 505 W 12th St Suite 200 Austin TX 78701

MALONEY, PHILIP DENNIS, lawyer; b. Salt Lake City, Nov. 14, 1947; s. Robert Vincent and Doris Anne (Crowe) M.; m. Deborah Kay Daughenbaugh, Jan. 3, 1981; 1 child, Bridget Anne. BA in Econs., George Washington U., 1970, JD, 1974. Bar: Alaska 1974, U.S. Dist. Ct. Alaska 1974. Assoc. Covington & Burling, Washington, 1974-75; sole practice Anchorage, 1975-77, 83—; gen. counsel Wien Air Alaska, Anchorage, 1977-83; instr. labor negotiations Stanford/Airline Transport Assn., exec. counsel, 1983; cons. Continental Airlines, Houston, Tex., 1982-83. Founding pres. Sta. KSKA Pub. Radio, Anchorage, 1980; bd. dirs. Citizens Adv. U. Alaska, Anchorage, 1983-86. Mem. ABA, Anchorage Labor Lawyers Assn. (pres. 1981), Assn. Trial Lawyers Am., Prime Number Soc. (bd. dirs., sustaining 1982—). Roman Catholic. State civil litigation, Labor, General corporate. Office: 405 W 36th Ave Anchorage AK 99503

MALONEY, ROBERT B., federal judge; b. 1933. BBA, So. Meth. U., 1956, JD, 1960. Asst. dist. atty. City of Dallas, 1961-62; ptnr. Watts, Stallings & Maloney, 1962-65, Maloney, Miller & McDowell, 1966-75, Maloney & McDowell, 1976-78, Maloney & Hardcastle, 1979-80, Maloney & Maloney, 1981-84; assoc. judge U.S. Ct. Appeals (5th cir.), Tex., 1983-85; judge U.S. Dist. Ct. (no. dist.) Tex., Dallas, 1985—. State rep., Austin, Tex., 1973-82. Mem. Tex. Bar Assn. Office: US Courthouse 1100 Commerce St Room 15-D-24 Dallas TX 75242 *

MALONEY, THOMAS JOSEPH, lawyer; b. Boston, July 6, 1953; s. Joseph Louis and Paulina Agnes (McKevitt) M.; m. Nancy Elizabeth Nedeau, Aug. 16, 1975; 1 child, John Joseph. BA, Boston Coll., 1976; JD, Fordham U., 1979. Assoc. Dunnington, Bartholow & Miller, N.Y.C., 1979-83, Finley, Kumble, Wagner et al, N.Y.C., 1983—; bd. dirs. TRL, Inc., Muskegon, Mich. Mem. ABA (subcom. on fgn. investments in U.S.), Iona Prep Alumni Assn. (bd. dirs. 1984—). General corporate, Securities, Contracts commercial. Office: Finley Kumble Wagner et al 425 Park Ave New York NY 10022

MALOOF, FARAHE PAUL, lawyer; b. Boston, Feb. 10, 1950; s. Farahe and Emily Suzanna (Puchy) M.; m. Brigitte Lucienne DeLugré. BS, Georgetown U., 1975, JD, 1978. Bar: Washington 1978, Va. 1981. Assoc. Corcoran & Rowe, Washington, 1978-81; sole practice Washington, 1982, 86—; ptnr. Berliner & Maloney, Washington, 1983-85; spl. counsel Advocacia Oliveira Ribeiro, Sao Paulo, Brazil, 1985-86; lectr. Am. U., Washington, 1984-85, Internat. Law Inst., Washington, 1986—. Served to cpl. USMC, 1968-70, Vietnam. Mem. ABA, Va. Bar Assn., D.C. Bar Assn., Georgetown U. Alumni Assn. (co-chmn. 1983-84). Republican. Roman Catholic. Avocations: Tennis, Water skiing. Private international, Real property, Legislative. Home: 1404 N 12th St #23 Arlington VA 22209 Office: 1825 Eye St NW Suite 300 Washington DC 20006-5486

MALOUF, STEPHEN FERRIS, lawyer; b. Dallas, Nov. 14, 1953; s. Edward Junior and Marie (Moossy) M. BA, U. Dallas, 1977; JD, St. Mary's U., San Antonio, 1982. Bar: Tex., U.S. Dist. Ct. (no. dist.) Tex., U.S. Ct. Appeals (5th cir.). Atty. Tex. Ct. Appeals, Dallas, 1982; assoc. Windle Turley Law Office, Dallas, 1983-84, Boyd Waggoner Law Office, Dallas, 1984-85, Windle, Turley Law Office, 1985—. Author: Criminal Appellate Rights of the United States. Mem. ABA, Assn. Trial Lawyers Am., Dallas Trial Lawyers Assn., Tex. Trial Lawyers Assn. (new membership com. 1986-87), Tex. Bar Assn., Dallas Assn. Young Lawyers (interest on lawyers' trust accounts com. com., chmn. continuing legal edn. program 1985, dir. continuing legal edn. programs 1986—). Roman Catholic. Avocations: painting, music. Personal injury. Home: 5726 Winton Dallas TX 75206

MALVIK, JOHN, lawyer; b. St. Paul, Oct. 3, 1949; s. Sverre and Svanhild (Holum) M.; m. Shirley Jean Bindel, Dec. 20, 1970; children—Jean Elizabeth, Jon-Erik; m. Wanda Lee Paul, Dec. 16, 1983. B.A., Augustana Coll., Ill., 1971; J.D., DePaul U., 1974. Bar: Ill. 1974, U.S. Dist. Ct. (cen. dist.) Ill. 1977, U.S. Ct. Appeals (7th cir.) 1980. Asst. state's atty. Rock Island County, Ill., 1974-77, asst. pub. defender, 1977-79; instr. law Blackhawk Coll., Moline, Ill., 1977-79; ptnr. Braud, Warner, Neppl & Westensee Ltd., Rock Island, 1980-83; sole practice, Rock Island, 1983—; panelist, guest expert in law; lectr. in field. Vol. coach Augustana Coll. Wrestling

Team, 1974-76, 82-84; Mem. ABA (def. services com. 1983—, com. on Torts & Ins. 1986—, criminal justice com., 1986—), Am. Trial Lawyers Assn., Nat. Geog. Soc., Ill. Bar Assn. (com. on law related edn., 1986—, Meritorious Service award 1983), Ill. Trial Lawyers Assn., Rock Island County Bar Assn., Beta Omega Sigma (pres. 1977-79). Democrat. Lutheran. Club: Tribe of Vikings (Augustana Coll.). Personal injury, Criminal, Jurisprudence. Home: #13 Velie Dr Moline IL 61265 Office: 1800 3d Ave Suite 502 Rock Island IL 61201

MAMAT, FRANK TRUSTICK, lawyer; b. Syracuse, N.Y., Sept. 4, 1949; s. Harvey Sanford and Annette (Trustick) M.; m. Kathy Lou Winters, June 23, 1975; children—Jonathan Adam, Steven Kenneth. B.A., U. Rochester, 1971; J.D., Syracuse U., 1974. Bar: D.C. 1976, Fla. 1977, Mich. 1984, U.S. Dist. Ct. (no. dist.) Ind. 1984, U.S. Dist. Ct. (ea. dist.) Mich. 1983, U.S. Ct. Appeals (D.C. cir.) 1976, U.S. Dist. Ct. (D.C. cir.) 1976, U.S. Ct. Appeals (6th cir.) 1983, U.S. Supreme Ct. 1979. Atty., NLRB, Washington, 1975-79; assoc. Proskauer, Rose, Goetz & Mendelsohn, Washington, N.Y.C., and Los Angeles, 1979-83; assoc. Fishman Group, Bloomfield Hills, Mich., 1983-85, ptnr., 1985—. Gen. counsel Rep. Com. of Oakland County, 1987—, bd. dirs. 300 Club, Mich., 1984—; Rep. Nat. Com., Nat. Rep. Senatorial Com., Presdl. Task Force; City dir. West Bloomfield, 1985-87; pres. West Bloomfield Rep. Club, 1985-87; fin. com. Rep. Com. of Oakland County, 1985—; vice. chmn. lawyers for Reagan-Bush, 1984; gen. counsel Rep. Party of Oakland County, 1987—; v.p. Fruehauf Farms, West Bloomfield, Mich., 1985—; bd. dirs. B'nai B'rith Barristers Unit, Detroit, 1983—, pres. 1985—; mem. staff Exec. Office of Pres. Of U.S. Inquiries/Comments, Washington, 1981-83. Mem. ABA, Oakland County Bar Assn., D.C. Bar Assn., Fed. Bar Assn., Fla. Bar Assn. (Labor com. 1977—), Auburn Hills C. of C. (bd. dirs.), Founders Soc. (Detroit Inst. of Art). Club: Econ. of Detroit. Lodge: B'nai Brith (v.p. 1982-83, pres. 1985—). Labor. Office: Fishman Group 2050 N Woodward Ave Bloomfield Hills MI 48013

MAMER, STUART MIES, lawyer; b. East Hardin, Ill., Feb. 23, 1921; s. Louis H. and Anna (Mies) M.; m. Donna E. Jordan, Sept. 10, 1944; children: Richard A., John S., Bruce J. A.B., U. Ill., 1942, J.D., 1947. Bar: Ill. bar 1947. Assoc. Thomas & Mulliken, Champaign, 1947-55; partner firm Thomas, Mamer & Haughey, Champaign, 1955—; lectr. U. Ill. Coll. Law, Urbana, 1965-85; Mem. Atty. Registration and Disciplinary Commn. Ill., 1976-82. Chmn. fund drive Champaign County Community Chest, 1955; 1st pres. Champaign County United Fund, 1957; Pres., dir. U. Ill. McKinley Found., Champaign, 1957-69; trustee Children's Home and Aid Soc. of Ill., v.p., 1977—. Served as pilot USAAF, 1943-45. Mem. Am. Coll. Probate Counsel (bd. regents 1984—), Phi Beta Kappa, Phi Gamma Delta. Republican. Presbyterian. Probate, Real property, Estate taxation. Home: 6 Montclair Rd Urbana IL 61801 Office: Thomas Mamer & Haughey 30 Main St 5th Floor Champaign IL 61820

MAMORSKY, JEFFREY DEAN, lawyer; b. New Haven, Conn., Feb. 26, 1946; s. Paul and Mildred Rosaline (Krevolin) M. B.A., NYU, 1967, J.D., 1972, LL.M., 1975. Bar: N.Y. 1972, U.S. Tax Ct. 1974, U.S. Ct. Appeals 1974, D.C., 1978, U.S. Supreme Ct. 1978. Legal editor Prentice Hall Pension & Profit Sharing Library, Englewood Cliffs, N.J., 1968-72; corp. counsel Titan Actuarial Services, N.Y.C., 1972-73; benefits atty. Mobil Oil Corp., N.Y.C., 1973-75; compensation and benefits counsel W.R. Grace & Co., N.Y.C., 1975-77; ptnr. Vedder, Price, Kaufman, Kammholz & Day, N.Y.C., 1977-81; ptnr. Shea & Gould, N.Y.C., 1981-84, Wender, Murase & White, N.Y.C., 1984-86, Rubin Baum, Levin, Constant & Friedman, N.Y.C., 1986—. Served with AUS. Mem. ABA (com. on employee benefits tax sect.), N.Y. State Bar Assn. (com. on employee benefits tax sect.), U.S. C. of C. (employee benefits com.), Assn. Bar City N.Y. Author: Pension and Profit Sharing Plans: A Basic Guide, 1977, Employee Benefits Law, ERISA and Beyond, 1980, updated 1986; editor: Employee Benefits Hardbook; editor-in chief Jour. of Compensation and Benefits; contbr. articles to profl. jours. Pension, profit-sharing, and employee benefits. Office: Rubin Baum Levin Constant et al 645 Fifth Ave New York NY 10022 *

MANARD, ROBERT LYNN, III, lawyer; b. New Orleans, Sept. 18, 1947; s. Robert Lynn Jr. and Marguerite (Castex) M.; m. Brenda Bennett Bohrer, July 7, 1973; children: Robbie, Wendy. BS, Tulane U., 1969, JD, 1972. Bar: La. 1972, U.S. Dist. Ct. 1972, U.S. Ct. Appeals (5th cir.) La. 1972. Law clk. U.S. Ct. Appeals (4th cir.), New Orleans, 1972-74; instr. Tulane U. Law Sch., New Orleans, 1973-75; assoc. Hammett, Leake & Hammett, New Orleans, 1974-76; sr. ptnr. Manard & Schoenberger, New Orleans, 1976-81, Manard, McKearn & Ryan, New Orleans, 1981—; panelist legal clk. seminar, La. Ct. Appeals, 1975; adv. com. Legal Access, Inc., New Orleans, 1986. Author: (booklet) Proper Techniques in Interviewing Clients, 1974. Bd. dirs. Tulane Legal Asst. Program, New Orleans, 1974-76; Inst. ARC, Kenner, La., 1966-70. Mem. ABA, La. Bar Assn., Assn. Trial Lawyers Am., La. Trial Lawyers Assn. Democrat. Roman Catholic. Avocations: pole vaulting, running, tennis, golf. Personal injury, Federal civil litigation, State civil litigation. Home: 23 Waverly Pl Metairie LA 70002 Office: Manard McKearn & Ryan 221 Carondelet St Suite 400 New Orleans LA 70130

MANASHIL, NED WILLIAM, lawyer; b. Phila., Dec. 21, 1938; s. Albert S. and Cecelia E. (Criss) M.; m. Brigitte E. Banz, Apr. 16, 1968; 1 child, Kirsten Anka. BS, Pa. State U., 1960; JD, Villanova U., 1963. Bar: Pa. 1964, U.S. Ct. Claims 1964, U.S. Dist. Ct. D.C. 1969, U.S. Ct. Appeals (D.C. cir.) 1969, Ohio 1972, Calif. 1983. Trial atty. U.S. Dept. Justice, Washigton, 1963-66; assoc. Chadbourne, Parke, Whiteside & Wolff, Washington, 1967-69; counsel TRW Inc., Cleve., 1969-73; v.p. TRW Info. Systems Group, Long Beach, Calif., 1981—; sr. counsel TRW Europe Inc., London, 1973-81. Mem. Order of Coif. Office: TRW Info Systems Group 200 Oceangate Suite 1200 Long Beach CA 90802

MANBECK, HARRY FREDERICK, JR., lawyer; b. Honesdale, Pa., June 26, 1926; s. Harry Frederick Sr. and Pauline (Holley) M.; m. Lois Marie Lange, May 30, 1953 (dec. July 1973); children: Holley Manbeck Day, Peter Charles; m. Noma Green Satterfield, Aug. 30, 1975. BEE, Lehigh U., 1949; LLB, U. Louisville, 1955. Bar: Ky. 1955, Ind. 1962, Mass. 1965, U.S. Ct. Appeals (fed. cir.) 1982. From trainee to patent atty. Gen. Electric Co., various locations, 1950-57; counsel patent div. Gen. Electric Co., Ft. Wayne, Ind., 1957-64; counsel patent air eng. div. Gen. Electric Co., Lynn, Mass., 1964-67; patent counsel major appliance group Louisville, 1967-69; gen. patent counsel Fairfield, Conn., 1970—. Mem. ABA (council mem., patent trademark and copyright sect. 1985—), Bar Assn. Ct. Appeals for Fed. Cir. (bd. dirs. 1984—), Assn. Corp. Patent Counsel (pres. 1978-79), Am. Arbitration Assn. (recipient Whitney North Seymour Sr. award 1984). Club: Patterson (Fairfield). Avocations: golf, boating. Patent, Trademark and copyright. Home: 34 Old Easton Turnpike Weston CT 06883 Office: Gen Electric Co 3135 Easton Turnpike Fairfield CT 06431

MANCINI, LORENZO ANTHONY, lawyer; b. Mola di Bari, Puglia, Italy, July 15, 1946; came to U.S., 1955; s. Frank and Palmina (Santoro) M.; m. Carol Rose Kula, Sept. 20, 1968 (div. April 1984); children: Christian, Angela, Lisa; m. Marie Bacino, Feb. 14, 1987. BA, St. Marys Coll., Winona, Minn., 1968; JD with highest honors, DePaul U., 1977. Bar: Ill. 1977, U.S. Dist. Ct. (no. dist.) Ill. 1977. Assoc. Law Office of Thomas P. McLaughlin, Schaumburg, Ill., 1977-78; atty. Montgomery Ward Ins., Chgo., 1978-79; assoc. O'Reilly & Cunningham, Wheaton, Ill., 1979-85, ptnr., 1986—. Mem. ABA (tort and ins. law com.), Ill. Bar Assn., DuPage County Bar Assn. (civil practice com.), Ill. Def. Counsel, Assn. Trial Lawyers Am., Lex Legion. Roman Catholic. Avocations: photography, hiking, tennis. State civil litigation, Personal injury, Insurance. Home: 27 W 015 Tamarack Ct Winfield IL 60190 Office: O'Reilly & Cunningham 109 N Hale Wheaton IL 60187

MANCINO, DOUGLAS MICHAEL, lawyer; b. Cleve., May 8, 1949; s. Paul and Adele (Brazaitis) M.; m. Carol Keith, June 16, 1973. BA, Kent State U., 1971; JD, Ohio State U., 1974. Bar: Ohio 1974, U.S. Tax Ct. 1977; Calif. 1981, D.C. 1981. Assoc. Baker & Hostetler, Cleve., 1974-1980; ptnr. Memel & Ellsworth, Los Angeles, 1980-87, McDermott, Will & Emery, Los Angeles, 1987—. Author: (with others) Hospital Survival Guide, 1984; co-author quar. tax column Am. Hosp. Assn. publ. Health Law Vigil, (with L. Barnes) Joint Ventures Between Hosps. and Physicians, 1987; contbr. articles to profl. jours. Trustee Womens Gen. Polyclinic Hosp., Cleve., 1979-80. Mem. ABA (tax, bus., real property, probate and trust sects., chmn. health care subcom. 1986—), Calif. State Bar Assn. (tax, bus. law sects.), Ohio Bar Assn., Greater Cleve. Bar Assn., D.C. Bar Assn., Beverly Hills Bar Assn. (chmn. health law com. 1982-84), Nat. Health Lawyers Assn., Am. Soc. Hosp. Attys., Calif. Soc. for Healthcare Attys. Club: Bel Air Country (Los Angeles). Corporate taxation, Health. Home: 2727 Patricia Ave Los Angeles CA 90064 Office: McDermott Will & Emery 2027 Century Park E Los Angeles CA 90067

MANCO, DOMINICK MICHAEL, lawyer; b. Lakewood, N.J., Aug. 26, 1955; s. Frank and Maria Rose (Maccarone) M.; m. Vicki Lynn Parker, Nov. 23, 1980; children: Jennifer Michele, Eric Michael. BA, Seton Hall U., 1977, JD, 1980. Bar: N.J. 1980, U.S. Dist. Ct. N.J. 1980, U.S. Ct. Appeals (3d cir.) 1982. Assoc. Steven C. Rubin/Charles Frankel, Oakhurst, N.J., 1980, Paschon, Feurey & Kotzas, Toms River, N.J., 1981-82; asst. atty. Lakewood Twp., 1982-83, acting atty., 1983-84, mcpl. atty., 1984—. Mem. ABA, N.J. Bar Assn., Ocean County Bar Assn. Local government, Real property, General practice. Home: 33 Garfield St Lakewood NJ 08701 Office: Twp Lakewood Mcpl Bldg 231 3d St Lakewood NJ 08701

MANDEL, MARTIN LOUIS, lawyer; b. Los Angeles, May 17, 1944; s. Maurice S. and Florence (Byer) M.; m. Duree Dunn, Oct. 16, 1982. B.A., U. So. Calif., 1965, J.D., 1968; LL.M., George Washington U., 1971. Bar: Calif. 1969, U.S. dist. ct. (cen. dist.) Calif. 1972, U.S. Ct. Claims, 1971, U.S. Tax Ct. 1971, U.S. Supreme Ct. 1972. With office of gen. csl. IRS, Washington, 1968-72; ptnr. Stephens, Jones, LaFever & Smith, Los Angeles, 1972-77, Stephens, Martin & Mandel, 1977-79, Fields, Fehn, Feinstein & Mandel, 1979-83; sr. v.p., gen. counsel Investment Mortgage Internat., Inc., 1983-84; ptnr. Feinstein, Gourley & Mandel, 1984-85, Mandel & Handin, San Francisco, 1985—; gen. counsel L.A. Express Football Club, 1983-86; instr. corps. U. West Los Angeles, 1973-83. Mem. ABA, Los Angeles County Bar Assn. Club: Los Angeles Athletic. Personal income taxation, Real property, General corporate. Office: Mandel & Handin 400 Montgomery St Suite 710 San Francisco CA 94104

MANDEL, NEWTON W., lawyer; b. Bklyn., Aug. 27, 1926; s. Nathan and Rose (Tenenbaum) M.; m. Ellen Tannenbaum, Nov. 27, 1954; children: Sherry, Harlan. BS, N.C. State U., Raleigh, 1948; JD, N.Y. Law Sch., 1951. Bar: N.Y. 1951, U.S. Dist. Ct. (ea. and so. dists.) N.Y. 1951, U.S. Ct. Appeals (2d cir.) 1953. Ptnr. Mandel & Beck, 1951-58, Mandel & Blum, 1958-64; v.p., gen. counsel 1st Republic Corp. Am., N.Y.C., 1964-69; v.p., counsel G & W Realty Corp., Madison Sq. Garden Corp., 1969-72; sr. atty. Dreyer & Traub, 1973-78; prin. Zimton Group, real estate developers, 1978—; of counsel Lefrak, Fischer & Myerson, 1981-84; ptnr. Certilman, Haft, Lebow, Balin, Buckley & Kremer, 1984-87; of counsel Reavis & McGrath, N.Y.C., 1987—. Bd. govs. Long Island U. CW Post Ctr. for Real Estate and Community Devel.; trustee Cen. Synagogue, N.Y.C. Served with USNR. Mem. ABA (chmn. syndications com., real property div., tax sect., corp. sect.), N.Y. State Bar Assn. (real property sect., tax sect.), LIU Real Estate Inst. Clubs: Knickerbocker Yacht (Port Washington, N.Y.); Yacht Racing Assn. L.I. Sound. Lodge: B'nai Brith. Real property, Corporate taxation. Office: 345 Park Ave New York NY 10154

MANDEL, RICHARD GORDON, lawyer; b. N.Y.C., Jan. 17, 1949; s. Max and Ruth (Gordon) M.; m. Andrea Sue Polovsky, Aug. 30, 1970. BA, Queens Coll., 1970; JD, Columbia U., 1973. Bar: N.Y. 1974, U.S. Ct. Appeals (2d cir.) 1975, U.S. Dist. Ct. (so. dist.) N.J. 1976. Atty. Met. Life Ins. Co., N.Y.C., 1974-80, asst. gen. counsel, 1980-84, assoc. gen. counsel, 1984—. Contbr. articles to profl. jours. Mem. ABA (chmn. health ins. law com. 1982-83, vice chmn. employee benefits law com. 1984—, editor Tort and Ins. Practice Jour. 1984—), Soc. of Corp. Ins. Litigators, Assn. of Life Ins. Counsel. Republican. Avocations: sci. fiction, computer games. Insurance, Pension, profit-sharing, and employee benefits. Office: Met Life Ins Co 1 Madison Ave New York NY 10010

MANDELL, CRAIG JACK, lawyer; b. N.Y.C., Jan. 6, 1953; s. Stanley I. and Julia (Baena) M. BS in Mgmt., Boston U., 1975; MBA, JD, Fla. State U., 1979. Bar: Fla. 1979. Ptnr. Goldberg & Young, P.A., Ft. Lauderdale, Fla., 1980—. Mem. ABA (real property sect.), Fla. Bar Assn. (real property sect.). Jewish. Avocation: golf. Real property, Landlord-tenant, Contracts commercial. Office: Goldberg & Young PA 1630 N Federal Hwy Fort Lauderdale FL 33305

MANDELL, DAVID E., lawyer; b. Norwich, Conn., Jan. 1, 1955. BA, U. Vt., 1976; JD, Western New England Sch. Law, 1979. Bar: Conn. 1979, U.S. Dist. Ct. Conn. 1980, Fla. 1984. Sole practice Norwich, 1980—. Contbr. articles to profl. jours. Recipient Jeremiah Halsey award Norwich Free Acad., 1972. Mem. Fla. Bar Assn. (young lawyers div.). Probate, Health, Juvenile. Home: 1 Indian Spring Ln Norwich CT 06360 Office: 71 E Town Norwich CT 06360

MANDELL, HOWARD ALLYN, lawyer; b. Los Angeles, Feb. 21, 1945; s. Leonard Charles and Frances (Friedman) M.; m. Laurie Weil, June 24, 1972; children: Joshua Francis, Charles David. BA, U. Pa., 1967; JD, Georgetown U., 1970. Bar: Ala. 1971, D.C. 1972. Law clk. to U.S. Dist. Judge, Montgomery, Ala., 1970-71 sole practice, Montgomery, 1971-75; ptnr. Mandell & Boyd, Montgomery, 1975—; mem. adj. faculty U. Ala. Law Sch., 1982; atty. Central Ala. Girl Scouts U.S.A. Chmn. bd. Legal Services Corp. Ala.; chmn. Montgomery County Grievance Panel; pres. Jewish Fedn. Montgomery, 1986; bd. dirs. So. Poverty Law Ctr. Mem. ABA, Fed. Bar Assn., Montgomery County Trial Lawyers Assn. (pres.-elect), Ala. State Bar (character fitness com.), Assn. Trial Lawyers Am., Ala. Trial Lawyers Assn. (exec. com.), Assn. Reps. of Profl. Athletes. Personal injury, Civil rights, Entertainment. Office: 1120 Vaughn Rd Pike Road AL 36064 Office: Mandell & Boyd PO Box 4248 Montgomery AL 36103

MANDELL, MARK STEVEN, lawyer; b. Providence, R.I., June 27, 1949; s. Leonard Charles and Francis (Friedman) M.; m. Faye Irene Shapiro, July 11, 1982; children: Rachel, Zachary. BA, U. Ala., 1971; JD, Georgetown U., 1974. Bar: R.I. 1974, Ala. 1975, U.S. Dist. Ct. R.I. 1975, U.S. Ct. Appeals (1st cir.) 1975, U.S. Supreme Ct. 1975. Law clk. to presiding justice U.S. Dist. Ct. R.I., Providence, 1974-75; ptnr. Decof, Weinstein & Mandell, Providence, 1975-80; sr. ptnr. Mandell, Goodman, Famiglietti & Schwartz, Ltd., Providence, 1980—; lectr. in field; chmn. Bd. Bar Examiners U.S. Dist. Ct. R.I., 1985—, bar examiner. Author: Dermatology, 1986, Value of a Chance, 1986; contbg. author: Ambulatory Gynecology, 1985. Pres. Jewish Community Ctr., Providence, 1982—, bd. dirs. 1979-82, exec. com. 1980-84, chmn. handicapped services com., adult services com.; mem. exec. com. Jewish Fedn. R.I., 1982—, bd. dirs. 1982—; bd. dirs. Camp JORI, 1979—, Miriam Hosp., 1983—, Nat. Jewish Welfare Bd., 1984—. Mem. ABA, Fed. Bar Assn., R.I. Bar Assn. (active continuing legal edn., medico-legal com., ins. com., fed. ct. bench/bar com., young lawyers clerkship com.), Ala. Bar Assn., Assn. Trial Lawyers Am., R.I. Trial Lawyers Assn., Tex. Trial Lawyers Assn., Pa. Trial Lawyers Assn. Personal injury, Federal civil litigation, State civil litigation. Home: Quaker Rd Pole #4 Cumberland RI 02864 Office: Mandell Goodman Famiglietti & Schwartz Ltd One Park Row Providence RI 02903

MANDELL, SAMUEL W.W., corporate lawyer; b. 1943. AB, Harvard U., 1965; JD, U. Mich., 1969. Assoc. various law firms, 1969-74; dir. corp. law dept. Stop & Shop Cos. Inc., Boston, 1974-78, v.p. gen. counsel, 1978—. Office: Stop & Shop Cos Inc PO Box 369 Boston MA 02101 *

MANDELL, STEVE ALLEN, lawyer; b. Phila., Aug. 16, 1947; s. Morton Lester and Ethel (Klein) M.; m. Eileen Phyllis Cohen, Aug. 24, 1969; children: Joshua, Adam, Michael. BS, Drexel U., 1970; MBA, Temple U., 1972; JD, So. Meth. U., 1977. Bar: Tex. 1977, U.S. Dist. Ct. (no. dist.) Tex. 1980, U.S. Ct. Claims 1980, U.S. Ct. Appeals (5th cir.) 1980, U.S. Supreme Ct. 1981, Va. 1984. Gen. counsel, corp. officer Carterfone Communications Corp., Dallas, 1977-81; dir. market devel. MCI Communications Corp., Washington, 1982-84; pres. Steve Allen Mandell, P.C., Vienna, Va., 1984—; chmn. bd. Bus. Planning Corp., Tysons Corner, Va.; adj. lectr. U. Va., Falls Church, 1984—, U. Md., Coll. Park, 1984—. Editor: Lawyer Marketing, 1985-86; (newsletter) Market Planning and Devel. for Lawyers, 1984-86; also articles. Bd. dirs. Temple Rodef Shalom, 1986—, pres. Brotherhood Club 1986—. Served to capt. U.S. Army, 1970-78. Mem. ABA, Fairfax County C. of C. Avocations: racquetball, exploring. General corporate, Contracts commercial. Home: 1645 Montmorency Dr Vienna VA 22180 Office: Steve Allen Mandell PC 8321 Old Court House Rd Suite 230 Tysons Corner Vienna VA 22180

MANDELL-RICE, BONNIE STARR, lawyer; b. Union City, N.J., Aug. 4, 1951; d. Sidney Norton and Roberta (Jones) M.; m. Brian Robbins Mandell-Rice, Aug. 23, 1980; 1 child, Rachel. BA with highest honors, U. Fla., 1973; JD, U. Colo., 1976. Bar: Colo. 1976, U.S. Dist. Ct. Colo. 1976, U.S. Ct. Appeals (10th cir.) 1978. Assoc. Holland & Hart, Denver, 1976-79, Parcel, Mauro, Hultin & Spaanstra (and predecessor firms), Denver, 1979—. Trustee The Nature Conservancy, Boulder, Colo., 1977-83; bd. dirs. North Am. Wildlife Ctr., Golden, Colo., 1980—; bd. dirs., officer Minerals Exploration Coalition, Englewood, Colo., 1986—. Mem. ABA, Colo. Bar Assn., Denver Bar Assn., Ind. Petroleum Assn. (sec. 1986—). Avocations: family, swimming, running, hiking, reading. Oil and gas leasing, Public lands law, Mining and natural resources. Office: Parcel Mauro Hultin & Spaanstra 1801 California #3600 Denver CO 80202

MANECKJI, BHIKHAJI MANECK, lawyer; b. Bombay, Nov. 15, 1948; came to U.S., 1966; s. Maneck Jehangir and Piloo Maneck (Sethna) M. BBA, U. Wash., 1969, MBA, 1970; JD, George Washington U., 1973. Bar: R.I. 1974. Corp. counsel Textron, Inc., Providence, 1973-79, corp. counsel, asst. sec., 1979-81, group counsel, asst. sec., 1981—; mem. Nat. Com. for U.S.-China Trade, N.Y.C., 1979—. Candidate R.I. Constitutional Convention, 1986. Mem. ABA. Club: Brown Faculty Providence Athenaeum (bd. dirs. 1978-80). General corporate, Antitrust, Private international. Home: 38 Adelphi Ave Providence RI 02906 Office: Textron Inc 40 Westminster St Providence RI 02903

MANEY, MICHAEL MASON, lawyer; b. Taihoku, Japan, Aug. 13, 1936; s. Edward Strait and Helen M. M.; m. Suzanne Cochran, Oct. 22, 1960; 1 child, Michele. B.A., Yale U., 1956; M.A., Fletcher Sch. Law and Diplomacy, Tufts U., 1957; LL.B., U. Pa., 1964. Bar: N.Y. 1966, D.C. 1977. Case officer CIA, 1957-61; law clk. Justice John Harlan, Supreme Ct. U.S., Washington, 1964-65; asso. Sullivan & Cromwell, N.Y.C., 1965-70; partner Sullivan & Cromwell, 1971-77, 81—; mng. partner Sullivan & Cromwell, Washington, 1977-81; law fellow Salzburg Seminar in Am. Studies, 1967. Served to lt. USAF, 1958-60. Mem. Am. Law Inst., Am. Coll. Trial Lawyers, ABA, N.Y. State Bar Assn., Assn. Bar. City N.Y., D.C. Bar Assn. Clubs: Metropolitan (Washington); Union, Players, Yale (N.Y.C.); Down Town Assn., Madison Beach, Madison Country, Met. Opera. Banking, Bankruptcy, Federal civil litigation. Home: 1220 Park Ave New York NY 10128 also: 48 Neptune Ave Madison CT 06443 Office: Sullivan & Cromwell 125 Broad St New York NY 10004

MANFREDA, MICHAEL JOSEPH, lawyer, cons.; b. New Haven, Dec. 28, 1951; s. Joseph Michael and Margaret Mary (Dunn) M. B.A. in History, Coll. of Holy Cross, 1974; J.D., Suffolk U., 1977. Bar: Mass. 1977, U.S. dist. ct. Mass. 1978, U.S. Ct. Appeals (1st cir.) 1978, Conn. 1980, U.S. Supreme Ct. 1982. Substitute tchr. Wallingford (Conn.) Pub. Schs., 1974-77; prosecutor Boston Juvenile Ct., 1976-77; law clk. to dist. atty., Boston, 1977; asst. dist. atty. Suffolk County, Boston 1977-79; prin. Michael J. Manfreda & Assocs., Boston and Wallingford, Conn., 1979—; cons. and lectr. in field; dir. Cele-Nav Industries, Inc. Ward coordinator Democratic campaign, 1978, coordinator, 1980, active other campaigns, 1978—. Recipient Am. Jurisprudence award, 1976. Mem. ABA, Mass. Bar Assn., Conn. Bar Assn., Boston Bar Assn., New Haven County Bar Assn. Roman Catholic. Criminal, General practice, Federal civil litigation. Office: 101 Tremont St Boston MA 02108

MANG, DOUGLAS A., lawyer; b. Little Falls, N.Y., Mar. 25, 1942; s. Willard D. and Mary L. (Murray) M.; m. Nora Ladeane Geren, Feb. 7, 1984; 1 child, Brittany Nandeana. BS, Cornell U., 1964; LLB, Syracuse U., 1967. Bar: N.Y. 1971, Fla. 1971, U.S. Dist. Ct. (no. dist.) Fla. 1977, U.S. Ct. Appeals (5th and 11th cirs.) 1981, U.S. Dist. Ct. (mid. dist.) Fla. 1982. Atty. Mut. Life Ins. Co., N.Y.C., 1971-73; asst. gen. counsel Am. Gen. Capital Mgmt., N.Y.C., 1973-77; gen. counsel Fla. Dept. of Ins., Tallahassee, 1977-79; ptnr. Mang & Stowell PA, Tallahassee, 1979-86, Mang, Rett & Collette, P.A., Tallahassee, 1986—. Served to 1st lt. U.S. Army, 1968-70, Vietnam. Mem. Assn. Trial Lawyers Am., Fla. Def. Lawyers Assn. Methodist. Clubs: Tiger Bay, Fla. Econs. (Tallahassee). Avocations: sailing, golf. Administrative and regulatory, Federal civil litigation, Insurance. Office: Mang Rett & Collette PA 315 S Calhoun St Suite 740 Tallahassee FL 32302

MANGAN, GEORGE EDWARD, lawyer; b. Lucas, Arkansas, Oct. 31, 1937; s. Louis F. and Iris Lee (James) M.; m. Kathryn Mortensen, Dec. 28, 1960; children: MaryLou, Keith G., Steven B., James M., JoLee, Katrina, Martin A., Janesse A. BS, Brigham Young U., 1961; JD, U. Utah, 1965. Bar: Utah 1965, U.S. Dist. Ct. Utah 1965, U.S. Ct. Appeals (10th cir.) 1968. Dep. atty. Duchesne (Utah) County, 1971-74; atty. City of Roosevelt, Utah, 1973-76; sole practice Roosevelt, 1976—; gen. counsel Moon Lake Electric Co., Roosevelt, 1982—; bd. dirs. Eldredge Enterprises, Greely, Colo., El Dorado Mining Co., Roosevelt. Mem. United Fund, Salt Lake City, 1966; chmn. Bi-Centenial Celebration, Roosevelt, 1976, Boy Scouts Am., Roosevelt, 1976-81; pres. Fine Arts Council, Roosevelt, 1977—. Mem. ABA, Utah Bar Assn., Uintah Basin Bar Assn. (pres. 1973-76), Nat. Rural Electric Coop. Assn. (pres. standing com. 1984—). Republican. Mormon. Avocations: gardening, fishing, hunting, camping. General practice, Public utilities, Probate. Home: 57 N Skyline Dr 54-1 Roosevelt UT 84066 Office: 47 N 200 E Roosevelt UT 84066

MANGANO, JOSEPH S., lawyer; b. Mellili, Italy, Oct. 3, 1952; came to U.S., 1958; s. Sebastian and Giuseppa (Airo) M. BS in Econs. summa cum laude, U. Pa., 1975, MBA, 1976; JD, Columbia U., 1979. Bar: N.Y. 1980, U.S. Dist. Ct. (so. and ea. dists.) N.Y. 1980, Conn. 1984. Assoc. Shearman & Sterling, N.Y.C., 1979-86, Willkie Farr & Gallagher, N.Y.C., 1986—. Mng. editor Columbia Jour. of Law and Social Problems, 1978-79. Harlan Fiske Stone scholar Columbia U., 1978, Charles Evans Hughes fellow Columbia U., 1979. Mem. ABA, N.Y. State Bar Assn., Council N.Y. Law Assocs., Columbia U. Alumni Assn. Roman Catholic. Club: U. Pa. General corporate, Securities. Home: 45 E End Ave Apt 5D New York NY 10028 Office: Willkie Farr & Gallagher 153 E 53d St New York NY 10022

MANGET, FREDERIC FAIRFIELD, lawyer; b. Quonset Point, R.I., Oct. 14, 1951; s. Henry Fairfield and Maie McKoy (Watkins) M.; m. Lesle Charlese Black, June 12, 1982; 1 child, Felice Ann. BA, U. Ga., 1973; MA, Oxford U., 1975; JD, Vanderbilt U., 1979. Bar: Ga. 1979, U.S. Dist. Ct. (no. dist.) Ga. 1979, U.S. Ct. Appeals (11th cir.) 1979. Assoc. Hicks, Maloof & Campbell, Atlanta, 1980-86; asst. gen. counsel CIA, Washington, 1986—; pres., bd. dirs. Village Writers Group Inc., Decatur, Ga., 1984-85. Author numerous poems. Served to capt. USAFR, 1975-76, with JAGC, USAR, 1984—. Rhodes scholar Oxford U., 1973; Patric Wilson scholar Vanderbilt U., 1976. Mem. ABA, U. Ga. Alumni Assn. (founding pres. honors program 1983), Phi Beta Kappa, Phi Kappa Phi. Republican. Methodist. Club: Atlanta Fencers (armorer 1980-84). Avocations: writing, fencing, archery. Federal civil litigation, National security matters.

MANGIA, ANGELO JAMES, lawyer; b. Bklyn., Mar. 12, 1954. AB in Govt. cum laude, Georgetown U., 1975; JD, St. Johns U., 1978. Bar: N.Y. 1979, U.S. Dist. Ct. (so. and ea. dists.) N.Y. 1979, U.S. Ct. Appeals (2d cir.) 1985. Asst. atty. Town of North Hempstead, N.Y., 1979-81; assoc. Ain, Libert & Weinstein, Garden City, N.Y., 1981; atty. Town of North Hempstead, N.Y., 1982; counsel senate com. on crime State of N.Y., N.Y.C., 1983-85; counsel com. on banks State of N.Y., 1985—. Recipient Outstanding Work in Field of Criminal Justice Legis. award, N.Y. Bar Assn., 1985. Mem. ABA, Nassau County Bar Assn. Office: 68 W Main St Oyster Bay NY 11771 Office: Legis Office Bldg Room 412 Albany NY 12247

MANGONE, LOUIS A., lawyer; b. N.Y.C., May 5, 1936; s. Alfred A. and Ida (Silvestri) M.; divorced, Sept. 1981. BA, Hunter Coll., 1959; postgrad., U. Chgo., 1959-60; LLB, Yale U., 1967. Mgmt. trainee U.S. Dept. of Navy, Washington, 1960-61; adminstrn. asst. New Haven Redevel. Agy., Conn., 1961-64; assoc. Breed, Abbott & Morgan, N.Y.C., 1967; ptnr. Mangone &

Schnapp, N.Y.C., 1976—. Mem. Phi Beta Kappa. Democrat. Federal civil litigation, State civil litigation. Home: Box 132 RD 4 Hudson NY 12534 Office: 32 E 57th St New York NY 10022

MANGUM, JOHN K., lawyer; b. Phoenix, Mar. 7, 1942; s. Otto K. and Catherine F. Mangum; m. Deidre Jansen, Jan. 10, 1969; children—John Jansen, Jeffery Jansen. Student Phoenix Coll. 1960-62; B.S., U. Ariz., 1965, J.D., 1969. Bar: Ariz. 1969. Sr. trial atty. criminal div. Maricopa County Atty.'s Office, Phoenix, 1969-71; ptnr. Carmichael, McClue and Stephens, P.C., Phoenix, 1972-74; ct. commr., judge pro tem Maricopa County super. ct., Phoenix, 1974-78, spl. commr., 1979-82; legal csl. to speaker of Ariz. Ho. of Reps., Phoenix, 1975-86; mem. John K. Mangum and Assocs., P.C., Phoenix, 1974—. Mem. Maricopa County Bd. Health, 1974-79; chmn. curriculum com., mem. legal asst. adv. com. Phoenix Coll., 1973-75; legal counsel Maricopa County Rep. Com., 1986—; mem. task force com. on career edn. Phoenix Mayor's Youth Commn., 1972-73; v.p. The Samaritans, 1984—. Mem. State Bar Ariz. (exec. bd. young lawyers sect. 1974-76), Maricopa County Bar Assn. (pres. young lawyers sect. 1974-75, dir. 1973-75), Ariz. C. of C. (dir. 1974-79). Republican. Clubs: Phoenix Country, Ariz. (Phoenix). Lodge: Rotary. General corporate, Probate, Real property. Office: 340 E Palm Lane Suite 280 Phoenix AZ 85007

MANIATIS, CHARLYNN CAROL, lawyer, physician, consultant; b. Bridgeport, Conn., Nov. 23, 1949; d. William Richard and Ada Mae (Wicks) M. BA, Wellesley Coll., 1969; JD, Harvard U., 1972; MPH, Johns Hopkins U., 1978, MD, 1979. Bar: N.Y. 1973, Md. 1975, U.S. Ct. Mil. Appeals 1976, U.S. Supreme Ct. 1977, U.S. Dist. Ct. Md. 1978. Assoc. Dewey, Ballantine, Bushby, et al., N.Y.C., 1972-74, Semmes, Bowen & Semmes, Balt., 1975-80, Garbarini, Scher & DeCicco, P.C., N.Y.C., 1980-83, Morris J. Eisen, P.C., N.Y.C., 1983-84; cons. Med. Malpractice and Negligence, Cos Cob, Conn., 1984—; asst. prof. radiology Cornell U. Med. Coll., N.Y.C., 1983—; attending radiologist N.Y. Hosp., N.Y.C., 1983—, St. Vincents Med. Ctr., S.I., N.Y., 1984-85, Bayley-Seton Hosp., S.I., 1984-85, Our Lady of Mercy Med. Ctr., Bronx, N.Y., 1984—. Served with USNR, 1975—. Fellow Am. Coll. Legal Med.; mem. ABA. Republican. Episcopalian. Clubs: N.Y. Wellesley Coll. (bd. dirs. 1983—, v.p. 1985—); Harvard (N.Y.C.); Army and Navy (Washington). Personal injury, Insurance, Health. Home: 11 River Rd Cos Cob CT 06807

MANIATTY, PHILIP WARD, lawyer; b. Burlington, Vt., Apr. 3, 1952; s. Philip George and Mary Elizabeth (Ward) M. BA, U. Vt., 1974; JD, U. Miami, 1977. Bar: Fla. 1977, D.C. 1978, U.S. Dist. Ct. (so. dist.) Fla. Asst. state atty. State Atty's Office, 11th cir., Miami, 1977—. Mem. adv. council Southeast Fla. Acad. Fire Sci., Miami, 1983-86; bd. dirs. Country Club of Miami Condominium Inc., Hialeah, Fla., 1985—, pres., 1986—. Mem. ABA, D.C. Bar Assn., Fla. Bar Assn. (chmn. criminal procedure rules com. 1986—, exec. council 1983—). Democrat. Roman Catholic. Club: Country of Miami. Avocation: golf. Criminal. Home: 6847 Brookline Dr Hialeah FL 33015 Office: State Atty 11th Jud Cir Fla 1351 NW 12 St Miami FL 33126

MANIKAS, PETER MICHAEL, lawyer, consultant; b. Kankakee, Ill., Dec. 31, 1946; s. Alphonse J. and Helen (Gorz) M. BA, Roosevelt U., 1969; MA, George Washington U., 1974; JD, DePaul U., 1977; cert. sr. mgrs. in govt. program, Harvard U., 1982. Bar: Ill. 1977, U.S. Dist. Ct. (no. dist.) Ill. 1977. Legis. asst. to congressman Sidney R. Yates U.S. Ho. of Reps., Washington, 1970-73; research coordinator Better Govt. Assn., Chgo., 1974-79; legis. counsel Better Govt. Assn., Washington, 1980-84; legal counsel John Howard Assn., Chgo., 1979-80; exec. dir. Spl. Commn. Adminstrn. of Justice, Chgo., 1984—; lectr. Loyola U., Chgo., 1976; cons. Essential Info., Washington, 1984. Ill. State scholar Roosevelt U., 1968. Mem. ABA, Ill. Bar Assn., Chgo. Bar Assn., Chgo. Council Lawyers (sec., bd. govs. 1979-80). Jurisprudence, Legislative, Judicial administration. Home: 2352 N Cleveland Chicago IL 60614 Office: Spl Commn Adminstrn of Justice 36 S Wabash Chicago IL 60603

MANION, DANIEL A., judge; b. South Bend, Ind., Feb. 1, 1942; s. Clarence E. and Virginia (O'Brien) M.; m. Ann Murphy, June 29, 1984. BA, U. Notre Dame, 1964; JD, Ind. U., 1973. Dep. atty. gen. State of Ind., 1973-74; from assoc. to ptnr. Doran, Manion, Boynton, Kamm & Esmont, South Bend, 1974-86; judge U.S. Ct. Appeals (7th cir.), South Bend, 1986—. Mem. Ind. State Senate, Indpls., 1978-82. Home: 51081 Laurel Rd South Bend IN 46637 Office: US Ct Appeals (7th cir) 204 S Main St 310 Fed Bldg South Bend IN 46601

MANION, HARRY LEO, lawyer; b. St. Louis, May 8, 1952; s. Harry Leo Manion Sr. and Constance (Mastorakas) Brencick; m. Clare Dunsford, Feb. 23, 1979; 1 child, John Patrick. BA, Ariz. State U., 1974; JD, Boston Coll., 1978. Bar: Mass. 1978, U.S. Dist. Ct. Mass. 1978, U.S. Ct. Appeals (1st cir.) 1978. Assoc. Hale & Dorr, Boston, 1978-83; ptnr. Cooley, Manion, Moore & Jones P.C., Boston, 1983—. Author: Loss of Center, 1974. Co-chmn. Citizens for Conv. Ctr., St. Louis, 1973. Mem. Mass. Bar Assn., Phi Beta Kappa. Democrat. Roman Catholic. Criminal, Family and matrimonial. Home: 115 Commonwealth Ave Chestnut Hill MA 02167 Office: Cooley Manion Moore & Jones PC 530 Atlantic Ave Boston MA 02210

MANION, PAUL THOMAS, lawyer; b. Decatur, Ill., Apr. 7, 1940; s. Charles F. and Jeannette (Kaufman) M.; m. Bonnie J. Rivard, Aug. 12, 1961; children: Christine (Manion) Henning, Sheila, Tessy, Michael, Brian, Daniel. BBA in Fin., Notre Dame U., 1961; JD, DePaul U., 1964. Bar: Ill 1964, U.S. Ct. Appeals (7th cir.) 1975. Ins. investigator Hooper Holmes Bur., South Bend, Ind., 1958-61; supr. U.S. Dist. Ct., Chgo., 1961-64; asst. states atty. Iroquois County, Watseka, Ill., 1964-67; sr. ptnr. Manion, Janov, Edgar, Devens & Fahey Ltd., Hoopeston, Ill., 1967—. Author: With Friends Like These, 1985. Mem. exec. com. Vermilion County Dem. Party, Danville, Ill., 1974—, county chmn. 1983—; pres. Vermilion Mental Health Ctr., Danville, 1975-78. Mem. Ill. Bar Assn., Assn. Trial Lawyers Am., Ill. Trial Lawyers Assn. Democrat. Roman Catholic. Personal injury, Workers' compensation, General practice. Home: Rt 2 PO Box 80 Hoopeston IL 60942 Office: Manion Janov Edgar Devens & Fahey 216 S Market Hoopeston IL 60942

MANIRE, JAMES MCDONNELL, lawyer; b. Memphis, Feb. 22, 1918; s. Clarence Herbert and Elizabeth (McDonnell) M.; m. Nathalie Davant Latham, Nov. 21, 1951 (div. Jan. 1979); children: James McDonnell, Michael Latham, Nathalie Latham; m. Virginia Nelson Self, Aug. 2, 1986. LL.B., U. Va., 1948. Bar: Tenn. 1948, U.S. Supreme Ct. 1957. Practice law Memphis; counsel Waring Cox; city atty. Memphis, 1968-71. Editor-in-chief Va. Law Rev., 1947-48. Served to lt. comdr. USNR, 1941-46. Fellow Am. Coll. Trial Lawyers, Am. Bar Found. (life); mem. ABA, Tenn. Bar Assn. (pres. 1966-67), Memphis and Shelby County Bar Assn. (pres. 1963-64), Tenn. Bar Found. (charter), 6th Circuit Jud. Conf. (life), Raven Soc. Clubs: Memphis Country, Memphis Hunt and Polo. General practice. Home: 318 Lancaster Sq #1 Memphis TN 38117 Office: Morgan Keegan Tower 50 N Front St Suite 1300 Memphis TN 38103

MANIS, STEPHANIE BRODIE, lawyer; b. Denver, Jan. 8, 1940; d. Dudley David and Amelia (Marx) Brodie; m. Robert S. Manis, Dec. 17, 1967; children: Lisa, Tamara, Valerie. BA, U. Fla., 1961, MA, 1967; JD, Emory U., 1977. Bar: Ga., U.S. Dist. Ct. (no. and mid. dists.) Ga., U.S. Ct. Appeals (5th and 11th cirs.), U.S. Supreme Ct. Law clk. to presiding justice Ga. Supreme Ct., Atlanta, 1977-79; sr. asst. atty. gen. Ga. Atty. Gen.'s Office, Atlanta, 1979—; adj. prof. law Emory U., Atlanta, 1980-82. Mem. ABA, Ga. Bar Assn., Atlanta Lawyer's Club. Avocation: family. Family and matrimonial. Home: 4202 Paran Pines Dr NW Atlanta GA 30327 Office: State Law Dept 132 Judicial Bldg Atlanta GA 30334

MANKES, KAREN MARCOUX, lawyer; b. Troy, N.Y., Feb. 18, 1950; d. A. Donald and Helen C. (Champo) Marcoux; m. Russell F. Mankes, June 16, 1972; children—Kristina, Gregory. B.A., SUNY-Albany, 1971; J.D., Albany Law Sch., 1974. Bar: N.Y. 1975, U.S. Dist. Ct. (no. dist.) N.Y. 1975. Atty., Farm Family Life/Mut. Ins. Co., Glenmont, N.Y., 1974-77; sole practice, Albany, 1977-82; legal counsel N.Y. Farm Bur., Glenmont, 1982-84; asst. atty. gen. for agrl. and rural affairs N.Y. State Dept. Law, Albany, 1984—. Chmn., N.Y. State Legis. Forum, Albany, 1981-82, co-chmn. legis. workshop, 1986; mem. adv. bd. Alternative Service Sentencing Program, Albany, 1982-84; bd. dirs. Vol. Ctr., Albany. Mem. N.Y. State Bar Assn., Am. Agrl. Law Assn., Women's Bar Assn. N.Y. Democrat. Roman Catholic. Club: Junior League of Albany (chmn. pub. affairs com. 1982-83). Agricultural. Office: Dept Law State of New York The Capitol Albany NY 12224

MANKIN, HART TILLER, lawyer; b. Cleve., Dec. 26, 1933; s. Howard Edmonn and Fantine (Tiller) M.; m. Ruth A. Larson, Aug. 14, 1954; children—Margaret, Theodore, Susan. Student, Northwestern U., 1950-52; B.A., U. South, 1954, cert. edn. for ministry, 1982; J.D., U. Houston, 1960. Bar: Tex. bar 1960, U.S. Supreme Ct. bar 1968, D.C. bar 1971. Individual practice law Houston, 1960-67; counsel, asst. to pres. Triumph Industries, Houston, 1967-69; gen. counsel GSA, Washington, 1969-71, Dept. Navy, Washington, 1971-73; Adminstrv. conf. of U.S. U.S., 1970-71; v.p., gen. counsel Columbia Gas System, Wilmington, Del., 1973—; dir. Del. Trust Co. Bd. dirs. Del. Law Sch., Del. Humanities Council, chmn., 1980-82, Am. Ctr. for Enterprise Edn., Inc., chmn. 1985—. Served with USAF, 1954-57. Recipient spl. achievement award GSA, 1970, Disting. Pub. Service award Dept. Navy, 1973. Mem. State Bar Tex., D.C. Bar Assn., Del. State Bar Assn., Am. Bar Assn., Fed. Bar Assn., Maritime Law Assn., U.S., Del. State C. of C. (chmn. 1981-83), Am. Gas Assn. Episcopalian. Clubs: Army and Navy (Washington); Greenville Country, Univ. and Whist., Del. Croquet. General corporate, Legislative, Jurisprudence. Home: 1101 Westover Rd Wilmington DE 19807 Office: 20 Montchanin Rd Wilmington DE 19807

MANKOFF, RONALD MORTON, lawyer; b. Gettysburg, S.D., Oct. 13, 1931; s. Harry B. and Sarah (Frank) M.; m. Joy Faith Shechtman, Nov. 3, 1959; children: Jeffrey Walker, Douglas Frank. B.S.L., U. Minn., J.D., 1954; LL.M. in Taxation, N.Y. U., 1959. Bar: Minn. 1954, Tex. 1959. With Leonard, Street & Deinard, Mpls., 1957-58, Lyne, Blanchette, Smith & Shelton, Dallas, 1959-60; partner firm Durant and Mankoff, Dallas, 1960-85; pres. firm Brice & Mankoff P.C., Dallas, 1985—; lectr. law So. Methodist U. Sch. Law, 1974-77; assocj. bd. dirs. Bank of Dallas, 1986—. Contbr. legal jours. Chmn. bd. Dallas chpt. Am. Cancer Soc., 1976-77; chmn. Dallas crusade, 1974-75, bd. dirs., mem. exec. com., 1963—; bd. dirs. Tex. div. Am. Cancer Soc., 1981—; mem. bd. Dallas Mcpl. Library, 1973-75, Am. Jewish Com., 1982—, v.p. Dallas chpt. 1986—; exec. com. Dallas Citizens Charter Assn., 1971-75; pres. Dallas Arts Found., Inc., 1973-75; mem. exec. com. Nat. Pooled Income Fund, Council Jewish Welfare Fedns. and Funds, 1975-77; adv. dir. Dallas Community Chest Trust Fund, 1976-78; chmn. Found. Dallas Jewish Fedn., 1976-77; pres. Temple Emanu-el, Dallas, 1977-79; bd. dirs. Jewish Fedn. Greater Dallas, 1977-79, Dallas Civic Opera, 1981-83, World Union Progressive Judaism, 1981—; mem. S.W. regional liaison com. Internat. Rev. Service, 1980-83; vice chmn., bd. dirs. Union Am. Hebrew Congregations, 1984—, exec. com., 1979—, nat. coll. com. 1983—, trustee 1979—; sec. Dallas Assembly, 1979-84; exec. com. Jewish Community Relations Council 1982-83, Com. for Qualified Judiciary, 1982— sec. Child Care Partnership, 1984-86, bd. dirs. 1986—; bd. dirs. Dallas Women's Found., 1985—, Am. Jewish Com., 1982—, v.p. Dallas chpt. 1986—; bd. dirs. Girl Scouts of U.S., Tejas council 1982-85, Goodwill Industries of Greater Dallas, 1979-83; mem. Mayor's Task Force on Child Care, regulations com. 1984. Served to lt. (j.g.) USNR, 1954-57. Mem. ABA, State Bar Tex., Dallas Bar Assn., North Dallas C. of C. (adv. bd. 1986—), Zeta Beta Tau, Delta Sigma Rho. Democrat. Clubs: Columbia Country (bd. govs.), T-Bar, Crescent (Dallas). Home: 5839 Colhurst St Dallas TX 75230 Office: Brice & Mankoff 300 Crescent Ct Dallas TX 75202

MANLEY, DOUGLAS REMPET, lawyer, educator; b. Denver, May 2, 1952; s. James Nelson and Audrey (Rempet) M.; m. Linda K. Rizzutto, Dec. 26, 1980; children: Rebecca, LeeAnna. BA, U. Denver, 1974; JD, U. Colo., 1977. Bar: Colo. 1977, U.S. Dist. Ct. Colo. 1977. Assoc. Holm & Dill P.C., Denver, 1977-78; asst. dist. atty. State of Colo., La Junta, 1978-82; sole practice La Junta, 1982—; instr. bus. law Otero Jr. Coll., La Junta, 1984—. Mem. La Junta City Council, 1983—. Mem. ABA, Colo. Bar Assn., 16th Jud. Dist. Bar Assn. (pres. 1984-85), Jaycees Internat. (senatorship 1984, recipient Charles Culp award 1981), La Junta Jaycees (pres. 1980-81, state dir. 1981-82). Democrat. Methodist. Lodge: Rotary. General practice, Criminal, Family and matrimonial. Home: 10 Chaparral Ct La Junta CO 81050 Office: 111 W 3d St Box 331 La Junta CO 81050

MANLEY, LARRY PAUL, lawyer; b. Houston, Aug. 22, 1947; s. James Olaf and Jaynelle (Christian) M. BBA in Fin., U. Tex., 1969, JD with honors, 1973. Bar: Tex. 1973. Assoc. Vinson & Elkins, Houston, 1973-79; ptnr., dir. Ross, Griggs & Harrison, Houston, 1979—; dir. Ross, Griggs & Harrison, Austin, Tex., 1985—. Assoc. editor Tex. Law Rev., 1973. Bd. dirs. Delia Stewart Dance Co., Houston, 1985—. Served as specialist 5th class USNG, 1969-75. Recipient Dist. Speaker award Houston Bar Assn., 1984. Mem. ABA (corp., banking and bus. law sect.), Tex. State Bar, Houston Young Lawyers Assn. (bd. dirs. 1975-76), Tex. Assn. of Bank Counsel, Houston C. of C. (life, Golden Key award 1974). Clubs: Austin, Metropolitan. Avocations: scuba diving, hunting, travel, reading. General corporate, Securities, Banking. Office: Ross Griggs & Harrison 1950 One American Ctr 600 Congress Ave Austin TX 78701

MANLEY, MARSHALL, insurance company executive, lawyer; b. Newark, May 3, 1940; s. Nathan and Faye (Rosen) M.; m. Johanna Kallenberg, June 26, 1986; 1 child, Chase. BA, Bklyn. Coll., 1962; JD cum laude, NYU, 1965. Bar: Calif. 1966, D.C. 1985, N.Y. Chmn. mgmt. com. Finley, Kumble, Wagner, Heine, Underberg, Manley, Myerson & Casey, 1978—; pres., dir. The Home Group, Inc., Newark, Del., 1985—; chief exec. officer The Home Group, Inc., Newark, 1986—; chmn. bd. dirs. The Home Ins. Co.; dir. Gen. Devel. Corp., Work Wear Corp.; chmn. bd. dirs. US Internat. Re DeLaurentiis; mem. adv. bd. Fed. Home Loan Mortgage Corp.; mem. Calif. State Senate Adv. Council on Ins. Problems of Fin. Insts., 1984—. Mem. Motion Picture Devel. Council, 1977-79, Commn. of Califs., from 1980, trustee Bklyn. Coll., adv. bd. Intrepid Sea-Air Space Mus., from 1982; Am. Mus. Nat. History; co-chmn. bus. com. N.Y. Zoological Soc.; mem. bus. com. Met. Mus. Art. Mem. ABA, Calif. Bar Assn.; trustee Am. Mus. Nat. Hist., N.Y.C.; assoc. Hayden Planetarium, N.Y. Clubs: Bd. Room, Regency. Federal civil litigation, State civil litigation, General corporate. Office: Home Group Inc 300 Continental Dr Box 8067 Newark DE 19714 also: Finley Kumble Wagner Heine Underberg Manley & Casey 9100 Wilshire Blvd Beverly Hills CA 90212

MANLEY, MICHAEL ALEXANDER, lawyer; b. Oakland, Calif., Dec. 29, 1938; s. John L. and Barbara J. (Alexander) M.; m. Lestelle Johns; children—Kevin, Lisa; m. 2d, Beverlee Reid, Nov. 7, 1970. B.A. with honors, U. Calif., Berkeley, 1960; J.D. with distinction, U. Pacific, 1970. Bar: Calif., 1971; U.S. dist. ct. (ea. dist.), Calif., 1971. Sole practice, 1971-73; ptnr. Coombs, Manley & Root, Sacramento, 1973-77, Memel, Jacobs, Pierno, Gersh & Ellsworth, Sacramento, 1977-82; corp. counsel Eskaton Health Corp., Carmichael, Calif., 1982—; lectr. medico-legal topics U. Calif. extension. Former mem. Calif. Democratic Central Com.; del Dem. Nat. Conv., 1968; former mem. Sacramento Recreation and Parks Commn.; mem. County Planning Commn. Served to capt. U.S. Army, 1960-62. Mem. ABA, Nat. Health Lawyers Assn., Calif. Bar Assn (chmn. com. to confer with Calif. Med. Assn. Club: Sacramento Yacht (commodore). Health, Legislative, Administrative and regulatory. Office: Eskaton Health Corp 5105 Manzanita Carmichael CA 95608

MANLEY, RICHARD SHANNON, lawyer; b. Birmingham, Ala., June 23, 1932; s. Richard Sabine and Alice (Hughes) M.; m. Lillian Grace Cardwell, Aug. 23, 1953 (div.); m. Rosemary Rankin, May 18, 1977; children: Richard Shannon, Alyce Hughes; 1 child, Brian K. Moseley. BS, U. Ala., 1953, LLB, 1958. Bar: Ala. 1958, U.S. Ct. Mil. Appeals 1963, U.S. Supreme Ct. 1963. Sole practice, Demopolis, Ala., beginning 1958; now ptnr. Manley and Traeger, Demopolis; mem. Ala. Ho. of Reps., 1966-83, chmn. house judiciary com., 8 yrs., speaker pro tem, 4 yrs.; mem. Ala. State Senate, 1986-90; mem. bd. bar commrs. Ala. State Bar, 1972—, v.p., 1979-80, 83-84; bd. dirs. New Southland Nat. Ins. Co. Past trustee Demopolis dist. Ala.-West Fla. Conf. Methodist Ch.; past mem. and pres. Demopolis Bd. Edn.; mem. Tenn.-Tombigbee Waterway Devel. Authority, 1975—, vice chmn., 1981; del. Democratic Nat. Conv., N.Y.C., 1976. Served to col. USMCR. Mem. ABA, Ala. State Bar Assn., Assn. Trial Lawyers Am., Am. Judicature Soc., Comml. Law League Am., U. Ala. Alumni Assn. (past pres. Marengo County), U. Ala. Nat. Alumni Assn. (past v.p.), Nat. Soc. State Legislators, Demopolis Jaycees (past pres.), Ala. Jaycees (past v.p.), U.S. Jaycees (past dir.), Demopolis C. of C. (past pres. and bd. dirs.), Farrah Law Soc., Phi Delta Phi. Club: Rotary (Demopolis). State civil litigation, Personal injury, General practice. Office: PO Box U Demopolis AL 36732

MANLEY, ROBERT EDWARD, lawyer, economist; b. Cin., Nov. 24, 1935; s. John M. and Helen Catherine (McCarthy) M.; m. Roberta L. Anzinger, Oct. 21, 1971 (div. 1980); 1 child, Robert Edward. Sc.B. in Econs, Xavier U., 1956; A.M. in Econ. Theory, U. Cin., 1957; J.D., Harvard U., 1960; postgrad., London Sch. Econs. and Polit. Sci., 1960, MIT, 1972. Bar: Ohio 1960, U.S. Supreme Ct. 1970. Practice law Cin., 1960—; pres. Manley, Burke & Fischer; Taft teaching fellow econs. U. Cin., 1956-57, vis. lectr. community planning law Coll. Design, Architecture and Art, 1967-73, adj. assoc. prof. urban planning Coll. Design, Architecture and Art, 1972-81, adj. prof., 1981—, adj. prof. law, 1980—. Author: Metropolitan School Desegregation, 1978, (with Robert N. Cook) Management of Land and Environment, 1981, others; chmn. editorial adv. bd. Urban Lawyer, 1986—. Mem. Hamilton County Public Defender Commn., 1976-79; trustee HOPE, Cin., Albert J. Ryan Found.; counsel, co-founder Action Housing for Greater Cin.; mem. Spl. Commn. on Formation U. Cin. Health Maintenance Orgn., Mayor Cin. Spl. Com. on Housing; chmn. Cin. Environ. Adv. Council, 1975-76. Mem. Cin. Bar Assn., ABA (council sect. local govt. law 1976-80, 81-85), Ohio Bar Assn., Am. Judicature Soc., Law and Soc. Assn., Nat. Council Crime and Delinquency, Harvard Law Sch. Assn. Cin. (pres. 1970-71), Am. Econ. Assn., Am. Acad. Polit. and Social Sci., Ohio Planning Conf. (trustee 1984—). Republican. Roman Catholic. Clubs: Queen City; Explorers (N.Y.C.); Athenaeum (Phila.); S.Am. Explorers (Lima, Peru). Federal civil litigation, State civil litigation, Real property. Home: 1861 Dexter Ave Cincinnati OH 45206 Office: Manley Burke & Fischer 4100 Carew Tower Cincinnati OH 45202

MANLY, CHARLES M., III, lawyer; b. Spencer, Iowa, July 18, 1950; s. Charles M. and B.A. (Lippold) M.; m. Debra Jo Yellick, May 22, 1982. B.A., Simpson Coll., 1972; J.D., Hamline U., 1976. Bar: Iowa 1976. Gen. practice law, Grinnell, Iowa, 1976—; ptnr. Manly Law Firm. Mng. editor Iowa Trial Lawyer, 1982—. Trustee Simpson Coll., Indianola, Iowa, 1984-86. Chmn. campaign Robert Ray for Gov., Poweshiek County, 1978, Jud. Magistrate Nominating Commn., Poweshiek County, 1979—, chmn., 1979—; chmn. Rep. Cen. Com., Poweshiek County, 1986—; pres. Grinnell Area Arts Council, 1982-83. Mem. ABA, Iowa Bar Assn., Poweshiek County Bar Assn. (pres. 1978-79), Assn. Trial Lawyers Am., Assn. Trial Lawyers Iowa (bd. govs. 1981-86), Simpson Coll. Alumni Assn. (pres. 1984-86), Am. Agrl. Law Assn., Iowa Mcpl. Attys. Assn. Club: Okoboji Yacht. Avocations: reading, sailboat racing, sports. State civil litigation, Family and matrimonial, General practice. Home: 917 10th Ave Grinnell IA 50112 Office: 720 4th Ave Grinnell IA 50112

MANLY, CHARLES M., lawyer; b. Grinnell, Iowa, Mar. 6, 1928; s. C.M. and Nell C. (Cooper) M.; m. Bernadette A. Lippold, Aug. 21, 1949; children: Charles M. III, John Thomas, Michael L. JD, Drake U., 1951. Bar: Iowa 1951, U.S. Dist. Ct. (so. dist.) Iowa 1964, U.S. Dist. Ct. (no. dist.) Iowa 1975, U.S. Ct. Appeals (8th cir.) 1975. Ptnr. Manly Law Firm, Grinnell, 1951—; atty. City of Grinnell, 1957—; mem. jud. nominating com. Iowa Supreme Ct., Des Moines, 1977-83. Mem. ABA, Iowa Bar Assn., Poweshiek County Bar Assn., Assn. Trial Lawyers Am., Assn. Trial Lawyers Iowa (pres. 1975-76). Republican. Lodge: Lions (Grinnell pres. 1960-61). Personal injury, Probate, General practice. Office: Manly Law Firm 720 4th Ave Grinnell IA 50112

MANLY, MARC EDWARD, lawyer; b. Knoxville, Tenn., Mar. 11, 1952; s. William Donald and Jane (Wilden) M.; m. Colby A. Chapman, July 20, 1974; children: Justin C., Allison C. BA, Amherst Coll., 1974; JD, U. Mich., 1977. Bar: Ill. 1978, U.S. Dist. Ct. (no. dist.) Ill. 1978. Assoc. Sidley & Austin, Chgo., 1978-84, ptnr., 1985—. Mem. ABA, Order of Coif, Phi Beta Kappa. Antitrust, Federal civil litigation, Public utilities. Office: Sidley & Austin 1722 Eye St NW Washington DC 20006

MANN, DONALD J., lawyer; b. Evanston, Ill., Feb. 9, 1949; s. Aloysius J. and Anne C. (Guilfoyle) M.; m. Darrlyn D'Ippolito, Aug. 31, 1974. B.S.B.A., Georgetown U., 1971; J.D., Yale U., 1974. Bar: Pa. 1974, U.S. Ct. Appeals (3d cir.) 1974, U.S. Dist. Ct. (ea. dist.) Pa. 1974, N.J. 1975, U.S. Dist Ct. N.J. 1975. Sole practice, Cherry Hill, N.J., 1974-78; ptnr. Flaster, Greenberg, Mann & Wallenstein, P.C. (formerly Liebman & Flaster), Marlton, N.J., 1978—, also bd. dirs. Contbr. chpt. to N.J. Family Law Practice, Tax Aspects of Separation and Divorce, 1985; lectr. profl. orgns. Mem. ABA, N.J. Bar Assn., Camden County Bar Assn. (chmn. tax sect. 1985-86). Roman Catholic. Personal income taxation, Corporate taxation, State and local taxation. Home: 271 Moore Ln Haddonfield NJ 08033 Office: Flaster Greenberg Mann & Wallenstein Five Greentree Centre Suite 200 Marlton NJ 08053

MANN, DOUGLAS FLOYD, lawyer; b. Platteville, Wis., Apr. 21, 1951. BA, Wartburg Coll., 1973; JD, Marquette U., 1976. Bar: Wis. 1976, U.S. Dist. Ct. (ea. and we. dists.) Wis. 1976, U.S. Ct. Appeals (7th cir.) 1977. Sole practice Milw., 1976—. Thomas More scholar Marquette U., 1973. Mem. Wis. Bar Assn., Milw. Bar Assn., Comml. Law League. Bankruptcy, Consumer commercial, State court receiverships. Office: 740 N Plankinton Ave Milwaukee WI 53203

MANN, J. KEITH, consultant to provost, arbitrator, law educator, lawyer; b. May 28, 1924; s. William Young and Lillian Myrle (Bailey) M.; m. Virginia McKinnon, July 7, 1950; children: William Christopher, Marilyn Keith Mann Leitch, John Kevin, Susan Bailey, Andrew Curry. B.S., U. Ind., 1948, LL.B., 1949. Bar: Ind. 1949, D.C. 1951. Law clk. Justice Wiley Rutledge and Justice Sherman Minton, 1949-50; practice, Washington, 1950; mem. Wage Stblzn. Bd., 1951; asst. prof. U. Wis., 1952; asst. prof. Stanford U. Law Sch., 1952-54, assoc. prof., 1954-58, prof., 1958—, assoc. dean, 1961-85, acting dean, 1976, 81-82; vis. prof. U. Chgo., 1953; mem. Sec. of Labor's Adv. Com., 1955-57; mem. Pres.'s Commn. Airlines Controversy, 1961; mem. COLC Aerospace Spl. Panel, 1973-74; chmn. and mem. Presdl. Emergency Bds. or Bds. of Inquiry, 1962-63, 67, 71-72; spl. master U.S. vs. Alaska, U.S. Supreme Ct., 1980—. Served to ensign USNR, 1944-46. Sunderland fellow U. Mich., 1959-60; scholar in residence Duke U., 1972. Mem. Nat. Acad. Arbitrators, ABA, Am. Assn. Univ. Profs., Indsl. Relations Research Assn., Order of Coif. Past articles and book rev. editor Ind. U. Law Jour. Legal education. Home: 872 Lathrop Dr Stanford CA 94305 Office: Stanford U Law Sch Stanford CA 94305-8610

MANN, JOHN RAYMOND, III, lawyer; b. Detroit, May 27, 1951; s. John Raymond Jr. and Mary Louise (Willoughby) M.; m. Lois Jean Noble, June 10, 1972 (Sept. 1983) (divorced); 1 child, Lindsay Corinne. BA, U. Mich., 1973; JD, Detroit Coll. Law, 1976. Bar: Mich. 1977, U.S. Dist. Ct. (ea. dist.) Mich. 1977, U.S. Ct. Appeals (6th cir.) 1977. Law clk. to presiding justice Mich. Ct. of Appeals, Detroit, 1977-78; law clk. U.S. Dist. Ct., Detroit, 1978-80; assoc. Beier, Howlett, McConnell & Googasian, Bloomfield Hills, Mich., 1980-81, Fildew, Hinks, Gilbride, Miller & Todd, Detroit, 1981-86; sole practice Detroit, 1986—; tchr. Detroit Coll. of Law, 1977-81, Cranbrook Prep. Sch., Bloomfield, 1981; bd. dirs. Thompson Svgs. Bank, Hudson, Mich., 1982—. Mem. ABA, Detroit Bar Assn., Oakland County Bar Assn., U. Mich. Alumni Assn. Club: Detroit Athletic. Avocations: handball, golf, hiking, basketball. Federal civil litigation, Environment, Criminal. Office: 3263 Penobscot Bldg Detroit MI 48226

MANN, KENNETH L., lawyer; b. Long Beach, N.Y., Feb. 16, 1946; s. Robert G. and Riva (Garson) M.; m. Janet Hurvitz, Aug. 16, 1967; children: Russell, Wendy. BSBA, U. N.C., 1966; JD magna cum laude, Mercer U., 1973. Bar: Fla. 1973, U.S. Ct. Claims 1973, U.S. Tax Ct. 1973, U.S. Dist. Ct. (mid. dist.) Fla. 1974, U.S. Ct. Appeals (11th cir.) 1982. From jr. to sr. auditor Price Waterhouse and Co., CPA's, Miami, Fla., 1966-70; assoc. Deutsch, Deutsch et al, Ft. Lauderdale, Fla., 1973-74, Subin, Shams, Rosenbluth, Orlando, Fla., 1974-82; sole practice Orlando, 1982—. Hearing officer Citizens Settlement Ctr., Orlando, 1976—; sunday sch. tchr. Congregation Liberal Judaism, Orlando, 1975-76, 80, trustee, 1984-85; bd. dirs. Holocaust Resource and Edn. Ctr. Cen. Fla., Orlando, 1982—. Mem. ABA, Fla. Bar Assn. (vice chmn. standing com. unlicensed practice law 1983—),

Orange County Bar Assn. (chmn. law week com. 1986), Am. Inst. CPAs, Fla. Inst. CPAs, Tax Roundtable (bd. dirs. 1979-80), Fla. Motion Picture and Television Assn. (exec. v.p. 1982-83). Lodge: Rotary. State civil litigation, General corporate, Real property. Office: 1231 Mt Vernon St Orlando FL 32803

MANN, MICHAEL BOND, lawyer; b. Balt., Oct. 16, 1951; s. James Lutz and Ruth Catherine (Moran) M.; m. Laurie Ellen Darroch, Aug. 6, 1976; children: Lindsay Beth, Michael Bond, Christian Chambers. BS, Washington Coll., 1973; JD, U. Md., 1976. Bar: U.S. Ct. Appeals (4th cir.) 1979, U.S. Dist. Ct. Md. 1982. Ptnr. Merriman & Mann P.A., Balt., 1976—. Mem. ABA, Md. Bar Assn., Balt. Bar Assn., Def. Trial Lawyers of Md. Republican. Roman Catholic. Personal injury, Insurance, Workers' compensation. Home: 38 Dulaney Hills Ct Cockeysville MD 21030 Office: Merriman & Mann PA 409 Washington Ave Towson MD 21204

MANN, PHILIP ROY, lawyer; b. N.Y.C., Jan. 31, 1948; s. Elias and Gertrude Esther (Levbarg) M. AB, Cornell U., 1968; JD, NYU, 1971, LLM, 1975. Bar: N.Y. 1972, U.S. Dist. Ct. (so. and ea. dists.) N.Y. 1983, U.S. Ct. Appeals (2nd cir.) 1973, U.S. Dist. Ct. (no. dist.) N.Y. 1974, U.S. Ct. Mil. Appeals 1974, U.S. Supreme Ct. 1975, D.C. 1976, U.S. Dist. Ct. (we. dist.) N.Y. 1976, U.S. Tax Ct. 1976, U.S. Ct. Appeals (D.C. cir.) 1978, Conn. 1983, U.S. Dist. Ct. D.C. 1983, U.S. Ct. Claims 1983, U.S. Ct. Appeals (3rd and fed. cirs.) 1983. Assoc. Levin & Weintraub, N.Y.C., 1971-74; assoc. Shea & Gould, N.Y.C., 1974-79, ptnr., 1979-84; sole practice N.Y.C., 1984—. Served to maj. USAR 1969—. Mem. ABA, Fed. Bar Assn. Democrat. Jewish. Clubs: City Mid-Day, World Trade Ctr. (N.Y.C.). Bankruptcy, Contracts commercial. Home: 250 E 87th St Apt 26H New York NY 10128 Office: 250 E 87th St New York NY 10128

MANN, RICHARD ALLAN, law educator; b. N.Y.C., Dec. 9, 1946; s. Charles and Madeline (Vakshall) M.; m. Karlene Fogelin Knebel. BS in Math., U. N.C., 1968; JD, Yale U., 1973. Bar: N.C. 1975. Asst. prof. law McMasters U., Hamilton, Ont., Can., 1973-74; prof. U. N.C., Chapel Hill, 1974—. Author: Business Law, 1985, Essentials of Business Law, 1986, Business Law and Regulation of Business, 1987; contbr. articles to profl. jours. Named one of Outstanding Young Men in Am., U.S. Jaycees, 1978. Mem. ABA, N.C. Bar Assn., Am. Bus. Law Assn. (del. 1981-82), Southeastern Regional Bus. Law Assn. (pres. 1980-81). Legal education. Office: U NC Sch Bus Adminstrn Chapel Hill NC 27514

MANN, RICHARD LYNN, lawyer; b. Columbus, Ohio, June 22, 1946; s. Clyde Earl and Kathryn Ann (Mock) M.; children: Richard Sean, Shannon Michele. BS, Ohio State U., 1968; JD, 1971. Bar: Ohio 1972, U.S. Dist. Ct. (so. dist.) Ohio 1979. Ptnr. Bolla, Mann & Caulfield, Columbus, 1973-76, Caulfield & Mann, Columbus, 1976-78, Mann & Stuhr, Columbus, 1978-81; ptnr. White, Rankin, Co., L.P.A., Columbus, 1981—, also prin.; state counsel Ohio Assn. Secondary Adminstrs., Columbus, 1976-86. Author article series Legal Notes, 1976-86; co-author pamphlet Due Process in Schools, 1977. Trustee Worthington Civic Ballet, Jazz North, Worthington, Ohio, 1978—. Served to 1st lt. U.S. Army, 1971-73. Decorated Army Commendation medal. Mem. Ohio Bar Assn., Columbus Bar Assn., Nat. Assn. Legal Problems in Edn. Republican. Club: Little Turtle Country (Westerville, Ohio). Real property, Legal education, Administrative and regulatory. Office: 175 S 3d St Suite 900 Columbus OH 43215

MANN, ROBERT BARNEY, lawyer; b. Bremerhaven, Germany, Apr. 5, 1948; s. Lionel and Miriam (Mills) M. B.A., Yale U., 1968, J.D., 1973. Bar: R.I. 1973, U.S. Ct. Appeals (1st cir.) 1976, U.S. Supreme Ct. 1979, U.S. Ct. Mil. Rev. 1982. VISTA atty. R.I. Legal Service, Providence, 1973-74; sole practice, Providence, 1974-78, 1982—; ptnr. Mann & Roney, Providence, 1978-82. Served to 1st lt. U.S. Army, 1968-70, Vietnam. Mem. R.I. Bar Assn., ABA, Nat. Assn. Criminal Def. Lawyers. Democrat. Jewish. Criminal, Civil rights. Home: 254 4th St Providence RI 02906 Office: 501 Turks Head Pl Providence RI 02903

MANN, ROBERT TRASK, lawyer, educator; b. Tarpon Springs, Fla., June 5, 1924; s. William Edgar and Lenora Eunice (Trask) M.; m. Elizabeth Brown, Dec. 27, 1947; children: Robert Trask, Margaret Elizabeth. BSBA, U. Fla., 1946, JD, 1951; MA in Govt., George Washington U., 1948; LLM, Harvard U., 1953, Yale U., 1968; LLD (hon.), Stetson U., 1979. Bar: Fla. 1951, Mass. 1952, U.S. Supreme Ct. 1960. Asst. prof. law Northeastern U., 1951-53; sole practice Tampa, Fla., 1953-68; judge 2d dist. Fla. Ct. Appeal, 1968-74, chief judge, 1973-74; prof. law U. Fla., Gainesville, 1974-86, prof. emeritus, 1986—; vis. prof. Herbert Herff chair excellence in law Memphis State U., 1987—. Editor-in-Chief U. Fla. Law Rev., 1951; contbr. articles to profl. jours. Mem. Fla. Pub. Service Commn., Tallahassee, 1978-81, chmn. 1979-81, Fla. Ho. of Reps., 1956-68; mem. Gen. Bd. Christian Social Concerns, 1960-70, treas., 1960-64; mem. Commn. on Status and Role of Women, United Meth. Ch., 1972-76, S.E. jurisdictional council, 1960-68; del. gen. conf., 1960, 64, 68, 72, lay leader Tampa dist., 1956-66; trustee Lake Junaluska Assembly, 1972-80. Recipient Most Outstanding Rep. award St. Petersburg (Fla.) Times, 1967, Disting. Service award Tampa Jaycees, 1958. Fellow Am. Bar Found. (life); mem. ABA, Am. Law Inst., Am. Judicature Soc. Democrat. Club: Rotary. Office: U Fla Holland Law Ctr Gainesville FL 32611

MANNE, HENRY GIRARD, educator, lawyer; b. New Orleans, May 10, 1928; s. Geoffrey and Eva (Shainberg) M.; m. Bobbette Lee Taxer, Aug. 19, 1968; children: Emily Kay, Geoffrey Adam. B.A., Vanderbilt U., 1950; J.D., U. Chgo., 1952; LL.M., Yale U., 1953, J.S.D., 1966. Bar: Ill. 1952, N.Y. 1969. Practice in Chgo., 1953-54; asso. prof. Law Sch., St. Louis U., 1956-57, 59-62; prof. Law Sch., George Washington U., 1962-68; Kenan prof. law and polit. sci. U. Rochester, 1968-74; Disting. prof. law, dir. Law and Econs. Center, U. Miami Law Sch., 1974-80; prof. law, dir. Law and Econs. Center, Emory U., Atlanta, 1980-86; dean, univ. prof. George Mason U. Sch. Law, 1986—; vis. prof. law U. Wis., Madison, 1957-59, Stanford (Calif.) Law Sch., 1971-72; dir. Econs. Insts. Fed. Judges, 1976—. Author: Insider Trading and the Stock Market, 1966, (with H. Wallich) The Modern Corporation and Social Responsibility, 1973, (with E. Solomon) Wall Street in Transition, 1974, Med. Malpractice Guidebook: Law and Economics, 1985; editor: (with Roger LeRoy Miller) Gold, Money and the Law, 1975; editor: (with Roger LeRoy Miller) Auto Safety Regulation: The Cure or the Problem, 1976, Economic Policy and the Regulation of Corporate Securities, 1968, The Economics of Legal Relationships, 1975; editor: (with James Dorn) Econ. Liberties and the Judiciary, 1987. Patron L'Institute Economique de Paris. Served to 1st lt. USAF, 1954-56. Mem. ABA, Am. Law Inst., Am. Econs. Assn., Phila. Soc., Mont Pelerin Soc., Found. Econ. Edn., Inst. for Humane Studies, Manhatten Inst. for Policy Research, Nat. Legal Ctr. for the Pub. Interest, Order of Coif, Phi Beta Kappa.

MANNE, ROBERT JAY, lawyer; b. N.Y.C., May 8, 1953; s. Alvin and Mildred (Harris) M.; m. Grace A. Nixon, Oct. 31, 1981; children: Jennifer, Michael. BA magna cum laude, SUNY, Albany, 1974; JD cum laude, Bklyn. Law Sch., 1977. Bar: Fla. 1977, U.S. Dist. Ct. (so. dist.) Fla. 1977, U.S. Ct. Appeals (5th cir.) 1978, U.S. Ct. Appeals (11th cir.) 1981. Ptnr. Becker, Poliakoff & Streitfeld, P.A., Ft. Lauderdale, Fla., 1978—. Contbr. articles to profl. jours. Mem. ABA (forum com. on constrn. industry), Broward County Bar Assn., Am. Arbitration Assn. (panel of arbitrators). Construction. Office: Becker Poliakoff & Streitfeld 6520 N Andrews Ave Fort Lauderdale FL 33310

MANNERINO, JOHN DAVID, lawyer; b. Fontana, Calif., Nov. 16, 1949; s. Nick and Alberine (DiPillo) M.; m. Susan Gail Puhek, June 22, 1975; children; John Nicholas, Nicole Michelle. BA cum laude, UCLA, 1971; JD cum laude, Loyola U., Los Angeles, 1974. Bar: Calif. 1974, U.S. Dist. Ct. (cen. dist.) Calif. 1975. Ptnr. Mannerino & Briguglio, Rancho Cucamonga, Calif., 1974—. Mem. Casa Colina Hosp. Found., Pomona, Calif., 1983, San Antonio Community Hosp. Found., Upland, Calif., 1984—; mem. citizens adv. com. Calif. Inst. for Women, Chino, Calif., 1985—; v.p. Prado Tiro Found., Chino, 1985—. Mem. ABA, Calif. Trial Lawyers Assn., San Bernardino County Bar Assn., West San Bernardino County Bar Assn. (pres. 1979-80). Club: West End Gun (Ontario, Calif.). Lodge: Elks. Avocations: shooting, hunting, fishing, cars. General corporate, Federal civil litigation, Personal injury. Office: Mannerino & Briguglio 9333 Baseline Rd #110 Rancho Cucamonga CA 91730

MANNI, KENNETH ALLEN, lawyer; b. Providence, July 26, 1948; s. Peter and Lucy (Chirico) M.; m. Eleanor Theresa Piccolo, June 28, 1975; children: Nathan Matthew, Jessica Marie, David Michael. Student, Cite Universite, Dijon, France, 1969; BA, George Washington U., 1970; MA, Mich. State U., 1973; JD, U. Idaho, 1979. Bar: Wash. 1979, U.S. Dist. Ct. (we. dist.) Wash. 1979, U.S. Supreme Ct. 1983. Specialist environ. edn. Harkness Creek Environ. Edn. Ctr., Pocatello, Idaho, 1975-76; tchr. sci. Our Lady of Mt. Carmel Sch., Waterbury, Conn., 1973-75; ptnr. Cohen, Manni & Theune, Oak Harbor, Wash., 1979—; bd. dirs. Island County Pub. Defenders, Oak Harbor. Cons. Our Lady of Rock Monastery Order of St. Benedict, Shaw Island, Wash., 1979—; parliamentarian Island County Rep. Conv., 1984—; bd. dirs. Evergreen Legal Services, 1979-82, Citizens Against Domestic Abuse, Oak Harbor, 1979-84, Crisis Pregnancy Ctr. of Whidbey Island, Oak Harbor, 1985—. Named one of Outstanding Young Men Am., 1985. Mem. ABA, Wash. State Bar Assn., Island County Bar Assn. (treas. 1984-85), Wash. State Trial Lawyers Assn., Assn. Trial Lawyers Am., Order of Barristers. Roman Catholic. Club: Navy League (judge adv.) (Oak Harbor). Lodges: Rotary (bd. dirs.), KC. Avocations: winter mountaineering, landscape architecture, music, sailing. Personal injury, State civil litigation, Family and matrimonial. Home: 4463 400 Ave SW Oak Harbor WA 98277 Office: Cohen Manni & Theune PO Box 889 Oak Harbor WA 98277

MANNING, B. HERBERT, lawyer, consultant; b. Yoakum, Tex., Sept. 14, 1914; s. Bernard Herbert and Linda (McDonnell) M.; m. Mary Elizabeth Cooke, children—Barbara Ann Manning Wood, Jean Elizabeth Manning Snelus. Ed. Tex. Christian U., So. Meth. U., U. Tex.-Arlington, Georgetown U.; LL.B., Cath. U. Am., 1939. Bar: D.C. 1939, Tex. 1946. Atty. SEC, Washington, 1939-42; asst. regional counsel USPHS-HUD, Ft. Worth, until 1971; spl. asst. atty. gen. State of La., 1972-77; ptnr. Groce, Manning & Groce, Ft. Worth; now sole practice, Ft. Worth; cons. housing fin. Recipient various certs. of appreciation. Mem. Fed. Bar Assn. (nat. v.p. 5th jud. dist. 1961-62, pres. Ft. Worth 1959-60), State Bar Tex., Nat. Assn. Housing and Redevel. Ofcls., Fed. Bus. Assn. Governmental assistance and financing elderly housing. Home: 6100 Winifred Dr Fort Worth TX 76133 Office: 1525 Merrimac Suite 204 Fort Worth TX 76107

MANNING, DONNA KASER, lawyer; b. Kansas City, Mo., Aug. 27, 1955; d. Robert Lee and Alice Marie (Burns) Lenington; m. Robert Richard Manning, Feb. 2, 1985. AA, Penn Valley Community Coll., 1975; BA, U. Mo., Kansas City, 1977; JD, U. Kans., 1981. Bar: Kans. 1981, U.S. Dist. Ct. Kans. 1981. Assoc. Schagel & Assocs., Olathe, Kans., 1981—; asst. prosecutor City of Olathe, Kans., 1981-82. Bd. dirs. Santa Fe Trail council Girl Scouts U.S., Kansas City, Kans., 1984—. Mem. Kans. Bar Assn., Johnson County Bar Assn., Olathe Jaycees (v.p. community devel. 1986—). Avocation: golf. Family and matrimonial, Criminal, General practice. Office: Schlagel & Assocs 124 N Cherry PO Box 683 Olathe KS 66061

MANNING, JAMES HAMINGTON, JR., lawyer; b. New Bern, N.C., Dec. 2, 1938; s. James Vernon and Alfreda (Sutton) M.; m. Cynthia Seth, Dec. 19, 1964; children: Clinton Seth, Kynya Verdette. BS in Edn. with honors, Cheyney (Pa.) State Coll., 1964; JD, U. Pa., 1971. Bar: Pa. 1971. Law clk. to presiding judge U.S. Dist. Ct. (ea. dist.) Pa., Phila., 1971-73; asst. states atty. U.S. Dist. Ct., Phila., 1973-75; trial atty. regional office EEOC, Phila., 1975-77; prof. law Villanova (Pa.) U., 1977-82; sr. counsel Sun Refining and Mktg., Phila., 1980—; law examiner Pa. Supreme Ct., 1982—; commr. Pa. Crime Commn. Served to sgt. USAF, 1957-61. Mem. Am. Corp. Counsel Assn., Barristers Phila. Federal civil litigation, State civil litigation, Premise security litigation. Home: 15 Waterview Rd Dounington PA 19335 Office: Sun Refining & Mktg 10 Penn Ctr Philadelphia PA 19103

MANNING, JEROME ALAN, lawyer; b. Bklyn., Dec. 31, 1929; s. Emanuel J. and Dorothy (Levine) M.; m. Naomi Jacobs, Oct. 31, 1954; children—Joy, Stephen, Susan. B.A., NYU, 1950, LL.B., 1952; LL.M., Yale U., 1953. Bar: N.Y. 1953, Fla. 1977. Assoc. Joseph Trachtman, N.Y.C., 1957-61; ptnr. Stroock & Stroock & Lavan, N.Y.C., 1961—; instr. NYU Sch. Law, 1956—. Dir., chmn. legal and tax panel United Jewish Appeal-Fedn. Jewish Philanthropies N.Y. Served to capt. USAF, 1953-56. Mem. ABA, N.Y. State Bar Assn., Am. Coll. Probate Counsel, Internat. Acad. Estate and Trust Law. Author: Estate Planning, 1982. Probate, Estate planning, Estate taxation. Home: 35 E 75th St New York NY 10021 Office: Stroock & Stroock & Lavan 7 Hanover Sq New York NY 10004

MANNING, JOHN PATRICK, V, lawyer; b. Urbana, Ill., Aug. 11, 1956; s. John Patrick and Sybellee (Overholser) M.; m. Lillian Louise O'Neal, Dec. 4, 1982. BS in Psychology, U. Ill., JD, 1981. Bar: Ill. 1981, Mo. 1982, U.S. Dist. Ct. (we. dist.) Mo. 1982. Assoc. atty. Fed. Land Bank St. Louis, 1981-85, atty., 1985; assoc. counsel The Equitable Life Assurance Soc. U.S., St. Louis, 1985—. Mem. ABA, Ill. Bar Assn., Mo. Bar Assn., St. Louis Bar Assn., Am. Agrl. Law Assn. Roman Catholic. Avocation: swimming. Real property, General corporate. Office: Equitable Life Assurance Soc US PO Box 12910 12747 Olive Suite 250 Saint Louis MO 63141

MANNING, WILLIAM JOSEPH, lawyer; b. N.Y.C., Aug. 11, 1926; s. Joseph Michael and Eileen Johanna (Walsh) M.; m. Maryanne Cullen, June 23, 1956; children—William Joseph, Michael P., Maura G., Marian T., John A., Mary E. B.B.A. magna cum laude, St. John's U., N.Y.C., 1949, LL.B. magna cum laude, 1952. Bar: N.Y. 1952. Asso. firm Simpson Thacher & Bartlett, N.Y.C., 1952-62; partner Simpson Thacher & Bartlett, 1962—, sr. partner, 1968—; dir. Brascan Ltd., Toronto, Ont., Can., 1970-79; bd. dirs. N.Y. Lawyers for Public Interest, 1977—. Notes editor: St. John's Law Rev, 1951-52. Trustee Inst. for Muscle Disease, N.Y.C., 1963-70; bd. dirs. Mercy Hosp., Rockville Centre, N.Y., 1975—. Served with inf. U.S. Army, 1944-46. Fellow Am. Coll. Trial Lawyers, Am. Law Inst., Am. Bar Found.; mem. Am. Bar Assn. (chmn. sect. litigation 1977-78, founding mem. council 1973), Assn. Bar City N.Y., N.Y. State Bar Assn., N.Y. County Lawyers Assn., Am. Judicature Soc. Roman Catholic. Clubs: Downtown Assn., Garden City Golf, Westhampton Country, Cherry Valley. Home: 18 Lefferts Rd Garden City NY 11530 also: 156 Dune Rd Westhampton Beach NY 11978 Office: One Battery Park Plaza New York NY 10004

MANNINO, EDWARD FRANCIS, lawyer; b. Abington, Pa., Dec. 5, 1941; s. Sante Francis and Martha Anne (Hines) M.; m. Mary Ann Vigilante, July 17, 1965; children—Robert John, Jennifer Elizabeth. B.A. with distinction, U. Pa., 1963, LL.B. magna cum laude, 1966. Bar: Pa. 1967. Law clk. U.S. Ct. Appeals 3d Circuit, 1966-67; assoc. firm Dilworth, Paxson, Kalish & Kauffman, Phila., 1967-71; ptnr. Dilworth, Paxson, Kalish & Kauffman, 1972-86, co-chmn. litigation dept., 1980-86, sr. ptnr., 1982-86; sr. prin. Baskin, Flaherty, Elliott & Mannino, P.C., Phila., 1986—; hearing examiner, disciplinary bd. Supreme Ct. Pa., 1986—; lectr. Temple U. Law Sch., 1968-69, 71-72; mem. Phila. Mayor's Sci. and Tech. Adv. Com., 1976-79; project mgr. Commonwealth of Pa. Environ. Master Plan, 1973; chmn. Pa. Land Use Policy Study Adv. Com., 1973-75; henry examiner disciplinary bd. Supreme Ct. Pa., 1986—. Mem. editorial bd. Litigation mag., 1985-87; contbr. articles to profl. jours. Pres. parish council Our Mother of Consolation Ch., 1977-79; chmn. adv. com., hon. faculty mem. U. Pa. History Dept., 1980-85; bd. overseers U. Pa. Sch. Arts and Scis. 1985—. Mem. ABA (fellow young lawyers 1977—, co-chmn. bus. torts litigation com., 1985—, mem. spl. RICO coordinating com., 1986—), Pa. Bar Assn., Phila. Bar Assn. (gov. 1975), Am. Law Inst., Hist. Soc. of U.S. Dist. Ct. Eastern Dist. Pa. (bd. dirs.), Justinian Soc., Order of Coif, Phi Beta Kappa, Phi Beta Kappa Assocs. Democrat. Clubs: Racquet, Sharswood Law, U. Pa. Faculty. Antitrust, Banking, Federal civil litigation. Office: 3 Mellon Bank Ctr 18th Floor Philadelphia PA 19102

MANNIS, BOB DAVIS, lawyer; b. N.Y.C., Aug. 16, 1949. AB, Rutgers U., 1971; JD, Georgetown U., 1974—. Bar: N.Y. 1975, U.S. Dist. Ct. (so. and ea. dist.) N.Y., U.S. Ct. Appeals (2d, 3d and 10th cirs.). Assoc. atty. Dewey, Ballantine, Bushby, Palmer & Wood, N.Y.C., 1974-83; corp. atty. Sterling Drug Inc., N.Y.C., 1983-86, asst. gen. counsel, 1986—; lead articles editor, exec. bd. dirs. Law and Policy in Internat. Bus., Washington, 1973-74. Nat. Merit scholar, 1967-71; recipient Georgetown U. Law Ctr. scholarship, 1971-74. Mem. ABA. General corporate, Mergers and acquisitions, Personal injury. Office: Sterling Drug Inc 90 Park Ave New York NY 10016

MANNIX, CHARLES RAYMOND, lawyer, law educator; b. Elizabeth, N.J., Aug. 2, 1950; s. Charles Raymond and Helen Joan (French) M.; m. Sherry Anne Stetson, May 6, 1979. B.A., Duquesne U., 1972, M.A., 1976, J.D., 1976. Bar: Iowa 1976, U.S. Ct. Claims 1976, U.S. Tax Ct. 1976, U.S. Ct. Mil. Appeals 1976, U.S. Ct. Internat. Trade 1976, U.S. Ct. Appeals (4th and 5th cirs.) 1977, U.S. Ct. Appeals (D.C. cir.) 1977, U.S. Dist. Ct. Va. 1980, U.S. Supreme Ct. 1980, Va. 1980, D.C. 1980, U.S. Ct. Appeals (D.C. cir.) 1980, U.S. Ct. Appeals (fed. cir.) 1982, Commd. 2d lt. U.S. Air Force, 1973, advanced through grades to maj., 1982; intern UN Office of Legal Affairs, N.Y.C., 1975; various legal assignments; law clk. McCrady, Kreimer, Ravick, Bonistalli, Pitts., 1973-76; lectr. bus. law, crim. law, internat. law and philosphy, 1976-80, St. Leo Coll. Fla., City Coll. Chgo.; lectr. USAF Med. Law Cons. Program, 1981-83; adj. faculty Georgetown U., Washington, 1984—; asst. prof. Health Law U. Md. Grad. Sch. Decorated Meritorious Service medal, Air Force Commendation medal with Oak Leaf clusters. Mem. ABA, Assn. Trial Lawyers Am., D.C. Bar Assn., Va. State Bar Assn., Am. Judicature Soc., Fed. Bar Assn., Am. Soc. Internat. Law, Inter-Am. Bar Assn., Internat. Bar Assn., Am. Soc. Law and Medicine, Am. Arbitration Assn. (arbitrator). Federal civil litigation, Legal education, Private international. Home: 10205 Walker Lake Dr Great Falls VA 22066 Office: 3132 N 10th St Arlington VA 22201

MANNIX, KEVIN LEESE, lawyer; b. Queens, N.Y., Nov. 26, 1949; s. John Warren Sr. and Editta Gorrell M.; m. Susanna Bernadette Chiocca, June 1, 1974; children: Nicholas Chiocca, Gabriel Leese. BA, U. Va., 1971, JD, 1974. Bar: Oreg. 1974, U.S. Ct. Appeals (9th cir.) 1976, U.S. Supreme Ct. 1978, Guam 1979. Law clk. to judge Oreg. Ct. Appeals, Salem, 1974-75; asst. atty. gen. Oreg. Dept. Justice, Salem, 1975-77, Govt. of Guam, Agana, 1977-79; judge adminstrv. law Oreg. Workers' Compensation Bd., Salem, 1980-83; assoc. Lindsay, Hart, Neil & Weigler, Portland, Oreg., 1983-86; sole practice Kevin L. Mannix Profl. Corp., Salem, 1986—. Chmn. St. Joseph Sch. Bd., Salem, 1981-86; pres. Salem Cath. Schs. Corp., 1985; v.p. Salem Cath. Schs. Found., 1985—. Mem. ABA, Inter-Am. Bar Assn., Multnomah Bar Assn., Marion Bar Assn. Democrat. Lodges: Rotary (bd. dirs. East Salem 1985—), KC, Grange. Avocations: photography, scuba diving, travel. Insurance, State civil litigation, Workers' compensation. Home: 375 18th St NE Salem OR 97301 Office: 2003 State St Salem OR 97301

MANOS, JOHN M., federal judge; b. 1922. BS, Case Inst. Tech., 1944; JD, Cleve.-Marshall Coll. Law, 1950. Bar: Ohio. Judge Ohio Ct. Common Pleas, 1963-69, Ohio Ct. Appeals, 1969-76, U.S. Dist. Ct. (no. dist.) Ohio, Cleve., 1976—. Mem. ABA, Fed. Bar Assn., Ohio Bar Assn. Judicial administration. Office: US Dist Ct 250 US Courthouse Cleveland OH 44114

MANRING, DANIEL LEE, lawyer; b. Marion, Ohio, Aug. 31, 1951; s. Charles Daniel and Geneva Nellie (Persinger) M.; m. Beth Ann Bender, June 25, 1971; children: Julianne Marie, Jillian Diana. BA, Ohio State U., 1973, JD, 1976. Bar: Ohio 1976, U.S. Dist. Ct. (so. dist.) Ohio, U.S. Ct. Appeals (6th cir.) 1977, U.S. Ct. Appeals (4th and 5th cirs.) 1980, U.S. Ct. Appeals (11th cir.) 1983, Tex. 1987. Assoc. Barkan, Barkan & Neff, Columbus, Ohio, 1976-79; atty., sec. Barkan & Neff & Co. L.P.A., Columbus, Ohio, 1980—. Mem. ABA, Assn. Trial Lawyers Am., Ohio State Bar Assn., Nat. Orgn. of Social Security Claimants Representatives. Democrat. Pension, profit-sharing, and employee benefits. Office: Barkan & Neff PO Box 1969 Columbus OH 43216

MANSBACH, ROBERT ALLEN, lawyer; b. N.Y.C., Dec. 30, 1949; m. Linda C. Mansbach, Aug. 23, 1982. BA with honors, SUNY, Cortland, 1970; JD, Am. U., 1974. Bar: D.C. 1975, N.Y. 1975, U.S. Ct. Appeals (D.C. cir.) 1982, U.S. Supreme Ct. 1983. Atty. advisor FCC, Washington, 1974-79; gen. atty. Communications Satellite Commn., Washington, 1979—. Mem. Fed. Communications Bar Assn., Washington Metropolitan Area Corp. Counsel Assn., Am. Corp. Counsel Assn. Avocation: antique books. Administrative and regulatory, General corporate. Office: Communications Satellite Commn 950 L'Enfant Plaza Washington DC 20024

MANSBACH, ROBERT EARL, JR., lawyer; b. Cheverly, Md., July 27, 1957; s. Robert Earl and Maryalice (McCue) M.; m. Daisy Valdivia, Aug. 21, 1982; 1 child, Alexandria Marie. BA in History with honors, Trinity Coll., 1979; JD, Vanderbilt U., 1982. Bar: Fla. 1982, U.S. Dist. Ct. (mid. dist.) Fla. 1983, U.S. Ct. Appeals (11th cir.) 1983. Assoc. van den Berg, Gay & Burke, Orlando, Fla., 1982-84; assoc. Zimmerman, Shuffield, Kiser & Sutcliffe, Orlando, 1984-86, ptnr., 1987—. Mem. Citrus Bowl Athletic Com., Orlando, 1986, serving com. St. John Luth. Ch., Orlando, 1984—. Mem. ABA (tort and ins. practice sect., litigation sect., products liability subsect.), Fla. Bar, Orange County Bar Assn., Fla. Def. Lawyers Assn., Def. Research Inst., Orlando C. of C., Cen. Fla. Vanderbilt U./Orlando Alumni Assn., Pi Gamma Mu, Phi Delta Phi. Democrat. Avocations: reading, running, racquetball, music. State civil litigation, Personal injury, Insurance. Home: 4308 Neko Ct Orlando FL 32825 Office: Zimmerman Shuffield Kiser & Sutcliffe PO Box 3000 Orlando FL 32802

MANSFIELD, JAMES NORMAN, III, lawyer; b. Chattanooga, Feb. 15, 1951; s. James Norman and Doris June (Hilliard) M.; m. Terry Ann Thomas, Dec. 28, 1975; children: Seth Thomas, James Norman. BA, U. Tenn., Chattanooga, 1973; MA, La. State U., 1976, JD, 1979. Bar: La. 1979, U.S. Dist. Ct. (we. dist.), La. 1979. Ptnr. Liskow and Lewis, Lafayette and New Orleans, La., 1979—. Pres. Raven Soc., Chattanooga, 1973. Mem. ABA, La. Bar Assn., Am. Assn. Petroleum Landmen, Lafayette Assn. Petroleum Landmen, Order of Coif. Methodist. Avocations: photography, jogging, fishing. Oil and gas leasing, Probate, Real property. Home: 419 Live Oak Dr Lafayette LA 70503 Office: Liskow and Lewis PO Box 52008 Lafayette LA 70505

MANSFIELD, JOHN H., legal educator; b. 1928. A.B., Harvard U., 1952, LL.B., 1956. Bar: Calif., Mass. Law clk. Justice Roger Traynor, U.S. Supreme Ct., 1956-57, Justice Felix Frankfurter, 1957-58; prof. law Harvard U., Cambridge, Mass. Mem. Assn. for Asian Studies (com. on Asian law). Editor: (with Maguire, Weinstein and Chadbourn) Cases and Materials on Evidence, 1973; book rev. editor Harvard U. Law Rev. Legal education. Office: Harvard U Sch Law Cambridge MA 02138 *

MANSFIELD, KAREN LEE, lawyer; b. Chgo., Mar. 17, 1942; d. Ralph and Hilda (Blum) Mansfield. B.A. in Polit. Sci., Roosevelt U., 1963; J.D., DePaul U., 1971; student U. Chgo., 1959-60. Bar: Ill. 1972, U.S. Dist. Ct. (no. dist.) Ill. 1972. Legis. intern Ill. State Senate, Springfield, 1966-67; tchr. Chgo. Pub. Schs., 1967-70; atty. CNA Ins., Chgo., 1971-73; law clk. Ill. Apellate Ct., Chgo., 1973-75; sr. trial atty U.S. Dept. Labor, Chgo., 1975—. Contbr. articles to profl. jours. Vol. Big Sister, 1975-81; bd. dirs. A. Hgeld Nursery Sch., 1963-66, Hull House Jane Addams Ctr., 1977-82, Broadway Children's Ctr., 1986—; research asst. Citizens for Gov. Otto Kerner, Chgo., 1964; com. mem. Ill. Commn. on Status of Women, Chgo., 1964-70; del. Nat. Conf. on Status of Women, 1968; candidate for del. Ill. Constl. Conv., 1969. Bd. dirs. Broadway Children's Ctr., 1986—. Mem. Chgo. Council Lawyers, Women's Bar Assn. Ill., Lawyer Pilots Bar Assn., Fed. Bar Assn. Unitarian. Clubs: Friends of Gamelan (performer, legis. chmn Chgo. area chpt. 1983-86, legis. chmn. N. Cen. sect., 1986—, legis. award 99's 1983, 86). Labor. Home: 2970 Lake Shore Dr Chicago IL 60657 Office: 8th Fl Office of Solicitor US Dept Labor 230 S Dearborn St Chicago IL 60604

MANSFIELD, SEYMOUR J., lawyer; b. Chgo., Mar. 30, 1945; s. Albert H. and Anne I. (Mittleman) M.; m. Susan Ann Bronner, Jan. 21, 1968; children—Justin, Alexis. B.S. in Sociology, U. Ill., 1966; J.D., DePaul U., 1969. Bar: Minn. 1978, Ill. 1969, U.S. Dist. Ct. (no. dist.) Ill. 1969, U.S. Dist. Ct. Minn. 1978, U.S. Ct. Appeals (7th cir.) 1971, U.S. Supreme Ct. 1976. Staff counsel Northwestern U. Legal Asst. Clinic, Chgo., 1969-70, Uptown Neighborhood Legal Services, 1970-72, Legal Asst. Found. Chgo., 1972-73; supervising atty. housing law reform team, 1973-78; exec. dir. Central Minn. Legal Services/Legal Aid Soc. Mpls., Inc., 1978-81; exec. dir., pres. Fund For Legal Aid Soc., 1981-82; adj. prof. civil practice skills William Mitchell Coll. Law, St. Paul, Minn., 1982—; owner, pres. Seymour J. Mansfield & Assocs., Mpls., 1981—; del. Minn. State Bar Assn. Gen. Assembly, 1982—; lectr. in field; speaker, Panelist on various TV Stas. Editor in chief, contbr. author Tenant's Rights, rev. edit., 1978, Judgment Landlord: A Study of the Evicion Court in Chicago, 1978. Contbr. articles to law review jours. Bd. dirs. Chgo. Council Lawyers, 1976-78, Nat. Clearinghouse for

Legal Services, 1973-80; Minn. Coalition for Protection of Youth Rights, 1978-81, Minn. Legal Services Coalition, 1980-81, also founder; vice chmn. FHA com. Ill. Commn. Mortgage Practices, 1975. Mem. ABA, Assn. Trial Lawyers Am., Minn. State Bar Assn., Loose Assn. Legal Services Housing Attys. and Clients, Minn. Trial Lawyers Assn., Hennepin County Bar Assn., Chgo. Council Lawyers. Jewish. State civil litigation, Federal civil litigation, Civil rights. Office: Seymour J Mansfield & Assocs National City Bank Bldg 6th Floor Minneapolis MN 55402

MANSFIELD, WILLIAM AMOS, lawyer; b. Redmond, Oreg., Oct. 23, 1929; s. Ellithorpe Garrett and Constance G. (Loney) M.; children—Johathan E., Frederick W., Paul F. B.S., U. Oreg., 1951, J.D., 1953. Bar: Oreg. 1953, U.S. Supreme Ct. 1960, U.S. Dist. Ct. Oreg. 1966, U.S. Ct. Appeals (9th cir.) 1982. Asst. atty. gen. State of Oreg., Salem, 1955-60; staff atty., gen. counsel U.S. Bur. Pub. Roads, Washington, 1961; city atty. City of Medford (Oreg.), 1962-64; sole practice, Medford, 1965—. Bd. dirs. Peter Britt Festival, 1963-65, Planned Parenthood, Jackson County, Oreg., 1978; bd. dirs. Rogue Valley Transp. Dist., 1976-81, chmn., 1977-78; trustee Children's Farm Home, 1970-76; bd. dirs. ACLU, 1971-77; mem. city council, City of Medford, 1985—. Served as 1st lt. USAF, 1953-55. Democrat. Congregationalist. Personal injury, State civil litigation, General practice. Address: 901 W 8th St PO Box 1721 Medford OR 97501

MANSHEL, ANDREW MAXIMILIAN, lawyer; b. Newark, Mar. 6, 1956; s. Milton Maximilian and Bernice (Lewitter) M.; m. Heidi Waleson, Sept. 16, 1984. BA with honors, Oberlin Coll., 1978; MBA with distinction, JD, N.Y.U., 1982. Bar: N.J. 1982, U.S. Dist. Ct. N.J. 1982, N.Y. 1983, U.S. Dist. Ct. (so. dist.) N.Y. 1987. Assoc. Riker, Danzig, Scherer & Hyland, Newark, 1982-83; counsel Birch Tree Group Ltd., N.Y.C., 1983-85; assoc. Wachtell, Manheim et al, N.Y.C., 1985—; counsel Nat. Music Council, N.Y.C., 1985—. N.Y. Alumni Convenor, Oberlin Coll., 1986—; spl. counsel Pres. Com. on the Arts and the Humanities, Washington, 1983-84. Hopf fellow NYU, 1978, 79. Mem. ABA (legislation com., copyright div., patent copyright trademark sect.), Copyright Soc., Assn. Bar of City of New York, Am. Symphony Orch. League, Chamber Music Am. (bd. dirs.). Democrat. Jewish. Avocations: opera, chamber music. Trademark and copyright, General corporate, Entertainment. Home: 60 W 66th St 20C New York NY 10023 Office: Wachtell Manheim et al 30 Rockefeller Plaza Suite 3325 New York NY 10112

MANSHEL, MAX, lawyer; b. Orange, N.J., Apr. 10, 1928; s. Milton Maximilian and Ruth Manshel; m. Bernice Lewitter, Dec. 22, 1952; children: Andrew M., Roberta S., Catherine L. BSME, U. Mo., 1950; JD, Rutgers U., 1977. Bar: N.J. 1977, U.S. Dist. Ct. N.J. 1977, U.S. Ct. Appeals (3d cir.) 1979, N.Y. 1985. V.p. Internat. Ticket, Newark, 1950-73; sec., treas. Due Max Internat., West Orange, N.J., 1973-77; assoc. Gladstone Hart, Hackensack, N.J., 1977-81; sole practice South Orange, N.J., 1981—. Chmn., mem. West Orange Planning Bd., 1967-74, West Orange Adv. Comm., 1965-71; mem. West Orange Dem. County Com., 1964—. Served to lt. comdr. USNR, 1950-74. Mem. ABA, Assn. Trial Lawyers Am. (bd. govs. Atlantic City chpt. 1980-84). Civil rights, State civil litigation, Consumer commercial. Home: 34 Collamore Terr West Orange NJ 07052 Office: 76 S Orange Ave Suite 202 South Orange NJ 07079

MANSMANN, CAROL LOS, judge; b. Pitts., Aug. 7, 1942; d. Walter Joseph and Regina Mary (Pilarski) Los; m. J. Jerome Mansmann, June 27, 1970; children—Michael, Casey, Megan, Patrick. B.A., J.D., Duquesne U.; LL.D., Seton Hill Coll., Greensburg, Pa., 1985. Asst. dist. atty. Allegheny County, Pitts., 1968-72; assoc. McVerry Baxter & Mansmann, Pitts., 1973-79; assoc. prof. law Duquesne U., Pitts., 1973-82; judge U.S. Dist. Ct. Pa., Pitts., 1982-85, U.S. Ct. Appeals, Phila., 1985—; mem. Pa. Criminal Procedural Rules Com., Pitts., 1972-77; spl. asst. atty. gen. Commonwealth of Pa., 1974-79; bd. dirs. Pa. Bar Inst., Harrisburg, 1984—. Mem. adv. bd. Villanova U. Law Sch., 1985—. Recipient St. Thomas More award, 1983. Mem. Nat. Assn. Women Judges, ABA, Pa. Bar Assn., Fed. Judges Assn., Am. Judicature Soc., Allegheny County Bar Assn., Phi Alpha Delta. Republican. Roman Catholic. Office: US Ct Appeals for 3d Cir 402 US PO and Courthouse 7th & Grant Sts Pittsburgh PA 15219

MANSORI, ZUBAIR S., lawyer, accountant; b. Lahore, Punjab, Pakistan, Nov. 30, 1934; came to U.S., 1973; s. Mohammad Saeed and Maryam (Hussain) M.; m. Tasneem Rafique, Nov. 23, 1957 (div. Apr. 1970); children: Aniqua, Najia; m. Kauser Amir, Sept. 6, 1972; children: Maaz, Hasan, Hena. B in Commerce, Punjab U., Pakistan, 1954, LLB, 1957, MA, 1965; JD, Duquesne U., 1981. Bar: Pa. 1981. Pvt. practice acctg. Johnstown, Pa., 1975—; sole practice Johnstown, 1981—. Mem. ABA, Pa. Bar Assn., Am. Inst. CPA's, Pa. Inst. CPA's. Lodge: Rotary (pres. Johnstown chpt. 1984-85). Corporate taxation, Pension, profit-sharing, and employee benefits, Bankruptcy. Home: Rd #1 Box 3A Sidman PA 15901 Office: 114 Lincoln ST Johnstown PA 15901

MANSOUR, NADIM NED, lawyer; b. Beirut, Lebanon, July 25, 1948; came to U.S., 1956.; s. Bishara and Mary (Hakim) M.; m. Dianne Elaine Elmer, May 27, 1972; 1 child, Ryan. BS in Fin., U. So. Calif., 1970; JD magna cum laude, U. San Diego, 1973. Bar: Calif. 1973. Acct. Touche Ross & Co., San Diego, 1973-74; sr. atty. Getty Oil Co., Los Angeles, 1974-78; v.p., asst. gen. counsel Mattel, Inc., Hawthorne, Calif., 1978—; bd. dirs. Mattel Credit Union, Hawthorne. Mem. ABA, Calif. Bar Assn., Los Angeles County Bar Assn., Beta Gamma Sigma. Republican. General corporate, Private international, Real property. Office: Mattel Inc 5150 Rosecrans Ave Hawthorne CA 90250

MANTEL, ALLAN DAVID, lawyer; b. N.Y.C., June 27, 1951; s. Bernard and Ruth (Weichman) M.; m. Janet Mantel, June 17, 1985. BA, NYU, 1973; JD, SUNY, Buffalo, 1976. Bar: N.Y. 1977, U.S. Dist. Ct. (so. and ea. dists.) N.Y. 1977. Assoc. Rosenthal & Herman P.C., N.Y.C., 1977-82; ptnr. Rosenthal, Herman & Mantel, N.Y.C., 1983—. Fellow: Am. Acad. Matrimonial Lawyers; mem. ABA (family law sect.), N.Y. State Bar Assn. (equitable distbn. com.), Assn. of Bar of City of N.Y. (matrimonial law com.), N.Y. County Lawyers Assn. Jewish. Family and matrimonial, State civil litigation. Office: Rosenthal Herman & Mantel PC 310 Madison Ave New York NY 10017

MANTERFIELD, ERIC ALAN, banker, law educator; b. N.Y.C., Oct. 2, 1947; s. Erskine Walker and Louise Ruth (Wild) M.; m. Valerie Jane Siegel, July 18, 1969; children—Brian W., Elyse A., Wesley A., Sean P. B.A., Denison U., 1969; J.D., U. Mich., 1972. Bar: Ind. 1972, U.S. Dist. Ct. (so. dist.) Ind. 1972, U.S. Tax Ct. 1979. Assoc. Barnes, Hickam, Pantzer & Boyd (now Barnes & Thornburg), Indpls., 1972-74; trust officer Bank One, Indpls., N.Am. (formerly Am. Fletcher Nat. Bank), Indpls., 1975-76, mgr. probate dept., 1976-82, mgr. personal trust div., 1982—; adj. prof. law Ind. U. Sch. Law, Bloomington, Ind., 1977—. Author: Basic Estate Planning, 1980, Fundamentals of Estate Planning, 1982 Estate Planning for Married Couples, 1982. Contbr. articles to profl. jours. Chmn. bd. Am. Heart Assn., Ind. Affiliate, Indpls., 1978-82, Festival Music Soc., Indpls., 1982; mem. deferred giving com. Crossroads Rehab. Ctr., Indpls., 1984—; Ind. del. North Central Regional Heart com. Am. Heart Assn., Dallas, Tex., 1981—; exec. com. Estate Planning Council Indpls. (treas. 1983-84, sec. 1984-85, v.p. 1985-86, pres. 1986-87). Mem. Ind. Bar Assn., Indpls. Bar Assn., Phi Beta Kappa. Estate planning, Probate, Estate taxation. Home: 5730 Carrollton Ave Indianapolis IN 46220 Office: Bank One Indpls N Am 111 Monument Circle Indianapolis IN 46277

MANTHEI, GAYL MARIE, lawyer; b. Kenosha, Wis.; d. Lothar Arthur and Cora (DeVries) M.; m. Gordon R. Barner, Aug. 2, 1980. BA cum laude, U. Wis., Eau Claire, 1976; JD cum laude, U. Wis., Madison, 1980. Bar: Wis. 1980, N.C. 1980. Assoc. Hollowell & Silverstein, P.A., Raleigh, N.C., 1980-84; asst. atty. gen. N.C. Dept. of Justice, Raleigh, 1984—. Contbr. articles to profl. jours. Mem. N.C. Bar Assn. (exec. com. health sect., sec. 1982-84), N.C. Soc. Health Care Attys. (mem. chmn. 1983-84). General corporate, Administrative and regulatory, Health. Home: 6513 Battleford Dr Raleigh NC 27612 Office: NC Dept Justice PO Box 629 Raleigh NC 27602-0629

MANTHEI, RICHARD DALE, health care company executive, lawyer; b. Olivia, Minn., Dec. 23, 1935; s. Alvin R. and Sidonia (Klatt) M.; m. Karen J. Peterson, Sept. 6, 1959 (dec. Mar. 1985); children: Steven, Jana, Kari, John, Rebecca; m. Lynn E. Graham, Aug. 9, 1986. B.S. in Pharmacy (Rexall award 1960), S.D. State U., 1960; J.D., U. Minn., 1967. Bar: Ind. 1967, Ill. 1970. Sales rep. Eli Lilly & Co., Indpls., 1962-64, atty., 1967-70; atty., then asst. corp. sec., dir. regulatory affairs Am. Hosp. Supply Corp., Evanston, Ill., 1970-79, corp. sec., dep. gen. counsel, 1979-85; assoc. gen. counsel Baxter Travenol Labs., Deerfield, Ill., 1986-87; ptnr. Burditt, Bowles & Radzius, Washington, 1987—. Author articles in field.; Editorial adv. staff: Med. Devices and Diagnostic Industry, 1979. Pres. Grace Lutheran Ch., Libertyville, Ill., 1978; mem. bd. edn. Libertyville High Sch., 1984-87; mem. governing bd. Spl. Edn. Dist. of Lake County, Ill., 1985-87. Served with AUS, 1954-56. Mem. ABA, Health Industry Mfrs. Assn. (chmn. law sect. 1976), Health Industry Assn. (chmn. legal com. 1973), Am. Soc. Corp. Secs. (corp. practices com. 1983—, pres. Chgo. regional group 1986-87), Ill. Bar Assn., Ind. Bar Assn., Chgo. Bar Assn. Club: University (Evanston, Ill.) (bd. dirs. 1984-86). Administrative and regulatory, General corporate, Health. Home: 884 Scott Pl Libertyville IL 60048 Office: Burditt Bowles & Radzius 1029 Vermont Ave NW Suite 200 Washington DC 20005

MANTLE, RAYMOND ALLAN, lawyer; b. Painesville, Ohio, Oct. 15, 1937; s. Junius Dow and Ada Louise (Stinchcomb) M.; m. Judith Ann LaGrange, Nov. 26, 1967; children—Amanda Lee, Rachel Ann, Leah Amy. B.S. in B.A. summa cum laude, Kent State U., 1961, B.A. summa cum laude, 1961; LL.B. cum laude, NYU, 1964. Bar: N.Y. 1964, N.J. 1976, U.S. Supreme Ct. Asst. counsel Gov. Nelson A. Rockefeller, N.Y., 1964-65; assoc. Paul Weiss Rifkind Wharton & Garrison, 1967-69; mem. firm Milgrim Thomajan & Lee, P.C., N.Y.C., 1969—. Served to capt. U.S. Army, 1965-67. Mem. N.Y. State Bar Assn., N.J. Bar Assn. Republican. Methodist. Contracts commercial, General corporate, Trademark and copyright. Office: 405 Lexington Ave 18th Floor New York NY 10174

MANTONYA, JOHN BUTCHER, lawyer; b. Columbus, Ohio, May 26, 1922; s. Elroy Letts and Blanche (Butcher) M.; m. Mary E. Reynolds, June 14, 1947; children: Elizabeth Claire, Mary Kay, Lee Ann. A.B. cum laude, Washington and Jefferson Coll., 1943; postgrad., U. Mich. Law Sch., 1946-47; J.D., Ohio State U., 1949. Bar: Ohio 1949. Assoc. A.S. Mitchell (Atty.), Newark, Ohio, 1949-50; asso. C.D. Lindrooth, Newark, 1950-57; partner firm Lindrooth & Mantonya, Newark, 1957-74; firm John B. Mantonya, 1974-81, John B. Mantonya, L.P.A., 1981—. Mem. North Fork Local Bd. Edn., 1962-69; adv. com. Salvation Army, Licking County, 1965—, Mayor of, Utica, Ohio, 1953-59. Served with AUS, 1943-45. Mem. Am. Bar Assn., Ohio Bar Assn., Licking County Bar Assn. (pres. 1967), Phi Delta Phi, Beta Theta Pi. Probate, Real property. Home: 11055 Reynolds Rd NE Utica OH 43080 Office: 3 N 3rd St Newark OH 43055

MANTOOTH, JOHN ALBERT, judge; b. Oklahoma City, June 13, 1947; s. Albert and Thelma (Kerr) M.; m. Eilene M. Meredith, Apr. 7, 1982; children: Susan, Jan, Meredith. BA, Okla. U., 1969, JD, 1972. Bar: Okla. 1973, U.S. Dist. Ct. (we. dist.) Okla. 1973, U.S. Ct. Appeals (10th cir.) 1975, U.S. Supreme Ct. 1976. Sole practice Purcell, Okla., 1973-79; ptnr. Elder, Mantooth & Haxel, Purcell, 1979-85, Mantooth & Haxel, Purcell, 1985—; judge City of Purcell, 1974, City of Lexington, Okla., 1980—; owner, bd. dirs. M-Quad Land Devel., Purcell, 1979-82, Cartier Jewelry, Dallas, 1982—; mem. com. on uniform jury instructions civil Okla. Supreme Ct. Mem. Gov.'s Task Force on Vocat.-Tech. Edn., 1975; chmn. Purcell Mcpl. Hosp., Purcell, 1974-76. Served to maj. JAGC U.S. Army, 1976—. Mem. Okla. Trial Lawyers Assn. (editor mag. 1976-80), Phi Alpha Delta. Democrat. Baptist. Clubs: University (Dallas); Whitehall Oklahoma City). Lodge: Rotary (pres. Purcell club 1978-79). Avocations: tennis, skiing, hunting, fishing, traveling. State civil litigation, Probate, Real property. Office: Mantooth & Haxel 310 Washington Purcell OK 73080-0677

MANZANARES, DENNIS, lawyer; b. Santa Fe, N.Mex., Sept. 20, 1950; s. Ercilia E. Martinez; m. Patricia C. Wallace, July 21, 1973. BA, Coll. Santa Fe, 1973; JD, Georgetown U., 1976. Bar: N.Mex. 1976, U.S. Dist. Ct. N.Mex. 1976, U.S. Ct. Appeals (10th cir.) 1979, U.S. Supreme Ct. 1981. Asst. pub. defender State of N.Mex., Albuquerque, 1976-79; gen. counsel to auditor State of N.Mex., Santa Fe, 1979-82; sole practice Santa Fe, 1983—; clin. law dir. N.Mex. Dept. Corrections, Santa Fe, 1983-84; adminstrv. law judge N.Mex. Alcoholic Beverage Control, Santa Fe, 1984—; spl. prosecutor 1st jud. dist. atty., Santa Fe, 1984-86. V.p. N.Mex. Young Dems., 1979-82; judge, adv. Marriage Tribunal Archdiocese Santa Fe, 1978—; mem. jud. council N.Mex. Dems., 1981-85, Santa Fe Airport Adv. Bd., 1985—. Mem. N.Mex. Bar Assn. (chmn. pub. advocacy sect. 1983-84), Lawyer-Pilot Bar Assn., Nat. Transp. Bd. Bar Assn., Nat. Dist. Attys. Assn., N.Mex. Civil Air Patrol (wing legal officer 1983-85, squadron comdr. Santa Fe chpt. 1985—, Outstanding Sr. Mem. award 1983-84, Gill Robb Wilson award 1985, Search & Rescue Find award 1984-85), N.Mex. Pilots Assn. (Leadership and Safety awards 1985—), N.Mex. Woodworkers Guild (v.p. 1983-85), Young Astronaut Program (chpt. sponsor). Avocations: aviation, politics, youth leadership, emergency services, amateru radio. General practice, Criminal, Aviation. Home: 2169 Ojo Ct Santa Fe NM 87505 Office: PO Box 4992 Santa Fe NM 87502-4992

MANZO, PETER THOMAS, lawyer, deacon; b. Bayonne, N.J., Feb. 16, 1947; s. Valentine Salvatore and Rita (Zito) M.; m. Linda A. Palazzolo, Aug. 21, 1977 (annulled Dec. 1983). A.B., Georgetown U., 1968; M.B.A., Columbia U., 1972; J.D., Cornell U., 1972. Bar: N.J. 1972. Asst. corp. counsel N.Y. Hosp., Cornell Med. Ctr., N.Y.C., 1972-75, asst. sec.-treas., asst. dir. for corp. and legal affairs; dep. pub. adv., mng. atty. in health N.J. Pub. Advocate, Newark and Trenton, 1976—. Brief writer Kessler Hosp. Case. Deacon, Roman Catholic Ch., St. Patrick Roman Cath. Ch., Chatham, N.J., 1982—. Served to capt. U.S. Army. Mem. ABA, N.J. State Bar Assn., Nat. Health Lawyers Assn. Lodge: K.C. (spiritual adviser 1983—). Health, Insurance, Public utilities. Home: 1701 Deerfield Dr Edison NJ 08820 Office: NJ Pub Advocate 407 Main St Chatham NJ 07928 Office: 974 Inman Ave Edison NJ 08820

MAPES, WILLIAM RODGERS, JR., lawyer; b. Cleve., Nov. 29, 1952; s. William R. and Marian (Atkins) M.; m. Patricia Soochan, Sept. 3, 1984. BS in Bus. Adminstrn., Miami U., Oxford, Ohio, 1974; JD, Am. U., 1977. Bar: D.C. 1978, U.S. Ct. Appeals (3d, 4th, 5th and D.C. cirs.), U.S. Supreme Ct. Ptnr. Ross, Marsh & Foster, Washington, 1978—. Mem. ABA (editor nat. resources sect. newsletter 1984—), Fed. Energy Bar Assn. Avocations: sailing, tennis, cycling. FERC practice, Administrative and regulatory. Home: 6916 Greenvale St NW Washington DC 20015 Office: Ross Marsh & Foster 888 16th St NW Washington DC 20006

MAR, EUGENE, lawyer, financial consultant; b. Hong Kong, July 5, 1940; s. Timothy T. and Shuh Yin L. (Lu) M.; came to U.S., 1946, naturalized, 1963; m. Sara C., Aug. 5, 1965; children—Christopher E., Jonathan M. B.S. in Metall. Engring., U. Md., 1964; J.D., Cath. U. Am., 1969. Bar: Va. 1970, U.S. Ct. Mil. Appeals, U.S. Supreme Ct., U.S. Tax Ct., U.S. Ct. Appeals D.C. Assoc. Philpitt, Steininger & Priddy, 1964-65; examiner U.S. Patent Office 1965-68; assoc. Arthur Schwartz, Arlington, Va., 1968-72; ptnr. Bacon & Thomas, Arlington, 1978—, mng. ptnr., 1981—; bus./fin. cons., 1978—. Mem. ABA, Am. Intellectual Property Law Assn., Licensing Execs. Soc., Phi Alpha Delta, Phi Kappa Sigma. Patent, General corporate. Home: 5133 Woodmire Ln Alexandria VA 22311 Office: 625 Slaters Ln Fourth Floor Alexandria VA 22314

MARAMES, WILLIAM ETHEME, lawyer; b. N.Y.C., Dec. 26, 1955; s. Gregory and Stella (Popescu) M. BA, Queens Coll., Flushing, N.Y., 1977; JD, Fordham U., 1980. Bar: N.Y. 1981, U.S. Dist. Ct. (so. and ea. dists.) N.Y. 1982. Assoc. Wyatt, Gerber, Shoup, Scobey and Badie, N.Y.C., 1981—. Asst. editor: Committee Reports--ABA Patent, Trademark and Copyright Section, 1985, 1986. J. Geist Law fellow Queen's Coll., 1977. Mem. ABA (patent, trademark and copyright law sect., sports and entertainment sect., vice-chmn. com. on publs. 1985—), N.Y. State Bar Assn., Phi Beta Kappa. Trademark and copyright, Antitrust, Entertainment. Home: 58-24 192nd St Flushing NY 11365 Office: Wyatt Gerber Shoup et al 261 Madison Ave New York NY 10016

MARAN, JOE, lawyer; b. Jersey City, Nov. 16, 1933; s. Joseph and Beatrice (Margolin) M.; m. Paula Schwartz, June 16, 1956 (div. Oct. 1979); children: David, Jodi & Erik; m. Joy Breen, July 10, 1980. BS, Fairleigh Dickinson U., 1957; LLB, Rutgers U., 1959. Bar: N.J. 1960; cert. trial atty., N.J. Sole practice Jersey City, 1960-64, Newark, 1984—; ptnr. Zarin & Maran, Newark, 1964-83, Maran & Maran, Newark, 1987—. Mem. Essex County Bar Assn. Personal injury, State civil litigation. Home: 329 W 108th St New York NY 10017 Office: Gateway I Newark NJ 07102

MARANDAS, JOHN STEVE, lawyer; b. Portland, Oreg., June 3, 1940; s. Steve George and Vasiliki (Paravantis) M.; m. Susan Margaret Bushnell, July 25, 1964; children—Stephanie Anne, John Steve John, Jason John. B.S., Lewis and Clark Coll., 1962; J.D., Willamette U., 1965. Bar: Oreg. 1966, U.S. Dist. Ct. Oreg. 1966, U.S. Ct. Appeals (9th cir.) 1968, U.S. Supreme Ct. 1972. Hearings referee Oreg. Dept. Motor Vehicles, Salem, 1965-66; asst. atty. gen. Dept. Justice, 1966-69; assoc. Lekas, Dicey & Sherwood, Portland, 1969-72; ptnr. Lekas, Dicey & Marandas, Portland, 1972-75, Bloom, Chaivoe, Ruben, Marandas, Berg, Sly & Barnett, Portland, 1975-79; sole practice, Portland; ptnr. Bloom, Marandas and Sly, P.C., Portland, 1979—; judge pro tem Circuit Ct., 1984—. Bd. dirs. Oreg. NCCJ, 1975-82, 86—, chmn., 1980-81, nat. bd. dirs., 1979-85; pres. Greek Civic Club Oreg., 1975-76, World Affairs Council, 1977—; regional v.p. United Hellenic Am. Congress, 1977—; trustee Northwestern Sch. Law Lewis & Clark Coll., 1971-73; chmn. bd. dirs. Project Stop, Alcohol Rehab. Clinic, 1976-84; bd. dirs. Oreg. Spl. Olympics, 1983—, Lewis & Clark Coll. Alumni Bd., 1969-73, 86—. Served to capt. JAGC, Army N.G., 1965-76. Mem. ABA (family law and econs. of laws sects.), Oreg. Bar Assn. (com. fgn. and internat. law, bar trial counsel), Am. Judicature Soc., Am. Immigration Lawyers Assn., Multnomah County Bar Assn. (com. dist. ct. liaison), Am. Hellenic C. of C., Delta Theta Phi. Democrat. Greek Orthodox. Clubs: Portland City, Am. Hellenic Ednl. and Progressive Assn. (Portland). Lodge: Kiwanis. Author: Miscellaneous Opinions of the Attorney General, 1966-69; Tort Liability of Government Officials, 1969; Duties, Tariffs and Import Controls, 1982. Immigration, naturalization, and customs, State civil litigation, General practice. Home: 17950 Royce Way Lake Oswego OR 97034 Office: 1600 SW 4th Ave Suite 667 Portland OR 97201

MARANS, J. EUGENE, lawyer; b. Butte, Mont., May 26, 1940; s. Edward and Florence M.; m. Anne Marie Borger, Sept. 3, 1978; children: Julia C., John E. A.B., Harvard U., 1962, LL.B., 1965. Bar: N.Y. 1966, D.C. 1971. Law clk. to Judge John M. Wisdom U.S. Ct. Appeals (5th cir.), New Orleans, 1965-66; assoc. Cleary, Gottlieb, Steen & Hamilton, N.Y.C., 1966-70, Paris, 1970-71; assoc. Cleary, Gottlieb, Steen & Hamilton, Washington, 1971-74, ptnr., 1975—; mem. N.Y. State adv. com. U.S. Commn. Civil Rights, 1969-70; mem. nat. eval. com. on. simplified method of determining eligibility in pub. assistance HEW, 1969-70; sec., counsel Bipartisan Com. on Absentee Voting, 1973—. Contbr. articles to legal jours. Bd. dirs. New Leadership Fund, chmn., 1977-79. Mem. Assn. Ams. Resident Overseas, Ripon Soc. (nat. governing bd. 1962—, chmn. chmn. 1969-70, council on fgn. relations), ABA, D.C. Bar Assn. (chmn. internat. sect. 1978-79), Assn. of Bar of City of N.Y., Am. Soc. Internat. Law, Union Internat. des Avocats, Washington Fgn. Law Soc. (pres. 1985-86), Am. Law Inst. Banking, General corporate, Private international. Office: Cleary Gottlieb Steen & Hamilton 1752 N St NW Washington DC 20036

MARAZITI, JOSEPH JAMES, JR., lawyer; b. Morristown, N.J., May 20, 1940; s. Joseph James and Margaret Eileen (Hopkins) M.; m. Claudette A. Awn, June 23, 1968; children—Jacqueline, Michele. B.S., Fordham U., 1962, J.D., 1965. Bar: N.J. 1965, U.S. Dist. Ct. N.J. 1965, U.S. Ct. Apls. (3rd cir.) 1980, U.S. Sup. Ct. 1969. Ptnr. Maraziti & Maraziti, Boonton, N.J., 1965-76; sr. mem. Maraziti, Kalish & Gregory, Morristown, N.J., 1976-84, Maraziti, Falcon & Gregory, 1985—; atty. Town of Boonton, N.J., 1965—; atty. Bd. Edn. Twp. of Jefferson, 1965—, Twp. of Mine Hill, 1975-83; atty. Rockaway Valley Regional Sewerage Authority, 1971—; mem. indsl. pretreatment task force N.J. Dept. Environ. Protection, 1982, subcom. 21st century task force Gen. Assembly State of N.J. Contbr. articles to profl. jours. Chmn. environ. task force MORRIS 2000. Mem. ABA, N.J. Bar Assn. (environ. law sect.), Assn. Trial Lawyers Am., N.J. Inst. for Mcpl. Attys., N.J. Sch. Bds. Assn., Morris County Bar Assn., Authorities Assn. N.J., Environ. Law Inst. of Washington. Environment, Local government, Federal civil litigation. Office: Maraziti Falcon & Gregory 65 Madison Ave Morristown NJ 07960

MARBUT, SYRIAN ERASMUS, lawyer; b. Verona, Mo., Apr. 30, 1907; s. John Franklin and Viola Ann (Walker) M.; m. Elizabeth Carolyn Gardner, Apr. 1, 1933. AB, Okla. U., 1931, LLB, 1932. Bar: Okla. 1931, Tex. 1932. Sole practice 1935-40, 41-42; ptnr. Anderson & Marbut, 1940-41; county atty. Lubbock County, Tex., 1942-46; asst. atty. City of Lubbock, 1947-49; ptnr. Crenshaw, Marbut & Charness, 1950-53; sole practice Lubbock, 1953—; asst. mcpl. judge City of Lubbock, 1960. Mem. Tex. Bar Assn. (50 yr. gold certificate 1952), Lubbock County Bar Assn. (past pres.), Sigma Mu Sigma, Phi Alpha Delta. Democrat. Episcopalian. Lodges: Masons (32 degree) (past high priest, past thrice illustrious master), Shriners, Yellowhouse (past master), KT, Knights of York, Order of Eastern Star (past patron), KP, Optimists (past pres., past dist. gov.). Federal civil litigation, General corporate, Probate. Home: 1922 24th St Lubbock TX 79411 Office: 1409 Metro Tower 1220 Broadway Lubbock TX 79401

MARCELLINO, STEPHEN MICHAEL, lawyer; b. Bklyn., July 11, 1950; s. Frank Joseph and Marie Leah (Lyda) M.; m. Karen Eileen Kelly, July 24, 1976; 1 child, Bridget. BA in English, Fordham U., 1972, JD, 1975. Bar: N.Y. 1976, U.S. Dist. Ct. (so. and ea. dists.) N.Y. 1977,. U.S. Ct. Internat. Trade 1983, U.S. Dist. Ct. (we. dist.) N.Y. 1985, U.S. Ct. Appeals (2d cir.) 1986. Ptnr. Wilson Elser Moskowitz Edelman & Dicker, N.Y.C., 1975—. Mem. ABA (forum com. on constrn. law, torts and ins. practice sect.), N.Y. State Bar Assn. (com. on trial lawyers). Republican. Roman Catholic. Avocations: basketball, tennis, skiing. Federal civil litigation, Construction, Insurance. Office: Wilson Elser Moskowitz et al 420 Lexington Ave New York NY 10170

MARCELLO, DAVID ANTHONY, lawyer; b. Thibodaux, La., June 14, 1946; s. Benny A. and Betty (Mims) M.; m. Jane L. Johnson, Apr. 3, 1980. BA, Williams Coll., 1968; JD, Tulane U., 1971. Bar: La. 1971, U.S. Dist. Ct. (ea. dist.) La., U.S. Ct. Appeals (5th cir.), U.S. Supreme Ct. Exec. dir. La. Ctr. for Pub. Interest, New Orleans, 1974-78; exec. counsel to mayor City of New Orleans, 1978-80; dir. Barham & Churchill, New Orleans, 1980-85; of counsel Stone, Pigman, Walter, Wittman & Hutchinson, New Orleans, 1985—; instr. Tulane U. Sch. Social Work, New Orleans, 1972-74, Law Sch., 1985-87; gen. counsel Regional Transit Authority, New Orleans, 1980—. Author: Lawyer Referral Services: An Organizer's Manual and Materials, 1976, Program Development Manual, 1976. Legal counsel Garden Dist. Assn., New Orleans, 1973-78; cons. New Orleans Council on Aging, 1974; vice chmn. Mayor's Criminal Justice Coordinating Council, New Orleans, 1979-80; chmn. bd. dirs. French Market Corp., New Orleans, 1980-82; bd. dirs. Urban League Greater New Orleans, 1974-76, Preservation Resource Ctr., 1974-76, La. Nature and Science Ctr., New Orleans, 1984-86. Loyola Inst. Politics fellow, 1970. Mem. ABA, Assn. Trial Lawyers Am., La. Trial Lawyers Assn., Order of Coif, Phi Beta Kappa. Democrat. Roman Catholic. Administrative and regulatory, Legislative, Local government. Office: Stone Pigman et al 546 Carondelet St New Orleans LA 70130

MARCHESO, JOSEPH JAMES, lawyer; b. Bklyn., Dec. 14, 1927; s. Vito and Jennie (DeCesare) M.; m. Marcella Evelyn Charles-Williams, Dec. 21, 1972; 1 child, Joseph J. Jr. BA, NYU, 1959; JD, St. Johns U., 1959, LLD, 1972. Bar: N.Y. 1959, U.S. Ct. Appeals (2d cir.), U.S. Dist. Ct. (ea. and so. dists.) N.Y. 1965, U.S. Supreme Ct. 1973. Asst. atty. U.S. Dept. Justice, Bklyn, 1959-63, spl. pros., 1964; ptnr. Christy, Bauman & Marcheso, N.Y.C., 1964-68, Bauman & Marcheso, N.Y.C., 1968-72, Law Offices of J.J. Marcheso, N.Y.C., 1972—; bd. dirs. Imperial Sterling Ltd., N.Y.C. Bd. dirs. N.Y. Foundling Home, N.Y.C., 1983-86; mem. pres.'s circle Metropolitan Opera, 1981-86. Served with U.S. Army, 1950-53. Mem. ABA, Fed. Bar Council, Assn. of Bar of City of N.Y. Clubs: Columbus (dir. 1979-83), N.Y. Athletic. Criminal, Probate, Real property. Office: 1290 Ave of Americas New York NY 10104

MARCO, RICHARD JOSEPH, JR., lawyer; b. Cleve., Mar. 13, 1957; s. Richard Joseph Sr. and Shirley Ann (Berna) M.; m. Cynthia Dusbiber, Mar.

17, 1979; children: Nathaniel (dec.), Nicholas Joseph. BA in Acctg., Ohio Northern U., 1978; JD, Cleveland-Marshall U., 1981. Bar: Ohio 1981, U.S. Dist. Ct. (no. dist.) Ohio 1981, U.S. Ct. Appeals (6th cir.) 1981. Ptnr. Marco & Marco, Medina, Ohio, 1982—. Editor-in-chief Cleveland-Marshall U. Law Rev., 1980-81. Mem. United Way of Medina, Ohio, 1983—. Mem. Fed. Bar Assn., Ohio Bar Assn., Medina Bar Assn., Jaycees, Key Club. Democrat. Lodge: Kiwanis. Avocations: softball, basketball, golf. Federal civil litigation, State civil litigation, Personal injury. Home: 404 Hampden Ct Medina OH 44256 Office: Marco & Marco 52 Public Sq Medina OH 44256

MARCOUX, WILLIAM JOSEPH, lawyer; b. Detroit, Jan. 20, 1927; s. Lona J. and Anna (Ransom) C.; m. Kae Marie Sanborn, Aug. 23, 1952; children: Ann K., William C. B.A., U. Mich., 1949, LL.B., 1952. Bar: Mich. 1953. Practiced in Pontiac, 1953, Jackson, 1953—; pres. Marcoux, Allen, Abbott & McQuillan (P.C.), 1965—. Mem. exec. bd. Land O'Lakes council Boy Scouts Am., pres., 1965-66; bd. dirs. Jackson County United Way, pres., 1983-84. Served with USNR, 1945-46. Recipient Silver Beaver award Boy Scouts Am., 1969. Fellow Am. Coll. Trial Lawyers; mem. ABA, Mich. Bar Assn., Jackson County Bar Assn. (pres. 1979-80). Methodist (chmn. adminstrv. bd., chmn. bd. trustees 1976-78). Clubs: Rotarian (pres. 1963-64), Town, Country, Clark Lake Yacht (hon. mem.; commodore 1959). State civil litigation, General practice. Home: 1745 Malvern St Jackson MI 49203 Office: 145 S Jackson St Jackson MI 49201

MARCOVSKY, GERALD BENNETT, lawyer; b. Pitts., Apr. 27, 1944; s. Abraham S. and Rosalind Francis (Marks) M.; m. Robin Gail Gilden, Aug. 21, 1966; children: Andrew S., Stephen M. BS, Pa. State U., 1966; JD, U. Pitts., 1969. Bar: Pa. 1969. Assoc. Rothman, Gordon, Foreman, Pitts., 1969-70; with Westinghouse Electric Corp., Pitts., 1970—, sr. counsel, 1978, chief counsel, 1980. Mem. Allegheny County Bar Assn. General corporate, Contracts commercial, Consumer commercial. Office: Westinghouse Law Dept 11 Stanwix St Pittsburgh PA 15222

MARCUS, ERIC PETER, lawyer; b. Newark, Aug. 31, 1950; s. John J. and Alice M. (Zeldin) M.; m. Terry R. Toll, Oct. 9, 1983. BA, Brown U., 1972; JD, Stanford U., 1976. Bar: N.Y. 1977, N.J. 1977. Assoc. Kaye, Scholer, Fierman, Hays & Handler, N.Y.C., 1976-84, ptnr., 1985—. Contbr. articles to profl. jours. Mem. Phi Beta Kappa. Banking, Contracts commercial. Office: Kaye Scholer Fierman Hays & Handler 425 Park Ave New York NY 10022

MARCUS, GARY, lawyer, educator; b. N.Y.C., Mar. 12, 1947; s. Nathan and Shirley (Miller) M.; m. Saundra Iris Gutterman, June 27, 1971; children: Jamye Ln, Neil Scott. BS in Acctg., Hunter Coll., 1969; JD, Bklyn. Law Sch., 1973; LLM, NYU, 1984. Bar: N.Y. 1974. Assoc. N.Y.C. Transit, Bklyn., 1973-76; corp. atty. Frigitemp, N.Y.C., 1976-78; dir. legal services The Flying Tiger, Jamaica, N.Y., 1978-81; dir. contract and govt. counsel Hazeltine Corp., Greenlawn, N.Y., 1981—; adj. prof., lectr., presenter seminars and workshops Hofstra U., Hempstead, N.Y. Mem. N.Y. State Bar Assn., ABA.

MARCUS, HARRY RICHARD, lawyer; b. Tifton, Ga., May 19, 1949; s. Murray and Shirley (Kulbersh) M.; m. Bonnie Carl, Sept. 2, 1973; children: Erin Leigh, Kimberly Ilene. BBA, U. Ga., 1971; JD, Emory U., 1974. Bar: Tenn. 1974, Ga. 1975, U.S. Dist. Ct. (ea. dist.) Tenn. 1975, U.S. Dist. Ct. Ga. (no. dist.) Ga. 1975, U.S. Ct. Appeals (5th and 6th cirs.) 1975, U.S. Supreme Ct. 1979. Trust adminstr. Hamilton Nat. Bank, Chattanooga, 1974-75; ptnr. Luther, Anderson, Cleary & Cooper, Chattanooga, 1975-82; counsel, v.p. The Sherwood Corp., Spring City, Tenn., 1982-83; ptnr. Fleissner, Cooper & Marcus, Chattanooga, 1983—; instr. bus. law and fin. McKenzie Coll. , Chattanooga, 1976-78,; bus. law and acctg. Chattanooga State Coll., 1978-80, bus. law Draughtons Bus. Coll., 1986—. Bd. dirs. B'Nai Zion Congregation, Chattanooga, 1979—, Jewish Community Ctr., Chattanooga, 1984—, Tenn. Humane League, Chattanooga, 1984—. Mem. ABA, Tenn. Trial Lawyers Assn., Lookout Mountain Bar Assn., Atlanta Claims Assn., Chatanoooga Bar Assn. (editor jour. 1979-80), Chattanooga Claims Assn. (assoc.). Republican. Clubs: The Colonial (Chattanooga) (pres. 1984-85), Valley Brook Golf. (bd. dirs. 1986—). Avocations: golf, playing cards, old automobiles, family. Insurance, Workers' compensation, Personal injury. Office: Fleissner Cooper & Marcus 555 River St Suite 200 Chattanooga TN 37405

MARCUS, IRA, lawyer; b. Newark, Oct. 27, 1948; s. William and Gertrude (Katz) M. BA, SUNY, Buffalo, 1970; JD magna cum laude, New Eng. Sch. Law, 1973. Bar: Mass. 1973, N.J. 1974, Fla. 1974, U.S. Dist. Ct. (so. dist.) Fla. 1974, U.S. Dist. Ct. N.J. 1974, U.S. Dist. Ct. Mass. 1974, U.S. Ct. Appeals (1st cir.) 1974. Assoc. Arnoloy & Portnoy, Boston, 1973-77; sole practice Ft. Lauderdale, Fla., 1977—. Mem. ABA (com. on bus. torts litigation 1985—), Mass. Bar Assn., N.J. Bar Assn., Fla. Bar Assn. Democrat. Jewish. Lodge: Fraternal Order Police (Ft. Lauderdale sec. 1979—, Citizen of Yr. 1982). Avocations: sailing, tennis, walking. State civil litigation. Office: 625 NE 3d Ave Fort Lauderdale FL 33304

MARCUS, JONATHAN SETH, lawyer; b. Jersey City, Feb. 27, 1956; s. Arthur Morton and Rhoda (Bressman) M.; m. Diane Carole Joblove, June 9, 1985. BA magna cum laude, Fairleigh Dickinson U., 1978; JD, U. Fla., 1981. Law clk. to U.S. magistrate State of Fla., Miami, 1981-84; assoc. McDermott, Will & Emery and predecessor firms, Miami, 1984-87, Goldberg, Young & Borkson, P.A., Ft. Lauderdale, Fla., 1987—. Mem. exec. com. Broward County Dems., Hollywood, Fla., 1982-83. Mem. ABA, Fla. Bar Assn., Dade County Bar Assn., Anti-Defamation League. Jewish. Lodge: B'nai B'rith. Avocations: golf, tennis, racquetball, spectator sports, reading. Real property, Contracts commercial, Banking. Home: 1313 NW 122d Terr Pembroke Pines FL 33026 Office: McDermott Will & Emery 1630 N Federal Hwy Fort Lauderdale FL 33305

MARCUS, KENNETH BEN, lawyer; b. Bklyn., June 17, 1952; s. Dolphe Marcus and Jacqueline Foil; m. Gail Elizabeth Hillman, June 27, 1976; children: Joshua B., Richard D. BS, U. Pa., 1972; JD, NYU, 1975. Assoc. Golenbock & Barell, N.Y.C., 1976-78, Paskus, Gordon & Hyman, N.Y.C., 1978-79; ptnr. Carro, Spanbock, Fass, Geller, Kaster & Cuiffo, N.Y.C., 1979—. Mem. ABA, Assn. Bar of City of N.Y., Internat. Council Shopping Ctrs. Avocations: hockey, games, historical simulations. Real property. Office: Carro Spanbock Fass Geller Kaster & Cuiffo 1345 Ave of Americas New York NY 10105

MARCUS, MYRON, lawyer; b. Bklyn., Feb. 4, 1933; s. Louis and Bess M.; m. Anlee Fischler, Aug. 10, 1956; children—Lauren, Helene. B.A., Alfred U., 1954; J.D., Cornell U., 1960. Bar: N.Y. 1960, U.S. Supreme Ct. 1974. Mem. firm Rippa, Marcus & Gould, White Plains, N.Y., 1980—. Mem. adv. bd. Tile Guarantee Co., 1982; counsel, exec. sec. Apartment Owners Adv. Council of Westchester, 1960; assoc. counsel Builders Inst. of Westchester and Putnam Counties, Inc., 1960; counsel, Cooperative and Condominuim Council of Westchester County. Served with U.S. Army, 1956-58. Mem. ABA, N.Y. Bar Assn., Yonkers Lawyers Assn., Westchester County Bar Assn., White Plains Bar Assn. (dir. 1977-85, pres. 1983-84), Westchester County Assn. Real property, Contracts commercial, Banking. Office: Marcus Rippa & Gould 4 Cromwell Place PO Box 1193 White Plains NY 10601

MARCUS, NORMAN, lawyer; b. N.Y.C., Aug. 31, 1932; s. David and Evelyn (Freed) M.; m. Maria Eleanor Lenhoff, Dec. 23, 1956; children: Valerie, Nicole, Eric. BA, Columbia U., 1953; LLB, Yale U., 1957. Bar: N.Y. 1958, U.S. Dist. Ct. (so. dist.) 1960, U.S. Supreme Ct. 1964. Assoc. LaPorte & Meyers, N.Y.C., 1957-61; assoc. counsel Stanley Warner Corp., N.Y.C., 1961-63; gen. counsel N.Y.C. Planning Commn. and Dept. of City Planning, 1963-85; ptnr. Finley, Kumble, Wagner, Heine, Underberg, Manley, Myerson & Casey, N.Y.C., 1985—; adj. prof. Pratt Inst., Bklyn., 1965-85, NYU Law Sch., 1977—, Benjamin N. Cardozo Sch. Law, N.Y.C., 1983-85. Contbr. articles to profl. jours. Recipient Meritorious Achievement award Am. Planning Assn., 1986. Mem. N.Y. State Bar Assn., Assn. of Bar of City of N.Y. Avocations: antique books, swimming, drama criticism. Real property, Local government, Environment. Home: 91 Central Park W New York NY 10023 Office: Finley Kumble Wagner Heine et al 425 Park Ave New York NY 10022

MARCUS, PAUL, university dean, lawyer; b. N.Y.C., Dec. 8, 1946; s. Edward and Lillian (Rubin) M.; m. Rebecca Nimmer, Dec. 22, 1968; children: Emily, Beth. A.B., UCLA, 1968, J.D., 1971. Bar: Calif. 1971, U.S. Ct. Apls. (D.C. cir.) 1972, U.S. Dist. Ct. (cent. dist.) Calif. 1972, U.S. Ct. Apls. (7th cir.) 1976. Law clk. U.S. Ct. Apls. D.C., 1971-72; assoc. Loeb & Loeb, Los Angeles, 1972-74; prof. law U. Ill., Urbana, 1974-83; dean Coll. Law U. Ariz., Tucson, 1983—; reporter, cons. Fed. Jud. Ctr. Commn. Author: The Prosecution and Defense of Criminal Conspiracy, 1978, (with others) Criminal Procedure: Cases and Materials, 1981, 2d edit., 1986, Gilbert Law Summary, 1982, Criminal Law: Cases and Materials. Mem. accreditation com. Am. Assn. Law Schs., 1978-81; nat. reporter on privacy U.S. Congress, 1978-86. Legal education, Criminal. Home: 5930 Placita Tecolote Tucson AZ 85718 Office: U Ariz Coll Law Tucson AZ 85721

MARCUS, RICHARD LEON, lawyer; b. San Francisco, Jan. 28, 1948; s. Irving Harry and Elizabeth (McEvoy) M.; m. Andrea June Saltzman, Apr. 26, 1981; 1 child, Ruth Emily. BA, Pomona Coll., 1969; JD, U. Calif., Berkeley, 1972. Bar: Calif. 1973, U.S. Dist. Ct. (no. dist.) Calif. 1976, U.S. Dist. Ct. (cen. dist.) Calif. 1978, U.S. Ct. Appeals (9th cir.) 1981. Law clk. to judge Calif. Supreme Ct., San Francisco, 1972; assoc. Boalt Hall U. Calif., 1973-74; law clk. to judge U.S. Dist. Ct. Calif., San Francisco, 1974-75; from assoc. to ptnr. Dinkelspiel, Pelavin, Steefel & Levitt, San Francisco, 1976-81; assoc. prof. law U. Ill., Champaign, 1981-84, prof. law, 1984—; reporter com. civil motions Ill. Jud. Conf., Chgo., 1984, com. on eivdence, 1985. Research editor U. Calif. Law Rev., 1971-72; author: Complex Litigation, 1985; contbr. articles to profl. jours. Mem. ABA, Am. Law Inst., Order of Coif. Democrat. Federal civil litigation, Judicial administration, State civil litigation. Home: 612 W Oregon Urbana IL 61801 Office: U Ill Coll Law 504 E Pennsylvania Champaign IL 61820

MARCUS, STANLEY, federal judge; b. 1946. BA, CUNY, 1967; JD, Harvard U., 1971. Assoc. Botein, Hays, Sklar & Herzberg, N.Y.C., 1974-75; asst. atty. U.S. Dist. Ct. (ea. dist.) N.Y., 1975-78; spl. atty., dep. chief U.S. organized crime sect. Detroit Strike Force, 1978-79, chief U.S. organized crime sect., 1980-82; atty. U.S. Dist. Ct. (so. dist.) Fla., Miami, 1982-85, judge, 1985—. Office: US Courthouse 301 N Miami AVe Miami FL 33128-7788 *

MARCUS, STEVEN EZRA, lawyer; b. Bklyn., May 19, 1946; s. Morris Aaron and Ruth (Hillman) M.; m. Arlene Lipsky, Dec. 28, 1969; children: Myra Amy, Seth Benjamin. BA in History with honors, NYU, 1968, JD, 1971; LLM in Taxation, Emory U., 1975. Bar: N.Y. 1972, Ga. 1972, U.S. Dist. Ct. (no. dist.) Ga. 1972, U.S. Ct. Appeals (11th cir.) 1981. Assoc. Kleiner & Herman, Atlanta, 1971-72; house counsel Travelers Ins. Co., Atlanta, 1972-75; sole practice Atlanta, 1975-77, 80—; ptnr. Marcus & Gingold, Atlanta, 1977-80. Served to capt. U.S. Army, 1971-72. Mem. ABA, Assn. Trial Lawyers Am., Ga. Trial Lawyers Assn. Democrat. Jewish. Lodge: Fulton (master 1983-84). Avocations: tennis, boating. Workers' compensation. Home: 5270 Meadowcreek Dr Dunwoody GA 30338 Office: PO Box 1328 613 Church St Decatur GA 30031

MARCUS, WALTER F., JR., state justice; b. 1927. B.A., Yale U.; J.D., Tulane U. Bar: La. 1955. Now assoc. justice Supreme Ct. La. Mem. ABA. Office: Supreme Ct La 301 Loyola Ave New Orleans LA 70112 also: Supreme Ct La Baton Rouge LA 70804 *

MARDINLY, PETER ALAN, lawyer, educator; b. Phila., Apr. 30, 1952; s. Ashe John and Jane Elizabeth (Fish) M.; m. Susan D. Pulver, Sept. 6, 1981; 1 child, Alan Robert. BA, Yale U., 1974; JD, Boston U., 1977; LLM in Taxation, Temple U., 1981. Bar: Pa. 1977, Mass. 1977, U.S. Dist. Ct. (ea. dist.) Pa. 1977, U.S. Tax Ct. 1978. Ptnr. Nilon, Paul & Mardinly, Media, Pa., 1977—; adj. asst. prof. Widener U., Chester, Pa., 1981—. Bd. dirs. Darlington Fine Arts Ctr., Wawa, Pa., 1978-83, Rotary Found., Media, 1983—. Mem. ABA, Pa. State Bar Assn., Del. County Bar Assn. Republican. Avocations: sailing, classical piano. General practice, Probate, Corporate taxation. Home: 311 S Ave Media PA 19063 Office: Nilon Paul & Mardinly 320 W Front St PO Box D Media PA 19063

MARGER, EDWIN, lawyer; b. N.Y.C., Mar. 18, 1928; s. William and Fannie (Cohen) M.; m. Kaye Sanderson, Oct. 1, 1951; children—Shari Ann, Diane Elaine, Sandy Ben, m. 2d, L. Suzanne Smyth, July 5, 1968; 1 son, George Phinney; m. 3d, Mary Susan Hamel, Sept. 23, 1987. B.A., U. Miami, 1951, J.D. 1953. Bar: Fla. 1953, Ga. 1971, D.C. 1978. Sole practice, Miami Beach, Fla., 1953-67, Atlanta, 1971—; spl. asst. atty. gen. Fla., 1960-61; of counsel Richard Burns, Miami, 1967—. Tchr. Nat. Inst. Trial Advocacy. Mem. Miami Beach Social Service Commn., 1957; chmn. Fulton County Aviation Adv. Com., 1980—; trustee Forensic Scis. Found., 1984—; lt. col., a.d.c. Gov. Ga., 1971-74, 80—; col., a.d.c. Gov. La., 1977—. Served with USAAF, 1946-47. Fellow Am. Acad. Forensic Scis. (chmn. jurisprudence sect. 1977-78, sec. 1976-77, exec. com. 1983-86); mem. ABA, Fla. Bar Assn. (aerospace com. 1971-83, bd. govs. 1983-87), State Bar Ga. (chmn. sect. environ. law 1974-75, aviation law sect. 1978), Ga. Trial Lawyers Assn., Nat. Assn. Criminal Def. Lawyers, Ga. Assn. Criminal Def. Lawyers, Assn. Trial Lawyers Am., Am. Judicature Soc., Am. Arbitration Assn. (comml. panel 1978—), Inter-Am. Bar Assn. (sr.), World Assn. Lawyers (founding), Advocates Club, Lawyer-Pilots Bar Assn. (founding; v.p. 1959-62), VFW. Contbr. articles to legal jours. Criminal, Public international, Private international. Office: 6666 Powers Ferry Rd Atlanta GA 30339

MARGOLIN, ERIC MITCHELL, lawyer; b. N.Y.C., Mar. 31, 1953; s. Benjamin and Muriel (Leibowitz) M. BA, SUNY, Buffalo, 1974; JD, Georgetown U., 1977. Bar: N.Y. 1978. Staff atty. Met. Life Ins. Co., N.Y.C., 1977-79; atty. Chesebrough-Ponds Inc., Greenwich, Conn., 1979-82; sr. atty. Cheeseborough-Ponds Inc., Greenwich, Conn., 1983-85; v.p., gen. counsel, sec., Health-tex Inc., N.Y.C., 1985—; bd. trustees, mem. exec. com., investment com., appeals com. Garment and Allied Industries Fund, N.Y.C., 1986—. Mem. ABA, N.Y. State Bar Assn. Democrat. Jewish. Avocation: running, basketball. General corporate, Labor, Contracts commercial. Office: Health-tex Inc 1411 Broadway New York NY 10018

MARGOLIN, STEPHEN M., lawyer; b. Chgo., Dec. 23, 1935; s. Albert and Mae Dorothy (Kaufman) M.; m. Hedy L. Freed, Oct. 27, 1966; children—Jocelyn, Holly, Jonathan. B.S., U. Ill., 1957; J.D., John Marshall Law Sch., 1964. Bar: Ill. 1964, U.S. Dist. Ct. (no. dist.) Ill. 1964. Field agt., lectr. IRS, 1957-62; ptnr. Brainerd, Brydges and Margolin, Chgo., 1965-68; sole practice, Chgo., 1968-77; sr. ptnr. Margolin, Zeitlin & Aronson, Chgo., 1977—. Co-chmn. lawyers div. Jewish United Fund, 1982—. Served to 1st lt. U.S. Army, 1958. Mem. ABA (employee benefit com., taxation com.), Ill. State Bar Assn. (employee benefit sect.), Midwest Pension Conf., Chgo. Assn. Commerce and Industry (employee benefit sub-com. 1981—). Clubs: League Am. Wheelmen, Wheeling Wheelmen. Contbr. articles to profl. jours. Pension, profit-sharing, and employee benefits, Corporate taxation. Office: 180 N LaSalle St Suite 1910 Chicago IL 60601

MARGOLIS, EMANUEL, lawyer, educator; b. Bklyn., Mar. 18, 1926; s. Abraham and Esther (Levin) M.; m. Edith Cushing; m. 2d, Estelle Thompson, Mar. 1, 1959; children—Elizabeth Margolis-Pineo, Catherine, Abby, Joshua, Sarah. B.A., U. N.C., 1947; M.A., Harvard U., 1948, Ph.D., 1951; J.D., Yale U., 1956. Bar: Conn. 1957, U.S. Dist. Ct. Conn. 1958, U.S. Sup. Ct. 1969. Instr. dept. govt. U. Conn. 1951-53; assoc. Sllberberg & Silverstein, Ansonia, Conn. 1956-60; assoc. Wofsey Rosen Kweskin & Kuriansky Stamford, Conn. 1960-66, ptnr. 1966—; arbitrator State of Conn., 1984-85; trial referee, 1985—. adj. prof. U. Bridgeport Law Sch., 1986—. Mem. nat. bd. ACLU, 1975-79; mem. Westport (Conn.) Planning & Zoning Commn., 1971-75. Served with U.S. Army, 1944-46. Decorated Purple Heart. Mem. ABA, Conn. Bar Assn. (chmn. human rights sect. 1970-73), Nat. Assn. Criminal Def. Lawyers. Sr. editor: Conn. Bar Jour. 1971-80, 83— editor in chief 1980-83; contbr. to legal jours. Federal civil litigation, Civil rights, Criminal. Home: 72 Myrtle Ave Westport CT 06880 Office: 600 Summer St Stamford Ct 06901

MARGOLIS, JOHN GILBERT, lawyer; b. N.Y.C., Mar. 15, 1947; s. Leo M. and Sara Ethel (Frohwirth) M.; m. Gail Barbara Gelber, Mar. 4, 1973; children: Sara Felice, Jaynee Morgan. AB in Acctg., Queens Coll., 1968; JD, St. John's U., Jamaica, N.Y., 1971. Bar: N.Y. 1973, U.S. Tax Ct. 1974. Commd. 2d lt. USMC, 1968, advanced through grades to 1st lt., resigned, 1977; tax atty. Am. Express Co., N.Y., 1973-75, IBM Corp., N.Y. and Paris, 1975-83; mgr. internat. tax EG&G, Wellesley, Mass., 1983-84; assoc. Packman, Neuwahl et al, Coral Gables, Fla., 1985-86; v.p. fin. and adminstrn. Churchill Mortgage Corp., Miami, Fla., 1986—; cons., Boston, 1984-85; cons., fin. planner, Fla., 1987—. Mem. ABA, N.Y. State Bar Assn. Democrat. Jewish. Avocations: photography, cooking, wine appreciation. Corporate taxation, Personal income taxation, State and local taxation. Home: 13440 SW 92d St Miami FL 33186

MARGOLIS, JONATHAN J., lawyer; b. Boston, Aug. 7, 1945; s. Leon and Rose (Loubet) M.; children: Amanda, Hillary. AB, Brandeis U., 1967; JD, Harvard U., 1970. Bar: Mass. 1970, U.S. Dist. Ct. Mass. 1970, U.S. Tax Ct., U.S. Ct. Appeals (1st and fed. cirs.). Assoc. Lourie & Cutler, Boston, 1970-77; sole practice Boston, 1977—. Producer plays including American Buffalo, 1979, Key Exchange, 1983; contbr. articles to gen. publs. Founder Am. Premiere Stage, Boston, 1980. Mem. Mass. Bar Assn., Am. Trial Lawyers Assn., Brandeis U. Alumni Assn. (v.p., bd. dirs. 1979—). State civil litigation, Entertainment, Federal civil litigation. Office: 1 State St Boston MA 02109

MARGOLIS, LAWRENCE STANLEY, judge; b. Phila., Mar. 13, 1935; s. Reuben and Mollie (Manus) M.; m. Doris May Rosenberg, Jan. 30, 1960; children: Mary Aleta, Paul Oliver. B.S.M.E., Drexel U., 1957; J.D., George Washington U., 1961. Bar: D.C. 1963. Patent examiner U. S. Patent Office, Washington, 1957-62; patent counsel Naval Ordnance Lab., White Oak, Md., 1962-63; asst. corp. counsel D.C., 1963-66; atty. criminal div., spl. asst. U.S. atty. Dept. of Justice, Washington, 1966-68; asst. U.S. atty. for D.C. 1968-71; U.S. magistrate U.S. Dist. Ct., Washington, 1971-82; judge U.S. Claims Ct., Washington, 1982—; mem. faculty Fed. Jud. Ctr., 1973—. Editor-in-chief: The Young Lawyer, 1965-66, D.C. Bar. Jour., 1967-73; bd. editor: The Dist. Lawyer, 1978-82. Assoc. trustee Drexel U., 1983—; bd. govs. George Washington U. Alumni Assn., 1978-85. Recipient Contbn. award D.C. Jaycees, 1966; recipient Service award Boy Scouts Am., 1970, Alumni Service award George Washington U., 1976, Disting. Alumni Achievement award, 1985. Fellow Inst. Jud. Adminstrn., Am. Bar Found.; mem. D.C. Jud. Conf., ABA (award for disting. service as chmn. Jud. Adminstrn. div. 1981), Bar Assn. D.C. (dir. 1970-72 award for contbn., young lawyers sect. award for contbns. 1983), Fed. Bar Assn., George Washington U. Nat Law Assn. (pres. D.C. chpt. 1974-76, pres. 1983-84), Nat. Conf. Spl. Ct. Judges (award for disting. service as chmn. 1978). Club: Nat. Lawyers (Washington). Lodge: Rotary (dir. 1984—, Rotarian of Yr. 1984, v.p. 1987—). Office: US Claims Ct 717 Madison Pl NW Suite 703 Washington DC 20005

MARGULIES, MARTIN B., legal educator, lawyer; b. N.Y.C., Oct. 6, 1940; s. Max N. and Mae (Cohen) M.; m. Beth Ellen Zeldes, July 26, 1981. A.B., Columbia Coll., 1961; LL.B., Harvard U., 1964; LL.M., NYU, 1966. Bar: N.D. 1968, N.Y. 1974, Mass. 1977, U.S. Dist. Ct. Mass. 1977, Conn. 1984, U.S. Ct. Appeals (2d cir.) 1984. Asst. prof. law U. N.D., Grand Forks, 1966-69; editor-in-chief Columbia Coll. Today, Columbia U., N.Y.C., 1969-71; assoc. editor Parade Mag., N.Y.C., 1971-72; assoc. prof. law Western New Eng. Law Sch., Springfield, Mass., 1973-76; Bernard Hersher prof. law U. Bridgeport, Conn., 1977—. Author: The Early Life of Sean O'Casey, 1970. Contbr. articles to profl. jours. Cooperating atty. Conn. Civil Liberties Union, Hartford, 1979—, bd. dirs., 1982—; bd. dirs. Conn. Attys. for Progressive Legislation, New Haven, 1982—; chmn. bd. dirs. Fairfield County Civil Liberties Union, 1982—, Hampden County Civil Liberties Union, 1976-78; bd. dirs. Civil Liberties Union Mass., Boston, 1975-78, Greater Springfield Urban League, 1976-78, Conn. Civil Liberties Union, 1982—. Recipient Media award N.Y. State Bar Assn., 1972; Gavel award ABA, 1973. Mem. Mass. Bar Assn., N.Y. State Bar Assn. Jewish. Civil rights, Legal education. Home: 79 High Rock Rd Sandy Hook CT 06482 Office: Univ Bridgeport Law Sch 303 University Ave Bridgeport CT 06601

MARIANES, WILLIAM BYRON, lawyer; b. East Chicago, Ind., Apr. 30, 1955; s. William Charles and Bess (Vambakas) M.; m. Audrey Jean May, Aug. 22, 1981; 1 child, Alexis Elaine. BA, Northwestern U., 1977; MBA, Emory U., 1981, JD, 1981. Bar: Ga. 1981, U.S. Dist. Ct. (no. dist.) Ga., 1981, U.S. Ct. Appeals (5th and 11th cir.) 1981. Assoc. Troutman, Sanders, Lockerman & Ashmore, Atlanta, 1981—; bd. advs. Atlanta Legal Aid Soc., 1987. Author and Editor: High Tech Legal Guide, 1985. Loaned exec. United Way of Atlanta, 1982, bd. dirs. 1986—; bd. dirs. United Way Loaned Execs. Assn., 1983—; fund raiser Atlanta Arts Alliance, 1985; mem. Robert Woodruff Scholarship Selection Com., Atlanta, 1985; bd. dirs. Greek Orthodox Cathedral of the Annunciation, also asst. treas., 1986—. Recipient Loaned Exec. of Yr. award United Way of Atlanta, 1982, Outstanding Service award, United Way of Atlanta, 1986, Service and Leadership award, Emory U. Sch. Bus. Adminstrn., 1981, . Mem. ABA, Ga. Bar Assn., Atlanta Bar Assn., Order of Am. Hellenic Ednl. Progressive Assn. (sec. 1983-85, v.p. 1985-86, pres. 1986—), Order of Coif. Avocations: music, athletics. General corporate, Computer, Trademark and copyright. Home: 1534 Idlehour Dr Tucker GA 30084 Office: Troutman Sanders et al One Ravinia Dr Suite 1600 Atlanta GA 30346

MARIANI, MICHAEL MATTHEW, lawyer; b. West Pittston, Pa., Sept. 25, 1950; s. Stephen Francis and Tulia Felicia (DelCorso) M.; m. Patricia Mary Leptak, June 26, 1976; children: Kathryn Elizabeth, Michael Joseph. BS with honors, Wilkes Coll., 1972; JD, St. John's U., Jamaica, N.Y., 1975; LLM, NYU, 1980. Bar: N.Y. 1976, U.S. Dist. Ct. (so. and ea. dists.) N.Y. 1976, U.S. Tax Ct. 1980. Law sec. to presiding judge Surrogate's Ct., New City, N.Y., 1976-80; assoc. Law offices of Edward S. Schlesinger P.C., N.Y.C., 1981—; instr. paralegal studies program Queens Coll., CUNY, Flushing, N.Y., 1984—. Author: (with Edward S. Schlesinger) New York Probate, 1986; contbr. articles to profl. jours. Trustee Cath. Charities, Diocese of Bklyn., 1981—, treas. 1985—. Mem. ABA (real property, probate and trust law sects.), N.Y. State Bar Assn. (trusts and estates sects.). Democrat. Probate, Estate taxation. Home: 53-32 215th St Bayside NY 11364 Office: Law offices of Edward S Schlesinger PC 630 Third Ave New York NY 10017

MARICK, MICHAEL MIRON, lawyer; b. Chgo., Nov. 20, 1957; s. Miron Michael and Geraldyne Marilyn (Lid) M.; m. Lisa Amy Gelman, May 17, 1986; B.A., Denison U., 1979; J.D., Ill. Inst. Tech./Chgo.-Kent Coll. Law, 1982. Bar: Ill. 1982, U.S. Dist. Ct. (no. dist.) Ill. 1982, Fla. 1983. Mem. firm Hinshaw, Culbertson, Moelmann, Hoban & Fuller, Chgo., 1982-85; mem. Phelan, Pope & John, Chgo., 1985—; instr. Ill. Inst. Tech./Chgo.-Kent Coll. Law, 1983-84, 87; comml. arbitrator Am. Arbitration Assn., Chgo., 1983—. Treas., exec. com. 42d Ward Rep. Orgn., 1984—. Econs. fellow Denison U., Granville, Ohio, 1978; Govs. fellow State of Ill., Springfield, 1978. Mem. ABA (exec. com., com. on legis. action young lawyers div. 1983-84), Ill. Bar Assn., Fla. Bar Assn., Chgo. Bar Assn., Omicron Delta Upsilon, Pi Sigma Alpha, Alpha Tau Omega. Republican. Presbyterian. Clubs: East Bank, Trial Lawyers. Contbr. articles on ins. law and litigation to profl. jours.; mem. writing staff Ill. Inst. Tech./Chgo.-Kent Law Rev., 1980-82. Federal civil litigation, State civil litigation, Insurance. Home: 260 E Chestnut Apt 3604 Chicago IL 60611 Office: Phelan Pope & John Ltd 180 N Wacker Dr Chicago IL 60606

MARIN, BAYARD, lawyer, legal educator; b. Newark, Del., June 2, 1941; s. Arnold and Sophia (Pollock) M.; m. Sonia Kathryn Sullivan, Feb. 24, 1968; children: Anne-Melanie, William. BA, U. Del., 1963; JD, Syracuse U., 1966; PhD, U. London, Eng., 1980. Bar: D.C. 1967, Del. 1973. Atty. E.I. DuPont deNemours and Co., Wilmington, Del., 1975-77; ptnr. Marin & Hudson, Wilmington, 1979—; instr. legal assistance program U. Del. Author: Inside Justice, 1983. Mem. Gov.'s Adv. Council on Corrections, Del., 1979-82; candidate U.S. Congress, 1982. Served to capt. U.S. Army, 1968-72. Mem. ABA, Del. Bar Assn., Assn. Trial Lawyers Am., Del. Trial Lawyers Assn., ACLU (bd. dirs. 1984—). Club: Wilmington T'affic. Personal injury, Federal civil litigation, State civil litigation. Home: 7 Willing Way Westhaven Wilmington DE 19807 Office: Marin & Hudson 521 West St Wilmington DE 19801

MARIN, PAUL MARTIN, lawyer; b. Marquette, Mich., July 18, 1951; s. Martin J. and Luella L. (Latola) M.; m. Mary Beth Little, Oct. 30, 1976; 1 child, Matthew Paul. BA, Mich. State U., 1973; JD, Wayne State U., 1976. Bar: Mich. 1976, U.S. Dist. Ct. (we. dist.) Mich. 1976. Assoc. Jason & Jason, Marquette, 1976-79; sole practice Marquette, 1979-84; ptnr. McDonald, Collins & Marin, Marquette, 1984-87, McDonald & Marin, Marquette, 1987—. Atty. ACLU, Marquette, 1978—; mem. Bd. of Zoning Appeals, Marquette City, 1980—; chairperson ARC, Marquette County, 1983-84. Mem. ABA, Mich. Bar Assn. (rep. state assembly 1983—), Fed. Bar Assn., Assn. Trial Lawyers Am., Mich. Trial Lawyers Assn. Lutheran. General practice, Family and matrimonial, Insurance. Office: McDonald & Marin 316 N Front Marquette MI 49855

MARINACCIO, CHARLES LINDBERGH, lawyer; b. Stratford, Conn., Dec. 10, 1933; m. Meta Lupin; children: Louisa, Heidi. BA, U. Conn., 1957; JD with honors, George Washington U., 1962. Bar: Conn. 1962, D.C. 1982. Trial lawyer U.S. Dept. Justice, Washington, 1963-69; advisor supervisory and regulation div. Fed. Res. Bd., Washington, 1969-73; dir., exec. sec. law enforcement asstistance adminstrn. U.S. Dept. Justice, Washington, 1973-75; gen. counsel banking housing and urban affairs com. U.S. Senate, Washington, 1975-84; commr. SEC, Washington, 1984-85; ptnr. Kelley, Drye & Warren, Washington, 1985—. Mem. Fed. Bar Assn. (banking law com.), Nat. Assn. Corp. Dirs. Banking, Securities. Home: 4911 Massachusetts Washington DC 20016 Office: Kelley Drye & Warren 1330 Connecticut Ave NW Washington DC 20036

MARINIS, THOMAS PAUL, JR., lawyer; b. Jacksonville, Tex., May 31, 1943; s. Thomas Paul and Betty Sue (Garner) M.; m. Lucinda Cruse, June 25, 1969; children—Courtney, Kathryn, Megan. B.A., Yale U., 1965; LL.B., U. Tex., 1968. Bar: Tex. Assoc. Vinson & Elkins, Houston, 1969-76, ptnr., 1977—. Served with USAR, 1968-74. Fellow Tex. Bar Found; mem. ABA (sec. taxation sect. 1984-85), Tex. Bar Assn. (chmn. taxation sect. 1986-87). Clubs: Houston Country, Houston Ctr., Coronado. Corporate taxation, Personal income taxation. Office: 3418 First City Tower 1001 Fannin Houston TX 77002

MARINSTEIN, ELLIOTT F., lawyer; b. N.Y.C., June 15, 1928; s. Joseph and Rose (Zessman) M.; m. Leita A. Adeson, Dec. 1, 1957; children: Edward Ross, Jay Drew. BA, Bklyn. Coll., 1950; JD, NYU, 1953. Bar: N.Y. 1955, U.S. Dist. Ct. (no. dist.) N.Y. 1956, U.S. Supreme Ct. 1970, U.S. Dist. Ct. (so. and ea. dists.) N.Y. 1986. Sole practice Troy, N.Y., 1956—; asst. dist. atty. County of Rensselaer, Troy, 1965-67; ptnr. Marinstein & Marinstein, Troy; counsel charter rev. com. City of Troy, 1972-73. Committeeman Rensselaer County Dem. Com., Troy, 1960-65; del. jud. convention Dem. State Com., Troy, 1978-81; chmn. housing bd. rev. City of Troy, 1979—. Served to cpl. U.S. Army, 1953-55. Mem. ABA (corp., banking and bus. law sect.,), N.Y. State Bar Assn. (count courts com., lectr. 1978-83), Rensselaer County Bar Assn. (chmn. grievance com. 1972-75, pres. 1979-80), N.Y. State Dist. Attys. Assn., Comml. Law League Am. (practice com.). Club: Tri City Raquet (Latham, N.Y.). Lodges: Knights of Pythias (past chancellor), Masons. Avocation: tennis. Consumer commercial, Bankruptcy, Probate. Home: 2354 Burdett Ave Troy NY 12180 Office: Marinstein & Marinstein 251 River St Troy NY 12181

MARK, DENIS HUGH, lawyer; b. N.Y.C., May 27, 1951; s. Murray Samuel and Roslyn (Strauchler) M.; m. Laurel Frances Lester, May 15, 1983. BS, Tufts U., 1972; postgrad., Washington U., St. Louis, 1975-76; JD, U. Colo., 1978. Bar: Colo. 1978, U.S. Dist. Ct. Colo. 1978, U.S. Ct. Appeals (10th cir.) 1980, U.S. Tax Ct. 1983, U.S. Ct. Appeals (9th and 6th cirs.) 1985, U.S. Supreme Ct. 1985. Law clk. to presiding judge Colo. Ct. Appeals, Denver, 1978-79; assoc. Wagner, D'Onofrio, Waller & Stouffer, Denver, 1979-80; assoc. Wagner & Waller, P.C., Englewood, Colo., 1980-83, ptnr., 1983-84; ptnr. Waller, Mark & Allen, P.C., Denver, 1985—. Editor: U. Colo. Law Rev., 1978. Del. Colo. State Dem. Assembly, Denver, 1980, 86. Mem. ABA, Colo. Bar Assn., Denver Bar Assn., Nat. Assn. Criminal Def. Lawyers, Assn. Trial Lawyers Am., Colo. Trial Lawyers Assn. (bd. dirs. 1984—), Order of Coif. Jewish. Avocation: skiing. Federal civil litigation, State civil litigation, Criminal. Home: 6257 E Mineral Pl Englewood CO 80112 Office: Waller Mark & Allen PC 2800 Arco Tower 707 17th St Denver CO 80202

MARK, HENRY ALLEN, lawyer; b. Bklyn., May 16, 1909; s. Henry Adam and Mary Clyde (McCarroll) M.; m. Isobel Ross Arnold, June 26, 1940; B.A., Williams Coll., 1932; J.D., Cornell U., 1935. Bars: N.Y. 1936, Conn. 1981, U.S. Dist. Ct. (so. dist.) N.Y. 1943. Assoc. firm Allin & Tucker, N.Y.C., 1935-40; mng. atty. Indemnity Ins. Co. of N.Am., N.Y.C., 1940-43; assoc. firm Mudge, Stern, Williams & Tucker, N.Y.C., 1943-50, Cadwalder, Wickersham & Taft, N.Y.C., 1950-53; ptnr. Cadwalader, Wickersham & Taft, 1953-74, of counsel, 1974—; lectr. Practicing Law Inst., N.Y.C., 1955-68. Mem. adv. com. zoning Village of Garden City (N.Y.), 1952-54, planning commn., 1957-59, zoning bd. appeals, 1959-61, trustee, 1961-65, mayor, 1965-67; chmn. planning commn. Town of Washington (Conn.), 1980-84. Mem. ABA, N.Y. Bar Assn., Assn. Bar City of N.Y., Conn. Bar Assn., Litchfield County Bar Assn., Cornell Law Assn. (pres. 1971-73), St. Andrew's Soc., Phi Beta Kappa. Republican. Congregationalist. Lodge: Masons. Landlord-tenant, Real property. Address: 10 Millay Ct Litchfield CT 06759

MARK, JONATHAN I., lawyer; b. N.Y.C., Oct. 18, 1947; s. Sandor and Ruth (Weiss) M.; m. B. Kathleen Munguia, May 25, 1986. AB, Dartmouth Coll., 1969; JD, Columbia U., 1974. Bar: N.Y., Calif., U.S. Dist. Ct. (so. and ea. dists.) N.Y., U.S. Ct. Appeals (2d cir.). Law clk. to presiding justice U.S. Dist. Ct. (so. dist.) N.Y., N.Y.C., 1974-75; assoc. Cahill Gordon & Reindel, N.Y.C., 1975-82; ptnr. Cahill, Gordon & Reindel, N.Y.C., 1982—. General corporate, Securities. Office: Cahill Gordon & Reindel 80 Pine St New York NY 10005

MARK, RICHARD STEVE, educator, consultant; b. Denver, June 19, 1948; s. Stephen Frank and Hilda (Cavarra) M.; m. Barbara Lester, June 1, 1974. B.S. in Mech. Engring., U. Colo., 1971, J.D., 1974; LL.M. in Taxation, U. Denver, 1977. Bar: Colo. 1974, Tex. 1978, U.S. Dist. Ct. Colo. 1974. Sole practice, Denver, 1974-77; trust officer United Bank Denver, 1977-79; tax cons. Atlantic Richfield, Dallas, 1979-80; prof. U. Tex., Arlington, 1980—; dir. Quantum Resources Corp., Denver, 1979-82. Author: Current Updates in Oil Tax, 1984, Royalty Trusts, 1984; contbg. author: Handbook of Oil and Gas Accounting, 1985. Contbr. articles to profl. jours. Mem. Council Petroleum Accts. (chmn. edn. com. Ft. Worth 1984), ABA (natural resources com. 1982-84), Tex. Bar Assn., Colo. Bar Assn., Am. Inst. C.P.A.s (edn. com. 1982-84), Ind. Producers Assn. Am., Omicron Delta Kappa, Tau Beta Pi. Corporate taxation, Personal income taxation, Pension, profit-sharing, and employee benefits. Home and Office: 125 Hunter's Hill Ct Argyle TX 76226

MARKE, JULIUS JAY, educator, law librarian; b. N.Y.C., Jan. 12, 1913; s. Isidore and Anna (Taylor) M.; m. Sylvia Bolotin, Dec. 15, 1946; 1 dau., Elisa Hope. B.S., CCNY, 1934; LL.B., NYU, 1937; B.S. in L.S., Columbia U., 1942. Bar: N.Y. 1938. Reference asst. N.Y. Pub. Library, 1937-42; pvt. practice N.Y.C., 1939-41; prof. law, law librarian NYU, 1949-83, prof. law emeritus, 1983—, interim dean of libraries, 1975-77; prof., dir. law library St. John's U. Sch. Law, 1983—; lectr. Columbia Sch. Library Service, 1962-78, adj. prof., 1978-85; Cons. Orientation Program Am. Law, 1965-68, Found. Overseas Law Libraries Am. Law, 1968-79 ; cons. copyright Ford Found.; cons. to law libraries, others. Author: Vignettes of Legal History, 1965, 2d Series, 1977, Copyright and Intellectual Property, 1967, (with R. Sloane) Legal Research and Law Library Management, 1982, supplement, 1986; editor: Modern Legal Forms, 1953, The Holmes Reader, 1955, The Docket Series, 1955—, Bender's Legal Business Forms, 4 vols, 1962; compiler, editor: A Catalogue of the Law Collection at NYU with Selected Annotations, 1953, Dean's List of Recommended Reading for Pre-Law and Law Students, 1958, 2d edit., 1984; co-editor, contbr.: Internat. Seminar on Constl. Rev, 1963, Coordinated Law Research, 1977; editor: Holmes Reader, rev. edit, 1964; co-editor: Commerical Law Information Sources, 1971; chmn. editorial bd.: Oceana Group, 1977—; chmn. editorial adv. bd.: Index to Legal Periodicals, 1978—. Contbr. articles to profl. jours. Mem. publs. council N.Y. U., 1964-80. Served to sgt. AUS, 1943-45. Decorated Bronze Star. Mem. Am. Assn. Law Libraries (pres. 1962-63, Disting. Service award 1986), Am. Bar Assn., Assn. Am. Law Schs., Council of Nat. Library Assns. (exec. bd., v.p. 1959, 60), Law Library Assn. Greater N.Y. (pres. 1949, 50, chmn. joint com. on library edn. 1950-52, 60-61), NYU Law Alumni Assn. (Judge Edward Weinfeld award 1987), Columbia Sch. Library Service Alumni Assn. (pres. 1973-75), Order of Coif (pres. NYU Law Sch. br. 1970-83), Phi Delta Phi, Field Inn 1966—). Club: N.Y. University Faculty (pres. 1965-66). Librarianship, Legal history, Trademark and copyright. Home: 4 Peter Cooper Rd #8F New York NY 10010

MARKEL, ROBERT EDWIN, lawyer; b. Denver, Feb. 23, 1957; s. John Edward and Mary Ellen (Seep) M. BA, Colo. Coll., 1979; JD, U. Colo., 1982. Bar: Colo. 1982, U.S. Dist. Ct. Colo. 1982. Assoc. Scheid & Horlbeck P.C., Denver, 1982-85, Hellerstein, Hellerstein & Shore P.C., Denver, 1985—. Mem. ABA, Colo. Bar Assn. (bankruptcy subcom.), Phi Beta Kappa. Bankruptcy, Consumer commercial. Home: 555 E 10th Ave Suite 216 Denver CO 80203 Office: Hellerstein Hellerstein & Shore PC 1139 Delaware Denver CO 80204

MARKEL, SHELDON MARTIN, lawyer; b. Bklyn., Jan. 22, 1929; s. Murray and Rebecca (Pickelsky) M.; m. Barbara Ellen Ladis, Aug. 7, 1960; children: Douglas C., Ann F., Karen S. BS, Bklyn, Coll., 1951; JD, Cornell U., 1958. BAr: N.Y. 1958, U.S. Dist. Ct. (we. dist.) N.Y. 1959, U.S. Supreme Ct. 1964. Sole practice Buffalo, 1959-63, 66-82; sr. asst. dist. atty. Erie County, Buffalo, 1963-66; sr. ptnr. Sheldon M. Markel & Assocs. P.C., Buffalo and Rochester, N.Y., 1982—; asst. to counsel N.Y. State Senate Minority Leader, Albany, 1965. V.p. N.Y. State Amateur Hockey Assn., 1985-86, pres. 1986—. Served to comdr. USN, 1951-55, with res., 1955-78. Fellow Am. Acad. Matrimonial Lawyers; mem. N.Y. State Bar Assn., Erie County Bar Assn., Assn. Trial Lawyers Am., N.Y. State Trial Lawyers Assn., Am. Soc. Law and Medicine, Nat. Bd. Trial Advocacy (cert.). State civil litigation, Personal injury, Family and matrimonial. Office: Sheldon M Markel & Assocs 888 Statler Towers Buffalo NY 14202

MARKER, MARC LINTHACUM, lawyer, leasing company executive; b. Los Angeles, July 19, 1941; s. Clifford Harry and Voris (Linthacum) M.; m. Sandra Yocom, Aug. 29, 1965; children—Victor, Gwendolyn. B.A. in Econs. and Geography, U. Calif.-Riverside, 1964; J.D., U. So. Calif., 1967. Bar: Calif. 1971, U.S. Dist. Ct. (cen. dist.) Calif. 1971, U.S. Tax Ct. 1972, U.S. Dist. Ct. (ea. dist.) Calif. 1977, U.S. Ct. Appeals (D.C. cir.) 1977, U.S. Ct. Appeals (9th cir.) 1978, U.S. Dist. Ct. (no. and so. dists.) Calif. 1984. Asst. v.p., asst. sec. Security Pacific Nat. Bank, Los Angeles, 1970-73; sr. v.p., chief counsel, sec. Security Pacific Leasing Corp., San Francisco, 1973—; pres. Security Pacific Leasing Services Corp., San Francisco, 1977-85, dir., 1977—; bd. dirs., sec. Voris, Inc., 1973-86; bd. dirs. Refiners Petroleum Corp., 1977-81, Security Pacific Leasing Singapore Ptc Ltd., 1983-85; lectr. in field. Served to comdr. USCGR. Mem. ABA, Calif. Bar Assn., San Francisco Bar Assn., Am. Assn. Equipment Lessors. Republican. Lutheran. Club: University (Los Angeles). Contracts commercial, Banking. Office: Security Pacific Leasing Corp 4 Embarcadero Ctr #1200 San Francisco CA 94111

MARKEWICH, ROBERT, lawyer; b. N.Y.C., Apr. 20, 1919; s. Samuel and Ida (Kaelis) M.; m. Iris Alexandra Grass, Feb. 20, 1949; children: Deborah, Judith, Ida, Jeremiah, Eve. AB, Harvard U., 1940; LLB, Columbia U., 1946. Bar: N.Y. 1947, U.S. Dist. Ct. (so. and ea. dists.) N.Y. 1950, U.S. Ct. Appeals (2d cir.) 1950, U.S. Supreme Ct. 1953. Ptnr. Markewich, Friedman and Markewich, N.Y.C., 1947—. Mem. ABA, N.Y. State Bar Assn., Bar Assn. of City of N.Y., N.Y. County Lawyers Assn., Fed. Bar Council. Democrat. Jewish. Club: Harvard (N.Y.C.). Lodge: Masons. Federal civil litigation, State civil litigation, Entertainment.

MARKEY, CHRISTIAN EDWARD, JR., superior court judge; b. Montebello, Calif., Oct. 27, 1929; s. Christian Edward and Mercy Adrienne (Morrison) M.; m. Sharri Lee Rodecker, June 27, 1953; children—Michelle, Melinda, Christian, Jill Marie. A.B., U. Calif.-Berkeley, 1951; J.D., UCLA, 1958. Bar: Calif. 1959, U.S. Dist. Ct. (cen. dist.) Calif. 1959, U.S. Supreme Ct. 1968. Trial lawyer, assoc. firm McClosky, Mitchell & Markey, Los Angeles, 1959-60; ptnr. Olson & Markey, Los Angeles, 1960-63, Munger, Tolles, Hills & Rickershauser, Los Angeles, 1964-74; judge Superior Ct., Los Angeles, 1974—; lectr. law, adj. prof. law U. So. Calif., 1978-79, Whittier Coll., 1979-83, Loyola Law Sch., 1983—. Chmn. bd. So. Calif. Ctr. for Law in Pub. Interest, 1971-74; mem., bd. regents U. Calif., 1969-72. Served to capt. USMC, 1951-54. Recipient Berkeley citation, 1972; named Alumnus of Yr., UCLA Sch. Law, 1972. Fellow Am. Bar Found., Berkeley Fellows; mem. Los Angeles County Bar Assn., ABA, Calif. Judges Assn. Democrat. Episcopalian. Club: Chancery. Author: California Family Law, Practice and Procedure, 7 vols. Contbr. articles to profl. jours. State civil litigation, Family and matrimonial. Office: Superior Ct 111 N Hill St Los Angeles CA 90012

MARKEY, E. LOWELL, lawyer; b. York, Pa., Mar. 22, 1946; s. Ernest L. and Carmen Lenore (Wilson) M.; m. Teryl Davis; children: Michelle Brett, Nathan Davis. BA, Lycoming Coll., 1968; MS, U. Louisville, 1971; JD, West Va. U., 1981. Bar: W.Va. 1981, U.S. Dist. Ct. (no. dist.) W.Va. 1981. Dir. pub. relations Alice Lloyd Coll., Pippa Passes, Ky., 1969-71; assoc. dean Potomac State Coll., Keyser, W.Va., 1971-78; law clk. to presiding justice U.S. Dist. Ct., Elkins, W.Va., 1981-84, clk., 1984-86; assoc. Rice, Douglas & Shingleton, Martinsburg, W.Va., 1986—. V.p. W.Va. Highlands Conservancy, 1976-80; bd. dirs. Friends of Library, Elkins, 1981-83; adminstrv. bd. dirs. 1st United Meth. Ch., Elkins, 1982—. Mem. ABA, Order of Coif. Democrat. Avocations: automobiles, hiking, cooking. Administrative and regulatory, General practice, Bankruptcy. Home: 109 Fulks Terr Martinsburg WV 25401 Office: Rice Douglas & Shingleton PO Drawer 1419 Martinsburg WV 25401

MARKEY, HOWARD THOMAS, judge; b. Chgo., Nov. 10, 1920; s. Thomas Joseph and Vera Marie (Dryden) M.; m. Elizabeth Catherine Pelletier, Mar. 17, 1942; children: Jeffrey, Christopher, Thomas (dec.), Mary Frances. J.D. cum laude, Loyola U., Chgo., 1949; M. Patent Law, John Marshall Law Sch., 1950; LL.D., N.Y. Law Sch., 1977. Bar: Ill. 1950. Practice law Chgo., 1950-72; partner Parker & Carter, 1949-50, then Parker, Markey & Plyer, 1952-72; chief judge U.S. Ct. Fed. Cir. Appeals, Washington, 1972—; lectr. on jets, rockets, missiles and space, 1946-50, on U.S. Constn., 1950—; instr. patent law Loyola U., 1970-71. Bd. advisers Loyola U. Sch. Law, 1978—. Served to lt. col. USAAF, 1941-46; to lt. col. USAF, 1950-52; pioneer jet test pilot 1944-46; maj. gen. Res. Decorated Legion of Merit, D.F.C., Soldier's medal, Air medal, Bronze Star (U.S.); Mil. Merit Ulchi medal (Korea); Recipient George Washington Honor medal Freedoms Found., 1964. Mem. ABA, Am. Bar Found., Fed. Bar Assn., Am. Judicature Soc., Am. Legion (post comdr.), Air Force Assn. (pres. 1960-61, chmn. 1961-62). Republican. Office: US Ct Appeals 717 Madison Pl NW Washington DC 20439 *

MARKEY, JAMES KEVIN, lawyer; b. Springfield, Ill., July 15, 1956; s. James Owen and Marjorie Jean (Diesness) M. BBA with highest honors, U. Notre Dame, 1977; JD cum laude, U. Mich., 1980; MBA, U. Chgo., 1987. Bar: Ill. 1980; CPA, Ill. Assoc. Chapman & Cutler, Chgo., 1980-81; atty. Quaker Oats Co., Chgo., 1981-84; corp. counsel Travenol Labs., Inc., Deerfield, Ill., 1984—. Mem. ABA, Ill. Bar Assn., Beta Alpha Psi, Beta Gamma Sigma. Avocations: racquetball, swimming, bridge. General corporate, Securities, Computer. Home: 1405 E Central Arlington Heights IL 60005 Office: Travenol Labs Inc 1 Baxter Pkwy Deerfield IL 60015

MARKEY, ROBERT GUY, lawyer; b. Cleve., Feb. 25, 1939; s. Nate and Rhoda (Gross) M.; divorced;children—Robert Jr., Randolph. A.B., Brown U., 1961; J.D., Case Western Reserve, 1964. Bar: Ohio 1964. Assoc., ptnr. Kahn and Kleinman, Cleve., 1964-75; ptnr. Arter & Hadden, Cleve., 1975-83, Baker & Hostetler, Cleve., 1983—; dir., sec. Blue Coral, Inc., Cleve.; dir. Matrix Essentials, Inc., Simoniz Internat. Ltd., London, Fox & Assocs., Inc., Cleve., McKay Chem. Co., Los Angeles. Chmn. attys. div. United Way Services, Cleve., 1978; trustee Fedn. Community Planning, Cleve., 1980—. Mem. ABA, Bar Assn. Greater Cleve. (chmn. securities law com. 1974-75), Ohio State Bar Assn. Republican. Jewish. Clubs: Union (Cleve.); Chagrin Valley Hunt (Gates Mills, Ohio). General corporate, Securities. Office: Baker & Hostetler 3200 Nat City Ctr Cleveland OH 44114

MARKHAM, CHARLES BUCHANAN, lawyer; b. Durham, N.C., Sept. 15, 1926; s. Charles Blackwell and Sadie Helen (Hackney) M. A.B., Duke U., Durham, N.C., 1945; postgrad., U. N.C. Law Sch., Chapel Hill, 1945-46; LL.B., George Washington U., Washington, 1951. Bar: D.C. 1951, N.Y. 1961, N.C. 1980, U.S. Ct. Appeals (2d cir.) 1962, U.S. Ct. Appeals (D.C. cir.) 1955, U.S. Supreme Ct. 1964. Reporter Durham Sun, N.C., 1945; asst. state editor, editorial writer Charlotte News, N.C., 1947-48; dir. publicity and research Young Democratic Clubs Am., Washington, 1948-49, exec. sec., 1949-50; polit. analyst Dem. Senatorial Campaign Com., Washington, 1950-51; spl. atty. IRS, Washington and N.Y.C., 1952-60; assoc. Battle, Fowler, Stokes and Kheel, N.Y.C., 1960-65; dir. research U.S. Equal Employment Opportunity Commn., Washington, 1965-68; dep. asst. sec. U.S. Dept. Housing and Urban Devel., Washington, 1969-72; asst. dean Rutgers U. Law Sch., Newark, 1974-76; assoc. prof. law N.C. Central U., Durham, 1976-81, prof. law, 1981-83; mayor City of Durham, N.C., 1981-85; ptnr. Markham and Wickham, Durham, 1984-86; Trustee Hist. Preservation Soc. Durham, 1982-86; bd. dirs. Stagville Ctr., 1984-86; mem. Gov's Crime Commn., Raleigh, 1985; dep. commr. N.C. Indsl. Commn., Raleigh, 1986—. Editor: Jobs, Men and Machines: The Problems of Automation, 1964. Mem. ABA, Durham County Bar Assn., Greater Durham C. of C. (bd. dirs. 1982-86), Phi Beta Kappa, Omicron Delta Kappa, Phi Delta Theta. Republican. Episcopalian. Club: Chapel Hill Country. Administrative and regulatory, Personal injury, Workers' compensation. Home: 204 N Dillard St Durham NC 27701 Office: NC Indsl Commn Dobbs Bldg Raleigh NC 27611

MARKHAM, JERRY WAYNE, lawyer; b. Louisville, Aug. 20, 1948; s. John and Marie (Deveny) M.; m. Marcia Harris; children: Sean, Mollie. BS, Western Ky. U., 1969; JD, U. Ky., 1971; LLM, Georgetown U., 1974. Bar: Ky. 1972, D.C. 1973, Ill. 1974, N.Y. 1982. Atty. SEC, Washington, 1972-74; sec., counsel Chgo. Bd. Options Exchange, 1974-75; chief counsel Commodity Futures Trading Commn., Washington, 1975-78; ptnr. Rogers & Wells, Washington, 1978—; adj. prof. Georgetown U., Washington; arbitrator NASD Inc. Contbr. articles to profl. jours. Mem. Carter-Mondale Legal Adv. Com., 1979-80. Mem. ABA, Ky. Bar Assn., Futures Industry Assn. Securities, Federal civil litigation, Commodities. Office: Rogers & Wells 1737 H St NW Washington DC 20006

MARKHAM, ROSEMARY, lawyer; b. Pitts., June 12, 1946; d. Chester James and Elizabeth Helen (Seger) Markham; m. Wayne Joseph Pfrimmer, Sept. 11, 1965 (div. 1975); 1 dau., Adriene. B.A., U. Pitts., 1968; J.D., Duquesne U., 1978. Bar: Pa. 1978; adminstrv. asst. West Pa. Conservancy, Pitts., 1969-70; law clk. Girman & DelSole, 1975-76, Watzman & DeAngelis, 1976-78; serious injury rep. Travelors Ins., 1978-79; assoc. Manifesto & Doherty, 1979-81; individual practice law, 1981—. Mem. ABA, Assn. Trial Lawyers Am., Pa. Bar Assn., Pa. Trial Lawyers Assn., Allegheny County Bar Assn. Democrat. Roman Catholic. Club: Rivers. Family and matrimonial, Real property. Office: 320 Allegheny Bldg 429 Forbes Ave Pittsburgh PA 15219

MARKMAN, STEPHEN W., lawyer; b. Detroit, June 4, 1949; s. Julius and Pauline Markman; m. Mary Kathleen Sites, Aug. 25, 1974. B.A., Duke U., 1971; postgrad., U. Va., 1972; J.D., U. Cin., 1974. Asst. to Rep. Edward Hutchinson, Mich., 1975; legis. asst. to Rep. Tom Hagedorn, Minn., 1976-78; chief counsel Senate Com. on Judiciary, 1978-83, chief counsel, staff dir. subcom. on constn., 1983-85, dep. chief counsel, 1983; asst. atty. gen. Office Legal Policy, Dept. Justice, Washington, 1985—. Office: Office Legal Policy Dept Justice 10th St and Constitution Ave NW Room 5111 Washington DC 20530

MARKOVICH, STEPHEN EDWARD, lawyer; b. Waynesburg, Pa., Sept. 20, 1951; s. Stephen Robert and Irene Frances (Kensic) M. BA, St. Vincent Coll., Latrobe, Pa., 1973; JD, Ohio No. U., 1976. Bar: Fla. 1977, D.C. 1985. Contract specialist U.S. Dept. of Energy, Washington, 1976-77, U.S. EPA, Washington, 1977-78; contracts counsel Systems Engr. Labs., Ft. Lauderdale, Fla., 1978-80, Booz, Allen & Hamilton, Bethesda, Md., 1980-82; atty. Datapoint Corp., Arlington, Va., 1982—; corp. sec. Fed. Integrated Systems Corp., Alexandria, Va., 1985—. Mem. ABA (pub. contract law sect.), Broward County Bar Assn., Delta Theta Phi. Democrat. Roman Catholic. Avocations: computers, bicycling, travel. Government contracts and claims, General corporate, Contracts commercial. Home: 4741 Kandel Ct Annandale VA 22003 Office: Datapoint Corp 1655 N Ft Myer Dr Arlington VA 22209

MARKOWITZ, DAVID BENJAMIN, lawyer; b. Chgo., July 27, 1949; s. Harry Max Markowitz and Louella (Johnson) Manganello; m. Ann Laurie Smith, Mar. 19, 1969; children: Rebecca, Michalina, Benjamin, Lee. BS, Calif. State Poly. Coll., San Luis Obispo, 1971; JD, U. Pacific, 1974. Bar: Oreg. 1974, U.S. Dist. Ct. Oreg. 1974, U.S. Ct. Appeals (9th cir.) 1983. Spl. legal asst. Nevada Supreme Ct., Carson City, 1974; ptnr. Spears, Lubersky, Campbell & Bledsoe, Portland, Oreg., 1974-83, Markowitz & Herbold, P.C., Portland, 1983—. Mem. Oreg. Bar Assn., Multnomah County Bar Assn., Oreg. Assn. Def. Counsel, Traynor Soc. Democrat. Federal civil litigation, State civil litigation, Insurance. Office: Markowitz & Herbold PC 300 Benjamin Franklin Plaza One SW Columbia Portland OR 97258

MARKOWITZ, MICHAEL JAY, lawyer; b. Suffern, N.Y., Jan. 15, 1951; s. Barbara (Orland) M.; m. Mady M. Aferiat, Aug. 11, 1974; children: Joshua A., Jacob M. AA, Rockland Community Coll., 1971; BS, SUNY Coll., Brockport, 1973; JD, Golden Gate U., 1982. Bar: Calif. 1982, U.S. Dist. Ct. (no. dist.) Calif. 1985, U.S. Dist. Ct. (ea. dist.) Calif. 1986. Dep. dist. atty. Contra Costa County, Martinez, Calif., 1982-85; assoc. Thiessen, Gagen & McCoy, Danville, Calif., 1985—. Mem. ABA, Calif. Bar Assn., Contra Costa County Bar Assn., Assn. Trial Lawyers Am., Calif. Trial Lawyers Assn., Alameda-Contra Costa Trial Lawyers Assn. (bd. govs. 1986—). Democrat. Jewish. Avocations: sports, music, camping, reading. Criminal, State civil litigation, Personal injury. Home: 1855 Carlotta Dr Concord CA 94519 Office: Thiessen Gagen & McCoy 279 Front St Danville CA 94526

MARKS, ALFRED MITCHELL, lawyer; b. N.Y.C., May 12, 1926; s. Mitchell Bennett and Estelle (Phillips) M.; m. Ruth Croog, May 17, 1959; children: Erica L., John M. BS in Econs., U. Pa., 1947; LLB, Columbia U., 1953. Bar: N.Y. 1953, U.S. Dist. Ct. (so. dist.) N.Y., U.S. Ct. Appeals (2d cir.) N.Y. With credit dept. United Mchts. and Mfrs., N.Y.C., 1947-50; assoc. Law Offices of Harold Orenstein, N.Y.C., 1953-55, Davis & Gilbert, N.Y.C., 1955-65; atty. law dept. CBS Inc., N.Y.C., 1965-74, asst. gen. atty., 1974-80, trademark counsel, 1980-86; of counsel Brumbaugh, Graves, Donohue & Raymond, N.Y.C., 1987—. Served with U.S. Army, 1944-46. Mem. ABA, Assn. of Bar of City of N.Y. (sec. trademark com. 1985—), U.S. Trademark Assn. (sec. 1978-81, bd. dirs. 1978-81, 1985—, mem. editorial bd. of jours., editor book revs. 1985—). Democrat. Trademark and copyright, Entertainment, Contracts commercial. Office: Brumbaugh Graves Donohue & Raymond 30 Rockefeller Plaza 44th Floor New York NY 10112

MARKS, ANDREW JAMES, lawyer; b. Mt. Pleasant, Mich., May 19, 1948; s. George James and Stella A. (Althouse) M. B.S. magna cum laude, Central Mich. U., 1969; J.D., U. Mich., 1972. Bar: Mich. 1973, U.S. Dist. Ct. (we. dist.) Mich. 1975. Sole practice, Mt. Pleasant, 1973—; assoc. John A. Watts, Allegan, Mich., 1983—; dir. grants, contracts Central Mich. U., Mt. Pleasant, Mich., 1972-82. Dir. research U.S. Senate campaign for Mich. candidate, 1982; treas., cons. State YMCA Mich., 1979, bd. dirs. Lansing, Central Lake, 1975-81; candidate Mich. Ho. Reps., 1982; bd. dirs. Arts Reach of Mid-Michigan, Mt. Pleasant, 1979-83, Middle Mich. Devel. Corp., Mt. Pleasant, 1981-83. Grantee NSF, 1978, NEH, Mem. Isabella County Bar Assn. (sec. 1978-79), ABA, Mich. Bar Assn. Government contracts and claims, Legislative, Non-profit organizations. Home: 300 Mill St Millbrook MI 49334 Office: Law Offices of John A Watts 245 Hubbard Ave Allegan MI 49010

MARKS, GARY LEE, lawyer; b. N.Y.C., July 8, 1951; s. George Lee and Mary Katherine (Clark) M.; m. Susan Ellen Woner, July 20, 1974; children: Gregory Laurence, Alan Lee. BA with honors, U. Tex., 1973, JD, 1976. Bar: Tex. 1976, U.S. Dist. Ct. (so. dist.) Tex. 1977, U.S. Supreme Ct. 1979, U.S. Ct. Appeals (5th cir.) 1979, U.S. Ct. Appeals (11th cir.) 1981, U.S. Dist. Ct. (no. dist.) Tex. 1982. Atty. Tex. Ct. Civil Appeals, 14th Supreme Jud. Dist., Houston, 1976-77; assoc. Crain, Winters, Deaton, James & Briggs, Houston, 1977-79; atty. Texaco, Inc., Houston, 1979-86; sr. atty., 1986—;

adj. prof. law Bates Coll. Law, U. Houston, 1981. Fundraiser Am. Cancer Soc., Houston, 1983-87. Mem. ABA, Houston Bar Assn., Houston Young Lawyers Assn., Phi Delta Phi. Contracts commercial, General corporate, Antitrust. Home: 1230 Wisterwood Houston TX 77043 Office: Texaco Inc 1111 Rusk St Houston TX 77002

MARKS, J(OHN) BARRETT, lawyer; b. Havre, Mont., Dec. 3, 1946; s. John Brady and Anne Camden (Barrett) M.; m. JoAnn Rosenthal, June 15, 1969; children: Robert Myer, Anne Camden. BA, Harvard U., 1969; postgrad., U. Calif., Irvine, 1969-70; JD, U. Calif., Berkeley, 1975. Bar: Oreg. 1975, U.S. Dist. Ct. Oreg. 1975, U.S. Ct. Appeals (9th cir.) 1980, Wash. 1986. Exec. asst. Orange County Bd. of Suprs., Santa Ana, Calif., 1970-72; assoc. Miller, Nash, Wiener, Hager & Carlsen, Portland, 1975-81, ptnr., 1981—; speaker med. and hosp. personnel on legal topics. Campaign coordinator for lawyers United Way of Oreg., Portland, 1983; bd. dirs. Luth. Family Services Oreg. and S.W. Wash., 1987—, Westside Youth Service Ctr., Portland, 1985-86, co-chmn., 1986—. Mem. ABA (health law forum), Multnomah County Bar Assn., Nat. Health Lawyers Assn., Am. Acad. Hosp. Attys., Oreg. Soc. Hosp. Attys. (bd. dirs. 1977-85, pres. 1978-79). Democrat. Episcopalian. Club: Harvard (Portland). Avocations: river running, skiing, reading. Health, Computer, Administrative and regulatory. Home: 7045 SW 84th Ave Portland OR 97223 Office: Miller Nash Wiener Hager & Carlsen 111 SW Fifth Ave Portland OR 97204-3699

MARKS, LEON, law educator; b. Ft. Smith, Ark., Mar. 23, 1951; s. Armand Morton and Lee (Eisen) M.; m. Patti Hudson, Mar. 9, 1975; children: Sarah, Jessica. BA, Tulane U., 1973; JD, U. Ark., 1976; LLM in Taxation, U. Denver, 1982. Bar: Ark. 1976, Colo. 1983, U.S. Dist. Ct. (ea. dist.) Ark. 1976, U.S. Dist. Ct. Colo. 1983, U.S. Tax Ct. 1983, U.S. Ct. Appeals (10th cir.) 1983. Staff atty. Cen. Ark. Legal Services, Little Rock, 1976-77; ptnr. Kaplan, Brewer & Marks, Little Rock, 1977-79; staff counsel Ark. Real Estate Commn., Little Rock, 1979-81; assoc. prof. law Met. State Coll., Denver, 1982-86, adv. acctg. honor soc., 1982-86; atty. U.S. West, Inc., Denver, 1986—; atty. Mountain Bell, Denver, 1985-86; dir. vol. income tax assistance IRS, Denver, 1983-86; cooperating atty. ACLU, Little Rock, 1977-81. Del. Denver Dem. Conv., 1986; bd. dirs. Legal Services Ark., 1979-81. Recipient Teaching Excellence award Met. State Coll. Alumni Assn., 1985, Meritorious Community Service award Commr. IRS, 1987. Mem. ABA, Ark. Bar Assn., Denver Bar Assn., U.S. Tennis Assn. Democrat. Jewish. Legal education, Corporate taxation, Pension, profit-sharing, and employee benefits.

MARKS, RAMON PAUL, lawyer; b. Washington, Dec. 9, 1948; s. Matthew J. and Simone V. (Vande Meulebroeke) M.; m. Susan Eleanor MacCarthy; children—Robert Justin, Timothy Matthews. A.B. magna cum laude, Dartmouth Coll., 1971; M.A., Johns Hopkins U., 1973; J.D., U. Va., 1976. Bar: N.Y. 1977, Tex. 1983, U.S. Dist. Ct. (so. dist.) Tex. 1984, U.S. Ct. Appeals (5th cir.) 1984. Assoc., Alexander & Green, N.Y.C., 1976-77; corporate atty. Schlumberger Ltd., N.Y.C., 1978; asst. legal counsel services, techniques Schlumberger Paris, 1978-80; gen. counsel Schlumberger Well Services, Houston, 1980-84; sec., gen. counsel Dowell Schlumberger, Inc., Houston, 1984-85; asst. gen. counsel Schlumberger Ltd., Houston, 1986-87; ptnr. Marks, Murase & White, N.Y.C., 1987—. Mem. ABA, Assn. Bar City N.Y., Tex. Bar Assn., Maritime Law Assn. U.S. (assoc.), Petroleum Equipment Suppliers Assn. (chmn. legal affairs steering com. 1984-85), Am. Corp. Counsel Assn. (litigation steering com. Houston chpt. 1985), Phi Beta Kappa. General corporate, Private international. Office: Marks Murase & White 400 Park Ave New York NY 10022

MARKS, ROGER HARRIS, lawyer; b. Cleve., Oct. 30, 1951; s. Leonard Morton and Elaine (Block) M. BS, BA, U. Pa., 1973; JD, Cornell U., 1976. Bar: Ill. 1976, U.S. Dist. Ct. (no. dist.) Ill. 1977. Assoc. atty. Seyfarth, Shaw, et.al., Chgo., 1976-77; atty. U.S. Gypsum Corp., Chgo., 1977-84, Morton Salt div. Morton Thiokol, Chgo., 1984—. Contbr. articles to law jours. Mem. ABA, Chgo. Bar Assn., Phi Beta Kappa, Pi Gamma Mu, Beta Gamma Sigma. Avocations: tennis, photography, music, travel. Contracts commercial, General corporate, Trademark and copyright. Office: Morton Salt div Morton Thiokol 110 N Wacker Dr Chicago IL 60606

MARKS, THEODORE LEE, lawyer; b. N.Y.C., Oct. 18, 1935; s. Irving Edward and Isabel (Goodman) M.; m. Benita Cooper, July 13, 1958; children—Eric, Robert, Jennifer. B.S., NYU, 1956, LL.B., 1958. Bar: N.Y. 1959, U.S. Dist. Ct. (so. dist.) N.Y. 1963, U.S. Supreme Ct. 1964, U.S. Ct. Appeals (2d cir.) 1975, U.S. Dist. Ct. (ea. dist.) N.Y. 1978. Assoc. Silver, Bernstein, Seawell & Kaplan, N.Y.C., 1959-65; sole practice, N.Y.C., 1965-70; ptnr. Lee, Cash & Marks, N.Y.C., 1970-76, Vogel, Marks & Rosenberg, N.Y.C., 1976-79, Bromberg, Gloger, Lifschultz & Marks, N.Y.C., 1979-85, Epstein Becker Borsody & Green, P.C., N.Y.C., 1985-86, Gelberg & Abrams, 1986—. Founder, bd. dirs., past pres. Citizens Assn. Larchmont-Mamaroneck (N.Y.), 1980—; trustee Congregation Emanu-El of Westchester, 1984—. Served with Army N.G., 1958-61. Mem. N.Y. State Bar Assn. (mem. real property, banking, corp. and bus. law sects.), N.Y. County Lawyers Assn., Fed. Bar Council. Jewish. Club: The Wings (N.Y.C.). Real property, General practice, General corporate. Office: Gelberg & Abrams 711 3d Ave New York NY 10017

MARKSTROM, WILBUR JACK, lawyer; b. South Haven, Mich., Sept. 29, 1930; s. Frank Otto and Lillie Lenore (Jensen) M. B.B.A., U. Mich., 1953, J.D., 1959. Bar: Ohio 1959, N.Y. 1983. Assoc. Squire, Sanders & Dempsey, Cleve., 1959-69, gen. ptnr., 1969—. Trustee Cleve. Play House, 1978—, Cleve. Scholarship Programs, Inc., 1982—, Huron Rd. Hosp., 1983-85, Univ. Circle Inc., 1984—, Community Circle Inc., 1984-87. Served to lt. (j.g.) U.S. Navy, 1953-56, PTO. Mem. ABA, Ohio Bar Assn., Greater Cleve. Bar Assn. Democrat. Clubs: Union, Cleve., Cleve. Play House (pres. 1979-82). Home: 1620 Oakwood Dr Cleveland Heights OH 44121 Office: Squire Sanders & Dempsey 1800 Huntington Bldg Cleveland OH 44115

MARKUS, ALLAN LEWIS, lawyer; b. Newark, Nov. 8, 1948; s. Seymour Bernard and Pearl (Weiss) M.; m. Debra J. Ross, Jan. 6, 1973; children—Dara, Lindsey. B.A. Monmouth Coll., 1970; J.D., Western New Eng. Sch. Law, 1975. Bar: N.J. 1976, U.S. Dist. Ct. N.J. 1976, U.S. Supreme Ct. 1985. Assoc. Miller & Platt, Paterson, N.J., 1976-78; sr. ptnr. Markus, Kuller & Cohen, Parsippany, N.J., 1978—; asst. atty. Pub. Defender Essex County, Newark, 1978-81, asst. pub. defender Morris County, Morristown, N.J., 1979-82; mcpl. prosecutor Twp. of Parsippany Troy-Hills, 1981-82. Committeeman Parsippany-Troy Hills Democratic Com., 1977-80, com. treas., mayoral campaign treas., 1979-80; leader organizing rent control Tenants Assn., Parsippany-Troy Hills, 1977-80. Recipient Bancroft-Whitney award Lawyers Coop. Pub. Co., 1974, 75. Mem. N.J. Bar Assn., Morris County Bar Assn., Zeta Beta Tau. Republican. Jewish. Real property, Family and matrimonial, General practice. Home: 6 Normandy Rd Pine Brook NJ 07058 Office: Markus Kuller & Cohen 322 Route 46 Suite 210 Parsippany NJ 07054

MARKUS, ANDREW JOSHUA, lawyer; b. Akron, Ohio, Nov. 24, 1948; s. Marion and Gale Bernice (Schimmel) M.; m. Wendy Ann Wurtz, Apr. 8, 1984; 1 child, Benjamin Marion. BA, Duke U., 1970; JD, U. Fla., 1973; LLM, Vrije Universiteit, Brussels, 1974. Bar: Fla. 1974, U.S. Dist. Ct. (so. dist.) Fla. 1976, D.C. 1977, U.S. Supreme Ct. 1982, U.S. Ct. Appeals (11th cir.) 1984. Intern EEC, Brussels, 1974; assoc. Mahoney, Hadlow & Adams, Miami, Fla., 1976-80, Barron & Lehman, Miami, 1980-82; assoc. Payton & Rachlin, P.A., Miami, 1982-84, ptnr., 1984—. Articles editor: U. Fla. Law Rev., 1972-73. Chmn. Community Devel. Bd., South Miami. Mem. ABA, Dade County Bar Assn., Order of the Coif, Phi Kappa Phi. Club: Grove Isle (Miami). Avocations: golf, tennis, internat. affairs. Private international, Real property, General corporate. Office: Payton & Rachlin PA 100 N Biscayne Blvd Suite 1810 Miami FL 33132

MARKWARDT, JOHN JAMES, lawyer; b. Phila., Jan. 12, 1950; s. John Frederick and Rita Mary (Lafferty) M.; m. Joann Marie Olivo, Aug. 16, 1969; 1 child, Kelly Ann. Student, Rutgers U., 1968-71; JD cum laude, Albany Law Sch., 1974. Bar: N.Y. 1975, U.S. Dist. Ct. (no. dist.) N.Y. 1975, N.J. 1976, U.S. Dist. Ct. N.J. 1976, Pa. 1977, U.S. Supreme Ct. 1978, U.S. Dist. Ct. (ea. dist.) Pa. 1978, U.S. Ct. Appeals (3d cir.) 1981, Fla. 1984. Staff atty. N.Y. State Law Revision Commn., Albany, 1974-75; assoc. Richard M. Meyers, Albany, 1975-76; sole practice Blackwood, N.J., 1976-82; ptnr. Horn, Kaplan, Goldberg, Gorny & Daniels, Atlantic City, 1982—; legis. aide N.J. State Senate, Trenton, 1976. Mem. Gloucester Twp. Council, Camden County, N.J., 1979-81; mem. Gloucester Twp. Rent Control Bd., 1979-81, solicitor, 1977; mem. Gloucester Twp. Planning Bd., 1980. Recipient Forneron Career award Highland Regional High Sch., 1981. Mem. ABA, N.J. State Bar Assn., Atlantic County Bar Assn. Roman Catholic. Avocations: reading, writing, golf. State civil litigation, Real property, Contracts commercial. Home: 100 Wesley Rd Ocean City NJ 08226 Office: Horn Kaplan Goldberg Gorny & Daniels 1300 Atlantic Ave Atlantic City NJ 08401

MARLATT, JERRY RONALD, lawyer; b. Vancouver, B.C., Can., Apr. 13, 1942; s. Edgerton Myron and Marion Christina (MacLeod) M.; m. Linda Susan Vaughn, Nov. 25, 1972 (div. 1985); children: Catherine Anne, Lindsey Alexandra, Christopher David. BA, U. So. Calif., 1967; JD, Southwestern U., 1977. Bar: Calif. 1977, D.C. 1979, N.Y. 1985. Systems analyst U. So. Calif., Los Angeles, 1964-72, City of Los Angeles, 1972-73, Rand Corp., Santa Monica, Calif., 1973-78; staff atty. SEC, Washington, 1978-81, spl. counsel, 1981, legal asst. to commr. P.A. Loomis, 1981-82, to commr. J.C. Treadway, 1982-84, asst. gen. counsel, 1984, assoc. Seward & Kissel, N.Y.C., 1984-87; assoc. Skadden, Arps, Slate, Meagher & Flom, N.Y.C., 1987—. Assoc. editor Law Rev., 1976-77; contbr. articles to profl. jours. Mem. ABA, Assn. Computing Machinery. Securities, Administrative and regulatory, Banking. Home: 49 W 12th St #4F New York NY 10011 Office: Skadden Arps Slate Meagher & Flom 919 3d Ave New York NY 10022

MARLER, DIRK ALAN, lawyer; b. Yakima, Wash., Jan. 29, 1955; s. Donald D. and Sylvia M. (Koch) M.; m. Brenda M. Buckingham, Oct. 11, 1980; children: Danielle Marie, Stephanie Lyn. BA in Polit. Sci., Wash. State U., 1977; JD, Idaho U., 1980. Bar: Wash. 1981, U.S. Dist. Ct. (ea. dist.) Wash. 1983. Assoc. Porter, Schwab & Royal, Yakima, 1980-84; mng. ptnr. Porter, Buren & Marler, Yakima, 1984—; adminstr. pub. defender program Yakima County Dist. Ct., 1984—. Mentor Yakima Pub. Schs., 1985; active Yakima PTA; vol. Am. Heart Assn., Yakima, 1986; chmn. publicity 1986 Law Day, Yakima chmn. Law Week 1987, chmn. Yakima County Democrats. Mem. ABA, Wash. Trial Lawyers Assn., Wash. State Bar Assn (alcoholism com., legis. com.), Yakima C.of C. (leadership tng. program). Democrat. Avocations: golf, politics. Criminal, Personal injury, Probate. Office: Porter Buren & Marler 402 N 4th St #202 Yakima WA 98901

MARLIN, JEFFREY STUART, lawyer; b. Chgo., Apr. 15, 1948; s. Kenton S. and Geraldine (Thompson) M.; m. Kathleen K. Kask, Mar. 5, 1977. AB, Ind. U., 1970, JD, 1973. Bar: Ind. 1973, U.S. Dist. Ct. (no. and so. dists.) Ind. 1973, Del. 1975, U.S. Dist. Ct. Del. 1975. Law clk. to presiding justice Superior Ct. State of Del.; atty. City of East Chicago, Ind., 1973-74; assoc. Given, Dawson & Cappas, East Chicago, 1974; atty. Register of Wills, Wilmington, Del., 1974-76; assoc. Tybout, Redfearn, Casarino & Pell, Wilmington, 1977-86, ptnr., 1986—; gen. counsel Contact Lens Soc., Lexington, Ky., Med. Eye Bank, Wilmington, Kuhwald Contact Lens Co., Wilmington, 1979—; legis. liason State Farm Ins. Co., Del. Gen. counsel Shipley Woods Civic Assn., Wilmington, 1984—; liason counsel Asbestos Claims Facility, Wilmington; mem. Gov.'s Circle, Wilmington, 1984. Served to 1st lt. U.S. Army, 1973-74. Mem. ABA, Ind. Bar Assn., Del. Bar Assn. Methodist. Avocations: jogging, cycling, reading, travel. State civil litigation, Personal injury, Legislative. Home: 120 Parrish Ln Wilmington DE 19810 Office: Tybout Redfearn Casarino & Pell 300 Delaware Ave Wilmington DE 19899

MARLOW, H(OBSON) MCKINLEY, JR., lawyer; b. Cookeville, Tenn., Sept. 20, 1931; s. H.M. and Birtha (Bryant) M.; m. Dorothy Fay Teal, June 18, 1960 (dec. Dec. 1981), children—Darryl McKinley, Stephen Teal, Eric Martin. B.S., Tenn. Tech. U., 1954; J.D., Vanderbilt U., 1957. Bar: Tenn., 1957. Sole practice law, Nashville, 1957—; pres. Newsletters, Inc., Ashwood Music Co. Mem. ABA (copyright com.), Nashville Bar Assn., Tenn. Bar Assn. Lodges: Masons, Shriners. Author: ABC's of Copyright Law for Songwriters, 1960. Trademark and copyright. Office: PO Box 111235 Executive Park Nashville TN 37222

MARLOW, ORVAL LEE, II, lawyer; b. Denver, May 1, 1956; s. Jack Conger and Barbara A. (Stolzenburg) M.; m. Paige Wood, June 8, 1985. BA, U. Nebr., 1978, JD, 1981. Bar: Tex. 1981, U.S. Dist. Ct. (so. dist.) Tex. 1984, U.S. Ct. Appeals (5th cir.) 1984. Assoc. Krist & Scott, Houston, 1981-82, Marlow & Assocs., Houston, 1982-83; ptnr. Lendais & Assocs., Houston, 1983—. Sustaining mem. Rep. Nat. Com., 1985—. Mem. ABA, Tex. Bar Assn., Houston Bar Assn., Phi Delta Phi. Lutheran. Avocations: golf, snow skiing, water skiing, chess. Private international, Real property, General corporate. Office: Lendais & Assocs 5718 Westheimer Suite 2121 Houston TX 77057

MARLOW, WILLIAM FREEMAN COALE, JR., lawyer; b. Balt., May 4, 1944; s. William Freeman Coale and Frances N. (Foote) M.; m. Monique Y. van Rootselaar, Oct. 7, 1972; children—Cameron Nelson, Adam Wheeler. B.S., U. Va., 1966; J.D., U. Md., 1969. Bar: Md. 1969, D.C. 1980, U.S. dist. ct. Md. 1974, U.S. Ct. Apls. (4th cir.) 1975, U.S. Supreme Ct. 1976. Ptnr., Covahey & Boozer, Towson, Md., 1970-78; ptnr. Marlow & Peddicord, Towson, 1978—. Bd. dirs. Md. State Fair and Agrl. Soc., 1982—. Mem. ABA, Md. Bar Assn., Baltimore County Bar Assn., D.C. Bar Assn., Phi Alpha Delta. Editor: Baltimore County Bar Quar., 1979—. Private international, Contracts commercial, Real property. Office: Marlow & Peddicord 404 Allegheny Ave Towson MD 21204

MARMER, RONALD LOUIS, lawyer; b. Miami, Fla., July 24, 1952; s. Albert and Marian (Luhrs) M. BS, MA, Northwestern U., Evanston, Ill., 1974; JD, U. Va., 1977. Bar: Ill. 1977, U.S. Dist. Ct. (no. dist.) Ill. 1978, U.S. Ct. Appeals (7th cir.) 1979. Assoc. Jenner & Block, Chgo., 1977-83, ptnr., 1983—. Hardy scholar Northwestern U., 1974. Mem. ABA (litigation sect.), Ill. Bar Assn. (civil practice sect., corp. and securities sect.), Chgo. Council of Lawyers, Order of Coif. Federal civil litigation, Securities, State civil litigation. Office: Jenner & Block One IBM Plaza Chicago IL 60611

MARMET, GOTTLIEB JOHN, lawyer; b. Chgo., Mar. 24, 1946; s. Gottlieb John and Margaret Ann (Saylor) M.; m. Jane Marie Borkowski, Sept. 12, 1970; children: Gottlieb John, Philip Stanley, Thomas Jacob. BS with distinction in Acctg., San Diego State U., 1967; JD, Northwestern U., 1970. Bar: Ill. 1970, U.S. Dist. Ct. (no. dist.) Ill. 1970, U.S. Tax Ct. 1981; CPA, Calif., Ill., Minn. Tax acct. Touche Ross & Co., Chgo., 1970-75; assoc. atty. Howington, Elworth, Osswald & Hough, Chgo., 1975-79; tax mgr. Peat, Marwick, Mitchell & Co., Mpls., 1979-81; assoc. Shefsky, Saitlin & Froelich, Ltd., Chgo., 1981-83; prin. G. John Marmet, Glenview, Ill., 1983—; lectr. corp. law William Rainey Harper Coll., Arlington Heights, Ill., 1984; instr. Ill. Soc. CPA's, 1976, 77, Minn. Soc. CPA's, 1980. Active Northeast Ill. Council Boy Scouts Am., 1984—. Recipient Hon. Mention, Chgo. Bar Assn. Art Show, 1972. Mem. ABA (fed. tax com.) Ill. Bar Assn., Chgo. Bar Assn., Am. Inst. Cert. Pub. Accts., Beta Gamma Sigma, Beta Alpha Psi, Phi Alpha Delta. Lodge: Rotary (Service Above Self award 1985-86). Author: Farm Corporations and Their Income Tax Treatment, 1970, 1974; contbr. articles to jours., publs. Probate, Corporate taxation, Personal income taxation. Office: 950 Milwaukee Ave Suite 318 Glenview IL 60025

MARMON, DAVID GLENN, lawyer; b. Kansas City, Mo., June 19, 1940; s. Glenn Marmon and Ruth Ferguson (Garrigues) Fox; 1 child, Temil. BA, U. Calif., Berkeley, 1963; JD, Harvard U., 1966; LLD (hon.), Cornerstone Christian U., 1982. Bar: Kans. 1966, Calif. 1979. Gen. ptnr. Christian Lawyers of Am., San Diego, 1981—. Mem. San Diego Bar Assn. Republican. Mem. Christian Ch. Family and matrimonial. Office: Christian Lawyers of Am 1200 3d Ave Suite 1402 San Diego CA 92101

MARMOR, THEODORE RICHARD, political science and public management educator; b. Bklyn., Feb. 24, 1939; s. James and Mira Bernice (Karpf) M.; m. Jan Schmidt, Oct. 20, 1961; children—Laura Carleton, Sarah Rogers. B.A., Harvard U., Cambridge, Mass., 1960, Ph.D., 1966; postgrad., Wadham Coll., Oxford U., Eng., 1961-62. Asst. and assoc. prof. polit. sci. U. Wis.-Madison, 1967-69; assoc. prof. pub. affairs U. Minn.-Mpls., 1970-73; prof. U. Chgo., 1973-79; prof. polit. sci. Yale U., New Haven, 1979—, chmn. Ctr. Health Studies, 1979—; prof. pub. mgmt. Yale U. Sch. Orgn. & Mgmt., New Haven, 1983—; cons., lectr. in field. Author: The Politics of Medicare, 1970, 73; Political Analysis & American Medical Care, 1983; co-author: Health Care Policy, 1982. Editor: Poverty Policy, 1971; National Health Insurance, 1980; Jour. Health Politics Policy and Law, 1980-84. Contbr. articles to profl. jours. Mem. Council on Fgn. Relations, N.Y.C., 1979-80, Pres.' Commn. on 1980s, 1980; social policy adviser Walter Mondale Presdl. Campaign, 1984. Fellow Adlai Stevenson Inst., JFK Inst. of Politics; mem. U.S. Squash Racquets Assn. (bd. dirs. 1983—). Democrat. Jewish. Clubs: United Oxford and Cambridge (London); Lawn (New Haven); Yale (N.Y.C.). Administrative and regulatory, Legal education, Health. Home: 139 Armory St Hamden CT 06511 Office: Yale Univ Sch Orgn & Mgmt 111 Prospect St New Haven CT 06520

MARNIK, MICHAEL PETER, lawyer; b. Albany, Calif., Mar. 12, 1945; children: Matthew, Daniel, Rachel. AB, Coll. of the Holy Cross, 1966; JD, Villanova U., 1969. Bar: Mass. 1969, U.S. Ct. Mil. Appeals 1970, U.S. Dist. Ct. Mass. 1972. Ptnr. Marnik & Sullivan, Peabody, Mass., 1985—. Pres. Neighborhood Legal Services, Inc., Lynn, Mass., 1980-82. Served to lt. JAGC USN, 1970-72. Mem. ABA, Mass. Bar Assn., Essex Bar Assn., Mass. Def. Lawyers Assn., Def. Research Inst. State civil litigation, Real property, Personal injury. Office: Marnik & Sullivan 1 Newbury St Peabody MA 01960

MAROHL, DAVID WILLIAM, lawyer; b. Beaver Dam, Wis., Jan. 25, 1955; s. John Ralph and Mary Elizabeth (Knop) M. B.A., U. Wis.-Madison, 1976; J.D., DePaul U., 1980. Bar: Ill. 1980, U.S. Dist. Ct. (no. dist.) Ill. 1980, Wis. 1981. Editor Commerce Clearing House, Chgo., 1980-81; sole practice, Chgo., 1981-84; adminstr. Nat. Bus. Inst., 1984-85; asst. dist. atty. Shawano (Wis.) County, 1985; atty. office hearings and appeals Social Security Adminstrn., 1987—. Mem. Wis. Bar Assn., Chgo. Bar Assn., Ill. State Bar Assn., ABA, Am. Judicature Assn. Republican. Lutheran. Avocations: book collecting, theatre. Librarianship, Criminal, Jurisprudence. Address: Marohl Constrn 103 S Hubbard Horicon WI 53032

MAROTTA, JAMES STEVEN, lawyer, educator; b. Paterson, N.J., Jan. 18, 1952; s. Adolph Ralph and Ida Florence (Soldoveri) M. BA in Govt., Seton Hall U., 1974, JD, 1977; postgrad., Fordham U., 1974-75. Bar: N.J. 1977, D.C. 1979. Law sec. to presiding justice Superior Ct., Paterson, 1977-78; legis. aide U.S. Congressman Robert A. Roe, Washington, 1978-79; staff atty. com. on narcotics abuse and control U.S. Ho. of Reps., Washington, 1979; assoc. Jeffer, Hopkinson & Vogel, Hawthorne, N.J., 1980; sole practice Totowa, N.J., 1980—; adj. prof. polit. sci. dept. Seton Hall U., South Orange, N.J., 1985—; legis. aide Assemblyman S.M. La Corte, 1980-82. Atty. Totowa Bd. Health, 1980-86, Totowa Planning Bd., 1983-86; mem. adv. com. Passaic County Family Ct., Paterson, 1982—, Totowa Reps., Rep. Nat. Com., Washington. Mem. N.J. State Bar Assn., D.C. Bar Assn., Passaic County Bar Assn. (chmn. legis. com. 1982—, journalistic and media law com. 1985—), Rep. Lawyers Assn. N.J., Rep. Nat. Lawyers Assn., Passaic Valley Jaycees, NAACP (Paterson br.), Seton Hall Law Sch. Alumni Assn., Nat. Italian-Am. Found., Italian-Am. Ind. Club, UNICO (Passaic Valley chpt.). Roman Catholic. Lodge: KC. Avocations: sports, music, politics. Legislative, Entertainment, Legal education. Home: 10 Cambridge St Totowa NJ 07512 Office: 248 Union Blvd Totowa NJ 07512

MAROTTA, ROBERT, lawyer; b. Bklyn., Mar. 17, 1943; s. Anne (Vinci) M.; m. Kathleen Jane Marsh, May 22, 1966; children: Marc, Jason, Peter. BA in Econs., CUNY, Queens, 1964; JD, St. John's U., Queens, 1970. Bar: N.Y. 1971, U.S. Dist. Ct. (so. and ea. dists.) N.Y. 1971, Mich. 1981. Various positions Gen. Motors Corp., N.Y.C., 1964-70, atty. overseas ops., 1970-75; atty. gen. counsel office Gen. Motors Corp., N.Y.C. and Detroit, 1975—; asst. gen. counsel Motors Ins. Corp., Detroit, 1980-86; gen. counsel Gen. Internat. Ltd., Hamilton, Bermuda, 1983-86. Mem. ABA, Mich. Bar Assn., N.Y. State Bar Assn. Roman Catholic. Avocations: amateur theatre, tennis, cooking. Insurance, Contracts commercial, Securities. Home: 25414 Tweed Dr Franklin MI 48025 Office: Gen Motors Corp 3041 W Grand Blvd Detroit MI 48232

MAROUSEK, ROBERT JOSEPH, retired corporation attorney; b. Chgo., Jan. 14, 1935; s. Joseph James and Marie Catherine (Kearney) M. B.A., U. Mich., 1955; J.D., Northwestern U., 1958; M. Comparative Law, U. Chgo./U. Munich, W.Ger., 1965. Bar: Mich. 1958, Ill. 1969. Atty., Lawyers Title Ins. Co., Mt. Clemens, Mich., 1958-60, Gen. Motors Corp., Detroit, 1960-63; internat. atty. Fed.-Mogul Corp., Southfield, Mich., 1965-67; regional csl. Abbott Labs., North Chicago, Ill., 1967-77; asst. co. csl.-internat. Intersoll-Rand Co., Woodcliff, N.J., 1978-81; sr. atty.-internat. Internat. Multifoods Corp., Mpls., 1981-86. Bayer-Farben fellow U. Chgo., 1963. Mem. ABA, Phi Delta Phi. Private international, General corporate, Trademark and copyright. Home: Apt 1107 1225 LaSalle Ave S Minneapolis MN 55403

MAROVITZ, JAMES LEE, lawyer; b. Chgo., Feb. 21, 1939; s. Harold and Gertrude (Luster) M.; m. Gail Helene Florsheim, June 17, 1962; children: Andrew, Scott. BS, Northwestern U., 1960, JD, 1963. Bar: Ill. 1963, U.S. Dist. Ct. (no. dist.) Ill. 1963. Assoc. Leibman, Williams, Bennett, Baird & Minow, Chgo., 1963-70, ptnr., 1970-72; ptnr. Sidley & Austin, Chgo., 1972—; bd. dirs. Dynascan Corp., Chgo. Plan commr. Village of Deerfield, Ill., 1972-79, trustee, 1983—. Mem. ABA, Ill. Bar Assn., Chgo. Bar Assn. Club: Univ. (Chgo.). Real property, Landlord-tenant, Contracts commercial. Office: Sidley & Austin One First National Plaza Chicago IL 60603

MARQUARD, HENRY FRANCIS, lawyer; b. Highwood, Ill., Dec. 5, 1954; s. Henry James and Dorothy M. (Stewart) M.; m. Sharon B. Lyons, June 18, 1977. BA with highest honors, De Paul U., 1972-76, JD, 1976-79. Bar: Ill. 1979, U.S. Dist. Ct. (no. dist.) Ill. 1980, U.S. Ct. Appeals (7th cir.) 1981. Assoc. Kiesler & Berman, Chgo., 1980-82; assoc. Snyder, Clarke, Dalziel & Johnson, Waukegan, 1982-83, ptnr., 1983—; lectr. Kendall Coll., Evanston, 1983. Mem. Northbrook Civic Found., 1982—; Northbrook (Ill.) Safety Commr., 1983—. Mem. Ill. Bar Assn. (assembly mem., del. 1986—), Chgo. Bar Assn., Lake County Bar Assn. Roman Catholic. Club: Waukegan (Ill.) Yacht. Avocation: sailing. State civil litigation, Insurance, Personal injury. Office: Snyder Clarke Dalziel & Johnson 301 Washington St #201 Waukegan IL 60085

MARQUARDT, CHRISTEL ELISABETH, lawyer; b. Chgo., Aug. 26, 1935; d. Herman Albert and Christine Marie (Geringer) Trolenberg; children: Eric, Philip, Andrew, Joel. BS in Edn., Mo. Western Coll., 1970; JD with honors, Washburn U., 1974. Bar: Kans. 1974, U.S. Dist. Ct. Kans. 1974, U.S. Supreme Ct. 1979, U.S. Ct. Appeals (10th cir.) 1980. Tchr. St. John's Ch., Tigerton, Wis., 1955-56; personnel asst. Columbia Records, Los Angeles, 1958-59; ptnr. Cosgrove, Webb & Oman, Topeka, 1974-86, Palmer, Marquardt & Snyder, Topeka, 1986—; mem. atty. bd. discipline Kans. Supreme Ct., 1984-86; lectr. in field. Contbr. articles to legal jours. Asst. treas., mem. exec. Rep. com., Kansas, 1983-87; dist. bd. adjudication Mo. Synod Luth. Ch., Kans., 1982—; bd. dirs. Topeka Civic Symphony, 1983—; hearing examiner Human Relations Com., Topeka, 1974-76; local advisor Boy Scouts Am., 1973-74; bd. dirs., nominating com. YWCA, Topeka, 1979-81; trustee Washburn U. Law Sch., 1987—. Named Women of Yr., Topeka Mayor, 1982; Mabee scholar Washburn U., 1972-74. Mem. ABA (labor law, family sects.), Kans. Bar Assn. (sec., treas. 1981-82, 83-85, v.p. 1985-86, pres. elect 1986-87, pres. 1987-88, lectr. 1974—, Disting. Service award 1980), Kans. Trial Lawyers Assn. (bd. govs. 1982-86, lectr.), Topeka Bar Assn., Am. Bus. Women's Assn. (lectr., corr. sec. 1983-84, pres. 1986-87, one of Top Ten Bus. Women of Yr. 1985), Golden City Forum, Greater Topeka C. of C. (v.p., bd. dirs. 1983-87). Labor, Family and matrimonial. Home: 3121 Briarwood Circle Topeka KS 66611 Office: Palmer Marquardt Snyder 112 SW 6th St Topeka KS 66603

MARQUARDT, MERRITT RENO, lawyer; b. Wausau, Wis., Dec. 5, 1934; s. Reno Henry and Nora (Tesch) M.; m. Betty Ann Marfell, Dec. 8, 1956; children: Andrew Scott, Lisa Ann, Amy Beth. BS, U. Wis., 1956; JD, George Washington U., 1963. Bar: Minn. 1966, U.S. Ct. Appeals (8th cir.) 1969. Contract adminstr. Bur. Naval Weapons, Washington, 1962-64; atty. office of gen. counsel 3M Co., St. Paul, 1966—; lectr. St. Thomas Coll., St. Paul, 1978-81. Mem. Gustavus Adolphus Luth. Ch. council, St. Paul, 1974-80; chmn. bd. Minn. Continuing Legal Edn., St. Paul, 1981-84. Served to lt. j.g. USN, 1956-59. Mem. ABA, Minn. Bar Assn. (bd. govs. 1979-80), Nat. Contract Mgmt. Assn. (v.p. 1981-82). Republican. Avocations: skiing,

sailing, golf, reading. Government contracts and claims, General corporate, Antitrust. Home: 3984 Birch Knoll Dr White Bear Lake MN 55110 Office: 3M Co Office of Gen Counsel PO Box 33428 3M Ctr 220-12E-02 Saint Paul MN 55133

MARQUARDT, ROBERT RICHARD, lawyer; b. Columbus, Ohio, Aug. 22, 1943; s. Robert Gustave and Ethel M. (Augur) M.; m. Alice Grant, Sept. 9, 1966 (div. Feb. 1985); children: Theresa, Robert, Christopher. BS in Commerce, Rider Coll., 1965; MBA, Fairleigh Dickinson, 1966; JD, U. Ark., 1973; LLM, Temple U., 1977. Bar: Iowa 1973, Ark. 1973, U.S. Dist. Ct. (ea. dist.) Ark. 1973, N.J. 1975, U.S. Supreme Ct. 1979. Counsel RCA Corp., Camden, N.J., 1973-77; assoc. counsel Occidental Chem. Corp., Niagara Falls, N.Y., 1977-79, div. counsel, 1979-80, counsel, 1980-81, assoc. gen. counsel, 1981—; instr. bus. law Niagara U., 1978-82. Contbr. legal essays to profl. publs. Chmn. Youngstown (N.Y.) Environ. Com., 1980-84; mil. chmn. UN Operation Horshoe, Niagara Falls, 1981; staff judge adv. USAFR, 1974—. Served to maj. USAFR, 1967—. Recipient United Way awards, 1968-76, Corp. award Am. Jurisprudence, 1972; named Judge Adv. of Yr., USAFR, 1980. Antitrust, Contracts commercial, General corporate. Office: 351 Phelps Ct Irving TX 75015

MARQUART, STEVEN LEONARD, lawyer; b. Georgetown, Minn., Feb. 2, 1954; s. Leonard Matthew and Gladys Viola (Myhre) M.; m. Cynthia Lou Smerud, June 21, 1975; children: Stephanie Lynn, Angela Marie, Andrew Steven. BA in Polit. Sci., Moorhead State U., 1976; JD with distinction, U. N.D., 1979. Bar: Minn. 1979, N.D. 1979, U.S. Dist. Ct. N.D. 1979, U.S. Dist. Ct. Minn. 1981, U.S. Ct. Appeals (8th cir.) 1981. Law Clk. U.S. Dist. Ct. N.D., Fargo, 1979-81; assoc. Cahill & Maring, PA, Moorhead, Minn., 1981-85, ptnr., bd. dirs., 1985. Mem. ABA, Minn. Bar Assn., N.D. Bar Assn., Order of Coif. Roman Catholic. Insurance, Federal civil litigation, State civil litigation. Home: 1913 S 23d St Fargo ND 58103 Office: Cahill & Maring PA 403 Center Ave Moorhead MN 56560

MARQUESS, LAWRENCE WADE, lawyer; b. Bloomington, Ind., Mar. 2, 1950; s. Earl Lawrence and Mary Louise (Coberly) M.; m. Barbara Ann Bailey, June 17, 1978; children: Alexander Lawrence, Michael Wade. B.S. in Elec. Engring., Purdue U., 1973; J.D., W.Va. U., 1977. Bar: W.Va. 1977, U.S. Dist. Ct. (so. dist.) W.Va. 1977, Tex. 1977, U.S. Dist. Ct. (no. dist.) Tex. 1977, Colo. 1980, U.S. Dist. Ct. Colo. 1980, U.S. Ct. Appeals (10th cir.) 1980, U.S. Supreme Ct. 1984. Assoc. Johnson, Bromberg, Leeds & Riggs, Dallas, 1977-79; assoc. Bradley, Campbell & Carney, Golden, Colo., 1979-82, ptnr., 1983-84; assoc. Stettner, Miller & Cohn P.C., Denver, 1984-85, ptnr., 1985—. Mem faculty Am. Law Inst.-ABA Advanced Labor and Employment Law Course, 1986, 87. Mem. ABA (labor and litigation sects.), Colo. Bar Assn. (program com., labor law com.), Denver Bar Assn. (program com., labor law com.), 1st Jud. Dist. Bar Assn. Sierra Club, Nat. Ry. Hist. Soc., ACLU. Democrat. Methodist. Labor, Pension, profit-sharing, and employee benefits, Federal civil litigation. Home: 2293 Yellowstone St Golden CO 80401 Office: Stettner Miller & Cohn PC 1380 Lawrence St Suite 1000 Denver CO 80204

MARQUEZ, ALFREDO C., federal judge; b. 1922; m. Linda Marquez. B.S., U. Ariz., 1948, J.D., 1950. Bar: Ariz. Practice law Mesch Marquez & Rothschild, 1957-80; asst. atty. gen. State of Ariz., 1951-52; asst. county atty. Pima County, Ariz., 1953-54; adminstrv. asst. to Congressman Stewart Udall 1955; judge U.S. Dist. Ct. Ariz., Tucson, 1980—. Served with USN, 1942-45. Judicial administration. Office: US Dist Ct 55 E Broadway Tucson AZ 85701

MARQUIS, HAROLD LIONEL, corporate lawyer; b. Osceola, Iowa, Oct. 9, 1931; s. Olin and Eula (Robins) M.; m. Shirley Weber, Nov. 15, 1952; children: Angela, Brett. BA, U. Iowa, 1954, JD, 1960; LLM, U. Mich., 1963. Bar: Iowa 1960, Mich. 1962, U.S. Patent Office 1962, Ga. 1972. Atty. patent and legal dept. Dow Corning Corp., Midland, Mich., 1960-62; asst. prof. law Temple U., Phila., 1963-65; prof. Emory U., Atlanta, 1965-82; v.p. legal affairs Mead Packaging Co., Atlanta, 1982—; Bd. dirs. Inst. Continuing Legal Edn.; vis. prof. U. Houston, 1970-71. Contbr. articles to profl. jours. Served to 1st lt. USAF, 1954-57. Fellow Inst. Law and Econs., 1974, Sociol. Methodology in Legal Edn., 1972; W.W. Cook fellow U. Mich., 1962-63. Mem. Ga. State Bar, Lawyers Club. Antitrust, General corporate, Private international. Home: 1858 Castleway Ln NE Atlanta GA 30345 Office: Mead Packaging 1040 W Marietta St NW Atlanta GA 30318

MARQUIS, JOSHUA KAI, lawyer; b. Los Angeles, Oct. 28, 1952; s. Lucian Charles and Elizabeth Jane (Slater) M. BA, U. Oreg., 1977, JD, 1980. Bar: Oreg. 1981, U.S. Dist. Ct. Oreg. 1981, U.S. Ct. Appeals (9th cir.) 1981. Dep. dist. atty. Lane County, Eugene, Oreg., 1974-84, Linclon County, Newport, Oreg., 1984-85—; spl. asst. to atty. gen. Calif. Dept. of Justice, Los Angeles, 1984-85. Bd. dirs. nat. ARC, Newport, 1986—. Mem. ABA, Lincoln County Peace Officer Assn. (v.p. 1986—). Criminal. Home: PO Box 732 Newport OR 97365 Office: Lincoln County 225 W Olive Newport OR 97365

MARQUIS, ROBERT STILLWELL, lawyer; b. Knoxville, Tenn., Jan. 16, 1943; s. Robert Henry and Ruth (Belden) M.; m. Mariana Spruhde, Aug. 23, 1969 (div. Jan. 1985); m. Gloria Nelson, Oct. 21, 1985; children: Alicea, Alison, Elaine. BS, Davidson Coll., 1963; JD, Duke U., 1968; LLM in Taxation, NYU, 1969. Tax atty. Norfolk & Western Ry., Roanoke, Va., 1969-73; ptnr. McCampbell & Young, Knoxville, 1973—. Bd. mem. St. Mary's Med. Found., Knoxville, 1985—; enrolled U. Tenn. Chancellors Assn., 1984—. Mem. ABA, Tenn. Bar Assn., Va. Bar Assn., Knoxville Bar Assn. (pres. tax sect. 1983), Knoxville Estate Planning Council (pres. 1985—), Phi Beta Kappa. Presbyterian. Clubs: LeConte, Cherokee Country (Knoxville). Avocations: jogging, tennis, history. Estate planning, Pension, profit-sharing, and employee benefits, Probate. Home: 3819 Oakhurst Dr Knoxville TN 37919 Office: McCampbell & Young 2021 Plaza Tower Knoxville TN 37901

MARR, DAVID ERSKINE, lawyer; b. Quincy, Mass., Aug. 20, 1939; s. Ralph G. and Ethel (Beals) M.; m. Patricia Ann Houghton, July 28, 1939; children—Bonnie J., Shelly A., David Scott. B.A., Colby Coll., 1961; M.A., Wesleyan U., 1967; J.D. with honors, U. Conn., 1970. Bar: Conn. 1970, Mass. 1974, U.S. Dist. Ct. Conn. 1971, U.S. Dist. Ct. Mass. 1975, U.S. Ct. Appeals (2d cir.) 1971, U.S. Supreme Ct. 1974. Assoc. Day, Berry & Howard, Hartford, Conn., 1970-73; counsel Honeywell Info. Systems, Inc., Waltham, Mass., 1973-75; sole practice, Boston, 1975-76, Natick, Mass., 1976—. Rep., Regional Vocat. Sch.; chmn. Hist. Dist. Com.; dir. Hist. Soc. & Museum. Mem. ABA, Mass. Bar Assn., Am. Trial Lawyers Assn. Club: Rotary (Natick). Opinion editor: Mass. Lawyers Weekly. General practice, Family, Personal injury. Office: 12 W Central St Natick MA 01760

MARRERO, LOUIS JOHN, lawyer; b. Bklyn., May 9, 1936; s. George William and Mamie (Zafonte) M.; m. Maria Louise, June 28, 1958; children: Lisa Anne, Louis Jr. BA in Polit. Sci., CCNY, 1958; LLB, St. John's U., 1963. Bar: N.Y. 1963, U.S. Dist. Ct. (ea. dist.) N.Y. 1966, U.S. Supreme Ct. 1967, U.S. Tax Ct. 1973, U.S. Dist. Ct. (so. dist.) N.Y. Sole practice, Bklyn., 1963. Mem. N.Y. State Rep. Com. Mem. Bklyn. Bar Assn., Kings County Criminal Bar Assn., N.Y. State Defenders Assn. Roman Catholic. Criminal, Family and matrimonial. Home: 2225 Royce St Brooklyn NY 11234 Office: 1409 E 92d St Brooklyn NY 11236

MARRINAN, TIMOTHY DAVID, lawyer; b. Detroit, Oct. 7, 1945; s. James Harry and Shirley Blanche (Amunson) M.; m. Patrice Cassady, May 31, 1985; children: Molly Elizabeth, Cara Lindsay, Timothy David Jr. BA, U. Minn., 1967, JD, 1970. Bar: Minn. 1972. Trust counsel First Nat. Bank of Mpls., 1972-74, assoc. gen. counsel, 1974-84; sr. corp. counsel First Bank System, Inc., Mpls., 1984-87, gen. counsel consumer and small bus. banking, 1987—; instr. Stonier Grad. Sch. Rutgers U., N.J., 1979-80, Grad. Banking Sch. U. Colo., Boulder, 1980-84, Grad. Sch. Banking U. Wis., Madison, 1982—; mem. consumer adv. council Fed. Res. Bd., Washington, 1983, vice chmn. 1984, chmn. 1985. Author: Truth-in-Lending Simplification, 1981. Recipient Exec. Com. award ABA. Mem. ABA, Minn. Bar Assn., Hennepin County Bar Assn., Am. Corp. Counsel Assn., Am. Bankers Assn. (author Compliance Sourcebook 1983), Delta Theta Phi. Roman Catholic. Club: Mpls. Athletic. Banking, General corporate. Home: 3332 W 56th St Edina MN 55410 Office: First Bank System Inc 1200 First Bank Pl E Minneapolis MN 55480

MARSCHING, RONALD LIONEL, lawyer; b. N.Y.C., Mar. 30, 1927; m. Marjory Fleming Duncan, Dec. 31, 1964; children: Christine, Jane. BA, Princeton U., 1950; JD, Harvard U., 1953. Bar: N.Y. 1954. With Timex Corp. Waterbury, Conn., 1967; vice chmn., gen. counsel Timex Corp., Waterbury, Conn., 1980—, also bd. dirs. Served with U.S. Army, 1953-54. Mem. ABA, Nat. Assn. Dirs., Assn. of Bar of City of N.Y., Westchester-Fairfield Corp. Counsel Bar Assn. Club: University (N.Y.C.); Waterbury. General corporate, Private international, Corporate taxation. Office: Timex Corp Park Rd Extension Waterbury CT 06720

MARSH, NORMAN JAMES, JR., lawyer; b. N.Y.C., Jan. 11, 1936; s. Norman James Sr. and Cornelia V.R. (King) M.; m. Margaret P. Ballard, Feb. 7, 1962 (div. Aug. 1977); children: Cornelia, Jane, Jamie, Anne; m. Mitzi Byrne, Aug. 16, 1986. AB, Harvard U., 1957; LLB, NYU, 1964. Bar: N.Y. 1964, N.H. 1974. Assoc. Bleakly, Platt, Hart & Fritz, N.Y.C., 1964-67; staff atty. Sanders Assocs., Inc., Nashua, N.H., 1967-72; asst. corp. counsel Sanders Assocs. Inc., Nashua, N.H., 1972-83, fed. systems group counsel, 1983-86, asst. co. counsel, 1986—. Served with USN, 1957-60. Mem. ABA, N.H. Bar Assn. Government contracts and claims, Private international, General corporate. Home: 15 Lakemans Ln Ipswich MA 01938 Office: Sanders Assocs Inc Daniel Webster Hwy S Nsashua NH 03061

MARSH, PAMELA ALISON, lawyer; b. Glen Ridge, N.J., Nov. 2, 1954; s. Peter Roland and Helen Louise (Pellman) M.; m. Lawrence C. Maier, Sept. 21, 1981; children: Rhys Michael, Kelly McAuslan. BA, Middlebury Coll., 1976; cert., Pushkin Inst., Moscow, 1976; JD, Harvard U., 1979. Bar: Vt. 1980, U.S. Dist. Ct. Vt. 1980. Law clk. to presiding justice Superior Ct. of Vt., Rutland, 1979-80; staff atty. Vt. Legal Aid, Brandon and Burlington, 1980-83; ptnr. Nuovo & Marsh, Middlebury, Vt., 1983—. Mem. New Haven Planning Commn., Vt., 1982-85, Addison County Dem. Com., Vt., 1985—; chairwoman New Haven Dems., 1985—; moderator Union Sch. Dist. #28, Bristol, Vt., 1985—; bd. dirs. Otter Creek Child Ctr., Middlebury, 1983—. Mem. ABA, Vt. Bar Assn. (bd. bar mgrs. 1981-83), Addison County Bar Assn. Avocations: gardening, hiking, sailing, swimming, reading. General practice, Mental health. Home: RD 1 Middlebury VT 05753 Office: Nuovo & Marsh 6 S Pleasant St Drawer 190 Middlebury VT 05753

MARSH, RICHARD MELVIN, lawyer; b. South Gate, Calif., Sept. 19, 1948; s. Clyde Francis and Velma Ransom (Crim) M.; m. Rae Anne Becker, Mar. 20, 1971; children: Melissa Grace, Gretchen Ette. AB, UCLA, 1971; JD, Southwestern U. Sch. Law, 1976. Bar: Calif. 1970, U.S. Dist. Ct. (so. and cen. dists.) Calif. 1985. Assoc. claims counsel Ticor Title Ins. Co., Los Angeles, 1976-79, asst. v.p., assoc. counsel, 1979-82; asst. v.p., sr. claims counsel Commonwealth Land Title Ins. Co., Los Angeles, 1982-85, v.p., regional counsel, 1985-86; ptnr. Miller, Feldman & Marsh, Los Angeles, 1986—. Mem. Town Hall of Calif., Los Angeles, 1985—; bd. dirs. San Fernando Valley Girl Scout Council, Chatsworth, Calif., 1985—. Served with USMC, 1968-70. Mem. Los Angeles County Bar Assn. (chmn. title ins. subcom. 1984-85), Assn. Real Estate Attys. (pres. 1986—), Mortgage Banking Assn. Calif., Am. Land Title Assn., Calif. Land Title Assn. Democrat. Jewish. Avocations: backpacking, camping. Real property, General corporate, Title Insurance. Office: Miller Feldman & Marsh 10100 Santa Monica Blvd Los Angeles CA 90067

MARSH, WILLIAM ROBERT, lawyer; b. Denver, Apr. 21, 1945; s. Robert William and Alice Belle (Walton) M.; m. Geraldine A. Evans, Jan. 13, 1967; children: Jack, Amy, Robert. BS in Geology, Colo. State U., 1970; JD, Denver U., 1974. Bar: Colo. 1974, U.S. Dist. Ct. Colo. 1974, U.S. Ct. Appeals (10th cir.) 1976. Geologist U.S. Geol. Survey, Denver, 1970-74; ptnr. Sherman & Howard, Denver, 1974—; instr. law Denver U., 1984—; adj. prof. Colo. Sch. Mines, Golden, 1985—; spl. counsel subcom. mines and mining U.S. Ho. of Reps., Washington, 1979-80. Contbr. articles on mining law to profl. jours. Mobile Oil fellow, 1973-74. Mem. ABA, Colo. Bar Assn., Denver Bar Assn., Colo. Mining Assn (chmn. mineral law com. 1985—, bd. dirs. 1985—). Avocations: hunting, writing. Federal civil litigation, Condemnation, Mineral law. Office: Sherman & Howard 633 17th St 2900 1st Interstate Tower N Denver CO 80202

MARSHALL, ANTHONY PARR, lawyer; b. N.Y.C., Aug. 7, 1937; s. Joseph Parr and Mildred Yoder (Heimbach) M.; m. Betsy Harbison, Sept. 28, 1963; children—Charles Christopher, Katharine Elizabeth. A.B., Princeton U., 1959; J.D., Columbia U., 1962. Bar: N.Y. 1963, U.S. Supreme Ct. 1968, U.S. Dist. Cts. (so. and ea. dists.) N.Y. 1973, N.J. 1979, U.S. Dist. Ct. N.J. 1979. Assoc., Davies, Hardy & Schenck, N.Y.C., 1964-68, Goldstein, Judd & Gurfein, N.Y.C., 1968-72; assoc. Kirlin, Campbell & Keating, N.Y.C., 1972-73, ptnr., 1973-85; v.p., mgr. estate planning sect. U.S. Trust Co. N.Y., 1985—. Past pres., chmn. bd. trustees The Hosp. Chaplaincy, Inc., N.Y.C.; pres. Retiring Fund for Women in Diaconate of Episcopal Ch. in U.S., N.Y.C.; warden St. Bartholomew's Ch., N.Y.C. Fellow Am. Coll. Probate Counsel (editor probate notes 1982-83); mem. ABA (past editor probate and property, chmn. coms. on modification, revocation and termination of trusts, tax legislation and regulations: interrelationship of gifts and estates), N.Y. State Bar Assn. (former chmn. com. on fed. legislation, estate and trust adminstrn.), Assn. Bar City N.Y. Clubs: Princeton of N.Y.C., Pilgrims. Contbr. articles to legal jours. Probate, Estate taxation, Personal income taxation. Home: 6 Carriage Dr Middletown NJ 07748

MARSHALL, ARTHUR K., lawyer, judge, arbitrator, educator, writer; b. N.Y.C., Oct. 7, 1911. B.S., CCNY, 1933; LL.B., St. John's U., N.Y.C., 1936; LL.M., U. So. Calif., 1952. Bar: N.Y. State 1937, Calif. 1947. Practice law N.Y.C., 1937-43, Los Angeles, 1947-50; atty. VA, Los Angeles, 1947-50; tax counsel Calif. Bd. Equalization, Sacramento, 1950-51; inheritance tax atty. State Controller, Los Angeles, 1951-53; commr. Superior Ct. Los Angeles County, 1953-62; judge Municipal Ct., Los Angeles jud. dist., 1962-63, Superior Ct., Los Angeles, 1963-81,; supervising judge probate dept. Superior Ct., 1968-69, appellate dept., 1973-77; presiding judge Appellate Dept., 1976-77; pvt. practice 1981—, arbitrator, referee, judge protem, 1981—; Acting asst. prof. law U. Calif. at Los Angeles, 1954-59; mem. grad. faculty U. So. Calif., 1955-75; lectr. Continuing Edn. of Bar; vice chmn. Calif. Law Revision Commn., 1984-86, chmn. 1986—. Author: Joint Tenancy Taxwise & Otherwise, 1953, Branch Courts, 1959, California State and Local Taxation, Text, 2 vols, 1962, rev. edit., 1969, supplement, 1979, 2d edit., 1981, California State and Local Taxation Forms, 2 vols, 1961-75, rev. edit., 1979, California Probate Procedure, 1961, 9th rev. edit., 1986, Guide to Procedure Before Trial, 1975. Served with AUS, 1943-46; lt. col. Res. ret. Named Judge of Yr. Lawyers Club of Los Angeles County, 1975; Arthur K. Marshall Award established by estate planning, trust and probate sect. Los Angeles Bar Assn., 1981; Disting. Jud. Career award Los Angeles Lawyers Club. Fellow Am. Bar Found.; mem. Internat. Acad. Estate and Trust Law (academician, founder, 1st pres., now chancellor), ABA (probate litigation com. real property, probate and trust sect.), Calif. State Bar (adv. to exec. com. estate planning, probate and trust sect. 1970-83), Santa Monica Bar Assn. (pres. 1960), Westwood Bar Assn. (pres. 1959), Los Angeles Bar Assn., Lawyers Club, Am. Judicature Soc., Am. Legion (comdr. 1971-72), U. So. Calif. Law Alumni Assn. (pres. 1969-70), Phi Alpha Delta (1st justice alumni chpt. 1976-77). Probate. Office: 300 S Grand Ave 29th Floor Los Angeles CA 90071

MARSHALL, BURKE, lawyer; b. Plainfield, N.J., Oct. 1, 1922. A.B., Yale U., 1944, LL.B., 1951, M.A., 1970. Bar: D.C. bar 1952. Assoc., then partner firm Covington and Burlington, Washington, 1951-61; asst. atty. gen. U.S., 1961-65; gen. counsel IBM Corp., Armonk, N.Y., 1965-69; sr. v.p. IBM Corp., 1969-70; prof. law Yale U. Law Sch., 1970—, Nicholas deB. Katzenbach prof.; chmn. Nat. Adv. Commn. SSS, 1967; chmn. bd. Vera Inst. Justice, N.Y.C., 1965—. Author: Federalism and Civil Rights, 1965; co-author: The Mylai Massacre and Its Cover-up, 1975; editor: The Supreme Court and Human Rights, 1982; Contbr. articles, revs. to legal pubs. Chmn. bd. dirs. Center Community Change, Washington, 1968—, Robert F. Kennedy Meml., 1975—. Home: Castle Meadow Rd Newtown CT 06470 Office: Law Sch Yale U New Haven CT 06520

MARSHALL, CONSUELO BLAND, U.S. district judge; b. Knoxville, Tenn., Sept. 28, 1936; d. Clyde Theodore and Annie (Brown) Arnold; m. George Edward Marshall, Aug. 30, 1959; children: Michael Edward, Laurie Ann. A.A., Los Angeles City Coll., 1956; B.A., Howard U., 1958, LL.B., 1961. Bar: Calif. 1962. Dep. atty. City of Los Angeles, 1962-67; assoc. Cochran & Atkins, Los Angeles, 1968-70; commr. Los Angeles Superior Ct., 1971-76; judge Inglewood Mcpl. Ct., 1976-77, Los Angeles Superior Ct., 1977-80, U.S. Dist. Ct. Central Dist. Calif., Los Angeles, 1980—. Contbr. articles to profl. jours.; notes editor Law Jour. Howard U. Mem. adv. bd. Richstone Child Abuse Center. Research fellow Howard U. Law Sch., 1959-60. Mem. State Bar Calif., Calif. Women Lawyers Assn., Calif. Assn. Black Lawyers, Calif. Judges Assn., Black Women Lawyers Assn., Los Angeles County Bar Assn., Nat. Assn. Women Judges, NAACP, Urban League, Beta Phi Sigma. Mem. Ch. Religious Science. Jurisprudence. Office: US Courthouse 312 N Spring St Los Angeles CA 90012

MARSHALL, DOUGLAS ANTON, lawyer; b. Santa Monica, Calif., Sept. 24, 1950; s. Douglas G. and Marjorie A. (Hadfield) M.; m. Cynthia K. Page, July 12, 1975; children: Jonathon P., Jeffrey R. BA, U. Calif., Davis, 1972; JD, Calif. Western Sch. Law, 1979. Bar: Calif. 1979, Utah 1980, U.S. Dist. Ct. (no. dist.) Calif., U.S. Dist. Ct. Utah, U.S. Ct. Appeals (9th and 10th cirs.). Law clk. to presiding justice U.S. Dist. Ct., Salt Lake City, 1979-80; assoc. Law Offices ofJosef D. Cooper, San Francisco, 1980—. Contbr. articles to profl. jours. Served to capt. U.S. Army, 1972-76. Mem. ABA, San Francisco Bar Assn., Assn. Trial Lawyers Am. Federal civil litigation, Securities, Antitrust. Office: Josef D Cooper Law Office 100 The Embarcadero Penthouse San Francisco CA 94105

MARSHALL, ELLEN RUTH, lawyer; b. N.Y.C., Apr. 23, 1949; d. Louis and Faith (Gladstone) M. AB, Yale U., 1971; JD, Harvard U., 1974. Bar: Calif. 1975, D.C. 1981. Assoc. McKenna & Fitting, Los Angeles, 1975-80; ptnr. McKenna, Conner & Cuneo, Los Angeles and Orange County, Calif., 1980—. Mem. ABA (corp., banking and bus. law sect., tax sect., employee benefits com.), Orange County Bar Assn. Club: Center (Costa Mesa, Calif.). Banking, Pension, profit-sharing, and employee benefits, General corporate. Office: McKenna Conner & Cuneo 611 Anton Blvd Costa Mesa CA 92626

MARSHALL, HERBERT A., lawyer; b. Clinton, Ill., Aug. 20, 1917; s. Harry A. and Andrea (Pederson) M.; m. Helen Christman, May 3, 1941; children—James A., Thomas O., Mary (Mrs. William Nichols). A.B., Washburn U., 1940, LL.B., J.D., 1943. Bar: Kans. bar 1943. Law clk. U.S. Ct. Appeals, 1943-44; asst. county atty. Shawnee County, Kans., 1944-50; practiced in Topeka, 1944—; mem. firm Mashall, Davis, Bennett & Hendrix, 1946—; instr. practice ct. Washburn U. Law Sch., 1963—; mem. Kans. Supreme Ct. Nominating Commn., 1968-79. Trustee, elder Presbyn. Ch. Fellow Am. Bar Found. (life), Kans. Bar Found. (life), Am. Coll. Trial Lawyers; mem. ABA, Kans. Bar Assn. (exec. council 1968—, v.p. 1977, pres. 1979), Am. Judicature Soc., Topeka Bar Assn. (pres. 1968), Topeka C. of C. Clubs: Masons, Elks, Moose, Topeka Optimist. Insurance, Federal civil litigation, State civil litigation. Home: 4722 Brentwood St Topeka KS 66606 Office: 210 Commerce Bank Bldg 31st and S Topeka Blvd Topeka KS 66611

MARSHALL, J. STEPHEN, lawyer; b. Grand Rapids, Mich., Mar. 19, 1948; s. Harry D. and Judy (Corrigan) M.; m. Pamela K. Bergmans, June 17, 1972; children: Sarah Aubrey, Heather Elizabeth. AA, Grand Rapids Jr. Coll., 1968; BBA, U. Mich., 1970; JD, Ind. U., 1975. Bar: Mich. 1975, U.S. Dist. Ct. (we. dist.) Mich. 1975. Ptnr. Norris, Keyser & Marshall, Grand Rapids, 1975-80; sole practice Grand Rapids, 1980—; bd. dirs. Med. Personnel Pool, Grand Rapids. Mem. ABA, Mich. Bar Assn., Grand Rapids Bar Assn., U. Mich. Alumni Assn. (pres., bd. dirs. 1984—). Presbyterian. Club: U. Mich. (Grand Rapids) (pres., bd. dirs. 1977—). General practice, Insurance, Personal injury. Office: 922 Trust Bldg Grand Rapids MI 49503

MARSHALL, JAMES MARKHAM, lawyer; b. Long Beach, Calif., Aug. 30, 1940; s. Henry Morris and Eleanor Thompson (Wallace) M.; m. Cheryl Suzanne Chance, Nov. 27, 1971; children: Edith, Robert, Carolyn. AB, Whitman Coll., 1962; LLB, Stanford U., 1966. Bar: Wash. 1966, D.C. 1979, U.S. Dist. Ct. (we. dist.) Wash., U.S. Ct. Appeals (9th and Fed. cirs.). Field atty. NLRB, Seattle, 1966-67; assoc. McMullen, Brooke et al, Seattle, 1967-69, Clodfelter, Lindell & Carr, Seattle, 1969-72; sole practice Seattle, 1973; ptnr. Preston, Thorgrimson,Ellis & Holman, Seattle, 1973—. Served with U.S. Army, 1963-64. Episcopalian. Labor, State civil litigation. Office: Preston Thorgrimson Ellis & Holman 5400 Columbia Seafirst Ctr Seattle WA 98104-7011

MARSHALL, JOHN DAVID, lawyer; b. Chgo., May 19, 1940; s. John Howard and Sophie (Brezenk) M.; m. Marcia A. Podlasinski, Aug. 26, 1961; children: Jacquelyn, David, Jason, Patricia, Brian, Denise, Michael, Catherine. BS in Acctg., U. Ill., 1961; JD, Ill. Inst. Tech., 1965. Bar: Ill. 1965, U.S. Tax Ct. 1968, U.S. Dist. Ct. (no. dist.) Ill. 1971; CPA, Ill. Ptnr. Mayer, Brown & Platt, Chgo., 1961—. Bd. dirs. Levinson Ctr. for Handicapped Children, Chgo., 1970-75. Fellow Am. Coll. Probate Counsel; mem. Ill. Bar Assn., Chgo. Bar Assn. (agribus. com. 1978—, trust law com. 1969—, probate practice com. 1969—, com. on coms. 1983—, legis. com. of probate practice com. 1983—, chmn. and vice chmn. legis. com. of probate practice com. 1983-84, chmn. exec. com. probate practice com. 1982-83, vice chmn. exec. com. 1981-82, sec. exec. com. 1980-81, div. chmn. 78-79, div. vice chmn. 1977-78, div. sec. 1976-77, Appreciation award 1982-83), Chgo. Estate Planning Council. Roman Catholic. Club: Union League (Chgo.). Estate planning, Probate, Estate taxation. Home: 429 Willow Wood Dr Palatine IL 60067 Office: Mayer Brown & Platt 190 S LaSalle St Chicago IL 60603

MARSHALL, JOHN HENRY, lawyer; b. Paterson, N.J., July 31, 1949; s. Henry Leland and Elizabeth Marion (Bates) M.; m. Jan Eastman, May 4, 1979. AB, Dartmouth Coll., 1971; BA, Cambridge U., Eng., 1973; JD, Yale U., 1977. Bar: Vt. 1977, U.S. Dist. Ct. Vt. 1978. Assoc. Downs Rachlin & Martin, St. Johnsbury, Vt., 1977-82, ptnr., 1982—. Chmn. Dist. Environ. Commn., St. Johnsbury, 1981—. Served to capt. U.S. Army, 1973-74. Public utilities, General corporate, Administrative and regulatory. Home: RFD 1-70 Barnet VT 05821 Office: Downs Rachlin & Martin 9 Prospect St Saint Johnsbury VT 05819-0099

MARSHALL, KATHRYN SUE, lawyer; b. Decatur, Ill., Sept. 12, 1942; d. Edward Elda, Jr. and Frances Maxine (Minor) Lahniers; m. Robert Stephen Marshall, Sept. 5, 1964; children—Stephen Edward, Christine Elizabeth. B.A., Lake Forest Coll., 1964; J.D., John Marshall Law Sch., 1976. Bar: Ill. 1976, U.S. Dist. Ct. (no. dist.) Ill. 1976, U.S. Ct. Mil. Appeals 1977, U.S. Supreme Ct. 1979; lic. real estate agt., Ill. Intern Office of U.S. Atty. No. Dist. Chgo., Ill., 1974-76; mng. ptnr. Marshall and Marshall, Ltd., Waukegan, Ill., 1976-84; sole practice, Waukegan, 1984—; adj. tchr. John Marshall Law Sch., Chgo., 1980-81, Nat. Coll. Edn., Evanston, Ill., 1981—; legal adviser Nat. Coll. Paralegal Program, Evanston, Ill., 1981—; lectr. on various subjects internationally, 1978—. Contbg. author: New Tricks for Old Dogs: Managing A Family Law Practice; Flying Solo, 1984; also articles, manuals. Mem. alumni council John Marshall Law Sch., Chgo., 1977-81; mem. adv. com. on vets. for Senator Adeline J. Geo-Karis; intervenor Lawyer's Assistance Program, Inc. Fellow Ill. Bar Found.; mem. ABA (rep. ho. of dels., chmn. various coms. sect of econs. of law practice 1976—, chmn. com. on econs. of practice 1981, mem. long planning com. 1982—, sect. family law), Ill. Bar Assn. (com. on econs. of law practice 1981-82), Women's Bar Assn. Ill. (com. on family law 1980-82), Ill. Trial Lawyers Assn., Lake County Bar Assn (com on circuit clk.'s office 1976-77, com. on family law 1977—, chmn. com. on econs. of law practice 1979-80, chmn. com. on fee grievances 1979-80), Chgo. Bar Assn., Assn. Women Attys. of Lake County (com. on award of reasonable atty.'s fees 1982, bd. dirs. 1983—, chmn. com. on family law 1984—), Internat. Bar Assn., Solicitor's Family Law Assn. Family and matrimonial, Military.

MARSHALL, PRENTICE H., fed. judge; b. 1926. B.S., 1949; J.D., U. Ill., 1951. Bar: Ill. bar 1951. Judge U.S. Dist. Ct. for No. Ill., 1973—; assoc. firm Johnston Thompson Raymond & Mayer, Chgo., 1953-60; ptnr. Raymond Mayer Jenner & Block, Chgo., 1961-67; spl. asst. atty. gen. State of Ill., 1964-67; hearing officer Ill. Fair Employment Practices Commn., 1967-72; faculty Am. Law Inst.; adj. prof. law Ill. Inst. Tech., Chgo.-Kent Coll. Law, 1975—; prof. law U. Ill., 1967-73. Served with USN, 1944-46. Mem. Am. Coll. Trial Lawyers, Am. Law Inst., ABA, Am. Judicature Soc.,

Ill., Chgo. bar assns., Bar Assn. of Seventh Cir., Phi Beta Kappa. Office: US Courthouse 219 S Dearborn St Chicago IL 60604 *

MARSHALL, RICHARD TREEGER, lawyer; b. N.Y.C., May 17, 1925; s. Edward and Sydney (Treeger) M.; m. Dorothy M. Goodman, June 4, 1950; children—Abigail Ruth Marshall Bergerson, Daniel Brooks; m. 2d, Sylvia J. Kelley, June 10, 1979. B.S., Cornell U., 1948; J.D., Yale U., 1951. Bar: Tex. 1952, U.S. Ct. Appeals (5th cir.) 1966, U.S. Ct. Appeals (10th cir.) 1980, U.S. Supreme Ct., 1959. Sole practice, El Paso, Tex., 1952-59, 61-79; assoc. Fryer & Milstead, El Paso, 1952; sr. ptnr. Marshall & Wendorf, El Paso, 1959-61; sr. ptnr. Marshall & Volk, El Paso, 1979-81; sr. atty. Richard T. Marshall & Assocs., P.C., El Paso, 1981-85; sr. ptnr. Marshall, Thomas & Winters, El Paso, 1985—; instr. ins. law C.L.U. tng. course Am. Coll.; officer, dir. Advance Funding, Inc., El Paso. Mem. ABA, State Bar Tex., El Paso Bar Assn., El Paso Trial Lawyers Assn. (pres. 1965-66), Tex. Trial Lawyers Assn., Assn. Trial Lawyers Am. (sec. personal injury law sect. 1967-68, nat. sec. 1969-70, sec.-treas. environ. law sect. 1970-71, vice chmn. family law litigation sect. 1971-72); Roscoe Pound-Am. Trial Lawyers Found. (Commn. on Profl. Responsibility 1979-82), Am. Arbitration Assn. (nat. panel arbitrators). Editor: El Paso Trial Lawyers Rev., 1973-80; contbr. articles to legal jours. Personal injury, Federal civil litigation, State civil litigation. Office: 6070 Gateway E Suite 306 El Paso TX 79905

MARSHALL, SYLVAN MITCHELL, lawyer, former ambassador, TV producer; b. N.Y.C., May 14, 1917; s. Louis H. and Kitty Markowitz; m. Mara Byron, Feb. 11, 1951; children: Douglas Wayne, Bradley Ross. B.A., CCNY, 1938; J.D., Harvard U., 1941. Bar: N.Y. State bar 1946, D.C. bar 1953. Mem. firm Garey & Garey, N.Y.C., 1946-51; spl. asst. to chief counsel OPS, Washington, 1951-53; partner firm Granik & Marshall, Washington, 1953-58; spl. dep. atty. gen. N.Y. State, 1946-50; pvt. practice law Washington, 1953—; sr. ptnr. law firm Marshall, Leon Weill & Mahony; counsel Leon, Weill & Mahony, N.Y.C., 1974-84; sr. Washington ptnr. Marshall, Tenzer, Greenblatt, Fallon & Kaplan, 1984—; Washington counsel Community Fed. Savs. & Loan Assn., St. Louis, First Fed., Jacksonville, Fla.; Washington counsel Southgate Fed. Savs. & Loan Assn., Newport, Ky., Diamond & Precious Stone Bourse, Idar-Oberstein, W. Ger.; also fgn. embassies; presdl. ambassador to Inauguration of pres. of Mexico, 1976; spl. counsel for internat. affairs to dir. Los Angeles County Mus. Natural History. Assoc. producer: Youth Wants to Know and Am. Forum, NBC-TV and radio, 1953-58. con. dep. police commr., N.Y.C., 1950-53, hon. consul, Finland; adv. trustee Am. U., Washington. Served from 2d lt. to lt. col. U.S. Army, 1941-46. Decorated knight comdr. Order of Falcon (Iceland), Order of Vasco Nunez de Balboa (Republic of Panama); comdr. Order of Lion (Finland); Order of Taj (Iran); Order Aztec Eagle (Mexico); Order So. Cross (Brazil); Order Ruben Dario (Nicaragua); Order of Lion and Sun (Iran); Nat. Order Merit (Mauritania). Order of Crown (Thailand); Order Strong Right Arm of Kingdom of Gurkhas (Nepal); Order or Republic (Tunisia). Club: Cosmos (Washington). Administrative and regulatory, Banking, Private international. Office: 4545 42d St NW Suite 214 Washington DC 20016 also: 405 Lexington Ave New York NY 10174

MARSHALL, THOMAS OLIVER, JR., judge; b. Americus, Ga., June 24, 1920; s. Thomas Oliver and Mattie Louise (Hunter) M.; m. Angie Ellen Fitts, Dec. 20, 1946; children—Ellen Irwin Marshall Beard, Anne Hunter Marshall Peagler, Mary Olivia Marshall Crook. B.S. in Engring, U.S. Naval Acad., 1941; J.D., U. Ga., 1948. Bar: Ga. bar 1947. Individual practice law Americus, Ga., 1948-60; judge S.W. Judicial Circuit, Americus, 1960-74, Ga. Ct. Appeals, Atlanta, 1974-77; justice Ga. Supreme Ct., Atlanta, 1977-86, chief justice, 1986—; chmn. bd. visitors U. Ga. Law Sch., 1970. Trustee Andrew Coll., So. Ga. Meth. Home for Aged; active ARC, 1948-60, United Givers Fund, 1948-54. Served with USN, World War II, Korean War. Decorated Bronze Star; named Young Man of Yr. Americus, 1953. Mem. ABA, Ga. Bar Assn. (bd. govs. 1958-60), Atlanta Bar Assn., State Bar Ga., Am. Judicature Soc., Nat. Jud. Coll., Jud. Coll. Ga., VFW, Am. Legion. Methodist. Lodges: Elks, Kiwanis, Masons, Shriners. Home: 238 15th St NE Condominium 3 Atlanta GA 30309 Office: Ga Supreme Ct 514 State Judicial Bldg Atlanta GA 30334

MARSHALL, THURGOOD, asso. justice U.S. Supreme Ct.; b. Balt., July 2, 1908; s. William and Norma (Williams) M.; m. Vivian Burey, Sept. 4, 1929 (dec. Feb. 1955); m. Cecilia S. Suyat, Dec. 17, 1955; children—Thurgood, John. A.B., Lincoln U., 1930, LL.D., 1947; LL.B., Howard U., 1933, LL.D., 1954; LL.D., Va. State Coll., 1948, Morgan State Coll., 1952, Grinnell Coll., 1954, Syracuse U., 1956, N.Y. Sch. Social Research, 1956, U. Liberia, 1960, Brandeis U., 1960, U. Mass., 1962, Jewish Theol. Sem., 1962, Wayne U., 1963, Princeton U., 1963, U. Mich., 1964, Johns Hopkins U., 1966; LL.D. hon. degree, Far Eastern Univ., Manila, 1968, Victoria U. of Wellington, 1968, U. Calif., 1968, U. Otago, Dunedin, New Zealand, 1968. Bar: Md. bar 1933. Practiced in Balt., 1933-37; asst. spl. counsel N.A.A.C.P., 1936-38, spl. counsel, 1938-50, dir., counsel legal def. and ednl. fund, 1940-61; U.S. circuit judge for 2d Jud. Circuit, 1961-65; solicitor gen. U.S., 1965-67; justice U.S. Supreme Ct., 1967—; Civil rights cases argued include Tex. Primary Case, 1944, Restrictive Covenant Cases, 1948, U. Tex. and Okla. Cases, 1950, sch. segregation cases, 1952-53; visited Japan and Korea to make investigation of ct. martial cases involving Negro soldiers, 1951; Cons. Constl. Conf. on Kenya, London, 1960; rep. White House Conf. Youth and Children. Recipient Spingarn medal, 1946; Living History award Research Inst. Mem. Nat. Bar Assn., N.Y. County Lawyers Assn., Am. Bar Assn., Bar Assn. D.C., Alpha Phi Alpha. Episcopalian. Club: Mason (33 deg.). Jurisprudence. Home: Falls Church VA Office: Supreme Ct US Washington DC 20543

MARSHALL, VALERIE ANN, lawyer; b. Evansville, Ind., Aug. 26, 1954; d. Arthur E. and Jacqueline J. (Maixner) M. BBA, Stetson U., 1976, JD, 1979. Bar: Fla. 1979. Assoc. Clayton & Landis, Orlando, Fla., 1980-81; in-house counsel Walt Disneyworld Co., Lake Buena Vista, Fla., 1981-83; assoc. Haas, Boehm, Brown, Rigdon & Seacrest, Orlando, 1983-84; jr. ptnr., workers compensation supr. Haas, Boehm, Brown, Rigdon, Seacrest & Fischer, Orlando, 1984—. Mem. ABA, Orange County Bar (vice chmn. worker's compensation com. 1984—), Fla. Bar (workers compensation rules com. 1985—), Fla. Assn. for Women Lawyers (sec. 1982-84), NOW, Alpha Chi Omega (v.p. 1974-76). Methodist. Avocations: music, writing, cooking, tennis, needlework. Workers' compensation, Insurance. Office: Haas Boehm Brown Rigdon Seacrest & Fischer 801 N Magnolia Orlando FL 32806

MARSICO, LEONARD JOSEPH, lawyer; b. Pitts., Sept. 7, 1955; s. Francis A. and Teresa (Constantini) M.; m. Mildred Farrar Williams, Dec. 3, 1983; 1 child, Megan Farrar. BA, U. Va., 1977; JD, U. Pitts., 1980. Bar: Pa. 1980, U.S. Dist. Ct. (we. dist.) Pa. 1980. Assoc. Buchanan Ingersoll, Pitts., 1980—; bd. dirs. Fin. Mgmt. and Analysis Group Inc. Staff mem. U. Pitts. Law Rev., 1979-80. Mem. ABA, Pa. Bar Assn., Allegheny County Bar Assn. Republican. Roman Catholic. Avocations: golf, squash, skiing, sailing. Commercial litigation, General corporate. Office: Buchanan Ingersoll Prof Corp 57th Floor 600 Grant St Pittsburgh PA 15219

MARSTELLER, THOMAS FRANKLIN, JR., lawyer; b. Phila., Oct. 18, 1951; s. Thomas Franklin and Hannah Henrietta (Bender) M.; B.S. in Physics, Rensselaer Poly. Inst., 1973; J.D., U. Houston, 1979. Bar: Tex. 1980, U.S. Ct. Claims 1980, U.S. Ct. Internat. Trade 1980, U.S. Patent Office 1980, U.S. Dist. Ct. (ea. and no. dist.) Tex. 1981, U.S. Ct. Appeals (5th and 11th cir.) 1981, U.S. Ct. Appeals (fed. cir.) 1982, U.S. Supreme Ct. 1983, U.S. Dist. Ct. (we. dist.) Tex. 1984, U.S. Dist. Ct. (so. dist.) Tex. 1985. Assoc., Pravel, Gambrell, Hewitt, Kirk & Kimball, Houston, 1979— ; shareholder Marsteller & Assocs., P.C., 1984—; panelist Am. Arbiration Assn. Host, Houston Grand Opera. Served with USAF, 1973-77. Decorated Air Force Commendation medal; recipient Am. Jurisprudence award U. Houston, 1978. Mem. ABA, Internat. Bar Assn., Fed. Bar Assn. (treas. local chpt. 1984-87), Tex. Young Lawyers Assn., Houston Bar Assn. (sec. Internat. law sect. 1983-84), Houston Engring. and Sci. Soc., Houston Young Lawyers Assn. (chmn. Bill of Rights com. 1980-81). Clubs: Masons, Shriners. Editor Houston Jour. Internat. Law, 1978-79. Contbr. articles to profl. jours. Patent, Trademark and copyright, General corporate. Home: PO Box 27580 Houston TX 77227 Office: Marsteller & Assocs PC 3000 Post Oak Blvd Suite 1400 Houston TX 77056

MARTAN, JOSEPH RUDOLF, lawyer; b. Oak Park, Ill., Mar. 28, 1949; s. Joseph John and Margarete Paulina (Rothenbock) M.; BA with honors, U. Ill., 1971; JD with honors, Ill. Inst. Tech., Chgo.-Kent Coll. Law, 1977. Admitted to Ill. bar, 1977, U.S. dist. ct. for No. dist. Ill., 1977; assoc. firm V. C. Lopez, Chgo., 1978-80; litigation counsel Goldblatt Bros., Inc., Chgo., 1980-81; br. counsel Ill. br. Am. Family Ins. Group, Schaumburg, 1981-87; atty. Judge & Knight Ltd., Park Ridge, Ill., 1987—. Mem. West Suburban Community Band, Inc., Western Springs, Ill., 1975—, pres., 1979-81. Served with U.S. Army, 1972-74, to capt. USAR, 1974-85. Decorated Army Commendation medal. Mem. Ill. State Bar Assn., Chgo. Bar Assn., Du Page County Bar Assn. (mem. civil practice com.), Bohemian Lawyer's Assn. Chgo., Def. Research Inst., Assn. Trial Lawyers Am., Res. Officer's Assn., Assn. U.S. Army, Met. Opera Guild, Pi Sigma Alpha, Pi Sigma Alpha. Insurance, State civil litigation, Personal injury. Home: 4056 Gilbert Ave Western Springs IL 60558 Office: Judge & Knight 422 N Northwest Hwy Park Ridge IL 60068

MARTEN, JUDD ROBERT, lawyer; b. Winfield, Kans., Mar. 2, 1946; s. John Alexander and Mary Ann (Bair) M.; m. Susanne E. Miller, June 22, 1974. BA, U. Calif., Santa Barbara, 1969; JD, U. Puget Sound, 1977; LLM in Taxation, Boston U., 1979. Bar: Wash. 1979. Assoc. Dahlgren & Dauenhauer, Seattle, 1979-83; ptnr. LeSourd & Patten, Seattle, 1983—; faculty Golden Gate U., Seattle, 1986—. Mem. ABA, Wash. State Bar Assn. (speaker 1986), Seattle Pension Round Table (speaker 1984-85), Wash. Women in Tax (speaker 1983), Wash. Soc. CPA's (speaker 1984). Avocation: Arabian horses. Pension, profit-sharing, and employee benefits, Corporate taxation, Estate taxation. Home: 5435 S Bell St Tacoma WA 98408 Office: LeSourd & Patten PS 2400 Columbia Ctr Seattle WA 98104-7005

MARTIN, ALAN JAY, lawyer; b. N.Y.C., Nov. 8, 1934; s. Julius and Mabel (Gettinger) M.; m. Carole Sheila Goldman, Sept. 7, 1962; children: Paul, David, Amy. BA, NYU, 1956, JD, 1962. Bar: U.S. Ct. Appeals (2d cir.) 1962, U.S. Supreme Ct. 1971. Claims mgr. Mission Ins. Group, N.Y.C., 1958-62; assoc. Honey H. Abrams, N.Y.C., 1962-64; ptnr. Abrams & Martin P.C., N.Y.C., 1964—; arbitrator N.Y.C. Small Claims Ct., Queens, 1970—, N.Y. Ins. Exchange, 1981—, Am. Arbitration Assn., N.Y.C., 1978—; counsel Profl. Ins. Wholesalers Assn., 1980—; panelist Property Loss Research Assn, Chgo., 1982—. Named Man of Yr., Anti Defamation League, 1983, Ins. Sq. Club, 1980. Mem. N.Y. State Bar Assn., Queens County Bar Assn., N.Y. County Bar Assn., Am. Judges Assn., Supreme Ct. Hist. Soc., Young Men's Philanthropic League. Jewish. Avocations: photography, stamps, coins. Insurance, General practice. Home: 415 Chestnut Dr East Hills NY 11576

MARTIN, ALLAN A., lawyer; b. N.Y.C., Feb. 16, 1945; s. Robert and Beatrice (Cohen) M.; m. Sheryl A. Spector, Oct. 19, 1969; children—Gregg, Kevin Rachel. B.B.A., CCNY, 1966; J.D., George Washington U., 1969, LL.M., 1973. Bar: N.Y. 1970, U.S. Dist. Ct. (so. dist.) N.Y. 1972, U.S. Ct. Appeals (2d, D.C. cirs.) 1972, U.S. Supreme Ct. 1974. Br. chief, trial atty. SEC, Washington, 1969-73; ptnr. firm Wachtell, Lipton, Rosen & Katz, N.Y.C., 1973—. Mem. Assn. Trial Lawyers Am., ABA, Nassau County Bar Assn., Fed. Bar Council, Beta Alpha Psi, Phi Alpha Delta. Securities, Federal civil litigation, Banking. Home: 21 Maple Dr Port Washington NY 11050 Office: Wachtell Lipton Rosen & Katz 229 Park Ave New York NY 10171

MARTIN, ALSON ROBERT, lawyer; b. Kansas City, Mo., Jan. 19, 1946; s. Keith U. and Hulda (Tully) M.; m. Dorian Doherty, May 26, 1979; children: Scott Alson, Bradley A. BA, U. Kans., 1968; JD cum laude, NYU, 1971, LLM in Taxation, 1976. Bar: N.Y. 1972, Kans. 1976, U.S. Supreme Ct. 1976, U.S. Ct. Appeals (10th cir.) 1979, U.S. Tax Ct. 1979. Assoc. Payne & Jones, Olathe, Kans., 1976-80; ptnr. Logan & Martin, Overland Park, Kans., 1980-85, Shook, Hardy & Bacon, Overland Park, 1986; mem. legal adv. bd. Small Bus. Counsel of Am.; speaker at numerous confs. Co-author: Kansas Corporation Law and Practice, 1977, rev. ed., 1983. Bd. dirs. Arthritis Found., Kans.; legal counsel Olathe Community Theatre Assn.; trustee Johnson County Community Coll.; exec. mem. profl. adv. com. Mid-Am. Arts Alliance, 1976-78. Served to lt. USN. Mem. ABA, Kans. Bar Assn. (exec. com. tax sect.), Johnson County Bar Assn., Estate Planning Council of Kansas City, Internat. Assn. Fin. Planning (adv. bd., regulatory com.). General corporate, Pension, profit-sharing, and employee benefits, Corporate taxation. Office: Shook Hardy & Bacon #40 Corporate Woods #650 9401 Indian Creek Pkwy PO Box 95128 Overland Park KS 66225

MARTIN, ARTHUR LEE, JR., lawyer; b. Montgomery, Ala., Jan. 13, 1949; s. Arthur Lee and Blanche (Bush) M.; m. Mary Lynne Ortmeyer, Sept. 29, 1973; children—Elizabeth Leah, Rachel Blanche. B.A. cum laude, Vanderbilt U., 1971; J.D. U. Chgo., 1974. Bar: U.S. Dist. Ct. (no. dist.) Ill. 1972, U.S. Ct. Appeals (7th cir.) 1972, Ill. 1975, Ala. 1979, U.S. Dist. Ct. (no. dist.) Ala. 1979, U.S. Ct. Appeals (5th cir.) 1979. Law clk. to Sr. judge U.S. Ct. Appeals (5th cir.), Montgomery, 1974-75; assoc. D'Ancona & Pflaum, Chgo., 1975-78; ptnr. Haskell, Slaughter & Young, Birmingham, Ala., 1978—. Trustee Arlington Hist. Mus., Birmingham, 1980—; dir. Birmingham Housing Devel. Corp., Ala., 1981—. Mem. Nat. Assn. Bond Lawyers, ABA, Ala. State Bar, Birmingham Bar Assn., Phi Delta Phi. Democrat. Congregationalist. Clubs: Relay House, Downtown Democratic. Local government, Health, Municipal bonds. Home: 4501 10th Ave S Birmingham AL 35222 Office: Haskell Slaughter & Young 800 1st Nat-So Nat Bldg Birmingham AL 35203

MARTIN, BARRY DOUGLAS, lawyer; b. Emporia, Kans., Jan. 8, 1951; s. Glenn F. and Dorthy (Lucker) M.; m. Mollie Pickford, June 20, 1978; children: Amanda, Carrie, Lisa. BS in Acctg., U. Kans., 1974; JD, Washburn U., 1976; LLM in Taxation, U. Mo., Kansas City, 1979. Bar: Kans. 1977, U.S. Dist. Ct. Kans. 1977, U.S. Ct. Claims 1979, U.S. Tax Ct. 1979. Staff auditor Price Waterhouse & Co., Kansas City, Mo., 1974; with tax dept. Arthur Andersen & Co., Kansas City, 1977-78; ptnr. Hackler, Londerholm, Corder, Martin & Hackler, Olathe, Kans., 1979—; Instr. Johnson Community Coll., Overland Park, Kans., 1985—. Contbr. articles to profl. jours. Mem. ABA (com. mem. sect. of taxation-domestic relations 1984—), Kans. Bar Assn., Johnson County Bar Assn., Kans. Trial Lawyers Assn. Republican. Methodist. Avocations: sports, teaching college classes, hunting. General corporate, Estate planning, Probate. Office: Hackler Londerholm Corder Martin 201 N Cherry Olathe KS 66061

MARTIN, BOYCE FICKLEN, JR., federal judge; b. Boston, Oct. 23, 1935; s. Boyce Ficklen and Helen Artt M.; m. Mavin Hamilton Brown, July 8, 1961; children: Mary V. H., Julia H.C. ,Boyce Ficklen III, Robert C. G. II. A.B., Davidson Coll., 1957; J.D., U. Va., 1963. Bar: Ky. 1963. Law clk. to Shackelford Miller, Jr., chief judge U.S. Ct. Appeals for 6th Circuit, Cin., 1963-64; asst. U.S. atty. Western Dist. Ky., Louisville, 1964; U.S. atty. U.S. atty. Western Dist. Ky., 1965; practiced in Louisville, 1966-74; judge Jefferson Circuit Ct., Louisville, 1974-76; chief judge Ct. Appeals Ky., Louisville, 1976-79; judge U.S. Ct. Appeals 6th Circuit Ohio, Cin., 1979—. Mem. vestry St. Francis in the Fields Episc. Ch., Harrods Creek, Ky., 1979-83; bd. visitors Davidson (N.C.) Coll., 1980-86; trustee Isaac W. Bernheim Found., Louisville, 1981—, Blackacre Found., Inc., Louisville, 1983—, Hanover Coll., Ind., 1983—; mem. exec. bd. Old Ky. Home council Boy Scouts Am., 1968-72; pres. Louisville Zool. Commn., 1971-74. Served to capt. JAGC, U.S. Army, 1958-66. Fellow Am. Bar Found.; mem. Inst. Jud. Adminstrn., Am. Judicature Soc., Fed Bar Assn., ABA (com. effective appellate advocacy Conf. Appellate Judges), Ky. Bar Assn., Louisville Bar Assn. Jurisprudence. Office: 601 W Broadway Louisville KY 40202

MARTIN, CHARLES HOWARD, law educator; b. Washington, Nov. 13, 1952; s. John Thomas and Hestlene Lee (Brooks) M. BA, Harvard U., 1974; JD, U. Calif., Berkeley, 1977. Bar: D.C. 1977, Fla. 1982. Assoc. Hogan & Hartson, Washington, 1977-78; asst. to gen. counsel Dept. Navy, Washington, 1978-79; asst. corp. counsel D.C. Corp. Counsel, Washington, 1979-82; asst. atty. gen. State of Fla., Tallahassee, 1982-84; asst. prof. Fla. State U. Law Sch., Tallahassee, 1984-85; assoc. prof. law Villanova (Pa.) U. Law Sch., 1985—; cons. Fisk U., Nashville, 1982—, Waskers Corp. Author: (with others) Media Access, 1981. Mem. ABA, Nat. Bar Assn. Administrative and regulatory, Personal injury, Workers' compensation. Home: 2740 N 46th St Philadelphia PA 19131 Office: Villanova U Sch of Law Villanova PA 19085

MARTIN, CHARLES LEE, lawyer; b. Birmingham, Ala., Apr. 22, 1952; s. John Owen and Mary King (Bridgers) M.; m. Gabrielle Manigault Northington, Mar. 17, 1973 (div. Mar. 1976); m. Valerie Lynn Duncan, Sept. 15, 1984; 1 child, Charles Maxwell. Student, Ga. Coll., 1970-72; AB, Mercer U., 1974, JD, 1977. Bar: Ga. 1977, U.S. Dist. Ct. (mid. and no. dists.) Ga. 1977, U.S. Ct. Appeals (5th and 11th cirs.) 1977. Sole practice Macon, Ga., 1977-84, Atlanta, 1983—. Mem. Community Devel. Hist. Dist. Program Commn., Macon, 1975-77, Atlanta Vol. Lawyers Found., 1983—, DeKalb Vol. Lawyers Found., Decatur, Ga., 1984—; chmn. membership com. Ga. Trust for Hist. Preservation, 1978. Mem. Nat. Orgn. Social Security Claimants Reps. Episcopalian. Pension, profit-sharing, and employee benefits, Civil rights, Federal civil litigation. Office: 119 N McDonough St Decatur GA 30030

MARTIN, CLIFFORD, lawyer; b. Bypro, Ky., Jan. 29, 1929; s. Milt and Ethel Martin; m. Helen Jeanne Huddleston, May 30, 1955; m. 2d, Rose Marie Hawkins, May 20, 1972; children—Daryll W., Isabel, Sandra. Student, Caney Jr. Coll. 1947-49, U. Ky. 1949-50; LL.B., St. Mary's U., 1954, J.D. 1970. Bar: Tex. 1953, Ky. 1954, Md. 1957. Claims adjuster Nationwide Ins. Co., Balt., 1954-60; sole practice, Ky., 1953-54, Balt., 1960—. Served with USAF, 1950-53. Mem. ABA, Md. Bar Assn., Md. Trial Lawyers Assn., Baltimore County Bar Assn. Democrat. Clubs: Luncheon Optimists (pres. 1982, 83), Omega, Gray Manor Sportsmen's (Dundalk, Md.). Criminal, Personal injury, Workers' compensation. Home: 12 King Charles Circle Baltimore MD 21237 Office: 2507 Old North Point Rd Baltimore MD 21222

MARTIN, CONNIE RUTH, lawyer; b. Clovis, N.Mex., Sept. 9, 1955; d. Lynn Latimer and Marian Ruth (Pierce) M. BA, Eastern N.Mex. U., 1976, MEd, 1977; JD, U. Mo., 1981. Bar: N.Mex. 1981, U.S. Dist. Ct. N.Mex. 1981. Asst. dist. atty. State of N.Mex., Farmington, 1981-84; from assoc. to ptnr. Tansey, Rosebrough, Roberts & Gerding, P.C., Farmington, 1984—; dep. med. investigator, State of N.Mex., Farmington, 1981-84; instr. San Juan Coll., 1987—. Bd. dirs., exec. com. San Juan County Econ. Opportunity Council, Farmington, 1982-83; bd. dirs. Four Corners Substance Abuse Council, Farmington, 1984. Recipient Distinguished Service award San Juan County, 1984; named Outstanding Young Woman in Am. Jaycees. Mem. ABA, San Juan County Bar Assn. (treas. 1985—, v.p. 1987), N.Mex. Bar Assn. (assistance to new lawyers com. 1986—), Christian Legal Soc. Democrat. Baptist. Avocations: skiing, camping. Real property, General corporate, Criminal. Office: Tansey Rosebrough Roberts & Gerding 621 W Arrington Farmington NM 87401

MARTIN, DAVID LUTHER, lawyer; b. Providence, Feb. 4, 1947; s. George J. and Helen I. Martin. BA, U. R.I., 1968; JD, U. Va., 1973. Bar: R.I. 1973, U.S. Dist. Ct. R.I. 1974, U.S. Ct. Appeals (1st cir.) 1986. Assoc. Connors & Kilguss, Providence, 1973-74; asst. pub. defender Providence, 1974-81; sole practice Cranston, R.I., 1981-85, Providence, 1985—. Served to lt. USAR, 1969-71. Mem. R.I. Bar Assn., Nat. Assn. Criminal Def. Atty.'s, Assn. Trial Lawyers Am. Lutheran. Criminal, General practice. Home: 77 Vancouver Ave Warwick RI 02886 Office: 808 Hospital Trust Bldg Providence RI 02903

MARTIN, E. GREGORY, lawyer; b. Warsaw, Mo., Mar. 17, 1931; s. E.R. and Orpha (Mitchener) M.; m. Betty Beal, Dec. 26, 1954; children: Michael Gregory, Scot Douglas, Brent Mitchener, Susan Elizabeth. LLB, U. Colo., 1959. Bar: Colo. 1959, U.S. Dist. Ct. Colo. 1959. Sole practice Boulder, Colo., 1959—; chmn. adv. commn. on crime classification and sentencing State of Colo., 1979-82. Fellow Am. Coll. Trial Lawyers; mem. Colo. Bar Assn. (sr. v.p. 1980-81), Boulder County Bar Assn. (pres. 1971-72). Democrat. Avocations: running, bicycling, skiing. Federal civil litigation, State civil litigation, Personal injury. Home: 7415 Panorama Dr Boulder CO 80303 Office: 2010 14th St Boulder CO 80302

MARTIN, FAYE SANDERS, judge; b. Brooklet, Ga., Feb. 6, 1934; d. Carroll Eugene and Addie L. (Prosser) Sanders; m. J. Hollis Martin, Feb. 26, 1961; children—Janna, Jenny Lynn. Student, Ga. So. Coll., 1952-54; J.D., Woodrow Wilson Coll. Law, Atlanta, 1956. Bar: Ga. 1956, U.S. Dist. Ct. (so. dist.) Ga. 1971, U.S. Supreme Ct. 1978. Ptnr., Anderson & Sanders, Statesboro, Ga., 1956-78; judge Superior Ct. Ga., Statesboro, 1978—. Recipient Disting. Alumni award Ga. So. Coll. Alumni Assn., 1984. Judicial administration. Home: RFD 6 Box 58 A Statesboro GA 30458 Office: PO Box 803 Statesboro GA 30458

MARTIN, GARY DUNCAN, lawyer; b. Montgomery, Ala., June 9, 1954; s. Andrew Franklin and Mary Alice (Duncan) M.; m. Karen Jean Hampsten, Aug. 1, 1981; children: Jessica Ruth, Jennifer Helen. BA, Okla. State U., 1976; JD, U. Okla., 1979. Assoc. McKnight & Gasaway, Enid, Okla., 1979-81; ptnr. Mitchell & Declerck, P.C., Enid, 1981—. bd. dirs. Greater Enid C. of C., 1986—, Cimarron Sch., Inc., 1983—; pres. Downtown Enid, Inc., 1984—; lay leader First United Meth. Ch., 1984-85. Mem. ABA, Okla. Bar Assn., Garfield County Bar Assn. (sec. 1984). Republican. Methodist. Lodge: Rotary. Avocations: travel, reading, golf. Oil and gas leasing, General practice, State civil litigation. Office: Mitchell & DeClerck PC 202 W Broadway Enid OK 73702

MARTIN, GEORGE GILMORE, lawyer; b. New Orleans, July 8, 1944; s. George Harris and Barbara (Gilmore) M.; m. Rowland Weir Jones, June 1, 1968; 1 son, Charles Gilmore. B.A., U. Miss., 1966, J.D., 1969. Bar: Miss. 1969. Assoc. Brunini, Everett, Grantham & Quin, Vicksburg, Miss., 1969-74; ptnr. Brunini, Everett, Beanland & Wheeless, Vicksburg, 1974-78; sole practice, Vicksburg, 1978-86; ptnr. Martin & Sherard, 1986—. Pres. Youth Services Ctr. Vicksburg, 1972-76; pres. Warren County (Miss.) Heart Assn., 1974-82; chmn. Vicksburg Mcpl. Elections Commn., 1977—. Named Outstanding Young Man of Vicksburg, 1974. Mem. ABA, Miss. Bar Assn., Warren County Bar Assn. Episcopalian. Clubs: Vicksburg Y Men's (pres. 1977), The Hundred (pres. 1975—). Lodge: Kiwanis (pres. 1985). Probate, State civil litigation, Consumer commercial. Home: 609 Pittman Ave Vicksburg MS 39180 Office: 1010 Monroe St PO Box 1334 Vicksburg MS 39180

MARTIN, HARRY CORPENING, judge; b. Lenoir, N.C., Jan. 13, 1920; s. Hal C. and Johnsie Harshaw (Nelson) M.; m. Nancy Robiou Dallam, Apr. 16, 1955; children: John, Matthew, Mary. A.B., U. N.C., 1942; LL.B., Harvard U., 1948; LL.M., U. Va., 1982. Bar: N.C. 1948. Sole practice Asheville, N.C., 1948-62; judge N.C. Superior Ct., Asheville, 1962-78, N.C. Ct. Appeals, Raleigh, 1978-82; justice N.C. Supreme Ct., 1982—. Served with U.S. Army, 1942-45, South Pacific. Democrat. Episcopalian. Judicial administration, Jurisprudence. Home: 2112 St James Rd Raleigh NC 27607 Office: Supreme Ct of NC Morgan St Raleigh NC 27602

MARTIN, HARRY STRATTON, III, law educator; b. 1943. AB, Harvard U., 1965; JD, U. Minn., 1968; MLS, U. Pitts., 1971. Instr. U. Liberia, Monrovia, 1969-71; asst. librarian U. Tex., Austin, 1972-74, assoc. librarian, 1975-76; librarian, asst. prof. Georgetown U., Washington, 1976-81; librarian, prof. Harvard U., Cambridge, Mass., 1981—. Office: Harvard Univ Harvard Law School Cambridge MA 02138 *

MARTIN, J. LANDIS, lawyer; b. Grand Island, Nebr., Nov. 5, 1945; s. John Charles and Lucile (Cooley) M.; m. Sharon Penn Smith, Sept. 23, 1978; children: Mary Frances, Sarah Landis, Emily Penn. BS in Bus. Adminstrn., Northwestern U., 1968, JD cum laude, 1973. Bar: Ill. 1974, D.C. 1978, Colo. 1982. Assoc. Kirkland & Ellis, Chgo., 1973-77; ptnr. Kirkland & Ellis, Washington, 1978-81; mng. ptnr. Kirkland & Ellis, Denver, 1981—; firm com. mem. Kirkland & Ellis, Chgo., 1983—. Editor-in-chief: Exchange Act Guide to SEC Rule 144, 1973; articles editor Northwestern U. Law Rev., 1972-73. Pres. Cen. City Opera House Assn., Denver, 1986—, bd. dirs., 1984—. Served with U.S. Army, 1969-71. Mem. ABA, Ill. Bar Assn., Colo. Bar Assn., D.C. Bar Assn. Clubs: Chevy Chase (Md.), John Evans (Evanston, Ill.), Denver. General corporate, Securities, Federal civil litigation. Office: Kirkland & Ellis 1999 Broadway Suite 4000 Denver CO 80202

MARTIN, JAMES ADDISON, JR., lawyer; b. Danville, Va., Nov. 8, 1945. AB, Duke U., 1967; AM, Brown U., 1972; JD, Emory U., 1973. Bar:

Fla. 1973, U.S. Dist. Ct. (mid., so. and dists.) Fla. 1974, U.S. Ct. Appeals (5th and 11th cirs.) 1974, U.S. Supreme Ct. 1980, U.S. Dist. Ct. (we. dist.) Okla. 1983, U.S. Ct. Claims 1985. Law clk. to presiding justice U.S. Ct. Appeals (5th cir.), St. Petersburg, Fla., 1973-74; ptnr. McMullen, Everett, Logan, Marquardt & Cline P.A., Clearwater, Fla., 1974—. Served as spl. agt., U.S. Army Mil. Intelligence, 1968-72. Mem. Fla. Bar Assn., Am. Acad. Hosp. Attys. (various coms.) Nat. Health Care Lawyers Assn., Fla. Soc. Hosp. Attys. Lodge: Masons, Shriners. Health, State civil litigation, Federal civil litigation. Office: McMullen Everett Logan et al PO Box 1669 Clearwater FL 33517

MARTIN, JAMES HENRY, lawyer; b. Deer River, Minn., Jan. 11, 1926; s. John M. and Marie Agatha (Carey) M.; m. Kathleen M. Crosby, Aug. 9, 1952; children—Liz Morrison, John, James, Thomas, Mary, Ruth. B.A., St. John's U., Collegeview, Minn., 1948; LL.D., U. Minn., 1951. Bar: Minn. 1951. Assoc. Rudy Saltness, Dawson, Minn., 1951-52; assoc. Gay and Martin, Morris, Minn., 1955-58; ptnr. Martin and Nelson, Morris, 1958—; atty. Stevens County, Minn., 1962-74, 80—. Bd. dirs. Lakeland Mental Health Center, 1962-74, Minn. State Bar Found., 1980-83. Served with USAF, 1943-45. Mem. Nat. Trial Lawyers Assn., Minn. Trial Lawyers Assn., Acad. Cert. Trial Lawyers of Minn., Nat. Bd. Trial Adv. (cert. specialist in trial adv.), Nat. Dist. Attys. Assn., Minn. Bar Assn. (bd. govs. 1979-83), 16th Dist. Bar Assn., Morris C. of C. (past pres.). Roman Catholic. Clubs: Kiwanis (past pres.), KC (past state advocate). State civil litigation, Probate, Personal injury.

MARTIN, JAMES RUSSELL, lawyer; b. Columbus, Ohio, June 24, 1947; s. Robert Wells and Gwendolyn (Collins) M.; m. Susan Virginia Jarman, Aug. 4, 1973; children: James Russell Jr., Elizabeth Collins. BA in History, Denison U., 1969; JD, U. Denver, 1972. Bar: Colo. 1972, U.S. Dist. Ct. Colo. 1972. Sole practice Denver, 1972-74, 76-78, 1983-85; asst. atty. gen. State of Colo., Denver, 1974-76; v.p. Butterwick Enterprises Ltd., Denver, 1978-81, pres., 1981-83; ptnr. Baker & Hostetler, Denver, 1985—. Mem. ABA, Colo. Bar Assn., Denver Bar Assn. Club: Hiwan Golf (Evergreen, Colo.). Avocations: skiing, tennis, golf, cycling. Real property, General corporate. Office: Baker & Hostetler 303 E 17th Ave Suite 1100 Denver CO 80203

MARTIN, JAMES WILLIAM, lawyer; b. Turlock, Calif., Dec. 20, 1949; s. George William and Mary Bob (Henderson) M.; m. Lynda Hodges Martin, July 18, 1969. Student, Ga. Inst. Tech., 1967-69; BS, Stetson U., 1971, JD, 1974. Bar: Fla. 1974, U.S. Dist. Ct. (mid. dist) Fla. 1974, U.S. Ct. Appeals (5th cir.) 1974, U.S. Supreme Ct. 1978. Ptnr. Brickley & Martin, St. Petersburg, Fla., 1974-79; pres. James W. Martin, P.A., St. Petersburg, 1979—; gen. counsel Salvador Dali Mus., St. Petersburg, 1980—, sec., trustee 1980-86. Author: West's Florida Corporation System, 1981, 1984, West's Legal Forms, 2d edit., Non Profit Corporations; contbr. articles to profl. jours. Mem. St. Petersburg City Council, 1982-83. Recipient Outstanding Young Man award Jaycees, 1982, Outstanding Contbn. to City award St. Petersburg C. of C., 1980. Mem. ABA, Fla. Bar Assn., St. Petersburg Bar Assn., Commerce Club Pinellas County (dir., sec. 1980-82). Club: St. Petersburg Yacht; Pres. (founding, hon. dir. 1985—). General practice, State civil litigation, Real property. Home: Suite C 201-2d Ave N Saint Petersburg FL 33701

MARTIN, JOEL CLARK, lawyer; b. Goshen, N.Y., Mar. 17, 1944; s. Harold Clark and Elma (Hicks) M.; m. Joyce Ellen Barron, Sept. 9, 1973; children: Eric Barron, Abigail Taylor. BA, Harvard U., 1965; JD, U. Chgo., 1977. Bar: Maine 1977, U.S. Dist. Ct. Maine 1977, U.S. Ct. Appeals (1st cir.) 1984. Assoc. Preti, Flaherty & Beliveau, Portland, Maine, 1977-80; ptnr. Petruccelli, Cohen, Erler & Cox, Portland, 1980—. Pres., trustee Portland Symphony Orch., 1978—. Mem. ABA, Maine Bar Assn., Maine Trial Lawyers Assn., Assn. Trial Lawyers Am. Episcopalian. State civil litigation, Contracts commercial, Real property. Home: 143 Scamman St South Portland ME 04106 Office: Petruccelli Cohen Erler & Cox 50 Monument Sq 6th Floor Portland ME 04101

MARTIN, JOHN CHARLES, judge; b. Durham, N.C., Nov. 9, 1943; s. Chester Barton and Mary Blackwell (Pridgen) M.; m. Talitha N. Conant, Dec. 23, 1967; children—Lauren Blackwell, Sarah Conant, Mary Susan. BA, Wake Forest U., 1965, JD, 1967; postgrad. Nat. Judicial Coll., Reno, 1979. Bar: N.C. 1967, U.S. Dist. Ct. (mid. dist.) N.C. 1967, U.S. Dist. Ct. (ea. dist.) N.C. 1972, U.S. Dist. (we. dist.) N.C. 1975, U.S. Ct. Appeals (4th cir.) 1976. Assoc., Haywood, Denny & Miller, Durham, N.C., 1970-72; ptnr. Haywood, Denny & Miller, 1973-77; resident judge Superior Ct. 14th Jud. Dist. N.C., Durham, 1977-84; judge N.C. Ct. Appeals, Raleigh, 1985—; mem. study com. rules of evidence and comparative negligence N.C. Legis. Research Commn., 1980; mem. N.C. Pattern Jury Instrn. drafting com., 1978-84, N.C. Trial Judge's Bench Book Drafting Com., 1984; mem. bd. visitors Wake Forest U. Sch. Law, 1985—; mem. state/fed. Judicial Council of N.C., 1985—. Mem. Durham City Council, 1975-77. Served with U.S. Army, 1967-69. Recipient Disting. Service award Durham Jaycees, 1976. Mem. ABA, N.C. Bar Assn., N.C. Conf. Superior Ct. Judges. Democrat. Methodist. Club: Hope Valley Country. Jurisprudence. Office: PO Box 888 Raleigh NC 27602

MARTIN, JOHN RANDOLPH, lawyer; b. Lexington, Ky., May 26, 1948; s. Harry and Geraldine (Gray) M.; m. Jacqueline Lauren Snyder, Apr. 24, 1976; 1 child, Lauren Elizabeth. BA, U. Okla., 1973, MA, 1976, JD, 1980. Bar: Okla. 1981, U.S. Ct. Mil. Appeals 1981, U.S. Dist. Ct. (we. dist.) Okla. 1982, S.C. 1983, U.S. Ct. Appeals (10th cir.) 1983, U.S. Dist. Ct. S.C. 1984, U.S. Ct. Appeals (4th cir.) 1984. Assoc. Finkel, Georgakilis et al, Columbia, S.C., 1984-86; ptnr. Mumford, Wishart & Martin, North Myrtle Beach, S.C., 1986-87, Gertz, Kastames, Moore & Martin, North Myrtle Beach, 1987—. Served to capt. U.S. Army, 1967-70, Vietnam, with Res. 1975-78, JAGC, 1981-84. Mem. ABA, Assn. Trial Lawyers Am., Pi Kappa Alpha, Nat. Rifle Assn. Republican. Episcopalian. Lodge: Masons. Avocations: singing, shooting, jogging. State civil litigation, Family and matrimonial, Real property. Office: Gertz Kastames Moore & Martin PO Box 46 North Myrtle Beach SC 29597

MARTIN, JOSEPH, JR., lawyer, diplomat; b. San Francisco, May 21, 1915; m. Ellen Chamberlain Martin, July 5, 1946; children: Luther Greene, Ellen Myers. AB, Yale U., 1936, LLB, 1939. Assoc. Cadwalader, Wickersham & Taft, N.Y.C., 1939-41; ptnr. Wallace, Garrison, Norton & Ray, San Francisco, 1946-55, Pettit & Martin, San Francisco, 1955-70, 73—; gen. counsel FTC, Washington, 1970-71; ambassador, U.S. rep. Disarmament Conf., Geneva, 1971-76; mem. Pres.'s Adv. Com. for Arms Control and Disarmament, 1974-78; bd. dirs. Arcata Corp., Shaughnessy Holdings Inc., Astec Industries, Inc. Pres. Pub. Utilities Commn., San Francisco, 1956-60; Rep. nat. committeeman for Calif., 1960-64; treas. Rep. Party Calif., 1956-58; bd. dirs. Patrons of Art and Music, Calif. Palace of Legion of Honor, 1958-70, pres., 1963-68; bd. dirs. Arms Control Assn., 1977—; pres. Friends of Legal Assistance to Elderly, 1983—. Served to lt. comdr. USNR, 1941-46. Recipient Ofcl. commendation for Outstanding Service as Gen. Counsel FTC, 1973, Distinguished Honor award U.S. ACDA, 1973, Lifetime Achievement award Legal Assistance to the Elderly, 1981. Fellow Am. Bar Found. Clubs: Burlingame Country, Pacific Union. Antitrust, General corporate. Home: 2580 Broadway San Francisco CA 94115 Office: 101 California St San Francisco CA 94111

MARTIN, JUDITH MORAN, lawyer, tax and financial planner; b. Ann Arbor, Mich., Feb. 10, 1943; d. D. Lawrence and Donna E. (Webb) Moran; divorced; children: Laura C., Paul M., A. Lindsay; m. Daniel B. Ventres Jr., Dec. 27, 1984. BA, U. Mich., 1963; postgrad., Universite de Jean Moulin, Institut du Droit, Lyon, France, 1982; JD, U. Minn., 1982; cert., Am. Coll. 1986. Bar: Minn. 1982. Tax supr., dir. fin. planning, asst. nat. dir. Coopers & Lybrand, Mpls., 1981-84; dir. fin. planning Investors Diversified Services subs. Am. Express, Mpls. and N.Y.C., 1984-85; tax mgr., dir. fin. planning KPMG Peat Marwick Main & Co. (merger KMG Main Hurdman and Peat Marwick), Mpls., 1985—; active Metro Tax Planning Group, Mpls., 1984—. Author contg. edn. materials on taxation and income and estate planning. Mem. Downtown Council Coms., Mpls., 1982-84, Mpl. Estate Planning Council, 1985—; class chmn. fundraising campaign U. Minn. Law Sch., Mpls., 1985; usher Christ Presbyn. Ch., Edina, Minn., 1983—. Mem. ABA (task force on legal fin. planning), Minn. Bar Assn., Hennepin County Bar Assn., Minn. Soc. CPA's (instr. continuing legal edn. 1983-84, continuing profl. edn. 1986—, individual trust and estate provisions 1986 tax reform act, author, instr. IRS Valuation Tables on Income and estate Tax Planning), Am. Soc. CLU's, Minn. Women Lawyers, U. Mich. Alumni Assn., U. Minn. Alumni Assn., Minn. World Trade Assn., Internat. Assn. Fin. Planners, Twin Cities Assn. Fin. Planners, Kappa Kappa Gamma. Clubs: Interlachen (Mpls.), Lafayette (Mpls.). Probate, Personal income taxation, Pension, profit-sharing, and employee benefits. Home: 1355 Vine Place Orono MN 55364 Office: KPMG Peat Marwick Main & Co IDS Tower Suite 1700 Minneapolis MN 55402

MARTIN, KATHLEEN MINDER, lawyer; b. Ludlow, Mass., Mar. 16, 1957; d. Norbert F. and Gladys Minder; m. Thomas O. Martin, May 21, 1982; 1 child, Matthew Thomas. BA, U. Minn., 1978, JD cum laude, 1981. Bar: Minn. 1981, U.S. Dist. Ct. Minn. 1981. Sr. atty. Popham, Haik, Schnobrich, Kaufman & Doty, Ltd., Mpls., 1981—. Mem. ABA, Minn. Bar Assn., Hennepin County Bar Assn. Lodge: Mpls. Women's Rotary (pres. 1986—, v.p. 1985-86). Lending, secured transactions, Construction, Real property. Home: 10386 Rich Rd Bloomington MN 55437 Office: Popham Haik Schnobrich Kaufman & Doty Ltd 4344 IDS Center Minneapolis MN 55402

MARTIN, KEITH, lawyer; b. Mpls., May 5, 1953; s. L. John and Lois Ann (Henze) M. BA, Wesleyan U., Middletown, Conn., 1974; JD, George Washington U., 1977; MS, London Sch. Econs., 1978. Bar: D.C. 1977, N.Y. 1986. Legis. counsel to hon. Daniel Patrick Moynihan Washington, 1979-82; ptnr. Chadbourne & Parke, Washington, 1983—; legis. asst. to Henry M. Jackson, Washington, 1974-77. Mem. ABA, Fed. Bar Assn., D.C. Bar Assn. Avocations: soccer, tennis, skiing. Corporate taxation, General corporate, Legislative. Home: 5227 Massachusetts Ave Bethesda MD 20816 Office: Chadbourne & Parke 1101 Vermont Ave NW Washington DC 20005

MARTIN, LOWELL FRANK, lawyer; b. Providence, R.I., Feb. 10, 1945; s. Frank Stephen and Vera Dawson (Lavonne) M.; m. Danea Kehoe, Oct. 6, 1982 (div.); children: Philip, Andrew. BS, Cornell U., 1967, M in Engrng., 1971; JD cum laude, Georgetown U., 1982. Bar: D.C. 1982, U.S. Dist. Ct. D.C. 1983, U.S. Ct. Appeals (D.C. cir.) 1983, U.S. Supreme Ct. 1987. Regulatory program mgr. USCG, Washington, 1974-78, NOAA, Washington, 1978-82; assoc. Morgan, Lewis & Bockius, Washington, 1982—; lectr. environ. law USDA Grad. Sch., Washington, 1983, Washington Summer Campus Program, 1984, Govt. Insts., Inc., Washington, 1986. Served to lt. USN, 1968-72. Mem. ABA (natural resources law sect.), D.C. Bar Assn., Pi Kappa Alpha. Avocations: sailing, collecting British sports cars. Environment, Administrative and regulatory, General corporate. Office: Morgan Lewis & Bockius 1800 M St NW Washington DC 20036

MARTIN, LUDGER D., lawyer; b. Clay County, Ala., Dec. 28, 1920; s. Dewitt and Emma (Smith) M.; m. Gayle Joyner, Feb. 19, 1944; 1 son, Charles Dewitt. A.B., Piedmont Coll., 1942; LL.B., U. Ala.-Tuscaloosa, 1948. Bar: Ala. 1948. Mem. firm Martin & Martin dep. dist. atty., Gadsden, Ala., 1973—; mem. State Bar Commn. of Ala., 1975—. Served with USAAF, 1942-45; ETO. Named Outstanding Grad., Piedmont Coll., 1967. Mem. Sigma Delta Kappa. Methodist. Criminal, Family and matrimonial, Personal injury. Home: 1024 Bellevue Dr Gadsden AL 35901 Office: 823 Forrest Ave Gadsden AL 35901

MARTIN, MALCOLM ELLIOT, lawyer; b. Buffalo, Dec. 11, 1935; s. Carl Edward and Pearl Maude (Elliot) M.; m. Judith Hill Harley, June 27, 1964; children—Jennifer, Elizabeth, Christina, Katherine. A.B., U. Mich., Ann Arbor, 1958, J.D., 1962. Bar: N.Y. 1963, U.S. Ct. Appeals (2d cir.) 1966, U.S. Supreme Ct. 1967. Assoc., Chadbourne, Parke, Whiteside & Wolff, N.Y.C., 1962-73, ptnr., 1974—, now Chadbourne and Parke, 1986; dir., sec. Carl and Dorothy Bennett Found., Inc.; sec. Copper Devel. Assn., Inc.; sec. Jute Carpet Backing Council, Inc.; sec., dir. Jute Mfg. Devel. Council, Inc. Served with U.S. Army, 1958-60. Mem. ABA, N.Y. State Bar Assn., Assn. Bar City N.Y., St. Andrew's Soc. of State of N.Y. Clubs: Oratamin (Blauvelt, N.Y.); Nyack (N.Y.) Field; Rockefeller Center Luncheon, Copper (N.Y.C.). Estate planning, Probate. Home: 74 S Highland Ave Nyack NY 10960 Office: Chadbourne & Parke 30 Rockefeller Plaza New York NY 10112

MARTIN, MARY KAY, lawyer; b. Perham, Minn., Apr. 25, 1954; d. Walter L. and Mildred D. (Johnson) M.; m. Dean W. Kalmoe, July 22, 1978; children: Megan Elizabeth Kalmoe, Ryan Martin Kalmoe. BA in Psychology, U. Minn., Morris, 1975; JD, U. Minn., Mpls., 1981. Bar: U.S. Dist. Ct. Minn. 1985, U.S. Ct. Appeals (8th cir.) 1985. Exec. dir. Ret. Sr. Vol. Program, Elbow Lake, Minn., 1975-76, Southwest Minn. Arts & Humanities Council, Marshall, Minn., 1976-78; research asst. Minn. Legislature, St. Paul, 1979-81; staff counsel Minn. Assn. Health Care Facilities, Mpls., 1981-82; govt. relations specialist Assn. Residential Resources Minn., St. Paul, 1982-84; sole practice West St. Paul, 1984—. Editor and pub. Administrv. Law Reports, 1984—. Mem. Met. Council of the Twin Cities, St. Paul and Mpls., 1985—. Mem. ABA (ad law sect.), Minn. State Bar Assn. (ad law sect.), Ramsey County Bar Assn., Dakota County Bar Assn. Democrat. Unitarian. Administrative and regulatory, Legislative, Health. Home: 2411 Francis St South Saint Paul MN 55075 Office: 1551 Livingston Ave Suite 102 West Saint Paul MN 55118

MARTIN, MICHAEL DAVID, lawyer; b. Lakeland, Fla., Jan. 4, 1944; s. E. Snow and Mary Y. (Yelvington) M.; divorced; children—Michael David, Mallory Thomas. B.A., U. of South, 1964; J.D., U. Fla., 1967. Bar: Fla. 1968, U.S. Dist. Ct. Fla. 1968, U.S. Ct. Appeals (5th cir.) 1975, U.S. Supreme Ct. 1974, U.S. Ct. Appeals (11th cir.) 1982. Mem. Martin & Martin, Lakeland, Fla., 1968—; lectr. on estate planning and trial practice, pub. seminars, 1974-83. Bd. dirs. Boys Clubs of Lakeland, 1972-73; mem. Tampa Bay area Com. on Fgn. Relations; pres. Lakeland Spl. Events Inc., 1982-85; trustee John Marshall House. Named Outstanding Young Man of Yr., Lakeland Jaycees, 1969. Mem. ABA, Fla. Bar, Acad. Fla. Trial Lawyers, Assn. Trial Lawyers Am., Am. Judicature Soc., Polk County Trial Lawyers Assn. (pres. 1976-77), Lakeland C. of C. (v.p. 1980, pres. 1982, chmn. bd. 1983—). Clubs: Rotary (dir. club 1972-73), Lakeland Yacht and Country (pres. 1978-79). State civil litigation, Environment, Estate planning. Office: 200 Lake Morton Dr Suite 300 Lakeland FL 33801

MARTIN, MICHAEL REX, lawyer; b. Lawton, Okla., Feb. 16, 1952; s. Rex R. and Mary L. (Smith) M.; m. Janet E. Becker, Aug. 25, 1979; children: Katy, Donnie, Melissa. BS in Bus. Adminstrn., Tulsa U., 1974, JD, 1979. Bar: Okla. 1979, U.S. Dist. Ct. (we. dist.) Okla. 1984. Ptnr. Musser, Musser & Martin, Enid, Okla., 1981-85, Crowley, Butler, Pickens & Martin, Enid, Okla., 1985—. Mem. Am. Trial Lawyers Assn., Okla. Trial Lawyers Assn., Garfield Co. Bar Assn. Republican. Methodist. Lodge: Lions (Enid). General practice. Office: PO Box 3487 Enid OK 73702

MARTIN, OSCAR THADDEUS, lawyer; b. Springfield, Ohio, Jan. 27, 1908; s. Harrie B. and Margaret L. (Buchwalter) M.; m. Dorothy Traquair, June 15, 1937; children: Cecily T., Nancy S. (Mrs. Roger L. Saunders), David M., Robert M.; m. Lydia Kauffman, July 15, 1966. A.B., Princeton, 1929; J.D. cum laude, Harvard, 1932. Bar: Ohio 1932. Practiced in Springfield, 1932-86; asso. firm Martin & Corry, 1932-40; partner in successor firms and sr. partner Martin, Browne, Hull & Harper, 1960-86, of counsel, 1986—; past sec., bd. dirs. Vernay Labs., Inc., The Kissell Co., Robbins & Meyers, Inc. Vice pres. nat. council YMCA, 1979-81, mem. nat. bd., 1958-83; trustee Springfield Found., Springfield Symphony. Mem. ABA, Ohio Bar Assn., Springfield Bar Assn. (past pres.), Am. Law Inst. (life), Am. Coll. Probate Counsel, Nat. Assn. Coll. and Univs. Attys., Phi Beta Kappa. Clubs: Springfield Country (past pres.), Sea Island Golf. General corporate, Probate, Estate taxation. Home: 119 Jacobs Rd Saint Simons Island GA 31522 Office: 203 BancOhio Springfield OH 45502

MARTIN, PAUL E(DWARD), lawyer; b. Atchison, Kans., Feb. 5, 1928; s. Harres C. and Thelma F. (Wilson) M.; m. Betty Lou Crawford, Feb. 23, 1934; children—Cherry G., Paul A., Marylou. B.B.A., Baylor U., 1955, LL.B., 1956; LL.M., Harvard U., 1957. Bar: Tex. 1956, Pa. 1958. Assoc. Ballard, Spahr, Andrews & Ingersoll, Phila., 1957-58; ptnr. Fulbright & Jaworski, Houston, 1959-77; sr. ptnr. Chamberlain, Hrdlicka, White, Johnson & Williams, Houston, 1977—; instr. in estate planning U. Houston. Exec. com. Met. Houston March of Dimes, 1980-82 ; chmn. deacons West Meml. Baptist Ch., 1979-80; trustee Baylor U., 1970—, Meml. Hosp. System, 1980—, Fgn. Mission Bd., So. Bapt. Conv.; pres. Baylor U. Devel. Council, 1973-74. Served to lt. comdr. USN, 1947-53. Fellow Am. Coll. Probate Council; mem. ABA (sect. real property, probate and trust law and sect. taxation), State Bar Tex., Houston Bar Assn., Houston Estate and Fin. Forum (pres. 1965-66), Houston Bus. and Estate Planning Council, Phi Delta Phi. Republican. Club: Houston. Co-author: How to Live and Die with Texas Probate. Probate, Estate taxation, Estate planning. Office: 1400 Citicorp Ctr 1200 Smith St Houston TX 77002

MARTIN, PETER WILLIAM, lawyer, university dean; b. Cin., Apr. 11, 1939; s. Wilfred Samuel and Elizabeth (Myers) M.; m. Ann Wadsworth, Nov. 28, 1964; children: Leah, Elliot, Isaac. B.A., Cornell U., 1961; J.D., Harvard U., 1964. Bar: Ohio 1964. Atty. AF Gen. Counsel's Office, 1964-67; asso. prof. law U. Minn., 1967-71; vis. asso. prof. law Cornell U., 1971-72, prof. law, 1972—; dean Cornell U. (Law Sch.), 1980—; pres. Ctr. for Computer Assisted Legal Instrn., 1986—; cons. Adminstrv. Conf. U.S., 1977-79; reporter Am. Bar Assn. Task Force on Lawyer Competency and the Role of the Law Schs.; pres. Ctr. for Computer Assisted Legal Instrn., 1986—. Author: The Ill-Housed, 1971, (with others) Social Welfare and the Individual, 1971, Cases and Materials on Property, 1974, 2d edit., 1983; editor: Jour. Legal Edn., 1985. Chmn. Ithaca Bd. Zoning Appeals, 1974-79. Served to capt. USAF, 1964-67. Mem. ABA, Am. Bar Found. (vis. com.), Am. Assn. Law Schs. (chmn. law and computers sect. 1987—). Real property, Pension, profit-sharing, and employee benefits. Office: Cornell Law School Myron Taylor Hall Ithaca NY 14853

MARTIN, QUINN WILLIAM, lawyer; b. Fond du Lac, Wis., Jan. 12, 1948; s. Quinn W. and Marcia E. (Petrie) M.; m. Jane E. Nehmer; children: Quinn W., William J. BSME, Purdue U., 1969; postgrad., U. Santa Clara, 1969-70; JD, U. Mich., 1973. Bar: Wis. 1973, U.S. Dist. Ct. (ea. dist.) Wis. 1973, U.S. Ct. Appeals (7th cir.) 1973. Sales support mgr. Hewlett-Packard, Palo Alto, Calif., 1969-70; assoc. Quarles & Brady, Milw., 1973-80, ptnr., 1980—; bd. dirs. Bolens Corp., Port Washington, Wis., Cruisers Inc., Oconto, Wis., Martin Communications, Inc., Kaukauna, Wis., Gen. Timber and Land, Inc., Fond du Lac. Treas. Citizens for Tom Petri, Wis., 1973; mem. steering com. Ford for Pres., Wis., 1973-74; active Wis. Rep. Fin. Com., 1984-85, McCallum for Lt. Gov., Wis., 1986. Mem. ABA, Wis. Bar Assn., Milw. Bar Assn. Clubs: University (Milw.), Milwaukee; Ozaukee Country (Mequon). Contracts commercial, General corporate, Computer. Office: Quarles & Brady 411 E Wisconsin Ave Milwaukee WI 53202

MARTIN, RICHARD KELLEY, lawyer; b. Tulsa, June 30, 1952; s. Richard Loye and Maxine (Kelley) M.; m. Laura Clare Burgett, Aug. 10, 1974; children: R. Kyle, Andrew J. BA, Westminster Coll., 1974; JD, So. Meth. U., 1977. Bar: Tex. 1977, U.S. Tax Ct. 1979. Ptnr. Akin, Gump, Strauss, Hauer & Feld, Dallas, 1977—. bd. dirs. Goodwill Industries, Dallas, 1986—. Mem. Tex. Bar Assn., Dallas Bar Assn. Republican. Methodist. Real property, Contracts commercial. Office: Akin Gump Strauss Hauer & Feld 4100 First City Cen 1700 Pacific Ave Dallas TX 75201

MARTIN, RONALD ALLEN, lawyer; b. Richmond, Va., Sept. 29, 1952; s. George Thomas Martin and Thelma May (Stanley) Moore; m. Debra Elaine Bodsford, May 27, 1978; 1 child, Kristin Adele. BA in Polit. Sci. and Sociology, U. Richmond, 1974; JD, T.C. Williams Sch. Law, 1977. Bar: Va. 1977, U.S. Dist. Ct. (ea. dist.) Va. 1977, U.S. Ct. Appeals (4th cir.) 1977. Sole practice Mechanicsville, Va., 1977-82; ptnr. McCaul, Martin, Evans & Cook, P.C. and predecessor firm Martin & Evans, P.C., Mechanicsville, 1982—. Active Hanover Dem. Com., Hanover County, Va., 1983—; Hanover Youth Basketball Assn., Mechanicsville, 1980-85. Named One of Outstanding Young Men Am., Jaycees, 1982. Mem. ABA, Hanover Bar Assn. (past pres., v.p., sec. treas. 1978—), Va. Trial Lawyers Assn., Fifteenth Jud. Cir. Bar Assn. (sec., treas. 1985, v.p. 1986, pres. 1987—), Mechanicsville Businessmen's Assn. (bd. dirs. 1985-86), Hanover Businessmen's Assn., Phi Delta Phi., Pi Sigma Alpha. United Methodist. Clubs: Spider (Richmond) (bd. dirs. 1981-82). Real property, Personal injury, State civil litigation. Office: McCaul Martin Evans & Cook PC 5716 Mechanicsville Pike Mechanicsville VA 23111

MARTIN, RONALD M., lawyer; b. Colorado Springs, Colo., Feb. 7, 1948; s. Ronald and Maryanne Martin; m. Jere Hughes, June 7, 1969; children: Christopher, Courtney. BS with Distinction, Colo. State U., 1970; JD, U. Colo., 1973. Bar: Colo. 1973, U.S. Dist. Ct. Colo. 1973, U.S. Ct. Appeals 1976. From assoc. to ptnr. Haney, Howbert & Akers, Colorado Springs, 1973-76; pres. Spurgeon, Haney & Howbert P.C., Colorado Springs, 1976-86; ptnr. Holland & Hart, Colorado Springs, 1986—. Co-author: Corpus Juris Secundum, Bankruptcy Table of Contents, 1985, West's Federal Practice and Procedure (Bankruptcy rules), 1985. Mem. Colo. Bar Assn., Denver Bar Assn., El Paso Bar Assn., Comml. Law League, Colorado Springs C. of C. Club: El Paso. Avocations: classic cars, travel, reading. Bankruptcy, Banking, Consumer commercial. Office: Holland & Hart 1400 Holly Sugar Bldg Colorado Springs CO 80901

MARTIN, RUSSELL WHITE, lawyer; b. Abington, Pa., Nov. 22, 1933; s. Russell W. and Margaret (Tull) M.; m. Dorothy Langer, Jan. 14, 1961; children: Jennifer, Bryan. BS in Econs., U. Pa., 1956; JD, NYU, 1959. Bar: N.Y. 1959. Law clk. to presiding justice U.S. Ct. Appeals (2d cir.), N.Y.C., 1959-60; atty. Gen. Electric Co., N.Y.C., 1960-64; spl. asst. pres. N.Y. Stock Exchange, N.Y.C., 1964-66; asst. treas., asst. gen counsel, assoc. gen. counsel Endl. Testing Service, Princeton, N.J., 1966—. Mem. ABA, N.Y. State Bar Assn., N.J. State Bar Assn., Princeton Bar Assn. (assoc.). Trademark and copyright, Contracts commercial, Government contracts and claims. Home: 45 Van Kirk Rd Princeton NJ 08540 Office: Ednl Testing Service Princeton NJ 08541

MARTIN, SERGE GREGORY, lawyer; b. Milw., May 1, 1956; s. Benjamin and Nataly (Fesino) M. BM with honors, Berklee Coll. Music, 1977; JD with honors, George Washington U., 1981. Bar: Fla. 1981. Assoc. Mershon, Sawyer, Johnston, Dunwody & Cole, Miami, Fla., 1981-83; corp. counsel Ryder System, Inc., Miami, 1983—. Mem. ABA, Dade County Bar Assn., Am. Corp. Counsel Assn. General corporate, Securities, State civil litigation. Home: 7445 SW 105th Terr Miami FL 33156 Office: Ryder System Inc 3600 NW 82d Ave Miami FL 33166

MARTIN, TERENCE ALAN, lawyer; b. Cooperstown, N.Y., Oct. 17, 1954; s. Theodore Alan and Betty Jane (Collins) M.; m. Linda Lee Litton, May 22, 1982; children: Lauren Elizabeth, Nicole Leigh. BS in Polit. Sci., Ariz. State U., 1976; JD, U. Ky., 1979. Bar: Ky. 1979, U.S. Dist. Ct. (ea. dist.) Ky. 1979, Ga. 1982, U.S. Dist. Ct. (no. dist.) Ga. 1982. Assoc. Wyatt, Tarrant & Combs, Lexington, Ky., 1979-82, Pierce, Goldner & Sommers, Atlanta, 1982-85; staff counsel Fireman's Fund Ins. Cos., Atlanta, 1985—. Mem. ABA, Atlanta Bar Assn., Ga. Bar Assn., Ky. Bar Assn. Avocation: automobile rallying. Insurance, Personal injury.

MARTIN, TERRENCE, lawyer; b. Aurora, Ill., Aug. 30, 1942; s. James and Margaret (Fithian) M.; children—Rolf Lyle. A.B., W. Ga. Coll., 1974; M.A., West Ga. Coll., 1976; J.D., Woodrow Wilson Coll. Law, 1980; LL.M., Atlanta Law Sch., 1983. Bar: Ga. 1981, U.S. Patent Office 1981. Assoc. engr. Automatic Electric Labs., Northlake, Ill., 1963-65; tech. writer RMS Engring., Atlanta, 1967-68; tech. writer Sci. Atlanta, 1968-73; patent atty. Southwire Co., Carrollton, Ga., 1981-83; corp. patent atty. The Foxboro Co., Mass., 1983—; cons. in field. Served with U.S. Army, 1965-67. Hirsch scholar 1975-76. Mem. ABA, Ga. Bar Assn., Intellectual Property Law Assn., Boston Patent Law Assn., Am. Radio Relay League (WD4AON). Patent, Trademark and copyright. Home: PO Box 540 Foxboro MA 02035 Office: 38 Neponset Ave (M/S BP-52-1J) Foxboro MA 02035

MARTIN, THOMAS L., lawyer. AB, Seton Hall U., 1971; JD, Rutgers U., 1974; cert., NYU Real Estate Inst., 1985. Bar: N.J. 1974. Atty. Mut. Benefit Life Ins. Co., 1977-79, asst. counsel, 1979-82, assoc. counsel, 1982-87, asst. sec., 1986—, counsel, 1987—; asst. sec., asst. treas. Muben Realty Co., 1981-87, sec., asst. treas., 1987—; instr. Upsala Coll. Paralegal Sch., East

Orange, N.J., 1981. Mem. Am. Arbitration Assn. General corporate, Real property. Office: 520 Broad St 14th Floor Newark NJ 07102

MARTIN, WALTER, lawyer; b. Crookston, Minn., Nov. 7, 1912; s. Frederick and Rosalie (Mertz) M.; m. Catherine Mary Severin, May 1, 1942 (dec. May 1979); children: Frederick H., Jacqueline K., Patricia, Priscilla, Walter Jr., John E.; m. Lois Laverne Seeman. BA, Albion Coll., 1937; JD, U. Mich., 1939. Bar: Mich. 1939, U.S. Dist. Ct. (fed. dist.) 1939, U.S. Ct. Appeals (6th cir.) 1947, U.S. Supreme Ct. 1958. Ptnr. Martin & Martin, Saginaw, Mich., 1952—. Fellow Mich. Bar Assn., Saginaw County Bar Assn. (pres. 1958). Lutheran. Avocations: hunting, fishing. Personal injury, Probate, Condemnation. Office: 803 809 Court St Saginaw MI 48602

MARTIN, WAYNE MALLOTT, lawyer, real estate company executive; b. Chgo., Jan. 9, 1950; s. Mallott Caldwell and Helen (Honkisz) M.; m. Josephine Ann Giordano, Mar. 18, 1978; 1 child, Bradley. BA, Drake U., 1972; JD, De Paul U., 1977. Bar: Ill. 1978. Loan officer Clyde Savs. & Loan Assn., Chgo., 1972-75, Am. Nat. Bank, Chgo., 1976-77; sales dir., atty. financing Inland Real Estate Corp., Chgo., Oak Brook, then Palatine, Ill., 1977-83; pres. Inland Property Sales, Inc., Palatine, 1983-84, Oak Brook, Ill., 1984-86; Dome Investments, Inc., Northbrook, Ill., 1986—; Quest Mortgage Co., Rolling Meadows, Ill., 1986—. Mem. ABA, Ill. Bar Assn., Chgo. Bar Assn., Nat. Bd. Realtors, Ill. Bd. Realtors, Chgo. Bd. Realtors (bd. dirs. 1986—, trustee action com. 1986—, fin. com. 1986—), Westside Bd. Realtors (bd. dirs. 1983-84, pres. 1984—). Real property, Securities, Landlord-tenant. Home: 1618 RFD Picardy Ct Long Grove IL 60047 Office: Quest Mortgage Co 1833 Hicks Rd Suite A Rolling Meadows IL 60008

MARTIN, WILLIAM CHARLES, lawyer; b. Shenandoah, Iowa, May 25, 1923; s. J. Stuart and Chloe Irene (Anderson) M.; m. Marilyn Forbes, Oct. 18, 1947 (div. 1979); children—Ann, James; m. 2d, Kathryn Ann Fehr, Sept. 17, 1979. B.A., U. Iowa, 1946, J.D., 1947. Bar: Iowa 1947, Oreg. 1948. Sr. ptnr. Martin Bischoff, Templeton, Biggs & Ericsson, Portland, Oreg., 1951—; mem. Oreg. Bd. Bar Examiners, 1966-69; instr. Lewis and Clark Coll. Law, 1973-75. Bd. dirs. Eastmoreland Gen. Hosp., Portland, 1960-84, chmn., 1978-81; mem. Lawyers Com. for Civil Rights Under Law, Jackson, Miss., 1965; bd. dirs. Lake Oswego (Oreg.) Pub. Library, 1981-84, chmn., 1982-84. Served to 1st lt. USAAF, World War II. Mem. Iowa State Bar, Oreg. State Bar, ABA, Phi Delta Phi, Sigma Nu. Democrat. Presbyterian. Clubs: University (Portland); Mt. Park Tennis, Portland Heights. Probate, Insurance, General practice. Home: 3915 S Shore Blvd Lake Oswego OR 97034 Office: Martin Bischoff Templeton Biggs & Ericsson 2908 1st Interstate Tower Portland OR 97201

MARTINEZ, CARLOS GUILLERMO, lawyer; b. San Antonio, Tex., June 21, 1947; s. Eloy E. and Livia Elia (Magnon) M.; m. Maria Guadalupe, July 18, 1975; children: Carlos Eloy, Maria Ysabel, Ruben Guillermo. BS, U. San Francisco, 1969; JD, U. Calif., Berkeley, 1972. From assoc. to ptnr. Butt, Thornton & Baehr P.C., Albuquerque, 1977—, also bd. dirs. Bd. dirs., past pres. Big Bros./Big Sisters Albuquerque. Served to capt. JAGC, U.S. Army, 1973-77. Recipient Bancroft Whitney award, 1973. Mem. ABA, N.Mex. Bar Assn. (fee arbitration com.), Albuquerque Bar Assn., N.Mex. Def. Lawyers, N.Mex. Workmen's Compensation Assn., Jud. Selection Com. Democrat. Roman Catholic. Avocation: skiing. Workers' compensation, State civil litigation. Office: Butt Thornton & Baehr PC 2155 Louisiana NE #7000 Albuquerque NM 87110

MARTINEZ, MEL R., lawyer; b. Sagua La Grande, Cuba, Oct. 23, 1946; came to U.S., 1962; naturalized, 1971; s. Melquiades C. and Gladys V. (Ruiz) M.; m. Kathryn Tindal, June 13, 1970; children—Lauren Elizabeth, John Melquiades. BA, Fla. State U., 1969, JD, 1973. Bar: Fla. 1973, U.S. Dist. Ct. (mid. dist.) Fla. 1973, U.S. Supreme Ct. 1979, U.S. Dist. Ct. (so. dist.) Fla. 1986; cert. Nat. Bd. Trial Advocacy, civil trial atty. Fla. Ptnr., Connor & Martinez (and predecessor firms), Tallahassee and Orlando, Fla., 1973—. Bd. dirs. Catholic Social Services Orlando, 1978-86 ; founder, chmn. Mayor's Hispanic Adv. Com., Orlando, 1981-82; chmn. bd. commrs. Orlando Housing Authority, 1983-86. Mem. Fla. Bar (bd. govs. young lawyers sect. 1980-81), Acad. Fla. Trial Lawyers (dir. 1981-85, treas. 1986-87), 9th Jud. Cir. (jud. nomination commn. 1986). Roman Catholic. Federal civil litigation, State civil litigation, Personal injury. Office: PO Box 2447 Orlando FL 32802

MARTINEZ-CID, RICARDO, lawyer; b. Havana, Cuba, May 9, 1950; came to U.S., 1962; s. Ricardo Martinez Balado and Pastora Cid Gonzalez; divorced; children: Maricer, Ricardo, Maite, Jordi. BA, U. Fla., 1970, JD, 1972. Bar: Fla. 1973. Assoc. Steel, Hector & Davis, Miami, Fla., 1972-76; ptnr. Martinez-Cid, Suarez & Amador, Miami, 1976-80; sole practice Miami, 1980—; bd. dirs. Belen Jesuit Prep. Sch., Miami, Casino Espanol de la Habana, Miami. Republican. Roman Catholic. Contracts commercial, General corporate, Real property. Office: 4000 SE Financial Ctr Miami FL 33131

MARTINI, GEORGE HENRY, lawyer; b. Parkersburg, W.Va., Aug. 5, 1949; s. Bernard A. and Lillian (Martini) Newsome; m. Rosemary Gallina, Apr. 25, 1980; children: Jennifer Marie, Jeffrey George. BS ChemE, Tufts U., 1971; JD, George Washington U., 1975. Bar: N.J. 1975, U.S. Dist. Ct. N.J. 1975. Law clk. U.S. Superior Ct. N.J., Newark, 1975-76; assoc. Wiley, Malehorn & Sirota, Morristown, N.J., 1976-78; sr. counsel Hoffman-La Roche, Inc., Nutley, N.J., 1978—. Mem. ABA, N.J. Bar Assn. General corporate, Health. Office: Hoffman La Roche Inc 340 Kingsland St Nutley NJ 07110

MARTIRANO, JOHN JOSEPH, lawyer, construction company executive; b. Yonkers, N.Y., Feb. 28, 1929; s. Alexander Augustus Martirano and Mary (Lauren) Mazzullo; divorced; children: John Alexander, Christopher Nevin, Lynn Marie. BS, Ithaca Coll.; JD, Cornell U. Bar: N.Y. 1955, U.S. Ct. Appeals (2d cir.) 1960. Sec., treas. Mar-Mes Constrn. Co. Inc., Eastchester, N.Y., 1952—; ptnr. McGoey & Martirano, New Rochelle, N.Y., 1957—; atty. Village of Mamaronek, N.Y., 1969-82. Chmn. North Eastchester Civic Assn., 1958-65. Mem. Am. Arbitration Assn. (panelist 1970—), Am. Fedn. Musicians. Club: Cornell (N.Y.C.). Construction, Federal civil litigation, State civil litigation. Office: McGoey & Martirano 301 North Ave New Rochelle NY 10801

MARTOCCIO, JULIA PALERMO, lawyer; b. Chgo., May 21, 1910; d. Eugene Louis and Lucy Mary (Russo) Palermo; married; children: John, Gina. AA, Crane Coll.; LLB, Loyola U., Chgo.; PhB, Loyola U. Tchr. comml. law Chgo. Pub. Sch., 1938-41; ptnr. Martoccio & Martoccio, Chgo., 1945-84, Des Plaines, Ill., 1945—; lectr. in field. Journalist Paddock Publs., 1974—. Mem. pta North Sch., Des Plaines; v.p. Maine Twp. Rep. Womens Club, 1946, 52-54, 54-56). Mem. Ill. Bar Assn., North Suburban Bar Assn., Ill. Womens Press Corr. (sec. 1963, Mate E. Palmer Writing award), Nat. Womens Press Corr., Nat. League of Pen Women, Kappa Beta Pi, Kappa Gamma Pi. Office: Martoccio & Martoccio 1984 Big Bend Dr Des Plaines IL 60016

MARTOCHE, SALVATORE RICHARD, lawyer; b. Buffalo, Oct. 12, 1940; s. Charles L. and Grace (Pignone) M.; m. Mary Dee Benesh, Oct. 17, 1945; children: Amy Catherine, Claire Elizabeth, Christopher Charles. B.S., Canisius Coll., 1962; J.D., U. N.D., 1967. Bar: N.Y. 1968. Atty. Legal Aid Bur., Buffalo, 1968-72; practice law Buffalo, 1968-82; asst. counsel to the majority N.Y. State Senate, Albany, 1974-82; U.S. atty. Western Dist. N.Y., Buffalo, 1982-86; asst. sec. labor mgmt. standards U.S. Dept. Labor, Washington, DC, 1986—. Author: (with B. Grahl) Guilty of Poverty: A Study of Bail and Pretrial Detention in Buffalo, N.Y., 1977; contbr. articles to profl. jours. Mem. Erie County Charter Revision Commn., Buffalo, 1980-81; bd. dirs. United Way of Buffalo and Erie County, 1980-82, The William Paca Soc., 1981-84, One Hundred Club, Buffalo, 1982—, NCCJ, 1982—. Recipient Brotherhood award NCCJ, 1981; recipient Man of Yr. award William Paca Anti-Defamation Soc., 1980; recipient LaSalle Medal Canisus Coll., 1979, Disting. Alumnus, Canisius Coll., 1986, Friend of Law Enforcement award N.Y. State Sheriff's Assn., 1978, Man of Yr. award Dwight D. Eisenhower Club, 1973, Vol. of Yr. award Addicts in Distress, 1974. Mem. State N.Y. Bar Assn., ABA, Erie County Bar Assn. Republican. Roman Catholic. Criminal, Federal civil litigation. Home: 288 Lincoln Pkwy Buffalo NY 14216 Office: US Dept Labor 200 Constitution Ave NW Washington DC 20210

MARTON, EMERY, chem. co. exec.; b. Nasna, Rumania, Aug. 11, 1922; s. Julius and Esther (Fritsch) M.; m. Marian C. Pruden, Dec. 25, 1948; children—Peter D., Elise J., Eric M., Susan A. B.S., U. Mich., 1947; M.S., Harvard, 1948; LL.B., N.Y. U., 1953, J.D., 1968. Bar: N.Y. bar 1954. Instr. civil engring. Newark Coll. Engring., 1948-51; project engr. Belco Indsl. Equipment, Paterson, N.J., 1951-53; asst. gen. counsel Dorr-Oliver, Inc., Stamford, Conn., 1953-63; sec., house counsel Foster Grant Co., Inc. subs. Am. Hoechst Corp., Somerville, N.J., 1963-77; v.p. Foster Grant Co., Inc. subs. Am. Hoechst Corp., 1973-77; v.p., gen. counsel Am. Hoechst Corp., 1978—. Served with AUS, 1942-46. Kellogg Found. fellow pub. health, 1947. Mem. Am. Bar Assn., N.Y. Acad. Scis., Harvard Engring. Soc. General corporate. Home: 40 Montadale Dr Princeton NJ 08540 Office: Route 202-206 N Somerville NJ 08876

MARTONE, PATRICIA ANN, lawyer; b. Bklyn., Apr. 28, 1947; d. David Andrew and Rita Mary (Dullmeyer) M. B.A. in Chemistry, NYU, 1968, J.D., 1973; M.A. in Phys. Chemistry, Johns Hopkins U., 1969. Bar: N.Y. 1974, U.S. Dist. Ct. (so. and ea. dists.) N.Y. 1975, U.S. Ct. Appeals (2d cir.) 1975, U.S. Ct. Appeals (1st cir.) 1981, U.S. Ct. Appeals (fed. cir.) 1984, U.S. Patent and Trademark Office 1983, U.S. Supreme Ct. 1984, U.S. Dist. Ct. (ea. dist.) Mich. 1985. Tech. rep. computer timesharing On-Line Systems, Inc., N.Y.C., 1969-70; assoc. Kelley Drye & Warren, N.Y.C., 1973-77; assoc. Fish & Neave, N.Y.C., 1977-82, ptnr., 1983—; participating atty. Community Law Offices, N.Y.C., 1974-78; atty. Pro Bono Panel U.S. Dist. Ct. (so. dist.) N.Y., 1982-84; lectr. Practising Law Inst., N.Y.C., 1984; dir. N.Y. Lawyers for the Pub. Interest, 1987—. Mng. editor NYU Law Sch. Rev. Law and Social Change, 1972-73. Contbr. articles to profl. jours. Recipient Founder's Day award NYU Sch. Law, 1973; NSF grad. trainee John Hopkins U., 1968-69; NYU scholar, 1964-68. Mem. ABA, Assn. Bar City N.Y. (mem. environ. law com. 1978-83, trademarks, unfair competition com. 1983-86), Am. Chem. Soc., N.Y. Patent, Trademark and Copyright Law Assn. Club: The Club at Citicorp Ctr. (N.Y.C.). Federal civil litigation, Patent, Trademark and copyright. Office: Fish & Neave 875 Third Ave New York NY 10022

MARTORI, JOSEPH PETER, lawyer; b. N.Y.C., Aug. 19, 1941; s. Joseph and Teresa Susan (Fezza) M.; m. Julia Ann D'Orlando, Mar. 7, 1964 (div. Mar. 1978); children: Joseph Peter, Christina Ann; m. Terres Edith Wolff, Dec. 23, 1980; 1 child, Arianne Terres. B.S. summa cum laude, NYU, 1964, M.B.A., 1968; J.D. cum laude U. Notre Dame, 1967; Bar: D.C. 1968, U.S. Dist. Ct. D.C. 1968, U.S. Dist. Ct. Ariz. 1968, U.S. Ct. Appeals (9th cir.) 1969, U.S. Supreme Ct. 1977. Assoc. Sullivan & Cromwell, N.Y.C., 1967-68, Snell & Wilmer, Phoenix, 1968-69; pres. Goldmar Inc., Phoenix, 1969-71; ptnr. Martori, Meyer, Hendricks & Victor, P.A., Phoenix, 1971-85; ptnr. Brown & Bain, P.A., Phoenix, 1985—; bd. dirs. Met. Bank, Phoenix, Internat. Leisure Enterprises, Phoenix, El Pollo Asado, Phoenix. Author: Street Fights, 1987; also articles, 1966-70. Bd. dirs. Men's Arts Council, Phoenix, 1972—; trustee Boys' Clubs Met. Phoenix, 1974—. Mem. ABA, State Bar Ariz., Maricopa County Bar Assn., Lawyers Com. for Civil Rights Under Law (trustee 1976—). Republican. Roman Catholic. Clubs: Phoenix Country, Plaza (founding bd. govs. 1979—) (Phoenix). General corporate, Probate, Corporate taxation. Office: Brown & Bain PA 222 N Central Ave Phoenix AZ 85001

MARTOWSKI, DAVID WILLIAM, lawyer, marine insurance company executive; b. Waltham, Mass., May 7, 1939; s. William Thomas and Beatrice (Doiron) M.; m. Jeanne Gossman, Aug. 7, 1965; children—Joanna, Sara. B.S. cum laude, Boston Coll., 1961; J.D., Fordham U., 1968; LL.M. in Internat. Legal Studies, NYU, 1973. Bar: N.Y. 1968, U.S. Dist. Ct. (so. dist.) N.Y. 1968. Fed. narcotics agent U.S. Dept. Treasury, Boston and N.Y.C., 1962-65; assoc. Kirlin, Campbell & Keating, N.Y.C., 1968-73, ptnr., 1974-79; pres. Transport Mut. Services Inc., N.Y.C., 1979—. Served in USMC. Recipient Amjur Prize in Admiralty, Fordham Law Sch., 1968. Mem. ABA (vice chmn. admiralty and maritime law com. sect. tort and ins. practice 1983-86), Assn. Bar City N.Y. (admiralty com. 1983-86), Assn. Average Adjusters (London), Assn. Average Adjusters U.S., Maritime Law Assn. U.S. (exec. com. 1982-85, sec. 1986—), Soc. Maritime Arbitrators (bd. govs. 1986—) . Clubs: Whitehall, Nippon (N.Y.C.); Marine (London). Admiralty, Insurance, Private international. Home: 91 Central Park W Apt 12-B New York NY 10023

MARTS, ANTHONY CHARLES, lawyer; b. Buffalo, Aug. 22, 1956; m. Theresa L. LaBrack, July 22, 1978; children: Charles A., Katie N., Alison M. BA, Eisenhower Coll., 1978; JD, SUNY, Buffalo, 1982. Bar: N.H. 1982, U.S. Dist. Ct. N.H. 1982. Assoc. Wiggin & Nourie, Manchester, N.H., 1982—. Mem. endowment com. Boy Scouts Am., Manchester, 1983—; mem. Goffstown (N.H.) budget com., 1986—, chmn., 1987—. Mem. ABA (corps., bus. and banking sects.), N.H. Bar Assn. (vice chmn. new lawyers com. 1985-86, chmn. 1986-87). Bankruptcy, Contracts commercial, General corporate. Office: Wiggin & Nourie Franklin & Market Sts. Manchester NH 03105

MARTUCCI, WILLIAM CHRISTOPHER, lawyer; b. Asbury Park, N.J., Mar. 10, 1952; s. Frank and Evelyn (Gerrity) M.; m. Julie Sessions, Aug. 2, 1980; children: Daniel Robert, William Sessions. AB magna cum laude, Rutgers U., 1974; JD with honors, U. Ark., 1977; LLM, Georgetown U., 1981. Bar: Mo. 1977. Law clk. to presiding justice Mo. Ct. Appeals, Kansas City, 1977-78; assoc. Spencer, Fane, Britt & Browne, Kansas City, 1981-86, ptnr., 1987—; mem. practice and procedure com. Nat. Labor Relations Act. Editor-in-chief Ark. Law Rev., 1976-77; contbr. articles to profl. jours. Chmn. adv. council Urban League Greater Kansas City Tng. Ctr. Served to lt. JAGC, USN, 1978-81. Mem. ABA, Mo. Bar Assn., Kansas City Bar Assn. (chmn. continuing legal edn. 1984-86, mem. exec. com. 1985—, leadership award 1985), Lawyers Assn. Kansas City (mem. exec. com. young lawyers sect. 1981-82). Republican. Roman Catholic. Club: Kansas City. Labor, Federal civil litigation, State civil litigation. Home: 6825 Cherry Kansas City MO 64131 Office: Spencer Fane Britt & Browne 1400 Commerce Bank Bldg 1000 Walnut St Kansas City MO 64106

MARTY, JAMES OWEN, lawyer; b. Bonne Terre, Mo., Aug. 5, 1942; s. Herbert Shelton and Glenda Mae (Burcham) M.; m. Jeanine Marie Gansmann, Oct. 27, 1964 (div. June 1981); children: Alaine Marie, Heather Cathleen. B in Mktg., Southeast Mo. State Coll., 1964; JD, Memphis State U., 1971. Bar: Tenn. 1972. Sr. ptnr. Marty & Todd, Memphis, 1972-83, Marty & Holloman, Memphis, 1983—. Candidate to Memphis City Council, 1976; past pres. West Tenn. Cerebral Palsey Council; spl. judge Memphis City Ct., 1972—. Served to sgt. USAR, 1966-72. Democrat. Presbyterian. Criminal, Civil rights. Office: 212 Adams Ave Memphis TN 38103

MARTZ, CLYDE OLLEN, lawyer, educator; b. Lincoln, Nebr., Aug. 14, 1920; s. Clyde O. and Elizabeth Mary (Anderson) M.; m. Ann Spieker, May 29, 1947; children: Robert Graham, Nancy. AB, U. Nebr., 1941; LLB, Harvard U., 1947. Bar: Colo. 1948, U.S. Ct. Appeals (10th cir.) 1968, U.S. Supreme Ct. 1969. Profl. U. Colo., Boulder, 1947-58, 60-62; jud. adminstr. State of Colo., Denver, 1959-60; ptnr. Davis, Graham & Stubbs, Denver, 1962-67, 69-80, 81-87; asst. atty. gen. U.S. Dept. Justice, Washington, 1967-69; solicitor U.S Dept. Interior, Washington, 1980-81; exec. dir. dept. natural resources State of Colo., 1987—; adj. prof. U. Denver, 1961-79; cons. Pres. Materials Policy Commn., 1951; mem. Colo. Adv. Bd. Bur. Land Mgmt., 1967-69. Author: Cases and Materials on Natural Resources Law, 1951, Water for Mushrooming Populations, 1954; co-author: American Law of Property, 1953, Water and Water Rights, 1963; editor, co-author: American Law of Mining, 1960. Co-chmn. Jud. Reorganization Commn., 1961-63; elder Presbyn. Ch., Boulder. Served to comdr. USN, 1942-58, PTO, with Res. Mem. ABA (chmn. natural resources sect. 1985-86), Fed. Bar Assn., Colo. Bar Assn. (chmn. water sect. 1957, chmn. mineral sect. 1961, award of merit 1962), Order of Coif. Democrat. Avocations: horticulture, woodworking, mountaineering, skiing. Oil and gas leasing, Environment, Real property. Home: 755 6th St Boulder CO 80302 Office: Davis Graham & Stubbs 370 17th St Suite 4700 Denver CO 80202

MARULLO, STEVEN JEFFREY, lawyer; b. New Haven, July 23, 1950; s. Joseph and Maria A. (Coppola) M.; m. Jo-Ann Szalay, Aug. 19, 1972; children: Dominic, Anthony. BA, U. Conn., 1972; JD, Suffolk U., 1975. Bar: Mass. 1975, U.S. Dist. Ct. Mass. 1976, U.S. Tax Ct. 1978. Sr. ptnr. Marullo & Barnes, Boston, 1975—; bd. dirs. Mead Devel. Corp., Boston. Bd. dirs. Harbor Area Community Service, Boston, 1984—; chmn. Zoning Bd. Appeals, Hanson, Mass., 1977—, Growth Policy Com., Hanson, 1976-77, Conservation Commn., Hanson, 1977-78; trustee Boston Opera Co., 1985—; counsel Town of Pembroke, Mass., 1986—; participant U.S./People's Republic of China Joint Session on Trade, Investment and Econ. Law, Beijing. Served to 1st lt. USAR, 1972-80. Mem. Mass. Bar Assn., Vol. Lawyers Project, Boston Bar Assn., Hanson Jaycees (pres. 1980), Justinian Law Soc. Republican. Catholic. Club: Halifax Country. Avocations: golf, softball. General corporate, Bankruptcy, Local government. Home: 24 Greenbrier Ln Hanson MA 02341 Office: Marullo & Barnes 141 Tremont St Boston MA 02111

MARVEL, WAYNE ANDREW, lawyer; b. Wilmington, Del., Oct. 11, 1955; s. Henry Medford and Olive Margaret (Lobban) M.; m. Joanne Margaret Hopkins, Apr. 25, 1973; children: Scott Andrew, Sara Beth. BS in Sociology, U. Del., 1977; JD, Villanova U., 1980. Bar: Del. 1981, Pa. 1981, U.S. Dist. Ct. Del. 1981. Law clk. to judge Del. Superior Ct., Wilmington, 1980-81; assoc. Biggs & Battaglia, Wilmington, 1981—; mem. Superior Ct. Civil Rules Adv. Com., Wilmington, 1984—; barrister Richard Rodney Inns of Ct., Wilmington, 1985—. Mem. ABA, Del. Bar Assn. Republican. State civil litigation, Federal civil litigation, Personal injury. Office: Biggs & Battaglia 1206 Mellon Bank Ctr PO Box 1489 Wilmington DE 19899

MARVIN, CHARLES ARTHUR, lawyer, educator; b. Chgo., July 14, 1942; s. Burton Wright and Margaret Fiske (Medlar) M.; m. Elizabeth Maureen Woodrow, July 4, 1970; children—Colin, Kristin. B.A., U. Kans., 1964; postgrad. (Fulbright scholar) U. Toulouse (France), 1964-65; J.D., U. Chgo., 1968, M.Comparative Law, 1970. Bar: Ill. 1969. Legal intern EEC, Brussels, 1970; lectr. law U. Kent, Canterbury, Eng., 1970-71; asst. prof. law Laval U., Quebec City, Que., Can., 1971-73; legal adv. constl., internat. and adminstrv. law sect. Can. Dept. Justice, Ottawa, Ont., 1973-76; assoc. prof. law U. Man., Winnipeg, Can., 1976-77; dir. adminstrv. law project Law Reform Commn. Can., Ottawa, 1977-80; prof. law Villanova (Pa.) U., 1980-83; dir. Adminstrv. Law Reform Project, Can. Dept. Justice, 1983-85; prof. law Ga. State U., 1985—; assoc. dean, 1987—. Summerfield scholar, 1961-64; Fulbright fellow, 1964-65; U. Chgo. scholar, 1965-68; Ford Found. Comparative Law fellow, 1968-70. Mem. ABA, Ill. Bar Assn., Chgo. Bar Assn., Am. Soc. Internat. Law, Am. Fgn. Law Assn., Internat. Law Assn., Can. Bar Assn., Can. Council on Internat. Law, Phi Beta Kappa. Methodist. Administrative and regulatory, Public international, Legal education. Office: Georgia State U Coll Law Atlanta GA 30303

MARVIN, CHARLES RAYMOND, lawyer, association administrator; b. Zanesville, Ohio, July 22, 1938; s. Bertia Hull. BA in Polit. Sci., Bowling Green State U., 1960; LLB, U. Mich., 1963. Bar: Ohio 1963, D.C. 1976, U.S. Dist. Ct., U.S. Ct. Mil. Appeals, U.S. Ct. Appeals (6th cir.), U.S. Supreme Ct. Assoc. Baker, Hostetler & Patterson, Cleve., 1966-71; asst. atty. gen. State of Ohio, Columbus, 1971-74; asst. dir. litigation bur. competition FTC, Washington, 1974-75; exec. dir., gen. counsel Nat. Assn. Atty. Gen., Washington, 1975-86; sole practice Washington, 1986—. Served to capt. USAF, 1963-66. Legislative, General corporate, Real property. Office: 1615 L St NW Washington DC 20036

MARVIN, DAVID EDWARD SHREVE, lawyer; b. Lansing, Mich., Jan. 6, 1950; s. George Charles Marvin and Shirley Mae (Martin) Schaible; m. Mary Anne Kennedy, Sept. 16, 1972; 1 child, John. BS cum laude, Mich. State U., 1972; JD cum laude, Wayne State U., 1976. Bar: Mich. 1976, U.S. Dist. Ct. (ea. dist.) Mich. 1976, U.S. Dist. Ct. (we. dist.) Mich. 1978, U.S. Ct. Appeals (7th cir.) 1977, U.S. Ct. Appeals (6th cir.) 1979, U.S. Supreme Ct. 1979, U.S. Ct. Appeals (D.C. cir.) 1982. Asst. mgr. Alta Supply Co., Lansing, 1972-73; research asst. Wayne State U., Detroit, fall 1975; jud. intern. U.S. Dist. Ct., Detroit, summer, 1975; ptnr. Fraser Trebilcock Davis & Foster, P.C., Lansing, 1976—. Exec. editor: Wayne Law Rev., 1975-76; contbr. articles to law jours. Commr. Mich. Solar Resource Adv. Panel, Lansing, 1978-81, Mich. Commn. Profl. & Occupational Licensure, 1981-83; chmn. Ingham County Energy Commn., Mason, Mich., 1978-80 (state bar rep. assembly 1985—); treas. Lansing Lawyer Referral Service, 1981; state del. Nat. Solar Congress, Washington, 1978; hearing officer City of East Lansing, 1985; Tri-County Council of Bar Leaders (chmn. 1986—). Named Outstanding Young Man Am., 1984, The Outstanding Young Lawyer in Mich., 1985-86; Wm. D. Traitel scholar, 1975. Mem. ABA, State Bar Mich. (com. chmn., sect. council 1982—), Ingham County Bar Assn. (pres. 1985-86), Pro Bono Lawyers Service (pres. 1982-83), Lansing Regional C. of C. (v.p. 1987), Phi Alpha Delta, Phi Eta Sigma, Theta Delta Chi (pres. 1972). Republican. Clubs: Downtown Coaches (bd. dirs., pres. 1987), Mich. State U. Pres.'s. Administrative and regulatory, State civil litigation, Public utilities. Home: 1959 Groton Way East Lansing MI 48823 Office: Fraser Trebilcock Davis & Foster PC Michigan Nat Tower 10th Floor Lansing MI 48933

MARX, DIANNE FRANCES, lawyer; b. Hamilton, Ohio, Nov. 22, 1956; d. Frank J. and Patricia (Crouch) M. AB magna cum laude, Miami U., Oxford, Ohio, 1979; JD, U. Notre Dame, 1982. Bar: Ohio 1982, U.S. Dist. Ct. (so. dist.) Ohio 1982. Assoc. Estabrook, Finn, McKee, Porter, Wright, Morris & Arthur, Dayton, Ohio, 1982-85; ptnr. Rieser & Marx, Dayton, 1985—. Thomas J. and Alberta White scholar U. Notre Dame, 1981-82. Mem. ABA, Ohio Bar Assn., Dayton Bar Assn., Phi Beta Kappa. Democrat. Insurance, Contracts commercial, Federal civil litigation. Office: Rieser & Marx 40 W 4th St Dayton OH 45402

MARX, GARY SAMUEL, lawyer; b. Monroe, La., Sept. 18, 1954; s. Joe E. and Wilma Elaine (Zavelo) M. BA, Washington U., 1975; JD, Washingotn and Lee U., 1979; LLM, Georgetown U., 1985. Bar: Ala. 1979, D.C. 1982. Assoc. Berkowitz, Lefkowitz & Patrick, Birmingham, Ala., 1979-82, Arent, Fox, Kintner & Kahn, Washington, 1982-86; asst. gen. counsel Dutko & Assocs., Washington, 1986—; bd. dirs. So. Hardware Supply, Monroe. Editor in chief Human Resource Mgmt. Reporter, 1986—. Asst. counsel Ams. with Hart, Washington, 1984; tech. adv. com. Dem. Nat. Com., Washington, 1985; nat. law com., regional bd. Anti-Defamation League B'nai B'rith, Washington, 1985; regional co-chmn. Am. Israel Pub. Affairs Com. New Israel Fund; bd. dirs. New Dem. Forum, Washington, 1986—. Mem. Phi Beta Kappa. Labor, Antitrust, Private international.

MARX, PAULA JEANNETTE, lawyer; b. Ringgold, La., Oct. 30, 1956; d. Robert Powell and Jeannette Ann (Thomas) Corley; m. Gregory Paul Marx, May 2, 1980; children: Sarah Jeannette, Lauren Elizabeth. BA, La. Tech. U., 1977; JD, La. State U., 1980. Bar: La. 1980., U.S. Dist. Ct. (we. dist.) La. 1980, U.S. Ct. Appeals (5th cir.) 1981. Assoc. David S. Foster III P.C., Lafayette, 1980-84; ptnr. Marx & Marx, Lafayette, 1984—. Chmn. notary exam. com. Lafayette Parish, 1983-85; bd. dirs., legal counsel Big Bros./Big Sisters of Acadiana, Lafayette, 1985—. Mem. Assn. Trial Am. Lawyers, La. Trial Lawyers Assn., Acadiana Assn. for Women Attys. (treas. 1981-83), Phi Delta Phi (clk. 1979), Phi Kappa Phi, Sigma Kappa. Democrat. General practice, Family and matrimonial, Probate. Office: Marx & Marx PO Drawer GG Lafayette LA 70502

MARX, ROBERT PHILLIP, lawyer; b. Oregon City, Oreg., Jan. 23, 1949; s. Joseph Wesley and Louise Roseline (Belen) M.; m. Paula Jayne Fisher, Sept. 14, 1968; children: Rachel Elizabeth, Justin Robert, Jordan Thomas. BS in Polit. Sci., Oreg. State U., 1971; JD, Northwestern U., 1979. Bar: Hawaii, 1980. Rep. Oreg. State Legis., Salem, 1973-79, vice chmn. com. on revenue, 1974-75, co-chmn. interim com. on judiciary, 1975; sole practice Hilo, Hawaii, 1980—. Recipient Star and Lamp Key award Phi Kappa Phi, Corvallis, Oreg., 1968; named Sr. Advocate of Yr., Nat. Retired Tchrs. Assn. and Am. Assn. Retired People, 1978. Mem. ABA, Assn. Trial Lawyers Am. Democrat. Personal injury, State civil litigation. Office: 688 Kinoole St Suite 105B Hilo HI 96720

MARZLOFF, GEORGE ERNEST, lawyer; b. New Orleans, Aug. 16, 1950; s. George Edward and Shirley (Zansler) M.; m. Linda Cox, Sept. 1, 1983; children: George Edward II, Gillian Elizabeth. JD, La. State U., 1974; LLM, George Washington U., 1977. Bar: La. 1974, U.S. Ct. Appeals (4th

and 5th cirs.) 1975, Va. 1978, U.S. Dist. Ct. (ea. dist.) Va. 1979, U.S. Bankruptcy Ct. 1979. Trial atty. FCC, Washington, 1974-79; sole practice Stafford, Va., 1979—. Mem. ABA, Assn. Trial Lawyers Am., Va. Trial Lawyers Assn. Bankruptcy, Personal injury, Real property. Office: PO Box 494 Stafford VA 22554

MASANOFF, MICHAEL DAVID, lawyer; b. Jersey City, N.J., May 5, 1951; s. Abraham and Rose (Markowitz) M.; m. Faye Ann Sander, Aug. 7, 1977. BA, Am. Internat. Coll., 1972; JD, Hofstra U., 1977. Bar: N.J. 1977, Pa. 1977, U.S. Dist. Ct. N.J. 1977, U.S. Dist. Ct. (ea. dist.) Pa. 1977, U.S. Tax Ct. 1979. Law clk. SEC, N.Y.C., 1976, Community Legal Asst. Corp., Hempstead, N.Y., 1977; research asst. Tax Analysts & Advocates, Washington, 1976; ptnr. Brener Wallack & Hill, Princeton, N.J., 1977—; v.p., dir. La Haem Co., Princeton, N.J., 1979—; ptnr. Ch. Street Properties, 1981—; asst. sec. Environ. Disposal Corp., Pluckemin, N.J., 1984—; sec. Systime, Inc., Columbia, Md., 1984—, Systime Ltd., Leeds, England, 1984—; dir. U.S. Power Constrn., Inc., Worldwide Energy Devel. Corp.; gen. counsel Cabot Med. Corp., 1983—. Research editor Tax Notes, 1976. Trustee, pres. Village Homeowners Assn., Lawrenceville, N.J., 1980-81. Hofstra Law fellow, 1977; Hofstra Moot Ct. Honor, 1975; Shalan Found. Tax fellow, 1976. Mem. Princeton Bar Assn., Mercer County Bar Assn., N.J. State Bar, ABA. Real property, General corporate, Corporate taxation. Home: 99 Poe Rd Princeton NJ 08540 Office: Brener Wallack & Hill 210 Carnegie Ctr Princeton NJ 08543-5226

MASCHER, GILBERT ERNSTING, lawyer; b. Indpls., Dec. 17, 1945; s. Gilbert William and Hermine (Ernsting) M.; m. Mary Jo Cooke, May 3, 1980; children: Lauren, Andrea. BS, Ind. U., 1967; JD, Ind. U., Indpls., 1973. Bar: Ind. 1974. Chief hearing officer Ind. Dept. Revenue, Indpls., 1972-75; ptnr. Elrod, Rees, Mascher & Whitham, Indpls., 1975—. Active Calvary Luth. Ch., Indpls.; bd. dirs. Ind. Arthritis Found., Indpls., 1985—. Served to capt. U.S. Army, 1968-71. Mem. ABA, Ind. Bar Assn., Indpls. Bar Assn., Johnson County Bar Assn., Sigma Pi (pres. Beta alumni chpt. 1973-86). Republican. Family and matrimonial, General corporate, Probate. Home: 5455 Camden St Indianapolis IN 46227 Office: Elrod Rees Mascher & Whitham 2 Market Ctr Indianapolis IN 46204 also: 6960 S Gray Rd Suite A Indianapolis IN 46237

MASEK, RAYMOND JOHN, lawyer; b. Cleve., Sept. 1, 1946; s. Raymond Clement and Rita Ann (Kalous) M.; m. Lynn Katherine Ramsey, May 1984. BBA, Cleve. State U., 1969, JD, 1975. Bar: Ohio 1977. Internal auditor, asst. to acctg. mgr. Procter & Gamble Co., Balt. and Cin., 1969-71; cost/fin. analyst Ford Motor Co., Toledo and Cleve., 1971-75; corp. auditor Harris Corp., Cleve., 1975-77; sr. corp. auditor Midland-Ross Corp., Cleve., 1977-78; mgr. internat. audits, corp. counsel Reliance Electric Co., Cleve., 1978—; bd. dirs. Toledo Espanola S.A. Named Outstanding Coop. Edn. Student in Sch. Bus., Cleve. State U., 1969. Mem. Cleve. State U. Bus. Alumni Assn. (dir. 1979-82), Bar Assn. of Greater Cleve., Ohio Bar Assn., Inst. Internal Auditors, ABA (internat. law sect.). Private international, Administrative and regulatory, Legislative. Home: 8500 Lucerne Dr Chagrin Falls OH 44022-4606 Office: Reliance Electric Co 29325 Chagrin Blvd Pepper Pike OH 44122

MASERITZ, GUY B., lawyer; b. Balt., June 5, 1937; s. Isadore H. and Gertrude (Miller) M.; m. Sally Jane Sugar, Mar. 30, 1961; children—Marjorie Ellen, Michael Louis. BA Johns Hopkins U., 1959, M.A. in Econs., 1961; LL.B., U. Md., 1966. Bar: Md. 1966, D.C. 1968, U.S. Sup. Ct. 1975, U.S. Dist. Ct. Md. 1979. Atty., SEC, Washington, 1966-70; asst. gen. counsel securities Am. Life Ins. Assn., Washington, 1971-74; atty. eval. sect., chief legis. unit Antitrust div. U.S. Dept. Justice, Washington, 1974-78; spl. asst. U.S. atty. Alexandria, Va., 1978; sole practice, Columbia, Md., 1978—. Mem. Howard County (Md.) Charter Revision Commn., 1979. Served with USAR, 1960-66. Recipient U.S. Dept. Justice award for spl. achievement 1977. Mem. ABA, Md. Bar Assn. (securities law com.), D.C. Bar Assn., Howard County Bar Assn., Greater Howard County C. of C. (dir., gen. counsel 1981-84). Democrat. Author: U.S. Department of Justice Antitrust Report, 1977. General corporate, Real property, Securities. Home: 10510 Green Mountain Circle Columbia MD 21044 Office: 2000 Century Plaza Suite 125 Columbia MD 21044

MASH, JERRY L., lawyer, minister; b. Oklahoma City, July 9, 1937; s. Mary Irene Scott; m. Beverly Anne Cain, Aug. 3, 1958; children—Deborah Ruth, John Mark, James Michael; m. Cuba Deann Corbin, Feb. 14, 1977. A.B. in Philosophy, Phillips U.; student Grad. Sem., 1960-62; J.D., Oklahoma City U., 1967; postgrad. Fuller Theol. Sem., 1984—; Bar: Okla. 1968, U.S. Dist. Ct. (we. dist.) Okla. 1974, U.S. Dist. Ct. (ea. dist.) Okla. 1981. Adminstrv. asst., legal staff officer to Gov. of Okla., 1962-67; investment specialist, Okla. counsel Ling & Co., Dallas, 1967-68; sole practice, Oklahoma City and Guthrie, Okla., 1969—; lic. to ministry Okla. region Christian Ch., 1957—; minister Okla. region Christian Ch. (Disciples of Christ), 1957—, sec. Okla. region, 1984—. speaker daily radio program in Okla., Ark., Kans. and Mo., The Way to Confident Living; contbr. article to legal jour. Pres. Okla. County-City Community Action Program, 1970-72; Republican candidate for Gov. of Okla., 1978; Rep. state committeeman, 1979-82. Mem. Okla. Bar Assn., ABA, Okla. County Bar Assn., Logan County Bar Assn., Oklahoma City Securities Lawyers Group, Blue Key, Phi Delta Phi. General corporate, Securities, Federal civil litigation. Home: 18 Bramble Bush Ln Crescent OK 73028

MASHAW, JERRY L., law educator, lawyer; b. 1941. B.A., Tulane U., 1962, LL.B., 1964; Ph.D., U. Edinburgh, 1969. Bar: La. 1964, Va. 1975. Asst. prof. Tulane U., 1966-68; asst. prof. U. Va., 1968-69, assoc. prof., 1969-72, prof., 1972-76; prof. Yale U. Law Sch., 1976—; cons. Ctr. Adminstrn. Justice. Mem. Order of Coif, Phi Beta Kappa. Author: (with Merrill) Introduction to the American Public Law System, 1975; (with others) Social Security Hearings and Appeals, 1978; past editor-in-chief Tulane Law Rev. Legal education. Office: Yale U Law Sch Drawer 401A Yale Sta New Haven CT 06520 *

MASHITA, LLOYD ISAO, lawyer; b. Honolulu, Nov. 20, 1949; s. Katsumi and Mabel Masaye (Nii) M.; m. Sarah Jane Western, Aug. 7, 1971 (div.); children: Melissa S., Mark W. BA, Ripon Coll., 1971; JD, Washington U., 1975. Bar: Hawaii 1975, U.S. Dist. Ct. Hawaii 1975, Wash. 1976, U.S. Dist. Ct. (we. dist.) Wash. 1976, U.S. Ct. Appeals (9th cir.) 1977. Assoc. Joseph Geden Law Offices, Honolulu, 1975, Watson, Grosse & Kelly, Seattle, 1976-80; ptnr. Schmidt & Linde, Friday Habor, Wash., 1980-82, Linde, Boyer & Mashita, Friday Habor, 1982—. Mem. ABA, Hawaii Bar Assn., Wash. State Bar Assn., San Juan County Bar Assn. Avocation: 2d degree black belt. General practice, Family and matrimonial, Real property. Office: Linde Boyer & Mashita PO Box668 Friday Harbor WA 98250

MASICA, MARK ALEXIS, lawyer; b. Mpls., Dec. 24, 1955; s. Steven and Helen Agatha (Bieza) M. Student, St. John's U., Collegeville, Minn., 1973-74; AA, Golden Valley Luth. Coll., 1975; BA, U. Minn., 1977, JD, 1981. Bar: Minn. 1981, U.S. Dist. Ct. Minn. 1982. Sole practice Mpls., 1982—. Active Loaves and Fishes Program, Mpls., 1983—; 5th Congl. Dist. Dem.-Farmer Labor Party, 1984—, bd. dirs. Mpls. chpt., 1985—; Northside Residents Redevel. Council, Mpls., 1985—. Mem. ABA, Minn. State Bar Assn., Hennepin County Bar Assn., Legal Advice Clinics Ltd., Phi Beta Kappa. Roman Catholic. Probate, State civil litigation, Family and matrimonial. Office: 4725 Olson Meml Hwy Minneapolis MN 55422-0197

MASINTER, EDGAR MARTIN, lawyer; b. Huntington, W.Va., Jan. 2, 1931; s. Ralph Leon and Gazella (Schlossberg) M.; m. Margery Flocks, July 9, 1962; children: Robert Andrew, Catherine Diane. BA, Princeton U., 1952; LLB, Harvard U., 1955. Bar: D.C. 1955, N.Y. 1958. Assoc. Simpson Thacher & Bartlett, N.Y.C., 1957-65, ptnr., 1966—; sec., 1966—, bd. dirs. Atlas Corp., Princeton, N.J. V.p., trustee Grand St. Settlement, N.Y.C. Served with U.S. Army, 1955-57. Mem. ABA, Assn. of Bar of City of N.Y. Banking, General corporate, Securities. Office: Simpson Thacher & Bartlett 270 Park Ave New York NY 10017

MASLIANSKY, NECHAMA, editor; b. Haifa, Israel, Dec. 21, 1947; came to U.S., 1948; d. Joseph and Clara Florence (Bogopulsky) M. Student, Bklyn. Coll., 1965-69; BA, Pace U., 1973; JD, Hofstra U., 1978. Bar: N.Y. 1979, U.S. Dist. Ct. (ea. and so. dists.) N.Y. 1980. Legal writer Matthew Bender & Co., N.Y.C., 1979-81, sr. legal writer, 1981-83, asst. publ. mgr., 1983-84, asst. exec. editor, 1984-86, exec. editor, 1986—. Editor: (4 volumes) Family Law and Practice, 1985; also articles. Co-founder Coalition for Abused Women Inc., East Meadow, N.Y., 1976-79, shelter planner, 1979, cons. 1983-84; founder City Coalition on Child Sexual Abuse, N.Y.C., 1981—; co-dir. Annual Confs. on Legal Rights of Battered Women, N.Y.C., 1981—; mem. N.Y.C. Task Force Against Sexual Assault, 1980—; bd. dirs. Support for Orthodox Victims of Rape and Incest, N.Y.C., 1982—. Mem. ABA, N.Y. State Bar Assn., N.Y. Women's Bar Assn. (bd. dirs. 1983—, chair com. on battered women 1979-85), Assn. of Bar of City of N.Y., Council of N.Y. Law Assocs., N.Y. County Lawyers Assn., Am. Orthopsychatric Assn. Family and matrimonial, Criminal, Civil rights. Home: 215 E Broadway Roslyn NY 11576 Office: Matthew Bender & Co Inc 11 Penn Plaza New York NY 10001

MASON, HENRY LOWELL, III, lawyer; b. Boston, Feb. 10, 1941; s. Henry Lowell and Fanny Crowninshield (Homans) M.; m. Elaine Bobrowicz, June 7, 1969. A.B., Harvard U., 1963, LL.B., 1967. Bar: Ill. 1967. Assoc. Leibman, Williams, Bennett, Baird & Minow, Chgo., 1967-72; assoc. Sidley & Austin, 1972-73, ptnr., 1973—. Mem. Ill. Bar Assn., Chgo. Bar Assn. Republican. Federal civil litigation, State civil litigation, Antitrust. Office: One First National Plaza Chicago IL 60603

MASON, JAMES WALTER, JR., lawyer; b. Laurinburg, N.C., Feb. 8, 1916; s. James Walter and Marie (Cornelius) M.; m. Nell Celeste Adams, June 1, 1940; children—Celeste M. Pittman, James Walter. L.L.B., Wake Forest U., 1938. Bar: N.C. 1938, U.S. Dist. Ct. (mid. dist.) N.C. 1942, U.S. Supreme Ct. 1946, U.S. Dist. Ct. (ea. dist.) N.C. 1951, U.S. Dist. Ct. (we. dist.) N.C. 1955, U.S. Ct. Appeals (4th cir.) 1960. Sole practice, Laurinburg, N.C., 1938-42; spl. agt. FBI, Los Angeles and San Francisco, 1942-46; pres. Mason, Williamson, Etheridge and Moser, P.A., Laurinburg, N.C., 1946-84; ptnr. Williamson, Dean, Brown & Williams, 1984— . Mem. N.C. State Senate, 1957-58; mem. N.C. State Hwy. Commn., 1958-61; del. Dem. Nat. Conv., 1968; trustee, Wake Forest U., chmn., 1978-79; bd. visitors Wake Forest U. Sch. Law. Mem. N.C. Bar Assn. (past bd. govs.). Democrat. Baptist. General practice. Home: 407 Prince St Laurinburg NC 28352 Office: Williamson Dean Brown & Williamson 231 E Cronly St PO Box 1627 Laurinburg NC 28352

MASON, JON GERARD, lawyer; b. Waukegan, Ill., Mar. 24, 1947; s. Horace Vernon Mason and Mary Beatrice (Smith) Jordan; m. Charlotte A. Davis, Aug. 16, 1969 (div. 1974); m. Barbara Elaine Wagner, Apr. 5, 1975; children: Tara, Stephanie, Shannon. BA, Carthage Coll., 1969; JD, Marquette U., 1972. Bar: Wis. 1972, U.S. Dist. Ct. (ea. and we. dists.) Wis. 1972. Sole practice Kenosha, Wis., 1972-73; ptnr. Greco & Mason, Kenosha, 1973-76, Wokwicz, Greco & Mason, Kenosha, 1976-79, Plous, Plous & Mason, Kenosha, 1979—. Mem. exec. bd. Kenosha Youth Devel. Service, 1978. Served to 2d lt. USMC, 1969-72. Mem. ABA, Kenosha County Bar Assn. (pres. 1979-80, exec. bd. 1979-82, cir. ct. commr. 1976—), Assn. Trial Lawyers Am., Wis. Trial Lawyers Assn. Lutheran. Lodge: Elks. Avocations: racquetball, tennis, skiing, wind surfing, baseball. State civil litigation, Criminal, Family and matrimonial. Home: 7817 7th Ave Kenosha WI 53140 Office: Plous Plous & Mason 1020 56th St Kenosha WI 53140

MASON, MARGARET PENDLETON PEARSON, lawyer; b. Radford, Va., Mar. 6, 1944; d. Charles Almond, Jr. and Margaret (Keller) Pearson; children: Sarah St. Clair, Amy Grey. Student Randolph-Macon Woman's Coll., 1962-63; B.A., Goucher Coll., 1975; J.D., Yale U., 1978. Bar: Conn., 1978, U.S. Dist. Ct. Conn., 1978, U.S. Ct. Appeals (2d cir.) 1980, U.S. Supreme Ct., 1982. Mem. firm Tyler Cooper & Alcorn, New Haven, 1978—; sec. Weaver Bros., Inc., Washington, 1963-66; dir. Madison & Madison, Inc., Bethany, Conn., 1976-86; trustee Orchestra New Eng., 1986—. Jr. sec. Haddonfield (N.J.) Fortnightly, 1970-72; dir. Del. Valley Citizens Council Clean Air, Phila., 1970-72; mem. Democratic Town Com., 1980-82. Danforth Found. fellow, 1975; Eleanor Voss fellow Goucher Coll./Voss Trust, 1975; NSF grantee, 1973. Mem. ABA, Conn. Bar Assn., New Haven County Bar Assn. (dir. 1980—), Conn. Def. Lawyers Assn. Democrat. Lutheran. Federal civil litigation, State civil litigation. Office: Tyler Cooper & Alcorn 205 Church St PO Box 1936 New Haven CT 06509

MASON, PAUL ERIC, lawyer; b. New Rochelle, N.Y., Sept. 25, 1945; s. Albert C. and Bertha (Blum) M.; m. Judith C. Wiegand, Aug. 10, 1980. BA, Yale U., 1967; MA in Internat. Relations with distinction, Johns Hopkins U., Washington and Bologna, Italy, 1969; JD, U. Maine, 1976. Bar: Maine 1977, U.S. Dist. Ct. Maine 1977, Mass. 1984, U.S. Dist. Ct. Mass. 1984. Cons. UN Fund for Population Activities, N.Y.C., 1977-84, Harvard Law Sch., Cambridge, Mass., 1984-85; counsellor at law Internat. Law Collaborative, Cambridge, 1985—. Contbr. articles to profl. jours. Mem. ABA (chmn. UN activities com. 1983-84, internat. law and practice sect., chmn. subcom. on dispute resolution 1981-84), Boston Bar Assn. (internat. law sect. 1984—). Private international, Trademark and copyright, Contracts commercial. Home: 2 Mason St Winchester MA 01890 Office: Internat Law Collaborative 6 Story St Penthouse Cambridge MA 02138

MASON, PETER IAN, lawyer; b. Bellfonte, Pa., Mar. 20, 1952; s. Robert Stanley and Abelle (Dinkowitz) M.; m. Margaret Ellen Bremner, July 9, 1983; 1 child, Henry Graham. AB Brad Coll., 1973; JD cum laude, Boston U., 1976. Bar: Ill. 1976, U.S. Dist. Ct. (no. dist.) Ill. 1976, N.Y. 1981. Assoc. Rooks, Pitts, Fullagar and Poust, Chgo., 1976-80, 81-83, Shearman & Sterling, N.Y.C., 1980; mng. ptnr. Freeborn & Peters, Chgo., 1983—; dir. U.S. Robotics, Inc., Chgo., 1983—; gen. counsel Graphisphere Corp., Bradley Printing Co. Mem. ABA, Ill. State Bar Assn., Chgo. Bar Assn., Ill. Oil and Gas Assn. Republican. Episcopalian. Clubs: The Attic, Union League of Chgo. General corporate, Securities, Oil and gas leasing. Office: Freeborn & Peters 11 S LaSalle St Chicago IL 60603

MASON, RONALD LEE, lawyer; b. Huntington, W.Va., May 16, 1951. BA, Ohio Dominican Coll., 1975; JD summa cum laude, U. Datyon, 1978; LLM in Labor Law, Georgetown U., 1981. Bar: Ohio 1978, Ga. 1982. Atty. in civil div. Montgomery County Prosecutor's Office, Dayton, Ohio, 1978-80; atty. in div. enforcement litigation Nat. Labor Relations Bd., Washington, 1980-82; assoc. Troutman, Sanders, Lockerman and Ashmore, Atlanta, 1982-85, Smith and Schnacke, Columbus, Ohio, 1985—. Mem. ABA, Ohio Bar Assn., Ga. Bar Assn., Atlanta Bar Assn., Columbus Bar Assn., Upper Arlington C. of C., Dublin C. of C. Republican. Club: Capitol (Columbus). Labor. Home: 3087 Scioto Trace Columbus OH 43220 Office: Smith and Schnacke 41 S High St Suite 2250 Columbus OH 43215-6199

MASQUELETTE, PHILIP EDWARD, lawyer; b. Houston, Aug. 9, 1952; s. Philip Abbott and Elizabeth Daggett (Simmons) M.; m. Melissa Simpson Fancher, Nov. 25, 1978; 1 child, Grace Fancher. Student French civilization course Sorbonne, 1972-73; student Institut d'Etudes Politiques de Paris, 1972-73; BA, Tulane U., 1974; JD, U. Houston, 1976. Bar: Tex. 1977, U.S. Tax Ct. 1980, D.C. 1982. Assoc. Dillingham, Masquelette & Boerstler, Houston, 1977-79; officer Masquelette & Masquelette P.C., Houston, 1979-84, ptnr., 1984—, also bd. dirs. Founder, co-chmn. docents Episc. High Sch., Houston, 1984; chmn. Prisoner Services Com. of Houston Met. Ministries, 1987, bd. dirs., 1987—. Recipient Service award Ch. St. John the Divine, Houston, 1983. Mem. Houston Bar Assn., ABA, D.C. Bar Assn., Tex. Bar Assn., Houston Young Lawyers Assn. (bd. dirs. 1982-83, Outstanding Service award 1981-82), Tulane Alumni Council of Houston (pres. 1984-86), Tulane Alumni Assn. (Vol. of Yr. award 1987), Sons of Republic of Tex. Republican. Episcopalian. Club: Houston. General practice. Office: 3463 W Alabama Houston TX 77027

MASS, ALLEN ROBERT, lawyer; b. Bklyn., May 12, 1950; s. George and Evelyn (Trachtman) M.; m. Maripat Jean Quinn, June 22, 1980; children: Aaron, Alexandra. BA, Colgate U., 1972; JD, NYU, 1975. Bar: N.Y. 1976, U.S. Dist. Ct. (ea. and so. dists.) N.Y. 1976, U.S. Ct. Appeals (2d cir.) 1979, U.S. Supreme Ct. 1980, U.S. Ct. Claims 1982, U.S. Tax Ct. 1982, Ga. 1985, U.S. Dist. Ct. (no. dist.) Ga. 1985. Assoc. Rosenman, Colin, Freund, Lewis & Cohen, N.Y.C., 1975-79; trial atty. U.S. Dept. Justice, Washington, 1979-84; atty. AT&T, N.Y.C. and Atlanta, 1984—. Editor NYU Law Rev., 1975. Mem. ABA (assn. and litigation sect.), Atlanta Bar Assn. (corp. counsel sect., litigation sect.), Phi Beta Kappa. Avocations: tennis, reading, swimming. Federal civil litigation, State civil litigation, Contracts commercial. Office: AT&T 1200 Peachtree St NE Atlanta GA 30357

MASSENGALE, JOHN EDWARD, 3D, lawyer; b. Kansas City, Mo., Nov. 18, 1921; s. John Edward, Jr. and Frances (Haig) M.; m. Jean Mitchell Montague, Dec. 8, 1942; children: Sarah Choate Massengale Gregg, John Edward IV, Thomas Haig. A.B., Harvard U., 1942, LL.B., 1948. Bar: N.Y. 1949, D.C. 1971. Practice law N.Y.C., 1948—; partner firm Paul, Weiss, Rifkind, Wharton & Garrison, 1958—; bd. dirs. Cullman Ventures Inc., Wellington Industries, Inc. Rep. town meeting, Darien, Conn., 1955-61, 63-70; mem. Zoning Bd. Appeals, 1985-86, Darien Planning and Zoning Commn., 1986—. Served to lt. USNR, 1942-45. Mem. Assn. Bar City N.Y., N.Y. State Bar Assn., ABA. Club: Noroton Yacht. General corporate, Private international. Home: Goodwives River Rd Noroton CT 06820 Office: 1285 Ave of the Americas New York NY 10019

MASSENGALE, ROGER LEE, lawyer; b. Somerset, Ky., Mar. 23, 1953; s. Wendell Howard and Norma Jean (Neely) M.; m. Debra Kaye Marcum, Mar. 19, 1978; children: Sarah Anne, Jessica Claire. BA, U. Ky., 1975; JD, Capitol U., 1979. Bar: Ky., U.S. Dist. Ct. (ea. dist.) Ky. 1980, U.S. Ct. Appeals (6th cir.) 1986. Assoc. Lovelace, Carroll & Peck, Monticello, Ky., 1979-80; asst. county atty. Wayne County, Monticello, 1979-80; region counsel Ashland (Ky.) Exploration, Inc., 1980-83; atty. Ashland Oil, Inc., 1983-85; assoc. Wells, Porter, Schmitt & Walker, Paintsville, Ky., 1985—. bd. mem. Parents Anonymous of Eastern Ky., Ashland, 1984, Tri-State Fair and Regatta, Ashland, 1983-85. Mem. ABA, Ky. Bar Assn., Boyd County Bar Assn., Ky. Acad. Trial Attys. Avocations: camping, backpacking, poetry writing, wood working. Oil and gas leasing, Personal injury, Insurance. Home: 1601 Lawrence Av Ashland KY 41101

MASSEY, ARTHUR BLANTON, lawyer; b. Richmond, Va., Feb. 27, 1943; s. C. Rosser and Kathryn (Harlin) M.; m. Betty Faye Branscome, Oct. 21, 1978; children: Gina Suzanne, James Anthony, Ann Garnett. BS, Randolph-Macon Coll., 1965; LLB, U. Va., 1968; LLM, Georgetown U., 1976. Bar: Va. 1968, U.S. Tax Ct. 1973. Ptnr. Massey & Nuckols, Fredericksburg, Va., 1970—; commonwealth's atty. King George County, Va., 1976. Author: Lawyer's Role in Financial Planning, 1986. Served to capt. JAGC, Va. N.G., 1976-78. Mem. ABA, Inst. Cert. Fin. Planners (cert.), Nat. Assn. Bond Lawyers, Fredericksburg Estate Planning Council (pres. 1977), Fredericksburg C. of C. (v.p. 1983, legal counsel 1984—). Episcopalian. Lodge: Rotary (sec. Fredericksburg 1985). Estate planning, General practice, Personal financial management law. Office: Massey & Nuckols PC 1119 Caroline St Fredericksburg VA 22401

MASSEY, DONALD TERHUNE, lawyer; b. Ridgewood, N.J., Dec. 15, 1951; s. Harold Jr. and Ann (Terhune) M.; m. Pamela Willis Waite, Oct. 2, 1982. BA, Yale U., 1974; JD, U. Conn., 1977. Bar: Conn. 1978, U.S. Dist. Ct. Conn. 1978, Maine 1983, U.S. Dist. Ct. Maine 1984, U.S. Ct. Appeals (1st cir.) 1985. Assoc. Fazzano & McGrail, Hartford, Conn., 1977-80; atty. Conn. Laborers Legal Services, Bridgeport, Conn., 1980-83; ptnr. Legal Ctr. Maine, P.A., Lewiston, 1983—. Mem. Chester (Conn.) Zoning Bd., 1977-78. Mem. Am. Judicature Soc., Assn. Trial Lawyers Am., Maine Trial Lawyers Assn. Criminal, Family and matrimonial, Real property. Home: Rural Rt 265A Yarmouth ME 04096 Office: Legal Ctr Maine PA Promenade Mall Lewiston ME 04240

MASSEY, JAMES BUCKNER, III, lawyer; b. Washington, Nov. 3, 1944; s. James Buckner Jr. and Helen (Collings) M.; m. Donna Carolyn Parker, Apr. 3, 1971; 1 child, Andrew Davies. BA, U. Va., 1966, JD, 1979. Bar: Va. 1979, U.S. Dist. Ct. (we. dist.) Va. 1979, U.S. Tax Ct. 1979, U.S. Ct. Appeals (4th cir.). Ptnr. Woods, Rogers & Hazlegrove, Roanoke, Va., 1979—. Served to lt. USN, 1966-73. Mem. ABA (taxation and corp. banking and bus. law sect.), Va. Bar Assn. (taxation com.), Roanoke Bar Assn., Order of Coif. Presbyterian. Lodge: Kiwanis. Avocation: flying. General corporate, Contracts commercial, Probate. Office: Woods Rogers & Hazlegrove 105 Franklin Rd SW Roanoke VA 24011

MASSEY, RAYMOND DAVID, lawyer; b. Goldsboro, N.C., Oct. 13, 1946; s. Raymond L. and Dorris L. (Grant) M.; m. Barbara A. Warner, Aug. 16, 1967; children—Suzanne, Christine. B.A., Wofford Coll., Spartanburg, S.C., 1968; J.D., U. S.C., 1971; L.L.M. in Taxation, Emory U., 1985. Bar: S.C. 1971, U.S. Dist. Ct. S.C. 1971. Assoc. Perrin, Perrin & Mann, Spartanburg, 1971-74; trust officer Bankers Trust of S.C., Columbia and Greenville, 1974-78; ptnr. Brown & Hagins, P.A., Greenville, S.C., 1978—; pres. Greenville Estate Planning Council, 1982. Mem. Greenville Bar Assn. (pres. tax sect. 1980-81), S.C. Bar Assn. (chmn. probate, estate planning and trust sect. 1983). Presbyterian. Clubs: Greenville Country, Poinsett. Probate, Estate taxation, State civil litigation. Office: PO Box 2464 Greenville SC 29602

MASSIE, JOEL LEE, lawyer; b. Bessemer, Mich., Mar. 6, 1954; s. Leo Oliver and Ann Matilda (Salmi) M.; m. Janice Marie Busch, Dec. 12, 1976; children: Jessica Lee, Jordan Andrew, Justin Paul. BS, Western Mich. U., 1976; JD, Marquette U., 1979. Bar: Mich. 1979, Wis. 1979, U.S. Dist. Ct. (ea. and we. dists.) Wis. 1979, U.S. Dist. Ct. (we. dist.) Mich. 1985. Asst. dist. atty. Iron County, Wis., 1979-80; sole practice Bessemer, 1980—; bd. dirs. Upper Penninsula Legal Services, Sault Sainte. Marie, Mich.; city atty. Bessemer, 1981—. Bd. dirs. Gogebic County Econ. Devel. Commn., Bessemer, 1984—; pres. Bessemer Centennial Com., 1984—. Mem. Mich. Bar Assn., Wis. Bar Assn., Gogebic Ontonagon Bar Assn. (sec., treas. 1981-84). Lodge: Lions (pres. 1985—). Local government, General practice, Banking. Home: 200 W Lead St Bessemer MI 49911 Office: 300 S Clayberg St Bessemer MI 49911

MASSLER, HOWARD ARNOLD, lawyer; b. Newark, July 22, 1946; s. Abraham I. and Sylvia (Botwin) M.; m. Randee Elyce Karch, July 1, 1977; children: Justin Scott, Jeremy Ross. BA, U. Pa., 1969; JD, Rutgers U., 1973; LLM in Taxation, NYU, 1977. Bar: N.J. 1974, U.S. Dist. Ct. N.J. 1974, D.C. 1975, U.S. Ct. Appeals (D.C. cir.) 1975, N.Y. 1977, U.S. Dist. Ct. (we. dist.) N.Y. 1977, U.S. Tax Ct. 1977. Counsel house banking, currency and housing com. U.S. Ho. Reps., Washington, 1974-76; tax atty. Lipsitz, Green, Fahringer, Roll, Schuller & James, N.Y.C. and Buffalo, 1977-79; sole practice Mountainside, N.J., 1979—; arbitrator U.S. Dist. Ct. N.J., 1985—; instr. taxation Seton Hall U., South Orange, N.J., 1984-85, N.J. Inst. for Continuing Legal Edn., 1986; chmn. bd. dirs. Bestway Group Inc.; lectr. N.J. Inst. for Continuing Legal Edn., 1986—; assoc. dir. United Jersey Bank/Franklin State Bank. Author: QDROs (Tax and Drafting Considerations), 1986; contbg. author: Contemporary Matrimonial Law Issues: A Guide to Divorce Economics and Practice, 1985; contbg. editor Pensions and Ins. Problems, 1984—, Taxation, 1984—, FairShare, 1984—, Law & Bus., Inc., 1984—; regular contbr. N.J. Law Jour., 1986—; contbr. articles to profl. jours. Bd. dirs., legal counsel western N.Y. chpt. Nat. Handicapped Sports and Recreation Assn., 1977-79; counsel Union County, N.J., 1984-85; candidate Springfield (N.J.) Twp. Commn., 1986. Mem. ABA, N.J. Bar Assn., N.Y. Bar Assn. (taxation com., subcom. on criminal and civil penalties), D.C. Bar Assn., N.Y. County Lawyers Assn. (taxation com. 1979—), Erie County Bar Assn. (sec. taxation com. 1977-79, continuing edn. lectr. taxation 1977—), Essex County Bar Assn. (tax com. 1981—), Union County Bar Assn. (chmn. tax com. 1984—). Republican. Lodge: Kiwanis. Avocation: SCCA formula Ford racing. Corporate taxation, Estate taxation, Personal income taxation. Office: 1125 Globe Ave Mountainside NJ 07092

MASSUCCO, LAWRENCE RAYMOND, lawyer; b. Waterbury, Conn., Sept. 6, 1947; s. Lawrence Philip and Marion Elizabeth (Bigelow) M.; m. Virginia L. Johnson, Sept. 6, 1969; children—Neil Raymond, Julie Lynn, Kathryn Rose. B.A., U. Vt., 1970; J.D., Suffolk U., 1973. Bar: Vt. 1973, U.S. Dist. Ct. Vt. 1973. Assoc. Kissell Law Offices, Bellows Falls, Vt., 1973-74; ptnr. Kissell & Massucco, Bellows Falls, 1975—; counsel Bellows Falls Village Corp., 1983—. Pres., v.p., sec. Fall Mountain YMCA, Bellows Falls, 1975—; chmn. St. Charles Parish Council, Bellows Falls, 1977; pres. Rockingham Townscape, Inc., Bellows Falls, 1977-83. Mem. ABA, Am. Trial Lawyers Assn., Vt. Bar Assn., Vt. Trial Lawyers Assn., Windham County Bar Assn. Roman Catholic. Lodges: KC (advocate 1980—), Elks. State civil litigation, General practice, Personal injury. Office: Kissell & Massucco 90 Westminster St Bellows Falls VT 05101

MASTERS, CLAUDE BIVIN, lawyer; b. Cleburne, Tex., July 25, 1930; s. Claude Pinkney and Ola Mae (Rollins) M.; m. Jenita Whites, June 1, 1949 (div.); children: C. Thomas, C. Danette Masters McClanahan, Teresa Masters Lebeck; m. Cynthia McCormack, Nov. 4, 1983. BS, U. Houston, 1953, JD, 1969, LLM, 1985. Bar: Tex. 1969, U.S. Dist. Ct. (so. dist.) Tex. 1971, U.S. Dist. Ct. (we. dist.) Tex. 1972, U.S. Ct. Appeals (5th cir.) 1971, U.S. Ct. Appeals (11th cir.) 1983, U.S. Supreme Ct. 1978. Ptnr. Martin & Masters, Houston, 1971-73; v.p., gen. counsel Summit Ins. Co. N.Y., N.Y.C., 1973-75; sr. atty. Ashland Oil Co., Ky., 1975-78; v.p. Houston Oil & Minerals Co., Houston, 1978-84; assoc. Dunnam & Strong, Houston, 1984-85; risk-mgmt. cons. Masters & Assocs., Houston, 1975—; bd. dirs. Alford & Assocs., Houston; adj. prof. law U. Houston, 1984—. Dir.-gen. Tex. Safety Assn., Austin, 1959. Served with U.S. Army, 1946-47. Named Outstanding Speaker, Southwest Ins. Info. Service, Dallas, 1961-62. Fellow Houston Bar Found; mem. Jaycees (bd. dirs. Tulsa 1962; named Outstanding Mem. Tex. 1960), Phi Delta Phi. Republican. Mem. Ch. of Christ. Private international, Oil and gas leasing, Insurance. Home: 3084 Holly Hall Houston TX 77054 Office: Halla & Masters 2200 Post Oak Blvd Suite 712 Houston TX 77056

MASTERS, KENNETH HALLS, lawyer; b. Washington, Aug. 16, 1943; s. Kenneth Hubert and Kathleen Elizabeth (Maloney) M.; m. Patricia Ann Pound, June 10, 1967; children: Maura Patricia, Kathleen St. John Masters. BA, Towson State Coll., 1965; JD, U. Md., 1972. Bar: Md. 1972, U.S. Dist. Ct. Md. 1973, U.S. Supreme Ct. 1976, U.S. Ct. Appeals (4th cir.) 1977. Assoc. Nolan, Plumhoff & Williams, Towson, 1972-82; sole practice Catonsville, Md., 1983-84; ptnr. McFarland, Weinkam, O'Connell & Masters, Catonsville, 1984—. Mem. Dem. State Cen. Com., Balt., 1974-78; del. Gen. Assembly of Md., Balt., 1979—. Served to 1st lt. U.S. Army, 1966-69. Decorated Bronze Star with oak leaf clusters, Air medal. Mem. ABA, Md. Bar Assn., Balt. Bar Assn., Balt. County Bar Assn. Democrat. Roman Catholic. General practice. Home: 1809 Edmondson Ave Catonsville MD 21228 Office: McFarland Weinkam O'Connell & Masters 1002 Frederick Rd Catonsville MD 21228

MASTERS, RICHARD L., lawyer; b. Lexington, Ky., June 13, 1954; s. Ronald Joseph and Marian Louise (Orcutt) M.; m. Susan Jean Kinlaw, May 13, 1978; children: Hannah Elisabeth, Sally Anne. BA, Asbury Coll., 1976; JD, U. Louisville, 1979. Bar: Ky. 1979, U.S. Dist. Ct. (we. dist.) Ky. 1980, U.S. Dist. Ct. (ea. dist.) Ky. 1982, U.S. Ct. Appeals (6th cir.) 1985. Sr. legal asst. Nat. Industries, Louisville, 1977-79; asst. atty. gen. Commonwealth of Ky., Frankfort, 1979-82; gen. counsel Council State Govts., Lexington, 1982-83; counsel Ky. Revenue Cabinet, Frankfort, 1983-84; ptnr. Amshoff, Amshoff & Searcy, Louisville, 1984—. Author: Suggested State Legislation, 1982, 2d rev. edition, 1983, Interstate Compacts, 1983. Mem. Rep. Nat. Com., Washington, 1985-86, Trail's End Homeowners Assn., Goshen, Ky., 1985-86; pres. Christian Conciliation Ministries, Louisville, 1986. Recipient Cert. Appreciation Freedom Council, 1985; named to Hon. Order of Ky. Cols., 1981. Mem. ABA, Ky. Bar Assn. (continuing legal edn. award 1981), Assn. Trial Lawyers Am., Christian Legal Soc., Am. Judicature Soc., Practitioners of State Tax Assn., Asbury Alumni Assn. (pres. 1986), Francis Asbury Soc. (sec. 1983—). Democrat. Methodist. Avocations: travel, racquetball, tennis. Federal civil litigation, State civil litigation, State and local taxation. Home: 13110 Settlers Point Trail Goshen KY 40026 Office: Amshoff Amshoff & Searcy 1012 S 4th Stldg Louisville KY 40202

MASTERSON, BERNARD JOSEPH, lawyer; b. Chgo., Mar. 19, 1919; s. Bernard Joseph and Katherine Mary (Murphy) Donovan; m. Stella Dennis, Mar. 27, 1943; children: Stephen M., Thomas Dennis, Sharon Svabek, Michael Daniel. BBA, U. Fla., 1941, LLB, 1952. Bar: Fla. 1952, U.S. Dist. Ct. Fla. 1953, U.S. Ct. Appeals (5th cir.) 1953. Sole practice St. Petersburg, Fla., 1952-53; ptnr. Mann, Harrison, Roney, Mann & Masterson, St. Petersburg, 1953-57, Masterson & Meros, St. Petersburg, 1957-60, Masterson, Rogers, Patterson & Masterson, P.A. and predecessor firms, St. Petersburg, 1960—; mem. com. on standard jury instrns. Fla. Supreme Ct., Tallahassee, 1981—, jud. nominating com. U.S. Ct. Appeals (2d cir.), Tallahassee, 1984—. Served to sgt. U.S. Army, 1942-46, PTO. Fellow Am. Coll. Trial Lawyers, 1973—; mem. ABA, Acad. Fla. Trial Lawyers (pres. 1975-76), Am. Judicature Soc., Pinellas Trial Lawyers Assn. (pres. 1959). Democrat. Avocations: travel, tennis, reading. Personal injury, State civil litigation, Federal civil litigation. Home: 416 Villa Grande Ave S Saint Petersburg FL 33707 Office: Masterson Rogers et al 699 1st Ave N PO Box 31517 Saint Petersburg FL 33732-1517

MASTERSON, KENNETH RHODES, courier company executive, lawyer; b. Memphis, Feb. 22, 1944; s. H. Byron and Mary (Rhodes) M.; m. Nancy Frederickson, Feb. 28, 1980; children—Michael K., Elizabeth Megel, Grace Megel. B.A., Westminster Coll., 1966; J.D., Vanderbilt U., 1970. Bar: Mo. 1970, Tenn. 1976. Ptnr. Thomason, Crawford & Hendrix, Memphis, 1976-79; v.p. legal Fed. Express Corp., Memphis, 1980-81, sr. v.p., gen. counsel, 1981—. Mem. ABA, Mo. Bar Assn., Am. Corp. Counsel Assn., Memphis and Shelby County Bar Assn. General corporate. Home: 2461 Brandemere Dr Germantown TN 38138 Office: Fed Express Corp 2005 Corporate Ave Memphis TN 38132

MASTERSON, RICHARD ARTHUR, lawyer; b. Norwich, N.Y., May 23, 1937; s. Willard Christopher and Helen Ann (Byrne) M.; m. Juliana Elizabeth Daily, Sept. 3, 1977. Student, Dartmouth Coll., 1955-58; BA, Colgate U., 1964; postgrad., NYU, 1965-67; JD, John Marshall Law Sch., 1973. Bar: N.Y. 1976, U.S. Dist. Ct. (no. dist.) N.Y. 1976. Asst. employment mgr. Union Carbide Corp., Kokomo, Ind., 1967-69; supvr. employee relations Pioneer Screw and Nut Co., Elk Grove Village, Ill., 1969-70; with Monroe County (N.Y.) Legal Assistance Corp., Rochester, 1973-74; personnel mgmt. specialist U.S. Immigration and Naturalization Service, N.Y.C., 1977-78; gen. atty. office of rev. and appeals EEOC, Washington, 1979-86; specialist equal employment Def. Logistics Agy., Alexandria, Va., 1986—; mem. handicapped employee adv. com., EEOC, Washington, 1983-86, personnel mgmt. evaluation team, U.S. Immigration and Naturalization Service , N.Y.C., 1978, Def. Logistics Agy., 1986—. contbr. writer 1984-85 cumulative ann. supplement to Employment Discrimination Law. Served with USAF, 1961-62. Recipient spl. achievement awards EEOC, 1980, 81. Mem. ABA (labor and employment law sect., EEO subcom.) Fed. Bar Assn. (sect. labor law and labor relations, EEOC subcom.), Dartmouth Coll. Lawyers Assn.. Republican. Roman Catholic. Clubs: Dartmouth (Washington), Toastmasters (Kokomo) (pres. 1966). Avocation: golf. Labor. Home: 2209 Coffeewood Ct Silver Spring MD 20906

MASTRANGELO, RICHARD EDWARD, lawyer; b. Watertown, Mass., May 14, 1938; s. Louis and Helen G. (DeCost) M.; m. Lois Jean Ficker, Aug. 30, 1973; children: Elizabeth Helen, James Elliot Ficker, Edward Lawrence Ficker. AA, Boston U., 1957, BS in Pub. Relations, 1959, JD, 1962. Bar: Mass. 1962, D.C. 1974, U.S. Dist. Ct. Mass. 1965, U.S. Ct. Appeals (1st Cir.) 1967, U.S. Supreme Ct. 1966. Sole practice, Watertown, Boston, Washington various times 1962—; asst. atty. gen. Commonwealth of Mass., Boston, 1967-69; exec. dir. Mass. Rep. State Com., Boston, 1969, Sargent Com., Boston, 1969-70; asst. to sec. HEW, Washington, 1970-73, Dept. Def., 1973; assoc. dep. atty. gen. Dept. Justice, Washington, 1973; exec. asst. Hon. Elliot L. Richardson, Washington, 1974; sec. President's Council Environ. Quality, Washington, 1975; dep. campaign dir. Pres. Ford Com., 1975-76; legal cons. to sec., gen. counsel Dept. Transp., Washington, 1976-77; pres., founding dir. Washington Group, 1977; campaign mgr. Hatch Com., Boston, 1977-78; dir. pub. affairs Associated Industries Mass., Boston, 1979-81, assoc. counsel, 1981-86, gen. counsel, 1986—. Selectman Town of Watertown, 1968-70, 79-81, chmn. bd. selectmen, 1970, chmn. redevel. authority, 1982-84, mem., 1978—, charter commn., 1979-80, town meeting mem., 1961-71, 78-81, clk. mcpl. personnel bd., 1960-61, 62-64, mem. mcpl. personnel bd., 1968-69; co-pres. Phillips Sch. Community Orgn., Watertown, 1982-85; treas. Russell Cooperative Preschool, Watertown, 1983-84; cubmaster Pack 202 Minuteman council Boy Scouts Am., 1984-86; mem. Watertown Rep. Town Com., 1960—, chmn. 1966-68; nat. committeeman Mass. Young Reps., 1965-67, chmn. 1963-65; alternate del.-at-large Rep. Nat. Conv., San Francisco, 1964; mem. council human concerns Rep. Nat. Com., Washington, 1977-80. Named Outstanding Young Men in Am., U.S. Jaycees, 1970, Man of Yr., Boston U., 1959. Mem. Mass. Selectmen's Assn., Boston U. Nat. Alumni Council, Scarlet Key, Alpha Phi Omega, Zeta Upsilon (leadership award 1959, Brother of Yr. 1958, disting. service key 1959), Tau Mu Epsilon, Chi Gamma Epsilon. Roman Catholic. Clubs: Middlesex (Boston); Federal City (Washington). Lodges: Sons of Italy (Watertown chpt. lodge orator 1967-68), Elks. General practice, Legislative, Local government. Home: 109 Barnard Ave Watertown MA 02172 Office: Associated Industries Mass 462 Boylston St Boston MA 02116

MASUCCI, LOUIS M., JR., lawyer; b. Newark, Oct. 1, 1956; s. Louis M. and Mary T. (DePaola) M. BS, Seton Hall U., 1978, JD, 1981. Bar: N.J., U.S. Dist. Ct. N.J., U.S. Supreme Ct. Law sec. to presiding justice N.J. Supreme Ct., Newark, 1981-82; ptnr. Masucci & Commisa, Nutley, N.J., 1982—. Mem. Essex County Bar Assn. (exec. com. young lawyers sect. 1984—, chmn. speaker's bur. 1985—). Roman Catholic. Criminal, Family and matrimonial, Personal injury. Office: Masucci & Commisa 234 Franklin Ave Nutley NJ 07110

MATANKY, ROBERT WILLIAM, lawyer; b. Chgo., Dec. 26, 1955; s. Eugene and Gertrude (Shiner) M.; m. Lee Mindy Frankel, Sept. 1, 1985. BS in Engring., U. Ill., 1977; JD, Ill. Inst. Tech., 1980; A in Hebrew Lit., Hebrew Theol. Coll., 1980; postdoctoral, U. Chgo., 1986—. Bar: Ill. 1980, U.S. Dist. Ct. (no. dist.) Ill. 1980, U.S. Ct. Appeals (7th cir.) 1980, U.S. Supreme Ct. 1984; lic. real estate broker, Ill., lic. ins. broker, Ill.; lic. prin. Nat. Assn. Securities Dealers. Traffic coordinator Chgo. Rock Island & Pacific R.R. Co., Chgo., 1978-79; assoc. Hollobow & Taslitz, Chgo., 1980-81; corp. counsel Matanky Realty Group, Chgo., 1981-84, asst. v.p., 1984-86, v.p., 1987—; bd. dirs. Community Bank and Trust Co. Edgewater, Chgo. Editor Decalogue Jour., 1985—. Co-chmn. lawyers div. Jewish United Fund, 1983—; bd. dirs. Hebrew Theol. Coll., Skokie, Ill., 1985—, Jewish Nat. Fund., Chgo., 1984—, Congregation Ezras Israel, Chgo., 1983—, Associated Talmud Torahs Chgo., 1982—, v.p. 1986—. Mem. ABA, Ill. Bar Assn., Chgo. Bar Assn. (real property law com.), Decalogue Soc. Lawyers (bd. mgrs. 1979—, pres. 1986-87, intra-soc. award 1985), Inst. Indsl. Engrs., Chgo. Bd. Realtors (active prin. 1985—), Real Estate Securities and Syndication Inst. (designations rev. bd.). Avocations: study of talmud, carpentry, elec. and plumbing work, golf. Real property, Real estate securities. Office: Matanky Realty Group Inc 1901 N Halsted St Chicago IL 60614-5008

MATCHETT, HUGH MOORE, lawyer; b. Chgo., Apr. 24, 1912; s. David Fleming and Jennie E. (Moore) M.; m. Ilo Venona Wolff, May 12, 1956. AB, Monmouth (Ill.) Coll., 1934; JD, U. Chgo., 1937. Bar: Ill. 1937. Practice, Chgo., 1937—. Served with USNR, 1942-46, MTO, PTO; lt. comdr. JAGC, USNR. Mem. Fed. Bar Assn. (chmn. mil. law com. Chgo. chpt. 1954-55, mem. com. 1960-61), ABA, Ill. Bar Assn. (mem. assembly 1980-86), Chgo. Bar Assn., Judge Advs. Assn., Tau Kappa Epsilon, Phi Alpha Delta. Republican. Presbyterian. Counsel in litigation establishing rule that charitable instns. are liable in tort to extent of their non-trust funds. State civil litigation, Federal civil litigation, General practice. Home and Office: 5834 S Stony Island Ave Chicago IL 60637

MATEAS, KENNETH EDWARD, lawyer; b. Aurora, Ill., May 7, 1949; s. Victor Joseph and Lois Rose (Carder) M. BA, U. Ill., 1971; JD, John Marshall Sch. of Law, 1982. Bar: Ill. 1982. Assoc. Law Offices of J. Timothy Loats, Aurora, 1982-83, Law Offices of Michael Marsh, Aurora, 1983-84; atty. Kane County States Atty.'s Office, Geneva, Ill., 1985; assoc. Law Offices of Gerard Kepple, St. Charles, Ill., 1985—. Mem. ABA, Ill. Bar Assn., Nat. Assn. Criminal Def. Lawyers. Republican. Roman Catholic. Lodge: KC. Criminal, Family and matrimonial. Office: Law Offices Gerard Kepple 619 W Main St Saint Charles IL 60174

MATEER, DON METZ, lawyer; b. Evanston, Ill., July 29, 1945; s. Bruce DeLoss and Ann (Timson) M.; m. Dawn Rebecca Hallsten, Oct. 4, 1981 children—Andrew, Alexandra; m. Jacquelyn Susan Henkin, June 7, 1969 (div. Apr. 1981); children—Kristin, Julie. B.A., U. Mich., 1967; J.D., U. Ill., 1971. Bar: Ill. 1971, U.S. Dist. Ct. (no. dist.) Ill. 1972, U.S. Ct. Appeals (7th cir.) 1974, U.S. Supreme Ct. 1981. Assoc., Gilbert & Powers, Rockford, Ill., 1971-73; ptnr. Gilbert, Powers & Mateer, Rockford, 1974, Gilbert, Powers, Mateer & Erickson, 1975, Mateer & Erickson, 1976—. Precinct and ward coordinator, mayoral campaign, Rockford, 1980-84; chmn. bd. Christian edn. Bethesda Covenant Ch., 1987; bd. dirs. Protestant Community Services, 1986—; chmn. christian edn., bd. Bethesda Covenant Ch. 1986—. Mem. Am. Arbitration Assn., Winnebago County Bar Assn. (chmn. jud. liaison com. 1986-87), Ill. Bar Assn., Assn. Trial Lawyers Am., Def. Research Inst., Ill. Def. Counsel, Am. Judicature Soc. Democrat. Mem. Covenant Ch. Club: Forest Hills Country, U. Mich. (bd. dirs. 1986—). Federal civil litigation, State civil litigation, Personal injury. Home: 2006 Oxford St Rockford IL 61103 Office: Mateer & Erickson 401 W State St Suite 400 Enterprise Bldg Rockford IL 61101

MATHENY, TOM HARRELL, lawyer; b. Houston; s. Whitman and Lorene (Harrell) M. B.A., Southeastern La. U., 1954; J.D., Tulane U., 1957; LL.D. (hon.), Centenary Coll., 1979, DePauw U. Bar: La. 1957. Ptnr. firm Pittman & Matheny, Hammond, La., 1957—; trust counsel, chmn. bd. 1st Guaranty Bank, Hammond; v.p. Edwards & Assocs., So. Brick Supply, Inc.; faculty Southeastern La. U., 5 yrs., Holy Cross Coll., New Orleans, 3 yrs.; lectr. Union Theol. Sem., Law Sci. Acad.; mem. com. on conciliation and mediation of disputes World Peace through Law Ctr. Chmn. advancement com. Boy Scouts Am., Hammond, 1960-64, mem. dist. council, 1957-66, mem. exec. bd. Istrouma council, 1966—, adv. com. to dist. area council; pres. Tangipahoa Parish Mental Health Assn.; mem. La. Mental Health Advocacy Service; co-chmn. La. Mental Health Advocacy Bd.; sec. Chep Morrison Scholarship Found.; mem. men's com. Japan Internat. Christian U. Found; chmn. speakers com., mem. com. on community action and crime prevention, La. Commn. on Law Enforcement and Adminstrn. Criminal Justice; campaign mgr. for Dem. gov. La., 1959-60, 63-64; bd. dirs. La. Moral and Civic Found., Tangipahoa Parish ARC, 1957-67, Hammond United Givers Fund, 1957-68, La. Council Chs., Southeastern Devel. Found., La. Mental Health Assn.; bd. dirs. Wesley Found., La. State U., 1965-68, 70—, chmn. bd.; trustee Centenary Coll., 1964-70, Scarritt Coll., 1975-81; hon. trustee John F. Kennedy Coll.; hon. sec. U.S. com. Audenshaw Found.; pres. jud. council United Meth. Ch., 1976—, trustee La. annual conf., pres. bd. trustees, 1984—, del. world conf. in London, 1966, Denver, 1971, Dublin, 1976, Hawaii, 1981, del. to gen. confs., 1968, 70, 72. Recipient Man of Yr. award Hammond, 1961, 64, also La. Jaycees, 1964, Layman of Yr. award La. Ann. Conf. United Meth. Ch., 1966, 73, Disting. Alumnus award Southeastern La. U., 1981, W.L. "Bill" May Outstanding Christian Bus. award La. Moral and Civic Found., 1986. Fellow Harry S. Truman Library Inst (hon.); mem. ABA (com. on probate), La. Bar Assn. (past gen. chmn. com. on legal aid, com. prison reform), 21st Jud. Dist. Bar Assn. (past sec.-treas., v.p. 1967-68, 71), Comml. Law League Am. (past mem. com. on ethics), La. Alumni Council (pres. 1963-65), Acad. Religion and Mental Health, La. Assn. Claimant Compensation Attys., Southeastern La. U. Alumni Assn. (dir., pres. 1961-62, dir. spl. fund 1959-62, dir. Tongipahoa chpt.), Tulane Sch. Law Alumni Assn., Assn. Trial Lawyers Am., Am. Judicature Soc., Law-Sci. Inst., World Peace Through Law Acad., Acad. Polit. Sci., Am. Acad. Polit. and Social Sci., Internat. Acad. Law and Sci., Common Cause, Internat. Platform Assn., UN Assn., La. Hist. Assn., Friends of Cabildo, Gideons Internat., Nat. Assn. Conf. Lay Leaders of United Meth. Ch. (pres. 1966-82), Assn. Conf. Lay Leaders South Central Jurisdiction (pres.), Hammond Assn. Commerce (dir. 1960-65), Intern Soc. Barristers, Intern Assn. Valuers, Phi Delta Phi, Phi Alpha Delta. Democrat. Methodist. Lodges: Masons, DeMolay (dist. dep. to supreme council 1964—, Legion of Honor), Kiwanis (v.p., dir., Layman of Yr. award for La., Miss. and West Tenn. 1972), Rotary. Mental health. Home: PO Box 221 Hammond LA 70404 Office: 401 E Thomas St PO Box 1598 Hammond LA 70401

MATHERS, ALLEN STANLEY, lawyer, arbitrator, consultant; b. Elmhurst, N.Y., Jan. 20, 1949; s. William Albert and Agnes (Przeniczny) M.; m. Mary Elizabeth Breslin, Oct. 1, 1977; children—Matthew Allen, Sarah Anne, Amanda Mary. B.A., St. Francis Coll., 1970; J.D., St. John's U., Jamaica, N.Y., 1973. Bar: N.Y. 1974, U.S. Dist. Ct. (so. and ea. dists.) N.Y. 1974, U.S. Ct. Appeals (2d cir.) 1974, U.S. Supreme Ct. 1983. Assoc. Israelson & Streit, N.Y.C., 1973-80; dir. labor relations Trans World Airlines, Inc., N.Y.C., 1980-82; dir. legal services fund, gen. counsel local 74 Service Employees Internat. Union, AFL-CIO, Long Island City, N.Y., 1982—; mem. faculty St. Francis Coll., Bklyn., 1979—. V.p. Garden City Dem. Club, N.Y., 1984—; bd. dirs. Garden City Estates Property Owners. Mem. Am. Prepaid Legal Service Inst., ABA, N.Y. State Bar Assn., Queens County Bar Assn., Am. Arbitration Assn. Democrat. Roman Catholic. General practice, Labor, Pension, profit-sharing, and employee benefits. Home: 30 Kensington Rd Garden City NY 11530 Office: Service Employees Internat Union Local 74 25-09 38 Ave Long Island NY 11101

MATHERS, PETER ROBERT, lawyer; b. Camden, N.J., Jan. 12, 1955; s. Edward Ronald and Gertrude Louise (Pennypacker) M.; m. Patti Lynn Mitchell, May 24, 1984. BS, Rensselaer Poly. Inst., 1976; JD, Yale U., 1979. Bar: D.C. 1979, U.S. Dist. Ct. (D.C. dist.) 1983, U.S. Ct. Appeals (D.C. Cir.) 1983, U.S. Supreme Ct. 1987. Assoc. Kleinfeld, Kaplan & Becker, Washington, 1979-87, ptnr., 1987—. Contbr. articles to profl. jours. Mem. ABA (corp. banking and bus. law sect., food and drug law com.), D.C. Bar Assn., Food and Drug Law Inst., Drug Info. Assn. Administrative and regulatory, Federal civil litigation, Food and Drug. Home: 1029 N Stuart St Arlington VA 22201 Office: Kleinfeld Kaplan & Becker 1140 19th St NW Washington DC 20036

MATHERS, STEPHEN CHARLES, judge; b. Galesburg, Ill., Nov. 1, 1946; s. Gale Albert and Viola Marie (Beecher) M.; m. Patricia Ann Wachunas, Sept. 16, 1978; 1 child, Jonathan Gale. BA, Northwestern U., 1968; JD, U. Ill., 1974. Bar: Ill. 1974, U.S. Supreme Ct. 1978. Asst. states atty. Kane County, Geneva, Ill., 1974-75; ptnr. Peel, Henning, Mathers et al, Galesburg, 1975-78; assoc. judge 9th Jud. Cir., Galesburg, 1978-80, cir. judge, 1980—; instr. criminal law Carl Sandburg Community Coll., 1975—; asst. atty. City of Galesburg, 1976-77; lectr. Trial Advocacy Course, U. Ill., 1979-83. Trustee Galesburg Cottage Hosp., 1980—; trustee Galesburg Hosps. Ambulance Service, 1981—, chmn. bd. dirs., 1984-85, 1986-87; chmn. bd. dirs. Cottage Care Corp., Galesburg, 1984—. Served with U.S. Army, 1968-71, Vietnam. Recipient citation for Outstanding Community Achievement by Vietnam Vet., Pres. U.S., 1979. Mem. ABA, Ill. Bar Assn., County Bar Assn. Office: Knox County Courthouse Cherry & Tompkins Sts Galesburg IL 61401

MATHESON, ALAN ADAMS, law educator; b. Cedar City, Utah, Feb. 2, 1932; s. Scott Milne and Adele (Adams) M.; m. Milicent Holbrook, Aug. 15, 1960; children—Alan, David Scott, John Robert. B.A., U. Utah, 1953, M.S., 1957, J.D., 1959; postgrad. asso. in law, Columbia U. Bar: Utah 1960, Ariz. 1975. Asst. to pres. Utah State U., 1961-67; mem. faculty Ariz. State U., Tempe, 1967—; prof. law Ariz. State U., 1970—, dean, 1978-84; bd. dirs. Ariz. Center Law in Public Interest, 1979-81; bd. dirs. DNA Navajo Legal Services, 1984—. Pres. Tri-City Mental Health Citizens Bd., 1973-74. Served with AUS, 1953-55. Mem. Utah Bar Assn., Ariz. Bar Assn., Maricopa County Bar Assn., Phi Beta Kappa, Order of Coif. Democrat. Mormon. Administrative and regulatory, Legal education. Home: 720 E Geneva Dr Tempe AZ 85282 Office: Coll Law Ariz State U Tempe AZ 85281

MATHEWS, BYRON B., JR., lawyer; b. Andalusia, Ala., Aug. 24, 1948; s. Byron Burnett and Georgia Ruth (Lowman) M.; m. Carol Ann Mathews, June 19, 1971; children: Wiley, Ann. BA, Birmingham-So. Coll., 1970; JD, U. Ala., 1975. Bar: Ala. 1975, Fla. 1976. Law clk. to presiding justice U.S. Ct. Appeals, Montgomery, Ala., 1975-76; assoc. Merson, Sawyer et al, Miami, Fla., 1976-78, Lane, Mitchell & Harris, Miami, 1978-80; ptnr. McDermott, Will & Emery, Tallahassee, 1980—. Served with U.S. Army, 1970-72. Democrat. Methodist. Clubs: Gov.'s, Capital City Country (Tallahassee). Avocations: golf, cinema, travel. Health, Administrative and regulatory. Home: 2523 Harriman Circle Tallahassee FL 32312 Office: McDermott Will & Emery 101 N Monroe St Tallahassee FL 32301

MATHEWS, CRAIG, lawyer; b. Columbus, Ohio, Oct. 19, 1929; s. Robert Elden and Grace Greenwood (Caie) M. BA, Yale U., 1951, JD, 1954; LLM, Georgetown U., 1967. Bar: Ohio 1954, D.C. 1959, U.S. Supreme Ct. 1963, U.S. Ct. Internat. Trade 1970. Assoc. Leva, Hawes, Symington, Martin & Oppenheimer, Washington, 1959-62, ptnr., 1962-83; sole practice Washington, 1983—; speaker, faculty mem. symposia and seminars on environ. and internat. law. Contbr. articles to legal jours. Served to 1st lt. U.S. Army, 1954-57. Recipient Andrew White History prize Yale U., 1949, Thomas Chetwood Law prize Georgetown U., 1967. Mem. ABA, D.C. Bar Assn., Am. Soc. Internat. Law, Yale Law Sch. Assn. D.C., Assn. Yale Alumni (past nat. bd. govs.), Environ. Law Inst. (chmn. exec. com. bd. dirs.), Phi Beta Kappa, Phi Delta Phi. Clubs: Yale (past pres.), Chevy Chase, Metropolitan (Washington); Multnomah Athletic (Portland, Oreg.); Yale (N.Y.C.). Environment, Private international, Public international. Office: 1919 Pennsylvania Ave NW Suite 300 Washington DC 20006

MATHEWS, MELINDA MCEACHERN, lawyer; b. Tampa, Fla., Nov. 5, 1943; d. Myron L. and Mildred (Smith) McEachern; m. Joseph W. Mathews, Jan. 17, 1965; children: Joseph W., Melanie April. AB, Birmingham So. Coll., 1965; MA in Teaching, Vanderbilt U., 1969; JD, Cumberland Law Sch., 1975-78; M Laws in Taxation, U. Fla., 1980-81. Bar: Ala. 1978. Assoc. Sirote, Permutt, Friend, Friedman, Held & Apolinsky, P.A., Birmingham, Ala., 1978-81; ptnr Sirote, Permutt, McDermott, Slepian, Friend, Friedman, Held & Apolinsky, P.A., Birmingham, 1981—. Author: (with others) Tax Planning for Professionals, 1986. Mem. Birmingham Tax Club (treas. 1986—), Estate Planning Council Birmingham. Republican. Episcopalian. Estate planning, Probate, Estate taxation. Office: Sirote, Permutt et al 2222 Arlington Ave S Birmingham AL 35255

MATHEWS, RODERICK BELL, lawyer; b. Lawton, Okla., Mar. 12, 1941; s. James Malcolm and Sallie Lee (Bell) M.; m. Karla Kurbjin, Apr. 26, 1980; children: Roderick B. Jr., Andrew Crittenden, Malcolm Timothy. BA, Hampden Sydney Coll., 1963; LLB, U. Richmond, 1966. Bar: Va. 1966. From assoc. to ptnr. Christian, Barton, Epps, Brent & Chappell, Richmond, Va., 1966—. Trustee Children's Hosp., Richmond, 1980—. Mem. Va. Bar Assn. (chmn. young lawyers div. 1972-73, pres.-elect 1986-87). Home: 404 N Meadow St Richmond VA 23220 Office: 909 E Main St 1200 Mutual Bldg Richmond VA 23219

MATHEWS, S. PAUL, lawyer; b. Cin., Nov. 27, 1914; s. J. Stanley and Margaret (Knell) M.; m. Thelma Cornm, June 19, 1942; children: Stanley A., John P. LLB, U. Cin., 1938, JD, 1967. Bar: Ohio 1938. Pres. Meier & Mathews, Cin., 1947—; bd. dirs. Provident Bank, Cin., 1980—. Gen. bd. Am. Baptist Chs. USA, Valley Forge, Pa., 1976-82; trustee No. Baptist Seminary, Lombard, Ill., 1984—; bd. dirs. Norwood YMCA, 1950—, Judson Village Baptist Home and Ctr., Cin., 1960—. Served to sgt. USAAF, 1942-45. Mem. ABA, Cin. Bar Assn., Cin. Lawyers Club. Republican. Lodges: Masons, KP. Probate, Real property, General practice. Home: 3928 Davemamt Ave Cincinnati OH 45213 Office: Meier & Mathews 4557 Montgomery Rd Cincinnati OH 45212

MATHEWSON, GEORGE ATTERBURY, lawyer, educator; b. Paterson, N.J., Mar. 31, 1935; s. Joseph B. and Christina A. (Atterbury) M.; m. Ann Elizabeth McVeigh, July 31, 1975; 1 son, James Lemuel. A.B., Amherst Coll., 1957; LL.B., Cornell U., 1960; LL.M., U. Mich., 1961. Bar: N.Y. 1963. Atty. office spl. legal assts., trial atty. FTC, Washington, 1963-65; regional atty. N.Y. State Dept. Environ. Conservation, Liverpool, 1972-73; sole practice, Syracuse, N.Y., 1967-72, 73—; adj. instr. bus. law Onondaga Community Coll., Syracuse, 1979-84. Bd. dirs. South Side Businessmen, 1971-72. Mem. Fed. Bar Assn., N.Y. State Bar Assn., Onondaga County Bar Assn., Am. Judicature Soc., Assn. Trial Lawyers Am., N.Y. State Trial Lawyers Assn. Presbyterian. Patentee safety device for disabled airplanes. General practice. Office: 4302 S Salina St Syracuse NY 13205

MATHIAS, JOSEPH MARSHALL, lawyer, judge; b. Frankfort, Ky., Jan. 23, 1914; s. Harry L. and Catherine Snead (Marshall) M.; children—Mark Wellington, Marcia Ann Mathias Wilson, Marilyn Roberta. A.B., U. Md., 1935; J.D., Southeastern U., 1942. Bar: Md. 1942, U.S. Supreme Ct. 1949, U.S. Dist. Ct. Md. 1963. Ptnr. Moorman and Mathias, 1946-50, Jones, Mathias and O'Brien and predecessor firms, 1950-65; judge Md. Tax Ct., 1959-65; assoc. judge Circuit Ct. of Montgomery County (Md.), 1965-80; chief judge 6th Jud. Circuit of Md., 1980-81, spl. assignments, 1981-83; spl. counsel Beckett, Cromwell & Myers, P.A., 1983—; past dir. Nat. Bank Md., Bank So. Md.; former mem. adv. bd. Citizens Bank and Trust Co. Md. Served with USN, 1942-46. Recipient cert. of disting. citizenship Gov. of Md., 1981. Mem. ABA, Md. State Bar Assn., Md. Bar Found., Am. Judica-

ture Soc. Democrat. Roman Catholic. Club: Nat. Press (Washington). Real property, Banking, General practice. Home: 10011 Summit Ave Kensington MD 20895

MATHIEU, RICHARD LOUIS, lawyer; b. Hanover, N.H., May 22, 1950; s. Thomas Joseph and Colomba Rachel (Simeone) M.; m. Debra Cameron, Mar. 31, 1979; children: Jessica, Alexandra. BA, Syracuse U., 1972; cert. teaching, Cen. Wash. U., 1974; JD, Willamette U., 1982. Bar: Wash. 1982. Tchr. Yakima (Wash.) Sch. Dist., 1974-79; assoc. Weeks, Dietzen & Skala, Yakima, 1982-86; sole practice Yakima, 1986—. Mem. ABA (tort and ins. practices), Wash. State Bar Assn., Yakima County Bar Assn., Wash. State Trial Lawyers Assn. Lodge: Rotary. Avocations: flying, bicycling. Insurance, Family and matrimonial, Bankruptcy. Home: 205 S 35th Ave Yakima WA 98902 Office: 1420 Summitview Ave Yakima WA 98902

MATHIS, JOHN PRENTISS, lawyer; b. New Orleans, Feb. 10, 1944; s. Robert Prentess and Lena (Horton) M.; m. Karen Elizabeth McHugh, May 31, 1966; children—Lisa Lynne, Andrew P. B.A. magna cum laude, So. Meth. U., 1966; J.D. cum laude, Harvard U., 1969. Bar: Calif. 1970, D.C. 1975, U.S. Ct. Appeals (5th cir.) 1975, U.S. Ct. Appeals (3rd cir.) 1980, U.S. Ct. Appeals (D.C. cir.) 1972, Temporary Emergency Ct. Appeals 1977, U.S. Supreme Ct. 1982. Assoc. Latham & Watkins, Los Angeles, 1969-71; spl. asst. to gen. counsel, FPC, Washington, 1971-72; gen. counsel Calif. Pub. Utilities Commn., San Francisco, 1972-74; ptnr. Baker & Botts, Washington, 1974—. Mem. ABA (co-chmn. energy litigation com.), Fed. Bar Assn., Fed. Energy Bar Assn., Harvard Law Sch. Assn. (D.C. pres.). Republican. Methodist. Clubs: City of Washington, Harvard, Congl. Country (Washington). Administrative and regulatory, Federal civil litigation, Public utilities. Office: 1701 Pennsylvania Ave NW Washington DC 20006

MATHISON, HARRY LEE, lawyer; b. Louisville, Dec. 26, 1952; s. Harry Lee Sr. and Mildred Helen (Clark) M. BA, U. Notre Dame, 1974; JD, U. Ky., 1976. Assoc. King, Deep & Branaman, Henderson, Ky., 1977-82, ptnr., 1982—; lectr. U. Evansville. Contbr. articles to profl. jours. Pres. Tri-State Landmen's Assn., Evansville, Ind., 1980-81. Mem. ABA, Ky. Bar Assn., Henderson County Bar Assn. (pres. 1980-81), Henderson C. of C. (bd. dirs. 1981-84). Democrat. Roman Catholic. State civil litigation, Federal civil litigation, Oil and gas leasing. Home: 111 Dixon St Henderson KY 42420 Office: King Deep & Branaman 140 N Main St Henderson KY 42420

MATIAS, THOMAS REDMOND, judge; b. Binghamton, N.Y., May 26, 1931; s. Frank Andrew and Margaret Anne (Redmond) M.; m. Joanne Mary Foody, Sept. 3, 1955; children—James Redmond, Timothy Redmond. Student Syracuse U., 1952; B.A., SUNY-Binghamton, 1953; M.B.A., Cornell U., 1958, J.D., 1959. Bar: N.Y. 1960. With Exec. Office of Pres., Washington, 1957; with IRS, Washington, 1958; atty. Gen. Acctg. Office, Washington, 1960-62; trial atty. Fed. Maritime Commn., Washington, 1962-65; regulatory atty. Western Union Telegraph Co., N.Y.C., 1965-68; regulatory atty. Internat. Telephone & Telegraph Co., N.Y.C., 1969-72; adminstrv. law judge Dept. Pub. Service State of N.Y., Albany, 1972—. Served with U.S. Army, 1953-55. Mem. N.Y. State Bar Assn., Cornell Law Assn., Phi Delta Phi. Public utilities, Administrative and regulatory, Environment. Home: 37 Douglas Rd Delmar NY 12054 Office: Three Empire State Plaza Albany NY 12223

MATLACK, DON(ALD) (CLYDE), lawyer; b. Halstead, Kans., June 18, 1929; s. Orval and Blanche (Harris) M.; m. Ardena Williams, June 10, 1951; children: Lucinda M. Manley, Roxanne M. Hitt, Terry C., Rex, Timothy. BBA, Kans. State U., 1951; JD, Washburn U., 1957. Bar: Kans. 1957, U.S. Dist. Ct. Kans. 1957, U.S. Ct. Appeals (10th cir.) 1962, U.S. Supreme Ct. 1969. Dep. county atty. Sedgwick County, Kans., 1957-59; city atty. City of Clearwater, Kans., 1958—; city atty. Bentley, Kans., 1960-64, Viola, Kans., 1965-79, Belle Plaine, Kans., 1975-82, Valley Ctr., Kans., 1977-81; ptnr. Blair, Matlack, Rogg, Foote & Scott, P.A. and predecessor firms, Wichita, Kans., 1959-77, Matlack & Foote, P.A. and predecessor firms, Wichita, 1977—; mem. Kans. Jud. Study Adv. Commn., 1973-74; legis. liason for Gov. Robert Docking, 1969-74; arbitrator Wichita Small Claims Arbitration Bd., 1973. Co-chmn. Clearwater March of Dimes, 1980, Clearwater Area United Fund, 1980, 83; Dem. precinct committeeman 1964—; treas. Kans. 5th dist. Dem. Com., 1966-68; Mem. Kans. Civil Service Commn., 1969-70; Kans. state senator, 1965-69; chmn. Docking for Gov. campaigns in Sedgwick County, 1970-72; chmn. and treas. Ardena Matlack for state rep. campaigns 1974, 76, 78, 80, 82; del. Dem. Nat. Conv., 1976; lay leader, trustee, adminstrv. bd. chmn. Clearwater United Meth. Ch.; Mem. Kans. West Conf. com. on Spl. Ministries United Meth. Ch. 1972-80, chmn. 1972-76. Served with USNR, 1951-57. Mem. ABA, Kans. Bar Assn. (profl. econs. com. 1983-84), Wichita Bar Assn. (chmn. legis. com. 1981-82, chmn. domestic relations com. 1979-81, mem. 1979-83, prepaid legal services com., fee disputes com. 1976-80), Assn. Trial Lawyers Am., Kans. Trial Lawyers Assn., Am. Legion, VFW, Delta Tau Delta, Alpha Kappa Psi. Methodist. Lodges: Masons, Shriners, Order Eastern Star, Lions (Clearwater pres. 1963-64). Banking, State civil litigation, Personal injury. Home: 615 Elaine Clearwater KS 67026 Office: 301 N Market Wichita KS 67202

MATLIN, DAVID STUART, lawyer; b. Rotterdam, The Netherlands, July 11, 1957; came to U.S., 1958; s. Jordon Sanders and Denise Phyllis (Van Der Roer) M.; m. Stephanie Robin Dloss, Nov. 28, 1981; children: Joshua Steven, Jeffrey Michael. AA, U. Fla., 1976, BA, 1978; JD, John Marshall Law Sch., 1981. Bar: N.J. 1981, Ill. 1981, U.S. Dist. Ct. N.J. 1981. Assoc. Heilbrunn, Finkelstein, Heilbrunn, Garutto, & Galex, Old Bridge, N.J., 1981-82, Hayt, Hayt & Landau, Shrewsbury, N.J., 1982-83; ptnr. Kahn, Reiter & Matlin, Somerset, N.J., 1983—; adj. prof. Middlesex County Coll., Edison, N.J., 1985—. Mem. ABA, N.J. State Bar Assn., Ill. State Bar Assn., Middlesex County Bar Assn., East Brunswick C. of C. Democrat. Jewish. Club: East Brunswick (N.J.) Jewish Ctr. Men's. Avocations: tennis, softball, racquetball. Real property, Personal injury, Consumer commercial. Office: Kahn Reiter & Matlin 1527 Hwy 27 Suite 2800 Somerset NJ 08873

MATOVICH, CAREY E., lawyer; b. Jordan, Mont., June 6, 1952; d. Philip Donald and Bette Lucille (Sult) M. Student, Mont. State U., 1970-72; BA, U. Mont., 1975; postgrad., U. Wyo., 1978-80; JD, U. Mont., 1981. Editor Mont. Kaimin, Missoula, 1974-75; news dir. Sta. KMTX Radio, Helena, Mont., 1976-78; freelance writer, staff mem. AP, Mont. and Wyo., 1972-79; assoc. Hoilt & Hart, Denver and Billings, Mont., 1981-83; sole practice Billings, 1983-84; ptnr. Matovich, Addy & Keller, P.C., Billings, 1984—; contbg. atty. ACLU, Billings, 1981—. Treas. Chet Blaylock Congl. Campaign, Billings, 1984. Mem. ABA (chmn. econ. com. on sole practice and small firms 1986), Am. Trial Lawyers Assn., Mont. Trial Lawyers Assn., Yellowstone Bar Assn. (bd. dirs. 1985-87), Mont. Assn. Female Exec., Order of Barristers. Federal civil litigation, Bankruptcy, Labor. Office: Matovich Addy & Keller PC 313 Hart-Albin Bldg Billings MT 59101

MATSCH, RICHARD P., federal judge; b. 1930. A.B., U. Mich., 1951, J.D., 1953. Bar: Colo. Asst. U.S. atty. Colo., 1959-61; dep. city atty. City and County of Denver, 1961-63; judge U.S. Bankruptcy Ct., Colo., 1965-74, U.S. Dist. Ct. for Colo., 1974—. Served with U.S. Army, 1953-55. Mem. ABA, Am. Judicature Soc. Judicial administration. Office: US Dist Ct US Courthouse 1929 Stout St Room C-226 Denver CO 80294 *

MATSUSHIGE, CARY SHIGERU, lawyer; b. Honolulu, Feb. 27, 1953; s. Howard Katsumi and Haruko (Niimi) M. BA in Econs., Stanford U., 1975, MA in Econs., 1975; JD, U. Hawaii, 1979. Bar: Hawaii 1979, U.S. Dist. Ct. Hawaii 1979. Assoc. Bendet & Fidell, Honolulu, 1979-80; assoc. Cades, Schutte, Fleming & Wright, Honolulu, 1980-86, ptnr., 1986—; atty. ways and means com. Hawaii Senate, Honolulu, 1980. Mem. ABA (corp. sect., real property and probate sect.), Hawaii Bar Assn. Avocations: surfing, bowling, golf. Real property, Banking, Contracts commercial. Office: Cades Schutte Fleming & Wright 1000 Bishop St 11th Floor Honolulu HI 96813

MATT, PETER KENT, lawyer; b. Bklyn., June 25, 1947; s. Benjamin and Frances (Shady) M.; m. Ruth Newman, May 1, 1971; children: Andrea, Lauren, Rebecca. BA, U. Pitts., 1969; JD with honors, George Washington U., 1973. Bar: Va. 1973, D.C. 1973, U.S. Ct. Appeals (D.C. cir.) 1973, U.S. Ct. Appeals (7th and 9th cirs.) 1977. Assoc. Spiegel & McDiarmid, Washington, 1973-78, ptnr., 1978—. Bd. dirs. The Langles Sch., McLean, Va., 1985-86. Mem. ABA, Fed. Energy Bar Assn. Democrat. Jewish. Avocations: tennis, swimming, reading, am. history. Administrative and regulatory, Antitrust, FERC practice. Office: Spiegel & McDiarmid 1350 New York Ave NW Washington DC 20005-4798

MATTAR, LAWRENCE JOSEPH, lawyer; b. Buffalo, Apr. 17, 1934; s. Joseph and Anne (Abraham) M.; m. Elaine Emma Kolbe, Aug. 1, children. Canisius Coll., 1956; J.D., SUNY-Buffalo, 1959. Bar: N.Y. 1959, Fla. 1977, U.S. Supreme Ct. 1972. Sole practice, Buffalo, 1959-62; sr. ptnr. Mattar, D'Agostino, Kogler and Runfola, Buffalo, 1962—; asst. to county ct. judge, 1961-66; counsel N.Y. State Senate Pub. Utilties Com., 1969-71. Bd. dirs. Better Bus. Bur. Western N.Y.; mem. exec. com. pres.'s council Canisius Coll.; mem. ho. of dels. United Way of Buffalo and Erie County; mem. Nat. Maronite Bishops' Adv. Council, U.S. Congl. Adv. Bd., Selective Service Bd. Western N.Y., Republican Presdl. Task Force. Decorated Knight of St. Charbiel, highest honor available to a Maronite Catholic; recipient award for outstanding service Buffalo Eye Bank, 1962; Leadership award Lions Club Buffalo, 1963; Citizen's award Erie Community Coll., 1982. Mem. Erie County Bar Assn., Erie County Trial Lawyers Assn., N.Y. State Bar Assn., Fla. Bar Assn., N.Y. State Trial Lawyers Assn., Buffalo C. of C., NFL Players Alumni Assn. (assoc.), Di Gamma (life). Roman Catholic. Clubs: Rotary (sec. 1978-79, dir. 1978-80, trustee, sec., mem. exec. com. Buffalo Rotary Found.), Buffalo (Buffalo); Transit Valley Country (East Amherst, N.Y.). Federal civil litigation, State civil litigation, General corporate. Office: 17 Court St Buffalo NY 14202

MATTER, BRUCE E., lawyer; b. Washington, Dec. 13, 1955; s. Harold Eugene and Cornelia Ethel (Dunn) M. BA, Salisbury State Coll., 1977; JD, George Mason U., 1982. Bar: Md. 1982, D.C. 1983, U.S. Dist. Ct. (D.C. dist.) 1983, Va. 1984, Fla. 1986. Assoc. Law Office William D. Stokes, Alexandria, Va., 1982-85; assoc. Harcourt, Brace Jovanovich, Inc., Orlando, Fla., 1985-86, San Diego, 1986—. Mng. editor George Mason U. Law Rev., 1981-82. Republican. Methodist. Avocation: tennis. Real property, Trademark and copyright, Entertainment. Office: Harcourt Brace Jovnovich Inc 1250 Sixth Ave San Diego CA 92101

MATTERN, KEITH EDWARD, lawyer; b. Savanna, Ill., Apr. 24, 1931; s. Harvey and Caroline (Miller) M.; m. Sue D. Cuquet, Oct. 12, 1963; children—Scott, David, Melissa. B.S. in Mgmt., U. Ill., 1953; J.D., U. Mo., 1958. Bar: Mo. 1958, U.S. Supreme Ct. 1971. Sole practice, St. Louis, 1958-66; atty. Interco, Inc., St. Louis, 1966-69, asst. gen. counsel, 1969-80, assoc. gen. counsel, 1980-82, gen. counsel, 1982—. Served to capt. USAF, 1953-55. Mem. St. Louis Bar Assn. Roman Catholic. General corporate, Labor, Federal civil litigation. Office: Interco Inc 101 S Hanley Rd Saint Louis MO 63105

MATTERN, PATRICIA ANN, lawyer; b. Wilkes-Barre, Pa., Apr. 16, 1950; d. Harry Joseph and Ann Marie (Jones) M. Student, Marywood Coll., 1968-70; BA magna cum laude, U. Pa., 1970-72, MA in Sociology, 1972; JD, Villanova U., 1975. Bar: Pa. 1975, U.S. Dist. Ct. (ea. dist.) Pa. 1978, U.S. Ct. Appeals (3d cir.) 1980, U.S. Supreme Ct. 1980. Law clk. to presiding justice Pa. Supreme Ct., Phila., 1975-76; assoc. Solo & Padova, Phila., 1976-77; assoc. Rawle & Henderson, Phila., 1977-83, ptnr., 1984—. Assoc. editor Villanova U. Law Rev., 1975. Mem. zoning com. Ctr. City Residents Assn., Phila., 1984—, World Affairs Council, Phila, 1984—, Friends of Independence Nat. Park, Phila., 1984—. Mem. ABA, Pa. Bar Assn., Workers' Compensation Claims Assn., Phila. Bar Assn., Phila. Assn. Def. Counsel, Order of Coif. Club: The Racquet (Phila.). Insurance, Federal civil litigation, Workers' compensation. Office: Rawle & Henderson 211 S Broad St Philadelphia PA 19107

MATTESON, WILLIAM BLEECKER, lawyer; b. N.Y.C., Oct. 20, 1928; s. Leonard Jerome and Mary Jo (Harwell) M.; m. Marilee Brill, Aug. 26, 1950; children: Lynn, Sandra, Holly. B.A., Yale U., 1950; J.D., Harvard U., 1953. Bar: N.Y. 1954. Clk. to judge Augustus N. Hand U.S. Ct. Appeals, 1953-54; clk. to U.S. Supreme Ct. Justice Harold H. Burton, 1954-55; asso. firm Debevoise & Plimpton (and predecessors), N.Y.C., 1955-61; partner Debevoise & Plimpton (and predecessors), 1961—, Debevoise & Plimpton (European office), Paris, 1973-78; lectr. Columbia U. Law Sch., 1972-73, 78-80. Trustee Peddie Sch., Highstown, N.J., 1968-73, Kalamazoo Coll., 1972-77, Miss Porter's Sch., Farmington, Conn., 1977-83, Nat. Council of Salk Inst., La Jolla, Calif., 1977—; trustee, chmn. fin. com. N.Y. Inst. for Spl. Edn., 1981—; chmn. USA BIAC, 1986—. Mem. Internat., Am., Fed., N.Y. State bar assns., Assn. Bar City N.Y. (chmn. securities regulation com. 1968-71), Harvard U. Law Sch. Assn. N.Y.C. (trustee 1968-73). Clubs: Union, River, Sky, Yale (N.Y.C.); Sankaty Head (Nantucket, Mass.); Circle Interallie (Paris). General corporate, Private international. Home: 201 E 62d St New York NY 10021 Office: 875 3d Ave New York NY 10022

MATTEUCCI, SHERRY SCHEEL, lawyer; b. Columbus, Mont., Aug. 17, 1947; d. Gerald F. and Shirley Scheel; m. William L. Matteucci, Dec. 26, 1969 (div. June 1976); children: Cory, Cody. Student, Kinman Bus. U., Mont. State U., Gonzaga U.; BS, Eastern Wash. State U.; JD, U. Mont. Bar: Mont., U.S. Dist. Ct. Mont., U.S. Ct. Appeals (9th cir.). Spl. asst. Commr. Higher Edn., 1974-76; assoc. Crowley, Haughey, Hanson, Toole & Dietrich, Billings, Mont., 1979-83, ptnr., 1984—. Mem. editorial bd. U. Mont. Law Rev., 1977-78, contbg. editor, 1978-79. Bd. dirs. Big Bros. & Sisters, Billings, 1982-85, City/County Library Bd., Billings, 1983—, Billings Community Cable Corp., 1986, chmn. Named one of Outstanding Young Women in Am., 1983. Mem. ABA, Mont. Bar Assn. (chmn. jud. polling com. 1985-87, chmn. women's law sect. 1985-86), Yellowstone County Bar Assn. (bd. dirs. 1984—, pres.-elect 1986-87), Billings C. of C. (leadership com. 1986, pres. 1987-88, legis. affairs com. 1984), Mont. Assn. for Female Execs., Mont. Lawyers for Peace. Democrat. Mem. Unitarian Ch. Federal civil litigation, State civil litigation, Consumer commercial. Home: 3035 Kincaid Rd Billings MT 59101 Office: Crowley Haughey Hanson Toole & Dietrich 490 N 31st St Billings MT 59103-2529

MATTHEWS, DAN GUS, lawyer; b. Jacksonville, Tex., Feb. 6, 1939; s. A.N. and Charlie Pryor (Morton) M.; m. Mary Ellen Whittredge, Dec. 12, 1959; children: Mark H., Daniel W. BS, Stephen F. Austin State U., 1960; LLB, U. Houston, 1964. Bar: Tex. 1964, U.S. Dist. Ct. (so. dist.) Tex. 1964, U.S. Dist. Ct. (we. dist.) Tex. 1984, U.S. Ct. Appeals (5th cir.) 1981, U.S. Ct. Appeals (11th cir.) 1981, U.S. Supreme Ct. 1967. Law clk. U.S. Dist. Ct. So. Dist. Tex., 1964-66; assoc. Fulbright & Jaworski, Houston, 1966-73, ptnr., 1973—. Mem. ABA, Tex. Bar Assn., Houston Bar Assn., San Antonio Bar Assn. Republican. Presbyterian. Federal civil litigation, State civil litigation. Office: 2200 InterFirst Plaza 300 Convent St San Antonio TX 78205

MATTHEWS, JAMES BERNARD, lawyer; b. Newton, Mass., Apr. 4, 1950; s. Gerard Joseph Sr. and Charlotte (Boisvert) M.; m. Susan Mary Gullage, June 9, 1973; 1 child, Gregory F. BA, Assumption Coll., Worcester, Mass., 1972; JD, U. Miami, 1976. Bar: Fla. 1976, U.S. Dist. Ct. (so. dist.) Fla. 1976, U.S. Ct. Appeals (11th cir.) 1982, Mass. 1983. Assoc. Groland, Brown & Huysman, Miami, Fla., 1976-77; ptnr. Huysman & Matthews, Miami, Fla., 1977-83; v.p., corp. counsel King's Dept. Stores, Newton, Mass., 1982-84, Strik Co. (formerly Multinat. Trading Co.), Auburndale, Mass., 1982—. Mem. ABA, Dade County Bar Assn. Democrat. Roman Catholic. Real property, Landlord-tenant, General corporate. Office: Strik Co 430 Lexington St Auburndale MA 02166

MATTHEWS, JAMES MICHAEL, lawyer; b. St. Louis, Aug. 10, 1948; s. John Immel and Delma Rita (Ostenfeld) M.; m. Jeanne M. McGinnis, Aug. 21, 1971; 1 child, Brendan Patrick. BA, Washington U., St. Louis, 1970; JD, St. Louis U., 1974; LLM in Taxation, Georgetown U., 1976. Bar: Mo. 1974, U.S. Tax Ct. 1978. Tax law specialist IRS, Washington, 1975-77; ptnr. Linde Thomson Fairchild Langworthy Kohn & Van Dyke, PC, Kansas City, Mo., 1977—. Contbr. articles to profl. jours. Roman Catholic. Avocation: sailing. Pension, profit-sharing, and employee benefits, Corporate taxation, State and local taxation. Home: 13006 W 84th St Lenexa KS 66215 Office: Linde Thomson Fairchild et al 2700 City Center Sq PO Box 26010 Kansas City MO 64196

MATTHEWS, MARIAN, lawyer; b. Springfield, Mo., Dec. 7, 1945; d. Morris and Julia Mae (Hill) Goodman; m. Daniel B. Matthews, July 1, 1967; 1 child, Adam Christopher. BA, S.W. Mo. State Coll., 1967; JD, U. N.Mex., 1974. Bar: N.Mex. 1974, U.S. Dist. Ct. N.Mex. 1974, U.S. Ct. Appeals (10th cir.) 1977, U.S. Supreme Ct. 1980. Ptnr. Matthews, Crider, Calvert & Bingham P.C. and predecessor firms, Albuquerque, 1974—; vice chmn. rules of civil procedure com. N.Mex. Supreme Ct., 1984—; mem. Equal Rights Legis. Com., Albuquerque, 1971-73, Fed. Magistrate Panel, 1980. Author: Collection Law in New Mexico, 1978. Mem. N.Mex. Women's Polit. Caucus, 1974—. Recipient service awards N.Mex. Supreme Ct. Mem. ABA, N.Mex. Bar Assn. (jud. selection panel, hearing officer disciplinary bd.), Albuquerque Bar Assn. (service awards), Order of Coif. Democrat. Avocations: golf, reading. State civil litigation, Federal civil litigation, Contracts commercial. Office: Matthews Crider Calvert & Bingham PC 3908 Carlisle NE Albuquerque NM 87107

MATTHEWS, PHILIP RICHARD, lawyer; b. San Francisco, Aug. 27, 1952; s. Richard Thomas and Marjorie Hilda (Dean) M.; m. Dana Lynn Meer, Aug. 8, 1981; 1 child, Lauren. BA, George Washington U., 1974; JD, U. Calif., San Francisco, 1977. Bar: Calif. 1978, U.S. Dist. Ct. (no., ea. and so. dists.) Calif. 1978, U.S. Ct. Appeals (9th cir.) 1978. Assoc. Dinkelspiel, Pelavin et al, San Francisco, 1978-80; assoc. Hancock, Rothert & Bushoft, San Francisco, 1980-85, ptnr., 1985—. Mem. ABA, Calif. Bar Assn., San Francisco Bar Assn. Democrat. Episcopal. Club: Commonwealth (San Francisco). State civil litigation, Insurance, Environment. Office: Hancock Ruthert & Bushoft 4 Embarcadero Ctr San Francisco CA 94111

MATTHEWS, ROGER HARDIN, lawyer; b. Greensboro, N.C., Sept. 16, 1948; s. Shuford Roger and Jacqueline (Hardin) M.; m. Jane Elizabeth Dougan, Aug. 7, 1982; children: Christopher Hardin, Marielle Aimée. AB, Harvard U., 1970, JD, 1974. Bar: Mass. 1974. Assoc. Ropes & Gray, Boston, 1974-84, ptnr., 1984—. Mem. ABA (employee benefits com., tax sect.), Boston Bar Assn. (co-chmn. Employee Retirement Income Security Act com. 1985—). Avocation: piano. Municipal bonds, Pension, profit-sharing, and employee benefits, Corporate taxation. Office: Ropes & Gray 225 Franklin St Boston MA 02110

MATTHEWS, STEPHEN ROSS, lawyer; b. Salt Lake City, Nov. 27, 1956; s. George Ronald Matthews and Nellie Carolyn (Sessions) Olafson; m. Lorie McFarland, Aug. 23, 1977; children: Brandon S., Winston R., Trevor W. BA, Brigham Young U., 1977, MA, JD, 1981. Bar: U.S. Dist. Ct. (ea. dist.) Washington, 1982, U.S. Ct. Claims, 1986. Legal counsel MONY Fin. Services, Spokane County, Wash., 1981-82; dep. pros. atty. Spokane County, 1982-85; assoc. Underwood, Campbell, Brock & Cerutti, P.S., Spokane, 1985—; instr. Spokane Community Coll., 1984—; bd. dirs., v.p. Brigham Young U. Mgmt. Soc., Spokane, 1986—; spl. dep. pros. atty. Spokane County, 1985-87. Pres. bd. dirs. Hospice of Spokane, 1986—. Mem. ABA, Wash. State Bar Assn., Spokane County Bar Assn., Lincoln County Bar Assn. Criminal, Labor, State civil litigation. Home: 4106 S Stone Spokane WA 99203 Office: Underwood Campbell Brock & Cerutti PS 820 Lincoln Bldg Spokane WA 99201

MATTHEWS, STEVE ALLEN, lawyer; b. Columbia, S.C., Oct. 11, 1955; s. Phillip Garland and Vernecia Neely (Wilson) M. BA in History, U. S.C., 1977; JD, Yale U., 1980. Bar: S.C. 1980, D.C. 1982. Assoc. Boyd, Knowlton, Tate & Finlay, Columbia, 1980-81, Dewey, Ballantine, Bushby, Palmer & Wood, Washington, 1981-85; spl. counsel to asst. atty. gen. Civil Rights div. U.S. Dept. Justice, Washington, 1985-86, dep. asst. atty. gen. for jud. selection, Office of Legal Policy, 1986—. Mem. Federalist Soc., Party of the Right, Euphradian Soc. Securities, General corporate, Civil rights. Office: Dep of Justice Legal Policy 10th & Constitution Ave NW Washington DC 20530

MATTHEWS, WARREN WAYNE, state supreme court justice; b. Santa Cruz, Calif., Apr. 5, 1939; s. Warren Wayne and Ruth Ann (Maginnis) M.; m. Donna Stearns, Aug. 17, 1963; children: Holly Maginnis, Meredith Sample. A.B., Stanford U., 1961; LL.B., Harvard U., 1964. Bar: Alaska 1965. Assoc. firm Burr, Boney & Pease, Anchorage, 1964-69, Matthews & Dunn, Matthews, Dunn and Baily, Anchorage, 1969-77; justice Alaska Supreme Ct., Anchorage, 1977—. Bd. dirs. Alaska Legal Services Corp., 1969-70. Mem. Alaska Bar Assn. (bd. govs. 1974-77), ABA, Anchorage Bar Assn., Assn. Trial Lawyers Am. also: Alaska Supreme Ct Juneau AK 99811

MATTHEWS, WILBUR LEE, lawyer; b. Big Spring, Tex., Jan. 20, 1903; s. Robert D. and Sallie (Bourland) M.; m. Mary LeNoir Kenney, June 22, 1932 (dec. Oct. 1972); children: Wilbur Lee, John Kenney; m. Helen P. Davis, May 28, 1976. LL.B. with highest honors, U. Tex., 1926. Bar: Tex. 1926. Since practiced in San Antonio; with Matthews & Branscomb (and predecessors firms), 1926—, partner, 1930—. Contbr. articles to legal publs.; author: San Antonio Lawyer, 1983. Mayor City of Terrell Hills, 1939-41; mem. Tex. Finance Adv. Commn., 1960; trustee, chmn. San Antonio Med. Found. Fellow Am. Coll. Trial Lawyers; mem. Am. Law Inst., Am. Judicature Soc., ABA. Clubs: San Antonio Country, Argyle, San Antonio. Antitrust, Federal civil litigation, General corporate. Home: 200 Patterson Ave #806 San Antonio TX 78209 Office: One Alamo Center 106 S St Mary's St San Antonio TX 78205

MATTHIAS, ROBERT CHARLES, lawyer; b. Evanston, Ill., May 4, 1943; s. Russell Howard and Helene (Seibold) M.; m. Barbara Madden, Aug. 28, 1965; children—Jennifer Anita, Robert Charles, Jr., Richard Russell. B.A., Northwestern U., 1965; J.D., U. Fla., 1968. Bar: Fla. 1968, U.S. Dist. Ct. (mid. dist.) Fla., 1968. Clk. to Justice Campbell Thornal Supreme Ct. Fla., Tallahassee, 1968-70; assoc. Carlton, Fields, Ward, Emmanuel, Smith and Cutler, Orlando, Fla., 1970-74, Law Offices Robert C. Matthias, Orlando, 1974-77, Robert C. Matthias, P.A., 1977-80; ptnr. Matthias and Matthias, Orlando, 1980-85, Matthias, DeLancett, Morse & Robb, P.A., Orlando, 1985—; dir. Old Orchard Bank & Trust Co., Skokie, Ill., First Am. Bank Corp., Dundee, Ill., First Am. Data Services, Elk Grove Village, Ill., Louis Joliet Bank and Trust Co., Joliet, Ill.; chmn. bd. dirs. 1st Am. Bank of Lake County, Buffalo Grove, Ill. Trustee Matthias Enterprises, Orlando, 1977—, First United Meth. Ch. Winter Park (Fla.), 1985—. Bd. dirs., Matthias Found., Inc., 1981—, Fla. Symphony Soc., Inc., 1976-85, Mental Health Services of Orange County, Inc., 1983-85. Alumni Regent Northwestern U., Orlando Area, 1985—. Mem. Orange County Bar Assn. Republican. Methodist. Clubs: Country of Orlando, Citrus, Interlachen (Orlando); John Evans at Northwestern U. Mem. staff U. Fla. Law Rev., 1968. Real property, Personal income taxation, Probate. Home: 2359 Forrest Rd Winter Park FL 32789 Office: Matthias Delancett Morse Robb 501 N Magnolia Ave Suite A Orlando FL 32801

MATTHIES, MARY CONSTANCE T., lawyer; b. Baton Rouge, Mar. 22, 1948; d. Allen Douglas and Mazie (Poche) Tillman. B.S., Okla. State U., 1969; J.D., U. Tulsa, 1972. Bar: Okla. 1973, U.S. Ct. Appeals (10th cir.) 1974, U.S. Ct. Appeals (8th and D.C. cirs.) 1975, U.S. Supreme Ct. 1976. Assoc., ptnr. Kothe, Nichols & Wolfe, Inc., Tulsa, 1972-78; pres. sr. prin. Matthies Law Firm, P.C., Tulsa, 1978—; guest lectr. U. Tulsa Coll. Law, U. Okla. Sch. Law, Oral Roberts U. Sch. Law. Mem. Women's Task Force, Tulsa Community Relations Commn., 1972-73; Recipient Tom Brett Criminal Law award, 1971; Am. Jurisprudence awards, 1971. Mem. ABA (mem. spl. subcom. for liaison with EEOC, 1974—, spl. subcom. for liaison with OFCCP, 1979—, mgmt. co-chmn. equal employment law subcoms. on nat. origin discrimination 1974-75, class actions and remedies 1975-80), Okla. Bar Assn. (council mem. labor law sect. 1974-80, chmn. 1978-79), Women's Law Caucus, Phi Delta Phi. Presbyterian. Contbr. articles on law to profl. jours.; mem. staff Tulsa Law Jour., 1971-72. Labor, Civil rights, Federal civil litigation. Office: Suite 300 Reunion Center Tulsa OK 74103

MATTIACCIO, RICHARD L., lawyer, consultant; b. N.Y.C., Oct. 10, 1953. BA, Columbia U., 1975, JD, 1978. Bar: N.Y. 1979, U.S. Dist. Ct. (so. and ea. dists.) N.Y. 1979, U.S. Ct. Appeals (fed. and 7th cirs.) 1979, U.S. Supreme Ct., 1986. Law clk. to presiding justice Washington, 1978-79; assoc. Simpson, Thacher & Bartlett, N.Y.C., 1979-83; assoc. Pavia & Harcourt, N.Y.C., 1983-86, ptnr., 1987—; bd. dirs. adv. council Product Liability, Detroit., 1986. Spl. asst. U.S. Embassy, Rome, 1977. Mem. ABA, Assn. of Bar of City of N.Y., Phi Beta Kappa. Avocations: travel, langs., automobiles. Private international, Federal civil litigation, State civil litigation. Home: 440 E 85th St New York NY 10028 Office: Pavia & Harcourt 600 Madison Ave New York NY 10022

MATTINGLY, WILLIAM EARL, lawyer; b. Decatur, Ill., Mar. 6, 1948; s. Woodrow W. and Lena (Dayhuff) M.; 1 child, Claire E. BS in Indsl. Engring., Purdue U., 1971, MSE, 1972; JD cum laude, Ind. U., Indpls., 1975. Bar: Ind. 1975, Ill. 1978, Okla. 1980. Assoc. Sonnenschein, Carlin, Nath & Rosenthall, Chgo., 1978-80, Hall, Estill, et al., Tulsa, 1980-83; head, employee benefits dept. Katten, Muchin, Zavis, Pearl, Greenberger & Galler, Chgo., 1984—; lectr. tax inst. conf. U. So. Calif., 1985, U. Ill. Conf. on Employee Stock Ownership Plans, 1987, Inst. for Health Law Loyola U., Chgo., 1987. Mem. ABA (subcom. chmn. corp., banking and bus. law sects.), Chgo. Bar Assn., Ill. State Bar Assn., Okla. Bar Assn. Pension, profit-sharing, and employee benefits.

MATTIONI, JOHN, lawyer; b. Phila., Dec. 18, 1935; s. Domenico and Concetta Maria (Tenisci) M.; m. Mary Elizabeth Amey; children—Michael J., Concetta M., Anne E., Christopher F. B.S., U.S. Mcht. Marine Acad., 1957; J.D., Temple U., 1964. Bar: Pa. 1965, D.C. 1965, U.S. Dist. Ct. (ea. dist.) Pa. 1966, U.S. Supreme Ct. 1971, N.J. 1983, U.S. Dist. Ct. N.J. 1983, U.S. Ct. Claims. Clk., Common Pleas Ct., Phila., 1964-67; asst. city solicitor Phila., 1967-71, dep. city solicitor appeals and spl. litigation, 1971-72, dep. city solicitor litigation div. 1972-74; ptnr. firm Mattioni, Mattioni & Mattioni, Phila., 1965-74; dir., corp. sec. Mattioni, Mattioni & Mattioni, Ltd., P.C., Phila., 1974—; instr. in law Temple U., 1974-76, Del. Law Sch., 1975-76; chief mate Oceans Unlimited, USCG, 1960. Trustee First United Methodist Ch. Roxborough, Phila. Served to lt. j.g. USNR, 1957-58. Temple U. Barenkopf Scholar, 1963-64; Thomas Skelton Harrison Found. grantee, 1963; recipient J. Howard Reber Meml. award, 1964, Sarah A. Schull award, 1964, A.J. Davis award, 1964, Robert E. Lamberton award, 1964, Phi Alpha Delta award, 1962. Mem. ABA, Pa. Bar Assn., Phila. Bar Assn. (com. chmn.), Assn. Trial Lawyers Am., Pa. Trial Lawyers Assn., Phila. Trial Lawyers Assn., Maritime Law Assn., Mcht. Marine Acad. Alumni Assn. (pres. Phila. chpt. 1979-81), Marine Tech. Soc., Port of Phila., Maritime Soc., Justinian Soc. Club: Downtown (Phila.). Editor-in-chief Temple Law Quarterly, 1963-64; contbr. articles to legal jours. Admiralty, Federal civil litigation, State civil litigation. Home: 2052 Spring Mill Rd Lafayette Hill PA 19444 Office: 330 Market St E Suite 200 Philadelphia PA 19106

MATTOX, JAMES ALBON, State official; b. Dallas, Aug. 29, 1943; s. Norman and Mary Kathryn (Harrison) M. B.B.A. magna cum laude, Baylor U., 1965; J.D., So. Meth. U., 1968. Bar: Tex. 1968. Asst. dist. atty. Dallas County, 1968-70; partner firm Crowder & Mattox, Dallas, 1970-83; mem. Tex. Ho. of Reps. from 33d Dallas Dist., 1972-76, 95th-97th Congresses from 5th Tex. Dist., 1977-83; atty gen. State of Tex., 1983—. Named Outstanding Freshman Rep. Tex. Intercollegiate Students Assn., 1973; Legislator of Yr. Dallas County Women's Polit. Caucus. Baptist. Criminal. Office: Office of the Atty Gen Supreme Ct Bldg PO 12548 Austin TX 78711

MATTSON, JAMES STEWART, lawyer; b. Providence, July 22, 1945; s. Irving Carl and Virginia (Lutey) M.; m. Carol Sandry, Aug. 15, 1964 (div. 1979); children—James, Birgitta; m. 2d Rana A. Fine, Jan. 5, 1983. B.S. in Chemistry, U. Mich., 1966, M.S., 1969, Ph.D., 1970; J.D., George Washington U., 1979. Bar: D.C. 1979, Fla. 1983, U.S. Dist. Ct. D.C. 1979, U.S. Dist. Ct. (so. dist.) Fla. 1984, U.S. Ct. Appeals (D.C. cir.) 1979, U.S. Ct. Claims 1985, U.S. Supreme Ct. 1985, U.S. Ct. Appeals (11th cir.) 1986. Staff scientist Gulf Gen. Atomic Co., San Diego, 1970-71; dir. research devel. Ouachita Industries, Inc., Monroe, La., 1971-72; asst. prof. chem. oceanography Rosenstiel Sch. Marine & Atmospheric Sci., U. Miami (Fla.), 1972-76; phys. scientist NOAA, Washington, 1976-78, Nat. Adv. Commn. on Oceans and Atmosphere, 1978-80; ptnr. Mattson & Pave, Washington, Miami and Key Largo, Fla., 1980—, adj. prof. law U. Miami, 1983—; cons. Alaska Dept. Environ. Conservation, 1981—. Editor (with others): Computers in Chemistry and Instrumentation, 8 vols., 1972-76; The Argo Merchant Oil Spill: A Preliminary Scientific Report, writer numerous monographs and tech. papers. Fellow Fed. Water Pollution Control Adminstrn., 1967-68; recipient Spl. Achievement award U.S. Dept. Commerce, 1976-77; Regents Alumni scholar U. Mich., 1963. Mem. ABA, Am. Chem. Soc. (chmn. Symposium on Oil Spill Indentification 1971), Fla. Keys Bar Assn. (pres. 1984-85), Order of Coif. Environment, Administrative and regulatory, Admiralty.

MATTSON, MARCUS, lawyer; b. Ogden, Utah, July 3, 1904; s. David and Blanche (Allison) M.; m. Eleanor L. Hynding, Dec. 30, 1933; 1 son, Peter H. A.B., U. Calif. at Berkeley, 1927, J.D., 1930. Bar: Calif. bar 1930. Since practiced in Los Angeles; sr. partner firm Lawler, Felix & Hall, 1942-86; lectr. antitrust law. Mem. Jud. Council Calif., 1969-73; adv. council FTC, 1970-74. Fellow Am. Bar Found., Am. Coll. Trial Lawyers (bd. regents 1973-77, pres. 1978-79); mem. ABA (chmn. antitrust law sect. 1965-66, mem. com. on multi-dist. litigation 1968-74), Los Angeles Bar Assn., State Bar Calif. (v.p., gov. 1959-60, chmn. com. bar examiners 1962-63, chmn. com. law sch. edn. 1960-67), U. Calif. Law Sch. Alumni Assn. (pres. 1958, citation award 1980). Mem. Ch. of Jesus Christ of Latter-day Saints. Clubs: California (Los Angeles), Los Angeles Country (Los Angeles); Pacific-Union (San Francisco). Antitrust, Federal civil litigation. Office: Lawler Felix et al 700 S Flower St 31st Floor Los Angeles CA 90017

MATTY, ROBERT JAY, lawyer; b. N.Y.C., July 6, 1948; s. Newton and Beatrice (Mituck) M.; m. Kathy Sirota, May 25, 1974; children—Jeffrey Scott, Lesley Jill. B.A., Queens Coll., 1970; J.D., Am. U., 1974. Bar: Md. 1975, U.S. Dist. Ct. Md. 1975, D.C. 1976, U.S. Dist. Ct. D.C. 1979, N.Y. 1984. Law clk. 7th Jud. Cir. Ct., Upper Marlboro, Md., 1974-75; asst. state's atty. Office Md. State's Atty., Upper Marlboro, 1975-78; asst. public defender Office Public Defender, Upper Marlboro, 1978-79; mng. atty. Robert A. Ades & Assocs., Landover, Md., 1979—. Co-chmn. lawyers div. United Way, Washington, 1981. Mem. Nat. Dist. Attys. Assn., Nat. Assn. Criminal Def. Lawyers, Assn. Trial Lawyers Am., ABA. Democrat. Jewish. Criminal, Personal injury, State civil litigation. Home: 6212 Mazwood Rd Rockville MD 20852 Office: Robert A Ades & Assocs PC 4301 Garden City Dr #300 Landover MD 20785

MATUS, WAYNE CHARLES, lawyer; b. N.Y.C., Mar. 10, 1950; s. Eli and Alma (Platt) M.; m. Marsha Rothblum, Jan. 16, 1982; 1 child, Marshall Scott. B.A., Johns Hopkins U., 1972; J.D., NYU, 1975. Law clk. Superior Ct. D.C., 1975-76; assoc. Marshall, Bratter, Greene, Allison and Tucker, N.Y.C., 1976-79; assoc. Christy & Viener, N.Y.C., 1979-83, ptnr., 1984—; spl. asst. dist. atty. New York County Dist. Atty's Office, 1980-81. Mem. Assn. Bar City N.Y.(com. on computer law 1985—, chmn. com. on state cts., subcom. on motion practice 1982-84), N.Y. State Bar Assn., Fed. Bar Council, N.Y. Litigators Club (steering com. 1985—), Johns Hopkins U. Alumni Assn. (bd. dirs. met. N.Y. chpt. 1987—). Construction, State civil litigation, Computer. Office: Christy & Viener 620 Fifth Ave New York NY 10020

MATUSHEK, EDWARD J., III, lawyer; b. Chgo., Feb. 2, 1954; s. Edward J. Jr. and Phyllis A. (Roseto) M.; m. Alisa M. Bombassi, Aug. 2, 1980. BA, Ill. Wesleyan U., 1975; JD, John Marshall Law Sch., 1982. Bar: Ill. 1982, U.S. Dist. Ct. (no. dist.) Ill. 1982. Claims adjuster Comml. Union Assurance Co., Oakbrook Terr., IL, 1976-79; assoc. Haskell & Perrin, Chgo., 1982—. Instr. Chgo. Coalition for Law Related Edn., 1983-84; comm. Zoning Bd. Appeals, Vill. Tinley Park, Ill., 1985-86, trustee, 1986—. Mem. ABA, Ill. Bar Assn., Chgo. Bar Assn. (vice-chmn. bench-bar relations com. 1985-86, chmn. bench-bar relations 1986—, dir. young lawyers sect., 1987—). State civil litigation, Environment, Insurance. Home: 8035 W Chippewa Trail Tinley Park IL 60477 Office: Haskell & Perrin 200 W Adams St Chicago IL 60604

MAUER, WILLIAM F., judge; b. Kansas City, Mo., Oct. 3, 1930; s. James A. and Anna Mae (Thompson) M.; m. Pamala Joan Grimm, Oct. 23, 1980; children: William F., John Hogan, David Christopher. BBA, Rockhurts Coll., 1953; JD, U. Mo., 1959. Bar: Mo. 1959. Trial atty. Krings, Stewart & Mauer, Kansas City, 1959-79; judge Cir. Ct. of Mo., Kansas City, 1979—. Serves as capt. USNR, 1953—. Fellow ABA; mem. Mo. Bar Assn., Assn. Trial Lawyers Am., Greater Kansas City C. of C., Navy League U.S., Navy Res. Assn. Democrat. Roman Catholic. Judicial administration. Home: 901 Burning Tree Dr Kansas City MO 64145 Office: Circuit Ct Mo Div 7 16th Jud Cir 415 E 12th St Kansas City MO 64106

MAUGER, LEE FILLMEN, lawyer; b. Pottstown, Pa., May 15, 1956; s. L. Stanley and Betty L. (Johnson) M.; m. Elizabeth Norris Mauger, June 4, 1983; 1 child, Sarah Elizabeth. BA in Biology, U. Pa., 1974-78; JD, Dickinson Law Sch., 1981. Bar: Pa. 1981, U.S. Dist. Ct. (ea. dist.) Pa. 1982. Parole atty. Montgomery County Pub. Defenders Office, Norristown, Pa., 1983-84; assoc. Mauger & Spare, Pottstown, 1981—; bd. dirs. Edgewood Cemetary, Pottstown, 1983—. Committeeman Montgomery County Republican Party, 1982-86; sec. Old Hill Boys of Pottstown, 1984-86; v.p. Pottstown Pub. Library, 1986-87; internal dir. Pottstown Jaycees, 1984-85. Mem. ABA, Pa. Bar Assn., Montgomery County Bar Assn., Montgomery County Probate & Tax Commn., Pottstown Lawyers Assn. (treas. 1984—). Lodges: Rotary (bd. dirs. local club 1984-85), Masons. Avocations: running, tennis. Probate, Estate planning, Real property. Home: 817 W Cedarville Rd Pottstown PA 19464 Office: 240 King St Pottstown PA 19464

MAUK, WILLIAM LLOYD, lawyer, investor; b. Pocatello, Idaho, Mar. 15, 1947; s. Jack Lawrence and Doris Lloyd (Shaw) M.; m. Susan Powell Ducker, May 10, 1975; children—Steven Allen and Jonathan Shaw. B.A., U. So. Calif., 1969; M.A., Columbia U., 1971; J.D., Antioch Coll., 1975. Bar: Idaho 1975, U.S. Dist. Ct. Idaho 1975, U.S. Ct. Appeals (9th cir.) 1979. Law clk to assoc. justice Idaho Supreme Ct, Boise, 1975-76; assoc. Eberle, Berlin, Kading, Turbow & Gillespi, Boise, 1976-78; sole practice William L. Mauk, Esq., Boise, 1978-80; ptnr. Skinner, Fawcett & Mauk, Boise, 1980—; assoc. appellate justice Shoshone-Bannock Tribes, Fort Hall, Idaho, 1977-80; gen. counsel Shoshone-Painte Tribes, Owyhee, Nev., 1980—; mem. faculty Nat. Coll. Advocacy. Mem. govs. adv. bd. on worker's compensation, 1985—; mgr. Idaho Indsl. Spl. Indemnity Fund, 1985—; bd. dirs. Idaho Conservation League, Boise, 1976-80; mem. Idaho U.S. Constl. Bicentennial com. Mem. Boise Bar Assn., Idaho Bar Assn., ABA, Idaho Trial Lawyers Assn. (sec., bd. dir. 1978, v.p. 1985-86, pres. 1986—), Assn. Trial Lawyers Am. Democrat. Unitarian. Contbr. articles to profl. jours. Personal injury, Labor, Workers' compensation. Office: Skinner Fawcett & Mauk 515 S 6th St Boise ID 83701

MAULDIN, JOHN INGLIS, lawyer; b. Atlanta, Nov. 6, 1947; s. Earle and Isabel (Inglis) M.; m. Cynthia Ann Balchin, Apr. 15, 1967 (div. Dec. 1985); children: Tracy Rutherford, Abigail Inglis. BA, Wofford Coll., 1970; JD, Emory U., 1973. Bar: S.C. 1974, U.S. Ct. Appeals (4th cir.) 1974, U.S. Dist. Ct. S.C. 1975, U.S. Supreme Ct. 1978. Asst. pub. def. Defender Corp. Greenville County, S.C., 1974-76; ptnr. Mauldin & Allison, Greenville, 1977—; adj. prof. Greenville Tech. Coll., 1975-80; sec., treas. Def. Corp. Greenville County, 1979—, bd. dirs. Bd. dirs. Speech Hearing and Learning Ctr., Greenville, 1977—, pres., 1982. Served to capt. USAR, 1970-78. Named S.C. Atty. Yr. ACLU, S.C., 1986. Mem. Sigma Delta Psi. Democrat. Methodist. Club: Harlequins (Greenville) (pres. 1978-79). Lodge: Sertoma (pres. Wade Hampton 1974—). Personal injury, Criminal, Workers' compensation. Office: Mauldin & Allison 710 E McBee Ave Greenville SC 29601

MAULDING, BARRY CLIFFORD, lawyer; b. McMinnville, Oreg., Sept. 3, 1945; s. Clifford L. and Mildred (Fisher) M.; m. Reva J. Zachow, Dec. 27, 1965; children—Phillip B., John C. B.A. in Psychology, U. Oreg., 1967, J.D., 1970. Bar: Oreg. 1970, U.S. Dist. Ct. (we. dist.) Oreg. 1970. Sec., gen. counsel Alaska Continental Devel. Corp., Portland, also Seattle, 1970-75; gen. counsel Alaska Airlines, Seattle, 1975-84; dir. legal services, corp. sec. Univar Corp., Seattle, 1984—; dir. Alaska N.W. Properties, Inc., Seattle. Trustee Cosgrave Found., Seattle. Republican. Contracts commercial, General corporate, Environment. Office: Univar Corp 1600 Norton Bldg Seattle WA 98104

MAULSBY, ALLEN FARISH, lawyer; b. Balt., May 21, 1922. A.B., Williams Coll., Williamstown, Mass., 1944; LL.B., U. Va., 1946. Bar: Md. 1947, N.Y. 1950. Law clk. to judge U.S. Circuit Ct. Appeals 4th Circuit, 1946-47; assoc. firm Cravath Swaine & Moore, N.Y.C., 1947-57; partner Cravath Swaine & Moore, 1958—. Vestryman St. James' Episcopal Ch., N.Y.C., 1962-68, 80-85, warden, 1986—; trustee Greer-Woodycrest Child Care, 1961-82; bd. dirs. Episc. Ch. Found., 1973-86. Mem. Am. Bar Found., N.Y. Bar Found., Am. Coll. Trial Lawyers, Am. Bar Assn., N.Y. State Bar Assn., Fed. Bar Assn., Assn. Bar City N.Y., N.Y. County Lawyers Assn. Federal civil litigation, State civil litigation. Office: Cravath Swaine & Moore One Chase Manhattan Plaza New York NY 10005

MAURER, HENRY STEPHEN, JR., lawyer; b. N.Y.C., Dec. 9, 1950; s. Henry Stephen Sr. and Emilia (Sherman) M.; m. Linda Sue Rosen, Aug. 11, 1974; 1 child, David Louis. BS, CCNY, 1971; MA, U. Pa., 1972; JD, Temple U., 1980. Bar: N.J. 1980, Pa. 1980, U.S. Dist. Ct. N.J. 1980, U.S. Dist. Ct. (ea. dist.) Pa. 1982. Editor The Phila. Fedn. Tchrs. Reporter, 1972-79; assoc. Selikoff & Cohen, Cherry Hill, N.J., 1979-81, Novack & Trobman, Cherry Hill, 1982-83; legis. specialist N.J. Dept. Personnel, Trenton, 1984—; arbitrator Better Bus. Bur. So. N.J., 1984—. Mem. Twp. Planning Bd. Cherry Hill, 1984—; chmn. individual rights com. Jewish Community Relations Council, So. N.J., 1982—. Mem. ABA (labor law sect.). Democrat. Jewish. Labor, Administrative and regulatory, Legislative. Home: 219 Drake Rd Cherry Hill NJ 08034 Office: NJ Dept Personnel CN 312 Trenton NJ 08625

MAURER, IRA MARK, lawyer; b. Manhasset, N.Y., May 21, 1954; s. Herbert and Phoebe (Horowitz) M.; m. Audrey Dankner, Aug. 26, 1979; 1 child, Lauren Danielle. BA, Harpur Coll., 1976; JD, St. John's U., Jamaica, N.Y., 1979. Bar: N.Y. 1980, U.S. Dist. Ct. (so. and ea. dists.) N.Y. 1980, U.S. Dist. Ct. (no. dist.) N.Y. 1984, U.S. Dist. Ct. Conn. 1985. Assoc. Elkind & Lampson, N.Y.C., 1979-82; assoc. Elkind, Flynn & Maurer, N.Y.C., 1982-84, ptnr., 1985—; designated counsel Brotherhood R.R. Signalmen, 1985—. Mem. N.Y. State Bar Assn., Assn. Trial Lawyers Am., N.Y. State Trial Lawyers Assn. Democrat. Avocations: tennis, video. Personal injury, Federal civil litigation, Labor. Office: Elkind Flynn & Maurer PC 122 E 42d St Suite 1515 New York NY 10168

MAURER, JOHN WILLIAM, judge; b. Joliet, Ill., Sept. 11, 1941; s. John Arthur and Magdalena Anna (Foesch) M.; divorced; 1 child, Jennifer. BS in Acctg. magna cum laude, U. Akron, 1973, JD, 1978. Bar: Ohio 1979. Tax auditor State of Ohio, 1970-78; prof. U. Akron, Ohio, 1978-79; adminstrv. law judge Ohio Bureau Employment Services Bd. Rev., Columbus, Ohio, 1979—; initiator tng. program for state adminstrv. law judges in Ohio, 1986. Author: Ohio Administrative Law Handbook, 1985. Served with USMC, 1959-64. Mem. Ohio State Bar Assn. (chmn. spl. com. 1983-86), ABA (conf. adminstrv. law judges, chmn. cen. panel com. 1984—, chmn. state legis. com.), Mensa. Avocation: barber shop singing. Administrative and regulatory, Judicial administration, Labor. Home: 1803 B King Ave Columbus OH 43212 Office: Ohio Bureau Employment Services Bd Rev 145 S Front St Columbus OH 43216

MAURER, VIRGINIA GALLAHER, legal educator; b. Shawnee, Okla., Nov. 7, 1946; d. Paul Clark Gallaher and Virginia Ruth (Watson) Abernathy; m. Ralph Gerald Maurer, July 31, 1971; children—Ralph Emmett, William Edward. B.A., Northwestern U., 1968; M.A., Stanford U., 1969, J.D., 1975. Bar: Iowa 1976. Tchr. social studies San Mateo (Calif.) High Sch. Dist., 1969-71; spl. asst. to pres. U. Iowa, Iowa City, 1976-80, adj. asst. prof. law, 1979-80; affiliate asst. prof. law U. Fla., Gainesville, 1981, asst. prof. bus. law, 1980-85, assoc. prof., 1985—, interim dir. MBA Program, 1987—; cons. Gov.'s Com. on Iowa 2000, Iowa City, 1976-77, Fla. Banker's Assn., Gainesville, 1982. Contbr. articles to profl. jours. Mem. fundraising com. Pro Arte Musica, Gainesville, 1980-84. Mem. ABA, Am. Bus. Law Assn., Southeastern Bus. Law Assn. (Proc. editor 1984—, treas. 1985-86, v.p. 1986—), Iowa Bar Assn., LWV, U. Fla. Athletic Assn. (bd. dirs. 1982—; v.p., chmn. fin. com.), Gainesville Womens' Forum, Beta Gamma Sigma, Kappa Alpha Theta, Delta Sigma Pi. Club: Univ. Women's (Gainesville, Fla.). Antitrust, Contracts commercial, General corporate. Home: 2210 NW 6th Pl Gainesville FL 32603 Office: U Fla Grad Sch Business Gainesville FL 32603

MAURO, RICHARD FRANK, lawyer, educator, businessman; b. Hawthorne, Nev., July 21, 1945; s. Frank Joseph and Dolores D. (Kreimeyer) M.; m. LaVonne M. Madden, Aug. 28, 1965; 1 child, Lindsay Anne. AB, Brown U., 1967; JD summa cum laude, U. Denver, 1970. Bar: Colo. 1970. Assoc. Dawson, Nagel, Sherman & Howard, Denver, 1970-72; assoc. Van Cise, Freeman, Tooley & McClearn, Denver, 1972-73, ptnr., 1973-74; ptnr. Hall & Evans, Denver, 1974-81, Morrison & Forester, Denver, 1981-84, Parcel, Mauro, Hultin & Spaanstra, Denver, 1984—; pres. Sundance Oil Exploration Co., 1985—; adj. prof. U. Denver Coll. Law, 1981—. Symposium editor: Denver Law Jour., 1969-70; editor: Colorado Corporation Systems Manual; contbr. articles to legal jours. Pres. Colo. Open Space Council, 1974. Francis Wayland scholar, 1967; recipient various Am. jurisprudence awards. Mem. ABA, Colo. Bar Assn., Denver Bar Assn., Colo. Assn. Corp. Counsel. (pres. 1974-75), Am. Arbitration Assn. (comml. arbitrator), Order St. Ives. Club: Denver Athletic (bd. dirs. 1986—). General corporate, Contracts commercial, Securities. Home: 3264 Taft Ct Wheat Ridge CO 80033 Office: 1801 California St Suite 3600 Denver CO 80202

MAUS, ROBERT MICHAEL, lawyer; b. Austin, Minn., July 31, 1952; s. Elbert Philip and Victoria (Omitanski) M.; m. Susan Kay Swift, May 20, 1978. BA, U. Minn., 1974; JD, Drake U., 1977. Bar: Minn. 1978, U.S. Dist. Ct. Minn. 1985. Ptnr. Baudler, Baudler & Maus, Austin, 1978—. Mem. Minn. Bar Assn., Mower County Bar Assn. (pres. 1985-86). Roman Catholic. Lodge: Rotary. Avocations: jogging, hiking, golf, tennis, cross-country skiing. Consumer commercial, General practice, State civil litigation. Home: 2005 8th Ave NW Austin MN 55912 Office: Baudler Baudler & Maus 110 N Main St Austin MN 55912

MAWER, WILLIAM THOMAS, lawyer; b. Toledo, May 11, 1948; s. Clifford M. and Mary E. (Avey) M.; m. Catherine M. Greenler, Aug. 16, 1969; children—Jennifer M., Melinda J., Ryanne E. BS., U. Toledo, 1970; J.D., Ohio No. U., 1973. Bar: Ohio 1973. Ptnr. FHM&D Co., L.P.A., Eaton, Ohio, 1973—; instr. Sinclair Coll., Dayton, Ohio, 1975-82; judge pro tem Eaton Municipal Ct., 1975-83. Trustee West Central Ohio council Boy Scouts Am., 1973-78; active Republican Central Com., Eaton, Ohio, 1980-84; pres. Rural Legal Aid Soc., Eaton, 1982-83; active Eaton Bd. Edn., 1984. Recipient Outstanding Jaycees award Eaton Jaycees, 1974; award of Merit, Boy Scouts Am., 1977. Mem. Ohio State Bar Assn. (taxation com.), ABA, Preble County Bar Assn. (pres. 1984-85). Lutheran. Lodges: Masons (chaplain 1974-75), Rotary. Avocations: downhill skiing; woodworking. General practice, Probate, Estate taxation. Home: 1409 East Ave Eaton OH 45320 Office: FHM&D Co 111 S Barron St Eaton OH 45320

MAX, HERBERT (BERTRAM), lawyer; b. Newark, May 24, 1931. BA, Columbia U., 1952, LLB, 1954. Bar: N.Y. 1958. Assoc. Delson & Gordon, N.Y.C., 1960-65; sole practice N.Y.C., 1965-84; ptnr. Mayer, Brown & Platt, N.Y.C., 1984—. Author: Raising Capital: Private Placement Form and Techniques, 1982; assoc. editor N.Y. State Annual, 1958-59. Mem. ABA, N.Y. State Bar Assn., Assn. of Bar of City of N.Y. Office: 10th Flr 520 Madison Ave New York NY 10022

MAX, RODNEY ANDREW, lawyer; b. Cin., Jan. 28, 1947; s. Howard Nelson and Ruth Max; m. Laurie Gilbert; children: Adam Keith, Jeffery Aaron. Student, Am. U.; BA, U. Fla., 1970; JD cum laude, Cumberland Sch., 1975. Bar: Ala. 1975, Fla. 1975, U.S. Ct. Appeals (5th and 11th cirs.) 1975, U.S. Supreme Ct. 1982. From assoc. to ptnr. Najjar, Denaburg, Meyerson, Zarzaur, Max, Boyd & Schwartz, Birmingham, Ala., 1975—; chmn. Ala. State Adv. Com. U.S. Civil Rights Commn., 1985—. Mem. project custody Birmingham Children's Hosp., 1985—; officer, bd. dirs. Jewish Community Ctr., Birmingham, 1980—, Family and Child Services, Birmingham, 1984—. Served to specialist grade 4 U.S. Army, 1970-72. Fellow Am. Matrimonial Lawyers; mem. Ala. Bar Assn. (task force for alternative dispute), Ala. Am. Trial Lawyers Assn., Ala. Def. Lawyers Assn., Am. Arbitration Assn., Birmingham Bar Assn. (trustee legal aid 1985—), Birmingham C. of C. (sports devel. com.). Democrat. Lodge: B'nai B'rith (pres. bd. of govs. 1978—). Avocations: sports, politics, children's athletics, religion, internat. relations, interfaith dialogue. Federal civil litigation, Contracts commercial, Construction. Office: Najjar Denaburg Meyerson Zarzaur et al 2125 Morris Ave Birmingham AL 35203

MAXEINER, JAMES RANDOLPH, lawyer; b. St. Louis, Sept. 7, 1952; s. Philip Arthur and Elaine (Foerster) M.; m. Andrea Dianne Bessac, Aug. 14, 1976. BA, Carleton Coll., 1974; JD in Internat. Legal Affairs, Cornell U., 1977; LLM, Georgetown U., 1981; D in Jurisprudence, U. Munich, Fed. Republic Germany, 1985. Bar: Mo. 1977, D.C. 1978, Ill. 1979, N.Y. 1983, U.S. Dist. Ct. (so. dist.) N.Y. 1983, U.S. Dist. Ct. (ea. dist.) N.Y. 1984, U.S. Ct. Appeals (3d and fed. cirs.) 1985. Trial atty. antitrust div. Dept. Justice, Washington, 1977-80; assoc. Walter, Conston, Alexander & Green P.C. and predecessor firm Walter, Conston & Schurtman P.C., N.Y.C., 1982—. Author: Policy and Methods in German and American Antitrust Law, 1986. Max Rheinstein fellow Max Planck Inst., Munich, 1980-82. Mem. ABA, Am. Fgn. Law Assn., German Am. Law Assn., Am. Soc. for Legal History, Selden Soc. Lutheran. Antitrust, Federal civil litigation, Private international. Office: Walter Conston Alexander & Green PC 90 Park Ave New York NY 10016

MAXFIELD, PETER C., law educator, university dean, lawyer; b. 1941. A.B., Regis Coll., 1963; J.D., U. Denver, 1966; LL.M., Harvard U., 1968. Bar: Colo. 1966, Wyo. 1969. Trial atty. Dept. Justice, 1966-67; assoc. Hindry, Erickson & Meyer, Denver, 1968-69; asst. prof. U. Wyo. Coll. Law, 1969-72, assoc. prof., 1972-76, prof., 1976—, dean, 1979—; vis. assoc. prof. U. N.Mex., 1972-73; Raymond F. Rice Disting. prof. U. Kans., fall, 1984, Chapman vis. Disting. prof., U. Tulsa, spring, 1987. Mem. Order St. Ives, Omicron Delta Kappa, Pi Delta Phi. Author: (with Bloomenthal) Cases and Materials on the Federal Income Taxation of Natural Resources, 1971, 72, 77; (with Houghton) Taxation of Mining Operations, 1973, 76; (with Trelease and Dietrich) Natural Resources Law on American Indian Lands, 1977. Legal education. Office: U Wyo Coll Law PO Box 3035 Laramie WY 82071

MAXSON, R. JAMES, lawyer; b. Thief River Falls, Minn., Dec. 12, 1947; s. Raymond G. and Loretta (Kruse) M.; m. Janet Lee Gunning, Dec. 28, 1973; children: Jesse R., Jacob C. BA, Moorhead (Minn.) State U., 1970; JD, U. N.D., 1973. Bar: N.D. 1973, U.S. Dist. Ct. N.D. 1973, U.S. Ct. Appeals (8th cir.) 1973. Asst. state's atty. Ward County, N.D., 1974-76; assoc. Farhart et al P.C., Minot, N.D., 1976—; spl. prosecuter Ward County State's Atty.'s Office, 1978; instr. Minot State U., 1981-84; senator State of N.D., 1986—. Mem. Minot Cable TV Com., 1983—, Minot City Planning Commn., 1984—; chmn. N.D. Parole Bd., 1985-86. Served with USAR, 1968-74. Mem. N.D. Bar Assn., Ward County Bar Assn., Assn. Trial Lawyers Am. (state del.), N.D. Trial Lawyers Assn. (pres. 1983-84), Nat. Assn. Criminal Def. Lawyers. Democrat. Methodist. Club: Exchange (Minot) (pres. 1980-81). Avocations: marathon running, skiing. State civil litigation, Probate, Criminal. Office: Farhart et al PC 600 22d Ave NW Minot ND 58701

MAXWELL, JAMES BECKETT, lawyer; b. Hampton, Va., Aug. 22, 1941; s. Harold Irvin and Lydia Grant (Beckett) M.; m. Elizabeth Holland, Sept. 5, 1964; children: Jonathan B., Scott H., Tracey E. BA, Randolph-Macon Coll., 1963; LLB, Duke U., 1966. Bar: N.C. 1966, U.S. Dist. Ct. (ea., mid. and we. dists.) N.C. 1967, U.S. Ct. Appeals (4th cir.) 1967. Assoc. Bryant, Lipton, Bryant & Battle, Durham, N.C., 1966-70, ptnr., 1970-75; ptnr. Maxwell, Freeman & Beason, Durham, 1975—. Pres. Durham YMCA, 1974, Durham Arts Council, 1977-79. Named one of Outstanding Young Men in Am., 1975, Father of Yr. Durham Merchants Assn., 1984, Southeastern Laymen of Yr. Southeastern YMCA, 1982. Mem. N.C. Acad. Trial Lawyers (pres. 1986—), Am. Bd. Trial Advs. (assoc.), Am. Assn. Matrimonial Attys. Democrat. Presbyterian. Avocation: swimming coach. Federal civil litigation, State civil litigation, Personal injury. Home: 3900 Wentworth Dr Durham NC 27707 Office: Maxwell Freeman & Beason PA 2741 University Dr Durham NC 27707

MAXWELL, RICHARDS DENYSE, JR., lawyer; b. Miami, Fla., Nov. 25, 1911; s. Richards DeNyse and Cora (Seward) M.; m. Evelyn Faye Grubbs, June 29, 1934; children—Richards DeNyse III, Jerry Lee Maxwell Chafin. B.A., U. Va., 1933, LL.B., 1935; LL.M., U. Miami, 1971. Bar: Fla. 1935, U.S. Dist. Ct. (so. dist.) Fla. 1936, U.S. Ct. Appeals 1956, U.S. Supreme Ct. 1946. Ptnr., Sanders & Maxwell, Miami, 1935-40, Smathers, Thompson, Maxwell & Dyer, Miami, 1941-55; sole practice, Miami, 1955—. Served to lt. comdr. USNR, 1942-45. Mem. ABA, Fla. Bar Assn., Dade County Bar Assn., Am. Coll. Probate Counsel, Raven Soc., Phi Beta Kappa. Episcopalian. Clubs: Biscayne Bay (Fla.) Yacht; Riviera Country, Miami, Bath;

Farmington Country (Charlottesville, Va.); Commonwealth (Richmond, Va.). General corporate, Probate, Estate taxation. Office: Room 821 Du-Pont Bldg Miami FL 33131

MAXWELL, ROBERT ALEXANDER, lawyer; b. Detroit, May 29, 1943; s. Earl and Betsy (Callender) M.; m. Vickie McCord, Sept. 25, 1982; children by previous marriage: Betsy Kay, Lauren McAllister. B.A. with honors, Denison U., 1965; J.D., U. Mich., 1968. Bar: Mich. 1969. sr. ptnr. Maxwell, Smith, Hanson & Mulvoy, 1968—; exec. v.p. Seamco, Inc., Bloomfield Hills, Mich., 1979—. Mem. Mich. Bar Assn., Sigma Chi. Republican. Presbyterian. Federal civil litigation, State civil litigation, Civil rights. Address: 300 Long Lake Rd Suite 300 Bloomfield Hill MI 48013

MAXWELL, ROBERT EARL, judge; b. Elkins, W.Va., Mar. 15, 1924; s. Earl L. and Nellie E. (Rexstrew) M.; m. Ann Marie Grabowski, Mar. 29, 1948; children—Mary Ann, Carol Lynn, Ellen Lindsay, Earl Wilson. Student, Davis and Elkins Coll.; LL.B., W.Va. U., 1949. Bar: W.Va. bar 1949. Practiced in Randolph County, 1949, pros. atty., 1952-61; U.S. atty. for No. Dist. W.Va., 1961-64; judge U.S. Dist. Ct. for No. Dist. W.Va., Elkins, 1965—, Temporary Emergency Ct. of Appeals, 1980; past chmn. budget com. Jud. Conf. U.S. Recipient Alumni Disting. Service award Davis and Elkins Coll., 1969; award Religious Heritage Am., 1979. Mem. Dist. Judges Assn. 4th Circuit (past pres.). Jurisprudence. Home: Elkins WV 26241 Office: US Courthouse PO Box 1275 Elkins WV 26241

MAXWELL, ROBERT WALLACE, II, lawyer; b. Waynesburg, Pa., Sept. 6, 1943; s. Robert Wallace and Margaret M.; m. Mamie Lee Payne, June 18, 1966; children—Virginia, Robert William. B.S. magna cum laude, Hampden-Sydney Coll., 1965; J.D. with honors, Duke U., 1968. Bar: Ohio 1968. Assoc. Taft, Stettinius & Hollister, Cin., 1968-75, ptnr., 1975—; part-time instr. U. Cin. Sch. Law, 1975-76. Bd. dirs. Comtemporary Arts Ctr. of Cin; bd. dirs. Cin. Ballet Co.; trustee, elder Covenant First Presbyterian Ch. Mem. ABA, Am. Assn. Mus. Trustees. Republican. Labor, Federal civil litigation, State civil litigation. Home: 535 Larchmont Dr Wyoming OH 45215 Office: First Nat Bank Center Suite 1800 Cincinnati OH 45202

MAY, ALAN ALFRED, lawyer; b. Detroit, Apr. 7, 1942; s. Alfred Albert and Sylvia (Sheer) M.; m. Elizabeth Miller; children—Stacy Ann, Julie Beth. B.A., U. Mich., 1963, J.D., 1966. Bar: Mich. 1967, D.C. 1976; registered nursing home adminstr., Mich. Ptnr. May and May, Detroit, 1967-79, pres. May & May, P.C., 1979—; spl. asst. atty. gen. State of Mich., 1970—; of counsel Charfoos & Christensen P.C. and predecessor firm Charfoos, Christensen & Archer, P.C., Detroit, 1970—; pres., instr. Med-Leg Seminars, Inc., 1978; lectr. Wayne State U., 1974; instr. Oakland U., 1969. Chmn. Rep. 18th Congl. Dist. Com., 1983-87, now chmn. emeritus; chmn. 19th Congl. Dist. Com., 1981-83; mem. Mich. Rep. Com., 1976-84; del. Rep. Nat. Conv., 1984; former chmn. Mich. Civil Rights Commn.; mem. Mich. Civil Service Commn.; trustee NCCJ, Mich. Cancer Found.; mem. Electoral Coll.; bd. dirs. Detroit Round Table, Charfoos Charitable Found., Temple Beth El, Birmingham, Mich. Mem. Detroit Bar Assn., Oakland County Bar Assn. Clubs: Victors, Franklin Hills Country (bd. dirs.), Presidents (trustee). Contbr. article to profl. jours. Probate, State civil litigation, Workers' compensation. Home: 4140 Echo Rd Bloomfield Hills MI 48013 Office: May & May PC 3000 Town Ctr Suite 2600 Southfield MI 48075

MAY, BRUCE BARNETT, lawyer; b. Portland, Oreg., Apr. 16, 1948; s. Ralph Barnett May and Barbara (Newton) Evans; m. Deborah Sue Wright, Jan. 22, 1972; children: Alexander, Christopher, Elizabeth, Andrew. BA, Princeton U., 1971; JD, U. Oreg., 1978. Bar: Ariz. 1978. Ptnr. Streich, Lang, Weeks & Cardon, Phoenix, 1978—; lectr. various bar and trade assns. Contbr. articles to profl. jours. V.p. Phoenix Mountain Preservation Council, 1985—; mem. Paradise Valley Urban Village Planning Com., Phoenix, 1985—. Served to lt. j.g. USN, 1972-75. Mem. ABA (vice chmn. land sales regulation com.), Order of Coif. Republican. Episcopalian. Avocations: book collecting, running. Real property. Home: 4616 E Shadow Rock Phoenix AZ 85028 Office: Streich Lang Weeks & Cardon 2100 1st Interstate Bank Plaza PO Box 471 Phoenix AZ 85003

MAY, DAVID P., lawyer; b. Wichita, Kans., Jan. 6, 1954; s. Ernest C. and Verlee R. (Bouska) M.; m. Mary E. May, Mar. 8, 1975. BA, Kans. Wesleyan U., 1975; JD, Drake U., 1978. Bar: Iowa 1979, U.S. Dist. Ct. (no. and so. dists.) Iowa 1980, U.S. Ct. Appeals (8th cir.) 1980. Ptnr. McMurry & May Law Firm, Ankeny, Iowa, 1979-83; staff atty. ITT Consumer Fin., Mpls., 1983-85; asst. gen. counsel Assocs. Corp. N. A., Dallas, 1985—. Mem. ABA. Bankruptcy, Consumer commercial, General corporate. Home: 3728 Walnut Dr Bedford TX 76021 Office: Assocs Corp NA PO Box 660237 Dallas TX 75266

MAY, GREGORY EVERS, lawyer; b. Harrisonburg, Va., Sept. 17, 1953; s. Russell J. and Arlene Virginia (Ringgold) M. AB, Coll. of William and Mary, 1975; JD, Harvard U., 1978. Bar: Va. 1978, U.S. Dist. Ct. (ea. dist.) Va. 1979, U.S. Ct. Appeals (4th cir.) 1979, U.S. Claims Ct. 1981, U.S. Tax Ct. 1981, D.C. 1985. Law clk. to presiding justice U.S. Ct. Appeals (4th cir.), Richmond, Va., 1978-79; law clk. to Justice Powell U.S. Supreme Ct., Washington, 1979-80; assoc. Hunton & Williams, Richmond, 1980-83; assoc. Hunton & Williams, Washington, 1984-86, ptnr., 1986—. Articles editor Harvard Law Rev., 1977-78. Mem. ABA, Va. State Bar, Va. Bar Assn. Corporate taxation. Office: Hunton & Williams 2000 Pennsylvania Ave NW Washington DC 20006

MAY, HENRY S., JR., lawyer; b. Greensboro, N.C., May 12, 1947; s. Henry Stratford and Doris (Richardson) M.; m. Jean Eros, May 5, 1979; children: Henry Stratford III, Benjamin Alexander. BA, U. Tex., 1969, JD, 1971. Bar: Tex. 1972, U.S. Ct. Appeals (D.C. cir.) 1974, U.S. Supreme Ct. 1977, U.S. Ct. Appeals (5th and 11th cirs.) 1981, U.S. Dist. Ct. (so. dist.) Tex. 1985. Law clk. to presiding justice U.S. Ct. Appeals (D.C. cir.), Washington, 1972-73; assoc. Vinson & Elkins, Houston, 1973—. Mem. ABA, Tex. Bar Assn. Republican. FERC practice. Home: 2315 Robinhood Houston TX 77005 Office: Vinson & Elkins 3300 First City Tower 1001 Fannin Houston TX 77002

MAY, JAMES, JR., judge; b. American Falls, Idaho, Dec. 16, 1925; s. James Alfred and Naomi Jane (Tolman) M.; m. Barbara Egbert, Oct. 21, 1945; children—Monte May Barney, J. Dee, Shawno Egbert. B.A., U. Idaho, 1949, J.D., 1951. Bar: Idaho 1953, Wash. 1952, U.S. Supreme Ct. 1960. Pros. atty. Twin Falls County (Idaho), 1961-66; sr. ptnr. Shindurling , Stubbs & Mitchell, Twin Falls, 1952-86; apptd. dist. judge, 1986; commr. Idaho State Bar 1978-80, pres. 1980. Served with USN, 1944-47. Mem. ABA (membership chmn. sect. ins., negligence and compensation law 1971-72), Wash. State Bar Assn., 5th Jud. Dist. Bar Assn., Nat. Dist. Attys. Assn., Calif. Trail Lawyers Assn., Nat. Criminal Def. Lawyers Assn., Assn. Trial Lawyers Am. (bd. govs. 1981—), Idaho Trial Lawyers Assn. (pres. 1971-74, bd. govs. 1971-86), Western Trial Lawyers Assn. (bd. govs. 1972-86, pres. 1984), Twin Falls C. of C. (1 dir. 1983-86, v.p. 1984, pres. 1985-86). Republican. Mormon. State civil litigation, Criminal, Personal injury. Home: PO Box 1630 Hailey ID 83333 Office: PO Box 1846 Twin Falls ID 83301

MAY, LAWRENCE EDWARD, lawyer; b. N.Y.C., Aug. 7, 1947; s. Jack and Ann Marie (Schnell) M.; m. Rosalind Marsha Israel, Feb. 3, 1979; children: Jeremy, Lindsey. BA, UCLA, 1969, JD, 1972. Bar: Calif. 1972, N.Y. 1973. Assoc. Paul, Weiss, Rifkind, Wharton & Garrison, N.Y.C., 1972-76, Levine, Krom & Unger, Beverly Hills, Calif., 1976-79, Weissburg & Aronson, Los Angeles, 1979-81, Valensi & Rose, Los Angeles, 1981-83; ptnr. Pollet & May, Los Angeles, 1983-84; Prin. Lawrence E. May, P. C., Los Angeles, 1984—. Bd. dirs. Jewish Publs., Inc., Los Angeles, 1985—, Boy Scouts Am., Los Angeles, 1985—. Mem. State Bar Calif., Los Angeles County Bar Assn. Beverly Hills Bar Assn. (bd. of govs. 1981—, v.p. 1986—, chmn. bus. law sect. 1984-85). Democrat. Avocations: tennis, current events, family. General corporate, Real property, Securities. Office: 10920 Wilshire Blvd Suite 650 Los Angeles CA 90024

MAY, RANDOLPH JOSEPH, lawyer; b. Wilmington, N.C., Aug. 11, 1946; s. Aaron and Norma (Eisen) M.; m. Laurie Eisenberg, Mar. 28, 1971; children—Joshua, Brooke. A.B., Duke U., 1968, J.D., 1971. Bar: D.C. 1973: U.S. Dist. Ct. D.C. 1973, U.S. Ct. Appeals (D.C. cir.) 1973, U.S. Supreme Ct. 1980. Law clk. U.S. Ct. Appeals (D.C. cir.), Washington, 1972-73; assoc. Steptoe and Johnson, Washington, 1973-78; assoc. gen. counsel FCC, Washington, 1978-81; ptnr. McKenna, Wilkinson & Kittner, Washington, 1981-86, Bishop, Liberman, Cook, Purcell & Reynolds, Washington, 1986—. Pres. Chancellor Farms Civic Assn., Springfield, Va., 1975, Voluntary Action Ctr., Fairfax, Va., 1976. Named Outstanding Sr. Exec. FCC, 1980. Mem. ABA, D.C. Bar Assn., Fed. Bar Assn. (communications com. 1979-81), Fed. Communications Bar Assn. (jud. rev. com. 1981-83). Jewish. Administrative and regulatory, Public utilities, Entertainment. Home: 10701 Stapleford Hall Dr Potomac MD 20854 Office: Bishop Liberman et al 1200 17th NW Washington DC 20036

MAY, RICHARD EDWARD, lawyer; b. Austin, Tex., Feb. 5, 1946; s. Howard Curtis and Gertrude E. (Wallace) M.; m. Elynor Maguire Stephens, June 16, 1984; 1 child, Elynor Lee. AB, U. Md., 1967; JD, Georgetown U., 1973. Bar: D.C. 1973, Va. 1984. Assoc. Steptoe & Johnson, Washington, 1973-79; spl. asst. to chief counsel IRS, Washington, 1979-81; ptnr. Jenkens & Gilchrist, Dallas, 1981-83, Hunton & Williams, Washington and Richmond, Va., 1983—. Served to lt. USN, 1968-71. Mem. ABA (taxation sect., chmn. corp. stockholder relationships com. 1984—). Episcopalian. Clubs: Metropolitan (Washington); Commonwealth (Richmond). Corporate taxation. Office: Hunton & Williams 2000 Pennsylvania Ave NW PO Box 19230 Washington DC 20036

MAY, ROBERT A., lawyer; b. Grand Rapids, Mich., May 8, 1911; s. Adam F. and Myra Ethel (Shedden) M.; m. Margrethe Holm, Aug. 30, 1934 (dec. Dec. 1970); children: Marcia, Margrethe; m. Virginia L. Salisbury, Mar. 20, 1973. A.B., U. Mich., 1933, J.D., 1936. Bar: Mich. 1936, Ariz. 1941, U.S. Supreme Ct. 1960. Practised in Grand Rapids, 1936-41; practised law Tucson, 1941-86, retired; partner Robert A. May, P.C. (and predecessors); mem. State Bar Ariz., vice chmn., 1952-53, chmn. group ins. com., 1953-72; co-founder, chmn. bd. trustees Client's Security Fund, 1961-81; mem. ABA standing com. Clients Security Fund, 1968-73; mem. com. on revision probate code Ariz. State Bar, 1970-72; Ariz. chmn. Joint Editorial Bd. for Uniform Probate Code, 1972-80; mem. com. on revision Ariz. probate code Ariz. Legis. Council, 1970-72; founding mem. Ariz. com. jud. selection, tenure, and discipline, 1957-72, chmn., 1957-67; co-founder Def. Info. Office; charter mem. Def. Research Inst. Bd. dirs. St. Luke's in the Desert, 1944-80, pres., 1964-77, pres. emeritus, 1977—, gen. counsel, 1944-82; bd. dirs. St. Luke's Chest Disease Clinic at U. Ariz. Med. Center; bd. dirs. Pima County Legal Aid Soc., 1952-77, emeritus, 1977—, pres., 1958-60; adv. bd. Tucson Med. Center, 1946-49; co-founder Tucson C. of C. Conv. Bur., 1945-74, exec. bd., 1957-67; regional chmn. U. Mich. Law Sch. Fund, 1963-66, mem. nat. com., 1967-72, now emeritus; vice chmn. so. Ariz. mil. base hosps. com. ARC, 1942-45; mem. Citizens Adv. Com. for Pub. Schs., 1944-46; vis. com. U. Mich. Law Sch., 1964-67. Recipient Outstanding Service award Ariz. State Bar Assn., 1977. Fellow Am. Coll. Probate Counsel (bd. regents 1966-69, 73-77); mem. Nat. Coll. Probate Judges (life), Internat. Acad. Law and Sci., Tucson C. of C., Ariz. Pioneers Hist. Soc., ABA (vice chmn. health ins. com. 1958-70, chmn. 1970-72), Am. Bar Found. (life), Internat. Bar Assn., Mich. Bar Assn., Pima County Bar Assn. (pres. 1955-56), Fed. Bar Assn., Am. Bar Found. (life), Found for Temple Bar (London), So. Ariz. Estate Planning Council (co-founder, pres. 1956), U. Mich. Alumni Assn. (dist. dir. 1943-46), Internat. Assn. Ins. Counsel, Am. Bar Inst., Tucson Council Chs. (mem. exec. bd., chmn. fin. com. 1948-64, pres. 1956-58), Ariz. Council Chs. (v.p. 1956-58), Internat. Acad. Law and Sci., Am. Judicature Soc. (nat. dir. 1963-67), Assn. Ins. Attys., Phi Sigma Kappa Found., Phi Sigma Kappa (pres. Tucson Alumni Club 1960-74), Alpha Epsilon Mu (hon.). Episcopalian (parish chancellor 1943-78, chancellor emeritus 1978—, vestryman 1943-73, 74-77, rector's warden 1977-78, vice chancellor Ariz. diocese 1959-71). Clubs: Round Table Internat. (pres. 1944-46), Old Pueblo, U. Mich. Alumni (pres. Grand Rapids 1938-41, pres. Tucson 1945-50, 76-77, bd. govs. 1942-79, hon. gov. 1983—); Inst. for Dirs., Wig and Pen (London). Estate planning, Probate. Home: 1915 E 3d St Tucson AZ 85719

MAY, WILLIAM LEOPOLD, JR., lawyer; b. Winthrop, Mass., Aug. 24, 1942; m. Claude Lamarque d'Arrouzat, June 10, 1981. BSCE, Cornell U., 1964; BL, Boston Coll., 1967; LLM, Harvard U., 1969. Bar: Vt. 1967, U.S. Dist. Ct. Vt. 1967, Mass. 1969, U.S. Tax Ct. 1969. Law clk. to presiding justice U.S. Dist. Ct. Vt., Burlington, 1967-68; assoc. Ely Bartlett, Boston, 1969-71; atty. Cabot Corp., Boston, 1971-74, tax counsel, 1974-76; counsel European div. Cabot Corp., Paris, 1976-84; sr. counsel Cabot Corp., Boston, 1984-86; chief counsel ops. Cabot Corp., Waltham, Mass., 1987—. General corporate, Private international, Corporate taxation. Office: Cabot Corp 890 Winter St Waltham MA 02254

MAYANS, STEVEN ANTHONY, lawyer; b. N.Y.C., July 6, 1956; s. Frank and Anna Elizabeth (Piselli) M.; m. Terry Ellen Resk, May 25, 1987. BA magna cum laude, Vanderbilt U., 1978; JD, Duke U., 1981. Bar: Ohio 1981, U.S. Dist. Ct. (so. dist.) Ohio 1981, U.S. Ct. Appeals (6th cir.) 1981, U.S. Supreme Ct. 1984, Fla. 1985, U.S. Dist. Ct. (so. dist.) Fla. 1986, U.S. Ct. Appeals (11th cir.) 1986. Assoc. Smith & Schnacke, Cin., 1981-85, Moyle, Flanigan, Katz, FitzGerald & Sheehan, West Palm Beach, Fla., 1985—. Mem. Norton Gallery and Sch. of Art, West Palm Beach, 1985—, Hist. Soc. of Palm Beach, Fla., 1985—. Mem. ABA, Acad. of Fla. Trial Lawyers, Assn. Trial Lawyers Am., Palm Beach County Bar Assn., Phi Beta Kappa, Omicron Delta Epsilon. Democrat. Roman Catholic. State civil litigation, Federal civil litigation. Home: 3000 N Ocean Dr No 22-E Singer Island FL 33404 Office: Moyle Flanigan Katz FitzGerald & Sheehan 625 W Flagler Dr West Palm Beach FL 33401

MAYBERRY, ALAN REED, assistant prosecuting attorney; b. Akron, Ohio, Mar. 15, 1954; s. Franklin Reed Mayberry and Mary K. (Kissane) Mayberry Alexander; m. Lisa Renee Rush, Dec. 19, 1981. B.S. in Edn., Bowling Green State U., 1975; J.D., U. Toledo, 1978. Bar: Ohio 1979, U.S. Dist. Ct. (no. dist.) Ohio 1981. Asst. prosecutor Wood County Pros. Atty.'s Office, Bowling Green, Ohio, 1980-81, chief criminal div., asst. pros. atty., 1981—; small claims ct. referee Bowling Green Mcpl. Ct., 1981. Mem. Bowling Green City Council, 1984—; chmn. Bowling Green Planning, Zoning and Econ. Devel. Com., 1984-85. Named to Outstanding Young Men Am., U.S. Jaycees, 1983, 84. Mem. Bowling Green Jaycees (bd. dirs. 1983—). Republican. Presbyterian. Lodges: Fraternal Order Police, Optimists (local program chmn.). Criminal. Office: Wood County Pros Atty's Office Courthouse Bowling 1 Courthouse Bldg Bowling Green OH 43402

MAYER, ANN ELIZABETH, legal educator; b. Seguin, Tex., May 5, 1945; d. William Vernon and Margaret Esther (Laird) M.; m. Jose Miguel Cobian, Dec. 23, 1967 (div. Oct. 1970). BA, U. Mich., 1964, MA, 1966, PhD, 1978; JD, U. Pa., 1975; cert., U. London, 1977. Bar: Pa. 1978. Asst. prof. Wharton Sch., U. Pa., Phila., 1979-82, assoc. prof. legal studies, 1982—; lectr. U. Pa. Law Sch., Phila., 1982—; vis. prof. Princeton U., 1983—; cons. Aga Khan Found., Aiglemont, France, 1983; mem. Middle East Research Cons., Stony Brook, N.Y., 1985—; bd. dirs. Am. Council for Study of Islamic Socs., Villanova, Pa., 1983—. Editor: Property, Social Stucture and Law in the Modern Middle East; mem. editorial bd. The Arab Law Quar., London, 1985—; contbr. chpts. to books, articles to profl. jours. Mem. Lawyers Alliance for Nuclear Arms Control, Phila., 1985—. Fellow U. Pa. Law Sch., 1975-77, U. Pa., 1978, Am. Research Ctr. in Egypt, N.Y.C. 1980, 84. Mem. ABA, Internat. Law Assn., Soc. Arab and Comperative Law, Am. Bus. Law Assn., Am. Soc. Polit. and Legal Philosophy. Democrat. Unitarian. Club: Oriental (Phila.). Avocations: opera, skiing, swimming. Islamic law, Middle Eastern Law, Legal history. Office: U Pa Wharton Sch Legal Studies Philadelphia PA 19104

MAYER, JOHN WILLIAM, lawyer; b. Houston, Nov. 17, 1941; s. Maurice William and Julie Eldee (Borddofsky) M.; m. Ann Jodoin, July 30, 1972; children—Norbert, Kristin, Mara. B.A. in Econs., Vanderbilt U., 1963; J.D., U. Chgo., 1966; postgrad. Nat. Jud. Coll., 1984. Bar: Ill. 1966, U.S. Ct. Mil. Appeals 1971, Colo. 1987. Assoc. Lorenz & Stamler, Newark, 1963-66; estate tax atty. IRS, Chgo., 1966-67; commd. U.S. Air Force, 1967, advanced through grades to lt. col., 1980; judge advocate U.S. Air Force, 1967— . Nat. Honor scholar U. Chgo., 1963; recipient Nat. Pub. Defender's award, Chgo., 1966. Mem. ABA (chmn. mil. judges com. 1984—), Assn. Trial Lawyer's Am., Zeta Beta Tau, Phi Delta Phi. Jewish. Club: Standard (Montgomery, Ala.). Military, Criminal, General practice. Office: KTTC/JA Keesler AFB MS 39534

MAYER, NEAL MICHAEL, lawyer; b. N.Y.C., Dec. 4, 1941; s. Joseph Henry and Cele (Brodsky) M.; m. Jane Ellen Greenberg, Aug. 24, 1963; children: Andrew Warren, Amy Lynn, Rebecca Ann, Jenny Leigh. BA in History with honors, Kenyon Coll., 1963; JD, Georgetown U., 1966. Bar: D.C. 1967, U.S. Dist. Ct. D.C. 1967, U.S. Ct. Appeals (D.C. cir.) 1967, U.S. Customs Ct. 1967, U.S. Supreme Ct. 1970, U.S. Ct. Appeals (5th cir.) 1975. Assoc. Coles & Goertner, Washington, 1966-71; ptnr., 1971-82; sr. ptnr. Hoppel, Mayer & Coleman, Washington, 1982—. Mem. ABA, Fed. Bar Assn. D.C., D.C. Bar Assn., Maritime Adminstrv. Bar Assn. (pres. 1979), Assn. Transp. Practioners, Phi Alpha Delta. Clubs: Nat. Lawyers, Propeller of U.S. (Washington). Administrative and regulatory, Admiralty. Office: Hoppel Mayer Coleman 1000 Connecticut Ave NW Washington DC 20036

MAYER, THOMAS MOERS, lawyer; b. N.Y.C., Sept. 23, 1955; s. Martin Prager and Ellen (Moers) M.; m. Jerri Sines. AB summa cum laude, Dartmouth Coll., 1977; JD magna cum laude, Harvard U., 1981. Bar: N.Y. 1982, U.S. Dist. Ct. (so. dist.) N.Y. 1982. Law clk. to judge U.S. Ct. Appeals (2d cir.), N.Y.C., 1981-82; assoc. Willkie, Farr & Gallagher, N.Y.C., 1982-84, Wachtell, Lipton, Rosen & Katz, N.Y.C., 1984—. Editor Harvard Law Rev., 1980-81. Mem. Phi Beta Kappa. Democrat. Jewish. Avocations: bridge, golf, opera. Bankruptcy. Office: Wachtell Lipton Rosen & Katz 299 Park Ave New York NY 10171

MAYERLE, THOMAS MICHAEL, lawyer; b. Grand Rapids, Minn., Jan. 5, 1948; s. James Raphael and Frances (Kosher) M.; m. Susan Terry Potter, Oct. 9, 1976; children—Jennifer Leigh, Scott Michael, Robert Michael. A.B., Dartmouth Coll., 1970; J.D. magna cum laude, U. Minn., 1973. Bar: Minn. 1973, U.S. Ct. Appeals (D.C. cir.) 1973. Law clk. to justice U.S. Ct. Appeals (D.C. cir.), Washington, 1973-74; ptnr. Faegre & Benson, Mpls., 1974—. Note and articles editor Minn. Law Rev., 1972-73. Mem. Minn. State Bar Assn., Hennepin County Bar Assn., Order of Coif. Real property, Landlord-tenant, Construction. Home: 5905 Chapel Dr Edina MN 55435 Office: Faegre & Benson 2300 Multifoods Tower Minneapolis MN 55402

MAYERSOHN, ARNOLD LINN, JR., lawyer; b. Little Rock, Mar. 26, 1955; s. Arnold Linn and Janet (Grundfest) M.; m. Elizabeth Hardin Rudel, May 31, 1981; 1 child, Sarah Kathleen. BS in Bus., U. Colo., 1977; JD, U. Ark., 1981. Bar: Ark. 1981, U.S. Dist. Ct. (ea. and we. dists.) Ark. 1984. House counsel, dir. real estate Sterling Stores Co., Inc., Little Rock, 1981-83; assoc. Prince & Ivester P.C., Little Rock, 1984-86; asst. legal counsel Worthen Banking Corp, Little Rock, 1986—; asst. sec. Forbing Investments Inc., Little Rock, 1983—; bd. dirs. Baconia Plantation, Inc. Cary, Miss., Baconia Farms, Cary, ALMB Plantation, Inc., Cary. Bd. dirs. Henry S. Jacobs Camp for Living Judiasm, Utica, Miss., 1983-85, Ark. Epilepsy Soc., Little Rock, 1984-85. Mem. ABA, Ark. Bar Assn., Pulaski County Bar Assn. Democrat. Jewish. Avocations: music, sports, family. General corporate, Securities, Real property. Home: 19 Mohawk Circle Little ROck AR 72207 Office: Worthen Banking Corp PO Box 1681 Little Rock AR 72203-1681

MAYERSON, SANDRA ELAINE, lawyer; b. Dayton, Ohio, Feb. 8, 1952; d. Manuel David and Florence Louise (Tepper) M.; m. Scott Burns, May 29, 1977 (div. Oct. 1978). BA cum laude, Yale U., 1973; JD, Northwestern U., 1976. Bar: Ill. 1976, U.S. Ct. Appeals (7th cir.) 1976, U.S. Dist. Ct. (no. dist.) Ill. 1977. Assoc. gen. counsel JMB Realty Corp., Chgo., 1979-80; assoc. Chatz, Sugarman, Abrams et al, Chgo., 1980-81; ptnr. Pollack, Mayerson & Berman, Chgo., 1981-83; dep. gen. counsel AM Internat., Inc., Chgo., 1983-85; ptnr. Kirkland & Ellis, Chgo., 1985—. Bd. dirs. Jr. Med. Research Inst. Council of Michael Reese Hosp., Chgo., 1981—. Mem. ABA (bus. bankruptcy com. 1976—), Ill. State Bar Assn. (governing council corp. and securities sect. 1983-86), Chgo. Bar Assn. (current events chmn. corp. sect. 1980-81), 7th Cir. Bar Assn. Democrat. Jewish. Clubs: Yale (N.Y.C.), Metropolitan, Eastbank (Chgo.). Bankruptcy, General corporate, Consumer commercial. Home: 1550 N Lake Shore Dr Apt 9B Chicago IL 60610 Office: Kirkland & Ellis 200 E Randolph Dr Chicago IL 60601

MAYES, S. HUBERT, JR., lawyer; b. Little Rock, Sept. 6, 1931; J.D., U. Ark., 1954. Bar: Ark. 1954. Asst. sec. Ark. State Senate, 1953; atty. Ark. State Revenue Dept., 1954-55; dep. pros. atty. 6th Jud. Dist., Ark., 1957-58; spl. asst. atty. gen. State of Ark., 1963; practice law, Little Rock. Fellow Ark. Bar Found., Am. Coll. Trial Lawyers; mem. ABA, Ark. Bar Assn., Pulaski County Bar Assn., Def. Research Inst., Assn. Trial Lawyers Am., Ark. Trial Lawyers Assn. Insurance, State civil litigation, Federal civil litigation. Home: 2021 Beechwood St Little Rock AR 72207 Office: Laser Sharp & Mayes PA One Spring St Little Rock AR 72201

MAYESH, JAY PHILIP, lawyer; b. Davenport, Iowa, July 22, 1947; s. Samuel and Dorothy (Katz) M.; m. Leslie Helene Haupt, June 1969; children: Stacey Janet, Beth Valerie. BA, U. Wis., 1969; JD, Columbia U., 1972. Bar: N.Y. 1973, U.S. Dist. Ct. (so. dist.) N.Y. 1973, U.S. Ct. Appeals (2d cir.) 1974. Assoc. Stroock & Stroock & Lavan, N.Y.C., 1972-80, ptnr., 1981—. Editor Product Liability Law and Strategy, 1984. Harlan Fiske Stone scholar Columbia U., 1971. Mem. ABA, N.Y. State Bar Assn., Assn. Trial Lawyers Am., Phi Beta Kappa. Federal civil litigation, State civil litigation, Product liability. Office: Stroock & Stroock & Lavan 7 Hanover Sq New York NY 10004

MAYFIELD, EDGAR, telephone company executive, lawyer; b. Lebanon, Mo., July 14, 1925; s. Winan I. and Mary J. (Turner) M.; m. Martha Ellen Burton, July 24, 1949; children—JoEllen Mayfield Essman, Cynthia Mayfield Dobbs, Andrew. Diploma Navy V-12 program, Central Meth. Coll., Fayette, Mo., 1944; LL.B., U. Mo., Columbia, 1949. Bar: Mo., 1949, Ark. 1960, Tex. 1965, N.Y. 1975. Pros. atty. Laclede County, Mo., 1949-52; atty. Southwestern Bell Telephone, St. Louis, 1956-60; gen. atty. Southwestern Bell Telephone, Little Rock, 1960-64; solicitor Southwestern Bell Telephone, Dallas, 1964-68; solicitor Southwestern Bell Telephone, St. Louis, 1968-69, gen. atty., 1970, gen. solicitor, 1970-74, v.p., 1980-81; v.p., gen. counsel Southwestern Bell Corp., St. Louis, 1981-86, sr. v.p. and gen. counsel, 1986—; v.p., gen. atty. AT&T, Long Lines, N.Y.C., Bedminster, N.J., 1975-80. Served to lt. (j.g.) USN, 1943-46. Recipient Disting. Alumni award Central Meth. Coll., 1981, Citation of Merit U. Mo. Law Sch, 1986. Mem. ABA, St. Louis Bar Assn. Clubs: Noonday, St. Louis, Bellerive Country (St. Louis). Lodge: Masons. General corporate, Administrative and regulatory, Public utilities. Office: Southwestern Bell Corp One Bell Ctr Saint Louis MO 63101

MAYKA, STEPHEN P., lawyer; b. Rochester, N.Y., Sept. 18, 1946; s. Stephen and Mary Jane (Laluppa) M.; m. Judith Holley Aitkin, July 26, 1981; children: Stephen I., Megan J., Judith Hope, Eric A. BA, U. Mich., 1968; JD, Union U., 1973. Bar: N.Y. 1973, U.S. Dist. Ct. (we. dist.) N.Y. 1973, U.S. Supreme Ct. 1973, U.S. Dist. Ct. (ea. and so. dists.) N.Y. 1984, U.S. Ct. Appeals (2d cir.) 1984, U.S. Dist. Ct. (no. dist.) N.Y. 1985. Assoc. Nixon & Hargrave, Rochester, 1973-75; gen. counsel Cen. Trust Co., Rochester, 1975-78; ops. counsel Gen. Electric Credit, Stamford, Conn., 1978-80; ptnr. Lacy, Katzen, Ryer & Nettleman, Rochester, 1980—. Mem. N.Y. State Bar Assn., Assn. Trial Lawyers Am., N.Y. Trial Lawyers Assn. Bankruptcy, Contracts commercial, Consumer commercial. Office: Lacy Katzen Ryer & Nettleman 130 Main St E Rochester NY 14604

MAYO, JOHN TYLER, lawyer; b. Goshen, N.Y., Sept. 10, 1933; s. William A. and Doris (Sinnott) M.; m. Ann Pettis, May 2, 1959; children: Susan C., Elizabeth T., John T. III. AB, Colgate U., 1954; postgrad., Ohio State U.; JD, Columbia U., 1960. Bar: N.Y. 1960, U.S. Supreme Ct. 1964. Assoc. Mayer, Kissel, Matz & Seward, N.Y.C., 1960-62; ptnr. Mayo & Mayo, Goshen, 1962—. Served to capt. USAF, 1954-57. Mem. ABA, N.Y. State Bar Assn., Orange County Bar Assn. (v.p. 1976-78, pres. 1979), Goshen Bar Assn. (pres. 1977), Middletown (N.Y.) Sports Club. Republican. Roman Catholic. Lodge: Rotary (pres. 1970-71). General business, Probate, Real property. Home: PO Box 22 Owens Rd Goshen NY 10924 Office: Mayo & Mayo 154 Main St PO Box 239 Goshen NY 10924

MAYOR, RICHARD BLAIR, lawyer; b. San Antonio, Mar. 27, 1934; s. E. Allan and Elizabeth Ann (Hastings) M.; m. Heather Donald, July 28, 1956; children: Diana Boyd, Philip Hastings. B.A., Yale U., 1955; postgrad., Melbourne U., (Australia), 1955-56; J.D., Harvard U., 1959. Bar: Tex. 1960.

Assoc. Butler, Binion, Rice, Cook & Knapp, Houston, 1959-67; ptnr. Butler, Binion, Rice, Cook & Knapp, 1967-82, Mayor, Day & Caldwell, Houston, 1982—. Trustee, mem. exec. com. Contemporary Arts Mus., Houston, 1972-78; Trustee Houston Ballet Found., 1983—. Fulbright scholar, 1955-56. Mem. ABA, Am. Law Inst., Tex. Bar Assn., Phi Beta Kappa. Home: 226 Pine Hollow St Houston TX 77056 Office: Mayor Day & Caldwell 1900 Republic Bank Ctr Houston TX 77002

MAYORAL, PAUL G., lawyer; b. New Orleans, Sept. 26, 1953; s. George A. and Yvonne (Viosca) M.; m. Susan Elizabeth Parr, June 14, 1975; children: John, Elise, Stephanie. BA, La. State U., 1976, JD, 1978. Bar: La. 1979, U.S. Dist. Ct. (ea. and mid. dists.) La. 1979. Asst. dist. atty. New Orleans Parish, 1979-85; asst. atty. Jefferson County Parish, Gretna, La., 1985—; legis. drafter New Orleans and Jefferson County Parish, Gretna, La., 1978—; chief of juvenile div. New Orleans Dist. Attys. Office, 1983-84; pub. collections New Orleans Dist. Attys. Office, 1984-85. Treas. La. Young Reps., Baton Rouge, 1976-77. Mem. Jefferson Parish Bar Assn., Jaycees, Greater New Orleans Football Officals (v.p. 1983-85). Republican. Roman Catholic. Avocations: football officiating. Estate planning, Probate, Real property. Office: Jefferson Parish Attys. Office PO Box 9 Gretna LA 70053

MAYOUE, JOHN CHARLES, lawyer; b. Avon, N.Y., Mar. 27, 1954; s. Vincent Henry and Mary (George) M. BA, Transylvania U., 1976; JD, Emory U., 1979. Bar: Ga. 1979. Assoc. Westmoreland, Hall, Atlanta, 1979-82; ptnr. Warner, Mayoue et al, Atlanta, 1982—. Vol. United Way, 1983-84; pro bono Atlanta Vol. Lawyers Found. 1982—. Mem. ABA (exec. council young lawyers div.), Ga. Bar Assn. (exec. council young lawyers sect.), Atlanta Council Younger Lawyers (bd. dirs. 1980—, pres. 1986—), Fed. Bar Assn., Am. Judicature Soc. (bd. dirs. 1986), Assn. Trial Lawyers Am., Ga. Trial Lawyers Assn., Atlanta Lawyers Club. Club: Capital City (Atlanta). Lodge: Kiwanis (pres. Buckhead, Ga. 1983). Avocations: tennis, art, home restoration. State civil litigation, Federal civil litigation, Jurisprudence. Home: 23 Brookhaven Dr Atlanta GA 30319

MAYS, CHARLES ANDREW, lawyer; b. Indian Head, Md., Dec. 31, 1939; s. Robert Bertrand and Elsie Lucille (Bedwell) M.; m. Marilyn Diane Costello; children—Christopher Andrew, Robert Davis. B.A. in Polit. Sci., George Washington U., 1961, J.D. 1964. Bar: D.C. 1965, Minn. 1969, U.S. Supreme Ct. 1969. Law clk. D.C. Ct. Appeals, 1964-65; asst. U.S. atty., Washington, 1965-69; assoc. Leonard, Street & Deinard, Mpls., 1969-70, ptnr., 1971—. Trustee Met. Med. Ctr., Mpls., 1981-84, U. Minn. Episcopal Ctr., Mpls., 1980-83. Minn. Episcopal Found., Mpls., 1981-83; chmn. bd. dirs. Inst. for Christian Living, 1983-87. Mem. ABA, Minn. Bar Assn., Hennepin County Bar Assn., U.S. Trademark Assn. Republican. Recent decisions editor George Washington Law Rev., 1964. Antitrust, Federal civil litigation, Trademark and copyright. Office: 100 S 5th St Minneapolis MN 55402

MAYS, WILLIAM GAY, II, lawyer; b. Washington, Mo., Apr. 8, 1947; s. Frank G. and Geneva Pauline (Brookhart) M.; m. Judith Ann Kriete, Oct. 5, 1974; 1 son, Daniel Brookhart. A.B., U. Mo., 1969, J.D., 1972. Bar: Mo. 1972, U.S. Dist. Ct. (we. dist.) Mo. 1972. Legis. researcher State of Mo., 1972; pub. defender 13th Jud. Cir. Mo., 1973-77; ptnr. Holt, Mays & Brady, Columbia, 1977—; ptnr. and gen. counsel comml. real estate devel. firm. Mem. Jud. Planning Commn., Mo., 1977. Served to capt. USAFR, 1969-82. Named Outstanding Young Man of Am., 1974. Mem. Mo. Bar Assn., Boone and Callaway County Bar Assn., Mo. Trial Lawyers Assn., Mo. Pub. Defender Assn. (pres. 1976-77), Beta Theta Pi. Republican. Club: Masons. Real property, Contracts commercial, Criminal. Office: 920 A East Broadway Columbia MO 65201

MAYWHORT, WILLIAM WALTER, lawyer; b. Phila., July 18, 1946; s. John Arthur and Helen Margaret (Wooten) M.; m. Diane Buchanan, June 29, 1968; children: Christopher Blair, Andrea Claire. BS, USAF Acad., 1968; JD with honors, U. N.C., 1972; LLM, Yale U., 1975. Bar: N.C. 1972, U.S. Ct. Claims 1975, U.S. Supreme Ct. 1977, Colo. 1978, U.S. Dist. Ct. Colo. 1978, U.S. Ct. Appeals (10th cir.) 1978. Commd. 2d lt. USAF, 1968, advanced through grades to capt., 1971, judge adv., 1969-78, resigned, 1978; assoc. Holland & Hart, Denver, 1978-83, ptnr., 1983—. Articles editor U. N.C. Law Rev., 1972. Mem. ABA, Denver Bar Assn., Colo. Bar Assn., Colo. Assn. Grads. (bd. dirs. 1978—), Centennial C. of C., Order of Coif. Republican. Presbyterian. Club: Met. (Englewood). Federal civil litigation, State civil litigation. Home: 5895 E Weaver Circle Englewood CO 80111 Office: Holland & Hart 7887 E Belleview Suite 1250 Englewood CO 80111

MAZADOORIAN, HARRY NICHOLAS, lawyer; b. New Britain, Conn., May 26, 1938; s. Nicholas G. and Elizabeth Mazadoorian; m. Janice R. Buckwell, May 15, 1965; children: Beth J., Lynne C. BA magna cum laude, Yale U., 1960, LLB, 1963. Bar: Conn. 1963, U.S. Dist. Ct. Conn. 1963. Ptnr. McCook, Kenyon & Bonee, Hartford, Conn., 1963-69, Ericson, Politis & Gleason, New Britain, 1969-76; atty. CIGNA Corp., Bloomfield, Conn., 1976—. Legis. commr. State of Conn., Hartford, 1973-74; chmn. eastern field office ARC, 1981. Served to 1st lt. USAR, 1963-68. Mem. Conn. Bar Assn. (chmn. corp. counsel sect. 1984-86), Am. Corp. Counsel Assn. (pres. Hartford chpt. 1987—). General corporate, Insurance. Home: 401 Monroe St New Britain CT 06052 Office: Cigna Corp W-26 Hartford CT 06152

MAZER, LAWRENCE, lawyer; b. Phila., Jan. 19, 1937; s. Manual and Sara (Kravitz) M.; children: Mindy Robin, Susan Elizabeth; m. Carol Ann Coppola, Oct. 7, 1984. BA magna cum laude, Temple U., 1958, JD, 1961. Bar: Pa. 1961, U.S. Dist. Ct. (ea. dist.) Pa. 1962, U.S. Ct. Appeals (3d cir.) 1962, U.S. Supreme Ct. 1976, U.S. Tax Ct. 1986; cert. in real estate. Assoc. Manchel, Lundy & Lessin, Phila., 1961-63; sole practice Phila., 1963-70; ptnr. Bogutz & Mazer, Phila., 1971-80, Lawrence Mazer & Assocs., Phila., 1980—; pres., bd. dirs. Am. Credit Inst. Inc., Zenith Abstract Co. Inc.; bd. dirs. Sales Aides Internat. Inc.; real estate developer. Editor-in-chief Temple Law Reporter, 1961; assoc. editor Temple Law Quarterly, 1961. Pres. Merion Park Civic Assn., 1974, sec., 1972, bd. dirs., 1969-70; hon. trustee Pop Warner Little League; bd. dirs. United Synagogue Del. Valley. Served with USAR, 1954-62. Recipient Gold medal Pop Warner Little League, 1985. Mem. ABA (asst. to dir. com. on continuing legal edn. Am. Law Inst.), Phila. Bar Assn. (chmn. joint com. lawyers and realtors, chmn. title ins. com., profl. edn., law office econs. and mcpl. ct. coms., real property, corp. banking and bus. law sects.), Comml. Law League Am., Order of Owl, Tau Epsilon Rho. Jewish. Real property, Contracts commercial, Family and matrimonial. Home: 1 Christian St #49 Philadelphia PA 19147 Office: Lawrence Mazer & Assocs 401 Lewis Tower Bldg Philadelphia PA 19102

MAZEWSKI, ALOYSIUS ALEX, lawyer; b. North Chicago, Ill., Jan. 5, 1916; s. Felix and Harriet (Konieczny) M.; m. Florence Wanda Heider, June 27, 1948; children—Aloysius, Marilyn. J.D., DePaul U., 1940; Litt.D., Daemen Coll., 1982, Coll. St. Rose, 1986. Bar: Ill. 1940, U.S. Dist. Ct. (no. dist.) Ill. 1940, U.S. Supreme Ct. 1961. Atty. Office of County Treas., Cook County, Ill., 1950-55; master in chancery Cir. Ct. Cook County, 1960-65; sole practice, Chgo., 1940-67; pres., legal counsel and exec. Polish Nat. Alliance Fraternal Ins.; U.S. del to UN, 1972. Mem. U.S. Holocaust Commn. Served to maj. AUS, 1942-46. Named Man of Yr. Italian Am. Joint Council, 1975; recipient Merit award Advs. Soc., 1983; Fidalitas award St. Mary's Coll., 1978. Mem. Chgo. Bar Assn., Ill. State Bar Assn., ABA, Fed. Bar Assn., Am. Judicature Soc., Chgo. Council Fgn. Relations, Nat. Fraternal Congress (law com.), Am. Arbitration Bd. Republican. Roman Catholic. Insurance, Probate, Legislative. Home: 3813 Medford Circle Northbrook IL 60062 Office: 6100 N Cicero Chicago IL 60638

MAZO, MARK ELLIOTT, lawyer; b. Phila., Jan. 12, 1950; s. Earl and Rita (Vane) M.; m. Fern Rosalyn Litman, Aug. 19, 1973; children: Samatha Lauren, Dana Suzanne, Ross Elliott, Courtney Litman. AB, Princeton U., 1971; JD, Harvard Law Sch., 1974. Bar: D.C. 1975, U.S. Dist. Ct. D.C. 1975, U.S. Claims Ct. 1975, U.S. Ct. Appeals (D.C. cir.) 1976, U.S. Supreme Ct. 1979. Assoc. Jones, Day, Revis & Pogue, Washington, 1974-79; Crowell & Moring, Washington, 1979-81; ptnr. 1981—. Contbr. articles to profl. jours. White House intern Exec. Office of Pres., Washington, 1972. Served to capt. USAR, 1971-79. Mem. Harvard Law Sch. Assn., ABA, D.C. Bar Assn., Phi Beta Kappa. Republican. Clubs: University (Washington); Columbia Country., Princeton, (N.Y.C.); Colonial. General corporate, Securities, Contracts commercial. Home: 3719 Cardiff Rd Chevy Chase MD 20815 Office: Crowell & Moring 1001 Pennsylvania Ave NW Washington DC 20004-2505

MAZUR, LAWRENCE JOSEPH, lawyer, banker; b. La Porte, Ind., May 17, 1948; s. Chester Stanley and Marie Jane (Ziarnek) M.; m. Laura Kay Alban, Oct. 17, 1981; 1 child, Lawrence Joseph II. BS, Ind. U., 1973; JD, John Marshall Sch. of Law, 1979; LLM, DePaul U., 1986; cert. in banking, U. Wis., 1986. Bar: Ind. 1979, U.S. Dist. Ct. (so. dist.) Ind. 1979, U.S. Tax Ct. 1985; licensed real estate broker, Ind.; CPA, Ind. Sr. auditor Alexander Grant, Chgo., 1972-75; sr. tax analyst Northwest Industries, Chgo., 1975-79; sr. v.p., sr. trust officer La Porte Bank and Trust Co., 1979—; sole practice La Porte, 1980—; lectr. Purdue U., Westville, Ind., 1979—. Bd. dirs. Planned Giving Com., La Porte, 1981, La Porte Estate Planning Council; past pres., bd. dirs. La Porte Area Lake Assn., 1982; past chmn. Main St. Bus. Assn., La Porte, 1986. Served with USMC, 1966-68, Vietnam. Mem. ABA, La Porte Bar Assn., Am. Inst. CPA's, Am. Assn. Attys. and CPA's, Ind. Soc. CPA's. Republican. Roman Catholic. Lodge: Rotary (bd. dirs. 1980-81). Avocations: historic preservation, real estate. Personal income taxation, Estate planning, Banking. Office: 326 Oak Dr La Porte IN 46350

MAZZAFERRI, KATHERINE AQUINO, lawyer; b. Phila., May 14, 1947; d. Joseph William and Rose (Aquino) M.; m. William Fox Bryan, May 5, 1984; 1 child, Josefine Mazzaferri. B.A., NYU, 1969; J.D., George Washington U., 1972. Bar: D.C., 1972. Trial atty. Equal Employment Opportunity Commn., Washington, 1972-75; dir. litigation LWV Edn. Fund, Washington, 1975-78; dep. asst. dir. for advt. practices FTC, Washington, 1978-80, asst. dir. for product liability, 1980-82, asst. dir. for advt. practices, 1982; exec. dir. D.C. Bar Assn., Washington, 1982—; dir. regulatory analysis project U.S. Regulatory Council, 1980; mediator D.C. Mediation Service, 1982; vis. instr. Antioch Law Sch., Washington, spring 1985. Recipient Superior Service award FTC, 1979. Mem. ABA, Womens Legal Def. (pres. 1971-75, bd. dirs. 1976-79). Home: 2410 Tunlaw Rd NW Washington DC 20007 Office: DC Bar Assn 1707 L St NW 6th Floor Washington DC 20036 *

MAZZONE, A. DAVID, judge; b. Everett, Mass., June 3, 1928; s. A. Marino and Philomena M.; m. Eleanor G. Stewart, May 10, 1951; children: Margaret Clark, Andrew David, John Stewart, Jan Eleanor, Martha Ann, Robert Joseph, Carolyn Cook. B.A., Harvard U., 1950; J.D., DePaul U., 1957. Bar: Ill. bar 1957, Mass. bar 1959, U.S. Supreme Ct. bar 1964. Asst. dist. atty. Middlesex County, Mass., 1961; asst. U.S. atty. Mass., 1961-65; partner firm Moulton, Looney & Mazzone, Boston, 1965-75; asso. justice Superior Ct., Boston, 1975-78; U.S. dist. judge Boston, 1978—. Served with U.S. Army, 1951-52. Mem. ABA, Mass. Trial Lawyers Assn., Am. Law Inst., Mass. Bar Assn., Boston Bar Assn., Middlesex Bar Assn., Fed. Bar Assn. Democrat. Roman Catholic. Office: US Dist Ct 2001 McCormack Post Office and Courthouse Bldg Boston MA 02109 *

MCADAMS, DON RANDALL, JR., lawyer. BSBA, La. State U., 1978, JD, 1980. Bar: La. 1981, U.S. Dist. Ct. (ea. dist.) La. 1982, U.S. Ct. Appeals (5th and 11th cirs.) 1982. Atty. Exxon Co. USA, Houston, 1981-83; v.p. La. Nat. Bank, Baton Rouge, 1983—. Mem. ABA, Fed. Bar Assn., La. Bar Assn., Baton Rouge Bar Assn. Oil and gas leasing, Probate, General practice. Office: La Nat Bank 451 Florida Baton Rouge LA 70801

MCADAMS, SHEILAH HELEN, lawyer, educator; b. Lima, Ohio, Aug. 27, 1951; d. Richard Albert and Mary Patricia (Burke) McA.; m. Michael W. Pettit, Sept. 24, 1976 (div. 1981). Student, Ohio Wesleyan U., 1969-70; B in Gen. Studies cum laude, Ohio U., 1973; postgrad., Emory U., 1973-74; JD cum laude, U. Toledo, 1978. Bar: Ohio 1978, U.S. Dist. Ct. (no. dist.) Ohio 1979. Assoc. Ritter, Boesel, Robinson & Marsh, Toledo, 1979—; pros. atty. City of Maumee, Ohio, 1979—, Village of Whitehouse, Ohio, 1981—; asst. solicitor City of Maumee, 1987—; adj. prof. law U. Toledo, 1985; asst. solicitor City of Maumee, 1986—. Mem. editorial bd. Toledo Law Rev. 1977-78. Emory U. fellow, 1973-74. Mem. ABA, Ohio Bar Assn., Lucas County Bar Assn., Ohio Mcpl. Attys. Assn., N.W. Ohio Suburban Mcpl. Prosecutors Assn. (pres. 1981-86), Toledo Bar Assn., Toledo Women's Bar Assn., Toledo Jr. Bar Assn. (exec. com. 1983)., Maumee C. of C. Lodge: Old Newsboys Goodfellows. Criminal, Local government. Office: Ritter Boesel et al 610 United Savs Bldg Toledo OH 43604

MCALILEY, THOMAS WATSON, lawyer; b. Jacksonville, Fla., June 7, 1932; s. Thomas W. and Dorothy J. McAliley; m. Janet Richards, June 14, 1955; children—Chris, Kevin, Neal. B.A., U. Fla., 1956, LL.B., J.D., 1959. Bar: Fla. 1959, U.S. Dist. Ct. (so. dist.) Fla. 1960, U.S. Ct. Appeals (5th cir.) 1961, (11th cir.) 1981, U.S. Supreme Ct. 1971. Assoc., Hector Faircloth & Rutledge, Miami, Fla., 1959-61; ptnr. Nichols Gaither Beckham Colson & Spence, Miami, 1961-66; sr. ptnr. Beckham, McAliley & Schultz, P.A., Miami, 1966—. Counsel to Fla. Senate, 1982; mem. investment adv. com. State Bd. Adjustment, 1980-83, chmn., 1980-82. Fla. Rural Legal Services, 1967-72, bd. dirs., 1970-76, pres., 1970-73. Served with U.S. Army, 1953-55. Fellow Internat. Acad. Trial Lawyers; mem. ABA, Fla. Bar, Dade County Bar Assn. (dir. 1979-83), Nat. Assn. Criminal Def. Lawyers, Inner Circle Advs., Internat. Soc. Barristers, Am. Trial Lawyers Assn., Fellows of Am. Bar Found., Acad. Fla. Trial Lawyers (dir. 1967-72), Maritime Law Assn. U.S., Am. Judicature Soc., Acad. Fla. Labor-Mgmt. Relations Attys., Dade County Trial Lawyers Assn., Blue Key, Phi Alpha Delta. Democrat. Unitarian Clubs: Miami, Bankers, Governors, Standard; Univ. (Jacksonville). Personal injury, State civil litigation, Federal civil litigation. Office: Concord Bldg 5th Floor 66 W Flagler St Miami FL 33130

MCALLISTER, KENNETH WAYNE, lawyer; b. High Point, N.C., Jan. 3, 1949; s. John Calhoun and Ruth Welch (Buie) McA.; m. Mary Gail Leonard, Jan. 2, 1972; 1 dau., Katherine Owen. B.A., U. N.C., 1971; J.D., Duke U., 1974. Bar: N.C. 1974, U.S. Dist. Ct. for Middle dist. N.C. 1974, U.S. Ct. Appeals for 4th circuit 1980, U.S. Supreme Ct. 1980. Assoc. firm Fisher, Fisher & McAllister, High Point, 1974-81; U.S. atty. for middle dist. N.C. U.S. Dept. Justice, Greensboro, 1981—. Pres. High Point Drug Action Council, 1977-78; chmn. High Point Republican Com., 1976-78; mem. adv. bd. Salvation Army, High Point, 1978-79. John Motley Morehead scholar Morehead Found., 1967; Arthur Priest scholar Phi Delta Theta, 1971. Mem. Phi Beta Kappa. Republican. Presbyterian. Club: Emerywood Country (High Point). Lodge: Kiwanis. Home: 116 Ferndale Blvd High Point NC 27262 Office: Dept Justic US Atty 324 W Market St Greensboro NC 27401 *

MCAMIS, EDWIN EARL, lawyer; b. Cape Girardeau, Mo., Aug. 8, 1934; s. Zenas Earl and Anna Louise (Miller) McA.; m. Malin Eklof, May 31, 1959 (div. 1979); 1 child, Andrew Bruce. A.B., Harvard U., 1956, LL.B., 1959. Bar: N.Y. 1960, U.S. Dist. Ct. N.Y., U.S. Supreme Ct. 1965, U.S. Ct. Appeals (2d, 3d and D.C. cirs.). Assoc. law firm Webster, Sheffield & Chrystie, N.Y.C., 1959-61, Regan Goldfarb Powell & Quinn, N.Y.C., 1962-65; assoc. law firm Lovejoy, Wasson, Lundgren & Ashton, N.Y.C., 1965-69, ptnr., 1969-77; ptnr. Skadden, Arps, Slate, Meagher & Flom, N.Y.C., 1977—; adj. prof. law Fordham U., 1984-85, Benjamin N. Cardozo Sch. Law, N.Y.C., 1985—. Bd. dirs. Aston Magna Found. for Music, Inc., 1982—. Served with U.S. Army, 1961-62. Mem. ABA, Assn. Bar City N.Y., Selden Soc. Club: Univ. (N.Y.C.). Federal civil litigation, State civil litigation. Office: 919 3d Ave New York NY 10022

MCANDREWS, JAMES PATRICK, lawyer; b. Carbondale, Pa., May 11, 1929; s. James Patrick and Mary Agnes (Walsh) McA.; m. Mona Marie Steinke, Sept. 4, 1954; children: James P., George A., Catherine McAndrews Lawlor, Joseph M., Anne Marie, Michael P., Edward R., Daniel P. B.S., U. Scranton, 1949; LL.B., Fordham U., 1952; grad., Real Estate Inst., NYU, 1972. Bar: N.Y. 1953, Ohio 1974. Assoc. law firm James F. McManus, Levittown, N.Y., 1955; atty. Emigrant Savs. Bank, N.Y.C., 1955-68; counsel Tchrs. Ins. and Annuity Assn., 1968-73; assoc. Thompson, Hine & Flory, 1973-74; ptnr. Thompson, Hine & Flory, Cleve., 1974-84, Benesch, Friedlander, Coplan & Aronoff, Cleve., 1984—; mem. law faculty Am. Inst. Banking, N.Y.C., 1968-69. Served to 1st lt. USAF, 1952-54. Fellow Am. Bar Found.; mem. ABA (past chmn. real estate financing com. 1985-87), Am. Coll. Real Estate Lawyers (gov. 1983-86, treas. 1986—, chmn. membership devel. com. 1985—), Ohio Bar Assn., Bar Assn. Greater Cleve. (past chmn. council real estate sect.), Am. Land Title Assn. (chmn. lenders counsel group 1978, chmn. membership com. 1983-84), Ohio Land Title Assn. (bd. trustees 1985—, chmn. lender's counsel group 1986), Internat. Council Shopping Ctrs., Urban Land Inst., Nat. Trust Hist. Preservation, Nat. Assn. Corp. Real Estate Execs. (chmn. nomination com. Ohio 1982, v.p. Ohio chpt. 1983-84), Nat. Assn. Indsl. and Office Parks, Am. Coll. Mortgage Attys., Am. Coll. Real Estate Lawyers (bd. govs. 1983-86). Roman Catholic. Real property, Landlord-tenant, Construction. Home: 2971 Litchfield Rd Shaker Heights OH 44120 Office: 1100 Citizens Bldg Cleveland OH 44114

MCANENY, EILEEN S., lawyer; b. Phila., May 31, 1952; d. William Patrick and Mary (DiBono) M.; m. Michael D. Gallagher, June 14, 1980. BA cum laude in Polit. Sci., Rosemont Coll., Pa., 1974; J.D., Villanova U., 1977. Bar: Pa. 1977. Assoc., LaBrum and Doak, Phila., 1977-80; sr. assoc. German, Gallagher & Murtaugh, Phila., 1980-81; sr. atty. SmithKline Beckman Corp., Phila., 1981—; lectr. in law. Contbr. articles to profl. and popular jours. Mem. ABA (health law, tort and ins. practice sect., products gen. liability and consumer law com., litigation sect., corp. banking and bus. law sect., antitrust, corp. gen. div.), Am. Corp. Counsel Assn. (product liability com.), Nat. Assn. Mfrs. (product liability and employee compensation sect.), Pa. Bar Assn., Phila. Bar Assn., Am. Clin. Labs. Assn., Delta Epsilon Sigma. Federal civil litigation, State civil litigation, General corporate. Home: 1106 Ivymont Rd Rosemont PA 19010 Office: Smith Kline Beckman Corp One Franklin Plaza PO Box 7929 Philadelphia PA 19101

MCANERNEY, ROBERT MOORE, lawyer; b. Greenwich, Conn., Jan. 29, 1924. B.A., Williams Coll., 1947; J.D., U. Va., 1953. Bar: Conn. 1954, U.S. Supreme Ct. 1969. Assoc. firm Sullivan & Cromwell, N.Y.C., 1953; assoc. Durey & Pierson, Stamford, Conn., 1953-63, ptnr., 1960-63; ptnr. McAnerney & Millar, Darien, Conn., 1963—; assoc. dir. Union Trust Co.; dir., mem. exec. com. Conn. Attys. Title Ins. Co. Fellow Am. Bar Found.; mem. ABA (del. 1978-81), Conn. Bar Assn. (bd. govs. 1964-67, chmn. family law com. 1967-71, chmn. law office econs. com. 1973-75, chmn. spl. com. legis. liaison 1977-78, pres. assn. 1980-81), Stamford Bar Assn., New Eng. Bar Assn. (dir. 1979-83). Home: Old Rock Ln Norwalk CT 06850 Office: 23 Old Kings Hwy S Darien CT 06820

MCANINCH, EDWIN LEE, lawyer; b. Key West, Fla., Apr. 22, 1956; s. Billy Edwin and Marjorie Lee (Moore) McA. BA, Rice U., 1978; JD, South Tex. Coll. Law, 1982. Bar: Tex. 1982, U.S. Dist. Ct. (so. and ea. dists.) Tex. 1982. Landman Tenex Corp., Houston, 1978-82; assoc. John O'Quinn & Assocs., Houston, 1982—. Mem. ABA, Tex. Bar Assn., Houston Bar Assn., Assn. Trial Lawyers Am., Tex. Trial Lawyers Assn., Houston Trial Lawyers Assn., Houston Young Lawyers Assn. Democrat. Episcopalian. Personal injury, Wrongful death, Workers' compensation. Home: 131 Pamellia Bellaire TX 77401 Office: John O'Quinn & Assocs 3200 Tex Commerce Tower Houston TX 77002

MCATEE, DAVID RAY, lawyer; b. Rosebud, Tex., Nov. 20, 1941; s. Lee Ray and Florine (Davis) McA.; m. Carole Kay Pendergraft, Jan. 28, 1967; children—David Ray, Kristin Carole. B.B.A. with honors, Baylor U., 1964; LL.B., U. Tex., 1967. Bar: Tex. 1967, U.S. Dist. Ct. (no. dist.) Tex. 1968, U.S. Ct. Appeals (5th cir.) 1969, U.S. Ct. Appeals (11th cir.) 1981. Briefing atty. Supreme Ct. Tex., Austin, 1967-68; ptnr. Thompson & Knight, Dallas, 1968—. Founder, bd. dirs. No. Hills Neighborhood Assocs., Inc., 1974-76; pres., bd. dirs. Montessori Sch. of Park Cities, 1975-78; mem. Goals for Dallas Com., City of Dallas Citizens Safety Adv. Com., 1975-77; chmn. City of Dallas Thoroughfare Com., 1979-81; mem. City of Dallas Plan Commn., 1979-83, vice-chmn., 1981-83. Mem. Dallas Bar Assn. (legal ethics com. 1979-81), Tex. Bar Assn. (legal ethics com. 1975-81), ABA (antitrust sect.). Democrat. Methodist. Antitrust, Federal civil litigation, State civil litigation. Office: Thompson & Knight 3300 1st City Ctr 1700 Pacific Ave Dallas TX 75201

MCAULIFFE, JOHN F., state judge; b. Washington, Nov. 4, 1932; m. Barbara McAuliffe, Nov. 4, 1955; children: John M., Mary K. JD, Am. U., 1955. Assoc. judge U.S. Ct. Appeals (6th cir.), Md., 1986; judge U.S. Ct. Appeals, Annapolis, Md., 1986—. Office: Ct Appeals Bldg 361 Rowe Blvd Annapolis MD 21401 *

MCAVOY, JOHN JOSEPH, lawyer; b. Worley, Idaho, June 28, 1933; s. Earl Francis and Florence (Mitchell) McA.; m. Joan Marjorie Zeldon, Sept. 20, 1964; children: Jason, Jon. B.A., U. Idaho, 1954, LL.B., 1958; LL.M., Yale U., 1959. Bar: Idaho 1958, U.S. Supreme Ct. 1962, N.Y. 1963, U.S. Tax Ct. 1969, D.C. 1976. Bd. dirs. N.Y. Civil Liberties Union, 1975-77; chmn. due process com. ACLU, 1971-75. Served with U.S. Army, 1954-56. Mem. Assn. Bar City N.Y., D.C. Bar Assn. (ethics com. 1982—, vice chmn. 1986—), Phi Beta Kappa, Phi Alpha Delta. Antitrust, Federal civil litigation, Trade. Home: 3110 Brandywine St NW Washington DC 20008 Office: 1747 Pennsylvania Ave NW Washington DC 20006

MCBAINE, JOHN NEYLAN, lawyer; b. San Francisco, Apr. 29, 1941; s. Turner H. and Jane Frances (Neylan) McB.; m. Alison Denny, Feb. 22, 1963 (div.); 1 child, Diana; m. Ariel Bybee, Nov. 24, 1972; 1 child, Neylan. B.A., Stanford U., 1962; J.D., U. Calif., 1967. Bar: D.C. 1968, Calif. 1970, N.Y. 1975. Assoc. law firm Covington & Burling, Washington, 1967-68; law clk. Hon. Gerhard A. Gesell U.S. Dist. Ct., D.C., 1968-69; assoc. law firm Pillsbury, Madison & Sutro, San Francisco, 1970-74; ptnr. Lord, Day & Lord, N.Y.C., 1975-86, Coudert Bros., N.Y.C., 1986—. Contbr. articles to profl. jours. Pres. Lincoln Plaza Tenants Corp., 1982-84, bd. dirs., 1982—; bd. visitors Brigham Young Law Sch., 1980-83. Served with AUS, 1963. Mem. ABA, Calif. Bar Assn., N.Y. Bar Assn. Mormon. Federal civil litigation, Antitrust, State civil litigation. Home: 44 W 62d St New York NY 10023 Office: Coudert Bros 200 Park Ave New York NY 10166

MCBEE, DONALD LAWRENCE, lawyer; b. Holyoke, Colo., Sept. 16, 1936; s. Virgil Woodrow and Mildred Irene (Gable) McB.; m. Janis Ruth Mason, Mar. 4, 1986; children: Stephanie, Deanna, Derek. BA, U.S. Mil. Acad., 1961; MS, Ohio State U., 1970; JD, Seton Hall U., 1981. Bar: Colo. 1981, U.S. Dist. Ct. Colo. 1982. Commd. 2d lt. U.S. Army, 1961, advanced through grades to lt. col., 1975, ret., 1981; ptnr. Harshman, Deister, Larson & McBee, Grand Junction, Colo., 1981—. Mem. ABA, Assn. Trial Lawyers Am., Colo. Bar Assn., Mesa County Bar Assn. Avocations: running, soccer referee. State civil litigation, Consumer commercial, Criminal. Office: Harshman Deister Larson & McBee 634 Main Grand Junction CO 81501

MCBRIDE, BEVERLY JEAN, lawyer; b. Greenville, Ohio, Apr. 5, 1941; d. Kenneth Birt and Glenna Louise (Ashman) Whited; m. Benjamin Gary McBride, Nov. 28, 1964; children—John David, Elizabeth Ann. B.A. magna cum laude, Wittenberg U., 1963; J.D. cum laude, U. Toledo, 1966. Bar: Ohio 1966. Intern Ohio Govs.' Office, Columbus, 1962; asst. dean of women U. Toledo, 1963-65; assoc. Title Guarantee and Trust Co., Toledo, 1966-69; spl. counsel Ohio Atty. Gen.'s Office, Toledo, 1975; assoc. Cobourn, Smith, Rohrbacher and Gibson, Toledo, 1969-76; gen. counsel The Andersons, Maumee, Ohio, 1976—. Exec. trustee, bd. dirs. Wittenberg U., Springfield, Ohio, 1980—; trustee Anderson Found., Maumee, 1981—; chmn. Sylvania Twp. Zoning Commn., Ohio, 1970-80; candidate for judge, Sylvania Mcpl. Ct., 1975; trustee Goodwill Industries, Toledo, 1976-82, Sylvania Community Services Ctr., 1976-78; founder Sylvania YWCA Program, 1973; active membership drives Toledo Mus. Art, 1977—. Recipient Toledo Women in Industry award YWCA, 1979; Outstanding Alumnus award, Wittenberg U., 1981. Mem. ABA, Ohio Bar Assn. Toledo Bar Assn. (treas. 1979-84, chmn., sec. various coms. 1985—), Toledo Women Attys. Forum (exec. com. 1978-82), AAUW. Club: Presidents (U. Toledo) (exec. com.). General corporate. Home: 5274 Cambrian St Toledo OH 43623 Office: The Andersons 1200 Dussel Dr Maumee OH 43537

MCBRIDE, JAMES FRANCIS, lawyer; b. N.Y.C., Aug. 7, 1946; s. Francis Patrick and Ruth Ann (Flynn) McB.; m. Catherine Lucille Schlick, Mar. 17, 1978; children: Brian, Mary Catherine, Elizabeth, Ann Marie. BS, Villanova U., 1968, JD, 1974. Bar: Pa. 1974, U.S. Dist. Ct. (ea. dist.) Pa. 1974, U.S. Ct. Appeals (3d cir.) 1976, U.S. Dist. Ct. (mid. dist.) Pa. 1980. Assoc. Nino V. Tinari, P.C., Phila., 1974-79, Donald J. Farage, Phila., 1979-82; ptnr. Farage and McBride, Phila., 1982—. Served with U.S. Army, 1968-71, Vietnam. Mem. ABA, Pa. Bar Assn. (co-author publs. on tort law in Pa.

1983—), Phila. Bar Assn., Assn. Trial Lawyers Am., Pa. Trial Lawyers Asssn., Phila. Trial Lawyers Assn., Brehon Law Soc., Phila. Lawyers Club, VFW. Democrat. Roman Catholic. Personal injury, Federal civil litigation, State civil litigation. Home: 13491 Trevose Rd Philadelphia PA 19116 Office: Farage and McBride 836 Suburban Sta Bldg Philadelphia PA 19103

MCBRIDE, KEITH WESLEY, lawyer; b. Sacramento, Dec. 25, 1944; s. Wesley L. and Miriam L. (Eastin) McB.; m. Kathleen Evelyn Crizer, Apr. 12, 1980; 1 child, Evelyn Ann. AB, U. Calif., Davis, 1966, MA, 1967, JD, 1973. Bar: Calif. 1973, U.S. Dist. Ct. (ea. dist.) Calif. 1973. Corps. counsel Dept. Corps., Sacramento, 1973-82; assoc. Diepenbrock, Wulff, Plant & Hannegan, Sacramento, 1982—. Contbg. editor-securities Calif. Bus. Law Reporter, 1984—. V.p. World Affairs Council Sacramento, 1985-86. Served to 1st lt. U.S. Army, 1968-70, Vietnam. Research fellow Western Interstate Commn. Higher Edn., 1972. Mem. ABA. Republican. Presbyterian. Securities, General corporate, Real property. Office: Diepenbrock Wulff Plant & Hannegan 300 Capitol Mall 17th Floor Sacramento CA 95814

MCBRIDE, MICHAEL FLYNN, lawyer; b. Milw., Mar. 27, 1951; s. Raymond Edward and Marian Dunne McBride; m. Karen Marie Wirth, May 29, 1976 (div. Dec. 1984). BS in Chem. and Biology, U. Wis., 1972, JD, 1976; MS in Environ. Engr. Sci., Calif. Inst. Tech., 1973. Bar: Wis. 1976, D.C. 1976. Assoc. LeBoeuf, Lamb, Leiby & MacRae, Washington, 1976-84, ptnr., 1985—. Mem. Fed. Energy Bar Assn., Assn. Transp. Practitioners (vice chmn. eastern transp. law seminar com. 1984, chmn. 1985). Roman Catholic. Club: Chantilly Nat. Golf and Country (Centerville, Va.). Avocations: golf, reading, travel. Federal civil litigation, FERC practice, Nuclear power. Home: 3628 Van Ness St NW Washington DC 20008 Office: LeBoeuf Lamb Leiby & MacRae 1333 New Hampshire Ave NW Washington DC 20036

MCBRIDE, MILFORD LAWRENCE, JR., lawyer; b. Grove City, Pa., July 16, 1923; s. Milford Lawrence and Elizabeth B. (Douthett) McB.; m. Madeleine Coulter, Aug. 6, 1947; children—Marta, Brenda, Trip, Randy, Barry. A.B., Grove City Coll., 1944; B.S., N.Y.U., 1944; J.D., U. Pa., 1949. Bar: Pa. 1949, U.S. Dist. Ct. (we. dist.) Pa. U.S. Supreme Ct. Ptnr., McBride & McBride, Grove City, 1949-77; ptnr. McBride and McNickle, Grove City, 1977-83, sr. ptnr., 1983—; dir., exec. com. 1st Seneca Bank. Served to 1st lt. USAAF, 1943-46. Mem. Mercer County Bar Assn. (state treas. 1970-77), ABA, Am. Bar Found. Republican. Clubs: Oakmont Country, University (Pitts.). Probate, Real property, General corporate. Office: 211 S Center St Grove City PA 16127

MCBROOM, DOUGLAS D., lawyer; b. Vancouver, Wash.; s. Richard Gordon and Mildred (Durgan) McB.; m. Judith Hall, July 9, 1966; children: Kathleen, Maurin. BA, U. Chgo., 1962, JD, 1965; LLM, Northwestern U., 1966. Bar: Wash. 1965, Pa. 1968, U.S. Dist. Ct. (we. dist.) Pa. 1968, U.S. Ct. Appeals (3d cir. 1968), U.S. Dist. Ct. (we. dist.) Wash. 1970, U.S. Ct. Appeals (9th cir.) 1970. Legal advisor Pitts. Bur. Police, 1966-69; asst. U.S. atty. U.S. Dist. Ct. (we. dist.) Pa., Pitts., 1969-70, U.S. Dist. Ct. (we. dist.) Wash., Seattle, 1970-72; chief dep. pros. atty. Pierce County, Tacoma, Wash., 1972-74; assoc. Schroter, Goldmark & Bender P.S., Seattle, 1975-76, ptnr., 1976—; staff counsel State of Ill Legis. Commn. on Low Income Housing, Chgo., 1965-66; cons. Pa. Crime Commn., Pitts., 1968-70; bd. dirs. Wash. State Commn. Law & Justice, Seattle, 1972-75. Author police tng. manual, 1969; contbr. articles to legal publs. Bd. dirs. Mt. Baker Housing Rehab., 1975-78, Downtown Emergency Service Ctr., Seattle, 1985—. Ford Found. fellow Northwestern U., 1965-66. Mem. Assn. Trial Lawyers Am., Wash. State Trial Lawyers Assn., King County Bar Assn., Wash. State Bar Assn. Personal injury, Criminal. Home: 2220 33d Ave S Seattle WA 98144 Office: Schroeter Goldmark & Bender PS 540 Central Bldg Seattle WA 98104

MCBURNEY, CHARLES WALKER, JR., lawyer; b. Orlando, Fla., June 6, 1957; s. Charles Walker McBurney and Jeane (Brown) McBurney Chappell. BA, U. Fla., 1979, JD, 1982. Bar: Fla. 1982, U.S. Dist. Ct. (mid. dist.) Fla. 1983, U.S. Ct. Appeals (11th cir.) 1984. Assoc. Mathews, Osborne, McNatt, Gobelman & Cobb, Jacksonville, Fla., 1982-84; asst. state's atty. State's Atty.'s Office, Jacksonville, 1984—; dir. Serious or Habitual Juvenile Offender Program, 1986—. Chmn. com. congl. campaigns, Jacksonville, 1982, 84. Mem. ABA, Jacksonville Bar Assn., Nat. Dist. Atty.'s Assn., Jacksonville Jaycees (pres. 1986). Democrat. Presbyterian. Juvenile, Criminal. Home: 1871 Dean Rd Jacksonville FL 32216 Office: State Atty's Office Duval County Courthouse Jacksonville FL 32202

MCBURNEY, GEORGE WILLIAM, lawyer; b. Ames, Iowa, Feb. 17, 1926; s. James William and Elfie Hazel (Jones) McB.; m. Georgianna Edwards, Aug. 28, 1949; children: Hollis Lynn, Jana Lee, John Edwards. B.A., State U. Iowa, 1950, J.D. with distinction, 1953. Bar: Iowa 1953, Ill. 1954, Calif. 1985. With Sidley & Austin and predecessor, Chgo., 1953—, ptnr., 1964—; resident ptnr. Singapore, 1982-84. Editor-in-chief: Iowa Law Rev., 1952-53. Mem. Chgo. Crime Commn., 1966-84; trustee Old People's Home of City of Chgo., 1968-83, sec., 1967-69, exec. v.p., 1969-74, pres., 1974-82, hon. life trustee, 1983—; hon. life trustee Georgian, Evanston, Ill., trustee, counsel, 1976-82, v.p., 1980-82. Served with inf. AUS, 1944-46. Fellow Am. Coll. Trial Lawyers; mem. ABA, State Bar of Calif., Los Angeles County Bar Assn., Am. Judicature Soc., Bar Assn. 7th Fed. Circuit, Am. Arbitration Assn. (panel), Assn. Bus. Trial Lawyers, The Los Angeles Ctr. for Internat. Comml. Arbitration Los Angeles (bd. dirs.), Nat. Coll. Edn. (bd. assocs. 1967-84), U.S. C. of C. (govt. and regulatory affairs com. of council on antitrust policy 1980-82), Phi Kappa Psi, Omicron Delta Kappa, Delta Sigma Rho, Phi Delta Phi. Republican. Presbyterian. Clubs: Union League, Mid-Day, Law, Legal (Chgo.); American, Cricket), Town (Singapore); Marina City (Marina del Rey, Calif.). Administrative and regulatory, Antitrust, Federal civil litigation. Home: Malibu Pacifica 13 3601 Vista Pacifica Malibu CA 90265 Office: Sidley & Austin 2049 Century Park E Los Angeles CA 90067

MCCABE, CHARLES KEVIN, lawyer, author; b. Springfield, Ill., Nov. 2, 1952; s. Charles Kenneth and Betty Lou (Williams) McC. B.S. in Aero. and Astronautical Engring. magna cum laude, U. Ill., 1975; J.D., U. Mich., 1978. Bar: Ill. 1978, U.S. Dist. Ct. (no. dist.) Ill. 1978, U.S. Ct. Appeals (7th cir.) 1980. Engring. co-op. student McDonnell Aircraft, St. Louis, 1972-74; chief aerodynamicist Vetter Fairing Co., Rantoul, Ill., 1974-75; assoc. Lord, Bissell, & Brook, Chgo., 1978—. Author: Qwiktran: Quick FORTRAN, 1979; FORTH Fundamentals, 1983; co-author: 32 BASIC Programs, 1981. Contbr. articles on aviation, computers to various mags., 1974—. Nat. Merit scholar U. Ill., Urbana, 1970. Mem. ABA, Ill. State Bar Assn., Chgo. Bar Assn. Aviation, Insurance, Personal injury. Office: Lord Bissell & Brook 115 S LaSalle St Chicago IL 60603

MCCABE, DAVID ALLEN, lawyer; b. N.Y.C., Aug. 2, 1940; s. Charles Bernard and Ruth (Starr) McC.; m. Georgiana Drake Hubbard, Aug. 6, 1966; children: Caroline F., Nicholas D. AB, Princeton U., 1962; LLB, Columbia U., 1966. Bar: N.Y. 1967, U.S. Dist. Ct. (so. dist.) N.Y. 1967. Assoc. Shearman & Sterling, N.Y.C., 1966-74, ptnr., 1974—; bd. dirs. Kanthal Corp., Bethel, Conn., Degussa Corp., Teterboro, N.J., fin. com., 1973—. Mem. ABA, N.Y. State Bar Assn., Assn. of Bar of City of N.Y., German-Am. C. of C. (bd. dirs. 1979-82, 83-86, sec. 1983-86). General corporate, Securities. Office: Shearman & Sterling 53 Wall St New York NY 10005

MCCABE, JAMES J., lawyer; b. Phila., May 8, 1929; A.B., LaSalle Coll., 1951; J.D., Temple U., 1955. Bar: Pa. and fed. cts., 1956, U.S. Supreme Ct. 1971. Assoc., Duane, Morris & Heckscher, Phila., 1955-64, ptnr. 1964—; chmn. litigation dept., 1984—; lectr. med. and ins. law, trial technique Practising Law Inst., N.Y. Law Jour. Seminars, Defense Research Inst.; adj. prof. family medicine Thomas Jefferson U. Sch. Medicine, Phila. Trustee Phila. Bar Found., 1979-81; past pres. St. Thomas More Soc.; vol. in Miss. Lawyers' Com. for Civil Rights, 1968. Fellow Am. Coll. Trial Lawyers, Am. Bd. Profl. Liability Attys.; mem. ABA, Pa. Bar Assn., Phila. Bar Assn., Am. Bd. Trial Advocates (pres. Pa. chpt.), Am. Coll. Legal Medicine, Assn. Ins. Attys., Assn. Defense Counsel Phila. (past pres.), Internat. Assn. Ins. Counsel, Defense Research Inst. (Pa. chmn. 1973-77, v.p. Atlantic region 1977-80, dir. 1980-83). Federal civil litigation, State civil litigation, Insurance. Office: Duane Morris Et Al 1 Franklin Plaza Philadelphia PA 19102

MCCABE, LAWRENCE JAMES, food products manufacturing company executive, lawyer; b. Uniontown, Pa., July 19, 1935; s. Patrick J. and Beatrice A. (Kane) McC.; m. Gretchen Ann Rittmeyer, Apr. 20, 1963; children—Susan M., Megan P., Kevin J., Heather K., Erin Kathleen. B.A., Pa. State U.-State College, 1957; J.D., U. Pitts., 1960. Bar: Pa. 1961, U.S. Dist. Ct. (we. dist.) Pa. 1961. Atty. Duquesne Light Co., Pitts., 1961-66; atty. H.J. Heinz Co., Pitts., 1966-72, asst. gen. counsel, 1972-75, dir. legal affairs, 1975-82, v.p., assoc. gen. counsel, 1982—; lectr. Conf. Am. Legal Execs., San Francisco, 1981, ABA, Boston, 1982. Bd. dirs. Pitts. Council for Internat. Visitors, 1980—, North Hills Passavant Hosp., Pitts., 1980—. Served with U.S. Army, 1960-61. Mem. ABA, Pa. Bar Assn., Allegheny County Bar Assn. Republican. Roman Catholic. Clubs: Wildwood Golf, Duquesne (Pitts.). General corporate, Securities, Private international. Home: 400 Gass Rd Wexford PA 15090 Office: H J Heinz Co 600 Grant St Pittsburgh PA 15219

MCCABE, ROBERT FOURCE, JR., lawyer; b. Pitcairn, Pa., Oct. 12, 1936; s. Robert Fource and Edith (Snee) McC.; m. Charlotte Overly, June 23, 1962; children: Marsha, Lea Anne, Julie. AB, U. Pitts., 1957, JD, 1960. Bar: Pa. 1961, U.S. Supreme Ct. 1969. Sole practice Pitts., 1961—; soliciter Pitcairn Borough, 1967—, Turtle Creek (Pa.) Valley Council Govts., 1976-86. Served with U.S. Army, 1960-63. Mem. ABA, Allegheny County Bar Assn. Club: University (Pitts.). Lodges: Kiwanis (pres. Pitcairn 1967), Masons. Construction, General practice. Home: 106 Himalaya Rd Monroeville PA 15146 Office: 345 4th Ave 200 Standard Life Bldg Pittsburgh PA 15222

MCCABE, STEPHEN M., lawyer; b. N.Y.C., Feb. 26, 1941; s. Henry Patrick and Helen M. (Murphy) McC.; m. Patricia Anne Giesen, Oct. 8, 1967; children—Stephen, William, Timothy, Maureen, Daniel. B.A., Seton Hall U., 1962, J.D., 1965. Bar: N.Y. 1966, U.S. Dist. Cts. (ea. and so. dists.) N.Y. 1967. Assoc., William H. Morris, N.Y.C., 1966-70; ptnr. McCabe & Cozzens, Mineola, N.Y., 1970—. Mem. ABA, N.Y. State Bar Assn., Nassau County Bar Assn., Def. Research Inst., Lawyer Pilots Bar Assn., Internat. Assn. Ins. Counsel. Club: Kiwanis (pres. Rockville Centre, N.Y. 1974-75). Federal civil litigation, Insurance, Personal injury. Office: 131 Mineola Blvd Mineola NY 11501

MCCABE, THOMAS JAMES, lawyer; b. Phila., May 21, 1946; s. James Bernard and Mary Elizabeth (Morton) McC. BA cum laude, La Salle Coll., 1968; JD, U. Idaho, 1979. Bar: Idaho 1980, U.S. Dist. Ct. Idaho 1980, U.S. Ct. Appeals (9th cir.) 1981. Law clk. to chief justice U.S. Dist. Ct. Idaho, Boise, 1980-81; assoc. Nelson & Westberg Chartered, Boise, 1981-82; ptnr. Nelson, Westberg & McCabe Chartered, Boise, 1982-85, Westberg & McCabe, Boise, 1985—; mem. Idaho misdemeanor rulesadv. com., 1984—, Criminal Ct. advisory commn., Boise, 1985—. Co-author: Advanced Drinking/Driving Litigation in Idaho, 1986. Served to capt. U.S. Army, 1968-71, Vietnam. Recipient Medal for Excellence in Adv. Am. Coll. Trial Lawyers, 1977. Mem. ABA, Idaho Bar Assn., Nat. Assn. Criminal Def. Lawyers, Nat. Orgn. Social Security Claimant's Reps., Idaho Trial Lawyers Assn., The Adv. (edit. adv. com. 1983, chmn. 1985—), Order of Barristers. Avocations: writing, skiing, bird watching, swimming. Criminal, Civil rights, Personal injury. Office: Westberg & McCabe PO Box 2836 Boise ID 83701

MCCAFFREY, CARLYN SUNDBERG, lawyer; b. N.Y.C., Jan. 7, 1942; d. Carl Andrew Lawrence and Evelyn (Back) Sundberg; m. John P. McCaffrey, May 24, 1967; children: John C., Patrick, Jennifer, Kathleen. AB in Econs., George Washington U., 1962; postgrad., Barnard Coll., 1962-63; LLB cum laude, NYU, 1967, LLM in Taxation, 1970. Bar: N.Y. 1974. Law clk. to presiding justice Calif. Supreme Ct., 1967-68; teaching fellow law NYU, N.Y.C., 1968-70, asst. prof. law, 1970-74; assoc. Weil, Gotshal & Manges, N.Y.C., 1974-80, ptnr., 1980—; prof. in residence Rubin Hall NYU, 1971-75; adj. prof. law NYU, 1975—, U. Miami, 1979-81, 83—; lectr. in field. Contbr. articles to profl. jours. Mem. ABA (chmn. generationskipping trusts-drafting 1979-81, real property probate and trust law sect.), N.Y. State Bar Assn. (exec. com. tax. sect. 1979-80, chmn. estate and gift tax com. 1976-78, life ins. com. 1983—, trusts and estates sect.), Assn. of Bar of City of N.Y. (matrimonial law com., chmn. tax subcom. 1984—). Probate, Family and matrimonial. Home: 38 Sidney Pl Brooklyn NY 11201 Office: Weil Gotshal & Manges 767 Fifth Ave New York NY 10153

MCCAFFREY, JUDITH E., lawyer; b. Providence, Apr. 26, 1944; d. Charles V. and Isadore Frances (Langford) McC.; m. Martin D. Minsker, Dec. 31, 1969 (div. May 1981); children: Ethan Hart Minsker, Natasha Langford Minsker. BA, Tufts U., 1966; JD, Boston U., 1970. Bar: Mass. 1970, D.C. 1972. Assoc. Sullivan & Worcester, Washington, 1970-76; atty. FDIC, Washington, 1976-78; assoc. Dechert, Price & Rhoads, Washington, 1978-82, McKenna, Conner & Cuneo, Washington, 1982-83; gen. counsel, corp. sec. Perpetual Savs. Bank, FSB, Alexandria, Va., 1983—. Contbr. articles to profl. jours. Mem. edn. com. Bd. Trade, Washington, 1986—; chairperson annual fundraising campaign Sch. Without Walls, Washington, 1987. Mem. ABA (chairperson subcom. thrift instns. 1985—), Feb. Bar Assn. (exec. com., banking law com. 1985—), U.S. League (vice chairperson lawyers' com. 1986), D.C. Bar Assn. (bd. govs. 1981-85), Women's Bar Assn. (pres. 1980-81). Democrat. Episcopalian. Club: Kenwood Country (Chevy Chase, Md.). Avocations: skiing, travel, tennis, reading, golf. Office: Perpetual Savs Bank FSB 2034 Eisenhower Ave Alexandria VA 22314

MCCAIN, LYNN, lawyer; b. Gadsden, Ala., Oct. 11, 1955; d. J.C. McCain Jr. and Nelta A. (Faulkner) McC.; m. Tony L. Walley, Apr. 25, 1986. BA, U. Ala., 1978, JD, 1982. Bar: Ala. 1982, Fla. 1983. Mem. ABA, Ala. Bar Assn. (exec. com. young lawyers sect. 1983—), Etowah County Bar Assn., Am. Assn. Univ. Women (pres. 1985—). Republican. Baptist. Avocations: running, swimming. Office: Simmons Ford & Brunson 1411 Rainbow Dr Gadsden AL 35902

MCCALEB, JOE WALLACE, lawyer; b. Nashville, Dec. 9, 1941; s. J.W. and Marjoire June (Hudson) McC.; m. Glenda Jean, June 26, 1965. B.A., Union U., Jackson, Tenn., 1964; postgrad. George Peabody Coll., 1965-66; J.D., Memphis State U., 1970. Bar: Tenn. 1971, U.S. Sup. Ct. 1978. Law clk. assoc. justice Tenn. Sup. Ct., 1970-71; staff atty. dept. pub. health bur. environ. service State of Tenn., 1971-77; sole practice, Hendersonville, Tenn., 1977—. Bd. dirs. Summer County (Tenn.) Humane Soc., chmn., 1980-81. Mem. ABA, Tenn. Bar Assn., Tenn. Trial Lawyers Assn., Summer County Bar Assn., Sierra Club (chmn. 1982), Phi Delta Phi. Baptist. Club: Exchange (pres. 1985-86) (Hendersonville). State civil litigation, Environment, Personal injury. Office: 118 Old Shackle Island Rd Hendersonville TN 37075

MCCALL, DAVID BLAIR, lawyer; b. Abilene, Tex., Sept. 24, 1948; s. C.W. and Clarice F. (Blair) McC.; m. Janet Hale, Feb. 13, 1982. B, McMurray Coll., 1971; JD, Tex. Tech U., 1974. Bar: Tex. 1974, U.S. Dist. Ct. (no. dist.) Tex. 1975, U.S. Supreme Ct. 1977. Staff atty. Phillips Petroleum Co., Amarillo, Tex., 1974-78, Tex. Oil and Gas Co., Dallas, 1978-80; mng. ptnr. Lynch, Chappell, Allday & Alsup, Austin, 1980—. Deacon Blu Bonnet Hills Christian Ch., Austin, 1985—; Rep. alt. del., Austin, 1986—. Mem. ABA, Tex. Bar Assn. Club: Lost Creek City, Barton Creek Ct. (Austin). Avocations: reading, swimming. Oil and gas leasing. Home: 1513 Ben Crenshaw Austin TX 78746 Office: Lynch Chappell Allday & Alsup 900 Littlefield Bldg Austin TX 78701

MCCALL, HARRY, lawyer; b. New Orleans, Nov. 27, 1915; s. Harry and Lilia (Kennard) McC.; m. Evelyn B. Peck, June 15, 1942; children: Richard E., Jonathan C. AB, Princeton U., 1936; LLB, Tulane U., 1939, ArtsD (hon.), 1985. Bar: La., U.S. Dist. Ct. La., U.S. Ct. Appeals (5th cir.), U.S. Supreme Ct. 1967. From assoc. to ptnr. Chaffe, McCall, Phillips, Toler & Sarpy, New Orleans, 1939—; bd. dirs. D.H. Holmes Co., New Orleans. Bd. govs. ARC, 1982—; Tulane Med. Ctr., New Orleans, 1969-83, chmn., 1977-83; mem. bd. Liquidation City Debt, Seerage and Water Bd., New Orleans, 1971-84, pres. pro tem, 1980-82; various philanthropic and ednl. insts. Served to capt. AGD, 1941-45. Mem. Am. Coll. Trial Lawyers, Am. Probate Counsel. Roman Catholic. Clubs: Boston, Pickwick, New Orleans Country (New Orleans); Princeton (N.Y.C.). Federal civil litigation, State civil litigation, General practice. Office: Chaffe McCall et al 1500 FNBC Bldg New Orleans LA 70112

MCCALL, PATRICK ANTHONY, lawyer, educator; b. Santa Barbara, Calif., Feb. 9, 1958; s. Verlin Ralph and Sally M. (Recupio) McC.; m. Christina M. (Campbell), Aug. 25, 1984; 1 child, Brittany Ann. BS, Calif. State U., Long Beach, 1979; JD, Western State U., 1982. Bar: Calif. 1983, U.S. Dist. Ct. (cen. and ea. dists.) Calif. 1983, U.S. Ct. Appeals (9th cir.) 1983. Ptnr. Lais & McCall, Santa Ana, Calif., 1982—; adj. prof. Saddleback Coll., Mission Viejo, Calif., 1985—; judge protempore Superior Ct. Calif., Riverside County, 1986—. Mem. Calif. Bar Assn., Orange County Bar Assn. (chmn. Bridging the Gap com. 1986), Orange County Barristers, Calif. Trial Lawyers Assn. (chmn. family law symposium com. 1985), Calif. Bd. Legal Specialization (cert. family law specialist). Republican. Roman Catholic. Avocations: commercial pilot, profl. skiier. Family and matrimonial, State civil litigation, Personal injury. Office: Lais & McCall 1200 N Main St #916 Santa Ana CA 92701

MCCALLIE, SPENCER WYATT, lawyer; b. Ft. Benning, Ga., July 11, 1944; s. Thomas Hooke and Eleanor Augusta (Wyatt) McC.; m. Joan M. Schwartz, Nov. 13, 1971; children: Katherine Rachel, Allison Elyse. AB, U. N.C., 1966; JD, Yale U., 1974. Bar: Colo. 1974. Commd. ensign USN, 1966, advanced through grades to lt., 1970, resigned, 1971; assoc. Holland & Hart, Denver, 1974-77; assoc. corp. counsel Manville Corp., Denver, 1977-84; gen. counsel CH2M Hill, Denver, 1984—; bd. dirs. Iotech, Inc., Northglenn, Colo. Mem. ABA, Am. Corp. Counsel Assn., Colo. Bar Assn., Denver Bar Assn., Denver C. of C. (chmn. surface transp. task force 1982—). Presbyterian. Clubs: Eastmoor, Metropolitan (Denver). General corporate, Engineering contracts and services, Insurance. Home: 4150 S Pontiac Denver CO 80237 Office: CH2M Hill PO Box 22508 Denver CO 80222

MCCALLUM, ALBERT DONALD, lawyer; b. Ottawa County, Mich., June 30, 1938; s. Homer Donald and B. Evelyn (Starks) McC.; m. Arlona L. Toman, Nov. 2, 1963; children: Adah, Donald, David. BCE, Mich. State U., 1962; JD cum laude, U. Mich., 1967. Bar: Mich. 1968. Assoc. Aten & Townsend, Jackson, Mich., 1967-70; engr. highway dept. State of Mich., Lansing, 1962-64; atty. Consumers Power Co., Jackson, 1970-86, sr. atty., 1986—. Trustee Napoleon (Mich.) Sch. Bd., 1969-70, v.p., 1970-71, pres. 1971-73; mem. Jackson Sch. Officials Assn., 1970-72. Mem. Mich. State Bar Assn. (oil and gas com. 1975-83), Chi Epsilon. Republican. Contracts commercial, Oil and gas leasing, Real property. Home: 18440 29 1/2 Mile Rd Springport MI 49284 Office: Consumers Power Co 212 W Michigan Ave Jackson MI 49201

MCCALLUM, BARBARA EILAND, lawyer; b. Fresno, Calif., Jan. 1, 1938; d. Edward Marvin Walker and Alma Bernice (Pratt) Rubes; m. Murray Lee Eiland, Feb. 25, 1955 (div. 1965); m. Donald George McCallum, Apr. 28, 1970. JD, U. Pacific, 1967. Bar: Calif., U.S. Dist. Ct. (no. and ea. dists.) Calif. 1967, U.S. Ct. Appeals (9th cir.). Atty. Coben & Eiland, Sacramento, 1967-68; sole practice Sacramento, 1968-70; ptnr. Wong, McCallum & McCallum, Sacramento, 1970-74, McCallum & McCallum, Sacramento, 1974—; atty. State Bar Vol. Legal Services, Sacramento, 1984—. Columnist: The Ethics Corner, Family Law News, 1970s. Mem., parliamentarian El Dorado Dem. Cen. Com., 1974-78; chairperson El Dorado County Commn. on Status of Women, 1978-79, 85—; mem. Calif. Senate Select Com. on Long Range Planning's Indsl. Competitiveness Task Force, 1985-86; mem. Nat. Panel Arbitrators Better Bus. Bur. Recipient Soroptimist Women Helping Women award, 1977, 79-80, 85-86. Mem. Women Lawyers Sacramento (past. pres.), Placerville Bus. and Profl. Women (pres. 1977-78), Capital Dist. Bus. and Profl. Women (pres. 1981-82, Woman of Achievement award 1980), El Dorado Women's Info. Ctr. (pres. 1979-84), Sacramento Community Commn. Women (past pres.), Calif. Legis. Roundtable (past vice chair), Nat. Women Lawyers, Calif. Women Lawyers, Sacramento County Bar Assn. (council mem. 1971-72, 80-82), Internat. Women Lawyers (past world council mem.), Calif. Fedn. Bus. Profl. Women (writer, editor newsletter 1980, writer legis. column 1980-85, writer newspaper 1986, legis. adv. 1975—). Club: Comstock (Calif.). Avocations: legis. advocacy, reading, oil painting, rug making. Family and matrimonial, Probate, Legislative. Office: 901 H St Suite 310 Sacramento CA 95814

MC CALLUM, CHARLES EDWARD, lawyer; b. Memphis, Mar. 13, 1939; s. Edward Payson and India Raimelle (Musick) McC.; m. Lois Ann Gowell Temple, Nov. 30, 1985; children—Florence Andrea, Printha Kyle, Chandler Ward Payson. B.S., MIT, 1960; J.D., Vanderbilt U., 1964. Bar: Mich. 1964. Assoc. Warner, Norcross & Judd, Grand Rapids, Mich., 1964-69, ptnr., 1969—; rep. assemblyman State Bar Mich., 1973-78; lectr. continuing legal edn. programs. Chmn. Grand Rapids Area Transit Authority, 1976-79, mem., 1972-79; regional v.p. Nat. Mcpl. League, 1978-86, mem. council, 1971-78; pres. Grand Rapids Art Mus., 1979-81, trustee, 1976-83; chmn. Butterworth Hosp., 1979—, trustee, 1977—; vice chmn. Citizens Com. for Consolidation of Govt. Services, 1981-82, chmn., 1984-86, ednl. counselor MIT, 1974—; nat. chmn. devel. com. Vanderbilt U. Law Sch., 1977-78; trustee Kent Med. Found., 1979-82; dir. Vol. Trustees of Not-for-Profit Hosps., 1983—, vice chmn., 1986—. Woodrow Wilson fellow, 1960-61; Fulbright scholar U. Manchester, Eng., 1960-61. Mem. ABA, Tenn. Bar Assn., Mich. Bar Assn. (sec., council mem., corp., fin. and bus. law sect.), Grand Rapids Bar Assn., Grand Rapids C. of C. (pres. 1975, dir. 1970-76), Order of Coif, Sigma Xi. Clubs: Kent Country, Grand Rapids Athletic, Peninsular, University. Securities, General corporate, Health. Home: 1346 Cornell Ave SE Grand Rapids MI 49506 Office: 900 Old Kent Bldg 1 Vandenberg Center Grand Rapids MI 49503

MCCALPIN, FRANCIS WILLIAM, lawyer; b. St. Louis, Nov. 8, 1921; s. George Ambrose and Marguerite (Miles) McC.; m. Margaret Wickes, Feb. 27, 1954; children: Martha McCalpin Boyd, William Francis, Katherine McCalpin Winfrey, Lucy McCalpin Hejlek, David Christopher. A.B., St. Louis U., 1943; LL.B., Harvard U., 1948. Bar: Mo. 1948, Ill. 1953. Since practiced in St. Louis; mem. firm Lewis & Rice, 1948—; sec., bd. dirs. Hardy Investment Co.; bd. dirs. Color Process Co.; mem. nat. adv. com. to legal services program Office Econ. Opportunity, 1965-73; mem. Mo. Coordinating Bd. Higher Edn., 1974-82, chmn., 1974; dir. Legal Services Corp., 1979-81, chmn. bd., 1980-81. Trustee, sec. St. Louis Ednl. TV Commn. KETC-TV, 1965-72; trustee Jr. Coll. Dist. St. Louis, 1962-65, St. Louis U., 1972-74; bd. dirs. Family and Childrens Service Greater St. Louis, 1972-78, 79-85, v.p., 1979-85; bd. dirs. Am. Bar Found., 1976-87, v.p., 1982-84, pres., 1984-86, chmn. fellows, 1976-77. Served with USMCR, 1942-46, 50-51. Mem. ABA (chmn. spl. com. on availabilty of legal services 1965-70, chmn. spl. com. on prepaid legal services 1970-73, chmn. standing com. on legal aid and indigent defendants 1973-76, 83-85, asst. sec. 1975-79, sec. 1979-83), Ill. Bar Assn., Mo. Bar Integrated (gov. 1967-73), Bar Assn. St. Louis (pres. 1961-62), Nat. Conf. Bar Presidents (treas. 1970-71, pres. 1973-74). Club: Harvard (St. Louis). Federal civil litigation, State civil litigation, General corporate. Home: 215 N Berry Rd St Louis MO 63122 Office: 611 Olive St Saint Louis MO 63101

MCCAMLEY, JOHN EDWARD, lawyer; b. Philipsburg, Pa., July 25, 1951; s. John Joseph and Miriam Louise (Burns) McC.; children: Lorien Shannon, Bryan William; m. Barbara Lynn Cantone, Mar. 17, 1984; children: Lori Lynn, Kerri Lee. BA, U. Colo., 1973; JD, Western State U., 1979. Bar: Vt. 1981, U.S. Dist. Ct. Vt. 1981. Assoc. Abatiell & Abatiell, Rutland, Vt., 1979-84, Law Offices of Carl O. Anderson PC, Rutland, 1984-85; sole practice Rutland, 1985—; mortgage loan officer Vt. Mortgage Group, Inc., Rutland, 1986. Adv. bd. Ret. Sr. Vol. Program, Rutland, 1986; advisor Green Mountain council Boy Scouts Am., Wallingford, Vt., 1986. Mem. ABA, Vt. Bar Assn. Real property, Personal injury, Contracts commercial. Office: 135 N Main St Rutland VT 05701

MCCANDLESS, JEFFRY SCOTT, lawyer; b. Kansas City, Mo., Apr. 14, 1954; s. Donald Eugene and June Marie (Winer) McC.; m. Elizabeth Ann Waugh, Nov. 3, 1984. JD, Washington & Lee U., 1979. Bar: Mo. 1979, U.S. Dist. Ct. (we. dist.) Mo. 1979. Assoc., then ptnr. Shook, Hardy & Bacon, Kansas City, Mo., 1979—. Contbr. articles to Kansas City Mag., 1985. Republican. Avocations: reading, writing, baseball. Real property, General corporate. Home: 629 W 63d Kansas City MO 64113 Office: Shook Hardy & Bacon 120 W 12th St Suite 600 Kansas City MO 64105

MCCANN, CLIFTON EVERETT, lawyer; b. Des Moines, July 11, 1950; s. George Lockhart and Evelyn Elizabeth (Miller) McC.; m. Marcia Ellen

Morrow, Feb. 19, 1984; 1 child, Gregory Lockhart. BA in Psychology, No. Ill. U., 1972; JD, Columbus Sch. Law, 1977; LLM in Intellectual Property, George Washington U., 1985. Bar: Va. 1978, U.S. Patent Office 1979, U.S. Ct. Appeals (fed. cir.) 1982, U.S. Supreme Ct. 1983, D.C. 1984, U.S. Dist. Ct. (ea. dist.) Va. 1984. Assoc. Beveridge, DeGrandi & Kline, Washington, 1977-83; ptnr. Lane & Aitken, Washington, 1983—; counsel intellectual property Am. Mensa, Ltd., N.Y.C., 1984—. Mem. ABA, Va. Bar Assn., D.C. Bar Assn. (chmn. trademark com. 1985—), Bar Assn. D.C. (steering com. 1986—), Am. Intellectual Property Law Assn., Patent Lawyer's Club, Delta Theta Phi. Trademark and copyright. Home: 3611 Quesada St NW Washington DC 20015 Office: Lane & Aitken 2600 Virginia Ave NW Washington DC 20037

MCCANN, JOHN ANTHONY, lawyer; b. N.Y.C., Sept. 23, 1954; s. Anthony Joseph and Margaret Theresa (Reiss) McC.; m. Jeanne Louise Marcarelli, Aug. 22, 1981; 1 child, Deirdre Jeanne. BA in Polit. Sci., SUNY, Binghampton, 1977; JD, Harvard U., 1980. Bar: D.C. 1981, Va. 1982. Atty. Dept. Health and Human Services, Washington, 1980-84; exec. dir. Affiliated Leadership League, Washington, 1984-86; commr. Va. Dept. Visually Handicapped, Richmond, 1986—. Pres. Old Dominion Council the Blind and Visually Impaired, Richmond, 1985. Mem. ABA. Democrat. Roman Catholic. Avocation: amateur radio operator. Advocacy. Office: Va Dept for Visually Handicapped 397 Azalea Ave Richmond VA 23227

MCCANN, JOSEPH LEO, lawyer, government official; b. Phila., Aug. 27, 1948; s. Joseph John and Christina Mary (Kirwan) McC.; m. Aida L. Kabigting, Dec. 6, 1986. B.A., St. Charles Sem., Phila., 1970, postgrad. in theology, 1970-71; M.A., Temple U., 1975, J.D., 1977. Bar: Pa. 1977, U.S. Dist. Ct. (ea. dist.) Pa. 1977, U.S. Dist. Ct. (mid. dist.) Pa. 1978, U.S. Ct. Appeals (3d cir.) 1978, D.C. 1986, U.S. Supreme Ct. 1986, Md. 1987. Law clk. to chief justice Pa. Supreme Ct., Phila., 1977-78; dep. atty. gen. Pa. Dept. Justice, Harrisburg, 1978-80; atty. U.S. GAO, Washington, 1980—. Mem. ABA, Pa. Bar Assn., Phila. Bar Assn., D.C. Bar Assn., Md. Bar Assn. Roman Catholic. Labor, Pension, profit-sharing, and employee benefits, Legislative. Home: 713 Monroe St Apt 301 Rockville MD 20850 Office: Office of Gen Counsel US Gen Acctg Office 441 G St NW Washington DC 20548

MCCANN, RICHARD EUGENE, lawyer; b. Billings, Mont., Aug. 14, 1939; s. Oakey O. and Edith May (Miller) McC.; m. Mona N. Miyagishima, Apr. 27, 1964; children: Tami, Todd, Jennifer. BA magna cum laude, Rocky Mountain Coll., 1965; JD with high honors, U. Mont., 1972. Bar: Mont. 1972, Washington 1977, Ala. 1982. Law clk. to presiding justice U.S. Dist. Ct., Billings, 1972-73; assoc. Crowley, Haughey, Hansen, Toole & Dietrich, Billings, 1973-77; assoc. Perkins Coie, Seattle, 1977-80, ptnr., 1980—; ptnr. Perkins Coie, Anchorage, 1982—. Contbr. articles to profl. jours. Trustee Rocky Mountain Coll., Billings, 1973-77. Served with USN, 1957-61. Mem. ABA, Mont. Bar Assn., Wash. Bar Assn., Alaska Bar Assn. Environment, Real property. Office: Perkins Coie 1029 W 3d Ave Anchorage AK 99501

MCCANN, WILLIAM ROBERT, lawyer, consultant; b. Tyndall, S.D., Dec. 4, 1909; s. William George and Emma Dean (Abbott) McC.; m. Elizabeth Joyce Sparks, Feb. 11, 1939; children: William Robert Jr., Michael S., Vernon Charles, James. BA, U. S.D., 1931, JD magna cum laude, 1939. Ptnr. McCann, Martin & McCann, Brookings, S.D.; chmn. bd. bar examiners S.D., 1958-63; pres. State Bar S.D., 1971; states atty. Brookings (S.D.) County, 1947-51, 57-59. Rep. S.D. Legis., Pierre, 1943-45; mem. Brookings Sch. Bd., 1953-59; v.p. local charities and corrections, State of S.D., 1961-73. Served with USN, 1944-46, PTO. Recipient McKusick award U. S.D. Fellow Am. Bar Found.; mem. ABA (ho. of dels. 1972-78). Republican. Presbyterian. Lodges: Kiwanis (pres. 1950), Masons. General practice. Home: 1007 6th Ave Brookings SD 57006

MCCANN, WILLIAM VERN, JR., lawyer; b. Lewiston, Idaho, June 10, 1943; s. William V. and Anna Gertrude (Hoss) McC.; m. Judith Anna Sodorff, June 26, 1966; children: Malinda Ann, William Vern III. BS in Bus., U. Idaho, 1966, JD, 1969. Bar: Idaho 1969, U.S. Dist. Ct. Idaho 1969, U.S. Supreme Ct. 1974. Sole practice Lewiston, 1969—. Pres. Lewiston Roundup Assn., 1978, 86. Mem. Idaho Bar Assn. (commr. 1983-86, pres. 1985-86), Clearwater Bar Assn. (v.p. 1980, pres. 1981-83), Lawyer-Pilot Bar Assn., Idaho Law Found. (sponsor), U.S. Jaycees (v.p. 1974-75, legal counsel 1975-76, ambassdor 1974, Hall of Leadership 1984), Jaycees Internat. (senator 1973) Idaho Jaycees (pres. 1973-74), Lewiston Jaycees (pres. 1971-72, Distinguished Services award 1979), Phoenix Jaycees (Sam Reed Meml. award 1981). Club: Lewiston Chamber (3d v.p. 1984-85, 2d v.p. 1985-86). Lodge: Elks. General corporate, Probate, Real property. Office: 1027 Bryden Lewiston ID 83501

MCCARTEN, PAUL VINCENT, lawyer; b. Alexandria, Minn., June 30, 1949; s. John James and Maureen A. (Riley) McC. BBA, Creighton U., 1971, JD, 1974. Bar: Minn. 1974, Nebr. 1974, U.S. Dist. Ct. Minn. 1976. Jud. law clk. Hennepin County Dist. Ct., Mpls., 1974-76; ptnr. Tillitt, McCarten, Johnson & Drummond Ltd. and predecessor firms, Alexandria, 1976—. Del., state cen. com. mem. Minn. Dems. Farmer-Labor Com. Mem. Minn. Bar Assn. (del. 1982-86), Nebr. Bar Assn., Douglas County Bar Assn. (pres. 1985—), Assn. Trial Lawyers Am., Minn. Trial Lawyers Assn. (bd. of govs. 1986—). Roman Catholic. Clubs: Mpls. Athletic, Alexandria Country. Avocations: running, sailing, skiing. Personal injury. Home: PO Box 506 Alexandria MN 56308 Office: Tillitt McCarten Johnson & Drummond Ltd 801 Broadway PO Box 188 Alexandria MN 56308

MCCARTER, CHARLES CHASE, lawyer; b. Pleasanton, Kans., Mar. 17, 1926; s. Charles Nelson and Donna (Chase) McC.; m. Clarice Blanchard, June 25, 1950; children—Charles Kevin, Cheryl Ann. B.A., Principia Coll., Elsah, Ill., 1950; J.D., Washburn U., Topeka, 1953; LL.M., Yale U., 1954, vis. scholar, 1980. Bar: Kans. 1953, Mo. 1968, U.S. Supreme Ct. 1962. Asst. atty. gen. State of Kans., 1954-57; lectr. law Washburn U. Law Sch., 1956-57; appellate counsel FCC, Washington, 1957-58; assoc. Weigand, Curfman, Brainerd, Harris & Kaufman, Wichita, 1958-61; gen. counsel Kans. Corp. Commn., 1961-63; ptnr. McCarter, Frizzel & Wettig, Wichita, 1963-68, McCarter & Badger, Wichita, 1968-73; pvt. practice St. Louis, 1968-76; ptnr. McCarter & Greenley, St. Louis, 1976—; mng. ptnr. Gage & Tucker, St. Louis, 1985—; prof. law, assoc. dir. Nat. Energy Law and Policy Inst., Tulsa U. Law Sch., 1977-79; prof. law, coach Nat. Moot Ct., Stetson U. Coll. Law, St. Petersburg, Fla., 1980-84; mem. govtl. adv. council Gulf Oil Corp., 1977—; legal com. Interstate Oil Compact Commn. Co-author: Missouri Lawyers Guide. Assoc. editor: Washburn U. Law Rev., 1952-53; contbr. articles to profl. jours. Chmn. Wichita Human Relations Devel. Adv. Bd., 1967-68; bd. dirs. Peace Haven Assn. Served with USNR, 1944-46. Recipient Nat. Moot Ct. award Washburn U., 1953, Excellent Prof. award U. Tulsa Law Sch., 1979. Mem. Am. Bar Assn., Kans. Bar Assn., Mo. Bar Assn., Am. Legion, VFW, Native Sons and Daus. Kans (pres. 1957-58), Kappa Sigma, Delta Theta Phi. Republican. Club: Principia Dads (pres.). Office: 7733 Forsyth Blvd Saint Louis MO 63105

MCCARTER, LOWELL HAROLD, lawyer; b. Alma, Mich., Aug. 4, 1934; s. Donal Liston and Ruby Anna (Porter) McC.; m. Mary Ann Dalton, Nov. 30, 1963; children: Martin Devroe, Michael Lowell. BS in Chem. Engring., Purdue U., 1957; JD, John Marshall Law Sch., 1962; MBA, Northeastern U., 1987. Bar: Ind. 1962, Ill. 1962, U.S. Patent Office 1963, Mich. 1965, Mass. 1968. Assoc. patent counsel BASF Wyandotte (Mich.) Chem. Co., 1964-67; patent counsel Kennecott Corp., Lexington, Mass., 1967-77, W.R. Grace & Co. Cambridge, Mass., 1977-80, Instrumentation Lab., Lexington, 1980-87; mgr. legal affairs Genzyme Corp., Boston, 1987—; instr. bus. law Middlesex Community Coll., Bedford, Mass., 1976. chmn. Town Bldg. Com., Carlisle, Mass., 1972-74; coach Town Recreation Program, Carlisle, 1974-79; umpire Town Recreation Baseball Program, Carlisle, 1980-82. Served with U.S. Army, 1959. Mem. Am. Intellectual Property Law Assn., Boston Patent Law Assn. (bd. govs. inventors, chmn. recognition com. 1982—), Inventors Assn. New Eng., Phi Alpha Delta. Patent, Trademark and copyright. Home: 150 Peter Hans Rd Carlisle MA 01741 Office: Genzyme Corp 75 Kneeland St Boston MA 02111

MCCARTHY, CATHERINE FRANCES, lawyer; b. N.Y.C., Feb. 13, 1921; d. Joseph J. and Eva E. (Berger) McC.; m. Peter Donald Andreoli, Aug. 25,

1945; children—Peter, Brian, Catherine, Christine, Francine. B.S., St. John's U., 1941, LL.B., 1943; Bar.: N.Y. 1943, U.S. Supreme Ct. 1966. Assoc. Spencer, Ordway & Wierum, 1942-50; sole practice, N.Y.C. and Pelham, N.Y., 1950-67; real estate atty. Gen. Foods Corp., White Plains, N.Y., 1967-68, trademark atty., 1968-73, chief trademark counsel, 1973-81, dir. legal services-trademarks, 1981—. Recent decisions editor St. John's Law Rev., 1942-43. Mem. ABA, Assn. Bar City N.Y., N.Y. State Bar Assn., Westchester County Bar Assn., Westchester-Fairfield Corp. Counsel Assn., U.S. Trademark Assn. (dir. 1976-80). Trademark and copyright, Federal civil litigation. Home: 134 Harmon Ave Pelham NY 10803 Office: 250 North St White Plains NY 10625

MCCARTHY, FRANCIS JAMES, insurance company executive; b. N.Y.C., Aug. 8, 1918; s. Eugene T. and Louise C. (Wacker) McC.; m. Barbara Ellen Cheney, Jan. 19, 1942; children—Morrison, Melissa. A.B. with honors and distinction, Wesleyan U., Middletown, Conn., 1940; J.D., Yale U., 1947; grad., Nat. Jud. Coll., 1975. Bar: Conn. bar 1947. With law dept. Travelers Ins. Cos., Hartford, 1947-74; asso. firm Maxwell & Dully, Hartford, 1947-62; judge Conn. Superior Ct., 1974-76; sr. v.p. gen. counsel Travelers Ins. Cos., 1976-85, legal cons., 1985—; counsel Skelley, Clifford, Vinkels, Williams & Rottner, Hartford, 1986—; chief counsel joint spl. com. inquiry into criminal investigation and intelligence Conn. Gen. Assembly, 1985-86, task force on jud. adminstrn., 1986-87; trial referee State of Conn., 1984—; lectr. U. Conn. Law Sch.; bd. dirs. Conn. Correctional Ombudsman Corp., 1987—, chmn. bd. dirs., 1987—. Contbr. articles to profl. jours. Chmn. Wethersfield (Conn.) Zoning Commn., 1958-59; charter mem. Capitol Region Planning Agy., 1958-60; mayor, chmn. Wethersfield Town Council, 1962-66; mem. Conn. Ho. of Reps. from 22d dist., 1967-71, chief counsel house and senate minority, 1972, majority, 1973; corporator St. Francis Hosp., Hartford.; adv. bd. Conn. Environ. Mediation Center; co-chmn. Conn. Atty. Gen.'s Blue Ribbon Commn.; bd. dirs. Neighborhood Legal Services, 1984—, chmn. bd. dirs., 1987. Fellow Am. Bar Found.; mem. ABA (lawyers conf. state rep. jud. adminstrn. div., v.p. lawyers responsibility com. tort and ins. practice sect.), Assn. Life Ins. Counsel, Conn. Bar Assn., Hartford County Bar Assn., Conn. Bar Found. (bd. dirs.), Sigma Chi. Republican. Club: Ocean Reef (Key Largo, Fla.). General corporate. Home: 19 Coleman Rd Wethersfield CT 06109 Office: Travelers Indemnity Co 1 Tower Sq Hartford CT 06115

MCCARTHY, J. THOMAS, lawyer, educator; b. Detroit, July 2, 1937; s. John E. and Virginia M. (Hanlon) McC.; m. Nancy Irene Orrell, July 10, 1976. B.S., U. Detroit, 1960; J.D., U. Mich., 1963. Bar: Calif. 1964. Assoc. Julian Caplan, San Francisco, 1963-66; prof. law U. San Francisco, 1966—; vis. prof. law Univ. Coll., Dublin, summer 1975; vis. prof. law U. Calif. Berkeley, 1976-77, Davis, 1979-80; vis. prof. law Monash U., Melbourne, Australia, 1985; cons. in field. Author: McCarthy on Trademarks and Unfair Competition, 2 vols., 1973, 2d edit., 1984; (with Oppenheim and Weston) Federal Antitrust Laws, 1981, McCarthy on Rights of Publicity and Privacy, 1987; mem. editorial bd. Trademark Reporter. Mem. Calif. Atty. Gen.'s Consumer Protection Task Force, 1970-78; mem. adv. bd. Bur. Nat. Affairs, 1978-87. Recipient Rossman award Patent Office Soc., 1979. Mem. Am. Intellectual Property Law Assn. (Watson award 1965), Internat. Assn. for Advancement of Teaching and Research in Intellectual Property, Am. Law Inst. (adv. com. on restatement of law of unfair competition), IEEE. Trademark and copyright, Antitrust, Patent.

MCCARTHY, JOHN CHARLES, lawyer; b. Chgo., Nov. 14, 1923; s. Thomas James and Margaret Mary (Schollmeyer) McC.; m. Lorraine Mary Donovan; children—Michael, Mary Pat, Sheila. Student Miami U., Oxford, Ohio, 1942-44; B.S. in Bus., U. So. Calif., 1947; J.D., UCLA, 1952. Bar: Calif. 1953, U.S. Dist. Ct. (cen. dist.) Calif. 1953, U.S. Ct. Appeals (9th cir.) 1973, U.S. Supreme Ct. 1964. Ptnr., Young, Henrie & McCarthy, Claremont, Calif., 1954-63, 66-75; sole practice, Claremont, 1975—; dir. Peace Corps, Thailand, 1963-66. Author: Successful Techniques in Handling Bad Faith Cases, 1973; Punitive Damages in Bad Faith Cases, 1976, 4th edit., 1987; Punitive Damages in Wrongful Discharge Cases, 1985. Named Alumnus of Yr., UCLA Law Sch., 1973. Insurance bad faith, Wrongful discharge, Commercial bad faith. Office: 401 Harvard Ave Claremont CA 91711

MCCARTHY, JOHN FRANCIS, lawyer; b. Providence, Jan. 14, 1909; s. John Henry and Alice Vincent (Degnan) McC.; m. Margaret Nancy Kane, Nov. 9, 1935; children—Nancy J., Mary A. McCarthy Spain, John J., James E. Ph.B., U. Chgo., 1930, J.D., 1932. Bar: Ill. 1932, U.S. Supt. Ct. 1949, U.S. Ct. Appeals (7th cir.) 1949, U.S. Dist. Ct. (no. dist.) Ill. 1932. Ptnr. McCarthy and Levin, Chgo., 1945—; gen. counsel Chgo. Bar Assn., 1973-85, spl. counsel, 1985—. Mem. Ill. Broker-Lawyer Accord Com., 1970-84. Mem. ABA, Fed. Bar Assn., Ill. Bar Assn., 7th Circuit Bar Assn., Chgo. Bar Assn. (sec. 1971-73, chmn. real property law com. 1969, chmn. grievance com. 1968-69, chmn. lawyer reference plan com. 1963-64). Roman Catholic. Clubs: Lawyers, Legal, Met. Real property (Chgo.). Probate, General practice. Home: 141 N LaGrange Rd Apt 405 LaGrange IL 60525 Office: 100 W Monroe Suite 2000 Chicago IL 60603

MCCARTHY, KITTY MONAGHAN, lawyer; b. Springfield, Mass., June 12, 1953; d. Ralph and Adrian (Chiste) Monaghan; m. D. Douglas McCarthy, Sept. 28,1979; Children: Keri Lynn, Katie Lynn. BS, Western Ill. U., 1975; JD, So. Ill. U., 1979. Bar: Ill. 1979, U.S. Dist. Ct., U.S. Supreme Ct. Asst. state's atty. Macon County, Decatur, Ill., 1979-81; ptnr. Fuller, Hopp, Barr, McCarthy & Quigg P.C., Decatur, 1981—. Bd. dirs. YMCA, Decatur, 1980-85, Macon County United Way, 1986—. Named one of Outstanding Young Women Am., 1984. Mem. Ill. Bar Assn., Assn. Trial lAwyers Am., Ill. Trial Lawyers Assn. (membership com. 1985—), Profl. Womens Network (bd. dirs. 1981-85). Democrat. Roman Catholic. Avocations: running, tennis. Personal injury, Workers' compensation, Insurance. Office: Fuller Hopp Barr McCarthy & Quigg PC 1301 E Mound Rd Decatur IL 62526

MCCARTHY, PATRICK JAMES, lawyer; b. Defiance, Iowa, Mar. 17, 1926; s. Thomas and Clara (Rushenberg) McC.; m. Margaret Ann O'Neill, June 17, 1950; children: Patrick, Theresa, Terrance, Colleen, Brian, Molly. LLB, Creighton U., 1952. Bar: Nebr. 1952; U.S. Ct. Appeals (3d, 5th, 8th and 10th cirs.), U.S. Supreme Ct. Ptnr. McCarthy & Shreves, Omaha, 1952-53; law clk. to presiding judge U.S. Ct. Appeals (8th cir.), Omaha, 1953-55; atty. No. Natural Gas Co., Omaha, 1955-86; ptnr. Adams & McCarthy, Omaha, 1986—; adj. prof. oil and gas law Creighton U. Served as cpl. USMC, 1943-45, PTO. Mem. ABA (vice-chmn. natural gas com. 1982-86). Democrat. Roman Catholic. Oil and gas leasing. Home: 304 S 56th Omaha NE 68132 Office: Adams & McCarthy Hist Library Plaza Suite 1016 1823 Harney St Omaha NE 68102

MCCARTHY, ROBERT EMMETT, lawyer; b. Bklyn., May 26, 1951; s. John Joseph and Leona Mary (Hart) McC.; m. Elizabeth Anne Naumoff, May 20, 1978; children: John Philip, Emily Jane. BS in Fgn. Studies, Georgetown U., 1973, MS in Fgn. Studies, JD, 1978. Bar: N.J. 1978, U.S. Dist. Ct. (ea. and so. dists.) N.Y. 1979. Assoc. Patterson, Belknap et al, N.Y.C., 1978-84; sr. counsel MTV Networks Inc., N.Y.C., 1984-86; communications counsel Viacom Internat., N.Y.C., 1986—; cons. UN Ctr. on Transnat. Corps., 1977, 80-82; exec. dir. Spl. Master Reapportionment of N.Y., 1982; term mem. Council Fgn. Relations, N.Y.C., 1980-84. Founder, pres. Elizabeth (N.J.) Dem. Assn., 1980; coordinator Florio for Gov., Union County, N.J., 1981. Mem. ABA, N.Y. Bar Assn., N.J. State Bar Assn., N.Y. County Lawyers Assn., Assn. Bar City N.Y. Democrat. Roman Catholic. Antitrust, Federal civil litigation, General corporate. Home: 1050 Harding Rd Elizabeth NJ 07208 Office: Viacom Internat Inc 1211 Ave of the Americas New York NY 10036

MCCARTHY, TIMOTHY MICHAEL, lawyer; b. Chgo., May 2, 1954; s. Daniel P. and Joanne (Sullivan) McC. BS, U. Ill., 1976; JD, U. Houston, 1981. Bar: Tex. 1981, U.S. Dist. Ct. (so. dist.) Tex. 1981, Ill. 1984, U.S. Dist. Ct. (no. dist.) Ill. 1984, U.S. Ct. Appeals (5th cir.) 1982, U.S. Ct. Appeals (7th cir.) 1984. Assoc. Childs, Fortenbach, Beck & Guyton, Houston, 1981-84, Law Offices of Dennis M. O'Brien, Chgo., 1984-85, Hinshaw, Culbertson, Moelmann, Hoban & Fuller, Chgo., 1985—. Recipient Fulbright Jaworski award U. Houston 1981, Butler Binion Rice Cook & Knapp award U. Houston 1981. Mem. Ill. Bar Assn., Chgo. Bar Assn., Tex. Bar Assn. Club: Derby (Chgo.). Personal injury. Home: 2330 Lincoln Park

W 1C Chicago IL 60614 Office: Hinshaw Culbertson et al 69 W Washington Suite 2800 Chicago IL 60602

MCCARTHY, VINCENT PAUL, lawyer; b. Boston, Sept. 25, 1940; s. John Patrick and Marion Priscilla (Buckley) McC.; children—Vincent, Sybil, Hope. A.B., Boston Coll., 1962; J.D., Harvard U., 1965. Bar: Mass. 1965. Mem. firm Hale and Dorr, Boston, 1965—, sr. ptnr., 1976—. Bd. dirs., sec. Pine St. Inn, Inc., Robert F. Kennedy Action Corps, Inc., Boston Alcohol Detoxification Project, Inc.; mem. Boston Landmarks Commn., Gov.'s Adv. Council on Alcoholism, Gov.'s Adv. Commn. Homeless; bd. dirs. Fund for Homeless, Fund for Boston Neighborhood; bd. dirs., sec. Charlesbank Apts.; trustee, sec. Franklin Sq. House. Mem. ABA, Mass. Bar Assn., Boston Bar Assn. Real property.

MCCARTHY, WILLIAM JOSEPH, lawyer, financial service executive; b. Bklyn., Feb. 13, 1923; s. William Joseph and Louise Ann (Malonson) M.; m. Carol E. Martin, Jan. 22, 1949 (dec. Jan. 1987); children—Christian, Mark, Margaret, Kelley, Mary. B.S., Georgetown U., 1944, LL.B., 1947; M.B.A., N.Y.U., 1965. Bar: D.C. 1947, U.S. Ct. Appeals (2d cir.) 1948, N.Y. 1947. Assoc., Hill, Rivkins & Middleton, 1947-49, Sullivan, Donovan, Heenehan & Hanrahan, 1949-52, Hawkins, Delafield & Wood, 1952-56; dep. U.S. mem. Validation Bd. for German Dollar Bond, 1956-60; mcpl. analyst Shearson, Hammill & Co., N.Y.C., 1960-62, sr. analyst, 1962-68, v.p., 1970, dir. new issue service, 1962-72; mcpl. bond research div., Moody's Investors Services, Inc., N.Y.C. 1972-75; v.p., mgr. mcpl. research Blyth, Eastman, Dillon & Co., NYC, 1975-80; v.p., mgr. mcpl. div. Fitch Investors Service, Inc., N.Y.C., 1980—. Active North East Yonkers Taxpayers Assn. (pres. 1970-71), Mohegan Heights Homeowners Assn. Mem. Soc. Mcpl. Analysts (pres. 1983), Assn. for Mcpl. Leasing and Fin. (dir. 1982-83), N.Y. Mcpl. Analysts (chmn. 1967-68), The Money Marketeers, Mun. Forum of N.Y., Met. Econ. Assn. Republican. Roman Catholic. Club: Mcpl. Bond (N.Y.C.). Lodge: K.C. Local government. Home: 36 Shawnee Ave Yonkers NY 10710 Office: 5 Hanover Sq New York NY 10004

MCCARTY, JACK DE, lawyer; b. Santa Fe, N.Mex., July 24, 1941; s. Jack and Marie (Benge) McC.; m. Kaye Eileen Ross, Feb. 1, 1964; children—Katherine, Joy, Kara. B.S., Okla. State U., 1963; J.D., U. Okla., 1968. Bar: Okla. 1968. Ptnr., Ross, McCarty & Rigdon, Newkirk, Okla., 1968—; pub. defender Kay County Dist. Ct., Newkirk, 1970-71. Mem. Okla. Crime Commn., Oklahoma City, 1975-79; mem. com. to Select Fed. Judges for Okla., 1979; chmn. Okla. State Bur. of Investigation, Oklahoma City, 1984; sec. Kay County Election Bd., Newkirk, 1973—. Served to 1st lt. U.S. Army, 1963-65. Mem. Okla. Bar Assn., Kay County Bar Assn. (pres. 1977), Phi Delta Phi (pres. 1967-68). Democrat. Methodist. Lodge: Rotary (pres.). Federal civil litigation, State civil litigation, Personal injury. Home: 701 W 8th St Newkirk OK 74647 Office: Ross McCarty & Rigdon 116 S Main St Newkirk OK 74647

MC CARTY, WILLIAM MICHAEL, JR., lawyer; Trenton, N.J., Jan. 17, 1938; s. William Michael and Mabel Virginia (Sears) Mc C.; m. Carlene Carver, July 30, 1976; children—William A., Allen M., Benjamin S., Brie A., Sean M., Scott C. A.B., Dickinson Coll., 1964, J.D., 1967. Bar: Vt. 1967, U.S. Dist. Ct. Vt. 1967, U.S. Ct. Appeals (2d cir.) 1973, U.S. Supreme Ct. 1978. Assoc., Fitts & Olson, Brattleboro, Vt., 1967-71; sole practice, Brattleboro, 1971-76; ptnr. Mc Carty & Rifkin, Brattleboro, 1976-80; sr. ptnr., Mc Carty Law Offices, 1980—; dir. various corps. Trustee, Vt. Legal Aid, 1970-80, pres. 1979-80; pres. Brattleboro Winter Carnival, 1971-72; rep. Windham Regional Planning Devel. Com., 1968-70. Served in USMC, 1956-60. Mem. ABA, Vt. Bar Assn., Windham County Bar Assn., Am. Judicature Soc., Am. Law Student Assn. (nat. v.p. all. govs.), Am. Trial Lawyers Assn., Brattleboro C. of C. (bd. mgrs., 1971-72). Republican. Congregationalist. Personal injury, Family and matrimonial, State civil litigation. Office: Mc Carty Law Offices 48 High St Brattleboro VT 05301

MCCASLIN, LEON, lawyer; b. Royal, Ark., Oct. 3, 1931; s. Robert O. and Gladys M. (Williamson) McC.; widowed; children: Robyn, Marcus, Jennifer, David, Ted. BS in Sci., U. Oreg., 1956; LLB, LaSalle Extension U., 1968. Bar: U.S. Dist. Ct. (no. dist.) Calif. 1968, U.S. Dist. Ct. (ea. dist.) Calif. 1969, U.S. Ct. Appeals (9th cir.) 1973, U.S. Tax Ct. 1974, U.S. Dist. Ct. (cen. dist.) Calif. 1980. Police officer Marysville Police Dept., Calif., 1956-59; adjuster CalFarm Ins. Co., Yuba City, Calif., 1959-68; sole practice Yuba City, 1968—; dist. claims mgr. CalFarm Ins. Co., 1968-69; dep. dist. atty. Yuba City, 1970-74. Past pres., bd. dirs. Sutter Buttes Regional Theatre; treas. Sutter County Dem. Cen. Com., Buttes Area Counsel. Mem. ABA, Calif. Bar Assn., Am. Trial Lawyers Am., Calif. Trial Lawyers Assn. Am. Arbitration Assn., Am. Judicature Soc., Ducks Unltd., Lambda Chi Alpha. Club: Toastmasters. Lodges: Masons, Shriners, Elks. Avocations: travel, marathon running, tennis, reading. Criminal, Personal injury, General practice. OFFICE: 1289 A Lincoln Rd Yuba City CA 95991

MCCAULEY, CLEYBURN LYCURGUS, lawyer; b. Houston, Feb. 8, 1929; s. Reese Stephens and Elizabeth Ann (Burleson) McC.; m. Elizabeth Kelton McKoy, June 7, 1950; children—Stephens Francis, Lillian Elizabeth, Cleyburn, Lucy Annette. B.S., U.S. Mil. Acad., 1950; M.S. in Engring. Econ., Statistical Quality Control and Indsl. Engring., Stanford U., 1959; J.D., Coll. William and Mary, 1970. Bar: D.C. 1971, Va. 1970, Tex. 1970, U.S. Ct. Claims 1971, U.S. Tax Ct. 1971, U.S. Supreme Ct. 1973. Commd. 2d lt. U.S. Air Force, 1950, advanced through grades to lt. col., 1971; ret., 1971; sole practice, Washington, 1975—. Mem. Fed. Bar Assn., Va. Bar Assn., Tex. Bar Assn., D.C. Bar Assn., IEEE, AIAA, Am. Soc. Quality Control, Phi Alpha Delta. Corporate taxation, Banking, General corporate. Office: 1900 S Eads St Suite 1007 Crystal House 1 Arlington VA 22202

MCCAULEY, RICHARD GRAY, real estate developer, lawyer; b. Balt., June 17, 1940. B.A. cum laude, Williams Coll., 1962; LL.B., U. Va., 1965. Bar: Md. 1969, U.S. Supreme Ct. 1969. Assoc. firm Piper & Marbury, Balt., 1965-69; asst. atty. gen. Md., 1969-71; sr. v.p., gen. counsel, sec. Rouse Co. and subs.'s, Columbia, Md., 1971—; chmn. bd. Md. Deposit Ins. Fund Corp., 1985-86; gen. counsel Howard Research and Devel. Corp., Columbia, 1972—; lectr. Am. Law Inst.; bd. dirs. First Atlanta Bank N.Am. Bd. dirs. Columbia Park and Recreation Assn., 1972—, chmn. exec. com. 1972-78, chmn. bd.; 1978-83; trustee The Columbia Found., 1984—, v.p., 1986—; trustee Howard Community Coll. Ednl. Found., 1982—, vice chair, 1985—. Mem. Md. Bar Assn., Am. Bar Assn., Balt. City Bar Assn., Am. Judicature Soc., Urban Land Inst., Am. Corporate Counsel Assn. General corporate, Real property. Office: Rouse Co Little Patuxent Pkwy Columbia MD 21044

MCCHESNEY, PAUL TOWNSEND, lawyer; b. Spartanburg, S.C., Mar. 4, 1953; s. Paul Stanley Jr. and Margaret (Coleman) McC.; m. Anne Tisdale, Dec. 30, 1978; 1 child, Sarah Caroline. BS, The Citadel, 1975; JD, Duke U., 1978. Bar: S.C. 1978, U.S. Dist. Ct. S.C. 1979, U.S. Ct. Appeals (4th cir.) 1982. Law clk. to presiding justice S.C. Supreme Ct., Columbia, 1978-79; ptnr. Fraley, McChesney & McChesney, Spartanburg, 1979—. Mem. Nat. Orgn. Social Security Reps. (sustaining), Am. Trial Lawyers Assn. Pension, profit-sharing, and employee benefits, Workers' compensation, Personal injury. Home: 241 Briarcliff Rd Spartanburg SC 29301 Office: Fraley & McChesney & McChesney 175 Magnolia St Suite 2 Spartanburg SC 29301

MCCHESNEY, PETER BROOKS, lawyer; b. Palo Alto, Calif., Jan. 27, 1948; s. Francis William and Jean Ellen (Coghlan) McC.; 1 child, Heather M. BA in History with distinction, BA in Polit. Sci. with distinction, Stanford U., 1970, postgrad. 1973; JD, Cornell U., 1973. Bar: Calif. 1973. Assoc. Cotton, Seligman & Ray, San Francisco, 1973-77; corp. counsel Saga Corp., Menlo Park, Calif., 1977-83; v.p., gen. counsel, sec. Businessland, San Jose, Calif., 1983—. Bd. editors Cornell Internat. Law Rev. Bd. dirs. Mgmt. Ctr., San Francisco, 1982—, pres., 1983-85; bd. dirs. J.P. Mktg. Co., Inc., 1986—. Mem. ABA (antitrust com.), Calif. Bar Assn., San Francisco Bar Assn. (client affairs com.), Peninsula Assn. Gen. Counsel, Am. Soc. Corp. Secs., Am. Corp. Counsel Assn. Club: Bohemian. General corporate. Office: 1001 Ridder Park Dr San Jose CA 95131

MCCLAIN, VAUGHN LEON, lawyer; b. Detroit, Jan. 6, 1948; s. Paul Bradford and Mary Antonia (Rizzo) McC.; m. Preyanoot Mesinsat, Nov. 30, 1980; 1 child, Virgilia. BS, Eastern Mich. U., 1970; JD, U. Mich., 1974.

Bar: Mich. 1975, U.S. Dist. Ct. (ea. dist.) Mich. 1975, Colo. 1985. Assoc. Sempliner, Thomas & Ruth, Plymouth, Mich., 1974-76, McDermott & Kiehnhoff, Canon City, Colo., 1984-86; sole proprietor South Lyon, Mich., 1977-84, Canon City, Colo., 1986—; mediator Oakland County Dist. Ct., Walled Lake, Mich., 1983-84; of counsel to Augspurger and Assocs., Southfield, Mich., 1984—. Bd. dirs. Econ. Devel. Corp., South Lyon, 1981-83. Mem. Mich. Bar Assn., Colo. Bar Assn. (real estate law sect.), 11th Jud. Dist. Bar Assn., Canon City Hist. Soc. Lodges: Kiwanis (pres. South Lyon chpt. 1982-83), Elks, Masons. Avocations: astronomy, physics, conservation, skiing, reading. Private international, Real property, Environment. Home: 1304 Mountain View Dr Canon City CO 81212 Office: First Nat Bank Bldg Suite D 531 Main St Canon City CO 81212

MCCLAIN, WILLIAM ANDREW, lawyer; b. Sanford, N.C., Jan. 11, 1913; s. Frank and Blanche (Leslie) McC.; m. Roberta White, Nov. 11, 1944. A.B., Wittenberg U., 1934; J.D., U. Mich., 1937; LL.D. (hon.), Wilberforce U., 1963, U. Cin., 1971; L.H.D., Wittenberg U., 1972. Bar: Ohio 1938, U.S. Dist. Ct. (so. dist.) Ohio 1940, U.S. Ct. Appeals (6th cir.) 1946, U.S. Supreme Ct. 1946. Mem. Berry, McClain & White, 1937-58; dep. solicitor, City of Cin., 1957-63, city solicitor, 1963-72; mem. Keating, Muething & Klekamp, Cin., 1972-73; gen. counsel Cin. Br., SBA, 1973-75; judge Hamilton County Common Pleas Ct., 1975-76; judge Mcpl. Ct., 1976-80; of counsel Manley, Jordan & Fischer, Cin., 1980—; adj. prof. U. Cin., 1963-72, Salmon P. Chase Law Sch., 1965-72. Exec. com. ARC, Cin., 1978—; bd. dirs. NCCJ, 1975—. Served to 1st lt. JAGC, U.S. Army, 1943-46. Decorated Army Commendation award; recipient Nat. Layman award, A.M.E. Ch., 1963; Alumni award Wittenberg U., 1966; Nat. Inst. Mcpl. Law Officers award, 1971. Fellow Am. Bar Found.; mem. Am. Judicature Soc., World Peace Through Law Ctr., Cin. Bar Assn., Ohio Bar Assn., ABA, Fed. Bar assn., Nat. Bar Assn., Alpha Phi Alpha, Sigma Pi Phi. Republican. Methodist. Clubs: Bankers, Friendly Sons of St. Patrick Lodge: Masons (33 deg.). Federal civil litigation, Administrative and regulatory, Local government. Address: 2101 Grandin Rd Apt 904 Cincinnati OH 45208

MCCLAIN, WILLIAM ASBURY, lawyer; b. Sweetwater, Tenn., Apr. 1, 1901; s. William Asbury and Annie Lynn (Bachman) McC.; m. Catherine Flagler, Nov. 15, 1933; children: Catherine McClain Hand, Annie Lynn, William Asbury III. BS, Davidson Coll., 1924; LLB, U. Va., 1927. Bar: Tenn. 1927, Ga. 1928. Assoc. Watkins, Asbell & Watkins, Atlanta, 1928-31, Hooper & Hooper, Atlanta, 1931-35; with Office Gen. Csl., SEC, Washington, 1935-38, Washington, 1938-46; ptnr. Candler, Cox, McClain & Andrews, Atlanta, 1946-70, McClain, Mellen, Bowling & Hickman, Atlanta, 1970-81, Smith Cohen, Ringel, Kohler & Martin, 1981-85, Smith Gambrell & Russell, 1985—; spl. asst. atty. gen. Ga., 1934, U.S., 1942. Mem. ABA, Ga. Bar Assn. Republican. Episcopalian. Clubs: Piedmont Driving, Nine O'Clocks, Atlanta Lawyers, Commerce. General corporate, Corporate Finance. Home: 1776 W Wesley Rd Atlanta GA 30327 Office: Smith Gambrell & Russell 2400 1st National Tower Atlanta GA 30383

MCCLANNAHAN, CINDY ANN, lawyer; b. Kansas City, Kans., Dec. 18, 1956; d. William C. and Edith M. (Halverhout) Brunker. BA in Polit. Sci., U. Kansa., 1978; JD, U. Kans., 1981; LLM in Taxation, NYU, 1983. Bar: Kans. 1981, U.S. Dist. Ct. Kans. 1981, Mo. 1982, U.S. Dist. Ct. (we. dist.) Mo. 1982. Assoc. Sullivan, Bodney & Hammond, Kansas City, 1981-82, Burrell, Seigfreid & Bingham, Kansas City, 1983—. Mem. ABA, Mo. Bar Assn., Kansas City Bar Assn., Lawyers Assn. (liason young lawyers sect.), Pi Sigma Alpha. Republican. Corporate taxation, Estate planning, Estate taxation. Office: Burrell Seigfreid & Bingham 2800 Commerce Tower Kansas City MO 64105

MCCLARD, JACK EDWARD, lawyer; b. Lafayette, La., May 13, 1946; s. Lee Franklin and Mercedes Cecile (Landry) McC.; m. Marilyn Kay O'Gorman, June 3, 1972; 1 child, Lauren Minton. BA in Hist., Rice U., 1968; JD, U. Tex., 1974. Bar: Va. 1974, U.S. Dist. Ct. (ea. and we. dists.) Va. 1974, D.C. 1981, U.S. Dist. Ct. D.C. 1981, N.Y. 1985, U.S. Dist. Ct. (so. and ea. dists.) N.Y. 1985, U.S. Ct. Appeals (4th cir.) 1978, U.S. Ct. Appeals (D.C. cir.) 1980. Assoc. Hunton & Williams, Richmond, Va., 1974-81; ptnr. Hunton & Williams, Richmond, 1981—. Served to lt. (j.g.) USN, 1968-71. Mem. ABA, Va. Bar Assn., Richmond Bar Assn., Va. Trial Lawyers Assn. Democrat. Episcopalian. Avocations: bridge, gardening. Federal civil litigation, State civil litigation, Private international. Home: 100 Trowbridge Rd Richmond VA 23233 Office: Hunton & Williams 707 E Main St PO Box 1535 Richmond VA 23219

MCCLARTY, JOHN WESTLEY, lawyer; b. Chattanooga, June 5, 1948; s. Pleas McClarty and Beulah (Jackson) McClarty Vasser; m. Doris Hendrick; children—Brian, Patrick. B.A., Austin Peay U., 1971; J.D., So. U., 1976; postdoctoral study Nat. Coll. Criminal Def. Lawyers, 1978. Bar: Tenn. Assoc. Jerry Summers Law Office, Chattanooga, 1976-78; sole practice, Chattanooga, 1978-80; sr. ptnr. McClarty & Williams, Chattanooga, 1981—. Articles editor So. U. Law Rev., 1975-76. Mem. Hamilton County Police Dept. Civil Service Bd., Chattanooga; past chmn. governing bd. Alton Park/Dodson Ave Health Ctrs., Chattanooga; mem. ofcl. bd. NAACP, Chattanooga. Mem. ABA, Nat. Bar Assn., Chattanooga Trial Lawyers, Tenn. Bar Assn., Chattanooga Bar Assn., Delta Theta Phi, Alpha Phi Omega, Omega Psi Phi. Democrat. Mem. African Methodist. Episcopal Ch. General practice, Criminal, Personal injury. Home: 2402 Haven Cove Ln Chattanooga TN 37421 Office: McLarty & Williams 18 Patten Pkwy Chattanooga TN 37402

MCCLASKEY, NORMAN DEAN, lawyer; b. Green City, Mo., Aug. 5, 1936; s. James Franklin and Bernice Wilson (Walters) McC.; m. Anna Dale Armsbury, Feb. 11, 1962; children: Kimberly Ann, Melinda Sue, Brendan Dale. BA in Math., U. Iowa, 1962, JD with high distinction, 1966. Bar: Iowa 1966, U.S. Patent Office 1967, U.S. Ct. Appeals (fed. cir.) 1967, Ill. 1970, N.Y. 1975. Patent atty. Bell Telephone Labs., Murray Hill, N.J., 1966-70, Naperville, Ill., 1970-72; patent atty. Eastman Kodak Co., Rochester, N.Y., 1972-74, atty. litigation, 1974-83, dir. patent litigation, 1983—. Served with USAF, 1955-58. Mem. ABA (subcom. chmn. computer program protection, patent, trademark and copyright sect. 1974-76), Order of Coif, Phi Delta Phi. Republican. Federal civil litigation, State civil litigation. Home: 6 Sand Brook Rd Pittsford NY 14534 Office: Eastman Kodak Co 343 State St Rochester NY 14650

MCCLAUGHERTY, JOE L., lawyer, educator; b. Luling, Tex., June 1, 1951; s. Frank Lee and Elease (Terrell) McC.; m. Katherine Morrison Witte, Feb. 24, 1980. B.B.A. with honors, U. Tex., 1973, J.D. with honors, 1976. Bar: Tex. 1976, N.Mex. 1976, U.S. Dist. Ct. N.Mex. 1976, U.S. Ct. Appeals (10th cir.) 1976, U.S. Supreme Ct. 1979. Assoc. firm Rodey, Dickason, Sloan, Akin & Robb, P.A., Albuquerque, 1976-81, ptnr., dir., 1981-87, resident ptnr., Santa Fe, 1983-87, mng. ptnr., 1985-87, ptnr. Kemp, Smith, Duncan & Hammond, P.C., 1987—, resident ptnr., Santa Fe, 1987—, mng. ptnr., 1987—; adj. prof. law U. N.Mex., Albuquerque, 1983—; faculty Nat. Inst. Trial Advocacy, so. regional, So. Meth. U. Law Sch., 1983—, Rocky Mt. regional, U. Denver Law Sch., 1986—, nat. session U. Colo. Law Sch., 1987— ; faculty Hastings Ctr. for Trial and Appellate Advocacy, 1985—; bd. dirs. MCM Corp., Raleigh, N.C., Brit.-Am. Ins. Co., Ltd., Nassau, The Bahamas, 1985—. Mem. N.Mex. Bar Assn. (bd. dirs. trial practice sect. 1976—, chairperson 1983-84, dir. young lawyers div. 1978-80), N.Mex. Assn. Def. Lawyers (pres. 1982-83, bd. dirs. 1982-85). Federal civil litigation, State civil litigation, Personal injury. Office: Kemp Smith Duncan & Hammond PC 123 E Marcy Suite 208 PO Box 8680 Santa Fe NM 87504

MCCLEAR, NICHOLAS WILLARD, lawyer; b. Newark, May 14, 1948; s. Willard John and Edythe (Sivolella) McC.; m. JoAnn Conroy, May 19, 1973; 1 dau., Kate. B.A. magna cum laude, Fordham U., 1970; J.D., Columbia U., 1973. Bar: N.J. 1973, U.S. Dist. Ct. N.J. 1973, U.S. Ct. Appeals (3d cir.) 1981. Assoc., Hellring, Lindeman & Landau, Newark, 1973-76; assoc. Wilentz, Goldman & Spitzer, Perth Amboy and Woodbridge, N.J., 1976-81, mem., 1981—. Mem. Bd. Trial Attys. (cert.), Middlesex County Bar Assn., N.J. State Bar Assn. (spl. com. on equity jurisprudence), ABA, Phi Beta Kappa. Federal civil litigation, State civil litigation. Address: PO Box 10 Woodbridge NJ 07095

MCCLELLAN, JANET ELAINE, law educator; b. Salina, Kans., June 30, 1951; d. William Francis and Ethel Mary (Rinebold) McC.; m. Richard Morris Rolfsness, Dec. 17, 1969 (div.). B.A. in Govt., Adminstrn., Park Coll., Parkville, Mo., 1976; M.P.A., U. Dayton (Ohio), 1978; postgrad. U. Kans., 1982-86; Police officer City of Leavenworth, Kans., 1970-71; narcotics agt. Kans. Bur. Investigation, Topeka, 1971-73; asst. to chief Police Dept., Ellensburg, Wash., 1973-76; dir. juvenile div. Police Dept., Centerville, Ohio, 1976-79; watch comdr. Police Dept., Douglas, Wyo., 1978-79; dir. criminal justice adminstrn. Park Coll., Parkville, Mo., 1979—; directing advisor Tau Lambda Alpha Epsilon and Alpha Phi Omega, Park Coll., 1980—; cons. Probation-Parole Dept., Kansas City, Mo., 1979-80, Police Dept., Leavenworth, 1981-82, Sheriff's Dept., Liberty, Mo., 1984—. Contbr. articles to profl. jours. Reviewer criminal justice textbooks, jours., reviewing editor book Introduction to Criminal Justice, 1984, Modern Police Management, Criminal Justice and Public Policy. Chmn. Southwest Montgomery County Youth Commn., Dayton, Ohio, 1977-79; bd. dirs. Synergy Youth Half-way House, Parkville, 1980—. Mem. Internat. Assn. Chiefs of Police, Am. Soc. Criminology, Am. Criminal Justice Soc., Am. Correctional Assn., Mo. Polit. Sci. Assn., Am. Soc. Pub. Adminstrn., Mo. Acad. Sci., Pi Gamma Mu, Pi Sigma Alpha, Delta Tau Kappa. Democrat. Methodist. Legal education, Criminal. Office: Criminal Justice Adminstrn Dept Park College Parkville MO 64152

MCCLELLAND, JAMES RAY, lawyer; b. Eunice, La., June 21, 1946; s. Rufus Ray and Homer Florene (Nunn) McC.; m. Sandra Faye Tate, Feb. 6, 1971; children—Joseph Ray, Jeffrey Ross. B.S., La. State U., 1969, M.B.A., 1971, J.D., 1975. Bar: La. 1975, U.S. Ct. Appeals (5th cir.) 1976, U.S. Dist. Ct. (ea. dist.) La. 1976, U.S. Dist. Ct. (we. dist.) La. 1976. Assoc. Aycock, Horne, Caldwell, Coleman & Duncan, Franklin, La., 1975-78, ptnr., 1978—; dir. Bayou Bouillon Corp., Cotten Land Corp. Mem. exec. com. Democratic Party, St. Mary Parish, 1980—; del. La. Dem. Party, 1982, 84. Mem. La. State Bar Assn. (ho. of dels. 1982—, law reform com. 1984—), St. Mary Parish Bar Assn. (pres. 1978-79), Order of Coif. Club: Rotary (pres. 1981-82). Criminal, State civil litigation, Personal injury. Home: PO Box 268 Franklin LA 70538 Office: PO Box 592 Franklin LA 70538

MC CLINTOCK, ARCHIE GLENN, semi-retired State attorney general, lawyer; b. Sheridan, Wyo., Mar. 26, 1911; s. James Porter and Martie E. (Glenn) McC.; m. Ina Jean Robinson, May 27, 1939 (dec. 1974); children: Ellery, Jeffry, Kathleen. B.A., U. Wyo., 1933, LL.B., 1935. Bar: Wyo. 1935, Calif. 1982. Pvt. practice law Cheyenne, Wyo., 1935-73, 81-83; justice Wyo. Supreme Ct., Cheyenne, 1973-81; atty. gen. State of Wyo., 1982-87; semi-ret. Mem. Wyo. Fair Employment Practices Commn., 1965-71. Served with USNR, 1944-45. Mem. Wyo. State Bar (pres. 1950-51), Am. Judicature Soc., Sigma Nu. Democrat. Club: Elks. Home: 1211 Richardson Ct Cheyenne WY 82001

MCCLINTOCK, GORDON EDWIN, lawyer; b. Salinas, Calif., Nov. 21, 1942; s. Edwin Herschel and Ruth Isabelle (Graves) McC.; m. Nancy Howe Kreuter, Dec. 1, 1943; children—Pamela Ann, Patricia E. B.A., Whitman Coll., 1964; J.D., Hastings Coll., 1967. Bar: Calif. 1967, U.S. Dist. Ct. (no. dist.) Calif. 1967, U.S. Tax Ct. 1969, U.S. Dist. Ct. (ea. dist.) Calif. 1986. Staff mem. Calif. Law Revision Commn., Stanford, 1967-68, assoc. Hession, Robb, Creedon, Hamlin & Kelly, San Mateo, 1968-72; mem. firm Hession, Creedon, Hamlin, Kelly, Hanson & Brown, P.C., San Mateo, 1972-85, Hession & Creedon, 1985—; judge pro tempore San Mateo County Superior Ct.; mem. judicial arbitration panels San Mateo, Santa Clara County Superior Cts. Leader faculty workshop Hastings Ctr. Trial and Appellate Advocacy, 1983. Mem. ABA, Calif. Bar Assn., San Mateo County Bar Assn., Santa Clara County Bar Assn., Calif. State Bar (exec. com. law office mgmt. sect. 1983-86), Associated Gen. Contractors No. Calif. (legal adv. com.), Def. Research Inst., Assn. Def. Counsel, Assn. Trial Lawyers Am., Order of Coif. Democrat. Club: Palo Alto Hills Golf & Country (bd. dirs.). State civil litigation, Real property, Insurance. Office: Hession & Creedon 1400 Fashion Island Blvd Suite 800 PO Box 4909 San Mateo CA 94404-0909

MCCLOSKEY, MICHAEL PATRICK, lawyer; b. Inglewood, Calif., Oct. 30, 1955; s. James Francis and Myrtle Helena (Hill) McC.; m. Diane Eleanore Bregand, June 12, 1976; children: Michael Patrick Jr., Jason Andrew. BS, U. So. Calif., 1976. Bar: Calif. 1982, U.S. Dist. Ct. (so. dist.) Calif. 1982. Of trial counsel Office of Staff Judge Adv., Camp Pendleton, Calif., 1982-85; litigation atty. Office of Judge Adv. Gen., Alexandria, Va., 1985—. Editor Pacific Law Jour., 1981-82. Served to capt. USMC, 1976—. Mem. ABA, Am. Trial Lawyers Assn., Phi Delta Phi. Democrat. Avocations: running, weight lifting. Federal civil litigation, Criminal, Military. Home: 7585 Seabrook Ln Springfield VA 22153-2118 Office: Office Judge Adv Gen 200 Stovall St Alexandria VA 22332-2400

MCCLOSKEY, PATRICK LAWRENCE, lawyer, author, educator; b. Elizabeth, N.J., Oct. 4, 1944; s. Lawrence Patrick and Marie Eleanor (McMahon) McC.; m. Carol Ann Flanagan, Aug. 23, 1969; children—Christopher Paul, Lynn Ann. B.A. in English, Villanova U., 1965; J.D., St. John's U., 1968. Bar: N.Y. 1969, U.S. Dist. Ct. (so. and ea. dists.) N.Y. 1970, U.S. Ct. Appeals (2d cir.) 1970, U.S. Supreme Ct. 1972. Assoc. McHugh, Heckman, Smith & Leonard, N.Y.C., 1968-71; ptnr. Borowka & McCloskey, Mineola, N.Y., 1971-75; asst. dist. atty. Nassau County, N.Y., Mineola, 1975-76, adminstrv. asst. dist. atty., 1976-81, exec. asst. dist. atty., 1981—; spl. prof. law Hofstra U., Hempstead, N.Y., 1980—; faculty N.E. Region Nat. Inst. Trial Advocacy, Hempstead, 1978—. Author: vols. 4 and 5, Criminal Law Advocacy, 1982, vol. 7, 1986; The Criminal Law Deskbook, 1984. Roman Catholic. Criminal. Office: 262 Old Country Rd Mineola NY 11501

MCCLOSKEY, STEPHEN PAUL, lawyer; b. Pitts., July 19, 1951; s. D. Paul and Joan H. (Harris) McC.; m. Shelley Beth Levy, July 22, 1978; children: Michael David, Rachel Meryl. BS in Fin., Pa. State U., 1973; JD, Duquesne U., 1976. Bar: Pa. 1976, U.S. Dist. Ct. (we. dist.) Pa. 1976. Staff atty. Southwestern Pa. Legal Aid Soc., Washington, Pa., 1977-79; assoc. Phillips and Faldowski, Washington, 1979-82, ptnr., 1982—; cons. to ins. carriers, Phillips and Faldowski, Washington, 1981—. Lectr. local high schs., Washington County, 1981-83, chmn. edn. com. 1982; bd. dirs. Beth Israel Synagogue, Washington, 1985—. Mem. ABA, Pa. Bar Assn., Washington County Bar Assn., Allegheny County Bar Assn., Assn. Trial Lawyers of Am., Pa. Def. Inst., Pa. Trial Lawyers Assn., Pa. Claims Assn., Pitts. Claims Assn., Assn. Ins. Attys. Democrat. Jewish. Avocations: golf, reading, writing. State civil litigation, Insurance, Personal injury. Home: 17 Wilmont Ave Washington PA 15301 Office: Phillips and Faldowski 29 E Beau St Washington PA 15301

MCCLOW, THOMAS ALAN, lawyer; b. Detroit, Apr. 25, 1944; s. Kenneth Ray and Rita Beatrice (Periard) McC.; B.S., Mich. State U., 1966; J.D., Loyola U., 1969; m. Diana L. McClow, Oct. 16, 1982; children—Amy Christine, Adam Andrew. Bar: Ill. 1969, U.S. Supreme Ct. 1973. Assoc. Douglas F. Comstock, Geneva, Ill., 1970-73, John L. Nickels, Elburn, Ill., 1973-78; ptnr. Nickels & McClow, Elburn, 1978-82; ptnr. McClow & Britz, Elburn, 1982-84; prin. Law Offices of Thomas A. McClow Ltd., Geneva, Ill., 1985—; pub. conservator, guardian, adminstr. Kane County, 1975-78. Bd. dirs. Kane County Council Econ. Opportunity, 1st vice chmn., 1971-73; bd. dirs. Tri City Youth Project, 1972-73; faculty dean Parent Edn. Center, 1974-76. Mem. ABA, Ill. Bar Assn., Kane County Bar Assn. (chmn. membership and admissions com. 1979-84), Fox Valley Estate Planning Council, Mensa. Probate, Family and matrimonial, Real property. Home: 919 Arbor Ave Wheaton IL 60187 Office: PO Box 721 Geneva IL 60134

MCCLUNG, MERLE STEVEN, lawyer; b. Clara City, Minn., June 30, 1943. BA, Harvard U., 1965, JD, 1972; AB, MA, Oxford U., Eng., 1967. Bar: Mass. 1973. Instr. Miles Coll., Birmingham, Ala., 1969-70; staff atty. Harvard Ctr. Law & Edn., Cambridge, Mass., 1972-79; dir. law and edn. ctr. Edn. Commn. States, Denver, 1979-81; gen. counsel Pendleton Land & Exploration, Inc., Denver, 1981—; legal cons. Conn. Dept. Edn., Hartford, 1974-77, Calif. Dept. Edn., Sacramento, 1978-81. Contbr. articles to profl. jours. Rhodes scholar Oxford U., Eng., 1965. Mem. ABA, Mass. Bar Assn., Phi Beta Kappa. Avocations: tennis, antique books, art. General corporate, Real property, Civil rights. Home: 838 Leyden St Denver CO 80220 Office: Pendleton Land and Exploration Inc 8085 S Chester St Englewood CO 80112

MCCLURE, DONALD JOHN, lawyer; b. Pitts., Mar. 31, 1940; s. Edward L. and Anna McC.; m. Judith Linda Richards, Sept. 2, 1961; children—Ian J., Sean M. Student El Dorado Jr. Coll., Kans., 1958-60; B.A., U. Denver, 1964, J.D., 1966. Bar: Colo. 1967, Ill. 1973, Tex. 1978, Kans. 1985. Ptnr. Robert J. Flynn Assocs., Englewood, Colo., 1967-68; with law dept. PepsiCo., Inc., 1968—, v.p., div. counsel Wilson Sporting Goods div., River Grove, Ill., 1972-77, v.p., div. counsel Frito-Lay, Inc. div., Dallas, 1977-84, Pizza Hut, Inc. div., 1984-87, Pepsico Food Services, Inc., 1987— . Mem. Dallas Bar Assn. (chmn. council antitrust and trade regulation sect.), ABA, Tex. Bar Assn., Colo. Bar Assn., Ill. Bar Assn., Denver Bar Assn., Chgo. Bar Assn., Kans. Bar Assn., Wichita Bar Assn. Antitrust, General corporate, Private international. Home: 14330 Donegal Circle Wichita KS 67230 Office: Pepsico Food Services Inc 13455 Noel Rd Dallas TX 75240

MCCLURE, JOHN CAMPBELL, lawyer; b. Englewood, N.J., Sept. 13, 1954; s. Starling Virgil and Mary Jane (Campbell) McC.; m. Julie Anne Cirksena, Nov. 28, 1981. BA, U. Nebr., 1977, JD, 1980. Bar: Nebr. 1980, U.S. Dist. Ct. Nebr. 1980. Staff atty. Nebr. Pub. Power Dist., Columbus, 1980-86, sr. staff atty., 1986—; real estate law instr. Cen. Community Coll., Columbus, 1985—; chmn. Nuclear Transp. Group R.R. Task Force, Washington, 1986—. Bd. dirs. Columbus Pub. Library and Found., 1985—; bd. dirs. Columbus Area Arts Council, 1985—. Mem. ABA, Nebr. Bar Assn., Platte County Bar Assn. Republican. Presbyterian. Avocations: gardening, golfing. Public utilities, Nuclear power, Real property. Home: 101 E Parkway Columbus NE 68601 Office: Nebr Pub Power Dist PO Box 499 Columbus NE 68601

MCCLURE, LAWRENCE RAY, lawyer, former judge; b. Moberly, Mo., Mar. 14, 1948; s. Ray C. and Jean R. (Ream) McC.; m. Carol N. McClure, Nov. 30, 1968; 1 dau.: Jennifer Lynn. B.S. in Edn., U. Mo.-Columbia, 1971, J.D., 1974. Bar: Mo. 1974. Ptnr. Harris, Reid & McClure, Marshall, Mo., 1975; city counselor Marshall, 1975; probate and ex-officio magistrate judge Saline County, Mo., 1975-78; assoc. cir. judge probate div. Cir. Ct. of Saline County, 1979-82; mem. state cts. data processing com.; lectr. Office of State Cts. Adminstr., Mo.; reporter Mo. Bar subcom. on pub. guardians, 1981—; mem. legis. steering com. Mo. Jud. Conf., 1981-82; com. council Mo. Bar, probate and trust com., 1981—; treas. Saline County Law Library; dir. Region XII Council on Criminal Justice, 1975-79. Bd. dirs., exec. com. Arrow Rock Lyceum Theatre; mem. Friends of Arrow Rock; bd. dirs. Saline County ARC, 1976-78; trustee Sappington Sch. Fund; mem. adv. bd. Butterfield Youth Services; active Saline County Assn. for Mental Health; chmn. Marshall Planning and Zoning Commn. 1976-78. Mem. Mo. Bar Assn., Saline County Bar Assn., Am. Judicature Soc., Mo. Mcpl. and Assoc. Cir. Judges Assn., Mo. Assn. Probate and Assoc. Cir. Judges (pres. 1981-82, bd. dirs. 1976-82), Saline County Hist. Soc. (bd. dirs. 1979-81). Republican. Methodist. Club: Marshall Kiwanis. Jurisprudence, Probate. Home: 750 E Eastwood Marshall MO 65340 Office: 171 Court St PO Box 719 Marshall MO 65340

MCCLURE, ROGER JOHN, lawyer; b. Cleve., Nov. 22, 1943; s. Theron R. and Colene (Irwin) McC. BA, Ohio State U., 1965, JD, 1972; MA, Northwestern U., 1966. Bar: U.S. Ct. Appeals (D.C. cir.) 1974, U.S. Supreme Ct. 1978, Va. 1983, Md. 1983, Ohio, U.S. Ct. Appeals (4th, 5th & 10th cirs.). Asst. atty. gen. State of Ohio, Columbus, 1972; trial atty. FTC, Washington, 1972-76; sr. assoc. Law Offices of A.D. Berkeley, Washington, 1976-81; sole practice Alexandria, Va., 1981-86; pres. Roger J. McClure & Assocs., P.C., Alexandria, 1987—; adj. prof. Antioch Sch. Law, Washington, 1982-84. Bd. editors Ohio State U. Law Rev., 1970-72. Contbr. numerous articles to profl. jours. Served with U.S. Army, 1967-69. Decorated Bronze Star. Mem. ABA, D.C. Bar Assn. (mem. real estate steering com. 1982-84, chmn. antitrust div. 1975-76), Real Estate Syndication & Securities Inst., Northern Va. Builders Assn., No. Va. Apt. Assn. (dir. 1986—). Avocation: sailing. Real property, Personal income taxation, Estate planning. Office: 1317 King St Alexandria VA 22314

MCCLURE, THOMAS EDWARD, lawyer; b. Urbana, Ill., Nov. 8, 1954; s. William Leslie McClure and Carolyn Jean (Hovey) McClure Byrnes; m. Karen Leah Zinn, Dec. 14, 1985. BS, Ill. State U., 1976; JD, DePaul U., 1979. Bar: Ill. 1979, U.S. Dist. Ct. (no. dist.) Ill. 1979, U.S. Ct. Appeals (7th cir.) 1980, U.S. Dist. Ct. (cen. dist.) Ill. 1983. Law clk. to presiding justice Ill. Ct. Appeals (1st dist.), Chgo., 1979-81; mem. Elliott & McClure, Bourbonnais and Momence, Ill., 1981—; legal counsel Ill. Jaycees, 1985-86. Editor DePaul Law Rev., 1978-79; contbr. articles to profl. jours. Recipient Outstanding Instruction award Dale Carnegie & Assocs., 1982, 83; named Outstanding Local Dir., East Region Jaycees, 1984, Outstanding Local Pres. Ill. Jaycees, 1985. Mem. ABA, Ill. Bar Assn. (cert. of recognition 1983), Chgo. Bar Assn., Kankakee County Bar Assn., Bourbonnais Bar Assn., Appellate Lawyers Assn., Kankakee Jaycees (pres. 1984-85, bd. dirs. 1983-86). Personal injury, Federal civil litigation, Civil rights. Office: Elliott & McClure 18 Briarcliff Profl Ctr Bourbonnais IL 60914

MCCLURG, ANDREW JAY, lawyer; b. East Lansing, Mich., Oct. 15, 1954; s. Donald W. McClurg and Helen (Tulin) Rohloff; m. Sharon Alane Hooper, Aug. 8, 1981; 1 child, Caitlin Lee. AA, Broward Community Coll., 1975; BS in Journlism, U. Fla., 1977, JD, 1980. Bar: Fla. 1981, U.S. Dist. Ct. (mid. dist.) Fla. 1981, U.S. Ct. Appeals (11th cir.) 1981, U.S. Dist. Ct. (so. dist.) Fla. 1984. Law clk. to presiding justice U.S. Dist. Ct. (mid. dist.), Jacksonville, Fla., 1980-82; assoc. Bedell, Dittmar, Devault, Pillans & Gentry, Jacksonville, 1982-86; asst. prof. law U. Ark. Sch. of Law, Little Rock, 1986—. Ombudsman Fed. Ct., 1980-82; vol. Spl. Olympics, 1986, Jacksonville Pro Bono Panel, 1986. Mem. ABA, Fla. Bar Assn. (code and rules of evidence com. 1985—), Jacksonville Bar Assn. (fee arbitration com. 1985—, profl. ethics com. 1985—, law and the elderly com. 1985—), Fed. Bar Assn., Assn. Trial Lawyers Am., Acad. Fla. Trial Lawyers. Criminal, Federal civil litigation. Office: U Ark Sch of Law 400 W Markham Little Rock AR 72201

MCCOBB, JOHN BRADFORD, JR., lawyer; b. Orange, N.J., Oct. 14, 1939; s. John Bradford and Dorothea Joyce (Hoffman) M.; m. Maureen Kelly, Oct. 6, 1973; 1 dau., Carrie Elizabeth. A.B., Princeton U. cum laude, 1961; J.D., Stanford U., 1966; LL.M., NYU, 1973. Bar: Calif. 1967. Assoc., IBM, Armonk, N.Y., 1966-1974, gen. counsel, Tokyo, 1974-77, lab. counsel, Endicott, N.Y., 1977-79, sr. atty., White Plains, N.Y., 1979-81, regional counsel, Dallas, 1981-83; counsel, sec. IBM Instruments, Inc., Danbury, Conn., 1983—. Trustee Princeton-in-Asia, Inc., 1970—. Princeton-in-Asia-teaching fellow at Chinese Univ. of Hong Kong, 1963-65. Mem. State Bar of Calif., World Peace through World Law, ABA, Phi Beta Kappa. Contbr. articles to profl. jours. Private international, Computer, Antitrust. Home: 7 Hedgerow Common Weston CT 06883 Office: IBM Instruments Inc Orchard Park Danbury CT 06810

MCCOLLAM, M. E., lawyer; b. Des Moines, Oct. 1, 1954; s. Max E. and Polly A. (Owens) McC.; m. Elizabeth Ann Meyer, Aug. 27, 1976; children: Megan Elayne, Katherine Owens. BBA, U. Kans., 1976; JD with honors, Washburn U., 1982. Bar: Kans. 1982, Okla. 1982. Bank examiner Office of Comptroller of Currency, U.S. Dept. Treasury, Topeka, 1976-79; assoc. Lemon & Hatley, Oklahoma City, 1982-83, Norman, Wohlgemuth & Thompson, Tulsa, 1983-85, Conner & Winters, Tulsa, 1985—; mem. spl. task force Office of Comptroller of Currency, U.S. Dept. Treasury, 1978. Mem. editorial bd. Washburn U. Law Jour., 1982. Harry K. Allen fellow Washburn U. Sch. Law, Topeka, 1981; George A. Kline scholar Washburn U. Sch. Law, 1982. Mem. ABA, Kans. Bar Assn., Okla. Bar Assn., Tulsa Bar Assn. (mem. vol. lawyers program 1983—), Christian Lawyers Prayer Breakfast Group, Alpha Tau Omega (bd. dirs., v.p. bldg. corp. 1978-82). Presbyterian. Clubs: Tulsa Running, Tulsa Wheelmen (pres. 1987—). Banking, Consumer commercial, State civil litigation. Office: Conner & Winters 2400 1st Nat Tower Tulsa OK 74103

MCCOLLOCH, MURRAY MICHAEL, lawyer; b. Los Angeles, June 9, 1926; s. Carrick L. and Irma (Shelton) McC.; m. Jane Frye, Oct. 17, 1953; children: Sidney Michael, Mark Lindsey. BA, U. Md., 1949; JD, Harvard U., 1952. Bar: U.S. Dist. Ct. D.C. 1953, U.S. Ct. Appeals (D.C. cir.) 1953, U.S. Ct. Claims 1953, U.S. Ct. Customs and Patent Appeals 1953, U.S. Tax Ct. 1953, Calif. 1954, U.S. Dist. Ct. (so. dist.) Calif. 1954, Va. 1963, N.Y. 1969, Tex. 1979, U.S. Dist. Ct. (no. dist.) Tex. 1980. Law clk. to presiding judge U.S. Ct. Appeals, Washington, 1952-53; atty. subcom. adminstrn.

internal revenue laws U.S. Ho. Reps., Washington, 1953; assoc. Gray, Binkley & Pfaelzer, Los Angeles, 1953-55; asst. counsel Occidental Life Co. Calif., Los Angeles, 1955-62; v.p. and counsel Fidelity Bankers Life Ins. Co., Richmond, Va., 1962-67; v.p., sec. and counsel J.C. Penney Life Ins. Co. subs. J.C. Penney Co., Inc., N.Y.C., 1967-76; sr. v.p., sec. and counsel J.C. Penney Life Ins. Co. subs. J.C. Penney Co., Inc., Plano, Tex., 1982—, J.C. Penney Life Ins. Co., Great Am. Res. Ins. Co., Dallas, 1976-82; chmn. industry adv. com. conf. ins. legislators, 1982-83. Author: Group Insurance Trusts, 1962, You Don't Say, 1986. Served as cpl. AC U.S. Army, 1944-45. Mem. ABA, Dallas Bar Assn., Assn. Life Ins. Counsel, Am. Council Life Ins. (chmn. legal sect. 1984-85). Republican. Methodist. Insurance, Legislative. Home: 3013 Jomar Dr Plano TX 75075 Office: JC Penney Life Ins Co 2700 W Plano Pkwy Plano TX 75075

MCCOLLUM, JAMES FOUNTAIN, lawyer; b. Reidsville, N.C., Mar. 24, 1946; s. James F. and Dell (Frazier) McC.; m. Susan Shasek, Apr. 26, 1969; children—Audra Lynn, Amy Elizabeth. B.S., Fla. Atlantic U., 1968; J.D., Fla. State U., 1972. Bar: U.S. Ct. Appeals (5th cir.) 1973, Fla. 1972, U.S. Ct. Appeals (11th cir.) 1982. Assoc., Kennedy & McCollum, 1972-73, James F. McCollum, P.A., 1973-77, McCollum & Oberhausen, P.A., 1977-80, McCollum & Rhoades, Sebring, Fla., 1980-86, McCollum & Waite, P.A., 1986—; pres. Highlands Devel. Concepts, Inc., Sebring, 1982—; sec. Focus Broadcast Communications, Inc., Sebring, 1982—; mng. ptnr. Highlands Investment Service. Treas., Highlands County chpt. ARC, 1973-76; vestryman St. Agnes Episcopal Ch., 1973-83, chancellor, 1978—; mem. Com. 100 of Highlands County, 1975-83, bd. dirs., 1985-87; chmn. bd., treas. Central Fla. Racing Assn., 1976-78; chmn. Leadership Sebring; life mem., past pres. Highlands Little Theatre, Inc. Recipient citation ARC, 1974; Presdl. award of appreciation Fla. Jaycees, 1980-81, 82, 85; named Jaycee of Year, Sebring Jaycees, 1981; Outstanding Local Chpt. Pres., U.S. Jaycees, 1977. Mem. ABA, Am. Trial Lawyers Assn., Commercial Law League Am., Am. Arbitration Assn. (comml. arbitration panel), Fla. Bar (Fla. Bar Jour. com.), Highlands County Bar Assn. (past chmn. legal aid com.), Greater Sebring C. of C. (bd. dirs. 1982—, pres. 1986-87), Fla. Jaycees (life mem. internat. senate 1977—). Republican. Episcopalian. Club: Lions (dir. 1972-73, Disting. award 1984). Probate, Real property. Office: 129 S Commerce St Sebring FL 33870

MCCOLLUM, SUSAN HILL, lawyer; b. Ogden, Utah, Aug. 16, 1955; d. George Junior and Marion Ella (Watson) Hill; m. Thomas David McCollum, Jan. 16, 1982. AAS in Radiol. Tech., Weber State Coll., 1975, BS in Acctg., 1979; JD, Brigham Young U., 1982. Bar: Utah 1982, U.S. Dist. Ct. Utah 1982, Calif. 1983, U.S. Ct. Appeals (9th cir.) 1984, U.S. Dist. Ct. (cen. dist.) Calif. 1985. X-ray technician Drs. West & McKay, Ogden, 1975-77; tax examiner IRS, Ogden, 1977-79; assoc. Craig P. Orrock P.C., Salt Lake City, 1982-83, Hollister & Brace, Santa Barbara, Calif., 1983—. Mem. ABA, Assn. Trial Lawyers Am., Calif. Trial Lawyers Assn., Phi Delta Phi. Democrat. Mormon. State civil litigation, Personal injury, Landlord-tenant. Office: Hollister & Brace 1126 Santa Barbara St PO Box 630 Santa Barbara CA 93102

MCCOMAS, ALBERT LAUN, lawyer; b. Balt., Aug. 28, 1952; s. Francis Marion and Marguerite Christina (Laun) McC. BA, Loyola Coll., Balt., 1974, MBA with honors, 1976; JD with honors, U. Md., 1979. Bar: Md. 1980, U.S. Dist. Ct. Md. 1980. Law clk. Md. Cir. Ct., Westminster, 1979-81; assoc. Lord, Whip, Coughlan & Green, P.A., Balt., 1981-85; claims counsel Md. Casualty Co., Balt., 1986—. Mem. Md. Law Rev., 1977-79. Mem. Chesapeake Bay Found., Annapolis, 1985—. Asper fellow U. Md., 1978. Mem. ABA, Md. Bar Assn., Bar Assn. Balt. City, Met. Assn. Def. Trial Counsel. Democrat. Roman Catholic. Insurance, Environment. Office: Md Casualty Co 3910 Keswick Rd Baltimore MD 21211

MCCOMB, JOHN PAUL, lawyer; b. Bellevue, Pa., Oct. 7, 1922; s. John Paul and Kathryn Elizabeth (McKinnon) M.; m. Anne Nutting Mercur, Nov. 8, 1944; children—Sarah, Stewart, David, Richard. B.A., Princeton U., 1944; J.D., Harvard U., 1948. Bar: Pa. 1949, U.S. Supreme Ct. 1980. Assoc. Griggs, Moreland, Blair & Douglass, 1949-53; ptnr. McComb & Wolfe, 1953-58; sec., counsel J.H. Hillman & Sons, 1958-63; ptnr. Buchanan Ingersoll and predecessor firm Moorhead & Knox, 1963—; trustee Hosp. Assn. Pa., 1983—; chmn., trustee Shadyside Hosp.; sec., bd. dirs. Action, Housing Inc. Served to capt. USMCR, 1944-46, 1951-52. Mem. ABA, Pa. Bar Assn., Allegheny County Bar Assn., Am. Judicature Soc. Republican. Presbyterian. Clubs: HYP, Duquesne, Pitts. Golf. Health, Federal civil litigation, Libel. Home: 207 Farmington Rd Pittsburgh PA 15215 Office: 57th Floor 600 Grant St Pittsburgh PA 15219

MCCONATY, BRIAN GILMOUR, lawyer; b. Denver, Sept. 15, 1949; s. Joseph Paul and Helen (Gilmour) McC.; m. Patricia Hughes, Sept. 28, 1953; children: Joseph, Matthew, Molly. Student, Gonzaga U., Florence, Italy, 1968-70; BA, Colo. U., 1972, JD, 1975. Dep. dist. atty. Aspen, Colo., 1977; dep. dist. atty. Denver, 1978-80, asst. U.S. atty., 1980-81; assoc. Halaby & Bahr, Denver, 1981-83, Johnson Mahoney & Scott, Denver, 1983—. Mem. ABA, Am. Trial Lawyers Assn., Colo. Trial Lawyers Assn., Colo. Def. Lawyers Assn., Def. Research Inst. Personal injury. Office: Johnson Mahoney & Scott 3773 Cherry Creek Dr N Denver CO 80209

MCCONKIE, OSCAR WALTER, lawyer; b. Moad, Utah, May 26, 1926; s. Oscar Walter and Margaret Vivian (Redd) M.; m. Judith Stoddard, Mar. 17, 1951; children—Oscar III, Ann, Daniel, Gail, Clair, Pace Jefferson, Roger James, Edward. B.S. in Polit. Sci., U. Utah, 1949, J.D., 1952. Bar: Utah 1952, U.S. Ct. Appeals (10th cir.) 1952, U.S. Supreme Ct. 1981. County atty. Summit County (Utah), 1959-63; instr. bus. law Stevens Henager Coll., Salt Lake City, 1952-67; ptnr. Kirton, McConkie & Bushnell, Salt Lake City, 1967. Served with USN, 1944-46. Mem. Utah House of Reps., 1955-57; pres. Utah State Senate, 1965-66; chmn. Utah Bd. Edn., 1983-85. Mem. ABA, Utah Bar Assn., Salt Lake County Bar Assn. Democrat. Mormon. Author: The Kingdom of God, 1962; God and Man, 1963; The Priest in the Aaronic Priesthood, 1964; Angels, 1975; Aaronic Priesthood, 1977; She Shall Be Called Woman, 1979. Legislative, Legal education, General practice. Home: 1954 Laird Dr Salt Lake City UT 84108 Office: 330 S 300 East Salt Lake City UT 84111

MC CONNAUGHEY, GEORGE CARLTON, JR., lawyer, utility company executive; b. Hillsboro, Ohio, Aug. 9, 1925; s. George Carlton and Nelle (Morse) McC.; m. Carolyn Schlieper, June 16, 1951; children: Elizabeth, Susan, Nancy. B.A., Denison U., 1949; LL.B., Ohio State U., 1951, J.D., 1967. Bar: Ohio 1951. Sole practice Columbus; ptnr. McConnaughey & McConnaughey, 1954-57, McConnaughey, McConnaughey & Stradley, 1957-62, Laylin, McConnaughey & Stradley, 1962-67, George, Greek, King, McMahon & McConnaughey, 1967-79, McConnaughey, Stradley, Mone & Moul, 1979-81, Thompson, Hine & Flory (merger McConnaughey, Stradley, Mone & Moul with Thompson, Hine & Flory), Cleve., Columbus and Washington, 1981—; sec., gen. counsel Alltel Corp., Hudson, Ohio, 1960—; also dir.; bd. dirs. N.Am. Broadcasting Co. (WMNI and WMGG Radio); asst. atty. gen. State of Ohio, 1951-54. Pres. Upper Arlington (Ohio) Bd. Edn., 1967-69, Columbus Town Meeting Assn., 1974-76; chmn. Ohio Young Reps., 1956; U.S. presdl. elector, 1956; trustee Buckeye Boys Ranch, Columbus, 1967-73, 75-81, Ohio Council Econ. Edn.; elder Covenant Presbyn. Ch., Columbus. Served with U.S. Army, 1943-45, ETO. Mem. ABA (council pub. utility law sect.), Ohio Bar Assn., Columbus Bar Assn., Am. Judicature Soc. Clubs: Columbus, Scioto Country, Athletic (Columbus). Lodges: Rotary, Masons. Public utilities, General corporate. Home: 1969 Andover Rd Columbus OH 43212 Office: 100 E Broad St Columbus OH 43215

MCCONNELL, DAVID KELSO, lawyer; b. N.Y.C., July 12, 1932; s. David and Caroline Hanna (Kelso) McC.; m. Alice Schmitt, Dec. 26, 1953; children—Elissa Anne, Kathleen Anne, David Willet. B.C.E., CCNY, 1954; LL.B., Yale U., 1962. Bar: Conn. 1962, Pa. 1975, U.S. dist. Ct. Conn. 1963, U.S. Dist. Ct. (ea. dist.) Pa. 1971, U.S. Ct. Appeals. (2d cir.) 1964, U.S. Ct. Appeals. (3d cir.) 1966, U.S. Sup. Ct. 1970, N.Y. 1985. Asst. counsel N.Y.N.H. & H. R.R., New Haven, 1962-65, counsel., 1966-68; asst. atty. gen. U.S. Virgin Islands, 1965-66; asst. gen. atty. Pa. Central Transp. Co., New Haven, 1969-70, asst. gen. counsel, Phila, 1970-71, sr. reorganization atty., 1971, adminstrv. officer and spl. counsel to trustees, 1971-76, gen. atty., 1977-78; asst. to chmn, chief exec. officer The Penn Central Corp., N.Y.C., 1979-80, corp. sec., 1980-82; v.p., gen. counsel Gen. Cable Co., Greenwich, Conn., 1982-85; of counsel McCarthy, Fingar, Donovan, Drazen & Smith, White Plains, N.Y. and Greenwich, Conn., 1985—. councilman Town of Pelham, N.Y., 1985—; dir. numerous cos. including Ft. Wayne Union R.R. Co., Gen. Cable Internat., Inc., Gen. Cable Licensing Corp., Mich. Central R.R. Co., Telsta Network Services, Inc., Pa.-Reading Seashore Lines, Dayton Union Railway Co., Waynesburg So. R.R. Co., United Railroad Corp. Trustee Huguenot Meml. Ch., Pelham N.Y. Served with U.S. Navy, 1954-59, USNR, 1959-79. Mem. ABA, Conn. Bar Assn., Assn. of Bar City of N.Y. Clubs: Yale Phila., Corinthians, St. Andrews Soc. N.Y. (bd. mgrs. 1986—). Private international, Legislative, General corporate. Home: 29 Storer Ave Pelham NY 10803 Office: 1 E Putnam Ave Greenwich CT 06830

MCCONNELL, JACK LEWIS, air lines executive, lawyer; b. Butler, Mo., Aug. 28, 1934; s. Virgil and Helen Hannah (Harris) McC.; m. Nancy Carolyn Roy, June 18, 1960; children—Thomas High, Christine Carolyn. B.S., U. Denver, 1957, J.D., 1965; M.B.A., Northwestern U., 1958. Bar: Colo. 1965, Ill. 1965, U.S. Dist. Ct. (no. dist.) Ill. 1965, U.S. Ct. Appeals (10th cir.) 1965. Asst. advt. staff Procter & Gamble, Cin., 1958-60; account exec. N.W. Ayer & Son, San Francisco, 1960-62; atty. Ill. Tool Works, Chgo., 1965-70; v.p., asst. gen. counsel Apeco Corp., Evanston, Ill., 1970-74; v.p. Vendo Corp., Kansas City, Mo., 1974-75; v.p., assoc. gen. counsel United Airlines, Inc., Chgo., 1975—. Mem. ABA (chmn. aviation com. 1977—). Presbyterian. Club: Thorngate Country. Administrative and regulatory, Antitrust, General corporate. Home: 4 Nottingham Dr Lincolnshire IL 60015 Office: United Air Lines Inc PO Box 66100 Chicago IL 60666

MCCONNELL, JAMES DAVID, lawyer; b. Edina, Mo., Oct. 31, 1955; s. Howard Weldon and Norma Eileen (Echternacht) McC.; m. Mary Lu Wilson, Nov. 12, 1983. BS, Northeast Mo. State U., 1976; JD, U. Mo., 1979. Bar: Mo. 1979, U.S. Dist. Ct. (ea. dist.) Mo. 1981. Ptnr. Bollow Wallace & McConnell, Shelbina, Mo., 1979—; atty. City of Shelbina, 1980-85, City of Clarence, Mo., 1983—; pros. atty. Shelby County, Mo., 1987—; pres. bd. dirs. Legal Services of N.E. Mo. 1985-86. Com. chair Cub Scouts Am., Shelbina, 1984—; bd. dirs. Shelby County (Mo.) Fair, 1985—. Mem. ABA (dist. rep. for Mo. and Tenn. young lawyers div. 1983-85, editorial bd. Barrister mag., 1985—, Chair Person's award 1984-85), Mo. Assn. Trial Lawyers, Mo. Bar Assn. (treas. young lawyers sect. council 1983-85, sec. 1984-85, chmn. 1986—, Pres.'s award 1982), Shelbina Jaycees. Democrat. Lodge: Lions (pres. Shelbina club 1985-86). Avocations: coin collecting, softball, hunting, skiing. General practice, Family and matrimonial, Criminal. Home: 205 E Spruce Shelbina MO 63468 Office: Bollow Wallace & McConnell 308 E Walnut Shelbina MO 63468

MCCONNELL, JAMES GUY, lawyer; b. Hinsdale, Ill., Sept. 24, 1947; s. William F. and Virginia (Brown) McC.; m. Debra Drue Wax, May 30, 1976; children: Colin, Nicholas, Joanna. BS in Journalism, Iowa State U., 1969; JD, Northwestern U., 1973. Bar: Ill. 1973, U.S. Dist. Ct. (no. dist.) Ill. 1973, U.S. Ct. Appeals (7th cir.) 1973, U.S. Supreme Ct. 1977. Assoc. Rooks, Pitts & Poust, Chgo., 1973-80, ptnr., 1980-85; ptnr. Bell, Boyd & Lloyd, Chgo., 1985—; adj. prof. Kent Coll. Law Ill. Inst. Tech., Chgo., 1978—. Author: Comparative Negligence Defense Tactics, 1985; contbg. editor jour. Hazardous Waste & Toxic Torts Law & Strategy. Mem. dist. 102 Sch. Bd., LaGrange Park. Ill., 1975-76. Mem. ABA, Ill. Bar Assn., Chgo. Bar Assn., Legal Club Chgo., Soc. Trial Lawyers, Union League. Federal civil litigation, State civil litigation, Insurance. Office: Bell Boyd & Lloyd Three First Nat Plaza Chicago IL 60602

MCCONNELL, JOHN HAY, lawyer; b. N.Y.C., Aug. 3, 1939; s. Frank J. and Dorothy (Hay) McC.; m. Diana Wallace; 1 child, Barnet Wallace. AB, U. Pa., 1962; JD, St. John's U., 1970; LLM in Internat. Legal Studies, NYU, 1975. Bar: N.Y. 1971, U.S. Dist. Ct. (so. and ea. dists.) N.Y. 1972, U.S. Ct. Appeals (2d cir.) 1975, U.S. Supreme Ct. 1976. Ptnr. Purrington, McConnell & Agus, N.Y.C., 1971—. Assoc. editor St. John's U. Law Rev., 1969-70. Served to capt. USCGR, 1962—. Mem. Maritime Law Assn. U.S., Phi Delta Phi. Clubs: India House (N.Y.C.), Indian Harbor Yacht (Greenwich, Ct.). Avocation: sailing. Admiralty, Consumer commercial, Private international. Office: Purrington McConnell & Agus 82 Wall St New York NY 10005

MCCONNELL, MICHAEL T., Lawyer; b. San Francisco, June 18, 1954; s. Lawrence V. and Ann (Poland) McC. BS, U. Oreg., 1977; JD, U. Denver, 1980. Bar: Colo., U.S. Dist. Ct. Colo., U.S. Ct. Appeals (10th cir.). Ptnr. Long & Jaudon, Denver, 1980—; lectr. U. Denver Coll. Law, 1985—. Mem. Assn. Trial Lawyers Am., ABA, Colo. Bar Assn., Denver Bar Assn., Colo. Def. Lawyers Assn. State civil litigation, Federal civil litigation, Insurance. Office: Long & Jaudon 1600 Ogden Denver CO 80218

MCCONNELL, PAUL STEWART, lawyer; b. Vancouver, B.C., Can., Sept. 2, 1955; came to U.S., 1978; s. Bruce Victor and Jewel Winnifred (Stewart) McC.; m. Patricia Jean Minthorn, Dec. 23, 1977; children: Audrey Dawn, Perry William, Nathanael Patrick. BA, Asbury Coll., 1977; JD, Oral Roberts U., 1982. Bar: Wash. 1982, U.S. Dist. Ct. (we. dist.) Wash. 1983, U.S. Supreme Ct. 1986, Va. 1987. Assoc. Moren, Lageschulte & Cornell, P.S., Seattle, 1982-84; asst. prof., dir. policy research Christian Broadcasting Network U., Virginia Beach, Va., 1984-86; staff atty. Nat. Legal Found., Virginia Beach, 1986—; policy cons. Christian Broadcasting Assn., Scarborough, Ont., Can., 1985—. Mem. resource bank Family Research Council, Washington, 1986—. Mem. ABA (corp. bus. and banking, internat. law sects.). Avocations: travel, family. Civil rights, Legal history. Office: Nat Legal Found 6477 College Park Sq Suite 306 Virginia Beach VA 23464

MCCONNICO, STEPHEN E., lawyer; b. Jacksonville, Tex., Apr. 8, 1950; s. Charles Kit and Ruth (Nettle) McC.; m. Deborah May, June 23, 1973; children: David Kit, Stephen Andrew. BA with honors, U. Tex., 1972; JD with honors, Baylor U., 1976. Bar: Tex. 1976. Briefing atty. Tex. Supreme Ct., Austin, 1976-77; assoc. Andrews & Kurth, Houston, 1977-81; ptnr. Scott, Douglass & Luton, Austin, 1981—; mem. Tex. Supreme Ct. Adv. Com., Austin, 1982—. Friend Laguna Gloria Mus., Austin, 1984; contbr. Austin Symphony, 1984; mem. St. Theresa Cath. Ch. Parish Counsel, Austin, 1984; mem. Austin Dem. Forum, 1984. Fellow Tex. Bar Found.; mem. ABA, Travis County Bar Assn. (bd. dirs. 1986), Tex. Young Lawyers Assn., Austin Young Lawyers Assn. (outstanding young lawyer 1984). Clubs: Austin, Westwood. State civil litigation, Personal injury. Home: 6106 Mountain Climb Austin TX 78731 Office: Scott Douglass & Luton 1st City Bank Bldg 12th Floor Austin TX 78701

MCCONOMY, JAMES HERBERT, lawyer; b. Pitts., Mar. 24, 1937; s. Murray Michael and Catherine Elizabeth (Herbert) McC.; m. Jeanne Margaret Cronin, Sept. 3, 1960; children: Margaret Jeanne, Michael Murray. AB cum laude, Harvard U., 1959, LLB, 1962. Bar: Pa. 1963, U.S. Ct. Appeals (3d cir.) 1972, U.S. Supreme Ct. 1977. Ptnr. Reed, Smith, Shaw & McClay, Pitts., 1962—. Fellow Am. Coll. Trial Lawyers; mem. ABA, Pa. Bar Assn. (chmn. comml. litigation sect. 1986—), Allegheny County Acad. Trial Lawyers. Republican. Roman Catholic. Clubs: Duquesne, Harvard-Yale-Princeton (Pitts.). Avocations: photography, travel. Federal civil litigation, State civil litigation, Contracts commercial. Home: 1117 Harvard Rd Pittsburgh PA 15205 Office: Reed Smith Shaw & McClay 435 6th Ave Pittsburgh PA 15219

MCCORKLE, LINDA ANN, lawyer; b. Raymond, Wash., Nov. 13, 1947; d. Marcus Eugene and Mary Lynn (Lamping) McC.; m. Michael George Wandell, Jan. 2, 1983; 1 child, Marcus Patrick Wandell. BA, U. Washington, 1969; MPA, Syracuse U., 1970; JD, Georgetown U., 1974. Bar: Washington 1974, D.C. 1977, U.S. Ct. Appeals (D.C. cir.) 1977, U.S. Supreme Ct. 1979, U.S. Dist. Ct. (we. dist.) Wash. 1984. Staff counsel commn. on commerce, sci. and transp. U.S. Senate, Washington, 1973-77; assoc. Blum & Nash, Washington, 1977-79; northwest counsel ITT Rayonier Inc., Seattle, 1980-86; assoc. Bogle & Gates, Seattle, 1986—; vol. guardian ad litem ct. appointed King County Superior Ct., Seattle, 1986—. Bd. dirs. Children's Trust Found., 1987—. Mem. ABA, D.C. Bar Assn., Wash. State Bar Assn., Wash. Women Lawyers. Episcopalian. Health, General corporate, Administrative and regulatory. Office: Bogle & Gates The Bank of Calif Ctr Seattle WA 98164

MCCORKLE, LUCY VIRGINIA, lawyer, consultant; b. White Pine, Tenn., May 12, 1951; d. William Moore and Gertrude (Huggins) McC. BS in Pathology, U. Ala., 1973; JD, Stamford U., 1980. Bar: Ala. 1980. Assoc., cons. Hardin & Hollis, Birmingham, Ala., 1980-83; sole practice Birmingham, 1983-85; atty., cons., pres. Southeastern Medicolegal Assocs., Inc., Birmingham, 1985—; cons. pvt. practitioners, Birmingham, 1980—, Ala. Med. Examiners Assn., 1980-82. Officer Birmingham Humane Soc. Bd., 1973-78, Ala. Animal League, bd. dirs.; coordinator Jefferson-Jackson Day Dinner Dems., Birmingham, 1979; nat. com. woman Ala. Young Dems., 1979; bd. dirs. Birmingham Festival Theater Bd., 1984-87. Mem. ABA (health law forum com.), Ala. Bar Assn. (young lawyers sect., exec. com., chmn. medicolegal com.'s subcom. pub. interest death investigation), Birmingham Bar Assn. (law day com., med. liaison com., interprofl. com. with Jefferson County Med. Soc.), Ala. Trial Lawyers Assn., ACLU, Am. Soc. Law and Medicine, Nat. Health Lawyers Assn., Young Men's Bus., Birmingham Bus. and Profl. Women's (nominated Outstanding Young Career Woman of Yr. 1978), Phi Beta Phi. Jewish. Avocations: cooking, fishing, sailing, hiking. Personal injury, Health, State civil litigation. Home: 4322 10th Ave S Birmingham AL 35222 Office: Southeastern Medicolegal Assocs Inc PO Box 550129 Birmingham AL 35255

MCCORMACK, DONNELL JAMES, lawyer; b. Memphis, Dec. 29, 1952; s. Donnell James and Mary Heath (Butler) McC.; m. Helen Lawrence Bozeman, Sept. 6, 1980; children: Helen Lawrence, Mary Butler. BA, Rhodes Coll., 1974; JD, Memphis State U., 1979. Bar: Tenn. 1979, U.S. Dist. Ct. (we. dist.) Tenn. 1979. Project coordinator engring. dept. Conwood Corp., Memphis, 1975-76; assoc. McDonald, Kuhn, Smith, Miller & Tait, Memphis, 1979-84; atty. Holiday Inns, Inc., Memphis, 1984-85, Holiday Corp., Memphis, 1985—; bd. dirs. Woodson & Bozeman Inc., Memphis. Chmn. law and adjudication com. Mayor's Task Rorce on Drunk Driving, Memphis, 1984-85, task force chmn., 1985—. Named Col. Aide de Camp Gov.'s Staff, 1979. Mem. ABA (tort and ins. practice subcom., deceptive unfair trade practices subcom., various sects.), Tenn. Bar Assn., Memphis Bar Assn., Shelby County Bar Assn. Federal civil litigation, State civil litigation, General corporate. Home: 27 Lynnfield Memphis TN 38119 Office: Holiday Corp Law Dept 3796 Lamar Ave Memphis TN 38195

MC CORMACK, EDWARD JOSEPH, JR., lawyer; b. Boston, Aug. 29, 1923; s. Edward J. and Mary T. (Coffey) McC.; m. Emily Rupils, Oct. 19, 1946; children—Edward Joseph III, John W. Student, Colby Coll., 1941-42; B.S., U.S. Naval Acad., 1946; JD cum laude, Boston U., 1952. Bar: Mass. 1952. Atty. Gen. Commonwealth of Mass., 1958-63. Mem. city council, Boston, 1953-58, pres., 1956; Chmn. Com. for Boston; trustee New Eng. Sch. Law., Boston Pvt. Industry Council, Boston Access Cable Commn. Served with USN, 1946-49. Club: 100 of Mass. (dir.). Administrative and regulatory, Real property, General practice. Home: Jamaicaway Tower 111 Perkins St Boston MA 02130 Office: 265 Franklin St Boston MA 02110

MC CORMACK, FRANCIS XAVIER, oil co. exec.; b. Bklyn., July 9, 1929; s. Joseph and Blanche V. (Dengel) McC.; m. Margaret V. Hynes, Apr. 24, 1954; children—Marguerite, Francis Xavier, Sean Michael, Keith John, Cecelia Blanche, Christopher Thomas. A.B. cum laude, St. Francis Coll., Bklyn., 1951; LL.B., Columbia, 1954. Bar: N.Y. bar 1955, Mich. bar 1963, Calif. bar 1974, Pa. bar 1975. Asso. firm Cravath, Swaine & Moore, N.Y.C., 1956-62; sr. atty. Ford Motor Co., 1962-64, asst. gen. counsel, 1970-72; v.p., gen. counsel, sec. Philco-Ford Corp., 1964-72; v.p., gen. counsel Atlantic Richfield Co., 1972-73, sr. v.p., gen. counsel, 1973—. Decorated commendatore Ordine al Merito della Republica Italiana. General corporate. Home: 975 Singing Wood Dr Arcadia CA 91006 Office: 515 S Flower St Los Angeles CA 90071

MCCORMICK, DAVID ARTHUR, lawyer; b. McKeesport, Pa., Oct. 26, 1946; s. Arthur Paul and Eleanor Irene (Gibson) McC. BA, Westminster Coll., 1967; JD, Duquesne U., 1973; MBA, U. Pa., 1975. Bar: Pa. 1973, D.C. 1978, U.S. Ct. Appeals (3d cir.) 1977, U.S. Ct. Appeals (4th and D.C. cirs.) 1980, U.S. Supreme Ct. 1980. Asst. commerce counsel Penn Cen. R.R., Phila., 1973-76; assoc. labor counsel Consol. Rail Corp., Phila., 1976-78; atty. Dept. Army, Washington, 1978—. Mem. ABA, Pa. Bar Assn., Phila. Bar Assn., D.C. Bar Assn., Soc. Cin. (Del. chpt.), SAR (Pitts. chpt.), Phi Alpha Delta. Presbyterian. Lodge: Masons. General practice, Public utilities.

MCCORMICK, EDWARD JAMES, JR., lawyer; b. Toledo, May 11, 1921; s. Edward James and Josephine (Beck) McC.; m. Mary Jane Blank, Jan. 27, 1951; children—Mary McCormick Krueger, Edward James III, Patrick William, Michael J. B.S., John Carroll U., 1942; J.D., Western Res. U., 1948. Bar: Ohio 1948, U.S. Supreme Ct. 1980. Ptnr., office mgr. McCormick, Pommeranz & Perlman and predecessor firm McCormick & Pommeranz, Toledo; mem. teaching staff St. Vincent Hosp. Sch. Nursing, 1951-67. Trustee Toledo Small Bus. Assn., 1950-75, pres., 1954-55, 56-58, 67-68; trustee Goodwill Industries Toledo, 1961-74, chmn. meml. gifts com., mem. exec. com., 1965-70; trustee Lucas County unit Am. Cancer Soc., 1950-61, sec., 1953, v.p., 1954-56, pres., 1957-58; founder, incorporator, sec., trustee Cancer Cytology Research Fund Toledo, Inc., 1956-79; trustee Ohio Cerebral Palsy Assn., 1963-70; incorporator, sec., trustee N.W. Ohio Clin. Engring. Ctr., 1972-74; trustee Friendly Ctr., 1973-83, Ohio Blind Assn., 1970-79; founder-incorporator, trustee, sec. Western Lake Erie Hist. Soc., 1978-85; mem. Toledo Deanery Diocesan Council Catholic Men; asst. gen. counsel U.S. Power and Sail Squadrons. Named Outstanding Young Man of Yr., Toledo Jr. C. of C., 1951; Man of Nation, Woodmen of World, Omaha, 1952. Mem. ABA (corp., banking and bus. law sect., sr. mem. sect.), Ohio Bar Assn. (chmn. Am. citizenship com. 1958-67, mem. pub. relations com. 1967-72), Toledo Bar Assn. (chmn. pub. relations com. 1979, mem. grievance com. 1975—), Lucas County Bar Assn. (chmn. Am. citizenship com.), Assn. Trial Lawyers Am., Am. Judicature Soc., Am. Arbitration Assn., Conf. Pvt. Orgns. (sec.-treas.), Toledo C. of C. Clubs: Toledo Torch, Toledo, Blue Gavel. Lodges: Elks (grand esteemed leading knight 1964-65, mem. grand forum 1965-70), Lions (trustee, legal advisor Ohio Eye Research Found. 1956-70; pres. 1957-58, chmn. permanent membership com. 1961-85, hon. mem. 1984, pres. 1957, A.B. Snyder award 1979), KC. Office: Nat Bank Bldg Suite 824 Toledo OH 43604

MCCORMICK, GEORGE PAUL, JR., lawyer; b. Ingelwood, Calif., Mar. 6, 1947; s. George Paul Sr. and Emma Marie (Price) McC.; m. Kay Ellen Cottingham, Sept. 10, 1968; Michael Paul, Aaron Robert. BS in Psychology, Ohio State U., 1969; JD, U. Colo., 1972. Bar: Colo. 1972, U.S. Dist. Ct. Colo. 1972. Dep. dist. atty. City of Denver, 1972-73; dep. state pub. defender State of Colo., Denver, 1973-76; dep. state pub. defender, head regional office State of Colo., Boulder, 1976-79; sole practice Boulder, 1979—; guest lectr. Colo. Pub. Defender Office, Coppermountain, Colo., 1984. Bd. dirs. Boulder County Community Corrections Bd., 1978-79. Mem. ABA, Colo. Bar Assn., Boulder County Bar Assn. (chmn. criminal law com. 1986-87), Assn. Trial Lawyers Am., Colo. Trial Lawyers Assn., Colo. Criminal Def. Bar Assn. Avocations: swimming, bicycling, running, triathlon, hiking. Criminal, Personal injury, Family and matrimonial. Home: Sugarloaf Star Rt Boulder CO 80302 Office: 1426 Pearl Suite 206 Boulder CO 80302

MCCORMICK, HUGH THOMAS, lawyer; b. McAlester, Okla., Nov. 24, 1944; s. Hugh O. and Lois (McGucken) McC.; m. Suzanna G. Weingarten, Dec. 5, 1975; 1 child, John B. BA, U. Mich., 1968; JD, Rutgers U., 1977; LLM in Taxation, Georgetown U., 1980. Bar: N.Y. 1977, D.C. 1979, Maine 1981. Atty. office chief counsel interpretative div. IRS, Washington, 1977-81; assoc. Perkins, Thompson, Hinkley & Keddy, Portland, Maine, 1981-83, LeBoeuf, Lamb, Leiby & MacRae, N.Y.C., 1983—. Trustee U.S. Team Handball Found., N.J., 1985—. Served to 1st lt. U.S. Army, 1966-69. Mem. ABA, D.C. Bar Assn., N.Y. State Bar Assn. (tax sect., exec. com., co-chmn. ins. co. com. 1986—). Democrat. Corporate taxation, Insurance. Home: 206 Ancon Ave Pelham NY 10803 Office: LeBoeuf Lamb Leiby & MacRae 520 Madison Ave New York NY 10022

MCCORMICK, JOHN HOYLE, lawyer; b. Pensacola, Fla., July 30, 1933; s. Clyde Hoyle and Orrie Brooks (Frink) McC.; m. Patricia McCall, Dec. 27, 1974. BS, U. Fla., 1955; JD, Stetson U., 1958. Bar: Fla. 1958. Ptnr. McCormick, Drury & Scaff, Jasper, Fla., 1958-74; sr. ptnr. McCormick, Drury & Scaff, Jasper, Fla., 1974—; county judge, Hamilton County, Fla., 1960-

72, atty., 1970—; local counsel So. Ry. System, 1968—, CSX, Ry., 1972—; atty. Hamilton County Devel. Authority, 1970—; bd. dirs. 1st Fed. Savs. Bank Fla. Mayor City of White Springs, Fla., 1959; pres. Hamilton County C. of C., Jasper, 1961. Mem. Phi Delta Phi. Democrat. Methodist. Lodges: Masons, Shriners. Avocations: gardening, motorhome camping, college football. Local government, Banking, Family and matrimonial. Home: 403 2d St NW Jasper FL 32052 Mailing Address: PO Drawer O Jasper FL 32052 Office: McCormick Drury & Scaff 215 2d St NE Jasper FL 32052

MCCORMICK, J(OSEPH) BURKE, lawyer; b. Port Washington, N.Y., Mar. 27, 1957; s. Raymond Daniel and Miriam (Lynch) McC.; m. Sallie Trigg Graham, Oct. 8, 1983; 1 child, Graham Keating. BSBA, Georgetown U., 1978; JD, Fordham U., 1981. Bar: N.Y. 1982, Tex. 1982, U.S. Dist. Ct. (no., so. and ea. dists.) Tex. 1982, U.S. Ct. Appeals (5th cir.) 1982, U.S. Dist. Ct. (we. dist.) Tex. 1984, U.S. Supreme Ct. 1986. Atty. legal dept. Texaco Inc., Houston, 1981-85; assoc. Butler & Binion, Houston, 1985—. Mng. editor: Fordham Urban Law Jour., 1980-81. Mem. ABA (litigation sect.), State Bar of Tex. (litigation sect.), Houston Bar Assn. (litigation sect.), Houston Young Lawyers Assn. Republican. Clubs: Georgetown Univ. Alumni of Houston (v.p. 1985-86, pres. 1986), Texas (Houston); N.Y. Athletic. Avocations: sailing, golf, running. Federal civil litigation, State civil litigation, Insurance. Home: 2116 Quenby Houston TX 77005 Office: Butler & Binion 1600 Allied Bank Plaza Houston TX 77002

MCCORMICK, SHAWN CHARLES, lawyer; b. Covington, Ky., July 31, 1954; s. Michael and Jeanette (Hemmerle) McC. B.S., Xavier U., Cin., 1974, M.B.A., 1978; J.D., No. Ky. U., 1978; LL.M., Georgetown U., 1981. Bar: Ky. 1978, Ohio 1979, Mich. 1981, U.S. Ct. Appeals (6th cir.) 1978, U.S. Tax Ct. 1979. Asst. plant engr. Texo Corp., Norwood, Ohio, 1972-78; tax cons. Touche Ross & Co., Cin., 1979-80; assoc. Dykema, Gossett, Spencer, Goodnow & Trigg, Detroit, 1981-85, Cors Bassett Kohlhepp Halloran & Moran, Cin., 1985—; cons. Tax Mgmt., Inc. Mem. ABA, Ky. Bar, Ohio Bar, Mich. Bar Assn. (employee benefits com.), No. Ky. Bar Assn. (chmn. tax sect. 1986—). Co-author: Tax Management Portfolio 61-4th Taxfree Exchanges Under Section 1031. Corporate taxation, Pension, profit-sharing, and employee benefits. Office: 1700 Carew Tower Cincinnati OH 45202

MCCOTTER, CHARLES KENNEDY, JR., United States magistrate; b. New Bern, N.C., Oct. 29, 1946; s. Charles Kennedy and Lucy (Dunn) McC.; m. Patricia Byrum, Aug. 3, 1968; children—Virginia Byrum, Patricia Dunn. B.S. in Bus., U. N.C.-Chapel Hill, 1968, J.D., 1971. Bar: N.C. 1971, U.S. Dist. Ct. (ea. dist.) N.C. 1971, U.S. Ct. Appeals (4th cir.) 1973. Law clk. to judge U.S. Dist. Ct. (ea. dist.) N.C. 1971-72; sole practice, New Bern, 1973; ptnr. McCotter and Mayo, New Bern, 1974-79; U.S. magistrate Eastern Dist. N.C., 1979—; lectr. in field; permanent del. to 4th Cir. Jud. Conf. Mem. ABA, N.C. Bar Assn., Craven County Bar Assn., N.C. Trial Lawyers Assn., Nat. Council U.S. Magistrates. Episcopalian. Lodges: Rotary, Lions (New Bern). Federal civil litigation. Office: PO Drawer 1029 New Bern NC 28560

MCCOTTER, JAMES RAWSON, lawyer; b. Denver, May 19, 1943; s. Charles R. and Jane M. (Ballantine) McC.; m. Carole Lee Hand, Sept. 5, 1965; children—Heidi M., Sage B. B.A., Stanford U., 1965; J.D., U. Colo., 1969. Bar: Colo. 1969, D.C. 1970, U.S. Dist. Ct. Colo. 1969, U.S. Ct. Appeals (10th and D.C. cirs.) 1970, U.S. Ct. Appeals (5th cir.) 1972, U.S. Supreme Ct. 1974. Law clk. U.S. Ct. Appeals (10th cir.), Denver, 1969-70; assoc. Covington & Burling, Washington, 1970-75; assoc. Kelly, Stansfield & O'Donnell, Denver, 1975-76, ptnr., 1977-86; assoc. gen. counsel Pub. Service Co. Colo., 1986—; . Editor-in-chief U. Colo. Law Rev. (Outstanding Achievement award 1969), 1968-69. Democratic precinct committeeman, Denver, 1983-84; bd. dirs. Sewall Rehab. Ctr., Denver, 1979-84, Porter Meml. Hosp. Found., 1986—. Named to Outstanding Young Men Am., U.S. Jaycees, 1971; Storke scholar U. Colo., Boulder, 1967. Mem. ABA, Colo. Bar Assn. (adminstrv. law com. 1979-84), Fed. Energy Bar Assn. (chmn. com. on environment 1982-83), Order of Coif. Episcopalian. Clubs: Law, University (admission com. 1981—), Denver Country (Denver). Public utilities, Juvenile, Federal civil litigation. Home: 345 Lafayette St Denver CO 80218 Office: Pub Service Co Colo 550 15th St Suite 830 Denver CO 80202

MCCOY, BRIAN LLOYD, lawyer, clergyman; b. Spokane, Wash., July 18, 1946; s. Robert Lloyd and Vera Jenny (Ellis) McC.; m. Janet Louise Harston, May 29, 1969; children: Brandon, Erin, Marschell, Jason, Spencer, Darek, Shannon, Garlan, Sharla. BA, Brigham Young U., 1970; MA, U. Okla., 1976; JD, U. Puget Sound, 1979. Bar: Wash. 1979, U.S. Dist. Ct. (we. dist.) Wash. 1979. Assoc. Law Offices of A. Knodel, Tacoma, 1979-80; sole practice Puyallup, Wash., 1980—. Bishop Mormon Ch., Puyallup, 1983—; Rep. State Conv., 1984; mem. parent-tchr. com. Bethel Sch. Bd., Tacoma, 1984-85. Served to capt. Spl. Forces, U.S. Army, 1970-75. Mem. ABA, Fed. Bar Assn. Western Wash., Wash. State Bar Assn., Assn. Trial Lawyers Am., Wash. State Trial Lawyers Assn., Pi Sigma Alpha. Lodge: Kiwanis. Avocations: basketball, skiing, reading. Personal injury, Insurance, State and federal civil litigation. Office: 12515 S Meridian Suite C Puyallup WA 98373

MCCOY, FRANCIS TYRONE, law educator; b. N.Y.C., Oct. 15, 1922; s. Francis Thomas and Gladys (Parker) M.; m. Mary Caldwell Watson, June 28, 1975. B.A., U. Fla., 1944, M.A., 1947, J.D., 1955. Bar: Fla. 1955. Faculty mem. U. Fla. Coll. Law, Gainesville, 1955—, prof., 1971—. Contbr. articles to profl. jours. Served to lt. U.S. Army, 1943-45. Mem. 8th Jud. Cir. Fla. Bar (sec. 1956—), Phi Beta Kappa (hon.). Episcopalian. Admiralty, Family and matrimonial, Legal history. Home: 2841 SW 1st Ave Gainesville FL 32607 Office: Coll of Law U Fla Gainesville FL 32611

MCCOY, HENRY DREWRY, II, lawyer; b. Pearisburg, Va., July 30, 1935; s. Henry Drewry and Valerie (Morris) M.; m. Jane Seed Pattie, Aug. 10, 1957 (div. Aug. 1965); 1 child, Julia Caperton. B.S., N.C. State U., 1956; LL.B., U. Va., 1962. Bar: N.Y. 1963. Assoc., Thacher, Proffitt & Wood, N.Y.C., 1962-64, Conboy, Hewitt, O'Brien & Boardman, N.Y.C., 1964-75; sole practice, N.Y.C., 1975—; cons. to attys. Project editor, co-founder Va. Jour. Internat. Law, 1961-62, also articles. Mem. Biafra Relief Com., N.Y.C., 1968; vol. Gubernatorial Campaign, Nelson Rockefeller, N.Y.C., 1966, Mayoralty Campaign, John Lindsay, N.Y.C., 1969. Served to capt. U.S. Army, 1957-59. Mem. Assn. of the Bar (sec. art law com., 1968-71, med. and law com., 1969-72). Republican. Episcopalian. Private international, Federal civil litigation, General corporate.

MCCOY, JOHN JOSEPH, lawyer; b. Cin., Mar. 15, 1952; s. Raymond F. and Margaret T. (Hohmann) McC. BS in Math. summa cum laude, Xavier U., 1974; JD, U. Chgo., 1977. Bar: Ohio 1977, D.C. 1980. Ptnr. Taft, Stettinius & Hollister, Cin., 1977—; lectr. Greater Cin. C. of C., 1984. Pro bono rep. Jr. Achievement Greater Cin., 1978; fund raiser Dan Beard council Boy Scouts Am., 1983; fund raising team leader Cin. Regatta, Cin. Ctr. Devel. Disorders, 1983; account mgr. United Appeal, Cin., 1984. Mem. ABA, Ohio State Bar Assn., Cin. Bar Assn. (fed. cts., common pleas cts. and negligence law coms. 1984), Cin. Inn of Ct. (barrister 1984-86, sec. bd. trustees 1986—). Clubs: Cin. Athletic (sec. bd. of trustees 1986—), Fairfield Sportsmen's (Cin.). Federal civil litigation, State civil litigation, General corporate. Home: 2567 Perkins Ln Cincinnati OH 45208

MCCOY, JOHN THOMAS, lawyer; b. Texarkana, Ark., Feb. 15, 1950. BA in Govt., U. Notre Dame, 1972; JD with honors, U. Iowa, 1977. Bar: Iowa 1977, U.S. Dist. Ct. (no. and so. dists.) Iowa 1978. Assoc. White, Wenzel & Piersall, Cedar Rapids, Iowa, 1977-78; from assoc. to ptnr. Lindeman & Yagla, Waterloo, Iowa, 1978—. Editor The Jour. Corp. Law, 1976-77. Pres. Columbus High Sch. Booster Club, Waterloo, 1985-87; judge adv. Amvet Post #11, Waterloo, 1986—. Served with U.S. Army, 1972-74. Mem. ABA, Iowa State Bar Assn., Black Hawk County Bar Assn. Roman Catholic. Lodge: KC. State civil litigation, Insurance, Personal injury. Home: 411 Carolina Ave Waterloo IA 50702 Office: Lindeman & Yagla 500 First Nat Bldg Waterloo IA 50703

MCCOY, REAGAN SCOTT, oil company executive, lawyer; b. Port Arthur, Tex., Nov. 25, 1945; s. William Murray and Elizabeth (Gilbert) McC.; m. Pat Kowalski, June 21, 1969; 1 child, Traci. BCE, Ga. Inst. Tech., 1968; JD, Loyola U., 1972. Bar: Tex. 1972, La. 1978. Structural engr. McDermott Inc., New Orleans, 1966-72; data processing mgr. McDermott Inc., London, 1972-76; cons. engr. McDermott Inc., New Orleans, 1976-79; adminstrv. mgr. Concord Oil Co., San Antonio, 1979-81, v.p., 1981—. Treas. Countryside San Pedro Recreation Club, 1981-82; bd. dirs. Countryside San Pedro Homeowners Assn., 1984-86. Fellow Tau Beta Pi; mem. ABA, San Antonio Bar Assn. (natural resources com. treas. 1986-87), NSPE, ASCE, Soc. Mining Engrs., Am. Assn. Petroleum Landmen, Real Estate Fin. Soc. (bd. dirs. 1986-87), Adminstrv. Mgmt. Soc. (pres. 1985-86). Presbyterian. Club: Plaza, Sonterra. Avocations: water sports, running, reading, woodworking. Oil and gas leasing, Real property, Construction. Home: 13015 Country Pass San Antonio TX 78216 Office: Concord Oil Co 1500 Alamo Bldg San Antonio TX 78205

MCCOY, THOMAS RAYMOND, lawyer, educator; b. Cin., Apr. 14, 1943; s. Raymond F. and Margaret T. (Hohmann) McC.; m. Judith A. Huth, July 27, 1968; children—Jennifer A., Ellen M. B.S., Xavier U., Cin., 1964; J.D., U. Cin., 1967; LL.M., Harvard U., 1968. Bar: Ohio 1967. Asst. prof. law Vanderbilt U., Nashville, 1968-71, assoc. prof., assoc. dean for acad. affairs, 1971-75, prof., 1975—. Bd. dirs. Opportunity House, Inc., Nashville, 1969-81, pres. bd., 1978-80. Mem. Am. Assn. Law Schs. (editorial bd. Soundings 1972-85). Civil rights, Jurisprudence, Oil and gas leasing. Home: 1502 Lynhurst Ct Brentwood TN 37027 Office: Vanderbilt U Law Sch Nashville TN 37240

MCCOY, WILLIAM CHARLES, JR., lawyer; b. Akron, Ohio, Dec. 10, 1923; s. William Charles and Katharine Raynolds (Bell) McC.; m. Julia Millikin Nash, June 21, 1952; children—Sarah, Louise, William, Peter. B.S. in Basic Engring., Princeton U., 1944; LL.B., Western Res. U., 1949. Bar: Ohio 1950. Ptnr. Bosworth, Sessions & McCoy, Cleve., 1973-79, Pearne, Gordon, McCoy & Granger, Cleve., 1979—; bd. dirs. Bicron Corp., Midwest Plastic Fabricators, Sparkle Wash Inc. Trustee Hawken Sch., 1970—, Ohio chpt. The Nature Conservatory. Councilman Hunting Valley Village. Served to lt. (j.g.) USNR, 1943-46. Mem. ABA, Cleve. Bar Assn., Am. Patent Law Assn., Fedn. Internationale des Counseils en Propriete Industrielle (council U.S. sect.). Club: Union (Cleve.). Patent, Trademark and copyright. Home: 36001 Shaker Blvd Chagrin Falls OH 44022 Office: Pearne Gordon McCoy & Granger 120 Leader Bldg Cleveland OH 44114

MCCRACKEN, CAROL WEAVER, lawyer, educator; b. Newark, Aug. 7, 1946; d. John Louis and Catherine (Keane) Weaver; m. Richard A. McCracken, June 15, 1968 (div. Feb. 1986); children: Megan S., Heather K. BA, Rutgers U., 1968; JD, Seton Hall U., 1977. Bar: N.J. 1977, U.S. Dist. Ct. N.J. 1977. Staff atty. Greenstone & Sokol, Hackensack, N.J., 1977-79; trial atty. Office of Pub. Defender, Paterson, N.J., 1979-82; ptnr. Barbarula, McCracken & Masessa, Butler, N.J., 1982—; adj. faculty William Paterson Coll., Wayne, N.J., 1983—. Council woman Borough of Butler, 1982-84. Mem. ABA, N.J. Bar Assn., N.J. Assn. Trial Attys., Phi Beta Kappa. Democrat. Roman Catholic. Avocation: piano. Criminal, Family and matrimonial, Juvenile. Home: 15 Woodward AVe Bloomingdale NJ 07403 Office: Barbarula McCracken & Massessa 1242 Rt 23 Butler NJ 07405

MCCRACKEN, CHRISTOPHER CORNELL, lawyer; b. Canton, Ohio, Dec. 18, 1951; s. William Edward and Clara (Berger) McC.; m. Gaylee June Rossi, May 6, 1973; children: Matthew, Caroline. BA, Bowling Green (Ohio) State U., 1973; JD, Case Western Res. U., 1977. Bar: Ohio 1977, U.S. Dist. Ct. (no. dist.) Ohio 1977. Assoc. Ulmer, Berne, Laronge, Glickman & Curtis, Cleve., 1977-84, ptnr., 1984—. Mem. ABA, Ohio Bar Assn., Cleve. Bar Assn. (council securities law sect. 1985—). Democrat. Presbyterian. General corporate, Securities, Contracts commercial. Home: 2528 Stratford Rd Cleveland Heights OH 44118 Office: Ulmer Berne Laronge Glickman & Curtis 900 Bond Ct Bldg Cleveland OH 44114

MCCRACKEN, EUGENE LUKE, lawyer; b. Savannah, Ga., Aug. 9, 1932; s. John and Estelle (Powers) M.; m. Helen Kelly Morekis, May 9, 1964; A.A., Armstrong State Coll., 1952; B.A., Mercer U., 1954; LL.B., U. Ga., 1957. Bar: Ga. 1958, U.S. Dist. Ct. (so. dist.) Ga. 1959, U.S. Ct. Appeals (5th cir.) 1961, U.S. Supreme Ct. 1978. Assoc. Brannen, Clark & Hester, Savannah, 1958-64; sole practice, Savannah, 1964-80, 84—; ptnr. Maurice & McCracken, Savannah, 1980-84; asst. dist. atty. Chatham County, Ga., 1963-64; asst. city atty. City of Savannah, 1970-74; judge pro tem Juvenile Ct. of Chatham County, 1974-80. Bd. dirs. United Way of Savannah, 1973-74; mem. Chatham County Zoning Bd. Appeals, 1967-70; chmn. Chatham County Reps., 1985-87, 1st congl. dist. Ga. Reps., 1987—. Named Savannah's Outstanding Young Man of Yr., Jaycees, 1966; recipient Sword of Hope award Am. Cancer Soc., 1968. Mem. Savannah Bar Assn., Armstrong State Coll. Alumni Assn. (pres. 1973, 83), Hibernian Soc. Roman Catholic. Club: First City. General practice, Personal injury, Insurance. Home: 16 Brightwater Dr Savannah GA 31410 Office: PO Box 8102 Savannah GA 31412

MCCRACKEN, SARAH ELIZABETH, lawyer; b. Cambridge, Mass., May 24, 1950; d. Frank Smith and Jane (Spencer) Fussner; m. Kenneth Russell McCracken, Mar. 21, 1981; 1 child, John Russell. BA, Harvard U., 1972; JD, U. Oreg., 1975. Bar: Alaska 1976, U.S. Dist. Ct. Alaska 1976, U.S. Ct. Appeals (9th cir.) 1976, U.S. Supreme Ct. 1980. Assoc. Ely, Guess & Rudd, Anchorage, 1975-77; asst. atty. gen. State of Alaska, Anchorage, 1977—. Mem. citizens adv. bd. Oreg. Land Conservation & Devel. Commn., Salem, 1975. Mem. Alaska Bar Assn. (law examiners com.), Assn. Trial Lawyers Am., Lawyer-Pilots Bar Assn. Administrative and regulatory, State civil litigation, Environment. Office: Office Atty Gen 1031 W 4th Suite 200 Anchorage AK 99501

MCCRARY, TONI MAREE, lawyer; b. Lake City, Tex., Oct. 23, 1952; d. Warren Ashton and Marilyn Maree (Fountain) McC.; m. Louis Huszar, Sept. 11, 1983. BA, Drake U., 1975; JD, Calif. Western Sch. Law, San Diego, 1978. Bar: Iowa 1978, D.C. 1979, Calif. 1985. Cons. Sci. Applications Internat. Corp., LaJolla, Calif. and McLean, Va., 1977-81; counsel Am. Mining Congress, Washington, 1981-83; assoc. Sullivan, McWilliams, Lewin & Markham, San Diego, 1985—. Mem. ABA, San Diego County Bar Assn., Calif. Bar Assn., D.C. Bar Assn., Iowa Bar Assn. Bankruptcy, Consumer commercial. Office: Sullivan McWilliams Lewin & Markham 600 B St Suite 1400 San Diego CA 92101

MCCRAY, SANDRA BROOMFIELD, lawyer; b. Los Angeles, May 24, 1938; d. Raymond Arthur and Betty (Gildner) Broomfield; m. Richard Alan McCray, Apr. 10, 1960; children: Julia Michelle, Carla Marie. BA magna cum laude, U. Calif., Los Angeles, 1967; JD, U. Colo., 1975; LLM, Georgetown U., 1985. Asst. atty. gen. State of Colo., 1976-80; adminstr. Colo. Uniform Consumer Credit Code, 1980-83; counsel Multistate Tax Commn., Boulder, Colo., 1984—; gov. appointee mem. Colo. State Banking Bd., 1985—. Exec. com. mem., bd. dirs. Boulder County Hospice. Mem. ABA, Colo. Bar Assn., Phi Beta Kappa. Democrat. Avocations: bicycling, hiking. Administrative and regulatory, Banking, State and local taxation. Home: 1900 Baseline Rd Boulder CO 80302 Office: Multistate Tax Commn 1790 30th St Suite 314 Boulder CO 80302

MCCREADY, LEO STEPHEN, lawyer; b. Medford, Mass., Apr. 14, 1956; s. Leo Patrick and Terese Rose (Kiely) McC.; m. Deborah Nancy Cardolino, Sept. 27, 1986. BBA magna cum laude, Suffolk U., 1978, JD, 1981. Bar: Mass. 1981, U.S. Dist. Ct. Mass. 1982, U.S. Supreme Ct. 1986. Contract specialist missile systems div. Raytheon Co., Andover, Mass., 1982-85; staff atty. Simplex Time Recorder Co., Gardner, Mass., 1985-87; asst. gen. counsel Simplex Time Recorder Co., Gardner, 1987—; tax title cons., Medford, 1980-82; real estate broker, Mass., 1982—. Notary pub. Commonwealth of Mass., Boston, 1980—. Mem. ABA, Mass. Bar Assn. Roman Catholic. Avocations: tennis, nautilus. General corporate, Government contracts and claims, Real property. Home: 701 A Ridgefield Circle Clinton MA 01510 Office: Simplex Time Recorder Co Legal Dept Simplex Plaza Gardner MA 01441

MCCREARY, FRANK E., III, lawyer; b. Santa Monica, Calif., Mar. 25, 1943; s. Frank Elijah and Irma (Holland) McC.; m. Jacqueline Moehlman, Feb. 15, 1969; children: Jennifer Claire, Frank Ward. BA, Cornell U., 1965; LLB with honors, U. Tex., 1968. Bar: Tex. 1968. Ptnr. Vinson & Elkins, Houston, 1970—. Chmn. admissions United Way of Tex. Gulf Coast, Houston, 1985—. Served to capt. U.S. Army, 1968-70, Vietnam. Mem. Houston Bar Found., Nat. Assn. Bond Lawyers. Municipal bonds, Administrative and regulatory, Local government. Office: Vinson & Elkins 1001 Fannin Suite 2828 Houston TX 77002-6760

MCCRORY, JOHN BROOKS, lawyer; b. St. Cloud, Minn., Oct. 23, 1925; s. John Raymond and Mary Lee (Rutter) McC.; m. Margaret Joan Dickson, Sept. 4, 1954 (dec. Apr. 1957); 1 child, William B.; m. Elizabeth Ann Quick, June 27, 1959; children—John B., Ann Elizabeth. B.A., Swarthmore Coll., 1948; J.D., U. Pa., 1951. Bar: N.Y., D.C. Assoc. Donovan, Leisure, Newton, Lumbard & Irvine, N.Y.C., 1951-52; assoc. Nixon, Hargrave, Devans & Doyle, Rochester, N.Y., 1952-62, ptnr., 1963—. Author: Constitutional Privilege in Libel Law, 1977-86. Served to lt. comdr. USNR, 1943-47, PTO. Fellow Am. Coll. Trial Lawyers; mem. ABA, Monroe County Bar Assn., N.Y. State Bar Assn., D.C. Bar Assn. Republican. Presbyterian. Libel, Personal injury, State civil litigation. Home: 210 Whitewood Ln Rochester NY 14618 Office: Nixon Hargrave Devans & Doyle Lincoln First Tower PO Box 1051 Rochester NY 14603

MCCROSKEY, ELIZABETH WEAR, lawyer; b. Dallas, Oct. 19, 1937; d. J. B. and Helen Elizabeth (Ginn) Wear; m. William James McCroskey, Jan. 31, 1960; children—Nancy Elizabeth, Susan Carol. B.A., U. Tex.-Austin, 1959; M.A., Rutgers U., 1965; J.D., U. Santa Clara, 1981. Bar: Calif. 1981. Coordinator low-moderate income housing Mid-Peninsula Citizens for Fair Housing, Palo Alto, Calif., 1972; assoc. Fuller, Glickman, Mousalam & Barton, Palo Alto, 1981-82; ptnr. Gullixson, Hollman & McCroskey, Palo Alto, 1983-87. Incorporator, bd. dirs. Mid-Peninsula Access Corp., Santa Clara County, Calif.; co-chmn. City Cupertino (Calif.) Goals Com. Housing Task Force, 1970-71. Mem. ABA, Calif. State Bar Assn., Santa Clara County Bar Assn., AAUW (dir. 1983-84). Democrat. Presbyterian. Family and matrimonial, Probate, General corporate. Office: 720 University Ave PO Box 1041 Palo Alto CA 94302

MCCUBBIN, GARRY, lawyer; b. St. Louis, Sept. 23, 1951; s. Giles H. and Margaret June (Handke) McC.; m. Sharron L. Mullins, June 10, 1978. BA, U. Mo., 1975; JD with honors, Washburn U., 1981. Bar: Kans. 1981, U.S. Dist. Ct. Kans. 1981, Mo. 1983, U.S. Dist. Ct. (ea. dist.) Mo. 1983, U.S. Ct. Appeals (8th cir.) 1983. Staff atty. Kans. Appellate Cts., Topeka, 1981-83; atty. Fed. Land Bank, St. Louis, 1984—. Contbr. articles to law jours. Mem. ABA, Mo. Bar Assn., Bar Assn. Met. St. Louis. Democrat. Roman Catholic. Contracts commercial, Federal civil litigation, Bankruptcy. Office: Fed Land Bank 1415 Olive St Saint Louis MO 63106

MCCUEN, JOHN FRANCIS, JR., auto parts manufacturing executive, lawyer; b. N.Y.C., Mar. 11, 1944; s. John Francis and Elizabeth Agnes (Corbett) McC.; children: Sarah, Mary, John. A.B., U. Notre Dame, 1966; J.D., U. Detroit, 1969. Bar: Mich. 1970, Fla. 1970, Ohio 1978. Legal counsel Kelsey-Hayes Co., Romulus, Mich., 1970-77; corp. counsel Sheller-Globe Corp., Toledo, 1977-79; sr. v.p., gen. counsel Sheller-Globe Corp., 1979—. Trustee Kidney Found. N.W. Ohio, 1979—, pres., 1984-86. Mem. Am. Bar Assn., Ohio Bar Assn., Fla. State Bar. Clubs: Toledo, Inverness, Catawba Island. Administrative and regulatory, Antitrust, General corporate. Home: 2745 Westowne Ct Toledo OH 43615 Office: Sheller Globe Corp 1505 Jefferson Ave Toledo OH 43697

MCCULLOUGH, GEORGE ELWOOD, lawyer; b. Coffeyville, Kans., Dec. 20, 1923; s. Harry Ernest and Gladys Margarite (Stoneking) McC.; m. Bonnie Moorehouse, June 2, 1950 (div. July 1967); children: George Elwood Jr., Kristy Lynn Jackson; m. Vivian Austin, Oct. 7, 1967. BA, Washburn Mcpl. U., 1949, JD, 1950. Bar: Kans. 1950, U.S. Dist. Ct. Kans. 1950, U.S. Ct. Appeals (10th cir.) 1958, U.S. Supreme Ct. 1964. Sr. ptnr. McCullough & Kimbrough, Topeka, 1950-55; sr. ptnr. McCullough, Wareheim & LaBunker and predecessor firms McCullough, Parker Wareheim LaBunker & Rose and McCullough, Parker & Wareheim, Topeka, 1955-86, of counsel, 1986—; lectr. law seminars U. Kans., Lawrence. Chmn. Topeka Urban Renewal Agency, Met. Topeka Airport Authority. Served with USNR, 1943-46. Mem. Kans. Bar Assn., Topeka Bar Assn., Assn. Trial Lawyers Am., Kans. Trial Lawyers Assn., Am. Arbitration Assn., Am. Judicature Soc., Law Sci. Acad. Found., Am. Legion, VFW. Republican. Lodges: Masons, Shriners. Avocations: fishing, golf, travel. Workers' compensation, Legislative. Office: McCullough Wareheim & LaBunker 1507 Topeka Blvd PO Box 1453 Topeka KS 66601

MCCULLOUGH, JOHN THOMAS, judge; b. Streator, Ill., June 15, 1931; s. Mark M. and Margaret J. (Manes) McC.; m. B. Joann McCullough; children: Shawn, Bridget, Molly, Anna, Katherine. BS, U. Ill., 1953, JD, 1955. Bar: Ill. 1955, U.S. Dist. Ct. (so. dist.) Ill. 1957. Sole practice Lincoln, Ill., 1955-62; judge Lincoln, 1962-74, chief judge, 1974-84; judge Ill. Ct. Appeals (4th cir.), Lincoln, 1984—. Past chmn. All Am. City Com., Lincoln, budget and admission com. United Fund, Lincoln, Prairie Trails Dist. Boy Scouts Am., Lincoln. Served with U.S. Army, 1955-57. Named Man of Month Lincoln Courier, 1961. Mem. Ill. Bar Assn., Logan County Bar Assn., Mt. Pulaski C. of C. (past chmn.), Lincoln Jaycees (Disting. Service award 1962), Phi Delta Phi, Alpha Kappa Lambda. Republican. Roman Catholic. Lodges: Elks, KC, Eagles, Moose, Ancient Order Hibernians in Am. State civil litigation, Criminal, Family and matrimonial. Office: Ill Appellate Ct 111 1/2 N Sangamon Lincoln IL 62656

MC CULLOUGH, RALPH CLAYTON, II, lawyer; b. Daytona Beach, Fla., Mar. 28, 1941; s. Ralph C. and Doris (Johnson) McC.; m. Elizabeth Grier Henderson, Apr. 5, 1986; children from previous marriage: Melissa Wells, Clayton Baldwin. B.A., Erskine Coll., 1962; J.D., Tulane U., 1965. Bar: La. 1965, S.C. 1974. Assoc. Baldwin, Haspel, Maloney, Rainold and Meyer, New Orleans, 1965-68; asst. prof. law U. S.C., 1968-71, asso. prof., 1971-75, prof., 1975—, chair prof. of advocacy, 1982—, asst. dean Sch. Law, 1970-75, instr. Med. Sch., 1970-79, adj. prof. law and medicine Med. Sch., 1979—; adj. prof. medicine Med. U. of S.C., 1984—; of counsel Finkel, Georgaklis, Goldberg, Sheftman & Korn, 1978—; adj. prof. pathology Med. U. S.C., 1985—; asst. dean U. S.C. Sch. Law 1970-75. Author: (with J. L. Underwood) The Civil Trial Manual, 1974 supplements, 1976, 77, 78, 80, 81, 82, The Civil Trial Manual II, 1984, (with Myers & Felix) New Directions in Legal Education, 1970, S.C. Torts II, 1986; co-reporter: (with Myers & Felix) S.C. Criminal Code, 1977, S.C. Study Sentencing, 1977. Trustee S.C. dist. U.S. Bankruptcy Ct., 1979—; exec. dir. S.C. Continuing Legal Edn. Program.; bd. visitors Erskine Coll. Mem. ABA, La. Bar Assn., S.C. Bar (sec. 1975-76, exec. dir. 1972-76, award of service 1978), New Orleans Bar Assn., Am. Trial Lawyers Assn., Am. Law Inst., Southeastern Assn. Am. Law Schs. (pres.), S.C. Trial Lawyers Assn. (bd. govs. 1984—), Phi Alpha Delta. Republican. Episcopalian. Club: Forest Lake. Bankruptcy, Federal civil litigation, General corporate. Home: PO Box 1799 Columbia SC 29202 Office: U SC Sch Law Columbia SC 29208

MCCULLOUGH, WILLIAM ANDREW, lawyer; b. Albany, N.Y., July 6, 1948; s. Harold and Betty Jane (Beiermeister) McC. BA, Brigham Young U., 1970; JD, U. Utah, 1973. Bar: Utah 1973, U.S. Dist. Ct. Utah 1973, U.S. Ct. Appeals (10th cir.) 1979, U.S. Supreme Ct. 1979, N.Y. 1986. Ptnr. Mulliner & McCullough, Orem, Utah, 1973-79; sr. ptnr. McCullough, Jones, Jensen & Ivins, Orem, 1979—. Mem. exec. com. Utah County Rep. Party, Provo, 1977-79, treas. Young Rep. Fedn., Salt Lake City, 1979-81, chmn. Young Reps., Provo, 1977-79; chmn. Utah County Council on Drug Abuse, Orem, 1981. Named one of Outstanding Young Men Am., 1985. Mem. ABA. Mormon. Lodge: Sertoma (v.p. Orem chpt. 1982). Avocations: tennis, travel, guitar, photography. Criminal, Family and matrimonial, General corporate. Office: 930 S State Suite 10 Orem UT 84058

MCCURDY, ROBERT CLARK, lawyer, consultant; b. Cin., Sept. 23, 1939; s. Edward Robert and Martha (Moul) McC.; m. Marjorie Ann Boehm, Oct. 7, 1967; children—Jonathan, Melinda. B.S. in Pharmacy, U. Fla., 1962; J.D., Stetson U. Coll. Law, 1973; M.S. in Hygiene, U. Pitts., 1974. Bar: Fla. 1973. House counsel Lee Meml. Hosp., Fort Myers, Fla., 1975—. Author, cons.; Hospital Law Manual, Aspen Systems, 1977-83. Served with U.S. Army, 1963-66. Mem. Am. Coll. Healthcare Execs., Am. Acad. Hosp. Attys., Fla. Assn. Hosp. Attys., Fla. Soc. Healthcare Risk Mgmt. (bd. dirs. 1985—, pres.-elect 1986-87). Health, Personal injury, Local government. Office: Lee Meml Hosp 2776 Cleveland Ave Fort Myers FL 33901

MCCURN, NEAL PETERS, federal judge; b. Syracuse, N.Y., Apr. 6, 1926. LL.B., Syracuse U., 1952, J.D., 1960. Bar: N.Y. 1952. Ptnr. Mackenzie Smith Lewis Mitchell & Hughes, Syracuse, 1957-79; judge U.S. Dist. Ct. (no. dist.) N.Y., 1979—; del. N.Y. State Constl. Conv., 1976; mem. 2d Cir. Jud. Council. Pres. Syracuse Common Council, 1970-78; mem. adv. council Maria Regina Coll. Mem. ABA, N.Y. State Bar Assn. (chmn. state constn. com.), Onondaga County Bar Assn. (past pres.), Am. Coll. Trial Lawyers, Am. Judicature Soc. (bd. dirs. 1980-84), 2d Cir. Jud. Council. Jurisprudence. Office: 333 US Courthouse 100 S Clinton St Syracuse NY 13260

MCCUSKER, WILLIAM LAVALLE, lawyer; b. Mpls., July 27, 1918; s. John Thomas and Emma Ernestine (Helfman) McC.; m. Phyllis E. Kischel, June 19, 1943; children—Patricia, Barbara, Marcia (dec.), William James, Nancy. B.S., U. Wis.-Superior, 1941; postgrad. U. Minn. Law Sch., 1943-44; J.D., U. Wis., 1946. Bar: Wis. 1946, U.S. Dist. Ct. (ea and we. dists.) Wis. 1946, U.S. Ct. Appeals (7th cir.) 1970, U.S. Supreme Ct. 1974. Assoc. Hill, Beckwith & Harrington, Madison, Wis., 1945-48; dep. dist. atty. Dane County, Wis., 1945-48; ptnr. Wilkie, McCusker and Wilkie, Madison, 1950-53; sole practice, Madison, 1948-50; ptnr., pres., sr. mem. McCusker and Robertson, SC., Madison, 1953—; spl. asst. atty. gen., Wis., 1955; instr. seminars. Kellogg scholar, 1943-44. Recipient jud. achievement award Wis. Acad. Trial Lawyers. Fellow Internat. Soc. Barristers; mem. State Bar of Wis., Dane County Bar Assn., Wis. Acad. Trial Lawyers (pres. 1977-78), Assn. Trial Lawyers Am. Club: Madison, Elks. Personal injury, Workers' compensation. Home: 3018 Pelham Rd Madison WI 53713 Office: 25 W Main St Suite 731 Madison WI 53703

MCCUTCHAN, GORDON EUGENE, lawyer, insurance company executive; b. Buffalo, Sept. 30, 1935; s. George Lawrence and Mary Esther (De Puy) McC. B.A., Cornell U., 1956, M.B.A., 1958, LL.B., 1959. Bar: N.Y. 1959, Ohio 1964. Sole practice Rome, N.Y., 1959-61; atty., advisor SEC, Washington, 1961-64; mem. office of gen. counsel Nationwide Mut. Ins. Co., Columbus, Ohio, 1964—, sr. v.p., gen. counsel, 1982—; sr. v.p., gen. counsel Beaver Pacific Corp., 1985—, Employers Ins. of Wausau, a Mut. Co., 1985—; ptnr. McCutchan, Schmidt & Druen, 1964—. Mem. Fed. Bar Assn., Columbus Bar Assn., Ohio Bar Assn., ABA, Am. Corporate Counsel Assn., Assn. Life Ins. Counsel, Fedn. Ins. and Corp. Counsel Assn. Home: 2376 Oxford Rd Columbus OH 43221 Office: Nationwide Mutual Ins Co One Nationwide Plaza Columbus OH 43216

MCDANIEL, DAVID JAMISON, lawyer; b. Portland, Oreg., July 24, 1913; s. David Lester and Harriet LeConie (Jamison) McD.; m. Martha Eyre, Dec. 15, 1961. A.B., Stanford U., 1933; LL.B., Harvard U., 1936. Bar: Calif. 1936, U.S. Dist. Ct. (no. dist.) Calif. 1936, U.S. Ct. Appeals (9th cir.) 1936, U.S. Ct. Appeals (10th cir.) 1958, U.S. Supreme Ct. 1972. Assoc. Shelton, Gray & McWilliams, San Francisco, 1936-41; atty., gen. atty., sr. gen. atty. U.S. Steel Corp. and subs., Calif., 1946-78; ptnr. Jordan, Keeler & Seligman, San Francisco, 1980-81; of counsel Cotton Seligman & Ray, San Francisco, 1981—; ptnr. Jordan, Keeler & Seligman, 1978-81, of counsel, 1978-87; instr., asst. prof. Hastings Coll. Law, 1946-58, chmn. local adminstrv. com. 1964, bd. visitors, 1974. Trustee Pacific Sch. Religion, 1978-87; trustee Mechanics' Inst. of San Francisco, 1961-78, pres., 1974-76; trustee Golden Gate U., 1969-82, life trustee, 1982—; trustee Regional Cancer Found, 1982-85; regent U. Calif., 1974; bd. dirs. San Francisco YMCA, 1960-73, pres. and chmn., 1970-73; pres. San Francisco chpt. English Speaking Union, 1985-87, mem. nat. bd., 1982—. Served with AUS, 1941-46; to col. Res. Decorated Bronze Star with oak leaf cluster and V Device. Fellow Am. Bar Found.; mem. State Bar of Calif., Bar Assn. San Francisco (Award of Merit, 1984), ABA, Am. Judicature Soc., Order of Coif, Ft. Point and Army Mus. Assn. (pres. 1986-87). Democrat. Presbyterian. Clubs: Cercle de l'Union, Mchts. Exchange, Pacific-Union, San Francisco Golf, Commonwealth of Calif. (bd. govs. 1974-80, pres. 1977), University, Queen's; Lansdowne (London). Labor, Probate. Office: 1400 Alcoa Bldg 1 Maritime Plaza San Francisco CA 94111

MCDANIEL, JAMES ALAN, lawyer; b. St. Joseph, Mo., June 10, 1953; s. John Redmond and Mary Jane (Chiles) McD.; A.B. with distinction, Stanford U., 1975; J.D., Harvard U., 1978. Bar: Mass. 1978, U.S. Dist. Ct. Mass. 1979, U.S. Ct. Appeals (1st cir.) 1979. Assoc. Choate, Hall & Stewart, Boston, 1978-85; ptnr., 1986— . bd. dirs. DARE, Inc. Mem. Boston Bar Assn., Mass. Bar Assn., ABA, Phi Beta Kappa. Democrat. Episcopalian. Co-founder and editor-in-chief Harvard Environ. Law Rev., 1976-77. General corporate, Banking. Home: 40 Herford St Boston MA 02115 Office: 53 State St Boston MA 02109

MCDANIEL, MYRA ATWELL, state official, lawyer; b. Phila., Dec. 13, 1932; d. Toronto Canada, Jr. and Eva Lucinda (Yores) Atwell; m. Reuben Roosevelt McDaniel Jr., Feb. 20, 1955; children—Diane Lorraine, Reuben Roosevelt III. BA, U. Pa., 1954; JD, U. Tex., 1975; LLD, Huston-Tillotson Coll., 1984; postgrad., Jarvis Christian Coll., 1986. Bar: Tex. 1975, U.S. Dist. Ct. (we. dist.) Tex. 1977, U.S. Dist. Ct. (so. and no. dists.) Tex. 1978, U.S. Ct. Appeals (5th cir.) 1978, U.S. Supreme Ct. 1978, U.S. Dist. Ct. (ea. dist.) Tex. 1979. Asst atty. gen. State of Tex., Austin, 1975-81, chief taxation div., 1979-81, gen. counsel to gov., 1983-84, sec. of state, 1984-87; asst. gen. counsel Tex. R.R. Commn., Austin, 1981-82; gen. counsel Wilson Cos., San Antonio and Midland, Tex., 1982; assoc. Bickerstaff, Heath & Smiley, Austin, 1984, ptnr., 1987—; mem. asset mgmt. adv. com. State Treasury, Austin, 1984-86; mem. legal affairs com. Criminal Justice Policy Council, Austin, 1984-86; mem. legal affairs com. Inter-State Oil Compact, Oklahoma City, 1984-86; bd. dirs. Austin Cons. Group, Inc.; lectr. in field. contbr. articles to profl. jours., chpts. to books. Del. Tex. Conf. on Libraries and Info. Scis., Austin, 1978, White House Conf. on Libraries and Info. Scis., Washington, 1979; mem. Library Services and Constrn. Act Adv. Council, 1980-84, chmn., 1983-84; mem. long range plan task force Brackenridge Hosp., Austin, 1981; clk. vestry bd. St. James Episcopal Ch., Austin, 1981-83; bd. visitors U. Tex. Law Sch., 1983—, vice chmn., 1983-85; bd. dirs. Friends of Ronald McDonald House of Cen. Tex., Women's Advocacy, Inc., Capital Area Rehab. Ctr.; trustee Episcopal Found. Tex., 1986—, St. Edward's U., Austin, 1986—, Tex. Bar Found., 1986—; chmn. div. United Way/Capital area campaign, 1986. Recipient Tribute to 28 Black Women award Concepts Unltd., 1983; Focus on women honoree Serwa Yetu chpt. Mt. Olive grand chpt. Order of Eastern Star, 1979, Disting. Alumni U. Tex. at Austin, 1986, Woman of Yr. Longview Metro C of C, 1985, Woman of Yr. Austin chpt. Internat. Tng. in Communication, 1985, Citizen of Yr. Epsilon Iona chpt. Omega Psi Phi. Mem. ABA, Am. Bar Found., Tex. Bar Found., Travis County Bar Assn., Travis County Women Lawyers' Assn., Austin Black Lawyers Assn., State Bar Tex. (chmn. Profl. Efficiency and Econ. Research subcom. 1978-84), Golden Key Nat. Honor Soc., Omicron Delta Kappa, Delta Phi Alpha, Order Coif (hon. mem.). Democrat. Administrative and regulatory, State civil litigation, State and local taxation. Home: 3910 Knollwood Dr Austin TX 78731 Office: Secretary of State Room 127 State Capitol Bldg Austin TX 78711

MCDAVID, JANET LOUISE, lawyer; b. Mpls., Jan. 24, 1950; d. Robert Matthew and Lois May (Bratt) Kurzeka; m. John Gary McDavid, June 9, 1973; 1 child, Matthew Collins McDavid. B.A., Northwestern U., 1971; J.D., Georgetown U., 1974. Bar: D.C. 1975, U.S. Supreme Ct., 1980, U.S. Ct. Appeals D.C. 1976, U.S. Ct. Appeals (5th cir.) 1983. Assoc. Hogan & Hartson, Washington, 1974-83, ptnr., 1984—; gen. counsel ERAmerica, 1977-83. Contbr. articles to profl. jours. Mem. ABA (vice chmn. civil practice com. antitrust sect.), Washington Council Lawyers, D.C. Bar Assn., Fed. Bar Assn., Womens Legal Def. Fund, ACLU. Democrat. Antitrust, Federal civil litigation. Office: Hogan & Hartson 555 13th St NW Washington DC 20004

MCDERMITT, EDWARD VINCENT, lawyer; b. Hagerstown, Md., Nov. 29, 1953; s. Edward Bernard and Genevieve Natalie (Gallo) McD.; m. Jane Langmead Springmann, June 28, 1986; children: Edward S., Maureen K. BA, Georgetown U., 1975, MA, 1978; JD, U. Santa Clara, 1980; LLM, U. Pa., 1984. Bar: D.C. 1981, U.S. Dist. Ct. D.C. 1981. Research asst. U. Santa Clara, Calif., 1980; sole practice Washington, 1981-82; assoc. Law Offices of Miller & Loewinger, Washington, 1982; sole practice Washington, 1983; research asst. U. Pa., Phila., 1983-84; sole practice Washington, 1984—; congl. intern to rep. Pat Schroeder, Washington, 1975; vol. atty. ACLU Nat. Capital area, Washington, 1982—. Vol. McGovern for Pres. campaign, Washington and Md., 1972, United Farmworkers Union, Washington, 1973-77, Urban Coalition Basketball League, Washington, 1977-78, Sarbanes re-election campaign, Md., 1982. Mem. ABA (individual rights div.), Superior Ct. Trial Lawyers Assn., Washington Writers Group, Pi Sigma Alpha. Roman Catholic. Avocations: photography, poetry, fiction writing, military history, bridge. Constitutional law, Legal history, Jurisprudence. Home and Office: 8000 Wildwood Dr Takoma Park MD 20912

MCDERMOTT, JAMES T., justice state supreme court; b. Sept. 22, 1926; m. Mary Theresa McDermott; children: James, Thomas, Suzanne, Michael, John, Matthew. B.S., St. Joseph's Coll., 1947; LL.B., Temple U., 1950. Bar: Pa. Judge Pa. Ct. Common Pleas 1st Jud. Dist., 1965-82; justice Supreme Ct. Pa., Phila., 1982—. Chmn. Criminal Justice Com.; chmn. City Charter Revision Commn. Mem. Phila Bar Assn., Pa. Bar Assn. Judicial administration. Office: Pa Supreme Ct 560 City Hall Philadelphia PA 19107 *

MCDERMOTT, JOHN ALOYSIUS, II, lawyer; b. Midland, Tex., Nov. 1, 1943; s. John Aloysius and Vesta (Fisher) McD.; m. Marlena C. Caspers; children—James, Brian, Megan. B.B.A., U. Notre Dame, 1966; J.D., UCLA, 1969. Bar: Calif. 1970. Assoc. Flint & MacKay, 1969-71; mem. Tuohey, Barton & McDermott; founding ptnr. Mc Dermott & Trayner, 1979—; exec. bd. Moot Ct. Honors Program, UCLA, 1968-69. Bd. dirs. Orange County (Calif.) Music Ctr., Inc., 1974-77. Mem. Los Angeles County Bar Assn., Orange County Bar Assn., State Bar Calif. Administrative and regulatory, Antitrust. Office: 1201 Dove St 6th Floor Newport Beach CA 92660

MCDERMOTT, JOHN HENRY, lawyer; b. Evanston, Ill., June 23, 1931; s. Edward Henry and Goldie Lucile (Boso) McD.; m. Ann Elizabeth Pickard, Feb. 2, 1966; children: Elizabeth A., Mary L., Edward H. BA, Williams Coll., 1953; JD, U. Mich., 1956. Bar: Mich. 1955, Ill. 1956. Assoc. McDermott, Will & Emery, Chgo., 1958-64, ptnr., 1964—; bd. dirs. Patrick Industries Inc. Served to 1st lt. USAF, 1956-58. Mem. ABA, Ill. Bar Assn., Chgo. Bar Assn., Legal Club Chgo. (pres. 1981-82), Law Club Chgo. (v.p. 1986-87, pres. 1987—). General corporate, Securities, Banking. Home: 330 Willow Rd Winnetka IL 60093 Office: McDermott Will & Emery 111 W Monroe St Chicago IL 60603

MCDERMOTT, RENÉE R(ASSLER), lawyer; b. Danville, Pa., Sept. 26, 1950; d. Carl A. and Rose (Gaupp) Rassler; m. James A. McDermott, Jan. 1, 1986. BA, U. So. Fla., 1970, MA, 1972; JD, Ind. U., 1978. Bar: Ind. 1978, U.S. Dist. Ct. (so. and no. dists.) Ind. 1978, U.S. Dist. Ct. Ariz. 1984, U.S. Ct. Appeals (7th cir.) 1979, U.S. Ct. Appeals (9th cir.) 1985. Law clk. to presiding judge U.S. Dist. Ct. (no. dist.) Ind., Ft. Wayne, 1978-80; assoc. Barnes & Thornburg, Indpls., 1980-84, ptnr., 1985—. Bd. visitors Ind. U. Law Sch., Bloomington, 1979—; mem. Environ. Quality Control Inc., Indpls. Named one of Outstanding Young Women Am., 1986. Mem. ABA (chmn. hazardous substances subcom. 1985—, corp., banking & bus. law sect.), Ind. Bar Assn. (chmn. young lawyers sect. 1985-86), Bar Assn. for 7th Fed. Cir., Ind. Mfrs. Assn. (environ. affairs com.), Indpls. C. of C. (environ. affairs com.), Nat. Health Lawyers Assn. Avocations: scuba diving, horseback riding, music, reading, hiking. Environment, Health, Federal civil litigation. Home: Rural Rt 5 Box 598 Nashville IN 47448 Office: 11 S Meridian St Suite 1313 Indianapolis IN 46204

MCDERMOTT, RICHARD FRANCIS, JR., lawyer; b. Seattle, Feb. 18, 1948; s. Richard F. Sr. and Madeline (Frison) McD.; m. Susan Lynn Brandt, Feb. 19, 1977; children: Kelsey, Megan, Michael. BA in Polit. Sci., Seattle U., 1970; JD, U. Wash., 1973. Bar: Wash. 1973, U.S. Dist. Ct. (we. dist.) Wash. 1973, U.S. Ct. Appeals (9th cir.) 1973, U.S. Supreme Ct. 1981. Atty. King County, Seattle, 1973-76; assoc. Parks, Johnson & East, Bellevue, Wash., 1976-77; ptnr. Revelle, Ries & McDermott, Bellevue, 1978-86, McDermott & Jones, Bellevue, 1986—. Served to 1st lt. USAR, 1970-78. Named one of The Best of CLE Wash. State Bar Assn., 1985. Mem. Seattle King County Bar Assn., East King County Bar Assn., Assn. Trial Lawyers Am., Wash. State Trial Lawyers Am. (bd. dirs. 1982—). Roman Catholic. Club: Bellevue (Wash.) Athletic. Lodge: Rotary (chmn. greetors com.). Avocation: golf. Personal injury, Insurance, State civil litigation. Home: 11201-NE 58th Pl Kirkland WA 98033 Office: McDermott & Jones 600 108th NE PO Bos 3247 Bellevue WA 98009-3247

MCDERMOTT, ROBERT B., lawyer; b. Washington, June 16, 1927; s. Edward H. and Goldie Lucile (Boso) McD.; m. Julia Wood, Nov. 16, 1950; children: John, Jeanne, Charles; m. Jane McDermott, July 31, 1973. A.B., Princeton U., 1948; LL.B., Harvard U., 1951. Bar: D.C. 1951, Ill. 1955. Atty. Office Gen. Counsel, Navy Dept., Washington, 1951-52; assoc McDermott, Will & Emery, Chgo., 1954-60, ptnr., 1961—; chmn. 1986—; bd. dirs. The Cherry Corp., Waukegan, Ill., Furst-McNess Co., Freeport, Ill., Maynard Oil Co., Dallas, Vermont Am. Corp., Louisville. Trustee, Ill. Inst. Tech., Chgo., 1985—, bd. govs. IIT Research Inst., 1985—. Served to lt. USNR, 1945-46, 52-54. Mem. ABA, Ill. Bar Assn., Chgo. Bar Assn. Clubs: Chicago, Economic, Mid-Day; University (Chgo.). Corporate taxation, General corporate. Home: 990 N Lake Shore Dr Chicago IL 60611 Office: McDermott Will & Emery 111 W Monroe St Chicago IL 60603

MCDEVITT, MARY ELIZABETH, judge; b. Detroit, May 9, 1930; d. James Edward and Mildred Loretta (Wines) McD. Student U. Detroit, 1947-48, Wayne U., 1949-51; LL.B., Detroit Coll. Law, 1954, J.D., 1968. Bar: Mich., 1954, U.S. Supreme Ct. 1958. With legal dept. Lawyers Title Co., Detroit, 1954-55; aide juvenile div., Macomb County Probate Ct., 1955-56; sole practice, Roseville, Mich., 1956-69; justice of peace Erin Twp., Mich., 1957-58; mcpl. judge City of Roseville, 1958-68; judge 39th Dist., Roseville and Fraser, Mich., 1969—. Formerly active Democratic Party. Mem. ABA, Am. Judges Assn., Am. Judicature Soc., Mich. Dist. Judges Assn., State Bar Mich., Macomb County Bar Assn. (past dir.), Women Lawyers Assn. Macomb County, Macomb County Dist. Judges Assn. (sec. treas. 1982, pres. 1983-85). Criminal, Personal injury, State civil litigation. Address: 18060 Elizabeth St Roseville MI 48066

MCDEVITT, RAY EDWARD, lawyer; b. San Francisco, Nov. 15, 1943; s. Edward Anthony and Margaret Ann (Peterson) McD.; m. Mary Rolfs, July 1, 1967; children—Jessica, Devon. B.A., Stanford U., 1966, J.D., 1969; Diploma in Law, Oxford U., 1973. Bar: Calif., 1970, U.S. Supreme Ct., 1975. Teaching fellow Stanford U., 1969; law clk. Calif. Supreme Ct., 1970; atty. EPA, 1973-75, assoc. gen. counsel, 1975-76; ptnr. Hanson, Bridgett, Marcus, Vlahos & Rudy, San Francisco, 1976—. Mem. Marin County Conservation League, Marin Arts Council. Recipient Silver medal for outstanding service EPA, 1976. Mem. ABA, Calif. Bar Assn., Order of Coif. Club: Olympic (San Francisco). Environment, Local government, Real property. Office: 333 Market St Suite 2300 San Francisco CA 94105

MCDIARMID, ROBERT CAMPBELL, lawyer; b. N.Y.C., July 13, 1937; s. Norman Hugh and Dorothy (Shoemaker) McD.; m. Ruth Sussman, Dec. 22, 1963; children—Jennifer, Alexander Samuel. B.S. in Mech. Engring., Swarthmore Coll., 1958; M.S. in Engring. Physics, Cornell U., 1960; LL.B., Harvard U., 1963. Bar: D.C. 1964, Va. 1964, U.S. Supreme Ct. 1967, U.S. Ct. Appeals (1st, 2d, 3d, 4th, 5th, 6th, 7th, 8th, 9th, 10th, 11th, fed. cirs.). Assoc. Weaver & Glassie, Washington, 1963-64; trial atty. Civil Div., Appellate Sect., Dept. Justice, Washington, 1964-68; asst. to gen. counsel Fed. Power Commn., Washington, 1968-70; assoc. Law Office of George Spiegel, Washington, 1970-73; ptnr. Spiegel & McDiarmid, Washington, 1973—. Mem. ABA, Va. State Bar, Bar Assn. D.C., D.C. Bar, Fed. Energy Bar Assn. (exec. com. 1982-83), Swarthmore Coll. Alumni Council (elected mem. 1986—). Democrat. Mem. Soc. Friends. FERC practice, Antitrust, Federal civil litigation. Home: 3003 Van Ness St NW Apt W 933 Washington DC 20008 Office: Spiegel & McDiarmid 1350 New York Ave NW Washington DC 20005

MCDONALD, ALAN A., federal judge; b. 1937. BS, U. Wash., 1950, JD, 1952. Dep. pros. atty. Yakima County, Wash., 1952-54; assoc. Halverson & Applegate, Yakima, 1954-56; ptnr. Halverson, Applegate & McDonald, Yakima, 1956-85; judge U.S. Dist. Ct. (ea. dist.) Wash., Spokane, 1985—. Office: US Dist Ct PO Box 2186 Spokane WA 99210 *

MCDONALD, ALAN THOMAS, lawyer; b. Paterson, N.J., Aug. 16, 1949; s. James Francis and Jennie Eloise (Thomits) McD.; m. Joyce Ann Martin, Feb. 28, 1981. BSCE, Rutgers U., 1971; JD, U. Houston, 1973; LLM in Patent and Trade Regulation Law, George Washington U., 1976. Bar: Tex. 1974, Pa. 1977, Va. 1980, U.S. Ct. Customs and Patent Appeals 1974. Patent examiner U.S. Patent and Trademark Office, Arlington, Va., 1974-75; patent atty. PPG Industries, Inc., Pitts., 1975-78, Reynolds Metals Co., Richmond, Va., 1978—. Patentee method for producing slubbed yarn. Mem. adminstrv. bd. Dutilh United Meth. Ch., Cranberry, Pa., 1977-78; Sunday sch. tchr. Providence United Meth. Ch., Chesterfield County, Va., 1981-84, mem. adminstrv. bd., 1985—. Mem. ABA, Richmond Bar Assn., Am. Intellectual Property Law Assn., Mensa (vice local sec. Richmond chpt. 1981-82, adminstr., 1980-81), Phi Delta Phi. Republican. Patent, Trademark and copyright. Home: 3300 Springcreek Ct Midlothian VA 23113 Office: Reynolds Metals Co 6601 W Broad St Richmond VA 23261

MCDONALD, BRADLEY GEORGE, lawyer; b. Okla., Sept. 16, 1934; s. Lewis W. and Emma M. McD.; m. Ann Gilbert, Sept. 3, 1964; 1 child, Perry. BA, U. Okla., 1956; JD, Georgetown U., 1961. Bar: D.C. 1961, U.S. Ct. Appeals (D.C. cir.) 1961, U.S. Ct. Appeals (11th cir.) 1982, U.S. Supreme Ct. 1967. Assoc. McInnis, Wilson, Munson & Woods and predecessor Roberts & McInnis, Washington, 1961-69; ptnr. McDonald & Karl, Washington, 1979—; gen. counsel, sec. Close Up Found., Nat. Alumni Adv. Council U. Okla., 1979-87; presdl. counselor Georgetown U., 1983-87; mem. Arlington (Va.) Com. of 100, 1970-87; bd. dirs. McLean (Va.) Montessori, Young Writers Contest Found., Parent's Council Randolph-Macon Acad. Served to 1st lt. USMC, 1956-58. Named to Legion of Honor, Delta Epsilon chpt. Sigma Nu, 1982. Mem. Bar Assn. D.C., D.C. Bar Assn., Fed. Bar Assn. Club: Washington Golf and Country (Arlington). Office: 1919 Pennsylvania Ave NW Washington DC 20006

MCDONALD, DARYL PATRICK, lawyer; b. Detroit, Aug. 27, 1950; s. Donald Angus and Rita Martha (Tymoszek) McD.; m. Deborah Ann Wenzinger, Dec. 29, 1972; children: Andrea, Laura. BA, U. Toledo, 1972; JD, Tulane U., 1975. Bar: Mich. 1975, U.S. Dist. Ct. (we. dist.) Mich. 1975, U.S. Dist. Ct. (ea. dist.) Mich. 1982. Magistrate 93d Dist. Ct., Munising, Mich., 1976-78; sole practice Munising, 1977-82; assoc. Patterson & Patterson, Whitfield, Manikoff, Ternan & White, Bloomfield Hills, Mich., 1982-85, ptnr., 1986; asst. corp. counsel Tecumseh (Mich.) Products Co., 1986—; city atty., City of Munising, 1978-82. Asst. editor Tulane U. Law Rev., 1973-75. Trustee Munising Meml. Hosp., 1980-82. Recipient Oustanding Service award Alger County Hist. Soc., Munising, 1982. Mem. ABA, Mich. Bar Assn., Oakland County Bar Assn., Am. Trial Lawyers Assn., Order of the Coif. Roman Catholic. Lodges: Rotary (Munising sec. 1975-76), KC (centennial chmn. 1982). Avocations: jogging, reading, family activities. Personal injury, General corporate, State civil litigation. Home: 707 W Chicago Blvd Tecumseh MI 49286 Office: Tecumseh Products Co Legal Dept Tecumseh MI 49286

MCDONALD, GABRIELLE ANNE KIRK, judge; b. St. Paul, Apr. 12, 1942; d. James G. and Frances R. Kirk; m. Mark T. McDonald; children: Michael, Stacy. LL.B., Howard U., 1966. Bar: Tex. Staff atty. NAACP Legal Def. and Ednl. Fund, N.Y.C., 1966-69; ptnr. McDonald & McDonald, Houston, 1969-79; judge U.S. Dist. Ct., Houston, 1979—; asst. prof. Tex. So. U., Houston, 1970, adj. prof., 1975-77; lectr. U. Tex., Houston, 1977-78. Bd. dirs. Community Service Option Program; bd. dirs. Alley Theatre, Houston, Nat. Coalition of 100 Black Women, ARC; trustee Howard U., from 1983; bd. vistors Thurgood Marshall Sch. Law, Houston. Mem. ABA, Nat. Bar Assn., Houston Bar Assn., Houston Lawyers Assn., Black Women Lawyers Assn. Democrat. Congregationalist. Judicial administration. Office: U S Dist Ct 9535 U S Courthouse 515 Rusk Ave Houston TX 77002 *

MCDONALD, JAMES DANIEL, JR., lawyer; b. Erie, Pa., Apr. 7, 1940; s. James Daniel and Joanna Bowman (Myers) McD.; m. Mary Helen Hamilton, June 30, 1962; children: Shannon Hamilton, Erin Brady. BS, Pa. State U., 1961; JD, Dickinson Sch. Law, 1964. Bar: Pa. 1965, U.S. Dist. Ct. (we. dist.) Pa. 1965, U.S. Ct. Appeals (3d cir.) 1967, U.S. Supreme Ct. 1972. Assoc. Curtze, Gent & McCullough, Erie, 1964-67, Quinn, Gent, Buseck & Leemhuis, Erie, 1967-72; prin. Quinn, Gent, Buseck & Leemhuis, Inc., Erie, 1972-86; sole practice Erie, 1986—; mem. Disciplinary Bd. Supreme Ct. Pa., 1983—. Bd. dirs. Hamot Health Systems, Erie, 1982—, Hamot Med. Ctr., Erie, 1982—. Mem. ABA, Pa. Bar Assn., Erie County Bar Assn. (pres. 1983), Assn. Trial Lawyers Am., Pa. Trial Lawyers Am. (bd. govs. 1980-85), Def. Research Inst., Pa. State Behrend (council of fellows 1984). Democrat. Presbyterian. Avocation: beef cattle farming. Federal civil litigation, State civil litigation, Personal injury. Home: 7467 W Grubb Rd McKean PA 16426 Office: 456 W 6th St Erie PA 16507

MCDONALD, JAMES DOUGLAS, lawyer; b. Chgo., Aug. 2, 1932; s. Elmer and Gladys (Bogner) McD.; m. Jacquelyn Milligan, Aug. 24, 1957; children: Mark D., Julia M., Maria B., Alexandra H., Anne P. AB, Cornell U., 1954, JD, 1958; LLM, NYU, 1964. Bar: N.Y. 1958, U.S. Dist. Ct. (ea. and so. dists.) N.Y. 1958, U.S. Supreme Ct. 1984. Assoc. Cadwalader, Wickersham & Taft, N.Y.C., 1958-67; atty. legal dept. Am. Cyanamid Co., Wayne, N.J., 1967-78; mgr. legal dept. Am. Cyanamid Co., Wayne, 1978—. Mem. ABA, N.Y. State Bar Assn., Assn. Corp. Counsel of N.J., Am. Arbitration Assn. Roman Catholic. Antitrust, Private international, General corporate. Home: 9 McKernan Ct Wayne NJ 07470 Office: Am Cyanamid Co One Cyanamid Plaza Wayne NJ 07470

MCDONALD, JOHN FRANKLIN, III, lawyer; b. New Orleans, May 29, 1950; s. John Franklin Jr. and Mary Elane (Coleman) McD.; m. Cathy Jean Fontenelle, Aug. 7, 1971; children: Jeffery Everett, Christopher Corcoran, Kathleen Anne. BA, Tulane U., 1972, JD, 1974. Bar: La. 1974, U.S. Dist. Ct (ea. dist.) La. 1974. Assoc. Bagert & Bagert, New Orleans, 1974-76; ptnr. Bagert, Bagert & McDonald, New Orleans, 1976-81; sole practice Metairie, La., 1981-84; prin. Brandt, Alarcon & McDonald, Metairie, 1984—. Mem. pres. adv. council Jesuit High Sch., New Orleans, 1983—; bd. dirs., sec. La. HLA Registry Found., Mandeville, La., 1984—. Mem. ABA, La. Bar Assn. Democrat. Catholic. Avocation: music. Real property, Probate, General practice. Home: 120 Belle Terre Covington LA 70433

MCDONALD, JULIA CAROL, lawyer; b. Macon, Ga., June 21, 1950; s. James Harold and Julia (Wiggins) McD. AB in Journalism magna cum laude, U. Ga., 1972; M in Communications, U. N.C., 1975, JD, 1980. Bar: N.C. 1980, Fla. 1985, U.S. Dist. Ct. (mid. dist.) Fla. 1986, U.S. Ct. Appeals (11th cir.) 1986. Editor Army Research Office, Research Triangle Park, N.C., 1972-75, Inst. Govt. U. N.C., Chapel Hill, 1976-77; assoc. Mitchell, Pickup & Rallings, Charlotte, N.C., 1980-82, Wahl & Gabel, Jacksonville, Fla., 1985—. Served as lt. JAGC, USN, 1982-85. Merit scholar Converse Coll., 1968-70. Mem. N.C. Bar Assn., Fla. Bar Assn., Jacksonville Bar Assn., Jacksonville Women Lawyers Assn., Maritime Law Assn., Southeast Admiralty Law Inst., Navy League, Phi Kappa Phi. Admiralty, State civil litigation, Workers' compensation. Office: Wahl & Gabel 920 Barnett Bank Bldg Jacksonville FL 32202

MCDONALD, LAURIER BERNARD, lawyer; b. Memphis, Oct. 3, 1931. BA, Tex. A&I U., 1957; JD, U. Tex., 1961. Bar: Tex. 1961, U.S. Supreme Ct. 1964. Agt. FBI, various cities, 1961-65; ptnr. Pena, McDonald, Prestia & Ibanez, Edinburg, Tex., 1966—; vis. lectr., prof. Pan Am. U., Edinburg, Tex.; guest lectr. Immigration and Nationality symposiums and seminars; del. to joint confs. USSR-U.S., Moscow, 1974, 76. Mem. ABA, Assn. Immigration and Nationality Lawyers (past pres. Tex. chpt.). Immigration, naturalization, and customs. Home: 1122 S 9th St Edinburg TX 78539 Office: Pena McDonald et al 600 S Hwy 281 Edinburg TX 78539

MCDONALD, PARKER LEE, state supreme court justice; b. Sebring., Fla., May 23, 1924; s. Monroe R. and Mattie (Etheredge) McD.; m. Velma Ruth McDonald, Dec. 17, 1949; children: Martha Rebecca, Bruce Lee, Robert Reid, Ruth Ann. B.S., B.A., LL.B., U. Fla. Individual practice law Sebring, Fla., 1950-51, Orlando, Fla., 1951-61; judge Fla. Circuit Ct., 9th Judicial Dist., Orlando, 1961-79; assoc. justice Fla. Supreme Ct., Tallahassee, 1979-86, chief justice, 1986—. Methodist. Office: Supreme Ct Bldg Tallahassee FL 32301 *

MCDONALD, THOMAS ALEXANDER, lawyer; b. Chgo., Aug. 20, 1942; s. Owen Gerard and Lois (Gray) McD.; m. Sharon Diane Hirk, Nov. 25,

1967; children: Cristin, Katie, Courtney, Thomas Jr. AB, Georgetown U., 1965; JD, Loyola U., Chgo., 1968. Bar: Ill. 1969, U.S. Dist. Ct. (no. dist.) Ill. 1969. Ptnr. Clausen, Miller, Gorman, Caffrey & Witous, P.C., Chgo., 1969—. Mem. ABA, Ill. Bar Assn., Chgo. Bar Assn. Federal civil litigation, State civil litigation, Insurance. Office: Clausen Miller Gorman et al 5400 Sears Tower Chicago IL 60606

MCDONALD, TOM, judge; b. Louisville, Feb. 10, 1955; s. Thomas Edward Jr. and Mary Thelma (Vogel) McD.; m. Susan Gingles, May 21, 1977; 1 child, Megan Claire. BA cum laude, U. Louisville, 1977; postgrad. law studies, U. London, Eng., 1979; JD, U. Louisville, 1980; postgrad., Nat. Coll. Juvenile Justice, 1985. Bar: Ky., U.S. Dist. Ct. (we. dist.) Ky., U.S. Supreme Ct. Sole practice Louisville, 1980-83; prosecuter Office of County Atty., Louisville, 1981-83; dep. chief judge Adminstrv. Office of Ct., Louisville, 1983—; Cons., lectr., various locations throughout U.S., 1983—; chmn. bd. dirs. Ct. Appointed Spl. Adv. Project Ky., Louisville, 1984—; adj. faculty U. Louisville, 1985—; mem. Jefferson County Juvenile Justice Commn., Louisville, 1985—; 2d v.p. Nat. Ct. Apptd. Spl. Adv. Assn., Seattle, 1986—; faculty Nat. Coll. Juvenile and Family Law. Bd. dirs. Jefferson County Spouse Abuse Ctr., Louisville, 1983—, KIPDA Council on Aging, Louisville, 1984—; mem. Nat. Eagle Scout Assn., 1983—; commn. mem. Ky. Task Force on Permanency Planning, Frankfort, Ky., 1985—, Ky. Task Force on Dispositional Alternatives for Foster Children, Frankfort, 1985—. Mem. ABA, Nat. Council Juvenile and Family Ct. Judges, Ky. Bar Assn., Louisville Bar Assn. Democrat. Roman Catholic. Avocations: sailing, tennis. Juvenile, Criminal.

MCDONALD, WILLIAM HENRY, lawyer; b. Niangua, Mo., Feb. 27, 1946; s. Milburn and Fannie M. McDonald; m. Janice E. Robinson, July 13, 1968; children: Melissa L., Meghan M. BS in Pub. Adminstrn., Southwest Mo. State U., 1968; JD, U. Mo., 1971. Bar: Mo. 1971, U.S. Dist. Ct. (we. dist.) Mo. 1973, U.S. Supreme Ct. 1978, U.S. Ct. Appeals (8th cir.) 1982. Ptnr. Woolsey, Fisher, Whiteaker & McDonald, Springfield, Mo., 1973—. Chmn. blue ribbon task force on Delivery of Mental Health Services to Southwest Mo., Mo. Commn. Continuing Legal Edn.; pres. Tan Oaks Homeowners Assn.; mem. fin. com. Child Adv. Council, Rep. Nat. Com., Mo. Rep. Com., Greene County Nat. Com.; active various Southwest Mo. State U. Clubs; bd. dirs. Greene County div. Am. Heart Assn., Ozarks regional Am. Athletic Union Jr. Olympics. Served to capt. U.S. Army, 1971-73. Named one of Outstanding Young Men Am., 1978, 81, Outstanding Young Men Springfield, 1980. Mem. ABA (litigation and torts and ins. sects., fellow young lawyers sect.), Mo. Bar Assn. (chmn. spl. com. on mandatory continuing edn., various coms.), Greene County Bar Assn. (chmn. pub. edn. speakers bur.), Met. Bar Assn. St. Louis, Fed. Bar Assn., Assn. Trial Lawyers Am., Mo. Trial Lawyers Assn., Am. Judicature Soc., Am. Bd. Trial Advs., Nat. Bd. Trial Advs., 31st Jud. Cir. Bar Com. (chmn.), Supreme Ct. Hist. Soc., U. Mo.-Kansas City Sch. Law Found., C.of C., Beta Omega Tau, Kappa Epsilon. Presbyterian. Federal civil litigation, State civil litigation, Personal injury. Home: 4857 Royal Dr Springfield MO 65804 Office: Woolsy Fisher Whiteaker & McDonald 300 S Jefferson Suite 600 Springfield MO 65806

MC DONALD, WILLIAM J., corporation executive, lawyer; b. N.Y.C., Apr. 17, 1927; s. William J. and Adelaide (Morrisson) McD.; m. Diane A. Saxer, Apr. 19, 1958; children: Brian, Timothy, Megan, Christopher. BS, Holy Cross Coll., 1949; JD, Georgetown U., 1952. Bar: N.Y. 1952, U.S. Supreme Ct. 1960. Assoc. Clark, Carr & Ellis, N.Y.C., 1952-62; ptnr. Clark, Carr & Ellis, 1963-69; gen. counsel Union Pacific R.R. Corp., 1968, v.p. law dept., 1969; v.p., gen. counsel Union Pacific Corp., Union Pacific R.R. Co., 1969-73, sr. v.p. law, 1973—; dir. Pacific Rail Systems, Champlin Petroleum Co., Union Pacific Land Resources Corp., Upland Industries, Rocky Mountain Energy Co. Assoc. editor in chief Georgetown Law Rev., 1951-52. Trustee Mercy Coll., 1970-71; mem. Bd. Edn. Archdiocese N.Y., 1969-73, Cardinal's Com. of Laity for the 80's; bd. dirs. Union Settlement 1966-71. Served with USNR, 1945-46, PTO. Mem. ABA (chmn. R.R.s com. 1975-79, chmn. pub. utilities sect. 1980-81), Assn. Bar City N.Y. (com. state legis. 1959-61, securities regulation 1962-67, corp. law depts. 1979-80), Assn. Am. R.R. (legal affairs com., chmn. subcoms. on securities matters and fin. assistance to R.R.'s), Bus. Roundatable (chmn. staff services subcom. environ. task force 1978-80)., Am. Arbitration Assn. (dir. 1979-80). Republican. Clubs: Sky (N.Y.C.), Met. (Wash.), Winged Foot Golf (Mamaroneck, N.Y.), Westchester Country (Rye, N.Y.). General corporate, Antitrust, Federal civil litigation. Home: 48 Biltmore Ave Rye NY 10580 Office: Union Pacific Corp 345 Park Ave New York NY 10154

MCDONALD, WILLIS, IV, lawyer; b. N.Y.C., Aug. 25, 1926; s. Willis McDonald III and Elizabeth Beaumont (Pfaff) McD.; m. Mary Lou H. Bellows, May 12, 1967; children: stepchildren: Randall F. Bellows, Jr., Lisa L. Thorne. B.S., Yale U., 1949; LL.B., U. Va., 1953. Bar: Va. 1952, N.Y. 1955. Assoc. White & Case, N.Y.C., 1953-63, ptnr., 1963—. Chmn. exec. com., trustee First Ch. of Round Hill, Greenwich, Conn., 1980—. Fellow Am. Bar Found., Am. Coll. Investment Counsel (pres. 1981-82), Am Coll. Investment Counsel (trustee); mem. ABA, Va. Bar Assn., N.Y. State Bar Assn., Assn. Bar City N.Y., N.Y. County Lawyers Assn. Republican. Episcopalian. Clubs: N.Y. Yacht, Yale, Down Town Assn. (N.Y.C.); Indian Harbor Yacht, Stanwich (Greenwich); Wigwam Country (Litchfield Park, Ariz.). General corporate, Bankruptcy, Securities. Office: White & Case 1155 Ave of the Americas New York NY 10036

MCDONNELL, MICHAEL R. N., lawyer; b. Paterson, N.J., Sept. 24, 1940; s. Thomas Edward and Margaret (Chapline) McD.; m. Nina Carlotta Gray, Jan. 5, 1980; children—Amy Kathleen, Andrew Gray; children by previous marriage—Michael R.N., James Egan. B.S., U.S. Mil. Acad., 1962; J.D., Stetson U., 1970. Bar: Fla. 1970, U.S. Dist. Ct. (so. and mid. dists.) Fla. 1972, U.S. Dist. Ct. (no. dist.) Fla. 1976, U.S. Supreme Ct. 1974, U.S. Ct. Appeals (5th cir.) 1975; cert. civil trial lawyer Fla. Bar. Hearing officer Div. Adminstrv. Hearings, State of Fla., Tallahassee, 1977-79; pres. McDonnell & Berry, Naples, Fla., 1981—; pres., dir., lectr. Am. Trial Forum, Naples, 1983-84. Contbr. articles to legal jours. Pres., Voters League of Collier County, Naples, 1982. Served to capt. U.S. Army, 1962-66. Mem. Assn. Trial Lawyers Am., Acad. Fla. Trial Lawyers. Republican. Episcopalian. Club: Naples Athletic. State civil litigation, Personal injury, Criminal. Office: McDonnell & Berry 720 Goodlette Rd Suite 304 Naples FL 33940

MCDONNELL, RICHARD C., lawyer; b. Bklyn., June 18, 1937; m. Jane F., July 15, 1961; children: Susan, Michael, Diane, Nancie. BS, St. Peter's Coll., 1959; MBA cum laude, Fairleigh Dickinson U., 1963; JD, Seton Hall U., 1969. Bar: N.J. 1969, U.S. Supreme Ct. 1983. Ptnr. McDonnell and Whitaker, Ramsey, N.J.; adj. faculty Bergen Community Coll., Paramus, N.J., 1971. Councilman Borough of Upper Saddle River, N.J., 1980-82; presiding condemnation commr. appointed by Superior Ct. of N.J., 1975; commr. Upper Saddle River Sewer Assessmant Com., 1985-86; legal advisor Upper Saddle River Youth Guidance Council, 1971-75; counsel Upper Saddle River Bd. Edn., 1974-80, Upper Saddle River Planning Bd., 1975—; P.B.A. atty. Borough of Waldwick, N.J., 1975-76. Served to capt. USAR, 1959-60. Mem. ABA, Assn. Trial Lawyers Am., Am. Arbitration Assn., Bergen County Bar Assn. (del. to State Bar Assn. 1979-80, chmn. land use com. 1985-86, co-chmn. judician selection com. 1979, mem. judicial appointments com. 1977-78, 80-81, panelist early settlement matrimonial panel 1977—). Roman Catholic. General practice, Family and matrimonial, State civil litigation. Office: McDonnell and Whitaker 79 N Franklin Turnpike Ramsey NJ 07446

MCDONOUGH, JOHN MICHAEL, lawyer; b. Evanston, Ill., Dec. 30, 1944; s. John Justin and Anne Elizabeth (O'Brien) McD.; m. Susan J. Moran, Sept. 19, 1981. A.B., Princeton U., 1966; LL.B., Yale U., 1969. Bar: Ill. 1969. Assoc. Sidley & Austin, Chgo., 1969-75, ptnr., 1975—. Bd. dirs. Met. Housing and Planning Council, 1978—, pres., 1982-84; bd. dirs. Ctr. Am. Archeology, 1980-85, chmn., 1982-84; bd. dirs. Leadership Greater Chgo., 1984—, sec.-treas., 1987—; bd. dirs. Lakefront Gardens, Inc., also sec.-treas.; bd. dirs. Brain Research Found. Served with JAGC, USAR, 1969-75. Mem. ABA, Ill. Bar Assn., Chgo. Bar Assn. Democrat. Roman Catholic. Clubs: Chicago, University (pres. 1979-81), Racquet, Economic, Chikaming Country. Probate, Estate planning, Estate taxation. Home: 1209 N Astor St Chicago IL 60610 Office: Sidley & Austin 1 First Nat Plaza Suite 4800 Chicago IL 60603

MC DONOUGH, JOHN RICHARD, lawyer; b. St. Paul, May 16, 1919; s. John Richard and Gena (Olson) McD.; m. Margaret Poot, Sept. 10, 1944; children—Jana Margaret, John Jacobus. Student, U. Wash., 1937-40; LL.B., Columbia U., 1946. Bar: Calif. bar 1949. Asst. prof. law Stanford U., 1946-49, prof., 1952-69; asso. firm Brobeck, Phleger & Harrison, San Francisco, 1949-52; asst. dep. atty. gen. U.S. Dept. Justice, Washington, 1967-68; asso. dep. atty. gen. U.S. Dept. Justice, 1968-69; of counsel and partner firm Keatinge & Sterling, Los Angeles, 1969-70; partner firm Ball, Hunt, Hart, Brown and Baerwitz, 1970—; exec. sec. Calif. Law Revision Commn., 1954-59, mem. commn., 1959-67, vice chmn., 1960-64, chmn., 1964-65; participant various continuing edn. programs. Served with U.S. Army, 1942-46. Mem. State Bar Calif., Am. Bar Assn., Los Angeles County Bar Assn., Am. Coll. Trial Lawyers. Democrat. Federal civil litigation, State civil litigation. Office: Ball Hunt Hart Brown & Baerwitz 4525 Wilshire Blvd 3d Floor Los Angeles CA 90010-3886

MCDONOUGH, JOSEPH RICHARD, lawyer; b. Newark, July 7, 1950; s. Richard Thomas and Catherine M. (Burns) McD.; m. Susan H. Fenske, Feb. 17, 1985. BA, Middlebury Coll., 1972; JD, Rutgers U., 1978. Bar: N.J. 1978, U.S. Ct. Appeals (3d cir.) 1983, U.S. Supreme Ct. 1985. Law sec. appellate div. N.J. Superior Ct., 1978-79; assoc. Carpenter, Bennett & Morrissey, Newark, 1979—. Pres. Delbarton Sch. Alumni Assn., Morristown, N.J., 1986-87. Recipient Outstanding Achievement in Oral Advocacy award Internat. Acad. Trial Lawyers, 1978. Mem. ABA, N.J. Bar Assn., Essex County Bar Assn. Federal civil litigation, State civil litigation. Home: 214 Brooklake Rd Florham Park NJ 07932 Office: Carpenter Bennett & Morrissey Three Gateway Ctr Newark NJ 07102

MCDONOUGH, PATRICK JOSEPH, lawyer; b. Los Angeles, Oct. 11, 1943; s. Thomas John and Cecilia Veronica (Roach) McD.; m. Susan Ann Singletary, Dec. 30, 1967; 1 child, Colleen Marie. BA, Calif. State U., Northridge, 1967; JD, Loyola U., Los Angeles, 1971. Bar: Calif. 1971, U.S. Dist. Ct. (cen. dist.) Calif. 1971. Assoc. counsel. Auto Club So. Calif., Los Angeles, 1971-77, sec., assoc. counsel, 1977-86; v.p., gen. counsel Johnson & Higgens Calif., Los Angeles, 1986—. Mem. ABA, Calif. Bar Assn., Los Angeles Bar Assn. (chmn. corp. law sect. 1987—), Inst. Corp Counsel (chmn. 1986—), Am. Corp. Counsel Assn. Southern Calif. (bd. dirs. 1985—), Assn. Calif. Tort Reform (bd. dirs. 1986—), Town Hall Calif. Roman Catholic. Avocations: boating, sailing, fishing. Insurance, General corporate, Legislative. Office: Johnson & Higgins Calif 2029 Century Park E 24th Fl Los Angeles CA 90067

MCDONOUGH, THOMAS JOSEPH, lawyer; b. N.Y.C., Jan. 20, 1934; s. Thomas Joseph and Kathleen (Casey) McD.; m. Marianne Amoia, Feb. 6, 1965; children: Catherine, Susan, Joanne. Student, Manhattan Coll.; BA, CUNY, 1956; LLB, NYU, 1962. Bar: N.Y. 1962, U.S. Dist. Ct. (so. and ea. dists.) N.Y. 1962, U.S. Ct. Appeals (2d cir.) 1967, U.S. Dist. Ct. (no. dist.) N.Y. 1969. Assoc. J. Robert Morris Law Offices, N.Y.C., 1962-65, Bigham, Englar, Jones & Houston, N.Y.C., 1965-70; ptnr. Miller & Mannix, Glen Falls, N.Y., 1970-76; sole practice Glen Falls, 1976—. Served to capt. USAF, 1956-60. Mem. ABA (ins. neglegence sect.), N.Y. State Bar Assn. (criminal law, food and drug, ins. neglegence and aviation sects), Warren County Bar Assn. (pres. 1985—, bd. dirs. 1978, 81, 84-85, 86-87), Maritime Law Assn. of the U.S., Def. Research Inst., N.Y. Defenders Assn. Democrat. Roman Catholic. Avocation: gardening. Personal injury, State civil litigation, Criminal. Home: 28 Twicwood Ln Glen Falls NY 12801 Office: Lake George Rd Rural Rt #5 Box 14 Glen Falls NY 12801

MCDOWELL, DOCK, JR., lawyer; b. Mobile, Ala., Apr. 16, 1950; s. Dock Sr. and Willie Pearl (Matthew) McD.; m. Cherie Denise McDowell, April 20, 1974 (div. Oct. 1982); children: LaShun Denise, Dock III. BA in Polit. Sci., Wabash Coll., 1972; JD, Valparaiso U., 1975; postgrad., John Marshall Law Sch., 1984. Bar: Tenn. 1976, Ind. 1976, U.S. Dist. Ct. (no. and so. dists.) Ind. 1976, U.S. Dist. Ct. (mid. dist.) Tenn. 1976, U.S. Tax Ct. 1982. With Legal Aid of Gary (Ind.), 1974-76; sole practice Gary, 1976—. Legal counsel Gary Police CSC, 1977—; pub. defender Lake County Criminal Ct., Crown Point, Ind., 1977-81, 84-86; pres. Bd. of Urban League Northwest, Ind., 1983; mem. Bd. of Project Justice and Equality. McIntosh fellow Wabash Coll., 1972, Reginald Heber Smith fellow, 1975-76. Mem. ABA, Ind. Bar Assn., Assn. Trial Lawyers Am. Democrat. Roman Catholic. Personal injury, Criminal, Probate. Office: 4746 Broadway Gary IN 46408

MCDOWELL, KAREN ANN, lawyer; b. Ruston, La., Oct. 4, 1945; d. Paul and Opal Elizabeth (Davis) Bauer; m. Norman McKay MacDonald, Aug. 10, 1970 (div. Dec. 1977); m. Gary Lee McDowell, Dec. 22, 1979. BA, N.E. La. U., 1967; JD, U. Mich., 1971. Bar: Ill. 1973, U.S. Dist. Ct. (so. dist.) Ill. 1973, Colo. 1977, U.S. Dist. Ct. Colo. 1977. Reference library assoc. Ill. State Library, Springfield, 1972-73; asst. atty. gen. State of Ill., Springfield, 1973-75; sole practice Boulder, Colo., 1978-79, Denver, 1979—. Mem. ABA, Colo. Bar Assn., Denver Bar Assn., Colo. Womens Bar Assn. (editor newsletter 1982-84), Colo. Trial Lawyers' Assn. Republican. Club: Toastmasters (Aurora, Colo.) (pres. 1981). Avocations: philately, needlework. Criminal, Bankruptcy, Family and matrimonial. Office: 1614 Gaylord St Denver CO 80206

MCDOWELL, MICHAEL DAVID, lawyer; b. Lewisburg, Pa., May 10, 1948; s. David Leonard and Mary Ellen (Scallan) McD.; m. Martha LaMantia, Aug. 4, 1973; 1 child, Daniel Joseph. B.S. in Bus. Mgmt., U. Dayton, 1970; J.D., U. Pitts., 1973. Bar: Pa. 1973, U.S. Dist. Ct. (mid. dist.) Pa. 1973, U.S. Tax Ct. 1974, U.S. Ct. Appeals (3d cir.) 1974, U.S. Dist. Ct. (we. dist.) Pa. 1975, U.S. Supreme Ct. 1977, U.S. Ct. Internat. Trade 1981, U.S. Ct. Appeals (fed. cir.) 1982. Asst. U.S. atty. Dept. Justice, Lewisburg, Pa., 1973-75; assoc. Hirsch, Weise & Tillman, Pitts., 1975-76, Plowman & Spiegel, Pitts., 1976-80; counsel Dravo Corp., Pitts., 1980-86, sr. counsel, 1987—; mem. panel of arbitrators Am. Arbitration Assn., 1978—, Pa. Bur. Mediation, 1983—, Pa. Labor Relations Bd., 1985—. Contbr. articles to profl. jours. Mem. Union County Child Welfare adv. com., 1974-75; account exec. Southwestern Pa. United Way, Pitts., 1983; bd. govs. Pine Run Homeowners Assn., 1986—; mem. nat. panel consumer arbitrators Better Bus. Bur.; mem. supervisory com. ALCOBAR Credit Union, 1986—. Recipient Dravo Corp. Editorial Achievement awards, 1982, 83, 85, 86; nominated as one of Outstanding Young Men. Am., 1983,84. Mem. ABA (Ho. of Dels. 1985—, exec. council sect. labor and employment law 1983-85, exec. council young lawyers div. 1982-84, chmn. YLD Labor Law Com. 1981-83), Pa. Bar Assn. (ho. of dels. 1980—, chmn. special rules subcom. Disciplinary Bd. Study Com. 1985—, com. on legal ethics and profl. responsibility, 1985—, Outstanding Young Lawyer award 1984, Spl. Achievement award 1986), Allegheny County Bar Assn. (profl. ethics com. 1980—, bd. govs. 1979, 85—, asst. sec.-treas. 1979, chmn. young lawyers sect. 1978, award for outstanding leadership and valuable contbns. to bar 1979), Nat. Constructors Assn. (gen. counsels com. 1983—), Am. Corp. Counsel Assn., Phi Alpha Delta (justice 1972-73, cert. Outstanding Service 1973). Republican. Roman Catholic. Club: McCandless Swimming (Pitts.) (bd. govs. 1982-85). Labor, Federal civil litigation, State civil litigation. Office: Dravo Corp Law Dept 33d Floor One Oliver Plaza Pittsburgh PA 15222

MCDUFFEE, PAUL GERARD, II, lawyer; b. Concord, N.C., Dec. 6, 1945; s. Paul G. and Sarah (Crooks) McD.; m. Betsy H. Huntington, Apr. 5, 1966; children: Matthew, Michele, Rachael. AA in Police Adminstrn., St. Petersburg Jr. Coll., 1970; BS in Criminology, U. Tampa, 1972; JD with honors, South Tex. Coll. Law, 1978. Bar: Fla. 1978., U.S. Dist. Ct. (mid. dist.) Fla. 1978, U.S. Ct. (5th cir.) 1978; licensed USCG ocean operator. Police officer, detective Tampa (Fla.) Police Dept., 1967-73; legal asst., investigator Levine, Freedman & Hirsch, Tampa, 1973-75; asst. state atty. Hills County, Tampa, 1977-80; ptnr. Langford, Mooney & McDuffee, P.A., Tampa, 1980—. Republican. Roman Catholic. Avocations: fishing, boating. Personal injury, State civil litigation, General practice. Home: 16137 Sandcrest Way Tampa FL 33618 Office: Langford Mooney & McDuffee PA 3321 Henderson Blvd Tampa FL 33609

MCDUFFEE, RENÉE RENAUD, lawyer; b. Detroit, Dec. 29, 1951; d. Daniel Webster Scott McDuffee and Renée (Renaud) Sankar; m. Bruce H. Kiernan, June 11, 1977. Student, Mich. State U., 1970-71; BA, Wayne State U., 1974; M in Criminology, U. Edinburgh, Scotland, 1976; JD, U. Detroit, 1979. Bar: Mich. 1979, U.S. Dist. Ct. (ea. dist.) Mich. 1980, Ill. 1983, U.S. Dist. Ct. (no. dist.) Ill. 1983, N.Y. 1986. Trial atty. Auto Club Mich., Detroit, 1980-83, 84-85; assoc. Pretzel & Stouffer, Chgo., 1983, James N. Hite & Assocs., Buffalo, 1986—. Rotary Found. fellow, 1975-76. Mem. ABA, Mich. Bar Assn., N.Y. State Bar Assn., Bar Assn. Erie County, Women's Bar Assn. of N.Y. (western chpt.), N.Y. State Trial Lawyers Assn., Women Lawyers of Western N.Y. Republican. Roman Catholic. Clubs: University (Buffalo); Indian Village Tennis (Detroit). Avocation: squash. State civil litigation, Personal injury, Real property. Home: 329 N Ellicott Creek Rd Amherst NY 14150 Office: James N Hite & Assocs 257 Elmwood Ave Buffalo NY 14222

MCDUNN, SUSAN JEANINE, lawyer; b. Chgo., Aug. 8, 1955; d. William Dorcey and Evelyn (Drabik) McD. BS, DePaul U., 1976, JD, 1980. Bar: Ill. 1980, U.S. Dist. Ct. (no. dist.) Ill. 1980, U.S. Ct. Appeals (7th cir.) 1981. Law clk. to presiding justice U.S. Dist. Ct. (no. dist.) Ill., 1981-82; assoc. Kirkland & Ellis, Chgo., 1982—. Mem. ABA, Fed. Bar Assn., Chgo. Bar Assn. Roman Catholic. Federal civil litigation, Bankruptcy, Contracts commercial. Home: 5362 S Maplewood Chicago IL 60632 Office: Kirkland & Ellis 200 E Randolph Dr Chicago IL 60601

MC ELHANEY, JAMES WILLSON, educator, lawyer; b. N.Y.C., Dec. 10, 1937; s. Lewis Keck and Sara Jane (Hess) McE.; m. Maxine Dennis Jones, Aug. 17, 1961; children: David, Benjamin. A.B., Duke U., 1960; LL.B., 1962. Bar: Wis. 1962. Assoc. firm Wickham, Borgelt, Skogstad & Powell, 1966; asst. prof. U. Md. Law Sch., 1966-69, assoc. prof., 1969-72; vis. prof. So. Meth. U. Sch. of Law, Dallas, 1973-74; prof. So. Meth. U. Sch. of Law, 1974-76; Joseph C. Hostetler prof. trial practice and advocacy Case Western Res. U. Sch. of Law, Cleve., 1976—; mem. faculty Nat. Inst. Trial Advocacy, Boulder, Colo., 1975—; vis. prof. U. Tulsa Coll. Law, summer 1977, 79, Ind. U. Law Sch., summer 1980; cons. to U.S. Atty. Gen. on Justice Dept. Advocacy Tng. Programs, 1979—; lectr. in field. Author: Effective Litigation: Trials, Problems and Materials, 1974, Trial Notebook, 1981, 2d edit., 1987; editor in chief Litigation mag., 1984-86; author: column Trial Notebook; contbr. articles to profl. jours. Recipient Outstanding Prof. award So. Meth. U., 1976. Mem. ABA, Assn. Am. Law Schs. (chmn. sect. trial advocacy 1974-76, chmn. sect. evidence 1978). Legal education, Federal civil litigation, State civil litigation. Home: 2842 E Overlook Cleveland Heights OH 44118 Office: Case Western Res U 11075 E Boulevard Cleveland OH 44106

MC ELHANEY, JOHN HESS, lawyer; b. Milw., Apr. 16, 1934; s. Lewis Keck and Sara Jane (Hess) McE.; m. Jacquelyn Masur, Aug. 4, 1962; children—Scott, Victoria. B.B.A., So. Meth. U., 1956, J.D., 1958. Bar: Tex. bar 1958. Pvt. practice law Dallas, 1958—; partner Locke Purnell Boren Laney & Neely, 1977—; lectr. law So. Meth. U., 1967-76. Contbr. articles to legal jours. Trustee St. Mark's Sch. Tex., 1980-86. Fellow Am. Coll. Trial Lawyers; mem. Am. Bd. Trial Advs., Am. Bar Assn., Tex. Bar Assn., So. Meth. U. Law Alumni Assn. (pres. 1972-73, dir. 1970-73). Presbyterian. Clubs: Town and Gown (pres. 1981-82), Masons. Federal civil litigation, State civil litigation, Libel. Home: 5340 Tanbark Dallas TX 75229 Office: 3600 Republic Bank Tower Dallas TX 75201

MCELLIGOTT, JAMES PATRICK, JR., lawyer; b. Chgo., Jan. 11, 1948; s. James Patrick and Helen Cecelia (Hogan) McE.; children: Michael Sean, Andrew David; m. Trina Reff, Aug. 25, 1985. BA, U. Ill., Urbana, 1970; JD, Harvard U., 1973. Bar: Va. 1974, U.S. Dist. Ct. (ea. and we. dists.) Va. 1974, U.S. Ct. Appeals (4th cir.) 1974, U.S. Supreme Ct. 1979. Research asst. U. Ill., 1970; assoc. McGuire, Woods & Battle, Richmond, 1973-79; ptnr. McGuire, Woods, Battle & Boothe, Richmond, 1979—. Mem. exec. com. Va. Home for Boys, Richmond, 1976—, pres. bd. govs. 1981-83; mem. Leadership Metro Richmond-Met. C. of C., 1984-85. Mem. ABA, Va. Bar Assn. (exec. com., chmn. pub. relations com. 1978-82, producer pub. service message 1973, Hot Spot award 1973), Richmond Bar Assn., Fed. Bar Assn. (v.p. Richmond chpt. 1984—), Nat. Sch. Bds. Assn., Council of Sch. Attys., Phi Beta Kappa, Phi Kappa Phi, Omicron Delta Epsilon. Federal civil litigation, Labor. Home: 203 Cyril Ln Richmond VA 23229 Office: McGuire Woods Battle & Boothe One James Ctr Richmond VA 23219

MCELROY, BERT COLYAR, lawyer; b. Pearl River, N.Y., Nov. 22, 1943; s. Bert and Nella Fae (Colyar) McE.; m. Mary Marcellyn Seal, Oct. 19, 1979; children: Stephanie, Sean. Student, U. Okla., 1961-64; LLB, U. Tulsa, 1967. Bar: Okla. 1967, U.S. Dist. Ct. (no. dist.) Okla. 1967, U.S. Ct. Appeals (10th cir.) 1967, U.S. Supreme Ct. 1974, U.S. Dist. Ct. (we. dist.) Ark. 1982, U.S. Dist. Ct. (we. dist.) Okla. 1982. Assoc. Sanders and McElroy, Tulsa, 1967-73; ptnr. McElroy, Naylor and Williams, Tulsa, 1973-77; sole practice Tulsa, 1977-78; spl. judge Tulsa County Dist. Ct., 1979-81; ptnr. Pray, Walker, Jackman, Williamson and Marlar, Tulsa, 1981—; bd. dirs. Lakeside State Bank, Oologah, Okla. State committeeman Okla. Rep. Party, Tulsa County, 1976-78; mem. Charter Revision Commn., Tulsa, 1973. Served to 1st lt. USAF, 1974-76. Named to Order of the Curule Chair U. Tulsa Coll. of Law, 1967. Mem. Okla. Bar Assn. (chmn. gen. practice sect. 1974), Tulsa County Bar Assn. (Outstanding Jr. Mem. 1974). Republican. Presbyterian. Clubs: Summit (Tulsa); Coves Golf (Afton, Okla.). Lodge: Masons. Administrative and regulatory, Banking, Federal civil litigation. Home: 1712 E 31st St Tulsa OK 74105 Office: Pray Walker Jackman Williamson and Marlar 100 W 5th St Tulsa OK 74103

MCELROY, HOWARD CHOWNING, lawyer; b. Shreveport, La., Mar. 26, 1946; s. Charles Imogene and Verna Mae (Snow) McE.; m. Heidi Margot Hansen, June 17, 1970; children—Christopher, Karen. B.S., U.S. Mil. Acad., 1968; J.D., Georgetown U., 1977. Bar: Va. 1977, U.S. Dist. Ct. (we. dist.) Va. 1977, U.S. Ct. Appeals (4th cir.) 1977. Ptnr. White, Elliott & Bundy, Abingdon, Va., 1977—; mem. mandatory continuing legal edn. bd. Va. State Bar 1986—. Served from 2d lt. to capt. M.I., U.S. Army, 1968-73, Vietnam. Mem. ABA, Def. Research Inst., Va. Bar Assn., Va. Assn. Def. Attys. Episcopalian. Lodge: Rotary (pres. local club 1983-84) Federal civil litigation, State civil litigation, Insurance. Home: 160 Crestview Dr Abingdon VA 24210 Office: White Elliott & Bundy 160 E Main St Abingdon VA 24210

MCELROY, MICHAEL ROBERT, lawyer, public utility consultant; b. Providence, Feb. 7, 1951; s. Gerald Robert and Jeannette (Belanger) McE.; m. Christine Anne O'Donnell, June 5, 1976; children—Brian Robert, Dianne Elizabeth, Erin Christine. B.A. with highest distinction, U. R.I., 1973; J.D. cum laude, Boston U., 1976; M.S. in Taxation, Bryant Coll., 1987. Bar: Tenn. 1976, U.S. Dist. Ct. (ea. dist.) Tenn. 1977, U.S. Ct. Appeals (5th cir.) 1977, U.S. Supreme Ct. 1979, U.S. Ct. Appeals (6th cir.) 1980, R.I. 1981, U.S. Dist. Ct. R.I. 1981, U.S. Ct. Appeals (1st cir.) 1981, Mass. 1985. Trial atty. TVA, Knoxville, 1976-81; counsel R.I. Pub. Utilities Commn., Providence, 1982-83; spl. asst. atty. gen. Office Atty. Gen., Providence, 1982-83; ptnr. O'Leary & McElroy, Providence, 1981-85; sole practice, Providence, 1985—; pres. Utility Cons., Inc., Providence, 1983; ptnr. McElroy, Lawrence, Edge & Assocs., Providence, 1983—. Legal counsel for candidate Congl. campaign, Providence, 1982; legal counsel Pawtuxet Valley Preservation and Hist. Soc., West Warwick, R.I., 1983—; chief speech writer for candidate gubernatorial campaign, R.I., 1983-84. Danforth Found. hon. fellow, 1973; Rhodes Scholar nominee, 1973; honoree for life-saving CPR, TVA, 1980. Mem. Assn. Trial Lawyers Am., Assn. Trial Lawyers R.I., R.I. Bar Assn. Democrat. Roman Catholic. Federal civil litigation, Contracts commercial, General practice. Home: 345 Sharon St Providence RI 02908 Office: 128 Dorrance St Suite 400 Providence RI 02903

MCELVEIN, THOMAS I., JR., lawyer; b. Buffalo, Apr. 19, 1936; s. Thomas I. and Edith Marian (Bowen) McE.; m. Ernesta F. McElvein, June 26, 1965; children—Christopher, Andrew, Kathryn. B.A., Antioch Coll., 1959; J.D., Yale U., 1962. Bar: N.Y. 1962, U.S. Dist. Ct. (we. dist.) N.Y. 1969. Ptnr. Nesper, McElvein, Ferber & DiGiacomo and predecessors, Buffalo, 1963—; atty. Village Akron (N.Y.); dir. Pollack Printing Corp., Reppenhagen Roller Corp.; trustee Yager Found. Mem. ABA, N.Y. State Bar Assn., Erie County Bar Assn. General corporate, Probate. Home: 295 Nottingham Terr Buffalo NY 14216 Office: 1220 Liberty Bldg Buffalo NY 14202

MC ELWAIN, LESTER STAFFORD, lawyer; b. San Mateo, Calif., Jan. 1, 1910; s. George Walter and Ethel (Dickson) McE.; m. Loretta F. Barksdale,

July 12, 1977; children from previous marriage: Roderick, Malcolm, Douglas. B.A., Stanford U., 1931, J.D., 1934. Bar: Calif. 1934, U.S. Supreme Ct. 1955. Assoc. Donahue, Richards & Hamlin, Oakland, Calif., 1934-41; sole practice, Oakland, 1946—. Past pres. Alameda County Rep. Assembly. Served with USN, 1941-46, to comdr. USNR. Mem. ABA, Calif. Bar Assn., Alameda County Bar Assn., Assn. Trial Lawyers Am., Am. Arbitration Assn., Ret. Officers Assn. (past pres.), Phi Alpha Delta, Phi Sigma Kappa, Jr. C. of C. (state v.p. 1940). Clubs: Athenian-Nile. Lodges: Kiwanis (past lt. gov.), Masons (past grand master), Elks. Family and matrimonial, Personal injury, Probate. Home: 4557 Mayfield Ct Fremont CA 94536 Office: 436 14th St Oakland CA 94612

MCELWRATH, MICHAEL ROGERS, lawyer; b. San Benito, Tex., Jan. 15, 1952; s. Albert Ransom and Sara Louise (McCammon) McE.; m. Mary Patricia Northern, Aug. 28, 1976; children—Mac McCammon, Sean Michael. B.A., U. Tex., 1974, J.D., 1977. Bar: Tex. 1977, U.S. Dist. Ct. (we. dist.) Tex. 1980. Assoc. Cotton, Bledsoe, Tighe, Morrow & Dawson, Midland, Tex., 1977-78; atty. Lone Star Abstract, Midland, 1978-80; assoc. Freeman & Hyde, Midland, 1980-82; assoc. Turpin, Smith, Dyer & Saxe, Midland, 1982-85, ptnr., 1985—. Vice chmn. Planning and Zoning Commn., City of Midland, 1982-84, chmn., 1985—; deacon First Presbyterian Ch., Midland, 1984—, chmn. service com., 1984—, chmn. bd. deacons, 1986, elder, 1987—; mem. Leadership Midland, 1981-82, Midland Com., 1983—, Leadership Midland Alumni Assn., 1982—; pres. Leadership Midland Alumni Assn., 1985-86; pres. Am. Heart Assn., Midland, 1984—, state v.p. Tex. div., 1985—, devel. chmn., 1982-83. Named Outstanding Young Lawyer of Midland County, 1986; recipient Exceptional Vol. Service honor State of Tex., 1986; Nat. Finalist White House Fellowship Competition, 1986. Mem. ABA, Tex. Bar Assn., Midland County Bar Assn., West Tex. Young Lawyers Assn. (treas. 1985—), Midland County Young Lawyers Assn. (v.p. 1984-85, pres. 1985—), Internat. Platform Assn., U. Tex. Law Alumni Assn. (bd. dirs. 1986—), Midland C. of C., Phi Delta Phi. Republican. Club: Midland Republican Men's. Oil and gas leasing, Probate, General corporate. Home: 2402 Sinclair Midland TX 79705 Office: Turpin Smith Dyer & Saxe PO Box 913 Midland TX 79702

MCENROE, JOHN PATRICK, lawyer; b. N.Y.C., Mar. 25, 1935; s. John Joseph and Kathleen C. (Kellaghan) McE.; m. Katherine Callender Tresham, Dec. 7, 1957; children: John, Mark T., Patrick W. BA, Cath. U. Am., 1955; JD, Fordham U., 1964. Bar: N.Y. 1975, U.S. Dist. Ct. (so. dist.) 1966, D.C. 1982. Assoc. Kelley, Drye, Newhall, Maginess & Warren, N.Y.C., 1964-67; assoc. Paul, Weiss, Rifkind, Wharton & Garrison, N.Y.C., 1967-74, ptnr., 1974—. Served to 1st lt. USAF, 1955-59. Mem. ABA, Assn. of Bar of City of N.Y. General corporate, Securities, Sports law. Office: Paul Weiss Rifkind Wharton & Garrison 345 Park Ave New York NY 10154

MCENROE, MICHAEL LOUIS, lawyer, judicial magistrate; b. Fort Dodge, Iowa, July 31, 1951; s. C. Louis and Mary C. (Cain) McE. B.A. magna cum laude, Loras Coll., 1973; J.D., Creighton U., 1976. Bar: Ill. 1976, Iowa 1977, U.S. Dist. Ct. (no. dist.) Iowa 1977. Assoc. McMahon & Cassel, Algona, Iowa, 1977-78, ptnr. McMahon, Cassel, McMahon, McEnroe & MacDonald, 1979—; judicial magistrate 3rd Judicial Dist. State of Iowa., Algona, 1981—. Mem. ABA, Ill. State Bar Assn., Iowa Bar Assn. (agrl. law com., exec. council young lawyers sect.), Kossuth County Bar Assn., Delta Epsilon Sigma. Democrat. Roman Catholic. Lodge: KC. General practice, Consumer commercial, Agricultural. Home: 408 N Harlan Algona IA 50511 Office: McMahon McEnroe & MacDonald & MacDonald 120 N Thorningon St Algona IA 50511

MCERLEAN, CHARLES F., JR., lawyer; b. Detroit, Nov. 23, 1938; s. Charles F. and Theodora L. (Emerson) McE.; m. Heather L. MacLeod, Oct. 28, 1979; children: James, Laura, Patrick, Kelly. BS, Georgetown U., 1960; JD, U. Notre Dame, 1963. Bar: Ill. 1963, Ind. 1963, D.C. 1964, U.S. Supreme Ct. 1966. Assoc. Mayer, Brown & Platt, Chgo., 1963; sr. counsel United Airlines, Chgo., 1967—. bd. dirs. Sacred Heart of Mary High Sch., Rolling Meadows, Ill. 1978-81. Served to lt. USNR, 1963-67. Mem ABA, D.C. Bar Assn. Republican. Club: Georgetown. Avocations: woodworking, golf. Contracts commercial, General corporate, Pension, profit-sharing, and employee benefits. Office: United Air Lines Inc PO Box 66100 Chicago IL 60666

MCEVERS, DUFF STEVEN, lawyer; b. Los Angeles, Apr. 21, 1954; s. Milton Stoddard and Virginia Mary (Tongue) McE.; m. Jeannine Marie Matthews, July 14, 1984; 1 child, Tay Colleen. BA, U. So. Calif., 1976; JD, Western State U., 1980. Bar: Calif. 1981, U.S. Dist. Ct. (cen. dist.) Calif. Assoc. Donald B. Black Inc., Laguna Beach, Calif., 1981-85; sole practice Laguna Beach, 1985-87, Newport Beach, Calif., 1987—. Editor: Law Review, 1979. Mem. ABA, Calif. Bar Assn., Am. Soc. Internat. Law, Assn. Trial Lawyers Am., Orange County Bar Assn., Orange County Trial Lawyers, Orange County Barristers. Club: Breakfast Club of Newport Beach. State civil litigation, General corporate, Private international. Office: 1300 Bristol St N Suite 280 Newport Beach CA 92660

MCEVILLY, JAMES PATRICK, lawyer; b. Phila., July 30, 1943; s. James P. and Virginia Frances (Madden) McE.; m. Joan Elizabeth O'Connor; children: James III, Christopher, Sara, Michael. BS, St. Joesph's U., 1965; JD, Temple U., 1971. Bar: Pa. 1971, U.S. Dist. Ct. (ea. dist.) Pa. 1972, U.S. Ct. Appeals (3d cir.) 1975, U.S. Supreme Ct. 1982. Law clk. presiding justice Phila. Mcpl. Ct., 1971-73; assoc. Galfand, Berger, Senesky, Lurie & March, Phila., 1973-76; asst. dist. atty. Phila. Dist. Atty., 1976-79; sole practice, Feasterville, Pa., 1979—; pres. Buck Village Profl. Commons, Southampton, 1983-86. Editor Temple U. Law Rev., 1971. Mem. Pa. Trial Lawyers Assn., Bucks County Bar Assn., Phila. Bar Assn., Brehon Law Soc., Assn. Trial Lawyers Am. Personal injury, Criminal, General practice. Home: 1401 Silo Rd Yardley PA 19067 Office: James P McEvilly 1200 Bustleton Pike Suite One B Feasterville PA 19047

MCEWAN, OSWALD BEVERLEY, lawyer; b. Orlando, Fla., Dec. 31, 1913; s. John Singer and Roberta (Dunn) McE.; m. Mary Ann Walker, May 14, 1941 (dec.); children—Christopher Gaillard, Nancy Fletcher, James Walker; m. 2d, Betty Wilson, June 14, 1975. A.B., U. Fla., 1936; J.D., Washington and Lee U., 1940. Bar: Fla. 1940, U.S. Ct. Appeals (5th cir.) 1946, U.S. Ct. Mil. Appeals 1956, U.S. Supreme Ct. 1956, U.S. Ct. Appeals (11th cir.) 1981. Assoc. Giles & Gurney, Orlando, 1940-41; sole practice, Orlando, 1945-47; city atty. City of Orlando, 1947-52 ptnr. Sanders, McEwan, Mims, and Martinez, Orlando, 1947—, pres.; gen. Counsel Fla. Real Estate Commn., 1952-53; trustee, Atty. Title Ins. Fund, 1960-82. Chmn. Mcpl. Planning Bd., Orlando, 1975; mem. Orange County Budget Com., 1946-48. Served to lt. col. JAGC, AUS, 1941-45. Decorated Legion of Merit. Recipient Disting. Service award Stetson Law Sch., 1959. Mem. Fla. Bar (Pres. 1958-59), ABA (ho. of dels. 1962-72), Am. Law Inst., Am. Coll. Probate Counsel, Fedn. of Ins. Counsel, Am. Bar Found., Internat. Assn. Ins. Counsel, Order of Coif. Republican. Episcopalian. Clubs: Country of Orlando, Univ. (Orlando), Rotary. Real property, Probate, Banking. Office: 108 E Central Blvd Orlando FL 32802

MCFADDEN, FRANK HAMPTON, former judge, business executive; b. Oxford, Miss., Nov. 20, 1925; s. John Angus and Ruby (Roy) McF.; m. Jane Porter Nabers, Sept. 30, 1960; children—Frank Hampton, Angus Nabers, Jane Porter. B.A., U. Miss., 1950; LL.B., Yale U., 1955. Bar: N.Y. 1956, Ala. 1959. Assoc. firm Lord, Day & Lord, N.Y.C., 1955-58, Bradley, Arant, Rose & White, Birmingham, Ala., 1958-63; partner Bradley, Arant, Rose & White, 1963-69; judge U.S. Dist. Ct. No. Dist. Ala., Birmingham, 1969-73; chief judge U.S. Dist. Ct. No. Dist. Ala., 1973-81; sr. v.p., gen. counsel Blount, Inc., Montgomery, Ala., 1982—; chmn. Blount Energy Resource Corp., Montgomery, 1983—. Served from ensign to lt. USNR, 1944-49, 51-53. Office: Blount Inc 4520 Executive Park Dr PO Box 949 Montgomery AL 36192-1201

MCFADDEN, JOSEPH R., JR., lawyer; b. Darby, Pa., Sept. 16, 1944; s. Joseph R. and Edith (Madden) McF.; m. Helene Sprows, Nov. 4, 1972; children: Christian, Ryan, Courtney. BS, U. Dayton, 1967, M.B.A., 1969; JD, U. Notre Dame, 1972. Bar: U.S. Dist. Ct. (ea. dist.) Pa. 1972, Pa. 1972, U.S. Supreme Ct. 1976. Assoc. Kassab, Cherry, Archbold, Ferrara & Mutzel, Media, Pa., 1972-78, ptnr., 1978—. Fellow Acad. Advocacy; mem. Assn. Trial Lawyers Am., Pa. Trial Lawyers Assn., Delaware County Bar Assn. Republican. Roman Catholic. Labor, Personal injury, Workers' compensation. Office: Kassab Cherry Archbold Ferrara & Mutzel 214 N Jackson St Media PA 19063

MCFALL, DONALD BEURY, lawyer; b. Charleston, W.Va., Aug. 2, 1941; s. Henry Tucker and Elizabeth Katharine (Beury) McF.; m. Donna Glenn Binion, May 27, 1972; children—Katharine Atkinson, Mary Crawford. B.A., Washington and Lee U., 1964, J.D., 1969. Bar: Va. 1969, Tex. 1969, U.S. Supreme Ct. 1979, U.S. Dist. Ct. (we., so. and ea. dist.) Tex. 1975. Asst. U.S. atty. U.S. Dept. Justice, Houston, 1970-71; assoc. firm Butler & Binion, Houston, 1971-77, ptnr., 1977-85, Cook, Davis & McFall, Houston, 1985—. Trustee Humana Hosp. Sharpstown, Houston, 1984-85; bd. dirs. Planned Parenthood of Houston and S.E. Tex., 1978—; trustee Woodberry Forest Sch., Orange, Va., 1984—. Served to capt. U.S. Army, 1964-66. Fellow Tex. Bar Found.; mem. Internat. Assn. Def. Counsel, Va. State Bar, Tex. State Bar, Fedn. Ins. and Corp. Counsel. Episcopalian. State civil litigation, Personal injury, Federal civil litigation. Home: 6058 Riverview Way Houston TX 77057 Office: Cook Davis & McFall 909 Fannin 2600 Two Houston Ctr Houston TX 77010-1003

MCFARLAND, ANNE SOUTHWORTH, law librarian, lawyer; b. Cleve., Mar. 12, 1940; d. Edward and Barbara Anne (Eberth) Southworth; m. Charles Warren, June 9, 1964; 1 child, Michael Edward. AB, Oberlin Coll., 1962; MLS, Case Western Res. U., 1964; JD, Cleve. State U., 1974. Bar: Ohio 1974, U.S. Dist. Ct. (no. dist.) Ohio 1974. Adminstrv. asst. Cleve. Pub. Library, 1970-72; caseworker Cleve. Soc. for the Blind, 1972-74; instr. Cleve.-Marshall Coll. Law, 1985-86; sole practice Cleve., 1974-86; assoc. law librarian U. Akron, Ohio, 1986—; library cons. Juvenile Ct. Cuyahoga County, 1973-86, Cleve. Soc. for the Blind, 1974-86. Author: Next Friend, 1986; contbr. articles to mags. and newspapers, 1982-84. Bd. dirs. Heights Community Congress, Cleve; bd. dirs. New Day Press, Cleve.; mem. City Planning Commn., 1983—. Mem. ABA, Ohio Regional Assn. Law Librarians, Guardian Ad Litem Project Cuyahoga County Juvenile Ct. Avocation: foster parenting. Legal education, Juvenile, Librarianship.

MCFARLAND, CAROL ANNE, lawyer; b. Eugene, Oreg., Aug. 25, 1951; s. Harvey John and Muriel Anne (Walker) McF.; m. Thomas E. Miller, July 29, 1982; children: Annette Catherine, Miles Patrick. BS, Oreg. State U., 1973; JD, Western State U., 1977. Bar: Calif. 1977, U.S. Dist. Ct. (so. dist.) Calif. 1977. Assoc. Sankary & Sankary, San Diego, 1977-81; sole practice San Diego, 1981—. Vol. atty. Supervision Ctr. Women's Studies-Clinic Domestic Violence Restraining Orders, 1983—, San Diego Vol. Lawyers Assn., 1986—. Mem. ABA, Calif. Bar Assn., San Diego County Bar Assn., San Diego Trial Lawyers Assn., Delta Theta Phi. Family and matrimonial, General practice, Probate. Office: 902 W University Ave Suite #8 San Diego CA 92103

MCFARLAND, JACLANEL MOORE, lawyer; b. Dawson, Tex., June 6, 1952; d. Jack Leon and Frances Junell (Linch) Moore; m. Allen Keith McFarland, Aug. 14, 1976; children—Allen Keith, Linch Moore. B.A., Baylor U., 1974, J.D., 1977; postgrad. Oxford U., 1974. Bar: Tex. 1977, U.S. Dist. Ct. (so. dist.) Tex. 1979. Atty. Tarrant Title Co., Ft. Worth, 1977-78; assoc. Gerald L. King and Assocs., Inc., Spring, Tex., 1978-79; sole practice, Houston, 1979—; prof. govt., bus. law North Harris County Coll., 1979-80. Campaign mgr. Gerald L. King for State Rep., 1982; mem. legal com. South Main Bapt. Ch., 1979-83, guest lectr., 1987. Mem. ABA, Tex. Bar (continuing law focused edn. com.), Houston Bar Assn., Criminal Def. Lawyers Assn., Baylor U. Alumni Assn., Harvey M. Richey Moot Ct. Soc., Assn. Women Attys., Phi Alpha Delta, Pi Sigma Alpha. General corporate, Family and matrimonial, Personal injury. Home: 542 Pine Walk Trail Spring TX 77373 Office: 400 FM 1960 W Suite 111 Houston TX 77090

MCFARLAND, KAY ELEANOR, state justice; b. Coffeyville, Kans., July 20, 1935; d. Kenneth W. and Margaret E. (Thrall) McF. BA magna cum laude, Washburn U., Topeka, 1957, JD, 1964. Bar: Kans. 1964. Sole practice Topeka, 1964-71; probate and juvenile judge Shawnee County, Topeka, 1971-73; dist. judge Topeka, 1973-77; justice Kans. Supreme Ct., 1977—. Mem. ABA, Kans. Bar Assn., Topeka Bar Assn. Office: Supreme Ct Kansas State House Topeka KS 66612

MCFARLAND, ROBERT EDWIN, lawyer; b. St. Louis, July 25, 1946; s. Francis Taylor and Kathryne (Stevens) M.; m. Jeannine M. Ghekiere, Feb. 26, 1982. B.A., U. Mich. 1968, J.D., 1971. Bar: Mich. 1971, U.S. Dist. Ct. (ea. dist.) Mich. 1971, U.S. Ct. Appeals (6th cir.) 1974, U.S. Supreme Ct. 1975, U.S. Ct. Appeals (D.C.) 1978. Law clk. to chief judge Mich. Ct. Appeals, 1971-72; assoc. William B. Elmer, St. Clair Shores, Mich., 1972-74, James Elsman, Birmingham, Mich., 1974-75; ptnr. McFarland, Schmier, Stoneman & Singer, Troy, Mich. 1975-77; sr. ptnr. McFarland & Bullard, Bloomfield Hills, Mich., 1977—. Chmn. bd. of govs. Transp. Law Jour., U. Denver Coll. of Law, 1981-83; mem. rulemaking study com. Mich. Pub. Service Commn., 1983—; mem. Motor Carrier Adv. Bd., Mich. Pub. Service Commn., 1984—; mem. bd. of control Intercollegiate Athletics, U. Mich., 1966-68. Served to capt. USAR, 1971-80. Mem. Transp. Lawyers Assn., Assn. Interstate Commn. Practioners, ABA, State Bar Mich., Am. Judicature Soc., Oakland County Bar Assn. Administrative and regulatory, Civil rights, Labor.

MCFARLANE, WALTER ALEXANDER, lawyer; b. Richlands, Va., May 4, 1940; s. James Albert and Frances Mae (Padbury) McF.; m. Judith Louise Copenhaver, Aug. 31, 1962; children—Brennan Alexander, Heather Copenhaver. B.A., Emory and Henry Coll., 1962; J.D., T.C. Williams Sch. Law, U. Richmond, 1966. Bar: Va. 1966, U.S. Supreme Ct. 1970, U.S. Ct. Appeals (4th cir.) 1973, U.S. Ct. Appeals (D.C. cir.) 1977, U.S. Dist. Ct. (ea. dist.) Va. 1973. Asst. atty. gen. Office Va. Atty. Gen., Richmond, 1969-73, dep. atty. gen., 1973—; adj. assoc. prof. U. Richmond, 1978—. Contbr. articles to profl. jours. Chmn. transp. law com. Transp. Research Bd., Nat. Research Bd. Nat. Acads. Scis. and Engring., Washington, 1977-85, chmn. legal affairs com., 1978-85, chmn. environ., archeological and hist. com., 1985—; pres., Windsor Forest Civic Assn., Midlothian, Va., 1975-76; bd. dirs. Greater Midlothian Civic League, 1981-86, v.p., 1980; instr. water safety ARC, 1962—; chmn. bldg. com. Mt. Pisgah United Meth. Ch., 1980-85, pres. men's club, 1980-81. Served to capt. JAGC, USAF, 1966-69. Recipient J.D. Buscher Disting. Atty. award Am. Assn. State Hwy. and Transp. Ofcls., 1983, John C. Vance legal writing award Nat. Acads. Sci. and Engring., 4th ann. outstanding evening lectr. award Student Body U. Richmond, 1980. Mem. Va. Trial Lawyers Assn., Richmond Bar Assn., Am. Assn. of State Hwys. and Transp. Ofcls., Richmond Scottish Soc. (bd. dirs. 1980-82), Emory and Henry Coll. Alumni Assn. (exec. com. bd. of govs., chpt. pres. 1971-73, regional v.p. 1974-77, pres. 1981-83). Club: Meadowbrook Country Club (Richmond). General practice, State civil litigation, Legislative. Home: 9001 Wideglow Way Chesterfield VA 23832 Office: Office Atty Gen 8th St Richmond VA 23219

MCGAHREN, EUGENE DEWEY, JR., lawyer; b. Jersey City, Oct. 4, 1926; s. Eugene D. and Cecelia (Paulsen) McG.; m. Elizabeth M. Connellan, Oct. 19, 1957; children—Eugene, Thomas, Kevin, Brian, Paul, Peter. A.B., Columbia U., 1949, J.D., 1952; LL.M., NYU, 1960. Bar: N.Y. 1955. Assoc. Willkie Farr & Gallagher, N.Y.C., 1954-56; assoc. McGovern, Vincent & Connelly, N.Y.C., 1956-60; asst. div. counsel Sperry Corp., N.Y.C., 1960-69, div. counsel, 1969-72, asst. gen. counsel, 1972-80, staff v.p., asst. gen. counsel, 1980—. Vice pres. Lincoln Park Taxpayers Assn., Yonkers, N.Y., 1974-78. Served to lt. USNR, 1952-54; Korea. Mem. ABA, N.Y. State Bar Assn., Bar Assn. City of N.Y. Club: Hemisphere (N.Y.C.). General corporate, Contracts commercial, Government contracts and claims. Office: 1290 Ave of Americas New York NY 10104

MCGANNON, ROBERT EUGENE, lawyer; b. Humboldt, Kans., Jan. 24, 1928; s. Patrick Joseph and Jane Clare (Barry) McG.; m. Mary C. Cavanaugh, Sept. 16, 1953; children: Molly, Maureen, Bob, John, Pat. AB, Rockhurst Coll.; JD, Georgetown U. Bar: Mo. 1951, D.C. 1951. Ptnr. Hoskins, King, McGannon, Kansas City, Mo., 1951—; former rep. Mo. Bar.; bd. dirs. Wire Rope Corp., St. Joseph, Mo., Fidelity Security Life, Kansas City, Rycom Instruments, Kansas City. Founding dir. Human Rescue Inc.; bd. dirs. St. Joseph Hosp., Geogetown Law Ctr. Served with USN, 1946. Mem. ABA, Kansas City Bar Assn., Lawyers Assn. Kansas City, Am. Judicature Soc. Clubs: Kansas City; Indian Hills Country (pres.). Lodge: Sertoma (bd. dirs. Kansas City club). General practice, Corporate taxation. Home: 2308 W 70th St Shawnee Mission KS 66208 Office: Hoskins King McGannon & Hahn 922 Walnut Kansas City MO 64106

MC GARR, FRANK J., federal judge; b. 1921. A.B., Loyola U., Chgo., 1942; J.D., Loyola U., 1950. Bar: Ill. 1950. Assoc. firm Dallstream Schiff Stern & Hardin, Chgo., 1952-54; asst. U.S. atty. No. dist. of Ill., 1954-55, first asst. U.S. atty., 1955-58; ptnr. firm McKay Solum & McGarr, Chgo., 1958-70; first asst. atty. gen. State of Ill., 1969-70; judge U.S. Dist. Ct. for No. Ill., 1970—, sr. judge, 1980-86; sr. judge 1986—. Recipient medal of Excellence, Loyola Law Alumni Assn., 1964. Served with USN, 1942-45. Mem. Am. Coll. Trial Lawyers, 7th Cir. Bar Assn., Chgo. Bar Assn. Jurisprudence. Office: US Dist Ct Rm 1846 US Courthouse 219 S Dearborn St Chicago IL 60604

MCGARRY, ALEXANDER BANTING, lawyer; b. Detroit, July 27, 1940; s. Patrick Joseph and Marne Elizabeth (Banting) McG.; m. Diane Lee Fisher, Feb. 10, 1940; children—Erin Kathleen, Molly Anne, Megan Catherine. B.S., Drake U., 1962; J.D., U. Minn., 1965. Bar: Minn. 1965, Mich. 1966, U.S. Supreme Ct. 1978. Labor relations atty. Ford Motor Co., 1965-66; asst. pros. atty. Oakland County (Mich.), 1967-69; assoc. Condit, Denison, Devine, Porter & Bartush, Bloomfield Hills, Mich., 1969-71; ptnr. Condit & McGarry, Birmingham, Mich. and sucessor Condit, McGarry & Schloff, P.C., 1971—. Chmn. City of Troy Irish Heritage Group and Bicentennial, 1976; mem. citizens adv. com. Troy Sch. Bd., 1978; chmn. Oakland County Cir. Ct. Com., 1973, 74, 76. Recipient Disting. Service award Oakland County, 1970. Mem. State Bar Mich., Oakland County Bar Assn. (dir.), Assn. Trial Lawyers Am., ABA, Inc. Soc. Irish Am. Lawyers (dir.), Minn. Bar Assn. Lodges: KC, Ancient Order Hibernians (state pres. 1972-76, nat. dir. 1976-78, nat. chmn. Notre Dame Fund 1978-82, Hibernian of Yr. 1980). Criminal, State civil litigation, Family and matrimonial. Office: Suite 215 6905 Telegraph Rd Birmingham MI 48010

MCGARRY, ARTHUR DANIEL, lawyer; b. Seattle, Sept. 22, 1948; s. James Frances and Bernice Lorraine (Harmon) McG.; m. Mary Matson, June 21, 1975; children: Maria, Lillian. BA with honors, U. Wash., 1969, JD, 1972. Bar: Wash. 1972, U.S. Dist. Ct. (ea. and we. dists.) Wash. 1973, U.S. Ct. Appeals (9th cir.) 1973. Assoc. Oles, Morrison, Rinker, Stanislaw & Ashbaugh, Seattle, 1972-79, ptnr., 1979—. Mem. Phi Beta Kappa. Federal civil litigation, State civil litigation, General corporate. Home: 2267 NE 62d Seattle WA 98115

MCGAUGHEY, JERRY JOSEPH, lawyer, educator; b. Vincennes, Ind., Dec. 8, 1937; s. Robert William and Vera Elizabeth (Leinbach) McG.; m. Barbara F. O'Neill, June 15, 1978; 1 child, L. Scott. A.A., Vincennes U., 1957; B.S. in Bus., Ind. U., 1959, LL.B., 1962. Bar: Ind. 1963, U.S. Dist. Ct. (so. dist.) Ind. 1963, U.S. Supreme Ct. 1973. Law Clerk to presiding justice Ind. Supreme Ct., Indpls., 1963-64; ptnr. Hornbrook, Stratton & McGaughey, Petersburg, Ind., 1964-70; prosecuting atty. 83rd Jud. Ct., Petersburg, 1970-82; dept. head abstracting and bus. law Vincennes U., Ind., 1982-86; prosecuting atty. 12th Jud. Ct., Vincennes, 1987—; dir. First Nat. Bank Spurgeon, Ind., 1965-72. Com. mem. Ind. Criminal Law Study Commn., Indpls., 1971-76; bd. dirs. Ind. Criminal Justice Planning Agy., Dist. 8, Evansville, 1972-80, Ind. Prosecuting Attys. Council, Indpls., 1975-77. Fellow Ind. Bar Found. Republican. Lodge: Kiwanis Internat. (pres. 1970-71). Criminal. Office: Knox County Courthouse Vincennes IN 47591

MCGAVICK, DONALD HUGH, lawyer; b. Tacoma, May 27, 1927; s. Hugh Cambridge and Frances A. (Rigney) McG.; children: Phyllis, Hugh, Mary, Kathleen, Mark, Karen, Mathew, James; m. Sharon M. Gorenson, Sept. 29, 1984. JD, Gonzaga U., 1955. Bar: Wash. 1955, U.S. Dist. Ct. (we. dist.) Wash. 1955, U.S. Ct. Appeals (9th cir.) 1958, U.S. Ct. Appeals (5th cir.) 1966, U.S. Supreme Ct. 1976. Ptnr. Scott, Longhorne & McGavick, Tacoma, 1955-62, McGavick & Sauriol, Tacoma, 1962-65, McGavick & Bottiger, Tacoma, 1965-68, Tanner & McGavick, Tacoma, 1976-78, McGavick & McGavick, Tacoma, 1985—. Mem. Young Dem., Spokane and Tacoma, Wash., 1950—. Served to sgt. USMC, 1945-49. Mem. Tacoma Pierce County Bar Assn. (trustee 1986—, Wash. State bar disciplinary bd. 1986—), Assn. Trial Lawyers Am., Wash. State Trial Lawyers Assn. Roman Catholic. Lodges: Eagles (pres., trustee). Avocations: skiing, golfing, gardening. Legislative, General practice, Personal injury. Home: 640 Vista Dr Tacoma WA 98465 Office: McGavick & McGavick 625 Commerce St Suite 250 Tacoma WA 98402

MCGAVIN, JOHN DAVID, lawyer; b. Arlington, Va., Apr. 15, 1957; s. Thomas A. and Jane Louise (Haupt) McG.; m. Linda Judith Peele, Oct. 6, 1984. BA with distinction, U. Va., 1979; JD, Coll. William and Mary, 1982. Bar: Va. 1982, U.S. Dist. Ct. (ea. dist.) Va. 1983, U.S. Ct. Appeals (4th cir.) 1983, U.S. Dist. Ct. (we. dist.) Va. 1985. Law clk. to presiding justice U.S. Dist. Ct. (ea. dist.) Va., Alexandria, 1982-83; assoc. Lewis, Tydings, Bryan & Trichilo, P.C., Fairfax, Va., 1983—. Mem. Va. Bar Assn., Fairfax Bar Assn. (law and medicine com.), No. Va. Def. Lawyers Assn., No. Va. Young Lawyers Assn (sec. 1986, pres. 1987), Va. Assn. Def. Attys. Republican. Methodist. Club: Wash. Golf and Country (Arlington, Va.). Avocations: basketball, tennis, golf. Federal civil litigation, State civil litigation, Insurance. Home: 2917 Village Spring Ln Vienna VA 22108 Office: Lewis Tydings Bryan & Trichilo 4114 Leonard Dr Fairfax VA 22030

MCGEADY, PAUL JOSEPH, lawyer; b. Jersey City, Nov. 12, 1920; s. Patrick and Mary (Ferry) McG.; m. Margaret Viola Mulligan, May 27, 1944; children: Margaret Mary, Rosemary, Paul. BSS, St. Peters Coll., 1942; LLD, Fordham U., 1948. Bar: N.Y. 1949. Asst. v.p., counsel Continental Corp., N.Y.C., 1950-78; gen. counsel Morality in Media, N.Y.C., 1978—; dir. Nat. Obscenity Law Ctr., N.Y.C., 1978—. Author: Rise and Fall of the ACA, 1972, ABC Statutes and Regulations, 1977; editor Obscenity Law Bull., 1978—. Served to 1st lt. USAAF, 1943-45, MTO. Decorated Air medal, Knight of Holy Sepulchre. Mem. Fed. Communication Bar Assn., Am. Arbitration Assn. Republican. Roman Catholic. Lodge: K.C. Criminal, Legislative. Office: Morality in Media Inc 475 Riverside Dr New York NY 10115

MCGEE, C(LARENCE) EDWARD, JR., lawyer; b. Atlanta, May 29, 1949; s. Clarence Edward Sr. and Kathleen (Porter) McG.; m. M. Monica Arends, Aug. 28, 1971; children: Andrea Leigh, Lauren Marie. BA in Polit. Sci., Fla. Atlantic U., 1971; JD, Fla. State U., 1973. Bar: Fla. 1974, U.S. Ct. Appeals (5th cir.) 1974, U.S. Dist. Ct. (so. dist.) Fla. 1975, U.S. Ct. Appeals (11th cir.) 1982. Asst. state atty. State Atty.'s Office, Ft. Lauderdale, Fla., 1974-79; ptnr. Gillespie & McGee, Ft. Lauderdale, 1979-81, Gillespie, McCormick, McFall, Gilbert & McGee, Ft. Lauderdale, 1981—. Mem. adv. bd. Cardinal Gibbons Edn. Endowment Fund, com. to re-elect William Herring, Ft. Lauderdale, 1986—; treas. campaign to re-elect Brian P. Kay, Ft. Lauderdale, 1986—; bd. dirs. Kids in Distress, Inc., Ft. Lauderdale, 1982-86, pres., 1984-85. Mem. ABA, Fla. Bar Assn. (grievance com. 1986—, UPH com. 1986—), Broward County Bar Assn. (chmn. criminal law sect. 1981-83, vice chmn. 1986-87, exec. com. young lawyers sect. 1984-85), Assn. Trial Lawyers Am., Broward County Criminal Def. Attys. Assn., Nat. Assn. Criminal Def. Lawyers, Nat. Inst. Trial Adv., Greater Ft. Lauderdale C. of C., Pompano Beach C. of C. Democrat. Roman Catholic. Avocations: snow skiing, boating, sports. State civil litigation, Personal injury, Criminal. Office: Gillespie McCormick McFall Gilbert & McGee 790 E Broward Blvd #302 Fort Lauderdale FL 33301

MCGEE, FRANCIS PARKER, II, lawyer; b. Los Angeles, Jan. 9, 1949; s. Francis P. and Regina H. (Hardeman) McG. B.S., U. San Francisco, 1969; J.D., U. Utah 1972. Bar: Calif. 1972, D.C. 1982, U.S. Ct. Clms. 1981, U.S. Tax Ct. 1981, U.S. Sup. Ct. 1977. Dep. pub. defender County of Los Angeles, 1973-75; sole practice, Whittier, Calif., 1975-82, Fullerton, Calif., 1982-85, Los Angeles, 1985—; judge pro tempore Southeast South Mcpl. Ct., South Gate, Calif., 1975—; mem. paralegal adv. com. Rio Hondo Coll., 1976-82. Bd. dirs. ARC, Rio Hondo, 1976-82, vice chmn., 1980-82. Mem. ABA, Southeast Dist. Bar Assn. (trustee 1977-81), Whittier Bar Assn. (pres. 1981), U. San Francisco Alumni Assn. (bd. govs. 1980-82). Democrat. Roman Catholic. Clubs: Kiwanis (pres. 1980-81) (South Gate, Calif); Los Angeles Athletic. Lodge: KC. General corporate, Probate, State and local taxation. Office: 800 S Figueroa St Suite 760 Los Angeles CA 90017

MCGEE, HENRY W., JR., legal educator, lawyer; b. 1932; B.S. in Journalism, Northwestern U., 1954; J.D., DePaul U., 1957; LL.M., Columbia U., 1970. Bar: Ill. 1957, Calif. 1975. Asst. state's atty. Cook County (Ill.), 1958-61; assoc. Jesmer & Harris, Chgo., 1962-66; regional dir. OEO Legal Service Program, Gt. Lakes Region, 1966-67; legal dir. Juvenile Delinquency Research Project, Ctr. for Studies in Criminal Justice, U. Chgo., 1967-68; acting prof. UCLA Law Sch., 1969-72, prof., 1972—; vis. fellow Wolfson Coll., Oxford (Eng.) U., 1973; vis. prof. U. Florence Inst. Comparative Law and Proc., 1976; Fulbright research prof. and vis. prof. law U. Madrid, 1982; mem. ABA-Am. Assn. Law Schs. Clin. Guidelines Com., 1977—. Mem. Blue Key. Co-author: Housing and Community Development, 1981. Office: UCLA Law Sch 405 Hilgard Ave Los Angeles CA 90024

MCGEE, JACK BRIAN, lawyer; b. Milw., Feb. 14, 1947; s. John Joseph and Francis (Ringler) McG.; 1 child, Colin. BS, U. Wis., Milw., 1965, MA, 1973; JD, U. Wis., Madison, 1968. Bar: Wis. 1968, U.S. Dist. Ct. (we. dist.) Wis. 1974, Alaska 1976, U.S. Dist./ Ct. Alaska 1978, U.S. Ct. Appeals (9th cir.) 1981, U.S. Supreme Ct. 1983. Asst. atty. City of Milw., 1968-71; VISTA atty. Alaska Legal Services, Fairbanks, 1971-72; hearing officer Wis. Dept. Industry Labor, Madison, 1974-76; asst. atty. Alaska Atty. Gens. Office, Juneau, 1976—; lectr. in philosophy U. Alaska, Juneau, 1980-83, adj. prof. philosophy, 1983—. Mem. ABA, Wis. Bar Assn., Alaska Bar Assn., Nat. Assn. Trial Lawyers. Roman Catholic. Avocations: skiing, hiking, boating. Administrative and regulatory, Legislative, Government contracts and claims. Home: 445 Nelson Juneau AK 99801 Office: State Alaska Dept Law PO Box K Juneau AK 99811

MCGEE, JOHN FRANCIS, lawyer; b. Independence, Kans., Aug. 18, 1945; s. Francis J. and Bonnell Maxine (La Duke) McG. BS in Edn., U. Kans., 1968, MBA, JD, 1977. Bar: Kans. 1977, U.S. Ct. Appeals (10th cir.) 1980. Ptnr. Williamson, McGee, Griggs & DeMoss Chartered, Wichita, Kans., 1978—; bd. dirs. 1st Nat. Bank, Independence, Kans. Mem. ABA, Kans. Bar Assn., Wichita Bar Assn., Assn. Trial Lawyers Am., Kans. Trial Lawyers Assn. Republican. Methodist. Bankruptcy, Contracts commercial, Real property. Office: Williamson McGee Griggs & DeMoss Chartered 200 W Douglas 9th Floor Wichita KS 67202

MCGEE, ROBERT LEON, JR., lawyer; b. Salt Lake City, July 25, 1946; s. Robert Leon and Ann (Cottrell) McG.; m. Alice McClelland, June 6, 1970 (div. Aug. 1974); m. Anne Robinson, Apr. 2, 1977 (div. Mar. 1982); m. Kathleen Rovegno, Feb. 15, 1986. Student, U. Bridgeport, 1966; AB in History with honors, Dartmouth Coll., 1968; JD, U. Colo., 1972. Bar: Colo. 1972, U.S. Dist. Ct. Colo. 1972, U.S. Tax Ct. 1976, U.S. Ct. Appeals (10th cir.) 1977. Prof. Athens (Greece) Coll., 1968-69; assoc. Sheldon, Bayer, McLean & Glasman, Denver, 1972-74, ptnr., 1975-77; ptnr. Bayer, Carey & McGee, Denver, 1977—; lectr. Ctr. for Law and Edn., Denver, 1980. Mem. appeals com. U.S. Sr. Soccer Div., N.Y.C.; bd. dirs., v.p. Colo. State Soccer Assn. Denver. Served to 1st lt. U.S. Army, 1972. Fellow Athens Coll., 1968-69, Ford Found., 1971. Mem. ABA, Colo. Bar Assn. (interdisciplinary com., domestic relations com.), Colo. Def. Lawyers Assn., Denver Bar Assn., Order of Coif. Democrat. Mormon. Club: Cherry Creek Coloradans (Denver) (pres. 1977—), Denver Athletic. Avocations: soccer, tennis, golf, skiing, stamp collecting. Family and matrimonial, Insurance, State civil litigation. Office: Bayer Carey & McGee PC 1660 Downing St Denver CO 80218

MCGEHEE, JACK EDWARD, JR., lawyer; b. Chambersburg, Pa., May 5, 1952; s. Jack E. Sr. and Janet L. (Wenger) McG.; m. Catherine E. Juergens; 1 child, Jennifer. BS, U.S. Mil. Acad., 1974; JD, St. Mary's U., San Antonio, 1980. Criminal prosecutor U.S. Govt., Killeen, Tex., 1980-84; med. malpractice trial atty. U.S. Govt., Washington, 1985—. Served to maj. U.S. Army, 1974-87, with res., 1974—. Mem. ABA, Assn. Trial Lawyers Am. Federal civil litigation, Personal injury. Office: 5225 Katy Freeway Suite 610 Houston TX 77007

MC GIFFERT, DAVID ELIOT, lawyer, former government official; b. Boston, June 27, 1926; s. Arthur Cushman and Elizabeth (Eliot) McG.; m. Enud De Kibedi-Varga, Jan. 21, 1966; children: Laura, Carola.; m. Nelse Greenway, Apr. 9, 1983. Student, U. Calif.-Berkeley, 1944; B.A., Harvard U., 1949, LL.B., 1953; postgrad., Cambridge (Eng.) U., 1950. Bar: D.C. 1954. With firm Covington & Burling, Washington, 1953-55, 57-61; ptnr. Covington & Burling, 1969-77, 81—; lectr. law U. Wis., 1956; asst. to sec. def. for legis. affairs Dept. Def., 1962-65, undersec. army, 1965-69, asst. sec. for internat. security affairs, 1977-81. Served with USNR, 1944-46. Mem. Am. Bar Assn., Am. Soc. Internat. Law, Council Fgn. Relations, Alpha Delta Phi. Club: Metropolitan (Washington). Home: 204 Primrose St Chevy Chase MD 20815 Office: 1201 Pennsylvania Ave NW Washington DC 20004

MCGILL, GERALD ALLEN, lawyer; b. Pensacola, Fla., June 11, 1943; s. Wilbur and Emogene (Brown) McG.; m. Maureen Logue, Dec. 18, 1971; children: Erin Mary, Stephanie Ann. BS in Engring., USCG Acad., 1965; JD, Cath. U., Washington, 1972. Bar: Fla. 1972, N.Y. 1980, Miss. 1986. Commd. line officer USCG, 1965, advanced through grades to lt., 1969, resigned, 1974; asst. states atty. State of Fla., West Palm Beach, 1974-76; assoc. Jones, Payne & Foster, West Palm Beach, 1976-78, Wells, Brown & Brady P.A., Pensacola, 1978-83; ptnr. Southworth & McGill P.A., Pensacola, 1983—. Contbr. articles to profl. jours. Mem. fin. com. Escambia County Utilities Authority, Pensacola, 1985-87. Decorated Bronze Star; Vietnamese Cross of Gallantry. Mem. Assn. Trial Lawyers Am., Fla. Trial Lawyers Assn. Democrat. Episcopalian. Avocations: golf, tennis. Admiralty, Personal injury. Home: 8621 Rosemont Dr Pensacola FL 32514 Office: Southworth & McGill 202 W Jackson Pensacola FL 32501

MCGILL, GILBERT WILLIAM, lawyer; b. Glen Cove, N.Y., Mar. 28, 1947; B.S., L.I. U., 1972; J.D., Hofstra U., 1975. Bar: N.Y. 1975, U.S. dist. ct. 1976, U.S. Supreme Ct. 1979. Sole practice, Huntington, N.Y., 1975-76; ptnr. Dunne & McGill, Huntington and Sea Cliff, N.Y., 1976-81; sole practice, 1981—. Mem. citizens adv. com. North Shore Schs., Glen Head, N.Y., 1977-79; chmn. legal adv. com. Sea Cliff Civic Assn., 1978-79; adv. com. North Shore Republican Club, Glen Head, 1979—; trustee Sea Cliff Village Library, 1980—, Angelo J. Melillo Ctr. for Mental Health, 1984—. Mem. ABA, N.Y. State Bar Assn., Nassau County Bar Assn., Nassau County Lawyers Assn., North Shore Lawyers Assn. (chmn. 1977-78), Sea Cliff Bus. Assn. (pres. 1979—). Lodge; Rotary (pres. Glen Head 1983-84). General practice. Office: 228 Sea Cliff Ave Sea Cliff NY 11579

MCGILL, SCOTT A., lawyer; b. Indpls., Apr. 3, 1951; s. Bert H. and Virginia (Koops) McG.; m. Margaret Montgomery, 1985. AB, Amherst Coll., 1973; JD, U. Maine, 1977. Bar: Colo. 1977. Assoc. Sharp & Black, Steamboat Springs, Colo., 1977-80; ptnr., founder Graves & McGill P.C., Steamboat Springs, 1980-85; prin. McGill Law Corp., Steamboat Springs, 1985—; bd. dirs. Juri, Ltd., Mpls. Real property, Contracts commercial, State civil litigation. Office: McGill Law Corp PO Drawer 772810 Steamboat Springs CO 80477

MCGINLEY, JOHN REGIS, JR., lawyer; b. Pitts., Nov. 26, 1943; s. John R. and Marie E. (Rooney) McG.; m. Nancy Carey, Aug. 15, 1968; children: John, Cathleen, Mary. BS, St. Bonaventure U., 1965; JD, Duquesne U., 1968. Bar: Pa. 1968, U.S. Dist. Ct. (we. dist.) Pa. 1968, U.S. Ct. Appeals (3d cir.) 1973, U.S. Supreme Ct. 1983. Asst. dist. atty. Allegheny County (Pa.), 1968-70; assoc. Duff Grogan & Doyle and Duff, Grogan Graffam, Pitts., 1970-71; ptnr. Grogan, Graffam, McGinley & Lucchino, Pitts., 1971—; mem. disciplinary bd. Pa. Supreme Ct.; mem. Pa. Ind. Regulatory Rev. Commn. Contbr. articles to legal jours.; contbr. to Duquesne U. Law Rev., 1968. Trustee, chmn. Mercy Hosp. Found. Bd. dirs. Easter Seals Soc. of Allegheny County, 1981—. Mem. ABA, Pa. Bar Assn., Allegheny County Bar Assn., Maritime Law Assn. (bd. dirs.), Acad. Trial Lawyers (Allegheny County chpt.). Democrat. Roman Catholic. Club: Allegheny (Pitts.). Federal civil litigation, State civil litigation. Office: Three Gateway Center 22nd Fl Pittsburgh PA 15222

MCGINLEY, NANCY ELIZABETH, lawyer; b. Columbia, Mo., Feb. 29, 1952; d. Robert Joseph and Ruth Evangeline (Garnett) McG. B.A. with high honors, U. Tex., 1974, J.D., 1977. Bar: Tex. 1977, U.S. Dist. Ct. (no. dist.) Tex. 1979. Law clk. U.S. Dist. Ct. (no. dist.) Tex., Fort Worth, 1977-79; assoc. Crumley, Murphy and Shrull, Fort Worth, 1979-81; staff atty. SEC, Fort Worth, 1981—. Mem. editorial staff Urban Law Rev. Mem. Tarrant County Young Lawyer's Assn., Women Lawyers of Tarrant County, Fort Worth Bus. and Profl. Women's Assn., Mortar Bd., Phi Beta Kappa, Phi Kappa Phi, Alpha Lambda Delta. Methodist. Securities, Federal civil litigation, Administrative and regulatory. Home: 432 S Norton Ave #311 Los Angeles CA 90020 Office: SEC 5757 Wilshire Blvd Suite 500 E Los Angeles CA 90036-3648

MCGINN, HOWARD ANTHONY, lawyer; b. Hartford, Conn., Jan. 11, 1944; s. Frank P. and Dorothy A. (Wissick) McG.; m. Judith A. Farrar, June, 10, 1967; children: Daniel F., Patricia A. BA, Rutgers U., 1965, JD, 1968. Bar: N.J. 1968, U.S. Dist. Ct. N.J. 1968, U.S. Tax Ct. 1971. Assoc. Law Offices of A.L. Alexander Esq., Washington, N.J., 1969-72; sole practice Washington, 1972—; ptnr. McGinn & Ours, Washington; prosecutor Warren County, Belvidere, N.J., 1981-86. Mem. ABA, N.J. Bar Assn., Warren County Bar Assn. Democrat. Lodge: Kiwanis (pres. Washington Club 1980-81). Avocations: photography, skiing, reading. General practice, Local government. Office: McGinn & Ours 21 Broad St Washington NJ 07882-0308

MCGINNIS, ANDREW MOSHER, lawyer; b. Madison, Wis., Nov. 18, 1946; s. John and Sarah McGinnis. AB in Chemistry and Physics cum laude, Harvard U., 1968, JD cum laude, 1973. Bar: Mass. 1973, U.S. Patent Office 1974. Computer programmer and analyst various cos., 1964-70; pub. policy cons. Somerville (Mass.), 1972; assoc. Fish & Richardson, Boston, 1973; legal asst. dist. atty.'s office Middlesex County, Cambridge, Mass., 1974-77; sole practice Belmont, Mass., 1974—; mediator Assocs. for Human Resources, Concord, Mass., 1977—. bd. dirs. North Cambridge Health and Social Service Ctr., 1972-80; mem. Fernald Sch. Human Rights Treatment com., Waltham, Mass., 1978-81. Mem. Mass. Bar Assn. (family law sect., civil litigation sect.), Middlesex County Bar Assn., Boston Bar Assn., Mass. Acad. Trial Attys., Boston Computer Soc., Harry Benjamin Internat. Gender Dysphoria Assn. Avocation: bird photography. General practice, Family and matrimonial, Real property. Home: 212 Bellevue Rd Watertown MA 02172 Office: 489 Common St Belmont MA 02178

MCGINNIS, ROBERT CAMPBELL, lawyer; b. Dallas, Jan. 1, 1918; s. Edward Karl and Helen Louise (Campbell) McG.; m. Ethel Clift, May 14, 1945; cihldren: Mary, Campbell, John, Robert, Michael. AB, U. Tex., 1938; LLB, Yale U., 1941. Bar: Tex. 1941, Ohio 1942, U.S. Dist. Ct. (no. dist.) Tex. 1948, U.S. Dist. Ct. (we. dist.) Tex. 1950. Assoc. Squires, Sanders & Dempsey, Cleve., 1941-42, Carrington, Gowan, Dallas, 1946-49; ptnr. McGinnis, Lochridge & Kilgore and predecessor firm Powell, Wirtz & Rauhut, Austin, Tex., 1950—; chmn. Tex. Com. Jud. Ethics, 1972-78; bd. dirs. Republic Bank, Austin. Served to lt. USNR, 1942-46, PTO. Fellow Am. Bar Found.; mem. ABA, Tex. Bar Assn. Democrat. Presbyterian. Administrative and regulatory, Oil and gas leasing, State civil litigation. Home: 2708 Scenic Dr Austin TX 78703 Office: McGinnis Lochridge & Kilgore 919 Congress Ave Austin TX 78701

MCGINNIS, THOMAS MICHAEL, lawyer; b. Royal Oak, Mich., July 13, 1954; s. Donald Edward and Marijane Carney (Jex) McG. BA, Regis Coll., 1976; JD, Thomas M. Cooley Sch. Law, 1980. Bar: Mich. 1981, U.S. Dist. Ct. (ea. dist.) Mich. 1981, U.S. Ct. Appeals (6th cir.) 1981. Law clk. to presiding justice Oakland County Cir. Ct., Pontiac, Mich., 1978-80; assoc. Wilson, Portnoy & Leader, Bloomfield Hills, Mich., 1980-83; sole practice Birmingham, Mich., 1983—. Advisor Boys Club of Royal Oak, 1981—. Mem. ABA, Mich. Bar Assn., Oakland County Bar Assn. (committeeperson 1983—, chairperson 1985—), Assn. Trial Lawyers Am., Mich. Trial Lawyers Assn. Personal injury, Criminal, Probate. Office: 1600 N Woodard Suite 224 Birmingham MI 48011

MCGINTY, BRIAN DONALD, lawyer, author; b. Santa Barbara, Calif., June 22, 1937; s. Donald Bruce and Natalia Vallejo (Haraszthy) M. A.B., U. Calif.-Berkeley, 1959, J.D., 1962. Bar: Calif. 1963. Assoc. Twohig, Weingarten & Haas, Seaside, Calif., 1962-63; ptnr. Weingarten & McGinty, Seaside, 1963-70; sole practice, Monterey, Calif., 1970-73, San Francisco, 1973-83; legal writer Matthew Bender & Co., San Francisco and Oakland, Calif., 1984—. Author: Haraszthy at the Mint, 1975; The Palace Inns, 1978, The Craft of Essay, Historial Times Illustrated, Encyclopedia of the Civil War, California Real Estate Law and Practice, California Legal Forums, California Insurance Law; editor: Napa Wine (Rounce and Coffin Club award 1975), 1974. Contbr. numerous articles to profl. jours. Recipient Excellence in Writing award Nat. Hist. Soc., 1976. Mem. Calif. Hist. Soc. Real property, Legal history, Estate planning. Office: 2101 Webster St Oakland CA 94612

MCGIRT, SHERRI LYNN, lawyer; b. Charlotte, N.C., May 3, 1949; d. Joseph Ward and S. Pearl (Gasaway) McG.; m. Lawrence D. Farber, Sept. 9, 1984. BA, U. N.C., 1971, JD, 1974. Bar: N.C 1974, U.S. Dist. Ct. (we. dist.) N.C. 1979, U.S. Tax Ct. 1982, N.C. 1984, U.S. Dist. Ct. (mid. dist.) N.C. 1974. Atty. estate and gift tax IRS, Greensboro, N.C., 1974-79; tax supr. Touche, Ross & Co., Charlotte, 1979-81; assoc. Weinstein & Sturges, Charlotte, 1981-83, ptnr., 1983—; mem. planning com. J. Nelson Young Ann. Tax Inst.; mem. planning com. U. N.C. Sch. Law, Chapel Hill, 1980-86, bd. dirs., 1987—. Mem. Mecklenburg County Young Dems., Charlotte, 1980-82; bd. dirs. Latta Pl. Inc., Charlotte, 1982-84. Mem. ABA, N.C. Bar Assn., N.C. Assn. CPA's, Am. Inst. CPA's, Mecklenburg County Bar Assn. (chmn. legal services for elderly 1983-85, nominating com. 1984-86, ad hoc pro bono com. 1985, vol. lawyers program 1986—). Presbyterian. Estate planning, Pension, profit-sharing, and employee benefits, Corporate taxation. Office: Weinstein & Sturges 810 Baxter St Charlotte NC 28202

MC GIVERIN, ARTHUR A., state justice; b. Iowa City, Iowa, Nov. 10, 1928; s. Joseph J. and Mary B. McG.; m. Mary Joan McGiverin, Apr. 20, 1951; children: Teresa, Thomas, Bruce, Nancy. B.S.C. with high honors, U. Iowa, 1951, J.D., 1956. Bar: Iowa 1956. Practice law Ottumwa, Iowa, 1956; alt. mcpl. judge Ottumwa, 1960-65; judge Iowa Dist. Ct. 8th Jud. Dist., 1965-78; asso. justice Iowa Supreme Ct., Des Moines, 1978—. Mem. Iowa Supreme Ct. Commn. on Continuing Legal Edn., 1975. Served to 1st lt. U.S. Army, 1946-48, 51-53. Mem. Iowa State Bar Assn., Am. Law Inst. Roman Catholic. Jurisprudence. Office: Supreme Ct of Iowa Capitol Bldg 10th and Grand Des Moines IA 50319 *

MCGIVERN, THOMAS MICHAEL, lawyer; b. Cedar Rapids, Iowa, Dec. 5, 1956; s. Edward Joseph and Lillian Joanne (Jagim) McG. BS in Econs. and Internat. Studies, Iowa State U., 1978; JD, Creighton U., 1981; LLM, U. Ark., 1986. Bar: Iowa 1981, Nebr. 1982. Atty. Fed. Land Bank, Omaha, 1981-82; atty. Commodity Futures Trading Commn., Washington, 1983—, asst. dir. div. of trading and markets, 1986—; law lectr. U. Ark., Fayetteville, 1982-83, Drake U., Des Moines, 1985. Contbr. articles to law rev. Mem. ABA (Internat. law and practice sect.), Iowa Bar Assn., Nebr. Bar Assn., Am. Agrl. Law Assn. (reporter, editor jour.). Commodities law, Private international, Public international. Office: Commodity Futures Trading Commn 2033 K St NW Washington DC 20581

MCGLINCHEY, DERMOT SHEEHAN, lawyer; b. N.Y.C., Mar. 21, 1933; s. Patrick J. and Ellen S. McGlinchey; m. Ellen F. Murphy, Aug. 19, 1967; children: Ellen F., Deirdre. BA, Tulane U., 1954, JD, 1957. Bar: La. 1957, U.S. Dist. Ct. (ea., mid., we. dists.) La. 1957, U.S. Ct. Appeals (5th and 11th cirs.) 1957, D.C. 1984, U.S. Supreme Ct. 1984. Pres. McGlinchey, Stafford, Mintz, Cellini & Lang, 1974—. Pres. Tulane U. Law Dean's Council, New Orleans, 1982-84; bd. dirs. World Trade Ctr., New Orleans, 1981-83, New Orleans Opera Assn., 1985—. Mem. ABA, La. Bar Found. (chmn. 1986—), Fedn. Ins. and Corp. Counsel, Internat. Assn. Ins. Counsel, Maritime Law Assn. of U.S., Phi Alpha Delta. Roman Catholic. Club: Round Table. Federal civil litigation, State civil litigation. Home: 533 Audubon St New Orleans LA 70118 Office: 643 Magazine St New Orleans LA 70130

MCGLORY, WILLIE EDWARD, lawyer; b. Fayette, Miss., Apr. 26, 1953; s. Geannetta (Woods) McG.; m. Lolita D. Marcus, Sept. 5, 1982; 1 child, Marcus. Bar: Mich. 1980, U.S. Dist. Ct. (ea. dist.) Mich. 1981, U.S. Ct. Appeals (6th cir.) 1986, U.S. Supreme Ct. 1984. Staff atty. Ford Motor Co., Dearborn, Mich., 1979—; bd. dirs. Nat. Tech. Unlimited, Detail, Inc.; cons. Avon Investment Group, Detroit, 1985—; sec. Comprehensive Youth Tng. and Community Involvement Program, Detroit, 1985—. Mem. ABA, Mich. Bar Assn., Wolverine Bar Assn., Nat. Bar Assn. Democrat. Baptist. Avocations: basketball, tennis, golf. State civil litigation, Federal civil litigation, Labor. Home: 16718 Avon Detroit MI 48219 Office: Ford Motor Co The American Rd Room 1088 Dearborn MI 48121-1899

MCGLOTHLIN, MICHAEL GORDON, lawyer; b. Richlands, Va., Oct. 31, 1951; s. Woodrow Wilson and Sally Ann (Cook) McG.; m. Sandra Lee Keen, Oct. 1, 1983; 1 child, Michael Alexander. BA, U. Va., 1974; JD, Coll. William and Mary, 1976. Bar: Va. 1977, U.S. Dist. Ct. (we. dist.) Va. 1978. Ptnr. McGlothlin, McGlothlin, Grundy, Va., 1977-79; commonwealth atty. Buchanan County, Grundy, 1980-83; ptnr. McGlothlin & Wife, Grundy, 1984—; county atty., Buchanan County, 1984—; bd. dirs. Gt. Southwest Home Commn. Mem. adv. bd. Clinch Valley Coll. Mem. ABA, Va. State Bar Assn., Buchanan County Bar Assn. (pres. 1984), Phi Alpha Delta. Democrat. Presbyterian. General practice, Criminal, State civil litigation. Home: PO Drawer 810 Grundy VA 24614 Office: PO Drawer 810 Grundy VA 24614

MCGLYNN, JOSEPH LEO, JR., judge; b. Phila., Feb. 13, 1925; s. Joseph Leo and Margaret Loretta (Ryan) McG.; m. Jocelyn M. Gates, Aug. 26, 1950; children: Jocelyn, Leo, Timothy, Suzanne, Alisa, Deirdre, Caroline, Elizabeth, Meghan, Brendan. B.S., Mt. St. Mary's Coll., 1948; LL.B., U. Pa., 1951. Bar: Pa. bar 1952. Asst. U.S. atty. Phila., 1953-60; asso., partner firm Blank Rudenko Klaus & Rome, Phila., 1960-65; judge County Ct. of Phila., 1965-68, Ct. of Common Pleas, 1st Jud. Dist. of Pa., 1968-74, U.S. Dist. Ct. for Eastern Dist. Pa., Phila., 1974—. Served with USN, 1943-46, PTO. Mem. Phila. Bar Assn. Jurisprudence. Office: US District Court 8614 US Courthouse Independence Mall W 601 Market St Philadelphia PA 19106 *

MCGLYNN, JOSEPH MICHAEL, lawyer; b. Detroit, Jan. 15, 1937; s. Frank J. and Germaine J. (Ackermann) McG.; m. Kathryn A. Montie, June 23, 1962; children—Julianne, Timothy, Kevin, Kathleen. B.S. in Acctg., U. Detroit, 1958, J.D., 1960. Bar: Mich. 1961, U.S. Dist. Ct. (ea. dist.) Mich. 1961, U.S. Supreme Ct. 1971. Sole practice, Detroit, 1961-67; ptnr. McGlynn, Dettmer & Spaulding, Detroit, and predecessor McGlynn & Dettmer, 1967-74; sole practice in assn. with Welday, Rosenthal, Reilly & McGlynn, Southfield, Mich., 1974-75, Welday, Klyman, Fortescue, Burau & McGlynn, Southfield, Mich., 1975-82, Brown, McGlynn, Charters & Thomas, Bloomfield Hills, 1982-87, Powers, Chapman & Deagostino, P.C., 1987—; dir., sec. UFORMA/Shelby Bus. Forms Inc. (Ohio); dir. Adray Appliance & Photo Ctr., Inc., Dearborn, Mich. Served with USAR, 1960-66. Recipient First prize Nathan Burkan Meml. Competition, 1959. Mem. ABA, State Bar Mich., Oakland County Bar Assn., Fin. and Estate Planning Council Detroit, Oakland County Estate Planning Council, Delta Sigma Pi, Alpha Sigma Nu (hon.), Beta Gamma Sigma (hon.). Roman Catholic. Editor U. Detroit Law Jour., 1958-60. Probate, General corporate, Real property. Office: Powers Chapman & DeAgostino 3001 W Big Beaver Rd Suite 704 Troy MI 48084

MC GOLDRICK, JOHN GARDINER, lawyer; b. Grand View-on-Hudson, N.Y., July 25, 1932; s. Francis Michael and Elizabeth Theresa (Leitner) McG.; m. Cathleen Elinor Cloney, June 5, 1965; children: John Francis, Ann Cathleen. Student, Coll. of Holy Cross, Worcester, Mass., 1950-51; seminarian, S.J., 1951-58; A.B., Fordham U., 1957; J.D., Georgetown U., 1961. Bar: N.Y. 1962, U.S. Dist. Ct (so. and ea. dists.) N.Y. 1975, U.S. Ct. Appeals (2d cir.) 1975, U.S. Supreme Ct. 1975. Assoc. Lowenstein, Pitcher, Hotchkiss, Amann & Parr, N.Y.C., 1961-66, Kaye, Scholer, Fierman, Hays & Handler, N.Y.C., 1966-69; ptnr. Schulte & McGoldrick, N.Y.C., 1969-81; counsel to Gov. Hugh L. Carey, N.Y., 1981-82; partner Schulte Roth & Zabel, 1983—; commr. Port Authority N.Y. and N.J., 1982—, chmn. audit com., 1985—. Bd. dirs., mem. exec. com. Georgetown U., 1973-79, vice chmn. bd., 1975-79; bd. dirs. Com. Modern Cts., Inc., 1983—. Mem. ABA, N.Y. State Bar Assn. (com. on state constitution), Assn. Bar City N.Y. (com. on profl. responsibilities 1974-76, com. on grievances 1976-79, com. profl. discipline 1980, com. 2d century 1982—, treas., mem. exec. com. 1984-87). Clubs: Board Room (N.Y.C.), University (N.Y.C.). General corporate, Municipal bonds, Securities. Home: 111 E 80th St New York NY 10021 Office: Schulte Roth & Zabel 900 Third Ave New York NY 10022

MCGONAGLE, SHIRLEE ANN, lawyer; b. Boston, Sept. 24, 1954; d. John Patrick and Shirley Joan (Brosnahan) McG.; m. Peter Alexander Campagna, July 15, 1978; 1 child, Alexander William. BA, Boston Coll., 1977; JD, Suffolk U., 1981; MBA, Western New Eng. Coll., 1987. Bar: Mass. 1977, U.S. Dist. Ct. Mass. 1978. Contract adminstr. Signatron, Inc., Lexington, Mass., 1981-83; contract counsel Input Output Computer Services Inc., Waltham, Mass., 1983-86; sr. contract negotiatior Digital Equipment Corp., Merrimack, N.H., 1986—. Mem. Mass. Devel. Disability Counsel, Boston, 1983—; bd. dirs. Ctr. for Living and Working, Worcester, Mass., 1981—, past pres. Mem. ABA, Nat. Contract Mgmt. Assn. Avocation: sailing. Government contracts and claims. Office: Digital Equipment Corp Continental Blvd Merrimack NH 03054

MCGONEGLE, TIMOTHY J., lawyer; b. Ft. Dodge, Iowa, Aug. 22, 1952; s. Eugene Francis and Margaret Ann (Chambers) McG.; m. Barbara Jo Sullivan, Oct. 6, 1979; children: Melissa Jo, Erin Kathleen. AA, Iowa Cen. Coll., 1972; BA, U. Iowa, 1974; JD, Loyola U., Chgo., 1977. Bar: Ill. 1977, U.S. Dist. Ct. (no. dist.) Ill. 1977, U.S. Dist. Ct. (cen. dist.) Ill. 1978, U.S. Ct. Appeals (7th cir.) 1978, U.S. Supreme Ct. 1981, U.S. Tax Ct. 1984, U.S. Ct. Appeals (D.C. cir.) 1987. Law clk. to presiding justice Ill. Supreme Ct., Chgo., 1977-78, Ill. Appellate Ct., Chgo., 1978; assoc. O'Brien, Carey, McNamara, Scheuneman & Campbell Ltd., Chgo., 1978-82; ptnr. Ashcraft & Ashcraft Ltd., Chgo., 1982—; instr. legal writing Loyola U., Chgo., 1978-81, appellate advocacy Loyola U., 1984—. Bd. dirs. Graceland West Community Assn., Chgo., 1983—; clinic atty. Chgo. Vol. Legal Services Found., 1982—. Mem. ABA, Ill. Bar Assn., Chgo. Bar Assn. (investigator jud. evaluation com. 1983-86, hearings div. 1987—), Fed. Bar Assn. State civil litigation, Federal civil litigation. Home: 4117 N Greenview Ave Chicago IL 60613 Office: Ashcraft & Ashcraft Ltd 200 E Randolph Dr 77th Fl Chicago IL 60601

MCGONIGLE, JOHN WILLIAM, lawyer, investment company executive; b. Pitts., Oct. 26, 1938; s. Henry J. and Madeline I. (Jones) McG.; m. Mary Ita Smith, July 13, 1963; children: Kevin M., Christine I., Michael J. B.S., Duquesne U., Pitts., 1960, J.D., 1965. Bar: Pa. 1965. Atty. SEC, Washington, 1965-66; sec., gen. counsel Federated Investors, Inc., Pitts., 1967—; v.p., counsel investment cos. Federated Funds, 1966—; dir. Liberty Bank & Trust,, Gibbsboro,, N.J. Editor: Duquesne Law Rev., 1963-65. Mem. Catholic Social Services Bd., Pitts., 1975-78. Served to 1st lt. U.S. Army, 1960-62. Mem. ABA, Pa. Bar Assn. (chmn. com. on corp. law depts. 1979-80), Allegheny County Bar Assn., Am. Soc. Corp. Secs. Clubs: Athletic Assn., Duquesne, Rivers, Pitts. Field. Securities. Office: Federated Investors Tower Pittsburgh PA 15222

MC GOUGH, WALTER THOMAS, lawyer; b. Steubenville, Ohio, June 4, 1919; s. Frank C. and Nellie C. (Curran) McG.; m. Jane Fitzpatrick, Nov. 24, 1949; children—Jane Ellen, Walter T., Hugh F., Marita. Student, Duquesne U., 1936-41; LL.B., U. Pitts., 1948. Bar: Pa. 1948, U.S. Dist. Ct. 1948. Asso. Reed Smith Shaw & McClay, Pitts., 1948-58; partner Reed Smith Shaw & McClay, 1958—, head litigation dept., 1965-79. Case editor U. Pitts. Law Rev. Served to capt. USAAF, 1941-46. Mem. ABA, Am. Law Inst., Pa. Bar Assn., Allegheny County Bar Assn., Am. Judicature Soc. (dir. 1981—), Acad. Trial Lawyers Allegheny County, 3d Circuit Jud. Conf., Order of Coif. Republican. Roman Catholic. Clubs: Duquesne, Press, Ross Mountain, Pitts. Athletic. Federal civil litigation, State civil litigation, Libel. Home: 825-D Morewood Ave Pittsburgh PA 15213 Office: Reed Smith Shaw & McClay James H Reed Bldg 435 6th Ave Pittsburgh PA 15219

MCGOVERN, DAVID TALMAGE, lawyer; b. N.Y.C., Apr. 3, 1928; s. Coleman Benedict and Doris (Mangam) McG.; m. Margery White, June 28, 1958; children: Alexandra, Justine. BS, Yale U., 1950; LLB, Columbia U., 1955. Bar: N.Y. 1955. Assoc. Shearman & Sterling, N.Y.C., 1955-67; ptnr. Shearman & Sterling, Paris, 1967—. Served to 1st lt. U.S. Army, 1951-53. Named to French Legion of Honor, 1983. Mem. Am. C. of C. in France

(pres. 1979-82, bd. dirs.). Private international, General corporate. Office: Shearman & Sterling, 21 Ave George V, Paris 75116, France

MCGOVERN, GLENN CHARLES, lawyer; b. New Orleans, Feb. 19, 1952; s. Daniel Allen and Shirley Catherine (Prattini) McG.; m. Elizabeth Sarah Sharp, Nov. 11, 1979; children: Celeste E., Megan H. BS in Econs., U. New Orleans, 1974; JD, Loyola U., New Orleans, 1977. Bar: La. 1977, U.S. Dist. Ct. (ea. dist.) La., U.S. Ct. Appeals (5th cir.), U.S. Supreme Ct. Sole practice New Orleans, 1977—. Mem. Eastern Govtl. Action League, New Orleans, 1977—; bd. dirs. Venetian Isle Civic Improvement Assn., 1985—. Mem. ABA (aviation litigation com. 1985-86), La. Bar Assn., New Orleans Bar Assn. (sole practitioners com. 1986), La. Trial Lawyers Assn. (adv. bd. 1985—), New Orleans Acad. Trial Lawyers Assn. (sec. 1985-86, barrister 1986-87), New Orleans East Bus. Assn., Lawyers Pilots Bar Assn. Democrat. Roman Catholic. Lodge: Kiwanis (local sec. 1980—). Avocations: flying airplanes, water skiing, boating. Federal civil litigation, State civil litigation, Personal injury. Office: Deer Park 10555 Lake Forest Rd Suite 5E New Orleans LA 70189-0569

MCGOVERN, KEVIN MICHAEL, lawyer; b. N.Y.C., July 16, 1948; s. Thomas Edward and Margaret (Smith) McG.; m. Lisa Camerota, Nov. 21, 1979; children: Jarrett, Ashley. Student, U. London, England, 1968; BA, Cornell U., 1970; JD, St. John's U., 1975. Bar: Conn. 1975, U.S. Dist. Ct. (so. dist.) 1980, Pa. 1981. Assoc. Ivey, Barnum & Omara, Greenwich, Conn., 1975-77; assoc. gen. counsel Clabir Corp., Greenwich, 1977-79; ptnr. Duel & Holland, Greenwich, 1979-81, Kaye, Effron & McGovern, Greenwich, 1981-84; sole practice law, Greenwich, 1984—; dir. Savant Group, Phila., Globe Ticket Co., Phila., Conn. Venture Mgmt. Corp., Stamford. Chmn. edn. task force Southwest Conn. Industry Assn., Stamford, 1979; chmn. spl. gifts Greenwich United Way, 1981, chmn. profl., 1980. Mem. Am. Judicature Soc. (dir. 1974-75, mem. com. 1974-77), Pa. Bar Assn., Conn. Bar Assn. (exec. com. on corps., 1982—), Greenwich Bar Assn. Roman Catholic. Clubs: Venture Capital Group (Stamford) (chmn. research and devel.); Burning Tree Country (Greenwich). General corporate, Private international, Securities. Home: 333 Webbs Hill Rd Stamford CT 06903 Office: 165 W Putnam Ave Greenwich CT 06836

MCGOVERN, PETER JOHN, law educator; b. N.Y.C., Dec. 6, 1938; s. John Phillip and Helen Marie (Gaisser) McG.; m. Catherine Bigley, Aug. 31, 1963; children—Brian Peter, Sean Daniel. A.B., Notre Dame U., 1961; J.D., Fordham U., 1964; Ed.D., U. S.D., 1980. Bar: N.Y. 1964, S.D. 1972, Ind. 1983, U.S. Supreme Ct. 1968. Atty. criminal div. Dept. Justice, 1971-72; prof. law U. S.D., Vermillion, 1972-83, asst. dean Sch. Law, 1972-75, acting dean, 1975, assoc. dean, 1977, dir. programs and planning, 1979-83; dean Sch. Law, Valparaiso (Ind.) U., 1983-85, Sch. Law St. Thomas U., Fla., 1985-87, John Marshall Law Sch., Chgo., 1987—; dir. continuing legal edn. State Bar S.D., 1972-83; mem., past chmn. S.D. Family Law Com.; bd. dirs. Legal Services of Greater Gary Inc. Past pres. Vermillion Area Arts Council. Served to lt. comdr. JAGC, USN, 1965-71. Recipient Legal Writing award Fed. Bar Assn., 1969. Fellow Ind. Bar Found. (bd. dirs.); mem. Nat. Assn. Coll. and Univ. Counsel, Am. Bar Assn., State Bar Ind. (ho. of dels.). Republican. Roman Catholic. Legal education, Family and matrimonial, Criminal. Home: 19415 E Lake Dr Country Club of Miami FL 33015

MCGOVERN, TERRY, lawyer, investment consultant; b. Boston, Sept. 6, 1951; d. Elwynn J. Miller and Margaret F. McGovern; m. Malvin Tyler, Aug., 1985. B.A., U. Mass., 1973; J.D., Northeastern U., 1976; LL.M., London Sch. Econs., 1978; M.B.A., Imede, Lausanne, Switzerland, 1983. Bar: Mass. 1980, Calif. 1980, N.Y. 1980. Pvt. practice legal cons., San Francisco, London, 1978-80; atty. Indo U.S. Subcommn., New Delhi, India, 1980-82; legal cons. Am. consulate, New Delhi, 1982; ptnr. Miller McGovern, San Francisco, 1980-83; cons. Service 800 SA, Nyon, Switzerland, 1983; sole practice, N.Y.C., 1984—; banker Merrill Lynch Internat., London, 1986—; atty., investment cons. E.F. Hutton, London, 1986—. NSF fellow, 1981-82; Indo-Am. Subcommn. grantee, 1981-82. Mem. ABA, World Peace Through Law Center, Hague Acad. Internat. Law, Nat. Women's Law Assn. (state del. 1984—). Home: 15 Bracknell Gardens, London NW3, England also: 310 Commonwealth Ave Chestnut Hill MA 02167 Office: 230 Park Ave Suite 1260 New York NY 10169

MC GOVERN, WALTER T., judge; b. Seattle, May 24, 1922; s. C. Arthur and Anne Marie (Thies) McG.; m. Rita Marie Olsen, June 29, 1946; children: Katrina M., Shawn E., A. Renee. B.A., U. Wash., 1949, LL.B., 1950. Bar: Wash. 1950. Practiced law in Seattle, 1950-59; mem. firm Kerr, McCord, Greenleaf & Moen; judge Municipal Ct., Seattle, 1959-65, Superior Ct., Wash., 1965-68, Wash. Supreme Ct. 1968-71, U.S. Dist. Ct. (we. dist.) Wash., 1971—; chief judge 1975—; mem. subcom. on supporting personnel Jud. Conf. U.S., 1981—, chmn. subcom., 1983, mem. adminstrn. com., 1983. Mem. Am. Judicature Soc., Wash. State Superior Ct. Judges Assn., Seattle King County Bar Assn. (treas.), Phi Delta Phi. Club: Seattle Tennis (pres. 1968). Office: 705 US Courthouse Seattle WA 98104

MC GOVERN, WILLIAM MONTGOMERY, JR., legal educator; b. Evanston, Ill., July 9, 1934; s. William Montgomery and Margaret (Montgomery) McG.; m. m Katharine Watts, Sept. 20, 1958; children: William Montgomery III, Elizabeth Lee, Katharine Margaret. A.B., Princeton U., 1955; LL.B., Harvard U., 1958. Bar: Ill. 1959. Assoc. Sidley, Austin, Burgess & Smith, Chgo., 1959-63; asst. prof. law Northwestern U. Sch. of Law, Chgo., 1963-66; assoc. prof. Northwestern U. Sch. of Law, 1966-68, prof., 1968-72; prof. law Sch. Law, UCLA, 1972—; vis. prof. U. Minn. Law Sch., 1979-80, U. Va. Law Sch., 1983. Author: Wills, Trusts and Future Interests: An Introduction to Estate Planning, 1983; (with Lary Lawrence) Cases and Problems on Contracts and Sales, 1986; bd. editors: Harvard Law Rev, 1956-58; Contbr. articles profl. jours. Served with U.S. Army, 1958-59. Legal education, Probate, Legal history. Home: 17319 Magnolia Blvd Encino CA 91316 Office: UCLA 405 Hilgard Los Angeles CA 90024 *

MCGOWAN, GARY V., lawyer; b. Houston, Apr. 2, 1948; s. Virgil Clarence and Mary Lucille (Reavis) McG.; m. Agelia Mercedes Perez, July 14, 1979; children: Leslie Anne, Kathryn Elizabeth. BA, U. Tex., 1970, JD, 1973. Bar: Va. 1974, Tex. 1977. Assoc. Hunton & Williams, Richmond, Tex., 1973-76; assoc. Mandell & Wright, Houston, 1976-78, ptnr., 1978-80; ptnr. Susman, Godfrey & McGowan, Houston, 1980—. Assoc. editor U. Tex. Law Rev., 1972-73. Fellow Houston Bar Found.; mem. ABA (antitrust sect.), Tex. Bar Assn. (chmn. antitrust and trade regulation sect. 1983-84, governing council 1977-79, 82-85). Clubs: Briar, Plaza (Houston); Tower (Dallas). Federal civil litigation, State civil litigation, Antitrust. Office: Susman Godfrey & McGowan 2400 Allied Bank Plaza Houston TX 77002

MCGOWAN, KEVIN MURRAY, lawyer; b. Drexel Hill, Pa., Mar. 7, 1953; s. Robert Walter Jr. and Gladys (Murray) McG.; m. Joan Katherine Hicks, Aug. 2, 1980; 1 child, Andrew Scott. BA, Belmont Abbey Coll., 1975; JD, U. Va., 1978. Bar: Va. 1978, U.S. Dist. Ct. (ea. dist.) Va. 1978, U.S. Ct. Appeals (4th cir.) 1978. Assoc. Marks, Stokes & Harrison, Hopewell, Va., 1978-81; sole practice Chesterfield, Va., 1982—. Legis. aide Va. Gen. Assembly, Richmond, 1981. Mem. ABA, Nat. Orgn. Soc. Security Claimant's Reps. (state chmn. 1982—), Jaycees. Roman Catholic. Lodge: Optimists. General practice. Home: 1602 S Esther Ct Chester VA 23831 Office: 9510 Ironbridge Rd Chesterfield VA 23832

MCGOWAN, PATRICK FRANCIS, lawyer; b. N.Y.C., July 23, 1940; s. Francis Patrick and Sonia Veronica (Koslow) M.; m. Patricia Neil, June 6, 1964; children—Susan Claire, Kathleen Anne. B.A., Rice U., 1962; J.D., U. Tex.-Austin, 1965. Bar: Tex. 1965, U.S. Supreme Ct. 1971. Briefing atty. Tex. Supreme Ct., Austin, Tex., 1965-66; ptnr. Strasburger & Price, Dallas, 1966—; mem. continuing legal edn. com. State Bar Tex.; dir. Tex Lex, Inc. Mem. ABA, Dallas Bar Assn., Tex. Law Review Editors Assn., Phi Delta Phi. Antitrust, Federal civil litigation, Trademark and copyright. Office: 4300 InterFirst Plaza Dallas TX 75202

MCGOWAN, RODNEY RALPH, lawyer; b. Goodland, Kans., Jan. 7, 1952; s. Ralph Eugene and Anita (Cook) McG.; m. Clarisse Jean Roberson, Nov. 3, 1974; children: Leslie, Ryan. BS, Colo. State U., 1974; JD, U. Colo., 1978. Bar: Colo. 1979, U.S. Dist. Ct. Colo. 1979. Assoc. Baker & Cazier, Granby, Colo., 1979-84; ptnr. Baker, Cazier & McGowan, Granby, 1984—. Mem. ABA, Colo. Bar Assn. (Pro Bono award 1984), Grand-Jackson County Bar Assn. (pres. 1980), Northwest Colo. Bar Assn., Phi Kappa Phi. Real property, Construction, Probate. Office: Baker Cazier & McGowan PO Box 588 Granby CO 80446

MCGOWIN, NICHOLAS STALLWORTH, lawyer; b. Chapman, Ala., May 17, 1912; s. James Greeley and Essie (Stallworth) McG.; m. Elizabeth Brittain Smith, Apr. 21, 1945; children: Nicholas Stallworth (dec.), Peter H., Elizabeth. A.B., U. Ala., 1933; postgrad., Pembroke Coll., Oxford U., Eng., 1933-34; LL.B., Harvard, 1937. Bar: Ala. bar 1937, Pa. bar 1939. Practice in Greenville, Ala., 1937-39, Phila., 1939-41, Washington, 1941-42, Mobile, Ala., 1946—; asso. Drinker, Biddle & Reath, 1939-41; mem. legal staff Brit. Purchasing Commn., 1941-42; mem. firm Thornton & McGowin, 1956—; Chmn. Ala. Fulbright Scholarship Com., 1951-72. Pres. Mobile Symphony, 1956-58; chmn. bd. trustees Lyman Ward Mil. Acad., Mobile Public Library, 1969-70. Served to lt. comdr. USNR, 1942-45, PTO. Decorated Order of Vasa Sweden, Order of North Star. Mem. ABA, Ala. Bar Assn. (chmn. real property, probate and trust sect. 1970-71), Mobile Bar Assn. (pres. 1974), Phi Beta Kappa, Delta Kappa Epsilon. Clubs: Country (Mobile), Athelstan (Mobile); Boston (New Orleans). General corporate, Probate, Real property. Home: 3604 Spring Hill Ave Mobile AL 36608 Office: 56 St Joseph St Mobile AL 36602

MCGRAIL, ALBERT JAMES, lawyer; b. New Haven, June 23, 1948; s. Albert Charles and Miriam Inez (O'Connor) McG.; m. Kristen Lee Gillmore, June 19, 1971; children: David, Katherine, John. BA, Johns Hopkins U., 1971; JD, U. Conn., 1974. Bar: Conn. 1974, U.S. Dist. Ct. Conn. 1975. Ptnr. Fazzano & McGrail, Hartford, Conn., 1974-81, McEleney & McGrail, Hartford, 1982—; arbitrator Dept. Edn. State of Conn., 1983—. Commr. Glastonbury (Conn.) Basketball Assn., 1983—; mem. Town of Glastonbury Parks and Recreation Commn. Mem. Conn. Bar Assn., Assn. Trial Lawyers Am., Conn. Trial Lawyers Assn. Democrat. Club: Irish/American (Glastonbury). Labor, State civil litigation, Criminal. Home: 148 Williams St Glastonbury CT 06033 Office: McEleney & McGrail 363 Main St Hartford CT 06106

MC GRATH, JOHN FRANCIS, judge; b. Chgo., Apr. 13, 1926; B.A., Loyola U., Chgo., 1947; J.D., U. Colo., 1950. Bar: Colo. 1950, Ill. 1950; partner firm Kettelkamp, McGrath, Vento, Pueblo, Colo., 1950-67; judge U.S. Bankruptcy Ct., Denver, 1967—; dep. dist. atty. Pueblo County (Colo.), 1953-57. Pres. Pueblo Symphony, Pueblo Broadway Theatre League. Mem. Colo., Pueblo County (sec.) bar assns., Phi Alpha Delta, Alpha Delta Gamma. Home: 1490 Findlay Way Boulder CO 80303 Office: 1845 Sherman St Courthouse 400 Columbine Bldg. Denver CO 80203

MCGRATH, JOHN NICHOLAS, JR., lawyer; b. Hollywood, Calif., Feb. 12, 1940; m. Margaret Crowley, Oct. 4, 1980; children: Nicholas Gerald, Molly Inez. BA with honors, Lehigh U., 1962; LLB magna cum laude, Columbia U., 1965. Bar: D.C. 1966, Calif. 1969, U.S. Supreme Ct. 1970, Colo. 1971. Law clk. to presiding justice U.S. Ct. Appeals (D.C. cir.), 1965-66; law clk. to assoc. justice Thurgood Marshall U.S. Supreme Ct., Washington, 1967-68; assoc. Pillsbury, Madison & Sutro, San Francisco, 1968-70; from assoc. to ptnr. Oates, Austin, McGrath, Aspen, Colo., 1970-80; ptnr. Austin, McGrath & Jordan, Aspen, 1980-82; sole practice Aspen, 1982—. Mem. Colo. Bar Assn., Colo. Supreme Ct. Grievance Com., Assn. Trial Lawyers Am., Pitkin County Bar Assn. (pres. 1977). Democrat. Avocations: skiing, tennis, computers. General practice, State civil litigation, Real property. Office: 600 E Hopkins Suite 203 Aspen CO 81611

MCGRATH, THOMAS J., lawyer, writer, film producer; b. N.Y.C., Oct. 8, 1932; m. Mary Lee McGrath, Aug. 4, 1956 (dec.); children: Maura Lee, J. Connell; m. Diahn Williams, Sept. 28, 1974; 1 dau., Courtney C. B.A., NYU, 1956, J.D., 1960. Bar: N.Y. 1960. Assoc. Milbank, Tweed, Hadley & McCloy, N.Y.C., 1960-69; ptnr. Simpson Thacher & Bartlett, N.Y.C., 1970—; lectr., writer Practicing Law Inst., 1976—, Am. Law Inst.-ABA, 1976-81. Author: Carryover Basis Under Tax Reform Act, 1977; contbg. author: Estate and Gift Tax After ERTA, 1982; producer: feature film Deadly Hero, 1977. Served with U.S. Army, 1952-54, Korea. Fellow Am. Coll. Probate Counsel; mem. N.Y. State Bar Assn., ABA, Assn. Bar City N.Y. Estate planning, Probate, Estate taxation. Office: Simpson Thacher & Bartlett 1 Battery Park Plaza New York NY 10004

MCGRATH, WILLIAM ARTHUR, lawyer; b. Hackensack, N.J., Jan. 31, 1941; s. Donald Marble and Elinor (Peck) M.; m. Diane Gurley, Apr. 25, 1965 (div. Nov. 1978); children: Philip M., Christian P.; m. Merlynn Miller, Dec. 14, 1980. B.S., Calif. U.-Long Beach, 1963. Bar: Colo. 1972, U.S. Dist. Ct. Colo. 1972. Sole practice, Breckenridge, Colo., 1972-75, Aurora, Colo., 1980-84; ptnr. McGrath & Callan, P.C., Breckenridge, 1975-80, McGrath & Lavenhar, Esq., Denver, 1984-85, prin. William A. McGrath & Assocs., Denver, 1985—; vocat. instr. Colo. Mountain Coll., 1972-80. Mem. ABA, Colo. Trial Lawyers Assn., Colo. Assn. Realtors. Republican. Episcopalian. Real property, State civil litigation, General practice. Home: 11647 E Cornell Circle Aurora CO 80014 Office: 1832 Clarkson St Denver CO 80218

MCGRATH, WILLIAM JOSEPH, lawyer; b. Cleve., July 6, 1943; s. William Peter and Marie Agnes (Wolf) McG.; m. Mary Ann Ostrenga; children: William Peter, Geoffrey Walton, Megan Joy. AB, John Carroll U., 1965; MA, Loyola U., 1967; JD, Harvard U., 1970. Bar: Ill. 1970. Assoc. McDermott, Will & Emery, Chgo., 1970-75, ptnr., 1976—; bd. dirs. Hobart-McIntosh Paper Co., Elk Grove, Ill. Mem. ABA. Democrat. Roman Catholic. Clubs: Evanston (Ill.) Golf; Union League (Chgo.) (trustee Boy Club Found. 1983). General corporate, Securities, Contracts commercial. Home: 1021 Greenwood Evanston IL 60201 Office: McDermott Will & Emery 111 W Monroe St Chicago IL 60603

MCGRAW, CHARLENE EVERTZ, lawyer; b. Syracuse, N.Y., June 2, 1956; d. George G. and Sally (Hogan) Evertz; m. Edward L. McGraw, July 29, 1978; children: Katherine, Elizabeth. BS in Acctg., SUNY, Binghamton, 1978; JD, Syracuse U., 1981. Bar: N.Y. 1982, U.S. Dist. Ct. (no. dist.) N.Y. 1982, U.S. Ct. Appeals (2d cir.) 1983. Assoc. MacKenzie, Smith, Lewis, Michell & Hughes, Syracuse, 1981—. Mem. ABA (del. 1984—), N.Y. State Bar Assn. (del. 1984—, exec. com. young lawyers sect.), Onondaga County Bar Assn., Order of Coif. Federal civil litigation, State civil litigation, Personal injury. Office: MacKenzie Smith Lewis Michell & Hughes 600 Onbank Bldg Syracuse NY 13202

MC GRAW, DARRELL VIVIAN, JR., judge; b. Wyoming County, W.Va., Nov. 8, 1936; s. Darrell Vivian and Julia (ZeKany) McG.; m. Jorea Marple; children: Elizabeth, Sarah, Darrell, Elliott. A.B., W.Va. U., 1961, LL.B., J.D., 1964, M.A., 1977. Bar: W.Va. 1964. Gen. atty. Fgn. Claims Settlement Commn., Dept. State, 1964; counsel to Gov. State of W.Va., 1965-68; practice law Shepherdstown, Morgantown and Charleston, 1968-76; judge W.Va. Supreme Ct. Appeals, Charleston, 1977—, chief justice, 1983, 87. Served with U.S. Army, 1954-57. Democrat. Jurisprudence. Office: Supreme Ct State Capitol Bldg Charleston WV 25305

MCGRAW, PATRICK JOHN, lawyer; b. Detroit, Feb. 3, 1956; s. John William and Elizabeth Kay (Foley) McG.; m. Susan Elaine Borowiak, Jan. 14, 1978; children: Kelly Elizabeth, Ryan Patrick, Brandon David. BS, Cen. Mich. U., 1979; JD, Cooley Law Sch., 1982. Bar: Mich. 1982. Ptnr. McGraw, Borchard & Martin, P.C., Saginaw, Mich., 1982—; advisor Cooley Law Sch., Lansing, Mich., 1984-85; lectr. Advanced Cardiac Life Support Legal Implications, Saginaw, 1985; instr. Cen. Mich. U., Mt. Pleasant, Mich, 1986—; speaker Sponsor of Malpractice Issues Delta Coll. and Saginaw Valley State Coll., 1986—. Atty. Sch. Program, Saginaw, 1986—; mem. YMCA. Mem. ABA, Mich. Bar Assn., Saginaw County Bar Assn., Am. Trial Lawyers Assn., Mich. Soc. of Hosp. Attys., Mich. Def. Trial Counsel, Phi Alpha Delta. Avocations: black belt karate, hunting, fishing. State civil litigation, Insurance, Personal injury. Home: 5220 Overhill Saginaw MI 48603 Office: McGraw Borchard & Martin 5200 State St Saginaw MI 48603

MCGREEVY, TERRENCE GERARD, lawyer; b. Flushing, N.Y., Aug. 15, 1932; s. Martin Gerard and Eileen Bridget (O'Connor) McG.; m. Elizabeth Ann Connelly, Sept. 6, 1958; children: Terrence G., Elizabeth C., Martha E., Connelly T., Daniel M. B.S. in Econs., Fordham U., 1954; LL.B., U. Tex., 1959. Mem. firm Vinson & Elkins, Houston, 1959—, ptnr., 1968—. Bd. dirs. St. Joseph Hosp. Found., U. St. Thomas. Served to capt. USAF, 1955-57. Mem. ABA, Tex. Bar Assn., Houston Bar Assn. Roman Catholic. Clubs: Houston Country, Petroleum. General corporate, Oil and gas leasing. Office: Vinson & Elkins 2701 First City Tower Houston TX 77002

MCGREW, THOMAS JAMES, lawyer; b. Wilkes-Barre, Pa., Jan. 21, 1942; s. James Albert and Mary Alice (Cavan) McG.; children—Jessica Lynn, Benjamin Cavan. A.B. cum laude in English Lit. and Philosophy, U. Scranton, 1963; J.D. cum laude, U. Pa., 1970. Bar: D.C. 1970, U.S. Ct. Appeals (D.C., 5th, 8th, 10th cirs.) 1974, U.S. Supreme Ct. 1974. With Arnold & Porter, Washington, 1970—, ptnr., 1978—; first holder Disting. Visitor from Practice chair Georgetown U. Law Ctr., 1985-86, adj. prof. fed. econ. regulation and deregulation, 1986—. Author: Principles of Advertising Law; monthly columnist The Legal Times, 1981-84; Adweek mag., 1986—; contbr. book revs. to profl. jours. Vol., Peace Corps, Nigeria, 1964-67; mem. nat. council Returned Peace Corps Vols. Mem. ABA, D.C. Bar Assn., Washington Council Lawyers. Administrative and regulatory, Antitrust, Advertising. Office: Arnold & Porter 1200 New Hampshire Ave Washington DC 20036

MCGUANE, FRANK L., JR., lawyer; b. White Plains, N.Y., July 10, 1939; s. Frank L. and Dorothy P. (McGrath) McG.; m. Mari Devers, Oct. 25, 1969 (div.); 1 dau., Lauri Elizabeth. B.A., U. Notre Dame, 1961; J.D., U. Cin., 1968. Bar: Colo. 1968, U.S. Dist. Ct. Colo. 1968, U.S. Ct. Apls. (10th cir.) 1970, U.S. Sup. Ct. 1971. Assoc., Long, Jaudon & Johnson, Denver, 1968-72; assoc. Donald M. Lesher, Denver, 1972-73; ptnr. McGuane and Malone, Denver, 1973—; lectr. in field. Chmn. Denver area chpt. Nat. Eagle Scout Assn. Boy Scouts Am., 1980—; Served with USMC, 1961-63. Fellow Am. Acad. Matrimonial Lawyers; mem. ABA, Colo. Bar Assn., Denver Bar Assn., Arapahoe County Bar Assn., Cath. Lawyers Guild. Club: Heather Ridge Country. Author: Domestic Relations-Colorado Methods of Practice, 1983; contbr. articles to profl. jours. Family and matrimonial. Office: 3773 Cherry Creek N Dr Suite 640 Denver CO 80209

MCGUINN, JOHN FRANCIS, lawyer; b. Chgo., Oct. 29, 1940; s. Martin F. and Margaret (O'Grady) McG.; m. Karen Nuzum, Sept. 27, 1969. BA in Lit., Ill. Benedictine Coll., 1962; JD, U. Ill., 1965. Bar: Ill. 1965, Calif. 1968. Assoc. Jurgensmeyer, McGuinn, Chase & Wotan, Elgin, Ill., 1965-67; dep. mng. atty. internat. legal dept. Bechtel Power Corp., Paris, 1974-76; counsel Middle East legal dept. Bechtel Power Corp., Kuwait City, Kuwait, 1976-78; mgr. internat. auditing Bechtel Power Corp., San Francisco, 1978-80, chief counsel legal dept., 1980—. Mem. ABA (chmn., editor Trends in Contrn. Law, governing com., forum com. on constrn. industry). Club: World Trade, Commonwealth (San Francisco). Avocations: fine arts, ballet, theatre, sports, horse races. Construction, General corporate, Nuclear power. Office: Bechtel Power Corp Legal Dept 50 Beale St San Francisco CA 94105

MCGUIRE, E. JAMES, lawyer; b. Kansas City, Mo., Feb. 10, 1914. AB, U. Calif., 1936, JD, 1948. Bar: Calif. 1948. Jr. acct. exec. McCann-Erickson Inc., San Francisco, 1938-39; mgr. advt. and sales promotion Calif. Almond Growers Exchange, Sacramento, 1939-41; asst. advt. mgr. Pacific Rural Press, San Francisco, 1941-42; officer Dist. Legal Office 12th Naval Dist., San Francisco, 1946-49; ptnr. O'Gara and McGuire, San Francisco, 1949—; lectr. Calif. Continuing Edn. of Bar, 1964. Served to lt. comdr. USNR, 1942-46. Mem. ABA, San Francisco Bar Assn., Alameda County Bar Assn., Phi Delta Phi. Clubs: Commonwealth of Calif.; Sequoyah Country (Oakland) (dir. 1970-74, v.p. 1973-74). Federal civil litigation, State civil litigation, General practice. Home: 889 Longridge Rd Oakland CA 94610 Office: Alcoa Bldg 1 Maritime Plaza Suite 950 San Francisco CA 94111

MCGUIRE, EDWARD DAVID, JR., lawyer; b. Waynesboro, Va., Apr. 11, 1948; s. Edward David and Mary Estelle (Angus) McG.; m. Georgia Ann Charuhas, Aug. 15, 1971; children: Matthew Edward, Kathryn Ann. BS in Commerce, U. Va., 1970; JD, Coll. William and Mary, 1973. Bar: Va. 1973, D.C. 1974, U.S. Dist. Ct. (ea. dist.) Va. 1974, U.S. Dist. Ct. D.C. 1974, U.S. Ct. Appeals (4th cir.) 1974, U.S. Ct. Appeals (D.C. cir.) 1974. Assoc. Wilkes and Artis, Washington, 1973-78; gen. corp counsel Mark Winkler Mgmt., Alexandria, Va., 1978-80; sr. contracts officer Amtrak, Washington, 1980-81; sr. real estate atty., asst. corp. sec. Peoples Drug Stores, Inc., Alexandria, 1981—. Bd. dirs. Dist. XVI Va. Student Aid Found., 1978—, George Washington Dist. Boy Scouts Am., 1986. Served to capt. JAGC, USANG, 1973-79. Mem. ABA, Va. Bar Assn., D.C. Bar Assn., Alexandria Bar Assn., Assn. Trial Lawyers Am., Va. Trial Lawyers Assn., Internat. Council Shopping Ctrs., William and Mary Law Sch. Assn. (bd. dirs., pres.-elect 1986-87). Greek Orthodox. Lodge: Rotary (Springfield, Va. treas. 1985-86, sec. 1986-87, pres.-elect 1987—, named Outstanding Rotarian 1984-85). Avocations: raquetball, softball, spectator sports. Real property, Contracts commercial, General corporate. Home: 31 Myrtle St Alexandria VA 22301 Office: Peoples Drug Stores Inc Legal Dept 6315 Bren Mar Dr Alexandria VA 22312

MCGUIRE, EUGENE GUENARD, lawyer; b. N.Y.C., Apr. 1, 1945; s. Edward Joseph and Carmen Isabel (Guenard) McG.; m. Pamela Jean Cottam, Sept. 14, 1969; children—Lauren Lambert, Christopher Cottam. B.Arch., Cornell U., 1967; J.D., Columbia U., 1970. Bar: N.Y. 1971, U.S. Ct. Appeals (2d cir.) 1974, U.S. Dist. Ct. (so. dist.) N.Y. 1972, U.S. Dist. Ct. (ea. dist.) N.Y. 1972. Assoc., Winthrop, Stimson, Putnam & Roberts, N.Y.C., 1970-79; counsel Texasgulf, Inc., Stamford, Conn., 1979-81, sr. counsel, asst. sec., 1981—; sr. counsel, asst. sec., Elf Aquitaine Inc., Stamford, 1983—, v.p.-law, 1987—. Mem. ABA, Westchester-Fairfield Corp. Counsel Assn. Quaker. Club: Am. Yacht (Rye, N.Y.). Antitrust, General corporate, Securities. Office: Elf Aquitaine Inc High Ridge Park Stamford CT 06904

MCGUIRE, HAROLD FREDERICK, lawyer; b. N.Y.C., Nov. 8, 1937; s. Harold Frederick and Lillian Virginia (Jones) McG.; m. Iris Horn, Sept. 23, 1972; 1 child, Daniel. AB, Princeton U., 1959; LLB, Columbia U., 1962. Bar: N.Y. 1962, U.S. Dist. Ct. (so. and ea. dists.) N.Y. 1964, U.S. Ct. Appeals (2d, 3d and 5th cirs.) 1966, U.S. Supreme Ct. 1966. Assoc. Cravath, Swaine & Moore, N.Y.C., 1963-69; asst. U.S. atty. U.S. Dist. Ct. (so. dist.) N.Y., N.Y.C., 1969-74; ptnr. Gilbert, Segall & Young, N.Y.C., 1974-77, McGuire & Tiernan and predecessor firms, N.Y.C., 1978—. Served with U.S. Army, 1962-63. Mem. ABA, N.Y. State Bar Assn., Assn. of Bar of City of N.Y., Fed. Bar Council. Democrat. Club: University (N.Y.C.). Federal civil litigation, Criminal, Antitrust. Home: 150 E 77th St New York NY 10021 Office: McGuire & Tiernan 230 Park Ave New York NY 10169

MCGUIRE, JOHN FRANCIS, lawyer; b. N.Y.C., Aug. 29, 1945; s. John F. Sr. and Gertrude (Quast) McG.; m. Lynne Marie Randazzo, June 9, 1968; children: Kerry L., John F. III, Patrice M., Brian F. BS, U.S. Naval Acad., 1968; MS, So. Ill. U., 1971; JD, Marquette U., 1975. Bar: Calif. 1976, Wis. 1976. Assoc. McInnis, Fitzgerald, Rees, Sharkey & McIntyre, San Diego, 1975-78; ptnr. Thorsnes, Bartolotta, McGuire & Padilla, San Diego, 1978—; bd. dirs. Bank Rancho Bernardo, San Diego. Thomas Moore scholar Marquette Bd. Govs., 1975; decorated Purple Heart. Mem. Calif. Bar Assn., Wis. Bar Assn., San Diego County Bar Assn., Calif. Trial Lawyers Assn., San Diego Trial Lawyers Assn. (Outstanding Trial Lawyer 1982, Trial Lawyer of Yr. 1983), Order of Barristers. Democrat. Roman Catholic. Avocations: surfing, golf. Construction, State civil litigation, Insurance. Home: PO Box 2492 Rancho Santa Fe CA 92067 Office: Thorsnes Bartolotta McGuire & Padilla 2550 Fifth Ave Suite 1100 San Diego CA 92103

MCGUIRE, PATRICIA A., lawyer; b. Phila.; d. Edward J. and Mary R. McGuire. BA cum laude, Trinity Coll., 1974; JD, Georgetown U., 1977. Bar: Pa. 1977, U.S. Ct. Appeals (D.C. cir.) 1979. Program dir. Georgetown U. St. Law Clinic, Washington, 1977-82; asst. dean for devel. and external affairs Georgetown U. Law Ctr., Washington, 1982—; adj. prof. law Georgetown U., 1977-82; legal commentator CBS News 30 Minutes, N.Y.C., 1978-80, WTTG "Panorama", Washington, 1980-82. Editor: Street Law Mock Trial Manual, 1984; contbr. articles to profl. jours. Recipient Daytime Emmy, TV Acad., N.Y.C., 1979-80. Mem. ABA, Assn. Am. Law Schs. (instl. advancement 1985—), Council for the Advancement and Support of Edn., Trinity Coll. Alumnae Assn. (pres. 1986—). Democrat. Roman Catholic. Legal education, Probate, Estate planning. Office: Georgetown U Law Ctr 600 New Jersey NW Washington DC 20001

MCGUIRE, WILLIAM B(ENEDICT), lawyer; b. Newark, Feb. 14, 1929; m. Joan Glinane, June 3, 1968; children—Joan Ellen, Ralph R., James C., Keith P., Grant W. B.S., Fordham U., 1950; J.D., Seton Hall U., 1958; LL.M. in Taxation, NYU, 1963. Bar: N.J. 1958, U.S. Dist. Ct. N.J. 1958, U.S. Supreme Ct. 1971, U.S. Ct. Appeals (3rd cir.) 1980, N.Y. 1982. Chief acct. Hanover Fire Ins. Co., N.Y.C., 1950-58; sr. ptnr. Lum, Biunno & Tompkins, Newark, 1958-83, Tompkins, Mc Guire & Wachenfeld, 1984—; asst. prosecutor Essex County, N.J., 1964-65; mem. bds. Ind. Coll. Fund of N.J., St. Peter's Coll.; trustee St. Barnabas Hosp.; mem. Essex County Ethics Com., 1974-77; mem. com. to review State Commn. of Investigation, 1982. Fellow Am. Coll. Trial Lawyers, Am. Bar Found., Am. Bd. Trial Advocates; mem. ABA, N.J. State Bar Assn. (trustee 1982—), Essex County Bar Assn. (pres. 1975-76), Internat. Assn. Ins. Counsel, Fedn. Ins. Counsel, Def. Research Inst., Maritime Law Assn. U.S., Am. Arbitration Assn., Trial Attys. N.J., Assn. Fed. Bar N.J. (1st v.p. 1983—). Roman Catholic. Club: Essex County Country (pres. 1983), Essex. Federal civil litigation, Insurance, State civil litigation. Home: 15 Tioga Pass Short Hills NJ 07078 Office: 550 Broad St Newark NJ 07102

MCGUIRL, MARLENE DANA CALLIS, law educator, law librarian; b. Hammond, Ind., Mar. 22, 1938; d. Daniel David and Helen Elizabeth (Baludis) Callis; m. James Franklin McGuirl, Apr. 24, 1965. A.B., Ind. U., 1959; J.D., DePaul U., 1963; M.A.L.S., Rosary Coll., 1965; LL.M., George Washington U., 1978, postgrad. Harvard U., 1985. Bar: Ill. 1963, Ind. 1964, D.C. 1972. Asst., DePaul Coll. of Law Library, 1961-62, asst. law librarian, 1962-65; ref. law librarian Boston Coll. Sch. Law, 1965-66; library dir. D.C. Bar Library, 1966-70; asst. chief Am.-Brit. Law div. Law Library of Library of Congress, Washington, 1970, chief Am.-Brit. Law div., 1970—; library cons. Nat. Clearinghouse on Poverty Law, OEO, Washington, 1967-69, Northwestern U. Nat. Inst. Edn. in Law and Poverty, 1969, D.C. Office of Corp. Counsel, 1969-70; instr. law librarianship Grad. Sch. of U.S. Dept. of Agr., 1968-72; lectr. legal lit. Cath. U., 1972; adj. asst. prof., 1973—; lectr. environ. law George Washington U., 1979—; judge Nat. and Internat. Law Moot Ct. Competition, 1976-78; pres. Hamburger Heaven, Inc., Palm Beach, Fla., 1981—, L'Image de Marlene, Inc., 1986—; dir. Stoneridge Farm Inc., Gt. Falls, Va., 1984—. Mem. Georgetown Citizens Assn.; trustee D.C. Law Students in Ct.; del. Ind. Democratic Conv., 1964. Recipient Meritorious Service award Library of Congress, 1974, letter of commendation Dir. of Personnel, 1976, cert. of appreciation, 1981-84. Mem. ABA (facilities law library Congress com. 1976—), Fed. Bar Assn. (chpt. council 1972-76), Ill. Bar Assn., Women's Bar Assn. (pres. 1972-73, exec. bd. 1973-77, Outstanding Contbn. to Human Rights award 1975), D.C. Bar Assn., Am. Bar Found., Nat. Assn. Women Lawyers, Internat. Assn. Law Libraries, (exec. bd. 1973-77), Law Librarians Soc. of Washington (pres. 1971-73), Exec. Women in Govt. Clubs: Nat. Lawyers, Zonta. Contbr. articles profl. jours. Private international, Environment, Librarianship. Home: 3416 P St NW Washington DC 20007 Office: American British Law Div Library of Congress Washington DC 20540

MCGUIRL, SUSAN ELIZABETH, lawyer; b. Providence, Sept. 10, 1952; d. John Raymond and Rita Mary (Ryan) McG. BA, R.I. Coll., 1974; JD, Suffolk U., 1977. Bar: R.I. 1977, U.S. Dist. Ct. R.I. 1977, U.S. Ct. Appeals (1st cir.) 1983, U.S. Supreme Ct. 1983. Spl. asst. atty. gen. State of R.I., Providence, 1977-80, dep. atty. gen., 1980-84; assoc. Lipsey & Skolnik, Providence, 1985-87; ptnr. Cerilli, McGuirl, Hustwit & Bicki, Providence, 1987—. Pres. R.I. Young Dems., 1974-76; mem. R.I. Coll. Found., 1984—, Providence 350 Jubilee Commn., 1986—; chmn. R.I. Coll. Ann. Drive, 1986—. Recipient Woman's Achievement award Gov.'s Adv. Com. on Women, 1980; Named Hon. Capt. R.I. State Police, 1982, Woman of Yr., R.I. Jaycees, 1983. Mem. ABA, R.I. Bar Assn., R.I. Women's Bar Assn. (chmn. 1985—), Assn. Trial Lawyers Am., R.I. Trial Lawyers Assn. Democrat. Roman Catholic. Avocation: photography. Personal injury, State civil litigation, Family and matrimonial. Office: Cerilli McGuirl Hustwit & Bicki 56 Pine St Providence RI 02903

MCGURK, EUGENE DAVID, JR., lawyer; b. Phila., Feb. 27, 1951; s. Eugene David and Mary Rose (O'Donnell) McG.; m. Kathleen Mary Murphy, Dec. 28, 1973 (dec. Aug. 1978). B.A., LaSalle Coll., 1973; J.D., Del. Law Sch., 1978. Bar: Pa. 1978, N.J. 1978, U.S. Dist. Ct. (ea. dist.) Pa. 1978, U.S. Dist. Ct. N.J. 1978, U.S. Ct. Appeals (3d cir.) 1981, U.S. Supreme Ct. 1982. Mgmt. analyst Mng. Dirs. Office, Phila., 1974-76; adminstr. Dept. Commerce, Phila., 1976-78; asst. city solicitor law dept. City of Phila., 1978-81; assoc. Raynes, McCarty, Binder, Ross & Mundy, Phila., 1981—; mem. Bench Bar com., 1982—, Legis. Liaison com., 1982—, Profl. Responsibility com., 1982—; guest lectr. Thomas Jefferson U. Med. Sch., 1983, 84, Del. Law Sch., 1980, Med. Coll. Pa., 1983, 84; vis. instr. Dept. Community and Preventive Medicine, 1983—. Mem. Camden County Bd. Elections, 1970; bd. of overseers Del. Law Sch., 1985—. Recipient award Fed. Bar Assn., 1978, Mayoral award City of Phila. Mem. ABA, Assn. Trial Lawyers Am., Pa. Bar Assn., N.J. Bar Assn., Camden County Bar Assn., Phila. Bar Assn., Del. Law Sch. Alumni (bd. dirs. 1980—, v.p. 1982-85, pres. 1985—), Phi Kappa Phi. State civil litigation, Federal civil litigation. Home: 144 Embassy Row Uxbridge Cherry Hill NJ 08034 Office: Raynes McCarty Binder Ross & Mundy PA 1845 Walnut St Philadelphia PA 19103 Office: Raynes McCarty Binder Ross & Mundy PA 9 Tanner St Haddonfield NJ 08033

MC HENRY, POWELL, lawyer; b. Cin., May 14, 1926; s. L. Lee and Marguerite L. (Powell) McH.; m. Venna Mae Guerrea, Aug. 27, 1948; children: Scott, Marshall, Jody Lee, Gale Lynn. A.B., U. Cin., 1949; LL.B., Harvard U., 1951, J.D., 1969. Bar: Ohio 1951. Assoc. Dinsmore, Shohl, Sawyer & Dinsmore, Cin., 1951-58; ptnr. Dinsmore, Shohl, Coates & Deupree (and predecessors), Cin., 1958-75; gen. counsel Federated Dept. Stores, Inc., 1971-75; assoc. gen. counsel Procter & Gamble Co., 1975-76, v.p., gen. counsel, 1976-83, sr. v.p., gen. counsel, 1983—; Dir. Republican Club of Hamilton County, Ohio, 1957-58. Served with USNR, 1944-46. Recipient award of merit Ohio Legal Center Inst., 1969. Mem. Am. Judicature Soc., ABA, Ohio Bar Assn., Cin. Bar Assn. (pres. 1979), Harvard Law Sch. Assn. Cin. (pres. 1960-61), Def. Research Inst., Cin. Council on World Affairs, Assn. of Gen. Counsel (pres. 1986—), Hamilton County Defender Commn. Methodist. Clubs: Harvard, Western Hill Country (dir. 1964-70, sec. 1966-69, treas. 1969-70), Queen City, Commonwealth, Diogenese. General corporate. Home: 1960 Beech Grove Dr Cincinnati OH 45238 Office: PO Box 599 Cincinnati OH 45201

MCHUGH, JAMES BERNARD, lawyer; b. Camden, N.J., Nov. 23, 1950; s. Bernard Joseph and Rosemary (Patterson) McH.; m. Lindsay Jean Campbell, Jan. 7, 1975; 1 child, Katherine. BA, Syracuse U., 1971; JD, U. Chgo., 1974. Bar: N.Y. 1975, U.S. Dist. Ct. (so. dist.) N.Y. 1975. Assoc. Cleary, Gottlieb, Steen & Hamilton, N.Y.C., 1974-81; v.p., assoc. gen. counsel Goldman, Sachs & Co., N.Y.C., 1981—. Mem. ABA, N.Y. State Bar Assn., Assn. of Bar of City of N.Y., Internat. Bar Assn. Securities, Private international, General corporate. Home: 11 Roosevelt Rd Maplewood NJ 07040 Office: Goldman Sachs & Co 85 Broad St New York NY 10004

MCHUGH, MARGARET COLLEEN, lawyer; b. Cleve., Nov. 10, 1946; d. James Anthony and Donella (Hostler) McH.; 1 child, Gregg McHugh Smolenski. BJ, So. Meth. U., 1969; JD, St. Mary's U., San Antonio, 1981. Bar: Tex. 1981, U.S. Dist. Ct. (so. dist.) Tex. 1982, U.S. Ct. Appeals (5th cir.) 1983, U.S. Dist. Ct. (ea. dist.) Tex. 1985. Assoc. Sorrell, Anderson, Lehrman & Wanner, Corpus Christi, Tex., 1981-84, Head & Kendrick, Corpus Christi, 1984—; mem. com. alternative dispute resolution Tex. State Bar, Austin, 1985—, chmn., 1987—; pres., bd, dirs. Nueces County Dispute Resolution Ctr., Corpus Christi, 1985—. Mem. Jr. League Corpus Christi, 1983—; mem. adv. bd., bd. dirs. Gulf Coast Council Boy Scouts Am., Corpus Christi, 1985—. Fellow Tex. Bar Found.; mem. ABA, Tex. Bar Assn., Nueces County Bar Assn. (sec. 1984-85, treas. 1985-86, v.p. 1986-87), Tex. Assn. Def. Counsel. Avocations: ballet, tennis. Labor, Personal injury, Insurance. Home: 311 Montclair Corpus Christi TX 78412 Office: Head & Kendrick 1020 1st City Bank Tower Corpus Christi TX 78477

MCHUGH, THOMAS EDWARD, state supreme court justice; b. Charleston, W.Va., Mar. 26, 1936; s. Paul and Melba McH.; m. Judith McHugh, Mar. 14, 1959; children: Karen, Cindy, James, John. A.B., W.Va. U., 1958, LL.B., 1964. Bar: W.Va. 1964. Individual practice law Charleston, 1964-66; law clk. to Judge Harlan Calhoun, W.Va. Supreme Ct. of Appeals, 1966-68; individual practice law Charleston, 1969-74; chief judge W.Va. Circuit Ct., 13th Jud. Circuit, Fairmont, W.Va., 1974-80; asso. justice W.Va. Supreme Ct., Charleston, 1980—. Bd. dirs. Goodwill Industries. Served to 1st lt. U.S. Army, 1958-61. Mem. W.Va. Jud. Assn., Am. Judicature Soc., W.Va. Bar Assn., Order of the Coif. Democrat. Roman Catholic. Club: Serra (Charleston). Jurisprudence. Office: Supreme Ct Bldg Charleston WV 25305 *

MCHUGH, WILLIAM F., legal educator; b. Stamford, Conn., June 23, 1933; s. William Thomas and Dorothy Amelia (Hanson) M.; m. Donna Hubbard, Apr. 10, 1960; children—William, Holly, Brian. B.A. in English Lit., Colgate U., 1956; J.D., Union U., Albany, N.Y., 1959. Bar: N.Y. 1960. Law clk. N.Y. State Supreme Ct., 1960-61; assoc. counsel Cornell U., Ithaca, N.Y., 1962-64; assoc. counsel SUNY, 1964-71; prof. law Am. U., Washington, 1971-73; prof. law Fla. State U., Tallahassee, 1973—; cons. and lectr. in law. Named Prof. of Yr., Fla. State U. Law Sch., 1976. Mem. N.Y. State Bar Assn., Nat. Assn. Coll. and Univ. Attys., Am. Assn. Law Schs., Soc. Profls. in Dispute Resolution. Episcopalian. Author: Contract Law for Electrical Contractors; contbr. articles to profl. jours. Contracts commercial, Labor, Legal education. Office: Fla State U Coll Law Tallahassee FL 32306

MCILVAINE, JAMES ROSS, lawyer; b. Youngstown, Ohio, July 22, 1944; s. Earl Eugene and Caroline E. (Clawson) McI.; m. Carol Beth Boyer, June 24, 1967; children—Andrew S., Katherine Erin. B.A., Muskingum Coll., 1966; J.D. cum laude, Ohio State Coll. Law, 1969. Bar: Ohio 1969, U.S. Dist. Ct. (no. dist.) Ohio 1971. Assoc. Oestricher, Seamon, Newman & Knoll, Akron, 1969-70; asst. pros. atty. Summit County Prosecutor's Office, Akron, 1970-71; ptnr. law firm Palecek, McIlvaine, Foreman & Paul, Wadsworth, Ohio, 1971—. Bd. dirs. Medina County Law Library, 1979-83, Wadsworth chpt. ARC, 1981—; mem. Citizen's Adv. Bd., Medina County Correctional Facility Study, 1983. Mem. Ohio Acad. Trial Lawyers (editor profl. newsletter 1982—, chairperson regional trial seminars 1980-81, sec. 1981-83, lectr. criminal law seminar 1981, ins. law seminar 1980, 84, 86, negligence law seminar 1984, 86, chairperson Student Advocacy div. 1976-78, pres. 1984-85, trustee, bd. dirs. 1976-83), Medina County Bar Assn. (pres. 1983, dir.), Assn. Trial Lawyers Am. (state del. 1985-87, bd. govs. 1987), Ohio State Bar Assn. Club: Lions. Personal injury, State civil litigation, Family and matrimonial. Office: Palecek McIlvaine Foreman & Paul 210 Bank One Bldg Wadsworth OH 44281

MCILVAINE, STEPHEN BROWNLEE, lawyer; b. Dover, Ohio, Feb. 28, 1953; s. Earl Eugene and Caroline Elmira (Clawson) McI.; m. Sarah Sue Aubihl, June 4, 1977; children: Jacob Ross, Alexander Jentes. BA, Muskingum Coll., 1975; JD, Ohio No. U., 1978. Bar: Ohio 1978, U.S. Dist. Ct. (no. dist.) Ohio 1982. Asst. pros. atty. Tuscarawas County Prosecutor's Office, New Philadelphia, Ohio, 1978-79; assoc. Luck, Palecek, McIlvaine & Foreman, Wadsworth, Ohio, 1979-81, Palecek, McIlvaine & Foreman, Wadsworth, 1981-83; ptnr. Palecek, McIlvaine, Foreman & Paul, Wadsworth, Ohio, 1983—. Campaign chmn. Wadsworth Rep. Com., Ohio, 1982—; trustee Wadsworth-Rittman Hosp., Ohio, 1983—; mem. Fair Housing and Human Relations Commn., Wadsworth, 1984—; adv. bd. Salvation Army, Wadsworth, 1986. Mem. Ohio State Bar Assn., Medina County Bar Assn., Ohio Acad. Trial Lawyers. Lutheran. Lodge: Lions. State civil litigation, Probate, Criminal. Home: 303 Dohner Dr Wadsworth OH 44281 Office: Palecek McIlvaine Foreman & Paul 210 Bank One Bldg Wadsworth OH 44281

MC INERNEY, DENIS, lawyer; b. N.Y.C., May 31, 1925; s. Denis and Ann (Keane) McI.; m. Mary Irene Murphy, Nov. 14, 1953; children: Kathleen, Denis J., Maura. B.S.S., Fordham U., 1948, J.D. cum laude, 1951. Bar: N.Y. 1951, D.C. 1961. Instr. philosophy Fordham U., 1948-51; since practiced in N.Y.C.; sr. partner firm Cahill Gordon & Reindel; vice chmn. Com. Character and Fitness Admission State Bar N.Y., 1st Jud. Dept., 1979—; lectr. in field. Co-author: Practitioners Handbook for Appeals to the Appellate Divisions of the State of New York, 1979, Practitioners Handbook for Appeals to the Court of Appeals of the State of New York, 1981. Served with AUS, 1943-46. Decorated knight of Malta; recipient Achievement in Law award Fordham U., 1977. Fellow Am. Coll. Trial Lawyers (state chmn. 1980-82); mem. ABA, N.Y. State Bar Assn., New York County Lawyers Assn. (pres. 1982-84), Fordham U. Law Alumni Assn. (pres. 1968-72, medal of achievement 1975). Roman Catholic. Clubs: Westchester Country, Univ. Home: Bellevue Ave Rye NY 10580 Office: 80 Pine St New York NY 10005

MCINERNEY, GARY JOHN, lawyer; b. Grand Rapids, Mich., Oct. 4, 1948; s. James Martin and Margery (Dumas) McI.; m. Juliet McInerney, Nov. 27, 1970; children: Ryan, John, Patrick, Kevin, Molly. BA, Notre Dame U., 1970, JD, 1973. Bar: Mich. 1973, U.S. Dist. Ct. (we. and ea. dists.) Mich. 1973, U.S. Supreme Ct. 1976. Assoc. Varnum, Riddering et al, Grand Rapids, 1973-74; ptnr. Murphy, Burns et al, Grand Rapids, 1974-86; pres. Gary J. McInerney, P.C., Grand Rapids, 1986—. Pres. Cath. Social Services, Grand Rapids; v.p. Kent County Legal Aid Soc., Grand Rapids; mem. devel. bd. St. Mary's Hosp., Grand Rapids; 5th congl. dist. chmn. Sesquicentenniel commn. State of Mich., 1984-86; Dem. nominee 5th dist. U.S. Congress, 1984. Mem. Am. Trial Lawyers Assn., Mich. Trial Lawyers Assn., Mich. Bar Assn. (criminal jurisprudence, med. legal, atty. arbitration coms.), Mich. BC/BS (bd. dirs.), Kent County Bar Assn., Grand Rapids Bar Assn., Grand Rapids C. of C. (pres. 1985-86). Roman Catholic. Clubs: Kent County, Peninsular (Grand Rapids). Federal civil litigation, State civil litigation, General corporate.

MCINNIS, EMMETT EMORY, JR., lawyer; b. McAlester, Okla., Sept. 12, 1920; s. Emmett Emory and Helen Franc (Kohler) M.; m. Howardine Muse McAteer, Nov. 5, 1949; children—Howard Emmett (dec.), Guy Bruce, Susan Muse. B.S. in History, Northwestern U., 1945; LL.B., Yale U., 1948. Bar: Wash. 1951, Seattle-King County 1951, U.S. Supreme Ct. 1958. Sole practice Seattle, 1951—; lectr. in trust and probate. Mem., Exchange Club, Seattle, pres., 1956; mem. Republican Nat. Com., 1981—; mem. Estate Planning Council, Seattle, 1954—, pres., 1973. Mem. Seattle Power Squadron (comdr. 1971), Northwestern U. Alumni Assn. Western Wash. (pres. 1965), Nat. Rifle Assn., Delta Tau Delta. Republican. Presbyterian. (elder 1961—). Club: Wash. Athletic (Seattle). Probate, Estate taxation, General corporate. Home: 5515 NE Penrith Rd Seattle WA 98105

MCINTOSH, BRUCE TERENCE, lawyer; b. Pasadena, Calif., May 9, 1948; s. Thomas William and Agnes (Schemmer) McI.; m. Susan Bosler, Nov. 20, 1982; 1 child, Ashley Marie. BA, U. San Francisco, 1970; JD, UCLA, 1973. Bar: Calif. 1974, U.S. Dist. Ct. (cen. dist.) Calif. 1974, U.S. Dist. Ct. (so. dist.) Calif. 1979, U.S. Dist. Ct. (ea. dist.) Calif. 1986. Assoc. Loeb & Loeb, Los Angeles, 1974-75, Murchison & Cumming, Los Angeles, 1975-80, Fogel, Rothschild, Feldman &Ostrov, Los Angeles, 1980-84; ptnr. Brown, Reed & Gibson, Pasadena, 1984—. Vol. Pasadena (Calif.) Tournament of Roses, 1973—. Served to capt. U.S. Army, 1973-74. Mem. Los Angeles County Bar Assn. (chmn. arbitration com. 1985—, constl. rights found., Lawyer of Yr. 1978, 86), Beverly Hills Bar Assn., Wilshire Bar Assn. (bd. of govs. 1979-85), Calif. Bar Assn., Assn. Trial Lawyers Am., Calif. Trial Lawyers Assn., Los Angeles Trial Lawyers Assn., Breakfast Roundtable. Democrat. Roman Catholic. Lodge: Optimists. Avocations: golf, tennis. State civil litigation, Real property, Personal injury. Office: Brown Reed & Gibson 600 S Lake Ave #300 Pasadena CA 91106

MCINTOSH, DOUGLAS MALCOLM, lawyer; b. Miami, Fla., Aug. 23, 1955; s. Donald Winston and Patricia (Mapleton) McI.; m. Theresa Tomey, Feb. 26, 1983. BA, Boston Coll., 1977; JD, Nova U., 1981. Bar: Fla. 1981, U.S. Dist. Ct. (so. dist.) Fla. 1981, U.S. Ct. Appeals (5th and 11th cirs.) 1981, U.S. Supreme Ct. 1986. Assoc. Dixon, Dixon, Hurst & Nicklaus, Miami, 1981-84, ptnr., 1984—. Pres. Bayberry Village Homeowners Assn., Plantation, Fla., 1984-85. Mem. ABA, Dade County Bar Assn., Fla. Def. Lawyers Assn., Southeastern Admiralty Law Inst., Nova U. Law Alumni Assn. (sec. 1984-85, pres.-elect 1985-86, pres. 1986—). Democrat. Roman Catholic. Club: Tower (Ft. Lauderdale). Avocations: sports, exercise, fishing, golf. State civil litigation, Federal civil litigation, Personal injury. Office: Dixon Dixon Hurst & Nicklaus 100 N Biscayne Blvd #1500 Miami FL 33132

MCINTOSH, JAMES ALBERT, lawyer; b. Long Beach, Calif., Nov. 2, 1933; s. James H. and Grace I. (Greenwell) McI.; m. Earlene Rae Bagley, June 22, 1956; children—Richard, Robert, Debra, Bruce, Linda, Sheri, Diane. B.S., U.S. Mil. Acad., 1955; J.D., U. Utah Law Sch., 1961. Bar: Utah 1961. Law clk. to justice Utah Supreme Ct., 1960-61; dep. county atty. Salt Lake County, 1962-66; legal adv. flood control and storm drainage matters Bd. Salt Lake County Commrs., 1967-73; prin. James A. McIntosh & Assocs., Salt Lake City, 1974-77; sole practice, Salt Lake City, 1961-74; ptnr. McMurray & McIntosh, 1977-84; sole practice, Salt Lake City, 1984-85, officer, ptnr. James A. McIntosh Assocs., P.C., 1985—. Trustee, U.S. Bankruptcy Ct. Utah, 1962-69. Served to 1st lt. U.S. Army, 1955-58. Recipient Am. Jurisprudence award, 1961. Mem. ABA, Fla. Bar Assn., Utah State Bar, Utah Trial Lawyers Assn., Salt Lake County Bar Assn., Assn. Trial Lawyers Am., Phi Delta Phi. Mem. Ch. Jesus Christ of Latter-day Saints. Club: Exchange (dist. pres. 1980-81). State civil litigation, General corporate, Real property. Office: James A McIntosh & Assocs PC Intrade Bldg S 1399 South 700 East Suite 14 Salt Lake City UT 84105

MCINTOSH, JAMES ARTHUR, lawyer; b. Terre Haute, Ind., Sept. 11, 1948; s. John Arthur and Norma Francis (Leaf) McI.; m. Sharon Kay Edwards, Mar. 21, 1970; children: Brian David, Jeffery Allen. Student, Creighton U., 1968-69; BS, U. Tenn., 1971, JD, 1974. Bar: Tenn. 1974, U.S. Dist. Ct. (ea. dist.) Tenn. 1974, U.S. Supreme Ct. 1979, U.S. Ct. Appeals (6th cir.) 1984. Ptnr. Ambrose, Wilson & Grimm, Knoxville, Tenn., 1974-81, Lockridge & Becker, P.C., Knoxville, 1981-84; prin. Robertson, Williams, Ingram & Overbey, Knoxville, 1984—; trustee in bankruptcy U.S. Bankruptcy Ct., Eastern Dist. Tenn., Knoxville, 1977-79. Mem. ABA, Tenn. Bar Assn., Knoxville Assn. Republican. Episcopalian. Avocations: running, hiking. Bankruptcy, Contracts commercial, Insurance. Office: Robertson Williams et al 10th Fl Andrew Johnson Plaza Knoxville TN 37901

MCINTYRE, ANITA GRACE, lawyer; b. Louisville, Jan. 29, 1947; d. Blakely Gordon and Shirley Evans (Grubbs) Jordan; m. Kenneth J. McIntyre, Oct. 11, 1969; children: Abigail, Jordan Kenneth. BA, Smith Coll., 1969; JD, U. Detroit, 1975. Bar: Mich. 1975, U.S. Dist. Ct. (ea. dist.) Mich. 1975, U.S. Ct. Appeals (6th cir.) 1976, U.S. Dist. Ct. (we. dist.) Mich. 1977. Atty. Motor Vehicle Mfrs. Assn., Detroit, 1975; ptnr. Prekel, Pacquette, Keida & White, Troy, Mich., 1975-79; vis. prof. Detroit Coll. Law, 1979-81; assoc. Tyler & Canham, P.C., Detroit, 1981-83; sole practice Grosse Pointe, Mich., 1983—. Sec. Berry Hist. Dist., 1975-79. Mem. ABA, Women Lawyers Assn. Mich., Smith Coll. Club Detroit (chairperson candidates com. 1982—). Club: Detroit Boat. Construction, Federal civil litigation, Bankruptcy.

MCINTYRE, BERNARD, lawyer, public administrator; b. Wilmington, N.C., Aug. 4, 1955; s. Arnold McIntyre and Hattie (Moore) McIntyre Sidbury; m. Beverly Dore, Aug. 8, 1981; 1 child, Emily Brooke. BA, U. N.C., 1977; MA in Pub. Adminstrn., Atlanta U., 1979; JD, U. S.C., 1982. Bar: S.C. 1982, U.S. Dist. Ct. S.C. 1983, U.S. Ct. Appeals (4th cir.) 1985. Staff/mng. atty. Neighborhood Legal Assistance Program Inc., Beaufort, S.C., 1982-84; judicature panel atty. Neighborhood Legal Assistance Program Inc., Charleston, S.C., 1984—; assoc. Moss, Bailey, Dore & Kuhn, P.A., Beaufort, 1984—; atty. Coastal Speech and Hearing Clinic, Beaufort, 1985, Beaufort County Dept. Social Services, 1986—. Contbr. articles to newspapers and profl. jours. Regent Beaufort County Meml. Hosp., 1984—; 2d v.p. Boys Club of Greater Beaufort, 1985—; mem. long range planning com. City of Beaufort, 1985—; panel mem. Guardian Ad Litem Tng. Program Abused and Neglected Children, 1986—; team tutor Beaufort County Acad. Olympics, 1984, 1987; candidate Beaufort City Council, 1987. Recipient Outstanding Service award Rocky Point (N.C.) Bd. Trustees, 1983; named one of Outstanding Young Men of Am., U.S. Jaycees, 1983; Ford fellow, 1978, 79. Mem. ABA, Assn. Trial Lawyers' Am., S.C. Bar Assn., S.C. Trial Lawyers Assn., Beaufort County Bar Assn. Democrat. Baptist. Avocations: basketball, reading, backgammon, jogging. Personal injury, Criminal, Family and matrimonial. Home: 2002 Roper St Beaufort SC 29902 Office: Moss Bailey Dore & Kuhn PA 1501 North St Beaufort SC 29902

MCINTYRE, DOUGLAS CARMICHAEL, II, lawyer; b. Lumberton, N.C., Aug. 6, 1956; s. Douglas Carmichael and Thelma Riley (Hedgpeth) McI.; m. Lola Denise Strickland, June 26, 1982; children: Joshua Carmichael, Stephen Christopher. BA, U. N.C., 1978, JD, 1981. Bar: N.C. 1981, U.S. Dist. Ct. (ea. dist.) N.C. 1984, U.S. Dist. Ct. (mid. dist.) N.C. 1985. Assoc. Law Office Bruce Higgins, Lumberton, 1981-82, McLean, Stacy, Henry & McLean, Lumberton, 1982-86; ptnr. Price & McIntyre P.A., Lumberton, 1987—; mem. law-focused edn. adv. com. N.C. Dept. Pub. Instrn., 1986-87. Del. Dem. Nat. Conv., N.Y.C., 1980, N.C. Dems., Raleigh, 1974—; pres. Robeson County Young Dems., Lumberton, 1982; sec., treas. 7th Congl. Dist. Young Dems., N.C., 1983, chmn., 1984; 2d vice chmn. 7th Congl. Dist. Dems. So. N.C., 1986—; mem. state adv. bd. North Carolinians Against Drug and Alcohol Abuse, Raleigh, 1984-85; chmn. Morehead Scholarship Selection Com., Robeson County, 1985—; deacon Presbyn. Ch.; active Boy Scouts Am., Lumberton, 1983; chmn. Robeson County U.S. Constn. Bicentennial com., 1986-87; mem. lawyers' adv. com. to N.C. Commn. on Bicentennial of U.S. Constn., 1986—; bd. dirs. Robeson County Group Home, Lumberton, 1984—, Lumberton Econ. Advancement for Downtown, Inc., 1987—; mem. N.C. Mus. of History Assocs., 1987—. Morehead Found. scholar, 1974-78; named one of Outstanding Young Men in Am., 1981, 84, 85; Outstanding Young Dem. Robeson County Young Dems., 1984-85; one of State's Outstanding Young Dems. Young Dems. N.C., 1984, 85. Mem. ABA (exec. com. citizenship edn. com. 1985—, nat. community law week com.), N.C. Bar Assn. (chmn. youth edn. and constn. bicentennial com. 1986—, youth edn. com., exec. council young lawyers div. 1986—), Robeson County Bar Assn. (founder, chmn. citizenship edn. com. 1983—, law day com.), 16th Jud. Dist. Bar Assn., N.C. Acad. Trial Lawyers, N.C. Coll. Advocacy, Eastern N.C. Social Security Claimants' Reps. Orgn., Christian Legal Soc. (state adv. bd. 1986, state pres. 1987), Lumberton C. of C. (legis. affairs and edn. coms., membership drive), Order of Old Well, Phi Beta Kappa, Phi Eta Sigma. Avocations: tennis, snow skiing, softball, dancing, Bible study. General practice, Personal injury, Real property. Home: 1701 N Chestnut St Lumberton NC 28358 Office: Price & McIntyre PA 102 Elizabeth Rd Lumberton NC 28358

MCIVER, ROBERT GILMOUR, lawyer; b. Greensboro, N.C., Nov. 2, 1952; s. John Jones and Ann (Evans) McI.; m. Mary Bohme, Mar. 1, 1986. BA, Harvard U., 1975; JD, U. Va., 1980. Bar: La. 1981, U.S. Dist. Ct. (ea. dist.) La. 1982, U.S. Ct. Appeals (5th cir.) 1982, U.S. Dist. Ct. (we. dist.) La. 1985, U.S. Dist. Ct. (mid. and ea. dists.) N.C. 1986, U.S. Ct. Appeals (4th cir.) 1986. Assoc. Lemle, Kelleher, Kohlmeyer, Hunley, Moss & Frilot, New Orleans, 1980-85, Foster, Conner, Robson & Gumbiner, Greensboro, 1985—. Mem. ABA, La. Bar Assn., N.C. Bar Assn. Avocations: reading, fishing, basketball. Construction, Federal civil litigation, State civil litigation. Office: Foster Conner Robson & Gumbiner 104 N Elm St PO Drawer 20004 Greensboro NC 27420

MCKAY, D. BRIAN, lawyer, attorney general; b. Billings, Mont., Jan. 18, 1945. A.B., Colgate U., 1971; J.D., Albany Law Sch., 1974. Bar: Nev., U.S. Dist. Ct. Nev., N.Y., U.S. Dist. Ct. (no. dist.) N.Y., U.S. Ct. Appeals (9th cir.) 1978, U.S. Supreme Ct. Former mem. Sully, McKay & Lenhard, Las Vegas, Nev.; atty. gen. State of Nev., Carson City, 1983—; mem. adv. policy bd. Nat. Crime Info. Ctr., 1986—. Alt. mem. Western States Water Council, from 1978; mem. Clark County Air Pollution Control Bd., from 1979, adv. policy bd. Nat. Crime Info. Ctr., 1986—. Served with USAF, 1966-69. Mem. ABA, State Bar Nev., N.Y. State Bar Assn. Criminal. Office: Office Atty Gen Heroes Meml Bdlg 198 S Carson St Capitol Complex Carson City NV 89710

MCKAY, DAN BOIES, JR., lawyer; b. Monroe, La., Aug. 31, 1948; s. Dan Boies and Joanna Irwin (McCoy) McK.; m. Adrienne Lee, Aug. 20, 1977; children: Holly, Managan. BA, N.E. La. U., 1970; BS, U. Tex., 1975; JD, La. State U., 1980. Bar: La. 1980, U.S. Dist. Ct. (mid. dist.) La. 1981, U.S. Dist. Ct. (we. and ea. dists.) La. 1982, U.S. Ct. Appeals (5th cir.) 1982. Assoc. N.M. Lee & Assocs., Bunkie, La., 1980-83; sole practice Bunkie, 1984—; atty. Town of Bunkie, 1982—; magistrate, atty. Village of Hessmer, La., 1984—. Defender indigents Avoyelles Parish, Marksville, La., 1984—. Served to capt. U.S. Army, 1970-73, Vietnam. Mem. ABA, La. State Bar

Assn., (ho. of dels. 1984—), Assn. Trial Lawyers Am., La. Trial Lawyers Assn. Democrat. Southern Baptist. Family and matrimonial, General practice, Real property. Home: 701 Lake St Bunkie LA 71322 Office: 1100 Shirley Rd PO Box 720 Bunkie LA 71322

MCKAY, DAVID LAWRENCE, lawyer; b. Ogden, Utah, Sept. 30, 1901; s. David Oman and Emma Ray (Riggs) McK.; m. Mildred Dean Calderwood, June 28, 1928; children—Midene Anderson, Teddy Lyn Parmley, Catherine Iba, Joyce Bennett. Cert., Sorbonne, France; A.B., U. Utah; J.D., George Washington U.; LL.M., Harvard U. Bar: D.C., Utah. Ptnr., McKay, Burton, Thurman & Condie, and predecessor firms, Salt Lake City, from 1936, former counsel; counsel, dir. Utah-Idaho Sugar Co., KIRO Inc., Zions Utah Bancorp. Vice-pres. Utah State Bd. Higher Edn., Utah Symphony; mem. Utah Fine Arts Commn.; sec. Utah Rep. Council, 1937. Mem. Salt Lake County Bar Assn., Utah State Bar Assn., ABA. Republican. Mem. Ch. Jesus Christ of Latter-day Saints. Club: Knife and Fork. General corporate, Oil and gas leasing.

MCKAY, JOHN EDWARD, lawyer; b. Great Lakes, Ill., Sept. 21, 1951; s. James Robert and Helen (Tilley) McK.; m. Carol Ann Petren, Aug. 21, 1976 (div. April 1982); m. Elisa Ann Beltz Adams, Mar. 21, 1987. BA, DePauw U., 1973; JD, Valparaiso U., 1976. Bar: Ind. 1976, Mo. 1976, U.S. Supreme Ct. 1981. Assoc. Deacy & Deacy, Kansas City, Mo., 1976; ptnr. Benson & McKay, Kansas City, 1976—. Articles editor Valparaiso U. Law Rev., 1975-76. Speaker Met. Orgn. to Combat Sexual Assault, Kansas City, 1985—. Recipient Disting. Achievement in the Art and Sci. of Adv. award Internat. Acad. Trial Lawyers, 1976. Mem. ABA, Ind. Bar Assn., Mo. Bar Assn., Kansas City Bar Assn., Assn. Trial Lawyers Am., Mo. Assn. Trial Attys., Nat. Eagle Scout Orgn. Avocations: karate, running, shooting. Personal injury, Workers' compensation. Home: 7051 Ward Pkwy Kansas City MO 64113 Office: Benson & McKay 911 Main 1430 Commerce Tower Kansas City MO 64105

MCKAY, JOHN JUDSON, JR., lawyer; b. Anderson, S.C., Aug. 13, 1939; s. John Judson and Polly (Plowden) McK.; m. Jill Hall Ryon, Aug. 3, 1961 (div. Dec. 1980); children—Julia Plowden, Katherine Henry, William Ryon, Elizabeth Hall; m. Jane Leahey, Feb. 18, 1982; 1 son, Andrew Leahey. A.B. in History, U. S.C., 1960, J.D. cum laude, 1966. Bar: S.C. 1966, U.S. Dist. Ct. S.C. 1966, U.S. Ct. Appeals (4th cir.) 1974, U.S. Supreme Ct. 1981. Assoc. Haynsworth, Perry, Bryant, Marion & Johnstone, Greenville, S.C., 1966-70; ptnr. Rainey, McKay, Britton, Gibbes & Clarkson, P.A., and predecessor, Greenville, 1970-78; sole practice, Hilton Head Island, S.C., 1978-80; ptnr. McKay & Gertz, P.A., Hilton Head Island, 1980-81, McKay & Mullen, P.A., Hilton Head Island, 1981—. Served to lt. (j.g.) USNR, 1961-64; lt. comdr. Res. (ret.). Mem. ABA, S.C. Bar Assn. (pres. young lawyers sect. 1970, exec. com. 1971-72, assoc. mem. grievance and disciplinary com. 1983-87), S.C. Bar, Beaufort County Bar Assn., Hilton Head Bar Assn., Assn. Trial Lawyers Am., S.C. Def. Attys. Assn., S.C. Trial Lawyers Assn., S.C. Bar Found. (pres. 1977), Blue Key, Wig and Robe, Phi Delta Phi. Episcopalian. Clubs: Poinsett (Greenville); Sea Pines (Hilton Head Island). Editor-in-chief U. S.C. Law Rev., 1966; contbr. articles to legal jours. Federal civil litigation, State civil litigation, Personal injury. Home: 6 Rice Ln Sea Pines Plantation Hilton Head Island SC 29928 Office: Suite 203 Watersedge PO Box 5066 Hilton Head Island SC 29938

MCKAY, MICHAEL DENNIS, lawyer; b. Omaha, May 12, 1951; s. John Larkin and Kathleen (Tierney) McK.; m. Christy Ann Cordwin, Apr. 22, 1978; children: Kevin Tierney, Kathleen Lindsay, John Larkin. B in Polit. Sci. with distinction, U. Wash., 1973; JD, Creighton U., 1976. Bar: Wash. 1976, U.S. Dist. Ct. (we. dist.) Wash. 1978, U.S. Dist Ct. (ea. dist.) Wash. 1982, U.S. Ct. Appeals (9th cir.) 1982. Sr. dep. pros. atty. King County, Seattle, 1976-81; ptnr. McKay & Gaitan, Seattle, 1981—; judge pro tem Seattle Dist Ct., 1982, King County Superior Ct., 1982—. Bd. dirs. Mental Health N., Seattle, 1982-85, St. Joseph Sch. Bd., 1984—, Tim Hill County Exec. Campaign, 1985, Fund for Am.'s Future, 1986, Norm Maleng Pros. Atty. Campaign, 1986. Republican. Roman Catholic. Clubs: Wash. Athletic, Columbia Tower (Seattle). Federal civil litigation, State civil litigation. Home: 1801 30th Ave W Seattle WA 98199 Office: McKay & Gaitan Columbia Ctr 49th Floor Seattle WA 98104

MCKAY, MONROE GUNN, judge; b. Huntsville, Utah, May 30, 1928; s. James Gunn and Elizabeth (Peterson) McK.; m. Lucile A. Kinnison, Aug. 6, 1954; children: Michele, Valanne, Margaret, James, Melanie, Nathan, Bruce, Lisa, Monroe. B.S., Brigham Young U., 1957; J.D., U. Chgo., 1960. Bar: Ariz. 1961. Law clk. Ariz. Supreme Ct., 1960-61; asso. firm Lewis & Roca, Phoenix, 1961-66; partner Lewis & Roca, 1968-74; asso. prof. Brigham Young U., 1974-76, prof., 1976-77; judge U.S. Circuit Ct. Appeals, 10th circuit, Denver, 1977—. Mem. Phoenix Community Council Juvenile Problems, 1968-74; pres. Ariz. Assn. for Health and Welfare, 1970-72; dir. Peace Corps, Malawi, Africa, 1966-68; bd. dirs., pres. Maricopa county Legal Aid Soc., 1972-74. Served with USMCR, 1946-48. Mem. ABA, Ariz., Maricopa County bar assns., Am. Law Inst., Am. Judicature Soc., Order Coif, Blue Key, Phi Kappa Phi. Mem. Ch. Jesus Christ of Latter-day Saints. Address: US Ct Appeals 6012 Federal Bldg 125 S State St Salt Lake City UT 84138 *

MC KAY, ROBERT BUDGE, legal educator; b. Wichita, Kans., Aug. 11, 1919; s. John Budge and Ruth Irene (Gelsthorpe) McK.; m. Sara Kate Warmack, Nov. 20, 1954 (dec. Oct. 1986); children: Kathryn Lee, Sara Margaret. B.S., U. Kans., 1940; J.D., Yale, 1947; LL.D., Emory U., 1973, Seton Hall U., 1975, U. Tulsa, 1981, John Jay Coll. Criminal Justice, 1983, Pace U., 1981, U. San Diego, 1982, N.Y. Law Sch., 1985; L.H.D., Mt. St. Mary Coll., 1973. Bar: Kans. 1948, D.C. 1948, N.Y. 1973. With Dept. Justice, 1947-50; asst., then assoc. prof. law Emory U., 1950-53; prof. law N.Y. U., 1953—; dean N.Y. U. (Sch. Law), 1967-75; bd. dirs. Loews Corp; mem. exec. com. Assn. Am. Law Schs., 1964-65; mem. exec. com. Lawyers Com. for Civil Rights Under Law; chmn. N.Y. State Spl. Commn. on Attica, 1971-72, N.Y.C. Bd. Correction, 1973-74; dir. program on justice, society and individual Aspen Inst. for Humanistic Studies, 1975-80, sr. fellow, 1980—. Author: Reapportionment: The Law and Politics of Equal Representation, 1965; Editor: Annual Survey of American Law, 1953-56, An American Constitutional Law Reader, 1958, Time-Life Family Legal Guide, 1971. Chmn. bd. dirs. Citizens Union, 1971-77; pres. Legal Aid Soc. of N.Y.C., 1975-77; vice chmn. Nat. News Council, 1973-80; bd. dirs. Inst. Jud. Adminstrn., 1980-83, Am. Arbitration Assn., Mexican-Am. Legal Def. Fund, Revlon Found., Vera Inst. of Justice; v.p. Am. Judicature Soc., 1980-85. Recipient award Am. Friends Hebrew U. Law Sch., 1972, William Nelson Cromwell medal New York County Lawyers Assn., 1973, Arthur T. Vanderbilt medal N.Y. U. Sch. Law, 1974, Albert Gallatin medal N.Y. U., 1975, Disting. Service medal U. Kans., 1983, Justice award Am. Judicature Soc., 1986. Mem. ABA (chmn. commn. on correctional facilities and services 1974-78, sect. legal edn. and admissions to bar 1983-84, action commn. to improve tort liability system 1985-86, bd. govs. 1986—, ho. of dels. 1985—), N.Y. State Bar Assn. (Gold Medal award 1987), Assn. Bar City N.Y. (chmn. exec. com. 1975-76, v.p. 1976-77, pres. 1984-86, chmn. council criminal justice 1982-84), Delta Upsilon. Presbyterian. Legal education, Labor. Home: 29 Washington Sq W New York NY 10011

MCKAY, ROBERT CONNALLY, lawyer; b. Tyler, Tex., Apr. 28, 1950; s. Connally and Glee (McCrary) McK.; m. Bonnie Swain, Mar. 31, 1979; children—Robert Connally, Sarah Catherine, Caroline Swain. B.A., Baylor U., 1972, J.D., 1975. Bar: Tex., U.S. Dist. Ct. (so. dist.) Tex. Asst. counsel com. on pub. works and transp. U.S. Ho. of Reps., Washington, 1975-77; dir. McKay, Smith, Robins, Russell & Rigsby, Victoria, Tex., 1977-85; chmn., chief exec. officer McKay, Smith, Robins, Russell & Rigsby, 1986—; pres. Victoria Savs. Assn., 1985; mem. Tex. State Ethics Adv. Commn., 1983—. Bd. dirs. Victoria Regional Mus. Assn., 1981-84, Victoria Econ. Devel. Corp., 1983—; mem. Mayor's Image Com., Victoria, 1983-84. Presbyterian. Club: Rotary. Oil and gas leasing, Real property, Banking. Home: 301 Woodway Dr Victoria TX 77904 Office: McKay Smith et al 5606 Hallettsville Hwy Victoria TX 77904

MCKAY, TIMOTHY JOHN, lawyer; b. Ottumwa, Iowa, June 10, 1950; s. Charles A. and Lucille D. (Pechacek) McK. BA, U. Notre Dame, 1972; JD, U. Iowa, 1975. Bar: Iowa 1975, Ill. 1976, U.S. Dist. Ct. (no. dist) Ill. 1976, U.S. Dist. Ct. (so. dist.) Iowa 1980. Law clk. to presiding justice Supreme Ct. Iowa, Des Moines, 1975-76; assoc. Franz, Naughton & Leahy, Crystal Lake, Ill., 1976-79; ptnr. McKay & Moreland, Ottumwa, 1979—. Bd. dirs. So. Iowa Mental Health Ctr., Ottumwa, 1980—, pres. 1982-84. Mem. ABA, Iowa Bar Assn., Wapello County Bar Assn., 8th Jud. Dist. Bar Assn. Republican. Roman Catholic. Lodge: KC (adv. 1982-83, 85-86). Avocation: tennis. State civil litigation, Insurance, Personal injury. Office: McKay & Moreland PC 129 W 4th St PO Box 250 Ottumwa IA 52501

MCKEAN, ROBERT JACKSON, JR., retired lawyer; b. N.Y.C., Dec. 21, 1925; s. Robert Jackson and Isabel (Murphy) McK.; m. Jean McMath, Aug. 18, 1951; children: Katherine, Douglas, Lauren, Andrew. B.A., Amherst Coll., 1950; LL.B., Harvard U., 1953. Bar: N.Y. 1954. Assoc. Simpson Thacher & Bartlett, N.Y.C., 1953-62, ptnr., 1962-85; pres. Nat. Bldg. Mus., Washington, 1986. Trustee Amherst Coll., Mass., Rye Free Reading Room, N.Y., Folger Shakespeare Library, Washington. Served with U.S. Army, 1944-46, ETO. Recipient medal for eminent service Amherst Coll., 1968. Mem. N.Y. State Bar Assn., Assn. Bar City N.Y., Phi Beta Kappa Assocs. Democrat. Presbyterian. Clubs: Apawamis; Am. Yacht (Rye); Sky (N.Y.C.). Home: 70 Island Dr Rye NY 10580 also: 2126 Connecticut Ave NW Washington DC 20008

MCKECHNIE, C. LOGAN, lawyer; b. Monticello, Ky., Sept. 29, 1942; s. Glenn Logan and Jean Alva (Eads) McK.; m. Barbara J. Allen, Apr. 3, 1971; children—B. Roxanne, Amanda J. Student W. Tex. State U., 1960-61, Amarillo Coll., 1961, Goethe Inst., Fed. Republic Germany, 1964-67; L.L.B., J.D., Western State U., San Diego, 1977. Reporter, editor News-Texan, Grand Prairie, Tex., 1959-60, KGNC-TV, Globe News, Amarillo, Tex., 1960-61; cryptologist Army Security Agy., Nat. Security Agy., 1962-64; corr. UPI, Europe, 1964-67; reporter Ariz. Republic, Phoenix, 1967-71; reporter, editor The Tribune, San Diego, 1971-72; spl. asst. to dist. atty., San Diego, 1972-80; sole practice, San Diego, 1981—; lectr. San Diego State U., Western State U., San Diego, Nat. Coll. Dist. Attys., U. Houston. Contbr. articles to Am., European and S.Am. mags. Pres. Tierrasanta Community Council, San Diego, 1974; life mem., advisor, counsel Tierrasanta Friends of Library, San Diego, 1979—; advisor Mudd for Judge Campaign, San Diego, 1984, Calif. Legis. Sports Law Com., 1983—; bd. dirs. Lakeside Cityhood Com., 1987—, East County Bus. Council. Served to capt. U.S. Army, 1961-67. Recipient cert. of Merit, U.S. Jaycees, 1969, Appreciation award Santee Lions Club, 1983. Mem. ABA (sports and entertainment com., vice chmn. criminal justice subcom. 1985—, disting. pub. service award 1970), Nat. Dist. Attys. Assn., Calif. Bar Assn., Calif. Dist. Attys. Assn., San Diego Bar Assn., Foothills Bar Assn., Trial Lawyers Assn., Lakeside C. of C. (bd. dirs. 1987—), Nu Beta Epsilon. Republican. Lodges: Lions (pres. Lakeside club 1984, officer 1985—), Kiwanis. Criminal, Entertainment, Family and matrimonial. Home: 11875 Rocoso Rd Lakeside CA 92040 Office: 9820 Maine Ave Lakeside CA 92040

MCKECHNIE, WILLIAM ELLIOTT, lawyer; b. Gloucester, Mass., Jan. 6, 1952; s. Robert Elliott and Catherine Margaret (Friend) McK.; m. Sharron Lynn McKechnie, Dec. 10, 1977; children: Mariah Robyn, Kaitlyn Rose. BA in History, The Citadel, 1974; MA, JD, U. N.D., 1981. Bar: N.D. 1981, Mont. 1985. Assoc. Bjella, Neff, Rathert, Wahl & Eiken, Williston, N.D., 1981-84, ptnr., 1984—; bd. dirs. Citizens State Bank, Ray, N.D. Dist. chmn. Boy Scouts Am., Williston, 1982—, Reps. Williston, 1984—. Served to capt. USAF, 1974-78. Mem. N.D. Bar Assn., Assn. Trial Lawyers Am., N.D. Trial Lawyers Assn. (bd. govs. 1986), Nat. Assn. Criminal Def. Attys., Ducks Unltd. Lodges: Lions (bd. dirs. 1986), Masons (sec. 1986), Elks. Avocations: golf, cross country skiing, bird hunting. State civil litigation, Personal injury, Criminal. Home: 621 University Ave Williston ND 58801

MCKEE, BARNET M., lawyer; b. St. Louis, Dec. 29, 1952; s. Donald Vernon and Juanita Antoinette (Seibert) McK.; m. Ellen H. Hiatt, Dec. 31, 1978; children: Kathleen, Jonathan. Student, U. Stirling, Scotland, 1973-74; BA cum laude, Kalamazoo Coll., 1975; postgrad., Yale U., 1977-79; MDiv., Yale Divinity Sch., 1979; JD cum laude, St. Louis U., 1980. Bar: Mo. 1980, U.S. Dist. Ct. (ea. and we. dists.) Mo. 1980, U.S. Ct. Appeals (8th cir.) 1980. Legal adivsor, dep. clk. St. Louis County Probate Ct., Clayton, Mo., 1980-83; assoc. Husch, Eppenberger et al, St. Louis, 1983—; founder Lawyers Ecumenical Cooperative, St. Louis, 1982—. Legal counsel Mo. Conf. United Ch. of Christ, St. Louis, 1985—; del. Gen. Synod. United Ch. of Christ, N.Y.C., 1985—. Mem. ABA, Mo. Bar Assn. (Mo. Pro Bono award 1986), St. Louis Met. Bar Assn. (grievance com.). Republican. Avocation: sailing. Probate, Estate taxation, Estate planning. Office: Husch Eppenberger 100 N Broadway Suite 1800 Saint Louis MO 63102

MCKEE, FRANCIS JOHN, association executive, lawyer; b. Bklyn., Aug. 31, 1943; s. Francis Joseph and Catherine (Giles) McK.; m. Antoinette Mary Sancis; children: Lisa Ann, Francis Dominick, Michael Christopher, Thomas Joseph. AB, Stonehill Coll., 1965; JD, St. John's U., 1970. Bar: N.Y. 1971. Assoc. firm Samuel Weinberg, Esquire, Bklyn., 1970-71, firm Finch & Finch, Esquire, Long Island City, N.Y., 1971-72; staff atty. Med. Soc. of State of N.Y., Lake Success, 1972-77; exec. dir. Suffolk Physicians Rev. Orgn., East Islip, N.Y., 1977-81, N.Y. State Soc. Surgeons, Inc., New Hartford, 1981—, Med. Socs. of Counties of Oneida, Herkimer, Madison and Chenango, New Hartford, 1981—, N.Y. State Soc. Orthopaedic Surgeons, Inc., New Hartford, 1981—, Upstate N.Y. chpt. ACS, Inc., New Hartford, 1981—, Central N.Y. Acad. Medicine, Inc., New Hartford, 1981—, N.Y. State Ophthalmol. Soc., 1985—; exec. v.p. Four County Mgmt. Corp., New Hartford, 1983—. bd. dirs. Med Econs. Bur., New Hartford. Served with U.S. Army, 1966-68. Mem. Oneida County Bar Assn., N.Y. State Bar Assn., Am. Soc. Assn. Execs., Am. Assn. Med. Soc. Execs., Utica C. of C. (chmn. health subcom.) Republican. Roman Catholic. Clubs: Engine Eleven, Nightstick (Utica). Health, General corporate. Home: 19 Mulberry St Clinton NY 13323 Office: Francis J McKee Assocs 210 Clinton Rd New Hartford NY 13413

MCKEE, THOMAS FREDERICK, lawyer; b. Cleve., Oct. 27, 1948; s. Harry Wilbert and Virginia (Light) McK.; m. Linda Miller, Aug. 22, 1970. B.A. with high distinction, U. Mich., 1970; J.D., Case Western Res. U., 1975. Bar: Ohio 1975, U.S. Dist. Ct. (no. dist.) Ohio 1975, U.S. Supreme Ct. 1979. Assoc. firm Calfee, Halter & Griswold, Cleve., 1975-81, ptnr., 1982—. Contbg. editor Going Public, 1985. Mem. ABA (com. fed. regulation securities law sect.), Bar Assn. Greater Cleve., Order of Coif. Clubs: Hermit, Country (Cleve.). General corporate, Securities. Home: 2947 Torrington Rd Shaker Heights OH 44122 Office: 1800 Society Bldg Cleveland OH 44114

MCKEEVER, JOHN EUGENE, lawyer; b. Phila., Oct. 24, 1947; s. John James and Marie Julia (Supper) McK.; m. Kathleen Marie McGuigan, June 5, 1971; children: John Joseph, Jeannine Marie. BA magna cum laude with distinction, U. Pa., 1969, JD magna cum laude, 1972. Bar: Pa. 1972, U.S. U.S. Dist. Ct. (ea. dist.) Pa. 1972, U.S. Dist. Ct. (mid. dist.) Pa. 1977, U.S. Ct. Appeals (3d cir.) 1979, U.S. Ct. Appeals (D.C. cir.) 1981, U.S. Supreme Ct. 1981. Assoc. Schnader, Harrison, Segal & Lewis, Phila., 1972-80, ptnr., 1980—. Mem. Pres. Council Allentown Coll. of St. Francis De Sales, Center Valley, Pa., 1980—, Bus. Leadership Organized for Cath. Schs., Phila., 1984—; capt. spl. gifts com. Cath. Charities Appeal, Phila., 1986—; bd. dirs. Jr. Achievement, Phila., 1986—. Mem. ABA, Pa. Bar Assn., Phila. Bar Assn., Pro-LIfe Lawyers' Guild (bd. dirs. 1983-84, chancellor 1984—), St. Thomas More Soc. (gov. 1979—), Order of Coif, Phi Beta Kappa, Pi Gamma Mu, Cath. Philopatrian Literary Inst. Republican. Roman Catholic. Administrative and regulatory, Federal civil litigation, Postal law. Office: Schnader Harrison Segal & Lewis 1600 Market St Suite 3600 Philadelphia PA 19103

MCKELVEY WRIGHT, ANNE FARRELL, circuit judge; b. Camden, Ala., Aug. 14, 1953; d. Cornelius Clifton and Susan Cherry (Ervin) McK.; m. Tom Wright. BA, Auburn U., 1975; JD, Samford U., 1978. Bar: Ala. 1979, U.S. Dist. Ct. (mid. dist.) Ala. 1979. Asst. atty. gen. State of Ala., Montgomery, 1979; dist. judge Wilcox County, Camden, 1979-84; cir. judge Ala. Appellate Ct. (4th cir.), Selma, 1984-87. Mem. 1st Presbyn. Ch. Choir, Camden, 1969—; leader Christian Youth Fellowship, Camden, 1980-84. Recipient Cert. of Merit Ala. Dept. Conservation and Natural Resources, 1980, Wildlife Conservationist of Yr. Ala. Wildlife Fedn., 1982; named one of Outstanding Young Women in Am. Selma Jaycees, 1986. Mem. ABA, Ala. Bar Assn., Dallas County Bar Assn., Assn. Trial Lawyers Am., Assn. Ala. Cir. Judges, Assn. Ala. Dist. Judges (sec. 1981-82), Christian Legal Soc., Ala. Hist. Soc., Wilcox County Hist. Soc., Alpha Gamma Delta. Lodge: DAR. Judicial administration. Home: PO Box 67 Camden AL 36726 Office: Dallas County Courthouse Selma AL 36701

MCKENDRY, JOHN H., JR., lawyer, educator; b. Grand Rapids, Mich., Mar. 24, 1950; s. John H. and Lois R. (Brandel) McK.; m. Linda A. Schmalzer, Aug. 11, 1973; children: Heather Lynn, Shannon Dawn, Sean William. BA cum laude, Albion Coll., 1972; JD cum laude, U. Mich., 1975. Bar: Mich. 1975. Assoc., then ptnr. Landman, Hathaway, Latimer, Clink & Robb, Muskegon, Mich., 1976-85; ptnr. Warner, Norcross & Judd, Muskegon, 1985—; dir. debate Mona Shores High Sch., Muskegon. pres. local chpt. Am. Cancer Soc., 1979. Recipient Disting. Service award Muskegon Jaycees, 1981; named 1 of 5 Outstanding Young Men in Mich., Mich. Jaycees. 1982; named to Hall of Fame, Mich. Speech Coaches, 1986, Diamond Key Coach Nat. Forensic League, 1987. Mem. ABA, Mich. Bar Assn., Muskegon C. of C. (bd. dirs. 1982—), Mich. Interscholastic Forensic Assn. (treas. 1979-86). Republican. Roman Catholic. Lodge: Optimists. Pension, profit-sharing, and employee benefits, Corporate taxation, Personal income taxation. Home: 1575 Brookwood Dr Muskegon MI 49441 Office: Warner Norcross & Judd 801 W Norton Muskegon MI 49441

MCKENNA, DAVID WILLIAM, lawyer; b. Rushville, Nebr., Sept. 7, 1945; s. Walter L. and Mary L. (McCloud) McK.; m. Rebecca Lynn Kissling, Aug. 31, 1968; children: Molly Colleen, Emily Ann. BA, Macalester Coll., 1967; JD, U. Minn., 1970. Bar: Minn. 1970, U.S. Dist. Ct. Minn. 1976. Ptnr. Erickson, Zierke, Kuderer, Utermarck & McKenna, Fairmont, Minn., 1971-76; asst. atty. Martin County, Fairmont, 1971-76; spl. asst. atty. gen. State of Minn., St. Paul, 1976-84; mgr. tort claims div. Minn. Atty. Gen.'s Office, 1979-84; assoc. Robins, Zelle, Larson & Kaplan, St. Paul, 1984—; dir. Econ. Crimes Control Project, St. Paul, 1976-79. Chmn. Martin County Democratic Farm Labor Party, Fairmont, 1976. Served to 2d lt. U.S. Army, 1970. Mem. ABA, Minn. Bar Assn., Ramsey County Bar Assn., Assn. Trial Lawyers Am., Minn. Trial Lawyers Assn. Democrat. Unitarian. Avocations: photography, music, art. Federal civil litigation, State civil litigation, Personal injury. Home: 330 Maple Lane Ct Roseville MN 55113 Office: Robins Zelle Larson & Kaplan 345 St Peter St 1500 Amhoist Tower Saint Paul MN 55102-1638

MCKENNA, EDWARD JAMES, JR., lawyer; b. Red Bank, N.J., Apr. 7, 1950; s. Edward J. and Rita L. (Spence) McK.; m. Christine J. Gerrard, Aug. 12, 1973; 1 child, Sean Edward. BS in Bus. Adminstrn., Villanova U., 1972; JD, Fordham U., 1975. Bar: N.J. 1975, U.S. Dist. Ct. N.J. 1975, D.C. 1978, U.S. Tax Ct. 1978, U.S. Ct. Claims 1979, U.S. Ct. Appeals (D.C. cir.) 1979, U.S. Ct. Appeals (3d cir.) 1980, N.Y. 1982. Ptnr. Vernon, McKenna & Liska, Shrewsbury, N.J., 1976-80, McKenna, Liska & Leone P.C., Red Bank, 1980—; asst. council Monmouth County, 1978-79. Trustee Legal Aid Soc., Monmouth County, 1978-82; bd. dirs. Ocean-Monmouth Legal Services, Red Bank, 1978-83. Fellow Monmouth Bar Found.; Monmouth Bar Assn. (trustee 1983—). Democrat. Roman Catholic. Real property, Contracts commercial, Entertainment.

MCKENNA, J. FRANK, III, lawyer; b. Pitts., Nov. 9, 1948; s. J. Frank Jr. and Antoinette (Schlafly) McK.; m. Colleen Shaughnessy, Mar. 25, 1972; children: Collette M., J. Frank IV, Laura J., Stephen J. BA, Williams Coll., 1970; JD, U. Pitts., 1973. Bar: Pa. 1973. Assoc. Thorp, Reed & Armstrong, Pitts., 1973-82, ptnr., 1982—. Served to lt. USAFR, 1973-74. Named one of Outstanding Young Men In Am., 1982. Mem. ABA, Pa. Bar Assn., Allegheny County Bar Assn. (chmn. young lawyers sect. 1980, v.p. 1987), Am. Law Inst., Am. Judicature Soc. Clubs: Pitts. Field, Pitts. Athletic Assn. Construction, Contracts commercial, Federal civil litigation. Home: 1402 Browning Rd Pittsburgh PA 15206 Office: Thorp Reed & Armstrong One Riverfront Ctr Pittsburgh PA 15222

MC KENNA, JAMES ALOYSIUS, JR., broadcasting executive; b. Poughkeepsie, N.Y., July 1, 1918; s. James Aloysius and Eleanor Frances (Mahoney) McK.; m. Rebekah Ann Rial, Sept. 1, 1941; children: Michelle Marie McKenna Nassif, James Aloysius, Dennis M., Matthew M., Marc W., Aileen M. Student, Manhattan Coll., 1934-35; B.S., Cath. U., 1938; LL.B., Georgetown U., 1942. Bar: D.C. bar 1941, U.S. Supreme Ct. 1947. Counsel Civil Aeronautics Bd., 1941-42; asst. to gen. counsel Office Alien Property Custodian, 1942-44; practicing lawyer Washington, 1946-87; ptnr. McKenna, Wilkinson & Kittner, 1952-87; pres., dir., owner radio stas. WCMB and WSFM, Harrisburg, Pa.; pres. and dir., owner radio stas. WHIT and WWQM-FM, Madison, Wis. Served as lt. (j.g.) USNR; active duty 1944-46. Named Outstanding Alumni Cath. U. Am., 1978; recipient DuBois medal Mt. St. Mary's Coll., 1966. Mem. FCC Bar Assn., Inst. Radio Engrs., Georgetown U. Alumni Assn., Delta Theta Phi. Clubs: Internat. (Washington), Army and Navy (Washington). Home: 5219 Oakland Rd Chevy Chase MD 20815 Office: 17th St NW Suite 810 3 Bethesda Metro Ctr Bethesda MD 20814

MCKENNA, JAMES L., lawyer; b. Elizabeth, N.J., May 9, 1954; s. James P. and Lucy M. (Perretti) McK.; m. Jaon M. Sweeny, June 26, 1982. AB, Brown U., 1976; JD, Villanova U., 1979. Bar: Pa. 1979, U.S. Dist. Ct. (ea. dist.) Pa. 1979, U.S. Ct. Appeals (3d cir.) 1981, N.J. 1985, U.S. Dist. Ct. N.J. 1985, D.C. 1987. Assoc. Feldman & Feldman, P.A., Phila., 1979-81, Deasey, Scalan & Bender, Ltd., Phila., 1981-86; ptnr. Deasey, Mahoney & Bender, Ltd., Phila., Cherry Hill, N.J., 1986—; gen. counsel Eastern Nat. Park & Monument Assn., Phila., 1982—. Assoc. editor: (book) Phila. Country Reporter, 1983—. Mem. William Penn Sch. Dist. Authority, Yeason, Pa. Named Eagle Scout with bronze palm, Boy Scouts Am., 1968. Mem. ABA, Pa. Bar Assn. (rules com. 1984—), Phila. Bar Assn., Def. Research Inst., Phila. Assn. Def. Counsel, N.J. Bar Assn. Avocations: music, reading, running, softball, spectator sports. State civil litigation, Environment, Computer. Office: Deasey Mahoney & Bender Ltd 215 S Broad St Suite 700 Philadelphia PA 19107

MCKENNA, MICHAEL FRANCIS, lawyer; b. N.Y.C., June 17, 1951; s. Thomas Joseph and Mary Kathleen (Reynolds) McK.; m. Marta Regina Diorio, Sept. 28, 1974; children: John, Jason. BSCE, Manhattan Coll., 1973; JD, Pace U., 1980. Bar: N.J. 1980, U.S. Dist. Ct. N.J. 1980, N.Y. 1981, U.S. Dist. Ct. (ea. dist.) N.Y. 1981, Fla. 1982, U.S. Dist. Ct. (mid. dist.) Fla. 1985, U.S. Ct. Appeals (11th cir.) 1985. Cons. engr. Chas. H. Sells, Inc., Pleasantville, N.Y., 1973-77; project mgr. William A. Kelly Co., Katonah, N.Y., 1977-80; assoc. Lewis & DeClemente, Union City, N.J., 1980-81, Law Office of Paul Lewis, Paramus, N.J., 1981-84; ptnr. Lewis & McKenna, Saddle River, N.J., 1984—. Mem. ABA (com. pub. contract law, com. torts and ins. practice). Republican. Roman Catholic. Construction, Government contracts and claims, Federal civil litigation. Home: 101 Deerfield Ln N Pleasantville NY 10570 Office: Lewis & McKenna 82 E Allendale Rd Saddle River NJ 07458

MCKENNEY, EDWARD JEROME, JR., lawyer; b. Memphis, Dec. 20, 1952; s. Edward J. Sr. and Cecelia Teresa (Maley) McK.; m. Barbara Walker, Apr. 13, 1974. BBA, Memphis State U., 1974, JD, 1976. Bar: Tenn. 1977, U.S. Dist. Ct. (we. dist.) Tenn. 1977, U.S. Ct. Appeals (6th cir.) 1980, U.S. Supreme Ct. 1984. Staff atty. Memphis Area Legal Services, 1977-79; from assoc. to ptnr. Hanover, Walsh, Jalenak & Blair, Memphis, 1979—; lectr. labor, mgmt. law State Tech. Inst., Memphis, 1984-85. Bd. dirs. Northeast Community Mental Health Ctr., Memphis, 1981—, United Cerebral Palsy, Memphis, 1982-85. Named VIP United Cerebral Palsy, 1983-85. Mem. ABA, Tenn. Bar Assn., Memphis Bar Assn., Shelby County Bar Assn., Tenn. Trial Lawyers Assn., Internat. Found. of Employee Benefits, Memphis Jr. C. of C. (exec. v.p., v.p., bd. dirs. 1978-83, Key Man, Dir. of Yr. 1978-83). Roman Catholic. State civil litigation, Labor, Personal injury. Home: 5966 Diplomat Place Bartlett TN 38134 Office: Hanover Walsh Jalenak & Blair 219 Adams Ave Memphis TN 38103

MCKENRY, JAMES REINHARDT, lawyer; b. Richmond, Va., Apr. 27, 1935; s. James S. and Margaret McKenry; m. Susan Elizabeth Winters, Oct. 11, 1974. BS, U. Va., 1959, BL, 1962. Bar: Va. 1962, U.S. Dist. Ct. Va. 1972, U.S. Ct. Appeals (4th cir.) Va. 1972, U.S. Supreme Ct. 1972. Sole practice Virginia Beach, Va.; sr. ptnr. Rixey, Heilig & McKenry, Virginia Beach, Heilig, McKenry, Fraim & Lollar, Virginia Beach, 1980—. Mem. Va. Bar Assn. (mem. exec. com., chmn. criminal law com. 1974-76), Virginia

Beach Bar Assn. (pres. 1973), Va. Trial Lawyers Assn. (lectr. continuing edn. porgram). Episcopalian. Family and matrimonial, Criminal, State civil litigation. Home: 1109 York Ln Virginia Beach VA 23451 Office: Heilig McKenry Fraim & Lollar 700 Newtown Rd Norfolk VA 23502

MCKENZIE, HORACE HOUSTON, lawyer; b. Prescott, Ark., Mar. 6, 1905; s. Henry Bernard and Fannie (Pittman) McK.; m. Lawrence Britt, Nov. 23, 1940; 1 child, James H. Bar: Ark., U.S. Dist. Ct. Ark., U.S. Supreme Ct. Sole practice Prescott, 1933-42, 46-49; ptnr. McKenzie, McRae & Vasser and predecessor firm Tompkins, McKenzie & McRae, Prescott, 1949—; mem. Ark. State Bar Examining Bd., spl. Ark. Supreme Ct., Ark. Statute Revision Com.; bd. dirs. Ozan Lumber Co., Prescott. Pres. Prescott Sch. Bd. Served to maj. USAF, 1942-46. Mem. ABA, Ark. Bar Assn., Am. Coll. Trial Lawyers. Methodist. Lodge: Rotary (pres. Prescott club 1935). Personal injury, Insurance, Probate. Office: McKenzie McRae & Vasser #122 E 2d South St McKenzie Bldg Lock Drawer #599 Prescott AR 71857

MCKENZIE, JAMES FRANKLIN, lawyer; b. Mobile, Ala., May 3, 1948; s. Frank L. McKenzie and Mary K. (Crow) McKenzie O'Neal; m. Randy Jo Jones, June 25, 1977; children—Katherine J., J. Alistair. B.A. magna cum laude, U. W. Fla., 1970; J.D. with honors, U. Fla., 1973. Bar: Fla. 1973, U.S. Dist. Ct. (no. dist.) Fla. 1973, U.S. Ct. Appeals (5th cir.) 1975, U.S. Ct. Appeals (11th cir.) 1982. Lectr. bus. law U. Fla., Gainesville, 1972-73; assoc. Levin, Warfield et al, Pensacola, Fla., 1973-76; ptnr. Myrick & McKenzie, P.A., Pensacola, 1976-82, McKenzie & Assocs., P.A., Pensacola, 1982—. Contbr. chpts. to books, articles to profl. jours. Pres. NW Fla. Easter Seal Soc., Pensacola, 1975; bd. dirs. Five Flags Sertoma Club, 1977; fund devel. chmn. Fla. Lawyers Action Group, Tallahassee, 1977—. Recipient Am. Jurisprudence award U. Fla., 1971, 72, 73. Mem. Acad. Fla. Trial Lawyers (coll. diplomates), 1st Circuit Acad. Trial Lawyers (founding mem., pres. 1984), Fla. Bar Assn., ABA, Am. Trial Lawyers Assn., Acad. Fla. Trial Lawyers (bd. dirs. 1986—, diplomate, cert. in civil trial law), Escambia-Santa Rosa Bar Assn., Pensacola C. of C., Order of Coif, Phi Kappa Phi, Omicron Delta Kappa, Phi Delta Phi. Republican. Presbyterian. Clubs: Pensacola Country, Executive. Personal injury, Insurance, State civil litigation. Home: 4546 Lassassier Pensacola FL 32504 Office: McKenzie & Assocs PA 900 E Scott St Pensacola FL 32503

MCKENZIE, ROBERT E., lawyer; b. Cheboygan, Mich., Dec. 7, 1947; s. Alexander Orlando and Edna Jean (Burt) McK.; m. Theresia Wolf, Apr. 26, 1975; 1 child, Robert A. BA in Personnel Adminstrn., Mich. State U., 1970; JD, Ill. Inst. Tech., 1979. Bar: Ill. 1979, U.S. Dist. Ct. (no. dist.) Ill. 1979, U.S. Tax Ct. 1979, U.S. Ct. Appeals (7th cir.) 1979, U.S. Supreme Ct. 1984. Revenue officer IRS, Chgo., 1972-78; ptnr. McKenzie & McKenzie, Chgo., 1979—; lectr. Tax Seminars Inst., Chgo., 1984—. Author: Representation Before the Division of IRS, 1984. Mem. vocat. adv. bd. Ridgewood High, Norridge, Ill., 1981-86; Lake Briarwood Bd. dirs., Arlington Heights, 1985-86; coordinator John Anderson for Pres., 1980; del. Rep. Nat. Conv., Detroit, 1980, Ill. State Rep. Conv., Peoria, 1980. Served with U.S. Army, 1970. Recipient scholarship Mich. State U., 1966-70, Stata of Mich., 1966-70, Silas Strawn scholarship ITT, 1977. Mem. ABA (tax com.), Chgo. Bar Assn. (tax com.), Northwest Suburban Bar Assn. (chmn. econs. of law com. 1986—). Lodge: Rotary (pres. Norridge club 1985-86). Avocations: flight tng., fishing. Personal income taxation, Corporate taxation. Office: 5151 N Harlem Chicago IL 60656

MCKEON, JOHN CARL, lawyer; b. Havre, Mont., Nov. 1, 1950; s. Willis M. and Laura (Svendson) McK.; m. Teresa R. Hould, Aug. 19, 1972; children: Erica, Katie. BA in Polit. Sci, Gonzaga U., 1972; JD, U. Mont., 1975. Bar: Mont. 1975, U.S. Dist. Ct. Mont. 1975. Ptnr. McKeon and McKeon, Malta, Mont., 1975-82, Bosch, Kuhr, Dugdale and McKeon, Malta and Havre, 1982—; dep. county atty. Phillips County, Mont., 1977-82, part-time county atty., 1986—; retained atty. Big Flat Electric Coop., Malta, 1983—. Mem. ABA, Mont. State Bar Assn., 17th Judicial Dist. Bar Assn. (sec. 1982—), Mont. Trial Lawyers Assn., Malta C. of C. (bd. dirs. 1980). Democrat. Roman Catholic. Lodge: KC (Grand Knight 1983). Avocations: fishing, camping, hunting. Health, Criminal, State civil litigation. Office: Bosch Kuhr Dugdale McKeon 155 S 1st Ave E Malta MT 59538

MCKEON, THOMAS JOSEPH, lawyer, broadcaster, detective; b. Indpls., Feb. 3, 1948; s. Thomas Michael and Mary Rose (Luzar) McK. B.A., Ind. U., 1970; J.D. cum laude, Ind. U.- Indpls., 1974. Bar: Ind. 1974, U.S. Dist. Ct. (so. dist.) Ind. 1974, U.S. Supreme Ct. 1979. Assoc. Nisenbaum & Brown, Indpls., 1974-76, Osborn & Hiner, Indpls., 1976-82; counsel Am. Family Ins., Indpls., 1982—; asst. counsel Radio Earth Internat. Inc., Radio Earth Curacao, Netherlands Antilles, 1985—. Author: Post Traumatic Stress Disorder: Real or Imagined, 1976, Repetition Strain As A Compensable Injury, 1987; contbr. articles to profl. jours. Mem. ABA, Assn. Trial Lawyers Am. (assoc.), Ind. Bar Assn., Ind. Def. Lawyers Assn. Inc., Ind. Trial Lawyers Assn., Indpls. Bar Assn., Def. Research & Trial Lawyers Assn., Am. Corp. Counsel Assn., Ind. Assn. Pvt. Detectives. Insurance, Communications, Entertainment. Office: Am Family Ins Group 1625 N Post Rd Indianapolis IN 46219

MCKEOWN, FRANK JAMES, lawyer; b. New Haven, Feb. 22, 1931. AB, U. N.C., 1957, JD, 1960. Bar: Fla. 1960, U.S. Dist. Ct. (so. dist.) Fla. 1960. Ptnr. McKeown & Gamot P.A., Palm Beach, Fla., 1960—. Chmn. bd. of trustees Palm Beach County Scholarship Found., Inc., 1965-80; pres. Palm Beach County Safety Council, 1977-79; bd. trustees Palm Beach Jr. Coll., 1970-73; bd. dirs. YMCA of Palm Beach, 1967-71, Palm Beach County Area Health Planning Council, 1973-75, Palm Beach County Emergency Med. Services Council, 1970-74. Served with USMC, 1950-54. Decorated Bronze Star, Purple Heart. Mem. ABA, Fla. Bar Assn. (trial law sect.), Palm Beach County Bar Assn., Assn. Trial Lawyers Am. (diplomate), Acad. Fla. Trial Lawyers (bd. dirs. 1973-76), Am. Judicature Soc., Lawyer-Pilot Bar Assn., Fla. Assn. Police Attys., Soc. Hosp. Attys., Am. Soc. of Law and Medicine, Am. Coll. Legal Medicine, Rep. Lawyers Assn. Palm County (chmn. 1965-80), Fla. Jaycees (state legal counsel 1965), World Assn. Lawyers (founding mem.), Phi Alpha Delta. Personal injury, Federal civil litigation, State civil litigation. Office: McKeown & Gamot PA 340 Royal Palm Way Palm Beach FL 33480

MCKIBBEN, DALE HARBOUR, lawyer; b. Pine Valley, Miss., Aug. 21, 1923; s. John Monroe McKibben and Lois Elizabeth (Morgan) Murphree; m. Margaret Fondren Striger, Aug. 26, 1950; children: Rob, Doug, Julie, Charles. Student, U. Miss., JD, 1949. Bar: Miss. 1949, U.S. Supreme Ct. 1954. Ptnr. McKibben & Spencer, Jackson, 1949—. Served to lt. col. JAGC USAFR, 1950-72. Mem. ABA, Miss. Bar Assn., Miss. Oil and Gas Lawyers Assn. (pres. 1971-72). Methodist. Oil and gas law, General practice. Home: 1545 Lelia Dr Jackson MS 39216 Office: McKibben & Spencer 1675 Lakeland Dr Suite 505 Jackson MS 39216

MCKIBBEN, HOWARD D., United States district judge; b. Apr. 1, 1940; s. James D. and Bernice (Brown) McK.; m. Mary Ann McKibben, July 2, 1966; children: Mark, Susan. B.S., Bradley U., 1962; M.P.A., U. Pitts., 1964; J.D., U. Mich., 1967. Assoc. George W. Abbott Law Office, 1967-71; dep. dist. atty. Douglas County, Nev., 1969-71, dist. atty., 1971-77; dist. ct. judge State of Nev., 1977-84; judge U.S. Dist. Ct. Nev., Las Vegas, 1984—. Mem. ABA, Nev. Bar Assn., Am. Inns of Ct. (pres. Nev. chpt. 1986—). Methodist. Avocations: tennis, golf. Home: Box 307 Minden NV 89423 Office: US Dist Ct 300 Las Vegas Blvd S Las Vegas NV 89101

MCKIE, EDWARD FOSS, lawyer; b. Albany, N.Y., Oct. 29, 1924; s. Edward F. and Helen (Carmody) McK.; m. Sarah Boyles, Nov. 29, 1952; children—Ann Phelps, Mary, John, Michael, William. B.E.E., Rensselaer Poly. Inst., 1948; LL.B., Georgetown U., 1952. Bar: D.C. 1952, U.S. Sup. Ct. Assoc., Pennie Edmonds, Washington, 1949-52; assoc., Stone, Boyden & Mack, Washington, 1952-56; assoc. Burns, Doane, Benedict & Irons, Washington, 1956-60; ptnr. Banner, Birch, McKie & Beckett, Washington, 1960—; adj. prof. law Georgetown U., 1962-67, 85—. Served with USNR, 1943-46. Fellow Am. Coll. Trial Lawyers, Am. Bar Found; mem. ABA (chmn. sect. patent, trademark and copyright law 1967-68), Am. Patent Law Assn. (pres. 1976-77), D.C. Bar Assn. Republican. Roman Catholic. Clubs: Burning Tree (Bethesda, Md.); Kiwanis (Washington). Contbr. articles to profl. jours. Patent, Trademark and copyright. Office: One Thomas Circle NW Washington DC 20005

MCKIM, LOWELL E., lawyer; b. Huffman, Ind., Oct. 29, 1930; s. Delbert and Glessie May (Rickenbaugh) McK.; m. Janet L. Stewart, Feb. 2, 1952 (div. 1975); children: Gregory L., Sharon L., Elizabeth A., Allison Jones, Douglas K., Julie C. BS in Bus., Ind. U., 1952; LLB, U. N.Mex., 1959. Bar: N.Mex. 1959, U.S. Dist. Ct. N.Mex. 1959. Assoc. Denny & Galascock, Gallup, N.Mex., 1959-72, Denny, Galascock & McKim, Gallup, 1972-85; ptnr. Galascock, McKim, Head & Kozeliski P.C., Gallup, 1985-87, McKim, Head & Ionta P.C., Gallup, 1987—. Mem. water com. City of Gallup, 1970-81, jail constrn. com., 1975. Served to cpl. U.S. Army, 1952-54. Mem. N.Mex. Bar Assn., Assn. Trial Lawyers Am. Democrat. Lodge: Elks. Avocations: hunting, fishing, outdoor photography. Contracts commercial, Family and matrimonial, Insurance. Office: 219 W Aztec PO Box 1059 Gallup NM 87301

MCKIM, SAMUEL JOHN, III, lawyer; b. Pitts., Dec. 31, 1938; s. Samuel John and Harriet Frieda (Roehl) McK.; children—David Hunt, Andrew John; m. Eugenia A. Leverich. A.A. with distinction, Port Huron Jr. Coll., 1959; B.A. with distinction, U. Mich., 1961, J.D. with distinction, 1964. Bar: Mich. 1965, U.S. Dist. Ct. (so. dist.) Mich. 1965, U.S. Ct. Appeals (6th cir.) 1969. Assoc., Miller, Canfield, Paddock and Stone, Detroit, Birmingham, Kalamazoo, Lansing, Monroe, Traverse City and Grand Rapids, Mich., Washington, Boca Raton, Fla., 1964-71, ptnr., 1971—, mng. ptnr., 1979-85, chmn., mng. ptnr., 1984-85; mem. tax council State Bar Mich., 1981-84, chmn. state and local tax coms. Real Property sect., 1982—. Trustee, past chmn. Goodwill Industries; mem. exec. bd. Detroit Area council Boy Scouts Am. Mem. ABA, Detroit Bar Assn., Oakland County Bar Assn., Barrister's Soc., Order of Coif, Phi Delta Phi. Presbyterian. Club: Detroit Yacht. Assoc. editor Mich. Law Rev. State and local taxation, General corporate. Office: 1400 N Woodward Ave PO Box 2014 Bloomfield Hills MI 48303-2014

MCKINLAY, DONALD CARL, lawyer; b. Chgo., June 3, 1916; s. Donald Sinclair and Frances (Wielenberg) McK.; m. Helen Stevenson Moore, Oct. 14, 1967; children by previous marriage: Susan Harried, David, Thomas. B.A., Dartmouth Coll., 1937, A.M., 1974; J.D., U. Chgo., 1940. Bar: Ill. 1940, Colo. bar 1946. With firm Taylor, Miller, Busch & Boyden, Chgo., 1940-42; atty. in gen. practice Denver, 1946-51; asst. atty. gen. State of Colo., 1948-50; partner firm Holme Roberts & Owen, Denver, 1951-81; sr. partner Denver office firm Mayer, Brown & Platt, Chgo., Washington, N.Y.C., London, Houston, Los Angeles, Tokyo, 1981—; gen. counsel, sec. Aspen Inst. for Humanistic Studies, 1963—. Trustee Dartmouth Coll., 1974-84; mem. Colo. Commn. on Higher Edn., 1966-75, chmn., 1968-72. Served to lt. U.S. Navy, 1942-46, PTO. Fellow Am. Coll. Trial Lawyers. Democrat. Presbyterian. Office: 600 17th St Suite 2800 Denver CO 80202

MCKINLEY, EDMON HOWARD, lawyer; b. Mobile, Ala., June 14, 1949; s. George Harold and Mary Rose (Goff) McK.; m. Margaret Lucile McPhail, Dec. 18, 1983; children: Elizabeth Mechel, Mary Jacob. BA, Birmingham So. Coll., 1971; JD, U. Ala., 1974. Bar: Ala. 1974, U.S. Dist. Ct. (so. dist.) Ala. 1976, U.S. Ct. Appeals (1st cir.) 1975. Sole practice Thomasville, Ala., 1975—; atty. Ala. Council Sch. Bd. Dir. S.W. Ala. Mental Health Bd., Monroeville, 1976-77; chmn. Clarke County Dem. Exec. Com., 1984—, So. Dist. Ala. SSS Appeal Bd., 1985—. Fellow Young Lawyers Am. Bar Assn.; mem. ABA (mem. exec. council young lawyers div. 1983-85), Ala. Bar Assn. (lectr. Continuing Legal Edn. Assn., mem. young lawyers sect. 1978-85, pres. young lawyers sect. 1983-85), 1st Jud. Cir. Bar Assn., Ala. Bond Issuers Council. Methodist. Lodge: Rotary (pres. Thomasville 1982-83). Avocations: reading, flower gardening, travel. Real property, Probate, Banking. Home: 220 Wilson Ave Thomasville AL 36784 Office: 117 Wilson Ave Thomasville AL 36784

MCKINLEY, MICHAEL ROBERT, judge; b. Ashland, Ohio, Nov. 13, 1936; s. Robert Steele and Amy Louise (Snyder) M.; m. Norma Elizabeth Anderson, June 8, 1959; 1 child, Scott. B.A., Ohio U., 1959; J.D., Ohio State U., 1962. Bar: Ohio 1962, U.S. Supreme Ct. 1973, U.S. Dist. Ct. (no. dist.) Ohio 1975. Dir. law City of Ashland, 1964-75; sole practice, Ashland, 1963-73; ptnr. Scheaffer & McKinley, Loudonville, Ohio, 1974-80; judge probate and juvenile divs. Ct. of Common Pleas, Ashland County, 1981—; dir. instl. research Ashland Coll., 1968-73. Pres. Ashland Nat. Little League, 1965-66; chmn. bd. trustees 1st Presbyterian Ch. of Ashland, 1970. Recipient Superior Jud. Service award, Ohio Supreme Ct., 1981, 82, 83, 84, 85, Cert. of Distinction, Ohio State U., 1983. Mem. Ohio Mcpl. Attys. Assn. (pres. 1975-76), Ashland County Bar Assn. (pres. 1976-77), Ohio State Bar Assn. (chmn. local law com. 1978-80), ABA, Ohio Assn. Probate Judges (chmn. edn. com. 1983), Ohio Juvenile Judges Assn. Republican. Presbyterian. Avocations: golf; boating; swimming; traveling. Home: 404 Lake Shore Rd RFD 4 Ashland OH 44805 Office: Ashland County Courthouse W 2d St Ashland OH 44805

MCKINNEY, IVY THOMAS, lawyer; b. Lynchburg, Va., Apr. 24, 1956; d. Payton R. and Esther V. (Chambers) Thomas; m. Frederick W. McKinney; 1 child, Warren Thomas. BA, Princeton U., 1977; JD, Yale U., 1980. Bar: N.Y., U.S. Dist. Ct. (so. and ea. dists.) N.Y., U.S. Dist. Ct. Conn. Assoc. Dewey, Ballantine, Bushby, Palmer & Wood, N.Y.C., 1980-84; regional atty. Xerox Corp., Stamford, Conn., 1984—. Mem. ABA, Nat. Bar Assn., So. Conn. Lawyers Assn. (parliamentarian 1985—), Assn. Black Princeton Alumni (bd. dirs. 1985—). Avocations: ceramics, bicycling, reading, aerobics. Federal civil litigation, State civil litigation, Labor. Office: Xerox Corp 200 First Stamford Pl PO Box 10345 Stamford CT 06904-2345

MCKINNEY, JAMES BERNARD, JR., lawyer; b. Hackensack, N.J., Sept. 16, 1950; s. James Bernard and Mathilda Frances (Graef) McK.; m. Linda Anita McClanahan, Aug. 12, 1978; 1 child, Brian James. AB magna cum laude, Dartmouth Coll., 1972, MBA, 1973; JD, Fordham U., 1981. Bar: N.J. 1981, U.S. Dist. Ct. N.J. 1981, N.Y. 1982, U.S. Dist. Ct. (so. and ea. dist.) N.Y. 1982. Litigation assoc. Donovan Leisure Newton & Irvine, N.Y.C., 1981-83; prosecutor N.Y. County Dist. Atty.'s Office, N.Y.C., 1983-86; litigation assoc. Morgan, Lewis & Bockius, N.Y.C., 1986—. Editor Fordham U. Internat. Law Rev., 1980-81. Served to lt. USN, 1973-78. Rotary fellow, 1973. Mem. N.Y. County Lawyer's Assn., Phi Beta Kappa. Federal civil litigation, Securities, Antitrust. Home: 917 Melrose Ave Trenton NJ 08629 Office: Morgan Lewis & Bockius 101 Park Ave New York NY 10178

MCKINNEY, JAMES DEVAINE, JR., lawyer; b. Muscatine, Iowa, Dec. 13, 1931; s. James D. and Jeffie Lillian Eblen McK.; m. Betty A. Guy, June 10, 1966; children—James D., Cynthia Dee, Jennifer. B.A., U. Iowa, 1956, LL.B., 1958. Bar: Iowa 1958, D.C. 1960, U.S. Ct. Appeals (D.C. cir.) 1961, U.S. Supreme Ct. 1962. Trial atty. FPC, 1958-60; ptnr. Ross, Marsh & Foster, Washington, 1965—. Mem. ABA, Iowa Bar Assn., D.C. Bar Assn., Fed Energy Bar Assn. (exec. com. 1979-82), Nat. Lawyers Club. FERC practice, Administrative and regulatory. Home: 6105 Lee Highway Arlington VA 22205 Office: 888 16th St NW Washington DC 20006

MCKINNEY, JOHN ADAMS, JR., lawyer; b. Washington, Mar. 10, 1948; s. John A. and Cleo G. (Turner) McK.; m. Carol A. Cowen, Dec. 22, 1970; children: John III, Thomas. BA, Principia Coll., 1970; JD, Coll. William and Mary, 1973. Bar: N.J. 1973. Assoc. Mason, Griffin & Pierson, Princeton, N.J., 1973-77; atty. Nabisco, Inc., East Hanover, N.J., 1977-79; asst. counsel Republic Steel Corp., Cleve., 1979-84; atty. AT&T, Berkeley Heights, N.J., 1984—. Mem. ABA, N.J. Bar Assn., Am. Corp. Counsel Assn. Environment. Office: AT&T One Oak Way Berkeley Heights NJ 07922

MCKINNEY, LUTHER C., corporate lawyer; b. 1931. BS, Iowa State U., 1953; LLB, U. Ill., 1959. Assoc. Chadwell, Kayser, Ruggles et al, 1959-74; v.p. spl. counsel Quaker Oats Co., Chgo., 1974-75, sr. v.p., sec. of law, 1977-81, sr. v.p., corp. sec. law and corp. affairs, 1981—, also bd. dirs. Served to capt. AUS, 1953-55. Office: Quaker Oats Co Merchandise Mart Plaza Chicago IL 60654 *

MCKINNON, DANIEL ANGUS, III, lawyer; b. Rochester, Minn., June 27, 1939; s. Daniel Angus Jr. and Mary Love (Walker) McK.; m. Karen Kristine McKinnon, June 5, 1961; children: Barbara, Daniel Ian. BS, U. N.Mex., 1962; LLB, U. Colo., 1965. Bar: N.Mex. 1966, U.S. Dist. Ct. N.Mex. 1966, U.S. Ct. Appeals (10th cir.) 1967. Assoc. Marron & Houk, Albuquerque, 1966-70; ptnr. Marron, Houk & McKinnon, Albuquerque, 1970-74, Marron, McKinnon & Ewing and predecessor firm, Albuquerque, 1974—. Mem. Albuquerque Bd. Edn., 1971-77, Albuquerque Tech. Vocat. Inst. Governing Bd., 1971-77; coop. atty. N.Mex. Civil Liberties Union 1967—; mem. Commn. on Pub. Broadcasting, N.Mex., 1975-79. Mem. N.Mex. Bar Assn. (bd. commrs. 1983-89, outstanding contbn. award 1983), Albuquerque Bar Assn., N.Mex. Trial Lawyers Assn., Am. Judicature Soc., Am. Arbitration Assn. (panel of arbitrators 1979—). Avocation: jazz musician. State civil litigation, Family and matrimonial, Estate planning. Home: 4101 Dietz Loop NW Albuquerque NM 87107 Office: Marron McKinnon & Ewing 300 Central SW Suite 1000 W Albuquerque NM 87102

MCKNEW, NATALMA M., lawyer; b. Los Angeles, Apr. 1, 1949; d. Teck Albert Wilson and Elizabeth (Morse) Morison; m. Mark Alfred McKnew, June 19, 1971; 1 child, Bronwyn Kelson. BA, U. Calif., Santa Barbara, 1971; MA, UCLA, 1973; JD, Northeastern U., 1978. Bar: S.C. 1978, U.S. Dist. Ct. S.C. 1978, U.S. Ct. Appeals 1979, U.S. Supreme Ct. 1980. From assoc. to ptnr. Leatherwood, Walker, Todd & Mann, Greenville, S.C., 1978—. Mem. ABA (fgn. franchising com., antitrust sect.). Republican. Roman Catholic. Avocation: aviation. Antitrust, General corporate. Home: Rt 2 Box 149AA Central SC 29630 Office: Leatherwood Walker Todd & Mann 217 E Coffee St Greenville SC 29601

MCKNIGHT, HENRY JAMES, lawyer; b. Pitts., Nov. 23, 1944; s. Harry George and Elizabeth Caroline (Reinhart) McK.; m. Patti Ann Lydic; 1 child, Robert Shawn. BA, Pa. State U., 1968; JD, Duquesne U., 1974. Bar: Pa. 1974, U.S. Dist. Ct. (we. dist.) Pa. 1974, U.S. Supreme Ct. 1979. Spl. asst. county solicitor div. air pollution control Allegheny County, Pitts., 1974; assoc. counsel Pullman Swindell, Pitts., 1975-79; counsel Dravo Corp., Pitts., 1979-84, group gen. counsel mfg., 1984-85, group gen. counsel materials handling and systems, 1985—. Mem. ABA, Allegheny County Bar Assn., Internat. Bar Assn. Republican. Avocations: tennis, skiing. Contracts commercial, General corporate, Private international. Office: Dravo Corp One Oliver Plaza Pittsburgh PA 15222

MCKNIGHT, RUFUS NICOLAUS, JR., lawyer; b. Dallas, Oct 27, 1921; s. Rufus N. and Ida L. McK.; m. Louise Ferguson, Aug. 7, 1953; children—Thomas R., Mary L., Monty L. B.A., So. Meth. U., 1942, J.D., 1947; LL.M., N.Y.U., 1948. Bar: Tex. 1947, Okla. 1954, U.S. Supreme Ct. 1977. Asst. dist. atty. Dallas County, 1948-50, 1953-54; assoc. Johnson, Bohannon, Prescott & Abney, Dallas, 1950-51; ptnr. McKnight & McKnight, Dallas, 1951-53, 83—; atty. Sunray Oil Co., Tulsa, 1954-64, sr. atty., 1964-70; sr. atty. Sun Exploration and Prodn. Co.-Sun Prodn. div., Dallas, 1970-78, chief staff atty., 1978-82, spl. counsel, 1982-83. Bd. dirs. WEGO, Inc., Dallas, 1974—; cert. lay speaker United Methodist Ch., 1969—, dir. legal counsel div. ch. extension North Tex. Conf. Served with USAAF, 1942-45; to capt. Judge Adv. Gen. USAR, 1948-56. Mem. ABA, State Bar of Tex., Okla. Bar Assn., Dallas Bar Assn., Delta Theta Phi. Club: Masons. Probate, Real property, General corporate. Home and Office: 3628 Cragmont Ave Dallas TX 75205

MCKUNE, INA RUTH, lawyer; b. Cheyenne, Wyo., May 18, 1955; d. William Harold and Carol Ann (Burch) Bigham; m. Jeffrey Lee Mckune, Dec. 3, 1983. BA in English, Vanderbilt U., 1977, JD, 1981. Assoc. Rain, Harrell, Emery, Young & Doke, Dallas, 1981-85; asst. pros. atty. Dent County, Salem, Mo., 1986—. Mem. ABA, Tex. State Bar Assn., Dallas Bar Assn., Mo. Bar Assn. Republican. Mem. Ch. of Christ. Avocations: photography, gardening, cooking. Criminal. Office: Dent County Courthouse Salem MO 65560

MC KUSICK, VINCENT LEE, state chief justice; b. Parkman, Maine, Oct. 21, 1921; s. Carroll Lee and Ethel (Buzzell) McK.; m. Nancy Elizabeth Green, June 23, 1951; children: Barbara Jane McKusick Liscord, James Emory, Katherine McKusick Ralston, Anne Elizabeth. A.B., Bates Coll., 1943; S.B., S.M., Mass. Inst. Tech., 1947; LL.B., Harvard U., 1950; LL.D., Colby Coll., 1976, Nasson Coll., 1978, Bates Coll., 1979, Bowdoin Colls., 1979, Suffolk U., 1983; L.H.D., U. So. Maine, 1978, Thomas Coll., 1981. Bar: Maine 1952. Law clk. to Chief Judge Learned Hand, 1950-51; to Justice Felix Frankfurter, 1951-52; partner Pierce, Atwood, Scribner, Allen & McKusick and predecessors, Portland, Maine, 1953-77; chief justice Maine Supreme Jud. Ct., 1977—; mem. Supreme Jud. Ct. Adv. Com. Maine Rules of Civil Procedure, 1957-59, chmn., 1966-75; commr. on uniform state laws, 1968-76, sec. nat. conf., 1975-77; mem. exec. com. Conf. of Chief Justices, 1980-82; leader Am. appellate judges del. to China, 1983. Author: Patent Policy of Educational Institutions, 1947, (with Richard H. Field) Maine Civil Practice, 1959; supplements, 1962, 67, (with Richard H. Field and L. Kinvin Wroth), 2d edit., 1970, supplements, 1972, 74, 77, also articles in legal publs. Trustee Bates Coll.; mem. adv. com. on pvt. internat. law U.S. State Dept., 1980-85; mem. ABA, Ho. of Dels., 1983—. Served with AUS, 1943-46; Served with Manhattan Project, 1945-46, Los Alamos. Fellow Am. Bar. Found. (dir. 1977—), Am. Philosophical Soc.; mem. ABA (chmn. fed. rules com. 1966-71, bd. editors Jour. 1971-80, chmn. bd. editors 1976-77, mem. study group to China 1978), Maine Bar Assn., Cumberland County Bar Assn., Am. Judicature Soc. (dir. 1976-78), Am. Law Inst. (council 1968—), Maine Jud. Council (chmn. 1977—), Inst. Judicial Adminstrn., Supreme Ct. Hist. Soc., Am. Philos. Soc., Phi Beta Kappa, Sigma Xi, Tau Beta Pi. Republican. Unitarian. Clubs: Rotary (hon.); Rotary (Portland) (past pres.); Harvard of N.Y. Home: 1152 Shore Rd Cape Elizabeth ME 04107 Office: Cumberland County Courthouse PO Box 4910 Portland ME 04112

MCLAIN, CHRISTOPHER, lawyer; b. San Luis Obispo, Calif., July 21, 1943; s. James Latane and Marjorie Patricia (McNalley) McL.; m. Barbara McFarland, Nov. 23, 1968; children—Beth, Brian, Amy. B.S. in Bus. Adminstrn., U. Calif.-Berkeley, 1965, J.D., 1968. Assoc. Knox, Goforth & Ricksen, Oakland, Calif., 1968-69; assoc. Donahue, Gallagher, Thomas & Woods, Oakland, Calif., 1969-73, ptnr., 1973-83; sec., counsel Lucky Stores, Inc., Dublin, Calif., 1984—, v.p., 1985—. Mem. ABA, State Bar Calif., Alameda County Bar Assn., Am. Soc. Corp. Secs. Avocation: skiing. General corporate. Office: Lucky Stores Inc 6300 Clark Ave Dublin CA 94568

MCLAIN, DENNIS O., lawyer; b. Detroit, Aug. 11, 1945; s. Francis William McLain and Hazel Joyce (Owen) Hortop. B.A., U. Mich., 1971; J.D., Detroit Coll. Law, 1975. Bar: Mich. 1975. Assoc. Collins & McCormick, Ypsilanti, Mich., 1972-77; gen. ptnr. McLain & Winters, Ypsilanti, 1977—. Mem. Fed. Bar Assn., Mich. Bar Assn., Wastenau County Bar Assn., Ypsilanti Bar Assn., Ypsilanti C. of C. Democrat. Roman Catholic. Personal injury, General practice, Public utilities. Office: McLain & Winters 61 N Huron St Ypsilanti MI 48197

MCLAIN, SUSAN LYNN, legal educator; b. Chestertown, Md., May 6, 1949; d. Joseph Howard and Margaret Ann (Hollingsworth) McL.; m. Donald Howard Pohl, July 5, 1974 (div. 1977); m. Bryson Leitch Cook, May 21, 1977. BA, U. Pa., 1971; JD, Duke U., 1974. Bar: Md. 1974, U.S. Dist. Ct. Md. 1975. Assoc. Piper & Marbury, Balt., 1974-76; John S. Bradway grad. fellow Duke U. Law Sch., Durham, N.C., 1976-77; asst. prof. U. Balt., 1977-80, assoc. prof. law, 1980-83, prof. law, 1983—; reporter on evidence Md. Trial Judge's Bench Book, 1981—; hearing officer Consumer Protection div. Md. Atty. Gen.'s Office, 1981-84. Contbr. chpt. to book, articles to profl. jours. Bd. dirs. Orchards Assn. Neighborhood Group, Balt., 1984-86. Recipient Best Full-Time Faculty Mem. award Student Bar Assn., U. Balt., 1984. Mem. ABA (sect. patent, trademark and copyright law, 1982—, chmn. subcom. 1983-84, sect. litigation trial evidence com. 1982—), Md. Bar Assn. (sect. litigation fed. bar cts. com. 1982—, co-chmn. 1982-83, chmn. com. and subcom. edn!. fed. practice program 1982-84), Balt. City Bar Found. (bd. dirs. 1984—). Republican. Episcopalian. Legal education, Trademark and copyright, Federal civil litigation. Home: 5704 Stony Run Dr Baltimore MD 21210 Office: U Balt Law Sch 1420 N Charles St Baltimore MD 21201

MCLAIN, WILLIAM ALLEN, lawyer; b. Chgo., Oct. 19, 1942; s. William Rex and Wilma L. (Raschka) McL.; m. Cynthia Lee Szatkowski, Sept. 3, 1966; children—William A., David M., Heather A. B.S., So. Ill. U., 1966; J.D., Loyola U., Chgo., 1971. Bar: Ill. 1971, U.S. Dist. Ct. (no. dist.) Ill. 1971, U.S. Ct. Appeals (7th cir.) 1971, Colo. 1975, U.S. Dist. Ct. Colo. 1975, U.S. Ct. Appeals (10th cir.) 1975. Law clk. U.S. Dist. Ct. (no. dist.) Ill.,

Chgo., 1971-72; assoc. Sidley & Austin, Chgo., 1972-75; ptnr. Welborn, Dufford, Brown & Tooley, Denver, 1975-86; pres. William A. McLain PC, 1986—, Interact, Inc., 1986—. Mem. Dist. 10 Legis. Vacancy Commn., Denver, 1984-86. Served with U.S. Army, 1966-68. Recipient Leadership and Scholastic Achievement award Loyola U. Alumni Assn., 1971. Mem. ABA, Colo. Bar Assn. (lobbyist 1983-85), Denver Bar Assn., Assn. Trial Lawyers Am., Colo. Assn. Commerce and Industry (legis. policy council 1983—), Colo. Mining Assn. (state and local affairs com. 1978—). Republican. Clubs: Denver Athletic; Pueblo Country (Colo.), Roundup Riders of the Rockies. Lodges: Masons, Shriners, Scottish Rite, York Rite. Legislative, Federal civil litigation, State civil litigation. Home: 8679 Doane Pl Denver CO 80231 Office: 1700 Broadway Suite 500 Denver CO 80290

MCLANE, DAVID GLENN, lawyer; b. Dallas, Jan. 17, 1943; s. Alfred Ervin and Dixie Marie (Martin) McL.; m. Sally Ruth Payne, Apr. 5, 1963; children—Cynthia Lynn, Kathleen Michelle, Michael Scott, Morgan Elizabeth; m. 2d, Beverly Anne Bledsoe, Feb. 5, 1983; 1 child, Morgan Elizabeth. B.A., So. Meth. U., 1963, LL.B., 1966. Bar: Tex. 1966, U.S. Supreme Ct. Briefing atty. Supreme Ct. Tex., 1966-67; assoc., then ptnr. Gardere & Wynne and predecessors, Dallas, 1967—; mem. faculty So. Meth. U.; lectr. in field. Bd. dirs. Urban Services br. Dallas YMCA, 1977-84, Dallas Symphony Assn., 1980—. Mem. Tex. Bar Assn., ABA, Dallas Bar Assn., S.W. Pension Conf. (dir. 1975-80, pres. 1978-79), So. Meth. U. Law Alumni Assn. (sec., dir. 1981-85, Vol. of Yr. award 1984), So. Meth. U. Alumni Assn. (dir. 1972-77). Presbyterian. Contbg. author: Texas Corporations—Law and Practice, 1984; editor: Incorporation Planning in Texas, 1977. General corporate, Pension, profit-sharing, and employee benefits, Securities. Office: 1500 Diamond Shamrock Tower Dallas TX 75201

MCLANE, FREDERICK BERG, lawyer; b. Long Beach, Calif., July 24, 1941; s. Adrian B. and Arlie K. (Burrell) McL.; m. Lois C. Roberts, Jan. 28, 1967; children: Willard, Anita. BA, Stanford U., 1963; LLB, Yale U., 1966. Bar: Calif. 1967, U.S. Dist. Ct. (cen. dist.) Calif. 1967. Assoc. prof. law U. Miss., Oxford, 1966-68; assoc. O'Melveny & Meyers, Los Angeles, 1968-74, ptnr., 1975—; com. of counsel HUD, Los Angeles, 1979-84; lectr. in field. Pres., bd. dirs. Legal Aid Found., Los Angeles, 1974-83; deacon Congl. Ch., Sherman Oaks, Calif., 1979-83. Mem. ABA (banking com.), Calif. Bar Assn. (fin. insts. com.), Los Angeles Bar Assn., Order of Coif. Democrat. Clubs: Lakeside Golf (Los Angeles), Lake Arrowhead Country (Calif.). Avocations: golf, skiing, walking, reading. Banking, General corporate, Securities. Office: O'Melveny & Myers 400 S Hope St #1500 Los Angeles CA 90071

MCLANE, JOHN THOMAS, lawyer; b. Scranton, Pa., Dec. 8, 1948; s. John T. and Mariam R. (Gilroy) McL.; m. Jane Elizabeth Earley, July 22, 1978; children: Jessica, Noreen, Melissa. BS in English and Edn. cum laude, U. Scranton, 1970; postgrad., Villanova U., 1971; JD cum laude, Duquesne U., 1975. Bar: Pa. 1976, U.S. Dist. Ct. (mid. dist.) Pa. 1977, U.S. Ct. Appeals (3d cir.) 1985. Law clk. to assoc. justice Pa. Supreme Ct., Phila., 1975-76, adminstrv. asst. to chief justice, 1977-80; assoc. Thomas J. Foley Jr. and Assocs., P.C., Scranton, Pa., 1980—. Assoc. editor Duquesne U. Law Rev., 1975. Trustee St. Michaels's Sch. for Boys, Hoban Heights, Pa., 1979—, pres. 1984—. Mem. ABA, Pa. Bar Assn., Lackawanna County Bar Assn. (vice chmn. civil rules com. 1985-86, chmn. civil procedural com. 1986—), Assn. Trial Lawyers Am., Pa. Trial Lawyers Assn. (amicus curiae com. 1984—), Order of Barristers, Duquesne U. Alumni Assn., U. Scranton Alumni Assn., St. Patrick's Parade Assn. (exec. com.), Irish Cultural Soc. Democrat. Roman Catholic. Lodges: Elks (lecturing knight 1985—), Lions, Friendly Sons of St. Patrick. Avocations: gardening, tennis. Federal civil litigation, State civil litigation, Personal injury. Home: 1208 Schlager St Scranton PA 18504 Office: Thomas J Foley Jr and Assocs PC PO Box 1108 Scranton PA 18501

MCLAREN, MICHAEL GLENN, lawyer; b. Joliet, Ill., Jan. 29, 1950; s. Robert G. and Ann (Gaffke) McL.; m. Karen Yandell, Dec. 20, 1976; children: Ann Marie, Michael. BA in History, Yale U., 1972; JD, Loyola U., Chgo., 1976. Bar: Tenn. 1976, U.S. Dist. Ct. (we. dist.) Tenn. 1977, U.S. Dist. Ct. (no. dist.) Ky. 1978, U.S. Supreme Ct. 1980. Assoc. Rickey Shankman, Memphis, 1976-80; ptnr. Thomason & Hendrix, Memphis, 1980—; cons. Inter City Homeowners Assn., Memphis, 1980—; gen. counsel Chgo. Balls Inc., 1976—, Deer Island Club Corp., Alexander Bay, N.Y., 1976—. Gen. counsel Cir. Playhouse, Inc., Memphis, 1980—, bd. dirs., 1977—. Mem. ABA, Tenn. Bar Assn., Memphis Bar Assn., Shelby County Bar Assn. Roman Catholic. Club: Yale (Memphis) (pres. 1984-86). Federal civil litigation, State civil litigation, Insurance. Office: Thomason & Hendrix 44 N 2d Memphis TN 38103

MCLAREN, RICHARD WELLINGTON, JR., lawyer; b. Cin., May 15, 1945; s. Richard Wellington and Edith (Gillett) McL.; m. Ann Lynn Zachrich, Sept. 4, 1974; children: Christine, Richard, Charles. BA, Yale U., 1967; JD, Northwestern U., 1973. Bar: Ohio 1973, U.S. Dist. Ct. (no. dist.) Ohio, 1973, U.S. Ct. Appeals (6th cir.) 1978, U.S. Supreme Ct. 1981. Assoc. Squire, Sanders & Dempsey, Cleve., 1973-82, ptnr., 1983—. Served to 1st lt. U.S. Army, 1967-70. Mem. ABA (litigation and pub. utilities sect.), Am. Judicature Soc., Ohio Bar Assn. (pub. utilities com.), Defense Research Inst. Club: Cleve. Athletic. Federal civil litigation, Public utilities, Legislative. Home: 20 River Stone Dr Moreland Hills OH 44022 Office: Squire Sanders & Dempsey 1800 Huntington Bldg Cleveland OH 44115

MCLAUGHLIN, DOUGLAS RAY, lawyer; b. Deadwood, S.D., Sept. 16, 1949; s. Alfred R. and Phyllis (Lynn) McL.; m. Beverly C. Mathisen, Feb. 5, 1983. B.S., U. Wyo., 1974, J.D., 1977. Bar: Wyo. 1977, U.S. Dist. Ct. Wyo. 1977, U.S. Ct. Appeals (10th cir.) 1977. Assoc. Hamilton & Hursh, Riverton, Wyo., 1977-78; shareholder Central Wyo. Law Assn., Riverton, 1978-80; ptnr. Hollon & McLaughlin, Douglas, Wyo., 1980—; legal del. People-to-People ambassador program, People's Republic of China and Republic of China, 1986. Dir., chmn. Douglas chpt. Ducks Unlimited, 1983-84; treas. Converse County Crimestoppers, Douglas, 1983-84. Mem. Wyo. Trial Lawyers Assn., Assn. Trial Lawyers Am., ABA, Wyo. Bar Assn. (com. for resolution of fee disputes 1986—), Converse County Bar Assn. (pres. 1986-87), Douglas C. of C. (bd. dirs. 1984-87). Republican. Methodist. Lodge: Rotary Internat. (sec. 1983-84, pres. 1985-86, PolioPlus com. local dist. 1986—). State civil litigation, Personal injury, Banking. Office: Hollon & McLaughlin 227 S 2d Douglas WY 82633

MCLAUGHLIN, JOHN SHERMAN, lawyer; b. Pitts., Apr. 1, 1932; s. John H. and Dorothy I. (Schrecongost) McL.; m. Suzanne Shaver, June 5, 1971; children—Dorothy, Sarah, Martha. A.B., Harvard U., 1954, LL.B., 1957. Bar: Pa. 1958, U.S. Supreme Ct. 1967. Assoc. Reed, Smith, Shaw & McClay, Pitts., 1957-71; ptnr. Reed, Smith, Shaw & McClay, 1971—. Trustee Harmarville Rehab. Ctr., Inc., 1980-87 ; pres. Pa. NG Assn., 1976-78; justice of peace Borough of Edgewood, 1963-73. Served to lt. col. Air NG, 1957-79. Mem. Allegheny County Bar Assn., Pa. Bar Assn., ABA, Soc. Hosp. Attys., Western Pa. Judicature Soc., Am. Judicature Soc., Am. Law Inst., Am. Coll. Probate Counsel. Clubs: Duquesne (Pitts.); Rolling Rock (Ligonier, Pa.). Probate, General practice. Office: 435 Sixth Ave Pittsburgh PA 15219

MC LAUGHLIN, JOSEPH MAILEY, lawyer; b. Los Angeles, July 10, 1928; s. James Aloysius and Cecilia Ann (Mailey) McL.; m. Beverly Jane Walker, July 24, 1949; children: Stephen Joseph, Lawrence James, Suzanne Carol, Eileen Louise. J.D., Loyola U., Los Angeles, 1955. Bar: Calif. 1955, U.S. Supreme Ct. 1959. Mem. firm McLaughlin and Irvin, Los Angeles, 1955—, San Francisco, 1969—, Newport Beach, Calif., 1980—; lectr. labor relations Loyola U., Los Angeles, 1958-60, pres. Food Employers Council, Inc., 1984—. Contbg. author: Labor Law for General Practitioners, 1960. Served to 1st lt. USAF, 1951-53. Mem. San Francisco, Long Beach, Los Angeles County, Fed., Am., Internat., Inter-Am. bar assns., State Bar Calif., Am. Judicature Soc., Assn. Bus. Trial Lawyers, Am. Soc. Internat. Law. Clubs: California, Los Angeles Stock Exchange (pres. 1972). Judicial administration. Office: 801 S Grand Ave 3d Floor Los Angeles CA 90017 also: 100 Pine St Suite 770 San Francisco CA 94111 also: 5000 Birch St 9th Floor Newport Beach CA 92660 *

MCLAUGHLIN, JOSEPH MICHAEL, judge, law educator; b. Bklyn., Mar. 20, 1933; s. Joseph Michael and Mary Catherine (Flanagan) McL.; m. Frances Elizabeth Lynch, Oct. 10, 1959; children: Joseph, Mary Jo, Matthew, Andrew. A.B., Fordham Coll., 1954, LL.B., 1959; LL.M., NYU, 1964; LL.D., Mercy Coll., White Plains, N.Y., 1981. Bar: N.Y. 1959. Assoc. Cahill, Gordon, N.Y.C., 1959-61; prof. law Fordham U., N.Y.C., 1961-71, dean Sch. of Law, 1971-81, adj. prof., 1981—; judge U.S. Dist. Ct. Eastern Dist. N.Y., Bklyn., 1981—; adj. prof. St. John's Law Sch., N.Y.C., 1982—; chmn. N.Y. Law Revision Commn., Albany, 1975-82. Author: (with Peterfreund) New York Practice, 1964, Evidence, 1979; also articles. Served to capt. U.S. Army, 1955-57, Korea. Mem. ABA, N.Y.C. Bar Assn., N.Y. State Bar Assn. Roman Catholic. Club: Lotos. Office: US Courthouse 225 Cadman Plaza E Brooklyn NY 11201 *

MCLAUGHLIN, JOSEPH THOMAS, lawyer; b. Boston, Mar. 30, 1944; s. James Francis and Madeline Louise (Hickman) McL.; m. Christine E. Mullen, Sept. 2, 1967; children: Amy Melissa, Caitlin Christine, Ian Michael. BA magna cum laude, Boston Coll., 1965; JD, Cornell U., 1968. Bar: Mass. 1969, N.Y. State 1968, U.S. Supreme Ct. 1974. Research asst. Brit. Council of Archaeology, Winchester, Eng., 1964; site supr. Brit. Council of Archaeology, 1966; legis. asst. Rep. Thomas P. O'Neill, Washington, 1967; research asst. Cornell U., 1967-68; law clk. to chief justice Mass. Superior Ct., 1968-69; assoc. Shearman & Sterling, N.Y.C., 1969-76, ptnr., 1976—; adj. prof. Fordham Law Sch., 1981—. Author: Federal Class Action Digests, 1974, 1976; contbr. articles to profl. jours. Exec. dir. Brooklyn Heights Draft Counseling Service, 1970-74, Presbyn. Task Force for Justice Counseling Service, 1973-75; v.p., bd. dirs. Brooklyn Heights Assn., 1973-77; bd. dirs. Willoughby Settlement House, Inc., Ingersoll-Willoughby Community Ctr., Inc., 1970-75, United Neighborhood Houses, 1976-78, Good Shepherd Residences, Resources for Children with Spl. Needs Inc. Mem. ABA, Assn. Bar City N.Y. (mem. com. on profl. discord 1986—), N.Y. State Bar Assn. (chmn. com. on marijuana and drug abuse 1972-75), Am. Law Inst. , Am. Arbitration Assn., N.Y. Lawyers for the Pub. Interest (chmn. bd. dirs. com. on promoting settlements), World Arbitration Assn. Club: Heights Casino. Federal civil litigation, Private international, Banking. Home: 174 State St Brooklyn NY 11201 Office: Shearman & Sterling 53 Wall St New York NY 10005

MCLAUGHLIN, PATRICK MICHAEL, lawyer, government official; b. Monahans, Tex., July 23, 1946; s. Patrick John and Ann (Donnelly) M.; m. Christine Manos, Aug. 21, 1970; children—Brian Patrick, Christopher Michael, Conor Andrew. B.Gen. Studies, Ohio U., 1972; J.D., Case Western Res. U., 1976. Bar: Ohio 1976, U.S. Dist. Ct. (no. dist.) Ohio 1978, U.S. Ct. Appeals (6th cir.) 1979, U.S. Supreme Ct. 1980. Dir. vets. edn. project. Am. Assn. Community and Jr. Colls., Washington, 1972-73; law clk. Common Pleas Ct., Cleve., 1976-77; law clk. to judge 8th Jud. Dist. Ct. of Appeals, Cleve., 1977-78; asst. U.S. atty. No. Dist. Ohio, Cleve., 1978-82; chief civil div. No. Dist. Ohio, 1982-84, U.S. atty., 1984—; cons. Nat. League of Cities, U.S. Conf. Mayors, 1971-72; co-creator Opportunity Fair for Veterans Concept, 1971. Editor-in-chief Case Western Res. Jour. Internat. Law, 1975-76. Chmn. N. Ohio Drug Abuse Task Force, 1986—. Served to staff sgt. U.S. Army, 1966-68, Vietnam; maj. JAGC, USAR. Decorated Silver Star, Bronze Star, Purple Heart, Army Commendation medal, Vietnamese Cross of Gallantry with Silver and Bronze Stars. Mem. ABA, Fed. Bar Assn. (chmn. ad hoc com. on drug abuse 1987—, pres. Cleve. chpt. 1987—), Res. Officers Assn. U.S., Soc. First Div., Order of Ahepa, Nat. Vietnam Vets. Network (Disting. Vietnam Vet. award 1985), Nat. Assn. Concerned Vets. (nat. v.p. external affairs 1971-72, exec. dir. 1972-73), Cuyahoga County Vets. (award 1985). Republican. Roman Catholic. Federal civil litigation, Personal injury. Office: US Atty No Dist Ohio 1404 E 9th St Suite 500 Cleveland OH 44114

MCLAUGHLIN, ROBERT FRANCIS, retired lawyer; b. Mountain Home, Idaho, July 11, 1920; s. Daniel and Mary C. McLaughlin; m. Patty McLaughlin, June 5, 1946; children—James D., John Patrick, Michael R., Mary, Anne Crim. B.A., U. Idaho, 1948, LL.B., 1950, J.D., 1969. Bar: Idaho 1950, U.S. Supreme Ct. 1958, U.S. Ct. Appeals (9th cir.) 1970. Pros. atty. Elmore County, Idaho, 1950-60; pvt. practice, Mountain Home, 1960-84, ret., 1984; city atty. Glenns Ferry, Idaho, 1952-54, Mountain Home, 1962-66; atty. Idaho State Land Bd., 1967-68. Democratic nominee U.S. Senate, 1960; mem. Kennedy-Johnson Natural Resources Com., 1960; active Boy Scouts Am. Served with U.S. Army, 1941-46. Mem. Am. Judicature Soc., Idaho Pros. Atty. Assn. (pres. 1959-60), Internat. Platform Soc., Idaho Trial Lawyers Assn. (pres. 1968-70), U. Idaho Law Sch. Alumni Assn. (pres. 1962-64). Democrat. Roman Catholic. Author: Idaho Magistrate Manual, 1958. Civil rights, General practice, Personal injury. Home: 875 Galena Ct Mountain Home ID 83647

MCLAUGHLIN, T. MARK, lawyer; b. Salem, Mass., Apr. 20, 1953; s. Terrence E. and Mary E. (Donlon) McL.; m. Sandra L. Roman, Oct. 16, 1982; 1 child, Daniel. BA in Econs., U. Notre Dame, 1975, JD, 1978. Bar: Ill. 1978, U.S. Dist. Ct. (no. dist.) Ill. 1978, U.S. Ct. Appeals (7th) 1982, U.S. Ct. Appeals (11th cir.) 1983. Assoc. Mayer, Brown & Platt, Chgo., 1978-84, ptnr., 1985—; adj. faculty law Loyola U., Chgo., 1983, 86—. Bd. dirs. no. Ill. affiliate Am. Diabetes Assn., Chgo., 1985—. Mem. ABA (franchising forum com. antitrust law sect.), Phi Beta Kappa. Antitrust, Federal civil litigation, Franchise law. Office: Mayer Brown & Platt 190 S LaSalle St Chicago IL 60603

MCLAUGHLIN, THOMAS ORVILLE, lawyer; b. Corvallis, Oreg., Mar. 17, 1940; s. Willard Thomas and Mabel Sarah (Mills) McL.; m. Sonya Jane Hanson, Sept. 20, 1969; children: Jay Thomas, Katharine Tyler. BA in Econs., Dartmouth Coll., 1961; LLB, U. Wash., 1964. Bar: Wash. 1964, Alaska 1983, U.S. Dist. Ct. (we. dist.) Wash., U.S. Dist. Ct. Alaska. Asst. corp. counsel City of Seattle, 1964, 67; assoc. Chadwick, Chadwick & Mills, Seattle, 1968-71; ptnr. Chadwick, Mills & McLaughlin, Seattle, 1971-74, LeSourd & Patten, Seattle and Anchorage, 1974-85, Copple, McLaughlin, Ferm & Wade, Seattle, 1985—. Elder Presbyn. Ch., Anchorage, 1985; vice chmn. Bainbridge (Wash.) Island Planning Commn., 1973-74. Served to capt. U.S. Army, 1964-66. Mem. ABA, Wash. State Bar Assn., Alaska Bar Assn., Seattle King County Bar Assn., Anchorage Bar Assn. Clubs: Seattle, Wing Point Golf and Country (bd. dirs. 1979-81, pres. 1981). General corporate, Securities, Estate planning. Office: Copple McLaughlin Ferm & Wade 2001 Western Ave Suite 510 Seattle WA 98121

MCLAWHORN, RICHARD EDWARD, lawyer; b. Rocky Mt., N.C., Mar. 4, 1947; s. Richard Earl And Dorothy Hale (Nichols) McL.; m. Jo Ann Martin, May 27, 1972; children: Dorothy, Mary, Richard, Joshua. AA with honors, Montgomery Coll., 1972; BA with high honors, U. Md., 1974; MPA, U. S.C., 1976, JD, 1977. Supr. communications U.S. FBI, Washington, 1969-72; dir. research S.C. Legis. Council, Columbia, 1977-85; exec. v.p., gen. counsel Nat. Coalition Against Pornography, Columbia, 1985-87; dir. research and spl. projects Office of Gov. of S.C., Columbia, 1987—. Featured in Pornography A Human Tragedy, 1986. Mem. speakers bur. United Way of Midlands, Columbia, 1983; bd. dirs. Citizens Advocating Decency and Revival of Ethics, Columbia, Citizens Concerned for Community Values, Cin., Am. Christian TV System, Columbia. Served to sgt. U.S. Army, 1966-69. Named One of Outstanding Young Men Am., 1980, 82, 84. Mem. ABA, S.C. Bar Assn., East Columbia Jaycees (pres. 1982), Wig & Robe, Phi Kappa Phi, Pi Sigma Alpha, John Marshall Pre-Law Soc. Southern Baptist. Club: Toastmasters (Columbia) (state chmn. pub. relations com.1983-84, v.p. local chpt. 1984). Avocations: reading, family activities, religion. General corporate, Legislative, Executive. Office: Office of Gov of SC PO Box 11369 Suite 9248 Columbia SC 29211

MCLEAN, CHRISTOPHER ANTHONY, lawyer; b. Chgo., Mar. 21, 1958; s. Earl James and Joan A. (Wolski) McL. BBA, Creighton U., 1980, JD, 1982; LLM, Georgetown U., 1985. Bar: Nebr. 1982, U.S. Dist. Ct. Nebr. 1982, D.C. 1985. Legis. asst. to Senator J. James Exon U.S. Senate, Washington, 1982—. Assoc. editor Creighton U. Law Rev., 1982. Pres. Creighton Dems., Omaha, 1977-79; vol. various polit. campaigns, Omaha and Washington, 1973—. Mem. ABA, Nebr. Bar Assn., D.C. Bar Assn., Creighton U. Alumni Assn. Washington D.C., Alpha Sigma Nu, Am. Film Inst. Democrat. Roman Catholic. Avocations: travel, photography, polit. memorabilia. Home: 1620 S 138th St Omaha NE 68144 Office: c/o Senator J James Exon US Senate Washington DC 20510

MCLEAN, DAVID LYLE, lawyer; b. Longview, Wash., May 5, 1941; s. David Edward and Helen Margaret (Andrews) McL.; m. Sheila Marsha Avrin, Apr. 27, 1968; children—Alexandra Andrews, David Benjamin Avrin. A.B., Princeton U., 1963; LL.B., Yale U., 1966. Bar: N.Y. 1967, D.C. 1980, U.S. Dist. Ct. (so. dist.) N.Y. 1968, U.S. Dist. Ct. (ea. dist.) N.Y. 1969, U.S. Ct. Appeals (2d cir.) 1969, U.S. Supreme Ct. 1973. Assoc. Sullivan & Cromwell, N.Y.C., 1967-73; asst. gen. counsel Coopers & Lybrand, N.Y.C., 1973-76, assoc. gen. counsel and prin., 1976—. Treas, Bellamy for State Senate campaigns 1970-76. Served with USMCR, 1966-72. Mem. ABA (com. law and acctg. 1981—), Assn. Bar City N.Y. (com. mil. justice 1971-75, com. corp. law dept's., 1986—). Democrat. Club: Hemisphere (N.Y.C.). Contbr. articles to legal jours. General corporate, Securities, Federal civil litigation. Office: Coopers & Lybrand 1251 Ave of Americas New York NY 10020

MCLEAN, ROBERT DAVID, lawyer; b. Mar. 1, 1945; s. Edward D. McLean; m. Rosemary P. McLean; children: Ann P., Robert P. BA, Northwestern U.; JD, Yale U. Law clk. to Justice Thurgood Marshall U.S. Supreme Ct.; ptnr. Sidley & Austin, Chgo. Note and comment editor Yale U. Law Rev. Home: 1235 Astor St Chicago IL 60610 Office: Sidley & Austin One First National Plaza Chicago IL 60603

MCLEAN, SHEILA AVRIN, lawyer, consultant; b. Phila., Nov. 1, 1941; d. Alexander A. and Pauline (Cross) Avrin; m. David L. McLean, Apr. 27, 1968; children: Alexandra Andrews, David Benjamin. AB, Smith Coll., 1963; LLB, Yale U., 1966. Bar: N.Y. 1968. Assoc. Cravain, Swaine & Moore, N.Y.C., 1966-70; assoc. gen. counsel The Ford Found., N.Y.C., 1970-79; gen. counsel U.S. Internat. Devel. Coop. Agy., Washington, 1979-80; pres. McLean & Co. Ltd., N.Y.C., 1980—. Contbr. articles to profl. jours. Mem. planning com. Allen-Stevenson Sch., 1983-84; bd. counsellors Smith Coll., Northampton, Mass., 1978-81; bd. dirs. Ctr. for Effective Philanthropy, Cambridge, Mass., 1982—, U.S. Com. for Refugees, 1983—, Am. Council for Nationalities Services, 1983—, Internat. Social Service, 1983—, OEF Internat., Washington, 1984—, Police Athletic League, 1985—. Mem. ABA, Assn. Bar of City of N.Y. (exec. com. 1971-75), Council Foreign Relations. Private international, Public international. Office: 809 UN Plaza New York NY 10017

MCLEMORE, GILBERT CARMICHAEL, JR., lawyer; b. Savannah, Dec. 15, 1942; s. Gilbert Carmichael and Jeannie Elizabeth (Gulley) McL.; m. Susan Ellen Hair, Nov. 21, 1965; children—Kimberly Bates, Gilbert Carmichael, Erin Frances. A.B. in Polit. Sci., U. N.C., 1965; J.D., U. Ga., 1970. Bar: Ga. 1970, U.S. Dist. Ct. (so. dist.) Ga. 1970. Assoc. Fendig, Dickey, Fendig & Whelchel, Brunswick, Ga., 1970-74, ptnr., 1974-77; ptnr. Fendig, Fendig & McLemore, Brunswick, 1977-81; ptnr. Fendig, McLemore, Taylor & Whitworth, Brunswick, 1981—. Bd. dirs. ARC, Glyn County chpt., Ga.; bd. dirs. Humane Soc. of South Coastal Ga. Served to lt. USNR, 1965-67. Mem. Glynn County Bar Assn. (pres. 1974-75, v.p. 1973-74, treas. 1972-73), State Bar Ga. (com. chmn. younger lawyers sect. 1977), Brunswick-Golden Isles Estate Planning Council (pres. 1980-81), Brunswick-Golden Isles C. of C. (chmn. com. 1975). Democrat. Methodist. Lodge: Rotary. Probate, Banking, Real property. Home: 545 Old Plantation Rd Jekyll Island GA 35120 Office: PO Box 1996 Brunswick GA 31521

MCLEMORE, MICHAEL KERR, lawyer; b. Atlanta, May 19, 1949; s. Gilbert Carmichael Sr. and Jeannie (Gulley) M.; m. Colleen Owen, Aug. 19, 1972; children: Megan, Shannon. BA, Haverford Coll., 1971; JD, U. Ga., 1974. Bar: Fla. 1974, U.S. Dist. Ct. (mid. and so. dists.) Fla. 1974, U.S. Ct. Appeals (5th cir.) 1974, U.S. Ct. Appeals (11th cir.) 1981, U.S. Supreme Ct. 1984. From assoc. to ptnr. Kimbrell and Hamann P.A., Miami, Fla., 1974—. Pres. Haverford Soc. South Fla., Miami, 1978—; lay leader First United Meth. Ch., South Miami, 1986—. Served to 1st lt. USAR, 1976-78. Mem. ABA, Fla. Bar Assn. (aviation sect.), Dade County Def. Bar Assn., Nat. Transp. Safety Bd. Assn. Democrat. Methodist. Federal civil litigation, State civil litigation. Home: 9430 SW 181st St Miami FL 33157 Office: Kimbrell and Hamann PA 799 Brickell Plaza Miami FL 33131

MCLENNAN, ROBERT BRUCE, lawyer; b. San Francisco, Aug. 5, 1948; s. Ronald and Ruth Eileen (Pierson) McL.; m. Suzanne Patricia Kirby, May 26, 1979; children: Amelia Suzanne, Alison Claire. AB, U. Calif., Berkeley, 1970; JD, Harvard U., 1975. Bar: Calif. 1975, U.S. Ct. Appeals (D.C. cir.) 1979, U.S. Ct. Appeals (5th cir.) 1982, U.S. Supreme Ct. 1982. Atty. FTC, Washington, 1975-77, Pacific Gas & Electric Co., San Francisco, 1978. Commr. Mill Valley (Calif.) Parks and Recreation Com., 1979-85; dir. Marin County (Calif.) ACLU, 1983-84; mem. Marin Dem. Cen. Com., 1982-83. Served with U.S. Army, 1970-73. Mem. Fed. Energy Bar Assn., Marin County Bar Assn. Avocations: running, backpacking, climbing. Administrative and regulatory, FERC practice, Public utilities. Home: 99 Sycamore Ave Mill Valley CA 94941 Office: Pacific Gas & Electric Co PO Box 7442 San Francisco CA 94120

MCLEOD, ROBERT MACFARLAN, lawyer, arbitrator, real estate executive; b. Toronto, Ont., Can., Oct. 13, 1925; s. William Green and Eliza Vest (Macfarlan) McL.; m. Siddney Anne Mercer, June 21, 1950; children—Ann Payne, William Mercer, Elizabeth Macfarlan. B.S., U. Wis.-Madison, 1950; J.D., U. Va., 1952. Bar: Calif. 1953, Va. 1952. Assoc. faculty U. Calif. Law Sch., Berkeley, 1952-53; assoc. then ptnr. Thelen Marrin Johnson & Bridges, San Francisco, 1953-86; real estate broker Hill & Co., San Francisco, 1986—; vis. lectr. U. Calif. Law Sch., Berkeley, 1965-86; arbitrator Calif. State Constrn. Arbitration Panel, 1978—, Am. Arbitration Assn. Constrn. Industry Panel, 1982—; judge pro tem San Francisco Mcpl. Ct., 1980-81; mem. Calif. Pub. Contract Code Com., 1980-85. Contbr. chpts. to books, articles to profl. jours.; bd. editors Va. Law Rev., 1951-52. Sustaining mem. The Museum Soc., San Francisco, 1974—; mem. the Nat. Trust, London, 1982—, Smithsonian Assocs., 1974—, U.S. Golf Assocs., 1978—, Forum for Architecture, N.Y.C., 1984-86, Found. for San Francisco's Archtl. Heritage, 1987—. Served with inf. U.S. Army, 1943-46, ETO. Mem. Internat. Bar Assn. (vice-chmn. internat. constrn. contracts com. 1984-86), ABA, State Bar Calif., Va. State Bar, Bar Assn. San Francisco, Nat. Assn. Realtors, Calif. Assn. Realtors, San Francisco Bd. Realtors, Order of Coif, Phi Alpha Delta, Delta Kappa Epsilon, English Speaking Union. Republican. Clubs: San Francisco Golf, Guardsmen, Commonwealth (San Francisco); Beefeater (N.Y.C.). Avocations: travel; golf. Construction, Government contracts and claims, Private international. Office: Hill & Co 2107 Union St San Francisco CA 94123 also: Thelen Marrin et al 2 Embarcadero Ctr San Francisco CA 94111

MCMAHON, COLLEEN, lawyer; b. Columbus, Ohio, July 18, 1951; d. John Patrick and Patricia Patterson (McDanel) McM.; m. Frank V. Sica, May 16, 1981; children: Moira, Catherine, Patrick McMahon. BA summa cum laude, Ohio State U., 1973; JD cum laude, Harvard U., 1976. Bar: N.Y. 1977, U.S. Dist. Ct. (so. and ea. dists.) N.Y. 1977, U.S. Ct. Appeals (2d cir.) 1978, U.S. Supreme Ct. 1980, U.S. Ct. Appeals (5th and D.C. cirs.) 1985. Assoc. Paul, Weiss, Rifkind, Wharton & Garrison, N.Y.C., 1976-79, 80-84, ptnr., 1984—; spl. asst. U.S. Mission to the UN, N.Y.C., 1979-80. Gen. Counsel, bd. dirs. Danceworks Inc., N.Y.C., 1977-83; bd. dirs. Dance Theatre Workshop, N.Y.C., 1978—, Vol. Lawyers for the Arts, N.Y.C., 1978-85. Mem. ABA, Assn. of Bar of City of N.Y. (chmn. state cts. superior jurisdiction com. 1983—), Fed. Bar Council, N.Y. State Bar Assn. (del. Ho. of Dels. 1987—). Republican. Federal civil litigation, State civil litigation. Home: 3 Westway Bronxville NY 10708 Office: Paul Weiss Rifkind Wharton & Garrison 1285 Ave of Americas New York NY 10020

MCMAHON, EDWARD RICHARD, lawyer; b. Jersey City, June 7, 1949; s. Edward Barnawall and Jean (Sullivan) McM.; m. Ellen Mary Bosek; children: Meghan Jean, Kerry Eileen. AB, Colgate U., 1972; JD, Seton Hall U., 1975. Bar: N.J. 1975, U.S. Dist. Ct. N.J. 1975, U.S. Ct. of Appeals (3rd circ.) 1980. Law clk. to presiding judge U.S. Dist. Ct., Newark, 1975-77; assoc. Lum, Biunno & Tompkins, Newark, 1977-83; ptnr. Lum, Hoens, Abeles, Conant, & Danzis, Roseland, 1983—. Mem. Morris County Rep. Com., N.J., 1982—, Chatham Boro Rep. Com., Chatham, N.J., 1982—, chmn. 1986—. Mem. ABA (litigation and banking sects.), N.J. Bar Assn., Assn. Fed. Bar N.J., Am. Judicature Soc., Morris County Bar Assn., Essex County Bar Assn., Chatham Boro Jaycees (pres. 1985-86), Delbarton Sch. Alumni Assn. (class rep. 1984—), Delta Upsilon, Phi Alpha Delta . Republican. Roman Catholic. Club: Colgate (No. N.J.). Banking, Federal civil litigation, State civil litigation. Home: 18 Orchard Rd Chatham NJ 07928

Office: Lum Hoens Abeles Conant & Danzis 103 Eisenhower Pkwy Roseland NJ 07068-1049

MCMAHON, JOHN JOSEPH, lawyer; b. N.Y.C., Aug. 23, 1949; s. John Joseph and Elizabeth Mary (Rowland) McM.; m. Susan Bernice Mullen, Dec. 2, 1978; children—John Joseph IV, Christopher Jordon, James Matthew. B.A. in History, Fordham U., 1971, J.D., 1974; M.A. in Human Devel., SalveRegina-Newport Coll., 1980. Bar: N.Y. 1975, U.S. Ct. Mil. Appeals 1975, R.I. 1978, U.S. Dist. Ct. R.I. 1978. Trial, def. counsel U.S. Marine Corps, Judge Adv. Div., Quantico, Va. Okinowa, Newport, R.I., 1974-79; staff judge adv. HQ 2nd MAB, 4th Marine Div., U.S. Marine Corps Res., Camp Edwards, Mass., 1979-81; state prosecutor Dept. of Atty. Gen., Providence, 1979-84, 86—; ptnr. Faerber & McMahon, Newport, 1985; exec. officer Trans Co., 6th MTBN, U.S. Marine Corps Res., Providence, 1981-84, comdg. officer, 1985-86; lectr. Roger Williams Coll., 1985; dir., juvenile prosecutor unit Dept. of Atty. Gen., Criminal Div., Providence, 1982-84; mem. Delinquency Prevention Task Force, Providence, 1983, Juvenile Probation Standards Task Force, Providence, 1983-84. Counselor St. Joseph's Catholic Youth Orgn., Newport, 1980-81; team capt. Catholic Charities, 1974-79. Served to lt. col. USMCR. Named Jr. Officer of Yr., U.S. Navy Base, Newport, 1979; Outstanding Young Am. award, 1981. Mem. Nat. Dist. Atty. Assn. (state dir. 1986—), ABA, Fed. Bar Assn. (v.p. R.I. chpt. 1980-81), N.Y. Bar Assn., R.I. Bar Assn., Marine Corps Res. Officers Assn. Criminal, Juvenile, Military. Home: 179 Third St Newport RI 02840 Office: Dept Atty Gen 222 Quaker Ln West Warwick RI 02893

MCMAHON, KATHERINE ELLEN, lawyer; b. Holyoke, Mass., Oct. 4, 1955; d. Thomas Emmanuel and Noreen Ellen (Kennedy) McM. BA, Fairfield U., 1977; JD, Western New England Coll., 1982. Bar: Mass. 1982, U.S. Dist. Ct. Mass. 1982, N.H. 1985. Legal asst. to dist. atty. No. Dist. Mass., Cambridge, 1982-83; spl. asst. dist. atty. Plymouth Dist. Mass., Brockton, 1983; asst. div. counsel Mass. Dept. Social Services, Worcester, 1983-85; asst. dist. atty. Mid. Dist. Mass., Worcester, 1985—. Mem. Mass. Bar Assn., Worcester County Bar Assn., Women's Bar Assn. Mass., Mass. Assn Women Lawyers, League of Women Voters. Democrat. Roman Catholic. Criminal. Office: Dist Atty Mid Dist 2 Main St Courthouse Room 220 Worcester MA 01608

MCMAHON, MARTIN JAMES, JR., law educator; b. Phila., May 3, 1949; s. Martin James and Doris (Raymond) McM.; m. Pamela Sue Zogbaum, June 26, 1971; children: Conor M., Timothy J. BA, Rutgers U., 1971; JD, Boston Coll., 1974; LLM, Boston U., 1979. Bar: N.H. 1974, U.S. Dist. Ct. N.H. 1974, U.S. Tax Ct. 1979, U.S. Supreme Ct. 1979, Ky. 1981. Assoc. Hambett & Kerrigan, Nashua, N.H., 1974-79; prof. law U. Ky., Lexington, 1979—; vis. assoc. prof. law U. Va., Charlottesville, 1982-83; prof. in residence, chief counsel IRS, Washington, 1986-87. Author: (with others) Coal Law and Regulation vol. 3, 1983, Fundamentals of Federal Income Taxation Study Problems, 1986; editor: (with others) Fundamentals of Federal Income Tax, 1983; contbr. articles to profl. jours. Mem. ABA, Ky. Bar Assn., N.H. Bar Assn., Eastern Mineral Law Found., Nat. Tax Assn., Tax Inst. Am., Order of Coif. Legal education, Corporate taxation, Personal income taxation. Home: 357 Ashmoor Dr Lexington KY 40503 Office: U Ky Coll Law Lexington KY 40506-0048

MCMAHON, MICHAEL JOSEPH, lawyer; b. Omaha, June 13, 1951; s. Thomas Jean McMahon and Donna Marion Dow;. Student, U. Calif., San Diego, 1969-71; BA, UCLA, 1973; JD cum laude, Gonzaga U., 1976. Bar: Wash. 1976, U.S. Dist. Ct. (ea. dist.) Wash. 1976, U.S. Ct. Appeals (9th cir.) 1978. Ptnr. Randall & Danskin P.S., Spokane, Wash., 1976-85, Etter & McMahon P.S., Spokane, 1985—. Mem. ABA, Wash. State Bar Assn., Spokane County Bar Assn., Wash. State Trial Lawyers Assn. Republican. Club: Spokane. Avocations: running, golf, volleyball. Insurance, Labor, Personal injury. Office: Etter & McMahon W 505 Riverside Ave 450 Fernwell Bldg Spokane WA 99201

MCMAHON, MICHAEL SEAN, lawyer; b. Mansfield, Ohio, Oct. 18, 1955; s. Walter Francis and Patricia Ann (Meyers) McM.; m. Melody Layton, Aug. 21, 1982. BA, John Carroll U., 1978; JD, Columbia U., 1981. Bar: Ohio 1981, U.S. Dist. Ct. (no. dist.) Ohio 1982, U.S. Dist. Ct. (ea. dist.) Wis. 1983, U.S. Ct. Appeals (6th cir.) 1985. Assoc. Guren, Merritt, Cleve., 1981-84, Benesch, Friedlander, Cleve., 1984—. Co-author: The Silent Alliance, 1984; also articles. Mem. ABA, Ohio Bar Assn., Fed. Bar Assn. Environment, Civil rights, Election and campaign finance law. Office: Benesch Friedlander 850 Euclid Ave Cleveland OH 44118

MCMAHON, THOMAS MICHAEL, lawyer; b. Evanston, Ill., May 11, 1941; s. Robert C. and Kathryn D. (Dwyer) McM.; m. M. Ann Kaufman, July 11, 1964; children—Michael, Patrick. Student, U. Notre Dame, 1959-61; B.A., Marquette U., 1963; J.D. magna cum laude, Northwestern U., 1970. Bar: Ill. 1970. Mgr. legal adv. sect. Ill. EPA, Springfield, 1970-72; assoc. firm Sidley & Austin, Chgo., 1972-75; ptnr., chmn. environ. group Sidley & Austin, 1975—; lectr. environ. law Practicing Law Inst., Calif. Bus. Law Inst., Chgo. Bar Assn., Inst. Continuing Legal Edn., Ill. State Bar Assn.; mem. City of Evanston Environ. Control Bd., 1981-83. Served to lt. USN, 1963-67. Decorated Republic of Vietnam Campaign medal. Mem. ABA (lectr. environ. law, chmn. subcom. environ. aspects bus. transactions natural resources com.), Ill. State Bar Assn., Chgo. Bar Assn., Chgo. Assn. Commerce and Industry. Environment, General corporate, Real property. Office: Sidley & Austin Suite 4500 One First Nat Plaza Chicago IL 60603

MCMAHON, WILLIAM ROBERT, lawyer, judge; b. Rochester, N.Y., Jan. 12, 1944; s. John Emmett and Kathryn F. (Hayes) McM.; m. Diane Sue Ballreich, Aug. 3, 1968; children: Lisa Marie, Timothy. BS in Bus. Adminstrn., Tri-State U., 1967; JD, Toledo U., 1970. Bar: Ohio 1971, U.S. Dist. Ct. (no. dist.) Ohio 1972, U.S. Supreme Ct. 1975. With Seneca County (Ohio) Pros. Atty.'s Office, 1970-73, asst. prosecutor, 1971, spl. asst. prosecutor, 1971-73; sole practice, Tiffin, Ohio and Toledo, 1970-79; ptnr. McMahon & Kelbley, Tiffin, 1979-80; judge Fostoria (Ohio) mcpl. ct., 1980—; mem. rules adv. com. Ohio Supreme Ct., 1982—. Co-author (videotape edn. series) Your Rights on the Job, Ohio Dept. Edn., 1986. Bd. dirs. Tiffin U., 1975—, sec., 1978-80, vice chmn. bd., 1980—; founding pres. bd. trustees Sandusky Valley Domestic Violence Shelter Inc., 1982; bd. dirs., pres. adv. bd. Seneca County Domestic Violence Shelter, 1980-82; bd. dirs. Sandusky Valley Bd. Substance Abuse, 1973-75, Big Bros./Big Sisters Seneca County, 1980-81, Fostoria Literacy Council, 1987—; bd. dirs., chmn. allocation com. United Way Seneca County, 1973-75; trustee Ohio Ctr. Law-Related Edn., 1984—; pres. Seneca County Young Reps., 1973-75; formerly active various polit. campaigns including Pres. Nixon, Pres. Ford, Pres. Reagan. Fellow Ohio Bar Found.; mem. ABA (Public Service award-Second Place Judiciary Lawday U.S.A. 1983, Nat. Conf. Spl. Ct. Judges 1982—, Nat. Conf. Bar Pres. 1980—, coms. on edn. and law-related edn. 1983—), Ohio Bar Assn. (jud. adminstrn. and legal reform com. 1981—, chmn. 1981-85, com. on law-related edn. 1980—, vice chmn. 1984-85), Seneca County Bar Assn. (pres. 1980), (trustee, treas. 1983—, chmn. Bar Assn., Am. Judicature Soc., Am. Judges Assn., Ohio Jud. Conf. (exec. com. 1986—), Ohio Mcpl. Ct. Judges (exec. adv. bd. 1980-81, trustee 1983—), Ohio County and Mcpl. Judges Assn. (trustee 1983—, treas. 1983-84, chmn. jud. adminstrn. rev. com., 2d. v.p. 1985-86, 1st v.p. 1985-87, pres. 1987—), Tiffin Area C. of C. (dir. 1972-75), Toledo Old Newsboys Assn., Horatio Alger Soc., Internat. Platform Assn. Club: Exchange (Exchangite of Yr. 1984, dist. pres. 1985-86). Lodges: KC (4th, advocate 1976-80), Kiwanis. Co-author: Scripts and Teachers Guide-State v. Gold E. Locks and B.B. Wolf v. Curly Pig, 1984, (film series) Your Rights on the Job, 1986, Ohio Trial Judges Resource Manual, 1986. Jurisprudence. Office: Fostoria Mcpl Ct 213 S Main St Fostoria OH 44830-1126

MCMAKIN, J. GARY, lawyer; b. Dothan, Ala., Jan. 11, 1947; s. William Coleman and Mary Lou (Sikes) McM.; m. Linda Louise Shoe, Sept. 13, 1970 (div.); children: Whitney Paige, Courtney Shay; m. Debra Ann Hoffman, July 5, 1986. BS in Bus., U. Tenn., 1969; JD, Memphis State U., 1974. Bar: Fla. 1974, U.S. Dist. Ct. (mid. dist.) Fla. 1974, U.S. Ct. Appeals (5th cir.) 1975. Asst. state's atty. 13th Jud. Cir., Tampa, Fla., 1974-76; ptnr. Goodrich & McMakin P.A., Tampa, 1976-79; sole practice Tampa, 1979—. Family and matrimonial, Personal injury. Office: 304 Plant Ave Tampa FL 33606

MCMANAMAN, KENNETH CHARLES, lawyer, judge, educator, naval officer; b. Fairfield, Calif., Jan. 25, 1950; s. Charles James and Frances J. (Holys) McM.; m. Carol Ann Wilson, Apr. 15, 1972; children—Evan John, Kinsey Bridget, Kierin Rose. B.A. cum laude, S.E. Mo. State U., 1972; J.D., U. Mo.-Kansas City, 1974; grad. Naval Justice Sch., Newport, RI., 1975; M.S. in Bus. Mgmt. summa cum laude, Troy State U., Montgomery, Ala., 1978. Bar: Mo. 1975, U.S. Dist. Ct. (we. dist.) Mo. 1975, U.S. Dist. Ct. (ea. Dist.) Mo. 1978, Fla. 1976, U.S. Dist. Ct. (no., mid. dists.) Fla. 1976, U.S. Ct. Mil. Appeals 1977, U.S. Ct. Appeals (5th, 8th cirs.) 1977, U.S. Supreme Ct. 1978, Ill, 1987. Ptnr. firm O'Loughlin, O'Loughlin & McManaman, Cape Girardeau, Mo., 1978—; prof. bus. law Troy State U., Ala., 1976-78; prof. bus. law S.E. Mo. State U., Cape Girardeau, 1978-84; instr. law Mo. Dept. Pub. Safety, S.E. Mo. Regional Law Enforcement Tng. Acad., 1979—; instr. law Cape Girardeau Police Res., 1983—; mcpl. judge City of Jackson, Mo., 1980—; spl. mcpl. judge City of Cape Girardeau, 1981—. Mem. Cape Girardeau County Council on Child Abuse, 1980-81; membership dir. S.E. Mo. Scouting council Boy Scouts Am., 1980-82; mem. Cape Girardeau County Mental Health Assn., 1982—; active local and state Dem. Party, del. Nat. Dem. Conv., San Francisco, 1984, chmn. County Dem. Com., 1984-86; mem. 8th Congl. Dist. Dem. Com., 1984-86, 27th State Dem. Senatorial Com., 1984-86; bd. dirs. Areawide Task Force on Drug and Alcohol Abuse, 1984—. Served to lt. JAGC, USN, 1975, lt. commdr. USNR, 1985—. Named One of Outstanding Young Men of Am. 1981, 82, 84, 85. Mem. ABA (Mo. del. for young lawyers div. 1982-83)., Mo. Bar Assn. (chmn. trial advocacy task force 1982, psychology and the law task force 1983), Mo. Bar (young lawyers sect. council, rep. dist. 13, 1980-85), Fla. Bar Assn., Kansas City Bar Assn., Assn. Trial Lawyers Am., Fed. Bar Assn., Nat. Coll. Dist. Attys., Cape Girardeau County Bar Assn. (founder, pres. young lawyers sect. 1981-82), Mo. Mcpl. and Assoc. Cir. Judges Assn., Naval Res. Assn. (v.p. Southeast Mo.-So. Ill. chpt. 1980-85), Southeast Mo. State Alumni Council, Sigma Chi (numerous awards), Sigma Tau Delta, Pi Delta Epsilon. Roman Catholic. General practice, Insurance, Workers' compensation. Home: 1135 Shawnee Jackson MO 63755 Office: O'Loughlin O'Loughlin and McManaman 1736 N Kingshighway Cape Girardeau MO 63701

MCMANUS, CLARENCE ELBURN, judge; b. New Orleans, June 3, 1934; s. Otis Clarence and Odell (Hawsey) McM.; m. Barbara Isabella Edmundson, Apr. 3, 1976; children—Elizabeth Ann, Bryan Stephen. B.B.A., Tulane U., 1958; J.D., 1961. Bar: La. 1961, U.S. Ct. Appeals (5th cir.) 1961, U.S. Dist. Ct. (ea. dist.) La. 1961. Sole practice, Metairie, La., 1961-69; asst. dist. atty. Jefferson Parish, La., 1969-82; state dist. 24th Jud. Dist. Ct., Gretna, La., 1982—. Democrat. State civil litigation, Criminal, Family and matrimonial. Home: 824 Bonnabel Blvd Metairie LA 70005 Office: Gretna Courthouse Annex Gretna LA 70053

MCMEEN, ELMER ELLSWORTH, III, lawyer; b. Lewistown, Pa., June 3, 1947; s. Elmer Ellsworth II and Frances Josephine (Biddle) McM.; m. Sheila Ann Taenzler, July 31, 1971; children—Jonathan Ellsworth, Daniel Biddle, James Cunningham and Mary Josephine (twins). A.B. cum laude, Harvard U., 1969; J.D. cum laude, U. Pa., 1972. Bar: 1973, U.S. Ct. Appeals (2d cir.) 1973, U.S. Dist. Ct. (so. and ea. dists.) N.Y. 1975. Assoc. Cravath, Swaine & Moore, N.Y.C., 1972-75; assoc. LeBoeuf, Lamb, Leiby & MacRae, N.Y.C., 1975-78, ptnr., 1979—; lectr. Editor U. Pa. Law Rev., 1970-72. Contbr. articles to profl. jours. Chmn. N.Y.C. regional com. for U. Pa. Law Sch., 1984-86; class sec. Mt. Hermon Sch. Class of 1965, Mass., 1984—. Fellow Am. Coll. Investment Counsel; mem. ABA, N.Y. State Bar Assn. (mem. corp. law com.). Democrat. Clubs: Wall Street, Marco Polo (N.Y.C.); Rockaway River Country (Denville, N.J.). General corporate, Securities, Public utilities. Home: 30 Oak Ln Mountain Lakes NJ 07046 Office: LeBoeuf Lamb Leiby & MacRae 28th Floor 520 Madison Ave New York NY 10022

MCMENAMIN, JOHN ROBERT, lawyer; b. Evanston, Ill., Sept. 30, 1946. BA, U. Notre Dame, 1968, JD, 1971. Bar: Ill. 1971. Law clk. to presiding judge U.S. Ct. Appeals (7th cir.), 1971-72; ptnr. Mayer, Brown & Platt, Chgo., 1978—. Chmn. adv. bd. Holy Trinity High Sch., Chgo., 1986. Mem. ABA, Chgo. Bar Assn., Mid-Am. Com. Roman Catholic. Clubs: Legal, Execs. of Chgo., University (Chgo.). Banking, General corporate. Office: Mayer Brown & Platt 190 S LaSalle St Chicago IL 60603

MCMENAMIN, MICHAEL TERRENCE, lawyer, author; b. Akron, Ohio, Nov. 11, 1943; s. John Joseph and Maxine Ann (Lipp) McM.; m. Carol Anne Breckenridge, June 27, 1967; children—Kathleen Heather, Colleen Cara, Patrick Rankin. B.A. with honors in Polit. Sci., Western Res. U., 1965; LL.B., U. Pa., 1968. Bar: Ohio 1968, U.S. Dist. Ct. (no. dist.) Ohio 1969, U.S. Ct. Appeals (6th cir.) 1971, U.S. Supreme Ct. 1981, U.S. Ct. Appeals (3d and 4th cirs.) 1986. Assoc. Walter, Harverfield, Buescher & Chockley, Cleve., 1968-74, ptnr., 1975—. Co-author: Milking the Public: Political Scandals of the Dairy Lobby from LBJ to Jimmy Carter, 1980. Contbg. editor Inquiry Mag., 1980-84, Reason Mag., 1983—. Trustee Fairmont Montessori Assn., 1979-87, sec., 1979-80, 81-82, treas., 1980-81, pres., 1982-85; trustee, sec. Inst. for Child Advocacy, 1977-80; active Citizens League Greater Cleve., 1968—, Council for a Competitive Economy, 1981—. Served to 1st lt. USAR, 1968-74. Mem. ABA, Ohio State Bar Assn., Greater Cleve. Bar Assn., Amnesty Internat. Labor, Federal civil litigation, Libel. Home: 3386 Ingleside Rd Shaker Heights OH 44122 Office: 1215 Terminal Tower Cleveland OH 44113

MCMENAMIN, ROBERT WILLIAM, lawyer, newspaper columnist; b. Portland, Oreg., Nov. 20, 1926; s. Frank Aloyious and Justice Hortense (Pessemier) McM.; m. Patricia Ann Wentworth, June 4, 1949; children—Michael, Maureen, Brian, Nancy. B.A. cum laude, U. Portland, 1947; J.D., Northwestern Coll. Law, 1951. Bar: Oreg. 1951. Founding ptnr. McMenamin & Assocs., Portland, Oreg., 1951—; newspaper columnist Oregonian, Daily Jour. of Commerce, Hillsboro Argus. Pres. City Club of Portland, 1977-78; presiding co-chmn. NCCJ, 1974-75; past pres. Cath. Charities; past pres. Friends of Library U. Portland. Mem. ABA, Oreg. Bar Assn. (merit award 1976, bd. govs. 1976-79, treas. 1978-79, mem., chmn. coms.), Multnomah County Bar Assn. Republican. Roman Catholic. Clubs: Riverside Golf and Country, Arlington, Multnomah Athletic. Author: Clergy Malpractice, 1986; contbg. editor: Law Office Economics and Management; contbr. articles to legal. publs. U.S., Can., Australia. General corporate and Clergy malpractice, Contracts commercial, Insurance. Home: 4435 SW 75th Portland OR 97225 Office: 621 SW Morrison Suite 1450 Portland OR 97205

MCMICHAEL, DONALD EARL, lawyer; b. Denver, Aug. 8, 1931; s. Earl L. and Charlotte F. McM.; m. Zeta Hammond, July 6, 1955; children—Lauren A. McMichael Gleason, Thomas D., Susan E. McMichael Markle. A.B., Dartmouth Coll., 1953; LL.B., U. Colo., 1956. Bar: Colo. 1956, U.S. Dist. Ct. Colo. 1956, U.S. Ct. Appeals (10th cir.) 1956. Assoc. Holme Roberts & Owen, 1956-58; pres. Corp. Ins. Assocs., 1958-70; dir. trust devel. Central Bank Denver, 1970-72; ptnr. Brenman, Sobol & Baum, Denver, 1972-74; ptnr. McMichael, Benedict & Multz (formerly McMichael, Wallace & Benedict), Denver, 1974—. Chmn. Denver Central YMCA, 1971-73. Served to capt. USAR, 1956-64. Named Layman of Yr., Denver Central YMCA, 1973. Mem. Colo. Bar Assn., Denver Bar Assn., Denver Estate Planning Council (sec. 1971-73). Republican. Methodist. Estate planning, Oil and gas leasing, General corporate. Office: 1580 Lincoln St Denver CO 80203

MCMICHAEL, JAMES DAVID, lawyer; b. Baton Rouge, Oct. 17, 1956. BA, La. State U., 1979; JD, U. Tex., 1982. Bar: La. 1982, U.S. Dist. Ct. (ea. dist.) La. 1982, U.S. Ct. Appeals (5th cir.) 1982. Assoc. Liskow & Lewis, New Orleans, 1982—. Mem. ABA, La. Bar Assn., Order of Coif. Federal civil litigation, State civil litigation. Office: Liskow & Lewis 1 Shell Sq 50th Floor New Orleans LA 70139

MCMILLAN, JAMES BRYAN, judge; b. Goldsboro, N.C., Dec. 19, 1916; s. Robert Hunter and Louise (Outlaw) McM.; m. Margaret Blair Miles, Feb. 27, 1944 (dec. Mar. 1985); children: James Bryan, Marjorie Miles Rodell. Grad., Presbyn. Jr. Coll., 1934; A.B., U. N.C., 1937; LL.B., Harvard, 1940; LL.D. (hon.), Belmont Abbey Coll., 1982, Davidson Coll., 1984, Johnson C. Smith Coll., 1985. Bar: N.C. bar 1941. Mem. staff N.C. atty.-gen., 1940-42; partner Helms, Mulliss, McMillan & Johnston, Charlotte, 1946-68; U.S. dist. judge Western Dist. N.C., Charlotte, 1968—; judge pro tem Charlotte City Ct., 1947-51; mem. faculty Nat. Inst. Trial Advocacy, Boulder, Colo., 1973-81; instr. trial advocacy course Harvard Law Sch., 1975—, U. N.C. Law Sch., 1976-78, U. Fla. Law Sch., 1978-80; mem. N.C. Cts. Commn., 1963-71. Pres. Travelers Aid Soc., 1957-59; bd. visitors Davidson Coll. Served from apprentice seaman to lt. USNR, 1942-46, ETO. Recipient Algernon Sydney Sullivan award St. Andrews Presbyn. Coll. Fellow Internat. Acad. Trial Lawyers; mem. ABA, 26th Dist. Bar Assn. (pres. 1957-58), N.C. Bar Assn. (pres. 1960-61), Am. Judicature Soc. (dir. 1984—). United World Federalists, Newcomen Soc., St. Andrews Coll. Alumni Assn. (pres. 1965-66), Order of Coif, Golden Fleece, Omicron Delta Kappa. Democrat. Presbyn. Clubs: Charlotte City, Charlotte Country, Charlotte Philosophers. Home: 1930 Mecklenburg Ave Charlotte NC 28205 Office: US Dist Ct US Courthouse 401 W Trade St Room 254 Charlotte NC 28202

MCMILLAN, LEE RICHARDS, II, lawyer; b. New Orleans, Aug. 26, 1947; s. John H. and Phoebe (Skillman) McM.; m. Lynne Clark Pottharst, June 27, 1970; children: Leslie Clark, Hillary Anne, Lee Richards III. BS in Commerce, Washington and Lee U., 1969; JD, Tulane U., 1972; LLm in Taxation, NYU, 1976. Bar: La. 1972. Assoc. Jones, Walker, Waechter, Poitevent, Carrere & Denegre, New Orleans, 1976-79, ptnr., 1979—; bd. dirs. Mech. Equipment Co., Inc., New Orleans, vice chmn., 1980-86, chmn. bd., 1986—. Bd. dirs. Louise S. McGehee Sch., New Orleans, 1982—, co-chmn. capital fund drive 1984-86, pres. bd. dirs. 1986—. Served to lt. JAGC USNR, 1972-75. Mem. ABA (ad hoc com. on negotiated acquisition 1986—), La. State Bar Assn. (chmn. corp. and bus. law sect., mem. com. on bar admissions). Republican. Episcopalian. Avocation: sailing. Securities, Banking, General corporate. Office: Jones Walker et al 201 St Charles Ave New Orleans LA 70170

MCMILLAN, M. SEAN, lawyer. Diploma U. Munich, 1963; cert. Internat. Sch., Copenhagen, Denmark, 1962; B.S., U. So. Calif., 1967; J.D., Harvard U., 1970. Bar: Calif. 1971. Spl. projects dir. Mass. Gen. Hosp., Boston, 1967-70; ptnr. Keatinge, Libbott, Bates & Loo, Los Angeles, 1970-74, Loo, Merideth & McMillan, Los Angeles, 1974-85, Bryan, Cave, McPheeters & McRoberts, Los Angeles, 1986—. Assoc. dir. U. So. Calif. Corp. Law and Fin. Inst., 1974—. Mem. Assn. Computing Machinery, ABA, Am. Soc. Internat. Law, Phi Beta Kappa, Phi Kappa Phi. Editor: Harvard Internat. Law Jour., 1968-70. Private international, General corporate. Office: Bryan Cave McPheeters & McRoberts 333 S Grand Suite 3100 Los Angeles CA 90017

MCMILLAN, RICHARD, JR., lawyer; b. Opa-Locka, Fla., June 16, 1944; s. Richard and Mary Allison (Bigelow) McM.; m. Barbara Ann Dillon, Dec. 20, 1969; children: Molly Bigelow, Karen Gilbert, Mark Richard. AB, Princeton U., 1966; JD, U. Minn., 1972. Bar: Minn. 1972, D.C. 1973, U.S. Supreme Ct. 1980, U.S. Ct. of Appeals (3rd, 5th, and D.C. cirs.). Assoc. Jones, Day, Reavis & Pogue, Washington, 1972-79, ptnr., 1979; ptnr. Crowell & Moring, Washington, 1979—. Contbr. articles to profl. jours. Served to 1st lt. U.S. Army, 1966-69. Mem. ABA (litigation and antitrust sects.). Presbyterian. Avocations: sports, bridge, theater. Federal civil litigation, State civil litigation, Antitrust. Home: 2 Newlands St Chevy Chase MD 20815 Office: Crowell & Moring 1001 Pennsylvania Ave Washington DC 20005

MCMILLEN, LINDA LOUISE, lawyer; b. Ft. Worth, Dec. 20, 1947; d. James M. and Helen Dorrace (Taylor) McM.; m. Burke William Biow, Dec., 1968 (div. 1973); 1 child, Heather Lyn McMillen. B.S. with high honors, Tex. Wesleyan Coll., 1977; J.D., Baylor U., 1980. Bar: Tex. 1980, U.S. Dist. Ct. (no. dist.) Tex. With Ryan Mortgage Co., Arlington, Tex., 1973-75; law clk. Wash, Hodges & Segrest, Waco, Tex., 1978-79; assoc. Kinkead Law Offices, Amarillo, 1980-81; lectr. bus. law, U. Tex.-Arlington, 1984-86; sole practice, Arlington, 1981—. Mem. Am. Thai Found. Edn. (sec., bd. dirs.), Arlington, 1982—, Am.-Thai Christian Found., Arlington, 1982-85. Author: The Shadow of Man, 1983; Eiphaun, 1986. Mem. State Bar Tex., ABA, Tarrant County Family Bar Assn., Tarrant County Women Lawyers, Tarrant County Bar Assn., Arlington Bar Assn., others. Mem. Christian Ch. General practice, Family and matrimonial, Consumer commercial. Home: 2904 Friendswood Arlington TX 76013 Office: Linda McMillen Atty at Law 1408 W Abram Arlington TX 76013

MCMILLIAN, ROGER LEE, lawyer; b. Oklahoma City, Sept. 4, 1947; s. Elbert L. and Majorie M. (Perkins) McM.; m. Martha Jane Martin, Sept. 27, 1969; children—Michol Leigh, Morgan Marie. B.S. in Acctg., Okla. State U., 1969; J.D., U. Tulsa, 1973. Bar: Okla. 1973, U.S. Dist. Ct. (we. dist.) Okla. 1975, U.S. Supreme Ct. 1978. City atty., Stillwater, Okla., 1973-78; ptnr. McMillian & Winters, Stillwater, 1978—. Sec., bd. dirs. YMCA, Stillwater, 1979; bd. dirs. United Way, Stillwater, 1975-78, Okla. Athletic Hall of Fame, 1975-76; bd. dirs. Okla. State Golf Assn., Oklahoma City, 1976-77. Mem. Okla. Mcpl. Attys. Assn. (pres. 1981-82), Payne County Bar Assn. (pres. 1982), Nat. Inst. Mcpl. Law Officers (state chmn. 1976-78). Democrat. Methodist. Local government, Consumer commercial, Landlord-tenant. Office: McMillian & Winters 720 S Husband Suite 3 Stillwater OK 74074

MCMILLIAN, THEODORE, federal judge; b. St. Louis, Jan. 28, 1919; m. Minnie E. Foster, Dec. 8, 1941. B.S., Lincoln U., 1941, H.H.D. (hon.), 1981; LL.D., St. Louis U., 1949; H.H.D. (hon.), U. Mo., St. Louis, 1978. Mem. firm Lynch & McMillian, St. Louis, 1949-53; asst. circuit atty. City of St. Louis, 1953-56; judge U.S. Ct. Appeals (8th cir.), 1978—; judge Circuit Ct. for City St. Louis, 1956-72, Mo. Ct. Appeals eastern div., 1972-78; asso. prof. adminstrn. justice U. Mo., St. Louis, 1970—; asso. prof. Webster Coll. Grad. Program, 1977; mem. faculty Nat. Coll. Juvenile Justice, U. Nev., 1972—. Served to 1st lt. Signal Corps U.S. Army, 1942-46. Recipient Alumni Merit award St. Louis U., 1965. Mem. Lawyers Assn., Mo., Mound City bar assns., Am. Judicature Soc., Phi Beta Kappa, Alpha Sigma Nu. Jurisprudence. Office: US Courthouse 1114 Market St Room 526 Saint Louis MO 63101 and: US Court of Appeals US Ct & Customs House Saint Louis MO 63101 *

MCMORROW, WILLIAM JOHN, lawyer; b. N.Y.C., June 25, 1928; s. William F. and Ruth (Hullinger) McM.; m. Bernadette Decouzon, Apr. 28, 1951; children: william D., James D., Nicole D. AB in Eng. Lit., Dartmouth Coll., 1949; LLB, Yale U., 1952. Bar: N.Y. 1956, U.S. Dist. Ct. (so. and ea. dists.) N.Y. 1956, U.S. Ct. Appeals (2d cir.) 1956. Labor counsel Sperry Corp., Great Neck, N.Y., 1955-72; asst. gen. counsel Sperry Corp., N.Y.C., 1975-85; gen. operations counsel aerospace and marine groups Sperry Corp., Phoenix, 1986—; assoc. Moskowitz & Flood, N.Y.C., 1972-75. Served to lt. USNR, 1952-55, Korea. Mem. ABA (labor sect.), Assn. of Bar of City of N.Y., Am. Arbitration Assn. (labor arbitrator). Labor, Government contracts and claims, Contracts commercial. Office: Sperry Corp Aerospace & Marine Group PO Box 21111 Phoenix AZ 85036

MCMURRY, ROBERT I., lawyer, educator; b. Sterling, Ill., Aug. 5, 1947; s. Robert Curtis and Vivian (Wolf) McM.; 1 child, Evan David. BS, U. Denver, 1970; MS, Ill. State U., 1971; postgrad., U. So. Calif., 1972-74; JD, UCLA, 1982. Bar: Calif. 1982, Ill. 1983, U.S. Dist. Ct. (cen. dist.) Calif. 1983, U.S. Dist. Ct. (no. dist.) Ill. 1984, U.S. Dist. Ct. (no. dist.) Calif. 1985. Law clk. U.S. Dist. Ct., Los Angeles, 1982-83; atty. Sidley & Austin, Los Angeles, 1983-87; prof. law Loyola Sch. of Law, Los Angeles, 1984—; Mem. com. on environment State Bar Calif. Mem. Los Angeles County Bar Assn. (exec. com., internat. law sect.), Chgo. Bar Assn., Assn. Bus. Trial Lawyers, Japanese-Am. Bar Assn. Environment, State civil litigation, Condemnation. Office: Haines Russ McMurry & deRecat 10920 Wilshire Blvd Suite 1000 Los Angeles CA 90024

MCNABNEY, RONALD LADD, lawyer; b. Anderson, Ind., Dec. 9, 1939; s. William S. and Leah F. (Richardson) M.; m. Patricia F. Maddox, May, 1960 (div. Nov. 1969); m. Sharon Jo Sourland, Apr. 3, 1971; children—Barbara, Ronald Jay, Justin, Joshua, Joel. B.S., Ball State U., 1965, M.S., 1971; J.D., Ind. U., Indpls., 1976. Bar: Ind. 1976. Tchr., Muncie Schs., Ind., 1965-71, dir. adult edn., 1970-71; prof. Anderson Coll., 1977-82; felony trial dep. pros. Madison County, Anderson, 1976-78, chief trial dep. pros., 1983-85; atty. Madison County Bar, Anderson, 1976—; police tng. Madison County Pros., 1983-85; cons. Parents without Ptnrs., 1978; Mem. bd. mgmt. YMCA, Anderson, 1980-82; mem. adminstrv. council First Meth. Ch., 1985—; com. mem. March of Dimes, 1981. Mem. ABA, Assn. Trial Lawyers

Am., Madison County Bar Assn., Ind. Bar Assn., Ind. Assn. Trial Lawyers. Democrat. Club: Anderson Country. Lodges: Elks, Lions. General practice. Office: Ronald L McNabney & Assocs Attys at Law One Citizens Plaza Suite 306 Anderson IN 46016

MCNAGNY, PATRICIA ANN, state judge; b. Ft. Wayne, Ind., June 29, 1926; d. Ralph F. and Helene Julia (Edwards) Gates; m. Phil M. McNagny Jr., Feb. 24, 1951 (dec. Mar. 1981); children: Julia, Elizabeth, Carolyn, Marcia. AB, Ind. U., 1948, JD, 1951. Bar: Ind. 1951, U.S. Dist. Ct. (no. and so. dists.) Ind. 1951. Atty. Columbia City, Ind., 1951-83; judge Whitley County Superior Ct., Columbia City, 1983—. Bd. trustees Peabody Library, Columbia City, 1958—; bd. elders First Presbyn. Ch., Columbia City, 1986—; vice chmn. Rep. com. Whitley County, Columbia City, 1952-60. Mem. Ind. Bar Assn., Ind. Judges Assn., Whitley County Bar Assn., Parliamentary Law Club (pres. 1960), Kappa Kappa Kappa. Office: Whitley County Superior Ct Columbia City IN 46725

MCNAIR, MICHAEL STEPHEN, lawyer; b. Montgomery, Ala., Sept. 30, 1952; s. William Hooten and Norma Jean (Hickman) McN.; m. Susan Stuart, Dec. 30, 1972; children—Stuart Michael, Michael Stephen. B.S. in Fin., U. South Ala., 1975; J.D., U. Ala., 1978, LL.M., 1983. Bar: Ala. 1978, U.S. Dist. Ct. (so. dist.) Ala. 1979. Atty. Mobile Police Dept., Ala., 1978-80; ptnr. Noojin & McNair, Mobile, 1980-86; sole practice, Mobile, 1986—; atty. Mobile Police Dept., 1986—. Editor Jour. of Legal Profession, 1976-77. Contbr. articles to profl. jours. Pres. Exchange Club Mobile, 1980-81; v.p. Ala. Dist. Exchange Clubs, 1983-84, 84-85, dir. 1981-83; named to Selective Service Bd., 1982. Hugo L. Black scholar U. Ala. Sch. Law, 1977. Mem. Ala. State Bar, Mobile Bar Assn., ABA, Ala. Trial Lawyers Assn., Am. Trial Lawyers Assn., Bench and Bar. Baptist. Home: 224 Walshwood Ave Mobile AL 36604 Office: 51 Government St Mobile AL 36602

MCNALLY, JAMES JOSEPH, lawyer; b. Saratoga Springs, N.Y., Nov. 15, 1955; s. Joseph F. and Rita J. (Powers) McN.; m. Ana Maria Iglesias, May 30, 1981; children: Sarah, Robert, Megan. BA, Boston Coll., 1977; JD, U. Md., 1980. Bar: Md. 1980, Fla. 1980, U.S. Dist. Ct. (so. dist.) Fla. 1981. Jr. ptnr. Blackwell, Walker, Fascell & Hohel, Miami, Fla., 1980—. Mem. ABA, Fla. Bar Assn., Md. Bar Assn., Assn. Trial Lawyers Am., Dade County Def. Bar Assn. Avocation: sports car restoration. Personal injury, Insurance, State civil litigation. Home: 8775 SW 61st Ave Miami FL 33143

MCNALLY, JOHN JOSEPH, lawyer; b. N.Y.C., July 1, 1927; s. Edward E. and Virginia L. (O'Brien) McN.; m. Sally Vose Greeley, Jan. 25, 1958; children: Martha, Sarah, Elizabeth, Julie, Thomas. A.B., Coll. Holy Cross, 1950; LL.B., Harvard U., 1953. Bar: N.Y. 1953. Assoc. White & Case, N.Y.C., 1953-63, ptnr., 1964—; dir. Waterman Marine Corp., N.Y.C.; panelist in field. Trustee Caedmon Sch., N.Y.C., 1968—; bd. dirs. Community Fund of Bronxville-Eastchester-Tuckahoe, Inc., 1986—. Fellow Am. Bar Found.; mem. ABA, N.Y. State Bar Assn., N.Y. County Lawyers Assn., Bar Assn. City N.Y. General corporate, Securities. Home: 58 Avon Rd Bronxville NY 10708

MCNALLY, PIERCE ALDRICH, corporate finance lawyer; b. Mpls., Jan. 23, 1949; s. William James Lois Marie (Aldrich) McN.; m. Deborah Zack, Oct. 16, 1976; children: Caitlin Barrett, Mary Murphy. AB, Stanford U., 1971; cert., U. Paris III, 1972; JD, U. Wis., 1978. Bar: Wis. 1978, Minn. 1978, U.S. Dist. Ct. Minn. 1978, U.S. Dist. Ct. (we. dist.) Wis. 1979, U.S. Ct. Appeals (8th cir.) 1979. Law clk. to sr. judge U.S. Dist. Ct. Minn., Mpls., 1978-79; assoc. Oppenheimer, Wolff and Donnelly, Mpls., 1979-85; v.p. FBS Mcht. Banking Group, Mpls., 1985—; bd. dirs. Midwest Communications, Inc., Mpls. Bd. dirs. New Dance Ensemble, Mpls., 1985—, Minn. Orchestral Assn., Mpls., 1986—. Mem. ABA, Minn. Bar Assn., Hennepin County Bar Assn., State Bar Wis. (bd. govs. 1984—, past pres., bd. dirs. nonresident lawyers div. 1980—), Wis. Law Alumni Assn. (bd. dirs. 1982-86), U. Wis. Madison Twin Cities Alumni Club (bd. dirs., past pres.), Bascom Hill Soc., Order of Coif. Club: Minnesota, Minneapolis, Minikahda. Avocations: skiing, squash, history. Corporate finance, General corporate. Office: FBS Mcht Banking Group 1300 1st Bank Pl W Minneapolis MN 55402

MCNALLY, SUSAN FOWLER, lawyer; b. Portsmouth, Va., Jan. 10, 1957; d. Joseph D. and Marie C. Fowler; m. James Edward McNally, Mar. 23, 1985. BA, U. Pacific, 1978; JD, UCLA, 1981. Bar: Calif. 1981, U.S. Dist. Ct. (cen. dist.) Calif. 1982, U.S. Ct. Appeals (9th cir.) 1982. Assoc. Hahn, Cazier & Smaltz, Los Angeles, 1982-85, Gilchrist & Rutter, Santa Monica, Calif., 1985—; moot ct. judge UCLA Moot Ct. honors program, 1982—. Mem. ABA (com. on real property litigation), Calif. Bar Assn., Los Angeles County Bar Assn. (law day speaker Roosevelt High Sch. 1986), Santa Monica Bar Assn., Women Lawyers Assn. (speaker Pepperdine U. 1985), Jaycees (speaker UCLA Grad. Sch. Mgmt. 1985), Assn. Bus. Trial Lawyers. Avocations: hiking, bicycling, skiing, running. Real property, Contracts commercial, State civil litigation. Office: Gilchrist & Rutter 1299 Ocean Ave Suite 9000 Santa Monica CA 90401

MCNAMARA, A. J., U.S. district judge; b. 1936. B.S., La. State U., 1959; J.D., Loyola U., New Orleans, 1968. Bailiff, law clk. U.S. Dist. Ct., New Orleans, 1966-68; individual practice law, New Orleans, 1968-72; mem. firm Monton, Roy, Carmouche, Hailey, Bivins & McNamara, New Orleans, 1972-78, Hailey, McNamara, McNamara & Hall, 1978-82; U.S. dist. judge Eastern dist. La., New Orleans, 1982—. Mem. La. Ho. of Reps., 1976-80. Judicial administration. Office: US District Court Chambers C-316 US Courthouse 500 Camp St New Orleans LA 70130 *

MCNAMARA, BARRY THOMAS, lawyer; b. New Haven, May 15, 1944; s. Joseph Thomas and Ann Winifred (Hannan) McN.; m. Paddy O'Donnell Harris, Aug. 19, 1972. A.B., U. Notre Dame, 1966; J.D., Northwestern U., 1969. Bar: Ill. 1969, U.S. Dist. Ct. (no. dist.) Ill. 1969, U.S. Ct. Appeals (7th cir.) 1969, U.S. Supreme Ct. 1974, U.S. Dist. Ct. (cen. dist.) Ill. 1979, U.S. Ct. Appeals (2d, 5th and 9th cirs.) 1980. Assoc. Gardner, Carton & Douglas, Chgo., 1969-75; ptnr. O'Brien, Carey, McNamara, 1975-82; ptnr. D'Ancona & Pflaum, Chgo., 1982—. adj. prof. Ill. Inst. Tech.-Kent Coll. Law, 1986—. Chmn. Chgo. Area Project; pres. Mental Health Assn. Greater Chgo.; fin. co-chmn. Stevenson for Gov., 1982. Mem. ABA (litigation sect. nat. task force on punitive damages, antitrust sect.), Ill. Bar Assn. (chmn. antitrust law council), Chgo. Bar Assn., Chgo. Council Lawyers, Fed. Bar Assn., 7th Cir. Bar Assn. Club: University (Chgo.). Contbr. articles to legal jours. Antitrust, Federal civil litigation. Home: Apt 20G 1550 N Lake Shore Dr Chicago IL 60610 Office: 30 N LaSalle St Chicago IL 60602

MCNAMARA, FRANK LUKE, JR., lawyer; b. Providence, Nov. 4, 1947; s. Frank Leo and Kathryn (Reardon) McN.; m. Elizabeth Jay Bacon, Sept. 16, 1978; children: Luke (dec.), Robert, Kate, Peter, Elizabeth. AB, Harvard U., 1969; JD, U. Va., 1976. Bar: Mass. 1977, U.S. Dist. Ct. Mass. 1977, U.S. Ct. Appeals (1st and D.C. cirs.) 1979. Assoc. Choate, Hall & Stewart, Boston, 1976-79; atty. Boston Bar Co., 1979-82; ptnr. Vena, McNamara, Truelove & Lahey, Boston, 1982—. Served as lt. USNR, 1969-73, Vietnam. Republican. Roman Catholic. Federal civil litigation, Real property, State civil litigation. Home: 52 Wilder Rd Boston MA 01740 Office: Vena McNamara Truelove Lahey 100 Boylston St Boston MA 02116

MCNAMARA, JOHN BOLIVAR, JR., lawyer; b. Waco, Tex., Nov. 24, 1914; s. John B. Sr. and Alice (Goodrich) McN.; m. Nancy Wallis, Sept. 16, 1939; children: John B. III, Nancy W. McNamara Groover. BA, Baylor U., 1936, LLB, 1938. Bar: Tex. 1938. Asst. atty. City of Waco, Tex., 1938-41; spl. agt. FBI, Washington, 1941-45; ptnr. McNamara & McNamara, Waco, 1945—. Mem. Waco Charter Commn., 1977-86; pres. United Fund of Waco, 1949-50. Mem. ABA, Tex. Bar Assn., Tex. Bar Found., Waco-McLennan County Bar Assn. (pres. 1950-51). Clubs: Ridgewood Country (Pres.), Brazos (Waco). Lodge: Kiwanis (pres. 1950-51). Avocations: hunting, fishing, boating, travel. Real property, Probate, Banking. Home: 5425 Lakecrest Dr Waco TX 76710 Office: McNamara & McNamara 500 Republic Bank Tower Waco TX 76701

MCNAMARA, LAWRENCE JOHN, lawyer; b. Evergreen Park, Ill., Aug. 10, 1950; s. William Francis and Florence M. (Nicholson) McN.; m. Julia Melton Wagner, Mar. 25, 1978. BA, Ill. Coll.; JD, Vanderbilt U. Bar: Tex. 1976, U.S. Ct. Appeals (5th cir.) 1976, U.S. Dist. Ct. (so. dist.) Tex. 1977, U.S. Dist. Ct. (ea. dist.) Tex. 1978, U.S. Supreme Ct. 1979, U.S. Ct. Appeals (11th cir.) 1981, U.S. Dist. Ct. (no. dist.) Tex. 1985. Assoc. Baker & Botts, Houston, 1976-85; ptnr. Baker, Smith & Mills, Dallas, 1985—. Mem. ABA, Tex. Bd. Legal Specialization (cert.), Phi Beta Kappa. Roman Catholic. Avocations: golf, running. Labor, Federal civil litigation, Trade secret litigation. Office: Baker Smith & Mills 500 LTV Ctr Dallas TX 75201-2916

MCNAMARA, MARTIN BURR, oil and gas company executive, lawyer; b. Danbury, Conn., Sept. 10, 1947; s. William Joseph and Geraldine Margaret (Young) McN.; m. Anne Rose Hogan, Jan. 15, 1977. BA in English, Providence Coll., 1969; JD, Yale U., 1972. Bar: N.Y. 1973, U.S. Dist. Ct. (so. and ea. dists.) N.Y. 1973, U.S. Ct. Appeals (2d cir.) 1973, Tex. 1980, U.S. Ct. Appeals (5th and 11th cirs.) 1980. Assoc. Shea & Gould, N.Y.C., 1972-76; asst. U.S. atty. (so. dist.) N.Y., N.Y.C., 1976-79; v.p., gen. counsel, sec. Tex. Oil & Gas Corp., Dallas, 1979—; gen. counsel Delhi Gas Pipeline Corp. subs. Tex. Oil & Gas Corp., Dallas; bd. dirs. Ala. Interstate Gas Corp., Calif. Natural Gas Pipeline, Inc., Delhi Gas Pipeline Corp., The Nueces Co., Ozark Gas Pipeline Corp., Red River Gas Pipeline Corp., various others. Co-contbr. articles to Yale Law Jour. Mem. exec. com. Yale Law Sch. Assn., 1983—. Mem. State Bar of Tex. (vice chmn. corp. counsel bd. 1984—), Assn. Bar. City of N.Y., N.Y. State Bar Assn., Fed. Energy Bar Assn. Republican. Roman Catholic. Clubs: Chaparral, Lancers (Dallas). General corporate, Oil and gas leasing, FERC practice. Office: Texas Oil & Gas Corp 1700 Pacific St Dallas TX 75201

MCNAMARA, RICHARD BEDLE, lawyer; b. Elizabeth, N.J., July 4, 1950; s. Robert Daniel and Doris (Bedle) McN.; m. Linda Battista, June 10, 1973; children: Jennifer Beth, Christopher Brendan, Julie Bridget. AB, Boston Coll., 1972, JD, 1975. Bar: N.H. 1975, U.S. Dist. Ct. N.H. 1975, U.S. Ct. Appeals (1st cir.) 1978, U.S. Supreme Ct. 1979. With Atty. Gen.'s Office, Concord, N.H., 1975-77, asst. atty. gen., 1977-79; assoc. Wiggin & Nourie, Manchester, N.H., 1979-82; ptnr. Wiggin & Nourie, Manchester, 1983—. Author: New Hampshire Criminal Practice and Procedure, 1980, Constitutional Limitations on Criminal Procedure, 1982. Mem. ABA, N.H. Bar Assn. (chmn. com. on rules of criminal procedure 1985—), Manchester Bar Assn. Republican. Roman Catholic. Federal civil litigation, State civil litigation, Criminal. Home: 52 Buttonwood Rd Bedford NH 03102 Office: Wiggin & Nourie Franklin and Market Sts Manchester NH 03105

MCNAMARA, ROGER THOMAS, lawyer; b. Balt., Feb. 13, 1939; s. Leonard Thomas and Regina Anne (Besche) M.; m. Sara Jane Jones, Sept. 5, 1975. B.S., U.S. Mil. Acad., 1962; J.D. with honors, George Washington U., 1973; LL.M. in Labor Law, Georgetown U., 1980. Bar: Va. 1974, U.S. Ct. Mil. Appeals 1974, U.S. Ct. Appeals (9th cir.) 1974, U.S. Ct. Appeals (3d cir.) 1986, U.S. Supreme Ct. 1986. Atty., U.S. Air Force, worldwide, 1974-83; dep. counsel U.S. Dept. Navy, Washington, 1983-85, counsel office civilian personnel mgmt. USN, 1985-86, asst. gen. counsel, 1987—. Served to maj. USAF, 1962-68, Vietnam; lt. col. USAFR. Decorated D.F.C., Air medal with 12 oak leaf clusters, Meritorious Service medal, Air Force Commendation medal with 3 oak leaf clusters; Presdl. Service Badge White House, 1965-67. Mem. ABA, Va. Bar Assn., Fed. Bar Assn. Roman Catholic. Labor, Military, Federal civil litigation. Home: 5501 Seminary Rd No 106-South Falls Church VA 22041 Office: Office of Gen Counsel Dept Navy Washington DC 20360-5110

MCNAMARA, THOMAS NEAL, lawyer; b. Washington, Dec. 1, 1930; s. Philip Joseph and Louise Loretta (Ryan) McN.; children: John Michael, George Denison, Mary Louise; m. Deana Hollingsworth, Dec. 21, 1987. B.A., Duke U., 1952; J.D. with honors, George Washington U., 1959. Bar: Va. 1959, Calif. 1960. Assoc. Pillsbury, Madison & Sutro, San Francisco, 1959-66, ptnr., 1967—; mng. ptnr. Pillsbury, Madison & Sutro, Los Angeles. Contbr. articles to profl. jours. Trustee Dixie Sch. Dist., San Rafael, Calif., 1964-76; dir. San Francisco Home Health Service, 1975-82. Served to lt. comdr. USNR, 1952-56, Korea. Mem. Am. Bar Found., Calif. Bar Assn., San Francisco Bar Assn., ABA, VA Bar Assn., Internat. Game Fish Assn. (Calif. rep. 1983—), Order of Coif. Republican. Roman Catholic. Clubs: San Francisco Stock Exchange, San Francisco Tennis, Pacific Union, The Family (San Francisco). Home: 11053 Strathmore Dr Los Angeles CA 90024 Office: Pillsbury Madison & Sutro 225 Bush St San Francisco CA 94104 also: 333 S Grand Ave Los Angeles CA 90071

MCNAMEE, STEPHEN M., lawyer. U.S. atty. State of Ariz., Phoenix. Office: 4000 US Courthouse 230 North First Ave Phoenix AZ 85025 *

MC NAUGHT, JOHN J., fed. judge; b. 1921. B.A., Boston Coll., 1943, J.D., 1949. Bar: Mass. 1949. Sole practice Malden, Mass., 1949-50; mem. Esdaile Morris & McKenney, 1954-58, 1958-72; assoc. justice Superior Ct. Mass., 1972-79; judge U.S. Dist. Ct. Mass., 1979—; mem. faculty Nat. Jud. Coll., 1978—. Served with AUS, 1943-46. Judicial fellow Am. Coll. Trial Lawyers; mem. ABA, Mass. Bar Assn. Jurisprudence. Office: care US Dist Ct 1525 US McCormack PO and Courthouse Bldg Boston MA 02109

MCNAUGHTON, GEORGE THEODORE, lawyer; b. Coldwater, Mich., Apr. 17, 1951; s. Ford Blaine and Lena Mae (Mulchahey) McN.; m. Beth Hadene Tredway, Mar. 23, 1973; children—Justin, Nathan, Heidi, Ethan, Zachary, Brigham. B.S., U. Oreg., 1973; J.D. cum laude, Ind. U., 1976. Bar: Ind. 1976, U.S. Dist. Ct. (so. dist.) Ind. 1976, U.S. Dist. Ct. (no. dist.) Ind. 1977, U.S. Supreme Ct. 1984. Sole practice, Fremont, Ind., 1976—. Editor: Ind. Law Jour., 1976. Town atty., Town of Fremont, 1978—, Town of Hamilton, Ind., Town of Orland, Ind.; bd. dirs. Fremont Community Schs., 1982-86 . Mem. ABA, Ind. Mcpl. Lawyers Assn., Ind. Bar Assn., Internat. Platform Assn. Republican. Mormon. Lodges: Masons, Shriners. General practice, Local government, Consumer commercial. Home and Office: PO Box A Fremont IN 46737

MC NEAL, HARLEY JOHN, lawyer; b. Birmingham, Ala.; s. John Harley and Alfretta (Frederick) McN.; m. Virginia Marie Hutzel, Feb. 8, 1936; children: Virginia Ann, Sandra Jean McNeal Highley. A.B., U. Mich., 1932, student Law Sch., 1934, student Med. Sch., 1936; LL.B., Western Res. U., 1936, LL.M., 1966; student, Case Sch. Applied Sci., 1938-39, student Med. Sch., 1940; student, U. Wis. Law Sch., 1935, Cleve. Coll., 1938. Bar: Ohio 1935. Mem. firm John H. McNeal and Harley J. McNeal, Cleve., 1935-45; partner Burgess, Fulton & Fullmer, Cleve., 1945-50, McNeal & Schick, Cleve., 1950-69; sr. partner McNeal & Schick, 1969—; lectr. Western Res. U. Med. Sch., also Dental Sch., 1945-62, Cleve. Marshall Law Sch., 1958-60, Western Res. U. Law Sch., 1958-62; mem. Nat. Bd. Trial Advocacy, 1979—. Author numerous articles profl. jours.; co-author: Personal Injury Litigation in Ohio; asso. editor: The Forum, 1965-69. Mem. council, Bay Village, Ohio, 1950-52; mem. center com. on law and environ. World Peace Through Law Center, Belgrade, Yugoslavia, 1971; mem. adminstrn. of justice adv. com. Greater Cleve. Asso. Found.; mem. com. for justice Greater Cleve. Growth Assn.; bd. dirs. Def. Research Inst. Served to capt. JAGD, USAAF, 1942-45, ETO. Fellow Am. Coll. Trial Lawyers (chmn. com. procedures and preservation oral argument), Internat. Acad. Trial Lawyers, Am. Acad. Forensic Scis., Am., Ohio bar founds.; mem. Am. Bd. Profl. Attys. (trustee), Internat. Assn. Ins. Counsel (pres. 1966-67), Fedn. Ins. Counsel Assn., ABA (chmn. rules and procedure and trial technique coms. ins. sect., co-chmn. profl. liability com. litigation sect., mem. council litigation sect. 1978—), Internat. Bar Assn., Fed. Bar Assn., Inter-Am. Bar Assn., Ohio Bar Assn. (chmn. individual rights and responsibilities com.), Cleve. Bar Assn. (chmn. modern jud. system com., trustee), Bar Assn. Greater Cleve. (pres. 1980-81), Cuyahoga County Bar Assn., World Peace Through Law (maritime com., chmn. litigation sect.), Am. Judicature Soc., Ohio Jud. Conf. (rules adv. com.), Maritime Law Assn. U.S., Nat. Assn. R.R. Trial Lawyers, Am. Soc. Internat. Law, U. Mich. Alumni Assn., Internat. Acad. Law and Sci., Greater Cleve. Growth Assn., Phi Delta Phi, Sigma Alpha Epsilon, Druids. Republican. Presbyn. Clubs: Westwood Country (Rocky River, Ohio); Union, Nisi Prius, Hermit (Cleve.). Lodge: Mason (Rocky River, Ohio) (32, K.T.). Federal civil litigation, State civil litigation, Personal injury. Home: 26828 W Lake Rd Bay Village OH 44140 Office: 10th Floor Illuminating Bldg Cleveland OH 44113

MCNEAL, JOHN EDWARD, lawyer; b. Mifflin, Pa., Feb. 15, 1935; s. William Clark and Margaret Evon (Smeal) McN.; m. Suzanne Fulton, Aug. 19, 1957; children: Pamela Jean, Gregg Fulton, Steven John. BS, Millersville State Coll., 1961; MA, U. Del., 1965; PhD, U. Va., 1970; JD, W.Va. U., 1981. Bar: W.Va. 1981, U.S. Dist. Ct. (so. dist.) W.Va., U.S. Ct. Appeals (D.C. cir.) 1986. Tchr. Solanco Jr. and Sr. High Sch., Quarryville, Pa., 1961-63, J.P. McCaskey High Sch., Lancaster, Pa., 1963-64; assoc. prof. history St. Francis Coll., Loretto, Pa., 1968-75; legis. advisor Council of D.C., Washington, 1981-86; staff asst. Office of Adjudication Dept. Consumer and Regulatory Affairs, Washington, 1986—. Coach elem. sch. football, Ebensburg, Pa., 1969-71, Little League baseball, Ebensburg, 1969-71, Pony League football, Ebensburg, 1971. Served as sgt. USMC, 1954-57. Mem. ABA, ACLU, W.Va. State Bar Assn., D.C. Bar, So. Poverty Law Ctr. Democrat. Avocations: running, reading, touch football, weight lifting. Administrative and regulatory, Legislative, Local government. Home: 1324 Jonquil St NW Washington DC 20012 Office: Office of Adjudication 613 G St NW Washington DC 20001

MCNEELY, J. LEE, lawyer; b. Shelbyville, Ind., May 4, 1940; s. Carl R. and Elizabeth J. (Orebaugh) McN.; m. Rose M. Wisker, Sept. 5, 1977; children: Angela, Susan, Meg, Matt. AB, Wabash Coll., 1962; JD, Ind. U., 1965. Bar: Ind. 1965, U.S. Dist. Ct. (so. dist.) Ind. 1965, U.S. Ct. Appeals (7th cir.) 1970. Assoc. Pell & Matchett, Shelbyville, 1965-70; ptnr. Matchet & McNeely, Shelbyville, 1970-74; sole practice Shelbyville, 1974-76; sr. ptnr. McNeely & Sanders, Shelbyville, 1976—; guest lectr. Franklin Coll., Ind., 1965-72; judge Shelbyville City Ct., 1967-71. Chmn. Shelbyville County Rep. Cen. Com., 1968—; bd. dirs. Ind. Lung Assn., 1972-75, Crossroads Council Boy Scouts Am., 1982; bd. dirs., pres. Shelbyville Girls Club. Named Sagamore of the Wabash, gov. Otis Bowen, 1977, gov. Robert Orr, 1986. Fellow Ind. Bar Found. (patron); mem. ABA, Ind. Bar Assn. (sec. 1985—, bd. dirs. 1976-78), Shelby County Bar Assn. (pres. 1975), Ind. Lawyers Commn. (pres. 1975), Fed. Merit Selection Commn., Shelbyville Jaycees (Distinguished Service award 1969, Good Govt. award 1970), Wabash Coll. Alumni Bd. (bd. dirs. 1983-85, 86—). Methodist. Lodges: Lions, Elks, Eagles. Avocations: golf, travel. Labor, Insurance, State civil litigation. Home: RR1 Box 510 Shelbyville IN 46176 Office: McNeely & Sanders PO Box 457 Shelbyville IN 46176

MCNEELY, MARK WRIGHT, lawyer; b. Shelbyville, Ind., Mar. 26, 1947; s. Carl R. and Elizabeth J. (Orebaugh) McN.; children—Patrick, Mary. Student Wabash Coll., 1965-67; A.B., Franklin Coll., 1970; J.D., Ind. U., 1974. Bar: Ind. 1974. Dep. state pub. defender State of Ind., 1972, pub. defender Shelby Superior Ct., 1973-76, Shelby County Ct., 1976—; atty. Shelby County Dept. Pub. Welfare, 1976—; ptnr. McNeely & Sanders, Shelbyville, Ind., 1976—; pres. Land Title & Abstract Co. Author: System Book for Family Law: Post Trial Enforcement of Decree, 1983. Mem. parish council, 1982-85, pres. 1983-85. Served with U.S. Army. Fellow Ind. State Bar Assn. (family law sect.); mem. ABA, Shelby County Bar Assn. (sec.-treas. 1985, pres. 1986), Ind. Pub. Defender Council (pres. 1983-84, sec. 1986-87). Democrat. Roman Catholic. Clubs: Lions, Elks. Family and matrimonial, Criminal, Bankruptcy. Home: Rural Rt #2 PO Box 408 Shelbyville IN 46176-9488 Office: McNeely & Sanders 611 S Harrison PO Box 457 Shelbyville IN 46176

MCNEIL, ALEXANDER MALLORY, lawyer, state court administrator; b. Washington, Jan. 20, 1948; s. Donald Southworth and Doris (Mallory) McN.; m. Mary Spencer, June 6, 1970; children: Joanna, Jeffrey. BA, Yale U., 1970; JD, Boston Coll., 1973. Bar: Mass. 1973, U.S. Dist. Ct. Mass 1982, U.S. Ct. Appeals (1st cir.) 1982. Law clk. Mass. Appeals Ct., Boston, 1973-74, adminstrv. asst., 1974—. Author: Total Television, 1980, 1st rev. ed., 1985. Mem. Mass. Bar Assn., Order of Coif. Judicial administration. Office: Mass Appeals Ct 1500 New Courthouse Boston MA 02108

MCNEIL, BUCK W., lawyer; b. Sevier County, Ark., Sept. 21, 1916; s. Benjamin Alexander and Mary Arthusa (Dillard) McN.; m. Betty Jo Watson, May 1, 1941; children—Kenneth E., Dan H., Buck Wayne, Diane McNeil Dittrich. B.A., Tex. Tech U., 1939; postgrad. Tulane U., 1939-41, Ohio State U., 1944; J.D., George Washington U., 1944. Bar: Tex. 1946, U.S. Ct. Appeals (5th cir.) 1947, U.S. Supreme Ct. 1950. Clk. FBI, Washington, 1941-42, spl. agt., 1942-46; ptnr. Burks & McNeil, Lubbock, Tex., 1946-53; prin. Buck W. McNeil Law Office, Lubbock, 1953—; v.p., sr. v.p. 1st Nat. Bank, Lubbock, 1960-79. Mem. ABA, Tex. Bar Assn., Am. Bankers Assn. Democrat. Baptist. Probate, Oil and gas leasing. Home and Office: 3310 54th St Lubbock TX 79413

MCNEIL, JEAN ANNE, lawyer; b. Boone, Iowa, June 23, 1954; d. Ronald Dean and Marjorie Ruth (Minson) McNeil; m. David W. Dunn. B.S. in Microbiology, U. Iowa, 1976; J.D., U. Ill., 1981. Bar: Iowa 1981. Ptnr., Davis, Hockenberg, Wine, Brown, Koehn & Shors, Des Moines, 1981—; part-time instr. Des Moines Area Community Coll., Ankeny campus, 1983. Mem. instnl. rev. com. Mercy Hosp. Med. Ctr., Des Moines, 1983—; active YMCA. Recipient Freshman Chemistry award Des Moines Area Community Coll., 1973. Mem. ABA, Iowa State Bar Assn., Polk County Bar Assn., Polk County Women's Bar Assn., Phi Delta Phi. Democrat. Baptist. State civil litigation, Federal civil litigation, Health. Office: Davis Hockenberg Wine et al 2300 Financial Ctr Des Moines IA 50309

MCNEILL, FREDERICK WALLACE, lawyer, writer, aviation consultant, pilot; b. Chgo., Jan. 4, 1932; s. James Joseph and Irene Gertrude (Stevenson) McN.; m. Judith Carol Austin, Feb. 9, 1957; children: Marjorie, Tamelyn, Kenneth, Patricia, Darcy, Sean, Meghan. BBA, U. Ariz., 1974, JD, 1977. Bar: Ariz. 1977, U.S. Dist. Ct. Ariz., 1977. Served to maj. USAF, 1949-73; ret., 1973; bus. mgr. Engring. & Research Assocs., Inc., Tucson, 1973-74; mng. ptnr. ERA Shopping Ctr., Tucson, 1973-75; chief pilot, spl. agt. Narcotics Strike Force, Ariz., 1975-77; dep. county atty. Pima County, Ariz., 1977-79; atty. Ariz. Drug Control Dist., 1977-79; ptnr. Rees & McNeill, Tucson, 1979-84; writer, 1984—; lectr. air smuggling seminars, organized crime seminars, Ariz., 1977-79. Vice pres. Indian Ridge Homeowners Assn., 1980-82; bd. dirs. Tucson Boys Chorus Bldg. Fund Com., 1972-74. Decorated DFC, Air medal (5), Air Force Commendation medal (2). Mem. ABA, Ariz. Bar Assn., Pima County Bar Assn., Assn. Trial Lawyers Am., Ariz. Trial Lawyers Assn., Lawyer Pilots Bar Assn., Ret. Officers Assn., Air Force Assn. Club: Order of Daedelians. Criminal, General practice, Air. Office: PSC Box 845 APO Miami FL 34002

MCNEILL, JOHN HENDERSON, government official, lawyer; b. Phila., Jan. 31, 1941; s. John Henderson and Cecilia Marie (Murphy) McN.; m. Helen Elizabeth Foley, June 18, 1966; children—John Henderson III, Bronwyn Jane Foley, Andrew Patrick Joseph. B.A., U. Notre Dame, 1962; J.D., Villanova U., 1965; LL.M., London Sch. Econs., 1971, Ph.D., 1974; diploma Hague Acad. Internat. Law, 1973. Bar: Pa. 1966, U.S. Supreme Ct. 1970, D.C. 1981. Assoc. Sheer & Mazzocone, Phila., 1966; asst. defender Defender Assn. Phila., 1966-67; law clk. to presiding justice, U.S. Ct. Common Pleas, Montgomery County, Pa., 1969-70; internat. relations officer ACDA, 1974-75, atty. adv., 1975-78, asst. gen. counsel, 1979-83; asst. gen. counsel (internat.) U.S. Dept. Def., 1983—; legal adv. U.S. del. SALT, 1977-79, Intermediate Range Nuclear Forces Negotiations with USSR, 1981-82, Strategic Arms Reduction Talks with USSR, 1983, Dept. Defense. rep. Maritime Boundary Talks with USSR, 1984— ; cons. Amnesty Internat., London, 1971-73, IAEA, Vienna, 1976; lectr. Notre Dame U. London Centre Legal Studies, 1973-74; adj. prof. law Georgetown U., 1987—. Bd. dirs. Crusade D.C. div. Am. Cancer Soc., 1976-77, recipient Leadership Honor award Nat. Capital Area Combined Fed. Campaign, 1982; bd. consultors Villanova U. Law Sch., 1978—. Served to 2d lt. USAF, 1967-68. Career mem. U.S. Sr. Exec. Service, 1983—. Recipient Meritorious Honor award ACDA, 1979; Centre Studies and Research in Internat Law and Internat. Relations, Hague Acad. Internat. Law scholar, 1974; London Sch. Econs. Internat. Law scholar, 1973. Mem. Am. Soc. Internat. Law. (exec. council 1986—), Internat. Inst. Strategic Studies, ABA, Fed. Bar Assn., Internat. Bar Assn. Club: Cosmos. Contbr. articles to legal jours. including Am. Jour. Internat. Law Public international, Legal education. Office: Pentagon Rm 3E963 Washington DC 20301

MCNEILL, PAUL SPURGEON, JR., state official; b. St. Louis, July 20, 1948; s. Paul Spurgeon and Lucille Elizabeth (Werner) McN.; m. Brandy Rachele Siegel, Sept. 23, 1982. BS, U. Mo., 1970, JD, 1974, MBA, 1975; LLM, Washington U., St. Louis, 1978. Bar: Mo. 1974, U.S. Tax Ct. 1975. Asst. county counselor St. Louis County, 1975-76; commr. Mo. Tax Commn., Jefferson City, 1976-77; sr. mgr. Peat, Marwick, Mitchell, N.Y.C.,

1977-85; dir. revenue State of Mo., Jefferson City, 1985—. Author: (with others) Administrative Law Handbook, 1978. Spl. asst. Mo. Gubernatorial Transition Commn., Jefferson City, 1979-80. Mem. ABA, Mo. Bar Assn., Bar Assn. Met. St. Louis, Am. Assn. CPA's, Mo. Soc. CPA's, Lambda Chi Alpha. Republican. Lutheran. Avocation: sailing. State and local taxation, Corporate taxation, Legislative. Home: 1448 Satinwood Dr Jefferson City MO 65101 Office: State of Missouri Dir Revenue PO Box 311 Jefferson City MO 65105

MCNEILL, THOMAS B., lawyer; b. Chgo., Oct. 28, 1934; s. Donald T. and Katherine M. (Bennett) McN.; m. Ingrid Sieder, May 11, 1963; children: Christine, Thomas, Stephanie. B.A., U. Notre Dame, 1956, J.D., 1958. Ptnr. Mayer, Brown & Platt, Chgo., 1962—; dir. Deltona Corp., Miami, Fla., Marley Holdings (U.S.A.) Inc. Served to capt. JAGC USAF, 1959-62. Mem. Chgo. Bar Assn., Chgo. Council Lawyers, Law Club Chgo., Legal Club Chgo. Club: Indian Hill (Winnetka, Ill.). Home: 930 Fisher Ln Winnetka IL 60093 Office: Mayer Brown & Platt 190 S LaSalle St Chicago IL 60603

MCNEILL, WALTER GILES, lawyer; b. Mt. Vernon, N.Y., Oct. 13, 1935; s. John Carroll and Amy (Giles) McN.; m. Roberta L'Heureux Gagnon, June 29, 1963; children: W. Giles, Mark, Leslie. BS, Tufts U., 1957; LLB, NYU, 1960. Bar: N.Y. 1960, U.S. Dist. Ct. (ea. dist.) N.Y. 1968, U.S. Supreme Ct. 1968. Assoc. Healy, Baillie & Burke, N.Y.C., 1960-64; assoc., then ptnr. Brown, Wood, Ivey, Mitchell & Petty, N.Y.C., 1964-84; ptnr. Skadden, Arps, Slate, Meagher & Flom, N.Y.C., 1984—. Contbr. articles on structured and mortgage related fin. to profl. jours. Mem. ABA, Assn. of Bar of City of N.Y. Avocations: tennis, skiing, sailing. Securities, Mortgage finance. Office: Skadden Arps Slate Meagher & Flom 919 3d Ave New York NY 10022-9931

MCNEILY, CURTLAN ROGER, lawyer; b. Columbus, Ohio, July 25, 1951; s. Roger and Lillian Louise (Birbeck-Robinson) McN.; m. Mary Zora Maletin, Aug. 26, 1973; children: Shannon, Colin. Student, Columbia Union Coll., 1969-71; BA, George Washington U., 1973; JD magna cum laude, Georgetown U., 1981. Bar: U.S. Ct. Appeals (D.C. cir.) 1981. Assoc. Cohen & Uretz, Washington, 1981-83; ptnr. Malley, Rosenfeld & Scott, Washington, 1983-85, McNeily & Rosenfeld, Washington, 1986—; bd. dirs. Washington Pvt. Capital, Ltd. Served to capt. USMC, 1973-78. Mem. ABA (editor in chief law rev. 1980-81). Republican. Club: Army and Navy (Washington). Personal income taxation, Corporate taxation, Securities. Home: 6104 Kennedy Dr Chevy Chase MD 20815 Office: McNeily & Rosenfeld 1747 Pennsylvania Ave Washington DC 20006

MCNEW, ROBERT A., lawyer; b. Mt. Vernon, Ohio, July 31, 1938; s. Virgil H. and Margaret (Johnston) McN.; m. Judith Ann Graffius, Sept. 4, 1964; children: Erin Margaret, Tracy Delores. BS, La. State U., 1961; JD, George Washington U., 1968. Bar: Ohio 1968, N.Y. 1979. Trial atty. antitrust div. U.S. Dept. of Justice Cleve. Regional Office, Cleve., 1968-75; asst. chief antitrust div. U.S. Dept. of Justice N.Y. Regional Office, N.Y.C., 1975-80; counsel trade regulation Eaton Corp., Cleve., 1980-87, sen. counsel, 1987—; adj. lectr. law Cleve. State U., 1985—. Editor: Jury Instruction in Criminal Antitrust Cases, 1982. Bd. dirs. Plainview-Old Bethpage Bd. of Edn., N.Y., 1975-80, pres., 1979; bd. dirs., trustee Alzheimers Disease and Related Disorders Assn., Cleve., 1985—, pres. 1986—. Served to lt. commdr. USCGR, 1961-68. Mem. ABA (chmn. criminal practice and procedure com. 1985-86), Fed. Bar Assn. (pres. Cleve. chpt. 1985-86, chmn. antitrust and trade regulation sect. 1986—). Democrat. Antitrust, Criminal. Home: 2926 Torrington Rd Shaker Heights OH 44122 Office: Eaton Corp 1111 Superior Ave Eaton Center Cleveland OH 44114

MCNEW, ROBERT BRUCE, lawyer; b. Augusta, Ga., Oct. 13, 1953; s. Robert Homer and Dorothy (Hesselbacher) McN.; m. Denise M. Goss, May 10, 1980. BA, U. Va., 1975; JD, Coll. William and Mary, 1979. Bar: Del. 1979, U.S. Dist. Ct. Del. 1980, U.S. Ct. Appeals (3d cir.) 1981, Pa. 1983, U.S. Dist. Ct. (ea. dist.) Pa. 1983, U.S. Ct. Appeals (10th and 11th cirs.) 1985. Law clk. to justice Del. Supreme Ct., Wilmington, 1979-80; assoc. Bayard, Handleman & Murdoch, Wilmington, 1980-83; ptnr. Greenfield & Chimicles, Haverford, Pa., 1983—. Mem. ABA, Del. Bar Assn., Pa. Bar Assn. Securities, Federal civil litigation. Office: Greenfield & Chimicles 361 W Lancaster Ave Haverford PA 19041

MCNICHOLS, ROBERT J., federal judge; b. 1922. Student, Wash. State U., 1946-48; J.D., Gonzaga U., 1952. Bar: Wash. 1952. Chief judge U.S. Dist. Ct. for Eastern Dist. Wash., Spokane. Office: US Dist Ct PO Box 2136 Spokane WA 99210 *

MCNICHOLS, STEPHEN LUCID ROBERT, JR., lawyer; b. Denver, June 5, 1943; s. Stephen Lucid Robert and Marjorie Roberta (Hart) McN.; children: Justin, Chelsea. Student, Monterey Inst. Fgn. Studies, 1964-65; BA, Pomona Coll., 1965; JD, U. Calif., Berkeley, 1968. Bar: Colo. 1968, Calif. 1969. Dep. dist. atty. San Luis Obispo County, Calif., 1970-73; assoc. Varni, Fraser, Hartwell & Van Blois, Hayward, Calif., 1973-76; ptnr. Varni, Fraser, Hartwell, McNichols & Rodgers, Hayward, 1976-86, McNichols, McCann, Seibel & Inderb, San Ramon, Calif., 1987—. Mem. Morro Bay (Calif.) Planning Commn., 1970-72, chmn. 1972; bd. dirs. Children's Hosp. Found., 1980-83. Mem. ABA (litigation sect.), Calif. Bar Assn. (adminstrn. justice com.), Alameda County (Calif.) Bar Assn. (bd. dirs. 1986—), So. Alameda County Bar Assn. (bd. dirs. 1978-80), Assn. Trial Laywers Am., Calif. Trial Lawyers Assn., Alameda-Contra Costa County Trial Lawyers Assn. (bd. dirs. 1977-78). Democrat. Club: Barristers (Alameda County)(bd. dirs. 1974-77); Blackhawk Country (Calif.). Avocations: skiing, running, golfing. State civil litigation, General business, Real property. Home: 947 Redwood Dr Danville CA 94526 Office: McNichols McCann Seibel & Inderbitzen 18 Crow Canyon Ct Suite 395 San Ramon CA 94583

MC NICOL, DONALD EDWARD, lawyer; b. Kew Gardens, N.Y., Aug. 11, 1921; s. William J. and Margaret (McGirr) McN.; m. Doris C. Egues, Apr. 3, 1943; children: Elaine McNicol Postley, Janet McNicol Barton, Donald Edward, Paul Mansfield. A.B., Harvard U., 1943, LL.B., 1948. Bar: N.Y. 1949. Assoc. Davis, Polk, Wardwell, Sunderland & Kiendl, N.Y.C., 1948-54, Hall, Patterson, Taylor, McNicol & Marett, N.Y.C., 1954-56; partner Hall, Patterson, Taylor, McNicol & Marett (now Hall, McNicol, Hamilton & Clark), 1956—; sec., dir. Am. Maize-Products Co.; bd. dirs. Am. Fructose Corp., Thomas Pub. Co., Thomson McKinnon Securities Inc., Westbury Fed. Savs. and Loan Assn. Trustee, sec. Boys Club Am. Served with AUS, 1942-46. Mem. N.Y. State Bar Assn., Assn. Bar City N.Y. Club: Harvard (bd. mgrs. N.Y.C. 1967-69). Home: 461 Berry Hill Rd Oyster Bay Cove NY 11791 Office: Hall McNicol Hamilton & Clark 220 E 42d St New York NY 10017

MCNIDER, JAMES SMALL, III, lawyer; b. Richmond, Va., Aug. 23, 1956; s. James Small Jr. and Phoebe Warwick (Johnston) McN.; m. Anna Mary Van Buren, Apr. 30, 1983; 1 child, Anna Lee. BS, Washington & Lee U., 1978, JD, 1981. Bar: Va. 1981, U.S. Tax Ct. 1981, U.S. Dist. Ct. (ea. dist.) Va. 1986. Assoc. Kaufman & Canoles, Norfolk, Va., 1981-85; assoc. Willcox & Savage, Norfolk, 1985-87, ptnr., 1987—. Mem. governing bd. Rights of Disabled, Richmond, 1985—; bd. dirs. Cultural Alliance of Hampton Roads, Norfolk. Mem. ABA, Va. Bar Assn., Omicron Delta Kappa. Episcopalian. Club: James River Country (Newport News, Va.). Avocations: pvt. pilot, tennis, golf, photography, computers. Corporate taxation, State and local taxation, General corporate. Home: 1108 Brunswick Ave Norfolk VA 23508 Office: Willcox & Savage 1800 Sovran Ctr Norfolk VA 23510-2197

MCNITT, DAVID GARVER, lawyer; b. Lewistown, Pa., Sept. 26, 1949; s. Garver M. and H. Faith (Harbeson) McN.; m. Mary Ellen Davis, Oct. 2, 1971; 1 child, David. B.S., Juniata Coll., 1971; J.D., Hamline U., 1976; cert. U. Exeter, Eng., 1976. Bar: Pa. 1977, U.S. Tax Ct. 1977, U.S. Dist. Ct. (ea. dist.) Pa. 1978, U.S. Supreme Ct. 1985. Sales assoc. Fin. Planning Assocs., Harrisburg, Pa., 1971-72; account supr. FMBAS, Inc., Camp Hill, Pa., 1972-74; tax acct. Stradley, Ronan, Stevens & Young, Phila., 1977; shareholder, dir. Cramp, D'Iorio, McConchie & Forbes, P.C., Media, Pa., 1977—; dir. Term-Tronics, Inc., San Diego, Vend-a-Video, Inc., San Diego, RDC Ventures, Inc., Chester, Pa., William Penn Seed Capital Fund, Phila.; guest lectr. Wharton Sch., U. Pa., Phila., 1982-84, 87; adj. prof. Del. Law Sch. at Widener U., Wilmington. Mem. ABA, Pa. Bar Assn., Del. County Bar Assn., Nat. Assn. Coll. and Univ. Attys. Republican. Mem. Society of Friends. Securities, General corporate, Corporate taxation. Home: 311 Smithfield Rd Wallingford PA 19086 Office: Cramp D'Iorio McConchie & Forbes PC 215 N Olive St Media PA 19063

MCNULTY, JOHN KENT, lawyer, educator; b. Buffalo, Oct. 13, 1934; s. Robert William and Margaret Ellen (Duthie) McN.; m. Linda Conner, Aug. 20, 1955 (div. Feb. 1977); children: Martha Jane, Jennifer, John K. Jr.; m. Babette B. Barton, Mar. 23, 1978. A.B. with high honors, Swarthmore Coll., 1956; LL.B., Yale U., 1959. Bar: Ohio 1961, U.S. Supreme Ct. 1964. Law clk. Justice Hugo L. Black, U.S. Supreme Ct., Washington, 1959-60; vis. prof. Sch. Law, U. Tex., summer 1960; asso. firm Jones, Day, Cockley & Reavis, Cleve., 1960-64; prof. law Sch. Law, U. Calif., Berkeley, 1964—; of counsel Baker & McKenzie, San Francisco, 1974-75; acad. visitor London Sch. Econs., 1985; lectr. univs. Cologne, Hamburg, London, Munich, Tokyo, Tilburg, Amsterdam, Rotterdam, Econs. U. Vienna, also others; mem. adv. bd. Carolina Acad. Press. Author: (with Kragen) Federal Income Taxation (Individuals, Corporations, Partnerships), 1985, 4th edit., Federal Income Taxation of Individuals, 3d edit., 1983, Federal Estate and Gift Taxation, 3d edit., 1983; mem. adv. bd. Carolina Academic Press. Guggenheim fellow, 1977. Mem. Am. Bar Assn., Am. Law Inst., Internat. Fiscal Assn. (council U.S. br.), Internat. Tax and Bus. Lawyers (mem. bd. overseers), Order of Coif, Phi Beta Kappa. International taxation, Personal income taxation, Corporate taxation. Home: 620 Spruce St Berkeley CA 94707 Office: 389 Boalt Hall Sch of Law U Calif Berkeley CA 94720

MCNULTY, THOMAS JOSEPH, JR., lawyer; b. Lawrence, Mass., Sept. 10, 1940; s. Thomas J. and Grace Elizabeth (Broderick) McN.; m. Maureen Ann Linehan, July 16, 1966; children: Shaela Ann, Sean Thomas, Kevin William. Student, Merrimack Coll., 1958-59, U.S. Naval Acad., 1959-60; BA, Boston U., 1963, JD, 1966. Bar: Mass. 1967, U.S. Dist. Ct. Mass. 1968, N.H. 1977, U.S. Supreme Ct. 1977. Assoc. Law Offices of Charles J. Ardito, West Yarmouth, Mass., 1966-68; staff atty. Legal Services Cape Cod & Islands Inc., Hyannis, Mass., 1968-69; ptnr. Holland, Farrel and McNulty, Falmouth, Mass., 1969-71; sr. atty., pres. McNulty and Hopkins, Barnstable, Mass., 1971—; master Mass. Superior Ct., examiner Mass. Land Ct. Mem. editorial bd. Mass. Lawyers Weekly, Boston, 1979-84; contbr. column to Barnstable Patriot, 1982-83. Chmn. Barnstable Mcpl. Airport Commn., 1973-76; pres. Centerville Civic Assn.; village chmn. United Fund, 1980—. Served with USN, 1959-60, with Res., 1960-66. Mem. ABA, Mass. Bar Assn., Mass. Trial Lawyers Assn., Mass. Assn. Town Counsel, Barnstable County Bar Assn. (editor newsletter 1976-81, 84-86, law day and chmn. pub. relations 1976-81, 1984-86). Avocations: writing, sailing. Contracts commercial, Probate, Real property. Office: McNulty and Hopkins PC 1441 Rt 132 PO Box 457 Barnstable MA 02630

MCPHAIL, ROBERT WILSON, lawyer; b. Jacksonville, Tex., Feb. 2, 1930; s. Charles Wesley and Bernice (Lee) McP.; m. Ann Radenz, June 6, 1953; children—Marilyn, Mark. B.B.A., Southwestern U., Georgetown, Tex., 1951; J.D., U. Houston, 1956. Bar: Tex. 1956, U.S. Dist. Ct. (so. dist.) Tex. 1983; cert. real estate law Tex. Bd. Specialization. Sole practice, Houston, 1960-68; mgr. exploration and prodn. contracts Conoco, Inc., Houston, 1968-70; pres. Tex. Republic Title Co., Houston, 1970-81; assoc. McPhail & Tennant, Houston, 1981-83; prin. McPhail Law Firm P.C., Houston and Fredericksburg, Tex., 1983—. Served with U.S. Army, 1952-54. Mem. Kappa Sigma. Methodist. Oil and gas leasing, Real property. Home: Route 3 Box 433 Fredericksburg TX 78624 Office: McPhail Law Firm PC PO Box 875 Fredericksburg TX 78624

MCPHERSON, BROCK RICHARD, lawyer; b. Salina, Kans., July 15, 1930; s. Boyd Richard and Thelma Myrtle (Jones) McP.; m. Barbara Jean Wasson, Mar. 25, 1951; children: Brad, Brit, Blair, Boyd. BA, U. Kansas City, 1955, JD, 1956. Bar: Kans. 1956, U.S. Dist. Ct. Kans. 1956. Clk., agt. FBI, Kansas City, Mo., 1948-57; ptnr. McPherson, Bauer, Pike & Pike, Great Bend, Kans.; atty. Barton County, Great Bend, 1965-67. Bd. dirs. Community Concert Assn., Great Bend, 1964-71, Heart Assn., Barton County, 1965-71. Mem. Kans. Bar Assn., Barton County Bar Assn., Jaycees (pres. Great Bend 1959-60, v.p. Kans. 1961-62, disting. service award 1962), County Attys. Assn. (v.p. 1965-66), Nat. Dist. Attys. Assn. (state bd. dirs. 1966-67), Interstate Oil Compact Commn. Democrat. Methodist. Club: Petroleum (Great Bend) (bd. dirs. 1965-67). Lodges: Elks (exalted ruler 1969-70), Shriners (bd. dirs. 1963-65). Avocations: restoring classic cars, snow skiing. Consumer commercial, Oil and gas leasing, Workers' compensation. Home: 2715 Broadway Great Bend KS 67530 Office: McPherson Bauer Pike & Pike 2109 12th Great Bend KS 67530

MCPHERSON, EDWIN FRANCIS, lawyer; b. Boston, Jan. 16, 1957; s. Henry Charles McPherson and Lucille (Gallacher) Davis. AB, U. So. Calif., 1978, MusB, 1978; JD, U. San Diego, 1982. Bar: Calif. 1982, U.S. Dist. Ct. (so., cen., we. and ea. dists.) Calif. 1983, U.S. Ct. Appeals (9th cir.) 1983, Hawaii 1983. Assoc. Booth, Mitchel, Strange & Smith, Los Angeles, 1982-85, Cooper, Epstein & Hurewitz, Beverly Hills, Calif., 1985—. Recipient Nathan Burkan Copyright Law award ASCAP, 1982. Mem. Calif. Bar Assn., Los Angeles County Bar Assn., Hawaii Bar Assn., Beverly Hills Bar Assn., Delta Chi (pres. 1976-77). Republican. Avocations: sports, music. Federal civil litigation, State civil litigation, Entertainment. Home: 11750 Sunset Blvd #219 Los Angeles CA 90049 Office: Cooper Epstein & Hurewitz 9465 Wilshire Blvd 8th Floor Beverly Hills CA 90012

MCPHERSON, JAMES AUBREY, lawyer, farmer; b. El Dorado, Ark., Dec. 11, 1931; s. Henry A. and Floye (Wheelus) McP.; m. Jacqueline Poet, Nov. 10, 1962 (div. 1972); children—Michael, David; m. 2d Julia Freeland, 1973 (dec. 1984); children—Jenipher, Matthew, Jessica. B.S. in Bus. Adminstrn., La. Poly. Inst., 1953; LL.B., Loyola U. of South, New Orleans, 1962. Bar: La. 1962. Law clk. to Robert A. Ainsworth, U.S. dist. ct. ea. dist. La., 1961-63; ptnr DuPlantier & McPherson, New Orleans, 1966-70, McPherson & Zainey, New Orleans, 1970—; lectr. legal seminars. Served with USMC, 1949-50. Mem. ABA, La. Bar Assn., Am. Trial Lawyers Assn., Nat. Assn. Criminal Def. Lawyers. Democrat. Unitarian. Criminal, Federal civil litigation.

MCPHERSON, NANCY JO BUENZLI, lawyer; b. Madison, Wis., Nov. 13, 1939; d. Philip Benedict and Helen Elizabeth (Welch) Buenzli; m. Robert Donald McPherson, Aug. 17, 1957; children: Sean Kelly, Eileen Patricia, Maureen Teresa, Cathleen Marie. Student, Tex. Western Coll., 1960-61, San Jacinto Jr. Coll., 1972-73; BA with honors, U. Houston, 1974; JD, So. Tex. Coll. Law, 1977. Bar: Tex. 1978. Assoc. Law Office R.D. McPherson, Houston, 1978-80; ptnr. McPherson & McPherson, Houston, 1980—. Mem. ABA, Tex. Bar Assn. Avocation: gardening. Personal injury, Workers' compensation, State civil litigation. Office: McPherson & McPherson 3818 Garrott St Houston TX 77006-5095

MCPHILLIPPS, JULIAN LENWOOD, JR., lawyer; b. Birmingham, Ala., Nov. 13, 1946; s. Julian and Eleanor E. (Dixon) McP.; m. Jeanne Leslie Burton, June 22, 1974; children—Rachel, Grace. A.B. with honors, Princeton U., 1968; J.D., Columbia U., 1971. Bar: N.Y. 1972, Ala. 1975, U.S. Sup. Ct. 1975, others. Assoc., Davis, Polk & Wardwell, N.Y.C., 1971-73; assoc. csl. Am. Express Co., N.Y.C., 1973-75; asst. atty. gen. Ala. and chief csl. Ala. Securities Commn. and Ala. State Banking Dept., Montgomery, 1975-77; sole practice, Montgomery, 1977-83, sr. ptnr. McPhillipps, De Bardelaben & Hawthorne, 1983-86. Vestryman, Episcopal Ch.; bd. dirs. YMCA, Montgomery Crime Prevention Program; del. Democratic Nat. Conv., 1980. Mem. ABA, Ala. Bar Assn., Ala. Trial Lawyers Assn., Montgomery County Bar Assn., Assn. Bar City N.Y. Clubs: Lions; Ivy (Princeton, N.J.). State civil litigation, Federal civil litigation. Home: 831 Felder Ave Montgomery AL 36106 Office: PO Box 64 Montgomery AL 36101

MCPHILLIPS, JOSEPH WILLIAM, lawyer; b. Glens Falls, N.Y., Feb. 18, 1951; s. W. Joseph and Margery (Ford) McP.; m. Nadine Trombly, June 8, 1974; children: Devin Ford, Blaine David. BS, SUNY, Oneonta, 1973; JD, Albany Law Sch., 1976. Bar: N.Y. 1977, U.S. Dist. Ct. (no. dist.) N.Y. 1977. Assoc. Corbett & Mercure, Ft. Edward, N.Y., 1977-78; sole practice South Glens Falls, N.Y., 1978—; justice Town of Moreau, South Glens Falls, 1980-86, Village of South Glens Falls, 1981-86; prosecutor Stop Driving While Intoxicated program Saratoga County Dist. Atty. Office, Ballston Spa, N.Y., 1986—. Pro bono atty. Legal Aid Soc. of Northeastern N.Y., Albany, 1986—; bd. dirs. Adirondack Samaritan Counseling Ctr., Inc., Glens Falls, 1984—. Mem. ABA, N.Y. State Bar Assn., Warren County Bar Assn., Saratoga County Bar Assn., South Glens Falls/Moreau C. of C. (bd. dirs. 1979—). Republican. Roman Catholic. Avocations: canoeing, cross country skiing. General practice, Real property, Family and matrimonial. Home: 7732 Oakwood Dr South Glens Falls NY 12803 Office: 55 Saratoga Ave South Glens Falls NY 12803

MCQUARRIE, CLAUDE MONROE, III, lawyer; b. Ft. Benning, Ga., Oct. 15, 1950; s. Claude Monroe Jr. and Rosanne (Sprinkle) McQ.; m. Patricia Elaine Swanson, Dec. 23, 1977; children: Kevin Andrew, Ryan Christopher, Erin Elizabeth. BS, U.S. Mil. Acad., 1972; JD with distinction, St. Mary's U., San Antonio, 1978. Bar: Tex. 1978, U.S. Dist. Ct. (so. dist.) Tex. 1982, U.S. Ct. Mil. Appeals 1979. Commd. 2d lt. U.S. Army, 1972, advanced through grades to capt., 1976, resigned, 1982; assoc. Fulbright & Jaworski, Houston, 1982—. Editor Law Rev., 1977-78. Mem. ABA, Houston Bar Assn., John M. Harlan Soc., Phi Delta Phi. Avocations: golf, skiing. State civil litigation, Insurance, Personal injury. Home: 2802 Eagle Creek Dr Kingwood TX 77345 Office: Fulbright & Jaworski 1301 McKinney Houston TX 77010

MCQUIGG, JOHN DOLPH, lawyer; b. Abilene, Tex., Oct. 19, 1931; s. John Lyman and Dorothy Elinor (King) McQ.; m. Sandra Elainea Duke, Oct. 18, 1969; 1 son, John Revel. B.A., Denison U., 1953; LL.B., U. Tex., Austin, 1962. Bar: Fla. 1962, U.S. Supreme Ct. 1971. Asso., Shackleford, Farrior, Stallings & Evans, 1962-66, ptnr., Tampa, Fla., 1966-73; pres. John McQuigg, P.A., Tampa, 1973-80; shareholder Fowler, White, Gillen, Boggs, Villareal & Banker, P.A., Tampa, 1980—. Bd. dirs. Fla. Gulf Coast R.R. Mus., Inc., 1985—. Served to 1st lt. USAF, 1953-57. Mem. Fla. Bar, ABA. Episcopalian. Club: Tampa. Federal civil litigation, State civil litigation, Workers' compensation. Home: 10114 Lindelaan Tampa FL 33618 Office: PO Box 1438 Tampa FL 33601

MCQUISTON, JOHN WARD, II, lawyer; b. Memphis, Sept. 19, 1943; s. John Ward and Anna Vance (Hall) McQ.; m. Robbie Walker, Aug. 20, 1966; children—Anna Stewart, Katherine Walker. B.A., Rhodes Coll., Memphis, 1965; J.D., Vanderbilt U., 1968; hon. grad. U.S. Naval Justice Sch., 1969. Bar: Tenn. 1968. Ptnr., Goodman, Glazer, Greener, Schneider & McQuiston, Memphis, 1972—; instr. constrn. contract law Memphis State U., 1982. Pres., Les Passes Rehab. Center, 1982; pres. St. Mary's Episcopal Sch., 1986, chmn. 1986-88, bd. dirs. NCCJ. Served with USCG, 1968-72. Mem. ABA, Tenn. Bar Assn. (chmn. sect. on antitrust 1983-84) Memphis and Shelby County Bar Assn. (dir. 1987), Forum Com. on Constrn. Law, Order of Coif. Episcopalian. Club: University (Memphis). Contbr. article to Tenn Bar Jour., 1983. Federal civil litigation, General corporate, Antitrust. Office: Goodman Glazer Greener et al 1 Tennessee Bank Bldg Suite 1500 Memphis TN 38103

MCRAE, DONALD JAMES, lawyer; b. Kewanee, Ill., May 5, 1926; s. Ross J. and Wilna Louise (Warner) McR. B.S., Northwestern U., 1948, J.D., 1951. Bar: Ill. 1951, U.S. Dist. Ct. (cen. dist.) Ill. 1954. Law office of D.J. McRae, Kewanee, Ill., 1951—; dir. Peoples Nat. Bank, Kewanee. Served with USN, 1944-46; to lt. comdr. USNR ret. Mem. Assn. Trial Lawyers Am., Ill. Trial Lawyers Assn., Ill. State Bar Assn., Henry County Bar Assn., Kewanee C. of C. Republican. Presbyterian. Club: Midland Country (pres. 1974—), Rotary (pres. 1974), Elks, Masons (Kewanee, Ill.). State civil litigation, Probate, Federal civil litigation. Home: Rural Route 2 Kewanee IL 61443 Office: 217 W 2d St Kewanee IL 61443

MCRAE, HAMILTON EUGENE, III, lawyer; b. Midland, Tex., Oct. 29, 1937; s. Hamilton Eugene and Adrian (Hagaman) McR.; m. Betty Hawkins, Aug. 27, 1960; children—Elizabeth Ann, Stephanie Adrian, Scott Hawkins. BSEE, U. Ariz., 1961; student, USAF Electronics Sch., 1961-62; postgrad., U. Redlands, Calif., 1962-63; JD with honors and distinction, U. Ariz., 1967. Bar: Ariz. 1967, U.S. Supreme Ct. 1979. Elec. engr. Salt River Project, Phoenix, 1961; assoc. Jennings, Strouss & Salmon, Phoenix, 1967-71, ptnr., 1971-85, chmn. real estate dept., 1980-85, mem. policy com., 1982-85, mem. fin. com., 1981-85, chmn. bus. devel. com., 1982-85; ptnr. and co-founder Stuckey & McRae, Phoenix, 1985—; co-founder, chmn. bd. Republic Cos., Phoenix, 1985—; magistrate Paradise Valley, Ariz., 1983-85; juvenile referee Superior Ct., 1983-85; pres., dir. Phoenix Realty & Trust Co., 1970—; officer Indsl. Devel. Corp. Maricopa County, 1972-86; instr. and lectr. in real estate; officer, bd. dirs. other corps. Contbr. articles to profl. jours. Elder Valley Presbyterian Ch., Scottsdale, Ariz., 1973-75, 82-85, corp. pres., 1974-75, 84-85, trustee, 1973-75, 82-85, chmn. exec. com., 1984; trustee Upward Found., Phoenix, 1977-80, Valley Presbyn. Found., 1982-83, Ariz. Acad., 1971—; trustee, mem. exec. com. Phi Gamma Delta Ednl. Found., Washington, 1974-84; trustee Phi Gamma Delta Internat., 1984-86, Archon, 1986-87, bd. dirs.; founder, trustee McRae Found.; trustee, mem. exec. com. Ariz. Mus. Sci. and Tech., 1984—, 1st v.p., 1985-86, pres., 1986—; vol. fund raiser YMCA, Salvation Army, others; mem. Taliesin Council, Frank Lloyd Wright Found., 1985—; dir. Food for Hungry (Internat. Relief), 1985—, exec. com., 1986—, chmn. bd. dirs. 1987—; mem. Ariz. State U. Council of 100, 1985—, investment com., 1985—; U. Ariz. Pres.'s Club, 1984—. Served with USAF, 1961-64. Recipient various mil. awards. Mem. ABA, Ariz. Bar Assn., Maricopa County Bar Assn., AIME, Ariz. Acad., U. Ariz. Alumni Assn., Clan McRae Soc. N.Am., Tau Beta Pi. Republican. Clubs: Phoenix Exec., Phoenix Country, Arizona, Continental Country; Jackson Hole Racquet (Wyo.). Real property, Contracts commercial, Condemnation. Home: 8101 N 47th St Paradise Valley AZ 85253 Office: Republic Cos 5500 N 24th St Phoenix AZ 85016

MCRAE, HAMILTON EUGENE, JR., lawyer; b. Arkadelphia, Ark., Feb. 9, 1905; s. Hamilton Eugene and Katherine (Old) McR.; m. Adrian Hagaman, Dec. 1, 1933; children: Mary Ann McRae Sloan, Hamilton Eugene III. Student, U. Ark., 1922-24; LL.B., U. Tex., 1928. Bar: Tex. 1928. Practice in Eastland, 1928-36, Midland, 1936—; mem. firm Conner & McRae, 1928-32, McRae & McRae, 1932-36, Stubbeman, McRae & Sealy, 1936-57, Stubbeman, McRae, Sealy & Laughlin, 1957-70, Stubbeman, McRae, Sealy, Laughlin & Browder, 1970—; dir. Midland Southwest Corp.; former dir. Depco, Inc. subs. DeKalb AgResearch, Inc., Santander Oil Co., Guanipa Oil Co. Pres. Midland Bd. Edn., 1943-44; Former trustee Austin (Tex.) Presbyn. Theol. Sem., Tex. Presbyn. Found.; past dir. Mus. of S.W.; bd. dirs. Permian Basin Petroleum Mus. Library and Hall of Fame, Midland Coll. Found.; formerly mem. fin. adv. com. United Way; mem. fin. adv. com. Jr. League. Mem. Am., Tex., Midland bar assns., Midland C. of C., Sigma Chi, Phi Delta Phi. Democrat. Presbyn. (elder). Clubs: Petroleum (past dir.), Midland Country (past pres., dir.), Racquet, Plaza. Nuclear power, Probate, Real property. Home: 406 South L St Midland TX 79701 Office: PO Box 1540 Midland TX 79702

MCRAE, ROBERT MALCOLM, JR., federal judge; b. Memphis, Dec. 31, 1921; s. Robert Malcolm and Irene (Pontius) McR.; m. Louise Howry, July 31, 1943; children: Susan Campbell, Robert Malcolm III, Duncan Farquhar, Thomas Alexander Todd. BA, Vanderbilt U., 1943; LLB, U. Va., 1948. Bar: Tenn. 1948. Sole practice Memphis, 1948-64; ptnr. Apperson, Crump, Duzane & McRae, 1955-59, Larkey, Dudley, Blanchard & McRae, 1959-64; judge Tenn. Circuit Ct., 1964-66; judge U.S. Dist. Ct. (we. dist.) Tenn., Memphis, 1966—, chief judge, 1979-86, sr. judge, 1987—; mem. Jud. Council 6th Cir., 1982-85, sr. dist. judge, 1987—; mem. Jud. Conf. Commn. Adminstrn. Criminal Law, 1979-86, Jud. Conf. U.S., 1984-87. Pres. Episcopal Ch. men of Tenn., 1964-65. Served to lt. USNR, 1943-46. Mem. Dist. Judges Assn. 6th Circuit (pres.), Phi Delta Phi, Omicron Delta Kappa. Office: 1107 Federal Bldg 167 N Main St Memphis TN 38103

MCREYNOLDS, MARY ARMILDA, lawyer; b. Carthage, Mo., Sept. 2, 1946; d. Allen and Virginia Madeliene (Hensley) McR.; m. John DeQuedville Briggs, III, Jan. 1, 1972. B.A., Mt. Holyoke Coll., 1968; J.D., Georgetown U., 1971; LL.M., Harvard U., 1973. Bar: D.C. 1971, U.S. Ct. Appeals (D.C. cir.) 1971, U.S. Ct. Appeals (2d cir.) 1975, U.S. Ct. Apls. (4th cir.) 1979, U.S. Ct. Apls. (1st, 5th, 6th, 9th, 10th cirs.) 1980, U.S. Supreme Ct. 1980, U.S. Ct. Apls. (11th cir.) 1981, U.S. Ct. Appeals (3d, 7th, 8th cirs.) 1983. Law clk. U.S. Ct. Appeals for D.C. circuit, 1971-72; assoc. Wilmer, Cutler & Pickering, Washington, 1973-77; sr. trial atty. civil div. fed. program br. U.S.

Dept. Justice, 1977-79, mem. appellate staff, 1979-81; ptnr. McReynolds & Mutterperl, Washington, 1981-83; ptnr. Wilner & Scheiner, 1983—. Mem. bd. dirs., gen. counsel Washington Bach Consort, 1985—. Mem. ABA, Bar Assn. D.C., Fed. Bar Assn., Am. Soc. Legal History. Episcopalian. Clubs: Racquet (Washington); Kenwood (Bethesda, Md.). Contbr. articles to profl. jours. Administrative and regulatory, Federal civil litigation, General corporate. Home: 2101 Connecticut Ave Apt 26 Washington DC 20008

MCREYNOLDS, MICHAEL PATRICK, lawyer; b. Omaha, Aug. 1, 1951; s. Clinton Andrew and Marie Margaret (Shields) McR.; m. Barbara Jean Carter, June 16, 1973; 1 child, Molly Ann. BA, Mich. State U., 1973; JD, U. Mich., 1976. Bar: Nebr. 1977, U.S. Dist. Ct. Nebr. 1977, U.S. Ct. Appeals (8th cir.) 1979, U.S. Supreme Ct. 1980, Minn. 1984, U.S. Dist. Ct. Minn. 1984. Gen. atty. Union Pacific R.R. Co., Omaha, 1976-83; asst. gen. solicitor Burlington No. R.R. Co., St. Paul, 1983-86; assoc. Rerat Law Firm P.A., Mpls., 1986—. Coach Cottage Grove (Minn.) Athletic Assn., 1984—. Mem. ABA, Minn. Bar Assn., Nebr. Bar Assn., Ramsey County Bar Assn. (vol. atty.), Def. Research Inst. Avocations: softball, basketball, golf, music, videotape prodn. Personal injury, Federal civil litigation, State civil litigation. Home: 7505 Immanuel Ave S Cottage Grove MN 55016 Office: Rerat Law Firm PA 222 S 9th St 1735 Piper Jaffray Tower Minneapolis MN 55402

MCREYNOLDS, STEPHEN PAUL, lawyer; b. Sacramento, Oct. 16, 1938; s. Leslie N. and Mary C. McR.; m. Chodi D. Greeno, Sept. 29, 1970. A.B., U. Calif.-Davis, 1969, J.D., 1972. Bar: Calif. 1972. Sole practice, Sunnyvale, Calif., 1972—. Served with U.S. Navy, 1956-62. Mem. Mensa Internat. General practice. Address: 27110 Moody Ct Los Altos Hills CA 94022

MCSHANE, BRUCE WINTHROP, lawyer; b. Montclair, N.J., Sept. 26, 1949; s. Gordon and Mary Elizabeth (Tiernan) McS.; m. Celeste Marie Bertucci, Nov. 21, 1981; children: Jessica Elizabeth, Kelly Ann. BA, Castleton State Coll., 1974; JD, Vt. Law Sch., 1977. Bar: N.Y. 1979, U.S. Dist. Ct. (so. and so. dists.) N.Y. 1980. Acct. rep. Marsh & McLennan, Inc., N.Y.C., 1977-79; assoc. Rogers, Hoge & Hills, N.Y.C., 1979-85; ptnr. Johnston, McShane & Kilgannon, N.Y.C., 1985—. Mem. Rep. Nat. Com., Washington, 1983. Served with U.S. Army, 1969-71, Vietnam. Mem. ABA, Assn. of Bar of City of N.Y., Nat. Assn. R.R. Trial Counsel. Roman Catholic. Clubs: Racquet and Tennis (N.Y.C.); Somerset Hills Country (Bernardsville, N.J.). Avocations: golf, tennis, swimming, squash, skiing. Federal civil litigation, State civil litigation, Insurance. Home: 42 Harbor Rd Westport CT 06880 Office: Johnston McShane & Kilgannon 420 Lexington Ave Suite 1701 New York NY 10017

MCSHERRY, WILLIAM JOHN, JR., lawyer, consultant; b. N.Y.C., Oct. 28, 1947; s. William John Sr. and Mary Elizabeth (Dunphy) McS.; m. Elizabeth Ann Crosby, June 8, 1974; children: Brendan, Sean, Rory. AB cum laude, Fordham U., 1969; JD cum laude, Harvard U., 1973. Bar: N.Y. 1974, U.S. Dist. Ct. (so. dist.) N.Y. 1975, U.S. Ct. Appeals (2d cir.) 1977. Assoc. Spengler, Carlson, Gubar, Brodsky & Frischling, N.Y.C., 1973-78, ptnr., 1979—; exec. dir. U.S. Football League, N.Y.C., 1985-86. Author: (with others) Tender Offer Regulation: The Federal SEC's Challenge and New York State's Response. Served with USAR, 1980-85. Mem. ABA (litigation and antitrust sects., subcom. litigation 1940 Act), Assn. of Bar of City of N.Y., Assn. Trial Lawyers Am., Fed. Bar Council, Council N.Y. Law Assocs. (bd. dirs., treas. 1975), Phi Beta Kappa. Roman Catholic. Avocations: community involvement, sports. Federal civil litigation, State civil litigation, Entertainment. Home: 2 Summit Ave Larchmont NY 10538 Office: Spengler Carlson Gubar et al 280 Park Ave New York NY 10017

MCSORLEY, BERNARD THOMAS, lawyer; b. N.Y.C., May 6, 1935; s. Bernard J. and Katherine (Harrigan) McS.; m. Clarice R. Biancaniello, Jan. 24, 1959; children: Janet K., Karen L., Lauren J. BA, St. John's U., Bklyn., 1961, JD, 1965. Bar: N.Y. 1966, U.S. Dist. Ct. (so. and ea. dists.) N.Y. 1967. Fin. analyst Dun & Bradstreet, Inc., N.Y.C., 1956-66; sr. appellate and litigation atty. Housing and Devel. Adminstrn. City of N.Y., 1966-78; prin. law sec. N.Y. Supreme Ct., Riverhead, 1978—. Bd. dirs., counsel New Eng. Village Civic Assn., Hauppauge, N.Y., 1968—; pres. Hauppauge Pub. Sch. Dist. Bd. Edn., 1972-75; Dem. committeeman Suffolk County, N.Y., 1974—; del. 10th Judicial Dist. Conv., Suffolk County, 1980—. Served as sgt. USMC, 1952-56. Mem. N.Y. Bar Assn., Suffolk County Criminal Bar Assn., Aircraft Owners and Pilots Assn., Phi Alpha Delta. Roman Catholic. Club: Aerocats Flying (treas. 1984—). Lodge: K.C. Criminal, State civil litigation, Administrative and regulatory. Home: 72 Pinedale Rd Hauppauge NY 11788 Office: NY State Supreme Ct Griffing Ave Riverhead NY 11901

MCSORLEY, CISCO, lawyer; b. Albuquerque, July 8, 1950; s. Frank N. and Virginia E. (Norton) McS. BA, U. N.Mex., 1974, JD, 1979; postdoctoral sch. govt., Harvard U., 1986. Bar: N.Mex. 1980, U.S. Dist. Ct. N.Mex. 1980. Tchr. Academia Cotopaxi, Quito, Ecuador, S. Am., 1973-76; sole practice Albuquerque, 1980—. State rep. N.Mex. Ho. Reps., Sante Fe, 1984—. Democrat. Mem. Soc. of Friends. Office: 5400 Phoenix NE Suite 100 Albuquerque NM 87110

MCVISK, WILLIAM KILBURN, lawyer; b. Chgo., Oct. 8, 1953; s. Felix Kilburn and June (DePear) Visk; m. Marlaine Joyce McDonough, June 20, 1975. BA, U. Ill, 1974; JD, Northwestern U., 1977. Bar: Ill. 1977, U.S. Dist. Ct. (no. dist.) Ill. 1977, U.S. Ct. Appeals (7th cir.) 1978. Assoc. Jerome H. Torshen, Ltd., Chgo., 1977-80, Silets & Martin, Chgo., 1980-81; assoc. Peterson, Ross, Schloerb & Seidel, Chgo., 1981-85, ptnr., 1985—. Contbr. articles to Jour. of Criminal Law and Criminology. Mem. ABA, Chgo. Bar Assn., Def. Research Inst., Am. Assn. Hosp. Attys., Ill. Assn. Hosp. Attys. Insurance, Personal injury, Health. Office: Peterson Ross Schloerb & Seidel 200 E Randolph Dr Chicago IL 60601

MCWHIRTER, BRUCE J., lawyer; b. Chgo., Sept. 11, 1931; s. Sydney William and Martha (Krucks) McW.; m. Judith Elizabeth Hallett, Apr. 14, 1960; children—Cameron, Andrew. B.A., Northwestern U., 1952; LL.B., Harvard U., 1955. Bar: D.C. 1955, Ill. 1955, U.S. Ct. Appeals (7th cir.) 1963, U.S. Dist. Ct. (no. dist.) Ill. 1958. Assoc. Lord, Bissell & Brook, Chgo., 1958-62; assoc., then ptnr. Ross & Hardies, Chgo., 1962—, now sr. ptnr. Editor: SEC Handbook, 1972—; contbr. articles to profl. publs. Served with U.S. Army, 1955-57, Japan. Mem. Harvard Law Soc. Ill. (bd. dirs. 1984), Phi Beta Kappa. Democrat. Contracts commercial, General corporate, Securities. Home: 111 Sheridan Rd Winnetka IL 60093 Office: Ross & Hardies 150 N Michigan Ave Suite 2500 Chicago IL 60601

MCWHIRTER, J(AMES) CECIL, lawyer; b. Marion County, Ala., Apr. 28, 1937; s. Grady Jackson and Anna Florence (Roby) McW.; m. Patricia Davis, Aug. 16, 1961; children—Warren Douglas, Barry Jason, Wenda Gail. B.S., Miss. State U., 1960; J.D., Memphis State U., 1969. Bar: Tenn. 1969, U.S. Dist. Ct. (we. dist.) Tenn. 1969, U.S. Ct. Appeals (6th cir.), 1978, U.S. Supreme Ct. 1975. Assoc., Neely, Green & Fargarson, Memphis, 1969, Holt, Batchelor, Taylor & Spicer, Memphis, 1970; ptnr. Sisson, McWhirter, Lowrance & Austin, Memphis, 1971-80, Walsh, McWhirter & Wyatt, Memphis, 1980—. Pres. several civic or similar groups including PTA, 1974-75, Scenic Hills Action Com., 1975-76. Mem. ABA, Tenn. Bar Assn., Memphis and Shelby County Assn. (assoc. editor Syllabus 1981—, editor 1982—). State civil litigation, Federal civil litigation, Insurance. Office: Walsh McWhirter & Wyatt Suite 3404 100 N Main Bldg Memphis TN 38103

MCWHORTER, ROBERT DALE, JR., lawyer; b. Ft. Benning, Ga., Jan. 6, 1953; s. Robert Dale Sr. and Martha Jo (Gilstrap) McW.; m. Terri Ann Pritchett, Dec. 6, 1980. BS in Acctg., U. Ala., 1975, MBA, JD, 1979. Bar: Ala. 1979, U.S. Dist. Ct. (no. dist.) Ala. 1980. Assoc. Law Offices of J.D. Pruett, Gadsden, Ala., 1979-80; ptnr. Pruett & McWhorter, Gadsden, 1981-82, Buttram & McWhorter, Centre, Ala., 1983—. Atty. commn. Cherokee County, Centre, 1983—; atty. city town council, Cedar Bluff, Ala., 1985—. Mem. ABA, Ala. Bar Assn., Assn. Trial Lawyers Am., Ala. Trial Lawyers Assn. Methodist. Avocations: woodworking, fishing, game hunting. General practice, State civil litigation, Bankruptcy. Home: PO Box 56 Centre AL 35960 Office: Buttram & McWhorter PO Box 603 Centre AL 35960

MCWILLIAMS, JOHN LAWRENCE, III, lawyer; b. Phila., Dec. 21, 1943; s. John Lawrence and Elizabeth Dolores (Chevalier) McW., Jr.; m. Paula Ann Root, July 19, 1969; children—John Lawrence, IV, Robert Root, Anne Elizabeth, David Stanford, Peter Farrell. B.S., St. Joseph's Coll., 1965; J.D., Seton Hall U., 1969. Bar: N.J. 1969, N.Y. 1975, U.S. Supreme Ct. 1975, Fla. 1977. Trial atty. regional office SEC, N.Y.C., 1969-72; assoc. Mudge Rose Guthrie & Alexander, N.Y.C., 1972-77; mem. Freeman, Richardson, Watson & Kelly, P.A., Jacksonville, Fla., 1977—, chmn., pres., 1984—; apptd. spl. asst. to U.S. atty. Dist. of N.J., 1971. Trustee Mcpl. Service Dist. Ponte Vedra Beach, 1981—, chmn. bd. trustees, 1984—; treas. Ponte Vedra Community Assn., 1980-82; mem. Leadership Jacksonville, 1981, mem. steering com., 1982; dir. Jacksonville Country Day Sch., 1985—. Mem. ABA, Assn. Bar City N.Y., N.J. Bar Assn., Nat. Assn. Mcpl. Bond Lawyers, Fla. Bar Assn. Republican. Roman Catholic. Clubs: Ponte Vedra, Sawgrass, University, River, Seminole (Jacksonville). Local government, State and local taxation. Home: 3040 Timberlake Point Ponte Vedra Beach FL 32082 Office: 3040 Timberlake Point Jacksonville FL 32202

MEACHAM, JERALD SAMUEL, lawyer; b. Tuscaloosa, Ala., July 28, 1952; s. Matt and Ruth Kate (Works) M.; m. Verna June Stroman, June 30, 1979; children: Bradford Paul, Jonathan David. BA, Tufts U., 1974; JD, U. Ala., 1979. Bar: Ind. 1979, U.S. Dist. Ct. (no. and so. dists.) Ind. 1979, U.S. Supreme Ct. 1982, U.S. Ct. Appeals (7th cir.) 1984. Referee, judge City Ct. of Gary, Ind., 1980-83, dep. corp. counsel, 1984-85; sole practice Law Offices of Jerald S. Meacham, P.C., Gary, 1980—. Mem. adv. bd. Urban League of N.W. Ind., 1981-83; bd. dirs. John Will Anderson Boys Club, 1983—. Mem. ABA, Ind. Bar Assn., Assn. Trial Lawyers of Am., Ind. Trial Lawyers Assn. (sustaining). Club: Frontiers, Inc. Personal injury, Consumer commercial, Federal civil litigation. Office: 504 Broadway Suite 320 Gary IN 46402

MEADE, RUSSELL ARTHUR, lawyer; b. N.Y.C., May 10, 1946; s. Robert Linthicum and Eleanor (Kagel) M.; m. Joan Sedita, Aug. 26, 1967; children: Suzanne, Michelle. AA, Nassau Coll., 1966; BA, Adelphi U., 1968; JD, St. John's U., N.Y.C., 1975. Bar: Fla. 1975, U.S. Supreme Ct. 1979. Ptnr. Meade & Kramer, Sarasota, Fla., 1975—. Bd. dirs. Fame Charities, Sarasota, 1978—. Served to sgt. USAF, 1968-72. Mem. ABA, Assn. Trial Lawyers Am., N.Y. State Trial Lawyers Assn., Christian Legal Soc., Fellowship of Fin. Advisors. Republican. Baptist. Lodge: Elks. Avocations: golf, travel. Federal civil litigation, Criminal, Probate. Office: Meade & Kramer 1620 Main St Sarasota FL 33577

MEADER, JOHN DANIEL, engineering company executive, lawyer; b. Ballston Spa, N.Y., Oct. 22, 1931; s. Jerome Clement and Doris Luella (Conner) M.; m. Joyce Margaret Cowin, Mar. 2, 1963; children—John Daniel, Julia Rae, Keith Alan. B.A., Yale U., 1954; J.D., Cornell U., 1962. Bar: N.Y. 1963, U.S. Dist. Ct. (no. dist.) N.Y. 1963, U.S. Ct. Appeals (2d cir.) 1966, U.S. Supreme Ct. 1967, U.S. Ct. Mil. Appeals 1973, Ohio 1978, U.S. Dist. Ct. (no. dist.) Ohio 1979, Fla. 1983. Sales engr. Albany Internat., Inc. (N.Y.), 1954-59; asst. track coach Cornell U., 1959-62; asst. sec., asst. to pres. Albany Internat., Inc., 1962-65; asst. atty. gen. state N.Y., Albany, 1965-68; ops. counsel, attesting sec. Gen. Electric Co., Schenectady, 1968-77; gen. counsel, asst. sec. SCM Corp., Glidden Div., Cleve., 1977-81; chmn. bd., pres. Applied Power Tech. Co., Fernandina Beach, Fla., 1981-84; pres. Applied Energy, Inc., Ballston Spa, N.Y., 1984—; dir. Saratoga Mut. Fire Ins. Co. Candidate, U.S. Ho. of Reps., 29th Dist. N.Y., 1964, N.Y. Supreme Ct., 1975. Serve to col. JAGC, USAR, 1968—, dep. staff judge adv. 3d U.S. Army, 1984. Nat. AAU High Sch. Cross Country Champion, 1948; Nat. AAU High Sch. Indoor Track 1000 Yard Champion 1949; Nat. AAU Prep. Sch. Indoor Track 440 and 880 Yard Champion, 1950; Nat. AAU Prep. sch. Track and Field Indoor Championships Outstanding Performer award Melrose Games Assn., 1950; Heptagonal Track 880 Yard Champion 1954; recipient Gardner Mallett award for courage, inspiration and sportsmanship Yale U., 1954. Mem. ABA, N.Y. State Bar Assn., Fla. Bar. Republican. Presbyterian. Clubs: Amelia Island Plantation (Fernandina Beach); Cyprus Temple, Masons (Schenectady); Yale of Jacksonville (Fla.) (pres.). Author: Labor Law Manual, 1972; Contract Law Manual, 1974. Administrative and regulatory, General corporate, Government contracts and claims. Home: Round Lake Rd Ballston Lake NY 12019 Office: Applied Energy Inc PO Box 1127 Albany NY 12201

MEADERS, PAUL LE SOURD, lawyer; b. Amarillo, Tex., Feb. 1, 1930; s. Paul Le Sourd and Lorna Irene (Pumroy) M.; m. Patricia Rockefeller, Mar. 21, 1953 (dec.); m. 2d Jane W. Dickely, Apr. 2, 1966; children—Phyllis P., Paul Le Sourd III. B.A., U. Va., 1952; LL.B., U. Tex., 1957; LL.M., NYU, 1961. Atty. office chief counsel IRS, 1957-59; asst. U.S. atty. So. Dist. N.Y., 1951-61; assoc. Breed Abbott & Morgan, N.Y.C., 1961-63, Reid & Priest, N.Y.C., 1963-67; ptnr. Morris & McVeigh, N.Y.C., 1967-77, McKenzie, Meaders & Ives, N.Y.C., 1977—. Active Vet. Corps of Arty., N.Y.C. Served to 1st lt. U.S. Army, 1952-54. Mem. ABA, (estate tax com. tax sect.) N.Y. State Bar Assn., Tex. Bar Assn., Seldon Soc., Brit. Inst. Internat. and Comparative Law, Internat. Bar Assn., U. Va. Alumni Assn. (pres. N.Y.C. chpt. 1982-84). Episcopalian. Clubs: Metropolitan, Church, Bronxville Field; Carlton (London); Southampton Bath and Tennis. Probate, Personal income taxation, Estate planning. Office: Suite 3105 535 Fifth Ave New York NY 10017

MEADOR, JAMES LEWIS, lawyer; b. Roanoke, Va., June 28, 1946; s. Lewis Morton and Nell Scott (Harris) M.; m. Barbara Janet Winn, July 26, 1975; children: Sarah Nelson, Andrew Harris. BA, U. Va., 1968; JD, Coll. of William and Mary, 1977. Bar: Va. 1977, U.S. Dist. Ct. (ea. dist.) Va. 1977, U.S. Ct. Appeals (4th cir.) 1977. Atty. FDIC, Washington, 1977-85; spl. counsel Continental Ill. Nat. Bank FDIC, Chgo., 1985—. Russell Cox scholar, 1976. Mem. ABA, Va. Bar Assn. Republican. Club: University (Chgo.). Avocation: golf. Banking, Contracts commercial. Office: FDIC 30 S Wacker Dr Chicago IL 60606

MEADORS, GAYLE MARLEEN, lawyer; b. Chgo., Sept. 13, 1946; d. Howard C. and Eileen M. (Baker) M.; m. William Frank Fortuna II, June 11, 1983. AB in English Lit. with honors, U. Ill., 1969; MA in Library Sci., U. Chgo., 1973; JD magna cum laude, DePaul U., 1977. Bar: Ill. 1977. Cons. Hewitt Assocs., Lincolnshire, Ill., 1976-83; sr. counsel Am. Hosp. Supply Corp., Evanston, Ill. 1983-84; assoc. Katten, Muchin, Zavis, Pearl, Greenberger & Galler, Chgo., 1984—. Mem. ABA, Chgo. Heart Assn. (vol. mgmt. services), Ill. State Bar Assn., Chgo. Bar Assn., Women in Employee Benefits, Phi Beta Kappa. Pension, profit-sharing, and employee benefits. Home: 530 E Prospect Lake Bluff IL 60044 Office: Katten Muchin Zavis Pearl & Galler 525 W Monroe Suite 1600 Chicago IL 60603

MEADOW, CLAIRE SAMUELSON, lawyer, educator; b. N.Y.C., Nov. 27, 1938; d. Aaron and Sylvia (Heller) Samuelson; m. Myron J. Meadow, June 25, 1961; children—Andrea, Roxanne, Aaron. B.A. cum laude, Hunter Coll., 1959; J.D., Columbia U., 1962. Bar: N.Y. 1963, U.S. Dist. Ct. (so. dist.) N.Y. 1964. Enforcement atty. SEC, N.Y.C., 1964-67; sole practice, Larchmont, N.Y. 1967—; mem. Arbitrators' Panels, Bronx and Westchester Civil Ct., 1976—; mem. indigent defendants' legal panel Appellate div. N.Y. Supreme Ct., 1969—; cons. in real property; sales coordinator L&H Abstract Corp., White Plains, N.Y., 1986—. Mem. editorial staff Bronx Bar Assn. Jour., 1963-69. Chmn. Larchmont area Columbia Law Sch. Fund, 1967—; moot ct. judge Columbia Law Sch., N.Y.C., 1967, 69, 78, 83. Mem. Bronx Women's Bar Assn. (rec. sec. 1964-65), N.Y. Women's Bar Assn. (rec. sec. local chpt. 1975-76) Nat. Assoc. Temple Educators, Westchester Jewish Conf. (mem. Warsaw ghetto commemoration com. 1981—), Hadassah Women's Orgn., B'nai Brith Women, Nat. Council Jewish Women, Phi Beta Kappa. Real property, Probate. Home and Office: 4 Virginia Pl Larchmont NY 10538

MEADOWS, JOHN FREDERICK, lawyer; b. Manila, Philippines, Mar. 7, 1926; s. Grover Cleveland and Millie M.; m. Karen Lee Morris, Nov. 17, 1962; children—Ian Joseph, Marie Irene. A.A., U. Mich., 1944; B.A. (Freshman Alumni Scholar, 1943), U. Calif., Berkeley, 1948, LL.B., Boalt Hall, 1951. Bar: Calif. 1952, U.S. Dist. Ct. (no. dist.) Calif 1952, U.S. Ct. Apls. (9th cir.) 1952, U.S. Sup. Ct. 1958. Assoc. Wallace, Garrison, Norton & Ray, San Francisco, 1952-56; atty. advisor Maritime Adminstrn., U.S. Dept. Commerce, Washington, 1956; trial atty. Admiralty and Shipping Sect., U.S. Dept. Justice, West Coast Office, San Francisco, 1956-64, atty. in charge, 1964-72; sr. resident ptnr. Acret & Perrochet, San Francisco, 1972-76; sr. ptnr. Meadows, Smith & Brown (formerly known as Meadows & Dorris), San Francisco, 1976—; cons. maritime law, UN, lectr. seminar Taipei, Taiwan, 1968; Served to lt. M.I. AUS, 1944-46. Mem. ABA, Assn. Def. Counsel, Maritime Law Assn., San Francisco Bar Assn., Council Am. Master Mariners. Republican. Roman Catholic. Clubs: San Francisco Comml., Merchants Exchange. Assoc. editor Am. Maritime Cases; contbr. articles to legal publs. Admiralty, Insurance, Federal civil litigation. Home: 205 The Uplands Berkeley CA 94705 Office: 425 California St Suite 1700 San Francisco CA 94104

MEADWAY, JAY KENNETH, lawyer; b. Kingston, Pa., May 31, 1953; s. Harold K. and Doris A. (Spencer) M.; m. Roberta L. Jacobs, June 27, 1982; 1 child, Hana K. BA, U. Pa., 1975; JD, George Washington U., 1978. Bar: D.C. 1978, Va. 1979, Pa. 1981, N.Y. 1986. Assoc. Jackson & Wells, Arlington, Va., 1979-81, Panitch, Schwarze, Jacobs & Nadel, Phila., 1981-85; trademark atty. Pfizer Inc., N.Y.C., 1985—. Mem. ABA, D.C. Bar Assn., Va. Bar Assn., Pa. Bar Assn., Phila. Bar Assn. Trademark and copyright. Office: Pfizer Inc 235 E 42d St New York NY 10017

MEAGHER, VIRGINIA MURNANE, lawyer; b. Harriman, Tenn., Aug. 9, 1949; d. James Louis and Floy Gates (Terstegge) M.; m. Chester William Sygiel, Dec. 31, 1984. BA, St. Mary's Coll., 1971; JD, U. Louisville, 1979. Bar: Ky. 1979, U.S. Dist. Ct. (ea. dist.) Ky. 1979. Staff atty. Ky. Legal Services, Jackson, 1979-81; sole practice Jackson, Ky., 1981-84, 85—; judge dist. ct. State of Ky., Jackson, 1984; trial commr. State of Ky., 1986. Dir. play My Three Angels, 1981. Pres. Red Masque Players, Inc., Jackson, 1981-83. Mem. Ky. Bar Assn., Louisville Bar Assn., Bus. and Profl. Women's Club. Democrat. Avocations: swimming, tennis, ballet, guitar, singing. General practice, Personal injury, Real property. Home: 101 River St Jackson KY 41339

MEANEY, MICHAEL LAWRENCE, lawyer; b. Louisville, June 19, 1949; s. Lawrence Dominic and Dorothy Mary (Brown) M.; m. Marie Antoinnette Texeira, Dec. 8, 1971; 1 child, Marcus J. BA cum laude, Spalding Coll., 1975; JD, U. Louisville, 1979. Bar: Hawaii 1980, U.S. Dist. Ct. Hawaii 1980, U.S. Ct. Appeals (9th cir.) 1985. Dep. pros. atty. City and County of Honolulu, 1981-84, dep. corp. counsel, 1984—. Bd. dirs. Am. Youth Soccer Assn., Honolulu. Served with USN, 1970-72, as lt. USNR, 1981—. Named to Hon. Order Ky. Cols., 1975. Mem. ABA, Assn. Trial Lawyers Am., Phi Alpha Delta, Delta Epsilon Sigma. Republican. Roman Catholic. Avocations: computers, softball, volleyball, fishing, soccer. State civil litigation, Local government, Military. Home: 1510 Haloa Dr Honolulu HI 96818 Office: City & County of Honolulu Dept Corp Counsel Honolulu Hale Honolulu HI 96813

MEANS, THOMAS CORNELL, lawyer; b. Charleston, S.C., Oct. 3, 1947; s. Thomas Lucas and Dean (Cornell) M.; m. Judith Faye Perlmutter, Sept. 10, 1977; children: Benjamin Thomas, Samuel Thomas. AB, Dartmouth Coll., 1969; postgrad., Princeton Theol. Sem., 1970-71; M of Pub. Adminstrn., U. Colo., 1975; JD, George Washington U., 1978. Bar: D.C. 1978, U.S. Dist. Ct. (D.C. dist.), U.S. Ct. Appeals (4th, 10th and D.C. cirs.). Social worker Vinyard Childcare, Ann Arbor, Mich., 1969-70; research analyst, registered lobbyist Colo. Counties, Inc., Denver, 1972-75; assoc. Jones, Day, Reavis and Pogue, Washington, 1978-79; assoc. then ptnr. Crowell and Moring, Washington, 1979—; mem. state adv. council on Pub. Personnel Mgmt., Colo. State Govt., Denver, 1974-75. Contbr. articles to profl. jours. Mem. George Washington U. Law Sch. Alumni Assn. (bd. dirs. 1986—), Order of the Coif, Phi Beta Kappa. Administrative and regulatory, Federal civil litigation, Mining and natural resources. Home: 6411 Dahlonega Rd Bethesda MD 20816 Office: Crowell and Moring 1001 Pennslyvania Ave NW Washington DC 20004

MEANS, TYRONE CARLTON, lawyer; b. Chgo., Mar. 3, 1954; s. Jerry Taft and Sarah (Foster) M.; m. Lillie Kay Banks, June 2, 1979. B.A., Morehouse Coll., 1974; J.D., U. Kans., 1976. Bar: Kans. 1976, Ala. 1977. Assoc. Gray, Seay & Langford, Montgomery and Tuskegee, Ala., 1976-81; ptnr. Massey, Means & Thomas, Montgomery, 1981—; spl. asst. atty. gen. State of Ala. Trustee Lilly Baptist Ch., Inc., 1980; bd. dirs. Jacksonville State U. Mem. Ala. State Bar Assn., Kans. Bar Assn., Assn. Trial Lawyers Am., Nat. Bar Assn., ABA, Ala. Trial Lawyers Assn. (exec. com.), Montgomery County Bar Assn., Montgomery County Trial Lawyers Assn. (treas., dir., pres.), Ala. Lawyers Assn. (treas.). Personal injury, Family and matrimonial. Office: 901 S Hull St PO Box 5058 Montgomery AL 36102

MEANY, BERNARD ANTHONY, lawyer, consultant; b. Jersey City, Jan. 20, 1935; s. Walter S. and Cecilia H. (Haidler) M.; children—Bernard A., James W., Mary T. B.M.E., Marquette U., 1956; postgrad. Syracuse U. Grad. Sch. Engring., 1956-57; J.D., Georgetown U., 1965. Bar: Calif. 1966, U.S. Dist. Ct. (no. dist.) Calif. 1966, U.S. Ct. Appeals (9th cir.) 1966, U.S. Ct. Appeals (Fed. cir.) 1973. Assoc. engr. IBM, Poughkeepsie, N.Y., 1956-58, sr. assoc. engr., 1958-61, atty.-in-tng., Washington, 1961-65, patent atty., San Jose, Calif., 1965-67, patent counsel Advanced Computing Systems Lab., Menlo Park, Calif., 1967-68, contract rep. corp. hdqrs., Armonk, N.Y., 1968-71, dir. licensing, 1971-74, dir. contracts and licensing, 1974-75, mgr. Latin Am. Patent Ops., Rio de Janeiro, 1978-81; asst. commr. patents and trademarks U.S. Patent and Trademark Office, Washington, 1975-78; of counsel for tech. contracts and licensing Mason, Fenwick & Lawrence, Washington, 1982-83; of counsel Ward, Lazarus, Grow & Cihlar, Washington, 1983—, ptnr. tech. transfer, 1984—; exec. ptnr. Internat. Technology Assocs., N.Y.C., Washington and Tokyo, 1982—; lectr. and author in field. Mem. pres.'s adv. bd. Fairfield U.; mem. Georgetown U. Law Center Dean's adv. com., chmn. D.C. Alumni Fund, also Nat. Alumni Fund. (vice chmn. law alumni affairs bd.); bd. dirs. community corps. and orgns. Recipient IBM Outstanding Contbn. award, 1971; Am. Jurisprudence award, 1963; hon. mem. League United Latin Am. Citizens for Disting. Contbns. Mem. ABA, Calif. Bar Assn., Am. Intellectual Property Law Assn., ASME, Lic. Execs. Soc., Latin Am. Indsl. Property Assn., U.S. Execs. of Rio de Janeiro, U.S. Naval League, U.S. Brazil C. of C., Pharm. Trademarks Group (hon.) (London). Clubs: Paisando (Rio de Janeiro); Farmington Golf and Country (Charlottesville, Va.); Washington Golf and Country (Arlington, Va.). Private international, Patent, Trademark and copyright. Home: 4455 N 33d St Arlington VA 22207 Office: 1711 N St NW Washington DC 20036

MEARS, MICHAEL, lawyer; b. Tupelo, Miss., Aug. 14, 1943; s. James Nash and Victoria (Taylor) M.; m. Sue Ellen Owens, May 25, 1973; 1 child, Alexander Taylor. B.S., Miss. State U., 1968, M.A., 1969; J.D., U. Ga., 1977. Bar: Ga. 1977, U.S. Dist. Ct. (no. dist.) Ga. 1977, U.S. Ct. Appeals (5th cir.) 1977, U.S. Ct. Appeals (11th cir.) 1981, U.S. Supreme Ct. 1980. Tchr., asst. prin. Decatur (Ga.) City Schs., 1969-74; assoc. firm McCurdy & Candler, Attys., Decatur, 1977-81, ptnr., 1981—. Author: Teaching Russian History, 1971; contbr. articles to profl. jours. Mem. bd. appeals City of Decatur, 1977-83; bd. dirs. Decatur-DeKalb YMCA, 1982—; commr. City of Decatur, 1983-84, mayor, 1984—. Served with USN, 1961-67. Fellow U.S. Coll. Mortgage Attys.; mem. Atlanta Lawyers Club, DeKalb C. of C. (dir. 1982—), Phi Kappa Phi, Kappa Delta Pi. Democrat. Baptist. State civil litigation, State and local taxation, Local government. Home: 303 Adams St Decatur GA 30030 Office: McCurdy & Candler PO Box 57 Decatur GA 30031

MEARS, PATRICK EDWARD, lawyer; b. Flint, Mich., Oct. 3, 1951; s. Edward Patrick and Estelle Veronica (Mislik) M.; m. Geraldine O'Connor, July 18, 1981. B.A., U. Mich., 1973, J.D., 1976. Bar: N.Y. 1977, U.S. Dist. Ct. (so. and ea. dists.) N.Y. 1977, Mich. 1980, U.S. Dist. Ct. (we. and ea. dists.) Mich. 1980, U.S. Ct. Appeals (6th cir.) 1983. Assoc. firm Milbank, Tweed, Hadley & McCloy, N.Y.C., 1976-79, ptnr. Warner, Norcross & Judd, Grand Rapids, Mich., 1980—; adj. prof. Grand Valley State Coll., Allendale, Mich., 1981-84. Author: Michigan Collection Law, 1981, 2d edit., 1983, Bankruptcy Law and Practice in Michigan, 1987, Bankruptcy Law and Practice in Michigan, 1987; also articles. Med. coordinator basketball tournament Mich. Spl. Olympics, Grand Rapids, 1983. Mem. ABA, Mich. State Bar Assn., Comml. Law League Am., Irish Heritage Soc. Republican. Roman Catholic. Clubs: Peninsular (Grand Rapids); Downtown Athletic (N.Y.C.). Bankruptcy, Consumer commercial, Federal civil litigation. Office: Warner Norcross and Judd 900 Old Kent Bldg Grand Rapids MI 49503

MEATH, BRIAN PATRICK, lawyer; b. Canandaigua, N.Y., Aug. 21, 1957; s. Gerald Barry and Ann Marie (Dobbins) M.; m. Kelly Diane Diver, Aug. 14, 1982. BS in Mgmt. Sci. magna cum laude, SUNY, Geneseo, 1978; JD, U. Buffalo, 1981; MBA, U. Rochester, 1985; ILR, Cornell U., 1987. Bar: N.Y., U.S. Dist. (we. dist.) N.Y. 1982, U.S. Bankruptcy Ct. 1982. Assoc. Sutton, Deleeuw, Clark & Darcy, Rochester, N.Y., 1981-85; corp. atty. Rochester Telephone Corp., Rochester, 1985—. Trustee Ontario County Hist. Soc., Canandaigua, 1984-85; vice-chmn. Ontario County 911 Com., 1984-85. Mem. ABA (pub. utility sect., labor and employment law sect., entertainment and sports law com.), N.Y. State Bar Assn. (labor and employment law sect., trial lawyers sect.), Monroe County Bar Assn. (labor law com.), Ontario County Bar Assn., Granger Homestead Soc., Omicron Delta Epsilon. Republican. Roman Catholic. Avocations: football, basketball, weightlifting, tennis, baseball. Labor, Public utilities, General corporate. Home: 197 N Main St Canandaigua NY 14424 Office: Rochester Telephone Corp 100 Midtown Plaza Rochester NY 14646

MEBANE, JULIE SHAFFER, lawyer; b. San Antonio, Mar. 13, 1957; d. John Cummins and Mildred (Hill) M.; m. Kenneth Jerome Stipanov, Jan. 21, 1984. BA in Polit. Sci., UCLA, 1978, JD, 1981. Bar: Calif. 1981, U.S. Dist. Ct. (so. dist.) Calif. 1981. Assoc. Gray, Cary, Ames & Frye, San Diego, 1981-85, Sheppard, Mullin, Richter & Hampton, San Diego, 1986—. Vol., intern for Hawaii County Councilwoman Merle K. Lai, Hilo. Mem. San Diego County Bar Assn., San Diego Barristers Club, San Diego Lawyers Club, Phi Beta Kappa. Democrat. Clubs: San Diego Tennis and Racquet, Bruins (San Diego). Avocations: sports, travel. Real property, Trademark and copyright. Office: Sheppard Mullin Richter & Hampton 701 B St 10th Floor San Diego CA 92101

MECHANIC, GENE BARRY, lawyer; b. N.Y.C., July 2, 1947; s. Arthur and Eveline (Zebrowitz) M.; m. Ruth Elizabeth Chapin, Feb. 3, 1973; children: Eli, Lianna. BA, U. Rochester, 1969; JD, George Washington U., 1972. Bar: N.Y. 1973, U.S. Dist. Ct. (so. and ea. dists.) N.Y. 1974, U.S. Dist. Ct. (we. dist.) N.Y. 1975, U.S. Ct. Appeals (2d cir.) 1975, U.S. Supreme Ct. 1976, Oreg. 1977, U.S. Dist. Ct. Oreg. 1977, U.S. Ct. Appeals (9th cir.) 1978. Dep. asst. atty. gen. Dept. Justice, N.Y.C., 1973-74; spl. litigator Legal Aid Soc., N.Y.C., 1974-76; dir. Prisoner's Legal Services, Salem, Oreg., 1977-79; ptnr. Goldberg, Mechanic & Goldstein, Portland, Oreg., 1979—; spl. lectr. U. Oreg. Law Sch., Eugene, 1978-79; lectr. Labor Edn. Research Ctr., Eugene, 1985—. Portland City Club, 1980, Oreg. Human Rights Rev. Commn., 1979; adj. prof. Lewis & Clark Coll. Law Sch., Portland, 1980-81. Contbr. articles to profl. jours. Mem. Dem. Bus. Forum, Portland, 1983—, adv. bd. lawyers com. AFL-CIO, Washington, 1983—. Recipient Service award Legal Aid Service Sr. Law Project, 1980-83; named Hon. Assoc. Pacific NW Labor Coll., 1981. Mem. Oreg. Bar Assn., Assn. Trial Lawyers Am., Oreg. Trial Lawyers Assn., ACLU (lawyer com. Oreg. chpt.). Avocations: photography, skiing, tennis, hiking. Labor, Pension, profit-sharing, and employee benefits, Federal civil litigation. Office: Goldberg Mechanic & Goldstein 808 SW Adler #200 Portland OR 97205

MECZ, JANE BELTZER, lawyer; b. Troy, N.Y., July 19, 1953; s. Harold and Zelma (Mark) Beltzer; m. Adrian Mecz, Mar. 26, 1978; 1 child, Karen Isabel. BA, Skidmore Coll., 1975; JD, Albany Law Sch., 1978. Bar: N.Y. 1979. Counsel Chem. Bank, N.Y.C., 1979-82, London, 1982—. Mem. ABA, N.Y. State Bar Assn., Phi Beta Kappa. Avocations: photography, skiing, horseback riding. Banking, General corporate, Contracts commercial. Office: Chem Bank, 180 Strand, London WC2R 1EX, England

MEDAGLIA, MARY-ELIZABETH, lawyer; b. Suffern, N.Y., Oct. 13, 1947; s. Joseph Mario and Edith Elizabeth (Price) M. BA, Sweet Briar Coll., 1969; JD, U. Va., 1972. Bar: Va. 1972, D.C. 1974, U.S. Ct. Appeals (D.C. cir.) 1974, U.S. Supreme Ct. 1980, U.S. Ct. Appeals (4th, 5th, 9th and 11th cirs.) 1981, U.S. Ct. Appeals (10th cir.) 1982. Law clk. to judge D.C. Ct. Appeals, Washington, 1972-74; asst. atty. U.S. Atty.'s Office, Washington, 1974-79; assoc. solicitor Fed. Labor Relations Authority, Washington, 1979-82, acting solicitor, 1982; assoc. Jackson & Campbell P.C., Washington, 1982-84, ptnr., 1984—; sec. D.C. Bar, 1983-84, bd. govs. 1984—. Fellow Am. Bar Found.; mem. ABA (ho. of dels. 1981-83), D.C. Bar Assn. (bd. dirs. 1980-83, chmn. young lawyers sect. 1980-81), Women's Bar Assn. D.C. (pres. 1982-83), Phi Beta Kappa. State civil litigation, Insurance, Federal civil litigation. Home: 3039 N Peary St Arlington VA 22207 Office: Jackson & Campbell PC 120 20th St NW Suite 300 S Washington DC 20036

MEDALIE, RICHARD JAMES, lawyer; b. Duluth, Minn., July 21, 1929; s. William Louis and Mona (Kolad) M.; m. Susan Diane Abrams, June 5, 1960; children: Samuel David, Daniel Alexander. B.A. summa cum laude, U. Minn., 1952; cert., U. London, 1953; A.M., Harvard U., 1955, J.D. cum laude, 1958. Bar: D.C. 1958, N.Y. 1963. Law clk. U.S. Ct. Appeals, Washington, 1958-59; asst. solicitor gen. U.S. 1960-62; asso. Kaye, Scholer, Fierman, Hays & Handler, N.Y.C., 1962-65; dep. dir. Ford Found. Inst. Criminal Law and Procedure, Georgetown U. Law Center, 1965-68; prin. Friedman and Medalie (P.C., and predecessors), Washington, 1968—; adj. prof. adminstrv. and criminal law Georgetown U. Law Center, 1967-70; Mem. D.C. Law Revision Commn., 1975-87, chmn. Criminal Law Task Force, mem. exec. com., 1978-82; panel comml. arbitrators Am. Arbitration Assn., 1964—; vice chmn. Harvard Law Sch. Fund, 1981-84, chmn. nat. maj. gifts, 1984-86, dep. chmn., 1986-87, chmn. 1987-89. Author: From Escobedo to Miranda: The Anatomy of a Supreme Court Decision, 1966; co-author: Federal Consumer Safety Legislation, 1970; contbr. to legal jours.; co-editor: Crime: A Community Responds, 1967; staff: Harvard Law Rev., 1956-58; case editor, 1957-58. Bd. dirs. alumni assn. Expt. in Internat. Living, Brattleboro, Vt., 1961-64, pres., 1962-63. Fulbright scholar, 1952-53; Ford fellow, 1954-55. Mem. Am. Law Inst., ABA (program co-chmn. 1983-84, chmn. legis. subcom. arbitration com. litigation sect. 1984—), D.C. Unified Bar, Assn. Bar City N.Y., N.Y. State Bar Assn., Harvard Law Sch. Assn. D.C. (pres. 1976-77, nat. v.p. 1977-78), Phi Beta Kappa, Phi Alpha Theta. Clubs: Harvard of D.C. (v.p. 1979-82), Harvard of N.Y.C. Federal civil litigation, Contracts commercial, Estate planning. Home: 3113 Macomb St NW Washington DC 20008 Office: 1899 L St NW Washington DC 20036

MEDD, JOEL DOUGLAS, judge; b. Langdon, N.D., Apr. 30, 1947; s. Ralph Rea and Elsie H. (Grossman) M. BA, U. of N.D., 1969, JD, 1975; postdoctoral, Nat. Jud. Coll., Reno, 1975, 78, 84. Bar: N.D. 1975, U.S. Dist. Ct. N.D. 1975. Judge Benson county, Minnewaukan, N.D., 1975-79, Williams County, Williston, N.D., 1979; tribal appeals judge Belcourt Reservation, Belcourt, N.D., 1979; mcpl. judge City of Minnewaukan, 1978-79; mem. N.D. Jud. Planning Commn., Bismarck, 1975—; chmn. Jud. Council Program Planning Commn., Bismarck, 1978-85; chmn. Civil Legal Services Commn., Bismark, 1985—. Contbr. articles to profl. jours. Bd. dirs. City Mission, Grand Forks, N.D., 1979—; chmn. Lake Agassiz council Boy Scouts Am., Grand Forks, 1981-84; comdr. Disabled Am. Vets., Grand Forks, 1985-86. Served to capt. U.S. Army, 1969-72, Vietnam. Decorated Bronze Star; recipient Outstanding Alumni award Phi Alpha Delta, Grand Forks, 1977; named Outstanding Young North Dakotan N.D. Jaycees, 1982; recipient Dist. Award of Merit, Boy Scouts Am., 1984, Silver Beaver award. Mem. ABA, Am. Judicature Soc. (bd. dirs.). Lodges: Lions (bd. dirs. Grand Forks chpt. 1982-84, v.p. 1986), Elks. Avocations: table tennis, tennis, photography. Judicial administration. Home: 1203 S 22d St Grand Folks ND 58201 Office: County Courthouse Dist Ct Grand Forks ND 58206

MEDEIROS, MATTHEW FRANCIS, lawyer; b. Little Compton, R.I., Apr. 30, 1945; s. Manuel S. and Marie F. (Goulart) M.; m. Sarah Judith Medjuck, July 26, 1970. AB, Brown U., 1967; JD, NYU, 1970. Bar: R.I. 1970, Mass. 1985, U.S. Dist. Ct. R.I. 1971, D.C. 1971, U.S. Dist. Ct. D.C. 1971, U.S. Ct. Appeals (1st cir.) 1972, U.S. Ct. Appeals (D.C. cir.) 1972, U.S. Supreme Ct. 1974. Summer assoc. Lewis & Roca, Phoenix, 1969; law clk. to chief judge U.S. Dist. Ct. R.I., 1970-71; assoc. Covington & Burling, Washington, 1971-76, on leave with Neighborhood Legal Services Program, Washington, 1973; ptnr. Edwards & Angell, Providence, 1977—; chmn. planning com. 1st Cir. Jud. Conf., 1980-81; mem. jud. screening coms. U.S. Bankruptcy Judge and U.S. Magistrate, 1981-82; mem. adv. com. for U.S. Ct. Appeals (1st cir.), 1983; adj. prof. fed. trial practice So. New Eng. Sch. Law, 1986. Editor: NYU Law Rev., 1969-70. Bd. dirs. Associated Alumni Brown U., 1969-71; bd. dirs. R.I. br. ACLU, 1977-79. Mem. ABA, Fed. Bar Assn. (pres. R.I. chpt. 1978-80), R.I. Bar Assn. Antitrust, Civil rights, Federal civil litigation. Office: Edwards & Angell 2700 Hospital Trust Tower Providence RI 02903

MEDFORD-ROSOW, TRACI, lawyer; b. Alexandria, Va., June 6, 1955; d. Charles Eugene and Jean (Tully) M.; m. Joel Rosow, Aug. 12, 1978; 1 child, Chad. BS, Va. Poly. Inst. and State U., 1977; JD, Bklyn. Law Sch., 1980; LLM, NYU, 1984. Bar: N.Y. 1981, D.C. 1981. Atty. Pfizer Inc., N.Y.C., 1980-81, mgr. health care, 1981-84, corp. counsel Europe, 1984—. Named to People to Watch list Fortune Mag., N.Y.C., 1986. Mem. ABA, N.Y. Bar Assn., D.C. Bar Assn., Phi Beta Kappa. Episcopalian. Avocation: chess. Private international, Patent, Contracts commercial. Home: 2 Candlewood Ct Scarsdale NY 10583 Office: Pfizer Inc 235 E 42d St New York NY 10017

MEDINA, STANDISH FORDE, JR., lawyer; b. Orange, N.J., June 16, 1940; s. Standish F. and Hope Tyler (Kiesewetter) M.; m. Kathryn L. Bach, Apr. 20, 1968; 1 child, Nathaniel Forde. A.B. cum laude, Princeton U., 1962; LL.B. magna cum laude, Columbia U., 1965, LL.M., 1966. Bar: N.Y. 1965, U.S. Supreme Ct. 1970, U.S. Dist. Ct. Appeals (2d, 3d, 4th, 5th, 7th, 11th, D.C. cirs.). Assoc. in law Columbia Law Sch., 1965-66; instr. law orientation program in Am. law Princeton U., 1966; assoc. Debevoise & Plimpton, N.Y.C., 1966-72, ptnr., 1973—. Trustee Hill Sch., Pottstown, Pa., 1976—. Mem. ABA (vice-chmn. com. on fed. cts., litigation sect. 1981-82, co-chmn. com. pleadings motions and pretrial 1986—), Fed. Bar Council, N.Y. State Bar Assn., Assn. of Bar of City of N.Y. (mem. exec. com. 1982-86, mem. judiciary com. 1978-81, mem. nominating com. 1986-87, mem. com. on ct. requirements 1978-81, fed. legis. com. 1971-75, chmn. membership com. 1986—, chmn. com. on fed. cts. 1978-81), Am. Law Inst., 2d Cir. Com. on Improvement Civil Litigation (chmn. 1986—), Civil Litigation Com. Ea. Dist. N.Y., Legal Aid Soc. (chmn. assoc. and young lawyers com. 1972). Federal civil litigation, State civil litigation. Home: 1105 Park Ave Apt 9A New York NY 10128 Office: Debevoise & Plimpton 875 3d Ave New York NY 10022

MEDLOCK, THOMAS TRAVIS, state attorney general, lawyer; b. Joanna, S.C., Aug. 28, 1934; s. Melvin Kelly and Mayme (DuBose) M.; m. Laura Virginia Orr, Oct. 11, 1969; children: Tom, Glenn. A.B., Wofford Coll., 1956, LLD, 1985; LL.B., U. S.C., 1959; DL (hon.), Wofford Coll., 1985. Bar: S.C. 1960, U.S. Supreme Ct. 1976. Asst. atty. gen. S.C. Atty. Gen.'s Office, Columbia, 1961-62; mem. S.C. Ho. of Reps., 1965-72, S.C. Senate, 1973-76; atty gen. S.C., 1983—; chmn. Gov. sub.-com. on econ. devel. for S.C., 1975-76; legis. com. S.C. State Bar Assn., 1979-80. Mem. S.C. State Tri-Centennial Commn., 1967-71; chmn. U.S. Pres.'s Com. on Children and Youth, S.C., 1971; mem. Wofford Coll. Alumni Bd., Spartanburg, S.C., 1972; bd. vistors Winthrop Coll., Rock Hill, S.C., 1975. Served to capt. U.S Army, 1975. Mem. S.C. Bar Assn., Richland County Bar Assn., Assn. Trial Lawyers Am., Phi Beta Kappa, Phi Alpha Delta. Democrat. Methodist. Administrative and regulatory, Criminal, Legislative. Office: Atty Gen SC PO Box 11549 Columbia SC 29211

MEDNICK, GLENN MYLES, lawyer; b. Phila., Sept. 9, 1953; s. Herbert Sheldon and Gertrude (Weitzner) M.; m. Linda Joy Packman, Dec. 28, 1975; children: Stacey Regan, Danielle Leigh. BBA cum laude, Temple U., 1975; JD, U. Miami, 1979. Bar: Fla. 1979, N.J. 1986. Assoc. Sandler & Sandler P.A., Miami, Fla., 1979-80; asst. city atty. City of Hollywood, Fla., 1980-82; assoc. Miller, Shapiro & Miller, Boca Raton, Fla., 1982-85; ptnr. Gutkin, Miller, Shapiro, Selesner & Shoobe, Boca Raton, 1986—. Mem. Fla. Bar Assn. (vice chmn. com. consumer protection law), Broward County Bar Assn., South Palm Beach County Bar Assn., Assn. Trial Lawyers Am., Delta Theta Phi. Real property, State civil litigation, Contracts commercial. Office: Gutkin Miller Shapiro et al 1300 N Federal Hwy Suite 108 Boca Raton FL 33432

MEDNICK, RICHARD, judge; b. Los Angeles, Nov. 28, 1933; B.A., UCLA, 1954; M.S. in Edn., U. So. Calif., 1955; J.D., Loyola U., Los Angeles, 1966. Bar: Calif. 1966, U.S. dist. Ct. (cen. dist.) Calif. 1966, U.S. Supreme Ct. 1972. Teaching fellow Loyola U.-Los Angeles, 1965-66; gen. practice, 1966-73; supr. litigation dept. Title Ins. and Trust Corp., Los Angeles, 1973-75; judge U.S. Bankruptcy Ct., U.S. Dist. (cen. dist.) Calif., Los Angeles, 1976—. Served to lt. U.S. Army, 1955-57. Mem. Nat. Conf. Bankruptcy Judges, Loyola Alumni Assn. (bd. govs.), Fin. Lawyers Assn. (bd. govs.), Los Angeles County Bar Assn. Contbr. chpt., articles to law publs. Bankruptcy. Office: US Courthouse Room 833 312 N Spring St Los Angeles CA 90012

MEDVECKY, THOMAS EDWARD, lawyer; b. Bridgeport, Conn., Apr. 22, 1937; s. Stephen and Elizabeth P. Medvecky; m. Patricia Conneally, Aug. 25, 1967; 1 son, Thomas Edward, II. A.B., Bowdoin Coll., 1959; LL.B., St. John's U., 1962. Bar: Conn. 1962. Assoc., Louis Katz, Danbury, Conn., 1963-68; sole practice, Bethel, Conn., 1968—; asst. town counsel Town of Bethel, 1963-67; assoc. dir. State Nat. Bank Conn. Mem. budget com. Danbury (Conn.) Community Chest, 1966-68. Served with USAR, 1962-68. Recipient Am. Jurisprudence award 1962. Mem. ABA, Conn. Bar Assn., Danbury Bar Assn. Democrat. Lutheran. Probate, Real property, General practice. Office: 99 Greenwood Ave PO Box 272 Bethel CT 06801

MEDVED, ROBERT ALLEN, lawyer; b. Cleve., July 22, 1945; s. Joseph Jack and Mary (Blasko) M. BBA, Kent State U., 1968; JD cum laude, U. Puget Sound, 1975. Bar: Wash. 1976, U.S. Ct. Appeals (9th cir.) 1976, U.S. Dist. Ct. (we. dist.) Wash. 1976, U.S. Dist. Ct. (ea. dist.) Wash. 1979, U.S. Supreme Ct. 1981. Fin. analyst Ford Motor Co., Sandusky, Ohio, 1972; research asst. U. Puget Sound, 1973; arbitration asst. to labor arbitrator, Tacoma, 1975; law clk. to judge U.S. Ct. Appeals 9th Circuit, Seattle, 1974, to judge U.S. Dist. Ct. Central Dist. Calif., Los Angeles, 1976; assoc. Graham & Dunn, Seattle, 1976-82, ptnr., 1982-83; ptnr. Drake and Whiteley, Bellevue, Wash., 1983-86, Foster, Pepper & Riviera, Seattle, 1986—; spl. dist. counsel 8th Congl. Dist. Wash., 1983—. Editor-in-chief U. Puget Sound Law Rev. Bd. dirs. Bellevue Community Coll. Found., 1986—. Served to lt., USN, 1968-71. U. Puget Sound scholar, 1974. Mem. ABA, Wash. State Bar Assn., Seattle C. of C., Bellevue C. of C. Roman Catholic. Corporate taxation, General corporate, Environment. Address: 212 108th Ave SE Bellevue WA 98004

MEDVIN, ALAN YORK, lawyer; b. N.Y.C., Sept. 13, 1947; s. Murray and Leona (Alpert) M.; m. Harriet A. Kass, July 11, 1976; children—Michelle K., Michael J. A.B., Colgate U., 1969; J.D., Rutgers U., 1972. Bar: N.J. 1972, U.S. Dist. Ct. N.J. 1972, U.S. Supreme Ct. 1981. Assoc., Horowitz, Bross & Sinins, Newark, 1972-75; ptnr. Horowitz, Bross, Sinins, Imperial & Medvin, 1976-83, Medvin & Elberg, Newark, 1983—; adj. prof. law Rutgers U., 1987. Fellow Roscoe Pound Found.; mem. Assn. Trial Lawyers Am. (state del. 1980, pres. N.J. affiliate, mem. bd. govs.), Am. Arbitration Assn., N.J. State Bar Assn. (Outstanding Profl. Achievement award 1982), Essex County Bar Assn., Mercer County Bar Assn. Democrat. Jewish. Personal injury, State civil litigation, Federal civil litigation. Home: 165 Bertrand Dr Princeton NJ 08540 Office: Medvin & Elberg Gateway 1 Newark NJ 07102

MEDZIE, KENNETH STEPHEN, lawyer, educator; b. Philipsburg, Pa., Dec. 22, 1947; s. George E. and Louise (Bilanich) M.; m. Deena Mickelberg, Aug. 17, 1974. A.S., Harrisburg Area Community Coll., 1968; B.S., U. Rochester, 1970; J.D., Dela. Law Sch., 1975; cert. in practice and advocacy Temple U., 1980. Bar: Pa. 1978, U.S. Dist. Ct. (ea. dist.) Pa. 1979, U.S. Supreme Ct. 1981. Sole practice Wallingford, Pa., 1978—; asst. prof. law U. Bridgeport, Conn., 1978—; vis. scholar Yale U., New Haven, Spring 1984, fall 1984. Contbr. articles to profl. jours. Mem. ABA, Pa. Bar Assn., Delaware County Bar Assn., Assn. Trial Lawyers Am., Pa. Trial Lawyers Assn., Nat. Assn. Estate Planning Council, Delaware County Estate Planning Council, Am. Judicature Soc., Comml. Law League Am., AAUP, Northeast Assn. Pre-Law Advs., Assn. Fed. Investigators, Internat. Assn. Chiefs Police, Internat. Assn. Auto Theft Investigators, Am. Soc. for Indsl. Security. Republican. Russian Orthodox. Clubs: Irish Am., West End Boat (Chester, Pa.). Criminal, Federal civil litigation, General practice. Home: 307 Hastings Ave Wallingford PA 19086 Office: Univ Bridgeport/Law 302 Mandeville Hall Bridgeport CT 06602

MEEHAN, JAMES FRANCIS, lawyer; b. Northampton, Mass., Feb. 9, 1930; s. James W. and Margaret M. (Henchey) M.; m. Dorothy Ring Kelleher, Oct. 24, 1953; children: Johanna, Margaret, Suzanne, Michaela. BS, Coll. of the Holy Cross, 1951; LLB, Boston Coll., 1954. Bar: Mass. 1954, U.S. Dist. Ct. Mass. 1956, U.S. Supreme Ct. 1969. Assoc. Law Office of John P. Donnelly, Malden, Mass., 1956-59; assoc. Parker, Coulter, Daley & White, Boston, 1959-62, ptnr., 1962-84; pres. Meehan, Boyle & Cohen, P.C., Boston, 1984—. Served with U.S. Army, 1954-56. Fellow Am. Coll. Trial Lawyers; mem. Mass. Acad. Trial Lawyers (pres. 1984-86). Federal civil litigation, Personal injury, Insurance. Home: 217 W Canton St Boston MA 02116

MEEHAN, MICHAEL JAN, lawyer; b. Columbus, Ohio, July 27, 1949; s. John Howard and Margaret Amelia (Maeder) M.; m. Ellen Kirwin, Mar. 15, 1975; children: Brian, Kevin. AB, John Carroll U., 1972; JD, U. Toledo, 1981. Bar: Mich. 1981, Ohio 1982, U.S. Dist. Ct. (ea. dist.) Mich. 1981, U.S. Dist. Ct. (no. dist.) Ohio 1982. Acct. Cleve. Clinic Found., 1972-74, acctg. supr., 1974-77, asst. sec., assoc. counsel, 1982—; fin. mgr. Toledo Hosp., 1977-81; assoc. Oykema, Gossett, Spencer, Goodnow & Trigg, Detroit, 1981-82; bus. mgr. Our House Assocs., Cleve., 1982-86. Mem. ABA, Ohio Bar Assn., Mich. Bar Assn., Am. Acad. Hosp. Attys., Assn. Ohio Hosp. Attys. Roman Catholic. Club: Coronary (Cleve.) (trustee, sec. 1985—). Avocations: music, sports. Health, Personal injury, General corporate. Home: 1733 Sperry's Forge Trail Westlake OH 44145 Office: Cleve Clinic Found 9500 Euclid Ave Cleveland OH 44106

MEEHAN, RICHARD THOMAS, JR., lawyer; b. Bridgeport, Conn., Jan. 11, 1949; s. Richard Thomas and Elvira (Avola) M.; m. Kathy Lynn Mucci, Aug. 23, 1969; children—Michael, Brian, Daniel, Timothy. B.A., U. Notre Dame, 1970; J.D. with honors, U. Conn., 1974. Bar: Conn. 1974, U.S. Dist. Ct. Conn. 1975, U.S. Ct. Appeals (2d cir.) 1975, U.S. Supreme Ct. 1980. Clk., Conn. Supreme Ct., Hartford, 1974-75; ptnr. Meehan and Meehan, Bridgeport, Conn., 1975—; adj. assoc. prof. paralegal program Sacred Heart U., Fairfield, Conn., 1976-79; dir. Coldwell Wilcox, Inc., Fairfield. Bd. editors U. Conn. Law Rev., 1972-73, research and spl. projects editor, 1973-74. Alderman, City of Bridgeport, 1975-79; commr. Airport Commn., Bridgeport, 1977-79; pres. Common Council, Bridgeport, 1977-79; mem. exec. bd. North End Little League, Bridgeport, 1983. Recipient Am. Jurisprudence award for torts Lawyers Coop, 1972; Am. Jurisprudence award advance criminal procedure Lawyers Coop, 1972; Am. Jurisprudence award contracts Lawyers Coop, 1972. Mem. Assn. Trial Lawyers Am., Conn. Bar Assn. (exec. com. criminal law 1981-83), Conn. Trial Lawyers Assn., Bridgeport Bar Assn. (exec. com. 1982-85, chmn. criminal law sect. 1981-82, 84-85, pres.-elect 1985-86, pres. 1986-87), Nat. Council Bar Pres., Conn. Council Bar Pres's. Democrat. Roman Catholic. Criminal, State civil litigation, Family and matrimonial. Home: 28 Elderberry Ln Shelton CT 06484 Office: Meehan and Meehan 76 Lyon Terr Bridgeport CT 06604

MEEK, LESLIE APPLEGATE, lawyer; b. Covington, Ky., July 31, 1913; s. John Risk and Louise Menzies (Applegate) M.; m. Elizabeth Katherine Nottingham, Sept. 14, 1938; m. 2d, Margaret Louisa Watkins, Jan. 3, 1963; 9 children. Student Centre Coll., 1930-32; A.B., U. Cin., 1934, LL.B., 1936. Bar: Ohio 1936, U.S. Dist. Ct. (so. dist.) Ohio 1939, U.S. Ct. Appeals (6th cir.) 1939. Assoc., Graydon, Head & Ritchey, Cin., 1936-49, ptnr., 1950—; dir. various corps. Served to lt. USNR, 1944-46. Mem. ABA, Cin. Bar Assn. Republican. Episcopalian. General corporate, Corporate taxation, Pension, profit-sharing, and employee benefits. Office: Suite 1900 Fifth Third Center Cincinnati OH 45202

MEEK, MARCELLUS ROBERT, lawyer, business consultant; b. N.Y.C., Nov. 20, 1929; s. Marcellus W. and Lillian D. (Hilward-Younes) M.; children—Susan J., Marcellus W. II, Mary F., Adam M. Student U. Ill., 1948-51; J.D., DePaul U., 1954; LL.M. (James Nelson Raymond fellow), Northwestern U., 1955. Bar: Ill. 1955, U.S. Supreme Ct. 1971, U.S. Dist. Ct. (no. dist.) Ill. 1955, U.S. Ct. Appeals (7th cir.) 1955, U.S. Ct. Appeals (5th cir.) 1971. Ptnr. Baker & McKenzie, firm specializing in internat. law, Chgo., 1956-77; sole practice, Chgo., 1977—; cons. fed. tax, bus., related fields to former internat. law practice; lectr. internat. law Marquette U., Milw., 1959-65; instr., dir. internat. law dept. John Marshall Law Sch., Chgo., 1964-69. Founder, chmn. bd. dirs. Tucson Jazz Soc., 1979—. Recipient citation for work with law rev. DePaul Law Sch., 1954; hon. justice Chgo. chpt. Moot Ct. competition, 1955; Nathan Burkan Meml. first award, ASCAP, 1954; Cert. contbg. author recognition DePaul Law Rev., 1966; Cert. distinction DePaul U., 1980. Mem. Ill. Bar Assn., ABA, Am. Judicature Soc., Am. Fgn. Law Assn., Celtic Legal Soc. Chgo., Am. Soc. Internat. Law, Chgo. Natural History Mus., Chgo. Hist. Soc., Art Inst. Chgo., Artists Guild Chgo. Republican. Presbyterian. Clubs: Mountain Oyster, Racquet, MG T Registry, Rod and Gun, Gun, Le Group, Foothills Yacht, Jaguar of So. Ariz. (Tucson); Racquet (Chgo.), Pima (Ariz.) County Polo. Author: Antiques, the Law and Taxes, 1964; Cases and Materials--International Commercial Transactions, 1964; (with H.J. Stitt) International Transactions, Commentaries and Forms, 1967; International Commercial Agreements, 1977; contbr. articles to profl. jours. Private international, Jurisprudence, Corporate taxation. Home: 3020 E Weymouth St Tucson AZ 85716

MEEK, WALTER BUCHANAN, lawyer; b. Memphis, Jan. 13, 1926; s. Arthur Maurice and Sarah Christine (Buchanan) M.; m. Patsy Joyce Haynes, June 26, 1949; children—Christine Thrasher, Buchanan, Joyce Yates. B.B.A., U. Miss., 1948, LL.B., 1950. Bar: Miss. 1950, U.S. Dist. Ct. (no. dist.) Miss. 1950, U.S. Ct. Appeals (5th cir.) 1972. Practice, Eupora, Miss., 1950—; mem. Meek and Meek, Eupora, 1975—; atty. Webster County Bd. Suprs., 1968—; dir. Security State Bank, Bank of Webster County. Served with USAAF, 1943-45. Mem. ABA, Miss. State Bar. Methodist. General practice, Family and matrimonial. Office: PO Box 555 Eupora MS 39744

MEEKINS, SAMUEL WARRENTON, JR., lawyer; b. Norfolk, Va., Aug. 1, 1945; s. Samuel Warrenton Sr. and Sarah Inez (Parker) M.; m. Robin Ross, Nov. 29, 1971; children: Samuel III, Erica, Audrey, Sarah. BS in Mktg., Old Dominion U., 1972; JD, Campbell U., 1980. Bar: Va., U.S. Dist. Ct. (ea. and we. dists.) Va., U.S. Ct. Appeals (4th cir.), U.S. Supreme Ct. Asst. atty. Commonwealth of Va., Portsmouth, 1980-82; assoc. Wolcott, Rivers, Wheary, Basnight & Kelly, P.C., Norfolk, Va., 1982-85; ptnr., office mgr. Wolcott, Rivers, Wheary, Basnight & Kelly, P.C., Virginia Beach, Va., 1985-87, pres., 1987—. Contbg. editor Campbell U. Law Rev., 1979. Chmn. bus. Am. Heart Assn., Norfolk, 1983, campaign chmn. Tidewater (Va.) chpt., 1984, bd. dirs., Tidewater, 1984-85. Served with USAF, 1965-68, Vietnam. Mem. ABA, Norfolk/Portsmouth Bar Assn., Portsmouth Bar Assn., Assn. Trial Lawyers Am., Va. Trial Lawyers Assn., Omicron Delta Kappa. Methodist. Clubs: Big Blue; Carolanne Farm Racquet & Swim (Virginia Beach). Avocation: sports. Criminal, State civil litigation, Federal civil litigation. Office: Wolcott Rivers Wheary Basnight & Kelly PC 1100 Sovran Bank Bldg One Colmubus Ctr Virginia Beach VA 23462

MEEKS, CORDELL DAVID, JR., state judge; b. Kansas City, Kans., Dec. 17, 1942; s. Cordell David and Cellastine Dora (Brown) M.; m. Mary Ann Sutherland, July 15, 1967; 1 child, Cordell D. III. B.A., U. Kans., 1964, J.D., 1967; postgrad., U. Pa., 1968. Bar: Kans. 1968, U.S. Dist. Ct. Kans. 1968, U.S. Mil. Ct. Appeals 1971, U.S. Ct. Appeals (10th cir.) 1971, U.S. Supreme Ct. 1971. Staff counsel Wyandotte County Legal Aid Soc., Kansas City, Kans., 1968-70; spl. asst. atty. gen. State of Kans., Kansas City, 1975; sr. ptnr. Meeks, Sutherland, and McIntosh, Kansas City, 1972-81; judge Mcpl. Ct. Kansas City, 1976-81; dist. ct. judge 29th Judicial Dist. Kans., Kansas City, 1981—; mem. govs. com. crime prevention, Kans., 1984—; mem. Kans. adv. com. overcrowded prisons, 1983-84, Kans. Com. on Bicentennial of U.S. Constn., 1987—; pres. Wyandotte County Law Library Com., 1982-83; staff judge adv. 35th Inf. Div. Kans. N.G., 1984—. Vice pres. Jr. Achievement Greater Kansas City, 1975- 76; pres. Wyandotte County chpt. ARC, 1971-73, Mental Health Assn., 1981-83, Legal Aid Soc., 1971-73, Econ. Opportunity Found., Inc., Kansas City, 1981-83; bd. dirs. Family and Childrens Service, 1983—; pres. Substance Abuse Ctr. Eastern Kans., 1985—; mem. exec. com. NCCJ, Kansas City, 1984—; mem. Kansas Commn. on Bicentennial of U.S. Constitution, 1987—. Recipient Outstanding Service award Kansas City United Way, 1979. Mem. Kans. Mcpl. Judges Assn. (pres. 1980-81), U. Kans. Law Soc. (pres. bd. govs. 1984-85), Nat. Conf. State Trial Judges (ethics and profl. responsibility com.), Am. Judicature Soc., Am. Judges Assn., ABA, Kans. Bar Assn., Am. Royal

Assn. (bd. govs. 1981—). Democrat. Mem. A. M. E. Ch. (gov. 1981-87). Lodge: Optimists (bd. dirs. 1977). Avocations: jazz piano; table tennis; swimming. Jurisprudence. Home: 7915 Walker Kansas City KS 66112 Office: Wyandotte County Courthouse 701 N 7th St Kansas City KS 66101

MEEKS, WILLIAM HERMAN, III, lawyer; b. Ft. Lauderdale, Fla., Dec. 30, 1939; s. Walter Herman, Jr. and Elise Walker (McGuire) M.; m. Patricia Ann Rayburn, July 30, 1965; 1 son, William Herman IV; m. 2d, Miriam Andrea Bedsole, Dec. 28, 1971; 1 dau., Julie Marie. A.B., Princeton U., 1961; LL.B., U. Fla., 1964; LL.M., NYU, 1965. Bar: Fla. 1964, U.S. Dist. Ct. (so. dist.) Fla. 1965, U.S. Tax Ct. 1966, U.S. Ct. Appeals (11th cir.) 1981, U.S. Supreme Ct. 1985. Ptnr. McCune, Hiaasen, Crum, Ferris & Gardner, Ft. Lauderdale, 1964—; dir. Attys. Title Services, Inc., 1978-79, Attys. Title Services of Broward County, Inc., 1971—, chmn. 1976-77. Active Ft. Lauderdale Mus., 1976—. Mem. ABA, Fla. Bar Assn., Broward County Bar Assn., Attys. Title Ins. Fund, Ft. Lauderdale Hist. Soc., Phi Delta Phi. Democrat. Presbyterian. Clubs: Kiwanis, Lauderdale Yacht, Tower (Ft. Lauderdale). Probate, Real property, General corporate. Office: McCune Hiassen et al PO Box 14636 Penthouse Barnett Bank Plaza Fort Lauderdale FL 33302

MEER, JULIAN MILTON, lawyer; b. Trinidad, Colo., Feb. 17, 1916; s. Jerome and Anna (Frank) M.; m. Clarice Sylvia Arbetter, Oct. 1, 1940; children: Janice Elaine, Jeralyn. BBA, U. Tex., 1939, JD, 1940; LLM, So. Meth. U., 1958. Bar: Tex. 1940, U.S. Dist. Ct. (no. dist.) Tex. 1947, U.S. Supreme Ct. 1947, U.S. Ct. Appeals (5th cir.) 1948. Atty., U.S. SEC, 1940-47; sole practice, Dallas, 1947-52; ptnr. Turner, White, Atwood Meer & Francis, Dallas, 1952-66, Meer, Chandler & Carlton, Dallas, 1967-72, Elliott, Meer, Vetter, Denton & Bates, Dallas, 1972-79, Steinberg, Solomon & Meer (formerly Steinberg & Meer), Dallas, 1980—. Contbr. articles to profl. jours. Served with USN, 1946-47. Mem. ABA, Fed. Bar Assn., Tex. State Bar, Dallas Bar Assn., Am. Assn. Attys.-CPA's. Jewish. Clubs: Brookhaven Country, Lancers (Dallas). Lodge: B'nai B'rith. General corporate, Securities, Administrative and regulatory. Office: 1120 One Galleria Tower 13355 Noel Rd Dallas TX 75240

MEERSMAN, ROBERT FRANCIS, lawyer; b. Evanston, Ill., Sept. 28, 1929; s. Joseph A. and Virginia G. (Grey) M.; widowed; children: Kathleen, Carole, Maribeth, Maureen. PhB, Marquette U., 1951; JD, DePaul U., 1958. Bar: Ill. 1958, U.S. Dist. Ct. (no. dist.) Ill. 1958, U.S. Ct. Appeals (7th and 10th cirs.) 1960, U.S. Supreme Ct. 1963. Ptnr. Moore & Meersman, Mt. Prospect, Ill., 1969-76; sole practice Mt. Prospect, 1976-84; ptnr. Meersman & Meersman, Mt. Prospect, 1984—; tech. advisor law State of Ill., Chgo., 1969-79. Served with U.S. Army, 1951-53, Korea. Mem. ABA, Ill. Bar Assn., Chgo. Bar Assn., Northwest Suburban Bar Assn. Democrat. Roman Catholic. General practice. Home: 201 N Russell St Mount Prospect IL 60056 Office: Meersman & Meersman 16 W Northwest Hwy Mount Prospect IL 60056

MEESE, EDWIN, III, lawyer, attorney general; b. Oakland, Calif., 1931; s. Edwin and Leone M. Meese; m. Ursula Herrick, 1958; children: Michael James, Dana Lynne. BA, Yale U., 1953; J.D., U. Calif., Berkeley, 1958; LLD, Del. Law Sch., Widener U., U. San Diego, Valparaiso U., Calif. Luth. Coll. Dep. dist. atty. Alameda County, Calif., 1959-67; sec. of legal affairs Gov. Reagan Calif., Sacramento, 1967-69, exec. asst., chief staff, 1969-75; v.p. Rohr Industries, Chula Vista, Calif., 1975-76; sole pratice law 1976-80; dir. ctr. criminal justice policy and mgmt. U. Calif., San Diego, 1977-81; counselor U.S. Pres., 1981-85; counselor to Pres. Reagan, Washington, 1981-85; U.S. atty. gen. Washington, 1985—; prof. law U. San Diego, 1978-81. V.p. Lutheran Ch., El Cajon, Calif. Served with U.S. Army. Criminal. Office: US Dept Justice 10th and Constitution Ave Washington DC 20530

MEGAARD, SUSAN LYNNE, lawyer, accounting educator; b. Washington, June 19, 1954; d. David Richard and Bette Jane (Ferkler) Brennan; m. Michael Martin Megaard, Apr. 4, 1981; 1 child, Megan Michelle. BA in History, U. of Pacific, 1976; JD, U. Wash., 1979; ML in Taxation, Georgetown U., 1982. Bar: Wash. 1979, U.S. Dist. Ct. (we. dist.) Wash. Atty., advisor U.S Tax Ct., Washington, 1979-82; assoc. Sax and MacIver, Seattle, 1982-83, MacGillivray and Jones, Spokane, Wash., 1983-84; asst. prof. taxation and accounting Eastern Wash. U., Spokane and Cheney, 1984—; CPA, atty. Tax Clinic, Spokane, 1983-84; staff author Tax Mgmt. Inc., Washington, 1984—. Author: (with Michael M. Megaard) Depreciation Recapture (portfolio), 1985. Mem. ABA (tax sect. 1983—), Wash. State Bar Assn., Phi Beta Kappa. Democrat. Avocations: aerobics, cross-country skiing, hiking, fishing. Corporate taxation, Personal income taxation, Contracts commercial. Office: Eastern Wash U Rm 203 Kingston Hall Cheney WA 99004

MEGAN, THOMAS IGNATIUS, judge; b. Chgo., Dec. 24, 1913; s. Charles P. and May M. (Magan) M.; m. Lucyanne Flaherty, Apr. 17, 1948; children: Anne, Thomas, Jane, Sarah, William, Molly. A.B., U. Ill., 1935; J.D., U. Chgo., 1938. Bar: Ill. 1939, N.Y. 1941. Mem. firm Pruitt & Grealis, Chgo., 1939-40, Pruitt, Hale & MacIntyre, N.Y.C., 1941; atty. U.S. Ordnance Dept., Chgo., 1941-42, Chgo., Rock Island and Pacific R.R. Co., Chgo., 1945-70; v.p. to gen. counsel Chgo., Rock Island and Pacific R.R. Co., 1970-74, v.p. law, 1974-75; adminstrv. law judge ICC, Washington, 1975-81, HHS, Washington, 1981, FERC, Washington, 1981—. Served to maj. AUS, 1942-45. Mem. ABA, Soc. Trial Lawyers Chgo., Chgo. Law Club, Phi Kappa Tau, Phi Delta Phi. Clubs: Union League (Chgo.); Nat. Lawyers (Washington). Home: 11108 Waycroft Way Rockville MD 20852 Office: 825 N Capital St Washington DC 20426

MEGIBOW, TOD DOUGLAS, lawyer; b. N.Y.C., Mar. 29, 1951; s. Samuel Jacob and Linnea (Wenberg) M.; m. Laura Ethel Brown, July 17, 1983; 1 child, Rachel Nicole. BA, Ky. Wesleyan Coll., 1973; JD, Loyola U., New Orleans, 1978. Bar: Ky. 1979, U.S. Dist. Ct. (we. dist.) Ky. 1980, U.S. Ct. Appeals (6th cir.) 1980, U.S. Supreme Ct. 1984. Asst. pub. adv. Ky. Dept. Pub. Advocacy, Eddyville, 1979-80; assoc. Owens & Graves, Paducah, Ky., 1980-81; sole practice Paducah, 1981-83; mng. ptnr. Freeland, Glanville & Megibow, Paducah, 1983—; adminstr. Graves County Pub. Defenders Inc., Mayfield, Ky., 1982-85; bd. dirs. West Ky. Services, Paducah. Mem. Ky. Bar Assn., McCrachen County Bar Assn., Assn. Trial Lawyers Am., Ky. Acad. Trial Atty.'s, Ky. Criminal Lawyer Def. Assn. (charter, founding bd. dirs.). Democrat. Jewish. Personal injury, Criminal, Family and matrimonial. Home: Rt 6 Box 620 Paducah KY 42001 Office: Freeland Glanville & Megibow 910 Citizens Bldg Paducah KY 42001

MEHLHAFF, ROBERT, lawyer; b. Friedrichshoff, Fed. Republic Germany, May 12, 1948; s. Waldemar and Veronica Mehlhaff; m. Mary Lynn Larsson, Aug. 31, 1969; children: James, Kristin, Matthew. Student, Delta Jr. Coll., 1965-67; BA, U. Calif., Berkeley, 1969; JD, San Francisco Law Sch., 1975. Bar: Calif. 1975, U.S. Dist. Ct. (no. dist.) Calif. 1975, U.S. Ct. Appeals (9th cir.) 1975, U.S. Dist. Ct. (ea. dist.) Calif. 1976. Ptnr. Souza, Coats, McInnis & Mehlhaff, Tracy, Calif., 1978—; asst. atty. City of Tracy, 1976—. Trustee Tracy Elem. Sch. Dist., 1984—. Served with N.G U.S. Army, 1968-74. Mem. Calif. Bar Assn., Calif. Trial Lawyers Assn., San Joaquin County Bar Assn. Lutheran. Lodge: Elks. Avocations: golf, guitar, fishing. State civil litigation, Condemnation, Personal injury. Office: Souza Coats McInnis & Mehlhaff 1011 Parker Ave Tracy CA 95376

MEHRTENS, WILLIAM OSBORNE, JR., lawyer; b. Miami Beach, Fla., Nov. 20, 1945; s. William Osborne and Jaime (Hancock) M. B.S., U. Fla., 1968; J.D. magna cum laude, Fla. State U., 1971. Bar admittee: Fla., 1971, U.S. Dist. Ct. (so. dist.) Fla., 1971, U.S. Dist. Ct. (no. and mid dists.) Fla., 1973, U.S. Customs Ct. 1977, U.S. Ct. Appeals (5th cir.), 1971, U.S. Ct. Appeals (11th cir.), 1981, U.S. Supreme Ct., 1974. Assoc., Smathers & Thompson, Miami, Fla., 1971-78; sole practice, Miami, 1978-79, 82—; mng. atty. Hartford Accident & Indemnity Co., Miami, 1979-82. Mem. ABA, Fla. Bar Assn. (fed. rules com. 1971-72, appellate rules subcom. 1973-77, admiralty law com. 1977, aviation and space law com. 1978), Dade County Bar Assn. (dir. 1973-77, co-chmn. fed. ct. com. 1971-72, mem. fed. ct. com. 1977-78, circuit ct. gen. div. com. 1978, fed. ct. com. 1983-84), Dade County Def. Bar Assn., Am. Judicature Soc., Phi Delta Phi, Pi Kappa Phi. Baptist. Federal civil litigation, State civil litigation, Personal injury. Home: 1441 SW 11th St Miami FL 33135 Office: 99 NW 183d St Suite 224 PO Box 4340 Miami FL 33169

MEIER, CARL CARSTEN, lawyer; b. New Orleans, Dec. 19, 1944; s. Merlyn P. and Leone (Frois) M.; m. Sharon Ann Huber, Aug. 17, 1968; children: Kristian, Clifton. AB, U. Notre Dame, 1966; JD, U. Ill., 1970. Bar: Ill. 1970, Iowa 1970, Minn. 1977. Assoc. Jurgemeyer & Eddy, Clinton, Iowa, 1970-72; atty. Bankers Life Co., Des Moines, 1972-77; sr. counsel Honeywell Inc., Mpls., 1977—. Mem. ABA, Minn. Bar Assn., Hennepin County Bar Assn., Am. Corp. Counsel Assn. Environment, Pension, profit-sharing, and employee benefits. Home: 4888 Edgewater Dr Mound MN 55364 Office: Honeywell Inc Honeywell Plaza Minneapolis MN 55408

MEIGS, JOHN FORSYTH, lawyer; b. Boston, Dec. 4, 1941; s. Charles H. and Florence S. (Truitt) M.; m. Faith C. Watson; children—Amy, Perry. B.A., Yale U., 1964; LL.B., U. Pa., 1969. Bar: Pa. 1969, U.S. Supreme Ct. 1977. Assoc. Saul, Ewing, Remick & Saul, Phila., 1969-76, ptnr., 1976—. Sec. Phila. Maritime Mus., 1978—; mem. Com. of 70, 1976—; trustee Woodmere Art Mus., 1987—. Mem. ABA, Pa. Bar Assn., Phila. Bar Assn. Episcopalian. Probate, General corporate, Estate planning. Home: 6 Norman Ln Philadelphia PA 19118 Office: 38th Floor Centre Sq W Philadelphia PA 19102

MEIGS, WALTER RALPH, lawyer, dry dock and shipbuilding company executive; b. Macon, Ga., Sept. 7, 1948; s. Ralph and Alice (Lee) M.; B.A., Birmingham So. Coll., 1970; J.D., U. Ala., 1973, postgrad., 1982; postgrad. Auburn U., 1974; m. Gloria Sharmon Eddins, Sept. 17, 1977; children—Nancy Sharmon, Stephen Walter, Christopher. Admitted to Ala. bar, 1973; law clk. Jud. br. State of Ala., 1973-74; assoc. firm Hubbard, Waldrop and Jenkins, Tuscaloosa, Ala., 1974-75; house counsel Ala. Dry Dock and Shipbldg. Co., Mobile., 1975—, asst. sec., 1978—, asst. v.p. adminstrn., 1981—; corp. sec. Addsco Industries Inc., 1985—. Bd. dirs. Mobile Pre-sch. for Deaf, Mobile chpt. ARC. Mem. ABA, Ala. State Bar Assn., Mobile Bar Assn., Maritime Law Assn., Propeller Club U.S., Mobile C. of C., Leadership Mobile, Ala. Forestry Assn., Am. Forestry Assn., Ala. Hist. Soc., So. Hist. Soc. Methodist (adminstrv. bd.). Club: Kiwanis. Admiralty, General corporate, Labor. Home: 313 Brawood Dr Mobile AL 36608 Office: ADDSCO Industries Inc PO Box 190 Mobile AL 36608

MEIKLE, WILLIAM MACKAY, lawyer; b. Wilkinsburg, Pa., July 13, 1933; s. William and Martha (Bohlender) M.; m. Mary Eileen Luth, Mar. 12, 1966; children—Elizabeth Ellen, Martha Pauline. B.B.A., U. Mich., 1955, J.D., 1959. Bar: Ohio 1959. Sole practice, Celina, Ohio, 1959-63; ptnr. Knapke & Meikle, Celina, 1964-76; ptnr. Meikle & Tesno, Celina, 1977-81; ptnr. Meikle, Tesno & Luth, Celina, 1982—; also asst. pros. atty. Mercer County (Ohio) 1959-74, pros. atty., 1975-76; sec., treas. Mercer County Civic Found., 1961—; pres. Mercer County Health Care Found., 1980—; sec. Western Ohio Ednl. Found., 1975—; trustee Auglaize County Family Y Inc., 1981-84. Served to capt. USAR, 1959. Mem. Ohio State Bar Assn., Ohio Assn. Civil Trial Attys. Democrat. Methodist. General practice, Probate, State civil litigation. Home: 209 Mercer St Celina OH 45822 Office: 100 N Main St Celina OH 45822

MEIKLEJOHN, ALVIN J., JR., state senator, lawyer, acct.; b. Omaha, June 18, 1923; B.S., J.D., U. Denver, 1951; m. Lorraine J. Meiklejohn; children—Pamela Ann, Shelley Lou, Bruce Ian, Scott Alvin. Mem. Colo. Senate from 19th dist., 1976—, chmn. com.; edn.; mem. Edn. Commn. of States, 1981—. Mem. Jefferson Sch. Dist. No. R-1 Bd. Edn., 1971-77, pres., 1973-77. Served to capt. U.S. Army, 1940-46; to maj. USAF, 1947-51. Mem. Colo. Bar Assn., Denver Bar Assn., Colo. Soc. C.P.A., Arvada C. of C. Republican. Clubs: Masons, Shriners. Administrative and regulatory, Antitrust, Public utilities. Home: 7540 Kline Dr Arvada CO 80005 Office: Jones Meiklejohn Kehl & Lyons 1600 Lincoln Ctr Bldg Denver CO 80264

MEIKLEJOHN, DONALD STUART, lawyer; b. Chgo., Oct. 27, 1950; s. Donald and Elizabeth (Moore) M.; m. Rebecca Schneider, Aug. 9, 1975; children: David Alexander, Sarah. AB, Harvard U., 1971, JD, 1975. Bar: N.Y. 1976, U.S. Dist. Ct. (so. and ea. dists.) N.Y. 1976, U.S. Ct. Appeals (2d cir.) 1981, U.S. Ct. Appeals (5th cir.) 1982, U.S. Supreme Ct. 1986. Assoc. Sullivan & Cromwell, N.Y.C., 1975-83, ptnr., 1983—; bd. dirs. Union Settlement, N.Y.C. Mem. Assn. of Bar of City of N.Y. Antitrust, Securities, Federal civil litigation. Office: Sullivan & Cromwell 125 Broad St New York NY 10004

MEIKLEJOHN, PAUL THOMAS, lawyer; b. Phila., Mar. 13, 1944; s. James Joseph and Helen Gertrude (Morrissey) M.; m. Dawn Lucille Hutchins, June 26, 1972; children: Heather, Matthew, Neil. BS in Chemistry, Allentown Coll., 1969; JD, Am. U., 1975; MS in Chem., Georgetown U., 1983. Bar: Va. 1976, D.C. 1976, U.S. Dist. Ct. D.C. 1977, U.S. Dist. Ct. (ea. dist.) La. 1980, U.S. Ct. Appeals (4th cir.) 1980, N.Y. 1981, U.S. Dist. Ct. (ea. and so. dists.) N.Y. 1981, U.S. Ct. Appeals (2d cir.) 1981, U.S. Ct. Appeals (D.C. cir.) 1982, U.S. Dist. Ct. N.J. 1983, U.S. Ct. Appeals (5th cir.) 1985. Tech. advisor U.S. Ct. Customs & Patent Appeals, Washington, 1976-77; assoc. Burns, Doane et al, Alexandria, Va., 1977-78; assoc. Hopgood, Calimafde et al, N.Y.C., 1978-82, ptnr., 1982—; instr. Practicing Law Inst., N.Y.C., 1978—. Contbr. articles on patents to profl. jours. Mem. ABA, Am. Intellectual Property Assn. Roman Catholic. Patent, Federal civil litigation, Trademark and copyright. Office: Hopgood Calimafde et al 60 E 42d St New York NY 10165

MEILY, WILLIAM DAVIS, lawyer; b. South Bend, Ind., July 4, 1949; s. William Amos Meily and Leslie Jean (Davis) Dickey; m. Linda Ellen Frazier, Sept. 9, 1972; 1 child, William Matthew. BA, U. Cin., 1971; JD, U. Dayton, 1978. Bar: Ohio 1978, U.S. Dist. Ct. (so. and we. dists.) Ohio 1978. Assoc. Legler, Lang & Kuhns, Dayton, Ohio, 1978-79, Biegel, Kirkland & Berger, Dayton, 1979-81; ptnr. Meily & Mues, Dayton, 1981—; acting referee Montgomery County Common Pleas Ct., Dayton, 1981—; acting prosecutor Oakwood (Ohio) Mcpl. Ct., 1985—. Vol. Dayton Art Inst. Oktoberfest, 1985-86; legal counsel Montgomery County Juvenile Ct. Rev. Bd., Dayton, 1984-85. Mem. ABA, Ohio Bar Assn., Dayton Bar Assn. (chmn. family law com. 1986—, co-chmn. instant child support com.), Greene County Bar Assn. Avocation: golf. State civil litigation, Family and matrimonial, Personal injury. Office: Meily & Mues 22 Clay St Dayton OH 45402

MEININGER, JOHN ALEXANDER, lawyer; b. Ft. Morgan, Colo., Jan. 17, 1948; s. Frederick and Miriam (Amen) M.; m. Barbara Cook, Sept. 24, 1976 (div. 14, 1984); children: Alexander Kent, Benjamin Todd. BA, Yale U., 1971; JD, U. Calif., Berkeley, 1974. Bar: Calif. 1974, Colo., 1975, U.S. Dist. Ct. (10th cir.) 1981. Sole practice Englewood, Colo., 1984-86; ptnr. Meininger & Assocs. P.C., Englewood, 1987—; author, cons. Agr. Homestead Protection and Rural Econ. Stabilization Act of 1986. V.p. Colo. Young Reps., 1975-76; coordinator Study Colo. & Fire Pension Reform, Colo., 1977-79. Mem. ABA, Calif. Bar Assn., Colo. Bar Assn. Episcopalian. Republican. Clubs: Metropolitan (Englewood). Real property, General corporate, Farmer and rancher debtor representation. Office: Meininger & Assocs PC 5990 Greenwood Plaza Blvd #205 Englewood CO 80111

MEISEL, ALAN, law educator; b. Newark, Dec. 24, 1946; s. Stanley and Beatrice (Katz) M.; m. Linda S. Serody, Mar. 6, 1982; 1 child, Matthew. BA, Yale U., 1968, JD, 1972. Bar: Conn. 1972, Pa. 1973, U.S. Dist. Ct. Conn. 1972, U.S. Dist. Ct. (we. dist.) Pa. 1973, U.S. Ct. Appeals (3d cir.) 1985. Assoc. Goldstein & Peck, P.C., Bridgeport, Conn., 1972-73; prof. psychiatry U. Pitts., 1973—, prof. law, 1976—, co-dir. Ctr. Med. Ethics, 1986—; of counsel Berkman, Ruslander, Pohl, Lieber & Engel, Pitts., 1983—; asst. dir. for legal studies Pres.'s Commn. for Study of Ethical Problems in Medicine and Biomed. and Behavioral Research, Washington, 1982. Co-author: Informed Consent: A Study of Decision Making in Psychiatry, 1984, Informed Consent: Legal Theory and Clinical Practice, 1987; contbr. articles to legal and med. jours. Grantee NIMH, grantee Pres.'s Commn. for Study of Ethical Problems in Medicine and Biomed. and Behavioral Research, 1981-82, Founds. Fund for Research in Psychiatry grantee, 1979-82, Legal Services Corp. grantee, 1985-87; fellow Hastings Ctr. Mem. Assn. Am. Law Schs. (chmn. law and medicine sect. 1984). Health, Legal education, Mental health. Office: U Pitts Sch Law Pittsburgh PA 15260

MEISELMAN, DAVID J., lawyer; b. Bklyn., May 15, 1947; s. Murray L. and Edith A. (Silverman) M.; m. Myra I. Packman, Feb. 9, 1974; 1 child, Rebecca. BS, Bklyn. Coll., 1970; JD N.Y. Law Sch. 1973. Bar: N.Y. 1974. Assoc. Barry, McTiernan & Moore, N.Y.C., 1974-75, Finkelstein, Mauriello, Kaplan & Levine, P.C., Newburgh, N.Y., 1975-76; mng. ptnr. Meiselman, Farber, Packman & Eberz, P.C., Poughkeepsie, N.Y., 1976—. Served with USMC 1968-70. Mem. ABA, Mid-Hudson Trial Lawyers Assn. (pres.), N.Y. State Trial Lawyers Assn. (dir., dist. gov.), Dutchess County Bar Assn., Orange County Bar Assn. (award 1976), N.Y. County Bar Assn., N.Y. State Bar Assn., Am. Trial Lawyers Assn. Author: Attorney Malpractice: Law and Procedure; contbr. articles to profl. jours. Personal injury, State civil litigation, General practice. Office: Two Jefferson St Poughkeepsie NY 12602

MEISER, KENNETH EDWARD, lawyer; b. Cin., Apr. 21, 1945; s. Edward M. and Margaret (Lowe) M.; m. Mirelynne Gisser, Sept. 2, 1979; children—Rebecca Anne, Michelle Jo. A.B. summa cum laude, Xavier U., 1967; J.D. cum laude, Harvard U., 1973. Bar: N.J. 1973, U.S. Dist. Ct. N.J. 1973, U.S. Ct. Appeals (3d cir.) 1974. Staff atty. Camden Regional Legal Services, N.J., 1973-74; asst. dep. pub. advocate N.J. Dept. Pub. Advocate, Trenton, 1974-80; dep. dir., Trenton, 1980-85; ptnr. Frizell and Pozycki, Metuchen, N.J., 1985—; lectr. N.J. Inst. Continuing Legal Edn., Newark, 1979—. Author: Tenant-Landlord Law in N.J., 1979. Vol. VISTA, Camden, N.J., 1970-72; mem. mobile home adv. com. HUD, Washington, 1976-77. Mem. Accts. for Pub. Interest (bd. dirs. 1975-76), N.J. Bar Assn., N.J. Tenant Orgn. (bd. dirs. 1972-74, v.p. 1973-74, pres. Alliance for Affordable Housing 1986), Alpha Sigma Nu. Democrat. Roman Catholic. Real property, Landlord-tenant, Land use and planning. Home: 8 Frost Ave East Brunswick NJ 08816 Office: Frizell & Pozycki 296 Amboy Ave Metuchen NJ 08840

MEISLAHN, HARRY POST, bank holding company executive, lawyer; b. Bklyn., Apr. 5, 1938; s. Harry E.P. and Marjorie I. (Findley) M.; m. Meredith Lee Gowdy, May 2, 1970; children—Brooke Louise, Leigh Marjorie, Christopher Post. A.B. in Classics cum laude, Princeton U., 1960; LL.B., Cornell U., 1966. Bar: N.Y. 1966, U.S. Supreme Ct. 1974. Ptnr. McNamee, Lochner, Titus & Williams, P.C., and predecessor firms, Albany, N.Y., 1966-80; v.p., gen. counsel Norstar Bancorp Inc., Albany, N.Y., 1980—, sec., 1982—. Vice pres. Albany Boys Clubs, 1974-81; pres. Legal Aid Soc. Northeastern N.Y., 1980-82, bd. dirs., 1972-83; trustee Albany Acad., 1980—. Served to lt. (j.g.) USN, 1960-63. Mem. ABA, N.Y. State Bar Assn. (exec. com. corp. counsel sect. 1981-84, 87—), Am. Soc. Corp. Secs., N.Y. State Bankers Assn. (lawyers adv. com. 1981—). Banking, Securities, General corporate. Home: 16 Axbridge Ln Delmar NY 12054 Office: Norstar Bancorp Inc One Norstar Plaza Albany NY 12207

MEISTER, FREDERICK WILLIAM, state official, lawyer; b. Waterbury, Conn., May 21, 1938; s. William Frederick and Marion Callender (Tracy) M.; m. Joanne Marie Babich, June 12, 1982. B.A., Swarthmore Coll., 1960; M.B.A., Harvard U., 1962; J.D., U. Pitts., 1975. Bar: Pa. 1975, D.C. 1980. Fin. analyst First Pa. Bank, Phila., 1966-67; asst. comptroller Am. Friends Service Com., Phila., 1967-72; program analyst HEW, Washington, 1976-77; project mgr., program analyst Health Care Financing Adminstrn., Balt., 1977-82; chief Bur. of Fiscal and Contract Mgmt., Ariz. Health Care Cost Containment System, Phoenix, 1982-84, chief policy, planning and research, 1984—. Founding chmn. troop com. Valley Forge council Boy Scouts Am., Media, Pa., 1966-68; bd. dirs., mem. bus. com. Fellowship House and Farm, Inc., Phila., 1968-72; county dir. U.S. Senate Primary Campaign for H. John Heinz, Montgomery County, Pa., 1976., mem. fin. com. Am. Friends Sevice Com., Balt., 1980-82; mem. contracts task force Ariz. Dept. Health Services, Phoenix, 1983-84. Served to lt. USNR, 1962-65. Recipient Bur. Dirs. citation Bur. Quality Control, Health Care Financing Adminstrn., 1982. Mem. ABA, Fed. Bar Assn., Am. Soc. Pub. Adminstrn. Republican. Mem. Soc. Friends. Club: Harvard Bus. Sch., Harvard of Phoenix, Phoenix City. Administrative and regulatory, Health, Local government. Home: 1722 W Earll Dr Phoenix AZ 85015 Office: Ariz Health Care Cost Containment System 801 E Jefferson St Phoenix AZ 85034

MEISTER, RONALD WILLIAM, lawyer; b. Bklyn., Mar. 19, 1947; s. Marvin and Helen Selma (Schwartz) M.; m. Carol Rita Sherman, June 20, 1976; 1 child, Beth Rose. BA summa cum laude, Yale U., 1967, JD, 1970. Bar: D.C. 1970, U.S. Ct. Mil. Appeals 1971, U.S. Ct. Appeals (1st cir.) 1972, N.Y. 1975, U.S. Dist. Ct. (so. and ea. dists.) N.Y. 1975, U.S. Ct. Appeals (2d cir.) 1975, U.S. Ct. Claims 1977, U.S. Supreme Ct. 1977, U.S. Ct. Appeals (5th cir.) 1979. Assoc. Paul, Weiss, Rifkind, Wharton & Garrison, N.Y.C., 1974-80; ptnr. Kornstein, Meister & Veisz, N.Y.C., 1980-84, Meister, Leventhal & Slade, N.Y.C., 1984—. contbr. articles to profl. jours. Served to lt. JAGC, USNR, 1970-74. Mem. Fed. Bar Council. Federal civil litigation, State civil litigation, Criminal. Home: 21 Stuyvesant Ave Larchmont NY 10538 Office: Meister Leventhal & Slade 777 3d Ave New York NY 10017

MEIVES, JOSEPH RICHARD, lawyer; b. St. Louis, Nov. 5, 1947; s. Albert Louis and Loretta (Barrett) M. BA, Washington U., St. Louis, 1970, JD, 1973, LLM, 1978. Bar: Mo. 1973. Assoc. Greensfelder, Hemker, Wiese, Gale & Chappelow, St. Louis, 1973-80, ptnr., 1980—; bd. dirs. Legal Services Eastern Mo. Inc., St. Louis; lectr. legal writing Washington U. Law Sch., St. Louis, 1976-80. Mem. ABA (tax sect.), Mo. Bar Assn., Order of Coif. Corporate taxation, Personal income taxation. Home: 512 Old Bonhomme Saint Louis MO 63130 Office: Greensfelder Hemker Wiese et al 10 S Broadway Suite 1800 Saint Louis MO 63102

MEKLER, ARLEN B., lawyer, chemist; b. N.Y.C., May 4, 1943; s. Lev A. and Ethel (Fox) M.; m. Deborah Kay Nagle, Aug. 6, 1983; children—Jeffrey Arlen, Rebecca Ann, Ann-Marie Laura, Victoria Arlene, Lamar Adam, Lars Arlen. B.S. in Chemistry, Reed Coll.-San Jose State U., 1953; M.S. in Organic Chemistry, Iowa State U., 1955; Ph.D., Ohio State U., 1958; J.D., Temple U., 1972. Bar: Del. 1972, Pa. 1972, U.S. Supreme Ct. 1976. Sr. research chemist E.I. du Pont de Nemours & Co., Wilmington, Del., 1958-69; sole practice Wilmington, 1972—; mem. Mekler and Tos, 1986—; chief appellate div. Office Pub. Defender, State of Del., 1973-77; pres. Del. Law Ctr., Wilmington, 1973—; instr. constl. law Wilmington Coll., 1976—; dir. Bar Rev. Del., 1972—; mem. 3d Circuit Ct. Appeal Jud. Nominating Commn., 1977—, 3d Circuit Ct. Appeals Jud. Conf. Contbr. monographs to legal publs. Pres. Mental Health Aux. for Gov. Bacon Health Ctr., 1964-66; mem. Citizens Conf. for Modernization of State Legislatures, 1964-68; state chmn., Reform Commn. for Modernization Polit. Party Rules, 1965-68; pres. Del. Citizens for Fair Housing, 1965-69; state commr. Nat. Conf. on Uniform State Laws, 1972—; pres. Democratic Forum Del., 1966-70; mem. Del. Dem. Platform Com., 1966, 68, 72, 76; research dir. Del. Citizens for Humphrey-Muskie, 1968, Citizens for Biden, 1972, 78, 84, Citizens for McDowell, 1986—; del. Dem. Nat. Conv., 1980; mem. social action com. Unitarian Ch., Wilmington, 1962-68. Recipient Keyman award, 1964, 65; State Govtl. Affairs award, 1964, 65. Mem. ABA, Del. Bar Assn. (com. on rules of criminal procedure 1973-74, supreme ct. com. on revision of criminal law 1973—, supreme ct. com. on rules of evidence 1976—, com. on revised rules of evidence 1976—, com. on revised rules of Del. Supreme Ct. 1974—, family law com. 1979—, continuing legal edn. com. 1981—), Pa. Bar Assn., Am. Chem. Soc., N.Y. Acad. Scis., Chem. Soc. (London), AAAS, Catalyst Club Phila., Wilmington Organic Chemists Club, ACLU (bd. dirs.), Sigma Xi, Phi Alpha Delta. Civil rights, Criminal, Family and matrimonial. Home: 714 W Matson Pkwy Brandywine Hills Wilmington DE 19802 Office: PO Box 1570 264 Delaware Trust Bldg Wilmington DE 19899

MELAMED, ARTHUR DOUGLAS, lawyer; b. Mpls., Dec. 3, 1945; s. Arthur Charles and Helen Beatrix (Rosenberg) M.; m. Carol Drescher Weisman, May 26, 1983; children: Kathryn Henrie, Elizabeth Allyn. B.A., Yale U., 1967; J.D., Harvard U., 1970. Bar: D.C. 1970, U.S. Ct. Appeals (9th cir.) 1971, U.S. Ct. Appeals (2d cir.) 1975, U.S. Ct. Appeals (D.C. cir.) 1978, U.S. Ct. Appeals (8th cir.) 1981, U.S. Supreme Ct. 1981, U.S. Ct. Appeals (fed. cir.) 1985, U.S. Ct. Internat. Trade 1985. Law clk. U.S. Ct. Appeals for 9th Circuit, 1970-71; assoc. Wilmer, Cutler & Pickering, Washington, 1971-77, ptnr., 1978—. Contbr. articles to profl. jours. Class agt. alumni fund Yale U. Mem. ABA, D.C. Bar Assn. Antitrust, Federal civil litigation. Office: 2445 M St NW Washington DC 20037

MELAMED, CAROL DRESCHER, lawyer; b. N.Y.C., July 12, 1946; d. Raymond A. and Ruth W. (Schwartz) Drescher; children—Stephanie Weisman, Deborah Weisman; m. Arthur Douglas Melamed, May 26, 1983;

children: Kathryn, Elizabeth. A.B. magna cum laude with high honors in English Lit., Brown U., 1967; M.A.T., Harvard U., 1969; J.D., Catholic U. Am., 1974. Bar: Md. 1974, D.C. 1975, U.S. Ct. Appeals, (D.C. cir.) 1975, U.S. Dist. Ct. D.C. 1981, U.S. Supreme Ct. 1982. Tchr. English, Wellesley High Sch., Mass., 1968-69; law clk. U.S. Ct. Appeals, (D.C. cir.), Washington, 1974-75; assoc. Wilmer, Cutler & Pickering, Washington, 1975-79; assoc. counsel The Washington Post, 1979—. Mem. Phi Beta Kappa. Libel, Trademark and copyright, Contracts commercial. Office: The Washington Post 1150 15th St NW Washington DC 20071

MELAMED, RICHARD, lawyer; b. Houston, Dec. 22, 1952; s. Gerald Sylvan and Elaine (Rubenstein) M.; m. Ann Roosth, Sept. 17, 1978; 1 child, Faith Elizabeth. BA, U. Tex., 1975; JD, S. Tex. U., 1978. Bar: Tex. 1978, U.S. Dist. Ct. (so. dist.) Tex. 1979, U.S. Ct. Claims 1981, U.S. Tax Ct. 1981, U.S. Ct. Customes and Patent Appeals 1981, U.S. Ct. Appeals (5th cir.) 1981, U.S. Supreme Ct. 1981. Assoc. Evans & Birnberg, Houston, 1978-80; counsel Stewart Title Co., Houston, 1980-83; sole practice Houston, 1984-85; ptnr. Jacobus & Melamed, Houston, 1986—; assoc. prof. Houston Community Coll., continuing edn. U. Houston. Mem. ABA, Fed. Bar Assn., State Bar Tex., Assn. Trial Lawyers Am., Houston Trial Lawyers Assn. Jewish. Real property. Home: 5403 Queensloch Houston TX 77096 Office: Jacobus & Melamed 4265 San Felipe Suite 360 Houston TX 77027

MELBARDIS, WOLFGANG ALEXANDER, lawyer; b. Bayreuth, Ger., June 21, 1946. BA, Hartwick Coll., 1968; JD, St. John's U., 1971; MBA, L.I. U., 1977. Bar: N.Y. 1972, U.S. Dist. Ct. (ea., no. and so. dists.) N.Y. 1979, U.S. Ct. Mil. Appeals 1972, U.S. Supreme Ct. 1977. Asst. prof. law U.S. Mil. Acad., 1974-77; asst. atty. gen. Appeals and Opinions Bur. State of N.Y., Albany 1977-79; ptnr. Gramer & Melbardis, Coram, N.Y., 1979—. Author: Legal Rights When Hospital Appointment Denied, The Suffolk County Med. Soc. Bull., vol. 61, 1983. Served to capt. U.S. Army, 1972-77. N.Y. State Regents scholar, 1964. Mem. ABA, N.Y. State Bar Assn., Suffolk County Bar Assn., Nat. Health Lawyers Assn., Hartwick Coll. Alumni Assn. (bd. dirs.). Club: Old Field (Stony Brook, N.Y.). State civil litigation, Health, Personal injury. Office: 625 Middle Country Rd Coram NY 11727

MELBYE, RICHARD BRENTON, lawyer; b. Berkeley, Calif., Dec. 8, 1933; s. Roy Marland and Bessie Christina (Williamson) M.; m. Anne Knowles Chew, June 20, 1958; children—Richard Brenton II, Mark William, Catherine Christina, Kristin Anne. A.B. cum laude, U. Calif., 1955; J.D. Boalt Hall, U. Calif., 1958. Bar: Calif. 1959, U.S. Dist. Ct. (no. dist.) Calif. 1959, U.S. Ct. Appeals (9th cir.) 1959, U.S. Dist. Ct. (cen. dist.) Calif. 1984. Assoc., James P. Shovlin, Jr., San Francisco, 1958-63; ptnr. Owen, Melbye & Rohlff and predecessor Kane, Owen & Melbye, Redwood City, Calif., 1963—. Active Atherton (Calif.) Little League, Republican Party, Sproul Assocs. Calif. Mem. State Bar Calif., Lawyers Club San Francisco, Assn. Def. Counsel (dir.), San Francisco Bar, San Mateo Bar, Santa Clara Bar, Bench and Bar Assn. San Mateo County. Lutheran. Clubs: Olympic, Pacific Union, San Francisco Grid (pres.) San Francisco); Sequoia (Redwood City, Calif.); Elks (Palo Alto, Calif.); Sharon Heights Country (Menlo Park, Calif.). Federal civil litigation, State civil litigation, Insurance. Address: 700 Jefferson Ave Redwood City CA 94063

MELCHERT, LORI LAYNE MCLARIO, lawyer; b. Milw., Dec. 15, 1956; d. John J. and Lois Jean (Kleist) McLario; m. Randall George Melchert, June 23, 1984; 1 child, Randall Ryan. BS, Bob Jones U., 1978; JD, Valparaiso U., 1981. Bar: Wis. 1982, U.S. Dist. Ct. (ea. dist.) Wis. 1982. Assoc. Offices of John McLario, Menomonee Falls, Wis., 1981—; legal advisor Law Explorers, Menomonee Falls, 1983-84. Mem. Wis. Bar Assn., Milw. Bar Assn., Christian Legal Soc. Baptist. Family and matrimonial, Juvenile, Personal injury. Office: Office of John McLario N88 W16783 Main St Menomonee Falls WI 53051

MELDMAN, CLIFFORD KAY, lawyer; b. Milw., July 27, 1931; s. Edward H. and Rose (Bortin) M.; children: Mindy, David, Linda, James, Noah. JD, Marquette U., 1956. Bar: Wis. 1956. Ptnr. Meldman & Meldman, Milw., 1956-73; pres. Meldman & Meldman S.C., Milw., 1973—. Contbr. articles to profl. jours., also editor. Fellow Am. Acad. Matrimonial Lawyers (pres. 1982); mem. Milw. Bar Assn. (bd. dirs. 1984-86, pres. 1986-87, chmn. family law sect.), Wis. Bar Assn. (chmn. family law sect.). Family and matrimonial. Home: 170 W Cherokee Circle Milwaukee WI 53217 Office: Meldman & Meldman SC PO Box 17397 Milwaukee WI 53217

MELDMAN, ROBERT EDWARD, lawyer; b. Milw., Aug. 5; s. Louis Leo and Lillian (Gollusch) M.; m. Sandra Jane Setlick, July 24, 1960; children—Saree Beth, Richard Samuel. B.S., U. Wis., 1959; LL.B., Marquette U., 1962; LL.M. in Taxation, NYU, 1963. Bar: Wis. 1962, U.S. Tax Ct. 1963, U.S. Supreme Ct. 1970, U.S. Ct. Claims 1971. Practice tax law Milw., 1963—; pres. Meldman, Case & Weine, Ltd., Milw., 1975-85; dir. Meldman & Weine div. Mulcahy & Wherry, S.C., Milw., 1985—; Adj. prof. taxation U. Wis., Milw., 1968—, mem. tax adv. council, 1978—; sec. Profl. Inst. Tax Study, Inc., 1978—. Author: (with Tom Mountin) Federal Taxation Practice & Procedure, 1983, 86; contbr. articles to legal jours. Mem. ABA, Fed. Bar Assn. (pres. Milw. 1966-67), Milw. Bar Assn. (chmn. tax sect. 1970-71), Wis. State Bar (dir. tax sect. 1964—, chmn. 1973-74), Marquette Law Alumni (dir. 1972-77), Phi Delta Phi, Tau Epsilon Rho (chancellor Milw. 1969-71, supreme nat. chancellor 1975-76). Jewish (trustee congregation 1972-77). Clubs: Milw. Athletic, Wisconsin. Lodge: B'nai B'rith (Ralph Harris meml. award Century Lodge, 1969-70, trustee). Corporate taxation, Estate taxation, Personal income taxation. Home: 7455 N Skyline Ln Milwaukee WI 53217 Office: 815 E Mason St Milwaukee WI 53202

MELI, SALVATORE ANDREW, lawyer; b. N.Y.C., Sept. 18, 1947; s. Andrew and Marie (Ruggiero) M.; m. Barbara Ann Chiesa, Aug. 16, 1970. BA, St. John's U., Jamaica, N.Y., 1969, JD, 1975. Bar: N.Y. 1976, Fla. 1976, U.S. Dist. Ct. (ea. and so. dist.) N.Y. 1976. Sole practice Flushing, N.Y., 1976-78; ptnr. Muratori & Meli, Flushing, 1978—, Lake Worth, Fla., 1978—; lectr. Lawyers in the Classroom program, N.Y.C., 1977-81; mem. ins. co. adv. council, Queens, N.Y., 1985—. Recipient Regents Scholarship, N.Y. State Bd. Regents. Mem. ABA, N.Y. State Bar Assn., Fla. Bar Assn., Queens County Bar Assn., Columbian Lawyers. Real property, Probate. Office: Muratori & Meli 189-05 Crocheron Ave Flushing NY 11358

MELIA, JAMES PATRICK, lawyer; b. Pitts., May 5, 1955; s. Martin Joseph and Anne Katherine (Kelly) M.; m. Luanne Kay Herb, June 7, 1986. BS in Biology, U. Notre Dame, 1977, BA in Psychology, 1978; JD, U. Pitts., 1981. Bar: Pa. 1981, U.S. Dist. Ct. (we. dist.) Pa. 1981, U.S. Dist. Ct. (mid. dist.) Pa. 1984, U.S. Ct. Appeals (D.C. cir.) 1985, Mich. 1986. Asst. counsel Pa. Pub. Utility Commn., Harrisburg, 1982-85; atty. Consumers Power Co., Jackson, Mich., 1985—; instr. legal research & writing U. Pitts., 1978-81, Pa. State U., Middletown, 1983-84. Mem. ABA (adminstrv. law sect., pub. utility law sect.), Fed. Energy Bar Assn. (, Mich. Bar Assn., Pa. Bar Assn. (chmn. law sch. com., young lawyer's div., governing bd., pub. utility law sect.), Allegheny Bar Assn., Phi Alpha Delta. Avocations: travel, cycling, swimming, jogging. Public utilities, Nuclear power, Administrative and regulatory. Home: 2762 Granada Dr 2B Jackson MI 49202 Office: Consumers Power Co 212 W Michigan Ave Jackson MI 48201

MELICAN, JAMES PATRICK, JR., lawyer; b. Worcester, Mass., Sept. 8, 1940; s. James Patrick and Abigail Helen (Donahue) M.; m. Debra A. Burns, Dec. 2, 1978; children: Marlane, James P., David, Molly, Megan. BA, Fordham U., 1962; JD, Harvard U., 1965; MBA, Mich. State U., 1971. Bar: Mich 1966. Supervising atty. product liability sect. Gen. Motors Corp., Detroit, 1971-73; atty.-in-charge trade regulation Gen. Motors Corp., 1973-77, atty.-in-charge mktg. and purchasing, 1977-80, asst. gen. counsel, 1980-81; gen. counsel Toyota Motor Sales, U.S.A., Inc., Torrance, Calif., 1981-82, v.p., gen. counsel, 1982—. Mem. ABA, Am. Law Inst. Roman Catholic. General corporate, Antitrust, Personal injury. Home: 17 Turtleback Ln West New Canaan CT 06830 Office: Internat Paper Co 77 W 45th St New York NY 10036

MELICAN, JOHN JOSEPH, lawyer; b. Worcester, Mass., Mar. 12, 1916; s. Martin J. and Helen E. (Grady) M.; m. Pauline B. O'Brien, Apr. 24, 1948; children: Paula M., Jack, Mary, E. AB, Holy Cross U., 1937; JD, Boston Coll., 1943; LLB, Northeastern U., 1948. Bar: Mass. 1949, U.S. Dist. Ct. 1950, U.S. Ct. Appeals 1950. Sole practice Worcester, 1948-1970; judge Mass. Trial Ct., 1969-76; chief counsel Mass. Dept. Pub. Health, 1977—. Mem. sch. com. Worcester, 1950-59, city council, Worcester, 1959-65. Served to lt. USN, 1943-45. Democrat. Roman Catholic. Judicial administration. Home: PO Box 1861 Cotoit MA 02635

MELICH, MITCHELL, lawyer; b. Bingham Canyon, Utah, Feb. 1, 1912; s. Joseph and Mary (Kalembar) M.; m. Doris M. Snyder, June 3, 1935; children: Tanya (Mrs. Noel L. Silverman), Michael, Nancy, Robert A. LL.B., U. Utah, 1934. Bar: Utah bar 1934. Pvt. practice Moab, 1934-63, city atty., 1934-55; county atty. Grand County, 1940-42; sec., dir. Utex Exploration Co., Moab, 1953-62; pres., dir. Uranium Reduction Co., Moab, 1954-62; cons. to pres. Atlas Minerals, div. Atlas Corp., 1962-67; dir., treas. New Park Mining Co., 1962-65; partner firm Ray, Quinney & Nebeker, 1973—; solicitor Dept. Interior, Washington, 1969-73;. Mem. of Colorado River Com. of Utah, 1945-47; mem. Utah Water and Power Bd., 1947; chmn. Citizens Adv. Com. on Higher Edn., 1968; mem. nat. adv. council U. Utah, 1976—; Mem. Utah Senate, 1942-50, minority leader, 1949-50; mem. Utah Legislative Council, 1949-54; del. Republican Nat. Conv., 1952-72; mem. Rep. Nat. Com. for Utah, 1961-64; Rep. candidate for gov., 1964; cons. on staff Congressman Sherman P. Lloyd, Utah, 1967-68; Bd. dirs. St. Marks Hosp., 1973—; bd. regents U. Utah, 1961-65, also mem. devel. fund com., mem. nat. adv. council, 1968-73, 76—; mem. Utah Statewide Health Coordinating Council, 1985—. Recipient Distinguished Alumni award U. Utah, 1969. Mem. Am. Bar Assn., Utah State Bar, Utah Mining Assn. (pres. 1962-63), Kappa Sigma. Republican. Club: Alta Salt Lake Country (Salt Lake City). Lodges: Masons; Shriners. Administrative and regulatory, Oil and gas leasing, General practice. Home: 900 Donner Way Apt 708 Salt Lake City UT 84108 Office: 400 Deseret Bldg 79 S Main St Salt Lake City UT 84111

MELIN, ROBERT ARTHUR, lawyer; b. Milw., Sept. 13, 1940; s. Arthur John and Frances Magdalena (Lanser) M.; m. Mary Magdalen Melin, July 8, 1967; children—Arthur Walden, Robert Dismas, Nicholas O'Brien, Madalyn Mary. B.A. summa cum laude, Marquette U., 1962, J.D., 1967. Bar: Wis. 1966, U.S. Dist. Ct. (ea. dist.) Wis. 1966, U.S. Ct. Appeals (7th cir.) 1966, U.S. Ct. Mil. Appeals 1967, U.S. Supreme Ct. 1975. Law clk. U.S. Dist. Ct. Eastern Dist. Wis., 1966; instr. bus. law U. Ga., Hinesville, 1968, also lectr. bus. law U. Md., Asmara, 1970; lectr. law Haile Selassie I U. Law Faculty, Addis Ababa, Ethiopia, 1971-72; mem. firm Walther & Halling, Milw., 1973-74, Schroeder, Gedlen, Riester & Moerke, Milw., 1974-82; ptnr. Schroeder, Gedlen, Riester & Melin, Milw., 1982-84, Schroeder, Riester, Melin & Smith, 1984—. lectr. charitable solicitations and contracts Philanthropy Monthly 9th Ann. Policy Conf., N.Y.C., 1985. Chmn. Milw. Young Democrats, 1963-64. Served to capt. JAGC, AUS, 1967-70. Mem. Wis. Acad. Trial Lawyers, ABA, Wis. Bar Assn., Milw. Bar Assn., Am. Legion, Friends of Ethiopia, Delta Theta Phi, Phi Alpha Theta, Pi Gamma Mu. Roman Catholic. Author: Evidence in Ethiopia, 1972; contbg. author to Annual Survey of African Law, 1974; contbr. numerous articles to legal jours. State civil litigation, Federal civil litigation, Charitable organizations. Home: 8108 N Whitney Rd Milwaukee WI 53217 Office: 135 W Wells St Milwaukee WI 53203

MELL, PATRICIA, legal educator; b. Cleve., Dec. 15, 1953; d. Julian Cooper and Thelma (Webb) M. AB with honors, Wellesley Coll., 1975; JD, Case Western Res. U., 1978. Bar: Ohio 1979, U.S. Dist. Ct. (so. and no. dists.) Ohio 1979. Asst. atty. gen. State of Ohio, Columbus, 1978-82, sec. of state corps. counsel, 1982-84; vis. asst. prof. Capital U. Law Sch., Columbus, 1984-85, U. Toledo Law Sch., 1985-86; asst. prof. law Widener U., Wilmington, 1986—, Del. Law Sch., Wilmington, 1986—; mediator night prosecutor's program, Columbus, 1984-85. Mem. scholarship screening com. Black Am. Law Student Assn. U. Toledo Law Sch., 1985-86, governing bd. Case Western Res. U. Law Sch., Cleve., 1985—, Alliance of Black Women, Columbus, 1983-85, Capers for Judge com., Cleve., 1980-86, century club Ohio Dems., 1985-86; chmn. law student com. Young Black Dems., Columbus, 1982-84; coordinator minority affiliations subcom. Citizens for Brown for Gov., Columbus, 1981-82. Recipient award Internat. Assn. Corps. Adminstrs., 1983. Mem. ABA, Nat. Bar Assn., Nat. Conf. Black Lawyers, Am. Arbitration Assn. (comml. arbitrator 1986—). Lutheran. Avocations: modern languages, stained glass work, fencing, tennis, piano. Consumer commercial, General corporate, Alternative dispute resolution.

MELLEY, STEVEN MICHAEL, lawyer; b. Rhinebeck, N.Y., Jan. 3, 1950; s. James Christopher and Virginia (Madonna) M.; m. Nancy Elaine Southard, June 15, 1985; children: Aliza Nicolina, Steven Jonathan. Cert., Moscow U., 1970; BA in Russian Studies with honors, Colgate U., 1972; JD, Tulane U., 1975. Bar: N.Y. 1976, U.S. Dist. Ct. 1976, U.S. Supreme Ct. 1980. Assoc. Woody N. Klose Law Offices, Red Hook, N.Y., 1975-78; ptnr. Klose & Melley, Rhinebeck, 1978-83; sole Practice Rhinebeck, 1983—; atty. Village of Tivoli, N.Y., 1977-78. Mem. lawyers com. Internat. League Human Rights UN, N.Y.C., 1977—; dist. rep. dem. com. Town of Rhinebeck. Mem. ABA, N.Y. State Bar Assn. (com. on specialization 1984—), Pa. Bar Assn., Dutchess County Bar Assn., Assn. Trial Lawyers Am., N.Y. State Trial Lawyer Assn., Melvin Belli Soc., Phi Alpha Delta, Kappa Delta Rho. Democrat. Club: Red Hook Businessmen's. Personal injury. Office: 22 E Market St Rhinebeck NY 12572

MELLINKOFF, DAVID, lawyer, educator; b. 1914. A.B., Stanford U., 1935; LL.B., Harvard U., 1939. Bar: Calif. 1939. Sole practice Calif., 1939-41, 46-64; lectr. UCLA Law Sch., 1964-65, prof., 1965-85, prof. emeritus, 1985—. Author: The Language of the Law, 1963, 9th edit., 1983, The Conscience of a Lawyer, 1973, Lawyers and the System of Justice, 1976, Legal Writing: Sense and Nonsense, 1982; contbr. articles to profl. jours. Served to capt. U.S. Army, 1941-46. Legal education. Home: 744 Holmby Ave Los Angeles CA 90024 Office: UCLA Law Sch 405 Hilgard Ave Los Angeles CA 90024

MELLO, SUSAN H., lawyer; b. South Bend, Ind., May 3, 1955. Student, Beloit Coll., 1972-74; AB, Washington U., St. Louis, 1976; JD magna cum laude, U. Ind., 1979. Bar: Mass. 1979, Ariz. 1981, Mo. 1981, U.S. Dist. Ct. Ariz. 1981, U.S. Ct. Appeals (9th cir.) 1981, U.S. Dist. Ct. (ea. dist.) Mo. 1983, U.S. Ct. Appeals (8th cir.) 1983. Assoc. Nutter, McClennen & Fish, Boston, 1979-80, Lewis and Roca, Phoenix, 1981-82, Louis Gilden, St. Louis, 1983-84, Green, Kehr & Kanefield, Clayton, Mo., 1984; sole practice Clayton and St. Louis, 1984—; assoc. housing research Rand Corp., Washington, 1974, Westat Corp., Washington, 1974, Trans Century Corp., Washington, 1975; legis. analyst U.S. Dept. Labor, Washington, 1976. Congl. asst. to Office of Congressman John Brademas, Washington, 1973. Named Lawyer of Month Maricopa County Bar Assn., Phoenix, 1982. Mem. Mo. Bar Assn., St. Louis Bar Assn. (treas. young lawyers sect. 1986, com. chmn. 1986—), St. Louis County Bar Assn., Mo. Womens Network, Am. Trial Lawyers Assn., Women Lawyers Assn. St. Louis, Washington U. Alumni Assn., Order of Coif, Pi Sigma Alpha. State civil litigation, Labor, General practice. Office: 111 S Bemiston Clayton MO 63105

MELLON, THOMAS EDWARD, JR., lawyer; b. Phila., July 24, 1947; s. Thomas Edward and Honor (McCormick) M.; m. Marilyn Joan Scott, Dec. 28, 1968; children—Thomas E. III, Christopher Scott, Ryan Scott. B.S., St. Joseph's U., 1969; J.D., Georgetown U., 1972; LL.M., Harvard U., 1974. Bar: Pa. 1973, D.C. 1973, U.S. Dist. Ct. (ea. dist.) Pa. 1974, U.S. Ct. Appeals (3d cir.) 1973, U.S. Supreme Ct. 1980. Law clerk to judge U.S. Ct. Appeals, Phila., 1972-73; asst. U.S. atty. Eastern Dist. Pa., Phila., 1974-80, chief narcotics unit, 1977-78, chief criminal div., 1978-80; atty. gen. Advocacy Inst., Washington, 1978-80; ptnr. Grim and Grim, Perkasie, Pa., 1980-81; asst. solicitor Bucks County, Doylestown, Pa., 1984—; founding ptnr. Mellon & Mellon, Doylestown, 1982—; mem. hearing com. Supreme Ct. Disciplinary Bd., Phila., 1984—. Counsel Democratic Party Bucks County, 1982—; active Dem. State Exec. Com., Harrisburg, Pa., 1984. Recipient Outstanding U.S. Atty. award for Eastern Dist. Pa., Atty. Gen. of U.S., 1980. Mem. ABA, Am. Trial Lawyers Assn., Pa. Bar Assn., Bucks County Bar Assn. Roman Catholic. Criminal, General practice, Personal injury. Office: Mellon & Mellon 50 E Court St Doylestown PA 18901

MELLOR, ROBERT E., corporate lawyer; b. 1943. BA, Westminster Coll., 1965; JD, So. Meth. U., 1968. Atty. legal dept. Union Oil Co. of Calif., 1968-73; atty. U.S. Leasing Internat. Inc., 1973-75; v.p. dir. Alexander & Bolton Inc., 1975-76; with Di Giorgio Corp., San Francisco, 1976-79, v.p., 1979-80, v.p. gen. counsel, 1980-81, v.p. sec. gen. counsel, 1981—. Office: Di Giorgio Corp 1 Maritime Plaza San Francisco CA 94111 *

MELTON, BARRY, lawyer, musician; b. N.Y.C., June 14, 1947; s. James Gerald and Terry Melton; m. Barbara Joy Langer; children: Kingsley, Kyle. Bar: Calif. 1982, U.S. Dist. Ct. (no. dist.) Calif. 1982, U.S. Dist. Ct. (cen. dist.) Calif. 1983, U.S. Ct. Appeals (9th cir.) 1983, U.S. Dist. Ct. (ea. dist.) Calif. 1985. Sole practice San Francisco, 1982-84; ptnr. Melton, Duncan & Hirshbein, San Francisco, 1984—; musician, pub. Seafood Music, San Francisco, 1965—. Musician, composer various phonograph records, 1965—. Mem. adv. bd. Freedom Found., San Rafael, Calif., 1981—. Mem. ABA, Calif. Bar Assn. (vol. legal service award 1983-85), San Francisco Bar Assn. (vol. legal service award 1985), Assn. Trial Lawyers Am., Police Activities League. Avocation: coaching baseball. Criminal, Juvenile, Landlord-tenant. Office: Melton Duncan & Hirshbein 1 Haight St San Francisco CA 94102

MELTON, HOWELL WEBSTER, judge; b. Atlanta, Dec. 15, 1923; s. Holmes and Alma (Combee) M.; m. Margaret Catherine Wolfe, Mar. 4, 1950; children—Howell Webster, Carol Anne. J.D., U. Fla., 1948. Bar: Fla. 1948. Mem. firm Upchurch, Melton & Upchurch, St. Augustine, 1948-61; judge 7th Jud. Circuit of Fla., St. Augustine, 1961-77, U.S. Dist. Ct. Middle Dist. Fla., Jacksonville, 1977—; Past chmn. Fla. Conf. Circuit Judges, 1974; past chmn. council bar pres.'s Fla. Bar. Trustee Flagler Coll., St. Augustine. Served with U.S. Army, 1943-46. Recipient Disting. Service award St. Augustine Jaycees, 1953. Mem. ABA, St. Johns County Bar Assn., Jacksonville Bar Assn., Fed. Bar Assn., Am. Judicature Soc., Fla. Blue Key, Phi Delta Theta, Phi Delta Phi. Methodist (past chmn. bd. trustees). Clubs: Ponce de Leon Country (St. Augustine), Sawgrass (Ponte Vedra, Fla.), Fla. Yacht (Jacksonville), St. Augustine Fla. Officer's. Lodges: Masons, Kiwanis (past pres.). Office: US Dist Ct PO Box 52201 Jacksonville FL 32201

MELTSNER, MICHAEL C(HARLES), legal educator; b. N.Y.C., Mar. 29, 1937; s. Ira D. and Alice G. M.; m. Heli Spiegel, Sept. 10, 1961; children: Jessica, Molly. A.B., Oberlin Coll., 1957; J.D., Yale U., 1960. Bar: N.Y. 1961, Mass. 1982. First asst. counsel NAACP Legal Def. and Ednl. Fund, N.Y.C., 1961-70; prof. law Columbia U., 1970-79; prof. Northeastern U. Sch. Law, 1979—, dean law, 1979-84. Author: Cruel and Unusual: The Supreme Court and Capital Punishment, 1973, (with P. Schrag) Public Interest Advocacy, 1974, (with P. Schrag) Toward Simulation in Legal Education, 1975, Short Takes, 1980. Bd. dirs. Legal Action Center N.Y.C. Simon Guggenheim fellow, 1977-78. Mem. Assn. Bar City N.Y., Soc. Am. Law Tchrs. Office: 400 Huntington Ave Boston MA 02115

MELTZER, BERNARD DAVID, legal educator; b. Phila., Nov. 21, 1914; s. Julius and Rose (Welkov) M.; m. Jean Sulzberger, Jan. 17, 1947; children: Joan, Daniel, Susan. A.B., U. Chgo., 1935, J.D., 1937; LL.M., Harvard U., 1938. Bar: Ill. 1938. Atty., spl. asst. to chmn. SEC, 1938-40; assoc. firm Mayer, Meyer, Austrian & Platt, Chgo., 1940; spl. asst. to asst. sec. state, also acting chief fgn. funds control div. State 1941-43; trial counsel U.S. staff Internat. Nuremberg War Trials, 1945-46; from professorial lectr. to disting. service prof. law emeritus U. Chgo. Law Sch., 1946—; hearing commr. NPA, 1952-53; labor arbitrator; spl. master U.S. Ct. Appeals for D.C., 1963-64; bd. publs. U. Chgo., 1965-67, chmn., 1967-68; mem. Gov. Ill. Adv. Commn. Labor-Mgmt. Policy for Pub. Employees in Ill., 1966-67, Ill. Civil Service Commn., 1968-69; cons. U.S. Dept. Labor, 1969-70. Author: (with W.G. Katz) Cases and Materials on Business Corporations, 1949, Labor Law Cases, Materials and Problems, 1970, supplement, 1972, 75, 2d edit., 1977, supplements, 1980, 82 (with S. Henderson), 3d edit. (with S. Henderson), 1985; also articles. Bd. dirs. Hyde Park Community Conf., 1954-56, S.E. Chgo. Commn., 1956-57. Served to lt. (j.g.) USNR, 1943-46. Decorated Army Commendation medal. Mem. ABA (co-chmn. com. devel. law under NLRA 1959-60, mem. spl. com. transp. strikes), Ill. Bar Assn., Chgo. Bar Assn. (bd. mgrs. 1972-73), Nat. Acad. Arbitrators, Am. Law Inst., Am. Acad. Arts and Scis., Order of Coif, Phi Beta Kappa. Labor. Home: 1219 E 50th St Chicago IL 60615

MELTZER, KRIS, lawyer; b. Shelbyville, Ind., Oct. 31, 1955; s. Phillip E. and Charlene (Jordan) M.; m. Sandra Everitt, Aug. 16, 1979; 1 child, Trent Everitt. B.S., Ball State U., 1976; J.D., Ind. U., 1980. Bar: Ind. 1980, U.S. Dist. Ct. (so. dist.) Ind. 1980, U.S. Supreme Ct. 1984. Assoc. Bate, Harrold & Meltzer, Shelbyville. 1980-86; ptnr. Bate, Harrold & Meltzer, Shelbyville, 1986—. Bd. dirs. Shelby County Youth Shelter, Shelbyville, 1982—. Mem. ABA, Assn. Trial Lawyers Am., Ind. State Bar Assn., Ind. Trial Lawyers Assn., Shelby County Bar Assn. (chmn. Law Day activities 1983, 84), Shelby County Jaycees (legal adviser 1982). Democrat. Roman Catholic. Lodge: Sertoma (pres. local club 1984). Criminal, Family and matrimonial, General practice. Home: 230 W Mechanic St Shelbyville IN 46176 Office: Bate Harrold & Meltzer 505 S Harrison St Shelbyville IN 46176

MELTZER, ROGER, lawyer; b. N.Y.C., Jan. 31, 1951; s. Irwin Samuel and Bewa (Jacobs) M.; m. Robin Hirtz, July 20, 1975; children: Justin, Martin, Elizabeth. BA cum laude, Harvard U., 1973; postgrad., Tulane U., 1974-75; JD cum laude, NYU, 1977. Bar: N.Y. 1978, D.C. 1979. Assoc. Cahill, Gordon & Reindel, N.Y.C., 1977-84, ptnr., 1984—; bd. dirs. Rogosin Enterprises Inc., Israel, Hirtz and Traubner Inc., N.Y.C. Mem. ABA. General corporate, Securities. Office: Cahill Gordon & Reindel 80 Pine St New York NY 10005

MELTZER, SANFORD, lawyer, educator; b. Syracuse, N.Y., July 4, 1933; s. Mose and Gertrude (Hodes) M.; m. Elaine Lois Levine, July 8, 1962; children: Robin Alisa, Marna Denise. BA, Syracuse U., 1957, JD, 1959. Bar: N.Y. 1959, U.S. Dist. Ct. (no. dist.) N.Y. 1959, U.S. Tax Ct. 1960, U.S. Dist. Ct. (so. dist.) N.Y. 1978, U.S. Ct. Appeals (2d cir.) 1978, U.S. Supreme Ct. 1978. Sole practice Syracuse; instr. community internship in family law Syracuse U., 1970—. Mem. council N.Y. State Legis. Syracuse, 1968-72; committeeman Onondaga County Rep. Com., Syracuse, 1959—. Mem. ABA, Assn. Trial Lawyers Am., Bar Assn. of Supreme Ct. of. U.S., N.Y. State Bar Assn., N.Y. State Trial Lawyers Assn., Onondaga County Bar Assn. (bd. dirs. 1981-83), Upstate Trial Lawyers Assn., Nat. Rifle Assn. Jewish. Club: University (Syracuse). Lodge: Masons (master 1970, 74). Avocations: target pistol shooting, photography, coin collecting. Criminal, Family and matrimonial, Legal education. Home: 120 Clearview Rd Dewitt NY 13214 Office: 472 Salina St Syracuse NY 13202

MEMEL, SHERWIN LEONARD, lawyer; b. Buffalo, Mar. 28, 1930; s. Maurice Memel and Nellie (Munshen) Katz; m. Iris C. Gittleman, Aug. 17, 1952; children: Jana Sue, Steven Keith, David Scott, Mara Jean. BA, UCLA, 1951, JD with honors, 1954. Bar: Calif. 1955, U.S. Ct. Appeals (9th cir.) 1955, U.S. Dist. Ct. (cen. dist.) Calif. 1959, U.S. Supreme Ct. 1963, D.C. 1979. Sr. ptnr. Memel & Ellsworth (formerly Memel, Jacobs, Pierno & Gersh and Memel, Jacobs, Pierno, Gersh & Ellsworth), Los Angeles, 1975-87; ptnr., chmn. health law dept. Manatt, Phelps, Rothenberg & Phillips, Los Angeles, 1987—; former instr. health law UCLA; former mem. Fed Health Ins. Benefits Adv. Counsel; cons. to major indsl. corps. on health bus. matters; lectr. in field. Contbr. numerous articles on health law to profl. jours. Chmn. Los Angeles Arts Council, 1986-87; vice chmn. Dem. Bus. Council, Washington, 1985-86; past pres. Calif. Bd. Med. Quality Assurance. Recipient Disting. Service award Fedn. Am. Hosps., 1970. Mem. ABA (forum com. health law), Am. Hosp. Assn. (life, Award of Honor 1971), Am. Acad. Hosp. Attys., Am. Soc. Law and Medicine, Nat. Health Lawyers Assn., Calif. Soc. for Healthcare Attys. (pres. 1983), Vista Del Mar Atty. Guild (pres. 1976—). Democrat. Health, Legislative, Administrative and regulatory. Office: Manatt Phelps Rothenberg & Phillips 11355 W Olympic Blvd Los Angeles CA 90064

MENAKER, BONNIE DOUGLASS, lawyer; b. Harrisburg, Pa., Sept. 26, 1939; d. William Tyler Jr. and Mary Alice (Hicks) D.; m. J. Thomas Menaker, June 18, 1960. BA, U. N.C., 1961; JD, Dickinson Sch. Law, 1964. Bar: Pa. 1965, U.S. Supreme Ct. 1976. Law clk. to presiding judge Ct. Common Pleas, Harrisburg, Pa., 1964-65; assoc. Hepford, Zimmerman & Swartz, Harrisburg, 1965-72, ptnr., 1972-81; ptnr. Hepford, Swartz, Menaker

& Morgan, Harrisburg, 1981—. Editor U. N.C. Law Rev., 1963; also articles. Bd. dirs. Harrisburg chpt. task force on divorce reform ACLU, 1979. Fellow Am. Bar Found., Am. Acad. Matrimonial Lawyers; mem. ABA, Pa. Bar Assn. (chmn. ERA com. 1972—), Dauphin County Bar Assn. (pres. young lawyers assn. 1976-77, chmn. family law sect. 1982—), Pa. Appellate Ct. Nomination Commn., Women's Networking Orgn. (founder Monday Club), Greater Harrisburg Area C. of C. (bd. dirs.). Republican. Avocations: sailing, traveling, reading. Family and matrimonial. Home: 4707 N Galen Rd Harrisburg PA 17110 Office: Hepford Swartz Menaker & Morgan 111 N Front St Harrisburg PA 17110

MENAKER, FRANK H., JR., lawyer; b. Harrisburg, Pa., Aug. 23, 1940; s. Frank H. and Romaine (Sadler) M.; m. Sharon Ann Lynch, Feb. 21, 1981; 1 dau., Denise L.; children by previous marriage: David C., Michelle R. A.B., Wilkes Coll., 1962; J.D., Am. U., 1965. Bar: D.C. 1966, Md. 1975, U.S. Supreme Ct. 1975. Staff counsel Office Gen. Counsel, GAO, Washington, 1965-67; atty., asst. corp. sec. Dynalectron Corp., Washington, 1968-70; asst. counsel Martin Marietta Aerospace, Balt., 1970-72, gen. counsel, 1977-81; asst. gen. counsel Martin Marietta Corp., 1973-77, dep. gen. counsel, 1981, gen. counsel, 1981—, v.p., 1982—; spl. counsel U.S. Commn. on Govt. Procurement, 1971; dir. PGM Systems Ltd., London. Vice pres., dir. Pinemere Camp Assn., Stroudsburg, Pa., 1978—; trustee Wilkes Coll., 1983—. Mem. ABA, Md. Bar Assn., Am. Corp. Counsel Assn. (bd. dirs. 1987—). Office: Martin Marietta Corp 6801 Rockledge Dr Bethesda MD 20817 *

MENARD, ARTHUR PATRICK, lawyer; b. Washington, Sept. 23, 1938; s. Arthur M. and Stella M. (Perreault) M.; m. Cecilia Husbands, May 5, 1962 (div.); m. Priscilla Glidden, Dec. 30, 1977; children: Deirdre Cecile, Arthur Christian. BS, Coll. Holy Cross, 1960; LLB with honors, Boston Coll., 1965. Bar: Mass. 1965, U.S. Dist. Ct. Mass. 1968, U.S. Dist. Ct. Conn. 1971, U.S. Ct. Apls. (1st cir.) 1972, U.S. Sup. Ct. 1972. Spl. legal intern U.S. Pub. Housing Authority, Phila., 1965; assoc. Morgan, Brown & Joy, Boston, 1965-72, ptnr., 1973-86; of counsel Hale and Dorr, Boston, 1986—. Pres., bd. dirs. Big Bros. Assn. Boston. Served to lt. comdr. USNR, 1960-72. Mem. ABA, Mass. Bar Assn., Boston Bar Assn., Nat. Assn. Coll. and Univ. Attys., Assn. Trial Lawyers Am. Clubs: Essex County (Manchester, Mass.); Algonquin (Boston). Contbr. articles to legal jours. Labor. Office: Hale and Dorr 60 State St Boston MA 02109

MENASHE, ALBERT ALAN, lawyer; b. Portland, Oreg., Apr. 24, 1950; s. Solomon A. and Faye F. (Hasson) M.; m. Laura L. Richenstein, July 23, 1972 (div. Oct. 1979); 1 child, Shawn Nathan; m. Sandra J. Laniado, June 28, 1980. B.S. in Polit. Sci., U. Oreg., 1971; J.D., Willamette U., 1976. Bar: Oreg. 1977, U.S. Dist. Ct. Oreg. 1977, U.S. Ct. Appeals (9th cir.) 1977, U.S. Supreme Ct. 1980. Assoc. Bullivant, Wright, et al, Portland, 1976-79; ptnr. Samuels, Samuels, et al, Portland, 1979-80; sr. ptnr., shareholder Gevurtz & Menashe P.C., Portland, 1981—; arbitrator Multnomah County Circuit Ct., Portland, 1983—; lectr. family law Lewis and Clark Law Sch., Portland, 1980—; frequent speaker on family law, 1979—. Editor-in-chief Willamette Law Jour. 1975-76. Bd. dirs. Solo Ctr., Portland, 1976-79; pres. Oreg. Club, Portland, 1981-82. Served to 1st lt. U.S. Army, 1971-73. Mem. U. Oreg. Alumni Assn. (dir. 1981-82), Am. Arbitration Assn. (mem. family dispute panel 1979—), Assn. Family Conciliation Cts., Am. Acad. Matrimonial Law, Oreg. State Bar Assn., Multnomah County Bar Assn., Oreg. Trial Lawyers Assn., ABA. Republican. Jewish. Family and matrimonial. Home: 1630 NE Brazee Portland OR 97212 Office: Gevurtz & Menashe PC 1515 SW 5th Ave Suite 808 Portland OR 97201

MENCER, GLENN EVERELL, judge; b. Smethport, Pa., May 18, 1925; s. Glenn Hezekiah and Ruth Leona (Rice) M.; m. Hannah Jane Freyer, June 24, 1950; children—Ruth Ann, Cora Jane, Glenn John. B.B.A., U. Mich., 1949, J.D., 1952. Bar: Pa. 1953, U.S. Dist. Ct. (we. dist.) Pa. 1953, U.S. Supreme Ct. 1958. Sole practice Eldred, Pa., 1953-64; dist. atty. McKean County, Pa., 1956-64; judge 48th Jud. Dist. Ct., Smethport, 1964-70, Commonwealth Ct. of Pa., Harrisburg, 1970-82, U.S. Dist. Ct., Erie, Pa., 1982—. Served with U.S. Army, 1943-45, ETO. Mem. ABA, Fed. Judges Assn., Pa. Bar Assn., McKean County Bar Assn. Republican. Methodist. Lodge: Masons (33 degree). Judicial administration. Home: 30 W Willow Smethport PA 16749 Office: US Dist Ct 6th and State Sts Erie PA 16501

MENCHEL, ARNOLD IRA, lawyer; b. Hartford, Conn., June 21, 1950; s. Philip and Dorothy (Kletsky) M.; m. Shereen F. Edelson; 1 child, Robert Joshua. BA magna cum laude, U. Miami, 1972; JD with honors, U. Conn., 1975. Bar: Conn. 1975, U.S. Dist. Ct. Conn. 1975, U.S. Ct. Appeals (2d cir.) 1975, U.S. Supreme Ct. 1981. Corp. counsel Conn. State Employees Assn., Hartford, 1976-79; asst. atty. gen. State of Conn., Hartford, 1979—; sole practice Plainville, Conn., 1985—. Mem. Plainville (Conn.) Dems., 1981-86; alt. Plainville Zoning Bd. of Appeals, 1981-83; councilman Plainville Town Council, 1983-85. Mem. Conn. Bar Assn. (computer law sect., adminstrv. law sect.), Conn. Health Lawyers Assn., Nat. Health Lawyers Assn. Democrat. Avocations: tennis, photography, guitar. Administrative and regulatory, Computer, Health. Home: 14 Roma Dr Farmington CT 06032 Office: PO Box 7011 Plainville CT 06062

MENDALES, RICHARD EPHRAIM, lawyer; b. N.Y.C., Mar. 12, 1950; s. Arnold and Helen Shirley (Milk) M. AB, U. Chgo., 1969, AM, 1970; JD, Yale U., 1981. Bar: N.Y. 1982, U.S. Dist. Ct. (so. and ea. dist.) N.Y. 1982. Research asst. Mus. of Sci. and Industry, Chgo., 1973-74; quality claims analyst Social Security Adminstrn., Chgo., 1975-78; assoc. Cravath, Swaine & Moore, N.Y.C., 1981-84, Skadden, Arps, Slate, Meagher & Flom, N.Y.C., 1984—. Ford Found. fellow, 1969-73. Mem. ABA, N.Y. County Lawyer's Assn., Assn. Internat. des Jeunes Avocats, Am. Hist. Assn., AAAS. Democrat. Avocations: hist. research and writing, photography. Bankruptcy, Private international, Contracts commercial. Home: 211 W 56th St Apt 4M New York NY 10019 Office: Skadden Arps et al 919 3d Ave New York NY 10022

MENDEL, M. MARK, lawyer; b. Gmuend, Germany, Aug. 23, 1929; came to U.S., 1939; s. Richard and Erna (Lindauer) M.; m. Grace A. Bastian, Feb. 7, 1959; children—Kathryn Mendel Sorkin, Richard Charles, Sigrid Arlene. B.S., Temple U., 1952, M.A., 1953, J.D., 1957; Cordell Hull scholar Cumberland U., 1955-56. Bar: Pa. 1957, U.S. Supreme Ct. 1959, U.S. Ct. Appeals (3d cir.) 1959. Formerly ptnr. Mendel & Killeen, and successor firm Mendel, Schwartz & Smith; solicitor pub. utilities City of Phila., 1957-68; now sr. mng. ptnr. M. Mark Mendel, Ltd., Phila.; chmn. bd. dirs. Barton Engring., Phila., Motorcrafters, Inc., Phila.; pres. 1620 Group, Inc., Aspen, Colo. and Phila.; lectr. trial law, continuing edn. programs; lectr. forensic medicine Grad. Sch. Medicine, Temple U., Jefferson Med. Coll., Med. Coll. Pa. Trustee Phila. Prisons, 1974—; commonwealth and alumni trustee Temple U., 1976-85; mem. Jud. Selection Commn. Pa., 1980-83. Mem. Phila. Trial Lawyers Assn. (past pres.), Phila. Bar Assn. (bd. govs.), Assn. Trial Lawyers Am., ABA, Pa. Trial Lawyers Assn. (pres. 1984-85, chmn. nominating com.). Democrat. Jewish. Contbr. articles in negligence, med. malpractice, trial law to profl. jours. Public utilities, Personal injury. Home: 465 Highview Dr Radnor PA 19087 Office: 1620 Locust St Philadelphia PA 19103

MENDEL, STEPHEN FRANK, lawyer; b. Memphis, Dec. 20, 1947; s. Walter H. and Gisela (Silton) M.; m. Emily Weinberg, Sept. 14, 1979; children: Sarah, Madeleine. BA in Philosophy, U. Rochester, 1970; JD with highest honors, Hofstra U., 1977. Bar: Calif. 1977, U.S. Dist. Ct. (no. dist.) Calif. 1977, U.S. Ct. Appeals (9th cir.) 1978, U.S. Supreme Ct. 1982. Atty. ACLU, N.Y.C., 1977, Feldman, Waldman & Kline, San Francisco, 1977-82; exec. v.p., gen. counsel Molecular Design Ltd., San Leandro, Calif., 1982—. Martin Greiner scholar, 1977. General corporate, Private international, Trademark and copyright.

MENDELSOHN, MARTIN, lawyer; b. Bklyn., Sept. 6, 1942; s. Hyman and Gertrude Mendelsohn; m. Syma Barbara Rossman, Aug. 15, 1964; children—Alice S., James D. B.A., Bklyn. Coll., 1963; LL.B., George Washington U., 1966. Bar: D.C. 1967, U.S. Supreme Ct. 1970, U.S. Ct. Appeals (D.C. cir.) 1967, (3d cir.) 1971, (7th cir.) 1973, Ill. 1973. With Gen. Counsel's Office, HEW, Washington, 1966-67; legal services, Washington, 1967-70, Pa., 1971-72, Ill., 1973-75; counsel Legal Services Corp., Washington, 1976; adminstrv. asst. U.S. Congress, Washington, 1977; chief spl. litigation U.S. Dept. Justice, Washington, 1977-79, dep. dir. office spl. investigations, 1979-80; counsel House Judiciary Com., 1980; sole practice, Washington, 1980—. Mem. ABA, D.C. Bar Assn. Jewish. Private international, Public international, Legislative. Home: 5705 McKinley St Bethesda MD 20817 Office: 1700 K St NW Suite 1100 Washington DC 20006

MENDELSOHN, SUSAN RAE, lawyer; b. Washington, Jan. 2, 1946; d. Harold and Lillian (Lipp) M. BS, Pa. State U., 1967; MSW, U. Ill., 1973; JD, U. San Francisco, 1980. Bar: Calif. 1980. Field rep. Pa. Human Relations Commn., Pittsburgh, 1967-68; liaison officer EEOC, Washington, 1968-69; on job training coordinator EEOC, San Francisco, 1970-71; project dir. No. Calif. Assn. Human Relations, San Francisco, 1969-70; cons. fair employment practices commn. State of Calif., San Francisco, 1973-74, hearing dep. div. labor standards enforcement, 1974-80; assoc. Pillsbury, Madison & Sutro, San Francisco, 1980—. Mem. ABA, Calif. Bar Assn., San Francisco Bar Assn., Alumnae Resources, NOW (1st pres., organizer 1971). Labor. Office: Pillsbury Madison & Sutro 225 Bush St San Francisco CA 94104

MENDELSON, ALAN CHARLES, lawyer; b. San Francisco, Mar. 27, 1948; s. Samuel Mendelson and Rita Rosalie (Spindel) Brown; divorced; children: Jonathan Daniel, David Gary. BA with great distinction, U. Calif., Berkeley, 1969; JD cum laude, Harvard U., 1973. Bar: Calif. 1973. Assoc. Cooley, Godward et al., San Francisco, 1973-80; ptnr. Cooley, Godward, Castro, Huddleson & Tatum, Palo Alto, Calif., 1980—; bd. dirs. Sanmina Corp., San Jose, Calif.; sec, Acuson, Mountain View, Calif., 1982—, Chisholm, Campbell, Calif., 1985—, Zoran Corp., Santa Clara, Calif., 1983—. Chmn. Piedmont (Calif.) Civil Service Commn., 1978-80; den leader Boy Scouts Am., Menlo Park, Calif.; coach Menlo Park Little League, 1982—; mem. exec. com., bd. dirs. No. Calif. chpt. Nat. Kidney Found. Served with USAR, 1969-75. Named U. Calif. Berkeley Alumni scholar, 1966, Scaife Found. scholar, 1966. Mem. Harvard U. Law Sch. Alumni Assn. (area rep. funds com. 1978—), Phi Beta Kappa. Democrat. Jewish. Avocations: golf, tennis, softball, basketball, photography. Home: 665 San Mateo Dr Menlo Park CA 94025 Office: Cooley Godward Castro et al 5 Palo Alto Sq 400 Palo Alto CA 94306

MENDELSON, LEONARD (MELVIN), lawyer; b. Pitts., May 20, 1923; s. Jacob I. and Anna R. M.; m. Emily Solomon, Dec. 2, 1956; children: Ann, James R., Kathy S. AB, U. Mich., 1947; JD, Yale U., 1950. Bar: Pa. 1951, U.S. Supreme Ct. 1955. Mem., Hollinshead and Mendelson, Pitts., chmn. bd., 1974—; chmn. Lawyer-Realty Joint Com., Pitts., 1971-72. Mem. Pitts. Bd. Pub. Edn., 1975-76. Mem. ABA, Pa. Bar Assn., Allegheny County Bar Assn. Condemnation, Real property, State and local taxation. Office: 230 Grant Bldg Pittsburgh PA 15219

MENDELSON, STEVEN EARLE, lawyer; b. Los Angeles, Mar. 24, 1948; s. Robert Alexander and Nell Earle (Jacobs) M.; divorced; 1 child, Laurel. BA, U. Calif., Santa Cruz, 1971; JD, Golden Gate U., 1975. Bar: Calif. 1975, U.S. Dist. Ct. (no. dist.) Calif. 1975. Assoc. Law Offices Robert A. Mendelson, Los Angeles, 1975-76, Law Offices Paul A. Eisler, San Francisco, 1976-77; sole practice Oakland, Calif., 1977-84; ptnr. Mendelson & Mendelson, Oakland, 1985—. Founding sponsor Civil Justice Found., 1986; mem. Com for Preservation of Coll. Life at U. Calif. Santa Cruz. Mem. Assn. Trial Lawyers Am., Calif. Trial Lawyers Assn. (speaker), Alameda Contra Costa Trial Lawyers Assn., Calif. Applicant Atty's Assn., Am. Back Soc. (workshop dir., speaker, bd. dirs. com. on programs and interprofl. relations, incorporator, legal counsel 1981—). Personal injury, Workers' compensation, State civil litigation. Office: Mendelson & Mendelson 120 11th St Oakland CA 94607

MENDEZ, WILLIAM, JR., lawyer; b. N.Y.C., Feb. 19, 1948; s. William Sr. and Esther (Davila) M.; m. Rosa Iris Ubides, Oct. 7, 1947; 1 child, Edmond Morgan. BA, CCNY, 1978; JD, Hofstra U., 1980. Bar: N.Y. 1981, U.S. Dist. Ct. (ea. dist.) 1981. Atty. trainee U.S. Dept. Transp., Fed. Hwy. Adminstrn., Washington, 1980-81; asst. atty. gen. N.Y. State Dept. Law, N.Y.C., 1981-85; asst. gen. counsel Office of Insp. Gen. Met. Transp. Authority, N.Y.C., 1985—. Vice pres. Goddard Riverside Community Ctr., N.Y.C., 1985—. Mem. ABA, Puerto Rican Bar Assn. of N.Y., N.Y. State Bar Assn. (vice chmn. minorities in profession com.), Hispanic Nat. Bar Assn. (treas. and conv. chmn. 1984-85, pres. elect 1985-86, pres. 1986—). Democrat. Avocations: boating, skiing, hiking. Civil rights, Criminal, Administrative and regulatory. Office: Met Transp Authority Office Insp Gen 100 Park Ave 14th Floor New York NY 10017

MENEILLY, JAMES KEVIN, lawyer; b. Astoria, N.Y., Dec. 26, 1934; s. Lester J. and Marion (Smith) M.; m. Mary J., July 9, 1960; 2 sons, Kevin, James. B.B.A., St. Johns U., 1956, J.D. cum laude, 1959. Bar: N.Y. 1959, U.S. Supreme Ct. 1963. Law sec. Chief Judge N.Y. State Ct. Appeals, 1959-60; gen. counsel Lord & Taylor div. Associated Dry Goods Corp., N.Y.C., 1960-68; gen. counsel Massapequa (N.Y.) Gen. Hosp., 1969-87; sole practice, Jericho, N.Y., 1969—; counsel N.Y. State Assn. Osteo. Hosps. and Physicians. Pres., United Cerebral Palsy Assn. N.Y. State. Mem. N.Y. State Bar Assn., Nassau County Bar Assn. Roman Catholic. Contracts commercial, Health, General corporate. Office: 99 Jericho Turnpike Jericho NY 11753

MENENDEZ, KENNETH GARY, lawyer; b. San Juan, P.R., Dec. 18, 1954; s. Henry and Joan Christine (Becker) M.; m. Lisa Marie Camacho, Apr. 11, 1981. BA in History magna cum laude, Vanderbilt U., 1977; JD, Northwestern U., 1980. Bar: Ga. 1980. Assoc. Powell, Goldstein, Frazer & Murphy, Atlanta, 1980-85; assoc. Phillips, Hinchey & Reid, Atlanta, 1985-86, ptnr., 1986—; lectr. Northwest Ctr. Profl. Edn., Seattle, 1985—, Nat. Banking Inst., N.Y.C., 1986—. Mem. Ga. Rep. Found., Atlanta, 1986—. Mem. ABA, Ga. Bar Assn. (adv. opinion bd., code profl. responsibility com.), Atlanta Bar Assn., Atlanta Vanderbilt Alumni Assn. (pres. 1986—). Episcopalian. Club: Lawyers (Atlanta). Avocations: racquetball, reading, tennis, film, running. Construction, Federal civil litigation, State civil litigation. Home: 4520 Candler Lake E Atlanta GA 30319 Office: Phillips Hinchey & Reid 3414 Peachtree Rd NE 340 Monarch Plaza Atlanta GA 30326

MENENDEZ, MANUEL, JR., judge; b. Tampa, Fla., Aug. 2, 1947; s. Manuel and Clara (Marin) M.; m. Linda Lee Stewart, Aug. 31, 1969; children: Jennifer Kay, Christine Marie. AA, U. Fla., 1967, BA, 1969, JD with Honors, 1972. Bar: Fla. 1972, U.S. Dist. Ct. (mid. dist.) Fla. 1973, U.S. Ct. Appeals (5th cir.) 1973, U.S. Ct. Claims 1974, U.S. Tax Ct. 1974, U.S. Ct. Customs and Patent Appeals 1974, U.S. Supreme Ct. 1976, U.S. Ct. Appeals (11th cir.) 1983, U.S. Ct. Appeals (D.C. cir.) 1984. Asst. U.S. atty. Dept. Justice, Jacksonville, Fla., 1973-77; chief asst. U.S. atty. Dept. Justice, Tampa, 1978-83; assoc. Law Office Jack Culp, Jacksonville, 1977-78; ptnr. Culp & Menendez, P.A., Jacksonville, 1978; county judge jud. br. State of Fla., Tampa, 1983-84, cir. judge jud. br., 1984—. Exec. editor U. Fla. Law Rev., 1971-72. Served to capt. USAR, 1971-83. Recipient Pub. Service Meritorious Achievement award West Tampa Civic Clubs Assn., 1983. Mem. ABA, Fla. Bar Assn., Fed. Bar Assn. (v.p. Jacksonville chpt. 1974-75, pres. Tampa Bay chpt. 1980-85), Hillsborough County Bar Assn. (media law com. 1984—, trial lawyers sect. 1985—), Am. Judicature Soc., Am. Judges Assn., Univ. Fla. Alumni Assn., Univ. Fla. Law Ctr. Assn., Phi Delta Phi. Clubs: Propellor (Port of Tampa); Tampa Gator; Gator Boosters. Avocations: fishing, golf, Univ. Fla. athletics. Criminal, State civil litigation. Office: Hillsborough County Courthouse Annex #124 Tampa FL 33602

MENENDEZ, ROBERT, lawyer; b. N.Y.C., Jan. 1, 1954; s. Mario and Evangelina (Lopez) M.; m. Jane Jacobsen, June 5; children: Alicia, Robert. BA, St. Peter's Coll., 1976; JD, Rutgers U., 1979. Bar: N.J. 1984. Sole practice Union City, N.J., 1980—. Sr. pub. info. officer U.N.C. City Hall., Union City, 1974-78, mayor 1986—; sec. U.N.C. Bd. Edn., Union City, 1978-82, elected trustee, 1974; pres. Alliance Civic Orgn., 1982—; mem. U.N. Hill High Sch. Edn., Union City, 1978-70, Gov.'s Hispanic Adv. Com., trenton, N.J. 1984—, Gov.'s Ethnic Adv. Com., Washington, 1985—. Recipient Community Service award Gran Logia del Norte, 1981, Outstanding Service award Hispanic Law Enforcement, 1981, Outstanding Community Service Revista Actualidades, 1982; named Father of Elected Bd. Citizens for Community Action, 1981. Mem. ABA, N.J. Bar Assn., Hudson County Bar Assn., Hispanic Bar Assn., NOrth Hudson Lawyers Club. Democrat. Roman Catholic. Avocations: chess, racquetball. Criminal, Family and matrimonial, Real property. Home: 535 41st St Union City NJ 07087

MENGEL, CHRISTOPHER EMILE, lawyer, educator; b. Holyoke, Mass., Sept. 11, 1952; s. Emile Oscar and Rose Ann (O'Donnell) M.; m. Sandra Lee Schultz, July 16, 1981; children: Meredith Anne, Celia Claire. Student, U. Notre Dame, 1970-71; BA, Holy Cross Coll., 1974; JD, Detroit Coll. Law, 1979. Bar: Mich. 1979, U.S. Dist. Ct. (ea. dist.) Mich. 1980. Tchr. Holyoke Pub. Schs., 1974-76; assoc. Fried & Sniokaitis P.C., Detroit, 1980-82; prof. law Detroit Coll. Law, 1982-85; sole practice Detroit, 1982—. Mem. council St. Ambrose Parish, Grosse Pointe Park, Mich., 1985—. Matthew J. Ryan scholar, 1970. Mem. ABA, Mich. Bar Assn., Detroit Bar Assn. Democrat. Roman Catholic. Avocations: baseball, sailing, photography. General practice, Personal injury, Criminal. Home: 1063 Somerset Rd Grosse Pointe Park MI 48230 Office: 4372 Penobscot Bldg Detroit MI 48226

MENGES, EUGENE CLIFFORD, lawyer; b. East St. Louis, Ill., Feb. 3, 1952; s. Eugene Varley and Carol Lee (Kane) M.; m. Joan Carol Westrich, July 22, 1980; children: Carson Clifford, Sarah Elizabeth, Grant Tyler. BS in Econs., Boston Coll., 1974; JD, St. Louis U., 1977, MBA in Fin., 1979. Bar: Ill. 1977, U.S. dist. ct. (so. dist.) Ill. 1977, U.S. Ct. Appeals (7th cir.) 1981. Ptnr. Wagner, Bertrand, Bauman & Schmieder, 1977-86, Hinshaw, Culbertson, Moelman, Hoban & Fuller, 1986—; assoc. prof. Belleville Area Coll., 1977-80; sec.-treas. Goehner & Eaves, Inc.; invited atty. AIA. Mem. dist. com. Okaw Valley council Boy Scouts Am., 1981—. Fellow St. Louis U., 1975-76, 76-77. Mem. East St. Louis Bar Assn. (sec./treas.), ABA, St. Clair County Bar Assn. (chmn.), Ill. Bar Assn., Belleville Jaycees, Phi Delta Phi. Roman Catholic. Federal civil litigation, State civil litigation, Personal injury. Address: 105 LaMoine Ln Belleville IL 62223

MENGES, JOHN KENNETH, JR., lawyer; b. Louisville, Sept. 23, 1957; s. John Kenneth and Barbara Jean (Vick) M.; m. Jennifer Lynn Skipworth, Jan. 5, 1985. BBA, Boston U., 1979; JD, Harvard U., 1982. Bar: Tex. 1982. Assoc. Akin, Gump, Strauss, Hauer & Feld, Dallas, 1982—. Co-chmn. commn. on ch. and soc. 1st United Meth. Ch., Dallas, 1986—; pres. Dallas County Young Dems., 1985-86; bd. dirs. Dallas Dem. Forum, 1986. Mem. Dallas Assn. Young Lawyers, Harvard U. Law Sch. Assn. Tex. (bd. dirs. 1984—). General corporate, Securities, Contracts commercial. Home: 4823 Tremont St Dallas TX 75246 Office: Akin Gump Strauss Hauer & Feld 4100 First City Ctr Dallas TX 75201

MENHALL, DALTON WINN, lawyer, insurance executive, director national programs; b. Edgerton, Wis., Aug. 1, 1939; s. Joseph Laurence and Mary Winn (Dalton) M.; m. Lilian Marilyn Christie, Oct. 19, 1968; children—Dalton Winn, Rebecca Lynn, Katherine Elizabeth. B.A., Ill. Coll., 1962; J.D., Vanderbilt U., 1965. Bar: Wis. 1965. Staff asst. State Bar of Wis., Madison, 1965-72, dir., 1972-76; exec. dir. N.J. State Bar Assn., Trenton, 1976-86. Fellow Am. Bar Found.; mem. ABA (cons.), Nat. Assn. Bar Execs. (pres. 1985-86), N.J. State Bar Assn., State Bar Wis., Am. Soc. Assn. Execs., Am. Judicature Soc. Office: Herbert L Jamison & Co 300 Exec Dr West Orange NJ 07052

MENKE, WILLIAM CHARLES, lawyer, consultant; b. Cin., Aug. 30, 1939; s. William Garhardt and Margaret Philomena (Mercurio) M.; m. Mary Lou Lapan, Jan. 7, 1967; children—William Leo II, Lorelei Louise. B.S., U. Detroit, 1961; M.B.A., Ind. No. U., 1972; J.D., U. Detroit, 1976. Bar: Ohio 1977, U.S. Ct. Appeals (6th cir.) 1977. Sr. engr. Gen. Electric Co., Cin., 1964-67; v.p., gen. mgr. Preventicare Systems, Inc., Dearborn Mich., 1967-71; dir. Comshare, Inc., Ann Arbor, Mich., 1971-76; chief exec. officer William C. Menke & Assocs., Inc., New Richmond, Ohio, 1976—; dir. New Richmond Nat. Bank; city atty. City of New Richmond, 1979-81. Served to lt. (j.g.) USN, 1961-64. Fellow Lawyers in Mensa; mem. ABA, Assn. Trial Lawyers Am., Ohio State Bar. Republican. Roman Catholic. Club: Mensa. Lodge: KC. General corporate, Jurisprudence, Corporate taxation. Home: 1432 Indian Ridge Trail New Richmond OH 45157 Office: William C Menke & Assocs Inc PO Box 10 New Richmond OH 45157

MENKEN, DAVID A., lawyer; b. N.Y.C., Sept. 6, 1955; s. Julian and Joan B. (Dissick) M. BA, Johns Hopkins U., 1977; JD, NYU, 1981. Bar: N.Y. 1982. Assoc. Spengler, Carlson, Gubar, Brodsky & Rosenthal, N.Y.C., 1981-83, Pavia & Harcourt, N.Y.C., 1983—; bd. govs. NYU Jour. Internat. Law and Politics, 1984—. Private international, General corporate, Contracts commercial. Office: Pavia & Harcourt 600 Madison Ave New York NY 10022

MENKIN, LITA SUE, lawyer; b. Newark, Feb. 6, 1954; d. Harold and Rita (Laufer) M.; m. John Israel Spangler III, May 18, 1980; children: Jennifer Lynn Spangler, John Israel Spangler IV. BA, MSW, Washington U., St. Louis, 1976, JD, 1980. Bar: Ga. 1981, U.S. Dist. Ct. (no. dist.) Ga. 1981, U.S. Ct. Appeals (11th cir.) 1981, U.S. Tax Ct. 1982. Staff atty. Ga. lawyers for Arts, Atlanta, 1980-82, Ga. Legal Services, Conyers, 1982-83; advocacy coordinator Sr. Citizens Law Project, Atlanta, 1983—. Co-author: Senior Citizens Handbook, 1985 (Pres. award 1984-85); editor: Elderly Crime Victims Assistance Handbook, 1986. Legis. counsel Silver Haired Legislature, Atlanta, 1983, 85; v.p. bd. dirs. Council on Elder Abuse, Atlanta, 1985-87. Grantee Population Inst., 1975. Mem. ABA, Ga. Bar Assn. (chairperson elderly legal services com. young lawyers sect. 1984—), Atlanta Bar Assn., League Women Voters. Avocations: skiing, sailing. Legislative, Administrative and regulatory, Health. Office: Sr Citizens Law Project 151 Spring St NW Atlanta GA 30335

MENNELL, ROBERT L., lawyer, educator; b. Boston, Mar. 5, 1934; s. Herbert R. and Irene Marie (Callahan) M.; m. Antoinette Y. Mennell, June 11, 1960; children—Ann, John, James, T. Elizabeth. B.A., UCLA, 1955; J.D., Harvard U., 1962. Bar: Calif. 1963, Minn. 1978. Assoc. Voegelin, Barton, Harris & Callister, Los Angeles, 1962-68; sole practice, Encino, Calif., 1968-70; prof. law Southwestern U., Los Angeles, 1968-78, Hamline U. Sch. Law, St. Paul, 1977-84; vis. prof. law Notre Dame Sch. Law, 1975-76. Served with U.S. Army, 1955-58. Cert. specialist in taxation law, Calif. Author: California Decedents Estates, 1973; Wills and Trusts in a Nutshell, 1979; Community Property in a Nutshell, 1982; mem. editorial bd. Community Property Jour., 1975—. Personal income taxation, Probate, Estate taxation. Home and Office: 75 Mid Oaks Ln Roseville MN 55113

MENNINGER, HENRY EDWARD, JR., lawyer; b. Cin., May 16, 1950; s. Henry Edward and Frances Henrietta (Stadtmiller) M.; m. Deborah Joe Saupe, Sept. 9, 1972; children—Henry Edward, Joseph Gilbert, Michael Jonathan. B.A., U. Cin., 1972; J.D., No. Ky. U., 1977. Bar: Ohio 1977, U.S. Dist. Ct. (so. dist.) Ohio 1977, U.S. Ct. Appeals (6th cir.) 1977, U.S. Ct. Customs and Patent Appeals 1979, U.S. Tax Ct. 1979, U.S. Ct. Claims 1979, U.S. Ct. Internat. Trade 1980, U.S. Supreme Ct., 1981. Assoc., Nieman, Aug, Elder & Jacobs, Cin., 1978-82, ptnr., 1982—; instr. real estate law practice Practical Law Inst., Cin. Bar Assn., 1979-81. Mem. Harrison (Ohio) Planning Com., 1979. Mem. ABA, Ohio Bar Assn., Cin. Bar Assn., Fed. Bar Assn., Assn. Trial Lawyers Am., Bar Assn. Found. (bd. trustees Cin. chpt.), Nat. Mullie Loading Rifle Assn. (bd. dirs.), Salmon P. Chase Coll. of Law Alumni Assn. (bd. of govs.) Phi Alpha Delta. Democrat. Roman Catholic. Clubs: Nat. Muzzle Loading Rifle Assn., Cin. Muzzle Loading Rifle, Lawyers, K.C. (Harrison, Ohio). Real property, Bankruptcy, Probate. Office: 1000 Atlas Bank Bldg 524 Walnut St Cincinnati OH 45202

MENTO, MARY ANN, patent agent, researcher; b. Orange, N.J., Aug. 12, 1933; d. Alfred James and Mary Ann (Winch) Quimby; m. Anthony Ronald Mento, Dec. 14, 1957; children—Ronald Kevin, Dale Austin. B.S. in Chemistry, Tufts Coll., 1954; postgrad. Columbia U., 1956-57; M.Ed., Rutgers U., 1967; M. Natural Sci., U. Okla., 1973. Registered U.S. patent agt. Research chemist Esso Research and Engring. Co., Linden, N.J., 1954-59, tech. writer, editor, 1959-63, patent info. specialist, Elizabeth and Linden, N.J., 1963-67; tchr. Arlington Meml. High Sch., Vt., 1967-73; chemist, patent agt. Univ. Engrs., Inc., Norman, Okla., 1973-76; patent agt. Sprague Electric Co., North Adams, Mass., 1977-87; cons. Am. Petroleum Inst., N.Y.C., 1959-60. Contbr. articles to profl. jours. Scholar NSF, Ford Found. Mem. Vt. Geol. Soc. Democrat. Episcopalian. Club: Arlington Chorale. Patent.

MENTON, FRANCIS JAMES, JR., lawyer; b. Glen Ridge, N.J., Nov. 21, 1950; s. Francis James and Katherine Lees (Durbrow) M.; m. Denise Dorothy Wilson, Aug. 18, 1985. BA, Yale U., 1972; JD, Harvard U., 1975. Bar: N.Y. 1976, U.S. Dist. Ct. (so. and ea. dists.) N.Y. 1976, U.S. Ct. Appeals (2d cir.) 1986. Assoc. Willkie, Farr & Gallagher, N.Y.C., 1975-83; ptnr. Willkie Farr & Gallagher, N.Y.C., 1984—. Mem. ABA, Harvard Law Sch. Assn. N.Y.C. (trustee 1983—). Federal civil litigation, State civil litigation. Home: 15 E 10th St Apt 3E/F New York NY 10003 Office: Willkie Farr & Gallagher One Citicorp Cen 153 East 53d St New York NY 10022

MENTZ, HENRY ALVAN, JR., federal judge; b. New Orleans, Nov. 10, 1920; s. Henry Alvan and Lulla (Bridewell) M.; m. Ann Lamantia, June 23, 1956; children—Ann, Carli, Hal, Frederick, George. B.A., Tulane U., 1941; J.D., La. State U., 1943. Bar: La. 1943, U.S. Dist. Ct. (ea. dist.) La. 1944. Assoc. Reid & Reid, Hammond, La., 1946-47; with legal dept. Shell Oil, New Orleans, 1947-48; sole practice Hammond, 1948-82; judge U.S. Dist. Ct. (ea. dist.) La., 1982—. Editor: Combined Gospels, 1976. Vestryman Christ Ch. Cath.; bd. dirs. Sta. WYES-TV Found., Southeastern La. U., Salvation Army. Served as sgt. inf. U.S. Army, 1943-46, ETO. Recipient Disting. Service award AMVETS, 1950, Delta Tau Delta, 1976. Mem. SAR, Royal Soc. St. George. Republican. Episcopalian. Clubs: Boston, Essex (New Orleans). Home: 2105 State St New Orleans LA 70118 Office: US Courthouse Chambers C-456 500 Camp St New Orleans LA 70130

MENTZ, J. ROGER, lawyer, government official; b. N.Y.C., Mar. 10, 1942; s. John Louis and Margaret Catherine (Spelyng) M.; m. Marilyn I. Knerr, Aug. 10, 1963; children—Steven Roger, Tanna Marie. B.S.E., Princeton U., 1963; LL.B., U. Va., 1966. Bar: N.Y. 1967, D.C. 1976. Assoc. Mudge, Rose, Guthrie, Alexander & Ferdon, N.Y.C., 1966-74, ptnr., 1974-85; acting asst. sec. for tax policy U.S. Treasury Dept., Washington, 1985; asst. sec. for tax policy U.S. Treasury Dept., 1986—. Contbr. articles to profl. jours. Chmn., Cub Scouts Pack 60, Summit, N.J., 1976-77. Mem. ABA (taxation sect.), Internat. Fiscal Assn., N.Y. State Bar Assn. (chmn. tax sect. 1982-83). Republican. Episcopalian. Clubs: Seaview Country (Absecon, N.J.); Canoe Brook Country (Summit, N.J.); The George Town (Washington). Avocations: skiing; golf; tennis; fishing. Corporate taxation, Personal income taxation, State and local taxation. Home: 2718 27th St NW Washington DC 20008 Office: U S Dept Treasury 15th & Pennsylvania Ave NW Room 3120 Washington DC 20220

MERAN, HARRY BRUCE, lawyer; b. Phila., May 27, 1948; s. Albert and Elsie Diane (Bowman) M.; m. Linda J. Plotnick, Nov. 24, 1971; children: Andrew, Jeffrey, Marc. BS in Econs., U. Pa., 1969; JD, Temple U., 1972. Bar: Pa. 1972, U.S. Tax Ct. 1972, U.S. Supreme Ct. 1972, U.S. Dist. Ct. (ea. dist.) Pa. 1979. Assoc. Dechert, Price & Rhoads, Phila., 1972-74; sr. atty. IU Internat. Corp., Phila., 1974-79; gen. counsel, exec. com. Internat. Mill Service, Phila., 1979—, also bd. dirs.; exec. com. Internat. Mill Service, Phila., 1979—. Coach Upper Dublin Jr. Athletic Assn., Ambler, 1979—; bd. dirs. Upper Dublin Athletic Assn., Ambler, 1984—. Mem. ABA, Phila. Bar Assn., Am. Corp. Counsel Assn. Avocations: tennis, basketball, coaching all sports. General corporate, Private international.

MERCER, EDWIN WAYNE, lawyer; b. Kingsport, Tenn., July 19, 1940; s. Ernest LaFayette and Geneva (Frye) M. B.B.A., Tex. Tech U., Lubbock, 1963; J.D., S. Tex. Coll. Law, Houston, 1971. Bar: Tex. 1971, U.S. Dist. Ct. for No. Dist. Tex 1975, U.S. Supreme Ct. 1976, U.S. Ct. Appeals for 5th Circuit 1979. With Lone Star Gas Co., Dallas, 1963-65, Continental Oil Co., Houston, 1965-71; pvt. practice Houston, 1971-73; gen. counsel, corp. sec. Alcon Labs., Inc., Ft. Worth, 1973-81; ptnr. Gandy Michener Swindle Whitaker Pratt & Mercer, Ft. Worth, 1981-84; v.p., gen. counsel, corp. sec. Pengo Industries, Inc., Ft. Worth, 1984—. Bd. dirs. Soc. for Prevention of Blindness, 1979-81, v.p. fin. planning, 1980-81, pres., 1984-86. Mem. Am. Bar Assn., State Bar Tex., Ft. Worth-Tarrant County Bar Assn., S. Tex. Coll. Law Alumni Assn., Tex. Tech. Ex-Assn., Delta Theta Phi, Phi Delta Theta. Methodist. Clubs: Ft. Worth, Ft. Worth Boat. General practice, Private international, Public international. Office: Pengs Industries Inc 1400 Everman Rd Fort Worth TX 76140

MERCER, RICHARD JAMES, lawyer; b. New London, Conn., Oct. 2, 1950; s. James Wilson and Marianne (Wieczorek) M.; m. Ann Holly Gutting, Oct. 9, 1970 (div. 1977); m. Harriet Allston Jopson, May 1, 1982; 1 child, James. BBA, Old Dominion U., 1972; JD, Coll. William and Mary, 1975; LLM in Taxation, Boston U., 1977, LLM in Banking, 1986. Assoc. Epstein & Epstein, Norfolk, Va., 1975, Bernard A. Kaplan, Boston, 1975-76; sole practice, 1976-78, 1979-80; ptnr. Shagory & Shagory, Boston, 1978-79, Alpert, Thurman & Mercer, Boston, 1980-82; assoc. counsel First Nat. Bank Boston, 1983-85, asst. v.p., assoc. counsel, 1985-86, sr. counsel, 1986—. Town coordinator George Bush Presdl. Campaign, Weston, 1980. Mem. ABA, Boston Bar Assn., Am. Arbitration Assn. (arbitrator 1978), Mass. Bar Assn., Va. Bar Assn. Republican. Episcopalian. Federal civil litigation, State civil litigation, Banking. Office: First Nat Bank Boston 100 Federal St Boston MA 02110

MERCY, JOHN R., lawyer; b. Sacramento, Jan. 17, 1957; s. John W. and Marjorie L. (Chappell) M.; m. Dona Kelly Stringfellow, July 28, 1979 (div. Jan. 1986); m. Susan Wright, Aug. 22, 1986. BA, Austin Coll., 1979; JD, Baylor U., 1982. Bar: Tex. 1982, U.S. Dist. Ct. (ea. and no. dists.) Tex. 1982, Ark. 1983, U.S. Dist. Ct. (we. dist.) Ark. 1983, U.S. Supreme Ct. 1985, U.S. Ct. Appeals (5th and 8th cirs.). Briefing atty. Tex. Ct. Appeals (6th cir.), Texarkana, Tex., 1982-83; ptnr. Atchley, Russell, Waldrop & Hlavinka, Texarkana, 1983—. Mem. ABA, Tex. Bar Assn., Tex. Young Lawyers Assn. (chmn. profl. ethics com. 1985—, bd. dirs. 1985—), Tex. Assn. Def. Counsel, Northeast Tex. Bar Assn., Texarkana Bar Assn., Jaycees (bd. dirs. Texarkansas 1986—). Democrat. Presbyterian. Avocations: softball, gardening, outdoors, painting. State civil litigation, Federal civil litigation, General practice. Home: 910 Japonica Wake Village TX 75501 Office: Atchley Russell Waldrop & Hlavinka 803 Spruce St Texarkansas TX 75501

MERDEK, ANDREW AUSTIN, publishing executive, lawyer; b. Portland, Maine, Oct. 11, 1950; s. Philip and Eleanor (Weiss) M.; m. Jeanne Mullen, July 22, 1983; 1 child, David. AB, Middlebury Coll., 1972; JD, U. Va., 1978. Bar: D.C. 1978, U.S. Dist. Ct. D.C. 1979, U.S. Ct. Appeals (D.C. cir.) 1979, U.S. Supreme Ct. 1982. Reporter, editor Portland Press Herald, 1973-75; assoc. Dow, Lohnes & Albertson, Washington, 1978-86, ptnr., 1986-87; v.p., gen. mgr. Atlanta Constitution and Journal, 1987—. Mem. Order of Coif, Phi Beta Kappa. Libel, Antitrust. Home: 7418 Lynnhurst St Chevy Chase MD 20815 Office: Atlanta Constitution and Jour 72 Marietta St Atlanta GA 30303

MEREDITH, JENNINGS BRYAN, judge; b. Pioneer, Tenn., Nov. 29, 1939; s. Sterling and Mary Matilda (Douglas) M.; m. Phyllis Ann Strong, Dec. 16, 1967; 1 child, Ashley Deanne. B.S., U. Tenn., 1961, J.D., 1961. Bar: Tenn. 1962, U.S. Dist. Ct. (ea. dist.) Tenn. 1966, U.S. Ct. Mil. Appeals 1980. Assoc. law offices W. Lawrence Tunnell, Oak Ridge, 1966-67; ptnr. Tunnell and Meredith, Oak Ridge, 1967-77; judge Trial Justice and Juvenile Cts., Clinton, 1977—; pub. defender Anderson County, Clinton, Tenn., 1972-75; guest lectr. Pub. Law Inst., Knoxville, Tenn., 1978—; cons., hearing officer Dept. Energy, Oak Ridge, 1981—; cons., hearing rev. examiner Maxima Corp., Clinton, 1984—. Contbr. articles to profl. jours. Mem. Tenn. Statewide Task Force on Citizenship through Law Related Edn., Nashville, 1983—, Gen. Sessions Ct. Reform Liaison Com., Nashville, 1984—; mem. subs. ANderson County Adult Literacy Council, Child Abuse Council Anderson County. Served to capt. USAF, 1962-66, Korea, col. Res. Mem. Tenn. Council Juvenile and Family Ct. Judges (pres. 1982-83), Tenn. Gen. Sessions Judges Conf., Nat. Council Juvenile and Family Ct. Judges, Anderson County Bar Assn., Phi Delta Phi. Democrat. Baptist. Club: Tri-County Sportsman (Oliver Springs, Tenn.) (pres. 1978). Juvenile, Judicial administration, General practice. Home: Route 7 Box 451 Clinton TN 37716 Office: Juvenile Ct Courthouse Room 127 Clinton TN 37716

MEREDITH, RONALD EDWARD, U.S. District Court judge; b. Clarkson, Ky., Jan. 30, 1946; s. Ralph and Mary (Anderson) M.; m. Joanne Marie Berry, Apr. 23, 1973; children: Kelly, Jamie, Ronee, Mark. BA, Georgetown Coll., Ky., 1967; JD, George Washington U., 1971. Bar: D.C. 1971, Ky. 1971. Minority counsel U.S. Senate Jud. Subcom., Washington, 1971-72; legis. asst. Senator Marlow W. Cook, Washington, 1973-74; ptnr. Kelley & Meredith, Elizabethtown, Ky., 1975-81; U.S. atty. U.S. Dept. Justice We. Dist. Ky., Louisville, 1981-85; judge U.S. Dist. Ct. (we. dist.) Ky., 1985—. Bd. trustees Georgetown Coll., 1983—; deacon Severns Valley Baptist Ch., Elizabethtown, 1977—; dist. chmn. Rep. Party of Ky., 2d Congl. Dist., 1976-80, state campaign chmn., 1979; exec. bd. Old Ky. Council Boy Scouts Am., Louisville, 1982—. Mem. ABA, Fed. Bar Assn., D.C. Bar Assn., Ky. Bar Assn. Lodge: Rotary (bd. dirs. 1976-81). Criminal, Federal civil litigation. Home: 2935 Goose Creek Rd Louisville KY 40222 Office: US Fed Courthouse 601 W Broadway Room 268 Louisville KY 40202

MERHIGE, ROBERT REYNOLD, JR., U.S. judge; b. N.Y.C., Feb. 5, 1919; s. Robert Reynold and Eleanor (Donovan) M.; m. Shirley Galleher, Apr. 24, 1957; children: Robert Reynold III, Mark Reynold. LL.B., U. Richmond, 1942, LL.D., 1976; LL.M., U. Va., 1982. Bar: Va. 1942. Ptnr. firm Bremner Merhige Montgomery & Baber, Richmond, 1945-67; judge U.S. Dist. Ct., Richmond, 1967—; guest lectr. trial tactics U. Va. Law Sch.; adj. prof. U. Richmond Law Sch., 1973—; appeal agt. Henrico County Draft Bd., 1954-67. Co-author: Virginia Jury Instructions. Mem. Richmond Citizens Assn.; mem. citizens adv. com. San. Dist. A, Henrico County. Served with USAAF, World War II. Decorated Air medal with 4 clusters; recipient Amara Civic Club award, 1968; spl. award, jud. council Nat. Bar Assn., 1972; citation City Richmond, 1967; named Citizen of Yr. 3d dist. Omega Psi Phi, 1972, Citizen of Yr. Richmond Urban League, 1977; Disting. Alumni award U. Richmond, 1979; Disting. Service award Nat. Alumni Council, U. Richmond, 1979; Herbert T. Harley award Am. Judicature Soc., 1982; Athenian Citizen medal, 1979; Torch of Liberty award Antidefamation League of B'nai B'rith, 1982; T.C. Williams Sch. of Law Disting. Service award, 1983; President's award Old Dominion Bar Assn., 1986, William J. Brennan award 1986; named Ewalt Disting. Prof. of Law U. Va., 1987—. Mem. ABA (Herbert Harley award), Va. Bar Assn., Richmond Bar Assn. (pres. 1963-64), Va. Trial Lawyers Assn. (chmn. membership com. 1964-65, distinguished service award 1977), Jud. Conf. U.S., Omicron Delta Kappa. Jurisprudence. Office: US Courthouse Richmond VA 23219 *

MERIGAN, GARY DOUGLAS, lawyer, consultant; b. Detroit, Mar. 4, 1950; s. Harry and Estelle Doris (Rautio) M. B.Social Sci., Mich. State U., 1971; J.D., Detroit Coll. Law, 1974. Bar: Mich. 1975, U.S. Dist. Ct. (ea. dist.) Mich. 1977. Senate aide Mich. Senate, Lansing, 1975-76; assoc. Thomas Guastello P.C., Mt. Clemens, Mich., 1976-79; legal counsel Dallas Devel. Co., Warren, Mich., 1979-85, Schwartz, Juneau & Sotz, Sterling Heights, Mich. Author legal forms. Inventor portable pipe stand. Sec., legal counsel Econ. Devel. Corp., Clinton Twp., Mich., 1977; legal counsel, Econ. Devel. Corp., Warren, 1980; bd. dirs. Bldg. Authority, Clinton Twp., 1978. Recipient Eagle Scout award Northridge council Boy Scouts Am., 1962, Pro Deo Et Patria award, 1983. Mem. Internat. Platform Assn., State Bar Mich. (real estate law sect.), Oakland county Bar Assn., Macomb County Bar Assn., Delta Theta Phi, Sigma Alpha Mu. Democrat. Lutheran. Real property. Office: Schwartz Juneau & Sotz 38900 Van Dyke Ave Sterling Heights MI 48077

MERKEL, ALBERT BENTON, lawyer; b. Jackson, Tenn., May 19, 1944; s. Melvin Raymond and Johnye Lee (Vestal) M.; m. Pamela Kay Grimmer, June 21, 1971; children: Jennifer G., Albert Benton Jr., Joseph Lee. BS, Lambuth Coll., 1968; JD, Memphis State U., 1975. Bar : Tenn. 1975, U.S. Dist. Ct. (we. dist.) Tenn. 1975. Assoc. Spragins & Murchison, Jackson, 1976-79; ptnr. Merkel & Tabor, Jackson, 1979—. Mem. ABA, Tenn. Bar Assn., Jackson-Madison County Bar Assn. (pres. 1985-86). Democrat. Lodge: Elks. Bankruptcy, Family and matrimonial, General practice. Home: 258 Old Humboldt Rd Jackson TN 38305 Office: Merkel & Tabor 202 W Baltimore Jackson TN 38301

MERKEL, ROLAND PETER, lawyer; b. Oceanside, N.Y., Oct. 7, 1954; s. Andrew K. and Frieda (Kraker) M.; m. Joni Carol Brumbaugh, Mar. 17, 1984. BA, Rider Coll., 1977; JD, U. TUlsa, 1982. Bar: Okla. 1982, U.S. Dist. Ct. (no. dist.) Okla. 1982, Ky. 1983, U.S. Ct. Appeals (10th cir.) 1984, U.S. Supreme Ct. 1986. Sole practice Tulsa, 1982-84, Hominy, Okla., 1984-86, Frankfort, Ky., 1987—. Mem. Tulsa County Bar Assn., Osage County Bar Assn., Okla. Bar Assn., Ky. Bar Assn., Assn. Trial Lawyers Am., Franklin County Bar Assn., Franfort/Franklin County C. of C. General practice, Consumer commercial, Probate. Office: 409 W Broadway Frankfort KY 40601

MERKER, STEVEN JOSEPH, lawyer; b. Cleve., Feb. 21, 1947; s. Steven Joseph and Laverne (Zamenik) M.; children: Steven, Rena. BS, Case Inst. Tech., 1968; MS, U. Fla., 1973. Bar: Ohio 1976, U.S. Dist. Ct. (no. dist.) Ohio 1976, U.S. Dist. Ct. Colo. 1979, U.S. Ct. Appeals (10th cir.) 1979. Assoc. Jones, Day, Reavis & Pogue, Cleve., 1976-78; assoc. Davis, Graham & Stubbs, Denver, 1978-82, ptnr., 1983—. Legal counsel Coloradans for Lamm-Dick campaign, Denver, 1982, Nancy Dick for U.S. Senate Com., Denver, 1984, Cantrell for Dist. Atty., Jefferson County, Colo., 1984. Served as capt. USAF, 1969-72. Mem. ABA, Colo. Bar Assn., Denver Bar Assn. Federal civil litigation, State civil litigation, Labor. Office: 370 17th St Suite 4700 Denver CO 80202

MERLIN, WILLIAM FIRMAN, JR., lawyer; b. St. Petersburg, Fla., Mar. 19, 1959; s. William Firman and Alice (Volk) M. BS, U. Fla., 1980, JD, 1982. Bar: Fla. 1983, U.S. Dist. Ct. (mid. dist.) Fla. 1983. Assoc. Butler & Burnette, Tampa, Fla., 1982-85; sole practice Tampa, 1985—. Pres. Career Assn. Fla. Orchestra, Tampa, 1986—. Mem. ABA (asst. editor property ins. annotations, home owners annotations), Assn. Trial Lawyers Am., Fla. Trial Lawyers Assn., Fla. Blue Key, Delta Chi, Omicron Delta Kappa. Republican. Roman Catholic. Club: Tampa Sports. Avocations: yacht racing, golf. Personal injury, Insurance. Home: 5221 Bayshore Blvd #7 Tampa FL 33611 Office: 1100 N Florida Ave #200 Tampa FL 33602

MERMELSTEIN, JULES JOSHUA, lawyer, political consultant; b. Phila., Apr. 25, 1955; s. Harry and Ellen Jane (Greenberg) M.; m. Ruth Susan Applebaum, Aug. 18, 1974; children—Hannah Leona, Benjamin Isaac. B.A., Temple U., 1977; J.D., Washington Coll. Law, 1979. Bar: Pa. 1980, U.S. Dist. Ct. (ea. dist.) Pa. 1980, U.S. Ct. Appeals (3d cir.) 1982, U.S. Supreme Ct. 1983. Ptnr. Mermelstein & Light, Norristown and Hatboro, Pa., 1980-83; v.p., gen. counsel Am. Ins. Cons., Feasterville, Pa., 1983; vol. atty. ACLU, Phila., 1980—; staff atty. Hyatt Legal Services, Phila., 1983-84, mng. atty., 1984-85; sole practice, Phila. and Montgomery County, 1985—; part-time prof. law, St. Matthew Sch. Law, Phila., 1985—. Area rep. Montgomery County Democratic Exec. Com., 1982-85, candidate coordinator, 1982, nominee for dist. atty., 1983, committeeman, 1973-77, 82-85. Mem. ABA, Assn. Trial Lawyers Am., Montgomery County Bar Assn., Pa. Bar Assn., Pa. Trial Lawyers Assn. Jewish. Civil rights, Criminal, State civil litigation. Home: 18 Northview Dr Glenside PA 19038 Office: 901 N York Rd Willow Grove PA 19090-1387 also: 201 S 18th St Suite 300 Philadelphia PA 19103

MEROLA, MARIO, lawyer; b. Bronx, N.Y., Feb. 1, 1922; s. Michael and Lucia (Morano) M.; m. Tullia Palermo, Aug. 21, 1949; children—Michael, Marylou Merola Zappa, Elizabeth. B.A., NYU, 1947, LL.B., 1948; LL.D. (hon.), Coll. Mt. St. Vincent, 1980. Bar: N.Y. 1949, U.S. Ct. Appeals (2d cir.) 1982, U.S. Dist. Ct. (so. dist.) N.Y. 1982. Sole practice Bronx, N.Y., 1949-57; atty. Dept. of Investigations, N.Y.C., 1957-60; asst. dist. atty. Bronx Dist. Attys' Office, 1960-64, dist. atty., 1973—; councilman City Council, N.Y.C., 1964-72. Served to lt. USAAF, 1942-45. Mem. N.Y. State Bar Assn., Bronx County Bar Assn., Bronx County Criminal Bar Assn. Democrat. Roman Catholic. Criminal. Office: Dist Atty's Office 215 E 161st St Bronx NY 10451

MEROW, JAMES F., federal judge; b. Salamanca, N.Y., Mar. 16, 1932; s. Walter and Helen (Smith) M. AB, George Washington U., 1953, JD, 1956. Bar: Va. Judge U.S. Claims Ct., Washington; trial atty. U.S. Dept. Justice, Washington, 1959-78; trial judge U.S. Ct. Claims, Washington, 1978-82, judge, 1982—. Served with JAGC, U.S. Army, 1956-59. Mem. Va. Bar Assn., ABA. Office: US Ct of Claims 713 Madison Pl NW Washington DC 20005 *

MEROW, JOHN EDWARD, lawyer; b. Little Valley, N.Y., Dec. 20, 1929; s. Luin George and Mildred Elizabeth (Stoll) M.; m. Mary Alyce Smith, June 19, 1957; 1 dau., Alison Rasmussen. Student, UCLA, 1947-48; B.S.E., U. Mich., 1952; J.D., Harvard U., 1958. Bar: N.Y. 1958, U.S. Supreme Ct. 1971. Assoc. Sullivan & Cromwell, N.Y.C., 1958-64, ptnr., 1965—, vice chmn. bd., 1986—; dir. Kaiser Aluminum & Chem. Corp., Seligman Group mut. funds. Mem. adv. council Ctr. for Study Fin. Instns., U. Pa Law Sch., 1974-83; mem. adv. bd. N.Y. Hosp.-Cornell Med. Ctr.; bd. dirs., sec. Met. Opera; warden St. Thomas Ch., N.Y.C., 1971-78; trustee Am. Friends of Australian Nat. Gallery Found., Inc.; bd. dirs. Mcpl. Art. Soc. N.Y. Served to lt. USN, 1952-55. Mem. ABA, N.Y. State Bar Assn., Assn. Bar City N.Y. (chmn. com. on securities regulation 1974-77), Am. Law Inst. (advisor project on corp. governance), Union Internationale des Avocats, Council on Fgn. Relations, Am. Australian Assn. (bd. dirs.), Internat. Bar Assn. Clubs: Links, Piping Rock, Down Town, Church, Chatham Beach and Tennis, The Calif. General corporate, Private international, Securities. Home: 350 E 69th St New York NY 10021 also: 51 Fruitledge St Brookville NY 11545 Office: Sullivan & Cromwell 125 Broad St New York NY 10004

MERRIAM, LAUREN EVERT, III, lawyer; b. Panama City, Fla., Dec. 17, 1957; s. Lauren Evert Jr. and Margaret E. (Nalle) M.; m. Darlene M. Merriam, Feb. 13, 1982. BS in Bus. Adminstrn., U. Fla., 1978, JD, 1980. Bar: Fla. 1981, U.S. Dist. Ct. (mid. dist.) Fla. 1982, U.S. Ct. Appeals (11th cir.) 1985, U.S. Supreme Ct. 1986. Ptnr. Blanchard, Custureri & Merriam P.A., Ocala, Fla., 1981—. Elder Fort King Presbyn. Ch., Ocala, 1984—. Real property, Probate, General corporate. Home: 713 SE 2d St Ocala FL 32671 Office: Blanchard Custureri & Merriam PA PO Box 24 Ocala FL 32678

MERRICK, GLENN WARREN, lawyer; b. Ft. Devens, Mass., Oct. 5, 1954; s. Clyde Douglas and Gloria Pauline (Alix) M. BA magna cum laude, U. Colo., 1976; JD with high honors, U. Tex., 1979. Bar: Colo. 1979, D.C. 1979, U.S. Ct. Appeals (5th and 10th cirs.) 1980, Tex., 1986. Law clk. to presiding judge U.S. Ct. Appeals (5th cir.), Austin, Tex., 1979-80; assoc. Davis, Graham & Stubbs, Denver, 1980-85, ptnr., 1985—; faculty mem. Nat. Bus. Inst., Denver, 1985—; chmn. 1st ann. real estate reorganization and foreclosure conf., Denver, 1987. Contbr. articles to profl. jours. Counsel Colo. Open Space Council, Denver, 1984-85, Concerned Friends and Relatives of Nursing Home Residents, Ft. Collins, Colo., 1984-85; speaker, author Rocky Mountain Mineral Law Found. Spl. Inst., Denver, 1986. Mem. ABA (bus. bankruptcy com.), Denver Bar Assn., Colo. Bar Assn. (bus. bankruptcy subcom.), Am. Bankruptcy Inst., Phi Beta Kappa. Republican. Roman Catholic. Club: Law (Denver). Avocations: running, golf, skiing. Bankruptcy, Consumer commercial, Federal civil litigation. Home: 10021 E Grand Ave Englewood CO 80111 Office: Davis Graham & Stubbs 370 17th St Suite 4700 Denver CO 80202

MERRIGAN, WILLIAM JOSEPH, lawyer; b. Conception Junction, Mo., Sept. 28, 1934; s. Patrick James and Irene Anna (McLaughlin) M.; m. Sandra Craig Bartolina, Oct. 22, 1977. B.S., Creighton U., 1956; LL.B., Georgetown U., 1961. Bar: Va. 1961, Mo. 1961. Legis. asst. Congressman W. R. Hull, Jr., U.S. Ho. of Reps., 1958-59; legal counsel, asst. sec. Civil Air Transport, Southern Air Transport and Air America, Inc., Taipei, Taiwan, 1962-74; legis. counsel Dept. Army, Washington, 1974—. Served with AC, USN. Mem. ABA, Mo. Bar Assn., Va. Bar Assn., Supreme Ct. Hist. Soc. Republican. Roman Catholic. Legislative, Administrative and regulatory, Government contracts and claims. Home: 4931 Old Dominion Dr Arlington VA 22207 Office: Hdqrs Mil Traffic Mgmt Command Washington DC 20315

MERRILL, ABEL JAY, lawyer; b. Balt., Mar. 25, 1938; s. Yale and Evelyn (Cordish) M.; m. Susan Stein, June 15, 1963; children: Adam L., Julie F. BA, Colgate U., 1959; LLB, U. Md., 1964. Bar: Md. 1964. Law clk. U.S. Ct. Appeals, Balt., 1964-65; assoc. Gordon, Feinblatt & Rothman, Balt., 1965-70; sole practice, Annapolis, Md., 1970-78, 83—; prin. Blumenthal, May, Downs & Merrill, P.A., Annapolis, 1979-83; mem. inquiry com. Atty. Grievance Commn. Md., 1975-85, character com. Ct. of Appeals. Fellow Am. Coll. Probate Counsel; mem. ABA, Md. Bar Assn., Anne Arundel County Bar Assn. Probate, Estate planning, General corporate.

MERRILL, BYRON ROBERT, lawyer; b. Palo Alto, Calif., June 23, 1947; s. George L. and Carma (Flake) M.; m. Patricia L. England, June 30, 1972; children: Aimee, Seth, Rachel, Timothy. BA, Brigham Young U., 1972; JD, U. Calif., Davis, 1975. Bar: Calif. 1975. Assoc. Thomas, Snell, et al, Fresno, Calif., 1975-76, Anderson, Nearon & Falco Inc., Walnut Creek, Calif., 1976-78; pres. Byron R. Merrill, Fresno, Calif., 1978-83, Citrus Heights, Calif., 1983—. Probate, Estate planning, Estate taxation. Office: 8391 Auburn Blvd #3 Citrus Hieghts CA 95610

MERRILL, GEORGE VANDERNETH, lawyer; b. N.Y.C., July 2, 1947; s. James Edward and Claire (Leness) M.; m. Janice Anne Humes, May 11, 1985. A.B., Harvard U., 1968, J.D., 1972; M.B.A., Columbia U., 1973. Bar: N.Y. 1973, U.S. Dist. Cts. (so. and ea. dists.) N.Y. 1974, U.S. Ct. Appeals (2d cir.) 1974. Assoc., Cleary, Gottlieb, Steen & Hamilton, N.Y.C., 1974-77, Hawkins, Delafield & Wood, N.Y.C., 1977-79; v.p. Irving Trust Co., N.Y.C., 1980-82; v.p., gen. counsel Listowel Inc., N.Y.C., 1982-84, exec. v.p., gen. counsel, 1984—, also bd. dirs. Pres. Arell Found., N.Y.C., 1985—, also bd. dirs.; pres. Northfield Charitable Trust Corp., N.Y.C., 1986—; v.p., sec. Brougham Prodn. Co., N.Y.C., 1986—, Cabriolet Prodn. Co., N.Y.C., 1986—. Recipient Detur Award Harvard U., 1968. Mem. ABA, Am. Mgmt. Assn. Clubs: The Brook, Union, Down Town, Knickerbocker, Racquet and Tennis, Players , Pilgrims of U.S. (all N.Y.C.). General corporate, General practice. Home: 50 Glenbrook Rd Stamford CT 06902 Office: Listowel Inc 2 Park Ave New York NY 10016

MERRILL, RICHARD AUSTIN, lawyer; b. Logan, Utah, May 20, 1937; s. Milton Rees and Bessie (Austin) M.; m. Elizabeth Duvall, Aug. 26, 1961; children—Patricia, John. A.B., Columbia U., 1959, LL.B., 1964; B.A. (Rhodes scholar), Oxford (Eng.) U., 1961, M.A., 1965. Bar: N.Y. 1964, D.C. 1965. Law clk. to Hon. Carl McGowan, U.S. Ct. Appeals for D.C., 1964-65, Va. bar, 1980; assoc. firm Covington & Burling, Washington, 1965-69; assoc. prof. law U. Va., 1969-72, prof., 1972-75, Daniel Caplin prof. law, 1977-85, Arnold Leon prof., 1985—; dean U. Va. (Sch. Law), 1980—; gen. counsel FDA, Washington, 1975-77; cons. in field. Mem. Inst. Medicine (council), Nat. Acad. Scis., 1977—, Bd. on Toxicology and Environ. Health Hazards, 1979-85. Author: (with Jerry L. Mashaw) American Administrative Law, 2d edit. (with Peter B. Hutt) Food and Drug Law, 1980. Mem. Am. Bar Found., Va. Bar Found., Am. Law Inst., Environ. Law Inst. (bd. trustees), Food and Drug Inst. (bd. trustees), So. Environ. Law Ctr. (bd. trustees). Administrative and regulatory, Environment, Health. Office: U Va Sch Law Charlottesville VA 22901

MERRILL, STEPHEN E., state official. Atty. gen. State of N.H., Concord, 1987—. Office: Atty Gen 208 State House Annex Concord NH 03301 *

MERRILL, THOMAS WENDELL, lawyer, law educator; b. Bartlesville, Okla., May 3, 1949; s. William McGill and Dorothy (Glasener) M.; m. Kimberly Ann Evans, Sept. 8, 1973; children: Jessica, Margaret, Elizabeth. BA, Grinnell Coll., 1971, Oxford U., 1973; JD, U. Chgo., 1977. Bar: Ill. 1980, U.S. Dist Ct. (no. dist.) Ill. 1980, U.S. Ct. Appeals (5th cir.) 1982, U.S. Ct. Appeals (7th cir.) 1983, U.S. Ct. Appeals (9th and D.C. cirs.) 1984, U.S. Supreme Ct. 1985. Clk. U.S. Ct. Appeals (D.C. cir.), Washington, 1977-78, U.S. Supreme Ct., Washington, 1978-79; assoc. Sidley & Austin, Chgo., 1979-81, councel, 1981—; prof. law Northwestern U., Chgo., 1981—. Contbr. articles to profl. jours. Rhodes scholar Oxford U., 1971; Danforth fellow, 1971. Mem. ABA, Chgo. Bar Assn. Legal education, Public utilities, Environment. Home: 939 Maple Evanston IL 60202 Office: Northwestern U Sch Law 357 E Chicago Ave Chicago IL 60611

MERRILL, WALTER JAMES, lawyer; b. Anniston, Ala., Sept. 30, 1912; s. Walter B. and Lilla (Jones) M.; m. Polly McCarty, Sept. 6, 1941; children: Martha, Mary M. Williams. BA, U. Ala., 1931, LLB, 1934. Bar: Ala. 1934, U.S. Dist. Ct. (no. dist.) Ala. 1934, U.S. Ct. Appeals (5th and 11th cirs.) 1934, U.S. Supreme Ct. 1934. Ptnr. Merrill, Jones & Merrill, Anniston,

1934-46, Knox, Jones, Woolf & Merrill, Anniston, 1946-72, Merrill, Porch, Doster & Dillon, Anniston, 1972—; bd. dirs. Comml. Nat. Bank, Anniston, 1947—. Served to lt. col. JAGC, USAF, 1942-46, ETO. Fellow Am. Coll. Trial Lawyers; mem. ABA, Ala. Bar Assn. Democrat. Baptist. Club: Anniston Country. Lodge: Rotary. Avocations: hunting, tennis. State civil litigation, Insurance, Probate. Home: 226 Crestview Rd Anniston AL 36201 Office: Merrill Porch Doster & Dillon PO Box 580 Anniston AL 36202

MERRING, ROBERT ALAN, lawyer; b. Middletown, N.Y., Oct. 5, 1951; s. Merton Joseph and Mabel Ruth M. Student Ohio Wesleyan U., 1969-70; A.B. with distinction and dept. honors, Stanford U., 1973; J.D. with honors in Internat. and Fgn. Law, Columbia U., 1977. Bar: Calif. 1977, U.S. Dist. Ct. (cen. dist.) Calif. 1978, U.S. Dist. Ct. (so. and ea. dists.) Calif. 1980, U.S. Ct. Appeals (9th cir.) 1980, U.S. Dist. Ct. (no. dist.) Calif. 1983, U.S. Supreme Ct. 1987. Assoc. Pacht, Ross, Warne, Bernhard & Sears, Inc., Los Angeles, 1977-79, Donovan Leisure Newton & Irvine, Los Angeles, 1979-81, Cutler and Cutler, Los Angeles, 1983—; clin. prof. Loyola U. Law Sch., Los Angeles, 1981-82. Columbia U. Internat. fellow, 1975-76. Mem. ABA, Los Angeles County Bar Assn., Assn. Bus. Trial Lawyers. editor Columbia Jour. Transnat. Law, 1976-77. Federal civil litigation, State civil litigation, Antitrust. Home: 4119 Via Marina Marina Del Rey CA 90292

MERRITT, GILBERT STROUD, federal judge; b. Nashville, Jan. 17, 1936; s. Gilbert Stroud and Angie Fields (Cantrell) M.; m. Louise Clark Fort, July 10, 1964 (dec.); children: Stroud, Louise Clark, Eli. B.A., Yale U., 1957; LL.B., Vanderbilt U., 1960; LL.M., Harvard U., 1962. Bar: Tenn. 1960. Asst. dean, instr. Vanderbilt Law Sch., 1960-61, lectr., 1973-75, assoc. prof. law, 1969-70; assoc. firm Boult Hunt Cummings & Conners, Nashville, 1962-63; assoc. met. atty. Nashville, 1963-66; U.S. dist. atty. for Middle Tenn. 1966-69; partner firm Gullett, Steele, Sanford, Robinson & Merritt, Nashville, 1970-77; judge U.S. Ct. of Appeals for 6th Circuit, Nashville, 1977—; exec. sec. Tenn. Code Commn., 1977. Mng. editor: Vanderbilt Law Rev, 1959-60; contbr. articles to law jours. Del. Tenn. Constl. Conv., 1965. Mem. ABA, Fed., Tenn., Nashville bar assns., Vanderbilt Law Alumni Assn. (pres. 1979-80), Am. Law Inst., Order of Coif. Episcopalian. Jurisprudence. Office: US Court Appeals 801 Broadway Nashville TN 37203 *

MERRITT, THOMAS BUTLER, lawyer; b. Toledo, Apr. 3, 1939; s. George Robert and Bernice (Gerwin) M.; m. Mary Jane Bothfeld, July 23, 1966; children—Thomas Butler, Haidee Soule, Theodore Bothfeld. A.B. magna cum laude, Harvard U., 1961, LL.B. cum laude, 1966. Bar: Mass. 1966, U.S. Supreme Ct. 1974. Law clk. to assoc. justice Supreme Jud. Ct. Mass., Boston, 1966-67, reporter of decisions, 1974—; assoc. Nutter, McClennen & Fish, Boston, 1967-69, Palmer & Dodge, Boston, 1969-73; asst. counsel to Gov. Mass. 1973. Mem. Conservation Commn. Town of Sherborn, Mass., 1969-74, chmn., 1972-74; mem. corp. Tenacre Country Day Sch., Wellesley, Mass., 1972-84, trustee, 1973-78. Served to 1st lt. U.S. Army, 1962-63, capt. USAR, 1963-69. Mem. Am. Law Inst., ABA, Mass. Bar Assn., Boston Bar Assn., Fed. Bar Assn., Am. Soc. Internat. Law, Internat. Law Assn. (Am. br.), Nat. Assn. Reporters of Jud. Decisions (pres. 1983-84). Episcopalian. Clubs: Union, Harvard (Boston). Jurisprudence, Public international. Office: 1407 New Court House Boston MA 02108

MERRITT, VALERIE JORGENSEN, lawyer; b. Palo Alto, Calif., Oct. 13, 1947; d. James Harold and Evelyn Marie (Flora) Jorgensen; m. Bruce Gordon Merritt, Dec. 28, 1969; children: Benjamin Carlyle, Alicia Marie. AB cum laude, Occidental Coll., 1969; JD, UCLA, 1976. Bar: Calif. 1977, U.S. Tax Ct. 1986. Assoc. Agnew, Miller & Carlson, Los Angeles, 1977-81, Hufstedler, Miller, Carlson & Beardsley, Los Angeles, 1981-82; ptnr. Dreisen, Kassoy & Freiberg, Los Angeles, 1982—. Contbr. articles to profl. jours. Treas. Los Angeles Family Sch., 1979-80. Mem. ABA (tax and real property and probate and trust sects.), Calif. Bar Assn. (estate planning probate and trust sect.), Los Angeles County Assn. (chmn. probate and trust sect. 1985-86, del. to state bar conf. and exec. com. 1983-86, tax sect.). Democrat. Avocations: mystery novels, travel. Probate, Estate planning, Estate taxation. Office: Dreisen Kassoy & Freiberg 1801 Century Park E Suite 740 Los Angeles CA 90067

MERRYMAN, JOHN HENRY, legal educator; b. Portland, Oreg., Feb. 24, 1920; s. Joseph M. and Bertha (Hale) M.; m. Nancy Dyer, Apr. 1, 1953; stepchildren: Leonard Perry Edwards, Samuel Dyer Edwards, Bruce Haven Edwards. BS, U. Portland, 1943; MS, U. Notre Dame, 1944, JD, 1947; LLM, N.Y. U., 1950, JSD, 1955; Docteur (hon.), U. Aix-Marseilles, France, 1982. Mem. faculty U. Santa Clara, Calif., 1948-53; mem. faculty Stanford U. Sch. Law, 1953—, prof., 1960—, Nelson B. and Marie B. Sweitzer prof., 1971—, affiliated prof. art, 1980—, prof emeritus, 1986—; vis. prof. law schs. NYU, 1950, 82, U. Rome, Italy, 1963-64, U. Aix-Marseilles III, France, 1983; vis. research prof. Center Planning and Econ. Research, Athens, Greece, 1962, 64; mem. Internat. Faculty Comparative Law, Strasbourg, France, 1964, 69, Mexico, 1965; Fulbright research scholar, vis. research prof. Max Planck Institut für ausländisches und internationales Privatrecht, Hamburg, Germany, 1968-69. Editor-in-chief N.D. Lawyer, 1947; author: The Civil Law Tradition, 1969, 2d edit., 1985, (with M. Cappelletti and J. Perillo) The Italian Legal System; An Introduction, 1967, (with D. Clark) Comparative Law: Western Europe and Latin American Legal Systems, 1978, (with A. Elsen) Law, Ethics and the Visual Arts, 1979 (2d edit. 1987), (with Barton, Gibbs and Li) Law in Radically Different Cultures, 1983; contbr. articles to profl. jours. Mem. Atty. Gen. Calif. Adv. Com. on Civil Rights, 1960-63; Bd. dirs. No. Calif. chpt. ACLU, 1955-68, chmn., 1957-61. Recipient Silver medal U. Rome, 1964; decorated officer Order Merit Italian Republic, 1971; Guggenheim fellow, 1985-86. Legal education. Home: 34 Peter Coutts Circle Stanford CA 94305

MERTENS, EDWARD JOSEPH, II, lawyer; b. N.Y.C., Dec. 11, 1949; s. Edward Joseph and Loretta (Clark) M.; m. Laurie Shea, Apr. 6, 1968; children—Mary, Susan, Edward. B.A., U. N.H., 1975; J.D., Franklin Pierce Law Ctr., Concord, N.H., 1978. Bar: N.H., U.S. Dist. Ct. N.H. Ptnr. Shea, Mertens, Sager & Sager, P.A., Wolfeboro, N.H., 1978—. Bd. dirs. Wolfeboro Ctr. of Hope, 1984. Mem. Assn. Trial Lawyers Am., N.H. Trial Lawyers Assn. (past gov.). Personal injury. Home: Main St Wolfeboro NH 03894 Office: Shea Mertens Sager & Sager Box 1508 Wolfeboro NH 03894

MERTHAN, LAWRENCE CASPER, lawyer; b. St. Paul, Sept. 25, 1918; s. Casper Matthew and Theresia Martha (Laber) M.; 1 dau., Mary Elizabeth. B.A. cum laude, Coll. St. Thomas, 1941; J.D., U. Minn., 1949; LL.D., Iowa Wesleyan Coll., 1967. Bar: Minn. 1949, D.C. 1954, U.S. Ct. Appeals 1946, U.S. Supreme Ct. 1959. Assoc. Thomas M. Walsh, St. Paul, 1949-55; ptnr. Hedrick and Lane, Washington, 1979-80; ptnr. Zuckert, Scoutt, Rasenberger & Johnson, Washington, 1980—. Vice-pres. St. Paul Housing and Redevel. Authority, 1953-55. Served with USAF, 1941-45. Decorated D.F.C., Air medal with 3 clusters, Legion of Merit. Mem. ABA, Minn. State Bar Assn., D.C. Bar. Roman Catholic. Clubs: George Town, Capitol Hill (Washington). Estate taxation, Private international. Home: 2230 46th St NW Washington DC 20007

MERTING, JOHN WEBSTER, lawyer; b. Pensacola, Fla., June 17, 1943; s. Fritz and Elizabeth (Webster) M.; m. Linda Claytor, Jan. 12, 1974; children—Courtney Kristin, Shannon Michelle. B.A. cum laude, Fla. State U., 1965; LL.B., U. Va., 1968, J.D., 1970. Bar: Fla. 1968, U.S. Dist. Ct. (no. dist.) Fla. 1969, U.S. Dist. Ct. (mid. dist.) Fla. 1984. Assoc. Merritt & Merting, Pensacola, Fla., 1968-70, Jones Latham, Liberis & Merting, Pensacola, 1970-75, Liberis & Merting, Pensacola, 1975-78; sole practice, Pensacola, 1978; ptnr. Merting & Davis, P.A., 1978-86 ; pres. Merting & Denison, P.A., 1986—; adj. prof. U. W. Fla., 1968-69. Legis. asst. Sen. John Spottswood, Fla., 1965. Served with Fla. N.G., 1968-74. Recipient Spl. Recognition award Pensacola Sports Assn., 1970-71. Mem. Fla. Bar Assn., Acad. Fla. Trial Lawyers (sustaining), Am. Trial Lawyers Assn. (sustaining), N.Y. Trial Lawyers Assn., ABA, Southeastern Admiralty Law Inst. (dir. 1985-87), Maritime Law Assn. of U.S., Escambia-Santa Bar Assn., Phi Beta Kappa, Phi Kappa Phi, Omicron Delta Kappa. Republican. Episcopalian. Clubs: Sertoma (pres. 1979-80, chmn. 1980-81), Pensacola Yacht, Order of Tristan, Krewe of Lafitte, Rebellaires, Hildagos, Pensacola Ski, Pensacola Sports Assn., Gold Key. Founding editor The Summation, 1974-77; editor-in-chief The Va. Law Weekly, 1967-68; patentee in field. Personal injury, Admiralty, General practice. Home: 258 Sabine Dr Pensacola Beach FL 32561 Office: 421 N Palafox St Pensacola FL 32501

MERTZ, DOUGLAS KEMP, lawyer; b. Albany, N.Y., Jan. 1, 1949; s. John Sherman and Virginia (Kemp) M.; m. Margo Wasserman Waring, Sept. 9, 1984; 1 child, Edward Nathan. BA, Yale U., 1971; JD, Harvard U., 1974. Bar: Alaska 1975, U.S. Dist. Ct. Alaska 1976, U.S. Ct. Appeals (9th cir.) 1981, U.S. Supreme Ct. 1982. Law clk. to presiding justice Alaska Supreme Ct., Fairbanks, 1974-75; asst. atty. gen. Alaska Dept. Law, Fairbanks, 1975-77, chief asst. atty. gen., 1977-80; asst. atty. gen. Alaska Dept. Law, Juneau, 1980—. V.p. Fairbanks Community Mental Health Ctr., 1978-80. Mem. ABA, Alaska Bar Assn., Alaska Admirality Bar Assn., Juneau Bar Assn. Environment, Indian law. Home: 1215 Fifth St Douglas AK 99824 Office: Office of the Atty Gen Box K Juneau AK 99811

MERZ, DANIEL LEE, lawyer; b. Brenham, Tex., Oct. 15, 1952; s. Stanley and Viola Merz; m. Sandra Kay Briles, Aug. 20, 1977; children: Carrie, Eli, Macie. BA with honors, Tex. A&M U., 1978; JD, U. Houston, 1982. Bar: Tex. 1982, U.S. Ct. Appeals (5th cir.) 1983, U.S. Dist. Ct. (so. dist.) Tex. 1984. Atty. Transco Energy Co., Houston, 1981-84, corp. atty., 1984-86, sr. atty., 1986—; bd. dirs. Inns Ct. Club. Vol. legal counsel Nelsonville Brethren Ch., 1984—, Cy-Fair Community Ch., 1984—; asst. coach Katy Am. Little League, 1986—. Served with U.S. Army, 1972-74. Mem. Tex. Bar Assn. (conv. planning com. 1985-86), Houston Bar Assn. (ex officio, bd. dirs. 1986, alternative dispute resolutions and jud. liaison coms.), Tex. Young Lawyers Assn. (bd. dirs. 1985-87, chmn. moot ct. competition com. 1985-86, chmn. pub. service program com. 1986-87), Houston Young Lawyers Assn. (bd. dirs. 1984-85, sec. 1985-86, pres. 1986-87, chmn. courthouse visitation com. 1982-84, outstanding com. chmn. award 1983, outstanding service award 1984), Am. Legion, Phi Kappa Phi, Phi Kappa Alpha. Federal civil litigation, State civil litigation, Insurance. Office: Transco Energy Co PO Box 1396 Houston TX 77251

MERZ, MICHAEL, judge; b. Dayton, Ohio, Mar. 29, 1945; s. Robert Louis and Hazel (Appleton) M., m. Marguerite Logan Lebreton, Sept. 7, 1968; children: Peter Henry, Nicholas George. AB cum laude, Harvard U., 1967, JD, 1970. Bar: Ohio 1970, U.S. Dist. Ct. (so. dist.) Ohio 1971, U.S Supreme Ct. 1974, U.S. Ct. Appeals (6th cir.) 1975. Assoc. Smith & Schnacke, Dayton, Ohio, 1970-75, ptnr., 1976-77; judge Dayton Mcpl. Ct., 1977-84; adj. prof. U. Dayton Law Sch., 1979—. Bd. dirs., v.p. United Way, Dayton, 1981—. Mem ABA, Fed. Bar Assn. (sec.), Am. Judicature Soc., Ohio State Bar Assn. Republican. Roman Catholic. Federal civil litigation, Judicial administration, Jurisprudence. Home: 1532 Bryn Mawr Dayton OH 45406 Office: US Dist Ct 200 W Second St Dayton OH 45402

MERZ, STUART OSCAR HAROLD, lawyer; b. South Orange, N.J., Feb. 6, 1930; s. Harold Oscar Merz and Mildred (Cyphers) M.; m. Joan LeCount Ahlgren, Dec. 27, 1952; children: Jeffrey Stuart, Melinda Joan Merz Gabarik, Wendy Carolyn Merz. B.S., Cornell U., 1952, LL.B., 1957. Bar: Ohio 1958. Ptnr. Jones, Day, Reavis & Pogue, Cleve., 1957—. Served to 1st lt. U.S. Army, 1952-54. Mem. ABA, Bar Assn. Greater Cleve., Cornell Law Assn. Republican. Presbyterian. Club: Mayfield Country (South Euclid, Ohio). Office: Jones Day Reavis & Pogue North Point 901 Lakeside Ave Cleveland OH 44114

MESCHKE, HERBERT L., state supreme court justice; b. Belfield, N.D., Mar. 18, 1928; s. G.E. and Dorothy E. Meschke; m. Shirley Ruth McNeil; children: Marie, Jean, Michael, Jill. B.A., Jamestown Coll., 1950; J.D., U. Mich., 1953. Bar: N.D. Law clk. U.S. Dist. Ct. N.D., 1953-54; practice law Minot, N.D., 1954-85; justice N.D. State Supreme Ct., 1985—; mem. N.D. Ho. of Reps., 1965-66, N.D. Senate, 1967-70. Mem. ABA, Am. Judicature Soc., N.D. Bar Assn. Judicial administration. Office: ND Supreme Ct State Capitol Bismarck ND 58505 *

MESERVE, RICHARD ANDREW, lawyer; b. Medford, Mass., Nov. 20, 1944; s. Robert William and Gladys Evangeline (Swenson) M.; m. Martha Ann Richards, Sept. 20, 1966; children: Amy, Lauren. BA, Tufts U., 1966; JD, Harvard U., 1975; PhD in Applied Physics, Stanford U., 1976. Bar: Mass. 1975, D.C. 1981, U.S. Supreme Ct. 1982. Law clk. Mass. Supreme Jud. Ct., Boston, 1975-76; law clk. to presiding justice U.S. Supreme Ct., Washington, 1976-77; legal counsel Pres. Sci. Adviser, Washington, 1977-81; ptnr. Covington & Burling, Washington, 1981—; mem. Nat. Acad. Scis. panel on nat. security controls on tech. transfer, Washington, 1985-87. Mem. Am. Physical Soc. Democrat. Avocations: tennis, sailing, hiking. Environment, Administrative and regulatory, Federal civil litigation. Home: 708 Berry St Falls Church VA 22042 Office: Covington & Burling 1201 Pennsylvania Ave NW PO Box 7566 Washington DC 20044

MESERVE, ROBERT WILLIAM, lawyer; b. Chelsea, Mass., Jan. 12, 1909; s. George Harris and Florence Elizabeth (Small) M.; m. Gladys E. Swenson, Oct. 17, 1936; children—Roberta Ann (Mrs. Gordon Weil), William George, Richard Andrew, John Eric, Jeanne-Marthe. A.B., Tufts Coll., 1931; LL.B., Harvard, 1934; LL.D., Villanova U., 1972, Drury Coll., 1972, Suffolk U., 1972, St. Michael's Coll., 1972, Wm. Mitchell Law Sch., 1977, Tufts U., 1979, Vt. Law Sch., 1984. Bar: Mass. bar 1934. Asst. U.S. atty. Boston, 1936-41, 83-85; lectr. Boston Coll. Law Sch., 1938-40, Harvard Law Sch., 1957-61; assoc., then partner firm Nutter, McClennen & Fish, Boston, 1934-36, 41-43, 46-73; ptnr. firm Newman & Meserve, 1973-78; ptnr. Palmer & Dodge, 1978-83, of counsel, 1986—; Mem. Mass. Bd. Bar Examiners, 1961-71, sec., 1964-71; chmn. Mass. Bd. Bar Overseers, 1974-77; Mem. sch. com., Medford, Mass., 1936-40, chmn., 1940. Editor: Harvard Law Rev, 1933-34. Mem. bd. aldermen, Medford, 1941-43; Trustee Tufts Coll., 1955-79, chmn., 1965-70, emeritus, 1979—. Served to lt. (s.g.) USNR, 1943-46. Mem. ABA (past chmn. standing com. fed. judiciary, pres. 1972-73), Mass. Bar Assn., Boston Bar Assn. (past pres.), Am. Bar Found. (pres. 1978-80), Am. Acad. Arts and Sci., Am. Coll. Trial Lawyers (regent, pres. 1968-69), Inst. Jud. Adminstrn. (pres. 1980-82), Phi Beta Kappa (pres. assocs. 1983-85). Democrat. Unitarian. Antitrust, Federal civil litigation, Condemnation. Home: 109 Worcester Lane Waltham MA 02154 Office: 1 Beacon St Boston MA 02108

MESIROV, LEON I., lawyer; b. Phila., Jan. 19, 1912; s. Isaac and Zippa (Robbins) M.; m. Sylvia W. Portner, June 25, 1935; children—Joan C. (Mrs. Thomas Rondell), Judy Lynn (Mrs. Hans B. Greenberg), Jill P. A.B., U. Pa., 1931, LL.B., 1934. Bar: Pa. 1934, U.S. Dist. Ct. (ea. dist.) Pa. 1934, U.S. Ct. Appeals (3d and Fed. cirs.) 1948, U.S. Ct. Internat. Trade 1948. Since practiced in Phila.; partner firm Mesirov, Gelman, Jaffe, Cramer & Jamieson, 1960—. Commr. Phila. Civil Service, 1952-70; pres. Jewish Community Relations Council, 1952-55, hon. pres., 1955—; commr. Phila. Fellowship Commn., 1952—, counsel, 1959—; sec. Jewish Y's and Centers, 1967-71; Trustee Fedn. Jewish Agencies, 1960-71, Com. of Seventy, 1972—. Mem. ABA, Pa., Phila. bar assns., Am. Judicature Soc., Order of Coif, Beta Sigma Rho. Jewish. Clubs: Racquet (Phila.), Peale (Phila.). General corporate, Labor, Real property. Home: 2131 St James Pl Philadelphia PA 19103 Office: Mesirov Gelman Jaffe Cramer & Jamieson Fidelity Bldg 15th Floor Philadelphia PA 19109

MESKILL, THOMAS J., judge; b. New Britain, Conn., Jan. 30, 1928; s. Thomas J. M.; m. Mary T. Grady; children—Maureen Meskill Heneghan, John, Peter, Eileen, Thomas. B.S., Trinity Coll., Hartford, Conn., 1950, LL.D., 1972; J.D., U. Conn., 1956; postgrad., Sch. Law, NYU; LL.D., U. Bridgeport, 1971, U. New Haven, 1974. Bar: Conn., Fla, Fed. bars, U.S. Supreme Ct. Former mem. firm Meskill, Dorsey, Sledzik and Walsh, New Britain; mem. 90th-91st Congresses 6th Conn. Dist.; gov. Conn. 1971-75; judge U.S. Circuit Ct., 1975—. Pres. New Britain Council Social Agys.; Asst. corp. council City of New Britain, 1960-62, mayor, 1962-64, corp. counsel, 1965-67; mem. Constl. Conv., Hartford, 1965. Served to 1st lt. USAF, 1950-53. Recipient Distinguished Service award Jr. C. of C., 1964, Jud. Achievement award Assn. Trial Lawyers Am., 1983. Mem. Conn., Hartford County, Fla., New Britain bar assns., New Britain Jr. C. of C. (pres.). Republican. Clubs: K.C, Elks. Jurisprudence.

MESSER, HOWARD FRANCIS, lawyer; b. Pitts., Feb. 23, 1945; s. Howard and Eva Louise (Baumgartel) M.; m. Linda Louise Schurr, Mar. 12, 1977; children—Matthew Howard, Valerie Ann. B.A., U. Pitts., 1968, J.D., 1971. Bar: Pa. 1971, U.S. Dist. Ct. (we. dist.) Pa. 1971, U.S. Ct. Appeals (3d cir.) 1971, U.S. Supreme Ct. 1979. Assoc. Sikov & Love, Pitts., 1971-74, Messer & Shilobod, Pitts., 1974-80; ptnr. Stassberger, McKenna, Messer, Shilobod & Crenney, 1980-86, Messer, Shilbod & Crenney, 1986—; adj. prof. law, 1986—, U. Pitts. Sch. Law. Fellow Acad. Trial Lawyers Allegheny County; mem. Pa. Bar Assn., ABA, Assn. Trial Lawyers of Am., Pa. Trial Lawyers Assn. (gov. 1983—), Western Pa. Trial Lawyers Assn. (pres. 1987—), Allegheny County Bar Assn. (council civil litigation sect.). Democrat. Presbyterian. Personal injury, Federal civil litigation, State civil litigation. Home: 115 Black Oak Dr Pittsburgh PA 15220 Office: Messer Shilobod & Crenney One Gateway Ctr 12th Floor Pittsburgh PA 15222

MESSINA, JOSEPH F., JR., lawyer, educator; b. Phila., May 8, 1954; s. Joseph F. Sr. and Gemma (Santonastasi) M. BS in Acctg., St. Joseph's U., Phila., 1976; JD, Duquesne U., 1979; LLM in Taxation, Temple U., 1980. Bar: Pa. 1979, U.S. Dist. Ct. (ea. dist.) Pa. 1979, U.S. Supreme Ct 1983, D.C. 1985. Assoc. Pincus, Verlin, Hahn & Reich, Phila., 1979—; asst. prof. Rutgers U., Camden, N.J., 1980—. Mem. Duquesne Law Alumni Assmn. (treas. Phila. chpt.). Roman Catholic. Avocation: coin collecting. Real property, Personal income taxation, Estate taxation. Office: Pincus Verlin Hahn & Reich PC 1710 Spruce St Philadelphia PA 19103

MESSING, ARNOLD PHILIP, lawyer; b. N.Y.C., Sept. 2, 1941; s. Louis Messing and Ruth Aaron; m. Esther S. Buchman, Oct. 1, 1967; 1 child, Noah. BA magna cum laude, NYU, 1962; JD, Yale U., 1965. Bar: N.Y. 1966, Mass. 1976, Pa. 1985, U.S. Dist. Ct. (so. and ea. dists.) N.Y., U.S. Dist. Ct. Mass. 1976, U.S. Ct. Internat. Trade 1977, U.S. Ct. Appeals (1st, 2d and D.C. cirs.), U.S. Supreme Ct. 1977, U.S. Tax Ct. 1984. Assoc. Cravath, Swaine & Moore, N.Y.C., 1967-76; ptnr. Csaplar & Bok, Boston, 1976—. Served to sgt. USAFR, 1965-71. Mem. ABA, Assn. of Bar of City of N.Y., Boston Bar Assn., Mass. Bar Assn., Internat. Bar Assn. Republican. Jewish. Clubs: Federal (Boston); Reform (London). Federal civil litigation, State civil litigation, Antitrust. Home: 271 Mill St Newtonville MA 02160 Office: Csaplar & Bok One Winthrop Sq Boston MA 02110

MESSING, HAROLD, lawyer, theatrical producer, educator; b. N.Y.C., May 4, 1935; s. Paul and Mary (Bromberg) M.; m. Marcia Yoffe, Feb. 18, 1984. B.A., NYU, 1956, J.D., 1966; M.A., Stanford U., 1958. Bar: N.Y. 1966, U.S. Supreme Ct. 1970, U.S. Ct. Appeals (2d cir.) 1972, U.S. Dist. Ct. (so. and ea. dists.) N.Y. 1974, Calif. 1977, Fla. 1977. Atty., asst. gen. counsel Embassy Pictures, N.Y.C., 1967-68; assoc. law firm Katz, Moselle & Schier, N.Y.C., 1968-69, Greenbaum, Wolff & Ernst, N.Y.C., 1969-70; ptnr. law firm Bomser & Messing, N.Y.C., 1970-72; sole practice law, N.Y.C., 1972-74; ptnr. law firm Kosmas & Messing, N.Y.C., 1974-76; sole practice law, N.Y.C., 1976—; mem. faculty New Sch., 1974—; lectr. Am. Film Inst., Washington, 1979—; producer: Herringbone, 1982. Contbg. author: Your Legal Rights, 1970. Mem. N.Y. State Bar Assn., ABA, League of Off Broadway Theatres and Producers, Dirs. Guild Am. Club: Friars. Entertainment, Trademark and copyright, Libel. Home: 33 Cavalry Rd Westport CT 06880 Office: Harold Messing 10 Columbus Circle New York NY 10019

MESSING, HOWARD ROBERT, law educator; b. N.Y.C., Apr. 2, 1943; s. Lewis George and Selma (Jarmel) M.; m. Jean Ann Ryan, Dec. 3, 1977. AB, Syracuse U., 1963, JD, 1973. Bar: Fla. 1973, U.S. Supreme Ct. 1976, U.S. Ct. Appeals (11th cir.) 1981, N.Y. 1982. Commr. consumer affairs City of Syracuse, N.Y., 1973-74; asst. pub. defender State of Fla., Ft. Lauderdale, 1974-76, asst. state atty., 1976-80; assoc. prof. law Nova Law Ctr., Ft. Lauderdale, 1980—; fed. master U.S. Dist. Ct., Miami, Fla., 1982—. Co-author: Pretrial Practice in Fla., 1985; contbr. articles to profl. jours. Served with USAF, 1965-66. Mem. ABA (criminal justice, prison and jails com. 1985—), Fla. Bar Assn. (chmn. grivance com. 1984, ethics com. 1983—, grantee 1982), Nat. Inst. of Correction (cons. 1982—, grantee 1984). Avocations: running, tennis, reading. Criminal, Legal education, Jurisprudence. Office: Nova Law Ctr 3100 SW 9th Ave Fort Lauderdale FL 33315

MESSINGER, J. HENRY, lawyer; b. N.Y.C., Sept. 7, 1944; s. Benjamin and Edna (Balser) M.; m. Karen Gilbert D'Abo, Feb. 5, 1977 (div.); 1 son, Alan Toby. B.A., Union Coll., 1965; J.D., NYU, 1968, M.A., 1969. Bar: N.Y. 1968, N.Mex. 1973, U.S. Tax Ct. 1973. Sole practice, Woodstock, N.Y., 1970-72; assoc. Stephen Natelson, Esq., Taos, 1972-73; ptnr. Natelson & Messinger, Taos, 1974-75; sole practice, Taos, 1976—. Bd. dirs. Taos Sch. Music, 1982—; bd. dirs. Taos Valley Sch., 1979-82, pres. 1980-81. Mem. ABA (agrl. com. of tax sect.; com. tax legis. of real propery probate and trust sect.). Personal income taxation, Estate planning. Office: PO Box 2596 Taos NM 87571

MESSINGER, SHELDON L(EOPOLD), law educator; b. Chgo., Aug. 26, 1925; s. Leopold J. and Cornelia (Eichel) M.; m. Mildred Handler, June 30, 1947; children—Adam J., Eli B. Ph.D. in Sociology, UCLA, 1969. Asso. research sociologist Center Study Law and Soc., U. Calif. at Berkeley, 1961-69, research sociologist, 1969-70, vice chmn., 1961-69, prof. criminology, 1970-77, acting dean criminology, 1970-71, dean criminology, 1971-75, prof. law jurisprudence and social policy program, 1977—, chmn. program, 1983-87. Author, co-author numerous books, articles. Legal education, Criminal, Legal history. Home: 860 Indian Rock Ave Berkeley CA 94707

MESSMER, KIRK DANIEL, lawyer; b. Saginaw, Mich., May 31, 1957; s. Ernest Dan and JoAnn (Fredrick) M. BA in Math., Mich. State U., 1979; JD, U. Mich., 1982. Bar: Mich. 1982, U.S. Dist. Ct. (we. dist.) Mich. 1982, U.S. Ct. Appeals (6th cir.) 1982, U.S. Dist. Ct. (ea. dist.) Mich. 1983. Assoc. Miller, Canfield, Paddock & Stone, Lansing, Mich., 1982—. Mem. ACLU (exec. bd. Lansing chpt. 1985-86). Election law, Environment, Federal civil litigation. Office: Miller Canfield Paddock & Stone 1 Michigan Ave Suite 900 Lansing MI 48933

MESTEL, MARK DAVID, lawyer; b. Bklyn., May 15, 1951; s. Oscar L. and Katherine (Waldner) M.; m. Linda Antonik, Jan. 6, 1984; 1 child, Brenton V. BA, Northwestern U., 1973; JD, U. Mich., 1976. Bar: Mich. 1976, D.C. 1977, Wash. 1978, U.S. Dist. Ct. (we. dist.) Wash. 1979, U.S. Ct. Appeals (9th cir.) 1984, U.S. Dist. Ct. (ea. dist.) Wash. 1986. Atty., EPA, Washington, 1976-77; sole practice, Washington, 1977-78, Everett, 1981-84; staff atty. Snohomish County Pub. Defender, Everett, Wash., 1978-80, dir., atty., 1980-81; ptnr. Mestel & Muenster, Everett, 1984—. Cert. criminal trial specialist Nat. Bd. Trial Advocacy, 1982, 86. Mem. Assn. Trial Lawyers Am., Nat. Assn. Criminal Def. Lawyers, Wash. Trial Lawyers Assn. Criminal. Office: Mestel & Muenster 1613 Smith Tower Seattle WA 98104 Office: 3221 Oakes Ave Everett WA 98201

METCALF, WILLIAM EVANS, lawyer, consultant; b. Phila., Jan. 20, 1944; s. William Evans and Evelyn (Bowen) M.; m. Kathryn Amayo, Sept. 12, 1970; 1 son, William. B.A., Park Coll., 1967; postgrad. U. Iowa, 1967-68; J.D., Washburn U., 1977. Bar: Kans. 1977, U.S. Dist. Ct. Kans. 1977, U.S. Ct. Appeals (10th cir.) 1978, U.S. Supreme Ct. 1980, U.S. Ct. Claims, 1985. Dir. community orgn. and planning Eckan, Inc., Ottawa, Kans., 1969-70; exec. dir. Nekcap Inc., Horton, Kans., 1970-74; asst. to mayor of Topeka, 1974-77; asst. atty. gen. Kans., 1977-78; project dir. Legal Services of S.E. Kans., Pittsburg, 1978-82; dep. dir. Kans. Legal Service, Topeka, 1982-84; ptnr. Metcalf and Justus, Topeka, 1984—. Mem. Kans. Health Planning Council, 1973-75; chmn. State Health Plan Devel. Commn., 1974; mem. N.E. Kans. Health Planning Council, 1972-74. Recipient Service to Mankind award Centro de Servicios para Hispanos, 1981; Community Service award Nek-Cap Inc., 1975, S.C.C.A.A., 1976; medal City of Topeka, 1971. Mem. ABA, Kans. Bar Assn., Kans. Community Action Dirs. Assn. (chmn. 1972-74). Democrat. Public international, Immigration, naturalization, and customs, General practice. Office: 801 Western St Topeka KS 66606

METCALFE, JAMES ASHFORD, lawyer; b. Washington, Nov. 8, 1940; s. Edward Conrad and Agnes Malcolm (Ashford) M.; m. Claire Elizabeth Madison, Dec. 23, 1963; children: Luta Marguerite, James Madison. BS, U.S. Naval Acad., 1963; JD, Coll. William and Mary, 1975. Bar: Va. 1975, U.S. Dist. Ct. (ea. dist.) Va. 1975, U.S. Ct. Appeals (4th cir.) 1975, U.S. Ct. Claims 1979, U.S. Supreme Ct. 1979, U.S. Ct. Appeals (5th cir.) 1983. Commd. ensign USN, 1963; advanced through grades to capt. USNR, 1986; resigned USN, 1972; law clk. to presiding justice U.S. Dist. Ct. (ea. dist.) Va., Norfolk, 1975-76; assoc. Seawell, McCoy et al, Norfolk, 1976-80; asst. U.S. atty. Dept. Justice, Norfolk, 1980—. Mng. editor William and Mary

Law Rev., Williamsburg, Va., 1974-75. Bd. dirs. Thalia Civic League, Virginia Beach, Va., 1973-78, Friends Sch., Virginia Beach, 1977-86. Commd. lt. USNR, 1972, advanced to capt. 1986. Mem. Fed. Bar Assn., U.S. Naval Inst., Aircraft Owners and Pilots Assn., Norfolk-Portsmouth Bar Assn. Episcopalian. Club: YMCA. Criminal, Federal civil litigation, Admiralty. Office: US Atty Walter E Hoffman US Courthouse 600 Granby St Suite 401 Norfolk VA 23510

METCALFE, ROBERT DAVIS, III, lawyer; b. Bridgeport, Conn., July 2, 1956; s. Robert Davis Jr. and Barbara Ann (Peaslee) M. BA summa cum laude, U. Conn., 1978, JD, 1981; MA, Trinity Coll., 1982. Bar: Conn. 1981, U.S. Supreme Ct. 1986. Judge adv. USN, Norfolk, Va., 1982-85; spl. asst. U.S. atty. U.S. Dept. Justice, Norfolk, 1985; trial atty. U.S. Dept. Justice, Washington, 1985—. Instr. ARC, Hartford, Conn., 1976-80; legis. asst. Conn. Gen. Assembly, Hartford, 1977. Served to lt. USN, 1982-85. Mem. Fed. Bar Assn., Conn. Bar Assn., Judge Adv. Assn., Mensa, Phi Beta Kappa. Republican. Episcopalian. Avocations: martial arts, reading, sailing, trap and skeet shooting, philately. Federal civil litigation, Corporate taxation, Military. Home: 833 S Frederick St Apt 301 Arlington VA 22204 Office: US Dept of Justice Washington DC 20530

METCALFE, WALTER GEOFFREY, lawyer; b. Chgo., Apr. 22, 1940; s. Jerome Walter and Patricia (Landy) M.; m. Nancy Louise Bingaman, May 22, 1964; children: Robert Edward, Jerome Walter. BA, U. S.C., 1969, JD, 1974. Bar: S.C. 1974, U.S. Dist. Ct. S.C. 1974, U.S. Ct. Appeals (4th cir.) 1975, U.S. Tax Ct. 1975, U.S. Ct. Mil. Appeals 1975, U.S. Ct. Claims 1976, U.S. Supreme Ct. 1979. State counsel Lawyers Title Ins. Co., Columbia, S.C., 1974-76; sole practice Cayce, S.C., 1976—. Bd. mem. Brothers & Sisters of Midlands, Columbia, 1982-85; precinct chmn. Lexington County Reps., S.C., 1984. Served to sgt. USMC, 1958-67. Mem. Assn. Trial Lawyers Am., Am. Judicature Soc., Nat. Orgn. Social Security Claimant's Reps. (chmn. S.C. 1981-83), S.C. Trial Lawyers Assn. Baptist. Club: Columbia Area Model Railroad Club. Avocations: jogging, swimming. Family and matrimonial, Personal injury, Workers' compensation. Home: 401 Ravenscroft Rd West Columbia SC 29169 Office: 1524 L Ave PO Box 2082 Cayce SC 29171

METRAILER, ANN MARIE, lawyer; b. Little Rock, June 15, 1950; d. William Joseph and Anna Jane (Fulmer) M.; m. Bernard Joseph Sharkey, Jr., June 11, 1983. B.F.A., Newcomb Coll., Tulane U., 1972; M.P.A., La. State U., 1981, J.D., 1981. Bar: La. 1981. Claims examiner State of La., Baton Rouge, 1974-76, research statistician, 1976-77; atty. U.C.C.S., Inc., Baton Rouge, 1981-84; in-house counsel Sentry Ins. Co., Baton Rouge, 1984—. Teagle scholar U.S. Dept. Edn. 1968-72; fellow U.S. Dept. Edn. 1977-78. Mem. Baton Rouge Assn. Women Attys. (treas. 1984, pres. 1985), Baton Rouge Bar Assn., La. State Bar Assn., ABA, La. Trial Lawyers Assn., La. Ins. Guaranty Assn. (bd. dirs.), Phi Alpha Delta. Democrat. Insurance. Office: PO Box 80013 2237 S Acadian St Baton Rouge LA 70898

METZ, JEROME JOSEPH, JR., lawyer; b. Cin., Dec. 25, 1950; s. Jerome Joseph Sr. and Loretta Ellen (Donnellon) M.; m. Deborah Carolyn Hundemer, July 2, 1976; children: Andrew Thomas, Matthew Jerome. BA, Xavier U., 1976; JD, U. Cin., 1980. Bar: Ohio 1980, U.S. Dist. Ct. (so. dist.) Ohio 1980, U.S. Ct. Appeals (6th cir.) 1980. Law clk. to judge U.S. Dist. Ct. (so. dist.) Ohio, Cin., 1980-82; assoc. Hartsock, Harris & Schneider, Cin., 1982-83, Porter, Wright, Morris & Arthur, Cin., 1983—; trustee Winton Pl. Devel. Corp., Cin., 1982—. Mem. ABA, Ohio Bar Assn., Cin. Bar Assn. Democrat. Roman Catholic. Federal civil litigation, State civil litigation, Contracts commercial. Office: Porter Wright Morris & Arthur 250 E 5th St 2200 Columbia Plaza Cincinnati OH 45202

METZ, ROBERT ERNEST, lawyer; b. Berkeley, Calif., Nov. 13, 1935; s. Ernest Estel and Margorie Marie (Gallagher) M.; m. Barbro Vera Kullgren, Oct. 3, 1959; children: Elisabeth Barbro Cueto, Annika Marie, Patrick Michael. AB, U. Calif., Berkeley, 1957, LLB, 1963. Bar: Calif. 1963, U.S. Dist. Ct. (no. dist.) Calif. 1964, U.S. Ct. Appeals (9th cir.) 1964. Assoc. Brobeck, Phleger & Harrison, San Francisco, 1963-69, ptnr., 1970—; sec. Andros Analyzers Inc., Berkeley, 1970—, Novacor Med. Corp., Oakland, Calif., 1980—; bd. dirs. Wollongong Group Inc., Palo Alto, Calif. Co-author: Financing California Business, 1976; note and comment editor U. Calif. Law Rev., 1962-63. Served to capt. USAF, 1957-60. Mem. ABA, Calif. Bar Assn., San Francisco Bar Assn., U.S. Council on Intellectual Property, U.S. Council Internat. Bus., Order of Coif. Republican. Club: Olympic (San Francisco). Avocations: cooking, fishing, skiing, swimming. General corporate, Securities, Intellectual property. Office: Brobeck Phleger & Harrison Spear St Tower One Market Plaza San Francisco CA 94105

METZGER, ALAN GLEN, lawyer; b. Amarillo, Tex., June 1, 1954; s. Carl Glen and Shirley Beth (Noble) M.; m. Emily B. Drexler, June 5, 1976; children: Alan Glenn, Carl Glen. BS, U. Kans., 1976, JD, 1979. Asst. dist. atty. Sedgwick County Dist. Atty.'s Office, Wichita, Kans., 1979; ptnr. Robbins, Tinker, Smith & Metzger, Wichita, 1979—. Co-chairperson Sedgwick County Dems. for John Glenn, Wichita, 1983-84. Mem. ABA, Kans. Bar Assn., Wichita Bar Assn., Wichita Young Lawyers Assn. (tres. 1982-83, pres. 1986-87), Am. Judicature Soc., Kans. Assn. Def. Counsel, Psi Kappa Psi. Democrat. Avocations: golf, running, reading, gunsmithing. Federal civil litigation, State civil litigation, Insurance. Home: 7211 Suncrest Wichita KS 67212 Office: Robbins Tinker Smith & Metzger 111 W Douglas Wichita KS 67202

METZGER, JEFFREY PAUL, lawyer; b. St. Louis, Oct. 13, 1950; s. John E. and Ellen M. Metzger; m. Stephanie Ann Stahr, Dec. 27, 1977. B.A. magna cum laude, Amherst Coll., 1973; J.D., Georgetown U., 1976. Bar admittee: D.C., 1977. Legis. asst. to U.S. Senator Joseph Biden, Jr. of Del., 1973; assoc. Collier, Shannon, Rill and Scott, Washington, 1976-79, Cole and Groner, P.C., Washington, 1979-82; trial atty. comml. litigation br. civil div. U.S. Dept. Justice, Washington, 1982-85; mem. profl. staff Pres.'s Blue Ribbon Commn. on Def. Mgmt., 1985-86; asst. gen. counsel Unisys Corp., McLean, Va., 1986—. Mem. ABA. Federal civil litigation, Public international, Government contracts and claims.

METZGER, JOHN MACKAY, lawyer; b. Princeton, N.J., Mar. 8, 1948; s. Bruce Manning and Isobel Elizabeth (Mackay) M. BA cum laude, Harvard U., 1970; JD, NYU, 1973; postgrad., London Sch. Econs., 1973-74. Bar: Pa. 1976, N.J. 1976, U.S. Dist. Ct. N.J. 1976, U.S. Tax Ct. 1977, D.C. 1978, U.S. Ct. Appeals (fed. cir.) 1982. Tax counselor N.J. Div. Taxation, Trenton, 1976-86; atty. McCarthy & Schatzman P.A., Princeton, 1986—. Contbr. articles to profl. jours. Mem. ABA, Mercer County Bar Assn., Princeton Bar Assn., Am. Soc. Internat. Law. Republican. Episcopalian. Club: Harvard (Phila.). State and local taxation, General corporate, General practice. Home: 112 Mandon Ct Princeton NJ 08540 Office: McCarthy & Schatzman PA 228 Alexander St Princeton NJ 08540

METZGER, KAREN SUSAN, judge, educator; b. Denver, Sept. 13, 1945; d. John William and Betty Berniece (Amen) M.; m. Roger Lee Keithley, Apr. 1, 1973; children—Livingston, Christopher, Katharyn Keithley. Student U. Santa Clara, 1963-64; B.A., Colo. Coll., 1967; J.D., U. Denver, 1970; LL.M., Harvard U., 1973. Bar: Colo. 1970, U.S. dist. ct. Colo. 1971, U.S. Ct. Appeals (10th cir.) 1971. Dep. state pub. defender, Denver, 1970-71; grad. teaching fellow Harvard U. Law Sch., 1971-73; assoc. prof. law U. Utah, 1973-74; practice law, Denver, 1973-77; judge county ct., Denver, 1977-79; judge Dist. Ct., Denver, 1979-83, Ct. Appeals, 1983—; lectr. law U. Colo. Grad. Sch. Nursing, 1975—; mem. community corrections bd., 1979—. Trustee Marycrest High Sch., Denver, 1982—. U. Denver Coll. Law Merit scholar, 1967-70. Mem. ABA, Colo. Bar Assn. (gov. 1979-81, council family law sect. 1980-84), Denver Bar Assn. (exec. bd. young lawyers sect. 1980-82, trustee 1985—), Colo. Women's Bar Assn., Denver Catholic Lawyers Guild (pres. 1980-81), Sigma Alpha Iota. Democrat. Roman Catholic. Family and matrimonial, Criminal, General practice. Address: 5239 E 17th Ave Denver CO 80220

METZGER, ROBERT STREICHER, lawyer; b. St. Louis, Sept. 27, 1950; s. Robert Stanley and Jean Harriet (Streicher) M.; m. Stephanie Joy Morgan, Nov. 16, 1980; children: Michael, Kristen. BA, Middlebury Coll., 1974; JD, Georgetown U., 1977. Bar: Calif. 1978, D.C. 1978. Legis. aide U.S. Rep. Robert F. Drinan, Washington, 1972-73; legis. asst. U.S. Rep. Michael J. Harrington, Washington, 1973-75; research fellow Ctr. for Sci. and Internat. Affairs Harvard U., Cambridge, Mass., 1977-78; assoc. Latham & Watkins, Los Angeles, 1978-84, ptnr., 1984—; cons. Congl. Research Service, Washington, 1977-78. Contbr. articles to profl. jours. Mem. ABA (pub. contracts sect.), Internat. Inst. for Strategic Studies. Government contracts and claims, Computer. Office: Latham & Watkins 555 S Flower St Los Angeles CA 90071

MEYER, ANDREW C., JR., lawyer; b. N.Y.C., June 28, 1949; s. Andrew and Myra Meyer; m. Kathleen A. Sullivan, May 7, 1982; children—Joshua Andrew, Daniel Gregory. B.S., C.W. Post Coll., 1971; J.D., Suffolk U., 1974. Bar: Mass. 1974, U.S. Dist. Ct. Mass. 1974, U.S. Ct. Appeals (1st cir.) 1974. Ptnr. Lubin & Meyer, P.C., Boston, 1974—. Contbr. articles to law jours. Mem. Mass. Bar Assn. (chmn. trial practice com. 1983-84, award 1984, seminar speaker, 21st Century Club award 1984, Continuing Legal Edn. Faculty award 1984), Mass. Acad. Trial Attys., Boston Bar Assn. Federal civil litigation, State civil litigation, Personal injury. Office: Lubin & Meyer PC 141 Tremont St Boston MA 02111

MEYER, BERNARD STERN, judge; b. Balt., June 7, 1916; s. Benjamin and Josephine Meyer; m. Elaine Strass, June 25, 1939; children—Patricia, Susan; m. Edythe Birnbaum, Apr. 18, 1975. B.S., Johns Hopkins U., 1936; LL.B., U. Md., 1938; LL.D., Hofstra U., 1980, Western State U. Coll. Law, 1982, Union U., 1984. Bar: Md. 1938, D.C., N.Y. 1947. Practiced in Balt., 1938-41; sole practice N.Y.C., 1948-58; with Office Gen. Counsel Treasury Dept., Washington, 1941-43; justice N.Y. State Supreme Ct., 1958-72; mem. Meyer, English & Cianciulli, P.C., Mineola, N.Y., 1975-79; counsel Fink, Weinberger, Fredman & Charney, P.C., N.Y.C., 1973-79; assoc. judge N.Y. Ct. Appeals, Albany, 1979-86; spl. dep. atty. gen. N.Y. State in charge spl. Attica investigation, 1975; mem. Meyer, Suozzi, English & Klein P.C., Mineola, N.Y., 1987—; assoc. counsel, spl. counsel Moreland Commn. to Study Workmen's Compensation Adminstrn. and Costs, 1955-57. Contbr. articles to profl. jours. Founder United Fund L.I.; former mem. adv. bd. Commn. Law and Social Action, Am. Jewish Congress; bd. dirs. Health and Welfare Council Nassau County, Nassau-Suffolk region NCCJ, Nassau County council Boy Scouts Am., Nat. Ctr. for State Cts. Served to lt. USNR, World War II. Recipient Disting. Service award L.I. Press. Mem. Am. Law Inst., ABA, N.Y. Bar Assn. (chmn. jud. sect.), Assn. Bar City of N.Y. (chmn. matrimonial law com.), Nassau County Bar Assn. (disting. service medallion 1982), Nat. Conf. Trial Judges (exec. com., past chmn.), Nat. Coll. State Judiciary (bd. dirs.), Assn. Supreme Ct. Justices (past pres. com. chmn.), Nassau County Lawyers Assn. (recipient award), Scribes, Order of Coif, Omicron Delta Kappa. State civil litigation, Family and matrimonial, Real property. Office: Meyer Suozzi English & Klein PC 1505 Kellum Pl Mineola NY 11501

MEYER, CATHY LYNN, lawyer; b. Springfield, Ill., Oct. 29, 1957; d. William Harold and Sandra Joan (Unsell) Meyer. BA, Sangamon State U., 1979; JD, St. Louis U., 1982. Bar: Tex. 1982. Assoc. firm George Chandler & Assoc., Baytown, Tex., 1982; asst. city atty. City of Abilene, Tex., 1983-84, City of Irving, Tex., 1984—. Mem. ABA, Tex. Bar Assn., Dallas Bar Assn., Tex. Young Lawyers Assn. State and local taxation. Office: City of Irving 825 W Irving Blvd Irving TX 75060

MEYER, CHARLES MULVIHILL, lawyer; b. Cin., Dec. 31, 1951; s. Charles Louis and Camilla Kathryn (Mulvihill) M.; m. Jacqueline L. Conner, July 5, 1975; children: Philip, Katherine, Evan. AB in English, Boston Coll., 1974, JD, 1977. Bar: Mass. 1977, Ohio 1978, Fla. 1978, U.S. Dist. Ct. (so. dist.) Ohio 1978. Law clk. City of Boston Law Dept., 1976-77; assoc. Curhan & Curhan, Boston, 1977-78, Waite, Schneider, Bayless & Chesley, Cin., 1978-81, Santen, Shaffer & Hughes, Cin., 1981—; instr. Great Oaks Vocat. Schs., Cin., 1983-86, Cin. Tech. Coll., Cin., 1984-85; legal advisor St. James Day Care Ctr., Cin., 1985-86. Sec. Cin. Opera Guild, 1983-85. Mem. ABA, Ohio Bar Assn., Cin. Bar Assn. Roman Catholic. Club: Boston Coll. of Cin. (pres. 1979-80). Avocation: long distance running. Contracts commercial, Bankruptcy, Real property. Office: Santen Shaffer & Hughes 105 E 4th St Cincinnati OH 45202

MEYER, CHRISTOPHER HAWKINS, lawyer, educator; b. Springfield, Mo., Sept. 29, 1952; s. Richard DeWitt and Nancy (Hawkins) M.; m. Karen Anne Adams, Aug. 8, 1987. Student, New Coll., 1971-72; BA in Econs. magna cum laude, U. Mich., 1977, JD cum laude, 1981. Bar: D.C. 1981, U.S. Dist. Ct. D.C. 1982, U.S. Ct. Appeals (D.C. cir.) 1982, U.S. Ct. Appeals (9th cir.) 1983, Colo. 1985, U.S. Dist. Ct. Colo. 1985, U.S. Ct. Appeals (10th cir.) 1985. Counsel water resources program Nat. Wildlife Fedn., Washington, 1981-84; assoc. prof. adjoint, counsel Rocky Mountain Natural Resources Clinic Nat. Wildlife Fedn., Boulder, Colo., 1984—. Contbr. articles to profl. publs. Mem. ABA (water resources com.), Phi Beta Kappa. Democrat. Roman Catholic. Avocations: backpacking, squash, acting, spelunking. Environment, Administrative and regulatory, Legal education. Home: 850 Twentieth St #702 Boulder CO 80302 Office: Nat Wildlife Fedn Campus Box 401 Fleming Law Bldg Boulder CO 80309

MEYER, DONALD ROBERT, banker, lawyer; b. Phoenix, June 4, 1942; s. Donald Duncan and Eleanor M.; m. Virginia Whitesel, Sept. 3, 1966; 2 children. AB, U. Calif., Berkeley, 1964, JD, 1967; postgrad. Harvard U. Sch. Bus. Adminstrn., 1968. Bar: Calif. 1972. Lectr. Seoul Nat. Univ., Korea, 1969-70; assoc. Graham & James, San Francisco, 1971-76; asst. sec. Calif. First Bank, San Francisco, 1973—, v.p., 1976-78, gen. counsel, 1976—, sr. v.p., 1978—. Contbr.: Intro to the Law & Legal System of Korea, 1983. Mem. World Affairs Council, San Francisco, Sierra Club; co-chmn. San Francisco/Seoul Sister City Com.; mem. Asian Art Commn. of San Francisco, 1985—. Recipient Key to Seoul, Korea, 1984. Mem. Am. Bankers Assn. (v.p. Calif. State 1982-83), Calif. Bankers Assn. (chmn. legal affairs com. 1982-84), Korean-Am. C. of C. (San Francisco sec., bd. dirs. 1974—), Soc. Calif. Pioneers. Republican. Episcopalian. Club: University. Banking, General corporate, Private international. Office: California First Bank 350 California St San Francisco CA 94104-1476

MEYER, DOUGLAS ALEXANDER, judge; b. Chattanooga, Nov. 30, 1932; s. Frank Marion and Katherine (Alexander) M.; m. Ximena Del Carmen Tagle, Sept. 1, 1962 (div. Dec. 1966); 1 child, Alexander Manuel; m. Linda Carolyn Burkhart, Jan. 24, 1969; 1 child, William Robinson. BA, U. Chattanooga, 1954; JD, U. Tenn., 1956. Bar: Tenn. 1957, U.S. Dist. Ct. (ea. dist.) Tenn. 1957, U.S. Ct. Appeals (6th cir.) 1957. Sole practice Chattanooga, 1957-61, 65-77; asst. dist. atty. gen. State of Tenn., Chattanooga, 1961-65; asst. atty. Hamilton County, Tenn., 1965-66; city ct. judge 1st div. 11th Jud. Dist., Chattanooga, 1977-82; criminal ct. judge 1st div. City of Chattanooga, 1982—. Democrat. Episcopalian. Avocations: golf, running, geneology, local history. Home: 1062 Carter Dr Chattanooga TN 37415 Office: Criminal Ct div 1 Hamilton County Justice Bldg Chattanooga TN 37415

MEYER, DOUGLAS OLIVER, banker, lawyer; b. Port Clinton, Ohio, Apr. 8, 1939; s. Leslie Evan and Ada Marie (Schrock) M.; m. Janith Adele Ellithorpe, June 28, 1969; children: Adrienne Renee, Tracey Leigh. BA, U. Mich., 1961, JD, 1964. Bar: Ohio 1964, U.S. Dist. Ct. (no. dist.) 1965, U.S. Ct. Appeals (6th cir.) 1972. Law dir. City of Port Clinton, Ohio, 1965-74; pros. atty. Ottawa County, Port Clinton, 1985—; sec., treas., trustee George F. Lonz Found., Put-in-Bay, Ohio, 1976. Mem. Ohio Bar Assn., Ottawa County Bar Assn. (pres. 1966), Ohio Community Theatre Assn. (pres. 1978). Republican. Lutheran. Club: Port Clinton Yacht (commodore 1984). Lodges: Rotary (pres. 1978), Masons. Avocation: theatre. General practice, Criminal, Insurance. Home: 1150 Lee Ave Port Clinton OH 43452 Office: Meyer & Kocher 101 1/2 Madison Port Clinton OH 43452

MEYER, GEORGE HERBERT, lawyer; b. Detroit, Feb. 19, 1928; s. Herbert M. and Agnes F. (Eaton) M.; m. Carol Ann Jones, June 28, 1958 (div. 1981); children: Karen Ann, George Herbert Jr. A.B., U. Mich., 1949; J.D., Harvard U., 1952; cert., Oxford (Eng.) U., 1955; LL.M. in Taxation, Wayne State U., 1962. Bar: D.C. bar 1952, Mich. bar 1953. Asso. firm Fischer, Franklin & Ford, Detroit, 1956-63; mem. firm Fischer, Franklin & Ford, 1963-74; established firm George H. Meyer, 1974-78; sr. mem. firm Meyer and Kirk, 1978-85; sr. ptnr. Meyer, Kirk, Snyder & Safford, Bloomfield Hills and Detroit, Mich., 1985—. Author: Equalization in Michigan and Its Effect on Local Assessments, 1963, Folk Artists Biographical Index, 1986. Chmn. Birmingham (Mich.) Bd. Housing Appeals, 1964-68; vice chmn. Birmingham Bd. Zoning Appeals, 1966-69; mem. Birmingham Planning Bd., 1968-70; trustee Bloomfield Village, Mich., 1976-80, pres., 1979-80; mem. exec. bd. Detroit Area council Boy Scouts Am., 1976—, asst. counsel, 1979-85, counsel, 1986—; chmn. Detroit area council Eagle Scout Recognition Dinner Com., 1978; mem. nat. adv. bd. Mus. Am. Folk Art, N.Y.C., 1985—; trustee Detroit Sci. Ctr., 1985—. Served as 1st lt. JAG USAF, 1952-55; maj. Res. ret. Recipient William Jennings Bryant prize in polit. sci. U. Mich., 1949. Mem. Am., Detroit, Oakland County bar assns., State Bar Mich., Harvard Law Sch. Assn. Mich. (dir. 1959—, pres. 1970-78), Detroit Sci. Mus. Soc. (pres. 1961-74, chmn. 1974—), Phi Beta Kappa, Alpha Phi Omega. Republican. Unitarian. Clubs: Masons, Rotary, Detroit Boat, Prismatic, Scarab, Harvard of N.Y.C., Detroit. General corporate, Corporate taxation, Trademark and copyright. Home: 1228 Sandringham Way Birmingham MI 48010 Office: 100 W Long Lake Rd Suite 100 Bloomfield Hills MI 48013

MEYER, HENRY THEODORE, III, lawyer; b. N.Y.C., Oct. 5, 1951; s. Henry Theodore Jr. and Joan Inez (Mussmann) M.; m. Barbara Susan Ball, Jan. 10, 1981. BA, Syracuse U., 1973; JD, Columbia U., 1976. Bar: N.Y. 1977. Assoc. Brauner, Baron, Rosenzweig, Kligler, Sparber & Bauman, N.Y.C., 1977-81, Parker, Duryee, Zunino, Malone & Carter, N.Y.C., 1981-84, Ruffa & Hanover P.C., N.Y.C., 1984—. Mem. ABA, N.Y. County Lawyers Assn., Phi Beta Kappa, Phi Kappa Phi, Phi Alpha Theta. Republican. Lutheran. General corporate, Securities, Contracts commercial. Office: Ruffa & Hanover PC 90 Park Ave New York NY 10016

MEYER, IRWIN STEPHAN, lawyer, accountant; b. Monticello, N.Y., Nov. 14, 1941; s. Ralph and Janice (Cohen) M.; m. Leslie J. Mazor, July 10, 1977; children—Kimberly B., Joshua A. B.S., Rider Coll., 1963; J.D., Cornell U., 1966. Bar: N.Y. 1966. Tax mgr. Lybrand Ross Bros. & Montgomery, N.Y.C., 1966-71; mem. firm Ehrenkranz, Ehrenkranz & Schultz, N.Y.C., 1971-74; prin. Irwin S. Meyer, 1974-77, 82—; mem. firm Levine, Honig, Eisenberg & Meyer, 1977-78, Eisenberg, Honig & Meyer, 1978-81, Eisenberg, Honig, Meyer & Fogler, 1981-82. Served with U.S. Army, 1966-71. C.P.A., N.J. Mem. ABA, N.Y. Bar Assn., Am. Assn. Atty.-C.P.A.s, N.Y. Assn. Atty.-C.P.A.s, Am. Inst. C.P.A.s, N.J. Soc. C.P.A.s. Personal income taxation, Estate taxation, Corporate taxation. Home: 19 Woodhaven Dr New City NY 10956 also: One Blue Hill Plaza Pearl River NY 10965

MEYER, JOSEPH B., state attorney general; b. Casper, Wyo., 1941; m. Mary Meyer; children: Vincent, Warren. Student, Colo. Sch. Mines; BA, U. Wyo., 1964, JD, 1967; postgrad., Northwestern U., 1968. Dep. county atty. Fremont County, Wyo., 1967-69; ptnr. Smith and Meyer, 1968-71; asst. dir. legis. service office State of Wyo., Cheyenne, 1971-87, atty. gen., 1987—; conductor numerous govt. studies on state codes including Wyo. probate, criminal, state adminstrn., banking, domestic relations, game and fish, state instn., employment security, worker's compensation, motor vehicle, others; conductor legis. rev. of adminstrv. rules; negotiator with Office of Surface Mining for Wyo. state preemption; instr. Wyo. Coll. Law, fall 1986; lectr. Rocky Mountain Mineral Law Found., 1977. Bd. dirs. Cheyenne Jr. League, 1982-85, Jessup PTO, 1980-81; instr. Boy Scouts Am. Congregationalist. Club: Cheyenne Country. Lodge: Rotary. Avocations: golf, tennis, gardening, wood carving, rock hunting. Office: Attorney Generals Office 123 Capitol Building Cheyenne WY 82002

MEYER, LAWRENCE GEORGE, lawyer; b. East Grand Rapids, Mich., Oct. 2, 1940; s. George and Evangeline (Boerma) M.; children from previous marriage—David Lawrence, Jenifer Lynne; m. 2d, Linda Elizabeth Buck, May 31, 1980; children—Elizabeth Tilden, Travis Henley. B.A. with honor, Mich. State U., 1961; J.D. with distinction, U. Mich., 1964. Bar: Wis., Ill. 1965, U.S. Supreme Ct. 1968, D.C. 1972. Assoc., Whyte, Hirschboeck, Minahan, Hardin & Harland, Milw., 1964-66; atty. antitrust div. U.S. Dept. Justice, 1966-68; legal counsel U.S. Senator Robert P. Griffin from Mich., 1968-70; dir. policy planning FTC, 1970-72; ptnr. Patton, Boggs & Blow, Washington, 1972-85, Arent, Fox, Kintner, Plotkin & Kahn, Washington, 1985—. Recipient Disting. Service Award, FTC, 1972. Mem. ABA, D.C. Bar Assn. Clubs: U.S. Senate Ex S.O.B.'s City Tavern, Congl. Country, Pisces (Washington); The Bayhill (Orlando). Contbr. articles on antitrust and trial practice to law jours.; asst. editor. U. Mich. Law Rev., 1960-61. Antitrust, Federal civil litigation, Administrative and regulatory. Home: 11832 Beekman Pl Potomac MD 20854 Office: 1050 Connecticut Ave Washington DC 20036

MEYER, LEE GORDON, attorney, fuel company executive; b. Washington, Oct. 22, 1943; s. Edmond Gerald and Betty (Knobloch) M.; m. Lynn Nix, Mar. 14, 1980; children—Veronica, Victoria, David. B.S. in Chemistry, U. Wyo., 1966, M.B.A., 1969, J.D. (hon.), 1973. Bar: Wyo. 1973, Tex. 1973, Ohio 1981, Ky. 1982, Colo. 1985, U.S. Patent Office, U.S. Supreme Ct. Patent atty. Texaco Corp., Austin, Tex., 1974-77; chief patent and trademark counsel Alcan Aluminum Co., Cleve., 1977-79; gen. counsel Donn, Inc., Cleve., 1979-81; asst. gen. counsel Diamond Shamrock Co., Lexington, Ky., 1981-83; v.p. fin. and adminstrn. Fort Union Coal Co., Denver, 1983-84; pres., chief exec. officer Carbon Fuels Corp., Denver, 1984—. Patentee in field. Mem. ABA, Am. Mgmt. Assn., Am. Chem. Soc., Licensing Exec. Soc., Ops. Research Soc., Denver C. of C. Republican. Patent, Licensing, General corporate. Home: 10487 E Ida Ave Englewood CO 80111 Office: Carbon Fuels Corp 5105 DTC Pkwy #317 Englewood CO 80111

MEYER, LEONARD JAMES, lawyer; b. Lockhart, Tex., Feb. 7, 1954; s. Erwin Henry and Martha Deleslyn (Wilburn) M.; m. Rose Ann Milheim, Nov. 14, 1981. BBA in Acctg., Southwest Tex. State U., 1978; JD, U. Houston, 1981. Bar: Tex. 1981, U.S. Dist. Ct. (so. dist.) Tex. 1982, U.S. Ct. Appeals (5th cir.) 1983, U.S. Dist. Ct. (ea. dist.) 1984, U.S. Dist. Ct. (no. dist.) 1984. Investigator Juarez & Scanio, San Marcos, Tex., 1976-78; mem. T. Cullen Davis Def. Team Pvt. Investigators, Houston, 1978-79; pvt. investigator Bri-Lab Def. Team, Houston, 1980; practice pvt. investigation Houston, 1978-81; prin. mem. Sellers & Berg, P.C., Houston, 1981—. Mem. ABA, Houston Bar Assn., Houston Young Lawyers Assn. Republican. Presbyterian. Avocations: reading, jogging, aerobics. State civil litigation, Construction, Consumer commercial. Office: Sellers & Berg PC 4120 SW Freeway Suite 111 Houston TX 77027-5790

MEYER, LOUIS B., state supreme court justice; b. Marion, N.C., July 15, 1933; s. Louis B. and Beulah (Smith) M.; m. Evelyn Spradlin, Dec. 29, 1956; children: Louis B., Patricia Shannon, Adam Burden. B.A., Wake Forest U., 1955, J.D., 1960. Bar: N.C. 1960, U.S. Dist. Ct. (ea. dist.) N.C. 1960, U.S. Ct. Appeals (4th cir.) 1960, U.S. Supreme Ct. 1962. Law clk. Supreme Ct. N.C., Raleigh, 1960; spl. agent FBI, 1961-62; atty. Lucas, Rand, Rose, Meyer, Jones & Orcutt P.A., Wilson, N.C., 1962-81; assoc. justice Supreme St. N.C., Raleigh, 1981—. Former county chmn. N.C. Democratic Com.; former mem. N.C. State Exec. Com. Dem. Party. Served to 1st lt. U.S. Army, 1955-57. Mem. Wilson County Bar Assn. (former pres.), Wake County Bar Assn., 7th Jud. Dist. Bar Assn. (former pres.), N.C. Bar Assn. (former v.p.). Baptist. Lodge: Masons. Jurisprudence. Office: North Carolina Supreme Ct PO Box 1841 Raleigh NC 27602

MEYER, LYNN NIX, lawyer; b. Vinita, Okla., Aug. 10, 1948; d. William Armour and Joan Ross Nix; m. Lee Gordon Meyer; children: Veronica, Victoria, David. BA, Baldwin Wallace Coll., 1978; JD, Case Western Res. U., 1981. Bar: Ky., Colo. Paralegal Texaco Devel., Austin, Tex., 1976-77; legal asst. Alcan Aluminum, Cleve., 1977-79; assoc. Wyatt, Tarrant & Combs, Lexington, Ky., 1982-83; ptnr. Meyer Legal Advisors, Denver, 1984—; bd. dirs. Carbon Fuels Corp. Denver, Craig Technologies Internat., Ltd., Denver. Mem. ABA, Am. Trial Lawyers Assn., Colo. Bar Assn., Ky. Bar Assn., Arapahoe County Bar Assn., Denver C. of C. Republican. General corporate, Trademark and copyright. Home: 10487 E Ida Ave Englewood CO 80111 Office: 5105 DTC Pkwy# 317 Englewood CO 80111

MEYER, MARTIN ARTHUR, lawyer; b. Saratoga Springs, N.Y., Mar. 17, 1934; s. Edward and Ann Rita (Mintzer) M.; m. Lynn Greenberg, Apr. 16, 1961; 1 child, Steven. B.A., Union Coll., Schenectady, N.Y., 1955; LL.B., Columbia U., 1958. Bar: N.Y. 1959, U.S. Dist. Ct. (no. dist.) N.Y. 1959, U.S. Tax Ct. 1966, U.S. Ct. Apls. (2d cir.) 1978. Assoc., McPhillips,

Fitzgerald & McCarthy, Glens Falls, N.Y., 1958-60; ptnr. McPhillips, Fitzgerald & Meyer, Glen Falls, 1961-70, McPhillips, Fitzgerald, Meyer & McLenithan, Glens Falls, 1971—; atty. City of Glens Falls, 1970-74. Bd. govs. Glens Falls Hosp., 1976—; mem. Glens Falls Civic Ctr. Commn., 1977-79; bd. edn. City of Glens Falls, 1984—; past pres., bd. trustees Congregation Shaaray Tefila, Glens Falls, 1961-81; pres. Glens Falls Area Council Chs.; committeeman N.Y. State Democratic Party, 1969-70. Mem. ABA, N.Y. State Bar Assn. (trial lawyers sect. mem. exec. com. 1986—), Warren County Bar Assn. (pres. 1974-75), Union Coll. Alumni Assn. Lodge: Bnai Brith State civil litigation, Personal injury, Probate. Home: 22 Roosevelt Ave Glens Falls NY 12801 Office: McPhillips Fitzgerald Meyer & McLenithan 288 Glen St PO Box 309 Glens Falls NY 12801

MEYER, MARTIN JAY, lawyer; b. Wilkes-Barre, Pa., Aug. 1, 1932; s. Max and Rose (Wruble) M.; m. Joan Rosenthal, Aug. 24, 1954; children—Leah, Gary. B.A., Wilkes Coll., 1954; postgrad. U. Miami, 1956-57; LL.B., Temple U., 1959. Bar: Pa. 1960, U.S. Dist. Ct. (mid. dist.) Pa. 1961, U.S. Ct. Appeals (3d cir.) 1966, U.S. Supreme Ct., 1978. Assoc., Mack, Kasper & Meyer, Wilkes-Barre, 1961-66; assoc. Mack & Meyer, Wilkes-Barre, 1966-68, ptnr., 1968-80; ptnr. Meyer & Swatkoski, Kingston, Pa., 1980—, sr. ptnr., 1980—. mem. disciplinary hearing bd. Pa. Supreme Ct.; Co-author weekly article You Be the Jury, Times Leader. Chmn., Muscular Dystrophy Assn., 1960; co-chmn. March of Dimes, 1962; trustee Temple Israel Wilkes-Barre; bd. dirs. Jewish Home Scranton, Family Service Assn. Served with U.S. Army, 1955-56. Mem. ABA, Assn. Trial Lawyers Am., Am. Arbitration Assn., Pa. Bar Assn. (co-chmn. adoption com. family law sect.), County Bar Officers Assn., Pa. Trial Lawyers Assn., Luzerne County Bar Assn. (pres. 1984, 85), DAV. Republican. Lodges: Elks (trustee), Masons (32 deg.), B'nai B'rith (pres. 1967). Federal civil litigation, Family and matrimonial, Workers' compensation. Home: 178 Joseph Dr Kingston PA 18704 Office: 401 3d Ave Kingston PA 18704

MEYER, MICHAEL ALAN, lawyer; b. Lebanon, Pa., Mar. 14, 1954; s. Simon J. and Dolores P. (Griscavage) M.; m. Martha Jo Cox, Apr. 30, 1983. BA, Wake Forest U., 1976; JD, Samford U., 1980. Bar: Ala. 1980, Tenn. 1981, U.S. Dist. Ct. (mid. dist.) Tenn. 1985. Atty. commerce and ins. State of Tenn. Dept. Commerce, Nashville, 1980-85; ptnr. Burn & Meyer, Nashville, 1985—. Mem. ABA, Tenn. Bar Assn., Nashville Bar Assn., Assn. Trial Lawyers Am., Federalist Soc. Law and Pub. Policy Studies. Republican. Roman Catholic. Securities, General corporate, Federal civil litigation. Home: 516 Saddle Dr Nashville TN 37221 Office: Burn & Meyer 172 2d Ave N Suite 202 Nashville TN 37201

MEYER, MICHAEL BROEKER, lawyer, consultant; b. Boston, July 12, 1946; s. Edward Carl and Marjory (Morse) M.; m. Barbara Rachel Beatty, June 23, 1977; children—Douglas Beatty, Lucy Beatty. B.A., Harvard U., 1967; J.D. cum laude, Boston Coll., 1973. Bar: Mass. 1973, U.S. Dist. Ct. Mass. 1974, U.S. Ct. Appeals (1st cir.) 1978, U.S. Ct. Appeals (D.C. cir.) 1978, U.S. Supreme Ct. 1978. Law clk. to chief justice Mass. Superior Ct., Boston, 1973-74; staff atty. Mass. Defenders Com., New Bedford, 1974-75; asst. atty. gen. Mass. Atty. Gen., Boston, 1975-79; cons., prin. Analysis & Inference, Inc., Boston, 1979-86; ptnr. Meyer, Connolly & Armstrong, Boston, 1986—. Editor-in-chief Environ. Affairs Law Rev., 1972-73. Contbr. articles to profl. jours. Served to capt. USMC, 1967-70. Decorated Bronze Star. Mem. ABA, AAAS, Soc. Risk Analysis, Mass. Bar Assn., N.Y. Acad. Scis., Boston Bar Assn., Order of Coif. Public utilities, Administrative and regulatory, Nuclear power. Home: 33 Beverly Rd Newton Highlands MA 02161 Office: Meyer Connolly & Armstrong 10 Post Office Sq Suite 955 Boston MA 02109

MEYER, PAUL JOSEPH, lawyer; b. Oak Park, Ill., Nov. 27, 1942; s. Paul Gilbert and Frances Marie (O'Shea) M.; m. Rosemary Anton, June 4, 1966. B.A. summa cum laude, St. Mary's Coll., 1964; J.D. cum laude, U. Notre Dame, 1967. Bar: Ill. 1967, Ariz. 1970, U.S. Tax Ct. 1975, U.S. Supreme Ct. 1980. Law clk. Ill. Supreme Ct., 1967-68; sr. law clk. to Chief Justice Earl Warren U.S. Supreme Ct., Washington, 1968-69; assoc. Snell & Wilmer, Phoenix, 1969-71; mem. Meyer, Hendricks, Victor, Osborn & Maledon, Phoenix, 1971—. Trustee, Ariz. Heart Inst. Found.; bd. dirs. St. Mary's Coll., Winona, Minn. Ill. State scholar, 1960; Weymouth Kirkland scholar, 1964; William J. Brennan Law scholar, 1964. Mem. Am. Law Inst., ABA, Ariz. Bar Assn., Maricopa County Bar Assn., Notre Dame Law Assn. (bd. dirs.). Club: Phoenix Country, Arizona (Phoenix). General corporate, Contracts commercial, Corporate taxation. Home: 3301 N Manor Dr Phoenix AZ 85014 Office: 2700 N 3d St Suite 4000 Phoenix AZ 85004

MEYER, PAUL RICHARD, lawyer; b. St. Louis, Apr. 12, 1925; s. Abraham Paul and Adele (Rosenfeld) M.; m. Alice Turtledove., Mar. 16, 1958; David Paul, Sarah Elizabeth, Andrea Ruth. BA, Columbia U., 1949; JD, Yale U., 1952. Bar: Oreg. 1953, Calif. 1953, N.Y. 1953, U.S. Dist.Ct. Oreg. 1953, U.S. Dist. Ct. (no. dist.) Calif. 1953, U.S. Ct. Appeals (9th cir.) 1953, U.S. Supreme Ct. 1958, U.S. Ct. Claims 1958, U.S. Tax Ct. 1958, U.S. Ct. Appeals (fed. cir.) 1958. Assoc. law sch. U. Calif., Berkeley, 1952-53; assoc. King, Miller et al, Portland, Oreg., 1953-60; ptnr. Kobin & Meyer, Portland, 1960-85, Meyer, Seifer & Stewart, P.C., Portland, 1985-86; sole practice Portland, 1986—. Mem. exec. com. ACLU, N.Y.C., 1971—. Served with U.S. Army, 1943-46, ETO. Decorated Purple Heart. Home: 602 NW Skyline Crest Portland OR 97229 Office: 900 SW 5th Ave Suite 1900 Portland OR 97204

MEYER, PHILIP GILBERT, lawyer; b. Louisville, June 26, 1945; s. Henry Gilbert and Adele (Gutermuth) M.; m. Jackie Darlene Watson, Jan. 30, 1971 (div. Apr. 1976); m. Sylvia Saunders, Oct. 9, 1976. B.B.A., U. Mich., 1967; J.D., U. Tex. 1970. Bar: Tex. 1970, Mich. 1971, U.S. Tax Ct. 1972, U.S. Dist. Ct. (ea. dist.) Mich. 1971, U.S. Ct. Appeals (6th cir.) 1972, U.S. Dist. Ct. (no. dist.) Ohio 1976. Clk., Wayne County Cir. Ct., Detroit, 1970-72; atty. Leonard C. Jaques, Detroit, 1972; assoc. Christy & Robbins, Dearborn, Mich., 1972-73; ptnr. Foster, Meadows & Ballard, Detroit, 1973-79; of counsel Christy, Rogers & Gantz, Dearborn, 1979-81, Rogers & Gantz, Dearborn, 1981-86, prin. Philip G. Meyer and Assocs., 1986—; adj. prof. U. Detroit Sch. Law, 1979. Mem. ABA (com. vice chmn. rules and procedure 1982—), Maritime Law Assn. U.S., Mich. Bar Assn. (vice chmn. admiralty sect. 1978), Tex. Bar Assn., Detroit Bar Assn. Republican. Club: Propeller-Port of Detroit (pres. 1984-85).). Personal injury, General practice, Admiralty. Home: 5905 Independence Ln West Bloomfield MI 48033 Office: 5767 W Maple Rd Suite 100 West Bloomfield MI 48033

MEYER, SCOTT JOHN, lawyer; b. Chgo., Sept. 16, 1927; s. Edward Alfred and Gertrude (Kohn) M.; m. Eunice Margaret Helmreich, July 23, 1955; children—William, Richard. Student Stevens Inst. Tech., 1945-46; B.S., Purdue U., 1952; M.B.A., Ind. U., 1953; J.D., Northwestern U., 1961. Bar: Ohio 1963, Ill. 1963, U.S. Dist. Ct. (no. dist.) Ill. 1963, U.S. Ct. Appeals (fed. cir.) 1982, U.S. Supreme Ct. 1969. Chemist, statistician, pricing engr. Dow Chem. Co., Midland, Mich., 1953-58; patent atty. Procter & Gamble Co., Cin., 1961-65, Baxter-Travenol Labs, Deerfield, Ill., 1965-75, Monsanto Co., St. Louis, 1975—. Author: Biography of W.C. Kohn, 1983. Chmn. Midland County Young Republican Club, 1956. Served to sgt. USMC and USN, 1945-49. Recipient Commendation award Concordia Hist. Inst., St. Louis, 1984. Mem. Am. Chem. Soc., AAAS, Chgo. Patent Law Assn., Ill. State Bar Assn., Am. Patent Law Assn. Lutheran. Patent. Office: Monsanto Co 800 N Lindbergh Blvd Saint Louis MO 63167

MEYER, SIDNEY L., lawyer; b. Bronx, Apr. 18, 1948; s. Curt and Florence (Zeremba) M.; m. Marian Wood, Jan. 18, 1976; 1 child, Michael. AB magna cum laude, Southampton Coll., 1971; JD, Bklyn. U., 1978. Bar: N.Y. 1978, U.S. Dist. Ct. (so. and ea. dists.) N.Y. 1981. Labor counsel Korvettes, N.Y.C., 1978-80, v.p. adminstrn., 1980-82; gen. counsel Local 810, N.Y.C., 1982—; trustee Local 888, N.Y.C., 1978-82, Local 21, Newark, 1979-82. Mem. ABA, N.Y. State Bar Assn., Bklyn. Bar Assn., N.Y. County Bar Assn. Democrat. Jewish. Avocation: travel. Labor, Pension, profit-sharing, and employee benefits. Home: 169 Bergen St Brooklyn NY 11217 Office: Local 810 10 E 15th St New York NY 11217

MEYER, STANLEY RUSSELL, lawyer; b. Alton, Ill., Mar. 16, 1945; s. Stanley E. and Julia M. (Stutz) M.; m. Carloyn M. Keane, Oct. 24, 1970; Amy. M. BA, So. Ill. U., 1972, JD, 1976. Bar: Ill. 1976, U.S. Dist. Ct. (so. dist.) Ill. 1977. Assoc. Wiseman Law Firm, Alton, 1976-78; sole practice Alton, 1978-79; ptnr. Wyss, Meyer & Stillwell, Alton, 1979-81, Stalker & Meyer, Alton, 1986—; bd. dirs. Veterans Outreach Investment Counseling Ednl. Services, Edwardsville, Ill. Served with U.S. Army, 1965-67. Mem. ABA, Madison County Bar Assn., Alton-Wood River Bar Assn. Democrat. Roman Catholic. Avocations: boating, classic car restoration. Personal injury, Family and matrimonial, Criminal. Home: 450 Bluff Alton IL 62002 Office: #4 Front St Alton IL 62002

MEYER, STEPHEN LEONARD, lawyer; b. Bristol, Pa., June 1, 1948; s. Harland Leonard and Lucille Leona (Sedler) M.; m. Jeanne Marie Bell, Aug. 21, 1971; children: Thomas, Richard. BA, Fordham U., 1970; JD, Vanderbilt U., 1973. Bar: Tenn. 1973. Staff atty. Legis. Council, Nashville, 1973-74; gen. counsel Tenn. Housing Devel. Agcy., Nashville, 1974-80; project dir. Am. Retirement Corp., Nashville, 1981-84; asst. gen. counsel Health Group, Nashville, 1984; spl. counsel Am. Gen. Corp., Nashville, 1985—. Mem. exec. com. Davidson County Dems., Nashville, 1980—, facilities bd. Met. Health and Edn., Nashville, 1983—, Met. Bd. Zoning Appeals, Nashville, 1980-81. Mem. ABA, Nashville Bar Assn. Roman Catholic. Lodge: KC. Real property, Local government, Municipal bonds. Home: 1112 Draughon Ave Nashville TN 37204

MEYER, WILLIAM DALE, lawyer; b. Waterloo, Iowa, July 21, 1948; s. George Derold and Gladys Charlene (Van Horsen) M.; m. Jane Ann Jackson, Dec. 2, 1967; children: Mikka Sue, G. Christian. BS, Iowa State U., 1970; JD magna cum laude, U. Mich., 1973. Bar: Mo. 1973, Colo. 1975, U.S. Dist. Ct. Colo. 1975, U.S. Ct. Appeals (10th cir.) 1975. Law clk. to presiding justice U.S. Dist. Ct. (we. dist.), Kansas City, 1973-75; ptnr. Hutchinson, Black, Hill & Cook, Boulder, Colo., 1975—. Note and comment editor U. Mich. Law Rev., 1972. Mem. ABA, Colo. Bar Assn., Boulder County Bar Assn., Assn. Trial Lawyers Am. Avocations: licensed river guide, sailing, youth coaching. Federal civil litigation, State civil litigation, Personal injury. Home: 1830 Elder Boulder CO 80302 Office: Hutchinson Black Hill & Cook PO Box 1170 Boulder CO 80306

MEYER, WILLIAM GEORGE, III, lawyer; b. N.Y.C., Aug. 29, 1954; s. William George and Joan Patricia (McClaury) M.; m. Lisa Louise Carlson; children: Ryan William, Rayna Joan. BA, Gonzaga U., 1975, MBA, 1979, JD magna cum laude, 1979. Bar: Hawaii 1979, U.S. Dist. Ct. Hawaii 1979. Assoc. Carlsmith & Dwyer, Honolulu, 1979-84; counsel Dwyer, Imanaka, Neeley & Peterson, Honolulu, 1984—; v.p., gen. counsel Capri Resorts, Inc., Portland, Oreg., 1985-87; pres. Meyer Corp., Stateline, Nev., 1985—. Mem. ABA (constrn. law and corp., bus., and banking sects.), Assn. Trial Lawyers Am., Hawaii Bar Assn. (young lawyer sect.), Phi Delta Phi (magistrate 1978-79). Construction, General corporate, Real property. Home: 688 Milokai St Kailua HI 96734 Office: Dwyer Imanaka Neeley & Peterson 900 Fort St Mall Suite 1800 Honolulu HI 96813

MEYER, WILLIAM LORNE, lawyer; b. Long Beach, Calif., Oct. 25, 1946; s. Harris Embury and Dorothy (Dinning) M.; m. Virginia Bell, Sept. 7, 1974; children: William Dinning, Lauren Elizabeth. BA, Vanderbilt U., 1968; JD, Emory U., 1975. Bar: Ga. 1975. Assoc. Smith, Gambrell & Russell and predecessor firm, Atlanta, 1975-82, ptnr., 1982—. Served to lt. USNR, 1968-72. Mem. Nat. Assn. Bond Lawyers, Nat. Health Lawyers Assn., ABA, State Bar Ga., Atlanta Bar Assn., Atlanta C. of C., Order of Coif. Democrat. Securities, General corporate, Municipal bonds. Home: 4050 Keswick Dr Atlanta GA 30339 Office: Smith Gambrell & Russell 2400 First Atlanta Tower Atlanta GA 30383

MEYERS, ANTHONY JAMES, lawyer, legal educator; b. Seattle, July 7, 1950; s. Henry Joseph and Catherine Luella (McGeough) M. B.A. in Philosophy and Polit. Sci. magna cum laude, Seattle U., 1972; M.A. in Polit. Sci., Boston Coll., 1973; J.D., U. Wash., 1976. Bar: Wash. 1977, U.S. Dist. Ct. Wash. 1977, U.S. Ct. Appeals (9th cir.) 1979, U.S. Supreme Ct. 1981. Grad. research asst. Boston Coll.; law clk. presiding justice Superior Ct., King County, Seattle, 1978; assoc. Joseph S. Kane, Seattle, 1977-78; ptnr. Kane & Meyers, Seattle, 1978-81, pres. Kane & Meyers, Inc., P.S., Seattle, 1981—; legal instr. City U. of Seattle; judge pro tem King County Superior Ct., Seattle. Mem. ABA, Seattle-King County Bar Assn., Wash. State Trial Lawyers Assn., Am. Trial Lawyers Assn., Nat. Assn. Criminal Def. Attys., Am. Soc. Internat. Law, Nat. Assn. Criminal Def. Lawyers, Phi Alpha Delta, Alpha Sigma Nu. Roman Catholic. Criminal, Personal injury, Public international. Home: 5113-1st Ave NE Seattle WA 98105 Office: Kane & Meyers Inc PS 607 3d Ave 306 Lyon Bldg Seattle WA 98104

MEYERS, ARTHUR S., JR., lawyer; b. Detroit, Aug. 30, 1956; m. Mary L. Bilovus, Sept. 11, 1981. BA, U. Mich., 1977, JD, 1981. Bar: Mich. 1981, U.S. Dist. Ct. (ea. dist.) Mich. 1981, Fla. 1983, U.S. Ct. Appeals (6th cir.) 1986. Assoc. Dickinson, Wright, Moon, Van Dusen & Freeman, Detroit, 1981-84, 85—, Akerman, Senterlitt & Eidson, Orlando, Fla., 1984-85. Mem. Mich. Bar Assn. (employee benefits com.), Detroit Bar Assn. Pension, profit-sharing, and employee benefits. Home: 718 Washington Rd Grosse Pointe MI 48230 Office: Dickinson Wright Moon et al 800 1st Nat Bldg Detroit MI 48226

MEYERS, BRUCE FRANCE, lawyer, former military officer; b. Seattle, Aug. 10, 1925; s. Herbert Walter and Bess (France) M.; m. JoAnne Hopf, Mar. 20, 1948; children: Craig F., Bruce F. Jr., Christopher F. BS in Geology, U. Wash., 1948, BA in Law, 1950; JD with honors, George Washington U., 1963; LLM, Yale U., 1980. Bar: Va. 1970, Wash. 1971, U.S. Dist. Ct. (we. dist.) Wash. 1970, U.S. Ct. Appeals (4th and 9th cirs.) 1970, U.S. Supreme Ct. 1974, U.S. Dist. Ct. (ea. dist.) Wash. 1986. Commd. 2d lt. USMC, 1943, advanced through grades to col., 1968; co. comdr. combat 5th Marine Regt., Korea, 1951; co. force reconnaissance co. 5th Marine Regt., Asia, 1957-59; comdr. 3d bn. 2d Marine Regt., Europe, 1965-66; regtl. comdr. 26th Marine Regt., Khe Sahh, Vietnam, 1967-68; ret. 26th Marine Regt., 1970; sole practice Seattle, 1981—; White House aide, Washington, 1961; dep. asst. legis. affairs Office Security Def., Washington, 1961-63; assoc. dean, prof. law U. Puget Sound, Tacoma, 1974-81. Editorial bd. George Washington U. Law Rev., 1962-63. Mem. ABA, Seattle-King County Bar Assn. (chmn. med. legal com. 1983, chmn. aviation sect. 1984), Order of Coif, Phi Delta Phi. Republican. Episcopalian. Club: Yale (Seattle). Avocations: flying, aircraft building. Insurance, Personal injury, Military. Home and Office: 6914 W Mercer Way Mercer Island WA 98040

MEYERS, ERIK JON, lawyer; b. Oak Park, Ill., Sept. 17, 1949; s. Ralph Edwin and Grace Marjorie (Georg) M.; m. Claire McCarthy, June 16, 1973; 1 child, Faith McCarthy. BS of Fgn. Service, Georgetown U., 1971; JD, Fordham U., 1974. Bar: N.Y. 1975, D.C. 1977, Va. 1982. Sole practice Arlington, Va. and Washington, 1975—; dir. devel., sr. staff atty. Environ. Law Inst., Washington, 1982—; cons. Action, Office of Recruitment & Communication, Washington, 1979-80. Editor, co-author: The Facts About Drug Abuse, 1980, The Wetlands of the Chesapeake, 1985; advisor Nat. Wetlands Newsletter, 1983—. Gen. counsel, sr. program officer Drug Abuse Council, Washington, 1974-80; mem. athletic bd. Georgetown U., Washington, 1976—; treas., bd. dirs. Potomac River Sports Found., Washington, 1978—; pres. Pub. Com. Mental Health, Washington, 1980-81; counsel Nat. Assn. for City Drug and Alcohol Coordination, Washington, 1978—; bd. dirs. Urban Preservation Trust, Washington, 1983—. Named to Georgetown U. Athletic Hall of Fame, 1982. Mem. ABA (exempt orgns. com. tax sect.), N.Y. State Bar Assn., Va. Bar Assn., D.C. Bar Assn., Environ. Law Inst. Assocs. Program (bd. dirs. 1982—, editor newsletter 1983—). Democrat. Club: Potomac Boat (Washington) (pres. 1983—). Environment, Corporate taxation, Non-profit exempt organization corporate. Home: 2002 N Lincoln St Arlington VA 22207 Office: Environ Law Inst 1616 P St NW Washington DC 20036

MEYERS, JAMES WILLIAM, judge; b. Natick, Mass., Sept. 16, 1942. B.S.A. with high honors, Bentley Coll., 1964; J.D., Harvard U., 1970. Bar: Mass. Sr. acct. Ernst & Ernst, Boston, 1964-67; trial atty. criminal div. Dept. Justice, Washington, 1970-72; chief appellate sect. Office U.S. Atty., So. Dist. Calif., 1972-76; judge U.S. bankruptcy judge So. Dist. Calif., San Diego, 1976—. Mem. ABA. Bankruptcy. Office: 5th Floor US Courthouse San Diego CA 92189 *

MEYERS, JEFFREY, lawyer; b. Phila., Jan. 11, 1952; s. Louis L. and Rhoda (Crowell) M.; m. Marcia D. Pintzuk, Feb. 9, 1976. BA summa cum laude, Temple U., 1973; JD, NYU, 1976. Bar: Pa. 1976, U.S. Dist. Ct. (ea. dist.) Pa. 1976, Fla. 1978, U.S. Ct. Appeals (3d cir.). Staff atty. Community Legal Services, Phila., 1976-79; assoc. Leonard M. Sagot & Assocs., Phila., 1979-81, Charleston & Fenerty, P.C., Phila., 1981-84; ptnr. Charleston & Meyers, P.C., Phila., 1984—; adj. lectr. law and real estate Temple U. Sch. Bus., Phila., 1984—. Mem. ABA, Phila. Bar Assn. Avocations: scuba diving, alping and cross country skiing, tennis, bird watching. Consumer commercial, Bankruptcy, Federal civil litigation. Home: 3730 Levy Ln Huntingdon Valley PA 19006-3108 Office: Charleston & Meyers PC 8304 Bustleton Ave Philadelphia PA 19152

MEYERS, JERRY IVAN, lawyer; b. McKeesport, Pa., Mar. 26, 1946; s. Eugene J. and Gladys Claire (Rubenstein) M.; m. Judith Drake Aughenbaugh, Feb. 26, 1971; 1 child, Lindsey Drake. BA in Philosophy and Rhetoric, U. Pitts., 1972; JD, U. Miami, 1975. Bar: Pa. 1975, U.S. Dist. Ct. (we. dist.) Pa. 1975. Assoc. Berger & Kapetan, Pitts., 1975-78; ptnr. Berger, Kapetan, Malakoff & Meyers P.C., Pitts., 1978—. Mem. Assn. Trial Lawyers Am., Pa. Trial Lawyers Assn. (med. legal com., bd. govs. western Pa. chpt. 1984-85, treas. 1986—), Acad. Trial Lawyers Allegheny County. Personal injury. Office: Berger Kapetan Malakoff & Meyers PC Law and Fin Bldg 5th Floor Pittsburgh PA 15219

MEYERS, KAREN DIANE, lawyer, educator; b. Cin., July 8, 1950; d. Willard Paul and Camille Jeannette (Schutte) M.; m. William J. Jones, Mar. 27, 1977. BA summa cum laude, Thomas More Coll., 1971; MBA, MEd, Xavier U., 1978; JD, U. Ky., Covington, 1978. Bar: Ohio 1978, Ky. 1978; CLU. Clk. to mgr. Baldwin Co., Cin., 1966-78; instr. bus. Thomas More Coll., Crestview Hill, Ky., 1978—; asst. sec., asst. v.p., sr. counsel The Ohio Life Ins. Co., Hamilton, 1978—. Bd. dirs. ARC, Hamilton, 1978-83, vol. 1978—; bd. dirs. YWCA, Hamilton, 1985—. Gardner Found. fellow, 1968-71, CLU Am. Coll., 1981. Fellow Life Mgmt. Inst. Atlanta; mem. ABA, Cin. Bar Assn., Butler County Bar Assn. Roman Catholic. Avocations: aerobics, jogging, crafts. Insurance, General corporate, Legal education. Home: 7903 Hickory Hill Ln Cincinnati OH 45241 Office: Ohio Life Ins Co 136 N 3d St Hamilton OH 45241

MEYERSON, STANLEY PHILLIP, lawyer; b. Spartanburg, S.C., Apr. 13, 1916; s. Louis A. and Ella Meyerson; m. Marion Legg, Feb. 6, 1941; children—Marianne Martin, Camilla Jurskis, Margot Ellis, Stanley P. A.B., Duke U., 1937, J.D., 1939. Bar: S.C. 1939, N.Y. 1940, Ga. 1945. Assoc. Edward L. Coffey, 1939-41; ptnr. Johnson Hatcher & Meyerson, Atlanta, 1945-55, Hatcher, Meyerson, Oxford & Irvin, Atlanta, 1955-78, Westmoreland, Hall, McGee, Oxford & Meyerson, Atlanta, 1978—; dir., officer various corps. Mem. Am. Coll. Mortgage Attys., Atlanta Estate Planning Council. Served to lt. cmdr. USNR, 1941-45. General corporate, Entertainment, Estate planning.

MEZZULLO, LOUIS ALBERT, lawyer; b. Balt., Sept. 20, 1944; m. Judith Scales, Jan. 2, 1970. BA, U. Md., 1967, MA, 1976; JD, T.C. Williams Law Sch., 1976. Bar: Va. 1976. Sales rep. Humble Oil (name now Exxon), 1970-72; acctg. Marcoin, Inc., 1972-73; pvt. practice bookkeeping, tax preparation 1973-76; assoc. McGuire, Woods & Battle, Richmond, Va., 1976-79; dir. Mezzullo, McCandlish & Framme, Richmond, 1979—. Contbr. articles to profl. jours. Bd. dirs. Richmond Symphony, pres. Southampton Citizens Assn., Richmond, 1986. Served with USAR, 1969-75. Mem. ABA (tax sect.), Va. State Bar (tax sect.), Va. Bar Assn., Estate Planning Council Richmond, Trust Adminstrs. Council. Republican. Roman Catholic. General corporate, Estate planning, Corporate taxation. Home: 3811 Custis Rd Richmond VA 23225 Office: Mezzullo McCandlish & Framme 700 E Main St Suite 804 Richmond VA 23219

MIANO, FREDERICK JOSEPH, lawyer; b. N.Y.C., Apr. 13, 1956; s. Frederick Phillip and Anne Mary (Cribben) M.; m. Nancy Ruth Crowley, May 16, 1981; children: Stephanie Irene, Matthew James. BS, Fairfield U., 1978; JD, Washington U., St. Louis, 1981. Bar: Conn. 1981, U.S. Dist. Ct. Conn. 1982. Assoc. Beebe & O'Neil, Norwich, Conn., 1981-84, Dzialo, Pickett & Allen, Middletown, Conn., 1984—. Dir. profl. sect. United Way, Middletown, 1985. Mem. ABA, Conn. Bar Assn., Conn. Trial Lawyers Assn. Roman Catholic. Avocations: golf, tennis. State civil litigation, Personal injury, General practice. Home: 82 Burr Ave Middletown CT 06457 Office: Dzialo Pickett & Allen PC 55 High St Middletown CT 06457

MICALE, FRANK JUDE, lawyer; b. Pitts., Jan. 10, 1949; s. Frank Jacob and Catherine Anna (Wagner) M. B.A., Duquesne U., 1971, J.D., 1977. Bar: Pa. 1977, U.S. Dist. Ct. (we. dist.) Pa. 1977, U.S. Ct. Appeals (3d cir.) 1978; U.S. Supreme Ct., 1986. Law clk. judge U.S. Ct. Appeals (3d cir.), 1977-78; law clk. to judge U.S. Dist. Ct. (we. dist. Pa.), 1978-79; assoc. Egler & Reinstadtler, Pitts., 1979-80; dep. atty. gen., sr. dep. atty. gen. in charge torts litigation sect. western region Office of Atty. Gen., Commonwealth of Pa., 1980—; Mem. ABA, Pa. Bar Assn., Allegheny County Bar Assn. State civil litigation, Personal injury. Home: 5816 Elmer St Pittsburgh PA 15232 Office: 400 Manor Bldg Pittsburgh PA 15219

MICCI, EUGENE D., lawyer; b. Derby, Conn., Aug. 17, 1945; s. Guerino J. and Elizabeth (Rondini) M.; m. Dianne H. Hanson, July 31, 1971; children—Elizabeth Denise, Christopher Hanson. B.A., Fairfield U., 1967; J.D., Boston U., 1970. Bar: Conn. 1970, N.Y. 1980, U.S. Supreme Ct. 1975. With firm Cohen, Finn and Sylvester, Shelton, Conn., 1971-76; ptnr. Cohen, Sylvester & Micci, Derby, 1976—; dir. Housatonic Bank & Trust Co., Ansonia-Derby Water Co. Trustee Griffin Hosp., 1980—; mayor City of Derby, 1974-76; legis. commr. State of Conn., 1976—. Mem. ABA, Conn. Bar Assn., Lower Naugatuck Valley Bar Assn. Democrat. Roman Catholic. General practice. Office: 315 Main St Derby CT 06418

MICEK, TERRANCE DEAN, lawyer; b. Fremont, Nebr., Oct. 9, 1949; s. Adrian Eli and June Ann (Blaser) M.; m. Helen Kay Connelly, June 10, 1972; children: Timothy Patick, Benjamin Terrance, Allison Marie, Katie Colleen. BS, U. Nebr., 1971, JD, 1973. Bar: Nebr. 1974, U.S. Dist. Ct. Nebr. 1974, D.C. 1984. Assoc. Padley & Dudden P.C., Grant, Nebr., 1973-75; dir. Nebr. Liquor Control Commn., Lincoln, 1975-84; exec. sec. Nat. Conference State Liquor Adminstrn., Lincoln, 1979-84; v.p., counsel U.S. Brewers Assn., Washington, 1984-86; assoc. Buchman, Buchman & O'Brien, Washington, 1986—. Mem. ABA, D.C. Bar Assn., Nebr. Bar Assn. Republican. Roman Catholic. Lodge: Optimists (pres. 1981, Optimist of Yr. southeast dist. 1981). Avocations: youth sports, education. Administrative and regulatory, Legislative, Intoxicating liquors. Home: 10611 Burr Oak Way Burke VA 22015 Office: Buchman Buchman & O'Brien 1275 Pennsylvania Ave NW Washington DC 20006

MICHAEL, JAMES HARRY, JR., judge; b. Charlottesville, Va., Oct. 17, 1918; s. James Harry and Reuben (Shelton) m. Barbara E. Puryear, Dec. 18, 1946; children: Jarrett Michael Stephens, Victoria von der Au. B.S., U. Va., 1940, LL.B., 1942. Bar: Va. bar 1942. Sole practice Charlottesville; ptnr. Michael & Musselman, 1946-54, J.H. Michael, Jr., 1954-59, Michael & Dent, 1959-72, Michael, Dent & Brooks Ltd., 1972-74, Michael & Dent, Ltd., 1974-80; assoc. judge Juvenile and Domestic Relations Ct., Charlottesville, 1954-68; judge U.S. Dist. Ct., Charlottesville, 1980—; mem. Va. Senate, 1968-80; exec. dir. Inst. Pub. Affairs, U. Va., 1952; chmn. Council State Govts., 1975-76, also mem. exec. com.; chmn. So. Legis. Conf., 1974-75. Mem. Charlottesville Sch. Bd., 1951-62; bd. govs. St. Anne-Belfield Sch., 1952-76. Served with USNR, 1942-46; comdr. Res. ret. Wilton Park fellow Wilton Park Conf., Sussex, Eng., 1971. Mem. ABA, Va. Bar Assn. (v.p. 1956-57), Charlottesville-Albemarle Bar Assn. (pres. 1966-67), C. of C., Am. Judicature Soc., Nat. Consumer Fin. Assn., 4th Jud. Conf., Va. Trial Lawyers Assn., Am. Trial Lawyers Assn., Raven Soc., Sigma Nu Phi, Omicron Delta Kappa. Episcopalian (lay reader). Jurisprudence. Office: US Dist Ct 255 W Main St Room 320 Charlottesville VA 22901

MICHAEL, MARK A., lawyer; b. Washington, Jan. 31, 1948; s. James Robert and Eileen (Sheridan) M.; m. Karen Caraniss, May 16, 1981; 1 child, John. BS, Providence Coll., 1969; JD, Duke U., 1975. Bar: N.C. 1975, U.S. Dist. Ct. (ea. and we. dists.) N.C. 1975, U.S. Ct. Appeals (4th cir.), U.S. Supreme Ct. Ptnr. Bishop & Michael, Charlotte, N.C., 1976-77, Mraz,

Michael & Boner, Charlotte, 1980-83, Badger, Johnson, Chapman & Michael, Charlotte, 1984-86; staff atty. Office Pub. Defender, Charlotte, 1977-80; sole practice Charlotte, 1986—; instr. Nat. Inst. for Trial Advocacy, 1978, 82, 86. Co-author (4 vols. index) United States Treaties and Other International Agreements, 1975. Served to 1st lt. U.S. Army, 1972-75. Mem. N.C. Bar Assn., N.C. Acad. Trial Lawyers. Democrat. Roman Catholic. Federal civil litigation, State civil litigation. Office: 312 W Trade St Suite 401 Charlotte NC 28202

MICHAELS, DAVID SETH, lawyer; b. Newark, Oct. 9, 1946; s. Melvin L. and Winifred (Elkes) M.; m. Jill R. Sachs, Sept. 17, 1978; children: Benjamin Isaac, Jeremy Ezra. BA, Amherst Coll., 1968; JD, U. Mich., 1972. Bar: Miss. 1973, Tenn. 1973, N.Y. 1981, U.S. Ct. Appeals (6th cir.) 1974, U.S. Ct. Appeals (2d cir.) 1979, U.S. Ct. Appeals (5th and 11th cirs.) 1981, U.S. Ct. Appeals (9th cir.) 1987, U.S. Supreme Ct. 1979. Counsel Miss. Mental Health Project, Jackson, 1974-77, So. Prisoners' Def. Com., Nashville, 1977-78; assoc. appellate counsel Fed. Defender Services Unit, N.Y.C., 1978-82; sole practice N.Y.C., 1982-87, Spencertown, N.Y., 1987—. Mem. ABA, N.Y. State Bar Assn. (civil rights com.), N.Y. County Lawyers Assn. (civil rights com.), N.Y. County Criminal Bar Assn. Avocation: marathon running. Criminal, Civil rights, Federal civil litigation.

MICHAELS, GARY DAVID, lawyer; b. Pitts., Apr. 27, 1955; s. Edgar Wolfe and Norma Flora (Barker) M.; m. Joan Marie Kelly, June 9, 1984. BA, U. Pa., 1977; JD, George Washington U., 1980. Bar: D.C. 1980, U.S. Dist. Ct. D.C. 1981, U.S. Ct. Appeals (D.C. cir.) 1981, U.S. Ct. Appeals (4th cir.) 1985, U.S. Supreme Ct. 1985. Assoc. Troy, Malin & Pottinger, Washington, 1981-82, Ballard, Spahr, Andrews & Ingersoll, Washington, 1982-84, Krivit & Krivit P.C., Washington, 1984—; bd. dirs. Hinkel-Hofmann Supply Co. Inc., Pitts., 1976—. Mem. The George Washington Law Rev., 1978-80. Vol. legal staff Gary Hart Presdl. Campaign, Washington, 1983, field coordinator, N.H. and Pa., 1984; bd. dirs., v.p. Van Ness South Tenants Assn., Inc., 1986—. Mem. ABA, D.C. Bar Assn. Democrat. Jewish. Administrative and regulatory, Federal civil litigation, Local government. Home: 3003 Van Ness St NW Washington DC 20008 Office: Krivit & Krivit 50 E St SE Washington DC 20003

MICHAELS, GEORGE, lawyer; b. Boston, Sept. 16, 1923; s. Arthur and Ida M.; m. Barbara G., Jan. 26, 1955 (div.); children—Julia S., Faith I. Grad. Coll. Bus. Adminstrn., Boston, 1943, LL.B., 1948. Bar: Mass. 1949, U.S. Dist. Ct. Mass. 1951, U.S. Sup. Ct. 1960. Asst. atty. gen. in charge constrn. litigation, 1955-58; ptnr. Michaels, Adler & Wilcon, Boston, 1965-77; sole practice George Michaels, P.C., Boston, 1977-85; ptnr. Edwards & Angell, 1985—; lectr. Grad. Sch. Design Harvard U., 1975-76; bd. dirs. Voicetek, Inc., N.Am. Plastics Corp., Lease Comm Corp., Computer Telephone Corp. New Eng.; clk. Abt Assos. Inc., ALS Corp., Appex, Inc., Med. Intermet, Inc., Voicetek, Inc., Boston Communications Group, Inc. Rep. candidate for atty. gen. Served with U.S. Army, 1943-45. Recipient award Am. Freedom Train Found., 1976. Mem. ABA, Mass. Bar Assn., Boston Bar Assn. Contbr. articles to publs. Federal civil litigation, State civil litigation, General corporate.

MICHAELS, JANE, lawyer; b. Pitts., Jan. 7, 1947; d. Bernard Irvin and Pauline (Liebling) M.; m. Neil G. Macey, Sept. 24, 1983; 1 child, Todd Michaels. BA, Wellesley Coll., 1968; MAT, Harvard U., 1970; JD, Boston U., 1973. Bar: Colo. 1973, U.S. Dist. Ct. Colo. 1973, U.S. Ct. Appeals (10th cir.0 1973, U.S. Supreme Ct. 1981. Law clk. to presiding judge U.S. Ct. Appeals (10th cir.), Denver, 1973-74; assoc. Holland & Hart, Denver, 1974-80, ptnr., 1980—. Pres. Women's Forum of Colo., Denver, 1984; bd. dirs. Nat. Women;s Forum, Washington, 1984-86. Mem. ABA, Colo. Bar Assn., Women's Bar Assn., Denver Bar Assn. (trustee 1981-84). Federal civil litigation, State civil litigation, Construction. Office: Holland & Hart 555 17th St Suite 2900 Denver CO 80202

MICHAELS, MICHAEL DANIEL, lawyer; b. Los Angeles, Sept. 1, 1954; s. Michael Daniel and Olga Milicent (Petkovich) M. BA magna cum laude, U. So. Calif., 1976; JD, Loyola U., Los Angeles, 1979. Bar: Calif. 1981, U.S. Dist. Ct. (cen. dist.) Calif. 1983, U.S. Ct. Appeals (9th cir.) 1986. Law clk. to presiding judge Calif. Ct. Appeals, Los Angeles, 1981-82; assoc. Law Offices of Ned Good, Pasadena, Calif., 1982-86, Robinson, Robinson, Di-Caro, D'Antony & Phillips, Santa Ana, Calif., 1986—; lectr. on tort litigation UCLA extension, Los Angeles, 1986. Researcher Californians for Brown, Los Angeles, 1978; mem., fundraiser Lawyers with Hart, Los Angeles, 1984; contrbg. mem. Dem. Nat. Com. Mem. ABA, Calif. Bar Assn., Los Angeles Bar Assn., Calif. Trial Lawyers Assn., Phi Beta Kappa, Phi Kappa Phi. Mem. Serbian Orthodox Ch. Club: YMCA (Pasadena). Avocations: distance running, weightlifting, volleyball. Federal civil litigation, State civil litigation, Personal injury. Home: 1621 S Pomona Ave D23 Fullerton CA 92632

MICHAELS, RICHARD EDWARD, lawyer; b. Chgo., June 10, 1952; s. Benjamin and Lillian (Borawski) Mikolajczewski; m. Karen Lynn Belau Michaels, May 17, 1980; children: Jonathan R., Timothy R. BS in Commerce summa cum laude, DePaul U., 1973; JD, Northwestern U., 1977. Bar: Ill. 1977, U.S. Dist. Ct. (no. dist.) Ill. 1977, U.S. Ct. Appeals (7th cir.) 1977; CPA, Ill. Acct. Touche Ross & Co., Chgo., 1973-74; assoc. Schuyler, Roche & Zwirner and predecessor firm Hubachek & Kelly Ltd., Chgo., 1977-83; ptnr. Schuyler, Roche & Zwirner, Chgo., 1983—. Mem. Northwestern U. Law Rev., 1976-77. Mem. mission bd. St. Andrews Luth. Ch., Park Ridge, Ill., 1983—. Mem. ABA, Internat. Bar Assn., Ill. Bar Assn., Chgo. Bar Assn., Beta Gamma Sigma, Pi Gamma Mu, Beta Alpha Psi, Phi Eta Sigma, Delta Epsilon Sigma, DePaul U. Alumni Assn., DePaul U. Boosters, Chgo. Athletic Assn. Lutheran. Clubs: Plaza, Northwestern U. (Chgo.). Avocations: photography, golf, softball. General corporate, Private international, Antitrust. Home: 832 Wilkinson Pkwy Park Ridge IL 60068 Office: Schuyler Roche & Zwirner 3100 Prudential Plaza Chicago IL 60601

MICHAELS, SHELDON, lawyer; b. Bklyn., May 19, 1941; s. Benjamin and Mildred (Kapler) Moscowitz; m. Maxine Stecker, June 14, 1964; children: Ariella Elizabeth, David Aaron. BA, Bklyn. Coll., CUNY, 1964; JD, UCLA, 1967. Bar: N.Y. 1968, U.S. Dist. Ct. (so. dist.) N.Y. 1969, U.S. Ct. Appeals (2d cir.) 1969, Calif. 1984, U.S. Dist. Ct. (no. dist.) Calif. 1984. Atty. FTC, N.Y.C., 1967-70, Western Electric Co., N.Y.C., 1970-84, AT&T Communications Inc., San Francisco, 1984—; arbitrator N.Y.C. Civil Ct., 1977-83; judge pro tem Alameda County Mcpl. Ct., Berkeley, Calif., 1985—. Bd. dirs. Village Greens Residents Assn., Staten Island, N.Y., 1978-79. Mem. Calif. Bar Assn. Democrat. Jewish. Antitrust, Consumer commercial, Public utilities. Home: 2749 Mountaingate Way Oakland CA 94611 Office: AT&T Communications Inc 1000 Broadway Suite 612 Oakland CA 94607

MICHAELSON, BENJAMIN, JR., lawyer; b. Annapolis, Md., May 30, 1936; s. Benjamin and Naomi Madora (Dill) M.; m. Frances Means Blackwell, Apr. 12, 1986; children—Benjamin, Robert Wendell. B.A., U. Va., 1957; J.D., U. Md., 1962. Bar: Md. 1962, U.S. Dist. Ct. Md. 1976. Assoc. Goodman, Bloom & Michaelson, Annapolis, 1962-63; sole practice, Annapolis, 1963-73; sr. ptnr. Michaelson & Christhilf, P.A., Annapolis, 1973-77, Benjamin Michaelson, Jr., P.A., Annapolis, 1977-81, Michaelson & Simmons, P.A., Annapolis, 1982-86, Michaelson & Newell, P.A., 1987—; gen. counsel, dir. Annapolis Fed. Savs. & Loan Assn., 1965—; counsel Anne Arundel County (Md.) Bd. Edn., 1966-76. Served to lt. U.S. Army, 1957-59. Named one of Outstanding Young Men Am., Severna Park chpt. U.S. Jaycees, 1965. Fellow Am. Coll. Mortgage Attys. mem. ABA, Md. Bar Assn. (chmn. real property, planning and zoning sect. council 1982-84, grievance commn. inquiry panel 1976-85, vice-chmn. 1983-85, grievance commn. review bd. 1985—), Anne Arundel County Bar Assn., Delta Theta Phi. Republican. Presbyterian. Clubs: Jaycees (Md. state legal counsel 1964-65, nat. dir. 1965-66); Sailing of Chesapeake (commodore 1982), Annapolis Yacht, Rotary (pres. 1975-76, Paul Harris fellow). Real property, Probate, Banking. Home: 3 Southgate Ave Annapolis MD 21401 Office: 215 Main St PO Box 11 Annapolis MD 21404

MICHAELSON, MELVIN, lawyer; b. N.Y.C., Dec. 28, 1928; s. Benjamin and Celia (Schwartz) M.; m. Judith R. Panush, Jan. 23, 1960; children: Carol, Helen. A.B., NYU, 1950; J.D., Harvard U., 1953. Bar: N.Y. 1955. Ptnr. Kaye, Scholer, Fierman, Hays & Handler, N.Y.C., 1969—. Served to 1st lt. USAF, 1953-55. Mem. ABA, Assn. Bar City N.Y., N.Y. State Bar Assn. Club: Old Westbury Golf and Country (N.Y.). Real property, Landlord-tenant. Home: Sands Point Rd Sands Point NY 11050 Office: Kaye Scholer Fierman Hays & Handler 425 Park Ave New York NY 10022

MICHAELSON, PETER LEE, lawyer; b. N.Y.C., Aug. 29, 1952; s. Henry W. and Pauline (Rosenzweig) M. B.S. in Elec. Engring. and Econs., Carnegie-Mellon U., 1974, M.S. in E.E., 1975; J.D., Duquesne U., 1979; LL.M. in Trade Regulation, NYU, 1985. Bar: Pa. 1979, N.J. 1980, U.S. Patent and Trademark Office 1980, U.S. Dist. Ct. N.J. 1980, U.S. Circuit Ct. Customs and Patent Appeals 1980, U.S. Ct. Claims 1980, U.S. Ct. Mil. Appeals 1980, N.Y. 1986, U.S. Tax Ct. 1980, U.S. Ct. Appeals (3d cir.) 1981, N.Y. 1986. Electronics project engr. Control Systems Research, Inc., Pitts., 1975-76; electronics devel. engr. Aluminum Co. Am., Alcoa Tech. Ctr., Prodn. Equip. Lab., Pitts., 1976-77, Rockwell Internat. Corp., Pitts., 1977-79; corp. patent atty., mem. patent and legal staff Bell Telephone Labs., Holmdel, N.J., 1979-82; patent atty. Pennie & Edmonds, N.Y.C., 1982-84; ptnr., atty. Stanger, Michaelson & Eischlag, Counsellors at Law, Red Bank, N.J., 1984—. Contbr. articles to profl. jours. Mem. Sch. Budget adv. com., Rumson, N.J., 1981—. Mem. ABA, N.J. State Bar Assn., Monmouth County Bar Assn. Patent, Trademark and copyright, Antitrust. Home: 33 Church St Rumson NJ 07760 Office: Stanger Michaelson & Einschlag 208 Maple Ave PO Box 8489 Red Bank NJ 07701

MICHALAK, EDWARD FRANCIS, lawyer; b. Evanston, Ill., Sept. 6, 1937; s. Leo Francis Michalak and Helen Sopie (Wolinski) Krakowski; m. Margaret Mary Minx, Jan. 2, 1978. BSBA, Northwestern U., 1959; LLB, Harvard U., 1962. Bar: Ill. 1962. Assoc. McDermott, Will & Emery, Chgo., 1963-69, ptnr., 1969—. Served to sgt. USAR, 1962-68. Mem. Ill. Bar Assn., Chgo. Bar Assn., Beta Gamma Sigma, Beta Alpha Psi. Roman Catholic. Club: Mid-Day (Chgo.). Avocations: golf, opera. Corporate taxation, Personal income taxation. Home: 3409 Summit Ave Highland Park IL 60035 Office: McDermott Will & Emery 111 W Monroe St Chicago IL 60603

MICHALAK, WILLIAM STEVEN, lawyer, restaurant executive, oil and gas consultant; b. Los Angeles, Oct. 19, 1947; s. William Vincent Michalak and Marcelle (Burns) Reynolds; m. Lizabeth Berner, Aug. 8, 1970; 1 child, Mark William. BA, U. Houston, 1970, JD, 1975. Bar: Tex. 1976, Okla. 1981, U.S. Dist. Ct. (no. dist.) Okla. 1981, U.S. Ct. Appeals (10th cir.) 1981. Staff landman Cities Service Co., Tulsa, 1976-81, lease records mgr. south, southwest and Canada, 1981-82; mgr. contracts and lease records Clayton W. Williams Jr., Tulsa, 1982-84; pres. Eclipse Investment Enterprises, Inc., Tulsa, 1985—; owner Vito's Pizza, Sand Springs, Okla., 1986—, Tulsa, 1987—; cons. oil and gas, Tulsa, 1984—; title atty., 1984—. Del. Rep. County Convention, Tulsa, 1984, Rep. Dist. Convention, 1984, Rep. State Convention, 1984. Mem. ABA, Tex. Bar Assn., Okla. Bar Assn., Am. Assn. Petroleum Landmen, Okla. Assn. Petroleum Landmen (chmn. forms com. 1984-85), Ft. Smith, Ark. Assn. Petroleum Landmen, Okla. Restaurant Assn., Order of Barons, Phi Theta Kappa, Delta Phi Alpha. Lutheran. Club: Summit (Tulsa). Avocations: bowling, tennis, computers, humorous writing. Oil and gas leasing. Home: 6502 S 32d W Ave Tulsa OK 74132-1709 Office: Eclipse Investment Enterprises Inc PO Box 9945 Tulsa OK 74157-0945

MICHALIK, JOHN JAMES, bar association executive; b. Bemidji, Minn., Aug. 1, 1945; s. John and Margaret Helen (Pafko) M.; m. Diane Marie Olson, Dec. 21, 1968; children: Matthew John, Nicole, Shane. BA, U. Minn., 1967, JD, 1970. Legal editor Lawyers Coop. Publishing Co., Rochester, N.Y., 1970-75; dir. continuing legal edn. Wash. State Bar Assn., Seattle, 1975-81, exec. dir., 1981—. Mem. Am. Soc. Assn. Execs., Nat. Assn. Bar Execs., Am. Mgmt. Assn., Am. Judicature Soc. Lutheran. Club: Seattle Coll. Office: Wash State Bar Assn 2001 6th Ave Seattle WA 98121-2599

MICHEAELS, JOHN ALLAN, lawyer; b. Pasadena, Calif., Oct. 19, 1952; s. Gregory John and Jean Marie (Somerindyke) M.; m. Marylou Micheaels, May 26, 1979; children: Jeffrey Charles, Carrie Ann. BA with highest honors, U. Calif., Santa Barbara, 1974; JD, U. Calif., Davis, 1979. Bar: Ariz. 1979, U.S. Dist. Ct. Ariz. 1979, U.S. Ct. Appeals (9th cir.) 1982, U.S. Supreme Ct. 1982. Assoc. Jennings, Strouss & Salmon, Phoenix, Ariz., 1979-83, ptnr., 1983-85; ptnr. Lowe & Berman P.A., Phoenix, 1985—; mem. jud. civil study com. Maricopa County, Phoenix, 1984—. Mem. Ariz. Bar Assn. (chmn. trial practice sect. 1985-86), Ariz. Coll. Trial Adv. (mem. adv. bd. 1986—), Phoenix Assn. Def. Council, Def. Research Inst. (products liability com. 1984—). Congregationalist. Clubs: Plaza, La Mancha Racquet (Phoenix). Avocations: fishing, hunting, basketball. Insurance, Personal injury. Office: Lowe & Berman PA 3300 N Central Ave Suite 2350 Phoenix AZ 85012

MICHEEL, RICHARD ARTHUR, lawyer; b. Davenport, Iowa, Dec. 19, 1920; s. Herman Peter and Katherine Mary M.; m. Patricia Shipe, Nov. 13, 1926; 1 child, Mary Pamela Micheel Tiernan. LL.B., Georgetown U., 1947. Bar: D.C. 1951, Iowa 1951. Practice law, Washington; ptnr. Speights, Pearce & Micheel, Washington. Served to lt. USN, 1943-46. Mem. Counsellors, D.C. Bar (chmn. continuing legal edn.). Roman Catholic. Club: Congl. Country. Bankruptcy, Criminal, Personal injury. Office: 1000 Connecticut Ave NW Washington DC 20036

MICHEL, CLIFFORD LLOYD, lawyer, investment executive; b. N.Y.C., Aug. 9, 1939; s. Clifford William and Barbara Lloyd (Richards) M.; m. Betsy Shirley, June 6, 1964; children: Clifford Fredrick, Jason Lloyd, Katherine Beinecke. A.B. cum laude, Princeton U., 1961; J.D., Yale U., 1964. Bar: N.Y. 1964, U.S. Dist. Ct. (so. dist.) N.Y. 1968, U.S. Ct. Appeals (2d cir.) 1967, U.S. Supreme Ct. 1972. Assoc. Cahill, Gordon & Reindel, N.Y.C., 1964-67, Paris, 1967-69, N.Y.C., 1969-71; ptnr. Cahill, Gordon & Reindel, Paris, 1972-76, N.Y.C., 1976—; pres., dir. Wenonah Devel. Co., 1975—; dir. Chem. Fund, Inc., Surveyor Fund, Inc., Dome Mines Ltd., Sigma Mines (Que.) Ltd. Bd. dirs. Jockey Hollow Found., Michel Found., St. Mark's Sch., Morristown Meml. Hosp., Alliance Counterpoint Fund, Alliance Convertible Fund, Fiduciary Growth Assocs., Quasar Assocs. Mem. ABA, N.Y. State Bar Assn., N.Y. County Lawyers Assn., Fed. Bar Assn., Am. Soc. Internat. Law. Republican. Clubs: City Midday, Racquet and Tennis, River; Shinnecock Hills Golf (N.Y.); Somerset Hills Country; Essex Hunt (N.J.); Polo, Golf de Morfontaine, Travellers (Paris). General corporate, Private international, Securities. Home: St Bernard's Rd Gladstone NJ 07934 Office: 80 Pine St New York NY 10005

MICHEL, TRUDI LOUISE, lawyer; b. Los Angeles, Mar. 4, 1958; d. Hubert Charles and Barbra Rae (Henrichs) M.; m. Alan Howard Painter, Aug. 13, 1983. BA, UCLA, 1978, JD, 1982. Bar: Calif. 1982, U.S. Dist. Ct. (mid. and cen. dists.) Calif. 1982, U.S. Tax Ct. 1983. Assoc. O'Melveny & Myers, Newport Beach, Calif., 1982—. Mem. ABA, Orange County Bar Assn. Corporate taxation, Personal income taxation, Estate taxation. Office: O'Melveny & Myers 610 Newport Center Dr Suite 1700 Newport Beach CA 92660-6429

MICHELMAN, FRANK I., lawyer, educator; b. 1936. B.A., Yale U., 1957; LL.B., Harvard U., 1960. Bar: N.Y. 1961, Mass. 1967. Law clk to assoc. justice William J. Brennan, U.S. Supreme Ct., Washington, 1961-62; asst. to asst. atty. gen., Tax Div., Dept. Justice, 1962-63; asst. prof. Harvard U., Cambridge, Mass., 1963-66, prof., 1966—; cons. HUD, 1966; cons. Boston Model City Program, 1968-69; mem. Boston Home Rule Commn., 1969-71; mem. Gov.'s Task Force on Met. Devel., 1974-75. Mem. Am. Soc. for Polit. and Legal Philosophy. Author: (with Sandalow) Materials on Government in Urban Areas, 1970. Real property, Local government, Jurisprudence. Office: Harvard U Law Sch Cambridge MA 02138 *

MICHELS, JOHN RUDOLF, lawyer; b. White Plains, N.Y., June 16, 1944; s. Rudolf Karl and Ilse (Gruner) M.; m. Nancy Hocker, Feb. 3, 1973; children: Christine, Robert, Anne. AB, Holy Cross Coll., 1966; MBA, Harvard U., 1971; JD, Suffolk U., 1979. Sr. adminstrv. officer Cabot, Cabot & Forbes Land Trust, Boston, 1971-75; trustee bankruptcy Stewart Meyers Co., Manchester, N.H., 1980-83; ptnr. Michels & Michels, Londondorry, N.H., 1983—; pres. Michels Devel. Co., Londondorry, 1976-80. Mem. N.H. Ho. of Reps., Concord, 1969-72, U.S. Adv. Commn. on Oceans and Atmosphere, Washington, 1977; del. N.H. Constl. Conv., Concord, 1974, Rep. Nat. Conv., Detroit, 1980; moderator Town of Danbury, N.H., 1976-80. Served as 1st lt. U.S. Army, 1966-68, Vietnam. Recipient Pub. Service award U.S. Dept. Justice, 1983. Republican. Roman Catholic. Avocations: sailing, skiing. Bankruptcy, General corporate, Real property. Home: 40 Shasta Dr Londonderry NH 03053 Office: Michels & Michels 25 Nashua Rd Londonderry NH 03053

MICHELSON, MARK A., lawyer; b. Cambridge, Mass., Apr. 28, 1935; s. Morris and Harriet (Steinberg) M.; m. Kadimah Freedman, June 27, 1963; children—Ruth Leah, Jessica Rachel, Emily Deborah. A.B. magna cum laude, Harvard U., 1957, LL.B. cum laude, 1962. Bar: Mass. 1962. Summer clk. FTC, 1961; law clk. to justice Supreme Jud. Ct. Mass., 1962-63; instr. Boston U. Law Sch., 1963-65; assoc. Choate, Hall & Stewart, Boston, 1963-69, ptnr., 1970—; owner Social Law Library; dir. METCO, 1970—; owner Boston Athenaeum. Regional v.p. New Eng. region Am. Jewish Congress, 1969—, mem. commn. on Law and Social Action, 1963—; mem. town meeting Town of Brookline (Mass.), 1972—; gen. counsel Civil Liberties Union Mass., 1978-81, 1st v.p., 1981-83. Mem. Am. Law Inst., Phi Beta Kappa. Democrat. Jewish. Federal civil litigation, State civil litigation. Home: 78 Evans Rd Brookline MA 02146 Office: Choate Hall & Stewart 53 State St Exchange Pl 33d Floor Boston MA 02109

MICHENER, JOHN ATHOL, lawyer; b. St. Louis, Mar. 17, 1947; s. Athol John and Anne Everett (Purnell) M.; m. Kibble Lee Jackson, June 19, 1970; children: Christopher Athol, Amelia Morgan, Dorian Everett. BA, Vanderbilt U., 1969; JD, U. Mo., Columbia, 1974. Bar: Mo. 1974, U.S. Dist. Ct. (ea. dist.) Mo. 1975, U.S. Ct. Appeals (8th cir.) 1985. Assoc. Evans & Dixon, St. Louis, 1974-81, ptnr., 1982—. Recipient Lon O. Hocker Meml. Trial Lawyer award Mo. Bar Found. 1980. Mem. 22d Jud. Cir. Bar Com. Insurance, State civil litigation, Federal civil litigation. Office: Evans & Dixon 314 N Broadway Saint Louis MO 63102

MICHIE, DANIEL BOORSE, JR., lawyer; b. Phila., July 28, 1922; s. Daniel Boorse and Mae (Mueller) M.; m. Barbara F. Maddox, Aug. 29, 1970. B.S., Harvard U., 1943; LL.B., U. Va., 1948. Bar: Pa. 1949. Practiced law Phila., 1949—; asso. firm Harry J. Alker (Esq.), 1949, Kephart & Kephart, 1950-51; asso. firm Fell & Spalding, 1952-53, partner, 1954-68; partner Fell, Spalding, Goff & Rubin, 1969-82, Fell & Spalding, 1982—; spl. master U.S. Ct. Appeals for 3d Circuit, 1970—; solicitor Twp. Abington, Pa., 1958-78; Pres. Phila. Council Internat. Visitors, 1957-60, chmn., 1979-81; pres. Phila. Crime Commn., 1960-63, Phila. Fellowship Commn., 1970-71; chmn. Pa. Adv. Com. on Probation, 1966—, Bd. Phila. Prisons, 1968-71. Pres. Nat. Assn. Citizens Crime Commns., 1961-62; pres. Unitarian Universalist Service Com., 1969-72; regional co-chmn. NCCJ, 1967-71, nat. bd. govs., 1971—, nat. exec. bd., 1981—; vice chmn. Southeastern Pa. chpt. ARC, 1978-82; bd. dirs. Urban League Phila., 1981-83; bd. dirs. Valley Forge council Boy Scouts Am., 1955-84, mem. adv. bd., 1984—. Served to lt. USNR, 1943-46. Mem. Phila. Bar Assn. (gov. 1970-72), Pa. Bar Assn. (ho. of dels. 1971—), ABA (chmn. organized crime com. 1964-65), Fed. Bar Assn., Am. Judicature Soc., Navy League (dir. Phila. 1967-73, v.p. 1973-76, pres. 1976-78, nat. dir. 1977-83), St. Andrew's Soc., Friendly Sons of St. Patrick, SAR. Republican. Unitarian Universalist (ch. pres. 1961-62, dist. pres. 1966-69). Clubs: Union League (Phila.); Sombrero Country (Fla.); Marathon Yacht (Fla.). General corporate, Probate, Real property. Home: 1129 Wrack Rd PO Box 8 Meadowbrook PA 19046 Office: 211 S Broad St 8th Floor Philadelphia PA 19107

MICKEL, JOSEPH THOMAS, lawyer; b. Monroe, La., Nov. 12, 1951; s. Toufick and Ruth Ella (Phelps) M.; m. Carlene Elise Nickens, Dec. 10, 1981; children: Leo, Thomas, Matthew. BA, La. State U., 1975; postgrad., Tulane U., 1977-78; JD, So. U., 1979. Bar: La. 1979, U.S. Dist. Ct. (mid. dist.) La. 1981, U.S. Ct. Appeals (5th cir.) 1981, U.S. Dist. Ct. (we. dist.) La. 1983, U.S. Ct. Mil. Appeals 1985, U.S. Supreme Ct. 1985. Staff atty. Pub. Defenders Office, Baton Rouge, La., 1979-80; assoc. Law Offices of Michael Fugler, Baton Rouge, 1981; asst. dist. atty. La. 4th Jud. Dist. Atty.'s Office, Monroe, 1982-84, 85—; ptnr. Bruscato, Loomis & Street, Monroe, 1984-85. Mem. ABA, Assn. Trial Lawyers Am., La. Trial Lawyers Assn. Democrat. Presbyterian. Avocations: trapshooting, skeetshooting, bird hunting, fishing. Criminal, Personal injury, General practice. Home: 209 Auburn Ave Monroe LA 71201 Office: Office of the Dist Atty 400 St John Monroe LA 71210

MICKELSON, HAL M., lawyer; b. San Pedro, Calif., Feb. 17, 1950; s. Norman S. and Olive Y. Mickelson. A.B., Stanford U., 1971; J.D., Harvard U., 1974. Bar: Calif. 1974, U.S. Dist. Ct. (no. dist.) Calif. 1975. Assoc. Athearn, Chandler & Hoffman, San Francisco, 1975-79; atty. Hewlett-Packard Co., Palo Alto, Calif., 1979-81, sr. atty., 1981-87, regional counsel, 1987—; dir. Stanford Daily Pub. Corp. U.S. Presdl. scholar, 1967. Mem. ABA, Am. Corp. Counsel Assn., Phi Beta Kappa. Republican. Presbyterian. Club: Commonwealth of Calif. General corporate, Labor. Address: PO Box 3662 Stanford CA 94305

MICKLEY, RICHARD STROUD, lawyer; b. Marion, Ohio, Apr. 21, 1939; s. Henry Arthur and Miriam Laura (Stroud) M.; m. Carolyn Latham, Sept. 6, 1964; children—Bruce Latham, Andrew Kenneth. B.A., Coll. Wooster, 1961; J.D., Ohio State U., 1970. Bar: Ohio 1971, U.S. Dist. Ct. (so. dist.) Ohio 1973, U.S. Dist. Ct. (no. dist.) Ohio 1980, U.S. Tax Ct. 1975. Assoc., Grigsby & Allen, Marysville, Ohio, 1971-73; sole practice, Marysville, 1973-77, 79; asst. county prosecutor Union County (Ohio), 1973-75, 78; ptnr. Mckinley & Mickley, 1978, Mickley & McNemar, Marysville, 1980-85; estate adminstr. U.S. Bankruptcy Ct., 1986—; city law dir. City of Marysville, 1982-85. Pres. Serve Inc., 1981, 84. Served to capt. USAF, 1962-68. Mem. Union County Bar Assn. (pres. 1973), Ohio State Bar Assn. Republican. Presbyterian. Lodges: Lions (pres. 1979), Masons (master 1977). Avocations: church committee work; woodworking; gardening. Bankruptcy. Home: 891 Catalpa Pl Marysville OH 43040

MICKS, D. FRED, lawyer; b. Balt., July 3, 1947. B.A., U. Tex., 1969, J.D., 1972. Bar: Tex. 1972, U.S. Dist. Ct. (so. dist.) Tex. 1973, U.S. Ct. Appeals (5th cir.) 1973, U.S. Supreme Ct. 1978, U.S. Ct. Apls. (11th cir.) 1981. Practice, Galveston, Tex.; ptnr. Martin, Cruse, Micks, Garza & Bunce. Fellow Tex. Bar Found. (life, dir. 1976-77); mem. ABA (ho. dels. 1980-84), Tex. Young Lawyers Assn. (pres. 1977-78), State Bar Tex. (dir. 1976-79), Galveston County Bar Assn. (Outstanding Young Lawyer 1977, pres. elect 1986-87), Assn. Trial Lawyers Am., Tex. Trial Lawyers Assn., Tex. Bd. Legal Specialization (cert. personal injury trial law), U. Tex. Law Alumni Assn. (bd. dirs. 1986—). Personal injury, State civil litigation, Federal civil litigation. Home: 7758 Beaudelaire Galveston TX 77550 Office: 1100 Rosenberg Galveston TX 77550

MICSAK, ROBERT WILLIAM, lawyer; b. Lorain, Ohio, Jan. 25, 1955; s. Robert Victor and Agnes Alvesta (Bloom) M.; m. Stephanie Bires, Sept. 3, 1977; 1 child, Robert Victor II. Student, Wittenberg U., 1973-74; BS, Ohio State U., 1977; M of Landscape Architecture, Harvard U., 1980; JD, U. Colo., 1981. Bar: Colo. 1981, U.S. Dist. Ct. Colo. 1981, U.S. Ct. Appeals (10th cir.) 1984. Atty. Gulf Oil Corp., Denver, 1981-85, registered lobbyist, 1982-85; atty. Chevron USA Inc., Denver, 1985-86; asst. gen. counsel Meridian Minerals Co., Englewood, Colo., 1986—. Contbr. articles to profl. jours. Instr. Handicapped Ski Program, Winter Park, Colo., 1981—. Mem. ABA, Colo. Bar Assn. (chmn. adminstrv. law subcom. 1981—), Denver Bar Assn., Nat. Coal Assn. (rep. joint com. 1984-86), Am. Mining Congress (rep. joint com. 1984-86), Rocky Mountain Oil and Gas Assn. (rep. oil shale com. 1981-84). Republican. Episcopalian. Avocations: skiing, fishing, hiking, bicycling. Real property, Environment, Mining. Office: Meridian Minerals Co 5613 DTC Parkway Englewood CO 80111

MIDDLEBROOK, STEPHEN BEACH, insurance company executive; b. Hartford, Conn., Jan. 30, 1937; s. Louis Frank and Eugenia Gertrude (Caravatt) M.; m. Patricia Niles, June 9, 1964. B.A., Yale U., 1958, LL.B., 1961. Bar: Conn. 1961. With Aetna Life & Casualty Co., Hartford, 1962—; counsel Aetna Life & Casualty Co., 1969-71, asst. gen. counsel, 1971—, corp. sec., 1973—, gen. counsel, 1978—, v.p., 1981—. Trustee, pres. Wadsworth Atheneum, Hartford; chmn. New Eng. Legal Found. Served to 1st lt. AUS, 1961-67. Mem. Assn. Life Ins. Counsel, ABA, Conn. Bar Assn., Am. Corp. Counsel Assn. (dir., exec. com.). Club: Farmington (Conn.) Country. In-

surance, General corporate. Home: 21 Guernsey Ln Avon CT 06001 Office: The Aetna Casualty and Surety Co 151 Farmington Ave Hartford CT 06156

MIDDLEKAUFF, ROGER DAVID, lawyer; b. Cleve., May 6, 1935; s. Roger David and Ella Marie (Holan) M.; m. Gail Palmer, Apr. 19, 1963; children: Roger David, Arthur Henry. BChemE, Cornell U., 1958; JD cum laude, Northwestern U., 1964. Bar: Ohio 1964, D.C. 1966, U.S. Supreme Ct. 1974. Assoc., Roetzel & Andress, Akron, Ohio, 1964-66, Kirkland, Ellis & Rowe, Washington, 1966-69; assoc. Thompson, and Middlekauff and predecessor firms, Washington, 1969-72, ptnr., 1973-83; ptnr. McKenna, Conner & Cuneo, 1983—; mem. adv. com. extension service project Dept. Agr., 1976; mem. adv. com. solar energy project ERDA, 1975; indsl. observer Codex Alimentarius Commn., FAO/WHO and com. meetings; project rev. group control tech. assessment of fermentation processes, Nat. Inst. Occupational Safety and Health. Contbr. articles to legal jours.; editor handbooks, Practising Law Inst.; mem. editorial bd. Jour. Regulatory Pharmacology and Toxicology. Vice chmn. bur. Greater Washington Bd. Trade; trustee Internat. Life Scis. Inst., Nutrition Found., Inc.; chmn. Arthur S. Fleming Awards Commn., 1969-70; vol. gen. counsel Episcopal Found. for Drama, 1976-77, Scotland Community Devel. Assn., 1971-73, Congregations United for Shelter, 1971-73, Iona House, 1974-77; sr. warden St. Columbia's Episc. Ch., Washington, 1975-77; sec., bd. dirs. Episc. Ch. Homes, Washington; mem. lawyers' panel Pres. Ford's Com., 1976; chmn. pres.'s chpt. Nat. Capital Area council Nat. Eagle Scout Assn. Served with USN, 1958-61. Recipient Silver Wreath award local chpt. Boy Scouts Am. Mem. ABA (chmn. subcom. on food and color additives and pesticide residues, food, drug and cosmetic com. 1977—), Bar Assn. D.C. (chmn. corp. and bus. law com. 1977-82), Am. Chem. Soc. (sec., treas. biotech. secretariat, 1986—), Order of Coif. Episcopalian. Clubs: Metropolitan, Rotary. Administrative and regulatory, Health, General corporate. Office: McKenna Conner & Cuneo 1575 Eye St NW Washington DC 20005

MIDDLETON, ELWYN LINTON, lawyer; b. Pomona, Fla., Oct. 16, 1914; s. William Spencer and Lizzie A. (Williams) M.; m. Annie L. Fielding, Dec. 7, 1942; children—Elwyn Linton, Mary Ann, John David, Phillip Fielding. LL.B., Stetson U., 1939. Bar: Fla. 1939. Assoc., E. Harris Drew, Palm Beach, Fla., 1939-42; ptnr. firm Steel, Hector, Davis, Burns & Middleton (formerly Burns, Middleton, Farrell & Faust), Palm Beach, 1946—; town atty., Palm Beach, 1953-81; dir. Bank of Palm Beach & Trust Co., Palm Beach. Trustee Eckerd Coll. Served from ensign to lt. USNR, 1942-46. Mem. ABA, Palm Beach County Bar Assn. (pres. 1951), Fla. Bar (gov. 1954-56), Phi Alpha Delta. Democrat. Presbyterian. Probate, Real property, General practice. Home: 242 Dunbar Rd Palm Beach FL 33480 Office: 440 Royal Palm Way Palm Beach FL 33480

MIDDLETON, HARLOW CLESTER, lawyer; b. Jacksonville, Fla., Sept. 24, 1939; s. Clyde Downing Sr. and Laurie Jane (Buck) M.; m. Anita Brigita Premfors, Dec. 31, 1967 (div. Oct. 1985); children: Elizabeth Anna, Anna Brita. BS in Journalism, U. Fla., 1963; JD, Stetson U., 1967. Bar: Fla. 1967. Ptnr. Bryan & Middleton, Palatka, Fla., 1968-70, Mt. Dora, Fla., 1970-76; sole practice Mt. Dora, 1976-84, 85-86; ptnr. Middleton & Benson, Mt. Dora, 1984-85; corp. counsel AuClair Corp., Mt. Dora, 1986—; corp. counsel City Mt. Dora, 1981—. Mem. Fla. Leadership Network, 1983-86; pres. Mt. Dora Cultural Council, Inc., 1984-86. Served with USCG, 1960-61. Mem. Lake County Bar Assn. Democrat. Avocations: sailing, cooking, jogging. General corporate, Real property, Local government.

MIDDLETON, J. HOWARD, JR., lawyer; b. Camden, N.J., Mar. 1, 1939; s. J. Howard and Helen Marie (Casper) M.; m. Betty Jo Bittinger, Aug. 22, 1965; children: J. Howard III, Lucia Katherine. BA, Haverford Coll., 1962; MDiv., Union Theol. Sem., 1965; JD, Georgetown U., 1972. Bar: Va. 1972, U.S. Dist. Ct. (ea. dist.) Va. 1973, U.S. Ct. Appeals (D.C. cir.) 1974, U.S. Supreme Ct. 1976, U.S. Ct. Claims 1978; ordained minister. Manpower analyst U.S. Dept. Labor, Washington, 1971-72; asst. atty. City of Alexandria, Va., 1972-76, dep. atty., 1976-78; sole practice Alexandria, Va., 1978-81; ptnr. Thomas & Fiske P.C., Alexandria, Va., 1981—; chmn. Alexandria mcpl. liaison com. Northern Va. Builders, 1986; active Va. legis. com. Washington Bd. Trade, Alexandria, 1986. Bd. dirs. Circle Terr. Hosp., Alexandria, 1986. Mem. ABA, Va. State Bar Assn., Alexandria Bar Assn., Am. Arbitration Assn. (panel of arbitrators), Unitarian Universalists Ministers Assn. Democrat. Real property, Local government, Environment. Office: Thomas & Fiske PC 510 King St Suite 200 Alexandria VA 22314

MIDDLETON, JACK BAER, lawyer; b. Phila., Jan. 13, 1929; s. Harry C. and Mildred Cornell (Baer) M.; m. Ann Dodge, Aug. 22, 1953; children: Susan D., Jack B. Jr., Peter C. AB, Lafayette Coll., 1950; JD cum laude, Boston U., 1956. Bar: N.H. 1956, U.S. Ct. Appeals (1st cir.) 1957, U.S. Supreme Ct. 1972. Assoc. McLane, Graf, Raulerson & Middleton, Manchester, N.H., 1956-62; ptnr., dir. McLane, Graf, Raulerson & Middleton, Manchester, 1962—; spl. justice Merrimack (N.H.) Dist. Ct., 1962-86; mem. Greater Manchester Devel. corp., 1983—. Author: (with others) Summary of NH Law, 1964, Compendium of New Hampshire Law, 1969, Trial of a Wrongful Death Action in NH, 1977; editor Boston U. Law Rev., 1954-56. Mem. Mount Washington Commn., 1969—, Bedford (N.H.) Sch. Bd., 1960-66, N.H. Jud. Council, 1978-83, adv. bd. Merrimack Valley Coll.; trustee Mount Washington Observatory, New Eng. Law Inst., 1977-80; commr. Uniform State Laws, 1971-75; chmn. bd. of trustees White Mountain Sch., 1976-79. Served to sgt. USMCR, 1950-52. Fellow ABA, Am. Coll. Trial Lawyers; mem. New Eng. Bar Assn. (bd. dirs. 1977-84, pres. 1982-83), N.H. Bar Assn. (pres. 1979-80), Manchester Bar Assn., Boston U. Law Sch. Alumni Assn. (exec. com., pres. 1979-80), N.H. Bar Found. (chmn.). Office: McLane Graf Raulerson & Middleton 40 Stark St Box 326 Manchester NH 03105

MIDDLETON, JAMES BOLAND, lawyer; b. Columbus, Ga., Aug. 19, 1934; s. Riley Kimbrough and Annie Ruth (Boland) M.; B.A. in Psychology, Ga. State U., 1964; J.D., Woodrow Wilson Coll. Law, 1972; m. Martha Ann Martin, June 27, 1965; 1 dau., Cynthia. Draftsman, paralegal and office mgr. to patent atty., Atlanta, 1955-68, for Jones & Thomas, Atlanta, 1968-72; admitted to Ga. bar, 1972, also U.S. Patent Office; assoc. firm Jones and Thomas, Atlanta, 1972-76; individual practice law, Decatur, Ga., 1976—. Served with U.S. Army, 1957-59. Mem. ABA, Am. Intellectual Property Law Assn., Atlanta Bar Assn., Decatur-DeKalb Bar Assn., State Bar of Ga. (editorial bd. jour. 1985—), Fed. Circuit Bar Assn., Am. Arbitration Assn. (comml. panel 1983—). Editor-in-chief: Atlanta Lawyer, 1981-82; contbr. articles on law to profl. jours. Patent, Trademark and copyright. Home: 1155 McConnell Dr Decatur GA 30033 Office: PO Box 1968 Decatur GA 30031

MIDDLETON, LINDA GREATHOUSE, lawyer; b. Poplar Bluff, Mo., Sept. 22, 1950; d. Casper Scott and Anna Garnelle (Qualls) Greathouse; m. Roy L. Middleton, Sept. 27, 1969. BS cum laude, Ark. State U.; JD, Baylor U. Asst. v.p., asst. sec., atty. Equitable Gen. Ins. Co., Ft. Worth, 1977-81; gen. counsel, corp. sec. Chilton Corp., Dallas, 1981-83; asst. corp. sec., sr. atty., mgr. pub. affairs Am. Petrofina Inc., Dallas, 1983—. Sec. Homeowners Assn., Dallas, 1981—. Mem. Tex. Bar Assn., Dallas Bar Assn. Baptist. Avocations: oil painting, sewing, piano. Office: Am Petrofina Inc 8350 N Central Expressway Dallas TX 75221

MIDDLETON, STEPHANIE ADELE, lawyer; b. Bethesda, Md.; d. Roderick Osgood and Ethel Adele (Bellows) M.; m. William G. Kussmaul III, Aug. 28, 1970 (div. Apr. 1981); children: Mary, Susannah; m. William B. Carr, Oct. 9, 1983; 1 child, Adele. BA, Yale U., 1972; JD, U. Pa., 1981. Bar: Pa. 1981, U.S. Dist. Ct. (ea. dist.) Pa. 1981. Assoc. Morgan, Lewis & Bockius, Phila., 1981-85; atty. corp. law dept. CIGNA Corp., Phila., 1985—. Labor, Federal civil litigation, General corporate. Home: 115 Vernon Ln Rose Valley PA 19063 Office: CIGNA 2600 One Logan Sq Philadelphia PA 19103

MIDGETT, JAMES CLAYTON, JR., lawyer; b. Nashville, June 19, 1950; s. James Clayton Sr. and Helen Marie (Baxter) M. BS with high honors, U. Tenn., 1972; JD, Emory U., 1975. Bar: Tenn. 1975, U.S. Ct. Mil. Appeals 1976, U.S. Dist. Ct. (mid. dist.) Tenn. 1983, U.S. Supreme Ct. 1986. Assoc. Finch & McBroom, Nashville, 1983-86, Miles, Dozier, Spann & Midgett, Nashville, 1986—; instr. bus. law U. Tampa, 1977-78, Tenn. State U., Nashville, 1984. Served with JAGC, USAF, 1976-80. Recipient Torchbearer award U. Tenn., 1972. Mem. ABA, Tenn. Bar Assn., Nashville Bar Assn., Arnold Air Soc., Scabbard and Blade, Phi Beta Kappa, Phi Delta Phi, Pi Sigma Alpha, Omicron Delta Kappa, Phi Kappa Phi. Lodge: Elks. Avocations: traveling, flying. General corporate, State civil litigation, Insurance. Office: Miles Dozier Spann & Midgett Dominion Bank Bldg Suite 707 Nashville TN 37201

MIDGLEY, DOUGLAS MERRITT, lawyer; b. Hamilton, Ont., Can., Feb. 17, 1940; came to U.S., 1952; s. James Arthur and E. Lois (Merritt) M.; m. Marilena Muller; children: Scott Douglas, Diana Lynne. BA, U. Fla., 1962, JD, 1964. Bar: Fla. 1965. Pub. def. 20th Jud. Cir., Lee, Charlotte, Collier, Hendry and Glades Counties, 1969—; chmn. steering com. for Integration of Criminal Justice Info. Sys. and CJIS Mgmt. Council, 1985—; mem. Criminal Justice Adv. Com., subcoms. on Disorder and Terrorism and Organized Crime, 1974-80, Fla. Supreme Ct. Com. Study of Ct. Documents Disposal, 1980, State Med. Examiners Com. Fla. Dept. Law Enforcement, 1981—, citizens adv. bd. Ft. Myers Community Correction Ctr., 1986—; chmn. Case Conflict Com., 20th Jud. Cir., 1982—. Mem. Fla. Bar Assn., Lee County Bar Assn., Fla. Pub. Def. Assn. (pres. 1981-82). Democrat. Episcopalian. Lodges: Masons, Shriners, Brotherhood of St. Andrew. Criminal. Office: Pub Def 20th Jud Cir PO Drawer 1980 Fort Myers FL 33902-1980

MIDKIFF, CHARLES FRANKLIN, lawyer; b. Charleston, S.C., Mar. 27, 1947; s. Leslie S. and Virginia M. (DeBord) M.; m. Sue A. Samuelson; 1 child, Alyssa Boyd. B.S., Old Dominion U., 1968; J.D., Coll. William and Mary, 1970. Bars: Va. 1970, D.C. Ct. Appeals 1975. Mem. law firm Christian, Barton, Epps, Brent & Chappell, Richmond, Va., 1972-87, ptnr., 1978-87, prin. Midkiff & Assocs., P.C., 1987—; panelist energy issues ABA, Washington, 1979; prin. speaker annual meeting Va. Soc. CPA's, 1986; Gen. counsel campaign com. Atty. Gen. Gerald Baliles of Va., 1981; v.p., bd. dirs. Big Bros. of Richmond, Inc., 1974-78. Served to 1st lt., U.S. Army, 1970-71. Mem. ABA (chmn. young lawyers div. com. on assoc. lawyers 1981, vice chmn. natural gas transp. com. natural resources sect. 1986—), Va. Bar Assn. (chmn. Young lawyers sect. 1980), Va. State Bar (bd. govs. adminstrv. law sect. 1981-85, chmn. 1984), Richmond Bar Assn., Va. Assn. Def. Attys., Am. Judicature Soc. Episcopalian. Clubs: Bull and Bear (Richmond). Editor-in-chief Coll. William and Mary Law Review, 1969-70. Administrative and regulatory, Federal civil litigation, State civil litigation.

MIDLEN, JOHN HOLBROOK, JR., lawyer; b. Washington, Oct. 1, 1942; s. John Holbrook and Gertrude Holcolmbe (Robertson) M. BS in Econs., U. Pa., 1964; JD, Am. U., 1969. Bar: D.C. 1969, U.S. Ct. Appeals (D.C. cir.) 1970, U.S. Supreme Ct. 1975, U.S. Ct. Appeals (2d and 4th cirs.) 1986. Ptnr. Midlen & Reddy, Washington, 1970-82; pres. John H. Midlen, Jr., Chartered, Washington, 1983—; mng. atty. Pacific Legal Found., Washington, 1975-76; chmn. Alpha-Omega Engring. Inc., Knoxville, Tenn., 1983—. Patentee cir. detector and noise reduction network with cir. detector, 1985, special vestigial sideband signal, 1987, panpotted to natural stereo transformation circuitry, 1987; editor-in-chief Am. U. Law Rev., 1968-69. Served to 1st lt. U.S. Army, 1964-66. Mem. ABA, D.C. Bar Assn., Fed. Communications Bar Assn. Presbyterian. Club: Chevy Chase (Md.). Communications, Trademark and copyright, Administrative and regulatory. Home: 7618 Lynn Dr Chevy Chase MD 20815 Office: 1050 Wisconsin Ave NW Washington DC 20007-3633

MIELA, DEBORAH LYNN, lawyer; b. Hamtramck, Mich., May 4, 1949; d. Vincent Miela and Martha Virginia Mason. BA, Mich. State U., 1971; JD, Detroit Coll. Law, 1975. Bar: Mich. 1976, U.S. Dist. Ct. (ea. dist.) Mich. 1976, U.S. Dist. Ct. (so. dist.) Ind. 1986. Atty. K mart Corp., Troy, Mich., 1976-85, counsel trade regulation, 1985—; mem. hearing panel Atty. Discipline Bd., spl. investigator Atty. Grievance Commn., 1980-81. Mem. ABA (antitrust, litigation and sci. and tech. sects. 1976—), Detroit Bar Assn., Women Lawyers Assn. Mich. (pres. 1985-86). Antitrust, Federal civil litigation, State civil litigation. Office: K Mart Corp 3100 W Big Beaver Rd Troy MI 48084

MIERS, JAMES WILLIAM, lawyer; b. Wichita, Kans., Jan. 6, 1953; s. C.E. and Anna M. (Grigsby) M.; m. Patricia K. Pastrich, Mar. 10, 1986. BA, Dartmouth Coll., 1975; JD, U. San Diego, 1981. Bar: Colo. 1981. Assoc. Calkins, Kramer, Grimshaw & Harring, Denver, 1981-82; ptnr. Knudson, Davine & Miers, Denver, 1982-85, Woods, Kinney & Miers, Denver, 1985—. Mem. ABA (fed. regulation of securities task force on integration), Colo. Bar Assn. Avocations: skiing, scuba diving, hiking. General corporate, Securities, Contracts commercial. Home: 6667 E Dorado Ave Greenwood Village CO 80111 Office: Woods Kinney & Miers 8400 E Prentice Englewood CO 80111

MIES, JAMES EDWARD, lawyer; b. Garrett, Ind., July 21, 1928; s. Edward A. and Mildred E. (Heatley) M.; m. Mary P. McBride, Feb. 4, 1950; children: Edward T., James E. Jr., Thomas G., Gerald P., Jean Ann, Catherine E., Michael F. Student, U. Detroit, 1948, JD, 1951. Bar: Mich. 1952, U.S. Dist. Ct. (ea. dist.) Mich. 1952, U.S. Ct. Appeals (6th cir.) 1960, U.S. Supreme Ct. 1963. Ptnr. Brashear, Brashear, Mies & Duggan, Livonia, Mich., 1953-68; judge 16th dist. Mich. Dist. Ct., Livonia, 1969-81; judge 3d cir. Mich. Cir. Ct., Detroit, 1981—; mem. Jud. Tenure Commn., Detroit, 1975-81. Bd. dirs. Community Opportunity Ctr., Livonia, 1961—; trustee Mich. Cancer Found., Detroit, 1963-84, Wayne Ctr., Detroit, 1978—. Named 1st Citizen of Livonia, Livonia Observer, 1977. Mem. Mich. Bar Assn., Detroit Bar Assn., Livonia Bar Assn. (pres. 1963), Am. Acad Jud. Edn. (faculty 1972—), Mich. Jud. Inst. (faculty 1978—), Mich. Dist. Judge Assn. (pres. 1974). Personal injury, State civil litigation. Office: 1019 City County Bldg 2 Woodward Ave Detroit MI 48226

MIGDEN-OSTRANDER, JANINE LEE, lawyer, consultant; b. Yonkers, N.Y., June 24, 1953; d. Nathan Howard and Simonne Noële Armande (Moutarlier) Migden; m. Stephen John Ostrander, Dec. 10, 1977; children: Catherine Madeleine, David Ansel. Certificat de la Lanque et Civilization Francaise, La Sorbonne, Paris, 1974; BA, SUNY, Plattsburgh, 1974; cert. paralegal, Adelphi U., 1976; JD, Capital U., 1981. Bar: Ohio 1981, U.S. Dist. Ct. (so. dist.) Ohio 1984. Assoc. consumers counsel Office of Consumers Counsel, Columbus, Ohio, 1981-85; sole practice Columbus, 1985—; spl. asst. prosecutor Montgomery County Utility Coalition, Columbus, 1985-86, asst. prosecutor, 1986—; cons. Lubow, McKay, Lewis & Stevens, Columbus, 1986. Vol. Choices Shelter for Battered Women, Columbus, 1978-81; mem. Amnesty Internat., Columbus, 1985—. Mem. ABA (pub. utilities and natural resources subcoms. 1985—), Sierra Club (vice-chmn. 1982-83). Avocations: ice skating, writing, gourmet cooking, racquetball, traveling. Public utilities, Nuclear power, Environment. Home and Office: 1415 Inglis Ave Columbus OH 43212

MIGHDOLL, STEPHEN J., lawyer; b. Amityville, N.Y., Jan. 3, 1952; s. Manuel J. and Virginia (Edelman) M.; m. Joan Kirstein, June 9, 1974; children: Andrea, Julie. BA, 1974, JD, 1977. Bar: N.Y. 1978. Assoc. Shea & Gould, N.Y.C., 1978-80, Reavis & McCrath, N.Y.C., 1980-83; assoc. Berwin Leighton, N.Y.C., 1983-85, ptnr., 1985—. Real property, General corporate. Home: 73 Cardinal Dr East Hills NY 11576 Office: Berwin Leighton 767 Fifth Ave New York NY 10153

MIHAL, THOMAS HARLAN, lawyer; b. Milw., Sept. 27, 1949; s. Milan and Dorothy Mae (Wegner) M.; m. Renee R. Shebesta, June 26, 1971; children: Jennifer Jae, Jeffrey Harlan. BBA, U. Wis., 1971, JD, 1974. Bar: Wis. 1974, U. Dist. Ct. (ea. and we. dists.) Wis. 1983. Staff atty. AU div. Northwestern Mut. Life Ins. Co., Milw., 1974-77; assoc. Hinners and Niemann, Milw., 1977-79; sr. assoc. Hinners, Guyette & Mihal, Milw., 1979-81; sr. ptnr. Hinners and Mihal, S.C., Milw., 1981-85, Mihal & Steffens S.C., Milw., 1986—. Pres. Pebble Valley Homeowners Assn., Waukesha, Wis., 1981; chmn. day Waukesha Wis. Sesquicentennial, Inc., Waukesha, 1984; bd. visitors U. Wis. Ctr. System, Madison, 1985—; trustee Gethsemane United Meth. Ch., Pewaukee, Wis., 1982-84. Mem. ABA, Wis. Bar Assn., Milw. Young Lawyers Assn., Vol. U. Wis. Waukesha Alumni Assn. (bd. dirs. 1980-85, pres. 1985, named outstanding alumnus 1986). Club: The Wisconsin. Avocations: cross country skiing, biking, canoeing, fishing, racquetball, reading. General corporate, Estate planning, Probate. Home: 2700 Newcastle Ct Waukesha WI 53188 Office: Mihal & Steffens SC 735 W Wisconsin Ave Suite 1177 Milwaukee WI 53233

MIKKELSEN, CHARLES R., lawyer, educator; b. Superior, Nebr., Jan. 24, 1954; s. Robert E. and Eileen H. (Shaw) M.; m. T.J. Reilley, Dec. 29, 1978. Student, Nebr. Wesleyan U., 1972-73; BBA, U. Nebr., 1975, MA in Econs., JD, 1979. Bar: Nebr. 1980, U.S. Dist. Ct. Nebr. 1980, Iowa 1982. Asst. prof. bus. law Ill. State U., Normal, 1979-80; trust officer 1st Nat. Bank Sioux City, Iowa, 1981-84, Farmers State Bank and Trust Co., Hays, Kans., 1984—; instr. econs. Fort Hays State U., Hays, 1984; bd. dirs. Bank of Inman, Kans. Mem. Nebr. State Bar Assn. Libertarian. Lodge: Lions. Probate, Estate taxation, Personal income taxation. Office: Farmers State Bank and Trust Co PO Box 10 Hays KS 67601-0010

MIKVA, ABNER JOSEPH, judge; b. Milw., Jan. 21, 1926; s. Henry Abraham and Ida (Fishman) M.; m. Zoe Wise, Sept. 19, 1948; children: Mary, Laurie, Rachel. J.D. cum laude, U. Chgo., 1951; LL.D. (hon.), U. Ill. Bar: Ill. 1951, D.C. 1978. Law clk. to U.S. Supreme Ct. Justice Sherman Minton, 1951; partner firm Devoe, Shadur, Mikva & Plotkin, Chgo., 1952-68, D'Ancona, Pflaum, Wyatt & Riskind, 1973-74; lectr. Northwestern U. Law Sch., Chgo., 1973-75, U. Pa. Law Sch., 1983-85, Georgetown Law Sch., 1986—; mem. Ill. Gen. Assembly from 23d Dist., 1956-66, 91st-92d Congresses from 2d Dist. Ill., 94th-96th Congresses from 10th Dist. Ill., ways and means com., judiciary com.; chmn. Dem. Study Group; resigned, 1979; judge U.S. Circuit Ct. Appeals D.C., 1979—; chmn. Ill. Bd. Ethics, 1973. Author: The American Congress: The First Branch, 1983. Served with USAAF, World War II. Recipient Page One award Chgo. Newspaper Guild, 1964; Best Legislator award Ind. Voters Ill., 1956-66; named One of Ten Outstanding Young Men in Chgo. Jr. Assn. Commerce and Industry, 1961. Mem. ABA, Chgo. Bar Assn. (bd. mgrs. 1962-64), Phi Beta Kappa, Order of Coif. Office: US Ct Appeals 3d and Constitution Ave NW Washington DC 20001

MILAN, EDWIN RAMON, lawyer, real estate broker, foreign language educator; b. Aguadilla, P.R., July 30, 1950; s. Luis Antonio and Tomasa (Perez) M.; m. Maureen Ann Kennedy, June 26, 1976. B.A., Fairfield U., 1972; M.A., U. Va., 1974; J.D., Boston Coll., 1978. Bar: Mass. 1979, U.S. Dist. Ct. Mass. 1981, U.S. Ct. Appeals (1st cir.) 1981. Student atty. Mass. Defenders Com., Boston, 1977-78; counsel Mass. Consumers Council, Boston, 1979-81; asst. counsel New Eng. Mut. Life Ins. Co., Boston, 1981—. Mem. Gov.'s Council on Hispanic and Puerto Rican Affairs, 1978-79; mem. adv. bd. Cardinal Cushing Ctr. for Spanish-Speaking, Boston, 1981-83, Recipient Excellence in Spanish award Am. Assn. Tchrs. Spanish, 1972. Mem. Boston Bar Assn. (mem. real estate com.), Mass. Bar Assn. Democrat. Mem. Christian Ch. Insurance, Real property, General corporate. Office: New England Mutual Life Ins Co 501 Boylston St Boston MA 02117

MILBERG, LAWRENCE, lawyer; b. Bklyn., Oct. 3, 1913; s. Samuel and Mollye (Felsenfeld) M.; m. Madeline Doris Marcus, Aug. 9, 1942; children—Susan J. Milberg Weissman, Frederic J. B.A. cum laude, N.Y.U., 1933; J.D., Harvard U., 1936. Bar: N.Y. 1937, U.S. Ct. Appeals (2d cir.) 1941, U.S. Supreme Ct. 1961. Ptnr. Blumberg, Singer, Ross & Gordon, N.Y.C., 1959-61, Milberg & Levy, N.Y.C., 1961-66; sr. ptnr. Milberg, Weiss, Bershad, Specthrie & Lerach, N.Y.C., 1966—. Served in U.S. Army, 1943-46. Mem. ABA, Bar Assn. N.Y.C., N.Y. County Lawyers Assn., Fed. Bar Council., Phi Beta Kappa. Federal civil litigation, Probate, Class actions. Address: 1 Pennsylvania Plaza New York NY 10119

MILBOURNE, WALTER ROBERTSON, lawyer; b. Phila., Aug. 27, 1933; s. Charles Gordon and Florie Henderson (Robertson) M.; m. Georgena Sue Dyer, June 19, 1965; children: Gregory Broughton, Karen Elizabeth, Walter Robertson, Margaret Henderson. A.B., Princeton U., 1955; LL.B., Harvard U., 1958. Bar: Pa. 1959. Assoc. firm Pepper, Hamilton & Sheetz, Phila., 1959-65, Obermayer, Rebmann, Maxwell & Hippel, Phila., 1965-67; ptnr. Obermayer, Rebmann, Maxwell & Hippel, 1968-84, Saul, Ewing, Remick & Saul, 1984—; dir. Pa. Lumbermen's Mut. Ins. Co., 1972—, Phila. Reins. Corp., 1976—; co-chmn. Nat. Conf. Lawyers and Collection Agys., 1979—; chmn. bus. litigation com. Def. Research Inst., 1986—. Chmn. mental health budget sect. Phila. United Fund, 1967-70. Served with Army N.G., 1958-64. Fellow Am. Coll. Trial Lawyers; mem. Am. Bar Assn., Pa. Bar Assn., Phila. Bar Assn., Internat. Assn. Def. Counsel (exec. com. 1985—), Assn. Def. Counsel. Republican. Clubs: Union League (Phila.); Merion Cricket, Princeton, Idle Hour Tennis (pres. 1968-69), Phila. Lawn Tennis Assn. (pres. 1969-70). Federal civil litigation, State civil litigation, Insurance. Home: 689 Fernfield Circle Strafford PA 19087 Office: 3800 Center Square W Philadelphia PA 19102

MILBRATH, DENNIS HENRY, lawyer; b. Milw., May 10, 1948; s. Earl and Alice (Wendt) M. BA in Econs., U. Wis., Milw., 1972; JD, New England Sch. Law, 1979. Bar: Idaho 1979, U.S. Dist. Ct. Idaho 1979, U.S. Ct. Appeals (9th cir.) 1979, U.S. Ct. Claims 1982, U.S. Tax Ct. 1984, U.S. Ct. Appeals (fed. cir.) 1986, Wis. 1987. Staff atty., counsel Idaho Migrant Council Inc., Boise, 1979-83; sole practice Boise, 1983-87; assoc. Hyatt Legal Services, Milw., 1987—. Bd. dirs. Ada County Parents Annonymous, Boise, 1984-85, Assn. for Retarded Citizens, Boise, ARC Living Inc., Boise. Bar: ABA, Idaho Bar Assn., Ada County Bar Assn., Idaho Trial Lawyers Assn., Nat. Health Lawyers Assn. Democrat. Lutheran. Avocations: hiking, writing essays. Administrative and regulatory, Labor, Government contracts and claims.

MILBURN, HERBERT THEODORE, judge; b. Cleveland, Tenn., May 26, 1931; s. J.E. and Hazel (Shanks) M.; m. Elaine Dillow, Aug. 23, 1957; children—Blair Douglas, Elizabeth Elaine. Student, U. Chattanooga, 1949-50, Boston U., 1950-51; B.S., East Tenn. State U., 1953; J.D., U. Tenn., 1959. Bar: Tenn. 1959, U.S. Supreme Ct. 1971. Assoc. Folts, Bishop, Thomas, Leitner & Mann, Chattanooga, 1959-63; ptnr. Bishop, Thomas, Leitner, Mann & Milburn, Chattanooga, 1963-73; judge Hamilton County Cir. Ct., Chattanooga, 1973-83, U.S. Dist. Ct. (ea. dist.) Tenn., Chattanooga, 1983-84, U.S. Ct. Appeals (6th cir.), Chattanooga, 1984—; mem. faculty Nat. Jud. Coll. U. Nev., Reno, 1980, Tenn. Jud. Acad., Vanderbilt U., Nashville, 1982. pres. Hamilton County Young Republicans, Chattanooga, 1965 (Outstanding Young Rep. 1965); mem. Chancellor's Roundtable U. Tenn., Chattanooga, 1983-86; pres. Lakeside Kiwanis, 1964. Served with U.S. Army Security Agy., 1953-56. Mem. Chattanooga Bar Assn. (sec.-treas. 1967), Tenn. Bar Assn. (commr. 1971-73, profl. ethics and grievance com.), ABA, Fed. Bar Assn. (life), Am. Legion, East Tenn. State U. Found., Golden Key Nat. Honor Soc. at U. Tenn.-Chattanooga (hon.), Alpha Scholastic Honor Soc. at U. Tenn.-Chattanooga (hon.). Republican. Episcopalian. Clubs: Chattanooga Yacht (Chattanooga), Signal Mountain Golf and Country (Tenn.); University (Cin.). Lodges: Masons, Kiwanis (pres. Lakeside club 1964). Office: U S Ct Appeals PO Box 750 Chattanooga TN 37401

MILCHAK, MICHAEL EDWARD, lawyer; b. Annapolis, Md., Nov. 19, 1949; s. Edward Joseph and Anna Bell (Harrison) M.; m. Catherine Louise Hicks, June 3, 1972; children: Michael Christopher, Catherine Elizabeth, Brian Alexander. BS in History, George Mason U., Fairfax, Va., 1975; JD, George Mason U., Arlington, Va., 1978. Bar: Va. 1978, U.S. Dist. Ct. (ea. dist.) Va., U.S. Ct. Appeals (4th cir.). Assoc. S & M Legal Clinic, Arlington, 1980-81, McGinnis & Assocs., Falls Church, Va., 1981-85; ptnr. McGinnis, Milchak & Assocs. Ltd., Falls Church, 1985—. Served with USAR, 1969-75. Mem. ABA. Real property. Home: 6091 N 9th Rd Arlington VA 22205 Office: McGinnis Milchak & Assocs Ltd 120 N Lee St Falls Church VA 22046

MILES, DANA BRENT, lawyer; b. Toronto, Ont., Can., Sept. 24, 1955; came to U.S. 1958; s. George Z. and Joan B. (Britton) M.; m. Bebe D. Crosby, Sept. 8, 1979; children: Britton Kirkland, Trenton Crosby. BA, Emory U., 1977; JD, U. Ga., 1980. Bar: Ga. 1980, U.S. Dist. Ct. (no. dist.) Ga. 1980, U.S. Ct. Appeals (11th cir) 1980. Law clk. to presiding justice Tallapoosa Jud. Cir., Douglasville, Ga., 1980-81; assoc. Lipscomb, Johnson, Miles & Ashway, Cumming, Ga., 1981-83; ptnr. Lipscomb, Johnson, Miles & Ashway, Cumming, 1984—; bd. dirs. Bank South, Cumming, Atlanta Millworks, Cumming, Wilson Clinic, Cumming. Trustee Cumming United Meth. Ch., 1985—. Recipient Appreciation award Concerned Citizens, S.E. Forsyth County, 1984. Mem. Ga. Bar Assn.(exec. com. young lawyers sect. 1982—, bd. dirs.), Blue Ridge Bar Assn. (sec.-treas. 1984, v.p. 1985, pres. 1986), Cumming-Forsyth Bar Assn. (treas. 1984-85). Democrat. Methodist. Lodge: Rotary (Appreciation award 1985). Federal civil litigation, State civil

litigation, Contracts commercial. Home: Lanier Rt 7 Box 955 Cumming GA 30130 Office: Lipscomb Johnson Miles & Ashway 112 N Main St Cumming GA 30130

MILES, DORI ELIZABETH, lawyer; b. Bklyn., Jan. 3, 1953; d. Sidney and Beatrice (Lehman) Miles. B.A., NYU, 1974; J.D., Southwestern U., Los Angeles, 1982. Bar: Calif. 1982, U.S. Ct. Appeals (9th cir.) 1982, U.S. Dist. Ct. (cen. dist.) Calif. 1982. Student extern U.S. Dist. Ct. (cen. dist.) Calif., Los Angeles, summer 1981, U.S. Ct. Appeals (9th cir.), Los Angeles, 1982; assoc. Fonda & Garrard, Los Angeles, 1982-85, Memel, Jacobs, Pierno, Gersh & Ellsworth, Los Angeles, 1985—. Mem. ABA, Calif. Bar Assn., Los Angeles Bar Assn., Southwestern U. Sch. Law Dean's Circle (founding). State civil litigation, Personal injury, Insurance. Home: 3400 Centinela Ave #13 Los Angeles CA 90066 Office: Fonda & Garrard 11150 W Olympic Blvd Suite 1000 Los Angeles CA 90064

MILES, GERARD FRANCES, lawyer; b. Balt., Nov. 12, 1954; s. Eugene Langrall and Anne (Noeth) M.; m. Katherine Hohman, July 30, 1977; 1 child, Gerard F. Jr. BA summa cum laude, Loyola Coll., Balt., 1975; JD with honors, U. Md., 1978. Bar: Md. 1978, U.S. Dist. Ct. Md. 1978, U.S. Ct. Appeals (4th cir.) 1978. Clk. to presiding justice U.S. Dist. Ct. Md., Balt., 1978-79; assoc. Baker & Baker, Balt., 1979-82; assoc. Lerch and Huesman, Balt., 1982-85, ptnr., 1986—. Nat. Merit Scholar Loyola Coll., 1972. Mem. ABA, Md. State Bar Assn., Balt. City Bar Assn., Md. Assn. Def. Trial Counsel, Def. Research and Trial Lawyer Assn., Order of Coif. Democrat. Roman Catholic. Club: Winters Run Golf (Belair, Md.) (bd. govs. 1980-82). Avocations: golf, bridge, tennis. Insurance, Personal injury, Federal civil litigation. Home: 1821 Leadburn Rd Baltimore MD 21204 Office: Lerch and Huesman 16 S Calvert St Suite 504 Baltimore MD 21202

MILES, HARRY LEHMAN, lawyer, educator; b. Bklyn., May 4, 1944; s. Sidney and Beatrice (Lehman) M.; m. Judith E. Bernstein, Oct. 20, 1967; children—Gary, Sarah. A.B., Dartmouth Coll., 1965; J.D., Bklyn. Law Sch., 1969; M.A. in Communications, U. Mass., Amherst, 1972. Bar: Mass. 1971, U.S. dist. ct. Mass. 1972. Tchr., James Madison High Sch., Bklyn., 1966-70; instr. U. Mass., Amherst, 1970-72; practice law, Amherst, 1971-75; asst. dist. atty. Northwestern Dist. Mass., 1975-79, 1st asst. dist. atty., 1979-80; ptnr. Growhoski, Callahan, Howard & Miles, Northampton, Mass., 1980—; adj. prof. law Western New Eng. Coll. Sch. Law; v.p., dir. Western Mass. Legal Services Corp. Mem. Shutesbury (Mass.) Bd. Health, 1972-74, Shutesbury Fin. Com., 1973-74. Mem. Mass. Assn. Law-Related Edn. (dir.), ABA, Mass. Bar Assn., Hampshire County Bar Assn., Franklin County Bar Assn., Am. Acad. Forensic Scis., Democrat. Jewish. Club: Pioneer Valley Dartmouth (former pres.). State civil litigation, Personal injury, Civil rights. Office: Growhoski Callahan Howard & Miles 60 State St Northampton MA 01060

MILES, JEROLD LANE, lawyer; b. Rocky Ford, Colo., Aug. 4, 1936; s. Virgil Mortimer and Lucy Corinne (Lane) M.; m. Jacquelyn Joyce Kavan, Feb. 2, 1957; children: Judith Candice, Jeffrey Douglas. BS in Bus., U. Colo., 1960; JD, UCLA, 1966. Bar: Calif. 1967. Assoc. O'Melveny & Myers, Los Angeles, 1966-72; from assoc. to ptnr. Agnew, Miller & Carlson, Los Angeles, 1972-81; ptnr. Finley, Kumble, Wagner, Heine, Underberg, Manley & Casey, Los Angeles, 1981-86, Newport Beach, Calif., 1986-87; of counsel Pettit & Martin, Costa Mesa, Calif., 1987—; panelist numerous orgns.; speaker various orgns. Mng. editor UCLA Law Rev., 1965-66. Treas. 1st Christian Ch. North Hollywood, chmn. bd. trustees, 1978-80; v.p., bd. dirs. Travelers Aid Soc. Los Angeles, 1973-77, 84-86; bd. dirs. United Services Orgn., Los Angeles Area, 1970-84, pres. 1977-79, Disciples Home Corp., 1978-81, Calif. Wine Patrons Calif. Mus. Sci. and Industry, 1983—, pres. 1986-87, Braille Inst. Am. Inc., 1984-86. Mem. Calif. Bar Assn. (exec. com. real property sect. 1979-82), Los Angeles Bar Assn. (symposium chmn. 1976-77, program chmn. 1977-78, retreat chmn. 1978-79, newsletter chmn. 1979-80, chmn. exec. com., real property sect. 1984-85, past chmn. real property subsect. 1976-77), Order of Coif, Wine and Food Soc. So. Calif., Am. Coll. Real Estate Lawyers. Republican. Clubs: Regency, Ironwood Country, Chevaliers du Tastevin, Center of Costa Mesa. Real property. Home: 32 Morro Bay Dr Corona del Mar CA 92625 Office: Pettit & Martin 3200 Park Center Dr Costa Mesa CA 92626

MILES, JUDITH ELLEN, lawyer, educator; b. Washington, Oct. 22, 1943; d. Louis Morton and Sylvia L. (Livingston) Bernstein; m. Harry Lehman Miles, Aug. 20, 1967; children—Gary David, Sarah Lynn. B.A., Sarah Lawrence Coll., 1965; J.D. magna cum laude, Western New Eng. Coll., 1977. Bar: Mass. 1977, U.S. Dist. Ct. Mass. 1978. Intern dist. atty. for northwestern dist. Commonwealth of Mass., 1976-77; assoc. firm Richard M. Howland, P.C., Amherst, Mass., 1977-79; law clk. Mass. Appeals Ct., Springfield and Boston, 1979-80, criminal staff atty., 1980-85, sr. criminal staff atty., 1985—; adj. prof. law Western New Eng. Coll., Springfield, 1980—. Assoc. editor Mass. Law Rev., 1981—. Recipient Am. Jurisprudence awards 1974-75, 76, 77. Mem. Mass. Assn. Law Related Edn. (lectr. 1982—), ABA, Mass. Bar Assn., Women's Bar Assn. Mass (v.p. 1984-85), Mass. Assn. Women Lawyers, Mass. Trial Lawyers Assn., Hampshire County Bar Assn., Franklin County Bar Assn., Hampden County Bar Assn. Democrat. Criminal, Legal education, Judicial administration. Home: 33 Fisher St Amherst MA 01002 Office: Mass Appeals Ct 80 State St Springfield MA 01103

MILES, LAWRENCE WILLIAM, JR., lawyer; b. San Antonio, July 8, 1953; s. Lawrence William and Aurora (Perales) M.; m. Marsha A. Bedwell, July 7, 1979; children: Jonathan, Katherine. BA in Polit. Sci., UCLA, 1975; MA in Urban Affairs, Occidental Coll., 1976; JD, U. Calif., Davis, 1980. Bar: Calif. 1980, U.S. Ct. Appeals (9th cir.) 1980. Ptnr. Bedwell & Miles Inc., Yuba City, Calif., 1980-84, Brown, Hill, Bedwell & Miles, Yuba City, 1984-85; v.p., gen. counsel Worthington Oil and Gas Corp., Sacramento, 1986—. Author: Hanging Up Your Shingle, 1986. CORO fellow, 1976. Mem. ABA, Calif. Bar Assn. (del. 1983), Calif. Trial Lawyers Assn. Democrat. Roman Catholic. Lodge: Kiwanis (v.p. Yuba City 1985—, Kiwanian of Yr. 1985). Avocations: flying, sports. General corporate, Insurance, Real property. Office: Worthington Oil and Gas Corp 3815 Florin Rd Sacramento CA 95823

MILES, WENDELL A., federal judge; b. Holland, Mich., Apr. 17, 1916; s. Fred T. and Dena Del (Alverson) M.; m. Mariette Bruckert, June 8, 1946; children: Lorraine Miles Rector, Michelle Miles Kopinski, Thomas Paul. A.B., Hope Coll., 1938, LL.D. (hon.), 1980; M.A., U. Wyo., 1939; J.D., U. Mich., 1942; LL.D. (hon.), Detroit Coll. Law, 1979. Bar: Mich. Ptnr. Miles & Miles, Holland, 1948-53, Miles, Mika, Meyers, Beckett & Jones, Grand Rapids, Mich., 1961-70; pros. atty. County of Ottawa, Mich., 1949-53; U.S. dist. atty. Western Dist. Mich., Grand Rapids, 1953-60; U.S. dist. judge Western Dist. Mich., 1974—, chief judge, 1979-86, sr. chief judge, 1986—; circuit judge 20th Jud. Circuit Ct. Mich., 1970-74; instr. Hope Coll., 1948-53, Am. Inst. Banking, 1953-60; adj. prof. am. constl. history Hope Coll., Holland, Mich., 1979—; mem. Mich. Higher Edn. Commn. Pres. Holland Bd. Edn., 1952-63. Served to capt. U.S. Army, 1942-47. Recipient Liberty Bell award, 1986. Fellow Am. Bar Found.; mem. Am., Mich., Fed., Ottawa County bar assns., Grand Rapids Bar, Am. Judicature Soc. Club: Torch. Lodges: Rotary; Masons. Jurisprudence. Office: US Dist Ct 482 Fed Bldg 110 Michigan St NW Grand Rapids MI 49503

MILIMAN, DAVID JAY, lawyer; b. Balt., Jan. 19, 1957; s. Theodore and Marcia Merle (Levin) M.; m. Hinda Miriam Leikach, July 24, 1980; children: Heather Rose, Louis Scott. BA, U. Md., 1978; JD, U. Balt., 1981. Bar: Md. 1981, U.S. Dist. Ct. Md. 1981, U.S. Ct. Appeals (4th cir.) 1982. Assoc. Law Offices of I. Elliott Goldberg, Balt., 1982-84, Rochlin & Settleman P.A., Balt., 1984—. Mem. ABA, Md. Bar Assn., Md. Trial Lawyers Assn., Nat. Orgn. Social Security Claimants Reps., Md. Criminal Def. Attys. Assn., Nat. Rifle Assn. (class C pistol coach 1984—). Republican. Jewish. Club: Arlington Rifle and Pistol Club (sec. 1982-83). Pension, profit-sharing, and employee benefits, Personal injury, Criminal. Office: Rochlin & Settleman PA 110 E Lexington St Suite 300 Baltimore MD 21202

MILITELLO, SAMUEL PHILIP, lawyer; b. Buffalo, Dec. 16, 1947; s. Samuel Anthony and Katherine (Pesono) M.; m. Anne Little, May 27, 1972; children—Matthew Samuel, Rebecca Anne, Caitlin Frances. BA, Canisius Coll., 1969; JD, SUNY-Buffalo, 1972. Bar: N.Y. 1972, U.S. Ct. Mil. Appeals 1973, U.S. Ct. Claims 1977, U.S. Supreme Ct. 1977, U.S. Dist. Ct. (we. dist.) N.Y. 1986. Assoc., Williams & Katzman, Watertown, N.Y., 1978-79; legal counsel Parsons Corp., Pasadena, Calif., 1979-84, mgr. litigation, 1981-84; gen. counsel, sec. Envirogas, Inc., Hamburg, N.Y., 1984-86 ; sole practice, Watertown, 1986—; counsel Parsons Gilbane, New Orleans, 1979-81; gen. counsel Graham Constrn. & Maintenance Corp., Watertown, 1979—, Law Bros. Contracting Corp., 1986—, C&C Infared, 1986—. Served to capt. JAGC, U.S. Army, 1973-78. Decorated Army Commendation medal with one oak leaf cluster, Meritorious Service medal. Mem. ABA (pub. contracts sect. oil and gas), Fed. Bar Assn., N.Y. State Bar Assn., Am. Judicature Soc., No. N.Y. Builders Exchange, Assoc. Gen. Contractors Am., Associated Bldg. Contractors, Am. Legion. Republican. Roman Catholic. Lodge: KC (advocate 1978-79). Construction, Oil and gas leasing, General corporate. Office: 215 Washington St PO Box 6158 Watertown NY 13601

MILKMAN, MURRAY, lawyer; b. Scranton, Pa., Dec. 6, 1929; s. Harry Robert and Rose (Marcus) M.; m. Irene Capin, Dec. 20, 1959; children: Harry, Samuel. BA, Temple U., 1951; LLB, U. Pa., 1954. Bar: U.S. Dist. Ct. D.C. 1954, PA. 1955, N.J. 1965. Assoc. Berger & Gelman, Phila., 1957-58, Ochman & Greenberg, Phila., 1958-59, Berger & Stein, Phila., 1960-64; asst. counsel Ronson Corp., Woodbridge, N.J., 1964-66, Pa. Power & Light Co., Allentown, 1966—. Mem. Allentown Human Relations Commn., 1974-80; bd. dirs. High Sch. in Israel, Miami, Fla., 1978-80; pres. Congregation Sons of Israel, Allentown, 1979-81; chmn. community relations council Jewish Fedn. Allentown, 1983-85. Served with U.S. Army, 1954-56. Mem. Pa. Bar Assn., Lehigh County Bar Assn. General corporate, Public utilities, Administrative and regulatory. Home: 3044 Greenleaf St Allentown PA 18104 Office: Pa Power & Light Co 2 N 9th St Allentown PA 18104

MILLANE, JOHN VAUGHAN, JR., lawyer; b. Buffalo, May 7, 1926; s. John Vaughan and Margaret Melvin (Hays) M.; m. Lynn Millane, Aug. 16, 1952; children: Maureen, Michele Millane Campanella, John Vaughan III, Kathleen Millane McConnell, Mark Robert. Grad., U. Buffalo, 1950, LLB, 1954; JD, SUNY, Buffalo, 1968. Sole practice Amherst, N.Y., 1955—. Mem., vol. Cath. Charities, United Fund Appeal, United Jewish Appeal; mem. exec. com. Erie County Rep. Party, Buffalo, 1976-86, Lawyers Helping Lawyers, Buffalo, 1982-86; bd. dirs. NAACP. Served to lt. USAAF, 1943-46, ETO. Paul Harris fellow. Mem. ABA (sustaining), N.Y. State Bar Assn., Erie County Bar Assn. (life, com. chmn. 1955-86), Am. Trial Assn., Erie County Bar Found., U. Buffalo Alumni Assn. (bd. dirs.), Amherst C. of C. Republican. Roman Catholic. Clubs: Buffalo Country (Amherst); Buffalo Athletic. Lodges: Rotary, KC. Avocations: reading, tennis. State civil litigation, Personal injury, Criminal. Office: 5500 Main St Amherst NY 14221

MILLAR, RICHARD WILLIAM, JR., lawyer; b. Los Angeles, May 11, 1938. LLB, U. San Francisco, 1966. Bar: Calif. 1967, U.S. Dist. Ct. (cen. dist.) Calif. 1967, U.S. Dist. Ct. (no. dist.) Calif. 1969, U.S. Dist. Ct. (so. dist.) Calif. 1973, U.S. Supreme Ct. Assoc. Iverson & Hogoboom, Los Angeles, 1967-72; ptnr. Eilers, Stewart, Pangman & Millar, Newport Beach, Calif., 1973-75, Millar & Heckman, Newport Beach, 1975-77, Millar, Hodges & Bemis, Newport Beach, 1979—. Mem. ABA (bus. litigation sect., trial practice com.), Calif. Bar Assn. (lectr. continuing legal edn.), Orange County Bar Assn. (chmn. bus. litigation sect. 1981), Am. Judicature Soc. Club: Balboa Bay (Newport Beach). State civil litigation, Federal civil litigation. Home: 2546 Crestview Dr Newport Beach CA 92663 Office: Millar Hodges & Bemis One Newport Pl Suite 900 Newport Beach CA 92660

MILLARD, DAVID B., lawyer; b. Kokomo, Ind., Aug. 31, 1955; s. Howard J. and E. Mary (Brubaker) M.; m. Elizabeth A. Gunyon, Jan. 8, 1984. BS summa cum laude, Ind. U., 1977, JD magna cum laude, 1979. Bar: Ind. 1979, U.S. Dist. Ct. (so. dist.) Ind. 1979. Assoc. Dutton, Kappes & Overman, Indpls., 1979-85, Davies & Leagre, Indpls., 1985—. Mem. Order of Coif, Beta Gamma Sigma, Sigma Iota Epsilon. Securities, Banking, General corporate. Home: 5155 E 74th Ct Indianapolis IN 46250 Office: Davies & Leagre 9100 Keystone Crossing Suite 800 Indianapolis IN 46240

MILLARD, JOHN ALDEN, lawyer; b. Buenos Aires, Argentina, Nov. 4, 1940; s. Alden Shultz and Lois (Guthrie) M.; m. Carey Barbara French, Sept. 7, 1966; children—John Alden, James Guthrie, Alexander French. B.A., Harvard U., 1963, LL.B., 1967. Bar: N.Y. 1968. Assoc., Shearman & Sterling, N.Y.C., 1967-75, ptnr., 1976—. Served with U.S. Army, 1963-64. Mem. Assn. Bar City N.Y. Banking, General corporate. Office: Shearman & Sterling 153 E 53d St New York NY 10022

MILLARD, NEAL STEVEN, lawyer; b. Dallas, June 6, 1947; s. Bernard and Adele (Marks) M.; m. Holly Ann Hinman, Dec. 30, 1970. BA cum laude, UCLA, 1969; JD, U. Chgo., 1972. Bar: Calif. 1972, U.S. Dist. Ct. (cen. dist.) Calif. 1973, U.S. Tax Ct. 1973, U.S. Ct. Appeals (9th cir.) 1987. Assoc. Willis, Butler & Schiefly, Los Angeles, 1972-75; ptnr. Morrison & Foerster, Los Angeles, 1975-84, Jones, Day, Reavis & Pogue, Los Angeles, 1984—; instr. Calif. State Coll., San Bernardino, 1975-76; lectr. Practising Law Inst., N.Y.C., 1983—. Mem. citizens adv. com. Los Angeles Olympics, 1982-84; trustee Altadena (Calif.) Library Dist., 1985—; bd. dirs. Woodcraft Rangers, Los Angeles, 1982—. Served to capt. U.S. Army, 1970-72. Mem. ABA, Calif. Bar Assn., Los Angeles County Bar Assn. (trustee 1985—), Pub. Counsel (bd. dirs. 1984—), U. Chgo. Law Alumni Assn. (So. Calif. chpt. bd. dirs. 1981—), Phi Beta Kappa, Pi Gamma Mu, Phi Delta Phi. Clubs: Los Angeles Athletic; Altadena Town and County. Banking, Private international, Real property. Office: Jones Day Reavis & Pogue 355 S Grand Ave Los Angeles CA 90071

MILLARD, RICHARD STEVEN, lawyer; b. Pasadena, Calif., Feb. 6, 1952; s. Kenneth A. and Kathryn Mary (Paden) M.; m. Jessica Ann Edwards, May 15, 1977;children: Victoria, Elizabeth. AB, Stanford U., 1974; JD magna cum laude, U. Mich., 1977. Bar: Calif. 1977, Colo. 1982, Ill. 1985. Ptnr. Mayer, Brown & Platt, Chgo. Mem. ABA, Order of Coif. Securities, General corporate, Real property. Office: Mayer Brown & Platt 190 S LaSalle St Chicago IL 60604

MILLER, ALAN LEIGH, lawyer; b. Lorain, Ohio, Dec. 5, 1950; s. Edwin Earl and Louise (Komlosi) M.; m. Joan Raynovich, Dec. 20, 1975; children: Ryan Joseph, Jeffrey Alan. BBA, U. Akron, 1973, JD, 1976. Bar: Ohio 1977. Mgr. fin. analysis and planning, truck group White Motor Corp., Eastlake, Ohio; v.p., sec., gen. counsel The Lamson & Sessions Co., Cleve. General corporate. Office: The Lamson & Sessions Co 1600 Bond Ct Cleveland OH 44114

MILLER, ALFRED MONTAGUE, lawyer; b. Augusta, Ga., Jan. 5, 1940; s. Dessie Ford and May Belle (Power) M.; m. Lynthia Wofford, Aug. 25, 1962 (div. 1979); children—William Montague, Stephen Mathews; m. Peggy Elaine Mays, July 26, 1980. B.B.A., U. Ga., 1961, J.D., 1963. Bar: Ga. 1962, Superior Ct. Ga. 1962, U.S. Dist. Ct. (so. dist.) Ga. 1963, U.S. Ct. Appeal (11th cir.) 1981, U.S. Supreme Ct. 1978. Ptnr. Fulcher, Fulcher, Hagler, Harper and Reed, Augusta, 1963-71, Dye, Miller, Tucker and Everitt, P.A., Augusta, 1971—; dir. First Nat. Bank Atlanta, Augusta, Cohen-Walker, Inc., Augusta. Bd. dirs. Ga. Student Ednl. Fund, Athens. Fellow Ga. Bar Found., Am. Coll. Trial Lawyers; mem. Am. Judicature Soc., ABA, Lawyers-Pilot Bar Assn., State Bar Ga. (bd. govs. 1977-85), Augusta Bar Assn. (pres. 1985), Internat. Assn. Ins. Counsel, Ga. Def. Lawyers Assn., Augusta Area Trial Lawyers Assn. (pres. 1974-76), Beta Gamma Sigma, Chi Phi (pres. 1960-61), Phi Delta Phi. Presbyterian. Personal injury, Federal civil litigation, State civil litigation. Home: 4384 Deer Run Evans GA 30809 Office: Dye Miller Tucker & Everitt PA 453 Greene St PO Box 2426 Augusta GA 30903

MILLER, ARTHUR HAROLD, lawyer; b. Plainfield, N.J., Sept. 21, 1935; s. Leon Daniel and Bertha Zelda (Madoff) M.; m. Lynn Fieldman, Aug. 24, 1958; children—Jennifer, Jonathan. B.A., Princeton U., 1957; J.D., Columbia U., 1960. Bar: N.Y. 1961, U.S. Supreme Ct. 1965, N.J. 1969. Assoc. Wachtel & Michaelson, N.Y.C., 1961-65, Netter, Lewy, Dowd, N.Y.C., 1965-67, Dannenberg Hazen & Lake, N.Y.C., 1967-69; ptnr. Clarick, Clarick & Miller, New Brunswick, N.J., 1971-78, Miller & Littman, New Brunswick, 1979—; chmn. Middlesex County Legal Services Corp., New Brunswick, 1975-83. Mem. Sch. Bd. Highland Park, N.J., 1981-84. Democrat. Jewish. Mem. N.J. Bar Assn. (chmn. availibility legal services com. 1983-85, lawyer referral com. 1986—), N.Y. State Bar Assn., Middlesex County Bar Assn. (trustee 1987—). Bankruptcy, State civil litigation, General corporate. Home: 145 N 9th Ave Highland Park NJ 08904 Office: Miller & Littman 96 Paterson St New Brunswick NJ 08901

MILLER, ARTHUR MADDEN, investment banker, lawyer; b. Greenville, S.C., Apr. 10, 1953; s. Charles Frederick and Kathryn Irene (Madden) M. AB in History, Princeton U., 1973; MA in History, U. N.C., 1976; JD with distinction, Duke U., 1978; LLM in Taxation, NYU, 1982. Bar: N.Y. 1979, U.S. Dist. Ct. (so. dist.) N.Y. 1979. Assoc. Mudge Rose Guthrie Alexander & Ferdon, N.Y.C., 1978-85; v.p. pub. fin. Goldman, Sachs & Co., N.Y.C., 1985—. Mem. adv. bd. Mary Baldwin Coll., Staunton, Va., 1982-86; trustee Princeton U. Rowing Assn., N.J., 1980—, pres., 1986—; trustee Rebecca Kelly Dance Co., N.Y.C., 1984-86. Mem. ABA (tax sect. com. on tax exempt financing 1985-86), Nat. Assn. Bond Lawyers (lectr. 1985—), Pub. Securities Assn. (cons. 1985—), Practising Law Inst. (lectr. 1980, editor/author course materials 1980), Bond Attys. Workshop (editor/author course material 1983—, lectr. 1983—). Clubs: Princeton, Downtown Athletic (N.Y.C.). Municipal bonds, Personal income taxation, Banking. Home: 145 W 86th St Apt 14C New York NY 10024 Office: Goldman Sachs & Co 85 Broad St New York NY 10004

MILLER, ARTHUR RAPHAEL, legal educator; b. N.Y.C., June 22, 1934; s. Murray and Mary (Schapin) M.; m. Ellen Monica Joachim, June 8, 1958 (div. 1978); 1 child, Matthew Richard.; m. Marilyn Tarmy, 1982 (separated 1984). A.B., U. Rochester, 1955; LL.B., Harvard U., 1958; student, Bklyn. Coll., 1952, 55, CCNY, 1955. Bar: N.Y. 1959, U.S. Supreme Ct 1959. With Cleary, Gottlieb, Steen & Hamilton, N.Y.C., 1958-61; assoc. dir. Columbia Law Sch. Project Internat. Procedure, N.Y.C., 1961-62; instr. Columbia U. Law Sch., 1961-62; asso. prof. U. Minn. Law Sch., 1962-65; prof. law U. Mich. Law Sch., 1965-72; vis. prof. Harvard U. Law Sch., 1971-72, prof., 1972—; research asso. Mental Health Research Inst., 1966-68; dir. project computer assisted instn. Am. Assn. Law Schs., 1968—; spl. rapporteur State Dept. concerning chpt. II of Hague Conv., 1967; del. U.S.-Italian Conf. Internat. Jud. Assistance, 1961, 62; chmn. task force external affairs Interuniv. Communications Council, 1966-70; mem. law panel, com. sci. and tech. info. Fed. Council Sci. and Tech., Pres.'s Office Sci. and Tech., 1969-72; mem. adv. group Nat. Acad. Sci. Project on Computer Data Banks, 1970—; mem. spl. adv. group to chief justice Supreme Ct. on Fed. Civil Litigation; mem. com. on automated personal data systems HEW, 1972-73; chmn. Mass. Security and Privacy Council, Mass. Commn. on Privacy; mem. U.S. Commn. New Technol. Uses Copyrighted Works, 1975-79; reporter U.S. Supreme Ct.'s Adv. Com. on Civil Rules; faculty Fed. Jud. Center; reporter study on complex litigation Am. Law Inst.; host syndicated TV show Miller's Court.; legal expert Good Morning America; Bd. dirs. Research Found. on Complex Litigations, 1975—. Author: (with others) New York Civil Practice, 8 vols, Civil Procedure Cases and Materials, (with C.A. Wright) Federal Practice and Procedure: Civil, 22 vols, 1969-85, (with others) CPLR Manual, 1967, The Assault on Privacy: Computers, Data Banks, and Dossiers, 1971, Miller's Court, 1982. Served with AUS, 1958-59. Mem. ABA, Am. Law Inst. Legal education. Office: Harvard U Sch Law Cambridge MA 02138 *

MILLER, ARTHUR ROBERT, lawyer; b. Chgo., June 19, 1950; s. Elmer and Rose Miller; m. Shirley J. Miller, Jan. 30, 1982; children: Allison Lynn, Adrianne Elizabeth. BA in Econs. with honors, U. Mich., 1971, JD, 1974. From assoc. to ptnr. Quinn, Jacobs, Barry & Miller, Chgo., 1974-85, sr. ptnr., 1985—. Mem. ABA, Ill. Bar Assn., Chgo. Bar Assn. Clubs: Met., Attic (Chgo.). General corporate, Corporate taxation, Personal income taxation. Office: Quinn Jacobs Barry & Miller 135 S LaSalle St #1425 Chicago IL 60603

MILLER, BARBARA CURRIE, lawyer; b. Port Huron, Mich., Jan. 3, 1930; s. Richard S. and Pearl Hattie (Schiel) Currie; divorced Nov. 1977; children: Kathleen, Peter, Melanie. BA, Mich. State U., 1952; MA, U. Ala., 1975; JD, Mercer U., 1981; grad. with honors, U.S. Army Missle Sch., 1982. Bar: Ga. 1981, Ala. 1982. Contract specialist U.S. Army Missle Command, Redstone Arsenal, Ala., 1981; sole practice Huntsville, Ala., 1982, 85—; contract adminstr. Sci Systems, Inc., Huntsville, 1982-83, Martin Marietta, Orlando, Fla., 1984-85. Mem. Huntsville Alliance for Mentally Ill. Mem. ABA, Ga. Bar Assn., Ala. Bar Assn., Huntsville Bar Assn., Nat. Contract Mgmt. Assn. (cert.), NOW, Women's Network. Avocations: sewing, reading, bicycling. Government contracts and claims, General practice, State civil litigation. Home: 341 Chateau Dr SW Huntsville AL 35801 Office: 101 N Clinton Ave 703 Terry Hutchens Bldg Box 4 Huntsville AL 35804

MILLER, BARRY ALAN, lawyer; b. Chgo., June 28, 1954; s. Bernard and Helene Iris (Lieberman) M. BA, Yale U., 1975; JD, Harvard U., 1978. Bar: Ill. 1978, U.S. Dist. Ct. (no. dist.) Ill. 1978, U.S. Ct. Appeals (7th cir.) 1979, D.C. 1981, U.S. Ct. Appeals (D.C. cir.) 1981. Law clk. U.S. Dist. Ct. (no. dist.) Ill., Chgo., 1978-79; trial atty. civil rights div. U.S. Dept. Justice, Washington, 1979-82; assoc. Miller, Shakman, Nathan & Hamilton, Chgo., 1982—. Sr. editor Harvard Civil Rights-Civil Liberties Law Rev., 1977-78. Mem. ABA, Chgo. Bar Assn., Cook County Legal Assistance Found. (bd. dirs. 1982-83), Chgo. Council Lawyers (bd. govs. 1985—). Federal civil litigation, State civil litigation, Civil rights. Office: Miller Shakman Nathan & Hamilton 208 S LaSalle St Chicago IL 60604

MILLER, CARL THEODORE, lawyer; b. Lewistown, Pa., July 17, 1953; s. Clifford R. Jr. and Pauline (Baker) M.; m. Lisa Williams, June 4, 1977; children: Emily Elizabeth, Timothy Stephen. AB, Coll. William and Mary, 1975, JD, 1978. Bar: Ky. 1979, U.S. Dist. Ct. (we. dist.) Ky. 1979. Assoc. Greenebaum Doll & McDonald, Louisville, 1978-80; atty. Ky. Ct. Appeals, Frankfort, 1980-83, Ky. Supreme Ct., Frankfort, 1983—; speaker workshops, Louisville, Denver. Pres. council and congregation Calvary Luth. Ch., Louisville, 1980-82; mem. fin. com. Hopeful Luth. Ch., Florence, Ky., 1984—, ch. council, 1987—. Mem. ABA (jud. adminstrn. div.), Ky. Govt. Bar Assn., Com. Appellate Staff Attys., Ky. Bar Assn. Avocation: sports. State civil litigation, Judicial administration, Administrative and regulatory. Home: 60 Miriam Dr Florence KY 41042 Office: Ky Supreme Ct 204 State Capitol Frankfort KY 40601

MILLER, CARLA DOROTHY, lawyer; b. Honesdale, Pa., Jan. 15, 1951; d. Carl K. Miller and Dorothy Ruth (Schubert) Jones. BA in Criminology, Fla. State U., 1972; JD, U. Fla., 1979. Bar: Fla. 1980. Asst. atty. U.S. Justice Dept., Jacksonville, Fla., 1980-83; sole practice Jacksonville, 1983—. Mem. Leadership Jacksonville, 1985, Jr. League, 1983—. Mem. Jax Bar Assn., Fed. Bar Assn. Computer, Criminal, Personal injury. Home: 1911 Hickory Ln Atlantic Beach FL 32233 Office: 221 E Church St Jacksonville FL 32202

MILLER, CHARLES E., judge; b. Washington, Sept. 26, 1944; s. Charles Edward Miller and Mary (Cox) M.; m. Katherine McGill Kelley, Dec. 24, 1983. B.A., So. Meth. U., 1971, J.D., 1972. Bar: Tex. 1972. Assoc., Roseborough & Curlee, Dallas, 1972-77; judge County Criminal Ct. #7, Dallas, 1977-82, Ct. Criminal Appeals, Austin, Tex., 1983—; adj. prof. criminal law So. Meth. U. Law Sch., Dallas, 1980-82. Served with U.S. Army, 1966-70. Named Disting. Mil. Grad., Officer Candidate Sch., Ft. Sill, Okla., 1968; decorated Army Commendation medal, 1970. Mem. State Bar Tex. (chmn. criminal law sect. 1981-82). Democrat. Criminal. Home: 1705 Wild Basin Ledge Austin TX 78746 Office: Ct Criminal Appeals Supreme Ct Bldg Austin TX 78711

MILLER, CHARLES JOSEPH, lawyer; b. Providence, Nov. 3, 1947; s. Edward and Marie Christine (Cameron) M.; m. Ashley Rives Rush, July 2, 1985; children: Anthony Lee, Christina Louise. BA, U. R.I., 1969; JD, The Cath. U. of Am., 1982. Bar: D.C. 1982, U.S. Ct. Appeals (Fed. cir.) 1985, U.S. Supreme Ct. 1986. Tchr. Providence Pub. Schs., 1969-70; vol. VISTA, Bronx, N.Y., 1970-72; investigator U.S. CSC, Washington, 1972-76, personnel mgmt. specialist, 1976-78; personnel mgmt. specialist U.S. Dept. Navy, Arlington, Va., 1970-80; mem. Employee Appeals Rev. Bd., Arlington, 1980-87; dep. chief office equal employment opportunity Def. Logistics Agy., Alexandria, Va., 1987—; guest instr. Office of Personnel Mgmt., Washington, 1978—; instr. Administrv. Law Inst., Washington, 1985. Mem. ABA, D.C. Bar Assn., Capital P.C. User Group Inc. Republi-

can. Roman Catholic. Avocations: micro computers, wine collecting. Administrative and regulatory, Civil rights, Labor. Home: 1346 Lynnbrook Dr Arlington VA 22201 Office: Def Logistics Agy Office Equal Employment Opportunity Alexandria VA 22304-6100

MILLER, DAMON CRADDOCK, lawyer; b. Summit, N.J., Jan. 26, 1947; s. Richard Lawrence and Gene (Williams) M. AB cum laude, Princeton U., 1968; JD, U. Pa., 1975. Bar: Pa. 1975, U.S. Dist. Ct. (ea. dist.) Pa. 1975, U.S. Ct. Appeals (3d cir.) 1975, U.S. Ct. Appeals (5th cir.) 1987. Assoc. Rawle & Henderson, Phila., 1975-83, Stassen, Kostos & Mason, Phila., 1983-84; trial atty. civil div., torts br. U.S. Dept. of Justice, Washington, 1984—. Served to lt. (j.g.) USNR, 1968-72. Mem. ABA, Maritime Law Assn. U.S. Democrat. Mem. Unitarian Ch. Avocations: choral singing. Admiralty, Federal civil litigation. Home: 4435 Fessenden St NW Washington DC 20016 Office: US Dept Justice Civil Div Torts Br PO Box 14271 Washington DC 20044

MILLER, DAVID, lawyer; b. Portsmouth, N.H., Nov. 1, 1905; s. Jacob Robert and Rebecca (Apteker) M.; m. Helen Oser, Jan. 15, 1944; children: Robin Miller Holbrook, Jay Robert, Brant Oser. B, U. N.H., 1926; LLB, Boston U., 1929; D in Polit. Sci. (hon.), U. San Antonio, 1967; LLD (hon.), U. Tex., 1969. Lic. real estate agt. N.H., Mass., Conn., R.I., N.J., Md., Va., Tex. Sole practice San Antonio, 1929—; asst. atty. City of Boston; asst. atty. gen. State of Mass., Boston. Mem. Hemisphere Tower Com., San Antonio, 1968, Bexar County Crime Commn., San Antonio, Tex. World Fair Com., San Antonio, 1962, N.Y. World Fair Com., San Antonio, 1964; bd. dirs. San Antonio Better Bus. Bur., San Antonio, Bexar County Mental Health Assn., San Antonio. Mem. Mass. Bar Assn. Jewish. Club: St. Anthony, University (San Antonio). Lodge: B'nai B'rith. Home: 174 Schreiner Pl San Antonio TX 78212 Office: 1003 NE Loop 410 San Antonio TX 78209

MILLER, DAVID ANTHONY, states attorney; b. Linton, Ind., Oct. 6, 1946; s. Edward I. and Jane M. (O'Hern) M.; m. Carol E. Martin, Aug. 9, 1970. Student, Murray State U., 1965; BS, Ind. State U., 1969; JD, Ind. U., Indpls., 1973. Bar: Ind. 1973, U.S. Dist. Ct. (so. dist.) Ind. 1973, U.S. Supreme Ct., U.S. Ct. Appeals (7th cir.) 1982. Dep. atty. gen. State of Ind., Indpls., 1973-76, dir. consumer protection div. office atty. gen.'s, 1976—, asst. atty. gen., 1977-80, chief counsel office atty. gen., 1981—. Youth dir. Emmanuel Luth. Ch., Indpls., 1981-85. Mem. ABA, Ind. State Bar. Assn., Ind. State U. Alumni Assn., Lambda Chi Alpha. Republican. Avocations: numismatics, golfing. Contracts commercial, Legislative, Civil rights. Home: 5320 E Fall Creek Pkwy N Dr Indianapolis IN 46220 Office: Office of Atty Gen 219 State House Indianapolis IN 46204

MILLER, DAVID KENNETH, lawyer; b. Newberg, Oreg., Oct. 10, 1955; s. Edgar Robert and Barbara Jean (Newberg) M.; m. Victoria Lynn Gernhart, June 25, 1977; children: Gabriel, Jessica. BS, U. Oreg., 1978, JD, 1982. Bar: Oreg. 1982, U.S. Dist. Ct. Oreg. 1982. Assoc. Schwabe, Williamson, Wyatt, Moore & Roberts, Portland, Oreg., 1982—. Mem. Oreg. Bar Assn. (continuing legal edn. com. 1985—), Multnomah County Bar Assn. (bd. dirs. young lawyers div. 1983-85, award of merit 1985), Oreg. Assn. Def. Counsel. Democrat. Presbyterian. Clubs: Multnomah Athletic (Portland); Willamette Valley Country (Canby, Oreg.). Avocations: golf, sports. State civil litigation, Insurance, Medical malpractice defense. Home: 13890 SE 115th Clackamas OR 97015 Office: Schwabe Williamson Wyatt et al 1211 SW Fifth Ave Portland OR 97204

MILLER, DAVID WILLIAM, lawyer; b. Denver, May 16, 1955; s. William Henry and Virginia Marie (Urban) M. BA in Polit. Sci., U. Denver, 1976, JD, 1979. Bar: Colo. 1979, U.S. Dist. Ct. Colo. 1979, U.S. Ct. Appeals (5th and 11th cirs.) 1979. Staff atty. Tenn. Valley Authority, Knoxville, 1979-83; assoc. Roath & Brega P.C., Denver, 1983-84; corp. counsel Ch 2M Hill, Denver, 1984—. Bd. dirs. Big Bros./Big Sisters of Knoxville, 1981-83, pres., 1982-83; bd. dirs. Big Bros., Inc. of Denver, 1986—. Mem. ABA, Colo. Bar Assn., Denver Bar Assn. Democrat. Roman Catholic. Avocations: skiing, tennis, movies, books, theater. General corporate, Insurance, Federal civil litigation. Home: 1780 S Washington St Denver CO 80210 Office: CH 2M Hill PO Box 22508 Denver CO 80222

MILLER, DONALD EUGENE, lawyer; b. Providence, Mar. 20, 1947; s. Meyer Samuel and Beatrice (Wattman) M. A.B., Boston U., 1968; J.D., U. Pa., 1972. Bar: R.I. 1974, U.S. Dist. Ct. R.I. 1974, Mass. 1985. Law clk. to assoc. justice R.I. Supreme Ct., Providence, 1972-73; prin. Temkin & Miller, Ltd., Providence, 1973—; legal counsel Jewish Home for Aged of R.I., 1973—, Camp Ruggles, Providence, 1980—; legal counsel, trustee 1st Night Providence, 1985—. Author: Buying and Selling a Small Business, 1984. Mem. exec. com., trustee Jewish Home for Aged of R.I., Providence, 1974—; trustee Camp Ruggles, Providence, 1980—. Mem. R.I. Bar Assn., Mass. Bar Assn. General corporate, Real property. Home: 320 Slater Ave Providence RI 02906 Office: Temkin & Miller Ltd 1400 Turks Head Pl Providence RI 02903

MILLER, DONN BIDDLE, lawyer; b. Gallipolis, Ohio, July 10, 1929; s. Harry M. and Ernestine (Biddle) M.; m. Margaret P. Sibert, Nov. 6, 1959; children: Robin, Karen, Arthur. B.A., Ohio Wesleyan U., 1951; J.D., U. Mich., 1954; grad., Advanced Mgmt. Program, Harvard, 1974. Bar: Ohio 1954, Calif. 1960. With firm Squire, Sanders & Dempsey, Cleve., 1956-59; from assoc. to ptnr. O'Melveny & Myers, Los Angeles, 1960—; exec. v.p. Carter Hawley Hale Stores, Inc., Los Angeles, 1974-77, gen. counsel, 1977—; also dir.; dir. Pacific Mut. Life Ins. Co., Security Pacific Corp., Security Pacific Nat. Bank, Automobile Club So. Calif. Mem. Los Angeles County Pub. Commn. on County Govt., 1975-76; pres. Conf. Calif. Pub. Utility Counsel, 1969; Trustee Ohio Wesleyan U., 1975-78, Sch. Theology at Claremont, Calif., 1976-78, Occidental Coll., 1981—, John R. and Dora Haines Found., 1987—; bd. dirs. United Way; chmn. Marlborough Sch., 1984-86, trustee, 1980—, John R. and Dora Haines Found., 1987—; mem. com. visitors U. Mich. Law Sch., 1971-74. Served with USAF, 1954-56. Rotary Found. fellow, 1951. Mem. ABA (mem. council pub. utilities sect., mem. spl. com. lawyers' pub. responsibility), Calif. Bar Assn., Ohio Bar Assn., Los Angeles Bar Assn., Los Angeles C. of C. (v.p. 1976-78, dir. 1973-78), Phi Beta Kappa, Order of Coif, Sigma Chi, Omicron Delta Kappa, Delta Sigma Rho, Pi Sigma Alpha, Phi Delta Phi. Methodist. Clubs: California (Los Angeles), Stock Exchange (Los Angeles), Los Angeles Country (Los Angeles), Chancery (Los Angeles), Bel Air Bay (Los Angeles). Home: 308 Loring Ave Los Angeles CA 90024 Office: 400 S Hope St Los Angeles CA 90071

MILLER, EDWARD DOUGLAS, lawyer; b. Covington, Ky., Apr. 8, 1954; s. Edwin Earl and Alberta Faye (King) M.; m. Lynnette Sue Robinson, Dec. 27, 1977; 1 child, Lauren Paige. BA in Polit. Sci. with high distinction, Eastern Ky. U., 1976; JD, U. Louisville, 1978. Bar: Ky. 1979, U.S. Dist. Ct. (ea. dist.) Ky. 1980, U.S. Ct. Appeals (6th cir.) 1982. Ptnr. Swinford & Sims, P.S.C., Cynthiana, Ky., 1979—. Mem. Ed Miller for Congress Com., Cynthiana and Lexington, Ky., 1980-82; treas. John Swinford for Senate Com., Cynthiana, 1981; bd. dirs. Harrison County Edn. Assn., Cynthiana, 1983—, v.p. 1987—; Child Day Care Bd., Cynthiana, 1984; county campaign chmn. Paul, Patton for Lt. Gov., 1987—. Mem. ABA, Ky. Bar Assn. (mem. ho. of dels. 1986—), Harrison County Bar Assn., Assn. Trial Lawyers Am., Ky. Acad. Trial Attys. Democrat. Baptist. Club: Cynthiana Country (bd. dirs. 1984). Lodge: Lions. State civil litigation, Criminal, Personal injury. Home: 126 Taylor Dr Cynthiana KY 41031 Office: Swinford & Sims PSC 34 E Pike St PO Box 397 Cynthiana KY 41031

MILLER, ELLIOT I., lawyer; b. Bklyn., June 4, 1934; children—Hope, Stuart, Abby. B.A. magna cum laude, Tufts U., 1955; LL.B. (Harlan Fiske Stone Scholar), Columbia U., 1958 Bar: N.Y. 1958, U.S. Dist. Ct. (ea. and so. dists.) N.Y. 1960, U.S. Ct. Appeals 1961, U.S. Supreme Ct. 1964. Sole practice, N.Y.C. and Pawling, N.Y., 1981—; mem. nat. adv. council Practising Law Inst., 1973-79. Trustee, Jewish Child Care Assn., 1970-80. Mem. ABA, N.Y. State Bar Assn., N.Y. County Lawyers Assn. Contbr. numerous articles to profl. jours. Corporate taxation, Personal income taxation. Office: 1 Memorial Ave Pawling NY 12564

MILLER, EUGENE PAUL, lawyer; b. Winchester, Va., June 17, 1937; s. Eugene Page and Julia Katherine (Miller) M.; m. Judith Kaye Hollenbank, Aug. 14, 1965; children—Paul Gregory, Heather Hollen. B.A. with honors, U. Va., 1959; J.D., Harvard U., 1962. Bar: D.C. 1962, U.S. Dist. Ct. D.C., 1962, U.S. Ct. Appeals (D.C. cir.) 1963. Trial atty. Dept. Justice, 1962; counsel Export Import Bank U.S., Washington, 1966-73; assoc. Kominers, Fort & Schlefer, Washington, 1973-76, ptnr., 1976—; instr. in bus. law U. Md., Atlantic Div., Lajes, Azores, 1963-64. Served as capt. USAF, 1963-66. Mem. D.C. Bar Assn., ABA, Fed. Bar Assn., Internat. Bar Assn. Club: Army Navy Country (Arlington, Va.). Administrative and regulatory, Contracts commercial, Private international. Office: 1401 New York Ave NW Washington DC 20005

MILLER, EVAN, lawyer; b. Bklyn., Sept. 18, 1956; s. Richard and Lois Pearl (Hirsch) M. BA, Columbia U., 1978; JD, Georgetown U., 1981. Bar: N.Y. 1982, D.C. 1983, U.S. Dist. Ct. D.C. 1984, U.S. Ct. Appeals (D.C. cir.) 1985. Law clk. to presiding justice U.S. Dist. Ct. (so. dist.) Ga., Brunswick, 1981-82; assoc. Pepper, Hamilton & Scheetz, Washington, 1982—. Class chmn. Columbia U. Club of Washington, 1985—. Mem. ABA (task force on prohibited transactions, tax sect., employee benefits com., labor sect., corp. and bus. sect.). Pension, profit-sharing, and employee benefits. Office: Pepper Hamilton & Scheetz 1777 F St NW Washington DC 20006

MILLER, FREDERICK LLOYD, lawyer; b. Cedar Rapids, Iowa, May 6, 1945; s. Howard L. and Fredericka Ann (Pachiarek) M. BA cum laude, Harvard U., 1968; JD, U. Chgo., 1971. Bar: Calif. 1972, N.Y. 1974. Assoc. Arthur, Dry & Kalish, N.Y.C., 1973-78; asst. counsel CIT Fin. Corp., N.Y.C., 1978-80; assoc. counsel Restaurant Assocs. Inc., N.Y.C., 1980-81; asst. sec. Chgo. Pneumatic Tool Co., N.Y.C., 1981—. Served with Army N.G., 1964-70. Securities, General corporate, State civil litigation. Home: 60 E 12th St #14J New York NY 10003 Office: Chgo Pneumatic Tool Co 6 East 44th St New York NY 10017

MILLER, GALE TIMOTHY, lawyer; b. Kalamazoo, Sept. 15, 1946; s. Arthur H. and Eleanor (Johnson) M.; m. Janice Lindvall, Mar. 23, 1946; children—Jeremy L., Amanda E., Timothy W. A.B., Augustana Coll., 1968; J.D., U. Mich., 1971. Bar: Mich. 1971, Colo. 1973, U.S. Dist. Ct. Colo. 1973, U.S. Ct. Appeals (10th cir.) 1979. Trial atty. FTC, Washington, 1971-73; assoc. Davis, Graham & Stubbs, Denver, 1973-77, ptnr., 1978—. Pres., bd. dirs. Ecumenical Housing Corp., 1984—. Mem. ABA (antitrust sect. task force on model civil antitrust jury instrns. 1984-86), Colo. Bar. Assn., Denver Bar Assn. Democrat. Lutheran. Antitrust, Federal civil litigation, State civil litigation. Office: Davis Graham & Stubbs PO Box 185 Denver CO 80201

MILLER, GEOFFREY CHARLES, lawyer; b. Chgo., Jan. 27, 1943; s. Eugene William and Helen Therese (Schwartz) M.; m. Eileen Beth Richmond, Feb. 4, 1978; children—Kimberly Anne, Bret Charles Robinson, Laura Suzanne. B.S. in Accountancy, U. Ill., 1965, J.D. with honors, 1968. Bar: Ill. 1968, U.S. Dist. Ct. (no. dist.) Ill. 1968, U.S. Supreme Ct. 1974. Assoc. Prince, Schoenberg & Fisher, Chgo., 1968-71; ptnr. Eisner, Miller & Frank, Chgo., Park Forest, Ill., 1971-76; prin. Law Offices of Geoffrey C. Miller, Matteson, Ill., 1976—. Pres. Park Forest-Richton Park Community Chest, Ill., 1972-74. Mem. ABA, Ill. State Bar Assn., Chgo. Bar Assn., Order of Coif. Family and matrimonial, Real property, General practice. Office: 930 W 175th St Homewood IL 60430

MILLER, HARRY DANIEL, lawyer, educator, writer; b. Oakland, Calif., Apr. 17, 1931; s. Ralph Daniel and Lucille Grace (Snaveley) M.; m. Jean Gustafson, Mar. 19, 1950; children: Kjerstein Lisa, Daniel Nelson, Carl Blake. BA, U. Calif.-Berkeley, 1952, JD, 1957; student U. Stockholm, 1957-58. Bar: Calif. 1958, U.S. Supreme Ct. 1981. Ptnr., Miller, Starr & Regalia, Oakland, San Francisco and Walnut Creek, Calif., 1964—; adj. prof. U. San Francisco Sch. Law, 1979-83. Trustee, Alta Bates Found. Served with USNR, 1952-54. Co-author: Current Law of California Real Estate, 2d edit., 1973. Real property. Office: Miller Starr & Regalia 2150 Valdez St 16th Floor Oakland CA 94612 Office: 101 California St San Francisco CA 94111

MILLER, HERBERT ALLAN, JR., lawyer; b. Spokane, Wash., Sept. 10, 1951; s. Herbert Allan Miller and Martha Townsend (Koppius) Hall; m. Cynthia Kay Harbett, Aug. 9, 1975; children: W. Stinson, Townsend Allan. BA, U. Ky., 1972, JD, 1976. Bar: Ky. 1976, D.C. 1979, U.S. Dist. Ct. (ea. dist.) Ky. 1977. Atty. chief counsel's office U.S. Customs Service, Washington, 1976-77; corp. counsel Lexington-Fayette (Ky.) Urban County Govt., 1977-80, First Security Nat. Bank, Lexington, 1980—; instr. Coll. of Bus. U. Ky., Lexington, 1984—; legal advisor Gov.'s Banking Task Force, Frankfort, Ky., 1984; bd. dirs. First Security Mortgage Co. Charter mem. Leadership of Lexington, 1980, mem. Lexington Bd. of Zoning Adjustments, 1982—, Lexington Forum, 1984—; bd. dirs. United Cerebral Palsy of Ky. Inc., 1981-85. Mem. ABA, Ky. Bar Assn. (chmn. corp. counsel sect. 1983-84), Ky. Bankers Assn. (legis. com.). Clubs: Lexington Country, Lafayette. Banking, General corporate, Legislative. Office: First Security Nat Bank & Trust Co One First Security Plaza Lexington KY 40507

MILLER, IRWIN ROBERT, lawyer; b. Mt. Vernon, N.Y., May 19, 1942; s. Hyman A. and Sylvia (Lash) M.; children—Jeffrey Brian, Daniel Stewart. B.B.A., Woodbury Coll., 1964; J.D., U. Cin., 1968. Bar: Calif. bar 1969. Since practiced in Los Angeles; propr. Irwin R. Miller (P.C.), 1976—. Contbr. to legal jours. Mem. Los Angeles County Bar Assn., Hollywood Bar Assn. (pres. 1978), Calif. Trial Lawyers Assn., Los Angeles Trial Lawyers Assn., Calif. State Bar (com. on maintenance of profl. competence). Office: 16133 Ventura Blvd #920 Encino CA 91436

MILLER, IVAN LAWRENCE, lawyer; b. Cleve., Feb. 2, 1914; s. Ralph and Sarah (Kichler) M. B.A., Case Western Res. U., 1936, LL.B., J.D., 1938; postgrad., Grad. Sch. Bus. Adminstrn., Harvard U., 1943, Inns of Ct. (Middle Temple), London, Eng., 1945. Bar: Ohio 1938, U.S. Supreme Ct 1960. Sole practice Cleve., 1938-63; ptnr. Ziegler, Metzger & Miller, 1968—; consul of Belgium, Ohio, 1962—; legal adviser Brit. Consulate Gen., 1947—, Canadian Consulate Gen. and Trade Commn., 1964—; v.p., trustee, legal counsel Maison Francaise. Bd. overseers Case Western Res. U., 1973-76. Served to maj., Judge Adv. Gen. Dept. AUS, 1941-46. Decorated Bronze Star medal, Exec. Order Ohio Commodore, Belgian Mil. Cross 1st Class, Knight Order Crown Belgium; officer Order of Brit. Empire, Knight Order of Leopold (Belgium); named Consul of Year in U.S., 1974; recipient Law Alumni Ys. award, 1986. Fellow Royal Soc. Arts (Brit.); mem. ABA, Fed. Bar Assn. (pres. Cleve. 1974-75), Ohio Bar Assn., Cleve. Bar Assn. (past trustee), English Speaking Union (past pres., nat. dir.), Consular Corps Coll., Sch. of Law Alumni Assn. (past pres.), Nat. Alumni Assn. Case Western Res. U. (past pres.), No. Ohio Golf Assn. (legal counsel), World Trade Assn., Assn. Ohio Commodores, Soc. Benchers (chmn.). Clubs: Union; Lake Forest Country (Hudson, Ohio); Commerce, Mid-day, Ohio Commodores, Wig and Pen (Eng.); Link. Lodge: Rotary. Home: 2482 Derbyshire Rd Cleveland Heights OH 44106 Office: 1900 Huntington Bldg Cleveland OH 44115

MILLER, J. BRUCE, lawyer; b. Louisville, Oct. 7, 1940; s. J. R. and Marceline S. (Shanklin) M.; m. Norma Carter Osborne, Feb. 14, 1983; children from previous marriage—Jamie, Alexis, Sarah. B.A. cum laude (Ford Found. scholar), Vanderbilt U., 1962, LL.B. cum laude (scholar), 1965. Bar: Ky. 1965, U.S. Sup. Ct. 1972. Sr. ptnr. Carroll & Miller, Louisville, 1965-79; sr. ptnr. Miller, Conliffe, Sandman, Sullivan & Gorman, 1979-85; sr. ptnr. Nold, Miller, Mosley, 1986—; county atty. Jefferson County (Ky.), 1969-85. Bd. dirs. Leukemia Soc., So. Growth Policies Bd. Named Outstanding Young Man, Louisville Jaycees, 1972. Mem. ABA, Ky. Bar Assn., Nat. Assn. Dist. Attys., Am. Assn. Trial Lawyers, Louisville C. of C. (dir.). Democrat. Club: Big Spring Country (Louisville). General corporate, Local government, Sports. Office: 730 W Main St Suite 500 Louisville KY 40202

MILLER, JACK BURLESON, legal educator, former mayor; b. San Saba, Tex., Oct. 21, 1921; s. Richard and Armour Leigh (Burleson) M.; m. Betty Jo Turner, June 20, 1943; children—Richard Turner, Joe Rogan, Martha Leigh. B.S., Tex. A&M U., 1943; J.D., U. Tex., 1948. Bar: Tex. 1948. County judge San Saba County, 1948-51; sole practice, San Saba, 1953-54; dist. atty. 33d Jud. Dist., 1954-60, dist. judge, 1960-76; assoc. prof. law St. Mary's U. Sch. Law, San Antonio, 1977-80, prof., 1982—; dir. Valero Energy Corp., Lower Colo. River Authority, 1985—. Mayor, City of San Saba, 1977-84. Served to capt. U.S. Army, 1943-46, 51-53. Decorated Bronze Star with oak leaf cluster, Purple Heart. Mem. State Bar Tex., Hill Country Bar Assn. (pres. 1967-68), Tex. Aggie Bar Assn. (pres. 1976-77). Democrat. Presbyterian. Club: Masons. Legal education. Home: 502 W Commerce San Saba TX 76877 Office: St Mary's U Sch Law One Camino Santa Maria San Antonio TX

MILLER, JACK EVERETT, lawyer; b. Monroe, La., Dec. 10, 1921; s. Herman M. and Sybil (Harrison) M.; m. Vivian G., May 13, 1945; m. 2d, Kathryn G., Dec. 23, 1970; children—Jack Everett, John A. Attended Ga. Inst. Tech., Gilbert Johnson Law Sch. Bar: U.S. Ct. Claims, U.S. Tax Ct., U.S. Ct. Mil. Appeals, U.S. Supreme Ct. Assoc. Lewis & Sullivan, Savannah, Ga., 1948-52; ptnr. Glass & Miller, Savannah, 1954-57; ptnr. Duffy, Miller & Duffy, Savannah, 1957-69; sole practice, Savannah, 1969—. Served with JAGC, USAF, 1952-54. Decorated Meritorious Service medal. Mem. Ga. Bar Assn., Am. Bus. Clubs (pres. 1959, dist. gov. 1964), Nat. Bus. Clubs. Criminal, General practice, Personal injury. Home: 2 Stillwood Ct Savannah GA 31406 Office: 122 E Oglethorpe Ave Savannah GA 31401

MILLER, JACK LEE, lawyer; b. Parkersburg, W.Va., Mar. 26, 1928; s. William Guy and Rosetta Pearle (Batten) M.; m. Roseanne K. Williams, Dec. 28, 1954; children—Glenn, Gaylene. AB., W.Va. U., 1950; LL.B., U. Mich., 1954. Bar: W.Va. 1954, Mo. 1955, U.S. Dist. Ct. (no. dist.) W.Va. 1956, U.S. Dist. Ct. (so. dist.) W.Va. 1963, U.S. Ct. Apls. (4th cir.) 1975. Mem. firm Miller, Goldenberg and Brown, Parkersburg, 1955; fin. commr. State W.Va., Charleston, 1969-70; sole practice Parkersburg, 1971-78; chmn. bd., chief exec. officer Appalachian Life Ins. Co., Huntington, W.Va., 1979—. Treas., dir. W.Va. Life & Health Guaranty Assn., Huntington, 1978—; dir. Nat. Brokers, Inc., Huntington, 1980—. Mem. W.Va. Ho. Dels., Charleston, 1960-62; mem. W.Va. Senate, 1962-69. Served to capt. USN, 1946-48, USAF, 1950-52. Chmn. state conv. State Republican Com. 1964. Mem. Am. Legion (state comdr. 1975-76), W.Va. Ins. Fed., Nat. Assn. Life Co.'s (treas. 1983-86). Republican. Methodist. Insurance. Office: Appalachian Life Ins Co 1124 4th Ave Huntington WV 25707

MILLER, JACK RICHARD, senior federal judge; b. Chgo., June 6, 1916; s. Forest W. and Blanche M.; m. Isabelle M. Browning, Aug. 1, 1942; children: Janice Lee (Mrs. Robert Amott), Judy Ann (Mrs. Robert Flynn), James Forrest, Jaynie Kay (Mrs. A.H. Studenmund). A.B. cum laude, Creighton U., 1938, LL.D. (hon.), 1966; M.A., Cath. U., Washington, 1939; J.D., Columbia U., 1946; postgrad., State U. Iowa Coll. Law, 1946; LL.D. (hon.), Loras Coll., 1967, Iowa Wesleyan Coll., 1969, Yonsei U., South Korea, 1976. Bar: Iowa 1946, Nebr. 1946, D.C. 1949. Atty. Office Chief Counsel, IRS, Washington, 1947-48; professorial lectr. taxation George Washington U., 1948; asst. prof. law U. Notre Dame, 1948-49; pvt. practice tax law Sioux City, Iowa, 1949-60; mem. Iowa Ho. of Reps., 1955-56, Iowa Senate, 1957-60; U.S. senator from Iowa 1961-73; judge U.S. Ct. Customs and Patent Appeals, Washington, 1973-82, U.S. Ct. Appeals (fed. cir.), Washington, 1982—; now sr. judge U.S. Ct. Appeals (fed. cir.). Contbr. articles on tax and patent law to legal periodicals. Served from lt. to lt. col. USAAF, 1942-46; brig. gen. USAF Res. (ret.). Mem. ABA, Iowa, Nebr., D.C. bar assns., Am. Law Inst. (life), Am. Patent Law Assn., Am. Legion, VFW, Amvets. Lodges: K.C., Rotary. Corporate taxation, Patent, Trademark and copyright. Office: US Cir Ct of Appeals 717 Madison Pl NW Washington DC 20439

MILLER, JAMES L., lawyer; b. Fairmont, W.Va., June 1, 1951; s. Robert Ogden Jr. and Dora Alice (Ward) M.; m. Maureen Clancy, Apr. 16, 1983; 1 child, James Clancy. BA, Calif. State u., Arcata, 1973; JD, U. Calif., Berkeley, 1976. From assoc. to ptnr. Brobeck, Phleger & Harrison, San Francisco, 1976—. Republican. Club: Athenian Nile (Oakland. Calif.). Avocation: fishing. Federal civil litigation, State civil litigation, Product Liability Litigation. Home: 11 La Bolsita Way Orinda CA 94563 Office: Brobeck Phleger & Harrison One Market Plaza San Francisco CA 94105

MILLER, JAMES ROGERS, JR., federal judge; b. Montgomery County, Md., June 15, 1931; s. James Rogers and Mary Ada (Cecil) M.; m. Jo Anne Trice, Apr. 27, 1957; children: James Rogers III, Andrew Cecil, Merrie H., Katherine T. B.A., Wesleyan U., 1953; LL.B., Georgetown U., 1955. Bar: D.C. 1955, Md. 1956. Practiced in Rockville, 1956-70; mem. firm Miller, Miller & Canby, 1956-70; judge U.S. Dist. Ct. Md., Balt., 1970-86; Mem. ho. of dels. Md. Gen. Assembly, 1962-66; mem. Legislative Council Md., 1963-66; chmn. Montgomery County del. Md. Gen. Assembly, Republican Central Com. for Montgomery County, 1966-67; mem. Jud. Conf. Com. To Consider Standards of Admission To Practice in Fed. Cts., 1977-79, Jud. Conf. Com. To Implement Standards of Admission To Practice in Fed. Cts., 1979-85, Jud. Conf. Com. on Operation of Jury System, 1983-86. Trustee Landon Sch. for Boys, Bethesda, Md., 1966-69. Mem. ABA, Md. Bar Assn., Montgomery County Bar Assn. (pres. 1969-70), Alpha Delta Phi. Jurisprudence. Office: US Courthouse Baltimore MD 21201

MILLER, JEREMY MATTHEW, lawyer, legal educator; b. Boston, Apr. 2, 1954; s. Harold Irving and Maida (Rosenburg) M.; m. Barbara Anderson, June 11, 1977; children: Rachelle Clara, Peter Jason, Nathaniel Perceval. BA, Yale U., 1976; BS, Meru, Switzerland, 1977; JD, Tulane U., 1980; LLM, U. Pa., 1981. Bar: Mass. 1980, U.S. Ct. Appeals (1st, 3d and 10th cirs.) 1981, U.S. Supreme Ct. 1985. Staff atty. Newcomb Fin., Ft. Collins, Colo., 1981; law clk. to presiding justice Colo. Supreme Ct., Denver, 1982-83; prof. Western State U. Coll. of Law, Fullerton, Calif., 1983—. Contbr. articles to profl. jours. Mem. ABA, Mass. Bar Assn. Republican. Avocations: playwriting, lecturing, sports, family. Jurisprudence, Criminal, General corporate. Home: 19761 Carmania Ln Huntington Beach CA 92646-4315 Office: Western State U Coll of Law 1111 N State College Blvd Fullerton CA 92631

MILLER, JOHN EDDIE, lawyer; b. Wayne, Mich., Nov. 14, 1945; s. George Hayden and Georgia Irene (Stevenson) M.; m. Nancy Carol Sanders, Jan. 7, 1968; children—Andrea Christine, Matthew Kit. B.A., Baylor U., 1967; J.D., Memphis State U., 1973; LL.M., U. Mo., 1980. Bar: Mo. 1974, U.S. Dist. Ct. (we. dist.) Mo. 1974, Tex. 1982. Asst. prof. Central Mo. State U., Warrensburg, 1973-74; sole practice, Sedalia, Mo., 1974-79; sr. contract adminstr. Midwest Research Inst., Kansas City, Mo., 1979-81; sr. contract adminstr Tracor Inc., Austin, Tex., 1981-84; contract negotiator Tex. Instruments, Austin, 1984-86; sr. contract adminstr., Tracor Aerospace Inc., Austin, 1986-87, Radian Corp., Austin, 1987—. instr., bus. law State Fair Community Coll., Sedalia, 1974-79, Austin Community Coll., 1983-84. Bd. dirs. Legal Aid Western Mo., 1977-79, Boy's Club, Sedalia, 1974-79, Austin Lawyers Care, 1987—. Served with U.S. Army, 1968-71. Mem. Mo. Bar Assn. Tex. Bar Assn., Nat. Contract Mgmt. Assn., Travis County Bar Assn., Austin Young Lawyers Assn., U.S. Tennis Assn., Phi Alpha Delta. Baptist. Club: AM Tennis (Austin). Government contracts and claims, Contracts commercial, Computer. Home: 12404 Mossy Bark Trail Austin TX 78750 Office: Radian Corp 8501 Mo-Pac Blvd Austin TX 78766

MILLER, JOHN LEED, lawyer; b. Geneva, Ill., May 7, 1949; s. John Axel and Martha Mary (Masilunis) M.; B.A., Northwestern U., 1971; J.D., U. Chgo., 1975. Bar: Ill. 1975. Assoc. counsel Profl. Ind. Mass-Mktg. Adminstrs., Chgo., 1975-76; legis. counsel to minority leader Ill. Ho. of Reps., Chgo. and Springfield (Ill.), 1977-80; chief legal counsel, 1980, chief counsel to speaker of Ho. of Reps., 1981-83; ptnr. Shaw and Miller, P.C., Chgo., 1981-84, Theodore A. Woerthwein, P.C., 1984-85, Woerthwein & Miller P.C., 1985—. Statewide chmn. Ill. Young Voters for the Pres., 1972; dir. Ill. Ho. Republican campaign com., 1976, 78, cons., 1982. Served with USNG, 1969-75. James scholar, 1970. Mem. ABA, Inter-Am. Bar Assn., Lawyers for the Creative Arts, Primitive Art Soc. Chgo. (treas. 1984-86, v.p. 1987—), Phi Eta Sigma, Phi Beta Kappa. Lutheran. Clubs: S.Am. Explorers (Lima, Peru), Elks (DeKalb, Ill.). Legislative, General corporate, Local government. Home: 1030 N State Apt 9D Chicago IL 60610 Office: Woerthwein & Miller 401 S LaSalle St Suite 1200 Chicago IL 60605

MILLER, JOHN RANDOLPH, lawyer; b. Balt., Oct. 1946; s. Alan Randolph and Martha Virginia (Mercer) M.; m. Margaret Rose McGrane, July 20, 1969; children—John Randolph, Joseph Alan. A.B., Duke U., 1968, J.D., 1975. Bar: N.C. 1975, U.S. Dist. Ct. (we. and mid. dists.) N.C. Ptnr. Robinson, Bradshaw & Hinson, P.A., Charlotte, N.C., 1975—; dir. GAAP Investment Co., Charlotte. Author: North Carolina Construction Law, 5th

edit., 1986. Editorial asst. Law and Contemporary Problems, 1974; article editor Duke Law Jour., 1975. Mem. Duke U. Alumni Council, Mecklenburg County, N.C., 1976—; vol. Charlotte Jr. Soccer Found., 1976—. Served to lt. USN, 1969-72. Angier Biddle Duke scholar, 1964. Mem. ABA, N.C. Bar Assn., Am. Arbitration Assn. (panel arbitrators 1986—), Order of Coif, Phi Delta Phi, Sigma Pi Sigma, Pi Mu Epsilon. Democrat. Episcopalian. Club: Tower (Charlotte). Securities, Construction. Home: 1644 Myers Park Dr Charlotte NC 28207 Office: Robinson Bradshaw & Hinson PA 1900 Independence Ctr 101 N Tryon St Charlotte NC 28246

MILLER, JOHN T., JR., lawyer; educator; b. Waterbury, Conn., Aug. 10, 1922; s. John T. and Anna (Purdy) M.; children—Kent, Lauren, Clare, Miriam, Michael, Sheila, Lisa, Colin, Margaret. A.B. with high honors, Clark U., 1944; J.D., Georgetown U., 1948; Docteur en Deoit, U. Geneva (Switzerland), 1951; postgrad. U. Paris, 1951. Bar: Conn. 1949, D.C. 1950, U.S. Ct. Appeals (3d cir.) 1958, U.S. Ct. Appeals (D.C. cir.) 1952, U.S. Ct. Appeals (5th cir.) 1957, U.S. Supreme Ct. 1952. With Econ. Cooperation Adminstrn., Am. embassy, London, 1950-51; assoc. Covington & Burling, 1952-53; Gallagher, Connor & Boland, 1953-62; sole practice, Washington, 1962—; adj. prof. law Georgetown U. Law Center, Washington, 1959—; mem. Panel on Future of Internat. Ct. Justice. Trustee Clark U., 1970-76; bd. advs. Georgetown Visitation Prep. Sch., 1972—; former fin. chmn. troop 46 Nat. Capital Area council Boy Scouts Am. Served with U.S. Army, 1943-46, to 1st lt. C.E., 1948-49. Recipient 10 yr. teaching award Nat. Jud. Coll., 1983. Mem. ABA (council mem., chmn. adminstrv. law sect.), D.C. Bar Assn., Fed. Energy Bar Assn., Internat. Bar Assn., Internat. Law Assn., AAUP. Republican. Roman Catholic. Clubs: International (Washington), Congressional Country (Bethesda, Md.). Co-author: Regulation of Trade, 1953, Modern American Antitrust Law, 1948, Major American Antitrust Laws, 1965; author: Foreign Trade in Gas and Electricity in North America: A Legal and Historical Study, 1970, Energy Problems and the Federal Government: Cases and Material, 1979, 2d edit. 1981; contbr. articles, book revs. to legal publs. FERC practice, Administrative and regulatory, Antitrust. Home: 4721 Rodman St NW Washington DC 20016 Office: 1001 Connecticut Ave NW Washington DC 20036

MILLER, JULES FREDERICK, lawyer; b. St. Louis; married. BA, St. Louis U., 1972, JD, 1975; LLM in Govt. Procurement Law, George Washington U., 1983. Bar: Mo. 1975, Calif. 1986. Atty., advisor Naval Research Lab., Washington, 1981-82; gen. counsel Def. Audiovisual Agy., San Bernardino, Calif., 1983-84; atty. Ford Aerospace, Newport Beach, Calif., 1985—. Served to capt. JAGC, USAF, 1975-80. Mem. ABA, Air Force Assn., Sigma Pi. Government contracts and claims, Federal civil litigation, General corporate. Office: Ford Aerospace Ford Rd Newport Beach CA 92658

MILLER, KEITH LLOYD, lawyer; b. Harvey, N.D., July 27, 1951; s. Lloyd Vernie and Marian A. (Leintz) M.; m. Linda Suzanne Nelson, Aug. 7, 1971; children—Christopher Nelson, Ann Elizabeth. B.A., Concordia Coll., Moorhead, Minn., 1972; J.D., U. N.D., 1975. Bar: Minn. 1976, U.S. Dist. Ct. Minn. 1976, U.S. Ct. Appeals (8th cir.) 1976, N.D. 1982, U.S. Dist. Ct. N.D. 1982. Assoc. Stefanson, Landberg & Alm, Moorhead, 1976-78; ptnr. Miller, Norman, Kenney, & Williams Ltd., Moorhead, 1978—; cons. Nat. Legal Services Corp., Washington, 1984—; dir. Northwestern Minn. Legal Services Corp., Moorhead, 1981-87, chmn. bd., 1983-86 . Bd. dirs. Clay County Democratic Farm Labor Party, Moorhead, 1984-86; advisor Nat. Moot Trial Competition Team Concordia Coll., 1987. Mem. Minn. Trial Lawyers Assn., Assn. Trial Lawyers Am., Minn. State Bar Assn. (state support policy bd. on legal assistance to disadvantaged), State Bar Assn. N.D. Lutheran. Personal injury, State civil litigation, Workers' compensation. Office: Miller Norman Kenney & Williams Ltd 403 S 8th St PO Box 1066 Moorhead MN 56560

MILLER, KENNETH CHARLES, lawyer; b. N.Y.C., Sept. 29, 1943; s. Henry Charles and Helen Miller; m. Mary Patricia Luken, Dec. 28, 1968; children: Jennifer, Charles. BS in Aero. Engring., St. Louis U., 1965, MS, 1969; JD, U. Cin., 1972. Bar: Ill. 1972, U.S. Dist. Ct. (no. dist.) Ill. 1972, U.S. Ct. Appeals (7th cir.) 1972, U.S. Dist. Ct. (so. dist.) Ala. 1975, U.S. Dist. Ct. Idaho 1975, U.S. Ct. Appeals (9th cir.) 1976, U.S. Dist. Ct. (so. dist.) Fla. 1977, U.S. Dist. Ct. N.Mex. 1984, U.S. Dist. Ct. Nev. 1985, U.S. Ct. Appeals (10th cir.) 1985. Engr. Cessna Aircraft, Wichita, Kans., 1965-66; sr. engr. McDonnell Douglas, St. Louis, 1966-69; assoc. Lord, Bissell & Brook, Chgo., 1972-79, Corboy & Demetrio, P.C., Chgo., 1985—; sole practice Chgo., 1979-85. Pres. Nat. Assn. Down Syndrome, Chgo., 1981-85. Mem. ABA, Chgo. Bar Assn. (pres. aviation law com. 1983-84), Assn. Trial Lawyers Am., Ill. Trial Lawyers Assn. Personal injury, Insurance, Aviation. Office: Corboy & Demetrio PC 33 N Dearborn Chicago IL 60602

MILLER, KENNETH MICHAEL, lawyer; b. Los Angeles, Sept. 10, 1941; s. Daniel D. and Lillian R. (Resnick) M.; m. Sheri Holmes, Sept. 4, 1966; children: Sean, Casey. BA, UCLA, 1963; JD, U. Calif., Berkeley, 1966. Bar: Calif. 1966. Spl. agt. FBI, Washington, Miami and San Antonio, 1967-70; assoc. Miller, Starr & Regalia, Oakland, Calif., 1970-75; ptnr. Kass, Morgan, Miller & Wilson, Oakland, 1965-85; & Morgan, Miller & Blair, Oakland, 1985—. Cons.: (book) California Real Property Remedies, 1982. Mem. ABA, Calif. Trial Lawyers Assn., Alameda County Bar Assn. (chmn. law office econs. com. 1983), Alameda Contra Costa Trial Lawyers Assn., Alameda Bar Assn., AIA. Real property, State civil litigation, Construction. Home: 59 Silverwood Dr Lafayette CA 94549 Office: Morgan Miller & Blair 1901 Harrison Suite 900 Oakland CA 94612

MILLER, LEE EDWARD, lawyer; b. Newark, July 12, 1951; s. Joseph and Rose (Fuchs) M.; m. Lesley Gwenn Osman, Nov. 27, 1974; children: Alexander David, Jessica Francine. BA summa cum laude, Rutgers U., 1973; JD magna cum laude, Harvard U., 1976. Bar: Wash. 1976, D.C. 1980, Fla. 1984, N.Y. 1985, U.S. Dist. Ct. (we. dist.) Wash., U.S. Dist. Ct. (mid. and so. dists.) Fla., U.S. Dist. Ct. D.C., U.S. Dist. Ct. (so. and ea. dists.) N.Y., U.S. Ct. Appeals (4th, 6th, 11th and D.C. cirs.), U.S. Supreme Ct. Assoc. Perkins, Coie, Stone, Olsen & Williams, Seattle, 1976-80; from assoc. to ptnr. Seyfarth, Shaw, Fairweather & Geraldson, Washington, 1980-84; v.p. labor relations, labor counsel R.H. Macy & Co., N.Y.C., 1984—. Mem. ABA (individual rights and responsiblities in the work place com. 1982—). Labor, Pension, profit-sharing, and employee benefits. Office: RH Macy & Co 151 W 34th St New York NY 10001

MILLER, LINDA SUZANNE, lawyer; b. Boulder, Colo., Mar. 26, 1953; d. J. Robert and Dorothy Miller; m. George L. Blau, Aug. 30, 1980. BS, Colo. State U., 1975; JD, U. Wyo., 1980. Bar: Wyo., U.S. Dist. Ct. Wyo. Atty. Legal Services, Casper, Wyo., 1980, Office Pub. Defender, Casper, 1981-85; ptnr. Miller & Blau, Casper, 1985—. Bd. dirs. Mercer House, Casper, 1985. Mem. ABA, Nat. Assn. Criminal Def. Lawyers, Nat. Assn. Women Lawyers, Assn. Trial Lawyers Am., Wyo. Trial Lawyers Assn. Personal injury, Labor, Criminal. Office: Miller & Blau PC 123 W 1st St Suite 830 Casper WY 82601

MILLER, MARY JANE, lawyer; b. Salinas, Calif., Apr. 19, 1953; d. Edward Frank and Mary D. (Bigolli) Espitallier; m. Alan D. Miller, Mar. 4, 1978; children: Colin Edward, Andrew Duncan, Bailey Alan. BA in Philosophy, Calif. State U., 1975; JD, So. Calif. Inst. Law, 1982. Bar: Calif. 1982, U.S. Dist. Ct. (cen. dist.) Calif. 1983, U.S. Ct. Appeals (9th cir.) 1983, U.S. Tax Ct. 1984. Assoc. Ambrecht & Worsley, Santa Barbara, Calif., 1982-83; ptnr. Cook, Berryhill, Edwards & Miller, Santa Barbara, 1983—. Mem. ABA, Calif. Bar Assn., Santa Barbara Bar Assn., Barrister's Club Santa Barbara (bd. dirs. 1985—, treas. 1986—). Probate, Real property, General practice. Home: 1474 Anita St Carpinteria CA 93013 Office: Cook Berryhill Edwards & Miller 120 E De la Guerra Santa Barbara CA 93101

MILLER, MAX DUNHAM, JR., lawyer; b. Des Moines, Oct. 17, 1946; s. Max Dunham and Beulah (Head) M.; m. Melissa Ann Dart, Jan. 10, 1969 (div. July 1975); 1 child, Ann Marie Victoria; m. Caroline Jean Armendt, Sept. 19, 1981; children: Alexander Bradshaw, Benjamin Everett. BS with high honors, Mich. State U., 1968; postgrad., George Washington U., 1970-71; JD, U. Md., 1975. Bar: Md. 1976, U.S. Dist. Ct. Md. 1976, U.S. Ct. Appeals (4th cir.) 1981, U.S. Supreme Ct. 1982. Engr. U.S. Dept. of Def., Aberdeen Proving Ground, Md., 1968-72; law clk. to presiding judge Md. Cir. Ct., Higinbothom in Bel Air, Md., 1975-76; asst. atty. Hartford County, Bel Air, 1976-79; assoc. Lentz & Hooper P.A., Balt., 1979-81; ptnr. Miller, Fry & Protokowicz, Bel Air, 1981—; atty. Harford County, 1983—. Mem. Md. Bar Assn., Assn. Trial Lawyers Am., Md. Trial Lawyers Assn., Hartford County Bar Assn., Phi Kappa Phi, Phi Eta Sigma. Avocations: carpentry, sailing, kyacking. Personal injury, Workers' compensation, Real property. Home: 308 Whetstone Rd Forest Hill MD 21050 Office: Miller Fry & Protokowicz 5 S Hickory Ave Bel Air MD 21014

MILLER, MICHAEL JOHN, lawyer; b. Alameda, Calif., Jan. 26, 1951; s. George Louis and Reta Wynona (Huitt) M.; m. Trijeanna Jo Nelson, Sept. 1, 1974; children: Christopher, Jennifer. BS in Police Sci., Wash. State U., 1973; JD, Oklahoma City U., 1982. Bar: Okla. 1982. Asst. dist. Atty. Lawton, Okla., 1982-83, 1st asst. dist. atty., 1984-86; assoc. Wade & Mackey, Lawton, 1986—. Pres. Western Hills Booster Club, Lawton, 1985—. Served to 1st lt. U.S. Army, 1973-76. Mem. ABA, Okla. Bar Assn., Comanche County Bar Assn. (v.p. 1986). Democrat. Baptist. Avocations: soccer coach, reading. Criminal, Juvenile, Mental health. Office: 431 Caveourthouse Lawton OK 73501

MILLER, MICHAEL PATIKY, lawyer; b. Huntington, N.Y., Apr. 16, 1944; s. George J. and Alida (Patiky) M.; m. Dorothy Denn, Dec. 25, 1966; children: Lauren M., Jonathan M., Rachel B. AB, Rutgers U., 1965; JD, NYU, 1968. Bar: N.J. 1968, U.S. Dist. Ct. N.J. 1968, Calif. 1975, U.S. Dist. Ct. (no. dist.) Calif. 1975, U.S. Tax Ct. 1977, U.S. Ct. Appeals (9th cir.) 1977, U.S. Ct. Appeals (fed. cir.) 1984, U.S. Dist. Ct. (cen. dist.) Calif. 1982, U.S. Supreme Ct. 1983, U.S. Claims Ct. 1986. Atty. Electric Power Research Inst., Palo Alto, Calif., 1974-77; assoc. Weinberg, Ziff & Kaye, Palo Alto, 1977-78; ptnr. Weinberg, Ziff & Miller, Palo Alto, 1978—; lectr. on tax and estate planning U. Calif. Extension, 1980—. Contbr. articles to profl. jours. Treas. No. Calif. region United Synagogue Am., 1985—. Served to capt. U.S. Army, 1968-74, Vietnam, Ethiopia. Recipient Lion of Judah award, 1984. Mem. ABA (chmn. region VI pub. contract law sect. 1975-78, commn. tax practice in small law firms taxation sect. 1986—), N.J. State Bar, State Bar of Calif., Santa Clara County Bar Assn. (chmn. estate planning, probate and trust sect. 1982, trustee 1983-84). Personal income taxation, Probate, Estate taxation. Office: Weinberg Ziff & Miller 400 Cambridge Ave Palo Alto CA 94306

MILLER, MILTON ALLEN, lawyer; b. Los Angeles, Jan. 15, 1954; s. Samuel C. and Sylvia Mary Jane (Silver) M. AB with distinction and honors in Econs., Stanford U., 1976; JD with honors, Harvard U., 1979. Bar: Calif. 1979, U.S. Ct. Appeals (9th cir.) 1979, U.S. Dist. Ct. (cen., no. and so. dists.) Calif. Law clk. U.S. Ct. Appeals (9th cir.), Sacramento, 1979-80; assoc. firm Latham & Watkins, Los Angeles, 1979-86, ptnr., 1986—. Articles editor Harvard Law Rev., 1978-79. Mem. Am. Cancer Soc., Los Angeles. Mem. ABA, Los Angeles County Bar Assn. (profl. responsibility and ethics com.), Assn. Trial Lawyers Am., Phi Beta Kappa. Federal civil litigation, State civil litigation, Insurance. Home: 1674 Clear View Dr Beverly Hills CA 90210 Office: Latham & Watkins 555 S Flower St Los Angeles CA 90071

MILLER, MIRIAM TURTELTAUB, academic administrator; b. Orange, N.J., July 1, 1924; s. John J. and Dora Ruth (Bloom) Turteltaub; m. Wade Miller, Mar. 3, 1946 (div. April 1973); children: Ellen Miller Eisenberg, Gail H., Theodore Max, Sara Miller. BA, Wellesley Coll., 1946; JD, Rutgers U., 1975. Bar: N.J. 1975, U.S. Dist. Ct. N.J. 1975. Assoc. Hellring, Lindeman, Goldstein & Siegal, Newark, 1975-78; asst. dean Rutgers U. Sch. of Law, Newark, 1978—. Mem. ABA, N.J. Bar Assn., Essex County Bar Assn., Essex County Women Lawyers Assn., Nat. Assn. for Law Placement (chmn. bylaws com. 1982-85, nat. adv. bd. 1983-85, bd. dirs. 1987—). Office: Rutger U Law Sch 15 Washington St Newark NJ 07102

MILLER, MONA JOY DEUTSCH, lawyer; b. Coral Gables, Fla., Feb. 9, 1953; s. Irvin and Freda (Smukler) Deutsch; m. Steven Jeffrey Miller, Aug. 21, 1977. AB witn distinction, Cornell U., 1973; JD, Stanford U., 1977. Bar: Calif. 1977, U.S. Dist. Ct. (cen. dist.) Calif. 1978. Assoc. McKenna, Conner & Cuneo, Los Angeles, 1977-83, ptnr., 1983—. Mem. Univ. Synagogue, Brentwood, Calif., 1980—. Mem. Los Angeles County Bar Assn. (real property and comml. law and bankruptcy sects.), Calif. Attys. Fed. Credit Union (bd. dirs. 1982), Phi Beta Kappa. Jewish. Avocations: piano, movies, reading, swimming. Federal civil litigation, State civil litigation, Banking. Office: McKenna Conner & Cuneo 444 S Flower St 9th Floor Los Angeles CA 90010

MILLER, NORMAN RICHARD, lawyer; b. Oak Ridge, Tenn., Apr. 4, 1948; s. Francis J. and Sylvia R. Miller; m. Carol Golden, Aug. 15, 1971; children: Russell, Adam, Jordan. BA, Northwestern U., 1970; JD, Harvard U., 1973. Bar: Ill. 1973, Ga. 1974, Tex. 1976. Law clk. to presiding justice U.S. Ct. Appeals (7th cir.), Chgo., 1973-74; assoc. Powell, Goldstein, Frazer & Murphy, Atlanta, 1974-76; assoc. Akin, Gump, Strauss, Hauer & Feld, Dallas, 1976-79, ptnr., 1980—. Trustee Temple Shalom, 1982-84. Mem. ABA, Tex. Bar Assn., Dallas Bar Assn. General corporate, Securities, Public international. Office: Akin Gump Strauss et al 4100 First City Cen 7100 Pacific Ave Dallas TX 75201-4618

MILLER, OWENS O'KEEFE, lawyer; b. Santa Monica, Calif., June 6, 1950; s. W. Owens and Margaret Mary (Howard) M.; m. Ann-Marie Pianta, Sept. 7, 1974 (div. Apr. 1984); m. Sara E. Miller, Jan. 5, 1985; 1 child, Patrick O'Keefe. BS, U. So. Calif., 1976; JD, Southwestern U., 1979. Bar: Calif. 1980, U.S. Dist. Ct. (cen. dist.) Calif. 1980. Assoc. Kendig, Stockwell & Gleason, Beverly Hills, Calif., 1977-83, Stockwell, Gleason, Anderson & Harris, Santa Ana, 1983-85, Sacks, Rivera & Soloman, Los Angeles, 1985—. Served to sgt. Calif. NG, 1970-76. Mem. ABA, Los Angeles Bar Assn., Orange County Bar Assn., Assn. Trial Lawyers Am., Calif. Worker's Compensation Assn., Calif. Worker's Compensation Def. Attys. Assn. Democrat. Roman Catholic. Workers' compensation, Insurance, State civil litigation. Office: Sacks Rivera & Soloman 1849 Sawtelle Blvd #700 Los Angeles CA 90025

MILLER, PATRICK EUGENE, lawyer; b. Spirit Lake, Idaho, Feb. 1, 1950; s. Eugene Lantz and Mary Ellen (Muehlethaler) M.; m. Renee Bright, Apr. 16, 1977; children: Charles Eugene, Keith Howard. BA, Willamette U., 1972; JD, U. Idaho, 1975. Bar: Idaho 1975, U.S. Ct. Mil. Appeals 1976, U.S. Dist. Ct. Idaho 1979, U.S. Ct. Appeals (9th cir.) 1985. Assoc. Miller, Knudson & Eismann, Coeur d'Alene, Idaho, 1980-81; ptnr. Miller & Miller, Coeur d'Alene, 1981-85, Paine, Hamblen, Coffin, Brooke & Miller, Coeur d'Alene, 1986—. Served to capt. USAF, 1976-80. Mem. Idaho Bar Assn. Roman Catholic. Lodges: Rotary, Elks. Insurance, State civil litigation, Federal civil litigation. Office: Paine Hamblen Coffin et al 816 Sherman Ave PO Box E Coeur d'Alene ID 83814

MILLER, PATRICK LYNN, lawyer; b. Lake Charles, La., Sept. 29, 1953; s. Robert Leroy Sr. and Mary Jean (Keith) M.; m. Virginia Faye Comeaux, Apr. 11, 1973 (div. 1978) m. Carla Rae Cadenhead, Oct. 11, 1980; 1 child, Natalie Renee.. BS, McNeese State U., 1976; JD, La. State U., 1980. La. 1981, U.S. Dist. Ct. (mid. dist.) La. 1983. Assoc. Ervin & Waguespack, Baton Rouge, 1981—; gen. counsel Presbytery South La.-Presbyn. Ch., Baton Rouge, 1986. Mem. ABA (probate property and trust law sects., econs. of law practice sects.), La. State Bar Assn., Baton Rouge Bar Assn. Presbyterian. Real property, General practice, Entertainment. Office: Ervin & Waguespack 8126 One Calais Ave Ste Suite 1C Baton Rouge LA 70809

MILLER, PAUL J., lawyer; b. Boston, Mar. 27, 1929; s. Edward and Esther (Kalis) M.; children by previous marriage—Robin, Jonathan; m. Michal Davis, Sept. 1, 1965; children—Anthony, Douglas. B.A., Yale U., 1950; LL.B., Harvard U., 1953. Bar: Mass. 1953, Ill. 1957. Assoc. Miller & Miller, Boston, 1953-54; assoc. Sonnenschein Carlin Nath & Rosenthal, Chgo., 1957-63, ptnr., 1963—; dir. Oil-Dri Corp. Am., Chgo. Trustee, Latin Sch. Chgo., 1985. Served to 1st lt. JAGC, U.S. Army, 1954-57. Mem. Phi Beta Kappa. Clubs: Tavern, Saddle and Cycle, Law (Chgo.). Avocations: jogging; sailing. Office: Sonnenschein Carlin Nath & Rosenthal 8000 Sears Tower Chicago IL 60606

MILLER, PETER DAVID, lawyer; b. Muncie, Ind., Apr. 23, 1947; s. Dewey E. and Alta A. (Summers) M.; m. Joyce C. Eden, Sept. 10, 1983. BS with honors, Ball State U., 1976; JD cum laude, Ind. U., 1982. Bar: Ind. 1982, U.S. Dist. Ct. (no. and so. dists.) Ind. 1982, Calif. 1984, U.S. Ct. Appeals (7th cir.) 1984. Counsel First Bank & Trust Co., Indpls., 1982—. Mem. ABA, Calif. Bar Assn., Ind. Bar Assn., Indpls. Bar Assn. Republican. Banking, Bankruptcy, Consumer commercial. Home: 645 Eastern Ave Indianapolis IN 46201 Office: First Bank & Trust Co 5300 Crawfordsville Rd Indianapolis IN 46224

MILLER, PETER PUTNAM, lawyer; b. N.Y.C., May 11, 1938; s. Robert Floyd and Dolores Madeleine (Putnam) M.; m. Gloria Jean Everson, July 26, 1968; children: Jonathan Putnam, Kristen Iversen. BA, Yale U., 1960; JD, Stanford U., 1968. Bar: N.Y. 1969. Assoc. Sullivan & Cromwell, N.Y.C., 1968-74; counsel Mobil Oil Corp., N.Y.C., 1974; counsel Producing NW Europe div. Mobil Oil Corp., London, 1974-76; gen. counsel Exploration Norway div. Mobil Oil Corp., Stavanger, 1976-79; gen. counsel Mobil Oil Indonesia div. Mobil Oil Corp., Jakarta, 1979-83; asst. gen. counsel E & D div. Mobil Oil Corp., N.Y.C., 1983—; lectr. numerous internat. bar assn. seminars; co-founder Indonesian Assn. Petroleum Lawyers, 1982-83. Cubmaster Cub Scouts Am., Jakarta, 1980-83, Darien, Conn., 1984-86, Weston, Conn., 1986—. Served to capt. U.S. Army, 1962-67, Vietnam. Recipient Dist. Award of Merit, Boy Scouts Am., Jakarta, 1983. Mem. ABA, Internat. Bar Assn. (officer oil and gas com. energy law sect. 1986—). Episcopalian. Avocations: skiing, hiking, sailing, collecting. Oil and gas leasing, General corporate, Private international. Home: 10 Cedar Ln Weston CT 06883 Office: Mobil Oil Corp 150 E 42d St New York NY 10017

MILLER, PHEBE CONDICT, lawyer, financial executive; b. Columbus, Ohio, Dec. 18, 1949; d. A. Fullerton and Mary Dixon (Sayre) M.; m. O. John Olcay. BA, Princeton U., 1971; JD, Harvard U., 1974. Bar: N.Y. 1975, U.S. Dist. Ct. (so. dist.) N.Y. 1975, U.S. Ct. Appeals (2nd cir.) 1975. Law clk. to judge U.S. Dist. Ct. (so. dist.) N.Y., N.Y.C., 1974-75; spl. asst. to deputy atty. gen. Dept. of Justice, Washington, 1975-76; assoc. Davis Polk & Wardwell, N.Y.C. and London, 1976-83; v.p. and counsel DCNY Corp., N.Y.C., 1983—. mem. ABA. General corporate, Securities. Office: DCNY Corp 58 Pine St New York NY 10005

MILLER, PHILIP R., federal judge; b. N.Y.C., Mar. 12, 1918; s. Louis and Minnie (Yatzkan) M.; m. Eunice Rothenberg, Nov. 1, 1941; children: Carolyn Ann, Ellen. B.B.A., CCNY, 1937; LL.B., Columbia U., 1940. Bar: N.Y. 1941, D.C. 1942. Assoc. Covington & Burling, Washington, 1941-42, Fulton, Walter & Halley, N.Y.C. and Washington, 1951-52; atty. criminal div. Justice Dept., Washington, 1942-45; atty. tax div. Justice Dept., 1945-51, 52-59, asst. sect. chief tax div., 1959-67, sect. chief, 1967-72; trial judge U.S. Claims Ct., 1972-82, chief trial div., 1980-82, judge, 1982—. Home: 8502 Donnybrook Dr Chevy Chase MD 20815 Office: US Claims Ct 717 Madison Pl Washington DC 20005 *

MILLER, RALPH WILLIAM, JR., lawyer; b. Chgo., Mar. 9, 1931; s. Ralph William and Pearl Mae (Bauer) M.; m. Jean Lois Gromer; children—Darlene Miller Martinez, Ralph William, Dean. B.S., Northwestern U., 1952, J.D., 1955. Bar: Ill. 1956. With firm Taylor, Miller, Magner, Sprowl & Hutchings, 1946-55; sole practice, Elgin, Ill., 1957-58; asst. counsel Jewel Cos., Inc., Melrose Park, Ill., 1958-67, ins. atty., 1967-71, sr. atty., 1971-72, gen. atty., 1972-74, v.p. regulatory research and planning Jewel Food Stores div., 1974-80, also gen. counsel, 1975-80; sole practice, Elmhurst, Ill., 1980-81; mem. Indsl. Commn. State of Ill., Chgo., 1981-86; sole practice, Oak Brook, Ill., 1986—. Mem. Gov.'s Agreed Bill Process Com. for Workers' Compensation in Ill., 1979-81. Served with inf. U.S. Army, 1955-57. Mem. ABA, Ill. Bar Assn. (chmn. ins. program com. 1971-73), Chgo. Bar Assn. (chmn. food, drug and consumer product safety com. 1975-76), DuPage County Bar Assn., Am. Judicature Soc., Chgo. Assn. of Commerce and Industry, Ill. Self-Insurers Assn., Ill. Def. Counsel, Def. Research Inst., Nat. Conf. Weights and Measures, Assn. Food and Drug Ofcls., Industry Com. Packaging and Labeling (chmn. 1977-79), Food Mktg. Inst. (chmn. metric com. 1978-80), Am. Nat. Metric Council (chmn. retailers sector, vice-chmn. legal adv. com. 1978-80), Ill. State C. of C. (chmn. workers compensation com. 1973-78). Workers' compensation, Administrative and regulatory, General practice. Home: 936 Spring Rd Elmhurst IL 60126-4928 Office: 2021 Midwest Rd Oak Brook IL 60521-1324

MILLER, RAYMOND VINCENT, JR., lawyer; b. Providence, July 1, 1954; s. Raymond Vincent and Mary Eunice (Mullen) M.; m. Elizabeth Ann White, May 31, 1980; 1 child, Travis. BA, U. R.I., 1976; JD, U. Miami, 1981. Bar: Fla. 1981, U.S. Dist. Ct. (so. dist.) Fla. 1981, U.S. Ct. Appeals (11th cir.) 1986. Area supr. job devel. and tng. div. R.I. Dept. Econ. Devel., Providence, 1977-78; assoc. Thornton & Herndon, Miami, Fla., 1981-83, Britton, Cohen et al, Miami, 1983-85, Law Office of Edward A. Kaufman, P.A., Miami, 1985—. ABA, Fla. Bar Assn., Nat. Order Barristers, Soc. Bar and Gavel. Federal civil litigation, State civil litigation, Personal injury. Home: 5045 SW 66 Ave South Miami FL 33155 Office: Edward A Kaufman PA 200 S Biscayne Blvd Suite 4950 Miami FL 33131

MILLER, RICHARD ALLAN, lawyer; b. N.Y.C., Oct. 28, 1947; s. Harold B. and Helen (Schwartz) M.; m. Karen R. Mangold, July, 5, 1970; children: David, Matthew. BA, SUNY, Buffalo, 1969; MA, Ohio State U., 1970; JD, NYU, 1973. Bar: N.Y. 1974, U.S. Dist. Ct. (so. and ea. dists.) N.Y. 1974, U.S. Ct. Appeals (2d cir.) 1977, U.S. Supreme Ct. 1980. Assoc. Paul Weiss et al, N.Y.C., 1973-75; asst. dist. atty. N.Y. County, N.Y.C., 1975-77, Kostelanetz & Ritholz, N.Y.C., 1977-79; ptnr. Newman, Tannenbaum et al, N.Y.C., 1980—. Editor Commodities Law Letter, 1981—. Mem. Assn. of the Bar of the City of N.Y. (commodities regulations com.). Jewish. Avocations: skiing, tennis. Administrative and regulatory, Federal civil litigation, Securities. Home: 22 Roosevelt Rd Maplewood NJ 07040 Office: Newman Tannenbaum Helpern et al 900 Third Ave New York NY 10022

MILLER, RICHARD CLARK, JR., lawyer; b. St. Charles, La., Sept. 8, 1953; s. Richard C. Sr. and Leslie P. (Mann) M.; married; children: Keenan C., Cyrus A. BS, Cornell U., 1975; JD, Union U., 1978. Bar: N.Y. 1979, U.S. Dist. Ct. (no. dist.) N.Y. 1979. Assoc. Herbert B. Sunshine, Latham, N.Y., 1979, Joseph A. Barbetta, Clifton Park, N.Y., 1979-81; ptnr. Barbetta & Miller, Clifton Park, 1981-83, Miller & Williams, Clifton Park, 1983-85; sole practice Clifton Park, 1985—; asst. atty. Town of Clifton Park, 1980-87; atty. Rexford (N.Y.) Water Dist., 1983—. Mem. Com. on Zoning, Clifton Park, 1984-85, Cable TV Com., Clifton Park, 1986; treas. Clifton Park Rep. Com., 1982-86; mem. master plan tech. adv. com. Clifton Park, 1987—. Mem. ABA, N.Y. State Bar Assn., Saratoga County Bar Assn. (exec. com. 1985). Republican. Methodist. Avocations: sailing, tennis. Real property, Local government, General corporate. Home: PO Box 438 Rt 9 Clifton Park NY 12065 Office: PO Box 438 Rt 9 Clifton Park NY 12065

MILLER, RICHARD STEVEN, lawyer; b. Mt. Vernon, N.Y., Dec. 5, 1951; s. Norman and Mildred (Curtis) M. BA, U. Pa., 1974; JD, NYU, 1977. Bar: N.Y. 1978, U.S. Dist. Ct. (so. and ea. dists.) N.Y. 1978, U.S. Ct. Appeals (2d cir.) 1978. Asst. dist. atty. Kings County, N.Y., 1977-79; assoc. Hahn & Hessen, N.Y.C., 1979-82, Levin & Weintraub & Crames, N.Y.C., 1982—. Mem. ABA, N.Y. County Lawyers Assn. Bankruptcy, Corporate reorganizations. Home: 130 Barrow St Apt 106 New York NY 10014 Office: Levin & Weintraub & Crames 225 Broadway New York NY 10007

MILLER, RICHARD WILLIAM, JR., lawyer; b. Pittsburgh, Mar. 17, 1949; s. Richard William and Mary Margaret (Pollack) M.; m. Mary Jane Angela Cosari, Sept. 2, 1972; children: Katherine Marie, Margaret Helen. BA cum laude, Allegheny Coll., 1971; JD, Georgetown U., 1978. Bar: D.C. 1978, U.S. Ct. Appeals (D.C. cir.) 1978, Md. 1979, U.S. Ct. Appeals (5th, 10th and 11th cirs.) 1981, U.S. Supreme Ct. 1983. Assoc. Sanders, Schnabel, Joseph & Powell, Washington, 1978-80, Brackett & Collins, P.C., Washington, 1980-86; sr. atty. ANR Pipeline Co. and Colo. Interstate Gas Co., Washington, 1986—. Served to capt. USAF, 1971-75. Mem. ABA, Fed. Bar Assn., Fed. Energy Bar Assn., Bar Assn. D.C., Phi Beta Kappa. Republican. Club: Nat. Lawyers. FERC practice, Public utilities, Administrative and regulatory. Office: Coastal Corp 1899 L St NW #501 Washington DC 20036

MILLER, ROBERT CHARLES, lawyer; b. Pottstown, Pa., Feb. 17, 1950; s. Charles Edward and Dorothy Ruth (Souder) M.; m. Kathleen Jo Stoner, Aug. 18, 1973 (div. Sept. 1978); m. Linda Rose Maggiore, Jan. 26,

1980. BA, Susquehanna U., 1973; JD, U. Fla., 1976. Bar: Fla. 1976, U.S. Dist. Ct. (mid. dist.) Fla. 1976. Assoc. Law Office of Jerry Hussey, Bradenton, Fla., 1976-78; dir. child support, clk. of ct. Cir. Ct. (12th jud. cir.) Manatee County, Bradenton, 1978-82; sole practice Bradenton, 1982—; pres. Fla. Family Support Council, 1981-82; mem. Mediation Panel, Sarasota, Fla., 1986. v.p. Civitan, Bradenton, 1977, pres. 1978; mem. 12th Jud. Cir. Visitation Rights Guidelines Panel, 1987. Mem. Fla. Bar Assn. (support enforcement panel, 1986, family and criminal law sects.), Manatee County Bar Assn., Phi Delta Phi. Democrat. Lutheran. Club: Local Group of Deep Sky Observers (Bradenton). Avocations: astronomy, photography, fishing. Family and matrimonial, Criminal, Landlord-tenant. Home: 2304 Falcon Ct Bradenton FL 33529 Office: 717 12th St W Bradenton FL 33505

MILLER, ROBERT HASKINS, state justice; b. Columbus, Ohio, Mar. 3, 1919; s. George L. and Marian Alice (Haskins) M.; m. Audene Fausett, Mar. 14, 1943; children: Stephen F., Thomas G., David W., Stacey Ann. A.B., Kans. U., 1940, LL.B., 1942; grad., Nat. Coll. State Trial Judges, Phila., 1967. Bar: Kans. 1943. Practice in Paola, 1946-60; judge 6th Jud. Dist. Kans., Paola, 1961-69; U.S. magistrate Kans. Dist., Kansas City, 1969-75; justice Kans. Supreme Ct., 1975—; chmn. Kans. Jud. Council, 1987—. Contbg. author: Pattern (Civil Jury) Instructions for Kansas, 2d edit, 1969. Served with AUS, 1942-46. Mem. Kans. Bar Assn., Wyandotte County Bar Assn., Shawnee County Bar Assn., ABA, Am. Legion, Phi Gamma Delta, Phi Delta Phi. Presbyterian. Judicial administration. Office: Kansas Supreme Ct Kans Jud Ctr Topeka KS 66612

MILLER, ROBERT M., lawyer; b. N.Y.C., July 13, 1951; s. Bertram Miller and Ruth (Benkow) Weintraub; m. Debra A. Taragan, Aug. 23, 1975; children: Carly, Samantha. BS in Communications, Boston U., 1968-73; JD, St. John's U., 1975-77. Bar: N.Y. 1978, U.S. Dist. Ct. (so. and ea. dists.) N.Y. Assoc. Mudge Rose Guthrie et al, N.Y.C., 1977-80; ptnr. Anderson Russell, N.Y.C., 1980-84, Bishop, Liberman & Cook, N.Y.C., 1984—. Notes and comments editor St. John's U. Law Rev.; Contbr. articles to profl. jours. Mem. ABA, N.Y. State Bar Assn. Bankruptcy, Consumer commercial. Office: Bishop Liberman & Cook 1155 6th Ave New York NY 10036

MILLER, ROBERT NOLEN, lawyer; b. Monmouth, Ill., May 30, 1940; s. Robert Clinton and Doris Margaret (Nolen) M.; m. Diane Wilmarth, Aug. 21, 1965; children—Robert Wilmarth, Anne Elizabeth. B.A., Cornell Coll., Mt. Vernon, Iowa, 1962; J.D., U. Colo., 1965. Bar: Colo. Assoc. firm M. Quiat, Denver, 1965-66; assoc. Fischer & Beaty, Ft. Collins, Colo., 1969-70; dist. atty. Weld County Dist. Atty's. Office, Greeley, Colo., 1971-81; U.S. atty. U.S. Dept. Justice, Denver, 1981—; instr. bus. law Am. U., U. S.C., Myrtle Beach, 1966-69. Co-author: Deathroads, 1978. Bd. dirs. Boys Club, Greeley, 1974-78, 1st Congl. Ch., Greeley, 1975-78; Republican candidate for atty. gen. Colo., 1977-78. Served to capt. USAF, 1966-69. Recipient Citizen of Yr. award Elks Club, Greeley. Mem. Fed. Bar Assn. (pres. Colo. chpt. 1983-84), Colo. Dist. Atty's Council (pres. 1976-77), Colo. Bar Assn., Weld County Bar Assn. Republican. Congregationalist, Rotary (pres. 1980-81). Avocations: fishing; hunting; golf; tennis; reading. Criminal. Office: U S Atty's Office 1961 Stout St Denver CO 80634

MILLER, ROGER JAMES, lawyer; b. Yankton, S.D., Oct. 6, 1947; s. Kenneth LeRoy and Bernice Mildred (Peterson) M.; m. Kristine Olga Christensen, June 12, 1971; children: David, Adam, Luke. BS, U. Nebr., 1970, JD, 1973. Bar: Nebr. 1973, U.S. Dist. Ct. Nebr. 1973, U.S. Ct. Appeals (5th, 8th and 10th cirs.) 1973, U.S. Ct. Appeals (D.C. cir.) 1974, U.S. Dist. Ct. (no. dist.) Calif. 1984. Assoc. Nelson & Harding, Lincoln, Nebr., 1973-74; ptnr. Nelson & Harding, Omaha, 1974-84, McGrath, North, O'Malley & Kratz, P.C., Omaha, 1984—. Adv. bd. Douglas County Rep. Party, Omaha, 1984. Mem. ABA (labor law sect., litigation sect.), Nebr. Bar Assn. Methodist. Clubs: Cosmopolitan, Highland Country. Avocations: golf, racquetball, jogging, fishing. Labor. Home: 13626 Seward Omaha NE 68154 Office: McGrath North et al 1100 One Central Park Plaza Omaha NE 68102

MILLER, RONALD STUART, lawyer; b. Chgo., Sept. 28, 1931; s. Manuel and Ruth (Romack) M.; m. Patricia Ann Murphy, Dec. 14, 1962; children—Michelle Ann, Lynn Elizabeth. B.S., U. Ill., 1953, LL.B., 1955. Bar: Ill. 1955, N.Y. 1960. Assoc., Devoe, Shadur & Mikva, Chgo., 1961-65; ptnr. Miller, Shakman, Nathan & Hamilton, Chgo., 1965—; trustee, bd. dirs. Lawyers Com. for Civil Rights, Washington, 1977—; mem. Ill. Speakers Task Force, Springfield, 1984. Bd. visitors U. Ill. Law Sch., Champaign, 1984—. Mem. ABA, Ill. Bar Assn., Chgo. Bar Assn., Chgo. Council Lawyers, Legal Club Chgo. Jewish. General corporate, Real property, Securities. Home: 330 W Diversey Pkwy Chicago IL 60657 Office: Miller Shakman Nathan & Hamilton 208 S LaSalle St Chicago IL 60604

MILLER, RUSSELL GEORGE, lawyer; b. Chgo., Sept. 1, 1932; s. Leon Norman and Marion (Rubenstein) M.; m. Nancie Lewis, Jan. 31, 1954; children—Lael Scott, Diane Elaine. B.S., U. Wis., 1954; J.D., DePaul U., 1955. Bar: Ill. 1955, U.S. Dist. Ct. (no. dist.) Ill. 1958, U.S. Ct. Appeals (7th cir.) 1959, U.S. Supreme Ct. 1969. With trust dept. Cosmopolitan Nat. Bank, Chgo., 1954-56; assoc. Leon N. Miller, Chgo., 1958-62; ptnr. Miller and Miller, Chgo., 1962-68; ptnr. Mass and Miller, Chgo., 1968-71; ptnr. Mass Miller & Josephson, Chgo., 1971-80; pres., prin. Mass Miller & Josephson, Ltd., Chgo., 1980—. Mem. Sch. Dist. 73 1/2, Skokie, Ill., 1961-71, pres., 1968-69; bd. dirs. Niles Twp. Dept. Spl. Edn., 1965-71, pres., 1967-71. Served with U.S. Army, 1956-58. Mem. Chgo. Bar Assn. (past chmn. com. profl. responsibility and adoption com., vice chmn. legis. com.), Ill. State Bar Assn., ABA, Am. Inst. Parliamentarians (past dir., v.p., parliamentarian, now adv. bd.), Decalogue Soc. Chgo. Jewish. Real property, General corporate, Probate. Home: 2055 N Howe St Chicago IL 60614 Office: 333 W Wacker Dr Suite 810 Chicago IL 60606

MILLER, SAM SCOTT, lawyer; b. Ft. Worth, July 26, 1938; s. Percy Vernon and Mildred Lois (MacDowell) M.; m. Mary Harrison FitzHugh, May 10, 1969. B.A., Mich. State U., 1960; J.D., Tulane U., 1964; LL.M., Yale U., 1965. Bar: La. 1965, N.Y. 1966, Minn. 1969. Assoc. Simpson Thacher & Bartlett, N.Y.C., 1965-68; sr. counsel Investors Diversified Services, Mpls., 1968-73; partner Ireland Gibson Reams & Miller, Memphis, 1973-74; gen. counsel Paine Webber Group, Inc., N.Y.C., 1974—; sr. v.p. Paine Webber Group, Inc., 1976—; adj. prof. NYU Law Sch., 1986—; vis. lectr. Yale Law Sch., 1980-85, Inst. for Internat. Econs. and Trade, Wuhan, China, 1983, U. Calif., 1986—; Mem. dean's council Tulane U. Law Sch., 1979—. Contbr. articles to profl. jours.; editor-in-chief: Tulane Law Rev, 1964-65; bd. editors Securities Regulation Law Jour., 1982—. Bd. dirs. Guthrie Theatre Found., Mpls., 1971-74; bd. dirs. Minn. Opera Co., 1971-74, Yale U. Law Sch. Fund, 1981—; bd. govs. Investment Co. Inst., 1980—. Mem. Assn. Bar City N.Y. (chmn. broker-dealer regulations subcom. 1982-83), ABA (chmn. subcom. broker-dealer matters 1985—), Internat. Bar Assn., Securities Industry Assn. (chmn. fed. regulation com. 1976-78), Order of Coif, Omicron Delta Kappa. Democrat. Baptist. Clubs: Down Town Assn., Knickerbocker. Administrative and regulatory, General corporate, Legislative. Office: 1285 Ave of the Americas New York NY 10019

MILLER, SAMUEL AARON, lawyer; b. Providence, June 4, 1955; s. Max and Miriam (Siperstein) M.; m. Pamela Lynn Kaitin, May 26, 1980; children: Shoshana Dina, David Daniel. Grad., Clark U., 1977; JD, Western New Eng. Coll., 1980. Bar: R.I. 1980, Mass. 1980, U.S. Dist. Ct. R.I. 1980, U.S. Dist. Ct. Mass. 1981, U.S. Ct. Appeals (1st cir.) 1981. Assoc. Quinn, Cuzzone & Geremia, Providence, 1980—. Mem. ABA, Mass. Bar Assn., Assn. Trial Lawyers Am., R.I. Trial Lawyers Assn., Am. Judicature Soc., Def. Research Assn. Jewish. State civil litigation, Environment, Personal injury. Home: 68 Ogden St Providence RI 02906 Office: Quinn Cuzzone & Geremia 189 Canal St Providence RI 02903

MILLER, SCOTT MITCHELL, lawyer; b. Phila., Apr. 30, 1953; s. Sylvan Hirsh and Natalie Lorraine (Neff) M. B.A., Pa. State U., 1974; J.D., U. Louisville, 1977. Bar: Pa. 1977, Ky. 1978, U.S. Dist. Ct. (ea. and we. dists.) Ky. 1979, Colo. 1981, U.S. Dist. Ct. Colo. 1981. Atty. felony prosecutor Jefferson County Atty.'s Office, Louisville, 1978-80; ptnr. Hoge & Erler, Louisville, 1978-80, Duncan & Miller, Durango, Colo., 1981-86; mcpl. judge Town of Bayfield, Colo., 1982-86; ptnr. Hoge and Miller, Louisville, 1987—. Mem. ABA, Colo. Bar Assn., Ky. Bar Assn., Pa. Bar Assn. Democrat. Jewish. Labor, Criminal. Home: 6709 Six Mile Ln Louisville KY 40218 Office: Hoge & Miller 1770 Bardstown Rd Louisville KY 40205

MILLER, SHELDON LEE, lawyer; b. Detroit, Apr. 19, 1936; s. Jack and Rose (Steinberg) M; m. Elaine Jo Schweitzer, Dec. 17; children: Randall, Lisa. Grad., Wayne State U., 1958, LLB, 1961. Bar: Mich. 1962, U.S. Dist. Ct., U.S. Ct. Appeals (6th cir.), U.S. Supreme Ct. Ptnr. Lopatin, Miller, P.C., Detroit. Served with U.S. Army, 1954-56. Mem. Assn. Trial Lawyers Am. (pres. Detroit chpt., nat. v.p. 1984-85, bd. govs. 1977—), Mich. Trial Lawyers Assn. (pres. 1975-76), Wayne County Mediation Tribunal Assn. (founder, bd. dirs. 1978—). Democrat. Jewish. State civil litigation, Federal civil litigation, Environment. Home: 7449 Stony River Ct Birmingham MI 48010 Office: Lopatin Miller PC 547 E Jefferson Detroit MI 48226

MILLER, STANTON BERNETT, lawyer; b. Chgo., Mar. 5, 1944; s. Nathan and Isabel P. (Edelman) M.; m. Peggy G. Goodkind, Dec. 11, 1971; 1 dau., Margaret Katherine. A.B., Miami U., Oxford, Ohio, 1965; J.D., U. Ill., 1968; LL.M. in Taxation, John Marshall Law Sch., 1979. Bar: Ill. 1969, U.S. Dist. Ct. (no. dist.) Ill. 1969, U.S. Ct. Mil. Appeals 1972. Assoc., Edelman & Rappaport, Chgo., 1969-76; ptnr. Anderson, McDonnell, Miller & Tabis, Chgo., 1976—; instr. IIT, 1980-82. Pres. Chgo. chpt. Dysautonomia Found., 1980-81; active Chgo. Estate Planning Council, 1979—. Served with USAR, 1968-74. Mem. Chgo. Bar Assn., Ill. Bar Assn., ABA. Contbr. articles to profl. jours. General corporate, Probate. Office: Anderson Mc Donnell Miller & Tabis 200 S Wacker Dr Chicago IL 60606

MILLER, STEPHEN, lawyer; b. Boston, May 21, 1937; s. Morris and Vera (Yassen) M.; m. Susan May Blacher, Dec. 15, 1965; children: Stacey Beth, Gregg Victor. BA, Mich. State U., 1959; LLB, George Washington U., 1962; cert., Nat. Inst. Trial Advocacy, U. Colo., 1975. Bar: U.S. Ct. Appeals (1st. cir.) 1963. Atty Fed. Trade Commn., Washington, 1968-78; asst. gen. counsel Interco Inc., St. Louis, 1978—. Mem. ABA, D.C. Bar Assn. Avocations: handball, jogging. Antitrust, General corporate, Employee termination. Home: 234 Stablestone Dr Chesterfield MO 63017 Office: Interco Inc 101 S Hanley Rd Saint Louis MO 63105

MILLER, STEVEN JEFFREY, lawyer; b. Chgo., Feb. 13, 1954; s. Hadley A. and Carol J. (Prince) M.; m. Mona Deutsch, Aug. 21, 1977. B.A. magna cum laude, U. Pa., 1974; J.D., Stanford U., 1977. Bar: Calif. 1977, U.S. Supreme Ct. 1982, U.S. Ct. Appeals (9th cir.) 1979, U.S. Ct. Appeals (10th cir.) 1981, U.S. Dist. Ct. (cent. dist.) Calif. 1978, U.S. Dist. Ct. (so. dist.) Calif. 1982, U.S. Dist. Ct. (no. dist.) Calif., 1987, U.S. Dist. Ct. (ea. dist.) Calif. 1987. Assoc. Lawler, Felix & Hall, Los Angeles, 1977-84, Wyman, Bautzer, Christensen, Kuchel & Silbert, Los Angeles, 1984-86; of counsel Law Offices of Peter J. McNulty, 1986—. Mem. ABA, State Bar of Calif., Los Angeles County Bar Assn., Am. Judicature Soc., Internat. Assn. Jewish Lawyers and Jurists, Phi Beta Kappa. Federal civil litigation, State civil litigation, Antitrust. Office: Law Offices of Peter J McNulty 827 Moraga Dr Los Angeles CA 90049

MILLER, STEVEN SCOTT, lawyer; b. N.Y.C., May 28, 1947; s. Stanley Irwin and Corinne (Mass) M.; m. Nina Catherine Augello, Apr. 24, 1983. BA cum laude, U. Pa., 1967; JD cum laude, NYU, 1970. Bar: N.Y. 1971, U.S. Dist. Ct. (so. and ea. dists.) N.Y. 1972, U.S. Ct. Appeals (2d cir.) 1974. Law clk. to judge U.S. Dist. Ct. (so. dist.) N.Y., N.Y.C., 1970-71; assoc. Proskauer Rose Goetz & Mendelsohn, N.Y.C., 1971-78; assoc. Rosenman & Colin, N.Y.C., 1978-81, ptnr., 1981—. Editor NYU Law Rev., 1968-70. Mem. ABA (litigation sect.), Assn. of Bar of City of N.Y. Federal civil litigation, State civil litigation. Office: Ronsenman & Colin 575 Madison St New York NY 10022 Home: 425 W 23rd St New York NY 10011

MILLER, STEWART RANSOM, lawyer; b. Dallas, June 11, 1945; s. Giles Edwin and Betty Jane (Stewart) M.; m. Ann Wilson Pugh, Dec. 7, 1963; children—Rhett, Ross, Christi. B.A., Austin Coll., 1968; J.D., U. Tex., 1970. Bar: Tex. 1970, U.S. Dist. Ct. (ea. dist.) Tex. 1971, U.S. Dist. Ct. (no. dist.) Tex. 1972, U.S. Dist. Ct. (so. dist.) Tex. 1980, U.S. Tax Ct. 1977, U.S. Ct. Appeals (5th cir.) 1977, U.S. Ct. Appeals (11th cir.) 1981, U.S. Supreme Ct. 1977. Assoc., Wade & Thomas, Dallas, 1970, 71, Sammons Enterprises, Inc., Dallas, 1971-78; ptnr. Smith, Miller & Carlton, Dallas, 1978—; dir. Legal Security Life Ins. Co., Dallas, 1971-78. Mem. Charter Commn., Town of Highland Park; bd. dirs., sec. Aberrant Behavior Ctr., Inc., Dallas, 1978—, Behavioral Research Ctr., Inc., Dallas, 1980—. Named Outstanding Student Delta Theta Phi, 1970; cert. comml. real estate law specialist Tex. Bd. Legal Specialization. Mem. State Bar Tex., Dallas Bar Assn., Dallas Bus. Assn. (past pres.). Episcopalian. Real property, Landlord-tenant, State civil litigation. Home: 3219 Mockingbird Dallas TX 75205 Office: Smith Miller & Carlton 5949 Sherry Ln Sterling Plaza Suite 900 Dallas TX 75225

MILLER, THOMAS BURK, state justice; b. Buffalo, May 4, 1929; s. Clarence Edwin and Helen Elizabeth (Burk) M.; m. Vaughn Carol Nolte, Apr. 17, 1954; children—Kenneth L. Goudy, George H. Goudy, Brian D. Miller, Bradley R. Miller. A.B., U. Va., 1950; LL.B., W.Va. U., 1956. Bar: W.Va. bar 1956. Sr. ptnr. firm Schrader, Miller, Stamp & Recht, Wheeling, 1959-76; justice W.Va. Supreme Ct. Appeals, 1977—, chief justice, 1982, 85-86. Served with USNR, 1950-53. Mem. Am., W.Va. bar assns., Assn. Trial Lawyers Am., W.Va. Trial Lawyers Assn. Democrat. Methodist. Office: W Va Supreme Ct Appeals Room E301 State Capitol Charleston WV 25305

MILLER, THOMAS EUGENE, legal editor, writer; b. Bryan, Tex., Jan. 4, 1929; s. Eugene Adam and Ella Lucille (Schroeder) M. B.A., Tex. A&M U., 1950; M.A., U. Tex., 1956, J.D., 1966; postgrad. U. Houston, 1957-58, U Calif.-Berkeley, 1983. Bar: Tex. 1966. Research technician M.D. Anderson Hosp., Houston, 1956-58; claims examiner trainee Sec. Security Adminstrn., New Orleans, 1964; trademark examiner trainee Dept. Commerce, Washington, 1966; editor Bancroft-Whitney Co., San Francisco, 1966—; author book under pseudonym. Contbg. mem. Democratic Nat. Com., 1981-87. Fellow Internat. Biog. Assn. (life); mem. ABA, Internat. Platform Assn., Phi Kappa Phi, Psi Chi, Phi Eta Sigma. Methodist. Clubs: Nat. Writers, Press, Commonwealth. Legal writing, Personal injury. Home: 2293 Turk Blvd Apt 5 San Francisco CA 94118 Office: Bancroft-Whitney Co 301 Brannan St San Francisco CA 94107

MILLER, THOMAS J., atty. gen. Iowa; b. Dubuque, Iowa, Aug. 11, 1944; s. Elmer John and Betty Maude (Kross) M.; m. Linda Cottington, Jan. 10, 1981; 1 child, Matthew. B.A., Loras Coll., Dubuque, 1966; J.D., Harvard U., 1969. Bar: Iowa bar 1969. With VISTA, 1969-70; legis. asst. to U.S. congressman, 1970-71; legal edn. dir. Balt. Legal Aid Bur., also mem. part-time faculty U. Md. Sch. Law, 1971-73; pvt. practice McGregor, Iowa, 1973-78; city atty. McGregor, 1975-78; atty. gen. of Iowa 1978—. Pres. 2d Dist. New Democratic Club, Balt., 1972. Mem. Am. Bar Assn., Iowa Bar Assn., Common Cause. Roman Catholic. Office: Attorney Generals Office Hoover Bldg 2d Floor Des Moines IA 50319 *

MILLER, THOMAS RAYMOND, lawyer, employee relations executive; b. Madison, Wis., Mar. 22, 1949; s. Raymond G. and Bernadette K. (Finnegan) M.; m. Susan K. Ahrensmeyer, May 20, 1978; children: Ryan, Jessica. BA, U. Wis., 1971, MA, 1972, JD, 1978. Bar: Wis. 1978, U.S. Dist. Ct. (we. dist.) Wis. 1979, U.S. Ct. Appeals (7th cir.) 1979. Atty. labor relations Nat. Airlines, Miami, Fla., 1978-80; dir. employee relations Am. Airlines, Dallas, 1980—. Labor. Home: 1113 Hidden Oaks Dr Bedford TX 76022

MILLER, WESLEY A. LOONEY, lawyer; b. Pitts., Oct. 16, 1917; s. William Evans and Elisabeth P. (Looney) M.; m. Jean Stanton, Aug. 28, 1948 (dec.); m. Carol Rockhold, Mar. 4, 1967; 1 dau., Elisabeth Carol. A.B., Amherst Coll., 1939; LL.B., NYU, 1965. Bar: N.Y. 1966, N.H. 1972, U.S. Dist. Ct. N.H. 1972. Assoc., Jillson, Bedford and Hoppen, N.Y.C., 1966-71; sole practice, Concord, N.H., 1972-76; adminstr. Com. on Profl. Conduct, N.H. Supreme Ct., 1976-83; exec. adminstr. Christian Sci. Instl. Com. for N.Y. State, 1985—. Served to it. USNR, 1941-46. Mem. ABA, N.H. State Bar Assn., N.Y. State Bar Assn. Republican. Christian Scientist. Administrative and regulatory, Professional responsibility, Jurisprudence. Home: 40 E 94th St Apt 8F New York NY 10128 Office: 342 Madison Ave Room 526 New York NY 10173

MILLER, WILLIAM BAYARD, JR., lawyer; b. Phila., Feb. 21, 1951; s. William Bayard Sr. and Jean (Keck) M.; m. Constance Sophocles, June 4, 1972; children: Kirstin, Erin, Timothy. BA summa cum laude, Amherst Coll., 1973; JD cum laude, Harvard U., 1976. Bar: Pa. 1976, U.S. Dist. Ct. (ea. dist.) Pa. 1976, Vt. 1980, U.S. Dist. Ct. Vt. 1980, U.S. Ct. Appeals (2d cir.) 1981. Assoc. Dilworth, Paxson, Kalish & Levy, Phila., 1976-80; ptnr. Langrock, Sperry, Parker & Wool, Middlebury, Vt., 1980—; lectr. Middlebury Coll, 1982—. Bd. dirs., counsel Bridge Sch., Inc., Middlebury, 1982—; bd. dirs. Addison County Hospice, Middlebury, 1982-84. Mem. ABA, Vt. Bar Assn. (chmn. jud. systems com. 1982-84), Assn. Trial Lawyers Am., Phi Beta Kappa. State civil litigation, Federal civil litigation, Real property. Home: RD #1 Middlebury VT 05753 Office: Langrock Sperry Parker & Wool 15 S Pleasant St Middlebury VT 05753

MILLER, WILLIAM EVANS, JR., lawyer; b. Pitts., May 8, 1923; s. William Evans and Elisabeth (Looney) M.; m. Phyllis Evans, Sept. 9, 1950 (dec. Oct. 7, 1982); children: Jonathan, David; m. Sandra Hawkins, June 14, 1986. A.B., Amherst Coll.; LL.B., U. Pa. Bar: Pa. Assoc. Reed Smith Shaw McClay, Pitts., 1949-64, ptnr., 1964—. Served to lt. (j.g.) USN, 1943-46, PTO. Republican. Christian Scientist. Clubs: Wildwood (Allison Park, Pa.); University (Pitts.). Lodge: Masons. Home: 4554 William Flynn Hwy Allison Park PA 15101 Office: Reed Smith Shaw and McClay PO Box 2009 Pittsburgh PA 15230

MILLER, WILLIAM FREDERICK, lawyer; b. Washington, July 18, 1946; s. Benjamin and Mary Frances (Zarbock) M.; m. Suzanne Lee Christmas, Dec. 21, 1975; children: Christopher McKenzie, Lindsay Noelle. BA, Coll. William & Mary, 1968, JD, 1974. Bar: Va. 1974, U.S. Dist. Ct. (ea. dist.) Va. 1974, U.S. Ct. Appeals (4th cir.) 1982. Ptnr. Loring & Miller, Williamsburg, Va., 1974-76, Rideout & Miller, Williamsburg, 1976—; spl. justice 9th Jud. Dist., Williamsburg, 1976—; commr. in chancery Cir. Ct., Williamsburg, 1983—. Pres. Williamsburg unit Am. Cancer Soc., 1977; state pres. Va. JCI Senate, 1984-85; chpt. pres., state officer Va. Jaycees, 1972-82; trustee Coll. William & Mary Athletic Ednl. Found., Williamsburg, 1984—. Served to maj. U.S. Army, 1968-71, Vietnam. Decorated Bronze Star. Mem. ABA, Omicron Delta Kappa. Episcopalian. General practice, Family and matrimonial, Real property. Home: 417 Hempstead Rd Williamsburg VA 23185 Office: Rideout & Miller 210 Parkway Dr Williamsburg VA 23185

MILLER, WILLIAM NAPIER CRIPPS, lawyer; b. Long Branch, N.J., June 7, 1930; adopted s. Julia (Erwin) M.; m. Carolyn Anderson, Jan. 19, 1951 (div. 1963); children: Bruce Douglass, Jennifer Erwin; m. Hannelore Steinbeck, Dec. 4, 1970;. A.A., Coll. Marin, 1949; student, U. Calif.-Berkeley, 1949-51, J.D., 1955. Bar: N.Y., Calif. 1956, U.S. Supreme Ct. 1983. Assoc. Mudge, Stern, Baldwin & Todd, N.Y.C., 1955-58; assoc. Pillsbury, Madison & Sutro, San Francisco, 1959-65, ptnr., 1966—; staff NYU Law Sch., 1957-58; ct. adv. com. Calif. State Assembly Judiciary Com., 1979-80. Bd. dirs. Laguna Honda Hosp., San Francisco, 1966—; bd. visitors U. Calif.-Hastings Law Sch. Served with USAF, 1951-52. Recipient Bur. Nat. Affairs award U. Calif.-Hastings, 1955; recipient Thurston Soc. award, 1953. Fellow Am. Coll. Trial Lawyers; mem. ABA, San Francisco Bar Assn., Order of Coif. Clubs: St. Francis Yacht; Stock Exchange (San Francisco); Silverado Country (Napa, Calif.). Antitrust, Federal civil litigation, Water law. Home: 16 George Ln Sausalito CA 94965 Office: Pillsbury Madison & Sutro 225 Bush St San Francisco CA 94104

MILLER-WACHTEL, ELLEN, lawyer; b. N.Y.C., Nov. 7, 1952; m. Alan B. Wachtel, June 20, 1976; 1 child, Carlyn. BS, Cornell U., 1974; postgrad., Columbia U. Law Sch., 1976-77; JD, Boston Coll., 1977. Bar: N.Y. 1978, U.S. Dist. Ct. (so. and ea. dists.) N.Y. 1978, U.S. Ct. Appeals (2d cir.) 1982, U.S. Supreme Ct. 1982. Assoc. Shearman & Sterling, N.Y.C., 1977-79, Barovick, Konecky, N.Y.C., 1979-83; gen. atty. NBC, N.Y.C., 1983—. Mem. Assn. of Bar of City of N.Y. Entertainment, Federal civil litigation. Office: NBC 30 Rockefeller Plaza Room 1022 New York NY 10020

MILLET, JOHN PORATH, lawyer; b. Detroit, Feb. 3, 1943; s. John Pettigrew and Doris Frieda (Porath) M.; m. Cecelia Fay McCallister, Apr. 14, 1973; children—Karen Anne, John Christopher. B.B.A., N. Tex. State U., 1966; J.D., So. Meth. U., 1969. Bar: Tex. 1969, U.S. Dist. Ct. (no. dist.) Tex. 1971. Examining atty. Fidelity Title Co., Dallas, 1970-72; atty., plant mgr., 1973-75; atty., plant mgr. Chgo. Title Co., Dallas, 1975-76; sr. v.p. USLIFE Title Co., San Antonio, 1976-83; v.p., chief title officer Dallas & Tex. Title Companies, Dallas, 1984-85; exec. v.p., Dallas Title Co., 1985-87, v.p. ops. Comml. Title Co., San Antonio, 1987—. Instr. law Eastfield Coll., Dallas, 1975-76; instr. Tex. Land Title Sch., San Antonio, 1982, 84, 86. Mem. Tex Bar Assn. Republican. Methodist. Club: Early Ford V-8 (chmn. com. So. Tex. region 1983). Real property. Home: 1500 Bamburgh Dr Plano TX 75075 Office: Comml Title Co 111 Soledad Suite 210 San Antonio TX 78205

MILLHAUSER, MARGUERITE SUE, lawyer; b. Balt., Dec. 30, 1953; d. Ernest and Gusti (Rosner) M. BS, U. Md., 1974, JD, 1977. Bar: Md. 1977, D.C. 1978. Instr. U. Md., College Park, 1975; from assoc. to ptnr. Steptoe & Johnson, Washington, 1977—; instr. family counseling U. Md.; mediator Supr. Ct. of D.C. Multi-Door Dispute Resolution program. Author: Voluntary Admission of Children to Mental Hospitals: A Conflict of Interest Between Parent and Child,The Unspoken Resistance to Alternative Dispute Resolution. Mem. ABA (litigation sect., alt. dispute resolution com.), Am. Arbitration Assn. (panel of arbitrators and mediators), Soc. Profls. in Dispute Resolution (BNA adv. panel for the alt. dispute resolution reporter), D.C. Bar (alternate dispute resolution com.), Order of Coif. Alternative dispute resolution, Negotiation. Office: Steptoe & Johnson 1330 Connecticut Ave NW Washington DC 20036

MILLHOFF, PATRICIA ANN, lawyer; b. Barberton, Ohio, Apr. 16, 1950; d. Kenneth Henry and Jeanne (Brand) M.; m. Ronald L. Piatt, Mar. 24, 1982. BA in Biology, Kent State U., 1972; JD, Akron U., 1979. Bar: Ohio 1979, U.S. Dist. Ct. (no. dist.) Ohio 1980. Staff atty. ABLE Legal Services, Toledo, 1979-80; sole practice Akron, 1980—; coordinator U. Akron (Ohio) Legal Clinic, 1983-84. Mem. investigation com. County Mental Health Bd., Akron, 1985. Recipient Vol. award Western Res. Legal Services, Akron, 1984, Summit County Mental Health Assn., Akron, 1986. Mem. Assn. Trial Lawyers Am., Ohio Acad. Trial Lawyers, Ohio Bar Assn., Akron Bar Assn. (chmn. young lawyers com. 1980, criminal law com. 1984—, chmn. law office mgmt. 1986-87), Kent State Alumni Assn. (sec. 1984-85, v.p. 1986—). Democrat. Methodist. Club: Women's Network (Akron). Avocations: tennis, needlepoint. Criminal, Personal injury, Mental health. Home: 1406 Stratofrd Dr Kent OH 44240-4638 Office: 501 Evans Savs Bldg Akron OH 44308

MILLIGAN, EDWARD JOSEPH, JR., lawyer; b. Bunkie, La., Sept. 23, 1945; s. Edward Joseph Sr. and Ann (Leger) M.; m. Denise DuPuis, Aug. 22, 1970; children: Denee, Joey, Case. BA, U. Southwestern La., 1971; LLB, So. U., 1974. Bar: La. 1975, U.S. Dist. Ct. (we., ea and mid. dists.) La. 1976, U.S. Ct. Appeals (5th cir.) 1977. Supr. La. Dept. Edn., Baton Rouge, 1974-75; from assoc. to ptnr. J. Minos Simon, Ltd., Lafayette, La., 1976-79; sole practice Lafayette, 1979—. Served to staff sgt. USAF, 1965-69. Named one of Outstanding Young Men of Am. Outstanding Young Men of Am., 1981. Mem. ABA, La. Bar Assn., La. Trial Lawyers Assn., Lafayette Trial Lawyers Assn., Lafayette C. of C., Lafayette Jaycees (legal counsel 1979-81, Officer of the Month award 1980, Jaycee of the Month and Quarter 1979). Democrat. Roman Catholic. Federal civil litigation, State civil litigation, General practice. Home: 125 Thrasher Dr Lafayette LA 70506 Office: 210 N Magnolia St Lafayette LA 70501

MILLIGAN, FRANCIS JOSEPH, JR., lawyer; b. Chgo., Aug. 19, 1924; s. Francis J. and Julia (Ryan) M.; m. Catherine Jeanne Collopy, July 10, 1954; children: Mary Ellen, Catherine Marie, Francis Joseph III, Elizabeth Marie, Anne Mary. Student, Loyola U., Chgo., U. Notre Dame; J.D., Harvard U., 1949. Bar: Ill. 1950. Trust officer Continental Ill. Nat. Bank & Trust Co., Chgo., 1949-58; practiced in Chgo., 1958—; mem. Arnstein, Gluck, Lehr & Milligan, 1965—. Pres. council Mundelein Coll., 1956-66, pres., 1963-66, trustee, 1967-73; trustee St. Marys Coll., Winona, Minn., 1969-73, Blue Army of Our Lady of Fatima, Chgo., 1975—; bd. dirs., exec. com. NCCJ, 1959—, co-chmn., 1964-69, nat. dir., 1966-74, 87—; bd. dirs. Scholarship Found., U. Notre Dame Club, Chgo., 1955—, sec., 1959-64, pres., 1965-73;

bd. dirs. John G. Symons YMCA, 1969-85, Inst. for Religious Life, 1978—; bd. dirs. Madonna Center, 1955-85, v.p., 1966-85; bd. govs. Thomas Aquinas Coll., Santa Paula, Calif., 1978—; v.p., mem. adv. bd. Apostolate for Family Consecration, 1978—, Cath. Charities Chgo., 1975—. Served to ensign USNR, 1943-46. Mem. Ill., Chgo. bar assns., Am. Coll. Probate Counsel, Chgo. Estate Planning Council, Harvard Law Sch. Assn., Notre Dame Law Assn., Cath. Lawyers Guild Chgo. (bd. dirs. 1955—, v.p. 1974-80, pres. 1980-86). Clubs: Serra, Legal, Notre Dame Alumni (pres. 1957-58), Metropolitan, Chicago, Economic (Chgo.). Lodge: Knights of the Equestrian Order of the Holy Sepulchre of Jerusalem. Estate planning, Probate. Home: 1721 Wagner Rd Glenview IL 60025 Office: Sears Tower Chicago IL 60606

MILLIGAN, MICHAEL ROY, lawyer; b. Houston, Nov. 2, 1941; s. Gaymond Eugene and Hilda Frances (Vaughan) M.; m. Elaine Kocian, Dec. 28, 1968 (div. 1977); m. Linda Herman, Dec. 1978 (dec. Feb. 1984); m. Gail Abraham, July 5, 1986. Student, Southwestern U., 1959-60; B.B.A., U. Tex., 1964; J.D., U. Houston, 1968. Bar: Tex. bar 1968. Assoc. Sigel & Simms, Houston, 1968-69, Roane & Milligan, Houston, 1970-74; ptnr. Johnson & Milligan, Houston, 1974-81; sole practice El Paso, Tex., 1981—. Assoc. editor: Houston Law Rev, 1967-68. Mem. Tex., Bar Assn., Houston Bar Assn., El Paso Bar Assn., Soc. Preservation and Encouragement of Barber Shop Quartet Singing in Am. (treas. 1977-78, dir. 1979), Phi Delta Phi. Personal injury, Family and matrimonial. Home: 6404 Los Altos El Paso TX 79912 Office: 5845 Onix #104 El Paso TX 79912

MILLIGRAM, STEVEN IRWIN, lawyer; b. N.Y.C., July 16, 1953; s. Harry William and Judith Edith (Soffen) M.; m. Michele Palamidy, Feb. 25, 1984. BA, SUNY, Buffalo, 1976; JD, Pace U., 1981. Bar: N.Y. 1982, U.S. Dist. Ct. (ea. and so. dists.) N.Y. 1982, N.J. 1982, U.S. Dist. Ct. N.J. 1982. Asst. dist. atty. State of N.Y., Bronx, 1982-86; assoc. Meiselman, Farber, Packman & Eberz, Poughkeepsie, N.Y., 1986—; founding atty. Bedford (N.Y.) Mt. Kisco Youth Ct., 1984-85. Mem. ABA, N.Y. State Bar Assn., Fed. Bar Council, Pace U. Alumni Assn. Democrat. Jewish. State civil litigation, Personal injury, Insurance. Home: 103 Crescent Dr Thiells NY 10984 Office: Meiselman Farber Packman & Eberz 2 Jefferson St Poughkeepsie NY 12602

MILLIKEN, CHARLES BUCKLAND, lawyer; b. New Haven, June 2, 1931; s. Arthur and Susan Lord (Buckland) M.; m. Sandra Stewart, July 6, 1957; children—Susan S., Andrew S. B.A., Yale U., 1952; J.D., Harvard U., 1957. Bar: Conn. 1957. Asso., Shipman & Goodwin, Hartford, Conn., 1957-60, ptnr., 1961—; lectr. law corp. taxation U. Conn.; dir. Acromold Products Corp. Trustee, Westminster Sch., Simsbury, Conn., 1969—, sec., 1970-74, chmn., 1974-80; bd. dirs. Hartford Symphony, 1959-74, 1980—, sec., 1960-62, pres., 1962-64; bd. dirs. Greater Hartford Arts Council, 1971—. Served with U.S. Army, 1952-54. Fellow Am. Coll. Probate Counsel, Am. Coll. Tax Counsel; mem. ABA, Conn. Bar Assn. (chmn. tax sect. 1979-82), Hartford County Bar Assn. Contbr. articles on law to profl. jours. Pension, profit-sharing, and employee benefits, Corporate taxation, General corporate. Home: 56 Ely Rd Farmington CT 06032 Office: 799 Main St Hartford CT 06103

MILLIMET, ERWIN, lawyer; b. N.Y.C., Oct. 7, 1925; s. Maurice and Henrietta (Cohen) M.; m. Renee Yudell, June 27, 1948; children—Robert, James. B.A. magna cum laude, Amherst Coll., 1948; LL.B. cum laude, Harvard U., 1951. Bar: N.Y. 1952. Mem. firm Stroock, Stroock & Lavan, N.Y.C., now sr. ptnr.; dir. Tosco Corp., Los Angeles. Bd. visitors U. San Diego Law Sch.; active Nat. Support Group for Africa; trustee Hebrew Home for Aged, Riverdale, N.Y.; founder Citizens for Am., Washington, 1984; mem. Rep. Club, N.Y.C. and Washington. Served with inf. U.S. Army, 1943-46. Mem. N.Y. State Bar Assn., Assn. of Bar of City of N.Y., Fed. Bar Assn., Phi Beta Kappa. General corporate, Securities. Office: Stroock & Stroock & Lavan 7 Hanover Sq New York NY 10004-2594

MILLINGER, DONALD MICHAEL, lawyer; b. N.Y.C., Nov. 17, 1954; s. Harvey I. and Sylva Dee (Gladstone) M. BA magna cum laude, U. Rochester, 1976; JD cum laude, U. Pa., 1979. Bar: Pa. 1979, U.S. Dist. Ct. (ea. dist.) Pa. 1979. Assoc. Wolf, Block, Schorr & Solis-Cohen, Phila., 1979-87, ptnr., 1987—; adj. assoc. prof. Drexel U., Phila., 1983—. Editor Sports Lawyers Newsletter, 1986—. Bd. of govs. Friends of Artists Equity, Phila., 1981—; bd. dirs. Am. Music Theater Festival, Phila., 1983—, Phila. Dance Alliance, 1986—. Mem. ABA (common entertainment and sports law forum), Pa. Bar Assn., Phila. Bar Assn., Sports Lawyers Assn., N.Y. Vol. Lawyers for the Arts, Phila. Vol. Lawyers for the Arts. Entertainment, General corporate, Trademark and copyright. Office: Wolf Block Schorr & Solis-Cohen Packard Bldg 12th Floor Philadelphia PA 19102

MILLION, STEPHEN A., lawyer; b. Elmhurst, Ill., Dec. 29, 1951; s. Elmer Garr and Ruth Aulick (Hatfield) M.; m. Karen Sue Grundhauser, July 28, 1971; children: Ryan, Evan, Elizabeth. BA, Portland State U., 1973, MA, 1979; JD, U. Mich., 1977. Bar: Calif. 1977, U.S. Dist. Ct. (no. dist.) Calif. 1977, U.S. Ct. Appeals (9th cir.) 1979. Assoc. Brobeck, Phleger & Harrison, San Francisco, 1977-84, ptnr., 1984—; bd. dirs. Laurel Resources Inc., Walnut Creek, Calif. Mem. ABA (partnership com. 1983—), Calif. Bar Assn. (partnership com. 1986—), San Francisco Bar Assn. (vice chmn. corp. sect. 1984—). General corporate, Securities. Office: Brobeck Phleger & Harrison One Market Plaza San Francisco CA 94105

MILLISOR, KENNETH RAY, lawyer; b. Belle Center, Ohio, Jan. 31, 1937; s. Darrel R. and Clara Sue (Miller) M.; m. Shirley A. Curtis, June 8, 1948 (div.); children—Diana, Michael, Robert, Richard; m. Annette M. Seigert Ross, June 7, 1985. B.A., Ohio Wesleyan U., 1959; J.D., Ohio State U., 1960. Bar: Ohio 1960, U.S. Dist Ct. (no. dist.) Ohio 1965, U.S. Ct. Appeals (6th cir.) 1966, U.S. Supreme Ct. 1970, U.S. Ct. Appeals (D.C. cir.) 1975. Ptnr. Poetzel & Andress, Akron, Ohio, 1960-75, Millisor & Nobil, Akron and Cleve., 1975—. Vice pres. Akron Area Council, Boy Scouts Am., active United Way. Mem. ABA, Ohio Bar Assn. (chmn. labor sect. 1978-81), Akron Bar Assn., Order of Coif. Democrat. Clubs: Akron City, Cascade, Rotary, Masons. Labor. Home: 1750 Brookwood Dr Akron OH 44313 Office: 430 Quaker Sq Akron OH 44308

MILLMAN, BRUCE RUSSELL, lawyer; b. Bronx, N.Y., June 4, 1948; s. Meyer and Garie (Solomon) M.; m. Lorrie Jan Liss, Aug. 12, 1973; children—Noemi, Avi. A.B., Princeton U., 1970; J.D., Columbia U., 1973. Bar: N.Y. 1974, U.S. Dist. Ct. (ea. and so. dists.) N.Y. 1975, U.S. Ct. Appeals (2d cir.) 1978, U.S. Supreme Ct. 1978. Assoc. Rains & Pogrebin and predecessors Rains, Pogrebin & Scher, Mineola, N.Y., 1973-79, ptnr., 1980—; arbitrator Nassau County Dist. Ct., Mineola, 1981-83. Contbr. to: Labor and Employment Law for the General Practitioner, 1983, Updating Issues in Employment Law, 1986. Bd. dirs. West Side Montessori Sch., N.Y.C., 1984—, sec. 1985—. Harlan Fiske Stone scholar Columbia U. Law Sch., N.Y.C., 1971, 73. Mem. ABA, N.Y. State Bar Assn., Nassau County Bar Assn., Indsl. Relations Research Assn. (bd. dirs. L.I. chpt. 1984—). Club: Princeton (N.Y.C.). Labor, Civil rights, Local government. Home: 60 Riverside Dr New York NY 10024 Office: Rains & Pogrebin PC 210 Old Country Rd Mineola NY 11501 Office: 425 Park Ave New York NY 10022

MILLMAN, RICHARD MARTIN, lawyer; b. Newark, July 7, 1937; s. Emmanuel and Leona Edith (Schachtel) M.; divorced. BA, Brandeis U., 1957; LLB, Georgetown U., 1960. Bar: D.C. 1961, U.S. Supreme Ct. 1965, Md. 1968. Law clk. to chief justice U.S. Ct. Appeals (4th cir.), Balt., 1960; sole practice Washington, 1961—. Mem. Montgomery County (Md.) Council Fin. Advising, 1967-69, Adminstrn. Justice in D.C., 1967, Md. Gov.'s Com. on Employment of Handicapped, 1967, Nat. Council Sr. Citizens Task Force on Housing, 1972, Montgomery County Council Task Force on Taxation, 1967, Md. Commn. Jud. Reform, 1974-75; co-chmn. Brandeis U. Annual Givers Fund, greater Washington area, 1971; bd. dirs. Mid div. Am. Trauma Soc., 1974, treas. 1975. Mid-career fellow Georgetown U. Grad. Sch. Fgn. Service, 1981-82. Mem. Md. Bar Assn., D.C. Bar Assn., Phi Delta Phi. Private international. Office: 1234 31st St NW Washington DC 20007

MILLS, ANDRE MICHEAUX, labor lawyer; b. Chgo., Dec. 1, 1946; s. Charles Elliott and Ruby Beatrice (Compton) M.; m. Robyn Fisher, June 21, 1986. BA in Polit. Sci., UCLA, 1974; JD, DePaul U., 1980. Bar: Ill. 1980. Labor counsel Beatrice Foods Co., Chgo., 1980-85; dir. labor relations John Sexton & Co., Chgo., 1985—. Served with USAF, 1963-67. Mem. ABA, Chgo. Bar Assn. Democrat. Methodist. Avocations: raising horses, tennis. Labor, General corporate, Workers' compensation. Office: John Sexton & Co 1050 Warrenville Rd Lisle IL 60532

MILLS, ANTHONY BELDEN, lawyer; b. Greensboro, N.C., Aug. 22, 1951; s. Burdette Belden and Patricia Ann (Buxton) M.; m. Cathy Lynn Gates, Aug. 20, 1977; children: Zachary Tucker, Jacob Whittaker. B in Gen. Studies, Ohio U., 1973; postgrad., Drake U., 1976-77; JD, Hamline U., 1979. Bar: Minn. 1980, N.D. 1981, U.S. Dist. Ct. Minn. 1981, U.S. Ct. Appeals (8th cir.) 1982, U.S. Dist. Ct. N.D. 1983. Sole practice Edina, Minn., 1980-81; assoc. Cahill, Jeffries & Maring P.A., Moorhead, Minn., 1981—; instr. Moorhead State U., 1985—. Mem. ABA, Minn. Bar Assn., N.D. Bar Assn., Def. Research Assn., Am. Arbitration Assn. Personal injury, Federal civil litigation, State civil litigation. Office: Jeffries & Mills PA 403 Center Ave Suite 302 Moorhead MN 56560

MILLS, DON HARPER, pathology and psychiatry educator; b. Peking, Republic of China, July 27, 1927; came to U.S., 1928; s. Clarence Alonzo and Edith Clarissa (Parott) M.; m. Lillian Frances Snyder, June 11, 1949; children: Frances Jo, Jon Snyder. BS, U. Cin., 1950, MD, 1953; JD, U. So. Calif., 1958. Diplomate Am. Bd. Law in Medicine. Intern Los Angeles County Gen. Hosp., 1953-54, admitting physician, 1954-57, attending staff pathologist, 1959—; pathology fellow U. So. Calif., Los Angeles, 1954-55, instr. pathology, 1958-62, asst. clin. prof., 1962-65, assoc. clin. prof., 1965-69, clin. prof., 1969—, clin. prof. psychiatry and behavioral sci., 1986—; asst. in pathology Hosp. Good Samatarian, Los Angeles, 1956-65, cons. staff, 1962-72, affiliating staff, 1972—; dep. med. examiner Office of Los Angeles County Med. Examiner, 1957-61; instr. legal medicine Loma Linda (Calif.) U. Sch. Medicine, 1960-66, assoc. clin. prof. humanities, 1966—; cons. HEW, 1972-73, 75-76, Dept. of Def., 1975-80; bd. dirs. Am. Bd. Law in Medicine, Inc., Chgo., 1980-86. Column editor Newsletter of the Long Beach Med. Assn., 1960-75, Jour. Am. Osteopathic Assn., 1965-77, Ortho Panel, 1970-78; exec. editor Trauma, 1964—; mem. editorial bd. Aspects of Med. Practice, 1972—, Med. Alert Communications, 1973-75, Am. Jour. Forensic Medicine and Pathology, 1979-87, Hosp. Risk Control, 1981—; contbr. numerous articles to profl. jours. Fellow Am. Coll. Legal Medicine (pres. 1974-76, bd. govs. 1970-78, v.p. 1972-74, chmn. malpractice com. 1973-74, mem. jour. editorial bd. 1984—), Am. Acad. Forensic Scis. (pres. 1986-87, v.p. 1984-85, exec. com. 1971-74, gen. program chmn. 1966-67, chmn. jurisprudence sect. 1966-67, 73-74, mem. jour. editorial bd. 1965-79); mem. AMA (mem. jour. editorial bd. 1973-77), Calif. Med. Assn., Los Angeles County Med. Assn., AAAS, ABA, State Bar Calif., Los Angeles County Bar Assn., Am. Judicature Soc., Drug Info. Assn., Am. Soc. Hosp. Attys., Calif. Soc. Hosp. Attys. Office: 1141 Los Altos Ave Long Beach CA 90815

MILLS, EDWARD WARREN, corporation executive, lawyer; b. N.Y.C., Apr. 7, 1941; m. Maria Parascandolo, Sept. 19, 1971; children: Edward Warren, Foy Fitzhugh, Joseph V.O. B.S., Washington and Lee U., 1962; M.B.A., Hofstra U., 1974; J.D., N.Y. Law Sch., 1977. Bar: N.Y. 1978. Acct., Wasserman & Taten, N.Y.C., 1962-69; exec. v.p. L.H. Keller, Inc. and Hugo P. Keller, Inc., N.Y.C., 1969-73; pres. Gen. Ruby & Sapphire Corp., 1973—, Qualistar Corp., 1973—; sole practice, N.Y.C., 1978—. Mem. ABA, N.Y. State Bar Assn., D.C. Bar Assn., N.Y. County Lawyers Assn., Am. Inst. CPAs, N.Y. State Soc. CPAs. Personal income taxation. Home: 1913 Ingersol Pl New Port Richey FL 33552 Office: 60 E 42d St New York NY 10017

MILLS, JOHN WELCH, lawyer; b. Cleve., June 4, 1931; s. Thoburn and Margaret (Welch) M.; m. Louise Cantwell Connell, Oct. 19, 1963; children: Carolyn, James, Jennifer. A.B., Princeton U., 1953; LL.B., Harvard U., 1958. Bar: N.Y. 1959, Ohio 1965, Ill. 1973. Asso. firm White & Case, N.Y.C., 1958-61; asst. U.S. atty. So. Dist. N.Y., 1961-64; asst. gen. counsel Republic Steel Corp., Cleve., 1964-72; v.p., gen. counsel Maremont Corp., Chgo., 1972-78, Tenneco Automotive, Lincolnshire, Ill., 1978—. Mem. sch. bd. Sears Sch., Kenilworth, Ill., 1975-81; trustee Univ. Sch., Cleve., 1970-72, Kenilworth Union Ch., 1982—; pres. Kenilworth Citizens Adv. Com., 1986—. Served to 1st lt. arty. AUS, 1953-55. Clubs: Kirtland Country (Cleve.); Indian Hill, Economic (Chgo.). General corporate, Contracts commercial, Antitrust. Home: 211 Essex Rd Kenilworth IL 60043 Office: 2275 Half Day Rd Bannockburn IL 60015

MILLS, KATHLEEN ANNE MERRY, lawyer; b. Pitts., Dec. 29, 1944; d. Eugene Webster and Mary Sara (Hall) Merry; m. Daniel Clay Mills, June 22, 1973; children: Stuart Jennings Doyle, Eugene Bernard, Frances Sarah, Kathryn Blaine. BA, Trinity Coll., Washington, 1966; JD, Duke U., 1969. Bar: Pa. 1969, U.S. Dist. Ct. (we. dist.) Pa. 1969, U.S. Ct. Appeals (3d cir.) 1972, U.S. Dist. Ct. (ea. dist.) Pa. 1975, U.S. Dist. Ct. (mid. dist.) Pa. 1980, U.S. Ct. Appeals (4th cir.) 1986. Assoc. Reed, Smith, Shaw & McClay, Pitts., 1969-73; atty. Bethlehem (Pa.) Steel Corp., 1973-78, gen. atty., 1978—; mem. legal adv. com. Washington Bus. Group on Health, 1985—. Bd. dirs. Sayre Child Ctr., Bethlehem, 1978-81. Mem. ABA, Pa. Bar Assn., Northampton County Bar Assn., Allegheny County Bar Assn. (sec. bd. govs. 1972-74), Women in Employee Benefits, Bethlehem Vis. Nurses Assn. (pres. 1980-84, bd. dirs. 1976—). Republican. Roman Catholic. Avocations: needlework, aerobics, reading. Labor, Antitrust, Pension, profit-sharing, and employee benefits. Home: 1370 Armstrong Rd Bethlehem PA 18017 Office: Bethlehem Steel Corp 2086 Martin Tower Bethlehem PA 18016

MILLS, MARCIA JOAN, lawyer; b. Evanston, Ill., Dec. 14, 1948; d. Fred Edward and Faye K. (Kohn) Ryherd; m. Gerald Edward Mills; children: Michael Edward, Amanda Susan. BA in English, U. Ill., 1970; JD cum laude, Fla. State U., 1975. Bar: Fla. 1975, Wis. 1977, U.S. Dist. Ct. (we. dist.) Wis. 1977, Tex. 1986. Research asst. Fla. State Ct. Appeals 1st Dist., Tallahassee, 1975-76; ptnr. Glinski, Haferman, Ilten, Mills, Dreier, SC, Stevens Point, Wis., 1976-85; asst. gen. counsel Res. Life Ins. Co., Dallas, 1985—. Bd. dirs. Womens Resource Ctr., Stevens Point, 1978-85; Cen. Wis. Alcohol and Drug Abuse Ctr., Stevens Point, 1978-85; Bd. dirs. Cen. Wis. Pvt. Industry Council, Wisconsin Rapids, 1981-85. James scholar U. Ill., 1966. Mem ABA, Dallas Council Insurance Attys. General corporate. Home: 1911 Espinosa Dr Carrollton TX 75007 Office: Reserve Life Ins Co 403 S Akard St Dallas TX 75202

MILLS, MICHAEL FRANCIS, lawyer; b. Medford, Mass., Sept. 22, 1957; s. Frank Richard and Lena Marie (Andreottola) M. BS, Boston U., 1979; JD, New Eng. Sch. Law, 1982. Bar: Mass. 1982, U.S. Dist. Ct. Mass. 1983, U.S. Ct. Appeals (1st cir.) 1984, U.S. Tax Ct. 1985, U.S. Ct. Claims 1986, U.S. Supreme Ct. 1986, D.C. 1987. Asst. dist. atty. Middlesex County, Cambridge, Mass., 1982-83; atty. Rifkin Law Offices, Salem, Mass., 1983-85; gen. counsel Computech Publ., Inc., Randolph, Mass., 1985-86; trial atty. Am. Transp. Ins. Co., Boston, 1986—; real estate broker, Boston, 1985—. Recipient Am. Jurisprudence award New Eng. Sch. Law, Boston, 1981. Mem. ABA, Mass. Bar Assn. General corporate, Personal injury, General practice. Home: 23 Alden Ln Medford MA 02155 Office: Am Transp Ins Co 142 Berkeley St 5th Floor Boston MA 02116

MILLS, PAUL HARLAND, lawyer; b. Farmington, Maine, Apr. 5, 1952; s. Sumner Peter Jr. and Katherine (Coffin) M. BA, Harvard U., 1974; JD, U. Maine, 1977. Bar: Maine 1977, U.S. Dist. Ct. Maine 1977, U.S. Ct. Appeals (1st cir.) 1986. Ptnr. Mills & Mills, Farmington, 1977—. Chmn. Town of Farmington Budget Com., 1979-85; moderator Town of Farmington, 1985—, Town of Kingfield, Maine, 1984—. Mem. ABA, Maine Bar Assn., Franklin County Bar and Law Library Assn. (librarian 1979-86, pres. 1986—), Assn. Trial Lawyers Am., Maine Trial Lawyers Assn., Farmington Area Alumni Inc. (pres. 1985—). Republican. Congregationalist. Lodges: Masons, Elks, Odd Fellows, Grange, SAD #58 (moderator 1981—). Real property. Home: 55 Main St Farmington ME 04938 Office: Mills & Mills 55 Main St PO Box 608 Farmington ME 04938

MILLS, RICHARD HENRY, judge; b. Beardstown, Ill., July 19, 1929; s. Myron Epler and Helen Christine (Greve) M.; m. Rachel Ann Keagle, June 16, 1962; children: Jonathan K., Daniel Cass. BA, Ill. Coll., 1951; JD, Mercer U., 1957; LLM, U. Va., 1982. Bar: Ill. 1957, U.S. Dist. Ct. Ill. 1958, U.S. Ct. Appeals 1959, U.S. Ct. Mil. Appeals 1963, U.S. Supreme Ct. 1963. Legal advisor Ill. Youth Commn., 1958-60; state's atty. Cass County, Virginia, Ill., 1960-64; judge Ill. 8th Jud. Cir., Virginia, 1966-76, Ill. 4th Dist. Appellate Ct., Virginia, 1976-85, U.S. Dist. Ct. (cen. dist.) Ill., Springfield, 1985—; adj. prof. So. Ill. U. Sch. Medicine, 1985—; mem. adv. bd. Nat. Inst. Corrections, Washington, 1984—, Ill. Supreme Ct. Rules Com., Chgo., 1963-85. Contbr. articles to profl. jours. Pres. Abraham Lincoln council Boy Scouts Am., Springfield, 1978-80. Served to col. USAR, 1952-85, Korea, Brigadier Gen., Ill. Militia, 1986—. Recipient George Washington Honor medal Freedoms Found., 1969, 73, 75, 82, Disting. Eagle Scout Boy Scouts Am., 1985. Fellow Am. Bar Found.; mem. ABA (joint com. profl. sanctions 1984—), Ill. Bar Assn., Chgo. Bar Assn., Cass County Bar Assn. (pres. 1962-64, 75-76), 7th Cir. Bar Assn., Fed. Judges Assn. Republican. Clubs: Army & Navy (Washington); The Sangamo (Springfield). Lodge: Masons. Home: 132 Oakmont Dr Springfield IL 62704 Office: US Dist Ct 319 U S Courthouse 600 E Monroe St Springfield IL 62701

MILLS, SUMNER PETER, III, lawyer; b. Farmington, Maine, June 3, 1943; s. Sumner Peter and Katherine (Coffin) M.; m. Margaret Thompson, June 16, 1965 (div. Mar. 1982); children: Katherine, Alice, Ruth; m. Nancy Lynn Diesel, Dec. 18, 1982. BA, Harvard U., 1965; JD cum laude, U. Maine, 1973. Bar: Maine 1973, Mass. 1973, U.S. Dist. Ct. Maine 1983. Assoc. Richardson, Tyler, Portland, 1973-82; ptnr. Wright & Mills, Skowhegan, Maine, 1982—. Served to lt. USN, 1965-70. Mem. ABA, Maine Bar Assn., Somerset Bar Assn., Assn. Trial Lawyers Am., Maine Trial Lawyers Assn. (bd. govs. 1983—). Republican. State civil litigation, Personal injury, Workers' compensation. Office: Wright & Mills PA 218 Water St Skowhegan ME 04976

MILLS, WILLIAM HAYES, lawyer; b. Gordo, Ala., Mar. 30, 1931; s. Early S. and Bama (Cameron) M. LL.B., U. Ala., 1956. Bar: Ala. 1956. Since practiced in Birmingha; partner Rogers, Howard, Redden & Mills, 1961-79, Redden, Mills & Clark, 1979—; arbitrator Fed. Mediation and Conciliation Service, Am. Arbitration Assn. Served with USAF, 1948-50, 50-51. Mem. ABA, Ala., Birmingham bar assns., Am., Ala. trial lawyers assns. Baptist. Club: Birmingham Optimist. Federal civil litigation, State civil litigation, General practice. Home: 2105 Williamsburg Way Birmingham AL 35223 Office: Redden Mills & Clark 940 1st Alabama Bank Bldg Birmingham AL 35203

MILLS, WILLIAM MICHAEL, lawyer; b. McAllen, Tex., Dec. 11, 1950; s. Clarence Young and Margaret Jo (Smith) M.; m. Kathy Jo Kirkpatrick, Feb. 6, 1982; children: Gregory Cy, Lucas William. BA with honors, U. Tex., 1973, JD, 1976. Bar: Tex. 1976, U.S. Dist. Ct. (so. dist.) Tex. 1977, U.S. Supreme Ct. 1980, U.S. Ct. Appeals (5th and 11th cirs.) 1981. Assoc. Atlas & Hall, McAllen, 1976-82, ptnr., 1982—. Mem. ABA, Hidalgo County Bar Assn. (bd. dirs. 1985—), Tex. Assn. Def. Counsel, Phi Beta Kappa, Phi Delta Phi. Federal civil litigation, State civil litigation, Insurance. Home: 309 Primrose McAllen TX 78504 Office: Atlas & Hall 818 Pecan St McAllen TX 78501

MILLS, WILLIAM S., lawyer; b. Roanoke, Va., Nov. 12, 1952; s. Wendell Ward and Norma Louise (Ayers) M.; m. Janice M. Rolli, June 22, 1985; 1 child, Ryan David. AB, U. N.C., 1975, JD with honors, 1979. Bar: N.C. 1979, U.S. Dist. Ct. (we., mid., and ea. dists.) N.C. 1979. Prin. William S. Mills & Assocs., Durham, N.C., 1979—; pres. 14th jud. dist. Durham County Bar, 1987—. Federal civil litigation, State civil litigation. Office: William S Mills & Assocs 104 E Main St Durham NC 27701

MILLSTEIN, DAVID J., lawyer; b. N.Y.C., Apr. 15, 1953; s. Stanley and Irma (Klein) M.; m. Barbara Louise Steger, Apr. 13, 1984; 1 child, Jesse Aaron. AB, U. Calif., Berkeley, 1975, JD, 1979. Bar: Calif. 1979, U.S. Dist. Ct. (no. dist.) Calif. 1979, U.S. Dist. Ct. (ea. dist.) Calif. 1984. Assoc. Bostwick & Tehin, San Francisco, 1980-82; asst. dist. atty. San Francisco Dist. Atty.'s Office, 1981-82; sole practice San Francisco, 1982—; judge pro tem San Francisco Mcpl. Ct., 1983—. Pres. Dem. League San Francisco, 1982-84. Regents scholar, 1973. Mem. Assn. Trial Lawyers Am., Calif. Trial Lawyers Assn., Phi Beta Kappa. Personal injury, Criminal. Office: 629 Bryant St San Francisco CA 94107

MILLSTEIN, LEO LEE, lawyer; b. China, Apr. 3, 1947; came to U.S., 1966; s. Benjamin and Jessie M.; m. Linda Sue Finkelman, Feb. 17, 1979. B.S. in Aero. Engring., Purdue U., 1970; J.D., George Washington U., 1975. Bar: D.C. 1975, U.S. Dist. Ct. D.C. 1975. Counsel corp. devel. Communications Satellite Corp., Washington, 1974-84; ptnr. Rothblatt & Millstein, Washington, 1984-85, Dyer, Ellis, Joseph & Mills, Washington, 1985—; v.p., gen. mgr. Whitman Assocs., Inc., Washington, 1983—. Mem. ABA, D.C. Bar Assn., Fed. Communications Bar Assn. General corporate, Private international, Communications. Home: 2736 Woodley Pl NW Washington DC 20008 Office: Dyer Ellis Joseph & Mills 600 New Hampshire Ave NW Suite 1000 Washington DC 20037

MILLY, LAWRENCE ARTHUR, lawyer; b. Pitts., Aug. 1, 1932; s. Paul Peter Milly and Julianna Yavorsky. BA, La. State U., New Orleans, 1970; student, U. Pitts., 1955-56; JD, Loyola U., New Orleans, 1973. Bar: La. 1973, U.S. Dist. Ct. (ea. dist.) La. 1973, U.S. Ct. Appeals (5th cir.) 1975, U.S. Supreme Ct. 1983. Sole practice New Orleans, 1973—. Served with USN, 1950-54, Korea. Avocation: artist. Personal injury, Family and matrimonial, Workers' compensation. Office: 333 St Charles Ave Suite 1004 New Orleans LA 70130

MILLY, RAYMOND ANTHONY, lawyer; b. Pitts., Aug. 29, 1930; s. Paul Peter and Juliana (Yavorsky) M. B.A., Duquesne U., 1956; J.D., Loyola U., New Orleans, 1974. Bar: La. 1975, U.S. Dist. Ct. (ea. dist.) La. 1975, U.S. Supreme Ct. 1978, U.S. Ct. Appeals (5th cir.) 1982. Sole practice, Metairie, La., 1985—. Served with USMC, 1948-52. Democrat. Roman Catholic. Admiralty, General corporate, Personal injury. Office: 117 Focis St Suite 202 Metairie LA 70005

MILNE, JACK FAGERLAND, lawyer; b. Jacksonville, Fla., May 23, 1953; s. Douglas Bisset and Betty L. (Fagerland) M.; m. Sharon J. Bald, Mar. 31, 1979; 1 child, Caroline Marie. BA, Vanderbilt U., 1975; JD, U. Fla., 1978. Bar: Fla. 1979, U.S. Dist. Ct. (mid. dist.) Fla. 1979. Assoc. Freeman, Richardson, Watson et al, Jacksonville, 1978-80; ptnr. Milne & Milne, P.A., Jacksonville, 1980—; bd. dirs. First Trust Savs. Bank, Jacksonville. Chmn. Jacksonville Environ. Protection Bd., 1984-85, bd. dirs. 1982—; pres. Jacksonville Hist. Soc., 1985-86; vestry St. Marks Episc. Ch., Jacksonville, 1983-86; bd. dirs. Jacksonville Humane Soc., 1983—. Mem. ABA, Fla. Bar Assn., Jacksonville Bar Assn., Fellowship Christian Athletes (pres. 1984-85). Democrat. Clubs: Timuquana Country, Seminole (Jacksonville). Lodge: Rotary. Avocations: Am. history, hunting, fishing, collecting duck decoys. General practice. Home: 1843 Challen Ave Jacksonville FL 32205 Office: Milne & Milne 100 Riverside Ave PO Box 41222 Jacksonville FL 32203

MILNER, CHRISTY ELIZABETH, lawyer; b. Ft. Worth, Tex., Jan. 17, 1953; d. George Henry and Pauline Elizabeth (Martin) M.; m. Hanford Michael Farrell, May 26, 1983; 1 child, Sean Michael. BA with honors, U. Tex., 1974, JD with honors, 1978. Bar: Tex. 1979. Assoc. Richie & Greenburg P.C., Houston, 1978-80; atty. Conoco Inc., Houston, 1980-84; assoc. Andrews & Kurth, Houston, 1984-86, Fizer, Beck, Webster & Bentley, Houston, 1986—; speaker on legal topics various instns. Contbr. articles on tax to profl. jours. Mem. ABA, Tex. Bar Assn., Houston Bar Assn. Pension, profit-sharing, and employee benefits, Estate taxation, State and local taxation. Home: 2406 Lazybrook Houston TX 77008 Office: Fizer Beck Webster & Bentley 1360 Post Oak Blvd Houston TX 77506

MILONE, FRANCIS MICHAEL, lawyer; b. Phila., June 18, 1947; s. Michael Nicholas and Frances Theresa (Fair) M.; m. Dorothy Therese Walters, Sept. 13, 1969; 1 child, Michael. BA, LaSalle Coll., 1969; MS, Pa. State U., 1971; JD, U. Pa., 1974. Bar: Pa. 1974, U.S. Dist. Ct. (ea dist.) Pa. 1974, U.S. Dist. Ct. (mid. dist.) Pa. 1979, U.S. Dist. Ct. (ea. dist.) Mich. 1983, U.S. Ct. Appeals (3d cir.) 1978, U.S. Ct. Appeals (4th and 5th cirs.) 1979, U.S. Supreme Ct. 1979. Assoc. Montgomery, McCraken, Walker & Rhoads, Phila., 1974-77; ptnr. Morgan, Lewis & Bockius, Phila., 1977—. Mem. ABA (labor and litigation sects.), Pa. Bar Assn., Phila. Bar Assn. Labor, Federal civil litigation, State civil litigation. Office: Morgan Lewis &

Bockius 2000 One Logan Sq Philadelphia PA 19103 Home: 89 Woodstone Ln Villanova PA 19085

MILSTEIN, EDWARD PHILIP, lawyer; b. N.Y.C., Apr. 20, 1949; s. Paul and Sylvia Milstein; m. Andrea Kay Wintner, Aug. 16, 1970; children—Scott, Erika. B.A., NYU, 1970; J.D., Bklyn. Law Sch., 1974. Bar: N.Y. 1975, U.S. Dist. Ct. (so. and ea. dists.) N.Y. 1975, U.S. Ct. Appeals (2d cir.) 1975, U.S. Supreme Ct. 1978, N.J. 1983. Assoc. Lipsig, Sullivan & Liapakis, P.C., N.Y.C., 1975-80, ptnr., 1980—. Mem. Assn. Trial Lawyers Am., ABA, N.Y. County Lawyers Assn., Acad. Sci., N.Y. Acad. Medicine, Am. Soc. Medicine and Law, N.Y. State Bar Assn., N.J. Bar Assn., Bergen County Bar Assn., N.Y. County Trial Lawyers Assn. Personal injury. Home: 30 Mountain Rd Tenafly NJ 07670 Office: 157 Engle St Englewood NJ 07631

MILSTEIN, RICHARD CRAIG, lawyer; b. N.Y.C., July 16, 1946; s. Max and Hattie (Jacobson) Worchel; m. SuAnn Leiken, May 30, 1971; children—Brian Matthew, Rachel Helanie. A.A. with honors, Miami-Dade Jr. Coll., 1966, A.B. cum laude, U. Miami, Fla., 1968, J.D., 1973. Bar: Fla. 1974, U.S. Dist. Ct. Fla. 1974, U.S. Ct. Appeals (5th cir.) 1974, U.S. Supreme Ct. 1977, U.S. Ct. Appeals (11th cir.) 1982. Assoc., August, Nimkoff & Pohlig, Miami, Fla., 1974-76; mng. ptnr. Jepeway, August, Gassen & Pohlig, Miami, 1976-78, August, Gassen, Pohlig & Milstein, Miami, 1978-80, August, Pohlig & Milstein, P.A., Coral Gables, Fla., 1980-83; sr. ptnr. Milstein & Wayne, Coral Gables, 1983-85; ptnr. Tescher & Milstein, PA, Coral Gables, 1986—. Co-founder Dade County Vol. Lawyers for Arts; mem. Met. Dade County Ind. Rev. Panel, 1984-86; councilor Metro Dade County Council of Arts and Scis., 1986—; bd. dirs. South Fla. Mediation Ctr., 1982—, chmn. bd. dirs., 1985-86; bd. dirs. Ptnrs. for Youth, 1981—; bd. dirs. Bet Shira Congregation, 1980-85, asst. treas., 1982-85, pres., 1985-86, bd. dirs., 1986—; treas. South. Fla. Inter-Profl. Council Inc., 1983-84, sec., 1984-85, v.p., 1985-86, pres., 1986—; bd. dirs., v.p. Dance Umbrella Inc., 1984-86, treas., 1983-84; bd. dirs. South of Broadway Inc., 1985-86 . Mem. ABA, Am. Trial Lawyers Assn., Dade County Bar Assn. (dir. 1980-83, treas. 1983-84, sec. 1984-85, v.p. 1985-87, pres. elect 1986—), Coral Gables Bar Assn., Fla. Bar, Acad. Fla. Trial Lawyers, Phi Theta Kappa, Delta Theta Mu, Omicron Delta Kappa, Phi Alpha Theta, Kappa Delta Pi, Phi Kappa Phi, Alpha Kappa, Zeta Epsilon Nu. Democrat. General practice, Family and matrimonial, Probate. Home: 12225 SW 97th Ct Miami FL 33176 Office: Tescher & Milstein PA 2100 Ponce de Leon Blvd Penthouse Coral Gables FL 33134

MILTON, GABRIEL, lawyer; b. Los Angeles, Aug. 18, 1947; s. Nathaniel Bruce and Shirley (Fuchs) M.; m. Janet Weisberg, Apr. 1, 1973 (Nov. 1976); m. Beth Joy Hollender, Aug. 25, 1985. BA, U. Wis., 1969; JD, NYU, 1972, LLM, 1982. Bar: N.Y. 1973, N.J. 1983. Assoc. mgr. Ogilvy & Mather Inc., N.Y.C., 1973-75; sole practice N.Y.C., 1975-77; assoc. counsel Block Drug Co. Inc., Jersey City, 1977-83, asst. corp. counsel, 1983—. Mem. N.J. Bar Assn., Assn. of Bar of City of N.Y. Republican. Jewish. Avocations: painting, drawing, running, skiing, biking. Administrative and regulatory, State civil litigation, General corporate. Office: Block Drug Co Inc 257 Cornelison Ave Jersey City NJ 07302

MIMS, WILLIAM LOVANDA, lawyer; b. Winter Garden, Fla., Sept. 22, 1924; s. A.D. and Irena (Sharp) M.; m. Lucile L. Cadley, Mar. 24, 1946; children—Diane Mims Silkey, William L. Jr. B.S. in Bus. Adminstrn., U. Fla., 1952, J.D., 1954. Bar: Fla. 1955, U.S. Dist. Ct. (mid. dist.) Fla. 1955. Assoc. Sanders & McEwan, Orlando, Fla., 1955-58; ptnr. Sanders, McEwan, Mims & McDonald, Orlando, 1959—. Chmn. Orange County Democratic Exec. Com., 1958-63; mem. Com. of 100 Orange County. Served with USN, 1943-45. Named to U. Fla. Hall of Fame, 1954; recipient Outstanding Young Democrat of Fla. award, 1960. Fellow Am. Bar Found.; mem. ABA, Am. Judicature Soc., Phi Delta Phi. Democrat. Episcopalian. Clubs: Rotary, University, Errol Country (Orlando). General corporate, Real property. Office: PO Box 753 Orlando FL 32802

MINAHAN, DANIEL F., JR., lawyer; b. Waterbury, Conn., Jan. 11, 1955; s. Daniel Francis Sr. and Mary Jean (Gaffney) M.; m. Martha Anne Laycock, July 22, 1977; 1 child, Daniel Francis III. AB, Georgetown U., 1976; JD, U. Conn., 1979; LLM, Georgetown U., 1980. Bar: Conn. 1979, Wash. 1980, Colo. 1982, U.S. Dist. Ct. Colo. 1982, U.S. Ct. Appeals (10th, D.C. and Fed. cirs.) 1982. Atty. Fed. Mine Safety and Health Commn., Washington, 1980-81, Fed. Labor Relations Authority, Denver, 1981-85; ptnr. Minahan & Shapiro P.C., Denver, 1985—. Mem. ABA, Colo. Bar Assn., Fed. Bar Assn., Denver Bar Assn., Soc. Fed. Labor Relations Profls. Democrat. Roman Catholic. Avocations: history, music. Labor, Civil rights, Federal civil litigation. Office: Minahan & Shapiro PC 1370 Pennsylvania Suite 320 Denver CO 80203

MINAHAN, DANIEL FRANCIS, manufacturing company executive; b. Orange, N.J., Dec. 3, 1929; s. Alfred A. and Katherine (Kelly) M.; m. Mary Jean Gaffney, May 2, 1953; children: Daniel Francis, John Alfred. AB magna cum laude, U. Notre Dame, 1951; JD magna cum laude, U. Conn., 1964; grad., Advanced Mgmt. Program, Harvard, 1975. Bar: Conn. 1964, U.S. Supreme Ct 1964, U.S. Ct. of Appeals, U.S. Dist. Ct. Conn. Mgr. indsl. engring. Uniroyal, Inc., Naugatuck, Conn., 1952-59, mgr. indsl. relations, 1959-64; supr. labor relations Uniroyal, Inc., N.Y.C., 1964-66; v.p. indsl. relations and labor counsel Phillips Van Heusen Corp., N.Y.C., 1966-69; v.p. personnel-adminstrn. Broadway-Hale Stores, Inc., Los Angeles, 1969-70; v.p. employee relations, sec. Magnavox-N.Am., Philips Corp., 1970-73, v.p. ops., group exec., 1973-83, sr. v.p., 1984—. Co-author: The Developing Labor Law, 1971. Pres. Magnavox Found.; bd. dirs. Young Audiences Los Angeles; chmn. bd. Internat. Fedn. Keystone Youth Orgns., London and Chgo.; trustee U. Conn. Law Sch. Served with USMCR. Mem. ABA, Conn. Bar Assn., Assn. Bar City N.Y., NAM, Research Inst. Am., Harvard Advanced Mgmt. Assn., Japan Soc., Bur. Nat. Affairs, Internat. Platform Assn., Electronic Inst. Am. Clubs: Harvard, Bd. Room (N.Y.C.); Club Internat. (Chgo.); Belfrey (London); Landmark. General corporate, Labor. Office: 100 E 42d St New York NY 10017

MINAHAN, ROGER COPP, lawyer; b. Green Bay, Wis., Feb. 13, 1910; s. Eben R. and Jessie (Copp) M.; m. Myrna J. Knight; children by previous marriage: Barbara Minahan Low, William Stephens. Ph.B., U. Wis., 1932, LL.B., 1934, J.S.D., 1935. Bar: Wis. 1934. Ptnr. Minahan & Bassett Green Bay, 1935-43; practiced in Milw., 1943—; partner firm Whyte & Hirschboeck, 1943-78, Minahan & Peterson, 1978—; former sec., gen. counsel, dir. Post Corp.; dir. Vaportek, Inc., Hatco, Inc. Mem. Natural Resources Bd., 1969-75. Served to lt. (s.g.) USNR, 1944-46. Mem. Am., Wis., Milw. bar assns., Order of Coif. General corporate, Corporate taxation, Probate. Office: Minahan & Peterson SC 411 E Wisconsin Ave Milwaukee WI 53202-4499

MINAMYER, WILLIAM ERIC, lawyer; b. Salem, Ohio, June 26, 1953; s. Kenneth Dean and Donna Lou (Whitehouse) M.; m. Colleen Ann Moore, Aug. 11, 1979; children: Jennifer Dale, Lisa Colleen. BA, U. Akron, 1975; JD, Am. U., 1978; LLM in Labor Law, Georgetown U., 1982. Bar: Ohio 1979, U.S. Dist. Ct. (so. dist.) Ohio 1983, U.S. Ct. Appeals (6th cir.) 1984, U.S. Supreme Ct. 1984. Spl. asst. to Congressman Charles W. Whalen Jr., Washington, 1975-76; assoc. Porter, Wright, Morris & Arthur, Dayton, Ohio, 1983-85, Paxton & Seasongood, 1985—. Chmn. sign com. Donna Moon, Dayton, 1984; campaign chmn. Morr for Congress, 1986—; campaign coordinator Whalen for Congress, Dayton, 1976; bd. dirs. Young Reps., Dayton, 1985-87, active, 1983—; bd. dirs. Hamilton County Rep. Club, 1987. Served to lt. comdr. JAGC, USN, 1979-83, USNR, 1983—. Decorated Navy Achievement medal, Meritorious Unit commendation; recipient Nat. Sojourner's award USAFR, 1974. Mem. Ohio Bar Assn., Cin. Bar Assn., ABA. Presbyterian. Labor, Federal civil litigation, Military. Home: 5655 Bayberry Dr Cincinnati OH 45242 Office: Paxton & Seasongood 1700 Central Trust Tower Cincinnati OH 45202

MINCH, ROGER JAMES, lawyer; b. Fargo, N.D., June 28, 1952; s. A. R. and Lois (Thompson) M. BA, N.D. State U., 1975; JD, U. N.D., 1978. Bar: N.D. 1978, Minn. 1978, U.S. Dist. Ct. N.D., U.S. Dist. Ct. Minn., U.S. Ct. Appeals (8th cir.). Ptnr. Serkland, Lundberg, Erickson, Marcil & McLean Ltd., Fargo, 1978—; lectr. continuing legal edn. Nat. Bus. Inst., Eau Claire, Wis., 1983—. Mem. N.D. Bar Assn. (lectr. continuing legal edn. 1983—), Cass County Bar Assn., Comml. Law League Am., Am. Bankruptcy Inst. Republican. Avocations: travel, hunting, fishing, moth and butterfly collecting. Bankruptcy, Contracts commercial, Agricultural law. Office: Serkland Lundberg Erickson Marcil & McLean Ltd 10 Roberts St PO Box 6017 Fargo ND 58102

MINDUS, HOWARD VICTOR, lawyer; b. N.Y.C., Aug. 22, 1944; s. Henry Victor and Hilde (Eschwege) M.; m. Myriam Georgette Ellis, Oct. 15, 1972; 1 son, Daniel Ellis. B.A., Swarthmore Coll., 1966; LL.B., Yale U., 1969. Bar: N.Y. 1970. Assoc. Donovan, Leisure, Newton & Irvine, N.Y.C., 1969-71; asso. gen. counsel N.Y.C. EPA, 1971-73; assoc. Morgan, Lewis & Bockius, N.Y.C., 1973-78, ptnr., 1978—. Mem. ABA, N.Y. State Bar Assn., Assn. Bar City N.Y. Democrat. Jewish. Contracts commercial, General corporate. Office: Morgan Lewis & Bockius 45th Floor 101 Park Ave New York NY 10178

MINEO, ROBERT ANTHONY, lawyer, aerospace engineer; b. Orental, N.C., Nov. 30, 1948; s. Jacob Anthony and Carol (Truitt) M.; m. Athena Redmond, Sept. 18, 1982; children: Gabrielle, Robert. BS in Aerospace Engring., N.C. State U., 1970; postgrad., U. Notre Dame, 1980; JD, Campbell Law Sch., 1981. Bar: N.C. 1981, U.S. Dist. Ct. (ea. dist.) N.C. 1981, U.S. Dist. Ct. Md. 1982, U. S. Dist. Ct. (ea. dist.) Tex. 1982, U. S. Claims Ct. 1982, U.S. Ct. Appeals (D.C. and 4th cirs.) 1982,. Aerospace engr. Dept. of Navy, Cherry Point, N.C., 1970-78; assoc. Smiley, Olson, Gilman & Pangia, Washington, 1982-84; ptnr. Smiley, Olson, Gilman & Pangia, Raleigh, N.C., 1985—. Mem. ABA, AIAA, N.C. Bar Assn., N.C. Trial Lawyers Assn., Nat. Transp. Safety Bd. Bar Assn (mem. rules com. 1985—), Phi Alpha Delta. Avocations: tennis, sailing. Aviation, Federal civil litigation, State civil litigation. Office: Smiley Olson Gilman & Pangia 530 N Blount Raleigh NC 27604

MINER, DON JONES, lawyer; b. Blackfoot, Idaho, May 30, 1951; s. Carl F. and Geneva (Bergeson) M.; m. Elaine Marie Reed, Dec. 28, 1978; children: Garret William, Brian Dixon. BA in Econs., Brigham Young U., 1976, JD, 1979. Bar: Ariz. 1979, U.S. Dist. Ct. Ariz. 1979. Assoc. Evans, Kitchel & Jenckes, Phoenix, 1979-85, ptnr., 1986—; bd. dirs. Devcon Devel. Mem. Maricopa County Foster Care Rev. Bd., Phoenix, 1985—. Mem. ABA, State Bar of Ariz. Assn., Maricopa County Ariz. Bar Assn. Republican. Mormon. Avocations: tennis, jogging. Real property, Contracts commercial, General corporate. Home: 1756 E Mallory Mesa AZ 85203

MINER, JOSEPH BRIAN, lawyer; b. Ft. Morgan, Colo., Apr. 8, 1954; s. James Kenneth and Helen Philomena (Perlinger) M.; m. Wendydru Leisher, Oct. 15, 1982. BA, Colo. State U., 1979; JD, Okla. City U., 1982. Bar: Okla. 1982, U.S. Dist. Ct. (we. and ea. dists.) Okla. 1982. Assoc. Law Offices of B.J. Cooper, Oklahoma City, 1982-83, Ungerman, Conner & Little, Oklahoma City, 1983—. Mem. Okla. Bar Assn., Okla. County Bar Assn., Comml. Law League. Democrat. Roman Catholic. Lodge: K.C. Avocations: flying, gardening. Bankruptcy, Consumer commercial, Probate. Home: 6501 Fawn Canyon Dr Oklahoma City OK 73132 Office: Ungerman Conner & Little 623 W California Oklahoma City OK 73126-0568

MINER, RICHARD THOMAS, lawyer; b. N.Y.C., Mar. 31, 1987; s. Dwight Carroll and Marie Carol (Maulhardt) M.; m. Gail Spaller, Jan. 1, 1984. AB in Econs, Brown U., 1964; JD, Columbia U., 1967; LLM in Corp. Law, NYU, 1978, postdoctorate, 1982. Assoc. Donovan, Leisure, Newton & Irvine, N.Y.C., 1969-76; asst. gen. counsel Mohawk Data Scis. Corp., Parsippany, N.J., 1976-79, gen. counsel, 1979-86; gen. counsel Momentum Techs. Inc., Morris Plains, N.J., 1986—; bd. dirs. Computer Terminals Systems Inc., Commack N.Y.; account exec. (fin. planning) The Windmill Group Inc., Armonk, N.Y. Served to lt. (j.g.) USN, 1967-69. Mem. ABA, Corp. Counsel Assn. N.J., N.J. Gen. Counsels Group. Clubs: Lake Mohawk (N.J.) Country, Lake Mohawk Yacht (commodore 1984), Lake Mohawk Tennis. Avocations: yachting, tennis. Contracts commercial, Computer, General corporate. Office: Momentum Techs 201 Littleton Rd Morris Plains NJ 07950

MINER, ROGER JEFFREY, federal judge; b. Apr. 14, 1934; s. Abram and Anne M.; m. Jacqueline Mariani; 4 children. BS, SUNY; JD cum laude, N.Y. Law Sch., 1956; postgrad., Bklyn. Law Sch., JAG Sch. U. Va. Bar: N.Y. 1956, U.S. Ct. Mil. Appeals 1956, Republic of Korea 1958, U.S. Dist. Ct. (so. and ea. dists.) N.Y. 1959. Ptnr. Miner & Miner, Hudson, N.Y., 1959-75; justice N.Y. State Supreme Ct., 1976-81; judge U.S. Dist. Ct. for No. Dist. N.Y., 1981-85, U.S. Ct. Appeals for 2d Circuit, Albany, N.Y., 1985—; corp. counsel City of Hudson, 1961-64; asst. dist. atty. Columbia County, 1964, dist. atty., 1968-75; adj. assoc. prof. criminal law State Univ. System N.Y., 1974-79; adj. prof. law N.Y. Law Sch., 1986—; lectr. state and local bar assns.; moot ct. judge; lectr. SUNY-Albany. Editor Columbia County Dist. Atty.'s Newsletter, 1968-75; contbr. articles to law jours. Mem. adv. council N.Y. Law Sch.; former bd. dirs. United Way Columbia County. Served to 1st lt. JAGC, U.S. Army, 1956-59, to capt. Res., ret. Recipient Dean's medal for Disting. Profl. Service N.Y. Law Sch., Outstanding Alumnus award N.Y. Law Sch., Albany Jewish Fedn. award, Abraham Lincoln award, Community Service award Kiwinis, also others; named Columbia County Man of Yr., 1984. Mem. ABA, N.Y. State Bar Assn., Am. Judicature Soc., Fed. Judges Assn., Fed. Bar Council, Assn. Trial Lawyers Am., Columbia County Bar Assn., Columbia County Magistrates Assn., N.Y. Supreme Ct. Justices Assn., Assn. Trial Judges 3d Jud. Dist., Supreme Ct. Hist. Soc., 2d Circuit Hist. Com., No. Dist. Hist. Com., Columbia County Hist. Soc., N.Y. Law Sch. Alumni Assn. (hon. mem. bd. dirs.). Jewish. Lodges: B'nai B'rith, Elks (past exalted ruler). Judicial administration. Office: US Ct Appeals US Post Office and Courthouse Albany NY 12201

MINES, MICHAEL, lawyer; b. Seattle, May 4, 1929; s. Henry Walker and Dorothy Elizabeth (Bressler) M.; m. Phyllis Eastham, Aug. 24, 1957; children: Linda Mines Elliott, Sandra, Diane Paull, Michael Lister. Student Whitman Coll., 1947-49; BA, U. Wash., 1951, JD, 1954. Bar: Wash. 1954, U.S. Dist. Ct. (we. dist.) Wash. 1957, U.S. Dist. Ct. Mont. 1970, U.S. Ct. Appeals (9th cir.) 1961, U.S. Supreme Ct. Assoc. Skeel, McKelvy, Henke, Evenson & Uhlman, Seattle, 1956-66, ptnr., 1966-68, Hullin, Roberts, Mines, Fite & Riveland, Seattle, 1968-75, Skeel, McKelvy, Henke, Evenson & Betts, Seattle, 1975-79, Betts, Patterson & Mines, Seattle, 1978-82, bd. dirs., 1982—. Moderator Wash.-No. Idaho conf. United Ch. of Christ, 1975-76. Served with U.S. Army, 1954-56. Mem. ABA, Wash. State Bar Assn., Seattle-King County Bar Assn., Am. Coll. Trial Lawyers, Internat. Assn. Def. Counsel, Wash. Assn. Def. Counsel (pres. 1971-72), Internat. Acad. Trial Lawyers. Federal civil litigation, State civil litigation, Insurance. Home: 2474 Crestmont Pl Seattle WA 98199 Office: Betts Patterson Mines PS 800 Financial Ctr 1215 4th Ave Seattle WA 98161

MINGEE, JAMES CLYDE, III, lawyer; b. Natchez, Miss., Oct. 10, 1943; s. James Clyde and Vivian Annette (Gunning) M., Jr.; m. Donna Jean Jezek, Dec. 28, 1964; children—Timothy Shawn, Shae Lin. B.P.A., U. Miss., 1965, J.D., 1968. Bar: Miss. 1968, D.C. 1974, U.S. Supreme Ct. 1978. Atty., CIA, Washington, 1968-73; legal asst. to chancellor U. Md.-College Park, 1973-77; assoc. gen. counsel, asst. sec. Carling Nat. Breweries, Inc., Balt., 1977-78; assoc. gen. counsel Stokely-Van Camp, Inc., Indpls., 1978-80; pvt. practice, Jackson, Miss., 1980—; instr. bus. law U. Md., 1970-72; cons. counsel com. intelligence U.S. Ho. of Reps., 1975-76; legal bus. cons. U.S., fgn. corps., 1973—. Mem. ABA, Miss. State Bar Assn., Am. Arbitration Assn., Fed. Bar Assn., U.S. Trademark Assn. Roman Catholic. Co-author: Miss. Construction Law Seminar Coursebook, 1980. General corporate, Trademark and copyright, Private international. Home: 102 Coker Rd Jackson MS 39213 Office: PO Box 1291 Jackson MS 39205

MINGLE, JOHN ORVILLE, engineer, lawyer, administrator; b. Oakley, Kans., May 6, 1931; s. John Russell and Beulah Amelia (Johnson) M.; m. Patricia Ruth Schmitt, Aug. 17, 1957; children: Elizabeth Lorene, Stephen Roy. B.S., Kans. State U., Manhattan, 1953, M.S., 1958; Ph.D., Northwestern U., 1960; J.D., Washburn U., 1980. Bar: Kans., U.S. Patent Office bar; registered profl. engr., Kans. Tng. engr. Gen. Electric Co., Schenectady, 1953-54; mem. faculty Kans. State U., 1956—, prof. nuclear engring., 1965—, Black & Veatch disting. prof., 1973-78; dir. Inst. Computational Research in Engring., 1969—; exec. v.p., patent counsel Kans. State U. Research Found., 1983—; instr. Northwestern U., 1958-59; vis. prof. U. So. Calif., 1967-68; cons. to govt. and industry. Author: The Invarient Imbedding Theory of Nuclear Transport, 1973; also articles. Served as officer AUS, 1954-56. Mem. ABA (chairperson sci. and tech. phys. scis. com. 1982—), NSPE (sect. exec. com. 1985-87, chmn. 1985-86), Am. Nuclear Soc. (sect. pres. 1976-77), Am. Inst. Chem. Engrs. (profl. devel. com. 1982—), Am. Soc. Engring. Edn. (chmn. Midwest sect. 1984-87, exec. com. 1984-87), Profl. Engrs. in Edn. (vice chmn. 1978-80, workshop chairperson 1983), Kans. Engring. Soc. (past chpt. pres.), Kans. Bar Assn., Licensing Execs. Soc., Sigma Xi (past chpt. pres., lectr.), Soc. Univ. Patent Adminstrs. (exec. com. 1985-87, v.p. cen. region 1985-87). Patent, Trademark and copyright, Nuclear power. Home: 2408 Buena Vista Dr Manhattan KS 66502 Office: Fairchild Hall Kans State Univ Manhattan KS 66506

MINICH, MARK ANDREW, lawyer; b. Tulsa, Sept. 2, 1955; s. Allen Frank and Thelma Katherine (Karleskint) M.; m. Debra Sue Dykstra, Feb. 11, 1984. BA in Polit. Sci. and Econs., UCLA, 1977; JD, U. So. Calif., 1981. Bar: Calif. 1981, U.S. Dist. Ct. (cen. dist.) Calif. 1981, U.S. Ct. Appeals (9th cir.) 1981. Assoc. Overton, Lyman & Prince, Los Angeles, 1980-85; atty. Pacific Lighting Corp., Los Angeles, 1985—. Mem. Friends of UCLA Rowing, MArina del Rey, 1978—, UCLA Dean's Council, Westwood, 1984—. Mem. ABA, Los Angeles County Bar Assn., Fed. Energy Bar Assn., Los Angeles Barristers (chmn. com. 1985—). Democrat. Roman Catholic. Club: Los Angeles Athletic. Avocation: photography. Antitrust, State civil litigation, FERC practice. Office: Pacific Lighting Corp 810 S Flower St Los Angeles CA 90017

MINKEL, HERBERT PHILIP, JR., lawyer; b. Boston, Feb. 11, 1947; s. Herbert Philip and Helen (Sullivan) M. A.B., Holy Cross Coll., 1969; J.D., NYU, 1972. Bar: Mass. 1973, N.Y. 1976, U.S. Dist. Ct. Mass. 1973, U.S. Dist. Ct. (so. dist.) N.Y. 1976. Law clk. U.S. Dist. Ct. Mass., Boston, 1972-73; assoc. Milbank, Tweed, Hadley & McCloy, N.Y.C., 1973-79; ptnr. Fried, Frank, Harris, Shriver & Jacobson, N.Y.C., 1979—; adj. prof. NYU Law Sch., 1987—. Contbg. editor 5 Collier on Bankruptcy, 15th edit. 1979-87; contbr. articles to profl. jours.; author American Bankers Association Bankruptcy Manual, 1979. Root-Tilden scholar, NYU, 1969-72. Mem. Nat. Bankruptcy Conf., ABA, N.Y. Bar Assn., Assn. Bar City of N.Y. Bankruptcy. Home: 330 E 46th St New York NY 10017 Office: Fried Frank Harris Shriver & Jacobson One New York Plaza New York NY 10004

MINNEY, MICHAEL JAY, lawyer; b. Lancaster, Pa., Aug. 15, 1948; s. Jay W. and Mary Jane (Erisman) M.; m. Barbara Ann Dunlap, June 28, 1975; 1 child, Michael Jayson. Student, U.S. Mil. Acad., 1967; BA, Ohio Wesleyan U., 1970; JD, Villanova U., 1973. Bar: Pa. 1973, U.S. Dist. Ct. (ea. dist.) Pa. 1974, U.S. Supreme Ct. 1977, U.S. Ct. Appeals (3d cir.) 1979. Ptnr. Glazier, Minney, Mecum & Kohr, Lancaster, 1975-78, Minney, Mecum & Kohr, Lancaster, 1978-84; sole practice Lancaster, 1973-75, 84—; regional council Govs. Justice Commn., Harrisburg, Pa., 1975-78; commr. Pa. Commn. on Sentencing, Harrisburg, 1979-81. Candidate U.S. House of Reps., 16th Dist., Pa., 1974, 76; bd. dirs. United Cerebral Palsy, Lancaster, 1976-84, pres. 1983-84. Named one of Outstanding Young Men of Am., 1976. Mem. ABA, Lancaster County Bar Assn., Pa. Bar Assn. Republican. Lutheran. Clubs: Hamilton, Conestoga Country (Lancaster). Lodge: Elks. Avocations: running, golf, photography. Real property, Criminal sentencing. Home: 1011 Woods Ave Lancaster PA 17603 Office: 150 E Chestnut St Lancaster PA 17602

MINNICK, CRAIG ALAN, accountant, lawyer; b. Chgo., May 1, 1951; s. Harry Harold and Betty Lou (Morrison) M.; m. Janice Agrest, May 23, 1976; children: Adam Charles, Paula Rene. BS in Acctg., U. Ill., 1973, JD, 1976. Bar: Ill. 1976, U.S. Dist. Ct. (no. dist.) Ill. 1976. Tax specialist Peat Marwick Mitchell & Co., Chgo., 1976-80; tax mgr. Ostrow Reisen Berk & Abrams Ltd., Chgo., 1980-82; mgr. in charge tax dept. B.L. Rosenberg & Co., Chgo., 1982—. Bd. dirs. Children's Heart Assn., Streamwood, Ill., 1970—. Mem. ABA, Ill. State Bar Assn., Chgo. Bar Assn., Am. Inst. CPA's, Ill. Soc. CPA's, Chgo. Estate Planning Council. Avocations: camping, photography, sports. Personal income taxation, Corporate taxation, Estate taxation. Office: BL Rosenberg & Co 1 S Wacker Dr #1700 Chicago IL 60606

MINNICK, MALCOLM DAVID, lawyer; b. Indpls., July 5, 1946; s. Malcolm Dick and Frances Louise (Porter) M.; m. Heidi Rosemarie Klein, May 24, 1972. BA, U. Mich., 1968, JD, 1972. Bar: Calif. 1972, U.S. Dist. Ct. (cen. dist.) Calif. 1972, U.S. Ct. Appeals (9th cir.) 1984, U.S. Dist. Ct. (no. dist.) Calif. 1986, U.S. Supreme Ct. 1986. Assoc. Lillick McHose & Charles, Los Angeles, 1972-78, ptnr., 1978—; panelist Calif. Continuing Edn. of Bar, Los Angeles, 1982-86; bd. dirs. State Bank of India, Los Angeles, 1982—; bd. govs. Fin. Lawyers Conf., Los Angeles, 1981-84; mem. exec. com. Lillick McHose & Charles, Los Angeles, 1982-85. Co-author: Checklist for Secured Commercial Loans, 1983. Mem. ABA (corp., banking and bus. law sect.), Calif. Bar Assn. (Uniform Comml.Code com. 1983-86), Los Angeles County Bar Assn. Club: University (Los Angeles) (bd. dirs. 1983-86, pres. 1985-86). Avocation: golf. Contracts commercial, Bankruptcy, Banking. Office: Lillick McHose & Charles 725 S Figueroa 12th Floor Los Angeles CA 90017

MINNITI, JOSEPH A., lawyer; b. Port Chester, N.Y., Oct. 25, 1928; s. Joseph Frances and Santa (Surace) M.; m. Suzanne Woolsey, Aug. 10, 1957 (div. 1978); children: Kathleen S., J. Gerald. AB, St. Lawrence U., 1952; JD, Syracuse U., 1957. Bar: N.Y. 1958, U.S. Dist. Ct. (so. and ea. dists.) N.Y. 1959, U.S. Supreme Ct. Assoc. Thomas J. Flood Law Office, N.Y.C., 1957-62; sole practice Mamaroneck, N.Y., 1962-74, 82-84; ptnr. Minniti & Pirro, Mamaroneck, N.Y., 1975-77, Minniti, Pirro & Monsell, Mamaroneck, N.Y., 1978-82, Minniti & Benedict, Mamaroneck, N.Y., 1984—; adj. prof. Westchester Community Coll., Valhalla, N.Y., 1982-83, Mercy Coll., White Plains, N.Y., 1983—; lectr. Consolidated Edison Co., N.Y.C., 1978—. Mem. Zoning Bd. Appeals, New Rochelle, N.Y., 1964-65, Cen. Bus. Dist. Actions Com., Mamaroneck, 1967-72, Zoning Law Study Commn., Mamaroneck, 1976; pres. Westchester alumni council St. Lawrence U., 1965-72, mem. estate planning council, 1980—. Served to capt. U.S. Army, 1952-54. Mem. ABA, N.Y. State Bar Assn., Westchester County Bar Assn., Mamaroneck-Larchmont-Harrison Bar Assn., Assn. Trial Lawyers Am. Clubs: Manursing Island, Orienta Beach, Dolphin Yacht. Personal injury, Probate, Real property. Home: 22 Beechtree Dr Larchmont NY 10538 Office: Minniti & Benedict 100 Mamaroneck Ave Mamaroneck NY 10543

MINNO, FRANCES PATRICIA FRAHER, lawyer; b. Lynn, Mass., July 25, 1930; d. James Edward and Alice (Murphy) Fraher; m. Alexander M. Minno, July 16, 1955; children: Marlee Anne, Alexander, Matthew, Derek. BA, Manhattanville Coll., 1951; LLB, Harvard U., 1954. Bar: Mass. 1954, Pa. 1961, U.S. Supreme Ct. 1965. Assoc. Bicknell & Smith, Boston, 1954-55; assoc. prof. law U. Pitts., 1963-78; assoc. counsel Mellon Bank Corp., Pitts., 1978—. Author: The History and Law of Nursing, 1973. Recipient Distinguished Alumnae award Girls' Latin Sch., Boston, 1975. Mem. ABA (mem. internat. estate planning council, probate and trust sect.), Allegheny County Bar Assn. (mem. continuing legal edn. com., probate and trust sect.). Roman Catholic. Probate, Estate taxation, Health. Home: 650 Morewood Ave Pittsburgh PA 15213 Office: Mellon Bank NA One Mellon Bank Ctr Pittsburgh PA 15258

MINOGUE, THOMAS JOHN, lawyer; b. St. Louis, June 10, 1954; s. John Vincent and Patricia Marie (Naert) M.; m. Rebecca Catherine Irmscher, July 30, 1977; children: Elizabeth Catherine, Kristen Rebecca. BA in Econs. summa cum laude, U. Mo., 1976; JD cum laude, Harvard U., 1979. Bar: Mo. 1979, Ill. 1980. From assoc. to ptnr. Thompson & Mitchell, St. Louis, 1979—. Bd. dirs. Ranken-Jordan Home for Convalescent Crippled Children, St. Louis, 1984—, Am. Heart Assn. St. Louis chpt., 1986—. Democrat. Roman Catholic. Avocations: tennis, golf. Banking, Contracts commercial, General corporate. Home: 1575 Timberlake Manor Pkwy Chesterfield MO 63017 Office: Thompson & Mitchell 1 Mercantile Ctr Saint Louis MO 63101

MINOR, DAVID MICHAEL, lawyer; b. Bowie, Tex., Apr. 21, 1946; s. David Ritchie and Lillian (Ervin) M. B.A., Tex. Christian U., 1969; J.D., South Tex. Coll. Law, 1976. Bar: Tex., U.S. Tax Ct. Asst. county atty. Hale County (Tex.), 1978-79; asst. criminal dist. atty. Kaufman County (Tex.), 1979-81; ptnr. Chitty & Minor, Terrell, Tex., 1982—. rep. client, gen. counsel Shroud of Turin Research Project Inc. Mem. ABA, State Bar Tex., Tex.

County and Dist. Attys. Assn. Democrat. Roman Catholic. State civil litigation, Criminal, Personal injury. Home: PO Drawer 610 Terrell TX 75160 Office: Brin Opera House Bldg 3d Floor 102 E Moore Terrell TX 75160

MINOT, WINTHROP GARDNER, lawyer; b. Greenwich, Conn., Jan. 27, 1951; s. William Amory Gardner Minot and Molly (Cummings) Cook; m. Gale Oakley Winslow, June 12, 1976; children: Hilary Russell, Amory Cummings. AB magna cum laude, Harvard U., 1973, M in Pub. Adminstrn., JD magna cum laude, 1979; MA, University Coll., Oxford, Eng., 1975. Bar: Mass. 1979. Assoc. Ropes & Gray, Boston, 1979—. Editor Harvard U. Law Rev., 1978-79. Bd. dirs. Beacon Hill Civic Assn., Boston, 1981—. Mem. ABA, Mass. Bar Assn. General corporate, Banking, Securities. Office: Ropes & Gray 225 Franklin St Boston MA 02110

MINOW, NEWTON NORMAN, lawyer; b. Milw., Jan. 17, 1926; s. Jay A. and Doris (Stein) M.; m. Josephine Baskin, May 29, 1949; children: Nell, Martha, Mary. B.A., Northwestern U., 1949, J.D., 1950, LL.D. (hon.), 1965; LL.D. (hon.), U. Wis., Brandeis U., 1963, Columbia Coll., 1972. Bar: Wis. 1950, Ill. 1950. With firm Mayer, Brown & Platt, Chgo., 1950-51, 53-55; law clk. to chief justice Fred. M. Vinson, 1951-52; adminstrv. asst. to Ill. Gov. Stevenson, 1952-53; spl. asst. to Adlai E. Stevenson in presdl. campaign, 1952, 56; partner firm Adlai E. Stevenson, Chgo., 1955-57, Stevenson, Rifkind & Wirtz, Chgo., N.Y.C. and Washington, 1957-61; chmn. FCC, 1961-63; exec. v.p., gen. counsel, dir. Ency. Brit., Chgo., 1963-65; partner Sidley & Austin (and predecessor firms), Chgo., 1965—; trustee, former chmn. bd. Rand Corp.; former chmn. Chgo. Ednl. TV; now hon. chmn.; chmn. pub. review bd. Arthur Andersen & Co., 1974-83; dir., gen. counsel Aetna Casualty and Surety Co. Ill., Aetna Life Ins. Co. Ill.; bd. dirs. Foote, Cone & Belding Communications Inc., CBS Inc., Chgo. Pacific Corp., Ency. Brit. Inc., Carnegie Corp. N.Y.; mem. internat. advisory bd. Pan Am. World Airways.; Professorial lectr. Northwestern U. Medill Sch. Journalism. Author: Equal Time: The Private Broadcasters and the Public Interest, 1964; co-author: Presidential Television, 1973, Tomorrow's American: Electronics and the Future, 1977; contbr.: As We Knew Adlai. Trustee Notre Dame U., 1964-77, 83—; trustee Mayo Found., 1973-81, Northwestern U., William Benton Found., 1981-83; co-chmn. presdl. debates LWV, 1976, 80; bd. govs. Pub. Broadcasting Service, 1973-80; chmn. bd., 1978-80; chmn. bd. overseers Jewish Theol. Sem., 1974-77; trustee Chgo. Orchestral Assn. Served with AUS, 1944-46. Named One of Ten Outstanding Young Men in Chgo. Jr. Chamber Commerce and Industry, 1960; named 1 of Am.'s 10 Outstanding Young Men of, 1961; recipient George Foster Peabody Broadcasting award, 1961; Ralph Lowell award, 1982. Fellow Am. Bar Found.; mem. Am., Ill., Chgo. bar assns., Northwestern U. Alumni Assn. (Alumni medal 1978). Democrat. Clubs: Standard (Chgo.), Legal (Chgo.), Economic (Chgo.), Carlton (Chgo.), Casino (Chgo.), Law (Chgo.), Commercial (Chgo.), Chicago (Chgo.); Century (N.Y.C.); Northmoor Country (Highland Park, Ill.); Federal City (Washington). General practice, Communications. Office: 1 First National Plaza Chicago IL 60603

MINTEL, JUDITH KING, lawyer; b. San Francisco, Sept. 26, 1948. AB in Am. History, U. Chgo., 1970, JD, 1973. Bar: Ill. 1973, Md. 1975, Va. 1978; CPCU, 1983. Assoc. McDermott, Will, & Emery, Chgo., 1972-74; asst. gen. counsel Md. Casualty Co., Balt., 1974-76; dep. ins. commr. Commonwealth of Va., Richmond, 1976-79; counsel State Farm Ins. Cos., Bloomington, Ill., 1979—. Author: Insurance Rate Litigation, 1983; contbr. articles to Jour. of Ins. Regulation. Bd. dirs. Music of the Baroque, Chgo., 1971—. Mem. ABA. Administrative and regulatory, Insurance, General corporate. Office: State Farm Ins Cos 1 State Farm Plaza Bloomington IL 61701

MINTER, GREGORY BYRON, lawyer, educator; b. Omaha, Dec. 6, 1940; s. Byron H. and Martha E. (Nelson) M.; m. Jere Chieppo, Feb. 18, 1978; children—Deborah Anne, Brian Thomas, David Barton. B.S.B.A., Mcpl. U. Omaha, 1964; J.D., Creighton U., 1965. Bar: Nebr. 1965, U.S. Supreme Ct. 1972. Assoc., Fitzgerald & Brown, Omaha, 1965-71, ptnr., 1971—; adj. prof. Creighton U. Sch. Law, 1969—, U. Nebr. Sch. Law, 1981—; dir., v.p.-pres. elect, 1984-86, pres., 1986-88, chmn. curriculum com. Nebr. Continuing Legal Edn., Inc., 1980-86; dir. Nebr. Jud. Coll., chmn. seminars com., 1985—; cons. U.S. Dept. Justice, 1981—; mem. faculty SEC, 1969—. Pres., Omaha Ballet Soc., 1982-83, bd. dirs., 1980-84 ; v.p., sec. Omaha Symphony Council, 1980-83, pres., 1983-84; bd. dirs. Omaha Symphony Assn., 1984—, v.p., 1985—; chairperson community adv. bd. Sta KVNO Pub. Radio, 1983-84. Served to capt. JAGC, U.S. Army, 1967-78. Mem. ABA, Am. Judicature Soc., Nebr. Bar Assn., Omaha Bar Assn., Nat. Assn. Bond Lawyers, Alpha Sigma Nu. Republican. Presbyterian. Author legal publs. Securities, General corporate, Immigration, naturalization, and customs. Home: 2331 N 53d St Omaha NE 68104 Office: 1000 Woodmen Tower Omaha NE 68102

MINTON, GOODRIDGE VENABLE MORTON, lawyer; b. Ft. Worth, Aug. 1, 1933; d. Joseph Jarrett and Frances Watkins (Morton) M.; m. Lloyd McKee Minton, Sept. 7, 1957; children: Marian, Ellen Minton Richey, Susan. BA, U. Tex., JD, 1957. Bar: Tex. 1957, Mo. 1972. Asst. dist. atty. Tarrant County, Ft. Worth, 1961-64; assoc. Law Offices of Max E. Clark, Ft. Worth, 1964-66; assoc. counsel Gen. Dynamics Corp., Ft. Worth, 1966-71; assoc. counsel Gen. Dynamics Corp., St. Louis, 1971—, asst. sec., 1972—. Served to 1st lt. JAGC, USAF, 1954-60, with Res., 1960-80. Mem. ABA, St. Louis Met. Bar Assn., Am. Soc. Corp. Secs. Democrat. Episcopalian. Club: Ft. Worth. Lodge: Elks. Government contracts and claims, General corporate. Home: 9520 Clayton Rd Ladue MO 63124 Office: Gen Dynamics Corp Pierre Laclede Ctr Saint Louis MO 63105

MINTON, MICHAEL HARRY, lawyer, business exec.; b. Indpls., May 14, 1946; s. Bernard Jerome and Dorothy Louise (Groene) M.; children—Melanie, Michael. B.A., U. Notre Dame, 1968; intermediate degree London Sch. Econs., 1970; J.D., Northwestern U., 1971. Bar: Ill. 1971, U.S. Dist. Ct. (no. dist.) Ill. 1971, U.S. Supreme Ct. 1980; cert. civil trial advocacy specialist Nat. Bd. Trial Advocacy. Assoc. Biestek & Facchini, Arlington Heights, Ill., 1971-74; ptnr. Facchini & Minton, Schaumburg, Ill., 1974-85; sole practice, Chgo., 1985—. Trustee Village of Mt. Prospect (Ill.), 1974-78, chmn. fire and police com. 1977-78, bldg. com. 1978. Mem. ABA, Ill. Bar Assn., Chgo. Bar Assn. (matrimonial law com. 1972—), DuPage County Bar Assn., N.W. Suburban Bar Assn. (chmn. family law sect. 1979—), Assn. Trial Lawyers Am., Ill. Trial Lawyers Assn. Roman Catholic. Clubs: Meadow (Rolling Meadows, Ill.); Union League (Chgo.). Mem. bd. editors Fair Share, Newsletter of Divorce, 1981; author: What Is a Wife Worth?, 1983; contbr. numerous articles to legal jours. Family and matrimonial. Home: 1615 Central Rd Arlington Heights IL 60005 Office: 2 N LaSalle St Suite 700 Chicago IL 60602

MINTZ, JEFFRY ALAN, lawyer; b. N.Y.C., Sept. 15, 1943; s. Aaron Herbert and Lillian Betty (Greenspan) M.; m. Susan Politzer, Aug. 22, 1979; children—Jennifer, Melanie, Jonathan. A.B., Tufts U., 1964; LL.B., Rutgers U., 1967; postgrad. U. Pa. Law Sch., 1968-70. Bar: D.C. 1968, N.Y. 1970, N.J. 1973, U.S. Supreme Ct. 1972, Pa. 1983. Law clk. to judge U.S. Ct. Appeals, New Orleans, 1967-68; asst. defender Defender Assn. Phila., 1968-70; asst. counsel NAACP Legal Def. and Ednl. Fund, N.Y.C., 1970-74; dir. Office Inmate Advocacy, N.J. Dept. Pub. Advocate, Trenton, 1974-81; sole practice Haddonfield and Medford, N.J., 1982; ptnr. Stein & Shapiro, Medford, 1982-83, Cherry Hill, N.J., 1983-84, Mesirov, Gelman, Jaffe, Cramer & Jamieson, Cherry Hill, also Phila., 1984—; cons. jail design and constrn. Asst. counsel Florio for Gov. campaign, 1981. Mem. ABA, N.J. Bar Assn. (del., gen. council 1986—), Pa. Bar Assn., D.C. Bar Assn., Camden County Bar Assn., Burlington County Bar Assn. Democrat. Jewish. State civil litigation, Federal civil litigation, Personal injury. Home: 106 Union Mill Rd Mount Laurel NJ 08054 Office: 900 Kings Hwy N Cherry Hill NJ 08034

MINTZ, JOEL ALAN, law educator; b. N.Y.C., July 24, 1949; s. Samuel Isaiah and Eleanor (Streichler) M.; m. Meri-Jane Rochelson, Aug. 25, 1975; 1 child, Daniel Rochelson. BA, Columbia U., 1970, LLM, 1982; JD, NYU, 1974. Bar: N.Y. 1975, U.S. Dist. Ct. (so. and ea. dists.) N.Y. 1982, U.S. Ct. Appeals (2d cir.) 1982. Atty. enforcement div. EPA, Chgo., 1975-76, chief atty. case devel. unit, 1977-78, policy advisor to regional adminstr., 1979; sr. litigation atty. Office Enforcement, EPA, Washington, 1980-81; asst. prof. environ. law Nova U. Law Ctr., Ft. Lauderdale, Fla., 1982-85; assoc. prof. Nova U. Law Ctr., Ft. Lauderdale, 1985—. Contbr. columns to newspapers and articles to legal jours. Bd. dirs. Environ. Coalition of Broward County, Ft. Lauderdale, 1985—. Mem. ABA, N.Y. State Bar Assn., Environ. Law Assocs., Fla. Bar. (assoc.), Assn. Am. Law Schs. (exec. com. environ. law 1987—), Internat. Council Environ. Law. Jewish. Avocations: photography, sports, music, reading. Environment. Home: 18221 NE 7th Ct North Miami Beach FL 33162 Office: Nova U Law Ctr 3100 SW 9th Ave Fort Lauderdale FL 33315

MINTZ, RONALD STEVEN, lawyer; b. Bklyn., Aug. 16, 1947; s. Herbert and Phoebe (Gilman) M.; m. Estrella del Rosario; children: Raymond, Gloria. JD, Western State U., Fullerton, Calif., 1978. Bar: Calif. 1978, U.S. Dist. Ct. (no., so., ea. and cen. dists.) Calif. 1978, U.S. Ct. Appeals (9th cir.) 1979, U.S. Supreme Ct. 1982. Sole practice Berkeley, Calif., 1978-80, Canyon Country, Calif., 1980-83, Chino, Calif., 1983-84, Pomona, Calif., 1985—. Producer film on air pollution: State of Emergency, 1971; publisher opposition newspaper: Ten Penny Press. Recipient Am. Jurisprudence awards Bancroft Whitney Law Book Pub. Co., 1977, 78. Mem. Lawyers in Mensa (charter), State Bar Calif. (criminal law sect. 1983-84, police misconduct lawyer referral service), Mensa. Avocations: photography, film, video, guns. Civil rights, Criminal, Police abuse and official corruption. Office: 1287 N Hamilton Blvd PO Box 3151 Pomona CA 91769-3151

MINTZER, EDWARD CARL, JR., lawyer; b. Phila., Sept. 17, 1949; s. Edward Carl and Jean Marie (McGinnis) M.; m. Colleen Anne Marie Hanratty, June 6, 1975; children: Catherine Marie, Elizabeth Seton, Edward Carl III, Conor Andrew. BA, St. Charles Coll., 1971; MA, Villanova U., 1974; JD, Temple U., 1979. Bar: Pa. 1979, U.S. Dist. Ct. (ea. dist.) Pa. 1979, U.S. Ct. Appeals (3rd cir.) 1980, U.S. Supreme Ct. 1982. Exec. dir., program dir. Programs for Exceptional People, Inc., Phila., 1973-78; assoc. McWilliams and Sweeney, Phila., 1979-82; ptnr. McWilliams and Mintzer, Phila., 1982—. chmn. bd. CATCH, Inc., Phila., 1981—. Mem. Pa. Bar Assn., Phila. Bar Assn. (med. and legal sub-com.), Pa. Trial Lawyers Assn., Phila. Trial Lawyers Assn. Democrat. Roman Catholic. Avocations: reading, tennis. Personal injury, State civil litigation, General practice. Office: McWilliams & Mintzer PC 260 S Broad St Atlantic Bldg Suite 610 Philadelphia PA 19102

MINUSE, CATHERINE JEAN, lawyer; b. Port Jefferson, N.Y., Feb. 5, 1951; d. William Brewster and Jean (Fairservis) M. BA, SUNY-Stony Brook, 1972; JD, Cornell U., 1975. Bars: N.Y. 1976, U.S. Dist. Ct. (so. and ea. dists.) 1977, U.S. Ct. Appeals (2d and 11th cirs.) 1986. Law clk. to judge So. Dist. N.Y., 1975-77; assoc. Poletti, Freidin, Prashker, Feldman & Gartner, and successor firm Poletti, Freidin, Prashker & Gartner, N.Y.C., 1977-85; mgr. labor relations Trans World Airlines, 1985-86; assoc. O'Donnell & Schwartz, 1986—; adj. instr. legal writing and research Cardozo Sch. Law, fall 1983, 84, 85, 86, moot ct. spring 1986, 87, summer 1986. Mem. ABA, Assn. Bar City of N.Y., N.Y. Women's Bar Assn., Council of N.Y. Law Assocs., DAR, Greenwich Village Trust for Historic Preservation. Democrat. Episcopalian. Club: St. Bartholomew's. Note editor Cornell Law Rev., 1974-75. Labor, Federal civil litigation. Home: 11 Waverly Pl Apt 3I New York NY 10003

MIRABELLO, FRANCIS JOSEPH, lawyer; b. Ft. Lauderdale, Fla., Mar. 2, 1954; s. Frank Guy and Mary (Sorce) M.; m. Marianna Hay O'Neal, Aug. 5, 1978; childen: Diana H., A. Paul. BS in Civil Engring., Princeton U., 1975; JD, Harvard U., 1978. Bar: Calif. 1978, Pa. 1981, Fla. 1983. Assoc. Irell & Manella, Los Angeles, 1978-81; ptnr. Morgan, Lewis & Bockius, Phila., 1981—; lectr. law Villanova (Pa.) U. Law Sch., adj. prof. law U. Pa., Phila. Mem. ABA (chmn. tax sect. subcom.). Club: Martins Dam. Avocation: tennis. Probate, Private international, Personal income taxation. Office: Morgan Lewis & Bockius 2000 One Logan Sq Philadelphia PA 19103

MIRABILE, THOMAS KEITH, lawyer; b. Lancaster, Ohio, May 11, 1948; s. Joseph Anthony and Marie Johanna (Reynolds) M.; m. Margaret Sue Hughes, Feb. 11, 1981; children—Michael, Adrian, Joseph. B.A., No. Ill. U., 1972; M.A., Northeastern Ill. U., 1974; J.D., Oklahoma City U., 1975. Bar: Okla. 1976, Ill. 1977, U.S. Dist. Ct. (we. dist.) Okla. 1976, U.S. Ct. Appeals (10th cir.) 1980, U.S. Tax Ct. 1977, U.S. Supreme Ct. 1983, U.S. Ct. of Claims 1985. Prof. sociology Oklahoma City U., 1976-77; prof. bus. Central State U., Edmond, Okla., 1977-82; ptnr. firm Mirabile and Assocs. P.C., Oklahoma City, 1977—; bd. dirs. New World Sch., 1983—, Oklahoma City Counseling Ctr., 1977-81. Mem. Ill. Bar Assn., Okla. Trial Lawyers Assn., Okla. Bar Assn., Oklahoma County Bar Assn. Republican. Baptist. Federal civil litigation, Securities, Immigration, naturalization, and customs. Home: 5912 N Billen St Oklahoma City OK 73112 Office: Mirabile and Assocs PC 5100 N Brookline Oklahoma City OK 73112

MIRAN, CLAUDIA BERRY, lawyer; b. Toledo, Dec. 8, 1947; d. Claude Gordon and Catherine Louise (Thornton) Berry; m. David Elliot Miran, June 13, 1971; children: Sean Lewis, Douglas Gordon, Sonya Rebecca. BA, Mary Manse Coll., 1969; MA, U. Wis., 1970, JD, 1974. Bar: Wis. 1975, U.S. Dist. Ct. (we. dist.) Wis. 1975. Counsel ednl. approval bd. State of Wis., Madison, 1977—; pub. mem. Cosmetology Examining Bd., Madison, 1985—, chmn. 1986, 87. Mem. Madison Symphony Chorus, 1977—. Mem. ABA, Wis. Bar Assn., Dane County Bar Assn. Democrat. Avocations: needlework, sewing. Administrative and regulatory. Home: 1610 Lynndale Rd Madison WI 53711-3322 Office: Wis Ednl Approval Bd P O Box 7874 Madison WI 53707-7874

MIRANDA, NEAL JOSEPH, lawyer; b. N.Y.C., June 19, 1955; s. Joseph Charles and Joan Florence (Viggiani) M.; m. Maria Marchese, Sept. 8, 1984. BA in English, U. Scranton, 1977; JD, Fordham U., 1980. Bar: N.Y. 1981. V.p., counsel Ticor Title Ins. Co., N.Y.C., 1980—. Cons., bd. dirs. 30 Grace Ave. Apts. Corp., Great Neck, N.Y., 1983—. Mem. ABA, N.Y. State Bar Assn., Nassau County Bar Assn., Phi Alpha Delta. General practice, Real property. Home: 30 Grace Ave Great Neck NY 11021

MIRANDA, THOM BERNARD, lawyer; b. Teaneck, N.J., Mar. 31, 1953; s. Charles Robert and Jane Evelyn (Larson) M. AB, New Coll., 1975; JD, Boston U., 1978. Bar: Mass. 1978. Counsel labor com. U.S. Senate, Washington, 1978-80; assoc. regulatory counsel Nat. Rural Electric Coop. Assn., Washington, 1980; dir. legis. programs Am. Nuclear Energy Counsel, Washington, 1981-85; sr. mgr. govt. affairs St. Paul Cos., 1985-86, govtl. affairs officer, 1986—. Mem. Mid Atlantic Sailing Assn. Roman Catholic. Club: Shearwater Sailing (Annapolis, Md.). Nuclear power, Legislative, Insurance. Office: St Paul Cos 385 Washington St Saint Paul MN 55102

MIRANDOLA, LORETTA JEAN, lawyer; b. Tarentum, Pa., July 19, 1956; d. Ernest and Mary Marta (Livrone) M.; m. Timothy Michael Mullen, Oct. 9, 1982; 1 child, Martina Kathryn. BA in Govt. and History, U. Notre Dame, 1978; JD, Georgetown U., 1981. Bar: Ga. 1981, U.S. Dist. Ct. (mid. dist.) Ga. 1981, U.S. Dist. Ct. (no. dist.) Ga. 1986. Staff atty. Ga. Legal Services Program, Columbus, 1981-82; sole practice Columbus, 1983; v.p. legal affairs Blue Cross and Blue Shield Ga./Columbus, Inc., Columbus, 1983-84; corp. staff counsel Blue Cross and Blue Shield Ga., Inc., Columbus, 1985—. Mem. Rape Crisis Adv. Com., Columbus, 1983, Columbus Women's Network, 1984-85; team mem. Cath. Engaged Encounter, 1983—; legal cons. Columbus Alliance for Battered Women, 1981-85, bd. dirs. 1983-85, pres. 1983. Mem. ABA, Ga. Bar Assn., Atlanta Bar Assn., Gwinnett County Bar Assn., Ga. Assn. Women Lawyers (historian 1987). Democrat. Club: Notre Dame (Atlanta). Avocations: reading, camping. Insurance, General corporate, Labor. Office: Blue Cross and Blue Shield Ga Inc 3348 Peachtree Rd NE PO Box 4445 Atlanta GA 30302

MIRANTI, RICHARD FREDERICK, lawyer; b. Mattoon, Ill., Sept. 17, 1954; s. Joseph Peter and Mary Margaret (Douglas) M.; m. Elizabeth Anne Rieger, Sept. 1, 1973; children: Reylissa Dawn, Erika Bethany. BA in Social Scis. and Edn., Shimer Coll., 1975; MA in History, So. Ill. U., 1977; JD, John Marshall Law Sch., 1981. Bar: Ill. 1981, U.S. Dist. Ct. (no. dist.) Ill. 1981, U.S. Ct. Appeals (7th cir.) 1981. Counsel Kemper Group, Long Grove, Ill., 1981—. Mem. ABA, Ill. Bar Assn., Chgo. Bar Assn. Computer, General corporate, Securities. Home: 108 W Harbor Dr Lake Zurich IL 60047 Office: Kemper Group Kemper Ctr Long Grove IL 60049

MIRONE, ROBERT C(ARMELO), lawyer; b. N.Y.C., May 11, 1938; s. Rosario S. and Marie (Valcante) M.; m. Joann F. Perrotta; children: Dawn Marie, Kim Ann. BS in Bus. Adminstrn., Fordham U., 1960, LLB, 1963. Bar: N.Y. 1964, U.S. Dist. Ct. (so. and ea. dists.) N.Y. 1965, U.S. Ct. Appeals (2d cir.) 1966, U.S. Dist. Ct. Conn. 1979, Conn. 1982, U.S. Dist. Ct. (no. dist.) N.Y. 1982, U.S. Supreme Ct. 1983. Law clk. to judge U.S. Dist. Ct., N.Y., 1963-64; assoc. Kirlin, Campbell & Keating, N.Y.C., 1964-70, Kissam & Halpin, N.Y.C., 1971-73, LoFrisco & Gallagher, N.Y.C., 1973-74; prin. Robert C. Mirone, N.Y.C., 1975-77; mem. Albert, Pastore & Ward, P.C., N.Y.C. and Conn., 1977-82, Chalos, English & Brown, P.C., N.Y.C., Conn. and N.J., 1986—, Gilbride, Tusa, Mirone, Last & Spellane, N.Y.C. and Conn., 1983-86. Mem. Internat. Bar Assn. (maritime and transport com.), ABA, Assn. of Bar of City of N.Y. (chmn. com. on transp. 1983-85), N.Y. County Lawyers Assn., Bronx County Bar Assn. (joint com. on fee disputes and conciliation), Maritime Law Assn., Greenwich Bar Assn. Admiralty, Federal civil litigation, State civil litigation. Office: 300 E 42d St New York NY 10017

MIRSKY, ELLIS RICHARD, lawyer; b. San Diego, Nov. 22, 1947; s. Jacob Joseph and Lucille (Albert) M.; m. Renee Grundstein, Apr. 18, 1970; children—Jason, Lauren. B.Engring., CCNY, 1969, M.Eng., 1971; J.D., Fordham U., 1976. Bar: N.Y. 1977, U.S. Dist. Ct. (so. and ea. dists.) N.Y. 1978, U.S. Supreme Ct. 1986. Engr., Curtiss-Wright Corp., Woodridge, N.J., 1969-73, Ebasco Services, Inc., N.Y.C., 1973-75; assoc. Rosenman Colin Freund Lewis & Cohen, N.Y.C., 1975-83; asst. gen. counsel Combustion Engring., Inc., Stamford, Conn., 1983—, head litigation dept., 1985—. NSF grantee, 1968. Mem. Assn. Bar City of N.Y., ASME (assoc.), Engrs. Club (trustee 1976), Fedn. Ins. and Corp. Counsel. Federal civil litigation, General corporate, Insurance. Home: 10 Cupsaw Ct Nanuet NY 10954 Office: Combustion Engring Inc 900 Long Ridge Rd Stamford CT 06902

MIRSKY, MOSHE Z., lawyer; b. Bklyn., July 6, 1955; s. David and Sarrah (Appel) M. BA, Yeshiva U., 1977, JD, 1980. Bar: N.Y. 1981, U.S. Dist. Ct. (so. dist.) N.Y. 1981, U.S. Tax Ct. 1981, U.S. Dist. Ct. (ea. dist.) N.Y. 1982, U.S. Ct. Appeals (2d and 3d cirs.) 1985. Legal editor Prentice-Hall, Paramus, N.J., 1981-82; assoc. Law Offices Marvin Neiman, N.Y.C., 1982-87, Silverberg, Stonehill & Goldsmith, P.C., N.Y.C., 1987—. Mem. ind. jud. screening panel N.Y. State Dems., 1985. Mem. ABA, N.Y. County Lawyers Assn. Federal civil litigation, State civil litigation, Contracts commercial. Home: 258 Riverside Dr New York NY 10025 Office: Silverberg Stonehill & Goldsmith PC 111 W 40th St New York NY 10018

MIRVIS, THEODORE NEAL, lawyer; b. Hampton, Va., July 28, 1951; s. Allan and Lena Gilman (Sear) M.; m. Ruth Lynn Tersher, July 1, 1973; children: Jason Stephen, Michelle Beth, Eric Sear. BA, Yeshiva Coll., 1973; JD, Harvard U., 1976. Law clk. to presiding judge U.S. Ct. Appeals (2d cir.), 1976-77; assoc. Wachtell, Lipton, Rosen & Katz, N.Y.C., 1977-82, ptnr., 1982—. Co-author: New York Practice Under CPLR, 1986. Federal civil litigation, Securities. Office: Wachtell Lipton Rosen & Katz 299 Park Ave New York NY 10171

MISCH, PAUL MICHAEL, lawyer; b. Bloomington, Ill., Feb. 1, 1953; s. Harold E. and Helen F. (Fanghan) M. Student, Georgetown U., 1972; BS, U. Ill., 1975; JD, John Marshall Law Sch., 1978, postgrad., 1987—. Bar: Ill. 1978, U.S. Dist. Ct. (cen. dist.) Ill. 1979, U.S. Dist. Ct. (no. dist.) Ill. 1980, U.S. Tax Ct. 1980. Ptnr. Bane, Allison & Saint, Bloomington, 1978-82, Paul Misch & Assocs., Chtd., Tulsa, Cin., Chgo., Bloomington, 1982—. Author: Advising Churches for the 1980's, 1984; editor Ill. Student Lawyer, 1975-81. Mem. ABA (silver key award 1978), Ill. Bar Assn., Ill. Trial Lawyers Assn., Chgo. Bar Assn., McLean County Bar Assn., Chgo. Council Lawyers, Phi Delta Phi. Republican. Clubs: Lincoln (Bloomington) (pres. 1979-81); Racquet (Chgo.), Financial Club (Tulsa). Avocations: tennis, camping, travel. Home: Rural Rt 1 Walnut Creek Downs IL 61736 Office: 102 S East St #100A Bloomington IL 61701

MISHKIN, PAUL J., lawyer, educator; b. Trenton, N.J., Jan. 1, 1927; s. Mark Mordecai and Bella (Dworetsky) M.; m. Mildred Brofman Westover; 1 son, Jonathan Mills Westover. A.B., Columbia, 1947, LL.B., 1950; M.A. (hon.), U. Pa., 1971. Bar: N.Y. State bar 1950, U.S. Supreme Ct. bar 1958. Mem. faculty U. Pa. Law Sch., Phila., 1950-73; prof. law U. Calif. at Berkeley, 1973-75, Emanuel S. Heller prof., 1975—; Cons. City of Phila., 1953; reporter study div. jurisdiction between state and fed. cts. Am. Law Inst., 1960-65; mem. faculty Salzburg Seminar in Am. Studies, 1974; Charles Inglis Thompson guest prof. U. Colo., 1975; John Randolph Tucker lectr., 1978, Owen J. Roberts Meml. lectr., 1982; vis. fellow Wolfson Coll., Cambridge U., 1984. Author: (with Morris) On Law in Courts, 1965, (with Bator, Shapiro and Wechsler) Federal Courts and the Federal System, 2d edit, 1973, supplement, 1981; Contbr. articles to profl. jours. Trustee Jewish Publ. Soc. Am., 1966-75; mem. permanent com. Oliver Wendell Holmes Devise, 1979-87. Served with USNR 1945-46. Rockefeller Found. research grantee, 1956; Center for Advanced Study in Behavioral Scis. fellow, 1964-65. Fellow Am. Acad. Arts and Scis., Am. Bar Found.; mem. Am. Law Inst., Order of Coif, Phi Beta Kappa. Club: Cosmos (Washington). Constitutional law, Federal civil litigation, Legal education. Home: 91 Stonewall Rd Berkeley CA 94705 Office: Boalt Hall Berkeley CA 94720

MISKO, FRED M., JR., lawyer; b. Texarkana, Tex., Sept. 23, 1942; s. Fred Mitchell and Grace (Allen) M. B.A., U. Tex., 1964, LL.B., 1968; Bar: Tex. 1968. Assoc., Wright & Barber, Grand Prairie, Tex., 1968-74; assoc. Windell Turley, Dallas, 1975-79; ptnr. Branson & Misko, Dallas, 1980-83; sole practice, Dallas, 1983-86; prin. Fred Misko Jr. & Assocs., Dallas, 1986—. Author: Tex. Trial Lawyers Forum, 1978-85. Editor: Tex. Civil Trial Handbook, 1985. Vice chmn. Jud. Selection Com., Citizens for Qualified Judiciary, Dallas, 1982-86. Mem. Am. Bd. Trial Advocates (pres. Dallas chpt. 1985), Am. Coll. Legal Medicine, Tex. Trial Lawyers Assn., Dallas Bar Assn. Democrat. Am. Baptist. Personal injury. Office: 1100 LTV Ctr Dallas TX 75201

MISKOVSKY, GEORGE, SR., lawyer; b. Oklahoma City, Feb. 13, 1910; s. Frank and Mary (Bourek) M.; m. Nelly Oleta Donahue, Dec. 30, 1932; children: George, Gary, Grover, Gail Marie. LL.B., U. Okla., 1936. Bar: Okla. 1936. Sr. partner firm Miskovsky, Sullivan, Taylor & Manchester, Oklahoma City, 1936—; pub. defender Oklahoma City, 1936; county atty. Oklahoma County, 1943-44; of counsel Col. John Embry. Mem. Okla. Ho. of Reps., 1939-42; mem. Okla. Senate, 1950-60; pres., dir. Economy Square Inc. Mem. Am., Okla., Oklahoma County bar assns., Am. Judicature Soc., Am. Trial Lawyers Assn., Nat. Assn. Criminal Def. Lawyers, Am. Acad. Matrimonial Lawyers, U. Okla. Law Assn., Oklahoma City C. of C., Order of Coif, Pi Kappa Alpha, Phi Alpha Delta. Democrat. Episcopalian. Clubs: Lions, Oklahoma City Golf and Country, Sooner Dinner, Masons, Shriners, Pair de la Chaine, Bailli Honoraire d'Okla, Confrerie de la Chaine des Rotisseurs. State civil litigation, Condemnation, Criminal. Home: 1511 Drury Ln Oklahoma City OK 73116 Office: Miskovsky Sullivan Taylor & Manchester 302 Hightower Bldg Oklahoma City OK 73102

MISPAGEL, MARK FRANCIS, lawyer; b. Inglewood, Calif., Jan. 4, 1942; s. Francis Joseph and Marjorie (Thornton) M.; m. Ann Thomas, July 1, 1967; children: Heather, Patrick. BA, Loyola U., 1964; JD, U. Pacific, 1974. Bar: Calif. 1975, U.S. Supreme Ct. 1975, U.S. Dist. Ct. (cen. dist.) Calif. 1978, U.S. Ct. Appeals (9th cir.) 1979, U.S. Dist. Ct. (ea. dist.) Calif. 1985, U.S. Dist. Ct. (no. dist.) Calif. 1986. Atty. Calif. Dept. Transp., Sacramento, 1975-80; dir. Calif. Div. Aeronautics, Sacramento, 1980-84; ptnr. Gatzke & Mispagel, Sacramento, 1984—; chmn. coalition U.S. Congress Airport Task Force, 1981-85. Del. Com. of the Califs., 1981-82; mem. U.S. Congress Drug Interdiction Adv. Panel, 1985-86. Mem. Nat. Assn. State Aviation Officials (bd. dir. 1981-84), Am. Assn. Airport Execs., Calif. Assn. Airport Execs. Republican. Roman Catholic. Avocations: motorsports, swimming. Airport & Air Transportation Development, Administrative and regulatory, Legislative. Office: Gatzke & Mispagel 1121 L St Suite 800 Sacramento CA 95814

MISSAN, RICHARD SHERMAN, lawyer; b. New Haven, Oct. 5, 1933; s. Albert and Hannah (Hochberg) M.; children—Hilary, Andrew, Wendy. B.A., Yale U., 1955, J.D., 1958. Bar: N.Y. 1959, U.S. Dist. Ct. (so. and ea. dists.) N.Y. 1979. Assoc. Kaye, Scholer, Fierman, Hays & Handler, N.Y.C., 1962-67; ptnr. Schoenfeld & Jacobs, N.Y.C., 1968-78, Walsh & Frisch, N.Y.C., 1979-80, Gersten, Savage & Kaplowitz, N.Y.C., 1980—. Mem. ABA, N.Y. State Bar Assn., Fed. Bar Council, Assn. Bar City N.Y. (com. on corrections, chmn. subcom. on legis., com. on juvenile justice, chmn. sub-

com. on juvenile facilities, past com. corrections, com. on atomic energy, com. on mcpl. affairs, com. on housing and urban devel.). Club: Yale (N.Y.C.). General corporate, General practice, Real property. Office: 575 Lexington Ave New York NY 10022

MITBY, JOHN CHESTER, lawyer; b. Antigo, Wis., Jan. 7, 1944; s. Norman Peter and Luvern T. (Jensen) M.; m. Julie Kampen, June 10, 1972; children: Tana, Jenna. B.S., U. Wis., 1966, LL.D., 1971. Bar: Wis. 1971; cert. civil trial advocate. Ptnr. Brynelson, Herrick, Bucida, Dorschel & Armstrong, Madison, Wis., 1973—; lectr. U. Wis. Law Sch. Served to capt. C.E., U.S. Army, 1966-68. Mem. ABA, Wis. Bar Assn. (past chmn. litigation sect.), Dane County Bar Assn., Civil Trial Counsel Wis. (bd. dirs.), Wis. Acad. Trial Lawyers, Assn. Trial Lawyers Am. Club: Nakoma Country (Madison). State civil litigation, Federal civil litigation, General practice. Home: 726 Oneida Pl Madison WI 53714 Office: Brynelson Herrick Bucida Dorschel & Armstrong 122 W Washington St PO Box 1767 Madison WI 53701

MITCHAM, BOB ANDERSON, lawyer; b. Atlanta, July 16, 1933; s. George Anderson and Pearl (Bing) M.; m. Lupe M. Vazquez, Dec. 6, 1969; children—Robert Anderson, Tamara Lynn, Matthew Vazquez. B.S., Fla. So. Coll., Lakeland, 1959; J.D., Stetson U., 1962. Bar: Fla. 1963, U.S. Dist. Ct. (mid. dist.) Fla. 1963, U.S. Ct. Apls. (5th cir.) 1965, U.S. Ct. Apls. (11th cir.) 1983. Ptnr., Mitcham & Honig, Tampa, Fla., 1963-66, Mitcham. Leon & Guito, Tampa, 1966-68; sole practice, Tampa, 1968-82; ptnr. Mitcham, Weed & Barbas, Tampa, 1982—; lectr. Oxford U., Eng., 1981. Contbr. articles to profl. jours. Pres. Young Democrats of Fla., Tampa, 1968. Served with USAF, 1952-59. Perry Nicholas Trial scholar, 1961. Mem. Criminal Def. Lawyers of Hillsborough County (pres. 1981-82), Hillsborough County Bar Assn. (dir. 1981-85), Ybor City C. of C. (dir. 1981-82, chmn. Super Bowl XVIII). Democrat. Mem. Ch. of God. Criminal. Office: Mitcham Weed Barbas Allen & Morgan 1509 E 8th Ave Tampa FL 33605

MITCHELL, ALEXANDER BALDWIN, lawyer; b. Honolulu, Apr. 22, 1945; s. Alexander Clark and Ruth Evelyn (Kackley) M.; m. Virgie Fay Pierce, Nov. 11, 1967 (div. Dec. 1980); m. Trina Jo Liebl, June 2, 1984; children: Clark, Kylie. BS, Kans. U., 1971, JD, 1973. Bar: Kans., U.S. Dist. Ct. Kans., U.S. Ct. Appeals (10th cir.) 1973. Law clk. U.S. Dist. Ct. Kans., Wichita, 1973-75; assoc. Sargent & Klenda, Wichita, 1975-80; ptnr. Sargent, Klenda, Mitchell & Austerman, Wichita, 1980—. Served with U.S. Army, 1966-69. Mem. Kans. Bar Assn., ABA, Sedgwick County Bar Assn., Kans. Trial Lawyers Assn., Am. Trial Lawyers Assn., Wichita C. of C. Democrat. Avocations: sailing, snow skiing. Federal civil litigation, State civil litigation, Workers' compensation. Home: 4531 Norwood Ct Wichita KS 67220 Office: Sargent Klenda Mitchell & Austerman 100 N Main Suite 1000 Wichita KS 67202

MITCHELL, ALICE SCHAFFER, lawyer; b. Mobile, Ala., Jan. 23, 1950; d. William James and Alice Martii (Ford) Schaffer; m. Timothy Allen Mitchell, Mar. 6, 1976; children: Meghan Ann, Kathleen Christine. B.S., U. Ala.-Tuscaloosa, 1971, J.D., 1974. Bar: Ala. 1975, Okla. 1976, U.S. Dist. Ct. (we. dist.) Okla. 1980, U.S. Supreme Ct. 1981. Contractman, Texaco, Inc., Tulsa, 1974-77; landman, atty. Sabine Corp., Oklahoma City, 1977-79; trial examiner Corp. Commn., Oklahoma City, 1979, conservation atty., 1980-82; atty. Linn & Helms, Oklahoma City, 1979-80; div. atty. Inexco Oil Co., Oklahoma City, 1982-85; ptnr. Mitchell & Mitchell, Edmond, Okla., 1985—; lectr. Okla. U., Norman, 1982. Mem. Okla. Bar Assn. Interstate Oil Compact Commn., Oklahoma City Mineral Lawyers, Oklahoma City Title Attys., Jefferson Bryan State Dem. Club (pres.), Dem. Women's Club, DAR. Democrat. Roman Catholic. Club: Zonta. Oil and gas leasing, General practice, Probate. Office: 2 East 11 Suite 7 Edmond OK 73034

MITCHELL, ANN POE, lawyer; b. Greenville, S.C., Oct. 3, 1952; d. Thomas McConnell Poe and Barbara Marie (Williamson) Calmes; m. Robert Charles Mitchell, Apr. 12, 1975; 1 child, Charles Poe. BA in English and Psychology, Agnes Scott Coll., Decatur, Ga., 1974; JD, Boston U., 1978. Bar: Ga. 1978, U.S. Dist. Ct. (no. dist.) Ga., U.S. Ct. Appeals (11th cir.), Fla. 1985, U.S. Dist. Ct. (mid. dist.) Fla. Law clk. to corp. counsel City of Boston, 1977-78; chief legal counsel Racetrac Petroleum, Altanta, 1979-80; law clk. office regional counsel HUD, Atlanta, 1980; asst. dist. atty. Dekalb County, Ga., 1981-83, Fulton County, Ga., 1983-85; assoc. Pavese, Shields, Garner, Haverfield, Dalton & Harrison, Ft. Myers, Fla., 1985—; Mem. Pros. Atty.'s Council, Ga. 1981-85. Editor Topics and Devels. sect. Am. Jour. Law and Medicine, 1978. Mem. ABA, State Bar of Ga. (co-chmn. mental health law com. 1980-81), Ga. Assn. Women Lawyers, Atlanta Bar Assn., Lee County Bar Assn., Agnes Scott Coll. Alumni Assn. (class pres.). Presbyterian. Club: Pilot (Ft. Myers). Avocations: reading, needlecrafts. State civil litigation, Contracts commercial, Construction. Home: 872 N Town and River Dr Fort Myers FL 33907 Office: Pavese Shields Garner et al 1833 Hendry St Fort Myers FL 33901

MITCHELL, BURLEY BAYARD, JR., state supreme court justice; b. Oxford, N.C., Dec. 15, 1940; s. Burley Bayard and Dorothy Ford (Champion) M.; m. Mary Lou Willett, Aug. 3, 1962; children: David Bayard, Catherine Morris. B.A., N.C. State U., 1966; J.D., U. N.C., 1969. Bar: N.C. 1969, U.S. Ct. Appeals (4th cir.) 1970, U.S. Supreme Ct. 1972. Asst. atty. gen. State of N.C., Raleigh, 1969-72, dist. atty., 1973-77, judge Ct. Appeals, 1977-79, sec. crime control, 1979-82; justice Supreme Ct. N.C. Raleigh, 1982—. Served with USN, 1958-62, Asia. Recipient N.C. Nat. Guard Citizen Commendation award, 1982. Mem. ABA, N.C. Bar Assn., N.C. Acad. Trial Lawyers, Mensa. Democrat. Methodist. Lodge: Kiwanis (Raleigh). Home: 2505 Glenwood Ave Raleigh NC 27608 Office: Supreme Court of North Carolina PO Box 1841 Raleigh NC 27602

MITCHELL, CYNTHIA INIS, lawyer; b. Ackerman, Miss., Aug. 27, 1957; d. Melville E. and Gloria (Woods) M. BA, Ind. U., 1978; JD, Harvard U., 1981. Bar: Miss. 1982, U.S. Dist. Ct. (no. dist.) Miss. 1982. Law clk. to judge U.S. Dist. Ct. (mid. dist.) Ala., Montgomery, 1981-82; atty. Holcomb, Dunbar, Connell, Clarksdale, Miss., 1982-86, Merkel & Cocke, Clarksdale, 1986—; bd. dirs. North Miss. Rural Legal Services, Oxford. Mem. ABA, Miss. State Bar. Democrat. Episcopalian. Avocation: jogging. Personal injury, Federal civil litigation, Civil rights. Home: 333 Cherry Clarksdale MS 38614 Office: Merkel & Cocke 30 Delta Ave Clarksdale MS 38614

MITCHELL, GARY COLAS, lawyer; b. Santa Fe, Oct. 27, 1950; s. Arney C. and Flocy Manon (Switzer) M.; m. Sharon Lee Stidley, Sept. 2, 1973 (div. 1982); children—Colter Monroe Stidley Mitchell, Shilo Manon Stidley Mitchell; m. Patricia Anne Tully, Aug. 25, 1983; 1 child, Jessica Tricia Tully Mitchell. B.A., Ill. Wesleyan U., 1973; J.D., U. Puget Sound, 1976. Bar: N.Mex. 1977, U.S. Dist. Ct. N.Mex. 1977, U.S. Ct. Appeals (10th cir.) 1982, U.S. Supreme Ct. 1982. Ptnr. firm Payne & Mitchell, Ruidoso, N.Mex., 1977-83; pres. firm Gary C. Mitchell, P.C., Ruidoso, 1983—; mng. ptnr. Mitchell Bros. Enterprises, Aragon, N.Mex., 1978—; pres. Tully-Mitchell, Inc., Ruidoso, 1984—. Bd. dirs. Ruidoso Hondo Valley Hosp., 1981—; mem. exec. com. N.Mex. Democratic Party, 1982—; chmn. Lincoln County Dem. Party, 1982—; mem. N.Mex. State Racing Commn., Albuquerque, 1984-87. Mem. N.Mex. Criminal Lawyers Assn., N.Mex. Trial Lawyers Assn., Nat. Assn. Criminal Def. Lawyers, Assn. Trial Lawyers Am., ABA. Methodist. Criminal, Personal injury, Civil rights. Home: Hat T Ranch Glencoe NM 88324 Office: 111 Spring Rd PO Box 2460 Ruidoso NM 88345

MITCHELL, GEORGE OLES, lawyer; b. Youngstown, Ohio, Mar. 9, 1939; s. James Edward Mitchell and Georgia (Oles) Meade; m. Monika Jutta Eichholz, July 24, 1964; children: James Earl, George O. Jr. AB, Harvard U., 1961; JD, U. Miami, 1964. Bar: Fla. 1969, U.S. Ct. Appeals (5th cir.) 1969, U.S. Supreme Ct. 1969, U.S. Ct. Appeals (11th cir.) 1981. Assoc. Dixon, DeJarnett, Bradford, Williams, McKay & Kimbrell, Miami, Fla., 1964-69; ptnr. Mitchell, Harris, Horr & Assocs. P.A., Miami, 1969—; lectr. Comml. Maritime Seminar, 1983. Mem. ABA, Fla. Bar Assn., Dade County Bar Assn., Maritime Law Assn. U.S. (marine counsel), Southeast Admiralty Law Inst. Republican. Clubs: Miami, Bath, Com. 100 (Miami). Office: Mitchell Harris Horr & Assocs PA 2650 Biscayne Blvd Miami FL 33137

MITCHELL, GERARD ELLSWORTH, lawyer; b. Washington, Dec. 30, 1944; s. Howard Bundy and Alma Gertrude (Metcalf) M.; m. Germana Biondi; children: Julie, Denis, Patrick, John Paul, Robert, Mark, David. AB, Georgetown U., 1966; LLB, U. Va., 1969. Bar: Md. 1969, D.C. 1970, U.S. Dist. Ct. D.C. 1970, U.S. Dist. Ct. Md. 1975. Law clk. to presiding judge Montgomery County Cir. Ct., Potomac, Md., 1969-70; asst. state's atty. Montgomery County, Potomac, Md., 1971-72; ptnr. Stein, Mitchell & Mezines, Washington, 1972—; adj. prof. Washington Coll. Law, Am. U., Washington, 1973-74. Bd. dirs. The Heights Sch., Potomac, Md., 1986. Mem. Bar Assn. D.C. (bd. dirs. 1984-86), Trial Lawyers Assn. Met. Washington (pres. 1977-78, Lawyer of Yr. 1984). Republican. Roman Catholic. Clubs: Barristers, Counsellors (Washington). Personal injury, Federal civil litigation, State civil litigation. Home: 7116 Fairfax Rd Bethesda MD 20814 Office: Stein Mitchell & Mezines 1800 M St NW Washington DC 20036

MITCHELL, JAMES ALBEE, lawyer; b. Grand Rapids, Mich., Aug. 27, 1943; s. Charles Abram and Helen Eloise (Albee) M.; m. Helen Joan Segard, Dec. 29, 1967; children—Christopher Albee, Andrew Charles. B.S. in Chemistry, Mich. Technol. U., 1965; J.D., U. Mich., 1968. Bar: Mich. 1968, U.S. Ct. Customs and Patent Appeals 1974, U.S. Ct. Appeals (Fed. cir.) 1982, U.S. Ct. Appeals (6th cir.) 1974, U.S. Ct. Appeals (5th cir.) 1975, U.S. Ct. Appeals (8th cir.) 1981, U.S. Dist. Ct. (we. dist.) Mich. 1968, U.S. Supreme Ct. 1981. Assoc., Price, Heneveld, Huizenga & Cooper, Grand Rapids, Mich., 1968-73, ptnr., 1973—; speaker patent, trademark, copyright law; instr. seminar in field. Contbr. articles to legal jours. Exec. com. Kent County Reps., 1974-78, 80-82, 86—; chmn. Fifth Congl. Dist. Conservative Caucus; elder Garfield Park Reformed Ch.; trustee Mich. Tech. Fund. Mem. ABA, Mich. Bar Assn. (exec. council for patent and trademark sect.), Grand Rapids Bar Assn., L'Association International pour la Protection de la Propriete Industrial, U.S. Patent Law Assn., Mich. Patent Law Assn., Patent and Trademark Inst. Can. Patent, Trademark and copyright, Private international. Office: PO Box 2567 5740 Foremost Dr SE Grand Rapids MI 49501

MITCHELL, JAYNE FRANCIS, lawyer; b. Great Falls, Mont., Feb. 8, 1951; d. William Howard and Dorothy Elizabeth (Lane) Mitchell; m. Clair Russell Tempero, June 23, 1973 (div. 1978); m. Doug Randell James, June 26, 1981 (div. 1983). B.S., Mont. State U., 1973; J.D., U. Mont., 1981. Bar: Mont. 1981, U.S. Dist. Ct. Mont. 1981, U.S. Ct. Appeals (9th cir.) 1985. Tchr. Edgar (Mont.) Pub. Sch., 1973-78; legal intern Office Pub. Instrn., Helena, Mont., 1980; research asst. Mont. Criminal Law Research Info. Ctr., Missoula, 1979-81; assoc. Robinson & Doyle, Hamilton, Mont., 1981; chief counsel Mont. Ins. Dept., Helena, 1981-83; assoc. Mont. Dept. Adminstrn., Helena, 1983—. Mem. ABA, Mont. Bar Assn. Club: Toastmistress. State civil litigation, Administrative and regulatory. Office: Dept Adminstrn Mitchell Bldg Tort Claims Div Room 111 Helena MT 59620

MITCHELL, JOE DAY, lawyer; b. Waco, Tex., Jan. 30, 1951; s. Francis Douglas and Helen Adelaide (Day) M.; m. Josephine Marian Jenkins, Oct. 25, 1975; children—Elizabeth Josephine, Kristina Helen, Katherine Day. B.A. cum laude, Duke U., 1973; J.D., So. Meth. U., 1976. Bar: Tex. 1976, U.S. Dist. Ct. (no. dist.) Tex. 1976, U.S. Tax Ct. 1979, U.S. Ct. Claims 1980. Assoc., Witt, Vanberg & Wilson, Dallas, 1976-78, Eggers & Wylie, P.C., 1978-79; assoc. Moore & Peterson, P.C., Dallas, 1979-81, ptnr., 1981—. Notes and comments editor Southwestern Law Jour., 1975-76. Mem. urban services div. Downtown Dallas YMCA, 1982—. Mem. Dallas Mus. Fine Arts, Tex. Old Forts and Missons Restoration Assn., ABA, Dallas Bar Assn., Dallas Asn. Young Lawyers, Dallas Estate Planning Council, Duke U. Alumni Assn., So. Meth. U. Alumni Assn., Order of Coif, Phi Delta Phi. Presbyterian. Personal income taxation, General corporate, Corporate taxation. Home: 3420 Princeton St Dallas TX 75205 Office: Moore & Peterson PC 4901 LBJ Freeway Suite 200 Dallas TX 75234

MITCHELL, JOHN BRUCE, lawyer; b. Fall River, Mass., Nov. 17, 1946; s. Nicholas W. and Rita T. (Blake) M.; m. Joyce L. Jackson, Aug. 17, 1975; children: Anna, Nicholas. BS, Northeastern U., 1969; JD, Boston U., 1974; postgrad., U. Mich., 1976. Bar: U.S. Dist. Ct. Mass. 1975, Mich. 1976, U.S. Dist. Ct. Mich. 1976, Mass. 1979, U.S. Ct. Appeals (1st cir.) 1979, U.S. Supreme Ct. 1979. Atty. U.S. Army Corps. Eng., Waltham, Mass., 1975, Pub. Health Statute Revision Project, Lansing, Mich., 1975-76; asst. exec. dir. Am. Pharm. Assn., Washington, 1977-78; sole practice Fall River, 1978—; asst. corp. counsel City of Fall River, 1979-81. Served with U.S. Army, 1969-71, Vietnam. Mem. ABA, Mass. Bar Assn., Comml. Law League. Unitarian. Consumer commercial, Probate, Real property. Home: 340 Rochester St Fall River MA 02720 Office: 7 N Main St PO Box 2507 Fall River MA 02722

MITCHELL, JOHN JOSEPH, lawyer; b. East Liverpool, Ohio, Mar. 19, 1945; s. John Baptist and Dorothy (Vranes) M. BA, Monterey (Calif.) Inst. Internat. Studies, 1973; MA, U. Wash., 1975; JD, U. Puget Sound, 1982. Bar: Wash. 1982, U.S. Dist. Ct. (we. dist.) Wash. 1982. Assoc. Oles, Morrison, Rinker, Stanislaw & Ashbaugh, Seattle, 1982-85; law clk. to presiding justice U.S. Bankruptcy Ct., Seattle, 1985-86; assoc. Lane, Powell, Moss & Miller, Seattle, 1986—. Translator: The Bridge, 1977. Served with USN, 1966-70. Avocations: musician, performing Balkan folk music. Bankruptcy, Contracts commercial. Home: 2915 Warren Ave N Seattle WA 98109 Office: LAne Powell Moss & Miller 3800 Rainier Bank Tower Seattle WA 98101

MITCHELL, JOYCE A. GATES, lawyer; b. Memphis, Sept. 30; m. Frank Edward Mitchell, Apr. 17, 1968; 1 child, Felipe Erick. BA, Tenn. State U., 1966; JD, Howard U., 1974. Bar: D.C. 1975, U.S. Dist. Ct. D.C. 1975, Md. 1980, U.S. Ct. Appeals (12th and D.C. cirs.) 1980, U.S. Supreme Ct. 1980. Gen. atty. U.S. Dept. Commerce, Washington, 1974-78; ptnr. Topping, Sherer & Mitchell, Washington, 1979-81; pres. Joyce A. Mitchell and Assoc., P.C., Ft. Washington, Md., 1981—; gen. counsel Multivac, Inc., Mersel GMC Trucks. Mem. Hillcrest Children's Ctr., bd. dirs. 1976-80, v.p. 1978-80; v.p. Willing Workers of Oxon Hill, 1982-84; employer trustee Service Employees Internat. Union AFL-CIO Health and Welfare Fund, 1985—; mem. Washington area chpt. Coalition of 100 Black Women; bd. dirs. Potomac Elemntary Sch. PTA 1985-86; commr. Montgomery County (Md.) Human Relations Commn., 1986—. Mem. ABA (gen. practice sect.), Nat. Bar Assn. (v.p. 1985-86), Md. Bar Assn., D.C. Bar Assn., J. Franklin Bourne Law Club, Howard U. Law Alumni Assn. (treas. 1981-82), Delta Sigma Theta. Office: 10903 Indian Head Hwy Suite 303 Fort Washington MD 20744

MITCHELL, LEE MARK, communications executive, lawyer; b. Albany, N.Y., Apr. 16, 1943; s. Maurice B. and Mildred (Roth) M.; m. Barbara Lee Anderson, Aug. 27, 1966; children: Mark, Matthew. A.B., Wesleyan U., 1965; J.D., U. Chgo., 1968. Bar: Ill. 1968, D.C. 1969, U.S. Supreme Ct. 1972. Assoc. Leibman, Williams, Bennett, Baird & Minow, Chgo. and Washington, 1968-72; assoc. Sidley & Austin, Washington, 1972-74, ptnr., 1974-84, of counsel, 1984—; exec. v.p. and gen. counsel Field Enterprises, Inc., Chgo., 1981-83, pres. and chief exec. officer, 1983-84; pres., chief exec. officer Field Corp., 1984—; bd. dirs. Manistique Papers, Inc., Pioneer Press, Field Publs., Muzak, Cabot, Cabot & Forbes Co., Boston, Boulevard Bancorp, Blvd. Bank, Chgo. Author: Openly Arrived At, 1974, With the Nation Watching, 1979; co-author: Presidential Television, 1973. Mem. LWV Presdl. Debates adv. com., Washington, 1979-80, 83; U.S. del. Brit. Legislators' Conf. on Govt. and Media, Ditchley Park, Eng., 1974; bd. visitors U. Chgo. Law Sch., 1984-86, Medill Sch. Journalism, Northwestern U., 1984—; bd. govs. Chgo. Met. Planning Council. Mem. ABA, Fed. Communications Bar Assn., Fed. Bar Assn. Clubs: Econ., Mid-Am., Mid-Day, Chicago (Chgo.); Nat. Press (Washington). Administrative and regulatory, Antitrust, General corporate. Home: 135 Maple Hill Rd Glencoe IL 60022 Office: Field Corp 333 W Wacker Dr Chicago IL 60606

MITCHELL, MICHAEL CHARLES, lawyer; b. Los Angeles, Feb. 13, 1947; s. Dominic Chester and Dorothy Marie (Dolmage) M.; m. Ingrid Burkard, June 21, 1969; children: Daniel, Alicia. BA, Loyola U., Los Angeles, 1969, JD, 1972. Bar: Calif. 1972, U.S. Supreme Ct. 1977. Assoc. Hanna & Morton, Los Angeles, 1972-79; ptnr. Anglea & Burford, Pasadena, Calif., 1979-82; sr. ptnr. MacFarlane, Lambert & Mitchell, Pasadena, 1982-85; sole practice Pasadena, 1985—; lectr. various founds., chs., and service clubs. Columnist Pasadena Jour. of Bus., 1985—; guest appearances on TV. Legal counsel Lions Eye Found. So. Calif. Inc., Meml. Trust, Dorland Mountain Colony, Tournament of Toys and Star News Charities; area chmn. San Gabriel Valley Council Boy Scouts Am., 1982-83; bd. of govs. Arthritis Found. of So. Calif.; bd. dirs. Pasadena Dispensary of Huntington Hosp., Escalon, Altadena, Pasadena, 1985-86. Named Outstanding Vol. Advs. for the Quiet Minority, 1986. Mem. ABA, Calif. Bar Assn., Los Angeles County Bar Assn., Pasadena Bar Assn. (sec., bd. dirs. 1985-86), San Gabriel Valley Estate Planning Council, Tournament of Roses Assn., Pasadena C. of C., Phi Alpha Delta, Pasadena Jaycees (Dist. Service award 1982). Republican. Roman Catholic. Club: Univ. (bd. govs.), Quarterbacks (Pasadena). Lodge: Lions (pres. 1980-81, bd. dirs. 1985—). Avocations: philately, racquetball, photography. Estate planning, Probate, Estate taxation. Home: 1007 Entrada Way Glendora CA 91740 Office: 131 N El Molino Ave Suite 395 Pasadena CA 91101

MITCHELL, NEIL RALPH, lawyer; b. Salt Lake City, Apr. 20, 1938; s. Ralph J. and Elna (Stringfellow) M.; children from a previous marriage: Amy, Ian; m. Danièle Dumais. B.S. Ch.E., U. Utah, 1960; J.D., U. Mich., 1965. Bar: Mich. 1966, Ill. Supreme Ct. 1980. Mem. patent dept. Dow Chem. Co., Midland, Mich., summer 1964, European counsel Dow Corning Corp., Brussels, 1965-68; asst. gen. counsel Velsicol Chem. Corp., Chgo., 1968-70, gen. counsel, 1970-83; ptnr. Nisen, Elliott & Meier, Chgo., 1983—. Bd. dirs. Jane Addams Center, 1977-78. Mem. ABA, Ill. Bar Assn., Internat. Bar Assn., Mich. Bar Assn., Chgo. Bar Assn., Am. Judicature Soc., French-Am. C. of C. Republican. Club: Union League of Chgo. Environment, Private international. Home: 4751 N Beacon Chicago IL 60640 Office: Nisen Elliott & Meier One N LaSalle St Suite 2300 Chicago IL 60602

MITCHELL, RICHARD AUSTIN, lawyer; b. Poughkeepsie, N.Y., Jan. 1, 1949; s. Richard W. and Wanda (Austin) M.; m. Susan H. Hoder, July 1, 1972; children: Lindsay, Brian, Courtney. BA, U. Pa., 1971; JD, Union U., 1974. Bar: N.Y. 1975, U.S. Dist. Ct. (so. and ea. dists.) N.Y. 1975, U.S. Ct. Appeals (2d cir.) 1975, U.S. Dist. Ct. (no. dist.) N.Y. 1980. Assoc. McCabe & Mack, Poughkeepsie, 1974-79, ptnr., 1980—. Bd. dirs. Am. Heart Assn., Poughkeepsie, 1983—, Vassar-Warner Home, Poughkeepsie, 1984—, Area Fund of Dutchess County, 1986—, Bardavon 1869 Opera House, 1987—. Mem. ABA, N.Y. State Bar Assn. (bankruptcy com. 1984—), Dutchess County Bar Assn. (pres. young lawyers 1976), Fed. Bar Council. Clubs: Poughkeepsie Tennis (bd. dirs. 1976-81), Amrita (Poughkeepsie). Avocations: tennis, skiing, biking. Bankruptcy, Consumer commercial, Banking. Home: 10 Carriage Hill Ln Poughkeepsie NY 12603 Office: McCabe & Mack 63 Washington St Poughkeepsie NY 12602-0509

MITCHELL, ROBERT BERTELSON, lawyer; b. Grand Forks, N.D., Nov. 26, 1952; s. Robert Berlelson and Laura Mae (Fleming) M.; m. Grayce Adele Anderson, Aug. 30, 1975; children: Carrie Jane, Emily Elspeth. BA, U. N.D., 1974, Oxford U., Eng., 1976; JD, Yale U., 1979. Bar: Wash. 1980, U.S. Dist. Ct. (we. dist.) Wash. 1980, U.S. Ct. Appeals (9th cir.) 1985. Law clk. to judge U.S. Ct. Appeals (8th cir.), Fargo, N.D., 1979-80; assoc. Preston, Thorgrimson, Ellis & Holman, Seattle, 1980-85, ptnr., 1986—; chmn. bd. Southeast Asian Design, Seattle, 1985—. Mem. Mcpl. League Seattle and King County, 1980-86; del. Dem. caucus, Seattle, 1984; elder Bethany Presbyn. Ch., Seattle, 1986—. Rhodes scholar Oxford U., 1974. Mem. ABA, Am. Judicature Soc., Wash. State Bar Assn., Seattle-King County Bar Assn. Club: Columbia Tower (Seattle). Libel, State civil litigation, Federal civil litigation. Home: 7536 Earl Ave NW Seattle WA 98117 Office: Preston Thorgrimson Ellis & Holman 701 5th Ave Seattle WA 98104

MITCHELL, ROBERT BURDETTE, lawyer; b. Bremerton, Wash., Mar. 27, 1953; s. Ronald Burdette and Patricia Joan (Thompson) M.; m. Lois Jean Griffith, Aug. 24, 1974; children: Reese Burdette, Charles Franklin. BA, Ohio Wesleyan U., 1975; JD, Tulane U., 1978. Bar: N.Y. 1979, U.S. Dist. Ct. (so. dist.) N.Y. 1979, La. 1980, U.S. Dist. Ct. (ea. dist.) La. 1980, U.S. Ct. Appeals (5th cir.) 1981. Assoc. Haight, Gardner, Poor & Havens, N.Y.C., 1978-80, Kullman, Lang, Inman & Bee, New Orleans, 1980-83; ptnr. McGlinchey, Stafford, Mintz, Cellini & Lang, New Orleans, 1983—. Editor Tulane Law Rev., 1976-78. Mem. ABA (chmn. young lawyer div. labor com. 1985—), N.Y. Bar Assn., La. Bar Assn., New Orleans C. of C. (com. chmn. 1985—), Order of Coif. Republican. Presbyterian. Avocations: history, bicycling. Federal civil litigation, Labor, Civil rights. Home: 4170 Vincennes Pl New Orleans LA 70125 Office: McGlinchey Stafford Mintz Cellini & Lang 643 Magazine St New Orleans LA 70130

MITCHELL, ROBERT EVERITT, lawyer; b. Port Washington, N.Y., June 14, 1929; s. Everitt and Alice (Fay) M.; m. Anne Nordquist, Nov. 2, 1957; children: Anne C. Mitchell Coneys, Maura A., Michael E. BS, U. Mich., 1952; JD, Georgetown U., 1956. Bar: N.Y. 1957, U.S. Dist. Ct. (so. dist). N.Y. 1958, U.S. Supreme Ct. 1966. Assoc. Sullivan & Cromwell, N.Y.C., 1956-63; v.p., sec., gen. counsel Lambert & Co. Inc., N.Y.C., 1963-65; ptnr. Campbell & Mitchell, Manhasset, N.Y., 1965-80; asst. gen. counsel J.P. Stevens & Co. Inc., N.Y.C., 1980-82, gen. counsel, 1982—. Atty. Village Baxter Estates, Port Washington, 1967-83; Counsel Mobilized Community Resources, Roslyn, N.Y., 1969-80; asst. scout master Troop 1001 Boy Scouts Am., Port Washington, 1976-79; justice Village Sands Point, N.Y., 1986—. Served to lt. USNR, 1952-55. Mem. ABA, N.Y. State Bar Assn., Assn. of Bar of City of N.Y. Republican. Roman Catholic. Clubs: Manhasset Bay Yacht (Port Washington) (commodore 1972-73); N.Y. Yacht (N.Y.C.). Avocations: sailing, fishing, camping, platform tennis, music. General corporate, Securities, Antitrust. Home: Cow Neck Rd Sands Point NY 11050 Office: JP Stevens & Co Inc 1185 Ave of Americas New York NY 10036

MITCHELL, RONNIE MONROE, lawyer; b. Clinton, N.C., Nov. 10, 1952; s. Ondus Corneilius and Margaret Ronie (Johnson) M.; m. Martha Cheryl Coble, May 25, 1975; children—Grant Stephen, Mitchell, Meredith Elizabeth Mitchell. B.A., Wake Forest U., 1975, J.D., 1978. Bar: N.C. 1978, U.S. Dist. Ct. (ea. dist.) N.C. 1978, U.S. Ct. Appeals (4th cir.) 1983, U.S. Supreme Ct. 1984. Assoc. atty. Brown, Fox & Deaver, Fayetteville, N.C., 1978-81; ptnr. Harris, Sweeny & Mitchell, Fayetteville, 1981—. Contbr.: chpts. to books. Bd. dirs. Cumberland County Rescue Squad, Fayetteville, 1983—. Recipient U.S. Law Week award Bur. Nat. Affairs, 1978. Mem. N.C. Bar Assn. (councillor Young Lawyers div. 1982-85), Cumberland County Bar Assn., N.C. Acad. Trial Lawyers, Am. Trial Lawyers Assn. Democrat. Club: Fayetteville Ind. Light Infantry. Lodges: Moose, Masons. Home: Route 5 Box 8C Fayetteville NC 28301 Office: Harris Sweeny & Mitchell 308 Person St Fayetteville NC 28302

MITCHELL, THEO WALKER, lawyer; b. Greenville, S.C., July 2, 1938; s. Clyde DeWitt and Dothenia (Lomax) M.; m. Greta JoAnne Knight, Jan. 28, 1959; children: Emily Kaye Mitchell Smith, Tamara J., Megan Dawn. BA, Fisk U., 1960; JD, Howard U., 1969. Bar: S.C. 1970, U.S. Ct. Appeals (4th cir.) 1970, U.S. Supreme Ct. 1970. Ptnr. Mitchell, Smith & Pauling, Greenville, 1970—; bd. dirs. Piedmont Area Developers, Seneca, S.C. Rep. S.C. Ho. of Reps., Columbia, S.C., 1974; senator S.C. Senate, Columbia, 1984. Mem. ABA, S.C. Bar Assn., Phi Alpha Delta, Omega Psi Phi. Democrat. Mem. African Methodist Episcopalian Ch. Lodge: Masons. Avocations: swimming, reading, hunting. General practice, Civil rights, Labor. Home: 522 Woodland Way Greenville SC 29607 Office: Mitchell Smith & Pauling 9 Bradshaw St Greenville SC 29601

MITCHELL, THOMAS BRADFORD, lawyer; b. Springfield, Mass., May 4, 1956; s. John Houston Jr. and Joan Vail (Payne) M.; m. Sharon Louise Swol, Apr. 28, 1984. BA, Amherst Coll., 1978; JD, Vanderbilt U., 1981. Bar: Mass. 1981, U.S. Dist. Ct. Mass. 1982, Conn. 1985. Assoc. Warner and Stackpole, Boston, 1981-85, Hoberman and Pollack, P.C., Hartford, Conn., 1985—. Bd. dirs., counsel Hartford Neighborhood Housing Services, Inc., 1986—. Mem. ABA, Mass. Bar Assn., Conn. Bar Assn. Episcopalian. Avocations: golf, piano. Real property, Contracts commercial. Office: Hoberman and Pollack PC One State St Hartford CT 06103

MITCHEM, ALLEN P., lawyer; b. Burley, Idaho, Oct. 30, 1918; s. James Edgar and Adah Elizabeth (Allen) M.; m. K. Irene Egan, May 19, 1945; children—Allen P., James E., Lowell E. A.B., Ft. Hays State U., 1940; J.D. magna cum laude, Washburn U., 1947; LL.M., Columbia U., 1948. Bar: Kans. 1947, Colo. 1949. Assoc. prof. Coll. Law U. Denver, 1948-53; practice, Denver, 1953-60; minority counsel interior and insular affairs com. U.S. Senate, Washington, 1961-62; practice, Denver, 1963—; pres. Mitchem &

Mitchem, P.C., Denver, 1978—; vis. lectr. Sch. Law U. Colo., 1954, 57, 59; lectr. Sch. Law U. Denver, 1953-63; labor arbitrator, Denver, 1965—. Trustee Endowment Assn. Ft. Hays State U., 1968-78; dir. Colo. Christian Home, Denver, 1974-80; pres. Denver Civitan Club, 1955-56; dist. gov. Civitan Internat., 1957-58, judge adv., 1958-59; dir. Denver Area Council of Churches, 1955, 57; pres. Denver Execs. Club, 1986—; chmn. gen. bd. Central Christian Ch., 1963-65, 75-76. Served to capt. USMC, 1942-45. Recipient alumni achievement award Ft. Hays State U., 1970. Mem. ABA, Colo. Bar Assn., Denver Bar Assn., Denver Law Club. Contbr. article to legal review. State civil litigation, Real property, General practice. Home: 420 S Marion Pkwy Denver CO 80209 Office: 1700 Lincoln St Suite 3910 Denver CO 80203

MITNICK, HAROLD, lawyer, mediator; b. Balt., Oct. 8, 1923; s. Henry and Adeline (Ehrlich) M.; children—Hilary D., Judith Sue. J.D., U. Balt., 1952. Bar: Md. 1953, D.C. 1973; cert. effectiveness trainer, creative divorce instr. Title abstractor, 1949-53; sole practice, Bethesda, Md., 1953—; mediator family matters, 1970—; pres. Marital Mediation Service Agy., Inc.; vis. prof. Bowie State Coll.; tchr. creative divorce Montgomery Coll., Prince Georges Community Coll, George Mason U. Former post comdr. VFW. Served with U.S. Army, 1943-46; ETO. Mem. Md. Bar Assn. (family and juvenile sect.), ABA (family law sect., mediation and arbitration com.). Author: How to Handle Your Divorce, Step by Step, 1981; contbr. articles to mags. Family and matrimonial, General practice. Office: 10101 Old Georgetown Rd Bethesda MD 20814

MITRANI, ISAAC JAIME, lawyer; b. Havana, Cuba, Aug. 26, 1957; s. Jaime and Donna (Rousso) M. BS summa cum laude, Cooper Union, 1978; JD, Harvard U., 1981. Bar: Fla. 1982, U.S. Ct. Appeals (11th cir.) 1982, U.S. Dist. Ct. (so. dist.) Fla. 1986. Law clk. to justice U.S. Dist. Ct., Miami, Fla., 1981-82; asst. U.S. atty. U.S. Atty.'s Office, Miami, 1982-85; ptnr. Beasley, Olle & Downs, Miami, 1985—; spl. counsel Fla. Bar Assn., Miami, 1986—. Mem. ABA, Fla. Bar Assn., Fed. Bar Assn., Dade County Bar Assn. Avocations: running, basketball. Federal civil litigation, State civil litigation, Criminal. Home: 2333 Brickell Ave #1816 Miami FL 33129 Office: Beasley Olle & Downs 200 S Biscayne Blvd 2700 SE Fin Ctr Miami FL 33131-2395

MITTELMAN, IRWIN DAVID, lawyer; b. Hartford, Conn., June 24, 1918; s. Louis and Corinne (Lefkowitz) M.; m. Margot Krinsky, June 22, 1950; children—Judith, Sharon. B.A., U. Conn., 1939, LL.B., 1947. Bar: Conn. 1947. Councilman Middletown, Conn., 1954-58; pros. atty., Middletown, 1955-61; chief prosecutor, Conn. Cir. Ct. No. 9, 1961-63; mem. Statewide Grievance Com., 1979-81; mem. Panel Pub. Defenders for Superior Ct. Middlesex County State Conn., Middletown, 1963-70; mem. Conn. Bar Examining Com., 1974—, State Bar Examing Com., 1978—; Conn. trial referee. Chmn. bldg. com. Woodrow Wilson Jr. High Sch., Middletown, 1956-58, Middlesex County March Dimes, 1958; bd. dirs. Middlesex County Legal Assistance Assn., 1966-68. Corporator emeritus Middlesex Meml. Hosp., Middletown, 1960-80. Served with USAF, 1942-46; maj. Res. (ret.). Mem. Middletown Bar Assn. (pres. 1962), Middlesex County Grievance Assn. (chmn. 1964-79), Conn. Bar Assn. (judiciary com., chmn. profl. discipline com. 1983), Middlesex County Bar Assn. (pres. 1968-69). Probate, General corporate, Condemnation. Home: 311 Old Mill Rd Middletown CT 06457 Office: 73 Main St Middletown CT 06457

MITTELMAN, ROBERT HIRSCH, lawyer; b. Chgo., Jan. 10, 1949; s. George E. and Marian (Stern) M. BA, Am. U., 1971; JD, DePaul U., 1977. Bar: Ill. 1977. Law clk. to presiding justice Miss. Supreme Ct., Jackson, 1977-78; assoc. Clausen, Miller, Gorman et al, Chgo., 1978-83; sole practice Chgo., 1986—. Mem. ABA, Chgo. Bar Assn. Insurance, Real property, General practice. Home: 3823 N Fremont Chicago IL 60613 Office: 20 N Clark St Chicago IL 60602

MITTELSTADT, RUSSELL JAMES, lawyer; b. Eau Claire, Wis., Jan. 12, 1931; s. Frederick William and Pearl Hazel (White) M.; m. Marlys Rudd, June 28, 1953; children—Mary K., Marcus J., Miles S. B.S., U. Wis., 1952, J.D., 1960; grad. U.S. Army Command and Gen. Staff Coll., U.S. Army War Coll., U.S. Indsl. Coll. Bar: Wis. 1960, U.S. Supreme Ct. 1966, U.S. Dist. Ct. (we. dist.) Wis. 1960, U.S Ct Appeals (7th cir.) 1962. Assoc. Spohn, Ross, Stevens & Pick, Madison, Wis., 1960-62; judge Dane County (Wis.), 1966-72; sole practice, Madison, 1962-66, 72-76; pres. Russell J. Mittelstadt Law Offices, S.C., Madison, 1976—. Treas., 2d Dist. Republican Com., 1981-83, chmn., 1983-85; bd. dirs. Rep. Com. Dane County, 1981-82, treas., 1965-66, bd. dirs., 1962-66; founder Vols. in Probation in Dane County, 1970. Served with U.S. Army, 1952-57; to col. Res. Decorated Meritorious Service medal; named Disting. Mil. Grad., U. Wis., 1952; recipient Service awards Am. Legion, 40 and 8, CD, others; Rennebohm scholar, 1952; Wis. Law Alumnae scholar, 1959. Mem. State Bar Wis., Res. Officers Assn. (jr. v.p. 1966, nat. v.p. 1970, nat. Army com. 1967-69), Mil. Order World Wars (comdr. Madison chpt. 1973-84), VFW, Am. Legion. Wis. nat. councilman 1980-85, Wis. pres. 1965). Lutheran. Clubs: Exchange (past pres.), Madison. Real property, Family and matrimonial, Personal injury.

MITTENTHAL, FREEMAN LEE, lawyer; b. Dallas, Dec. 29, 1917; s. Albert Harry and Rae (Goldstein) M.; m. Evelyn Naomi Gates, May 3, 1947; children: Richard Charles, Brian Lee. Student, U. Tex., 1934-36; LL.B., So. Meth. U., 1940. Bar: Tex. bar 1940, U.S. Supreme Ct. and U.S. Ct. Mil. Appeals bars 1954. Practice law Dallas, 1940-42, 49—; chief enforcement atty. Office Price Adminstrn., Dallas, 1946-47; claims atty. VA, Dallas, 1947-49; dir., gen. counsel Purvin & Gertz Inc. Mem. Tex. Economy Commn., 1950; Mem. state exec. com. Tex. Young Democrats, 1940. Served to maj. USAAF, 1942-46. Mem. State Bar Tex., Dallas Bar Assn. (chmn. bicentennial com. 1975), ABA, Fed. Bar Assn. Clubs: Mason (32 deg., Shriner), Elk, Dallas Athletic, Metropolitan. General corporate, Oil and gas leasing, General practice. Home: 820 Overglen Dr Dallas TX 75218 Office: Coit Central Tower 12001 N Central Expressway Dallas TX 75243

MITZNER, MICHAEL JAY, lawyer; b. Paterson, N.J., July 4, 1944; s. Louis B. and Dora (Sandler) M.; m. Jere Peg Herzog, Dec. 23, 1967; children—Dawn Lee, Scott Clinton. A.B., NYU, 1965; J.D., Harvard U., 1968. Bar: N.J. 1968, U.S. Dist. Ct. N.J. 1968, U.S. Supreme Ct., 1972, N.Y. 1981. Law clk. appellate div. N.J. Superior Ct., Asbury Park, N.J., 1968-69; asst. prosecutor Union County Prosecutor's Office, Elizabeth, N.J., 1969-75; ptnr. Mitzner & Kaczorowski, P.A., Fanwood, N.J., 1975—; twp. atty. Township of Scotch Plains (N.J.), 1979-82, municipal prosecutor, Scotch Plains, 1983-85; municipal prosecutor Borough of Fanwood (N.J.), 1977—. Editor: Criminal Law, 1976. Bd. dirs. Watchung Hills Soccer Assn. (N.J.), 1983-85; coach Watchung Soccer League, 1979-85, Watchung Little League, 1979-85, Watchung Recreation Basketball League, 1983-85. Mem. Nat. Dist. Attys. Assn., N.J. Inst. Municipal Attys., N.J. Bar Assn., Union County Bar Assn. Republican. Jewish. General practice, Personal injury, Criminal. Home: 30 Brook Dr Watchung NJ 07060 Office: Mitzner & Kaczorowski PA 141 South Ave PO Box 157 Fanwood NJ 07023

MIX, GEORGE WARREN, lawyer; b. Wilmington, Del., July 9, 1937; s. George Lee and Katherine Lucille (Reinhardt) M.; m. Virginia Dorsey Peach, Jan. 30, 1960; children: George Warren Jr., Suzanne D'Arcy, Gregory Nelson, Rebecca Lee. BA, U. Md., 1960; JD, U. Balt., 1964. Bar: Md. 1965, U.S. Dist. Ct. Md. 1974, U.S. Ct. Appeals (4th cir.) 1974, U.S. Supreme Ct. 1980. Asst. county atty. Towson, Md., 1968-76; ptnr. Turnbull, Mix & Farmer, Towson, 1976—. Past pres. United Dems., Pikesville, Md., 1970-79. Mem. ABA, Md. Bar Assn., Balt. County Bar Assn. (exec. council 1986—), Assn. Trial Lawyers Am., Md. Trial Lawyer Assn., Md. Criminal Def. Attys. (treas. 1986), Am. Judicature Soc. Democrat. Club: Dissenter Lan (sec., treas.). Lodge: Lions (past pres.). Criminal, Family and matrimonial, State civil litigation. Office: 706 Washington Ave Towson MD 21204

MIYASAKI, SHUICHI, lawyer; b. Paauilo, Hawaii, Aug. 6, 1928; s. Torakichi and Teyo (Kimura) M.; m. Pearl Takeko Saiki, Sept. 11, 1954; children—Joy Michiko, Miles Tadashi, Jan Keiko, Ann Yoshie. B.S.C.E., U. Hawaii-Honolulu, 1951; J.D., U. Minn., 1957; LL.M. in Taxation, Georgetown U., 1959; grad. Army War Coll., 1973. Bar: Minn. 1957, Hawaii 1959, U.S. Supreme Ct. 1980. Examiner, U.S. Patent Office, 1957-59; dep. atty. gen. State of Hawaii, 1960-61; mem., dir., treas. Okumura Takushi Funaki & Wee, Honolulu, 1961—; atty. Hawaii Senate, 1961, chief counsel ways and means com., 1962, chief counsel judiciary com., 1967-70; civil engr. Japan Constrn. Agy., Tokyo, 1953-54; staff judge adv., col. USAR, Ft. DeRussy, Hawaii, 1968-79; local legal counsel Jaycees, 1962. Legis. chmn. armed services com. C. of C. of Hawaii, 1973; instl. rep. Aloha council Boy Scouts Am., 1963-78; exec. com., sec., dir. Legal Aid Soc. Hawaii, 1970-72; state v.p. Hawaii Jaycees, 1964-65; dir., legal counsel St. Louis Heights Community Assn., 1963, 65, 73; dir., legal counsel Citizens Study Club for Naturalization of Citizens, 1963-68; life mem. Res. Officers Assn. U.S. Served to 1st lt., AUS, 1951-54. Decorated Meritorious Service medal with oak leaf cluster. Mem. ABA, Hawaii Bar Assn., U.S. Patent Office Soc., Hawaii Estate Planning Council, Phi Delta Phi. Clubs: Central YMCA, Waikiki Athletic, Elks, Army Golf Assn. Estate planning, Corporate taxation, Estate taxation. Address: 1552 Bertram St Honolulu HI 96816

MIYOSHI, DAVID MASAO, lawyer, international investment consultant; b. Overton, Nev., Jan. 2, 1944; s. Joseph Masaru and Jean Michiye (Horikiri) M.; m. Teruko Ochiai, July 16, 1977; children: Mark Masahiro, Brandon Kouhei. BS, U. So. Calif., 1966; JD, U. Calif., San Francisco, 1973; cert. completion, Waseda U., Tokyo, 1976; MBA, Harvard U., 1978. Bar: Calif. 1973, U.S. Dist. Ct. (cen. dist.) Calif. 1973. Fgr. assoc. atty. Matsuo and Kosugi Law Offices, Tokyo, 1974-76; assoc. Mori & Ota, Los Angeles, 1978-80, Morgan, Lewis & Bockius, Los Angeles, 1980-82; pres., chief exec. officer Trans-Continental Investment, Los Angeles, 1982-84; sr. atty. Miyoshi Law Office, Los Angeles, 1983—; sr. cons. Miyoshi & Assocs., Los Angeles, 1984—; legal, investment cons. Itoman (U.S.A.) Inc., Los Angeles, 1979—; chmn. bd. Dai-I chi Mortgage Corp., Los Angeles, 1982-84. Author: U.S. Condominium Regulations, 1976, U.S. Real Property Investment, 1986; editor U.S. Trade Laws newsletter, 1978, U.S. Real Estate Report, 1987—. Bd. dirs. Am. Bapt. Soc., Los Angeles, 1986, Palos Verdes (Calif.) Bapt. Ch., 1986. Served to capt. USMC, 1966-69, Vietnam. Mem. ABA, Calif. Bar Assn., Am. Leading Execs., Japanese Am. Bar Assn., Japanese Am. Republicans (sustaining). Republican. Avocations: golf, flying, skiing. General corporate, Private international, Real property. Home: 4009 Via Largavista Palos Verdes Estates CA 90274 Office: 3250 Wilshire Blvd Suite 1610 Los Angeles CA 90010

MLSNA, KATHRYN KIMURA, lawyer; b. Yonkers, N.Y., Apr. 23, 1952; d. Eugene T. and Grace (Watanabe) Kimura; m. Timothy Martin Mlsna, Oct. 4, 1975; children: Lauren Marie, Matthew Christopher. BA, Northwestern U., 1974, JD, 1977. Bar: Ill. 1977, U.S. Dist. Ct. (no. dist.) Ill. 1977. Sr. counsel McDonald's Corp., Oak Brook, Ill., 1977—. Mem. ABA, Ill. Bar Assn., Chgo. Bar Assn., Promotion Mktg. Assn. Am. (bd. dirs. 1984—). Marketing, advertising (not trademarks). Office: McDonald's Corp One McDonald's Plaza Oak Brook IL 60521

MMAHAT, JOHN ANTHONY, lawyer; b. New Orleans, Sept. 5, 1931; s. Joseph and Mary M. m. Arlene Cecile Montgomery, Oct. 5, 1943; children—Arlene Cecile, Amy Montgomery, John A. J.D., Tulane U., 1958. Bar: La. 1958. Sr. ptnr. Mmahat, Duffy & Richards, Metairie, La., 1958—; chmn. bd. Medallion Mgmt., Inc. and Exec. Office Ctrs., Inc.; chmn. bd. Gulf Fed. Savs. Bank. Active La. Landmarks Soc., New Orleans Mus. Art. Fellow Am. Coll. Mortgage Attys. (bd. regents); mem. New Orleans Bar Assn., Jefferson Bar Assn., La. Bar Assn., ABA, Phi Sigma Alpha. Club: K.C. Administrative and regulatory, Landlord-tenant, Real property. Home: 1239 1st St New Orleans LA 70130 Office: NBC Bldg Suite 300 5500 Veterans Meml Blvd Metairie LA 70003

MNOOKIN, ROBERT HARRIS, lawyer, educator; b. Kansas City, Mo., Feb. 4, 1942; s. I.J. and Marion (Sittenfeld) M.; m. Dale Seigel, June 16, 1963; children—Jennifer Leigh, Allison Heather. A.B., Harvard U., 1964, LL.B., 1968. Bar: D.C. bar 1969, Calif. bar 1970. Fulbright scholar Econometric Inst., Netherland Sch. Econs., 1964-65; asso. Howard, Prim, Smith, Rice & Downs, San Francisco, 1970-72; of counsel Howard, Prim, Smith, Rice & Downs, 1972—; lectr. U. Calif., Berkeley, 1972, dir. childhood and govt. project, 1972-74, acting prof. law, 1973-75, prof. law, 1975-81; vis. prof. Stanford U. Sch. Law, Calif., 1980-81, prof. law, 1981—; vis. fellow Wolfson Coll. and Centre for Socio-Legal Studies, Oxford, Eng., 1978; fellow Center for Advanced Studies in Behavioral Scis., 1981-82. Author: Child, Family and State, 1978, In the Interest of Children, 1985. Contbr. articles in field to profl. jours. Mem. overseer's com. to visit Law Sch., Harvard U., 1972-78; trustee Berkeley Pub. Library, 1973-80, chmn., 1975-77, vice chmn., 1978-80. Mem. Am., Calif., San Francisco bar assns., Am. Law Inst. Home: 430 El Escarpado Stanford CA 94305 Office: Stanford U Law Sch Stanford CA 94305

MOATES, G. PAUL, lawyer; b. Los Angeles, May 26, 1947; s. Guy Hart and Virginia Rose (Mayolett) M.; m. Paulette Anita Minkus, Mar. 21, 1970; 1 child, Amanda Frances. B.A., Amherst Coll., 1969; J.D., U. Chgo., 1975. Bar: Ill. 1975, U.S. Ct. Appeals (D.C. cir.) 1976, U.S. Supreme Ct. 1980, U.S. Ct. Appeals (6th cir.) 1984. Assoc. firm Sidley & Austin, Washington, 1975-82, ptnr., 1982—. Contbr. articles to profl. jours. Served with U.S. Army, 1970-73. Mem. ABA, Ill. Bar Assn., D.C. Bar Assn. Administrative and regulatory, Antitrust. Office: Sidley & Austin 1722 Eye St NW Washington DC 20006

MOBILLE, GEORGE THOMAS, lawyer; b. South Bend, Ind., July 27, 1925; s. Thomas George and Anne N. (Psillas) M.; m. Diana Mezines; children—Jane, Barbara, Thomas, John. B.S. in Chem. Engring., U. Notre Dame, 1948; LL.B., Cornell U., 1951. Bar: N.Y. 1951, D.C. 1952. Assoc. Cushman, Darby & Cushman, Washington, 1951-55, ptnr., 1955—, sr. ptnr., 1965—; vis. lectr. patent and antitrust law Cath. U. Am. Law Sch., 1953-56. Served with USNR, 1943-45. Republican. Greek Orthodox. Clubs: Capitol Hill, Metropolitan. Contbr. articles to profl. jours. Antitrust, Federal civil litigation, Patent. Home: 5210 Portsmouth Rd Bethesda MD 20816 Office: Cushman Darby & Cushman 1615 L St NW Washington DC 20036

MOBLEY, GARY STEVEN, lawyer; b. San Francisco, Sept. 14, 1949; s. William Philo and Beatrice (Murchison) M.; m. Jeanette Biscay, June 28, 1980; children: Alison Jeanette, Erica Lynn. BA, UCLA, 1971; JD, U. San Francisco, 1976. Bar: Calif. 1976, U.S. Dist. Ct. (no., cen. and so. dists.) Calif. 1976, U.S. Ct. Claims 1978, U.S. Ct. Appeals (9th cir.) 1986. Assoc. Murchison & Davis, Beverly Hills, Calif., 1976-77, Weissburg & Aronson, Los Angeles, 1977-83, Wyman, Bautzer, Christensen, Kuchel & Silbert, Newport Beach, Calif., 1983-87; ptnr. Case, Schroeder, Knowlson, Mobley & Burnett, 1987—; mem. com. bar examiners Calif. Bar, San Francisco, 1977. Mem. Rep. Fin. Com., Orange County, Calif., 1985—. Mem. ABA, Orange County Bar Assn., McAuliffe Soc. Lodge: Rotary. Avocations: investments, tennis, golf. Federal civil litigation, State civil litigation, Health. Home: 6081 Jasonwood Dr Huntington Beach CA 92648 Office: Case Schroeder Knowlson Mobley & Burnett One Newport Pl Suite 260 Newport Beach CA 92660

MOCCIARO, PERRY D., lawyer; b. Lynwood, Calif., June 29, 1950; s. Peter N. Mocciaro and Betty Jean (Kreinbring) Le Sieur; Rebecca R. Bonanno, May 10, 1974; 1 child, Michael Charles. AB, U. So. Calif., 1972; JD, U. Calif., Berkeley, 1975. Bar: Calif. 1975, U.S. Supreme Ct. 1979, U.S. Dist. Ct. (cen. dist.) 1976, U.S. Calif. (so. dist.) Calif. 1978. U.S. Ct. Appeals (9th cir.) 1979, U.S. Dist. Ct. (ea. dist.) 1982. From assoc. to ptnr. Bushkin, Gaims, Gaines & Jonas, Los Angeles, 1975—. Mem. ABA, Century City Bar Assn., Assn. Trial Lawyers Am., Assn. Bus. Trial Lawyers, Am. Arbitration Assn. (nat. panel arbitrators 1986—). Federal civil litigation, State civil litigation. Office: Bushkin Gaims Gaines & Jonas 2121 Ave of the Stars 19th Floor Los Angeles CA 90067

MOCH, JOSEPH WILLIAM, lawyer; b. Grand Rapids, Mich., Jan. 19, 1947; s. Joseph Andrew and Francis (Firlik) M.; m. Sherry Lane Fisher, Apr. 26, 1975; children: Joseph Allan, Courtney Lane. BBA, Western Mich. U., 1970; JD, Western State U., 1974. Bar: Mich. 1974, U.S. Dist. Ct. (we. and ea. dists.) Mich. 1974. Assoc. Mike Comorre, Anaheim, Calif., 1974, Allaben & Massie, Grand Rapids, 1974-75, Twohey & Maggini, Grand Rapids, 1975-77, Catchick & Dodge, Grand Rapids, 1977-81; sole practice Grand Rapids, 1981—; trial atty. City of Orange, Calif., 1974. Author: (with Kenneth J. Sanders) Michigan Divorce Manual, 1982, Winning Motor Vehicle Accidents, 1984, (with Chris J. Roy) Winning All Terrain Vehicle Accidents, 1987. Mem. ABA, Mich. Bar Assn., Grand Rapids Bar Assn., West Mich. Trial Lawyers Assn. (pres. 1985-87), Assn. Trial Lawyers Am. (steering com. on all terrain vehicles), Traumatic Head Injury Profl. Assn. Mich. (bd. dirs.), Consumers Product Safety Commn. (exchange group on all terrain vehicles), Belli Soc. (trustee 1985, bd. dirs., editor internat. jour.), Authors League Am. , Authors Guild. Club: Peninsula. Avocations: Ferrari's, running, swimming, antiques. Personal injury, State civil litigation, Federal civil litigation. Home: 2950 Bonnell SE Grand Rapids MI 49506 Office: 121 Michigan Grand Rapids MI 49506

MOCZULA, BORIS, lawyer; b. Passaic, N.J., Nov. 16, 1956; s. Michael and Olga (Kuzyk) M.; m. Maureen Ann Varley, Oct. 13, 1984. BA in Polit. Sci. with high honors, Rutgers Coll., 1978; JD, Seton Hall U., 1981. Law clk. to judge N.J. Superior Ct., Paterson, 1981-82; dep. atty. gen. N.J. Div. Criminal Justice, Trenton, 1982—. Grad. Studies scholar Ukrainian Culture Ctr., 1978. Mem. ABA, N.J. Bar Assn., Assn. Govt. Attys. in Capital Litigation, Pi Sigma Alpha. Mem. Ukrainian Cath. Ch. Avocations: theatre, literature, sports. Criminal, Appellate, Legislative. Office: Div Criminal Justice Hughes Justice Complex CN 086 Trenton NJ 08625

MODELL, MICHAEL STEVEN, lawyer, business executive; b. Bklyn., Mar. 11, 1953; s. William D. and Shelby (Zaldin) M.; m. Abby Marcia Grossman, Sept. 5, 1981; 1 child, Alexander Henry. BA in Internat. Service, Govt. Pub. Adminstrsn., Am. U., 1974; JD, St. Johns U., Jamaica, N.Y., 1977. Bar: N.Y. 1978, Fla. 1978, U.S. Dist. Ct. (so. dist.) N.Y. 1979, U.S. Dist. Ct. (ea. dist.) N.Y. 1979. V.p., gen. counsel, asst. sec. Henry Modell and Co., Inc., N.Y.C., 1977-87, chief exec. officer, 1987—. Foster parent Save the Children Found., N.Y.C., 1970—; big brother Big Brother Orgn., N.Y.C., 1970-80; trustee Nat. Found. for Iletis and Colitis, N.Y.C., 1968—. Mem. ABA, Real Estate Bd. of N.Y., Pi Sigma Alpha. Clubs: Seawane (Hewlett); Friars (N.Y.C.). General corporate, Landlord-tenant, Real property. Office: Henry Modell and Co Inc 280 Broadway New York NY 10007

MODESITT, FRITZY DAL, lawyer; b. Brazil, Ind., Nov. 11, 1942; s. Chester D. Modesitt and Josephine (Haviland) Harrison; m. Mary Kathryn Sapp, June 12, 1965; children—Chad, Leslie. B.A. in Bus. Mgmt., Ind. State U., 1972; J.D., Ind. U., 1976. Bar: Ind., U.S. Dist. Ct. (so. dist.) Ind., U.S. Claims Ct., U.S. Tax Ct., U.S. Ct. Internat. Trade, U.S. Ct. Appeals (fed. and 7th cirs.), U.S. Mil. Ct. Appeals, U.S. Supreme Ct., U.S. Ct. Internat. Trade, U.S. Tax Ct. Microwave technologist AT&T Corp., Inpls., 1966-76; pros. atty. 13th Judicial Cir., Brazil, Ind., 1979—; sole practice, Brazil, 1976—. Mem. ABA, Nat. Dist. Attys. Assn., Ind. Trial Lawyers Assn., Am. Trial Lawyers Assn., Ind. Bar Assn., Clay County Bar Assn., Exchange (Brazil). Lodge: Masons. Democrat. Personal injury, General practice, Banking. Home: RR 14 Brazil IN 47834

MODLIN, HOWARD S., lawyer; b. N.Y.C., Apr. 10, 1931; s. Martin and Rose Modlin; m. Margot S., Oct. 18, 1956; children—James, Laura, Peter. A.B., Union Coll., Schenectady, 1952; J.D., Columbia U., 1955. Bar: N.Y. 1956, D.C. 1973. Assoc., Weisman, Celler, Spett & Modlin, N.Y.C., 1956-61, ptnr., 1961-76, mng. ptnr., 1976—; sec., dir. Fedders Corp., Peapack, N.J., Gen. DataComm Industries, Inc., Middlebury, Conn.; dir. Trans-Lux Corp., Norwalk, Conn., Fischbach Corp., N.Y.C., Am.-Book-Stratford Press, Inc., Jersey City, N.J. Vice chmn. bd. dirs. Daus. of Jacob Geriatric Ctr., Bronx, N.Y. Mem. ABA, Assn. Bar City N.Y., D.C. Bar Assn. Contracts commercial, General corporate, Securities. Office: Weisman Celler Spett & Modlin 425 Park Ave New York NY 10022

MODLIN, LOWELL RONALD, lawyer; b. Huntington, W.Va., Aug. 29, 1930; s. Lowell Gifford and Dela Mae (Proctor) M.; m. Jeanne Marie Thomas, Dec. 26, 1958 (div. Dec. 1985); children: Stacey Ann, Susan Lynne; m. Susan Faye Lowery, Feb. 22, 1986. BSME, U. Mich., 1952, JD, 1958. Bar: Ill. 1964, Wash. 1960, Mich. 1958. Engr. Reliance Electric, Cleve., 1954-56; law clk. to assoc. justice Supreme Ct. Oreg., Salem, 1958-59; assoc. Holman, Marion, Black, Perkins, & Coie, Seattle, 1959-64; atty. Deere & Co., Moline, Ill., 1964-69, sr. atty., 1969-74, asst. gen. counsel, 1974—. Bd. dirs. Vis. Nurses Assn., Moline, 1974-84. Served to 1st lt. U.S. Army, 1952-54. Republican. Club: Short Hills. Avocation: photography. Contracts commercial, General corporate, Insurance. Office: Deere & Co John Deere Rd Moline IL 61265

MOEHLMAN, MICHAEL SCOTT, lawyer; b. Columbus, Ohio, Apr. 11, 1938; s. Arthur Henry and Marguerite Caroline M.; m. Carol Jean Shafer, Sept. 28, 1963; 1 son, Matthew. B.A., Harvard U., 1960; LL.B., U. Tex., 1963. Bar: Tex. 1963. Ptnr. Baker & Botts, Houston, 1963—. Mem. ABA (com. bank securities, com. bus. bankruptcy, savs. instns. com.) Tex. Bar Assn. (com. revision corp. law), Houston Bar Assn. (judicature com.), Am. Judicature Soc., Houston Bar Found. (bd. dirs.), Phi Delta Phi. Episcopalian. Clubs: Houston, Houston Racquet, Houston Yacht; Harvard (Boston). General corporate, Securities, Banking. Office: 30th Floor One Shell Plaza Houston TX 77002

MOENSSENS, ANDRE ACHILLES, law educator; b. 1929; m. Susan Gedney; 8 children. JD with honors, Chgo.-Kent Coll. Law, 1966; LLM, Northwestern U., 1967. Bar: Ill. 1966, U.S. Dist. Ct. (no. dist.) Ill. 1966, Va. 1974, U.S. Dist. Ct. (ea. dist.) Va. 1974, U.S. Ct. Appeals (4th cir.) 1975, U.S. Supreme Ct. 1978. Prof. law Chgo.-Kent Coll Law, Ill. Inst. Tech., 1967-73, T.C. Williams Sch. Law, U. Richmond (Va.), 1973—; lectr. continuing legal edn. programs, 1967—. Assoc. editor Chgo.-Kent Law Rev., 1966; author: Fingerprints and the Law, 1969, Fingerprint Techniques, 1971, Cases on Agency, 1978; (with Inbau and Vitullo) Scientific Police Investigation, 1972; (with Inbau) Scientific Evidence in Criminal Cases, 1973, 3d edit. 1986; (with Inbau and Thompson) Cases and Materials in Criminal Law, 1973, 4th edit. 1987; (with Singer and Bacigal) Cases and Materials in Criminal Procedure, 1979, 2d edit. 1987; gen. editor: What's New in Forensic Scis., 1969-73, Sources of Proof in Preparing a Lawsuit, 1976, 83; mem. editorial bd. Jour. Forensic Scis., 1971—; editorial cons. Jour. Criminal Law, Criminology and Police Sci., 1968-73, Jour. Police Sci. and Adminstrn., 1973—; also articles. Recipient Excellence in Teaching award, Spl. Recognition award Chgo.-Kent Coll. Law, 1973, Disting. Educator award U. Richmond, 1979, Outstanding Law Rev. Alumnus award Chgo.-Kent Coll. Law and Chgo.-Kent Coll. Law Rev., 1983. Fellow Am. Acad. Forensic Scis.; mem. Va. Bar Assn. (bd. dirs. internat. law sect., com. legal edn. and admission to bar), Ill. Bar Assn., Henrico County Bar Assn. (charter), 17th Jud. Dist. Bar Assn., Richmond Bar Assn. Baptist. Home: Flowering Fields PO Box 160 Kilmarnock VA 22482 Office: Univ Richmond TC Williams Sch Law Richmond VA 23173

MOERDLER, CHARLES GERARD, lawyer; b. Paris, Nov. 15, 1934; came to U.S., 1946, naturalized, 1951; s. Herman and Erna Anna (Brandwein) M.; m. Pearl G. Hecht, Dec. 26, 1955; children: Jeffrey Alan, Mark Laurence, Sharon Michele. B.A., L.I.U., 1953; LL.B., J.D., Fordham U., 1956. Bar: N.Y. 1956. Asso. firm Cravath, Swaine & Moore, N.Y.C., 1956-65; spl. counsel coms. City of N.Y. and judiciary N.Y. State Assembly, 1960-61; commr. bldgs. City of N.Y., 1966-67; sr. partner Stroock & Stroock & Lavan, N.Y.C., 1967—; cons. housing, urban devel. and real estate to mayor City N.Y., 1967-73; commr. N.Y. State Ins. Fund, 1978—, vice chmn., 1986—. Mem. editorial bd. N.Y. Law Jour., 1985—. Pres. N.Y. Young Republican Club, 1965; asst. dir. Rockefeller nat. presdl. campaign com., 1964; adv. bd. Sch. Internat. Affairs, Columbia U., 1977-80; bd. govs. L.I. U., 1966, trustee, 1985—; chmn. Community Planning Bds. 8 and 14, Bronx County, 1977-78; nat. bd. govs. Am. Jewish Congress, 1966; bd. overseers Jewish Theol. Sem. Am., 1983—; trustee St. Barnabas Hosp., Bronx, N.Y., 1985—. Recipient Tristam Walker Metcalf award L.I.U., 1966, cert. N.Y.C. Planning Commn., 1979; named Riverdale (N.Y.) Man of Year Riverdale Community Council, 1980. Mem. Am. Bar Assn., N.Y. State Bar Assn., N.Y. County Lawyers Assn., Bar Assn. City N.Y., Free Sons of Israel. Club: World Trade Center (N.Y.C.). Federal civil litigation, Labor, Real property. Home: 7 Rivercrest Rd Riverdale NY 10471 Office: 7 Hanover Sq New York NY 10004

MOERDLER, JEFFREY ALAN, lawyer; b. N.Y.C., July 14, 1957; s. Charles G. and Pearl G. (Hecht) M.; m. Susan A. Berkowitz, Aug. 17, 1980; 1 child, Scott Adam. BA, Columbia Coll., 1978; JD, NYU, 1981. Bar: N.Y. 1982, Fla. 1982, U.S. Dist. Ct. (so. and ea. dists.) N.Y. 1982. Law clk. to presiding justice U.S. Dist Ct. (so. dist.), N.Y., 1981-82; assoc. Kaye,

Scholer, Fierman, Hays & Handler, N.Y.C., 1982—; mem. disciplinary com. Appellate Div. First Dept., N.Y.C., 1984—. Author book revs. Communications and the Law, 1982. V.p. Riverdale Jewish Community Council, Bronx, N.Y., 1981—; trustee, asst. sec. Young Men's and Young Women's Hebrew Assn. of the Bronx, 1983—. Mem. ABA, N.Y. State Bar Assn. (sec. com. on cts. and community 1987—). Democrat. Real property. Office: Kaye Scholer Fierman Hays & Handler 425 Park Ave New York NY 10022

MOFFITT, WILLIAM A., JR., lawyer; b. St. Louis, June 19, 1919; s. William Albert and Marie (Solien) M.; m. Dolores Finan, Apr. 27, 1946; children: Patricia Anne, Maureen Mary, William A. III and Terrence Finan (twins). BA magna cum laude, St. Louis U., 1941, JD, 1948. Bar: Mo. 1948, U.S. Supreme Ct. 1956, U.S. Tax Ct. 1968. Sole practice St. Louis, 1948—; lectr. phiosophy St. Louis U., 1948-53, law in modern social legis., 1960-61; spl. asst. atty. gen. State of Mo., 1968; mcpl. judge Village of Bel-Ridge, Mo., 1970-71. Mem., sec. planning and zoning commn. City of Bellefontaine Neighbors, Mo., 1959-65. Served with U.S. Army, 1942-46, PTO. Mem. ABA, Mo. Bar Assn. (chmn. civil practice and procedure com. 1963-64), Bar Assn. Met. St. Louis (lectr. continuing legal edn. programs), Lawyers Assn. St. Louis, West Port C. of C. (bd. dirs.), Maryland Heights-West Port C. of C., St. Vincent de Paul Soc. St. Anselm Parish. Lodges: Elks, Kiwanis. General practice, Probate, Estate planning. Home: 622 Chamblee Ln Saint Louis County MO 63141 Office: 12115 Lackland Rd Citadel Bldg Suite 382 Saint Louis MO 63146

MOFSKY, JAMES STEFFAN, legal educator, lawyer, consultant; b. Rochester, N.Y., May 16, 1935; s. Michael and Myna (Goldman) M.; m. Barbara Kaplan, Aug. 19, 1977; children: Russell David, Michael Benjamin, Jonathan Marshall, Allison Brooke. B.A., Wesleyan U., 1956; J.D., Cornell U., 1959; LL.M., U. Miami, Fla., 1968; J.S.D., George Washington U., 1971. Bar: N.Y. 1959, Fla. 1959, D.C. 1967. Sole practice Miami, 1960-66; asst. prof. U. Miami, 1968-70, assoc. prof., 1970-72, prof., 1972—; vis. assoc. prof. Ind. U., 1971; vis. prof. So. Meth. U., 1972; mem. securities law adv. council to state comptroller Fla., 1978-82, comptroller's task force on securities regulation 1985-86; cons. Nat. Assn. Realtors, 1972-75. Author: Blue Sky Restrictions on New Business Promotions, 1971; contbr. articles to legal jours. Earhart fellow, 1967-68. Mem. ABA, Am. Law Inst., Fla. Bar (exec. council sect. corp., banking and bus. law 1979-81), Assn. Am. Law Schs. (exec. council sect. bus. assns. 1973-80, chmn. 1973-75), Mont Pelerin Soc. Administrative and regulatory, General corporate, Legal education. Home: 5955 SW 129 Terr Miami FL 33156 Office: U Miami Sch Law Coral Gables FL 33124

MOGIL, BERNARD MARC, judge; b. N.Y.C., May 13, 1949; S. Roman and Musia (Mosiewicka) Mogilanski; m. Terry Gerbs, Dec. 21, 1975; 1 child, Matthew Scott. B.A., CCNY, 1970; student Ind. U. Law Sch., 1970-71; J.D., N.Y. Law Sch., 1974. Bar: N.Y. 1975, Fla. 1974, U.S. Ct. Appeals (2nd cir.) 1975, U.S. Dist. Ct. (so. dist. and ea. dist.) N.Y. 1975, D.C. 1978. Asst. gen. counsel N.Y.C. Health Dept., 1975-76; assoc. Hayt, Hayt & Landau, Gt. Neck, N.Y., 1976-81; spl. asst. atty. gen. N.Y. Medicaid fraud prosecutor, N.Y.C., 1981-84; sole practice, Garden City, 1984-86, former chief legal officer Conservative Party, 1984-86; judge Nassau County Dist. Ct., Mineola, N.Y., 1987—; chief legal officer, pilot CAP, Garden City, 1982-86; chief counsel Nassau County Conservative Party, 1984-86. Mem. N.Y. State Bar Assn., Fla. Bar Assn. Jewish. Home: 32 The Mews Syosset NY 11791 Office: Dist Ct Nassau County 272 Old Country Rd Mineola NY 11501

MOGIL, GARY MARC, lawyer; b. Phila., Mar. 14, 1949; s. Philip and Renee L. (Witkin) M. B.B.A. in Fin., Temple U., 1970; postgrad., 1970-72; J.D. cum laude, Delaware Law Sch., 1976. Bar: Pa. 1976, U.S. Dist. Ct. (ea. dist.) Pa. 1977, U.S. Ct. Appeals (3d cir.) 1981, U.S. Supreme Ct. 1982; cert. specialist criminal law. Asst. dist. atty. Dist. Atty. of Delaware County, Media, Pa., 1976-84; dep. atty. gen. Pa. Office of Atty. Gen., Phila., 1984—; guest speaker, cons. Pa. Assn. Arson Investigators, University Park, 1983. Bd. govs. Albert Einstein Med. Ctr., Phila., 1981—, trustee, 1985—. Recipient Outstanding Sr. award Temple U., 1970; Law Rev. Service award Del. Law Sch., 1976, Scholarship award, 1976. Mem. Pa. Assn. Arson Investigators, ABA, Pa. Bar Assn., Assn. Trial Lawyers Am., Phila. Bar Assn., Delta Theta Phi, Phi Kappa Phi, Phi Sigma Delta (treas. 1968-69). Republican. Jewish. Club: Lawyers of Phila. Criminal. Home: 1200 Disston St Philadelphia PA 19111 Office: Office of Atty Gen 2490 Blvd of the Generals Norristown PA 19403

MOGIN, DANIEL JAY, lawyer; b. Washington, May 16, 1955; s. Bert and Faye (Krenzen) M.; m. Laura Lynn Stacy, June 24, 1978. BA, Ind. U., 1976; JD, U. San Diego, 1980. Bar: Calif. 1980, U.S. Dist. Ct. (so. dist.) Calif. 1980, U.S. Dist. Ct. (cen. dist.) Calif. 1981, U.S. Dist. Ct. (no. dist.) Calif. 1982, U.S. Supreme Ct. 1984. Ptnr. Mogin & Noel, San Diego, 1981—. Contbr. articles to profl. jours. Recipient Cert. of Merit Fed. Defenders of San Diego, 1980. Mem. ABA (litigation sect. com. on complex crimes 1983—), Assn. Trial Lawyers of Am., Calif. Attys. for Criminal Justice. Republican. Jewish. Criminal, Federal civil litigation, Securities. Office: 101 W Broadway Suite 527 San Diego CA 92101

MOHEN, THOMAS PATRICK, lawyer; b. N.Y.C., July 5, 1957; s. Joseph Conrad and Virginia Ann (Kelly) M. AB, Boston Coll., 1979; JD, Suffolk U., 1982. Bar: Mass. 1982, N.Y. 1983, N.J. 1986, U.S. Supreme Ct. 1986. Assoc. Rich, May, Bilodeau & Flaherty, Boston, 1981-82, Fisher, Kelly, Fallon, et al., N.Y.C., 1982-84; ptnr. Kelly, Eckhaus & Mohen, N.Y.C., 1984—; counsel Nat. Assn. Catalog Showroom Merchandisers, N.Y., 1982—. Mem. ABA (vice-chmn. antitrust law com. young lawyers div. 1986-87, exec. com. corps. banking and bus. law sect. 1984-85), Mass. Bar Assn., Assn. Trial Lawyers Assn., N.Y. State Trial Lawyers Assn., Fed. Bar Council, Boston Coll. Club. N.Y., Inc. (bd. dirs. 1984—, pres. 1986). Antitrust, Federal civil litigation, General corporate. Home: 16 W 16th St Apt 1 D S New York NY 10011 Office: Kelly Eckhaus Mohen 230 Park Ave New York NY 10169

MOHER, THOMAS GERALD, lawyer; b. Sault Sainte Marie, Mich., Dec. 8, 1936; s. Clarence and Helen (Krol) M.; m. MaryLou Moher (dissolved); children: Timothy Sean, Laura Ann; m. Henrietta Marilee; 1 child, Grant Thomas. PhB, U. Detroit, 1958; JD, Wayne State U., 1962. Bar: Mich. 1963, Wis. 1985. Assoc. Veum & Veum, Sault Sainte Marie, 1962-64; sole pracitce Sault Sainte Marie, 1964-68, 73-80; assoc. Livingston, Gregory, VanLopik & Higle, Detroit, 1968, Kelman, Loria, Downing & Schneider, Detroit, 1969-73; ptnr. Moher, Andary & Cannello, Sault Sainte Marie, 1980-85, Moher & Cannello, Sault Sainte Marie, 1985—; atty. City of Sault Sainte Marie, 1973—. Personal injury, Workers' compensation. Home: 3330 Lakeshore Dr Sault Sainte Marie MI 49783 Office: Moher & Cannello 150 Water Sault Sainte Marie MI 49783

MOHR, ANTHONY JAMES, lawyer; b. Los Angeles, May 11, 1947; s. Gerald Leonard and Rita Lenore (Goldstein) M. B.A. in Govt. cum laude with honors, Wesleyan U., 1969; J.D., Columbia U., 1972; diploma with honors Faculté Internationale pour l'Enseignement du Droit Comparé, 1975. Bar: Calif. 1972, U.S. Dist. Ct. (cen. dist.) Calif. 1973, U.S. Ct. Appeals (4th cir.) 1974, D.C. 1976, U.S. Supreme Ct. 1981. Law clk. to judge U.S. Dist. Cent. Dist. Calif., 1972-73; assoc. Schwartz Alschuler & Grossman (now Alschuler Grossman & Pines), 1973-75; sole practice, Los Angeles, 1976—; judge pro-tem Los Angeles Mcpl. Ct. Small Claims and Traffic Div.; faculty atty. asst. tng. program UCLA, 1982—, bd. dirs. internat. student ctr., 1986—. Del., White House Conf. on Youth, 1971; nat. adv. council Ctr. for Study of Presidency, 1974—; mem. Los Angeles Dist. Atty.'s Adv. Council, 1976-82; hearing officer Los Angeles County Employees Retirement Assn., 1986—. Mem. Beverly Hills Bar Assn. (bd. govs. 1975-80, chmn. litigation sect. 1983-85), Barristers of Beverly Hills Bar Assn. (pres. 1979-80), Am. Judicature Soc. (dir.), ABA, Los Angeles County Bar Assn., Phi Beta Kappa, Phi Delta Phi. Contbr. articles to profl. jours.; editorial bd. Calif. Bar Jour., 1979-80. Federal civil litigation, State civil litigation, Real property. Office: 9300 Wilshire Blvd Suite 555 Beverly Hills CA 90212

MOHR, TERRY RICHARD, lawyer; b. Moline, Ill., Dec. 5, 1942; s. Robert George and Alberta Mary (Marre) M.; m. Roberta Lynn Rasmussen, Oct. 4, 1975; children—Jensina Anne, Richard Scott. B.S. in Indsl. Engring., Iowa State U., 1965; J.D., U. Fla., 1968. Bar: Ill. 1971, U.S. Patent Office, 1971, U.S. Dist. Ct. (no. dist.) Ill. 1971, U.S. Supreme Ct. 1982. Atty., examiner U.S. Patent Office, Washington, 1968-70; assoc. Hume, Clement, Brinks, William & Olds, Ltd., Chgo., 1970-72; sole practice, McHenry, Ill., 1972-78; sr. ptnr. Mohr & Lewis, McHenry, 1978-81, Mohr, Lewis & Reilly, McHenry, 1981—; instr. bus. law McHenry County Coll., 1978-79. Recipient Cert. Appreciation, Sr. Citizens Assn., 1980. Mem. ABA, Ill. State Bar Assn., McHenry County Bar Assn. (bd. govs. 1982-83), Assn. Trial Lawyers Am., Ill. Trial Lawyers Assn., Phi Delta Phi, Sigma Alpha Epsilon. Republican. Methodist. Clubs: Elks, Kiwanis. Contbr. articles in field. Family and matrimonial, Real property, State civil litigation. Home: 18 W Scott St Barrington IL 60010 Office: 420 N Front St McHenry IL 60050

MOJOCK, DAVID THEODORE, lawyer; b. Uniontown, Pa., Nov. 9, 1945; s. Charles Angelo and Mary Ann (Fabbri) M.; m. Colleen E. Creany, Aug. 10, 1968; children—David T., Angela, Todd, Eric. B.S., Duquesne U., 1967, J.D., 1972. Bar: Pa. 1972, U.S. Dist. Ct. (we. dist.) Pa. 1972, U.S. Ct. Appeals (3d cir.) 1976. Assoc. Cauley, Birsic & Conflenti, Pitts., 1972; law clk. presiding justices Ct. Common Pleas, Lawrence County, New Castle, Pa., 1973; assoc. Gamble & Verterano, New Castle, 1974-76; ptnr. Gamble, Verterano, Mojock, New Castle, 1976-81; ptnr. Gamble, Verterano, Mojock, Piccione & Green, New Castle, 1981—. Contbr. article to Scapel and Quill. Bd. dirs. Cath. Social Services, New Castle, 1981-83, Vis. Nurse Assn., New Castle, 1983-87, Allied Human Services Assn., New Castle, 1983—. Served with U.S. Army, 1969-71. Mem. Pa. Bar Assn., Pa. Trial Lawyers Assn., Assn. Trial Lawyers Am., Lawrence County Bar Assn., Allegheny County Bar Assn. Democrat. Roman Catholic. Lodge: KC (grand knight 1976-77, legis. chmn. state council 1980-82). State civil litigation, Personal injury, Insurance. Home: 811 Highland Ave New Castle PA 16101 Office: Gamble Verterano Mojock et al 12 W Washington St New Castle PA 16101

MOLAND, BRUCE, lawyer; b. Duluth, Minn., Apr. 21, 1945; s. Lothard Norman and Helen (Udclaire) M.; Elizabeth Anne Wolner, June, 17, 1967; children: Anne, Christopher. BA, U. Minn., Duluth, 1967; JD, U. Minn., Mpls., 1973. Bar: Minn. 1973, U.S. Dist. Ct. Minn. 1981. Asst. v.p. Norwest Bank, Mpls., 1973-80; asst. v.p. Norwest Corp., Mpls., 1980-81, asst. gen. counsel, 1981—, v.p., 1983—. Ski ofcl. U.S. Ski Assn. Colorado Springs, 1963, Fedn. De Internationale De Ski, Berne, Switzerland, 1984; trustee Episc. Diocese of Minn., Mpls., 1982. Served to 1st lt. U.S. Army, 1968-71. Banking, General corporate. Office: Norwest Corp 730 2d S Minneapolis MN 55479-1026

MOLER, ELIZABETH ANNE, lawyer; b. Salt Lake City, Jan. 24, 1949; d. Murray McClure and Eleanor Lorraine (Barry) M.; m. Thomas Blake Williams, Oct. 19, 1979; 1 child, Blake Martin Williams. BA, Am. U., 1971; postgrad., Johns Hopkins U., 1973; JD, George Wash. U., 1977. Bar: D.C. 1978. Law clk. Sharon, Pierson, Semmes, Crolius & Finley, Washington, 1975-76; chief legis. asst. Senator Floyd Haskell, Washington, 1973-75; sr. counsel com. on energy and natural resources U.S. Senate, Washington, 1976—; bd. dirs. Inst. Study of Regulation, Washington, 1985—. Mem. ABA. Democrat. Legislative, FERC practice, Public utilities. Home: 1537 Forest Ln McLean VA 22101 Office: Com Energy Natural Resources US Senate Washington DC 20510

MOLIERE, DONNA RENEE, lawyer; b. New Orleans, Feb. 16, 1958; d. Albert Francis Jr. and Joan Ann (Armstrong) M. BA, Loyola U., New Orleans, 1979, JD, 1982. Bar: La. 1982, U.S. Dist. Ct. (ea. dist.) La. 1982, U.S. Ct. Appeals (5th cir.) 1985. Extern to presiding justice U.S. Dist. Ct. (ea. dist.) La., New Orleans, 1981-82; assoc. Sessions, Fishman, Rosenson, Boisfontaine, Nathan & Winn, New Orleans, 1982—. Contbr. articles to Loyola Law Review. Mem. ABA, La. Bar Assn., New Orleans Bar Assn., Assn. for Women Attys., La. Assn. Def. Counsel, New Orleans Assn. Def. Counsel. Insurance, Personal injury, Errors and omissions. Home: 6727 Ave A New Orleans LA 70124 Office: Sessions Fishman et al 201 St Charles Ave New Orleans LA 70170

MOLINE, GARY L., bank executive; b. Elgin, Ill., July 26, 1952; s. Martin N. and Donna N. (Lange) M. BA, Western Ill. U., 1974; JD, St. Louis U., 1977. Bar: Ill. 1977, U.S. Dist. Ct. (no. dist.) Ill. 1980. Assoc. Geister, Schnell, Richards & Brown, Elgin, 1977-79, Hamer, Schuh & Baker, Woodstock, Ill., 1979-81; v.p., trust officer State Bank of Geneva, Ill., 1981—, also bd. dirs.; consumer compliance officer State Bank of Geneva, 1981—. Mem. ABA, Ill. Bar Assn., Kane County Bar Assn., Fox Valley Estate Planning Council, Land Trust Council, Geneva Jaycees (v.p. 1984-86). Lodges: Optimists (treas. Geneva club 1984-86), Moose. Probate, Banking, Pension, profit-sharing, and employee benefits. Home: 519 Anderson Blvd Geneva IL 60134 Office: State Bank of Geneva 4th and James Geneva IL 60134

MOLINEAUX, CHARLES BORROMEO, JR., lawyer; b. N.Y.C., Sept. 27, 1930; s. Charles Borromeo and Marion Frances (Belter) M.; m. Patricia Leo Devereux, July 2, 1960; children—Charles, Stephen, Christopher, Patricia, Peter, Elizabeth. B.S. cum laude, Sch. Fgn. Service, Georgetown U., 1950; J.D., St. John's U., N.Y.C., 1959. Bar: N.Y. 1959, Mass. 1981. Assoc., then ptnr. Nevius, Jarvis & Pilz and successor firms, N.Y.C., 1959-77; ptnr. Gadsby & Hannah, N.Y.C., 1978-80; v.p., gen. counsel Perini Corp., Framingham, Mass., 1980—. Committeeman Republican Party, Nassau County, N.Y., 1965-71, mem. exec. com., 1969. Served to 1st lt. U.S. Army, 1954-56. Mem. ASCE, ABA (chmn. region II pub. contracts sect, vice chmn. model procurement project constrn. and engring. services com.), Del. Hist. Soc. Roman Catholic. General corporate, Private international, Construction. Home: 127 Farm St Dover MA 02030 Office: Perini Corp 73 Mt Wayte Ave Framingham MA 01701

MOLLET, CHRIS JOHN, lawyer; b. Bottineau, N.D., Jan. 31, 1954; s. Lyle F. and Aileen C. (Murdoch) M.; m. Lynne M. La Jone, Sept. 20, 1980. B.A. with distinction, U. Wis., 1976, J.D., 1979. Bar: Wis. 1979, Ill. 1980, U.S. Ct. Appeals (7th cir.) 1979. Staff counsel Michael Reese Hosp. and Med. Ctr., Chgo., 1980-82; assoc. Gardner, Carton & Douglas, Chgo., 1982-85; assoc. gen. counsel, asst. sec. Luth. Gen. Health Care System, Park Ridge, Ill., 1985—; asst. sec. Parkside Home Health Services Inc., 1985—, Parkside Luth. Hosp., Augustana Hosp. Health Care Ctr., Luth. Gen. Hosp., Inc., bd. dirs., v.p. Norwood Park Citizens Assn., Chgo., 1983-84. Mem. ABA, Wis. Bar Assn., Chgo. Bar Assn., Am. Acad. Hosp. Attys. Democrat. Health, General corporate, Corporate taxation. Office: Luth Gen Health Care System 1775 Dempster Ave Park Ridge IL 60068

MOLLICA, SALVATORE DENNIS, lawyer; b. Waterbury, Conn., Nov. 27, 1948; s. Dennis Salvatore and Nellie (Albani) M. BA in History, St. Johns U., Jamaica, N.Y., 1970; JD, U. Fla., 1975. Bar: Fla. 1975, U.S. Dist. Ct. (no., mid. and so. dists.) Fla. 1975. Investigator State of Fla. Pub. Defenders Office, Gainesville, 1972-75; asst. pub. defender State of Fla., Gainesville, 1975-76; div. chief State of Fla. Pub. Defenders Office, Gainesville, 1976-80; sole practice Gainesville, 1980; ptnr. Mollica & Vipperman, Gainesville, 1981-82; sole practice Gainesville, 1982—. Democrat. Roman Catholic. Criminal, Juvenile, State civil litigation. Home: PO Box 694 Gainesville FL 32602 Office: 605 Northeast First St Gainesville FL 32602

MOLLINGER, JUDITH ELLEN, lawyer, industrial relations specialist; b. Phila., Nov. 20, 1943; d. Owen Samuel and Florence (Devinsky) M. BA, U. Conn., 1965; JD, Temple U., 1980. Bar: Pa. 1980, N.J. 1981, U.S. Dist. Ct. (ea dist.) Pa. 1981. Social worker Pa. Dept. Welfare, 1965-70; rep. Am. Fed. State, County and Mcpl. Employees, AFL-CIO, Phila., 1970-80; staff atty. Pub. Employment Relations Commn., Trenton, N.J., 1980-85; indsl. relations rep. Beverly Enterprises, Rockville, Md., 1986—; adj. prof. mgmt. Widener U., Chester, Pa., 1985-86. Mem. ABA, Pa. Bar Assn., N.J. Bar Assn., Indsl. Relations Research Assn., Coalition of Labor Union Women, Nat. Assn. Female Execs., Am. Health Care Assn., Temple U. Law Sch. Women's Caucus, Phi Kappa Phi. Avocations: aerobic dancing, tennis, community theater. Labor, General practice.

MOLLOY, BRIAN JOSEPH, lawyer; b. Jersey City, July 19, 1953; s. Joseph G. and Agnes L. (Mullaney) M.; m. Christina M. Cencek, June 14, 1975; children: Brooke Leigh, Evan Joseph. BA, Kean Coll. of N.J., 1975; JD, Seton Hall U., 1978. Bar: N.J. 1978, U.S. Dist. Ct. N.J. 1978. Ptnr. Wilentz, Goldman & Spitzer P.A., Woodbridge, N.J., 1978—. Mem. ABA, N.J. Bar Assn., Middlesex County Bar Assn. Administrative and regulatory, State civil litigation, Gambling law. Home: 321 Jefferson Ave Westfield NJ 07090 Office: Wilentz Goldman & Spitzer 900 Rt 9 PO Box 10 Woodbridge NJ 07095

MOLLOY, ROBERT JOSEPH, lawyer; b. Hartford, Conn., Aug. 26, 1953; s. Robert Joseph and Lorraine (Abbott) M. BA in English magna cum laude, Tufts U., 1975; JD, Boston U., 1980. Bar: Alaska, U.S. Dist. Ct. Alaska, U.S. Ct. Appeals (9th cir.), U.S. Supreme Ct. Ct. atty. State of Alaska, Kenai, 1980-81; sole practice Soldotna, Alaska, 1981-82; ptnr. Cusack & Molloy, Kenai, 1982—. Co-chmn. Shelter Steering Com., Kenai, 1982-85; bd. dirs. Women's Resource and Crisis Ctr., Kenai, 1982—. Mem. Alaska Bar Assn., Kenai Peninsula Bar Assn., Assn. Trial Lawyers Am., Kenai Peninsula Trial Lawyers Assn., Phi Beta Kappa. Avocations: backpacking, kayaking, skiing, music. State civil litigation, Personal injury, Contracts commercial. Office: Cusack & Molloy APC 110 S Willow St Suite 102 Kenai AK 99611

MOLOD, FREDERICK M., lawyer; b. Bklyn., May 20, 1930; s. Louis and Ida (Zuckerman) M.; m. Irene Klein, June 1, 1953; children: Andrea, Rise, Seth. BA, L.I. U.; LLB, Bklyn. Law Sch., LLM. Bar: N.Y. 1951, U.S. Dist. Ct. (so. and ea. dists.) N.Y. 1951, U.S. Immigration Ct. 1957. Ptnr. Weiss, Molod, Berkowitz & Godosky, N.Y.C., 1954—; bd. dirs. Am. Colonial Ins. Co., Portland, Maine, 1983—; lectr. in field. Mem. Assn. Trial Lawyers Am., N.Y. State Trial Lawyers Assn., N.Y. County Lawyers Assn., Nassau County Bar Assn., Jewish Lawyers Guild, Brit. Law Assn. Avocations: boating, fishing, photography. State civil litigation, Insurance, Personal injury. Home: 162 Remi Rd Manhasset NY 10030 Office: Weiss Molod Berkowitz & Godosky 12 E 41st New York NY 10017

MOLONEY, THOMAS JOSEPH, lawyer; b. Bklyn., Oct. 14, 1952; s. Thomas J. and Grace (Nelson) M.; m. Molly K. Heines, Dec. 26, 1976. AB, Columbia U., 1973; JD cum laude, NYU, 1976. Bar: N.Y. 1977, U.S. Dist. Ct. (so. dist.) N.Y. 1977, U.S. Dist. Ct. (ea. dist.) N.Y. 1978, U.S. Ct. Appeals (2d cir.) 1981. Assoc. Cleary, Gottlieb, Steen & Hamilton, N.Y.C., 1976-84, ptnr., 1984—; bd. dirs. N.Y. Lawyers for Pub. Interest, N.Y.C., 1986—. Asst. counsel Gov.'s Jud. Nominating Com., N.Y.C., 1981-85. Mem. ABA, N.Y. County Lawyers Assn., Assn. Bar City N.Y. (bankruptcy, corp. reorganization coms. 1983—), Order of Coif. Avocations: chess, golf, dance, travel, wine. Bankruptcy, Federal civil litigation, State civil litigation. Office: Cleary Gottlieb Steen & Hamilton One State St Plaza New York NY 10004

MOLONY, MICHAEL JANSSENS, JR., lawyer; b. New Orleans, Sept. 2, 1922; s. Michael Janssens and Marie Louise (Perret) M.; m. Jane Leslie Waguespack, Oct. 21, 1951; children—Michael Janssens III, Leslie, Megan, Kevin, Sara, Brian, Ian, Duncan. J.D., Tulane U., 1950. Bar: La. 1950, D.C. 1979. Practice law New Orleans. Ptnr., Molony & Baldwin, 1950; assoc. ptnr. Jones, Flanders, Waechter & Walker, 1951-56; ptnr. Jones, Walker, Waechter, Poitevent, Carrere & Denegre, 1956-75, Milling, Benson, Woodward, Hillyer, Pierson & Miller, 1975—; instr., lectr. Med. Sch. and Univ. Coll., Tulane U., 1953-59; mem. Eisenhower Legal Com., 1952. Bd. commrs. Port of New Orleans, 1975-85, pres., 1978, vice-chmn. past pres.' council, 1985—; bd. dirs. La. World Expn. Inc., 1974-84; bd. dirs., exec. com. New Orleans Tourist and Conv. Commn., 1971-74, 78, chmn. family attractions com. 1973-75; chmn. La. Gov.'s Task Force on Space Industry, 1971-73; chmn. Gov.'s Citizens' Adv. Com. Met. New Orleans Transp. and Planning Program, 1971-77; mem. La. Gov.'s Task Force Natural Gas Requirements, 1971-72; mem. Goals Found. Council and ex-officio mem. Goals Found., Met. New Orleans Goals Program, 1969-72, vice chmn. ad hoc planning com. Goals Met. New Orleans, 1969-73; vice chmn. Port of New Orleans Operation Impact, 1969-70; mem. Met. Area Com., New Orleans, 1970-84; trustee Pub. Affairs Research Council La., 1970-73; bd. dirs., mem. exec. com. Met. Council Continuing Higher Edn., U. New Orleans, 1980—; Mayor's Council on Internat. Trade and Econ. Devel., 1978; trustee Gulf South Research Inst., 1980—; trustee Loyola U., New Orleans, 1985—; bd. visitors Loyola U. Sch. Bus. Adminstrn., 1981—; bd. dirs., mem. exec. com. Internat. Trade Mart, chmn. internat. bus. com., 1983-85; chmn. Task Force on Internat. Banking, 1982; Acad. Sacred Heart, 1975-77, Internat. House, 1985—. Served with AUS, USAAF, 1942-46, PTO. Mem. Fed. Bar Assn., ABA (mgmt. co-chmn. com. devel. law union adminstrn. and procedures 1969), La. Bar Assn. (past sec.-treas., gov. 1959-60, editor jour. 1957-59, sec. spl. supreme ct. com. on drafting code jud. ethics), New Orleans Bar Assn. (dir. legal aid bur. 1954, vice chmn. standing com. pub. relations 1970-71), Am. Judicature Soc., La. Law Inst. (asst. sec.-treas. 1958-79), Am. Arbitration Assn. (bd. dirs., chmn. La. adv. council), So. Inst. Mgmt. (founder), World Trade Ctr.-New Orleans (bd. dirs. 1978—), AIM, U.S. C. of C. (urban and regional affairs com. 1970-72), La. C. of C. (bd. dirs. 1963-66), New Orleans Area C. of C. (v.p. met. devel. and urban affairs 1969, past chmn. council, bd. dirs. 1970-78, pres.-elect 1970, pres. 1971, exec. com. 1972), Sigma Chi (pres. alumni chpt. 1956). Roman Catholic. Clubs: Internat. House, Plimsoll, So. Yacht Serra, Lakewood Country, Pickwick, Bienville, City (New Orleans). Labor, Federal civil litigation, General corporate. Home: 3039 Hudson Pl New Orleans LA 70114 Office: 1100 Whitney Bldg New Orleans LA 70130

MOLTZ, MARSHALL JEROME, lawyer; b. Chgo., May 22, 1930; s. Nathan and Rose (Nathanson) M.; m. Rita G., Dec. 26, 1954; m. 2d, Mary Ann, Nov. 4, 1967; children—Alan J., Michelle S., Marilyn F., Julie A., Steven E., Rachel N. B.S., Northwestern U., 1951, J.D., 1954. Bar: Ill. 1954, Mo. 1954. Assoc., John B. Moser, Chgo., 1957; assoc. Goldberg, Devoe, Shadur & Mikva, Chgo., 1957-58; assoc. Lester Plotkin, Chgo., 1958-59; sole practice, Chgo., 1959-65; ptnr. Moltz & Spagat, Chgo., 1966-67; sole practice, Chgo., 1967-68; ptnr. Moltz & Wexler, Chgo., 1968-80; sole practice Chgo. 1980—; speaker real estate law. Atty., Lake View C. of C., Chgo., Lake View Neighborhood Devel. Corp., Chgo. Served with M.I., U.S. Army, 1955-56; ETO. Recipient Louden Wigmore prize Northwestern U. Law Sch., 1954. Mem. ABA, Ill. State Bar Assn., Chgo. Bar Assn. (mem. real property law com. 1958-82, chmn. Torrens sub-com. 1968-75, vice chmn. real property law com. 1974-75, chmn. real property law com. 1975-76, chmn. sub-com. on modernization recorders and Torrens office 1973-75), Phi Alpha Delta. Jewish. Club: VFW (Chgo.). Author course outlines Ill. Inst. Continuing Legal Edn., 1972, 73; editorial bd. Northwestern U. Law Rev., 1953-54. Real property, Banking, Contracts commercial. Home: 808 Westwood Ln Wilmette IL 60091 Office: 77 W Washington Suite 1620 Chicago IL 60602

MONACELLI, WALTER JOSEPH, patent lawyer; b. Albion, N.Y., Jan. 16, 1914; s. Horace and Hyacinth (Lombard) M.; m. Miriam E. Johnson, Sept. 7, 1947 (div.); children—Linda, Janet; m. Phyllis E. Fuhrman, 1973. BSChemE, U. Notre Dame, 1938, Ph.D. in Organic Chemistry, 1941; J.D., DePaul U., 1945. Bar: Ohio 1946, Ill. 1946, U.S. Supreme Ct. 1953. Research chemist Atlantic Refining Co., Phila., 1941-42, Sinclair Oil Co., East Chicago, Ind., 1942-43, Sherwin-Williams Co., Chgo., 1943-45; patent atty. Indsl. Rayon Corp., Cleve., 1946-47; mgr. patent dept. Koppers Co., Inc., Pitts., 1947-57; sole practice patent law, Cleve., 1957-72, St. Petersburg, Fla., 1972—; pres. Interlock Corp., Cleve., 1965—; v.p. Deltronix Corp., 1963—; pres. Waller Devel. Corp., St. Petersburg, 1986— ; Patentee in field. Mem. ABA, Intellectual Property Assn., Cleve. Patent Law Assn., Bar Assn. Greater Cleve., Phi Alpha Delta. Republican. Roman Catholic. Club: St. Petersburg Yacht. Patent, Trademark and copyright. Home and Office: 720 36th Ave N Saint Petersburg FL 33704

MONACO, DANIEL JOSEPH, lawyer; b. Easton, Pa., May 12, 1922; s. Federico and Maria (Romano) M.; m. Marian P., June 25, 1953 (div.); children—Denise E., Mimi D. A.B., Lafayette Coll., 1943; M.A., U. Chgo., 1946; J.D., Stanford U., 1951; postgrad., U. Mich., 1944-45. Bar: Calif. 1951, U.S. dist. ct. (no. dist.) Calif. 1951, U.S. Sup. Ct. 1961. Faculty U. Miami, Fla., 1946-47; assoc. Hession, Robb & Creedon, San Mateo, Calif., 1951-53; founder, sr. ptnr. Monaco, Anderlini & Finkelstein, San Mateo, 1953—; inheritance tax appraiser State of Calif., 1963-67. Chmn. San Mateo County Democratic Central Com., 1960-61, mem. Calif. State Exec. Bd.; founder, pres. Circlon Internat., 1980-81, Served with M.I. U.S. Army, 1943-46; served to lt. USAR, 1946-50. Mem. Calif. State Bar Assn., San Mateo County Bar Assn., Am. Trial Lawyers Assn., Calif. Trial Lawyers Assn., (bd. govs.), San Mateo County Trial Lawyers Assn. (pres.), Am. Bd. Trial Advocates, World Peace through Law. Club: Peninsula Golf and Country (San Mateo). Personal injury, State civil litigation, Product and malprac-

tice.. Home: 295 Darrell Rd Hillsborough CA 94010 Office: 400 S El Camino Real #700 San Mateo CA 94402

MONACO, GRACE POWERS, Lawyer; b. Union City, N.J., Sept. 3, 1938; d. Rea John and Grace Elizabeth (FitzGibbons) Powers; m. Lawrence Anthony Monaco, Aug. 10, 1963; children—Kathleen Rea (dec.), David Gordon, Stephen Michael, Peter Joseph. B.A., Coll. Misericordia-Pa., 1960, D.Letters(hon.), 1979; J.D., Georgetown U., 1963. Bar: D.C. 1964. Mem. honor law grad. program Dept. Justice, Washington, 1963-64; sole practice 1965-66; assoc. Wheatley & Wollesen, Washington, 1967-78; ptnr. Fairman, Frisk & Monaco, Washington, 1978-82; ptnr. White, Fine & Verville, Washington, 1983—. Chmn. bd. dirs. Candlelighters Childhood Cancer Found.; mem. Capitol Hill Restoration Soc.; chmn. bd. Capitol Hill Hosp., 1982-85; vice chairperson Medlantic Healthcare Group, 1982—. Recipient Nat. Award, Am. Cancer Soc., 1978. Mem. Women's Bar Assn., D.C. Bar Assn., Fed. Bar Assn., Nat. Health Lawyers Assn., Fed. Energy Regulatory Bar Assn. Democrat. Roman Catholic. Contbr. chpts. to books and articles in field to profl. jours. Health, Insurance, Administrative and regulatory. Home: 123 C St SE Washington DC 20003 Office: 1100 15th St NW Washington DC 20005

MONACO, MARIO ANTHONY, lawyer; b. N.Y.C., Oct. 19, 1931; s. Roger and Angela Monaco; m. Arline C. DiNapoli, Oct. 17, 1959; children: Gregory, Stephanie. BS in Chemistry, City Coll. of N.Y., 1953; MS in Chemistry, Bklyn. Coll., 1959; JD, N.Y. Law Sch., 1965. Bar: N.J. 1965. Dir. patents Merck and Co., Inc., Rahway, N.J., 1961—; instr. law Rutgers U., New Brunswick, N.J., 1966-67. Served to cpl. U.S. Army, 1953-55, ETO. Mem. ABA, N.J. Bar Assn. (chmn. patent com. 1978-79), Am. Intellectual Property Assn. Avocations: walking, golf, music. Patent, Legislative. Office: Merck and Co Inc PO Box 2000 Rahway NJ 07065

MONACO, NICHOLAS M., lawyer; b. St. Louis, Apr. 29, 1930; s. Michael and Conie (Bevi) M.; m. Mildred Ann Pickett, Oct. 23, 1954; children: Catherine Joan, Ann Marie, Micheal Eldon. BA, U. Mo., 1952, JD, 1958. Bar: Mo. 1958, U.S. Dist. Ct. (we. dist.) Mo. 1959, U.S. Ct. Appeals (9th cir.) 1979, U.S. Ct. Appeals (8th cir.) 1982. Gen. counsel Mo. Div. Ins., Jefferson City, 1958-62; ptnr. Carson, Monaco, Coil, Riley & McMillin, Jefferson City, 1962-85, Inglish, Riner & Lockenvitz, Jefferson City, 1985—; gen. counsel Comml. State Life Ins., St. Louis, 1962-79, Mo. Profl. Liability Ins. Assn., Jefferson City, 1976-81. Author: Missouri Suicide Statute, 1960; editor: Missouri Insurance Practice Manual, 1978-86. Dist. Chmn. 5 Rivers Dist. Boy Scouts Am., 1972. Recipient Silver Beaver award Boy Scouts Am., 1973. Mem. ABA, Mo. Bar Assn., Met. St. Louis Bar Assn., Cole County Bar Assn., Ins. Law Com. (chmn. 1958—), U. Mo. Alumni Alliance (chmn.), Order of Barristers. Democrat. Roman Catholic. Lodge: Rotary (dist. 605 gov. 1981-82, pres. Jefferson City club 1976-77). Avocation: investments. Administrative and regulatory, Insurance, Securities. Home: 1122 Moreau Dr Jefferson City MO 65101 Office: Inglish Monaco Riner & Lockenvitz 237 E High PO Box 1496 Jefferson City MO 65102

MONAGHAN, PETER GERARD, lawyer; b. Belfast, Ireland, July 12, 1949; came to U.S., 1961; s. William Liam and Elizabeth (Eccles) M.; m. Barbara Marie Farrenkopf, Sept. 24, 1972; children: Brian Patrick, Kevin James, Allison Mary. BS, Fordham U., 1970; JD, St. John's U., Jamaica, N.Y., 1977. Bar: N.Y. 1978, U.S. Dist. Ct. (so. dist.) N.Y. 1978, U.S. Dist. Ct. (ea. dist.) N.Y. 1979, U.S. Supreme Ct. 1986. Claims examiner Royal Ins. Co., N.Y.C., 1970-76; assoc. Kroll, Edelman, Elser and Dicker, N.Y.C., 1976; assoc. Bower and Gardner, N.Y.C., 1977-83, ptnr., 1984—. Cubmaster Boy Scouts Am., Bayside, N.Y., 1985—. Served to capt. U.S. Army, 1970-78. Mem. ABA, Queens County Bar Assn. Democrat. Roman Catholic. State civil litigation, Federal civil litigation, Personal injury. Office: Bower and Gardner 110 E 59 St New York NY 10022

MONAHAN, JOHN CONNOLLY, lawyer; b. Port chester, N.Y., Oct. 8, 1947; s. Henry Joseph and Catherine B. (Connolly) M.; m. Gail C. Harrison, May 1, 1982; 1 child, Ryan Michael. AB, Boston Coll., 1969; JD cum laude, Suffolk U., 1976. Bar: Md. 1977, D.C. 1978, U.S. Dist. Ct. Md. 1978, U.S. Dist. Ct. D.C. 1978, U.S. Ct. Appeals. (D.C. cir.) 1978. Law clk. to presiding justice Md. Cir. Ct., Rockville, Md., 1976-77; assoc. Law Offices of Henry J. Monahan, Rockville, 1977-79; asst. pub. defender Md. Pub. Defender's Office, Rockville, 1979-81; ptnr. Bours & Monahan, Rockville, 1981-86; pres. John C. Monahan, P.C., Rockville, 1986—. Mem. Am. Trial Lawyers Assn., Nat. Assn. Criminal Def. Lawyers, Md. State Bar Assn., Md. Criminal Def. Attys. Assn. (bd. dirs. 1983—), D.C. Bar Assn., Montgomery County Bar Assn. (exec. com. 1983-84, 85-86). Democrat. Roman Catholic. Club: Argyle Country. Avocations: golf, swimming, gardening. Personal injury, Criminal, State civil litigation. Home: 17709 Shady Mills Rd Derwood MD 20855 Office: 401 E Jefferson St #106 Rockville MD 20850

MONAHAN, MARIE TERRY, lawyer; b. Milford, Mass., June 26, 1927; d. Francis V. and Marie I. (Casey) Terry; m. John Henry Monahan, Aug. 25, 1951; children: Thomas F., Kathleen J., Patricia M., John Terry, Moira M., Deirdre M. AB, Radcliffe Coll., 1949; JD, New Eng. Sch. Law, 1975. Bar: Mass. 1977, U.S. Dist. Ct. Mass. 1978, U.S. Supreme Ct. 1982. Tchr. French and Spanish Holliston (Mass.) High Sch., 1949-52; sole practice Newton, Mass., 1977—. Mem. ABA, Mass. Bar Assn., Nat. Assn. Women Lawyers, Assn. Trial Lawyers Am., Mass. Assn. Women Lawyers (pres. 1986), Mass. Acad. Trial Attys., Boston Bar Assn. Avocations: reading, travel. State civil litigation, Family and matrimonial, Probate. Home and Office: 34 Foster St Newtonville MA 02160

MONCURE, JOHN LEWIS, lawyer; b. Houston, Nov. 4, 1930; s. Walter Raleigh Daniel and Margaret (Atkins) M.; m. Norma Steed, Dec. 29, 1954 (dec. June 1982); children—John Carter, Michael Lewis, Douglas Lee, Stuart Richard, Mary Margaret; m. Margaret Edmonston, Nov. 12, 1983. B.B.A., U. Houston, 1953; J.D., U. Tex., 1956. Bar: Tex. bar 1956. Assoc. Butler, Binion, Rice, Cook & Knapp, Houston, 1956-68; ptnr. Prappas, Moncure & Eidman, Houston, 1969-86, John L. Moncure and Assocs., Houston, 1987—; lectr. bus. law U. Houston, 1958-59, 68-69. Mem. sch. bd. St. Thomas Episcopal Sch., Houston, 1965-78; mem. vestry St. Thomas Episc. Ch., 1975-78. Named Distinguished Alumni Coll. Bus., U. Houston, 1968. Fellow Am. Coll. Probate Counsel; mem. Am., Tex., Houston bar assns., Assn. Christian Schs. (trustee), Coll. Bus. Alumni Assn. U. Houston (pres., dir.), U. Houston Alumni Fedn. (treas., dir.), Sigma Alpha Epsilon. Democrat. Club: Sugar Creek Country. Real property, Probate, Estate taxation. Home: 806 Merrick Dr Sugar Land TX 77478 Office: 9800 Richmond Suite 465 Houston TX 77042

MONE, MATHIAS EDWARD, lawyer; b. Bklyn., Dec. 29, 1940; s. Edward W. and Mary (Maloney) M.; m. Maureen Reidy, June 12, 1965; children: Christopher, Jennifer, Maureen, Gregory. AB, Villanova U., 1962; JD, Fordham U., 1965. Bar: N.Y. 1966, D.C. 1969. Assoc. Cahill, Gordon & Reindel, N.Y.C., 1965-72, ptnr., 1972—. Mem. ABA, N.Y. State Bar Assn., Nassau County Bar Assn., Fed. Bar Council. Republican. Roman Catholic. Federal civil litigation, State civil litigation. Home: 10 Cross Rd Plandome NY 11030 Office: Cahill Gordon & Reindel 80 Pine St New York NY 10005

MONE, PETER JOHN, lawyer; b. Brockton, Mass., Apr. 8, 1940; s. Edward Patrick and June E. (Kelliher) M.; m. Sharon Lee Bright, Oct. 9, 1965; children—Kathleen, Peter. A.B., Bowdoin Coll., 1962; J.D., U. Chgo., 1965. Ptnr., Baker & McKenzie, Chgo., 1968—. Mem. Winnetka Caucus, Ill., 1984-85. Served to capt. U.S. Army, 1966-67; Vietnam. Decorated Purple Heart, Bronze Star, Air medal. Fellow Am. Coll. Trial Lawyers; mem. Soc. Trial Lawyers, Chgo. Trial Lawyers Club, Internat. Assn. Def. Counsel (Ill. Supreme Ct. Ad Hoc Rules com.). Democrat. Roman Catholic. Club: Skokie Country (Glencoe, Ill.). Avocations: photography; golf; paddle tennis; softball. Federal civil litigation, State civil litigation, Personal injury. Home: 1035 Sunset Rd Winnetka IL 60093 Office: Baker & McKenzie Prudential Plaza Chicago IL 60601

MONES, PAUL ALAN, lawyer; b. Bronx, N.Y., May 5, 1952; s. Raymond and Gwen (Altman) M. BA magna cum laude, SUNY, Buffalo, 1974; M Regional Planning, JD, U. N.C., 1978. Bar: W.Va. 1978, U.S. Dist. Ct. (no. and so. dists.) W.Va. 1978, Mass. 1984. Staff atty. W.Va. Legal Services, Clarksburg, 1978-80; dir. Juvenile Advs. Inc., Morgantown, W.Va., 1980-83; cons. Boston, 1983-84; dir. legal Pub. Justice Found., Los Angeles, 1984-86; cons. Los Angeles, 1986—; adj. lectr. W.Va. Coll. Law., Morgantown, 1982-83; invited witness juvenile justice sucom. U.S. Senate Judiciary, Washington, 1983. Co-author: Juvenile Justice Practice Manual, 1982. Mem. ABA (juvenile justice com. criminal justice 1985—), Phi Beta Kappa. Juvenile, Intra-family homicide, emphasis on parricide with relation to child abuse. Home and Office: 2432 3d St Santa Monica CA 90405

MONHEIT, HERBERT, lawyer; b. Atlantic City N.J., Dec. 12, 1929; s. Philip and Yetta (Abel) M.; m. Patricia Silver, Mar. 13, 1959; children—Michael, Maryann. B.A., Rutgers Coll., 1951, LL.B., 1956; postgrad. Georgetown U., 1953-55. Bar: Pa. 1957, U.S. Dist. (ea. dist.) Pa. 1957, U.S. Supreme Ct. 1974. Pub. defender, Phila., 1957-58; sole practice, Phila., 1960—; spl. asst. atty. gen., 1968-70; mem. County Bd. Law Examiners, 1961; lectr. U. Del. Law Sch., 1975. Republican committeeman, 1964-70; bd. dirs. Cheltenham Twp. Sch. Authority, 1965. Jewish. Clubs: Philmont Country (Pa.); Atlantic City Country (N.J.); Linwood Country (N.J.); Golden Slipper Lodge: Masons. Home: 324 Rices Mill Rd Wyncote PA 19095 Office: Herbert Monheit PC 2010 Chestnut St Philadelphia PA 19103

MONIZ, DONNA MARIA, lawyer, nurse; b. Sept. 18, 1950; d. Frank and Gloria Camille (Mancino) M. BS magna cum laude, Cath. U. Am., 1972; M in Nursing, U. Wash., 1975, JD, 1982. Staff mem. Loeb Ctr. for Nursing and Rehab., Bronx, N.Y., 1973-74; family nurse practitioner Whatcom-Skagit Rural Health Clinics, Mt. Vernon, Wash., 1975-76, Providence Family Med. Ctr., Seattle, 1976-78; clin. instr. U. Wash., Seattle, 1977-78, instr. med. sch., 1978-80, clin. asst. prof. sch. nursing, 1986—; family nurse practitioner Seattle-King County Health Dept., 1978-83; assoc. Reed McClure Moceri Thonn & Moriarty, Seattle, 1982—; health care instr. U. Wash., 1978-80, City U., 1982—; cons. Internat. Childbirth Edn. Assn., 1986—; bd. dirs. Yesler Terrace Health Clinic. Mem. editorial bd. Region X Women's Health Care newsletter, 1977; contbr. articles to profl. jours. Mem. Childbirth Edn. Assn. Seattle, 1976-78; coordinator Law Women's Caucus, 1980-81. Mem. ABA, Am. Nurses Assn., Am. Assn. Nurse Attys., Wash. Assn. Def. Counsel, Sigma Theta Tau, Kappa Gamma Pi. Health, State civil litigation, Administrative and regulatory. Home: 422 McGraw St Seattle WA 98109

MONK, JAMES RUSSELL, lawyer, state senator; b. Sullivan, Ind., Oct. 5, 1947; s. Lyman Elihu and Charlotte May (Ellingsworth) M.; m. Sarah Jane Stewart, June 11, 1966; children—James Stewart, John Robert (dec.), Daniel Joshua. Student, Ind. State U., 1965-66; A.B., Ind. U., 1969; postgrad. U. Miami, 1974-75; J.D., U. Fla., 1977. Bar: Ind. 1978. Tchr. Plantation (Fla.) High Sch., 1969-71; tchr. South Plantation High Sch., 1971-76, dir. student activities, 1971-76; sole practice, Sullivan, 1978—; prosecutor Sullivan County, 1979-82, county atty., 1979-81; mem. Ind. State Senate, 1982—. Recipient Outstanding Freshman Legislator award Ind. Assn. Broadcasters, 1983, Legislator of Yr. award United Mine Workers Am., 1986. Mem. ABA, Ind. Bar Assn., Sullivan County Bar Assn. Democrat. Roman Catholic. Lodges: Kiwanis (past pres.), Elks, K.C. (Sullivan). Home: Rural Rt 1 Box 22 Sullivan IN 47882 Office: 110 S Main St Sullivan IN 47882 Office: 26 N 4th St Vincennes IN 47591

MONK, SAMUEL HOLT, II, judge; b. Anniston, Ala., July 14, 1946; s. Richard Hunley and Marjorie Louise (Schneider) M.; m. Mary Lou Gibbins, June 11, 1971; children—Carolyn Elizabeth, William Gibbins. B.A., Jacksonville State U., 1969; J.D., U. Ala., 1975. Bar: Ala. 1975, U.S. Dist. Ct. (no. dist.) Ala. 1976, U.S. Tax Ct. 1978. Sole practice, Anniston, 1975-78; asst. dist. atty. 7th Jud. Cir., Anniston, 1977-78, judge, 1979—; dist. judge Calhoun-Cleburne Counties, Anniston, Ala., 1978-79. Bd. dirs. YMCA, Anniston, 1979-86, Choccolocco council Boy Scouts Am., 1980—, Voluntary Action Agy., Anniston, 1981—; pres. Am. Cancer Soc., Calhoun County, 1984-86, bd. dirs., 1984—; pres, Vol. and Info. Ctr., Calhoun County, 1986. Served to capt. USAR, 1969-72, Vietnam. Mem. ABA, Ala. State Bar Assn., Calhoun County Bar Assn., Ala. Cir. Judges Assn., Ala. Jud. Coll. Faculty Assn., Order of Coif. Democrat. Episcopalian. Clubs: Rotary, Exchange (Anniston and Jacksonville). Lodges: Masons. Judicial administration. Home: 614 Ayers Dr Anniston AL 36201 Office: Cir Ct 7th Cir Ala PO Box 636 Anniston AL 36202

MONROE, CECIL BARLOW, judge; b. Mobile, Ala., May 15, 1952; s. Henry Evans and Sally (Barlow) M.; m. Patricia Ann Head, May 18, 1984. BA, U. So. Ala., 1978; JD, Tex. So. U., 1982. Bar: Ala. 1982. Sole practice Mobile, 1982—; pros. atty. City of Mobile, 1983-86, judge, 1986—. Served with USMC, 1970-74. Mem. ABA, Ala. Bar Assn., Mobile Bar Assn. Episcopalian. Personal injury, Judicial administration, General practice. Office: 951 Government St Suite 818 Mobile AL 36604

MONROE, JERALD JACOB, lawyer; b. Clayton, N.Mex., Feb. 4, 1938; s. Dottis Donald and Helen (Kurth) M. BS in Econs., Colo. State U., 1960; JD, U. N.Mex., 1963. Bar: N.Mex. 1963, U.S. Dist. Ct. N.Mex. 1963, U.S. Supreme Ct. 1971, Hawaii 1978, U.S. Dist. Ct. Hawaii 1978. Ptnr. Iden & Johnson, Albuquerque, 1963-73; v.p., counsel Hawaii Escrow, Honolulu, 1978; v.p., gen. counsel Honolulu Fed., 1979; assoc. Tarkildson-Katz, Honolulu, 1980; sole practice Alburquerque and Honolulu, 1981—; v.p. Advanced Legal Software, Honolulu, 1984. Mem. ABA (computer com.), State Bar N.Mex. (continuing legal edn. com., medical legal com.), State Bar Hawaii, NTSB Bar Assn., Alburquerque Bar Assn., Japan-Hawaii Lawyers' Assn., Lawyer-Pilot Assn. Episcopalian. Banking, Federal civil litigation, Real property. Office: 2730 San Pedro NE Suite H Albuquerque NM 87110

MONROE, KENDYL KURTH, lawyer; b. Clayton, N.Mex., Sept. 6, 1936; s. Dottis Donald and Helen (Kurth) M.; m. Barbara Sayre, Sept. 12, 1956; children: Sidney, Dean, Loren. AB, Stanford U., 1958, LLB, 1960. Bar: N.Y. 1961, Calif. 1961. Assoc. Sullivan & Cromwell, N.Y.C., 1960-67, ptnr., 1968—; chmn. Bata Land Co., Belcamp, Md.; bd. dirs. No. Minerals Co., Keesville, N.Y., CHB Corp, Belcamp. chmn. N.Y. Chamber Soloists, N.Y.C., Lambs Theatre, N.Y.C.; vice-chmn. Pub. Health Research Inst. N.Y., N.Y.C.; v.p., trustee Collegiate Sch., N.Y.C. Mem. ABA (tax sect.), N.Y. State Bar Assn. (past chmn. various coms., tax sect.), Assn. of Bar of City of N.Y. (sec. 1967-69), Multinat. Fiscal Assocs. (vice-chmn.). Clubs: Met., Down Town Assn., Downtown Athletic (N.Y.C.). Avocation: aviation. Corporate taxation, Corporate general, Securities, Real property. Home: 59 Charles St New York NY 10014 Office: Sullivan & Cromwell 125 Broad St New York NY 10004

MONSON, TERRY LEWIS, lawyer; b. Fargo, N.D., Jan. 5, 1947; s. Calmer M. and Marion Geneva (Lewis) M.; m. Ginger Gayle Culpepper, Aug. 23, 1970; children: Tara, Lindsey. BA, N.D. State U., 1969; JD, Northwestern U., 1972. Bar: Iowa 1972, U.S. Dist. Ct. (so. dist.) Iowa 1972, U.S. Ct. Appeals (8th cir.) 1977, U.S. Dist. Ct. (no. dist.) Iowa 1984. Assoc. Ahlers Law Firm, Des Moines, 1972-77; ptnr. Ahlers, Cooney, Dorweiler, Haynie, Smith & Allbee, Des Moines, 1978—. Served to 2d lt. U.S. Army, 1972. Mem. ABA, Iowa Bar Assn., Polk County Bar Assn., Iowa Assn. Workers' Compensation Lawyers, Iowa Def. Counsel Assn., West Des Moines C. of C. (edn. com. 1985—), Greater Des Moines Chamber Fedn. (exec. call com. 1985—). Real property, State civil litigation, Workers' compensation. Office: Ahlers Cooney et al 300 Liberty Bldg Des Moines IA 50309

MONSON, THOMAS LEE, lawyer; b. Salt Lake City, May 28, 1951; s. Thomas S. and Frances (Johnson) M.; m. Carma R. Rhodehouse, Apr. 26, 1974; children: Thomas P., Lauren A. BA, Brigham Young U., 1974; JD, U. Utah, 1978. Bar: Utah 1978. Assoc. Senior & Senior, Salt Lake City, 1978-83, Van Cott, Bagley, Cornwall & McCarthy, Salt Lake City, 1983—; bd. dirs. Geyser Marion Gold Mining Co., Salt Lake City, Sacramento Gold Mining Co., Salt Lake City. Mem. ABA (natural resources sect.), Utah Bar Assn. (chmn. client security fund com. 1983—), Rocky Mountain Mineral Law Inst. (oil and gas com.). General corporate, Oil and gas leasing, Real property. Office: Van Cott Bagley Cornwall & McCarthy 50 S Main Suite 1600 Salt Lake City UT 84144

MONTABON, DENNIS GENE, judge; b. Tomahawk, Wis., Sept. 30, 1943; s. Frank William and Laura Elizabeth (Krubsack) M.; m. Julie Ann Bishop, Nov. 4, 1967; children: Frank, Anthony, Sara. BS, U. Wis., 1965; JD, John Marshall Sch. Law, 1972. Bar: Ill. 1972, Wis. 1972, U.S. Dist. Ct. (we. dist.) Wis. 1978. Sr. inspector alcohol, tobacco and firearms U.S. Treasury Dept., Chgo., 1966-72; dist. atty. Lincoln County, Merrill, Wis., 1973-76; assoc. Bosshart & Assoc., LaCrosse, Wis., 1976-78; judge LaCrosse County Cir. Ct., 1978—; dep. chief judge 7th jud. adminstrv. dist., State of Wis., 1984—. Mem. legis. com. Wis. Jud. Conf., Supreme Ct., Madison, 1982—; mem. Cathedral Sch. Bd.; bd. dirs. Riverland Girl Scouts U.S. Council, chmn. com. fin. Mem. ABA (jud. adminstrn. sect.), Wis. Bar Assn. Lutheran. Lodges: Kiwanis (bd. dirs. LaCrosse 1982-85). Avocation: watching children's sporting events. Judicial administration, Personal injury, Criminal. Home: 1512 State St LaCrosse WI 54601 Office: Cir Ct Branch 3 Courthouse PO Box 637 LaCrosse WI 54601

MONTAGNA, ANTHONY LOUIS, JR., lawyer; b. Norfolk, Va., Apr. 17, 1940; s. Anthony Louis and Phoebe Estell (Selby) M.; m. Jane Angela McGrath, July 8, 1967; 1 child, Anthony Louis, III. B.A. in Psychology, U. Va., 1962, LL.B., 1965. Bar: Va. 1965, U.S. Dist. Ct. (ea. dist.) Va. 1968, U.S. Mil. Ct. 1965, U.S. Ct. Appeals (4th cir.) 1982, U.S. Supreme Ct. 1974. Law specialist U.S. Navy, 1965-68; asst. city atty. City of Norfolk, Va., 1968-73; sole practice, Norfolk, 1973—; instr. bus. law Onslow Tech. Inst., Jacksonville, N.C., 1967-68, Tidewater Community Coll., Portsmouth, Va., 1978. Legal advisor Little Creek Pony Baseball, Norfolk, 1980; vice chmn. bd. St. Mary's Cemetery, Norfolk, 1983. Mem. Va. State Bar (mem. com. for liason with armed forces 1982—), Va. Trial Lawyers, Va. Bar Assn., ABA, Assn. Trial Lawyers Am., Am. Judicature Soc., Norfolk/Portsmouth Bar Assn. Roman Catholic. Clubs: Ryans (pres. 1982-83), Mil. Order World Wars (judge adv. 1980-82) (Norfolk). Lodges: K.C. (adv. 1974-76), Elks. Family and matrimonial, State civil litigation, General practice. Home: 2111 Hollybriar Point Norfolk VA 23518 Office: 804 Plaza One Bldg Norfolk VA 23518

MONTANA, JANICE, lawyer; b. N.Y.C., May 23, 1954; d. John D. and Amelia Montana. BA, Fairleigh Dickinson U., 1976; JD, Ohio No. U., 1979. Bar: Pa. 1979, N.J. 1980, U.S. Dist. Ct. N.J. 1980, U.S. Dist. Ct. (so. and ea. dists.) N.J. 1983, U.S. Ct. Claims 1983, U.S. Ct. Internat. Trade 1983, U.S. Tax Ct. 1983, U.S. Ct. Appeals (2d and 3d cirs.) 1983, U.S. Supreme Ct. 1983, N.Y. 1987. Assoc. Law Offices of Milton M. and Adrian M. Unger, Newark, 1979-80; asst. corp. counsel dept. of law City of Newark, 1980-84; assoc. Pitney, Hardin, Kipp & Szuch, Morristown, N.J., 1984—. Assoc. editor Ohio No. U. Law Rev., 1977-79. Corr. sec., mem. Rep. County Com. for Twp. Springfield, N.J., 1985—; del. Union County Rep. Conv., Roselle Park, N.J., 1986; atty. Rent Leveling Bd., Twp. of Springfield, 1983-84, mem. 1982. Named one of Outstanding Young Women Am., 1985. Mem. ABA, N.J. Bar Assn., Pa. Bar Assn., Assn. Trial Lawyers Am., Rep. Lawyers Assn. N.J., Rep. Nat. Lawyers Assn., Phi Omega Epsilon. Roman Catholic. Club: Gov.'s (Trenton, N.J.). Avocations: tennis, jogging, skiing. Federal civil litigation, State civil litigation. Home: 565 S Springfield Ave Springfield NJ 07081 Office: Pitney Hardin Kipp & Szuch 163 Madison Ave Morristown NJ 07960-1945

MONTANTE, PHILIP JOSEPH, JR., lawyer; b. Buffalo, Jan. 30, 1945. B.B.A., Drake U., 1966; M.Ed., Fla. Atlantic U., 1967; J.D., Samford U., 1971. Bar: Fla. 1971, U.S. Dist. Ct. (so. dist.) Fla. 1971, U.S. Ct. Appeals (5th cir.) 1972, U.S. Supreme Ct. 1976, D.C. 1979, U.S. Ct. Appeals (11th cir.) 1982, N.Y. 1984. Asst. state atty., Ft. Lauderdale, Fla., 1971-75, spl. asst. atty. gen., 1975-76; chief judge Mcpl. Ct., Margate, Fla., 1976-77; sole practice, Ft. Lauderdale and Pompano Beach, Fla., 1975—; chmn. Jud. Nominating Commn., 1975-79; mem. ethics com. Fla. Bar, 1976-77, chmn. grievance com., 1981-83, spl. counsel to grievance com., 1985; mem. Atlanta Regional panel Pres.'s Commn. on White House Fellowships, 1980—; chief pros. atty. City of Pompano Beach, Lauderdale by the Sea and Lighthouse Point; adj. prof. Fla. Atlantic U., 1975-83, Nova U., 1975-77, Broward Community Coll., 1976-77, Coll. Boca Raton, 1977-78. Author: Florida Consumer Fraud Laws: A Compilation; (with others) Organized Crime Desk Book for Florida Prosecutors. Recipient Ft. Lauderdale Police Dept. commendation, 1974. Mem. ABA (jud. qualifications com. 1984-85), N.Y. State Bar Assn., D.C. Bar Assn., Nat. Dist. Attys. Assn., Am. Judicature Soc., Assn. Trial Lawyers Am., Acad. Fla. Trial Lawyers. Democrat. Roman Catholic. Criminal, State civil litigation, Legal education. Office: 1500 E Atlantic Blvd Pompano Beach FL 33060

MONTEE-CHAREST, KAREN ANN, legal historian; b. Montclair, N.J., May 15, 1957; d. Bobby Dean and Barbara Joyce (Thatcher) Montee; m. Stephen Glenn Charest, Aug. 14, 1982. BA, U. Nebr., 1979, JD, 1982. Bar: Nebr. 1982, U.S. Dist. Ct. Nebr. 1982, Ariz. 1984. Assoc. Elsken Law Offices, Lincoln, Nebr., 1984; ptnr. Elsken & Montee-Charest, Lincoln, 1985-86; grad. asst. dept. history U. Nebr., 1986—; adj. faculty Chapman Coll., Tucson, 1983-84; adj. prof. history and bus. law Park Coll., Tucson, 1983-84. Omaha Lawyers Wives' grantee, 1981; Mildred F. Thompson fellow, 1985-86. Mem. ABA, Nebr. Bar Assn., Ariz. Bar Assn., Am. Judicature Soc. Democrat. Roman Catholic. Avocations: photography, aerobics, drawing, reading. Legal history, General practice, Bankruptcy.

MONTEITH, ROBERT ALEXANDER, lawyer; b. Waterloo, Iowa, Feb. 7, 1952; s. Arnold Purdy and Virginia (Gould) M.; m. Ann Elizabeth Conorer, Aug. 18, 1979; children: Terry, Kevin. AA, Aims Community Coll., 1972; BA, U. N.C., 1975; JD, U. Wyoming, 1981. Bar: Wyo. 1981, U.S. Dist. Ct. Wyo. 1981, U.S. Ct. Appeals (10th cir.) 1982. Assoc. Russell, Greenhaw & Rummel, Casper, Wyo., 1980-82, Boynton & Monteith, Casper, 1982-85; sole practice Casper, 1985, 86—; ptnr. Monteith, Raymond & Brown P.C., Casper, 1986; lectr. bankruptcy various insts. Co-author: Bankruptcy Law Update in Wyoming, 1986; contbr. articles to mags. Press sec. Ostlund for Gov. campaign, Wyo., 1978. Mem. ABA (student liason pub. utility law 1980), Wyo. Bar Assn., Natrona County Bar Assn. Republican. Presbyterian. Avocations: hunting, fishing, boating, carpentry. Office: 246 S Center #101 Casper WY 82601

MONTEVERDE, TOM PETER, lawyer; b. Pitts., May 13, 1927; s. Joseph Earl and Josephine Agnes (Muldowney) M.; m. Catharine Louise Stauffer, Dec. 31, 1955 (dec. Jan. 1960); children: Margaret, Susan.; m. Dorothy S. Steidler, Aug. 11, 1962; children: Dorothy Scullin Kaplan, Robert S. Scullin, Michael E. Scullin. AB, U. Pitts., 1947; JD, Dickinson Sch. Law, 1951. Bar: Pa. 1951, U.S. Dist. Ct. (ea. dist.) Pa. 1952, U.S. Ct. Appeals (3d cir.) 1952, U.S. Supreme Ct. 1977. Assoc. James J. Burns, Jr., Pitts., 1951-55; assoc., then ptnr. Schnader, Harrison, Segal & Lewis, Phila., 1955-70; ptnr. Pelino, Wasserstrom, Chucas & Monteverde, Phila., 1970-77; pres. Monteverde, Hemphill, Maschmeyer & Obert, Phila., 1977—; co-chmn. Dickinson Forum, Carlisle, Pa., 1971-83. vol. lawyer com. for civil rights under law Miss. Program, 1967; lifetime trustee Dickinson Sch. Law, Carlisle, 1977. Served to cpl. U.S. Army, 1944-47, ETO. Mem. ABA, Pa. Bar Assn., Phila. Bar Assn., Phila. Trial Lawyers Assn., Dickinson Sch. Law Alumni Assn. (named outstanding alumnus 1980). Democrat. Roman Catholic. Club: Sky Top (Cresco), Union League; Pa. Soc. Banking, Federal civil litigation, State civil litigation. Home: 220 W Rittenhouse Sq Philadelphia PA 19103 Office: Monteverde Hemphill et al 2230 The Fidelity Bldg 123 S Broad St Philadelphia PA 19109

MONTGOMERIE, BRUCE MITCHELL, lawyer; b. South Bend, Ind., Feb. 9, 1946; s. Ralph H. and Dorothy (Larson) M.; m. Kathleen Ann McIntyre, June 21, 1969 (dissolved); m. Claire Desrosier, Nov. 28, 1985. BA, DePauw U., 1968; JD, MIA, Columbia U., 1972; LLM in Taxation, NYU, 1975. Bar: N.Y. 1973. From assoc. to ptnr. Milbank, Tweed, Hadley & McCloy, N.Y.C., 1972-83; ptnr. Willkie, Farr & Gallagher, N.Y.C., 1983—. Mem. Nat. Assn. Real Estate Investment Trusts (bd. govs. 1983-85). Corporate taxation, Real property. Home: 17 Windabout Dr Greenwich CT 06831 Office: Willkie Farr & Gallagher 153 E 53d St One Citicorp Ctr New York NY 10022

MONTGOMERY, DAVID PAUL, lawyer; b. Boulder City, Nev., May 1, 1953; s. Erwin Bert Montgomery Sr. and Giuliana (Bullo) Schuster; m. Deborah Ann Slisz, Nov. 25, 1972; children: Rebecca, David P. Jr. BA in Polit. Sci. and English, SUNY, Buffalo, 1974; JD, Stetson U., 1977. Bar: Fla. 1977, U.S. Dist. Ct. (mid. dist.) Fla. 1977, U.S. Ct. Appeals (5th cir.) 1977, U.S. Supreme Ct. 1980, U.S. Ct. Appeals (11th cir.) 1981. Law clk. to sr. judge Fla. Ct. Appeals (2d dist.), Lakeland, 1977-78; assoc. Mann & Fay,

Chartered, Bradenton, 1978-79; ptnr. Staab & Montgomery, Bradenton, 1979-81; sole practice Bradenton, 1981-82; sr. ptnr. Montgomery, Murrell & Boles, Chartered, Bradenton, 1982—; adj. prof. law Manatee Community Coll., Bradenton, 1982—. Author: (weekly article) The Manateean, 1983; editor: Internal Operations Manual 2d Dist. Ct. Appeals, 1978. Pres. Manatee Solve, Inc., Bradenton, 1980-81; mem. bd. zoning appeals Manatee County, Bradenton, 1983—, chmn. charter study com., 1984. Mem. Am. Jurisprudence Soc., Assn. Trial Lawyers Am., ABA, Fla. Bar Assn. (real property sect., spl. counsel unauthorized practice of law 1984, condominium com. 1985—). Democrat. Roman Catholic. Lodges: Lions (v.p. 1982, 85, 86), Sertoma, Moose, KC (adv. 1980-84). Avocation: bass fishing. Personal injury, Real property, State civil litigation. Office: Montgomery Murrell & Boles 2103 Manatee Ave W Bradenton FL 33529

MONTGOMERY, JOHN VINCENT, lawyer, small business owner; b. Lemmon, S.D., Oct. 22, 1947; s. Harry and Helen (Payne) M.; m. Ann D. Olsen; children: Molly, Meg. BA, U. Kans., 1970; JD, U. Minn., 1974. Bar: Minn. 1974, U.S. Dist. Ct. Minn. 1976, U.S. Ct. Appeals (8th cir.) 1976, U.S. Supreme Ct. 1978. Staff atty. Walter F. Mondale, Washington, 1974-76; asst. pub. defender Hennepin County, Mpls., 1976-79; owner Little Falls and Princeton, Minn., 1979—. Mem. ABA, Minn. Bar Assn., Nat. Assn. Broadcasters. General corporate, Federal communications commission. Home: 3843 Hubbard Ave N Minneapolis MN 55422

MONTGOMERY, JOHN WARWICK, legal educator, theologian; b. Warsaw, N.Y., Oct. 18, 1931; s. Maurice Warwick and Harriet (Smith) M.; m. Joyce Ann Bailer, Aug. 14, 1954; children—Elizabeth Ann, David Warwick, Catherine Ann. A.B. in Philosophy with distinction, Cornell U., 1952; B.L.S., U. Calif., Berkeley, 1954, M.A., 1958; B.D., Wittenberg U., 1958, M.S.T., 1960; Ph.D., U. Chgo., 1962; Docteur de l'Université, mention Théologie Protestante, U. Strasbourg, France, 1964; LLB, LaSalle Extension U., 1977; diplôme cum laude, Internat. Inst. Human Rights, Strasbourg, 1978; M. Phil. in Law, U. Essex, Eng., 1983. Bar: Va. 1978, Calif. 1979, D.C. 1985, U.S. Supreme Ct. 1981, Eng. 1984; cert. law librarian; diplomate Med. Library Assn.; ordained to Ministry Lutheran Ch., 1958. Librarian, gen. reference service U. Calif. Library, Berkeley, 1954-55; instr. Bibl. Hebrew, Hellenistic Greek, Medieval Latin Wittenberg U., Springfield, Ohio, 1956-59; head librarian, mem. federated theol. faculty Swift Library Div. and Philosophy, U. Chgo., 1959-60; assoc. prof., chmn. dept. history Waterloo Luth. U. (now Sir Wilfred Laurier U.), Ont., Can., 1960-64; prof., chmn. div. ch. history, history of Christian thought, dir. European Seminar program Trinity Evang. Div. Sch., Deerfield, Ill., 1964-74; prof. law and theology Internat. Sch. Law (now George Mason U. Sch. Law), Washington, 1974-75; theol. cons. Christian Legal Soc., 1975-76; dir. studies Internat. Inst. Human Rights, Strasbourg, France, 1979-81; dean, prof. jurisprudence, dir. European program Simon Greenleaf Sch. Law, Anaheim, Calif., 1980—; vis. prof. Concordia Theol. Sem., Springfield, Ill., 1964-67, DePaul U., Chgo., 1967-70; hon. fellow Revelle Coll., U. Calif., San Diego, 1970; rector Freie Fakultaten Hamburg, Federal Republic Germany, 1981-82; participant Cons. on Evang. Concerns, Colorado Springs, 1965, numerous other invitational functions. Author: The Writing of Research Papers in Theology, 1959; A Union List of Serial Publications in Chicago Area Protestant Theological Libraries, 1960; A Seventeenth-Century View of European Libraries, 1962; Chytraeus on Sacrifice: A Reformation Treatise in Biblical Theology, 1962; The Shape of the Past: An Introduction to Philiosophical Historiography, 1962, rev. edition, 1975; The Is God Dead Controversy, 1966; (with Thomas J.J. Altizer) The Altizer-Montgomery Dialogue, 1967: Crisis in Lutheran Theology, 2 vols., 1967, rev. edit., 1973; Es confiable el Christianismo?, 1968; Ecumenicity, Evangelicals, and Rome, 1969; Where is History Going?, 1969; History & Christianity, 1970; Damned Through the Church, 1970; The Suicide of Christian Theology, 1970; Computers, Cultural Change and the Christ, 1970; In Defense of Martin Luther, 1970; La Mort de Dieu, 1971; (with Joseph Fletcher) Situation Ethics: True or False?, 1972; The Quest for Noah's Ark, 1972, rev. edit., 1974; Verdammt durch die Kirche, 1973; Christianity for the Toughminded, 1973; Cross and Crucible, 2 vols., 1973; Principalities and Powers: The World of the Occult, 1973, rev. edit., 1975; How Do We Know There is a God?, 1973; Myth, Allegory and Gospel, 1974; The Inerrant Word of God, 1974; Jurisprudence: A Book of Readings, 2d edit., 1980; The Law Above the Law, 1975; Cómo Sabemos Que Hay un Dios?; 1975; Demon Possession, 1975; The Shaping of America,11976; Faith Founded on Fact, 1978; Law and Gospel: A Study in Jurisprudence, 1978; Slaughter of the Innocents, 1981; the Marxist Approach to Human Rights: Analysis & Critique, 1984; Human Rights and Human Dignity, 1986. Editor: Lippincott's Evangelical Perspectives, 7 vols., 1970-72; International Scholars Directory, 1973. Editor-at large: Christianity Today, 1965-83. Films: Is Christianity Credible?, 1968; In Search of Noah's Ark, 1977; (videocassettes) Defending the Biblical Gospel, 1985. Contbr. articles to acad., theol., legal jours., chpts. to books. Nat. Luth. Ednl. Conf. fellow, 1959-60; Can. Council postdoctoral sr. research fellow, 1963-64; Am. Assn. Theol. Schs. faculty fellow, 1967-68. Fellow Académie de Gastronomie Brillat-Savarin (Paris); Victoria Inst. (London), Am. Sci. Affiliation (nat. philosophy sci. and history sci. commn. 1966-70); mem. World Assn. Law Profs., Am. Soc. Internat. Law, ABA, Internat. Bar Assn., Calif. Bar Assn. (human rights commn. 1980-83), Union Internat. des Avocats, Nat. Assn. Realtors, Tolkien Soc. Am., N.Y. C.S. Lewis Soc., Am. Hist. Assn., Soc. Reformation Research, Creation Research Soc., Luth. Acad. for Scholarship, Tyndale Fellowship (Eng.), Am. Theol. Library Assn., Bibliog. Soc. U. Va., Evang. Theol. Soc., Middle Temple and Lincoln's Inn (barrister mem.), Internat. Wine and Food Soc., Société des Amis des Arts (Strasbourg), Chaîne des Rôtisseurs (chevalier), Wig & Pen (London), Ordre du St.-Sépulcre Byzantin (commandeur), Phi Beta Kappa, Phi Kappa Phi, Beta Phi Mu. Public international, Jurisprudence, Legal education. Address: 1 rue de Palerme, Strasbourg France 67000 also: 2530 Shadow Ridge Ln Orange CA 92667 also: Flat 9, 4 Crane Ct, Fleet St, London England C4

MONTGOMERY, JOSEPH TUCKER, lawyer, physician; b. Knoxville, Tenn., July 15, 1946; s. John Lee and Agnes (Tucker) M.; m. Joyce Ellen Nicoll; children: Josh, Rachel, Larkin, Nic. BS, U. Tenn., Knoxville, 1969, JD, 1973; MD, U. Tenn., Memphis, 1972. Bar: Tenn. 1977, U.S. Dist. Ct. (ea. dist.) Tenn. 1977. Resident in family practice U. Tenn. Med. Ctr., Koxville, 1973-75; physician, dir. emergency dept. Erlanger Hosp., Chattanooga, 1975-77; physician Knoxville Emergency Physicians Group, 1977-82, Southeastern Emergency Partnership, Knoxville, 1982—; ptnr. Hogin, London, Montgomery, Knoxville, 1982—. Fellow Am. Coll. Legal Medicine, Am. Coll. Emergency Physicians; mem. AMA, Knoxville Acad. Medicine, Tenn. Med. Assn., Knoxville Bar Assn., Tenn. Bar Assn. Personal injury, Insurance. Home: 520 Dixon Rd Knoxville TN 37922 Office: Hogin London Montgomery 1716 Clinch Ave Knoxville TN 37916

MONTGOMERY, KENNETH FLOYD, lawyer; b. Apalachicola, Fla., Apr. 15, 1903; s. William H. and Henrietta (Pohlmann) M.; m. Lucile Hassell Harris, Apr. 17, 1947; m. 2d Harle Garth, June 23, 1973; children—Henrietta Montgomery Heydon, Kenneth H. A.B., Dartmouth Coll., 1925, D.H.L. (hon.); J.D., Harvard U., 1928; D.H.L. (hon.) Columbia Coll., Miles Coll. Bar. Ill. With Wilson & McIlvaine, Chgo., 1928—, ptnr., 1940—, of counsel; dir. Seaway Nat. Bank. Bd. dirs. Rush-Presbyterian-St. Luke's Hosp.; trustee Lake Forest Coll., Art Inst. Chgo.; bd. visitors Stanford U. Law Sch., U. Chgo. Law Sch. Mem. ABA, Ill. Bar Assn., Chgo. Bar Assn., Harvard Law Soc. (dir.). Clubs: Univ., Glen View Country, Attic, Legal, Law, Commonwealth, Chgo. Com. General practice.

MONTGOMERY, ROBERT CORNELIUS, III, lawyer; b. Stamford, Conn., Nov. 22, 1952; s. Robert Cornelius Jr. and Jane (Aldridge) M.; m. Josette Marie Casalnuovo, Aug. 25, 1984. BA, Colgate U., 1978; JD, MBA, Harvard U., 1982. Bar: Colo. 1982, U.S. Dist. Ct. Colo. 1982. Assoc. Parcel, Meyer, Schwartz, Ruttum & Mauro, P.C., Denver, 1982-85, Krendl & Krendl P.C., Denver, 1985-86, Ducker, Gurko & Roble, P.C., Denver, 1986—. Served to q.m. 2d class USN, 1971-74. Mem. ABA, Colo. Bar Assn., Denver Bar Assn., Phi Beta Kappa. Democrat. Presbyterian. Avocations: skiing, golf, computers. General corporate, Contracts commercial, Real property. Home: 57 1/2 S Pearl St Denver CO 80209

MONTGOMERY, ROBERT H., JR., lawyer; b. Kingsport, Tenn., Sept. 24, 1953; s. Robert H. Sr. and Ruth (Cline) M. BA, Vanderbilt U., 1975; JD, U. Tenn., 1979. Bar: Tenn. 1979, U.S. Dist. Ct. (ea. dist.) Tenn. 1980. Assoc. Hunter, Smith & Davis, Kingsport, 1979-82; atty. Tenn. Printing Co., Kingsport, 1982-86; assoc. Donelson, Stokes & Bartholomew, Kingsport and Nashville, Tenn., 1985-87; asst. dist. atty. Sullivan County, Tenn., 1987—. Pres. Kingsport Vanderbilt Club, 1983-86, Vol. Kingsport, 1984-85; vice chmn. Kingsport Pub. Library, 1985—; bd. dirs. Sullivan County Reps., 1981—. Named one of Outstanding Young Men of Am., 1984, 85, 86. Mem. ABA, Tenn. Bar Assn. (bd. dirs. young lawyers div. 1981—), Kingsport Bar Assn., Kingsport Jaycees (pres. 1985-86, Young Man of Yr. award 1985). Methodist. General corporate, Real property, Probate. Home: 3433 Park Cliffe Dr Kingsport TN 37664 Office: Office of Dist Atty Gen Main St Blountville TN 37617

MONTGOMERY, ROBERT MOREL, JR., lawyer; b. Birmingham, Ala., June 9, 1930; 2. Robert Morel and Ella Bernice (Smith) M.; m. Mary Lemerle McKenzie, Mar. 6, 1953; children—Scott McKenzie, Courtnay Elizabeth. B.S., U. Ala., 1952; LL.B., U. Fla., 1957. Bar: Fla. 1957; diplomate Acad. Fla. Trial Lawyers. Pres. Montgomery, Searcy & Denney, P.A., West Palm Beach, Fla; dir. First Am. Bank; lectr. continuing edn. of bar Fla. Bar.; civil trial adv. Nat. Bd. Trial Advocacy. Mem. adminstrv. bd., pres. Palm Beach Opera; bd. dirs. Goodwill Industries. Served as 1st lt. AUS, 1952-54. Mem. ABA, Palm Beach County Bar Assn., Trial Lawyers Assn. Am., Fla. Bd. Civil Trial Lawyers (inner circle advs.). Federal civil litigation, State civil litigation, Personal injury. Home: 2273 Ibis Isle Rd Palm Beach FL 33480 Office: PO Drawer 3626 West Palm Beach FL 33402

MONTGOMERY, THOMAS CHARLES, lawyer; b. Celina, Ohio, Mar. 22, 1955; s. Don W. Montgomery and Barbara S. (Sibbitt) Weirich. BA, DePauw U., 1977; JD, Ohio State U., 1980. Bar: Ohio 1980. Staff atty. Ohio Rehab. Services Commn., Columbus, Ohio, 1981; legis. counsel U.S. Rep. Michael G. Oxley, Washington, 1981-85, legis. dir., 1985-86; corp. counsel, sec. Celina Ins. Group, Celina, 1986—; bd. dirs. Buckeye Reinsurance Co., Ltd., Hamilton, Bermuda, Republic Mut. Ins. Co., Celina, Celina Mutual Ins., Nat. Mut. Ins. Co., Patrons Mut. Ins. Co., Nat. Term LIfe Ins. Co., First Nat. Indemnity Co., Congregation Ins. Co., Midwest Data Systems Inc., Nat. Tech. Services, First Ohio Fin. Corp. Mem. ABA, Ohio Bar Assn., Am. Performance Horse Assn. Inc. Republican. Methodist. Lodge: Lions. Avocations: running, weightlifting. General corporate, Insurance, Legislative. Home: 8250 State Rt 703 E Box 8 Celina OH 45882 Office: Celina Group One Ins Sq Celina OH 45882

MONTI, RENARD GEORGE, lawyer; b. Arlington, Va., Sept. 8, 1950; s. Renard R. and Julie (Skorich) M.; m. Lois L. Tafaro, Sept. 17, 1977; children: Julie, Robert. BA, U. Va., 1972; JD, NYU, 1979. Bar: N.J. 1979. Assoc. Stryker, Tams & Dill, Newark, 1979-82; asst. v.p., assoc. Crum & Forster Corp., Morristown, N.J., 1982-86; gen. counsel, sec. Mercantile and Gen. Reins. Co. of Am., Morristown, 1986—. Democrat. Roman Catholic. Club: Tostamasters (Morristown) (edn. v.p.). General corporate, Computer, Insurance. Home: 199 Watchung Ave Chatham NJ 07928 Office: Mercantile and Gen Reins Co Am 310 Madison Ave Morristown NJ 07960

MONTJOY, RICHARD WILSON, II, lawyer; b. Greenwood, Miss., Oct. 15, 1953; s. Paul Dyche and Dorothy (Sabin) M.; m. Stephanie Lynn Cooke, June 15, 1985. BA, U. Miss., 1975, JD, 1978. Bar: Miss. 1978, U.S. Dist. Ct. (no. and so. dists.) Miss. 1978, U.S. Ct. Appeals (5th cir.) 1978, U.S. Supreme Ct. 1984. Ptnr. Brunini, Grantham, Grower & Hewes, Jackson, Miss., 1978—. Articles editor U. Miss. Law Rev., 1977-78. Mem. ABA (young lawyers div., chmn. continuing legal edn. bd. 1985-87), Miss. Bar Assn. (bd. dirs. young lawyers sect. 1986—), Jackson Young Lawyer Assn. Inc. (bd. dirs. 1980-82, treas. 1984-85, sec. 1985-86, pres. elect 1986-87, pres. 1987-88), Hinds County Bar Assn. (bd. dirs. 1987—), Omicrom Delta Kappa, Phi Kappa Phi. Episcopalian. Avocations: golf, travel. Oil and gas leasing, Federal civil litigation, State civil litigation. Home: 2218 Sheffield Dr Jackson MS 39211 Office: Brunini Grantham Grower & Hewes 1400 Trustmark Bank Bldg Jackson MS 39201

MONTROSS, W. SCOTT, lawyer; b. Milw., Apr. 16, 1947; s. William Phillips and Gay (Altenhofen) M.; m. Janice Townsend, May 25, 1968; children—Eric, Christine. B.B.A., U. Mich., 1969; J.D., Ind. U., 1971. Bar: Ind. 1971, U.S. Dist. Ct. (so. dist.) Ind. 1971, U.S. Ct. Appeals (7th cir.) 1973, U.S. Dist. Ct. (so. dist.) Wis. 1978, U.S. Dist. Ct. (so. dist.) Ohio 1983. Assoc., Townsend, Hovde & Townsend, Indpls., 1971-76, ptnr. Townsend, Hovde, Townsend & Montross, Indpls., 1976-84; ptnr. Townsend, Hovde and Montross, 1984—. Contbr. articles to profl. jours. Fellow Indpls. Bar Found.; mem. Assn. Trial Lawyers Am., ABA, Am. Bd. Trial Advocates, Am. Judicature Soc., Am. Assn. Automotive Medicine, Am. Arbitration Assn., Ind. Trial Lawyers Assn. (bd. dirs. 1981—, treas. 1984, sec. 1985, 1st v.p., 1986, pres.-elect 1987). Republican. Clubs: Columbia, Crooked Stick. State civil litigation, Federal civil litigation, Personal injury. Office: Townsend Hovde & Montross 230 E Ohio St Indianapolis IN 46204

MOODY, JAMES SHELTON, JR., lawyer; b. Tampa, Fla., Mar. 31, 1947; s. James Shelton and Irma (Cone) M.; m. Carol Still, June 19, 1971; children: Ashley Brooke, James Shelton III, Patricia Noel. BS, BA, U. Fla., 1969, JD, 1972. Bar: Fla. 1972, U.S. Dist. Ct. (mid. dist.) Fla. 1972; CPA, Fla. Ptnr., officer Trinkle, Redman, Moody & Swanson P.A., Plant City, Fla., 1972—; bd. dirs. Hillsboro Sun Bank, Plant City. Chmn. profl. div. United Fund and Cancer Soc., East Hillsborough County; mem. Plant City Arts Council, 1974—, Plant City East Hillsborough Hist. Soc., 1983—, Hillsborough County Law Library com., 1978-85, chmn., 1983-85. Named one of Outstanding Young Men Am., U.S. Jaycees, 1982. Mem. ABA, Fla. Bar Assn. (jurisprudence com. 1975, vice-chmn. 1976, chmn. 1977, atty.'s fees com. 1978, vice-chmn. 1979, chmn. 1980-81, annual meeting com. 1978, chmn. legal runaround com. 1982—), Hillsborough County Bar Assn. (bd. dirs. 1983—, v.p./pres. elect 1986—, pres. 1986—, office study com., meml. service com., picnic com., social com., law week com., medical-legal com. 1982, chmn. law library com. 1980-83, bd. dirs. 1983—), Assn. Trial Lawyers Am., Fla. Trial Lawyers Assn., Order of Coif, Phi Kappa Phi, Beta Gamma Sigma, Omicron Delta Kappa. Democrat. Presbyterian. Lodge: Lions (past pres., past bd. dirs., past v.p., past tail twister and program dir. Plant City club, Golden Chain award 1980-82, 100% Pres. award 1981). Federal civil litigation, State civil litigation, Personal injury. Home: 2202 Country Club Ct Plant City FL 33566 Office: Trinkle Redman Moody & Swanson PA 121 N Collins St PO Box TT Plant City FL 34289-9040

MOODY, JAMES SHELTON, SR., former state legislator, circuit judge; b. Plant City, Fla., Dec. 29, 1914; s. Thomas Edwin and Anna Louise (Herron) M.; m. Irma Cone, Nov. 29, 1939; children: Carole, James Shelton Jr., William Cone. BS, U. Fla., 1936, JD with honors, 1939. Bar: Fla. Ptnr. Trinkle and Moody, Plant City, 1939-57; asst. county atty. Hillsborough County, Tampa, Fla., 1941-57, presiding judge, 1966-67; mem. House of Reps. State of Fla., Tallahassee, 1948-57, chmn. appropriations com., 1951-57, law clk. to presiding judge, 1963-65, mem. judicial qualifications com., 1969-75; sr. trust officer, bd. dirs. Hillsboro Bank, Plant City, 1977—; chmn. Conf. of Cir. Judges of Fla., 1970; dir. emeritus Sunshine State Fed. Scoutmaster Boy Scouts of U.S., Plant City, 1940-70, mem. exec. bd. Gulf Ridge council; deacon, elder, supt. First Presbyn. Ch., Plant City; bd. dirs. Strawberry Festival Assn. Served with U.S. Army, 1943-46, ETO. Mem. Fla. Bar Assn., Hillsborough Bar Assn., Fla. State Ret. Judge's Assn., Am. Legion, Phi Kappa Alpha (past pres.), Phi Delta Phi, Phi Kappa Phi. Democrat. Club: Walden Lake Country (bd. govs.). Lodge: Elks. Avocations: fishing, hunting, golf. Home: 803 N Collins St Plant City FL 33566

MOODY, JAMES T(YNE), federal judge; b. LaCenter, Ky., June 16, 1938; s. Harold B. and Dorothy M. (Simmons) M.; m. Kay A. Gillett, Dec. 26, 1960; children: Patrick, Jeffrey, Timothy, Kathleen. B.A., Ind. U., 1960, J.D., 1963. Bar: Ind. 1963, U.S. Dist. Ct. (no. and so. dists.) Ind. 1963, U.S. Supreme Ct. 1972. City atty. Cities of Hobart and Lake Station, Ind., 1963-73; sole practice Hobart, 1963-73; judge Lake County Superior Ct., Ind., 1973-79; magistrate U.S. Dist. for No. Dist. Ind., 1979-82, judge Hammond div., 1982—; mem. faculty bus. law Ind. U., 1977-80. Mem. ABA, Fed. Bar Assn., Ind. Bar Assn. Republican. Federal civil litigation, Criminal. Office: US Dist Ct 128 Fed Bldg 507 State St Hammond IN 46320 *

MOODY, RALPH E., judge; b. Vance, Ala., Nov. 23, 1915; s. Charles F. and Harriet (Youmans) M.; m. Carolyn R. Krebs, May 9, 1942. LL.D., U. Ala., 1940; grad., Nat. Coll. State Trial Judges, U. Colo., 1964. Bar: Alaska 1948. Atty. War Dept., Alaska Dist. Engrs., Fort Richardson, Alaska, 1946-47; asst. U.S. atty. (Dist. Alaska, 3d div.), 1947-51; atty. gen. Alaska, 1960-62; pvt. practice law Anchorage, 1951-60, city atty., 1951-54; judge Superior Ct. Alaska, 1962-85, presiding judge, 1964-69, 75-81. Mem. adv. bd. Salvation Army; mem. Alaska Senate, 1957-60, Alaska Legis. Council, 1957-60. Served from pvt. to lt. col., Signal Corps AUS, 1940- 46. Mem. ABA, Alaska Bar Assn., Am. Judicature Soc. Democrat. Baptist. Club: Kiwanian. Lodge: Elk. Judicial administration, Criminal, State civil litigation. Home: 1032 Cordova St Anchorage AK 99501

MOODY, WILLARD JAMES, SR., lawyer; b. Franklin, Va., June 16, 1924; s. Willie James and Mary (Bryant) M.; m. Betty Glenn Covert, Aug. 2, 1948; children: Sharon Paige Moody Edwards, Willard J. Jr., Paul Glenn. AB, Old Dominion U., 1946; LLB, U. Richmond, 1952. Bar: Va. 1952. Pres. Moody, Strople & Lawrence Ltd., Portsmouth, Va., 1952—; commr. Chancery, Portsmouth, 1960—, Accounts, 1960—. Del. Va. Ho. of Reps., Portsmouth, 1956-68; senator State of Va., 1968-83; chmn. Portsmouth Dems., 1983—. Recipient Friend of Edn. award Portsmouth Edn. Assn., 1981. Mem. ABA, Va. Bar Assn., Portsmouth-Norfolk County Bar Assn. (pres. 1960-61, lectr. seminars), Va. Trial Lawyers Assn. (pres. 1968-69), Hampton Roads C. of C. (bd. dirs. 1983-86), Portsmouth C. of C. (bd. dirs. 1960-61), Inner Circle Advs., VFW. Club: Cosmopolitan. Lodges: Moose, Elks. Personal injury, Workers' compensation. Home: 120 Riverpoint Crescent Portsmouth VA 23707 Office: Moody Strople & Lawrence Ltd 330 County St Portsmouth VA 23704

MOOG, MARY ANN PIMLEY, lawyer; b. Havre, Mont., May 29, 1952; d. Orville Leonard and Della Mae (Cole) Pimley; m. Daren Russell Moog, Apr. 15, 1978. BS, Mont. State U., 1975; JD, U. Mont., 1981; LLM, NYU, 1983. Bar: Mont. Law clk. Mont. Supreme Ct., Helena, 1981-82; assoc. Bosch, Kuhr, Dugdale, Warner, Martin & Kaze, Havre, 1984—. Recipient Am. Jurisprudence Book award Lawyers Coop. Publ. Co., 1980-81, Tax award Prentice Hall, Inc., 1981, Northwestern Union Trust Co. award, 1981. Mem. ABA, Mont. Bar Assn., 12th Jud. Bar Assn., Phi Delta Phi. Democrat. Roman Catholic. Avocations: sports, arts and crafts. Estate taxation, Personal income taxation, Estate planning. Home: 925 Wilson Havre MT 59501 Office: Bosch Kuhr et al PO Box 7152 Havre MT 59501

MOOMJIAN, CARY AVEDIS, JR., lawyer, drilling executive; b. Albany, N.Y., June 8, 1947; s. Cary A. and Ruth (Michael) M.; m. Laurian Sue Ingram, Aug. 11, 1984; 1 child, Chad Andrew. BA, Occidental Coll., 1969; JD, Duke U., 1972. Bar: Calif. 1972, U.S. Dist. Ct. (cen. dist.) Calif. 1972. Assoc. McCutcheon, Black et al., Los Angeles, 1972-76; counsel, v.p., dir. Santa Fe Drilling Co., Alhambra, Calif., 1976—. Chmn. Santa Fe Internat. Corp. Polit. Action Com., Calif., 1985—. Mem. ABA, Maritime Law Assn. U.S. (proctor), Internat. Assn. Drilling Contractors (dir.), Nat. Ocean Industries Assn., Duke Law Alumni Council (trustee 1984—). Republican. Club: Bicycle (charter) (Bell Gardens, Calif.). Avocations: antique gaming machines, investments. Admiralty, Contract drilling activities. Office: Sante Fe Drilling Co 1000 S Fremont Ave Alhambra CA 91802

MOOMJIAN, GARY THOMAS, lawyer; b. Flushing, N.Y., June 23, 1952; m. Judith A. Schoenwetter, May 22, 1982; children: Jessica, Eric, Justin. BA in Acctg., Queens Coll., Flushing, 1974; JD, NYU, 1977. Bar: N.Y. 1978. Assoc. Wachtell, Lipton, Rosen & Katz, N.Y.C., 1977-81; assoc. Breslow & Walker, N.Y.C., 1981-83, ptnr., 1983—. Editor NYU Law Rev., 1976-77. Mem. ABA, N.Y. State Bar Assn., Order of Coif. Republican. Armenian Orthodox. Securities, General corporate. Office: Breslow & Walker 875 3d Ave New York NY 10022

MOON, JOHN PAUL, lawyer; b. Honolulu, May 1, 1947; s. Daniel D.S. and Violet K. Moon; m. Frances Avison, Apr. 23, 1983. BA, U. Puget Sound, 1969; JD, Willamette U., 1972. Bar: Hawaii 1972, U.S. Dist. Ct. Hawaii 1972, U.S. Ct. Appeals (9th cir) 1974. Law clk. Supreme Ct. Hawaii, Honolulu, 1972-73; dep. prosecutor City and County of Honolulu, 1973-74; assoc. Anthony, Hoddick, Reinwald & O'Connor, Honolulu, 1974-76; ptnr. Hoddick, Reinwald, O'Connor & Marrick, Honolulu, 1976-80; sr. ptnr. Ezra, O'Connor, Moon & Tam, Honolulu, 1980—; mem. Hawaii Bd. Bar Examiners, Honolulu, 1981—; lectr. Bank of Hawaii, Honolulu, 1984-85. Assoc. editor Willamette Law Rev., 1972. Chmn. Hawaii Dem. Conv., Honolulu, 1980; mem. Bd. Veterinary Examiners, Honolulu, 1980-84. Reginald Heber Smith scholar Willamette u. Coll. Law, 1972. Mem. ABA, Hawaii Bar Assn., Delta Theta Phi, Theta Chi. Banking, Consumer commercial, General corporate. Office: Ezra O'Connor Moon & Tam 220 S King St 20th Floor Honolulu HI 96813

MOONEY, CHARLES W., JR., law educator; b. Shawnee, Okla., Aug. 13, 1947; s. Charles W. and Mary Jane (Jones) M.; m. Christina Eager Anderson, Dec. 31, 1973; children: Mia Elizabeth, Natasha Lea. BA with high honors, U. Okla., 1969; JD cum laude, Harvard U., 1972. Bar: Okla. 1972, U.S. Dist. Ct. (we. dist.) Okla. 1972, N.Y. 1982, U.S. Ct. Appeals (10th cir.) 1973. Assoc. Crowe & Dunlevy, Oklahoma City, 1972-77, ptnr., 1977-81; ptnr. Shearman & Sterling, N.Y.C., 1981-86; assoc. prof. law U. Pa., Phila., 1986—; assoc. bar examiner Okla. Bd. Examiners, Oklahoma City, 1978-81; del. U.S. Dept. State Internat. Inst. for Unification of Pvt. Internat. Law, Conv. on Internat. Fin. Leasing, Rome, 1986—. Contbr. articles to profl. jours. Mem. ABA (mem. council corp. banking and bus. law sect. 1987—, chmn. on uniform comml. code corp. banking and bus. law sect. 1982-87), Okla. Bar Assn., N.Y. State Bar Assn., Assn. of Bar of City of N.Y., Am. Law Inst. (ABA com. on continuing profl. edn., uniform comml. code adv. group, advisor to permanent edit. bd. for uniform comml. code 1987—), Phi Beta Kappa. Republican. Contracts commercial, Legal education, Private international. Office: U Pa Law Sch 3400 Chestnut St Philadelphia PA 19104

MOONEY, JEROME HENRI, lawyer; b. Salt Lake City, Aug. 7, 1944; s. Jerome Henri and Bonnie (Shepard) M.; m. Carolyn Lasrich, Aug. 10, 1965 (div. Dec. 1978); 1 child, Dierdre Nicole; m. Catherine Lee, May 3, 1986. BS, U. Utah, 1966, JD, 1972. Bar: Utah 1972, U.S. Ct. Appeals (10th cir.) 1974, U.S. Supreme 1984. Sole practice Salt Lake City, 1972-75, 79-83; sr. ptnr. Mooney, Jorgenson & Nakamura, Salt Lake City, 1975-78, Mooney & Smith, Salt Lake City, 1983—; bd. dirs. Mooney Real Estate, Salt Lake City. Mem. Gov.'s Council on Vet. Affairs, Salt Lake City, 1982—; trustee Project Realty, Salt Lake City, 1976—. Served to capt. U.S. Army, 1966-69, Vietnam, col. Utah NG, 1969—. Mem. ABA, Utah Bar Assn., Utah NG Assn. (trustee 1976), 1st Amendment Lawyers Assn. (v.p. 1966-69, 86—), VFW. Democrat. Jewish. Avocations: skiing. Real property, Entertainment, Criminal. Home: 128 I St Salt Lake City UT 84103 Office: Mooney & Smith 236 S 300 E Salt Lake City UT 84111

MOORE, ANDREW GIVEN TOBIAS, II, state supreme court justice; b. New Orleans, Nov. 25, 1935; m. Ann Elizabeth Dawson, June 5, 1965; children—Cecily Elizabeth, Marianne Dawson. B.B.A., Tulane U., 1958, J.D., 1960. Bar: La. 1960, Del. 1963. Law clk. to chief justice Del. Dover, 1963; assoc. firm Killoran & Van Brunt, Wilmington, Del., 1964-70; partner Killoran & Van Brunt, 1971-76; partner firm Connolly, Bove & Lodge, Wilmington, 1976-82; justice Del. Supreme Ct., Wilmington, 1982—; mem. Del. Bd. Accountancy, 1965-72, Del. Bd. Bar Examiners, 1975-82, Del. Jud. Selection Commn., 1977-82; mem. law com. Del. Gen. Corp., 1969-83; chmn. joint com. Del. Bar Assn.-Del. Bankers Assn., 1978-79; Chmn. Del. Jud. Proprieties Com., 1983—; trustee Del. Bar Found., 1984—. Trustee Del. Home and Hosp. for Chronically Ill., Smyrna, 1966-70, chmn., 1966-69; mem. New Castle County Hist. Rev. Bd., Wilmington, 1974-82; bd. visitors Walter F. George Sch. Law, Mercer U., 1985—. Served with Judge Adv. Gen. Dept. USAF, 1960-63. Mem. ABA, La. Bar Assn., Del. Bar Assn. (v.p. 1976-77, exec. com. 1982-83), Am. Judicature Soc. (bd. dirs. 1982-86), Order Barristers, Phi Delta Phi, Delta Theta Phi (hon.), Omicron Delta Kappa. Democrat. Presbyterian. Home: 11 Red Oak Rd Wilmington DE 19806 Office: Chambers of the Supreme Court 820 N French St Wilmington DE 19801

MOORE, CHARLES DUDLEY, JR., lawyer; b. Lexington, Ky., Aug. 27, 1946; s. Charles Dudley and Harriett Emily (Glascock) M.; m. Harriet Ellen Bowers, May 18, 1968; children: Jennifer Ellen, Emily Katherine, Zachary Charles. BSCE, U. Ky., 1969, JD, 1974. Bar: Ky. 1974, U.S. Dist. Ct. (ea. dist.) Ky. 1981. Civil engr. Ky. Transp. Cabinet, Lexington, 1968-74; legal counsel Ky. Transp. Cabinet, Frankfort, 1978-81, atty., 1981-82, atty. supr.,

1982-85, asst. gen. counsel, 1985—. Served with USAR. Mem. ABA, Franklin County Bar Assn., State Govt. Bar Assn., Ky. Assn. Transp. Engrs. (sec. 1979-81). Democrat. Baptist. Clubs: Bluegrass Striders (bd. dirs. 1985—), Capitol City Racquet (Frankfort) (pres. 1986—). Government contracts and claims, Construction, Administrative and regulatory. Home: 305 Farmbrook Circle Frankfort KY 40601 Office: Commonwealth Ky Transp Cabinet State Office Bldg Office Gen Counsel Frankfort KY 40622

MOORE, DAVID CHARLES, lawyer; b. Bellevue, Iowa, June 14, 1953; s. George Eugene and Lois Eileen (Hueneke) M.; m. Christine Anne Ericksen, July 9, 1977; children: Caroline Signe, Catherine Anne. BA, Luther Coll., 1975; JD, U. Wis., 1978. Bar: Wis. 1978, U.S. Dist. Ct. (we. dist.) Wis. 1978, U.S. Dist. Ct. (ea. dist.) Wis. 1980, U.S. Ct. Appeals (7th cir.) 1983. Assoc. Brennan, Steil, Ryan, Basting & McDougall, S.C., Janesville, Wis., 1978-83, ptnr., 1984; ptnr. Wesner, Fowler & Moore, Janesville, 1985—; lectr. debtor, creditor law U. Wis., Madison, 1984, bankruptcy Blackhawk Tech. Inst., Janesville, 1983—, consumer law U. Wis. Rock County, Janesville, 1983—. Pres. St. John Luth. Ch. Found., Inc., Janesville, 1983—. Mem. Wis. Bar Assn., Rock County Bar Assn. Avocation: basketball official. Consumer commercial, Bankruptcy, Contracts commercial. Home: 67 Campus Ln Janesville WI 53545 Office: Wesner Fowler & Moore 56 S River St Janesville WI 53545

MOORE, DAVID LEWIS, lawyer; b. Astoria, Oreg., May 8, 1943; s. Eugene Steven and Eleanor May (Wheelon) M.; m. Jean, May 6, 1978; children—Christina, Michael, Kathi. B.B.A., U. Oreg., 1966; J.D., Lewis and Clark Coll., 1971. Bar: Oreg., 1971; C.P.A., Oreg. Staff acct. Herzinger Ray Porter & Co., Eugene, Oreg., 1964-67; sr. acct. Haskins & Sells, Portland, Oreg., 1967-68; sr. acct., assoc. atty. Pattullo & Gleason, Portland, 1968-72; assoc. Frohnmayer & Deatherage, Medford, Oreg., 1972-74; sole practice, Medford, 1974—. Mem. ABA, Oreg. Bar, Am. Inst. C.P.A.s., Oreg. Soc. C.P.A.s. General corporate, General practice, Personal income taxation. Office: PO Box 1022 Medford OR 97501

MOORE, DONALD FRANCIS, lawyer; b. N.Y.C., Dec. 14, 1937; s. John F. and Helen A. (McLoughlin) M.; children: Christina M., Marianne, Karen L., Alison A. AB, Fordham U., 1959; JD, St. John's U., Bkyln., N.Y., 1962. Bar: N.Y. 1962, D.C. 1970. Assoc. Paul, Weiss, Rifking, Wharton & Garrison, N.Y.C., 1962-70, ptnr., 1970—. Editor in chief St. John's U. Law Rev., 1962. Served to 1st lt. U.S. Army, 1962-64. Mem. N.Y. State Bar Assn., Assn. of Bar of City of N.Y. Roman Catholic. Avocation: fishing. Pension, profit-sharing, and employee benefits, Probate. Home: 7 Wedgewood Ct Glen Head NY 11545 Office: Paul Weiss Rifkind Wharton & Garrison 1285 Ave of Americas New York NY 10019

MOORE, DOUGLAS MATTHEW, JR., lawyer; b. San Francisco, Apr. 21, 1939; s. Douglas Matthew Sr.and Jean (Kinzie) M.; m. Michael Earle Gardner, Sept. 12, 1965; children: Mary Kinzie, Maisey Shelton. BS, U. Calif., Berkeley, 1961; JD, U. Calif., San Francisco, 1966. From assoc. to ptnr. Sedgwick, Detert, Moran & Arnold, San Francisco, 1967—. Served to capt. USNR, 1961—. Mem. Internat. Assn. Ins. Counsel (exec. com.), Ins. Counsel Trial Acad. (dir. faculty U. Colo. 19826). Club: University. State civil litigation, Federal civil litigation, Insurance. Home: 1 Shanley Ln PO Box 1033 Ross CA 94957 Office: Sedgweick Detert Moran & Arnold One Embarcadero Ctr San Francisco CA 94111

MOORE, ELIZABETH REITZ, lawyer; b. Louisville, Oct. 29, 1952; d. Clifford Lincoln and Louise Henriette (Bussman) Reitz; m. Howard Edgar Moore, May 11, 1975. BA, Lebanon Valley Coll., Annville, Pa., 1974; JD, George Washington U., 1981. Bar: D.C. 1981, U.S. Dist. Ct. D.C. 1982, U.S. Ct. Appeals (D.C. cir.) 1982, U.S. Supreme Ct. 1985. Assoc. Baker & Hostetler, Washington, 1981-85; atty. U.S. Dept. Justice, Washington, 1985—. Mem. ABA, D.C. Bar Assn., Women's Bar Assn. of D.C. Methodist. Banking, Federal civil litigation, Civil rights.

MOORE, GARY ALAN, lawyer; b. Bainbridge, Ga., Apr. 24, 1953; s. Paul Bryan and Daisey Ray (Seale) M.; m. Kathy Hirz, May 19, 1984. BA cum laude, U. South Ala., 1975; JD cum laude, Cumberland Sch. Law, 1978. Bar: U.S. Dist. Ct. (so. dist.) Ala. 1978, U.S. Ct. Appeals (5th cir.) 1979, U.S. Ct. Appeals (11th cir.) 1981. Adminstrv. aide to Senator James B. Allen U.S. Senate, Washington, 1975; ptnr. Shores & Moore, Fairhope, Ala., 1978-83; sole practice Fairhope, 1983—. Mem. Baldwin County Dem. Exec. Com., 1978—. Mem. Ala. Bar Assn., Mobile County Bar Assn., Baldwin County Bar Assn., Assn. Am. Trial Lawyers, Ala. Trial Lawyers Assn. Episcopalian. Club: Fairhope Yacht (bd. govs. 1985-86, vice commodore 1987). Lodge: Rotary (pres. Fairhope chpt. 1984-85). Personal injury, Real property, Consumer commercial. Home and Office: 203 Fairhope Ave Fairhope AL 36532

MOORE, HAROLD FRANCIS, lawyer; b. Jersey City, Apr. 1, 1947; s. Harold J. and Mary K. (Mindrup) M.; m. Mary Ann Roberts, May 30, 1968; children: Melissa Ann, Jennifer Suzanne. BS, Fordham U., 1968, MA, PhD, 1971; JD, Notre Dame U., 1980. Bar: N.J. 1980, U.S. Dist. Ct. N.J. 1980, N.Y. 1981, U.S. Dist. Ct. (so. dist.) N.Y. 1981. Assoc. Milbank, Tweed, Hadley & McCloy, N.Y.C., 1980—. Author: Problems of Philosophy, 1976. Thomas White scholar Notre Dame U., 1978, Glenn Peters scholar Notre Dame U., 1979. General corporate, Banking, Securities. Home: 22 Curtiss Place Maplewood NJ 07040 Office: Milbank Tweed Hadley & McCloy 1 Chase Manhattan Pl New York NY 10005

MOORE, HENRY TRUMBULL, JR., judge; b. El Paso, Tex., Dec. 28, 1932; s. Henry Trumbull and Bonnie (Platt) M.; m. Lynda Doughty, Nov. 8, 1963; stepchildren—Kenneth S. Miller, Laura M. Sauck; 1 child, Michael S. B.A. magna cum laude, U. So. Calif., 1954, J.D., 1957; LL.M., Harvard U., 1958. Bar: Calif. 1957, U.S. Dist. Ct. (cen. dist.) Calif. 1957, U.S. Ct. Appeals (9th cir.) 1967, U.S. Supreme Ct. 1980. Assoc., then ptnr. Moore & Trinkaus, Los Angeles, 1958-62; ptnr. Moore & Moore, Los Angeles, 1962-76; sole practice, Los Angeles, 1976-79, Santa Ana, Calif., 1979-84; judge Calif. Superior Ct., Orange County, Santa Ana, 1984—; of counsel Ward & Heyler, Los Angeles, 1976-79; arbitrator Los Angeles Superior Ct., 1979-82; judge pro tem Los Angeles County Mcpl. Ct., 1979. Pres. Mandeville Canyon Property Owners Assn., 1971, 73; mem. Brentwood-Pacific Palisades Citizens Adv. Com. of Los Angeles Planning Dept., 1971-72. Assoc. editor So. Calif. Law Rev., 1957. Mem. State Bar Calif. (chmn. local adminstrv. com. 1972), Los Angeles County Bar Assn. (chmn. pub. relations com. 1972-74), Westwood Village Bar Assn. (pres. 1968), ABA, Beverly Hills Bar Assn., Orange County Bar Assn., Calif. Judges Assn., Assn. Trial Lawyers Am., Los Angeles Trial Lawyers Assn., Orange County Trial Lawyers Assn., Assn. Bus. Trial Lawyers, Internat. Acad. Law and Sci., Am. Judicature Soc., Phi Beta Kappa, Order of Coif. Republican. Presbyterian. Lodge: Rotary (Newport Beach, Calif.). Judicial administration. Office: Courthouse 700 Civic Center Dr W Santa Ana CA 92702

MOORE, HUGH JACOB, JR., lawyer; b. Norfolk, Va., June 29, 1944; s. Hugh Jacob and Ina Ruth (Hall) M.; B.A., Vanderbilt U., 1966; LL.B., Yale, 1969; m. Jean Garnett, June 10, 1972; children—Lela Miller, Sarah Garnett. Bar: Tenn. 1970, U.S. Dist. Ct. (mid. dist.) Tenn. 1970, U.S. Supreme Ct., 1973, U.S. Ct. Appeals (6th cir.) 1973, U.S. Dist. Ct. (ea. dist.) Tenn. 1973, U.S. Dist. Ct. (we. dist.) Tenn. 1982. Law clk. U.S. Dist. Court (mid. dist.) Tenn., Nashville, 1969-70; asst. U.S. atty., Eastern Dist. of Tenn., Chattanooga, 1973-76; assoc. Witt, Gaither & Whitaker, Chattanooga, 1976-77, partner, 1977—. Mem. bd. dirs. Adult Edn. Council, Chattanooga, 1976-81, pres., 1977-79; bd. dirs. Chattanooga Symphony and Opera Assn., 1981—, Riverbend Festival, 1983-85; Landmarks Chattanooga, 1983-84. Mem. alumni council McCallie Sch., 1980-85; trustee St. Nicholas Sch. 1983—, chmn. 1986—. Mem. ABA (bd. editors jour. 1983—), Tenn. Bar Assn., Chattanooga Bar Assn. (bd. govs. 1985-87). Methodist. Home: 101 Ridgeside Rd Chattanooga TN 37411 Office: Witt Gaither & Whitaker 1100 Am Nat Bank Bldg Chattanooga TN 37402

MOORE, JACQUELINE URSULA, lawyer; b. Palo Alto, Calif., Oct. 23, 1952; d. Ernest Julius and Ursula Susanne Moore; m. Steven R. Dantzker, June 20, 1981. AB, Stanford U., 1974, JD, 1977. Bar: Calif. 1977. Assoc. Morrison & Foerster, San Francisco, 1977-84; v.p., real estate counsel Triton Nat., Danville, Calif., 1984—. Mem. ABA, Bar Assn. San Francisco. Real property. Office: Triton Nat 375 Diablo Rd Suite 200 Danville CA 94526

MOORE, JAMES CLINTON, II, lawyer, data company executive; b. Pueblo, Colo., Aug. 2, 1946; s. James C. and Mary J. (Johnson) M.; m. Ann M. McWilliams, June 21, 1969. BA, Princeton U., 1968; JD, Harvard U., 1971. Bar: Vt. 1972, D.C. 1973, U.S. Dist. Ct. (so. and ea. dists.) N.Y, U.S. Tax Ct., U.S. Supreme Ct. Law clk. to presiding justice U.S. Ct. Appeals (2d cir.), N.Y.C., 1971-72; atty. Watergate com. U.S. Senate, Washington, 1973-74; assoc. Bierbower & Rockefeller, Washington, 1974-76; founding ptnr. Zuckerman, Spaeder et al, Washington, 1976-85; sr. dir. Mead Data Cen. Inc., Miamisburg, Ohio, 1985—. Office: Mead Data Cen Inc 9393 Springboro Pike Miamisburg OH 45342

MOORE, JAMES DALTON, lawyer; b. Danville, Ill., June 3, 1952; s. Harry Dalton and Margaret Katherine (Sandy) M.; m. Diana Kay Parker, Mar. 28, 1981; 1 child, Adam Dalton. BA high distinction, DePauw U., 1974; JD magna cum laude, Ind. U., 1977. Bar: Ind. 1977, U.S. Dist. Ct. (so. dist.) Ind. 1977. Assoc. Barnes, Hickam, Pantzer & Boyd, Indpls., 1977-81; assoc. Ryan, Hartzell & Ryan, Frankfort, Ind., 1981-82, ptnr., 1982—. Asst. articles editor Ind. U. Law Jour., 1976-77. Asst. city atty. Frankfort, 1981-82, city atty., 1983-84; bd. dirs. Frankfort Main St., Inc., 1985—. Recipient William Wallace Carson award Depauw U., 1973. Mem. ABA, Ind. State Bar Assn. (ho. dels. 1983—, ethics subcom. 1982—), Clinton County Bar Assn. (sec. 1983-84, pres. 1984-85), Order of the Coif. Republican. Contracts commercial, Bankruptcy, State civil litigation. Office: Ryan Hartzell Ryan & Moore 257 S Main St Frankfort IN 46041

MOORE, JAMES EVERETT, JR., lawyer; b. Georgetown, Del., July 23, 1950; s. James Everett Sr. and Dorothy (Wilson) M.; m. Deborah Chafin, June 9, 1973; children: Jennifer, Lara, Jaime, J. Everett III (Trey). AA, U. Del., Georgetown, 1970; BA, U. Del., Newark, 1972; JD, Marshall-Wythe Sch. Law, 1975. Bar: D.C. 1976, Del. 1976, U.S. Dist. Ct. Del. 1977. Assoc. Robert C. Wolhar, Jr., Georgetown, 1976; ptnr. Wolhar & Moore, Georgetown, 1976-84; dir. J. Everett Moore, Jr., P.A., Georgetown, 1984-86; ptnr. Moore & Hitchens, P.A., Georgetown, 1986—; issuing agt. Ticor Title, 1st Am. Title, Meridian Title. Pres. Active Young Reps., Sussex County, Del., 1976; chmn. Sussex County Rep. Exec. Com., 1985—. Named one of Outstanding Young Men Am., 1979. Mem. Sussex County Bar Assn., Del. Bar Assn., ABA. Methodist. Lodges: Masons, Elks. Avocations: politics, hunting, fishing. General practice, Real property. Home: RFD 5 Box 22 Georgetown DE 19947 Office: 108 N Bedford St Georgetown DE 19947

MOORE, JAMES M(ACK), JR., lawyer; b. Memphis, Feb. 21, 1945; s. James Mack and Lois Mildred (Norris) M.; m. Janice Lee Mahlman, Sept. 26, 1972; 1 child, Thomas Madison. BS in Engring. Physics, U. Tenn., 1971, JD, 1974. Bar: Tenn. 1974, U.S. Dist. Ct. (ea. dist.) Tenn. 1977, U.S. Ct. Appeals (6th cir.) 1979. Assoc. John H. Little, Livingston, Tenn., 1975-77; ptnr. Milligan and Moore, Knoxville, Tenn., 1977—. Served with U.S. Army, 1967-70, Vietnam. Mem. Am. Trial Lawyers Assn., Tenn. Trial Lawyers Assn., Tenn. Bar Assn., Knoxville Bar Assn. (assoc. program chmn. 1980-81). Club: W. Knoxville Exchange (treas. 1985-86). Federal civil litigation, Workers' compensation, Personal injury. Home: 933 High Springs Rd Knoxville TN 37932 Office: Valley Fidelity Bank Bldg 12th Floor Knoxville TN 37902

MOORE, JANET PATRICIA, lawyer, personnel executive; b. N.Y.C., Mar. 28, 1951; m. Robert J. Mischler Sr., May 19, 1984. BA, Douglass Coll., 1973; JD, Seton Hall U., 1976. Bar: N.J. 1976, U.S. Dist. Ct. N.J. 1976. Assoc. Enright, Porter & Leslie, Bloomfield, N.J., 1977-78; counsel, asst. sec. Integrity Ins. Co., Paramus, N.J., 1979-84; v.p., gen. counsel RJM Fin. Services, Glen Rock, N.J., 1984—; also bd. dirs. RJM Fin. Services, Glen Rock; exec. recruiter Phillips, Majewski & Assocs. Inc., Union, N.J., 1985—; bd. dirs. RJM Premium Contractors Inc., Glen Rock, Expert Resumes Inc., Glen Rock. Mem. ABA, N.J. Bar Assn. Insurance, General corporate, Contracts commercial. Home: 320 S Maple Ave Glen Rock NJ 07452 Office: Phillips Majewski & Assocs Inc 1961 Morris Ave Union NJ 07083

MOORE, JEAN BANTE, lawyer; b. St. Louis, Oct. 26, 1955; d. John Delbert and Mary Garvin (Quinn) Bante; m. Stephen James Moore, Aug. 4, 1979; children—Michelle Marie, Colleen Garvin. B.S. in Bus. Adminstrn., Rockhurst Coll., 1977; J.D., St. Louis U., 1980. Bar: Mo. 1980, U.S. Dist. Ct. (we. dist.) Mo. 1980, U.S. Ct. Appeals (D.C. cir.) 1984. Atty., Union Electric Co., St. Louis, 1980—. Adminstrv. editor St. Louis U. Law Jour., 1979-80. Mem. ABA, Mo. Bar, Bar Assn. St. Louis. Republican. Roman Catholic. Administrative and regulatory, General corporate. Office: Union Electric Co 1901 Gratiot Saint Louis MO 63166

MOORE, JOHN HENRY, II, U.S. judge; b. Atlantic City, Aug. 5, 1929; s. Harry Cordery and Gertrude (Wasleski) M.; m. Joan Claire Kraft, Dec. 29, 1951; children—Deborah Joan, Katherine Louise. Student, Cornell U., 1947; B.S., Syracuse U., 1952; J.D., U. Fla., 1961. Bar: Fla. 1961. Assoc. Fisher & Phillips, Atlanta, 1961; ptnr. Flemming O'Bryan & Fleming, Fort Lauderdale, Fla., 1961-67, Turner, Shaw & Moore, Fort Lauderdale, Fla., 1967; judge 17th Jud. Circuit, Fort Lauderdale, Fla., 1967-77, U.S. Dist. Ct. Appeals for 4th Circuit, West Palm Beach, Fla., 1977-81, U.S. Dist. Ct. for Middle Dist. Fla., Jacksonville, 1981—; mem. Fla. Constitution Revision Com., 1977-78; chmn. Fla. Jud. Qualifications Commn., 1977-81. Bd. dirs. Community Service Council, Fort Lauderdale, 1970-75; pres. Broward County Assn. for Retarded Children, Fort Lauderdale, 1962; hon. bd. trustees Broward Community Coll., Fort Lauderdale, 1970. Served to comdr. USNR, 1948-71, Korea. Named hon. Alumnus Nova U., 1977; recipient cert. of good govt. Gov. of Fla., 1967. Mem. ABA, Fla. Bar Assn., Fed. Bar Assn., Jacksonville Bar Assn., Fla. Conf. Circuit Judges (chmn.-elect 1977), Fla. Blue Key (hon.), U.S. Navy League, Naval Res. Assn., Ret. Officers Assn. Republican. Presbyterian. Clubs: Timuquana Country, Jacksonville Quarterback, Seminole (Jacksonville). Lodge: Rotary. Avocations: golf, tennis, boating. Judicial administration, Federal civil litigation, Criminal. Office: US District Court Middle Dist of Fla 311 W Monroe St Jacksonville FL 32201

MOORE, JOHN L., judge; b. Ortonville, Minn., Sept. 27, 1931; s. Harold L. and Lilian O. (Rudd) M.; m. Carol A. McDonald, Sept. 22, 1956; 1 dau., Mary Kathryn. B.A., Beloit (Wis.) Coll.; J.D., Northwestern U. Bar: Ill. 1957, U.S. Dist. Ct. (no. dist.) Ill. 1958, U.S. Ct. Apls. (7th cir.) 1961. Sole practice, 1957-64; state's atty. County of Ogle, Ill., 1964-68; magistrate 15th Cir., 1968-70, cir. judge, Oregon, Ill., 1970—; mem. faculty State's Atty.'s Law Tng. Assn. Mem. ABA, Ill. Bar Assn. Roman Catholic. State civil litigation, Criminal, Family and matrimonial. Office: PO Box 338 Oregon IL 61061

MOORE, JOHN PORFILIO, federal judge; b. Denver, Oct. 14, 1934; s. Edward Alphonso Porfilio and Caroline (Carbone) Moore; m. Joan West, Aug. 1, 1959 (div. 1983); children—Edward Miles, Joseph Arthur, Jeanne Kathrine; m. Theresa Louise Berger, Dec. 28, 1983; 1 stepchild, Katrina Ann Smith. Student, Stanford U., 1952-54; B.A., U. Denver, 1956, LL.B., 1959. Bar: Colo. 1959, U.S. Supreme Ct. 1965. Asst. atty. gen. State of Colo., Denver, 1962-68, dep. atty. gen., 1968-72, atty. gen., 1972-74; U.S. bankruptcy judge Dist. of Colo., Denver, 1975-82; judge U.S. Dist. Ct. Colo., Denver, 1982-85, U.S. Ct. Appeals for 10th Circuit, Denver, 1985—; instr. Colo. Law Enforcement Acad., Denver, 1965-70, State Patrol Acad., Denver, 1968-70; guest lectr. U. Denver Coll. Law, 1978. Committeeman Arapahoe County Republican Com., Aurora, Colo., 1968; mgr. Dunbar for Atty. Gen., Denver, 1970. Mem. ABA, Colo. Bar Assn., Denver Bar Assn. Roman Catholic. Office: US Courthouse 1929 Stout St Denver CO 80294

MOORE, JULIE E., lawyer; b. San Jose, Calif., May 14, 1957; d. Alan J. and M. Laverne (Galeener) M. BA, U. Calif., Davis, 1978, JD, 1981. Bar: Calif. 1981. Assoc. Law Office of Michael di Leonardo A.P.C., Sunnyvale, Calif., 1981-84, Heisler, Stewart & Daniels Inc., Monterey, Calif., 1984—; sec., bd. dirs. R. Talsorian Games, Aptos, Calif., 1985-86. Mem. Phi Beta Kappa, Phi Kappa Phi, Order of Coif, Delta Phi Alpha. General corporate, Family and matrimonial, Probate. Office: Heisler Stewart & Daniels Inc 563 Figueroa St Monterey CA 93940

MOORE, KATHLEEN ANN, lawyer; b. East St. Louis, Ill., June 23, 1958; s. David Lee and Margaret Ann (Kennedy) M. BA, So. Ill. U., Edwardsville, 1979; JD, St. Louis U., 1981. Bar: Ill. 1982, Mo. 1983, U.S. Dist. Ct. (so. dist.) Ill. 1983, U.S. Supreme Ct. 1985. Ptnr. Cueto, Daley, Williams, Moore & Cueto Ltd, Belleville, Ill., 1982—; guardian ad litem, part-time asst. St. Clair County, Belleville, 1984-85, pub. defender, 1985—. Mem. ABA, Ill. Bar Assn., Ill. Trial Lawyers Assn., Mo. Bar Assn., St. Clair County Bar Assn. Family and matrimonial, Consumer commercial, Personal injury. Office: Cueto Daley Williams Moore & Cueto Ltd 123 W Main St Belleville IL 62220

MOORE, KENNETH CAMERON, lawyer; b. Chgo., Oct. 25, 1947; s. Kenneth Edwards and Margaret Elizabeth (Cameron) M.; m. Karen M. Nelson, June 22, 1974; children—Roger Cameron, Kenneth Nelson. B.A. summa cum laude, Hiram Coll., 1969; J.D. cum laude, Harvard U., 1973. Bar: Ohio 1973, U.S. Dist. Ct. Md. 1974, U.S. Ct. Appeals (4th cir.) 1974, D.C. 1975, U.S. Dist. Ct. (no. dist.) Ohio 1976, U.S. Ct. Appeals (6th cir.) 1977, U.S. Ct. Appeals (D.C. cir.) 1979, U.S. Supreme Ct. 1980. Law clk. to judge U.S. Ct. Appeals, 4th Circuit, Balt., 1973-74; assoc. Squire, Sanders & Dempsey, Washington, 1974-75, Cleve., 1975-82, ptnr., 1982—. Chmn. Jimmy Carter Ohio Fin. Com., 1976; del. Democratic Nat. Conv., 1976; chief legal counsel Ohio Carter-Mondale Campaign, 1976; trustee, mem. com. Cleve. Council World Affairs. Served with AUS, 1970-76. Mem. ABA, Ohio Bar Assn., Greater Cleve. Bar Assn. Club: Cleve. City. Environment, Federal civil litigation, State civil litigation. Home: 15602 Edgewater Dr Lakewood OH 44107 Office: Squire Sanders & Dempsey 1800 Huntington Bldg Cleveland OH 44115

MOORE, KEVIN JOHN, lawyer; b. N.Y.C., Aug. 13, 1956; s. John Seymour and Maxine (Brown) M.; m. Mary Alice Fitzpatrick, May 18, 1985. BA, Drew U., 1978; JD, NYU, 1981. Bar: N.J. 1981, U.S. Dist. Ct. N.J. 1981. Assoc. Jamieson, Moore, Peskin & Spicer, Princeton, N.J., 1981-86, ptnr., 1986—. Participant Fenwick for Senate Campaign, Princeton, 1981. Trustee scholar Drew U., Madison, N.J., 1974-78. Mem. ABA, N.Y. State Bar Assn., N.J. Bar Assn., Mercer County Bar Assn., Princeton Bar Assn. (nominating and contract revision com.), Princeton C. of C. (W. Windsor div., legis. com.), Sigma Phi, Pi Sigma Alpha. Avocations: reading, theatre, art. Real property. Home: 291 Nassau St Princeton NJ 08540 Office: Jamieson Moore Peskin & Spicer 300 Alexander Park Princeton NJ 08543-5276

MOORE, KEVIN MICHAEL, lawyer; b. 1951. BA, Fla. State U.; JD, Fordham U. Bar: Fla. 1976. U.S. atty. no. dist. State of Fla., Tallahassee. Office: 227 N Bronough Street Suite 4014 Tallahassee FL 32301 *

MOORE, LARRY G., lawyer; b. Ogden, Utah, Dec. 11, 1954; s. Lawrence Gale and Ivy (Blalock) M.; married. BA, Brigham Young U., 1977; JD, Columbia U., 1980. Bar: Utah 1980, U.S. Dist. Ct. Utah 1980. Ptnr. Ray, Quinney & Nebeker, Salt Lake City, 1986—; faculty Am. Banker's Inst., 1981-83; lectr. Mortgage Banker's Assn., 1986—. Real property, Banking. Office: Ray Quinney & Nebeker 400 Deseret Bldg Salt Lake City UT 84111

MOORE, LAWRENCE JACK, oil company executive, lawyer; b. Brownwood, Tex., Jan. 24, 1926; s. Lawrence Houston and Lena Emily (Grantham) M.; m. Eloise Camille Dickinson, May 24, 1947; children: John L., James D., Jane E. Moore Horner. Student Howard Payne U., 1946-47, Tarleton State U., 1942-43; LLB, U. Tex., 1949. Bar: Tex. 1949, N.Y. 1980. Sole practice, 1949-57; city atty., Ballinger, Tex., 1950, 55-57; county atty. Runnels County, Tex., 1951-54; atty. Texaco Inc., 1957-70, assoc. gen. counsel, 1970-79; v.p., gen. counsel Caltex Petroleum Corp., Dallas, 1979—; adv. bd. Internat. and Comparative Law Ctr./Internat. Oil and Gas Ctr. of Southwestern Legal Found. Served to cpl. AUS, 1944-46. Mem. ABA, Am. Soc. Internat. Law, Internat. Bar Assn., Internat. Law Assn., State Bar Tex., Dallas Bar Assn., Assn. Bar City N.Y. Republican. Methodist. Clubs: University (N.Y.C.); Country of Darien (Conn.); Northwood, Dallas Petroleum, University (Dallas). Lodge: Masons. Oil and gas leasing, Private international, General corporate. Office: Caltex Petroleum Corp PO Box 619500 Dallas TX 75261-9500

MOORE, LLOYD EVANS, lawyer; b. Columbus, Ohio, Feb. 10, 1931; s. Bascom Sturgill and Julia M. (Martin) M.; m. Marilyn Moore, June 12, 1955; children—William, Erik, Julia. B.A., Ohio State U., 1957, J.D., 1958. Bar: Ohio 1959, U.S. Dist. Ct. (so. dist.) Ohio 1962, U.S. Ct. Appeals (6th cir.) 1962, U.S. Dist. Ct. (ea. dist.) Ky. 1965, U.S. Supreme Ct. 1963. Sole practice, Ironton, Ohio, 1959—; county prosecutor Lawrence County (Ohio), 1973-76. Mem. Ironton Sch. Bd., 1966-69, pres. 1968-69; bd. dirs. Lawrence County Joint Vocat. Sch., 1966-69. Served in USMC, 1950-54. Ohio Bar Assn., Lawrence County Bar Assn., Royal Photog. Soc. (fellow).Author: The Jury, 1973. Family and matrimonial, Personal injury. Office: 122 S 4th St Ironton OH 45638

MOORE, MARGARET ANN, lawyer; b. Orange, N.J., Oct. 17, 1955; d. Robert C. and Betty (Aierstock) M. BA, Dickinson Coll., 1977; JD, George Washington U., 1980. Bar: D.C. 1980, U.S. Dist. Ct. D.C. 1981, U.S. Ct. Appeals (D.C. cir.) 1986. Project mgr. ACEC Research and Mgmt. Found., Washington, 1980-82; atty.-advisor Fed. Energy Regulatory Commn., Washington, 1982-83; staff atty. electric rates FERC, Washington, 1983-85; assoc. VanNess, Feldman, Sutcliffe & Curtis, Washington, 1985—. Mem. ABA, Fed. Bar Assn., D.C. Bar Assn., Fed. Energy Bar Assn. Democrat. Avocation: crossword puzzles. FERC practice, Administrative and regulatory. Home: 2115-A N Monroe St Arlington VA 22207 Office: Van Ness Feldman Sutcliffe & Curtis 1050 Thomas Jefferson St NW Washington DC 20007

MOORE, MCPHERSON DORSETT, lawyer; b. Pine Bluff, Ark., Mar. 1, 1947; s. Arl Van and Jesse (Dorsett) M. B.S., U. Miss., 1970; J.D., U. Ark., 1974. Bar: Ark. 1974, Mo. 1975, U.S. Patent and Trademark Office 1977, U.S. Dist. Ct. (ea. dist.) Mo. 1977, U.S. Ct. Appeals (8th, 10th and D.C. cirs.). Design engr. Tenneco, Newport News, Va., 1970-71; assoc. Rogers, Eilers & Howell, St. Louis, 1974-80; ptnr. Rogers, Howell, Moore & Haferkamp, St. Louis, 1981—. Bd. dirs. Legal Services of Eastern Mo., 1984—. Served with USAR, 1970-76. Mem. ABA, Bar Assn. Met. St. Louis (chmn. young lawyers sect. 1981-82, sec. 1984-85, v.p. 1985-86, chmn. trial sect. 1986-87, pres.-elect 1987—), Ark. Bar Assn., St. Louis County Bar Assn., Am. Intellectual Property Law Assn., Assn. Trial Lawyers Am., Phi Delta Theta Alumni (treas. St. Louis chpt. 1987—). Episcopalian. Club: University (St. Louis). Patent, Trademark and copyright, Federal civil litigation. Home: 49 Godwin Ln Saint Louis MO 63124 Office: Rogers Howell Moore & Haferkamp 7777 Bonhomme Ave Suite 1700 Saint Louis MO 63105

MOORE, MITCHELL JAY, lawyer, law educator; b. Lincoln, Nebr., Aug. 29, 1954; s. Earl J. and Betty Marie (Zimmerlin) M. BS in Edn., U. Mo., Columbia, 1977, JD, 1981. Bar: Mo. 1981, U.S. Dist. Ct. (we. dist.) Mo. 1981, Tex. 1982. Sole practice Columbia, Mo., 1982—; instr. law U. Mo., Columbia, 1982—. Bd. dirs. Planned Parenthood of Cen. Mo., Columbia, 1984-86, Opportunities Unltd., Columbia, 1984-86. Mem. ABA, Assn. Trial Lawyers Am., Mo. Assn. Trial Attys., Phi Delta Phi. Democrat. Mem. Unitarian Ch. Avocations: softball, camping. Family and matrimonial, State civil litigation, Criminal. Office: 1104-A E Broadway Columbia MO 65201

MOORE, RAYMOND ROBERT, lawyer; b. Los Angeles, Oct. 15, 1943; s. Robert Forrest and Lilian Rae (Rennahan) M.; m. Karen Ann Lopez, Oct. 25, 1969; children: Collin Raymond, Christopher Forrest. BA, Calif. State U., Northridge, 1965; JD, U. So. Calif., 1968. Bar: Calif. 1969, U.S. Dist. Ct. (cen. dist.) Calif. 1969, U.S. Dist. Ct. (ea. dist.) Calif. 1985. Dep. counsel Los Angeles County, 1969-73; ptnr. Home & Clifford, N. Hollywood, Calif., 1973-80; from ptnr. to sr. ptnr. Hagenbaugh & Murphy, Los Angeles, 1980—. Mem. ABA, Am Bd. Trial Advs. (assoc.), Assn. So. Calif. Def. Counsel, Los Angeles County Bar Assn., Sigma Chi, Phi Delta Phi. Insurance, Personal injury, State civil litigation. Office: Hagenbaugh & Murphy 3701 Wilshire Blvd 400 Los Angeles CA 90010

MOORE, ROBERT ALLEN, lawyer; b. Rankin Tx., Sept. 21, 1943; s. Allen and Ellen Virginia (Shugart) M.; m. Tina Baker, Nov. 22, 1967; m.

Marie Elaine Smith, Jan. 22, 1977; m. Shelly Acquard, July 5, 1976; children—Kenny, Brenna, Meagen, Anthony. Student Odessa Coll., 1960-62; B.A., U. Tex., 1966; J.D. S. Tex. Coll. of Law, 1968. Bar: Tex. 1969, U.S. Dist. Ct. (we. dist.) Tex. 1970, U.S. Dist. Ct. (so. dist.) Tex. 1970, U.S. Ct. Appeals (5th cir.) 1974, U.S. Supreme Ct. 1978. Sole practice Moore & Assocs., Odessa Tex., 1969—. Mem. State Bar Tex., Houston Bar Assn., Ector County Bar Assn., Tex. Trial Lawyers Assn., ABA, Tex. Criminal Def. Bar, Nat. Assn. Criminal Def. Lawyers, Ector County Def. Bar Assn., Law Sci. Acad. Am., Odessa Jaycees, Phi Alpha Delta. Personal injury, Workers' compensation. Office: 307 N Grant Odessa TX 79761 also: 208 E 10th Ave Del Rio TX 78840

MOORE, ROBERT MADISON, food company executive; b. New Orleans, June 21, 1925; s. Clarence Greer and Anna Omega (Odendahl) M.; m. Evelyn Eileen Varva, Apr. 11, 1953; children: Eileen Alexandria Moore Wynne, John Greer. B.B.A., Tulane U., 1943; J.D., U. Va., 1952; LL.M. (Food Law Inst. fellow), NYU, 1953. Bar: La. 1956, Calif. 1972. Asst. to pres., gen. counsel Underwear Inst., N.Y.C., 1953-55; pvt. practice law New Orleans, 1955-56; asst. gen. atty., dir. Legal services, sec. and gen. atty. Standard Fruit & Steamship Co., New Orleans, 1957-72; v.p., gen. counsel Castle & Cooke Foods, 1972—; v.p., gen. counsel Castle & Cooke, Inc., 1973-81, sr. v.p. law and govt., 1981-82; pres. Internat. Banana Assn., 1983—; dir. Ferson Optics of Del., Inc., 1958-69, Baltime Securities Corp.; former dir. Standard Fruit Co., Compania Bananera Antillana, Castle & Cooke Food Co. Asst. atty. gen., La., 1958-63. Served with AUS, 1943-46. Mem. Am., Calif., Hawaii, La. bar assns., SAR (sec. 1960-61), Phi Delta Phi, Alpha Tau Omega. Democrat. Roman Catholic. Clubs: Essex (New Orleans), Orleans (New Orleans); St. Francis Yacht (San Francisco), Pacific Union (San Francisco); Cosmos (Washington), Washington Golf and Country. General corporate, Private international. Home: 3323 R St NW Washington DC 20007 Office: 1101 Vermont Ave Suite 306 Washington DC 20006

MOORE, ROY DEAN, lawyer; b. Chickasha, Okla., Jan. 15, 1940; s. Frank B. and Delia Pauline (Morgan) M.; m. Carolyn Kaye Wood, Aug. 10, 1962; children—Darla Kaye, Jared Dean, Amy Darise. B.A., Central State U., 1962, M. Teaching, 1966; J.D., Oklahoma City U., 1970; grad., Nat. Coll. State Trial Judges, 1972. Bar: Okla. bar 1970. Coach debate, instr. dramatics Kingfisher (Okla.) High Sch., 1962-67; instr. English and journalism, head dept. lang. arts. Jarman Jr. High Sch., Midwest City, Okla., 1967-70; pros. atty. City of Lawton, Okla., 1970; spl. dist. judge 5th Jud. Dist. Okla., 1971-72; practicing atty. Lawton, 1973—. Pres. Swinney PTA, 1975-76; Editor: Problems in Teaching in the Secondary School, 1966. Pres. Comanche County Mental Health Assn., 1973—, bd. dirs., 1972—; co-chmn. Kingfisher County Reps. for Congressman James V. Smith, 1966; mem. state exec. com. Okla. Republican Com., 1973-74, chmn. auditing com., 1977-78; del. Rep. Nat. Conv., 1976; chmn. cts. com. Assn. South Central Okla. Govts. Crime Commn.; chmn. Comanche County Reps. for Reagan for Pres., 1973-83; mem. adv. bd. Jim Taliferro Mental Health Center, 1977-78; del. Nat. Mental Health Assn. Conv., 1975; bd. dirs. Lawton Campfire Girls; elder N.W. Ch. of Christ, 1977—; dir. Back to Bible Campaigns, 1976—. Mem. Am., Okla., Comanche County bar assns., Okla. Trial Lawyers Assn., Lawton Antique Auto Club, Ford Retractible Club Am., Alpha Psi Omega, Delta Theta Phi. Republican. Mem. Ch. of Christ (elder). Clubs: Mem. Fraternal Order of Police, Lion. Personal injury, Family and matrimonial, Criminal. Home: 2114 Atlanta Ave Lawton OK 73501 Office: 810 C Ave Box 2095 Lawton OK 73501

MOORE, STANLEY RAY, lawyer; b. Dallas, July 20, 1946; s. Elzey and Heloise (Dillon) M.; m. Lindsay Kathleen Newton, July 3, 1969; children—Natalie, William. B.S.M.E., So. Meth. U., 1969, J.D., 1973. Bar: Tex. 1973; U.S. Dist. Ct. (no. dist.) Tex. 1974. Assoc. Clegg, Cantrell, Crisman, Dallas, 1973-75; ptnr. Crisman & Moore, Dallas, 1975-80, Schley Cantrell & Moore, Dallas, 1980-83, Schley, Cantrell, Kice & Moore, Dallas, 1983—; dir. F.S.O.A., Inc., Dallas, 1979-81, SMS Realty, 1983—; cons. Bus. Graphics, Inc., 1983—. Patentee in field. Precinct chmn. Democratic Party, Dallas, 1974; foster parent Hope Cottage, Dallas, 1982—; fund raiser Am. Heart Assn., Republican Party. Recipient Outstanding Leadership commendation ASME, 1969. Mem. Dallas Bar Assn., ABA, Am. Patent Law Assn. Baptist. Patent, Trademark and copyright. Home: 1005 W Main St Lancaster TX 75146 Office: Schley Cantrell Kice and Moore 5001 LBJ Suite 705 Dallas TX 75244

MOORE, THOMAS ADAIR, lawyer; b. Orlando, Fla., Sept. 22, 1953; s. John Alvin and Patricia Louise (Horning) M.; m. Sheryl Lynn Hepker, Sept. 7, 1974; children: Michael Andrew, Nicholas Alexander. AA cum laude, Seminole Jr. Coll.; BA, U. Fla.; DL, Cumberland Sch. Law. Bar: Fla. 1979, U.S. Dist. Ct. (mid. dist.) Fla. 1979. Assoc. Pitts, Eubanks & Ross, PA, Orlando, 1979-85; ptnr. Pitts, Eubanks, Hannah, Hilyard, & Marsee, P.A., Orlando, 1985-86; sole practice Orlando, 1986—; cons. Orange County Sch. Bd., Orlando, 1982—, Orlando Regional Med. Ctr. Mem. Fla. Bar Assn. (rules com. workers compensation sect.), Orange County Bar, Delta Theta Phi (Most Outstanding Student 1979). Republican. Methodist. Avocations: football, baseball, softball, golf. State civil litigation, Workers' compensation, Personal injury. Home: 1425 N Hampton Ave Orlando FL 32803 Office: Thomas A Moore PA 1224 E Concord St Orlando FL 32803

MOORE, THOMAS JEFF, JR., lawyer; b. Duluth, Ga., Jan. 28, 1949; s. Thomas J. Moore Sr. and Ponnie (McConnell) M.; m. Rhonda Ayers (div.); children: Jennett, Margie; m. Cathy Reed Gable, May 23, 1987. BS, Jacksonville State U., 1971; JD, Woodrow Wilson Coll., 1978. Bar: Ga. 1978. Sole practice Lawrenceville, Ga. Bd. dirs. Gwinnett County (Ga.) Bd. Edn., 1984—. Mem. Jaycee Internat. (Internat. Senatorship award). Republican. Southern Baptist. Lodges: Lions, Masons. Office: PO Box 1975 53 Crogan Lawrenceville GA 30246

MOORE, THOMAS MICHAEL, lawyer; b. Jersey City, May 25, 1955; s. Harold Joseph and Mary Kathleen (Mindrup) M. BA in English, U. Notre Dame, 1977; JD, Seton Hall U., 1980. Bar: N.J. 1981. Assoc. atty. Riker Danzig Scherer & Hyland, Newark, 1981-83, Carpenter Bennett & Morrissey, Newark, 1983—. Democrat. Roman Catholic. State civil litigation, Federal civil litigation. Home: 6 Altamont Ct Morristown NJ 07960 Office: Carpenter Bennett & Morrissey 100 Mulberry St Newark NJ 07102

MOORE, THOMAS R., lawyer; b. Duluth, Minn., Mar. 27, 1932; s. Ralph Henry and Estelle Marguerite (Hero) M.; m. Margaret C. King, Sept. 10, 1955; children: Willard S., Clarissa, Charles R.H. B.A. magna cum laude (scholar of the House), Yale U., 1954; J.D., Harvard U., 1957; LL.M. in Taxation, NYU, 1961. Bar: N.Y. 1958, U.S. Supreme Ct. 1958. Instr. Harvard Law Sch. Internat. Program in Taxation, 1956-57; assoc. Dewey, Ballantine, Bushby, Palmer & Wood, N.Y.C., 1957-65; ptnr. Breed, Abbott & Morgan, N.Y.C., 1965-84; sr. ptnr. Finley, Kumble, Wagner, Underberg, Heine, Manley, Myerson & Casey, N.Y.C., 1984—; lectr. on law Cornell Law Sch., NYU Inst. Fed. Taxation, So. Fed. Tax Inst., Condyne, U. Hartford Tax Inst., Practising Law Inst., N.Y.C., Las Vegas, New Orleans; lectr. Nat. Soc. to Prevent Blindness, N.Y.C., San Antonio, Tampa, Fla., Los Angeles, Moscow, Charlottesville, Va., Washington, Kansas City; bd. dirs. Millburn Corp. Co-author: Estate Planning and the Close Corporation, 1970; bd. editors: The Tax Lawyer; contbr. articles to profl. jours. Bd. dirs. Citymeals on Wheels; pres., bd. dirs. Nat. Soc. To Prevent Blindness, 1973-81, chmn., 1981-83, now hon. pres.; bd. dirs. Am. Found. Blind; sec.-treas., trustee A.D. Henderson Found., Del., trustee, Fla.; bd. dirs. Phoenix Theatre, Inst. Aegean Prehistory, Found. Future of Man, Am. and Internat. Friends of Victoria and Albert Mus., London; conservator N.Y. Pub. Library. Decorated Order of St. John; honoree Thomas R. Moore Dinner, Pub. Servant award Nat. Soc. Prevent Blindness. Mem. ABA, N.Y. State Bar Assn. (exec. com. sect. on taxation), Assn. Bar City N.Y., Confrerie de la Chaine des Rotisseurs (U.S. treas., dir., exec. com., world council Paris), Delta Sigma Rho. Republican. Episcopalian. Clubs: University, Lucullus Circle, Chevalier du Tastevin, Chaine des Rotisseurs. Corporate taxation, General corporate, Estate planning. Office: Finley Kumble Wagner 425 Park Ave New York NY 10022

MOORE, TYLER MOSES, lawyer; b. Reno, Aug. 6, 1955; s. Ronald Troy and Olga (Sananes) Hartman; m. Pamela Wimmer, Oct. 20, 1984; children: Christopher T., Emily M., Sarah T. BS in Fin., Va. Poly. Inst. & State U., 1977; JD summa cum laude, Washington & Lee U., 1981. Bar: Va. 1981. Fin. analyst and acct. Shell Oil Co., Houston, 1977-78; assoc. Gardner, Cranwell & Rocovich, Roanoke, Va., 1981-82; ptnr. Cranwell, Flora & Moore, Roanoke, 1982—. John Marshall fellow, 1979. Mem. Assn. Trial Lawyers Am., Assn. Trial Lawyers Va., Nat. Assn. Bond Lawyers, Order of Coif. General corporate, State civil litigation, Municipal bonds. Office: Cranwell Flora & Moore 111 Virginia Ave PO Box 91 Roanoke VA 24002

MOOREHEAD, TIMOTHY LUCAS, lawyer; b. Columbus, Ohio, Mar. 8, 1957; s. Lee Charles and Betty Moorehead; m. Tina Ann Lindsey. BA with highest honors, So. Ill. U., 1978; JD, U. Va., 1981. Bar: D.C. 1981, U.S. Dist. Ct. D.C. 1982, U.S. Ct. Appeals (D.C. cir.) 1982, U.S. Ct. Appeals (6th cir.) 1984, U.S. Supreme Ct. 1985, Ill. 1986, U.S. Dist. Ct. (no. dist.) 1987, U.S. Ct. Appeals (7th cir.) 1987. Assoc. Pepper, Hamilton & Scheetz, Washington, 1981-83, Piper & Marbury, Washington, 1983-85, McDermott, Will & Emery, Chgo., 1986—. Mem. ABA, Supreme Ct. Hist. Soc., Order of Coif. Methodist. Labor, Federal civil litigation, State civil litigation. Home: 827 Stewart St Batavia IL 60510 Office: McDermott Will & Emery 111 W Monroe Chicago IL 60603

MOORER, MAC MITCHELL, lawyer; b. Eufaula, Ala., Jan. 24, 1956; s. William Daniel and Lillie (Mitchell) M.; m. Angela Mary MacKinnon, Aug. 19, 1983. BA, U. Ala., 1978, JD, 1981. Bar: Ala. 1981, U.S. Dist. Ct. (mid. and no. dists.) Ala., U.S. Ct. Appeals (11th cir.) 1981. Law clk. to presiding judge U.S. Dist. Ct. (no. dist.) Ala., Birmingham, 1981-82; assoc. Bradley, Arant, Rose & White, Birmingham, 1982—. Mem. ABA, Ala. Bar Assn. (task force on jud. evaluation, task force on jud. evaluation on lawyer competency), Birmingham Bar Assn. Club: The Club (Birmingham). Federal civil litigation, State civil litigation, General practice. Home: 3736 Valley Head Rd Birmingham AL 35223 Office: Bradley Arant Rose & White 1400 Park Place Tower Birmingham AL 35203

MOORES, EDWARD HARRISON, lawyer, business executive; b. Berwyn, Ill., Sept. 22, 1926; s. Edward Millard and Vira Mary (Harrison) M.; m. Helen Louise Shutt, June 11, 1954; children—Blake Edward, Lisa Jeanne. A.B., U. Tulsa, 1948; LL.B., U. Okla., 1951. Bar: Okla. 1951, Pa. 1967. Law clk. U.S. Dist. Ct. No. Dist. Okla., 1951-53; partner firm Spradling & Moores, Tulsa, 1953-55; counsel Skelly Oil Co., Tulsa, 1955-59; gen. atty., asst. sec. Jones & Laughlin Steel Corp., and subs., Tulsa and Pitts., 1959-75; v.p. legal, gen. counsel, sec. Ampco-Pitts. Corp., Pitts., 1975—; dir. Ampco-Pitts. Found.; dir., sec. Ampco-Pitts. Ferrous and Nonferrous Export Sales Corps., 1975-85; v.p., sec. Pitts. Forgings Co., Greenville Steel Car Co., 1979-87, Greenlease Holding Co., 1986—, Janney Cylinder Co., 1979-85, Buffalo Forge Co. and Aerofin Corp., 1981—, Buffalo Pumps, Inc., 1986—, Ampco-Pitts. Securities Corp., Buffalo Forge S.A. (Mex.), Ampco-Pitts. Overseas Corp., Vulcan, Inc., 1983—, Union Electric Steel Corp. and Union Rolls Corp., 1984—, Shepard Niles Crane & Hoist Corp., 1983—, Parnell Precision Products, Inc., 1983—, AP Venture Corp. I, 1986—; asso. prof. U. Tulsa Law Sch., 1953. Pres. Tulsa Young Republicans, 1948; v.p. Northampton Civic Assn., Allison Park, Pa., 1974-75. Served with A.C. USNR, 1944-46. Mem. Am., Okla., Pa., Allegheny County bar assns., U. Okla. Assn. (life), Am. Corp. Counsel Assn. (dir. Western Pa. chpt. 1985-86), Assn. of President U. Tulsa, Assn. Trial Lawyers Am. (assoc.), Def. Research Inst., Phi Delta Phi, Delta Kappa Epsilon (past pres. U. Okla. Alumni chpt.). Methodist. General corporate, Litigation, Government contracts and claims. Home: 3073 Woodland Rd Allison Park PA 15101 Office: 700 Porter Bldg Pittsburgh PA 15219

MOORHEAD, JAMES BARR, lawyer; b. Pitts., Feb. 3, 1954; s. William Singer and Lucy (Galpin) M. BA, Harvard U., 1976; JD, Columbia U., 1981. Bar: D.C. 1982, N.Y. 1982, U.S. Dist. Ct. Md. 1982, U.S. Ct. Appeals (4th cir.) 1982. Law clk. to presiding justice U.S. Dist. Ct. Md., Balt., 1981-82; assoc. Williams & Connolly, Washington, 1982-83; asst. U.S. atty. State of Md., Balt., 1983-86; legal corr. Md. Pub. TV, 1986—. TV host Howard Cable TV, 1985—; contbr. articles to profl. jours. Co-chmn. Harvard Coll. Fund, Cambridge, Mass., 1980—; coordinator Howard COunty Just Say No anti-drug program, 1986—; bd. dirs. Am. Cancer Soc., Howard County, 1986—. Harlan Fiske Stone scholar Columbia U., 1980. Mem. ABA. Democrat. Federal civil litigation, State civil litigation. Home: 12030 Little Patuxent Pkwy Columbia MD 21044

MOORHEAD, WILLIAM DAVID, III, lawyer, corporate executive; b. Knoxville, Tenn., Aug. 13, 1952; s. William David and Virginia (Wood) M.; m. Thelma Rogena Murray, Sept. 4, 1976; children—John Murray, Virginia Salima. B.B.A., U. Ga., 1973, J.D., 1976. Bar: Tenn. 1976, U.S. Dist. Ct. (ea. dist.) Tenn. 1976, Ga. 1977, U.S. Tax Ct. 1977, U.S. Ct. Claims, 1985, U.S. Supreme Ct. 1985. Assoc. Stophel, Caldwell & Heggie, Chattanooga, 1976-77; ptnr. Murray & Moorhead, Americus, Ga., 1977-80, Vansant, Corriere & Moorhead, Albany, Ga., 1981-85, Hall & Moorhead, P.C., Albany, 1985—; pres. Continental Consol. Corp., Albany, 1983—, W.D. Moorhead & Co., Albany, 1984—; chmn. Moorhead & Farmer Inc., 1987—. Del. Ga. Dem. Com., 1978. Vassar Wooley scholar, 1973-76. Mem. ABA, Tenn. Bar Assn., Ga. Bar Assn., Dougherty County Bar Assn., Albany Estate Planning Council (v.p. 1982-83). Baptist. Estate taxation, Probate, General corporate. Home: 3509 Old Dawson Rd Albany GA 31707 Office: WD Moorhead & Co 314 Residence Ave Albany GA 31701

MOORMAN, ELLIOTT DUANE, lawyer; b. N.Y.C., Oct. 26, 1949; s. Clement Leroy and Beatrice Melba (Smith) M.; m. Jocelyn Petteway, Sept. 1, 1984; children: Rafiq Elliott, Kaliq Duane, Justin David. BA in Pub. and Internat. Affairs, Princeton U., 1971; JD, Columbia U., 1977. Bar: N.J. 1977, U.S. Dist. Ct. N.J. 1977, U.S. Supreme Ct. 1980, U.S. Ct. Appeals (3d cir.) 1986, U.S. Tax Ct. Assoc. McCarter & English, Newark, 1977-79; trial atty. AT&T, N.Y.C., 1979-81; assoc. Sills, Beck, Cummis, Zuckerman, Radin & Tischmann, P.A., Newark, 1981-82; sr. trial atty. Freeman & Bass, Newark, 1982-84; house counsel Gen. Accident Ins. Co., Cherry Hill, N.J., 1985—; bd. dirs., chmn. reorganization com. Essex-Newark Legal Services Project Inc.; mem. statewide com. civil case mgmt. and procedure, 1985, com. on bar admissions N.J. Supreme Ct., 1984. Contbr. articles to profl. jours. V.p. Internat. Affairs U.S. Youth Council; chmn. annual fund, v.p. fin. Columbia Law Sch. Class of 1977; pres. bd. dirs. Joint Connection Prison Reform Project; bd. dirs., pres. youth div. Nat. Bd. YMCA's; bd. dirs. World Council YMCA's. Mem. ABA (chmn. law day 1982, litigation and young lawyer sects., Am. Law Inst., nat. conf. of bar pres. 1984), N.J. Bar Assn. (vice chmn. young lawyers div. 1979-82, casino law, child abuse, civil practice and continuing legal edn. coms, outstanding service award 1981,82), Garden State Bar Assn. (pres., chmn. 1984), Camden County Bar Assn., Essex County Bar Assn., Assn. Trial Lawyers Am., Columbia Law Sch. Alumni Assn. N.J. (founding dir., v.p.). Roman Catholic. State civil litigation, Insurance, Personal injury. Home: 6 Ashwood Ct Maple Shade NJ 08052 Office: Gen Accident Ins Co 2 Executive Campus Suite 445 Cherry Hill NJ 08002

MOORMAN, HELEN LOUISE, lawyer; b. Chgo., Dec. 5, 1940; d. George Rhoades and Mary Louise (Dennison) Dean; m. G. Edward Moorman, Dec. 28, 1960 (div. Apr. 1983); children: Rebecca Lynn, Michael William. AB, U. Chgo., 1962; JD, Washington U., St. Louis, 1972; student, London Sch. Econs., 1982-83. Bar: Ill. 1973, Mo. 1973, U.S. Dist. Ct. (we. dist.) Mo. 1973, U.S. Dist. Ct. (so. dist.) Ill. 1973, U.S. Dist. Ct. (cen. dist.) Ill. 1979, U.S. Ct. Appeals (9th cir.) 1984, Oreg. 1985. Staff atty., directing atty. Land of Lincoln Legal Assistance Found., Alton, Ill., 1973-75, 79-80; asst. pub. defender Madison County, Edwardsville, Ill., 1975-79; law. clk. Ill. Ct. Appeals, Collinsville, 1980-82; atty., dir. litigation Marion-Polk Legal Aid Service, Salem, Oreg., 1984-86; mng. atty. Hyatt Legal Services, North Riverside, Ill., 1986, Natkin and Fish, PC, Chgo., 1987—; sole practice, Alton, 1977-79. Bd. dirs. YWCA, Quincy, Ill., 1979-81, Parents Anonymous, Quincy, 1979-81, Oasis Women's Shelter, Alton, 1977-84; v.p., bd. dirs. Mid-Valley Women's Crisis Service, Salem, 1984-86. dAm. Friends London Sch. Econs. scholar, 1983. Mem. ABA, Ill. State Bar Assn. (com. to revise juvenile ct. act 1978-82), Mo. Bar Assn., Oreg. Bar Assn., Mensa (pres. St. Louis chpt. 1973, 74, recipient scholarship ednl. and research found. 1983). Avocations: cross country skiing, camping, travel, theater, photography. General practice, Immigration, naturalization, and customs, Family and matrimonial. Home: 445 S Cleveland #301 Arlington Heights IL 60005 Office: Natkin and Fish PC 1045 N Ashland Ave Chicago IL 60522

MOORSTEIN, MARK ALAN, lawyer; b. Ann Arbor, Mich., June 27, 1949; s. Benjamin and Barbara Sue Moorstein; m. Georgia Sue Boyle, Apr. 29, 1978; children: Timothy Brandon, Kathryn Elizabeth. AB cum laude, Princeton U., 1971; JD, Temple U., 1974. Bar: Ohio 1974, U.S. Dist. Ct. (no. dist.) Ohio 1975, U.S. Ct. Appeals (6th cir.) 1975, U.S. Supreme Ct. 1977, D.C. 1980, Va. 1981, U.S. Dist. Ct. (ea. dist.) Va. 1982, U.S. Ct. Appeals (D.C. cir.) 1982, U.S. Ct. Appeals (4th cir.) 1984, U.S. Tax Ct. 1984. Assoc. Roetzel & Andress, Akron, Ohio, 1974-76; atty. HUD, Cleve. and Washington, 1976-80; v.p. Walker & Dunlop, Washington, 1980-84; ptnr. Dixon & Smith, Fairfax, Va., 1984-86, Watt, Tieder, Killian & Hoffar, Vienna, Va., 1986; bd. dirs. Raven Corp., Washington. Contbr. articles to profl. jours. Chmn. Coles Rep. Party, Prince William County, Va., 1985—; founder Mid-County Civic Assn., 1985; active Prince William Little Theatre, Manassas, Va. Recipient Silver Bird award No. Va. Soc. Newspaper Columnists, 1986. Mem. ABA, Va. State Bar Assn., Fed. Bar Assn., Fairfax Bar Assn., Aircraft Owners and Pilots Assn. (panelist 1984). Avocations: writing, musical compositions, flying, swimming, cycling. Municipal bonds, Real property, Real estate finance. Office: Watt Tieder Killian & Hoffar 8401 Old Courthouse Rd Vienna VA 22180

MOOTY, DAVID NELSON, lawyer; b. Mpls., June 18, 1953; s. John William and Virginia Mae (Nelson) M.; m. Jeanne Hirschey, Aug. 26, 1978; children: Virginia, Brianna, Alicia. BA, Amherst Coll., 1975; JD, U. Minn., 1978; postgrad., William Mitchell Coll. Law, 1986—. Bar: Minn. 1978, U.S. Dist. Ct. Minn. 1979. Ptnr. Gray, Plant, Mooty, Mooty & Bennett, Mpls., 1978—; bd. dirs. Brown Farms, Inc., Mpls., Traverse, Inc., Mpls. Vol. Amicus, Mpls., 1985. Mem. ABA, Minn. Bar Assn., Hennepin County Bar Assn. Clubs: Mpls. Athletic (mem. bowling com. 1984—, volleyball com. 1985—), Minikahda (Mpls.). Lodge: Kiwanis. Avocations: golf, bridge, soccer, volleyball, bowling. Estate planning, Probate, Estate taxation. Office: Gray Plant Mooty Mooty & Bennett 33 S 6th St Minneapolis MN 55402

MORA, DAVID BAUDILIO, lawyer; b. N.Y.C., Apr. 16, 1957; s. Rafael B. and Theresa (De Jesus) M.; m. Maria Elisa Rivera, Aug. 21, 1980; 1 child, David Michael. BBA, U. P.R., Rio Piedras, 1978; JD, SUNY, Buffalo, 1981; postdoctoral, George Washington U., 1982-83. Estate tax atty. trainee IRS, Buffalo, 1980-81; atty., chief counsel IRS, Washington, 1981-85; sr. atty. dist. counsel IRS, Houston, 1985—. Mem. ABA, Hispanic Nat. Bar Assn. Democrat. Avocation: trombone. Personal income taxation, Federal civil litigation, Bankruptcy. Home: 4711 Kilmarnoch Way Missouri City TX 77459 Office: IRS Dist Counsel 10850 Richmond Suite 350 Houston TX 77042

MORABITO, DAVID ROBERTSON, SR., lawyer; b. Rochester, N.Y., May 3, 1954; s. Nicholas and Patricia Ann (Robertson) M.; m. Colette Mariane Gagnier, Sept. 29, 1984; 1 child, David Robertson Jr. BA magna cum laude, U. Miami, 1975; JD, Nova U., 1979. Bar: N.Y. 1981, Fla. 1981, U.S. Tax Ct. 1982, U.S. Dist. Ct. (we. dist.) N.Y. 1985, U.S. Ct. Appeals (5th and 11th cirs.) 1985. Law clk. U.S. Dept. Justice, Miami, Fla., 1979; editor Lawyers Coop. Pub. Co., Rochester, 1981; pub. defender Monroe County, N.Y., 1981-85; sole practice East Rochester, N.Y., 1985—; instr. Rochester Inst. Tech., 1986—, Am. Paralegal Inst., 1985; real estate broker, Rochester, 1986—. Contbr. articles in Am. Law Reports Fed. Counselor Boy Scouts Am., Rochester, 1982—. Mem. ABA, Fla. Bar Assn., N.Y. State Bar Assn., Monroe County Bar Assn., N.Y. State Defenders Assn., Assn. Trial Lawyers of Am., N.Y. State Trial Lawyers Assn., Am. Judicare Soc., Phi Kappa Phi, Delta Theta Mu. Avocation: restoration of old homes. Criminal. Home: 1100 Main St East Rochester NY 14445 Office: 117 W Commercial St East Rochester NY 14445

MORALES, JULIO K., lawyer; b. Havana, Cuba, Jan. 17, 1948; came to U.S., 1960; s. Julio E. and Josephine (Holsters) M.; m. Suzette M. Dussault, May 31, 1970 (div. 1978); children: Julio E., Karel A.; m. Barbara A. Miller, July 14, 1979; 1 child, Nicolas W. BA, Carroll Coll., 1969; JD, U. Mont., 1972. Bar: Mont. 1972, U.S. Dist. Ct. Mont. 1972, U.S. Ct. Mil. Appeals 1972, U.S. Ct. Appeals (9th cir.) 1980. Law clk. to presiding justice Mont. Supreme Ct., Helena, 1972; sole practice Missoula, Mont., 1973-78; sr. ptnr. Morales & Volinkaty, Missoula, 1978—. Author: Estate Planning for the Handicapped, 1975. Pres. Rockmont, Inc., Missoula, 1985-87. Served to 2d lt. U.S. Army, 1972. Mem. ABA (dist. rep. 1975-79, exec. council young lawyer div. 1977-79), Mont. Bar Assn. (chmn. law day 1974, 75, 77), Am. Trial Lawyers Assn., Am. Judicature Soc., Am. Trial Lawyers Assn., World Assn. Lawyers, Phi Delta Phi. Roman Catholic. Clubs: Missoula Exchange (pres. 1985-86), Mont. Avocations: sports, coaching youth, boating, skiing, golf. Personal injury, Workers' compensation, Probate. Office: Morales & Volinkaty 316 W Spruce Missoula MT 59807-8272

MORALES, NESTOR, lawyer; b. Tampa, Fla., Mar. 25, 1909; LL.B., U. Fla., 1935. Bar: Fla. 1935. Sole practice, Miami, Fla., 1935-79; ptnr. Morales, Rudolph & Hevia, 1979-86, Morales and Rudolph, Miami, 1987—; co-founder Hemisphere Nat. Bank. Mem. ABA, Fla. Bar Assn., Am. Judicature Soc., Dade County Bar Assn. Author legal booklets. Real property, General corporate, Probate. Home: 645 Solano Prado Coral Gables FL 33156 Office: 2450 SW 137th Ave Suite 221 Miami FL 33175

MORAN, DONALD J., lawyer; b. Evanston, Ill., Nov. 30, 1951; m. Lisa Moran. BA, Northwestern U., Evanston, Ill.; MRP, JD, Syracuse U. Bar: Ill., U.S. Dist. Ct. (no. dist.) Ill. Ptnr. Pedersen & Houpt P.C., Chgo.; bd. dirs. Legal Assistance Found.; adj. faculty John Marshal Sch. Law, Chgo.; speaker various legal seminars. Contbr. articles to profl. jours. Bd. dirs. Legal Assistance Found., 1983-86. Mem. ABA (litigation sect.), Ill. Bar Assn. (civil practice com., Lincoln Legal Writing award 1980), Chgo. Bar Assn. (profl. fees com., constl. law com., exec. council young lawyers sect. 1981-83), Assn. Trial Lawyers Am. Federal civil litigation, State civil litigation. Home: 554 Longwood Glencoe IL 60022 Office: Pedersen & Houpt PC 180 N LaSalle St Suite 3400 Chicago IL 60601

MORAN, JAMES BYRON, judge; b. Evanston, Ill., June 20, 1930; s. James Edward and Kathryn (Horton) M.; m. Nancy Adam; children: John, Jennifer, Sarah, Polly. AB, U. Mich., 1952; LLB magna cum laude, Harvard U., 1957. Bar: Ill. 1958. Law clk. to presiding judge U.S. Ct. of Appeals (2d cir.), 1957-58; assoc. Bell, Boyd, Lloyd, Haddad & Burns, Chgo, 1958-66, ptnr., 1966-79; judge U.S. Dist. Ct.(no. dist.) Ill., Chgo., 1979—. Dir. Com. on Ill. Govt., 1960-78, chmn., 1968-70; vice chmn., sec. Ill. Dangerous Drug Adv. Counsel, 1967-74; chmn. sect. dir. Gateway Found., 1969—; mem. Ill. Ho. of Reps., 1965-67; mem. Evanston City Council, 1971-75. Served with AUS, 1952-54. Mem. Ill. Bar Assn., Chgo. Bar Assn., Chgo. Council Lawyers, Phi Beta Kappa. Clubs: Law, Legal. Jurisprudence. Home: 117 Kedzie St Evanston IL 60202 Office: US Courthouse 219 S Dearborn St Chicago IL 60604

MORAN, JAMES MICHAEL, lawyer; b. New Haven, Feb. 20, 1957; s. Francis Richard and Anne (Dugan) M.; m. Kathy Hildebrandt, Sept. 22, 1984. BA, Loyola U., New Orleans, 1979; JD, U. Fla., 1982. Bar: Fla. 1982. Assoc. Barton, Cox & Davis, Gainesville, Fla., 1982-85, Patterson, Turk & Hudson P.A., Cape Coral, Fla., 1985—. Mem. Acad. Trial Lawyers Am., Acad. Fla. Trial Lawyers, Phi Sigma Alpha, Beta Alpha Phi. Avocations: windsurfing, scuba diving. Banking, State civil litigation, Federal civil litigation. Office: Sun Bank Lee County 1612 E Cape Coral Pkwy Cape Coral FL 33904

MORAN, JOSEPH MILBERT, banker; b. Dentsville, Md., July 23, 1929; s. Thomas Roger and May Marianne (Montgomery) M.; m. Jacqueline V. Kines, Sept. 3, 1955; children: Susanne, Stacey, Siobain, Meghan. Ph.B., Loyola Coll., Balt., 1950; LL.B., U. Md., 1959. Bar: Md. 1959. Copy boy Balt. News Post, 1950-51; with INA, Balt., 1955-56; with aerospace div. Martin Marietta Co., Balt., 1956-59, with nuclear div., 1959-64; with Wilmington Trust Co., Del., 1964—; sr. v.p. Wilmington Trust Co., 1972—, sec., dir., 1979—; mem. Govs. Council on Banking, 1982—. Mem. bd. visitors Del. Law Sch., Weidner U., 1985—. Served to capt. USNR, 1951-73. Mem. ABA, Del. Bar Assn., Md. Bar, Navy League, Naval Res. Assn., Am. Banker's Assn. (legis. council 1979-82, leadership del. 1985-86), Del. Banker's Assn. (chmn. legis. com.). Democrat. Roman Catholic. Banking, Legislative, General corporate. Home: RD 4 Box 495D Hockessin DE 19707 Office: Rodney Square N Wilmington DE 19809

MORAN, THOMAS JOSEPH, justice Supreme Court Illinois; b. Waukegan, Ill., July 17, 1920; s. Cornelius Patrick and Avis Rose (Tyrrell) M.; m. Mary Jane Wasniewski, Oct. 4, 1941; children: Avis Marie, Kathleen, Mary Jane, Thomas G. B.A., Lake Forest Coll., 1947; J.D., Chgo. Kent Coll. Law, 1950; J.D. (hon.), Lake Forest Coll., 1977. Bar: Ill. Individual practice law Waukegan, Ill., 1950-56; state's atty. Lake County, Ill., 1956-58; probate ct. judge Lake County, 1958-61; judge 19th Circuit Ct., Lake and McHenry counties, Ill., 1961-64; appellate ct. judge 2d Dist., Elgin, Ill., 1964-76; justice Supreme Ct. Ill., 1976—; faculty appellate judges seminars NYU; continuing legal edn. seminars La. State U. Served with USCG, 1943-45. Mem. Inst. Jud. Adminstrn., Am. Judicature Soc., ABA, Ill., Lake County bar assns. Office: Supreme Ct Bldg Springfield IL 62756 *

MORANDO, MARTA LUCILE HOPE, lawyer; b. Portland, Oreg., June 20, 1952; d. Sil. S. and Jeanne Hope (Butler) M. AB summa cum laude, U. Calif., Berkeley, 1972, JD, 1975. Bar: Calif. 1975. Assoc. Ware & Freidenrich, Palo Alto, Calif., 1975-80, ptnr., 1980—, mem. exec. com., 1983-86; lectr. on various legal topics. Mem. ABA, Calif. Bar Assn., Calif. Women's Lawyers Assn. Republican. Lutheran. General corporate, Securities. Office: Ware & Freidenrich 400 Hamilton Ave Palo Alto CA 94301

MORANT, BLAKE DOMINIC, lawyer; b. Ft. Eustis, Va., Nov. 4, 1952; s. John Henry and Rosa Lee (Johnson) M.; m. Paulette Joyce Jones, Aug. 2, 1980. BA, U. Va., 1975, JD, 1978. Bar: Va. 1978, U.S. Dist. Ct. (ea. dist.) Va. 1985. Commd. 2d lt. U.S. Army, 1975; advanced through grades to capt. JAGC U.S. Army, 1978; govt. contract atty. JAGC U.S. Army, Ft. Bragg, N.C., 1979-82; recruiting atty. JAGC U.S. Army, Washington, 1982-84, adminstrv. law atty., 1984-85, resigned, 1985; assoc. Braude, Margulies, Sacks & Rephan, Washington, 1985—; asst. prof. Campbell U., Fayetteville, N.C., 1980-82; guest prof. Fayetteville State U., 1981; recruiting atty. U.S. Army, Washington, 1982-84. Active Cancer Vols. of Am., N.Y.C., 1980—; bd. dirs. Wesley Housing Devel. Corp., 1986—. Earl Warren scholar 1974-75, Ribble-Kennedy scholar, 1976, Army ROTC scholar; named one of Outstanding Young Men of Am., 1984. Mem. ABA, Nat. Bar Assn., Phi Beta Kappa. Methodist. Avocations: singing, clarinet, tennis. Government contracts and claims, Construction, Federal civil litigation. Home: 7307 Scarborough St Springfield VA 22153-1815 Office: Braude Margulies et al 1828 L St NW Suite 900 Washington DC 20036

MORAVSIK, ROBERT JAMES, lawyer; b. Jersey City, Sept. 21, 1942; s. Charles B. and Marie A. (Hoppe) M.; children: Barry, Athena; m. Anne B. Wyman, July 29, 1984. BS in Aero. Engring., Tri-State U., 1963; MMS, Stevens Inst. Tech., 1969; JD, Seton Hall U., 1978. Bar: N.J. 1978, U.S. Dist. Ct. N.J. 1978, U.S. Supreme Ct. 1986. Sr. engr. Curtiss Wright Corp., Fairfield, N.J., 1963-66; mgr. Fisher Stevens Inc., Totowa, N.J., 1966-78, v.p., gen. counsel, 1978-87; v.p., gen. counsel, sec. Biosearch Med. Products, Inc., Somerville, N.J., 1987—. Councilman Boro of Ringwood, N.J., 1974; pres. Par Troy Condominium Assn., Parsippany, N.J., 1984—. Mem. ABA, N.J. Bar Assn., (law com.), Am. Computer Law Assn., Passic Bar Assn. General practice, Computer, General corporate.

MORD, IRVING CONRAD, II, lawyer; b. Kentwood, La., Mar. 22, 1950; s. Irving Conrad and Lillie Viva (Chapman) M.; m. Julia Ann Russell, Aug. 22, 1970 (div. Apr. 22, 1980); children: Russell Conrad, Emily Ann; m. Kay E. McDaniel, Aug. 31, 1985. BS, Miss. State U., 1972; JD, U. Miss., 1974. Bar: Miss. 1974, U.S. Dist. Ct. (no. dist.) Miss. 1974, U.S. Dist. Ct. (so. dist.) Miss. 1984. Counsel to bd. suprs. Noxubee County, Miss., 1976-80, Walthall County, Miss. 1980—, Bd. Educ., Walthall County, 1980—. Trustee, Walthall County Gen. Hosp., 1982—; county pros. atty. Noxubee County, Miss., Macon, 1974-80, Walthall County, Tylertown, 1982—. Bd. dirs. East Miss. Council, Meridian, 1978-80, Trustmark Nat. Bank, Tylertown, 1986—; v.p. Macon council Boy Scouts Am., 1978, mem. council, 1979; county crusade chmn. Am. Cancer Soc., Macon, 1976-78, county pres., 1979; chmn. fund drive Miss. State U. Fine Arts Complex, Macon, 1979. Recipient Youth Leadership award Miss. Econ. Council, 1976. Mem. Miss. Prosecutors Assn., Miss. Assn. Board Attys. (v.p. 1985, pres. 1986), Miss. Assn. Sch. Bd. Attys., Miss. State Bar, Am. Judicature Soc. (Torts award 1972), Miss. Assn. Trial Lawyers, Assn. Trial Lawyers Am., Miss. Criminal Justice Planning Commn., Nat. Fed. Ind. Bus., Miss. State U. Alumni Assn., Macon-Noxubee County C. of C., Phi Kappa Tau (bd. govs. 1976-80, grad. council, 1972—, pres. grad. council 1977-80, pres. house corp. 1977-80, alumnus of yr. Alpha Chi chpt. 1979), Phi Delta Phi. Republican. Methodist. Lodge: Rotary (sec. treas. 1977, v.p. 1978, pres. Macon 1979, pres. Tylertown club 1986—) Local government, General practice, Criminal. Office: 816 Morse St Tylertown MS 39667

MOREHOUSE, ARTHUR ROGERS GRANT, lawyer; b. Utica, N.Y., June 3, 1929; s. George Crane Jr. and Priscilla (Grant) M.; m. Jean Ann Gutmann, Dec. 17, 1950; children: Abigail, A.R. Grant Jr., Mark, Priscilla. BA, St. Lawrence U., 1951; JD, Syracuse U., 1977. Bar: S.C. 1978, U.S. Dist. Ct. S.C. 1986. Dir. indsl. relations Carrier Corp., Syracuse, 1953-64; exec. asst., dir. personnel Alcan Aluminum, Oswego, N.Y., 1964-69; dir. indsl. relations TRW Inc., Cleve., 1969-73, also bd. dirs.; v.p. Sea Pine Corp., Hilton Head Island, S.C., 1973-75; sole practice Hilton Head Island, 1978—. Contbr. articles to profl. jours. Commr. Hilton Head Island Commn., 1981-83, Election Commn., Hilton Head Island, 1986—; mem. Pub. Employment Relations Bd., N.Y., 1965. Served to 1st lt. U.S. Army, 1951-54, Korea. Recipient Service Recognition award Salvation Army, 1966, Outstanding Service award Am. Cancer Soc., 1985. Mem. ABA, S.C. Bar Assn., Hilton Head Island Bar Assn. (pres. 1985—), Assn. Trial Lawyers Am., Am. Arbitration Assn. (arbitrator, labor panel 1978—). Republican. Episcopalian. Clubs: Yacht (Hilton Head Island) (commodore 1981-82), Sea Pines Golf (Hilton Head Island). Lodge: Rotary. Avocations: sailing, tennis, fishing, skiing. General corporate, General practice, Real property. Home: 19 Stoney Creek Rd Villa 297 Hilton Head Island SC 29928 Office: 49 D Bow Circle Hilton Head Island SC 29928

MORELLI, ARNOLD, lawyer; b. Cin., June 28, 1928; s. Zopito and Josephine (Nerone) M.; m. Gloria Keyes, Jan. 12, 1957; children—Michael, Lisa. B.A., U. Cin., 1951; LL.B., Harvard U., 1955. Bar: Ohio 1955. Assoc. Squire, Sanders & Dempsey, Cleve., 1955-57, Paxton & Seasongood, Cin., 1957-61; asst. U.S. atty. Office of U.S. Atty., Cin., 1961-66, 1st asst. U.S. atty. 1964-66; ptnr. Bauer, Morelli & Heyd, Cin., 1966—; lectr. law Chase Coll. Law, U. Cin. Law Sch. Mem. Mariemont (Ohio) Bd. Edn. 1972-76, pres. 1974; bd. dirs. Hamilton County (Ohio) Pub. Defenders; trustee Legal Aid Soc. Served with U.S. Army 1951-53. Fellow Am. Bd. Criminal Lawyers, Am. Coll. Trial Lawyers; mem. ABA, Ohio State Bar Assn., Cin. Bar Assn., Fed Bar Assn. State civil litigation, Criminal, Labor. Home: 6507 Mariemont Ave Cincinnati OH 45227 Office: 1029 Main St Cincinnati OH 45202

MORELLI, CARMEN, lawyer; b. Hartford, Conn., Oct. 30, 1922; s. Joseph and Helen (Carani) M.; m. Irene Edna Montminy, June 26, 1943; children: Richard A., Mark D., Carl J. BSBA, Boston U., 1949, JD, 1952. Bar: Conn. 1955, U.S. Dist. Ct. Conn. 1958. Sr. ptnr. Morelli & Morelli, Windsor, Conn.; mem. Conn. Ho. of Reps., 1959-61; rep. Capitol Regional Planning Agy., 1965-72; atty. Town of Windsor, 1961; asst. prosecutor Town of Windsor, 1957-58. Mem. Windsor Town Com., 1957-82, chmn. 1964-65, treas., 1960-64, mem. planning and zoning commn., 1965-74, mem. charter revision com., 1963-64, Rep. Presdl. Task Force. Served with USN, 1943-45. Mem. ABA, Conn. Bar Assn., Hartford Bar Assn., Windsor Bar Assn. (pres. 1979), Windsor C. of C. (v.p. 1978), Am. Arbitration Assn. Roman Catholic. Club: Elks, Rotary. General practice, Personal injury, Probate. Home: 41 Farmstead Ln Windsor CT 06095 Office: 66 Maple Ave Windsor CT 06095

MORELLI, JOSEPH CHRISTOPHER, lawyer; b. Hartford, Conn., June 20, 1956; s. Joseph Louis and Nancy (Petro) M.; m. Debra Ann Tarascio, Dec. 27, 1980; 1 child, Joseph William. BA, Fairfield U., 1978; JD cum laude, Western New Eng. Sch. of Law, 1981. Bar: Conn. 1981, U.S. Dist. Ct. Conn. 1981. Law clk. to presiding justice Conn. Supreme Ct., Hartford, 1981-82; assoc. Adinolfi, O'Brien & Hayes P.C., Hartford, 1982—. Mem. ABA, Conn. Bar Assn., Hartford County Bar Assn., Internat. Right of Way Assn., YMCA. Republican. Roman Catholic. Avocations: sports, woodworking. State civil litigation, Condemnation, General corporate. Office: Steier & Assocs 65 LaSalle Rd West Hartford CT 06103

MORELLI, RONALD JOSEPH, lawyer; b. N.Y.C., July 8, 1948; s. Samuel and Ruth (Freisen) M.; m. Catherine Theresa Mifsud, Aug. 13, 1972; children: Ronald, Robert, Russell. BA, Hofstra U., 1970; JD, St. John's U., Jamaica, N.Y., 1973. Bar: N.Y. 1974, U.S. Dist. Ct. (ea. and so. dists.) N.Y. 1976. Dep. county atty. Nassau County, Mineola, N.Y., 1974-81; assoc. J. Russell Clune P.C., Mineola, 1981-85, ptnr., 1985—. Mem. Rep. Law Com., Mineola, 1975-80. Served to 1st lt. USAR, 1974. Mem. N.Y. State Bar Assn., Columbian Lawyers Assn., Nassau County Bar Assn., Nassau-Suffolk Trial Lawyers Assn. Republican. Roman Catholic. State civil litigation, Insurance, Personal injury. Office: J Russell Clune PC 290 Old Country Rd Mineola NY 11501

MOREMEN, JOHN S., corporation executive, lawyer; b. Louisville, Jan. 25, 1930; s. John R. and Louise (Pilcher) M.; m. Frances Cummins, children—Lindsay, Holly, John R. B.A., U. Ky., 1954; LL.B., Washington & Lee U., 1957. Bar: Ky. 1957. Assoc., Bullitt, Dawson & Tarrant, Louisville, 1957-58; assoc. Sandidge, Holbrook & Craig, Owensboro, Ky., 1959-65; asst. gen. counsel Brown-Forman Distillers Corp., Louisville, 1965—, v.p., sec., gen. counsel, 1979—, sr. v.p., 1985—; dir. Fratelli Bolla Internat. Bd. dirs. Louisville Ballet, Arthritis Found, Louisville Water Co. Served as cpl. USMC, 1951-53; Korea. Mem. ABA, Ky. Bar Assn., Louisville Bar Assn., Filson Club Hist. Soc. Clubs: Filson, Pendennis, Harmony Landing (Louisville). Antitrust, Private international. Office: Brown-Forman Corp 850 Dixie Hwy Louisville KY 40210

MOREN, CHARLES VERNER, lawyer, judge; b. Webster, Wis., Jan. 29, 1920; s. John Arthur and Jennie Marie (Anderson) M.; m. Sylvia Jene Smith, Mar. 15, 1946 (div.); m. Donna Rae McFarland, Sept. 22, 1982; children—Marie, Leslie, Stephen, James, John, Daniel. B.A., U. Minn., 1942, LL.B., 1948. Bar: Minn. 1948, Wash. 1954, U.S. Dist. Ct. (we. dist.) Wash. 1956. Trial atty. Mpls. St. Ry. Co., 1948-50; sole practice, Anoka, Minn., 1951-52; assoc. Bundlie, Kelley, Finley & Maun, St. Paul, 1952-53; asst. city atty. City of Seattle, 1954-55; atty. Gen. Ins. Co., Seattle, 1955-56; ptnr. Keller, Rohrback, Waldo, Moren & Hiscock, Seattle, 1957-75, Moren Lageschulte & Cornell, Seattle, 1975—; city atty. City of Lake Forest Park, Wash., 1963-65, judge mcpl. ct., 1970—. Co-founder City of Lake Forest Park, Seattle, 1963, Served to lt. USN, 1942-46, PTO. Mem. ABA, Minn. Bar Assn., Wash. State Bar Assn., Am. Arbitration Assn., Assn. Trial Lawyers Am., Full Gospel Businessmens Fellowship (bd. dirs. Seattle chpt. 1975-78). Republican. State civil litigation, Personal injury. Home: 1213 SW 174th St Seattle WA 98166 Office: Moren Lageschulte & Cornell 11320 Roosevelt Way NE Seattle WA 98125

MORENO, FEDERICO ANTONIO, lawyer; b. Caracas, Venezuela, Apr. 10, 1952; came to U.S., 1963; s. Francisco Jose and Rejane Genevieve (Nogues) M.; m. M. Cristina M. Morales-Gomez, May 31, 1977; children: Cristi, Ricky. AB cum laude, U. Notre Dame, 1974; JD, U. Miami, 1974. Ptnr. Thornton, Rothhan & Moreno, Miami, 1982-86; judge Dade County, Miami, 1986. Recipient People Helping People award United Way, 1980, Pro Bono award Pub. Interest Law Bank, 1985. Mem. ABA, Fed. Bar Assn. Republican. Roman Catholic. Clubs: Big Five, Tiger Bay. Judicial administration, Criminal. Home: 1314 Castile Ave Coral Gables FL 33134 Office: Met Justice Bldg 1351 NW 12th St Miami FL 33125

MORENO, FERNANDO, legal educator; b. Santurce, P.R., Oct. 17, 1934; s. Esteban and Maria (Salas) M.; m. Rosario Gonzalez, Dec. 21, 1957; children—Rosario, Esteban, Marie, Fernando. B.A., U. P.R., 1955, postgrad. in pub. adminstrn., 1955-56, J.D. magna cum laude, 1973; LL.M. in Ocean and Coastal Law, U. Miami, 1982. Bar: P.R. 1974, U.S. Dist. Ct. P.R., 1974, U.S. Ct. Appeals (1st cir.) 1974. Teaching asst. U. P.R. Sch. Law, 1972-73; office mgr., personnel dir., house counselor at law, dir. Gonzalez Rodriguez Investment Corp., Catalan Gonzalez & Co., Inc., Indsl. Gonzalez, Inc., Santurce, 1958-79; lectr. Sch. Law, U. P.R., 1973-79; law lectr. marine sci. program U. Miami, Fla., 1982—; treas. Gonzalez R. Investment Corp., P.R., 1958-79, dir., 1958-83. Recipient Civil and Comparative Law award, 1973. Mem. U. P.R. Law Rev., 1971-73, chmn. San Juan Mail Users Council, 1968. Mem. ABA, P.R. Bar Assn., P.R. Philatelic Soc. (founder 1952, pres. 1967-68). Legal education, Public international, Private international. Home: 1811 SW 99th Pl Miami FL 33165

MORENO, M. CRISTINA, lawyer; b. La Habana, Cuba, Dec. 7, 1952; came to U.S., 1960; d. Manuel Rafael and Esther (Pando) Morales-Gomez; m. Federico Antonio Moreno, May 31, 1977; children: Cristina Maria, Federico Antonio Jr. BA magna cum laude, U. Miami, 1973, JD magna cum laude, 1978. Bar: Fla. 1978, U.S. Dist. Ct. (so. dist.) Fla. 1979. Assoc. Paul, Landy, Beiley & Harper, Miami, Fla., 1978-80; ptnr. Murai, Wald, Biondo, Matthews & Moreno, Miami, 1980—; instr. law U. Miami, Coral Gables, 1980-81. Mem. ABA, Fla. Bar Assn., Fla. Assn. Women Lawyers, Dade County Bar Assn., Cuban Am. Bar Assn. Republican. Roman Catholic. Club: Big 5 (Miami). Avocations: photography, travel, volleyball, softball. Real property, Banking, Contracts commercial. Office: Murai Wald Biondo Matthews & Moreno 25 SE 2d Ave Suite 900 Miami FL 33131

MORETTI, AUGUST JOSEPH, lawyer; b. Elmira, N.Y., Aug. 18, 1950; s. John Anthony and Dorothy M. (De Blasio) M.; m. Audrey B Kavka, Nov. 8, 1981;children: David Anthony, Matthew Alexander. BA, Princeton U., 1972; JD, Harvard U., 1975. Assoc. Heller, Ehrman, White and McAuliffe, San Francisco, 1976-82; ptnr. Heller, Ehrman, Whitey and McAuliffe, San Francisco, 1982—; lectr. bus. adminstrn. U. Calif. Berkeley, 1977-79. Mem. ABA. General corporate, Securities. Office: Heller Ehrman White & McAuliffe 525 University Ave Palo Alto CA 94301

MORF, DARREL ARLE, lawyer; b. Fredericksburg, Iowa, Dec. 24, 1943; s. Arle Eric and Ruth Dagne (Vaala) M.; m. Mildred Mae Petersen, 1968; children—Paul Petersen, Andrew Thomas, John Alexander. B.A., U. Iowa, 1966, J.D., 1969. Bar: Iowa, U.S. Dist. Ct. (no. and so. dists.) Iowa 1970, U.S. Tax Ct. 1980, U.S. Ct. Appeals (8th cir.) 1970. Clk. to chief judge U.S. Ct. Appeals (8th cir.), 1969-70; ptnr. Simmons, Perrine, Albright & Ellwood, Cedar Rapids, Iowa, 1970—; dir. Brucemore, Inc.; lectr. U. Iowa Coll. Law, 1973—. Bd. dirs., sec. Hall Found.; trustee Herbert Hoover Presdl. Library Assn.; bd. dirs. Am. Bapt. Homes of Midwest, Cornell Coll., Mt. Vernon, Iowa, Mercy Hosp., Cedar Rapids. Mem. ABA, Iowa State Bar Assn., Linn County Bar Assn., Order of Coif. Clubs: Rotary, Lions, Masons. Estate planning, General corporate, Probate. Office: Simmons Perrine Albright & Ellwood Suite 1200 Merchants Nat Bank Bldg Cedar Rapids IA 54201

MORGAN, BRUCE KENT, lawyer; b. Holdrege, Nebr., Mar. 2, 1953; s. Howard Winfield and Phyllis Lee (Floro) M.; m. Cheryl Dee Bulkley, Jan. 4, 1974 (div. Dec. 1976); 1 child, Nichole Andrea; m. Tamara Painter, Sept. 23, 1978; children: Tiffany Laele, Paul Kent. BS, U. Utah, 1979; JD, U. of Pacific, 1982. Bar: Calif. 1982, U.S. Dist. Ct. (ea. dist.) Calif. 1982, Utah 1983, U.S. Dist. Ct. Utah 1983. Asst. atty. Sandy (Utah) City, 1982-84; dep. atty. Salt Lake County Attys., 1984—. Served with USN, 1970-74, Vietnam. Mem. ABA, Salt Lake County Bar Assn. Avocations: art, trains. Criminal, Government contracts and claims, Local government. Home: 8426 S 3150 W West Jordan UT 84084 Office: Salt Lake County Attys Office 231 E 400 S Suite 300 Salt Lake City UT 84111

MORGAN, CECILIA HUFSTEDLER, lawyer; b. Lubbock, Tex., Mar. 20, 1952; d. Jethro Douglas and Kathleen Teresa (Walker) Hufstedler; m. John Robert Morgan Jr., Feb. 14, 1981. BA, Abilene Christian Coll., 1974; JD, Tex. Tech U., 1977. Bar: Tex. 1977, U.S. Dist. Ct. (no. dist.) Tex. 1978, U.S. Ct. Appeals (5th cir.) 1981, U.S. Supreme Ct. 1982, U.S. Dist. Ct. (so. and we. dists.) Tex. 1984. Assoc. Peter S. Chantilis, Dallas, 1977-84; ptnr. Chantilis & Morgan, Dallas, 1984—. Mem. ABA, Tex. Bar Assn., Dallas Bar Assn. (vice chmn. law in changing soc. com. 1984, chmn. 1985—), Dallas Assn. Young Lawyers, Bar of 5th Cir. Assn. Mem. Ch. of Christ. General practice, Federal civil litigation, State civil litigation. Home: 3140 Westminster Dallas TX 75205 Office: Chantilis & Morgan 1233 Campbell Centre II 8150 N Central Expressway Dallas TX 75206-1863

MORGAN, DANIEL LOUIS, lawyer, educator; b. Newark, Oct. 17, 1952; s. A. Henry and Eunice (Neubauer) M. BA in History, Tufts U., 1974; JD, U. Conn., 1977; LLM, Georgetown U., 1981. Bar: Conn. 1977, D.C. 1978. Atty., advisor, chief counsel IRS, Washington, 1977-81; assoc. Tucker, Flyer, Sanger, & Lewis PC, Washington, 1981-85, ptnr., 1985—; adj. prof. Cath. U. Law Sch., Washington, 1984—. Contbr. articles to profl. jours. Mem. ABA (chmn. tax sect. com. on social security and payroll tax problems 1986—). Pension, profit-sharing, and employee benefits, Corporate taxation, General corporate. Office: Tucker Flyer Sanger & Lewis 1615 L St NW Ste 400 Washington DC 20036

MORGAN, DARWIN EDWARD, legal examiner; b. Greenburg, Ind., Nov. 19, 1946; s. Frank N. and Juanita (Zaring) M.; m. Nancy Parsons; Nov.25, 1971; children: Benjamin, Abigail. BA, Purdue U., 1973; MBA, JD, Ind. U., 1978. Bar: Pa. 1979, U.S. Dist. Ct. (we. dist.) Pa. 1979. Sole practice Erie, Pa., 1979-81; asst. prof. bus. law Pa. State U., Erie, 1981-86; legal examiner Am. Interins. Exchange, Indpls., 1986—. Contbr. articles to profl. jours. Participant Leadership Erie, 1982; bd. dirs., solicitor Flagship Niagara League, Erie, 1982-86; bd. dirs. Lake Area Health Edn. Ctr., Erie, 1983-86. Served with U.S. Army, 1968-71. Named Vol. of Yr. Flagship Niagara League, 1982, Tri-State Music Organ., 1984. Mem. ABA, Pa. Bar Assn., Erie County Bar Assn., Am. Bus. Law Assn. Democrat. Club: The Landmen (Erie) (bd. dirs. 1985-86). Insurance. OFfice: Am Interins Exchange PO Box 7009 Indianapolis IN 46207

MORGAN, DAVID SCOTT, lawyer; b. Reading, Pa., July 5, 1951; s. Charles House and Barbara Ann (Fry) M.; m. Jean Lenski, May 20, 1972; children: Jennifer, Rebecca. BA in English, Journalism, U. N.C., 1973; JD, Dickinson Coll., 1976. Bar: Pa. 1976, U.S. Dist. Ct. (ea. dist.) Pa. 1979, U.S. Ct. Appeals (3d cir.) 1982. Law clk. to presiding justice U.S. Dist. Ct. (ea. dist.), Reading, 1976-79; litigation atty. Consol. Rail Corp., Phila., 1979-86, commerce atty., 1986—. Quincy Sharp Mills scholar U. N.C. Mem. Nat. Assn. R.R. Trial Counsel. Democrat. Lutheran. Avocation: model railroads. Contracts commercial. Home: 52 N New Ardmore Ave Broomall PA 19008 Office: Consol Rail Corp 1138 Six Penn Ctr Philadelphia PA 19103

MORGAN, DENNIS RICHARD, lawyer; b. Lexington, Va., Jan. 3, 1942; s. Benjamin Richard and Gladys Belle (Brown) M. B.A., Washington and Lee U., 1964; J.D., U. Va., 1967; LL.M. in Labor Law, NYU, 1971. Bar: Ohio 1967, Va. 1967, U.S. Ct. Appeals (4th cir.) 1968, U.S. Ct. Appeals (6th cir.) 1971, U.S. Supreme Ct. 1972. Law clk. to chief judge U.S. Dist. Ct. Ea. Dist. Va., 1967-68; mem. Marshman, Snyder & Seeley (now Marshman, Snyder & Corrigan), Cleve., 1971-72; dir. labor relations Ohio Dept. Adminstrv. Services, 1972-75; asst. city atty. Columbus, Ohio, 1975-77; dir. Ohio Legis. Reference Bur., 1979-81; assoc. Clemans, Nelson & Assocs., Columbus, 1981; sole practice, Columbus, 1978—; lectr. in field; guest lectr. Central Mich. U., 1975; judge moot ct. Ohio State U. Sch. Law, 1981, 83, grad. div., 1973, 74, 76, Baldwin-Wallace Coll., 1973; legal counsel Dist. IV Communications Workers Am. Vice chmn. Franklin County Democratic Party, 1976-82, dem. com. person Ward 58, Columbus, 1973—; chmn. rules com. Ohio State Dem. Conv., 1974; co-founder, trustee Greater West Side Dem. Club; negotiator Franklin County United Way, 1977-81; regional chmn. ann. alumni fund-raising program U. Va. Sch. Law; mem. Friends of the Library, Franklin County, 1976—. Robert E. Lee Research scholar, summer, 1965; recipient Am. Jurisprudence award, 1967. Served to capt. U.S. Army, 1968-70. Mem. Indsl. Relations Research Assn., ABA, Fed. Bar Assn., Am. Judicature Soc., Pi Sigma Alpha. Roman Catholic. Clubs: Shamrock, Columbus Metroplitan (charter). Labor, Administrative and regulatory, Legislative. Home: 1261 Woodbrook Ln #G Columbus OH 43223

MORGAN, EDDIE LAMONT, county prosecutor, writer; b. Warren, Ohio, Apr. 16, 1949; s. Philip Lamont and Dorothy Marie (Franklin) M.; m. Nancy Delight Jones, July 21, 1972; children—Rhett David, Tanya Lee, Cheryl Diane, Candice Suzanne, Carrie Melissa, Clinton Edward. B.S. in Polit. Sci., Ariz. State U., 1971; J.D., U. Ariz., 1974. Bar: Ariz. 1974, U.S. Dist. Ct. Ariz. 1976, U.S. Supreme Ct. 1980. Dep. county atty., prosecutor trial bur. Maricopa County Atty.'s Office, Phoenix, 1974-76, assigned to organized crime bur., 1976-77, spl. ops. bur., 1977-81, organized crime and racketeering unit, 1981-86, juvenile div., 1986—; legal adviser organized crime bur. Phoenix Police Dept., 1977-86; lectr., tchr. in field. Author (procedure manual): Electronic Surveillance, 1981; author short stories, poems, songs. Coach Little League Baseball, Scottsdale, Ariz., 1977-82; bd. dirs. Boy Scouts Am., 1984. Recipient letters of commendation, including from Maricopa County Atty., 1976, chief Phoenix Police Dept., 1978, 80, FBI Dir. William H. Webster, 1986. Mem. Ariz. State Bar (criminal justice sect.). Republican. Methodist. Criminal. Office: Maricopa County Atty's Office Organized Crime and Racketeering 3125 W Durango Phoenix AZ 85003

MORGAN, FRANK EDWARD, II, lawyer, resource company executive; b. Burlington, Vt., May 16, 1952; s. Robert Griggs and Ruth (Jepson) M. First Class Cert. Merit, U. Edinburgh, Scotland, 1973; A.B. with honors, Brown U., 1974; LL.M., Cambridge U., Eng., 1976; J.D., U. Va., 1978. Bar: Mass. 1978. Assoc. Gaston Snow & Ely Bartlett, Boston, 1978-82; v.p., gen. counsel Adobe Resources, Corp., N.Y.C., 1982—; dir. Trend Internat. Ltd., Hamilton, Bermuda. Mem. ABA, Am. Soc. Internat. Law, Am. Soc. Corp. Secs. Republican. Congregationalist. Avocation: private pilot. General corporate, Securities, Private international. Home: 400 E 70th St New York NY 10021 Office: Adobe Resources Corp 645 Madison Ave New York NY 10022

MORGAN, JACK COCHRAN, lawyer; b. Nolan County, Tex., Mar. 17, 1928; s. John Franklin and Tommie Lee (Cochran) M.; m. Millie E. Edmunds, Jan. 24, 1953; children—Millicent, Jack C. B.A., U. Tex., Austin, 1950, J.D., 1950; LL.D., U. Tex.-Tyler, 1979. Bar: Tex. 1950, U.S. Dist. Ct. (no. dist.) Tex. 1960, U.S. Dist. Ct. (ea. dist.) Tex. 1973, U.S. Supreme Ct. 1954. Sole practice, 1950-51; asst. dist. atty., Kaufman County, Tex., 1951-52; sole practice, Kaufman, Tex., 1952-68; ptnr. Morgan & Shumpert, Kaufman, 1968-72; ptnr. Morgan, Shumpert, Huff, Mosley & Co., Kaufman, 1972-80; ptnr. Morgan & Mosley, Kaufman, 1980—. Mem. Tex. Legislature, 1955. Served to capt. USAFR. Democrat. Clubs: Rotary, Masons. Family and matrimonial, General practice, State civil litigation. Home: 1506 S Houston Kaufman TX 75142 Office: 201 W Mulberry St Kaufman TX 75142

MORGAN, LEWIS RENDER, U.S. judge; b. LaGrange, Ga., July 14, 1913; s. William Ellington and Bettie (Render) M.; m. Sue Phillips, July 29, 1944; children: Parks Healy, Sue Ann. Student, U. Mich., 1930-32; LL.B., U. Ga., 1935; LL.B. hon. degrees, Atlanta Law Sch., 1963, La Grange Coll., 1977. Bar: Ga. bar 1935. Mem. firm Wyatt & Morgan, LaGrange, 1935-61; U.S. judge No. Dist. Ga., 1961-68, chief judge, 1965-68; U.S. judge 5th and 11th Circuit Ct. of Appeals, 1968—; mem. budget com. U.S. Courts, 1967—; Mem. Gen. Assembly Ga., 1937-39; exec. sec. A. Sidney Camp (congressman), 1939-42; Mem. visitors com. U. Ga. Law Sch., 1970-73; mem. spl. div. U.S. Ct. Appeals for D.C., 1978—; mem. Temporary Emergency Ct. Appeals, 1979—. Mem. Chi Psi, Phi Delta Phi. Presbyn. Home: Cameron Mill Rd LaGrange GA 30240 Office: US Court Appeals PO Box 759 Newnan GA 30264

MORGAN, LOUIS LINTON, lawyer; b. New Orleans, May 4, 1935; s. Linton L. and Leona (Flieller) M.; m. Sally Bisso, May 25, 1963; children: Martin Louis, Michael Linton, Lauren Lee. BA in Econs., Tulane U., 1957, LLB, 1965. Bar: La. 1965, U.S. Dist. Ct. (ea. dist.) La. 1965, U.S. Supreme Ct. 1967, U.S. Dist. Ct. (we. dist.) La. 1987. From assoc. to ptnr. Liskow & Lewis, New Orleans, 1965-83; ptnr. Morgan & Williams, New Orleans, 1983—; prof. Tulane Law Sch., New Orleans, 1975—; adv. bd. Tulane Law Rev., 1969—; adv. council La. Dept. Natural Resources, Baton Rouge, 1980-83. Bd. dirs. Ind. Petroleum Assn. Am., Dallas, 1972-74; mem. La. Energy Bd., Baton Rouge, 1978. Served to capt. USMC, 1957-62. Mem. Order of Coif (pres. Tulane chpt. 1986—). Democrat. Roman Catholic. Avocations: golfing, boating. Oil and gas leasing, Banking, General corporate. Home: 5660 Cherlyn Dr New Orleans LA 70124 Office: Morgan & Williams 336 Camp New Orleans LA 70130

MORGAN, MICHAEL VINCENT, lawyer; b. Detroit, July 31, 1947; s. Stanley William and Alice (Michalski) M.; m. Susan Wanda Staub, Aug. 21, 1970; children—Jason, Allison. B.A., U. Detroit, 1969, J.D., 1972. Bar: Mich. 1972, U.S. Dist. Ct. (ea. dist.) Mich., 1972. Chmn. Lic. Appeal Bd. Mich. Dept. State, Detroit, 1972-73; sole practice, Detroit, 1973-75, Troy,

Mich., 1975—; lectr. in field. Editor: Michigan Drunk Driving Law & Practice, 1986; contbr. articles to profl. publs. Bd. dirs. U. Detroit Nat. Alumni Bd., 1974-77. Recipient Athletic Dirs. award U. Detroit, 1983. Mem. State Bar Mich., Detroit Bar Assn. Roman Catholic. Clubs: Titan (bd. dirs. 1982-86), Advocates (Detroit). Criminal. Office: 2970 E Big Beaver St Troy MI 48083

MORGAN, REBECCA C., lawyer, educator; b. Clinton, Mo.. BSBA, Cen. Mo. State U., 1975; JD, Stetson U., 1980. Bar: Fla . 1981, U.S. Ct. Appeals (11th cir.) 1981, U.S. Dist. Ct. (mid. dist.) Fla. 1982. Staff atty. sr. unit Gulfcoast Legal Services, St. Petersburg, Fla., 1981-83; project dir. sr. citizens project Pinellas & Manatee (Fla.) Counties, 1984-85; vis. asst. prof. Stetson Coll. Law, St. Petersburg, 1985—. Dir. Stetson Elderlaw Clinic. Mem. ABA (exec. com. Young Lawyers div. delivery of legal services to elderly 1986—), Fla. Bar Assn. (chmn. com. on elderly 1986—), St. Petersburg Bar Assn. Legal problems of the elderly. Office: Stetson U Coll Law 1401 61st St S Saint Petersburg FL 33707

MORGAN, RICHARD HURSTON, JR., lawyer; b. Memphis, Feb. 12, 1944; s. Richard Hurston and Lula (Redditt) M.; m. Olga Elaine Jackson, Nov. 15, 1981; children: Nia Abena, Amirh Adzua, Darrin Allen, Heather Nicole. BA, Western Mich. U., 1968, MA, 1969; JD, U. Detroit, 1973. Bar: Mich. 1974, U.S. Dist. Ct. (ea. and so. dists.) Mich. 1974, U.S. Supreme Ct. 1981. Asst. v.p. Oakland U., Rochester, Mich., 1969-75; atty. Law Offices William Waterman, Pontiac, Mich., 1975-77, Law Offices Elbert Hatchett, Pontiac, 1978-83; sr. ptnr. Morgan & William, Pontiac, 1983—. Office: Morgan & William 47 Saginaw Ave Pontiac MI 48058

MORGAN, RICHARD MOORE, lawyer; b. Hamlet, N.C.; s. Zebulon Vance and Bertha Wilson (Moore) M.; m. Mary James Sutherland, May 14, 1965 (div. July 1985); children: Alice Lucinda, Mary Anita. AB, Davidson Coll., 1962; JD, Duke U., 1965. Bar: N.C. 1965, U.S. Dist. Ct. (ea. and mid. dists.) N.C. 1965, U.S. Ct. Appeals (4th cir.) 1965. From assoc. to ptnr. Stevens, McGhee, Morgan, Lennon & O'Quinn, Wilmington, N.C., 1968—. Trustee New Hanover County Retirement System, Wilmington; bd. dirs. Lower Cape Fear Arts Council, Wilmington, Wilmington Civic Ballet. Served to capt. U.S. Army, 1965-68, Vietnam. Decorated Bronze Star. Presbyterian. Clubs: Cape Fear (Wilmington, N.C.); Cape Fear Country Club. Office: Stevens McGhee Morgan Lennon & O'Quinn 409 Wachovia Bank Bldg PO Box 59 Wilmington NC 28402

MORGAN, ROBERT EDWARD, state justice; b. Mitchell, S.D., Aug. 13, 1924; s. Chester Lawrence and Phyllis Mae (Saterlie) M.; m. Mary Doyle, Oct. 28, 1950; children: Mary Alice, Michael Chester, Thomas Wayne, Margaret Jane; m. Mary Ann Ver Meulen, June 1, 1974; 1 child, Daniel James. Student, Creighton U., 1942, 46-47, 48; J.D., U. S.D., 1950. Bar: S.D. 1950. Mem. firm Mitchell & Chamberlain, S.D., 1950-76; justice S.D. Supreme Ct., Pierre, 1977—. Served with USAAF, 1943-45. Mem. ABA, S.D. Bar Assn. Judicial administration. Office: U SD Sch Law Vermillion SD 57069

MORGAN, ROBERT HALL, lawyer; b. San Jose, Calif., Oct. 14, 1950; s. William Robert and Willa June (Hall) M.; m. Susan Kay Meyer, June 16, 1972; children: Robert Scott, Ryan William, Cory Benjamin, Nathan Thomas, Katherine Linn. BA, U. Oreg., 1974; MBA, U. Santa Clara, 1975, JD summa cum laude, 1978. Bar: Calif. 1978, U.S. Dist. Ct. (no. dist.) Calif. 1978. Legal extern Supreme Ct. Calif., San Francisco, 1978; ptnr. Morgan & Towery (formerly Morgan, Morgan, Towery, Morgan & Spector), San Jose, Calif., 1978—; counsel Better Bus. Bur. Santa Clara Valley, Ltd., San Jose, 1980-86. Bd. dirs. Metro Pal Youth Soccer, San Jose, 1982, San Jose Am. Little League, 1983—. Mem. Santa Clara County Bar Assn., Assn. Trial Lawyers Am. Democrat. Federal civil litigation, State civil litigation, Probate. Office: Morgan & Towery 1651 N 1st St San Jose CA 95112

MORGAN, THOMAS JADA, lawyer; b. Raleigh, N.C., June 29, 1950; s. Walter Truett and Bessie Mae (Butt) M.; m. Karen Annette Johnston, Feb. 7, 1982. BS in Indsl. Relations, U. N.C., 1972; JD, Mercer U., 1976. Bar: Ga. 1976, N.C. 1976, U.S. Dist. Ct. (mid. dist.) Ga. 1976, U.S. Dist. Ct. (ea. dist.) N.C. 1977, U.S. Ct. Appeals (4th cir.) 1981. Assoc. Hunoval, Fullwood & Kingsley, Wilmington, N.C., 1976-81; ptnr. Fullwood & Morgan, Wilmington, 1981—. Mem. ABA, N.C. Bar Assn., N.C. Acad. Trial Lawyers, Phi Delta Phi. Democrat. Episcopalian. Club: Exchange (pres. 1985—). Avocation: water sports, fishing. Personal injury, Real property, Criminal. Office: Fullwood & Morgan 19 N 5th Ave Wilmington NC 28401

MORGAN, THOMAS SIDNEY, lawyer; b. Kansas City, Mo., Feb. 21, 1951; s. David Basil and Elsie Catherine (Cairns) M.; m. LaVerne Faye Teichelman, Dec. 29, 1973; Meredith Sheree, Brent Adam. U. Tex., 1972; JD, Baylor U., 1975. Bar: Tex. 1975, U.S. Dist. Ct. (we. and no. dists.) Tex. 1975, U.S. Ct. Appeals (5th cir.) 1975, U.S. Supreme Ct. 1975. Asst. atty. County of Bell, Tex., 1975-83; sr. staff atty. Tex. Ct. of Appeals, Dallas, 1983-84; adminstrv. asst. dist. atty. Dist. Atty.'s Office, Midland, Tex., 1984-86; assoc. Robert R. Truitt, Jr. P.C., Midland, 1986-87; sole practice Midland, 1987—. Author: Juvenile Law and Practice, 1985. Mem. ABA, Tex. Bar Assn. Republican. Lodge: Lions. Avocations: golf, tennis. Bankruptcy, Criminal, Juvenile. Home: 2826 Northtown Place Midland TX 79705 Office: 1701 N Big Spring Midland TX 79701

MORGAN, TIMI SUE, lawyer; b. Parsons, Kans., June 16, 1953; d. James Daniel and Iris Mae (Wilson) Baumgardner; m. Rex Michael Morgan, Oct. 28, 1983; 1 child, Tessa Anne. BS, U. Kans., 1974; JD, So. Meth. U., 1977. Bar: Tex. 1977, U.S. Dist. Ct. (no. dist.) Tex. 1978, U.S. Ct. Appeals (5th cir.) 1979, U.S. Tax Ct. 1980. Assoc. Gardere & Wynne, Dallas, 1977-79; assoc. Akin, Gump, Strauss, Hauer & Feld, Dallas, 1979-83, ptnr., 1984-86; of counsel Stinson, Mag & Fizzell, Dallas, 1986—. Mem. Dallas Symphony Orchestra League Innovators. Mem. State Bar Tex., Dallas Bar Assn., Tex. Young Lawyers Assn., Dallas Assn. Young Lawyers, So. Meth. U. Law Alumni Council (sec. 1985-86), Order of Coif, Beta Gamma Sigma. Republican. Episcopalian. Corporate taxation, Personal income taxation, State and local taxation. Home: 3416 Amherst Dallas TX 75225 Office: Stinson Mag & Fizzell 4000 Lincoln Plaza 500 N Akard Dallas TX 75201

MORGAN, WENDELL RICHMOND, medical association executive, lawyer; b. Mobile, Ala., Apr. 27, 1943; s. Thomas Wendell and Catherine (Lewis) M.; m. Joan Louise Cannon, June 5, 1965; children—Wendell Richmond, Thomas Brent, Bonnie Alice-Louise. B.A., Auburn U., 1965; J.D., U. Ala., 1969. Bar: Ala. 1969, U.S. Dist. Ct. (so. dist.) Ala. 1973, U.S. Dist. Ct. (mid. dist.) Ala., U.S. Dist. Ct. (no. dist.) Ala. 1974, U.S. Ct. Appeals (11th cir.) 1981. Sole practice, Montgomery, Ala., 1969-76; asst. atty. gen. Ala. Dept. Mental Health, Montgomery, 1976-80; gen. counsel Med. Assn. State of Ala., Montgomery, 1981—. Served to 1st lt. AUS, 1966-68. Decorated Bronze Star medal; recipient Am. Jurisprudence award Ban Croft-Whitney Co. and Lawyers Coop. Pub. Co., 1969. Mem. ABA (forum com. on health law 1982-85), Nat. Health Lawyers Assn., Am. Soc. Law and Medicine, Am. Assn. Med. Soc. Execs., Am. Assn. Corp. Counsel. Methodist. General corporate, Health, Federal civil litigation. Address: PO Box 1900-C Montgomery AL 36104

MORGAN, WILLIAM BORDEN, lawyer, educator; b. West Long Branch, N.J., May 17, 1944; s. Charles Lester and V. Claire (Johnson) M.; m. Marjorie M. Mitchell, Sept. 4, 1967; 1 child, Marjorie Claire. AB, Muhlenberg Coll., 1966; JD, U. Tulsa, 1971. Bar: Okla. 1972, U.S. Dist. Ct. (no. dist.) Okla. 1972, U.S. Ct. Appeals (10th cir.) 1972, U.S. Supreme Ct. 1977. Assoc. Doerner, Stuart, Saunders, Daniel & Anderson, Tulsa, 1972-76, ptnr., 1976—; adj. prof. law U. Tulsa, 1973—. Vice chmn. Town & Country Sch., Tulsa, 1982—; bd. dirs. Arts & Humanities Council of Tulsa, 1984—; pres. Theatre Tulsa, Inc., 1984—. Served to 1st lt. U.S. Army, 1966-69, Vietnam. Decorated Bronze Star. Mem. ABA, Okla. Bar Assn., Tulsa County Bar Assn. Republican. Unitarian. Club: Tulsa. Securities. Home: 1201 E 20th St Tulsa OK 74105 Office: Doerner Stuart et al 1000 Atlas Life Bldg Tulsa OK 74103

MORGAN, WILLIAM CASWELL, lawyer, computer specialist; b. Phila., Aug. 27, 1932; s. David Robert and Mary (Caswell) M.; m. Irmgard Helwing, June 15, 1957; children: Christel, Irvin, Michael. AB, Cornell U., 1954; JD, U. Balt., 1974. Bar: Pa. 1974, D.C. 1984. Mgmt. trainee U.S. Dept. Agriculture, Phila., 1962-63; mgmt. analyst U.S. Dept. Agriculture, Washington, 1963-66, U.S. Army, Washington, 1966-67; computer specialist USMC, Washington, 1967-71, U.S. Dept. Transp., Washington, 1971—; bd. dirs. Realty Engring Corp., Bowie, Md. Pres. Bowie chpt. U.S. Jaycees, 1969-70; J.C.I. hon. senator, 1969; bd. dirs. Ctr. for Community Devel., Riverdale, Md., 1985-86, bd. dirs. Fed. Exec. and Profl. Assn., Washington, 1984-86; mem. exec. com. Pub. Employees Roundtable, Washington, 1986. Served to 1st lt. U.S. Army, 1954-56. Mem. ABA, Pa. Bar Assn., D.C. Bar Assn. (computer law div., litigation div.). Republican. Methodist. Avocations: jogging, growing roses and other flowers. Computer, Federal civil litigation, Trademark and copyright. Home: 12304 Melling Ln Bowie MD 20715 Office: Office of Sec Dept Transp 400 7th St SW Washington DC 20850

MORGAN, WILLIAM ROBERT, lawyer; b. Arkansas City, Kans., Jan. 6, 1924; s. Louis and Betty (Starner) M.; m. Willa June Hall, Mar. 11, 1945; children: Marilyn, Robert. A.A., Arkansas City Jr. Coll., 1942; postgrad., U. Okla., 1942-43, Susquehanna U., 1943; B.A., Stanford U., 1948, LL.B., 1949. Bar: Calif. 1949, U.S. Supreme Ct. 1953. Assoc. Johnson, Morgan, Thorne, Speed & Bamford, San Jose, Calif., 1949-52; founder, partner Morgan, Beauzay, Hammer, Ezgar, Bledsoe & Rucka (and predecessors), San Jose, 1952-78; sr. ptnr. Morgan & Towery, San Jose, 1978—; pres., chmn. bd. Triton Corp.; owner, operator Sta. KRAD, Perry, Okla. Author: Chairman Mao's Big Red Book, 1976, Justin Morgan, Founder of the Breed, 1987, Morgan Horse of the West, 1985; editor Labor Code Annotated, 1960—, Twenty-Four Dramatic Cases of the International Academy of Trial Lawyers, 1974. Chmn. San Jose Fine Arts Commn., 1960-63; chmn., bd. dirs. Triton Mus. Art, 1963; mem. central com. Santa Clara County Democratic Party, 1958-60; campaign mgr. numerous Calif. Democrats; mem. San Martin Planning Commn., 1981, Calif. Jud. Council, 1980-83; Gideon elder Presbyn. Ch. Served with U.S. Army, 1943-46. W. Robert Morgan day proclaimed on March 14, 1972 by resolution of Calif. Senate. Mem. ABA (Bus. Frauds and Their Complexities, 1986), Calif. Bar Assn. (bd. govs. 1977-80), Santa Clara County Bar Assn. (pres.), Santa Clara County Bar Assn. (pres. sr. lawyers club 1986-87), Calif. State Bar (v.p. 1979-80, exec. bd. law office mgmt. sect. 1980—), Assn. Trial Lawyers Am. (jud. council), Internat. Acad. Trial Lawyers (past pres., past sec., Am. nat. dir. at large), No. Calif. Morgan Horse Clubs, Geranium Soc. Presbyterian (elder). Clubs: Masons, Shriners (v.p. club), Eastern Star, Rotary, Kiwanis. State civil litigation, Federal civil litigation, Personal injury. Home: 9500 New Ave PO Box 1507 Gilroy CA 95020 Office: 1651 N 1st St San Jose CA 95112

MORGANROTH, FRED, lawyer; b. Detroit, Mar. 26, 1938; s. Ben and Grace (Greenfield) M.; m. Janice Marilyn Cohn, June 23, 1963; children: Greg, Candi, Erik. BA, Wayne State U., 1959, JD with distinction, 1961. Bar: Mich. 1961, U.S. Dist. Ct. (ea. dist.) Mich. 1961, U.S. Supreme Ct. 1966, U.S. Ct. Claims 1967. Ptnr. Greenbaum, Greenbaum & Morganroth, Detroit, 1963-68, Lebenbom, Handler, Brody & Morganroth, Detroit, 1968-70, Lebenbom, Morganroth & Stern, Southfield, Mich., 1971-78; sole practice Southfield, 1979-83; ptnr. Morganroth & Morganroth P.C., Southfield, 1983—. Mem. Mich. Bar Assn. (hearing panelist grievance bd. 1975—), Detroit Bar Assn., Oakland Bar Assn. (cir. ct. mediator 1983—, dist. ct. mediator 1984—), Mich. Trial Lawyers Assn., Am. Arbitration Assn. Jewish. Clubs: Detroit Tennis (Farmington, Mich.) (pres. 1978-82); Admirals (N.Y.). Avocations: comml. pilot, tennis. Federal civil litigation, Family and matrimonial, Real property. Home: 30920 Woodcrest Ct Franklin MI 48025 Office: 4000 Town Center Suite 555 Southfield MI 48075

MORGANROTH, MAYER, lawyer; b. Detroit, Mar. 20, 1931; s. Maurice Jack Morganroth and Sophie (Reisman) Blum; m. Sheila Rubinstein, Aug. 16, 1958; children: Lauri, Jeffrey, Cherie. JD, Detroit Coll. Law, 1954. Bar: Mich. 1955, Ohio 1958, U.S. Ct. Appeals (6th cir.) 1968, U.S. Supreme Ct. 1971, N.Y. 1985, U.S. Tax Ct. 1985, U.S. Ct. Appeals (4th cir.) 1985, U.S. Ct. Claims 1986, U.S. Ct. Appeals (2d cir.) 1986. Sole practice Detroit, 1955—, N.Y.C., 1983—; cons. to lending instns.; lectr. on real estate NYU, 1980—, bus. entities and structures Wayne State U., 1981—. Served with USN, 1948-50. Mem. ABA, N.Y. State Bar Assn., Southfield Bar Assn., Assn. Trial Lawyers Am., Am. Judicature Soc. Republican. Jewish. Clubs: West Bloomfield (Mich.) Country; Fairlane (Dearborn, Mich.); Knollwood, Edgewood Athletic (pres. 1963-65). Federal civil litigation, State civil litigation, Criminal. Office: 24901 Northwestern #555 Southfield MI 48075 Also Office: 99 Park Ave New York NY 10016

MORGEN, RICHARD BURTON, corporate lawyer; b. Bklyn., Mar. 16, 1934; s. Sam M. and Anna (Lembeck) Morgenstern; m. Lorraine Alice Perry, Sept. 1, 1958; children: Allison F., Matthew S. BS in Acctg., L.I. U., 1955; LLB, Bklyn. Coll., 1958; LLM in Tax, NYU, 1962. Bar: N.Y. 1959, N.J. 1963. Ptnr. S.J. Perzanowski, Paterson, N.J., 1962-70, 75-77; v.p. The Aims Group Inc., N.Y.C., 1970-75; fin. planner Merrill, Lynch, Pierce, Fenner & Smith, N.Y.C., 1977-81; asst. tax counsel N.Y. Life Ins. Co., N.Y.C., 1981—. Trustee Temple Sharey Tefilo/Israel, South Orange, N.J., 1985—. Mem. Am. Council Life Ins. (editor information at source manual 1983, 85, mem. annuity task force), Com. Annuity Insurers, Domestic Preference Tax Group. Democrat. Jewish. Avocation: white water rafting. Corporate taxation, Estate taxation, State and local taxation. Home: 12 Fairway Dr West Orange NJ 07052 Office: NY Life Ins Co 51 Madison Ave New York NY 10010

MORGENSTERN, JONATHAN DAVID, lawyer; b. Cleve., Sept. 5, 1954; s. Conrad Jack and Renee (Saltzman) M. BA, Oberlin Coll., 1978; JD, Case Western Res. U., 1981. Bar: Ohio 1982, U.S. Dist. Ct. (no. dist.) Ohio 1982, Tex. 1985, U.S. Dist. Ct. (no. dist.) Tex. 1985, U.S. Ct. Appeals (6th cir.) 1986. Dir. advt. promotion Scene Mag., Cleve., 1975-77; asst. base mgr. Neptune Oil Co., A-Tur, Sinai Penisula, 1978-79; acct. rep. Ohio Bus. Jour., Cleve., 1979; assoc. Morgenstern & Assocs. Co., L.P.A., Cleve., 1982-85, Arter, Hadden & Witts, Dallas, 1985-86, Page & Addison, P.C., Dallas, 1986-87; sole practice Dallas, 1987—; of counsel Kaplan & Dowd, P.C., Dallas, 1987—, and Morgenstern & Assocs. Co. L.P.A., Cleve., 1985—; arbitrator Cuyahoga County Common Pleas Ct., Cleve., 1984—. Contbg. editor Health Matrix Jour., 1981-82. Mem. Dallas County Young Reps. Recipient Degrees of Excellence, Merit and Honor, Nat. Forensic League; fellow Eisendrath Internat. Exchange. Mem. ABA, Ohio Bar Assn. (author jour. and reports), Tex. Bar Assn., Dallas County Bar Assn. (unauthorized practice com., media relations com.), Cuyahoga County Bar Assn. (contbg. editor Law & Fact Jour. 1985), Ohio Bar Coll., Dallas Assn. Young Lawyers (exec. bd. mem., chairperson law talk com.), Ctr. for Automotive Safety, U.S. Arbirtation, Inc., Am. Arbitration Assn. Jewish. Club: Texas (Dallas). Avocations: squash, weightlifting, triathlons. Federal civil litigation, State civil litigation, Bankruptcy. Office: 3030 McKinney Suite #803 Dallas TX 75204 Also Office: Morgenstern and Assocs Co LPA 510 Leader Bldg Cleveland OH 44114

MORGENSTERN, ROBERT TERENCE, lawyer; b. N.Y.C., Aug. 23, 1944; s. Carl G. and Jean C. (Madden) M.; m. Nancy G. Golden, June 29, 1968; children: Cynthia, John, Katherine, Brian. BA, Villanova U., 1966, JD, 1969. Bar: N.J. 1969, U.S. Supreme Ct. 1986. Assoc. Dolan & Dolan, Newton, N.J., 1969-74, officer, dir., 1975—; bd. atty. Andover Twp. Planning Bd., Sussex County, N.J., 1977—, Andover Twp. Zoning Bd., 1977—, Hampton Twp. Planning Bd., Sussex County, 1979—, Branchville Boro Planning Bd., Sussex County, 1981—, Branchville Boro Zoning Bd., 1981—. Legacy chmn. Am. Cancer Soc., Newton, 1969-75; active Morris-Sussex area council Boy Scouts Am., 1969-71. Mem. ABA, Assn. Trial Lawyers Am., N.J. Fedn. Planning Officials, N.J. Inst. Mcpl. Attys., Sussex County Bar Assn., N.J. State Bar Assn., Newton C. of C. Roman Catholic. Lodge: Lions (sec. 1976-77), Rotary. Real property, State civil litigation, Probate. Home: 31 Westgate Dr Sparta NJ 07871 Office: Dolan & Dolan PA 53 Spring St & 1 Legal Ln PO Box D Newton NJ 07860

MORGENTHAU, ROBERT MORRIS, lawyer; b. N.Y.C., July 31, 1919; s. Henry, Jr. and Elinor (Fatman) M.; m. Martha Pattridge (dec.); children: Joan, Anne, Elinor, Robert P., Barbara; m. Lucinda Franks, Nov. 19, 1977. Grad., Deerfield (Mass.) Acad., 1937; B.A., Amherst Coll., 1941, LL.D. (hon.), 1966; LL.B., Yale U., 1948; LL.D. (hon.), N.Y. Law Sch., 1968, Syracuse Law Sch., 1976, Albany Law Sch., 1982. Bar: N.Y. 1949. Assoc. firm Patterson Belknap & Webb, N.Y.C., 1948-53; partner Patterson Belknap & Webb, 1954-61; U.S. atty. So. Dist. N.Y., 1961-62, 62-70; dist. atty. New York County, 1975—. Mem. N.Y. exec. com. State of Israel Bonds; pres. Police Athletic League.; Democratic candidate for gov., N.Y., 1962; Bd. dirs. P.R. Legal Def. and Edn. Fund; trustee Baron de Hirsch Fund, Lochland Sch., Fedn. Jewish Philanthropies, Temple Emanu-El, N.Y.C. Served with USNR, 1941-45. Fellow Am. Bar Found.; mem. Am., N.Y. State, Bronx County bar assns., Assn. Bar City N.Y., N.Y. County Lawyers Assn., Phi Beta Kappa Lodge: B'nai B'rith. Office: Office of Dist Atty 155 Leonard St New York NY 10013 *

MORI, JUN, lawyer; b. San Francisco, Dec. 13, 1929; s. Isamu Arthur and Hide (Nakae) M.; m. May Tsutsumoto, Apr. 25, 1954; children: Jean Kikuko, Richard Isamu, Ken Arthur. B.A., UCLA, 1955; LL.B., Waseda U., Tokyo, Japan, 1951; J.D., U. So. Calif., 1958. Bar: Calif. 1959, U.S. Supreme Ct. 1971, D.C. 1979. Dep. commr. of corp. State of Calif., 1959-60; sr. ptnr. firm Mori & Ota, Los Angeles, 1960-84, Kelly Drye & Warren, Los Angeles and N.Y.C., 1984—; dir. Yamaha Internat. Corp., Buena Park, Calif.; legal adviser Sumitomo Bank of Calif., Los Angeles, 1962—. Chmn. Los Angeles-Nagoya Sister City Affiliation, 1966-67; trustee UCLA Found.; mem. com. on Pacific Basin studies UCLA; pres. Bd. Harbor Commrs., City of Los Angeles, 1980-82; mem. adv. bd. Office Internat. Trade, Calif. Dept. Econ. and Bus. Devel.; mem. President's Export Council. Mem. Am. Bar Assn., Am. Judicature Soc., Japanese Am. Jr. C. of C. (pres. 1962-63), Japan Am. Soc. So. Calif., Los Angeles World Affairs Council. Home: 2219 Cheswic Ln Los Angeles CA 90027 Office: 624 S Grand Ave Suite 2600 Los Angeles CA 90017 also: 101 Park Ave New York NY 10178

MORIARITY, JOHN L., lawyer; b. North Hollywood, Calif., Oct. 23, 1932; s. William Joseph and Mary Elizabeth (Rising) M.; m. Maria Anne Tanzola, July 24, 1966; children: Donald, Lloyd, Lynda, Robert, Douglas, John Jr. BA in History, UCLA, 1957, JD, 1960; postdoctoral, U. So. Calif., 1961-62. Bar: Calif. 1961, U.S. Dist. Ct. (cen. dist.) Calif. 1961, U.S. Dist. Ct. D.C. 1984. Claims rep. Farmers Ins. Co., Los Angeles, 1960-61; dep. states atty. State of Calif., Los Angeles, 1960-63; sole practice Van Nuys, Calif., 1964—; commr. U.S. Dept. Transp., Washington, 1984—, Los Angeles County, 1985—. Del. Reagan for Pres., 1976, 80, 84; commdr. Mil. Order World Wars, 1979. Served to col. U.S. Army, 1954-56, with Res. 1951-54, 71—. Mem. San Fernando Valley Bar Assn. (trustee 1976), Calif. Trial Lawyers Assn. (polit. action com. bd. dirs. 1984-85), Los Angeles Trial Lawyer Assn. (trustee 1966-71), San Fernando Valley Bus. and Profl. Assn. (pres. 1983-85, bd. dirs. 1971—), Am. Ednl. League (bd. dirs. 1985—), Assn. U.S. Army (bd. dirs. 1977—), Granada Hills C. of C. (pres. 1969-71). Lutheran. Clubs: Lincoln (San Fernando Valley) (pres. 1978); Little League (Woodland Hills) (mgr. 1976-80). Avocation: world travel. Personal injury, Military. Office: 14123 Victory Blvd Van Nuys CA 91401

MORIARTY, HERBERT BERNARD, JR., lawyer; b. Memphis, June 5, 1929; s. Herbert Bernard and Kathleen (Prindaville) M.; 6 children. B.A., Vanderbilt, U., 1950, J.D., 1952. Bar: Tenn. 1952, U.S. Supreme Ct. 1956, U.S. Ct. Mil. Appeals 1956. commr. Shelby County, 1960-66; mem. firm Moriarty & Smith, Memphis; mem. Tenn. State Legislature, 1959-60, Democratic exec. com., 1959-62; lectr. ABA, Am. Law Inst., 1980. Pres., Muscular Dystrophy Assn., 1957-62; dir. Goodwill Industries, 1960-66; chmn. NCCJ, Memphis, 1962, life bd. dirs., 1963—. Served to capt. JAGC USAF, 1952-54. Recipient Disting. Service award, U.S. Jaycees, Memphis, 1963, Disting. Merit Citation, NCCJ, 1968. Mem. ABA, Tenn. Bar Assn., Shelby County Bar Assn., Memphis Bar Assn., Young Lawyers Assn. Memphis (v.p. 1957-58), Am. Legion (adj. Memphis Post 1 1959), Sigma Chi, Delta Theta Phi. Democrat. Roman Catholic. Clubs: University, Racquet (Memphis). Lodge: Kiwanis (bd. dirs. East Memphis chpt. 1974-75). Federal civil litigation, State civil litigation, Environment. Home: 222 Meadowgrove Ln Memphis TN 38119 Office: Moriarty & Smith 1420 White Station Tower Memphis TN 38157

MORIARTY, JAMES PAUL, lawyer; b. Boston, July 13, 1955; s. Robert D. Sr. and Irene (McCann) M.; m. Dawn Lin Lordan, Dec. 24, 1977; 1 child, Ian Jeffrey. AB cum laude, Suffolk U., 1977, JD, 1982. Bar: Mass. 1982, U.S. Dist. Ct. Mass. 1982, Maine 1983, U.S. Dist. Ct Maine 1983, U.S. Ct. Appeals (1st cir.) 1983. Sole practice Presque Isle, Maine, 1982—. Mem. ABA, Maine Bar Assn., Mass. Bar Assn., Presque Isle Bar Assn., Mass. Acad. Trial Attys. Lodge: Kiwanis. State civil litigation, Personal injury, General practice. Home and Office: 27 Mechanic St Presque Isle ME 04769

MORIBONDO, THOMAS PETER, lawyer; b. Darby, Pa., Oct. 22, 1954; s. Charles C. and Marie (Salvati) M.; m. Cynthia Del Sordo, Oct. 26, 1984. BA, Villanova U., 1976, JD, 1979. Bar: Pa. 1979, U.S. Dist. Ct. (ea. dist.) Pa. 1980, U.S. Ct. Appeals (3d cir.) 1980. Law clk. presiding justice U.S. Ct. Appeals (3d cir.), Phila., 1978; atty. Gustine Pelagatti, Phila., 1980-81; sole practice Phila., 1981—. Mem. Pa. Bar Assn., Assn. Trial Lawyers Am. Roman Catholic. Avocations: travel, WWII history. Personal injury, State civil litigation, Workers' compensation. Home: 1428 Linden Ln West Chester PA 19380 Office: 1616 Walnut St 22nd Floor Philadelphia PA 19103

MORIMOTO, MARY A., lawyer; b. San Diego, July 20, 1957. BA in Linguistics, Stanford U., 1979; JD, NYU, 1982. Bar: Tex. 1982, Calif. 1984. Assoc. Vinson & Elkins, Houston, 1982-83, Freshman, Marantz, Orlanski, Cooper & Klein, Beverly Hills, 1984—. Business, Securities.

MORITZ, PRESTON WILLIAM, lawyer; b. North Catasauqua, Pa., June 21, 1939; s. Preston James and Margaret (Bretz) M.; m. Nadine F. Paulnack, Oct. 25, 1962; children—Nadia A., Jennifer C., Preston T., Joshua M. Student U.S. Coast Guard Acad., 1958-60; B.A., Moravian Coll., 1963; J.D., Dickinson Sch. Law, 1966. Bar: Pa. 1966. Assoc. Brose, Poswistilo & LaBarr, Easton, Pa., 1966-70; v.p. Lehigh Valley Title Co., 1968-70; ptnr. Peters, Moritz, Peischl and Zulick, Nazareth, Pa., 1970—; guest lectr. Nazareth Area Sch. Dist. Pres. Lehigh Valley Football All-Star Game, 1981-82; coach youth group, 1977-79; vice-chmn. service Minsi Trail council Boy Scouts Am., 1975-76; mem. exec. bd. Northampton County chpt. Am. Cancer Soc.; Northampton County Young Republicans. Recipient City of Easton citation, 1968. Mem. ABA, Pa. Bar Assn., Northampton County Bar Assn., Nat. Sch. Bd. Solicitor Orgn., Nazareth Area C. of C. (pres. 1977), Nat. Hall of Fame and Football Found. (Lehigh Valley chpt.). Republican. Lutheran. Contbr. article to law jour.; author several fiction stories. State civil litigation, Family and matrimonial, Personal injury. Home: 305 E Center St Nazareth PA 18064 Office: Center Square Nazareth PA 18064

MORONEY, LINDA LELIA SUSAN, lawyer; b. Washington, May 27, 1943; d. Robert Emmet and Jessie (Robinson) M.; m. Clarence Renshaw II, Mar. 28, 1967 (div. 1977); children: Robert Milnor, Justin W.R. BA, Randolph-Macon Woman's Coll., 1965; JD cum laude, U. Houston, 1982. Bar: Tex. 1982, U.S. Ct. Appeals (5th cir.) 1982, U.S. Dist. Ct. (so. dist.) Tex. 1982. Law clk. to assoc. justice 14th Ct. Appeals, Houston, 1982-83; assoc. Pannill and Reynolds, Houston, 1983-85, Gilpin, Pohl & Bennett, Houston, 1985—; adj. prof. law U. Houston, 1986—. Mem. ABA, Tex. Bar Assn., Houston Bar Assn., Order of the Barons, Phi Delta Phi. Episcopalian. Federal civil litigation, State civil litigation, Real property. Home: 3730 Overbrook Houston TX 77027

MORONEY, MICHAEL JOHN, lawyer; b. Jamaica, N.Y., Nov. 8, 1940; s. Everard Vincent and Margaret Olga (Olson) M.; m. Sandra S.Y. Chun, Oct. 22, 1966; children: Sean, Megan, Matthew. BS in Polit. Sci., Villanova U., 1962; JD, Fordham U., 1965; Police Sci. (hon.), U. Guam, 1976. Bar: Hawaii 1974, U.S. Dist. Ct. Hawaii 1974, U.S. Ct. Appeals (9th cir.) 1974, Guam 1976, U.S. Dist. Ct. (Guam dist.) 1976, U.S. Ct. Claims 1976, U.S. Tax Ct. 1976, U.S. Ct. Mil. Appeals 1977, U.S. Supreme Ct. 1977, High Ct. Trust Ters. 1977, U.S. Dist. Ct. (No. Mariana Islands) 1983. Spl. agt. FBI, Memphis and Nashville, 1965-67, Cleve. and Elyria, Ohio, 1967-71; spl. agt., prin. legal advisor FBI, U.S. Dept. Justice, Honolulu, 1971—; bar examiner and applications rev. com. Supreme Ct. Hawaii, 1980—; pres. Hawaii State Law Enforcement Adminstrn., 1985-86. Recipient Govs. Award for Outstanding Contbns. to Law Enforcement, Gov. of Guam, 1974, 76, cert. of appreciation Supreme Ct. Hawaii, 1981, cert. of appreciation Honolulu Police Commn., 1984, 86. Mem. ABA, Fed. Bar Assn., Hawaii Bar Assn., Guam Bar Assn., Assn. Trial Lawyers Am., Inst. Jud. Adminstrn., Hawaii State

Law Enforcement Ofcls. Assn., Internat. Assn. Chiefs of Police. Club: Honolulu Press. Criminal, General corporate, Judicial administration. Office: US Dept Justice PO Box 50164 Honolulu HI 96850

MOROS, NICHOLAS PETER, railroad executive, lawyer; b. N.Y.C., Oct. 18, 1947; s. Nicholas F. and Mary M. (Sulima) M.; m. Susan Ann Girouard, Aug. 28, 1971; 1 child, Alexander N. B.A., Manhattan Coll., 1969; J.D. cum laude, Boston Coll., 1972. Bar: N.Y. 1973, Minn. 1976, Tex. 1985. Assoc. Dewey, Ballantine, Bushby, Palmer & Wood, N.Y.C., 1972-75; staff atty. Burlington No. R.R. Co., St. Paul, 1975-83, gen. counsel, Fort Worth, 1983-86, sr. asst. v.p. Coal & Taconite, 1986, v.p., 1987—. Editor Environ. Affairs Law Rev., 1971-72. Advisor, Boy Scouts Am., St. Paul, 1977-78; bd. dirs. Theatre Arlington, Tex., 1984—. Mem. ABA, Minn. Bar Assn., Tex. Bar Assn., Tarrant County Bar Assn., Ramsey County Bar Assn., N.Y. State Bar Assn . Republican. Roman Catholic. Antitrust, Administrative and regulatory, General corporate. Home: 4800 Villa Vera Dr Arlington TX 76017 Office: Burlington No RR Co 3700 Continental Plaza 777 Main St Fort Worth TX 76102

MOROSCO, B. ANTHONY, lawyer; b. Yonkers, N.Y., Nov. 29, 1936; s. Ben and Rita (Farrelly) M. m. Laurie Lee Scott, Nov. 12, 1983; children—Marina, Edith, Anthony, Benson, Lenore. A.B., Fordham U., 1958; LL.B., Columbia U., 1961. Bar: N.Y. 1962, Va. 1963, U.S. Ct. Mil. Appeals 1963, U.S. Dist. Ct. (so. dist.) N.Y. 1971, U.S. Ct. Appeals (2d cir.) N.Y. 1973, U.S. Supreme Ct. 1975. Asst. dist. atty., Westchester County, N.Y., 1965-78, chief of appeals, 1971-78; ptnr. Aurnou, Rubenstein, Morosco & Kelligrew, White Plains, N.Y., 1978-80; ptnr. Morosco & Cunard, White Plains, 1980—; counsel to spl. dist. atty. Dutchess County (N.Y.), 1981—; adj. assoc. prof. law Pace U., Pleasantville, N.Y. Editor Columbia Law Rev. Served to capt. JAGC, U.S. Army, 1962-65. Mem. N.Y. State Bar Assn., Westchester County Bar Assn. (bd. dirs. 1975-77), Yorktown Bar Assn. (pres. 1977-78), N.Y. State Dist. Attys. Assn. (legis. sec. 1969-78). Republican. Roman Catholic. Club: K.C. Author: Prosecution and Defense of Sex Crimes, 1976; chpts. in books. Criminal, State civil litigation, General practice. Office: 99 Court St White Plains NY 10601

MORRALL, MATTHEW EARL, lawyer; b. Lansing, Mich., May 27, 1957; s. Earl Edwin and Jane Marlene (Whitehead) M. BBA, U. Fla., 1979, JD, 1981. Bar: Fla. 1982. Assoc. Gillespie, McCormick, McFall, Gilbert & McGee, Pompano Beach, Fla., 1981—. Mem. ABA, Fla. Bar Assn., North Broward Bar Assn. (bd. dirs. 1985—). Democrat. Roman Catholic. Club: Broward County Gator (bd. dirs. 1984—, v.p. athletics 1985—). Securities, General corporate, Consumer commercial. Office: Gillespie McCormick McFall et al 2400 E Atlantic Blvd #300 Pompano Beach FL 33062

MORRELL, RIVERS JUDSON, III, lawyer; b. Los Angeles, Feb. 20, 1947; s. Rivers Judson Jr. and Iris Marie (Wood) M.; m. Jane Donaldson (div.); m. Nancy Susan Morrell, Oct. 1, 1982; children: Rivers, Brooke, Ryan, Rowan. BA in Econs., U. Calif., Berkeley, 1970; LLB, Golden Gate U., 1973. Bar: Calif. 1973, U.S. Dist. Ct. (no. and so. dists.) Calif. Assoc. Erickson Law Offices, Oakland, Calif., 1973-74, Daniel C. Miller, San Francisco, 1974-75, Low, Ball & Lynch, San Francisco, 1975-79, MacFarlane Law Office, Santa Ana, Calif., 1979-81; sole practice Santa Ana, 1982—. Republican. Insurance, Personal injury, State civil litigation. Office: 701 S Parker Suite 2600 Orange CA 92668

MORRIS, BENJAMIN HUME, lawyer; b. Louisville, Sept. 25, 1917; s. Benjamin Franklin and Mary (Hume) M.; m. Lacy Hibbs Abell, July 7, 1942; children—Benjamin Hume, Lacy Wayne; m. 2d, Mary Frances Fowler Gatlin, Nov. 9, 1968. J.D., U. Louisville, 1941. Bars: Ky. 1940, U.S. Supreme Ct. 1966. Assoc., Doolan, Helm, Stites & Wood, Louisville, 1941-50; atty. Brown-Forman Distillers Corp., Louisville, 1950-56; resident counsel, 1956-64, v.p., resident counsel, 1964-73, v.p., gen. counsel 1973-81, corp. sec. 1981; pres., dir. Canadian Mist Distillers, Ltd., Collingwood, Ont., Can., 1971-81; of counsel Morris, Nicolas, Welsh & Vandeventer, Louisville, 1982-86, Ray & Morris, 1986—. Trustee, sec. W. L. Lyons Brown Found., 1964—; trustee City of Riverwood, Ky., 1977-81; chmn. Jefferson County Social Service Adv. Com., 1959-62; bd. govs. Jefferson Alcohol and Drug Abuse Ctr., 1983—; past. bd. dirs. Ky. C. of C., Better Bus. Bur. Louisville. Served to capt. USAF, 1941-45; col. Res. ret. Decorated Air medal with oak leaf cluster; recipient Disting. Alumni award, U. Louisville, 1981. Mem. Ky. Bar Assn., Ky. Soc. S.A.R. (pres., 1978), Nat. Soc. S.A.R. (v.p. 1980, chancellor gen. 1982-83, sec. gen. 1984, pres. gen. 1985, Minuteman award 1984, Gold Good Citizenship medal 1986), Ky. Distillers Assn. (chmn. 1969), Distilled Spirits Council U.S. (pres. 1973, chmn. 1973-74, chmn. emeritus 1982—), Assn. Canadian Distillers (bd. dirs. 1971-81), Soc. Colonial Wars, Soc. of the War of 1812, Soc. Sons and Daus. of the Pilgrims, Mil. Order of World Wars. Republican. Presbyterian. Clubs: Louisville Boat, Filson, Army and Navy. Reviser, Corp. sect. Banks-Baldwin's Ky. Legal Forms Book, 1982. General corporate. Address: 2005 High Ridge Rd Louisville KY 40207

MORRIS, DAVID MICHAEL, lawyer; b. San Juan, P.R., Dec. 8, 1948; s. Edwin Thaddeus and Winifred Isabel (Walsh) M.; m. Carol Anderson Worden, Aug. 7, 1971; children: Laura H., John C. BA, U. Md., 1971; JD, U. Balt., 1975. Bar: Md. 1976, U.S. Dist. Ct. Md. 1977; CLU. Mng. ptnr. Franklin/Morris Assocs., Balt., 1976—. Columnist legal newspaper Daily Record, 1985—. Pres., trustee 2d Presbyn. Ch., Balt., 1980-86; vice chmn. Balt. div. United Way, 1981-84; fund raiser Johns Hopkins Children's Ctr., Balt., 1984—. Mem. ABA, Md. Bar Assn., Balt. Bar Assn., Assn. Advanced Life Underwriting, Balt. Life Underwriters Assn. (chmn. ethics 1977-80, bd. dirs. 1982-85), Million Dollar Round Table (life). Clubs: The Md. (Balt.), Merchants. Avocations: squash, tennis. Pension, profit-sharing, and employee benefits, Estate taxation, Probate. Home: 205 Paddington Rd Baltimore MD 21212 Office: Franklin/Morris Assocs 7 E Redwood St Baltimore MD 21202

MORRIS, DEWEY BLANTON, lawyer; b. Richmond, Va., Sept. 15, 1938; s. Thomas Cecil and Mary Katherine (Rowlett) M.; m. Nancy Edmunds, Aug. 27, 1960; children: Sally Pendleton, Katherine Archer. BA, U. Va., 1960, LLB, 1965. Bar: Md. 1965, Va. 1968, U.S. Dist. Ct. Md., U.S. Dist. Ct. (ea. dist.) Va., U.S. Ct. Appeals (4th cir.). Assoc. Piper & Marbury, Balt., 1965-67; ptnr. Hunton & Williams, Richmond, 1967—. Served to 1st lt., USMC, 1960-62. Mem. ABA (corp. banking and bus. law sect.), Va. Bar Assn. (bus. law sect.), Richmond Bar Assn., Phi Alpha Delta, Omicron Delta Kappa, Raven Soc. Presbyterian. Clubs: Commonwealth, Country Club Va. (Richmond). Lodge: Kiwanis. Avocations: golf, tennis, skiing, photgraphy. Banking, Contracts commercial, General corporate. Home: 302 Locke Ln Richmond VA 23226 Office: Hunton & Williams 707 E Main St PO Box 1535 Richmond VA 23219

MORRIS, EARL FRANKLIN, lawyer; b. Byesville, Ohio, Apr. 5, 1909; s. Thomas and Marietta (Bean) M.; m. Jean Esther Butcher, Aug. 1, 1942; 1 child, Ann Morris Sward. A.B., Wittenberg U., 1930, LL.D. (hon.), 1955; J.D., Harvard U., 1933; LL.D. (hon.), Willamette U., 1967, Valparaiso U., 1968, Findlay Coll., 1971, Dickinson Sch. Law, 1974, William Mitchell Coll. Law, 1980, Capital U., 1980. Bar: Ohio 1933, U.S. Dist. Ct. (so. dist.) Ohio, U.S. Ct. Appeals (6th cir.), U.S. Supreme Ct. Since practiced in Columbus; assoc. Porter, Wright, Morris & Arthur, 1933-34, ptnr., 1935-82, of counsel, 1983—; spl. counsel Midland Mut. Life Ins. Co. Contbr. articles to profl. jours. Bd. dirs. Wittenberg U., chmn., 1973-84; mem. exec. com., trustee Ohio Found. Ind. Colls., Assn. Ind. Colls. and Univs. Ohio. Mem. ABA (ho. dels. 1952—, bd. govs. 1962-65, pres. 1967-68, medal 1982), Ohio Bar Assn. (pres., medal 1968), Columbus Bar Assn. (pres., Disting. Service medal 1982), Nat. Conf. Bar Pres. (chmn. 1961-62), Am. Judicature Soc. (chmn. bd. dirs. 1970-72), Am., Ohio bar founds., Inst. Court Mgmt. (chmn. trustees 1973-86), Am. Coll. Trial Lawyers, Inst. Jud. Adminstrn., Sixth Circuit Jud. Conf. (life), Assn. Life Ins. Counsel. Republican. Episcopalian. Federal civil litigation, State civil litigation, Insurance. Home: 2531 Fair Ave Columbus OH 43209 Office: Porter Wright Morris & Arthur 41 S High St Columbus OH 43215

MORRIS, EDWARD WILLIAM, JR., lawyer; b. Medford, Oreg., Apr. 12, 1943; s. Edward William and Julia Loretta (Sullivan) M.; m. Margaret Ellen McKenna, 1976; children—John McKenna, Elizabeth Anne. B.S., Fordham Coll., 1965, J.D., 1971. Bar: N.Y. 1973. Dir. Drug Products Co., Inc., Union City, N.J., 1968-71; asst. arbitration dir. N.Y. Stock Exchange, N.Y.C., 1971-73, arbitration dir., 1973-74, asst. sec., arbitration dir., 1974—; dir. Stock Clearing Corp., N.Y.C.; mem. Securities Industry Conf. on Arbitration, N.Y.C., 1977—; lectr. in field. Served to sgt. U.S. Army, 1965-68, Vietnam. Mem. ABA, Am. Arbitration Assn. (comml. law com. 1983—), N.Y. County Lawyers Assn. (sec. com. on arbitration 1983—). Clubs: High Mountain Golf (Franklin Lakes, N.J.); New York Roadrunners (N.Y.C.). Arbitration, Securities. Home: 67 Arlton Ave Allendale NJ 07401 Office: NY Stock Exchange Inc 11 Wall St New York NY 10005

MORRIS, EUGENE JEROME, lawyer; b. N.Y.C., Oct. 14, 1910; s. Max and Regina (Cohn) M.; m. Terry Lesser, Mar. 28, 1934; 1 son, Richard S. B.S.S., CCNY, 1931; LL.B., St. John's U., 1934. Bar: N.Y. 1935. Practiced N.Y.C., 1935—; sr. and founding partner firm Demov, Morris & Hammerling, 1946—; adj. prof. land use regulation N.Y. U. Grad. Sch. Public Adminstrn., 1978-81; spl. master Supreme Ct. of State of N.Y., 1979—. Editor weekly column: N.Y. Law Jour, 1965—; Editor monthly column: It's the Law, Real Estate Forum, 1982—; editor-in-chief N.Y. Practice Guide: Real Estaste, 4 vols., 1986; Contbr. articles to profl. jours. Mem. N.Y.C. Rent Guidelines Bd., 1983-85. Served with AUS, 1943-45. Mem. Am. Bar Assn. (chmn. spl. com. housing and urban devel. 1970-73, council sect. real property, probate and trust law 1971-74, assoc. editor Real Property Probate and Trust Jour., editor Real Property, Probate and Property mag., article s editor 1986—), Assn. Bar City N.Y. (chmn. com. housing and urban devel. 1971-74, chmn. com. on lectures and continuing edn. 1980-83), N.Y. State Bar Assn. (exec. com. 1980—, chmn. com. meetings and lectures 1982—, continuing legal edn. com. 1984—, ho. of dels. 1986—), Citizens Union (dir.). Club: City (mem. com. landmarks and historic dists.). Real property, Landlord-tenant, State civil litigation. Home: 200 Central Park S New York NY 10019 Office: 40 W 57th St New York NY 10019

MORRIS, FRANK CHARLES, JR., lawyer, educator; b. Pitts., May 11, 1948; s. Frank Charles and Mary Louise (Veverka) M.; m. Kathleen; 1 child, Frank Charles III. B.S. with distinction, Northwestern U., 1970; J.D., U. Va., 1973. Bar: Pa. 1973, U.S. Ct. Appeals (4th and 7th cirs.) 1974, D.C. 1975, U.S. Ct. Appeals (1st, 2d and 9th cirs.) 1975, U.S. Ct. Appeals (10th cir.) 1976, U.S. Supreme Ct. 1976, U.S. Ct. Appeals (5th and D.C. cirs.) 1977, U.S. Dist. Ct. D.C. 1977, U.S. Dist. Ct. (ea. dist.) Wis. 1980, U.S. Ct. Appeals (11th cir.) 1981, U.S. Dist. Ct. (we. dist.) Pa. 1984, U.S. Dist. Ct. Md. 1985. Research asst. Bernard Dunau, Washington, 1972-73; appellate ct. br. atty. NLRB, Washington, 1973-76; assoc. McGuiness & Williams, Washington, 1976-78; mem. Epstein Becker Borsody & Green, P.C., Washington, 1978—; mem. adj. faculty Law Sch., Catholic U. Am., Washington, 1979-80, Law Sch., George Washington U., Washington, 1984—; mem. faculty Sch. Indsl. and Labor Relations EEO study program Cornell U., N.Y.C., 1979—, Inst. for Applied Mgmt. and Law, Newport Beach, Calif., 1982—; lectr. in field. Author: Current Trends in the Use (and Misuse) of Statistics in Employment Discrimination Litigation, 1977, 2d edit., 1978. Contbg. editor EEO Today, 1979-80; editor-in-chief The Equal Employer newsletter, 1981-86. Labor relations columnist Internat. Personnel Mgmt. Assn. News, 1980-81. Dir. Northwestern U. Alumni Admissions Council, Washington Area Council, 1978-81. Recipient Sustained Superior Performance award NLRB Gen. Counsel, 1974, cert. commendation for outstanding performance NLRB Gen. Counsel, 1975; named to Outstanding Young Men Am., U.S. Jaycees, 1982. Mem. ABA (labor and employment law, adminstrv. and litigation sects.), Pa. Bar Assn., D.C. Bar Assn. (administrv. law, labor relations and litigation divs.), Fed. Bar Assn., Northwestern U. Alumni Club (bd. govs. 1975—). Roman Catholic. Club: D.C. Rd. Runners. Labor, Federal civil litigation, Administrative and regulatory. Home: 6210 Homespun Ln Falls Church VA 22044 Office: Epstein Becker Borsody & Green PC 1140 19th St NW Suite 900 Washington DC 20036

MORRIS, FRANK LOWRY, lawyer; b. Atlanta, June 16, 1932; s. James Edward and Margaret (Dooley) M.; m. Carol Ware, Aug. 21, 1948; children—Brenda, Belinda, Lowry, Lisa, Brent. B.B.A., Loyola U., New Orleans, 1955, J.D., 1968. Bar: La. 1968, U.S. Dist. Ct. (ea. dist.) La. 1968, U.S. Ct. Appeals (5th cir.) 1968. Mem. F.L. Morris & Assocs., Metairie, La., 1968—; Pres. La. chpt. Cystic Fibrosis, New Orleans, 1976-78. Served to 1st lt. U.S. Army, 1955-57. Mem. Jefferson Parish Bar Assn. (pres. 1976-77), La. State Bar Assn. (ho. of dels. 1970-79, bd. govs. 1983—). Republican. Roman Catholic. Family and matrimonial, Personal injury, Probate. Home: 261 Walter Rd River Ridge LA 70123 Office: FL Morris & Assocs 2909 David Dr Metairie LA 70003

MORRIS, GREG ARTHUR, lawyer; b. Buffalo, Nov. 27, 1953; s. Arthur and Sylvia (Dorobant) M.; m. Mary Weiksnar, Aug. 6, 1977; children: Matthew, Megan. BGS, U. Mich., 1976; JD, U. Tulsa, 1979. Bar: Calif. 1979, U.S. Dist. Ct. (cen. dist.) Calif. 1980, U.S. Dist. Ct. (so. dist.) Calif. 1982, Okla. 1983, U.S. Dist. Ct. (no. dist.) Okla. 1984. Assoc. Reilly & Zell, Los Angeles, 1980-83; ptnr. Morris & Morris, Tulsa, 1983—. Mem. ABA, Okla. Bar Assn., Calif. Bar Assn., Assn. Trial Lawyers Am., Okla. Trial Lawyers Assn., Nat. Acad. Criminal Def. Lawyers. Personal injury, Criminal, Insurance. Office: Morris & Morris 201 W 5th St Suite 520 Tulsa OK 74127

MORRIS, HERBERT, educator; b. N.Y.C., July 28, 1928; s. Peter and Minnie (Miller) M.; m. Virginia Ann Grenier, Apr.3, 1956 (div. Nov. 1977); children: Jacob Jeremy, Benjamin John.; m. Margery Ruth Maslon, June 8, 1980. A.B., UCLA, 1951; LL.B., Yale, 1954; D. Phil., Oxford (Eng.) U., 1956. Bar: Calif. bar 1958. Mem. faculty UCLA, 1956—, prof. philosophy and law, 1962—, dean div. humanities, 1983—; research clin. assoc. So. Calif. Psychoanalytic Inst., 1977—. Editor: Freedom and Responsibility, 1961, The Masked Citadel, 1968, Guilt and Shame, 1971, On Guilt and Innocence, 1976. Mem. State Bar Calif. Legal education. Home: 233 S Medio Dr Los Angeles CA 90049

MORRIS, JAMES MALACHY, lawyer; b. Champaign, Ill., June 5, 1952; s. Walter Michael and Ellen Frances (Solon) M. Student Oxford U. (Eng.), 1972; B.A., Brown U., 1974; J.D., U. Pa.-Phila., 1977. Bar: N.Y. 1978, U.S. Dist. Ct. (so. and ea. dists.) N.Y. 1978, Ill. 1980, U.S. Tax Ct. 1982, U.S. Sup. Ct. 1983. Assoc., Reid & Priest, N.Y.C., 1977-80; sr. law clk. Sup. Ct. Ill., Springfield, 1980-81; assoc. Carter, Ledyard & Milburn, N.Y.C., 1981-83; sole practice, N.Y.C., 1983—; cons. Internat. Awards Found., Zurich, 1981—, Pritzker Architecture Prize Found., N.Y.C., 1981—, Herbert Oppenheimer, Nathan & VanDyck, London, 1985—. Contbr. articles to profl. jours. Mem. ABA, Ill. Bar Assn., N.Y. State Bar Assn., N.Y. County Lawyers Assn., Assn. Bar City N.Y., Brit. Inst. Internat. and Comparative Law. General practice, General corporate, Probate. Office: 150 E 39th St New York NY 10016

MORRIS, JAMES W., lawyer, mineral acquisitions consultant; b. Carbondale, Ill., Oct. 21, 1948; s. James and Emilyn (Snow) M.; m. Jan Dunning, June 5, 1970; children—Jennifer R., J. Hunter. B.A., So. Ill. U., 1969; J.D., U. Ill., 1972. Bar: Ill. Supreme Ct. 1972, U.S. Dist. Ct. (ea. dist.) Ill. 1976. Ptnr. Barrett, Twomey, Morris & Broom and predecessor firm Barrett & Morris, Carbondale, Ill., 1972—; v.p., Egyptian Mining Corp., Murphysboro, Ill., 1975-79, also dir.; v.p. So. Ill. Minerals Corp., Carbondale, 1977, also dir.; pvt. practice mineral acquisitions consulting, Carbondale, 1979—. Co-author: Illinois Mortgage and Farm Foreclosures, Professional Education Systems, 1986. Mem. ABA (real property, probate and trust law sect., Soc. Mining Engrs., Tri-State Profl. Landman's Assn., Eastern Mineral Law Found., Ill. State Bar Assn. (real estate sect. council, mineral law subcom. 1984—), Am. Arbitration Assn. (mem. panel arbitrators 1976—), Carbondale C. of C. (v.p. 1975). Republican. Club: Mo. Athletic. Lodge: Elks. Mining and minerals, Real property, Oil and gas leasing. Home: R R #3 Box 376 Carbondale IL 62901 Office: Barrett Twomey Morris & Broom 401 N Beadle Dr PO Box 1227 Carbondale IL 62901

MORRIS, JEFFREY LYONS, lawyer; b. Hartford, Conn., Nov. 16, 1950; s. John William Jr. and Mary Jane (Dore) M.; m. Joan Elizabeth DiDonato, Oct. 25, 1975; children: Jeffrey J., Jessica M. AB, St. Anselm Coll., 1972; JD, We. New Eng. Sch. of Law, 1982. Bar: Conn. 1982, U.S. Dist. Ct. Conn. 1983. With The Hartford Ins. Group, Ft. Lauderdale, Fla., 1972-83; staff atty. The Hartford (Conn.) Ins. Group, 1983-86, asst. counsel, 1986—. Mem. ABA, Conn. Bar Assn., Hartford County Bar Assn. Democrat. Roman Catholic. Avocations: golf, tennis, theater, music. Federal civil litigation, State civil litigation, Insurance. Home: 14 Maureen Dr Simsbury CT 06070 Office: The Hartford Ins Group Hartford Plaza Hartford CT 06115

MORRIS, JOHN E., lawyer; b. N.Y.C., Sept. 30, 1916; s. John and Honora C. (Long) M.; m. Patricia E. Grojean. A.B., CCNY; A.M., Columbia U.; J.D., Harvard U. Bar: N.Y. 1942, U.S. Dist. Ct. (so. and ea. dists.) N.Y. Trial lawyer Clarke & Reilly, 1946-50; ptnr. Morris & Duffy, N.Y.C., 1950—. Served to lt. USCG, 1942-46; ETO. Mem. ABA, N.Y. State Bar Assn., Airplane Owners & Pilots Assn., N.Y. County Lawyers Assn., Internat. Assn. Ins. Counsel. Roman Catholic. Clubs: Harvard, N.Y. Athletic (N.Y.C.), Great Dane Club Am. (bd. dirs.). Personal injury, Insurance, Federal civil litigation. Office: 233 Broadway 18th Floor New York NY 10279

MORRIS, JOSEPH DEAN, lawyer; b. Point Pleasant, N.J., Apr. 14, 1948; s. Samuel Esterbrook and Dorothy (Miller) M.; m. Elizabeth Loretta Crowe, Aug. 26, 1977; children: Dean, Tara, Lisa, Joseph Jr., Kevin. BS, Villanova U., 1970, MA, 1971; JD, Suffolk U., 1974. Bar: N.J. 1974, U.S. Dist. Ct. N.J. 1974. Law clk. to presiding justice Ocean County Superior Ct., N.J., 1974-75; sole practice Brick, N.J., 1975—. Mem. ABA, N.J. State Bar Assn., Ocean County Bar Assn. Avocation: golf. Criminal, Real property, Personal injury. Home and Office: 464 Mantoloking Rd Brick NJ 08723

MORRIS, KENNETH DONALD, chemical company executive, lawyer; b. Montclair, N.J., Apr. 5, 1946; s. Thomas Almerin and Katherine Louise (Jacobs) M.; m. Susan Sauer, Sept. 1, 1976; children: Ian, Jennifer. BA, Ohio Wesleyan U., 1968; MBA in Internat. Bus., George Washington U., 1971, JD, 1972. Bar: Pa. 1973, N.J. 1975. Atty. Westinghouse Electric, Pitts., 1972-74, Tenneco Chems., Inc., N.J., 1974-76; asst. corp. counsel Ronson Corp., Bound Brook, N.J., 1976-78; assoc. Walder, Sondak, Berkley & Brogan, Newark, 1978-81; sec., gen. counsel NOR-AM Chem. Co. subs. Schering AG, Wilmington, Del., 1981—; adj. prof. law Carnegie Mellon U., Pitts., 1972-73. Wolcott scholar Wolcott Found., 1969. Mem. ABA (antitrust sect., corp., banking and bus. law sect., multinational corps. subcom.), Del. Bar Assn., Am. Corp. Counsel Assn., Def. Research Inst., George Washington U. Sch. Govt. and Bus. Adminstrn. Alumni Assn. (Phila. chpt.), Phi Alpha Theta, Kappa Sigma. Republican. Presbyterian. Lodge: Rotary. General corporate, Personal injury, Contracts commercial. Office: NOR-AM Chem Co 3509 Silverside Rd Wilmington DE 19803

MORRIS, LARRY DEAN, lawyer, insurance company executive; b. Amarillo, Tex., Dec. 10, 1949; s. John P. and Wanda (Pennington) M.; m. Sara Lisbeth Blong, Apr. 29, 1977; children: Jeffrey Ryan, Hillary Anne. BA, Yale U., 1972; JD, So. Meth. U., 1975. Bar: Tex. 1975, U.S. Dist. Ct. (no. dist.) Tex. 1975, U.S. Dist. Ct. (ea. dist.) Tex. 1979, U.S. Ct. Appeals (5th cir.) 1980, U.S. Dist. Ct. (so. dist.) Tex. 1981. Assoc. Windle, Turley & Assocs., Dallas, 1975-78; ptnr. Bracken & Morris, Dallas, 1979-81; sole practice Dallas, 1981-84; v.p., claims counsel U.S. Ins. Group, Basking Ridge, N.J., 1984—. Chmn. Yale U. Undergrad. Schs. Com., Dallas, 1979-84; trustee Met. Baptist Ministries, N.Y.C., 1985—; deacon Wilshire Bapt. Ch., Dallas, 1980-84, Madison Bapt. Ch., Madison, N.J., 1984—. Mem. ABA, Tex. Bar Assn., Dallas Bar Assn., Young Lawyers of Tex. (chmn. speakers com. 1978-79). Republican. Baptist. Clubs: Yale (N.J.), Yale (Dallas) (v.p. 1981-84). Insurance, Personal injury, State civil litigation. Home: 29 Phyllis Pl Randolph NJ 07869 Office: US Ins Group 211 Mount Airy Rd Basking Ridge NJ 07920

MORRIS, MARC, lawyer; b. Bklyn., Apr. 6, 1953; s. Edward and Lillian (Stone) M. BS, Boloit COll., 1975; JD, New England Sch. Law, 1979; LLM, Boston U., 1980. Bar: Mass. 1979, U.S. Dist. Ct. Mass. 1979, U.S. Ct. Appeals (1st cir.) 1979, Colo. 1981, U.S. Dist. Ct. Colo. 1981. Ptnr. Shaw, Spangler & Roth, Denver, 1981—. Mem. ABA, Colo. Bar Assn., Assn. Trial Lawyers Am. Jewish. Federal civil litigation, State civil litigation, Labor. Home: 6355 W Portland Pl Littleton CO 80123 Office: Shaw Spangler & Roth 1700 Broadway Denver CO 80290

MORRIS, NEIL ALAN, lawyer; b. Phila., Mar. 11, 1954; m. Delight S. Pratt; children: Thomas, Richard, Christopher, Theresa, Heather. BA, Temple U., 1975, JD, 1979. Bar: Pa. 1979, U.S. Dist. Ct. (ea. dist.) Pa. 1979, U.S. Ct. Appeals (3d cir.) 1979. Sr. ptnr. Sidkoff, Pincus & Green, Phila., 1976—. Mem. ABA, Pa. Bar Assn., Phila. Bar Assn., Assn. Trial Lawyers Am., Pa. Trial Lawyers Assn. Republican. Jewish. Lodge: B'rith Shalom. Federal civil litigation, Civil rights, State civil litigation. Home: 6012 Buckingham Dr Bensalem PA 19020 Office: Sidkoff Pincus & Green PC 530 Walnut St Philadelphia PA 19106

MORRIS, NORVAL, criminologist, educator; b. Auckland, New Zealand, Oct. 1, 1923; s. Louis and Vera (Burke) M.; m. Elaine Richardson, Mar. 18, 1947; children: Gareth, Malcolm, Christopher. LL.B., U. Melbourne, Australia, 1946, LL.M., 1947; Ph.D. in Criminology (Hutchinson Silver medal 1950), London (Eng.) Sch. Econs., 1949. Bar: called to Australian bar 1953. Asst. lectr. London Sch. Econs., 1949-50; sr. lectr. law U. Melbourne, 1950-58, prof. criminology, 1955-58; Ezra Ripley Thayer teaching fellow Harvard Law Sch., 1955-56, vis. prof., 1961-62; Boynthon prof., dean faculty law U. Adelaide, Australia, 1958-62; dir. UN Inst. Prevention Crime and Treatment of Offenders, Tokyo, Japan, 1962-64; Julius Kreeger prof. law and criminology U. Chgo., 1964—, dean Law Sch., 1975-79; Chmn. Commn. Inquiry Capital Punishment in Ceylon, 1958-59; mem. Social Sci. Research Council Australia, 1958-59; Australian del. confs. div. human rights and sect. social def. UN, 1955-66; mem. standing adv. com. experts prevention crime and treatment offenders; chmn. com. on law enforcement and adminstrn. of justice Nat. Acad. Scis.; mem police bd. City of Chgo. Author: The Habitual Criminal, 1951, Report of the Commission of Inquiry on Capital Punishment, 1959, (with W. Morison and R. Sharwood) Cases in Torts, 1962, (with Colin Howard) Studies in Criminal Law, 1964, (with G. Hawkins) The Honest Politicians Guide to Crime Control, 1970, The Future of Imprisonment, 1974, Letter to the President on Crime Control, 1977, Madness and the Criminal Law, 1983. Served with Australian Army, World War II, PTO. Decorated Japanese Order Sacred Treasure 3d Class. Fellow Am. Acad. Arts and Scis. Legal education. Home: 1207 E 50th St Chicago IL 60615

MORRIS, REBECCA ROBINSON, lawyer; b. McKinney, Tex., July 27, 1945; d. Leland Howell and Grace Laverne (Stinson) Robinson; m. Jesse Eugene Morris, July 18, 1964; children: Jesse III, Susan, John. BBA in Acctg., So. Meth. U., 1974, JD, 1978. Bar: Tex. 1979, U.S. Dist. Ct. (no. dist.) Tex. Acct. Electronic Data Systems Corp., Dallas, 1975; assoc. atty. Dresser Industries, Inc., Dallas, 1978-81, staff atty., 1981-83, corp. atty., 1983-86, asst. sec., 1984—, sr. atty. corp. adminstrn., 1986—. Trustee Plano (Tex.) Ind. Sch. Dist., 1979—, pres. 1980-85, sec. 1986. Mem. Tex. State Bar, Tex. Soc. CPA's, Am. Soc. Corp. Secs. (membership chmn. Dallas chpt. 1986). Methodist. General corporate, Local government, Securities. Home: 1718 14th Pl Plano TX 75074 Office: Dresser Industries Inc 1600 Pacific Ave Dallas TX 75201

MORRIS, RICHARD PAUL, lawyer; b. N.Y.C., June 25, 1949; s. Aaron D. and Edith (Wolarsky) M.; m. Linda S. Bohm, Nov. 18, 1972; children: Evan L., Jamie R. BA, Adelphi U., 1970; JD, Bklyn. Law Sch., 1973. Bar: N.Y. 1974, U.S. Dist. Ct. (so. and ea. dists.) N.Y. 1975, U.S. Ct. Appeals (2d cir.) 1975. Atty. Mental Health Info. Service, Bklyn., 1973-76; from assoc. to ptnr. Klein, Wagner & Morris, N.Y.C., 1976—. Mem. N.Y. State Social Security Bar Assn. (sec., treas., trustee 1980—), Queens County Bar Assn., N.Y. County Lawyers Assn. Democrat. Jewish. Pension, profit-sharing, and employee benefits, Real property, Personal injury. Home: 80-39 189th St Jamaica NY 11423 Office: Klein Wagner & Morris 71 Murray St New York NY 10007

MORRIS, ROBERT SMITH, lawyer; b. Bethesda, Md., Feb. 6, 1952; s. Woodrow Bryan and Dorothy Inez (Smith) M.; m. Gizelle Suzan Master, Nov. 24, 1979; 1 child, Sarah Michelle. BA, John Hopkins U., 1974; JD, U. Tex., 1977. Bar: Tex. 1977, U.S. Dist. Ct. (we. dist.) Tex. 1980. Sole practice Austin, Tex., 1977-81; atty. Martin County, Stanton, Tex., 1981-85;

asst. dist. atty. 118th Jud. Dist., Big Spring, Tex., 1985-87; asst. criminal dist. attyl Denton County, Tex., 1987—. Mem. ABA, Tex. Dist. and County Atty.'s Assn. (bd. dirs. 1984-86). Methodist. Local government. Home: 3912 Waterford Way Denton TX 76205 Office: Criminal Dist Atty Denton County 5th Floor Carroll Courts Bldg PO Box 2344 Denton TX 76201

MORRIS, THOMAS HANSLEY, lawyer; b. Halifax, N.C., Apr. 25, 1936; s. E. Thomas and Dorothy (Hansley) M.; m. Ruby Hilda Hunter, May 30, 1964; children: Thomas Hunter, Jessica Leigh. BA, Wake Forest U., 1958, JD, 1963. Bar: N.C. 1963, U.S. Dist. Ct. (ea. dist.) N.C. 1975, U.S. Ct. Appeals (4th cir.) 1985. Assoc. Whitaker & Jeffress, Kinston, N.C., 1963-64; ptnr. Whitaker, Jeffress & Morris, Kinston, 1964-74, Morris, Rochelle, Duke & Braswell, Kinston, 1974-86, Wallace, Morris, Barwick & Rochelle P.A., Kinston, 1986—. Chmn. Lenoir County Dems., Kinston, 1975-80; pres. Lenoir County United Way, Kinston, 1981; pres. Lenoir County C. of C., 1985. Served to petty officer 3d class USN, 1958-60. Mem. N.C. Bar Assn. (bd. of govs. 1980-81), NC. Assn. Def. Attys., 8th Jud. Dist. Bar Assn. (pres. 1975). Democrat. Avocations: sailing, golf. Insurance, State civil litigation, General practice. Home: 1800 Emerson Rd Kinston NC 28501 Office: Wallace Morris Barwick Rochelle PA 131 S Queen St Kinston NC 28501

MORRIS, TRUDE MCMAHAN, lawyer; b. Los Angeles, July 11, 1946; d. Billy K. and Mary June (Marshall) McMahan; m. Kevin L. Morris, Jan. 15, 1973. BA, U. Nev., 1968; JD, McGeorge Sch. Law, 1980, LLM in Taxation, 1981. Bar: Nev. 1980, Calif. 1980, U.S. Dist. Ct. (ea. dist.) Calif. 1980. Ptnr. Rudiak, Oshins, Segal & Larsen, Las Vegas, Nev., 1981—. Chmn. So. Nev. div. affiliate Am. Heart Assn., Las Vegas, 1986-87. Served to sgt. U.S. Army, 1974-77. Mem. ABA, Clark County Bar Assn., Order of Coif. Democrat. Avocations: sailing, flying, reading. Pension, profit-sharing, and employee benefits, Probate, Estate taxation. Office: Rudiak Oshins Segal & Larsen 720 S 4th Suite 200 Las Vegas NV 89101

MORRIS, WILLIAM, lawyer; b. Lakewood, N.J., Sept. 2, 1941; s. Saul and Beatrice M. Morris; m. Susan Wolfbein, Feb. 13, 1965; children: David, Jonathan. AB, Rutgers U., 1963; JD, Georgetown U., 1966, LLM in Taxation, 1971. Bar: Va. 1966, N.J. 1967, D.C. 1981. Trial atty. IRS, Washington, 1966-70; atty., advisor U.S. Tax Ct., Washington, 1970-72; gen. counsel U.S. Senate, Washington, 1972-80; of counsel Reid & Priest, Washington, 1981-83; ptnr. Rogers & Wells, Washington, 1984—. Corporate taxation, Estate taxation. Office: Rogers & Wells 1737 H St NW Washington DC 20006

MORRISON, ALEXIA, lawyer; b. Los Angeles, Apr. 9, 1948; d. Alexander and Sarah Edith (Blayney) M.; m. Robert A. Shuker, Feb. 11, 1978; 1 child, Amanda Meighan. BA, Douglass Coll., 1969; JD, George Washington U., 1972. Bar: D.C. 1973, U.S. Dist. Ct. (D.C. dist.) 1975, U.S. Ct. Appeals (D.C. cir.) 1975, U.S. Supreme Ct. 1981. Legal asst. U.S. Dept. Justice, Washington, 1972-73; asst. U.S. Atty. Washington, 1973-78; chief grand jury sect. U.S. Dist. Ct. D.C., Washington, 1978-79, chief felony trial div., 1979-81; chief litigation counsel SEC, Washington, 1981-85; ptnr. Swidler & Berlin, Washington, 1985—; mem. adv. bd. Racketeer Influenced and Corrupt Orgns. Act Bur. Nat. Affairs, Washington, 1986—. Recipient U.S. Dept. Justice Dir.'s award, 1980, Sr. Exec. Service Performance bonus, 1983, Presdl. Rank award, 1985. Mem. ABA (litigation sect.), D.C. Bar (v.p. long range planning com. 1985—, chmn. steering com. litigation div. 1985-86). Republican. Federal civil litigation, Criminal, Securities. Office: Swidler & Berlin 1000 Thomas Jefferson St NW Washington DC 20007

MORRISON, DAVID PATRICK, lawyer; b. Portland, Oreg., Aug. 14, 1952; s. Este Jr. and Nancy Jean (Fitzmaurice) M.; m. Charlene Mary Vogel, Nov. 30, 1984; 1 child, Daniel Henry. BA, U. Oreg., 1974; JD, Lewis and Clark Coll., 1977. Bar: Oreg. 1977, U.S. Dist. Ct. Oreg., U.S. Ct. Appeals (9th cir.). From assoc. to ptnr. Cosgrave, Kestor, Crowe, Gidley & Lageser, Portland, 1977—. Mem. ABA, Oreg. Bar Assn., Multnomah County Bar Assn., Nat. Assn. R.R. Trial Counsel, Oreg. Assn. Def. Counsel, Phi Beta Kappa. Republican. Episcopalian. State civil litigation, Insurance, Personal injury. Office: Cosgrave Kestor Crowe Gidley & Lageser 1515 SW 5th Ave Portland OR 97201

MORRISON, EDMUND DUNHAM, JR., lawyer; b. Washington, Iowa, June 10, 1909; s. Edmund Dunham and Emeline (Warren) M.; m. Kathleen Wellman Coffey, June 18, 1934; children—Edmund Dunham, Thomas C., James N., Jean Morrison Macenski. Student Grinnell Coll., 1928-29; B.A., U. Iowa, 1931, J.D. with distinction, 1933. Bar: Iowa 1933, U.S. Dist. Ct. (so. dist.) Iowa 1933. Ptnr. Morrison, Lloyd & McConnell and predecessor Morrison & Morrison, Washington, 1933—; past dir., chmn. bd. Washington State Bank; Past pres. Washington YMCA, past pres. Men's Club: past trustee United Meth. Ch., Washington, former lay leader; bd. dirs., past pres. South Iowa Methodist Homes, Inc.; bd. dirs. Conger House, Inc.; past mem. Washington (Iowa) Pub. Library, Washington Community Theatre. Served as lt. USNR, 1944-45; PTO. Morrison Ctr. named in his honor Halcyon, Washington, Iowa, 1980. Fellow Am. Coll. Probate Counsel; mem. Iowa State Bar Assn. (gov., former chmn. legal forms com., past mem. probate com.), Dist. 8A Iowa Bar Assn. (pres. 1951-52), Washington County Bar Assn. (pres. 1947), ABA (mem. probate com.), Hoover Soc., Am. Legion, Phi Delta Phi, Beta Theta Pi, Republican. Clubs: Mason, Shriners, Rotary (Man of Yr. 1974, past pres.). Probate, Estate planning, Banking. Office: Morrison Lloyd & McConnell 211 W Washington St Washington IA 52353

MORRISON, FRANCIS HENRY, lawyer; b. Springfield, Mass., July 3, 1947; s. Frank and Jean (Conley) M.; m. Sally Murphy, Sept. 26, 1970; children—Brian, Matthew. A.B., Coll. of Holy Cross, 1969; J.D. with distinction, Duke U., 1975. Bar: Conn. 1975, U.S. Dist. Ct. Conn. 1975, U.S. Dist. Cts. (so. and ea. dists.) N.Y. 1975, U.S. Ct. Appeals (2d cir.) 1976. Assoc. Day, Berry & Howard, Hartford, Conn., 1975-81, ptnr., 1981—; corp. counsel Town of West Hartford (Conn.), 1983-85; spl. master U.S. Dist. Ct. Conn., 1983—; med. malpractice cons. various hosps., Con., 1983—. Pres., Buena Vista Property Owners, West Hartford, 1982-83; pres. parish council Ch. of St. Helena, West Hartford, 1987—. Served to lt. USN, 1969-72. Note and comments editor Duke Law Jour., 1974-75. Mem. Am. Bd. Trial Advocates (charter Conn. chpt.), Cert. as a Civil Trial Specialist by Nat. Bd. Trial Advocacy 1986, Conn. Bar Assn. (chmn. legis. and ednl. coms. civil justice sect. 1983—, task force on ct. delay 1984, moderator seminars), Fed. Bar Assn., ABA, Hartford County Bar Assn., Conn. Def. Lawyers Assn. (treas. 1987—), Conn. Conf. Municipalities. Democrat. Roman Catholic. Federal civil litigation, State civil litigation, Local government. Home: 57 Pheasant Hill Dr West Hartford CT 06107 Office: Day Berry & Howard Cityplace Hartford CT 06103

MORRISON, FRANK BRENNER, JR., state justice; b. McCook, Nebr., Sept. 27, 1937; s. Frank Brenner and Maxine Elizabeth (Hepp) M.; m. Sharon Romaine McDonald, June 28, 1959; children: John Martin, Anne Elizabeth. B.S., U. Nebr., 1959; LL.B., J.D., U. Denver, 1962. Bar: Nebr., Mont. Assoc. firm McGinley, Lane, Mueller & Shaanahan, Ogallala, Nebr., 1962-64; partner firm Eisenstatt, Higgins, Miller, Kinnamon & Morrison, Omaha, 1964-69, Morrison & Hedman, Whitefish, Mont., 1969-78, Morrison, Jonkel, Kemmis & Rossback, Missoula, Mont., 1978-80; justice Mont. Supreme Ct., 1981—; mem. part-time faculty Flathead Valley Community Coll., Kalispell, U. Mont. Law Sch. Past pres. Whitefish Community Devel.; past del. Democratic Nat. Conv. Recipient Disting. Service award Student Bar Assn. U. Mont. Law Sch., Disting. Service award Flathead County Bar Assn.; Gold medal award Law Sci. Acad. Am. Fellow Internat. Soc. Barristers; mem. Order St. Ives, Sigma Chi. Democrat. Episcopalian. Clubs: Toastmasters (past club pres., past area gov.), Kiwanis, Mont, Green Meadow Country. State civil litigation, Federal civil litigation. Home: 630 Monroe St Helena MT 59601 Address: Supreme Ct Mont State Capitol Helena MT 59620

MORRISON, HARVEY LEE, JR., lawyer; b. Hattiesburg, Miss., June 7, 1947; s. Harvey Lee Sr. and Tommye (Walker) M.; m. Norma Hairston, Aug. 21, 1976. BBA, U. Miss., 1970, JD, 1972. Bar: Miss. 1972, U.S. Dist. Ct. (no. dist.) Miss. 1982, U.S. Ct. Appeals (5th cir.) 1982. Ptnr. Tubb, Stevens & Morrison, West Point, Miss., 1972—. Mem. Miss. State Bar Assn., Miss. Def. Lawyers Assn., Clay County Bar Assn. (pres. 1986—). Presbyterian. Lodge: Rotary (sec. 1975, v.p. 1976, pres. 1977, dist. gov. Miss. and Tenn. 1984-85, Paul Harris fellow 1985). Avocations: jogging, tennis. Federal civil litigation, State civil litigation, Insurance. Home: 1206 Mapleview West Point MS 39773 Office: Tubb Stevens & Morrison PO Box 324 West Point MS 39773

MORRISON, JAMES LAWRENCE, lawyer, consultant; b. Decatur, Ill., Aug. 14, 1927. A.B., Millikin U., 1950; J.D., U. Ill., 1951; A.M.P., Harvard U., 1974. Bar: Ill. 1951, D.C. 1977, Va. 1985, . Atty. Swift & Co., 1951-57, tax counsel, 1957-68, mgr. tax div., 1968-73; dir. taxes Esmark, Inc., Chgo., 1973-74, asst. controller taxes, 1974-77, asst. gen. counsel, dir. govt. relations, 1977-82; mem. Esmark Pension Bd., 1975-77, Esmark Found. Bd., 1976-77. Vice pres., dir. Chgo. Jr. Assn. Commerce and Industry, 1957-62; bd. dirs. Joint Civic Com. on Elections, 1954-62; pres., chmn. bd. Citizens Greater Chgo., 1965-67; active Boy Scouts Am.; bd. dirs. Boys and Girls Clubs of Greater Washington, 1980-86. Recipient Disting. Service award Chgo. Jaycees, 1967, Trail Blazer award, Silver Beaver award Boy Scouts Am., 1974. Mem. ABA, Ill. Bar Assn., Chgo. Bar Assn., D.C. Bar Assn. Club: Harvard Bus. Sch. (v.p. 1982-84). Administrative and regulatory, Legislative, Corporate taxation. Home: 7348 Eldorado St McLean VA 22102 Office: 1901 N Moore St Suite 1204 Arlington VA 22209

MORRISON, JEANNE LUNSFORD, lawyer; b. Huntington, W.Va., Feb. 20, 1952; d. Harold Dennis and Dorothy Iola (Jones) Lunsford. B.S., W.Va. U., 1974; J.D., Oklahoma City U., 1977; M.B.A. in Fin., U. Tex. at El Paso, 1984. Bar: W.Va. 1977, Tex. 1979, U.S. Dist. Ct. (we. dist.) Tex. 1980, U.S. Supreme Ct. 1983. Staff atty. W.Va. Inheritance Tax div. State Tax Dept., 1977-78; atty. El Paso (Tex.) Exploration Co., 1978-85, El Paso City Atty. Office, 1985—. Bd. dirs. Big Bros./Big Sisters Corp., 1982-84, El Paso Shelter for Battered Wives, 1985—. Mem. ABA, W.Va. State Bar, Tex. State Bar, El Paso Women's Bar Assn. (v.p. 1979-80, pres. 1980-81), Tex. Young Lawyers Assn., Delta Delta Delta. Republican. Methodist. Oil and gas leasing, Banking, General corporate. Office: 2 Civic Center Plaza El Paso TX 79901

MORRISON, JOHN DITTGEN, lawyer; b. Ridgefield Park, N.J., Sept. 2, 1921; s. John D. and Florence C. (Davis) M.; m. Dorothy M. Veldran, May 8, 1944 (dec. Aug. 1977); m. Laraine C. Kopec, Nov. 15, 1981. Student, Bergen Jr. Coll., 1939-41; LLB, John Marshall Law Sch., Jersey City, 1947. Bar: N.J. 1949, U.S. Dist. Ct. N.J. 1949. Machine operator U.S. Rubber Co., Passaic, N.J., 1941-42, engr.'s asst., 1945-47; sole practice Wyckoff, N.J., 1950—; mcpl. judge Oakland, N.J., 1963-84, Mahwah, N.J., 1966-72, Montvale, N.J., 1971-80, Wyckoff, N.J., 1972-75. Served to lt. comdr. USN, 1942-45. Mem. Bergen County Bar Assn. (pres. 1979-80), ABA, N.J. State Bar Assn., N.J. Trial Lawyers Assn., Assn. Trial Lawyers Am. Republican. Roman Catholic. Lodge: Lions (pres. Wyckoff club). Avocation: boating. General practice, Probate, Real property. Home and Office: 232 Cresent Ave Wyckoff NJ 07481

MORRISON, JOHN HORTON, lawyer; b. St. Paul, Sept. 15, 1933. B.B.A., U. N.Mex., 1955; B.A., U. Oxford, 1957, M.A., 1961; J.D., Harvard U., 1962. Bar: Ill. 1962, U.S. Supreme Ct. 1966. Assoc., Kirkland & Ellis, Chgo., 1962-67, ptnr., 1968—. Mem. ABA, Ill. Bar Assn., Chgo. Bar Assn. Antitrust, Federal civil litigation. Home: 2717 Lincoln St Evanston IL 60201 Office: Kirkland & Ellis 200 E Randolph Dr Chicago IL 60601

MORRISON, JOHN STANLEY, lawyer; b. St. Louis, Dec. 9, 1943; s. Frank andrew and Theresa Marie (Bartos) M.; m. Elizabeth Frank, Aug. 23, 1969; children: Andrew, Kathryn, Jeffrey. AB, Colgate U., 1965; JD, U. Ill., 1968; LLM, NYU, 1969. Bar: Ill. 1968, Oreg. 1969, Mo. 1972, U.S. Dist. Ct. (ea. dist.) Mo. 1980, U.S. Claims Ct. 1980, U.S. Tax Ct. 1980, U.S. Ct. Appeals (8th cir.) 1980. Assoc. Cake, Jaureguy, Hardy, Buttler & McEwen, Portland, Oreg., 1969-71; tax atty. Ralston Purina Co., St. Louis, 1971-80; assoc. Thompson & Mitchell, St. Louis, 1980-82; employee benefits atty. Monsanto Co., St. Louis, 1982—. bd. dirs. Little Symphony Orchestra, St. Louis, 1973-80. Recipient Vol. Lawyer Program award Legal Services Eastern Mo., Inc., 1986. Mem. ABA (corp., banking and bus. law and taxation sects., employee benefits and exec. compensation com., interest in lawyer trust accts. commn., chmn. gen. income tax problems com. 1981-83), Bar Assn. Met. St. Louis (exec. com. 1976-81, v.p. 1977-78, treas. 1978-79), Mo. Lawyer Trust Account Found. (v.p., bd. dirs. 1984-86), Mid-Am. Tax Conf. (planning com.), Midwest Pension Conf. Pension, profit-sharing, and employee benefits, Corporate taxation, General corporate. Home: 9215 Ladue Rd Saint Louis MO 63124 Office: Monsanto Co 800 N Lindbergh Rd Saint Louis MO 63167

MORRISON, JOHNNY EDWARD, lawyer; b. Greenville, N.C., June 24, 1952; s. Mary Morrison; m. Cynthia Payton, Aug. 21, 1976; children—Melanie Yvette, Camille Yvonne. Bar: Va. 1977. Staff atty. Legal Aid. Soc., Roanoke Valley, Va., 1977-78; prosecutor Commonwealth's Atty.'s Office, Norfolk, Va., 1978-79, Portsmouth, Va., 1979-82, Commonwealth's atty., 1982—; ptnr. Overton, Sallee & Morrison, Portsmouth, 1982-83; bd. dirs. Tidewater Legal Aid Soc. Bd. dirs. Effingham Street Br. YMCA, Central Civic Forum, United Way. Named Young Man of Yr., Eureka, Inc., 1982; Man of Yr. local chpt. DAV, 1983, Outstanding Community Leader of Yr., Mt. Lebanon Bapt. Ch., 1984. Fellow Nat. Dist. Atty.'s Assn., Va. Assn. Commonwealth's Atty.'s (rep. 4th Congl. dist.), Tidewater Assn. Commonwealth's Attys. (rep.), Va. State Bar Assn., Old Dominion Bar Assn., Portsmouth Bar Assn. Democrat. Baptist. Club: Eureka. Lodge: Kiwanis. Criminal, General practice, Legislative. Home: 4105 Swannanoa Dr Portsmouth VA 23703 Office: Commonwealth's Attorney's Office 601 Crawford St PO Box 1417 Portsmouth VA 23704

MORRISON, PETER HENRY, lawyer; b. N.Y.C., Feb. 27, 1935; s. Milton A. and Sophia A. (Lipshitz) M.; m. Laura Torbet, June 19, 1983; children: Alix, Adam, Jennifer, Nicole. B.A., Colgate U., 1955; LL.B., Columbia U., 1958. Bar: N.Y. 1958, U.S. Ct. Appeals (1st cir.) 1960, U.S. Ct. Appeals (2d cir.) 1968, U.S. Supreme Ct. 1972, U.S. Ct. Appeals (3d cir.) 1978, U.S. Ct. Appeals (11th cir.) 1982, U.S. Ct. Appeals (9th cir.) 1985. Atty. office gen. counsel SEC, Washington, 1958-60; asst. U.S. atty. So. Dist. N.Y. Dept. Justice, 1960-64, chief securities fraud unit, 1963-64; sr. ptnr. Morrison, Paul & Beiley, P.C., N.Y.C., 1968-84, Morrison, Cohen & Singer, N.Y.C., 1984—; mem. faculty Insider Trading Panel-Law Jour. Seminars Press trial advocacy panel and broker-dealer liability Practicing Law Inst., Am Law Inst.-ABA Fraud and Fiduciary Duty Under Fed. Securities Laws. Contbr. articles to profl. jours. Mem. ABA (program panelist), Fed. Bar Council, N.Y. State Bar Assn. (chmn. fed. ct. practice seminars 1983, chmn. com. on fed. cts. 1979-83), Assn. Bar City N.Y. Clubs: Atrium (N.Y.C.); Sedgewood (Carmel, N.Y.). Federal civil litigation, State civil litigation, Criminal. Office: 110 E 59th St New York NY 10022

MORRISON, ROBERT DALE, lawyer; b. Fernbank, Ala., Apr. 24, 1942; s. William Clayton and Annie Ellen (Brock) M.; m. Louise F. Rose, Jan. 1, 1980; children—Andrew Stephen; m. Elizabeth Jane Gredinger, July 7, 1963 (div. June 1979); children—Jennifer Lynn, Teresa Beth. Student Miss. State U., 1960-61; B.A., U. Ala., 1964, LL.B., 1966. Bar: N.Mex. 1970, U.S. Dist. Ct. N.Mex. 1970, U.S. Ct. Appeals (10th cir.) 1975, U.S. Dist. Ct. Colo. 1978, Colo. 1978. Spl. agt. FBI, Washington, other locations, 1966-69; mgmt. trainee Met. Life Ins. Co., Albuquerque, 1969-71; assoc. Mitchell, Mitchell & Alley, Taos, N.Mex., 1971-73; ptnr. Mitchell, Mitchell, Alley & Morrison, Taos, 1973-77; sole practice, Taos, 1977—; asst. bar counsel N.Mex. Disciplinary Bd., 1973—. Pres. Taos Opera Guild, 1974-75; v.p. N.Mex. Opera Guild, 1975-76; cubmaster Boy Scouts Am., 1978-79. Mem. Taos County Bar Assn. (pres. 1971-75), ABA, N.Mex. Bar Assn., Colo. Bar Assn., Assn. Trial Lawyers Am., Am. Judicature Soc., N.Mex. Trial Lawyers Assn. Democrat. State civil litigation, Real property, Probate. Home: Upper Ranchitos Rd Taos NM 87571 Office: Upper Ranchitos Rd PO Box 648 Taos NM 87571

MORRISON, SHARON MCDONALD, lawyer; b. McCook, Nebr., May 10, 1937; s. Robert Martin and Eunice Fern (Stevens) McDonald; m. Frank B. Morrison Jr., June 28, 1959; children: John Martin, Anne Elizabeth. BS with honors, U. Nebr., 1959; JD with honors, U. Mont., 1979. Bar: Mont. 1979. Tchr. Jefferson County Schs., Littleton, Colo., 1959-61; ptnr. Morrison Law Office, Missoula, Mont., 1979-81, Morrison Law Offices, P.S.C., Helena, Mont., 1982—. Bd. dirs. Mont. Sch. Creative Arts, Helena, 1982-84. Mem. Mont. Trial Lawyers Assn. (pres. 1985-86), Western Trial Lawyers Assn. (bd. govs. 1981—). Democrat. Methodist. Federal civil litigation, State civil litigation. Office: Morrison Law Offices PSC 100 Neill Ave Helena MT 59601

MORRISON, SIDNEY EDER, lawyer; b. Chgo., Mar. 7, 1934; s. Gustave S. and Ruth (Birkenstein) M.; m. Diane M. Olszewski, Mar. 7, 1974; children: Barbara L., Andrew S., Leslie A., Robert S. BSL, Northwestern U., 1955, LLB with distinction, 1957. Bar: Ill. 1957, U.S. Dist. Ct. (no. dist.) Ill. 1959, U.S. Dist. Ct. (no. dist.) Miss. 1980. Assoc. Neistein, Richman & Hauslinger, Chgo., 1958-61; ptnr. Morrison, Shifris, Kovitz & Kamins and successor, Chicago, Ill., 1961-76; ptnr. Morrison, Kamins & Saltz, P.C., Chgo., 1976—; tchr. evening div. YMCA. Mem. Zoning Bd. Apls., Skokie, Ill., 1964-69; mem. Village of Skokie Human Relations Com., 1977-80. Served with USANG, 1957-58. Mem. Chgo. Bar Assn., Chgo. Bar Assn. Mech. Lien Subcommittee of Real Properties Committee Ill. State Bar Assn., Order of Coif. General corporate, Real property, General practice. Home: 8941 Forestview Skokie IL 60076 Office: 33 N LaSalle Suite 2030 Chicago IL 60602

MORRISON, WALTON STEPHEN, lawyer; b. Big Spring, Tex., June 16, 1907; s. Matthew Harmon and Ethel (Jackson) M.; m. Mary Lyon Bell, Dec. 19, 1932. Student Tex. A&M U., 1926-28; J.D., U. Tex., 1932. Bar: Tex. 1932. Asso., Morrison & Morrison, Big Spring, 1932-36, ptnr., 1939, 46; atty. County of Howard, 1937-39, judge, 1941-42, 47-48; atty. City of Big Spring, 1949-58; sole practice, Big Spring, 1953—; lectr. Am. Inst. Banking. Served with USAF, 1942-46. Fellow Tex. Bar Found., Am. Coll. Probate Counsel; mem. Tex. City Attys. Assn. (pres. 1955-56), Am. Judicature Soc., Tex. Bar Assn., ABA. Baptist. Clubs: Rotary (pres. 1949), Masons, Shriner. Probate, Real property, Estate taxation. Home: 1501 E 11th Pl Big Spring TX 79720 Office: 113 E 2d St PO Box 792 Big Spring TX 79720

MORRISON, WILLIAM DAVID, lawyer; b. Phila., Aug. 19, 1940; s. Maxey Neal and Mary Fuller (Chase) M.; m. Barbara Heath, Aug. 25, 1962; (div.); children—David Conrow, Stephen Munro, John Pomeroy; m. 2d., Sandra Elizabeth Butter, Mar. 16, 1983; children: Charles, Nicholas. B.A., Princeton U., 1962; LL.B., Yale U., 1965. Bar: N.Y. 1966, Calif. 1975. Assoc. firm Winthrop, Stimson, Putnam & Robert, N.Y.C., 1965-74; ptnr. Erickson & Morrison, and predecessor firms, Los Angeles, 1974-78; ptnr. LeBoeuf, Lamb, Leiby & Macrae, N.Y.C., 1978—; lectr. on Saudi Arabian law. Active Internat. Inst. for Strategic Studies. Mem. ABA, Assn. Bar City of N.Y., Calif. Bar Assn., Internat. Bar Assn. Clubs: Marks, Annabel's, RAC (London); Princeton (N.Y.C.). Author chpt. in Saudi Arabia: Keys to Business Success, 1981; contbr. articles to profl jours. Private international, General corporate, Contracts commercial. Home: 34 Norland Sq, London W11 England Office: LeBoeuf Lamb Leiby Macrae, 47 Berkeley Sq, London W1 England

MORRISSEY, GEORGE MICHAEL, lawyer; b. Chgo., Aug. 12, 1941; s. Joseph Edward and Mary Bernice (Shields) M.; m. Mary Kay McCarthy, Jan. 3, 1976; children: Meghan Catherine, Colleen Mary. BS, Ill. Inst. Tech., 1963; JD, De Paul U., 1971. Bar: Ill. 1972, U.S. Dist. Ct. (no. dist.) Ill. 1978, U.S. Supreme Ct. 1981. Auditor Touche Ross & Co., Chgo., 1963-68; sole practice Evergreen Park and Worth, Ill., 1972-77; 1st asst. suburban div. Cook County Pub. Defender, Chgo., 1978—; mem. spl commn. on adminstrn. of justice in Cook County, Chgo., 1984—. Mem. commn. on future of Ill. Inst. Tech., Chgo., 1976-77; bd. trustees Oak Lawn (Ill.) Library, 1979-85; bd. dirs. Crisis Ctr. for South Suburbia, Worth, 1979—. Served with U.S. Army, 1963-69. Mem. Chgo. Bar Assn. (jud. retention com., bar pres. com.), S.W. Bar Assn. (past pres.), Coalition of Suburban Bar Assn. (past pres.), Fed. Bar Assn., Alpha Sigma Phi. Democrat. Roman Catholic. Clubs: Columbia Yacht (commodore 1976-78) (Chgo.), Chgo. Yachting (commodore 1982). Lodge: Elks. Criminal. Office: Cook County Pub Defender 16501 Kedzie Pkwy Markham IL 60426

MORRISSEY, JAMES MALCOLM, lawyer; b. Hanover, N.H., Mar. 23, 1948; s. Leonard Eugene Jr. and Winifred Carol (White) M. BA, Yale U., 1970; JD, Stanford U., 1975. Bar: N.Y. 1976, Calif. 1976, U.S. Dist. Ct. (so. and ea. dists.) N.Y. 1977, U.S. Ct. Appeals (2d cir.) 1979. Assoc. Lord, Day & Lord, N.Y.C., 1975-79; assoc. appellate counsel The Legal Aid Soc., N.Y.C., 1979-82; asst. atty. gen. dept. law State of N.Y., N.Y.C., 1982-85; ptnr. Baer, Marks & Upham, N.Y.C., 1985—. Mem. Calif. Bar Assn., N.Y. State Bar Assn., Assn. of Bar of City of N.Y. Real property, State civil litigation, Securities. Office: Baer Marks & Upham 805 3d Ave New York NY 10022

MORRISSEY, PHILIP PATRICK, lawyer; b. Phila., Mar. 20, 1952; s. Philip Patrick and Gertrude (Foscio) M. BA, East Stroudsburg (Pa.) State Coll., 1974; JD, Ohio No. U., 1978. Bar: Pa. 1978, U.S. Dist. Ct. (mid. dist.) Pa. 1982. Sole practice Stroudsburg, Pa., 1978—; staff atty. Legal Services Northeastern Pa. Inc., Stroudsburg, 1982—. Sec. West End Rep. Club, Brodheadsville, Pa., 1983—. Mem. ABA, Pa. Bar Assn., Monroe County Bar Assn. (edn. com.). Roman Catholic. Avocations: art, music, gardening. Bankruptcy, Consumer commercial, General practice. Home: RD 1 PO Box 1466 Stroudsburg PA 18360 Office: Legal Services Northeastern Pa Inc 810 Monroe St Stroudsburg PA 18360

MORROW, EMILY RUBENSTEIN, lawyer; b. Poughkeepsie, N.Y., Sept. 14, 1952; d. Lewis W. and Erica (Beckh) Rubenstein; m. Paul L. Morrow; 1 child, Lillian. BA summa cum laude, Oberlin Coll., 1974; JD, U. Buffalo, 1977. Bar: N.Y. 1978, Ill. 1979, Vt. 1982. Law clk. Syracuse, N.Y., 1977-78; assoc. Altheimer & Gray, Chgo., 1978-80; sr. tax counsel Cen. Carolina Bank, Durham, N.C., 1980-81; assoc. Pierson, Attolter & Wadhams, Burlington, Vt., 1981-86; ptnr. Dinse, Erdmann & Clapp, Burlington, 1986—; adj. prof. bus. law Trinity Coll., Burlington, 1983-84; adj. prof. commercial law St. Michaels Coll., Burlington, 1984-85. Mem. edit. adv. bd. Vt. Woman Pubs., Burlington, 1986—. Bd. govs. Hosp. of Vt. Med. Ctr., Burlington, 1985-86; bd. dirs. Chittenden County United Way, Burlington, 1985-86; chmn. Vt. Whey Pollution Abatement Authority, Cabot, 1985-86; assoc. bd. trustees St. Michael's Coll, Winooski, 1986—. Mem. ABA (real property com., probate and trust law com., taxation com.), Vt. Bar Assn., Chittenden County Bar Assn., Internat. Assn. Fin. Planners, Women Bus. Owners of Vt., Phi Beta Kappa. Lodge: Zonta. Avocations: skiing, swimming, reading, sailing. Estate planning, Probate, General corporate. Home: 19 Pine Haven Shore Rd Shelburne VT 05482 Office: Dinse Erdmann & Clapp 209 Battery St Burlington VT 05401

MORROW, JOHN ELLSWORTH, lawyer; b. Los Angeles, Mar. 17, 1943; s. Charles Henry and Lillian (Harmon) M.; m. Rita Ann Gerrity, Sept. 24, 1966; children—David, Thomas, Kara. B.S., U. Southern Calif., 1965; J.D., U. Chgo., 1968; postgrad. U. Munich (Germany), 1969. Bar: Calif. 1969, Ill. 1971. Law clrk. to judge U.S. Dist. Ct. (cen. dist.) Calif., 1969-70; ptnr. Baker & McKenzie, Chgo., 1970-73, 75-76, 83—, Zurich, Switzerland, 1974-75, Hong Kong, 1976-82. Mem. ABA (subcom. on internat. banking and fin., internat. bus. law com. of corp. sect.; com. internat. fin. transactions of internat. law sect.). Banking, Private international. Office: Baker & McKenzie Prudential Plaza Chicago IL 60601

MORROW, PATRICK CRAIG, lawyer; b. Plaquemine, La., Jan. 15, 1948; s. Robert L. and Ruth (Wilbert) M.; m. Mary Alice Palazzo; children: Patrick Craig Jr., Celeste Marcelle, Charlotte Grace. BA in Govt., La. State U., 1969, JD, 1972. Bar: U.S. Dist. Ct. (ea., we. and mid. dists.) La., U.S. Dist. Ct. (so. dist.) Tex., U.S. Ct. Appeals (5th and 11th cirs.), U.S. Supreme Ct., 1982. Ptnr. Morrow & Morrow, Opelousas, La., 1972—. Mem. ABA, La. Bar Assn., St. Landry Parish Bar Assn. (sec./treas. 1974), Assn. Trial Lawyers Am., La. Trial Lawyers Assn. (adv. council 1981-82), La. City Attys. Assn. Home: 3175 London Dr Opelousas LA 70570 Office: Morrow & Morrow 324 W Landry St Opelousas LA 70570

MORROW, THOMAS CAMPBELL, lawyer; b. Cin., July 5, 1948; s. Worcester Beach Morrow & Alice Patricia (Faust) Bardon; m. Lynn Sharon Palatucci, July 5, 1974; children: Courtney Ann, Thomas Richard, John Campbell. BA, U. Cin., 1971; JD, U. Balt., 1975. Bar: Md. 1975, Fla. 1975, U.S. Dist. Ct. Md. 1979, U.S. Supreme Ct. 1979, U.S. Dist. Ct. (so. dist.) Fla. 1981, U.S. Ct. Appeals (4th cir.) 1981. Chief, adminstrv. services State's Atty.'s Office, Balt., 1972-75; asst. state's atty. Balt. County, 1975-78; asst. atty. gen. Md., Balt., 1978-79; asst. state atty. 11th Jud. Cir., Miami, Fla.,

1979-80; assoc. Weinberg & Green, Balt., 1980-84, ptnr., 1984—. Bd. dirs. Montessori Soc. Central Md., 1982, Kingsville Civic Assn., 1982-83. Mem. ABA, Assn. Trial Lawyers Am., Fed. Bar Assn., Md. Bar Assn., Md. Criminal Def. Attys. Assn., Heuisler Honor Soc. Criminal, Federal civil litigation, State civil litigation. Home: 12209 Kingswood Ln Kingsville MD 21087 Office: Weinberg & Green 100 S Charles St Baltimore MD 21201

MORSCH, THOMAS HARVEY, lawyer; b. Oak Park, Ill., Sept. 5, 1931; s. Harvey William and Gwenodyne (Maun) M.; m. Jacquelyn Casey, Dec. 27, 1954; children: Thomas H. Jr., Margaret, Mary Susan, James, Kathryn, Julia. Student, U. Notre Dame, 1949-52; B.S.L., Northwestern U., 1953, J.D., 1955. Bar: Ill. 1955, D.C. 1955. Assoc. Crowell & Leibman, Chgo., 1955-62; ptnr. Leibman, Williams, Bennett, Baird & Minow, Chgo., IL, 1962-72, Sidley & Austin, Chgo., 1972—; bd. dirs. Chgo. Lawyers Com. for Civil Rights under Law, Chgo., IL, 1970—, chmn., 1981-83. Pres. Republican Workshops of Ill., 1970; chmn. LaGrange Plan Commn., Ill., 1972-80, LaGrange Fire and Police Commn., 1968-72; bd. of advisors Legal Services Inst., 1982-85; trustee LaGrange Meml. Hosp., 1983—; bd. advs. Catholic Charities of Chgo., 1985—. Fellow Am. Coll. Trial Lawyers; mem. ABA, Am. Judicature Soc., Ill. State Bar Assn., Chgo. Bar Assn. (bd. mgrs. 1979-81), D.C. Bar Assn. Roman Catholic. Clubs: Legal, Univ. (Chgo.); LaGrange Country, Palisades Country (Mich.). State civil litigation, Antitrust, Trademark and copyright. Home: 301 S Edgewood Ave LaGrange IL 60525 Office: Sidley & Austin 1 First Nat Plaza Chicago IL 60603

MORSE, GEORGE WRAY, II, protective services official; b. Pensacola, Fla., Mar. 21, 1942; s. George Wray Morse and Sybil Annette (Newman) Kenngott; m. Susan Gene Loftin, Mar. 7, 1970; 1 child, George Wray III. BS, U. So. Miss., 1970; JD magna cum laude, Birmingham (Ala.) Sch. Law, 1982. Bar: Ala. 1982, U.S. Dist. Ct. (no. dist.) Ala. 1983. Spl. agent FBI, Denver, 1971-72, San Diego, 1972-73; spl. agent FBI, Birmingham, 1973-82, legal advisor, instr., 1982—; legal instr. Birmingham Police Acad., 1982—. Served with USAF, 1961-65. Mem. ABA, Ala. Bar Assn., Birmingham Bar. Assn., Hoover Athletic Assn., Sigma Delta Kappa. Methodist. Club: Chace Lake Country (Birmingham). Avocations: golf, tennis, flying, Little League coaching. Criminal, Civil rights, Legal education. Home: 2029 Shebia Dr Hoover AL 35216 Office: FBI 1400-2121 Bldg Birmingham AL 35203

MORSE, JACK CRAIG, lawyer; b. Evanston, Ill., Aug. 11, 1936; s. Leland Robert and Pauline (Pettibone) M.; children by former marriage—David Leland, Katherine Malia. B.A., Beloit Coll., 1958; J.D., Northwestern U., 1965. Bar: Hawaii 1967, U.S. Dist. Ct. Hawaii 1969, U.S. Ct. Appeals (9th cir.) 1977. Legal staff Bishop Estate, Honolulu, 1966-68; dep. atty. gen. State of Hawaii, Honolulu, 1968-71; ptnr. Saunders & Morse, Honolulu, 1971-73; assoc. Chuck & Wong, Honolulu, 1974-75; officer, dir. Morse, Nelson & Ross, Honolulu, 1976—; mem. Hawaii Med. Claim Conciliation Panel, Honolulu, 1977—, chmn., 1980—; mem. panel of arbitrators First Judicial Cir., Hawaii, 1986—. Served to lt. USN, 1959-62. Hardy scholar Northwestern U., 1962. Mem. Am. Judicature Soc., Assn. Trial Lawyers Am., Omicron Delta Kappa. Federal civil litigation, State civil litigation, Personal injury. Office: Morse Nelson & Ross 345 Queen St Suite 600 Honolulu HI 96813

MORSE, RICHARD ALLEN, lawyer; b. Manchester, N.H., Oct. 7, 1929; s. Emilus Allen and Rena (Philbrick) M.; m. Maxine Katz, Oct. 16, 1965. BA, U. N.H., 1951; JD, Harvard U., 1956. Bar: N.H. 1956. Assoc. Sheehan, Phinney, Bass & Green, P.A., Manchester, N.H., 1956—, mng. ptnr., 1963-74, treas., 1975—. Chmn. Charter Revision Commn., Manchester, 1962; vice-chmn. Rep. State Com., Concord, N.H., 1963-68; chancellor, trustee N.H. Meth. Conf., Concord, 1963—; trustee, treas. Tilton Sch., N.H., 1965—; chmn. bd. trustees Univ. System of N.H., Durham, 1977—. Mem. ABA, N.H. Bar Assn. Estate planning, Probate, Estate taxation. Home: Rd 5 Box 98 Laconia NH 03246 Office: Sheehan Phinney Bass & Green PA 1000 Elm St PO Box 3701 Manchester NH 03105

MORSE, SAUL JULIAN, lawyer; b. N.Y.C., Jan. 17, 1948; s. Leon William and Goldie (Kohn) M.; m. Anne Bruce Morgan, Aug. 21, 1982; 1 child, John Samuel Morgan. BA, U. Ill., 1969, JD, 1972. Bar: Ill. 1973, U.S. Dist. Ct. (so. dist.) Ill. 1976, U.S. Ct. Appeals (7th cir.) 1983, U.S. Supreme Ct. 1979, U.S. Tax Ct. 1982. Law clk. State of Ill. EPA, 1971-72; law clk. Ill. Commerce Commn., 1972, hearing examiner, 1972-73; trial atty. ICC, 1973-75; asst. minority legal counsel Ill. Senate, 1975, minority legal counsel, 1975-77; mem. Ill. Human Rights Commn.; gen. counsel Ill. Legis. Space Needs Commn., 1978—; sole practice, Springfield, Ill., 1977-79; ptnr. Gramlich & Morse, Springfield, Ill., 1980-85; prin. Saul J. Morse and Assocs., 1985—; gen. counsel Ill. State Med. Soc., lectr. in continuing med. edn. 1986; gen. counsel Ill. State Med. Ins. Exchange, Tele-Sav Communications, County Nursing Home Assn. Ill., Ill. Occupational Therapy Assn., Northeastern Ill. Rail Corp.; mem. faculty Ill. Inst. for Continuing Legal Edn., 3d Party Practice, 1978, also symposia; bd. dirs. Springfield Ctr. for Ind. Living, 1984—; mem. task force on transp. Republican Nat. Com., 1979-80, Springfield Jewish Community Relations Council, 1976-79, 82; mem. spl. com. on zoning and land use planning Sangamon County Bd., 1978. Named Disabled Adv. of Yr., Ill. Dept. Rehab. Services, 1985; recipient Chmn.'s Spl. award Ill. State Med. Soc., 1987. Fellow Internat. Acad. Law and Sci., Nat. Health Lawyers Assn., Am. Soc. Law and Medicine; mem. ABA (vice chmn. medicine and law com., tort and ins. practice sect., forum com. on health law), Ill. State Bar Assn. (spl. com. on reform of legis. process 1976-82, spl. com. on the disabled lawyer 1978-82, young lawyers sect. com. on role of govt. atty. 1977-80, chmn. 1982, sect. council adminstrv. law, vice chmn. 1981-82), Sangamon County Bar Assn., Phi Delta Phi. Lodge: B'nai B'rith. (bd. dirs.). Administrative and regulatory, Health, Legislative. Home: 2105 Noble Ave Springfield IL 62704 Office: Saul J Morse & Assocs 828 S 2d St Springfield IL 62701

MORTENSEN, PHILIP STEPHEN, lawyer; b. Orange, N.J., Sept. 6, 1947; s. Leonard R. and Marie Tobias M.; m. Patricia J. Randall, Aug. 23, 1969; children—Barnaby D., Heather L., Erin B., Benjamin P. B.S., Pa. State U., 1969; J.D., Suffolk U., 1972. Bar: N.Y. 1973, Fla. 1976, U.S. Dist. Ct. (ea. and so. dist.) N.Y. 1974, U.S. Dist. Ct. (mid. dist.) Fla. 1977, U.S. Ct. Appeals (5th cir.) 1978, U.S. Ct. Appeals (11th cir.) 1981, U.S. Ct. Appeals (7th cir.) 1981, U.S. Supreme Ct. 1978, U.S. Dist. Ct. 1985, U.S. Ct. Appeals (9th cir.) 1985. Assoc. firm Jackson, Lewis, Schnitzler & Krupman, N.Y.C., 1972-77; sole practice, Sarasota, Fla., 1977-80; ptnr. firm Kreitzman, Mortensen & Simon, N.Y.C., 1980—; mem. labor relations law sect. Fla. Bar. Mem. ABA (labor and employment law sect.), N.Y. State Bar Assn. (labor and employment law sect.), Assn. Bar City N.Y. Republican. Labor. Home: 256 Thayer Pond Rd Wilton CT 06897 Office: Kreitzman Mortensen & Simon 25 W 43d St New York NY 10036

MORTON, FRANKLIN WHEELER, JR., judge; b. Bklyn., May 17, 1920; s. Franklin Wheeler and Inez Eloise (Moore) M.; m. Gwendolyn Louise Irish, June 14, 1952; children: Franklin III, Sherill Patricia, Rebecca Inez, Catharine Louise. BA, L.I. U., 1941, LLD (hon.), 1975; JD, St. John's U., 1948, LLD (hon.), 1985. Bar: N.Y. 1948. Asst. atty. U.S. Dist. Ct. (ea. dist.) N.Y., 1949-51, King County Dist. Atty.'s Office, Bklyn., 1951-58; justice N.Y.C. Mcpl. Ct., 1958-62; judge N.Y.C. Civil Ct., 1962-68; justice N.Y. State Supreme Ct., N.Y.C., 1969—; Chmn. judiciary relations com. 2d Dept. N.Y. Judiciary, 1976-77. Contbr. articles to profl. jours. Trustee Bklyn. Psychiat. Ctr., 1958, Soc. Prevention of Cruelty to Children, Bklyn., 1960, Bklyn. Hosp., 1960—, St. John's U., Queens, 1985—, L.I. Diocese Episc. Found., 1965—. Named Hon. Citizen, City of Auburn, N.Y., 1975, State of Del., 1975. Mem. Assn. Justices Supreme Ct. State of N.Y. (pres. 1984-85, chmn. exec. com. 1985—), Kings County Criminal Bar Assn., Met. Black Lawyers Assn., Protestant Lawyers Assn. Club: Comus Soc. (Bklyn.). Avocations: bridge, reading, theater, spectator sports. Office: Supreme Ct State of NY 360 Adams St Brooklyn NY 11201

MORTON, ROBERT BALL, judge; b. Webb City, Mo., Oct. 26, 1912; s. Frank Percy and Grace Aurelia (Ball) M.; m. Dorothy Compton, July 25, 1942; 1 son, Robert Charles. J.D., U. Kans.-Lawrence, 1935. Bar: Kans. 1935, U.S. Dist. Ct. Kans. 1943, U.S. Ct. Appeals (10th cir.) 1951, U.S. Supreme Ct. 1955. Practice, Wichita, Kans., 1935-41; mem. Gardiner & Helsel, 1935-37; asst. probate judge Sedgwick County (Kans.), 1937-41; mem. Kidwell, Darrah & Morton, 1946-50; judge 18th Jud. Dist. Ct. Kans., 1950-51; mem. Aley, Morton & Darrah, Wichita, 1950-62; spl. counsel City of Wichita, 1955-62; judge U.S. Bankruptcy Ct. Dist. Kans., Wichita, 1962-86 , chief judge, 1979-82; lectr. profl. seminars; mem. faculty Fed. Jud. Center seminars for newly appointed bankruptcy judges. Bd. regents Wichita U., 1952-63, chmn., 1956, 62; trustee St. Francis Hosp., Wichita, 1964-66. Served to lt. col. USMC, 1942-46. Decorated Bronze Star; recipient Disting. Service Citation City of Wichita, 1962, recognition award Wichita State U. Alumni Assn., 1969. Mem. Nat. Conf. Bankruptcy Judges (pres. 1974-75). Republican. Congregationalist. Contbr. chpt., papers, articles to legal publs.; chmn. editorial adv. bd. Am. Bankruptcy Law Jour., 1976-86. Bankruptcy. Office: PO Box 1118 401 US Courthouse 401 N Market St Wichita KS 67202

MORTON, THOMAS EDWARD, JR., business executive, lawyer; b. Cleve., Aug. 30, 1936; s. Thomas Edward and Mary (Coakley) M.; m. Jean Inglis Gibbs, June 21, 1958; children: Douglas, Jennifer; m. Roxana Mitchell, Oct. 30, 1982. B.S. magna cum laude, John Carroll U., 1958; LL.B., Case Western Res. U., 1961, M.B.A., 1971. Bar: Ohio 1961, Tex. 1981. Tax counsel Pickands Mather & Co., Cleve., 1961-68, asst. sec., 1961-72; asst. sec. Diamond Shamrock Corp., Dallas, 1972-78, asst. gen. counsel, corp. sec., 1978-80; sr. v.p. So. Union Co., Dallas, 1981—, chmn. exec. mgmt. com., 1985—; adv. dir. Southwestern Legal Found., Dallas, 1982—. Author: American Jurisprudence Prize-Income Taxation, 1961 (cert. award 1961). Bd. dirs. Am. Cancer Soc., Cleve., 1978; bd. dirs. Jr. Achievement Cleve., 1976; patron Dallas Mus. Fine Arts, 1981, Southwest Legal Found.; rep. Eagle Republican Nat. Com., Dallas, 1983. Mem. ABA, State Bar Tex., Dallas Bar Assn., Am. Soc. Corporate Secs. (mem. securities law com.). Clubs: Dallas, Petroleum (Dallas). Antitrust, Oil and gas leasing, Public utilities. Home: 4415 Glenwood Ave Dallas TX 75205 Office: So Union Co 1800 InterFirst Two Dallas TX 75270

MORTON, WOOLRIDGE BROWN, JR., lawyer; b. N.Y.C., Nov. 11, 1914; s. W. Brown and Lucie Crommelin (Taylor) M.; m. Louisa Lay, June 10, 1935; children—Lisa Morton Chute, W. Brown III, Marion H. Morton Carroll, Lucie Morton Garrett. B.S., U. Va., 1936, LL.B., 1938. Bar: Va. 1938, N.Y. 1940, D.C. 1951. Assoc. Pennie, Davis, Marvin & Edmonds, and successor firms, N.Y.C. and Washington, 1938-50, ptnr., 1950-64; ptnr. McLean, Morton & Boustead, N.Y.C. and Washington, 1964-70, Morton, Bernard, Brown, Roberts & Sutherland, Washington, 1970-77, Morton and Roberts, Washington, 1977-78, sole practice, King George, Va., 1980-81, Warsaw, Va., 1981—; lectr. U. Va., Charlottesville, 1959-82. Served to maj. AUS, 1941-46. Decorated Croix de Guerre (France). Mem. ABA (ho. of dels. 1965-79), Va. Bar Assn., D.C. Bar Assn., Am. Intellectual Property Law Assn. (pres. 1964-65). Episcopalian. Federal civil litigation, Patent, Trademark and copyright. Home and office: RR1 Box 586 Warsaw VA 22572

MORTRUD, DAVID LLOYD, lawyer; b. Mpls., Oct. 2, 1940; s. Clarence Orrin and Helen Irene (Chase) M.; m. Cynthia Ruth Mariner, Dec. 30, 1967 (div. Dec. 1980); 1 child, Jonathan William; m. Sharon Lee Lindell, July 28, 1984. BA, Augsburg Coll., 1963; JD, U. Conn., 1974. Bar: Conn. 1974, U.S. Dist. Ct. Conn. 1974, U.S. Ct. Appeals (2d cir.) 1975, U.S. Tax Ct. 1977, Minn. 1983, U.S. Ct. Appeals (8th cir.) 1983, U.S. Dist. Ct. Minn. 1984. Commd. ensign USN, 1963, advanced through grades to lt. comdr., 1973, resigned from active duty, 1973; fin. analyst Traveler's Ins. Co., Hartford, Conn., 1973-76; counsel Aetna Life & Casualty Ins. Co., Hartford, 1976-83, Northwestern Nat. Life Ins. Co., Mpls., 1983—. Mem. Planning and Zoning Commn., Hebron. Conn., 1975-78, Planning Commn., Maple Grove, Minn., 1984—. Served to capt. USNR, 1973—. Contracts commercial, Real property, Securities. Home: 10203 Union Terr Ln Maple Grove MN 55369

MOSCHOS, DEMITRIOS MINA, lawyer; b. Worcester, Mass., Jan. 8, 1941; s. Constantine Mina and Vasiliky (Strates) M.; m. Celeste Thomaris, Sept. 28, 1975; children—Kristin M., Thomas W. B.A. magna cum laude, U. Mass., 1962; J.D. magna cum laude, Boston U., 1965; grad. basic course U.S. Army JAG Sch., Charlottesville, Va., 1966. Bar: Mass., 1965, U.S. dist. ct. Mass. 1975, U.S. Ct. Mil. Apls. 1966. Exec. asst. to city mgr., also spl. legal csl. City of Worcester (Mass.), 1966-75, asst. city mgr. and spl. legal csl., 1975-80; assoc. Mirick, O'Connell, DeMallie & Lougee, Worcester, 1980-81, ptnr., 1982—; lectr. labor relations Worcester State Coll., 1975—; lectr. labor relations Clark U., 1978—; bd. dirs. Consumers Savs. Bank, Guaranty Bank. Chmn. Worcester Housing Com., 1968-78, Worcester Energy Com., 1978-80; mem. Mass. Joint Labor Mgmt. Com., 1978-80; trustee United Way Hellenic Coll. and Mechanics Hall, Worcester; pres. Cath. Charities of Worcester. Served to capt. JAGC, U.S. Army, 1966-68. Decorated Army Commendation medal; recipient Alumni Acad. Achievement award Boston U. Law Sch., 1965; named Outstanding Young Man of Worcester County, Worcester County Jaycees, 1969; named in resolution of commendation Worcester City Council, 1980. Mem. ABA, Mass. Bar Assn., Worcester Bar Assn., Nat. Sch. Bds. Assn. Council Sch. Attys. Greek Orthodox. Club: Tatnuck Country. Drafter adminstrv. codes; contbr. articles to profl. jours. Labor, Local government, Administrative and regulatory. Office: 1700 Mechanics Bank Tower Worcester MA 01608

MOSCHOS, MICHAEL CHRISTOS, lawyer; b. Worcester, Mass., Jan. 8, 1941; s. Constantine Mina and Vasiliky (Strates) M.; m. Mary Patricia Dermody, Feb. 20, 1977; children: Charles, Michael Patrick. B.B.A. cum laude, U. Mass., 1962; J.D., Boston U., 1965. Bar: Mass. 1965, N.Y. 1970, U.S. Dist. Ct. Mass. 1981, U.S. Supreme Ct. 1982. Lawyer, Investors Group, N.Y.C., 1968-72; assoc., spl. counsel Cabot, Cabot, Forbes, Boston, 1972; sole practice, Boston, 1973, Worcester, 1979—; spl. counsel Esso-Pappas, S.A., Athens, Greece, 1969-70; investment banker Worcester Bancorp., 1974-79; cons. atty. Baskins-Sears Esq., N.Y.C., 1979, Downtown Worcester Bus. Devel. Corp., 1974-76. Legal officer Worcester Heritage Soc., 1975-82; of counsel Worcester Art Mus., 1975-83; incorporator Worcester Natural History Soc., 1977—; spl. counsel Hellenic Bottling Co., S.A., Hellenic Canning Industries, S.A., Internat. Canning Industry, S.A., Athens, Greece, 1973. Served to capt. U.S. Army, 1965-67. Mem. Mass. Bar Assn., Worcester County Bar Assn., Am. Judicature Soc. Greek Orthodox. Clubs: Worcester, Plaza; Union Boat of Boston. Contracts commercial, Construction, Real property. Home: 15 Massachusetts Ave Worcester MA 01609 Office: 131 Clarendon St Suite 300 Boston MA 02116 also: 446 Main St Suite 1300 Worcester MA 01608

MOSELEY, JAMES FRANCIS, lawyer; b. Charleston, S.C., Dec. 6, 1936; s. John Olin and Kathryn (Moran) M.; m. Anne McGehee, June 10, 1961; children: James Francis, John McGehee. A.B., The Citadel, 1958; J.D., U. Fla., 1961. Bar: Fla. 1961, U.S. Supreme Ct. 1970. Pres. Taylor, Moseley & Joyner, Jacksonville, Fla., 1963—; chmn. jud. nominating com. 4th Jud. Cir., 1978-80. Contbr. articles on admiralty, transp. and ins. law to legal jours. Pres. Civic Round Table, Jacksonville, 1974, United Way, 1979, Greater Jacksonville Community Found.; chmn. bd. trustees Jacksonville Pub. Library Found., sec.,1987—; chmn. Southeastern Admiralty Law Inst., 1980; dir. Nat. Young Life Found., 1987—. Fellow Am. Coll. Trial Lawyers, Am. Bar Found.; mem. Jacksonville Bar Assn. (pres. 1975), Fla. Council Bar Pres. (chmn.), Maritime Law Assn. (exec. com. 1978-81, chmn. navigation com. 1981—, del. Comite Maritime Internat. on Collision 1984—), Fed. Ins. Corp. Counsel (chmn. maritime law sect.), Internat. Assn. Def. Counsel. Clubs: Deerwood, River, Downtown Athletic (N.Y.C.), India House (N.Y.C.), St. John's Diner (pres.-elect). Admiralty, Federal civil litigation, Insurance. Home: 7780 Hollyridge Rd Jacksonville FL 32217 Office: Taylor Moseley & Joyner 1887 Bldg 501 W Bay St Jacksonville FL 32202

MOSELEY, PATRICIA ANN, lawyer; b. Rio Grande City, Tex., Apr. 19, 1946; d. Percy and Virginia Elizabeth (Gregg) M.; m. Richard M. Montgomery, July 1964 (div. Dec. 1967); m. Norman L. Williamson, Oct. 15, 1981; children: Norma Williamson Nash, W. Scott Williamson. BS in Secondary Edn., Tex. A&I, 1968; MA, U. Tex., 1972; JD, Tex. Tech U., 1978. Bar: Tex. 1978, U.S. Dist. Ct. (no. dist.) Tex. 1979, U.S. Ct. Appeals (5th cir.) 1981. Tchr. Galena Park Ind. Sch. Dist., Houston, 1968-70; teaching asst. journalism dept. U. Tex., Austin, 1970-71; tchr. Corsicana (Tex.) Ind. Sch. Dist., 1972-75; atty. West Tex. Legal Services, Lubbock, 1978-83; sole practice Lubbock, 1983—. Mem. Tex. Bar Assn. (family law sect.), Lubbock County Bar Assn. (family law sect.), Lubbock Women Lawyers Assn., Lubbock LWV (bd. dirs. 1981-84, v.p. 1986—), Women in Communications Inc. (bd. dirs. 1984—). Democrat. Baptist. Club: WIN (Lubbock). Family and matrimonial, Criminal, Juvenile. Home: PO Box 466 Lubbock TX 79408 Office: 1304 Texas Ave Lubbock TX 79401

MOSER, MELVIN LAVALLE, JR., lawyer; b. Pitts., Sept. 25, 1949; s. Melvin Lavalle and Mary (Conroy) M.; m. Madalyn Rice, Aug. 24, 1973; children: Ryan Patrick, Susan Leigh. BS in Math., U. Pitts., 1971, JD, 1976. Bar: Pa. 1976, U.S. Dist. Ct. (we. dist.) Pa. 1976, Fla. 1978, U.S. Ct. Appeals (3rd cir.) 1978, U.S. Ct. Appeals (D.C. cir.) 1986. Assoc. Buchanan Ingersoll P.C., Pitts., 1976-83, ptnr., 1983—. Contbr. articles to profl. jours. Served with U.S. Army, 1971-73. Mem. Am. Bar Assn. (litigation, coal and damages sects.), Pa. Bar Assn., Allegheny County Bar Assn. Democrat. Roman Catholic. Club: Longue Vue (Verona, Pa.) (entertainment com.). Avocations: golf, horse racing. Federal civil litigation, State civil litigation, Construction. Home: 209 Oakview Ave Pittsburgh PA 15218 Office: Buchanan Ingersoll Profl Corp 600 Grant St 57th Fl Pittsburgh PA 15219

MOSER, WILLIAM R., judge, legal educator; b. Chgo., Oct. 14, 1927; m. Mary Bernadette, July 2, 1956; children: William Reding, Mary Magdalan. BS in History, St. Norbert Coll., DePere, Wis., 1950; LLB, Marquette U., 1953; LLM, U. Va., 1982. Sole practice Milw., 1953-62; county judge State of Wis., Milw., 1962-66, cir. judge, 1966-78, appellate judge, 1978—; senator State of Wis., Milw., 1956-62; adj. prof. Marquette U. Law Sch. Contbr. articles to profl. jours. Mem. disciplinary disability com. Wis. Jud. Commn., Madison, 1978—. Served to cpl. U.S. Army, 1945-47, PTO. Mem. ABA, Wis. Bar Assn., Milw. Bar Assn., Wis. Bar Found. (life), Am. Judicature Soc. Roman Catholic. State civil litigation, Criminal, Legal education. Home: 1410 Lake Dr South Milwaukee WI 53172 Office: Wis Ct of Appeals Courthouse Milwaukee WI 53233

MOSES, CARL MICHAEL, lawyer; b. Sharon, Pa., Dec. 23, 1940; s. Joseph H. and Sophia (Schmier) M.; m. Paula Leslie Steinberg, June 17, 1973. BA, Pa. State U., 1962; LLD, Wayne State U., 1967. Bar: Mich. 1967, Pa. 1968, U.S. Ct. Appeals (3d cir.) 1975, U.S Supreme Ct. 1975, U.S. Dist. Ct. (we. dist.) Pa. 1979. Assoc. Irwin & Perfilio, Sharon, 1968-69, Rodgers, Marks, Irwin & Perfilio, Sharon, 1969-71; sole practice Sharon, 1971—. Bd. dirs. Am. Cancer Soc., Sharon, 1976—. Served as sgt. USMC, 1963-68. Recipient 10 Yrs. Vol. Services award Am. Cancer Soc., 1986. Mem. Mercer County Bar Assn. (chmn. edn. com. 1981-86), Allegheny County Bar Assn. (assoc.), Pa. Bar Assn., Pa. Trial Lawyers Assn., Mich. Bar Assn. Republican. Jewish. Club: Sharon Country. Lodge: Kiwanis (bd. dirs., sec., v.p. local chpt. 1986). Avocations: golf, racquetball,running, traveling, reading. Personal injury, Family and matrimonial, General practice. Home: 330 Rexford Dr Apt 17 Hermitage PA 16148 Office: 19 Jefferson Ave Sharon PA 16146

MOSES, GENE RONALD, lawyer; b. Yakima, Wash., Dec. 7, 1949; s. Gerald Louis Bradley and Norma Murial (Eastwood) M.; m. Jackie Lynn Burley, Ju.y 4, 1980; 1 child, Chad Corwin. BA in Polit. Sci., Western Wash. U., 1971; JD, Gonzaga U., 1975. Bar: Wash. 1976, U.S. Dist. Ct. (we. dist.) Wash. 1976, U.S. Tax Ct. 1976, U.S. Ct. Appeals (9th cir.) 1976, U.S. Supreme Ct. 1986. Assoc. Millhouse, Nelle Law Firm, Bellingham, Wash., 1975-76; chief civil dep. Whatcom County Prosecutor's Office, Bellingham, 1976-86; assoc. Hindman & Tasker, Bellingham, 1986—; assoc. prof. Western Wash. U., Bellingham, 1975-81. Bd. dirs. Planned Parenthood Whatcom County, Bellingham, 1976. Mem. Wash. State Bar Assn., Assn. Trial Lawyers Am., Wash. State Trial Lawyers, Wash. Assn. Ins. Def. Counsel, Wash. Assn. Pros. Attys. (lectr. 1976-86). Club: Bellingham Yacht. Avocations: yachting, fishing. State civil litigation, Insurance, Insurance defense litigation. Office: Hindman & Tasker 306 Flora St Bellingham WA 98225

MOSES, MARY HELEN, law educator, lawyer; b. Atlanta, Aug. 18, 1953; d. Jack and Jean Elizabeth (Tollison) M.; m. E. Michael Ruberti, Aug. 12, 1986. B.A., Furman U., 1975; J.D., U. Ga., 1978; LL.M., Georgetown U., 1981. Bar: Ga. 1978, D.C. 1980. Asst. prof. law N.C. Central U., Durham, 1978-79; counsel to John A. Penello, NLRB, Washington, 1979-81; asst. prof. law Albany Law Sch., N.Y., 1981-84, assoc. prof., 1984-87, prof. 1987—; cons. LSAT preparation Siena Coll., Londonville, N.Y., 1982—; cons. N.Y. State Sch. Indsl. and Labor Relations, 1985—, O'Connell & Aronowitz, P.C., Albany, Nelson A. Rockefeller Coll. Pub. Affairs, SUNY-Albany, 1985—; conf. speaker Cornell U. Sch. Indsl. and Labor Relations, Albany, N.Y., 1984; mem. com. on research involving human subjects Albany Med. Coll., 1981—. Author: (with others) A Guide to Research in the Common Law, 1982. Contbr. articles to profl. jours. Mem. Indsl. Relations Research Assn., ABA, Women's Bar Assn. N.Y., Order of Barristers. Legal education, Labor, Civil rights. Home: 233 Bentwood Ct W Albany NY 12203 Office: Albany Law Sch Union U 80 New Scotland Ave Albany NY 12208

MOSHER, RICHARD UNDERHILL, lawyer; b. Pontiac, Mich., Nov. 18, 1945; s. William Edwin and Jane (Underhill) M.; m. Gretchen Dorn, Aug. 23, 1967; children: Richard Andrew, Jane Amanda, Ashley Dorn. BA, Williams Coll., 1967; JD, Wayne State U., 1972. Bar: U.S. Dist. Ct. (ea. dist.) Mich. 1972, U.S. Ct. Appeals (6th cir.) 1972, U.S. Tax Ct. 1974. Ptnr. Butzel, Long, Gust, Klein & Van Zile, Detroit, 1972-81, May, Gowing, Mosher & Simpson, Bloomfield Hills, Mich., 1982-85, Mosher, Vondale & Gierak (formerly Mosher & Vondale), Bloomfield Hills, 1986—; bd. dirs. Phoenix Wire Cloth, Inc., Troy, Mich., Charles M. Campbell Co., Bloomfield Hills. Served to lt. USAFR, 1969-75. Mem. ABA, Mich. Bar Assn., Detroit Bar Assn., Oakland County Bar Assn. Episcopalian. Labor, Federal civil litigation, State civil litigation. Home: 280 Canterbury Bloomfield Hills MI 48013 Office: Mosher Vondale & Gierak 74 E Long Lake Bloomfield Hills MI 48013

MOSHOS, ARTHUR LEON, lawyer; b. N.Y.C., Apr. 28, 1938; s. Arthur and Pauline (Sobanko) M.; m. Sandra Marie West, Sept. 5, 1965; children: Candice, Arthur, April, Amber. BA, Lehigh U., 1960, BSME, 1961; LLB, U. Va., 1969. Bar: Va. 1969, U.S. Dist. Ct. (ea. dist.) Va. 1969. Assoc. Fitzgerald, Smith & Davis, Fairfax, Va., 1969-71; sole practice Fairfax, 1972; ptnr. Fortkort & Moshos, Fairfax, 1972-77, Moshos, Byrd, McClure, De Deo & Mische, P.C., Fairfax, 1979—. Pres. Young Dems., Fairfax, 1974, Fairfax High Sch. PTA, 1985; chmn. police adv. council, Fairfax, 1985. Mem. Va. Bar Assn. (council), Fairfax Bar Assn. (pres. 1984), Assn. Trial Lawyers Am., Va. Trial Lawyers Assn., Fairfax Law Found. Avocation: golf. Real property, General corporate, Negligence. Office: Moshos Byrd McClure De Deo & Mische PC 10521 Judicial Dr Suite 201 Fairfax VA 22030

MOSICH, NICHOLAS JOSEPH, Lawyer; b. San Pedro, Calif., July 2, 1951; s. Nicholas Andrew and Barbara Yvonne (Chutuk) M.; m. Susanne Melinda Wolf, Dec. 18, 1976; children: Nicholas Daniel, Andrea Michelle. BA, Santa Clara U., 1974; JD, Pepperdine U., 1977. Bar: Calif. 1977, U.S. Dist. Ct. (so. dist.) Calif. 1979, U.S. Dist. Ct. (cen. dist.) Calif. 1980. Assoc. Forgy & Inadomi, Santa Ana, Calif., 1978-83, ptnr., 1983—. Bd. dirs. Young Men's Christian Assn., Santa Ana, 1980—. Mem. ABA, Orange County Bar Assn., Am. Trial Lawyers' Assn. Republican. Roman Catholic. State civil litigation, Insurance, Real property. Office: Forgy Inadomi & Mosich 550 N Golden Circle Dr Santa Ana CA 92705

MOSK, RICHARD MITCHELL, lawyer; b. Los Angeles, May 18, 1939; s. Stanley and Edna M.; m. Sandra Lee Budnitz, Mar. 21, 1964; children: Julie, Matthew. AB with great distinction, Stanford U., 1960; JD cum laude, Harvard U., 1963. Bar: Calif. 1964, U.S. Supreme Ct. 1970, U.S. Ct. Mil. Appeals 1970, U.S. Dist. Ct. (no., so., ea., and cen. dists.) Calif 1964, U.S. Ct. Appeals (9th dist.) 1964. Mem. staff Pres.'s Commn. on Assassination Pres. Kennedy, 1964; research clk. Calif. Supreme Ct., 1964-65; assoc. Mitchell, Silberberg & Knupp, Los Angeles, 1965-87; mem. Sanders, Barnet, Jacobson, Goldman & Mosk, Los Angeles, 1987—, ptnr., 1987—; spl. dep. Fed. Pub. Defender, Los Angeles, 1975-76; instr. U. So. Calif. Law Sch., 1978; arbitrator Iran-U.S. Claims Tribunal, 1981-84, substitute arbitrator, 1984—; mem. Los Angeles County Jud. Procedures Commn., 1973-82, chmn., 1978; substitute arbitrator Iran-U.S. Claims Tribunal, 1984—. Contbr. articles to profl. jours. Mem. Los Angeles City-County Inquiry on Brush Fires, 1970; bd. dirs. Calif. Mus. Sci. and Industry, 1979-82, Vista Del Mar Child Ctr., 1979-82; trustee Los Angeles County Law Library, 1985-86;

bd. govs. Town Hall Calif, 1986—. Served with USNR. Hon. Woodrow Wilson fellow, 1960; recipient Roscoe Pound prize, 1961. Mem. ABA (internat. law sect. 1986—), Fed. Bar Assn. (pres. Los Angeles chpt. 1972), Los Angeles County Bar Assn., Beverly Hills Bar Assn., Los Angeles Assn. Bus. Trial Lawyers, Am. Film Mktg. Assn. (arbitration panel 1986—), Am. Arbitration Assn. (comml. panel and adv. council of Asia/Pacific Ctr. for resolution internat. trade disputes 1986—), Hong Kong Internat. Arbitration Ctr. (panel 1986—), Am. Film Mktg. Assn. (arbitration panel, adv. council Asia/Pacific ctr. for resolution internat. trade disputes 1986—), Los Angeles Ctr. for Internat. Comml. Arbitration, Phi Beta Kappa. State civil litigation, Federal civil litigation, Public international. Office: Sanders Barnet et al 1901 Ave of Stars Suite 850 Los Angeles CA 90067

MOSKATEL, IRA DENNIS, lawyer; b. Los Angeles, Nov. 18, 1950; s. Leon and Edith (Levin) M.; m. Barbara V. Schochet, Dec. 16, 1984. BS, Calif. Inst. Tech., 1972; JD, U. So. Calif., 1975. Bar: Calif., U.S. Dist. Ct. (cen. dist.) Calif. Assoc. Swerdlow, Glikbarg & Shimer, Beverly Hills, Calif., 1975-78, Gillin, Scott & Alperstein, Los Angeles, 1978; prin. Moskatel Law Corp., Beverly Hills, 1979—. Mem. Editorial Bd. U. So. Calif. Law Rev., 1974-75; assoc. editor Beverly Hills Bar Jour., 1976-82; contbr. articles to profl. jours. Sec. systems sect. Town Hall Calif., Los Angeles, 1983—. Mem. ABA (econs. of practice sect., chmn. com. on artificial intelligence 1984—, vice chmn. research and devel. 1986—), IEEE, Los Angeles County Bar Assn. (chmn. law and tech. sect. 1984-86), Assn. for Computing Machinery, Order of Coif. Club: Del Rey Yacht (Marina del Rey, Calif.). Corporate taxation, General corporate, Computer. Office: Moskatel Law Corp 10100 Santa Monica Blvd Los Angeles CA 90067

MOSKIN, MORTON, lawyer; b. N.Y.C., Mar. 28, 1927; s. Barnett and Sonia (Burr) M.; m. Rita Lee Goldberg, June 15, 1952; children: Tina, Ilene, Jonathan. B.A., Pa. State Coll., 1947; LL.B., Cornell U., 1950. Assoc. White & Case, N.Y.C., 1950-61, ptnr., 1962—; dir. Crum & Forster, Morristown, N.J., 1973-82, Internat. Minerals & Chem. Corp., Northbrook, Ill., 1973—; sec. BT Mortgage Investors, Garden City, N.J., 1975-82. Bd. dirs., pres. Henry M. Blackmer Found., N.Y.C., 1974—; bd. dirs., pres. Achievement Found., Stamford, Conn., 1975—; pres., bd. dirs. Jewish Community Services of L.I., 1982-87. Served to ensign USNR, 1945-46, 47. Fellow Am. Bar Found.; mem. ABA, N.Y. State Bar Assn., N.Y. County Lawyers Assn. (dir. 1981-86), Am. Judicature Soc. Clubs: Norfolk Country (Conn.). General corporate, Securities. Home: 1160 Park Ave Apt 15B New York NY 10128 Office: White & Case 1155 Ave of Americas New York NY 10036

MOSKOF, HOWARD RICHARD, lawyer, businessman; b. N.Y.C., May 19, 1935; s. Joseph Louis and Florence (Polesie) M.; m. Ruth Patricia Singer, Aug. 25, 1968; children: Melissa Hope, Adam Daniel. A.B., Colgate U., 1956; J.D., Yale U., 1959. Bar: Conn. 1960, N.Y. 1961, D.C. 1965. Asst. dir., dep. gen. counsel New Haven Redevel. Agy., 1960; legal asst. to mayor of New Haven, 1960; asst. U.S. atty. Dist. Conn., 1964; assoc. Donohue, Kaufmann and Shaw, Washington, 1965; dep. dir., gen. counsel D.C. Redevel. Land Agy., 1965-67; exec. dir. President's Com. Urban Housing, 1967-68; v.p. ops. Nat. Corp. Housing Partnerships, 1969-70; assoc. Hogan & Hartson, Washington, 1971; ptnr. Hogan & Hartson, 1972-84; gen. mgr. Flower Mound New Town, Dallas, 1972; pres. Oxford Nat. Properties Corp., 1984—; lectr. Yale U., 1968-70; adj. prof. Georgetown U. Law Ctr., 1980-84. Author reports, studies on urban housing. Exec. dir. New Haven Legal Aid Soc., 1964; bd. dirs. Com. for Responsible Budget; trustee Georgetown Day Sch. Served with AUS, 1959-60. Mem. ABA, Fed. Bar Assn., Bar Assn. D.C., Nat. Apt. Assn. (chmn. legis. com.), Nat. Assn. Securities Dealers (direct sales com.), Pi Sigma Alpha, Kappa Delta Rho, Phi Delta Phi. Democrat. Jewish. Club: Univ. Real property, Condemnation, Bankruptcy. Home: 4528 28th St NW Washington DC 20008 Office: 815 Connecticut Ave NW Washington DC 20006

MOSKOWITZ, STUART STANLEY, lawyer; b. N.Y.C., Aug. 27, 1955; s. Arthur Appel and Rebecca (Gordon) M. BS magna cum laude, SUNY, Albany, 1977; JD with honors, Union U., Albany, 1981. Bar: N.Y. 1982, U.S. Tax Ct. 1983, U.S. Dist. Ct. (so. dist.) N.Y. 1985. Law clk. to presiding judge U.S. Tax Ct., Washington, 1981-83, U.S. Ct. Appeals (2d cir.), N.Y.C., 1983-84; atty. IBM Corp., Armonk, N.Y., 1984—; research asst. fin. SUNY Sch. of Bus., Albany, 1976-77, corp. law Albany Law Sch., 1980-81; instr. acctg. Ednl. Oppurtunities Program SUNY, Albany, 1977-78. Tax counselor for elderly Am. Assn. Retired Persons, Westchester County, N.Y., 1986. Mem. ABA, N.Y. State Bar Assn., Westchester Fairfield Corp. Counsel Assn., Order of Justinian. Contracts commercial, General corporate, Computer. Home: 153 Princeton Dr Hartsdale NY 10530 Office: IBM Corp 590 Madison Ave New York NY 10022

MOSOFF, SERLE IAN, lawyer; b. Chgo., May 12, 1942; s. Sidney Simon and Helen (Weisbrod) M.; m. Barbara Jeanette Payne, Dec. 14, 1967 (div. Apr. 1986); children: Susan Sydney Creed Payne, Perrine Elizabeth Barrie Payne. BS in Physical Sci., Mich. State U., 1964; JD, De Paul U., 1967; LLM, U. London, Eng., 1968; cert., Hague Acad. Internat. Law, The Netherlands, 1968. Bar: Penn. 1969, U.S. Dist. Ct. (we. dist.) Penn. 1969, U.S. Patent Office 1971. Patent atty. U.S. Steel Corp., Pitts., 1968-72; mgr. legal services Diamond Shamrock Corp., Cleve., 1972-82; prin. Law Office of S.I. Mosoff, Beachwood, Ohio, 1982-84; sr. patent counsel Schering-Plough Corp., Madison, N.J., 1984-85; corp. counsel Enzo Biochem, Inc., N.Y.C., 1986—. Mem. ABA, N.Y. Patent Law Assn., Am. Intellectual Property Law Assn., Licensing Execs. Soc. Patent, Private international, General corporate. Home: 4 Exeter Ct Somerset NJ 08873 Office: Enzo Biochem Inc 325 Hudson St New York NY 10013

MOSS, HERBERT ALLEN, lawyer; b. N.Y.C., Jan. 18, 1934. BA, City Coll. N.Y., 1955; LLB, NYU, 1962, LLM in Labor Law, 1964. Bar: N.Y. 1962, Calif. 1965, U.S. Supreme Ct. 1977. Atty. NLRB, Newark and Los Angeles, 1962-67; sole practice Santa Ana, Calif., 1968—; lectr. labor law UCLA U., Irvine, Calif., 1969—. Contbr. articles to profl. jours. Mem. ABA, Orange County Bar Assn. (chmn. corp. law sect. 1978). Labor. Office: 888 N Main St Santa Ana CA 92701

MOSS, JOE ALBAUGH, petroleum company executive; b. Waco, Tex., July 26, 1925; s. Robert Edwin and Winnie (Hughes) M.; B.B.A., U. Tex., 1946, J.D., 1950; 1 child, Joe David. Bar: Tex. 1949, Supreme Ct. U.S. 1960, U.S. Dist. Ct. (we. dist.) Tex. 1956, U.S. Dist. Ct. (no. dist.) Tex. 1980. Asso. firm Moss & Prewett, Austin, Tex., 1950; atty. State of Tex., Abilene, 1952; sec., asst. gen. counsel Cosden Petroleum Corp., Big Spring, Tex., 1952-63, v.p., sec., gen. counsel Cosden Oil & Chem. Co., Big Spring, 1963-85; v.p., gen. counsel Am. Petrofina, Inc., Dallas, 1971—, sec., 1984—. v.p., dir. Trust P/L Co., 1957—, River P/L Co., 1958—, Fina Oil and Chem. Co., 1971—, Petrofina Delaware, Inc. 1979—; sec., dir. Cos-Mar, Inc., 1968—; v.p. Am. Petrofina Exploration Co., 1971—, v.p. Am. Petrofina Co. Norway, 1971—. Trustee, pres. Big Spring Ind. Sch. Dist., 1961-71; trustee Siblings Found., Permian Basin Petroleum Mus. Served with USNR, 1942-46, 50-52; PTO. Recipient Spl. Merit award Big Spring Ind. Sch. Dist., 1971. Fellow Tex. Bar Found.; mem. ABA, Dallas County Bar Assn., State Bar Tex., Ind. Petroleum Assn. Am. (dir. 1972—), Tex. Mfrs. Assn. (dir. 1971-72), Am. Petroleum Inst., Tex. Mid-Continent Oil and Gas Assn. Presbyn. Mason. Clubs: Petroleum, Lancers, (Dallas). General corporate, Antitrust, Oil and gas leasing. Home: 5230 Royal Crest Dr Dallas TX 75229

MOSS, JUDITH DOROTHY, lawyer, consultant, lecturer; b. Indpls., June 2, 1945; d. Frank Maxwell and Dorothy Grace (Wisnofske) M.; A. in Computer Sci., Electronic Computer Programming Inst., Columbus, Ohio, 1969; B.S.B.A., Ohio State U., 1975, J.D., 1977. Bar: Ohio 1978, U.S. Dist. Ct. (so. dist.) Ohio 1978. Organic chemistry research technician O.M. Scott and Sons, Marysville, Ohio, 1965-68; computer programmer/systems analyst State of Ohio, Columbus, 1969-75; pvt. practice, Columbus, 1978-81; pres. Barrett and Barrett Co., L.P.A., Columbus, 1982-85; pres. Barrett & Moss Co., L.P.A., 1985-86; ptnr. Brownfield, Cramer & Lewis, Columbus, 1986—; cons. to Pres. U.S. and Congress, Nat. Adv. Council on Women's Ednl. Programs, chmn. civil rights com., 1983-84, 86—; pub. speaker and guest lectr. on constl. integrity. Coordinator Ohio Eagle Forum, 1982, gen. counsel, 1978-82, 83—; mem. Ohio Gov.'s Coordinating Commn. for Ohio, White House Conf. on Families, 1980, also nat. task force, 1980; del. Central Regional White House Conf. on Families, 1980; ofcl. observer Internat. Women's Yr. Conf., Houston, 1977; adv. bd. Franklin County (Ohio) Extension Service, Area Soil Conservation Service, 1980—; trustee United Conservatives of Ohio, 1984—, 1st v.p. 1985—; mem. Chmn.'s Club, Franklin County Ohio Republican Com., 1981—; active leadership program Pvt. Industry Council of Columbus and Franklin County, Inc., 1985-86; adv. commn. Columbus Area Cable TV, 1985—, Ohio Elections Commn., 1986—; past pres., chmn. planning com. Ravine Condominium Unit Owners Assn.; trustee Friends of 4-H, Area Soil Conservation Service, Cen. Ohio Lung Assn., Crossroads Counseling; bd. dirs. Pvt. INdustry Council Columbus and Franklin County; mem. adv. council Columbus Area Cable TV. Recipient Eagle award Phyllis Schlafly and Eagle Forum, 1980, cert. appreciation Pres. Carter, White House Conf. on Families Nat. Task Force, 1980. Mem. Ohio Bar Assn., Columbus Bar Assn., Alpha Xi Delta. Author various positions papers, pamphlets on constl. integrity. State civil litigation, Jurisprudence, Probate. Office: 140 E Town St Suite 1200 Columbus OH 43215-5194

MOSS, KATHLEEN SUSAN, patent lawyer, geneticist; b. Washington, Dec. 21, 1950; d. Janet Daines McCowin; m. Dale Thomas Moss, Jan. 1, 1981; 1 child, Jan Alexis. BA in Genetics, U. Calif., Berkeley, 1971; MS in Human Genetics, George Washington U., 1978; postgrad. law program, U. Va., Exeter, Eng., 1978, Am. U., Warsaw, Poland, 1979; JD, George Mason U., 1980. Bar: D.C. 1980, U.S. Patent office 1980. Research fellow, asst. George Washington U. Med. Sch., Washington, 1971-75; assoc. Bernard & Brown, Washington, 1980-81; patent examiner U.S. Patent Office, Crystle City, Va., 1981-85; assoc. Wegner & Bretschneider, Washington, 1985—; lectr. George Washington U. Med. Sch., 1974-75. Pres. Marcheta Tenants Assn., Washington, 1981-83. Recipient letter of commendation chief adminstrv. law judge FDA, 1976. Mem. ABA, D.C. Bar Assn., Am. Patent Law Assn., Patent Office Profl. Assn., Woman's Patent Profl. Assn. Computer, Patent, Trademark and copyright. Home: 1 Scott Circle NW Washington DC 20036 Office: Wegner & Bretschneider 1233 20th St NW 3d Floor PO Box 18218 Washington DC 20036-8218

MOSS, KIRBY GLENN, lawyer; b. Elizabeth City, N.C., July 8, 1954; s. Lindy G. and Jeanne H. (Howie) M.; m. Barbara Ann Monroe, Sept. 6, 1986. B.S. in Acctg., Ind. U.-Bloomington, 1976; J.D., Ind. U.-Indpls., 1979. Bar: Ind. 1979, U.S. Dist. Ct. (no. and so. dists.) Ind. 1979, U.S. Supreme Ct. 1982. Assoc. Torborg, Miller, Moss, Harris & Yates and predecessors, Ft. Wayne, Ind., 1979-83, ptnr., 1984—. Bd. dirs. Harold W. McMillen Ctr. Health Edn., Ft. Wayne, 1980—, chmn. nominating com., treas., 1984-86, sec. 1986-87, v.p. 1987—. Mem. Allen County Bar Assn. (trial lawyers and young lawyers div. 1979—, lawyer referral com. 1984, pub. relations com. 1983), Ind. Bar Assn. (young lawyers div. 1979—), Ind. Trial Lawyers Assn., ABA (family law div. 1983-85, young lawyers div. 1979—, litigation sect., mem. trial practice com. 1980—, gen. practice sect. 1985—), Assn. Trial Lawyers Am. Lodge: Rotary (charter mem. Little Turtle club 1987—). Personal injury, State civil litigation, Federal civil litigation. Office: Torborg Miller Moss Harris & Yates 1800 Fort Wayne Bank Bldg PO Box 10839 Fort Wayne IN 46854-0839

MOSS, LOGAN VANSEN, lawyer; b. Atlanta, Apr. 17, 1957; s. Joseph Henry Moss and Elsie Louise (McCown) Daniels. BA, Bates Coll., 1979; JD, U. Tulsa, 1982. Bar: Okla. 1982, U.S. Dist. Ct. Okla. 1982, Maine 1984, U.S. Dist. Ct. Maine 1984, U.S. Supreme Ct. 1986. Law clk. to presiding justice Okla. Ct. Appeals, Tulsa, 1982-84; assoc. Strout, Payson et al, Rockland, Maine, 1984-87, Joseph M. Cloutier & Assocs., Camden, Maine, 1987—. Mem. Assn. Trial Lawyers Am. Republican. Presbyterian. Avocation: sports. Personal injury, Federal civil litigation, State civil litigation. Office: Joseph M Cloutier & Assocs 58 Bayview St Camden ME 04843

MOSS, RAYMOND GENE, II, lawyer; b. Duncan, Okla., Apr. 11, 1945; s. Raymond Gene and Jimmie Orene (Boyles) M.; m. Grenda Falene Penhollow, Mar. 29, 1969; children—Travis Penhollow, Clayton Boyles. B.A., U. Okla., 1967; postgrad. George Washington U., 1967-68; J.D., U. Okla., 1970. Bar: Okla. 1970, U.S. Dist. Ct. (we., no., ea. dists.) Okla. 1970, U.S. Ct. Appeals (10th cir.) 1970. Law clk. Pierce, Couch, Hendrickson, Johnston & Baysinger, 1968-69; legal intern Walker & Watson, 1969-70; assoc. McAffee & Taft, 1970-75, mem. firm, 1975-84; ptnr. De Spain & Moss, 1984-86, Daugherty, Bradford, Fowler & Moss, 1986—. Bd. dirs. Okla. div. Am. Cancer Soc., 1975-84. Served to capt. USAF, 1969-75. Mem. ABA, Okla. Bar Assn., Oklahoma County Bar Assn., Oklahoma City C. of C. (facilities com., Bicentennial com.), Phi Gamma Delta (pres. chpt. 1974-81). Democrat. Episcopalian. Club: Kiwanis. Bankruptcy, Contracts commercial, Federal civil litigation. Address: 900 First City Pl Oklahoma City OK 73102

MOSS, ROBERT WILLIAM, lawyer; b. Detroit, Mar. 2, 1928; s. Albert Roderick Moss and Vonda (Hartfelder) Gordon; m. Joan Therese Davis, Aug. 20, 1949 (div. July 1973); children: Andrea Edwards, Suzanne L. Qualls, Gary, Reid; m. Carol Jean Hartman, Oct. 10, 1973. BA, Wayne State U., 1951, LLB, 1953. Bar: Mich. 1954, U.S. Dist. Ct. (ea. and we. dists.) Mich., U.S. Ct. Appeals (3d cir.). Sole practice Detroit, 1954-69, Southfield and Bloomington, Mich., 1969—. Mem. Mich. Bar Assn., Detroit Bar Assn., Oakland County Bar Assn., Assn. Trial Lawyers Am., Mich. Def. Trial Counsel Inc., Def. Research Inst. Clubs: Pine Lake Country (Orchard Lake, Mich.) (treas. 1986); Cypress Lake Country (Ft. Myers, Fla.). Federal civil litigation, State civil litigation, Insurance. Home: 27760 W 14 Mile Rd West Bloomfield MI 48033 Office: 30400 Telegraph Suite 460 Birmingham AL 48010-3002

MOSS, VICTOR, lawyer; b. Poland, Feb. 11, 1944; s. Walter G. and Vladys Moss; m. Margaret Kuimoff, June 8, 1969; children—Paul, Kathy. Student U. Utah, 1963; B.S., N.Mex. Highlands U., 1967; J.D., U. N.Mex., 1971. Bar: N.Mex. 1971, Colo. 1972, U.S. Dist. Ct. N.Mex. 1971, U.S. Dist. Ct. Colo. 1972. Asst. atty. gen. State N.Mex., Santa Fe, 1972; asst. city atty. City of Pueblo, 1972-73; sole practice, Pueblo, 1973—; acting mcpl. judge City of Pueblo; city atty. Town of Boone, Colo., 1975-81. Bd. dirs. Girls Club, Pueblo; del. Democratic County Conv., 1980; bd. dirs. C.A.T. Spanish Peaks, Pueblo. Mem. Colo. Bar Assn., N.Mex. Bar Assn., Pueblo County Young Lawyers, ABA, Colo. Trial Lawyers Assn. Eastern Christian Orthodox. Lodges: Optimist, Elks, Kiwanis. Personal injury, Bankruptcy, Probate. Office: 311 W 24th St Suite A Pueblo CO 81003

MOSS, WILLIAM JOHN, lawyer; b. Duluth, Minn., Aug. 31, 1921; s. John Hugh and Mary (Quinn) M.; m. Kathryn Casale, June 14, 1947; children: Mary Appleton, Catherine Warner, Elizabeth Bradley, Amy Moss Brown, John, Gerard, Hugh, Patricia, Susan, Barbara. A.B., Harvard U., 1947, LL.B., 1949. Bar: N.Y. 1950. Assoc. firm Cadwalader, Wickersham & Taft, N.Y.C., 1949-58, ptnr., 1959—. Served to maj. AUS, 1942-45. Mem. ABA. Republican. Roman Catholic. Club: Down Town Assn. (N.Y.C.). General corporate. Home: Route 9D Garrison NY 10524 Office: Cadwalader Wickersham & Taft 100 Maiden Ln New York NY 10038

MOSSINGHOFF, GERALD JOSEPH, lawyer, industry association executive; b. St. Louis, Sept. 30, 1935; s. Aloysius Joseph and Gladys Marie (Gerwitz) M.; m. Jeanne Carole Jack, Dec. 29, 1958; children: Pamela Ann Mossinghoff France, Gregory Joseph, Melissa Louise. B.S. in Elec. Engring, St. Louis U., 1957; J.D. with honors, George Washington U., 1961. Bar: Mo. 1961, D.C. 1965, Va. 1981. Engr. Sachs Electric Corp., St. Louis, 1954-57; patent examiner U.S. Patent Office, Washington, 1957-61; dir. legis. planning U.S. Patent Office, 1965-66; atty. Koenig, Senniger, Powers & Leavitt, St. Louis, 1961-63; atty. NASA, Washington, 1963-65, dir. congl. liason, 1967-71, dep. asst. adminstr. for legis. affairs, 1971-73, asst. gen. counsel, 1973-76, dep. gen. counsel, 1976-81; asst. Sec. Commerce, commr. patents and trademarks U.S. Patent Office, 1981-85; pres. Pharm. Mfrs. Assn., Washington, 1985—; adj. prof. Am. U. Washington Coll. Law.; ambassador Paris Conv. Diplomatic Conf., 1982-85. Recipient Exceptional Service medal NASA, 1971, Disting. Service medal, 1980, Outstanding Leadership medal, 1981; granted presdl. rank of meritorious exec., 1980; Disting. Pub. Service award Sec. of Commerce, 1983. Assoc. fellow AIAA; mem. Am. Acad. Pub. Adminstrn., Internat. Inst. Space Law, Internat. Assn. Teaching and Research in Intellectual Property Law, Am. Bar Assn., Fed. Bar Assn. (nat. council), Order of Coif, Eta Kappa Nu, Pi Mu Epsilon. Patent, Trademark and copyright. Home: 1530 N Key Blvd #PH28 Arlington VA 22209 Office: Pharm Mfrs Assn 1100 15th St NW Washington DC 20005

MOSSNER, EUGENE DONALD, lawyer; b. Saginaw, Mich., May 27, 1930; s. Clarence William and Irma Gertrude (Schallhorn) M.; m. Yoko Ito, Jan. 12, 1957; children: Christine Mossner McGuinness, David Y., Peter J. AA, Bay City Jr. Coll., 1950; BA, U. Mich., 1952; JD, Wayne State U., 1955. Bar: Mich. 1957, U.S. Dist. Ct. (ea. dist.) Mich. 1957, U.S. Ct. Appeals (6th cir.) Mich. 1961, U.S. Supreme Ct. 1971. With Mossner, Majoros & Alexander, PC (formerly Cicinelli, Mossner, Majoros & Alexander, PC), Saginaw, Mich.; pres. Mich. Trial Lawyers Assn., Lansing, 1969-70; commr. State Bar of Mich., Lansing, 1973—. Alternate del., Dem. Nat. Conv., Chgo., 1968; del., Miami, Fla., 1972; chmn. Saginaw County Dem. Party, 1968-72. Served with U.S. Army, 1955-57. Fellow Am. Bar Found., State Bar of Mich. Found.; mem. Saginaw County Bar Assn. (pres. 1971-72), State Bar of Mich. (chmn. Negligence Law Sect. 1969-70, mem. Rep. Assembly 1973-76, 84—, chmn. Lawyers Profl. Liability Ins. Com. 1979—, spl. com. on Contingent Fees and No-Fault Ins. 1973-74, mem. com. on legis., 1979-83, com. on jud. qualifications 1980—, pres.-elect 1986-87), Wayne State U. Law Sch. Alumni Assn., Anthony Wayne Soc., Internat. Luth. Laymen's League, NAACP (life), Supreme Ct. of the U.S. Soc., Truman Library Assn., Nat. Trust for Hist. Preservation, Mich. Hist. Soc., Am. Bible Soc., Evang. Luths. in Mission, Ptnrs. in Mission. Clubs: People to People (Saginaw), Germania of Saginaw, Saginaw. Personal injury, State civil litigation. Home: 5320 Nottingham Dr N Saginaw MI 48603 Office: Mossner Majoros & Alexander PC 913 N Michigan Ave PO Box 3305 Saginaw MI 48605

MOST, JACK LAWRENCE, lawyer, consultant; b. N.Y.C., Sept. 24, 1935; s. Meyer Milton and Henrietta (Meyer) M.; children: Jeffery, Peter; m. Irma Freedman Robbins, Aug. 8, 1968; children: Ann, Jane. BA cum laude, Syracuse U., 1956; JD, Columbia U., 1960. Bar: N.Y. 1960, U.S. Dist. Ct. (so. and ea. dists.) N.Y. 1963. Assoc. Hale, Grant, Meyerson and O'Brien, N.Y.C., 1960-66; dep. assoc. dir. OEO, Exec. Office of The President, Washington, 1965-67; asst. to gen. counsel C.I.T. Fin. Corp., N.Y.C., 1968-70; corp. counsel PepsiCo, Inc., Purchase, N.Y., 1970-71; v.p. legal affairs Revlon, Inc., N.Y.C., 1971-76; asst. gen. counsel Norton Simon, Inc., N.Y.C., 1976-79; ptnr. Rogers Hoge and Hills, N.Y.C., 1979-86, Finkelstein Bruckman Wohl Most & Rothman, N.Y.C., 1986—; bd. dirs. Requa, Inc., Greenwich, Conn., Flowery Beauty Products, Inc.; corp. sec. and gen. counsel PharmaKinetics Labs, Inc., Balt., 1985—. Contbr. articles to profl. jour. and mags. Bd. dirs. Haym Salomon Home for Aged, 1978—, pres. 1981—. Served to sgt. USAR, 1959-65. Mem. ABA (Fed. Regulation of Securities Com.), N.Y. State Bar Assn. (food, drug and cosmetics sect.), Am. Soc. Pharmacy Law. Jewish. Clubs: Lords Valley Country (bd. govs. 1984—, corp. sec. 1986—) (Hawley, Pa.); 60 East (N.Y.C.). General corporate, Securities, Administrative and regulatory. Home: 1175 York Ave New York NY 10021 Office: Finkelstein Bruckman Wohl Most & Rothman 801 Second Ave New York NY 10017

MOTCHAN, BRENT L., lawyer; b. St. Louis, Sept. 19, 1949; s. Paul and Pauline (Sherman) M.; m. Marilynn A. Brody, June 3, 1973; children: Jessica, Kathryn, Blair. BSEE, Washington U., St. Louis, 1971; JD, Washington U., 1974, LLM in Taxation, 1978. Bar: Mo. 1974, U.S. Dist. Ct. (ea. and we. dists.) Mo. 1974, U.S. Supreme Ct. 1980. Sole practice St. Louis, 1974-77; asst. gen. counsel Arch Mineral Corp., St. Louis, 1977-85; v.p., gen. counsel Zeigler Coal Co., Fairview Heights, Ill., 1985—. Mem. editorial bd. American Law of Mining, 2d rev. edit., 1984. Bd. dirs. St. Louis Apt. Assn., 1985—. Served to maj. USAR, 1971—. Mem. ABA, St. Louis Bar Assn., St. Louis Trial Lawyers Assn. General corporate, Real property, Labor. Home: 14280 Forest Crest Chesterfield MO 63017 Office: Zeigler Coal Co 331 Salem Pl Fairview Heights IL 62208

MOTE, CLYDE A, lawyer; b. Vernon, Tex., Feb. 12, 1926; s. Neven and Lona (May) M.; m. Jean Henderson, Apr. 26, 1952; children—Terron, Bruce, Douglas. J.D., Baylor U., 1950. Bar: Tex. 1950, Okla. 1960. Ptnr. Cummings & Mote, Abilene, Tex., 1950-52; asst. city atty. City of Lubbock, Tex., 1952-54; ptnr. Napier & Mote, Lubbock, 1954-59; atty. Amoco Prodn. Co., Houston, 1959-86, regional atty., New Orleans Region, 1986—. Served to sgt. U.S. Army, 1943-46, ETO. Mem. Phi Alpha Delta. Republican. Baptist. Oil and gas leasing, General corporate. Home: 4 Grand Canyon Dr New Orleans LA 70114 Office: Amoco Prodn Co PO Box 50879 New Orleans LA 70150

MOTES, CARL DALTON, lawyer; b. Palatka, Fla., May 31, 1949; s. Carl Thomas and Orpha Jeanette (McGauley) M.; m. Maria Eugenia Aguirre, Apr. 19, 1975. A.A., St. Johns River Jr. Coll., 1969; B.A., Fla. State U., 1971, J.D., 1974. Bar: Fla. 1974, U.S. Dist. Ct. (cen., no. and so. dists.) Fla. 1975, U.S. Ct. Appeals (11th cir.) 1980. Asst. to pres. Fla. Bar, Tallahassee, 1974-75; assoc. Maguire, Voorhis & Wells P.A., Orlando, Fla., 1975-79, ptnr., 1979—; dir. Legal Aid Soc., Orlando, 1979-83, pres, 1983-84; lectr. at various Bar Assns. and ednl. insts. Contbr. articles to profl. jours. Mem. editorial bd. Jour. Trial Advocate Quarterly, 1981—. Active in Planning & Zoning Bd., Altamonte Springs, Fla., 1977-79, Capital Funds Project Review Com., Central Fla., 1983; bd. dirs. Cen. Fla. Council Boy Scouts Am. Mem. Orange County Bar Assn. (sec. 1979-80, exec. council 1980-83, named Outstanding Mem. 1981-82, Outstanding Com. Chmn. 1977), ABA, Fla. Def. Lawyer's Assn., Internat. Assn. Ins. Counsel, Fla. State U. Coll. Law Alumni Assn. (bd. dirs. 1975-78, pres. 1979), Def. Research Inst., Phi Delta Phi. Republican. Clubs: Univ. (Orlando), Citrus (Orlando). State civil litigation, Federal civil litigation, Professional liability. Office: Maguire Voorhis & Wells PA Two S Orange Plaza Orlando FL 32802

MOTSINGER, CARL DANIEL, lawyer; b. Ft. Wayne, Ind., Oct. 16, 1956; s. Harry E. and Miriam Rose (Katanich) M.; m. Deborah Ann Kirkland, Sept. 29, 1984. BA, Hillsdale Coll., 1979; JD, U. Mich., 1982. Bar: Ind. 1982, U.S. Dist. Ct. (no. and so. dists.) Ind. 1982, Fla. 1983, U.S. Dist. Ct. (so. and mid. dists.) Fla. 1983. Law. clk. to judge U.S. Dist. Ct. (so. dist.), Miami, Fla., 1982-83; assoc. Ice, Miller, Donadio & Ryan, Indpls., 1983—. Fund-raiser Ind. Repertory Theatre, Indpls., 1984-86, Family Support Ctr., Indpls., 1984. Glenn D. Peters scholar, 1981. Mem. Indpls. Bar Assn., Ind. Bar Assn., Fla. Bar. Republican. Eastern Orthodox. Avocation: jogging. Bankruptcy, Contracts commercial, Federal civil litigation. Office: Ice Miller Donadio & Ryan One American Sq Indianapolis IN 46282

MOTT, JOHN C., lawyer; b. LeRoy Twp., Pa., May 23, 1955; s. Charles S. and H. Grace (Spencer) M.; m. Brenda K. Bailey, Aug. 19, 1972; children—Reeve A., Nicholas H., Adam R. B.A. with high honors, Mansfield Univ., Pa., 1977; J.D., Dickinson Sch. of Law, Carlisle, Pa., 1980. Bar: Pa. 1980, U.S. Dist. Ct. (mid. dist.) Pa. 1983. Assoc. firm Vineski, Brann, Williams and Caldwell, Troy and Canton, Pa., 1980-83; ptnr. firm Vineski, Brann, Williams, Caldwell and Mott, Troy and Canton, 1984—. Committeeman Bradford County Republican Com., Pa., 1982—, chmn., 1984-85; deacon Canton Ch. of Christ (Disciples), 1982—, chmn. steward-ship com. 1983-84; Bradford County crusade chmn. Am. Cancer Soc., Sayre, Pa., 1983-84; dir. N.Y.-Pa. Health System Agy., Binghamton, N.Y., 1984-85, Troy Community Hosp., Inc., 1983-85. Mem. Bradford County Bar Assn. (sec.-treas. 1980-82), Pa. Bar Assn., ABA, Assn. Trial Lawyers Am., Pa. Trial Lawyers Assn. Lodges: Lions (pres. 1983-84), Moose, Elks. General practice, State civil litigation, Real property. Office: Vineski Brann Williams Caldwell & Mott 111 W Main St Troy PA 16947 also: 66 Troy St Canton PA 17724

MOTT, JOSEPH WILLIAM HOOGE, lawyer; b. Bethesda, Md., July 24, 1952; s. Charles Davis and Ellen Mary (Hooge) M.; m. Patricia Jay Garber, Mar. 14, 1971 (div. Feb. 1983); children: Patrick, Justin; m. Susan Creasy, Nov. 2, 1985. BBA, George Mason U., 1974; JD, U. Richmond, 1982. Bar: Va. 1982, D.C. 1983, U.S. Dist. Ct. (ea. and we. dists.) Va. 1983, U.S. Ct. Appeals (4th cir.) 1984. Private practice Vienna, Va., 1982-84; assoc. Woodward, Fox, Wooten & Hart, Roanoke, Va., 1984; asst. commonwealth's atty. Franklin County, Rocky Mount, Va., 1984—; instr. No. Va. Community Coll., Fairfax, 1983, Va. Western Community Coll., Roanoke, 1984—, Roanoke County Continuing Edn., Salem, Va., 1984—. Mem. Va. Bar Assn., D.C. Bar Assn., Vienna Jaycees (v.p. 1983). Criminal, Consumer commercial, Family and matrimonial. Office: Commonwealth Attys Office Courthouse Annex Rocky Mount VA 24151

MOTZ, JOHN FREDERICK, U.S. District Court judge; b. Balt., Dec. 30, 1942; s. John Eldered and Catherine (Grauel) M.; m. Diana Jane Gribbon, Sept. 20, 1968; children—Catherine Jane, Daniel Gribbon. A.B., Wesleyan

U., Conn., 1964; LL.B., U. Va., Charlottesville, 1967. Assoc. Venable, Baetjer & Howard, Balt., 1968-69; asst. U.S. atty. U.S. Atty.'s Office, Balt., 1969-71; assoc. Venable, Baetjer & Howard, Balt., 1971-75, ptnr., 1976-81; U.S. atty. U.S. Atty.'s Office, Balt., 1981-85; judge U.S. Dist. Ct. of Md., Balt., 1985—. Bd. trustees Friends Sch., Balt., 1970-77, 1981—. Mem. ABA, Am. Coll. Trial Lawyers, Md. State Bar Assn., Baltimore City Bar Assn. Republican. Quaker. Criminal. Office: US Dist Ct Room 510 101 W Lombard Baltimore MD 21201 *

MOUAT, WILLIAM GAVIN, lawyer; b. Myers, Mont., Apr. 5, 1919; s. Jeremiah James and Lena (Pedersen) M.; m. Shirley Manning, June 9, 1946; children: Martin, Marvin, William. BA, U. Idaho, 1944; JD, U. Mont., 1947. Bar: Mont. 1947, U.S. Dist. Ct. Mont. 1949, U.S. Ct. Appeals (9th cir.) 1955, U.S. Supreme Ct. 1977. Court reporter 13th Jud. Dist., Billings, Mont., 1947-50; sole practice Billings, 1950—. Co-inventor mining and smelting processes. Served to lt. USNR, 1943-45. Presbyterian. Avocations: mining, tennis. General practice, Federal civil litigation, State civil litigation. Home: 825 Parkhill Dr Billings MT 59102 Office: 317 First Fed Savs Bldg Billings MT 59101

MOUGHAN, PETER RICHARD, JR., lawyer; b. Phila., July 29, 1951; s. Peter R. and Catherine L. (Gavin) M.; m. Janice Billick, Aug. 3, 1974; children—Peter R. III, Gavin Patrick, Jacob Daniel. B.A., Wheeling Coll., 1973; M.S., Gonzaga U., 1975, M.B.A., 1977, J.D., 1977. Bar: Pa. 1977, N.Mex. 1980. Legal researcher Am. Law Inst.-ABA, Phila., 1977-78; claim rep. Allstate Ins., Phila., 1978-79; assoc. Larry D. Beall, P.A., Albuquerque, 1979-81; sole practice, Albuquerque, 1981—. Pres. Ancient Order of Hibernians, Albuquerque, 1984-85. Mem. Assn. Trial Lawyers Am., N.Mex. Trial Lawyers Assn., Albuquerque Bar Assn., Albuquerque Lawyers Club, Phi Alpha Delta. Democrat. Roman Catholic. Club: Albuquerque Aardvarks Rugby Football (chmn. 1980-84). Lodge: K.C. Consumer commercial, Personal injury, State civil litigation. Office: PO Box 715 Albuquerque NM 87103

MOULTON, HUGH GEOFFREY, lawyer, business executive; b. Boston, Sept. 18, 1933; s. Robert Selden and Florence (Bracq) M.; m. Catherine Anne Clark, Mar. 24, 1956; children: H. Geoffrey, Cynthia C., M. Bassett. B.A., Amherst Coll., 1955; LL.B., Yale U., 1958; postgrad. Advanced Mgmt. Program, Harvard U., 1984. Bar: Pa. 1959. Assoc. Montgomery, McCracken, Walker-Rhoads, Phila., 1958-66, ptnr., 1967-69; v.p., counsel Dolly Madison Industries, Inc., Phila., 1969-70; sec. Alco Standard Corp., Valley Forge, Pa., 1970-72, v.p. law, 1973-79, v.p., sec., gen. counsel, 1979-83, sr. v.p., gen. counsel, 1983—. Pres. Wissahickon Valley Watershed Assn., Ambler, Pa., 1975-78, treas., 1978—; mem. Area Council for Econ. Edn. (bd. dirs. 1985—). Mem. ABA, Phila. Bar Assn., Pa. Bar Assn., Am. Corp. Counsel Assn. (bd. dirs. Delaware Valley chpt. 1984—, pres. 1986-87). Club: Sunnybrook Golf (Plymouth Meeting, Pa.). Home: 300 Williams Rd Fort Washington PA 19034 Office: Alco Standard Corp Box 834 Valley Forge PA 19482

MOUNTAIN, C(LINTON) DELAINE, lawyer; b. Pisgah, Ala., Aug. 17, 1941; s. Albert Lyle and Winnie (Boak) M.; divorced; children: Jennifer Leigh, Clinton Delaine Jr.; m. Barbara Claire Woodley, Nov. 22, 1980; 1 child: Catherine Boak. BA, U. Ala., 1965, JD, 1968. Bar: Ala. 1968, U.S. Dist. Ct. (no. dist.) Ala. 1968, U.S. Ct. Appeals (5th and 11th cirs.) 1981. Sole practice Tuscaloosa, Ala., 1968—; instr. legal studies U. Ala., Tuscaloosa, 1964-84; prosecutor City of Tuscaloosa, 1970-72. Commr. pub. safety City of Tuscaloosa, 1972-76. Mem. Ala. Trial Lawyers Assn. (treas. 1985-86, sec. 1986—). Personal injury. Home: 50 Sherwood Dr Tuscaloosa AL 35401 Office: 2618 7th St Tuscaloosa AL 35401

MOURSUND, ALBERT WADEL, III, lawyer, rancher; b. Johnson City, Tex., May 23, 1919; s. Albert Wadel and Mary Frances (Stribling) M., Jr.; m. Mary Allen Moore, May 8, 1941; children: Will Stribling, Mary Moore Moursund DesChamps. LLB, U. Tex., 1941. Bar: Tex. 1941. Sole practice, Johnson City, 1946-63; mem. Moursund & Moursund Johnson City, Round Mountain and Llano, Tex., 1963-80; Moursund, Moursund, DesChamps & Moursund, 1980—; county judge Blanco County, Tex., 1953-59; bd. dirs., pres. 1st Llano Bank 1963—, Arrowhead Co., Arrowhead West, Inc., Am. Moursund Corp., S.W. Moursund Corp., Ranchlander Corp., Cattleman's Nat. Bank, Round Mountain. Mem. Parks and Wildlife Commn., 1963-67, Tex. Ho. reps., 1948-52. Served with USAAF, 1942-46. Mem. ABA, Tex. Bar Assn., Hill County Bar Assn. (past pres.), Blanco County Hist. Soc. (charter). Democrat. Lodges: Masons, Woodmen of World. General practice. Home: Johnson City TX 78636 Office: Moursund Moursund DesChamps & Moursund Llano TX 78643

MOW, ROBERT HENRY, JR., lawyer; b. Cape Girardeau, Mo., Dec. 10, 1938; s. Robert H., Sr. and Ann Elise (Beck) M.; m. Beverly Ann Decker, Aug. 28, 1960 (div. Oct. 1986); children—Robert Merritt, Brynn Ann, William Brett, Rebecca Marie. Student, Westminster Coll., 1956-57; A.B. with distinction, U. of Mo., 1960; LL.B. magna cum laude, So. Meth. U., 1963. Bar: Tex. 1963, U.S. Dist. Ct. (no. dist.) Tex. 1965, U.S. Dist. Ct. (so. dist.) Tex. 1969, U.S. Dist. Ct. (ea. dist.) Tex. 1976, U.S. Dist. Ct. (we. dist.) Tex. 1976, U.S. Ct. Claims 1973, U.S. Ct. Appeals (5th cir. 1972, U.S. Ct. Appeals (11th cir.) 1981, U.S. Supreme Ct. 1978. Assoc., Carrington, Johnson & Stephens, Dallas, 1963-69; ptnr. Carrington, Coleman, Sloman, & Blumenthal, Dallas, 1970-85; ptnr. Hughes & Luce, Dallas, 1985—. Editor-in-chief Southwestern Law Jour., 1962-63. Served to 1st lt. U.S. Army, 1963-65. Fellow Am. Coll. of Trial Lawyers, mem. Dallas Jr. Bar Assn. (pres. 1968), Dallas Assn. of Def. Counsel (chmn. 1976-77), Tex. Assn. of Def. Counsel (v.p. 1981-82), Am. Bd. of Trial Advocates (pres. Dallas chpt. 1983-84). Republican. Methodist. Club: Northwood (Dallas). Federal civil litigation, State civil litigation, Personal injury. Office: Hughes & Luce 1000 Dallas Bldg Dallas TX 75201

MOWBRAY, JOHN CODE, judge; b. Bradford, Ill., Sept. 20, 1918; s. Thomas John and Ellen Driscoll (Code) M.; m. Kathlyn Ann Hammes, Oct. 15, 1949; children: John, Romy, Jerry, Terry. B.A., Western Ill. U., 1940, L.H.D. (hon.), 1976, LL.D. (hon.), 1977; LL.D. (hon.), Far Eastern Civil Affairs Tng. Sch., Northwestern U., 1945; D.J. cum laude, U. Notre Dame, 1949; LL.D. (hon.), U. Nev., 1978. Bar: Nev. 1949, Ill. 1950. Dep. dist. atty. Clark County, Las Vegas, Nev., 1949-53; U.S. referee Fed. Cts. in Nev., 1955-59; dist. judge for Nev. 1959-67; justice Nev. Supreme Ct., Carson City, 1967—, chief justice, 1986—; founder 1st pub. defender program in Nev., 1967; mem. faculty Nat. Coll. State Judiciary, 1967. V.P. Boulder Dam Area council Boy Scouts Am., 1960-70; bd. dirs. Nev. Area council, 1967—; pres. City of Hope, 1963-64, NCCJ, 1965-66; v.p. YMCA, 1964—; chmn. Nev. Commn. on Bicentennial U.S. Constitution, 1986. Served to maj. AUS, 1942-46, PTO. Recipient Outstanding Alumni award Western Ill. U., 1971, Equal Justice award Western regional dept. NAACP, 1970, Minuteman award SAR, 1982, Silver Antelope award Boy Scouts Am., 1983, Jurist of Yr. award Nev. Trial Lawyers Assn., 1986, Judicial Officer of Yr. award State Sheriff and Police Assn., 1986; Mowbray Hall, Western Ill. U. named in his honor, 1974. Mem. ABA, Nev. Trial Lawyers Assn. (Jurist of Yr. award 1986), Am. Judicature Soc., State Sheriff and Police Assn. (Jud. Officer of Yr. award 1986), SAR (pres. Nev. 1969-70, Nat. Gen. MacArthur medal 1971, nat. trustee 1971—), VFW. Clubs: Rotarian (hon.), Elk. Jurisprudence. also: 189 Lake Glen Dr Carson City NV 89701 Office: Supreme Ct Bldg Capitol Complex Carson City NV 89710

MOWELL, GEORGE MITCHELL, lawyer; b. Balt., July 31, 1951; s. George Robert and Polly (Sattler) M.; m. Patricia Edith Forbes, Sept. 23, 1978; children: Rachel Elizabeth, George Robert. BA, Washington Coll., Chestertown, Md., 1973; JD, U. Balt., 1977. Bar: Md. 1978, U.S. Dist. Ct. Md. 1982, U.S. Bankruptcy Ct. 1982. Claims authorizer Social Security Adminstrn., Balt., 1973-79; law clk. to presiding justice Kent County Cir. Ct., Chestertown, 1979-81; ptnr. Boyer & Mowell, Chestertown, 1981—; atty. Kent County Planning Commn., Chestertown, 1982—. Bd. dirs. Kent County Heart Assn., Chestertown, 1983-84. Mem. ABA, Md. Bar Assn. (com. on laws 1984—), Kent County Bar Assn. (sec. 1985—), Balt. Bar Assn., Md. Trial Lawyers Assn. Democrat. Episcopalian. Lodges: Elks, Optimists. General practice, Land use and planning law. Home: RD 1 PO Box 382 Chestertown MD 21620 Office: Boyer & Mowell 107 Court St Chestertown MD 21620

MOWRY, KATHY SUZANNE, lawyer; b. Lancaster, Ohio, Dec. 28, 1952; d. Homer Edman and Eileen Joan (Love) Beavers; m. David Dee Mowry, Sept. 7, 1975; children: David E., Joan E. BA, Ohio U., 1974; JD, Capital U., Columbus, Ohio, 1980. Bar: Ohio 1981, U.S. Dist. Ct. (so. dist.) Ohio 1983. Probation officer Juvenile Ct., Lancaster, 1975-77; bailiff Mcpl. Ct., Lancaster, 1979; research clk. Common Pleas Ct., Lancaster, 1980; asst. prosecutor Fairfield County, Lancaster, 1983—; sole practice Bremen, Ohio, 1981—; lectr. retirement seminar Ohio U., Lancaster, 1984—. Advisor Bremen Sesquicentennial Com., 1982-85; officer United Presbyn. Womens Assn., 1983—; ruling elder Bremen Bethel Presbyn. Ch.; bd. mem., treas. New Horizons Drug Abuse, Prevention and Treatment Agts., Lancaster, 1984-86; mem. Welfare Adv. Bd., Lancaster, 1985-86; advisor, statutory agt. Bremen Activity Com., 1986, Bremen Hist. Soc., 1985. Named Young Careerist of Yr., Lancaster Bus. and Profl. Womens Assn., 1982. Republican. Avocations: travel, gardening, home restoration. Probate, General practice. Home and Office: 129 Strayer Ave Bremen OH 43107

MOXLEY, CHARLES JOSEPH, JR., lawyer; b. Balt., Feb. 22, 1944; s. Charles J. and Kathryn (Foley) M.; m. Norma Fox, Feb. 14, 1975. BA, Fordham U., 1965, MA, 1966; JD, Columbia U., 1969. Bar: U.S. Ct. Appeals (2d cir.) 1972, U.S. Dist. Ct. (so. and ea. dists.) N.Y. 1972, U.S. Supreme Ct. 1982, U.S Ct. Appeals (7th cir.) 1984. Law clk. to judge U.S. Dist. Ct. N.Y., N.Y.C., 1969-70; assoc. Davis Polk & Wardwell, N.Y.C., 1970-79; mem. Schwartz, Klink & Schreiber P.C., N.Y.C., 1979-87, Jones Hirsch Connors & Bull, N.Y.C., 1987—; spl. master N.Y. State Supreme Ct., N.Y.C. 1977-85; arbitrator N.Y.C. Civil Ct., 1982; adj. prof. law N.Y. Law Sch., 1986—. Mem. ABA, Assn. of Bar of City of N.Y. (com. on internat. arms control and sec. affairs 1986—), N.Y. State Bar Assn. (com. on civil practice law and rules 1977-85, com. on Constl. law 1985—), N.Y. County Lawyers Assn. (internat. law com. 1981-86), Am. Arbitration Assn. (arbitrator). Federal civil litigation, State civil litigation, Securities. Home: 2 Fifth Ave New York NY 10011 Office: Jones Hirsch Connors & Bull 101 E 52d St New York NY 10022

MOY, CELESTE MARIE, lawyer; b. Detroit, July 16, 1950; s. Melvin Bell and Hazel Vernice (Ridgell) M.; m. Richard J. Whitman, Sept. 2, 1972 (div. 1981); m. L. Edward Street, Aug. 25, 1984. B.A., Mich. State U., 1972; J.D., U. Detroit, 1976. Bar: Mich. 1976, Tex. 1983. Atty. IRS, 1973-76; ptnr. Kirk, Ellis & Moy, Detroit, 1976-78; sole practice, Detroit, 1979-80; atty. mktg. dept. Alexander Hamilton Life ins. Co. Am., Farmington Hills, Mich., 1980-81; atty. southwestern region Mut. of N.Y., Dallas, 1981-83; assoc. Mahomes & Assocs., Dallas, 1983; v.p., gen. counsel legal affairs for Dallas, Mesquite and Farmers Branch, Warner Amex Cable Communications-Dallas, 1984-85, gen. counsel Sphere Communication, Inc., Wescom Constrn. Co., 1986—. Mem. Dallas Black Exec. Assembly; officer Dallas Arboretum; bd. dirs. Botanical Soc. Recipient Pro Bono Service award North Tex. Legal Services, Dallas, 1983. Mem. State Bar Mich., State Bar Tex., Dallas Black Lawyers Assn., Dallas Bar Assn., LWV, NAACP, Internat. Bus. Fellows Soc., Alpha Kappa Alpha. Democrat. Methodist. Lodge: Zonta. General corporate, Entertainment, Estate planning. Office: Sphere Cable Communications Inc 3151 Turtle Creek Blvd Suite 700 Dallas TX 75219 also: Wescom Constrn Co 3131 Turtle Creek Blvd Suite 2224 Dallas TX 75219

MOY, DONALD RICHARD, lawyer; b. Portsmouth, Va., Feb. 8, 1953; s. Richard S. and Hazel (Yuen) M. JD, Albany Law Sch., 1977. Bar: N.Y. 1978. Atty. N.Y. State Med. Soc., Lake Success, 1978-82, gen. counsel, 1982—. Mem. Nat. Health Lawyers Assn., Soc. Med. Assn. Counsel. Health. Home: 91 Tulip Ave Floral Park NY 11041 Office: NY State Med Soc 420 Lakeville Rd Lake Success NY 11042

MOYE, CHARLES ALLEN, JR., U.S. judge; b. Atlanta, July 13, 1918; s. Charles Allen and Annie Luther (Williamson) M.; m. Sarah Ellen Johnston, Mar. 9, 1945; children: Henry Allen, Lucy Ellen. A.B., Emory U., 1939, J.D., 1943. Bar: Ga. 1943. Since practiced in Atlanta; partner firm Gambrell, Russell, Moye & Killorin (and predecessors), 1955-70; judge U.S. Dist. Ct. No. Dist. Ga., 1970—, chief judge, 1979—. Chmn. DeKalb County Republican Exec. Com., 1952-56; chmn. Rep. Exec. Com. 5th Congl. Dist. Ga., 1956-64; mem. Ga. Rep. Central Com., 1952-64; Rep. candidate for Congress, 1954; del. Rep. Nat. Conv., 1956, 60, 64; chmn. Rep. Exec. Com. 4th Congl. Dist., 1964, Rep. presdl. elector, 1964. Mem. ABA, Fed. Bar Assn., Atlanta Bar Assn., Ga. Bar Assn., Lawyers Club Atlanta, Am. Judicature Soc., Am. Bar Found., Am. Law Inst., Delta Tau Delta. Congregationalist. Clubs: Atlanta Athletic (Atlanta), Atlanta City (Atlanta); Nat. Lawyers (Washington). Home: 1317 Council Bluff Dr NE Atlanta GA 30345 Office: US Dist Court House 75 Spring St SW Atlanta GA 30303

MOYE, ERIC VAUGHN, lawyer; b. N.Y.C., Aug. 22, 1954; s. Lemuel Alexander and Florence (Miller) M. BA in Polit. Sci. with distinction, So. Meth. U., 1976; JD, Harvard U., 1979. Bar: Tex. 1979, U.S. Dist. Ct. (no. dist.) Tex. 1980, U.S. Ct. Appeals (5th cir.) 1980, N.Y. 1985, U.S. Supreme Ct. 1985, U.S. Dist. Ct. (no. dist.) Calif. 1986, U.S. Ct. Claims 1986. With Office Gen. Counsel CIA, McLean, Va., 1978; assoc. Akin, Gump, Strauss, Hauer & Feld, Dallas, 1979-83; prin. Law Office of Eric V. Moye, Dallas, 1983—. Mem. Permit and License Appeals Bd., 1984—; chmn. Mayor's Task Force on Housing and Econ. Devel., Dallas, 1983-85; bd. dirs. Dispute Mediation Service, Dallas, 1980—, Dallas Urban League, 1980-84, Pub. Utility Counsel Adv. Bd., 1984—. Mem. Assn. Bar of City of N.Y. Democrat. Methodist. Avocations: aikido, motorcycling, chess. Federal civil litigation, State civil litigation, Contracts commercial. Home: 3621 Turtle Creek Blvd Dallas TX 75219 Office: Law Offices of Eric V Moye 3505 Turtle Creek Blvd Dallas TX 75219

MOYE, JOHN EDWARD, lawyer; b. Deadwood, S.D., Aug. 15, 1944; s. Francis Joseph and Margaret (Roberts) M.; children: Kelly Maura, Mary Shannon, Megan Jane, Rachael Laura Portnoy. B.B.A., U. Notre Dame, 1965; J.D. with distinction, Cornell U., 1968. Bar: N.Y. 1968, Colo. 1971. Research asst. Cornell U., 1967-68; ptnr. Moye, Giles, O'Keefe, Vermeire & Gorrell, Denver, 1976—; mem. faculty U. Denver Coll. Law, 1969—, prof., 1972-79, asso. dean, 1974-76; adviser Denver Legal Aid Soc.; bd. advisers U. Denver Coll. Law, U. Denver Law Jours.; dir. United Bank Cherry Creek. Author: Cases and Materials on Federal Jurisdiction and Procedure, 3d edit., 1979, Problem Series on Commercial Transactions Under the Uniform Commercial Code, 1976, The Law of Business Organizations, 2d edit., 1981, Student Handbook to Corporations, 1974, Buying and Selling a Business, 1980, Financing with Personal Property as Collateral, 1981, Corporations, 1982, 85, Partnerships, 1983. Legis. revision com. Colo. Corp. Code, Uniform Comml. Code, and Land Use Legislation Bd.; Bd. dirs. Denver Symphony Assn., 1978-79, Colo. Ballet, Downtown Denver, Inc., Patten Inst. for Arts; bd. dirs., pres. Continuing Legal Edn. in Colo.; commr. consumer credit State of Colo., 1984—, Denver Urban Renewal Authority, 1985—. Served to capt. USAF, 1968-72. Decorated Meritorious Service medal, award of merit Denver U. Student Bar Assn., 1972; named Prof. of Yr., 1972-73, 75-76, 76-77, 78-79. Mem. ABA, Colo. Bar Assn. (chmn. long range planning com.), Denver County Bar Assn., Denver Bar Assn. (dir.), Comml. Law League Am., Order of Coif, Phi Kappa Phi, Beta Alpha Psi, Phi Alpha Delta. Republican. Roman Catholic. Office: Moye Giles O'Keefe Vermeire & Gorrell 730 17th St Suite 600 Denver CO 80202

MOYER, JAY EDWARD, lawyer, professional sports league executive; b. Sellersville, Pa., July 28, 1940; s. J. Edward and Frances (Apple) M.; m. Ellen W. Boldt, Sept. 20, 1960 (div. Sept. 1979); children—Sherrill Ann, Jennifer Lee, James Edward; m. Terry Jane Brown, Sept. 27, 1980. A.B. magna cum laude, Dartmouth Coll., 1962; J.D., Duke U., 1965. Bar: Ohio 1965, U.S. Dist. Ct. (no. dist.) Ohio 1967, U.S. Supreme Ct. 1972. Assoc. Squire, Sanders & Dempsey, Cleve., 1965-72; gen. counsel NFL, N.Y.C., 1972—, exec. v.p., 1985—; speaker numerous ednl. seminars, 1971—; witness various congl. and state legis. coms., 1980—. Contbr. articles to profl. jours. Mem. ABA, Am. Arbitration Assn. (regional adv. council 1970-72), Order of Coif. Phi Beta Kappa. Republican. Methodist. Entertainment, Antitrust. Office: NFL 410 Park Ave New York NY 10022

MOYER, THOMAS J., state judge; b. Sandusky, Ohio, Apr. 18, 1939; s. Clarence and Idamae (Hessler) M.; m. Mary Francis Moyer, Dec. 15, 1984; 1 child, Drew; stepchildren: Anne, Jack, Alaine, Elizabeth. BA, Ohio State U., 1961, JD, 1964. Asst. atty. gen. State of Ohio, Columbus, 1964-66; sole practice Columbus, 1966-69; dep. asst. Office Gov. State of Ohio, Columbus, 1969-71, exec. asst., 1975-79; assoc. Crabbe, Brown, Jones, Potts & Schmidt, Columbus, 1972-75; judge U.S. Ct. Appeals (10th cir.), Columbus, 1979-86; chief justice Ohio Supreme Ct., Columbus, 1987—. Sec. bd. trustees Franklin U., Columbus, 1986-87; trustee Univ. Club, Columbus, 1986; mem. nat. council adv. com. Ohio State U. Coll. Law, Columbus. Recipient Award of Merit, Ohio Legal Ctr. Inst.; named Outstanding Young Man of Columbus, Columbus Jaycees, 1969. Mem. Ohio State Bar Assn. (exec. com., council dels.), Columbus Bar Assn. (pres. 1980-81). Republican. Clubs: Crichton, Columbus Maennerchor (Columbus). Avocations: sailing, tennis. Office: Supreme Court of Ohio 30 E Broad St Columbus OH 43266-0419

MOYLAN, JAMES JOSEPH, lawyer; b. Forest Hills, N.Y., Feb. 3, 1948; s. James Gerard and Jessie Cora (Geary) M.; m. Barbara Chesrow, Aug. 29, 1970; children—James C., Joseph O., Alicia G. B.S.B.A., U. Denver, 1969, J.D., 1971. Bar: Colo. 1972, D.C. 1972, Ill. 1975, U.S. Dist. Ct. Colo. 1972, U.S. Supreme Ct. 1975. Trial atty. SEC, Washington, 1972-75; assoc. gen. counsel Chgo. Bd. Options Exchange, Ill., 1975-77; assoc. Abramson & Fox, Chgo., 1977-80; ptnr. Bowen, Knepper & Moylan Ltd., Chgo., 1980-82; ptnr. Moylan & Early, Ltd., Chgo., 1983-84; prin. James J. Moylan and Assocs., Ltd., Chgo., 1984—; adj. prof. law IIT Chgo. Kent Coll. Law, 1976—; pub. dir. MidAm. Commodity Exchange div. Chgo. Bd. Trade, Chgo., 1983-87. Contbr. articles to profl. jours. Precinct capt. Ann M. Stepan Campaign, Chgo., 1983. Mem. Ill. State Bar Assn. (sect. council mem.), Chgo. Bar Assn., D.C. Bar Assn., ABA (sect. corp., banking and bus. law, sect. litigation). Republican. Roman Catholic. Club: Chgo. Athletic Assn. Securities, General corporate.

MOYNIHAN, JOHN BIGNELL, assistant U.S. attorney; b. N.Y.C., July 25, 1933; s. Jerome J. and Stephanie (Bignell) M.; m. Odilia Marie Jacques, Nov. 13, 1965; children—Blair, Dana. B.S., Fordham U., 1955; J.D., St. John's U., N.Y.C., 1958. Bar: Tex. 1961, U.S. Supreme Ct. 1965, U.S. Dist. Ct. (we. dist.) Tex. 1968, U.S. Ct. Apls. (5th cir.) 1973. Sole practice Brownsville, Tex., 1961-62; asst. city atty. City of San Antonio, 1962-63; sole practice, San Antonio, 1963-65; estate tax atty. IRS, San Antonio, 1965-73; dist. counsel EEOC, San Antonio, 1973-79; asst. U.S. atty. Office U.S. Atty., San Antonio, 1980—; pres., dir. Mambo Restaurants, Inc., San Antonio, 1986—. Served with U.S. Army, 1958-60. Mem. San Antonio Bar Assn. (chmn. state and nat. legis. com. 1972-73, Meritorious Service award 1968), Fed. Bar Assn. (bd. dirs. 1983—, pres. elect 1986), Tex. Restaurant Assn. Chmn. reform and renewal com. San Antonio Roman Catholic Archdiocese, 1968. Democrat. Lodge: K.C. (pres. 1967).). Civil rights, Federal civil litigation, Labor. Home: 11011 Whispering Wind Rd San Antonio TX 78230 Office: US Attys Office US Court House 655 E Durango Blvd San Antonio TX 78206

MOZENA, PETER JOSEPH, lawyer; b. Portland, Oreg., May 16, 1948; s. Joseph I. Mozena and Mary Teresa (Delaney) Mozena-Hough; m. Jane E. Riggin, Mar. 3, 1973; children: Paul D., Claire E. Student, U. Notre Dame, 1966-67, Seattle U., 1973; BS, U. Puget Sound, 1976; JD, U. Wash., 1976. Bar: Wash. 1977, U.S. Dist. Ct. (we. dist.) Wash., U.S. Supreme Ct. From v.p. to pres. Med. Specialties Co., Seattle and Portland, 1970-80; ptnr. Mozena and Armstrong, Vancouver, Wash.; law instr. Clark Coll., Vancouver, 1981; chmn. of bd., pres. Vantech Enterprise Northwest, Vancouver, Wash., 1981-86. Served with U.S. Army, 1968-70. Real property, General corporate, Personal injury. Office: Mozena and Armstrong 2901 Main St Vancouver WA 98663

MOZER, MICHAEL THEODORE, lawyer; b. Great Falls, Mont., Oct. 23, 1948; s. John and Otylia Ann (Lund) M.; m. Roxanna Elizabeth Britten, Jan. 25, 1986; children: Connie, Jonathan; children from previous marriage: Katherine S., Joseph M. BA cum laude, U. Mont., 1971; postgrad., U. Minn., 1971-72; JD cum laude, William Mitchell Coll. Law, 1976. Bar: Minn. 1977, U.S. Dist. Ct. Minn. 1977. Assoc. Stephens & Morris, Edina, Minn., 1977-79; gen. counsel Banco Mortgage Co., Mpls., 1979-83; sr. v.p., mktg. FBS Mortgage Co., Mpls., 1983; sole practice Denver, 1983—; cons. First Interstate Mtg. Co., Denver, 1983—, Insilco Corp., Meriden, Conn., 1984—, All Valley Acceptance Co., Irvine, Calif., 1984—, Foremost Guaranty Ins. Co., 1984—, Cuna Mut. Ins. Group, Madison, Wis., 1986—, Miller & Schroeder Fin. Inc., Mpls., 1986—. Legis. lobbyist Minn. Mortgage Bankers Assn., St. Paul, 1980-83. Mem. Minn. Bar Assn., Hennepin County Bar Assn. Avocations: hiking, fishing, hunting. Development of marketing programs for lenders, Real property, Securities. Home: 13515 Oakland Dr Burnsville MN 55337 Office: 1660 S Highway 100 #331 Minneapolis MN 55416

MUCCIA, JOSEPH WILLIAM, lawyer; b. N.Y.C., May 31, 1948; s. Joseph Anthony and Charlotte (Mohring) M.; m. Margaret M. Reynolds, June 29, 1985. B.A. magna cum laude, Fordham U., 1970, J.D., 1973. Bar: N.Y. 1974, U.S. Dist. Ct. (so. dist.) N.Y. 1974, U.S. Dist. Ct. (ea. dist.) N.Y. 1980, U.S. Ct. Appeals (2d cir.) 1974, U.S. Ct. Appeals (D.C. cir.) 1980, U.S. Supreme Ct. 1980. Assoc. Cahill Gordon & Reindel, N.Y.C., 1973-82; ptnr. Corbin Silverman & Sanseverino, N.Y.C., 1983—. Assoc. editor Fordham Law Rev., 1972-73. Mem. ABA (litigation sect.), N.Y. County Lawyers Assn., Fed. Bar Council, Phi Beta Kappa, Pi Sigma Alpha. Federal civil litigation, State civil litigation, Securities. Office: Corbin Silverman & Sanseverino 805 3d Ave New York NY 10022

MUCHIN, ARDEN ARCHIE, lawyer; b. Manitowoc, Wis., Dec. 9, 1920; s. Alfred and Ida (Golden) M.; m. Bettie Lou Barenbaum, Dec. 19, 1948; children—Ann L., Efrem B., Jay. B.A., U. Wis., 1942, J.D., 1947; I.A., Harvard U. Grad. Sch. Bus. Adminstrn., 1943. Bar: Wis. 1947, U.S. Dist. Ct. (ea. dist.) Wis. 1948, U.S. Tax Ct. 1965. Pres. Muchin, Muchin & Bendix, S.C. and predecessors, Manitowoc, 1947—; sec. and/or dir. Chippewa Pub. Co., Inc., Register Pub. Corp., Portage, Wis., Foster Needle Co., Inc., Manitowoc, Foster Needle Ltd. (Eng.), Muchin Steel Supply Co. Inc., Manitowoc; sec. Lavine Media Inc., Chippewa Falls, Wis., Shawano Evening Leader Co.; sec., dir. WaterCare Corp., Granger Land and Mortgage Corp., Schwartz Mfg. Co., Heresite Saekaphen, Inc.; dir. CUB Radio, Inc., Manitowoc; gov. State Bar Wis., 1976-80. Bd. dirs. Manitowoc United Way Inc., 1968—; mem. Wis. adv. com. U.S. Commn. Civil Rights, 1985-86. Mem. ABA, Manitowoc County Bar Assn. (pres. 1972-73). General corporate, Estate taxation, Labor. Home: 1426 Arden Ln Manitowoc WI 54220 Office: Muchin Muchin & Bendix SC 1004 Washington St Manitowoc WI 54220

MUCKENFUSS, CANTWELL FAULKNER, III, lawyer; b. Montgomery, Ala., Apr. 25, 1945; s. Cantwell F. and Dorothy (Dauphine) M.; m. A. Angela Lancaster, June 25, 1978; 1 child, Alice Paran Lancaster. BA, Vanderbilt U., 1967; JD, Yale U., 1971. Bar: N.Y. 1973, D.C. 1976. Law clk. to presiding justice U.S. Ct. Appeals (6th cir.), 1971-72; atty., project developer Bedford Stuyvesant D and S Corp., Bklyn., 1972-73; spl. asst. to the dir. FDIC, Washington, 1974-77, counsel to the chmn., 1977-78; sr. dep. comptroller for policy Office of the Comptroller of the Currency, Washington, 1978-81; ptnr. Gibson, Dunn & Crutcher, Washington, 1981—; mem. editorial adv. bd. Issues in Bank Regulation, Rolling Meadows, Ill., 1977—; mem. bd. advisors Rev. Fin. Regulation, N.Y.C., 1985—. Served with USNG, 1968-70, USAR, 1970-74. Recipient Spl. Achievement award U.S. Dept. Treasury, 1979, Presdl. Rank award U.S. Govt., 1980. Mem. ABA, Fed. Bar Assn. Democrat. Episcopalian. Banking, Legislative. Office: Gibson Dunn & Crutcher 1050 Connecticut Ave NW Suite 900 Washington DC 20036

MUDD, JOHN O., lawyer, university dean; b. 1943. BA, Cath. U., 1965, MA, 1966; JD, U. Mont., 1973; LLM, Columbia U., 1986. Bar: Mont. 1973. Ptnr. Mulroney, Delaney, Dalby & Mudd, Missoula, Mont., 1973-79; lectr. U. Mont., Missoula, 1973-74, 75-76, prof. law, dean, 1979—; pres. Mid-Continent Assn. Law Schs., 1982-83. Mem. ABA, Am. Judicature Soc. (bd. dirs. 1985—), State Bar Mont. Editor Mont. Law Rev., 1972-73. Legal education. Office: U Mont Sch of Law Missoula MT 59812

MUDD, JOHN PHILIP, lawyer, real estate executive; b. Washington, Aug. 22, 1932; s. Thomas Paul and Frances Mary (Finotti) M.; m. Barbara Eve Sweeney, Aug. 10, 1957; children: Laura, Ellen, Philip, Clare, David. B.S.S., Georgetown U., 1954; J.D., Georgetown Law Center, 1956. Bar: Md. bar 1956, D.C. bar 1963, Fla. bar 1964, Calif. bar 1973. Individual practice law

Upper Marlboro, Md., 1956-66; v.p., sec., corporate atty. Deltona Corp., Miami, Fla., 1966-72; sec. Nat. Community Builders, San Diego, 1972-73; gen. counsel Continental Advisers (adviser to Continental Mortgage Investors), 1973-75, sr. v.p., gen. counsel, 1975-80; sr. v.p., corp. atty. Am. Hosp. Mgmt. Corp., Miami, 1980—; pres. Tropic Devel. Corp., 1979—. Former mem. Land Devel. Adv. Com. N.Y. State; chmn student interview com. Georgetown U.; bd. dirs. Lasalle High Sch., Miami; bd. dirs., corporate counsel Com. of Dade County, Fla. Mem. ABA, Fla. Bar Assn., Calif. Bar Assn., Md. Bar Assn, D.C. Bar Assn., Fla. State Bar (exec. com. of corp. counsel com. 1978—). Democrat. Roman Catholic. Real property, Health, General corporate. Home: 1211 Hardee Rd Coral Gables FL 33146 Office: 9405 NW 41st St Miami FL 33178

MUDGE, GEORGE ALFRED, lawyer; b. Orlando, Fla., Apr. 30, 1943; s. Gilbert Horton and Eleanor (Mackenzie) M. BA, Amherst Coll., 1965; postgrad., Grad. Inst. Internat. Studies, Geneva; JD, U. Mich., 1969. Bar: N.Y. 1970. Assoc. Shearman & Sterling, N.Y.C., 1969-76, ptnr., 1977—. Contbr. articles to profl. jours. Mem. ABA, N.Y.C. Lawyers Assn., Assn. of Bar of City of N.Y. (com. on InterAm. Affairs), Inst. Internat. Fin. (adv. com. to legal com.), Am. Soc. Internat. Law. Banking, Country debt restructure. Office: Shearman & Sterling 599 Lexington Ave New York NY 10022-6004

MUDRICK, DAVID PHILLIP, lawyer; b. Kansas City, Mo., Jan. 3, 1951; s. David S. and Bessie (Litwin) M.; m. Mary Beth Walker, Dec. 31, 1972; children: Jeffrey David, Clint Robert. BS in Journalism and Polit. Sci. summa cum laude, Kans. State U., 1973; postgrad., Duke U. Sch. Law, 1973-75; JD, U. Kans., 1976. Bar: Kans. 1976, U.S. Dist. Ct. Kans. 1976, U.S. Ct. Appeals (10th cir.) 1977. Atty. Southwestern Bell Telephone Co., Topeka, 1976—; bd. dirs. Legal Aid Soc., Topeka, 1984—, now v.p.; bd. dirs. Mudrick's of Litwin's Inc., Ottawa, Kans. Alt. del. Kans. Rep. Conv., Topeka, 1984; del. 2d Congl. Dist. Rep. Conv., Wetmore, Kans., 1984; mem. Helping Hands Humane Soc. and Friends of Zoo, Topeka, 1983—. Mem. Am. Judicature Soc., Kans. Bar Assn., Topeka Bar Assn., Order of Coif, Phi Kappa Phi, Phi Eta Sigma. Republican. Jewish. Club: Investments Ltd. (Topeka). Avocations: racquetball, snow skiing, flying, scuba diving, politics. Administrative and regulatory, Public utilities, Federal civil litigation. Home: 5837 SW Smith Pl Topeka KS 66614 Office: Southwestern Bell Telephone Co 220 E 6th Rm 515 Topeka KS 66603

MUELLER, BARRY SCOTT, lawyer; b. Moline, Ill., Dec. 25, 1954; s. Wayne H. and LuRae E. (Paridon) M.; m. C. Sue Delfs, June 12, 1976. BA, Ill. Wesleyan U., 1976; JD, Drake U., 1980. Bar: Iowa 1980, U.S. Dist. Ct. (so. and no. dists.) Iowa 1980, U.S. Ct. Appeals (8th cir.) 1980. Ptnr. Kelly & Mueller Law Office P.C., Postville, Iowa, 1980—; jud. magistrate State of Iowa, Waukon, 1981—. Sec. Conestoga Council Girl Scouts U.S., Waterloo, Iowa, 1985—, bd. dirs. 1983-84; council pres. St. Paul Luth. Ch., Postville, 1985, bd. dirs. 1982—. Named Super Spouse Conestoga Council Girl Scouts U.S., 1985. Mem. Allamakee County Bar Assn. (sec./treas. 1981-82, pres. 1982-83), Assn. Trial Lawyers Am., Assn. Trial Lawyers Iowa. Republican. Lodges: Lions (v.p. 1983—). Avocations: camping, working with youth, reading. State civil litigation, Personal injury, General practice. Home: PO Box 400 Postville IA 52162 Office: Kelly & Mueller Law Office PC PO Box 400 Postville IA 52162

MUELLER, FOORMAN LLOYD, lawyer; b. Chgo., Aug. 5, 1904; s. George Edgar and Bessie Dorothy (Foorman) M.; m. Isabel McFarland, Oct. 25, 1930; children—Georgeana (Mrs. Thomas J. McColloch), Foorman Lloyd. A.B., U. Mich., 1927; J.D., Kent. Coll. Law, Chgo., 1932. Bar: Ill. 1932, D.C. Assoc., George E. Mueller, Chgo., 1932-35; practice, Chgo., 1935-75; sole practice, Phoenix, 1975—; patent counsel Motorola, Schaumberg, Ill., 1935—. Chmn. Hinsdale (Ill.) Community Caucus, 1948, 49, Hinsdale Planning Commn., 1949-57. Mem. ABA, Ill. Bar Assn., Chgo. Bar Assn., Chgo. Patent Law Assn. (pres. 1967), Am. Patent Law Assn. (pres. 1953-54), Phi Gamma Delta, Phi Delta Phi. Presbyterian. Clubs: Union League (Chgo.); Hinsdale Golf; Paradise Valley Country. Patent, Trademark and copyright. Home: 6721 E Cheney Rd Paradise Valley AZ 85253 Office: 4250 E Camelback Rd Suite 390K Phoenix AZ 85018

MUELLER, JOSEPH HENRY, lawyer; b. St. Louis, Mar. 19, 1935; s. Thomas E. and Marie C. (Cleary) M.; m. Nancy K. Picraux, Nov. 5, 1960; children: James V., Christopher J., Gregory T., Anne C. BBA, St. Louis U., 1956, JD, 1959. Bar: Mo. 1959, U.S. Dist. Ct. (ea. dist.) Mo. 1960, U.S. Ct. Appeals (8th cir.) 1972, U.S. Supreme Ct. 1974. From assoc. to ptnr. Moser & Marsalek, St. Louis, 1959—. Bd. dirs. St. Vincent De Paul Soc., St. Louis, 1970—, Cath. Family Services, St. Louis, 1975—. Served to staff sgt. USAF, 1959-63. Mem. Am. Bd. Trial Advs., Internat. Assn. Ins. Counsel., Am. Coll. Trial Lawyers. Club: Media (St. Louis). Insurance, State civil litigation, Federal civil litigation. Home: 528 Olive Ct Saint Louis MO 63119 Office: Moser Marsalek et al 314 N Broadway Saint Louis MO 63102

MUELLER, MARK CHRISTOPHER, lawyer, accountant; b. Dallas, June 19, 1945; s. Herman August and Hazel Deane (Hatzenbuehler) M.; m. Linda Jane Reed. B.A. in Econs., So. Meth. U., 1967, M.B.A. in Acctg., 1969, J.D., 1971. Bar: Tex. 1971, U.S. Dist. Ct. (no. dist.) Tex. 1974, U.S. Tax Ct. 1974; C.P.A., Tex. Acct. Arthur Young & Co., Dallas, 1967-68, A.E. Krutilek, Dallas, 1968-71; sole practice law, Dallas, 1971—; assoc. L. Vance Stanton, Dallas, 1971-72; instr. legal writing and research So. Meth. U., Dallas, 1970-71, instr. legal acctg., 1975. Leading articles editor Southwestern Law Jour., 1970-71. Mem. ABA, Tex. Bar Assn., Tex. Soc. C.P.A.s, Nat. Rifle Assn., Order of Coif, Beta Alpha Psi, Phi Delta Phi, Sigma Chi. Lodges: Masons, Shriners. General practice, Real property. Home: 7310 Brennans St Dallas TX 75214 Office: 9854 Plano Rd Suite 100 Dallas TX 75238

MUELLER, RICHARD EDWARD, lawyer; b. Chgo., Mar. 23, 1927; s. Edward and Edith (Burman) M.; divorced; children: Keith, James. B.S., Northwestern U., 1949, LL.B., 1951. Bar: Ill. 1951. Ptnr. Lord, Bissell & Brook, Chgo., 1961—; specialist in ins. def. Selected as One of Best Lawyers in Am. Seaview Putman, 1983, One of Best Lawyers in Am. Town and Country, June 1985, One of Best Lawyers in Am. Woodward White, 1987. Mem. Ill. Appellate Lawyers Assn., Ill. State Bar Assn., Chgo. Bar Assn., Ill. Def. Counsel. Insurance, Personal injury, Federal civil litigation. Home: 5057 N Mango St Chicago IL 60630 Office: Lord Bissell & Brook Suites 3200-3500 Harris Bank Bldg 115 S LaSalle St Chicago IL 60603

MUELLER, ROBERT CLARE, lawyer; b. Sioux City, Iowa, May 17, 1946; s. Clare Robert and Betty Louise (Abker) M.; m. C. Brenda Rowland, Jan. 21, 1977; children—Martin, Clinton, Mitchell. A.B., U. S.D., 1968; J.D., Duke U., 1971; LL.M., George Washington U., 1974. Bar: Iowa 1971. Counsel to judge U.S. Ct. Mil. Appeals, Washington, 1975-80, counsel to chief judge, 1980—; mem. Joint-Service Com. Mil. Justice, Washington, 1977—, Working Group to Mil. Justice Act of 1983 Adv. Commn., Washington, 1984-85; judge Cath. U. Law Sch. Moot Ct. Competition, Washington, 1985-87. Co-author: Manual for Courts-Martial, U.S., 1984; Military Rules of Evidence. Contbr. articles to profl. publs. Editor Fed. Bar News & Jour., 1984, 86 (Disting. Service award 1984, 86). Sec. Mil. Law Inst., 1986—; mem. County Supr.'s Zoning Rev. com., Fairfax County, Va., 1982. Served to capt. U.S. Army, 1971-75. Decorated Meritorious Service medal; recipient Outstanding Achievement award Sec. Def., 1976—. Mem. Fed. Bar Assn. (cir. v.p. 1983-85, nat. membership chmn. 1985-87, dep. chmn. judiciary sect. 1985-86, chmn. mil. law com. 1985-86; chmn. career service sect., 1986—; Disting. Service award 1985, nat. council mem. 1983—). Clubs: Nat. Lawyers, Washington Duke Law (bd. dirs. 1984—). Military, Criminal. Home: 5446 Midship Ct Burke VA 22015 Office: US Ct Mil Appeals 450 E St NW Washington DC 20442

MUELLER, WILLIAM JEFFREY, lawyer; b. Omaha, Nebr., Dec. 21, 1954; s. William Paul and Martha Ann (Hatchett) M. BS, U. Nebr., 1977, JD, 1980. Bar: Nebr. 1980, U.S. Dist. Ct. Nebr. 1980, U.S. Ct. Appeals (8th cir.) 1980. Assoc. Sodoro, Daly & Sodoro, Omaha, 1981-84, Knudsen, Berkheimer, Richardson & Endacott, Lincoln, 1984—; bd. dirs. Nebr. Continuing Legal Edn., Lincoln. Nat. committeeman Nebr. Young Reps., Lincoln, 1980-83, state chmn. 1981-82; mem. com. United Way of Lincoln, 1986—. Schreiber-Hunter scholar U. Nebr., 1976. Mem. ABA (chmn. membership 1983-84), Nebr. Bar Assn. (exec. council 1983-84, legis. counsel 1984—, vice chmn. judiciary com. 1985—, pres. Young Lawyers div. 1983-84), Omaha Barristers (v.p. 1982-84), Assn. Trial Attys. Am., Nebr. Assn. Trial Attys., Sons of Am. Legion, Lincoln C. of C. Club: Updowntowners (Lincoln). Lodges: Lions, Elks. Legislative, Personal injury, Federal civil litigation. Home: 2917 S 20th St Lincoln NE 68502 Office: Knudsen Berkheimer et al 1327 H St 100 Capital Park Lincoln NE 68508

MUGLER, MOLLY SCOTT, lawyer; b. Buffalo, Oct. 16, 1951; d. Milton William and Margot (Rumsey) M.; m. John Charles Sullivan, Sept. 11, 1982; children: William Patrick, Margaret Scott. BA, U. Pa., 1973; JD, Boston U., 1980. Bar: N.H. 1980, U.S. Dist. Ct. N.H. 1980, Mass. 1981, U.S. Dist. Ct. Mass. 1981. Assoc. Devine, Millimet, Stahl & Branch, Manchester, N.H., 1980-82; atty. Wang Labs., Inc., Lowell, Mass., 1982—. Editor Boston U. Law Rev., 1979-80. Mem. ABA, Mass. Bar Assn., N.H. Bar Assn. Computer, Antitrust, Federal civil litigation. Office: Wang Labs Inc 1 Industrial Ave Lowell MA 01851

MUHLANGER, GILDA OLIVER, lawyer; b. Cienfuegos, Cuba, Sept. 26, 1951; came to U.S., 1969; d. Orlando J. and Gilda (Aloma) O.; m. Erich Muhlanger, July 13, 1973; 1 child, Erich Jr. AA, Hartford Coll. for Women, 1972; BA, Wesleyan U., 1974; JD, U. Conn., 1980. Bar: Conn. 1981. Tchr. Mercy High Sch., Middletown, Conn., 1974-79; law clk., then assoc. Williams & Brooke, P.C., Hartford, Conn., 1979-82; contract atty. The Travelers Ins. Co., Hartford, 1982, atty., 1983—. pro-bono atty. Legal Aid Soc., Hartford, 1982-83; chmn. Travelers Fin. Services dept. United Way Combined Health Appeal Campaign, Hartford, 1985. Mem. ABA, Conn. Bar Assn., Hartford County Bar Assn., Hartford Assn. Women Attys. Republican. Roman Catholic. Avocations: skiing, travel. Insurance. Home: 13 Clemens Ct Rocky Hill CT 06067 Office: The Travelers Ins Co One Tower Sq Hartford CT 06183

MUHLBACH, ROBERT ARTHUR, lawyer; b. Los Angeles, Apr. 13, 1946; s. Richard and Jeanette (Marcus) M.; m. Kerry Eldene Mahoney, July 26, 1986. BSME, U. Calif., Berkeley, 1967; JD, U. Calif., San Francisco, 1976; MME, Calif. State U., 1969; M in Pub. Adminstrn., U. So. Calif., 1976. Bar: Calif. 1976. Pub. defender County of Los Angeles, 1977-79; assoc. Kirtland & Packard, Los Angeles, 1979-85, ptnr., 1986—. Chmn. Santa Monica Airport Commn., Calif., 1984-87. Served to capt. USAF, 1969-73. Mem. ABA, AIAA. Federal civil litigation, Personal injury, Insurance. Office: Kirtland & Packard 626 Wilshire Blvd Los Angeles CA 90017

MUHLHEIM, WILSON C., lawyer; b. Hays, Kans., June 26, 1944; s. Wilson and Margaret Muhlheim; m. Nancy Colleen Collins, Sept. 11, 1965; children; Eric Wilson, Susan Elizabeth. Student, Claremont Mens Coll., 1962-64; BS, U. Oreg., 1966, JD, 1968. Bar: Oreg., U.S. Dist. Ct. Oreg. 1972. Assoc. Miller, Moulton & Andrews, Eugene, Oreg., 1972-75; ptnr. Miller, Moulton & Andrews, Eugene, 1975-76, Hershner, Hunter, Moulton, Andrews & Neill, Eugene, 1976—. Bd. dirs. Oreg. State Easter Seal Soc., Portland, Oreg., 1976-77. Served to capt. U.S. Army, 1968-72, Vietnam. Mem. Oreg. Bar Assn. (exec. com. 1984-86, debtor-creditor sect.). Republican. Avocations: skiing, fly fishing, flying, computer research. Banking, Pension, profit-sharing, and employee benefits, Contracts commercial. Office: Hershner Hunter Moulton et al 180 E 11th Eugene OR 97401

MUIR, J. DAPRAY, lawyer; b. Washington, Nov. 9, 1936; s. Brockett and Helen Cassin (Dapray) M.; m. Louise Rutherfurd Pierrepont, July 16, 1966. A.B., Williams Coll., 1958; J.D., U. Va., 1964. Bar: Md., Va., D.C. 1964, U.S. Supreme Ct. 1967. Ptnr. Muir & Ward; asst. legal adviser for econ. and bus. affairs U.S. Dept. State, 1971-73; mem. U.S. del. to Joint U.S./USSR Comml. Commn., 1972; chmn. D.C. Securities Adv. Com., 1981-82, mem. 1985—. Bd. editors Va. Law Rev, 1963-64; bd. advisers George Washington Jour. Internat. Law and Econs, 1974—; contbr. articles to profl. jours. Served to lt. (j.g.) USNR, 1958-61. Mem. ABA (co-chmn. com. internat. econ. orgns. Internat. Law sect. 1977-80), D.C. Bar (chmn. internat. law div. 1977-78, chmn. environ., energy and natural resources div. 1979-81), Washington Fgn. Law Soc. (pres. 1982-83). Clubs: Metropolitan (Washington); Union (N.Y.C.); Chevy Chase (Md.). General corporate, Private international, Securities. Home: 2905 Woodland Dr Washington DC 20008 Office: 888 17th St NW Washington DC 20006

MUIR, ROBERT EUGENE, lawyer; b. Olean, N.Y., Aug. 22, 1934; s. Hiram Abraham and Estelle Christine (Roscoe) M.; m. Gail Charlene Hendrickson, Aug. 31, 1957; children—Linda Sue, Karen Lee Muir Crane, Christine Marie, Nancy Anne, Steven Martin, Brian Robert. B.S. in Civil Engring., Valparaiso U., 1955; J.D., Ind. U., 1964. Bar: Ind. 1964, Ill. 1964, U.S. Patent Office, 1965, Can. Patent Office 1975. Engr., Ind. Hwy. Commn., Indpls., 1955-64; assoc. McCanna, Morsbach & Pillote, Rockford, 1964-68; ptnr. Morsbach, Pillote & Muir, 1968-74; sr. patent atty. Caterpillar Tractor Co., Peoria, Ill., 1974-86; asst. mgr. patent dept. Caterpillar, Inc., Peoria, 1986—. U.S. del. to transfer of technology discussions UNCTAD/Center for Applied Studies in Internat. Negotiations, Geneva, 1983; advisor State Dept., 1981—, Commerce Dept., 1982. Pres., Concordia Lutheran Ch., Rockford, 1971-72; vice chmn. City County Planning Commn., Rockford, 1973-74; pres. Peoria Civic Ballet Co., 1977-79; treas. Local Boy Scouts Am., 1981-82. Mem. Peoria County Bar Assn., Ill. Bar Assn., Internat. Patent and Trademark Assn., Licensing Execs. Soc., NAM, Pi Kappa Alpha. Patent, Licensing. Office: Caterpillar Inc 100 NE Adams St Peoria IL 61629

MUKA, BETTY LORAINE OAKES, lawyer; b. McAlester, Okla., Jan. 30, 1929; d. Herbert La Fern and Loraine Lillian (Coppedge) Oakes; m. Arthur Allen Muka, Sept. 6, 1952; children: Diane Loraine, Stephen Arthur, Christopher Herbert, Martha Ann, Deborah Susan. Student Monticello Coll., 1946-47; BS, Okla. U., 1950; MS, Cornell U., 1953, MBA, 1970; JD, Syracuse U. 1980. Bar: R.I. 1983, U.S. Dist. Ct. R.I. 1984. Mgr. dining room Anna Maude's Cafeteria, Oklahoma City, 1950-51; faculty dining room mgr. V.P.I., Blacksburg, Va., 1955-56; owner, mgr. The Cottage Restaurant, 1959-60; lectr., lab. instr. foods and organic chemistry Cornell U., 1961; owner, mgr. student housing, 1965-68; jr. acct. Maxfield, Randolph & Carpenter, CPA's, Ithaca, N.Y., 1970-71; income tax cons. H & R Block, Ithaca, 1971-73; attorney pro se, 1972—; hostess-bookkeeper Holiday Inn, Ithaca, 1972-73; salesperson Investors Diversified Services, Ithaca, 1972-73, NASD, 1973; agt. Inventory Control Co., 1975-78; law clk. 1978-79; sole practice, Providence, 1983-85; lectr. in fin. Tompkins Cortland Community Coll. Leader various youth groups, Ithaca, 1964-71. Mem. ABA, N.Y. State Bar Assn., R.I. Bar Assn., R.I. Trial Lawyer's Assn., Assn. Trial Lawyers Am., Mortar Bd., Delta Delta Alumnae (pres. 1974), Phi Delta Phi (bd. dirs. 1980, J. Mark McCarthy award 1980), Sigma Delta Epsilon. Club: Toastmasters. State civil litigation, Federal civil litigation, Personal injury. Home and Office: 113 Kay St Ithaca NY 14850

MUKAIDA, WAYNE HIDEO, lawyer; b. Honolulu, July 1, 1952; s. Tomio and Shizuko (Kohatsu) M. BBA, U. Hawaii, 1975; JD, Gonzaga U., 1978. Bar: Hawaii 1978, U.S. Dist. Ct. Hawaii 1978, U.S. Ct. Appeals (9th cir.) 1980. Law clk. Family Ct., Honolulu, 1978-80; assoc. Law Offices of Ronald Au, Honolulu, 1980-85, Law Offices of Rueben Wong, Honolulu, 1985—; arbitrator Supreme Ct. Hawaii, Honolulu, 1986; vol. atty. Hawaii Lawyers Care, Honolulu, 1985-86. Mem. ABA, Hawaii State Bar Assn. State civil litigation, Personal injury, Construction. Office: Law Offices of Rueben Wong 1001 Bishop St Pacific Tower Suite 1630 Honolulu HI 96813

MUKAMAL, STUART SASSOON, lawyer, educator; b. Kew Gardens, N.Y., July 10, 1951; s. Meir S. Mukamal and Florence S. Appel; m. Diane Edwards, June 29, 1984. BA, Brandeis U., 1973; JD, Yale U., 1976. Bar: Wis. 1976, D.C. 1979. Assoc. Foley & Lardner, Milw., 1976-78; mediator, arbitrator, examiner Wis. Employment Relations Commn., Milw., 1978-81; assoc. Brynelson, Herrick, Gehl & Bucaida, Madison, Wis., 1981-84; atty. City of Milw., 1984—; instr. mgmt. indsl. labor relations U. Wis., Milw., 1985—. Author: Federal Wage/Hour and Equal Pay Requirements, 1985; also articles. Mem. Wis. Bar Assn. (dir. labor law sect. 1983—), Wis. Pub. Employer Labor Relations Assn., Indsl. Relations Research Assn. (Wis. chpt.), Nat. Inst. Mcpl. Law Officers (chmn. personnel and labor relations sect. 1984—). Democrat. Jewish. Avocations: baseball, golf. Labor, Administrative and regulatory, Local government. Home: 240 N Pinecrest St Milwaukee WI 53208 Office: City Attys Office 200 E Wells St 800 City Hall Milwaukee WI 53202

MULACK, DONALD G., lawyer; b. Ladysmith, Wis., Jan. 3, 1942; s. Joseph and Bernice (Glowacki) M.; m. Rozanne Faraco, July 25, 1964; children—David Justin, Jason Daniel, Danielle Judith. B.S., No. Ill. U., 1963; J.D., ITT/Chgo. Kent Coll. Law, 1966. Bar: Ill. 1966, U.S. Dist. Ct. (no. dist.) Ill. 1967, Fla. 1976, U.S. Ct. Appeals (7th cir.) 1979, U.S. Supreme Ct. 1979. Asst. atty. gen. State of Ill., Chgo., 1969-74, chief fraud div. Office of Atty. Gen., 1976-78, chief charity div., 1974-76; ptnr. Keck, Mahin & Cate, Chgo., 1978—. Republican candidate for Cook County Sheriff, 1978; campaign. chmn. 10th congl. dist. Reagan for Pres. 1980; mem. Chgo. Crime Commn., 1983—; eagle scout coordinator Boy Scouts Am., Glencoe, Ill., 1983—. Mem. Chgo. Bar Assn., Phi Delta Phi. Club: Skokie Country (Glencoe). Federal civil litigation, State civil litigation, Contracts commercial. Office: Keck Mahin & Cate 8300 Sears Tower Chicago IL 60606

MULCAHY, DANIEL JOSEPH, JR., lawyer; b. Chgo., Feb. 19, 1947; s. Daniel J. Sr. and Phyllis A. (Terhune) M.; m. Patricia Manzel, July 28, 1985; children: Sarah, Beth. BA, St. Mary's Coll., 1969; JD, Loyola U., 1972. Bar: Ill. 1972, U.S. Dist. Ct. (no. dist.) Ill. 1972, U.S. Ct. Appeals (7th cir.) 1975. Assoc. Gilmartin, Schroeder & Hacker, Chgo., 1972-85; claims mgr. Scarborough and Co., Chgo., 1986-87, v.p. claims, 1987—. Mem. ABA, Ill. Bar Assn., Chgo. Bar Assn. Roman Catholic. Banking, Insurance, Federal civil litigation. Office: Scarborough and Co 123 N Wacker Dr Chicago IL 60606

MULHERN, EDWIN JOSEPH, lawyer; b. Bklyn., Mar. 8, 1927; s. Edward Thomas and Jennie (Keenan) M.; m. Maureen P. Purcell, Oct. 2, 1964; children—Edwin T., Deborah J., Kevin T. B.B.A., St. John's U., 1950, LL.B., 1954. Bar: N.Y. 1954, U.S. Dist. Ct. (ea. and so. dists.) N.Y. 1954, U.S. Supreme Ct. 1960. Sr. acct. Susquehanna Mills Inc., N.Y.C., 1947-53; chief acct. Rockwood Chocolate Co., Bklyn., 1953-54; trial atty. Allstate Ins. Co., Freeport, N.Y., 1954-57; claims rep. State Farm Ins. Co., Hempstead, N.Y., 1957-58; sole practice, Bellmore, N.Y., 1958-70, Mineola, N.Y., 1970-81, Carle Place, N.Y., 1981—; mem. joint grievance com. for 10th jud. dist. (N.Y.). Pres. Christian Bros. Boys' Assn., 1975-82; bd. dirs. Legal Aid Soc. of Nassau County. Served with USAAF, 1945-46. Mem. ABA, N.Y. State Bar Assn., Nassau Bar Assn. (bd. dirs. 1981-83), Suffolk County Bar Assn., Nassau Lawyers Assn. (pres. 1975, Man of Yr. 1981), Criminal Cts. Bar Assn. of Nassau County (pres. 1976), Criminal Cts. Bar Assn. of Suffolk County, Am. Assn. Trial Lawyers. Clubs: University of L.I. (Hempstead), K.C. (new Hyde Park, N.Y.). Criminal, Family and matrimonial, Personal injury. Office: 1 Old Country Rd Suite 145 Carle Place NY 11514

MULHERN, JOHN JOSEPH, lawyer; b. Buffalo, Aug. 11, 1919; s. Bernard and Johanna (O'Leary) M.; m. Jean Eileen Beecdgalupo, Sept. 11, 1948; children: Brian, Mary, Terence, John F., Ann, Patricia, Thomas. BA, Canisius Coll., 1947; JD, Fordham U., 1952. Bar: N.Y. 1953, U.S. Supreme Ct. 1964, N.Mex. 1971, U.S. Dist. Ct. N.Mex. 1979. Sole practice Albuquerque, 1952—. Served to 1st lt. AUS, 1943-46. Republican. Roman Catholic. Avocation: bridge. Consumer commercial, Real property, Probate. Home: 1404 Washington NE Albuquerque NM 87110 Office: 1101 Cardenas NE Albuquerque NM 87110

MULHERN, PATRICK J., lawyer, banker; b. N.Y.C., Mar. 17, 1928; s. John J. and Beatrice (Gilholly) M.; m. Joan F. Cassidy, June 14, 1952; children—Eileen, John, Barbara. B.S., Fordham U., 1952, J.D., 1955. Bar: N.Y. 1955, U.S. Dist. Ct. (so. dist.) N.Y. Assoc. counsel Shearman & Sterling, 1955-66; v.p. cashier's adminstrn. Citibank N.A., N.Y.C., 1966-79, sr. v.p. Office of Gen. Counsel, 1979-80, sr. v.p., gen. counsel, 1980—. Served with U.S. Army, 1946-47. Mem. Assn. Bar City of N.Y., Am. Soc. Corp. Secs., ABA, Fed. Bar Assn. Clubs: University (N.Y.C.); Unqua Corinthian Yacht (Massapequa, N.Y.). Lodges: K.C., Kiwanis. Office: Citicorp 399 Park Ave New York NY 10043

MULL, GALE W., lawyer; b. Hillsdale, Mich., Sept. 8, 1945; s. Wayne E. and Vivien M. (Bavin) M.; m. Holly Ann Allen, Aug. 2, 1969 (div. Nov. 1983); 1 child, Carter B.; m. Jeanne Anne Haughey, Aug. 18, 1985. BA, Mich. State U., 1967; MA in Sociology, Ind. U., 1969; JD, Emory U., 1972. Bar: Ga. 1972, U.S. Dist. Ct. (no. dist.) Ga. 1972, U.S. Ct. Appeals (5th cir.) 1973, U.S. Ct. Appeals (11th cir.) 1981. Sole practice Atlanta, 1972-75; ptnr. Mull & Sweet, Atlanta, 1975-81; pres. Gale W. Mull, P.C., Atlanta, 1981—; bd. dirs. BOND Community Fed. Credit Union, Atlanta, 1975-81; directing atty. Emory Student Legal Services, Atlanta, 1975—. Pres. Inman Park Restoration, Inc., Atlanta, 1972-74, BASS Orgn. for Neighborhood Devel., Inc., 1974-78; mem. Housing Appeals Bd., Atlanta, 1982-; mem. Mayor's Task Force on Prostitution, 1984—. Mem. ABA, Ga. Bar Assn., Atlanta Bar Assn. Clubs: East Lake Country; Quail Unltd. (bd. dirs., sec. 1984—). General practice, Family and matrimonial, Criminal. Office: 990 Edgewood Ave NE Atlanta GA 30307

MULL, RICHARD EUGENE, lawyer; b. Rock Island, Ill., Feb. 8, 1952; s. Eugene Gus and Alice Naomi (Irish) M.; m. Elise Mary Wright, July 7, 1979; children: Meredith Anne, Matthew David. BBA, U. Iowa, 1974, JD with distinction, 1977. Bar: Iowa 1977, U.S. Dist. Ct. (no. and so. dists.) Iowa 1978, U.S. Ct. Appeals (8th cir.) 1978. Dep. clk. Iowa Supreme Ct., Des Moines, 1977-78; asst. atty. gen. Iowa Dept. Justice, Ames, 1978—. Mem. ABA, Assn. Trial Lawyers Am., Def. Research Inst., Iowa State Bar Assn., Iowa Def. Counsel Assn., Assn. Trial Lawyers of Iowa, Iowa Alumni Assn., Story County Bar Assn., Phi Delta Phi. Methodist. Club: Iowa State U. Tennis (Ames). Avocations: tennis, music. State civil litigation, Personal injury, Condemnation. Home: 2515 Woodview Dr Ames IA 50010 Office: Iowa Dept JusticeTransp Div 800 Lincoln Way Ames IA 50010

MULLANE, JOHN FRANCIS, pharmaceutical company executive; b. N.Y.C., Mar. 10, 1937; s. John Gerard and Rita Ann (Hoben) M.; m. Ruth Ann Cecka, Nov. 17, 1962; children—Rosemarie, Michael, Kathleen, Therese, Thomas. M.D., SUNY, 1963, Ph.D., 1968; J.D., Fordham U., 1977. Bar: N.Y. 1978, D.C. 1979. Assoc. med. dir. Ayerst Labs. div. Am. Home Products Corp., N.Y.C., 1973-75, dir. clin. research, 1975-76, v.p. clin., 1977, v.p. sci., 1978-82, sr. v.p., 1982, exec. v.p., 1983—. Contbr. articles to profl. jours. Served to lt. col. U.S. Army, 1970-73. Recipient Upjohn Achievement award, 1970; N.Y. Heart Assn. Crawford-Maynard fellow, 1966-68. Fellow Am. Coll. Clin. Pharmacology; mem. Am. Soc. Nephrology, ABA, Am. Soc. Clin. Pharmacology and Therapeutics, Am. Assn. Study of Liver Diseases. Roman Catholic. Club: Pelham Country, Bald Head Island Golf. Avocation: golf. Home: 132 E 35th St Apt 7H New York NY 10016 Office: Ayerst Labs Am Home Products Corp 685 3d Ave New York NY 10017

MULLANEY, THOMAS JOSEPH, lawyer; b. N.Y.C., Feb. 9, 1946; s. James Joseph and Dorothy Mary (Fulling) M.; m. Christine E. Hampton, Aug. 16, 1969; children—Richard, Jennette. B.A., Fordham U., 1967; J.D., U. Va., 1970; LL.M., NYU, 1977. Bar: Va. 1970, N.Y. 1971, U.S. Dist. Ct. (so. and ea. dists.) N.Y. 1972, U.S. Ct. Appeals (2d cir.) 1972, U.S. Supreme Ct. 1975. Assoc. Brown, Wood, Ivey, Mitchell & Petty, N.Y.C., 1970-79; assoc. Law Offices of John M. Kenney, Garden City, N.Y., 1979-84; ptnr. Abrams & Thaw, N.Y.C. and Farmingdale, N.Y., 1985—. Served to capt. JAGC, U.S. Army, 1971-74. Mem. Va. State Bar Assn., N.Y. State Bar Assn., Republican. Roman Catholic. Federal civil litigation, State civil litigation, Securities. Home: 104 Huntington Rd Garden City NY 11530 Office: 45 Banfi Plaza Farmingdale NY 11735

MULLEN, JOHN CLANCY, lawyer; b. Falls City, Nebr., Sept. 26, 1919; s. John Clancy and Helen Agnes (Majerus) M.; m. Kathleen Florence Diesing, June 4, 1949; children—Michael, Clancy, Kathy, Dennis, Monica. AB., Creighton U., 1941; LL.B., Harvard U., 1948. Bar: Tex. 1948. Sole practice, Alice, Tex., 1948—; mcpl. judge City Alice, 1951-52; county atty. Jim Wells County, 1955-68; dist. atty. 79th Jud. Dist., Alice, 1974-76. Pres., Jim Wells Co. Master Plan, 1970-71. Chmn., United Fund, 1961. Served as sgt. AUS, 1942-46. Mem. Coastal Bend Bar Assn. (pres. 1969-70), Tex. Bar Assn. Democrat. Roman Catholic. Lodges: Rotary, Elks. State civil litigation, Criminal, Family and matrimonial. Home: 713 Schallert St Alice TX 78332 Office: 112 N Adams St Alice TX 78332

MULLEN, MARGARET JEAN, lawyer; b. Milw., Dec. 3, 1956; d. Richard John and Virginia Rita (Lahey) M.; m. Terry Wayne Campton, Mar. 31,

1977. BA, Ill. State U., Normal, 1977; JD with distinction, John Marshall Sch. of Law, 1980. Bar: Ill. 1980, U.S. Dist. Ct. (no. dist.) Ill. 1982. Law clk. to presiding justice Ill. Appellate Ct., Crystal Lake, 1980-81; asst. state's atty. Dupage County State's Atty.'s Office, Wheaton, Ill., 1981-82; prin. asst. state's atty. Lake County State's Atty.'s Office, Waukegan, Ill., 1982-87, chief juvenile trial div., 1987—; legal intern US Atty.'s Office, Chgo., 1980. Sustaining mem. Northern Ill. Blood Bank, Glenview, 1983—; mem. Lake County Rep. Fedn., Waukegan, 1984—. Recipient Resolution of Commendation Lake County Sheriff's Merit Commn., 1984, Letter of Commendation City of Libertyville, 1986. Mem. ABA, Ill. Bar Assn., Lake County Bar Assn. Club: Young Irish Fellowship (Chgo.). Avocations: horseback riding, waterskiing, golf, downhill skiing. Criminal. Home: 472 Mawman Lake Bluff IL 60044 Office: Lake County States Atty's Office 18 N County Waukegan IL 60085

MULLEN, MICHAEL FRANCIS, lawyer, judge; b. Bronx, N.Y., May 27, 1937; s. John Patrick and Mary Catherine (Coyle) M.; m. Ann Marie Casey, Dec. 30, 1961; children—Michael, Matthew, Maura, Margaret, Mary, Mark. A.B. in English, Fairfield U., 1959; LL.B., St. John's U., Bklyn., 1962. Bar: N.Y. 1963, U.S. Dist. Ct. (so. and ea. dists.) N.Y. 1975, U.S. Ct. Appeals (2d cir.) 1975. Assoc. Clare & Whitehead, N.Y.C. 1965-67; law sec. Appellate Div., 2d Dept., Bklyn., 1968-75; sole practice, Huntington, N.Y., 1976—; referee in incompetency N.Y. State Supreme Ct., Suffolk County, 1976—; judge N.Y. State Ct. Claims, 1987—; counsel N.Y. State Senate Environ. Conservation Com., Albany, 1977-78; asst. counsel N.Y. State Senate Majority Leader, Albany, 1979—. Mem. Suffolk County Bar Assn. (chmn. grievance com. 1981-83). Republican. Roman Catholic. Lodge: Elks. State civil litigation, Probate, General practice. Office: 425 New York Ave Huntington NY 11743

MULLEN, PETER P., lawyer; b. N.Y.C., Apr. 8, 1928. A.B., Georgetown U., 1948; LL.B., Columbia U., 1951. Bar: N.Y. 1951. Assoc. firm Dewey Ballantine Bushby Palmer & Wood, N.Y.C., 1951-61; partner firm Skadden Arps Slate Meagher & Flom, N.Y.C., 1961—, exec. ptnr., 1982—. Bd. dirs. Lawrence Hosp., Bronxville, N.Y., Project Orbis, Georgetown U., Washington, 1982—, chmn., 1985—; mem. Bd. Edn. Bronxville, N.Y., 1976—, pres., 1979-81. Mem. Am. Bar Assn., N.Y. State Bar Assn. (com. securities regulation 1980-83), Assn. Bar City N.Y. (com. corp. law 1964-67, com. admissions 1965-68, com. securities regulation 1970-73). Office: Skadden Arps Slate Meagher & Flom 919 3rd ave New York NY 10022

MULLEN, THOMAS MOORE, lawyer; b. Redding, Calif., June 20, 1915; s. Thomas B. and Enid (Moore) M.; m. Agnes Druecker, July 7, 1941; children: Thomas Moore, Patricia, Cheryl, Kathleen. B.S., U. San Francisco, 1937; J.D., Hastings Coll. Law, 1939. Bar: Calif. 1939. Practice in Redding, 1939-41; ptnr. firm Cavaletto, Webster, Mullen & McCaughey, Santa Barbara, Calif., 1946-82, Mullen, McCaughey & Henzell, Santa Barbara, Calif., 1982—; Bar Examiner State Bar of Calif., 1963-65. Del. Republican Nat. Conv., 1948; chmn. Rep. Central Com. Santa Barbara County, 1946-48. Served to col. AUS, 1941-46. Mem. Santa Barbara County Bar Assn. (pres. 1968-69). Club: Rotarian (pres. Santa Barbara 1949-50). Insurance, Personal injury. Home: 770 Mission Canyon Rd Santa Barbara CA 93105 Office: Mullen McCaughey & Henzell 112 E Victoria St Santa Barbara CA 93101

MULLEN, WILLIAM DAVID, lawyer; b. Walnut Ridge, Ark., Jan. 15, 1949; s. William Lemoyne and Margaret V. (Finley) M.; m. Judy C. McNamee, Jan. 24, 1970 (div. Aug. 1977); children: Gwen, Mary. Student, Harding U., 1967-68; BS, Ark. State U., 1970; JD, U. Ark., Little Rock, 1976. Bar: Ark. 1976, U.S. Dist. Ct. (Ark.) 1976. Owner, operator Walnut Ridge, 1970-71; abstracter Little Rock Abstract Co., 1972-76; sole practice Walnut Ridge, 1976—; agt. Chgo. Title Ins. Co., 1977—, So. Title Ins. Co., Knoxville, Tenn., 1982—; county atty., dep. prosecutor Lawrence County, Walnut Ridge, 1979; atty. City of Ravenden, Ark., 1980—; lectr. So. Bapt. Coll., Walnut Ridge, 1980—; cons. Lawrence County Bank, Portia, Ark., 1984—; sec. Northeast Ark. Legal Services, Newport, 1986—, bd. dirs. 1978-81, 86—. Coach Walnut Ridge Little League, 1979-84; dir. Walnut Ridge Christmas Parade, 1981—. Mem. ABA, Ark. Bar Assn. (named Outstanding Citizen 1982), Lawrence-Randolph County Bar Assn. (pres. 1983-85), Walnut Ridge Jaycees (pres. 1982, bd. dirs. 1981—, named Key Man 1981, named Outstanding Local Pres. Ark. Jaycees 1982, recipient BUBBA award 1983). Democrat. Mem. Christian Ch. Avocations: water skiing, quail hunting. General practice, State civil litigation, Criminal. Home: 1011 SE Front St Walnut Ridge AR 72476 Office: 119 SW 2d St PO Box 567 Walnut Ridge AR 72476

MULLENBACH, LINDA HERMAN, lawyer; b. Sioux City, Iowa, Dec. 25, 1948; d. Verner Wilhelm and Margaretta Victoria (Grant) Herman; m. Hugh James Mullenbach, Aug. 22, 1970; 1 child, Erika Lynn. BS in Speech, Northwestern U., 1971, MS in Speech, 1972, JD, 1979. Bar: Ill. 1979, U.S. Dist. Ct. (no. dist.) Ill. 1979, D.C. 1983, U.S. Dist. Ct. D.C. 1983, U.S. Ct. Appeals (7th, D.C. and fed. cirs.), 1983, U.S. Supreme Ct. 1984. Assoc. Jenner & Block, Chgo., 1979-83; assoc. Dickstein, Shapiro & Morin, Washington, 1983-85, prin., 1985—. Mem. ABA (litigation sect.), D.C. Bar Assn., Women's Bar Assn. D.C., Women's Legal Def. Fund, Assn. Trial Lawyer Am., Mortar Bd., Zeta Phi Eta. Federal civil litigation, Criminal. Home: 8201 Killean Way Potomac MD 20854

MULLENDORE, JAMES MYERS, lawyer; b. Charlottesville, Va., Mar. 21, 1946; s. James M. and Elaine (Gregg) M.; m. Kristine B. Mullendore; children—Margaret E., Sean T. B.S., W.Va. U., 1968; J.D., U. Va., 1975. Bar: Mich. 1975, U.S. Dist. Ct. (we. dist.) Mich. Ptnr. Frye, Mullendore & Carr, Greenville, Mich., 1975—; dir. Comml. Bank, Greenville, 1979—. Pres., v.p. Greenville Bd. Edn., 1978-82; ofcl. Mid-Am. Football Conf., 1985-86, Big Ten Football Conf., 1987—; bd. dirs. United Way of Greenville, 1978-83. Mem. ABA, Assn. Trial Lawyers Am., Mich. Trial Lawyers Assn., Ionia-Montcalm Bar Assn. (pres. 1982-83), U.S. Football League (ofcl. 1983). Congregationalist. Lodge: Rotary (v.p. 1983-84). Personal injury, Criminal, Family and matrimonial. Home: 5877 Fenwick Rd Greenville MI 48838 Office: PO Box 100 132 S Lafayette St Greenville MI 48838

MULLENIX, LINDA SUSAN, lawyer, educator; b. N.Y.C., Oct. 16, 1950; d. Andrew Michael and Roslyn (Rosenthal) Marasco; m. James William Mullenix, Sept. 26, 1981; children—Robert Bartholomew, John Theodore, William Joseph. B.A., CCNY, 1971; M. Philosophy, Columbia U., 1974, Ph.D. (Pres.'s fellow), 1977; J.D., Georgetown U., 1980. Bar: D.C. 1981, U.S. Dist Ct. D.C. 1981, U.S. Supreme Ct. 1986. U.S. Ct. Appeals (D.C. cir.) 1981. Assoc. prof., lectr. George Washington U., Washington, 1977-80; asst. prof. Am. U., Washington, 1979; clin. prof. Loyola U. Law Sch., Los Angeles, 1981-82, vis. asst. prof., 1982-83; vis. asst. prof. Catholic U. Law Sch., Washington, 1983-84, asst. prof., 1984-86, assoc. prof., 1986—; assoc. Pierson, Ball & Dowd, Washington, 1980-81; adj. instr. Fordham U., N.Y.C., 1975-76, adj. asst. prof. 1977; adj. asst. prof. CCNY, 1977; adj. instr., adj. asst. prof. Cooper Union Advancement Sci., Art, N.Y.C., 1977; instr. N.Y. Inst. Tech., N.Y.C., 1976, U. Md. European div., Ramstein, Germany, 1974. Editor bibliographies Political Theory, A Jour. Polit. Philosophy, 1972-74; The Tax Lawyer Jour., 1978-80; contbr. articles to profl. publs. Alt. del. Va. Democratic State Conv., 1980. Fellow NDEA, 1971-74, Georgetown U. Law Sch., 1978; N.Y. State Regents scholar, 1967-71. Mem. D.C. Bar Assn., Women's Bar Assn. D.C., ABA, Phi Beta Kappa, Phi Alpha Delta. Legal education, Jurisprudence, Federal civil litigation. Home: 6221 Redwing Rd Bethesda MD 20817 Office: Cath U Am Columbus Sch Law Washington DC 20064

MULLER, CARL FREDERICK, lawyer; b. Charlotte, N.C., Aug. 30, 1951; s. George Frederick and Catherine (McCuen) M.; m. Katherine Allison Gulick, Sept. 17, 1977; children: Katherine Allidah, Charles Wiley. AB magna cum laude, Harvard U., 1973, JD, MBA, 1977. Bar: S.C. 1978, U.S. Ct. Appeals (4th cir.) 1978, U.S. Ct. Appeals (5th cir.) 1983, U.S. Supreme Ct. 1984. Ptnr. Wyche, Burgess, Freeman & Parham P.A., Greenville, S.C., 1977—; bd. dirs. Legal Services Agy. of Western Carolina, Greenville. Pres. Phillis Wheatley Assn., Greenville, 1985-86; elder Westminster Presbyn. Ch., Greenville, 1986—; bd. dirs. Greenville Arts Festival, 1983—. Recipient Saltonstall prize Harvard U., 1973. Mem. S.C. Bar Assn., Greenville County Bar Assn., Phi Beta Kappa. Club: Piedmont Econs. (Greenville). Lodge: Masons. General corporate. Home: 130 Wilderness Ln Greenville SC 29607 Office: Wyche Burgess Freeman & Parham PA 44 E Camperdown Way Greenville SC 29603

MULLER, EDWARD ROBERT, lawyer; b. Phila., Mar. 26, 1952; s. Rudolph E. and Elizabeth (Steiner) M.; m. Patricia Eileen Bauer, Sept. 27, 1980; children—Margaret Anne, John Frederick. A.B. summa cum laude, Dartmouth Coll., Hanover, N.H., 1973; J.D., Yale U., New Haven, 1976. Assoc. Leva, Hawes, Symington, Martin & Oppenheimer, Washington, 1977-83; atty., health care exec. Whittaker Corp., Washington, 1983-85; v.p., gen. counsel, sec. Whittaker Corp., Los Angeles, 1985—. Mem. Phi Beta Kappa. General corporate, Federal civil litigation. Office: Whittaker Corp 10880 Wilshire Blvd Los Angeles CA 90024

MULLER, FREDERICK ARTHUR, legal editor, publisher; b. Center Moriches, N.Y., Dec. 18, 1937; s. Frederick Henry and Estelle May (Reeve) M.; m. Ellen Ruth Willard, Sept. 8, 1962; children—John F., Matthew R. B.A., U. Rochester, N.Y., 1960; J.D., U. Chgo., 1963. Bar: Ill. 1963, N.Y. 1964, U.S. Ct. Mil. Appeals 1965, U.S. Dist. Ct. (we. dist.) N.Y. 1971. Law clk. to judge N.Y. State. Ct. Appeals, 1968-69, 72; assoc. Hodgson, Russ, Andrews, Woods & Goodyear, Buffalo, 1969-72; asst. consultation clk. N.Y. State Ct. Apls., 1973-82; dep. state reporter State of N.Y., 1982—; cons. staff atty. N.Y. State Ct. on Judiciary, 1973; chmn. supervisory com. Stewart AFB Fed. Credit Union, 1964-65. Editor N.Y. State Official Style Manual, 1985, 87. Mem. budget and allocations com. United Way Northeastern N.Y., Inc., 1975-80. Served with JAGC USAF, 1964-67. Mem. N.Y. State Bar Assn., Nat. Assn. Reporters of Jud. Decisions, U. Chgo. Club (chmn. alumni schs. com., 1984-87, bd. dirs. 1986—), Phi Beta Kappa, Phi Delta Phi. Baptist. Club: Tri-City Racquet (Latham, N.Y.). legal editing and publishing. Home: 47 Hiawatha Dr Guilderland NY 12084 Office: One Commerce Plaza Suite 1750 Albany NY 12210

MULLER, JOHANNES JOSEPH, lawyer; b. Buch, Thurgau, Switzerland, Mar. 24, 1930; s. Josef and Anna (Wirth) M.; m. Jacqueline Vinatier, Dec. 26, 1964; children: Nicolas, Veronique, Jean-Marc. LLB, U. Fribourg, Switzerland, 1956, JD, 1960; LLM, Yale U., 1958; postdoctoral, Stanford U., 1958-59; JD, Ill. Inst. Tech., 1966. Bar: Ill. 1966. Assoc. Lehner-Homburger, Zurich, Switzerland, 1959-63; assoc. Baker & McKenzie, Chgo., 1963-67, ptnr., 1967—; ptnr. Homburger, Acherman, Muller & Heini, Zurich, 1966—. Author: Formation of a Corporation in the USA, 1978, Characteristics of Corporation Law in the USA, 1983. Active various polit. and ch. orgns. Mem. ABA, Ill. Bar Assn., Chgo. Bar Assn., Zurich Bar Assn. General corporate, General practice, Private international. Home: Rebhusstrasse 15, 8126 Zumikon, Canton of Zurich Switzerland 8126 Office: Baker & McKenzie, Zollikerstrasse 225, Zurich Switzerland 8008

MULLER, JOHN, lawyer; b. N.Y.C., Nov. 20, 1947; s. Paul Frederick and Ruth Ann (Courtney) M.; m. Susan M. Wente, May 14, 1980. BA, U. Notre Dame, 1969; JD, George Washington U., 1973. Assoc. Steers, Sullivan, McNamar & Rogers, Indpls., 1973-75; trial atty. Marion County Prosecutors, Indpls., 1975-77; pub. defender Marion County Criminal Ct., Indpls., 1977-80; ptnr. Mendelson, Kennedy, Miller, Muller & Hall, Indpls., 1980—; adj. prof. law Marian Coll., Indpls., 1979; cons. Ind. Pub. Defender Counsel, Indpls., 1980. Chmn. commn. Indpls. Nuclear Weapons Freeze, 1984; bd. dirs. United Way Budget Allocation Commn., Indpls., 1983; bd. dirs. exec. com. Marion County Dems., Indpls., 1983—, fin. com., 1983-86. Mem. Ind. Bar Assn., Indpls. Bar Assn., Assn. Trial Lawyers Am., Ind. Trial Lawyers Assn. Democrat. Roman Catholic. Avocation: computers. Federal civil litigation, State civil litigation, Personal injury. Home: 7502 N Pennsylvania St Indianapolis IN 46240 Office: Mendelson Kennedy Miller Muller & Hall 22 E Washington St Suite 600 Indianapolis IN 46204

MULLER, SCOTT WILLIAM, lawyer; b. Stamford, Conn., Feb. 15, 1950; s. Robert Sielke and Patricia (Harris) M.; m. Caroline Severance Adams, June 24, 1972; children: Christopher Adams, Robin McPherson, Peter Severance. BA, Princeton U., 1971; JD, Georgetown U., 1975. Bar: N.Y. 1976, U.S. Dist. Ct. (so. dist.) N.Y. 1977, U.S. Ct. Appeals (2d. cir.) 1978, U.S. Supreme Ct. 1978, U.S. Tax Ct. 1984, D.C. 1986. Law clk. to presiding justice U.S. Ct. Appeals (3d cir.), Phila., 1975-76; assoc. Davis, Polk & Wardwell, Washington, 1976-78, 82-84, ptnr., 1985—; asst. atty. criminal div. U.S. Atty.'s Office, N.Y.C., 1978-82. Served with NG, 1971-72. Mem. ABA, N.Y. State Bar Assn., Fed. Bar Assn., Assn. of Bar of City of N.Y. Republican. Episcopalian. Federal civil litigation, Criminal, Securities. Home: 20 Magnolia Chevy Chase MD 20815 Office: Davis Polk & Wardwell 1575 Eye St NW Washington DC 20005

MULLIGAN, ELINOR PATTERSON, lawyer; b. Bay City, Mich., Apr. 20, 1929; d. Frank Clark and Agnes (Murphy) P.; m. John C. O'Connor, Oct. 28, 1950; children—Christine O'Connor, Valerie O'Connor, Amy O'Connor, Christopher Criffan O'Connor; m. 2d, William G. Mulligan, Dec. 6, 1975. B.A., U. Mich. 1950; J.D., Seton Hall U., 1970. Bar: N.J., 1970. Assoc. firms Springfield and Newark, 1970-72; sole practice, Hackettstown, N.J., 1972; ptnr. Mulligan & Jacobson, N.Y.C., 1973—, Mulligan & Mulligan (now Mulligan, Mulligan & Gavin), Hackettstown, 1976—; atty. Hackettstown Planning Bd., 1973—, Blairstown Bd. Adjustment, 1973—; sec. Warren County Ethics Com., 1976-78, sec. Dist. X Fee Arbitration Com., 1979—; mem. spl. com. on atty. disciplinary structure N.J. Supreme Ct., 1981—. lectr. Nat. Assn. Women Judges. Named Vol. of Yr., Attys. Vols. in Parole Program, 1978. Fellow Am. Acad. Matrimonial Lawyers; mem. Warren County Bar Assn., N.J. State Bar Assn., ABA, Am. Mensa Soc., Kappa Alpha Theta. Republican. Clubs: Union League (N.Y.C.); Baltusrol Golf (Springfield, N.J.); Panther Valley Golf and Country (Allamuchy, N.J.). Family and matrimonial, State civil litigation, General practice. Home: 12 Goldfinch Way Panther Valley Hackettstown NJ 07840 Office: 480 Hwy 517 PO Box 211 Hackettstown NJ 07840

MULLIGAN, JAMES FRANCIS, business executive, lawyer; b. Attleboro, Mass., Aug. 27, 1925; s. Henry D. and Eleanor R. (Carey) M.; m. Mary Alice Mangels, Aug. 28, 1948; 1 son, Christopher. A.B., Tufts U., 1947; J.D., Columbia U., 1950. Bar: N.Y. 1950, Pa. 1968. Gen. atty. Erie-Lackawanna R.R., N.Y.C., 1950-61; gen. counsel Monroe Internat. div. Litton Industries, Orange, N.J., 1961-67; v.p., sec., gen. counsel Lukens Steel Co., Coatesville, Pa., 1967-83; v.p. law and corp. affairs, sec. Lukens, Inc., Coatesville, Pa., 1983—. Pres. United Way of Chester County. Served to ensign USN, 1943-46. Mem. Am. Bar Assn., Pa. Bar Assn., Am. Soc. Corp. Secs., Nat. Investor Relations Inst. Home: 1060 Squire Cheney Dr West Chester PA 19382 Office: Lukens Inc Coatesville PA 19320

MULLIGAN, JENNIFER, lawyer, law educator; b. Indpls., Mar. 16, 1954; d. William Albert and Joan Lucille (Frost) M. BA, Roanoke Coll., 1976; JD, Wake Forest U., 1979. Bar: Va. 1979, U.S. Dist. Ct. (we. dist.) Va. 1979, U.S. Ct. Appeals (4th cir.) 1979. Atty. Legal Clinic of Tonita Foster, Roanoke, Va., 1979-81; ptnr. Spencer & Mulligan, Roanoke, 1981-86; asst. prof. bus. law Va. Western Community Coll., Roanoke, Va., 1983—; sole practice Roanoke, 1986—; adj. faculty Roanoke Coll., Salem, Va., 1986—. Mem. ABA, Va. Bar Assn., Roanoke Bar Assn. (chmn. spl. events 1984—), Blue Ridge Soaring Soc. (tng. officer, v.p. 1984—). Avocations: flying sailplanes, airplanes. Legal education, Family and matrimonial, Bankruptcy. Home: 2328 Westover Ave SW Roanoke VA 24015 Office: PO Box 4419 Roanoke VA 24015

MULLIGAN, JOHN THOMAS, lawyer; b. Phila., Dec. 28, 1934; s. Martin A. and Mary Katherine (Glennon) M.; m. Marie A. Pinter, Aug. 22, 1959; children—Mary T., Lisa M. B.S. in Polit. Sci., St. Joseph's U., 1956; J.D. cum laude, U. Pa., 1959. Bar: N.Y. 1960, Pa. 1963, U.S. Dist. Ct. (so. and ea. dists.) N.Y. 1962, U.S. Dist. Ct. (ea. dist.) Pa. 1964, U.S. Tax Ct. 1962, U.S. Ct. Appeals (3d cir. 1965), U.S. Supreme Ct. 1965. Assoc. Dewey, Ballantine, Bushby, Palmer & Wood, N.Y.C., 1959-62; sr. atty. Western Electric Co., N.Y.C., 1962-63; ptnr. Lord & Mulligan, Media, Pa., 1963—; solicitor Marple Twp., Broomall, Pa., 1970-71, Haverford Twp., Havertown, Pa., 1972-73, Radnor-Haverford-Marple Sewer Authority, Wayne, Pa., 1974-83; panel mem. Fed. Ct. Arbitration, Phila., 1977—. Mem. Haverford Twp. Adult Sch., Haverford, Pa., 1965-66; fin. chmn. Haverford Twp. Democratic Com., Havertown, 1965-70. Recipient Commendation U.S. Dist Ct. (ea. dist.) Pa. 1983. Mem. Assn. Trial Lawyers Am., ABA, Pa. Trial Lawyers Assn., Pa. Bar Assn., N.Y. State Bar Assn., Delaware County Bar Assn., Assn. Bar City of N.Y. Democrat. Roman Catholic. Clubs: Llanerch Country (Havertown, Pa.) (sec. 1977-81); Seaview Country (Absecon, N.J.); Atlantic City Country (Northfield, N.J.). Federal civil litigation, State civil litigation, Environment. Home: 2728 N Kent Rd Broomall PA 19008 Office: Lord and Mulligan 15 W Front St Media PA 19063

MULLIGAN, WILLIAM G(EORGE), lawyer; b. N.Y.C., July 16, 1906; s. William George and Agnes (Murphy) M.; m. Dorothy K. Zimmer, Jan. 27, 1928; 1 dau., Maura Elaine; m. Mary Luciel McGookey, Sept. 6, 1942; children—Don John (dec.), Luciel Laurene; m. Elinor Patterson O'Connor, Dec. 6, 1975. A.B., Hamilton Coll., 1927; LL.B., Harvard U., 1930. Bar: N.Y. 1931, N.J. 1976. Asst. Wickersham Crime Commn., 1929-30; asst. to Hon. Hiram C. Todd, spl. dep. N.Y. atty. gen. pros. jud. frauds, 1930-31; asst. Hon. Samuel Seabury in proceedings before N.Y. State Gov. Franklin D. Roosevelt to remove James J. Walker as mayor of N.Y. City, 1931-32; assoc. White & Case, 1932-34; asst. corp. counsel City N.Y., 1934-38; chief div. transit 1936, chief div. franchises, 1938; asso. counsel Bd. Transportation, 1939-40; sr. ptnr. various law firms since 1940; now Mulligan, Jacobson & Langenus and predecessor firm Mulligan & Jacobson; defended N.Y. Curb Exchange in all litigations brought against it, 1943-50; gen. counsel War Materials, Inc. (fed. material procurement agy.), Pitts., 1942-43. Author, lectr. on legal topics. Mem. Assn. Bar City N.Y., Am. Coll. Trial Lawyers, N.Y. County Lawyers Assn., Am., N.Y. State, N.J. bar assns., S.A.R. (chancellor N.Y. chpt.), Theta Delta Chi (grad. treas. grand lodge 1964-66). Roman Catholic. Clubs: Union League (N.Y.C.), Harvard (N.Y.C.); Panther Valley Golf and Country (Allamuchy, N.J.); Baltusrol Golf (Springfield, N.J.). Family and matrimonial, State civil litigation, Federal civil litigation. Office: Mulligan Jacobson & Langenus 25 W 45th St Suite 1405 New York NY 10036

MULLIGAN, WILLIAM HUGHES, lawyer, former federal judge; b. N.Y.C., Mar. 5, 1918; s. Stephen Hughes and Jane (Donahue) M.; m. Roseanna Connelly, Oct. 20, 1945; children: Anne O'Boyle Mulligan Hartmere, William Hughes, Stephen Edward. A.B. cum laude, Fordham U., 1939, LL.B. cum laude, 1942, LL.D., 1975; LL.D., St. Peter's Coll., Jersey City, 1966, Bklyn. Law Sch., 1972, Iona Coll., 1972, Villanova U., 1974, Pace U., 1979; L.H.D., Siena Coll., 1967. Lectr. law Fordham U., 1946-52, assoc. prof., 1953-54, asst. dean. prof. law., 1954-56; dean Fordham U. (Law Sch.), 1956-71, Wilkinson prof. law, 1961-71; judge U.S. Ct. Appeals, 2d circuit, 1971-81; ptnr. firm Skadden, Arps, Slate, Meagher & Flom, N.Y.C., 1981—; Mem. Law Revision Commn. State N.Y., 1958-71; chmn. exam. bd. Manhattan and Bronx Surface Transit Operating Authority, 1964-71; mem. N.Y. State Commn. on Constl. Conv., 1965; mem. adv. council Labor and Mgmt. Improper Practices Act, 1968-71; mem. state Commn. Rev. Legislative and Jud. Salaries, 1970-71; mem. Com. Adminstrn. Cts., 1970-71; bd. dirs. Fed. Jud. Center, 1979-81; internat. arbitrator; legal cons. counsel various state and local coms.; chmn. Citizens Com. of Reapportionment Gov. Rockefeller, 1964; assoc. chmn. N.Y. State Com. on Sentencing Guidelines, 1984-86. Contbr. articles to profl. publs. Gen. counsel Republican delegation N.Y. State Constl. Conv., 1967; trustee St. Patrick's Cathedral, 1981—, Fordham U., 1982—, Catholic Charities, Archdiocese of N.Y., 1985—; mem. N.Y.C. Bd. Ethics, 1986-87. Served as spl. agt. CIC AUS, 1942-46. Recipient St. John de La Salle medal Manhattan Coll., 1967, Learned Hand award Am. Jewish Com., 1986; Encaenia medal Fordham Coll., 1966; Fordham Law Alumni medal, 1971; Gold medal N.Y. State Bar Assn., 1982. Mem. ABA, N.Y. State Bar Assn., Assn. of Bar of City of N.Y., Friendly Sons of St. Patrick (pres. 1983-85), Knights of Malta. Roman Catholic. Clubs: Merchants, Metropolitan. Office: Skadden Arps Slate Meagher & Flom 919 3d Ave New York NY 10022

MULLIN, MICHAEL JOSEPH, lawyer; b. Louisville, Ky., Feb. 13, 1950; s. John Joseph and Anna May (Stickels) M.; m. Christy Ann Michel, July 13, 1974. B.A., U. Dayton, 1972; J.D., Notre Dame U., Ind., 1975. Bar: Ohio 1975, U.S. Dist. Ct. (so. dist.) Ohio 1976, Fla. 1977, U.S. Supreme Ct. 1978, U.S. Ct. Appeals (5th cir.) 1979, U.S. Dist. Ct. (so. dist.) Fla. 1982. Trust adminstr. 1st Nat. Bank, Dayton, Ohio, 1975-76; atty. advisor contracts U.S. Air Force Logistics Command, Dayton, 1976-83; chief patents and data div. Hdqrs. U.S. Air Force Contract Law Ctr., Dayton, 1983-85, chief airlift, trainer, reconnaissance, and electronic warfare br., 1985-87, chief system programs div., 1987—. Mem. Fed. Bar Assn. (sec. Dayton Chpt. 1983-84), ABA, Ohio State Bar Assn., Dayton Bar Assn., Armed Services Contract Trial Lawyers Assn. (chartered). Government contracts and claims, Computer. Office: Hdqrs USAF Contract Law Ctr AFCLC/JANS Wright Patterson AFB OH 45433

MULLINIX, EDWARD WINGATE, lawyer; b. Balt., Feb. 25, 1924; s. Howard Earl and Elsie (Wingate) M.; m. Virginia Lee McGinnes, July 28, 1944; children: Marcia Lee (Mrs. James R. Ladd), Edward Wingate. Student, St. John's Coll., 1941-43; J.D. summa cum laude, U. Pa., 1949. Bar: Pa. 1950, U.S. Supreme Ct. 1955. Assoc. Schnader, Harrison, Segal & Lewis, Phila., 1950-55; ptnr. Schnader, Harrison, Segal & Lewis, 1956—; mem. adv. bds. Antitrust Bull., 1970-81, BNA Antitrust and Trade Regulation Report, 1981—. Trustee Sta. KYW-TV Project Homeless Fund, 1985-86. Served with USMCR, 1943-44; to lt. (j.g.) USNR, 1944-46. Fellow Am. Bar Found. (life), Am. Coll. Trial Lawyers (mem. complex litigation com. 1980—, vice-chmn. com. 1981-83); mem. Juristic Soc., Hist. Soc. U.S. Dist. Ct. for Eastern Dist. Pa. (dir. 1984—), Am. Judicature Soc., ABA (spl. com. complex and multidist. litigation 1969-73, co-chmn. com. 1971-73, council litigation sect. 1976-80), Pa. Bar Assn., Phila. Bar Assn. (hon. trustee Campaign for Qualified Judges 1985—), Order of Coif. Republican. Presbyterian. Clubs: Lawyers (Phila.), Union League (Phila.), Socialegal (Phila.), Down Town (Phila.); Aronimink Golf (Newtown Sq., Pa.); Bald Peak Colony (Melvin Village, N.H.). Antitrust, Federal civil litigation, Criminal. Home: 251 Chamounix Rd Saint Davids PA 19087 Office: 1600 Market St Suite 3600 Philadelphia PA 19103

MULLINS, GEORGE HOLLAND, judge; b. Yakima, Wash., Mar. 28, 1920; s. George Holland and Catherine Josephine (Ledwich) M.; m. Mary Virgil O'Leary, Dec. 28, 1942; 1 son, Joseph Dennis. B.A. magna cum laude, Gonzaga U., 1942; J.D., Georgetown U., 1948. Bar: Wash. 1948. Mem. firm Cheney & Hutcheson, 1948-50, sole practice, Yakima, Wash., 1952-67; mem. firm Edmondson & Mullins, 1952-54; judge Mcpl. Ct., City of Yakima, 1965-70, Dist. Ct., Dist. Yakima County, 1970—. Pres. Sundown M Ranch Corp., alcohol rehab. Ctr., 1969-72; justice of the peace Yakima precinct, 1965-70. Served with USN, 1942-46, 50-52. Mem. ABA, Wash. Bar Assn., Yakima County Bar Assn., Wash. Magistrates Assn. (pres. 1981), VFW, Cath. War Vets. (state judge advocate 1956-71). Clubs: Elks, Gyro, Footprint Internat. Judicial administration. Office: County Courthouse Suite 225 Yakima WA 98901

MULLINS, MARGARET-ANN FRANCES, lawyer; b. Jersey City, Feb. 3, 1953; d. William Francis Sr. and Ada Louise (Pellizzari) M.; m. Robert Laurence Tortoriello, Sept. 29, 1979; children: Lauren, Christopher. AB, Coll. of St. Elizabeth, 1975; JD, Seton Hall U., 1978. Bar: N.J. 1978, U.S. Dist. Ct. N.J. 1978, U.S. Ct. Appeals (3d cir.) 1982, U.S. Supreme Ct. 1982, N.Y. 1984, U.S. Dist. Ct. D.C. 1985, U.S. Ct. Appeals (D.C. cir.) 1986. Assoc. Edwin C. Eastwood Jr., North Bergen, N.J., 1978-79; asst. prosecutor Essex County Prosecutor's Office, Newark, 1980-82, Passaic County County Prosecutor's Office, Paterson, N.J., 1982-86; faculty mem. Seton Hall U., Newark, 1987—. Mem. ABA, N.J. Bar Assn., N.Y. State Bar Assn., Hudson County Bar Assn., Essex County Bar Assn. Republican. Roman Catholic. Criminal appellate practice, Legal education. Home: 91 Clarewill Ave Upper Montclair NJ 07043

MULLINS, MICHAEL ROYCE, lawyer; b. Houston, Mo., May 27, 1952; s. Roy Dwayne and Freda Jean (Shelton) M.; m. Regina Diane Smith, March 16, 1974; children: Matthew Royce, Diana Jean. BA, S.W. Bapt. U., 1974; MSW, U. Iowa, 1976; JD, Drake U., 1982. Bar: Iowa 1982, U.S. Dist. Ct. (so. dist.) Iowa 1982. Assoc. Day & Meeker, Washington, Iowa, 1982—. Editor-in-chief Drake Law Rev., 1981-82. Sec. bd. dirs. YMCA, Washington, Iowa, 1984-86, v.p. 1986-87; bd. dirs. Washington (Iowa) Community Theater, 1984—; pres. YMCA Men's Club, Washington, Iowa, 1985-86; bd. dirs. Welcom House, Inc., Washington, Iowa, 1986—. Mem. ABA, Iowa Bar Assn., Washington County Bar Assn., Assn. Trial Lawyers Am., Assn. Trial Lawyers Iowa, Fed. Bar Assn. Baptist. Avocations: golfing, hunting, camping, fishing. State civil litigation, Criminal, Consumer com-

mercial. Home: 1110 E Tyler Washington IA 52353 Office: Day & Meeker 112 S Avenue B Washington IA 52353

MULLINS, ROGER WAYNE, lawyer; b. Bluefield, Va., Feb. 6, 1944; s. Robert Ford and Gladys Mae (Stacy) M.; m. Lois Nan Barnett, Apr. 3, 1977; children: Stacey Marie, Alison Lea. BS, U. Ala., 1968, JD, 1971. Bar: Va. 1971, U.S. Dist. Ct. (we. dist.) Va. 1974, U.S. Ct. Appeals (4th cir.) 1980. Jr. ptnr. McClintock & Mullins, Tazewell, Va., 1971; commonwealth atty. State of Va., County of Tazewell, 1977-80; sole practice Tazewell, 1980-81; pres. Mullins & Mullins, Tazewell, 1981-84, Mullins & Henderson, Tazewell, 1984—. Served with USAF, 1962-66. Mem. Tazewell County Bar Assn. (pres. 1977), Va. State Bar, Va. Trial Lawyers Assn. (bd. govs. 1976, v.p. 1984). Democrat. Disciples of Christ. General practice. Home: 129 Schenley Ave Bluefield VA 24605 Office: Mullins & Henderson 227 W Main St Tazewell VA 24651

MULLOY, WILLIAM PATRICK, II, lawyer; b. Louisville, May 12, 1953; s. William P. and Katie (Lee) M.; m. Francie Lowe Olsen, May 15, 1976; children: Patrick, Mollie. BA, Vanderbilt U., 1974, JD, 1977. Bar: Ky. 1977, U.S. Dist. Ct. (we. dist.) Ky. 1977, N.Y. 1978, U.S. Ct. Appeals (6th cir.) 1985. Ptnr. Mulloy, Walz & Mulloy, Louisville, 1978—. Spl. counsel Dem. Nat. Com., Washington, 1982; candidate for U.S. congress, Louisville, 1984; chmn. Gov. John Y. Brown Campaign Com., Louisville, 1986. Mem. ABA, N.Y. State Bar Assn., Ky. Bar Assn., Louisville Bar Assn., Phi Beta Kappa, Omicron Delta Kappa. Democrat. Episcopalian. Avocations: politics, traveling, running. Federal civil litigation, State civil litigation, Real property. Home: 2015 Camargo Rd Louisville KY 40207 Office: Mulloy Walz & Mulloy 200 S 7th St Louisville KY 40202

MULROY, THOMAS ROBERT, JR., lawyer; b. Evanston, Ill., June 26, 1946; s. Thomas Robert and Dorothy (Reiner) M.; m. Elaine Mazzone, Aug. 16, 1969. Student Loyola U., Rome, 1966; B.A., U. Santa Clara, Calif., 1968; J.D., Loyola U., Chgo., 1972. Bar: Ill. 1973, U.S. Dist. Ct. (no. dist.) Ill. 1973, U.S. Ct. Appeals (7th cir.) 1973. Asst. U.S. atty. No. Dist. Ill., Chgo., 1972-76; ptnr. Jenner & Block, Chgo. 1976—. Adj. prof. Northwestern Sch. Law, Chgo., 1978-85, Loyola Sch. Law, Chgo., 1983—, DePaul U. Sch. Law, Chgo., Nova U. Ctr. for Study of Law; bd. dirs. Loyola U. Trial Advocacy Workshop, 1982—; mem. Fed. Defender Panel Adv. Bd., 1981—. Mem. Chgo. Crime Commn., 1978—. Mem. ABA, Assn. Trial Lawyers Am., Am. Judicature Soc., Fed. Bar Assn., Fed. Trial Bar Assn., Legal Club Chgo., Law Club, Nat. Assn. Criminal Def. Lawyers, Nat. Dist. Attys. Assn., 7th Fed. Cir. Bar Assn., Chgo. Bar Assn. Clubs: University, Executives of Chgo. Federal civil litigation, State civil litigation, Criminal. Office: Jenner & Block 1 IBM Plaza Chicago IL 60611

MULVEHILL, JOHN HENRY, lawyer; b. Louisville, Jan. 20, 1934; s. Vincent Lyman and Vera Marie (Sexton) M.; m. Kathleen Judith Ryan, Sept. 7, 1963; children: Richard, Mary, John. BA, St. John's Coll., Bklyn., 1955; LLB, Georgetown U., 1958; LLM, NYU, 1964. Bar: N.Y. 1960. Assoc. Casper & Ughetta, N.Y.C., 1959-61, Fogerty & Schreiber, Bklyn., 1961-64, Ponzan & Goldblum, Queens, N.Y., 1964-69; ptnr. Mulvehill & O'Brien, Smithtown, N.Y., 1970—. Chmn. N.Y. State Conservatives, Huntington, N.Y., 1968-85. Served with U.S. Army, 1957-59. Mem. ABA, N.Y. State Bar Assn., Suffolk County Bar Assn., Nassau-Suffolk Trial Lawyers Assn., Phi Delta Phi. Roman Catholic. State civil litigation, Insurance, Personal injury. Office: Mulvehill & O'Brien 260 Middle Country Rd Smithtown NY 11787

MULVEY, W. MICHAEL, lawyer, court administrator; b. Salem, Mass., May 2, 1945; s. William Keane and Mary Angela (MacDuffie) M.; m. Debra Anne Dalton, July 1984; children—Courtney K., Meredith M., Wynne M. B.A., Villanova U., 1967; J.D., Del. Sch. Law, 1975. Bar: Pa. 1976, U.S. Dist. Ct. (ea. dist.) Pa. 1976, U.S. Ct. Appeals (3d cir.) 1983. Court administr. Phila. Ct. Common Pleas, 1971-78, mental health master, 1978—; sole practice law, Phila., 1978-81; assoc. Sagot and Jennings, Phila., 1981-85; ptnr. Ritner, Mulvey & Flanagan, Phila., 1985—; instr. basic legal practices course, 1978, civil practices course Pa. Bar Inst., 1980. Bd. dirs. Sparrowhawk, Ltd., Phila., 1982—. Mem. Assn. Trial Lawyers Am., Pa. Trial Lawyers Assn., Phila. Trial Lawyers Assn., Phila. Bar Assn., LAWPAC. Democrat. Roman Catholic. State civil litigation, Personal injury, Workers' compensation. Office: Ritner Mulvey and Flanagan The Exchange Suite 600 1411 Walnut St Philadelphia PA 19102

MULVIHILL, DAVID BRIAN, lawyer; b. Pitts., Jan. 21, 1956; s. Mead J. Jr. and Margaret (O'Brien) M. BA, U. Pitts., 1977; JD, Duquesne U., 1981. Bar: Pa. 1981, U.S. Dist. Ct. (we. dist.) Pa. 1981, U.S. Ct. Appeals (3d cir.) 1985. Ptnr. Mansmann, Cindrich & Titus, Pitts., 1981—. Mem. wish com., speakers' bur. Make-a-Wish Found., Pitts., 1986. Mem. ABA, Pa. Bar Assn., Allegheny County Bar Assn., Order of Barristers. Avocations: flying, tennis, reading. Civil rights, Federal civil litigation, State civil litigation. Office: Mansmann Cindrich & Titus Two Chatham Ctr Suite 1510 Pittsburgh PA 15219

MULVIHILL, MEAD JAMES, JR., lawyer; b. Salt Lake City, Oct. 1927; s. Mead James and Lahela M. (Samuels) M.; m. Margaret Elizabeth O'Brien, June 19, 1950; children: David, Robert, Susan. BSBA, U. Pitts, 1951; JD, Duquesne U., 1955. Bar: Pa. 1956, U.S. Dist. Ct. (we. dist.) Pa., U.S. Ct. Appeals (3d cir.), U.S. Supreme Ct. Dep. city solicitor City of Pitts., 1970-74, city solicitor, 1974-82, dep. mayor, 1976-82; of counsel Mansmann Cindrich & Titus, 1983—. Mem. bd. public edn. Sch. Dist. Pitts., 1972-76. Served with USAAF, 1945-46. Mem. ABA, Pa. Bar Assn., Allegheny County Bar Assn., Mcpl. and Sch. Solicitors Assn. General practice, Probate, Local government. Office: Mansmann Cindrich & Titus Two Chatham Ctr Suite 1510 Pittsburgh PA 15219

MUMFORD, MANLY WHITMAN, lawyer; b. Evanston, Ill., Feb. 25, 1925; s. Manly Stearns and Helen (Whitman) M.; m. Luigi Thorne Horne, July 1, 1961; children—Shaw, Dodge. A.B., Harvard U., 1947; J.D., Northwestern U, Chgo., 1950. Bar: Ill. 1950, U.S. Supreme Ct. 1969. Assoc. Chapman and Cutler, Chgo., 1950-62, ptnr., 1963—. contbr. articles to profl. jours. Served with USNR, 1942-46. Mem. Nat. Assn. Bond Lawyers, ABA. Democrat. Clubs: Cliff Dwellers, Univ., Monroe, Chgo. Literary. Avocation: computers. Municipal bonds. Home: 399 W Fullerton Pkwy Chicago IL 60614 Office: Chapman and Cutler 111 W Monroe St Chicago IL 60603

MUNDAY, MELVIN WAYNE, lawyer; b. Granite Falls, N.C., Jan. 11, 1931; s. Connelly E. and Nora V. (Teague) M.; children—P. Erin, Michael W., Janet S. B.A., Lenoir Rhyne Coll., Hickory, N.C., 1952; J.D., Georgetown U., 1961. Bar: Md. 1962. Assoc. Mudd, Mudd & Munday, P.A., LaPlata, Md., 1962-65, ptnr., 1966-82; sole practice M. Wayne Munday, P.A., 1982-86; ptnr., Munday, Sturman & Everton, P.A., 1986—; spl. asst. atty. gen. Md. Public Constrn. Program Inquiry Panel, 1975-78; chmn. Panel to Investigate Propriety of Charter Govt. for Charles County (Md.), 1976. Trustee, St. Mary's Coll. Md., 1977-86. Served to maj. USMC, 1954-57. Fellow Am. Coll. Trial Lawyers; mem. Md. State Bar Assn. (chmn. ethics com. 1972-73), ABA, Baltimore County Bar Assn. Presbyterian. Trial practice. Home: Unit 2306 The Ridgely 205 E Joppa Rd Towson MD 21204 Office: The Exchange 1122 Kenilworth Dr Suite 417 Towson MD 21204

MUNDELL, JOHN ANDREW, JR., lawyer; b. Chgo., June 20, 1923; s. John Andrew Sr. and Ellen M. (Paterson) M.; m. Colleen Robson, Nov. 6, 1954; 1 child, John Andrew III. Student, Alma Coll., 1943; BA, Oberlin Coll., 1947; JD, U. Detroit, 1951. Bar: Mich. 1951, Ohio 1970, U.S. Dist. Ct. (ea. dist.) Mich. 1951, U.S. Ct. Appeals (6th cir.) 1970, U.S. Supreme Ct. 1970. Diplomatic courier U.S. Dept. of State, Washington, 1948; assoc. Foster, Meadows & Ballard, Washington, 1953, from ptnr. to sr. ptnr., 1960—; spl. asst. atty. gen. maritime affairs State of Mich., 1979—. Served to lt. j.g. USNR, 1942-46, 51-53, capt. Res. ret. Mem. U.S. Maritime Law Assn., Propeller Club of U.S. (pres. 1971-72). Republican. Presbyterian. Clubs: Detroit, Stonycroft Hills (Bloomfield, Mich.) (pres. 1971-72), Birmingham (Mich.) Athletic. Avocations: tennis, golf, gardening. Admiralty, Insurance, Personal injury. Home: 85 Cabot Pl Bloomfield Hills MI 48013 Office: Foster Meadows & Ballard 3200 Penobscot Bldg Detroit MI 48226

MUNDHEIM, ROBERT HARRY, legal educator; b. Hamburg, Germany, Feb. 24, 1933; m. Guna Smitchens; children—Susan, Peter. B.A., Harvard U., 1954, LL.B., 1957; M.A. (hon.), U. Pa., 1971. Bar: N.Y. 1958, Pa. 1979. Assoc. Shearman & Sterling, N.Y.C., 1958-61; spl. counsel to SEC, Washington, 1962-63; vis. prof. Duke Law Sch., Durham, N.C., 1964; prof. law U. Pa., Phila., 1965—, Univ. prof., 1980—, dean, 1982—; gen. counsel U.S. Dept. Treasury, Washington, 1977-80; dir. Ctr. for Study of Fin. Instns., U. Pa.; dir. 1st Pa. Corp., 1st Pa. Bank, Commerce Clearing House; gen. counsel Chrysler Loan Guarantee Bd., 1980. Served with USAF, 1961-62. Recipient Alexander Hamilton award U.S. Dept. Treasury, 1980. Mem. ABA (council bus. law sect.), Am. Law Inst. (council). Author: Outside Director of the Publicly Held Corporation, 1976; American Attitudes Toward Foreign Direct Investment in the United States, 1979; Conflict of Interest and the Former Government Employee: Re-thinking the Revolving Door, 1981. Banking, General corporate, Securities. Office: U Pa Law Sch 3400 Chestnut St Philadelphia PA 19104

MUNDT, DANIEL HENRY, lawyer, educator; b. Barron, Wis., July 28, 1927; s. William Herman and Mary Asenath (Cook) M.; m. Catherine L. Sulzbach, Mar. 24, 1951; children: Mary Lou, Dan, Martha, David, Sarah. BBA, U. Minn., 1951, JD, 1954, MA in Psychology, 1956. Bar: Minn., Wis., U.S. Dist. Ct. Wis., U.S. Dist. Ct. Minn., U.S. Supreme Ct. From assoc. to ptnr. McCabe, Van Evera, Duluth, Minn., 1954-79; ptnr. Mundt & Hall, Duluth, 1979-85; prin. Mundt & Assocs., Duluth, 1985—; lectr. regulation of bus. law, U. Minn., Duluth, 1955-74. Mem. Duluth Bd. Edn., 1961-64, bd. adminstrn. Presbyn. Ch., State of Minn.; bd. dirs. Duluth YMCA. Served to 1st lt. U.S. Army, 1945-48, PTO. Mem. U. Minn. Alumni Club, Phi Delta Phi. Club: Kitchi Gammi (Duluth). Lodges: Masons, Rotary. Avocations: hunting, fishing. General corporate, Antitrust, General practice. Home: 2001 Waverly Ave Duluth MN 55803 Office: Mundt & Assocs 715 W Superior St Duluth MN 55802

MUNN, FORD DENT, lawyer; b. Montgomery, Ala., Jan. 19, 1951; s. Ford Jr. and Eugene Dent (Maharrey) M. Student, Coll. of Desert, 1969-71, U. Ala., 1971-72; BA, U. Calif., Riverside, 1974; JD, Pepperdine U., 1978. Bar: Calif. 1979. Rep. patient accounts Desert Radiology, Palm Springs, Calif., 1979-81, Desert Hosp., Palm Springs, Calif., 1981; assoc. Law Offices of O. Brazelton, Palm Desert, Calif., 1981-82; ptnr. Casey & Munn, Palm Springs, 1982—. Mem. ABA, Riverside County Bar Assn., Assn. Trial Lawyers Am., Indio Jaycees (legal counsel 1984—). Democrat. Avocations: classic movies, travel, history. Landlord-tenant, Consumer commercial, Contracts commercial. Home: 2925 Escoba Dr #111 PO Box 605 Palm Springs CA 92262 Office: Law Offices of Casey & Munn 202 N Palm Canyon Dr Palm Springs CA 92262

MUNNEKE, GARY ARTHUR, legal educator, consultant; b. Cedar Rapids, Iowa, Dec. 29, 1947; s. Leslie Earl and Margaret Frances (Fortsch) M.; children—Richard Arthur, Matthew Frederick. B.A. in Psychology, U. Tex. 1970; J.D., 1973. Bar: Tex. 1973. Asst. dean, dir. placement U. Tex., Austin, 1978-80; asst. prof., asst. dean Del. Law Sch., Widener U., Wilmington, 1980-84, assoc. prof., 1984—. Contbr. articles to profl. jours. Mem. ABA (chmn. standing com. on profl. utilization and career devel. 1981—, articles editor Legal Econs. mag. 1984—), State Bar Tex., U. Tex. Law Sch. Assn. (bd. dirs.). Presbyterian. Legal education, Jurisprudence, General practice. Office: Del Law Sch PO Box 7474 Wilmington DE 19803

MUNOZ, ROBERT F., lawyer; b. Bklyn., Jan. 22, 1953; s. Robert I. and Joan A. (Fales) M.; m. Dolores A. Smith, June 21, 1975; children: Robert B., Melissa A. BA, NYU, 1975, JD, 1978. Bar: N.J. 1978, U.S. Dist. Ct. N.J. 1978, U.S. Supreme Ct. 1982, N.Y. 1985. Dep. atty. gen. N.J. Dept. Law and Pub. Safety, Newark, 1978-79; assoc. Kaye & Davison, Freehold, N.J., 1979-82; sr. assoc. Porzio, Bromberg & Newman, Morristown, N.J., 1982-84; ptnr. Bennett, Davison & Munoz, Freehold, N.J., 1984—; mcpl. prosecutor Borough of Keansburg, N.J., 1984—; planning bd. atty. Twp of Manalapan, N.J., 1985—. Atty. Bd. Edn., Keyport, N.J.; aAdult mem. Boy Scouts Am., Freehold, N.J., 1985—; coach Freehold Soccer League, 1986, Freehold Borough Little League, 1986. Mem. ABA, N.J. State Bar Assn., N.Y. State Bar Assn., Monmouth County Bar Assn., Monmouth County Mcpl. Prosecutors Assn., Rep. Nat. Lawyers Assn., Environ. Law Inst. Roman Catholic. Club: Republican. Real property, Local government, Environment. Home: 4 Crestwood Dr Freehold NJ 07728 Office: Bennett Davison & Munoz 8 Throckmorton St Freehold NJ 07728

MUNRO, ROBERT ALLAN, lawyer; b. Kearney, Nebr., June 16, 1932; s. George Allan and Alta Susan (Corn) M.; m. Patricia Lee Purcell, Apr. 29, 1961; children—Michael Duncan, Diane Purcell. Student Harvard U., 1950-53; B.S., U. Nebr., 1957, J.D., 1957. Bar: Nebr. 1957, U.S. Dist. Ct. Nebr. 1957, U.S. Ct. Appeals (8th cir.) 1975, U.S. Tax Ct. 1967. Assoc. Munro & Parker, Kearney, 1957-60; county atty. Buffalo County, Kearney, 1959-63; ptnr. Munro & Munro (and predecessor firms), Kearney, 1960-75, sr. ptnr., 1975—; sec., dir. J.F. Brandt Gen. Contracting Co., Kearney; pres., dir. The RAM Co., Kearney, 1982—, Husker Hostelries, Inc., Kearney, 1983—. Sec., dir. Kearney Conv. Ctr. Inc., 1963—, pres., dir. 1983—; sec., dir. Highland Park Devel. Co., Kearney, 1964—; chmn. Buffalo County Young Reps., 1958-62; co-chmn. Gov.'s Adv. Com. on Drug and Alcohol Abuse, 1980-84; bd. dirs. Nebr. Art Collection, 1984—, mem. exec. com., 1986—. Mem. ABA, Nebr. Assn. Trial Attys., Buffalo County Bar Assn., (pres. 1964), Cen. Nebr. Bar Assn. (pres. 1970-71), Am. Judicature Soc., Nat. Trust Hist. Preservation, Smithsonian Assocs., Nebr. Bar Assn. (chmn. com. on ethics 1972-73), Am. Arbitration Assn. (panel arbitrators 1974—). Presbyterian. Club: Kearney Country. Lodges: Masons, Shriners. Personal injury, General corporate, Probate. Home: 2915 5th Ave Kearney NE 68847 Office: 16th St at 3d Ave Munro & Munro PC PO Box 2375 Terrace Level Blackacre Pl Kearney NE 68848

MUNSEY, STANLEY EDWARD, lawyer; b. Brunswick, Maine, Mar. 12, 1934; s. Maynard Edward and Estelle Mary (Martin) M.; m. Elena Opal Munsey, Dec. 22, 1954; children—Stanley Edward, Michele E. B.A., Millsaps Coll., 1961; LL.B., Tulane U., 1964. Bar: Miss. 1965, Ala. 1970. With land dept. Shell Oil Co., New Orleans, 1964-66; sole practice, Picayune, Miss., 1966-67; exec. dir. Muscle Shoals Council Local Govts., Muscle Shoals, Ala., 1967-71; ptnr. Rosser & Munsey, Tuscumbia, Ala., 1971-85; sr. ptnr. Munsey & Ford, 1986—. Chmn. N. Ala. Health Systems Agy., 1981-82; vice chmn. Ala. Statewide Health Coordinating Council, 1981-82. Served with AUS, 1953-58. Mem. ABA, Miss. Bar Assn., Ala. Bar Assn. Am. Judicature Soc., Miss. Trial Lawyers Assn., Ala. Trial Lawyers Assn., Assn. Trial Lawyers Am. Presbyterian. General practice, Personal injury, Federal civil litigation. Office: PO Box 496 Tuscumbia AL 35674

MUNSING, PETER NICHOLAS, lawyer; b. Munich, Fed. Republic Germany, Jan. 21, 1952; s. Stefan P. and Juliana Munsing; m. Beverly Mae White, Oct. 6, 1984. BA, U. Mich., 1972; JD, Georgetown U., 1975. Bar: D.C. 1975, U.S. Ct. Appeals (2d cir.) 1975, Conn. 1976, U.S. Dist. Ct. Conn. 1976, Pa. 1982, U.S. Dist. Ct. (ea. dist.) Pa. 1982, U.S. Ct. Appeals (3d cir.) 1982, U.S. Ct. Appeals (1st cir.) 1984, Md. 1985, Mass. 1985, U.S. Ct. Appeals (4th cir.) 1985, U.S. Dist. Ct. Md. 1986. Atty. legal services State Ct. of Conn., Stamford, 1975-81; assoc. David Cohen P.C., Phila., 1982-84, Swartz & Swartz, Boston, 1984-85, Mayerson, Gerasimowicz & Munsing (formerly Mayerson, Shniper & Gerasimowicz), Spring City, Pa., 1985—. Active in polit. campaigns and community athletic orgns., 1968—. Mem. ABA (criminal justice sect., com. on grand jury, individual rights and responsibilities sect., com. on freedom of speech and freedom of press, program chmn. 1976-86, trial problems in high publicity cases com., criminal justice awards com., tort and ins. practice sect., com. excess liability coverage, chmn. consumer rights com. 1986—), Pa. Bar Assn., Phila. Bar Assn., Chester County Bar Assn., Berks County Bar Assn., Assn. Trial Lawyers Am., Pa. Trial Lawyers Assn., Phila. Trial Lawyers Assn. Avocations: photography, rowing, writing. Personal injury, Federal civil litigation, State civil litigation. Office: Mayerson Gerasimowicz & Munsing Meetinghouse Law Offices Spring City PA 19475

MUNSON, HOWARD G., judge; b. Claremont, N.H., July 26, 1924; s. Walter N. and Helena (O'Halloran) M.; m. Ruth Jaynes, Sept. 17, 1949; children: Walter N., Richard J., Pamela A. B.S. in Economics, U. Pa., 1948; LL.B., Syracuse U., 1952. Bar: N.Y. With Employers' Assurance Corp., Ltd., White Plains, N.Y., 1949-50; mem. firm Hiscock, Lee, Rogers, Henley & Barclay, Syracuse, N.Y., 1952-76; judge U.S. Dist. Ct. No. Dist. N.Y., Syracuse, 1976—. Mem., pres. Syracuse Bd. Edn.; bd. dirs. Sta. WCNY-TV; chmn. ethics com. Onondaga County Legislature. Served with U.S. Army, 1943-45, ETO. Decorated Bronze Star, Purple Heart. Mem. Am. Coll. Trial Lawyers, Nat. Assn. R.R. Trial Counsel, Am. Arbitration Assn., Justinian Soc., Alpha Tau Omega, Phi Delta Phi. Office: US Courthouse 100 S Clinton St Syracuse NY 13260

MUNSON, JAMES CALFEE, lawyer; b. Ashville, N.C., May 17, 1944; s. James B. and Margaret (Calfee) M.; children: Garrett, Ingrid Grove; m. Melinda Tippet, Sept. 14, 1985. BA, Yale U., 1966; JD, U. Wis., 1969. Bar: Wis. 1970, Ill. 1971. Law clk. to presiding justice U.S. Dist. Ct., Milw., 1969-70; assoc. Kirkland & Ellis, Chgo., 1970-75, ptnr., 1975—. Bd. dirs. Ronald Knox Montessori Sch., Wilmette, Ill., 1975-78, Trevian Youth Soccer Club, Wilmette, 1984—. Mem. ABA, Chgo. Bar Assn. Democrat. Clubs: Tavern, West Moreland Country (Chgo.). Federal civil litigation, State civil litigation, Utilities. Home: 1420 Sheridan Rd 2H Wilmette IL 60091 Office: Kirkland & Ellis 200 E Randolph Dr Chicago IL 60601

MUNSON, MARK PARR, lawyer; b. Yakima, Wash., Jan. 18, 1957; s. Ray Eugene and Christine (Parr) M.; m. Dawna Kay Worthington, June 28, 1980. BBA, U. Wash., 1979; JD, Harvard U., 1982. Bar: Wash. 1982. Assoc. Perkins Coie, Seattle, 1982—. General corporate, Corporate taxation, Real property. Office: Perkins Coie 1900 Washington Bldg Seattle WA 98101

MUNSON, NANCY KAY, lawyer; b. Huntington, N.Y., June 22, 1936; d. Howard H. and Edna M. (Keenan) Munson. Student Hofstra U., 1959-62; J.D., Bklyn. Law Sch., 1965. Bar: N.Y. 1966, U.S. Supreme Ct. 1970, U.S. Ct. Appeals (2d cir.) 1971, U.S. Dist. Ct. (ea. and so. dists.) N.Y. 1968. Law clk. to E. Merritt Weidner, Huntington, 1959-66; sole practice law, Huntington, 1966—; mem. legal adv. bd. Chgo. Title Ins. Co., Riverhead, N.Y., 1981—. Trustee Huntington Fire Dept. Death Benefit Fund; chmn. bd. Bklyn. Home for Aged Men Found. Mem. ABA, Suffolk County Bar Assn., Bklyn. Bar Assn., N.Y. State Bar Assn., Nat. Rifle Assn. Republican. Christian Scientist. Club: Soroptimist (past pres.). General practice, Probate, Real property. Office: 197 New York Ave Huntington NY 11743

MUNTZ, RICHARD KARL, lawyer; b. Clinton, Iowa, Apr. 22, 1951; s. Karl Huber and Lois Elizabeth (Lohberg) M.; m. Marianna Margaret Hupp, Sept. 4, 1971; children: Karl, David. BS in Engring., Purdue U., 1972; JD, Valparaiso U., 1975. Bar: Ind. 1975, Mich. 1978. Assoc. Petersen & Muntz, LaGrange, Ind., 1975-79; sole practice LaGrange, 1980-85; ptnr. Muntz & VanDerbeck, LaGrange, 1986—. Treas. LaGrange County Assn. for Retarded Citizens, 1986. Mem. ABA, Ind. Bar Assn., Mich. Bar Assn., Assn. Trial Lawyers Am., LaGrange County Bar Assn. (pres. 1979). Club: Exchange (LaGrange) (pres. 1979). Lodges: Masons, KT, Shriners. Avocations: farming, skiing. General practice, State civil litigation, Probate. Home: RR 5 Box 125 LaGrange IN 46761 Office: Muntz & VanDerbeck 109 S Detroit St LaGrange IN 46761

MUNZER, STEPHEN IRA, lawyer, real estate syndicator; b. N.Y.C., Mar. 15, 1939; s. Harry and Edith (Isacowitz) M.; m. Patricia Eve Munzer, Aug. 11, 1965; children—John, Margaret. A.B., Brown U., 1960; J.D., Cornell U., 1963. Bar: N.Y. 1964, U.S. Supreme Ct. 1974. Formerly assoc. Finley, Kimble & Underburg; formerly ptnr. Pincus Munzer Bizar & D'Alessandro; real estate investor; pres. Simon Mgmt. Corp., N.Y.C., Redstone Real Estate Corp., N.Y.C. Served to lt., USNR, 1965-75. Mem. Assn. Bar City N.Y., N.Y. State Bar Assn. Jewish. Club: City Athletic (N.Y.C.). Real property. Home: 850 Park Ave New York NY 10021 Office: One Citicorp Center New York NY 10022

MUNZER, STEPHEN R., law educator; b. 1944. BA, U. Kans., 1966; PhB, Oxford U., Eng., 1969; JD, Yale U., 1972. Assoc. Covington & Burling, Washington, 1972-73; staff atty. Columbia U., N.Y.C., 1973-74; asst. prof. philosophy Rutgers U., New Brunswick, N.J., 1974-77; assoc. prof. U. Minn., Mpls., 1977-80, prof., 1980-81; prof. UCLA, 1981—. Office: UCLA Sch Law 405 Hilgard Ave Los Angeles CA 90024 *

MUR, RAPHAEL, lawyer, aerospace manufacturing executive; b. Bklyn., Jan. 29, 1927; s. William and Celia (Greenwald) M.; m. Sonia Rose Sacks, Nov. 11, 1951; children: Laura Jacqueline McColgan, Susan Elynn Mur Rusciano, Alice Jennifer. Student, Middlebury Coll., 1944-45; B.S., Tufts U., 1946; LL.B., Harvard U., 1950; A.M.P., Harvard Bus. Sch., 1977; LL.M., NYU, 1955. Bar: N.Y. 1950, U.S. Supreme Ct. 1955, U.S. Ct. Claims 1982. With Office Gen. Counsel, Dept. Navy, 1950-61; counsel purchasing dept. Grumman Aircraft Engring. Corp., 1961-63, asst. gen. counsel, 1964-69; sec., gen. counsel Grumman Aerospace Corp., Bethpage, N.Y., 1969-82, v.p., 1982—; sec. Grumman Houston Corp., 1973—, Grumman St. Augustine Corp., 1980—, Grumman Tech. Services, Inc., 1983—; Spl. legal adviser Commn. Govt. Procurement. Served to ensign USNR, 1944-46; capt. JAGC Res. Mem. ABA (lawyers in armed forces com. 1981-87 , council sect. pub. contract law 1983-86), Fed. Bar Assn. (chmn. govt. contracts com. 1978), Maritime Law Assn. U.S., Judge Advs. Assn. (regional chmn. Mid-Atlantic region 1983-84), Nat. Security Indsl. Assn. (chmn. legal and spl. tasks subcom. 1969-70), Aerospace Industries Assn., Am. Arbitration Assn. (dir. 1983-87), Naval Res. Assn. (v.p. legal affairs 1982). Government contracts and claims, General corporate, Personal injury. Home: 3047 Johnson Pl Wantagh NY 11793-2838 Office: Grumman Aerospace Corp Mail Stop BO2-05 Bethpage NY 11714

MURACA, FRANK JOHN, lawyer; b. Scranton, Pa., Aug. 25, 1953; s. Frank Bruno and Grace Delores Muraca; m. Denise Elizabeth Moran, June 20, 1975; children: Frank John Jr., Leigh Nealon, Michael David. BS in Acctg., Pa. State U.; JD, Western New Eng. Coll. Bar: U.S. Supreme Ct. Assoc., ptnr. Dolphin, Solfanelli & Butler, Scranton, 1978-81; pntr. Kuha, Zipay & Muraca, Scranton, 1981—; mgr. Borough of Dunmore, Pa., 1982—; mem. bd. appeals SSS, Washington, 1983—. Mem. Pa. State Dem. Com., Harrisburg, 1982-84; bd. dirs. Lackawanna County Dem. Exec. Com., Scranton, 1984—; chmn. Dem. Party, Dunmore, 1983—; chmn. bd. Dunmore Sr. Citizens Ctr., 1984—; former chmn. bd. ACLU of Northeast Pa., Scranton, 1983-85. Recipient UN award UN Day Com., Scranton, 1984, Merit award Northeast Pa. Bus. Woman's Club, Scranton, 1985. Mem. ABA, Pa. Bar Assn., Lackawanna County Bar Assn., Assn. Trial Lawyers Am., Omicron Delta Kappa. Democrat. Roman Catholic. Clubs: Skull & Bones, Lion's Paw (University Park, Pa.). Lodge: Lions. Avocations: tennis, music, reading, boating. State civil litigation, Criminal, Local government. Home: 1622 Clay Ave Dunmore PA 18509 Office: 1st Eastern Bank Bldg Suite 1200 Scranton PA 18503

MURAKAMI, ALAN TOMOO, lawyer; b. Hilo, Hawaii, Nov. 4, 1949; s. Shigeo and Michie (Tatsuta) M. BA in Econs., U. Santa Clara, 1971; MA in Econs., U. Hawaii, 1075; JD, U. Calif., Davis, 1978. Bar: Hawaii 1978. Mng. atty. Legal Aid Soc., Kaunakakai, Hawaii, 1978-81, Waianae, Hawaii, 1981-83; staff atty. Native Hawaiian Legal Corp., Honolulu, 1983-86; dir. litigation Native Hawiian Legal Corp., Honolulu, 1986—; bd. dirs. Na Loio No Na Kanaka, Honolulu. Vol. Asian Legal Services, Sacremento, 1976-78, Asian Law Caucus, Oakland, Ca., 1976. Served to 1st lt., 1971-73. Federal civil litigation, State civil litigation, Public interest, native Hawaiian rights. Home: 3729 Pukalani Pl #900 Honolulu HI 96816 Office: Native Hawaiian Legal Corp 1164 Bishop St #900 Honolulu HI 96213

MURASKI, ANTHONY AUGUSTUS, lawyer; b. Cohoes, N.Y., July 28, 1946; s. Adam Joseph and Angeline Mary (Vozzy) M.; m. Janice Kay Selberg, Nov. 25, 1978; children: Adam Peter, Emily Jo. BA, MA in Speech/Hearing, Sacramento State Coll., 1970; PhD in Audiology/ Hearing Sci., U. Mich., 1977; JD, Detroit Coll. Law, 1979. Bar: Mich. 1980, U.S. Dist. Ct. (ea. dist.) Mich. 1981, U.S. Ct. Appeals (6th cir.) 1982. Asst. Kresge Hearing Research Inst. U. Mich., Ann Arbor, 1971-77; asst. prof. Wayne State U. Med. Sch., Detroit, 1979-82; assoc. Kitch, Suhrheinrich, Saurbier & Drutchas, Detroit, 1982-83; assoc. prof. Detroit Coll. Law, 1983-85; mng. ptnr. Vieweg & Muraski, P.C., Ann Arbor, 1985—; cons. audiology Ministry of Environment, Ont., Can., 1980-81; trustee Deaf, Speech and Hearing Ctr., Detroit, 1981—; legal adv. on air WWJ Radio, Detroit, 1984—; mem. mental health adv. bd. on deafness Dept. Mental Health,

1984, vis. com. U. Mich. Sch. Edn., 1986—. Author: Legal Aspects of Audiological Practice, 1982, Hearing Conservation in Industry: Licensure, Liability and Forensics, 1985. Mem. ABA, Mich. Bar Assn., Washtenaw County Bar Assn., Am. Speech-Lang.-Hearing Assn. (sci. merit award, 1981), Ann Arbor C. of C. Avocations: photography, running. Health, Private international, Labor. Home: 1603 Westminster Pl Ann Arbor MI 48104 Office: Vieweg & Muraski PC 300 N Fifth Ave Suite 240 Ann Arbor MI 48104

MURATIDES, JOHN NICHOLAS, lawyer; b. Massillon, Ohio, Dec. 6, 1955; s. George M. and Ann Muratides. BBA, Ohio No. U., 1978; JD, Am. U., 1981. Bar: Fla. 1981, D.C. 1982. Law clk. to presiding justice U.S. Dist. Ct. Fla., Jacksonville, 1981-83; assoc. Stearns, Weaver, Tampa, Fla., 1983—. Mem. ABA, Fla. Bar Assn., D.C. Bar Assn., Hillsborough County Bar Assn., Assn. Trial Lawyers Am. Federal civil litigation, State civil litigation. Office: Stearns Weaver Miller et al PO Box 3299 Tampa FL 33601

MURAWSKI, ROBERTA LEE, lawyer; b. Staunton, Va., June 6, 1958; d. Norbert Thomas and Germaine Felicia (Lipinski) M. BA in English magna cum laude, SUNY, Buffalo, 1979; JD, George Washington U., 1982. Bar: D.C. 1982, Md. 1984, Va. 1986. Legal researcher, writer Samuel Green & John V. Long, Washington, 1980-83; assoc. Herbert Rubenstein & Assocs., Washington, Md. and Va., 1986—. Author/editor: Marriage and Family Law Agreements, 1984, Dissolution of Marriage, 1986. Mem. Md. Bar Assn., Va. Bar Assn., D.C. Bar Assn., Women's Bar Assn. D.C., Phi Beta Kappa. Democrat. Roman Catholic. Family and matrimonial, General practice. Office: Herbert Rubenstein & Assocs 1818 N St NW West Lobby Washington DC 20036

MURCHISON, DAVID CLAUDIUS, lawyer; b. N.Y.C., Aug. 19, 1923; s. Claudius Temple and Constance (Waterman) M.; m. June Margaret Guilfoyle, Dec. 19, 1946; children—David Roderick, Brian, Courtney, Bradley, Stacy. Student, U. N.C., 1942-43; A.A., George Washington U., 1947, J.D. with honors, 1949. Bar: D.C. 1949, Supreme Ct. 1955. Asso. Dorr, Hand & Dawson, N.Y.C., 1949-50; partner Howrey, Simon, Baker & Murchison, Washington, 1956—; legal asst. under sec. army, 1949-51; counsel motor vehicle, textile, aircraft, ordnance and shipbldg. divs. Nat. Prodn. Authority, 1951-52; asso. gen. counsel Small Def. Plants Adminstrn., 1952-53; legal adv., asst. to chmn. FTC, 1953-55. Served with AUS, 1943-45. Mem. ABA (chmn. com. internat. restrictive bus. practices, sect. antitrust law 1954-55, sect. adminstrv. law, sect. litigation), Fed., D.C., N.Y. bar assns., Order of Coif, Phi Delta Phi. Republican. Clubs: Metropolitan, Chevy Chase. Administrative and regulatory, Antitrust, Federal civil litigation. Home: 5409 Spangler Ave Bethesda MD 20816 Office: 1730 Pennsylvania Ave NW Washington DC 20006

MURDOCH, DAVID ARMOR, lawyer; b. Pitts., May 30, 1942; s. Armor M. and N. Edna (Jones) M.; m. Joan Wilkie, Mar. 9, 1974; children—Christina, Timothy, Deborah. A.B. magna cum laude, Harvard U., 1964, LL.B., 1967. Bar: Pa. 1967, U.S. Dist. Ct. (we. dist.) Pa. 1967. Assoc. Kirkpatrick & Lockhart, Pitts., 1971-78, ptnr., 1978—. Vice pres., bd. dirs. Avonworth Sch. Dist., 1977-83; chmn. bd. dirs. Pitts. Expt., 1980-82; mem. Pa. Housing Fin. Agy., 1981—, vice chmn., 1983-87; alt. del. Republican Nat. Conv., 1980; mem. council legal advisors Rep. Nat. Com., 1981—; elder The Presby. Ch. of Sewickley, 1986—. Served to capt. U.S. Army, 1968-71. Mem. ABA, Pa. Bar Assn., Allegheny County Bar Assn. Republican. Club: Duquesne, Harvard-Yale-Princeton, Edgeworth (Pitts.). Creditors rights, Bankruptcy. Office: 1500 Oliver Bldg Pittsburgh PA 15222

MURDOCH, DONALD R., lawyer, pharmaceutical company executive; b. Chgo., May 29, 1942; s. Stuart M. and Olive K. Murdoch; m. Ellen Press, Aug. 14, 1971; 1 child, Catherine London. B.A., U. Wis., Madison, 1964, J.D., 1968. Bar: Wis. 1968, Pa. 1968. Spl. counsel to dir. OEO, Washington, 1969; spl. counsel to Pres. White House, Washington, 1969-71; dep. dir. bur. domestic commerce U.S. Dept. Commerce, Washington, 1971-72; asst. dir. Cost of Living Council for Program Devel., 1972-73; ptnr. firm DeWitt, Sundby, Huggett, Schumacher & Morgan, Madison, Wis., 1973-82; sr. v.p., law G.D. Searle & Co., Skokie, Ill., 1982—; cons. to White House, Washington, 1974-75; cons. to sec. def., Washington, 1981. Mem. adv. bd. Wis. Clin. Cancer Ctr., Madison, 1984—; alderman common council City of Madison, 1975-77. Mem. State Bar Assn. Wis., ABA, Def. Adv. Com. on Women in Service. Republican. Office: GD Searle & Co Box 1045 Skokie IL 60076

MURER, MICHAEL ANTON, lawyer, consultant; b. Joliet, Ill., Sept. 3, 1944; s. Sergio Arthur and Helen Ilene (Bolos) M.; m. Cherilyn G. DiSpirito, Nov. 19, 1966; children: Jeffrey, Sasha. BA, Purdue U., 1965; JD, Georgetown U., 1968. Bar: Ill. 1968. Ptnr. Vinson, Singer & Murer, Joliet, 1969-74, Murer, Bolden, Koslowski & Polito, Joliet, 1975-80; sole practice Joliet, 1980—; 1st asst. pub. defender Will County, 1970-78; adj. faculty Lewis U., Lockport, Ill., 1975-79; cons. Murer Cons., Joliet, 1980—. Mem. founding com. Lewis U. Sch. Law, Glen Ellyn, Ill., 1976-78; nominee 4th congl. dist. Ill. U.S. Congress, 1980-82; bd. dirs. Spanish Ctr., Joliet. Mem. ABA, Ill. Bar Assn., Will County Bar Assn., Ill. Trial Lawyers Assn. Democrat. Roman Catholic. Health, Family and matrimonial, Criminal. Home: 2601 Dougall Rd Joliet IL 60432 Office: 81 N Chicago St Joliet IL 60431

MURG, GARY EARL, lawyer, educator; b. Detroit, Nov. 2, 1947; s. Earl and Doris (Jensen) M.; m. Diane J. Biocchi, June 16, 1971; children—Stephanie Lynn and Bradley Jensen (twins), Cameron Natale. B.S., Eastern Mich. U., 1969; M.A., J.D., Wayne State U., 1972, postgrad. in labor law and econs. Bar: Mich., 1972, D.C., 1981, U.S. Dist. Ct. (ea. dist.) Mich., 1972. Assoc., Law Office George Gregory Mantho, Detroit and Chgo., 1971-74; sr. labor counsel Burroughs Corp., Detroit, 1974-79; Detroit mng. ptnr., mem. firm exec. com. and operating com., Pepper, Hamilton & Scheetz, 1979-87, Epstein, Becker, Borsody & Green, P.C., Detroit mng. ptnr., offices also in N.Y., Wasington, San Francisco, Dallas, Stamford, Conn.; adj. prof. comparative labor relations law Georgetown U. Law Ctr., Washington. Served to capt. JAG Corps, U.S. Army Res., 1971. Mem. ABA (internat. labor law com., subcom. on practice and procedure in class actions EEO labor sect., com. on EEO law as it affects labor relations devel. law, practice and procedure), Fed. Bar Assn., D.C. Bar Assn. Mich. Bar Assn., Detroit Bar Assn., NAM (internat. labor relations com.). Clubs: Grosse Pointe Yacht (Grosse Pointe Shores, Mich.); Old (Harsens Island, Mich.); Detroit, Economic, Renaissance (Detroit). Co-author: Labor Relations Law: Canada, Mexico and Western Europe, 2 vols., 1978; contbr. numerous articles on civil rights, occupational safety and health and labor relations to legal jours. Labor, Federal civil litigation. Home: 40 Oxford Rd Grosse Pointe Shores MI 48236 Office: 100 Renaissance Center 36th Floor Detroit MI 48243

MURIS, TIMOTHY JOSEPH, government official; b. Massillon, Ohio, Nov. 18, 1949; s. George William and Louise (Hood) M.; m. Susan Sexton, Aug. 10, 1974; children—Matthew Allen, Paul Austin. B.A., San Diego State U., 1971; J.D., UCLA, 1974. Bar: Calif. 1974, U.S. Supreme Ct. 1983. Asst. to dir. policy planning and evaluation FTC, Washington, 1974-76, dir. Bur. Consumer Protection, 1981-83, dir. Bur. Competition, 1983-85; exec. assoc. dir. Office Mgmt. and Budget, Washington, 1985—; policy planning and evaluation law and econs. fellow U. Chgo. Law Sch., 1979-80; asst. prof. antitrust and consumer law U. Miami Law Sch. and Law Econs. Ctr., Fla., 1976-79, assoc. prof., 1979-81, prof., 1981-83, on leave, 1981-83; dep. counsel Presdl. Task Force on Regulatory Relief, Washington, 1981. Editor: The Federal Trade Commission, 1970—, Economic Regulation and Bureaucratic Behavior, 1981. Mem. Reagan-Bush Transition Team for FTC, Washington, 1980. Am. Bar Found. affiliated scholar, 1979. Mem. State Bar Calif., Order of Coif. Administrative and regulatory, Antitrust, Consumer commercial. Office: Office of Mgmt and Budget 17th & Pennsylvania Ave NW Room 260 Old Exec Office Bldg Washington DC 20503

MURNAGHAN, FRANCIS DOMINIC, JR., judge; b. Balt., June 20, 1920; m. Diana Edwards; children: Sheila H., George A., Janet E. B.A., Johns Hopkins U., 1941; LL.B., Harvard U., 1948. Bar: Md. bar 1949. Asso. firm Barnes Dechert Price Smith & Clark, Phila., 1948-50; staff atty. Office of Gen. Counsel, U.S. High Commr. for Ger., 1950-52; asst. atty. gen. State of Md., 1952-54; asso. firm Venable Baetjer & Howard, Balt., 1952-57; partner Venable Baetjer & Howard, 1957-79; judge U.S. Ct. Appeals for 4th Circuit Balt., 1979—. Chmn. Balt. Charter Revision Commn., 1963-64; trustee Walters Art Gallery, 1961, pres., 1963-80, chmn., 1980-85, chmn. emeritus, 1985—; pres. Balt. Sch. Bd., 1967-70. Served to lt. USNR, 1942-46. Mem. Am. Bar Assn., Md. Bar Assn., Balt. Bar Assn., Am. Coll. Trial Lawyers. Office: US Courthouse 101 W Lombard St Rm 950 Baltimore MD 21201

MURPHY, ARTHUR JOHN, JR., lawyer; b. Aug. 13, 1950; s. Arthur John, Sr. and Joan Marie (von Albade) M.; m. Joanne Therese Blak, Dec. 18, 1976; children—Arthur John III, Matthew Newsom. B.A., U. San Diego, 1972, J.D., 1975. Bar: Calif. 1975. Atty., SEC, Washington, 1975-78; assoc. Bronson, Bronson & McKinnon, San Francisco, 1979-82, ptnr., 1983—; lectr.; arbitrator Nat. Assn. Securities Dealers, 1982—. Contbr. securities law articles to profl. jours. Recipient Franklin award for Outstanding Grad., U. San Diego, 1972. Mem. ABA, Calif. Bar Assn. (exec. com. bus. law sect. 1986—), San Francisco Bar Assn. Roman Catholic. Club: Olympic. Securities, General corporate. Home: 81 Rutherford Ave San Anselmo CA 94960 Office: Bronson Bronson & McKinnon 555 California St San Francisco CA 94104

MURPHY, ARTHUR WILLIAM, lawyer, educator; b. Boston, Jan. 25, 1922; s. Arthur W. and Rose (Spillane) M.; m. Jane Marks, Dec. 21, 1948 (dec. Sept. 1951); 1 dau., Lois; m. Jean C. Marks, Sept. 30, 1954; children—Rachel, Paul. A.B. cum laude, Harvard, 1943; LL.B., Columbia, 1948. Bar: N.Y. State bar 1949. Asso. in law Columbia Sch. Law, N.Y.C., 1948-49; asso. dir. Legislative Drafting Research Fund, 1956, prof. law, 1963—; trial atty. U.S. Dept. Justice, 1950-52; asso. firm Hughes, Hubbard, Blair & Reed, N.Y.C., 1953-56, 57-58; partner firm Baer, Marks, Friedman & Berliner, N.Y.C., 1959-63; Mem. safety and licensing panel AEC, 1962—; mem. spl. commn. on weather modification NSF, 1964-66; mem. N.Y. State Atomic and Space Devel. Authority, 1964—. Author: Financial Protection against Atomic Hazards, 1957, (with others) Cases on Gratuitous Transfers, 1968, The Nuclear Power Controversy, 1976. Served with AUS, 1943-46. Decorated Purple Heart. Mem. Am. Bar Assn., Assn. Bar City N.Y. (spl. com. on sci. and law). Office: Columbia School of Law New York NY 10027

MURPHY, BETTY JANE SOUTHARD (MRS. CORNELIUS F. MURPHY), lawyer; b. East Orange, N.J.; d. Floyd Theodore and Thelma (Casto) Southard; m. Cornelius F. Murphy, May 1, 1965; children: Ann Southard, Cornelius Francis Jr. AB, Ohio State U.; postgrad., Alliance Française and U. Sorbonne, Paris; J.D., Am. U., 1958; LL.D. (hon.), Eastern Mich. U., 1975, Capital U., 1976, U. Puget Sound, 1986. Bar: D.C. 1958. Corr., free lance journalist Europe and Asia, UPI, Washington; pub. relations counsellor Capital Properties, Inc. of Columbus (Ohio), Washington; atty. Appellatte Cts. br. NLRB, Washington, 1958-59; practiced in Washington, 1959-74; mem. firm McInnis, Wilson, Munson & Woods (and predecessor firm), 1959-70; gen. partner firm Wilson, Woods & Villalon, 1970-74; dep. asst. sec., adminstr. Wage and Hour div. Dept. Labor, 1974-75; chmn. and mem. NLRB, 1975-79; ptnr. firm Baker & Hostetler, 1980—; adj. prof. law Am. U., 1972—; mem. adv. com. on rights and responsibilities of women to sec. HEW; mem. panel conciliators Internat. Center Settlement Investment Disputes, 1974-85 ; mem. Adminstrv. Conf. U.S., 1976-80, Public Service Adv. Bd., 1976-79; mem. human resources com. Nat. Center for Productivity and Quality of Working Life, 1976-80; mem. Presdl. Commn. on Exec. Exchange, 1981-85. Trustee Am. U., Mary Baldwin Coll.; nat. bd. dirs. Med. Coll. Pa., bd. corporators, 1976-85; bd. dirs. Center for Women in Medicine; bd. govs. St. Agnes Sch., 1981—; mem. exec. com. Commn. on Bicentennial of U.S. Constn., chmn. instnl. adv. com. Recipient Ohio Gov.'s award, 1980; fellow award, 1981. Mem. Am. Bar Assn. (adminstrv. law sect., chmn. labor law com. 1980-83, chmn. internat. and comparative law adminstrv. law sect. 1983—), Fed. Bar Assn., Inter-Am. Bar Assn. (editor Newsletter 1960-69, Silver medal 1967, co-chmn. labor law com. 1975-83), Bar Assn. D.C., World Peace Through Law Center, Internat. Soc. for Labor Law and Social Security, Am. Arbitration Assn. (dir.), Am. U. Alumni Assn. (dir. 1964-65, sec. law sch. 1965-66, pres. 1966-69, chmn. bd. govs. law sch. alumni 1969-73), Mortar Board, Kappa Beta Pi, Delta Delta Delta., Order Eastern Star. Republican. Episcopalian. Office: Baker & Hostetler 1050 Connecticut Ave NW Washington DC 20036

MURPHY, BRIAN PAUL, lawyer; b. Providence, June 29, 1943; s. Robert Thomas and Anna Loise (Meenagh) M.; m. Julia Anna Leppea, Apr. 12, 1974; children: Brian Paul Jr., Hillary H. AB, Georgetown U., 1965; JD, Cath. U. Am., 1968. Bar: D.C. 1969, Md. 1979. Assoc. Reed, Smith, Shaw & McClay, Washington, 1968—. Democrat. Roman Catholic. Real property, Administrative and regulatory. Home: 3286 Arcadia Pl NW Washington DC 20015 Office: Reed Smith Shaw & McClay 1150 Connecticut Ave NW Washington DC 20036

MURPHY, CAROL C., judge; b. Chgo., June 17, 1933; d. James I. and Catherine F. (Glasgow) Gibbons; m. Frank P. Murphy, Sept. 13, 1952; children: Eileen, Catherine Cox, Frank Jr., Stephen, Daniel, Christine, Robert, E. Patricia, John. BA summa cum laude, Fla. So. Coll., 1975; JD with honors, Stetson U., 1978. Bar: Fla. 1979, U.S. Dist. Ct. (mid. and so. dists.) Fla. 1979, U.S. Dist. Ct. (no. dist.) Fla. 1981, U.S. Ct. Appeals (5th and 11th cirs.) 1981, U.S. Supreme Ct. 1984. Staff atty. Fla. Rural Legal Services, Bartow, Fla., 1979-82; sole practice Lakeland, Fla., 1982-84; judge Polk County Ct., Bartow, 1985—. Bd. dirs. Mental Health Assn., Polk County, 1984—, Cath. Social Services, Polk County, 1983—; mem. adv. bd. United Way Cen. Fla., 1984—; mem. Fla. Ctr. Children and Youth, Fla. Council Crime and Delinquency. Mem. ABA (nat. conf. spl. ct. judges), Am. Judges Assn., Fla. Bar Assn. (chmn. consumer protection law com. 1983-84), Lakeland Bar Assn., Nat. Assn. Women Lawyers, Nat. Assn. Women Judges, Fla. Assn. Women Lawyers (past. pres. 10th cir. chpt.), Conf. County Ct. Judges Fla. (bd. dirs. 1986-87), Pionette Bus. and Profl. Women, Polk County LWV, AAUW. Club: Toastmasters (Lakeland). Office: PO Box 928 Bartow FL 33830

MURPHY, CHARLES CONROW, JR., lawyer; b. Mount Holly, N.J., May 22, 1946; s. Charles Conrow Sr. and Theresa Margaret (Daddino) M.; m. Roberta Grace Everett (div.); 1 child, Pamela Anne; m. Laura Lee Martin. AB, Rutgers Coll., 1969; JD, U. Tenn., 1973. Bar: Tenn. 1973, Ga. 1975, U.S. Dist. Ct. (ea. dist.) Tenn., 1973, U.S. Dist. Ct. (no. dist.) Ga., 1981, U.S. Ct. Appeals (5th and 11th cirs.) 1981. Staff atty. FTC, Atlanta, 1973-75; trial atty. antitrust div. U.S. Dept. Justice, Atlanta, 1976-80; ptnr. Vaughan, Roach, Davis, Birch & Murphy, Atlanta, 1980—. Mem. ABA. Clubs: Druid Hills Golf (Atlanta). Antitrust, Federal civil litigation, Computer. Home: 1714 E Clifton Rd Atlanta GA 30307 Office: Vaughan Roach Davis Birch & Murphy One Ravinia Dr Suite 1500 Atlanta GA 30346

MURPHY, DANIEL HAYES, II, lawyer; b. Hartford, Conn., Jan. 8, 1941; s. Robert Henry and Jane Granville (Cook) M.; m. Deann Ellison, June 30, 1962; children—Edward Ellison, Jessica Jane. B.A., Yale U., 1962; LL.B., Columbia U., 1965. Bar: N.Y. 1965, U.S. Dist. Ct. (so. and ea. dists.) N.Y. 1967, U.S. Ct. Appeals (2d cir.) 1968, Conn. 1978, Calif. 1984, Fla. 1986. Assoc. White & Case, N.Y.C., 1965-70; asst. U.S. atty. So. Dist. N.Y., N.Y.C., 1970-74; sole practice N.Y.C., 1974-76; assoc. Mendes & Mount, N.Y.C., 1977-81, jr. ptnr., 1981-85; sole practice N.Y.C., 1985—; spl. master Supeme Ct. N.Y. County, 1981—. Chmn. planning commn., Groton Long Point, Conn., 1977-84. Mem. ABA, N.Y. State Bar Assn., N.Y. County Lawyers Assn., Assn. Bar City N.Y. Roman Catholic. Club: Yale (N.Y.C.), Ocean Reef (Key Largo, Fla.). Insurance, Federal civil litigation. Office: 123 William St Suite 2310 New York NY 10038

MURPHY, DIANA E., U.S. district judge; b. Faribault, Minn., Jan. 4, 1934; d. Albert W. and Adleyne (Heiker) Kuske; m. Joseph E. Murphy, Jr., July 24, 1958; children: Michael, John E. B.A. magna cum laude, U. Minn., 1954, J.D. magna cum laude, 1974; postgrad., Johannes Gutenberg U., Mainz, Germany, 1954-55, U. Minn., 1955-58. Bar: Minn. 1974. Mem. firm Lindquist & Vennum, 1974-76; mcpl. judge Hennepin County, 1976-78; Minn. dist. judge 1978-80; U.S. dist. judge Minn. Mpls., 1980—; instr. Law Sch. U. Minn., Atty. Gen.'s Advocacy Inst.;. Bd. editors: U. Minn. Law Rev. Bd. dirs. Spring Hill Conf. Ctr., 1978-84; bd. dirs. Bush Found., 1982—. chmn. bd., 1986—; bd. dirs. Amicus, 1976-80, organizer, 1st chmn. adv. council; mem. Mpls. Charter Commn., 1973-76, chmn., 1974-76; bd. dirs. Ops. De Novo, 1971-76, chmn., 1974-75; mem. Minn. Constl. Study Commn., chmn. bill of rights com., 1971-73; regent St. Johns U., 1978—, vice chmn. bd., 1985—; trustee Twin Cities Pub. TV, 1985—; bd. dirs. Mpls. United Way, 1985—. Fulbright scholar; recipient U. Minn. Outstanding Achievement award; Amicus Founders' award; YWCA Outstanding Achievement award. Fellow Am. Bar Found.; mem. Am. Bar Assn. (Ethics and Profl. Responsibility Judges Adv. Com. 1981—), Minn. Bar Assn. (bd. govs. 1977-81), Hennepin County Bar Assn. (gov. council 1976-81), Am. Law Inst., Am. Judicature Soc. (bd. dirs. 1982—, v.p. 1985—), Nat. Assn. Women Judges, Minn. Women Lawyers, U. Minn. Alumni Assn. (bd. dirs. 1975-83, pres. 1981-82), Fed. Judges Assn. (bd. dirs. 1982—, v.p. 1984—), Order of Coif, Phi Beta Kappa. Federal civil litigation, Criminal, Jurisprudence. Office: US District Court 670 US Courthouse 110 S 4th St Minneapolis MN 55401

MURPHY, EDWARD ELIAS, JR., lawyer; b. St. Louis, Dec. 21, 1925; s. Edward Elias Sr. and Mary Christine (Shelton) M.; m. Margaret Jean Berger, Sept. 10, 1949; children: Mary Anna Murphy Burroughs, Edward Elias III. AB, Washington U., St. Louis, 1947; JD, Harvard U., 1950. Bar: Mo. 1950, U.S. Dist. Ct. (ea. dist.) Mo. 1951, U.S. Supreme Ct. 1972. Assoc. Coburn, Croft & Putzell, St. Louis, 1950-55; sole practice St. Louis, 1955-60; ptnr. Kortenhof & Ely, St. Louis, 1960-73, Murphy & Assocs., Clayton, Mo., 1973-84, Murphy & Selzer, Clayton, 1984—. Councilman, chmn. St. Louis County Council, 1960-64; vice chmn. St. Louis County Charter Commn., 1967; chmn. St. Louis County Planning Commn., 1970-76. Mem. ABA, Mo. Bar Assn., Met. St. Louis Bar Assn. (exec. com. 1965-67). Republican. Roman Catholic. Avocations: history, travel. General corporate, Probate, State civil litigation. Home: 9967 Holliston Ct Saint Louis MO 63124 Office: Murphy & Seltzer 120 S Central Saint Louis MO 63105

MURPHY, EWELL EDWARD, JR., lawyer; b. Washington, Feb. 21, 1928; s. Ewell Edward and Lou (Phillips) M.; m. Patricia Bredell Purnell, June 26, 1954 (dec. 1964); children: Michaela, Megan Patricia, Harlan Ewell. B.A., U. Tex., 1946, LL.B., 1948; D.Phil., Oxford U., Eng., 1951. Bar: Tex. 1948. Assoc. Baker & Botts, Houston, 1954-63, ptnr., 1964—, head internat. dept., 1972—; pres. Houston World Trade Assn., 1972-74; trustee Southwestern Legal Found., 1978—; chmn. Houston Com. on Fgn. Relations, 1984-85, Inst. Transnational Arbitration, 1985—, Internat. and Comparative Law Ctr., 1986—. Contbr. articles to profl. jours. Served to lt. USAF, 1952-54. Recipient Carl H. Fulda award U. Tex. Internat. Law Jour., 1980; Rhodes scholar, 1948-51. Mem. ABA (chmn. sect. internat. law 1970-71), Houston Bar Assn. (chmn. internat. law com. 1963-64, 70-71), Inter-Am. Bar Assn., Am. Soc. Internat. Law, Houston Philos. Soc. (pres. 1976-77), Houston C. of C. (chmn. internat. bus. com. 1964, 65). Private international, General corporate. Home: 17 W Oak Dr Houston TX 77056 Office: Baker & Botts 1 Shell Plaza Houston TX 77002

MURPHY, GAVIN PALMER, lawyer, educator; b. Albany, N.Y., May 26, 1926; s. Vincent Bernard and Margaret (Palmer) M.; m. Margaretha Sällfors, Jan 5, 1968; 1 child, Palmer Wellington. AB, Tufts U., 1949; JD, Harvard U., 1954. Bar: N.Y. 1955, U.S. Dist. Ct. (so. dist.) N.Y. 1955. Assoc. Dewey, Ballantine, N.Y.C., 1954-61; internat. counsel Standard Brands, N.Y.C., 1961-72; asst. gen. counsel J.P. Stevens & Co. Inc., N.Y.C., 1972—; adj. asst. prof. NYU, 1974—, adj. prof. Cardozo Law Sch., 1983—. Editor the Am.-Irish Hist. Soc. annual Recorder, 1974-77. Treas./sec. J.P. Stevens' polit. action com., 1976—. Served with USN, 1944-46. Mem. Internat. Bar Assn., Assn. Bar City N.Y., Phi Beta Kappa. Republican. Roman Catholic. General corporate, Legal education. Office: JP Stevens & Co Inc 1185 Ave of Americas New York NY 10036

MURPHY, GREGORY G., lawyer; b. Helena, Mont., Feb. 3, 1954; s. Michael Anthony and Elizabeth (Cooney) M.; m. Katherine Joan Koch, Dec. 30, 1977; children: Megan, Brian, Allison. BA, U. Mont., 1976; JD, U. Notre Dame, 1979. Bar: Oreg. 1979, U.S. Dist. Ct. Oreg. 1979, U.S. Ct. Appeals (9th cir.) 1979, Mont. 1980, U.S. Dist. Ct. Mont. 1980. Clk. to judge U.S. Ct. Appeals (9th cir.), Portland, 1979-80; assoc. Moulton, Bellingham, Longo & Mather P.C., Billings, Mont., 1980-84; ptnr. Moulton, Bellingham, Longo & Mather, Billings, Mont., 1984—; trustee Mont. dist. U.S. Bankruptcy Ct., 1982-85; examiner Mont. Bd. Bar Examiners, 1985—; mem. multi state bar examination com. Nat. Conference Bar Examiners, 1986—. Assoc. editor Notre Dame Law Rev., 1978-79. bd. dirs. Billings Symphony Soc., 1982—. Thomas and Alberta White scholar U. Notre Dame, 1978-79. Mem. ABA, Mont. Bar Assn., Oreg. Bar Assn., Yellowstone County Bar Assn. Lodge: Rotary. Avocations: french horn, backpacking. Bankruptcy, Federal civil litigation, Insurance. Home: 3220 Fairmeadow Billings MT 59102 Office: Moulton Bellingham Longo & Mather PC 200 Securities Bldg PO Box 2545 Billings MT 59103-2545

MURPHY, HAROLD LOYD, judge; b. Haralson County, Ga., Mar. 31, 1927; s. James Loyd and Georgia Gladys (McBrayer) M.; m. Jacqueline Marie Ferri, Dec. 20, 1958; children: Mark Harold, Paul Bailey. Student, West Ga. Coll., 1944-45, U. Miss., 1945-46; LL.B., U. Ga., 1949. Bar: Ga. 1949. Practice law Buchanan, Ga., from 1949; partner firm Howe and Murphy, Buchanan, Tallapoosa, Ga., 1958-71; judge Superior Cts., Tallapoosa Circuit, 1971-77; U.S. dist. judge No. Dist. of Ga., Rome, 1977—; rep. Gen. Assembly of Ga., 1951-61; asst. solicitor gen. Tallapoosa Jud. Circuit, 1956; mem. Jud. Qualifications Commn., State of Ga., 1977. Served with USNR, 1945-46. Mem. Am. Bar Assn., Ga. Bar Assn., Dist. Judges Assn. for 11th Circuit, Am. Judicature Soc., Tallapoosa Circuit Bar Assn. Democrat. Methodist. Clubs: Lions, Gridiron Secret Soc, Masons. Home: Buchanan Rd Tallapoosa GA 30176 Office: PO Drawer 53 Rome GA 30161

MURPHY, JAMES PAUL, lawyer; b. Jackson, Tenn., Apr. 29, 1944; s. Paul Joseph and Marjorie Mary (Smyth) M.; m. Marcia Mae Gaughan, Sept. 5, 1975. B.A., U. Notre Dame, 1966; J.D., U. Mich., 1969. Bar: Ohio 1969, D.C. 1984, Md. 1984, U.S. Dist. Ct. (no. dist.) Ohio 1970, U.S. Ct. Appeals (6th cir.) 1972, U.S. Supreme Ct. 1976, U.S. Dist. Ct. Md., 1984, U.S. Dist. Ct. D.C., 1984, U.S. Dist. Ct. of Appeals (4th cir., D.C. cir.) 1984. Vol. VISTA, 1969-70; assoc. Squire, Sanders & Dempsey, Cleve., 1970-79, ptnr., 1979—. Mem. ABA (litigation, antitrust sects.), Greater Cleve. Bar Assn. (fed. ct. com.), Md. Bar Assn., D.C. Bar Assn., Ohio State Bar Assn. (antitrust sect.). Clubs: Mid-Day (Cleve.); Westwood Country (Rocky River, Ohio), City (Washington). Antitrust, Federal civil litigation, State civil litigation. Home: 4512 Weatherill Rd Bethesda MD 20816 Office: Squire Sanders & Dempsey 1201 Pennsylvania Ave NW Washington DC 20004

MURPHY, JOHN FRANCIS, law educator, consultant, lawyer; b. Portchester, N.Y., Apr. 25, 1937; s. Francis John and Emilie (Tourtellot) M.; children—Andrew, Robert. B.A., Cornell U., 1959, LL.B. in Internat. Affairs, 1962. Bar: D.C. 1963, Kans. 1970. Afro-Asia Public Service fellow, India, 1962-63; assoc. Winthrop, Stimson, Putnam & Roberts, N.Y.C., 1963-64; atty. Office Legal Adv., dept. state, Washington, 1964-67; assoc. Kirkland, Ellis, Hodson, Chaffetz & Masters, Washington, 1967-69; assoc. prof. law U. Kans., Lawrence, 1969-72, prof., 1972-84, assoc. dean Sch. Law, 1975-77; vis. prof. Villanova U., 1983-84, prof., 1984—; vis. prof. law Cornell U., fall 1979, Georgetown U., summer 1982; Charles H. Stockton prof. internat. law Naval War Coll., 1980-81. Recipient Raymond F. Rice prize Sch. Law, U. Kans., 1979, 83. Mem. ABA, Am. Soc. Internat. Law, Internat. Law Assn. Episcopalian. Author: Legal Aspects of International Terrorism: Summary Report of an International Conference, 1980, The United Nations and the Control of International Violence, 1982, Punishing International Terrorists, 1985; contbr. articles, comments, book revs. to profl., popular jours.; editor (with Alona E. Evans), contbg. author: Legal Aspects of International Terrorism, 1978; bd. editors Cornell Law Quar., 1961, 62; mem. bd. editors Terrorism: An Internat. Jour., 1981—. Legal education, Private international, Public international. Office: Villanova Law Sch Villanova PA 19085

MURPHY, JOHN PAUL, judge; b. Omaha, July 26, 1947; s. Albert V. and Mary (Martin) M.; m. Marie Ford, Oct. 25, 1969; children—Daniel Joseph, Timothy Ford, Patrick Martin. A.B., St. Louis U., 1969; J.D., Creighton U., 1974. Bar: Nebr. 1975, U.S. Dist. Ct. Nebr. 1975, U.S. Supreme Ct. 1979. Dep. county atty. Lincoln County, North Platte, Nebr., 1975-77; ptnr. Ruff & Murphy, North Platte, 1977-83; pub. defender Lincoln County, 1981-83; dist. judge 13th Dist. Nebr., North Platte, 1983—; instr. Kearney State Coll., Nebr., 1978-83, Mid Plains Community Coll., North Platte, 1977-83;

bd. dirs. Nebr. Ctr. on Sentencing Alternatives, Lincoln, 1983—. Contbr. articles to law revs. Mem. jud. nominating commn. Chief Justice Supreme Ct. Nebr., 1978-83, Nebr. Gov.'s Task Force on Sexual Assault, 1984; chmn. North Platte Planning Commn., 1982-83, Lincoln County Democratic Party, 1978-82. Served as 1st lt. USAF, 1969-72. Mem. Nebr. Dist. Judges Assn., ABA, Nebr. Bar Assn., Lincoln County Bar Assn., Assn. Trial Lawyers Am. (jud. mem.). Democrat. Roman Catholic. Judicial administration. Home: 510 W 4th St North Platte NE 69101 Office: Lincoln County Courthouse North Platte NE 69101

MURPHY, JOSEPH ALBERT, JR., lawyer; b. Grosse Pointe, Mich., May 29, 1934; s. Joseph Albert and Isabel C. (Callahan) M.; m. Joanne Becker, June 24, 1961; children: Michael, Joseph III. BS, Georgetown U., 1956; JD, Detroit Coll. Law, 1962. Bar: Mich. 1962. House counsel Blue Cross Mich., Detroit, 1964-69, gen. counsel, corp. sec., 1969-75; v.p., dep. gen. counsel Blue Cross & Blue Shield Mich., Detroit, 1975—; chmn. Health Care Network, Southfield, Mich., 1981-85; chmn. Blue Care Inc., Southfield, 1986—. Mem. Allocations panel United Found., Detroit, 1985—; treas. Grosse Pointe Dem. Club, 1972-73; chmn. Health and People's Polit. Action Commn., Detroit, 1978-84. Served with U.S. Army, 1957-59. Mem. ABA, Mich. Bar Assn., Detroit Bar Assn., Nat. Health Lawyers Assn. (pres. 1981-82), Am. Corp. Counsel Assn., Am. Arbitrators Assn. (panel of arbitrators). Roman Catholic. Administrative and regulatory, General corporate, Health. Home: 1419 Kensington Rd Grosse Pointe Park MI 48230 Office: Blue Cross Blue Shield of Mich 600 E Lafayette Detroit MI 48226

MURPHY, JOSEPH EDWARD, lawyer, legal educator; b. Chgo., Aug. 30, 1948; s. Edward J. and Rita E. (Huver) M.; m. Vicki L. Chavar, Ocy. 15, 1983; children: Kim, Isadora, Ira. BA, Rutgers U., 1970; JD, U. Pa., 1973. Bar: Pa. 1973, U.S. Dist. Ct. (ea. dist.) Pa. 1973, N.J. 1975, U.S. Dist. Ct. N.J. 1975. Assoc. Wolf, Block, Schorr & Solis-Cohen, Phila., 1973-76; atty. Bell Telephone of Pa., Phila., 1976-83; sr. atty. Bell Atlantic Corp., Phila., 1984—; instr. for Paralegal Tng., Phila., 1982—; adj. lectr. Rutgers U., 1986—. Mng. editor U. Pa. Law Rev., 1972-73; contbr. articles to profl. jours. Mem. ABA (antitrust sect.), Pa. Bar Assn., Phila. Bar Assn., Am. Corp. Counsel Assn., Order of Coif, Pi Sigma Alpha. Democrat. Avocation: family. Administrative and regulatory, Antitrust, Computer. Home: 612 Harper Ave Drexel Hill PA 19026 Office: Bell Atlantic Corp 1600 Market St Philadelphia PA 19103

MURPHY, JOSEPH F., lawyer, state insurance official; b. White Plains, N.Y., Apr. 4, 1915; s. Joseph Francis and Bessie L. (Madden) M.; m. Marion L. Barrett, Oct. 18, 1942; children: Elizabeth Ann, Kevin Barrett, Brian Sean. A.B., Fordham U., 1936, LL.B., 1938. Bar: N.Y. 1938. Eastern counsel Kemper Ins. Group, 1947-52; dep. supt. N.Y. Ins. Dept., 1952-55; with Continental Ins. Cos., 1955-80, v.p., gen. counsel, 1957-74, exec. v.p., 1974-80; exec. v.p. Continental Corp., 1974-80; partner Le Beouf, Lamb, Leiby & MacRae, N.Y.C., 1980-82, 84—; commr. of ins. State of N.J., 1982-84. Served to lt. comdr. USNR, 1942-45. Decorated Bronze Star. Administrative and regulatory. Home: 18 Bennington Rd Convent Station NJ 07961 Office: 520 Madison Ave New York NY 10022

MURPHY, KATHRYN COCHRANE, lawyer; b. Chatham, Ont., Can., Apr. 17, 1949; came to U.S., 1949; d. John Romaine and Mary Emma (Suchta) Cochrane; m. Glenn E. Murphy, Jr., Aug. 19, 1972; children: Glenn E. III, Emma Kathryn. Student Mt. Holyoke Coll., 1967-69; AB cum laude in Urban Studies, Yale U., 1971; postgrad. Georgetown U., 1971-72; JD magna cum laude, Boston Coll., 1975. Bar: Mass. 1975. Assoc. Csaplar and Bok, Boston, 1975-83, ptnr., 1983—. Former trustee Soc. for Preservation New Eng. Antiquities, Boston, Boston YWCA; incorporator Children's Mus., Boston, 1983—. Mem. Urban Land Inst., ABA, Mass. Bar Assn., Boston Bar Assn., Mass. Conveyancers Assn., New Eng. Women in Real Estate (steering com. 1982—), Order of Coif. Clubs: Yale (Boston) (bd. dirs. 1983-86), Boston Luncheon (bd. dirs. 1977-80). Real property, Environment. Office: Csaplar and Bok One Winthrop Sq Boston MA 02110

MURPHY, LESTER F(ULLER), lawyer; b. East Chgo., Ind., Nov. 28, 1936; s. Lester Fuller Sr. and Angelique (Molloy) M.; divorced; children: John Justin, Angelique, Lester Fuller III, Christopher, Colleen, Bridget, Erika, Shannon; m. Susan Olsen, Aug. 16, 1986. AB, U. Notre Dame, 1959, JD, 1960. Bar: Ind. 1960, U.S. Dist. Ct. (no. and so. dists.) Ind. 1960, U.S. Ct. Appeals (7th cir.) 1961, U.S. Supreme Ct. 1963, Ill. 1976, U.S. Dist. Ct. (no. dist.) Ill. 1983, U.S. Ct. Appeals (8th cir.) 1985. Assoc. Riley, Reed, Murphy & McAtee, East Chgo., Ind., 1960-64, ptnr., 1964-65; ptnr. Murphy, McAtee & Murphy, East Chgo., 1965-68, Murphy, McAtee, Murphy & Costanza, East Chgo., 1968—. Contbr. articles to profl. jours. Mem. ABA, Ind. Bar Assn., East Chgo. Bar Assn., World Peace Through Law Conf., Ind. Bar Found., Ind. Continuing Legal Edn. Found. (lectr.), Defense Research and Trial Lawyers Assn., Nat. Bd. Trial Advocacy (cert.), Am. Arbitration Assn. (panel arbitrators). Roman Catholic. Clubs: Woodmar Country (Hammond), Columbia Yacht (Chgo.). Federal civil litigation, State civil litigation, Insurance. Office: Murphy McAtee Murphy & Costanza 1st National Bank Bldg East Chicago IN 46312

MURPHY, LYNDA MARIE, lawyer; b. Boston, July 17, 1945; d. John E. and Marie Louise (Pierce) M.; m. Jon L. Boisclair, June 14, 1980; 1 child, Alexandra Marie. BA, U. So. Calif., 1970; JD, U. Calif., Berkeley, 1973; LLM, Harvard U., 1974. Bar: Calif. 1973, Mass. 1980, D.C. 1985. Office dir. HUD, Washington, 1978-82; ptnr. Dunnells, Duvall, Bennett & Porter, Washington, 1982-85; sr. ptnr. Barrett, Montgomery & Murphy, Washington, 1985—. Mem. exec. com. Dem. Fin. Counsel, Washington, 1985, exec. com. Potomac Group, 1983—. Mem. ABA, Calif. Bar Assn., Mass. Bar Assn., D.C Bar Assn. Roman Catholic. State and local taxation, Real property, Administrative and regulatory. Office: Barrett Montgomery & Murphy 2555 MST Suite 100 Washington DC 20037

MURPHY, MARCIA GAUGHAN, lawyer, educator; b. Cleve., Nov. 23, 1949; d. John James and Alma Marie (Friedman) Gaughan; m. James Paul Murphy, Sept. 5, 1975. A.B. with honors in English, Smith Coll., Northampton, Mass., 1972; J.D. summa cum laude, U. Notre Dame, 1975. Bar: Ohio 1975. Assoc. Jones, Day, Reavis & Pogue, Cleve., 1975-77; asst. prof. law Case Western Res. U., 1977-81, assoc. prof., 1981-83, prof., 1983; vis. prof. law Am. U., Washington Coll. Law, 1983, prof., 1984—, acting dep. dean, 1985-86; referee Ct. Common Pleas, Cleve., 1980; participant Law & Econs. Conf. for Lawyers, Hanover, N.H., 1983. Assoc. editor: Couse's Ohio Form Book, 1985; contbr. articles to law jours. Div. chmn. Campaign for Notre Dame U., 1979; mem. Women's Com. Nat. Symphony Orch., Washington. Mem. ABA, Women's Bar Assn. D.C. Roman Catholic. Legal education, Probate, Real property. Office: Am U Washington Coll Law 4400 Massachusetts Ave NW Washington DC 20016

MURPHY, MATTHEW M., lawyer; b. Chgo., July 18, 1956; s. Mathew Martin and Mary (Daly) M.; m. Carlene Heldt, Aug. 9, 1980; children: Megan, Jill. BA, U. Ill., 1977; JD, Ill. Inst. Tech., 1982. Bar: Ill. 1982, U.S. Dist. Ct. (no. dist.) Ill. 1982. Field claim investigator Sentry Ins. Co., Chgo., 1978-79; v.p. Internat. Surplus Lines Ins. Co., Chgo., 1979—. Insurance, General practice. Home: 1751 N Fern Ct Chicago IL 60614 Office: Internat Surplus Lines Ins 200 S Wacker Dr Chicago IL 60606

MURPHY, MICHAEL R., judge; b. Denver, Aug. 6, 1947; s. Roland and Mary Cecilia (Maloney) M.; m. Maureen Elizabeth Donnelly, Aug. 22, 1970; children: Amy Christina, Michael Donnelly. BA in History, Creighton U., 1969; JD, U. Wyo., 1972. Bar: Wyo. 1972, U.S. Ct. Appeals (10th cir.) 1972, Utah 1973, U.S. Dist. Ct. Utah 1974, U.S. Dist. Ct. Wyo. 1976, U.S. Ct. Appeals (5th cir.) 1976, U.S. Tax Ct. 1980, U.S. Ct. Appeals (9th cir.) 1981, U.S. Ct. Appeals (fed. cir.) 1984. Law clk. to judge U.S. Ct. Appeals (10th cir.), Salt Lake City, 1972-73; assoc. Jones, Waldo, Holbrook & McDonough, Salt Lake City, 1973-86; judge 3d Dist. Ct., Salt Lake City, 1986—; mem. adv. com. on rules of civil procedure Utah Supreme Ct., Salt Lake City, 1985—. Mem. ABA, Wyo. Bar Assn., Utah Bar Assn. (chmn. alternative dispute resolution com. 1985—), Salt Lake County Bar Assn. Roman Catholic. Office: Met Hall of Justice 240 E 400 S Salt Lake City UT 84111

MURPHY, NINA REBECCA, law educator; b. N.Y.C., Nov. 24, 1947; d. Krass and Estelle (Greenberg) Kestin; m. Eugene Paul Murphy, Sept. 3, 1967 (div. June 1978); children: Sarabeth Kestin, Sean Joseph. Student, U. Mass., 1965-67; BA, Hunter Coll., 1969; JD, NYU, 1972, LLM, 1976. Bar: N.Y. 1973, U.S. Ct. Appeals (2d cir.) 1977, Va. 1981. Assoc. Mead & Callan, Bay Shore, N.Y., 1972-74; sole practice Levittown, N.Y., 1974-76; prof. law U. of Richmond, Va., 1976—. Mem. Richmond (Va.) First Club, 1986; bd. dirs. Congregation Beth Ahabeth, Richmond, 1986. Mem. ABA (tax sect., Outstanding Woman Atty. 1986), Va. Bar Assn. (tax sect., Outstanding Woman Atty. 1986). Democrat. Club: Warsaw Women (Richmond, Va.). B'nai B'rith (adv. bd. Anti-Defamation League 1985—). Personal income taxation, State and local taxation, Legal education. Home: 7619 Bryn Mawr Rd Richmond VA 23229 Office: U Richmond TC Williams Sch of Law Richmond VA 23173

MURPHY, PATRICK JAMES, lawyer; b. Monroe, Mich., Sept. 20, 1953; s. Ralph B. and Jayleane M. Murphy; m. Gail F. Lechner, Oct. 5, 1985. BS summa cum laude, No. Mich. U., 1978; JD, U. Puget Sound, 1980. Bar: Nev. 1981, U.S. Dist. Ct. Nev. 1981, U.S. Ct. Appeals (9th cir.) 1981, U.S. Supreme Ct. 1986. Ptnr. Rawlings, Olson & Cannon, P.C., Las Vegas, Nev., 1981—. Mem. ABA (gov. law student div. 1978-79, gen. practice sect.), Nev. Bar Assn., Clark County Bar Assn., Am. Trial Lawyers Assn., Def. Research Inst. Republican. Roman Catholic. Avocations: raquetball, skiing. Insurance, Federal civil litigation, State civil litigation. Office: Rawlings Olson & Cannon 514 S 3d St Las Vegas NV 89101

MURPHY, PHILIP DEVER, lawyer; b. Boston, Dec. 28, 1951; s. David Loring Sr. and Dorothy V. (Dever) M.; m. Kate M. McCartin, June 26, 1982. AB, Dartmouth Coll., 1974; JD, Suffolk U., 1979; LLM in Taxation, Boston U., 1982. Bar: Mass. 1979, U.S. Dist. Ct. Mass. 1980, U.S. Tax Ct. 1981. Assoc. Liberty Mut. Ins. Co., Boston, 1980-83, sr. atty., 1983-84, asst. counsel, 1984-86, assoc. counsel, 1986—; chmn. legal commn. Mass. Auto Rating Bur., Boston, 1983—, N.C. Reins. Facility, Raleigh, 1984—; mem. legal commn. N.C. Rating Bur., Raleigh, 1984—, N.J. Auto Full Ins. Underwriting Assn., Newark, 1984—. Mem. Town Meeting, Milton, Mass., 1974-81. Mem. ABA (tort and ins. practice sect., vice chmn. pub. regulation of ins. com. 1986—, editor pub. regulation of ins. newsletter 1985—), Mass. Bar Assn., South Shore Dartmouth Club (dist. enrollment dir. 1985—). Democrat. Roman Catholic. Avocations: tennis, gardening, softball. Insurance, Corporate taxation. Home: 1050 Canton Ave Milton MA 02186 Office: Liberty Mut Ins Co 175 Berkeley St Boston MA 02117

MURPHY, R. ANTHONY, lawyer; b. Pittsburg, Kans., Oct. 25, 1947; s. Ronald Glenn and Geneva Esther (Mattingly) M.; m. Cheryl Louise Weaver, Mar. 8, 1975; children: Glyndon Genelle and Cullen Michael (twins). BA, U. Mo., Kansas City, 1969, MA, 1971, JD, 1979. Bar: Mo. 1980, U.S. Dist. Ct. (we. dist.) Mo. 1980, Ariz. 1984, U.S. Dist. Ct. Ariz. 1985. Field examiner labor mgmt. relations NLRB, Kansas City, Kans., 1971-75; officer labor relations IRS, Kansas City, Mo., 1975-77; assoc. Whipple & Kraft, P.C., Kansas City, 1980-83; sole practice Kansas City, 1983-84; assoc. Little, Fisher & Siegel, P.C., Tucson, 1984-85, Dunscomb & Shepherd, Tucson, 1985-87; sole practice Tucson, 1987—; adj. prof. Avila Coll., Kansas City, 1980-82. Asst. research editor The Urban Lawyer, 1977-78. Active Big Bros. of Greater Kansas City, 1971-76. Mem. ABA (labor law sect.), Ariz. Bar Assn., Mo. Bar Assn., Assn. Trial Lawyers Am. U. Mo. Kansas City Alumni Assn. (treas. 1983-84, bd. dirs. 1982-84), Phi Alpha Theta, Omicron Delta Kappa. Roman Catholic. Personal injury, Labor, General practice. Office: 323 S Gollob Rd Tucson AZ 85701

MURPHY, RICHARD PATRICK, lawyer; b. Elizabeth, N.J., Dec. 13, 1954; s. Richard Francis and Marie (Conlon) M.; m. Ana Alvarez. AB with distinction, Cornell U., 1976; JD cum laude, AM, U. Mich., 1980. Bar: D.C. 1980, U.S. Dist. Ct. D.C. 1981, U.S. Ct. Appeals (D.C. cir.) 1981, U.S. Supreme Ct. 1984. Assoc. Bergson, Borkland, Margolis & Adler, Washington, 1980-82; atty. enforcement div. SEC, Washington, 1982-84, br. chief enforcement div., 1984—. Mem. ABA, D.C. Bar Assn. Securities, Federal civil litigation, Antitrust. Home: 15710 Dorset Rd Apt 303 Laurel MD 20707 Office: US SEC Div Enforcement 450 5th St NW Washington DC 20549

MURPHY, RICHARD VANDERBURGH, lawyer; b. Syracuse, N.Y., May 9, 1951; s. Robert Drown and Reta (Vanderburgh) M.; m. Patricia Lynn Eades, May 18, 1973; 1 child, Alan Christopher. A.B., Dartmouth Coll., 1973; J.D., U. Ky., 1976. Bar: Ky. 1976, U.S. Dist. Ct. (ea. dist.) Ky. 1977, U.S. Supreme Ct. 1980. Corp. counsel Lexington-Fayette Urban County Govt., Lexington, 1976-82; asst. county atty. Fayette County, Lexington, 1982-84; assoc. H. Foster Pettit, Lexington, 1982-83; ptnr. Pettit & Murphy, Lexington, 1983-84; sr. atty. Wyatt, Tarrant & Combs, Lexington, 1984—; cons. zoning ordinance update Lexington-Fayette Urban County Govt., Lexington, 1982-83. Elder, vice chmn. bd. South Elkhorn Christian Ch., Lexington, 1982—. Mem. Am. Planning Assn., ABA, Ky. Bar Assn., Order of Coif, Phi Beta Kappa. Democrat. Real property, Administrative and regulatory, General corporate. Home: 3313 Otter Creek Dr Lexington KY 40502 Office: Wyatt Tarrant & Combs 1100 Kincaid Towers Lexington KY 40507

MURPHY, ROBERT ANTHONY, JR., lawyer; b. Albany, N.Y., Dec. 14, 1953; s. Robert A. Sr. and Mary Lourdes (Cosenke) M.; m. Paula J. Follett, Aug. 20, 1977; 1 child, Peter J. BS magna cum laude, SUNY, Albany, 1976; JD cum laude, Albany Law Sch., 1979. Bar: N.Y. 1980, U.S. Dist. Ct. (no. dist.) N.Y. 1980, U.S. Ct. Appeals (2d cir.) 1983. Law clk. N.Y. Supreme Ct. Appellate Div. (3d. dept.), Albany, 1979-80; assoc. Pentak, Brown & Tobin, Albany, 1980—. Mem. ABA, N.Y. State Bar Assn., Albany County Bar Assn. Democrat. Roman Catholic. Lodge: Optimists (v.p. Albany club 1984—). Federal civil litigation, State civil litigation, Personal injury. Home: 36 Palma Blvd Albany NY 12203 Office: Pentak Brown & Tobin 111 Pine St Albany NY 12207

MURPHY, ROBERT C(HARLES), judge; b. Balt., Oct. 9, 1926; (married); 3 children. J.D., U. Md., 1951, LL.D. (hon.), 1973; LL.D. (hon.), U. Balt., 1981. Bar: Md. 1952, D.C. 1952, U.S. Supreme Ct. 1957. Law clk. to Hon. William P. Cole, Jr., assoc. judge U.S. Ct. Customs and Patent Appeals, Washington, 1951-53; gen. counsel U. Md., 1955-57; apl. asst. atty. gen. Atty. Gen. Md., Balt., 1957-62; asst. atty. gen., then dep. atty. gen. Atty. Gen. Md., 1962-66; atty. gen. 1966-67; chief judge Md. Ct. Spl. Appeals, Annapolis, 1967-72, Md. Ct. Appeals, 1972—; adminstrv. head Md. Jud. Br., 1972—; chmn. Constl. Commn. on Jud. Disabilities, 1971-73; mem. Md. State-Fed. Jud. Council, Md. Gov.'s Commn. on Law Enforcement and Adminstrn. Justice; mem. governing bd., exec. com. Council of State Govts., 1984—; chmn.-elect. Nat. Ctr. State Cts., Williamsburg, Va., 1985-86. Chmn. bd. dirs. Nat. Ctr. for State Cts., Williamsburg, Va., 1986—. Served with USN, 1944-46. Fellow Md. Bar Found.; mem. U. Md. Alumni Assn.-Internat. (chmn., trustee), Conf. Chief Justices (pres. 1986), ABA, Md. State Bar Assn., Council State Govts., Order of Coif. Office: Ct Appeals Md Cts of Appeal Bldg Annapolis MD 21401

MURPHY, ROBERT MOORE, lawyer; b. Stillwater, Okla., May 23, 1920; s. Wyche Blakely and Mildred (Moore) M.; m. Shirley Bond Love, Apr. 19, 1947; children—Robert Moore, Terrence E., Shirley Love, Helen-Mary Shinn. Student Okla. State U.-Stillwater, 1938-40; J.D., U. Ark.-Fayetteville, 1943. Bar: Okla. 1943, Ark. 1943, U.S. Supreme Ct. 1978. County atty., Payne County, Okla., 1953; mem. Okla. Senate, 1963-81; mem. firm Berry, Murphy & Osborn, Stillwater, 1970-78; mem. firm Murphy & Murphy, P.C., Stillwater, 1978—, now pres. Served to lt. USNR, 1943-46. Mem. Stillwater C. of C. Democrat. Presbyterian. Club: Rotary. State civil litigation, Oil and gas leasing, Family and matrimonial. Office: Murphy & Murphy Box 1984 Stillwater OK 74076

MURPHY, SAMUEL WILSON, JR., lawyer; b. Orange, N.J., Dec. 18, 1927. B.A., Wesleyan U., 1948; LL.B., Harvard U., 1951. Bar: N.Y. 1954, U.S. Supreme Ct. 1962, Pa. 1984. Assoc. firm Donovan Leisure Newton & Irvine, N.Y.C., 1953-60; ptnr. Donovan Leisure Newton & Irvine, 1961-83; sr. v.p., counsel Gulf Corp., Pitts., 1983-84; sr. v.p., gen. counsel RCA Corp., N.Y.C., 1984-86; counsel Davis, Markel & Edwards, N.Y.C., 1986—; past pres. Fed. Bar Council. Fellow Am. Coll. Trial Lawyers; mem. ABA (commn. standards jud. adminstrn.), N.Y. State Bar Assn., Am. Judicature Soc., Assn. Bar City of N.Y., N.Y. County Lawyers Assn. Federal civil litigation, State civil litigation. Office: Davis Markel & Edwards 100 Park Ave New York NY 10017

MURPHY, SANDRA ROBISON, lawyer; b. Detroit, July 28, 1949; m. Richard Robin. BA, Northwestern U., 1971; JD, Loyola U., Chgo., 1976. Bar: U.S. Dist. Ct. (no. dist.) Ill. 1976. Assoc. Notz, Craven, Mead, Maloney & Price, Chgo., 1976-78; ptnr. McDermott, Will & Emery, Chgo., 1978—. Mem. ABA (family law sect.), Ill. Bar Assn. (chair sec. family law council 1985—), Chgo. Bar Assn. (chairperson matrimonial law com. 1985—), Am. Acad. Matrimonial Lawyers, Legal Club Chgo. Family and matrimonial. Home: 1727 N Fremont Chicago IL 60614 Office: McDermott Will & Emery 111 W Monroe Chicago IL 60603

MURPHY, SHARON FUNCHEON, lawyer; b. Lafayette, Ind., Jan. 8, 1954; s. Bernard Joseph and Helen M. (Bates) Funcheon; m. Daniel Ralph Murphy, June 14, 1980; 1 child, Megan Kathleen. BA, U. Dallas, 1976; JD, Ind. U., 1982. Bar: Ind. 1982, U.S. Dist. Ct. (no. and so. dists.) Ind. 1982. Assoc. Locke, Reynolds, Boyd & Weisell, Indpls., 1982-84, Bartlett & Robb, Lafayette, 1984—; active moot ct. practitioner adv. bd. Ind. U. Sch. of Law, 1985—. Assoc. editor Ind. U. Law Rev., 1981-82. Diocesan adv. Roman Cath. Diocese of Lafayette, 1984—. Mem. ABA (chairperson appellate adv. com. 1986-87, tort and ins. practice sect., litigation sect., 1st place Nat. Appellate Adv. Competition, 1982), Ind. Bar Assn., Tippecanoe County Bar Assn. (treas. 1984-85). Club: Lafayette (Ind.) Duplicate Bridge (bd. dirs. 1985—). General practice, Personal injury, Probate. Office: Bartlett & Robb 710 Brown St PO Box 407 Lafayette IN 47902

MURPHY, STEPHEN MICHAEL, lawyer; b. Boston, Dec. 28, 1955; s. Robert Francis and Teresa Ellen (Considine) M.; m. Patricia Ann McMahon, Aug. 6, 1983. BA, Holy Cross Coll., Worcester, Mass., 1977; JD, U. San Francisco, 1981. Bar: Calif., Mass., U.S. Dist. Ct. (no. dist.) Calif., 1982. Law clk. to justices N.H. Supreme Ct., Manchester, 1981-82; sr. assoc. Bianco, Brandi, Jones & Rudy, San Francisco, 1982—; prof. Unilex Coll., San Francisco, 1985—. Editor-in-chief San Francisco Barrister Law Jour., 1986, editor 1985. Vol. atty. Legal Advice and Referral Clinic, San Francisco, 1984—, Call-a-Lawyer, San Francisco, 1986, campaign Gary Hart for Pres., 1984; del. to State Bar conf. San Francisco Barristers Club, 1986, bd. dirs., 1987. Mem. ABA, Bar Assn. San Francisco (cert. 1985), San Francisco Trial Lawyers Assn., Calif. Trial Lawyers Assn., Assn. Trial Lawyers Am. Democrat. Roman Catholic. Avocations: photography, journalism, softball. Personal injury, Insurance, Landlord-tenant. Office: Bianco Brandi Jones & Rudy 44 Montgomery St #900 San Francisco CA 94104

MURPHY, STEPHEN P., corporate lawyer; b. 1926. Student, Mo. Valley U., 1948, U. Kans., 1949, Georgetown U., 1950. With Kansas City Star, 1951-56, Denver-Chgo. Truck Lines, Watson Wilson Transp. System, 1956-63; sr. v.p., sec. gen. counsel Yellow Freight System Inc., Overland Park, Kans., 1963—. Office: Yellow Freight System Inc of Del 10990 Roe Ave Box 7563 Overland Park KS 66207 *

MURPHY, TERENCE ROCHE, lawyer; b. Laurium, Mich., Oct. 20, 1937; s. M. Leonard and Alice Lenore (Roche) M.; m. Suzanne Kathryn Dupré, Oct. 14, 1967 (div. Apr. 1980); children—Braden Mathias, Fiona Elizabeth Dupré; m. Patricia Ann Sherman, May 21, 1983. A.B., Harvard Coll., 1959; J.D. with distinction, U. Mich., 1966. Bar: D.C. 1967, U.S. Supreme Ct. 1971. Trial atty. Dept. Justice, Washington, 1966-68; assoc. Wald, Harkrader & Ross, Washington, 1968-72, ptnr., 1972-83; ptnr. McDermott, Will & Emery, Washington, 1983-84, Adams, Duque & Hazeltine, Washington, 1984-86; founding ptnr. Murphy & DeLong, 1986—; lectr. on internat. trade, antitrust and administrv. law. Contbr. numerous articles to European and Am. legal publs. Mem. com. visitors U. Mich. Law Sch., 1975—. Served to lt. USN, 1959-63. Mem. ABA (council adminstrv. law sect. 1980-83), Am. Law Inst., Internat. Bar Assn. (sec. antitrust and monopolies com. 1981-83); Am. Soc. Internat. Law, Deutsch-Amerikanische Juristen-Vereinigung (Bonn). Clubs: Metropolitan (Washington); Harvard (N.Y.C.). Private international, Administrative and regulatory, General corporate. Home: 2737 Devonshire Pl NW Washington DC 20008 Office: Murphy & DeLong 1029 Vermont Ave NW Washington DC 20005

MURPHY, THOMAS HUGH, lawyer; b. Denver, Jan. 18, 1943; s. F. Allan and Anne Marie (Pettinger) M.; children—Matthew, Geoffrey. B.A., Colo. State U., 1965; J.D., Duke U., 1968. Bar: Wash. 1968. Assoc. Short Cressman & Cable, Seattle, 1968-71; sole practice, Seattle, 1972-73; ptnr. Kelleher & Murphy, Seattle, 1973-79; prin. Thomas H. Murphy and Assocs., Seattle, 1979-80; ptnr. Murphy & McGowan, Seattle, 1980-83, sr. ptnr., 1980-83; ptnr. Murphy & Elgot, 1984—. Mem. ABA, Fed. Bar Assn., Wash. State Bar, Seattle King County Bar, Assn. Trial Lawyers Am. Democrat. Banking, State civil litigation, Real property.

MURPHY, THOMAS LEE, lawyer; b. Topeka, Kans., Nov. 1, 1945; s. Thomas Jefferson and Barbara Lea (Riley) M.; m. Diane Marcella Jauch, Dec. 18, 1964; children: Steven Thomas, Melissa Anna. BA, Elmhurst Coll., 1967; JD, DePaul U., 1971. Bar: Ill. 1971, U.S. Dist. Ct. (no. dist.) Ill. 1971, U.S. Ct. Appeals (7th cir.) 1974, U.S. Tax Ct. 1981. Staff atty. Cen. Soya Co., Ft. Wayne, Ind., 1971-74; assoc. Moriarty, Rose & Hultquist Ltd., Chgo., 1974-78; atty. Andrew Corp., Orland Park, Ill., 1978—; asst. sec. Andrew Corp., Orland Park, 1982-84, sec., 1984—; instr. bus. law Keller Grad. Sch., Chgo., 1980-81. Arbitrator Better Bus. Bur., Chgo., 1980—. Ill. State Regents scholar, 1963-67. Mem. ABA, Ill. Bar Assn., Chgo. Bar Assn., Am. Corp. Counsel Assn. (v.p., bd. dirs. 1983—), Orland Park Area C. of C. (v.p., bd. dirs. 1983—). Lutheran. Lodge: Rotary. Avocations: jogging, swimming, reading, photography, collecting antique cars. General practice, General corporate, Pension, profit-sharing, and employee benefits. Office: Andrew Corp 10500 W 153d St Orland Park IL 60462

MURPHY, THOMAS PATRICK, lawyer; b. Syracuse, N.Y., Feb. 12, 1952; s. George Edward and Sara Eileen (Murphy) M.; m. Susan Hollis Francher, Oct. 19, 1974; 1 child, Casey Marie. BS, Clarkson U., 1974; JD, Vermont Law Sch., 1978. Bar: N.Y. 1978, D.C. 1981. Asst. U.S. atty. U.S. Atty.'s Office, Washington, 1982-85; assoc. Highsaw & Mahoney, Washington, 1985-87, McGuire, Woods, Battle & Boothe, Washington, 1987—. Served with USN, 1978-82, USNR, 1978—. Recipient Spl. Achievement Award U.S. Dept. Justice, 1984. Mem. ABA, Fed. Bar Assn., N.Y. State Bar Assn., D.C. Bar Assn., Assn. Trial Lawyers Am., Assn. Asst. U.S. Attys. Labor, Criminal. Office: McGuire Woods Battle & Boothe 2000 Pennsylvania Ave NW Washington DC 20006

MURPHY, THOMAS W., state judge. Judge High Ct. of Am. Samoa, Pago Pago. Office: High Court of Am Samoa Pago Pago AS 96799 *

MURPHY, WILLIAM CELESTIN, lawyer; b. Chgo., Dec. 5, 1920; s. William F. and Louise F. (Florence) M.; m. Mary G. Powers, July 7, 1951; children: William F. II, Maire Ann, Keelin J. BS with honors, Harvard U., 1942, JD, 1948. Bar: Ill. 1948. Ptnr. Reid, Ochsenschlager, Murphy & Hupp, Aurora, Ill., 1948-83, Murphy, Hupp, Foote & Mielke, Aurora, 1983—; atty. City of Aurora, 1984-52; chmn. com. on fed. judiciary and related appointments Ill. Bar Assn., 1981-83; mem. com. on standard civil jury instructions Ill. Supreme Ct., 1983—. Served to lt. USNR, 1942-46, PTO. Mem. ABA, Chgo. Bar Assn., Kane County Bar Assn., Am. Coll. Trial Lawyers. Club: Aurora Country. State civil litigation, Family and matrimonial, Personal injury. Office: Murphy Hupp Foote & Mielke 8 E Galena Blvd Suite 202 Aurora IL 60506

MURPHY, WILLIAM ROBERT, lawyer; b. New Haven, Oct. 6, 1927; s. Michael David and Loretta Dorothy (Murphy) M.; m. Virginia Anne Selfors, July 23, 1960; children: David M., Christopher W. B.A., Yale U., 1950, LL.B., 1953. Bar: Conn. 1953, U.S. Dist. Ct. Conn. 1957, U.S. Ct. Appeals (2d cir.) 1966, U.S Supreme Ct. 1956, U.S. Ct. Appeals (fed. cir.) 1986. Exec. editor: Yale Law Jour., 1952-53. Sec. John Brown Cook Found., 1971—; mem. Woodbridge Bd. Edn., Conn., 1969-75, Woodbridge Planning and Zoning Commn., 1967-69.Served to lt (j.g.) USNR, 1945-46, 53-56. Fellow Am. Coll. Trial Lawyers, Am. Bar Found.; mem. ABA, Conn. Bar Assn., New Haven County Bar Assn., Internat. Assn. Ins. Counsel. Clubs: Quinnipiack (New Haven); Mory's Assn.; Milford Yacht. Federal civil liti-

gation, State civil litigation, Antitrust. Home: 15 Ledge Rd Woodbridge CT 06525 Office: Tyler Cooper & Alcorn 205 Church St New Haven CT 06509

MURRAY, CONAL EUGENE, lawyer; b. N.Y.C., Oct. 12, 1937; s. Francis Joseph and Madge (O'Donnell) M.; m. Betty C. Lanzini, July 27, 1968; children: Conal, Heather. AB, Harvard U., 1959, MBA, 1961, JD, 1968; LLM, NYU, 1973. Bar: N.Y. 1969, U.S. Dist. Ct. (so. dist.) N.Y. 1973, U.S. Ct. Appeals (2d cir.) 1973, U.S. Supreme Ct. 1973. Dir. legal services Gen. Foods Corp., White Plains, N.Y., 1968—. Served to lt. USNR, 1961-65. Mem. ABA, N.Y. State Bar Assn. (chmn. corp. counsel sect. 1986—), Westchester Fairfield Corp. Counsel Assn. (pres. 1983). Clubs: Harvard (N.Y.C.), Harvard Faculty (Cambridge, Mass.). Antitrust, Contracts commercial, Securities. Home: 196 Croton Ave Mount Kisco NY 10549 Office: Gen Foods Corp 250 North St White Plains NY 10625

MURRAY, DAVID EUGENE, lawyer; b. Clinton, Iowa, Apr. 11, 1936; s. Eugene Paul and Margaret Lucille (Hicks) M.; m. Helen Nichols, July 5, 1958; children: Lisa, Heather, Michael. BA, U. Ill., 1957, LLB, 1960. Bar: Ill. 1960, U.S. Dist. Ct. (no. dist.) Ill. 1960, U.S. Supreme Ct. 1968. Ptnr. Ward, Murray, Pace & Johnson P.C., Sterling, Ill., 1961—; bd. dirs. Communitron, Inc., Sterling, Attys. Title Guaranty Fund, Champaign, Ill. Mem. Ill. State Bd. Elections, 1985—; chmn. Whiteside County Rep. Cen. Com., 1974-80, Ill. Bd. Regents, 1978-85. Served to staff sgt. USAF, 1960-61. Fellow Ill. Bar Found.; mem. ABA (Ho. of Dels. 1979-83), Ill. Bar Assn. (bd. of govs. 1971-74), Assn. Trial Lawyers Am., Ill. Trial Lawyers Assn. Congregationalist. Lodge: Rotary (pres. Sterling chpt. 1968-70). Avocations: skiing, flying, scuba diving. General practice, Labor, Workers' compensation. Home: 707 W 14th St Sterling IL 61081 Office: Ward Murray Pace & Johnson PC 202 E 5th St Sterling IL 61081

MURRAY, DAVID G., lawyer; b. Syracuse, N.Y., June 18, 1946; s. Ernest Charles and Dickron (Dumanian) M.; m. Elizabeth Graham Holt, July 27, 1968; children: Laura Ellen, Paul Graham. BBA in Fin., U. Miami, 1969; JD, Stetson Coll. Law, 1972. Bar: Fla. 1972. Asst. city atty. City of Ft. Lauderdale, Fla., 1972-75, chief city prosecutor, 1975-76; ptnr. Murray & Bush, P.A., Ft. Lauderdale, 1976-78, Huebner & Murray P.A., Ft. Lauderdale, 1978—; lectr. real estate law Fla. Bar, 1981, Attys. Title Ins. Fund, 1981—. Bd. dirs. Broward County chpt. ARC, 1975-77, Broward County chpt. Girl Scouts Am., 1979-80, Ft. Lauderdale YMCA, 1978-81. Mem. Phi Alpha Delta (past pres.). Republican. Presbyterian. Club: Fort Lauderdale Yacht. Real property, General corporate. Office: Huebner & Murray PA 321 SE 15th Ave Fort Lauderdale FL 33303

MURRAY, ELIZABETH ANN, lawyer; b. St. Louis, Sept. 9, 1947; d. Hugh Vincent and Jane (Hassett) M. BA, Manhattanville Coll., 1969; JD, Suffolk U., 1975. Bar: Mass. 1975, U.S. Dist. Ct. Mass. Legis. aide Mass. Senate, Boston, 1972-76; asst. dist. atty. Suffolk County, Boston, 1978-79; atty. Mass. Exec. Office Transp., Boston, 1979-83; assoc. Connolly, Feingold & McGrail, 1983-86; assoc. counsel Associated Industries of Mass., 1986—. Mem. ABA, Assn. Trial Lawyers Am., Mass. Bar Assn., Boston Bar Assn., Mus. Fine Arts, New Eng. Aquarium. Democrat. Roman Catholic. Real property, General practice. Home: 130 Bowdoin St Boston MA 02108 Office: Associated Industries of Mass 462 Boylston St Boston MA 02116

MURRAY, FREDERICK FRANKLIN, lawyer; b. Corpus Christi, Tex., Aug. 1, 1950; s. Marvin Frank and Suzanne Louise Murray; m. Susan McKeen. BA, Rice U., 1972; JD, U. Tex., 1974. Bar: Tex. 1975, N.Y. 1987, D.C. 1987, U.S. Dist. Ct. (so. dist.) Tex. 1976, U.S. Dist. Ct. (no. and we. dists.) Tex. 1986, U.S. Ct. Claims 1976, U.S. Tax Ct. 1976, U.S. Ct. Appeals (5th and D.C. cirs.) 1976, U.S. Supreme Ct. 1978, U.S. Ct. Internat. Trade 1985, U.S. Dist. Ct. (ea. dist.) Tex. 1987. Sr. assoc. Chamberlain, Hrdlicka, White, Johnson & Williams, Houston, 1984-85, ptnr., 1985—; mem. tax law adv. commn. Tex. Bd. Legal Specialization, 1984—, vice chmn., 1987—; mem. Commn. of Tax Law Examiners, 1984—; adj. prof. U. Houston Law Ctr., 1984—, U. Tex. Sch. Law, 1987—; speaker various assns. and univs. Author various publs; mem. bd. advisers Houston Jour. Internat. Law, 1986—, chmn., 1987—. Del. Bishop's Diocesan Pastoral Council, 1979-80; chmn. parish council Sacred Heart Cathedral, Cath. Diocese Galveston-Houston, 1979-81, mem. Red Mass Steering Com., 1986—; mem. bd. advisers, co-chmn. deferred giving com. Houston Symphony Soc., 1984—, bd. dirs., 1987—; mem. fund council Rice U., 1987—. Mem. Am. Arbitration Assn. (panels comml. and internat. arbitrators 1980—), ABA (various coms.), Internat. Bar Assn., Houston Bar Assn., State Bar of Tex. (various coms.), N.Y. State Bar Assn., D.C. Bar Assn., Am. Inst. CPA's, Tex. Soc. CPA's, Internat. Tax Forum of Houston (sec. 1981-84, pres. 1984—), Internat. Fiscal Assn., Am. Soc. Internat. Law., Am. Fgn. Law Assn., Union Internationale Des Avocats. Private international, Family and matrimonial, Corporate taxation. Office: Citicorp Ctr Suite 1400 1200 Smith St Houston TX 77002

MURRAY, GREGORY VINCENT, lawyer; b. Highland Park, Mich., July 30, 1949; s. James M. and Helen M. (Bader) M.; m. Connie S. Popa, May 29, 1977; 1 child, Daniel T. BA, U. Mich., 1971; JD cum laude, Detroit Coll. Law, 1978. Bar: Mich. 1978. Asst. adminstrv. officer Nat. Bank of Detroit, 1967-78; ptnr. Butzel, Long, Gust, Klein & Van Zile P.C., Detroit, 1978—. Mem. ABA, Mich. Bar Assn., Detroit Bar Assn., U. Detroit Jesuit High Sch. Alumni Assn. (pres. bd. dirs.). Roman Catholic. Labor, Federal civil litigation, State civil litigation. Office: Butzel Long Gust Klein & Van Zile PC 1881 1st National Bldg Detroit MI 48226

MURRAY, HERBERT FRAZIER, judge; b. Waltham, Mass., Dec. 29, 1923; s. Arnold Howatt and Hilda (Frazier) M.; m. Jane Ward, Sept. 4, 1948; 1 son, Douglas Frazier. B.A., Yale U., 1947; postgrad., Harvard Law Sch., 1947-48; LL.B., U. Md., 1951. Bar: Md. bar 1951. Law clk. to U.S. Dist. Judge W. Calvin Chesnut, 1951-52; asso. firm Ober, Grimes & Stinson, Balt., 1952-54; asst. U.S. atty. for Md., 1954-56; asso., partner firm Smith, Somerville & Case, Balt., 1956-71; U.S. dist. judge for Md., 1971—. Past bd. dirs. Union Meml. Hosp., Legal Aid Bur., Inc. of Balt. Served to capt. USAAF, World War II, MTO. Decorated Air medal with 3 oak leaf clusters, D.F.C. Mem. ABA, Md. Bar Assn., Balt. Bar Assn., Fed Bar Assn. (hon.mem.) Bar Assns.), Wednesday Law Club Balt., Nat. Lawyers Club of Washington (hon.). Judicial administration. Office: 530 US Courthouse Baltimore MD 21201

MURRAY, JAMES MICHAEL, law librarian, legal educator, lawyer; b. Seattle, Nov. 8, 1944; s. Clarence Nicholas and Della May (Snyder) M.; m. Linda Monthy Murray; M.Law Librarianship, U. Wash., 1978; J.D., Gonzaga U., 1971. Bar: Wash., 1974. Reference/reserve librarian U. Texas Law Library, Austin, 1978-81; assoc. law librarian Washington U. Law Library, St. Louis, 1981-84; law librarian, asst. prof. Gonzaga U. Sch. Law, Spokane, 1984—; cons. in field. Bd. dirs. ACLU, Spokane chpt., 1987—; Wash. Vol. Lawyers for the Arts, 1976-78. Mem. Am. Assn. Law Libraries, Western Pacific Assn. Law Libraries, ABA, Wash. State Bar Assn (law sch. liaison com., 1986—). Mem. state adv. bd. National Reporter on Legal Ethics and Professional Responsibility, 1982—; author: (with Reams and McDermott) American Legal Literature: Bibliography of Selected Legal Resources, 1985; editor Texas Bar Jour. (Books Appraisals Column), 1979-82; author revs., acknowledgements and bibliographies in field. Legal education, General practice, Librarianship. Home: W 921 29th Spokane WA 99203 Office: Gonzaga U Sch Law Library E 600 Sharp Ave Spokane WA 99202

MURRAY, JAMES THOMAS, JR., lawyer; b. Racine, Wis., July 3, 1949; s. James T. Sr. and Barbara (Buhler) M.; m. Mary Frances Gerler, Aug. 14, 1971; children: Eileen, Patrick, Daniel, Michael. BA, U. Wis., 1971; JD, Marquette U., 1974. Bar: Wis. 1974, U.S. Dist. Ct. (ea. and we. dists.) Wis. 1974, U.S. Ct. Appeals (7th cir.) 1977. Law clk. to presiding justice Wis. Supreme Ct., Madison, 1974-75; assoc. Borgelt, Powell, et al, Milw., 1975-80, ptnr., 1980-82; ptnr. Peterson, Johnson & Murray, S.C., Milw., 1982—. Mem. ABA, Wis. Bar Assn., Def. Research Inst., Civil Trial Counsel Wis. (bd. dirs., program chmn. 1984—), Marquette U. Law Alumni Assn. (bd. dirs. 1980—). Federal civil litigation, State civil litigation. Office: Peterson Johnson & Murray SC 733 N Van Buren Milwaukee WI 53202

MURRAY, JOHN CHARLES, lawyer; b. Detroit, Sept. 1, 1945; s. Francis James and Florence Eva (Howes) M.; m. Frances Tsirou, Sept. 1, 1973. B.B.A. with distinction, U. Mich., 1967, J.D., 1969. Bar: Mich. 1970, U.S. Dist. Ct. (ea. dist.) Mich. 1970, U.S. Tax Ct. 1971, U.S. Ct. Appeals (6th cir.) 1972, U.S. Supreme Ct. 1974, Ill. 1982. Assoc., Poole, Littell, Emery & Sutherland, Detroit, 1970-73; asst. resident atty. The Prudential Ins. Co., Southfield, Mich., 1973-77, assoc. resident atty., 1977-82, assoc. regional counsel, Chgo., 1982-83, regional counsel, 1983; regional counsel The Travelers Ins. Co., Oak Brook, Ill., 1983—. Contbr. articles to profl. jours. Mem. Mich. Bar Assn., Ill. Bar Assn., Chgo. Bar Assn., ABA, Chgo. Mortgage Attys. Assn., Am. Coll. Real Estate Lawyers, Am. Coll. Mortgage Attys. Roman Catholic. Club: Fairlane (Dearborn, Mich.). Real property. Home: 1 S 150 Spring Rd Oakbrook Terrace IL 60126 Office: The Travelers Ins Co 2215 York Rd Suite 504 Oak Brook IL 60521

MURRAY, JULIAN R., JR., lawyer; b. Atlanta, Jan. 30, 1938; s. Julian R. and Virginia (Horgan) M.; m. Kathleen Drown, May 26, 1964; children—Shawn Michael, Kathleen Margaret. BA in History, La. State U., 1965; JD, Tulane U., 1964. Bar: La. 1964, U.S. Dist. Ct. (ea. dist.) La., U.S. Ct. Appeals (5th and 6th cirs.) 1969, U.S. Ct. Appeals (11th cir.) 1982, U.S. Supreme Ct. 1972. Assoc. Hubert, Baldwin & Zibilich, New Orleans, 1964-65, Sidney W. Provensal, Slidell, La., 1965-66; asst. dist. atty. Orleans Parish, La., 1966-68; asst. U.S. atty. for Eastern Dist. La., New Orleans, 1968-70, 1st asst. U.S. atty., 1970-72; ptnr. Murray, Braden, Gonzalez & Richardson, P.C., New Orleans, 1972—; chief prosecutor organized crime and racketeering unit Office La. State's Atty. Gen., New Orleans, 1973-75; adj. assoc. prof. law Tulane U. Law Sch., 1975—; instr. trial practice and criminal law Inst. Continuing Edn., La. State U. Law Sch., Loyola U. Law Sch., New Orleans, New Orleans Police Acad., La. Police Acad.; mem. La. Gov.'s Commn. on Pardon, Parole and Rehab.; mem. Com. to Rev. Forensic Psychiatry System in La. Spl. counsel 1st and 2d congl. dists. presdl. campaigns La. Democratic Central Com., 1976, 80. Served with USN Air Res., 1955-63. Fellow Internat. Soc. Barristers, Am. Bd. Criminal Lawyers, La. Bar Assn. (chmn. criminal law sect. 1976-77); mem. Fed. Bar Assn. (past pres. New Orleans chpt.), New Orleans Bar Assn., Assn. Trial Lawyers Am., ABA (organized crime com. 1973-74, com. on liaison with state bar assns. 1976-77, RICO com. 1979-85, teaching of trial advocacy com. gen. litigation sect. 1981, grand jury com. 1985—), La. Law Inst. (adv. com. on evidence code), La. Assn. Criminal Def. Lawyers (pres. 1986—), Phi Alpha Delta. Democrat. Roman Catholic. Criminal, Personal injury. Office: 612 Gravier St New Orleans LA 70130

MURRAY, KATHLEEN ANNE, lawyer; b. Los Angeles, Feb. 14, 1946; s. Francis Albert and Dorothy (Thompson) M.; 1 child, Anne Murray Ladd. BA, U. Mich., 1967; JD, Hastings Coll. of Law, 1973. Bar: Calif. 1973, U.S. Dist. Ct. (no. dist.) Calif. 1973, U.S. Ct. Appeals (9th cir.) 1973. Sr. staff atty Child Care Law Ctr., San Francisco, 1979-84, cons. child day care law and regulation, 1984-86; atty Epstein & Harris, San Francisco, 1985-86; gen. counsel Fisher Friedman Assocs., San Francisco, 1986—; adv. bd. North of Market Child Devel. Ctr., San Francisco, 1983—; bd. dirs. San Francisco Infant Sch., Pacific Primary Sch.; exec. dir. editorial adv. bd. Parenting mag. San Francisco, 1985—. Editor: Tax Guide for California Child Care Providers, Child Care Center Legal Handbook; contbr. articles to profl. jours. Mem. adv. council Humanities West, Inc., San Francisco, 1986. Democrat. Episcopalian. General corporate, Construction.

MURRAY, LORENE FRANCES, lawyer; b. Evergreen Park, Ill., Nov. 6, 1953; d. Michael J. and Lorene (McMahon) M.; m. Thomas J. Shanahan, Nov. 29, 1985. BA, St. Mary's Coll., Notre Dame, Ind., 1975; JD, No. Ill. U., 1978. Bar: Ill. 1978, U.S. Dist. Ct. (no. dist.) Ill. 1978, U.S. Ct. Appeals (7th cir.) 1978. Acting dean students Lewis U., Lockport, Ill., 1978; dir. gen. law Chgo. Transit Authority, 1978—, also bd. dirs.; speaker Assn. Labor-Mgmt. Adminstrs. and Cons. Alcoholism, Chgo., 1984, Am. Pub. Transit Assn., Milw., 1983. Recipient Cert. of Leadership, YMCA, Chgo., 1984, Cert. of Appreciation, Assn. Labor-Mgmt. Adminstrs. and Cons. Alcoholism, 1984. Mem. ABA, Chgo. Bar Assn. (lectr. local govt. commn. 1986). Civil rights, Labor, Federal civil litigation. Office: Chgo Transit Authority 440 Merchandise Mart Chicago IL 60654

MURRAY, ROBERT FOX, lawyer; b. Burlington, Vt., Feb. 28, 1952; s. Robert and Mary (Fox) M. BA, Colgate U., 1974; JD, Boston U., 1978. Bar: Mass. 1978, U.S. Dist. Ct. Mass. 1979. Assoc. Law Offices of George Howard, Dedham, Mass., 1978-80, from assoc. to ptnr. Fairbanks & Silvia Koczera, Fountain, Murray, New Bedford, Mass., 1980-84; sole practice, New Bedford, 1984—. Bd. dirs., clk. New Bedford Downtown Bus. Assn., Inc. Mem. New Bedford C. of C., Downtown Bus. Man's Assn. (bd. dirs.), Waterfront Hist. Area League, Assn. Trial Lawyers Am., Mass. Acad. Trial Attys., Mass. Bar Assn., New Bedford Bar Assn., Bristol County Bar Assn., Bristol County Bar Advs. Democrat. State civil litigation, Environment, Personal injury. Office: 22 Centre St New Bedford MA 02740

MURRAY, WILLIAM JAMES, lawyer; b. N.Y.C., June 21, 1948; s. John Patrick and Elizabeth Madeline (Murtha) M.; m. Susan Audré Fash, Sept. 23, 1972; children: Kathryn, Margaret. Diploma, Girard Coll., 1965; BA, L.I. U., 1969; JD, St. John's U., Jamaica, N.Y., 1977. Bar: N.Y. 1978, U.S. Dist. Ct. (so. dist.) N.Y. 1978. Surety underwriter Chubb & Son Inc., Warren, N.J., 1968-77, from asst. to gen. counsel to asst. v.p. and assoc. counsel, 1977-85, v.p. and counsel, 1985—. Mem. ABA, N.Y. State Bar Assn., Am. Inst. Marine Underwriters, Nat. Assn. Ins. Commrs. (adv. com. fin. guarantees 1985—). Republican. Roman Catholic. Avocation: photography. Insurance, General corporate, Government relations. Home: Box 314 Lilac Dr Annandale NJ 08801 Office: Chubb & Son Inc 15 Mountain View Rd Warren NJ 07061

MURRAY, WILLIAM MICHAEL (MIKE), lawyer; b. Ottumwa, Iowa, Dec. 28, 1947; s. William Bernard and Thelma Jean (Hart) M.; m. Ann Elizabeth Wawzonek, Oct. 11, 1973; children—Kathleen Elizabeth, Daniel Webster. B.A., U. Iowa, 1970, J.D., 1973. Bar: Iowa 1973, U.S. Dist. Ct. (so. dist.) Iowa 1976, U.S. Dist. Ct. (no. dist.) Iowa 1978, U.S. Ct. Appeals (8th cir.) 1978. Staff counsel Iowa Civil Rights Commn., Des Moines, 1973-76; assoc. Bertroche & Hagen, Des Moines, 1976-78; ptnr. Murray, Davoren & Dudley, Des Moines, 1978—. Bd. dirs. Iowa Civil Liberties Union, Des Moines, 1978-83, pres., 1982-83; bd. dirs. Polk County Legal Aid Soc., Des Moines, 1984—. Mem. Assn. Trial Lawyers Am., Assn. Trial Lawyers Iowa, ABA, Iowa State Bar Assn., Polk County Bar Assn. Democrat. Club: Des Moines Jaycees (bd. dirs. legal counsel 1980-81). Lodge: Masons. State civil litigation, Personal injury, Workers' compensation. Home: 600 SW 42d St Des Moines IA 50312 Office: Murray Davoren & Dudley 5601 Hickman Rd Suites 3 & 4 Des Moines IA 50310

MURRAY, WILLIAM PETER, lawyer; b. Albany, N.Y., June 29, 1924; s. James Ryan and Hazel Mary (Kilroy) M. B.A., Siena Coll., 1948; J.D., Cath. U., 1951. Bar: D.C. 1951, U.S. Ct. Appeals D.C. 1951, N.Y. 1952, U.S. Dist. Ct. (so. dist.) N.Y. 1953, U.S. Ct. Appeals (2d cir.) 1973, U.S. Ct. Mil. Appeals 1956, U.S. Supreme Ct. 1980. Sole practice, N.Y.C. and Washington, 1951-69; assoc. McNally O'Brien & K, N.Y.C., 1951-56, Robert G. Burkhardt, Esq., N.Y.C., 1962-63, Donald F. Mooney, Esq., N.Y.C., 1967-68; counsel in charge and acting corp. counsel Water Supply Unit, N.Y.C. Law Dept., Kingston, 1969-79; sole practice, Kingston, 1979—. Casenote editor Cath. U. Am. Law Rev., 1950-51; contbr. articles to profl. jours. Spl. dep. atty. gen. Dept. Law, State of N.Y., 1952-57. Founding mem., law sch. rep. Cath U. Am. Grad. Student Council, 1951. Served with U.S. Army, 1943-45. Decorated Combat Infantryman's badge, Bronze Star. Mem. D.C. Bar Assn. Roman Catholic. Club: Century. Federal appellate litigation, State appellate litigation, Water rights. Home: 138 Washington Ave Kingston NY 12401

MURRELL, ALAN H., lawyer, state official. Pub. defender State of Md., Balt. Office: Pub Defender Office 222 E Baltimore St Baltimore MD 21202 *

MURRELL, JACK OLIVER, lawyer; b. Lafayette, Ind., Jan. 5, 1948; s. James Oliver and Patti J. (Patterson) M.; m. Barbara A. Elgin, Feb. 12, 1972; children: Jack, Sean. AB in Polit. Sci., Ind. U., 1970; JD, Ind. U., Indpls., 1977. Bar: Ind. 1977, U.S. Dist. Ct. (so. dist.) Ind. 1977, U.S. Ct. Mil. Appeals 1977, U.S. Supreme Ct. 1980, U.S. Ct. Claims 1985, U.S. Dist. Ct. (no. dist.) Ind. 1986. Commd. 2d lt. U.S. Army, 1970, advanced through grades to maj., 1982, resigned, 1985; def. atty. U.S. Army, Ft. Dix, N.J., 1977-80; asst. prof. JAG Sch. U.S. Army, Charlottesville, Va., 1981-84; trial atty. U.S. Army, Washington, 1984-85; assoc. gen. counsel Magnavox Govt. and Indsl. Electronics Co., Ft. Wayne, Ind., 1985—. Mem. ABA, Nat. Security and Indsl. Assn., Am. Corp. Counsel Assn., Allen County Bar Assn., Phi Kappa Psi. Republican. Methodist. Government contracts and claims, Labor, General corporate. Office: Magnavox Govt and Indsl Electronics Co 1313 Production Rd Fort Wayne IN 46808

MURRELL, ROBERT GEORGE, lawyer; b. Atlanta, Jan. 27, 1932; s. Samuel Edwin and Myrtle Josephine (Hailey) M.; m. Bonnie Bird Robinson, Nov. 11, 1961; children—Robert George, Michele Grace, Bonnie Melissa. B.A., U. Fla., 1952, J.D., 1953. Bar: Fla. 1953, U.S. Dist. Ct. (so. dist.) Fla. 1953, U.S. Ct. Appeals (5th cir.) 1953, U.S. Ct. Mil. Appeals 1958, U.S. Supreme Ct. 1958, U.S. Ct. Claims 1975, U.S. Tax Ct. 1975, U.S. Ct. Customs and Patent Appeals 1975, D.C. 1976, U.S. Ct. Internat. Trade 1980, U.S. Dist. Ct. (mid. dist.) Fla. 1980, N.Y. 1981, Pa. 1982, U.S. Ct. Appeals (11th cir.) 1982. Ptnr. Sam E. Murrell & Sons, Orlando, Fla., 1953—; mem. Citrus Assocs. of N.Y. Stock Exchange; pres. Colonial Mortgage Co. Fla., Inc.; dir. Weiss Realty Corp., Lake Margaret Co., We Care, Inc.; owner, Vista Travel, Inc.; arbitrator Am. Arbitration Assn. Served to sgt. U.S. Army, 1953-55. Mem. ABA, Fla. Bar, Orange County Bar Assn., Attys. Title Services, Inc. Republican. Baptist. Clubs: Univ. of Winter Park (Fla.); Masons, Shriners, Elks (Orlando). State civil litigation, Personal injury, Criminal. Home: 415 Raintree Ct Winter Park FL 32789 Office: 1 N Rosalind Ave Orlando FL 32801

MURRELL, SAM EDWIN, JR., lawyer; b. Sarasota, Fla., Sept. 28, 1927; s. Sam Edwin and Myrtle (Hailey) M.; m. Mercerdees Lawrence, Oct. 6, 1955; children: Joan, Katherine, Sarah, Sam. LLB, JD, U. Fla., 1948. Bar: Fla. 1948, D.C. 1975, N.Y. 1980, Pa. 1981, Wis. 1982, Mass. 1984, U.S. Supreme Ct. 1952. Ptnr. Sam E. Murrell & Sons, Orlando, Fla., 1948—. Served to 1st lt. JAG Corps, U.S. Army, 1951-52. Mem. ABA, Inter-Am. Bar Assn., Fla. Bar, D.C. Bar, Pa. Bar Assn., Wis. Bar, Assn. Bar City N.Y., Fed. Bar Assn., Assn. Trial Lawyers Am., Am. Immigration Lawyers Assn., Fla. Trial Lawyers Assn. Democrat. Presbyterian. Lodges: Elks, Moose (Orlando). General practice, Bankruptcy, State civil litigation. Home: 3041 Westchester Orlando FL 32803 Office: 1 N Rosalind Ave Orlando FL 32802

MURREN, PHILIP JOSEPH, lawyer; b. Hanover, Pa., Mar. 29, 1950; s. Joseph Edward and Jeune (Mathews) M.; m. Kathleen Mary Buckley, Oct. 28, 1978; children—Andrew, Patrick, David. B.A., LaSalle Univ., 1972; J.D., Villanova U., 1975. Ptnr., Ball & Skelly, Harrisburg, Pa., 1975—. Bar: Pa. 1975, U.S. Dist. Ct. (ea. dist.) Pa. 1976, U.S. Dist. Ct. (mid. dist.) Pa. 1978, U.S. Supreme Ct. 1978, U.S. Ct. Appeals (3d cir.) 1977, (5th cir.) 1979, (D.C. cir.) 1980, (6th cir.) 1984, (9th cir.) 1984. Mem. allocations exec. com. Tri-County United Way, Harrisburg, 1983—; mem. mental health adv. council Holy Spirit Hosp., 1985—. Mem. ABA (com. vice chmn. 1978), Pa. Bar Assn., Dauphin County Bar Assn. Republican. Roman Catholic. Constitutional, Legislation, Constitutional law, Nonprofit organizations, Legislative. Home: 206 Willow Ave Camp Hill PA 17011 Office: Ball & Skelly 511 N 2d St Harrisburg PA 17108

MURRIN, JOHN OWEN, lawyer; b. San Pedro, Calif., Sept. 22, 1950; s. John O. Murrin Jr. and Billie Crandell (Bucher) Beeler; m. Devonna Kae Quail, Aug. 2, 1980; children: Emily, John. BA, U. Calif., Los Angeles, 1972; JD, Duke U., 1975. Bar: Minn. 1976, Calif. 1977, U.S. Supreme Ct. 1985. Pres. Murrin Met., Attys. at Law, Mpls., 1977—; owner Dial L-A-W-Y-E-R-S, 1977—; mem. Alt. Dispute Resolution, Mpls., 1986; lectr. various seminars. Author: Minnesota Do-It-Yourself Divorce Book, 1982, How To Buy and Sell Real Estate, a Minnesota Guidebook, 1986; contbr. articles to profl. jours. Mem. Calif. Bar Assn., Minn. Bar Assn. (chmn. com. on legal services to the elderly young lawyers sect. 1985-86), Hennepin County Bar Assn. Episcopalian. Lodge: Lions (Mpls. treas. 1984-85, sec. 1985—). Avocations: running, racquetball, writing. Personal injury, Small business, Family and matrimonial. Home: 5506 Lakeview Edina MN 55424 Office: Murrin Met Attys at Law 3009 Holmes Ave S Minneapolis MN 55408

MURRY, HAROLD DAVID, JR., lawyer; b. Holdenville, Okla., June 30, 1943; s. Harold David Sr. and Willie Elizabeth (Dees) M.; m. Ann Moore Earnhardt, Nov. 1, 1975; children: Elizabeth Ann, Sarah Bryant. BA, Okla. U., 1965, JD, 1968. Bar: Okla. 1968, D.C. 1974. Asst. to v.p. U. Okla., Norman, 1968-71, legal counsel Research Inst., 1969-71; atty. U.S. Dept. Justice, Washington, 1971-74; spl. asst. U.S. Dist. Atty.'s Office, Washington, 1972; assoc. Clifford & Warnke, Washington, 1974-78, ptnr., 1978—. Mem. ABA, Okla. Bar Assn., D.C. Bar Assn., Fed. Bar Assn., Phi Alpha Delta. Democrat. Club: Metropolitan (Washington). General practice, Federal civil litigation, Administrative and regulatory. Home: 8931 Bel Air Pl Potomac MD 20854 Office: Clifford & Warnke 815 Connecticut Ave NW Washington DC 20006

MURTAGH, JAMES P., lawyer; b. N.Y.C., Feb. 26, 1911; s. Thomas and Mary (Mee) M.; m. Roberta Flaherty, Aug. 30, 1947; children—Melinda, James, Robert, Hilary, Richard, Kenneth. B.A. cum laude, CCNY, 1931; J.D., Harvard U., 1934. Bar: N.Y. 1935, U.S. Dist. Ct. (so. dist.) N.Y. 1935, U.S. Ct. Appeals (2d cir.). Spl. asst. U.S. atty. So. Dist. of N.Y., 1935-36; assoc., ptnr. Simpson Thacher & Bartlett, N.Y.C., 1936-78; of counsel Murtagh & Cohen, Garden City, N.Y., 1978—. Mem. Bd. Higher Edn., N.Y.C., 1948-52. Served to lt. col. AUS, 1942-45. Mem. Phi Beta Kappa. Democrat. Roman Catholic. Club: Larchmont Shore (N.Y.). Contbr. articles on tax law to profl. jours. Corporate taxation, General corporate. Home: 4301 Gulf Shore Blvd N Naples FL 33940 Office: 1122 Franklin Ave Garden City NY 11530

MURTAGH, JOHN WALTER, JR., lawyer; b. Bklyn., May 7, 1947; s. John Walter and Irene Anne (McCormack) M.; m. Sheila Horsman, Aug. 12, 1972; children: Kerin Leigh, John W. III. AB in Politics, St. Joseph's U., 1969; JD, U. Pa., 1972. Bar: Pa. 1972, U.S. Dist. Ct. (ea. dist.) Pa. 1973, U.S. Dist. Ct. (we. dist.) Pa. 1976, U.S. Ct. Appeals (3d cir.) 1977, U.S. Supreme Ct. 1977. Trial atty. U.S. Dept. Justice, Pitts., 1973-76; litigator Greenfield & Murtagh, Pitts., 1976—. Mem. Assn. Trial Lawyers Am., ABA, Pa. Bar Assn., Allegheny County Bar Assn., Gaelic League. Democrat. Roman Catholic. Lodge: KC. Labor, General practice, Civil rights. Home: Box 52 Bellcrest Rd Ingomar PA 15127 Office: Greenfield & Murtagh 728 5th Ave Pittsburgh PA 15219

MURTAUGH, JOHN PATRICK, lawyer; b. Orrville, Ohio, Feb. 23, 1952; s. Bernard Francis and Helen Jane (Ellsworth) M. BA summa cum laude, U. Notre Dame, 1974; JD, U. Mich., 1978. Bar: Calif. 1978, U.S. Dist. Ct. (no. dist.) Calif. 1979, U.S. Ct. Appeals (D.C. cir.) 1979, U.S. Dist. Ct. (ea. dist.) Calif. 1980, Ohio 1981, U.S. Dist. Ct. (no. dist.) Ohio 1981, U.S. Ct. Appeals (6th cir.) 1982. Law clk. to judge U.S. Ct. Appeals (D.C. cir.), Washington, 1978-79; assoc. Orrick, Herrington, Rowley & Sutcliffe, San Francisco, 1979-80, Calfee, Halter & Griswold, Cleve., 1980—. Assoc. editor U. Mich. Law Rev., 1976-77, sr. editor, 1977-78. Mem. ABA, Ohio Bar Assn., Cleve. Bar Assn., Young Profls. of Cleve., Notre Dame Club of Cleve., Phi Beta Kappa. Roman Catholic. Avocations: sailing, scuba diving, skiing. Federal civil litigation, State civil litigation. Home: 16207 Van Aken Blvd #103 Shaker Heights OH 44120 Office: Calfee Halter & Griswold 1800 Society Bldg Cleveland OH 44114

MURTHA, THOMAS MICHAEL, lawyer; b. Hartford, Con., Aug. 20, 1955; s. Robert F. and Mary C. (Urrichio) M.; m. Mary Ann Daily, July 5, 1980; children: Timothy, Stephen.. BA, Fairfield U., 1978; JD, U. Bridgeport, 1980. Bar: Conn. 1981, U.S. Dist. Ct. Conn. 1981. Assoc. Maher & Maher, Bridgeport, 1980-82; ptnr. Maher & Murtha, Bridgeport, 1982—; active Bench-Bar Com., Bridgeport, 1983-86. Mem. Am. Arbitration Assn., Ins. Commerce. Democrat. Roman Catholic. Avocation: running. State civil litigation, Federal civil litigation, Real property. Home: 5 Cadey Ln Newton CT 06470 Office: Maher & Murtha 540 Clinton Ave Bridgeport CT 06605

MUSACCHIO, KIRK ANTHONY, lawyer, financial and real estate consultant; b. Fresno, Calif., Nov. 11, 1955; s. Theodore Alphonsus and Darlene June (Mirigian) M.; m. Stephane-Leigh Haines, Sept. 22, 1984. BA cum

laude, U. San Francisco, 1977; JD, U. Santa Clara, 1980. Bar: Calif. 1982, U.S. Dist. Ct. (no. dist.) Calif. 1982. Legal writer Matthew Bender & Co., San Francisco, 1981-82; sr. v.p., legal counsel Centennial Savs. and Loan, Santa Rosa, Calif., 1983-84, exec. v.p., gen. counsel, asst. sec., 1984, exec. v.p. and gen. counsel/adminstrn., 1984-85; pres. KTM Corp., San Francisco, 1986—. Comments editor and mem. law rev. bd., U. Santa Clara, 1980. Jr. exec. com. mem. Boy's Town of Italy, San Francisco, 1986. Mem. ABA, Commonwealth Club Calif., Triple X fraternity. Republican. Roman Catholic. Lodge: Masons. Avocations: music, skiing, tennis. Real property, Banking, General corporate. Home: 4703 Tee View Ct Santa Rosa CA 95405 Office: KTM Corp 201 Spear St San Francisco CA 94105

MUSCATO, ANDREW, lawyer; b. Newark, Aug. 28, 1953; s. Salvatore and Bertha (Kubilus) M.; m. Ann Marie Hughes, Aug. 19, 1978; children: Amy, Andrew Joseph. AB magna cum laude, Brown U., 1975; JD, Seton Hall U., 1978. Bar: N.J. 1978, U.S. Dist. Ct. N.J. 1978, U.S. Ct. Appeals (3d cir.) 1981, N.Y. 1984, U.S. Dist. Ct. (so. and ea. dists.) N.Y. 1984. Law clk. to presiding judge, appellate div. N.J. Superior Ct., Somerville, 1978-79; staff atty. Adminstrv. Office of Cts., Trenton, N.J., 1979-80; assoc. Simon & Allen, Newark, 1980-86; ptnr. Kirsten, Simon, Friedman, Allen, Cherin & Linken, Newark, 1987—; atty. Irvington (N.J.) Rent Leveling Bd., 1980—. Author: Executing on a Debtor's Interest in a Tenancy by the Entirety, 1986. Mem. ABA, Essex County Bar Assn., Trial Attys. N.J., N.J. Inst. Mcpl. Attys. Republican. Roman Catholic. State civil litigation, Federal civil litigation, Contracts commercial. Home: 66 Addison Dr Basking Ridge NJ 07920 Office: Kirsten Simon Friedman Allen Cherin & Linken One Gateway Ctr Newark NJ 07102

MUSHKIN, MARTIN, lawyer; b. Boston, Nov. 21, 1931; s. William and Belle (Winer) M.; m. Ruth Benjamin, May 25, 1986; children: Elena, Hillary. BBA, U. Wis., 1953; LLB, Harvard U., 1956. Bar: N.Y. 1956, U.S. Dist. Ct. (so. and ea. dists.) N.Y. 1956, U.S. Ct. Appeals (2d cir.) 1962, Conn. 1977, U.S. Dist. Ct. Conn. 1978. Sr. atty. SEC, 1960-64; ptnr. Philips & Mushkin, P.C., N.Y.C., 1970-85, Blodnick, Pomeranz, Schultz & Abramowitz, P.C., N.Y.C. and Lake Success, N.Y., 1985—. Co-author: Am. Inst. CPA's Handbook on Accountants Liability, 1977; contbr. articles on corp. fin. to profl. jours. Served as 1st lt. JAGC, USAF, 1956-58. Mem. ABA (com. on devels. in investment services, chmn. subcom. on effect of tech. on investment services 1983-87), Assn. of Bar of City of N.Y. (com. on law and computers 1983-85), Fed. Bar Council (com. on 2d cir.). General corporate, Securities, Federal civil litigation. Office: Blodnick Pomeranz Schultz & Abramowitz Lake Success NY 11042-1273 Also Office: 477 Madison Ave New York NY 10022

MUSHKIN, MICHAEL ROBERT, lawyer; b. Las Vegas, Nev., Jan. 18, 1954; s. Lawrence and May (Barsky) M. BS, Ind. U., 1976; JD, Georgetown U., 1979. Bar: Nev. 1980. Assoc. Goodman, Oshins, Brown & Singer, Las Vegas, 1979-81; ptnr. Mushkin, Samuels & Assocs., Las Vegas, 1981-86, Michael Mushkin & Assocs., Las Vegas, 1986—; bd. dirs. Aztec Supply Corp., Las Vegas, MIKEMARK Inc., Las Vegas. Head coach tennis team U. Nev., Las Vegas, 1983; parlimentarian Nev. Dems., 1983. Mem. Nev. Bar Assn., Clark County Bar Assn., Ind. U. Alumni Assn., Georgetown U. Alumni Assn. Jewish. Avocations: tennis, scuba, cycling. General corporate, Consumer commercial, Corporate taxation. Office: Michael Mushkin & Assocs 930 S 3d #300 Las Vegas NV 89101

MUSKIN, VICTOR PHILIP, lawyer; b. N.Y.C., Mar. 1, 1942; s. Jacob Cecil and Fanya (Solomonoff) M.; m. Odette Cheryl Spreier, June 10, 1979; children: Adam James, Liana Jeanne. B.A., Oberlin Coll., 1963; J.D., NYU, 1966. Bar: N.Y. 1969, U.S. Dist. Ct. (so. and ea. dists.) N.Y. 1972, U.S. Ct. Appeals (2nd cir.) 1974, U.S. Ct. Appeals (9th and 10th cirs.) 1978, U.S. Supreme Ct. 1974. Asst. corp. csl. div. gen. litigation City of New York, 1969-73; assoc. Wolf, Popper, Ross, Wolf & Jones, 1973-74, Reavis & McGrath, 1974-78; sole practice, 1979; ptnr. Gruen & Muskin, 1980-81, Gruen, Muskin & Thau, 1981—. Served with Peace Corps, 1966-68. Mem. ABA, N.Y.C. Bar Assn. (com. computer law 1982-84). Federal civil litigation, State civil litigation, Private international. Address: 529 E 84th St New York NY 10028

MUSSELMAN, FRANCIS HAAS, lawyer; b. Utica, N.Y., Aug. 3, 1925; s. John Joseph and Kathryn Agnes (Haas) M.; m. Marjorie Louise Balme, June 22, 1948; children: Martha Musselman Sheridan, Kathryn Ann Musselman Bourbonniere, Carol Elizabeth Musselman Kuntz, John Francis. A.B., Hamilton Coll., Clinton, N.Y., 1950; J.D., Columbia U., 1953. Bar: N.Y. 1954. Assoc. firm Milbank, Tweed, Hadley & McCloy, N.Y.C., 1953-60; mem. Milbank, Tweed, Hadley & McCloy, 1960—; pres., dir. Panfield Corp., N.Y.C., 1961-82; dir. Panfield Nurseries, N.Y.C., 1961-82. Bd. dirs. Milbank Meml. Fund, 1960—, chmn., 1985—; bd. dirs. Memton Fund, 1958—; trustee Kirkland Coll., Clinton, 1971-78, chmn., 1972-78; trustee Nat. Center for Automated Info. Retrieval, 1979-80, Hamilton Coll., 1978—, Barnard Coll., 1979-81; trustee Wadhams Hall Sem. Coll., 1978—, vice chmn., 1979—. Served with USN, 1943-46. Fellow Am. Bar Found.; mem. Am. Judicature Soc., Am., N.Y. law insts., Internat., Am., Fed., N.Y. State, Nassau County bar assns., Assn. Bar City N.Y., Phi Delta Phi, Lambda Chi Alpha. Roman Catholic. Clubs: World Trade (N.Y.C.), Union League (N.Y.C.); Capitol Hill (Washington). Banking, Bankruptcy. Home: Oak Point Hammond NY 13646 Office: 1 Chase Manhattan Plaza New York NY 10005

MUSSELMAN, ROBERT METCALFE, lawyer, accountant; b. N.Y.C., June 12, 1914; s. Joseph Franklin and Susan (Metcalfe) M.; m. Lucie Carolyn Clarke, Sept. 6, 1958; 1 dau., Susan Carole. B.S., U. Va., 1934, M.A. in Polit. Sci., 1940, LL.B., 1945. Bar: Va. 1945, U.S. Dist. Cts. (ea. dist.) Va. 1948, U.S. Dist. Ct. (we. dist.) Va. 1951, U.S. Ct. Appeals (4th cir.) 1953, U.S. Tax Ct. 1948, U.S. Supreme Ct. 1964. Instr., lectr. U. Va., Charlottesville, 1936-59, chief acct., 1943-46; law clk. to judge U.S. Ct. Appeals (4th cir.), 1945-46; ptnr. Michael and Musselman, Charlottesville, 1946-53, Musselman and Drysdale, Charlottesville, 1953-56; sole practice, Charlottesville, 1956—; lectr. in field. Pres. Charlottesville-Albemarle Young Democratic Club, 1940-43; mem. Albemarle County Dem. Com., 1978—. Mem. Am. Assn. Atty.-C.P.A.s (charter mem., bd. dirs.), ABA, Va. Bar Assn., Charlottesville-Albemarle Bar Assn., Am. Inst. C.P.A.s, Va. Soc. C.P.A.s, Phi Sigma Kappa. Episcopalian. Editor-in-Chief: Alexander's Fed. Tax Handbook, 1955-61; bd. editors Jour. Taxation, 1954-73. Bankruptcy, Personal income taxation, Probate. Home: 306 Carrsbrook Dr Charlottesville VA 22901 Office: 413 7th St NE PO Box 254 Charlottesville VA 22902

MUSSER, JAMES WILLIAM, lawyer; b. Enid, Okla., Nov. 3, 1949; s. William Wesley and Estell Bee (Wiedeman) M.; m. Deborah Lynn Meier, May 2, 1981; children: Amber Dawn and Elizabeth Bee. BBA, U. Okla., 1971, JD, 1975. Bar: Okla. 1975, U.S. Dist. Ct. (we. dist.) Okla. 1975. Spl. dis. judge State of Okla., Enid, 1976-78; ptnr. Musser & Musser, Enid, 1979-80, Musser, Musser & Martin, Enid, 1981-85, Musser, Musser & Thomas, Enid, 1986. Served to capt. USAR. Named one of Outstanding Young Men Am., 1982. Mem. Am. Adjudicature Soc., Assn. Trial Lawyers Am., Okla. Trial Lawyers, Am. Bus. Club (pres. Enid 1979). Republican. Mem. Christian Ch. Avocations: scuba diving, gourmet cooking. State civil litigation, Criminal, Personal injury. Home: 1210 Cheyenne Enid OK 73703 Office: Musser Musser & Thomas 114 E Broadway Suite 1405 Enid OK 73702

MUSSER, R. CLARK, lawyer, educator; b. Oklahoma City, Aug. 21, 1945; s. Sidney Arthur and Mary Martha (Buecking) M.; m. Kay Louise, Aug. 24, 1968; children—Robert Clayton, Cara Lauren. B.B.A., U. Okla., 1967, J.D., 1970. Bar: Okla. 1970. Ptnr., Musser and Bunch, Oklahoma City, 1980-83, Musser, Bunch and Robinson, 1983—; adj. asso. prof. oil and gas law U. Okla., Norman, 1979—, lectr. bus. devel. programs. Served as capt. JAGC, USAF, 1970-75. Mem. Okla. Bar Assn. (guest lectr.), Oklahoma City Title Attys. Assn. (pres.), Phi Delta Phi. Contbg. editor Okla. Bar Jour., 1978—; contbr. articles to legal jours. Oil and gas leasing. Home: 6506 NW Grand Blvd Oklahoma City OK 73116 Office: 220 Oil and Gas Bldg Main and Robinson Oklahoma City OK 73102

MUSSER, WILLIAM WESLEY, JR., lawyer; b. Enid, Okla., July 17, 1918; s. William W. and Ethel R. (McElroy) M.; m. Estelle Bee Wiedeman, Jan. 19, 1947; children: James William, Mary Bee. B.A., U. Okla., 1939, LL.B., 1941. Bar: Okla. 1941. Partner firm Elam, Crowley & Musser, Enid, 1946-47; probate judge Garfield County, Okla., 1949-51; chmn. Bd. Tax Roll Corrections Garfield County, 1950-51; partner firm Otjen, Carter & Musser, Enid, 1952-54; pvt. practice, also asst. county atty. Garfield County, 1955-56; practice in Enid, 1957-79; mem. firm Musser, Musser & Martin, 1980-85; partner firm Musser & Green, 1965-77, Musser & Musser, 1977-86; sole practice Enid, 1987—; judge Okla. Ct. Appeals, 1982; Rep. 6th Congl. dist. Okla. Jud. Nominating Com., 1967-74. Pres. Am. Bus. Club Enid, 1947, Great Salt Plains council Boy Scouts Am., 1955; gen. chmn. St. Mary's Hosp. bldg. fund, 1949; Bd. dirs. Enid Community Chest, 1950-51; v.p. bd. trustees Phillips U., 1955-74, mem. exec. com., 1955-78, trustee, 1975-82; bd. dirs. Enid Estate Planning Council, 1971-74, sec., 1972, pres., 1973-74; bd. dirs. N.W. Okla. Pastoral Care Assn., 1978. Served to maj. AUS, 1941-46. Decorated Bronze Star. Fellow Okla. Bar Found.; mem. ABA., Okla. Bar Assn. (v.p., bd. govs. 1957), Garfield County Bar Assn. (pres. 1962), Okla. Trial Lawyers Assn., U. Okla. Alumni Assn. (exec. bd. 1959-61), Sons and Daus. of Cherokee, Strip Pioneers Assn. (exec. bd. dirs. 1967-70), Greater Enid C. of C. (dir. 1969-71), VFW, Am. Legion, Phi Delta Phi, Alpha Tau Omega. Republican. Mem. Christian Ch. (chmn. trustees 1968, elder 1967-70, 75-78, 79-82, 86—, deacon 1955-58, 61-64). Club: Oakwood Country. Probate, Real property, General practice. Home: 1301 Indian Dr Enid OK 73701 Office: 1405 Broadway Tower Bldg Enid OK 73701

MUSSMAN, WILLIAM EDWARD, III, lawyer; b. San Francisco, Jan. 31, 1951; s. William Edward and Janet Jonn (Skittone) M. B.S., Stanford U., 1973; J.D., U. Calif.-San Francisco, 1976. Bar: Calif. 1976, U.S. Dist. Ct. (no. dist.) Calif. 1976,, U.S. Dist. Ct. (cen. dist.) Calif. 1982, U.S. Supreme Ct., 1986. Assoc. Lasky, Haas, Cohler & Munter, San Francisco, 1980-82, Pillsbury, Madison & Sutro, San Francisco, 1982-84; assoc. Carr & Mussman, San Francisco, 1984—. Sustaining mem. Yosemite Area council Boy Scouts Am., 1981—; missionary Ch. Jesus Christ Latter Day Sts., Tokyo, 1977-78. Mem. ABA, San Francisco Bar Assn., Latter Day Saints Bus. Club (pres. 1982-84), Am. Horse Shows Assn., Brigham Young U. Mgmt. Soc. (bd. dirs., 1984-88, v.p. 1984-86, pres. 1986—), Stanford Alumni Assn. (life), Tau Beta Pi. Club: Commonwealth of Calif. Antitrust, Federal civil litigation, State civil litigation. Office: Carr & Mussman 3 Embarcadero Ctr Suite 1060 San Francisco CA 94111

MUSSMAN, WILLIAM EDWARD, lawyer, oil company executive; b. Mpls., Feb. 10, 1919; s. William Edward and Vera Marie (Chamberlain) M.; m. Janet Jonn Skittone, Dec. 19, 1948; children: William Edward III, Ann C. B.S. in Law, U. Minn., 1941, J.D., 1946. Bar: Minn. 1946, Calif. 1950, U.S. Supreme Ct. 1960. Asst. prof. law U. Minn., 1946-49; vis. prof. U. Calif., Berkeley, 1949; assoc. firm Pillsbury, Madison & Sutro, San Francisco, 1949-56; partner Pillsbury, Madison & Sutro, 1956-74; v.p., legal, dir. Standard Oil Co. of Calif., San Francisco, 1974-84. Served with USMCR, 1942-45. Decorated D.F.C. Fellow Southwestern Legal Found.; mem. ABA, Am. Arbitration Assn. Antitrust, Federal civil litigation, State civil litigation. Office: Three Embarcadero Ctr Suite 1060 San Francisco CA 94111

MUSTAIN, DOUGLAS DEE, lawyer; b. Shreveport, La., Nov. 2, 1945; s. Reginald K. and Dorothy J. (Green) M.; m. Sharon L. Tegarden, Aug. 19, 1967; children—Kristi Kaye, Kari Dee, Kenton Douglas, Kyle Robert, Kirk Stephen. Student Knox Coll., 1963-64, Murray State U., 1964-66; B.S., U. Ill., 1971; J.D., U. Iowa, 1974. Bar: Iowa 1974, Ill. 1974; U.S. Dist. Ct. (cen. dist.) Ill. 1974, U.S. Ct. Appeals (7th cir.) 1980, U.S. Supreme Ct. 1986. Law clk. Shulman, Phelan, Tucker, Boyle & Mullin, Iowa City, 1972-74; assoc. Stuart, Neagle & West, Galesburg, Ill., 1974-76; ptnr. West, Neagle & Williamson, Galesburg, 1977—; instr. real estate law Carl Sandburg Coll., Galesburg, 1977-81. Chmn. Citizens Referendum Com., Galesburg, 1983; bd. dirs. YMCA, Galesburg, 1984, Cottage Hosp. Care Corp., Galesburg, 1984; trustee 1st Presbyn. Ch., Galesburg, 1984; commr. Galesburg Pub. Transp. Commn., 1985. Served to SP5 U.S. Army, 1966-69, Vietnam. Decorated Army Commendation with oak leaf cluster. Mem. Knox County Bar Assn. (pres. 1980-82), ABA (comml. litigation com. 1971—), Am. Trial Lawyers Assn., Ill. Trial Lawyers Assn. Republican. State civil litigation, General practice. Home: 1234 N Prairie St Galesburg IL 61401 Office: West Neagle & Williamson 58 S Cherry St Galesburg IL 61401

MUSTER, DOUGLAS FREDERICK, engineering educator; b. Milw., Nov. 2, 1918; s. Ernst Frederick and Maye (White) M.; m. Jean Brown, Jan. 15, 1944; children: David, Randell, Scott, Gordon, Deborah. B.S., Marquette U., 1940; M.S., Ill. Inst. Tech., 1949, Ph.D., 1955. Diplomate Nat. Acad. Forensic Engrs. Asst. prof. Ill. Inst. Tech., 1950-53; mech. systems engr. Gen. Electric Co. Lab., Schenectady, 1953-61; prof. mech. enging. U. Houston, 1961—, chmn. dept., 1962-72, Brown and Root prof. mech. engring., 1967—; dir. Office of Engring. Practice Programs, 1976-79; adj. prof. law, 1981—. Editor: Theory of Shells, 1967; procs.: Internat. Symposium Lubrication and Wear, 1965. Served with AUS, 1943-47. Fellow Acoustical Soc. Am., ASME, Instn. Mech. Engrs., Inst. Acoustics, AAAS; mem. Am. Soc. Engring. Edn., Inst. Noise Control Engring., Nat. Council Acoustical Cons. Clubs: Cosmos; Naval (London). Legal education, Patent, Personal injury. Home: 4615 O'Meara Dr Houston TX 77035

MUSTO, JOSEPH J., lawyer; b. Pittston, Pa., Nov. 22, 1943; s. James and Rose (Frushon) M.; m. Fortunata Giudice, July 5, 1969; children: Laura, Joseph Robert. BA, King's Coll., Wilkes-Barre, Pa., 1965; JD, Dickinson Sch. Law, Carlisle, Pa., 1968. Bar: Pa. 1968, U.S. Ct. Appeals (3d cir.) 1968, U.S. Dist. Ct. (mid. dist.) Pa. 1971. Asst. dist. atty. City of Phila., 1968-69; assoc. Bedford, Waller, Griffith, Darling & Mitchell, Wilkes-Barre, 1969-73; ptnr. Griffith, Darling, Mitchell, Aponick & Musto, Wilkes-Barre, 1973-75; prin. Griffith, Aponick & Musto, Wilkes-Barre, 1975—; solicitor Yatesville (Pa.) Borough, 1973-80, Duryea (Pa.) Borough, 1975-80, Pittston Area Sch. Dist., 1973—. Mem. Luzerne County Gov. Study Com., Wilkes-Barre, 1973-74; mem., chmn. No. Luzerne Health Adv. Council, Wilkes-Barre, 1976-80; pres., mem. Health Systems Agy. of Northeast Pa., Avoca, 1980—; pres. Pa. Health Planning Assn., Harrisburg, 1985—. Mem. Pa. Bar Assn., Wilkes-Barre Law and Library Assn. Democrat. Roman Catholic. Federal civil litigation, State civil litigation, Insurance. Home: 7 Prospect Pl Pittston PA 18640 Office: Griffith Aponick & Musto 408 Wilkes-Barre Ctr 39 Public Sq Wilkes-Barre PA 18701

MUSTOKOFF, MICHAEL MARK, lawyer; b. Phila., Oct. 19, 1947; s. Harry and Ethel (Sobel) M.; m. Rae Janet Vogel, June 7, 1970; children: Matthew Leo, Jessica Beth. BA, Albright Coll., 1969; JD, U. Pa., 1972. Bar: Pa. 1972, U.S. Dist. Ct. (ea. dist.) 1980, U.S. Ct. Appeals (3d cir.) 1981, U.S. Supreme Ct. 1983. Asst. dist. atty. Office of Dist. Atty., Phila., 1972-79; ptnr. Duane, Morris, Heckscher, Phila., 1980—. Author: (manuals) Use of Search Warrants in White Collar Criminal Investigations, 1980, Prosecution of Hazardous Waste Cases, 1980. Candidate for U.S. Congress, 4th Congl. Dist. Phila., 1980. Mem. ABA, Pa. Bar Assn., Phila. Bar Assn., Nat. Assn. Criminal Def. Lawyers, Def. Research Inst., Pa. Def. Reserach Inst. Democrat. Jewish. Criminal, Federal civil litigation, Environment. Home: 1079 Hillview Turn Huntingdon Valley PA 19006 Office: Duane Morris Heckscher 16th & Race Sts. Philadelphia PA 19102

MUTEK, MICHAEL WENDELL, lawyer; b. Somerville, N.J., Sept. 20, 1951; s. Wendell Augustus and Sophia (Grigorifew) M.; m. Patricia Kay Steinwedel, Sept. 28, 1983. BA, U. Dayton, 1972, JD, 1979. Bar: Ohio 1979, U.S. Ct. Claims 1980, U.S. Tax Ct. 1980, U.S. Dist. Ct. (so. dist.) Ohio 1981, U.S. Ct. Appeals (6th cir.) 1981, U.S. Ct. Appeals (Fed. cir.) 1983, U.S. Supreme Ct. 1983, D.C. 1985, Calif. 1986. Trial atty. USAF, Wright-Patterson AFB, Calif., 1979-84; asst. div. counsel Litton Industries, Woodland Hills, 1984-85; div. counsel Litton Industries, Woodland Hills, 1985—. Mem. ABA (state chmn. pub. contract law sect. 1984-85), Fed. Bar Assn. (sec. 1982-83, pres. 1983-84), D.C. Bar Assn., Calif. Bar Assn., Los Angeles Bar Assn. Republican. Roman Catholic. Avocations: running, sailing. Government contracts and claims, Public international, General corporate. Home: 5515 Alfredo Ct Agoura Hills CA 91301 Office: Litton Industries Law Dept M/S24 5500 Canoga Ave Woodland Hills CA 91367

MUTH, MICHAEL RAYMOND, lawyer; b. Chgo., Dec. 28, 1950; s. Michael Jacob Muth and Mary (Birch) LaSpesa. B. in Gen. Studies, Ohio U., 1972; J.D., U. N.C., 1975. Bar: Ky. 1975, Pa. 1976, U.S. Dist. Ct. (mid. dist.) Pa. 1979. Chief pub. defender Monroe County, Stroudsburg, Pa., 1978—; sole practice, Stroudsburg, 1976-84; ptnr. Muth & Zulick, Stroudsburg, 1984—. Treas., bd. dirs. Women's Resources, Inc., Stroudsburg, 1981-86; pres., bd. dirs. Monroe County Youth Employment Service, Inc., Stroudsburg, 1977-81, Twin-Boro Teenage Baseball League, Inc., East Stroudsburg, 1982—; speech coach East Stroudsburg State Coll., 1977-79; campaign mgr. Com. to Elect Tom Shiffer, Stroud Twp., 1983; trustee Com. to Elect Dennis Deshler, 1979; vice chmn. Com. to Re-Elect Dale Keenhold, Stroudsburg, 1983. Mem. ABA, Ky. Bar Assn., Pa. Bar Assn., Pa. Trial Lawyers Assn., Assn. Trial Lawyers Am., Omicron Delta Kappa. Democrat. Roman Catholic. Club: Aardvark Enterprises (pres. 1977—) (Stroudsburg). Criminal, Family and matrimonial, Senior citizen advocacy. Home: 271 Prospect St East Stroudsburg PA 18301 Office: Muth and Zulick 729 Monroe St Stroudsburg PA 18360

MUTTALIB, KALAM, lawyer; b. Cleve., Apr. 21, 1943; s. Roy and Ruby (Pitts) Mathis; m. Bashirah, Dec. 12, 1970 (div. Jan. 1977); children—Khabir, Rasool; m. Kimetta Ann Davis, Sept. 12, 1980; children—Kalam, Aliyah, Meira. B.A., Cleve. State U., 1971; J.D., Case Western Res. U., 1974. Bar: Ohio 1974, U.S. Dist. Ct. (no. dist.) Ohio 1975, U.S. Ct. Appeals (6th cir.) 1980, U.S. Supreme Ct. 1980. Research technician Glidden Durkee div. of SCM Cleve., 1966-75; assoc. Carl J. Character Co. L.P.A., Cleve., 1975-78; sole practice, 1978-80, 84—; housing ct. referee Cleve. Municipal Ct., 1980-84. Editor, compiler: Cleveland Municipal Housing Court Rules, 1983; editor Vindicator, 1970; founding editor Kuwais, 1971. Mem. Big Bros. Greater Cleve., 1975, United Negro Coll. Fund, Cleve., 1983. Recipient Martin Luther King award Friends of East Side News, Cleve., 1982. Mem. NAACP, Norman S. Minor Bar Assn. (pres. 1981-82), Friends of Karamu, John Harlan Law Club (2d v.p. 1977-78), Young Lawyers Council, Cleve. Bar Assn. (bd. mem. 1976-79). Democrat. Muslim. Landlord-tenant, General practice, Real property. Home: 3693 Berkeley Cleveland Heights OH 44118 Office: 401 Euclid Ave #516 Cleveland OH 44114-2402

MUZZY, GRAY HOWARD, lawyer; b. Anderson, S.C., Jan. 7, 1954; s. Richard Wainwright and Robin (Hill) M.; m. Phoebe Welsh, Apr. 28, 1984. BA, Yale U.; JD, U. Tex. Bar: Tex. 1981. Assoc. Bracewell & Patterson, Houston, 1981—. Fellow Houston Bar Found. Republican. Episcopalian. Real property, Oil and gas leasing. Office: Bracewell & Patterson 2900 Pennzoil Pl South Tower Houston TX 77002

MYCOCK, FREDERICK CHARLES, lawyer; b. Columbus, Ga., Oct. 3, 1943; s. Edwin S. and Elaine M.M. B.S. in Bus. Adminstrn., Boston U., 1965, LL.B., 1968. Bar: Mass. 1968, U.S. Dist. Ct. Mass. 1974, U.S. Supreme Ct. 1980. Assoc. Roderick E. Smith, Hyannis, Mass., 1968-71; asst. atty. gen. Mass., 1972-73; ptnr. Mycock, Kilroy, Green & Mycock, Hyannis, 1972-77, Mycock, Newell & Morse, Barnstable, Mass., 1977—. Mem. Barnstable County Bar Assn., Mass. Bar Assn., ABA, Assn. Trial Lawyers Am., Mass. Acad. Trial Lawyers, Nat. Assn. Criminal Defense Lawyers. Republican. Methodist. Criminal. Home: Santuit Rd Cotuit MA 02635 Office: Mycock Newell & Morse 3291 Rt 6A Barnstable MA 02630

MYERS, EDWARD DORAN, lawyer; b. Pitts., Dec. 3, 1952; s. George Carl and Elizabeth Baird (Doran) M. BA, St. John's Coll., Annapolis, Md., 1974; BA in Journalism, George Washington U., 1975; JD, U. Pitts., 1978. Bar: Pa. 1978, U.S. Dist. Ct. (we. dist.) Pa. 1978, N.Mex. 1982, U.S. Dist. Ct. N.Mex. 1983, U.S. Ct. Appeals (10th cir.) 1983. Staff atty. Northwestern Legal Services, Inc., Erie, Pa., 1978-80; law clk. to presiding justice Ct. Common Pleas, Erie, 1980-82; assoc. Sarah Singleton Law Firm, Sante Fe, 1982-83, Marchiondo & Berry P.A., Albuquerque, 1983-84, Jennie Deden Behles P.A., Albuquerque, 1984—. Mem. ABA, N.Mex. Bar Assn. (bankruptcy sect.), Assn. Trial Lawyers Am., N.Mex. Trial Lawyers Assn. Avocations: white water rafting, photography, camping. Bankruptcy, Federal civil litigation, Contracts commercial. Home: 421 14th St SW Albuquerque NM 87102 Office: Jennie Deden Behles PA 1104 Park Ave SW Alburquerque NM 87102

MYERS, JAMES WOODROW, III, lawyer; b. Gary, Ind., Aug. 3, 1954; s. James Woodrow Jr. and Martha G. (Ladd) M.; m. Barbara Anne Johnson, Aug. 15, 1980. BA, Valparaiso U., 1976, JD, 1979. Bar: U.S. Dist. Ct. (so. and no. dists.) Ind. 1979, Ind. 1980, Ill. 1983, U.S. Dist. Ct. (no. dist.) Ill. Assoc. Law Offices of J. Diaz P.C., Portage, Ind., 1979-83, Leonard M. Ring & Assocs., Chgo., 1983-87; sole practice Crown Point, Ind., 1987—. Mem. ABA, Ind. Bar Assn., Ill. Bar Assn., Mich. Bar Assn., Chgo. Bar Assn., Assn. Trial Lawyers Am., Ill. Trial Lawyers Assn., Ind. Trial Lawyers Assn., Mich. Trial Lawyers Assn., Lake County Bar Assn. Federal civil litigation, State civil litigation, Personal injury. Home: 4004 Oak Grove Dr Valparaiso IN 46383 Office: 5221 Fountain Dr Suite A Crown Point IN 46307

MYERS, JESSE JEROME, lawyer, construction company executive; b. Anthony, Kans., Sept. 30, 1940; s. Claud Lewis and Lucille S. (Robertson) M.; m. Claire H. Conni, Nov., 1966; children: Timothy Todd, Jessica Joy. B.S., McPherson Coll., 1963; J.D., Washburn U., 1970. Bar: Kans. 1970, U.S. Dist. Ct. Kans. 1970. Law clk. U.S. Dist. Ct. Judge Frank Theis, Wichita, KS, 1970-72; individual practice law Wichita, KS, 1972-74; lawyer Cessna Aircraft Co., Wichita, KS, 1974-75; with Martin K. Eby Constrn. Co., Wichita, Kans., 1975—; now v.p., dir., gen. counsel. Martin K. Eby Constrn. Co. Served with USN, 1963-67. Mem. Am. Bar Assn., Kans. Bar Assn. Construction, Government contracts and claims, General corporate. Office: Martin K Eby Constrn Co Inc 610 N Main Wichita KS 67203

MYERS, J(OSEPH) MICHAEL, lawyer; b. Austin, Tex., Sept. 5, 1947; s. Joseph Marion and Constance Lorraine (Clarke) M.; m. Cindy Jean Sutherland, July 11, 1970; children—Joseph Merritt, Jordan Robertson. B.A., U. Tex., 1970; J.D., St. Mary's U., San Antonio, 1974. Bar: Tex. 1974, U.S. Dist. Ct. (we. dist.) Tex. 1975, U.S. Dist. Ct. (so. dist.) Tex. 1976, U.S. Ct. Appeals (5th cir.) 1976, U.S. Supreme Ct. 1976. Briefing atty. to chief judge U.S. Dist. Ct. (we. dist.) Tex., San Antonio, 1974-75; ptnr. Groce, Locke & Hebdon, San Antonio, 1975—. Editor, contbr. St. Mary's U. Law Sch. Rev., 1974. Mem. ABA, Fed. Bar Assn. (speaker 1982-84), San Antonio Bar Assn. (Outstanding Service award 1980), Am. Judicature Soc., Tex. Assn. Def. Counsel, Phi Delta Phi (historian 1974-75). Episcopalian. Federal civil litigation, State civil litigation, Personal injury. Home: 10818 Tioga San Antonio TX 78230 Office: Groce Locke Hebdon 2000 Frost Bank Tower San Antonio TX 78205

MYERS, LONN WILLIAM, lawyer; b. Rockford, Ill., Nov. 14, 1946; s. William H. and Leona V. (Janvrin) M.; m. Janet L. Forbes, May 14, 1968; children: Andrew, Hillary, Corwin. BA, Mich. State U., 1968; MBA, Ind. U., 1973; JD, Harvard U., 1976. Bar: Ill. 1976, U.S. Dist. Ct. (no. dist.) Ill., U.S. Ct. Claims, U.S. Ct. Appeals (7th cir.). Ptnr. McDermott, Will & Emery, Chgo., 1976—. Served to maj. USAR, 1968-80. Mem. ABA (chmn. subcom. on ACRS of capital recovery and leasing com. tax sect. 1986). Episcopalian. Club: Union League (Chgo.). Corporate taxation, Personal income taxation, Municipal bonds. Home: 1711 Highland Terr Glenview IL 60025 Office: McDermott Will & Emery 111 W Monroe St Chicago IL 60603

MYERS, PHILIP ERIC, lawyer, corporation executive; b. Erie, Pa., Feb. 21, 1952; s. George Alfred and Helen Louise (Walper) M.; m. Phyllis Evelyn Nordstrom, Jan. 1, 1983. BA, Stanford U., 1974; JD, UCLA, 1977. Bar: Calif. 1977, U.S. Dist. Ct. (no., mid., and ea. dists.) Calif. 1977. Assoc. West Favor & Woodruff, Santa Barbara, Calif., 1977-78; sole practice Santa Barbara, 1978—; pres. Montecito Trading Co., Santa Barbara, 1984—; cons. polit. polling and campaign strategy, Mycon Co., Venezuela, Brazil and Mex., 1980—. Vice chmn. Alliance Franchise of Santa Barbara, 1980—; vol. Stanford Ann. Fund., Santa Barbara, 1978—, chmn. Santa Barbara Ctr. Performing Arts, 1985—; vice chmn. U. Calif. Santa Barbara Affiliates, Santa Barbara, 1984-86; treas. Alzheimer's Disease Related Disorder Assn. of Santa Barbara, 1982—. Mem. ABA (internat. law sec.), Santa Barbara Com. Fgn. Relations, Wilton Park Alumni of So. Calif., Phi Beta Kappa, 1977. Republican. Methodist. Club: Santa Barbara Yacht. Avocation: French and Portuguese langs., sailing, tennis, oceanliner history. Private international, Estate planning. Home: 1701 Anacapa St #19 Santa Barbara CA 93101 Office: 6 E Arellagu St Santa Barbara CA 93101

MYERS, ROBERT DAVID, lawyer; b. Springfield, Mass., Nov. 20, 1937; s. William and Pearl (Weiss) M.; m. Judith G. Dickenman, July 1, 1962; children—Mandy Susan, Jay Brandt, Seth William. A.B., U. Mass., 1959; J.D., Boston U., 1962. Bar: Ariz. bar 1963. Practice in Phoenix, 1963—; mem. firm Hofmann, Salcito, Stevens & Myers, 1966—; pro tem judge Superior Ct. of, Maricopa County, Ariz., Ct. Appeals; Chmn. com. on exams. and admissions Ariz. Supreme Ct., 1974-75, chmn. com. on character and fitness, 1975-76, mem. multi-state bar exam. com., 1976—. Pres. Valley of Sun chpt. City of Hope, 1965-66, Community Orgn. for Drug Abuse Control, 1972-73, Valley Big Bros., 1975; chmn. Mayors Ad Hoc Com. on Drug Abuse, 1974-75; bd. dirs. Maricopa County Legal Aid Soc., 1978, Phoenix Jewish Community Center; sec. Jud. Selection Adv. Com. of City of Phoenix. Mem. Ariz. Bar Assn. (gov., com. chmn., sect. pres.), Maricopa County Bar Assn. (dir., pres. 1979-80), Am. Trial Lawyers Assn. (nat. chmn. gov.), Ariz. Trial Lawyers Assn. (pres., dir., co-editor Newsletter), Phoenix Trial Lawyers Assn. (pres., dir.), Western Trial Lawyers Assn. (pres. 1977), Am. Arbitration Assn. (nat. panel arbitrators), Am. Judicature Soc. (spl. merit citation outstanding service improvement of adminstrn. justice 1986), Am. Bd. Trial Advocates. State civil litigation, Federal civil litigation, Personal injury. Office: Hofmann Salcito Stevens & Myers 302 E Coronado St Phoenix AZ 85004

MYERS, ROBERT EARL, lawyer; b. Phila., Nov. 20, 1951; s. Stanley and Joan (Blumberg) M.; m. Sherrie Lynne Trautenberg, Sept. 24, 1978; children: Jennifer Rachel, Julie Lauren. BA, Temple U., 1973, LLM in Taxation, 1985; JD, Cath. U., 1976. Bar: Pa. 1976, D.C. 1977, N.J. 1986, U.S. Dist. Ct. N.J. 1986, U.S. Dist. Ct. (ea. dist.) Pa. 1976. Assoc. Dagui & Delcollo, Phila., 1976-78; asst. dist. atty. State of Pa., Phila., 1978-86; assoc. Sprague, Thall & Creamer, Phila., 1986-87; assoc. Law Offices of Marvin I. Barish, Phila., 1987—; ombudsman Dist. Atty. Office of Phila., 1978-86. Jewish. Federal civil litigation, State civil litigation, Personal injury. Home: 84 Woodstone Ln Villanova PA 19085 Office: Law Offices of Marvin I Barish 135 S 19th St #400 Philadelphia PA 19103

MYERS, RODMAN NATHANIEL, lawyer; b. Detroit, Oct. 27, 1920; s. Isaac Rodman and Fredericka (Hirschman) M.; m. Jeanette Polisei, Mar. 19, 1957; children: Jennifer Sue, Rodman Jay. BA, Wayne State U., 1941; LLB, U. Mich., 1943. Bar: Mich. 1943, U.S. Supreme Ct. 1962. Agt. IRS, Detroit, 1943; ptnr. Butzel, Keidan, Simon, Myers & Graham, Detroit, 1943—; bd. dirs. Mich. Nat. Bank North-Metro. Bd. dirs. United Community Services of Met. Detroit, 1978—, v.p., 1981—, chmn. social services div., 1982—; bd. dirs. Children's Ctr. of Wayne County (Mich.), 1963—, pres., 1969-72; founding mem., trustee Detroit Sci. Ctr.; pres., nat. trustee Mich. chpt. Leukemia Soc. Am.; commr. Detroit Mcpl. Parking Authority, 1963-71; trustee Temple Beth El, Birmingham; former trustee Jewish Vocat. Service and Community Workshop. Mem. ABA, State Bar Mich. (chmn. atty. discipline panel, past vice chmn. unauthorized practice of law com., past mem. character and fitness com.), Detroit Bar Assn. Club: Renaissance. General corporate. Home: 3833 Lakeland Ln Bloomfield Hills MI 48013 Office: 2490 1st Nat Bldg Detroit MI 48226

MYERS, RONALD LYNN, lawyer; b. Houston, Jan. 18, 1949; s. E. Carlton and Elizabeth Anne (Boyette) M.; m. Nancy G. Finney, May 20, 1972. B.S. in History, Kans. State U., 1971; J.D., U. Kans., 1974. Bar: Mo. 1974, U.S. Dist. Ct. (we. dist.) Mo. 1974, U.S. Ct. Appeals (8th cir.) 1977, U.S. Supreme Ct. 1978. Assoc. Strop, Watkins et al, St. Joseph, Mo., 1974-76; ptnr. Daniel, Clampett et al, Springfield, Mo., 1976-84; sole practice, Springfield, 1984—. Author: Exemplifying Punitive Damages, 1976. Mem. com. counsel Springfest '84, Springfield, 1984; dir., counsel Agape House Springfield, 1984. Mem. ABA, Mo. Bar Assn., Greene County Bar Assn., Springfield Claims Assn. (pres. 1984-85, bd. dirs. 1980-85), Assn. Trial Lawyers Am. Republican. Methodist. Personal injury, Insurance, Federal civil litigation. Home: 920 Northfield Rd Springfield MO 65803 Office: 1909 E Bennett Springfield MO 65804

MYERS, WILLIAM EDWARD, lawyer, educator; b. Johnson City, N.Y., Feb. 17, 1956; s. Kenneth R. and Janet M. (Grenier) M.; m. Karen R. Harwood, Oct. 12, 1985. BA in Polit. Sci., BA in History, SUNY, Buffalo, 1978; JD, U. Dayton, 1981. Bar: N.Y. 1982. Assoc. Sargent, Sargent, Martin & Levin, Syracuse, N.Y., 1982-84, William D. Weisberg, P.C., Syracuse, 1984-85; ptnr. Myers, Rose & Flynn, Syracuse, 1985—; instr. Am. Paralegal Inst., Syracuse, 1986—. Mem. ABA, N.Y. State Bar Assn., Onondaga County Bar Assn. Republican. Roman Catholic. Avocations: golf, coin collecting, woodworking. Real property, General practice, Criminal. Home: 8 Carol Dr Camillus NY 13031 Office: Myers Rose & Flynn 103 E Water St Suite 403 Syracuse NY 13202

MYERSON, HARVEY DANIEL, lawyer; b. Phila., Aug. 1, 1939; s, Morris and Rachel (Cohen) M.; m. Anne Borish, Aug. 20, 1961 (div. 1975); children: Karen Michelle, Jill Diane, Jessica Ann; m. Diane Clare Stukelman, Oct. 17, 1975; children: Rachel Clare, Emily Alicia. Student, U. Chgo., 1957-59; BS, Temple U., 1961; LLB, Columbia U., 1964. Bar: N.Y. 1964, U.S. Ct. Appeals (2d cir.) 1965, U.S. Dist. Ct. (so. dist.) N.Y. 1965, U.S. Supreme Ct. 1975, U.S. Ct. Appeals (4th cir.) 1975. Assoc. firm Hughes, Hubbard & Reed, N.Y.C., 1964-70; mng. ptnr. Webster & Sheffield, N.Y.C., 1970-84; mng. ptnr. Finley, Kumble, Wagner, Heine, Underberg, Manley, Myerson & Casey, N.Y.C., 1984-86, ptnr., 1986—; lectr. seminars. Mem. Fed. Bar Council, Assn. Bar City N.Y. Republican. Jewish. Clubs: University (N.Y.C.); Tryall Golf and Beach (Jamaica, W.I.); Mattakesett Tennis (Edgartown, Mass). Federal civil litigation, Administrative and regulatory, Securities and antitrust. Office: Finley Kumble Wagner Heine et al 425 Park Ave New York NY 10022

MYERSON, TOBY SALTER, lawyer; b. Chgo., July 20, 1949; s. Raymond King and Natalie Anita (Salter) M. BA, Yale U., 1971; JD, Harvard U., 1975. Bar: N.Y. 1977, Calif. 1977. Assoc. Coudert Bros., N.Y.C., 1975-77, 81, San Francisco, 1977-81; assoc. Paul, Weiss, Rifkind, Wharton & Garrison, N.Y.C., 1981-83, ptnr., 1983—; lectr. U. Calif. Berkeley, 1979-81, Harvard U., Cambridge, Mass., 1982-83; visiting lectr. Yale U., New Haven, Mass., 1983-84; bd. dirs. Myerson, Van Den Berg & Co., Santa Barbara. Contbg. editor: Doing Business in Japan, 1983. Sec. Japan Soc. Inc., N.Y.C., 1985—; bd. dirs. 1058 Corp., N.Y.C., 1985—. Mem. ABA (subcom. internat. banking, corp. banking and bus. law sect.), Internat. Bar Assn., Calif. Bar Assn., N.Y. State Bar Assn., Assn. of Bar of City of N.Y. (com. on fgn. and comparative law). Avocations: art, music, ballet, literature, tennis. General corporate, Banking, Private international. Office: Paul Weiss Rifkind Wharton & Garrison 1285 Ave of Americas New York NY 10019

MYGATT, ANN BLISS, lawyer; b. Chappaqua, N.Y., Sept. 16, 1942; d. Edward Elliott and Ruth Anne (Corkey) Bliss; m. Bruce Macdonald Mygatt, June 9, 1962 (div. Aug. 1976); children: Christopher McLean, Brian Macdonald. BS, Mont. State U., 1965; M in Pub. Adminstrn., U. Colo., 1976; JD, U. Wis., 1979. Bar: Colo. 1979. Dep. dist. atty. Boulder (Colo.) County, 1980-83; ptnr. Edwards, Terrill & Mygatt, Boulder, 1983—. Mem. Boulder County Women's Polit. Caucus. Mem. ABA, Colo. Bar Assn., Boulder Bar Assn. (sec.-treas. 1986, chmn. media law com. 1985—), Assn. Trial Lawyers Am., Colo. Trial Lawyers Am., Women's Internat. League for Peace and Freedom. Democrat. Avocations: backpacking, running, hiking. Criminal, Family and matrimonial. Home: 827 Maxwell Boulder CO 80302 Office: Edwards Terrill & Mygatt 1227 Spruce St Boulder CO 80302

MYLOTT, THOMAS RAYMOND, III, lawyer; b. Boston, Mar. 22, 1952; s. Thomas Raymond Jr. and Louise Margaret (Spencer) M. AB, Vassar Coll., 1974; JD, Boston U., 1977. Bar: Tex. 1978, U.S. Dist. Ct. (no. dist.) Tex. 1983; cert. data processor. Sole practice Dallas, 1978—; Author: Computer Law for Computer Professionals, 1984; contbr. articles to profl. jours. Fellow Vassar Coll., 1974. Mem. ABA (com. chmn. 1981—), Data Processing Mgmt. Assn., Tex. Bar Assn., Computer Law Assn., Mensa, Phi Beta Kappa, Omicron Delta Epsilon. Avocations: amatuer radio, gardening, long distance running. Computer. Home: 5417 Willis Dallas TX 75206 Office: 5925 Forest Ln Suite 501 Dallas TX 75230

MYREN, RICHARD ALBERT, university administrator; b. Madison, Wis., Aug. 9, 1924; s. Andrew Olaus and Olyanna (Olson) M.; m. Patricia Ross Hubin, June 12, 1948; children—Nina Ross Schroepfer, Tania Ellis Myren Sparks, Kristina Albee Myren Sheldon, Andrew James. B.S., U. Wis., 1948; LL.B., Harvard U., 1952; LL.D. (hon.), U. New Haven, 1976. Bar: N.C. 1954. Research chemist U.S. Dept. Agr., No. Regional Research Lab., Peoria, Ill., 1948-49; asst. to assoc. research prof. pub. law and govt. Inst. Govt., Chapel Hill, N.C., 1952-56; asst. to assoc. prof. Ind. U., 1956-66; dean, prof. Sch. Criminal Justice, State U. N.Y., Albany, 1966-76; dean, prof. Sch. Justice, Am. U., Washington, 1976-86, prof. emeritus, 1986; cons. 1987—; vis. prof. Inst. Criminology, Cambridge (Eng.) U., 1973-74; cons. law enforcement programs for children and youth Children's Bur., HEW, Washington, 1960-62; cons. Pres.'s Com. on Juvenile Delinquency and Youth Crime, 1962-64, Pres.'s Commn. on Law Enforcement and Adminstrn. Criminal Justice, 1966, U.S. Law Enforcement Assistance Adminstrn., 1968-82, N.Y. State Temp. Commn. on Constl. Conv., 1967, N.Y. State Dept. Edn., 1967, 69, Calif. Coordinating Council for Higher Edn., 1969-70, Nat. Adv. Commn. on Criminal Justice Standards and Goals, 1971-72, Tenn. Higher Edn. Commn., 1976, Ky. Dept. Justice, 1977-78, NSF, 1978—, U.S. Civil Rights Commn., 1978, others. Author: Coroners in North Carolina: A Discussion of Their Problems, 1953, Indiana Sheriffs' Manual of Law and Practice, rev. edit, 1959, Indiana Conservation Officers' Manual of Law and Practice, 1961, (with Lynn D. Swanson) Police Work With Children, 1962, (with Carroll L. Christenson) The Walsh-Healey Public Contracts Act: A Critical Review of Prevailing Minimum Wage Determinations, 1966, Education in Criminal Justice, 1970; contbr. to: Bases for Justice Systems: Law and the Social Sciences (Gordon E. Misner), 1980, Five Year Outlook: Problems, Opportunities and Constraints in Science and Technology, 1980; Asso. editor: Jour. Criminal Justice; editorial rev. bd.: Criminal Justice Rev; contbr. articles to profl. jours. Bd. dirs. Sex Info. and Edn. Council U.S., 1972-75. Served with inf. AUS, 1943-46, ETO; with USNR, 1954-68. Fulbright research scholar to Argentina Cordoba, 1964-65. Mem. Am. Soc. Criminology, N.C. Bar Assn., Sociedad Argentina de Sociología. Criminal, Legal education, Juvenile. Home: Route 1 Box 394 Purcellville VA 22132 Office: Nebraska and Massachusetts Aves Washington DC 20016

NAAR, ALAN S., lawyer; b. New Brunswick, N.J., May 12, 1951; s. Sam A. and Mary (Oziel) N. BA summa cum laude, Rutgers Coll., 1973; JD, Columbia U., 1976. Bar: N.J. 1976, U.S. Dist. Ct. N.J. 1976. Assoc. Pitney, Hardin, Kipp & Szuch, Morristown, N.J., 1976-81; assoc. Greenbaum, Rowe, Smith, Ravin, Davis & Bergstein, Newark, 1982-84, ptnr., 1984—. Henry Rutgers scholar, 1973. Mem. ABA, N.J. Bar Assn., Essex County Bar Assn. Avocations: tennis, reading. Federal civil litigation, State civil litigation, Bankruptcy. Office: Greenbaum Rowe Smith et al PO Box 5600 Woodbridge NJ 07095

NACE, BARRY JOHN, lawyer; b. York, Pa., Nov. 28, 1944; s. John Harrison and Mildred Louise (Orwig) N.; m. Andrea Marcia Giardini. Apr. 28, 1973; children: Christopher Thomas, Jonathan Barry, Matthew Andrew. BS, Dickinson Coll., 1965, JD, 1969. Bar: Md. 1970, D.C. 1971, Pa. 1972, U.S. Ct. Appeals (3d, 4th and D.C. cirs.), U.S. Supreme Ct. House counsel W.R. Grace & Co., Clarksville, Md., 1969-71; assoc. Sughrue, Rothwell et al, Washington, 1971-72; ptnr. Davis & Nace, Washington, 1972-78, Paulson & Nace, Bethesda, Md., 1978-85; sr, ptnr. Paulson, Nace & Norwind, Washington, 1986—. Fellow Roscoe Pound Found.; mem. D.C. Bar Assn., Montgomery County Bar Assn., Assn. Trial Lawyers Am. (gov. 1976—), Met. D.C. Trial Attys. (pres. 1977, 87, Atty. of Yr. 1976), Trial Lawyers for Pub. Justice, Am. Inns of Ct. Avocations: golf, tennis, reading, racquetball. Personal injury, State civil litigation, Federal civil litigation. Home: 6208 Garnett Dr Chevy Chase MD 20815 Office: Paulson Nace & Norwind 1814 N St NW Washington DC 20036

NACHMIAS, CAROLYN SHARENOW, law educator; b. Montclair, N.J., June 4, 1956; d. Joel Henry and Ethel (Bateman) Sharenow; m. Mark David Nachmias, Dec. 26, 1976; children: Adam Jeffrey, Rachel Beth. BA, Seton Hall U., 1976; JD, Rutgers U., 1980. Bar: Pa. 1980, N.J. 1981, U.S. Dist. Ct. N.J. 1981, U.S. Tax Ct. 1981. Assoc. Drinker, Biddle & Reath, Phila., 1980-86; asst. prof. Del. Law Sch., Wilmington, 1986—; cons. in field; v.p. Addent Enterprises, Livingston, N.J., 1983—. Mem. ABA (tax sect.), Pa. Bar Assn. (tax sect.), Phila. Bar Assn. (tax, corp., bus. and banking sects.), Phila. Tax Supper Group. Jewish. Avocations: gardening, cooking. Legal education, Personal income taxation, Municipal bonds. Home: 16 Blossom Ct Cherry Hill NJ 08003 Office: Del Law Sch Concord Pike PO Box 7474 Wilmington DE 19803

NACHWALTER, MICHAEL, lawyer; b. N.Y.C., Aug. 31, 1940; s. Samuel J. Nachwalter; m. Irene, Aug. 15, 1965; children—Helynn, Robert. B.S., Bucknell U., 1962; M.S., L.I. U., 1967; J.D. cum laude, U. Miami, 1967; LL.M., Yale U., 1968. Bar: Fla. 1967, D.C. 1979, U.S. Dist. Ct. (so., middle dists.) Fla., U.S. Ct. Appeals (5th and 11th cirs.), U.S. Supreme Ct. Law clk. U.S. Dist. Ct. (so. dist.) Fla.; ptnr. Kelly, Black, Black & Kenney; now ptnr. Kenny Nachwalter & Seymour, Miami; lectr. Law Sch. U. Miami. Mem. Fla. Bar Assn., ABA, Fed. Bar Assn., Dade County Bar Assn., Fla. Bar. (bd. govs.), Omicron Delta Kappa, Phi Kappa Phi, Phi Delta Phi, Iron Arrow, Soc. Wig and Robe. Democrat. Editor in chief U. Miami Law Rev., 1966-67. Antitrust, Federal civil litigation, State civil litigation. Office: 400 Edward Ball Bldg 100 Chopin Plaza Miami FL 33131

NADEL, ALAN STEVEN, lawyer; b. Milford, Conn., Apr. 1, 1949; s. Melvin J. and Rhoda S. (Levy) N.; m. Marcy R. Rettig, Aug. 5, 1972; children: Russel, Fran. BS in Chemistry, George Washington U., 1971, JD with honors, 1976. Bar: U.S. Dist. Ct. (ea. dist.) Pa. 1976, U.S. Patent Office 1976, U.S. Ct. Appeals (fed. cir.) 1982, U.S. Supreme Ct. 1984. Assoc. Seidel, Gonda, Goldhammer & Panitch, P.C., Phila., 1976-81, ptnr., 1981-83; ptnr. Panitch, Schwarze, Jacobs & Nadel, Phila., 1983—. Mem. ABA, Pa. Bar Assn., Phila. Bar Assn., Assn. Trial Lawyers Am., Am. Intellectual Property Law Assn., Phila. Patent Law Assn. (chmn. fed. practice and procedures com. 1982-84). Club: Wyncote Men's (v.p. 1986—). Patent, Trademark and copyright. Office: Panitch Schwarze Jacobs & Nadel 2000 Market St Suite 1400 Philadelphia PA 19103

NADITCH, RONALD MARVIN, lawyer; b. Balt., Oct. 3, 1937; s. Albert I. and Marion Naditch; m. Phyllis K. Naditch, Dec. 31, 1968; children—Robyn, Allison. B.A., Dickinson Coll., 1959; J.D. with honor, U. Md., 1962. Bar: Md. 1962. Law clk. to assoc. judge Md. Ct. Appeals, 1962-63; assoc. Goodman and Bloom, 1964-65; part-time asst. states atty. Anne Arundel County, Md., 1966—; atty. Anne Arundel County Dept. Social Services, 1979-85; sole practice, Annapolis, Md., 1964—; mem. grievance rev. bd. State of Md.; lectr. continuing legal edn. Served with USCG. Mem. ABA, Md. Trial Lawyers Assn., Am. Trial Lawyers Assn., Nat. Dist. Attys. Assn. (lectr.), Md. Dist. Attys. Assn. (lectr.). Assoc. editor Md. Law Rev. Family and matrimonial, General practice, State civil litigation. Home: 44 Southgate Ave Annapolis MD 21401 Office: 49 Cornhill St Annapolis MD 21401

NADKARNI, GIRISH VISHWANATH, lawyer; b. Beawar, India, Mar. 11, 1957; s. Vishwanath Nagesh and Vatsala (Wagle) N.; m. Catherine Cresson, Oct. 2, 1981; children: Sophie, Sumati. B.Com. with honors, Sydenham Coll., Bombay, India, 1977; LLB, U. Bombay, 1980; LLM, U. Va., 1981. Bar: N.Y. 1982. Adj. prof. Sydenham Coll., Bombay, 1977-80; advocate trainee Crawford Bayley & Co., Bombay, 1979-80; assoc. Coudert Bros., N.Y.C., 1981-83, Shearman & Sterling, N.Y.C., 1983—. Mem. ABA, Bar Assn. City N.Y., Bar Assn. of India. Banking, General corporate, Private international. Home: 25 Waterside Plaza Apt 22 New York NY 10010 Office: Shearman & Sterling 153 E 53d St New York NY 10010

NADLER, JEROME STEVEN, lawyer; b. Newark, Dec. 3, 1952; s. Roy Nadler and Audree Sheila Weil; m. Judith Marguerite Shasky, Aug. 10, 1974; 1 child, Sarah Evelyn. BA, George Washington U., 1974; JD, Santa Clara U., 1977. Bar: Calif. 1977. Atty. Charter Rev. Commn., San Jose, Calif., 1977-79, Office of County Exec., San Jose, 1979-83; dep. dist. atty. Dist. Atty.'s Office, San Jose, 1983—; chief environ. crimes Dist. Atty.'s Office, San Jose, Calif., 1984-86. Chmn. Santa Clara County Health Systems Agy., San Jose, 1983-86. Mem. Calif. Bar Assn., Santa Clara County Bar Assn. (trustee 1980-86, sec. 1986—), Calif. Dist. Atty.'s Assn. Democrat. Environment, Criminal. Office: Office of Dist Atty 70 W Hedding San Jose CA 95110

NADLER, RICHARD GREGORY, lawyer; b. St. Paul, May 7, 1946; s. Max and Estelle (Zouber) N.; m. Kathryn Elizabeth Daniel, Dec. 1, 1973; children: Anthony, Scott. BA, U. Minn., Morris, 1969; JD, Mercer U., 1972. Bar: Minn. 1972, U.S. Dist. Ct. Minn. 1972, U.S. Ct. Appeals (8th cir.) 1973, U.S. Supreme Ct. 1979. Atty., legal asst. Ramsey County, St. Paul, 1972-74; assoc. Friedman Law Offices, Duluth, Minn., 1974-75; sr. ptnr. Richard G. Nadler & Assocs., St. Paul, 1976—; community faculty mem. Met. State U., St. Paul, 1976—; adj. prof. law William Mitchell Coll. Law, St. Paul, 1983. Assoc. editor Mercer Law Rev., 1972. Precinct chmn. Minn. Dem. Farmer Labor Party, Mendota Heights, 1984—, state cen. mem. St.Paul, 1986; chief YMCA Indian Guide Program-Hawk Tribe, West St. Paul, 1985—. Mem. ABA, Minn. State Bar Assn., Ramsey County Bar Assn. (chmn. law office mgmt. com. 1986). Jewish. Avocations: photography, video photography, computer sci. Bankruptcy, Consumer law. Office: 510 Degree of Honor Bldg Saint Paul MN 55101

NADORFF, NORMAN J., lawyer; b. Grand Rapids, Mich., July 21, 1953; s. Carl J. and Mary L. (Vessels) N.; m. Kathryn Ann Kirch, June 9, 1979; children: Christopher, Carla. BA, St. Louis U., 1975, MA, 1976; JD, Ohio State U., 1980. Bar: Ohio, 1980. Sr. auditor E.I. duPont de Nemours and Co., Wilmington, Del., 1981-85; atty. Conoco Inc., Houston, 1985—. Fulbright scholar, 1980-81. Mem. ABA. Avocations: fgn. langs., Spanish guitar. Contracts commercial, Private international. Home: Conoco Inc 600 N Dairy Ashford Houston TX 77079

NAEGELE, JORI BLOOM, lawyer; b. Cleve., Nov. 29, 1953; d. Howard L. and Phyllis I. (Weissfeld) Bloom; m. Richard A. Naegele, Oct. 21, 1979; 1 child, Michael J. BA, U. Cin., 1976; JD, Case Western Res. U., 1979. Bar: Ohio 1980, U.S. Dist. Ct. (no. dist.) Ohio 1980, U.S. Supreme Ct. 1985, Colo. 1986. Staff atty. Legal Aid Soc. Lorain County, Elyria, Ohio, 1980-82; sole practice Lorain, Ohio, 1982—. Mem. ABA, Ohio Bar Assn., Lorain County Bar Assn., Assn. Trial Lawyers Am., Ohio Acad. Trial Lawyers. Avocations: water skiing, snow skiing, traveling, bicycling. Federal civil litigation, State civil litigation, Personal injury. Home: 5503 Hartford Ave Vermilion OH 44089 Office: 446 Broadway Lorain OH 44052

NAFTALIS, GARY PHILIP, lawyer; b. Newark, Nov. 23, 1941; s. Gilbert and Bertha Beatrice (Gruber) N.; m. Donna Arditi, June 30, 1974; children: Benjamin, Joshua, Daniel, Sarah. AB, Rutgers U., 1963; AM, Brown U., 1965; LLB, Columbia U., 1967. Bar: N.Y. 1967, U.S. Supreme Ct. 1974, U.S. Ct. Appeals (2d cir.) 1968, U.S. Ct. Appeals (3d cir.) 1973, U.S. Dist. Ct. (so. dist.) N.Y. 1969. Law clk. to judge U.S. Dist. Ct. So. Dist. N.Y., 1967-68; asst. U.S. atty. So. Dist. N.Y., 1968-74, asst. chief criminal div., 1972-74; spl. asst. U.S. atty. for V.I., 1972-73; spl. counsel U.S. Senate Subcom. on Long Term Care, 1975; spl. counsel N.Y. State Temp. Commn. on Living Costs and the Economy, 1975; ptnr. Orans, Elsen, Polstein & Naftalis, N.Y.C., 1974-81, Kramer, Levin, Nessen, Kamin & Frankel, N.Y.C., 1981—; lectr. in law Columbia U. Law Sch., 1976—; vis. lectr. Harvard U. Law Sch., 1979; mem. deptl. disciplinary com. Appellate div. 1st Dept., 1980—. Author: (with Marvin E. Frankel) The Grand Jury: An Institution on Trial, 1977, Considerations in Representing Attorneys in Civil and Criminal Enforcement Proceedings, 1981, Sentencing: Helping Judges Do Their Jobs, 1986; editor: White Collar Crimes, 1980. Trustee, Boys Brotherhood Republic, 1978—, Blueberry Treatment Center, 1981—. Mem. ABA, N.Y. City Bar Assn. (com. criminal cts. 1980-83, com. judiciary 1984—, council on criminal justice 1985—), Fed. Bar Council (com. cts. of 2d cir. 1974-77), N.Y. State Bar Assn. (com. state legis. 1974-76). Criminal, Federal civil litigation. Home: 336 West End Ave Apt 18-C New York NY 10023 Office: 919 3d Ave New York NY 10022

NAFZIGER, JAMES ALBERT RICHMOND, lawyer, educator; b. Mpls., Sept. 24, 1940; s. Ralph Otto and Charlotte Monona (Hamilton) N.; B.A., U. Wis., 1962, M.A., 1969; J.D., Harvard U., 1967. Bar: Wis. 1967. Law clk. to chief judge U.S. Dist. Ct. (ea. dist.) Wis., 1967-69; fellow Am. Soc. Internat. Law, Washington, 1969-70, adminstrv. dir., 1970-74; exec. sec. Assn. Student Internat. Law Socs., 1969-70; lectr. Sch. Law, Cath. U. Am., Washington, 1970-74; vis. assoc. prof. Sch. Law, U. Oreg., 1974-77; vis. prof. Nat. Autonomous U. Mex., 1978; assoc. prof. law Coll. Law, Willamette U., Salem, Oreg., 1977-80, prof., 1980—, assoc. dean, 1985-86, dir. China program, 1984—; scholar-in-residence Rockefeller Found. Ctr., Bellagio, Italy, 1985; lectr., tutor Inst. Pub. Internat. Law and Internat. Relations, Thessaloniki, Greece, 1982; mem. bd. advisors Harvard Internat. Law Jour., Denver Jour. Internat. Law and Policy, Am. Jour. Comparative Law (bd. dirs. 1985—). Mem. adv. bd. NW Regional China Council, 1986—. Served to 1st lt. U.S. Army, 1962-64. Mem. Am. Soc. Internat. Law (exec. council 1983-86, co-chmn. western region), Am. Assn. for Comparative Study of Law (bd. dirs., bd. editors Am. Jour. Comparative Law 1985—), Internat. Law Assn. (exec. com. 1986—, chmn. human rights com. Am. br. 1983—), Washington Fgn. Law Soc. (v.p. 1973-74), Internat. Studies Assn. (exec. bd. 1974-77, internat. law sect.), ACLU (pres. chpt. 1980-81, mem. state bd. 1982—, sec. 1983—), Assn. Am. Law Schs. (chmn. law and arts sect. 1981-83, chmn. internat. law sect. 1984-85, adv. bd. N.W. Regional China Council 1986—), Am. Law Inst., Oreg. Internat. Council (exec. com. 1985—, dir. 1982—), Phi Beta Kappa, Phi Kappa Phi. Editor Procs. of Am. Soc. Internat. Law, 1977; Am. author: Conflict of Laws: A Northwest Perspective, 1985; contbr. articles to profl. jours. Immigration, naturalization, and customs, Private international, Public international. Home: 3775 Saxon Dr S Salem OR 97302 Office: Willamette U Coll Law Salem OR 97301

NAGEL, STUART S., law educator, lawyer. BS; LLB Bar: Ill. Prof. dept. polit. sci. U. Ill., Urbana; atty. U.S. Senate Subcom. on Adminstrv. Practice and Procedure, NLRB, OEO Legal Services Program; cons. Nat. Acad. Scis. Water Quality Com., Acad. Contemporary Problems, Adminstrv. Conf. U.S., Nat. Assessment of Edn. Progress, Pres.'s Reorgn. Program, Office of Personnel Mgmt. Author: The Policy Studies Handbook, 1980, Policy Evaluation: Making Optimum Decisions, 1982, Public Policy: Goals, Means, and Methods, 1984, Contemporary Public Policy Analysis, 1984, Policy Evaluation and the Legal Process, 1984, Using Personal Computers for Decision-making in Law Practice, 1985, Evaluation Problems with Microcomputers, 1986, Law, Policy and Optimizing Analysis, 1986, Prediction, Causation and Legal Analysis, 1986, others; editor: The Political Science of Criminal Justice, 1982, Productivity and Public Policy, 1983, 2d edit., 1984, The Policy Studies Field: Its Basic Literature, 1983, 2d edit., 1984, Public Policy Studies: A Multi-Volume Treatise, 1983, Law and Policy Studies, 1986, Public Policy Analysis and Management, 1986, others; contbr. articles to polit. sci. and law jours.; mem. editorial bds. of jours. and book series. Legal education. Office: U Ill Coll Liberal Arts & Scis Dept Polit Sci 361 Lincoln Hall 702 S Wright St Urbana IL 61801

NAGEL, STUART SAMUEL, political science educator, lawyer; b. Chgo., Aug. 29, 1934; s. Leo I. and Florence (Pritikin) N.; m. Joyce Golub, Sept. 1, 1957; children: Brenda Ellen, Robert Franklin. Student, U. Chgo., 1954-55; B.S., Northwestern U., 1957, J.D., 1958, Ph.D., 1961. Bar: Ill. 1958. Instr. Pa. State U., 1960-61; asst. prof. U. Ariz., 1961-62; prof. polit. sci. U. Ill., 1962—; law and social sci. vis. fellow Yale Law Sch., 1970-71; vis. fellow Nat. Inst. Law Enforcement and Criminal Justice, 1974-75; Sr. scholar East-West Center, Honolulu, 1965; fellow Behavioral Scis. Center, Palo Alto, Calif., 1964-65; dir. O.E.O. Legal Services Agy. of Champaign, 1966-69; vol. atty. Lawyers Constl. Def. Com., Miss., 1967; asst. counsel U.S. Senate Jud. Com., 1966. Author: The Legal Process from a Behavioral Perspective, 1969, Law and Social Change, 1970, New Trends in Law and Politics Research, 1971, Rights of the Accused, 1972, Comparing Elected and Appointed Judicial Systems, 1973, Minimizing Costs and Maximizing Benefits in Providing Legal Services to the Poor, 1973, Improving the Legal Process: Effects of Alternatives, 1975, Operations Research Methods: As Applied to Political Science and The Legal Process, 1976, The Application of Mixed Strategies: Civil Rights and Other Multiple Activity Policies, 1976, Legal Policy Analysis: Finding an Optimum Level or Mix, 1977, Too Much or Too Little Policy: The Example of Pretrial Release, 1977, The Legal Process: Modeling the System, 1977, Decision Theory and the Legal Process, 1979, Policy Analysis: In Social Science Research, 1979, Policy Studies Handbook, 1980, Policy Evaluation: Making Optimum Decisions, 1982, Public Policy: Goals, Means and Methods, 1984, Contemporary Public Policy Analysis, 1984, Prediction Causation and Legal Analysis, 1986, Law, Policy and Optimizing Analysis, 1986, Evaluation Problems and Microcomputers, 1987; others; editor: Policy Studies Jour., The Policy Studies Directory, 1973, Environ-

mental Politics, 1974, Policy Studies in America and Elsewhere, 1975, Policy Studies and the Social Sciences, 1975, Sage Yearbooks in Politics and Public Policy, 1975—, Lexington-Heath Policy Studies Orgn. Series, 1975—, Political Science Utilization Directory, 1975, Policy Studies Review Annual, 1977, Policy Grants Directory, 1977, Modeling the Criminal Justice System, 1977, Policy Research Centers Directory, 1978, Policy Studies Personnel Directory, 1979, Improving Policy Analysis, 1980, Policy Publishers and Associations Directory, 1980, Encyclopedia of Policy Studies, 1982, The Political Science of Criminal Justice, 1982, Productivity and Public Policy, 1983, The Policy Studies Field: It's Basic Literature, 1983; editorial bd.: Law and Soc. Assn., 1966—, Law and Policy Studies, 1986—, Pub. Policy Analysis and Mgmt., 1986—. Grantee Social Sci. Research Council, 1959-60; Grantee Am. Council Learned Socs., 1964-65; Grantee NSF, 1970-73; Grantee Rockefeller Found., 1976; Grantee Dept. Transp., 1976; Grantee Ford Found., 1975—; Grantee ERDA, 1977; Grantee Dept. Agr., 1977; Grantee NIE, 1976; Grantee HUD, 1978; Grantee ILEC, 1978; Grantee Dept. Labor, 1978; Grantee NIJ, 1979; Grantee Am. Bar Assn., 1980. Mem. Am. Polit. Sci. Assn., Am. Bar Assn., Law and Soc. Assn. (trustee), Policy Studies Orgn. (sec.-treas.). Civil rights, Computer, General practice. Home: 1720 Park Haven Dr Champaign IL 61820

NAGELBERG, HOWARD ALLEN, lawyer; b. Oct. 31, 1947; s. Joseph Nagelberg and Freida Weiner; m. Sandra Richter, June 12, 1971; children: Allison, Robert. BA in Econs. with distinction, U. Mich., 1969; JD, U. Chgo., 1973. Bar: Ill. 1973. Ptnr. Sachnoff, Weaver & Rubenstein, Chgo., 1973-79, Fishman, Merrick, Perlman & Nagelberg, Chgo., 1979-82; prin. ptnr. Nagelberg & Resnick P.C., Chgo., 1982—. Assoc. editor U. Chgo. Law Rev., 1971-72. Mem. ABA, Ill. Bar Assn., Chgo. Bar Assn., Am. Coll. Real Estate Lawyers, Chgo. Council Lawyers, Am. Land Title Assn. (assoc.), Ill. Chpt. Real Estate Securities Syndication Inst. (bd. dirs. 1985—). Avocation: golf. Real property, General corporate. Office: Nagelberg & Resnick PC 200 S Wacker Dr Chicago IL 60606

NAGIN, STEPHEN E., lawyer, educator; b. Phila., Nov. 7, 1946; s. Harry S. and Dorothy R. (Pearlman) N.; m. Marjorie Riley. BBA, U. Miami, 1969, JD, 1974. Bar: Fla. 1974, D.C. 1976, U.S. Supreme Ct. 1978. Asst. atty. gen. State of Fla., Miami, 1974-75; atty., FTC, 1975-80; spl. asst. U.S. atty. D.C., 1980-81; pres. Ginsburg, Nagin, Rosin & Ginsburg, PA, 1982-84; ptnr. Law Office of Stephen E. Nagin, Miami, 1984—; adj. prof. St. Thomas U. Sch. Law, 1984—. Mem. ABA, Fed. Bar Assn., D.C. Bar Asn., Fla. Bar Assn. (editor, trial lawyers sect. 1983-84; mem. spl. antitrust task force 1983—, chmn. editorial bd., 1982-83), Coral Gables Bar Assn. (bd. dirs. 1983-87), Assn. Trial Lawyers Am., Acad. Fla. Trial Lawyers, Am. Arbitration Assn., Nat. Health Lawyers Assn. Antitrust, Federal civil litigation, Civil rights. Office: 3100 Southeast Financial Ctr Miami FL 33131-2327

NAGLE, JOHN JOSEPH, III, lawyer; b. Balt., Dec. 26, 1954; s. John Joseph Jr. and Eleanor Marie (Watkins) N.; m. Elizabeth Dixon Bagli, Oct. 10, 1981; 1 child, John Joseph IV. BA, Coll. of Holy Cross, 1976; JD, U. Balt., 1980. Bar: Md. 1981, U.S. Dist. Ct. Md. 1981, U.S. Bankruptcy Ct. 1981. Ptnr. Power and Mosner, Towson, Md., 1981—. Mem. ABA, Md. Bar Assn., Balt. County Bar Assn. Democrat. Roman Catholic. Avocations: golf, squash, reading. State civil litigation, Insurance, Personal injury. Home: 232 Blenheim Rd Baltimore MD 21212 Office: Power and Mosner 21 W Susquehanna Ave Towson MD 21204

NAGY, JILL HARRIET, lawyer; b. N.Y.C., Mar. 14, 1941; d. Samuel and Beatrice (Ehrlich) Beckoff; m. George Nagy, July 20, 1963; children: Naomi Gail, Edwin Neal. BS, Cornell U., 1961; JD, U. Nebr., 1977. Bar: Nebr. 1977, U.S. Dist. Ct. Nebr. 1977, U.S. Ct. Appeals (8th cir.) 1982, N.Y. 1985, U.S. Dist. Ct. (no. dist.) N.Y. 1985. Agency counsel Dept. Pub. Institutions, Lincoln, Nebr., 1978-80; reporter of decisions Nebr. State Supreme Ct., Lincoln, 1980; sole practice Lincoln, 1981-85; assoc. Lee & LeForestier P.C., Troy, N.Y., 1985—; cons. Nebr. Com. Status of Women, Lincoln, 1977; field investigator Lincoln Human Rights Commn., 1985. Treas. Cub Scout Pack 30, Lincoln, 1983-84, Lancaster County Dems., Lincoln, 1985. Mem. N.Y. State Bar Assn., Rensselaer County Bar Assn., Order of Coif. Club: RPI Womens (Troy) (sec. 1986—). Avocations: music, books, sports, gardening. Immigration, naturalization, and customs, Civil rights, General practice. Office: Lee & LeForestier PC 33 2d St PO Box 1054 Troy NY 12181

NAHLEN, DANA GAYLE, lawyer; b. Little Rock, Aug. 5, 1955; s. Andrew Edward Nahlen and Betty Jo (Ball) Taylor. Student, U. London, 1975; BA with high honors, U. Notre Dame, 1977; JD, Columbia U., 1980. Bar: N.Y., 1981, Ark., 1981, Tex., 1983. Law clk. to presiding judge U.S. Dist. Ct. (ea. dist.) Ark., Little Rock, 1980-82; assoc. banking real estate and internat. law Hughes & Luce, Dallas, 1982—. Private international, Real property, General corporate. Office: Hughes & Luce Dallas Bldg Suite 1000 Dallas TX 75201

NAJARIAN, MALCOLM ASKANAZ, lawyer; b. Providence, Oct. 23, 1955; s. Askanaz and Anna (Hanoian) N. BA, Boston Coll., 1977; JD, Suffolk U., 1980. Bar: R.I. 1980, Mass. 1980, U.S. Dist. Ct. R.I. 1980, U.S. Dist. Ct. Mass. 1984. Law clk. R.I. Superior Ct., Providence, 1980-81; atty. Nat. Assn. Govt. Employees, Cranston, R.I., 1981-84; assoc. Lipsey & Skolnik, Providence, 1984—; instr. bus. law U. R.I., Providence, 1984—. Mem. Armenian Apostolic Ch. Avocations: golfing, music, traveling. Labor, State civil litigation, Personal injury. Office: Lipsey & Skolnik Ltd 369 S Main St Providence RI 02903

NAJJOUM, LINDA LEMMON, lawyer; b. Washington, June 15, 1946; d. Alexis William and Elizabeth Jane (Button) Lemmon; m. Charles J. Najjoum, Jr., June 8, 1985. BS in Nursing, Ohio State U., 1970; MS in Nursing, Va. Commonwealth U., 1973; JD, U. S.C., 1981. Bar: S.C. 1981, Va. 1983. Law clk. S.C. Supreme Ct., Columbia, 1981-82; assoc. atty. Hunton & Williams, Richmond, Va., 1982-85, Fairfax, Va., 1985—. Contbr. articles to Law Rev. Mem. ABA (litigation sect.), Va. Bar Assn., S.C. Bar Assn., Fairfax County Bar Assn., Va. Trial Lawyers Assn. Federal civil litigation, State civil litigation, Personal injury. Office: Hunton & Williams 3050 Chain Bridge Rd Fairfax VA 22030

NAKAMURA, EDWARD H., state supreme court justice. Assoc. justice Hawaii Supreme Ct., Honolulu. Judicial administration. Office: Supreme Ct Hawaii 417 S King St Honolulu HI 96813 *

NAKARADO, GARY LEE, lawyer; b. Petosky, Mich., Aug. 30, 1949; s. Richard William and Helen Bedola (Campbell) N.; m. Christine M. Manchester, June 19, 1971; children: Kirtley Campbell, Christian Hart. AB with spl. honors, U. Chgo., 1971; JD, U. Mich., 1973. Bar: Ill. 1974, Colo. 1978. Ptnr. Head, Moye, Carver & Ray, Denver, 1981-83, Mineral Resources, Steamboat Springs, Colo., 1983-85; of counsel Moye, Giles, O'Keefe, Vermeire & Gorrell, Denver, 1985-86, ptnr., 1986—; bd. dirs. Loft House, Denver, 1984—. NSF grantee, 1970. Mem. ABA (com. on Nat. Resources), Colo. Bar Assn. (chmn. tax sect. 1984-85), Denver Bar Assn. Republican. Avocations: computers, skiing, kites. Corporate taxation, Oil and gas leasing, General corporate. Home: 864 Aster Way Golden CO 80401 Office: Moye Giles O'Keefe Vermeire Gorrell 730 17th St #600 Denver CO 80202-3582

NALLE, HORACE DISSTON, JR., lawyer; b. Phila., Aug. 1, 1956; s. Horace D. and Ethel (Benson) N. BA, Harvard U., 1978; JD, U. Pa., 1982. Bar: Pa. 1982, U.S. Dist. Ct. (ea. dist.) Pa. 1982, U.S. Ct. Appeals (3d cir.) 1982. Polit. researcher Com. to Protect Charter, Phila., 1978; writer grants Library Co. Phila., 1979; assoc. Drinker, Biddle & Reath, Phila., 1982—; mktg. cons. SEA Assocs., Phila., 1983. Mem. ABA, Pa. Bar Assn., Phila. Bar Assn. Democrat. Episcopalian. Club: Racquet (Phila.). Federal civil litigation, Securities, Antitrust. Home: 219 Delhi St Philadelphia PA 19107 Office: Drinker Biddle & Reath 1100 PNB Bldg Philadelphia PA 19107

NALLS, CLARENCE THEO, lawyer; b. Monroe, La., Sept. 23, 1948; s. Clarence Theo and Helen (Rushing) N.; m. Gloria Jean Foreman, Dec. 23, 1968; children: Corey, Chris, Charles, Michael. BA, U. Ark., 1970; JD, So. U., 1976. Bar: La. 1982, U.S. Dist. Ct. (ea. and mid. dists.) La. 1982. Job developer Opportunities Industries Ctr., Little Rock, 1970-73; adminstrv. law judge Ark. Employee Commn., Little Rock, 1977-81; asst. law librarian So. U. Law Sch., Baton Rouge, 1981-85; sole practice Baton Rouge, 1985—. Recipient Am. Jurisprudence award Lawyers Co-operative Pub., 1977. Mem. La. Bar Assn., Baton Rouge Bar Assn., La. Trial Lawyers Assn. Democrat. Avocations: reading, football, baseball. Personal injury, Probate, Civil rights. Home: 5432 Johnette Dr Baton Rouge LA 70812 Office: 1433 Harding Blvd Baton Rouge LA 70807

NAMANWORTH, ELI, lawyer; b. N.Y.C., Jan. 3, 1938; s. Robert and Lena (Eisen) N.; m. Isabelle Clampert, June 26, 1960; children: Jenny, Sheila, Julie. BS, CCNY, 1959; PhD, Yale U., 1965; JD, N. Ky. State U., 1976. Bar: Ohio 1965, U.S. Dist. Ct. (so. dist.) Ohio 1977, U.S. Ct. Appeals (6th cir.) 1978, U.S. Dist. Ct. (no. dist.) Ky. 1979, U.S. Supreme Ct. 1984. Asst. prof. Chemistry Case Western Res. U., Cleve., 1966-69; research chemist Sterling Drug Co. div. Hilton Davis, Cin., 1969-77; sole practice Cin., 1977-81; ptnr. Simon, Namanworth & Bohlen LPA, Cin., 1981—. Author research papers in physical chemistry and related fields, 1965-70. Post doctoral fellow Yale U., 1965, Case Western Res. U., 1965-66. Mem. ABA, Ohio Bar Assn., Cin. Bar Assn., Assn. Trial Lawyers Am., Ohio Trial Lawyers Assn., Am. Chem Soc. Avocations: swimming, biking. toxic tort litigation, state and federal, Federal civil litigation, Personal injury. Home: 9548 Linfield Dr Blue Ash OH 45242 Office: Simon Namanworth Bohlen 602 Main St Suite 408 Cincinnati OH 45202

NANGLE, JOHN FRANCIS, judge; b. St. Louis, June 8, 1922; s. Sylvester Austin and Thelma (Bank) N.; 1 child, John Francis Jr. A.A., Harris Tchrs. Coll., 1941; B.S., U. Mo., 1943; J.D., Washington U., St. Louis, 1948. Bar: Mo. 1948. Practiced in Clayton, 1948-73; chief judge U.S. Dist. Ct., St. Louis, 1973—; mem. jury com. U.S. Cts. Mem. Mo. Republican Com., 1958-73; mem. St. Louis County Rep. Central Com., 1958-73, chmn., 1960-61; pres. Mo. Assn. Reps., 1961, Reps. Vets. League, 1960; mem. Rep. Nat. Com., 1972—; Bd. dirs. Masonic Home Mo. Served with AUS, 1943-46. Named Mo. Republican of Year John Marshall Club, 1970, Mo. Republican of Year Mo. Assn. Reps., 1971; recipient Most Disting. Alumnus award Harris-Stowe Coll., Most Disting. Alumnus award Washington U. Sch. Law, 1986. Mem. Am. Judicature Soc., Legion of Honor DeMolay, Am., Mo., St. Louis, St. Louis County bar assn., 8th Circuit Jud. Council, Jud. Conf. U.S. Office: US District Court US Courthouse 1114 Market St Saint Louis MO 63101 *

NANGLE, THOMAS ROCKWELL, lawyer; b. New Haven, June 14, 1928; s. Benjamin Christie and Katharine Robb (Rawles) N.; m. Patricia Hamilton Littlejohn, Sept. 15, 1951 (div. 1968); m. Christiane Georgette DuPont, Dec. 14, 1968; children: Thomas Joseph, Emilie Katharine. B.A., Yale U., 1949; LL.B., U. Va., 1952. Bar: N.Y. 1953. Assoc. Shearman & Sterling, N.Y.C., 1952-62, ptnr., 1962—. Episcopalian. Clubs: City of London, Hurlingham. Home: 81 Eaton Terr, London England SW1W Office: 53 Basinghall St, London England EC2V 5DE

NAPIER, DOUGLAS WILLIAM, lawyer, county attorney; b. Alexandria, Va., Sept. 11, 1951; s. William Wilson and Leo Elizabeth (Moore) N.; m. Kathy Gwen Talbert, Aug. 24, 1974; children—Brian Douglas, Adam Scott. B.S., Va. Poly. Inst. and State U., 1973; J.D., Wake Forest U., 1976. Bar: Va. 1976, U.S. Ct. (ea. and we. dist.) Va. 1978, U.S. Ct. Appeals (4th cir.) 1983. Assoc., Ambrogi, Mote & Ritter, Winchester, Va., 1976-77; ptnr. Napier & Napier, Front Royal, Va., 1977—; county atty. Warren County (Va.), 1978—; atty. Chem. Abuse Task Force, 1983—. Author: The Cross, 1982. Mem. staff, contbr. Wake Forest Law Rev., 1976. Bd. dirs. United Way, Front Royal, 1978; parliamentarian Warren County Republican Com., 1981; cons. Council Domestic Violence, 1984. Mem. Warren County Bar Assn. (v.p., pres.), Va. Bar Assn., Va. Trial Lawyers Assn., ABA, Front Royal C. of C. (bd. dirs., v.p. 1986—). Baptist. Clubs: Optimist Internat. (sec. 1980-81, Achievement award 1980), Isaac Walton League. Federal civil litigation, State civil litigation, Local government. Home: 115 Accomac Rd Royal VA 22630 Office: Napier & Napier 10 Court House Sq Front Royal VA 22630

NAPOLI, JOSEPH ANTHONY, lawyer; b. Rochester, Pa., Aug. 24, 1956; s. Joseph Anthony and Rita Louise (Sylvester) N.; m. Sandra Marie Sekely, Nov. 6, 1982; 1 child, Laura Ann. BA, Duquesne U., 1977, JD, 1982. Bar: PA. 1982, U.S. Dist. Ct. (we. dist.) Pa. 1982, Fla. 1986. Assoc. Ruffin, Hazlett et al, Pitts., 1982-83, Eckerd, Seamaus et al, Pitts., 1983-85, Broad and Cassel, Miami, Fla., 1985—. Mem. ABA, Nat. Assn. Bond Lawyers, Fla. Bar Assn., Pa. Bar Assn. Democrat. Roman Catholic. Municipal bonds, Local government, General corporate. Office: Broad and Cassel One Biscayne Tower Miami FL 33131

NARBER, GREGG ROSS, lawyer; b. Iowa City, Sept. 4, 1946; s. James R. and Marguerite Maxine (Lasher) N.; m. Christopher Ann Kice, June 1, 1968; children: Joshua Ross, Zachary Edward. BA, Grinnell Coll., 1968; MA, JD, Washington U., St. Louis, 1971. Bar: Iowa 1971, U.S. Dist. Ct. (so. dist.) Iowa 1971, U.S. Ct. Mil. Appeals 1974, U.S. Supreme Ct. 1974. Atty. The Prin. Fin. Group, Des Moines, 1975-76; asst. counsel Prin. Fin. Group, Des Moines, 1976-80, assoc. counsel, 1980-85, counsel, 1985—; lectr. Iowa Humanities Bd., 1981-82. Co-author: New Deal Mural Projects in Iowa, 1982; also articles; artist various works. Pres. intercultural programs Am. Field Service Internat., West Des Moines, 1980-87. Mem. Iowa Bar Assn., Polk County Bar Assn. Democrat. Mem. Unitarian Ch. Clubs: Prairie (sec. 1982-84, 86-87), West Des Moines Soccer (coach 1982—, referee 1984—). Avocations: art history, collecting art, soccer. Pension, profit-sharing, and employee benefits, Corporate taxation, Insurance. Home: 309 Jordan Dr West Des Moines IA 50265 Office: The Prin Fin Group 711 High St Des Moines IA 50309

NARDONE, RICHARD, lawyer, consultant; b. Poughkeepsie, N.Y., Dec. 29, 1945; s. Michael and Rosemary (Murden) N.; m. Merry Lou Bennett, June 4, 1966; children: Richard David, Jorinda Suzanne. BA, Syracuse U., 1970; JD, Albany Law Sch., 1973. Bar: N.Y. 1974, U.S. Dist. Ct. (no. dist.) N.Y 1974, U.S. Dist. Ct. (so. dist.) N.Y. 1977. Ptnr. Nardone & Nardone, Highland, N.Y., 1977-79; sole practice Highland, 1979—; cons. Nardone Enterprises, Highland, 1973—, Nardone Farms, Highland, 1973—; pres. MLF Devel. Corp., Highland, 1986; v.p. Magnum Racing Corp., Pine Plains, N.Y., 1984—. Fellow mem. ABA, N.Y. State Bar Assn., N.Y. State Trial Lawyers Assn., Ulster County Bar Assn., Dutchess County Bar Assn., Nat. Rifle Assn. (life). Republican. Roman Catholic. Club: New Paltz (N.Y.) Rod & Gun. Avocations: gun collecting, fishing, hunting, boating, auto racing. Personal injury, State civil litigation, Criminal. Office: N Roberts Rd Highland NY 12528

NARISI, STELLA MARIA, heavy equipment mfg. co. exec.; b. Fort Smith, Ark., Oct. 24, 1950; d. Vincent J. and Norma J. Narisi; B.B.A., U. Tex., 1972, J.D., 1975. Admitted to Tex. bar, 1975; staff atty. enforcement div. Tex. State Securities Bd., Houston, 1975-79; corp. sec., in-house counsel Marathon Mfg. Co., Houston, 1979—. Mem. Am. Bar Assn., Tex. Bar Assn., Houston Bar Assn. Club: Houston. General corporate. Office: Marathon Mfg Co 600 Jefferson Suite 1900 Houston TX 77550

NARKO, MEDARD MARTIN, lawyer; b. Chgo., Sept. 14, 1941; s. Casimer and Stephanie (Wasylik) N.; m. Mary Kathleen Hanrahan, June 8, 1963; children—Kevin, Sue. B.S., Loyola U., 1963; J.D., Northwestern U., 1966. Bar: Ill. 1966, U.S. Dist. Ct. (no. dist.) Ill. 1967, U.S. Ct. Appeals (7th cir.) 1970. Instr., John Marshall Law Sch., Chgo., 1970-71; prof. lawyers assistance program Roosevelt U., Chgo., 1975-81; ptnr. Narko & Sonenthal, Chgo., 1974-79, Medard Narko & Assocs., Oak Forest, Ill., 1979—; arbitrator Am. Arbitration Assn., Chgo.; hearing officer Ill. Pollution Control Bd., Evanston, Civil Service Commn., Evanston, Ill. Dept. Edn., State Univ. Civil Service System. City atty. City of Oak Forest, 1985—, prosecutor City of Oak Forest, 1976-85 ; atty. Oak Forest Park Dist., 1974—, Bridgeview Park Dist., Ill., 1976-80, Midlothian Park Dist., Ill., 1983—. Contbr. articles to profl. jours. Mem. Ill. Bar Assn., Chgo. Bar Assn., Ill. Trial Lawyers Assn., Assn. Trial Lawyers Am., Ill. Mcpl. League, Nat. Inst. Mcpl. Law Officers. Lodge: Rotary. General practice, Local government, Personal injury. Home: 5 Equestrian Way Lemont IL 60439 Office: Medard M Narko and Assocs PC 15000 S Cicero Ave Oak Forest IL 60452

NARROW, NANCY HENTIG, lawyer; b. Chgo., May 16, 1954; d. William Hector and Geneva Jeanette (Hofer) H.; m. Steven Robert Narrow, Apr. 24, 1982; children: Megan Michelle, Timothy Charles. BA, Salem Coll., 1974; JD, Washington U., St. Louis, 1981. Bar: Mo. 1981. Asst. pub. defender State Mo., Jackson, 1981-82, pub. defender, Benton, Mo., 1983-87. Bd. dirs., chmn. fundraising WISER Inc. Women's Ctr. and Safehouse, Cape Girardeau, 1982-87. Mem. ABA, Mo. Bar Assn., Mo. Assn. Criminal Def. Lawyers, Scott County Bar Assn., Cape Girardeau County Bar Assn. Phi Delta Phi. Lutheran. Club: Zonta. Criminal, Juvenile. Home: 718 W Rodney Cape Girardeau MO 63701 Office: Public Defender Office PO Box 429 Benton MO 63736

NARUS, EDWARD R., lawyer; b. New Britain, Conn., July 22, 1956. BS in Acctg., U. Conn., 1978; LLB, Western New Eng. Coll., 1981. Bar: Conn. 1981, U.S. Dist. Ct. Conn. 1983. Tax specialist Coopers & Lybrand, CPAs, Springfield, Mass., 1981-82; asst. state's atty. econ. crime unit State of Conn., Wallingford, 1982—. Mem. Nat. Dist. Atty.'s Assn. Avocations: sports, films. Criminal.

NARUSIS, REGINA GYTÉFIRANT, lawyer; b. Kaunas, Lithuania, Oct. 12, 1936; d. Victor and Eugenia S. (Cesnavicius) Firant; brought to U.S., 1949, naturalized, 1955; B.A., U. Ill., 1957, J.D., 1959; m. Bernard V. Narusis, June 19, 1959; children—Victor John, Ellen Marie, Susan Marie. Bar: Ill. 1960. Partner firm Narusis & Narusis, Cary, Ill., 1961—; city atty. City of McHenry (Ill.), 1973—; village atty. Fox River Grove, Ill., 1967-73; asst. state's atty., McHenry County, Ill., 1968-75, head juvenile div., 1968-75. Mem. McHenry County Bd. Health, Woodstock, Ill., 1964-75; mem., pres. Dist. 46 Sch. Bd., McHenry County, 1964-79; mem. McHenry County Welfare Services Com., 1968-75; mem. adminstrv. council, mem. exec. bd. Marian Central Cath. High Sch., 1981—. Mem. Ill. Bar Assn., McHenry County Bar Assn., Women's Bar Assn., Am. Judicature Soc., Nat. Dist. Attys. Assn., Kappa Beta Pi. Family and matrimonial, General practice, Local government. Address: 213 W Lake Shore Dr Cary IL 60013

NASATIR, MICHAEL DAVID, lawyer; b. Los Angeles, Sept. 24, 1940; s. George and Nellie Nasatir; m. Delight Eastman, Dec. 31, 1967; 1 child, Matthew. JD, U. Calif., Berkeley, 1966. Bar: Calif. 1966, U.S. Dist. Ct., U.S. Ct. Appeals (1st, 2d, 5th and 9th cirs.), U.S. Supreme Ct. Staff atty. San Francisco Neighborhood Legal Assistance Found., 1969-70; asst. U.S. Atty. Office of U.S. Atty., Los Angeles, 1966-69; ptnr. Nasatir, Sherman and Hirsch, Los Angeles, 1970-83, Santa Monica, Calif., 1983—; lectr. UCLA, U. So. Calif., Los Angeles, Loyola Marymount U., various seminars. Mem. ABA, Fed. Bar Assn., Los Angeles County Bar Assn., Beverly Hills Bar Assn., Calif. Atty.'s for Criminal Justice. Criminal. Office: Nasatir and Hirsch 2115 Main St Santa Monica CA 90405

NASH, FRANK ERWIN, lawyer; b. Pendleton, Oreg., Feb. 27, 1916; s. Frank Lee and Gertrude (Walbridge) N.; m. Elizabeth Ann Kibbe, Apr. 20, 1943; children: Thomas K., Robert L., Carl F., Frances L. B.S., U. Oreg., 1937, J.D., 1939. Bar: Oreg. 1939. Since practiced in Portland; with firm Miller, Nash, Wiener, Hager & Carlsen (and predecessors), 1939—, partner, 1948—. Bd. dirs. Tri-County United Good Neighbors, 1961-66, pres., 1963-64; pres. U. Oreg. Found., 1979-81; bd. dirs. Med. Research Found., pres., 1980-81; bd. dirs. Library Assn. Portland, pres., 1978-81; bd. visitors U. Oreg. Law Sch. Served to lt. col., inf. AUS, 1941-46, PTO. Fellow Am. Bar Found.; mem. ABA, Multnomah Bar Assn. (pres. 1964-65), Oreg. State Bar, Order of Coif, Phi Delta Phi, Phi Delta Theta. Republican. Methodist (past chmn. ofcl. bd.). Clubs: Arlington (Portland) (dir. 1963-65), Multnomah Amateur Athletic (Portland) (dir. 1963-65, pres. 1965-66), Waverley (Portland) (pres. 1979-80). General corporate, Estate planning, General practice. Home: 1885 NW Ramsey Dr Portland OR 97229 Office: 35th Floor 111 SW 5th Ave Portland OR 97204

NASH, JAMES HARRY, lawyer; b. Toronto, Ont., Can., July 31, 1936; s. James Harry and Stella Annetta (Thompson) N.; m. Barbara Bergfield, Aug. 1985; children—Leslie, Meredith. B.A., Wabash Coll., 1959; J.D., Ill. Inst. Tech.-Kent Coll., 1968. Bar: Ill. 1969, U.S. Dist. Ct. (no. dist.) Ill. 1969, Ohio 1987, U.S. Dist. Ct. (no. dist.) Ohio 1987. Asst. counsel Fed. Res. Bank Chgo., 1969-79, gen. counsel, Cleve., 1979-81; ptnr. Seki, Jarvis & Lynch, Chgo., 1980-84; sole practice, Chgo., 1984—, Shaker Heights, Ohio, 1987—. Mem. ABA, Ill. Bar Assn., Chgo. Bar Assn. Republican. Banking, Bankruptcy, General corporate.

NASH, MELVIN SAMUEL, lawyer; b. Atlanta, Aug. 26, 1949; s. Ralph Samuel and Mary Pauline (Quarles) N.; m. Cynthia Joanna Hamrick, Aug. 21, 1980. A.B., Ga. State U., 1974; J.D., U. Fla., 1976. Bar: Ga. 1978, U.S. Ct. Claims 1983, U.S. Ct. Internat. Trade 1983, U.S. Tax Ct. 1982, U.S. Ct. Appeals (5th cir.) 1978, U.S. Ct. Appeals (11th cir.) 1981, U.S. Supreme Ct. 1985. Asst. solicitor State Ct., Cobb County, Marietta, Ga., 1977-78; assoc. Milam & Smith, Austell, Ga., 1978; ptnr. Milam, Smith & Nash, Austell, 1978-79; sole practice, Marietta, 1979—; dir. Nash Trucking Co., Inc., Marietta, Security Fiedelity Mortgage, Marietta, Nash Properties, Marietta. Magistrate Prohac Vice State Ct. Cobb County, Marietta, 1980-82; candidate state rep. State of Ga. Dist. 21, Marietta, 1982. Served with USAF, 1967-71. Mem. ABA, Acad. Fla. Trial Lawyers, Assn. Trial Lawyers Am., Nat. Assn. Criminal Def. Lawyers, Ga. Assn. Criminal Def. Lawyers, Cobb County Bar Assn. (com. 1983-84), Cobb Criminal Def. Bar Assn. (sec., Seminar award 1984), State Bar Ga. (fee arbitrator 1982—). Democrat. Baptist. Clubs: Atlanta Ski, Atlanta Track (Marathon finisher). Criminal, Personal injury.

NASH, PAUL LENOIR, lawyer; b. Poughkeepsie, N.Y., Jan. 29, 1931; s. George Matthew and Winifred (LeNoir) N.; m. Nancy Allyn Thouron, Dec. 30, 1961; children—Andrew Gray, Laurie LeNoir, Daphne Thouron. B.A., Yale U., 1953; LL.B., Harvard U., 1958. Bar: N.Y. 1959. Assoc., Dewey, Ballantine, Bushby, Palmer & Wood, N.Y.C., 1958-66, ptnr., 1966—. Pres. bd. trustees Peck Sch., Morristown, N.J., 1978-82. Served to capt. USMC, 1953-55; Japan. Mem. ABA, N.Y. State Bar Assn., Assn. Bar City of N.Y. Republican. Mergers and acquisitions, General corporate, Securities. Home: 4 Westminster Pl Morristown NJ 07960 Office: Dewey Ballantine Bushby Palmer & Wood 140 Broadway Room 4500 New York NY 10005

NASH, THOMAS ACTON, JR., lawyer; b. Washington, Ga., July 28, 1950; s. Thomas A. Sr. and Mary P.H. Nash; m. Deborah S. Sandefur, July 25, 1971; children: Lindsey, Jessica. BA, U. Ga., 1972, JD, 1975. Bar: Ga. 1976, U.S. Dist. Ct. (no. and mid. dists.) Ga. 1976, U.S. Ct. Appeals (11th cir.) 1976, U.S. Tax Ct. 1977, U.S. Supreme Ct. 1987. Of counsel Fortson, Bentley & Griffin, Athens, Ga., 1975-83; staff atty., gen. mgr. Carswell Ins. Group, Inc., Savannah, Ga., 1983-85; assoc. Adams, Gardner, Ellis & Inglesby, Savannah, 1985—. Co-chmn. lawyers sect. United Way, 1977-78, 78-79, chmn. commerce div., 1984; bd. dirs. Goodwill Industries, Savannah, 1983—. Mem. ABA, Ga. Bar Assn. (young lawyers assn., econs. com., law and the clergy com., clin. legal edn. com.), Athens Bar Assn. (chmn. law day com. 1976, pub. relations com.), Savannah Bar Assn., Western Bar Assn., Assn. Trial Lawyers Am., Ga. Trial Lawyers Assn., Savannah Bar Assn., Ind. Ins. Agts. of Savannah (bd. dirs. 1985), U. Ga. Alumni Assn. (1st dist. v.p. 1984-86), C. of C., Order of Coif, Phi Delta Phi, Phi Beta Kappa, Phi Kappa Phi. Clubs: Oglethorpe, Chatham, Athens, Athens Touchdown (bd. dirs. 1980-81, 2d v.p. 1982-83), Marshwood. Lodge: Rotary (bd. dirs. Athens chpt. 1980-81). Avocations: boating, tennis. Federal civil litigation, General practice, Insurance. Home: 12 Tidewater Way Savannah GA 31411 Office: Adams Gardner Ellis & Inglesby PC PO Box 2364 Savannah GA 31498-2364

NASRI, WILLIAM ZAKI, legal educator, copyright consultant; b. Tanta, Gharbeya, Egypt, Apr. 19, 1925; came to U.S., 1964, naturalized, 1967; s. Zaki F. and Nadima (Hanna) N.; m. Eunice McConkey, June 14, 1960; children—Nadine Elizabeth, William Peter. B.A., U. Alexandria, Egypt, 1953, LL.B., 1957; Ph.D., U. Pitts., 1975. Pvt. practice law, Cairo, 1957-64; asst. prof. library and info. service and law U. Pitts., 1970-75, assoc. prof., 1976—, copyright cons., 1976—; translator Dept. Justice, Pitts., 1973-74; copyright cons., Pitts., 1970—; speaker, lectr. nationwide, 1975—. Author: Crisis in Copyright, 1976, Legal Taxes for Library and Information Managers, 1987; editor: (monograph series) Communication, Information Technology and the Law, 1984, Legal Issues for Library and Nformation Managers, 1987; editor column Jour. Library Adminstrn., 1981; asst. editor Encyclopedia of Library and Information Science, 1968—. Bd. dirs. Col-

legiate YMCA, Pitts., 1978—, Greentree Pub. Library, Pa., 1978—. Mem. Nat. Assn. Coll. and Univ. Attys., Assn. Library and Info. Sci. Edn., AAUP. Republican. Presbyterian. Lodges: Oakland Rotary (bd. dirs. 1980-84, pres. 1986-87), Masons. Legal education, Trademark and copyright. Home: 179 Parkedge Rd Pittsburgh PA 15220 Office: U Pitts Sch Library and Info Sci 135 N Bellefield Ave Pittsburgh PA 15260

NASSBERG, RICHARD T., lawyer; b. N.Y.C., Mar. 30, 1942; s. Jules and Rhea (Steinglass) N.; m. Ellen Jane Silverman, Jan. 1, 1966; m. 2d Kathryn J. Schultz, May 2, 1981; children—Schuyler M. L., Kathryn Cupp. B.S. in Econs., Wharton Sch., U. Pa., 1963; J.D., U. Pa., 1968. Bar: N.Y. 1969, U.S. Ct. Appeals (2d cir.) 1970, Pa. 1972, Tex. 1983. Assoc. Milbank, Tweed, Hadley & McCloy, N.Y.C., 1968-70; assoc. Baer & McGoldrick, N.Y.C., 1970-71; assoc. Schnader, Harrison, Segal & Lewis, Phila., 1971-78, ptnr., 1978-82; ptnr. Mayor, Day & Caldwell, Houston, 1982—; planning chmn. courses of study on banking and comml. lending law Am. Law Inst.-ABA, 1979— mem. adv. com. to subcom. on continuing legal edn., 1982—. Served with Army N.G., 1963-65, USAR, 1965-66, USAFR, 1966-69. Mem. Am. Law Inst., ABA (adv. group on comml. law 1985—), Tex. Bar Assn., Houston Bar Assn. Clubs: Racquet, Franklin Inn (Phila.); Houston (Houston). Author: The Lender's Handbook. 1986; editor resource books on banking law; contbr. articles on banking law to profl. publs.; editor U. Pa. Law Rev., 1967-68, assoc. editor, 1966-67. Banking. Office: Mayor Day & Caldwell 1900 Republic Bank Center Houston TX 77002

NASSER, WOODROW SAM, lawyer; b. Terre Haute, Ind., July 17, 1931; s. Sam Jacob and Elvira (Luciana) N.; divorced; children—Stacy Ann, Woodrow Sam. B.S., Ind. State U.; J.D., Ind. U. Bar: U.S. Dist. Ct. (so. dist.) Ind., U.S. Ct. Appeals (7th cir.), U.S. Supreme Ct. Sole practice, Terre Haute, 1960-72; ptnr. Nasser & Felling, Terre Haute, 1972-74; sole practice, Terre Haute, 1974—. Served with USN. Mem. Ind. Bar Assn., Terre Haute Bar Assn. Democrat. Greek Orthodox. Clubs: Masons, Shriners. General practice, Criminal, Personal injury. Home: Rural Route 32 Terre Haute IN 47803 Office: 1446 S 7th St Terre Haute IN 47802

NASSIF, JOSEPH GERARD, lawyer; b. St. Louis, Jan. 9, 1949; s. John Michael and Frieda Marie (Mard) N.; m. Christina Ann Blumfelder, July 2, 1973; children: Meredith Ann, Jeffrey Alan. BA, St. Louis U., 1971, JD, 1974. Bar: Mo. 1974. Asst. counsel litigation Monsanto Co., St. Louis, 1974-86; ptnr. Coburn, Croft & Putzell, St. Louis, 1986—. Editor: Community Service Orders for Offenders, 1982. Pro bono atty. Legal Services of Eastern Mo., St. Louis, 1985—. Recipient Vol. Lawyers award Legal Services of Eastern Mo., 1985. Mem. ABA (co-chmn. young lawyers com., achievement award 1982), Mo. Bar Assn., Met. St. Louis Bar Assn. (co-chmn. young lawyers sect. 1980, chmn. 1981), Am. Corp. Counsel Assn. Democrat. Roman Catholic. Avocations: golf, basketball, swimming. Personal injury, Environment, Toxic tort law. Home: 10701 Kingsbridge Estates Dr Saint Louis MO 63141 Office: Coburn Croft & Putzell 1 Mercantile Ctr Saint Louis MO 63101

NASSIKAS, JOHN NICHOLAS, lawyer; b. Manchester, N.H., Apr. 29, 1917; s. Nicholas John and Constantina (Gagalis) N.; m. Constantina Andreson, Feb. 21, 1943; children: Constance (Mrs. John J. Hohenadel, Jr.), Marcy, Elizabeth (Mrs. William Cobbett), John Nicholas III. A.B., Dartmouth Coll., 1938; M.B.A., Harvard U., 1940, J.D., 1948; LL.D. (hon.), Notre Dame Coll., Manchester, N.H., 1972. Bar: N.H. and Mass. 1948, D.C. 1968, U.S. Supreme Ct. 1953, Va. 1986. Asst., dep. atty. gen. N.H., 1950-53; sr. partner firm Wiggin, Nourie, Sundeen, Nassikas & Pingree, Manchester, 1953-69; chmn. FPC, 1969-75; partner firm Squire, Sanders & Dempsey, Washington, 1975-86; spl. commr. N.H. Pub. Utilities Commn., 1984-86. Mem. Adminstrv. Conf. U.S., 1969-75; bd. dirs. U.S. Nat. Com. of World Energy Conf., 1970-74, 77-87; mem. Water Resources Council, 1969-75; mem. exec. com. NARUC, 1970-75; mem. Pres.'s Cabinet Task Force on Oil Import Control, 1969-70; mem. energy subcom. domestic council, 1969-73; mem. Pres.'s Joint Bd. on Fuel Supply and Transport, 1970-73, Pres.'s Energy Resources Council, 1974-75, Nat. Petroleum Council, 1975-79; bd. dirs. Ams. for Energy Independence, 1975-84; trustee Pathfinder Mines Corp., 1976-82; mem. adv. council Gas Research Inst., 1977-87; bd. dirs. corp. Madeira Sch., 1972-80. Served to lt. USNR, 1942-46. Mem. ABA, N.H. Bar Assn., Mass. Bar Assn., D.C. Bar Assn., Fed. Bar Assn., Va. Bar Assn., Energy Bar Assn., Ahepa, Kappa Kappa Kappa. Republican. Clubs: Cosmos, Met, Bald Peak Colony, Farmington Country. General practice, FERC practice. Home and Office: 1131 Litton Ln McLean VA 22101

NATCHER, STEPHEN DARLINGTON, lawyer, business executive; b. San Francisco, Nov. 19, 1940; s. Stanlus Zoch and Robena Lenore Collie (Goldring) N.; m. Carolyn Anne Bowman, Aug. 23, 1969; children: Tanya Michelle, Stephanie Elizabeth. A.B. in Polit. Sci., Stanford U., 1962; J.D., U. Calif., San Francisco, 1965. Bar: Calif. 1966. Asso. firm Pillsbury, Madison & Sutro, San Francisco, 1966-68; counsel Douglas Aircraft div. McDonnell Douglas Corp., Long Beach, Calif., 1968-70; asst. gen. counsel Electronic Memories & Magnetics Corp., Los Angeles, 1970-71; asst. sec. Security Pacific Nat. Bank, Los Angeles, 1971-72; v.p., asst. sec. Security Pacific Nat. Bank, 1972-76, v.p., sec., 1976-79; asst. gen. counsel Security Pacific Corp., 1979-80; v.p., sec., gen. counsel Lear Siegler, Inc., Santa Monica, Calif., 1980—. Served with USCG, 1965-66. Republican. Club: St. Francis Yacht (San Francisco). Office: Lear Siegler Inc 2850 Ocean Park Blvd Santa Monica CA 90406

NATEMAN, GARY M., lawyer; b. Columbus Ohio, Mar. 27, 1938; s. Raymond D. and Nanette (Kellner) N.; m. Nancy Ruth Frick, Apr. 26, 1968 (div.); 2d, Suzanne Cox, Nov. 23, 1979. B.B.A., Ohio U., 1959; LL.B. George Washington U., 1962. Bar: D.C. 1964. Counsel, Machinery and Allied Products Inst., Washington, 1964-66; assoc. gen. counsel, Nat. Assn. Life Underwriters, Washington, 1966-70, sr. v.p., gen. counsel Beer Inst., 1970—; dir. State Govtl. Affairs Council; mem. Adv. Com. to Adopt Model Liquor Laws, Joint Com. State. Mem. ABA, DC Bar Assn., Washington Met. Area Corp. Counsel Assn.; Phi Sigma Delta. Jewish. Clubs: Masons, Shriners. Restaurant and bar, Antitrust, Legislative. Home: 1929 N Woodley St Arlington VA 22207 Office: Beer Institute 1750 K St NW Washington DC 20006

NATES, JEROME HARVEY, publisher, lawyer; b. N.Y.C., Sept. 19, 1945; s. Louis and Lillian (Berger) N.; m. Marilyn Arlene Weiss, June 6, 1971; children: Lori Jennifer, Scott Eric. BA, Hunter Coll., 1968; JD, Bklyn. Law Sch., 1972. Bar: N.Y. 1973. Assoc. atty. Natiss & Rogers, Long Island, N.Y., 1972-73; editorial dir. Matthew Bender & Co., N.Y.C., 1973-84; editor-in-chief Kluwer Law Book Pub., N.Y.C., 1984—. Co-author: Damages in Tort Actions, 1982; editor: Personal Injury Deskbook-1983, Personal Injury Deskbook-1984. Mem. ABA, Assn. Trial Lawyers Am., N.Y. State Trial Lawyers Assn., Assn. of the Bar of City of N.Y. Lodge: KP. Avocations: tennis, golf. Legal publishing. Home: 8 Mitchell Ct Marlboro NJ 07746 Office: Kluwer Law Book Pub 36 W 44th St New York NY 10036

NATHAN, KENNETH SAWYER, SR., lawyer; b. Oshkosh, Wis., Feb. 8, 1906; s. Abraham Nathan and Jenny Blumenthal; m. Jean Hollander, Dec. 31, 1932 (div. July 26, 1962); children: Anthony, Meryl; m. Doris Jean Kahn, Sept. 26, 1962; 1 child, Kenneth Sawyer Jr.; stepchild: Jeffery Preucil. Student, U. Chgo., 1923-26; JD, DePaul U., 1930. Bar: Ill. 1930. Arbitrator indsl. commn. State of Ill., Chgo., 1939-41; asst. U.S. atty. Dept. Justice, Chgo., 1943-46; sole practice Chgo., 1946—. Pres. 49th Ward Dem. Orgn., Chgo., 1950-58. Mem. ABA, Ill. Bar Assn., Chgo. Bar Assn., 7th Dist. Bar Assn., Assn. Trial Lawyers Am., Am. Judicature Soc. Episcopalian. State and local taxation, Probate, Estate planning. Home: 7755 Kenway Pl E Boca Raton FL 33433 Office: 39 S LaSalle St Chicago IL 60603

NATION, HORACE HENDRIX, III, circuit court judge; b. Birmingham, Ala., Oct. 8, 1948; s. Horace Hendrix Nation Jr. and Lucy Faye (Diesker) Bearden; m. Jean Marie Lawley, Dec. 30, 1970; children—Horace Hendrix, IV, James Leighton. B.S., U. Ala., 1971; J.D., Cumberland Law Sch., 1974. Bar: Ala. 1974. Asst. dist. atty. Walker County, Jasper, Ala., 1975-77; judge dist. ct. State of Ala., Jasper, 1977-80, cir. ct., 1980—; instr. Walker Coll. Mem. ABA, Ala. State Bar Assn., Walker County Bar Assn., Law Enforcement Planning Agy. (adv. bd.), Ala. Assn. Cir. Judges, Phi Delta Phi. Democrat. Mem. Disciples of Christ Ch. Lodge: Rotary. Judicial administration. Home: 2300 Acadian Pl Jasper AL 35501 Office: Presiding Circuit Judge PO Box 1442 Jasper AL 35502

NATISS, GARY MITCHELL, lawyer; b. N.Y.C., Dec. 12, 1956; s. Marvin and Suzanne E. (Brodie) N.; m. Lisa Sue Maller, Sept. 6, 1981; 1 child, Lauren Beth. BS, Union Coll., Schnectady, N.Y., 1978; JD, N.Y. Law Sch., 1981. Bar: N.Y. 1982, Fla. 1982, U.S. Dist. Ct. (ea. and so. dists.) N.Y. 1982. Assoc. Natiss, Ferenzo & Barrocas P.C., Roslyn Heights, N.Y., 1981-83, Garbarini, Scher & DeCicco P.C., N.Y.C., 1983-87; of counsel Weinreb, Weinreb & Weinreb, West Babylon, N.Y., 1987—. Mem. ABA, Fla. Bar Assn., N.Y. State Bar Assn., Nassau County Bar Assn., Assn. Trial Lawyers Am. Republican. Jewish. Personal injury, General practice. Office: Weinreb Weinreb & Weinreb 475 Sunrise Hwy PO Box 1579 West Babylon NY 11704

NAUMAN, JOSEPH GEORGE, lawyer; b. Cleve., Jan. 1, 1928; s. George N. and Margaret M. (O'Dea) N.; m. Mary O'Donnell, July 28, 1951; children—George, Michael, Mary L., Nancy, Carolyn, Timothy, Patricia, William (dec.), Christine. B.S. in M.E., Notre Dame U., 1949; J.D, Georgetown U., 1953. Bar: Ohio 1953, U.S. Dist. Ct. (so. dist.) Ohio 1954. Patent examiner U.S. Patent Office, Washington, 1951-53; ptnr. Biebel, French & Nauman and predecessors, Dayton, Ohio, 1953—; adj. prof. U. Dayton, Law Sch., 1972-82. Bd. dirs., pres. Dayton Opera Assn., 1973-77. Mem. ABA, Ohio Bar Assn., Ohio Bar Found., Dayton Bar Assn., Am. Intellectual Property Assn., Engrs. Club Dayton (pres. 1979). Republican. Roman Catholic. Club: Dayton Racquet. Patent, Trademark and copyright, Computer. Home: 4624 Wing View Ln Kettering OH 45429 Office: Biebel French & Nauman 2500 Kettering Tower Dayton OH 45423

NAUMAN, SPENCER GILBERT, JR., lawyer; b. Bryn Mawr, Pa., Mar. 4, 1933; s. Spencer Gilbert and Gertrude Howard (Olmsted) N.; m. Helen Gibbon Trimble, Oct. 19, 1963; children—Spencer G., Helen G., John T. A.B., Princeton U., 1955; LL.B., U. Pa., 1961. Bar: Pa. 1962, U.S. dist. ct. (mid. dist.) Pa. 1968. Assoc. Nauman, Smith, Shissler & Hall, Harrisburg, Pa., 1962-66, ptnr, 1966—; asst. city solicitor City of Harrisburg, 1962-69. Dir. Wagner Bros. Containers, Inc., Balt. Past pres., trustee emeritus Harrisburg Acad.; bd. dirs. Harrisburg chpt. ARC; bd. mgrs. Harrisburg Cemetery Assn., Harrisburg Hosp., 1973-79. Served with U.S. Army, 1955-58. Mem. ABA, Pa. Bar Assn., Dauphin County Bar Assn. Republican. Episcopalian. Clubs: Racquet (Phila.); Princeton (N.Y.C.); W. Shore Country (Camp Hill, Pa.). Insurance, Probate, Corporate taxation. Home: Creek Farm Bowmansdale PA 17008 Office: 122 Market St PO Box 840 Harrisburg PA 17108

NAVE, THOMAS GEORGE, lawyer; b. Medford, Oreg., Mar. 12, 1950; s. Edward Clements and Marjorie May (Donahoe) N.; m. Susan Debra Cox, Sept. 8, 1984. BS, Oreg. State U., 1972; JD, Lewis and Clark U., 1976. Bar: Alaska 1977. Assoc. Douglas L. Gregg, Juneau, Alaska, 1977, Peter M. Page, Juneau, 1978; asst. pub. defender State of Alaska, Fairbanks, 1979; dep. dir. Alaska Pub. Defender's Office, Juneau, 1980-85; ptnr. Gullufsen and Nave, Juneau, 1985—; lectr. Legis. Affairs Agy., Juneau, 1982-83. Mem. Alaska Bar Assn., Am. Judicature Soc., Nat. Assn. Criminal Def. Lawyers, Assn. Trial Lawyers Am. Democrat. Roman Catholic. Avocations: skiing, hunting, fishing. Criminal, State civil litigation, General practice. Home: 625 W 10th St Juneau AK 99801 Office: Gullufsen and Nave PC 227 7th St Juneau AK 99801

NAYLOR, GEORGE LEROY, lawyer, railroad executive; b. Bountiful, Utah, May 11, 1915; s. Joseph Francis and Josephine Chase (Wood) N.; student U. Utah, 1934-36; student George Washington U., 1937; J.D. (Bancroft Whitney scholar), U. San Francisco, 1953; m. Maxine Elizabeth Lewis, Jan. 18, 1941; children—Georgia Naylor Price, RoseMaree Naylor Hammer, George LeRoy II. Admitted to Calif. bar, 1954, Ill. bar, 1968; v.p., sec., legis. rep. Internat. Union of Mine, Mill & Smelter Workers, CIO, Dist. Union 2, Utah-Nevada, 1942-44; examiner So. Pacific Co., San Francisco, 1949-54, chief examiner, 1955, asst. mgr., 1956-61; carrier mem. Nat. R.R. Adjustment Bd., Chgo., 1961-77, chmn., 1970-77; atty. Village of Fox River Valley Gardens, Ill., 1974-77; practice law, legal cons., Ill. and Calif., 1977—; gen. counsel for Can-Veyor, Inc., Mountain View, Calif., 1959-64; adj. instr. dept. mgmt. U. West Fla., 1981. Served with AUS, World War II. Mem. ABA, Ill. Bar Assn., Calif. Bar Assn., Chgo. Bar Assn., San Francisco Bar Assn. Mormon. Author: Defending Carriers Before the NRAB and Public Law Boards, 1969, Choice Morsels in Tax and Property Law, 1966, Underground at Bingham Canyon, 1944; National Railroad Adjustment Board Practice Manual, 1978. Labor, Probate, Real property. Home: Rural Rt #1 Box 255 Monticello IL 61856 Office: Round Barn Station PO Box 6323 Champaign IL 61821-8323 also: 2976 Camargo Ct San Jose CA 95132

NEAGLE, CHRISTOPHER SCOTT, lawyer; b. Braintree, Mass., Mar. 21, 1952; s. Philip A. Neagle and Karin I. (Hauge) Withington; m. Ruth Wyman Neagle, Oct. 11, 1981; children: Scott Wyman, Jeffrey Spiller. BA, Wesleyan U., Middletown, Conn., 1974; JD, Cornell U., 1977. Bar: Maine 1977, Mass. 1977, U.S. Dist. Ct. Maine 1977. Assoc. Verrill & Dana, Portland, Maine, 1977-81; ptnr. Verrill & Dana, Portland, 1982—; instr. real estate law U. So. Maine, Portland, 1979—. Author: (seminar book) Problem Loans, 1985. Mem. ABA, Maine Bar Assn. (chmn. real estate title standards com. 1984—, vice-chmn. real estate sect. 1985—), Mass. Bar Assn., Northeast Land Title Assn. Congregationalist. Avocations: running, hiking, soccer. Real property, Banking, Environment. Home: 21 Underwood Rd Falmath ME 04105 Office: Verrill & Dana Two Canal Plaza Portland ME 04112

NEAL, A. CURTIS, lawyer; b. Nacogdoches, Tex., Nov. 25, 1922; s. Berry W. and Mattie E. (Shepherd) N.; m. Martha E. Bishop, Apr. 16, 1942; children—A. Curtis, Patricia Ann, Dick (dec.). B.B.A., U. Tex. 1948, LL.B. 1952. Bar: Tex. 1951; CPA., Tex. With Office of Tex. Sec. of State 1948-52; practice law, Amarillo, Tex., 1952—. Counsel exec. com. Boy Scouts Am., 1957-67; past pres. Kids, Inc. Served with USN, 1942-45. Fellow Tex. Bar Found., mem. ABA, State Bar Tex. (chmn. assistance to local bar assns. 1982-83, com. on coordination with accts. 1979—, spl. services to membership div. 1982, state bar coll. of law), Amarillo Bar Assn. (pres. 1981-82), Amarillo C. of C. (legis. affairs com.), Delta Theta Phi, Beta Alpha Psi. Republican. Clubs: Amarillo, Masons, Shriners (Khiva Potentate 1970). Banking, Contracts commercial, General corporate. Home: 6205 Jameson St Amarillo TX 79106 Office: 1002 Plaza One Amarillo TX 79101

NEAL, ANNE DEHAYDEN, lawyer; b. Indpls., Mar. 22, 1955; d. James Thomas and Georgianne (Davis) N.; m. Thomas Evert Petri, Mar. 26, 1983. A.B. in Am. History and Lit., Harvard U., 1977, J.D., 1980. Bar: N.Y. 1981, U.S. Dist. Ct. (so. dist.) N.Y. 1981, U.S. Dist. Ct. (ea. dist.) N.Y. 1981, U.S. Ct. Claims 1982, U.S. Ct. Appeals (fed. cir.) 1982, D.C. 1984, Wis. 1986. Assoc., Rogers & Wells, N.Y.C., 1980-82; gen. counsel Office of Adminstrn., Exec. Office Pres., Washington, 1982-84; assoc. Wiley, Rein & Fielding, Washington, 1984-87; dep. gen counsel Recording Industry Assn. Am. Inc., 1987—. founding mem. Nat. Mus. of Women in Arts, 1984—; chmn. Com. on Nat. Mus. of Women in Arts, 1985—; chmn., bd. dirs., v.p., ho. of reps. Child Care Ctr. Inc., 1986—; chmn. New Leadership Fund, 1985—. Pulliam journalism fellow Indpls. News, 1977. Mem. Fed. Communications Bar Assn., ABA, Communications Law Forum, Colonial Dames Am., Phi Beta Kappa. Republican. Methodist. Club: Dramatic (Indpls.). Office: Rec Industry Assn of Am Inc 1020 19th St NW Suite 200 Washington DC 20006

NEAL, DAVID W., lawyer; b. Joliet, Ill., June 2, 1955; s. H. Wayne and Rosemary (Ronchetti) N.; m. Delia D. Cacia, Nov. 16, 1986. BA, Lewis U., Lockport, Ill., 1977; JD, No. Ill. U., 1980. Asst. state's atty. State's Atty.'s office of Will County, Joliet, 1980-82; sr. ptnr. Neal, Cortina & Assocs., Coal City, Ill., 1982—; instr. Joliet Jr. Coll., 1987—; cons. in field. Exec. dir. Grundy County Crimestoppers, Coal City, 1983—; vice-chmn. Grundy County chpt. Am. Cancer Soc., Morris, Ill., 1985—. Recipient Ronan award Young Dems. Ill., 1983. Mem. Ill. Trial Lawyers Assn., Ill. State Bar Assn., Fla. State Bar Assn. Democrat. Roman Catholic. Lodges: Lions, Moose. Office: Neal Cortina & Assocs Attys at Law 415 W Division St Coal City IL 60416

NEAL, JAMES F., lawyer; b. Sumner County, Tenn., Sept. 7, 1929; s. Robert Gus and Emma Clendenning N.; m. Victoria Jackson , Mar. 21, 1985; children: James F., Julie Ellen. B.S., U. Wyo., 1952; LL.B., Vanderbilt U., 1957; L.L.M., Georgetown U., 1960. Bar: Tenn. 1957, D.C. 1958. Asso. firm Turney & Turney, 1957-60; spl. asst. to Atty. Gen. U.S., 1961-64; U.S. atty. for Middle Dist. of Tenn., 1964-66; partner Cornelius, Collins, Neal & Higgins, Nashville, 1966-70; partner firm Neal & Harwell, Nashville, 1971—; assoc. spl. prosecutor Watergate prosecuting force, 1973, 74; lectr. law Vanderbilt U., 1966-79; chief counsel U.S. Senate Select Commn. on Undercover Ops., 1982; bd. dirs. Ingram Industries., Inc. Vice chmn. Nashville Human Rights Com., 1968-70; vice chmn. Nashville Urban League, 1969-71; dir. Lawyers Com. for Civil Rights Under Law, 1978—, Am. Bar Assn. Found. Served with USMCR, 1952-54. Mem. Am. Bar Assn., Tenn. Bar Assn., Fed. Bar Assn., Am. Coll. Trial Lawyers, Internat. Acad. Trial Lawyers, Bar Assn. D.C. Clubs: Richland Country, Nashville City. Office: 2000 One Nashville Pl 150 4th Ave N Nashville TN 37219

NEALER, KEVIN GLENN, lawyer; b. Johnstown, Pa., May 3, 1954; s. Kenneth Glenn and Norma June (Lane) N.; m. Stephanie Lee Mann, Jan. 4, 1986. AB, U. Mich., 1975; JD, Case Western Res. U., 1978. Bar: Ohio 1978, D.C. 1985. Counsel Diamond-Shamrock Co., Cleve., 1979; advisor indsl. relations Midland-Ross Corp., Cleve., 1979-80; officer fgn. service U.S. Dept. of State, Washington, 1980-82; trade advisor U.S. Senate Dem. Policy Com., Washington, 1982—87; sr. assoc. Arnold & Porter Cons. Group, Washington, 1987—. Mem. D.C. Bar Assn. (internat. div.). Private international, Public international, Legislative. Office: 1200 New Hampshire Ave NW Washington DC 20036

NEALON, WILLIAM JOSEPH, federal judge; b. Scranton, Pa., July 31, 1923; s. William Joseph and Ann Cannon (McNally) N.; m. Jean Sullivan, Nov. 15, 1947; children: Ann, Robert, William, John, Jean, Patricia, Kathleen, Terrence, Thomas, Timothy. Student, U. Miami, Fla., 1942-43; B.S. in Econs, Villanova U., 1947; LL.B., Cath. U. Am., 1950; LL.D. (hon.), U. Scranton, 1975. Bar: Pa. 1951. With firm Kennedy, O'Brien & O'Brien (and predecessor), Scranton, 1951-60; mem. Lackawanna County Ct. Common Pleas, 1960-62; U.S. dist. judge Middle Dist. Pa., 1962—, chief judge, 1976—; mem. com. on adminstrn. of criminal law Jud. Conf. U.S., 1979—; lectr. bus. law and labor law U. Scranton, 1951-59. Mem. Scranton Registration Commn., 1953-55; hearing examiner Pa. Liquor Control Bd., 1955-59; campaign dir. Lackawanna County chpt. Nat. Found., 1961-63; mem. Scranton-Lackawanna Health and Welfare Authority, 1963—; Asso. bd. Marywood Coll., Scranton; pres. bd. dirs. Cath. Youth Center; pres. Father's Club Scranton Prep. Sch., 1966; chmn. bd. trustees U. Scranton; vice chmn. bd. trustees Lackawanna Jr. Coll., Scranton; bd. dirs. St. Joseph's Children's and Maternity Hosp., 1963-66, Lackawanna County unit Am. Cancer Soc., Lackawanna County Heart Assn., Lackawanna County chpt. Pa. Assn. Retarded Children, Scranton chpt. A.R.C., Lackawanna United Fund, Mercy Hosp., Scranton, 1975—; trustee St. Michael's Sch. Boys, Hoban Heights; adv. com. Hosp. Service Assn. Northeastern Pa. Served to 1st lt. USMCR, 1942-45. Recipient Americanism award Amos Lodge B'nai B'rith, 1975; Cyrano award U. Scranton Grad. Sch., 1977; Disting. Service award Pa. Trial Lawyers Assn., 1979; named one of 50 Disting. Pennsylvanians Greater Phila. C. of C., 1980, Outstanding Fed. Trial Judge Assn. Trial Lawyers Am., 1983. Mem. Pa., Lackawanna County bar assns., Friendly Sons St. Patrick (pres. Lackawanna County 1963-64). Club: Scranton Country (Clarks Summit, Pa.) (bd. dirs.). Lodge: K.C. Office: Federal Bldg PO Box 1146 Scranton PA 18501 *

NEALS, FELIX, lawyer, parapsychologist; b. Jacksonville, Fla.; children—Felix R., Felice, Julien. B.S., Idaho State U., 1955; J.D., Washburn U., 1958. Bar: Kans. 1958, N.Y. 1961. Atty., adminstr. ITT, N.Y.C., 1964-67; adminstr. RCA, N.Y.C., 1967-69; gen. counsel Lovable Co., N.Y.C., 1969-74; sole practice, N.Y.C., 1975-80; adminstrv. law judge N.Y. State Dept. of State, N.Y.C., 1980—; owner, founder Jazz Hall of Fame Club. Author: Psychosystematics—A Method of Mental Control, 1975. Chmn. housing com. N.J. Gov's. Bi-Partisan Com. Equal Opportunity, 1965; mem. U.S. Vice-Pres.'s Spl. Task Force Edn., and Employment, 1968; co-chmn. Mayor's Com. on Edn., East Orange, N.J., 1975; arbitrator Community Dispute Service, Am. Arbitration Assn., N.Y.C., 1983. Served with U.S. Army, 1946-49, PTO. Mem. Nat. Bar Assn., Assn. of N.Y. State Civil Service Attys. Office: NY State Dept of State 270 Broadway New York NY 10007 Office: 21 Hudson St New York NY 10013

NEARING, VIVIENNE W., lawyer; b. N.Y.C.; d. Abraham M. and Edith Eunice (Webster) N. B.A., Queens Coll.; M.A., J.D., Columbia U. Bar: N.Y., D.C., U.S. Dist. Ct. (so. and ea. dists.) N.Y. Ptnr. Stroock, Stroock and Lavan, N.Y.C. Mem. editorial bd. Communications and the Law, 1978-82, adv. bd. 1982—; mem. editorial bd. U.S. Trademark Reporter, 1982-86. Bd. dirs. Light Opera of Manhattan, 1981-82; bd. dirs. Lyric Opera N.Y., 1984—. Mem. ABA, Fed. Bar Council, N.Y. State Bar Assn., U.S. Trademark Assn., Copyright Soc. U.S.A., N.Y. Lawyers for Pub. Interest (bd. dirs. 1983—), Commn. for Law and Social Justice. Federal civil litigation, Entertainment, Libel. Home: 1185 Park Ave New York NY 10128 Office: Stroock Stroock and Lavan 7 Hanover Sq New York NY 10004

NEARY, CHRISTOPHER J., lawyer; b. Miami Beach, Fla., Aug. 7, 1948; s. Ralph C. and Barbara J. (Ingram) N. BA in English, U. Pacific, 1970; JD, Humphreys Coll., 1975. Bar: Calif. 1976, U.S. Dist. Ct. (no. dist.) Calif. 1976. Sole practice Willits, Calif., 1976—. Gen. counsel Brooktrails Community Services Dist., Willits, 1977—; trustee Willits Unified Sch. Dist., 1980—; bd. dirs. Little Lake Water Dist., Willits, 1977-82. Mem. ABA, Mendocino County Bar Assn. Republican. Methodist. Lodge: Rotary (bd. dirs. Willits 1978-80). General practice, Government contracts and claims, Construction. Home: Sunnybrook Ranch Willits CA 95490 Office: 110 S Main St Suite C Willits CA 95490

NEARY, GERALD CLARKE, lawyer; b. N.Y.C., Dec. 27, 1932; s. Gerald Patrick and Rita Augusta (Cating) N.; m. Mary Alice Gerstell, May 26, 1962 (div. 1972); children—Elizabeth B., Mary Louise. Student Yale U., 1950-52, A.B., 1957; LL.B., NYU, 1963. Bar: N.Y. 1964, N.J. 1973. Assoc. Milbank, Tweed, Hadley & McCloy, N.Y.C., 1963-69, 71-72; staff tax atty. Rockefeller Family and Assocs., N.Y.C., 1969-71; ptnr. Pitney, Hardin, Kipp & Szuch, Morristown, N.J., 1973—. Mem. ABA (tax sect.), N.Y. State Bar Assn. (tax sect.), N.J. State Bar Assn. (tax sect., chmn. 1980-81). Republican. Roman Catholic. Corporate taxation, Personal income taxation, State and local taxation. Office: Pitney Hardin Kipp & Szuch 163 Madison Ave CN 1945 Morristown NJ 07960

NEBEKER, FRANK QUILL, federal judge; b. Salt Lake City, Apr. 23, 1930; s. J. Quill and Minnie (Holmgren) N.; m. Louana M. Visintainer, July 11, 1953; children: Cariamaria, Melia, William Mark. Student, Weber Coll., 1948-50; B.S. in Polit. Sci, U. Utah, 1953; J.D., Am. U., 1955. Bar: D.C. 1956. Corr. sec. The White House, 1953-56; trial atty. Internal Security div. Justice Dept., Washington, 1956-58; asst. U.S. atty. 1958-69; asso. judge D.C. Ct. Appeals, 1969—; Cons. Nat. Commn. on Reform of Fed. Criminal Laws, 1967-68; adj. prof. Am. U. Washington Coll. Law, from 1967. Mem. Am., D.C. bar assns. Office: DC Court of Appeals 500 Indiana Ave NW Washington DC 20001 *

NEBEL, MARY BETH, lawyer; b. Chgo., Sept. 14, 1956; d. Harry Albert and Emily Virginia (Gabriel) Moscinski; m. Gary L. Nebel, Aug. 17, 1984; 1 child, Timothy A. BS, So. Ill. U., JD. Bar: Ill. 1980. Claims atty. Shand, Morahan & Co. Inc., Evanston, Ill., 1981-84, counsel, 1984—. Mem. ABA (torts and ins. practice sect.), Chgo. Bar Assn. Insurance. Office: Shand Morahan & Co Inc Shand Morahan Plaza Evanston IL 60201

NEBLETT, STEWART LAWRENCE, lawyer; b. Houston, Dec. 8, 1948; s. Sterling A. and Esther G. (McLeroy) N.; m. Charlene Jordan, Jan. 12, 1985. Student Southwestern U., 1967-68; B.B.A., U. Tex., 1970; JD, South Tex. Coll. Law, 1975. Bar: Tex. 1976, U.S. Dist. Ct. (so. dist.) Tex. 1979, U.S. Ct. Appeals (5th cir.) 1979, U.S. Ct. Appeals (11th cir.) 1979, U.S. Supreme Ct. 1980. Sole practice, Houston, 1976-77; gen. counsel Fed. Intermediate Credit Bank, Austin, Tex., 1977-85; dep. gen. counsel Farm Credit Banks of Tex., Austin, 1985—. Mem. Coll. of State Bar Tex., State Bar Tex. (agrl. law com. 1984—). Republican. Presbyterian. Banking, General corporate, Ban-

kruptcy. Home: 600 Crystal Creek Dr Austin TX 78746 Office: Farm Credit Banks of Tex PO Box 15919 Austin TX 78761

NEBUSH, FRANK JOHN, JR., lawyer; b. Utica, N.Y., Nov. 25, 1948; s. Frank John and Bertha Mary (Mack) N.; m. Joyce Mary Chrupcala, July 5, 1971; children—Joshua, Christian, Seth, Luke. B.A., Northeastern U., Boston, 1971; J.D., New Eng. Sch. Law, 1974. Bar: N.Y. 1975, U.S. Dist. Ct. (no. dist.) N.Y. 1975, U.S. Tax Ct. 1980. Assoc. Joseph L. Fey, Utica, 1974-76; assoc. Penberthy & Kelly, Utica, 1976-78; sole practice, Utica, 1978-81; asst. Oneida County atty., Utica, 1980-81; pub. defender Oneida County, Utica, 1981—; adminstr. Assigned Counsel Plan, Utica, 1976-80; lectr. SUNY, Utica, 1974-83. Sr. editor New Jour. Prison Law, 1974. Pres. Young Republicans Oneida County, Utica, 1976; pres. Poland Central Bd. Edn., (N.Y.), 1984. Mem. Oneida County Bar Assn. (exec. sec. 1976-80), ABA (pub. def. com.). Roman Catholic. Lodge: K.C. Criminal, Legal education. Home: RD 2 Box 414 Utica NY 13502 Office: Oneida County Pub Defender Courthouse Utica NY 13501

NECHEMIAS, STEPHEN MURRAY, lawyer; b. St. Louis, July 27, 1944; s. Herbert Bernard and Toby Helen (Wax) N.; m. Marcia Rosentein, June 19, 1966, (div. Dec. 1981); children: Daniel Jay, Scott Michael; m. Linda Adams, Aug. 20, 1983. BS, Ohio State U., 1966; JD, U. Cin., 1969. Bar: Ohio 1969. Ptnr., Taft, Stettinius & Hollister, Cin., 1969— ; adj. prof. law No. Ky. U., Chase Coll. Law. Tax comment author: Couse's Ohio Form Book, 6th edit., 1984. Mem. Cin. Bar Assn. (chmn. taxation sect.). Democrat. Jewish. Corporate taxation, State and local taxation, Personal income taxation. Home: 777 Cedar Point Dr Cincinnati OH 45230 Office: Taft Stettinius & Hollister 1800 First National Bank Center Cincinnati OH 45202

NEDWEK, THOMAS WAYNE, association executive; b. Milw., Sept. 30, 1933; s. Thomas Anton and Josephine Ruth (Felski) N.; m. Charlotte A. Jager, June 16, 1956 (div. Jan. 1982); children: Thomas W. Jr., David J., Peter C., Annemarie R., Paul J. BSBA, Marquette U., 1955; postgrad. San Diego State Coll., 1958, Marquette U., 1960-61. Tchr., English Cathedral High Sch., San Diego, 1958-60; radio announcer Sta. WISN, Milw., 1960-65; instr. English Milw. Sch. Engring., 1960-62, Messmer High Sch., Milw., 1962-65; mem. pub. relations staff AC Electronics div., Gen. Motors Corp., Milw., 1965-70; sr. reporter Sta. WISN-TV, Milw., 1970-72, dir. pub. relations, 1972-76; v.p. pub. relations Milw. Sch. Engring., 1976-80; exec. dir. Milw. Bar Assn., 1980—; corp. mem. Milw. Sch. Engring. Alderman, City of Glendale (Wis.), 1976—, plan commr., 1976-84; bd. dirs. St. Joseph's Hosp., 1980-85, World Festivals, Inc., 1978-83; v.p. Milw. Council on Alcoholism, 1980—; sec. Milw. Bar Found., 1983—; dir. Florentine Opera Club, 1986—. Served to lt. (j.g.) USN, 1955-58. Mem. Pub. Relations Soc. Am. (past pres. Wis. chpt., assembly del.), Am. Soc. Assn. Execs., Nat. Assn. Bar Execs., Wis. Soc. Assn. Execs. Roman Catholic. Club: Milw. Press (sec. 1983-85). Home: 2620 W Custer Ave Glendale WI 53209 Office: 605 E Wisconsin Ave Milwaukee WI 53202

NEEDELL, RUSSELL LAWRENCE, lawyer; b. N.Y.C., Feb. 14, 1956; s. Stanley Howard Needell and Jo-Ann (Boltuch) Koons; m. Wanda Lassiter, Sept. 14, 1985. BA in History with honors, Franklin Pierce Coll., 1978; JD, Capital U., 1981. Bar: N.J. 1982, Ohio 1982, Pa. 1984. Law clk. to presiding justice N.J. Superior Ct., Mercer County, 1981-82; asst. atty. City of Columbus, Ohio, 1982-84; ptnr. Needell & Needell, Trenton, N.J., 1984—; bd. trustees Mercer County Legal Aid, 1985—. Mem. ABA, N.J. Bar Assn., Mercer County Bar Assn., N.J. Def. Assn., Assn. Trial Lawyers Am., Del. Valley Claims Assn. Avocations: hiking, climbing, photography. Insurance, Personal injury, General practice. Home: 107 Mulberry Dr Holland PA 18966 Office: 908 W State St Trenton NJ 08618

NEELEY, JOYCE YOUNT, lawyer; b. Cedar City, Utah, Aug. 18, 1947; d. Carl Riley and Norma (White) Y.; m. Phillip M. Neeley, Sept. 15, 1967 (div.); children: Slade Riley, Jenny Lynne. BA cum laude, Weber State Coll., 1973; JD magna cum laude, U. San Diego, 1978. Bar: Ariz. 1978, Calif. 1980, Hawaii 1982. Assoc. Evans, Kitchel and Jenckes, Phoenix, 1978-80, Carlsmith and Dwyer, Honolulu, 1980-84; dir. Dwyer, Imanaka, Neeley and Peterson, Honolulu, 1984—; instr. real estate U. Hawaii, Honolulu, 1983-85. Mem. Ariz. Women Lawyers Assn. (bd. dirs. 1979-80), Hawaii Women Lawyers Assn. (bd. dirs. 1983, v.p. 1984, pres. 1985), Phi Kappa Phi. State civil litigation, Contracts commercial, General corporate. Home: 914 Hokulani St Honolulu HI 96825 Office: Dwyer Imanaka Neeley & Peterson 1800 Pioneer Plaza Honolulu HI 96813

NEELY, RICHARD, state supreme court justice; b. Aug. 2, 1941; s. John Champ and Elinore (Forlani) N.; m. Carolyn Elaine Elmore, 1979; 1 child, John Champ. A.B., Dartmouth Coll., 1964; LL.B., Yale U., 1967. Bar: W.Va. 1967. Practiced in Fairmont, W.Va., 1969-73; chmn. Marion County Bd. Pub. Health, 1971-72; mem. W.Va. Ho. of Dels., 1971-72; justice W.Va. Supreme Ct. of Appeals, Charleston, 1973; chief justice W.Va. Supreme Ct., 1980-81, 85; chmn. bd. Kane & Keyser Co., Belington, W.Va. Author: How Courts Govern America, Why Courts Don't Work, 1983, The Divorce Decision, 1984, Judicial Jeopardy: When Business Collides With The Courts, 1986; contbr. articles to nat. mags. Served to capt. U.S. Army, 1967-69. Decorated Bronze Star, Vietnam Honor medal 1st Class. Mem. W.Va. Bar Assn., Am. Econ. Assn., Internat. Brotherhood Elec. Workers, VFW, Am. Legion, Phi Delta Phi, Phi Sigma Kappa. Episcopalian. Club: Moose. Jurisprudence. Office: WVa Supreme Ct of Appeals Charleston WV 25305 *

NEESE, SANDRA ANNE, lawyer; b. Lapel, Ind., Apr. 8, 1936; d. Oral Manfred and Alma Mae (Meeker) Neese. A.B., Ind. U., 1958, J.D., 1961. Bar: Ind. 1961, U.S. Dist. Ct. (so. dist.) Ind. 1961. Dep. atty. gen. State of Ind., Indpls., 1961-63; vol. atty. U.S. Peace Corps, Liberia, 1963-65; field rep., then dir. compliance, acting asst. dir. Mo. Commn. on Human Rights, Jefferson City, 1965-70; regional counsel EEOC, Kansas City, Mo., 1970-72, sr. trial atty., Chgo., 1973-74, supervisory trial atty., 1974-79, regional atty., Milw., 1979—. Mem. ACLU, Milw., 1979; mem. Amnesty Internat., 1981. Recipient Freedom Fund award NAACP, Jefferson City, 1970. Mem. Ind. State Bar Assn., ABA, Fed. Bar Assn., Am. Judicature Soc., Ind. U. Alumni Assn., Wis. Assn. Women Lawyers. Methodist. Labor, Federal civil litigation, Administrative and regulatory.

NEFF, FRED LEONARD, lawyer; b. St. Paul, Nov. 1, 1948; s. Elliott and Mollie (Poboisk) N. B.S. with high distinction, U. Minn., 1970; J.D., William Mitchell Coll. Law, 1976. Bar: Minn. 1976, U.S. Dist. Ct. Minn. 1977, U.S. Ct. Appeals (8th cir.) 1985, U.S. Supreme Ct. 1985, Wis. Supreme Ct. 1986. Tchr. Hopkins (Minn.) Pub. Schs., 1970-72; instr. Inver Hills Community Coll., St. Paul, 1973-76, U. Minn., Mpls., 1974-76; sole practice, Mpls., 1976-79; asst. county atty. Sibley County, Gaylord, Minn., 1979-80; mng. atty. Hyatt Legal Services, St. Paul, 1981-83, regional ptnr., 1983-85, profl. devel. ptnr., 1985-86; owner, dir. Neff Law Firm, Edina, Mpls. and St. Paul, 1986—; counsel Am. Tool Supply Co., St. Paul, 1976-78; cons. Nat. Detective Agy., Inc., St. Paul, 1980-83. Author: Fred Neff's Self-Defense Library, 1976, Everybody's Self-Defense Book, 1978, Karate Is for Me, 1980, Running Is for Me, 1980, Lessons from the Samurai, 1986, Lessons from the Art of Kempo, 1986, Lessons from the Western Warriors, 1986. Adviser to bd. Sibley County Commrs., 1979-80; speaker before civic groups, 1976-82; mem. Hennepin County Juvenile Justice Panel, 1980-82, Hennepin County Pub. Def. Conflict Panel, 1980-82, 86—, Edina Hist. Soc.; founding sponsor Civil Justice Found., 1986—. Recipient St. Paul Citizen of Month award, Citizens Group, 1975, Student Appreciation U. Minn. award, 1978, Commendation award Sibley County Attys. Office, 1980, Leadership award Hyatt Legal Services, 1984, Mgn. Attys. Guidance award 1985, Justice award 1986, Creative Thinker award regional staff 1986, Good Neighbor award WCCO Radio, 1985, Lamp of Knowledge award Twin Cities Lawyers Guild, 1986, numerous other awards and honors. Fellow Internat. Biog. Assn., Nat. Dist. Attys. Assn.; mem. ABA, Assn. Trial Lawyers Am., Minn. Bar Assn., Hennepin County Bar Assn., Wis. Bar. Assn., Ramsey County Bar Assn., Medina C. of C., Minn. Martial Arts Assn. (pres. 1974-78 Outstanding Instr. award 1973), Nippon Kobudo Rengokai (dir. N.Central States 1972-76), Edina C. of C., Sigma Alpha Mu. Lodge: Masons, Kiwanis. Criminal, General practice, Law firm management. Home: 4515 Andover Rd Edina MN 55435 Office: 7380 France Ave Edina MN 55435 also: 345 St Peter St Suite 800 Saint Paul MN 55102 also: 3407 Hazelton Rd Edina MN 55435

NEFF, MICHAEL ALAN, lawyer; b. Springfield, Ill., Sept. 4, 1940; s. Benjamin Ezra and Ann (Alpert) N.; m. Lin Laghi, Mar. 26, 1977; 1 son, Aaron Benjamin. Student U. Ill., 1958-61; B.A., U. Calif.-Berkeley, 1963, postgrad. 1963-64; J.D., Columbia U., 1967. Bar: N.Y. 1967, U.S. Dist. Ct. (so. and ea. dists.) N.Y. 1969. Assoc., Sage Gray Todd & Sims, N.Y.C., 1967-74, Fellner & Rovins, N.Y.C., 1974-75; ptnr. Polier Tulin Clark & Neff, N.Y.C., 1976-77; sole practice, N.Y.C., 1977—; counsel St. Dominic's Home, 1971-74, Louise Wise Services, 1976-77, Edwin Gould Service for Children, 1969-74, 76—, Family Services of Westchester, Inc., 1977—, The Children's Village, 1977-84, Puerto Rican Assn. for Community Affairs, Inc., 1979—, Brookwood Child Care, 1980—; teaching asst. U. Calif., 1963-64; congl. intern U.S. Ho. of Reps., summer 1965; instr. Marymount Manhattan Coll., 1973; mem. Indigent Defendant's Legal Panel, Appellate Div., First Dept., 1974—; participant N.Y. State Conf. on Children's Rights, 1974; tng. supr. EST, 1978-81; asst. sec. Edwin Gould Services for Children, 1977—; cons. N.Y. Task Force on Permanency Planning For Children in Foster Care, 1985— . Mem. Assn. Bar City of N.Y., ABA. Contbr. articles to profl. jours. Family and matrimonial, State civil litigation, General practice. Home: 5 W 86 St Apt 6B New York NY 10024 Office: 36 W 44th St Suite 805 New York NY 10036

NEFF, R. MATTHEW, lawyer; b. Huntington, Ind., Mar. 26, 1955; s. Robert Eugene and Ann (Bash) N.; m. Lee Ann Loving, Aug. 23, 1980. BA in English, DePauw U., 1977; JD, Ind. U., Indpls., 1980. Bar: Ind. 1980, U.S. Dist. Ct. (so. dist.) Ind. 1980. Assoc. Krieg, DeVault, Alexander & Capehart, Indpls., 1980-85, ptnr., 1986—; lectr. various bank groups, Indpls., 1982—, Ind. Continuing Legal Edn. Forum, Indpls., 1986—. Exec. editor Ind. Law Rev., 1979-80. Participant Lacy Exec. Leadership Conf., Indpls., 1985-86; trustee DePauw U., 1977-80. Mem. Ind. Bar Assn. (chmn.-elect corps. banking and bus. law sect. 1986-87), ABA (chmn. fin. instns. subcom. young lawyers div. 1987), DePauw Alumni Assn. (bd. dirs. 1982—), Phi Kappa Psi, Phi Beta Kappa. Club: Indpls. Athletic. Avocations: racquetball, tennis. Banking, General corporate, Securities. Home: 6455 N Olney St Indianapolis IN 46220 Office: Krieg DeVault et al One Indiana Sq Suite 2800 Indianapolis IN 46204

NEFF, ROBERT CLARK, lawyer; b. St. Marys, Ohio, Feb. 11, 1921; s. Homer Armstrong and Irene (McCulloch) N.; m. Betty Baker, July 3, 1954; children—Cynthia Lee Neff Schifer, Robert Clark, Abigail Lynn (dec.); m. 2d, Helen Picking, July 24, 1975. B.A., Coll. Wooster, 1943; postgrad. U. Mich., 1946-47; LL.B., Ohio No. U., 1950. Bar: Ohio 1950, U.S. Dist. Ct. (no. dist.) Ohio 1978. Sole practice, Bucyrus, Ohio, 1950—; law dir. City of Bucyrus, 1961—. Chmn. blood program Crawford County (Ohio) unit ARC, 1955—; mem. adv. bd. Salvation Army, 1962—; clk. of session 1st Presbyterian Ch., Bucyrus, 1958—. Served with USNR, World War II; comdr. Res. ret. Named Bucyrus Citizen of Yr., 1981; Mem. Ohio Bar Assn., Crawford County Bar Assn., Naval Res. Assn., Ret. Officers Assn., Nat. Inst. Mcpl. Law Officers, Am. Legion, Bucyrus Area C. of C. (bd. dirs., recipient Outstanding Citizen award, 1973), Bucyrus Citizen of Yr., 1981. Republican. Clubs: Kiwanis (past pres.), Masons. General practice, Probate, Local government. Home: 1085 Mary Ann Ln Box 406 Bucyrus OH 44820 Office: 840 S Sandusky Ave Box 406 Bucyrus OH 44820

NEGRON, DENNIS, lawyer, food company executive; b. N.Y.C., Dec. 4, 1948; s. Dionisio and Mercedes (Martinez) N.; m. Patricia Marie Gonzales, Dec. 10, 1970 (div. June 1975); 1 child, Shawna; m. Maurine Claudia Dohse, June 19, 1980; children: Thomas, Bambi, Dennis, Tappi. AA, Rio Hondo Coll., Whittier, Calif., 1974; BS, Western State U., 1977, JD, 1978; MS in Mgmt., Pacific Christian Coll., 1980. Bar: Calif. 1979, U.S. Dist. Ct. (cen. dist.) Calif., U.S. Ct. Claims, U.S. Ct. Internat. Trade, U.S. Tax Ct., U.S. Ct. Customs and Patent Appeals, U.S. Ct. Appeals (9th cir.); cert. purchasing mgr. Foreman Ford Motor Co., Pico Rivera, Calif., 1970-79; contracts adminstr. Fluor Engring. and Constrn. Inc., Irvine, Calif., 1979-81; contracts specialist Bechtel Power Corp., Norwalk, Calif., 1981-82; contracts mgr. Kal-Kan Foods, Inc., Vernon, Calif., 1982-86; assoc. Law Offices of Evan Ginsburg, Fullerton, Calif., 1986—; part time bus. instr. Cerritos (Calif.) Community Coll., 1981-85, U. La Verne, 1986—. Served with USN, 1967-70, Vietnam. Mem. Nat. Assn. Purchasing Mgmt., ABA, Calif. Bar Assn. Republican. Avocations: golf, tennis, shooting. State civil litigation, Construction, Personal injury. Office: Evan L Ginsburg Law Offices 704 N Harbor Blvd Fullerton CA 92632

NEGRON-GARCIA, ANTONIO S., justice P.R. Supreme Ct.; b. Rio Piedras, P.R., Dec. 31, 1940; s. Luis Negron-Fernandez and Rosa M. Garcia-Saldana; m. Gloria Villardefrancos-Vergara, May 26, 1962; 1 son, Antonio Rogelio. B.A., U. P.R., 1962, LL.B., 1964. Bar: P.R. bar 1964. Law aide and lawyer legal div. Water Resources Authority, 1962-64; judge Dist. Ct., 1964-69, Superior Ct., 1969-74; justice P.R. Supreme Ct., San Juan, 1974—; administrating judge 1969-71; exec. officer Constl. Bd. for Revision Senatorial and Rep. Dists., 1971-72; mem. Jud. Conf., 1974; first exec. sec. Council for Reform of System of Justice in P.R., 1973-74; chmn. Gov.'s Advisory Com. for Jud. Appointments, 1973-74; lectr. U. P.R. Law Sch., 1973-74. Mem. P.R. Bar Assn., Am. Judicature Soc. Roman Catholic. Office: Supreme Court of PR Box 3292 San Juan PR 00903

NEHRA, GERALD PETER, lawyer; b. Detroit, Mar. 25, 1940; s. Joseph P. and Jeanette M. (Bauer) N.; children—Teresa, Patricia. B.I.E., Gen. Motors Inst., Flint, Mich., 1962; J.D., Detroit Coll. Law, 1970. Bar: Mich. 1970, U.S. Dist. Ct. (ea. dist.) Mich. 1970, N.Y. 1972, U.S. Dist. Ct. (so. dist.) N.Y. 1972, U.S. Dist. Ct. (no. dist.) N.Y. 1976, U.S. Ct. Appeals (6th cir.) 1978. Successively engr., supr., gen. supr. Gen. Motors Corp., 1958-67; mktg. rep., to regional counsel IBM Corp., 1967-79; v.p., gen. counsel Church & Dwight Co., Inc. 1979-82; dep. chief atty-Amway Corp., 1982-83, dep. gen. counsel, 1983—; adj. instr. Dale Carnegie Courses, 1983—. Recipient Outstanding Contbn. award Am. Cancer Soc., 1976. Mem. Mich. Bar Assn., Grand Rapids Bar Assn., N.Y. State Bar Assn., ABA. Contbr. chpt. to book. Antitrust, Contracts commercial, General corporate. Home: 1710 Beach Muskegon MI 49441 Office: Amway Corp 7575 E Fulton Ada MI 49355

NEIBART, RALPH, lawyer; b. Orange, N.J., Mar. 23, 1923; s. Isaac and Esther (Beim) N.; m. Renee Levous, Feb. 26, 1950 (div.); children: Janet, Ivan; m. Marilyn Cook, Nov. 14, 1976. BA, Oberlin Coll., 1943; LLB, Harvard U., 1949; LLM, NYU, 1957. Bar: N.J. 1950, U.S. Dist. Ct. N.J. 1950, U.S. Ct. Appeals (3d cir.) 1958, U.S. Supreme Ct. 1986. Ptnr. Singer & Neibart, Orange, 1950-53; sole practice Newark, 1953-75, West Orange, N.J., 1975—; asst. prosecutor Essex County, Newark, 1963-65; mem. Essex County Ethics com. N.J. Supreme Ct., 1972-74, Fee Arbitration com., 1978-83; Trustee Edn. Law Ctr. Inc., Newark, 1977-83. Served to lt. USN, 1943-46, PTO. Mem. N.J. State Bar Assn., Essex County Bar Assn. (jud. selection com., chmn. adminstrv. law com., 1986—), Am. Judicature Soc. Jewish. Club: Orange Lawn Tennis. Probate, General corporate, State civil litigation. Home: 11 Lewis Dr Maplewood NJ 07040 Office: 80 Main St West Orange NJ 07052

NEIDELL, MARTIN H., lawyer; b. Bklyn., Apr. 5, 1946; s. Sidney B. and Sophie (Goldstein) N.; m. Suzan C. Rucker, June 23, 1968; children: Michael, Sari. BA magna cum laude, Lehigh U., 1968; JD cum laude, NYU, 1971. Bar: N.Y. 1972, U.S. Dist. Ct. (ea. and so. dists.) N.Y. 1973, U.S. Ct. Appeals (2d cir.) 1973. Law clk. to presiding justice U.S. Dist. Ct. (ea. dist.) N.Y., Bklyn., 1971-73; assoc. Stroock & Stroock & Lavan, N.Y.C., 1973-79, ptnr., 1980—; sec. Page Am. Group, Hackensack, N.J., 1983—. Editor NYU Law Rev., 1971. Trustee North Shore Synagogue, Syosset, N.Y., 1984—. Mem. ABA. General corporate, Securities. Office: Stroock & Stroock & Lavan 7 Hanover Sq NY NY 10004

NEIDICH, GEORGE ARTHUR, lawyer; b. N.Y.C., Feb. 22, 1950; s. Hyman and Rosalyn (Eisenberg) N.; m. Alene Wendrow, Jan. 10, 1982. B.A., SUNY-Binghamton, 1971; J.D. magna cum laude, SUNY-Buffalo, 1974; M.L.T., Georgetown U., 1981. Bar: N.Y. 1975, D.C. 1979, U.S. Ct. Appeals (2d cir.) 1975, U.S. Dist. Ct. (we. dist.) N.Y. 1975, U.S. Tax Ct. 1976. Assoc. Runfola & Birzon, Buffalo, 1973-75, Duke, Holzman, Yaeger, & Radlin, Buffalo, 1975-77; gen. counsel subcom. on capital, investments and bus. opportunity, com. on small bus. U.S. Ho. of Reps., Washington, 1977-79, subcom. on gen. oversight, 1979-80; sr. legal advisor Task Force Product Liability and Accident Compensation, Office of Gen. Counsel, Dept. Commerce, Washington, 1980-81; assoc. Steptoe & Johnson, Washington, 1981-86, spl. counsel, 1986—; adj. prof. Georgetown U. Law Ctr., 1985—. Author: Report on Product Liability, 1980. Contbr. articles to profl. jours. Mem. ABA, N.Y. State Bar Assn. Corporate taxation, Legislative. Home: 2008 N Brandywine Arlington VA 22207 Office: Steptoe & Johnson 1330 Connecticut Ave NW Washington DC 20036

NEIGHER, ALAN, lawyer; b. Bridgeport, Conn., July 5, 1941; s. Harry and Esther Adrien (Lev) N.; m. Sylvie Haber, Apr. 11, 1978; children—Leslie Sharon, Jeremy Robert. A.B. with distinction, Colby Coll., 1962; J.D., Boston Coll., 1965. Bar: Conn. 1965, U.S. Supreme Ct., 1969, U.S. Dist. Ct. Conn., 1969, U.S. Ct. Appeals (2nd cir.) 1974, U.S. Ct. Appeals (9th cir.) 1985. Atty., Office Gen. Counsel, HEW, Washington, 1965-67; asst. gen. counsel Hotel Corp. Am., Boston, 1967-68; campaign staff Vice-pres. Hubert Humphrey, Washington, 1968; asst. prosecutor Cir. Ct., Bridgeport, Conn., 1969-70; sole practice, Bridgeport, 1969-80, Westport, Conn., 1980—; adj. prof. U. Bridgeport, 1977—; dir., csl. Hartcom, Inc. Pres., Conn. Consumer Assn., 1971-73; dir. Consumer Fedn. Am., 1972-75; bd. dirs. Fairfield County Legal Services, 1974-76. Recipient Pub. Service award, FTC, 1972. Mem. ABA, Conn. Bar Assn. (exec. com. antitrust sect.), Fed. Communications Bar Assn., Libel Def. Resource Center. Democrat. Jewish. Contbr. articles to profl. jours. Libel, Antitrust, Federal civil litigation. Home: 272 Fleming Ln Fairfield CT 06430 Office: 1804 Post Rd E Westport CT 06880

NEIL, BENJAMIN ARTHUR, lawyer, educator; b. Chambersburg, Pa., Nov. 9, 1950; s. Donald Arthur Neil and Betty Elizabeth (Geedy) Chase; m. Janice Joyce Czosnowski, Aug. 11, 1973; children—Benjamin Arthur, Brian Andrew. B.A., U. Balt., 1973, J.D., 1978; M.S., Morgan State U., Balt., 1975. Bar: Md. 1978, U.S. Dist. Ct. Md. 1979, U.S. Ct. Appeals (4th cir.) 1980, U.S. Supreme Ct. 1982, U.S. Ct. Appeals (5th cir.) 1983. Sole propr. Benjamin A. Neil & Assocs., Balt., 1978—; pres. Ben Neil Realty Inc., Balt., 1984—; asst. prof. law Towson State U., Balt., 1979—; asst. state's atty. Carroll County, Westminster, Md., 1980-81. Pres. parish council Our Lady of Fatima, Balt., 1978-80, 83-85; legal counsel Highlandtown Mchts. Assn., Balt., 1980-84. Recipient Gov.'s citation, Annapolis, Md., 1983; Mayor's cert., City of Balt., 1982. Mem. ABA, Assn. Trial Lawyers Am., Md. State Bar Assn., Balt. City Bar Assn. (legislation com. 1983—), Md. State's Attys. Assn. (faculty 1981—), Nat. Inst. Trial Advocacy (faculty 1984). Democrat. Roman Catholic. Clubs: Exchange of Highlandtown (v.p. 1984, pres. 1985-86), St. Gerard's YMA (dir. 1980-81), Highland Clipper (Balt.). General practice, Criminal. Home: 324 Imla St Baltimore MD 21224 Office: Benjamin A Neil and Assocs 3500 Bank St Baltimore MD 21224

NEILES, JOSEPH, judge; b. Sioux Falls, S.D., May 21, 1951; s. Cyril Charles and Marise Annette (Ege) N.; m. Jane Maurine Christensen, Apr. 17, 1982; children: Lindsay Jo, Brittany Jaine. BS in Math., U. S.D., 1973, JD, 1976. Bar: S.D. 1976, U.S. Dist. Ct. S.D. 1978, U.S. Ct. Appeals (8th cir.) 1985. Asst. pub. defender Pennington County, Rapid City, S.D., 1976-81; chief pub. defender Minnehaha County, Sioux Falls, 1981-83; ptnr. Zimmer, Richter & Duncan, Parker, S.D., 1983-85; law trained magistrate judge United Jud. System, Sioux Falls, 1986—. Mem. ABA, S.D. Bar Assn. (pattern jury criminal com.). Democrat. Roman Catholic. Avocations: golf, skiing, camping, family. Judicial administration. Home: 6208 WestView Rd Sioux Falls SD 57107 Office: Magistrate Ct 415 N Dakota Sioux Falls SD 57102

NEILL, ROBERT, lawyer; b. Batesville, Ark., July 23, 1908; s. Robert and Ida (Wing) N.; m. Nancy Mitchell, Aug. 5, 1939; children—Robert III, Nancy Lee. A.B., U. Mo., 1929; LL.B., Harvard U., 1932. Bar: Mo. 1932. Since practiced in St. Louis; asso. Thompson & Mitchell, and predecessors, 1932-44, ptnr., 1944—; personal counsel to adminstr. RFC, 1953; counsel Adv. Com. Financial Instrns. Act, 1956-57; adv. com. Jordan Charitable Trust, 1958—; Mem. adv. com. to comptroller currency, 1962-63; cons. Mo. Commn. Finance on New Banking Code, 1966. Bd. curators U. Mo., 1956-69, pres., 1964-67. Fellow Am. Bar Found.; mem. ABA, Mo. Bar Assn., St. Louis Bar Assn. (past v.p.), Law Library Assn. St. Louis (dir., past pres.), Phi Delta Phi (hon.). Club: Bogey (St. Louis). Banking, Probate, General corporate. Home: 665 S Skinker Blvd Saint Louis MO 63105 Office: 1 Mercantile Center Saint Louis MO 63101

NEIMAN, JOHN HAMMOND, lawyer; b. Des Moines, Jan. 8, 1917; s. Donald Edwin and Bessie A. (White) N.; m. Madeline Clare Flint, July 2, 1941; children—Richard F., Donald F., Nancy J. Student, Grinnell Coll., 1935-37; B.A., Drake U., 1939, J.D., 1941. Bar: Iowa 1941. Ptnr. Neiman, Neiman, Stone & Spellman, Attys., Des Moines, 1946—; exec. v.p., sec. Nat. Assn. Credit Mgmt., Des Moines, 1956-83; mem., chmn. Client Security & Atty. Disciplinary Commn., Iowa, 1974-85. Pres. bd. councilors Drake U. Law Sch., 1968; pres. Northwest Community Hosp., Des Moines, 1974-77. Recipient Centennial award Drake U., 1981. Fellow Am. Bar Found., Comml. Law Found.; mem. ABA (bd. govs. 1984-85, ho. dels. 1978-87), Iowa Bar Assn. (bd. govs. 1963-67, pres. 1967-68, award of merit 1975), Polk County Bar Assn. (pres. 1960-61), Comml. Law League Am., Iowa State Bar Found. (sec. 1975—). Republican. Methodist. Clubs: Wakonda (pres. 1973), Bohemian (pres. 1981-82, 84-86), Des Moines. Home: 3514 Wakonda Ct Des Moines IA 50321 Office: Neiman Neiman Stone & Spellman PC Attys 1119 High St Des Moines IA 50308

NEIMAN, TANYA MARIE, lawyer; b. Pitts., June 28, 1949; d. Max and Helen (Lamaga) N. AB, Mills Coll., 1970; JD, U. Calif., San Francisco, 1974. Bar: Calif. 1975. Law assoc. Boalt Hall U. Calif., Berkeley, 1974-76; pub. defender State of Calif., San Francisco, 1976-81; assoc. gen. counsel, dir. vol. legal services Bar Assn. San Francisco, 1982—. Mem. ABA (speaker 1985—, Harrison Tweed award 1985), Calif. Bar Assn. (exec. com. 1984—), Golden Gate Bus. Assn. Found. (v.p. grant making 1985—), Nat. Conf. Women and Law (speaker 1975—)Nat. Lawyers Guild. Legal services to the poor, Bar association and legal services program administration. Office: Bar Assn San Francisco 685 Market St San Francisco CA 94105

NEITHERCUTT, MARCUS GIBBS, criminal justice educator, consultant; b. Hobbs, N.Mex., June 23, 1939; s. Marcus Cleo and Pauline (Gibbs) N.; m. Janice Grant, Aug. 12, 1962; children—Marcus Gibbs II, Jeffrey Scott. B.A., Baylor U., 1961; M.Criminology, U.Calif.-Berkeley, 1964, D.Criminology, 1968. Probation officer U.S. Probation/Parole, U.S. Dist. Ct., San Francisco, 1964-69; research criminologist Nat. Council on Crime and Delinquency Research Ctr., Davis, Calif., 1969-77; assoc. prof. Calif. State U., Hayward, 1977—; pres. Bay Area Research Design Assocs., San Francisco, 1977—; cons. to govt. agys. in Alaska, Ariz., Calif., Ky., Ohio, Ill., Utah, Pa., Wis., 1970—; cons. to law firms on criminal risk/correctional mgmt., 1976—. Author: Uniform Parole Reports: A National Correctional Data System, 1975. NIMH research fellow U. Calif., Berkeley, 1963. Mem. Am. Correctional Assn. (life), Assn. for Correctional Research and Info. Mgmt., Correctional Edn. Assn., Calif. Probation, Parole and Correction Assn. (life). Criminal, Juvenile, Legal education. Home: 21 Almond Ln Davis CA 95616 Office: Dept Criminal Justice Adminstrn Calif State U 25800 Hillary St Hayward CA 94542

NEIWIRTH, RONALD GEORGE, lawyer; b. Newark, Mar. 8, 1948; s. Leo and Miriam (Gross) N.; m. Judith Ellen Cohen, Feb. 19, 1984. BA, St. Francis Coll., 1970; JD, U. Fla., 1972. Bar: Fla., 1972, N.J., 1973, U.S. Dist. Ct. (so. and mid. dists.) Fla., U.S. Ct. Appeals (5th and 11th cirs.), U.S. Dist. Ct. N.J. Ptnr. Neiwirth and Neiwirth, Newark, 1972-78, Miami, Fla., 1978—; sole practice Miami, 1984-86; ptnr. Neiwirth & Nierenberg, Miami, 1986—. Bd. dirs. Consumer Credit Counseling Service, Miami, 1986—; trustee So. Fla. Theatre Co. Mem. ABA, So. Fla. Bankruptcy Bar Assn., Comml. Law League. Lodge: Masons. Bankruptcy, Contracts commercial, General corporate. Home: 20608 NE 7th Ct North Miami Beach FL 33179 Office: 825 S Bayshore Dr Suite 246 Miami FL 33131

NEKRITZ, BARRY B., lawyer; b. Chgo., Dec. 16, 1938; s. Irving M. and Mildred (Bernberg) N.; m. Susan Moss, Mar. 31, 1963; children—Edward, Michael, Felicia. B.A., U. Ill., 1959, LL.B., 1962. Bar: Ill. 1962, U.S. Dist. Ct. (no. dist.) Ill. 1962, U.S. Ct. Appeals (7th cir.) 1963, Fla. 1969. Assoc., Friedman & Koven, 1962-65; assoc. Mitchell Edelson, Sr., Chgo., 1965-68; assoc. Bernstein, Golan & Yalowitz, Chgo., 1968-69; ptnr. Aaron, Schimberg, Hess, Rusnak, Deutsch & Gilbert and predecessor firm Aaron, Aaron Schimberg & Hess, Chgo., 1969-83; ptnr. Altheimer & Gray, Chgo.,

1983—. Trustee, Village of Northbrook, 1973-81; mem. Northbrook Plan Commn., 1972-73; bd. dirs. Northbrook Civic Found., 1981-86 , pres., 1984. Served to sgt. U.S. Army, 1962-68. Mem. ABA, Ill. Bar Assn., Fla. Bar Assn., Chgo. Bar Assn. Jewish. Club: Standard (Chgo.). Contbr. articles to law review, Chgo. Lawyers Court Handbook. General practice, Contracts commercial, General corporate. Office: Suite 2600 333 W Wacker Dr Chicago IL 60606

NELON, ROBERT DALE, lawyer; b. Shawnee, Okla., Aug. 8, 1946; s. Cecil Eugene and Neata Madelyn (Fox) N.; m. Freddie Anne Tipton, Aug. 2, 1975; children—Lindsay Anne, Gregory Tipton. B.A., Northwestern U., 1968; J.D., U. Okla., 1971. Bar: Okla. 1971, U.S. Dist. Ct. (we., no. and ea. dists.) Okla. 1971, U.S. Mil. Ct. Appeals 1972, U.S. Ct. Appeals (10th cir.) 1971. Law clk. Okla. Atty. Gen., Oklahoma City, 1966-70; mem. Andrews, Davis, Legg, Bixler, Milsten & Murrah, Oklahoma City, 1971—. Served to capt. USMCR 1972-74. Mem. ABA, Am. Judicature Soc., AIAA, Okla. Bar Assn. Democrat. Methodist. Libel, Antitrust, Federal civil litigation. Office: Andrews Davis Legg Bixler Milsten & Murrah 500 Main Plaza Oklahoma City OK 73102

NELSON, ALICE K., lawyer; b. Bklyn., May 7, 1943; d. Irving J. and Sonia (Bookman) Katz; m. Carnst E. Nelson, Sept. 1, 1963; children: Jeremy Howard, Seth Robert. BA in History, City Coll. N.Y., 1965; MSW, U. Ga., 1967; postgrad., Johns Hopkins U., 1968-69; JD, Stetson U., 1976. Bar: Fla. 1976, U.S. Dist. Ct. (mid. dist.) Fla. 1976, D.C. 1976, U.S. Ct. Appeals (5th, 11th and D.C. cirs.) 1981, U.S. Dist. Ct. (so. dist.) Fla. 1983, U.S. Supreme Ct. 1983. Instr. U. Md. Sch. of Social Work, Balt., 1970-71; dir. social work devel. disabilities law project U. Md. Sch. of Law, Balt., 1976-78; unit head pub. benefits unit Bay Area Legal Services, Inc., Tampa, Fla., 1978-79; cons. John F. Kennedy Inst., Balt., 1979-80; law clk. to presiding justice U.S. Ct. Appeals (5th cir.), Tampa, 1980; sole practice Tampa, 1980—; clin. intern Legal Aid Soc. of St. Petersburg, Fla., 1975. Author: The Legal Rights of Handicapped Persons: Cases, Materials and Text, 1979, The Legal Needs of the Mentally and Developmentally Disabled Citizens of Florida, 1982; exec. editor Stetson U. Law Rev., 1975. Mem. Chief Justices Com. on Pro Bono Awards; co-chairperson pub. welfare com. Md. Conf. of Social Welfare, 1969-70, bd. dirs. 1969-71. Mem. ABA, D.C. Bar Assn., Fla. Bar Assn. (chmn. disability law com. 1983-85, active continuing legal edn. 1986—), Hillsborough County Bar Assn. (chmn. availability of legal services com. 1984-85), Nat. Assn. Social Workers, Acad. Cert. Social Workers. Home: 727 S Edison Tampa FL 33606 Office: 1410 N 21st St Tampa FL 33605

NELSON, BERNARD EDWARD, lawyer; b. Miles City, Mont., May 9, 1950; s. Theodore M. and Lucille K. (Cain) N.; m. Jane Walker, Sept. 8, 1978; children: Iain, Colin. BA, Yale U., 1972; JD, Harvard U., 1975. Bar: N.Y. 1976. Assoc. White & Case, N.Y.C., 1975-84, ptnr., 1984—. Mem. Union Internatioale Des Avocats (U.S. rep. permanent tax commn.). Democrat. Avocations: antique map collecting, antiquarian books. Corporate taxation, General corporate. Office: White & Case 1155 Ave of the Americas New York NY 10036

NELSON, BRYAN EUGENE, lawyer; b. Salina, Kans., Sept. 21, 1946; s. Merle Theodore and Winona Jean (Parsons) N. Student Kans. State U., 1968-72; B.S. in Polit. Sci., U. Kans., 1973, J.D., 1976. Bar: Kans. 1976, U.S. Dist. Ct. Kans. 1976, U.S. Ct. Appeals (10th cir.) 1981, U.S. Supreme Ct. 1981. Cert. civil trial adv. Nat. Bd. Trial Advocacy. Assoc. Weeks, Thomas, Lysaught, Bingham & Mustain, Overland Park, Kans., 1976, Alder & Zemites, Overland Park, 1977; ptnr. Alder Nelson & McKenna, Overland Park, 1978—; lectr. seminars. Served with USAF, 1976-79. Mem. Def. Research Inst., ABA, Kans. Bar Assn., Wyandotte County Bar Assn., Johnson County Bar Assn., ACLU, Kans. Assn. Def. Counsel, Kansas City Claims Assn. Republican. Methodist. Federal civil litigation, Civil rights, State civil litigation. Office: 9300 W 110th St Suite 690 Overland Park KS 66210

NELSON, CAROL SUSAN, lawyer; b. Miles City, Mont., Feb. 6, 1947; d. Eddie James and Anne (Kluksdal) S.; m. J. Dennis Nelson, July 12, 1969; children: Ryan Christopher, Jeremy Daniel. A in Bus., Valley City State Coll., 1977; JD, U. N.D., 1980. Bar: N.D. 1980, U.S. Dist. Ct. N.D. 1981. Asst. state's atty. Barnes County, Valley City, N.D., 1981-85; assoc. Simonson Law Office, Valley City, 1981-83; ptnr. Simonson & Nelson Law Offices, Valley City, 1983-85; state's atty. Barnes County, 1986—; sole practice Nelson & Huseby, Valley City, 1986; ptnr. Hooper and Nelson, Valley City, 1986—. Bd. dirs. Open Door Inc., Valley City, 1981-85, pres. of bd., 1985—; bd. dirs. Small World Daycare Inc., Valley City, 1981—, Barnes County Srs., Valley City, 1986—. Recipient Law Womens Recognition award Law Womens Caucus U. N.D., 1980. Mem. State Bar Assn. N.D., States Attys. Assn., Barnes County Bar Assn. Lutheran. Avocations: travel, walking, tennis, reading, family. Criminal, Personal income taxation, Family and matrimonial. Office: 411 W Main St PO Box 209 Valley City ND 58072

NELSON, DAVID ALDRICH, federal judge; b. Watertown, N.Y., Aug. 14, 1932; s. Carlton Low and Irene Demetria (Aldrich) N.; m. Mary Dickson, Aug. 25, 1956; children: Frederick Dickson, Claudia Baxter, Caleb Edward. A.B., Hamilton Coll., 1954; postgrad., Peterhouse, Cambridge, Eng., 1954-55; LL.B., Harvard U., 1958. Bar: Ohio 1958, N.Y. 1982. Assoc. Squire, Sanders & Dempsey, Cleve., 1958-67, ptnr., 1967-69, 72-85; circuit judge U.S. Ct. Appeals for 6th Circuit, Cin., 1985—; gen. counsel U.S. Post Office Dept., Washington, 1969-71; sr. asst. postmaster gen., gen. counsel U.S. Postal Service, Washington, 1971. Served to 1st lt. USAF, 1959-62; served to maj. USAFR, 1962-69. Fulbright scholar, 1954-55; recipient Benjamin Franklin award U.S. Post Office Dept., 1969. Fellow Am. Coll. Trial Lawyers; mem. Cleve. Bar Assn., Ohio Bar Assn., ABA, Fed. Bar Assn., Cin. Bar Assn., Phi Beta Kappa. Republican. Congregationalist. Clubs: University (Cin.); Emerson Lit. Soc. (Clinton, N.Y.). Office: 414 US Post Office & Courthouse 5th and Walnut Sts Cincinnati OH 45202

NELSON, DAVID EDWARD, lawyer; b. Passaic, N.J., Oct. 26, 1930; s. David Charles and Ann Ellen (Pardoe) N.; m. Stuart McKenna, May 28, 1953; children: Douglas, Kathryn, Ann; m. Elizabeth A. Carlston, Dec. 28, 1974; children: Lynn, Kathleen. A.B., UCLA; LL.B., U. Calif.-Berkeley; Diploma in Comparative Legal Studies, U. Cambridge, Eng., 1960. Bar: Calif. Assoc. Morrison & Foerster, San Francisco, 1960-65, ptnr., 1965—. Bd. dirs. Berkeley Bd. Edn., 1967-69; chmn. bd. Head-Royce Sch., Oakland, Calif., 1974-79. Served to lt. (j.g.) U.S. Navy, 1952-56. Mem. San Francisco Bar Assn. (pres. Barrister Club), ABA (chmn.-elect corp. banking and bus. law sect.), Calif. Bar Assn. (com. bar examiners 1973-77, chmn. 1976-77), Southwestern Legal Found. Clubs: Bankers (San Francisco), World Trade (San Francisco). Banking, General corporate, Private international. Office: Morrison & Foerster 345 California St San Francisco CA 94104

NELSON, DAVID S., federal judge; b. Boston, Mass., Dec. 2, 1933; s. Maston A. and Enid M.N. B.S., Boston Coll., 1957, J.D., 1960. Assoc. Crane, Inker & Oteri, 1960-73; U.S. commr. 1968-69; asst. atty. gen. State of Mass., 1971-73; justice Superior Ct. Mass., Boston, 1973-79; judge U.S. Dist. Ct. Mass., Boston, 1979—. Fellow Am. Bar Found.; mem. Am. Law Inst. Judicial administration. Office: US Dist Ct 1525 Post Office and Courthouse Boston MA 02109 *

NELSON, DAVID WAYNE, lawyer; b. Williston, N.D., Apr. 18, 1951; s. Ralph L. and Olga M. (Anderson) N.; m. Sherri E. Thorness, Aug. 11, 1973; children: Matthew, Steve. AA, U. N.D., Williston, 1971; BA, U. N.D., 1973; postgrad., Wartburg Theol. Sem., 1974; JD, U. N.D., 1981. Bar: N.D. 1981, U.S. Dist. Ct. N.D. 1983. Sole practice Williston, 1981—; spl. asst. atty. gen., N.D., 1984—; contract atty. Legal Aid N.D., Bismark, 1984—; judge N.D. Mcpl. Ct., Grenora, 1985—, Williston, 1986—. Leader Boy Scouts Am., Williston, 1984—; bd. dirs. Family Crisis Shelter, Williston, 1983—, pres., 1986—. Mem. ABA, N.D. Bar Assn. Lodges: Lions, Elks. Avocations: shooting pool, reading, restoring Packards (cars). General practice. Home: 705 4th Ave E Williston ND 58801 Office: 417 1st Ave E Williston ND 58801

NELSON, DOROTHY WRIGHT (MRS. JAMES F. NELSON), judge; b. San Pedro, Calif., Sept. 30, 1928; d. Harry Earl and Lorna Amy Wright; m. James Frank Nelson, Dec. 27, 1950; children: Franklin Wright, Lorna Jean. B.A., UCLA, 1950, J.D., 1953; LL.M., U. So. Calif., 1956. Bar: Calif. 1954. Research assoc. fellow U. So. Calif., 1953-56; instr. 1957, asst. prof., 1958-61, assoc. prof., 1961-67, prof., 1967, assoc. dean., 1965-67, dean., 1967-80; judge U.S. Ct. Appeals for 9th Circuit, 1980—; cons. Project STAR, Law Enforcement Assistance Adminstrn. Author: Judicial Administration and The Administration of Justice, 1973; Contbr. articles to profl. jours. Co-chmn. Confronting Myths in Edn. for Pres. Nixon's White House Conf. on Children, Pres. Carter's Commn. for Pension Policy, 1974-80; bd. visitors U.S. Air Force Acad., 1978; bd. dirs. Council on Legal Edn. for Profl. Responsibility, 1971-80, Constnl. Right Found., Am. Nat. Inst. for Social Advancement; adv. bd. Nat. Center for State Cts., 1971-73. Named Law Alumnus of Yr. UCLA, 1967; recipient Profl. Achievement award, 1969; named Times Woman of Yr., 1968; recipient U. Judaism Humanitarian award, 1973; AWARE Internat. award, 1970; Ernestine Stalhut Outstanding Woman Lawyer award, 1972; Coro award for edn., 1978. Fellow Am. Bar Found., Davenport Coll., Yale U.; mem. Bar Calif. (bd. dirs. continuing edn. bar commn. 1967-74), Am. Judicature Soc. (dir.), Assn. Am. Law Schs. (chmn. com. edn. in jud. adminstrn.), Am. Bar Assn. (sect. on jud. adminstrn., chmn. com. on edn. in jud. adminstrn. 1973—), Phi Beta Kappa, Order of Coif (nat. v.p. 1974-76), Jud. Conf. U.S. (com. to consider standards for admission to practice in fed. cts. 1976-79). Judicial administration. Office: US Court of Appeals 312 N Spring St Los Angeles CA 90012

NELSON, DOUGLAS THOMAS, lawyer, educator; b. New Brunswick, N.J., Mar. 9, 1946; s. Lloyd Alfred and Vivian Cathryn (Eden) N. AB summa cum laude, Rutgers U., 1968; MA, Columbia U., 1969, PhD, 1976, JD, 1980. Bar: N.J. 1980, N.Y. 1981. Asst. prof. history N.C. State U., Raleigh, 1974-77; project officer NEH, Washington, 1977; asst. to chmn. FTC, Washington, 1978; assoc. Coudert Bros., N.Y.C., 1980-82, Paul, Weiss, Rifkind, Wharton & Garrison, N.Y.C., 1982-85; asst. counsel acquistions and divestitures Union Carbide Corp., Danbury, Conn., 1985—; lectr. law New Sch. for Social Research, N.Y.C., 1983-84. Woodrow Wilson Dissertation fellow Columbia U., 1971, Stone scholar Columbia U. Law Sch., 1979. ABA, Assn. of the Bar of the City of N.Y., Westfacca, Phi Beta Kappa. Avocations: travel, singing, jogging, whitewater rafting. General corporate, Securities, Private international. Office: Union Carbide Corp Old Ridgebury Rd Danbury CT 06817

NELSON, GEOFFREY WILLIAM, lawyer; b. Colorado Springs., Colo., Jan. 7, 1932; s. William Franklin Cram and Margaret (Price) N.; m. Joan D. Eberle, May 1, 1965; m. 2d, Megan E. Hughes, May 7, 1976; children—Elizabeth P., Geoffrey W., Jr. B.A., Yale U., 1953, LL.B., 1959. Bar: Conn. 1960, U.S. Dist. Ct. Conn. 1961, U.S. Ct. Appeals (2d cir.) 1966. Assoc. Murtha, Cullina, Richter and Pinney and predecessor Shepherd Murtha & Merritt, Hartford Conn., 1959-64, ptnr. 1964—; dir. Erickson Metals Corp. Financing for Sci. and Industry, Inc., Stewart Therapy, Inc., Denominator Co., Inc. Past sec., treas., Hartford Urban Research Commn.; bd. dirs. Hartford Ballet Co., 1970-81, pres. bd. trustees, 1971-75; pres. Mt. Sinai Hosp. Assn., 1978-79; incorporator Mt. Sinai Hosp., St. Francis Hosp. and Med. Ctr. Mem. ABA, Conn. Bar Assn. (chmn. exec. com. sect. on corps. and other bus. orgns. 1982-84), Hartford County Bar Assn. Chi Psi, Phi Delta Phi. Republican. Clubs: Hartford, Univ. General corporate. Home: 8 Willow Ln West Hartford CT 06107 Office: Murtha Cullina Richter Pinney PO Box 3197 Hartford CT 06103

NELSON, JACK ODELL, JR., lawyer; b. Dallas, Oct. 8, 1947; s. Jack Odell and Rose Mary (Trepoy) N. B.B.A., Tex. Tech U., 1969; J.D., U. Tex., 1972. Bar: Tex. 1972, U.S. Dist. Ct. (no. dist.) Tex. 1973, U.S. Ct. Appeals (5th cir.) 1974, U.S. Supreme Ct. 1981. Assoc. firm Garner, Boulter, Jesko & Purdom and successor firms, Lubbock, Tex., 1972-76, 77-80, firm Gardere, Porter & DeHay, Dallas, 1976-77; ptnr. firm Nelson & Nelson, Lubbock, 1981—. Mem. Tex. Bar Assn. (dist. 16 grievance com.), Lubbock County Bar Assn., Tex. Assn. Def. Counsel, Internat. Assn. Def. Counsel, Sigma Chi, Phi Delta Phi. Mem. Disciples of Christ Ch. Club: Lubbock. Lodge: Rotary. State civil litigation, Banking, Insurance. Office: Nelson & Nelson 1220 Republic Bank Bldg 916 Main St Lubbock TX 79401

NELSON, JANE WANDEL, lawyer; b. Aberdeen, Wash., July 26, 1941; d. George Grosser and Kathryn Hettie (Callow) Wandel; 1 child, Sierra Kathryn. B.A. magna cum laude, U. Wash., 1959-63; M.A., Stanford U., 1965; J.D., U. Calif.-Berkeley, 1977. Bar: Calif. 1978, Nev. 1978, Wash. 1982. Law clk. presiding justice Supreme Ct. of Nev., 1977-79, spl. legal cons., 1981-82, supervising staff atty., 1979-81; dep. atty. gen. (civil) Office of Atty. Gen., Carson City, Nev., 1982; law clerk coordinator, spl. legal cons. Supreme Ct. of Nev., 1982, 84; acad. asst. to dean Nat. Jud. Coll., 1985, acad. co-dir., 1985-86, dir. degree program, spl. projects, 1986—; adj. faculty Old Coll. Sch. Law, 1982, 84; chmn., adv. com. Nev. Supreme Ct. Task Force on Gender Bias in the Courts. Woodrow Wilson teaching fellow, 1966-67; named Woman of the Yr. Reno Bus. and Profl. Women, 1986. Mem. ABA, Nev. Bar Assn., Washoe County Bar Assn., Calif. Bar Assn., Am. Judicature Soc., No. Nev. Women Lawyers, Wash. State Bar Assn., Phi Beta Kappa. Democrat. Episcopalian. Administrative and regulatory, State civil litigation, Labor. Home: 3270 Cashill Blvd Reno NV 89509 Office: U Nev Nat Jud Coll Reno NV 89557

NELSON, JAY SCOTT, lawyer; b. Chgo., Sept. 5, 1941; s. J.O. and Genevieve (Monson) N.; m. Gertrude Sturhahn, Aug. 29, 1970; children: Erik, Thea. BA, Parsons Coll., 1964; MBA, U. Iowa, 1967; JD, John Marshall Law Sch., 1975. Bar: Ill. 1975, U.S. Dist. Ct. (no. dist.) Ill. 1975, U.S. Ct. Appeals (7th cir.) 1978, U.S. Dist. Ct. (no. dist. trial) Ill. 1985. Auditor E.I. duPont Co., Wilmington, Del., 1969-71; assoc. Schaffenegger, Watson & Peterson Ltd., Chgo., 1975—. Served to sgt. U.S. Army, 1968-69. Mem. ABA, Ill. State Bar Assn., Chgo. Bar Assn., Trial Lawyers Club Chgo. Presbyterian. Federal civil litigation, State civil litigation, Insurance.

NELSON, JONI LYSETT, lawyer; b. Highland Park, Mich., June 3, 1938; d. Daniel Walton Lysett and Evelyn Sylvia (Ladd) Sorenson; children: A. Ladd, Derek A. BA cum laude, Mich. State U., 1959; JD, Harvard U., 1962. Bar: N.Y. 1963, U.S. Dist. Ct. (so. dist.) N.Y. 1963. Assoc. Shearman & Sterling, N.Y.C., 1962-65; atty. various orgns., N.Y.C., Washington, London and Athens, Greece, 1965-76; ptnr. Rogers & Wells, N.Y.C., 1977-82, 85—; mng. ptnr. Rogers & Wells, London, 1982-85; lectr. on fin. law. Editor: Current Issues in International Ship Finance, 1984; contbr. articles to profl. jours. Founder City Women's Network, London, 1978; chmn., gen. counsel Reps. Abroad, London and Washington, 1978-85; legal advisor Rep. Nat. Com., Washington, 1984—. Fellow Inst. of Dirs.; mem. ABA, Assn. of Bar of City of N.Y., Internat. Bar Assn. (chmn. electronic banking com.), World Trade Inst. (adv. bd. 1986—). Clubs: Harvard, Sky (N.Y.C.); University Womens (London). Avocation: running, sailing, skiing, tennis, quilting. Banking, Contracts commercial, Private international. Office: Rogers & Wells Pan Am Bldg 200 Park Ave New York NY 10166

NELSON, LEONARD JOHN, III, law educator; b. Spokane, Wash., July 31, 1949; s. Leonard John, Jr. and Lois Marian (McCuaig) N.; m. Janice Helen Linebarger, Aug. 15, 1970; children—Leonard John IV, Mary Beth, Monica Teresa. Student, Whitman Coll., 1967-68; B.A. magna cum laude, U. Wash., 1970; J.D. cum laude, Gonzaga U., 1974; LL.M., Yale U., 1984. Bar: Wash. 1974, Okla. 1979. Asst. prof. Gonzaga U. Law Sch., 1974; law clk. Wash. Supreme Ct., Olympia, 1975-76; ct. clk. Wash. Ct. Appeals, Spokane, 1976-78; from asst. to assoc. prof. O.W. Coburn Sch. Law, Tulsa, 1979-83; assoc. prof. Cumberland Sch. Law, Birmingham, Ala., 1984-87; prof., 1987—. Contbg. editor: The Death Decision, 1984; contbr. articles to law revs. Mem. instl. rev. bd. Samford U., 1986-87. Named Outstanding Young Man of Am., U.S. Jaycees, 1982; recipient Nat. Chmn.'s award Nat. Coll. Republican League, 1980. Mem. Am. Soc. Law and Medicine, Nat. Health Lawyers Assn., Phi Beta Kappa. Roman Catholic. Jurisprudence, Legal education. Home: 3140 Sunny Meadows Ln Birmingham AL 35243 Office: Cumberland Sch of Law 800 Lakeshore Dr Birmingham AL 35229

NELSON, LUELLA ELINE, lawyer; b. Portland, Oreg., Apr. 11, 1952; d. Alben Wayne and Geneva Esther (Larsen) N. BS in Econs. and Polit. Sci., Macalester Coll., 1973; JD, Harvard U., 1976. Bar: Oreg. 1976, Calif. 1984. Counsel to bd. mem. NLRB, Washington, 1976-80, sr. counsel to bd. mem., 1980-81; field atty. NLRB, Oakland, Calif., 1981-86; pvt. practice arbitrator Oakland, 1986—. Mem. Thomas Circle Singers, Washington, 1979-81, San Francisco Civic Chorale, 1982—. Mem. ABA, San Francisco Bar Assn., Oreg. Bar Assn., Calif. Bar Assn., Indsl. Relations Research Assn., Soc. Profls. in Dispute Resolution. Democrat. Methodist. Avocations: singing, hiking, swimming, cross-country skiing, reading. Labor. Home and Office: 64 Linda Ave Oakland CA 94611

NELSON, MARK DOUGLAS, lawyer; b. Rochester, Minn., Feb. 14, 1957; s. Douglas Wayne and Barbara Mary (Brown) N.; m. Jeanne Marie Clark, June 2, 1984. BA, U. Ill., 1979; postgrad. in law, Wake Forest U., 1979-80; JD, U. Ill., 1982. Bar: Ill. 1982, U.S. Dist. Ct. (no. dist.) Ill. 1982. Assoc. Wood, Lucksinger & Epstein, Chgo., 1982—; appointed mem. task force on AIDS Ill. Hosp. Assn., Naperville, 1986. Mem. ABA, Ill. Bar Assn. (labor law sect. council 1986—, task force on AIDS 1986—). Roman Catholic. Labor. Office: Wood Lucksinger & Epstein 333 W Wacker Dr #400 Chicago IL 60606

NELSON, MERRILL FRANCOM, lawyer; b. Grantsville, Utah, July 16, 1955; s. Russell A. and Ruth (Francom) N.; m. Karen Olpin, June 20, 1980; children: Aaron Merrill, Evan Olpin, Benjamin Marc. BS, Brigham Young U., 1979, JD cum laude, 1982. Bar: Utah 1982, U.S. Dist. Ct. Utah 1982, U.S. Ct. Appeals (10th cir.) 1984. Law clk. to presiding justice Utah Supreme Ct., Salt Lake City, 1982-83; assoc. Kirton, McConkie & Bushnell, Salt Lake City, 1983—; lectr. appellate practice U. Utah, Salt Lake City, 1985—; moot ct. judge Brigham Young U., 1985; judge pro tem 5th Cir. Ct., Salt Lake City, 1986—. Contbg. author: Guide to Utah Supreme Court, Appellate Practice Manual, 1986; editor Brigham Young U. Law Rev., 1981-82. Chmn. Rep. Voting Dist., Salt Lake City, 1984—; county del. Salt Lake County Conv., 1984; admnstrv. asst. Gov.'s Commn. on Bicentennial U.S. Constitution, Salt Lake City, 1986-87. Mem. ABA, Utah Bar Assn. (litigation, edn. law sects.), Salt Lake County Bar Assn. Mormon. Avocations: Am. hist., politics, baseball, racquetball, camping. Federal civil litigation, State civil litigation, Education, hospital and church law. Office: Kirton McConkie & Bushnell 330 S 300 E Salt Lake City UT 84111

NELSON, NORMAN ROY, lawyer; b. Quincy, Ill., July 13, 1944; s. Richard E. and Florine E. (Sharrow) N.; m. Sara Jones, Dec. 9, 1945; children—Matthew Edward, Clark Richard. A.B., U. Ill., 1966; J.D., Columbia U., 1969. Bar: N.Y. 1969, U.S. Dist. Ct. (so. and ea. dists.) N.Y. 1971, U.S. Ct. Appeals (2d cir.) 1971, U.S. Ct. Appeals (6th cir.) 1977, U.S. Dist. Ct. (ea. dist.) Ky. 1979, U.S. Supreme Ct. 1981. Law clk. to judge U.S. Ct. Appeals (2d cir.), N.Y.C., 1969-70; assoc. Milbank, Tweed, Hadley & McCloy, N.Y.C., 1970-78, ptnr., 1979—. Mem. ABA, N.Y. State Bar Assn., Assn. Bar City of N.Y., Fed. Bar Council, Am. Soc. Internat. Law. Episcopalian. Club: Down Town of N.Y.C. Federal civil litigation, State civil litigation. Office: Milbank Tweed Hadley & McCloy 1 Chase Manhattan Plaza New York NY 10005

NELSON, PAUL DOUGLAS, lawyer; b. Silverton, Oreg., Dec. 22, 1948; s. Robert Thorsen and Elene Lillie (Douglas) N.; m. Mary Linda Hilligoss, Feb. 28, 1981; children: Christopher R., Matthew D., Patrick D. BA cum laude, Lewis and Clark Coll., 1971; JD, U. Oreg., 1974. Bar: Calif. 1974, Oreg. 1975, U.S. Dist. Ct. (no., ea. and cen. dists.) 1975. Law clk. U.S. Atty.'s office U.S. Dist. Ct. Oreg., Portland, 1973; assoc. Hoge, Fenton, Jones & Appel, San Jose, 1974-75; ptnr. Hancock, Rothert & Bunshoft, San Francisco and London, 1975—. Nat. Presbyn. scholar Lewis and Clark Coll., Portland, 1967, Oreg. Trial Lawyers scholar U. Oreg., 1973. Mem. ABA, San Francisco Bar Assn., San Francisco Lawyers Club. Republican. Presbyterian. Avocations: skiing, sailing. Insurance, Private international, Sports injury. Office: Hancock Rothert & Bunshoft 4 Embarcadero Ctr San Francisco CA 94111

NELSON, PEGGY ANN, lawyer; b. Duluth, Minn., Sept. 14, 1954; d. Marvin Henning and Eileen Marie (Pettit) N. BA, Brown U., 1977; JD, NYU, 1981. Bar: Mass. 1981, U.S. Dist. Ct. Mass. 1981, Minn. 1983, U.S. Dist. Ct. Minn. 1983, U.S. Ct. Internat. Trade 1983. Atty. Peabody & Brown, Boston, 1981-83, Winthrop & Weinstine, 1983—. Del. Dem. Farmer Labor Party Dist. Caucus, 1984; treas., bd. dirs. Great Midwestern Bookshow, 1985-86. Mem. ABA (litigation sect.), Minn. State Bar Assn., Ramsey County Bar Assn. Club: St. Paul Athletic. Federal civil litigation, State civil litigation. Office: Winthrop & Weinstine 444 Cedar 1800 Conwed Tower Saint Paul MN 55101

NELSON, RICHARD S., lawyer; b. Pitts., June 22, 1931; s. Ben and Minna (Blumer) N.; m. Inez Joan Krouse, Oct. 17, 1954; children—David, Gary, Linda, Wendy. A.B., U. Mich., Ann Arbor, 1953, J.D., U. Pitts., 1956. Bar: Pa., 1956, Ky., 1961, U.S. Supreme Ct., 1971. Spl. agt. FBI, Louisville and Covington, Ky., 1958-61; ptnr. Bridges & Nelson, Covington, 1964-66; sole practice, Covington, 1966-69, 72-83; sr. ptnr. Davies, Nelson and Taliaferro, Covington 1969-72; ptnr. Nelson and McClure, 1984-86; sole practice, Covington, 1986—; trial commnr. Kenton County Ct. and judge pro-tem, 1964-69; asst. atty. Kenton County, 1978-82; adj. prof. law Chase Coll. Law, 1973-83; city atty., Ft. Mitchell, Ky., 1964-80. Fellow Am. Coll. Trial Lawyers; mem. Ky. Bar Assn. (bd. govs. 1976-81, v.p. 1982), Kenton County Bar Assn. (pres. 1971-72). Served with U.S. Army, 1956-58. Mem. Am. Arbitration Assn. State civil litigation, Federal civil litigation, General practice. Home: 201 Riverside Dr #304 Covington KY 41011 Office: 11 W 6th St Covington KY 41011

NELSON, ROBERT BRUCE, lawyer; b. Chgo., Feb. 21, 1935; s. Albert G. and Julia (Stevens) N.; m. Mary Louise Sauer, May 4, 1957 (div. Apr. 1986); children: Kimberley, Shane Nelson Frederick; m. Jeanne Bambas Denton, June 21, 1986. BA in Econs., U. Mich., 1957, JD, 1960. Bar: Ohio 1961, Fla. 1976. Assoc. Jones, Day, Reavis & Pogue, Cleve., 1960-68, ptnr., 1968—. Spl. counsel to atty. gen. Ohio for Litigation regarding Battelle Meml. Inst., Columbus, 1973-75; v.p. Children's Aid Soc., Cleve., 1977-79, pres., 1979-81, trustee, 1970—; chmn. Inner City Renewal Soc., Cleve., 1971-73, trustee, 1965—. Mem. ABA, Ohio Bar Assn., Cleve. Bar Assn., Am. Coll. Probate Counsel, Order of Coif, Phi Beta Kappa, Phi Kappa Phi, Phi Eta Sigma. Republican. Congregationalist. Avocation: jogging. Estate planning, Probate, Estate taxation. Home: 11421 Fitzwater Rd Brecksville OH 44141 Office: Jones Day Reavis & Pogue 901 Lakeside Ave Cleveland OH 44114

NELSON, ROBERT CHARLES, lawyer; b. Cedar Rapids, Iowa, Nov. 13, 1920; s. Charles A. and Lottie A. (Youngman) N.; m. Bernice M. Svoboda, Sept. 19, 1947; 1 child David S. BA, U. Iowa, 1949, JD, 1952. Bar: Iowa 1952, U.S. Dist Ct. (no. dist.) Iowa 1952, U.S. Ct. Appeals (8th cir.) 1974. Ptnr. Nelson & Nelson, Cedar Rapids, 1952—. Active various coms. City of Cedar Rapids. Served to capt. USAF, 1942-46; served with USAR, 1946-57. Mem. Iowa State Bar Assn. Episcopalian. Lodge: Shriners. Avocation: traveling. Personal injury, Probate, Condemnation. Home: 801 30th St NE Cedar Rapids IA 52402 Office: Nelson & Nelson 215 3d Ave SW Cedar Rapids IA 52404

NELSON, ROBERT LOUIS, lawyer; b. Dover, N.H., Aug. 10, 1931; S. Albert Louis and Alice (Rogers) N.; m. Rita Jean Hutchins, June 11, 1955; children: Karen, Robin Andrea. B.A., Bates Coll., Lewiston, Maine, 1956; LL.B., Georgetown U., 1959. Bar: D.C. 1960. With U.S. Commn. Civil Rights, 1958-63, AID, 1963-66; program sec. U.S. Mission to Brazil, 1965-66; exec. dir. Lawyers Com. Civil Rights Under Law, 1966-70; dep. campaign mgr. Muskie for Pres., 1970-72; v.p. Perpetual Corp., Houston, 1972-74; sr. v.p., gen. counsel Washington Star, 1974-76; pres. broadcast div. Washington Star Communications, Inc., 1976-77; asst. sec. of army U.S. Dept. Def., 1977-79; spl. advisor to chief N.G. Bur., Dept. Def., 1980-85; pres., dir. Mid-Md. Communications Corp., 1981-85; partner Verner, Liipfert, Bernhard, McPherson and Hand,, 1979—. Vice chmn. D.C. Redevel. Land Agy., 1976-77; bd. dirs. Community Found. Greater Washington, 1977-86 ; bd. dirs. Friends of Nat. Zoo, 1975—, pres., 1982-84; bd. dirs. Downtown Progress, 1976-77, Fed. City Council, 1976-77, 83—, Pennsylvania Ave. Devel. Corp., 1977-85. Served with AUS, 1953-54. Mem. ABA, D.C. bar assns. Democrat. Episcopalian. Club: University (Washington). General corporate, Law firm management. Home: 3819 Ingomar St NW Washington DC 20015 Office: 1660 L St NW Washington DC 20036

NELSON, ROGER MILTON, insurance company executive, lawyer; b. Detroit, Aug. 27, 1924; s. Milton and and Christine Florence (Rogers) N.; m. Nancy Marilyn Agy, Oct. 22, 1948; children—Gregory A., Halley A. Nelson McKinney. BS., Ohio U., 1948; J.D., Case-Western Res. U. Bar: Ohio bar 1950. With Shelby Mut. Ins. Co., Ohio, 1950-86; asst. gen. counsel Shelby Mut. Ins. Co., 1965-70, v.p., gen. counsel, 1970-74, sr. v.p., gen. counsel, 1974-81, exec. v.p., sec., gen. counsel, 1981-86, ret., 1986—, also dir. Trustee Shelby Meml. Hosp., Richland Alt. Plan, Mansfield, Ohio. Served with USAAF, 1943-45. Decorated D.F.C., Air medal with 5 oak leaf clusters. Mem. Am. Bar Assn., Ohio Bar Assn., Richland County Bar Assn., Internat. Assn. Ins. Counsel, Def. Research Inst., Am. Soc. Law and Medicine, Ohio Assn. Civil Trial Attys. (pres. 1978-79, trustee 1972-86), Alliance Am. Insurers, Am. Legion. Republican. Clubs: Rotary (Shelby), Masons (Shelby). General corporate, Insurance, Personal injury. Home: Route 2 Myers Rd Shelby OH 44875 Office: 175 Mansfield Ave Shelby OH 44875

NELSON, STEPHEN DALE, lawyer, legal consultant; b. Lawrence, Kans., Jan. 11, 1948; s. Homer Dale and Goldie Lee (Houghton) N.; m. Dianna Sue Johnson, Apr. 28, 1973; 1 child, Christopher; 1 stepchild, Donna Bins. BS in Fgn. Service, Georgetown U., 1970; JD, U. Kans. Law Sch., 1973. Bar: Kans. 1974, U.S. Dist. Ct. Kans. 1974. Sr. legis. asst. to Congressman Larry Winn, Jr. Washington, 1973-77; minority staff cons. House Fgn. Affairs Com., Washington, 1977—. v.p. Barcroft Terrace Citizens Assn., Fairfax County, Va., 1983-84, pres. 1984-85, bd. dirs. 1985-86. Served to capt. U.S. Army. Mem. ABA, Delta Phi Epsilon. Republican. Legislative. Home: 3904 Fairfax Pkwy Alexandria VA 22312 Office: US House of Reps Com on Fgn Affairs B-360 Rayburn HOBs Washington DC 20515

NELSON, STEVEN SIBLEY, lawyer; b. Huntington, W.Va., Aug. 7, 1943; s. Joseph C. Nelson and Betty (Sibley) Wagers; m. Ann Mecum, Jan. 25, 1964 (div.); children—Joseph B., S. Alexandra, Jessica N.; m. Sandra K. Baker, July 15, 1983. B.S., Marshall U., 1966; M.S. in Pub. Health, U. N.C., 1968; J.D., Ohio State U., 1975. Bar: Ohio 1975, U.S. Dist. Ct. (no. dist.) Ohio 1976, U.S. Dist. Ct. (so. dist.) Ohio 1979. Vol., Peace Corps, El Salvador, 1966-67; asst. dir. Regional Health Counsel Eastern Appalachia, Morganton, N.C., 1968-69; cons. Westinghouse Learning Corp., Bladensburg, Md., 1969; exec. dir. Planned Parenthood, Columbus, Ohio, 1970-72; ptnr. firm Mills, Nelson & Ramey, Mansfield, Ohio, 1975-78; assoc. firm Bradley & Ferris Co., L.P.A., Columbus, 1978-80; sole practice, Columbus, 1980-81; assoc., then ptnr. firm Dagger, Johnston, Ogilvie, Charles & Hampson, Lancaster, Ohio, 1981. Contbr. chpt. to Personal Injury Litigation in Ohio revised edit., 1984; contbr. articles to profl. jours. Mem. Welfare Adv. Com., Lancaster, 1982—; active youth and youth sports orgns., environ. orgns. and civic orgns. Named Boss of Yr., Fairfield County Legal Secs. Assn., 1984. Founding fellow Columbus Bar Found.; mem. ABA (litigation sect., family law sect.), Ohio State Bar Assn. (negligence law com. 1982—), Fairfield County Bar Assn., Columbus Bar Assn. (coordinator, speaker continuing legal edn. programs, co-chmn. trial advocacy inst. 1981, trial advocacy com. 1984-86, mem. continuing legal edn. com. 1978-82), Fairfield County Trial Lawyers Assn., Franklin County Trial Lawyers Assn., Assn. Trial Lawyers Am., Ohio Acad. Trial Lawyers, Phi Delta Phi. Republican. Methodist. State civil litigation, Federal civil litigation, Personal injury. Office: Dagger Johnston Ogilvie Charles & Hampson PO Box 1270 Lancaster OH 43130

NELSON, SUSAN RICHARD, lawyer; b. Buffalo, Oct. 26, 1952; d. Norman Bernard and Gloria (Hirsch) Richard; m. Thomas Franklin Nelson, Oct. 16, 1983; 1 child, Robert Edward. BA, Oberlin Coll., 1974; JD, U. Pitts., 1978. Bar: Pa. 1978, U.S. Dist. Ct. (we. dist.) Pa. 1978, Conn. 1981, U.S. Dist. Ct. Conn. 1981, Minn. 1984, U.S. Dist. Ct. Minn. 1985, U.S. Ct. Appeals (8th cir.) 1985, U.S. Supreme Ct. 1985. Assoc. Reed Smith Shaw & McClay, Pitts., 1978-80, Tyler, Cooper & Alcorn, New Haven, 1980-83, Robins, Zelle, Larson & Kaplan, Mpls., 1984—; pro bono juvenile representation, Pitts., 1978-80. Mem. ABA, Assn. Trial Lawyers Am., Minn. Bar Assn., Minn. Trial Lawyers Assn. Avocations: tennis, gourmet cooking, music. Federal civil litigation, State civil litigation, Personal injury. Office: Robins Zelle Larson & Kaplan 1800 Internat Ctr 900 2d Ave S Minneapolis MN 55402

NELSON, WARREN OWEN, lawyer; b. Roslyn, N.Y., May 8, 1955; s. Orville E. and Mary Ellen (Umbreit) N. BA, SUNY, Albany, 1977; JD, Rutgers U., 1980; student, NYU, 1981-83. Bar: N.J. 1980, U.S. Dist. Ct. N.J. 1980, U.S. Ct. Appeals (3d cir.) 1983, U.S. Tax Ct. 1983. Assoc. Hannoch Weisman, Newark, 1980-83, Skaddan, Arps, Slate, Meagher & Flom, N.Y.C., 1983-84; sr. exec. atty. Merck & Co., Inc., Rahway, N.J., 1984—. Editor, bus. mgr. Rutgers U. Law Rev., 1979-80. Coordinator, rep. United Way, Newark, 1982. Mem. N.J. Bar Assn. (employee benefits com.), Assn. of Bar of City of N.Y. (employee benefits com.). Pension, profit-sharing, and employee benefits, Executive compensation. Home: 417 Morris Ave #35 Summit NY 07901 Office: Merck and Co Inc R60-31 PO Box 2000 Rahway NJ 07065

NELSON, WILLIAM EUGENE, lawyer; b. Roland, Iowa, Sept. 23, 1927; s. Sam J. and Katherine A. (Coffey) N.; m. Sherlee M. Stanford, July 11, 1959; children—Anne, Kristin, William. B.A., U. Iowa, 1950; J.D., Drake U., 1957. Bar: Iowa 1957, D.C. 1965, Md. 1976. Trial atty. civil div. U.S. Dept. Justice, 1957-65, asst. chief tort sect., 1966-70, chief r.r. reorgn. unit 1970-71; gen. counsel Cost of Living Council Phase I, 1971, chief econ. stblzn. sect., 1971-74; ptnr. Qualley and Nelson, Washington, 1974-75, Nelson and Nelson, Washington, 1975—; dir. Robert Pierce Films, Inc., Washington, The Communicators, Inc., Rockville, Md. Served with USN, 1945-46. Recipient Atty. Gen.'s Disting. Service award, 1972. Mem. Am. Bar Assn., Assn. Trial Lawyers Am., Fed. Bar Assn., Md. Bar Assn., D.C. Bar, Order of Coif, Omicron Delta Kappa. Club: Edgemoor (Bethesda, Md.). Assoc. editor Drake Law Rev., 1955-57. Personal injury, Federal civil litigation, State civil litigation. Home: 4422 Ridge St Chevy Chase MD 20815 Office: Nelson & Nelson 1815 H St NW Washington DC 20006

NEMETH, CHARLES PAUL, lawyer, consultant; b. Pitts., July 30, 1951; s. Stephen J. and Rosemary M. (Mille) N.; m. Jean Marie Murray, May 14, 1981; children: Eleanor, Stephen, Ann Marie. BA, U. Del., 1972; JD, U. Balt.; MS, Niagara U., 1982; LLM, George Washington U., 1987. Bar: Pa. 1980. Prof. of criminal justice Niagara U., 1977-80; prof. law,justice U. Balt., 1979-80, Glassboro (N.J.) State Coll., 1980—; sole practice, Chadds Ford, Pa., 1980-86; writer, educator Nat. Ctr. for Continuing Edn., Chadds Ford, 1985—; mem. grad. faculty St. Joseph's U., 1985—. Author: Directory of Criminal Justice Education, 1986. Mem. ABA, Northeastern Assn. of Criminal Justice (bd. dirs. 1985—), Acad. Criminal Justices and Scis., Assn. Trial Lawyers Am., Pa. Bar Assn. Roman Catholic. Criminal, Corporate taxation. Home: 1100 Shadeland Ave Drexel Hill PA 19026 Office: 954 E Baltimore Pike Kennett Square PA 19348

NEMETZ, MARGARET NOTTINGHAM, lawyer; b. Waukegan, Ill., Apr. 7, 1942; d. Raymond James and Mary (Gantar) Nottingham; m. Robert Anthony Nemetz, Sept. 12, 1964. BA, U. Md., 1975; JD, Cath. U. Am., 1978. Bar: Md. 1978, U.S. Dist. Ct. Md. 1980, U.S. Ct. Appeals (4th cir.) 1985. Asst. state's atty. misdemeanors div. Prince George County, Upper Marlboro, Md., 1978-79, asst. state's atty. juvenile crime div., 1979-80, asst. state's atty. felony trials div., 1980-84, chief criminal trials div., 1984—. Mem. Child Abuse Team Prince George's County, 1983-84, atty. grievence commn., Annapolis, Md., 1983—, Task Force on Domestic Violence, Upper Marlboro, 1984-85, Women's Polit. Caucus, South Prince George's County, Chesapeake Area Group Women Historians, College Park, Md. Mem. ABA, Md. Bar Assn., Prince George's County Bar Assn. (bd. dirs. 1982—), Nat. Dist. Attys. Assn., Md. State's Attys. Assn., Women's Lawyers' Caucus (sec. 1980-81). Criminal, Juvenile, Civil rights. Office: Price George's County States Atty Court House Room 410 Upper Marlboro MD 20772

NEMIR, DONALD PHILIP, lawyer; b. Oakland, Calif., Oct. 31, 1931; s. Philip F. and Mary (Shavor) N.; A.B., U. Calif. at Berkeley, 1957, J.D., 1960. Admitted to Calif. bar, 1961; sole practice San Francisco, 1961—; pres. Law Offices Donald Nemir. Mem. ABA (litigation com.), Calif. State Bar Assn. (litigation com.). Phi Delta Phi. Club: Univ. (San Francisco). Real property. Office: One Maritime Plaza San Francisco CA 94111

NEMSER, EARL HAROLD, lawyer; b. N.Y.C., Jan. 17, 1947; s. Harold Sumers and Eleanor Patricia (Beckerman) N.; m. Randy Lynn Lehrer, June 17, 1974 (div.); children—Eliza Sarah, Maggie Lehrer. B.A., NYU, 1967; J.D. magna cum laude, Boston U., 1970. Bar: N.Y. 1970, U.S. Supreme Ct. 1975, U.S. Claims Ct. 1979, U.S. Tax Ct. 1985. Law clk. Hon. Collins J. Seitz, Chief Judge U.S. Ct. appeals 3rd Cir., 1970-71; ptnr. Cadwalader, Wickersham & Taft, N.Y.C., 1971—. Mem. ABA, Assn. Bar City of N.Y., Fed. Bar Council, Boston U. Law Sch. Alumni Assn. (pres.). Clubs: Downtown Assn.; Guana Island (British Virgin Islands) (soliciter gen.). Contbr. note to legal rev. State civil litigation, Contracts commercial, Securities. Office: Cadwalader Wickersham & Taft 100 Maiden Lane New York NY 10038

NERN, CHRISTOPHER CARL, lawyer; b. N.Y.C., Sept. 30, 1944; s. William Francis and Jule Anne (Allison) N.; m. Kathleen Jean Brogan, Aug. 24, 1974 (div. Nov. 1985). BA, Mich. State U., 1967; JD, Wayne State U., 1972. Bar: Mich. 1973, U.S. Dist. Ct. (ea. and we. dists.) Mich. 1973, U.S. Ct. Appeals (6th cir.) 1974, U.S. Supreme Ct. 1979. Asst. atty. gen. State of Mich., Lansing, 1972-73; staff atty. corp. affairs div. Detroit Edison Co., 1973-74, sr.atty. rates and regulatory div., 1975-78, gen. atty. regulatory affairs div., 1978-82, assoc. gen. counsel, mgr., 1982—. Mem. allocation com. United Found., Detroit, 1983, 86—; bd. dirs. Oakland Parks Found., Oakland County, Mich., 1985—. Served with USAF, 1967-69. Mem. ABA, Detroit Bar Assn., Am. Corp. Counsel Assn. (pres. Mich chpt. 1986—). Roman Catholic. Club: Econ. (Detroit). Public utilities, Administrative and regulatory, General corporate. Home: 910 Lakeside Birmingham MI 48009 Office: Detroit Edison Co 2000 2d Ave 688 WCB Detroit MI 48226

NESBIT, PHYLLIS SCHNEIDER, district judge; b. Newkirk, Okla., Sept. 21, 1919; d. Vernon Lee and Irma Mae (Biddle) Schneider; m. Peter Nicholas Nesbit, Sept. 14, 1939. B.S. in Chemistry, U. Ala., 1948, B.S. in Law, 1958, J.D., 1969. Bar: Ala. 1958. Ptnr. Wilters, Brantley and Nesbit, Robertsdale, Ala., 1958-74; sole practice, Robertsdale, 1974-76; dist. judge Baldwin County Juvenile Ct., 1977—. Ex-officio bd. dirs. Baldwin Youth Services; bd. dirs., v.p. women's activities So. Ala. chpt. Nat. Safety Council, 1978-83. Mem. Nat. Assn. Women Lawyers, Nat. Assn. Women Judges, N.Am. Judges Assn., Ala. Dist. Judges Assn., Ala. Council Juvenile Judges, Am. Judicature Soc., Baldwin County Bar Assn., Phi Alpha Delta. Democrat. Methodist. Clubs: Spanish Fort, Fairhope Bus. and Profl. Women's. Jurisprudence. Office: PO Box 1138 Bay Minette AL 36507

NESBITT, CHARLES RUDOLPH, lawyer; b. Miami, Okla., Aug. 30, 1921; s. Charles Rudolph and Irma Louise (Wilhelmi) N.; m. Margot Dorothy Lord, June 6, 1948; children: Nancy Margot Nesbitt Nagle, Douglas Charles, Carolyn Jane Nesbitt Gresham. B.A., U. Okla., 1942; LL.B., Yale, 1947. Bar: Okla. bar 1947, U.S. Supreme Ct 1957. Practice in Oklahoma City, 1948-62, 67-69, 75—; atty. gen. Okla., 1963-67; mem. Okla. Corp. Commn., 1968-75, chmn., 1969-75. Bd. dirs. endowment fund St. Gregory's Coll.; pres. Hist. Preservation, Inc.; pres. bd. trustees Okla. Mus. Art.; v.p., bd. dirs. Western History Collections Asocs., U. Okla. Libraries; mem. panel arbitrators Am. Arbitration Assn. Served with AUS, 1942-46. Mem. Am., Okla. bar assns., Oklahoma City C. of C., Phi Beta Kappa, Phi Delta Phi. Episcopalian. Oil and gas leasing. Home: 1703 N Hudson St Oklahoma City OK 73103 Office: 125 NW 6th St Oklahoma City OK 73102

NESBITT, FRANK WILBUR, lawyer; b. Miami, Okla., Dec. 26, 1916; s. Frank Wilbur and Nelle M. (Grayson) N.; m. Delores M. Shaw, 1950 (div. 1978); children: Mary Nelle Pearson, Kathleen Marie Smith; m. Mary Louise Turner Gardner, Aug. 22, 1982. AB, Okla. U., 1937; JD, U. Tex., 1939. Bar: Tex. 1939, U.S. Dist. Ct. (so. dist.) Tex. 1939, U.S. Ct. Appeals (5th cir.). Sole practice, Corpus Christi, Tex., 1939-41; asst. city atty. Corpus Christi, 1941-42; ptnr. King & Nesbitt, Corpus Christi, 1946-54, Wood & Burney, Corpus Christi, 1954—. Served to capt. AUS, 1942-46. Mem. ABA, State Bar Tex., Nueces County Bar Assn., Am. Coll. Trial Lawyers, Tex. Bar Found. Democrat. Episcopalian. Federal civil litigation, State civil litigation, Oil and gas leasing. Office: Wood & Burney 1700 First City Tower II Corpus Christi TX 78478

NESBITT, JOHN BENEDICT, lawyer; b. Clifton Springs, N.Y., Sept. 16, 1952; s. Henry Benedict and Jane (Free) N.; m. Sheryl Ann Vanderlinde, Feb. 18, 1984; 1 child, Jason Free. BA, St. Lawrence U., 1974; JD, Syracuse U., 1977. Bar: N.Y. 1978. Ptnr. Nesbitt & Williams, Newark, N.Y., 1978—; asst. dist. atty. Wayne County, N.Y., 1980-83; atty. Village of Sodus Point, N.Y., 1981—, Village of Palmyra, N.Y., 1984—, Palmyra Sch. Dist., 1985—, Town of Williamson, N.Y., 1986—. Articles editor Syracuse Law Rev., 1977. Bd. visitors Newark (N.Y.) Devel. Ctr., 1980—, Syracuse U. Coll. Law, 1982—. Mem. ABA, N.Y. Bar Assn., Order of Coif. Republican. Episcopalian. Avocations: reading, writing, yachting. Local government, Probate, General practice. Home: 122 Cuyler St Palmyra NY 14522 Office: Nesbitt & Williams 605 Mason St Newark NY 14513

NESBITT, JOHN ROBERT, lawyer; b. Rensselaer, Ind., Oct. 15, 1934; s. Edgar Darius and Annabel (Wartena) N.; children—Kathy Lynn, Judy Dawn. B.S., Purdue U., 1955; J.D., Ind. U., 1958. Bar: Wis. 1958, Ind. 1960, U.S. Dist. Ct. (no. dist.) Ind. 1958, U.S. Dist. Ct. (so. dist.) Ind. 1958, U.S. Supreme Ct. 1960, U.S. Ct. Appeals (D.C. cir.) 1985. Assoc., Michael Best Friedrich, Milw., 1958-60; sr. ptnr. Nesbitt Law Firm, Rensselaer, Ind., 1960—; patent counsel, dir. div. patents and copyrights Purdue Research Found., 1977-82. Chmn. bd. First Christian Ch., Rensselaer, 1974-75, 85-86. Mem. ABA, Ind. Bar Assn., Am. Intellectual Property Law Assn. Club: Rotary (pres. club 1976-77). Patent, Probate, General practice. Home: 325 N Front St Rensselear IN 47978 Office: 116 N Front St Rensselear IN 47978

NESBITT, MARK THOMAS, lawyer; b. Spokane, Wash., May 3, 1945; s. Thomas Eugene and Edna Mae (Florea) N.; m. Susanne Sokang Hwang, Apr. 6, 1971; 1 child, Brian Eugene. BS in Geology, Wash. State U., 1968; postgrad., Eastern Wash. State U., 1971; JD, Gonzaga U., 1975. Bar: Colo. 1978, U.S. Dist. Ct. Colo. 1978. Atty., land mgr. Pechiney Ugine Kuhlman Inc & Minatome Corp., Albuquerque and Denver, 1975-81; land supr. Amoco Minerals Co., Denver, 1981-85; supr., property records and land Cyprus Minerals Co., Denver, 1985-87; mgr. mineral lands Homestake Mining Co., San Francisco, 1987—. Served to 1st lt. U.S. Army, 1969-71. Mem. ABA, Colo. Bar Assn., Denver Bar Assn., Rocky Mountain Assn. Mineral Landmen. (pres. 1984-85), Rocky Mountain Mineral Law Found. (chmn. 32d ann. Rocky Mountain landmen's session, trustee 1987—). Avocations: ancient history, gardening, skiing, camping. Mining-land acquistion and management, Real property. Office: Homestake Mining Co 650 California St 9th Floor San Francisco CA 94108

NESMITH-ROSNER, JOANNA, lawyer; b. Thomasville, Ga., Dec. 18, 1938. B.A., Stetson U., 1960; M.A., U. Tex., 1962; J.D., Southwestern U., 1977. Bar: Ga. 1977, Fla. 1977, Calif. 1977, D.C., 1978, U.S. Dist. Ct. (mid. dist.) Ga. 1978, U.S. Dist. Ct. (mid. dist.) Fla. 1984. Criminal justice specialist Calif. Council Criminal Justice, 1970-73; criminal justice cons. nationwide, 1973-77; sole practice, Thomasville, Ga., 1978—. Author: The California Criminal Justice System, 1972; contbr. articles to profl. jours. Cons. Exec. Office of Pres., Washington, 1972, Nat. Govs. Conf., 1972-73; bd. dirs. Friends of Library, Inc. Mem. Selective Service (chmn. appeals bd. 1982—, vice chmn. local bd. 1982), Assn. Trial Lawyers Am. Personal injury, Contracts commercial, Probate. Office: 419 N Dawson St PO Box 1638 Thomasville GA 31799

NESS, JULIUS B., chief justice Supreme Ct. S.C.; b. Manning, S.C., Feb. 27, 1916; s. Morris P. and Raye L. N.; m. Katherine Rhoad, Jan. 25, 1946; children: Gail Ness Richardson, Richard B. B.S., U. S.C., 1938, LL.B., 1940, J.D., 1970. Bar: S.C. 1940. Practiced law Bamberg, S.C., 1940-58; judge S.C. Circuit Ct., 1958-74; assoc. justice S.C. Supreme Ct., 1974-85, chief justice, 1985—; mem. S.C. Senate, 1957-58; instr. Nat. Coll. State Judiciary, 1971. Mem. S.C. Hwy. Commn., 1954-56, chmn., 1956. Served to capt. U.S. Army, 1941-45. Named S.C. Judge of Yr. Assn. Trial Lawyers Am., S.C. Trial Lawyers Assn., 1973, 79. Mem. S.C. Bar, ABA. Democrat. Office: County Courthouse Bamberg SC 29003 also: SC Supreme Ct Columbia SC 29211

NESSELER, STEVEN EDWARD, lawyer, medical researcher; b. Rock Island, Ill., July 25, 1945; s. Henry Louis and Edith Doris (Johnson) N.; m. Kerry Paige Pierson, June 11, 1978; children: Naomi Catherine, Shea Kaiiwa, Kelly Pierson. BA in Psychology, U. Hawaii, 1968, M in Pub. Health, 1985; Baccalaureate of Sci. Nursing, Calif. State U., 1977; JD, Golden Gate U., 1979. Bar: Calif. 1980, U.S. Dist. Ct. (no. dist.) Calif. 1980, U.S. Ct. Appeals (9th cir.) 1981, Hawaii 1982, U.S. Dist. Ct. Hawaii 1982; RN. Sole practice Calif. and Hawaii, 1980—; direct care specialist John Muir Hosp., Walnut Creek, Calif., 1980-81; owner/pres. Medical Legal Research, Honolulu, 1982—. Served to capt. U.S. Army, 1983—. Mem. ABA, Calif. Bar Assn., Am. Assn. Nurse Attys. (exec. com. 1981), Am. Nurses Assn., Calif. Nurses Assn. (bd. dirs., edn. and welfare commr. 1979-81), Alameda County Nurses Assn., Hawaii State Pub. Health Nurses (Lectr. 1982), Am. Soc. Law and Medicine, Phi Alpha Delta. Democrat. Bahai. Club: Micro-Masters (Honolulu). Health, Family and matrimonial, Civil rights. Home and Office: 516 Chestnut St Cloquet MN 55720

NESSEN, MAURICE NORMAN, lawyer; b. Boston, Jan. 28, 1927; s. Samuel and Molly Nessen; m. Hermine Fuld, Feb. 1, 1953; children: Joshua Fuld, William Arthur, Elizbeth. BA, Yale U., 1950, LLB, 1953. Law clk. to judge U.S. Dist. Ct. (so. dist.) N.Y., N.Y.C., 1953-54; asst. U.S. atty. U.S. Justice Dept., N.Y.C., 1954-57; ptnr. Kramer, Levin, Nessen, Kamin & Frankel and predecessor firms, N.Y.C., 1957—; adj. prof. N.Y. Law Sch., N.Y.C., 1972-75; vis. prof. Columbia U. Law Sch., N.Y.C., 1975, lectr., 1975-80; lectr. Harvard U. Law Sch., Cambridge, Mass., 1979—. Author: Royal Flush. 1963, Orange Power/Black Juice, 1973. Bd. dirs. The Legal Aid Soc., N.Y.C., 1980—, pres. 1985—; bd. dirs. The Jewish Mus., N.Y.C., 1971—. Served with USN, 1945-46. Mem. N.Y. State Bar Assn. (ho. of dels. 1978-83), Am. Law Inst., N.Y. County Lawyers Assn. (bd. dirs. 1972-81). Democrat. Jewish. Home: 27 W 86th St Apt 10B New York NY 10024 Office: Kramer Levin Nessen Kamin & Frankel 919 Third Ave New York NY 10022

NESSON, CHARLES R., lawyer, educator; b. 1939. A.B., Harvard U., 1960, LL.B., 1963. Bar: D.C. 1964, Mass. 1971. Law clk. to assoc. justice Harlan, U.S. Supreme Ct., Washington, 1964-65; spl. asst. Civil Rights Div., Dept. Justice, 1965-66; asst. prof. Harvard U., Cambridge, Mass., 1966-69, prof., 1969—. Author: Green and Nesson, Evidence. Constitutional, Criminal. Office: Harvard U Law Sch Cambridge MA 02138 *

NESTRUD, CHARLES ROBERT, lawyer; b. Memphis, Dec. 10, 1951; s. Charles Arden and Loretta (Sheeran) N.; m. Suzanne Joan Gibbons, Feb. 1, 1955; children: Christopher Charles, Lauren Marie. BS in Indsl. Engring., U. Iowa, 1974; JD, U. Ark., 1976. Bar: Ark. 1977, U.S. Dist. Ct. (ea. and we. dist.) Ark. 1977, U.S. Ct. Appeals (8th cir.) 1977, U.S. Supreme Ct. 1983, U.S. Ct. Appeals (10th cir.) 1984. Ptnr. House, Wallace, Nelson & Jewell, PA, Little Rock, 1977—; bd. dirs. Ark. Fedn. Water and Air Users, Inc., Little Rock. Mem. ABA, Ark. Bar Assn. (chmn. environ. law com. 1983—). Lodge: Lions. Environment, Hospital law, State civil litigation. Office: House Wallace Nelson Jewell 1500 Tower Bldg Little Rock AR 72201

NETSCH, DAWN CLARK, state senator; b. Cin., Sept. 16, 1926; B.A. with distinction, Northwestern U., 1948, J.D. magna cum laude, 1952; m. Walter A. Netsch. Admitted to Ill. bar; individual practice law, Washington, Chgo.; law clk. U.S. Dist. Ct. Chgo.; adminstrv. and legal aide Ill. Gov. Otto Kerner, 1961-65; prof. law Northwestern U., 1965—; mem. Ill. Senate. Del. Ill. Constl. Conv.; adv. bd. Nat. Program Ednl Leadership, LWV, Mus. Contemporary Art, Ill. Welfare Assn. Democrat. Author: (with Daniel Mandelker) State and Local Government in a Federal System; contbr. articles to legal jours. Legal education, Antitrust, Local government. Office: State Capitol Room 121C Springfield IL 62706

NETTERVILLE, ROBERT LAVELLE, lawyer; b. Nathcez, Ms., Apr. 24, 1918; s. Charles T. and Jennie (McCraine) N.; m. Peggy Junk, July 31, 1948; children: Charmaine, Richard, Virginia, Elizabeth. Diploma, David Lipscomb Jr. Coll., 1938; BA, Pepperdine U., 1940; LLB, U. Ms., 1943. Bar: Miss. 1943, U.S. Dist. Ct. (no. and so. dists.) Miss., U.S. Dist. Ct. (ea. dist.) Ark. 1981, U.S. Ct. Appeals (5th cir.), U.S. Supreme Ct. Dist. atty. Ms. 6th Jud. Dist., Natchez, 1948-52; sole practice Natchez, 1954—; interim trial judge Ms. Cts. Served with USN, 1942-47. Mem. ABA, Ms. Bar Assn., Adams County Bar Assn., Assn. Trial Lawyers Am., Am. Judicature Soc. Democrat. Mem. Ch. Christ. Admiralty, Personal injury, General practice. Home: 401 N Commerce Natchez MS 39120 Office: 114 N Union PO Box 946 Natchez MS 39120

NETTESHEIM, CHRISTINE COOK, judge; b. Oakland, Calif., Aug. 25, 1944; d. Leo Marshall and Carolyn Grant (Odell) Cook; m. Paul Henry Nettesheim, Feb. 18, 1978. B.A., Stanford U., 1966; J.D., U. Utah, 1969. Bar: Utah 1969, D.C. 1972, Calif. 1982. Clk. to chief judge U.S. Ct. Appeals (10th cir.), 1969-70; trial atty. U.S. Dept. Justice, Washington, 1970-72, Fed. Trade Commn., Washington, 1972-74; litigation Hogan & Hartson, Washington, 1974-76; spl. counsel Pension Benefit Guaranty Corp., Washington, 1976-78; asst. gen. counsel U.S. Ry. Assn., Washington, 1978-80; litigation Shack & Kimball P.C., Washington, 1980-83; judge U.S. Claims Ct., Washington, 1983—. Mem. State Bar Assn. Calif., D.C. Bar Assn., Utah State Bar Assn., ABA (mem. tax, pub. contract and jud. adminstrv. div.), Order of Coif. Republican. Presbyterian. Club: City Tavern (Washington). Office: US Claims Ct 717 Madison Pl NW Washington DC 20005

NETTLES, ALAN ROSS, lawyer; b. Freeport, Ill., Jan. 17, 1948; s. Harold Ross and Garnet Lucille (Jeffrey) N.; m. Anne Terhune, Feb. 19, 1948; 1 child, Adam Ross. B.A., St. Olaf Coll., 1970; J.D., Washington U., St. Louis, 1973; student Am. U., 1969. Bar: Conn. 1973, Minn. 1976, U.S. Dist. Ct. Conn. 1976, U.S. Dist. Ct. Minn. 1977, U.S. Dist. Ct. (we. dist.) Wis., 1986. Assoc. Fredrik D. Holth, New London, Conn., 1973-76; ptnr. Nelson, Njus & Nettles, Mpls., 1977-81, Meyer, Njus, Johnson & Nettles, P.A., Mpls., 1981—; adminstrv. law judge Office Adminstrv. Hearings, Mpls., 1978—; mem. panel Legal Advice Clinic, Mpls., 1976—; bd. dirs. Twin Cities OIC, 1985—. Mem. Assn. Trial Lawyers Am., Minn. Trial Lawyers Assn. Mem. Democratic Farm Labor Party. Universalist. Personal injury, State civil litigation, Administrative and regulatory. Home: 1940 Shoreline Dr Orono MN 55409 Office: Meyer Njus Johnson & Nettles PA 701 Fourth Ave S Suite 1110 Minneapolis MN 55415

NETZORG, GORDON WEMPLE, lawyer; b. Alma, Mich., May 23, 1949; s. Gordon M. and Naomi N.; m. Jane Watson, Aug. 4, 1984. B.A., U. Pa., 1970; J.D. cum laude, Syracuse U., 1976. Bar: Colo. 1976, U.S. Dist. Ct. Colo. 1976, U.S. Ct. Appeals (10th cir.) 1977, U.S. Claims Ct. 1985. Law clk. Colo. Supreme Ct., Denver, 1976-77; assoc. Welborn, Dufford, Cook & Brown, Denver, 1977-79; sole practice, Denver, 1980-81; ptnr. Krendl & Netzorg, P.C., Denver, 1981-84, Netzorg & McKeever, P.C., Denver, 1984—. Co-author: Rights of Older Persons, 1977. Mem. Colo. Bar Assn. (ethics com.), Denver Bar Assn., Colo. Bar Assn., Colo. Trial Lawyers Assn., Assn. Trial Lawyers Am., ABA. Club: Denver Athletic. Federal civil litigation, State civil litigation, Securities. Office: Netzorg & McKeever PC 1410 Grant St Suite C-308 Denver CO 80203

NEUBECKER, EDWARD FREDERICK, lawyer, real estate investor, cattle breeder; b. Weidman, Mich., Mar. 1, 1937; s. Leo Michael and Elizabeth (Schmidt) N.; m. Vicki Neubecker; children: Chelsey, Edward F. III. B.S., Marquette U., 1959; J.D., Georgetown U., 1963. Bar: Wis. 1963, U.S. Dist. Ct. (ea. dist.) Wis. 1963, U.S. Dist. Ct. (no. dist.) Ill. 1966, U.S. Ct. Appeals (7th cir.) 1967. Sole practice, Milw., 1963-68; ptnr. Neubecker, Weiss & Schimsky, Milw., 1982—. Pres. Civil Service Commn., Milw., 1974—; chmn. search coms. for city execs., Milw., 1976—; co-chmn. Mayor Maier's polit. orgn., Milw., 1977-84. Mem. State Bar of Wis. Assn., Wis. Acad. Trial Lawyers, St. Thomas More Soc. (bd. dirs. Milw. chpt. 1982-84). Republican. Roman Catholic. Club: A.O.O.B. (Milw.) (chief exec. 1972—). General practice, Personal injury, Family and matrimonial. Home: 2585 N Summit Ave Milwaukee WI 53211 Office: 2649 N Downer Ave Milwaukee WI 53211

NEUBER, FRANK WILLIAM, JR., legal educator; b. Milw., May 4, 1927; s. Frank William Sr. and Ruby Pauline (Robinson) N.; m. Helen Jean Willever, Aug. 28, 1949; children: Melanie Ann, Frank William III, Chris-

topher Alan. BA summa cum laude, Beloit Coll., 1949; MA in Polit. Sci., U. Ill., Champaign, 1950; PhD, U. Oreg., Eugene, 1958; JD, U. Tenn., 1982. Bar: Ky. 1983, U.S. Dist. Ct. (we. dist.) Ky. 1984, U.S. Ct. Appeals (6th cir.) 1985. Instr. polit. sci. Whitman Coll., Walla Walla, Washington, 1952-53; asst. prof. polit. sci. Cen. Coll., Pella, Iowa, 1953-57; asst. prof. govt. Western Washington U., Bellingham, 1957-61; assoc. prof. social sci. Eastern Ill. U., Charleston, 1961-63; head polit. sci. dept. Parsons Coll., Fairfield, Iowa, 1964-65, prof., 1963-66; vis. prof. govt. Western Ky. U., Bowling Green, 1966-67, prof. govt., 1967—; tchr. law sch. admission test prep. course Community Edn. of Bowling Green (Ky.) and Warren County, 1982-86; treas. Assn. Western Faculty Western Ky. U., Bowling Green, 1984—. Mem. state bds. Ky. Civil Liberties Union, Louisville, 1974-80; exec. com., chmn. legal redress com. NAACP, Bowling Green, 1980-82; pres. Am. Assn. for the United Nations, Bellingham, Wash., 1959-60. Served with USN, 1945-46. Named to Hon. Order of Ky. Cols., 1982. Mem. ABA, Ky. Bar Assn., Bowling Green Bar Assn., Am. Polit. Sci. Assn., Ky. Polit. Sci. Assn., Phi Beta Kappa, Pi Sigma Alpha, Phi Eta Sigma. Avocations: TV, automobiles. Civil rights, Legal education, Federal civil litigation. Home: 1321 Willow Ln Bowling Green KY 42101 Office: Western Ky Univ College Heights Bowling Green KY 42101

NEUHAUS, MARY LYNN, lawyer; b. Dubuque, Iowa, Nov. 24, 1953; d. Kenneth A. and Mary J. (Dugan) N.; m. James L. Jarrard, Apr. 12, 1980; Children: Patrick, Thomas. BA in Polit. Sci. and Spl. Communication, Loras Coll., 1976; JD, Creighton U., 1979. Bar: Iowa 1980, U.S. Dist. Ct. (no. dist.) Iowa 1980. Mem. staff Iowa Senate, Des Moines, 1975; assoc. Sprengelmeyer and Henkels, Dubuque, 1979-81; ptnr. Kaufman, Lange, Hodge and Neuhaus, Dubuque, 1981-86; sole practice Dubuque, 1986—; lectr. Clarke Coll., Dubuque, 1981; adj. faculty Loras Coll., Dubuque Coll., and Cardinal Stritch Coll., Milw. Vice chmn. Dubuque Adv. Commn., 1971-75; v.p. Dubuque Symphony Orch., 1981—. Recipient Service award Dubuque Sch. Dist. 1983, Service award City of Dubuque 1975, Outstanding Youth Leadership award Seratoma 1972. Mem. ABA (del. young lawyers div. 1985-86, exec. com. health care 1987—), Iowa Bar Assn. (exec. council Young lawyers sect. 1980—), Dubuque County Bar Assn. (sec. 1981-82), Iowa Young Lawyers Assn. (chmn. legal writing competition 1980—), Iowa Orgn. Women Attys. (charter), Women in Mgmt. Inc. (Woman of Achievement award 1986), Dubuque Hist. Soc., Creighton U. Club, Loras Club. Democrat. Roman Catholic. Avocation: charity fundraising. Juvenile. Home and Office: 408 Burch St Dubuque IA 52001

NEUMEYER, RICHARD ALBERT, lawyer; b. Los Angeles, Oct. 7, 1944; s. Albert G. and Sally (Wohl) N.; children: Andrew Richard, Kari Elizabeth. BS, Northwestern U., 1966; JD, UCLA, 1969. Bar: Calif. 1970, U.S. Dist. Ct. (cen. dist.) Calif. 1970, U.S. Ct. Appeals (9th cir.) 1973, U.S. Supreme Ct. 1973, U.S. Dist. Ct. (no., so. and ea. dists.) Calif. 1983. Assoc. Youngman, Hungate & Leopold, Los Angeles, 1970-72, Spray, Gould & Bowers, Los Angeles, 1972-76; owner Grace, Neumeyer & Otto, Inc. and predecessor firms, Los Angeles, 1976; of counsel Grace, Neumeyer and Otto, Inc., Los Angeles, 1987—; judge pro tem Los Angeles Mcpl. Ct.; arbitrator Los Angeles Superior Ct. Mem. ABA, Calif. Bar Assn., Los Angeles County Bar Assn., Calif. Acad. Appellate Lawyers, Phi Delta Phi. Federal civil litigation, State civil litigation, Insurance. Office: Grace Neumeyer & Otto Inc 3200 Wilshire Blvd Suite 1300 Los Angeles CA 90010

NEUNER, GEORGE WILLIAM, lawyer; b. Buffalo, Oct. 3, 1943; s. George J. and Geraldine M. (O'Connor) N.; m. Kathleen M. Stoeckl, Aug. 28, 1965; children: George W., Kathleen E. BS in Chem. Engring., SUNY, Buffalo, 1965; SM, MIT, 1966; JD, George Washington U., 1975. Bar: Va. 1975, N.Y. 1976, D.C. 1976, Mass. 1978, U.S. Dist. Ct. Mass. 1978, U.S. Ct. Appeals (Fed. cir.) 1982. Engr. Eastman Kodak Co., Rochester, N.Y., 1966-71, patent agt., 1971-75, patent atty., 1975-77; assoc. Dike Bronstein, Boston, 1977-80, ptnr., 1980—; arbitration panelist 4th Judicial Dept., Rochester, 1976-77. Grantee Sun Oil Co., MIT, 1966. Mem. ABA, Mass. Bar Assn., Am. Intellectual Property Lawyers Assn., Boston Patent Law Assn. (v.p. 1986-87, treas. 1985-86), Fed. Cir. Bar Assn., Tau Beta Pi. Club: MIT (Rochester) (bd. dirs. 1976-77). Patent, Trademark and copyright. Home: 8 Ravenscroft Rd Winchester MA 01890 Office: Dike Bronstein et al 130 Water St Boston MA 02109

NEUREN, MICHAEL SCOTT, lawyer; b. Columbus, Ga., May 3, 1958; s. Elias and Arline Cynthia (Cooper) N.; m. Linda Ann Klein, Sept. 23, 1985. BA in History, Emory U., 1979; JD, U. Ga., 1982. Bar: Ga. 1982, U.S. Dist. Ct. (no. dist.) Ga. 1982, U.S. Ct. Appeals (11th cir.) 1986. Assoc. Sekulow & Assocs., Atlanta, 1982-83; sole practice Atlanta, 1983-84; assoc. McCurdy & Candler, Atlanta, 1984—. Mem. ABA, Ga. Bar Assn., Atlanta Bar Assn., Decatur-Dekalb Bar Assn. Democrat. Jewish. Avocations: photography, camping, travel, computers. Real property, Construction, General corporate. Home: 1218 Druid Knoll Dr Atlanta GA 30319 Office: McCurdy & Candler 1875 Century Blvd Suite 410 Atlanta GA 30345

NEUSTROM, PATRIK WILLIAM, lawyer; b. Kearney, Nebr., Dec. 15, 1951; s. Willys Edward and Geraldine (Slocum) N.; m. Debra Thornton, Aug. 3, 1974; children: Cassie, Emily, Nicholas. BA in English and History with honors, Kans. U., 1974; JD, Washburn U., 1976. Bar: Kans. 1977, U.S. Dist. Ct. Kans. 1977, U.S. Ct. Appeals (10th cir.) 1984. Assoc. Gilliland, Hayes & Goering, Hutchinson, Kans., 1976-78; ptnr. Achterberg & Neustrom, Salina, Kans., 1979—; asst. county counsellor, chief civil litigation Saline County, Salina, 1981—. Bd. editors Washburn U. Law Rev., 1976-77. Chmn. Salina Arts & Humanities Commn., 1983-85; mem. adv. bd. Salina Bus. Improvement Dist., 1985—; active Salina United Way, Christ Cathedral Vestry. Mem. ABA, Kans. Bar Assn., Northwest Kans. Bar Assn. (pres. 1982-83), Assn. Trial Lawyers Am., Kans. Trial Lawyers Assn., Salina C. of C., Salina Jaycees (pres. 1979), Kans. U. Gtr. Univ. Fund, Phi Alpha Theta, Phi Delta Phi. Republican. Episcopalian. Lodge: Elks. Avocations: hunting, fly fishing, running, art. General practice, Personal injury, Workers' compensation. Office: Achterberg & Neustrom 118 S 7th Salina KS 67401

NEUWIRTH, GLORIA S., lawyer; b. N.Y.C., Aug. 16, 1934; d. Nathan and Jennie (Leff) Salob; m. Robert S. Neuwirth, June 9, 1957; children: Susan Madeleine, Jessica Anne, Laura Helaine, Michael Jonathan. BA, Hunter Coll., 1955; JD, Yale U., 1958. Bar: N.Y. 1959, Fla. 1979, U.S. Supreme Ct. 1976, U.S. Dist. Ct. (so. and ea. dists.) N.Y. 1976. Assoc. dir. Joint Research Project on Ct. Calendar Congestion, Columbia U., N.Y.C., 1958-61; assoc. Kridel and Friou, N.Y.C., 1974-76; ptnr. Kridel, Slater and Neuwirth, N.Y.C., 1976-82; assoc. Kaye, Scholer, Fierman, Hays and Handler, N.Y.C., 1982-84; assoc. Graubard Moskovitz McGoldrick Dannett & Horowitz, N.Y.C., 1984-86; ptnr. Kridel & Neuwirth, N.Y.C., 1986—; vol. arbitrator Better Bus. Bur. Author: (with R.B. Hunting) Who Sues in New York City: A Study of Automobile Accident Claims, 1962; contbr. articles to law jours. Trustee Blueberry Inc., 1962-70, Riverdale Country Sch., 1981—; trustee, v.p., sec. Nat. Kidney Found. Inc., N.Y.C., 1980—, trustee nat. office, 1980—. Recipient C. LaRue Munson prize Yale Law Sch., 1958. Mem. ABA, N.Y. State Bar Assn. (vice chmn. com. on persons under disability), Assn. Bar City N.Y., Estate Planning Council of N.Y., Nat. Health Lawyers Assn., Fed. Bar Council, Sierra Club. Club: Appalacian Mountain. Estate planning, Probate, Estate taxation. Office: Kridel & Neuwirth 360 Lexington Ave New York NY 10017

NEVAS, ALAN HARRIS, U.S. attorney; b. Norwalk, Conn., Mar. 27, 1928; s. Nathan and Eva (Harris) N.; m. Janet S. Snyder, Sept. 13, 1959; children: Andrew, Debra, Nathaniel. B.A., Syracuse U., 1949; LL.B., NYU, 1951. Bar: Conn. 1951, U.S. Dist. Ct. Conn. 1955, U.S. Supreme Ct. 1959, U.S. Ct. Appeals for 2d circuit 1967, U.S. Tax Ct. 1981. Ptnr. firm Nevas Nevas & Rubin, Westport, Conn., 1954-81; U.S. atty. for Dist. of Conn. 1981-85; judge U.S. Dist. Ct., Hartford, 1986—. Mem. Conn. Ho. Reps., 1971-77, dep. house majority leader, 1973-75, dep. house minority leader, 1975-77. Served with AUS, 1952-54. Named One of 10 Most Outstanding Mems. Conn. Gen. Assembly Conn. Mag., 1975-77. Mem. Conn. Bar. Assn. (gov. 1978-81). Republican. Jewish. Criminal. Home: 4 Charcoal Ln Westport CT 06880 Office: US Dist Ct 450 Main St Hartford CT 06103 *

NEVAS, LEO, lawyer; b. Norwalk, Conn., Jan. 20, 1912; s. Morris and Ethel (Baron) Navasky; m. Libby Joseloff, Dec. 4, 1938; children: Jo-Ann, Bernard A., Marc L. BA, U. Mich., 1933; JD, Cornell U., 1936; postgrad., NYU, 1937-39; LLD (hon.), Sacred Heart U., 1981. Bar: Conn. 1936, U.S. Dist. Ct. Conn. 1939, U.S. Supreme Ct. 1959. Assoc. Nevas, Nevas and Rubin, Westport, Conn., 1936-42, sr. ptnr., 1942—; pros. atty. Mcpl. Ct. of Westport, 1943-45, judge, 1946-51. Contrbr. articles to profl. jours. Rep. UN World Peace Through Law Ctr., 1965-73; v.p. UN Internat. League for Human Rights, 1978-85; chmn. Conf. UN Reps., UN Assn./U.S.A., 1976-79, vice-chmn. bd. govs.; mem. U.S. Nat. Commn. for UNESCO, 1982; bd. trustees Norwalk Hosp., 1970-86; chmn. bd. Westport Nat. Bank, 1966-81; bd. dirs. Conn. Bank & Trust Co.; chmn. ARC campaign, 1944-46; mem. Conn. Human Rights Commn., 1973-77 pres. Norwalk Jewish Community Council, 1945-48; pres. Temple Beth El, Norwalk, 1950-53; chmn. bd. govs. Am. Jewish Com., 1986—; v.p. Home for the Elderly, Fairfield County, 1970-76; bd. govs. Jacob Blaustein Inst. Advancement of Human Rights. Mem. ABA, Internat. Bar Assn., Conn. Bar Assn., Westport Bar Assn. (pres. 1964-66), Am. Soc. Internat. Law, Am. Arbitration Assn., Am. Jewish Com. (steering com. Fgn. Affairs Commn.), Internat. Inst. Human Rights, Cornell Law Assn. (pres. 1979-81). Club: Birchwood Country (pres.). State civil litigation, Family and matrimonial, Real property. Office: Nevas Nevas & Rubin PO Box 791 Westport CT 06880

NEVELOFF, JAY A., lawyer; b. Bklyn., Oct. 11, 1950; s. Cydelle (Weber) Elrich; m. Arlene Sillman, Aug. 26, 1972; children: David, Kevin. BA, Bklyn. Coll., 1971; JD, NYU, 1974. Bar: N.Y. 1975, U.S. Dist. Ct. (so. and ea. dists.) N.Y. 1975, U.S. Ct. Appeals (2d cir.) 1975, U.S. Supreme Ct. 1982. Assoc. Marshall, Bratter, Greene, Allison & Tucker, N.Y.C., 1974-82; assoc. Rosenman, Colin, Freund, Lewis & Cohen, N.Y.C., 1982-83, ptnr., 1983—. Mem. N.Y. State Bar Assn. (condominium and cooperative law com. 1983—), Assn. of Bar of City of N.Y. (real property law com. 1984—, chmn. subcom. to prepare condominium unit resale contract 1984—), Practising Law Inst. (lectr. 1985), N.Y. County Lawyers Assn. (lectr. 1984), Am. Law Inst., Community Assns. Inst. (lectr. 1986). Real property. Home: 134 Alder Dr Briarcliff Manor NY 10510 Office: Rosenman & Colin 575 Madison Ave New York NY 10022

NEVILLE, JAMES MORTON, food company executive; b. Mpls., May 28, 1939; s. Philip and Maurene (Morton) N.; m. Judie Martha Proctor, Sept. 9, 1961; children: Stephen Warren, Martha Maurene. B.A., U. Minn., LL.B. magna cum laude, 1964. Bar: Minn. 1964. Assoc. firm Neville, Johnson & Thompson, Mpls., 1964-69; ptnr. Neville, Johnson & Thompson, 1969-70; assoc. counsel Gen. Mills, Inc., Mpls., 1970-77; sr. assoc. counsel Gen. Mills, Inc., 1977-83, asst. treas., 1971-79, corp. sec., 1976-83; v.p., sec., asst. gen. counsel Ralston Purina Co., St. Louis, 1983-84, v.p., gen. counsel, 1984—; lectr. bus. law. U. Minn., 1967-71. Mem. South Hennepin Human Services Council, 1977-78. Named Man of Year Edina Jaycees, 1967. Mem. ABA, Minn. Bar Assn., Hennepin County Bar Assn., Mo. Bar Assn., St. Louis Bar Assn., U. Minn. Law Alumni Assn., Am. Soc. Corp. Secs., Order of Coif, Phi Delta Phi, Psi Upsilon. Democrat. Episcopalian. Club: Mo. Athletic. Home: 11565 New London Dr Creve Coeur MO 63141 Office: Ralston Purina Company Checkerboard Square Saint Louis MO 64164

NEVILLE, MARTIN JOHN, lawyer; b. N.Y.C., Apr. 23, 1941; s. John James and Marguerite Bernadette (Fetten) N.; m. Susan Marie Duffner, Sept. 21, 1968; children: Kerry Beth, Erin Suzanne, Colin Martin. BA, Fordham Coll., 1963, JD, 1966. Bar: N.Y. 1969, U.S. Dist. Ct. (so. dist.) N.Y. 1971, U.S. Dist. Ct. (ea. dist.) N.Y. 1983, U.S. Ct. Appeals (3d cir.) 1979. Assoc. Burns Van Kirk, Greene & Kafer and predecessor Burns & Van Kirk, N.Y.C., 1969-77, ptnr., 1978-79; counsel Lovejoy, Wasson, Lundgren & Ashton, N.Y.C., 1979-81; counsel Joseph W. Burns, P.C., New Rochelle, N.Y., 1981-83; ptnr. Fanelli, Burns & Neville, 1983-86, Fanelli, Neville, Varian & Staker, 1986—. Served to lt. U.S. Army, 1966-69. Decorated Army Commendation medal. Mem. ABA, N.Y. State Bar Assn., Bar Assn. City N.Y., Westchester County Bar Assn., New Rochelle Bar Assn. Roman Catholic. Clubs: Wykagyl Country (New Rochelle); Manhasset (N.Y.) Country. Antitrust, Administrative and regulatory, Federal civil litigation. Office: 277 North Ave New Rochelle NY 10801

NEVIN, JACK FREDERICK, lawyer; b. Seattle, May 26, 1951; s. Stanley M. and Katheryne (Brandt) N.; m. Cheryl French, Sept. 2, 1978. BA, Wash. State U., 1973; MS, Gonzaga U., 1976, MBA and JD, 1978. Bar: Mont. 1978, U.S. Ct. Mil. Appeals 1979, Wash. 1980, U.S. Dist. Ct. (we. dist.) Wash. 1980. Assoc. Davies & Pearson P.C., Tacoma, 1981-84; dep. pros. atty. Pierce County, Tacoma, 1984—; adj. prof. U. Puget Sound, Tacoma, 1980-83, Ft. Steilawom Coll., Tacoma, 1984—, Cen. Wash. U., Ellensburg, 1984—. Served to capt. JAGC, U.S. Army, 1978-81. Avocations: skiing, mountain climbing. Criminal, Military, Personal injury. Home: 11108 North Star Way SW Tacoma WA 98498 Office: Pierce County Pros Office 946 County City Tacoma WA 98498

NEWACHECK, DAVID JOHN, lawyer; b. San Francisco, Dec. 8, 1953; s. John Elmer and Estere Ruth Sybil (Nelson) N. AB in English, U. Calif., Berkeley, 1976; JD, Pepperdine U., 1979; MBA, Calif. State U., Hayward, 1982. Bar: Calif. 1979, U.S. Dist. Ct. (no. dist.) Calif. 1979, U.S. Ct. Appeals (9th cir.) 1979, U.S. Supreme Ct. 1984, Washington D.C. 1985. Tax cons. Pannell, Kerr and Forster, San Francisco, 1982-83; lawyer, writer, editor Matthew Bender and Co., Oakland, 1983—; tax cons., Walnut Creek, Calif., 1983—; bd. dirs. Aztec Custom Co., Orinda, Calif., 1983—; cons. software Collier Bankruptcy Pricing System, 1984. Author/editor (treatises) Ill. Tax Service, 1985, Ohio State Taxation, 1985, N.J. Tax Service, 1986. Mem. youth com. Shepherd of the Valley Luth. Ch., Orinda, 1980-85, ch. council, 1980-82. Mem. ABA, State Bar Assn. Calif., Alameda County Bar Assn., U. Calif. Alumni Assn., U. Calif. Band Alumni Assn., Mensa. Republican. Club: Commonwealth (San Francisco). Avocations: music, competitive running, sports. Personal income taxation, Computer, State and local taxation. Home: 21 Tappan Ln Orinda CA 94563-1310 Office: Matthew Bender & Co 2101 Webster St Oakland CA 94612

NEWBERG, HERBERT BARKAN, lawyer; b. Phila., July 18, 1937; s. Samuel A. and Lillian (B.) N.; m. Babette Josephs, Jan. 28, 1962; children: Lee Aaron, Elizabeth. B.S., U. Pa., 1958; J.D., Harvard U., 1961. Bar: Pa. 1962, U.S. Dist. Ct. (ea. dist.) Pa. 1962, U.S. Ct. Appeals (3d cir.) 1962, U.S. Supreme Ct. 1966, U.S. Ct. Appeals (2d, 5th, 6th, 10th, 11th, D.C. cirs.) 1981-85. Asst. city solicitor City of Phila., 1962-64; assoc., then ptnr. firm Cohen, Shapiro, Berger, Polisher & Cohen, Phila., 1964-70; ptnr. firm David Berger Profl. Assn., Phila., 1971-72, cons., 1972—; ptnr. Herbert B. Newberg Law Offices, Phila., 1975-78; counsel Barrack, Rodos & McMahon, 1978-81; pres. Herbert B. Newberg, Esq. P.C., Phila., 1982—; cons., expert in field; mem. faculty Temple U. Law Sch., 1975; mem. faculty Advanced Advocacy Coll., Assn. Am. Trial Lawyers, 1977; bd. dirs. Phila. Community Legal Services, 1976, 78, Pa. Law Coordination Ctr., 1981—. Author: Newberg on Class Actions, 8 vols., 1977, 2d edit., 5 vols., 1985, Attorney Fee Awards, 1986, Action Decisions Checklist, 1977; editor: Court Awarded Fees in Public Interest Litigation, 1978; others. Bd. dirs. Pa. ACLU, 1982-84; bd. dirs. Sr. Citizens Judicare Project, 1978-85, Am. Jewish Com., Phila., 1970-85, Jewish Community Relations Council, 1976—; pres. Lawyers Alliance for Nuclear Arms Control, Phila., 1982—; orgn. rep. Phila. Council for Ednl. Priorities, 1980-81. Served with USAR, 1961-66. Beta Gamma Sigma scholar, 1958; Beta Alpha Psi scholar, 1958. Mem. ABA, Pa. Bar Assn., Phila. Bar Assn., Am. Law Inst., Fed. Bar Assn., Assn. Am. Trial Lawyers. Class actions, Antitrust, Civil rights. Office: 227 S 6th St Suite 200 Philadelphia PA 19106

NEWBERGER, STUART HENRY, lawyer; b. N.Y.C., Dec. 2, 1953; s. Sheldon Mayer and Lillian (Fisher) N.; m. Marcy Andrea Leon, May 28, 1978; children: Elana Sara, Rebecca Danielle. BA, George Washington U., 1974; JD, Georgetown U., 1979. Bar: D.C. 1980, U.S. Dist. Ct. D.C. 1980, U.S. Ct. Appeals (D.C. cir.) 1980. Law clk. to presiding judge U.S. Dist. Ct. D.C., 1979-80; assoc. Schwalb, Domenfeld, Bray & Silbert P.C., Washington, 1980-82; asst. U.S. atty. U.S. Atty. D.C., 1982—; adj. prof. law Georgetown U., 1984—. Mem. ABA. Jewish. Avocations: gourmet cooking, fishing, skiing, camping, basketball. Federal civil litigation, Government contracts and claims, Labor. Office: US Atty DC 555 4th St NW Washington DC 20001

NEWBERN, WILLIAM DAVID, justice; b. Oklahoma City, May 28, 1937; s. Charles Banks and Mary Frances (Harding) N.; m. Barbara Lee Rigsby, Aug. 19, 1961 (div. 1968); 1 child, Laura Harding; m. Carolyn Lewis, July 30, 1970; 1 child, Alistair Elizabeth. B.A., U. Ark., 1959, J.D., 1961; LL.M., George Washington U., 1963; M.A., Tufts U., 1967. Bar: Ark. Supreme Ct. 1961, U.S. Dist. Ct. (we. dist.) Ark. 1961, U.S. Supreme Ct. 1968, U.S. Ct. Appeals (8th cir.) 1983. Prof. law U. Ark., Fayetteville, 1970-85; adminstr. Ozark Folk Ctr., Mountain View, Ark., 1973; judge Ark. Ct. Appeals, Little Rock, 1979-81; assoc. justice Ark. Supreme Ct., Little Rock, 1985—; mem. faculty sr. appellate judges seminar NYU, 1987—. Editor Ark. Law Rev., 1961; author: Arkansas Civil Practice and Procedure, 1985. Mem. Fayetteville Bd. Adjustment, 1973-79; bd. dirs. Decision Point, Inc., Springdale, Ark. Served to maj. JAGC, U.S. Army, 1961-70. Mem. Ark. Bar Assn., Am. Judicature Soc. (bd. dirs.). Democrat. Avocation: string band music. Judicial administration. Office: Justice Bldg Little Rock AR 72201

NEWBERRY, JAMES H., JR., lawyer; b. Hiseville, Ky., Dec. 16, 1956; s. James H. Sr. and Carrie (Walker) N.; m. Cheryl Ann Harlow, Dec. 29, 1979. BA, U. Ky., 1978, JD, 1981. Bar: Ky. 1981, U.S. Dist. Ct. (ea. dist.) Ky. 1981. Assoc. Fowler, Measle & Bell, Lexington, Ky., 1981-84, of counsel, 1984—; gen. counsel Airdrie Stud, Inc., Midway, Ky., 1984—; sec. Newberry Broadcasting, Cave City, Ky., 1984—, bd. dirs. Advisor Ky. Tomorrow Commn., Frankfort, 1984-86; organizer, counsel Com. to Elect Brereton Jones Lt. Gov., Lexington, Ky., 1985—. Mem. ABA, Ky. Bar Assn., Fayette County Bar Assn., Lexington Forum, Sigma Nu, Omicron Delta Kappa (Nat. scholar 1979). Democrat. Baptist. Contracts commercial, Equine, General corporate. Home: 401 Henry Clay Blvd Lexington KY 40502 Office: Airdrie Stud Inc PO Box 487 Midway KY 40347

NEWBLATT, STEWART ALBERT, U.S. dist. judge; b. Detroit, Dec. 23, 1927; s. Robert Abraham and Fanny Ida (Grinberg) N.; m. Flora Irene Sandweiss, Mar. 5, 1965; children—David Jacob, Robert Abraham, Joshua Isaac. B.A. with distinction, U. Mich., 1950, J.D. with distinction, 1952. Bar: Mich. bar 1953. Partner firm White & Newblatt, Flint, Mich., 1953-62; judge 7th Jud. Circuit Mich., 1962-70; partner fir Newblatt & Grossman (and predecessor), Flint, 1970-79; U.S. dist. judge Eastern Dist. Mich., Flint, 1979—; adj. instr. U. Mich.-Flint, 1977-78, 86. Mem. Internat. Bridge Authority Mich., 1960-62. Served with AUS, 1946-47. Mem. Fed. Bar Assn., State Bar Mich., Dist. Judges Assn. 6th Circuit. Jewish. Judicial administration. Office: Federal Bldg 600 Church St Flint MI 48503

NEWBORN, SAMUEL R(EUBEN), lawyer; b. N.Y.C., June 9, 1954; s. Abraham and Joyce (Ringel) N.; m. Deborah W. Feinberg. BA, Barnard U., 1972; M in Environ. Studies, Yale U., 1974, BA, 1976; JD, Columbia U., 1982. Bar: N.Y. 1980, U.S. Dist. Ct. (so. dist.) N.Y. 1980. Ptnr. Janklow & Traum, N.Y.C., 1979—. Mem. ABA, Assn. of Bar of City of N.Y. General corporate, Entertainment, Trademark and copyright. Office: Janklow & Traum 598 Madison Ave New York NY 10022

NEWBY, FRED BRYANT, lawyer; b. Greensboro, N.C., Sept. 18, 1948; s. Fred Bulla and Ruth Truehart (Bryant) N.; m. Cheryl Lynn Moore, Aug. 29, 1970; children: Redding Elizabeth, Fred Bryant Jr. BA, U. S.C., 1971, JD, 1974. Bar: S.C. 1974, U.S. Dist. Ct. S.C., 1974, U.S. Ct. Appeals (4th cir.) 1983. Assoc. Moore & Swofford, Spartansburg, S.C., 1974-76; ptnr. Swofford, Turnipseed, Allen & Newby, Spartansburg, 1976-78; sole practice Myrtle Beach, S.C., 1978—; Founding dir. Internat. Affairs Council of the Carolinas, Myrtle Beach, 1985—. Exec. committeeman, Horry County (S.C.) Dems., 1986; youth soccer coach Horry County, 1985-86; scoutmaster Myrtle Beach council Boy Scouts Am., 1986—. Mem. ABA, S.C. Bar Assn., Assn. Trial Lawyers Am. Democrat. Methodist. Lodges: Kiwanis, Sertoma, Masons. Real property, Contracts commercial, State civil litigation. Office: 5001 Kings Hwy Suite 204 Myrtle Beach SC 29578

NEWBY, PAUL MARTIN, lawyer; b. Asheboro, N.C., May 5, 1955; s. Samuel O. and Ruth (Parks) N.; m. Macon Tucker, Apr. 16, 1983. BA, Duke U., 1977; JD, U. N.C., 1980. Bar: N.C. 1980, U.S. Dist. Ct. (we. dist.) N.C. 1981, U.S. Dist. Ct. (mid. dist.) N.C. 1983, U.S. Dist. Ct. (ea. dist.) N.C. 1985, U.S. Ct. Appeals (4th cir.) 1986. Assoc. Van Winkle, Buck, Wall, Starnes & Davis, P.A., Asheville, N.C., 1980-84; gen. counsel Cannon Mills Realty & Devel. Corp., Kannapolis, N.C., 1984-85; asst. atty. U.S. Attys Office (ea. dist.) N.C., Raleigh, 1985—. Chmn. bd. dirs. Pregnancy Life Care Ctr., Raleigh, 1986. Mem. N.C. Bar Assn., Christian Legal Soc. Avocation: tennis. Federal civil litigation, Real property, Civil rights. Home: 6108 Chowning Ct Raleigh NC 27612 Office: US Attys Office 310 New Bern Ave Room 874 Raleigh NC 27611

NEWCITY, MICHAEL ALBERT, legal educator; b. Washington, Dec. 12, 1950; s. Hayden Earle and Emily Frances (Sullivan) N. BA, George Washington U., 1972, MA, JD, 1975. Bar: N.Y. 1976, D.C. 1979. Assoc. Shearman & Sterling, N.Y.C., 1975-79, Graham & James, Singapore, 1979-82; lectr. in law Macquarie U., Sydney, Australia, 1982-85; asst. prof. of law U. Puget Sound, Tacoma, 1985—. Author: Copyright Law in the Soviet Union, 1978, Taxation in the Soviet Union, 1986. Recipient 1st Prize Nathan Burkan Meml. Competition ASCAP, 1974. Legal education, Legal history, Private international. Office: U Puget Sound Sch Law 950 Broadway Plaza Tacoma WA 98406

NEWCOMB, DANFORTH, lawyer; b. Tarrytown, N.Y., Jan. 24, 1943; s. Russell Ladd and Louise Munroe (Blazer) N.; m. Elizabeth W. Newcomb, Nov. 25, 1966; children—Alexander, Thomas. B.A., U. Vt., 1965; LL.B., Columbia U., 1968. Bar: N.Y. 1968, U.S. Dist. Ct. (so. and ea. dists.) N.Y. 1971, U.S. Ct. Claims 1971, U.S. Tax Ct. 1971, U.S. Ct. Appeals (2d and 3d cir.) 1971, U.S. Supreme Ct. 1981, U.S. Dist. Ct. (ea. dist.) Mich. 1983, U.S. Ct. Appeals (11th cir.) 1983, U.S. Ct. Appeals (6th cir.) 1986. Assoc., Shearman & Sterling, N.Y.C., 1968-69, 71-78, ptnr., 1979—. Served to capt. U.S. Army, 1969-70. Decorated Bronze Star. Mem. ABA, Fed. Bar Council, Am. Arbitration Assn. (panel of arbitrators). Federal civil litigation, Private international, Banking. Office: Shearman & Sterling 153 E 53d St New York NY 10022

NEWCOMBE, GEORGE MICHAEL, lawyer; b. Newark, Nov. 11, 1947; s. George Anthony and Mary Hellen (Ganon) N.; m. Joan Sharon Hanlon, May 30, 1969; children: Sean Michael, Scott Ryan, Jennifer Leigh. BS in Chem Engring., N.J. Inst. Tech., 1969; JD, Columbia U., 1975. Bar: N.J. 1975, U.S. Dist. Ct. N.J. 1975, U.S. Ct. Appeals (2d cir.) 1975, N.Y. 1976, U.S. Dist. Ct. (so. dist.) N.Y. 1976, U.S. Dist. Ct. (we. dist.) Tex. 1985, U.S. Ct. Appeals (5th cir.) 1986. Ptnr. Simpson, Thacher & Bartlett, N.Y.C., 1975—. Council mem. com. law offices vol. div. Legal Aid Soc., N.Y.C., 1980—. Served to lt. USPHS, 1970-72. James Kent scholar Columbia Law Sch., 1974, Harlan Fiske Stone scholar Columbia Law Sch., 1975. Mem. ABA, Assn. of Bar of City of N.Y., Am. Inst. Chem. Engrs., Tau Beta Epsilon, Omicrom Delta Kappa. Federal civil litigation, Environment, Securities. Home: 39 Inwood Circle Chatham NJ 07928 Office: Simpson Thacher & Bartlett One Battery Park Plaza New York NY 10004

NEWCOMER, CLARENCE CHARLES, judge; b. Mount Joy, Pa., Jan. 18, 1923; s. Clarence S. and Marion Clara (Charles) N.; m. Jane Moyer Martin, Oct. 2, 1948; children: Judy (Mrs. Kenneth N. Birkett, Jr.), Nancy Jane, Peggy Jo (Mrs. Russell Pollack). A.B., Franklin and Marshall Coll., 1944; LL.B., Dickinson Sch. Law, 1948. Bar: Pa. 1950. Practiced law Lancaster, 1950-57; partner firm Rohrer, Honaman, Newcomer & Musser, Lancaster, 1957-60; with Office of Dist. Atty., Lancaster, 1960-64; 1st asst. dist. atty. Office of Dist. Atty., 1964-68, dist. atty., 1968-72; partner Newcomer, Roda & Morgan, 1968-72; fed. dist. judge Eastern Dist. Pa., Phila., 1972—; Spl. dep. atty. gen. Pa. Dept. Justice, 1953-54. Served to lt. (j.g.) USNR, 1943-46, PTO. Office: 13th Floor US Courthouse Independence Mall Philadelphia PA 19106

NEWELL, THOMAS PETER, lawyer; b. Berkeley, Calif., Aug. 27, 1957; s. Peter Carroll and Nancy Barbara (Gwerder) N.; m. Deborah Lee Searles, May 24, 1980. BA, Stanford U., 1979; JD, U. So. Calif., 1979. Bar: Calif. 1982, U.S. Dist. Ct. (cen. dist.) Calif. 1982, U.S. Dist. Ct. (so. and no. dists.) Calif. 1983, U.S. Ct. Appeals (9th cir.) 1983, U.S. Dist. Ct. (ea. dist.) Calif. 1985. Assoc. O'Melveny & Myers, Newport Beach, Calif., 1982—. Co-pres., bd. dirs. Resolve of Orange County, Dana Point, Calif., 1984—. Mem. Order of Coif. Federal civil litigation, State civil litigation, Libel. Office: O'Melveny & Myers 610 Newport Ctr Dr #1700 Newport Beach CA 92660

NEWLIN, CHARLES FREMONT, lawyer; b. Palestine, Ill., Nov. 18, 1953; s. Charles Norris and Regina Helen (Correll) N.; m. Jean Bolt, Jan. 6, 1975; children: Christian N., Charles W., Ethan A. BA in Polit. Sci. summa cum laude, Ill. Wesleyan U., 1975; JD cum laude, Harvard U., 1978. Bar: Ill. 1978, U.S. Dist. Ct. (no. dist.) 1978, U.S. Tax Ct. 1980. Assoc. Mayer, Brown & Platt, Chgo., 1978-84, ptnr., 1985—; adj. prof. law DePaul U., Chgo., 1986—. Contbg. author: Am. Law of Property, 1975, Trust Adminstrn. Ill., 1983, 87, Bogert on Trusts, 1986—; contbr. articles to profl. jours. Scouting coordinator DuPage area council Boy Scouts Am., Woodridge, Ill., 1984-86; bishop's counselor Mormon Ch., Woodridge, 1984-86. Mem. Chgo. Bar Assn., Chgo. Estate Planning Council. Democrat. Club: University (Chgo.). Probate. Office: Mayer Brown & Platt 190 S LaSalle St Chicago IL 60603

NEWMAN, ALAN HARVEY, lawyer; b. Bklyn., June 10, 1946; s. Bernard Newman and Anne (Simon) Friedman; m. Julie Lois Lennard, Aug. 11, 1974; 1 child, Kimberly Joy. BA, Bklyn. Coll., 1969; MA, Bklyn. Coll, 1971; JD, St. Johns U., 1975. Bar: N.Y. 1976, U.S. Dist. Ct. (so. and ea. dists.) N.Y. 1976. Sole practice Oceanside, N.Y., 1976—; labor atty. N.Y.C. Bd. Edn., Bklyn., 1976—. Mem. ABA, N.Y. State Bar Assn. (labor law com.), Bar Assn. of Nassau County. Labor, Real property, General practice.

NEWMAN, BRUCE ALLEN, lawyer, educator; b. Muskogee, Okla., Oct. 9, 1943; s. Raymond Max and Delores Judy (Zielinski) N.; m. Mary Therese Lietelt, June 20, 1969; children—Brian B., Bradley R. A.B., U. Detroit, 1966, J.D., 1969; LL.M. in Taxation, George Washington U., 1979. Bar: Mich. 1970, U.S. Dist. Ct. (ea. dist.) Mich. 1970, U.S. Tax Ct. 1979, U.S. Ct. Mil. Appeals 1970, U.S. Supreme Ct. 1979, U.S. Ct. appeals (6th cir.) 1983. Asst. prosecutor Genesee County, Flint, Mich., 1969-72; ptnr. Crawford & Newman, Flint, 1972-78; ptnr., prin. Mansour, Newman & Thomas P.C., Flint, 1979-80; sole practice, Flint, 1980—; instr. C.S. Mott Community Coll., 1973—. Pres., Cath. Social Services, 1976-78, Ctr. for Ind. Living, 1981—; co-founder, past pres. Mich. Conf. for Law-Focused Edn.; bd. dirs. Genesee-Lapeer Counties ARC, 1986—. Served to 1st lt. AUS, 1970-71. Recipient Achievement award State Bar Mich. Young Lawyers Div., 1979. Mem. ABA (mem. com. adminstrv. practice, com. tax practice and procedures; Young Lawyers Div. Achievement award 1981), Mich. Bar Assn. (council legal econs. sect. 1986—, mem. com. practice and procedure), Genesee County Bar Assn. (chmn. legis. liaison com. 1974—, bd. dirs. 1985—). Roman Catholic. Author: (with R.J. Drew) American Law Sourcebook for the Classroom Teacher, 1981; contbr. numerous articles to profl. jours. Corporate taxation. Address: 444 Church St Suite 301 Flint MI 48502

NEWMAN, CAROL L., lawyer; b. Yonkers, N.Y., Aug. 7, 1949; d. Richard J. and Pauline Frances (Stoll) N. A.B./M.A. summa cum laude, Brown U., 1971; postgrad. Harvard U. Law Sch., 1972-73; J.D. cum laude, George Washington U., 1977. Bar: D.C., 1977, Calif., 1979. With antitrust div. U.S. Dept. Justice, Washington and Los Angeles, 1977-80; asso. Alschuler, Grossman & Pines, Los Angeles, 1980-82, Costello & Walcher, Los Angeles, 1982-85, Rosen, Wachtell & Gilbert, 1985—; adj. prof. Sch. Bus., Golden Gate U., spring 1982. Candidate for State Atty. Gen., 1986. Mem. ABA, State Bar Calif., Los Angeles County Bar Assn., Order of Coif, Phi Beta Kappa. Federal civil litigation, State civil litigation, Antitrust.

NEWMAN, CHARLES A., lawyer; b. Los Angeles, Mar. 18, 1949; s. Arthur and Gladys (Barnett) N.; m. Joan Kathleen Meskiel, Aug. 8, 1971; children: Anne R., Elyse S. BA magna cum laude, U. Calif., 1970; JD, Washington U., 1973. Bar: Mo. 1973, U.S. Dist. Ct. (ea. dist.) Mo. 1973, U.S. Ct. Appeals (8th cir.) 1973, U.S. Supreme Ct. 1976, D.C. 1981, U.S. Tax Ct. 1981, U.S. Claims Ct. 1981. From assoc. to ptnr. Thompson & Mitchell, St. Louis, 1973—; lectr. law Washington, U., St. Louis, 1976-78. Mem. United Jewish Appeal Young Leadership Cabinet, N.Y.C., 1985—; v.p. Repertory Theatre of St. Louis, 1986—; bd. dirs. Ctr. for Study of Dispute Resolution, 1985—, Legal Services Eastern Mo., 1985—, bd. dirs. Planned Parenthood of St. Louis, 1986—, Jewish fedn. of St. Louis, 1986—. Mem. ABA, Mo. Bar Found. (recipient Lon O. Hocker Meml. Trial award 1984), Mo. Bar Assn., Bar Assn. Met. St. Louis (Merit award 1976). Democrat. Club: Mo. Athletic (St. Louis). Avocations: golf, tennis, reading, music. Federal civil litigation, State civil litigation, Health. Office: Thompson & Mitchell One Mercantile Ctr Saint Louis MO 63101

NEWMAN, CHARLES FORREST, lawyer; b. Grenada, Miss., Jan. 15, 1937; s. Wiley Clifford and Lurene (Westbrook) N.; B.A. magna cum laude, Yale, 1959, J.D., 1963; postgrad. (Adenauer fellow) U. Bonn (Germany), 1959-60; m. Jeannette Kay Bailey, May 26, 1973. Admitted to Tenn. bar, 1964; law clk. U.S. Dist. Judge Bailey Brown, Western Dist. Tenn., 1963-64; mem. firm Burch Porter & Johnson, Attys., Memphis, 1965—, partner, 1966—; commr. Memphis Landmarks Commn.; assoc. Environ. Law Inst. Past bd. dirs. Tenn. Environ. Council, Environ. Action Fund, Inc., Tenn. Conservation League; bd. dirs. LeMoyne-Owen Coll., Memphis Acad. Arts, Wolf River Conservancy Inc.; mem. exec. com. Yale Law Sch. Assn., 1984—, Pres.'s Council Southwestern Coll.; Memphis-Shelby County chmn. Gary Hart Presdl. Campaign, 1984, Mondale Presdl. Campaign, 1984; mem. class council Class of '59, Yale Coll.; mem. ABA, Tenn., (corp. law revision com.) Memphis and Shelby County Bar Assns., Am. Judicature Soc., Am. Assn. Trial Lawyers, Memphis C. of C., Tenn. Environmental Council, Wilderness Soc., Memphis Pub. Affairs Council, Phi Beta Kappa. Clubs: Tennessee, Economic, Yale of Memphis (past pres.), Yale of N.Y. Federal civil litigation, State civil litigation, General practice. Home: 3880 Poplar Ave Memphis TN 38112 Office: Burch Porter & Johnson 130 N Court Memphis TN 38103

NEWMAN, GEORGE HENRY, lawyer; b. Cheverly, Md., Dec. 16, 1949; s. Leon and Ruth (Patt) N.; m. Linda Joan Fahy; children: Joshua Michael, David Peter. BA, U. Pa., 1971; JD, Temple U., 1975. Bar: Penn. 1975, U.S. Dist. Ct. (ea. dist.) Penn. 1976, U.S. Ct. Appeals (3d cir.) 1985, U.S. Supreme Ct. 1985. Staff atty. Defender Assn. Phila., 1975-79; law clk. to presiding judge Ct. of Common Pleas, Phila., 1979-82; ptnr. Ellis and Newman, P.C., Phila., 1982—. Mem. ABA, Internat. Assn. Young Lawyers, Nat. Assn. Criminal Def. Lawyers, Phila. Bar Assn. (elected chmn. criminal justice sect. 1986). Democrat. Avocations: skiing, sailing, tennis, swimming. Criminal, Immigration, naturalization, and customs. Office: Ellis and Newman PC The Benjamin Franklin Suite 400 Philadelphia PA 19107

NEWMAN, HOWARD JULIAN, lawyer; b. Bronx, N.Y., Dec. 11, 1950; m. Myrna Estrin, July 8, 1973; 1 child, Meredith. BS magna cum laude, N.Y. Inst. Tech., 1972; JD, Bklyn. Law Sch., 1975. Bar: N.Y. 1976, U.S. Dist. Ct. (ea. and so. dists.) N.Y. 1978. Ptnr. Rivkin, Radler, Dunne & Bayh, N.Y.C. and Uniondale (N.Y.), Washington, Los Angeles and Chgo., 1976—. Mem. ABA, N.Y. State Bar Assn., Nass County Bar Assn., Nass/Suffolk Trial Lawyers Assn. Avocations: athletics, music. Insurance, Construction, Professional liability litigation. Office: Rivkin Radler Dunne & Bayh EAB Plaza Uniondale NY 11556

NEWMAN, JAY HARTLEY, financial company executive; b. N.Y.C., Dec. 20, 1951; m. Connie Baum, Aug. 7, 1977. BA, Yale U., 1973; JD, Columbia U., 1976; LLM, NYU, 1981. Bar: N.J. 1976, N.Y. 1977, D.C. 1978. Assoc. Cravath Swaine & Moore, N.Y.C., 1977-79, Hughes Hubbard & Reed, N.Y.C., 1979-83; v.p. Lehman Bros., N.Y.C., 1983-85; sr. v.p. Shearson Lehman Bros., N.Y.C., 1985—. Editor notes and comments Columbia Law Rev., 1974-76. Office: Shearson Lehman Bros Inc 200 Vesey St New York NY 10285

NEWMAN, JEFFREY K., lawyer; b. Cleve., Jan. 11, 1951; s. Robert Joel and Rita Louise (Gray) N.; m. Sylvia Jeanne Sheret, June 8, 1975; children: Alexander Sheret, Harriet Gray. BA magna cum laude, Cornell U., 1973; JD, U. Tex., 1976. Bar: N.Y. 1977, U.S. Dist. Ct. (we. dist.) N.Y. 1977. Assoc. Chamberlain & D'Amanda, Rochester, N.Y., 1977-83, Gallo & Iacovangelo, Rochester, 1983-84; assoc. Remington, Gifford, Williams & Colicchio, Rochester, 1984—, ptnr., 1987—; bd. dirs. Writers and Books, Inc., Rochester, BOA Editions, Ltd., Rochester, INTAC Corp., Rochester, Nexus Personal Mgmt. Internat. Inc., Toronto, Rochester and N.Y.C. spl. counsel Bucket Dance Theatre, Rochester; pres. Perinton Performing Arts, Fairport, N.Y., 1983-85; bd. dirs. Arts for Greater Rochester, 1985—, sec., 1986—. Grantee NSF 1973. Mem. ABA, N.Y. State Bar Assn., Vol. Lawyers for The Arts, Lawyers for the Creative Arts, Sigma Alpha Mu. Democrat. Jewish. General corporate, Entertainment, Real property. Home: 53 Roselawn Ave Fairport NY 14450 Office: Remington Gifford Williams & Colicchio 183 E Main St Suite 1400 Rochester NY 14604

NEWMAN, JOHN ANDREW, lawyer; b. San Diego, May 16, 1956; s. Joan (Smith) Crotts; m. Lisa Ann Cherup, May 22, 1981; 1 child, Matthew Michael. BS with highest honors, Salisbury (Md.) State Coll., 1978; JD, Wake Forest U., 1981; LLM in Taxation, Georgetown U., 1982. Bar: Va. 1981, Mo. 1982, U.S. Ct. Appeals (8th cir.) 1982. Assoc. Bryan, Cave, et al, St. Louis, 1982-84, Husch, Eppenberger, et al, St. Louis, 1984-86; tax assoc. Reed, Smith, Shaw & McClay, Pitts., 1986—. Contbr. articles to profl. jours. Mem. Met. Bar Assn. St. Louis (chmn. media com. young lawyers sect. 1984-85), Phi Kappa Phi. Roman Catholic. Corporate taxation, Personal income taxation, Tax policy development. Office: Reed Smith Shaw & McClay 6th Ave & William Penn Way Pittsburgh PA 15219-1886

NEWMAN, JON O., U.S. judge; b. N.Y.C., May 2, 1932; s. Harold W., Jr. and Estelle L. (Ormond) N.; m. Martha G. Silberman, June 19, 1953; children: Leigh, Scott, David. Grad., Hotchkiss Sch., 1949; A.B. magna cum laude, Princeton U., 1953; LL.B., Yale U., 1956; LLD (hon.), U. Hartford, 1975, U. Bridgeport, 1980. Bar: Conn. and D.C. 1956. Law clk. to judge U.S. Ct. Appeals, 1956-57; sr. law clk. to Chief Justice Earl Warren, U.S. Supreme Ct., 1957-58; mem. firm Ritter, Satter & Newman, Hartford, Conn., 1958-60; counsel to majority Conn. Gen. Assembly, 1959; spl. counsel to gov. Conn., 1959-61; asst. to sec. HEW, 1961-62; adminstrv. asst. to U.S. senator, 1963-64; U.S. atty., Conn., 1964-69; pvt. law practice 1969-71; U.S. dist. judge Conn., 1972-79; U.S. circuit judge 2d Circuit Ct. of Appeals, 1979—. Co-author: Politics: The American Way. Chmn. bd. dirs. Hartford Inst. Criminal and Social Justice; mem. bd. regents U. Hartford. Served with USAR, 1954-62. Fellow Am. Bar Found.; mem. ABA, Am. Law Inst., Conn. Bar Assn., Am. Judicature Soc. Democrat. Jurisprudence. Office: US Courthouse 450 Main St Hartford CT 06103

NEWMAN, LAWRENCE GRAHAM, lawyer; b. Dallas, July 7, 1947; s. Frank Gene and Frances Helen (Graham) N.; m. Nancy Lynn Vanderkolk, June 14, 1969; children: Courtney Kolk, Torrey Peyton. BA cum laude, Colo. Coll., 1969; JD, U. Chgo., 1972. Bar: Colo. 1973, Tex. 1973, U.S. Dist. Ct. (no. dist.) Tex. 1973, U.S. Supreme Ct. 1979, U.S. Ct. Appeals (5th cir.) 1982. Ptnr. Newman, Shook & Newman, Dallas, 1973-79; sole practice Dallas, 1980—. Author: (book) Texas Corporation Law, 1986; assoc. editor U. Chgo. Law Rev., 1972. Chmn. Dallas chpt. Lawyers Alliance for Nuclear Arms Control. Mem. ABA, Colo. Bar Assn., Tex. Bar Assn., Dallas Bar Assn. (chmn. minority participation com. 1983-85). Avocations: sailing, snow skiing, athletics, artist. Federal civil litigation, General corporate, Private international. Home: 3529 Haynie Ave Dallas TX 75205 Office: 3402 McFarlin Suite 200 Dallas TX 75205

NEWMAN, LAWRENCE WALKER, lawyer; b. Boston, July 1, 1935; s. Leon Bettoney and Hazel W. (Walker) N.; m. Cecilia Isette Santos, Nov. 29, 1975; children: Reynaldo W., Timothy D., Virginia I.S., Isabel B., Thomas H. A.B., Harvard U., 1957, LL.B., 1960. Bar: D.C. 1961, N.Y. 1965. Atty. U.S. Dept. Justice, 1960-61, Spl. Study of Securities Markets and Office Spl. Counsel on Investment Co. Act Matters, U.S. SEC, 1961-64; asst. U.S. atty. So. Dist. N.Y., 1964-69; assoc. Baker & McKenzie, N.Y.C., 1969-71, ptnr., 1971—; mem. internat. adv. com. World Arbitration Inst., 1984—; mem. adv. council Asia/Pacific Ctr. for Resolution of Internat. Trade Disputes, 1986—. Co-author: column N.Y. Law Jour., 1982—, U.S. Iranian Claimants Com. (chmn. 1982—). Chmn. U.S. Iranian Claimants Com., 1982. Mem. ABA (com. internat. litigation), Internat. Bar Assn. (com. dispute resolution), Inter-Am. Bar Assn., Fed. Bar Council, Am. Fgn. Law Assn., Maritime Law Assn. U.S., Assn. of Bar of City of N.Y. (mem. com. on arbitration 1977-79). Federal civil litigation, Private international, Contracts commercial. Home: 1001 Park Ave New York NY 10028 Office: 805 3d Ave New York NY 10022

NEWMAN, MICHAEL RODNEY, lawyer; b. N.Y.C., Oct. 2, 1945; s. Morris and Helen Gloria (Hendler) N.; m. Cheryl Jeanne Anker, June 11, 1967; children—Hillary Abra, Nicole Brooke. B.A., U. Denver, 1967; J.D., John Marshall Law Sch., 1970. Bar: Calif. 1971, U.S. Dist. Ct. (cen. dist.) Calif. 1972, U.S. Dist. Ct. (no. dist.) Calif. 1975, U.S. Dist. Ct. (so. dist.) Calif. 1979, U.S. Dist. Ct. (ea. dist.) Calif. 1983, U.S. Ct. Appeals (9th cir.) 1974, U.S. Tax Ct. 1979, U.S. Supreme Ct. 1978. Assoc., David Daar, 1971-76; ptnr. Daar & Newman, 1976-78, Miller & Daar, 1978—; judge pro tem Los Angeles Mcpl. Ct., 1982—. Mem. Los Angeles Citizens Organizing Com. for Olympic Summer Games, 1984, mem. govtl. liaison adv. commn. 1984; mem. So. Calif. Com. for Olympic Summer Games, 1984; cert. ofcl. Athletics Congress of U.S., bd. dirs. So. Pacific Assn. Recipient NYU Bronze medal in Physics, 1962; U.S. Navy Sci. award in Math., 1963. Mem. ABA (multi-dist. litigation subcom., com. on class actions), Los Angeles County Bar Assn., Conf. of Ins. Counsel. Insurance, Federal civil litigation, State civil litigation. Office: 11500 W Olympic Blvd Suite 600 Los Angeles CA 90064

NEWMAN, PAULINE, federal judge; b. N.Y.C., June 20, 1927; d. Maxwell Henry and Rosella N. B.A., Vassar Coll., 1947; M.A., Columbia U., 1948; Ph.D., Yale U., 1952; LL.B., NYU, 1958. Bar: N.Y. 1958, U.S. Supreme Ct. 1972, U.S. Ct. Customs and Patent Appeals 1978, Pa. 1979, U.S. Ct. Appeals (3d cir.) 1981, U.S. Ct. Appeals (fed. cir.) 1982. Research chemist Am. Cyanamid Co., Bound Brook, N.J., 1951-54; mem. patent staff FMC Corp., N.Y.C., 1954-75; mem. patent staff FMC Corp., Phila., 1975-84, dir. dept. patent and licensing, 1969-84; judge U.S. Ct. Appeals (fed. cir.), Washington, 1984—; bd. dir. Research Corp., 1982-84; program specialist Dept. Natural Scis. UNESCO, Paris, 1961-62; mem. State Dept. Adv. Com. on Internat. Indsl. Property, 1974-84; lectr. in field. Contbr. articles to profl. jours. Bd. dirs. Med. Coll. Pa., 1975-84, Midgard Found., 1973-84; trustee Phila. Coll. Pharmacy and Sci., 1983-84. Mem. ABA (council sect. patent trademark and copyright 1983-84), Am. Patent Law Assn. (bd. dirs. 1981-84), U.S. Trademark Assn. (bd. dirs. 1975-79, v.p. 1978-79), Am. Chem. Soc. (bd. dirs. 1972-81), Am. Inst. Chemists (bd. dirs. 1960-66, 70-76), Pacific Indsl. Property Assn. (pres. 1979-80). Clubs: Vassar, Yale. Office: US Ct Appeals 717 Madison Pl NW Washington DC 20439

NEWMAN, ROBERT WILLIAM, lawyer; b. Chgo., Aug. 12, 1933; s. Henry and Marion (Riederman) N. LLB, DePaul U., 1957. Bar: Ill. 1957. Ptnr. Newman, Stahl & Shadur and predecessor firms, Chgo., 1960—, Newman & Stahl, Chgo., 1982-84, Arvey, Hodes, Costello & Burman, Chgo., 1984—. Mem. ABA, Ill. Bar Assn., Chgo. Bar Assn. Office: Arvey Hodes Costello & Burman 180 N LaSalle St Chicago IL 60601

NEWMAN, SCOTT DAVID, lawyer; b. N.Y.C., Nov. 5, 1947; s. Edwin Stanley and Evaline Ada (Lipp) N.; m. Judy Lynn Monchik, June 24, 1972; 1 child, Eric. B.A. magna cum laude, Yale U., 1969; J.D., Harvard U., 1973, M.B.A., 1973; LL.M. in Taxation, NYU, 1977. Bar: N.Y. 1974, U.S. Dist. Ct. (so. and ea. dists.) N.Y. 1975, U.S. Ct. Appeals (2d cir.) 1975, U.S. Ct. Claims 1976, U.S. Tax Ct. 1979. Assoc. Dewey, Ballantine, Bushby, Palmer & Wood, N.Y.C., 1973-76, Stroock & Stroock & Lavan, N.Y.C., 1976-78; assoc., ptnr. Zimet, Haines, Moss & Friedman, N.Y.C., 1978-81; tax counsel Phibro-Salomon Inc., N.Y.C., 1981-84; ptnr. Baer, Marks & Upham, N.Y.C., 1984—. Co-author tape cassettes: New Tax Reform Act of 1976, Tax Reform' '78, 1978. Tax Reform Act of 1984, 1986, Tax Reform Act of 1986, 1986; contbr. article to profl. jour. Mem. Phi Beta Kappa. Corporate taxation, Personal income taxation, Estate taxation. Home: 21 Kipp St Chappaqua NY 10514 Office: Baer Marks & Upham 805 3d Ave New York NY 10022

NEWMAN, STUART, lawyer; b. Hackensack, N.J., June 7, 1947; s. Joseph and Rose (Wilenski) N.; m. Vicki Einhorn, Dec. 28, 1969; children: Leslie, Dara, Mindy. BA, SUNY, Cortland, 1971; JD cum laude, Union U., 1974. Assoc. Dewey, Ballantine, Bushby, Palmer & Wood, N.Y.C., 1974-76; from assoc. to ptnr. Jackson, Lewis, Schnitzler & Krupman, Atlanta, 1976—; lectr. U. Ala., Tuscaloosa, 1980—. Dir. Ruth Mitchell Dance Co. of Atlanta, 1986—. Mem. ABA, Atlanta Bar Assn., Ga. Bar Assn., Lawyers Club of Atlanta. Clubs: Shakerag Hounds, Ansley Golf (Atlanta). Labor. Office: Jackson Lewis Schnitzler & Krupman 700 Peachtree Ctr South Tower 225 Peachtree St NE Atlanta GA 30303

NEWMAN, THEODORE R., JR., judge; b. Birmingham, Ala., July 5, 1934; s. Theodore R. and Ruth L. (Oliver) N. A.B., Brown U., 1955, LL.D., 1980; J.D., Harvard U., 1958. Bar: D.C. bar 1958, Ala. bar 1959. Atty. civil rights div. Dept. Justice, Washington, 1961-62; practiced law in Washington, 1962-70; asso. judge D.C. Superior Ct., 1970-76; judge D.C. Ct. of Appeals, 1976—, chief judge, 1978-84; Bd. dirs. Nat. Center for State Cts., v.p., 1980-81, pres., from 1981. Trustee Brown U. Served with USAF, 1958-61. Fellow Am. Bar Found.; mem. ABA, Nat. Bar Assn. (past pres. judicial council, C. Francis Stradford award 1984), Am. Judicature Soc. Jurisprudence.

NEWMAN, WILLIAM ARTHUR, lawyer; b. Dupont, Pa., Oct. 10, 1947; s. Jerome Mager and Doris Evelyn (Ross) N.; m. Pamela Jane Schneider, May 19, 1974; children: Romy S., T. R. BA, Yale U., 1969; JD, U. Mich., 1973. Bar: N.Y. 1973, U.S. Dist. Ct. (so. dist.) N.Y. 1973. Assoc. Debevoise & Plimpton, N.Y.C., 1973-77; assoc. Richards, O'Neil & Allegaert, N.Y.C., 1977-79, ptnr., 1979—. Pres. Vocations and Community Services for Blind, N.Y.C., 1981-85. General corporate, Securities, Mergers and acquisitions. Office: Richards O'Neil & Allegaert 660 Madison Ave New York NY 10021

NEWMAN, WILLIAM BERNARD, JR., railroad executive; b. Providence, Nov. 16, 1950; s. William Bernard and Virginia (Crosby) N.; m. Karen O'Connor, Jan. 11, 1951. B.A., Ohio Wesleyan U., 1972; J.D., George Mason U., Arlington, Va., 1977; attended advanced mgmt. program, Harvard U., 1987. Bar: Va., D.C. Atty. com. energy Ho. of Reps., Washington, 1978-81; v.p., Washington counsel Consol. Rail Corp., Washington, 1981—. Mem. ABA, Va. Bar Assn. Legislative. Home: 1009 Priory Place McLean VA 22101 Office: Consol Rail Corp 990 L'Enfant Plaza Washington DC 20026

NEWMARK, MILTON MAXWELL, lawyer; b. Oakland, Calif., Feb. 24, 1916; s. Milton and Mary (Maxwell) N.; m. Marion Irene Johnson, July 31, 1941; children—Mari Newmark Anderson, Lucy Newmark Sammons, Grace Newmark Lucini. A.B., U. Calif.-Berkeley, 1936, J.D., 1947. Bar: Calif. 1941, U.S. Supreme Ct. 1944. Ptnr. Milton Newmark, San Francisco, 1941-56; sole practice, 1956-62; sole practice, Lafayette, Calif., 1962-80, Walnut Creek, Calif., 1980—; lectr. bankruptcy State Bar of Calif. Continuing Edn. Program. Served with U.S. Army, 1942-46; to lt. col. USAR. Mem. Alameda County Rep. Cen. Com., 1940-41; pres. Alameda Rep. Assembly, 1950. Mem. Am. Legion, ABA, San Francisco Bar Assn., Contra Costa Bar Assn., Alameda County Bar Assn., Scabbard and Blade. Lodges: Masons, Shriners, Rotary. Bankruptcy. Home: 609 Terra California Dr No 6 Walnut Creek CA 94595 Office: 1900 Olympic Blvd Suite 103 Walnut Creek CA 94596

NEWSOM, DANIEL OREN, lawyer; b. Marlow, Okla., May 19, 1933; s. Edwin Parker and Frances (Haug) N.; m. Patricia Caldwell; children—Kathi, Chip, Cindy, Jed. B.S. in Indsl. Engring., U. Okla., 1957; J.D., U. Houston, 1962. Bar: Tex. 1962, U.S. Dist. Ct. (so. dist.) Tex., U.S. Ct. Appeals (5th cir.). Sole practice, Houston, 1962—. Mem. ABA, Tex. Bar Assn. State civil litigation, Family and matrimonial, General practice. Office: 1300 Texas Ave Suite 204 Houston TX 77002

NEWSOM, JAN LYNN REIMANN, lawyer; b. Madison, Wis., Feb. 28, 1947; d. Curtis Whitt and Doris Elizabeth (Jerde) Reimann; m. Neil Edward Newsom, Apr. 15, 1972; children—Kelly Ann, Loren Elizabeth. B.A., U. Tex., 1969, J.D., 1971. Bar: Tex., 1972, U.S. Dist. Ct. (no. dist.) Tex. 1982. Vice pres. legal Nat. Compliance Cons., Dallas, 1972; corp. atty. Blue Cross & Blue Shield of Tex., Dallas, 1972—. Bd. dirs., chmn. pub. edn. com. Dallas central unit, Am. Cancer Soc., 1978—; mem. Innovators, Dallas Symphony Orch. League, 1983—; sponsor 500, Inc. (arts support group), Dallas, 1980—. Recipient Outstanding Leadership award Am. Cancer Soc., 1977, Sword of Hope award, 1984. Mem. ABA, Dallas Bar Assn. (various coms. 1974—), State Bar of Tex., Nat. EEO Task Force, Blue Cross and Blue Shield Assn., Assn. for Retarded Citizens (edn. com.), Alpha Chi Omega. Republican. Methodist. General corporate, Health, Insurance. Home: 6040 Preston Haven Dallas TX 75230 Office: Blue Cross Blue Shield Tex Legal Div PO Box 655730 Dallas TX 75265

NEWSOM, NEIL EDWARD, lawyer; b. Ft. Worth, Nov. 24, 1945; s. Raymond E. and Alice Ruth (Daniel) N.; m. Jan Lynn Reimann, Apr. 15, 1972; children—Kelly Ann, Loren Elizabeth. B.B.A., Tex. Christian U., 1967; J.D., U. Tex.-Austin, 1970. Bar: Tex. 1970, U.S. Dist. Ct. (no. dist.) Tex. 1971. Assoc., Coke & Coke, Dallas, 1971-76; assoc. Hughes Luce Hennessy Smith & Castle, Dallas, 1977-78; assoc. Gardere Porter & Dehay, Dallas, 1978-79; ptnr. Gardere & Wynne, Dallas, 1979-84; ptnr. Freytag, LaForce, Rubinstein & Teofan, Dallas, 1984—. Bd. dirs. Dallas Assn. Retarded Citizens, 1987—. Served with USAR, 1970-78. Mem. ABA (steering com. design, devel. and financing of constrn. div. of forum com. on constrn. industry 1985—), State Bar Tex., Dallas Bar Assn., Tex. Assn. Bank Counsel, Tex. Law Rev. Assn., Tex. Christian U. Alumni Assn. (nat. bd. dirs. 1981—, pres. Dallas chpt. 1980-81, bd. dirs. Dallas chpt. 1977-83, 86—, recipient Pres. Service award 1981). Clubs: Exchange. Real property, General corporate, Banking. Office: Suite 2000 Lincoln Plaza 500 N Akard St Dallas TX 75201

NEWSOME, GEORGE MARVIN, lawyer; b. Phenix City, Ala., June 30, 1919; s. Thomas L. and Mary E. (Spivey) N.; m. Norma Elizabeth Hollomon, Aug. 19, 1941; children—Keith, Glenn, Carol. A.A., George Washington U., LL.B., 1949. Bar: D.C. Dist. Ct. With IBM 1945-83, office adminstrn., Washington, 1945-49, atty., N.Y.C., 1949-51, plant counsel, Poughkeepsie, Kingston, N.Y., 1951-59, div. counsel, White Plains, N.Y., 1959-68, staff counsel, Armonk, N.Y., 1968-79, staff counsel, Washington, 1979-83; pvt. practice, Washington, 1983—. Pres., United Way No. Westchester, 1974-79, v.p., 1977-79. Served with USAF, 1942-45. Recipient Marshall award United Way No. Westchester, 1977. Mem. ABA, Fed. Bar Assn. D.C. Bar Assn., Nat. Security Indsl. Assn., Nat. Lawyers Club. Administrative and regulatory, General corporate, Private international. Home: 10520 Wickens Rd Vienna VA 22180 Office: 1815 H St NW Suite 1010 Washington DC 20006

NEWTON, ALEXANDER WORTHY, lawyer; b. Birmingham, Ala., June 19, 1930; s. Jeff H. and Annis Lillian (Kelly) N.; m. Sue Aldridge, Dec. 22, 1952; children: Lamar Aldridge Newton, Kelly McClure Newton Hammond, Jane Worthy Newton, Robins Jeffry Newton. B.S., U. Ala., 1952, J.D., 1957. Bar: Ala. 1957. Sole practice Birmingham; ptnr. Hare, Wynn, Newell & Newton, 1957—; mem. Jefferson County Jud. Nominating Com., 1983—. Mem. Birmingham Racing Commn., 1984-87; v.p. U. Ala. Law Sch. Found., 1978-79, pres., 1980-82. Served to capt. inf. U.S. Army, 1952-54. Recipient Disting. Alumnus award Farrah Law Soc. U. Ala., 1982. Fellow Am. Coll. Trial Lawyers (state chmn. 1983-84, regents' nominatin com. 1984-85), Internat. Soc. Barristers (bd. dirs. 1974-75, sec.-treas. 1976-77, v.p. 1977-78, pres. 1979-80); mem. ABA, Am. Bar Found., Ala. State Bar (chmn. practices and proc. subsect. 1965, governance com. and pres.'s task force 1984—), Birmingham Bar Assn. (exec. com. 1967), Ala. Trial Lawyers Assn. (sec.-treas. 1958-65), Assn. Trial Lawyers Am., Am. Judicature Soc., Sigma Chi. Democrat. Presbyterian. Clubs: Shoal Creek, Birmingham Country (Birmingham); Capital City (Atlanta); Garden of the Gods (Colorado Springs, Colo.). Federal civil litigation, State civil litigation, Personal injury. Home: 2837 Canoe Brook Ln Birmingham AL 35243 Office: Hare Wynn Newell & Newton City Fed Bldg 7th Floor Birmingham AL 35203-3709

NEWTON, FRANCIS CHANDLER, JR., lawyer; b. Boston, Oct. 25, 1925; s. Francis C. and Helen L. (Prentiss) N.; m. Elizabeth White, June 8, 1950; children—James W., Francis C., III. B.A., Amherst Coll., 1949; J.D., Boston U., 1952. Bar: Mass. 1952, U.S. Dist. Ct. Mass. 1953, U.S. Ct. Claims 1969, U.S. Ct. Mil. Appeals, 1959, U.S. Ct. Appeals (1st cir.) 1969, U.S. Supreme Ct. 1959. Trial counsel Powers and Hall, P.C., Boston, 1952-61, ptnr., 1962-66; sole practice, Boston, 1966—. Served as col. JAGC, USAR, 1943-82. Mem. ABA, Boston Bar Assn., Assn. Trial Lawyers Am., Ancient and Hon. Arty. Co. State civil litigation, Federal civil litigation, Criminal. Office: 85 Merrimac St Boston MA 02114

NEWTON, GREGORY CLARK, lawyer; b. Salt Lake City, July 18, 1954; s. Jack Winston and Sylvia Ruth (Clark) N. BS cum laude with honors, Brigham Young U., 1978, BS, 1979, JD cum laude, 1982. Bar: Oreg. 1982,

Calif. 1985, U.S. Dist. Ct. (no. dist.) Calif. 1985. Assoc. Stoel, Rives, Boley, Fraser & Wyse, Portland, Oreg., 1982-85, Gaston, Snow & Ely, San Francisco and Palo Alto, Calif., 1985-86, Niehaus, Hanna, Murphy, Green, Osaka & Dunn, Portland, 1986—. Mem. Tigard Econ. Devel. Commn., Oreg., 1984-85, Tigard Planning Commn., 1986—. Mem. ABA, Oreg. Bar Assn., Calif. Bar Assn. Republican. Mormon. Avocations: golf, skiing, basketball, mathematics, piano. General corporate, Securities. Office: Niehaus Hanna Murphy Green Osaka & Dunn One Southwest Columbia Portland OR 97258

NEWTON, JOSEPH STEVEN, lawyer; b. Salt Lake City, Sept. 18, 1948; s. Joseph Raymond and Betsy Ross (Young) N.; m. Karen Ryser, Jan. 23, 1974; children: Andrea, Joseph Steven, Christopher. BA, U. Utah, 1973; JD, Brigham Young U., 1976. Bar: Utah 1976, U.S. Dist. Ct. Utah 1976, U.S. Ct. Appeals (10th cir.) 1978. Assoc. Romney, Nelson & Cassity, Salt Lake City, 1976-79; sole practice, Salt Lake City, 1979-81; ptnr. Newton & Ivins, Salt Lake City, 1981-85; mayor Sandy City, Utah, 1986—; v.p. Salt Lake County Council Govts., 1986—. Mem. Sandy City Council, Utah, 1980—, chmn., 1982—; chmn. Sandy Redevel. Agy, 1982, Alta Canyon Recreation Spl. Service Dist., Sandy, 1983-85; chmn. ad hoc com. for Excellent Edn., Sandy, 1984; Brigham Young Family Assn., 1985. Mem. Utah State Bar Assn., Salt Lake County Bar Assn., Assn. Trial Lawyers Am., Utah League Cities and Towns (bd. dirs.). Republican. Mormon. State civil litigation, Local government. Home: 8689 Treasure Mountain Dr Sandy UT 84092 Office: Sandy City Hall 440 E 8680 S Sandy UT 84070

NEWTON, MARY S., lawyer; b. Fond du Lac, Wis., Dec. 23, 1947; d. C. Baxter and M. Kathryn (Jones) N.; m. James R. Sanger, Aug. 28, 1971; children: Elizabeth J., Susan M. BA, U. Wis., 1970, MFA, 1973; JD, UCLA, 1979. Bar: Wis. 1979, U.S. Dist. Ct. (we. dist.) Wis. 1979. Assoc. Meissner, Tierney, Ehlinger & Whipp, S.C., Milw., 1979-85; ptnr. Meissner & Tierney S.C., Milw., 1986—. Bd. dirs. Bauer Contemporary Ballet, Milw., 1983—. Mem. Greater Milw. Employee Benefits Council, Wis. Retirement Plan Profls., Ltd. Pension, profit-sharing, and employee benefits, General corporate, Probate. Office: Meissner & Tierney SC 735 N Water St Milwaukee WI 53202

NG, PETER JOSEPH, lawyer; b. Monticello, N.Y., Oct. 26, 1949; s. Yen and Yuen Sun (Ying) N.; m. Marie Elizabeth LaPone, June 9, 1984. AS, Orange County (N.Y.) Community Coll., 1970; BS, SUNY, Albany, 1972; JD, Suffolk U., 1977. Bar: N.Y. 1978, U.S. Dist. Ct. (so., ea. and no. dists.) N.Y. 1979, U.S. Tax Ct. 1979, U.S. Ct. Appeals (2d cir.) 1981, U.S. Supreme Ct., 1982. Acct. Bachrach & Waschitz, Monticello, 1972-74; ptnr. Willis & Ng, Monticello, 1978—. Mem. Sullivan County Young Dems. Mem. ABA, Am. Judicature Soc., N.Y. Bar Assn., Sullivan County Bar Assn. (treas., sec. 1980-83, bd. dirs. 1984—). Democrat. Roman Catholic. Lodges: Elks, Kiwanis. Avocations: tennis, listening to music. General practice, Probate, Real property. Home: RD #2 Box 35B Monticello NY 12701 Office: Willis & Ng PO Box 632 262 Broadway Monticello NY 12701

NGUYEN, PAUL DUNG QUOC, lawyer; b. Hung Yen, Vietnam, Feb. 2, 1943; came to U.S., 1975; s. Trac Trong and Do Thi (Vu) N.; m. Kim-Dung T. Dang, Dec. 26, 1967; children: Theresa Thu, Catherine Bao-Chau, Jonathan Hung. LLB, Hue Law Sch., Vietnam, 1965; MA in Pub. Policy Adminstrn., U. Wis., 1973. Bar: N.Y. 1979. Prof. law Hue & Can Tho Law Schs., Vietnam, 197368-75; assoc. Proskauer, Rose, Getz & Mendelsohn, N.Y.C., 1979-80; sole practice N.Y.C., 1980-81; asst. corp. counsel law dept. City of New York, 1981—. Bd. dirs. N.Y.C. Indochinese Refugees, 1980—. Recipient Nat. Legion Honor award Office of Pres., Saigon, 1970. Mem. ABA, Assn. of Bar of City of N.Y. (Outstanding Performance prize com. on mcpl. affairs 1986). Avocations: tennis, reading, classical music. Real property, Local government, General corporate. Office: NYC Law Dept Office Corp Counsel 100 Church St New York NY 10007

NICHELSON, JAMES LEE, lawyer; b. Lima, Ohio, May 3, 1948; s. Donald J. and Donna E. (Neifer) N.; m. Mary Carolyn Pearl, Aug. 19, 1972; children—Thomas A., Lauren R., Ellen M. B.S., Ohio State U., 1971, M.S., 1971, J.D. cum laude, 1974. Bar: Ohio 1974. Assoc. Kinder, Kinder & Hanlon, St. Clairsville, Ohio, 1975-76; asst. pros. atty. Belmont County, Ohio, 1977-80; pub. defender, 1981—. Instr. Ohio Peace Officer Tng. Council, 1982—; mem. Martins Ferry Planning Commn., Ohio, 1982—; mem. central cim. Belmont County Democratic Party, 1983—; bd. dirs. Belmont County chpt. Am. cancer Soc., 1983—. Served to 1st lt. U.S. Army, 1974. Mem. Martins Ferry C. of C. (pres. and mem. bd. dirs. 1982). Lodges: Elks (exalted ruler 1979-80), Eagles, Redmen. Criminal, Probate, Real property. Office: 135 E Main St Saint Clairsville OH 43950

NICHOLAS, CAROL LYNN, lawyer; b. Berkeley, Calif., July 28, 1938; d. Frederick Mortimer and Carolyn (Wright) Nicholas; m. Donald Herrick Maffly, Aug. 24, 1958 (div. 1973); children: Donald Herrick, Brian A. E., Elizabeth Lynn. Student, Conn. Coll., 1956-58; AB, U. Calif., Berkeley, 1971; JD, U. San Francisco, 1975; LLM, Georgetown U., 1982. Bar: Calif. 1976. Staff atty. SEC, San Francisco, 1976-79, Crocker Nat. Bank, San Francisco, 1979-81, Fed. Home Loan Bank, San Francisco, 1983-84; assoc. Rosen, Wachtell & Gilbert, San Francisco and Los Angeles, 1984-86, Lewis, D'Amato, Brisbois & Bisgaard, Los Angeles, 1986—. Contbr. book revs. and articles to profl. jours. Mem. ABA (fed. regulation of securities com.). Democrat. Episcopalian. Securities, General corporate. Home: 2738 Webster St Berkeley CA 94705 Office: Lewis D'Amato Brisbois & Bisgaard 261 Figueroa St Suite 300 Los Angeles CA 90012

NICHOLAS, CHRISTOPHER PAUL, lawyer; b. Bklyn., Apr. 25, 1949; s. K. Calvin and Evelyn Constance (Nurkiewicz) N.; m. Mary Mee Yee, Aug. 16, 1974; children: Matthew, Michael, Gregory. AB, Princeton U., 1971; JD, Harvard U., 1974. Bar: N.Y. 1975, U.S. Dist. Ct. (so. dist.) N.Y. 1975. Assoc. Willkie, Farr & Gallagher, N.Y.C., 1974-79; asst. gen. counsel Prudential Ins. Co., Newark, 1979-84, Met. Life Ins. Co., N.Y.C., 1984—; sec. Met. Series Fund, N.Y.C., 1986—. Trustee, deacon Bklyn. Bapt. Ch., 1975—; alumni dir. Princeton (N.J.) U. Evang. Fellowship, 1976—. Mem. ABA. Republican. Avocations: sports, opera, Brit. history. Securities, Insurance, General corporate. Home: 961 Bay Ridge Pkwy Brooklyn NY 11228 Office: Met Life Ins Co One Madison Ave New York NY 10010

NICHOLAS, EDWARD ERNEST, III, lawyer; b. Washington, Jan. 5, 1955; s. Edward Ernest Jr. and Constance (Maybach) N.; m. Patricia Shaver, Aug. 9, 1980. BA, U. Va., 1977, JD, 1981. Bar: Va. 1981, U.S. Dist. Ct. (ea. and we. dists.) Va. 1982, U.S. Ct. Appeals (4th cir.) 1982. Assoc. McGuire, Woods & Battle, Richmond, Va., 1981-86, Wright, Robinson, McCommon & Tatum, P.C., Richmond, 1986—. Mem. ABA, Va. Bar Assn., Richmond Bar Assn., Phi Beta Kappa. Democrat. Club: Shenandoah Mountain (Richmond). Avocations: hiking, traveling, reading. Construction, State civil litigation, Federal civil litigation. Home: 607 W 34th St Richmond VA 23225 Office: Wright Robinson McCommon & Tatum PC 629 E Main St Suite 400 Richmond VA 23219

NICHOLAS, SAMUEL JOHN, JR., arbitrator; b. Yazoo City, Miss., July 4, 1937; s. Samuel J. and Mildred Lucille (Jefferies) N.; m. Olivia Thomas; children—Samuel John III, Christopher Walter, Patrick Peterson, John Thomas. B.A., U. Miss., 1959, M.B.A., 1962; J.D., Miss. Coll., 1966. Bar: Miss. 1966. Asst. prof. econs. Millsaps Coll., 1963-70; arbitrator, 1970—; adj. prof. law U. Miss., Miss. Coll., 1966. Labor. Home: 2668 Lake Circle Jackson MS 39211 Office: Box 22512 Jackson MS 39205

NICHOLES, STEVEN ATWATER, lawyer; b. Eugene, Oreg., Sept. 29, 1952; s. Bruce O. and Anita B. (Frost) N.; m. Laura J. Verling, July 30, 1977; children: Patrick S., Sarah E. BA in Psychology and BBA, Oreg. State U., 1975; JD, Gonzaga U., 1980; LLM in Taxation, U. Fla., 1981. Bar: Oreg. 1980, U.S. Dist. Ct. Oreg. 1982, U.S. Ct. Appeals (9th cir.) 1986. Comptroller Morrow Produce Co., Boardman, Oreg., 1975-77; atty. Duffy, Kekel & Jensen, Portland, Oreg., 1981—; speaker seminars on fed. estate tax. Mem. ABA, Aircraft Owners and Pilots Assn. Republican. Roman Catholic. Avocations: skiing, flying, sailing. Personal income taxation, Corporate taxation, Estate taxation. Home: 4940 SW Lowell St Portland OR 97221 Office: Duffy Kekel & Jensen 1404 Standard Plaza Portland OR 97204

NICHOLLS, JEFFREY MICHAEL, lawyer; b. Beloit, Wis., Dec. 26, 1953; s. Harold Edgar and Barbara Helen (Sommer) N.; m. Jackie Lee Anderson, June 12, 1976. BA in Philosophy, Valparaiso U., 1976, JD, 1979. Bar: Ind. 1979, U.S. Dist. Ct. (so. dist.) Ind. 1979, U.S. Dist. Ct. (no. dist.) Ind. 1980. Sole practice Lafayette, 1979-80; assoc. Law Office of George J. Heid, Lafayette, 1980-81; sole practice Anderson, Ind., 1982—. mem. Ind. Bar Assn., Madison County Bar Assn. Lutheran. Avocation: military history. Consumer commercial. Home: 1125 Crane Ct Anderson IN 46011 Office: 616 McArthur Blvd Anderson IN 46015

NICHOLLS, RICHARD H., lawyer; b. Toronto, Ont., Can., Oct. 27, 1938; s. Richard S. and Roberta N.; m. Judy Carter, Apr. 15, 1963; children—Christopher, Jamie C.; m. Anne Delaney, June 10, 1978. B.A. cum laude, Amherst Coll., 1960; LL.B., Stamford U., 1963; LL.M., NYU, 1964. Bar: Calif. 1964, N.Y. 1965, D.C. Assoc. Mudge Rose Guthrie, Alexander & Ferdon and predecessor, N.Y.C., 1964-70, ptnr., 1971—. Mem. N.Y. Bar Assn., ABA, Nat. Assn. Bond Lawyers (bd. dirs.). Club: Stamford Yacht. Corporate taxation, Personal income taxation. Address: 159 Ocean Dr W Stamford CT 06902 Office: Mudge Rose Guthrie Alexander & Ferdon 180 Maiden Ln New York NY 10038

NICHOLS, ALAN HAMMOND, lawyer; b. Palo Alto, Calif., Feb. 14, 1940; s. John Ralph and Shirley Weston (Charles) N.; children—Alan Hammon, Sharon Elizabeth, Shan Darwin. B.A., Stanford U., 1951, J.D., 1955; D.S. (hon.), Calif. Coll. Podiatric Medicine, 1980. Bar: Calif. 1955, U.S. Dist. Ct. (no. dist.) Calif. 1955, U.S. Dist. Ct. (cen. dist.) Calif. 1969, U.S. Dist. Ct. (ea. dist.) Calif. 1978, U.S. Dist. Ct. Ariz. 1978, U.S. Dist. Ct. Minn. 1979, U.S. Dist. Ct. (so. dist.) Calif. 1980, U.S. Tax Ct. 1981. Assoc. Lillick, Geary, Wheat, Adams & Charles, San Francisco, 1955-61; pres. Nichols & Rogers, San Francisco, 1961-74; pres. Nichols Law Corp., San Francisco, 1974-83, Nichols, Doi & Rapaport, San Francisco, 1983—; prof. forensic medicine Calif. Coll. Podiatric Medicine, 1975-77. Mem. San Francisco Library Commn., 1962-65; v.p. San Francisco Council Chs., 1965-68; pres. sch. bd. San Francisco Unified Sch. Dist., 1967-71; exec. com. Council Great City Schs. of U.S.; del. Calif. Sch. Bd. Assn. Assembly; mem. Civil Grand Jury, San Francisco, 1975-76; pres. Young Republicans San Francisco, 1957, Calif.; 1959, mem. Rep. Central Com., San Francisco, 1961—, pres., 1976; trustee City Coll. San Francisco, 1966-71, pres. bd. trustees, 1970-71; trustee Calif. Coll. Podiatric Medicine, 1973-85, Cathedral Sch., 1973-74, 83—; past trustee Prescott Center Coll. Served to lt. AUS, 1951-54. Decorated Commendation medal with 4 clusters; named Young Man of Yr., San Francisco newspapers, 1961. Mem. ABA (local govt. sect., real property probate and trust law sect., urban, state and local govt. sect., corp., banking and bus. law sect., forum com. on health law), San Francisco Bar Assn., State Bar Assn. Calif. (estate planning, trust and probate law sect.), Am. Arbitration Assn. (arbitrator), Phi Beta Kappa, Phi Delta Phi, Sigma Nu. Club: Bohemian. Author: (with Harold E. Rogers, Jr.) Water for California, 2 vols., 1967; (poetry) To Climb a Sacred Mountain, 1979, San Francisco Commuter, 1970; (play) Siddartha, 1977; A Gift from the Master, 1978; contbr. articles to profl. jours. including Stanford Law Rev., UCLA Law Rev., Am. Bar Rev. General corporate, Banking, Health. Office: Nichols Doi & Rapaport 1032 Broadway San Francisco CA 94133

NICHOLS, CHARLES LEONARD, lawyer; b. Sheboygan, Wis., June 10, 1943; s. Elias Nikolopulos and Lulu (Covolos) N.; children: Julie, Paul. BS in Chemistry, U. Mich., 1965; MS in Chemistry, Oakland U., Rochester, Mich., 1970-71; JD, Detroit Coll. Law, 1979. Bar: Mich. 1979, U.S. Dist. Ct. (so. dist.) Mich. 1979. Control chemist Sherwin-Williams Co., Cleve., 1965-66; chemist, mgr. Parke-Davis & Co., Detroit, 1971-80; ptnr. Charfoos & Christensen P.C., Detroit, 1980—. Served to lt. USN, 1966-70, Vietnam. Mem. ABA, Assn. Trial Lawyers Am., Mich. Trial Lawyers Assn., Downriver Bar Assn., Detroit Bar Assn., Hellenic Bar Assn. of Mich. (pres. 1985—, sec. 1983-84). Avocations: racquetball, golf. Personal injury, Federal civil litigation, State civil litigation. Home: 20 Middlebury Ct Dearborn MI 48120 Office: Charfoos & Christiansen PC 4000 Penobscott Bldg Detroit MI 48226

NICHOLS, CYNTHIA LEIGH, lawyer; b. Gainesville, Fla., Aug. 3, 1957; d. Donald Gilbert and Betty Catherine (Bullard) Nichols. B.S., Fla. State U., 1978; J.D., Stetson U., 1980. Bar: Fla. 1981. Law clk. Fla. Supreme Ct., Tallahassee, 1981; asst. state atty. State of Fla., Jacksonville, 1981-82; sole practice, Jacksonville, 1982-83; ptnr. Nichols & Nichols, Jacksonville, 1983—. Bd. dirs. P.A.C.E. Ctr. for Girls. Mem. ABA, Fla. Bar Assn., Jacksonville Bar Assn., Assn. Trial Lawyers Am. Democrat. Baptist. Juvenile, Personal injury, Probate. Office: Nichols & Nichols 340-1 E Adams St Jacksonville FL 32202

NICHOLS, DAVID ARTHUR, state justice; b. Lincolnville, Maine, Aug. 6, 1917; s. George E. and Flora E. (Pillsbury) N. A.B. magna cum laude, Bates Coll., 1942; J.D., U. Mich., 1949. Bar: Maine bar 1949, Mass. bar 1949, U.S. Supreme Ct 1954. Practice in Camden, Maine, 1949-75; justice Maine Superior Ct., 1975-77, Maine Supreme Jud. Ct., 1977—; Mem. Maine Exec. Council, 1955-57; moderator Lincolnville Town Meeting, 1950-74. Contbr. to legal and geneal. publs. Chmn. Maine Republican Com., 1960-64; mem. Rep. Nat. Com., 1960-68; chmn. Maine council Young Reps., 1950-54; New Eng. council Young Reps., 1952-54; trustee, past pres. Penobscot Bay Med. Center. Served with USAAF, 1942-45. Fellow Am. Bar Found., Am. Coll. Trial Lawyers; mem. Camden-Rockport C. of C. (past pres.), Maine Hist. Soc., Camden Hist. Soc. (past pres.), Camden Bus. Men's Assn. (past pres.), ABA (bd. govs. 1960-63, ho. dels. 1957-78), Maine Bar Assn., Am. Judicature Soc. (dir. 1960-64), New Eng. Historic Geneal. Soc. (trustee), Bates Coll. Alumni Assn. (past pres.), Maine Trial Lawyers Assn. (past pres.), Phi Beta Kappa, Delta Sigma Rho. Clubs: Odd Fellow, Rotary (past pres.). Evidence, State civil litigation, Probate. Home: Box 76 Lincolnville ME 04849 Office: Knox County Courthouse Rockland ME 04841

NICHOLS, ELAINE KILBURN, lawyer; b. New Haven, Oct. 27, 1955; d. Richard Flemmimg and Janet (Tousey) Kilburn; m. Jeffrey Spencer Nichols, Sept. 14, 1985. BA, U. Vt., 1977; JD, Boston Coll., 1981. Bar: Vt. 1981. Assoc. Downs, Rachlin & Mattin, Burlington and St. Johnsbury, Vt., 1981-85; sole practice Stowe, Vt., 1985—. Mem. ABA, Vt. Bar Assn., Lamille County Bar Assn. Administrative and regulatory, Contracts commercial, Real property. Home and Office: Birch Hill Rd Stowe VT 05672

NICHOLS, HENRY ELIOT, lawyer, savings and loan executive; b. N.Y.C., Jan. 3, 1924; s. William and Elizabeth (Lisse) N.; m. Frances Griffin Morrison, Aug. 12, 1950 (dec. July 1978); children—Clyde Whitney, Diane Spencer. B.A., Yale U., 1946; J.D., U. Va., 1948. Bar: D.C. 1950, U.S. Dist. Ct. 1950, U.S. Ct. Appeals 1952, U.S. Supreme Ct. 1969. Assoc. Frederick W. Berens, Washington, 1950-52; sole practice, Washington, 1952—; real estate columnist Washington Star, 1966-81; pres., gen. counsel Hamilton Fed. Savs. & Loan Assn., 1971-74; vice chmn. bd. Columbia 1st Fed. Savs. & Loan Assn., Washington, 1974—; pres. Century Fin. Corp., 1971—; regional v.p. Preview, Inc., 1972-78; dir., exec. com. Columbia Real Estate Title Ins. Co., Washington, 1968-78; dir. Greater Met. Bd. Trade, 1974-78, Dist. Realty Title Ins. Co., 1978-86. Nat. adv. bd. Harker Prep. Sch., 1975-80; exec. com. Father Walter E. Schmitz Meml. Fund, Cath. U., 1982=83; bd. dirs. Vincent T. Lombardi Cancer Research Ctr., 1979-84; del. Pres. Johnson's Conf. Law and Poverty, 1967; vice chmn. Mayor's Ad Hoc Com. Housing Code Problems, Washington, 1968-71; mem. Commn. Landlord-Tenant Affairs Washington City Council, 1970-71; vice chmn. Washington Area Realtors Council, 1970; exec. com., dir. Downtown Progress, 1970; bd. dirs. Washington Mental Health Assn., 1973, Washington Med Ctr., 1975. Served to capt. USAAF, 1942-46. Mem. Am. Land Devel. Assn., Nat. Assn. Realtors, Nat. Assn. Real Estate Editors, Washington Bd. Realtors (pres. 1970, Realtor of Yr. 1970, Martin Isen award 1981), Greater Met. Washington Bd. Trade (bd. dirs. 1974-80), U.S. League Savs. Assns. (attys. com. 1971—), Washington Savs. and Loan League, ABA, D.C. Bar Assn., Internat. Real Estate Fedn., Omega Tau Rho. Episcopalian. Clubs: Yale, Cosmos, Rolls Royce, Antique Auto, St. Elmo. Patentee med. inventions; contbr. articles profl. jours. Real property. Address: 1 Kittery Ct Bethesda MD 20817 Office: 1122 Connecticut Ave NW Washington DC 20036

NICHOLS, HOWARD MELVIN, lawyer; b. Glasgow, Mont., Apr. 25, 1951; s. James Donald and Gertrude Sarah (Rongstad) N.; m. Leslie Ann Downey, July 20, 1974; children: Dylan, Kord. BA in History and Polit. Sci., U. Mont., 1974; JD, Gonzaga U., 1978. Bar: Wash. 1978, U.S. Dist. Ct. (ea. dist.) Wash. 1979, U.S. Dist. Ct. (we. dist.) Wash. 1985. Dep. pros. atty. Spokane County, Wash., 1977-79; assoc. Sharpe, Ganz & Henderson, Spokane, 1979-81, Law Office James J. Workland, Spokane, 1981-84; ptnr. Henderson & Nichols P.S., Spokane, 1984—; judge pro-tem Spokane County Dist. Ct., 1984—. Bd. dirs. Friends Spokane Airport, 1984—. Mem. ABA, Wash. State Bar Assn. (spl. dist. counsel 1984—), Spokane County Bar Assn., Wash. State Trial Lawyers Assn., Wash. State Assn. Def. Counsel, Legal Services to Armed Com., Def. Research Inst. Democrat. Lutheran. Club: Spokane. Avocations: running, golf. Insurance, State civil litigation, Personal injury. Home: 4702 E Sumac Spokane WA 99223 Office: Henderson & Nichols PS W 601 Main St 715 Wash Mut Bldg Spokane WA 99201

NICHOLS, ROBERT HASTINGS, lawyer; b. Mpls., Aug. 12, 1941; s. James Hastings and Judith (Beach) N.; m. Jean Christy, Nov. 30, 1968; children—Marc O., Seth J., Ethan D., Rebecca J. A.B., Yale U., 1963; cert. in Pub. Affairs, CORO Found., 1964; J.D., U. Chgo., 1967. Bar: Ill. 1967, U.S. Dist Ct. (no. dist.) Ill. 1967, U.S. Dist. Ct. (ea. dist.) Wis. 1975; U.S. Ct. Appeals (7th cir.) 1972, U.S. Ct. Appeals (8th cir.) 1975, U.S. Ct. Appeals (D.C. cir.) 1976, U.S. Supreme Ct. 1986. Ptnr. Cotton, Watt, Jones & King, Chgo., 1967—; gen. counsel Air Line Employees Assn., Internat., Chgo., 1986—; chmn. United Airlines Pilots' System Bd. of Adjustment, Elk Grove Village, Ill., 1970—; cons. Govt. of New Zealand, Auckland, 1980; mem. Lawyers Coordinating Com., AFL-CIO. Contbr. articles to legal publs. Mem. ABA, Ill. State Bar Assn., Chgo. Council Lawyers. Democrat. Presbyterian. Club: Columbia Yacht. Labor, Federal civil litigation. Home: 1030 E 49th St Chicago IL 60615 Office: Cotton Watt Jones King One IBM Plaza Chicago IL 60611

NICHOLS, STEPHEN WAYNE, lawyer; b. Kansas City, Mo., May 16, 1955; s. Lee Richard and Catherine Virginia (Hitt) N.; m. Linda Marie Owsley, June 29, 1979; children: Audrey Lynn, Adam Joseph, Alex John. BA, U. Kans., 1977; JD, U. Mo., Kansas City, 1980. Bar: Mo. 1980, U.S. Dist. Ct. (we. dist.) Mo. 1980. Assoc. Law Office of Timothy H. Bosler, Liberty, Mo., 1980-86; ptnr. Panus & Nichols, Kansas City, 1986—. Mem. ABA, Kansas City Met. Bar Assn. (civil law and procedure com.), Mo. Bar Assn. (civil practice and procedure com.), Clay County Bar Assn., Assn. Trial Lawyers Am., Mo. Assn. Trial Attys., Phi Alpha Theta, Pi Sigma Alpha. Avocations: golf, softball. Personal injury, Federal civil litigation, State civil litigation. Home: 510 NE 98th Terr Kansas City MO 64155 Office: Panus & Nichols 2800 Rockcreek Pkwy Suite 500 North Kansas City MO 64117

NICHOLSON, BRENT BENTLEY, lawyer; b. Perrysburg, Ohio, Mar. 30, 1954; s. Donald Grant and Wilma Ione (Bentley) N.; m. Ann Elizabeth Loehrke, Sept. 1, 1978; children: Bradley, Lindsay. BS in Bus. Adminstrn., Bowling Green State U., 1976; JD, Ohio State U., 1979. Bar: Ohio 1979, U.S. Dist. Ct. (no. dist.) Ohio 1979, U.S. Tax Ct. 1984; CPA, Ohio. Tax atty. Arthur Young & Co., Toledo, 1979-83; assoc. Cobourn, Smith, Rohrbacher & Gibson, Toledo, 1983—; adj. asst. prof. Bowling Green State U., Ohio, 1984-85. Contbr. articles to profl. jours. Treas. N.W. Ohio chpt. March of Dimes, Toledo, 1983-85; mem. Toledo Estate Planning Council. Mem. ABA, Ohio Bar Assn., Toledo Bar Assn., Lucas County Bar Assn., Ohio Soc. CPA's, Toledo Estate Planning Council, Pi Sigma Alpha, Beta Gamma Sigma. Republican. Methodist. Avocations: reading, tennis. Probate, Personal income taxation, General corporate. Home: 3542 Mapleway Dr Toledo OH 43614 Office: Cobourn Smith Rohrbacher & Gibson 624 Adams St Toledo OH 43604

NICHOLSON, BRUCE ALLEN, lawyer; b. Phila., Nov. 12, 1949; s. Charles Glanz and Jean (Billman) N.; m. Linda King Barton, Apr. 22, 1972; children—Jessica Ann, James Barton. B.A., Cornell U., 1971; J.D. cum laude, Boston Coll., 1975. Bar: Pa. 1975. Staff asst. Mass. Bar Assn., Boston, 1973-75; assoc. Duffy, North, Wilson, Thomas & Nicholson, Hatboro, Pa., 1975-78, ptnr., 1978—. Mem. Hatboro Boro Council, 1984—; chmn. Hatboro Hist. Commn., 1981-83; bd. mgrs. Hatboro Area YMCA, 1984—. Mem. Pa. Bar Assn., Montgomery Bar Assn., Greater Hatboro C. of C. (v.p., bd. dirs.). Republican. Episcopalian. Lodge: Rotary. Banking, Real property, Probate. Office: Duffy North Wilson Thomas & Nicholson 104 N York Rd Hatboro PA 19040

NICHOLSON, FRANCIS JOSEPH, law educator, clergyman; b. Medford, Mass., Apr. 11, 1921; s. James Joseph and Eileen Cecilia (Dinan) N.;. AB, Boston Coll., 1942, AM, 1947; STL, Weston Coll., 1954; LLB, Georgetown U., 1949, LLM, 1951; LLM, Harvard U., 1956, SJD, 1963. Bar: D.C. 1950, U.S. Dist. Ct. D.C. 1950, U.S. Ct. Appeals (D.C. cir.) 1950, Mass. 1960. Mem. faculty Boston Coll. Law Sch., 1958—, prof. law, 1958—; rector Jesuit Community Coll., 1968-76. Contbr. articles to profl. jours. Mem. Mass. Maritime Commn., 1970-74, Mass. Bd. Regents of Higher Edn., 1980-84. Mem. ABA, Am. Soc. Internat. Law. Legal education, Private international, Public international. Home: Boston College Chestnut Hill MA 02167 Office: Boston Coll Law Sch 885 Centre St Newton MA 02159

NICHOLSON, MICHAEL, lawyer, engineer; b. Alexandroupolis, Greece, Nov. 26, 1936; m. Diana Long, June 21, 1964. B.S. in Civil Engring., Northwestern U., 1961; M.S. in Civil Engring., Columbia U., 1963; J.D., St. John's U., 1970. Bar: N.Y. 1971, U.S. Dist. Ct. (ea. dist.) N.Y. 1979. Counsel, George A. Fuller Co., N.Y.C., 1970-72, Leonard Wegman Cons. Engrs., N.Y.C., 1972-73; sr. ptnr. Corner, Finn, Nicholson & Charles, Bklyn., 1973—. Bd. dirs. Bklyn. Nephrology Found., 1979, Pelham Bay Gen. Hosp., 1979—. Mem. Am. Arbitration Assn., ABA, N.Y. State Bar Assn., N.Y. State Soc. Profl. Engrs., Nat. Soc. Profl. Engrs., Mcpl. Engrs. City of N.Y. (award 1971). Contbr. articles to profl. jours. Government contracts and claims, State civil litigation, Contracts commercial. Home: 35 Hilton Ave Garden City NY 11530 Office: 32 Court St 19th Floor Brooklyn NY 11201

NICHOLSON, THOMAS LAURENCE, lawyer; b. Evanston, Ill., Nov. 19, 1923; s. Thomas Laurence Nicholson and Nelle Braxton (Jones) McKittrick; m. Eleanor A. Kuester, Sept. 11, 1954; children: Anne Lindsey, John Chester, Sarah Stoney, Martha Kenyon. AB, Princeton U., 1944; student, U. Paris, 1949; JD, U. Chgo., 1954, M in Comparative Law, 1958; postdoctoral, U. Hamburg, 1958-59. Bar: Ill. 1955. From asst. to acting pub. affairs officer U.S. Consulate Gen., Algiers, Algeria, 1949-51; assoc. Isham, Lincoln & Beale, Chgo., 1954-61, ptnr., 1961-66; ptnr. Mayer, Brown & Platt, Chgo., 1967—; research assoc. law U. Mich., 1959-60. Trustee Inst. for Psychoanalyst, Chgo., 1974—, pres., 1979-83; bd. dirs. Pub. Interest Law Internship, Chgo., Chgo. Area Found. for Legal Services. Served to lt. USN, 1941-46. Named 1 amoung 10 Outstanding Chicagoans, Jaycees, 1963; Recipient Outstanding Citizen award U. Chgo., 1966; Woodrow Wilson fellow, 1948; Ford Found. grantee, 1958-59. Mem. ABA, Am. Law Inst., The Law Club, The Legal Club. Private international, General corporate. Home: 7 Swift Ln Lakeside MI 49116 Office: Mayer Brown & Platt 190 S LaSalle St Chicago IL 60603

NICKERSON, EUGENE H., judge; b. Orange, N.J., Aug. 2, 1918; m. Marie-Louise Steiner; children—Marie-Louise, Lawrie H., Stephanie W., Susan A. A.B., Harvard U., 1941; LL.B. (Kent scholar), Columbia U., 1943; LL.D. (hon.), Hofstra U., 1970. Bar: N.Y. 1944, U.S. Supreme Ct. 1948. Law clk. to Judge Augustus N. Hand, 2d circuit U.S. Ct. Appeals, 1943-44; to Chief Justice Harlan F. Stone U.S. Supreme Ct., 1944-46; county exec. Nassau County, N.Y., 1962-70; practice law N.Y.C., 1946-61, 71-77; judge U.S. Dist. Ct., Bklyn., 1977—; Counsel N.Y. Gov.'s Com. Pub. Employee Procedures, 1956-58; mem. N.Y. State Law Revision Commn., 1958-59, 77; mem. Met. Regional Council, 1962-70, chmn., 1969-70; mem. adv. council pub. welfare HEW, 1963-65; mem. pub. ofcls. adv. council OEO, 1968. Mem. Assn. Bar City N.Y. (com. fed. legislation 1971-74, com. on communication 1971-77, com. on judiciary 1974-77), Am., Nassau County bar assns., Am. Law Inst., Phi Delta Phi. Jurisprudence. Address: US Courthouse 225 Cadman Plaza E Brooklyn NY 11201

NICKERSON, MARK WILLIAM, lawyer; b. Boston, Nov. 23, 1948; s. Seth Connor and Genevieve (Lensing) N.; m. Mary Hannah, June 1, 1973; children: Scott, Stuart. BA in Psychology, U. Rochester, 1970; JD with

honors, George Washington U., 1977, LLM in Taxation with highest honors, 1979. Bar: Va. 1977, U.S. Dist. Ct. (no. dist.) Ga. 1978, U.S. Tax Ct. 1978, U.S.Supreme Ct. 1982, Ga. 1983, U.S. Dist. Ct. (no. dist.) Ga. 1983. Sr. staff atty. dist. counsel IRS, Atlanta, 1978-83; assoc. Merritt & Tenney, Atlanta, 1983; tax mgr. May Zima & Co. CPA, Atlanta, 1983-85; sole practice Atlanta, 1985—; exec. v.p., gen. counsel Lawmark Inc., Atlanta, 1985—. Served to lt. USNR, 1971-74. Mem. ABA (taxation sect.), Ga. Bar Assn., Va. Bar Assn. Corporate taxation, Estate taxation, Personal income taxation. Office: Northwind Profl Bldg Suite G 1495 Alpharetta Hwy Alpharetta GA 30201

NICKLIN, EMILY, lawyer; b. Cooperstown, N.Y., June 24, 1953; d. George Leslie Jr. and Katherine Mildred (Aronson) N.; m. Jay Schleusener, Dec. 28, 1974; children: Max, Lucas. BA, U. Chgo., 1975, JD, 1977. Bar: Ill. 1977, U.S. Dist. Ct. (no. dist.) Ill. 1979, U.S. Ct. Appeals (7th cir.) 1979. Law clk. to judge U.S. Dist. Ct. (no. dist.) Ill., Chgo., 1977-79; assoc. Kirkland & Ellis, Chgo., 1979-83, ptnr., 1983—; tchr. Ill. Continuing Legal Edn. Bar Program, Chgo., 1983—; fellow Salzburg Seminar, Austria, 1983. Mem. Nat. Inst. Trial Advocacy (tchr., team leader 1982—), Order of Coif, Phi Beta Kappa. Federal civil litigation, State civil litigation, Libel. Office: Kirkland & Ellis 200 E Randolph Dr Chicago IL 60601

NICKSON, MILTON SCOTT, JR., lawyer; b. Shawnee, Okla., May 7, 1934; s. Milton Scott and W.L. N.; m. Janice Ann Alexander, Dec. 22, 1956; children: Stephanie Ann, Suzanne, Ashley Ann. B.B.A., U. Okla., 1956, LL.B., 1961. Bar: Okla. 1961, Tex. 1981, U.S. Dist. Ct. (no. dist.) Tex. 1984, U.S. Ct. Appeals (fed. cir.) 1985. Practice law Oklahoma City, 1961-68; atty., law dept. Dresser Industries, Inc., Dallas, 1968-72; v.p., gen. counsel machinery group Dresser Industries, Inc., 1972-76; v.p. ops. Jeffrey Mfg. Div., 1976-79; staff v.p., gen. counsel Jeffrey Mfg. div. Dresser Industries, Inc., 1979-80, v.p. gen. counsel, 1980-85, v.p., gen. counsel, sec., 1985—, chmn. polit. action com., 1981-86; Adminstrv. asst. Gov. Okla., 1967; mem. adv. bd., treas. Internat. and Comparative Law Center, 1979—. Served with USAF, 1957-60. Research fellow Southwestern Legal Found., 1979—. Mem. Machinery and Allied Products Inst. (law council). Clubs: City, Bent Tree Country, Tower.

NICOLA, ROBERT JAMES, lawyer; b. Bridgeport, Conn., Oct. 16, 1942; s. Nicholas J. and Elizabeth (Mussi) N.; m. Diana R. Rozdilsky, July 14, 1968; children—Robert N., Allyson J., Jennifer M., Stephanie J. B.S., Franklin and Marshall Coll., 1964; J.D., U. Conn., 1967. Bar: Conn. 1967. Assoc. D'Amore, Jacobson & Janello, Bridgeport, 1967-68; ptnr. Owens & Schine, Bridgeport, 1969—; town atty., Easton, Conn., 1980-84. Mem. Fairfield Republican Town Com., 1968-74, Easton Rep. Town Com., 1984—; mem. Internat. Inst., 1968-84; pres. St. Dimitrie's Ch. Council, 1980-82; mem. Indian Affairs Council, State of Conn., 1973-82; mem. U. Bridgeport Bd. Assocs. Served with USAR, 1968-74. Mem. Conn. Bar Assn., Bridgeport Bar Assn., ABA, Assn. Conn. Trial Attys. Eastern Orthodox. Club: Easton Lions (sec. 1981-82). Family and matrimonial, Personal injury, Real property. Home: 480 Rock House Rd Easton CT 06612 Office: 10 Middle St Suite 1200 Bridgeport CT 06604

NICOLAIDES, MARY, lawyer; b. N.Y.C., June 7, 1927; d. George and Dorothy Nicolaides. BCE, CUNY, 1947; MBA, DePaul U., 1975, JD, 1981. Bar: Ill. 1982, U.S. Dist. Ct. (no. dist.) Ill. 1982, U.S. Patent Office 1983. Sr. design engr. cement subs. U.S. Steel Corp., N.Y.C., then Pitts., 1948-71; sole practice Chgo., 1982—. Mem. ABA. Republican. Greek Orthodox. State civil litigation, Patent, Probate.

NIEHANS, DANIEL, lawyer; b. Basel, Switzerland, July 9, 1949; came to U.S., 1966, naturalized, 1972; s. Jurg Max and Gertrud Helen (Heusler) N.; m. Patricia Delano Lazowska, July 14, 1979; 1 child, Christina Claire. AB, Johns Hopkins U., 1971; JD, U. Chgo., 1974. Bar: Calif. 1974, U.S. Dist. Ct. (no. dist.) Calif. 1974, U.S. Tax Ct. 1981. Assoc. Pillsbury, Madison & Sutro, San Francisco, 1974-81, ptnr., 1982—. Mem. ABA, Western Pension Conf. Republican. Pension, profit-sharing, and employee benefits. Home: 22 Harrington Rd Moraga CA 94556 Office: Pillsbury Madison & Sutro 235 Montgomery St San Francisco CA 94104

NIEHAUS, SUSAN PATRICIA, lawyer; b. Bklyn., May 11, 1941; d. Jules and Grace (Straim) Backman; m. Charles R. Frank, Jr., Mar. 9, 1963; (div. June 1976); children—Elizabeth Grace, Stephen Raphael; m. Edward L. Niehaus, Dec. 21, 1986. A.B., U. Mich., 1962; cert. in demography Princeton U., 1963; J.D., Georgetown U., 1975. Bar: D.C. 1975, Tex. 1986. Assoc., Wenchel, Schulman & Manning, Washington, 1975-77; assoc. Mercier, Sanders, Baker & Schnabel, P.C., Washington, 1978-79, Sanders, Schnabel, Joseph & Powell, P.C., Washington, 1979-82; assoc. Sanders, Schnabel & Brandenburg, P.C., Washington, 1982-83, mem. firm, 1983-85. Contbr. articles to legal jours. Mem. ABA, Phi Beta Kappa. Estate planning, Probate, Personal income taxation.

NIELSEN, ANITA SPECTOR, lawyer; b. Bklyn., Nov. 15, 1945; d. Nathan and Gertrude (Metkofsky) Spector; m. Donald Allen Nielsen, Aug. 27, 1967 (div.). BA, SUNY, Stony Brook, 1967; JD, Bklyn. Law Sch., 1975. Bar: Va. 1975, Conn. 1977. Tax technician IRS, Bklyn., 1967-69; research asst. Sir George Williams U., Montreal, Que., Can., 1969-71; assoc. Bai, Pollock & Dunnigan, Bridgeport, Conn., 1977-79; sole practice New Haven, 1979—. N.Y. State Regents scholar, Albany, 1963-67. Mem. NOW (bd. dirs. New Haven 1978-80), Assn. Trial Lawyers Am., Conn. Bar Assn. (Acad. Profl., Devel., 1984—), Va. Bar Assn., Conn. Trial Lawyers Assn., New Haven County Bar Assn. Democrat. Jewish. Avocations: cooking, tennis, bird watching, flower arranging. Personal injury, Probate, General practice. Home: 230 Treadwell St 804 Hamden CT 06517 Office: 246 Church St New Haven CT 06510

NIELSEN, RUTH, lawyer; b. Salt Lake City, Nov. 3, 1952; d. Arthur Hansen and Vera (Richards) N.; m. Christopher Whitman Moore, July 31, 1982. BA in English cum laude, U. Utah, 1977, JD, 1980. Bar: Wash. 1980, U.S. Dist. Ct. (we. dist.) Wash. 1980, U.S. Ct. Appeals (9th cir.) 1985. Assoc. Helsell & Fetterman, Seattle, 1980-82; law clk. to presiding justice King County, Seattle, 1983-84; assoc. Carney, Stephenson, Seattle, 1984—. Mem. ABA, Wash. State Bar Assn. (editorial adv. bd. 1984—), Wash. Women Lawyers Assn., Wash. Assn. of Def. Counsel, Seattle-King County Bar Assn. (vol. atty. 1985—). Avocations: skiing, mountain climbing, winter camping, soccer. State civil litigation, Federal civil litigation, Personal injury. Home: 1023 NE 71st St Seattle WA 98115 Office: Carney Stephenson 2300 Columbia Ctr Seattle WA 98115

NIELSEN, WILLIAM ROBERT, lawyer; b. Grand Rapids, Mich., Feb. 23, 1954; s. Robert Raymond and Donna Ann (Laundra) N.; m. Denise Diane Desprez, June 16, 1978. BA, Mich. State U., 1976; JD, Thomas M. Cooley Law Sch., 1981. Bar: Mich. 1982, Wis. 1984, Iowa 1986. Dir. Muscular Dystrophy Assn., Chgo., 1977-78; bus. mgr. Boarshead Theater, Lansing, Mich., 1979-81; labor counsel Mich. Assn. Sch. Bds., Lansing, 1981-83; staff atty., dir. personnel Beloit (Wis.) Sch. Dist., 1983-84; dir. employment relations State of Iowa, Des Moines, 1984-86; corp. labor counsel Gerber Products Inc, Fremont, Mich., 1986—; chmn. comparable worth legis. com., State of Iowa, Des Moines, 1984-85, mem. gov.'s legal task force to rev. and rewrite code of Iowa, 1985—. Mem. ABA, Wis. Bar Assn. (non-resident lawyers div.), Wis. Sch. Attys. Assn. Republican. Roman Catholic. Avocations: golf. Labor, Legislative, General corporate. Office: Gerber Products Inc 445 State St Fremont MI 49412

NIEMI, BRUCE ALAN, lawyer; b. Detroit, Jan. 15, 1950; s. Harold I. and Bernice L. (Durrand) N.; m. Rhonda Jean Crowdus, June 2, 1980. BA, DePauw U., 1972; JD, U. Louisville, 1975. Bar: Ky. 1976, U.S. Dist. Ct. (we. dist.) Ky. 1976, U.S. Supreme Ct. 1979, U.S. Ct. Appeals (6th cir.) 1986. Tchr. Ky. Acad., Lyndon, 1972-73; ptnr. Carey, Caye, Niemi & Clements, Louisville, 1976—. Named disting. citizen, Mayor of Louisville, 1976. Mem. ABA, Ky. Bar Assn. (CLE recognition award 1981, 86), Louisville Bar Assn. Republican. Presbyterian. Family and matrimonial, General corporate, Probate. Home: 4106 Alton Rd Louisville KY 40207 Office: Carey Caye Niemi & Clements One Riverfront Plaza Suite 2000 Louisville KY 40202

NIERENBERG, GERARD IRWIN, lawyer; b. N.Y.C., July 27, 1923; s. George T. and Sally (Siegel) N.; m. Juliet Low, Oct. 9, 1943; children: Roy, Roger, George. Grad., NYU, 1941; JD, Bklyn. Law Sch., 1946; hon. degree, La acadamie Mexicana de Derecho International, Mex., 1971. Bar: N.Y. 1946. Ptnr. Nierenberg, Zeif & Weinstein, N.Y.C.; counsel People for UN, 1971; pres. Negotiation Inst. Inc., N.Y.C., 1966—, Inst. Gen. Semantics, 1969-70. Author: Art of Negotiating, 1968, Creative Business Negotiating, 1971, How To Read A Person Like A Book, 1971, Meta Talk, 1973, Fundamentals of Negotiating, 1973, How To Give And Receive Advice, 1975, The Art Of Creative Thinking, 1982, Complete Negitiator, 1986, Workable Ethics, 1987. Served with USAF, 1943-45. Negotiation training. Home: 421 E 51st St New York NY 10022 Office: Nierenberg Zeif & Weinstein 230 Park Ave New York NY 10169

NIES, HELEN WILSON, federal judge; b. Birmingham, Ala., Aug. 7, 1925; d. George Earl and Lida Blanche (Erckert) Wilson; m. John Dirk Nies, July 10, 1948; children: Dirk, Nancy, Eric. B.A., U. Mich., 1946, J.D., 1948. Bar: Mich. 1948, D.C. 1961, U.S. Supreme Ct. 1962. Atty. Dept. Justice, Washington, 1948-51, Office Price Stblzn., Washington, 1951-52; assoc. Pattishall, McAuliffe and Hofstetter, Washington, 1960-66; resident ptnr. Pattishall, McAuliffe and Hofstetter, 1966-77; ptnr. Howrey & Simon, Washington, 1978-80; judge U.S. Ct. Customs and Patent Appeals, 1980-82, U.S. Ct. Appeals Fed. Circuit, 1982—; mem. judicial conf. U.S. Com. on Bicentennial of Constitution; mem. public adv. com. trademark affairs Dept. Commerce, 1976-80; mem. adv. bd. BNA's Patent Trademark and Copyright Jour., 1976-78; bd. visitors U. Mich. Law Sch., 1975-78; adv. for restatement of law of unfair competition Am. Law Isnt., 1986. Contbr. articles to legal jours.; lectr. in field. Anne E. Shipman Stevens scholar, 1945-47; recipient Athena Outstanding Alumna award U. Mich., 1987. Mem. ABA (chmn. com. 203, 1972-74, com. 504, 1975-76), Bar Assn. D.C. (chmn. patent trademark copyright sect. 1975-76, dir. 1976-78), U.S. Trademark Assn. (chmn. lawyers adv. com. 1974-76, dir. 1976-78), Am. Patent Law Assn., Fed. Bar Assn., Nat. Assn. Women Lawyers (Woman Lawyer of Year 1980), Order of Coif, Phi Beta Kappa, Phi Kappa Phi. Jurisprudence. Office: US Court of Appeals 717 Madison Pl NW Washington DC 20439 *

NIFONG, J. MICHAEL, lawyer; b. San Diego, May 20, 1950; s. James Milton and Evelyn (Smith) N. BA, U. Fla., 1971, JD, 1974. Bar: Fla. 1974, D.C. 1980, U.S. Dist. Ct. (so. no. and mid. dists.) Fla., U.S. Ct. Appeals (5th and 11th cirs.). Assoc., jr. ptnr. Blackwell, Walker & Gray, Miami, Fla., 1974-81; assoc. Squire, Sanders & Dempsey, Miami, 1981-83; sr. ptnr. Finley, Kumbly, Wagner, Heine, Miami, 1983—. Mem. Fla. Bar Assn. (civil procedures com.), Am. Trial Lawyers Assn., Fla. Def. Lawyers Assn., Tiger Bay Polit. Club, Fla. Acad. Trial Lawyers, Products Liability Adv. Council. Democrat. Clubs: Beta, Grove Isle (Miami). Federal civil litigation, State civil litigation. Home: 2449 S Bayshore Dr Miami FL 33133 Office: Finley Kumble Wagner et al 777 Brickell Ave Miami FL 33131

NIGG, KARL FREDERICK, lawyer; b. N.Y.C., July 6, 1930; s. Fred B. and Hedwig (Richter) N.; m. Mary E. Olguin, May 7, 1952; children—Karl, Susan, Bryan, Miriam. B.B.A., U. N.Mex., 1961; J.D., U. Santa Clara, 1970. Bar: Calif. 1971, U.S. Dist. Ct. (no. dist.) Calif. 1971. With IBM, 1954-76, mgr., 1976; sole practice law, San Jose, 1971—. Served with USAF, 1948-53. Mem. State Bar Calif., Santa Clara County Bar Assn., ABA. Democrat. Roman Catholic. Family and matrimonial, Estate planning, General corporate. Address: 6849 Hampton Dr San Jose CA 95120

NILES, JOHN GILBERT, lawyer; b. Dallas, Oct. 5, 1943; s. Paul Dickerman and Nedra Mary (Arendts) N.; m. Marian Higginbotham, Nov. 21, 1970; children: Paul Breckenridge, Matthew Higginbotham. BA in History, Stanford U., 1965; LLB, U. Tex., 1968. Bar: Tex. 1968, Calif. 1969, U.S. Dist. Ct. (cen. dist.) Calif. 1973, U.S. Ct. Appeals (9th cir.) 1973, U.S. Dist. Ct. (so. dist.) Calif. 1977, U.S. Supreme Ct. 1979, U.S. Dist. Ct. (no. dsit.) Calif. 1983. Assoc. O'Melveny & Myers, Los Angeles, 1973-77, ptnr., 1978—; judge pro tem mcpl. Ct., Los Angeles; speaker, panel mem. Praticing Law Inst., N.Y.C. and San Francisco, 1984, 86. Served to lt. comdr. USNR, 1968-72, Viet Nam. Mem. ABA, Los Angeles County Bar Assn., Am. Judicature Soc. Clubs: Bel-Air Bay (Pacific Palisades, Calif.); Los Angeles Athletic. Avocation: sailing. Federal civil litigation, State civil litigation, Insurance. Home: 1257 Villa Woods Dr Pacific Palisades CA 90272 Office: O'Melveny & Myers 400 S Hope St Los Angeles CA 90071-2899

NIMETZ, MATTHEW, lawyer, former govt. ofcl.; b. Bklyn., June 17, 1939; s. Joseph L. and Elsie (Botwinnik) N.; m. Gloria S. Lorch, June 24, 1975; children—Alexandra Elise, Lloyd. B.A., Williams Coll., 1960, LL.D. (hon.), 1979; B.A. (Rhodes scholar), Balliol Coll., Oxford (Eng.) U., 1962; M.A., Oxford (Eng.) U., 1966; LL.B., Harvard U., 1965. Bar: N.Y. State bar 1966, D.C. bar 1968. Law clk. to Justice John M. Harlan, U.S. Supreme Ct., 1965-67; staff asst. to Pres. Johnson, 1967-69; asso. firm Simpson Thacher & Bartlett, N.Y.C., 1969-71; partner Simpson Thacher & Bartlett, 1972-77; counselor Dept. of State, Washington, 1977-80; acting coordinator refugee affairs Dept. of State, 1979-80, under sec. of state for security assistance, sci. and tech., 1980; partner firm Paul, Weiss, Rifkind, Wharton & Garrison, N.Y.C., 1981—; Commr. Port Authority N.Y. and N.J., 1975-77; Chmn. World Resources Inst., 1982—; dir. Council for U.S. and Italy, Inc., 1982—. Trustee Williams Coll., 1981—; chmn. UN Devel. Corp., 1986—. Mem. Council Fgn. Relations, Assn. Bar City N.Y., Am. Assn. Internat. Commn. Jurists Inc. (dir. 1983—). Club: Harvard (N.Y.C.). General corporate, Private international, Securities. Office: Paul Weiss Rifkind Wharton & Garrison 1285 Ave of Americas New York NY 10019

NIMKIN, BERNARD WILLIAM, lawyer; b. N.Y.C., Apr. 15, 1923; s. Myron Benjamin and Anabel (Davidow) N.; m. Jean Horowitz, Feb. 9, 1947; children—David Andrew, Margaret Lee, Katherine. B.S. cum laude, Harvard U., 1943, LL.B. cum laude, 1949. Bar: N.Y. State bar 1949. Asso. firm Carter, Ledyard & Milburn, N.Y.C., 1949-58; asso. and partner firm Kaye, Scholer, Fierman, Hays & Handler, N.Y.C., 1958—; lectr. Practising Law Inst., Banking Law Inst.; Mem. Am. Law Inst.; vis. com. U. Miami Law Sch.; mem. adv. bd. Rev. of Securities Regulation. Contbr. articles to profl. jours. Mem. Conservation Commn., Town of Mamaroneck (N.Y.), 1970-74; bd. dirs., sec. United Way of Tri-State, 1985—. Served to 1st lt. U.S. Army, 1943-46. Mem. Am. Bar Assn. (mem. fed. regulation of securities com. 1975—, corp. laws com. 1984—), N.Y. State Bar Assn. (chmn. sect. banking, corp. and bus. law 1979-81, ho. of dels. 1981-84, chmn. corp. law com. 1976-79), Assn. Bar of City of N.Y. (chmn. uniform state laws com. 1962-65). Democrat. Jewish. Banking, General corporate, Securities. Home: 116 E 63d St New York NY 10021 Office: 425 Park Ave New York NY 10022

NIMMONS, RALPH WILSON, JR., judge; b. Dallas, Sept. 14, 1938; s. Ralph Wilson and Dorothy (Tucker) N.; m. Doris Penelope Pickels, Jan. 30, 1960; children—Bradley, Paige, Bonnie. B.A., U. Fla., 1960, J.D., 1963. Bar: Fla. 1963, U.S. Dist. Ct. (mid. dist.) Fla. 1963, U.S. Ct. Appeals (5th cir.) 1969, U.S. Supreme Ct. 1970. Assoc. Ulmer, Murchison, Ashby & Ball, Jacksonville, Fla., 1963-65, ptnr., 1973-77; asst. pub. defender Pub. Defender's Office, Jacksonville, 1965-69; first asst. state atty. State Atty.'s Office, Jacksonville, 1969-71; chief asst. gen. counsel City of Jacksonville, 1971-73; judge 4th Jud. Cir. Ct., Jacksonville, 1977-83, First Dist. Ct. of Appeal Fla., Tallahassee, 1983—; mem. faculty Fla. Jud. Coll., Tallahassee, 1985, 86; mem. Fla. Bar Grievance Com., 1973-76, vice chmn., 1975-76; mem. Fla. Conf. Cir. Judges, 1977-83, mem. exec. com., 1980-83; mem. Met. Criminal Justice Adv. Council, 1977-79; mem. Fla. Gov.'s Task Force on Prison Overcrowding, 1983. Chmn. lay bd. Riverside Baptist Ch., Jacksonville, 1982; trustee Jacksonville Wolfson Children's Hosp., 1973-83. Recipient Carroll award for Outstanding Mem. Judiciary Jacksonville Jr. C. of C., 1980, Disting. Service award Fla. Council on Crime and Delinquency, 1981; named Outstanding Judge in Duval County, Jacksonville Bar Assn. Young Lawyers Sect., 1981. Mem. Phi Alpha Delta (pres. chpt. 1962-63), Am. Inns of Ct. (master of bench), Delta Tau Delta (pres. chpt. 1959-60). Administrative and regulatory, State civil litigation, Criminal. Home: 5505 Touraine Dr Tallahassee FL 32308 Office: Dist Ct of Appeal Tallahassee FL 32301

NIMS, ARTHUR LEE, III, judge; b. Oklahoma City, Jan. 3, 1923; s. Arthur Lee and Edwina (Peckham) N.; m. Nancy Chloe Keyes, July 28, 1950; children: Chloe, Lucy. B.A., Williams Coll., 1945; LL.B., U. Ga., 1949; LL.M. in Taxation, NYU, 1954. Bar: Ga. 1949, N.J. 1955. Practice law Macon, Ga., 1949-51; spl. atty. Office Chief Counsel, IRS, N.Y.C. and Washington, 1951-55; assoc. McCarter & English, Newark, 1955-61; ptnr. McCarter & English, 1961-79; judge U.S. Tax Ct., Washington, 1979—. Mem. standing com. Episcopal Diocese of Newark, 1971-75; pres. Colonial Symphony Soc., Madison, N.J., 1975-78. Served to lt. (j.g.) USNR, 1943-46. Mem. ABA (sec. sect. taxation 1977-79), N.J. Bar Assn. (chmn. sect. taxation 1969-71), Am. Law Inst. Jurisprudence. Office: US Tax Ct 400 Second St NW Washington DC 20217

NINNIS, WILLIAM RAYMOND, JR., lawyer; b. San Francisco, Aug. 23, 1932; s. William Raymond and Oda Marie (Jensen) N.; m. Ethel Marie Willis; children: William Bradley, David Raymond. AB, San Francisco State U., 1958; LLB, JD, U. Calif., 1962. Bar: Calif. 1963, U.S. Dist. Ct. (no. dist.) Calif. 1963, U.S. Ct. Appeals (9th cir.) 1963, U.S. Dist. Ct. (ea. dist.) Calif. 1967, U.S. Dist. Ct. (cen. dist.) Calif. 1984. Assoc. house counsel Pacific Gas and Electric Co., San Francisco, 1962-67; trial atty., v.p. and sec. Dawson & Ninnis PLC, Fresno, Calif., 1967-84; ptnr., trial atty. Ninnis & Cribbs, Fresno, 1984—; chmn. worker's compensation com. San Francisco Bar Assn., 1965-67; bd. dirs. No. Calif. Def. Atty.'s Assn., San Francisco, 1973-83. Mem. Calif. State Bar Assn., San Francisco County Bar Assn., Fresno County Bar Assn. Republican. Methodist. Avocations: hunting, fishing. Workers' compensation, Personal injury, Civil rights. Home: 2747 W Beechwood Fresno CA 93711 Office: Ninnis & Cribbs 3106 Willow #101-104 Clovis CA 93612 Mailing Address: PO Box 5314 Fresno CA 93755

NIPE, CHRIS ALAN, lawyer; b. Watertown, S.D., Oct. 26, 1956; s. Harold Charles and Maricie Loretta (Curtis) N. BS, No. State U., 1978; JD, MA in Econs., U. S.D., 1981. Bar: S.D. 1981, U.S. Dist. Ct. S.D. 1982, U.S. Ct. Appeals (8th cir.) 1982, U.S. Ct. Mil. Appeals 1985. Ptnr. Heideptiam, Bridgman & Nipe, Wessington Springs, S.D., 1981-83, Bridgman, Larson & Nipe (and predecessor firms), Mitchell, S.D., 1983—; Spl. asst. atty. gen. S.D., 1983—; states atty. Jerauld County, Wessington Springs, 1983-86. Mem. S.D. Bar Assn. (sec. young lawyers sect. 1985—, bd. dirs. young lawyers sect. 1983-85, pres.-elect 1986—), Assn. Trial Lawyers Am., S.D. Trial Lawyers Assn., S.D. States Atty. Assn., S.D. City Attys. Assn., Jaycees . Republican. Lutheran. Lodges: Kiwanis, Masons. Personal injury, General practice, State civil litigation. Home: 1301 Firesteel Dr #2 Mitchell SD 57301 Office: Bridgman Larson & Nipe Box 396 200 E 5th Mitchell SD 57301

NIPPERT, ALFRED KUNO, JR., lawyer; b. Asheville, N.C., Mar. 15, 1951; s. Alfred Kuno Sr. and Leah Ecetra (Anderson) N.; m. Jean A. Wagner, May 12, 1984. BS in Polit. Sci., U. Southwestern at Memphis, 1973; JD, U. Cin., 1976. Bar: Ohio 1976, U.S. Dist. Ct. (so. dist.) Ohio 1976, U.S. Supreme Ct. 1986. Ptnr. Nippert and Nippert, Cin., 1976—; cons. passenger and freight rail transp.; guest lectr. Am. U., Washington, Xavier U., Cin. Pre-publ. reviewer numerous articles. Bd. dirs. Cin.-Hamilton County YMCA, 1978-86; active Christ Hosp., Cin., 1977-85. Mem. ABA, Cin. Bar Assn. (numerous com. 1986), Assn. Transp. Practitioners. Probate, Transportation, Construction. Office: 3510 Glenmore Ave Cincinnati OH 45211

NISBET, ALEXANDER WYCKLIFF, JR., lawyer; b. Chgo., Apr. 15, 1948; s. Alexander Wyckliff and Olivia (Owens) N.; m. Theresa Wilson, Aug. 8, 1970; children: Jane Embry, Alexis Olivia, Rebecca Gable. BBA, U. Ark., 1970, JD, 1973; LLM in Taxation, Georgetown U., 1974. Bar: Ark. 1973. Ptnr. Friday, Eldredge & Clark, Little Rock, 1974—; bd. dirs. SCAT, Inc., Little Rock. Bd. dirs. Am. Heart Assn. affiliate, Little Rock. Mem. ABA (tax. sect.). Republican. Episcopalian. Club: Little Rock Country. Pension, profit-sharing, and employee benefits, Corporate taxation. Home: #19 Edgehill Rd Little Rock AR 72207 Office: Friday Eldredge & Clark 2000 1st Comml Bldg Little Rock AR 72201

NISSAN, RANDY S., lawyer; b. Flushing, N.Y., Aug. 6, 1953; s. Edward D. and Mary (Murad) N.; m. Amy Solomon, Nov. 25, 1978; children: Jordana M, Jeremy D.. BA, SUNY, Albany, 1977; JD, Western New Eng. U., 1979. Bar: N.Y. 1980, U.S. Dist. Ct. (so. and ea. dists.) N.Y., 1980. Assoc. Siben & Siben, Bayshore, N.Y., 1980—. Mem. Suffolk County Bar Assn. Personal injury, Bankruptcy, Criminal. Home: 24 Lincoln Ave Dix Hills NY 11746 Office: Siben & Siben PO Box 146 P Bayshore NY 11706

NISSEN, WILLIAM FORBES, lawyer; b. Chgo., May 31, 1926; s. William J. and Virginia E. (Forbes) N.; children—Virginia Boyd, Douglas, William R., Betsy, Robin. J.D., John Marshall Law Sch., 1952. Bar: Ill. 1952, U.S. Dist. Ct. (no. dist.) Ill. 1952, U.S. Ct. Mil. Appeals, 1954, U.S. Dist. Ct. (so. dist.) Ill. 1955. Ptnr. Berns & Nissen, Chgo., 1952-55; assoc. Hunter & Walden, Quincy, Ill., 1955-57; sole practice, Quincy, 1957—; spl. asst. to Ill. atty. gen., 1960-74, standing trustee in bankruptcy, 1960—; cons. on bankruptcy. Republican candidate for state's atty., 1980. Mem. ABA, Ill. State Bar Assn., Comml. Law League Am. Club: Elks. Bankruptcy, General practice, Real property. Home: 13 Ridgewood Dr Quincy IL 62301 Office: 522 Vermont St Suite 2 Quincy IL 62301

NISSEN, WILLIAM JOHN, lawyer; b. Chgo., July 28, 1947; s. William Gordon Jr. and Ruth Carolyn (Banas) N.; m. Patricia Jane Press, Jan. 16, 1971; children: Meredith Warner, Edward William. BA, Northwestern U., 1969; JD magna cum laude, Harvard U., 1976. Bar: Ill. 1976, U.S. Dist. Ct. (no. dist.) Ill. 1976, U.S. Ct. Appeals (7th cir.) 1981. Assoc. Sidley & Austin, Chgo., 1976-83, ptnr., 1983—; gen. counsel Heinold Commodities, Inc., Chgo., 1982-84. Editor Harvard U. Internat. Law Jour., 1974-76. Served to lt. USN, 1969-73. Mem. ABA (co-chmn. futures regulation subcom. 1985—), Chgo. Bar Assn. (chmn. futures regulation com. 1985-86, continuing legal edn. program), Ill. Inst. Continuing Edn. (lectr. commodity futures law topics), IIT-Kent Commodities Law Inst. Commodity futures law and litigation. Home: 348 Foss Ct Lake Bluff IL 60044 Office: Sidley & Austin One First Nat Plaza Chicago IL 60603

NISSENBERG, MEREL GREY, lawyer; b. Chgo., May 24, 1948; s. Milton Kenneth and Rose (Karpin) G.; m. David Neil Nissenberg, Dec. 27, 1969; James Matthew, Brett Andrew, Ashley Michele. BA, UCLA, 1969; JD, U. Miami, 1973. Bar: Calif. 1974, Fla. 1974, U.S. Dist. Ct. (so. dist.) Calif. 1977, U.S. Ct. Appeals (9th cir.) 1985. Ptnr. Nissenberg & Nissenberg, La Jolla, Calif., 1974—. active various civic orgns. Mem. ABA, San Diego Bar Assn. (chair med.-legal com.), La Jolla Bar Assn. (co-founder, pres. 1986-87), Assn. Trial Lawyers Am., Am. Soc. Law and Medicine. Avocations: travel, art, antiques, cooking. Personal injury, Medical malpractice. Home: 8476 Cliffridge Ave La Jolla CA 92037 Office: 7855 Ivanhoe Ave Suite 224 La Jolla CA 92037

NISSL, COLLEEN KAYE, lawyer; b. McMinnville, Oreg., June 3, 1950; d. Anton Arthur and Luella Elaine (Kerr) N.; m. Roger Philip Sugarman; children: Jordan Elizabeth, Zachary Max. BA, Ohio Wesleyan U., 1972; JD, U. Toledo, 1975. Bar: Ohio 1975, U.S. Dist. Ct. (so. dist.) Ohio 1977, U.S. Supreme Ct. 1980. Litigation sect. chief Atty. Gen. Ohio, Columbus, 1976-82; sr. counsel Battelle Meml. Inst., Columbus, 1982-84; sr. litigation counsel Borden, Inc., Columbus, 1984—. Mem. ABA, Ohio Bar Assn., Columbus Bar Assn. (chmn. alt. dispute resolution com.). Democrat. Roman Catholic. Avocations: skiing, bicycling, antiques. Federal civil litigation, State civil litigation. Office: Borden Inc 180 E Broad St 27th Floor Columbus OH 43215

NISSLY, KENNETH L., lawyer; b. Mesa, Ariz., Oct. 25, 1952; m. Marjorie J. Nissly, Aug. 17, 1974; children: Jennifer, Peter. BA, San Diego State U., 1974; JD, U. Calif., San Francisco, 1977. Bar: Calif. 1977, U.S. Dist. Ct. (no. and ea. dist.) Calif., U.S. Ct. Appeals (9th cir.). Assoc. Thelen, Marrin, Johnson & Bridges, San Jose, Calif., 1977-85, ptnr., 1985—. Mem. ABA, Santa Clara County Bar Assn. (judge pro tem neighborhood small claims ct program 1985—), Order of Coif, Phi Beta Kappa. Avocation: flying. Federal civil litigation, State civil litigation, Labor. Office: Thelen Marrin Johnson & Bridges 1 Almaden Blvd Suite 1100 San Jose CA 95113

NISSON, TIMOTHY JAMES, lawyer; b. Ft. Lewis, Wash., Nov. 20, 1956; s. James Leonard and Sharon (Shepard) N.; m. Donna Marie Daly, Mar. 4, 1986. AB in Philosophy, U. Calif., Davis, 1979; JD, U. San Francisco, 1982.

Bar: Calif. 1982, U.S. Dist. Ct. (ea. dist.) Calif. 1982. Atty. Weintraub, Genshlea, Hardy, Erich & Brown, Reading, Calif., 1982-86. Mem. ABA, Shasta-Trinity Bar Assn., Assn. Def. Counsel. Insurance, Personal injury. Office: Weintraub Genshlea et al PO Box 1350 Redding CA 96099

NISWANDER, FRANK CLYDE, lawyer; b. Kansas City, Mo., Oct. 29, 1919; s. Paul N. and Emma M. (Sewald) N.; m. Shirley Eleanor Cotton, Mar. 21, 1943; children—Nancy J. Conard, F. Christopher. B.A., Colo. Coll., 1941; J.D., George Washington U., 1948. Bar: D.C. 1948, Ill. 1955, Mass. 1965. Ptnr. Nutter, McClennen & Fish, Boston, 1970—. Served to lt. comdr. USNR, 1942-46. Mem. ABA (tax sect.). Episcopalian. Corporate taxation, Personal income taxation. Home: 84 Furnace Brook Pkwy Quincy MA 02169 Office: Nutter McClennen & Fish 600 Atlantic Ave Boston MA 02210

NITIKMAN, FRANKLIN W., lawyer; b. Davenport, Iowa, Oct. 26, 1940; s. David A. and Janette (Gordon) N.; m. Adrienne C. Drell, Nov. 28, 1972. BA, Northwestern U., 1963; LLB, Yale U., 1966. Bar: Ill. 1966, U.S. Dist. Ct. (no. dist.) Ill. 1967, U.S. Tax Ct. 1972, Fla. 1977, D.C. 1981. Assoc. McDermott, Will & Emery, Chgo., 1966-72, ptnr., 1973—. Co-author: Drafting Wills and Trust Agreements, 1985. Chmn. bd. dirs. Sinfonia Orch. Chgo., 1982—; bvd. dirs. Owen Coon Found., Glenview, Ill., 1985—. Clubs: Standard, Arts, Monroe (Chgo.). Estate planning, Probate, Estate taxation. Home: 365 Lakeside Pl Highland Park IL 60035 Office: McDermott Will & Emery 111 W Monroe St Chicago IL 60603

NIX, MARIE LOUISE GUSTE, lawyer, humanist; b. New Orleans, Nov. 21, 1950; d. William Joseph Jr. and Dorothy (Schutten) Guste; m. Ralph Robert Nix III, Feb. 19, 1977; children: Raphael Robert IV, Peter Guste, Marie Louise. Diplôme Supèrieur des Etudes Françaises Modernes, Université Catholique de l'Ouest, Angers, France, 1970; BA in French, Manhattanville Coll., 1972; JD, Loyola U., New Orleans, 1980. Bar: La. 1980. Assoc. Guste, Barnett & Shushan, New Orleans, 1981—; researcher Inst. Human Relations, New Orleans, 1979—; mem. adv. commn. 50 States Project, Baton Rouge, 1984—, civil and criminal law coms. La. Notary Pub., 1985. Mem. ABA, La. Bar Assn., Young Women's Christian Assn. (3d v.p., bd. dirs. 1980—), Eye, Ear, Nose & Throat Hosp. Aux. (pres. 1985—), St. Thomas More Cath. Lawyers Assn., Literary Study Club, Blue Key. Democrat. Roman Catholic. Avocations: swimming, aerobics, gourmet cooking. General practice.

NIX, ROBERT NELSON CORNELIUS, JR., chief justice; b. Phila., July 13, 1928; s. Robert Nelson Cornelius and Ethel (Lanier) N.; m. Dorothy Lewis, July 3, 1954; children: Robert Nelson Cornelius 3d, Michael, Anthony, Jude. A.B., Villanova U.; J.D., U. Pa.; postgrad. bus. adminstrn. and econs., Temple U.; LLD (hon.), St. Charles Sem., Dickinson U. Sch. Law. Bar: Pa. 1956. Dep. atty. gen. Pa., 1956-58; partner firm Nix, Rhodes & Nix, Phila., 1958-68; judge Common Pleas Ct., Philadelphia County, 1968-71; justice Supreme Ct. Pa., 1972—; bd. dirs. Nat. Ctr. State Cts., 1985—. Bd. dirs. U.S.O., from 1969; bd. consultors Villanova U. Sch. Law, from 1973; bd. trustees Villanova U., 1986—. Served with AUS, 1953-55. Recipient First Pa. award, Benjamin Franklin award Poor Richard Club Pa., James Madison award Soc. Profl. Journalists; named Knight Comdr. Order of St. Gregory the Great. Mem. Omega Psi Phi. Lodge: KC. Office: Supreme Ct Pa City Hall Philadelphia PA 19107 also: Supreme Ct Pa Harrisburg PA 17120 *

NIXON, ELLIOTT BODLEY, lawyer; b. Balt., Aug. 21, 1921. AB, Princeton U., 1942; JD, Harvard U., 1948. Bar: N.Y. 1949, U.S. Supreme Ct. 1957. Ptnr. Burlingham Underwood & Lord and predecessor firms, N.Y.C., 1956—. Contbr. articles to encyclopaedias and profl. jours. Mem. ABA, Assn. of Bar of City of N.Y., Internat. Bar Assn., Maritime Law Assn. U.S. (editor Am. Maritime Law Cases 1969—). Admiralty, Private international. Home: 420 E 23d St New York NY 10010 Office: Burlingham Underwood & Lord 1 Battery Park Plaza New York NY 10004

NIXON, JOHN TRICE, federal judge; b. New Orleans, Jan. 9, 1933; s. H. C. and Anne (Trice) N.; m. Betty Chiles, Aug. 5, 1960; children: Mignon Elizabeth, Anne Trice. A.B. cum laude, Harvard Coll., 1955; LL.B., Vanderbilt U., 1960. Bar: Ala. bar 1960, Tenn. bar 1972. Individual practice law Anniston, Ala., 1960-62; city atty. Anniston, 1962-64; trial atty. Civil Rights Div., Dept. Justice, Washington, 1964-69; staff atty., comptroller of Treasury State of Tenn., 1971-76; individual practice law Nashville, 1976-77; circuit judge 1977-78, gen. sessions judge, 1978-80; U.S. dist. judge Middle Dist. Tenn., Nashville, 1980—. Served with U.S. Army, 1958. Mem. Am. Bar Assn., Tenn. Bar Assn., Nashville Bar Assn., Ala. State Bar. Democrat. Methodist. Clubs: D.U. (Cambridge); Harvard-Radcliffe (Nashville). Home: 1607 18th Ave N Nashville TN 37212 Office: US Dist Ct 825 US Courthouse Nashville TN 37203 *

NIXON, LEWIS MICHAEL, lawyer; b. Gallion, Ala., Feb. 1, 1949; s. John C. King and Alfredia (Nixon) Cobb; m. Evon Grant, Aug. 31, 1985; children—Michael Lewis, Jeremy Michael. B.A., St. John's U., 1971; J.D., DePaul U., 1974. Bar: Ill. 1975, U.S. Dist. Ct. (no. dist.) Ill. 1975, U.S. Ct. Appeals (7th cir.) 1976, U.S. Ct. Mil. Appeals 1978, U.S. Supreme Ct. 1979. Asst. U.S. atty. U.S. Dept. Justice, Chgo., 1975-79; assoc. Conklin & Adler, Chgo., 1979-80; atty. Burlington No. R.R., Chgo., 1980-83; regional counsel HUD, Chgo., 1983—. Federal civil litigation, Criminal, Personal injury. Office: HUD 300 S Wacker Suite 2306 Chicago IL 60606

NIZIO, FRANK, lawyer; b. Dearborn, Mich., May 15, 1948; s. Frank F. and Josephine (Morsillo) N.; m. Linda Allen, Aug. 21, 1976. BS in Mech. Engring., U. Mich., 1971; JD cum laude, Detroit Coll. Law, 1976. Bar: Mich. 1976, U.S. Dist. Ct. (ea. dist.) Mich. 1976, U.S. Dist. Ct. (no. dist.) Tex. 1984. Engr. product devel. Ford Motor Co., Dearborn, 1971-75; law clk. to presiding justice Wayne Cir. Ct., Detroit, 1975-76; ptnr. Dykema, Gossett, Spencer, Goodnow & Trigg, Detroit, 1976—; mediator Wayne County Mediation Tribunal, Detroit, 1981—; lectr. product liability U. Mich., Dearborn, 1985—; asst. prof. advocacy Detroit Coll. of Law, 1986—. Mem. ABA, Mich. Bar Assn., Detroit Bar Assn., Def. Research Inst., Mich. Def. Trial Counsel, Assn. Def. Trial Counsel. Avocations: bicycling, cross country skiing. Personal injury, State civil litigation, Federal civil litigation. Home: 570 Lakepointe Gross Pointe Park MI 48230 Office: Dykema Gossett Spencer et al 400 Renaissance Ctr 35th Floor Detroit MI 48243

NOACK, CHARLES ELROY, lawyer; b. Vernon, Tex., May 13, 1938; s. Carl Ernest and Frieda (Lingnau) N.; m. Judy Noack, Mar. 16, 1965 (div. Sept. 1977); children: Scott, Steven; m. Sherry Eddins, Feb. 14, 1981. BBA, N. Tex. State U., 1964; LLB, Baylor U., 1966. Bar: Tex. 1966, U.S. Dist. Ct. (no. dist.) Tex. 1968. Sole practice Dallas, 1966-74; assoc. gen. counsel Hunt Oil Co., Dallas, 1974—. City councilman, mem. planning and zoning com. City of Flower Mound, Tex., 1984-85. Served with Army N.G., 1959. Mem. Dallas Bar Assn., Sigma Nu. Republican. Lutheran. Avocation: sports. General corporate, Labor. Home: 118 Red Oak Flower Mound TX 75028 Office: Hunt Oil Co 2900 InterFirst One Bldg Dallas TX 75201-2970

NOALL, L. SCOTT, lawyer; b. Salt Lake City, Apr. 9, 1944; s. Harold F. and Sandra (Hawkes) N.; m. Barbara Anne Ernst, June 24, 1978; children: Debbie, Teri, Jeff. BS, U. Utah, 1966; JD, Denver U., 1976. Bar: Colo. 1977, U.S. Dist. Ct. Colo. 1977, U.S. Ct. Appeals (10th cir.) 1984. Assoc. Boulter & Hall, P.C., Denver, 1977-78; ptnr. Branney & Hillyard, Englewood, Colo., 1978-81, Van Horne, Vogt & Noall, Denver, 1981-84; pres. Van Horne, Vogt, Noall & Hodges, P.C., Denver, 1984—; gen. ptnr. NWB Enterprises, Denver, 1984—. Mem. Nat. Inst. for Trial Advocacy (diplomate). Republican. Avocations: flying, skiing, motorcycle racing, survivorship. Personal injury, Workers' compensation, Federal civil litigation. Office: Van Horne Vogt Noall & Hodges PC 5353 W Dartmouth Ave #410 Denver CO 80227-5569

NOCAS, ANDREW JAMES, lawyer; b. Los Angeles, Feb. 2, 1941; s. John Richard and Muriel Phyliss (Harvey) N.; m. Beverly De La Mare, June 27, 1964; 1 son, Scott Andrew. B.S., Stanford U., 1962, J.D., 1964. Bar: Calif. 1965. Assoc. Thelen, Marrin, Johnson & Bridges, Los Angeles, 1964-71, ptnr., 1972—; del. Calif. Bar Conv., 1972—. Served to capt. JAGC, USAR. Mem. Los Angeles County Bar Assn. (chmn. sect. law office mgmt. 1980-82), ABA (chmn. arbitration com. 1981). Club: San Marino City. State civil litigation, Federal civil litigation, Health. Office: 333 S Grand Ave Suite 3400 Los Angeles CA 90071

NOE, RALPH HENDERSON, JR., lawyer; b. Morristown, Tenn., Aug. 25, 1930; s. Ralph H. Sr. and Annie (Fort) N.; m. Fenn L. Wright, May 19, 1957; children: Lori, Rachael. Student, Carson Newman Coll., 1948-50; JD, U. Tenn., 1955. Bar: Tenn. 1955. Ptnr. Noe & Travis, Morristown; commr. Hambler County Cts. Tenn. 1982-85; atty. Hambler County, 1984-85. Served to sgt. U.S. Army, 1950-52. Mem. Hambler County Bar Assn. (pres. 1973-74). Democrat. Baptist. Horseback riding. Personal injury, Local government, General practice. Home: Rt 2 Slatehill Rd Moonesburg TN 37811 Office: Noe & Travis PO Box 7 Morristown CA 37815

NOE, RANDOLPH, lawyer; b. Indpls., Nov. 2, 1939; s. John H. and Bernice (Baker) Reiley; m. Anne Will, Mar. 2, 1968; children—J.H. Reiley, Anne Will, Randolph, Jonathan Baker. Student Franklin Coll. 1957-60; B.S., Ind. State U., 1964; J.D., Ind. U., 1967. Bar: Ind. 1968, Ky. 1970. Trust officer Citizens Fidelity Bank & Trust Co., Louisville, 1969-71; sole practice, Louisville, 1971-84; ptnr. Greenebaum, Young, Treitz & Maggiolo, 1984—; asst. county atty. Jefferson County, 1979-84. Mem. exec. bd. Louisville area Muscular Dystrophy Assn., 1971-73; chmn. Eagle Scout Assn., 1975-77; bd. dirs. Holy Rosary Acad., 1978-82. Mem. ABA, Ind. Bar Assn., Ky. Bar Assn. Democrat. Clubs: Pendennis, Wranglers. Author: Kentucky Probate Methods, 1976, supplement, 1985—. Editor: Kentucky Law Summary, 1985—. Probate, Real property, Estate taxation. Home: 3222 Crossbill Rd Louisville KY 40213 Office: 2700 First Nat Tower Louisville KY 40202

NOEL, DAVID BOBBITT, JR., lawyer; b. Dallas, July 28, 1950; s. David Bobbitt and Marion (Wunderle) N.; m. Karen Michelle Hankins, Aug. 10, 1985. BA, Bowdoin Coll.; JD, So. Meth. U. Law clk. to presiding justice U.S. Dist. Ct. Tex., Dallas, 1976, Houston, 1976-77; from assoc. to ptnr. Vinson & Elkins, Houston, 1977—. Mem. ABA, Tex. Bar Assn., Houston Bar Assn. Methodist. Bankruptcy, Federal civil litigation, State civil litigation. Home: 4623 Devon Houston TX 77027 Office: Vinson & Elkins 3209 1st City Tower 1001 Fannin Houston TX 77002

NOEL, EDWIN LAWRENCE, lawyer; b. St. Louis, July 11, 1946; s. Thomas Currie and Christine (Jones) N.; m. Nancy Carter Simpson, Feb. 7, 1970; children: Caroline, Edwin C. BA, Brown U., 1968; JD cum laude, St. Louis U., 1974. Bar: Mo. 1974, U.S. Dist. Ct. (ea. dist.) Mo. 1974, U.S. Ct. Appeals (8th cir.) 1974, U.S. Ct. Appeals (6th cir.) 1978, U.S. Ct. Appeals (7th cir.) 1982, U.S. Supreme Ct. 1986. Ptnr. Armstrong, Teasdale, Kramer, Vaughan & Schlafly, St. Louis, 1974—; bd. dirs. Elcom Industries, St. Louis. Bd. dirs. Edgewood Children's Ctr., St. Louis, 1982—, St. Louis Assn. for Retarded Citizens, 1984-; chmn. Mo. Clean Water Com., Jefferson City, 1982-86; chmn. environ. com. St. Louis Regional Commerce and Growth Assn., 1982—. Served to lt. USN, 1968-74, Vietnam. Mem. Mo. Bar Assn., Bar Assn. Met. St. Louis. Republican. Episcopalian. Environment, Federal civil litigation, State civil litigation. Home: 301 S McKnight Saint Louis MO 63124 Office: Armstrong Teasdale Kramer Vaughan & Schlafly 611 Olive St Suite 1900 Saint Louis MO 63101

NOEL, RANDALL DEANE, lawyer; b. Memphis, Oct. 19, 1953; s. D.A. and Patricia G. Noel; m. Lissa Johns, May 28, 1977; children: Lauren Elizabeth, Randall Walker. B in Pub. Adminstrn. with honors, U. Miss., 1975, JD, 1978. Bar: Miss. 1978, U.S. Dist. Ct. (no. dist.) Miss. 1978, Tenn. 1979, U.S. Dist. Ct. (we. dist.) Tenn. 1979, U.S. Ct. Appeals (6th cir.) 1984, U.S. Supreme Ct. 1986. Assoc. Armstrong, Allen, Braden, Goodman, McBride & Prewitt, Memphis, 1978-85, ptnr., 1985—. Mem. fin. com. Memphis in May Internat. Festival, Memphis, 1980-81; sec., gen. counsel Great River Carnival Assn., Memphis, 1981—; gen. counsel Tenn. Ballet Co., Memphis, 1983; bd. dirs. Christ United Meth. Ch., Memphis, 1984—. Mem. ABA (young lawyers div., assembly del., vice chmn. award of achievement com., 1986, editor The Affiliate newsletter, 1987—), Tenn. Bar Assn. (v.p. young lawyers conf. 1983-85, exec. council coordinator 1985—, litigation sect. sec., treas. 1986), Memphis and Shelby County Bar Assn. (jud. recommendations com., law week com.), Miss. Bar Assn., Fed. Bar Assn., Defense Research Inst., Omicron Delta Kappa (pres. 1978), Phi Delta Phi (legal fraternity), Phi Kappa Phi, Phi Eta Sigma, Phi Delta Theta (pres. 1975). Clubs: Petroleum, Osiris. Federal civil litigation, State civil litigation, Consumer commercial. Home: 2938 Tishomingo Ln Memphis TN 38111 Office: Armstrong Allen et al 1900 One Commerce Sq Memphis TN 38103

NOEL, SIMON, lawyer, educator; b. Eschwege, Germany, July 5, 1947; came to U.S., 1949; s. Wolf and Blanche (Elsner) N.; m. Donna Marie Del Cotto, Mar. 28, 1981; 1 child, Stephanie Michelle. A.B., Ohio U., 1969; J.D., U. Toledo 1972; LL.M. in Taxation, George Washington U., 1977. Bar: Pa. 1972, U.S. Dist. Ct. (we. dist.) Pa. 1972, U.S. Tax Ct. 1977, U.S. Ct. Appeals (3d cir.) 1986. Tax researcher Silverstein & Mullens, Washington, 1975-77; assoc. Lynch, Lynch, Carr, Pitts., 1977-78, Allegheny Internat., Pitts., 1978-82; tax profl. Coopers & Lybrand, Pitts., 1982-83; sole practice, Pitts., 1984—; instr. paralegal cert. program U. Pitts., 1984. Author publs. in field of tax law. Mem. Allegheny County Bar Assn. (continuing legal edn., pub. relations coms. 1984—). Democrat. Jewish. Personal income taxation, Corporate taxation, Real property. Home: 1871 Shaw Ave Pittsburgh PA 15217 Office: 2200 Lawyers Bldg 428 Forbes Ave Pittsburgh PA 15219

NOELKE, PAUL, lawyer; b. La Crosse, Wis., Feb. 10, 1915; s. Carl Bernard and Mary Amelia (O'Meara) N.; m. Mary Jo Kamps, May 4, 1943; children: Paul William, Mary Nesius, Ann Witt, Kate Helms. A.B. magna cum laude, Marquette U., 1936, J.D. cum laude, 1938; LL.M., U. Chgo., 1947; D.H.L. (hon.), Mt. Senario Coll., 1976. Bar: Wis. 1938, U.S. Dist. Ct. (ea. dist.) Wis. 1938, U.S. Supreme Ct. 1960, Ct. Appeals D.C. 1975. Assoc. firm Miller, Mack & Fairchild, 1938-40; asst. prof. law Marquette U., 1940-42; spl. agt. FBI, 1942-45; assoc. Quarles & Brady and predecessor firms, Milw., 1943-52, ptnr., 1952-85, of counsel, 1985—. Trustee Viterbo Coll., LaCrosse; chmn. Pres.'s Council Marquette U.; bd. dirs. Wis. region bd. NCCJ; counsel, trustee, past pres. Serra Internat. Found., Chgo.; past chmn. Bd. Tax Review, Village of Shorewood, Wis. Recipient Alumnus of Yr. award Marquette U., 1980; recipient Conf. award NCCJ, 1967. Mem. ABA, Wis. State Bar Assn., Milw. Bar Assn., D.C. Bar Assn., Am. Judicature Soc., Order Holy Sepulchre, Alpha Sigma Nu. Roman Catholic. Club: Univ. (Milw.). Home: 4440 N Farwell Ave Shorewood WI 53211 Office: 411 E Wisconsin Ave Milwaukee WI 53202

NOFER, GEORGE HANCOCK, lawyer; b. Phila., June 14, 1926. B.A., Haverford Coll., 1949; J.D., Yale U., 1952. Bar: Pa. 1953. Practice law Phila., 1953—; ptnr. Schnader, Harrison, Segal & Lewis, Phila., 1961—; lectr. probate law, 1955—. Pres. bd. sch. dirs. Upper Moreland Twp., Pa., 1965-73; trustee Beaver Coll., Glenside, Pa., 1969-76; elder, trustee, deacon Abington Presbyn. Ch., Pa. Fellow Am. Coll. Probate Counsel (regent 1975—, pres. 1983-84, chmn. Pa. 1973-78), Am. Law Inst., Am. Bar Found.; mem. ABA (standing com. on specialization 1980-86, chmn. 1983-86), Pa. Bar Assn., Phila. Bar Assn., Internat. Acad. Estate and Trust Law, Phi Beta Kappa, Phi Delta Phi. Probate. Home: 241 Pine St Philadelphia PA 19106 Office: Schnader Harrison Segal & Lewis 1600 Market St Suite 3600 Philadelphia PA 19103

NOGAL, RICHARD JOHN, lawyer; b. Chgo., Sept. 6, 1956; s. Richard Francis and Mary Jane (Grevens) N.; m. Kristine Lynn Holmes, June 26, 1983. BA, Northwestern U., Evanston, 1978; JD, Northwestern U., Chgo., 1981. Bar: Ill. 1981, U.S. Ct. Appeals (7th cir.) 1981, U.S. Dist. Ct. (no. dist.) Ill. 1982. Assoc. Jenner & Block, Chgo., 1981-86; sr. assoc. Lillig, Kemp & Thorsness, Ltd., Oak Brook, Ill., 1986—. Mem. Editorial bd. Northwestern U. Law Rev., 1980. Chmn. local polit. com., Orland Park, Ill., 1984—; bd. dirs. Woodcreek Condominium Assn., Clarendon Hills, Ill., 1985—. Recipient Ednl. Achievement award Lincoln Acad. of Ill., 1978. Mem. ABA, Ill. Bar Assn., Chgo. Bar Assn., DuPage County Bar Assn., Phi Beta Kappa. Federal civil litigation, State civil litigation. Home: 537 Willow Creek Ct Clarendon Hills IL 60514 Office: Lillig Kemp & Thorsness Ltd 1900 Spring Rd Oak Brook IL 60521

NOGEE, JEFFREY LAURENCE, lawyer; b. Schenectady, N.Y., Oct. 31, 1952; s. Rodney and Shirley Ruth (Mannes) N.; m. Freda Carolyn Wartel, Aug. 31, 1980; children: Rori Caitlen, Amara Sonia. BA cum laude, Bucknell U., 1974; JD, Boston U., 1977. Bar: N.Y. 1978, U.S. Dist. Ct. (so. and ea. dists.) 1978. Assoc. Hale Russell & Gray, N.Y.C., 1977-83; sr. atty. Ebasco Services Inc., N.Y.C., 1984—, dir. Countertrade unit, 1985—; pvt. counsellor for internat. bus. firms, 1987—. Mem. ABA, Assn. of Bar of City of N.Y., Phi Beta Kappa, Pi Sigma Alpha. Avocations: fencing, bassoon and saxophone music, racquet sports. Private international, Contracts commercial, Computer. Office: Ebasco Services Inc Two World Trade Ctr New York NY 10048-0752

NOHR, WILLIAM ARTHUR, lawyer; b. Merrill, Wis., July 6, 1938; s. Albert D. and Dorothy (Finn) N.; m. Marilyn H. Elliott, June 5, 1963; children: Melanie, Robert, Steven, Timothy. BA, U. Wis., 1960, LLB, 1964. Bar: Wis. 1964, U.S. Ct. Appeals (7th cir.) 1970, U.S. Supreme Ct. 1987. Assoc. Hoffman, Trembath & Gullickson, Wausau, Wis. 1964; mem. Quarles, Herriott & Clemons, Milw., 1964-69, Ebert & Ebert, Milw., 1969-79; ptnr. Walsh & Nohr, Milw., 1979-84; sole practice, Milw., 1985—. Served to lt. U.S. Army, 1960-61. Mem. Am. Arbitration Assn., Milw. Bar Assn., Wis. Acad. Trial Lawyers, Phi Beta Kappa, Order of Coif. Roman Catholic. Club: KC. Federal civil litigation, State civil litigation, General practice. Home: 10103 N Greenview Dr Mequon WI 53092 Office: 161 W Wisconsin Ave Milwaukee WI 53203

NOLAN, DAVID BRIAN, lawyer; b. Washington, Jan. 1, 1951; s. John Joseph and Mary Jane N.; m. Cheryl Ann Cottle, June 30, 1979; children: John Joseph II, David Brian II. BA, Duke U., 1973; MPA, Am. U., 1975; JD, U. San Fernando Valley, 1978; postgrad., Georgetown U., 1981—. Bar: Calif. 1978, U.S. Dist. Ct. (cen. dist.) Calif. 1979, D.C. 1981, U.S. Ct. Claims 1981, U.S. Tax Ct. 1981, U.S. Dist. Ct. D.C. 1984. Asst. dir. research Younger-Curb Campaign, Los Angeles, 1978; assoc. L. Rob Werner Law Offices, Encino, Calif., 1979-80; atty. conflicts Office of Pres. Elect, Washington, 1980-81; staff atty. office of counsel to th pres. White House, Washington, 1981; staff asst. office of sec. U.S. Dept. Treasury, Washington, 1981-85; spl. asst. office gen. counsel U.D. Dept. Energy, Washington, 1985—. Assoc. editor New Guard Mag., 1983-85. Steering com. Los Angeles Reps., 1979-80, Reagan for Pres., Los Angeles, 1980; chmn. 39th assembly, Rep. Cen. Com., 1979-80; alt. del. 1972 Rep. Nat. Conv.; pres. N.C. Coll. Rep. Com. 1972-73; nat. treas., bd. dirs. Young Americans for Freedon, Sterling, Va., 1983-85; corp. dir., sec. Am. Sovereignty Task Force, Vienna, Va., 1984—, State Dpet. Watch. Ltd., Vienna, 1984—. Charles Edison Youth Found. scholar, 1971; Named one of Outstanding Young Men Am., Jaycees, 1976—. Mem. ABA, Fed. Bar Assn., D.C. Bar Assn. (chmn. ethics com. young lawyers div. 1985—), Federalist Soc., U.S. Justice Found. (of counsel, co-founder 1979—), Nat. Lawyers Club. Club: Conservative (Washington). Administrative and regulatory, Personal income taxation. Home: 1805 Ingemar Ct Alexandria VA 22308 Office: US Dept Energy 1000 Independence Ave SW Washington DC 32399

NOLAN, JENELLE WHITE, lawyer; b. Gorman, Tex., Feb. 19, 1941; d. Bill Dixon and Ima Jennie (Harvey) White; m. Edwin Kirtley Nolan, Aug. 6, 1966 (div. Oct. 1971); 1 child, Jenny. BA cum laude, Abilene Christian U., 1963; JD cum laude, U. Houston, 1974. Bar: Tex. 1974, U.S. Dist. Ct. (so. dist.) Tex. 1975, U.S. Ct. Appeals (5th cir.) 1975, U.S. Supreme Ct. 1978, U.S. Dist. Ct. (no. dist.) Tex. 1981. Atty. Exxon Co. USA, Houston, 1974-78, 83, counsel, 1984—; atty. Exxon Co. USA, Corpus Christi, Tex., 1978-80, Dallas, 1980-83. Editor U. Houston Law Rev., 1974. Chmn. visiting com. on English, adv. bd. Abilene Christian U., Tex., 1983-84. Mem. ABA, Assn. Women Attys. Oil and gas leasing, Real property, General corporate. Home: 17711 Moss Point Dr Spring TX 77379 Office: Exxon Co USA PO Box 2180 Houston TX 77252-2180

NOLAN, JOHN MICHAEL, lawyer; b. Conway, Ark., June 21, 1948; s. Paul Thomas and Peggy (Hime) N.; m. Kathleen Ann Mitchell, May 26, 1983; children: Michelle, Stacy, Allison. BA, U. Tex., 1970, postgrad., 1971, JD, 1973; LLM in Taxation, George Washington U., 1976. Bar: Tex. 1973, U.S. Ct. Mil. Appeals 1973, U.S. Ct. Appeals (D.C. cir.) 1975, U.S. Tax Ct. 1975, U.S. Supreme Ct. 1975. Chief counsel to chief judge U.S. Ct. Mil. Appeals, Washington, 1976-77; assoc. Winstead, McGuire, Sechrest & Minick P.C., Dallas, 1977-81, dir., 1981—; also bd. dirs. Sechrest & Minick P.C., Dallas. Editor in chief The Advocate, 1973-76. Served as capt. JAGC, U.S. Army, 1973-76. Named one of Outstanding Young Men in Am., U.S. Jaycess, 1976. Mem. ABA (real property, probate and trust sect., real property com., partnerships, joint ventures, and other investment vehicles), Tex. Bar Assn. (real property, probate and trust sect.), D.C. Bar Assn., Dallas Bar Assn. (real estate group), YMCA. Democrat. Presbyterian. Club: City (Dallas). Real property, Bankruptcy, Contracts commercial. Home: 4201 Windsor Pkwy Dallas TX 75205 Office: Winstead McGuire Sechrest & Minick PC 1700 Dallas Bldg Dallas TX 75201

NOLAN, JOHN STEPHAN, lawyer; b. Cin., Jan. 12, 1926; s. Edward Leroy and Florence (Wetterer) N.; m. Adeline Jean Mosher, Sept. 5, 1949; children: Michael Christopher, Joyce Patricia, Matthew Mosher, John Giles, Elizabeth Ann. AB, BS in Commerce, U. N.C., 1947; LLB magna cum laude, Harvard U., 1951. Bar: D.C. 1951, U.S. Ct. Appeals (D.C. cir.) 1951, U.S. Supreme Ct. 1955, Md. 1959, U.S. Ct. Appeals (Fed. cir.) 1982, U.S. Ct. Appeals (11th and 9th cirs.) 1983. Assoc. Miller & Chevalier, Washington, 1951-58, ptnr., 1958-69; dep. asst. sec. for tax policy U.S. Treasury Dept., Washington, 1972-79; assoc. Miller & Chevalier Chartered, Washington, 1972—; adj. prof. law Georgetown U. Law Sch., Washington, 1955-59, 71-78; mem. adv. group to commr. IRS, Washington, 1967-68, 83-84. Contbr. articles to profl. jours. Vice chmn., gen. counsel D.C. chpt. ARC, Washington; bd. dirs. Connelly Sch. of Holy Child, Washington, Miller & Chevalier Charitable Found., Washington, 1962—. Served to lt. USN, 1944-46, 52-54. Fellow Am. Bar Found. (chmn. D.C. chpt.); mem. ABA (chmn. tax sect. 1981-82), Am. Law Inst. Roman Catholic. Clubs: Met., Georgetown (Washington). Corporate taxation, Estate taxation, Personal income taxation. Home: 10904 Stanmore Dr Potomac MD 20854 Office: Miller & Chevalier Chartered 655 15th St NW Washington DC 20005

NOLAN, JOSEPH RICHARD, justice Supreme Court Massachusettes; b. Boston, June 14, 1925; s. John Leo and Alma (Heimann) N.; m. Margaret M. Kelly, Aug. 23, 1947; children: Jacqueline, Janice, Leonard, Barbara, Maura, Martina, Joseph Richard. B.S., Boston Coll., 1950, J.D., 1954; LL.D. (hon.), Suffolk Law Sch., 1981, New Eng. Law Sch., 1983. Sole practice Boston, 1954-74; justice Mass. Supreme Jud. Ct., Boston, 1981—; asst. dist. atty. 1960-71; legal counsel Mass. Lottery, 1971-73. Author: Equitable Remedies, 1975, Civil Practice, 2 vols., 1975, Criminal Law, 1976, Tort Law, 1979, Trial Practice—Cases and Materials, 1981, Black's Law Dictionary, 5th edit., 1979. Mem. F. Flaschner Jud. Law Inst. (dean, pres.), Am. Law Inst., ABA, Mass. Bar Assn. Roman Catholic. Clubs: Belmont Hill (Mass.); Hatherly Country (North Scituate, Mass.). Jurisprudence. Home: 242 Common St Belmont MA 02178 Office: New Court Pemberton Sq Boston MA 02108 *

NOLAN, KENNETH PAUL, lawyer; b. Bklyn., June 11, 1949; s. John Joseph and Eleanor Joan (Cullinan) N.; m. Nancy C. Cirrito, June 23, 1973; children: Kenneth Paul Jr., Caitlin, Elizabeth. BA, Bklyn. Coll., 1971. Bar: N.Y. 1978, U.S. Dist. Ct. (so. and ea. dists.) N.Y. 1978, U.S. Supreme Ct. 1982. Journalist, editor N.Y. Times, N.Y.C., 1968-73; tchr. N.Y.C. Bd. Edn., 1972-77; ptnr. Speiser & Krause P.C., N.Y.C., 1977—. Contbr. articles to profl. jours. and newspapers. V.p. Bay Ridge Community Council, Bklyn., 1984-85; trustee Bishop Ford Cen. Cath. High Sch., Bklyn., 1980—. Recipient Appreciation Cup, Bay Ridge Community Council, 1985. Mem. ABA (editor Litigation Jour. 1982—), Assn. of Bar of City of N.Y. (aero. com.), Am. Arbitration Assn. (arbitrator 1980—). Democrat. Roman Catholic. Avocations: running, golf, gardening, reading, writing. Personal injury, Federal civil litigation. Home: 641 78th St Brooklyn NY 11209 Office: Speiser & Krause PC 200 Park Ave New York NY 10166

NOLAN, LAWRENCE PATRICK, lawyer; b. Mich., Dec. 31, 1948; s. Gerard P. and Katherine (Gluns) N.; m. Laurel Lee Blasi, Apr. 26, 1980; children: Bridget Blasi, Lawrence Patrick Jr. BA, Western Mich. U., 1971; JD, Thomas M. Cooley Law Sch., 1976. Bar: Mich. 1976, D.C. 1977. Pres. Lawrence P. Nolan & Assocs., P.C., Eaton Rapids, Mich., 1977—. Pres. Cooley Lawyers Credit Union; bd. dirs. Thomas M. Cooley Law Sch., 1983—. Named Outstanding Man of Yr., Eaton Rapids Jaycees, 1981.

Mem. ABA, Mich. Bar Assn. (chmn. young lawyers sect. 1982-83), Eaton County Bar Assn., Ingham County Bar Assn. Roman Catholic. Lodge: Rotary (v.p. Eaton Rapids chpt. 1984-85, pres. Eaton Rapids chpt. 1985-86). Home: 8974 Private Dr Springport MI 49284 Office: 239 S Main St Eaton Rapids MI 48827-1291

NOLAN, PAUL WILLIAM, lawyer; b. Covington, Ky., Jan. 4, 1955; s. John F. and Dorothy L. (Dwertman) N.; m. Katherine Thurlow, Apr. 7, 1984. BA, U. Notre Dame, 1975; JD, Georgetown U., 1978. Bar: D.C. 1978, U.S. Dist. Ct. Md. 1979, Md. 1980. Law clk. to presiding judge U.S. Dist. Ct. Md., Balt., 1978-80; assoc. Hogan & Hartson, Washington, 1980-81, Kramon & Graham, Balt., 1981-84; ptnr. Thurlow & Nolan P.A., Balt., 1984—. Editor: Estate and Gift Tax Letter and Revenue Rulings, 1985-86. Mem. D.C. Bar Assn., Md. Bar Assn., Nat. Orgn. Social Security Reps. (sustaining), Am. Arbitration Assn. (arbitrator 1981—), Phi Beta Kappa, Notre Dame Club (bd. dirs. 1984-86). Democrat. Roman Catholic. Insurance, Federal civil litigation, General practice. Office: Thurlow & Nolan PA 711 W 40th St Baltimore MD 21211

NOLAN, TERRANCE JOSEPH, JR., lawyer; b. Bklyn., Mar. 29, 1950; s. Terrance Joseph Sr. and Antonia (Pontecorvo) N.; m. Irene M. Rush, Aug. 2, 1980; 1 child, Maryjane Frances. BA, St. Francis Coll., Bklyn., 1971; JD, St. Johns U., Jamaica, N.Y., 1974; M in Law, NYU, 1982. Bar: N.Y. 1975, U.S. Dist. Ct. (ea. and so. dists.) N.Y. 1975, U.S. Ct. Appeals (2d cir.) 1975, U.S. Supreme Ct. 1980. Atty. N.Y.C. Transit Authority, Bklyn., 1974-77; specialist labor relations Pepsi-Cola Co., Purchase, N.Y., 1977-80; asst. gen. counsel, assoc. dir. labor relations NYU, N.Y.C., 1980—. Mem. ABA, N.Y. State Bar Assn., Indsl. Relations Research Assn., Nat. Assn. Coll. and Univ. Attys., N.Y.-N.J. Arbitration Group. Labor, Administrative and regulatory, Pension, profit-sharing, and employee benefits. Home: 1918 Ford St Brooklyn NY 11229 Office: NYU 70 Washington Sq South New York NY 10012

NOLAND, JAMES ELLSWORTH, U.S. judge; b. LaGrange, Mo., Apr. 22, 1920; s. Otto Arthur and Elzena (Ellsworth) N.; m. Helen Warvel, Feb. 4, 1948; children—Kathleen Kimberly, James Ellsworth, Christopher Warvel. A.B., Ind. U., 1942, LL.B., 1948; M.B.A., Harvard U., 1943. Bar: Ind. 1948. Since practiced in Bloomington; partner law firm of Hilgedag and Noland, Indpls., 1955-66, 1st asst. city atty., 1956-57; dep. atty. gen. Ind., 1952; spl. asst. U.S. atty. gen. 1953; appointed Ind. State Election Commr., 1954; U.S. judge So. Dist. Ind., 1966—, chief judge, 1984—; Mem. com. on magistrates system Jud. Conf. U.S., 1973-81; mem. 81st (1949-51) Congress, 7th Ind., Dist.; sec. Ind. Democratic Com., 1960-66; chmn. bd. visitors Ind. Law Sch., Indpls., 1974-76. Served as capt., Transp. Corps. AUS, 1943-46. Mem. ABA (chmn. jud. adminstrn. div. 1984-85), Ind. Bar Assn., Ind. Assn. Trial Lawyers (pres. 1956), Nat. Conf. Fed. Trial Judges (chmn. 1981-82), Phi Delta Phi, Phi Kappa Psi. Mem. Moravian Ch. Jurisprudence. Office: Federal Ct Bldg Indianapolis IN 46204

NOLEN, LYNN DEAN, lawyer; b. Wetumka, Okla., Sept. 16, 1940; s. James Everett and Ora Florence (Pierce) N.; m. Cynthia Kay Heath, May 7, 1971; children—Angela Kay, Jennifer Lynn. B.A., East Central State Coll., Ada, Okla., 1961; LL.B., U. Okla., 1964. Bar: Okla. Sole practice, 1964-69; asst. dist. atty. Muskogee County, Okla., 1971—. Served to capt. JAGC, U.S. Army, 1968-72. Mem. Okla. Bar Assn. Democrat. Baptist. Clubs: Masons, Shriners, Odd Fellows. General practice, Family and matrimonial, Probate. Address: 501 W Okmulgee Ave Muskogee OK 74401

NOLEN, ROY LEMUEL, lawyer; b. Montgomery, Ala., Nov. 29, 1937; s. Roy Lemuel Jr. and Elizabeth (Larkin) N.; m. Evelyn McNeil Thomas, Aug. 28, 1965; 1 child, Rives Rutledge. BArch, Rice U., 1961; LLB, Harvard U., 1967. Bar: Tex. 1968, U.S. Ct. Appeals (5th cir.) 1969. Law clk. to sr. judge U.S. Ct. Appeals (5th cir.), 1967-68; assoc. Baker & Botts, Houston, 1968-75, ptnr., 1976—. Trustee Houston Ballet Found., 1980—. Served to 1st lt. USMC, 1961-64. Mem. ABA, Tex. Bar Assn. (corp. law com.). Episcopalian. Clubs: Coronado, Forest (Houston). General corporate, Securities. Office: Baker & Botts One Shell Plaza Houston TX 77002

NOLTE, HENRY R., JR., automobile company executive, lawyer; b. N.Y.C., Mar. 3, 1924; s. Henry R. and Emily A. (Eisele) N.; m. Frances Messner, May 19, 1951; children: Gwynne Conn, Henry Reed III, Jennifer, Suzanne. BA, Duke U., 1947; LLB, U. Pa., 1949. Bar: N.Y. 1950, Mich. 1967. Assoc. Cravath, Swaine & Moore, N.Y.C., 1951-61; assoc. counsel Ford Motor Co., Dearborn, Mich., 1961; asst. gen. counsel Ford Motor Co., 1964-71, assoc. gen. counsel, 1971-74, v.p., gen. counsel fin. and ins. subsidiaries, 1974—; v.p., gen. counsel, sec. Philco-Ford Corp., Phila., 1961-64, Ford of Europe, Inc., Warley, Essex, Eng., 1967-69; mem. Ford Motor Co. Found.; bd. dirs. First Fed. of Mich. Trustee Cranbrook Ednl. Community; mem. Internat. and Comparative Law Ctr. of Southwestern Legal Found., Pres.'s Assn. Duke U., 1976; bd. dirs. Detroit Symphony Orch. Served to lt. USNR, 1943-46, PTO. Mem. ABA (past chmn. com. corp. law depts.), Mich. Bar Assn., Assn. Bar City of N.Y., Assn. Gen. Counsel., Mich. Gen. Counsels Assn. Episcopalian. Clubs: Orchard Lake Country, Bloomfield Hills Country (Mich.). Office: Ford Motor Co The American Rd Dearborn MI 48121

NOLTE, MELVIN, JR., lawyer; b. New Braunfels, Tex., Dec. 14, 1947; s. Melvin Sr. and Louise (Beaty) N.; m. Elizabeth C. Tolle, Aug. 26, 1972 (div. June 1980); 1 child, Melvin III; m. Sandra J. Prochazka, Dec. 4, 1984; 1 child, Chad Louis. BA, Southwest Tex. U., 1970; JD, St. Mary's U., San Antonio, 1972. Bar: Tex. 1973. Sole practice New Braunfels, 1973—; mem. adv. council Cibolo (Tex.) State Bank, 1982—; chmn. bd. dirs., pres. Garden Villa, Inc., New Braunfels; bd. dirs., v.p. Foerster Enterprises, Inc., New Braunfels; bd. dirs. New Braunfels Title Co. Mem. ABA, New Braunfels C. of C., Phi Delta Phi, Pi Gamma Mu. Lodges: Lions, Eagles (past pres. local chpt.). Avocations: hunting, fishing. Real property, Probate, Contracts commercial. Office: 175 N Market St New Braunfels TX 78130

NONET, PHILIPPE, law educator; b. Liège, Belgium, Feb. 25, 1939; s. Leon and Helene (Reginster) N.; m. Pamela Jean Utz, Mar. 21, 1978; children—Michael, Genevieve, Beatrice. Docteur en Droit, U. Liège, 1961; Ph.D., U. Calif.-Berkeley, 1966. Prof. law U. Calif.-Berkeley, 1966—. Author: Administrative Justice, 1969; (with others) Law and Society in Transition, 1978. Mem. Am. Soc. for Polit. and Legal Philosophy, Amintaphil, Law and Soc. Assn. Jurisprudence. Home: 885 Creed Rd Oakland CA 94610 Office: U Calif-Berkeley Sch of Law Berkeley CA 94720

NOOJIN, RAY OSCAR, JR., lawyer; b. Durham, N.C., Apr. 26, 1945; s. Ray O. and Martha (Gunning) N.; m. Janice Skinner, May 25, 1966; children: Catherine, Allison, Ronnie. BS, U. Ala., 1967, JD, 1970. Assoc. Sadler, Sadler, Sullivan & Sharp, Birmingham, Ala., 1970-73; ptnr. Hardin, Stuart, Moncus & Noojin, Birmingham, 1973-76, Noojin, Haley & Ashford, Birmingham, 1976-79, Hare, Wynn, Newell & Newton, Birmingham, 1979—. Mem. Am. Judicature Soc., Assn. Trial Lawyers Am., Ala. Trial Lawyers Assn. (bd. govs. 1980—), Ala. Bar Assn. (chmn. task force on legal services to poor 1986—), Birmingham Bar Assn. (exec. com. 1986), U. Ala. Alumni Assn. (pres. Jeff County chpt. 1976). Lodge: Rotary. Avocations: racquetball, jogging, tennis, golf. State civil litigation, Federal civil litigation. Home: 38 Stonehurst Green Birmingham AL 35213 Office: Hare Wynn Newell & Newton 700 City Federal Bldg Birmingham AL 35203

NOONAN, DENNIS CHARLES, lawyer; b. St. Paul, Sept. 1, 1940; s. Charles Francis and Helen (Fidelius) N.; m. Kathleen Kasper, Sept. 1, 1961 (div. Mar. 1978); children: Michael, Sara. BA, Coll. St. Thomas, 1962; JD, U. Calif., Berkeley, 1965. Bar: Calif. 1966, U.S. Dist. Ct. (no. dist.), U.S. Ct. Appeals (9th cir.). Ptnr. Rich, Fuidge et al, Marysville, Calif., 1965-71, Tweedy, Noonan et al, Sacramento, 1971-75; sole practice Sacramento, 1975—; bd. dirs. Re-Ed West, Sacramento, 1979—. Mem. Am. Trial Lawyers Assn., Calif. Trial Lawyers Assn., State Bar Calif., No. Calif. Def. Counsel, Sacramento County State Bar Assn. Democrat. State civil litigation. Home: 709 E Ranch Rd Sacramento CA 95825 Office: 1600 Sacramento Inn Way #229 Sacramento CA 95825

NOONAN, JOHN T., JR., federal judge, legal educator; b. Boston, Oct. 24, 1926; s. John T. and Maria (Shea) N.; m. Mary Lee Bennett, Dec. 27, 1967; children—John Kenneth, Rebecca Lee, Susanna Bain. B.A., Harvard U., 1946, LL.B., 1954; student, Cambridge U., 1946-47; M.A., Cath. U. Am., 1949, Ph.D., 1951, LHD, 1980; LL.D., U. Santa Clara, 1974, U. Notre Dame, 1976, Loyola U. South, 1978; LHD, Holy Cross Coll., 1980; LL.D., St. Louis U., 1981, U. San Francisco, 1985; student, Holy Cross Coll., 1980, Cath. U. Am., 1980, Gonzaga U., 1986, U. San Francisco, 1986. Bar: Mass. 1954, U.S. Supreme Ct. 1971. Mem. spl. staff Nat. Security Council, 1954-55; sole practice Boston, 1955-60; prof. law U. Notre Dame, 1961-66, U. Calif., Berkeley, 1967-86; judge U.S. Ct. Appeals (9th cir.), San Francisco, 1986—, chmn. religious studies, 1970-73, chmn. medieval studies, 1978-79; Oliver Wendell Holmes, Jr. lectr. Harvard U. Law Sch., 1972; chmn. bd. Games Research, Inc., 1961-76; Pope John XXIII lectr. Cath. U. Law Sch., 1973; Cardinal Bellarmine lectr. St. Louis U. Div. Sch., 1973. Author: The Scholastic Analyst of Usury, 1957; Contraception: A History of Its Treatment by the Catholic Theologians and Cononists, 1965; Power to Dissolve, 1972; Persons and Masks of the Law, 1976; The Antelope, 1977; A Private Choice, 1979; Bribes, 1984; editor: Natural Law Forum, 1961-70, Am. Jour. Jurisprudence, 1970, The Morality of Abortion, 1970. Chmn. Brookline Redevel. Authority, Mass., 1958-62; cons. Papal Commn. on Family, 1965-66, Ford Found., Indonesian Legal Program, 1968; NIH, 1973, NIH, 1974; expert Presdl. Commn. on Population and Am. Future, 1971; cons. U.S. Cath. Conf., 1979—; sec., treas. Inst. for Research in Medieval Canon Law, 1970—; pres. Thomas More-Jacques Maritain Inst., 1977—; trustee Population Council, 1969-76, Phi Kappa Found., 1970-76, Grad. Theol. Union, 1970-73, U. San Francisco, 1971-75; mem. com. theol. edn. Yale U., 1972-77; exec. com. Cath. Commn. Intellectual and Cultural Affairs, 1972-75; bd. dirs. Ctr. for Human Values in the Health Scis., 1969-71, S.W. Intergroup Relations Council, 1970-72, Inst. for Study Ethical Issues, 1971-73. Recipient St. Thomas More award U. San Francisco, 1974, 77, 78, Christian Culture medal, 1975; Guggenheim fellow, 1965-66, 79-80, Laetare medal U. Notre Dame, 1984, Campion medal, 1987; Ctr. for advanced Studies in Behavioral Scis. fellow, 1973-74; Wilson Ctr. fellow, 1979-80. Fellow Am. Acad. Arts and Scis.; mem. Am. Soc. Polit. and Legal Philosophy (v.p. 1964), Canon Law Soc. Am. (gov. 1970-72), Am. Law Inst., Phi Beta Kappa (senator United chpts. 1970-72, pres. Alpha of Calif. chpt. 1972-73). Office: US Ct Appeals 9th cir 7th and Mission Sts San Francisco CA 94101

NOONAN, PATRICK MATTHEW, lawyer; b. Bainbridge, Md., Oct. 6, 1952; s. Matthew Aloysius and Alice Jean (Flynn) N.; m. Denise Ann Doyle, Aug. 13, 1977; children: Colleen Doyle Noonan, Meghan Doyle Noonan. BA, Yale U., 1974; JD, U. Va., 1977. Bar: Conn. 1977, U.S. Dist. Ct. Conn. 1977, U.S. Ct. Appeals (2d cir.) 1981. Law clk. to presiding justice U.S. Dist. Ct., Hartford, Conn., 1977-79; assoc. Wiggin & Dana, New Haven, 1979-84, ptnr., 1984—. Mem. Personnel Rev. Bd., Meriden, Conn., 1979-81; v.p. Bd. Edn., Meriden, 1981-85. Mem. ABA, Conn. Bar Assn., Fed. Practice Com., Meriden Young Lawyers (pres. 1980-82). Democrat. Roman Catholic. Lodge: Ancient Order Hibernians in Am. (treas. 1979-84). Avocations: softball, racquetball, fishing. Federal civil litigation, Personal injury, Criminal. Home: 137 Overshores Dr W Madison CT 06443 Office: Wiggin & Dana PO Box 1832 New Haven CT 06508

NOONAN, THOMAS JOSEPH, lawyer; b. St. Louis, Feb. 8, 1955; s. Leo James and Gloria (Crane) N.; m. Kathryn Kindred Noonan, July 20, 1985. BA in Polit. Sci., U. Mo.; JD, Syracuse U. Bar: Mo. 1980, U.S. Dist. Ct. (ea. dist.) Mo. 1980, Ill. 1982. Assoc. Bamberger and Shea, St. Charles, Mo., 1980-82, Moser, Marsalek et al, St. Louis, 1982-86; ptnr. Noonan and Burke, St. Louis, 1986—. Avocations: winter sports, scuba diving. Insurance, General corporate, Contracts commercial. Office: Noonan and Burke 906 Olive St Suite 1010 Saint Louis MO 63101

NOONE, MICHAEL F., JR., legal educator; b. Los Angeles, Jan. 8, 1934; S. Michael F. and Beverly A. (Manis) N.; m. Ann Hackett, Sept. 16, 1961; children: Catherine, Elizabeth, Michael. BS, Georgetown U., 1955, LLB, 1957, LLM, 1962; SJD, George Washington U., 1965. Commd. USAF, 1957, advanced through grades to col., judge adv., 1957-77, ret., 1977; assoc. dean, assoc. prof. law Cath. U., Washington, 1978—. Chmn. supervisory com. credit union, Washington, 1963-66; chmn. parish fund council Bolling AFB, Washington, 1965-67; chmn. parish council S. Ruislip Air Sta., Eng., 1973-74; chmn. parish council Offutt AFB, Neb., 1975-77. Mem. ABA (young lawyers rep. 1964-67), Fed. Bar Assn. (torts sect. chmn. 1980, nat. council mem. 1973, Eng. chpt. pres. 1971, Outstanding Young Fed. Lawyer 1966), Judge Advs. Assn. (young lawyers rep. 1965-67). Republican. Roman Catholic. Club: RAF (London). Avocation: military history. Federal civil litigation, Military, Legal education. Home: 6025 Woodmont Rd Alexandria VA 22307 Office: Cath U Am Columbus Sch Law Washington DC 20064

NOPAR, ALAN SCOTT, lawyer; b. Chgo., Nov. 14, 1951; s. Myron E. and Evelyn R. (Millman) N. BS, U. Ill., 1976; JD, Stanford U., 1979. Bar: Ariz. 1979, U.S. Dist. Ct. Ariz. 1980, U.S. Ct. Appeals (9th cir.) 1980, U.S. Supreme Ct. 1982; CPA, Ill. Assoc. O'Connor, Cavanagh, Anderson, Westover, Killingsworth & Beshears P.A., Phoenix, 1979-85, ptnr., 1985—. Mem. Ariz. Rep. Caucus, Phoenix, 1984—. Mem. ABA (corp. banking and bus. law sect.), Ariz. Bar Assn. (corp. banking and bus. law sect.), Maricopa County Bar Assn. (corp. banking and bus. law sect.), Am. Inst. CPA's, Phoenix Met. C. of C. Avocations: skiing, water skiing. General corporate, Mergers and acquisitions, Franchise law. Office: O'Connor Cavanagh Anderson et al One E Camelback Rd Suite 1100 Phoenix AZ 85012

NORA, JOHN JOSEPH, lawyer; b. Norway, Mich., May 1, 1947; s. Joseph John and Amelia (Ziller) N.; married; children: Joseph John, Patrick William, Amanda Marie. BBA, Mich. State U., 1969; MBA, U. Detroit, 1974, JD summa cum laude, 1980. Bar: Mich. 1980, U.S. Ct. Appeals (6th cir.) 1980. Dir. human resources Gen. Motors Corp., Detroit, 1970-79; dir. plant personnel Gen. Motors Corp., Livonia, Mich., 1979-81; assoc. Dickinson, Wright, Moon, Van Dusen & Freeman, Detroit, 1981-83; ptnr. Nora, Hemming, Essad & Polaczyk P.C., Plymouth, Mich., 1983—; pres. Workplace Transformation, Inc., Plymouth, 1983—. Author: Transforming The Workplace, 1986. Mem. ABA, Mich. Bar Assn., Detroit Bar Assn., Suburban Bar Assn. Club: Ridgevale Holding, Inc. (Lachine, Mich.) (pres. 1986—). Labor, Local government, Pension, profit-sharing, and employee benefits. Office: Nora Hemming Essad & Polaczyk PC 40600 Ann Arbor Rd E Suite 200 Plymouth MI 48170

NORA, WENDY ALISON, lawyer; b. New Haven, Conn., Feb. 14, 1951; d. James Jackson Nora and Barbara June (Fluhrer) P.; m. Jay Robert Vercauteren, Aug. 21, 1973 (div. Nov. 1981); children: Lucas Jay, Eric Robert. BA, U. Wis., 1971, JD, 1975. Bar: Wis. 1975, U.S. Dist. Ct. (we. dist.) Wis. 1975, Minn. 1985, U.S. Dist. Ct. Minn. 1985, U.S. Supreme Ct. 1986. Sole practice Cross Plains, Wis., 1975-81, Madison, Wis., 1981-84, Mpls., 1985-86. Author: Wednesday's Child, 1984, The Mortal Shore, 1984. Hearing examiner, atty. State of Wis., 1977-81, asst. pub. defender, 1983-84; candidate for U.S. Atty. Gen., Minn., 1986—. Mem. ABA (vice chmn. adminstrv. law sect., criminal law and juvenile justice com. 1982—), Wis. Bar Assn., Soc. Agrarian Lawyers (chmn.). Civil rights, Contracts commercial, Bankruptcy. Home: 4349 Bryant Ave S #3 Minneapolis MN 55409

NORBERG, CHARLES ROBERT, lawyer; b. Cleve., July 25, 1912; s. Rudolf Carl and Ida Edith (Roberts) N. B.S. in Adminstrv. Engring, Cornell U., 1934; M.A. in Internat. Econs, U. Pa., 1937; LL.B., Harvard U., 1939. Bar: Pa. bar 1940, U.S. Supreme Ct. bar 1946, D.C. bar 1947. Lab. research asst. Willard Storage Battery Co., Cleve., 1934-35; asso. firm Hepburn and Norris, Phila., 1939-42; with Office of Assn. Sec. State for Public Affairs, Dept. State, 1948-51; asst. dir. psychol. strategy bd. Exec. Office of the Pres., 1952-54; mem. staff U.S. Delegation to UN Gen. Assembly, Paris, 1951; adviser U.S. Delegation to UNESCO Gen. Conf., Montevideo, 1954; assoc. firm Morgan, Lewis and Bockius, Washington, 1955-56; individual practice law Washington, 1956—; treas., gen. counsel Inter-Am. Comml. Arbitration Commn., 1968-83, dir. gen., 1983—; chief Spl. AID Mission to Ecuador, 1961; spl. Aid Mission to Uruguay, 1961; mem. U.S. delegation to Specialized Inter-Am. Conf. on pvt. internat. law, Panama, 1975. Chmn. Internat. Visitors Info. Service, Washington, 1965-69; chmn. Mayor's Com. on Internat. Visitors, 1971-78; chmn., pres. Bicentennial Commn. of D.C., Inc., 1975-81. Served with USAF, 1942-46. Mem. Phila. Bar Assn., Pa. Bar Assn., Inter-Am. Bar Assn., Washington Fgn. Law Soc. (pres. 1959-63), Am. Soc. Internat. Law, Am. Law Inst., Am. Bar Assn. (chmn. internat. legal exchange program 1974-79), Bar Assn. of D.C. (chmn. internat. law com. 1977-79), Inter-Am. Bar Found. (founder, dir. 1957, pres. 1969-84, chmn. bd. 1984—), Washington Inst. Fgn. Affairs, Academia Colombiana de Jurisprudencia, Inter-Am. Acad. Internat. and Comparative Law, Colegio de Abogados de Quito. Clubs: Metropolitan (Washington); Racquet (Phila.); Harvard (N.Y.C.). Private international, Public international. Home: 3104 N St NW Washington DC 20007 Office: 1819 H St NW Washington DC 20006

NORD, ROBERT EAMOR, lawyer; b. Ogden, Utah, Apr. 11, 1945; s. Eamor Carroll and Ella Carol (Winkler) N.; m. Sherryl Anne Smith, May 15, 1969; children: Kimberly, P. Ryan, Debra, Heather, Andrew, Elizabeth. BS, Brigham Young U., 1969; JD, U. Chgo., 1972. Bar: Ill. 1972, U.S. Dist. Ct. (no. dist.) Ill. 1972, U.S. Ct. Appeals (D.C. cir.) 1974, U.S. Dist. Ct. (mid. dist.) Fla. 1976, U.S. Ct. Appeals (7th cir.) 1977, U.S. Dist. Ct. (no. dist.) Ind. 1978, U.S. Dist. Ct. (no. dist.) Fla. 1979, U.S. Supreme Ct. 1981, U.S. Dist. Ct. (ea. dist.) Mich. 1984, U.S. Ct. Appeals (11th cir.) 1985. Assoc. Chadwell & Kayser, Chgo., 1972-75; from assoc. to ptnr. Hinshaw, Culbertson, Moelmann, Hoban & Fuller, Chgo., 1975—. Republican. Mormon. Club: University (Chgo.). Federal civil litigation, Antitrust. Home: 481 Woodlawn Glencoe IL 60022 Office: Hinshaw Culbertson Moelmann Hoban & Fuller 69 W Washington St Chicago IL 60602

NORDAHL, NORRIS GEORGE, lawyer; b. Milw., June 18, 1918; S. George E. and Lullie (Christenson) N.; m. Betty R. Papp, Dec. 17, 1949. Ph.B. cum laude, U. Wis., 1940; Ph.M., J.D., Marquette U., 1946. Bar: Wis. 1946. Assoc. Olwell & Brady, Milw., 1946-48; sole practice, Milw., 1948-51; sr. ptnr. Nordahl & Cimpl, Milw., 1951—; instr. U. Wis., Madison, 1940-42. Mem. Wis. Bar Assn., Alpha Sigma Nu, Delta Theta Phi. Editor Marquette Law Rev., 1945-46. Probate, Real property. Home: c/o Clover Leaf Farms 900-4318 US Hy 41 North Brooksville FL 33512

NORDAUNE, ROSELYN JEAN, lawyer; b. Montevideo, Minn., May 26, 1955; d. Herbert Palmer and Myrtle (Risdahl) N. BA, Augsburg Coll., 1977; JD, U. Minn., 1980. Bar: Minn. 1980, U.S. Dist. Ct. Minn. 1980, U.S. Ct. Appeals (8th cir.) 1980, U.S. Tax Ct. 1981. Assoc. Rossini, Cochran et al, Mpls., 1980-83; ptnr. Nodland, Conn, Nordaune & Perlman, Mpls., 1983—; bd. dirs. Augsburg Coll., Mpls., 1982—. Bd. dirs. Sr. Community Services, Mpls., 1984—. Mem. ABA, Minn. Bar Assn., Hennepin County Bar Assn., Minn. Women Lawyers, Augsburg Coll. Alumni Assn. (pres. 1984—). Democrat. Lutheran. Lodge: Zonta. General corporate, Family and matrimonial, Probate. Home: 3490 Pilgrim Ln Plymouth MN 55441 Office: Nodland Conn Nordaune & Perlman 550 Shelard Tower Minneapolis MN 55426

NORDBERG, JOHN ALBERT, federal judge; b. Evanston, Ill., June 18, 1926; s. Carl Albert and Judith Ranghild (Carlson) N.; m. Jane Spaulding, June 18, 1947; children—Carol, Mary, Janet, John. B.A., Carleton Coll., 1947; J.D., U. Mich., 1950. Bar: Ill. 1950, U.S. Dist. Ct. (no. dist.) Ill. 1957, U.S. Ct. Appeals (7th cir.) 1961. Assoc. Pope & Ballard, Chgo., 1950-57; ptnr. Pope, Ballard, Shepard & Fowle, Chgo., 1957-76; judge Cir. Ct. of Cook County, Ill., 1976-82, U.S. Dist. Ct. (no. dist.) Ill., Chgo., 1983—. Editor-in-chief, bd. editors Chgo. Bar Record, 1966-74. Magistrate of Cir. Ct. and justice of peace Ill., 1957-65. Served with USN, 1944-46; PTO. Mem. ABA, Chgo. Bar Assn., Ill. State Bar Assn. (assembly rep. 1971-76), Am. Judicature Soc., Law Club Chgo., Legal Club Chgo., Order of Coif. Clubs: Union League, University (Chgo.). Lodge: Rotary. Judicial administration. Office: US Dist Ct 219 S Dearborn St Chicago IL 60604

NORDEN, DENNIS ARTHUR, lawyer; b. Chgo., Mar. 3, 1945; s. Arthur Ferdinand and Alice Dorothea (Offerman) N.; m. Rhonda Lynn DeCardy, Aug. 15, 1965 (div. Apr. 1986); children: Catherine, Amy, Adam. BA, U. Ill., 1966, JD, 1969. Bar: Ill. 1969, U.S. Dist. Ct. (cen. dist.) Ill. 1969, U.S. Supreme Ct. 1969. Ptnr. Thacker & Norden, Kankakee, Ill., 1971-73, Beaupre, Norden & Barmann, Kankakee, 1973-75, Norden & Barmann, Kankakee, 1975-78, Blanke, Norden, Barmann & Bohlen, P.C., Kankakee, 1978—; bd. dirs. Attys. Title Guaranty Fund, Inc., Champaign, Ill. Mem. ABA, Ill. State Bar Assn. (chmn. real estate council, 1982-83), Am. Acad. Hosp. Attys., Kankakee Area C. of C. (bd. dirs. 1978-83). Club: Union League. Avocations: photography, golf. Health, Banking, Real property. Home: 620 Park Pl Kankakee IL 60901 Office: Blanke Norden Barmann & Bohlen PC 189 E Court Suite 500 Kankakee IL 60901

NORDIN, JOHN ERIC, II, lawyer; b. Cleve., Jan. 24, 1943; s. John Eric Albin and Garnett Sara (Hamilton) N.; m. Amanda Jill Felton, Nov. 19, 1977. B.A., San Diego State U., 1964; J.D., U. Calif.-Hastings Coll. of Law, Francisco, 1969. Bar: Calif. 1971, U.S. Ct. Appeals (9th cir.) 1971, U.S. Dist. Ct. (no. and cen. dists.) Calif. 1971, U.S. Supreme Ct. 1975, U.S. Tax Ct. 1980, U.S. Ct. Mil. Appeals 1980, U.S. Claims Ct. 1982. Asst. U.S. atty. civil div. U.S. Dept. Justice, Los Angeles, 1971-75; assoc. Gerald Lipsky, Inc., Beverly Hills, Calif., 1975-79, Bear, Kotob, Ruby & Gross, Downey, Calif., 1979-80; ptnr./litigation counsel Angela & Burford, Pasadena, Calif., 1981-82; assoc., Brown, Reed & Gibson, Pasadena, Calif., 1983-84, ptnr., 1985—; asst. to dean, placement dir. U. Calif. Hastings Coll. Law, San Francisco, 1970-71; instr. Calif. State U.-Long Beach, 1973; asst. prof. M.B.A. program Calif. State U.-Dominguez Hills, 1973-75; instr. Ctr. Trial and Appellate Advocacy, U. Calif. Hastings Coll. Law, 1974, trustee Hastings Coll. Law, 1066 Found. Recipient Am. Jurisprudence award Hastings Coll. Law, 1969. Mem. ABA, Fed. Bar Assn., Bus. Trial Lawyers Assn., Calif. State Bar Assn., Los Angeles County Bar Assn., Pasadena Bar Assn. Republican. Club: University. Federal civil litigation, State civil litigation. Office: 600 S Lake Ave Suite 300 Pasadena CA 91106

NORDLING, BERNARD ERICK, lawyer; b. Nekoma, Kans., June 14, 1921; A.B., McPherson Coll., 1947; student George Washington U., 1941-43; LL.B., J.D., Kans. U., 1949; m. Barbara Ann Burkholder, Mar. 26, 1949. Clerical employee FBI, 1941-44; admitted to Kans. bar, 1949, U.S. Dist. Ct. Kans. 1949, U.S. Ct. Appeals (10th cir.) 1970; practiced in Hugoton, Kans., 1949—; mem. firms Kramer & Nordling, 1950-65, Kramer, Nordling, Nordling & Tate, 1966—; city atty., Hugoton, 1951—; county atty. Stevens County (Kans.), 1957-63. exec. sec. S.W. Kans. Royalty Owners Assn., 1968—; Kans. mem. legal com. Interstate Oil Compact Commn., 1969—, mem. supply tech. adv. com. Nat. Gas Survey, FPC, 1975-77; mem. Kans. Energy Adv. Council, 1975-78, exec. com., 1976-78. Editor U. Kans. Law Rev. of Kans. Bar Jour., 1949. Mem. Hugoton Sch. Bds., 1954-68, pres. grade sch. bd., 1961-66; pres. Stevens County Library Bd., 1957-63. Trustee McPherson Coll., 1971-81, mem. exec. com., 1975-81; bd. govs. Kans. U. Law Soc., 1984—. Served with AUS, 1944-46. Mem. ABA, Kans. Bar Assn., SW Kans. Bar Assn., Am. Judicature Soc., City Attys. Assn. of Kans. (exec. com. 1975-83, pres. 1982-83), Nat. Honor Soc., Nat. Assn. Royalty Owners (bd. govs. 1980—), Order of Coif, Phi Alpha Delta. Oil and gas leasing, Probate, General practice. Home: 218 N Jackson St Hugoton KS 67951 Office: 209 E 6th St Hugoton KS 67951

NORDLINGER, DOUGLAS EDWARD, lawyer; b. Freeport, N.Y., Mar. 27, 1956; s. Lewis Emil and Joyce Marilyn (Strongwater) N.; m. Margaret Dick Meads, Aug. 10, 1979. AB, Duke U., 1978; JD, Harvard U., 1981. Bar: D.C. 1981, U.S. Dist. Ct. D.C. 1982, U.S. Ct. Appeals (D.C. cir.) 1986. Assoc. Hale & Dorr, Boston, 1980; atty. Pierson, Semmes, et al, Washington, 1981-84, Skadden, Arps, et al, Washington, 1984—. Mem. ABA, D.C. Bar. Democrat. Jewish. FERC practice, Federal civil litigation, Antitrust. Home: 6707 Bradley Blvd Bethesda MD 20817 Office: Skadden Arps et al 1440 New York Ave NW Washington DC 20005

NORDLUND, WILLIAM CHALMERS, lawyer; b. Chgo., Aug. 29, 1954; s. Donald E. and Jane H. (Houston) N.; m. Elizabeth A. Nordlund, Oct. 1, 1983; 1 child, William Chalmers Jr. BA, Vanderbilt U., 1976; JD, Duke U., 1979. Bar: Ill. 1979. Assoc. Winston & Strawn, Chgo., 1979—. Bd. dirs. Orchestra of Ill., Chgo., 1983-85; bd. dirs., sec. Literacy Vols. of Am.- Ill., Chgo., 1985—. Mem. ABA, Chgo. Bar Assn. Republican. Presbyterian. Club: University. Avocations: golf, tennis, skiing. General corporate, Securities. Home: 90 Warwick Rd Winnetka IL 60093 Office: Winston & Strawn One First National Plaza Chicago IL 60603

NORDYKE, STEPHEN KEITH, lawyer; b. Kansas City, Mo., Sept. 9, 1953; s. L. Keith and W. Jean (Pickering) N.; m. Debra J. Kirby, July 23, 1983. BS, Southwest Mo. State U., 1976; postgrad., Okla. City U., 1979-80; JD with distinction, U. Mo., Kansas City, 1981. Bar: Mo. 1982, U.S. Dist. Ct. (we. dist.) Mo. 1982. Ptnr. Bertram & Nordyke, Kansas City, 1982-83; sole practice Kansas City, 1983—. Mem. Kansas City Met. Bar Assn., Assn. Trial Lawyers Am., Mo. Assn. Trial Attys., Inns of Ct. Personal injury, Workers' compensation, State civil litigation. Home: 7401 Maywood Raytown MO 64133 Office: 324 E 11th Suite 1700 Kansas City MO 64106

NOREK, FRANCES THERESE, attorney; b. Chgo., Mar. 9, 1947; d. Michael S. and Viola C. (Harbecke) N.; m. John E. Flavin, Aug. 31, 1968 (div.); 1 child, John Michael. B.A., Loyola U., Chgo., 1969, J.D., 1973. Bar: Ill. 1973, U.S. Dist. Ct. (no. dist.) Ill. 1973, U.S. Ct. Appeals (7th cir.) 1974. Assoc. Alter, Weiss, Whitesel & Laff, Chgo., 1973-74; asst. states atty. Cook County, Chgo., 1974-86; assoc. Clausen, Miller, Gorman, Caffrey & Witous P.C., 1986—; mem. trial practice faculty Loyola U. Sch. Law, Chgo., 1980—; judge, evaluator mock trial competitions, Chgo., 1978—; lectr. in field. Recipient Emil Gumpert award Am. Coll. Trial Lawyers, 1982. Mem. Ill. State Bar Assn., Womens Bar Assn. Ill., Chgo. Bar Assn. (instr. fed. trial bar adv. program young lawyer's sect. 1983-84). Insurance, Federal civil litigation, State civil litigation. Office: Clausen Miller Gorman et al 5400 Sears Tower Chicago IL 60606

NORGLE, CHARLES RONALD, United States district judge; b. Mar. 3, 1937. B.B.A., Northwestern U., 1964; J.D., John Marshall Law Sch., Chgo., 1969. Asst. state's atty. DuPage County, Ill., 1969-71, dep. pub. defender, 1971-73, assoc. judge, 1973-77, circuit judge, 1978-84; U.S. dist. judge U.S. Dist. Ct. (no. dist.) Ill., Chgo., 1984—. Mem. ABA, DuPage Bar Assn., Ill. Bar Assn., Fed. Bar Assn., DuPage Assn. Women Attys., Nat. Attys. Assn., Chgo. Legal Club. Office: Federal Courthouse 219 S Dearborn St Chicago IL 60604

NORMAN, CHERIE SHELTON, lawyer; b. Ft. Collins, Colo., Sept. 25, 1950; d. Willie L. and Doris E. (Hoopes) Shelton; m. J. Thomas Norman, May 27, 1972; children—Elizabeth Ella, Robert Thomas, Victoria Cherie, Virginia Elaine. B.S., U. Wyo., 1973, M.S., 1974, J.D., 1979. Bar: Wyo. 1979, U.S. Dist. Ct. Wyo. Assoc. John Burk, P.C., Casper, Wyo., 1979-82; sole practice law, Casper, 1982-85; ptnr. Monroe & Norman, Casper, 1985—; trustee chpt. 7 in bankruptcy, Casper, 1982—. Co-author Bankruptcy Update in Wyoming, 1986. Pres. Ross Law Forum, Laramie, 1978-79. Dir. Community Recreation, Inc., Casper, 1980-84; 1st v.p. Casper Rep. Women, 1984; parliamentarian Wyo. Rep. Women, Casper, 1983—. Mem. ABA, Wyo. Bar Assn., Assn. Trial Lawyers Am., Wyo. Trial Lawyers, Assn. Bankruptcy Trustees, Bus. and Profl. Women., Sigma Alpha Eta (v.p. Laramie 1972). Episcopalian. Banking, Bankruptcy, Family and matrimonial. Home: 4361 S Ash Casper WY 82601 Office: 232 E 2nd Suite 200 Casper WY 82601

NORMAN, DONALD HAMILTON, lawyer; b. Bergen County, N.J., Mar. 6, 1930; s. William H. and Nellie S. N.; m. Joan Retta Blackledge, Aug. 28, 1954; 1 child, Carol Lynn. BA summa cum laude, Rutgers U., 1952; JD magna cum laude, U. Miami, 1955, LLM in Taxation, 1968. Bar: Fla. 1955. Asst. city atty. Ft. Lauderdale, Fla., 1955-59; ptnr. Ross, Norman & Cory, Ft. Lauderdale, 1959—; city atty. Hallandale, Fla., 1970-72; lectr. in taxation Law Sch. U. Miami, 1970-74; adj. prof. taxation Nova Law Sch., 1975-77. Recipient Roger Sorino Award, U. Miami, 1955; Henry Rutgers scholar, 1951-52, Root-Tilden scholar NYU Law Sch., 1952-53. Fellow Am. Coll. Probate Counsel; mem. Fla. Bar (bd. govs. 1974-78), Broward County Bar (pres. 1964-65). Democrat. Presbyterian. Clubs: Lauderdale Yacht. Lodge: Elks. Contbr. articles to legal publ. Condemnation, Probate, General practice. Office: 2720 E Oakland Park Blvd Fort Lauderdale FL 33306

NORMAN, JOHN WAYNE, lawyer; b. Duncan, Okla., Feb. 18, 1944; s. Clarence Dibrell and Mavis Flodess (Griffen) N.; m. Cecelia Ann Bentley, Nov. 27, 1963; children: John Bentley, Michael Wayne, Bradley Earl. BA in English, U. Okla., 1966, LLB, 1968. Bar: Okla. 1968, U.S. Dist. Ct. (we. dist.) Okla. 1970, U.S. Ct. Appeals (10th cir.) 1970, U.S. Dist. Ct. (ea. dist.) Okla. 1972, U.S. Supreme Ct. 1972, U.S. Ct. Appeals (5th cir.) 1974. Ptnr. Lampkin, Wolf, McCaffry & Norman, Oklahoma City, 1968-78, Norman, Hays & Mayfield, Oklahoma City, 1978—. Contbr. articles to profl. jours. Mem. ABA (ins. and negligence sect.), Okla. Bar Assn. (chmn. negligence sect. 1971, chmn. no-fault com. 1974), Assn. Trial Lawyers Am. (chmn. repair sta. com. aviation law 1971-73, chmn. Constl. rev. com. 1975-76, parliamentarian 1974-78, com. supr. 1975-76, bd. govs. 1971-74, chmn. state devel. fund 1985-86), Okla. Trial Lawyers Am. (chmn. legis. com. 1976-77, bd. dirs. 1970, editor torts sect. newsletter 1970), Am. Bd. Trial Advs. (v.p. Okla. chpt. 1986, pres. 1986-87), Inner Circle of Advs., Oklahoma City C. of C., Order of Coif. Democrat. Baptist. Clubs: Rooster (Okla.); Quail Untld. Avocations: flying, farming, hunting, scuba diving. Federal civil litigation, State civil litigation, Personal injury. Home: 8029 Golden Oaks Rd Oklahoma City OK 73127 Office: John Norman Inc 127 NW 10th St Oklahoma City OK 73103-4903

NORMAN, ROBERT DANIEL, lawyer; b. Birmingham, Ala., Mar. 16, 1924; s. Benjamin Daniel and Bernice A. (Cherry) N.; Joan Lorraine Moore, Apr. 13, 1946; married; children: Robert Daniel Jr., Carol Joan McWhorter. BSBA, U. Ala, 1947, JD, 1950. Bar: U.S. Dist. Ct. (no. and so. dists.) Ala. 1953, U.S. Ct. Appeals (5th and 11th cirs.) 1955, U.S. Supreme Ct. 1961. Ptnr. Mead & Norman, Birmingham, 1951-62, Mead, Norman & Fitzpatrick, Birmingham, 1962-68, Norman & Fitzpatrick, Birmingham, 1968-80, Norman, Fitzpatrick & Wood, Birmingham, 1980-86, Norman, Fitzpatrick, Wood, Wright, & Williams, Birmingham, 1986—. Served as lt. (j.g.) USNR, 1942-46, PTO. Fellow Internat. Acad. Trial Lawyers; mem. ABA, Am. Judicature Soc., Def. Research Inst., Internat. Assn. Ins. Counsel (pres. 1982-83), Birmingham Bar Assn. (pres. 1974), Phi Delta Phi. Republican. Clubs: Birmingham Country, Birmingham Ski (pres. 1974-75). Avocations: tennis, fishing, alpine skiing, hunting, boating. Federal civil litigation, State civil litigation, Personal injury. Home: 3925 Royal Oak Dr Birmingham AL 35243 Office: Norman Fitzpatrick et al 1800 City Federal Bldg Birmingham AL 35203

NORMAN, VICTOR CONRAD, lawyer; b. N.Y.C., Mar. 20, 1930; s. Maxwell Nicholas and Lucy (Serbin) N.; children—Marc Elliot, Neil Darryl, Allison Regina. B.A., Syracuse U., 1950; J.D., Bklyn. Law Sch., 1954. Bar: N.Y. 1954, U.S. Dist. Ct. (so. dist.) N.Y. 1965, U.S. Ct. Claims 1965, U.S. Tax Ct. 1965, U.S. Ct. Appeals (2d cir.) 1965, U.S. Supreme Ct. 1965, N.J. 1971, U.S. Dist. Ct. (3rd dist.) N.J. 1971. Sole practice, N.Y.C., 1957—, Rockaway, N.J., 1971—; land procurement negotiator Rockaway Valley Sewer Authority, Boonton, N.J., 1977—; atty. Rockaway Bd. Zoning Appeals, 1976-79. Bd. dirs. Morris County Democratic Orgn., N.J., 1975-79; vice chmn. Rockaway Twp. Dem. Orgn., 1974-75; mem. Rockaway Twp. Zoning Bd. Adjustment, 1973-75; chmn. Dem. County Conv., Morris County, 1974-75. Served with U.S. Army, 1954-56, ETO. Mem. N.Y. State Bar Assn., Morris County Bar Assn. Real property, Personal injury, Probate. Home and Office: 127 W Lakeshore Dr Rockaway NJ 07866

NORRIS, ALAN EUGENE, judge; b. Columbus, Ohio, Aug. 15, 1935; s. J. Russell and Dorothy A. (Shrader) N.; m. Nancy Jean Myers, Apr. 15, 1962 (dec. Jan. 1986); children: Tom Edward Jackson, Tracy Elaine. BA, Otterbein Coll., 1957; cert., U. Paris, 1956; LLB, NYU, 1960; LLM, U. Va., 1986. Bar: Ohio 1960, U.S. Dist. Ct. (so. dist) Ohio 1962, U.S. Dist. Ct. (no. dist) Ohio 1964. Law clk. to judge Ohio Supreme Ct., Columbus, 1960-61; assoc. Vorys, Sater, Seymour & Pease, Columbus, 1961-62; ptnr. Metz, Bailey, Norris & Spicer, Westerville, Ohio, 1962-80; judge Ohio Ct. Appeals (10th dist.), Columbus, 1981-86, U.S. Ct. Appeals (6th cir.), Columbus, 1986—. Contbr. articles to profl. jours. Mem. Ohio Ho. of Reps., Columbus, 1967-80. Named Outstanding Young Man, Westerville Jaycees, 1971; recipient Legislator of Yr. award Ohio Acad. Trial Lawyers, Columbus, 1972. Mem. ABA, Am. Judicature Soc., Inst. Jud. Adminstrn., Ohio Bar Assn., Columbus Bar Assn. Republican. Methodist. Lodge: Masons (master 1966-67). Office: US Ct Appeals 103 US Courthouse Columbus OH 43215

NORRIS, CYNTHIA ANN, lawyer; b. South Bend, Ind., Aug. 3, 1951. B.S., Ind. State U., 1973; J.D., South Tex. Coll. Law, 1977. Bar: Tex. 1977, La. 1979, U.S. Dist. Ct. (ea. dist.) La. 1979, Calif. 1984, U.S. Dist. Ct. (ea. dist.) Calif. 1984, U.S. Dist. Ct. (so. dist.) Tex. 1978, U.S. Ct. Appeals (5th cir.) 1979. Atty. Brill, Brooks, Gillis & Yount, Houston, 1977-78, L.R. Koerner, New Orleans, 1978-80; atty.-land Gulf Oil Corp., New Orleans, 1980-83, Bakersfield, Calif., 1983-84, Chevron U.S.A., Inc. Hdqrs., San Ramon, Ventura and San Francisco, 1984—; vis. scholar John Westburg & Assocs., Tehran, Iran, 1976; Mem. ABA, Tex. Bar Assn., La. Bar Assn., Calif. Bar Assn., Women in Law Assn. (pres. 1975-76), Phi Alpha Delta. Republican. Presbyterian. FERC practice, Oil and gas leasing, Environment. Office: Chevron USA Inc Hdqrs 575 Market St Rm 2738 San Francisco CA 94105-2856

NORRIS, JAMES ROBERT, lawyer; b. Rock Rapids, Iowa, Feb. 23, 1947; s. George Bryan and Katherine Virginia (Kerns) N.; m. Donna Jean Bedell, Aug. 7, 1971; children: Andrew, Betsy. Student, U.S. Mil. Acad., 1965-68; BS, Coe Coll., 1970; JD, Drake U., 1974. Bar: Iowa 1974, U.S. Dist. Ct. (no. dist.) Iowa 1974, U.S. Ct. Appeals (8th cir.) 1981, U.S. Dist. Ct. (so. dist.) Iowa 1984. Sole practice Cedar Rapids, Iowa, 1974—. Mem. Assn. Trial Lawyers Am. Personal injury, Criminal, Workers' compensation. Home: 4510 Deer View Rd Cedar Rapids IA 52401 Office: 8226 Cedar Point Rd NE Cedar Rapids IA 52402

NORRIS, JANET CLARE, lawyer; b. Chgo., Jan. 17, 1952; d. Wells Rudolph and Lois Joy (Klock) N.; m. Thomas Young Coleman, Aug. 30, 1980; 1 child, Dana. BA, Princeton U., 1973; JD, U. Va., 1976. Bar: Calif. 1976. Assoc. Pillsbury, Madison & Sutro, San Francisco, 1976-79, Dinkelspiel, Pelavin, Steefel & Levitt, San Francisco, 1979-80; from assoc. to ptnr. Steefel, Levitt & Weiss, San Francisco, 1981—. Mem. Jr. League, San Francisco, 1978—, Family Service Agy., San Francisco, 1980-81. Mem. ABA (real estate fin. com.), Calif. Bar Assn. (real property sect.), San Francisco Bar Assn. Republican. Episcopalian. Real property. Home: 54 Wildwood Gardens Piedmont CA 94611 Office: Steefel Levitt & Weiss 1 Embarcadero Ctr 29th Floor San Francisco CA 94111

NORRIS, JOHN ANTHONY, commissioner, lawyer, businessman, manager; b. Buffalo, Dec. 27, 1946; s. Joseph D. and Maria L. (Suite) N.; m. Kathleen Mullen, July 13, 1969; children: Patricia Marie, John Anthony II, Joseph Mullen, Mary Kathleen, Elizabeth Mary. BA, U. Rochester, 1968; JD, MBA with honors, Cornell U., 1973; cert., Harvard U. Sch. Govt., 1986. Bar: Mass. 1973. Assoc. Peabody, Brown, Boston, 1973-75; assoc. Power & Hall, Boston, 1975-76, ptnr., mem. exec. com., 1976-80, v.p., 1979-80, chmn. adminstrv. com., 1976-79, chmn. hiring com., 1979-80; pres., chief exec. officer Norris & Norris, Boston, 1980-85; dep. commr. and chief operating officer FDA, Washington, 1985—; mem. faculty Tufts Dental Sch., 1973-79, Boston Coll. Law Sch., 1976-80, Boston U. Law Sch., 1979-83; mem. bd. editors FDA Drug Bulletin and FDA Consumer Report, 1985—. Faculty editor-in-chief Am. Jour. Law and Medicine, 1973-81, emeritus 1981—; editor-in-chief Cornell Internat. Law Jour., 1972-73; reviewer New Eng. Jour. Medicine Law-Medicine Notes, 1980-81; assoc. editor Medicolegal News, 1973-76. Chmn. Mass. Statuatory Adv. Com. on Regulation of Clin. Labs., 1977-83; chmn. Boston Alumni and Scholarship Com., 1979-85; mem. trustees council U. Rochester, 1979-85; mem. exec. com. Cornell Law Sch. Assn., 1982-85;Mass. Gov.'s Blue Ribbon Task Force on DON, 1979-80, exec. com. bd. trustees Jordan Hosp., 1978-80; chmn. Joseph D. Norris Health, Law and Pub. Policy Fund, 1980—; chmn. bd. Boston Holiday Project, 1981-83; mem. Pres. Chernobyl Task Force, 1986, co-chmn. health affects sub-com., Intergovtl. AIDS Task Force, 1987. Served with U.S. Army, 1972-73, with res. Fed. Comprehensive Health Planning fellow, 1970-73; PHS Superior Service award FDA, 1986; recipient TOYL award, 1982. Mem. ABA (vice chmn. medicine and law com. 1977-80), Mass. Bar Assn., Am. Soc. Hosp. Attys., Nat. Health Lawyers, Am. Soc. Law and Medicine (life, 1st v.p. 1975-80, chmn. bd. 1981-85, mem. award 1981), Soc. Computer Applications to Medicare (mem. bd. 1984-85), Phi Kappa Phi. Home: 8460 Holly Leaf Dr McLean VA 22102 Office: FDA 5600 Fishers Ln Rockville MD 20857

NORRIS, JOHN HART, lawyer; b. New Bedford, Mass., Aug. 4, 1942; s. Edwin Arter and Harriet Joan (Winter) N.; m. Anne Kiley Monaghan, June 10, 1967; children—Kiley Anne, Amy O'Shea. B.A., Ind. U., 1964; J.D., U. Mich., 1967. Bar: Mich. 1968, U.S. Ct. Mil. Appeals 1969, U.S. Supreme Ct. 1974, U.S. Ct. Claims 1975, U.S. Tax Ct. 1979. Assoc., then ptnr. Monaghan, Campbell, LoPrete, McDonald and Norris, 1970-83; of counsel Dickinson, Wright, Moon, Van Dusen & Freeman, 1983-84, ptnr.1985—; bd. dirs. Holly's Hotsock, Prime Securities Corp., Ray M. Whyte Co., Ward-Williston Drilling Co., Bott Lodge Enterprises. Mem. Rep. State Fin. Com.; founder, co-chmn. Rep. majority club; bd. dirs. Boys and Girls Clubs of Southeastern Mich., 1979—, Mich. Wildlife Habitat Found., Mercy Coll., Detroit; mem. Detroit Hist. Soc., 1984—; trustee Nat. Council Salk Inst. Served with M.I., U.S. Army, 1968-70. Recipient numerous civic and non-profit assn. awards. Fellow Mich. State Bar Found.; mem. ABA (litigation and natural resources sects.), Mich. Oil and Gas Assn. (legal and legis. com.), State Bar Mich. (chmn. environ. law sect. 1982-83, probate and trust law sect., energy conservation task force, oil and gas com.), Oakland County Bar Assn., Detroit Bar Assn. (pub. adv. com.), Am. Arbitration Assn., Fin. and Estate Planning Council Detroit, Def. Orientation Conf. Assn., Detroit Zool. Soc., Blue Key Nat. Hon. Fraternity, Phi Delta Phi. Roman Catholic. Clubs: Bloomfield Hills Country; Thomas M. Cooley, Detroit Athletic, Economic (Detroit); Hundred, Prismatic, Turtle Lake, Yondotega. Contbr. articles to profl jours. State civil litigation, Oil and gas leasing, Estate planning. Home: 1325 Buckingham St Birmingham MI 48008 Office: 525 N Woodward Ave PO Box 509 Bloomfield Hills MI 48013

NORRIS, JOHN STEVENS, JR., lawyer; b. Alexandria, Va., Oct. 15, 1951; s. John Stevens and Mary Anna (Werner) N.; m. Amy Ann Kyker, Dec. 21, 1986; 1 stepchild, Amanda Leigh. AB, Coll. William and Mary, 1973; JD, Washington and Lee U., 1976. Bar: Va. 1976, U.S. Dist. Ct. (ea. dist.) Va. 1977, U.S. Ct. Appeals (4th cir.) 1979. Law clk. Va. Supreme Ct., Richmond, 1976-77; assoc. Williams Worrell, Kelly and Greer, P.C., Norfolk, Va., 1977-82; ptnr. Williams Worrell, Kelly and Greer, P.C., Norfolk, 1982-85, Anderson and Padrick, Virginia Beach, Va., 1986—. Burks Teaching scholar Washington and Lee U., 1976. Mem. Va. Bar Assn., Virginia Beach Bar Assn., Norfolk-Portsmouth Bar Assn., Fed. Bar Assn. (pres. 1985, nat. del. Tidewater chpt. 1986), Va. Assn. Def. Atty., Ocean Front Jaycees (bd. dirs. 1980-83). Roman Catholic. Club: Virginia Beach Exchange (bd. dirs. 1986—). Avocations: golf, racquet ball, scuba diving, reading, travel. Personal injury, Construction, Insurance. Home: 2312 Calvert St Virginia Beach VA 32451 Office: Anderson and Padrick 3330 Pacific Ave Suite 500 Virginia Beach VA 23451

NORRIS, LAWRENCE GEOFFREY, lawyer; b. Centralia, Ill., June 4, 1926; s. Patrick Iranaeus and Julia Catherine (Lordan) N.; m. Lauretta Shore, Feb. 7, 1953; children—Deborah, Lawrence, David Steven; m. Barbara H. deKorte, Sept. 28, 1979. B.S.E.E., U. Ill., 1947; M.S.E.E., Northeastern U., 1962; J.D., Boston Coll., 1953. Bar: Mass. 1953, Va. 1968. Div. patent counsel Gen. Electric Co., 1962-69; assoc. patent counsel, sr. corp. atty. Polaroid Corp., 1969-80; v.p., corp. counsel Energy Conversion Devices, Inc., Troy, Mich., 1980—. Sustaining mem. Republican Nat. Com. Served with U.S. Army, 1944-46. Mem. ABA, Am. Patent Law Assn., Mich. Patent Law Assn. Club: Fides Soc. Boston Coll. General corporate, Patent. Office: Energy Conversion Devices Inc 1675 W Maple Rd Troy MI 48084

NORRIS, ROBERT WHEELER, lawyer, air force officer; b. Birmingham, May 22, 1932; s. Hubert Lee and Georgia Irene (Parker) N.; m. Martha Katherine Cummins, Feb. 19, 1955; children—Lisha Katherine Norris Utt, Nathan Robert. B.A. in Bus. Adminstrn., U. Ala., 1954, LL.B., 1955; LL.M., George Washington U., 1979; postgrad., Air Command & Staff Coll., 1968, Nat. War Coll., 1975. Advanced through grades to maj. gen. U.S. Air Force; chief def. services div. HQ U.S. Air Force, Washington, 1976-78, chief internat. law, 1978-80, dir. civil law HQ, 1980-82; staff judge advocate SAC U.S. Air Force, Offutt AFB, Nebr., 1982-83; dep. judge advocate gen. HQ U.S. Air Force, Washington, 1983-85, judge advocate gen., 1985—. Decorated Legion of Merit, Meritorious Service award, Air Force Commendation medal. Mem. ABA, Inter-Am. Bar Assn., Internat. Inst. Space Law, Ala. Bar Assn. Methodist. Military, Estate taxation. Office: Office Judge Advocate Gen HQ US Air Force Washington DC 20330

NORRIS, WILLIAM ALBERT, judge; b. Turtle Creek, Pa., Aug. 30, 1927; s. George and Florence (Clive) N.; m. Merry Wright, Nov. 23, 1974; children—Barbara, Donald, Kim, Alison. Student, U. Wis., 1945; B.A., Princeton U., 1951; J.D., Stanford U., 1954. Bar: Calif. and D.C. 1955. Asso. firm Northcutt Ely, Washington, 1954-55; law clk. to Supreme Ct. Justice William O. Douglas, Washington, 1955-56; sr. mem. firm Tuttle & Taylor, Inc., Los Angeles, 1956-80; circuit judge U.S. Ct. Appeals, 9th Circuit, Los Angeles, 1980—; spl. counsel Pres.' Kennedy's Com. on Airlines Controversy, 1961; mem., v.p. Calif. State Bd. Edn., 1961-67. Trustee Calif. State Colls., 1967-72; pres. Los Angeles Bd. Police Commrs., 1973-74; Democratic nominee for atty. gen. State of Calif., 1974; founding pres. bd. trustees Mus. Contemporary Art, Los Angeles, 1979—; trustee Craft and Folk Art Mus., 1979—. Served with USN, 1945-47. Jurisprudence. Home: 1473 Oriole Dr Los Angeles CA 90069 Office: US Courthouse 17th Floor 312 N Spring St Los Angeles CA 90012

NORSTRAND, HANS PETER, lawyer, real estate investment co. exec.; b. Cambridge, Mass., Aug. 1, 1940; s. Hans Donald and Marion (Hardy) N.; m. Janet Hoover, Dec. 30, 1967; children—Rachel Bell, Hans Christopher. A.B., Dartmouth Coll., 1963; J.D., Boston Coll., 1966. Bar: Mass. 1966. Asst. atty. gen. Mass., 1966-69; assoc. Sullivan & Worcester, Boston, 1969-74; v.p., gen. csl. Kuras & Co., Inc., Boston, 1974-76; sole practice, Boston, 1977-80; v.p. Boston Co. Real Estate Counsel, Inc., 1980-81; prin. Aldrich, Eastman & Waltch, Inc., Boston, 1981—; mem. faculty Internat. Council Shopping Ctrs., 1981—; part-time mem. faculty Boston U. Sch. Mgmt., 1980—, Boston U. Sch. of Law, 1987—; corporator West Newton (Mass.) Savs. Bank, 1976-86. Served with USMCR, 1958-61. Mem. ABA, Boston Bar Assn. Democrat. Unitarian. Contbr. articles to legal jours. Real property. Office: Aldrich Eastman & Waltch Inc 265 Franklin St Boston MA 02110

NORTELL, BRUCE, lawyer; b. Oak Park, Ill., Nov. 19, 1946; s. Joseph and Dorothy Nortell; m. Joan Ott, Apr. 5, 1975; children—Adam, Daniel, Anthony. A.B., Boston U., 1968; J.D., U. Chgo., 1971. Bar: Ill. 1971, U.S. Dist. Ct. (no. dist.) Ill. 1971, U.S. Supreme Ct. 1979. Sole practice, Chgo., 1971-74; asst. dir. legal affairs AMA, Chgo., 1974-81, counsel, sec. jud. council, 1976-81; dir. tax and fin. planning Loyola U., Chgo., 1981—. Contbr. articles to profl. jours. Mem. ABA, Ill. Bar Assn. (Lincoln award 1975), Chgo. Bar Assn., Phi Beta Kappa. Estate planning, General practice, Estate taxation. Home: 48 Kinglet Ct Naperville IL 60565 Office: 820 N Michigan Ave Chicago IL 60611

NORTH, KENNETH EARL, lawyer; b. Chgo., Nov. 18, 1945; s. Earl and Marion (Temple) N.; m. Susan C. Gutzmer, June 6, 1970; children: Krista, Kari. AA with high honors, Coll. of DuPage, Glen Ellyn, Ill., 1970; BA with high honors, No. Ill. U., 1971; JD, Duke U., 1974. Bar: Ill. 1974, U.S. Dist. Ct. (no. dist.) Ill. 1974, Guam 1978, U.S. Tax Ct., 1975, U.S. Ct. Appeals (7th cir.), 1978, U.S. Supreme Ct., 1978, U.S. Ct. Internat. Trade 1978, U.S. Ct. Appeals (9th cir.) Ill. 1979. Div. chief DuPage County State's Attys. Office, Wheaton, 1976-78; spl. asst. U.S. atty. Terr. of Guam, Agana, 1978-79, atty. gen., 1979-80; ptnr. firm Solomon, Rosenfeld, Elliott & Stiefel Ltd., Chgo., 1982-86, Burke, Bosselman & Weaver, Chgo., 1986—; adj. prof. law John Marshall Law Sch., Chgo., 1985—, Keller Grad. Sch. Mgmt. Northwestern U.; instr. Northwestern U. Traffic Inst., 1985—; cons. Terr. of Guam, 1980-81; lectr., cons. regarding computer-aided litigation support, 1985—; counsel to various fin. instns. and domestic corps. Co-author: Criminal and Civil Tax Fraud, 1986; bd. editors Attorneys' Computer Report, 1986—; contbr. articles to legal publs. Trustee, mem. adv. bd. Ams. for Effective Law Enforcement, 1986—; v.p. Glen Ellyn Manor Civic Assn., 1981-84, pres., 1984—; police commr. Village of Glen Ellyn, 1982—. Mem. Assn. Trial Lawyers Am. (sec. criminal sect. 1986-87), ABA, Ill. Bar Assn., World Bar Assn., Chgo. Bar Assn., Chgo. Duke Bar Assn. (pres. 1986-87), Chgo. Council Fgn. Relations, Internat. Platform Assn., Mensa. Republican. Pioneer use of computer in ct. Federal civil litigation, Private international, Federal white collar criminal. Office: Burke Bosselman & Weaver Xerox Ctr 55 W Monroe St Chicago IL 60603

NORTH, THOMAS BRIAN, lawyer; b. Battle Creek, Mich., Mar. 2, 1956; s. Walter Harper and Sally Ann (Greensmith) N. BBA, Western Mich. U., 1977; JD, Thomas M. Cooley Law Sch., 1981. Bar: Mich. 1982, U.S. Dist. Ct. (we. dist.) Mich. 1982, U.S. Dist. Ct. (ea. dist.) Mich. 1983, U.S. Ct. Appeals (fed. cir.) 1986. Assoc. Law Offices of Peter Patrick P.C., Cheboygan, Mich., 1982—. Fellow Mich. Bar Found. Methodist. General practice. Home: 3787 Greenman's Point Rd Cheboygan MI 49721 Office: Law Offices of Peter Patrick PC 520 N Main St Cheboygan MI 49721

NORTHCUTT, CLARENCE DEWEY, lawyer; b. Guin, Ala., July 7, 1916; s. Walter G. and Nancy E. (Homer) N.; m. Ruth Eleanor Storms, May 25, 1941; children: Gayle Marie (Mrs. John J. Young), John E. A.B., U. Okla., 1939, LL.B., 1938. Bar: Okla. 1938. Practiced in Ponca City, 1938—; former gen. counsel Frontier Fed. Savs. and Loan Assn.; Mem. bd. visitors U. Okla. Served with AUS, 1941-46. Decorated Bronze Star, Air medal with oak leaf cluster., Order St. John of Jerusalem; named Outstanding Citizen of Ponca City, 1982. Fellow Am. Coll. Trial Lawyers, Am. Coll. Probate Counsel, Am. Bar Found.; mem. Acad. Univ. Fellows, Internat. Soc. Barristers, Am. Bd. Advocacy, Internat. Acad. Trial Lawyers, Okla. Bar Assn. (pres. 1975, bd. govs.), Ponca City C. of C. (past pres.). Democrat. Baptist. Clubs: Mason, Kiwanian. Probate, Personal injury. Home: 132 Whitworth St Ponca City OK 74601 Office: PO Box 1669 Ponca City OK 74601

NORTHROP, CARL WOODEN, lawyer; b. Princeton, N.J., Sept. 30, 1950; s. M. Starr and Margaret Leigh (Wooden) N.; m. Michaelanne Provencher, July 21, 1972; 1 child, Lisa Erin. BBA, U. Mich., 1972; JD, Georgetown U., 1976. Assoc. Norm Jorgensen Law Office, Washington, 1976-78; ptnr. Jorgensen, Johnson & Northrop, Washington, 1978-81; ptnr. Kadison, Pfaelzer, Woodard, Quinn & Rossi, Washington, 1981-85, mng. ptnr., 1985—. Editor Georgetown U. Law Jour., 1975-76. Mem. Fed. Communications Bar Assn. Administrative and regulatory. Office: Kadison Pfaelzer Woodard Quinn 2000 Pennsylvania Ave NW Washington DC 20006

NORTHROP, CYNTHIA ELLEN, lawyer, nurse, educator; b. North Tonawanda, N.Y., June 11, 1950; d. Francis Merle and Marjorie Imogene (Wion) N.; m. Harvey Cary Dzodin, Jan. 29, 1984. BS, Columbia Union Coll., 1972; MS, U. Md., 1975; JD, U. Balt., 1979. Bar: Md. 1980. Surgical team leader Wash. Adventist Hosp., Md., 1972; pub. health nurse health dept. Prince George's County, Md., 1972-75; instr. U. Md., Balt., 1975-77, asst. prof., 1977-84; sole practice Hyattsville, Md., 1980—; lectr. Georgetown U., Washington, 1983-85; adj. assoc. prof. Columbia U. Tchrs. Coll., N.Y.C., 1985—; cons. Office Tech. Assessment U.S. Congress, 1985. Contbr. articles to profl. jours. Fellow Nat. Endowment for Humanities, 1980; recipient Creative Achievement award Am. Pub. Health Assn., 1984, Disting. Service award Am. Soc. Law & Medicine, 1985; named one of Outstanding Young Women in Am., 1982. Mem. ABA, Md. Bar Assn., Am. Assn. Nurse Attys. (pres. 1982-84, bd. dirs. 1982—, disting. service award 1985), Am. Assn. Nurse Attys. Found. (pres., trustee 1984—), Am. Nurses Assn., N.Y. State Nurses Assn. Avocation: genealogy. Health, Administrative and regulatory, Legal education. Home and Office: 444 E 86th St #33B New York NY 10028

NORTON, FLOYD LIGON, IV, lawyer; b. Shreveport, La., Oct. 23, 1950; s. Floyd Ligon III and Grace Louise (Julian) N.; m. Kathleen Fair Patterson, Nov. 24, 1979; children: Caroline, Elizabeth. BA with honors, U. Va., 1972, JD, 1975. Bar: Va. 1975, D.C. 1975. Assoc. Reid & Priest, Washington, 1975-83, ptnr., 1983—. Mem. ABA, Fed. Energy Bar Assn. Episcopalian. FERC practice, Public utilities, Administrative and regulatory. Home: 1723 U St NW Washington DC 20009 Office: Reid & Priest 1111 19th St NW Washington DC 20036

NORTON, GERARD FRANCIS, JR., lawyer; b. N.Y.C., Feb. 5, 1937; s. Gerard Francis and Florence (Keane) N.; m. Margot Dessauer, Aug. 11, 1962; children—John G., David F., Katherine L., Maureen M., Michael X. B.A., Coll. of Holy Cross, 1959; J.D., Cornell U., 1962. Bar: N.Y. 1962, U.S. Dist. Ct. (so. and ea. dists.) N.Y. 1963, U.S. Customs Ct. 1963, U.S. Dist. Ct. (we. dist.) N.Y. 1968. Assoc. Hill, Betts, Yamaoka, Freehill & Longcope, N.Y.C., 1962-65; asst. atty. gen. N.Y. State, Poughkeepsie, 1965-67; ptnr.

Garrity & Dietz, Poughkeepsie, 1967-68; assoc., then ptnr. Culley, Marks, Corbett, Tanenbaum, Reifsteck & Potter, Rochester, N.Y., 1968-75; assoc. counsel Sybron Corp., Rochester, 1975-83; gen. counsel, sec. Champion Products, Inc., Rochester, N.Y., 1983—. Mem. Pittsford Central Sch. Bd., 1971-75, v.p. 1974-75. Mem. N.Y. State Bar Assn. (corp. law sect.). Republican. Roman Catholic. Clubs: Monroe Golf, Tennis of Rochester, Holy Cross of Rochester. General corporate, Private international, Federal civil litigation. Office: Champion Products Inc 3141 Monroe Ave Rochester NY 14603

NORTON, JANE MARIE, lawyer; b. Milw., Mar. 6, 1954; d. Richard Geiger and Betty Jane (Case) N.; m. William W. Wells Jr., Aug. 4, 1979. BA, U. Tex., 1975; JD, U. Puget Sound, 1978. Bar: Tex. 1979, Va. 1980, U.S. Dist. Ct. (we. dist.) Va., U.S. Ct. Appeals (4th cir.). Law editor Michie Co., Charlottesville, Va., 1979-81, sr. editor, 1981-83; sr. editor law library Library of Congress, Washington, 1984-86; sole practice. Legal editing & writing..

NORTON, JOHN EDWIN, lawyer; b. Rockford, Ill., Aug. 14, 1949; s. Joseph A. and Irene (O'Connell) N.; m. Ellen M. Feldner, Jan. 7, 1977; children: John J., Molly M., Donald J. BA, U. Notre Dame, 1971; JD, DePaul U., 1975. Bar: Ill. 1975, U.S. Ct. Appeals (7th cir.) 1975. From assoc. to ptnr. O'Reilly, Cunningham, Duncan & Norton, Wheaton, Ill., 1978—. Roman Catholic. Home: 6040 Brookbank Rd Downers Grove IL 60516 Office: O'Reilly Cunningham et al 109 N Hale St PO Box 846 Wheaton IL 60189

NORTON, JOHN WILLIAM, lawyer, investment advisory firm executive; b. St. Paul, Sept. 30, 1941; s. John William Jr. and Dorothy (Sheridan) N.; m. Kathleen L. Smith, Aug. 19, 1967 (div.); children—Tiffany, Sean. B.A. in Bus. Adminstrn., Marquette U., 1964; J.D., Stetson U., 1968. Bar: Fla. 1968, Minn. 1968. Atty. Minn. Mut. Life Ins. Co., St. Paul, 1968-73; asst. counsel IDS Life Ins. Co., Mpls., 1973; atty., adviser fin. SEC, Washington, 1973-78; gen. counsel, sec. AMEV Advisers, Inc., AMEV Investors, Inc., St. Paul, Minn., 1978—, AMEV Money Mgrs., Inc.; v.p. eight investment cos. including AMEV Securities, Inc., AMEV Capital Fund, Inc., AMEV Fiduciary Fund, Inc., others; corp. counsel Western Life Ins. Co. Mem. ABA, Minn. Bar Assn., Fla. Bar Assn. Securities, General corporate, Pension, profit-sharing, and employee benefits. Home: 7833 Cayenne Pl E Saint Paul MN 55125

NORVILLE, CRAIG HUBERT, lawyer; b. N.Y.C., June 10, 1944; s. Hubert G. and Harriett (Johnson) N.; m. Margaret Brent, Nov. 14, 1980; 1 child, Margaret Amelia. AB, Harvard U., 1966; LLB, U. Va., 1969. Bar: N.Y. 1971, Pa. 1979, Tenn. 1985. Instr. law U. Mich., 1969-70; assoc. Cravath, Swaine & Moore, N.Y.C., 1970-76; sr. atty. Bethlehem (Pa.) Steel Corp., 1976-80; v.p., assoc. gen. counsel Holiday Corp., Memphis, 1980-84, v.p., gen. counsel, 1984-86, sr. v.p., gen. counsel, 1986—. Articles editor U. Va. Law Rev. Mem. Raven Soc., Hasty Pudding Inst. of 1770, Order of Coif. Club: Harvard Varsity (Cambridge, Mass.). Avocations: tennis, skiing. General corporate, Real property, Securities. Home: 527 E Parkway S Memphis TN 38104 Office: Holiday Corp 1023 Cherry Rd Memphis TN 38117

NORWIND, EDWARD LEE, lawyer; b. Pitts., May 1, 1950; s. Sidney Norwind; m. Pamela Downs, May 30, 1982. BS, Mich. State U., 1972; JD, U. Calif., Santa Clara, 1976. Bar: Calif. 1976, D.C. 1977, U.S. Dist. Ct. (no. dist.) Calif. 1979, U.S. Dist. Ct. D.C. 1977, U.S. Ct. Appeals (D.C. cir.) 1981, Md. 1983, U.S. Dist. Ct. Md. 1984, U.S. Ct. Appeals (4th cir.) 1984. Assoc. Chapman, Norwind & Vaughters, Washington, 1978-85; ptnr. Paulson, Nace & Norwind, Washington, 1985—; arbitrator Am. Arbitration Assn. Mem. Assn. Trial Lawyers Am. (del. 1985-87, bd. of govs. 1987—), D.C. Bar Assn. (lectr. contining legal edn. com. 1984—), Met. Wash. Trial Lawyers Assn. (bd. of govs. 1984—, steering com. negligence div. 1984—, pres. 1984-85). Avocations: tennis, running, baseball. Personal injury, Federal civil litigation, State civil litigation. Office: Paulson Nace & Norwind 1814 N St NW Washington DC 20036

NORWOOD, DOROTHY F., Supreme Court deputy clerk; b. Prattville, Ala., July 31, 1943; d. Ralph L. and Gladys (Dawson) Ferrell; m. William R. Norwood, Apr. 2, 1965; children—Jay, Richard. B.S., Auburn U., 1978; J.D., Jones Law Inst., 1981. Steno clk. State Ala., Montgomery, 1961-71; asst. clk. Ala. Supreme Ct., Montgomery, 1971-77, acting dep. clk., 1977-82, acting clk., 1982-83, dep. clk., 1983—. Author Assignment of Cases, 1979, Assistance to Attorneys, 1981. Mem. Ala. State Bar (chmn. com.), Am. Bar Assn., Montgomery County Bar Assn., Nat. Conf. Appellate (sec., treas. 1978-82). Club: Zonta (rec. sec. 1985—). Judicial administration, State civil litigation, Appellate practice. Home: 1310 Magnolia Ave Montgomery AL 36101 Office: Ala Supreme Ct PO Box 157 Montgomery AL 36130

NOTOPOULOS, ALEXANDER ANASTASIOS, JR., lawyer; b. Altoona, Pa., Jan. 29, 1953; s. Alexander Anastasios Sr. and Christine (Economou) N.; m. Alexis J. Anderson, Aug. 4, 1984. BA, Amherst Coll., 1974; JD, Harvard U., 1977. Bar: Mass. 1978, U.S. Dist. Ct. Mass. 1979. Law clk. to judge U.S. Ct. Appeals (3d cir.), Phila., 1977-78; assoc. Sullivan & Worcester, Boston, 1978-85, ptnr., 1985—. General corporate, Municipal bonds, Securities. Home: 9C Russell St Cambridge MA 02140 Office: Sullivan & Worcester One Post Office Sq Boston MA 02109

NOTTINGHAM, EDWARD WILLIS, JR., lawyer; b. Denver, Jan. 9, 1948; s. Edward Willis and Willie Newton (Gullett) N.; m. Cheryl Ann Card, June 6, 1970 (div. Feb. 1981); children: Amelia Charlene, Edward Willis III; m. Janis Ellen Chapman, Aug. 18, 1984; 1 child, Spencer Chapman. AB, Cornell U., 1969; JD, U. Colo., 1972. Bar: Colo. 1972, U.S. Dist. Ct. Colo. 1972, U.S. Ct. Appeals (10th cir.) 1973. Law clk. to presiding judge U.S. Dist. Ct. Colo., Denver, 1972-73; assoc. Sherman & Howard, Denver, 1973-76, 78-80, ptnr., 1980-87; ptnr. Beckner & Nottingham, Grand Junction, Colo., 1987—; asst. U.S. atty. U.S. Dept. Justice, Denver, 1976-78. Bd. dirs. Beaver Creek Met. Dist., Avon, Colo., 1980—, Justice Info. Ctr., Denver, 1985—. Mem. ABA, Colo. Bar Assn. (chmn. criminal law sect. 1983-85), Assn. Trial Lawyers Am., Colo. Trial Lawyers Assn., Order of Coif, Delta Sigma Rho, Tau Kappa Alpha. Republican. Episcopalian. Clubs: Colo. Lincoln (Denver), Denver Athletic. Federal civil litigation, State civil litigation, Criminal. Home: 347 Harrison St Denver CO 80206 Office: Beckner & Nottingham 225 5th St #850 Grand Junction CO 81501

NOVACK, CATHERINE GAIL, lawyer; b. N.Y.C., July 6, 1944; d. James Francis and Dorothy Patricia (Kadish) Burke; m. James F. Smith, Feb. 14, 1979 (div. 1983). BA, Hunter Coll., 1974; JD, SUNY, Buffalo, 1977. Bar: Pa. 1977, U.S. Dist. Ct. (ea. dist.) Pa. 1977, Fla. 1979, U.S. Dist. Ct. (so. and mid. dists.) Fla. 1979. Field atty. NLRB, Phila., 1977-79; sec., treas. Jim Smith Electric Co., Inc., 1979-82; atty. vol. Fla. Rural Legal Services, Ft. Myers, Fla., 1979-82; dir. vol. lawyers program Bay Area Legal Services, Tampa, Fla., 1982-86; counsel litigation Jim Walter Corp., Tampa, 1986—. Contbr. articles to profl. jours. V.p. membership Hillsborough Polit. Caucus, Tampa, 1984; bd. dirs. The Tampa Players, 1986-87. Recipient Florence P. MooreHouse award Hunter Coll., 1974; Sea Grant Law fellow, 1975. Mem. ABA, Fla. Bar Assn. (vice-chmn. delivery legal services com., Pres.'s award 1986), Hillsborough County Bar Assn. (pro bono coordinator 1982-86, chmn. soc. com. 1984-86), Hillsborough Assn. for Women Lawyers (bd. dirs. 1984-86). Democrat. Episcopalian. Avocations: horseback riding, theater, dance, baking. General corporate, Federal civil litigation, State civil litigation. Home: 14205 Village View Dr Tampa FL 33624 Office: Jim Walter Corp PO Box 22601 Tampa FL 33622

NOVAK, MICHAEL ALAN, lawyer; b. Detroit, Apr. 25, 1955; s. Stanley C. and Rose M. (Szott) N.; m. Loretta Martha Ames, Oct. 9, 1982. BFA, NYU, 1977; JD, Wayne State U., 1980. Bar: Mich. 1980, U.S. Dist. Ct. (ea. dist.) Mich. 1980, Calif. 1985. Assoc. Freydl & Assocs., Birmingham, Mich., 1980—; v.p. Brass Ring Prodns., Royal Oak, Mich. Mem. ABA (entertainment and sports forum com. 1980). Club: Detroit Yacht. Avocations: musician., golf, tennis. Entertainment, Federal civil litigation, State civil litigation. Office: Freydl & Assocs 30200 Telegraph #221 Birmingham MI 48010

NOVAK, NINA, lawyer; b. Basking Ridge, N.J., Oct. 2, 1952; d. Edward Lawrence and Rita Virginia (Myers) N. B.A., Roanoke Coll., 1974; J.D., U. Richmond, 1976. Bar: Va. 1977, D.C. 1984. Assoc. Taylor, Walker & Adams, Norfolk, Va., 1977-80; asst. resident counsel Va. Hosp. Assn., Richmond, 1980-82; assoc. Miles & Stockbridge, Washington, 1982-85, health law cons., 1986—. Mem. ABA (governing com., forum com. on health law), Va. Bar Assn., Am. Acad. Hosp. Attys., Nat. Health Lawyers Assn., Roanoke Coll. Alumni Assn. (pres. 1981—). Republican. Health, Legislative. Office: 1701 Pennsylvania Ave NW Suite 500 Washington DC 20006

NOVAK, PETER JOHN, lawyer; b. Chgo., Apr. 16, 1939; s. Peter and Ann (Jakocko) N.; m. Sarah Ellen Tayntor, Sept. 18, 1965; children: Nancy Ann, Natalie Hastings. AB, U. Ill., 1960, LLB, 1962. Bar: Ill. 1963, Ariz. 1972. Regional atty. Great Atlantic & Pacific Tea Co., Chgo., 1963-68; from staff atty. to gen. solicitor Greyhound Corp., Phoenix, 1968—, v.p. brokerage, 1973-75. Served with U.S. Army, 1962-63. Mem. ABA, Ariz. Bar Assn., Maricopa County Bar Assn., Chgo. Bar Assn., Internat. Assn. Ins. Counsel, Fedn. Ins. and Corp. Counsel. Republican. Personal injury, Federal civil litigation, Contracts commercial. Home: 4309 E Palo Verde Dr Phoenix AZ 85018 Office: Greyhound Corp 111 W Clarendon Phoenix AZ 85077

NOVELLINO, LOUIS ANTHONY, lawyer; b. Jersey City, July 6, 1944. BA, St. Peter's Coll., 1966; MA, Georgetown U., 1972, New Sch., N.Y.C., 1976; JD, Rutgers U., 1980. Bar: N.J. 1981. Sole practice Newark, 1980-87; ptnr. Weeks & Novellino, P.A., Newark, 1987—. Trustee bankruptcy Newark Pvt. Panel Trustees, 1983—, Middletown (N.J.) Townhouses Assn., 1985—. Presdl. scholar St. Peter's Coll., 1962-66. Mem. N.J. Bar Assn., Rutgers U. Alumni Assn. Republican. Roman Catholic. Home: 522 Clubhouse Dr Middletown NJ 07748 Office: 972 Broad St Newark NJ 07102

NOVICK, MINDY, lawyer; b. Forest Hills, N.Y., Dec. 19, 1952; d. Murray D. and Arline (Wishengrad) Marin; m. Gary Laurence Novick, May 14, 1977; 1 child, Michael Seth. BA in History, SUNY, Buffalo, 1974; JD, St. John's U., Jamaica, N.Y., 1980. Bar: N.Y. 1981, U.S. Dist. Ct. (so. and ea. dists.) N.Y. 1981, U.S. Ct. Appeals (2d cir.) 1986. Assoc. Benetar, Issacs, Bernstein & Schair, N.Y.C., 1980-84; counsel labor Fairchild Republic Co., Farmingdale, N.Y., 1984—; bd. dirs. FRC Employees Assn., Farmingdale, N.Y. Mem. ABA, N.Y. State Bar Assn., Am. Corp. Counsel Assn., Nat. Mgmt. Assn. Avocation: reading. Labor. Office: Fairchild Republic Co Conklin St Farmingdale NY 11735

NOVOTNY, F. DOUGLAS, lawyer; b. Mineola, N.Y., Mar. 10, 1952; s. Frank Joseph and Eleanor Evans (Rose) N.; m. Susan Kathleen Frye, June 26, 1976. B.A. cum laude, SUNY-Albany, 1974; J.D. cum laude, Albany Law Sch., 1979. Bar: N.Y. 1980, U.S. Dist. Ct. (no. dist.) N.Y. 1980. Confidential law asst. Appellate Div. 3d Dept., Albany, 1979-80; ptnr. DeGraff, Foy, Conway, Holt-Harris & Mealey, Albany, 1980—. Editor Albany Law Rev., 1978-79; contbr. articles to profl. jours. Mem. Justinian Soc., Assn. Trial Lawyers Am., ABA, N.Y. State Bar Assn., Albany County Bar Assn., Columbia County Bar Assn., N.Y. State Trial Lawyers Assn. Presbyterian. Club: Winding Brook. State civil litigation, Federal civil litigation. Home: RD 2 Box 1K Chatham Center NY 12184 Office: DeGraff Foy Conway Holt-Harris & Mealey 90 State St Albany NY 12207

NOVOTNY, RONALD WAYNE, lawyer; b. San Diego, June 16, 1956; s. Paul Evart and Vivian Kathryn (Gill) N.; m. Heidi Elise Swinnerton, June 12, 1982. BA, U. Calif., Berkeley, 1978; JD, U. Calif., San Francisco, 1981. Bar: Calif. 1981. Assoc. Thierman, Simpson & Cook, San Francisco, 1981-85, Hill, Farrer & Burrill, Los Angeles, 1985—. Tony Patino fellow Hastings Coll. Law U. Calif., 1981. Mem. ABA, Los Angeles Bar Assn. Labor. Office: Hill Farrer & Burrill 445 S Figueroa 34th Floor Los Angeles CA 90071

NOWACKI, JAMES NELSON, lawyer; b. Columbus, Ohio, Sept. 12, 1947; s. Louis James and Betty Jane (Nelson) N.; m. Catherine Ann Holden, Aug. 1, 1970; children: Carrie, Anastasia, Emma. AB, Princeton U., 1969; JD, Yale U., 1973. Bar: Ill. 1973, U.S. Dist. Ct. (no. dist.) Ill. 1973, U.S. Ct. Appeals (7th cir.) 1978, N.Y. 1982. Assoc. Isham, Lincoln & Beale, Chgo., 1976-80; ptnr. Kirkland & Ellis, Chgo., 1980—. Mem. Winnetka Sch. Bd. Dist. 36, Ill., 1983—. Harlan Fiske Stone prize Yale U., 1972. Mem. ABA (forum com. on construction industry, litigation sect.). Club: Chgo. Athletic. Federal civil litigation, State civil litigation, Construction. Home: 738 Lincoln Ave Winnetka IL 60093 Office: Kirkland & Ellis 200 E Randolph Dr Chicago IL 60601

NOWADZKY, ROGER ALAN, lawyer, lobbyist; b. Cedar Rapids, Iowa, Dec. 28, 1949; s. James Richard and Harriet Marie (Kacer) N.; m. Karen Louise Urban, June 3, 1972 (div.); children—Robert, Jill, Brooke. B.A. summa cum laude, St. Mary's Coll., Winona, Minn., 1972; J.D. with distinction, U. Iowa, 1976. Bar: Iowa 1976, U.S. Dist. Ct. (no. and so. dists.) Iowa 1976, U.S. Ct. Appeals (8th cir.) 1976. Acct. Quaker Oats Co., Cedar Rapids, Iowa, 1972; legal clk. bankruptcy div. U.S. Dist. Ct. (no. dist.) Iowa, Cedar Rapids, 1976; legal counsel for Iowa Legislature, Legis. Service Bur., Des Moines, 1976-83; legis. counsel League Iowa Municipalities, Des Moines, 1983—; mem. state govt. issues and orgn. com. Assembly on the Legislature, Nat. Conf. State Legislatures, 1983; participant Iowa Key Decision Makers Correctional Policy Conf. of Nat. Council on Crime and Delinquency, Des Moines, 1982; mem. tort liability/ins. focus group Iowa Dept. Human Resources, 1986. Bd. dirs. Tatterdemalion Prodns. Theatre Prodn. Workshop, Des Moines, 1983—. Mem. Iowa Mcpl. Attys. Assn. (ex-officio bd. dirs. 1983—), Iowa State Bar Assn. (penal reform com. 1977), Phi Delta Phi McLain Inn (vice magister 1975-76, cert. appreciation U. Iowa chpt. 1976), Pi Gamma Mu. Legislative, Local government, Administrative and regulatory. Home: 3909 Hubbell Apt 44 Des Moines IA 50317 Office: League Iowa Municipalities 900 Des Moines St Suite 100 Des Moines IA 50309

NOWAK, DARLENE M., lawyer; b. Buffalo, Nov. 3, 1956. BA, Canisius Coll., 1978; JD, U. Mich., 1981. Bar: Pa. 1982, U.S. Dist. Ct. (we. dist.) Pa. 1982, N.Y. 1983, U.S. Ct. Appeals (3d cir.) 1985. Law clk. to presiding justice U.S. Bankruptcy Ct., Detroit, 1981-82; assoc. Marcus & Shapira, Pitts., 1982—. Mem. ABA, Pa. Bar Assn., Allegheny County Bar Assn., Comml. Law League. Bankruptcy, Contracts commercial, Federal civil litigation. Office: Marcus & Shapira 624 Oliver Bldg Pittsburgh PA 15222

NOWICKI, MICHAEL THOMAS, lawyer; b. Yonkers, N.Y., Aug. 28, 1955; s. Joseph Francis Xavier and Catherine (McLoughlin) N. BA, Fordham U., 1977, JD, 1980. Bar: N.Y. 1981, U.S. Dist. Ct. (ea. and so. dists.) N.Y. 1981. Asst. dist. atty. Rockland County, N.Y., 1981-83, sr. asst. dist. atty., 1983-86, exec. asst. dist. atty., 1986—. Mem. ABA, N.Y. State Bar Assn. Republican. Roman Catholic. Criminal, Local government, Prosecution. Home: 149 N Middletown Rd Nanuet NY 10954 Office: Rockland County Dist Atty County Office Bldg New York City NY 10956

NOWINSKI, THOMAS STEPHEN, lawyer; b. Alexandria, Minn., Apr. 5, 1946; s. John Joseph and Doris Louella (Coykendall) N.; m. Michaeline Rose Perfetti, Dec. 26, 1969; 1 child, Matthew. BSE in Mechanical Engring., U. Mich., 1968, JD, 1974. Bar: Mich. 1974, U.S. Dist. Ct. (ea. dist. 1974), Fla. 1985. Assoc. Clark, Klein & Beaumont, Detroit, 1974-80, ptnr., 1981—. Served with U.S Army, 1969-71. Club: Detroit Athletic. General corporate, Estate planning, Personal income taxation. Home: 1120 Audubon Grosse Pointe Park MI 48230 Office: Clark Klein & Beaumont 1600 First Fed Bldg Detroit MI 48226

NOWLIN, JAMES ROBERTSON, federal judge; b. San Antonio, Nov. 21, 1937; s. William Forney and Jeannette (Robertson) N.; m. Kirsten Wunderlich, Oct., 1973 (div. 1978). B.A., Trinity U., 1959, M.A., 1962; J.D., U. Tex., Austin, 1963. Bar: Tex. 1963, U.S. Dist. Ct. (we. dist.) Tex. 1971, U.S. Dist. Ct. D.C. 1966, U.S. Ct. Claims 1969, U.S. Supreme Ct. 1969. Assoc. Kelso, Locke, & King, San Antonio, 1963-65; assoc. Kelso, Locke & Lepick, San Antonio, 1966-69; legal counsel U.S. Senate, Washington, 1965-66; propr. Law Offices James R. Nowlin, San Antonio, 1969-81; mem. Tex. Ho. of Reps., Austin, 1967-71, 73-81; judge U.S. Dist. Ct. (we. dist.) Tex., Austin, 1981—; instr. Am. govt. and history San Antonio Coll., 1964-65, 71-73. Served to capt. U.S. Army, 1959-60, USAR, 1960-68. Fellow State Bar Found; mem. Travis County Bar Assn., San Antonio Bar Assn., ABA, Am. Judicature Soc. Republican. Presbyterian. Avocations: pilot; skiing; hiking; jogging. Office: U S Courthouse 200 W 8th St Austin TX 78701

NOWNEJAD, CYRUS SIROUSS, lawyer; b. Tehran, Iran, Nov. 30, 1929; came to U.S. 1950; s. Reza Nownejad and Soroor Kachanchi; children: Gita Marie, Jamshyd John. BSCE, U. Calif., Berkeley, 1956, JD, U. Calif., San Francisco, 1961. Bar: Calif. 1963, U.S. Patent and Trademark Office 1964, Can. Patent Office 1965, U.S. Supreme Ct. 1976, U.S. Dist. Ct. (cen. dist.) Calif. 1979, U.S. Ct. Appeals (9th cir.) 1979. Design engr. Bechtell Corp., San Francisco, 1956-58; patent counsel Crown Zellerback Corp., Camas, Wash., 1962-65; dir. law dept. Polymer Corp., Reading, Pa., 1965-69; internat. patent counsel Eastman Kodak Co., Rochester, N.Y., 1969-74; patent and licensing counsel Tosco Corp., Los Angeles, 1974-82; sole practice, Century City, Los Angeles, Calif., 1982—. Mem. ABA, Los Angeles County Bar Assn., Los Angeles Patent Law Assn., Am. Intellectual Law Assn., Licensing Exec. Soc. U.S.A. and Can. (v.p. 1980-81, trustee 1977-81), U. Calif. Alumni Assn., Phi Alpha Delta. Clubs: Toastmasters Internat. (chmn. speakers bur. 1967); Internat. Patent of Rochester (pres. 1972-74). Private international, Contracts commercial, Patent. Office: 10100 Santa Monica Blvd Suite 2500 Century City Los Angeles CA 90067

NOYES, MICHAEL LANCE, lawyer; b. Davenport, Iowa, Oct. 13, 1946; s. John Joseph Noyes and Marjorie Jean (Bell) Dierker; m. Barbara Ann Rehling, Dec. 19, 1970; children: David, Katherine, Andrew, Robert. BA, U. Iowa, 1968, JD, 1971. Bar: Iowa 1971, U.S. Dist. Ct. (no. and so. dists.) Iowa, U.S. Dist. Ct. (cen. dist.) Ill. Assoc. Rehling, Lindburg & Gosma, Davenport, 1971-72, ptnr., 1972—. Trustee Davenport Library Bd., 1984—; bd. dirs. Community Mental Health Ctr., Davenport, 1978-80. Fellow Iowa Acad. Trial Lawyers; mem. ABA, Iowa Bar Assn., Assn. Trial Lawyers Am., Assn. Trial Lawyers Iowa, Davenport C. of C. (bd. dirs. 1976-79). Republican. Presbyterian. Club: Davenport Country. Avocations: golf, fishing. Federal civil litigation, State civil litigation, Banking. Home: 24 Glenwood Ave Davenport IA 52803 Office: Rehling Lindburg & Gosma 617A Davenport Bank Bldg Davenport IA 52801

NTEPHE, AZIKE A., lawyer; b. Onitsha, Nigeria, Aug. 13, 1944; came to U.S. 1970; s. Robert and Zenebu (Irameh) N. BA in English, Pomona Coll., 1974; MA in Communications, Stanford U., 1975; JD, U. Calif., Berkeley, 1978. Bar: Calif. 1982, U.S. Dist. Ct. (cen., no. and so. dists.) Calif. 1983. Asst. dir. CLE program ABA, Chgo., 1978-84; dir. legal communications Am. Hosp. Assn., Chgo., 1984—. Contbr. articles to profl. jours. Mem. Hyde Park/Kenwood Community Health Ctr., Chgo., 1973—, Goodman Theatre, Chgo., 1981—, Chgo. Council on Fgn. Relations, 1980—, Internat. Visitors Ctr., Chgo., 1980. Mem. ABA, Calif. Bar Assn., Am. Soc. Law and Medicine, Chgo. Soc. of Assn. Execs., Beta Phi Gamma. Home: 1310 E 54th St 3W Chicago IL 60615 Office: Am Hosp Assn 840 N Lake Shore Dr Chicago IL 60611

NUANES, JOHN GILBERT, lawyer; b. Whittier, Calif., Nov. 22, 1953; s. Joseph and Margaret Nuanes; m. Dorothy Nuanes, Oct. 18, 1980. AB, Stanford U., 1975; JD, U. Mich., 1978. Bar: Calif. 1980. Atty., v.p. MCA Inc., Universal, Calif., 1978-87; atty. Chase, Rotchford, Drukker & Bogust, Los Angeles, 1987—; mem. internat. anti-counterfiting coalition. Mem. ABA, U.S. Trademark Assn. Democrat. Avocations: motion pictures, politics, sports, music. Entertainment, Trademark and copyright. Office: Chase Rotchford et al 700 S Flower St 5th Floor Los Angeles CA 90017

NUCCIARONE, A. PATRICK, lawyer; b. Denville, N.J., Aug. 29, 1947; s. H. Joseph and Alice Marie (McGuirk) N. BA, U. So. Calif., 1969; JD, George Washington U., 1973. Bar: N.J. 1973, U.S. Dist. Ct. N.J. 1973, U.S. Ct. Appeals (3d cir.) 1976, N.Y. 1981, Vt. 1984. Com. staff asst. U.S. House of Reps., Washington, 1971-72; staff asst. Exec. Office of Pres. of U.S., Washington, 1972-73; asst. U.S. Atty. Office of U.S. Atty., Newark, 1974-83, chief environ. sect., 1978-83; spl. asst. Atty. Gen. Office of Atty. Gen., Montpelier, Vt., 1984; ptnr. Hannoch Weisman, Roseland, N.J., 1984—; co-chmn. N.J. Hazardous Wast Task Force, Trenton, 1978-83; supr. Rutgers U. Environ. Law Clinic, Newark, 1978-83; mem. Environ. Exposition Adv. Bd., Trenton, 1985—. Contbr. articles to profl. jours. Recipient Outstanding Service award U.S. Dept. Justice, Washington, 1980, Spl. Achievement awards U.S. Dept. Justice, 1978, 79, Presdl. Citation for Excellent Performance Exec. Office of Pres., Washington, 1973. Mem. ABA, N.J. State Bar Assn. (bd. dirs. environ. law sect. 1985), Monmouth County Bar Assn. Avocations: sailing, skiing, hiking. Environment, Criminal. Office: Hannoch Weisman 4 Becker Farm Rd Roseland NJ 07068

NULL, DOUGLAS PETER, lawyer; b. N.Y.C., Nov. 11, 1926; s. William H. and Florence (Ostrow) N.; m. Marcia Tabor, Jan. 27, 1985; children: Lisa A. Holdeman, William S., Michael C. BS, Harvard U., 1945; JD, NYU, 1949, LLM, 1954. Bar: N.Y. 1950, U.S. Supreme Ct. 1963. Assoc. Poletti, Diamond, Roosevelt, Freidin & McKay, N.Y.C., 1949-50; asst. dist. atty. N.Y. County, N.Y., 1950-54; ptnr. Levy, Gutman, Goldberg & Null, N.Y.C., 1956-61; assoc. counsel CIT Fin. Corp., N.Y.C., 1954-56; sr. dep. county atty. Nassau County, N.Y., 1961-62; sr. ptnr. Null & Null, Garden City, N.Y., 1962-82; v.p. adminstrn., gen. counsel, bd. dirs. Kleartone, Inc., Westbury, N.Y., 1982—. Chmn. Great Neck Zone Dem. Party, 1960-67; bd. dirs. United Jewish Y's of L.I., 1983—; chmn. cultural Arts Com., 1983-86, v.p., 1986—. Served to lt. USNR, 1944-46. Mem. ABA, N.Y. State Bar Assn., Nassau Bar Assn., N.Y. State Trial Lawyers Assn., N.Y. Dist. Attys. Assn. Club: NYU (N.Y.C.). General corporate, Federal civil litigation, General practice. Office: 78 Mitchell Ave Plainview NY 11803

NULL, GREGORY B., lawyer; b. Waynesburg, Pa., Sept. 17, 1953; s. Neill N. and Marie A. (McDonald) N.; m. Mary B. Mayak, Oct. 25, 1979; 1 child, Matthew N. BSBA, W.Va. U., 1974, JD, 1979. Bar: W.Va. 1979, U.S. Dist. Ct. (so. dist.) W.Va. 1979, U.S. Ct. Appeals (4th cir.) 1981. Assoc. Breckinridge & Davis, Summersville, W.Va., 1979-81; ptnr. Breckinridge, Davis & Null, Summersville, 1982-84, Breckinridge, Davis, Null & Sproles, Summersville, 1985—; bd. dirs. Nicholas County Pub. Defender Corp., Summersville, 1981—. Bd. dirs. Nicholas County Sheltered Workshop, 1981-85. Mem. ABA, W.Va. Bar Assn., W.Va. Trial Lawyers Assn., Jaycees. Democrat. Mem. Ch. Christ. State civil litigation, Personal injury, Real property. Home: PO Box 166 Canvas WV 26662 Office: Breckinridge Davis Null & Sproles 509 Church St Summersville WV 26651

NULL, MICHAEL ELLIOT, lawyer; b. Chgo., Feb. 14, 1947; s. Samuel Joseph and Rose (Baren) N.; m. Eugenia Irene Frack, Dec. 21, 1969; 1 dau., Jennifer Susan. B.S. in Psychology, U. Ill., 1969; J.D., Ill. Inst. Tech. Chgo. Kent Law Sch., 1974. Bar: Ill. 1974, U.S. Dist. Ct. (no. dist.) Ill. 1974, U.S. Dist. Ct. (ea. dist.) Mich., 1985, U.S. Dist. Ct. (ea. dist.) Wis., 1986, U.S. Ct. Appeals (7th cir.) 1981, U.S. Ct. Appeals (6th cir.) 1985, U.S. Supreme Ct., 1985. Assoc. Adam Bourgeois Ltd., Chgo., 1974-76; ptnr. Null & Superfine, Chgo., 1976-77; pres. Michael Null, Ltd., Chgo., 1977—. Composer musical selections. Mem. ABA, 1st Amendment Lawyers Assn. Constitutional, Criminal. Office: 155 N Michigan Ave Chicago IL 60601

NUNGESSER, NANCY ANN, lawyer; b. New Orleans, Aug. 30, 1957; d. Willaim Aicklen and Ruth Amelia (Marks) N. Student, U. New Orleans, 1975, La. State U., 1975-76; BA, Tulane U., 1979, JD, 1982. Bar: La. 1982, U.S. Dist. Ct. (ea. dist.) La. 1984, U.S. Ct. Appeals (5th cir.) 1984. Law clk. to presiding justice U.S. Dist. Ct., New Orleans, 1982-83; asst. U.S. atty. U.S. Atty.'s Office (ea. dist.) La., New Orleans, 1983—. Mem. ABA, La. Bar Assn., New Orleans Bar Assn., Algiers Jaycees, PDP (historian 1981-82). Republican. Avocations: piano, boating, swimming. Federal civil litigation, Personal injury, Admiralty. Office: US Attys Office 500 Camp St New Orleans LA 70130

NUNN, LESLIE EDGAR, b. Evansville, Ind., Oct. 10, 1941. B.A., U. Evansville, 1964; J.D., U. Denver, 1967. Bar: Colo. 1967, N.Mex. 1977. Lawyer, adminstr. Navajo Tribe of Indians, 1973-76; sole practice, Silverton and Cortez, Colo., 1977-78; ptnr. Nunn & Dunlap, Farmington, N.Mex., 1978-84; sole practice, Denver, 1984—. Served with JAGC, USAF, 1967-73. Mem. ABA, Colo., N.Mex., S.W. Colo., San Juan County, Navajo Nation bar assns., World Peace Through Law Assn., World Assn. Lawyers (world

chmn. law and agr. com.). Decorated Bronze Star. Contbr. articles to legal jours. Agrricultural law, Bankruptcy. Home: 5296 Bristol Arvada CO 80002 Office: 4701 Marion St Suite 400 Denver CO 80216

NUNN, ROBERT WARNE, lawyer; b. Salem, Oreg., Sept. 20, 1950; s. Warne Harry and Delores (Netz) N.; 1 child, Hayley Elisabeth. Student, U. Vienna, Austria, 1971; BS, Willamette U., 1972; MS in Acctg., Northeastern U., Boston, 1973; JD, U. Oreg., 1976. Bar: Oreg 1977, U.S. Dist. Ct. Oreg. 1977, U.S. Ct. Appeals (9th cir.) 1976, U.S. Supreme Ct. 1982, Wash. 1986. Ptnr. Schwabe, Williamson, Wyatt, Moore & Roberts, Portland, Oreg., 1976—, vice chmn. internat. legal dept., 1986—. Bd. mgrs. Multnomah metro br. YMCA, Portland, 1983-86, chmn., 1984-85; pres. Oreg. div. Am. Cancer Soc., Portland, 1986—, bd. dirs. 1982—; legal counsel campaign Gwen Ericcsen, Portland, 1986; trustee Marylhurst Coll., Oreg., 1985—; bd. dirs. United Way of Columbia-Willamette, Portland, 1984-87. Am. Leadership fellow, 1987; named Order of Red Sword Am. Cancer Soc., 1985. Mem. ABA (chmn.), Oreg. Bar Assn. (chmn. legal assistants and legal investigators com., chmn. cert. subcom., fee arbitration panel), Internat. Bar Assn., Nat. Assn. Bond Lawyers (vice chmn. mcpl. utility obligations com.), Pacific Northwest Internat. Trade Assn. Republican. Lutheran. Clubs: University, Willamette Athletic (Portland). Avocations: skiing, sailing. General corporate, Private international, Real property. Home: PO Box 8459 Portland OR 97207 Office: Schwabe Williamson Wyatt et al 1211 SW 5th St Suite 1800 Portland OR 97204 also: 1800 Pacwest Cen Portland OR 97204

NUNNALLY, KNOX DILLON, lawyer; b. Haynesville, La., Jan. 26, 1943; s. Miles Dillon and Linnie Mat (Knox) N.; m. Kay Clyde Webb; 1 child, Kevin Knox. B.B.A., U. Tex., 1965, LL.B., 1968. Bar: Tex. 1968, U.S. Dist. Ct. (ea. dist.) Tex. 1970, U.S. Dist. Ct. (so. dist.) Tex. 1969, U.S. Dist. Ct. (we. dist.) Tex. 1976; U.S. Ct. Appeals (5th cir.) 1978. Diplomate Tex. Bd. Legal Specialization. Ptnr., Vinson & Elkins, Houston, 1976—. Mem. ABA, Tex. Bar Assn., Houston Bar Assn. Personal injury, State civil litigation, Federal civil litigation. Home: 1904 Albans Rd Houston TX 77005 Office: Vinson & Elkins 1st City Tower Houston TX 77002-6760

NUSBAUM, JACK HENRY, lawyer; b. Casablanca, Morocco, July 22, 1940; came to U.S., 1941; s. Simon and Regine (Kleefeld) N.; m. Ronni Danciger, June 10, 1962 (div. 1983); children: Lisa B., Gary D.; m. Margie Goldsmith, Feb. 5, 1984. BS, U. Pa., 1962; JD, Columbia U., 1965. Bar: N.Y. 1965. Assoc. Willkie, Farr & Gallagher, N.Y.C., 1965-70, ptnr., 1971—; bd. dirs. W.R. Berkley Corp., Greenwich, Conn., Nat. Guardian Corp., Greenwich, Hirschl & Adler Galleries, Inc., N.Y.C., United Mchts. and Mfrs. Inc., N.Y.C., Victoria Creations, Inc., N.Y.C., Shearson Lehman Bros., Inc., N.Y.C. Active Blythedale Children's Hosp., Valhalla, N.Y., 1970—. Mem. ABA, N.Y. State Bar Assn., N.Y. County Lawyers Assn. General corporate, Securities. Home: 300 E 56th St New York NY 10022 Office: Willkie Farr & Gallagher 153 E 53d St New York NY 10022

NUSSBAUM, PAUL ALLAN, lawyer; b. Bklyn., July 8, 1947; s. Theodore and Dorothy (Jones) N.; m. Anita D.; children: Craig and Ross (twins); m. Tara I. Stacom, June 8, 1985. BA, SUNY, Buffalo, 1967; JD, Georgetown U., 1971. Bar: N.Y. 1972. Assoc. Dreyer & Traub, N.Y.C., 1971-75, ptnr., 1975-79; ptnr. Schulte, Roth & Zabel, N.Y.C., 1979—; adj. asst. prof. NYU, 1978-85; panelist practicing law inst. Real Estate Inst.; bd. dirs. Hanover Cos. Inc., N.Y.C. Contbr. articles to profl. jours. Mem. North Salem (N.Y.) planning bd., 1974-76; trustee Westchester Exceptional Children, Purdys, N.Y., 1976—, pres. 1978-80. Served to 2d lt. USAR, 1968-73. Mem. ABA, N.Y. State Bar Assn., N.Y. County Bar Assn., Assn. of Bar of City of N.Y., Am. Coll. Real Estate Lawyers. Jewish. Real property, Banking. Home: 875 Park Ave Apt 7-B New York NY 10021 Office: Schulte Roth & Zabel 900 3d Ave New York NY 10022

NUSSBAUM, PETER DAVID, lawyer; b. Bklyn., June 26, 1942; s. Alfred and Olga (Thome) N.; m. Aleta Spaulding Wallace. B.S., Cornell U., 1959-63; LL.B. Harvard U., 1963-66; postgrad. (Fulbright Scholar) London Sch. of Econs., 1967-68. Bar: N.Y. 1967, Calif. 1971, U.S. Dist. Ct. (ea. and so. dists.) N.Y. 1968, U.S. Dist. Ct. (no., ea. and cen. dists.) Calif. 1971, U.S. Ct. Appeals (2d, 9th and D.C. cirs.). Law clk. U.S. Ct. Appeals, N.Y.C., 1966-67; staff atty. Vera Inst. of Justice, N.Y.C., 1968-69; staff atty. Ctr. for Soc. Welfare Policy and Law, N.Y.C., 1969-70; staff atty. Legal Aid Soc. of Alameda County, Oakland, Calif., 1971-74; ptnr. Neyhart, Anderson, Nussbaum, Reilly & Freitas, San Francisco, 1974—; lectr. in field. Dir. Kensington Community Services Dist., 1976-81; mem. fin. com. for Rep. George Miller; pres. Kensington Dem. Club; chmn. Contra Costa County Cen. Dem. Com. Recipient Borden Found. award, 1960. Mem. ABA, Calif. Bar Assn. (fed. cts. com.), San Francisco Barristers (co-chmn. labor law com.), Ninth Cir. Jud. Conf. (lawyer rep., chmn. No. Calif. del., exec. com.), Phi Eta Sigma, Phi Kappa Phi. Contbr. articles to profl. jours. Labor. Office: 568 Howard St San Francisco CA 94102

NUSSBAUM, RICHARD ANTON, II, lawyer; b. Pitts., Sept. 4, 1952; s. Richard A. and Mary (Oliver) N.; m. Mary Patricia Leyes, July 24, 1976; children: Matthew, Daniel, Kathryn. BA in English, U. Notre Dame, 1974, JD, 1977. Bar: Ind. 1977, U.S. Dist. Ct. (no. dist.) Ind. 1977, Mich. 1978. Assoc. Krisor & Assocs., South Bend, Ind., 1977-85; dep. prosecutor St. Joseph County, Ind., 1978—; ptnr. Krisur & Nussbaum, South Bend, 1985—. Pres. St. Anthony's Parish Pastoral Council, South Bend, 1983-86. Mem. ABA, Ind. Bar Assn., Mich. Bar Assn. Roman Catholic. Club: Notre Dame Monogram. Consumer commercial, Criminal, Real property. Office: Krisor & Nussbaum 211 W Washington Suite 2416 South Bend IN 46601

NUTTER, FRANKLIN WINSTON, lawyer; b. Charleston, W.Va., Apr. 17, 1946; s. Frank Hamilton and Marie Agnes (Pyles) N.; m. Linda Jean Davis, Sept. 2, 1972; children: Alycia Marie, Aaron Davis. BBA in Econs., U. Cin., 1968; JD, Georgetown U., 1974. Bar: D.C., Va., U.S. Dist. Ct. (no. dist.) Va., U.S. Ct. Appeals (9th and D.C. cirs.). Gen. counsel Nat. Flood Ins. Assn., Washington, 1975-78; gen. counsel Reins. Assn. Am., Washington, 1978-81, pres., 1981-84; pres. Alliance Am. Insurers, Schaumburg, Ill., 1984—, Property Loss Research Bur., Schaumburg, 1984—; bd. overseers Inst. Civil Justice subs. Rand Corp. Served to lt. (j.g.) USN, 1968-72. Mem. ABA (past chmn. excess, surplus lines and reins. com., chmn. internat. ins. law com. torts and ins. practice com.), Va. Bar Assn., Ins. Inst. Hwy. Safety (bd. dirs.), Workers' Compensation Research Inst. Insurance, Legislative. Home: 1467 Thor Dr Inverness IL 60067 Office: Alliance Am Insurers 1501 Woodfield Rd Suite 400W Schaumburg IL 60173

NUTTER, THOMAS EDWARD, lawyer; b. Jefferson City, Mo., Mar. 31, 1946; s. Waldo Edward and Helen Irene (Huth) N.; m. Shawn Lampkin, Oct. 12, 1985. BA in History, U. Mo., 1968, MA in History, 1971, PhD in History, 1974; JD, U. Mo., Kansas City, 1979. Bar: Kans. 1980, U.S. Dist. Ct. Kans. 1980, U.S. Ct. Appeals (fed. and 8th cirs.) 1983. Law clk. to presiding justice U.S. Dist. Ct. Kans., 1979-80; assoc. McDowell, Rice & Smith, Kansas City, Kans., 1980-82, Litman, Day & McMahon, Kansas City, Mo., 1982—; asst. dean St. Louis U., 1974-75. Author: American Telegraphy and the Open Door Policy in China, 1974. Viles scholar U. Mo., 1973. Mem. ABA, Kans. Bar Assn., Kansas City Met. Bar Assn., Mid Am. Rescue Dog Assn. (v.p. 1983—). Club: Cen. Exchange (Kansas City). Avocation: writing. Federal civil litigation, Patent, Trademark and copyright. Office: Litman Day & McMahon 922 Walnut Suite 1215 Kansas City MO 64106

NUTZHORN, CARL ROBBINS, lawyer; b. Rockville Centre, N.Y., Sept. 13, 1927; s. Carl William and Lorena Waite (Robbins) N.; m. Marta RoseMarie Larsson, Feb. 1965 (div. 1966). B.A. cum laude, Princeton U., 1951; J.D., Columbia U., 1955. Bar: N.Y. 1957, U.S. Dist. Ct. (so. and ea. dist.) N.Y. 1957, U.S. Supreme Ct. 1961, U.S. Ct. Appeals (2d cir.) 1962, U.S. Dist. Ct. (we. dist.) Okla. 1968, U.S. Dist. Ct. Colo. 1970, U.S. Ct. Appeals (10th cir.) 1971. Assoc. Carter, Ledyard & Milburn, N.Y.C., 1955-57; assoc. atty. to gen. counsel Am. Fore Loyalty Ins. Group, N.Y.C., 1959-60; assoc. Smith & Auslander, N.Y.C., 1960-61, Smith, Steibel & Alexander, N.Y.C., 1962-63; sole practice, Aspen, Colo., 1972-81; semi-retired, Ft. Lauderdale, Fla., 1983—; mem. U.S. Tenth Cir. Jud. Conf., 1973-81. Author: Wage-Price Spiral and the Presidential Tariff Power, 1956, Hydrogen-Oxygen Energy Systems, 1964, Constitutional Problems of Pardon for Presidential Crime, 1985. Mem. Pitikin County Bd. Adjustment, Aspen, 1972-80; auditor Summer Arms Control Workshops of Aspen Inst., 1976-82. Served with USMCR, 1945-46. Mem. Colo. Bar Assn., Am. Arbitration Assn. (panel of arbitrators), Phi Delta Phi. Democrat. Lutheran. General practice, Federal civil litigation, Constitutional. Home: 1900 S Ocean Dr N #1101 Fort Lauderdale FL 33316

NYBERG, WILLIAM ARTHUR, lawyer; b. Chgo., Aug. 27, 1947; s. E. Arthur and Lyna Marie (Palmer) N.; m. Margery Ann Lissner, Mar. 11, 1984. A.B., U. Ill., 1969, J.D., 1975; M.B.A., Columbia U., 1976. Bar: Ill. 1975, U.S. Dist. Ct. (so. and no. dists.) Ill. 1975, U.S. Ct. Appeals (7th cir.) 1975, U.S. Supreme Ct. 1981. Assoc. Winston & Strawn, Chgo., 1976-77; atty. AMSTED Industries, Inc., Chgo., 1977-81, The Richardson Co., Des Plaines, Ill., 1981-82; sr. atty. John Morrell & Co., Northfield, Ill., 1982-84; v.p., gen. counsel United States Can Co., Oak Brook, Ill., 1984-86; assoc.Laser, Schostok, Kolman and Frank, Chgo., 1986—. Served with U.S. Army, 1969-72; Vietnam. Decorated Bronze Star, Joint Service Commendation Medal. Mem. ABA, Ill. State Bar Assn., Chgo. Bar Assn. Methodist. General corporate, Contracts commercial, Securities. Home: 1325 N State Pkwy Apt 11B Chicago IL 60610 Office: Laser Schostok Kolman & Frank 189 W Madison St Chicago IL 60602

NYCE, JOHN DANIEL, lawyer; b. York, Pa., Sept. 7, 1947; s. Harry Lincoln and Dorothy (Wagner) N.; m. Karen Martzolf, Dec. 28, 1974; children—Joshua David, Laura Kimberly. B.A., SUNY-Buffalo, 1970; J.D., U. Miami, 1973. Bar: Fla. 1973, U.S. Dist. Ct. (so. dist.) Fla. 1973, U.S. Dist. Ct. (middle dist.) Fla. 1973, U.S. Ct. Appeals (5th and 11th cirs.) 1986, U.S. Supreme Ct. 1984. Assoc. Ralph P. Douglas, Pompano Beach, Fla., 1974, Coleman, Leonard & Morrison, Ft. Lauderdale, Fla., 1975-78; ptnr. Nyce and Smith, Ft. Lauderdale, 1979; sole practice, Ft. Lauderdale, 1980—. co-founder, dir. Rutherford Inst.; Bd. dirs. Alliance for Responsible Growth, Inc., Habitat for Humanity of Broward County, Inc.; bd. dirs., co-founder Fla. Family Adoption, Inc.; mem. Social Register Ft. Lauderdale; mem. Broward County Right to Life; mem. exec. com. Broward County Republican Party; bd. dirs. Shepherd Care Ministries, Inc., co-founder Christian Adoption Services of Shepherd Care Ministries, Inc.; cert. trainer Evangelism Explosion III Internat., Inc. Mem. Christian Lawyer's Assn. (founder, past pres., bd. dirs.), Atty's. Title Ins. Fund, Christian Legal Soc., Conservative Caucus of Broward County, Fla. Tennis Assn., The Gideons. Republican. Presbyterian. State civil litigation, Family and matrimonial, Real property. Home: 5910 NE 21st Ln Fort Lauderdale FL 33308 Office: 4367 N Federal Hwy Fort Lauderdale FL 33308

NYE, DANIEL ALAN, lawyer; b. Shelton, Wash., May 19, 1952; m. Amy M. Wayson; 1 child, Ingrid Marie. BA, U. Oreg., 1971-75; MA, U. Wash., 1977; spl. diploma in admiralty law and petroleum law, U. Oslo, 1979; JD, U. Oreg., 1980. Bar: Oreg. 1981. Law clk. U.S. Dist. Court Oreg., Portland, 1981-83; asst. prof. Scandinavian Inst. of Maritime Law, Oslo, 1983-85; lectr. Norwegian Shipping Acad., Oslo, 1984-85; atty. Christiania Bank og Kreditkasse, Oslo, 1985; assoc. Lindsay, Hart, Neil & Wegler, Portland, 1985—; cons. Trade Commn. Norway, San Francisco, 1985—. Am. Field Service scholarship, 1969, ITT Rayonier scholarship, 1971; Rotary Grad. fellow, 1978. Mem. ABA, Norwegian Petroleum Soc., Sons of Norway. Admiralty, Banking, Private international. Office: Lindsay Hart Neil & Wiegler 222 SW Columbia Suite 1800 Portland OR 97201

NYE, JERROLD LINDEN, lawyer; b. St. Joseph, Mich., June 6, 1939; s. Harry Hall and Leone (Becker) N.; m. Marcia L. Shepherd, Mar. 14, 1962 (div. June 1976) children: Cynthia, Jennifer; m. Joan Meyer, Nov. 19, 1984. BS, Mich. State U., 1962, MS, 1963; JD, U. Wyo., 1974. Bar: Mich. 1974, U.S. Dist. Ct. (we. dist.) Mich. 1975, Mont. 1978, U.S. Dist. Ct. Mont. 1978, U.S. Ct. Appeals (9th cir.) 1984. Commd. 2d lt. USAF, 1962, advanced through grades to col., 1984, retired, 1984; sole practice St. Joseph, Mich., 1974-78, Billings, Mont., 1978-82; ptnr. Nye and Meyer P.C., Billings, 1982—; staff judge adv. Ill. Air N.G., Chgo., 1975-84. Contbr. articles to profl. jours. Mem. Mont. Bar Assn., Mich. Bar Assn., Assn. Trial Lawyers Am., Mont. Trial Lawyers Assn., Mont. Rifle Assn. Republican. Congregationalist. Club: Toastmasters (Billings) (area gov.). Avocations: competitive shooting, fishing, camping. State civil litigation, Federal civil litigation, Bankruptcy. Home: 4 Locust St Billings MT 59101 Office: Nye and Meyer PC 3317 Third Ave N Billings MT 59101-1961

NYE, SANDRA GAYLE, lawyer, psychiatric social worker, consultant; b. Chgo., Jan. 12, 1935; d. Harry A. and Mildred (Blumenthal) Iseberg; children—Elizabeth Robin, Jonathan Douglas. J.D., DePaul U., 1962; M.S.W., Loyola U.-Chgo., 1974. Bar: Ill. 1963, U.S. Dist. Ct. (no. dist.) Ill. 1966, U.S. Supreme Ct. 1967. Ptnr., Nye and Nye, Chgo., 1962-74; dir. child and family law and psychiatry Inst. Juvenile Research, Chgo., 1974-78; dir. legal services Jewish Family and Community Services, Chgo., 1978-80; dir. Ill. Guardianship and Advocacy Commn., 1979-82; pres. Nye, Brent & Shoenberger, Ltd., Chgo., 1982-85, Sandra G. Nye & Assocs., Chgo., 1985—; asst. prof. psychiatry Abraham Lincoln Sch. Medicine, U. Ill., Chgo., 1978—; mem. faculty Inst. for Family Studies, Northwestern U. Sch. Medicine. Mem. com. on confidentiality Ill. Gov.'s Commn. to Revise the Mental Health Code, 1976-77; mem. Ill. Commn. on Children-Com. on Youth and the Law, 1975-79; mem. Oak Park (Ill.) Beautification Commn., 1969-73. Mem. ABA (chmn. mental health law com., family law sect.), Ill. State Bar Assn., Chgo. Bar Assn. (chmn. juvenile law com.), Women's Bar Assn., Am. Soc. Law and Medicine, Am. Orthopsychiat. Assn., Am. Assn. Psychiat. Services for Children. Health, Family and matrimonial, Mental Health. Home: 1150 N Lake Shore Dr Chicago IL 60611 Office: 180 N Michigan Ave Suite 1605 Chicago IL 60601

NYE, W. MARCUS W., lawyer; b. N.Y.C., Aug. 3, 1945; s. Walter R. and Nora (McLaren) N.; m. Eva Nye. BA, Harvard U., 1967; JD, U. Idaho, 1974. Bar: Idaho 1974, U.S. Dist. Ct. Idaho 1974, U.S. Ct. Appeals (9th cir.) 1980. Ptnr. Racine, Olson, Nye, Cooper and Budge, Pocatello, Idaho, 1974—; vis. prof. law U. Idaho, Moscow, 1984. Mem. ABA, Idaho State Bar Assn. (commr. 1985—), Idaho Def. Lawyers Assn. (pres. 1982), State Centennial Found. (commr. 1985), 6th Dist. Bar Assn. (pres. 1982), Idaho C. of C. (bd. dirs. 1985). Insurance, Personal injury. Home: 173 S 15th Pocatello ID 83201 Office: Racine Olson Nye Cooper Budge PO Box 1391 Pocatello ID 83201

NYESTE, JAMES THOMAS, lawyer; b. Port Huron, Mich., Nov. 18, 1955; s. Stephen John and Shirley June (Regling) N.; m. Marla Harriet Hand. BS, Mich. State U., 1976; JD, U. Chgo., 1979. Bar: Ill. 1979, U.S. Dist. Ct. (no. dist.) Ill. 1979, U.S. Ct. Claims, U.S. Ct. Appeals (7th cir.) 1983. Assoc. Peterson, Ross, Schloerb & Seidel, Chgo., 1979-80; from assoc. to ptnr. Wildman, Harold, Allen & Dixon, Chgo., 1980—. Vol. lawyer Pro Bono Advs., Chgo., 1982—. Mem. ABA, Ill. Bar Assn., Chgo. Bar Assn. (chmn. writing subcom. ins. com. young lawyers sect. 1985-86), Phi Beta Kappa. Insurance, Federal civil litigation, Nuclear power. Office: Wildman Harrold Allen & Dixon One IBM Plaza Chicago IL 60611

NYGAARD, DIANE ACKER, lawyer; b. Ames, Iowa, Feb. 15, 1953; d. Duane Calvin and Shirley (Hansen) Acker; m. Terrence W. Nygaard, Apr. 16, 1983; children: Eric, Clay. BA, Drake U., 1974; JD, Harvard U., 1977. Bar: Colo. 1977, U.S. Dist. Ct. Colo. 1977, Kans. 1982, U.S. Dist. Ct. 1982. Assoc. Ireland, Stapleton, Pryor & Pascoe, Denver, 1977-80; ptnr. Brown, Koralchik & Fingersh, Kansas City, Mo., 1982-86; sole practice Overland Park, Kans., 1986—; vis. prof. Washburn U. Law Sch., Topeka, Kans., 1980-82. Mem. ABA, Am. Trial Lawyers Assn., Kans. Bar Assn., Kansas Trial Lawyers Assn., Johnson County Bar Assn., Phi Beta Kappa. Personal injury, Federal civil litigation, State civil litigation. Office: 8000 Foster Overland Park KS 66204

NYGREN, KARL FRANCIS, lawyer; b. Wilkes-Barre, Pa., Mar. 9, 1927; s. Elmer F. N. and Stella P. (Rozmarek) Gernand; m. Elizabeth J. Parsons, Dec. 26, 1949; children: Phillip K., James F., Anne E. Student, DePaul U., 1946-48; J.D., U. Chgo., 1951. Bar: Ill. 1950, U.S. Dist. Ct. (no. dist.) Ill. 1951, U.S. Supreme Ct. 1972, U.S. Appeals (7th cir.) 1980, Calif. 1985. Assoc. Kirkland & Ellis, Chgo., 1951-58, ptnr., 1959-86, of counsel, 1987—. Bd. dirs. Chgo. Lung Assn., 1971—, exec. com., 1979—, pres., 1986-87; exec. com. Lawyers Com. for Civil Rights Under Law, 1964-76, co-chmn., 1972-74; mem. vis. com. Law Sch., U. Chgo., 1974-77; governing mem. Art Inst. Chgo., 1981-82, Chgo. Symphony, 1981-86; adv. bd. Chgo. Cath. Charities; trustee DePaul U., 1985—. Served with F.A. AUS, 1944-46. Mem. ABA, Ill. Bar Assn. (chmn. com. on fed. legis. 1965-66, vice chmn. antitrust sect. 1964-65), Chgo. Bar Assn., State Bar Calif., Am. Judicature Soc. (v.p., exec. com.), Bar Assn. 7th Fed. Cir., U. Chgo. Law Sch. Alumni Assn. Republican. Roman Catholic. Clubs: Law (Chgo.), Mid-Am. Arts (Chgo.), Commercial (Chgo.). General corporate, Health, Antitrust. Home: 360 Encinal Ave Menlo Park CA 94025 Office: Kirkland & Ellis Suite 5600 200 E Randolph Dr Chicago IL 60601

NYLAND, W(ILLIAM) DONALD, lawyer; b. N.Y.C., Jan. 12, 1930; s. Thomas A. and Margaret M. (Murphy) N.; m. Dorothy A. Shea, Nov. 28, 1953; children—Jeanne, Marianne, Claire. B.S., Manhattan Coll., 1951; LL.B., NYU, 1957. Bar: N.Y. 1958, U.S. Dist. Ct. (so. dist.) N.Y. 1980, U.S. Dist. Ct. (ea. dist.) N.Y. 1980, U.S. Ct. Appeals (2d cir.) 1985. With Morgan Guaranty Trust Co. N.Y., 1957-59; ptnr. Patterson, Eagle, Greenough & Day, N.Y.C., 1959-69; ptnr. Lambos, Flynn, Nyland & Giardino, N.Y.C., 1970-86, of counsel, 1987—. Served as lt. (j.g.) USCG, 1951-53. Mem. ABA, N.Y. State Bar Assn., N.Y. County Lawyers Assn. Democrat. Roman Catholic. Clubs: Downtown Athletic, Leewood Golf and Country (Eastchester, N.Y.). Probate, Estate taxation, General corporate. Office: 29 Broadway New York NY 10006

NYPAVER, STEPHEN, III, lawyer; b. Cleve., June 18, 1948; m. Carol Anne Dickson. BA, John Carroll U., 1970; JD, Ohio State U., 1978. Bar: Ohio 1978, U.S. Ct. Mil. Appeals 1978, U.S. Supreme Ct. 1982. Commd. 2d lt. U.S. Army, 1970, advanced through grades to maj., 1981; atty. 1978-83; sr. def. counsel U.S. Army, Schofield Barracks, Hawaii, 1983-85; dep. staff judge adv. Combined Field Army, Uijongbu, Republic of Korea, 1985-86; judge adv. 6th region crimianl investigation command U.S. Army, San Francisco, 1986—. Mem. Assn. Trial Lawyers Am., Assn. U.S. Army. (legal advisor 1985-86). Club: CG Mess (Uijongbu) (legal advisor 1985-86). Avocation: mountain hiking. Military, Criminal. Office: US Army 6th Region Criminal Investigation Command San Francisco CA 94129

NYQUIST, DEAN ALLEN, lawyer, mayor; b. Brule, Wis., Jan. 24, 1935; s. William Theodore and Lilly E. (Lindberg) N.; m. Marie Evangeline Nelson, Sept. 9, 1961; children: Leland, Jeanette, Frederick. BEE, N.D. State U., 1956; LLB, William Mitchell Coll. Law, 1961. Bar: Minn. 1961. Ptnr. Nyquist & Assocs., Brooklyn Center, Minn., 1968-84, Henderson, Hass, Nyquist P.A., Brooklyn Center, 1985—; mayor City of Brooklyn Center, 1978—; bd. dirs. for several retirement homes. Sen. Minn. Legis., Brooklyn Center, 1967-72; pres. Brooklyn. Peacemaker Ctr. Inc., Brooklyn Center, 1985—. Mem. ABA. Mem. Evangelical Covenant Ch. Family and matrimonial, General corporate, Real property. Home: 5701 June Ave N Brooklyn Center MN 55429 Office: Henderson Hass & Nyquist PA 5637 Brooklyn Blvd Brooklyn Center MN 55429

NYS, JOHN NIKKI, lawyer; b. Duluth, Minn., May 3, 1948; s. Leslie Leo and Kathleen Cecilia (Beaudin) N.; m. Sandra Ann Stephenson, Aug. 20, 1977; 1 child, John Stephenson. B.A., Dartmouth Coll., 1970; J.D., Stanford U., 1973. Bar: Minn. 1973, U.S. Dist. Ct. Minn. 1973, U.S. Dist. Ct. (we. dist.) Wis. 1984, Wis. 1985, U.S. Ct. Appeals (8th cir.) 1985. Dir. Johnson, Killen, Thibodeau & Seiler, P.A., Duluth, Minn., 1973—; dir., treas., pres. Duluth Regional Care Ctr., 1979—; mem. Lawyers Profl. Responsibility Bd., St. Paul, 1981-87. Precinct chmn. Democratic-Farmer-Labor Party, Duluth, 1976-82, alt. del. state central com., 1976-78; bd. dirs., pres. Morgan Park-Smithville Community Club, Duluth, 1978-84; v.p. Western Community Council, Duluth, 1980—. Mem. 11th Dist. Bar Assn., Minn. State Bar Assn. (chmn. lawyer referral com. 1986—), ABA, Duluth Young Lawyers (pres. 1974-75). Roman Catholic. Banking, Bankruptcy, General corporate. Home: 8506 Beverly Duluth MN 55808 Office: Johnson Killen Thibodeau & Seiler 811 Norwest Ctr Duluth MN 55802

NYSTROM, HAROLD CHARLES, lawyer, labor consultant; b. White, S.D., Apr. 6, 1906; s. Charles Alfred and Augusta Cornelia (Olson) N.; m. Ruth Greenwood, Sept. 30, 1931 (dec. Jan. 1974); children—Nancy Ann Nystrom Railton, Erik Linfred; m. Martha Ann Harper Pattison, Oct. 13, 1980. Student, S.D. State Sch. Mines and Tech., 1922-23; A.B. cum laude, U. S.D., 1926; J.D. with honors, George Washington U., 1931. Bar: S.D. 1931, U.S. Supreme Ct. 1947. Practiced in Rapid City, 1931-35; cons. Bethesda, Md., 1975-78, Rockville, Md., 1978—; editorial staff Lawyers Coop. Pub. Co., Rochester, N.Y., 1935-41; staff Office of Solicitor U.S. Dept. Labor, 1941-74, chief codification unit, chief interpretations sect., chief wage-hour hdqrs. sect., N.Y.C., chief interpretations br., Washington, acting asst. solicitor for legislation and gen. legal services, asst. solicitor, 1941-58, dep. solicitor, 1958-59, acting solicitor, 1959-61, dep. solicitor, 1961-62, asso. solicitor, 1962-74; cons. fed. labor standards, 1975—; Lectr. Labor Law Inst. Southwestern Legal Found., Dallas, 1960; lectr. Banking Law Inst., N.Y., 1967; speaker labor law sect. Assn. Bar City N.Y., 1967, Labor Relations Inst., Atlanta Lawyers Found., 1969, 73; Sec.-treas. Oakmont (Md.) Citizens Com., 1950-59. Contbr. articles to legal publs. Recipient award for meritorious service Dept. Labor, 1957, award for distinguished service, 1961, award for distinguished career service, 1973; certificate of appreciation Employment Standards Adminstrn., 1975; 50 Yr. award State Bar S.D., 1981. Mem. ABA (vice chmn. agy. liaison com. adminstrv. law sect. 1960-73), Fed. Bar Assn. (speaker BNA Labor Law briefing conf. 1967), Tenn. Bar Assn. (hon. life mem. labor law sect.), S.D. State Bar, Old Georgetown Road Citizens Assn. (exec. bd. 1958-60), Phi Beta Kappa, Phi Alpha Delta. Presbyn. (deacon). Club: National Lawyers. Labor, Administrative and regulatory, Government contracts and claims. Home and Office: 11425 Luxmanor Rd Rockville MD 20852

OAKES, JAMES L., federal judge; b. Springfield, Ill., Feb. 21, 1924; m. Evelena S. Kenworthy, Dec. 29, 1973; one son, two daus. by previous marriage. A.B., Harvard U., 1945, LL.B., 1947; LL.D. (hon.), New Eng. Coll., 1976, Suffolk U., 1980. Bar: Vt., Calif. Practiced in Brattleboro, Vt.; spl. counsel Vt. Pub. Service Commn., 1959-60; counsel Vt. Statutory Revision Commn., 1957-60; mem. Vt. Senate, 1961, 63; atty. gen. Vt. 1967-69, U.S. dist. judge, 1970-71; U.S. circuit judge 2d Circuit Ct. Appeals, 1971—. Jurisprudence. Address: Box 696 Brattleboro VT 05301

OAKEY, JAMES LEO, lawyer; b. Chgo., July 5, 1931; s. James L. and Josephine M. (Rogers) O.; m. Angeline Piscitello, June 28, 1980; children: James L., Brian J. BA, Loyola U., Chgo., 1951; JD, John Marshall Law Sch., 1955. Bar: Ill. 1955, U.S. Dist. Ct. (no. and ea. dists.) Ill. 1955. Asst. atty. gen. State of Ill., Chgo., 1957-59; asst. pub. defender Cook County, Chgo., 1959-61, asst. states atty., 1961; sole practice Chgo., 1961-66, 75—; judge Cir. Ct. Cook County, Chgo., 1966-75. Contbr. articles to profl. jours. Served with USN, 1955-57. Fed. fellow U.S. Juvenile Judges Assn., 1969. Mem. ABA, Ill. Bar Assn., Chgo. Bar Assn. Democrat. Roman Catholic. Club: Highsteppers (Highland Pk., Ill.) (sec. 1984—). State civil litigation, Criminal, General practice. Home: 951 St Johns Highland Park IL 60035 Office: 1150 N State Chicago IL 60610

OAKLEY, ROBERT LOUIS, law librarian; b. N.Y.C., Nov. 6, 1945; s. Bert Tuttle Oakley and Allese (Duffin) Vestigo; m. Madeleine Cohen, Aug. 13, 1971; children: Esther Shulamit, Daniel Isaac. BA, Cornell U., 1968; MLS, Syracuse U., 1972; JD, Cornell U., 1976. Bar: N.Y. 1977, U.S. Dist. Ct. (no. dist.) N.Y. 1977. Assoc. dir. Cornell U. Law Library, Ithaca, N.Y., 1976-79; dir., assoc. prof. Boston U. Law Library, 1979-82, Georgetown U. Law Library, Washington, 1982—; bd. advisors Huddleson-Brown Pubs., Port Washington, N.Y., 1985—. Mem. Rockville (Md.) Library Adv. com., 1985—. Mem. ABA, ALA, Am. Assn. Law Librarians, Library of Congress Network Adv. Com. Avocations: running, photography, music, personal computers. Librarianship, Legal education, Computer. Home: 1827 Greenplace Terr Rockville MD 20850 Office: Georgetown U Law Ctr 600 New Jersey Ave NW Washington DC 20001

OASTLER, BERT ROBERT, lawyer; b. Atlanta, Oct. 19, 1933; s. Thomas William and Verdrie May (Davis) O.; m. Belitje D. Bancker, Sept. 15, 1956 (div. May 1979); children: Elizabeth, Elaine, Thomas, Lola; m. Alexandria Paul Dowling, Dec. 26, 1979. BCE, Duke U., 1956; JD, Emory U., 1966. Bar: Ga. 1966, U.S. Dist. Ct. (no. dist.) Ga. 1966, U.S. Ct. Appeals (5th and 11th cirs.) 1966. V.p. Tri State Constn. Co., Atlanta, 1959-64; assoc. Smith, Currie & Hancock, Atlanta, 1964—. Served to 1st lt. USAF, 1956-59. Mem. ABA, Ga. Bar Assn., Assn. Trial Lawyers Am., Ga. Trial Lawyers Assn., Lawyers Club of Atlanta. Republican. Presbyterian. Club: Cher-

okee Town and Country Club (Atlanta). Construction. Home: 3131 Slaton Dr NW #22 Atlanta GA 30305 Office: Smith Currie & Hancock 233 Peachtree St Suite 2600 Atlanta GA 30043

OATES, CARL EVERETTE, lawyer; b. Harlingen, Tex., Apr. 8, 1931; s. Joseph William and Grace (Watson) O.; m. Nadine Marie Bosley McCreary, Mar. 3, 1984; children: Lisa Marie McCreary Morris, Carl William, Patricia Grace. BS, U.S. Naval Acad., 1955; LLB, So. Meth. U., 1962. Bar: Tex. 1962, D.C. 1977, Nebr. 1985. Assoc. Akin, Gump, Strauss, Hauer & Feld, Dallas, 1962-64, ptnr., 1965—; chmn. Meridian Svgs. Assn. Pres. S.W. Mus. Sci. and Tech., Dallas; v.p. S.W. Sci. Mus. Found., Dallas; bd. dirs. Kiwanis Wesley Dental Ctr., Inc., Dallas; pres. Wesley Dental Found., Dallas. Served to lt. USN, 1955-59. Mem. ABA, D.C. Bar Assn., Tex. Bar Assn., Dallas Bar Assn., Nebr. Bar Assn., Barristers, Delta Theta Phi. Clubs: Northwood, Dallas Country, Dallas. Banking, General corporate, Real property. Home: 6924 Stefani Dr Dallas TX 75225 Office: Akin Gump Strauss Hauer & Feld 4100 First City Ctr 1700 Pacific Ave Dallas TX 75201

OATES, KATHLEEN MARIE, lawyer; b. Chgo., Dec. 2, 1955; d. William Robert, Jr., and Ethelyn Rose (Calhoun) O. Student l'Université de Clermont-Ferrand, France, 1976-77; B.A., Kalamazoo Coll., 1978; J.D., U. Wis., 1981. Bar: Wis. 1981, Minn. 1981, U.S. Dist. Ct. Minn. 1981, U.S. Dist. Ct. (ea. dist.) Wis. 1983. Assoc. Larkin, Hoffman, Daly & Lindgren, Ltd., Mpls., 1981—. Mem. Assn. Trial Lawyers Am., Minn. Bar Assn., Wis. Bar Assn., Hennepin County Bar Assn., Minn. Trial Lawyers Assn., Phi Beta Kappa, Alpha Lambda Delta, Phi Eta Sigma. Antitrust, Labor, Federal civil litigation. Home: 2400 W 102nd St Apt 335 Bloomington MN 55431 Office: Larkin Hoffman Daly & Lindgren Ltd 7900 Xerxes Ave S Suite 1500 Minneapolis MN 55431

OBARA, PATRICIA EVELYN, banker, lawyer; b. Springfield, Mass., Sept. 26, 1952; d. Adam John and Evelyn Victoria (Pazik) O.; m. Walter W. Wronka, Jr., Oct. 8, 1977; children—Matthew Obara, Marissa Obara. B.A., Colgate U., 1974; J.D., Rutgers U., 1977. Bar: N.J. 1977. Vice-pres., asst. counsel, asst. sec. United Jersey Banks, Princeton, N.J., 1979—. Mem. ABA, N.J. Bar Assn., Somerset County Bar Assn., Princeton Bar Assn., Corp. Counsel Assn., Bank Counsel Group N.J., N.J. Bankers Assn. Roman Catholic. Consumer commercial, Contracts commercial, Labor. Office: United Jersey Banks 301 Carnegie Ctr Princeton NJ 08540

OBER, RUSSELL JOHN, JR., lawyer; b. Pitts., June 26, 1948; s. Russell J. and Marion C. (Hampson) O.; m. Kathleen A. Stein, Apr. 8, 1972; children—Lauren Elizabeth, Russell John III. B.A., U. Pitts., 1970, J.D., 1973. Bar: Pa. 1973, U.S. Dist. Ct. (we. dist.) Pa. 1973, U.S. Ct. Appeals (4th cir.) 1976, U.S. Supreme Ct. 1976, U.S. Dist. Ct. (ea. dist.) Pa. 1978, U.S. Ct. Appeals (3d cir.) 1979, U.S. Tax Ct. 1982, U.S. Ct. Appeals (D.C. cir.) 1985. Asst. dist. atty. Allegheny County, Pitts., 1973-75; ptnr. Wallace Chapas & Ober, Pitts., 1975-80, Rose, Schmidt, Chapman, Duff & Hasley, Pitts., 1980—. Bd. dirs. Parent and Child Guidance Ctr., Pitts., 1983—, treas., 1985-86, pres. 1986—; mem. Mt. Lebanon Traffic Commn., 1976-81. Mem. ABA (discovery com. litigation sect. 1982—, ho. of dels. young lawyers div. 1982-83), Nat. Bd. Trial Advocacy (diplomate), Pa. Bar Assn. (ho. of dels. 1983—), Acad. Trial Lawyers Allegheny County (fellow 1983—), Allegheny County Bar Assn. (chmn. young lawyers sect. 1983, bd. govs. 1984, fin. com. 1984—), U. Pitts. Law Alumni Assn. (bd. govs. 1984—, v.p. 1985-86, pres.-elect 1986—). Clubs: Pitts. Athletic, Rivers, Duquesne Golf, Chartiers Country. Federal civil litigation, State civil litigation, Insurance. Home: 393 Parker Dr Pittsburgh PA 15216 Office: Rose Schmidt Chapman Duff & Hasley 900 Oliver Bldg Pittsburgh PA 15222

OBERDORFER, LOUIS F., fed. judge; b. Birmingham, Ala., Feb. 21, 1919; s. A. Leo and Stella Maud (Falk) O.; m. Elizabeth Weil, July 31, 1941; children: John Louis, Kathryn Lee, Thomas Lee, William L. A.B., Dartmouth, 1939; LL.B., Yale, 1946. Bar: Ala. bar 1946, D.C. bar 1949. Law clk. to Justice Hugo L. Black, 1946-47; practiced Washington, 1947-77; pvt. practice 1947-51; mem. firm Wilmer, Cutler, & Pickering (and predecessors), 1951-61, 65-77; asst. atty. gen. tax div. Dept. of Justice, 1961-65; U.S. dist. judge for D.C., 1977—; Vis. lectr. Yale Law Sch., 1966-71; Adv. com. Fed. Rules Civil Procedure, 1962—; co-chmn. lawyers com. Civil Rights Under Law, 1967-69. Served to capt. AUS, 1941-46. Mem. ABA, D.C. Bar Assn. (bd. govs. 1972-77, pres. 1977), Ala. Bar Assns., Am. Law Inst., Yale Law Sch. Assn. (pres. 1971-73). Jurisprudence. Office: US District Court US Courthouse John Marshall Pl and Constitution Ave NW Washington DC 20001 *

OBERHAUSEN, FRANK CLAY, JR., lawyer; b. Charleston, W.Va., Aug. 28, 1947; s. Frank Clay and Lillian (Berterro) O.; m. Teresa Burdette, Nov. 19, 1968; children—Clay William, Chad Thomas. B.S. in Polit. Sci., U. Fla., 1969; J.D., 1972. Bar: Fla. 1972, U.S. Dist. Ct. (no. and so. dists.) Fla. 1980. Asst. state's atty., 10th Jud. Dist., Fla., 1972-74; city atty. Avon Park, Fla., 1979-83; sole practice, Sebring, Fla., 1974—. Bd. dirs., pres. Highlands Little Theatre, Inc., Sebring, 1974-84; mem. adv. council Grand Prix Race Sebring Internat., 1986—, bd. dirs. 1986—; bd. dirs. Sebring Jaycees, 1974-82, Salvation Army, Sebring, 1982. Served to capt. U.S. Army, 1972-73. Republican. Roman Catholic. Criminal, General corporate, Family and matrimonial. Home: 120 Parkview Dr Sebring FL 33870 Office: 241 S Commerce Ave Sebring FL 33870

OBERLY, CHARLES MONROE, III, attorney general of Delaware; b. Wilmington, Del., Nov. 9, 1946; s. Charles M. and Prudence Elizabeth (Curry) O.; children: Kimberly, Michael and Kristy Lyn (twins). A.A., Wesley Coll., 1966; B.A.A., Pa. State U., 1968; J.D., U. Va., 1971. Bar: Del. Clk. U.S. Dist. Ct., 1971-72; assoc. Morris, James, Hitchens & Williams, Wilmington, Del., 1972-75; dep. atty. gen. Del. Dept. Justice, 1974-82, state prosecutor, 1976-78; atty. gen. State of Del., Wilmington, 1982—; instr. U. Del. Contbr. articles to law jours. Mem. Phi Beta Kappa, Phi Kappa Phi. Democrat. Lutheran. Criminal. Office: Office of the Attorney General 829 N French St Wilmington DE 19801 *

OBERMAIER, OTTO GEORGE, lawyer; b. N.Y.C., Apr. 16, 1936; s. Joseph and Rosina (Abt) O.; m. Patricia Joan Favier, July 1, 1961; children: Thomas More, Patricia Lee, Joseph Favier, Karen Marie. BEE, Manhattan Coll., 1957; LLB, Georgetown U., 1960. Bar: D.C. 1960, N.Y. 1960, U.S. Dist. Ct. (so. and ea. dists.) N.Y. 1964, U.S. Ct. Appeals (2d cir.) N.Y. 1964, U.S. Supreme Ct. 1968. Law clk. to judge U.S. Dist. Ct. (so. dist.) N.Y., New York, 1962-64, asst. U.S. atty., 1964-67; chief trial counsel SEC, New York, 1968-70; assoc. counsel N.Y.C. Commn. to Invstigate Alleged Police Corruption, 1970-71; ptnr. Obermaier, Morvillo & Abramowitz, N.Y.C., 1970—; lectr. Practicing law inst., N.Y.C., 1975—, Law Jour. Seminar Press, N.Y.C., 1986—; adj. asst. prof. law St. John's U., N.Y.C., 1967-69. Coauthor: White Collar Crime, 1981, Securities Law Techniques, 1985; columnist N.Y. Jour., 1982—. Served with U.S. Army, 1960-62. Fellow Am. Bar Found.; mem. ABA, N.Y. State Bar Assn., Assn. of Bar of City of N.Y. Roman Catholic. Club: University (N.Y.C.). Avocations: tennis, skiing, marathon running. Federal civil litigation, Criminal, Securities. Office: Obermaier Morvillo & Abramowitz PC 1120 Ave of Americas New York NY 10036

OBERMAN, STEVEN, lawyer; b. St. Louis, Sept. 21, 1955; s. Albert and Marian (Kleg) O.; m. Evelyn Ann Simpson, Aug. 27, 1977; children: Rachael Diane, Benjamin Scott. BA, Auburn U., 1977; JD, U. Tenn., 1980. Bar: Tenn. 1980, U.S. Dist. Ct. (ea. dist.) Tenn. 1980, U.S. Ct. Appeals (4th cir.) 1981, U.S. Ct. Appeals (6th cir.) 1985, U.S. Supreme Ct. 1985. Assoc. Daniel, Claiborne & Lewallen, Knoxville, Tenn., 1980-82; ptnr. Daniel, Claiborne, Oberman & Buuck, Knoxville, 1983-85, Daniel & Oberman, Knoxville, 1986—; pres., Project First Offender, Knowville, 1983—; guest lectr. law U. Tenn., 1982-86; guest speaker Ct. Clk's Meeting, Cambridge, Eng., 1984; instr. legal clinic , trial advocacy program U. Tenn., 1987—. Contbr. legal articles on drunk driving to profl. jours. Bd. dirs. Knoxville Legal Aid Soc., Inc., 1986—. Mem. ABA, Am. Trial Lawyers Assn., Nat. Assn. Criminal Defense Lawyers, Tenn. Trial Lawyers Assn., Tenn. Assn. Criminal Defense Lawyers (bd. dirs. 1983—, featured speaker 1985), Knoxville Bar Assn. Republican. Jewish. Criminal, Personal injury. Office: Daniel & Oberman Suite 350 One Regency Sq Knoxville TN 37915-2594

OBREMSKI, CHARLES PETER, lawyer; b. Passaic, N.J., Sept. 11, 1946; s. Charles Joseph and Ann (Tichansky) O.; m. Nancy Gail Howell, May 13, 1973; children—Gregory, Christian. B.A., Boston U., 1968; J.D., NYU, 1972. Bar: N.Y. 1972, U.S. Dist. Ct. (so. and ea. dists.) N.Y. 1974, U.S. Ct. Appeals (2d cir.) 1974, U.S. Ct. Claims 1975, U.S. Supreme Ct. 1975. Account specialist IBM Corp., N.Y.C., 1968-69; atty. Home Life Ins. Co., N.Y.C., 1972-73; sole practice, Cornwall, N.Y., 1973—. V.p. Mus. Hudson Highlands, Cornwall-on-Hudson, N.Y., 1975-86; mayor Village of Cornwall, 1977-79. Served to maj. JAGC N.Y. Army N.G. Mem. N.Y. State Bar Assn. Consumer commercial, Real property. Home: PO Box 537 Cornwall NY 12518 Office: 320 Main St Cornwall NY 12520

O'BRIEN, CHRISTOPHER EDWARD, lawyer; b. N.Y.C., Sept. 30, 1955; s. Edward Joseph and Maureen Dorothy (Kelly) O'B.; m. Rita Rose McSweeney, Apr. 8, 1977; 1 child, Katrina. Student, Internat. Coll., 1975-76; BA, Fordham U., 1977; JD, U. Pa., 1980. Bar: N.Y. 1981, U.S. Dist. Ct. (so. and ea. dists.) N.Y. 1981. Assoc. Olwine, Connelly, Chase, O'Donnell & Weyher, N.Y.C., 1980-81, Gaston, Snow, Beekman & Bogue, N.Y.C., 1981—. Officer Concerned Property Owners of Mt. Vernon, N.Y., 1983-84, Fleetwood (N.Y.) Assn., 1983—. Mem. ABA, N.Y. State Bar Assn., East Side Conservative Club. Republican. Roman Catholic. Securities, Federal civil litigation, General corporate. Home: 183 Audobon Ave Mount Vernon NY 10552-2001 Office: Gaston Snow Beekman & Bogue 14 Wall St New York NY 10005

O'BRIEN, CLAUDINE MICHELE NIEDZIELSKI, lawyer; b. Wilmington, Del., July 24, 1953; d. Edmund Luke and Isabelle (Paradis) Niedzielski; m. Patrick Creighton O'Brien, Dec. 15, 1979. BA, U. Del., 1975; JD, Villanova U., 1979, LLM, 1983. Bar: Pa. 1979, U.S. Dist. Ct. (ea. dist.) Pa. 1979, Tex. 1984. With mktg. dept. GIGNA Corp., Phila., 1981-82; counsel mktg. dept. GIGNA Corp., Houston, 1983-85; counsel Southwest and Capital Fin. Groups, Houston, 1985—. Vol. A.I. duPont Inst., Wilmington, Del., 1969-72; atty. Vol. Lawyers for Arts, Houston, 1983—. Mem. ABA. Clubs: Houstonian, Alliance Francaise (Houston). Avocations: oil painting, piano, weightlifting, sailing, skiing. Personal income taxation, Estate taxation, Pension, profit-sharing, and employee benefits. Home: 3622 Pinemont Houston TX 77018 Office: Southwest Fin Group 1400 Post Oak Blvd Suite 300 Houston TX 77056

O'BRIEN, DANIEL LOUIS, lawyer; b. Pasco, Wash., Apr. 7, 1952; s. Louis Edmond and Irene Faye (West) O'B.; m. Marianne O'Brien, Oct. 5, 1974; children: Karen, Kelly. BA, Wash. State U., 1976; JD, Willamette U., 1981. Bar: Nev. 1981. Assoc. Beckley, Singleton, DeLanoy & Jemison, Las Vegas, Nev., 1981-84, Crowell, Crowell, Crowell & Susich Ltd., Carson City, Nev., 1984—; adj. prof. Clark County Community Coll., North Las Vegas, Nev., 1983. Served with USN, 1974-78. Mem. ABA, Washoe County Bar Assn., Clark County Bar Assn., Assn. Transp. Practitioners. Republican. Roman Catholic. Administrative and regulatory, Personal injury, State civil litigation. Home: 2407 Lewis Dr Carson City NV 89701 Office: Crowell Crowell Crowell & Susich Ltd PO Box 1000 Carson City NV 89702

O'BRIEN, DANIEL PAUL, lawyer; b. Long Beach, Calif., Mar. 14, 1942; s. Robert F. and Rita Elizabeth (Wurst) O'B.; m. Gloria Jean Floyd, Dec. 26, 1964; children: Michael, Laurie. Student, Diablo Valley Coll., 1961, Fresno State U., 1964; BA in Journalism, Bus., San Diego State U., 1969; JD, Southwestern U., 1974. Bar: Calif. 1974, U.S. Dist. Ct. (cen. dist.) Calif. 1974. Ptnr. Hanna, Brophy Maclean et al, Fresno, Calif., 1975—; instr. Ins. Edn. Assn., San Francisco, 1980-85. Mem. Fresno Mental Health Assn., 1984—; fund raiser Bulldog Found., 1982—. Served to lt. USNR, 1964-68, Vietnam. Mem. ABA (workers compensation com.), Fresno County Bar Assn., Calif. Compensation Def. Attys. Assn. (bd. dirs. 1983—), Calif. Worker Compensation Def. Attys. Assn. (legis. com.), Fresno Indsl. Claims Assn. (bd. dirs. 1982—), Sigma Chi, NFL Alumni Assn. Republican. Club: Bluegoose Internat. (Fresno, Calif.) (pres. 1986—). Workers' compensation. Office: Hanna Brophy Maclean et al 2310 Tulare St Suite 330 Fresno CA 93721

O'BRIEN, DARLENE ANNE, lawyer; b. Cleve., July 14, 1955; d. Joseph and Suzanne (Belica) Mason; m. Thomas C. O'Brien, Feb. 2, 1984; children: John Michael, Lauren Katherine. BA summa cum laude, U. Toledo, 1977; JD, U. Notre Dame, 1980. Bar: Ind. 1980, Mich. 1981. Law clk. to presiding justice U.S. Bankruptcy Ct. (no. dist.), Ind., 1980-81; assoc. Smith and Brooker P.C., Saginaw, Mich., 1981-84; ptnr. O'Brien and O'Brien, Ann Arbor, Mich., 1984—. Mem. ABA, Mich. Bar Assn., Women's Law Assn. Mich., Washtenaw County Bar Assn., Ind. Bar Assn. State civil litigation, Personal injury, General practice. Office: O'Brien and O'Brien 300 N Fifth Ave Ann Arbor MI 48104

O'BRIEN, DAVID VINCENT, judge; b. New Rochelle, N.Y., June 19, 1932; s. Donald R. and Florence L. (Duffy) O'B.; m. Barbara Mett, July 7, 1956 (dec. June 1974); children: Kathryn, Elizabeth, Kevin, David V., Daniel; m. Janet Burgess, July 18, 1974. B.A., U. Vt., 1956; J.D., Syracuse U., 1959. Bar: N.Y. 1960, V.I. 1971. Ptnr. Byrne, Costello & O'Brien, Syracuse, 1966-70, Mernin, Alexander & O'Brien, St. Croix, V.I., 1971-78, O'Brien & Moore, St. Croix, V.I., 1978-81; judge U.S. Dist. Ct. V.I., St. Croix, 1981—. Served with USMC, 1950-52. Republican. Roman Catholic. Judicial administration. Office: US District Ct PO Box 3439 Christiansted Saint Croix VI 00820 *

O'BRIEN, DENISE MARIE, lawyer; b. Boston, Nov. 1, 1953; d. Maurice Joseph and Elizabeth Marguerite (Sullivan) O'B. BA, Boston Coll., 1975, JD, 1978. Bar: Mass. 1978, D.C. 1979, U.S. Ct. Appeals (1st, 6th and D.C. cirs.) 1979, U.S. Ct. Appeals (5th and 9th cirs.) 1980, U.S. Dist. Ct. D.C. 1982, U.S. Ct. Appeals (10th and 11th cirs.) 1982, U.S. Ct. Appeals (7th and 8th cirs.) 1984, U.S. Supreme Ct. 1985. Trial and appellate atty. ICC, Washington, 1978-80; assoc. Hamel & Park, Washington, 1980-84, ptnr., 1984—. Co-author: Transportation Law Study Guide, 1984. Recipient Nat. Moot Ct. award for oral advocacy Bar Assn. N.Y., 1977, Alumni Assn. award Boston Coll., 1978. Mem. ABA, D.C. Bar Assn., Mass. Bar Assn., Assn. Transp. Practitioners (chmn. edn. com. 1984—, sec., treas. 1985-86, vice chmn. 1986—). Roman Catholic. Federal civil litigation, Administrative and regulatory, Antitrust. Home: 2825 D S Wakefield St Arlington VA 22206 Office: Hamel & Park 888 16th St NW Washington DC 20006

O'BRIEN, DENNIS FRANCIS, lawyer; b. Balt., Jan. 26, 1956; s. Francis Robert and Louise Teresa (Helewicz) O'B.; m. Linda Mae Hejl, Mar. 6, 1982; 1 child, Shana Louise. BS in History, U. Md., 1978; JD, U. Balt., 1981. Bar: Md. 1981, U.S. Dist. Ct. Md. 1981, U.S. Ct. Appeals (4th cir.) 1982. Ptnr. White, Mindel, Clarke & Hill, Towson, Md., 1981—. Mem. Md. State Bar Assn., Balt. County Bar Assn., Assn. Trial Lawyers Am., Md. Trial Lawyers Assn. Democrat. Roman Catholic. Avocations: athletics, reading, gardening. Personal injury, Insurance, State civil litigation. Home: 29 Pikehall Pl Baltimore MD 21236 Office: White Mindel Clarke & Hill 29 W Susquehanna Ave Towson MD 21204

O'BRIEN, DONALD EUGENE, dist. judge; b. Marcus, Iowa, Sept. 30, 1923; s. Michael John and Myrtle A. (Toomey) O'B.; m. Ruth Mahon, Apr. 15, 1950; children—Teresa, Brien, John, Shuivaun. LL.B., Creighton U., 1948. Bar: Iowa bar 1948, U.S. Supreme Ct. bar 1963. Asst. city atty. Sioux City, Iowa, 1949-53; county atty. Woodbury County, Iowa, 1955-58; mcple. judge Sioux City, Iowa, 1959-60; U.S. atty. No. Iowa, 1961-67; individual practice law Sioux City, 1967-78, U.S. dist. judge, 1978—. Served with USAAF, 1943-45. Decorated D.F.C., air medals. Mem. Woodbury County Bar Assn., Iowa State Bar Assn. Roman Catholic. Office: PO Box 267 Sioux City IA 51101

O'BRIEN, FRANCIS JOSEPH, lawyer; b. Bklyn., Mar. 25, 1926; s. Francis Casimir and Marjorie (MacKell) O'B.; m. Ellin Carley Amorosi, Feb. 4, 1956; children—Francis, Paul, Matthew, Christopher. B.S., Holy Cross Coll., 1947; LL.B., Fordham U., 1950. Bar: N.Y. 1950, U.S. Dist. Ct. (cen., so. and ea. dists.) N.Y. 1950, U.S. Ct. Appeals (2d cir.) 1951, U.S. Supreme Ct. 1960. Ptnr. Hill Rivkins, Carey, Loesberg, O'Brien & Mulroy, N.Y.C., 1972—; lectr. admiralty Tulane U., Practising Law Inst., ABA; chmn. U.S. del. Comité Maritime Internat. to Rio de Janeiro Charter Party (Laytime) Definitions. Mem. ABA (internat. sect. del. People's Republic of China 1978), Comite Maritime Internat., Assn. Average Adjusters, Maritime Law Assn. (sec., 1st and 2d v.p., chmn. maritime arbitration. pres. 1986—). Assoc. editor Am. Maritime Cases. Admiralty. Home: 166 80th St Brooklyn NY 11209 Office: 21 West St New York NY 10006

O'BRIEN, JOHN GRAHAM, lawyer; b. N.Y.C., May 12, 1948; s. John Edward and Marian Helen (FitzGerald) O'B.; m. Phyllis Mary Eyth, Apr. 10, 1976; children: John Jr., Jennifer Ann. BS cum laude, Mt. St. Mary's Coll., 1970; JD, Am. U., 1973. Bar: N.J. 1974, D.C. 1974, U.S. Dist. Ct. N.J. 1974, N.Y. 1982, U.S. Supreme Ct. 1982. Law clk. to presiding justice Union County Ct., Elizabeth, N.J., 1973-74; assoc. Carpenter, Bennett & Morrissey, Newark, 1975-81; assoc. counsel GAF Corp., N.Y.C., 1981-85; sr. counsel products liability litigation GAF Corp., Wayne, N.J., 1986—. Contbr. articles to profl. jours. Named Outstanding Young Alumnus, Mt. St. Mary's Coll., 1976. Mem. N.J. Bar Assn., D.C. Bar Assn. Roman Catholic. Club: Echo Lake Country (Westfield, N.J.). Insurance, Personal injury, Workers' compensation. Home: 1501 Rahway Ave Westfield NJ 07090 Office: GAF Corp 1361 Alps Rd Wayne NJ 07470

O'BRIEN, JOSEPH EDWARD, JR., lawyer; b. Keokuk, Iowa, July 27, 1933; s. Joseph Edward and Dorothy Maude (Dickinson) O'B.; m. Jeralyn Alice Nibler, Jan. 28, 1966; children—Joseph Edward III, Leslie Ann. B.S. cum laude, Georgetown U., 1955, J.D., 1963; M.B.A., Am. U., 1956. Bar: Md. 1964, D.C. 1964, U.S. Ct. Appeals (D.C. cir.) 1964, U.S. Tax Ct. 1973, U.S. Ct. Appeals (4th cir.) 1977. Law clk. Circuit Ct. Montgomery County, Md., 1963-64; assoc. Brodsky & Cuddy, Kensington, Md., 1964-66; sole practice Rockville, Md., 1966-79, Bethesda, Md., 1979—; judge Appeal Tax Ct. Montgomery County, 1967-69, chief judge, 1968-69; mem. Montgomery County Bd. Appeals 1969—, chmn. 1969-71, 81-83, vice chmn., 1972-80, 84—. Served to comdr. USN. Mem. Montgomery County Bar Assn., ABA, Am. Arbitration Assn., Soc. Mayflower Descendants, Phi Delta Phi, Phi Alpha Theta. Republican. Roman Catholic. Clubs: Congressional Country. (chmn. legal com. 1977, chmn. legal com. Kemper Open Golf Tournament, 1981, 83-86). Estate planning, Probate, Real property. Address: 6105 Madawaska Rd Bethesda MD 20816

O'BRIEN, KEVIN J., lawyer; b. N.Y.C., Mar. 12, 1934; s. George and Kathleen (Fox) O'B.; m. Winifred Gallagher, Aug. 23, 1958; children: Karen A., Kevin J., Susan M. BS, Fordham U., 1959; LLB, Columbia U., 1962. Bar: N.Y. 1962, U.S. Ct. Appeals (2d cir.) 1971, U.S. Dist. Ct. (so. dist.) N.Y. 1972, U.S. Tax Ct. 1972. Law clk. to presiding justice U.S. Ct. Appeals (2d. cir.), N.Y.C., 1962-63; assoc. Paul, Weiss, Rifkind, Wharton & Garrison, N.Y.C., 1963-70, ptnr., 1970—. Contbr. articles to profl. jours. Trustee Convent of Sacred Heart, Greenwich, Conn., 1979-82; mem. Cardinal's Com. of Laity, N.Y.C., 1986—. Served with USN, 1952-55. Mem. ABA, N.Y. State Bar Assn. (exec. com. tax sect. 1979-83), Assn. of Bar of City of N.Y., Nat. Assn. Real Estate Investment Trusts. Roman Catholic. Club: Westchester Country (Harrison, N.Y.). Corporate taxation, Personal income taxation. Office: Paul Weiss Rifkind Wharton & Garrison 1285 Ave of Americas New York NY 10019

O'BRIEN, PATRICK W., lawyer; b. Chgo., Dec. 5, 1927; s. Maurice Edward and Ellen (Fitzgerald) O'B.; m. Deborah Bissell, July 2, 1955; children: Kathleen, Mariellen, Patrick, James, Patricia. BS in Mech. Engring., Northwestern U., JD. Bar: Ill. 1951, U.S. Dist. Ct. (no. and so. dists.) Ill., U.S. Ct. Appeals (7th and 8th cirs.), U.S. Supreme Ct. Assoc. Bell, Boyd, Marshall & Lloyd, Chgo., 1950-51; assoc. Mayer, Brown & Platt, Chgo., 1953-62, ptnr., 1962—. Served to capt. USAF, 1951-53. Fellow Am. Coll. Trial Lawyers; mem. ABA, Ill. Bar Assn., Chgo. Bar Assn. Republican. Roman Catholic. Clubs: Chgo., Attic, University, Westmoreland Country, Cliff Dwellers, Dairymen's Country. Federal civil litigation, State civil litigation, Libel. Home: 1119 Judson Evanston IL 60202 Office: Mayer Brown & Platt 190 S LaSalle St Chicago IL 60604

O'BRIEN, RONALD JOSEPH, lawyer; b. Columbus, Ohio, Nov. 7, 1948; m. Paula O'Brien. BA, Ohio Dominican Coll., 1970; JD, Ohio State U., 1974. Asst. prosecutor Franklin County, Columbus, 1974-77; prosecutor City of Columbus, 1978-85, atty., 1986—. Mem. ABA, Ohio Bar Assn., Columbus Bar Assn., Nat. Dist. Atty. Assn. Republican. Roman Catholic. Federal civil litigation, State civil litigation, Criminal. Home: 543 Yaronia Columbus OH 43214 Office: City of Columbus 90 W Broad St Columbus OH 43215

O'BRIEN, THOMAS C., lawyer; b. Ann Arbor, Mich., Dec. 2, 1943; s. Francis Lewis and Irene Catherine (Hert) O'B.; m. Darlene Anne Mason, Feb. 2, 1984; children: John Michael, Lauren Katherine. BS, Eastern Mich. U., 1966; JD, U. Detroit, 1969. Bar: Mich. 1970, U.S. Dist. Ct. (ea. dist.) Mich. 1970. Law clk. Mich. Ct. Appeals, Lansing, 1969-70; assoc. Plunkett, Cooney, Rutt & Peacock, Detroit, 1970-74; prin. ptnr. O'Brien, Moran & Dimond, Ann Arbor, 1974-82; ptnr., pres. O'Brien, Moran & Stein, Ann Arbor, 1982-84; ptnr. O'Brien & O'Brien, Ann Arbor, 1984—; guest lectr. trial adv. U. Mich., Ann Arbor, 1977—; faculty mem. trial adv. skills workshop Inst. Continuing Legal Edn., Ann Arbor, 1978—, Nat. Inst. for Trial Adv. Midwest Regional Program, Chgo., 1979—, Nat. Session, Boulder, Colo., 1981, 86. Chmn. Bicentennial Commn., Ann Arbor, 1975-76; campaign dir. candidacy for gov. Jerome P. Cavanagh, 1974; campaign chmn. candidacy for Mich. Supreme Ct. Justice Dean Robb, 1986; bd. dirs. Parent/Infant Ctr., Ann Arbor, 1971-73, Spaulding for Children, Chelsea, Mich., 1980-84, Northfield Twp. Hist. Soc., Mich., 1982-84, COPE-O'Brien Ctr, Ann Arbor, 1985—. Mem. ABA, (trial practice com.), Mich. Bar Assn., Fed. Bar Assn., Washtenaw County Bar Assn., Mich. Trial Lawyers Assn., Washtenaw Trial Lawyers Assn., Nat. Assn. Criminal Def. Lawyers, Criminal Def. Lawyers Mich. (faculty 1984, 87). Democrat. Roman Catholic. State civil litigation, Criminal, Personal injury. Office: O'Brien & O'Brien 300 N 5th Ave Ann Arbor MI 48104

O'BRIEN, THOMAS GEORGE, III, lawyer; b. N.Y.C., Aug. 26, 1942; A.B. magna cum laude, U. Notre Dame, 1964; J.D., Yale U., 1967. Bar: N.Y. 1967. Assoc. Carter, Ledyard & Milburn, N.Y.C., 1971-78; assoc. gen. counsel Frank B. Hall & Co. Inc., Briarcliff Manor, N.Y., 1978-79, v.p., sec., gen. counsel, 1979-86; exec. v.p., sec., gen. counsel CenTrust Savs. Bank, Miami, 1986-87; of counsel Steel, Hector and Davis, Miami, 1987—. Mem. ABA, N.Y. State Bar Assn., Assn. Bar City N.Y. General corporate, Securities. Office: Steel Hector & Davis 4000 Southeast Fin Ctr Miami FL 33131 Office: Frank B Hall & Co Inc 549 Pleasantville Rd Briarcliff Manor NY 10510

O'BRIEN, TIMOTHY ANDREW, writer, journalist, lawyer; b. N.Y.C., July 11, 1943; s. Timothy Andrew and Hildegarde J. (Schenkel) O'B.; m. Maria de Guadalupe Margarita Moreno, Jan. 15, 1971; children: Theresa Marie, Tim A. B.A. in Communications, Mich. State U., 1967; M.A. in Polit. Sci., U. Md., 1972; postgrad., Tulane U. Law Sch., 1974-75; J.D., Loyola U., New Orleans, 1976. Bar: La. 1976, D.C. 1977, U.S. Supreme Ct 1981. News writer, reporter, anchorman WKBD-TV, Detroit, 1968-69, WTOP-TV, Washington, 1969-72, WDSU-TV, New Orleans, 1972-74, WVUE-TV, New Orleans, 1974-77; law corr. ABC News, Washington, 1977—. Contbr. articles to profl. jours. Bd. govs. Woodward Acad., College Park, Ga. Recipient AP award for outstanding reporting of extraordinary event, 1976; New Orleans Press Club award for non-spot news reporting, 1976; Emmy award for documentary on D.C.'s troubled schs., 1969; Am. Bar Assn. awards merit, 1979 (2); Am. Bar Assn. awards merit, 1980, 85; Gavel award for documentary, 1980; nat. award for human rights reporting Women-in-Communications, 1981. Mem. Radio-Television Corrs. Assn. Washington, Am. Judicature Soc., Sigma Delta Chi, Pi Sigma Alpha, Phi Kappa Phi. Jurisprudence, Supreme court constitutional law. Office: ABC News 1717 DeSales NW Washington DC 20036

O'BRIEN, TIMOTHY JAMES, lawyer; b. Detroit, Nov. 4, 1945; m. Hyon Baek, Jan. 31, 1970; children: Jean, Jane. AB, Yale U., 1967; JD, Harvard U., 1976. Bar: N.Y. 1977, U.S. Dist. Ct. (so., ea. and we. dists.) N.Y. 1978. Assoc. Cleary, Gottlieb, Steen & Hamilton, N.Y.C., 1976-80; ptnr. Coudert Bros., N.Y.C., 1980—. Assoc. dir., vol. Peace Corps, Republic of Korea, 1967-73. Mem. ABA, N.Y. State Bar Assn., Assn. of Bar of City of N.Y. (internat. law com.). Private international. Office: Coudert Bros 200 Park Ave New York NY 10166

O'BRIEN, WALTER JOSEPH, II, lawyer; b. Chgo., Apr. 22, 1939; s. Walter Joseph O'Brien and Lorayne (Stouffer) Steele; m. Dee Ann Dvorak, June 4, 1964 (div. Oct. 1977); children—Kelly A., Patrick W., Kathleen; m. Sharon Ann Curling, July 8, 1978; 1 child, John Joseph. B.B.A., U. Notre Dame, 1961; J.D., Northwestern U.-Chgo., 1964. Bar: Ill. 1965, U.S. Dist. Ct. (no. dist.) Ill. 1965, U.S. Supreme Ct. 1973. Assoc. Nicholson, Nisen, Elliott & Meier, Chgo., 1966-70; pres., Capstan Co., Chgo., 1970-73, Walter J. O'Brien II, Ltd., Oak Brook, Ill., 1973-78, O'Brien & Assocs., P.C., Oakbrook Terrace, Ill., 1978—; dir. Atty. Title Guaranty Fund, Inc., Champaign, Ill., 1980—. Contbr. articles to legal jours. Commr., Oak Brook Plan Commn., 1980-85 ; mem. Oak Brook Zoning Bd. Appeals, 1985—; v.p. Oak Brook Civic Assn., 1972; trustee St. Isaac Jogues Ch., Hinsdale, Ill., 1975-76. Served as capt. Q.M.C., U.S. Army, 1964-66. Fellow Ill. Bar Found.; mem. Ill. State Bar Assn. (mem. assembly), ABA, DuPage Bar Assn. Roman Catholic. Club: Butterfield Country (bd. dirs. 1982—) (Oak Brook). Real property, General corporate, Probate. Office: O'Brien & Assocs PC 17W200 22d St Oakbrook Terrace IL 60181

O'BRIEN, WILLIAM SCOTT, lawyer; b. Findlay, Ohio, Nov. 21, 1945; m. Jody B. Beall; children: Stephanie Louise, William Hosler. BCE, Mich. Tech. U., 1968; student, Findlay Coll., 1969, U. Toledo; JD, No. U., Ada, Ohio, 1972. Bar: Ohio 1972, U.S. Dist. Ct. (no. dist.) Ohio 1973, U.S. Supreme Ct. 1976; registered engr. in tng. Sole practice 1972-76; ptnr. O'Brien & Bauer Co. L.P.A., Findlay, 1976—; instr. real estate law Findlay Coll., 1975-78; instr. flight Eddie's Flying Service, Findlay, 1969-71; referee Common Pleas Ct., Hancock County, Ohio, 1977-79; trustee U.S. Bankruptcy Ct., no. dist. Ohio; arbitrator med. malpractice; lectr. in field. Solicitor Village of Arcadia, Ohio, 1973-75, Village of Van Buren, Ohio, 1975-79, Village of Arlington, Ohio, 1979-82; treas. Council on Domestic Violence, Inc., 1979—; founding pres. greater Ohio affiliate Am. Diabetes Assn., 1979-82; sec. Litter Landing Assn., 1983—. Mem. Ohio Bar Assn., Findlay/Hancock County Bar Assn. (chmn. unauthorized practice com. 1977-83, pres. elect 1986—), Northwest Ohio Bar Assn., Ohio Acad. Trial Lawyers. Republican. Presbyterian. Lodge: Rotary. Family and matrimonial, Construction, Bankruptcy. Home: 17228 County Rd 70 Jenera OH 45841 Office: O'Brien & Bauer Co LPA 410 W Sandusky PO Box 932 Findlay OH 45840

OBSTLER, HAROLD, lawyer, consumer products co. exec.; b. Bklyn., Nov. 7, 1925; s. Joseph and Belle (Fox) O.; m. Mimi Otto, Sept. 4, 1952; children—Peter, Andrew. B.A., Columbia U., 1948; LL.B., Yale U., 1952. Assoc., then partner firm Sherman & Golding, 1952-70; partner firm Leon, Weill & Mahony, 1970-77; asst. gen. counsel, asst. sec. Colgate-Palmolive Co., N.Y.C., 1977-85, v.p., sec., gen. counsel, 1985—. Served with USAAF, 1944-46. Club: Yale. General corporate. Address: Colgate-Palmolive Co 300 Park Ave New York NY 10022

O'CALLAGHAN, WILLIAM LAWRENCE, JR., lawyer; b. Atlanta, Aug. 6, 1941; s. William Lawrence and Martha Kathryn (Fitzpatrick) O'C.; m. Faye Whitmire, Dec. 18, 1964; children: Diana Lee, John Patrick, Michael Lawrence. BBA, U. Ga., 1963, JD cum laude, 1965; LLM in Taxation, Georgetown U., 1968. Bar: Ga. 1965, U.S. Supreme Ct. 1971. Ptnr. Gambrell, Russell et al, Atlanta, 1968-74, O'Callaghan, Saunders & Stumm, Atlanta, 1974—. Bd. dirs. Atlanta Jr. Golf Assn., 1984—, Phoenix Soc. of Atlanta, 1985—, Sandy Springs C. of C., Atlanta, 1982-83. Served as capt. U.S. Army, 1965-68. Mem. ABA (chmn. com. on fed. tax real property sect.), Internat. Bar Assn., Fed. Bar Assn., Ga. Bar Assn., North Atlanta Tax Council, Lawyers Club of Atlanta. Presbyterian. Clubs: Atlanta Athletic, Georgian. Lodges: Rotary (v.p. Sandy Springs chpt. 1986), Optimists (pres. Sandy Springs chpt. 1978). Avocations: golf, travel. Real property, Corporate taxation, General corporate. Home: 9350 Riverclub Pkwy Atlanta GA 30136 Office: O'Callaghan Saunders & Stumm 6201 Powers Ferry Rd Suite 330 Atlanta GA 30339

O'CARROLL, ANITA LOUISE, legal editor, lawyer; b. Jersey City, Nov. 19, 1953; d. Henry Patrick and Anita (Babikian) O'C. B.A., Rutgers U., 1975; J.D., N.Y. Law Sch., 1978. Bar: N.J. 1983, Pa. 1983, U.S. Dist. Ct. N.J. 1983. Legal asst. to Manhattan Dist. Atty., N.Y.C., 1977, to Bergen County Counsel, Hackensack, N.J., 1977; jud. clk. City of Hackensack, 1978-79; legal editor West Pub. Co., Mineola, N.Y., 1980-85; staff atty. Social Security Adminstrn. Office of Hearings and Appeals, Newark, 1985-86; staff atty. Aetna Life and Casualty Co., Parsippany, N.J., 1986—. Author: (with others) The Guide to American Law, 1981; A Synthesis of N.Y. Case Law on the Bill of Particulars and Pretrial Discovery, 1977. Mem. ABA, Assn. Trial Lawyers Am., N.J. State Bar Assn., Bergen County Bar Assn., Pa. Bar Assn. Republican. Pension, profit-sharing, and employee benefits, Real property, Workers' compensation. Home: 109 Edison Glen Terr Edison NJ 08837

OCHELTREE, RICHARD LAWRENCE, forest products company executive; b. Springfield, Ill., Oct. 9, 1931; s. Chalmer Myerly and Helen Margaret (Camm) O.; m. Ann Maureen Washburn, Apr. 11, 1958; children: Kirstin Ann, Lorraine Page, Tracy Lynn. A.B., Harvard U., 1953, LL.B., 1958. Bar: Calif. 1959. Sec., gen. counsel Am. Forest Products Corp./Bendix Forest Products Corp., San Francisco, 1961-81; v.p. adminstrn., sec., gen. counsel Am. Forest Products Co., 1981-87. Served with USAF, 1953-55. Mem. Am., San Francisco bar assns. General corporate, Contracts commercial. Home: 1446 Floribunda Ave Apt 102 Burlingame CA 94010 Office: 2740 Hyde St San Francisco CA 94109

OCHMANSKI, CHARLES JAMES, bar association executive; b. Augusta, Maine, Dec. 17, 1932; s. Frank and Michalina (Popowich) O.; m. Martha Lillian Masters, July 1, 1961; children—Lisa Ellen, Angela Joan. B.S. in Edn., U. Maine, 1960, M.Ed., 1963. Sales rep. L.G. Balfour Co., Rochester, N.Y., 1960-62; tchr. Bloomfield High Sch., Conn., 1963-68; asst. exec. dir. Maine Tchrs. Assn., Augusta, 1968-74; exec. dir. Vt. Edn. Assn., Montpelier, 1974-81; asst. exec. dir. Vt. Bar Assn., Montpelier, 1981-82, exec. dir., 1982—. Served with USAF, 1952-56. Mem. Vt. Soc. Assn. Execs., Am. Soc. Assn. Execs. Roman Catholic. Legal association executive. Office: Vt Bar Assn PO Box 100 Montpelier VT 05602

OCHS, ROBERT DUANE, lawyer; b. LaCrosse, Kans., June 16, 1942; s. Manuel and Marie Elizabeth (Koch) O.; m. Catherine Clemens Fockele, Dec. 18, 1971; children—Elizabeth Marie, Thomas Fockele. A.B., Ft. Hays State U., 1965; J.D., Washburn U., 1968. Bar: Kans. 1968, U.S. Dist. Ct. Kans. 1968, U.S. Ct. Appeals (10th cir.) 1968, U.S. Supreme Ct. 1973. Exec. dir. Kans. Constn. Revision Com., Topeka, 1968; research atty. Kans. Sup. Ct., Topeka, 1968; asst. pardon atty. Gov.'s Office, Topeka, 1968-69, legal counsel to gov., 1969; sr. ptnr. Ochs and Kelley, P.A., Topeka, 1985—. Author supplement: Kansas Practice Methods, 1977. Mem. Kans. Bar Assn. (profl. ethics and grievance com. 1982-87, Outstanding Service award 1987), Topeka Bar Assn. (chmn. profl. ethics and grievance com. 1981-87). Democrat. Lutheran. Federal civil litigation, State civil litigation, Personal injury. Home: 1936 Arrowhead Rd Topeka KS 66604 Office: Ochs and Kelley PA 5040 SW 28th St Topeka KS 66667

OCHS, ROBERT FRANCIS, lawyer; b. Chgo., Feb. 22, 1937; s. Benjamin M. and Florence (Gust) O.; m. Sharon Weiss, Sept. 6, 1958; children: Scott, Melinda, Christopher, Neil. Student, Duke U., 1955-56; BA, U. Toledo, 1958; JD, U. Mich., 1961. Bar: U.S. Dist. Ct. (no. dist.) Ohio 1966, U.S. Dist. Ct. (cen. dist.) Calif. 1974, U.S. Temporary Emergency Ct. Appeals 1976, U.S. Dist. Ct. (so. dist.) Tex. 1986. Atty. Hazeltine Corp., Little Neck, N.Y., 1961-64, Gulf Oil Corp., Chgo. and Los Angeles, 1964-75; counsel Gulf Oil Corp., Houston, 1975-82, asst. gen. counsel, 1982-86; sr. counsel Conoco Inc., Houston, 1986—. Mem. ABA (energy com.), Ohio Bar Assn., Calif. Bar Assn., Tex. Bar Assn. (chmn. law subcom. 1981-82), Am. Petroleum Inst., Phi Alpha Theta. Republican. Roman Catholic. Clubs: Pine Forest Country Club (bd. dirs. 1983-86), Plaza (entertainment com.) (Houston). Avocations: golf, church, travel. General corporate, Administrative and regulatory, Federal civil litigation. Home: 11720 Cobblestone Houston TX 77024 Office: Conoco Inc PO Box 2197 Houston TX 77252

OCKERMAN, EDWIN FOSTER, JR., lawyer; b. Lexington, Ky., June 17, 1952; s. Edwin Foster Sr. and Joyce Ann (Harris) O.; m. Martina Young. AB, U. Carolina, 1974; JD, U. Ky., 1977. Bar: Ky. 1978, U.S. Dist. Ct. (ea. dist.) Ky. 1978. From assoc. to ptnr. Martin, Ockerman & Brabant, Lexington, 1978—. Contbr. articles to profl. jours. Chartered class mem. Leadership Lexington, 1979-80, bd. dirs., 1981-82, Commonwealth Preservation Council, Frankfort, Ky., 1980-82, Ky. Citizens for the Arts, 1981-83, Lexington Council of the Arts, 1979-86, sec., 1980-82; co-chmn. Lawyers for the Arts, 1983-84. Named one of Outstanding Young Men in Am., 1985. Mem. ABA, Ky. Bar Assn., U.S. Supreme Ct. Hist. Soc., Dialectic and Philanthropic Literary Socs., Actors Guild of Lexington, Inc. (pres. 1986—). Democrat. Methodist. Club: Filson (Louisville, Ky.). Real property, General corporate, Equine law. Office: Martin Ockerman & Brabant 200 N Upper St Lexington KY 40507

OCKEY, RONALD J., lawyer; b. Green River, Wyo., June 12, 1934; s. Theron G. and Ruby O. (Sackett) O.; m. Arline M. Hawkins, Nov. 27, 1957; children—Carolyn S. Ockey Baggett, Deborah K. Ockey Christiansen, David, Kathleen M. Ockey Hellewell, Valerie, Robert. B.A., U. Utah, 1959, postgrad. 1959-60; J.D. with honors, George Washington U., 1966. Bar: Colo. 1967, Utah 1968, U.S. Dist. Ct. Colo. 1967, U.S. Dist. Ct. Utah 1968, U.S. Ct. Appeals (10th cir.) 1969. Missionary to France for Mormon Ch., 1954-57; law clk. to judge U.S. Dist. Ct. Colo., 1966-67; assoc. ptnr., shareholder Jones, Waldo, Holbrook & McDonough, Salt Lake City, 1967—. State govtl. affairs chmn. Utah Jaycees, 1969; state del. 1980-82, 84-86; Republican Convs., 1972-74, 1976-78, 1980-82, 84-86; del. Salt Lake County Rep. Conv., 1978-80; sec. Wright for Gov. campaign, 1980; legis. dist. chmn. Utah Rep. Party, 1983—; trustee Food for Poland, 1981—. Served to lt. U.S. Army, 1960-66; to capt. Judge Adv. Gen. USAR, 1966-81. Mem. Utah State Bar (various coms.), ABA (com. on public borrowing), Nat. Assn. Bond Lawyers (chmn. com. on state legislation 1982-85), George Washington U. Law Alumni Assn. (bd. dirs. 1981-85), Order of Coif, Phi Delta Phi. Contbr. articles on law to profl. jours.; mem. editorial bd. Utah Bar Jour., 1973-75; mem. staff and bd. editors George Washington Law Rev., 1964-66. Contracts commercial, Bankruptcy, Securities. Home: 4502 Crest Oak Circle Salt Lake City UT 84124 Office: 1500 First Interstate Plaza Salt Lake City UT 84101

O'CONNELL, CHARLES FRANCIS, lawyer; b. Boston, Jan. 31, 1955; s. Thomas Patrick and Florence E. (McCarthy) O'C. BS, Boston Coll., 1976; JD, Suffolk U., 1980; LLB, Cambridge U., 1982. Bar: Mass. 1980, U.S. Dist. Ct. Mass. 1981, U.S. Tax Ct. 1986. Tax cons. Touche Ross & Co., Boston, 1980-81; sole practice law Boston, 1982; assoc. Taylor, Ganson & Perrin, Boston, 1983—; bd. dirs. Textile Shield Co., Lawrence, Mass. Mem. adv. bd. History of South Boston Project, Boston, 1984—. Mem. ABA, Internat. Bar Assn., Am. Arbitration Assn., Internat. Bus. Ctr. New Eng., Beta Gamma Sigma, Phi Delta Phi. Club: United Oxford-Cambridge Univ. (London). Avocations: amateur ice hockey, music, history. Estate taxation, Real property, General corporate. Office: Taylor Ganson & Perrin 100 Franklin St Boston MA 02110

O'CONNELL, DANIEL HENRY, lawyer; b. Eugene, Oreg., Apr. 5, 1941; s. Kenneth J. and Evelyn (Wacksmuth) O'C.; m. Ellen E. Bryant, Dec. 17, 1976; children—Brian Daniel, Sarah Anne. B.S., U. Oreg., 1963; J.D., Boalt Hall Sch. Law, 1966; LL.M., NYU, 1967. Bar: Oreg. 1966, Ariz. 1970. Faculty, U. Ariz., Tucson, 1968-73; mem. firm Bilby, Thompson, et al, Tucson, 1973-75, Johnson, Johnson & Harrang, Eugene, Oreg., 1975-76, O'Connell & Hecker, Tucson, 1976-79, O'Connell, Wezelman, Poston and Boss', P.C., 1979—. Mem. Ariz. Bar Assn. (cert. tax specialist), ABA, Pima County Bar Assn. (dir. 1978—). Author, books, articles on tax/law-related topics. General corporate, Estate planning, State and local taxation. Office: 1840 E River Rd Suite 100 Tucson AZ 85718

O'CONNELL, HANS JAMES, lawyer; b. Teaneck, N.J., Aug. 14, 1947; s. James Anthony O'Connell and Margaret (Imhoff) O'Connell Romeo; m. Gisela Lorey, Feb. 3, 1977; children: Alexandra, Mark, Erik. BA in Philosophy magna cum laude, Fordham U., 1969, JD, 1972. Bar: N.Y. 1973, U.S. Dist. Ct. (so. and ea. dists.) N.Y. 1973, U.S. Ct. Appeals (2d cir.) 1973, N.J. 1974, U.S Dist. Ct. N.J. 1974, U.S. Supreme Ct. 1976. Asst. dist. atty. City of N.Y., Bronx, 1972-76; law clk. to presiding justice N.Y. Supreme Ct., Bronx, 1976; assoc. Moses & Singer, N.Y.C., 1977; ptnr. Griffiths & O'Connell, Hackensack, N.J., 1978—. Phi Beta Kappa. Roman Catholic. Personal injury, Federal civil litigation, State civil litigation. Office: Griffiths & O'Connell 2 University Plaza Hackensack NJ 07601

O'CONNELL, HENRY FRANCIS, lawyer; b. Winthrop, Mass., Jan. 4, 1922; s. Henry F. and Anna (Cunning) O'C. B.A., Boston Coll., 1943, J.D., 1948. Bar: Mass. 1948, U.S. Supreme Ct. 1956. House counsel electronics div. Am. Machine & Foundry Co., Boston, 1951-54; sole practice, Boston, 1954-60; assoc. Glynn & Dempsey, Boston, 1960-70, Avery, Dooley, Post & Avery, 1970—; asst. atty. gen. mcpls. affairs State of Mass., 1969—. Mem. Winthrop Bd. Selectmen, 1958-64, 68-72, chmn. 1960-61, 68-69, 71-72. Served to lt. USCGR, World War II. Mem. Mass. Bar Assn., Nat. Boating Fedn. (past pres.), Mass. Selectmen's Assn., Mass. Bay Yachts Clubs Assn. (past commodore). Local government, Admiralty, Condemnation. Home: 20 Belcher St Winthrop MA 02152

O'CONNELL, JOHN RYAN, lawyer; b. N.Y.C., July 4, 1951; s. John Joseph and Patricia (Smith) O'C.; m. Janet Bayard Keyes, Oct. 19, 1985. BA, Harvard U., 1973; JD, U. Pa., 1977. Bar: N.Y. 1978, U.S. Dict. Ct. (so. and ea. dists.) N.Y. 1978. Assoc. Whitman & Ransom, N.Y.C., 1977-80, Weil, Gotshal & Manges, N.Y.C., 1980-82, Burns, Summit, Rovins & Feldesman, N.Y.C., 1982-84; sr. corp. atty. Union Pacific Corp., N.Y.C., 1984—. Mem. ABA, Assn. of Bar of City of N.Y. Democrat. Roman Catholic. Clubs: Harvard (N.Y.C.), Maidstone (E. Hampton, N.Y.). Avocations: squash, tennis, reading, opera, theatre. General corporate, Securities. Home: 225 Central Park W Apt 1205 New York NY 10024 Office: Union Pacific Corp 345 Park Ave New York NY 10154

O'CONNELL, JOSEPH FRANCIS, III, lawyer; b. Boston, Apr. 18, 1948; s. Joseph Francis Jr. and Suzanne (O'Brien) O'C. B.S.B.A., Villanova U., 1970; M.B.A., So. Meth. U., 1975, J.D., 1975. Bar: Tex. 1975, Mass. 1975, U.S. Dist. Ct. Mass. 1976, D.C. 1978, U.S. Supreme Ct. 1979. Assoc. firm Epstein, Salloway & Kaplan, Boston, 1976-78; corp. counsel Thomas E. Sears, Inc., Boston, 1978—. Serving as maj. JAGC, USAR, 1979—. Mem. Boston Bar Assn., ABA. Clubs: University (Boston); Army and Navy (Washington). General corporate, Insurance. Office: Thomas E Sears Inc 200 Clarendon St Boston MA 02116

O'CONNELL, KEVIN MICHAEL, lawyer; b. N.Y.C., Sept. 10, 1948; s. George Francis and Marion (O'Connor) O'C.; m. Elizabeth Terlep, June 27, 1970; children: Brendan Matthew, Megan Lucy, Roderick George Francis, Daniel, Patrick Vincent. AB, Providence Coll., 1970; JD, Am. U., 1973; LLM, Georgetown U., 1984. Bar: Md. 1974, N.J. 1974, D.C. 1975, U.S. Dist. Ct. D.C. 1975, U.S. Ct. Appeals (D.C. cir.) 1975, Va. 1984. Mem. legis. staff U.S. Ho. of Reps., 1973-76; assoc. Betts, Clogg & Murdock, Rockville, Md., 1976-80; assoc., then ptnr. Kenary, Tietz & Hogan, Washington, 1980-84; asst. Commonwealth's atty. Loudoun County, Va., 1984-87; assoc. Hazel, Beckhorn & Hanes, Fairfax and Leesburg, Va., 1987—; Mem. Jud. Conf. of D.C., 1983, 84. Contbg. author The Lessons of Victory, 1969. Cubmaster Boy Scouts Am., Leesburg, Va., 1986—; chmn. bd. mgrs. Christ Child Inst. for Children, Rockville, 1977-81; bd. dirs. Christ Child Soc. of Washington, 1977-81; mem. Loudoun County Task Force on Alcohol Abuse, 1985-87. Mem. ABA, Va. State Bar Assn., Va. Bar Assn., D.C. Bar Assn., Nat. Dist. Attys. Assn., Va. Assn. Commonwealth's Attys., Loudoun County Bar Assn. Roman Catholic. Club: The Barristers. Lodge: KC. State civil litigation, General corporate, Securities. Home: Route 1 Box 346J Leesburg VA 22075 Office: 116G Edwards Ferry Rd NE Leesburg VA 22075

O'CONNOR, BRUCE EDWARD, lawyer; b. Cin., Dec. 12, 1942; s. John Joseph and Dorothy R. (Bishop) O'C.; m. Janet L. Wright, July 30, 1966; children: Matthew, Edward. BSEE, U. Cin., 1965; JD, Georgetown U., 1969. Bar: Wash. 1969, U.S. Dist. Ct. (we. dist.) Wash. 1969, U.S. Ct. Appeals (fed. cir.) 1972. Trainee Gen. Electric Co., Arlington, Va., 1965-69; assoc. Christensen, O'Connor, Johnson & Kindness, Seattle, 1969-72, ptnr., 1972-83, mng. ptnr., 1983—. Mem. ABA, Am. Intellectual Property Law Assn. Democrat. Roman Catholic. Club: Rainier. Avocations: piano, photography, fishing, car restoration. Patent, Trademark and copyright, Federal civil litigation. Home: 2021 First Ave Seattle WA 98121 Office: Christensen O'Connor et al 2700 Westin Bldg Seattle WA 98121

O'CONNOR, DONALD JOHN, lawyer; b. N.Y.C., Jan. 6, 1932; s. John Joseph and Eileen (O'Kelly) O'C; m. Susan Melvin, June 30, 1953; children: Davis Owen, Peter John, Susan, Richard Andrew. BA, Cornell U., 1953, JD, 1958. Bar: Colo. 1958, U.S. Dist. Ct. (Colo.) 1958, U.S. Tax Ct. 1958. Assoc. Davis, Graham & Stubbs, Denver, 1958-64, ptnr., 1964—, mng. ptnr., 1986—. Contbr. articles on income tax to profl. jours. Served in USAF, 1953-55. Mem. ABA, Colo. Bar Assn. (chmn. tax sect.), Denver Bar Assn., Greater Denver Tax Counsels Assn. (sec. 1969, pres. 1972), Colo. Bd. Psychologist Examiners, Colo. Assn. Commerce and Industry Ednl. Found. (bd. dirs., sec. 1984—, chmn. bd. dirs. 1987—). Roman Catholic. Clubs: Arapahoe Tennis (Denver) (membership com.), Arapahoe Hunt (Douglas County). Avocations: fox hunting, running. Corporate taxation, State and local taxation, General corporate. Home: 2841 E Geddes Pl Littleton CO 80122 Office: Davis Graham & Stubbs 370 17th St Denver CO 80202

O'CONNOR, EARL EUGENE, U.S. district judge; b. Paola, Kans., Oct. 6, 1922; s. Nelson and Mayme (Scheetz) O'C.; m. Florence M. Landis, Nov. 3, 1951 (dec. May 1962); children: Nelson, Clayton; m. Jean A. Timmons, May 24, 1963; 1 dau., Gayle. B.S., U. Kans., 1947, LL.B., 1950. Bar: Kans. 1950. Practiced in Mission, Kans., 1950-51; asst. county atty. Johnson County, Kans., 1951-53; probate and juvenile judge 1953-55; dist. judge 10th Jud. Dist., Olathe, Kans., 1955-65; justice Kans. Supreme Ct., 1965-71; judge U.S. Dist. Ct., Dist. of Kans., Kansas City, 1971—, chief judge, 1981—. Served with AUS, World War II, ETO. Mem. Am., Kans. bar assns., Nat. Conf. Fed. Trial Judges, Nat. Conf. State Trial Judges, Phi Alpha Delta. Clubs: Mason, Rotary. Jurisprudence. Office: US Courthouse Kansas City KS 66101

O'CONNOR, EDWARD GEARING, lawyer; b. Pitts., May 5, 1940; s. Timothy R. and Irene B. (Gearing) O'C.; m. Janet M. Showalter, June 17, 1972; children: Mark G., Susan M. BA, Duquesne U., 1962, JD, 1965. Bar: Pa. 1965, U.S. Dist. Ct. (we. dist.) Pa. 1965, U.S. Ct. Appeals (3d cir.) 1968, U.S. Supreme Ct. 1976. Assoc. Eckert, Seamans, Cherin & Mellott, Pitts., 1965-72, ptnr., 1973—; mem. adv. com. on appellate ct. rules Supreme Ct. Pa., 1986—. Editor Duquesne U. Law Rev., 1964-65. Chmn. Hampton Township (Pa.) Planning Commn., 1986-87; alumni bd. govs. Duquesne U., 1982—. Recipient Distinguished Alumni award Duquesne U., 1985; named Century Club Distinguished Alumni Duquesne U. Law Rev., 1985. Fellow Am. Bar Found.; mem. Pa. Bar Assn. (Ho. of Dels. 1985—), Acad. Trial Lawyers Allegheny County (bd. govs. 1984-86), Allegheny County Bar Assn. (bd. govs. 1986—), Duquesne U. Alumni Assn. (pres. 1980-82, v.p. 1986—). Republican. Roman Catholic. Clubs: Duquesne, Downtown, Pitts. Athletic Assn. Federal civil litigation, State civil litigation, Antitrust. Home: 4288 Green Glade Ct Allison Park PA 15101 Office: Eckert Seamans Cherin & Mellott 600 Grant St 42nd Floor Pittsburgh PA 15219

O'CONNOR, FRANCIS PATRICK, state supreme court justice; b. Boston, Dec. 12, 1927; s. Thomas Lane and Florence Mary (Hagerty) O'C.; m. Ann Elizabeth O'Brien; children: Kathleen, Francis P., Brien T., Maureen T., Ellen M., Ann E., Jane C., Joyce E., Thomas J., Matthew P. A.B., Holy Cross Coll., 1950; LL.B., Boston Coll., 1953; J.D. (hon.), Suffolk U., 1983, New Eng. Sch. Law, 1984. Bar: Mass. 1953. Assoc. Friedman, Atherton, Sisson & Kozol, Boston, 1954-57, Mason, Crotty, Dunn & O'Connor, Worcester, Mass., 1957-73, Wolfson, Moynihan, Dodson & O'Connor, Worcester, 1974-75; superior ct. judge, Mass., 1976-81; supreme jud. ct. justice, Mass., 1981—. Judicial administration. Office: Supreme Ct New Court House Boston MA 02108 *

O'CONNOR, JAMES EDWARD, lawyer; b. Omaha, Apr. 5, 1953; s. Edward Wilson and Virginia (Conry) O'C.; m. Diana Clare Fuller, Sept. 22, 1984. BA magna cum laude, U. Nebr., 1975; JD, U. Notre Dame, 1978. Bar: Wis. 1978, U.S. Dist. Ct. (ea. dist.) Wis. 1978, Nebr. 1982. Sec., gen. counsel Data Retrieval Corp., Milw., 1977-82; asst. gen. counsel Mut. Omaha Ins. Co., 1982—; lectr. Creighton U. Law Sch., Omaha, 1986—, U. Nebr. at Omaha, 1985—. Leader Boy Scouts Am. Explorers, Omaha, 1984—; adviser Jr. Achievement, Omaha and Milw., 1969-85; del. Douglas County Dem. Conv., Omaha, 1982—; mem. steering com. Interfaith Com. Archdiocese Omaha, 1986, dir. info. services, 1973-75. Kayser Found. scholar, 1975, Regents scholar U. Nebr., 1975; named one of Outstanding Young Men in Am., 1981. Mem. ABA (liaison 1977-79, governing council sect. sci. and tech. 1978-81, Silver Key award 1978), Omaha Bar Assn., Nebr. Bar Assn., Omaha Fin. Planners, Ralston Jaycees. Democrat. General corporate, Computer, Insurance. Home: 11406 Sahler St Omaha NE 68164-2325 Office: Mut Omaha Ins Co Mut Omaha Plaza Omaha NE 68175

O'CONNOR, JAMES MICHAEL, lawyer, educator; b. Cambridge, Mass., Nov. 14, 1943; s. Jeremiah Raphael and Nora Theresa (Enright) O'C.; m. Judith Ann Bourgault, June 17, 1967; children—James Arthur, Christopher Michael, Kevin Patrick. B.A., Boston Coll., Newton, Mass., 1966, J.D., 1969; M.P.H., Yale U., 1977. Bar: Conn. 1970, U.S. Dist. Ct. Conn. 1975. With Uarco, Depp River, Conn., 1969-70; asst. counsel Redevelopment Agy. City New Haven, 1970-75, dep. corp. counsel, 1975-81; ptnr. Marcus & Burns, New Haven, 1981-85, Ginsberg, Ginsburg and Alderman, 1985—. lectr. health law Quinnipiac Coll., Yale U. Mem. Health Systems Agy. South Central Conn. Bd.; chmn. Gov.'s Adv. Com. Long Term Care Commn. Served with USMC, 1963-65. Mem. ABA, Conn. Bar Assn., Am. Pub. Health Assn., Assn. Trial Lawyers Am., Nat. Environ. Health Assn., Conn. Environ. Health Assn. Roman Catholic. Lodge: Knights of St. Patrick. Real property, Personal injury. Office: Ginsberg Ginsburg & Alderman 377 Main St West Haven CT 06516-4310

O'CONNOR, JAMES MICHAEL, lawyer, educator; b. Cambridge, Mass., June 21, 1942; s. James Patrick and Mary Agnes (Coyne) O'C. AB, Providence Coll., 1964; MEd, U. Mass., 1971; JD, Suffolk U., 1972. Bar: Mass. 1973, U.S. Dist. Ct. Mass. 1973, U.S. Ct. Appeals (1st. cir.) 1973. Mgmt. coordinator Honeywell, Inc., Lawrence, Mass., 1967-69; instr. law Cambridge Latin Sch., 1970—; sole practice Cambridge, 1973—; lectr. Mass. Assn. of Law, 1981—. Founder Students Against Driving Drunk, Cambridge Rindge and Latin Sch, 1985, Key Club, 1981. Served to 1st lt. U.S. Army, 1965-67. Mem. ABA, Mass. Bar Assn., Middlesex County Bar Assn., Cambridge, Arlington, Belmont Bar Assn. Democrat. Roman Catholic. Clubs: Wychmere Harbor (Mass.). Lodge: Kiwanis. Legal education, General practice, Civil rights. Home: Blair Pond Estate 303 32 Normandy Ave Cambridge MA 02138

O'CONNOR, JOHN CHARLES, lawyer; b. Dubuque, Iowa, Jan. 28, 1949; s. Francis J. and Marion (Rhomberg) O'C.; m. Mary Beth Kelly, Sept. 16, 1977; children: Michael Kelly, Katherine Mary, John Kelly, Patrick Kelly. BBA, Loyola U., New Orleans, 1971; JD, Creighton U., 1974. Bar: Iowa, U.S. Dist. Ct. (no. dist.) Iowa, U.S. Tax Ct. Ptnr. O'Connor & Thomas, P.C., Dubuque, 1974—; bd. dirs. O'Connor & Assocs. Ins., Dubuque, Communications Properties, Inc., Dubuque; Klauer Mfg. Co., Dubuque. Bd. dirs. Dubuque Boys Club, 1983, Pastoral Marriage Counseling, 1980. Named Disting. Vol., March of Dimes, Dubuque, 1981. Fellow Am. Coll. of Probate Counsel; mem. ABA, Iowa Bar Assn., Iowa Probate, Property and Trust Commn., Dubuque County Bar Assn. Probate, General corporate, Contracts commercial. Office: O'Connor & Thomas PC 200 Dubuque Bldg Dubuque IA 52001

O'CONNOR, JOHN PAUL, judge; b. Evanston, Ill., Sept. 30, 1939; s. James C. and Alice (Daly) O'C.; m. Judith Byrne Dec. 27, 1961 (div. June 1976); children—John P., Kathleen A., James B.; m. Kathleen A. Ballinger, Nov. 29, 1985. B.S. Xavier Coll., Cin., 1963; J.D., Chase Law Sch., 1967. Bar: Ohio 1967, U.S. Ct. Appeals (6th cir.) 1968, U.S. Dist. Ct. (so. dist.) Ohio 1968. Ptnr., Schuch, Grossmann & O'Connor, Cin., 1967-73; referee Juvenile Ct. Cin., 1967-73, judge, 1979—; judge Mcpl. Ct., Cin., 1973-79; adj. asst. prof. Xavier U. Grad. Sch., Cin., 1969-78. Author: Juvenile Offenders and the Law, 1971. Bd. dirs. Regional Council on Alcoholism, Kids Helping Kids, Cin. Mem. ABA, Ohio Bar Assn., Am. Judges Assn., Cin. Bar Assn., Ohio Juvenile and Probate Judges. Republican. Roman Catholic. Juvenile, Family and matrimonial. Office: Juvenile Ct 222 E Central Pkwy Cincinnati OH 45202

O'CONNOR, KARL WILLIAM, lawyer, U.S. attorney; b. Washington, Aug. 1, 1931; s. Hector and Lucile (Johnson) O'C.; m. Sylvia Gasbarri, Mar.

23, 1951 (dec.); m. Judith Ann Byers, July 22, 1972 (div. 1983); m. Alma Hepner, Jan. 1, 1987; children: Blair, Frances, Brian, Brendan. B.A., U. Va., 1952, LL.B., 1958. Bar: Va. 1958, D.C. 1959, Am. Samoa 1976, Calif. 1977. Law clk. U.S. Dist. Ct. Va., Abingdon, 1958-59; practice law Washington, 1959-61; trial atty. U.S. Dept. Justice, Washington, 1961-65; dep. dir. Men's Job Corps OEO, Washington, 1965-67; mem. civil rights div. Dept. of Justice, chief criminal sect., prin. dep. asst. atty. gen., 1967-75; spl. counsel for intelligence coordination 1975; v.p., counsel Assn. of Motion Picture and Television Producers, Hollywood, Calif., 1975-76; assoc. justice Am. Samoa, 1976, chief justice, 1977-78; sr. trial atty. GSA Task Force, Dept. Justice, 1978-81; insp. gen. CSA, 1981-82; spl. counsel Merit Systems Protection Bd., Washington, 1983-86; U.S. atty. for Guam and the No. Marianas 1986—. Served with USMC, 1952-55. Mem. ABA, D.C., Va., Calif., Am. Samoa bar assns., Phi Alpha Delta, Sigma Nu. Federal civil litigation, Criminal, Labor. Office: 238 O'Hara St Agana GU 96910

O'CONNOR, LIAM T(HOMAS), lawyer; b. Bklyn., Apr. 24, 1954; s. Denis Patrick and Patricia (Young) O'C.; m. Elizabeth Marie Wring, Sept. 28, 1985. BA in Sociology, Bklyn. Coll., CUNY, 1976; JD, Bklyn. Law Sch., 1980. Bar: N.Y. 1981, U.S. Dist. Ct. (so. and ea. dists.) N.Y. 1981. Atty., fraud investigator Bur. Client Fraud Investigation, Dept. Social Services, N.Y.C., 1982-85, atty., adv., 1985-86; estate tax atty. IRS, N.Y.C., 1986—; instr. Bur. Client Fraud Investigation, 1985-86. Mem. ABA, Assn. Trial Lawyers Am., Soc. Profl. Investigators, N.Y. Welfare Fraud Investigators Assn. (instr. 1986), Bklyn. Law Sch. Alumni Assn. Libertarian. Roman Catholic. Avocations: mysteries, polit. history, gen. history. Estate taxation, Criminal, Family and matrimonial. Office: IRS Estate Tax Div PO Box 3100 Group 1527 Church St Sta New York NY 10008

O'CONNOR, MICHAEL E., lawyer; b. Syracuse, Sept. 15, 1948; s. Leo T. and Geraldine (Hager) O.; m. Margaret A. Soplop, June 3, 1972. A.A., Auburn Community Coll., N.Y., 1968; B.A., SUNY-Buffalo, 1970; J.D., Syracuse U., 1974. Bar: N.Y. 1975, U.S. Supreme Ct. 1983. Assoc., Coulter, Fraser, Ames, Bolton, Bird & Ventre, Syracuse, 1975-80, ptnr., 1981—. Pres., Onondaga Title Assn., 1979, Central N.Y. Estate Planning Council, 1981; legal counsel Syracuse Jaycees; v.p. Most Holy Rosary Home Sch. Assn., 1984-85, pres., 1985—. Mem. ABA, N.Y. State Bar Assn. (ho. of dels. 1982—, exec. com. trusts and estates sect. 1984—), Onondaga County Bar Assn. (chmn. estate and surrogate's ct. com. 1981—, bd. dirs. 1984—). Republican. Roman Catholic. Clubs: Syracuse Lions (pres. 1984-85), University. Estate planning, Probate, Estate taxation. Home: 154 Robineau Rd Syracuse NY 13207 Office: Coulter Fraser Ames Bolton Bird & Ventre 499 S Warren St Syracuse NY 13202

O'CONNOR, RAYMOND VINCENT, JR., lawyer; b. N.Y.C., Feb. 27, 1951; s. Raymond Vincent and Rita Margaret (McCarthy) O'C.; m. Patricia Ellen Bliss, June 7, 1975 (div. 1980). AB in History, Georgetown U., 1973; JD, St. John's U., N.Y.C., 1976. Bar: N.Y. 1977, U.S. Ct. Mil. Appeals 1981. Labor relations specialist Def. Communications Agy., Washington, 1985—; dep. gen. counsel U.S. Army Audit Agy., Alexandria, Va., 1986—. Served to capt. JAGC, U.S. Army, 1977-83. Named one of Outstanding Young Men Am., 1985. Mem. ABA, Soc. Fed. Labor Relations Profls., Nat. Pub. Employer Labor Relations Assn. Roman Catholic. Labor, Military, Workers' compensation. Home: 4000 Massachusetts Ave NW #1036 Washington DC 20016 Office: US Army Audit Agy 3101 Park Center Dr Alexandria VA 22302-1596

O'CONNOR, ROBERT EDWARD, JR., lawyer; b. Omaha, June 1, 1950; s. Robert Edward Sr. and Agnes (Flynn) O'C.; m. Jean Patricia Mergens; children: Maureen, Kathleen. Undergrad. degree, Creighton U., 1974, JD, 1974. Bar: Nebr. 1974. Sole practice Omaha, 1974—. Mem. Nebr. State Bar Assn. (del. 1982-84), Nebr. Assn. Trial Attys. (del.), Assn. Trial Lawyers Am. (del.). Democrat. Roman Catholic. Avocation: sailing. Labor, Personal injury, Workers' compensation. Office: 2437 S 130th Circle Omaha NE 68144

O'CONNOR, SANDRA DAY, justice U.S. Supreme Court; b. El Paso, Tex., Mar. 26, 1930; d. Harry A. and Ada Mae (Wilkey) Day; m. John Jay O'Connor, III, Dec. 1952; children: Scott, Brian, Jay. A.B. with gt. distinction in Econs., Stanford U., 1950, LL.B. (bd. editors Law Rev.), 1952. Bar: Calif. Dep. county atty. San Mateo, Calif., 1952-53; civil atty. Q.M. Market Center, Frankfurt/Main, W. Ger., 1954-57; pvt. practice law Phoenix, 1959-65; asst. atty. gen. State of Ariz., 1965-69; Ariz. state senator 1969-75; judge Maricopa County Superior Ct., 1975-79, Ariz. Ct. Appeals, 1979-81; assoc. justice Supreme Ct. U.S., 1981—; juvenile ct. referee, 1962-64; chmn. vis. bd. Maricopa County Juvenile Detention Home, 1963-64; chmn. com. to reorganize lower cts. Ariz. Supreme Ct., 1974-75; mem. Anglo-Am. Legal Exchange, 1980, Maricopa County Superior Ct. Judges Tng. and Edn. Com.; faculty Robert A. Taft Inst. Govt.; vice chmn. Select Law Enforcement Rev. Commn., 1979-80. Chmn. state, county and mcpl. affairs com. Ariz. Senate, 1972-73, majority leader, 1973-74; past Republican dist. chmn.; mem. Maricopa County Bd. Adjustments and Appeals, 1963-64, Ariz. Personnel Commn., 1968-69, Nat. Def. Adv. Com. Women in Services, 1974-76; mem. nat. bd. Smithsonian Assocs., 1981—; trustee Heard Mus., Phoenix, 1968-74, 76-81, pres., 1980-81; adv. bd. Phoenix Salvation Army, 1975-81; bd. dirs. Phoenix Community Council, Ariz. Acad., 1970-75, Jr. Achievement Ariz., 1975-79, Blue Cross/Blue Shield Ariz., 1975-79, Channel 8, 1975-79, Phoenix Hist. Soc., 1974-77, Maricopa County YMCA, 1978-81, Golden Gate Settlement; trustee Stanford U., 1976-80, Phoenix County Day Sch.; v.p. Soroptimist Club Phoenix, 1978-81; mem. Citizens Adv. Bd. Blood Services, 1975-77, Maricopa Ct. Study Com. Recipient Ann. award NCCJ, 1975, Disting. Achievement award Ariz. State U., 1980; named Woman of Yr. Phoenix Advt. Club, 1972. Jurisprudence. Address: Supreme Court of the US 1 1st St NE Washington DC 20543 *

O'CONNOR, TERESA MCCANN, lawyer; b. Culbertson, Mont., June 23, 1956; d. Thomas Paul and Sharon (Quigley) McCann; m. William J. O'Connor II, June 17, 1978; 1 child, Brendan Francis. BA Polit. Sci., Cath. U., 1977, MLS, JD, 1980. Bar: Mont. 1981, U.S. Dist. Ct. Mont. 1981. Legal intern enforcement dir. SEC, Washington, 1979-80; librarian U.S. Senate Library, Washington, 1980; staff counsel, lobbyist ALA, Washington, 1980-81; assoc. Law Offices of Robert Ryan, PC, Billings, Mont., 1981-82; dep. county atty. Yellowstone County, Billings, 1983—. County atty. liason Rape Task Force, Billings, Mont., 1983—, Sexual Abuse Task Force, 1984—; bd. dirs. Beta Imprisonment Alternatives, 1985—; singer Billings Symphony Chorale, 1981—; assoc. Yellowstone Art Ctr. Mem. ABA, ALA, Mont. Bar Assn., Yellowstone County Bar Assn., Mont. County Atty.'s Assn. (dep.). Democrat. Roman Catholic. Criminal. Home: 2720 Palm Dr Billings MT 59102 Office: County Attys Office Yellowstone County Courthouse Billings MT 59107

O'CONNOR, WILLIAM JENNINGS, JR., lawyer; b. Buffalo, Feb. 6, 1923; s. William Jennings and Elizabeth (Sweeney) O'C.; m. Dorothy May Dunn, July 9, 1949 (dec. Jan. 1971); children: Brian D., Kathleen A., Sheila M., Michael T., Eileen P., Bridget E.; m. Joan B. Wilbert, Mar. 10, 1973. BA, U. Toronto, 1943; LLB, Cornell U., 1948. From. assoc. to ptnr. Penney, Penney & Buerger, Buffalo, 1948-59; ptnr. Buerger & O'Connor, Buffalo, 1959-70, Phillips, Lytle, Hitchcock, Blaine & Huber, Buffalo, 1970-84; asst. gen. counsel Marine Midland Banks Inc, Buffalo, 1984—; mem. consumer adv. council Fed. Res. Bd., 1981-82, vice chmn. 1983. Co-author: Equal Credit Opportunity, 1979, Electronic Fund Transfers, 1981, Truth in Lending Manual, 1982; contbr. articles to profl. jours. Served to lt. U.S. Army, 1943-46. Mem. ABA (chmn. com. regulation of consumer credit 1974-78, council sect. corp. law 1978-81), N.Y. State Bar Assn. (chmn. sect. banking corp. and bus. law 1968-69). Clubs: Buffalo Canoe, Cherry Hill (Ridgeway, Ont., Can.). Banking, Consumer commercial, Contracts commercial. Home: 251 Middlesex Rd Buffalo NY 14216 Office: Marine Midland Banks Inc 1200 Marine Midland Centre Buffalo NY 14203

O'CONNOR, WILLIAM MATTHEW, lawyer; b. Pensacola, Fla., Apr. 5, 1955; s. William Francis and Rosalind (Shea) O'C.; m. Mary Patricia Keepnews, Oct. 13, 1984; 1 child, William Lawrence. B.S. in Psychology, Fordham Coll., 1977, J.D., 1980. Bar: N.Y. 1981, U.S. Dist. Ct. (so., ea., no. and we. dists.) N.Y., 1981, U.S. Ct. Appeals (2nd cir.) 1983. Intern, N.Y. Atty. Gen., N.Y.C., 1978-79; legis. intern Am. Lung Assn., N.Y.C., 1979; assoc. Keane & Butler, N.Y.C., 1979-81, Keane & Beane, White Plains, N.Y., 1981-83, Cooperman, Levitt & Winikoff, P.C., N.Y.C., 1983-86, sr. assoc. Sullivan, Donovan, Hanrahan & Silliere, N.Y.C., 1986-87; ptnr. Foyen & Peri, N.Y.C., 1987—. Author: Lobbying Guidebook Am. Lung Assn., 1979. Named to Jessup Moot Ct. team Fordham Law Sch., 1980. Contbr. articles to profl. jours. Mem. legis. com. pub. schs., White Plains, 1981-82; Democratic committeeman Village of Pelham Manor, N.Y., 1985—. Mem. Assn. Trial Lawyers Am., Fed. Bar Council, N.Y. State Bar Assn., Westchester Bar Assn. (editor in chief Jour. 1983, mem. labor law com. 1981—). Fordham ILJ Alumni Assn. (dir. 1984—), New Rochelle Bar Assn. Democrat. Roman Catholic. Club: N.Y. Roadrunners. Federal civil litigation, State civil litigation, Banking. Home: 933 Washington Ave Pelham Manor NY 10803 Office: Foyen & Peri 250 Park Ave New York NY 10177

O'CONOR, ANDREW JOSEPH, IV, lawyer; b. Ottawa, Ill., June 25, 1919; s. Andrew Joseph III and Mary Irma (Ryan) O'C.; m. Carol Grace Hedman, Sept. 13, 1952; children: Kathleen, Andrew V, Jane, Megan. BS, Georgetown U., 1941; JD, Northwestern U., 1945. Bar: Ill. 1946, U.S. Dist. Ct. (no. dist.) Ill. 1946, U.S. Dist. Ct. (so. dist.) Ill. 1948, U.S. Supreme Ct. 1960, U.S. Ct. Appeals (7th cir.) 1981. Assoc. Herman & Pollak, Chgo., 1946-49, jr. ptnr., 1946-49; ptnr. Berry & O'Conor, Ottawa, 1950-80; ptnr. O'Conor, Karaganis & Gail Ltd., Ottawa, 1981; ptnr. Myers, Daugherity, Berry & O'Conor, Ltd., Ottawa, 1982—; dir. First Nat. Bank of Ottawa. Mem. Ottawa Twp. High Sch. Bd. Edn., 1946-74; gen. co-chmn. campaign fund drive and v.p. bd. dirs. Community Hosp. Ottawa, 1964-76. Served with USMC, 1941-43. Fellow Am. Coll. Trial Lawyers (co-chmn. Ill. sect. 1977-78), Internat. Soc. Barristers; mem. Soc. Trial Lawyers Ill. (dir. 1968-70, 84-86), Appellate Lawyers Assn. Ill. (founding), ABA, Chgo. Bar Assn., La Salle County Bar Assn., Ill. Bar Assn. (chmn. sect. tort law 1966-67). Clubs: University (Chgo.); Ottawa Boat. Lodges: Elks, K.C. Co-author Ill. Pattern Jury Instrns.-Civil, 2d edit., 1966-71; bd. editors Northwestern U. Law Rev., 1943-45. State civil litigation, Insurance, Personal injury. Home: North Bluff Ottawa IL 61350 Office: 130 E Madison St Ottawa IL 61350

ODAHOWSKI, DAVID ANTHONY, foundation executive, lawyer; b. Chgo., Apr. 25, 1956; s. William Julian and Mary Jo (Korzienowski) O.; m. Heather Marie Friend, Aug. 7, 1982; children: Julianne Marie, Peter William. BS with honors, U. Wis., Stevens Point, 1978; JD, Hamline U., 1981. Bar: Minn., U.S. Dist. Ct. Minn. Exec. dir., gen. counsel The Wasie Found., Mpls., 1981—, also bd. dirs.; speaker to various groups on grantmaking, found. adminstrn. and other philanthropic issues. Editor-in-chief Pub. Law Research Ctr., Hamline U., 1981. Mem. Citizens League, Mpls., 1983-85; bd. dirs. Hamline U. Sch. Law, St. Paul, 1983—, Midwest Mental Health Inst., Mpls, 1984—, Na-way-ee Indian Sch., Mpls., 1985. Recipient Chancellor's and James H. Albertson awards, U. Wis., Stevens Point, 1978. Mem. ABA (found. com.), Minn. Bar Assn., Council Founds., Minn. Council Founds., Polish Nat. Alliance, U.S. Tennis Assn. (cert. linesman and chair). Roman Catholic. Clubs: NW Racquet (Mpls.). Avocations: antiques, non-fiction reading. Nationally rated tennis player. Exempt organizations, private foundations. Home: 7425 Oak Park Village Dr #10 Minneapolis MN 55426 Office: The Wasie Found 909 Foshay Tower Minneapolis MN 55402

O'DANIEL, JEAN ELIZABETH, lawyer; b. Louisville, Aug. 16, 1955; d. Philip Benedict and Clara Elizabeth (Scott) O'D.; m. Donald Gene Keach, II, Apr. 16, 1977. BA in Social Work, U. Ky., 1975; MSW, JD, Washington U., St. Louis, 1981. Bar: Ky. 1982, U.S. Dist. Ct. (we. dist.) Ky. 1982. Intern, atty. Fayette County Legal Aid, Inc., Lexington, Ky., 1981-82; atty. Adminstrv. Office Cts., Frankfort, Ky., 1982-84; staff atty. Ky. Ct. of Appeals, Frankfort, 1984-85, Lexington, 1985—. Author: (with others) Interstate Child Custody Disputes, 1982. Big sister to Big Bros./Big Sisters, Lexington, Ky., 1985-86; mem. Ky. Foster Care External Rev. Bd., State Exec. Bd.; mem. exec. bd. and chairperson Fayette County Bd., 1986—. Mem. ABA, Ky. Bar Assn., NOW. Democrat. Juvenile, Judicial administration, Family and matrimonial. Home: 3900 Sundart Dr Lexington KY 40502 Office: Ky Ct of Appeals 177 N Upper St Lexington KY 40507

ODAY, LARRY ALAN, lawyer; b. Chillicothe, Ohio, Nov. 27, 1947; s. Lawrence W. and Eva N. (Lewis) O.; m. Joan D. Loeb, Dec. 7, 1968; 1 child, Joy M. BA, Case Western Res. U., 1969; JD, Chgo.-Kent Coll. Law, 1973. Bar: Ill. 1973, U.S. Dist. Ct. (no. dist.) Ill. 1973, D.C. 1980. Counsel govt. relations Combined Ins. Co., Chgo., 1973-79; asst. v.p. fed. affairs Combined Ins. Co., Washington, 1979-81; dir. program policy Health Care Fin. Adminstrn., Balt., 1981-84; assoc. Wood, Lucksinger & Epstein, Washington, 1984-85, ptnr., 1985—; instr. Aspen Systems, Rockville, Md., 1984—. Bd. dirs. Asthma and Allergy Found., Washington, 1985-86. Recipient Adminstrs. Citation, Health Care Financing Adminstrn., Balt., 1983, 84. Mem. ABA, D.C. Bar Assn. Clubs: Capitol Hill, National Lawyers (Washington).

O'DELL, DEBBIE, lawyer; b. New Eagle, Pa., July 13, 1953; d. John and Margaret (Troncatti) O'D.; m. Anthony J. Seneca, Nov. 1, 1980; 1 child, Mario O'Dell. B, W.Va. U., 1974; JD, Duquesne U., 1977. Bar: Pa. 1977, U.S. Dist. Ct. (we. dist.) Pa. 1977. Sole practice Washington, Pa., 1977-78; sr. ptnr. Seneca & O'Dell, Washington, 1978—; asst. pub. defender Pub. Defenders Office, Washington, 1978; law clk. to presiding judge Washington County Common Pleas, 1978-80; chief of litigation Dist. Atty.'s Office, Washington, 1980-84. Del. Dem. Nat. Convention, San Francisco, 1984; bd. dirs. Daughters of Current Events, Washington, Pa., 1984, 85, 86. Named one of Outstanding Young Women in Am., 1978. Mem. Washington County Bar Assn. (exec. bd. dirs. 1980-84), Pa. Trial Lawyers Assn. (sustaining), Western Pa. Trial Lawyers Assn. (bd. dirs. 1984, 85, 86), Washington Bus. and Profl. Womens Club (pres. 1985-86, corr. sec. 1986—). Avocations: reading, swimming, politics, historic preservation. Family and matrimonial, Criminal, State civil litigation. Home: 333 N Main St Washington PA 15301

ODELL, HERBERT, lawyer; b. Phila., Oct. 20, 1937; s. Samuel and Selma (Kramer) O.; m. Anne Deborah Ilson, Sept. 13, 1959; children: Wesley, Jonathan, James. BS in Econs., U. Pa., 1959; LLB magna cum laude, U. Miami, 1962; LLM, Harvard U., 1963. Bar: Fla. 1963, Pa. 1968. Trial atty. tax div. U.S. Dept. Justice, Washington, 1963-65; assoc. Walton, Lantaff, Schroeder, Carson & Wahl, Miami, Fla., 1965-67; from assoc. to ptnr. Morgan, Lewis & Bockius, Phila., 1967—; adj. prof. U. Miami, Villanova U.; lectr. various tax insts. Contbr. articles to profl. jours. Ford fellow, 1962-63. Mem. ABA, Fla. Bar Assn., Pa. Bar Assn., Phila. Bar Assn., Pa. Economy League (bd. dirs. 1983-85), Phi Kappa Phi, Omicron Delta Kappa, Beta Alpha Psi. Club: Harvard (N.Y.C.). Avocations: sailing, running, tennis, scuba diving. Corporate taxation, Estate taxation, Personal income taxation. Office: Morgan Lewis & Bockius 2000 One Logan Sq Philadelphia PA 19103

ODELL, STUART IRWIN, lawyer; b. Phila., Jan. 1, 1940; s. P. Samuel and Selma Odell; m. Andrea L. Villegas; children—Stuart Irwin Jr., Benjamin Eaton. B.S. in Econ., U. Pa., 1961; LL.B. cum laude, U. Miami, 1964; LL.M., NYU, 1965. Bar: Fla. 1965, Pa. 1966, N.Y. 1982. Assoc., Morgan, Lewis & Bockius, 1966-70, ptnr. 1970—; dir. Gen. Resources Internat., Inc.; chmn. tax sect. Morgan, Lewis & Backus; lectr. law NYU, 1965-66, adj. prof. law, 1969-80; adj. lectr. Temple U. Law Sch., 1972. Recipient Harry J. Rudick award NYU. Mem. ABA, N.Y. State Bar Assn., Fla. Bar Assn. Club: Union League. Assoc. editor U. Miami Law Rev., 1963-64. Corporate taxation, Contracts commercial, Private international. Home: 5 Riverside Dr New York NY 10023 Office: Morgan Lewis & Bockius 101 Park Ave New York NY 10178

ODEN, WALDO TALMAGE, JR., lawyer; b. Altus, Okla., May 17, 1929; s. Waldo Talmage and Lily Juanita (Clark) O.; m. Rebecca Jane Hazlitt, Mar. 25, 1951; children: Waldo Talmage, Timothy Patrick, Amy Germaine Lindley, Jonathan Andrew. BA, U. Okla., 1950, LLB, 1952, JD, 1970. Bar: Okla. 1952, U.S. Supreme Ct. 1960. Sole practice, Altus, 1952—; mem. Robinson & Oden, 1952-53, Oden & Oden, 1954-67, 70-81; mng. ptnr. Oden Oden & Derryberry, 1967-70; asst. atty. Jackson County, 1953-54; dir. Farmers & Mchts. Bank; instr. bus. law Western Okla. State Coll., 1956-59; instr. criminology Altus AFB, 1958; instr. masters degree program Webster Coll., Altus AFB, 1975—; mem. Okla. Jud. Nominating Commn., 1967-71; lectr. agrl. law. County dir. Jackson County CD, 1959-68; chmn. Kicking Bird dist. Boy Scouts Am., 1969-78; del. Meth. Jurisdictional Confs., Meth. Gen. Confs.; lay leader Clinton Dist. of Okla. Conf. of United Meth. Ch., 1982—; dir. Gen. Bd. of Global Ministries, United Meth. Ch., 1984—; sec. exec. com. Meth. Series of Protestant Hour, 1968-72; chmn. dept. communications and pub. relations Okla. United Meth. Conf., 1976—; mem. United Meth. Nat. Bd. Higher Edn. and Ministry, 1980—; mem. exec. com. W.W. and Rosa Woodworth Estate; pres. U. Okla. Wesley Found., 1947, Okla. Meth. Student Movement, 1948; mem. Okla. Humanities Com., 1976-79; campaign chmn. Jackson County Dem. Com., 1954-60; trustee Altus Library Bd., 1965-72; chmn. Okla. Bar Assn. Task Force on Farm Crisis, 1985—. Mem. ABA (chmn. agrl. law com. gen. practice sect. 1976-84, sec. gen. practice sect. council 1982-83), Okla. Bar Assn. (chmn. gen. practice sect.), Jackson County Bar Assn., Assn. Trial Lawyers Am., Okla. Trial Lawyers Assn., Phi Delta Phi. Club: Masons, Rotary (pres. 1959-60). Mem. staff Okla. Law Rev., 1950-52. Probate, Real property, Consumer commercial. Home: 913 E Elm St Altus OK 73521 Office: PO Drawer J 209 N Hudson St Altus OK 73521

ODER, KENNETH WILLIAM, lawyer; b. Newport News, Va., July 9, 1947; s. Thomas William and Joy Reletta (McNeil) O.; m. Lucinda Ann Fox, July 20, 1969; children: Joshua, Devon, Chelsea. BA, U. Va., 1969, JD, 1975. Bar: Calif. 1975, U.S. Dist. Ct. (cen. dist.) Calif. 1975, U.S. Dist. Ct. (so. and no. dists.) Calif. 1977, U.S. Ct. Appeals (9th cir.) 1977, D.C. 1979. Assoc. Latham & Watkins, Los Angeles, 1975-77, 79-82, ptnr., 1982—; assoc. Latham & Watkins, Washington, 1978-79. Exec. editor U. Va. Law Rev., 1973-74. Coach San Marino Little League, Calif., 1983—, Am. Youth Soccer Orgn., Rosemeade, Calif., 1984—. Mem. Calif. Bar Assn. (employment law sect.), Los Angeles County Bar Assn., D.C. Bar Assn. Republican. Methodist. Avocations: jogging, hiking, fishing. Labor, Federal civil litigation, State civil litigation. Office: Latham & Watkins 555 S Flower St Los Angeles CA 90071

ODIORNE, JAMES THOMAS, lawyer, accountant; b. Austin, Tex., Mar. 9, 1947; s. Thomas King and Mary Ann (McInnis) O.; m. Alice Bell Soulek, Apr. 26, 1980; children—James Michael, Raymond Andrew. B.B.A., U. Tex.-Austin, 1969; J.D., Baylor U., 1973. Bar: Tex. 1973; C.P.A., Tex. Atty., acct. Bastrop, Tex., 1974-83; atty. Tex. State Bd. Ins., Austin, 1983-85, statutory liquidator and receiver, 1985—, statutory ins. liquidator, 1985—. Candidate for Sheriff Bastrop County, Tex., 1974, for County Judge Bastrop County, 1978; chmn. Bastrop County ARC, 1977. Mem. Bastrop County Bar Assn. (past sec.). Democrat. Methodist. Club: Kiwanis. Administrative and regulatory, Real property, Family and matrimonial. Home: Route 1 Box 408 Cedar Creek TX 78612 Office: Tex State Bd Ins Liquidation Div 7901 Cameron Rd Bldg 1 Austin TX 78753

ODOM, ELIZABETH ANN, lawyer; b. Lawrenceburg, Tenn., Dec. 14, 1949; d. Chester C. and Elizabeth Carolyn (Wesson) B.; m. Terry William Odom, June 13, 1971; children: William Andrew, Elizabeth Ruth, Gregory Thomas. Student, Middle Tenn. State U., 1967-70; BA, Memphis State U., 1970, JD, 1976. Bar: Miss. 1976, U.S. Dist. Ct. (no. dist.) Miss. 1977. Spl. edn. tchr. Lawrence (Tenn.) County Schs., 1971; social worker Tenn. Dept. Pub. Welfare, Memphis, 1971-73; taxpayer asst. IRS, Memphis, 1975; assoc. Patterson & Patterson, Aberdeen, Miss., 1976-79; sole practice Amory, 1979—; corp. counselor Magnolia State Ry., Amory, 1984—; bd. dirs. Haughton Place, Amory, 1980—. Chmn. Memphis State U. Law Day, 1976; justice Memphis State U. Moot Ct. Bd., 1975-76. Mem. ABA, Miss. Bar Assn., Monroe County Bar Assn., Am. Diabetes Assn. (chmn. bd. dirs. Miss. 1983-85, v.p. 1985—, nat. govt. relations com. 1986—, Outstanding Service Vol. 1986). Mem. Ch. of Christ. Club: Fidelia (Amory) (v.p. 1985—). Avocations: contract and duplicate bridge. Family and matrimonial, Real property, General practice. Home and Office: Rt 1 Box 321 Aberdeen MS 39730

O'DONNELL, HUGH DAVID, lawyer, educator; b. Ft. Lauderdale, Fla., May 5, 1955; s. James Edward and Martha Jean (Leavitt) O'D. BS, James Madison U., 1978; JD, George Mason U., 1981. Bar: Va. 1981, U.S. Ct. Appeals (4th cir.) 1982, U.S. Dist. Ct. (ea. and we. dists.) 1982. Sole practice Harrisonburg, Va., 1981-83; ptnr. Green & O'Donnell, Harrisonburg, 1983—; lectr., instr. polit. sci. James Madison U., Harrisonburg, 1984—. Pres. Lambda Sigma House Corp., James Madison U., 1982—. Mem. ABA, Assn. Trial Lawyers Am. Lodge: Elks. Consumer commercial, Personal injury, State civil litigation. Office: 245 N Liberty St PO Box 512 Harrisonburg VA 22801

O'DONNELL, JOHN JAMES, lawyer; b. White Plains, N.Y., Feb. 14, 1946; s. Hubert Bernard and Loretta Ann (Schmidt) O'D.; m. Francoise Dominique Joubert, Dec. 3, 1972; children: Sarah, Julia. BBA, U. Notre Dame, 1968; JD, NYU, 1971; LLM in Tax, Boston U., 1979. Bar: N.Y. 1972, Mass. 1975, U.S. Dist. Ct. Mass. 1975, Wash. 1979, U.S. Dist. Ct. (we. dist.) Wash. 1979. Tax supr. Ernst & Whinney, Boston, 1973-78; ptnr. Karr, Tuttle, Koch, Campbell, Mawer, Morrow & Sax, Seattle 1979—; faculty Golden Gate U., Seattle, Wash. Acctg. Seminars, Bellevue. Contbr. articles to profl. jours. Bd. dirs. Seattle-Nantes Sister City Assn., Seattle, 1986. Served with USN, 1971-73, Vietnam. Mem. Wash. State Bar Assn., Seattle King County Bar Assn., Seattle Estate Planning Council, Am. Assn. CPA's, Wash. Soc. CPA's. Clubs: City, Seattle. Avocations: squash, soccer. Corporate taxation, State and local taxation, Estate taxation. Office: Karr Tuttle et al 1111 3d Ave Suite 2500 Seattle WA 98101

O'DONNELL, MICHAEL LAWRENCE, lawyer; b. Chgo., Oct. 12, 1954; s. Lawrence James and Alice (Claire) O'D.; m. A. Brett Long, Dec. 22, 1979; children: Conor Lyons, Devon Kathleen. BA, U. Notre Dame, 1976; JD, U. Denver, 1979. Bar: Colo. 1980, U.S. Dist. Ct. Colo. 1980, U.S. Ct. Appeals (10th cir.) 1980. Ptnr. White and Steele, P.C., Denver, 1980—. Bd. dirs. Denver Met. Heart Assn., 1986. Mem. ABA (chmn. issues affecting legal profession com. young lawyers div. 1982-84, liason to standing com. on profl. discipline 1985—), Colo. Bar Assn., Denver Bar Assn. Democrat. Roman Catholic. Avocations: racquet sports, football, softball, travel, reading. Insurance, Federal civil litigation, State civil litigation. Home: 4081 S Cherry St Englewood CO 80110 Office: White and Steele PC 1120 Lincoln St #1400 Denver CO 80203-2112

O'DONNELL, PAUL EUGENE, JR., lawyer; b. Atlanta, Sept. 27, 1937; s. Paul E. and Annie Elizabeth (Boynton) O'D.; m. Mary Anne McShain, June 4, 1966; children—Mark C., Kevin H., Heather E. B.Ch.E., Ga. Inst. Tech., 1960; J.D., Georgetown U., 1964. Bar: D.C., 1965, N.Y., 1968. Patent agt. and atty. E.I. DuPont de Nemours & Co., Inc., Washington, 1960-64, Wilmington, Del., 1964-65; law clk. U.S. dist. ct. D.C., 1965-66, U.S. Ct. Cust. & Pat. Apls., Washington, 1966-67; practice in N.Y.C., 1967-76; pat. and trademark csl. Nabisco, Inc., East Hanover, N.J., 1976-80; ptnr. Vogt & O'Donnell, White Plains, N.Y., 1981—. Served to 1st lt. USAR, 1968. Mem. ABA, N.J. Patent Law Assn., Am. Intellectual Property Law Assn., N.Y. Patent Trademark and Copyright Law Assn., Republican. Roman Catholic. Patent, Trademark and copyright, Federal civil litigation. Home: 81 Lake Dr Mountain Lakes NJ 07046 Office: 707 Westchester Ave White Plains NY 10604

O'DONNELL, PIERCE HENRY, lawyer; b. Troy, N.Y., Mar. 5, 1947; s. Harry J. and Mary (Kane) O'D.; m. Connie Casey, June 28, 1970; children: Meghan Maureen, Brendan Casey. BA, Georgetown U., 1969, LLD, 1972; LLM, Yale U., 1975. Bar: D.C. 1973, U.S. Supreme Ct. 1975, Calif. 1978. Assoc. Williams & Connolly, Washington, 1975-78; ptnr. Beardlsey, Hufstedler & Kemble, Los Angeles, 1978-81, Beardsley, Miller, Carlson & Beardsley, Los Angeles, 1981-82, O'Donnell & Gordon, Los Angeles, 1982—; exec. asst. U.S. Sec. Edn., 1979; spl. counsel Commn. Judicial Performance, San Francisco, 1979; chmn. Nat. Media, Inc., 1984—. Contbr. articles to profl. jours. vice chmn. Friends of the Calif. Tech. U., 1983-84; chmn. Verduga-San Rafael Urban Mountain Park Fund, 1980-84; active Los Angeles World Affairs Council, Los Angeles Com. on Fgn. Relations; bd. dirs. Friends of the Altadena Library, 1979-81, Foothil Family Service 1979-85, chmn., 1984-85, Pasadena-Foothill Urban League, Rossi Youth Interfaith Ctr. to Reverse the Arms Law, 1984—. Mem. NAACP, Sierra Club, Am. Law Inst. Democrat. Roman Catholic. Clubs: University (Los Angeles), Gridiron (Georgetown U.). Federal civil litigation, Environment, Criminal.

O'DONNELL, ROBERT HARRY, lawyer; b. Phila., June 15, 1948; s. Robert Charles and Eunice (Gibbs) O'D.; m. Mary Bootle, June 24, 1972; children: Elizabeth Gibbs, Robert Charles II. BS in Edn., U. S.C., 1970, JD, 1973. Bar: S.C. 1974, U.S. Dist. Ct. S.C. 1974, U.S. Ct. Appeals (4th cir.)

1974. Ptnr. Schneider & O'Donnell P.A., Georgetown, S.C., 1974—; mcpl. judge City of Georgetown, S.C., 1975—. Served to ensign JAGC S.C. Militia, 1970-76. Mem. ABA, S.C. Bar Assn., Am. Judicature Soc., S.C. Trial Lawyers Assn. Presbyterian. Lodges: Rotary, Masons (treas.). State civil litigation, Probate, Real property. Home: 118 Queen St Georgetown SC 29440 Office: Schneider & O'Donnell 601 Front St Georgetown SC 29442

O'DONNELL, ROBERT JOHN, lawyer; b. Worcester, Mass., Aug. 3, 1943; s. Joseph C. and Nellie (Balrukaitis) O'D.; m. Joyce I. Thomas, June 30, 1969 (div. Feb. 1984); children: Gary T., Shaun K. BS in Bus. Adminstrn., U. Calif., Berkeley, 1965; JD, Boston Coll. Law, 1969; cert., Coro Found., San Francisco, 1969. Bar: Vt. 1970, U.S. Dist. Ct. Vt. 1970. Sole practice Woodstock, Vt., 1970—; adj. faculty Coll. Edn. and Social Services U. Vt.-Burlington, 1986—, Woodbury Coll., Montpelier, Vt., 1986—. Intern San Francisco Neighborhood Legal Assistance Found., 1967; assoc. Harvard Legal Aid bur., 1967-68; founding dir., pres. Boston Coll. Legal Assistance Bur., 1968-69; justice peace Windsor County, 1979; mem. planning commn. Town of Pomfret, Vt., 1980—, grand juror, 1985—; mem. council Episcopal Diocese of Vt., 1982-86; sch. dir. Woodstock Union High Sch., 1983—; bd. dirs. ARC Cen. Vt. chpt., 1983—; lay reader, vestryman St. James Episc. Ch., Woodstock, 1985—; chmn., pres. Nat. Ctr. for Collaborative Planning and Community Services, Inc.; sr. mediator Pvt. Peace-Mediation Services, Woodstock, 1985—. Mem. Vt. Bar Assn. (fee arbitration com. 1974-80), Windsor COunty Bar Assn. (pres.), Vt. Mediators Assn. (steering com. 1986—), N.H. Mediators Assn., Soc. for Profl. in Dispute Resolution, Assn. of Family and Conciliation Cts. Republican. Avocation: sailing. General practice, Mediation, Environment. Home: Donegal On the Stage Rd South Pomfret VT 05067 Office: 5 the Green Woodstock VT 05091

O'DONNELL, THOMAS PATRICK, lawyer, educator; b. St. Louis, Oct. 14, 1941; s. John James and Gertrude (Hamm) O'D. B.A., U. Mo.-Columbia, 1968, M.A., 1969, J.D., 1974. Bar: Mo. 1975, Ind. 1977, U.S. Dist. Ct. (we. dist.) Mo. 1975, U.S. Ct. Appeals 8th cir. 1982. Instr. Stephens Coll., Columbia, Mo., 1969-74; atty., prin. Larrimer & O'Donnell, Columbia, 1975-76; atty. Nat. Ctr. for Law and The Handicapped, South Bend, Ind., 1976-78; sr. atty. Legal Aid of Western Mo., Kansas City, 1978-80; project rev. dir. Mid-Am. Health Systems, Agy., Kansas City, 1981-82; adminstr. Providence, St. Margaret Health Ctr., Kansas City, 1982-83; atty. Mitchell, Kristl & Lieber, Kansas City, 1983—; cons. Kemp & Young, Inc., Kansas City, Kans., 1980-81; legal cons. Mo. Protection and Advocacy Services, Jefferson City, 1979-85. Pres. United Cerebral Palsy Assn., Kansas City, 1983-86, bd. dirs., 1982-86; cons. bd. dirs. Coll. Meadows Psychiat. Hosp., 1986—. U. Mo. Curators scholar, 1967, grad. fellow, 1968. Mem. ABA, Health Forum Com., Am. Soc. Law and Medicine, Nat. Health Lawyers Assn., ABA, (anti-trust com.), Phi Beta Kappa. Roman Catholic. Health, Antitrust, Administrative and regulatory. Office: Mitchell Kristl & Lieber PC 1220 Washington 3d Floor Kansas City MO 64105

O'DONNELL, WILLIAM KENNETH, lawyer; b. Glasgow, Scotland, July 29, 1946; came to U.S., 1953; s. Thomas and Margaret Dallas (Leitch) O'D.; m. Nancy E. Reynolds, Aug. 23, 1969 (div. Aug. 1978); 1 child, Thomas Howard; m. Janice Linda Olivo, Dec. 14, 1979; 1 child, Kerri Lynn. BS, Boston Coll., 1969; JD, Suffolk U., 1973. Bar: Mass. 1973, R.I. 1975, U.S. Dist. Ct. Mass. 1975, U.S. Dist. Ct. R.I. 1975, U.S. Supreme Ct. 1982. Staff auditor Price Waterhouse, Providence, 1973-75; spl. asst. atty. gen. Atty. Gen. R.I., Providence, 1975-78; assoc. Coffey, McGovern et.al., Providence, 1978-83; ptnr. D'Agostino & O'Donnell, Providence, 1983—; bd. dirs. Par Mfg., Inc., Providence, J. Callahan Engring., Middletown, Newport (R.I.) Navigation Co., Inc. Mem. ABA, Assn. Trial Lawyers Am., R.I. Bar Assn. Democrat. Roman Catholic. Club: Wannamoisett Country (East Providence, R.I.). Lodge: KC. Avocations: golf, bridge, reading, collecting, trivia. Personal injury, Criminal, Family and matrimonial. Office: D'Agostino & O'Donnell 1340 N Main St Providence RI 02904

O'DORISIO, JOHN WILLIAM, JR., lawyer; b. Denver, July 8, 1953; s. John William Sr. and Nancy Lou (Kennedy) O'D.; m. Pamela Dawn Jaragoske, Aug. 11, 1972; children: Daunine R., John William III, Joel E. BS in Bus. Adminstrn., U. Denver, 1974, JD, 1976. Bar: Colo. 1976, U.S. Dist. Ct. Colo. 1976. Appraiser People's Mortgage Co., Aurora, Colo., 1972-75; ptnr. Robinson, Waters, O'Dorisio & Rapson P.C., Denver, 1976—, also bd. dirs.; bd. dirs. Columbine Valley Bank & Trust, Littleton, Colo., 1983-85. Mem. ABA, Colo. Bar Assn., Denver Bar Assn. Republican. Club: Lakewood (Colo.) Country. Avocations: golf, tennis, coin collecting. Real property, General corporate. Home: 13867 West Cedar Ave Cherry Hills Village CO 80110 Office: Robinson Waters O'Dorisio & Rapson PC 1640 Grant St Denver CO 80203

O'DWYER, BRIAN, lawyer, educator; b. N.Y.C., Oct. 10, 1945; s. Paul and Kathleen (Rohan) O.; m. Marianna Page, Sept. 7, 1968; children—Brendan, Kathleen. A.B., George Washington U., 1967, LL.M., 1976; M.A., Middlebury Coll., 1968, J.D., Georgetown U., 1971. Bar: N.Y. 1972, U.S. Dist Ct. (so. ea. and no. dists.) N.Y. 1973, U.S. Ct. Appeals (2d cir.) 1975, U.S. Supreme Ct. 1983. Atty. NLRB, Newark, 1972-73, N.Y. State Labor Bd., 1973-74; mng. ptnr. O'Dwyer & Bernstein, N.Y.C., 1974—; dir. Queens Outreach, Queens, N.Y., 1983—; dir.-gen. counsel Malcom King Coll., 1980—; gen. counsel Kappa Sigma Frat. Charlottesville, Va., 1983—. Mem. ABA, Nat. Assn. Coll. and Univ. Attys., Brehon Law Soc. Democrat. Roman Catholic. Club: Downtown Athletic (N.Y.C.). Federal civil litigation, Labor, Pension, profit-sharing, and employee benefits. Home: 350 Central Park W New York NY 10025 Office: O'Dwyer & Bernstein 99 Wall St New York NY 10005

ODZA, RANDALL M., lawyer; b. Schnectady, May 6, 1942; s. Mitchell and Grace (Mannes) O.; m. Rita Ginness, June 19, 1966; children—Kenneth, Keith. B.S. in Indsl. and Labor Relations, Cornell U., 1964, LL.B., 1967. Bar: N.Y. 1967, U.S. Ct. Appeals (2d cir.) 1970, U.S. Dist. Ct. (so. and ea. dists.) N.Y. 1969, U.S. Dist. Ct. (we. dist.) N.Y. 1970. Assoc. Proskauer, Rose, Goetz & Mandelsohn, N.Y.C., 1967-69; assoc. Jaeckle, Fleischmann & Mugel, Buffalo, 1969-72, ptnr., 1972—. Trustee, legal counsel, treas. Temple Beth Am. Recipient Honor award Western N.Y. Retail Mchts. Assn., 1980. Mem. Indsl. Relations Research Assn. Western N.Y., ABA, Erie County Bar Assn., N.Y. State Bar Assn. Labor. Office: Jaeckle Fleischmann & Mugel Norstar Bldg 12 Fountain Plaza Buffalo NY 14202

OESTREICHER, MICHAEL ROBERT, lawyer; b. Cin., June 20, 1950; s. Robert Leopold Oestreicher and Ruth (Kraus) Lowenthal; m. Diane Mary Reif, Oct. 4, 1981; children: Robert Alan, David Jonathan. AB, Miami U., Oxford, Ohio, 1972; JD, Boston U., 1975. Bar: N.Y. 1976, U.S. Dist. Ct. (so. dist.) N.Y. 1976, Ohio 1978. Assoc. Haight, Gardner, Poor & Havens, N.Y.C., 1975-78; assoc. Strauss, Troy & Ruehlmann, Cin., 1978-81, ptnr., 1981-84; sole practice Cin., 1984-86; ptnr. Smith & Schnacke, Cin., 1986—. U.S. Rep. Canton of Neuchatel, Switzerland, 1982—. Mem. Internat. Bar Assn., ABA, Cin. Bar Assn. (chmn. internat. law com.), Asia-Pacific Lawyers Assn. Private international, General corporate. Office: Smith & Schnacke 511 Walnut 2900 Dubois Tower Cincinnati OH 45202-3163

OETTINGER, MARK DAVID, lawyer; b. Schenectady, N.Y., June 3, 1955; s. Walter Hans and Hanni Elizabeth (Frutiger) O.; BA, Dartmouth Coll., 1975; JD, Albany Law Sch., 1980. Bar: Vt. 1981, U.S. Dist. Ct. Vt. 1981. Jud. clk. to chief justice Vt. Supreme Ct., Montpelier, 1980-81; assoc. Robert J. O'Donnell, Woodstock, Vt., 1981-82, Bloomberg & Assocs., Burlington, 1982-86 Bloomberg & Oettinger, 1987— ; instr. bus. law Champlain Coll., Burlington, Vt., 1986—; chief auditor East Barnard (Vt.) Coop. Soc. Inc., 1980-82. Author newspaper column Vt. Standard 1976-77; author/editor Albany Law Rev., 1979-80. Sr. nat. ski patrolman Nat. Ski Patrol, 1984—; ski patrolman Sonnenberg Ski Area, Barnard, Vt., 1973—, patrol dir. 1975-77, 1985-87. Mem. Vt. Bar Assn. (author Jour. first prize 1st Annual Vt. Bar Assn. writing competition 1984), Assn. Trial Lawyers Am. Club: Vt. Bridge Assn. (pres. 1984-85). General corporate, Criminal, Family and matrimonial. Home: 18 Southwind Dr Burlington VT 05401 Office: Bloomberg & Oettinger 200 Battery St Burlington VT 05401

OFFER, STUART JAY, lawyer; b. Seattle, June 2, 1943; m. Judith Spitzer, Aug. 29, 1970; children: Rebecca, Kathryn. BA, U. Wash., 1964; LLB, Columbia U., 1967. Bar: D.C. 1968, U.S. Tax Ct. 1968, Calif. 1972. Atty., advisor U.S. Tax Ct., Washington, 1967-68; assoc. Morrison & Foerster, San Francisco, 1972-76, ptnr., 1976—. Mem. San Francisco Dir.'s Adv. Com. 1985. Served as capt. U.S. Army, 1968-72. Mem. ABA (vice chmn. taxation sect. 1987—, corp. tax com.), Internat. Fiscal Assn., Western Pension Conf. (steering com. San Francisco chpt. 1985—). Corporate taxation, Pension, profit-sharing, and employee benefits, Private international. Office: Morrison & Foerster 345 California St San Francisco CA 94104-2105

OFFICE, JAMES RICHARD, lawyer; b. Dayton, Ohio, May 12, 1955; s. Philip A. and Alaine (Ettlinger) O.; m. Jan Tremaine, Aug. 31, 1980; 1 child Lauren M. BS in Bus., Ind. U., 1977; JD, U. Dayton, 1980. Bar: Ill. 1980, Ohio 1982, U.S. Tax Ct. 1982, U.S. Dist. Ct. (so. dist.) Ohio 1983. Tax specialist Altschuler, Melvoin & Glasser, CPAs, Chgo., 1980-81; atty. Robins, Preston & Beckett, Co., LPA, Columbus, Ohio, 1981—. Trustee Happy Hearts Found., Columbus, 1984-87, Laser Med. Research Found., Columbus, 1985—; mem. citizen's adv. bd. Columbus Devel. Ctr., 1987—. Mem. ABA, Ohio Bar Assn. (tax com., health law com.), Ohio State Bar Assn. Col., Columbus Bar Assn., Cen. Region IRS (bar liaison com.). Republican. Jewish. Club: Capital (Columbus). Lodge: Lions. Personal income taxation, General corporate, Health. Home: 5232 Bandon Ct Columbus OH 43220 Office: Robins Preston & Beckett Co LPA 1328 Dublin Rd Columbus OH 43215-1090

OFFNER, ERIC DELMONTE, lawyer; b. Vienna, Austria, June 23, 1928; came to U.S., 1941, naturalized, 1949; s. Sigmund J. and Kathe (Delmonte) O.; m. Julie Cousins, 1955 (dec. 1959); m. Barbara Ann Shotton, July 2, 1961; 1 son, Gary Douglas; m. Carol Sue Marcus, Jan. 12, 1980 (dec. 1983). B.B.A., CCNY, 1949; LL.B. in Internat. Affairs, Cornell U., 1952. Bar: N.Y. 1952. Assoc. Langner, Parry, Card & Langner, N.Y.C., 1952-57; ptnr. Haseltine, Lake, Waters & Offner, N.Y.C., 1957-77; sr. ptnr. Offner & Kuhn, 1978-83; instr. George Washington U. Law Sch., Cornell U. Law Sch.; spl. prof. law Hofstra Law Sch., Cornell Law Sch., 1979. Author: International Trademark Protection, 1964, Japanese edit., 1977, International Trademark Service, Vols. I-III 1970, Vol. IV, 1972, Vol. V., 1973, Vol. VI, 1976, Vol. VII, 1981, Vols. I-VII, 2d edit., 1981, Legal Training Course on Trademarks, 1982; contbr. articles to profl. jours.; editor-in-chief: Cornell Law Forum, 1950-51; editorial bd.: Trademark Reporter, 1961-64, 69-72. Vice pres. Riverdale Mental Health Clinic, N.Y.C., 1966-67; pres. Riverdale Mental Health Assn., 1967-69, Ethical Culture Soc., Riverdale-Yonkers, 1964-67, Ethical Cultural Retirement Ctr., 1975—; trustee Am. Ethical Union, 1967-73. Mem. N.Y. Patent Law Assn. (assoc. editor Bull. 1961-66, gov. 1973-76), ABA, City N.Y. Bar Assn. (sec. 1962-64), U.S. Trademark Assn., World Peace Through Law (charter), Trademark Soc. Washington (charter), Inst. Trade Mark Agts. (London), Australian Patent Inst., Internat. Assn. Protection Indsl. Property, Nat. Council Patent Law Assn., Internat. Patent, Trademark Assn., Phi Alpha Delta. Trademark and copyright, Private international. Home: 20 Joy Dr Manhassat Hills NY 11040 Office: 1412 Broadway New York NY 10018

OFFRET, RONALD (ALVIN), lawyer; b. Los Angeles, Dec. 8, 1944; s. Alvin Joseph and Elaine (Houston) O.; m. Kathleen Bradley, Feb. 20, 1974; children: Rebecca Ann, Craig Ronald, Elizabeth Kathleen, Amy Patricia, Nicole Marie. BA in Acctg., Internat. Bus., U. Wash., 1970; JD, Lewis and Clark Coll., 1973; LLM, Boston U., 1974. Bar: Alaska 1974, U.S. Dist. Ct. Alaska 1974, U.S. Tax Ct. 1980, Utah 1981, U.S. Ct. Appeals (9th cir.) 1986. Assoc E.P. Boyko Assocs. P.C., Anchorage, 1974-76, ptnr., 1976-78; ptnr. Aglietti, Offret & Pennington, Anchorage, 1978-81; sole practice Salt Lake City, 1981-84; ptnr. Aglietti, Pennington & Rodey, Anchorage, 1984—. Mem. ABA, Assn. Trial Lawyers Am. Mormon. Personal injury, Personal income taxation, State civil litigation. Office: Aglietti Pennington & Rodey 733 W 4th Ave Suite 206 Anchorage AK 99501

O'FLAHERTY, DANIEL FAIRFAX, judge; b. Washington, June 26, 1925; s. Daniel and Isabel (Boyer) O'F.; m. Resa Hutt, July 15, 1950; children—D.F., Susan H., M. Lucelle. J.D., George Washington U., 1949; postgrad. Am. Acad. Jud. Edn., 1974, Nat. Jud. Coll., 1975-80, 1982-83. Bar: Va. 1949. Sole practice, 1949-73; substitute judge Alexandria (Va.) Civil and Police Ct., 1956-67; judge Alexandria Mcpl. Ct., 1967-70, sr., 1970-73; chief judge Alexandria Gen. Dist. Ct., 1973—. Mem. Alexandria City Council, 1953-55. Served with USAAF, 1944-45. Mem. Va. Bar, Va. Bar Assn., Am. Judges Assn., ABA. Democrat. Methodist. Home: 103 Summers Dr Alexandria VA 22301 Office: 520 King St Courthouse Alexandria VA 22314

O'FLAHERTY, PAUL BENEDICT, lawyer; b. Chgo., Feb. 11, 1925; s. Benedict Joseph and Margaret Celestine (Harrington) O'F.; m. Catherine Margaret Bigley, Feb. 13, 1954; children—Paul Benedict, Michael, Kathleen, Ann, Neil. J.D. cum laude, Loyola U., Chgo., 1949. Bar: Ill. 1949, U.S. Dist. Ct. (no. dist.) Ill. 1949, U.S. Ct. Appeals (7th cir.) 1956, U.S. Supreme Ct. 1959. Ptnr. Madden, Meccia, O'Flaherty & Freeman, Chgo., 1949-56; ptnr. Groble, O'Flaherty & Hayes, Chgo., 1956-63, Schiff Hardin & Waite, Chgo., 1963—; mem. adj. faculty Loyola U., 1959-65. Author: (with others) Illinois Estate Administration, 1983; contbr. articles to profl. jours. Bd. advisors Catholic Charities, Chgo., 1979—; trustee Clarke Coll., Dubuque, Iowa, 1982—. Served to 2d lt. U.S. Army, 1943-46. Fellow Am. Coll. Probate Counsel; mem. ABA, Ill. Bar Assn. (past chmn. fed. taxation sect. council), Chgo. Bar Assn. (past chmn. trust law com.), Chgo. Estate Planning Council. Clubs: Union League, Metropolitan (Chgo.). Estate planning, Probate, Estate taxation. Office: Schiff Hardin & Waite 7200 Sears Tower Chicago IL 60606

O'FLARITY, JAMES P., lawyer; b. Yazoo City, Miss., Oct. 15, 1923. B.S., Millsaps Coll., 1950; postgrad., Jackson Sch. Law, 1948, 53-54; J.D., U. Fla., 1965. Bar: Miss. 1954, U.S. Dist. Ct. (so. dist.) Miss. 1954, U.S. Supreme Ct. 1957, U.S. Ct. Mil. Appeals 1957, U.S. Ct. Appeals (5th Cir.) 1957, Fla. 1966, U.S. Dist. Ct. (so. and mid. dists.) Fla. 1966, U.S. Dist. Ct. (no. dist.) Fla. 1967, U.S. Ct. Appeals (11th cir.) 1981. Assoc. law firm Cone, Owen, Wagner, Nugent & Johnson, West Palm Beach, Fla., 1966-69; sole practice law Palm Beach, Fla., 1969—; mem. nat. panel arbitrators Am. Arbitration Assn., 1967—; mem. Supreme Ct. Matrimonial Law Commn. Fla., 1982—, procedure B com., 1982—; lectr. on marital and family la; observer family ct. proc. Nat. Jud. Coll., 1983; mem. U. Fla. Law Ctr. Council, 1972-78, mem. legal edn. com., 1973, chmn. membership and fin. com., 1977-78, mem. emeritus, 1978—; leader del. for legal exchange on family law to Ministry of Justice, Peoples Republic of China, 1984. Contbr. articles to profl. publs. Mem. U. Fla. Pres.'s Council; mem. Fla. Family Support Council Adv. Bd., 1976; mem. chmn.'s com. U.S. Senatorial Bus. Adv. Bd., 1980—; col. La. Gov.'s Staff, 1982—; dir. Delegation for Legal Exchange on Family Law to the Ministry of Justice, Peoples Republic China, 1984. Fellow Am. Bar Found. (life), Roscoe Pound-Am. Trial Lawyers Found. (life), Am. Acad. Matrimonial Lawyers (nat. bd. govs. 1977, bd. mgrs. Fla. chpt. 1976—, pres. 1976-80, nat. pres. 1985—, hon. permanent pres. emeritus 1982), Trusler Soc.; mem. Internat. Soc. Family Law, Internat. Bar Assn. (assoc.), Inter-Am. Bar Assn., Am. Law Inst., ABA (chmn. mem. 1972-76, chmn. coms. 1973-75, 78-81, 82-83, editor Family Law Newsletter 1975-77, mem. council family law sect. 1976-85, vice-chmn. sect. 1981-82, chmn. sect. 1983-84, mem. conf. sect. chairmen 1982-85, mem. adv. bd. jour. 1978-80), Assn. Trial Lawyers Am. (Fla. State committeeman 1973-75, 1st chmn. family law sect. 1971-72, 72-73), Am. Judicature Soc., Am. Soc. Legal History, Supreme Ct. Hist Soc., Fla. Council Bar Assn. Presidents, Fla. Bar Found. (life, exec. dir. screening com. 1976, chmn. projects com. 1976-77, asst. sect. 1973-79, dir. 1977-81), U. Fla. Law Ctr. Assn. (life), Acad Fla. Trial Lawyers (dir. 1974-77, coll. diplomates 1977), Fla. Bar Assn. (exec. council 1973-84, sec.-treas. family law sect. 1973-74, chmn. sect. 1974-75, 75-76, guest editor spl. issue jour. 1978, chmn. jour. and news editorial bd. 1978-79, mem. bd. cert., designation and advt. 1982—), Palm Beach County Bar Assn. (circuit ct. civil adv. com. 1981, mem. circuit ct. juvenile domestic relations adv. com. 1971-80, 81-83, adv. com. chmn. 1974-78), Solicitor's Family Law Assn. (Eng.), Phi Alpha Delta (life), Sigma Delta Kappa. Family and matrimonial, State civil litigation. Home: 908 Country Club Dr North Palm Beach FL 33408 Office: 215 5th St Suite 108 West Palm Beach FL 33401

O'FLINN, PETER RUSSELL, lawyer; b. Bklyn., Jan. 8, 1953; s. Russell William and Mary (Tavoulareus) O'F.; m. Kathleen Tracy, May 28, 1981; children: Peter Andrew, Michael Christopher. BA, Colgate U., 1974; JD, Columbia U., 1977. Bar: N.Y. 1978. Assoc. Dewey, Ballantine, Bushby, Palmer & Wood, N.Y.C., 1977-81; assoc. LeBoeuf, Lamb, Leiby & MacRae, N.Y.C., 1982-85, ptnr., 1986—. Securities, General corporate, Insurance. Office: LeBoeuf Lamb Leiby & MacRae 520 Madison Ave New York NY 10022

OFNER, WILLIAM BERNARD, lawyer; b. Los Angeles, Aug. 24, 1929; s. Harry D. and Gertrude (Skoss) Offner; m. Florence Ila Maxwell, Apr. 13, 1953 (div. 1956). A.A., Los Angeles City Coll., 1949; B.A., Calif. State U., Los Angeles, 1953; LL.B., Loyola U., Los Angeles, 1965; postgrad. Sorbonne, 1951, U. So. Calif., 1966. Bar: Calif. 1966, U.S. Dist. Ct. Calif. 1966, U.S. Supreme Ct. 1972. Assoc., Thomas Moore and Assocs., Los Angeles, 1967-69; sole practice, Los Angeles, 1969-70, 74—; assoc. Peter Lam, Los Angeles, 1981-86; assoc. C.M. Coronel, 1986—; lectr. Van Norman U., 1975. Served with USNR, 1947-54. Mem. Inst. Gen. Semantics, Inst. for Antiquity and Christianity, Shakespeare Soc. (bd. dirs. 1987). Democrat. Jewish. Clubs: Los Angeles Athletic Roadrunners, Soc. of Judgement, Toastmasters. Avocations: water color painting, photography, linguistics. Probate, Family and matrimonial, Jurisprudence. Home: 105 E Stocker St Glendale CA 91207 Office: 1102 Brand N Blvd #24 Glendale CA 91202

O'GARA, JAMES VINCENT, lawyer; b. Rockville Centre, N.Y., July 30, 1953; s. James Vincent and Marguerite (Rohmer), O'G; m. Elizabeth Ann Pavel, Apr. 8, 1979; children: Maureen Bevin, Michael James. BA, Fairfield U., 1975; JD, N.Y. Law Sch., 1979. Bar: N.Y. 1979, U.S. Dist. (so., ea., we. and no. dists.) 1979. Assoc. Bleakley, Platt, Schmidt & Fritz, N.Y.C, 1979-81, Patterson, Belknap, Webb & Tyler, N.Y.C., 1981-83, Kelley, Drye & Warren, N.Y.C., 1983—. Mem. Fed. Bar Counsel, N.Y. State Bar Assn., Nassau County Bar Assn., N.Y. County Lawyers. Personal injury, Insurance, Federal civil litigation. Office: 101 Park Ave New York NY 10178

OGBURN, ROBERT WILSON, judge; b. Detroit, Dec. 2, 1937; s. Wilson and Dorothy Edith (Hicks) O.; m. Ann Elizabeth Parkin, Jan. 27, 1962; children—Meredith Ann, Bret Wilson, Heather Leigh. A.B., U. Mich., 1959, J.D., 1962. Bar: Ill. 1962, Colo. 1964, U.S. Supreme Ct. 1970. Ptnr., Ouren & Ogburn, Monte Vista, Colo., 1966-68; sole practice, 1969-72; dist. atty. 12th Jud. Dist. Colo., 1970-73; ptnr. Ogburn & Wilder, 1972-76; dist. judge 12th Jud. Dist. Ct. Colo., 1976—, chief judge, 1981—; judge Water Div. 3, 1976—; faculty advisor Nat. Jud. Coll., 1985. Mem. adv. council Title I, Colo. Commn. on Higher Edn., 1968-76; delay reduction com. Colo. Supreme Ct., 1986-87 ; chmn. Monte Vista Centennial Commn., 1982-87 . Served to capt. JAGC, U.S. Army, 1963-66. Mem. San Luis Valley Bar Assn. (pres. 1968-69), Colo. Bar Assn. (bd. govs. 1979-85, v.p. 1983-84), ABA. Episcopalian. Jurisprudence, Judicial administration, Water law. Home: 317 1st Ave Monte Vista CO 81144

OGDEN, HARRY PEOPLES, lawyer; b. Memphis, Jan. 30, 1949; s. Harry K. and Mary (Peoples) O.; m. Amy Inklebarger, Aug. 5, 1972; children: Emily Rebecca, Sarah Ruth, Stephen Robinson. BA, Rhodes Coll. (formerly Southwestern at Memphis), 1971; JD, U. Tenn., 1975. Bar: Tenn. 1976, U.S. Dist. Ct. (we. dist.) Tenn. 1976, U.S. Dist. Ct. (ea. Dist.) Tenn. 1977, U.S. Supreme Ct. 1984, U.S. Ct. Appeals (6th cir.) 1986. Tchr. English, Knoxville City High Schs., Tenn., 1971-73; law clk. to judge western sect. Tenn. Ct. Appeals, Memphis, 1975-76; sole practice, Knoxville, 1977-79; mem., shareholder Egerton, McAfee, Armistead & Davis, P.C., Knoxville, 1980—; participant Tenn. Coll. Trial Advocacy, Knoxville, 1983. Mem. alumni adv. council U. Tenn., Knoxville, 1983—; bd. dirs., officer Goodwill Industries Knoxville, 1978—. Mem. ABA (litigation and econs. of law practice sects.), Tenn. Bar Assn., Knoxville Bar Assn., Def. Research Inst., Tenn. Def. Lawyers, Tenn. Trial Lawyers Assn. Presbyterian. Club: LeConte (Knoxville). Federal civil litigation, State civil litigation, Family and matrimonial. Home: 4704 Simona Rd Knoxville TN 37918 Office: First American Ctr Egerton McAfee Armistead & Davis PC PO Box 2047 Suite 500 Knoxville TN 37901

OGDEN, LEN WILLIS, JR., lawyer; b. Lexington, Ky., Feb. 1, 1949; s. Len Willis and Ellis Edna (Rayborn) O.; m. Ruth Ann Jackson, Aug. 15, 1975; 1 child, Seth Rayborn. BA, U. Va., 1971; JD, U. Louisville, 1974; student, Nat. Coll. Criminal Def. Lawyers and Pub. Defenders, Houston, 1975. Bar: Ky. 1974, U.S. Dist. Ct. (ea. and we. dists.) Ky. 1974, U.S. Ct. Appeals (6th cir.) 1975. Assoc. Frank E. Haddad, Jr., Louisville, Ky., 1974-86; ptnr. Williams, Housman, Sparks & Franklin, Paducah, Ky., 1986—. Mem. ABA, Assn. Trial Lawyers of Am., Nat. Assn. of Criminal Def. Lawyers, Ky. Acad. Justice (pres. 1984), Ky. Bar Assn., Louisville Bar Assn., McCracken County Bar Assn. Democrat. Baptist. Avocations: hunting, fishing, golf. Federal civil litigation, State civil litigation, Criminal. Office: Williams Housman Sparks & Franklin 1700 Kentucky Ave Paducah KY 42001

OGDEN, W. EDWIN, lawyer; b. Reading, Pa., Dec. 2, 1947; s. Walter Emerson and Ruby Lee (Spann) O.; m. Barbara June Grumbach, Aug. 11, 1973; children: Sarah Ellen, Cody Edwin. AB in Polit. Sci., Albright Coll., 1970; JD, U. Pitts., 1973. Bar: Pa. 1973, U.S. Dist. Ct. (ea. dist.) Pa. 1973, U.S. Supreme Ct. 1985. Assoc. Ryan, Russell & McConaghy, Reading, 1973-82, ptnr., 1982—. Asst. treas., bd. dirs. Berks County Vis. Nurse-Home Health Agy., Reading, 1984—. Mem. ABA, Pa. Bar Assn. (editorial staff pub. utility sect. newsletter 1985—), Berks County Bar Assn. (chmn. profl. econs. com. 1984, ad hoc found. com. 1985—)., Endlich Law Club, World Hobie Class Assn., U.S. Yacht Racing Union (commodore Hobie fleet 176, 1983—). Republican. Lodge: Masons. Avocations: sailing, karate, woodworking. Administrative and regulatory, General corporate, Public utilities. Home: 109 E 36th St Reading PA 19606 Office: Ryan Russell & McConaghy 530 Penn Sq Ctr Reading PA 19603

OGDEN, WARREN COX, lawyer; b. New Orleans, July 21, 1942; s. Warren Cox and Mary Frances (Johnson) O.; m. Susan Broz, Dec. 30, 1968; children—Corinne, Warren Cox, Suzanne. A.B. with honors, U. N.C., 1964; J.D., Cornell U., 1971. Bar: D.C. 1971, Wash. 1976. Law clk. to mem. NLRB, Washington, 1971-72, atty. NLRB, 1971-75; atty. Davis, Wright, Toss, Riese & Jones, Seattle, 1975-77; pres. Northwest Employee Relations Assocs., Seattle, 1978—; mem. Warren C. Ogden, Mercer Island, Wash., 1977-82; assoc. Williams, Kastner & Gibbs, Mercer Island, 1980-86; prin. Ogden & Assocs., Mercer Island, 1987—; exec. v.p. human resources Miller-Cascade; instr. labor relations Georgetown U., Washington, 1972-75. Served with USN, 1964-68; Vietnam. Mem. D.C. Bar Assn., Wash. State Bar Assn. Contbr. articles to profl. jours. Labor. Home: 3465 W Mercer Way Mercer Island WA 98040

OGG, ROBERT KELLEY, lawyer; b. Missoula, Mont., May 22, 1947; s. Robert Nelson and Dorothy Virginia (Kelley) O.; m. Toni Jane Mickey, Sept. 30, 1972; children: Mickey Kelley, Joseph Robert. BS, USAF Acad., 1969; JD with honors, U. Mont., 1981. Bar: Colo. 1981, Mont. 1981, U.S. Dist. Ct. Colo. 1981, U.S. Dist. Ct. Mont. 1981. Assoc. Wagner & Waller P.C., Denver, 1981-83; sole practice Whitefish, Mont., 1983-86; ptnr. McChesney, Grenfell & Ogg, Missoula, Mont., 1987—; corp. counsel Applied Information Services, Inc., Whitefish, 1985—. Councilman City of Whitefish, 1986—. Served to capt. USAF, 1965-74. Mem. ABA, Mont. Bar Assn., Whitefish Lake Golf Assn. (bd. dirs. 1985-86). Avocations: golf, skiing. Securities, General corporate, Federal civil litigation. Office: McChesney Grenfell & Ogg 412 W Adler Missoula MT 59802

OGG, WILSON REID, poet, lawyer, educator; b. Alhambra, Calif., Feb. 26, 1928; s. James Brooks and Mary (Wilson) O. Student Pasadena Jr. Coll., 1946; A.B., U. Calif. at Berkeley, 1949, J.D., 1952; Cultural D in Philosophy of Law, World Univ. Roundtable, 1983. Assoc. trust Dept. Wells Fargo Bank, San Francisco, 1954-55; admitted to Calif. bar; pvt. practice law, Berkeley, 1955-78; real estate broker, cons., 1974-78; curator-in-residence Pinebrook, 1964—; research atty., legal editor dept. of continuing edn. of bar U. Calif. Extension, 1958-63; psychology instr. 25th Sta. Hosp., Taegu, Korea, 1954; English instr. Taegu English Lang. Inst., Taegu, 1954. Trustee World U., 1976-80; dir. admissions Internat. Soc. for Phil. Enquiry, 1981-84; dep. dir. gen. Internat. Biographical Centre, Eng., 1986—; dep. gov. Am. Biographical Inst. Research Assn., 1986—. Served with AUS, 1952-54. Cert. community coll. instr. Fellow Internat. Acad. Law and Sci.; mem. ABA, State Bar Calif., San Francisco Bar Assn., Am. Arbitration Assn. (nat. panel arbitrators), World Univ. Round Table (cult. D. in Philosophy of Law 1983), World Future Soc. (profl. mem.), AAAS, Am. Assn. Fin. Profls., Am. Soc. Psychical Research, Calif. Soc. Psychical Study (pres., chmn. bd. 1963-65), Suomi Soc., Soc. for Phys. Research (London), Parapsychol. Assn. (asso.),

999 Soc., Internat. Soc. Unified Sci., Worldwide Acad. Scholars, Am. Acad. Polit. and Social Sci., Internat. Platform Assn., Intertel, Ina Coolbrith Circle, Am. Legion, VFW, Am. Mensa, Lawyers in Mensa, Psychic Sci. Spl. Interest Group, Am. Legion, VFW. Unitarian. Mason, Elk. Clubs: Faculty (U. Calif.), City Commons (Berkeley); Press (San Francisco); Commonwealth of Calif.; Town Hall Calif. Editor: Legal Aspects of Doing Business under Government Contracts and Subcontracts, 1958, Basic California Practice Handbook, 1959; contbr. numerous articles profl. jours; contbr. poetry to various mags. including American Poetry Anthology Vol. VI Number 5, New Voices in American Poetry, 1987. Administrative and regulatory, Jurisprudence, Real property. Home: 1104 Keith Ave Berkeley CA 94708-1607 Office: Eight Bret Harte Way Berkeley CA 94708-1611

OGGEL, STEPHEN PETER, lawyer; b. Monmouth, Ill., Apr. 18, 1942; s. Harold Paul and Olive Lois (Wilson) O.; m. Linda C. Oggel, Sept. 14, 1974; children—Gregg, Grant, Claire. B.A., Vanderbilt U., 1964; J.D. with honors, George Washington U., 1967. Bar: D.C. 1968, Calif. 1970, U.S. Dist. Ct. (no., so., cen. dists.) Calif. 1970, U.S. Ct. Appeals (9th cir. 1970), U.S. Ct. Appeals (2d cir.) 1972. Assoc. Pierson, Ball & Dowd, Washington, 1970-72; ptnr. Sullivan, Jones & Archer, San Diego 1972-82; ptnr. Christison, Martin & Oggel San Diego 1982—; adj. prof. U. Calif.-San Diego; lectr. in field. Bd. govs. Downtown San Diego YMCA. Served to capt. USMC 1967-70. Mem. ABA, San Diego County Bar Assn. Democrat. Presbyterian. Clubs: San Diego Country, Rotary, University (San Diego). Federal civil litigation, State civil litigation, Antitrust. Office: 450 B St Suite 1500 San Diego CA 92101

OGLE, JERRY MICHAEL, lawyer; b. Elgin, Ill., Nov. 17, 1954. BA, Northwestern U., 1976; JD, U. Ill., 1979. Bar: Ill. 1979, U.S. Dist. Ct. (no. dist.) Ill. 1979. Assoc. Arnstein, Gluck & Lehr, Chgo., 1979-80, Katten, Muchin, Zavis, Pearl & Galler, Chgo., 1980-82; v.p., legal assoc. Balcor Co., Skokie, Ill., 1982—. Bd. dirs. Chgo. Chamber Brass, 1981-82; docent Grosse Pointe Lighthouse, Evanston, Ill., 1982—. Mem. ABA, Chgo. Bar Assn., Nat. Assn. Realtors, Real Estate Securities and Syndication Inst., Evanston Environ. Assn. (docent 1982-86), Chgo. Acad. Scis. (docent 1983—). Episcopalian. Avocations: reading, travel. Securities, General corporate, Real property. Home: 1508 Oak St Evanston IL 60201 Office: The Balcor Co 4849 Golf Rd Skokie IL 60077

OGLESBY, PAUL LEONARD, JR., lawyer; b. Decatur, Ill., Aug. 17, 1955; s. Paul Leonard and Dorothy E. (Yeoman) O. B.A., U. Ill., 1977; J.D., So. Ill. U., 1980. Bar: Ill. 1980. Asst. state's atty. Coles County, Charleston, Ill., 1981-83; assoc. Dilsaver, Nelson & Ryan, Mattoon, Ill., 1983—. Mem. ABA, Res. Officers Assn., Ill. State Bar Assn., Coles-Cumberland Bar Assn. Republican. Methodist. State civil litigation, Consumer commercial, Criminal. Home: 1413 Lafayette Apt 4 Mattoon IL 61938 Office: Dilsaver Nelson & Ryan 1632 Broadway Mattoon IL 61938

OGLETREE, ANNE MEVE CALLAHAN, lawyer; b. N.Y.C., Nov. 15, 1944; d. Justin Thomas and Frances (Halsey) Callahan; m. Joseph L. Ogletree, Aug. 11, 1973 (div. Nov. 1982); children: Joseph Denning, Katharine A. Vermette. BA, Manhattanville Coll., 1966; JD with honors, U. Md., 1974. Md. 1974, U.S. Dist. Ct. Md. 1982. Assoc. Robert C. Thompson, Easton, Md., 1974-76, Roland C. Kent, Denton, Md., 1976-77; ptnr. Kent, Ogletree & Thornton, Denton, 1977-86; sole practice Denton, 1986—; bd. dirs. Legal Aid Bur. Inc., Balt.; mem. standing com. on rules, practice and procedure Md. Ct. of Appeals, 1979—. Mem. Md. Bar Assn. (real property sect.), Order of Coif. Real property, Probate, Family and matrimonial. Home: Rt 2 Box 175 Federalsburg MD 21629 Office: PO Box 559 Denton MD 21629

O'GRADY, JOHN JOSEPH, III, lawyer; b. N.Y.C., Mar. 21, 1933; s. John Joseph and Terese (O'Rourke) O'G.; m. Mary E. McHugh, June 28, 1958; children—Glennon, Ellen, Carol, Paul. A.B., Holy Cross Coll., 1954; J.D., Harvard U., 1957. Bar: N.Y. 1958. Assoc. Cadwalader, Wickersham & Taft, N.Y.C., 1958-66, ptnr., 1966—. Mem. ABA, N.Y. State Bar Assn. Probate. Office: 100 Maiden Ln New York NY 10038

OH, MATTHEW IN-SOO, lawyer; b. Seoul, Republic of Korea, Aug. 5, 1938; s. Young Whan and Jeom-soon (Kim) Oh; m. Young Ok, May 24, 1973; children: John Z., Amy J. LLB, Seoul Nat. U., 1963, LLM, 1968; LLM, Columbia U., 1972; JD, William Mitchell Coll. Law, St. Paul, 1982. Bar: Minn. 1982. Sr. planning researcher Ministry of Constrn., Seoul, 1968-71; planner Altamaha, Ga. Regional Planning Commn., 1972-74; sole practice St. Paul, Minn., 1982—. Legal advisor Korean Elderly Soc., St. Paul, 1984—; mem. North Korea Human Rights Project, Mpls., 1985—; chmn. State of Minn. Council on Asian-Pacific Relations, St. Paul, 1985—; v.p. Minn. Asian Advocacy Coalition, St. Paul, 1983-85; bd. dirs. Urban Concern Workshop, Inc., St. Paul, 1985-86. Fulbright fellow Fulbright Commn., Seoul, 1971. Mem. ABA, Fed. Bar Assn., Minn. Bar Assn., Ramsey County Bar Assn. (Yogi Berra award), Am. Immigration Lawyers Assn. Presbyterian. Immigration, naturalization, and customs, Contracts commercial, General practice. Home: 720 Mercury Dr Shoreview MN 55126 Office: 1430 Conwed Tower 444 Cedar St Saint Paul MN 55101

O'HAIR, JOHN D., lawyer, county prosecuting attorney; b. Detroit, Sept. 29, 1929; s. Walter R. and Willis W. (Watts) O.; m. Barbara Stanton, Jan. 15, 1966; 1 child: John Dennis. B.A., DePauw U., 1951; J.D., Detroit Coll. Law, 1954. Bar: Mich. 1954. Asst. corp. counsel City of Detroit, 1957-65; judge Common Pleas Ct., Detroit, 1965-68; judge Wayne County Cir. Ct., 1968-83; Wayne County pros. atty., 1983—; Wayne County counsel, 1983—; mem. Mich. Jud. Tenure Commn., 1977-82. Trustee, Detroit Coll. Law, 1982—. Served with Intelligence Corps, U.S. Army, 1955-56. Mem. ABA, Mich. Bar Assn. Democrat. Presbyterian. Office: 1441 St Antoine Prosecuting Atty's Office Frank Murphy Hall of Justice 12th Floor Detroit MI 48226

O'HALLORAN, ROBERT LUIS, lawyer; b. Annapolis, Md., Sept. 17, 1957; s. John William and Donna Marion (Kemnitzer) O'H.; m. Michele Ann Des Brisay. BS in Internat. Bus., U. Oreg., 1979; JD, Lewis and Clark Coll., 1982. Bar: Oreg. 1982, U.S. Dist. Ct. Oreg. 1982, U.S. Ct. Claims 1982. Assoc. Allen & Yazbeck, Portland, Oreg., 1982-85, Allen, Kilmer, Schrader, Yazbeck & Chenoweth P.C., Portland, 1985—. Mem. ABA (construction sect., ins. law sect.), Multnomah County Bar Assn., Associated Gen. Contractors (legal com. mid columbia chpt. 1985—). Construction, Federal civil litigation, Securities. Office: Allen Kilmer Schrader et al 1001 SW 5th Ave Portland OR 97204

O'HARA, JAMES THOMAS, lawyer; b. Hazelton, Pa., Oct. 11, 1936; s. Thomas James and Bridget Helen (Campbell) O'H.; m. Kathleen M. Shane, Aug. 3, 1963; children: Colleen, Michael, Brian. BS in Acctg., Kings Coll., 1958; LLB, Cath. U., 1962; LLM, Georgetown U., 1967. Bar: D.C. 1962. Section chief IRS, Washington, 1967-69; ptnr. Casey, Tyre et al, N.Y.C., 1969-73, Jones, Day, Reavis & Pogue, Washington, 1973—; adj. prof. tax Georgetown U., Washington, 1976—. Contbr. articles to profl. jours. Served with USAR, 1959. Mem. ABA (chmn. subcom. tax sect. 1982—). Democrat. Roman Catholic. Clubs: Metropolitan (Washington); Union (Cleve.). Corporate taxation. Home: 1610 44th St NW Washington DC 20007 Office: Jones Day Reavis & Pogue 655 15th St NW Washington DC 20005

O'HARA, MICHAEL JAMES, law educator, researcher; b. Detroit, Feb. 4, 1953; s. Edward Richard and Eileen Mary (Friel) O.; m. Mary Catherine Cortese, June 1, 1981. BA in Sociology, U. Nebr., 1975, JD, 1978, MA in Econs., 1979, PhD in Econs., 1983. Bar: Nebr. 1978, U.S. Dist. Ct. Nebr. 1978. Research asst. S.E. Nebr. Health Systems Agy., Lincoln, 1979; legis. aide State of Nebr., Lincoln, 1979-81; instr. econs. U. Nebr., Omaha, 1981-82; asst. prof. law, 1982—. Contbr. articles to profl. jours. Econs. advisor 2nd Congl. Dist. Campaign, Omaha, 1984; mem. Nebr. Power Rev. Bd., 1985—. Mem. ABA (corp., banking and bus. law sect., sci. and tech. sect., task force on uniform distbn. practices act), Am. Econs. Assn., Computer Law Assn., Nat. Gov.'s Assn. (task force on ecelectric transmission), Omicron Delta Epsilon, Beta Gamma Sigma. Franchising law and economics, Computer, Public utilities. Home: 6005 Charles St Omaha NE 68132 Office: Univ Nebr at Omaha 60th and Dodge Sts Omaha NE 68182

O'HARA, ROBERT SYDNEY, JR., lawyer; b. Englewood, N.J., Apr. 26, 1939; s. Robert Sydney and Katharine (Drayton) O'H.; m. Elizabeth Crocker, June 17, 1961; children—Jennifer, Isabelle; m. 2d Bonnie Durkin, July 19, 1975. A.B., Princeton U., 1960; J.D., U. Pa., 1963. Bar: N.Y. 1964. Ptnr. firm Milbank, Tweed, Hadley & McCloy, N.Y.C., 1965—. Served to capt. AUS 1963-65. General corporate, Banking. Office: Milbank Tweed Hadley & McCloy 1 Chase Manhattan Plaza New York NY 10005

O'HEARN, BARBARA ANN, lawyer; b. St. Paul, Nov. 11, 1950; s. Robert Emmet and Ada Ruth (French) O'H.; m. Henry P. Barnard III, June 10, 1985. AA, Bakersfield Coll., 1971; BA, U. Calif., Santa Barbara, 1973; JD, Antioch Sch. Law, 1979. Bar: Calif. 1980, D.C. 1985. Sole practice, cons. San Francisco, 1980-82; atty., hearing officer San Francisco Rent Bd., 1981-82, dep. dir., 1986—; atty., hearing officer Santa Monica Rent Bd., Calif., 1982-85; cons., writer Youth law Ctr., San Francisco, 1980-81, Legal Services Corp., Washington, 1980-81; cons., trainor Nat. Paralegal Inst., San Francisco, 1980. Author: Introduction to State Codes, 1981, Introduction to Case Reporters, 1981. Loepold Schepp Found. scholar, 1977-79. Mem. Calif. Bar Assn., D.C. Bar Assn., Calif. Women Lawyers Assn. (com. mem. 1983, bd. of govs. 1987—), Queens Bench. Local government, Administrative and regulatory, Housing. Office: San Francisco Rent Bd 170 Fell St Room 16 San Francisco CA 94102

O'HEARN, WILLIAM WILSON, judge; b. Memphis, Jan. 24, 1914; s. John Joseph and Molly (Kehoe) O'H.; 1 dau., Mary Ann Sawyer. LL.B., So. Law U., 1941. Bar: Tenn. 1941, U.S. Dist. Ct. (6th cir.) 1946, U.S. Supreme Ct. 1979. Pvt. practice, Memphis, 1941-48, 48-66; asst. dist. atty., Memphis, 1946-48; judge Tenn. 15th Jud. Cir., Memphis, 1966, sr. cir. judge, presiding judge, 1982-83; chmn. Tenn. Jury Pattern Instructions (civil), 1984—. Served to maj. U.S. Army, 1941-45. Decorated Bronze Star. Mem. Am. Judicature Soc., ABA, Tenn. Bar Assn., Memphis Bar Assn., Shelby County Bar Assn. Roman Catholic. Club: Tenn. Petroleum (Memphis). State civil litigation, Personal injury. Office: Circuit Ct Memphis TN 38103

O'HERN, DANIEL JOSEPH, state supreme court justice; b. Red Bank, N.J., May 23, 1930; s. J. Henry and Eugenia A. (Sansone) O'H.; m. Barbara Ronan, Aug. 8, 1959; children: Daniel J., Eileen, James, John, Molly. A.B., Fordham Coll., 1951; LL.B., Harvard U., 1957. Bar: N.J. 1958. Clk. U.S. Supreme Ct., Washington, 1957-58; assoc. Abramoff, Apy & O'Hern, Red Bank, N.J., 1966-78; commr. N.J. Dept. Environ. Protection, 1978-79; counsel to Gov. N.J. Trenton; justice N.J. Supreme Ct., Trenton, 1981—; former mem. adv. com. profl. ethics N.J. Supreme Ct. Past trustee Legal Aid Soc. Monmouth County, (N.J.); mayor City of Red Bank, 1969-78, councilman, 1962-69. Served as lt. (j.g.) USNR, 1951-54. Mem. N.J. Bar Assn., Monmouth County Bar Assn., Harvard Law Sch. Assn. N.J. (past pres.). Judicial administration. Office: NJ Supreme Ct State House Annex Trenton NJ 08625 *

OHLMAN, DOUGLAS RONALD, securities firm executive, lawyer; b. Rockville Centre, N.Y., Mar. 25, 1949; s. Maxwell and Miriam (Frucht) O.; m. Elat Menashe, Dec. 4, 1983. B.A., Columbia Coll., 1971; J.D., Hofstra U., 1974. Bar: N.Y. 1975, U.S. Dist. Ct. (so., ea., no. and we. dists.) N.Y. 1976, U.S. Tax Ct. 1978, U.S. Supreme Ct. 1978, U.S. Ct. Claims 1978, U.S. Customs Ct. 1978. Vice pres. Info. & Research Services, Inc., Roslyn, N.Y., 1975-81; assoc. Baer & Marks, N.Y.C., 1974-75, Rains, Pogrebin & Scher, Mineola, N.Y., 1975-76, Weisman, Celler, Spett, Modlin & Wertheimer, N.Y.C., 1976-79, Hoffberg, Gordon, Rabin & Engler, N.Y.C., 1979-80, Bergner & Bergner, Blum & Ruditz, N.Y.C., 1980-81; gen. counsel Greenfield Ptnrs., N.Y.C., 1981-86, gen. ptnr., 1982-86, dep. mng. ptnr., 1984-86, V.W. Investors, Inc., J.W. Investors, Inc., N.Y.C., 1985—, chief operating officer, sr. v.p., sec., dir.; allied mem. N.Y. Stock Exchange, Inc. Mem. radio news team WKCR-FM, N.Y.C. (Writers Guild award, Peabody nomination 1968). Communications dir., dep. radiol. officer Nassau County Civil Def., Town of Roslyn, N.Y., 1964-74; mem. com. Nassau County Liberal Party, 1982. Columbia U. grantee, 1968. Mem. ABA, N.Y. State Bar Assn., N.Y. County Lawyers Assn., Assn. Bar City N.Y. Securities, General corporate, State civil litigation. Home: 7 E 14th St Apt 602 New York NY 10003 Office: Greenfield Ptnrs 45 Broadway Atrium New York NY 10006

OHLY, D. CHRISTOPHER, lawyer; b. N.Y.C., Nov. 7, 1950; s. Bodo Charles and Ellen Charlotte (Nekolla) O.; m. Alma Lynn Borenstein, Sept. 11, 1978; 1 child, Sara Rebecca. AB, John Hopkins U., 1972; JD, U. Va., 1975. Bar: Md. 1975, U.S. Dist. Ct. Md. 1975, U.S. Ct. Appeals (2d and 4th cirs.) 1978, U.,S. Ct. Appeals (1st cir.) 1984, U.S. Tax Ct. Assoc. Melnicove, Kaufman, Weiner, Smouse & Garbis, Balt., 1975-78, 81-82, ptnr., 1982—; asst. U.S. Atty. U.S. Atty.'s Office, Balt., 1978-81. Contbr. articles to profl. jours. Mem. ABA (internat. law sect. 1973-74), Fed. Bar Assn., Md. Bar Assn. (internat. comml. law sect. 1986—), Am. Soc. Internat. Law, Phi Beta Kappa, Omicron Delta Kappa, Pi Sigma Alpha. Avocations: computers, amatuer radio. Private international, Federal civil litigation, Criminal. Home: 5714 St Albans Way Baltimore MD 21212 Office: Melnicove Kaufman Weiner et al 36 S Charles St 6th Floor Baltimore MD 30133-2858

OHMAN, JOHN MICHAEL, lawyer; b. Dec. 22, 1948; s. John W. and D. Jeanne (Forster) O.; m. Susan M. Samson; children: Brittany Michelle, Andrea Michaela. BSBA, Creighton U., 1971, JD, 1972. Bar: Idaho 1973, Nebr. 1973, U.S. Dist. Ct. Idaho 1973, U.S. Dist. Ct. Nebr. 1973, U.S. Ct. Appeals (9th cir.) 1978, U.S. Interstate Commerce Commn. 1975, U.S. Supreme Ct. 1978. Atty. Cox & Ohman, Idaho Falls, Idaho, 1978—; lectr. various locations. Contbr. articles to profl. jours. Bd. dirs. Idaho Transp. Dept.; chmn. Bonneville County Hist. Soc.; exec. bd. Assn. Humanities in Idaho, legal advisor; active United Way, YMCA; past pres. Am. Cancer Soc.; judge advocate Intermountain dist. Civitan Internat., also past pres. Idaho Falls chpt.; legal adv. Mayor's Com. for Handicapped, Mayor's Com. for Swimming Pool, Community Concert Assn., Idaho Falls Symphony Soc., Eastern Idaho Spl. Services Agy.; dir. Group Homes, Inc.; campaign coordinator Gov. Idaho; mem. State Dem. Cen. Com.; precinct committeeman. Served to capt. U.S. Army. Recipient Outstanding Pres. award Civitian Internat., Century Club mem. YMCA, Idaho Safe Pilot award; named del. to Hong Kong, to People's Republic of China and Japan by Idaho Bus. Leaders. Mem. ABA (litigation sect., family law sect., tort and ins. practice sect., div. law and procedures com.), Am. Soc. Law and Medicine, Am. Judicature Soc., Idaho State Bar Assn. (adv. council continuing legal edn.), Nebr. State Bar. Assn., Seventh Judicial Dist. Bar Assn., Assn. Trail Lawyers Am., Idaho Trail Lawyers Assn., Assn. Interstate Commerce Practitioners, Idaho Law Found., Unauthorized Practice Law Com., Western Assn. State Hwy. and Transp. Officials, Am. Assn. State Hwy. and Transp. Officials, Smithsonian Inst. (assoc.), Internat. Platform Assn., Am. Mus. Natural History, Airplane Owners and Pilots Assn., Nat. Arbor's Day Found., C. of C. (chmn. legis. com.), Phi Alpha Delta, Omicron Delta Epsilon, Phi Kappa Psi. Democrat. Roman Catholic. Club: Toastmasters. Lodge: Elks (legal advisor). Avocations: aquatic sports, numismatics, reading, aviation, racquetball. Office: Cox and Ohman PO Box 621 Idaho Falls ID 83402

O'KEEFE, KEVIN MICHAEL, lawyer; b. Vincennes, Ind., Sept. 24, 1946; s. Roy Daniel and Mildred (Pawlak) O'K.; m. Margaret Yvonne Green, Sept. 25, 1971; children—Kathleen, Kelly. B.S. in Communications, U. Ill., 1969; J.D., Ill. Inst. Tech., 1973. Bar: Ill. 1973, Fla. 1974. Assoc. O'Keefe, Ashenden, Lyons & Ward, Chgo., 1973-76; ptnr., 1976—; bd. dirs. Healthcorp Affiliates, Naperville, Ill. Bd. dirs. Central DuPage Hosp., Winfield, Ill., 1981—, B.R. Ryall YMCA, Glen Ellyn, Ill., 1979-81. Mem. Inst. Property Taxation, Internat. Assn. Assessing Officers. Democrat. Roman Catholic. State and local taxation. Home: 1730 Thompson Dr Wheaton IL 60687 Office: O'Keefe Ashenden Lyons & Ward 1 1st National Plaza Suite 5100 Chicago IL 60603

O'KEEFE, PATRICK FRANCIS, lawyer, insurance company executive, educator; b. Kansas City, Mo., Feb. 20, 1947; s. Bernard Joseph and Carmelita Teresa (McEvoy) O'K.; children: Denise, David, Melissa. BA, U. Mo., Kansas City, 1969; JD, Western State U., San Diego, 1977; MBA, Golden Gate U., 1985. Bar: Calif. 1978, U.S. Dist. Ct. (so. dist.) Calif. 1978, U.S. Dist. Ct. (no. dist.) Calif. 1979; CPCU; CLU; Chartered Fin. Cons. Underwriter ins. Safeco ins., Panorama City, Calif., 1972-73, Fireman's Fund Ins., San Diego, 1973-78; atty. Fireman's Fund Ins., San Francisco, 1978-79, asst. counsel, 1979-80, assoc. counsel, 1980-82, counsel, 1982-83, sr. counsel, 1983-85, asst. gen. counsel, asst. v.p., 1985—. Served to capt. USMC, 1969-72, Vietnam. Mem. Calif. Bar Assn. (bus. law sect.), Soc. CPCU's, Am. Soc. CLU's, Am. Corp. Counsel Assn., Ins. Ednl. Assn. (instr. 1981—). Administrative and regulatory, Insurance, General corporate. Office: Firemans Fund Ins 777 San Marin Dr Novato CA 94998

O'KEEFE, WILLIAM PATRICK, lawyer; b. Foxhome, Minn., May 18, 1938; s. William P. and Catherine (Hemenfent) O'K.; m. Eva I. O'Keefe; children: Erin I., Abbey L. AA, Santa Ana Coll., 1960; BA, Calif. State U., 1962; JD, U. So. Calif., 1967. Bar: Calif. 1968, U.S. Dist. Ct. (cen. dist.) Calif. 1968, U.S. Ct. Appeals (9th cir.) 1968, U.S. Supreme Ct. 1978. Sole practice Santa Ana, 1967—. Served with USMC, 1957-59. Mem. Orange County Bar Assn. (bd. dirs.). General corporate, Real property, Estate planning. Office: 1055 N Main Suite 401 Santa Ana CA 92701

O'KEEFFE, JOHN JOSEPH, JR., holding company executive, lawyer; b. Norwalk, Conn., Dec. 21, 1941; s. John Joseph and Mary Ellen (Snee) O'K.; m. Valerie Anne Moore, Sept. 2, 1967; children: Anna Gould, John Moore. B.A., Fairfield U., 1965; J.D., George Washington U., 1968. Bar: N.Y. 1969. Atty. Pan Am. World Airways, Inc., N.Y.C., 1968-72, Trans World Airlines, N.Y.C., 1972-77; corp. sec., asst. gen. counsel Trans World Airlines, 1977-83; asst. gen. counsel Transworld Corp., N.Y.C., 1979-86; corp. sec. Transworld Corp., 1979-86, v.p. adminstrn., gen. counsel, 1986, v.p. adminstrn., gen. counsel, corp. sec., 1986; v.p. adminstrn., gen. counsel, corp. sec. TW Services Inc., 1986—. Mem. N.Y. State Bar Assn. Republican. Roman Catholic. Club: Larchmont Yacht. General corporate. Home: 11 Dante St Larchmont NY 10538 Office: 605 3d Ave New York NY 10158

O'KELLEY, WILLIAM CLARK, judge; b. Atlanta, Jan. 2, 1930; s. Ezra Clark and Theo (Johnson) O'K.; m. Ernestine Allen, Mar. 28, 1953; children: Virginia Leigh O'Kelley Wood, William Clark Jr. A.B., Emory U., 1951, LL.B., 1953. Bar: Ga. 1952. Practiced in Atlanta, 1957-59; asst. U.S. atty. No. Dist. Ga., 1959-61; partner law firm O'Kelley, Hopkins & Van Gerpen, Atlanta, 1961-70; U.S. dist. judge No. Dist. Ga., Atlanta, 1970—; mem. com. on adminstrn. of criminal law Jud. Conf. U.S., 1979-82, exec. com., 1981-84, mem. adv. com. of fed. rules of criminal procedure, 1985—; mem. Fgn. Intelligence Surveillance Ct., 1980—; corp. sec., dir. Gwinnett Bank & Trust Co., Norcross, Ga., 1968-70. Mem. exec. com., gen. counsel Ga. Republican Com., 1968-70. Served as 1st lt. USAF, 1953-57; capt. Res. Mem. Am., Atlanta bar assns., Ga. State Bar, Am. Judicature Soc., Dist. Judges Assn. 5th Circuit (pres. 1979-80), Sigma Chi, Phi Delta Phi, Omicron Delta Kappa. Baptist. Clubs: Kiwanian (past pres.), Atlanta Athletic, Lawyers of Atlanta. Jurisprudence. Home: 550 Ridgecrest Dr Norcross GA 30071 Office: US DistrictCourt 1942 US Courthouse 75 Spring St SW Atlanta GA 30303 *

OKINAGA, LAWRENCE SHOJI, lawyer; b. Honolulu, July 7, 1941; s. Shohei and Hatsu (Kakimoto) O.; m. Carolyn Hisako Uesugi, Nov. 26, 1966; children—Caryn, Laurie. B.A., U. Hawaii, 1963; J.D., Georgetown U., 1972. Bar: Hawaii 1972, U.S. Dist. Ct. Hawaii 1972, U.S. Ct. Appeals (9th cir.) 1976. Administrv. asst. to Congressman Spark Matsunaga, Honolulu, 1964, 1965-69; law clk. to chief judge U.S. Dist. Ct. Hawaii, Honolulu, 1972-73; assoc. Carlsmith, Carlsmith, Wichman and Case, Honolulu, 1973-76, ptnr., 1976—; mem. Gov.'s Citizens Adv. Com. Coastal Zone Mgmt., 1974-79; sec. Hawaii Bicentennial Corp., 1975-77, chmn., 1985-87; vice chmn., mem. Jud. Selection Commn., State of Hawaii, 1979-87, vice chmn., 1986; mem. consumer adv. council Fed. Res. Bd. Bd. dirs. Moiliili Community Ctr., Honolulu, 1965-68, 1973-86; trustee Kuakini Med. Ctr., 1984-87. Served to capt. USAFR, 1964-72, 1974-76. Mem. ABA, Hawaii Bar Assn., Res. Officers Assn., Am. Judicature Soc. (bd. dirs. 1986—), Georgetown U. Law Alumni Assn. (bd. dirs. 1986—), Omicron Delta Kappa. Banking, Consumer commercial, General corporate. Office: PO Box 656 Honolulu HI 96809

OKRASINSKI, MARY ANN, lawyer; b. Huntington, W.Va., Mar. 22, 1954; d. Edward and Mirvine Byars (Garrett) O.; m. Bruce W. Pitt, Mar. 26, 1983; children: William Edward Okrasinski Pitt, Sean Bruce O'Garretty Pitt. BA with honors, U. Iowa, 1975, JD with high distinction, 1982. Bar: Iowa 1982, U.S. Dist. Ct. (no. dist.) Iowa 1982, U.S. Ct. Appeals (8th cir.) 1982, Tenn. 1985. Investigator Dept. Correctional Services, Iowa City, Iowa, 1976-79; atty. Bradley & Riley P.C., Cedar Rapids, Iowa, 1982-83; atty. investments Provident Cos., Chatanooga, 1983—; instr. paralegal tng. Cleveland (Tenn.) State Community Coll., 1983-85. Mem. ABA (real estate property sect., com. on creditor's rights in real estate financing), Tenn. Bar Assn., Tenn. Scenic Rivers Assn., Audubon Soc., Tenn. Conservation Assn. Avocations: farming, sailing, water sports. Real property, Landlord-tenant, Bankruptcy. Home: Rural Rt 3 Box 192C Decatur TN 37322 Office: Provident Cos Fountain Square Chattanooga TN 37402

OKUN, TODD ALAN, lawyer; b. N.Y.C., June 6, 1949; s. Irwin Leon and Lola Charlotte (Bonime) O.; m. Sheri Ann Edwards, Aug. 29, 1982 (dec. June 1985); children: Joshua, Sarah, Bailey. AB, Harvard U., 1971; JD, George Washington U., 1974. Bar: N.Y. 1975, D.C. 1976, U.S. Dist. Ct. D.C. 1977, U.S. Supreme Ct. 1977. Staff attyl. FDIC, Washington, 1974-76, Fed. Res. Bd., Washington, 1976-78; asst. gen. counsel NAt. Credit Union Adminstrn., Washington, 1978-84; sr. counsel Fed. Home Loan Mortgage Corp., Washington, 1984—. Mem. ABA, Fed. Bar Assn., Am. Corp. Counsel Assn., Washington Met. Area Corp. Counsel Assn. Jewish. Avocations: sports, children. General corporate, Contracts commercial, Banking. Home: 6204 Erman Ct Burke VA 22015 Office: Fed Home Loan Mortgage Crop 1776 G St NW Washington DC 20013

OLACK, NEIL PETER, lawyer; b. N.Y.C., June 6, 1956; s. Theodore James and Josephine (Giambrone) O.; m. Rebecca Lynn Mayhugh, May 26, 1979; 1 child, Kyle Andrew. BA, Lehigh U., 1978; JD, Emory U., 1981. Bar: Miss. 1981, Ga. 1981, U.S. Dist. Ct. (so. dist.) Miss. 1981, U.S. Ct. Appeals (5th and 11th cirs.) 1981, U.S. Dist. Ct. (no. dist.) Miss. 1986. From assoc. to ptnr. Watkins, Ludlam & Stennis, Jackson, Miss., 1981—. Mem. ABA (litigation sect.), Am. Bankruptcy Inst., Miss. Bankruptcy Conf. (chmn. legis. com.), Comml. Law League of Am. Bankruptcy, Federal civil litigation, State civil litigation. Home: 1440 Saint Ann St Jackson MS 39202 Office: Watkins Ludlam & Stennis PO Box 427 Jackson MS 39205

OLANDER, CHRISTOPHER DEAN, lawyer; b. Chgo., Dec. 14, 1948; s. Donald Richard and Betty (Fisher) O.; 1 child, Donald Richard II. BA, Johns Hopkins U., 1970; JD with honors, U. Md., 1973. Bar: Ill. 1973, U.S. Dist. Ct. (no. dist.) Ill. 1973, Md. 1977. Assoc. Schff, Hardin & Waite, Chgo., 1973-77; ptnr. Shapiro & Olander, Balt., 1977—, mng. ptnr., 1980—; bd. dirs., officer Premier Design Systems Inc., Towson, Md., Arbitrage & Compliance, Inc. Author: Securities Regulation, 1975. Adviser Talent Assistence Program, Chgo., 1974-78; bd. dirs. Friends Balt. Symphony, 1984-85, North Balt. Mental Health Ctr., 1986—. Mem. ABA (fed. regulation securities com.), Md. Bar Assn., Nat. Assn. Bond Lawyers. Democrat. Avocations: lit., computers, tennis. Securities, Banking, Municipal bonds. Office: Shapiro and Olander 36 S Charles St Baltimore MD 21201

OLANDER, RAY GUNNAR, mining and aerospace equipment company executive, lawyer; b. Buhl, Minn., May 15, 1926; s. Olof Gunnar and Margaret Esther (Meisner) O.; m. Audrey Joan Greenlaw, Aug. 1, 1959; children—Paul Robert, Mary Beth. B.E.E. with distinction, U. Minn., 1949, B.B.A. with distinction, 1949; J.D. cum laude, Harvard U., 1959. Bar: Minn. 1959, Wis. 1962, U.S. Patent Office 1968. Elec. engr. M. A. Hanna Co., Hibbing, Minn., 1950-56; assoc. Leonard, Street & Deinard, Mpls., 1959-61; comml. atty. Becor Western Inc. (formerly Bucyrus-Erie Co.), South Milwaukee, Wis., 1961-70, dir. contracts, 1970-76, v.p. comml., 1976—, gen.

atty., 1978-80, corp. sec., 1978—, gen. counsel, 1980—; dir. Western Gear Corp., Western Gear Machinery Co., Bucyrus Europe, Ltd., Becor Western FSC, Inc., Bucyrus Disc, Inc., Bucyrus Internat., Inc., Bucyrus (Africa) (Proprietary) Ltd., Bucyrus (Australia) Proprietary, Ltd. Bd. dirs. Ballet Found. Milw., Inc., 1978—, Pub. Expenditure Research Found., Inc., Madison, Wis., 1978—, Pub. Expenditure Survey Wis., Madison, 1978-82. Served with USN, 1944-46. Mem. ABA, Wis. Bar Assn., Wis. Intellectual Property Law Assn., Am. Soc. Corp. Secs., Inc., Am. Corp. Counsel Assn., VFW, Eta Kappa Nu, Tau Beta Pi, Beta Gamma Sigma. Republican. Roman Catholic. Clubs: Harvard (N.Y.C.), Harvard of Wis., University (Milw.), Tuckaway Country (Franklin, Wis.). Lodges: Masons, Shriners. Avocations: tennis; golf. Contracts commercial, General corporate. Home: 5881 Fleming Ct Greendale WI 53129 Office: Becor Western Inc 1100 Milwaukee Ave South Milwaukee WI 53172

OLDENETTEL, RICK LEE, lawyer; b. Alton, Ill., Aug. 1, 1953; s. Alvin Benhart and Florence Rebecca (Gilley) O.; m. Beverly Jackson, Mar. 20, 1982. Student, San Jacinto Jr. Coll., 1971-72, North Tex. State U., 1972-73; BS, Houston State U., 1975; JD, South Tex. Coll. Law, 1978. Bar: Tex. 1979, U.S. Dist. Ct. (so. dist.) Tex. 1979, U.S. Ct. Appeals (5th cir.) 1979, U.S. Ct. Appeals (11th cir.) 1981, U.S. Dist. Ct. (ea., we. and no. dists.) Tex. 1981. Atty. Exxon Corp., Houston, 1978-79; assoc. Boswell, O'Toole, Davis & Pickering, Houston, 1979-82; ptnr. Gilpin, Maynard, Parsons, Pohl & Bennett, Houston, 1982—. Mem. ABA, Tex. Bar Assn., Houston Bar Assn., Tex. Assn. Def. Counsel, Tex. Young Lawyers Assn. Republican. Federal civil litigation, State civil litigation, Personal injury. Office: Gilpin Maynard Parsons Pohl & Bennett 1300 Post Oak Blvd Allied Bank Tower 23d Floor Houston TX 77056

OLDER, JACK STANLEY, lawyer; b. Phila., Feb. 20, 1934; s. Morris and Lee (Goldstein) O.; m. Sondra Chait, June 21, 1959; children: Michael, Stephen, Elizabeth, Carolyn. B.S. in Econs., U. Pa., 1955, LL.B., 1958. Bar: N.Y. 1959. Atty. Office of Chief Counsel, IRS, 1960-66; editor Tax Research Inst. Am., 1966-68; asso. gen. counsel Nat. Assn. Mut. Savs. Banks, 1968-70; tax counsel Atlantic Richfield Co., 1970-72; sr. v.p., sec. Bowery Savs. Bank, N.Y.C., 1972; sec., office counsel Bowery Savs. Bank, 1973-76, sr. v.p., sec., office counsel, 1976-82; ptnr. Rogers & Wells, 1982—. Author: Employee Retirement Income Security Act of 1974, 1975, Conversion of Thrift Institutions, The Review of Securities Regulations, 1983; also articles. Treas. Bowery Ofcls. Nonpartisan Polit. Com., 1974—. Served with U.S. Army, 1958-59. Mem. ABA (author handbook), N.Y. State Bar Assn., Beta Gamma Sigma, Beta Alpha Psi. Home: 7 Stratton Rd Scarsdale NY 10583 Office: Rogers & Wells 200 Park Ave New York NY 10166

OLDFIELD, E. LAWRENCE, lawyer; b. Lake Forest, Ill., Dec. 21, 1944; s. W. Ernest and Evelyn Charlotte (Gyllenburg) O.; m. Kaaren Elaine Sabey, Aug. 24, 1974; 1 step child, Kimberly Jo; 1 child, Lauren Elizabeth. BA in Polit. Sci., No. Ill. U., 1969; JD, DePaul U., 1973. Bar: U.S. Dist. Ct. (no. dist.) Ill. 1973, U.S. Ct. Appeals (7th cir.) 1974, U.S. Supreme Ct. 1979, U.S. Ct. Appeals (3d cir.) 1985, U.S. Ct. Appeals (10th cir.) 1986. Assoc. Ruff & Grotefeld Ltd., Chgo., 1973-77; gen. counsel livestock dept. Hartford Fire Ins. Co., Chgo., 1977—; sole practice Glen Ellyn and Oak Brook, Ill., 1977—. Trustee Village of Glen Ellyn, 1981-85; committeeman Milton Twp., DuPage County Reps, Wheaton, Ill., 1985—; publicity chmn. Milton Twp. Reps., Wheaton, 1986—. Served with U.S. Army, 1964-67. Mem. ABA, Ill. Bar Assn., Chgo. Bar Assn., DuPage County Bar Assn., Fed. Trial Trial Bar Assn., VFW. Presbyterian. Lodges: Kiwanis, Moose. Avocations: camping, fishing, amateur radio. General practice, Federal civil litigation, State civil litigation. Home: 412 Kenilworth Glen Ellyn IL 60137 Office: 2021 Midwest Rd Suite 1105 Oak Brook IL 60521 Also Office: 22W 600 Butterfield Rd Glen Ellyn IL 60137

OLDFIELD, RUSSELL MILLER, lawyer; b. Salem, Ohio, Aug. 18, 1946; s. Donald W. and Virginia Alice (Harold) O.; m. Mary Lou Kubrin, May 28, 1966; children: Lindsey Marie, Grant Russell. AB, Youngstown State U., 1971; JD, Ohio No. U., 1974. Bar: Ohio 1974, U.S. Dist. Ct. (no. dist.) Tenn. 1984. Assoc. counsel Gulf. and Western Industries, Nashville, 1979-83; v.p., gen. counsel, sec. Rogers Group Inc., Nashville, 1983—. Served with U.S. Army, 1966-68. Mem. ABA. Episcopalian. Club: Indian Lake Swim and Tennis (Hendersonville, Tenn.). General corporate, Contracts commercial, Construction. Home: 129 Glen Hill Dr Hendersonville TN 37075 Office: Rogers Group Inc PO Box 25250 Nashville TN 37202

OLDHAM, DARIUS DUDLEY, lawyer; b. Beaumont, Tex., July 6, 1941; s. Darius Saran and Mary Francis (Carraway) O.; m. Judy J. White, Jan. 23, 1966; children—Steven, Michael. B.A., U. Tex., Austin, 1964; J.D., U. Tex., 1966. Bar: Tex. 1966, U.S. Dist. Ct. (so., no., ea. and we. dists.) Tex. 1966, U.S. Supreme Ct. 1974, U.S. Ct. Appeals (5th and 11th cirs.) 1968. Assoc. Fulbright & Jaworski, Houston, 1966-74, ptnr., 1974—; mem. faculty grad. litigation program U. Houston; lectr. on corp. def., aviation and product liability, chmn. aviation com. Def. Research Inst. Contbr. articles to profl. jours. Sec.-treas. FIC Found. Fellow Tex. Bar Found., Am. Bar Found., Houston Bar Found., Am. Bd. Trial Advocates; mem. ABA (chmn. aviation com. litigation sect.; vice chmn. aviation com. tort and ins. practice sect.), Fedn. Ins. and Corp. Counsel (bd. dirs., v.p., chmn. continuing legal edn. and aviation coms.) Tex. Assn. Def. Counsel, Maritime Law Assn. U.S., Am. Counsel Assn., Houston Pops Orchestra (bd. dirs.). Clubs: Lakeside Country, Houston Ctr., Inns of Court (Houston); Les Ambassadeurs (London). Federal civil litigation, State civil litigation, General corporate. Office: Gulf Tower 1301 McKinney 51st Floor Houston TX 77010

OLDHAM, STEVE ANTHONY, lawyer; b. Madisonville, Ky., Dec. 8, 1951; s. Maurice Eugene and Peggy Sue (Nance) O.; m. Sharon Leigh Pavach, June 24, 1974; children: Douglas, Patrick, Ashley. BA, Ind. U., 1973; JD, Harvard U., 1976. Bar: Ind. 1976, U.S. Dist. Ct. (so. dist.) Ind. 1976, U.S. Ct. Appeals (7th cir.) 1978. Assoc. Barnes, Hickam, Pantzer & Boyd, Indpls., 1976-79; atty. Hillenbrand Industries Inc., Batesville, Ind., 1979-82; sr. atty., asst. sec. Hillenbrand Industries Inc., Batesville, 1982-86, assoc. gen. counsel, asst. sec., 1986—. Mem. ABA, Ind. Bar Assn. General corporate, Labor, Real property. Home: Rural Rt #1 327-I Batesville IN 47006 Office: Hillenbrand Industries Inc Hwy 46 Batesville IN 47006

OLDMAN, OLIVER, legal educator; b. N.Y.C., July 19, 1920; s. Max and Rose (Meyers) O.; m. Barbara Lublin, May 2, 1943; children: Andrew, Margaret, Michele. Grad., Mercersburg Acad., 1938; S.B., Harvard, 1942, LL.B., 1953. Bar: N.Y. 1953. Jr. economist OPA, 1942; instr. econs. U. Buffalo, 1946-50; v.p. Lublin Constrn. Co., 1946-50; asso. firm Hodgson, Russ, Andrews, Woods & Goodyear, Buffalo, 1953-55; dir. tng. internat. tax program Harvard Law Sch., 1955-65, dir. internat. tax program, 1965—, prof. law, 1961-76, Learned Hand prof. law, 1976—, dir. East Asian Legal Studies, 1983—; cons. on taxation, Govts. of Argentina, Bolivia, Chile, Colombia, Egypt, El Salvador, Ethiopia, Indonesia, Jamaica, Senegal, Venezuela, Mass., N.Y., N.H., N.Y.C., R.I. and; UN Secretariat. Author: (with others) The Fiscal System of Venezuela, 1959, Financing Urban Development in Mexico City, 1967; Editor: (with R. Bird) Readings on Taxation in Developing Countries, 1964, rev. edit., 1967, 3d edit., 1975, (with P. Kelley) Readings on Income Tax Administration, 1973, (with F.P. Schoettle) State and Local Taxes and Finance, 1974. Served to 1st lt. AUS, 1943-46. Mem. Nat. Tax Assn., Am. Econ. Assn., ABA, Pacific Community Legal Research Seminar. Legal education, Corporate taxation, State and local taxation. Home: 15 Buckingham St Cambridge MA 02138 Office: Harvard Law Sch LW 332 Cambridge MA 02138

OLDS, DAVID MCNEIL, lawyer; b. New Haven, Vt., Jan. 16, 1919; s. Edwin G. and Marion (Knowles) O.; m. Lark Hargraves March; children: Jonathan D. March, Japheth March, Amy M.T. March. B.A. with highest honors, Swarthmore Coll., 1939; LL.B., Harvard U., 1946 (as of 1942). Bar: Pa. 1947. Assoc. firm Duane, Morris & Heckscher, Phila., 1946-48, Reed Smith Shaw & McClay, Pitts., 1948-58; ptnr. Reed Smith Shaw & McClay, 1958—, head environ. law group, 1970-79; mem. Pa. Joint State Govt. Commn. Task Force on Eminent Domain, 1959-72, 82—, chmn. adv. group, 1969—; dir. Pa. Bar Inst. Contbr. articles to profl. jours. Served to lt. comdr. USNR, World War II. Decorated Bronze Star with clasp. Fellow Am. Coll. Trial Lawyers; mem. ABA, Pa. Bar Assn. (chmn. jr. bar sect. 1952-53, chmn. sect. on real property, probate and trust law, chmn. eminent domain com.), Am. Law Inst., Phi Beta Kappa. Club: Harvard-Yale-Princeton. Home: 220 Beech St Edgewood PA 15218 Office: Reed Smith Shaw & McClay Mellon Sq 6th Ave and William Penn Way Pittsburgh PA 15219

O'LEARY, DANIEL BRIAN, lawyer; b. Syracuse, N.Y., May 20, 1947; s. John Patrick and Cecilia Frances (May) O'L.; m. Patricia Anne Adams, June 22, 1974. BA, U. Minn., 1972; JD, William Mitchell Coll. Law, 1976. Bar: Minn. 1976, U.S. Dist. Ct. Minn. 1977. Assoc. Mansur & Mansur, St. Paul, 1976-81; ptnr. Mansur O'Leary & Gabriel, P.A., St. Paul, 1981—; adj. prof. William Mitchell Coll. Law, St. Paul, 1981—. Mem. West St. Paul Charter Commn., 1984—. Served to 1st lt. U.S. Army, 1966-69. Mem. ABA, Assn. Trial Lawyers Am., Minn. Trial Lawyers Assn. (bd. govs. 1976—). Roman Catholic. Personal injury, Workers' compensation, State civil litigation. Home: 1660 Humboldt Ave West Saint Paul MN 55118 Office: Mansur O'Leary & Gabriel PA 300 Minnesota State Bank Bldg 200 S Robert St Saint Paul MN 55107

O'LEARY, MARILYN C., lawyer; b. Rockford, Ill., Sept. 22, 1940; s. Charles Samuel and Nell Theresa (Alongi) Cacciatore; m. James O'Leary, Aug. 4, 1962; children: James, Charles. BA, St. Mary's Coll., Notre Dame, Ind., 1962; MA, U. N.Mex., 1974, JD, 1981. Bar: N.Mex. 1981, U.S. Dist. Ct. (D.C.) 1981/. Campaign mgr. candidate for lt. gov. State of N.Mex., Albuquerque, 1977-78; law clk. Fed. Bankruptcy Ct., Albuquerque, 1981-82; asst. commn. counsel N.Mex. Pub. Service Commn., Santa Fe, 1982-84, exec. dir., 1984-85, commr., 1985-86, chmn., 1986-87; cons. Mgmt. Analysis Co., San Diego, 1987—. Author: Negotiated Settlements in Utility Regulation; co-author: Pueblo Indian Water Rights, 1981, Stay Provisions of the Bankruptcy Act, 1983. Mem. ABA, N.Mex. Bar Assn. (officer natural resources sect. 1983—), Oil Compact Commn., Nat. Assn. Regulatory Utility Commrs. Democrat. Avocations: skiing, music, karate, gourmet cooking. Administrative and regulatory, Public utilities.

O'LEARY, RICHARD PATRICK, lawyer; b. Bklyn., Aug. 9, 1956; s. Daniel Vincent and Mary Magdalen (Maxwell) O'L.; m. Kelly Shawn Patricia Healy, Apr. 28, 1984. AB, Georgetown U., 1978, JD, 1981. Bar: N.J. 1981, U.S. Dist. Ct. N.J. 1981, N.Y. 1982, U.S. Dist. Ct. (so. and ea. dists.) N.Y. 1982, Fla. 1983. Law clk. to presiding justice U.S. Dist. Ct., Newark, 1981-82; assoc. McCarter & English, Newark, 1982—. Coach Ocean Twp. Little League, Soccer, and Biddy Basketball, N.J., 1981—; moderator St. Mary's Youth Group, Deal, N.J., 1985—; tchr. St. Mary's Ch., Deal, 1985—. Mem. ABA, N.J. Bar Assn., N.Y. State Bar Assn., Fla. Bar Assn., Essex County Bar Assn. Republican. Roman Catholic. Avocations: tennis, sailing, bicycling, skiing, golf. Federal civil litigation, State civil litigation, General corporate. Home: 5 Jerome Smith Dr Wayside NJ 07712 Office: McCarter & English 550 Broad St Newark NJ 07102

O'LEARY, THOMAS MICHAEL, lawyer, army officer; b. N.Y.C., Aug. 16, 1948; s. James and Julia Ann (Conolly) O'L.; m. Luise Ann Williams, Jan. 13, 1978; 1 child, Richard Meridith. B.A., CUNY, 1974; J.D., U. Puget Sound., 1977. Bar: Wash. 1977, U.S. Ct. Mil. Appeals 1978, U.S. Supreme Ct. 1983. Dep. pros. atty. Pierce County Pros. Atty.'s Office, Tacoma, 1978; commd. 1st lt. U.S. Army, 1978, advanced through grades to capt., 1978; chief trial counsel Office of Staff Judge Adv., Fort Polk, La., 1978-79, trial def. counsel trial def. service, 1979-81; chief legal advisor Office Insp. Gen., Heidelberg, W.Ger., 1981-82; sr. def. counsel Trial Def. Service, Giessen, W.Ger., 1982-84; asst. chief adminstrv. law U.S. Army Armor Ctr., Fort Knox, Ky., 1984-85, chief adminstrv law, 1985, chief legal asst., 1985-86; sr. trial atty. Immingration and Naturalization Service, Phoenix, 1987—. Decorated Purple Heart; Cross of Gallantry (Vietnam). Mem. ABA, Assn. Trial Lawyers Am., Judge Advs. Assn., Wash. State Bar Assn., Pierce County Bar Assn. Military, Administrative and regulatory, Immigration, naturalization, and customs. Home: 4903 W Thomas Rd Phoenix AZ 85031 Office: Immigration and Naturalization Service 230 N 1st Ave Phoenix AZ 85025-0096

OLES, DOUGLAS S., lawyer; b. Seattle, Nov. 10, 1954; s. Stuart G. and Ilse (Hanewald) O.; m. Laura Treadgold, Dec. 18, 1979. AB in History with honors and distinction, Stanford U., 1976; JD with honors, U. Wash., 1979. Bar: Wash. 1979, U.S. Dist. Ct. (we. dist.) Wash. 1979. Law clk. to judge U.S. Dist. Ct. (we. dist.) Wash., Seattle, 1979-81; assoc. Oles, Morrison, Rinker, Stanislaw & Ashbaugh, Seattle, 1981—. Exec. editor U. Wash. Law Rev., 1978-79. Mem. Diocese Olympia Council, Western Wash., 1985—. Mem. ABA, Wash. State Bar Assn., Seattle King County Bar Assn., Japanese Am. Soc. for Legal Studies, Phi Beta Kappa. Episcopalian. Club: Rainier (Seattle). Avocation: classical archaeology. Construction, Government contracts and claims. Office: Oles Morrison Rinker et al 3300 Columbia Ctr Seattle WA 98104-7007

OLES, LAURA TREADGOLD, lawyer; b. Seattle, June 21, 1956; d. Donald Warren and Alva Adele (Granquist) Treadgold; m. Douglas Stuart Oles, Dec. 18, 1979. AB in History with honors and distinction, Stanford U., 1978; JD, U. Wash., 1981. Bar: Wash. 1981, U.S. Dist. Ct. (we. dist.) Wash. 1981. Assoc. Bogle & Gates, Seattle, 1981-83, Weinrich, Gilmore & Adolph, Seattle, 1983—; bd. dirs. MIT Enterprise Forum of Northwest. Assoc. editor Wash. Law Rev., 1980-81. Mem. ABA, Wash. Bar Assn., Seattle-King County Bar Assn., Japanese-Am. Soc. for Legal Studies. Episcopalian. Securities, General corporate. Home: 6442 NE 192d Pl Seattle WA 98155 Office: Weinrich Gilmore & Adolph 800 5th Ave Seattle WA 98104

OLESKE, MICHAEL MATTHEW, lawyer; b. N.Y.C., June 11, 1952; s. William F.X. and Mary V. (Tierney) O.; m. Mary E. Laspakis, Aug. 22, 1976; children: Timothy Michael, Paul Christian. BA cum laude, Fordham U., 1974; JD, St. John's U., 1977; LLM in Taxation, NYU, 1982. Bar: N.Y. 1978. Atty., editor Inst. for Bus. Planning, Port Washington, N.Y., 1978-82; assoc. Geller and Simon, P.C., N.Y.C., 1982-84; atty. Met. Life Ins. Co., N.Y.C., 1984-86; asst. tax counsel N.Y. Life Ins. Co., N.Y.C., 1986—. Mem. N.Y. Bar Assn. (tax sect., com. on ins. cos.). Democrat. Roman Catholic. Corporate taxation. Home: 30-85 30th St Astoria NY 11102 Office: NY Life Ins Co 51 Madison Ave New York NY 10010

OLEYER, GEORGE RICHARD, lawyer; b. New Britain, Conn., May 24, 1946; s. Michael and Ann (Pacinda) O.; m. Susan Wall, June 28, 1975. B.A., Tufts U., 1968; J.D., Boston U., 1971. Bar: Conn. 1971, U.S. Dist. Ct. Conn. 1971, U.S. Supreme Ct. 1976. Assoc., Lovejoy, Hefferan, Rimer & Curtis, Norwalk, Conn., 1971-74, Magilnick, Simko & Elstein, Bridgeport, Conn., 1974-77; pub. defender Pub. Defender Services, Bridgeport, 1977-86; supervising atty. Juvenile Matters Cts., 1986—; guest lectr. Yale U. Sch. Law, 1978—, U. Bridgeport Sch. Law, 1978—; supervising clin. atty. U. Conn. Sch. Law, 1978—; mem. juvenile justice adv. council Office of Policy and Mgmt.; chmn. juvenile justice subcom., 1985—; others. Co-editor Discovery mag., 1986—. Mem. ABA (chmn. serious juvenile offender com. 1986—, sect. individual rights, chmn. tng. programs subcom. of juvenile justice com., mem. adv. council on implementation of juvenile justice standards), Conn. Bar Assn. (exec. com. sect. human rights and responsibiliites 1979—); Nat. Legal Aid and Defenders Assn. Juvenile, Civil rights. Office: 784 Fairfield Ave Bridgeport CT 06604

OLIAN, ROBERT MARTIN, lawyer; b. Cleve., June 14, 1953; s. Robert Meade and Doris Isa (Hessing) O.; m. Terri Ellen Ruther, Aug. 10, 1980; 1 child, Andrew Zachary. AB, Harvard U., 1973, JD, M in Pub. Policy, 1977. Bar: Ill. 1977, U.S. Dist. Ct. (no. dist.) Ill. 1977, U.S. Ct. Appeals (7th cir.) 1983. Assoc. Sidley & Austin, Chgo., 1977-84, ptnr., 1985—. Panel atty. Chgo. Vol. Legal Services, Chgo., 1983—; mem. planning com. Alexian Bros. Hosp., Elk Grove, Ill., 1985—. Mem. ABA, Ill. Bar Assn., Chgo. Bar Assn., Ill. Assn. Environ. Profls. (bd. dirs. 1984-85). Democrat. Jewish. Clubs: Standard, Harvard (Chgo.). Environment. Home: 50 Pierce Rd Highland Park IL 60035 Office: Sidley & Austin One First Nat Plaza Chicago IL 60603

OLICK, ARTHUR SEYMOUR, lawyer; b. N.Y.C., June 15, 1931; s. Jack and Anita (Babsky) O.; m. Selma Ada Kaufman, June 27, 1954; children: Robert Scott, Karen Leslie. B.A., Yale U., 1952, LL.B., J.D., 1955. Bar: N.Y. 1956. Instr. polit. sci.-bus. law U. Ga., 1955-57; assoc. atty. Casey, Lane & Mittendorf, N.Y.C., 1957-62; asst. U.S. atty. So. Dist. N.Y., 1962-68; chief civil div. 1965-68; partner Otterbourg, Steindler, Houston & Rosen, N.Y.C., 1968-71, Kreindler, Relkin, Olick & Goldberg, N.Y.C., 1971-74; officer, dir. Anderson, Russell, Kill & Olick (P.C.), N.Y.C., 1974—; partner Anderson, Baker, Kill & Olick, Washington, 1979—; lectr. Practicing Law Inst., N.Y.C., 1965—, Comml. Law League; candidate N.Y. State Supreme Ct., 1971; counsel Tarrytown (N.Y.) Urban Renewal Agy., 1968-73, 75-77; town atty., Greenburgh, N.Y., 1974, spl. counsel, Town of New Castle, N.Y., 1979—, village atty., Tarrytown, 1968-73, 75-77, Dobbs Ferry, N.Y., 1975-77; dir. Westchester County (N.Y.) Legal Aid Soc., 1976-79. Pres. Hartsdale (N.Y.) Bd. Edn., 1968-72; bd. dirs. Westchester County Mcpl. Planning Fedn., 1976-78, Circle in the Sq. Theater, 1978—; trustee Calhoun Sch., N.Y.C., 1973-80. Served with U.S. Army, 1955-57. Mem. Am., N.Y. State, Westchester County bar assns., Assn. Bar City New York, Fed. Bar Council, Am. Arbitration Assn. (nat. panel arbitrators), Phi Beta Kappa. Club: Yale, Merchants (N.Y.C.); Nat. Lawyers (Washington). Bankruptcy, Federal civil litigation, State civil litigation. Home: 98 Harvard Dr Hartsdale NY 10530 also: Lake Oscawana Putnam Valley NY 10579 Office: 666 3d Ave New York NY 10017

OLIENSIS, SHELDON, lawyer; b. Phila., Mar. 19, 1922. A.B. with honors, U. Pa., 1943; LL.B. magna cum laude, Harvard U., 1948. Bar: N.Y. State bar 1949. Partner Kaye Scholer Fierman Hays & Handler, N.Y.C., 1960—. Pres.: Harvard Law Rev., 1948. Trustee Harvard Law Sch. Assn., 1973-77, 1st v.p., 1980-82, pres., 1982-84; trustee Harvard Law Sch. Assn. N.Y.C., 1962-65, v.p., 1972-73, pres., 1978-79; nat. chmn. Harvard Law Sch. Fund, 1973-75; mem. Harvard overseers com. to visit law sch., 1981-87; spl. master appellate div. 1st dept. N.Y. State Supreme Ct., 1983—; bd. dirs. Legal Aid Soc., 1969—, pres., 1973-75; vice-chmn. N.Y.C. Cultural Council, 1968-75; bd. dirs. Cultural Council Found., 1968—, pres., 1968-72, v.p., 1972-82; bd. dirs. Park Assn. N.Y.C., Inc., 1963-73, exec. com., 1967-73, pres., 1965-67; bd. dirs. Gateway Sch., N.Y.C., 1968-83, chmn. bd. trustees, 1968-70; dir., officer Wiltwyck Sch. for Boys, Inc., 1951-71; bd. dirs. East Harlem Tutorial Program, 1972-80, Fund for Modern Cts., 1979—, N.Y. Laywers for Pub. Interest, 1980-85; bd. dirs. Vols. of Legal Service Inc., 1984—, pres., 1984-87. Fellow Am. Coll. Trial Lawyers, Am. Bar Found.; mem. Lawyers' Com. Civil Rights Under Law, ABA, N.Y. State Bar Assn., N.Y. County Lawyers Assn., Assn. of Bar of City of N.Y. (exec. com. 1961-65, v.p. 1974-75, 86—, chmn. com. state legis. 1959-61, com. revision of constn. and by-laws 1965-66, com. electric power and environ. 1971-74, com. on grievances 1975-78, com. on access to legal services 1982-87 , com. on fee disputes and conciliation, 1987—, mem. com. on grievances 1966-69, com. judiciary 1969-71, environ. report 1972, ad hoc com. lawyer advt. 1977-78). Federal civil litigation, State civil litigation, Administrative and regulatory. Office: Kaye Scholer Fierman Hays & Handler 425 Park Ave New York NY 10022

OLINDE, JOHN FRANCIS, lawyer; b. Baton Rouge, Feb. 28, 1957. BBA, Emory U., 1979; JD, La. State U., 1982. Bar: La. 1982, U.S. Dist. Ct. (ea. and mid. dist.) La. 1982. Law clk. La. Supreme Ct., New Orleans, 1982-83; assoc. Chaffe, McCall, Phillips, Toler & Sarpy, New Orleans, 1983—. Mem. ABA, La. Bar Assn., Nat. Inst. Trial Advocacy, Order of the Coif. Insurance, Personal injury. Office: Chaffe McCall Phillips Toler & Sarpy 1500 FNBC Bldg New Orleans LA 70112

OLIVA, ROBERT ROGELIO, legal educator; b. Havana, Cuba, Jan. 5, 1946; came to U.S., 1962; s. Roberto J. Oliva and Juana (Ruiz) Gonzalez; m. Iris Borrok, Dec. 17, 1966. BS in Fin., Fla. Atlantic U., 1967; JD, Whittier Coll., 1980; LLM in Taxation, U. San Diego, 1983. Bar: Fla. 1981, Calif. 1981, U.S. Dist. Ct. (cen. dist.) Calif. 1981, U.S. Tax ct. 1983, U.S. Dist. Ct. (so. dist.) Fla. 1984, U.S. Ct. Appeals (11th cir.) 1984; CPA, Fla. Investment stockbroker Merrill Lynch, Los Angeles, 1973-77; assoc. prof. taxation Fla. Internat. U. Sch. of Acctg., Miami, 1981—. Contbr. articles to profl. jours. Pres. Reform Jewish Congregation, San Juan, P.R., 1975; legal advisor, bd. dirs. Dade-Broward Lupus Found., Miami, 1981—. Served to staff sgt. USAF, 1968-71, PTO. Mem. Calif. Bar Assn., Fla. Bar Assn., Am. Bus. Law Assn., Am. Taxation Assn., Am. Acctg. Assn. Republican. Jewish. Avocation: travel. Legal education, Corporate taxation, International taxation. Office: Fla Internat U Sch of Acctg DM 371A Miami FL 33199

OLIVAS, ADOLF, lawyer, city official; b. Hamilton, Ohio, Jan. 31, 1956; s. Henry and Eloina (Lopez) O.; m. Marian Jayne Hart, Dec. 7, 1985. B.A., U. Cin., 1978, J.D., 1981. Bar: Ohio 1981, U.S. Dist. Ct. (so. dist.) Ohio 1981. Law clk., U.S. Dist. Ct. Ea. Dist. Ky., Covington, 1981; assoc. Holbrock, Jonson, Bressler & Houser, Hamilton, Ohio, 1981-85; ptnr. Rogers & Olivas, 1985—. Mem. Hamilton City Council, 1983-85; vice mayor City of Hamilton, 1986—; mem. exec. com. Butler County Democatic Com., 1983—; bd. dirs. Open Door Food Pantry, Hamilton, 1982-85; county coordinator Ohio State Gov. Celeste, 1982—; bd. dirs. Hamilton Com. Improvement Corp., 1986— . Mem. Butler County Bar Assn., Cin. Bar Assn., ABA, Assn. Trial Lawyers Am., Ohio State Bar Coll., U.S. Jaycees. Roman Catholic. Avocations: racquetball, running, biking. Personal injury, State civil litigation, Criminal. Home: 130 W Fairway Dr Hamilton OH 45013 Office: Rogers & Olivas 6 Court St PO Box 1240 Hamilton OH 45012

OLIVE, SUSAN FREYA, lawyer; b. Durham, N.C., June 26, 1952; d. B.B. and Denyse L.A. (Edwards) O.; m. Richard Anthony Rall, June 28, 1980; children—Erin Alyssa, Park Anthony, Ashley Erica. A.B. in Med.-Legal Interface, Brown U., 1974; J.D. with distinction, Duke U., 1977. Bar: N.C. 1976, U.S. Ct. Mil. Appeals 1976, U.S. Dist. Ct. (ea. and mid. dists.) N.C. 1977, U.S. Dist. Ct. (we. dist.) N.C. 1984. Sole practice Durham, N.C., 1976-77; spl. counsel 9th Jud. Dist., Butner, N.C., 1977-79; ptnr. Olive, Faust & Olive, Durham, 1979-80; ptnr. Olive & Olive, P.A., Durham, 1980-86, v.p., 1986—; regional chmn. Brown U. Nat. Alumni Schs. Program, Central N.C., 1977—; guest lectr. Duke U. Sch. Law, Durham, 1982—, supervising atty. trial advocacy clinic outplacement, 1982-83; participant supervising atty. Duke U., 1982—; guest lectr. N.C. Sch. Sci. and Math., Durham, 1983—; lectr. continuing legal edn. program N.C. Bar Found., Raleigh, 1983, 85, 86; mem. N.C. Fed. Bar Adv. Council, 1984—; mem. merit selection panel U.S. Dist. Ct. (mid. dist.) N.C., 1984, mem. atty. qualifications rev. com., 1984—. Editor: The Durham Docket newsletter, 1977-83, Reference Guide for Area Mental Health, Mental Retardation and Substance Abuse Board Members in North Carolina, 1980. Bd. dirs. Mental Health Assn. Durham County, 1979-83, chmn. legis. com., 1980-82; bd. dirs. N.C. Prisoners' Legal Services, Inc., Raleigh, 1980—; fin. dir. Knox 1984 Gubernatorial Campaign, Durham County, 1984. Mem. N.C. Coll. Advocacy, N.C. Bar Found., Durham County Bar Assn. (sec. 1981-82, pres. 1983-84), Fourteenth Jud. Dist. Bar (pres. 1983-84), N.C. Bar Assn. (rep. to Dorothea Dix Hosp. med.-legal adv. com. 1980-84, chmn. com. on mental health law 1982-84, nominations com. 1983-84, chmn. Intellectual Property Law com. 1984-87), Carolina Patent, Trademark and Copyright Law Assn., N.C. Acad. Trial Lawyers (lectr. continuing legal edn. program 1983), N.C. Assn. Women Attys., ABA, Am. Soc. Law and Medicine, Assn. Trial Lawyers Am. Democrat. Episcopalian. Trademark and copyright, Patent, Computer. Home: Rt 2 Box 473 Durham NC 27705 Office: Olive & Olive PA 500 Memorial St PO Box 2049 Durham NC 27702

OLIVER, ANTHONY THOMAS, JR., lawyer; b. San Jose, Calif., July 19, 1929; s. Anthony Thomas and Josephine Gertrude (Bem) O.; m. Beverly J. Wirz, Jan. 27, 1952; children—Jeanne M. Hall, Marilyn M., Cynthia M. Eschardies, Michelle M. Rogan; m. Margaret E. Gurke, Mar. 31, 1984; 1 child, Christopher A. B.S., U. Santa Clara, 1951, J.D., 1953. Bar: Calif. 1954, U.S. Supreme Ct. 1979. Asst. counsel Bank Am. Legal Dept., Los Angeles, 1953-57; assoc. Taylor & Barker, Los Angeles, 1957-58, John F. O'Hara, Los Angeles, 1958-63; sr. pntr., chmn. labor dept. Parker, Milliken, Clark, O'Hara & Samuelian; Los Angeles, 1963—. Mem. Town Hall Calif., 1981—; bd. visitors U. Santa Clara Coll. Law, 1982—. Served to lt. col. USAR. Recipient Edwin J. Owens Lawyer of Year award U. Santa Clara Coll. Law, 1976. Mem. ABA (co-chmn. com. labor arbitration 1985—), Los Angeles County Bar Assn., Indsl. Relations Research Assn., Am. Arbitration Assn. (mem. adv. bd. Los Angeles), N.G. Assn. U.S., N.G. Assn. Calif., State Bar Calif. (chmn. labor law sect. 1985-86), Ariz. Indsl. Relations Assn. , Orange County Indsl. Relations Research Assn., Roman Catholic. Club: University, Chancery (Los Angeles). Labor. Home: 2606 Canada Blvd #201 Glendale CA 91208 Office: 333 S Hope St 27th Floor Los Angeles CA 90071

OLIVER, BONNIE CHESSHER, lawyer; b. Atlanta, Jan. 14, 1957; d. Albert Jack and Bonnie Faye (Richardson) C.; m. Michael Edward Oliver,

Oct. 15, 1983; 1 child, Jackson Edward. BA, Shorter Coll., 1978; JD, Mercer U., 1981. Bar: Ga. 1981, U.S. Dist. Ct. (no. dist.) Ga. 1981. Gen. counsel Peak Services, Inc., Gainesville, Ga., 1981-85; assoc. Wycliffe Orr, Gainesville, 1986—; bd. dirs. Dunlap Employment Tng. Services, Gainesville, 1985—. Author: Senior Citizens Handbook, 1984; editor Law for the Elderly Manual, 1983. Mem. ABA, Ga. Bar Assn. (exec. council 1983-87), Gainesville-Northeast Ga. Bar Assn. Democrat. Roman Catholic. Lodge: Civitan (bd. dirs. 1984-87). Avocations: water skiing, history. Insurance, Personal injury, State civil litigation. Home: Rt 6 Box 967 Maynard Circle Gainesville GA 30503 Office: 625 Green St Gainesville GA 30503

OLIVER, DALE HUGH, lawyer; b. Lansing, Mich., June 26, 1947; s. Alvin Earl and Jean Elizabeth (Stanton) O.; m. Mylbra Ann Chorney, Aug. 16, 1969; children—Nathan Corey, John Franklin. B.A., Mich. State U., 1969; J.D. cum laude, Harvard U., 1972. Bar: D.C. 1973, U.S. Dist. Ct. (D.C. dist.) 1973, U.S. Ct. Claims 1983, U.S. Ct. Appeals (D.C. cir.) 1976, U.S. Ct. Appeals (fed. cir.) 1983, U.S. Supreme Ct. 1980. Assoc., ptnr. Jones, Day, Reavis & Pogue, Washington, 1975-79; ptnr. Crowell & Moring, Washington, 1979-84; ptnr. Gibson, Dunn & Crutcher, Washington, 1984-87; ptnr. Jones, Day, Reavis & Pogue, Washington, 1987—. Contbr. articles to profl. jours. Editor jour. Pub. Contracts Law, 1980—. Spl. counsel 1980 Presdl. Inaugural Com., Washington, 1980. Served to capt. USAF, 1973-75. Mem. ABA (com. chmn. pub. contract section 1979—), Nat. Contract Mgmt. Assn., Nat. Security Indsl. Assn., Harvard Law Sch. Assn. Club: Mich. State U. Alumni of Washington (pres., dir. 1984—). Government contracts and claims, Federal civil litigation. Home: 8403 Honeywood Ct McLean VA 22102 Office: Jones Day Reavis & Pogue 655 15th St NW Washington DC 20005

OLIVER, DAVID FIELD, lawyer; b. Kansas City, Mo., Mar. 23, 1952; s. John Watkins and Gertrude (Field) O.; m. Mary Elizabeth Gresham, Mar. 26, 1983. BA, Haverford Coll., 1974; JD, Boston U., 1977. Bar: Mo. 1977, U.S. Dist. Ct. (we. dist.) Mo. 1977. Ptnr. Field, Gentry, Benjamin & Robertson, Kansas City, 1982—; pres. Greater Kansas City Mental Health Found., 1980-85, bd. dirs. 1981—; pres. Kansas City Eye Bank, 1983-86, bd. dirs. 1981—; bd. dirs. Edgar Snow Meml. Fund, 1982—, The Cross Found., 1982—, Choral Arts Ensemble of Kansas City, 1982—, Greater Kansas City Epilepsy League, 1984—, De La Salle Edn. Ctr., 1985—. Mem. ABA, Mo. Bar Assn., Kansas City Bar Assn., Lawyers Assn. Kansas City, Phi Beta Kappa. Clubs: Mission Hills Country, University (Kansas City). Federal civil litigation, State civil litigation, General practice. Office: Field Gentry Benjamin & Robertson 600 E 11th St Kansas City MO 64106

OLIVER, J. VAN, lawyer; b. Steubenville, Ohio, June 26, 1949; s. Paul E. and Barbara (Burke) O.; m. Anne Martin, June 12, 1971; children: Ashley Lauren, Linsay Brooke. BA, Vanderbilt U., 1971, JD, 1974; postdoctoral, So. Meth. U., 1975-77. Bar: Tex., U.S. Dist. Ct. (no. dist.) Tex., U.S. Tax Ct., U.S. Ct. Appeals (5th cir.). Law clk. to presiding justice U.S. Dist. Ct. (no. dist.) Tex., Dallas, 1974-75; ptnr. Thompson & Knight, Dallas, 1975-82, Akin, Gump, Strauss, Hauer & Feld, Dallas, 1983-87; of counsel Andrews & Kuath, Dallas, 1987—. Head usher St. Michael's and All Angels Ch., Dallas. Mem. ABA (corp. banking and comml. law sect., tax, secured creditors' and oil and gas subcoms., speaker), Dallas Bar Assn. (pres. comml. and bankruptcy law sect. 1980-81). Episcopalian. Club: Tower. Bankruptcy. Home: 3429 Southwestern Blvd Dallas TX 75225 Office: Andrews & Kuath 4400 Thanksgiving Tower Dallas TX 75201

OLIVER, JOHN LEACHMAN, lawyer; b. Carmel, Calif., Apr. 23, 1943; s. Jack L. and Elizabeth H. (Pierce) O.; 1 child, John L. III. BA with honors, Yale U., 1965; JD (valedictorian), U. Mo., 1968. Bar: Mo., U.S. Dist. Ct. (ea. and we. dists.) Mo., U.S. Dist. Ct. (so. dist.) Ill., U.S. Dist. Ct. D.C., U.S. Ct. Appeals (5th, 7th and 8th cirs.), U.S. Supreme Ct. Law clk. to presiding justice U.S. Dist. Ct. (ea. dist.) Mo., St. Louis, 1968-69; assoc. Oliver, Oliver, Waltz, Cape Giradeau, Mo., 1969-71; ptnr., pres. Oliver, Oliver, Waltz & Cook P.C., Cape Giradeau, 1971—; lectr. real estate, fed. and Mo. practice; mem. Mo. Supreme Ct. Com., Mo. Supreme Ct. Com. on Rules of Evidence, Mo. Supreme Ct. Com. on Advt.; mem. Mo. Bd. Law Examiners. Co-author: Missouri Evidence Revised; editor: Missouri Bar CLE Handbook; contbr. articles to legal jours. Fellow ABA, Am. Bar Found.; mem. Def. Research Inst., Mo. Orgn. Def. Lawyers (exec. com.), Bar Assn. Met. St. Louis, Mo. Bar Assn. (chmn. tort law com. 1982-84, chmn. client security fund 1986—), Internat. Assn. Ins. Counsel, Order of Coif, Phi Delta Phi. Federal civil litigation, State civil litigation. Home: #8 Terripan Ln Cape Girardeau MO 63701

OLIVER, MILTON MCKINNON, lawyer, German translator, patent database searcher; b. Columbia, S.C., Jan. 12, 1951; s. Caldwell Hardy and Eleanor (McKinnon) O.; m. Joan Nichols, July 12, 1981; children—John, James. B.A., Harvard U., 1972; J.D., Golden Gate U., 1975. Bar: Calif. 1975, Mass. 1975, Fla. 1978, D.C. 1983, N.Y. 1984, U.S. Supreme Ct. 1979, U.S. Ct. Appeals (Fed. cir.) 1982. Assoc. Wolf, Greenfield & Sacks, P.C., Boston and West Palm Beach, Fla., 1977-83, Frishauf, Holtz, Goodman & Woodward, P.C., N.Y.C., 1983—. Author Congl. testimony on offshore oil drilling, Dec. 1978. Mem. Am., N.Y., Boston Patent Law Assns., Calif. State Bar Patent-Trademark-Copyright Sect., Computer Law Assn., Lawyers in Mensa, Aircraft Owners and Pilots Assn., Fedn. Am. Scientists, Sierra Club (life, chmn. nat. oil and gas subcom. 1976-79). Episcopalian. Patent, Trademark and copyright, Private international. Home: 35 Alton Rd Stamford CT 06906 Office: 261 Madison Ave 19th Floor New York NY 10016-2363

OLIVER, RAYMOND A., lawyer; b. Paterson, N.J., Feb. 26, 1951; s. Nicholas Joseph and Mona (Fayad) O.; m. Katherine Osborne McCullough, Aug. 27, 1977; children—Kristine Bettcher, Bennet Raymond. Student Emporia Coll., 1969-71; A.B., Loyola U., Chgo., 1973; postgrad NYU, 1974; J.D., John Marshall Law Sch., 1979. Bar: N.J. 1979, U.S. Dist. Ct. N.J. 1979, D.C. 1980. Clinic atty. Ill. Office Atty. Gen., Chgo., 1978-79; chief investigative staff, asst. to dir. Somerset County Consumer Affairs Office, Somerville, N.J., 1979; sole practice, West Paterson, N.J., and Washington, 1979—; instr. Taylor Bus. Inst., Plainfield, N.J., 1981. Mem. N.J. Bar Assn. (bd. dirs. adminstrv. law sect. 1983—, sec. adminstrv. law sect. 1985—, editor adminstrv. law newsletter 1979—), Passaic County Bar Assn. (chmn. govt. law sect. 1983—, chmn. scholarship fund 1984—, chmn. constitutional law and civil rights com., chmn. internat. law com.), U.N. Internat. Progress Orgn., D.C. Bar Assn., Assn. Trial Lawyers Am. Democrat. Roman Catholic. Administrative and regulatory, Federal civil litigation, General practice. Home: 88 Rose Pl W Paterson NJ 07424 Office: Great Notch Ctr Notch Rd & Hwy 46W West Paterson NJ 07424

OLIVER, ROBERT HAROLD, lawyer; b. San Jose, Calif., June 21, 1943; s. Arthur S. and Elsa Mae (Sawyer) O.; m. Stephanie Yates, July 24, 1971; children: Charles A., Bradley R. BSBA, Calif. State U., Fresno, 1966; JD, Golden State U., 1973. CLU. Assoc. predecessor firm of Wild, Carter, Tipton & Oliver, Fresno, 1973-75; ptnr. Wild, Carter, Tipton & Oliver, Fresno, 1975—; instr. paralegal law San Joaquin Delta Coll., Stockton, Calif.; former instr. Humphreys Coll., Stockton. Mem. dist. hearing bd. Fresno County Air Pollution Control, 1975-77, adv. bd. Salvation Army Fresno Citadel, 1975, chmn. 1979-80; mem. adv. bd. YMCA, 1983, adv. bd. Leadership Fresno, 1984, steering com. 1985; bd. dirs. St. Agnes Hosp. Found., 1983; pres. Fresno Estate Planning Council, 1985-86. Served to lt. col. Calif. N.G., 1965—. Named Man Yr., Jr. C. of C., Fresno, 1970; recipient Service award Salvation Army, 1979. Mem. Calif. Bar Assn. (recognition award 1983-84, mem. various coms.), Fresno County Bar Assn. (pres. 1982, pres. young lawyers div.). Republican. Lodge: Rotary (pres. Fresno chpt. 1986—). Avocation: dixieland jazz. General corporate, Estate planning. Office: Wild Carter Tipton & Oliver 246 W Shaw Ave Fresno CA 93704

OLIVER, ROBERT SPENCER, lawyer; b. Newark, Nov. 1, 1937; s. Robert and Mary Louise (McClellan) O.; divorced; children: Jackie, Martha, Robert S. Jr. BA, Tex. Christian U., 1960; JD, George Washington U., 1967. Bar: D.C., 1974. Spl. asst., press sec. to Carl Hayden U.S. Senate, 1962-66; dep. chmn. Nat. Dem. Com., Washington, 1967-70; exec. dir. Assoc. of State Dem. Chmn., Washington, 1971-75; staff dir., gen. counsel Helsinki Commn. U.S. Congress, 1976-85; chief counsel fgn. affairs com. U.S. Ho. of Reps., 1985—; adminstrv. asst. to chmn. Dem Nat. Com., 1966-67. Pres. Young Polit. Leaders NATO, Brussels, 1971-74, Young Dems. Am., 1967-69; bd. dirs., trustee Nat. Dem. Inst. for Internat. Affairs, 1983-85. Mem. Am. Council Young Polit. Leaders (bd. dirs., trustee 1967—). Episcopalian. Public international, Legislative, Government contracts and claims. Office: US Ho of Reps Fgn Affairs Com 2170 Rayburn House Office Bldg Washington DC 20515

OLIVER, ROSEANN SELLANI, lawyer, nurse; b. Pittston, Pa., Sept. 12, 1939; d. Pasquale Ronaldo and Lucy (Potenza) Sellani; m. Karl J. Oliver, Nov. 22, 1960 (div. Mar. 1978); children: Karlene M., Patrick Sellani, Andrew Potenza Sellani. Diploma, Pittston Hosp. Sch of Nursing, 1960; BS in Nursing, U. Pa., 1969, MS in Nursing, 1972; JD, Rutgers U., 1979. Bar: Pa. 1979, N.J. 1980, U.S. Dist. Ct. N.J. 1980, U.S. Dist. Ct. (ea. dist.) Pa. 1981, U.S. Ct. Appeals (3d cir.) 1985, U.S. Supreme Ct. 1986. Various nursing positions hosps., N.J. and Pa., 1960-70; paralegal Brown, Connery, Camden, N.J., 1971-79; assoc. Brown, Connery, Camden, 1979-82; sole practice Phila., 1982—, Camden and Bridgeton, N.J., 1982—; cons. in field, 1972-79; lectr. on law and nursing various insts. Mem. ABA, Pa. Bar Assn., N.J. Bar Assn., Am. Soc. Law and Medicine, Am. Pub. Health Assn., Am. Nurses Assn., N.J. Nurses Assn. Avocations: mother, homemaker. Personal injury, Plaintiff medical malpractice. Home and Office: RD #9 Box 53 Finley Sta Rd Bridgeton NJ 08302

OLIVERI, PAUL FRANCIS, lawyer; b. Far Rockaway, N.Y., Feb. 27, 1954; s. Alphonse J. and Rita (Gregorace) O.; m. Debra Lynn Malkin, Aug. 7, 1977; 1 child, Jason Robert. BA, NYU, 1976; JD, St. John's U., Queens, N.Y., 1978. Bar: N.Y. 1979, U.S. Dist. Ct. (ea. and so. dists.) N.Y. 1980. Assoc. Fuchsberg & Fuchsberg, N.Y.C., 1979-83; ptnr. Oliveri & Schwartz, N.Y.C., 1983—; cons. atty. Alliance for Consumer Rights, N.Y.C., 1986—. Mem. ABA, N.Y. State Bar Assn., Assn. Trial Lawyers Am., N.Y. State Trial Lawyers Assn. Avocations: music, numismatics. Personal injury, Insurance. Office: Oliveri & Schwartz 30 Vesey St New York NY 10007

OLMER, LIONEL HERBERT, lawyer; b. New Haven, Nov. 11, 1934; s. Abraham and Gertrude (Jacobs) O.; m. Judith Sayler, 1962; children—Stuart A., Sally A. B.A., U. Conn., 1956; J.D., Am. U., 1963; postgrad., Nat. War Coll., 1972-73. Bar: Conn. 1963, D.C. 1975. Commd. ensign U.S. Navy, advanced through grades to capt., 1977; sea duty and shore assignments in Japan, Philippines, Hawaii, and the Atlantic; staff of chief of naval ops. 1969-72; staff exec. Pres.'s Fgn. Intelligence Adv. Bd., 1973-77; ret. 1977; dir. internat. programs Motorola Corp., Washington, 1977-81; undersec. internat. trade U.S. Dept. Commerce, Washington, 1981-85; ptnr. Paul, Weiss, Rifkind, Wharton & Garrison, Washington, 1985—. Bd. dirs. Internat. Rescue Com., 1980-85. Mem. Conn. Bar Assn., Fed. Bar Assn. Home: 6107 Neilwood Dr Rockville MD 20852 Office: 1615 L St NW Suite 1300 Washington DC 20036

OLMSTEAD, CECIL JAY, JR., lawyer; b. Jacksonville, Fla., Oct. 15, 1920; s. Cecil Jay Sr. and Bessie (Irby) O.; m. Frances Hughes; children: Cecil Jay III, Frank Hughes, Jane Olmstead Murphy, Amy Olmstead Vanecek. B.A., U. Ga., 1950, LL.B., 1951; Sterling Grad. fellow, Yale Law Sch., 1951-52; LL.D. (hon.), U. Hull, Eng., 1978. Bar: Ga. 1950, U.S. Supreme Ct 1964, D.C. 1978. Asst. to legal adviser Dept. State, counsel Mut. Security Agy., counsel Hoover Commn. on Orgn. Exec. Br. of Govt., 1952-55; prof. N.Y. U. Sch. Law, 1953-61; dir. Inter-Am. Law Inst., 1958-61, adj. prof. law, 1961—; atty. Texaco, Inc., N.Y.C., 1961-62; asst. to chmn. bd. Texaco, Inc., 1962-70, v.p., asst. to chmn. bd., 1970, v.p., asst. to pres., 1970-71, v.p., asst. to chief exec. officer, 1971-73, exec. dept., v.p., 1973-80; mem. firm Steptoe & Johnson, Washington, 1980—; Mem. adv. panel on internat. law to sec. state; adv. com. law of sea State Dept.; also adv. com. transnat. enterprise; U.S. del. UN Com. on Law of Sea, 1972-73; U.S. del. UN Conf. on Law of Sea, 1974-76; Eisenhower lectr. Nat. War Coll., 1973; mem. U.S. del. UN Conf. on Code of Conduct for Transnat. Corps., 1984, 85, 86; vis. fellow All Souls Coll., Oxford U., 1988. Mem. Internat. Law Assn. (pres. Am. br. 1966-73, pres. 1972-75, vice chmn. exec. council 1975-86, chmn. exec. council, 1986—), Am. Law Inst. (assoc. reporter Restatement of the Fgn. Relations Law of the U.S.), Council on Fgn. Relations, Washington Inst. Fgn. Relations, Am. Soc. Internat. Law, Nat. Petroleum Council, Nat. Fgn. Trade Council (dir.), Am. Council on Germany (dir). Episcopalian. Clubs: Knickerbocker, Yale (N.Y.C.); Fairfield County Hunt (Westport); 1925 F Street, Cosmos (Washington); Fla. Yacht (Jacksonville). Home: 4 Sprucewood Ln Westport CT 06880 Office: Steptoe & Johnson 1330 Connecticut Ave NW Washington DC 20036

OLMSTEAD, CLARENCE WALTER, JR., lawyer; b. Alexandria, Va., Jan. 24, 1943; s. Clarence Walter and Rhea Nancy (Donnelly) O.; m. Kathleen Frances Heenan, Sept. 7, 1973; children: Nicholas Heenan, Jonathan Heenan, Caitlin Heenan. AB, Stanford U., 1965; LLB, Columbia U., 1968. Bar: N.Y. 1970, U.S. Dist. Ct. (so. and ea. dists.) N.Y. 1970, U.S. Ct. Appeals (2d cir.) 1970, U.S. Supreme Ct. 1986. Law clk. to presiding justice U.S. Dist. Ct. (we. dist.) Wis., 1968-69; assoc. Shearman & Sterling, N.Y.C., 1969-76, ptnr., 1976—. Pres., bd. dirs. West Side Montessori Sch., N.Y.C., 1985—. Mem. ABA, N.Y. State Bar Assn., Phi Beta Kappa. Federal civil litigation, Real property. Home: 470 West End Ave New York NY 10024 Office: Shearman & Sterling 153 E 53d St New York NY 10005

OLMSTEAD, WILLIAM J., lawyer; b. Liberal, Kans., Aug. 17, 1944; s. Herschel Alonzo and Elsie Grace (Deuel) O.; m. Rebecca Joan Berthelsen, June 14, 1967; 1 child, Thomas Justin. Student, Am. U., 1965; BA, Southwestern Coll., 1966; JD, Washburn U., 1974. Dir. affirmative action Washburn U., Topeka, 1974; with U.S. Nuclear Regulatory Commn., Washington, 1974-80, dep. chief hearing counsel, 1980-81, dir. regulations, 1981-86, dir. hearings, 1986—. Notes editor Washburn U. Law Rev., 1974. Area v.p. Montgomery County Council of PTA's, Md., 1985-87; chair com. Hughes United Meth. Ch., Wheaton, Md., 1985—. Served to capt. USAF, 1966-71. Mem. ABA, Kans. Bar Assn., Delta Theta Phi. Democrat. Avocations: photography, journalism, computers. Nuclear power, Administrative and regulatory, Environment. Office: US Nuclear Regulatory Commn Hearings Div 1717 H St NW Washington DC 20555

O'LOUGHLIN, JOHN PATRICK, lawyer; b. Cape Girardeau, Mo., Nov. 21, 1950; s. Thomas King and Agnes (Schmuke) O'L. B.A., Southeast Mo. State U., 1973; J.D., U. Tulsa, 1976. Bar: Mo. 1977, U.S. Dist. Ct. (ea. dist.) Mo. 1977, U.S. Ct. Appeals (8th cir.) 1978. Asst. prosecutor Cape Girardeau County, Mo., 1977-79; ptnr. O'Loughlin, O'Loughlin & McManaman, Cape Girardeau, 1977—; faculty Southeast Mo. State U., Cape Girardeau, 1977. Contbr. articles to profl. jours. Democratic committeeman, Cape Girardeau County, 1984; active United Way, Cape Girardeau, 1977-78. Mem. Cape Girardeau County Bar Assn., Mo. Bar Assn., ABA, Bankruptcy Trustees Assn., Assn. Trial Lawyers Am., Cape Girardeau C. of C. (agr. com. 1980-82). Roman Catholic. Lodges: K.C., Elks. Bankruptcy, Contracts commercial, General corporate. Home: 3125 Themis Apt 2 Cape Girardeau MO 63701 Office: O'Loughlin O'Loughlin & McManaman 1736 N Kings Hwy Cape Girardeau MO 63701

OLSCHWANG, ALAN PAUL, lawyer; b. Chgo., Jan. 30, 1942; s. Morton James and Ida (Ginsberg) O.; m. Barbara Claire Miller, Aug. 22, 1965; children—Elliot, Deborah, Jeffrey. B.S., U. Ill., 1963, J.D., 1966. Bar: Ill. 1966. Law clk. Ill. Supreme Ct., Bloomington, 1966-67; assoc. Sidley & Austin, and predecessor, Chgo., 1967-73; with Montgomery Ward & Co., Inc., Chgo., 1973-81, assoc. gen. counsel, asst. sec., 1979-81; ptnr. Seki, Jarvis & Lynch, Chgo., 1981-84; v.p., gen. counsel Mitsubishi Electric Am., Inc., N.Y.C., 1983—. Mem. Am. Corp. Counsel Assn., ABA, Ill. Bar Assn., Chgo. Bar Assn., N.Y. State Bar Assn., Bar Assn. City of N.Y., Am. Arbitration Assn. (panel arbitrators). Contracts commercial, General corporate, Private international. Office: 645 Fifth Ave New York NY 10022

OLSEN, ALFRED JON, lawyer; b. Phoenix, Oct. 5, 1940; s. William Hans and Vera (Bearden) O.; m. Susan K. Smith, Apr. 15, 1979. B.A. in History, U. Ariz., 1962; M.S. in Acctg, Ariz. State U., 1964; J.D., Northwestern U., 1966. Bar: Ariz. 1966, Ill. 1966; C.P.A., Ariz., Ill. cert. tax specialist. Acct. Arthur Young & Co., C.P.A.s, Chgo., 1966-68; dir. firm Ehmann, Olsen & Lane (P.C.), Phoenix, 1969-76; dir. Streich, Lang, Weeks & Cardon (P.C.), Phoenix, 1977-78; v.p. Olsen-Smith, Ltd., Phoenix, 1978—. Bd. editors: Jour. Agrl. Law and Taxation, 1978—, Practical Real Estate Lawyer, 1983—. Mem. Phoenix adv. bd. Salvation Army., 1973-81. Fellow Am. Coll. Probate Counsel, Am. Coll. Tax Counsel; Mem. Central Ariz. Estate Planning Council (pres. 1972-73), State Bar Ariz. (chmn. tax sect. 1977-78), ABA (chmn. com. on agr., sect. taxation 1976-78, chmn. CLE com. sect. taxation 1982-84), Am. Law Inst. (chmn. tax planning for agr. 1973—), Nat. Cattlemen's Assn. (tax com. 1979—), Internat. Acad. Estate and Trust Law (academician), Sigma Nu Internat. (pres. 1986—). Estate planning, Probate, Corporate taxation. Office: 3300 Liberty Bank Plaza 301 E Virginia Ave Phoenix AZ 85004

OLSEN, ARNOLD, judge; b. Butte, Mont., Dec. 17, 1916; s. Albert and Anna G. (Vennes) O.; m. Margaret M. Olsen, Aug. 13, 1942; children—Margaret Rae Olsen Childs, Anna Kristine Olsen Graetz, Karin S. Olsen Billings. Student Mont. Sch. Mines, 1935-37; LL.B., U. Mont., 1940. Bar: Mont. 1940, U.S. Sup. Ct. 1952. Sole practice, Butte, 1940-42, 71-75; atty. gen. State of Mont., 1949-57; mem. U.S. Congress, 1960-71; dist. judge 2d Jud. Dist. State of Mont., County of Silver Bow, 1975—. Served with USNR, World War II. Mem. Am. Judicature Soc., Fed. Bar Assn., Mont. Bar Assn., Phi Delta Phi. Democrat. Methodist. Clubs: Am. Legion, VFW, Mason, Shriner, Elks. General practice. Home: 3160 Atherton Lane Butte MT 59701 Office: Silver Bow County Courthouse Butte MT 59701

OLSEN, HANS PETER, lawyer; b. Detroit, May 21, 1940; s. Hans Peter and Paula M. (Olsen) O.; m. Elizabeth Ann Gayton, Sept. 14, 1968; children—Hans Peter, Heidi Susanne, Stephanie Elizabeth. B.A., Mich. State U., 1962; J.D., Georgetown U., 1965; LL.M., NYU, 1966. Bar: Mich. 1967, Pa. 1969, R.I. 1974. Law clk. firm Monaghan, McCrone, Campbell & Crawmer, Detroit, 1964; law clk. U.S. Ct. of Claims, Fed. Appellate Ct., Washington, 1966-68; assoc. firm Pepper, Hamilton & Scheetz, Phila., 1968-72; ptnr. firm Hinckley, Allen, Tobin & Silverstein, Providence, 1972—; lectr. tax insts. and other profl. groups N.Y., Los Angeles, Phila., Boston, R.I. Contbr. numerous articles on taxation to legal jours. Fellow Am. Bar Found.; mem. ABA (sect. taxation), Fed. Bar Assn. (sect. taxation), R.I. Bar Assn. (sect. taxation, sec.-treas. 1977-80, mem. various coms.), U. R.I. Fed. Taxation Inst. (adv. planning com.), Bryant Coll. Fed. Taxation Inst. (adv. planning com.), R.I. Public Expenditures Council, R.I. Tax Adminstrs. Adv. Com., Providence C. of C., R.I. C. of C. (chmn. com. on taxes and public spending, mem. legis. action council). Club: Hope (Providence). Corporate taxation, Personal income taxation, State and local taxation. Home: 274 Olney St Providence RI 02906 Office: 1500 Fleet Ctr Providence RI 02903

OLSEN, KENNETH ALLEN, lawyer; b. Jersey City, June 6, 1953; s. George Anton and Dorothy (Mitschell) O. BA in Polit. Sci. and Pre-Law magna cum laude, Rutgers U., 1975; JD, Temple U., 1978. Bar: N.J. 1978, U.S. Dist. Ct. N.J. 1978, Pa. 1979, U.S. Ct. Appeals (3d cir.) 1979, U.S. Dist. Ct. (mid. dist.) Pa. 1980, U.S. Ct. Appeals (11th cir.) 1981, U.S. Ct. Appeals (D.C. cir.) 1982, U.S. Supreme Ct. 1983. Sole practice; gen. counsel Altus Freight Traffic Service Inc.; spl. counsel Chgo. Title Ins. Co.; atty. Chelsea Title and Guaranty Co., Commonwealth Land Title Co. Named to Presdl. Classroom Young Ams. Mem. ABA (various sects. and coms.), N.J. State Bar Assn., Pa. Bar Assn., Morris County Bar Assn., Am. Acad. Polit. Sci., Am. Acad. Polit. and Social Sci., Assn. Transp. Practitioners, Temple U. Alumni Assn., Rutgers U. Alumni Assn., Newark Coll. Alumni Assn., Traffic Club Newark Inc., Transp. Lawyers Assn., Phi Beta Kappa, Pi Sigma Alpha. Lutheran. Avocations: tennis, golf, bowling. General practice, Transportation, Real property.

OLSEN, ROGER MILTON, lawyer; b. San Jose, Calif., Mar. 27, 1942; s. Chester Milton and Alice Louise (Leland) O.; m. Joanne Lee Gordon, Sept. 7, 1974; 1 son, Nicholas. A.B., U. Calif.-Berkeley, 1964; postgrad. in Am. Govt., U. So. Calif., 1964-65; J.D., Boalt Hall, 1968; LL.M. in Taxation, George Washington U., 1976. Bar: Calif. 1969, D.C. 1977. Dept. dist. atty. Alameda County Dist. Atty.'s Office, Oakland, Calif., 1969-72; trial atty. tax div. Dept. Justice, Washington, 1972-76, dep. asst. atty. gen. criminal div., 1981-83, dep. asst. atty. gen. tax div., 1983-85, asst. atty. gen. tax div., 1985—; pvt. practice law San Francisco and Washington, 1977-81; adj. prof. Golden Gate U., San Francisco, 1977. Mem. U. Calif. Alumni Assn., Boalt Hall Alumni Assn., Big C Soc. Greek Orthodox. Home: 7004 Clemson Dr Alexandria VA 22307 Office: Office of Asst Atty Gen Tax Div US Dept Justice 10th and Constitution Ave NW Washington DC 20530 *

OLSEN, THEODORE ALAN, lawyer; b. El Paso, Tex., Oct. 23, 1953; s. Henry Edward and Elizabeth Lucille (Horan) O.; m. Sharon Eileen Kenna, May 27, 1978. BS, Boston U., 1975; JD, U. Colo., 1978. Bar: Colo. 1978, U.S. Dist. Ct. Colo. 1978. Assoc. DeMuth, Eiberger, Kemp & Backus, Denver, 1978-79; assoc. Sherman & Howard, Denver, 1979-84, ptnr., 1984—. Contbr. articles to profl. jours. Mem. ABA, Def. Research Inst., Colo. Bar Assn. (chmn. labor law com. 1986—), Denver Bar Assn., Order of Coif. Labor. Office: Sherman & Howard 633 17th St #2900 Denver CO 80202

OLSHAN, GARY STEVEN, lawyer; b. Birmingham, Ala., Dec. 6, 1953; s. Melvin and Irma Olshan. BA, U. Ill., 1976; JD, Loyola U., Chgo., 1979. Bar: Calif., Ala. Assoc. Kallen, Grant & Kosnett, Los Angeles, 1979-81; sole practice Birmingham, 1981—; bd. dirs. Mortgage Investors, Inc., Birmingham. Mem. Birmingham Bar Assn., Apple Bus. Club. Real property, Consumer commercial, Landlord-tenant. Office: 1211 S 28th St Birmingham AL 35205

OLSHAN, JOSEPH RAYMOND, lawyer, insurance company executive; b. Pottsville, Pa., May 28, 1929; s. Joseph and Theda (Warakomski) O.; m. Virginia I. Kuczin, Aug. 30, 1952; children—Gary P., Nancy Olshan Paige, David M., Patricia A. student Boston Coll., 1953; LL.B., New Eng. Sch. Law, 1958; postgrad. Grad. Law Sch., Suffolk U., 1959. Bar: Mass. 1958. Teller, Home Savs. Bank, Boston, 1954-55; chief adjuster Sentry Ins. Co., Boston, 1955-65; v.p., gen. counsel, sec. Factory Mut. Engring. Corp., Norwood, Mass., 1968—, Factory Mut. Engring. Assn., 1968—, Factory Mut. Research Corp., 1968— (all affiliates of Factory Mut. System). Mem. Norwood Sch. Com.; mem. Norwood Zoning Bd. Appeal, 1971—; mem. Norwood Democratic Town Com., 1960-70. Served with U.S. Army, 1952-54. Decorated Combat Infantryman's badge, Presdl. Unit citation. Mem. ABA (vice chmn. com. on property law sec. tort and ins. practice), Fedn. Ins. and Corp. Counsel (vice chmn. property ins. com. 1978-79, chmn. 1979-82, v.p. 1982-83, chmn. projects and objectives com. 1982-84, dir. 1983—), Norwood C. of C. Lodge: Lions (past pres.). Insurance, General corporate. Office: 1151 Boston-Providence Turnpike Norwood MA 02062

OLSON, CARL ERIC, lawyer; b. Center Moriches, N.Y., May 19, 1914; s. August William and Sophie (Maiwald) O.; m. Ila Dudley Yeatts, May 31, 1945; children—Carl Eric, William Yeatts, Nancy Dudley. A.B., Union Coll., 1936; J.D., Yale, 1940. Bar: Conn. 1941, N.Y. 1947. Assoc. Clark, Hall & Peck, New Haven, 1940-41; assoc. Reid & Priest, N.Y.C., 1946-56, ptnr. 1956-80; solo practice 1981—. Served to maj. U.S. Army, 1941-45. Mem. ABA, N.Y. State Bar Assn., Assn. Bar City of N.Y., Inter-Am. Bar Assn., Internat. Bar Assn. Republican. Congregationalist. Clubs: Yale (N.Y.C.). General corporate, Private international, General practice. Home and Office: 6 Surrey Rd Palm Beach Gardens FL 33418

OLSON, GEORGE ALBERT, lawyer; b. San Antonio, Dec. 31, 1936; s. Marion Alfred and Martha Walthal (Pancoast) O.; m. Margo L. Whitt, July 11, 1964, 86; children—Martha W., Minette W., George Pancoast, Scarlett Whitt. B.A., U. Tex., 1958, J.D., 1963. Bar: Tex. 1963. Assoc., Marion A. Olson; ptnr. Olson & Olson, San Antonio, 1963-65; prin. Olson & Olson, P.C., San Antonio, 1965-74; ptnr. Beckmann, Krenek, Olson & Quirk and predecessor firm Beckmann, Stanard & Olson, San Antonio, 1974-85, Foster, Lewis, Langley, Gardner & Banack Inc., San Antonio, 1985—; adv. dir. Nat. Bank of Fort Sam Houston, 1971-73, dir., 1973—; dir., Fort Sam Houston Bancshares Inc., 1974-80. Hon. counsel El Patronato De La Cultura Hispano Americana, 1977—; v.p., gen. counsel Humane Soc. Bexar County, Tex., 1978-82, prin. operating officer, 1981-83. Served to it. USN, 1958-61. Fellow Tex. Bar Found., San Antonio Bar Found.; mem. State Bar of Tex., San Antonio Bar Assn., San Antonio Jr. Bar Assn. (past pres.), ABA, Am. Judicature Soc., San Antonio Estate Planners, Republican. Episcopalian. Clubs: Order of the Alamo, San Antonio German, Conopus, San Antonio Country, Tex. Cavaliers, Giraud, El Patronato, Los Granaderos de Galves. Banking, Estate planning, General practice. Office: Suite 1600 Frost Bank Tower San Antonio TX 78205

OLSON, GERALD W., lawyer; b. Pocatello, Idaho, Sept. 17, 1925; s. Alma R. and Hazel C. Olson; m. Glenna M. Collier, Aug. 13, 1950; children—Diane Olson Thronson, Janine Olson Hall, G. David. B.A., Idaho State U., 1950; J.D. cum laude, Washburn U., 1953. Bar: Idaho 1953, U.S. Dist. Ct. Idaho, 1953; U.S. Supreme Ct. 1971. Sole practice, Pocatello, 1953-56; ptnr. Johnson and Olson, Pocatello, 1956-80, Johnson, Olson, Robison, Chartered, 1980—. Bd. dirs. Idaho State U. Mus. Found., Med. Ctr. Found.; city atty. City of Pocatello, 1957-79, spl. counsel, 1979—. Served with USN, 1943-46; PTO. Fellow Am. Bar Found., Am. Coll. Probate Counsel, Idaho State Bar Found. (life); mem. ABA (ho. of dels., nat. nominating com., standing com. nat. conf. groups), Idaho State Bar (pres. 1975-76), Am. Acad. Hosp. Attys., Pocatello Estate Planning Counsel (pres. 1969). Club: Juniper Hills Country. Lodges: Kiwanis, Masons, Elks. Estate planning, Probate. Office: PO Box 1725 Pocatello ID 83204-1725

OLSON, JAMES CALVIN, lawyer; b. Orange, N.J., Jan. 11, 1954; s. John Arthur and Mary Katherine (Wyrick) O.; m. Sharon Ann Stierwalt, Sept. 11, 1983; 1 child, Lindsay. BA, Lafayette Coll., 1976; JD, Wash. and Lee U., 1979. Bar: Pa. 1979, Calif. 1985. Assoc. Ballard, Spahr, Andrews & Ingersoll, Phila., 1979-84, Pillsbury, Madison & Sutro, San Francisco, Hong Kong, 1984—. Mem. ABA, Calif. Bar Assn., San Francisco Bar Assn., Pa. Bar Assn. Avocations: tennis, skiing, backpacking. Banking, General corporate, Private international. Home: 785 Arguello Blvd San Francisco CA 94118 Office: Pillsbury Madison & Sutro 225 Bush St San Francisco CA 94104

OLSON, JEFFREY SCOTT, lawyer; b. Augusta, Wis., Mar. 20, 1950; s. H. Robert and Genevieve (Scott) O. BA with honors, U. Wis., 1972, JD, 1976; postgrad., Yale U., 1972-73. Bar: Wis. 1976, U.S. Dist. Ct. (we. dist.) Wis. 1976, U.S. Dist. Ct. (ea. dist.) Wis. 1977, U.S. Ct. Appeals (7th and 8th cirs.) 1977, U.S. Supreme Ct. 1979. Assoc. Julian & Assocs., S.C., Madison, 1976-79; ptnr. Julian & Olson, S.C. and predecessor firm Julian, Olson & Crandall, S.C., Madison, Wis., 1979—; v.p. recruiting and training Unemployment Compensation Appeals Clinic, Madison, 1985—; supervising atty. community law office U. Wis. Law Sch., Madison, 1977—; lectr., panelist various orgns. and radio and tv shows, 1979—. Contbr. articles to profl. jours. Mem. ABA, Wis. Bar Assn. (gov. council indiv. rights sect. 1985—, lectr.), 7th Cir. Bar Assn., Dane County Bar Assn., Assn. Trial Lawyers Am., Wis. Acad. Trial Lawyers, Nat. Assn. Criminal Def. Lawyers, 1st Amendment Lawyers Assn., Dane County Criminal Def. Lawyers Assn. Baptist. Avocations: folk music, photography. Civil rights. Home: 727 Jenifer St Madison WI 53703 Office: Julian & Olson SC 330 E Wilson St Madison WI 53703

OLSON, JOHN FREDERICK, lawyer; b. Santa Monica, Calif., Dec. 24, 1939; s. Paul Frederick and Helen Elizabeth (Evans) O.; m. Elizabeth H. Callard, Feb. 22, 1966; children: Timothy Cooley, Peter Jacobus, Matthew Evans, Emily Merrell, Nicholas Porter. AB, U. Calif., Berkeley, 1961; LLB, Harvard U., 1964. Bar: Calif. 1965, U.S. Dist. Ct. (cen. dist.) Calif. 1965, D.C. 1977, U.S. Dist. Ct. (D.C.) 1977. Assoc. Gibson, Dunn & Crutcher, Los Angeles, 1964-71, ptnr., 1971—. Contbr. articles to profl. jours. Vestryman S. John's Ch., Lafayette Sq., Washington, 1981-86, chmn. Triennial Fund Drive, 1984; v.p. Combined Health Appeal Nat. Capital Area, Washington, 1985—; chmn. Lawyers Com. for Performing Arts, 1986—; mem. adv. com. to Senate Banking Com. on Insider Trading Legis., 1987—. Mem. ABA (chmn. task force regulation of insider trading 1983—, chmn. subcom. civil liabilities and litigation1985—, com. on fgn. claims 1982-86), Fed. Bar Assn. (exec. council securities com. 1985—), D.C. Bar Assn. (gen. counsel 1983-85), Am. Coll. Investment Counsel (founding trustee 1981-85). Democrat. Episcopalian. Clubs: University, Fed. City (Washington). Securities, Private international, General corporate. Home: 3719 Bradley Ln Chevy Chase MD 20815 Office: Gibson Dunn & Crutcher 1050 Connecticut Ave NW Suite 900 Washington DC 20036

OLSON, JOHN LOUIS, lawyer; b. Honolulu, Aug. 30, 1944; s. Robert Carroll and Maxine Marie (McQueery) O.; m. Jill Fredericka Roehrig, May 3, 1969; children: Robert K., Peter S. R. BA, U. Hawaii, 1969; JD, U. San Francisco, 1973. Bar: Hawaii 1973, U.S. Dist. Ct. Hawaii 1973. Assoc. Law Offices of R.I. Ishida, Kealakekua, Hawaii, 1973-75; dep. pub. defender Hawaii County, 1975-78; sole practice Captain Cook, Hawaii, 1978—; judge par diem dist. ct., Kona, Hawaii, 1979-80; mem. fed. indigent panel Fed. Pub. Defenders, Hawaii, 1984-86. Symposium editor U. San Francisco Law Rev., 1972. Candidate Hawaii Ho. Reps., Kona, 1974; bd. dirs. Keei Honaunau Community Assn., Kona, 1981. Served with USMC, 1962-67. Mem. ABA, Hawaii Bar Assn. (bd. dirs. 1982), West Hawaii Bar Assn. (pres. 1980, bd. dirs. 1981-82), Assn. Trial Lawyers Am., Kona Hist. Soc. Democrat. Club: Keoua Canoe (Kona) (pres. 1978-80, coach 1986—). Avocations: outrigger canoe paddling, kayaking, hiking. General practice. Home and Office: PO Box 129 Captain Cook HI 96704

OLSON, LYNN CLOONAN, judge; b. Pitts., Oct. 14, 1941; s. Richard Thomas and Kathleen (Aland) Cloonan; m. Thomas L. OLson, May 12, 1977. Bar: Minn. 1977, U.S. Dist. Ct. Minn. 1977, U.S. Dist. Ct. Appeals (8th cir.) 1977. Tchr. U.S. Peace Corps, Nigeria, 1964-66; asst. pub. defender State of Minn., Mpls., 1977-79; asst. county atty. Anoka County, Minn., 1979-80; assoc. Steffen, Munstenteiger P.A., Anoka, 1980-82; judge county ct. Anoka County, 1982-83; judge trial ct. Minn. Dist. Ct. (10th dist.), Anoka, 1983—; mem. panel jud. appeals Mentally Ill and Dangerous, Minn., 1985—. commr. Gov.'s hearing to Remove County Atty., 1985. Mem. bd. visitors U. Minn. Law Sch., Mpls., 1983—; chmn. Alexandra House, Anoka, 1985—; mem. Atty. Gen.'s Task Force Child Abuse, Minn., 1986—. Named Woman of Achievement Bus. & Profl. Women's Club, Mpls., 1985. Mem. ABA, Nat. Assn. Women Judges, Minn. Judges Assn. (exec. bd. 1985-86, v.p. 1986-87), Minn. Bar Assn. (chairperson criminal sect. 1982), Minn. Trial Lawyers Assn. (chairperson criminal com., Outstanding Service award 1982). Judicial administration. Home: 19827 Orchid St NW Anoka MN 55303 Office: Anoka County Courthouse Anoka MN 55303

OLSON, MARK DOUGLAS, lawyer; b. Johnson City, N.Y., Apr. 3, 1945; s. Nelson Leonard and Agnes Cecilia (Connelly) O.; m. Merrijane Pierce, Apr. 4, 1970; children: Kirsten, Andrew, Mia, Margit. BA, SUNY, Binghamton, 1973; JD, U. Pa., 1976. Bar: Del. 1976, U.S. Dist. Ct. Del. 1976. Assoc., dir. Bayard, Handelman & Murdoch P.A., Wilmington, Del., 1976—; officer, bd. dirs. Kalmar Nyckel Commemorative Commn., Wilmington, Del. Bd. dirs. Del. Swedish Colonial Soc., Wilmington, 1984—. Served to sgt. U.S. Army, 1967-69, Vietnam. Mem. ABA (tax sect.), Del. Bar Assn. (tax sect.), Phi Beta Kappa. Republican. Presbyterian. Avocations: gardening, church youth work. Corporate taxation, Personal income taxation, State and local taxation. Home: RFD 4 Box 16 Hockessin DE 19707 Office: Bayard Handelman & Murdoch PO Box 25130 Wilmington DE 19899

OLSON, M(ELVIN) RICHARD, banker, attorney; b. Chicago Heights, Ill., Dec. 26, 1942; s. Melvin Richard and Gwenyth (Hills) O.; m. Evelyn Gizella Kantor, June 19, 1965; children—Richard William, Eric Scott. B.A., Blackburn U., 1964; J.D., Chicago-Kent Coll. of Law, 1968. Bar: Ill. 1968, U.S. Dist. Ct. (no. dist.) Ill. 1968. Trust officer and sec. Evanston Trust & Savings, Ill., 1966-68; trust officer, Milw. Western Bank, 1969-73; with Mich. Nat. Bank of Detroit, Troy, 1973—, group v.p., 1978-82, sr. v.p., 1982—; dir. Centrevest REIT, Southfield, Mich., 1983—, Mich. Nat. Investment Corp., Bloomfield Hills, Mich., 1984—. Sec. Planning Commn., Planning Commn. Brandon Twp., Ortonville, Mich., 1980—; chmn. planned giving Am. Cancer Soc. of Southeast Mich., 1981-83, Crittendon Hosp., Rochester Mich., 1980-83. Recipient Achievement award Am. Cancer Soc., Southfield, 1983. Mem. Fiduciary and Estate Council of Detroit (dir. 1980-84), Troy C. of C. Probate, Banking, Estate taxation. Home: 3392 Breezewood Trail Ortonville MI 48462 Office: Mich Nat Bank PO Box 9065 Farmington Hills MI 48018-9065

OLSON, REBECCA J. MCGEE, lawyer; b. Norman, Okla., May 23, 1953; d. Howell Walton and Amy Eileen (Davison) McGee; m. Stephen Lynn Olson. Bar: Okla. 1980. Atty. Okla. State Senate, Oklahoma City, 1980—. co-chmn. Love Fund for Critically Ill Children, Norman, 1985. Mem. ABA, Okla. Bar Assn., Christian Legal So., Phi Alpha Delta (treas. 1980), Beta Sigma Phi (treas. 1984-85, pres. 1985-86). Legislative. Home: 1820 Auburn Ct Norman OK 73071 Office: Okla State Senate 309 State Capitol Oklahoma City OK 73105

OLSON, RONALD KEITH, lawyer; b. Burlington, Colo., Aug. 29, 1933; s. Oscar Albin O.; m. Marian Katherine Lahman, Oct. 27, 1956. B.A. in Polit. Sci., U. Colo., 1958; M.A. in English, 1962; J.D., U. Tulsa, 1969; LL.M., George Washington U., 1978. Bar: Mont. 1969, D.C. 1975, Okla. 1978, Colo. 1983. Assoc., Landoe & Gary, Bozeman, Mont., 1970-73; legis. counsel to U.S. Congressman, 1973-74; dep. county atty. Gallatin County, Mont., 1974-75; dep. minority counsel commerce com. U.S. Ho. of Reps., 1975; sr. atty. adv. U.S. Dept. Energy, litigation sect., 1975-79; counsel to Bartlesville (Okla.) Energy Tech. Center, Dept. Energy, 1979-83; sole practice, 1983—. Served with USMC, 1951-54. Recipient Dept. Energy Merit award, 1981, 82. Mem. ABA, Am. Judicature Soc., Assn. Trial Lawyers Am., Mont. Bar Assn., Okla. Bar Assn., D.C. Bar Assn. Contbr. articles on law to profl. jours. Oil and gas leasing, Federal civil litigation, Personal injury. Office: 1417 Richards Lake Rd Fort Collins CO 80524

OLSON, RONALD LEROY, lawyer; b. Carroll, Iowa, July 9, 1941; s. Clyde L. and Delpha C. (Boyens) O.; m. Jane Tenhulzen, June 21, 1964; children—Kristin, Steven, Amy. B.S., Drake U., 1963; J.D., U. Mich., 1966; Diploma in Law, Oxford U., Eng., 1967. Bar: Wis. 1966, Calif. 1969, U.S. Dist. Ct. (cen. dist.) Calif. 1969, U.S. Dist. Ct. (so. dist.) Calif. 1973, U.S. Ct. Appeals (9th cir.) 1974, U.S. Ct. Appeals (10th cir.) 1980, U.S. Ct. Appeals (5th cir.) 1982, U.S. Supreme Ct. 1976, U.S. Dist. Ct. Alaska 1983. Atty. U.S. Dept. Justice, 1967; clk. to chief judge U.S. Ct. Appeals (D.C. cir.), Washington, 1967-68; ptnr. Munger, Tolles & Olson, Los Angeles, 1968—; mem. adv. com. Corp. Dispute Resolution Inst., Ctr. for Pub. Resources and Northwestern U. Sch. Law, 1983, adv. bd. communications law program UCLA; lawyer del. Ann. 9th Cir. Conf., 1984; lectr. in field. Mem. editorial bd. Alternatives, 1983—. Contbr. numerous articles to legal jours. Mem. adv. com. Los Angeles and Orange Counties chpt. Lawyers Alliance for Nuclear Arms Control; mem. Los Angeles Olympic Citizens Adv. Commn., 1982-83; trustee Drake U., 1977—, Sequoia Nat. Park Natural History Assn., 1983—; bd. dirs., exec. v.p. Fraternity of Friends of Music Ctr., 1978—; pres. bd. fellows Claremont U. Ctr. and Grad. Sch., 1984—; bd. dirs. Legal Aid Found. Los Angeles, 1975—, pres., 1984; bd. dirs. Salzburg Seminar; com. visitors U. Mich. Law Sch., 1986—, sec. Los Angeles Arts Festival, 1985—; me. editorial bd. Alternatives, 1983—. Burton scholar U. Mich.; Ford Found. fellow Oxford U., 1967. Fellow Am. Coll. Trial Lawyers, Am. Bar Found.; mem. ABA (litigation sect. council 1976—, chmn. 1981-82, chmn. spl. com. on dispute resolution 1976-86, litigation sect. Soviet Exchange Program com. 1983—), Am. Judicature Soc., Los Angeles Bar Found. (bd. dirs. 1977—), Am. Arbitration Assn. (bd. dirs. 1983—, comml. panel 1983—), Los Angeles County Bar Assn., State Bar Calif. (bd. dirs. 1985—), Assn. Bus. Trial Lawyers, Democrat. Episcopalian. Clubs: Los Angeles Athletic, Chancery. Federal civil litigation, State civil litigation, Antitrust. Office: Munger Tolles & Olson 355 S Grand Ave 35 Floor Los Angeles CA 90071-1560

OLSON, STEPHEN M(ICHAEL), lawyer; b. Jamestown, N.Y., May 4, 1948; s. Charles R. and Marilyn (Dietzel) O.; m. Linda C. Hanson, Aug. 24, 1968; children: Kevin, Darren. AB cum laude, Princeton U., 1970; JD, U. Chgo., 1973. Bar: Pa. 1973, U.S. Dist. Ct. (we. dist.) Pa. 1973, U.S. Ct. Appeals (3d cir.) 1975, U.S. Ct. Appeals (1st and D.C. cirs.) 1986, U.S. Supreme Ct. 1986. Assoc. Kirkpatrick & Lockhart, Pitts., 1973-81, ptnr., 1981—. Chmn. nat. schs. com. Princeton U., 1985—. Mem. ABA (ry./ airline labor law com.), Pa. Bar Assn., Allegheny County Bar Assn. Clubs: Rivers, Shannopin Country (Pitts.). Avocations: photography, music, sports. Labor. Office: Kirkpatrick & Lockhart 1500 Oliver Bldg Pittsburgh PA 15222

OLSON, WALTER GILBERT, lawyer; b. Stanton, Nebr., Feb. 2, 1924; s. O.E. Olson and Mabel A. Asplin; m. Gloria Helen Bennett, June 26, 1949; children: Clifford Warner, Karen Rae Olson Gannon. BS, U. Calif., Berkeley, 1947, JD, 1949. Bar: Calif. 1950, U.S. Dist. Ct. (no. dist.) Calif. 1950, U.S. Tax Ct. 1950, U.S. Ct. Appeals (9th cir.) 1950. Assoc. Orrick, Herrington and Sutcliffe (formerly Orrick, Dahlquist, Herrington and Sutcliffe), San Francisco, 1949-54, ptnr., 1954—; bd. dirs. CP Nat. Corp. (formerly Calif.-Pacific Utilities Co.), San Francisco, chmn. bd. dirs. 1974-79, chmn. exec. com. 1979—; mem. Commn. to Revise Calif. Corp. Securities Law, 1967-69, Securities Regulatory Reform Panel, 1978-80; mem. corp. security adv. com. Calif. Commr. of Corps., 1975—. Editor-in-chief Calif. Law Review, 1948-49. Bd. dirs. Internat. Ho., Berkeley, 1981-86. Served to pvt. 1st class U.S. Army, 1943-46, ETO. Fellow Am. Bar Found.; mem. ABA (trust div. nat. conf. of lawyers and reps. of Am. Bankers Assn.), Calif. Bar Assn. (chmn. corps. com. 1975-76, exec. com. bus. law sect., 1977-78), San Francisco Bar Assn., U. Calif. Alumni Assn., Boalt Hall Alumni Assn. (bd. dirs. 1982—, sec. 1985, v.p. 1987), Order of Coif. Clubs: Menlo Country Club (Woodside, Calif.); Pacific-Union, Bankers (San Francisco). General corporate, Contracts commercial, Securities. Office: Orrick Herrington & Sutcliffe 600 Montgomery St 12th Floor San Francisco CA 94111

OLSSON, HARRY RUDOLPH, JR., lawyer; b. N.Y.C., May 2, 1923; s. Harry R. and Sigrid Victoria (Ek) O.; m. Mildred Louise Campbell, Aug. 1, 1947 (div. 1972); children: Harry Robertson, Randall Richard.; m. Diane T. Ramella, May 23, 1976. BS in Soc. Sci., CCNY, 1947; JD, Columbia U., 1948. Bar: N.Y. 1948, U.S. Dist. Ct. (so dist.) N.Y. 1948, U.S. Ct. Appeals (2d cir.) 1950, U.S. Ct. Appeals (10th cir.) 1951. Atty. Warner Bros. Pictures, N.Y.C., 1948-53; sr. atty. NBC, N.Y.C., 1953-62; gen. atty. ABC, N.Y.C., 1962-69, CBS Inc., N.Y.C., 1969-87; ptnr. Gilbert & Gilbert, N.Y.C., 1987—; Mem. Panel of Expert Cons. on Gen. Rev. of Copyright Law, 1955-76. Contbr. articles to profl. jours. Chmn. Stewart Manor (N.Y.) com. Boy Scouts Am., 1968-71. Served to 1st lt. inf. U.S. Army, 1943-46, ETO. Decorated Bronze Star, Purple Heart. Mem. Assn. of Bar of City of N.Y. (assn. chmn. 1974-77, copyright com.), N.Am. Nat. Broadcasters Assn. (chmn. legal com. 1978-83). Avocation: photography. Trademark and copyright, Legal education. Office: Gilbert & Gilbert 10 E 40th St New York NY 10016

OLSZAK, DANIEL DOMINIC, lawyer; b. Trenton, N.J., July 13, 1947; s. Daniel D. and Clara (Karpovage) O.; m. Jean A. Lombardo, July 25, 1970; 1 child, Christopher. BA, Trenton State Coll., 1969; JD, Fordham U., 1974; postgrad., U.S. Army JAG Sch., 1977-80. Bar: N.J. 1974, U.S. Dist. Ct. N.J. 1974, U.S. Supreme Ct. 1987. Estate tax atty. IRS, Bklyn., 1974, 77-80; assoc. counsel Mgmt. Planning, Princeton, N.J., 1980-83; sole practice Lakewood, N.J., 1983—; instr. Am. Tech. U., Killeen, Tex., 1975-77, Coll. for Fin. Planning, Denver, 1985—, Monmouth Coll., W. Long Branch, N.J., 1985—. Served to capt. U.S. Army, 1975-77. Mem. ABA, Ocean County Bar Assn. (chmn. tax com. 1983—), Internat. assn. Fin. Planners. Estate planning, Corporate taxation, Real property. Home: 1451 Cedarwood Dr Lakewood NJ 08701 Office: 1000 Hwy 70 Lakewood NJ 08701

OLSZEWSKI, KEVIN TRENT, lawyer; b. Balt., Dec. 2, 1957; s. Anthony Frank and Delores Elizabeth (Sprainis) O. AA, Harford Community Coll.; BS, U. Balt., JD. Bar: Md. 1982, U.S. Dist. Ct. Md. 1984. Jud. law clk. to presiding justice Harford County Cir. Ct., Bel Air, Md., 1982-83; assoc. Miller, Fry & Protokowicz, Bel Air, 1983—. Mem. Com. to re-elect judges Close and Whitfill, Harford County, 1984, Com. to re-elect judge William O. Carr, Harford County, 1986. Named one of Outstanding Young Men in Am., 1985. Mem. ABA, Md. Bar Assn., Harford County Bar Assn. (treas. 1985-86), Assn. Trial Lawyers Am., Md. Trial Lawyers Assn., Md. Jaycees (bd. dirs. 1986). Democrat. Roman Catholic. Avocations: tennis, reading, skiing, basketball, woodworking. General practice, Family and matrimonial, State civil litigation. Office: Miller Fry & Protokowicz 5 S Hickory Ave Bel Air MD 21014

OLSZEWSKI, PETER PAUL, judge; b. Plains, Pa., May 12, 1925; s. Alex J. and Sophie (Mohelski) O.; m. June M. Swantko, Aug. 4, 1956; children: Peter Paul Jr., Paul Peter II, John Alexander, Mary June. AB, Lafayette Coll., 1948; JD, St. John's U., Jamaica, N.Y., 1952. Bar: Pa. 1952, U.S. Dist. Ct. Pa. 1953. Sole practice Wilkes-Barre, Pa., 1952-67; judge Luzerne County Ct. Common Pleas, Wilkes-Barre, 1968-83, Pa. Superior Ct., 1984—; city atty. Wilkes-Barre, 1955-62; atty. Luzerne County, solicitor Redevel. Authority Wilkes-Barre, 1958-68; solicitor Parking Authority, Recreation Commn. Luzerne County; instr. King's Coll., Wilkes-Barre, 1969-70; mem. Nat. Judicial Coll., 1968, 71, 79, faculty advisor, 1985. Trustee Misericordia Coll., Dallas, Pa.; chmn. Wyo. Valley Interfaith Council; bd. dirs. Pa. State U. Wilkes-Barre campus. Recipient Liberty Under Law award Fraternal Order of Eagles, 1981, Disting. Law and Justice award Deputy Sheriff's Assn. Pa., 1984. Mem. ABA, Pa. Bar Assn., Wilkes-Barre Bar and Library Assn., Pa. Conf. State Trial Judges, Appellate Judges' Conf., St. John's U. Alumni Bd. (lifetime hon. dir.), Sigma Pi Mu, Pi Delta Epsilon. Roman Catholic. Judicial administration. Home: 56 Riverside Dr Wilkes-Barre PA 18702 Office: Superior Ct Pa 10 E South St Wilkes-Barre PA 18701

OLTARZ-SCHWARTZ, SARA, lawyer; b. Ostrow, Poland, May 5, 1945; came to U.S., 1950; d. Simon and Mindy (Salzburg) Oltarz; m. Michael Alan Schwartz, Dec. 8, 1973; children: Carl, Justin. BA, NYU, 1969, JD, N.Y. Law Sch., 1972. Bar: N.Y. 1973, Mich. 1980, U.S. Dist. Ct. (so. and ea. dists.) N.Y. 1974, U.S. Ct. Appeals (2d cir.) 1975, U.S. Ct. Mil. Appeals 1976, U.S. Dist. Ct. (ea. dist.) Mich. 1982, U.S. Ct. Appeals (6th cir.) 1983, U.S. Supreme Ct. 1976. Asst. dist. atty. Kings County, Bklyn., 1972-77; adj. prof. N.Y. Law Sch., 1978-79; of counsel David F. DuMouchel, P.C., Detroit, 1983—; sole practice, Detroit, 1983—. Recipient Am. Jurisprudence award Lawyers Coop. Pub. Co., 1972. Mem. State Bar Mich., Detroit Bar Assn., Oakland County Bar Assn., Women Lawyers of Mich., Internat. Assn. Jewish Lawyers and Jurists. Construction, Criminal, State civil litigation. Office: 1930 Buhl Bldg Detroit MI 48226

OLUP, LINDA ANN, lawyer; b. Paterson, N.J., Sept. 19, 1950; d. Victor Daniel and Ruth Patricia (Booss) O. B.A., Rutgers U., 1972; J.D., William Mitchell Coll. Law, St. Paul, 1977. Bar: Minn. 1977, U.S. Ct. Appeals (8th cir.) 1979. Sole practice, Edina, Minn., 1977-85; ptnr. Swaden-Olup Law Offices, 1985—; adj. faculty William Mitchell Coll. Law, 1979-85 ; speaker profl. orgn. seminars. Sec., chmn. internal affairs St. Paul Dist. 8 Planning Council, 1980-83. Recipient commendation for vol. services So. Minn. Regional Legal Services, St. Paul, 1984. Fellow Am. Acad. Matrimonial Lawyers (sec. Minn. chpt. 1986-88); mem. ABA (family law sect.), Minn. Bar Assn. (family law sect.), Minn. Trial Lawyers Assn. (family law sect.), Hennepin County Bar Assn. Family and matrimonial. Office: 7400 Metro Blvd Suite 450 Edina MN 55435

OLVER, MICHAEL LYNN, lawyer; b. Seattle, June 22, 1950; s. Manley Deforest and Geraldine (Robinson) O.; m. Wendy Kay Williams, July 6, 1974; children: Erin Marie, Christina Lynne. BA, U. Wash., 1972; JD, Calif. Western Sch. Law, 1976. Bar: Wash. 1976, U.S. Dist. Ct. (we. dist.) Wash. 1977. Assoc. Robbins, Merrick & Kraft, Seattle, 1976-77; sole practice Michael L. Olver, Seattle, 1977-80; ptnr. Merrick & Olver, P.S., Seattle, 1980—. Asst. mng. editor Calif. West. Internat. Law Jour., 1975-76. Lectr. Assumption Cath. Ch., Seattle, 1978—; mem. Full Gospel Businessmen Internat., Seattle, 1984, trust and investment com. Found. for the Handicapped. Mem. Seattle King County Bar Assn. (mem. internat. law sect. 1976—, judiciary and cts. com. 1986, family law sect. 1986), Wash. State Bar Assn. (mem. World Peace Through Law sect. 1980—), Alpha Theta Delta (dir., sec. 1977—). Catholic Evangelical. Estate planning, Probate, Personal injury. Home: 5545 33d NE Seattle WA 98105 Office: Merrick & Olver PS 1522 Seattle Tower Seattle WA 98101

O'MALLEY, JAMES TERENCE, lawyer; b. Omaha, Nov. 24, 1950; s. John Austin and Mayme Bernice (Zentner) O'M.; m. Colleen K. Kizer, May 22, 1972; children: Erin C., Michael B., James P. BA magna cum laude, U. Notre Dame, 1972; JD, Stanford U., 1975. Bar: Calif. 1975. Ptnr. Gray, Cary, Ames & Frye, San Diego, 1975-87, of counsel, 1987—; exec. v.p., gen. counsel Noble Broadcast Group, Inc., San Diego, 1987—. Bd. dirs. Children's Museum, San Diego, 1986—. Mem. Am. Judicature Soc., San Diego Taxpayers Assn. (pres. 1986—), Real Estate Securities and Syndication Inst., Order of Coif. Avocation: basketball. General corporate, Real property, Broadcasting. Office: Noble Broadcast Group Inc 4891 Pacific Hwy San Diego CA 92110

O'MALLEY, KEVIN FRANCIS, lawyer, educator; b. St. Louis, May 12, 1947; s. Peter Francis and Dorothy Margaret (Cradick) O'M.; m. Dena Hengen, Apr.2, 1971; children: Kevin Brendan, Ryan Michael. AB, St. Louis U., 1970, JD, 1973. Bar: Mo. Supreme Ct. 1973, U.S. Ct. Appeals (D.C. cir.) 1974. Trial lawyer U.S. Dept. Justice, Washington, 1973-74, Los Angeles, 1974-77, Phoenix, 1977-78, St. Louis, 1978-83; trial lawyer Shifrin & Treiman, St. Louis, 1987—; adj. prof. law St. Louis U., 1979—. Contbr. articles to law jours. Community ambassador Expt. in Internat. Living, Prague, Czechoslovakia, 1968. Served to capt. A.S. Army, 1973. Recipient Atty. Gen.'s Disting. Service award U.S. Dept. Justice, 1977, John J. Dwyer Meml. Scholarship award, 1967-70. Mem. ABA (chmn. govt. litigation counsel com. 1982-86, chmn. jud. com. 1986—), Met. Bar Assn. St. Louis. Roman Catholic. Club: Mo. Athletic. Home: 512 East Dr University City MO 63130 Office: Shifrin & Treiman 8182 Maryland Ave Saint Louis MO 63102

O'MALLEY, MICHAEL JOHN, lawyer; b. Honolulu, Jan. 15, 1954; s. Philip Buckley and Sara Margaret (Quick) O'M.; m. Nancy Joyce Dirrigl, May 24, 1981; children: Cristin Milla, Aislynn Joyce. BA, Claremont-McKenna Coll., 1977; JD, Harvard U., 1981. Bar: Hawaii 1981, U.S. Dist. Ct. Hawaii 1981, U.S. Ct. Appeals (9th cir.) 1981, N.Y. 1983, U.S. Dist. Ct. (so. dist.) N.Y. 1983, U.S. Ct. Claims 1983, U.S. Tax Ct. 1983. Engr.'s asst. Gen. Constrn. Co., Honolulu, 1977-78; assoc. Goodsill Anderson & Quinn, Honolulu, 1981-82, Dewey, Ballantine, Bushby, Palmer & Wood, N.Y.C., 1982-85, Goodsill Anderson Quinn & Stifel, Honolulu, 1985—; counsel Innervisions, Bklyn., 1983-85. Pres. Harvard Jour. Legislation. Vol. Aloha United Way; tax advisor Mufi Hanneman for Congress campaign, Honolulu, 1986; vol. Cec Heftel for Gov. campaign, Honolulu, 1986; chmn. fin. com. of gov.'s task force on long-term care for the elderly. Mem. N.Y. State Bar Assn., Hawaii State Bar Assn. (co-chmn. internat. law sect., activities com., mem. tax sect.), Hawaii C. of C. (tax com.). Avocations: snorkeling, softball, soccer, volleyball. State and local taxation, Securities, Personal income taxation. Home: 1659 Sherman Park Pl Honolulu HI 96817 Office: Goodsill Anderson Quinn & Stifel 130 Merchant St Honolulu HI 96813

OMAN, LAFEL EARL, former chief justice New Mexico Supreme Court; b. Price, Utah, May 7, 1912; s. Earl Andrew and Mabel (Larsen) O.; m. Arlie Edna Giles, June 3, 1936; children: Sharon O. Beck, Phyllis O. Bowman, Conrad LaFel, Kester LaFel. J.D., U. Utah, 1936. Bar: Utah bar 1936, N.Mex. 1947. Practiced in Salt Lake City and Helper, Utah, 1937-40; practiced law in Las Cruces, N.Mex., 1948-66; investigator, examiner CSC, Denver, 1941-43; with office chief atty. VA, Albuquerque, 1946-48; asst. city atty. Las Cruces, 1958-59; city atty. City of Truth or Consequences, N.Mex., 1959-61; judge N.Mex. Ct. Appeals, Santa Fe, 1966-70; justice N.Mex. Supreme Ct., 1971-77, chief justice, 1976-77; spl. master, dist. judge pro tem. in adjudication Suits of Waters of N.Mex. Rivers, 1977—; mem. firm Sutin, Thayer & Browne P.A., 1977-85, Oman & Carmody P.A., 1985-86; ptnr. Oman, Gentry & Yntema, P.A., 1986—; mem. N.Mex. Jud. Standards Commn., 1968-70, 71-72, N.Mex. Jud Council, 1972-77, N.Mex. Bd. Bar Examiners; bd. dirs. N.Mex. Continuing Legal Edn., Inc. Bd. dirs. N.Mex. Soc. Crippled Children; active Boy Scouts Am., Girl Scouts U.S.A., Polio Found.; chmn. ofcl. bd. St. John's United Methodist Ch., Santa Fe.; bd. dirs. Vis. Nurse Service, Inc., 1980-84, pres., 1983-84. Served to lt. USNR, 1943-46. Mem. ABA, Utah Bar Assn., N.Mex. Bar Assn., Dona Ana County (N.Mex.) Bar Assn. (pres. 1952-53), 1st Judicial Dist. Bar Assn., N.Mex., Santa Fe hist. socs., Santa Fe Opera Guild, Law-Sci. Acad., Def. Research Inst., Am. Trial Lawyers Assn., Inst. Jud. Adminstrn., Appellate Judges Conf., Nat. Legal Aid and Defender Assn., Am. Judicature Soc. (dir. 1970-74), Phi Alpha Delta. Lodge: Rotary (pres. Las Cruces club 1952-53, Santa Fe club 1976-77). State civil litigation, Personal injury. Home: 510 Camino Pinones Santa Fe NM 87501

OMAN, RALPH, lawyer; b. Huntington, N.Y., July 1, 1940; s. Henry Ferdinand and Annamarie (Reteldorf) O.; m. Anne K. Henehan, Oct. 21, 1967; children: Tabitha Russel, Caroline Adams, Charlotte Ericsson. Diploma, Sorbonne U., Paris, 1961; BA, Hamilton Coll., 1962; LLD, Georgetown U., 1973. Bar: D.C. 1973, U.S. Dist. Ct. Md., U.S. Ct. Appeals (4th cir.), U.S. Supreme Ct. Law clk. to presiding justice U.S. Dist. Ct. Md., Balt., 1973-74; trial atty U.S. Dept. Justice, Washington, 1974-75; chief minority counsel patents, trademarks and copyrights subcom. U.S. Senate, Washington, 1975-77; legis. dir. Senator Charles Mathias, Washington, 1977-

78; minority counsel judiciary com. U.S. Senate, Washington, 1978-81, chief counsel, staff dir. criminal law subcom., 1981-82, chief counsel patents, trademarks and copyrights subcom., 1982-85; register U.S. Copyright Office, Washington, 1985—. Served to lt. USN, 1965-70, Vietnam. Mem. Naval Res. Assn. (v.p. Patuxent River chpt. 1977-78). Episcopalian. Avocations: woodworking, sailing, tennis, squash. Trademark and copyright, Legislative, Public international. Home: 1110 E Capitol St NE Washington DC 20002 Office: Library of Congress Copyright Dept DS 1st & Independence Ave SE Washington DC 20540

O'MARA, WILLIAM MICHAEL, lawyer; b. Milw., May 8, 1938; s. Olivar Edward and Winifred Agnes (Morrisroe) O'M.; m. Maureen Teresa Lidster, Sept. 3, 1970; children—Timothy, Erin, Brian, David, Matthew, Catherine, Patrick, Bridget, Michael. B.A. in History, Loyola U., Los Angeles, 1960; J.D., Hastings Coll. Law, 1967. Bar: Calif. 1968, Nev. 1968. Assoc. Belford & Anglim, 1968-69, ptnr., 1969-74; ptnr. firm W.M. O'Mara, Reno, 1974-82, O'Mara and Kosinski, 1983—; tchr. bus. law Manogue High Sch., Chapman Coll., 1970-76. Candidate for U.S. Ho. of Reps., 1978. Served to capt., USNR, 1961—. Mem. ABA, Nev. Bar Assn., Calif. Bar Assn., Washoe Bar Assn., U.S. Navy League, Serra Internat. (past pres.), U.S. Naval Res. Assn., Air Force Assn. Republican. Roman Catholic. Lodges: Optimists, Toastmasters (Reno) (past pres.). Contracts commercial, Federal civil litigation, State civil litigation.

OMBRES, TERESA, lawyer; b. N.Y.C., Dec. 4, 1952; d. Joseph and Jaye (Rotolo) Gorgonzola; m. Frank Ombres, July 7, 1977; 1 child, Allie. BA, Fordham U., 1974; JD, New York Law Sch., 1981. Bar: N.Y. 1981, U.S. Dist. Ct. (so. and ea. dists.) N.Y. 1983. Counsel Alley Marketing, Inc., N.Y.C., 1983—. Mem. Promotion Mktg. Assn. Am. (assoc.). Democrat. Avocations: boating, waterskiing, reading, cooking. General corporate, promotion marketing. Office: Alley Mktg Inc 24 E 23 St New York NY 10010

OMER, MICHAEL LEE, lawyer; b. San Antonio, Feb. 23, 1954; s. George E. Jr. and Wendie (Vilven) O.; m. Marla L. Williams. BA, U. N.Mex.; JD, U. Houston. Bar: Tex. 1981, Hawaii 1981. Corp. counsel Gulf Interstate Engring., Houston, 1981-82, Amax Petroleum Corp., Houston, 1982-86; contract counsel Dresser Industries, Inc., Houston, 1986—. Mem ABA, Am. Assn. Petroleum Landmen, Houston Bar Assn. Private international, General corporate, Oil and gas leasing. Home: 3215 Meadway Ave Houston TX 77082 Office: Dresser Industries Inc 601 Jefferson Houston TX 77002

ONCKEN, HENRY K., lawyer; b. Shiner, Tex., Sept. 17, 1938; s. William Otto and Stella Helen (Kuck) O.; m. Jacqueline Ann Mansker, Aug. 6, 1960; 1 child, Leah Ann. BBA, U. Houston, 1965, JD, 1966. Bar: Tex. 1966, U.S. Dist. Ct. (so. dist.) Tex. 1968. Ptnr. Mabry & Oncken, Houston, 1966-69; asst. dist. atty. Harris County, Houston, 1969-81; judge Texas Dist. Ct. (248th jud. dist.), 1981-82; assoc. Gardner, Wald & Evans, Houston, 1983-84; atty. so. dist. U.S. Dept. Justice, Houston, 1985—. Pres. Mcpl. Utility Dist., Houston, 1976-81. Served with USNG, 1956-63. Republican. Avocations: hunting, fishing, pistol shooting, automobiles. Home: 9303 Godstone Ln Spring TX 77379 Office: US Attys Office 515 Rusk Houston TX 77002

O'NEAL, LESLIE KING, lawyer; b. Downey, Calif., Nov. 17, 1952; d. Lawrence Donald and Lilyan Mae (England) King. BA, U. Fla., 1974, JD, 1977. Bar: Fla. 1978, U.S. Dist. Ct. (mid. dist.) Fla. 1978, U.S. Ct. Appeals (11th cir.) 1984. Assoc. Markel, McDonough & O'Neal, Orlando, Fla., 1978-81; ptnr. Marker, McDonough & O'Neal, Orlando, Fla., 1981—. Chmn. bd. Christian edn. First Congl. Ch., Winter Park, Fla., 1980-82, trustee, 1982-85. Named one of Outstanding Young Women in Am., 1982. Mem. ABA (forum com. on construction industry, adminstrv. law sect., torts and ins. practice sect.), Fla. Bar Assn. (adminstrv. law sect.). Democrat. Construction, Public international, Insurance. Home: 1666 Forest Ave Winter Park FL 32789 Office: Markel McDonough & O'Neal 19 E Central Blvd Orlando FL 32802

O'NEAL, MICHAEL RALPH, lawyer, state representative; b. Kansas City, Mo., Jan. 16, 1951; s. Ralph O. and Margaret E. (McEuen) O'N.; m. Tammy E. Miller, Dec. 30, 1978. BA in English, U. Kans., 1973, JD, 1976. Bar: Kans. 1976, U.S. Dist. Ct. Kans. 1976, U.S. Ct. Appeals (10th cir.) 1979. Intern Legis. Counsel State of Kans., Topeka, 1975-76; assoc. Hodge, Reynolds, Smith, Peirce & Forker, Hutchinson, Kans., 1976-77; ptnr. Reynolds, Peirce, Forker, Suter, O'Neal & Myers, Hutchinson, 1980—; instr. Hutchinson Community Coll., 1977—; vice chmn. house judiciary and labor and industry coms. Kans. Ho. of Reps., Topeka, 1985—; adv. bd. dirs. Valley Fed. Savs. and Loan Assn., Hutchinson. Vice chmn. Rep. Party Reno County, Kans., 1982—; bd. dirs. Mental Health Assn. Reno County, Hutchinson, 1984—, YMCA, 1984-86, Crime Stoppers (ex-officio), Hutchinson; chmn. adv. bd. dirs. Wesley Towers Retirement Community, 1984—. Recipient Leadership award Kans. C. of C. and Industry, 1985; named one of Outstanding Young Men Am., 1986. Mem. Assn. Trial Lawyers Am., Nat. Conf. State Legislatures (criminal justice com.), Kans. Assn. Def. Counsel, Kans. Bar. Assn. (prospective legis. com., outstanding service award), Hutchinson C. of C. (ex-officio bd. dirs., Leadership award 1984. Lodge: Rotary. Avocations: basketball, tennis, golf. State civil litigation, Personal injury, Legislative. Home: 304 Crescent Hutchinson KS 67502 Office: Reynolds Peirce et al PO Box 1868 Hutchinson KS 67504-1868

O'NEAL, MICHAEL SCOTT, SR., lawyer; b. Jacksonville, Fla., Dec. 22, 1948; s. Jack Edwin and Lucille (Colvin) O'N.; m. Barbara Louise Hardie, Jan. 30, 1971 (div. Sept. 1974); 1 child, Jennifer Erin; m. Helen Margaret Joost, Mar. 18, 1985; children: Mary Helen, Angela Marie, Michael Scott O'Neal Jr. AA, Fla. Jr. Coll., 1975; BA in Econs. summa cum laude, U. No. Fla., 1977; JD cum laude, U. Fla., 1979. Bar: Fla. 1980, U.S. Dist. Ct. (mid. dist.) Fla. 1980, U.S. Dist. Ct. (no. dist.) Fla. 1981, U.S. Ct. Appeals (5th and 11th cirs.) 1981, U.S. Supreme Ct. 1986. Assoc. Howell, Liles, Braddock & Milton, Jacksonville, Fla., 1980-83; ptnr. Commander Legler Werber Sadler & Howell, Jacksonville, 1983—; pro bono atty. Legal Aid Soc., Jacksonville, 1980—; practicing atty. Lawyers Reference, Jacksonville, 1980—. Pres. Julington Landing Homeowners Assn., Jacksonville, 1980-83. Served to staff sgt. USAF, 1968-74. Mem. ABA, Jacksonville Bar Assn., Fed. Bar Assn., Assn. Trial Lawyers Am., Fla. Def. Lawyers Assn., Jacksonville Def. Lawyers Assn. Republican. Methodist. Clubs: Tournament Players (Ponte Vedra, Fla.); University (Jacksonville). Avocations: golf, music. Personal injury, Federal civil litigation, State civil litigation. Home: 1299 Norwich Rd Jacksonville FL 32207 Office: Commander Legler Werber et al 200 Laura St Jacksonville FL 32202

O'NEIL, JAMES E., lawyer; b. Mt. Vernon, N.Y., Feb. 28, 1939; s. John James and Miriam (Dillon) O'N.; m. Anne Worrell, May 4, 1985; 1 child, Katherine Reed. BS, Providence Coll., 1963; JD, New Eng. Sch. Law, 1967. Bar: R.I., Mass., U.S. Ct. Appeals (1st cir.), U.S. Supreme Ct. Advisor law enforcement assistance adminstrn. U.S. Dept. Justice, Boston, 1972-74; asst. U.S. atty. U.S. Dept. Justice, 1974-78; dep. chief U.S. Atty. Internat. Narcotics Unit, Mass., 1975-78; asst. U.S. atty. State of R.I., 1978-85; atty. gen. State of R.I., Providence, 1987—; head R.I. Drug Task Force, 1981-83; atty gen State of Rhode Island, Providence, 1987—. Trial Advocacy adv. Harvard U., Suffolk U., New Eng. Law Sch.; mem, counsel Save the Bay, Providence, 1972; bd. dirs. Conservation Law Found. Mem. R.I. Bar Assn., Mass. Bar Assn. Democrat. Criminal, Environment, Juvenile. Office: Dept Atty Gen 72 Pine St Providence RI 02903

O'NEIL, JOHN JOSEPH, lawyer; b. Detroit, July 20, 1943; s. John J. and Dora J. (Collins) O'N.; m. Margaret J. Walter, July 19, 1969; children: Meghan, Kathryn. BA, Trinity Coll., 1965; JD, U. Va., 1968. Bar: N.Y. 1969, U.S. Ct. Appeals (2d cir.) 1969, Fla. 1979, D.C. 1982. Assoc. Jackson & Nash, N.Y.C., 1968-71; assoc. Paul, Weiss, Rifkind, Wharton & Garrison, N.Y.C., 1971-77, ptnr., 1977—. Fellow Am. Coll. Probate Counsel; mem. ABA (com. on spl. problems of aged), N.Y. State Bar Assn., Assn. of Bar of City of N.Y. (com. on trusts and estates), Pi Gamma Mu. Probate, Family and matrimonial. Office: Paul Weiss Rifkind Wharton & Garrison 1285 Ave of Americas New York NY 10019

O'NEILL, BRIAN DENNIS, lawyer; b. Phila., Feb. 21, 1946; s. Harry William and Margaret Elizabeth (Miller) O'N.; m. Bonnie Anne Ryan, Aug. 17, 1968; children: Aimee Kathleen, Catherine Margaret. BA, Fla. State U., 1968, JD, 1971. Bar: Fla. 1971, D.C. 1975, U.S. Ct. Appeals (D.C. cir.) 1978, U.S. Ct. Appeals (5th and 11th cirs.) 1981, U.S. Ct. Appeals (10th cir.) 1985. Trial atty. Fed. Power Commn., Washington, 1972-75; assoc. Farmer, Shibley, McGuinn & Flood, Washington, 1975-80; ptnr. LeBoeuf, Lamb, Leiby & MacRae, Washington, 1980—; lectr. in field. Editorial bd. Energy Law Jour., Washington, 1983-84; contbr. articles to profl. jours. Served to 2d lt. USAF, 1971-72. Mem. Fla. Bar Assn. (energy com. 1985—), Fed. Energy Bar Assn. (chmn. coms. 1983-84), Phi Alpha Delta. Democrat. Roman Catholic. Club: Montgomery Village Golf (Gaithersburg, Md.) (bd. dirs. 1984—). FERC practice, Administrative and regulatory, Public utilities. Office: LeBoeuf Lamb Leiby & MacRae 1333 New Hampshire Ave NW Washington DC 20036

O'NEILL, JOHN IGNATIUS, lawyer; b. N.Y.C., Oct. 4, 1949; s. John Joseph and Margaret Mary (Gallagher) O'N.; m. Irene J. Daley, June 8, 1974. AB cum laude, U. Notre Dame, 1971; MA, Boston U., 1973; JD, SUNY, Buffalo, 1978. Bar: N.Y. 1979, U.S. Dist. Ct. (so. dist) N.Y. 1982. Instr. sociology Salve Regina Coll., Newport, R.I., 1973-75; ptnr. McCarthy, Fingar, Donovan, Drazen & Smith, White Plains, N.Y., 1978—. Editor Buffalo Law Rev., 1976-78. Mem. ABA, N.Y. State Bar Assn., Westchester County Bar Assn. Clubs: Winged Foot Golf, Shenorock Shore. State civil litigation. Home: 32 Fernwood Rd Larchmont NY 10538 Office: McCarthy Fingar Donovan Drazen & Smith 175 Main St White Plains NY 10601

O'NEILL, JOSEPH DEAN, lawyer; b. Bayonne, N.J., June 11, 1940; s. Austin Joseph and Ann (Lynch) O'N.; m. Susan Marie Clancy, Nov. 5, 1941; children—Kimberley Kelly. A.B., Allegheny Coll., Meadville, Pa., 1962; J.D., N.Y. Law Sch., 1967. Bar: N.J. 1968, U.S. Dist. Ct. N.J. 1968, U.S. Supreme Ct. 1974; cert. civil and criminal trial atty. Pres. Joseph D. O'Neill, P.A., Vineland, N.J., 1968—; lectr. trial tactics, personal injury and criminal law. Pres. Cumberland County Legal Aid Soc., 1974—; assoc. counsel N.J. Jaycees, 1970-71. Mem. ABA (mem. trial techniques com., products liability com.), N.J. State Bar Assn. (mem. spl. com. on cert. of trial attys.), Nat. Assn. Criminal Def. Lawyers (mem. nat. hotline panel of experts in homicide cases, outstanding contbn. award 1978), Assn. Trial Lawyers Am. (pres. elect, bd. govs. N.J. affiliate). Contbr. articles to legal jours. Personal injury, Criminal, State civil litigation. Address: 30 W Chestnut Ave PO Box 847 Vineland NJ 08360

O'NEILL, JOSEPH THOMAS, lawyer; b. St. Paul, Nov. 13, 1931; s. Joseph Thomas and Marie (O'Connell) O'N; m. Marianne Kenefick; children: Kathleen, Joseph, Maureen, Thomas, John, Michael, Kevin, Shelagh. BA, U. Notre Dame, 1953; LLB, U. Minn., 1956. Bar: Minn. 1956, D.C. 1959, U.S. Supreme Ct. 1977. Ptnr. Firestone, Fink, Krawetz, Miley & O'Neill, St. Paul, 1959-67, O'Neill, Burke and O'Neill, Ltd., St. Paul, 1970—. State rep. of State Minn., St. Paul, 1970-76, state senator 1971-77. Served with USAF, 1956-59; chmn. St. Joseph's Hosp. Named One of Outstanding Young Men St. Paul, U.S. Jaycees, 1967, Outstanding State Legislator, Rutgers U., 1971. Mem. St. Paul Charter Commn., St. Paul C. of C. (chmn. 1986), St. Paul Jr. C. of C. (pres. 1964-65). Republican. Roman Catholic. State civil litigation, Environment, Legislative. Home: 1381 Summit Saint Paul MN 55105 Office: O'Neill Burke and O'Neill Ltd 55 E 5th St Saint Paul MN 55101

O'NEILL, LAWRENCE DANIEL, lawyer, consultant, entrepreneur; b. Granite City, Ill., May 16, 1946; s. Lawrence Frederick and Dorthy Lee (Breckenridge) O'N.; m. Judith Dianne Ratinetz, July 5, 1969; children—Jaishri Erin, Tara Breckenridge. Student U. Mo., 1964-66; B.A., U. Md., 1970; postgrad. Georgetown U., 1970; J.D., U. Balt., 1975. Bar: Md. 1975, D.C. 1978, U.S. Supreme Ct. 1980, U.S. Ct. Claims 1982. Cryptologist/linguist Nat. Security Agy., Fort Meade, Md., 1966-70; fgn. service officer U.S. Info. Agy., Washington, New Delhi (India), 1970-73; budget officer U.S. Consumer Product Safety Commn., Washington, 1973-75; asst. to dir. then dir. policy White House Office Telecommunication Policy, 1975-78; assoc. chief counsel Nat. Telecommunications and Info. Adminstrn., U.S. Dept. Commerce, 1978-81; chmn., chief exec. Technology Analysis Group, Washington, 1981—; Washington counsel Fenwick, Stone, Davis & West, Palo Alto, Calif., 1982-86; ptnr. Winston & Strawn, Washington, 1986—; chmn. Pan Am Tech. Policy Forum, Miami, Fla., 1982—; dir. Teleport Internat., Washington, 1984—. Author: The Telecommunications Revolution, 1981, Five Top Technologies 1984-1995, 1982. Contbr. chpt. to Media Privacy, 1984. Mem. legis. adv. bd. Md. Senate, 1983-84. Served to sgt. U.S. Army, 1966-70. Mem. ABA (mem. council 1984—), AAAS, Md. Bar Assn., D.C. Bar Assn., Nat. Conf. Lawyers and Scientists. Democrat. Roman Catholic. Lodge: Order of Hibernians. Private international, Administrative and regulatory. Home: 316 Old Stone Rd Colesville MD 20904 Office: Winston and Strawn 2550 M St NW Washington DC 20037

O'NEILL, MARTHA EMMA, lawyer, educator; b. Nashua, N.H., June 10, 1957; d. Thomas Eugene and Katherine Mary (Clancy) O'N. AB, Wellesley Coll., 1979; JD, Georgetown U., 1982. Bar: N.H. 1982, U.S. Dist. Ct. N.H. 1982. Ptnr. Clancy & O'Neill P.A., Nashua, 1982—; part-time instr. Rivier Coll., Nashua, 1983—. Del. Constl. Conv., Concord, N.H., 1984. Mem. N.H. Bar Assn., Nashua Bar Assn., Assn. Trial Lawyers Am., N.H. Trial Lawyers Assn. Avocations: swimming, running, cross-country skiing, reading, drawing. Probate, Real property, Juvenile. Home and Office: 53 E Pearl St Nashua NH 03060

O'NEILL, MICHAEL JOSEPH, lawyer; b. Burtonwood, Eng., Mar. 3, 1956; s. John William and Doreathea Marie (Howley) O'N.; m. Erin Marie O'Donnell, May 14, 1984; children: Kerry Anne, Kathleen Marie. BA in Econs., Belmont Abbey Coll., 1978; JD, MBA in Fin., U. Balt., 1982. Bar: Md. 1982, U.S. Dist. Ct. Md. 1984, U.S. Ct. Appeals (5th cir.) 1984. Contracts mgr. Westinghouse, Balt., 1982-83, div. contract advisor, 1983-84; legal counsel Honeywell, Annapolis, Md., 1984-86; sr. legal counsel Honeywell, Clearwater, Fla., 1986—; contract advisor Small and Small Disadvantaged Bus. Programs, 1984. Mem. ABA, Md. Bar Assn., Anne Arundel County Bar Assn., Nat. Contract Mgrs. Assn., Pi Gamma Mu, Sigma Phi Epsilon. Democrat. Roman Catholic. Avocations: tennis, racquetball, soccer. Government contracts and claims, Computer, General corporate. Home: 820 Hillside Dr Palm Harbor FL 33563 Office: Honeywell Inc Legal Office 13350 US 19 Clearwater FL 33546

O'NEILL, PATRICK JOSEPH, publisher, lawyer; b. N.Y.C., Apr. 14, 1953; s. Patrick and Elizabeth (Feigl) O'N.; m. Mary Beth Gallagher, Aug. 12, 1978; 1 child, Mary Elizabeth. BA, CUNY, Bronx, 1976; JD, N.Y. Law Sch., 1979; postgrad. in law, NYU, 1983-85. Bar: N.Y. 1980, U.S. Tax Ct. 1980. Legal editor Prentice-Hall, Inc., Paramus, N.J., 1980-81, asst. dir., 1981-82; mgr. customer support PHINet, N.Y.C., 1984-85, v.p. ops., 1986-87; v.p., exec. dir. Josephson and Kluwer, N.Y.C., 1986&. Mem. ABA. Communications, Computer, Corporate taxation. Home: 94-D Edgewater Park Bronx NY 10465 Office: Josephson & Kluwer 10 E 21st St New York NY 10465

O'NEILL, PHOEBE JOAN, lawyer; b. Seattle, Sept. 5, 1934; d. Herald A. and Phoebe (Titus) O'N.; m. Edward Palfreyman, Sept. 20, 1981. BSE, Marylhurst Coll., 1959; MA, Seattle U., 1970; JD, Lewis & Clark U., 1975. Bar: Oreg. 1975, U.S. Dist. Ct. Oreg. 1975. Tchr. various schs., Portland and Eugene, Oreg., 1957-70; dean of students Marylhurst (Oreg.) Coll., 1970-72; law clk. to presiding justice Multnomah County Cir. Ct., Portland, 1972-75, pro tem judge, 1986—; law clk. to presiding justice U.S. Dist. Ct. Oreg., Portland, 1975-76; from assoc. to ptnr. Black, Tremaine et al, Portland, 1976-84; ptnr. Dunn, Carney, Allen, Higgins & Tongue, Portland, 1984—. Mem. ABA, Oreg. Bar Assn., Multnomah County Bar Assn., Assn. Trial Lawyers Am., Oreg. Trial Lawyers Assn., Oreg. Assn. Def. Counsel, Uniform Trial Ct. Rules Com., Oreg. Law Inst. (bd. dirs. 1986—), Phi Delta Delta. Club: City (Portland). Avocations: hiking, climbing. Federal civil litigation, State civil litigation. Office: Dunn Carney Allen Higgins & Tongue 851 SW 6th #1500 Portland OR 97204

O'NEILL, THOMAS NEWMAN, JR., federal judge; b. Hanover, Pa., July 6, 1928; s. Thomas Newman and Emma (Cornpropst) O'N.; m. Jeanne M. Corr., Feb. 4, 1961; children: Caroline Jeanne, Thomas Newman, III, Ellen Gitt. A.B. magna cum laude, Catholic U. Am., 1950; LL.B. magna cum laude, U. Pa., 1953; postgrad. (Fulbright grantee), London Sch. Econs., 1955-56. Bar: Pa. 1954, U.S. Supreme Ct. 1959. Law clk. to Judge Herbert F. Goodrich (U.S. Ct. Appeals 3d Circuit), 1953-54; to Justice Harold H. Burton (U.S. Supreme Ct.), 1954-55; assoc. firm Montgomery, McCracken, Walker & Rhoads, Phila., 1956-63; ptnr. Montgomery, McCracken, Walker & Rhoads, 1963-83; judge U.S. Dist. Ct. (eastern dist.) Pa., 1983—; counsel 1st and 2d Pa. Legis. Reapportionment Commns., 1971, 81; lectr. U. Pa. Law Sch., 1973. Articles editor: U. Pa. Law Rev, 1952-53. Former trustee Lawyers Com. for Civil Rights under Law; former mem. Gov.'s Trial Ct. Nominating Commn. for Philadelphia County; former mem., bd. overseers U. Pa. Mus.; trustee, v.p. Gladwyne Free Library. Fellow Am. Coll. Trial Lawyers; mem. Am. Law Inst., Phila. Bar Assn. (chancellor 1976), Pa. Bar Assn. (gov. 1978-81), U. Pa. Law Alumni Soc. (pres. 1976-77), Order of Coif (pres. U. Pa. chpt. 1971-73), Phi Beta Kappa. Clubs: Merion Cricket, Edgemere, Broadacres Trouting Assn. Office: US Courthouse Room 14613 601 Market St Philadelphia PA 19106

ONEK, JOSEPH NATHAN, lawyer; b. N.Y.C., Jan. 9, 1942; s. Jacob J. and Doris (Aaronson) O.; m. Margot Debra Piore, June 29, 1963; children—David, Matthew. A.B. magna cum laude, Harvard Coll., 1962; M.A., London Sch. Econs., 1964; LL.B. magna cum laude, Yale Law Sch., 1967. Bar: D.C. 1968. Law clk. to chief judge U.S. Ct. Appeals (D.C. cir.), 1967-68; law clk. Justice William J. Brennan, U.S. Supreme Ct., 1968-69; asst. counsel Senate Adminstrv. Practice and Procedure Subcom., 1969-71; dir., atty. Ctr. for Law and Social Policy, 1971-76; adj. prof. U. Md. Law Sch., Health Care Law, 1976-77; dir. health policy analysis Carter-Mondale Transition Planning Group, 1976-77; assoc. dir. for health and human resources Domestic Policy Staff, White House, 1977-79; dep. counsel to Pres., White House, 1979-81; ptnr. Onek, Klein & Farr, Washington, 1981—. Marshall scholar, 1962. Mem. ABA, Phi Beta Kappa. Health, Federal civil litigation, Libel. Home: 3723 Ingomar St NW Washington DC 20015 Office: Onek Klein & Farr 2550 M St NW Washington DC 20037

ONG, HENRY HOP, lawyer; b. Sze Hop Village, Kwangsi Province, China, Nov. 10, 1944; s. Albert June and Sue Kim (Wong) O.; m. Fidelina Tan, Jan. 10, 1976; children—Jennifer Lynn, Melissa Joy, Nicole Anne. B.S. with distinction, U. Ariz., 1966, J.D., 1969. Bar: Ariz. 1972. Dep. county atty. Maricopa County, Ariz., 1973—. Agnes Miller unit bd. dirs. Boys Club Am., Phoenix, 1974-78; mem. Chinese Am. Citizens Alliance, Phoenix, 1975—, parlimentarian, 1976, auditor, 1979-80, marshall, 1981—; legal officer Ong Ko Met Family Assn., Phoenix, 1973—. Served to capt. U.S. Army, 1969-71. Decorated Bronze Star. Mem. State Bar Ariz. (sec. young lawyers sect. 1974-75, mem. exec. council 1974-76, family law sect. 1983—), Maricopa County Bar Assn. (family law com. 1982—), Filipino Club Ariz. (bd. dirs. 1986-87), Phi Alpha Delta. Roman Catholic. Lodge: Phil.-Am. Lions. Local government, Family and matrimonial, State civil litigation. Home: 7222 N 18th Pl Phoenix AZ 85020 Office: 11 W Jefferson Suite 400 Phoenix AZ 85003

OPALA, MARIAN P(ETER), state supreme court justice; b. Lodz, Poland, Jan. 20, 1921. B.S. in Econs., Oklahoma City U., 1957, J.D., 1953, LL.D., 1980; LL.M., NYU, 1968. Bar: Okla. 1953, U.S. Supreme Ct. 1970. Asst. county atty. Oklahoma County, 1953-56; practiced law Oklahoma City, 1956-60, 65-69; referee Okla. Supreme Ct., Oklahoma City, 1960-65; prof. law Oklahoma City U. Sch. Law, 1967-68; prof. U. Okla. Coll. Law, 1969—, adj. prof., 1980—; jud. asst. Supreme Ct. Okla., adminstrv. dir. Cts. Okla., 1968-77; presiding judge Okla. State Indsl. Ct., 1977-78; judge Workers Compensation Ct., 1978; justice Okla. Supreme Ct., 1978—; mem. permanent faculty Am. Acad. Jud. Edn., 1970—; mem. NYU Inst. Jud. Adminstrn.; mem. faculty Nat. Jud. Coll., U. Nev., 1975—; chmn. Nat. Conf. State Ct. Adminstrs., 1976-77; mem. Nat. Conf. Commrs. on Uniform State Laws, 1982—. Co-author: Oklahoma Court Rules for Perfecting a Civil Appeal, 1969. Recipient Herbert Harley award Am. Judicature Soc., 1977; Disting. Alumni award Oklahoma City U., 1979; NSDAR Americanism medal, 1984; named Outstanding Okla. Pub. Adminstr., Am. Soc. Public Adminstrn., 1979; ABA/Am. Law Inst. Harrison Tweed Spl. Merit award, 1987. Mem. ABA, Okla. Bar Assn., Oklahoma County Bar Assn., Am. Soc. Legal History, Oklahoma City Title Lawyers Assn., Order of Coif, Phi Delta Phi (Oklahoma City U. Alumni award 1962). Legal history, Jurisprudence. Office: Supreme Ct Okla State Capitol Room 202 Oklahoma City OK 73105

OPALINSKI, CHRISTOPHER RICHARD, lawyer; b. Syosset, N.Y., May 19, 1956; s. Richard Eugene and Suzanne Patricia (Maguire) O.; m. Beth Ellen McLaughlin, Aug. 16, 1980. BS magna cum laude, Kent State U., 1978; JD magna cum laude, Wake Forest U., 1981. Bar: Pa. 1981, U.S. Dist. Ct. (we. dist.) Pa. 1981, U.S. Ct. Appeals (3d cir.) 1981. Assoc. Eckert, Seamans, Cherin & Mellott, Pitts., 1981—; speaker, lectr. Allegheny Community Coll., Pitts., 1986.; speaker Project Mgmt. Inst., 1986. Author: Arbitration or Litigation: Selecting the Best Method for the Resolution of Your Construction Dispute, 1986. Mem. ABA (forum com. on constrn. industry 1982—), Am. Arbitration Assn. (panel of arbitrators), Pa. Bar Assn. (constrn. litigation com.), Allegheny County Bar Assn. (alt. dispute resolution com.). Democrat. Roman Catholic. Avocations: sports, landscaping. Construction, Federal civil litigation, State civil litigation. Office: Eckert Seamans Cherin & Mellott 600 Grant St 42d Fl Pittsburgh PA 15219

OPERHALL, HARRIE MARIE POLLOK, lawyer; b. Floresville, Tex., Sept. 23, 1949; d. Harry Alexander and Dorothy (Niestroy) Pollok; m. Michael Edward Operhall, Apr. 4, 1971; 1 child, Lance. BBA in Acctg., U. Tex., 1971; JD, South Tex. Coll. Law, 1978. Bar: Tex. 1978, U.S. Dist. Ct. (so. dist.) Tex. 1984, U.S. Tax Ct. 1986. Tax acct. M.W. Kellogg Co., Houston, 1972-74; tax specialist Coastal State Gas Co., Houston, 1974-76; sr. analyst tax Allied Chem. Co., Houston, 1977-78; tax mgr. Dillashaw & Hawthrone, Houston, 1978-81; sole practice Houston, 1981—; pres. Oper-Vision Ltd., Houston, 1985. Pres., sec. Maplewood Sq. Council Co-owners, Houston, 1977-79. Mem. ABA, Tex. Bar Assn., Houston Bar Assn., Am. Inst. CPA's, Tex. Soc. CPA's, Tex. CPA's (Houston chpt.), Wednesday Tax Forum. Roman Catholic. Avocations: reading, sewing, TV. General corporate, Probate, Personal income taxation. Home: 10834 Sandpiper Houston TX 77096 Office: 6610 Harwin Dr Suite 118 Houston TX 77036

OPLINGER, JON CARL, lawyer; b. Berwick, Pa., June 3, 1948; s. Albert M. and Betty L. (Bower) O.; m. Janet L. Smith, Dec. 27, 1969; children: Brian, Ellen. AB, Dartmouth Coll., 1970; JD, Temple U., 1973. Bar: Pa. 1973, U.S. Dist. Ct. (ea. dist.) Pa. 1974, U.S. Dist. Ct. (mid. dist.) Pa. 1986. Assoc. Beasley, Henson & Casey, Phila., 1973-79; ptnr. Prewitt & Oplinger, Phila., 1979-80; assoc. Masterson, Braunfeld, Himsworth & Maguire, Norristown, Pa., 1980-81; atty. Bell of Pa., Phila. and Harrisburg, 1981—; adminstrv. asst. to speaker N.H. Ho. Reps., Concord, 1970. Chmn. Buck Scott for Gov. com., Pa., 1985-86. Served to lt. (j.g.) USNR, 1970-74. Mem. Pa. Bar Assn., Phila. Bar Assn. (chmn. young lawyers sect. 1980-81), Dauphin County Bar Assn., Montgomery Bar Assn. Clubs: Dartmouth Phila. (sec. 1980-86); Tuesday (Harrisburg). Public utilities, Administrative and regulatory, Legislative. Office: Bell of Pa 315 N 2d St Harrisburg PA 17101

OPPEDAHL, CARL W., lawyer; b. N.Mex., 1956. BA, Grinnell Coll., 1978; JD, Harvard U., 1981. Assoc. Kreindler & Kreindler, N.Y.C., 1981-87, Morgan & Finnegan, N.Y.C., 1987—. Author: Inside the Model 100, 1986, The Telephone Book: Getting What You Want and Paying Less for it, 1986; contbg. editor: Portable 100, 1986. Computer, Patent. Office: Morgan & Finnegan 345 Park Ave New York NY 10154

OPPENHEIMER, JERRY L., lawyer; b. Birmingham, Ala., Feb. 22, 1937; s. Jerome H. and Mina (Loveman) O.; m. Joan H. Chadwick-Collins, Feb. 23, 1963; children: Julia Cole, James Chadwick. BS, U. N.C., 1958; LLB, U. Va., 1961. Bar: D.C. 1961, Va. 1961. Assoc. Covington & Burling, Washington, 1961-69; atty., advisor U.S. Treasury Dept., Washington, 1969-70, assoc. tax legis. counsel, 1970-71, dep. tax legis. counsel, 1971-73; ptnr. Mayer, Brown & Platt, Washington, 1973—. Corporate taxation, Pension, profit-sharing, and employee benefits. Home: 4655 Garfield St NW Washington DC 20007 Office: Mayer Brown & Platt 2000 Pennsylvania Ave Washington DC 20006

OPPENHEIMER, JESSE HALFF, lawyer; b. San Antonio, Jan. 4, 1919; s. Jesse D. and Lillie (Halff) O.; m. Susan R. Rosenthal, July 31, 1946; children—David, Jean, Barbara. Student U. Tex., 1935-37; B.A. with honors in Econs., U. Ariz., 1939; J.D. cum laude, Harvard U., 1942, postgrad., 1946.

Bar: Tex. 1946. Ptnr. firm Oppenheimer, Rosenberg, Kelleher & Wheatley, Inc., San Antonio, 1970—; former instr. taxation St. Mary's Law Sch.; lectr. taxation; dir., organizer Southwest Tex. Nat. Bank; dir. Standard Electric Co. Editor Harvard Law Rev., 1942. Former mem. adv. council and UTSA Assocs., U. Tex.-San Antonio, v.p., 1977-78; bd. dirs., mem. exec. com. Symphony Soc. San Antonio, former pres., chmn. bd.; former trustee Robert B. Green Hosp., San Antonio, St. Mary's Hall girls' sch.; former bd. dirs. Santa Rosa Children's Hosp., United Fund, Children's Service Bur., Bexar County Mental Health Assn.; former mem. planning com. U. Tex. Law Sch. Ann. Tax Inst.; former mem. steering com. Met. San Antonio Urban Coalition; former adv. bd. trustees Southwest Found. for Research and Edn.; former mem. Adv. Hosp. Council, State of Tex.; former mem. adv. bd. Coll.-Community Creative Arts Ctr., Our Lady of the Lake Coll., San Antonio; former mem. Centro-21, San Antonio, 1975-77; mem. economy study group Adv. Council Elected Ofcls., Democratic Nat. Com., 1975-76; mem. chancellor's council, Centennial Commn., U. Tex.; trustee, pres. Marion Koogler McNay Art Mus., San Antonio; former mem. adv. bd. Ursuline Acad., San Antonio; mem. Kenwood Neighborhood Council; trustee The Woodrow Wilson Internat. Ctr. for Scholars, Washington, 1979—. Served to lt. col. U.S. Army; World War II; ETO, PTO. Mem. ABA (former mem. taxation com.). Clubs: Argyle (organizing bd., bd. dirs.), San Antonio Country. Estate planning, Real property, General practice. Office: Oppenheimer Rosenberg Kelleher Wheatley Inc 711 Navarro 6th Floor San Antonio TX 78205

OPPENHEIMER, LAURENCE BRIAN, lawyer; b. N.Y.C., June 18, 1952; s. Bennett and Sandra Joan (Haber) O.; m. Andrea Carol Meksin, Nov. 25, 1977; children: Philip, Andrew, Elizabeth. BA, U. Denver, 1974; JD cum laude, U. Miami, 1980. Bar: Fla. 1980, N.Y. 1981, U.S. Dist. Ct. (we. dist.) N.Y. 1981, U.S. Bankruptcy Ct. (we. dist.) N.Y. 1981, U.S. Ct. Appeals (5th and 11th cirs.) 1981. Assoc. Rachle, Banning, Weiss & Halpern, Buffalo, 1980-81; assoc. Cohen, Swados, Wright, Hanifin, Bradford & Brett, Buffalo, 1981-86, ptnr., 1986—. Editor Jour. Lawyers of the Americas, 1979, bus. mgr., 1980. Rep. committeeman, Amherst, N.Y., 1985-86. Recipient Book award-agy., Am. Jurisprudence, 1979. Mem. ABA, Fla. Bar Assn., N.Y. State Bar Assn., Erie County Bar Assn., Phi Delta Phi. General corporate, Environment, Labor. Office: Cohen Swados et al 70 Niagara St Buffalo NY 14202

OPPENHEIMER, RANDOLPH CARL, lawyer; b. N.Y.C., Feb. 5, 1954; s. Bennett and Sandra (Haber) O.; m. Cynthia Ellen Shatkin, June 19, 1976; children: Benjamin David, Adam Jeremy, Jacob Aaron, Jordan Michael, Daniel Corey. BA, U. Vt., 1976; JD, Case Western Res. U., 1979. Bar: N.Y. 1980, U.S. Dist. Ct. (we. dist.) N.Y. 1980, U.S. Bankruptcy Ct. 1980, U.S. Ct. Appeals (2d cir.) 1981. Assoc. Kavinoky & Cook, Buffalo, 1979-84, ptnr., 1984—; instr. legal research, writing and adv., Case Western Res. U., 1978-79. Mem. ABA, N.Y. Bar Assn., Erie County Bar Assn. Contracts commercial, General corporate, Labor. Home: 3772 Main St Eggertsville NY 14226 Office: Kavinoky & Cook 120 Delaware Ave Buffalo NY 14202

ORBAN, FRANK ANTON, III, lawyer; b. Johnstown, Pa.; s. Frank Anton Jr. and Mary (Servicky) O.; m. Gillian Anne Joseph, Mar. 25, 1972; children: Sarah Prentice, Michael Maurice. BA cum laude, Harvard U., 1966; JD, U. Pa., 1968. Bar: Pa. 1968, U.S. Ct. Appeals (D.C. cir.) 1976, U.S. Supreme Ct. 1983, U.S. Dist. Ct. (ea. dist.) Pa. 1984. Asst. to atty. gen. Kingdom of Swaziland, 1968-70; counsel, mng. dir. Satra Group Cos., N.Y.C., Moscow and Hamburg, Fed. Republic Germany, 1970-75; v.p. Research Group Internat., Charlottesville, Va., 1975-78; assoc. counsel, internat. legal affairs Armstrong World Industries Inc., Lancaster, Pa., 1978—; adj. prof. internat. law U. Va., Charlottesville, 1976-78; lectr. Mgmt. Ctr. Europe, Brussels, 1977—; advisor on product liability to fgn. govts. and industries; legal study interagy. task force on product liability, White House; mem. pvt. internat. law adv. com. U.S. State Dept., 1985—. Contbr. articles to profl jours. Founding mem. Swaziland Nat. Mus., 1968-70; mem. German Chamber Industry's com. on Soviet Trade, 1973-75; chmn. jud. appointments screening com., Lancaster County, 1985. Honory Harvard scholar, 1968, Emerson-Lowell scholar, 1968. Mem. ABA, Am. Soc. Internat. Law, Am. Corp. Counsel Assn. (chmn. internat. legal affairs com. 1983—), Pa. Bus. Roundtable Civil Justice Reform Working Group (chmn. 1986—), Pa. C. of C. (vice chmn. civil justice com. 1982—). Republican. Private international, General corporate, Personal injury. Home: 155 Wilson Dr Lancaster PA 17603 Office: Armstrong World Industries PO Box 3001 Lancaster PA 17604

ORBE, OCTAVIUS ANTHONY, lawyer; b. Passaic, N.J., Sept. 18, 1927. A.B., Princeton U., 1950; J.D., U. Va., 1953. Bar: Va. 1953, N.J. 1954. Assoc. Pitney, Hardin & Ward, Newark, 1953-55; ptnr. Orbe, Nugent, Collins & Darcy and predecessor firms, Ridgewood, N.J., 1955—; arbitrator Am. Arbitration Assn. Contbr. articles to profl. jours. Pres. Ridgewood Republican Club, 1971-72; mem. Bergen County Rep. Fin. Com., 1958-59. Served with U.S. Army, 1946-48. Fellow Am. Bar Found.; mem. ABA (ho. of dels.), N.J. Bar Assn. (past pres.) Bergen County Bar Assn. (past pres.), Va. Bar Assn., Essex County Bar Assn., Bergen County Mus., Blood Donors' Assn. Ridgewood (dir.), Princeton U. Alumni Assn. Roman Catholic. Clubs: Nassau, Saddle River Power Squadron, Ridgewood Golf, Ridgewood Exchange. General corporate, Probate, Real property. Office: 40 W Ridgewood Ave Ridgewood NJ 07450

ORDING, MICHAEL K., lawyer; b. Troy, Ohio, Aug. 2, 1955; s. Alton C. and Mary Ann (Huter) O.; m. Charlotte Eppich, Mar. 23, 1983. BS, Ohio No. U., 1977; JD, Ohio State U., 1980. Bar: Ohio 1980, Tex. 1982. Assoc. Jones, Day, Reavis & Pogue, Austin, Tex., 1980—. Municipal bonds, Real property, Securities. Office: Jones Day Reavis & Pogue 301 Congress Ave Suite 1200 Austin TX 78701

ORDMAN, HOWARD FRANCIS, lawyer; b. Bklyn., Oct. 12, 1914; s. Max D. and Anna (Wolpert) Ordmann; m. Sophie Janasz, Sept. 22, 1943; children—Robert, John, Aline. B.A., Cornell U., 1935; LL.B., Bklyn. Law Sch., St. Lawrence U., 1938. Bar: N.Y. 1938, U.S. Dist. Ct. (so. dist.) N.Y. 1941, U.S. Dist. Ct. (ea. dist.) N.Y. 1941, U.S. Ct. Appeals (2d cir.) 1964, U.S. Ct. Appeals (6th cir.) 1977, U.S. Ct. Appeals (8th cir.) 1967, U.S. Supreme Ct. 1978. Assoc. Putney, Twombly, Hall & Hirson and predecessor Putney, Twombly & Hall, N.Y.C., 1939-57, ptnr., 1957—; trustee Leopold Schepp Found. Served with USNR, 1942-46. Mem. ABA, Assn. Bar City N.Y., Am. Arbitration Assn. (nat. panel arbitrators, mem. arbitration practice com.). Club: Cornell of N.Y. Contracts commercial, Federal civil litigation, State civil litigation. Office: 36 W 44th St New York NY 10017

ORDONEZ, LUIS ENRIQUE, lawyer; b. Santiago, Cuba, June 24, 1955; came to U.S., 1961; s. Antonio Rafael and Lucilla Nieves (Castellvi) O.; m. Judith Ann Lakowski, Aug. 19, 1979. BBA with high honors, Eastern Ill. U., 1978; JD, U. Ill., 1981. Bar: Ill. 1981, U.S. Dist. Ct. (no. dist.) Ill. 1981, Fla. 1984. Assoc. Mckenna, Storer, Rowe, White & Farrug, Chgo., 1981-85; ptnr. Schwartz, Volpe & Ordonez, P.A., Miami, Fla., 1985—. Mem. ABA, Ill. Bar Assn., Chgo. Bar Assn., Assn. Trial Lawyers Am. Republican. Roman Catholic. Avocations: fishing, golfing, tennis, swimming, aquarium. Insurance, Contracts commercial. Home: 7545 E Treasure Dr #10G North Bay Village FL 33141 Office: Schwartz Volpe & Ordonez PA 200 S Biscayne Suite 3450 Miami FL 33131

ORDOVER, ABRAHAM PHILIP, legal educator; b. Far Rockaway, N.Y., Jan. 18, 1937; s. Joseph and Bertha (Fromberg) O.; m. Carol M. Ordover, Mar. 23, 1961; children: Andrew Charles, Thomas Edward. BA magna cum laude, Syracuse U., 1958; JD, Yale U., 1961. Bar: N.Y. 1961, U.S. Dist. Ct. (so. and ea. dists.) N.Y., U.S. Ct. Appeals (2d cir.), U.S. Supreme Ct. Assoc. Cahill, Gordon & Reindel, N.Y.C., 1961-71; prof. law Hofstra U., Hempstead, N.Y., 1971-81; L.Q.C. Lamar prof. law Emory U., Atlanta, 1981—; vis. prof. Cornell U., Ithaca, N.Y., 1977; team leader nat. program Nat. Inst. Trial Advocacy, Boulder, Colo., 1980, 82, 84, 86, tchr. program Cambridge, Mass., 1979-84, adv. program Gainesville, Fla., 1978-79, northeast regional dir., 1977-81. Author: Argument to the Jury, 1982, Problems and Cases in Trial Advocacy, 1983; contbr. articles to profl. jours. Bd. dirs. Atlanta Legal Aid Soc., 1984—. Recipient Gumpert award Am. Coll. Trial Lawyers, 1984, 85, Jacobsen award Roscoe Pound Am. Trial Lawyer Found., 1986. Mem. ABA, N.Y. State Bar Assn., Assn. Am. Law Schs. (chmn. litigation sect. 1986), Atlanta Lawyers Club. Avocations: photography, scuba diving, jogging. Legal education, Federal civil litigation, Criminal. Office: Emory U Law Sch Atlanta GA 30322

O'REILLY, JAMES THOMAS, lawyer, author; b. N.Y.C., Nov. 15, 1947; s. Matthew Richard and Regina (Casey) O'R.; m. Rosann Tagliaferro, Aug. 26, 1972; children: Jean, Ann. BA cum laude, Boston Coll., 1969; JD, U. Va., 1974. Bar: Va. 1974, Ohio, 1974, U.S. Supreme Ct. 1979, U.S. Ct. Appeals (6th cir.) 1980. Atty. Procter & Gamble Co., Cin., 1974-76, counsel, 1976-79, sr. counsel for food, drug and product safety, 1979-85, corp. counsel, 1985—; adj. prof. in adminstrv. law U. Cin., 1980—; cons. Adminstrv. Conf. U.S., 1981-82; mem. Ohio Bishop's Adv. Council. Author: Federal Information Disclosure, 1977, Food and Drug Administration Regulatory Manual, 1979, Unions' Rights to Company Information, 1980, Federal Regulation of the Chemical Industry, 1980, Administrative Rulemaking, 1983, Ohio Public Employee Collective Bargaining, 1984, Protecting Workplace Secrets, 1985, Emergency Response to Chemical Accidents, 1986, Product Defects and Hazards, 1987; contbr. articles to profl. jours.; editorial bd. Food and Drug Cosmetic Law Jour. Mem. Hamilton County Dem. Central Com. Served with U.S. Army, 1970-72. Mem. Food and Drug Law Inst., ABA (chmn. com. on food, drug and cosmetic law), Fed. Bar Assn. Democrat. Roman Catholic. Administrative and regulatory, Environment, Labor. Office: Procter & Gamble Co PO Box 599 Cincinnati OH 45201

O'REILLY, KEVIN THOMAS, lawyer; b. N.Y.C., Feb. 15, 1943; s. John James and Mary Ann (Bogue) O'R.; m. Loretta Ann Creaven, Jan. 11, 1969; children: Kevin J., Kathleen A., Timothy J., Daniel P., Mary P., Sean M. BS, Fordham U., 1964; MA in Math., U. Rochester, 1966; JD, NYU, 1970. Bar: N.Y. 1971, U.S. Dist. Ct. (so. and ea. dists.) N.Y. 1972, U.S. Ct. Appeals (2d cir.) 1972, U.S. Supreme Ct. 1974. Assoc. Breed, Abbott & Morgan, N.Y.C., 1970-75; sr. litigation counsel W.R. Grace & Co., N.Y.C., 1975-79, chief litigation counsel, 1979—. Bd. dirs., sec. The Greenwood Found., N.Y.C., 1985—. Mem. N.Y. State Bar Assn. Antitrust, Federal civil litigation, State civil litigation. Office: W R Grace & Co 1114 Ave of Americas New York NY 10036

O'REILLY, MICHAEL JAMES, lawyer; b. Lafayette, Ind., Sept. 15, 1946; s. Robert Edward and Lou (Tolan) O'R.; m. Jean Frances Jacob, Aug. 24, 1968; children: Kevin Robert, Mary Katherine. BA, U. Notre Dame, 1968; JD, St. John's Sch. of Law, N.Y.C., 1971. Bar: Ind. 1976, U.S. Dist. Ct. (so. dist.) Ind. 1976, U.S. Dist. Ct. (no. dist.) Ind. 1977. Trust officer Purdue Nat. Bank of Lafayette, Ind., 1974-77; sole practice Lafayette, 1977—. Candidate Tippecanoe County Rep. Nomination, 1984; century mem. Boy Scouts Am., Lafayette, 1984-86; mem. Lafayette Police Dept. Civil Service Merit Bd., 1983—, v.p. 1985-86, pres. 1986—. Served to 1st lt. U.S. Army, 1971-74, capt. USANG, 1977-80. Recipient Appreciation award Fraternal Order of Police, 1984, Cert. of Commendation Legal Corp. Tippecanoe County, 1985. Mem. Ind. Bar Assn., Tippecanoe County Bar Assn. (treas. criminal def. com. 1986—), Assn. Trial Lawyers Am., Nat. Assn. Criminal Def. Lawyers, Ind. Trial Lawyers Assn., Am. Legion. Roman Catholic. Club: Forty and Eight (Lafayette). Lodge: Optimists. Avocations: golf, flying, fishing. Criminal, Personal injury, State civil litigation. Home: 922 S 10th St Lafayette IN 47902 Office: 424 Columbia St PO Box 1158 Lafayette IN 47902

O'REILLY, TIMOTHY PATRICK, lawyer; b. Kingston, N.Y., July 18, 1948; s. William Joseph and Gertrude Elizabeth (Falvey) O'R.; m. Denise Maria Bianchetto, Apr. 3, 1971; children: Devin, Trevor. BA, Manhattan Coll., 1970; JD, New Eng. Sch. of Law, 1974. Bar: N.Y. 1975, U.S. Dist. Ct. (no. dist.) N.Y. 1975, U.S. Dist. Ct. (so. dist.) N.Y. 1977, U.S. Ct. Appeals (2d cir.) 1981, Pa. 1982, Ohio 1986. Assoc. Stewart T. Schantz P.C., Highland, N.Y., 1974-79; chief asst. atty. Dutchess County, Poughkeepsie, N.Y., 1979-82; gen. counsel Carlisle (Pa.) Tire and Rubber Co., 1982-84; staff counsel Carlisle Corp., Cin., 1984—. Served with USAR, 1970-76. Mem. Def. Research Inst. Roman Catholic. Avocations: family, tennis. Personal injury, General corporate, Federal civil litigation. Office: Carlisle Corp 1600 Columbia Plaza Cincinnati OH 45202

O'REILLY, TIMOTHY PATRICK, lawyer; b. San Lorenzo, Calif., Sept. 12, 1945; s. Thomas M. and Florence Ann (Ohlman) O'R.; m. Susan Ann Marshall, July 18, 1969; children: Patrick, Sean, Colleen. BS, Ohio State U., 1967; JD, NYU, 1971. Bar: U.S. Dist. Ct. (ea. dist.) Pa. 1971, U.S. Dist. Ct. (mid. dist.) Pa. 1972, U.S. Ct. Appeals (3d cir.) 1977. Ptnr. Morgan, Lewis & Bockius, Phila., 1978—. Mem. ABA, Pa. Bar Assn., Phila. Bar Assn. Labor, Pension, profit-sharing, and employee benefits. Home: 1127 Cymry Dr Berwyn PA 19312 Office: Morgan Lewis & Bockius 2000 One Logan Sq Philadelphia PA 19103

ORENBERG, ALLEN HOWARD, lawyer; b. Balt., May 18, 1954; s. Carl Saul and Cecilia (Katz) O. Student, Hebrew Union Coll., Jerusalem, 1975; BA, U. Md., 1977; JD, So. Tex. Coll. Law, 1980. Bar: Pa. 1982, U.S. Tax Ct. 1982, U.S. Ct. Mil. Appeals 1982, D.C. 1985, U.S. Dist. Ct. D.C. 1986. Sole practice Phila., 1982-85; assoc. Leitner, Greene & Christensen and predecessor firm Leitner & Martin, Washington, 1985—. Mem. ABA, D.C. Bar Assn., Assn. Trial Lawyers Am., Delta Theta Phi. Republican. Jewish. Lodge: B'nai B'rith (capital legal council 1986—). Trademark and copyright, Criminal, General practice. Home: 412 Branch Dr Silver Spring MD 20901 Office: Leitner Greene & Christensen 2201 Wisconsin Ave NW Washington DC 20007

ORESKOVICH, CARL JOSEPH, lawyer; b. Butte, Mont., Oct. 31, 1954; s. Steve John and Zorka (Masonovich) o.; m. Mitriann Popovich, Sept. 1, 1979. BA, Seattle U., 1976; JD, U. Mont., 1982. Bar: Wash. 1982, Mont. 1982, U.S. Dist. Ct. Mont., U.S. Dist. Ct. Wash. Assoc. Hemovich, Nappi & Oreskovich, Spokane, Wash., 1982-85, ptnr., 1985—. Criminal, Securities, Personal injury. Home: 1115 E Rockwood Blvd Spokane WA 99203 Office: Hemovich Nappi & Oreskovich 818 W Riverside 540 Lincoln Bldg Spokane WA 99201

ORESMAN, ROGER B., lawyer; b. N.Y.C., Oct. 26, 1920; s. A. Louis and Gertrude (Bergel) O.; m. Charlotte Stephenson, June 26, 1948 (div. Jan. 1970); m Janice Carlson Fortenbaugh, Mar 20, 1975; stepchildren: Samuel B. Fortenbaugh IV, Cristina C. Fortenbaugh. A.B., Harvard U., 1941, M.B.A., 1943; LL.B., Columbia U., 1952. Bar: N.Y 1952. Indsl. engr. Botany Mills, N.J., 1946-47; mgmt. cons. Aronson & Oresman, N.Y.C., 1947-49; assoc. Milbank, Tweed, Hadley & McCloy, N.Y.C., 1952-58, ptnr., 1958—; dir. Amerada Hess Corp., Thomas Jefferson Life Ins. Co. Trustee Randolph-Macon Woman's Coll., Lynchburg, Va. Served to lt. USNR, 1943-46. Mem. Assn. Bar City N.Y. (exec. com. 1959-62). Home: 1001 Park Ave New York NY 10028 Office: Milbank Tweed Hadley & McCloy 1 Chase Manhattan Plaza New York NY 10005

ORKIN, NEAL, law educator; b. Phila., Mar. 7, 1945; s. Jules and Sylvia Orkin; m. Nancy Carol Bookbinder, July 27, 1969; children: Elaine, David, Robert. BEE, Drexel U., 1967; JD, Temple U., 1975. Bar: Pa. 1976, U.S. Dist. Ct. (ea. dist.) Pa. 1979. Sole practice Pa., 1976—; asst. prof. Drexel U., Phila., 1985—; lectr. U. London, 1985, Stockholm Sch. Econ., 1986. Author: Employee Inventions, 1981. Avocations: photography. Labor. Home: 43 Lanfair Rd Cheltenham PA 19012

ORLEANS, NEIL JEFFREY, lawyer; b. N.Y.C., June 7, 1948; s. Fred Allan and Shirley (Kovner) O.; m. Joan Elizabeth Painter, Aug. 10, 1974; children: David Anthony, Kimberly Ann. BA with high honors, U. Tex., Austin, 1969, JD with honors, 1971. Bar: Tex. 1972, U.S. Ct. Mil. Appeals, 1972, U.S. Ct. Appeals (5th cir.) 1981, U.S. Dist. Ct. (no. dist.) Tex. 1978, U.S. Dist. Ct. (we. dist.) Tex. 1981, U.S. Dist. Ct. (ea. and so. dists.) Tex. 1983. Assoc. Eldridge, Goggans, Dallas, 1976-78, Baldwin & Assocs., Dallas, 1978-79; ptnr. Wise, Stuhl, Andrea, Orleans and Morris, 1979—. Contbr. to Tex. Law Rev., 1970. Ruling elder North Park Presbyn. Ch., Dallas, 1980-82. Served to capt. JAGC, USAF, 1972-76. Recipient Am. Jurisprudence award, 1969. Mem. ABA, Tex. Bar Assn., Dallas Bar Assn., Dallas Bankruptcy Bar Assn., Dallas Hist. Preservation Soc., Phi Beta Kappa. Republican. Clubs: Oakridge (Garland), Towne (Dallas). Bankruptcy, Contracts commercial. Office: Wise Stuhl Andrea Orleans & Morris 3434 Thanksgiving Tower Dallas TX 75201

ORLEBEKE, WILLIAM RONALD, lawyer; b. El Paso, Tex., Jan. 5, 1933; s. William Ronald and Frances Claire (Cook) O.; m. Barbara Raye Pike, Aug. 29, 1954; children—Michelle, Julene, David. B.A., Willamette U., 1956; M.A., Kans. U., 1957; J.D., Willamette U., 1966. Bar: Calif. 1966, U.S. Dist. Ct. (no. dist.) Calif. 1967, U.S. Ct. Appeals (9th cir.) 1967. Assoc. Eliassen & Postel, San Francisco, 1966-69; ptnr. Coll, Levy & Orlebeke, Concord, Calif., 1969-77, Orlebeke & Hutchings, Concord, 1977-86, Orlebeke, Hutchings & Pinkerton, 1986—; hearing officer Contra Costa County, Calif., 1981—; arbitrator Contra Costa County Superior Ct., 1977—, U.S. Dist. Ct. No. Calif., 1978—; judge pro tem Mt. Diablo Mcpl. Ct., 1973-77. Alumni bd. dirs. Willamette U., 1978-81, trustee, 1980-81; scholarship chmn. Concord Elks, 1977-79; del. Joint U.S/China Internat. Trade Law Conf., Beijing, Peoples Republic of China, 1987. Served with USMCR, 1952-59. Sr. scholar, Willamette U., 1955-56; Woodrow Wilson fellow, Kans. U., 1956-57; U.S. Bur. Nat. Affairs fellow, 1966, others. Mem. SAR. Republican. Clubs: Order Eastern Star, Masons, Shriners, Elks. Administrative and regulatory, General practice, State civil litigation. Office: 3330 Clayton Rd Suite F Concord CA 94519

ORLIN, KAREN J., lawyer; b. Washington, Apr. 2, 1948; d. Hyman and Lenore (Driller) O. AB summa cum laude, U. Pa., 1969; JD, Harvard U., 1972. Bar: N.Y. 1973, U.S. Dist. Ct. (so. and ea. dists.) N.Y. 1973, U.S. Ct. Appeals (2d cir.) 1973, Fla. 1982. Assoc. Kronish, Lieb, Weiner & Hellman, N.Y.C., 1972-81, Mahoney, Hadlow & Valdes-Fauli, P.A., Miami, Fla., 1981-82; ptnr. Valdes-Fauli, Richardson & Cobb, P.A., Miami, 1982-83; assoc. Ruden, Barnett, McClosky, Schuster & Russell, P.A., Miami, Fla., 1983-85, Shea & Gould, Miami, 1985—; mem. securities com. Fla. Bar, 1983—. Bd. dirs. Coop. Housing Corp., N.Y.C., 1980-81; bd. dirs. S. End Alternative Theatre, Miami, 1984—; mem. Com. of 100, Temple Beth Am. Mem. ABA, Fla. Assn. Women Lawyers, Dade County Bar Assn., Coral Gables Bar Assn., Assn. of Bar of City of N.Y. (com. securities regulation 1979-81), Mortar Bd. Soc., U. Pa. Dade Alumni Club (dir. 1985—, exec. com.), Wharton Club South Fla. (exec. com.), Phi Beta Kappa. Banking, General corporate, Securities. Office: Shea & Gould 801 Brickell Ave Miami FL 33131

ORLINS, PETER IRWIN, lawyer; b. Syracuse, N.Y., Apr. 5, 1947; s. Barney and Jane (Fink) O.; m. Janis P. Eskowits, June 17, 1967 (div.); children: Mia, Constance. BA, Hamline U., 1969; JD, William Mitchell Sch. Law, 1973. Bar: Minn., U.S. Dist. Ct. Minn., U.S. Ct. Appeals (8th cir.) 1973. Ptnr. Orlins & Brainerd, Richfield, Minn., 1973—. Mem. Hennepin County Bar Assn., Minn. Trial Lawyers Assn., Richfield C. of C. (pres. 1982). Jewish. Lodges: Masons, Shriners. Personal injury, Banking, State civil litigation.

ORLOFF, RONALD LEONARD, lawyer; b. N.Y.C., Oct. 2, 1932; s. Benjamin H. and Sydell (Schimmel) O.; m. June Yudenfreund, Sept. 3, 1955 (dec. 1981); children—Gordon M., Jeffrey K. B.A., Washington and Jefferson Coll., 1954; LL.B., Yale U., 1957. Bar: Conn. 1957, Oreg. 1958, N.Y. 1964, Ohio, 1966, Ill. 1985. Teaching fellow, instr. U. Chgo. Law Sch., 1957-58; assoc. Stoel, Rives, Boley, Fraser & Wyse, Portland, Oreg., 1958-63; atty. Western Electric Co., N.Y.C., 1963-65; gen. atty. Ohio Bell Tel. Co., Cleve., 1965-83; v.p., gen. counsel Ameritech Services, Inc., 1983—. Mem. ABA, Ohio State Bar Assn., N.Y. State Bar Assn., Oreg. Bar Assn., Ill. Bar Assn. General corporate, Public utilities, Administrative and regulatory. Office: 1900 E Golf Rd Schaumburg IL 60173

ORLOSKI, RICHARD J., lawyer; b. Taylor, Pa., Jan. 31, 1947; s. Joseph Bernard and Wanda (Chodnicki) O.; m. Kathy Law, Aug. 14, 1971; children: Richard Law, Rebecca Lee, Kevin Law, Joseph Law. BA cum laude, King's Coll., 1968; JD, Cornell U., 1971. Bar: Pa. 1971, Mich. 1971, U.S. Supreme Ct. 1975. Law clk. Mich. Ct. Appeals, Lansing, 1971-72; dep. atty. gen. Pa. Atty Gen.'s Office, Harrisburg, 1972-74; asst. dist. Atty. Office of Dist. Atty., Allentown, Pa., 1974-77; assoc. Stamberg, Caplan & Calnan, Allentown, 1977-81; ptnr. Calnan & Orloski, P.C., Allentown, 1981-85; mgr. Richard J. Orloski, Allentown, 1985—; commr. Pa. Commn. on Charitable Orgns., Harrisburg, 1972-74. Author: Criminal Law: An Indictment, 1976. Candidate for U.S. Ho. of Reps., Pa. 15th Dist., 1982; del. Dem. Nat. Conv., San Francisco, 1984. Mem. ABA, Pa. Bar Assn., Am. Trial Lawyers Assn., Pa. Trial Lawyers Assn. Democrat. Roman Catholic. Federal civil litigation, State civil litigation, Probate. Home: 3524 Patricia Dr Allentown PA 18103 Office: 1005 S Cedar Crest Blvd Allentown PA 18103

ORMAN, LEONARD ARNOLD, lawyer; b. Balt., June 15, 1930; s. Samuel and Bertie (Adler) O.; m. Barbara Gold, June 9, 1978; children: Richard Harold, Robert Barton. A.B. summa cum laude, U. Md., 1952, J.D., 1955. Bar: Md. 1955. Law clk. Hon. Frederick W. Brune, Chief Judge Md. Ct. of Appeals, 1955-56; mem. dept. legis. reference Md. Legislature, 1957-58; mem. Gov.'s Commn. to Revise Criminal Code, 1958-59; pvt. practice law Balt., 1956—. Mem. editorial bd.: Md. Law Rev, 1953-55; Contbr. articles to profl. jours. Pres. Young Democrats 2d Dist., Balt., 1960-63. Served with AUS, 1948-49; lt. col. USAF Res.; ret. Mem. Assn. Trial Lawyers Am. (nat. committeeman 1976-80, bd. govs. 1985—, liaison 1985-86, key man com. 1986—, ABA-ATLA liaison com. 1985-86, steering com. 1986—), Md. Trial Lawyers Assn. (bd. govs., pres. 1984-85), Md. Bar Assn., Balt. City Bar Assn. (legis. com., lectr. trial tactics), Order of Coif. Club: Masons. Personal injury, Federal civil litigation, State civil litigation. Home: 2 Celadon Rd Owings Mills MD 21117 Office: Orman & Dilli 5 Light St Suite 1100 Baltimore MD 21202

ORMOND, GREGG JOSEPH, lawyer; b. Phila., Oct. 5, 1955; s. Francis Joseph and Patricia Eileen (Toohey) O. BA, U. Pa., 1977; JD, U. Miami, 1980. Bar: Fla. 1980, U.S. Dist. Ct. (so. dist.) Fla. 1981, U.S. Ct. Appeals (fifth cir.) 1981, U.S. Ct. Appeals (11th cir.) 1982. Assoc. Law Offices of R. Stuart Huff P.A., Coral Gables, Fla., 1979-83; sole practice Coral Gables, 1983-84; ptnr. Lisk & Ormond P.A., Coral Gables, 1984—. Pres. young alumni group U. Miami, Coral Gables, 1981-82; bd. dirs. Dade County alumni U. Pa., Miami, Fla., 1981—. Mem. ABA, Fla. Bar Assn., Acad. Fla. Trial Lawyers, Assn. Trial Lawyers Am., Pi Kappa Alpha (pres. regional chpt. 1984—). State civil litigation, Federal civil litigation, Contracts commercial. Home: 624 Fluvia Ave Coral Gables FL 33134 Office: Lisk & Ormond PA 200 Aragon Ave Coral Gables FL 33134

ORMSBY, DAVID GEORGE, lawyer; b. Buffalo, Oct. 21, 1933; s. Charles C. and Katharine (Van Keuren) O.; m. Lindsay Walker, May 16, 1987; children: Peter, Thomas, Christopher. BA, Amherst Coll., 1955; LLD, Harvard U., 1961. Bar: N.Y. 1961, U.S. Dist. Ct. (so. dist.) N.Y. 1965. Assoc. Cravath, Swaine & Moore, N.Y.C., 1961-69, ptnr., 1969—. Bd. ethics Town of Greenwich, Conn., 1979—; pres., bd. mgrs. Camp Dudley YMCA, Westport, N.Y., 1980-86; bd. dirs. N.Y./N.J. Minority Purchasing Council, 1975—. Served to capt. USAF, 1955-58. Mem. ABA, N.Y. State Bar Assn., Assn. of Bar of City of N.Y. General corporate, Securities. Office: Cravath Swaine & Moore 1 Chase Manhattan Plaza New York NY 10005

ORMSETH, MILO E., lawyer; b. Wolf Point, Mont., July 28, 1932; m. Beverly Tuftedal, July 29, 1956. BA, St. Olaf Coll., 1954; LLB, Harvard U., 1959. Bar: Oreg. 1959. Assoc. Davies, Biggs et al, Portland, Oreg., 1959-65; ptnr. Stoel, Rives, Boley, Fraser & Wyse and predecessor firms, Portland, 1965—. Mem. Oreg. Bar Assn. (chmn. taxation sect.). Clubs: Multnomah (Oreg.) Athletic; Portland Yacht. General corporate, State and local taxation. Home: 6820 SE 29th Ave Portland OR 97202 Office: Stoel Rives Boley Fraser & Wyse 900 SW 5th Ave 23d Floor Portland OR 97204

ORN, CLAYTON LINCOLN, lawyer; b. Weatherford, Tex., June 20, 1902; s. Jacob J. and Etta (Hill) O.; m. Zara Laura Sims, July 27, 1927; 1 child, Camille (Mrs. W.R. Haynes). Student, Baylor U., 1921-23; J.D., George Washington U., 1925. Bar: Tex. 1925, Ohio 1954, D.C. 1954. Practice of law Cisco, Tex., 1925-31; mem. firm Phillips, Trammel, Estes, Edwards & Orn, Ft. Worth, 1931-42; div. atty. Marathon Oil Co., Houston, 1942-54; gen. atty. Marathon Oil Co., Findlay, Ohio, 1954-61; dir., gen. counsel Marathon Oil Co., 1961-67; sr. partner firm Anderson, Brown, Orn & Jones, 1967—; Mem. adv. bd. Southwestern Legal Found. Contbr. articles to legal jours. Mem. ABA (ho. dels. 1959-60, chmn. mineral sect. 1956-57), Tex. Bar Assn. (chmn. mineral sect. 1953-54), Mid-Continent Oil and Gas Assn. (distinguished service award 1965), Am. Petroleum Inst., Am. Judicature

Soc. Presbyterian. State civil litigation, FERC practice, Oil and gas leasing. Home: 2929 Buffalo Speedway Houston TX 77098 Office: Anderson Brown Orn & Jones 900 Tex Commerce Tower Houston TX 77002

ORNITZ, RICHARD MARTIN, lawyer, business executive; b. Annapolis, Md., July 4, 1945; s. Martin Nathaniel and Beatrice Cynthia (Swick) O.; m. Margareth Adams, June 15, 1971 (div. Apr. 1977); m. Janet Alma Steen, Dec. 5, 1981; children—Alexandra, Zachary, Darren. B.S. in Metall. Engring., Cornell U., 1967; J.D., NYU, 1970; grad. sr. exec. program, MIT, 1985. Bar: N.Y. 1971, U.S. Dist. Ct. (ea. dist.) 1972, U.S. Supreme Ct. 1984. Assoc. Cravath, Swaine & Moore, N.Y.C., 1972-77; v.p., gen. counsel, sec. Degussa Corp., Teterboro, N.J. 1977—; of counsel, Hughes, Hubbard & Reed, N.Y.C., 1985—; dir. Degussa Corp. subs., 1980—; dir. Metal Products Internat., Inc., Greenwich, Conn; speaker Risk Ins. Mgmt. Soc., 1984, 85, 86, IBA, 1986, ACCA, 1986, European Co. Lawyers Assn., 1986. Assoc. editor Ann. Survey of Law, NYU, 1970. Served to 1st lt. U.S. Army, 1970-72. Mem. ABA (sub-com. chmn. European law sect.), N.Y. State Bar Assn., Internat. Bar Assn., Am. Corp. Counsel Assn. (vice chmn. of internat. sect. com.), European Am. Gen. Counsels Group (chmn. 1986—), N.J. Gen. Counsels Group, Cornell Soc. Engrs. Republican. Jewish. Clubs: Old Greenwich Republican (Conn.), Innis Acden. General corporate, Private international, Insurance. Home: 18 Meadowbank Rd Old Greenwich CT 06870 Office: Degussa Corp Rt 46 at Hollister Rd Teterboro NJ 07608

ORNSTEIN, ALEXANDER THOMAS, lawyer; b. Detroit, Oct. 11, 1944; s. Charles and Martha (Lichter) O.; m. Harriet Rozenblum, July 5, 1970; children: Charles Allen, Deborah Rena. BS, Washburn U., 1969; postgrad., Detroit Coll. Law, 1970-72; JD, Wayne State U., 1974. Bar: Mich. 1972, U.S. Dist. Ct. (ea. dist.) Mich. 1972, U.S. Ct. Appeals (6th cir.) 1972, U.S. Supreme Ct. 1978. Counselor New Horizons of Oakland County, Pontiac, Mich., 1969-70; staff atty. Mich. Mut. Ins. Co., Detroit, 1973-74; assoc. Chambers, Steiner, Mazur, Ornstein & Amlin P.C., Detroit, 1974—; hearing officer Mich. Dept. Civil Rights, Detroit and Flint, Mich., 1980—. Editor: Metro Memo Newspaper, 1984, 86—. Bd. dirs. B'nai B'rith Youth Orgn., Detroit, 1984—. Bancroft-Whitney scholar, 1971. Mem. ABA, Mich. Bar Assn., Detroit Bar Assn., Fed. Bar Assn., Assn. Trial Lawyers Am., Mich. Trial Lawyers Assn., Am. Judicature Soc., Anti Defamation League (chmn. com., bd. dirs. 1984—). Lodge: B'nai B'rith (treas. Dist. 6, trustee barristers 1983—, pres. Centennial 1985, bd. dirs. youth orgn. 1984—, Hillel 1984—, resident atty.). Avocations: computers, vol. service, flute. Workers' compensation, Personal injury. Home: 32614 Olde Franklin Dr Farmington Hills MI 48018 Office: Chambers Steiner Mazur et al 2167 Orchard Lake Rd Pontiac MI 48053

ORNSTIL, MICHAEL GARY, lawyer; b. Bklyn., Oct. 29, 1956; s. Sydney Gary and Dorothy Ann (Braver) O.; m. Barrie Bulmore, Sept. 16, 1984. BA, U. Miami, 1978; JD, U. Calif., San Francisco, 1982. Bar: Calif. 1982, U.S. Dist. Ct. (no. dist.) Calif. 1982. Order book ofcl. Pacific Stock Exchange, San Francisco, 1978-79; assoc. Sedgwick, Detert, Moran & Arnold, San Francisco, 1982—. Named Athlete of Yr., U. Miami, 1978. Mem. San Francisco Bar Assn. Clubs: Telegraph Hill (San Francisco); Berkeley Tennis. Avocations: basketball, tennis, cycling, baseball. State civil litigation, Insurance, Consumer commercial. Office: Sedgwick Detert Moran & Arnold One Embarcadero Ctr 16th Floor San Francisco CA 94111-3765

O'RORKE, JAMES FRANCIS, JR., lawyer; b. N.Y.C., Dec. 4, 1936; s. James Francis and Helen (Weber) O'R.; m. Carla Phelps, Aug. 6, 1964. A.B., Princeton U., 1958; J.D., Yale U., 1961. Bar: N.Y. 1962. Assoc. Davies, Hardy & Schenck, 1962-69; ptnr. Davies, Hardy, Ives & Lawther, 1969-72, Skadden, Arps, Slate, Meagher & Flom, N.Y.C., 1972—; dir. Clinipad Corp., E.B. Meyrowitz, Inc. Trustee Mus. Am. Indiana-Heye Found., 1977-80. Mem. ABA, N.Y. State Bar Assn., Assn. Bar City N.Y., Am. Coll. Real Estate Lawyers. Club: City Midday (N.Y.C.). Real property, Contracts commercial, Environment. Office: 919 3d Ave New York NY 10022

OROSZ, RICHARD THOMAS, lawyer; b. Painesville, Ohio, Dec. 26, 1942; s. Gabriel John and Helen Anna (Black) O.; m. Elizabeth Ann Dempsey, June 28, 1969; Karen, Gregory, Megan. B.S., Lake Erie Coll., 1967; J.D., Cleve. State U., 1970. Bar: Ohio 1971, U.S. Dist. Ct. (no. dist.) Ohio 1976, U.S. Supreme Ct. 1977. Sole practice, Painesville, 1971—; acting judge Painesville Mcpl. Ct., 1977—; foreman Lake County Grand Jury, 1979. Trustee Morley Library Assn. Mem. ABA, Ohio State Bar Assn., Lake County Bar Assn., Lake County Law Library Assn. (sec. 1973—). Roman Catholic. Club: Exchange (pres. 1984) (Painesville). Lodge: Elks. Avocations: golf; jogging. General practice. Home: 7740 Mountain Ash Dr Concord Township OH 44060 Office: 56 Liberty St Suite 207 Painesville OH 44077

O'ROURKE, DANIEL, lawyer; b. Evanston, Ill., Mar. 22, 1947; s. Thomas Edward and Marion Helen (Mulligan) O'R.; m. Kathleen Wallace, May 19, 1977; children: Daniel, Maureen, Erin, Timothy, Elizabeth. AB in Econs., Coll. of Holy Cross, 1969; JD, Georgetown U., 1972. Bar: Ill. 1972. Assoc. McDermott, Will & Emery, Chgo., 1972-78, ptnr., 1978—. Served to 2d lt. U.S. Army, 1971-73. Mem. ABA. Roman Catholic. Banking, Securities, General corporate. Office: McDermott Will & Emery 111 W Monroe St Chicago IL 60603

O'ROURKE, PETER EDWARD, lawyer; b. Detroit, Nov. 14, 1933; s. Randall Michael and Alice Ellen (White) O'R.; m. Susan Ellen Gehrke, Sept. 30, 1968; children—Kathleen Ann, Peter Edward. B.A., Wayne State U., 1955; J.D., Detroit Coll. Law, 1958. Bar: Mich. bar 1958. Practiced in Detroit, 1961—; partner firm Porritt, Hegarty & O'Rourke, 1964-75; sr. partner firm O'Rourke, Fitzgerald, Kazul & Rutledge, 1975-80; prin. firm Peter E. O'Rourke, P.C., 1980—; TV host Law Forum, 1983-84; judge Grosse Pointe Farms Mcpl. Ct., Mich., 1985—. Chmn. Mich. Employment Security Appeal Bd., 1969-72; mem. Regional Export Expansion Council, 1971-76, Gov.'s Spl. Commn. on Energy, 1972-76; Republican candidate for Mich. Senate, 1966, U.S. Congress, 1968. Served to comdr. USCGR, 1958-81. Mem. Mich., Detroit bar assns., Mich. C. of C., Am. Judicature Soc. Roman Catholic. Clubs: Mackinac Island (Mich.); Yacht (commodore), Grosse Pointe Yacht (dir.). General corporate, Real property, Environment. Home: 241 Lewiston Rd Grosse Pointe Farms MI 48236 Office: 200 1st Federal Bldg Detroit MI 48226

ORR, DENNIS PATRICK, lawyer; b. N.Y.C., Dec. 29, 1952; s. Gerard Samuel and Mary Ellen (Dowd) O.; m. Laurie Louise Lawless, Jan. 15, 1977; children: Kathryn, Kristen, Megan. BA, Boston Coll., 1975; JD, St. John's U., 1978. Bar: N.Y., U.S. Dist. Ct. (so. and ea. dists.) N.Y., U.S. Ct. Appeals (2d cir.). Assoc. Shearman & Sterling, N.Y.C., 1978-86, ptnr., 1987—. St. Thomas More scholar St. John's Law Sch., Jamaica, N.Y., 1975. Mem. ABA, N.Y. State Bar Assn. Republican. Roman Catholic. Antitrust, Securities, Personal injury. Office: Shearman & Sterling 53 Wall St New York NY 10005

ORR, PARKER MURRAY, lawyer; b. Cleve., Mar. 29, 1927; s. Stanley Lutz and Katherine (Murray) O.; m. Joan Luttrell, June 8, 1946; children: Kathleen Orr Guzowski, Parker Murray, Louise Orr Black, Kevin J. B.A., Western Res. U., 1948, LL.B., 1950. Bar: Ohio 1950. Atty. Leckie, McCreary, Schlitz, Hinslea & Petersilge, Cleve., 1950-51; owner Orr Constrn. Co., Cleve., 1951-57; assoc. firm Baker & Hostetler, Cleve., 1957-67, ptnr., 1967—. Chmn. City of Willoughby Hills Planning Commn., Ohio, 1964-78. Mem. ABA, Ohio Bar Assn., Greater Cleve. Bar Assn. Republican. Club: Mayfield Country (Cleve.). Home: 37801 Rogers Rd Willoughby OH 44094 Office: Baker & Hostetler 3200 National City Ctr Cleveland OH 44114

ORR, ROBERT M., lawyer, law educator; b. Detroit, Aug. 31, 1954; s. Robert James and Lynn Gertrude (Avery) O.; m. Janet L. Loretz, June 3, 1978. BA, U. Calif., Irvine, 1976; JD, Pepperdine U., 1979. Assoc. Law Office of Leonard A. Matsuk, Long Beach, Calif., 1979-82; ptnr. Matsuk & Orr, Long Beach, Calif., 1982—; adj. prof. Am. Coll. of Law, Brea, Calif., 1982—, Pacific Coast Coll. of Law, Long Beach, 1986; judge pro tem Long Beach Mcpl. Ct., 1983—. Mem. ABA, Calif. Bar Assn. (voluntary investigator 1986), Los Angles County Bar Assn. (fee arbitrator), Long Beach County Bar Assn. (fee arbitrator), Sigma Chi. Republican. Avocations: wine collecting, carpentry, jogging. State civil litigation, Real property, General corporate. Home: 1402 Stonewood Ct San Pedro CA 90732 Office: Matsuk & Orr 100 Oceangate #1010 Long Beach CA 90802

ORR, THOMAS JOHN, lawyer; b. Jersey City, May 27, 1956; s. John Henry and Regina Barbara (Juralowicz) O.; m. Patricia Margaret Ryan, Apr. 16, 1983. BA, Rutgers U., 1978; JD, Rutgers U., Camden, N.J., 1981. Bar: N.J. 1981, U.S. Dist. Ct. N.J. 1981. Assoc. Bookbinder & Colaguori, Burlington, N.J., 1981-84; ptnr. Colaguori & Orr, Burlington, 1984—. Sec., treas. Endeavor Emergency Squad, Burlington, 1981—, atty. 22d dist. N.J. First Aid Council, Mt. Holly, N.J., 1984—, Burlington County First Aid Council, Mt. Holly, 1984—, N.J. Exempt Fireman's Assn., Piscataway, N.J., 1986—; dive rescue leader, 1985—; capt. Palmyra (N.J.) Ambulance Squad, 1986—. Mem. ABA, Comml. Law League Am., N.J. Bar Assn. (Service to Community award 1986), Burlington County Bar Assn. (trustee 1986—, Robert W. Crisuolo award 1986). Roman Catholic. Avocations: scuba diving, tennis, softball. Consumer commercial, Bankruptcy, General practice. Home: 1043 Harbour Dr Palmyra NJ 08065 Office: Colaguori and Orr 505 High St Po Box 1427 Burlington NJ 08016

ORRICK, WILLIAM HORSLEY, JR., judge; b. San Francisco, Oct. 10, 1915; s. William Horsley and Mary (Downey) O.; m. Marion Naffziger, Dec. 5, 1947; children: Mary-Louise, Marion, William Horsley III. Grad., Hotchkiss Sch., 1933; B.A., Yale, 1937; LL.B., U. Calif.-Berkeley, 1941. Bar: Calif. 1941. Partner Orrick, Dahlquist, Herrington & Sutcliffe, San Francisco, 1941-61; asst. atty. gen. civil div. Dept Justice, 1961-62, antitrust div., 1963-65; dep. under sec. state for adminstrn. Dept. State, 1962-63; practice law San Francisco, 1965-74; former partner firm Orrick, Herrington, Rowley & Sutcliffe; U.S. dist. judge No. Dist. Calif., 1974—. Past pres. San Francisco Opera Assn., Trustee, World Affairs Council; former trustee San Francisco Law Library, San Francisco Found., Children's Hosp. San Francisco, Grace Cathedral Corp. Served to capt. M.I. AUS, 1942-46. Fellow Am. Bar Found.; mem. Bar Assn. San Francisco (past trustee, treas.). Office: US Courthouse PO BOx 36060 San Francisco CA 94102

ORSATTI, ERNEST BENJAMIN, lawyer; b. Pitts., Nov. 14, 1949; s. Ernest Ubaldo and Dorothy Minerva (Pfeiffer) O.; m. Ingrid Zalman, May 3, 1975; 1 child, Benjamin E. B.A., Marquette U., 1971; J.D. Duquesne U., 1974; postgrad. Army Command and Gen. Staff Coll., 1984. Bar: Pa. 1974, U.S. Dist. Ct. (we. dist.) Pa. 1974, U.S. Ct. Appeals (3d cir.) 1977, U.S. Supreme Ct. 1978, Assoc. Jubelirer, Pass & Intrieri, Pitts., 1974-81, ptnr. 1981—; mil. justice officer 42d Mil. Law Ctr., Pitts., 1976—. Contbg. editor: The Developing Labor Law, 2d edit., 1983. Served to major U.S. Army, 1975, JAGC Res. Mem. ABA, Am. Arbitration Assn., Pa. Bar Assn., Indsl. Relations Research Assn., Assn. U.S. Army. Democrat. Roman Catholic. Labor, Workers' compensation. Home: 9343 N Florence Rd Pittsburgh PA 15237 Office: Jubelirer Pass & Intrieri 219 Ft Pitt Blvd Pittsburgh PA 15222

ORSBON, RICHARD ANTHONY, lawyer; b. North Wilkesboro, N.C., Sept. 23, 1947; s. Richard Chapman and Ruby Estelle (Wyatt) O.; m. Susan Cowan Shivers, June 13, 1970; children: Sarah Hollingsworth, Wyatt Benjamin, David Allison. BA disting. mil. grad. ROTC, Davidson Coll., 1969; JD, Vanderbilt U., 1972; honor grad. Officers Basic Course, U.S. Army, 1972. Bar: N.C. 1972, U.S. Dist. Ct. (we. dist.) N.C., 1972. Assoc. Kennedy, Covington, Lobdell & Hickman, Charlotte, N.C., 1972-75; assoc. Grier, Parker, Poe et. al., Charlotte, 1975-77, ptnr. 1978—. Assoc. editor, contbr. Vanderbilt Law Review, 1971-72. Pres. ECO, Inc., Charlotte, 1982—; bd. dirs. Charlotte United Way, 1983—; mem. planning bd. Queens Coll. Estate Planning Day, 1978—; active Myers Park United Methodist Ch.; mem. YMCA basketball com., Dem. precinct chmn., 1980-86; mem. Dem. state exec. com., 1980; bd. dirs. law explorer program Boy Scouts Am., Charlotte, 1976-78. Served to 1st lt. U.S. Army, 1972-73. Named Outstanding Vol., Charlotte Observer/United Way, 1984; Patrick Wilson Merit scholar Vanderbilt U. Law Sch., 1969-72. Mem. ABA (real property probate sect.), N.C. Bar Assn. (probate and fiduciary law sect., author, speaker 1987—), N.C. Bar Assn. Coll. of Advocacy, Mecklenburg County Bar Assn. (law day com., vol. lawyers program, bd. dirs.), Deans Assn. of Vanderbilt U. Law Sch. (bd. dirs.), Davidson Coll. Alumni Assn. (bd. dirs. 1983, class alumni sec. 1986—), Charlotte Estate Planning Council, Omicron Delta Kappa. Club: Foxcroft Swim and Racquet (pres. 1986-87, bd. dirs. 1985-88). Probate, Estate taxation, Estate planning. Home: 2819 Rothwood Dr Charlotte NC 28211 Office: Parker Poe Thompson et al 2600 Charlotte Plaza Charlotte NC 28244

ORSBURN, CHARLES CLAUDE, lawyer; b. Gainesville, Tex., Nov. 29, 1940; Student North Tex. State U., 1959-60; J.D., U. Houston, 1967. Bar: Tex. 1967. Prin. Orsburn & Holland, Houston; presiding judge Mcpl. Ct. of West University Place, 1976-84. Mem. State Bar Tex., Houston Bar Assn. (former officer and dir.), Tex. Trial Lawyers Assn., Tex. Criminal Def. Lawyers (former dir.). Criminal, Personal injury, Workers' compensation. Home: 5910 Fordham Houston TX 77005 Office: 320 Main Suite 200 Houston TX 77002

ORTEGA, CYNTHIA POTI, lawyer; b. Gary, Ind., Dec. 15, 1957; d. Julius Paul and Barbara Ann (Prokop) Poti; m. Michael Bruce Ortega, May 10, 1980. BS in Legal Adminstrn., U. Evansville, 1978; JD, Ind. U., 1981. Bar: Mich. 1981, U.S. Dist. Ct. (we. dist.) Mich. 1981. Law clk. to presiding justice Mich. Cir. Ct., Kalamazoo, 1981-82; assoc. Huff, Kreis & Enderle, Kalamazoo, 1982—. Mem. ABA, Kalamazoo County Bar Assn. (sec. 1985-86, bd. dirs. 1986—), Kalamazoo Network. Avocations: traveling, raquetball. State civil litigation, Landlord-tenant, Real property. Home: 2777 S 11th St Kalamazoo MI 49009 Office: Huff Kreis Enderle 800 Comerica Bldg Kalamazoo MI 49007

ORTH, BEVERLY JEAN, lawyer; b. Portland, Oreg., July 28, 1952; d. Leslie Russell and Marian Virginia (Trummer) O.; m. Tony Noe, Oct. 28, 1975. BS, Harvey Mudd Coll., 1974; JD, Harvard U., 1978. Bar: Calif. 1978. Assoc. Brawerman, Kopple & Lerner, Los Angeles, 1978-81, Adams, Duque & Hazeltine, Los Angeles, 1981-84; staff counsel William M. Mercer-Meidinger-Hansen, Inc., Los Angeles, 1984—; controller Software Spectrum, Culver City, Calif., 1980—. Trustee Harvey Mudd Coll., Claremont, Calif., 1985—. Mem. Los Angeles County Bar Assn., Women Lawyers Assn. Los Angeles, Assn. Pvt. Pension and Welfare Plans, Nat. Orgn. for Women, Harvey Mudd Coll. Alumni Assn. (gov. 1978—). Democrat. Pension, profit-sharing, and employee benefits, Corporate taxation, Personal income taxation. Office: William M Mercer-Meidinger-Hansen Inc 3303 Wilshire Blvd Los Angeles CA 90010

ORTH, CHARLES ADAM, JR., lawyer; b. Milw., Nov. 1, 1914; s. Charles Adam and Meta (Wefing) O.; m. Ruth L. Plenzke, Aug. 4, 1940; children: Charles Adam, Bonnie Vierthaler. PhB, U. Wis., 1935, JD, 1937. Bar: Wis. 1937, U.S. Dist. Ct. (ea. dist.) Wis. 1937. Ptnr. Orth & Orth, Milw., 1937-40, Orth, Riedl & Orth, Milw., 1945-84; pres. Orth, Finey & Laskowski, 1984—. Pres. Servite Woods Homes Assn. Inc., 1974-77, bd. dirs., 1974-78; pres. Milw. Council on Alcoholism, 1967-69, bd. dirs. 1962—; mem. Wis. Assn. on Alcoholism and Other Drug Abuse, 1963-82; mem. Wis. State Council on Alcoholism and Drug Abuse, 1979-82; mem. Wis. Gov.'s Council on Drug Abuse, 1973-76; chmn. Citizens Adv. Council on Alcohol and Drug Abuse, 1979-82; mem. Prison Health Care Adv. Com., 1977-78; treas. Nat. Assn. State Adv. Councils, 1978-82; bd. dirs. Milw. Psychiat. Hosp. Served with USNR, 1940-46. Recipient Alcohol and Drug Coalition of Wis. Outstanding Citizen award, 1981. Fellow Am. Coll. Probate Counsel; mem. ABA, Wis. Bar Assn. (bd. govs. 1965), Milw. Bar Assn. (mem. exec. com. 1964), Am. Judicature Soc., Milw. Estate Planning Council, Am. Legion, Am. Assn. Ret. Persons, Alpha Chi Rho, Phi Alpha Delta. Lodges: Kiwanis, Masons, Shriners. Probate, Estate planning, General practice. Office: 152 W Wisconsin Ave Milwaukee WI 53203

ORTH, JOHN VICTOR, legal history educator; b. Lancaster, Pa., Feb. 7, 1947; s. John and Mildred (Spalding) O.; m. Noreen Nolan, May 20, 1972; children—Katherine E., Zachary J. A.B. magna cum laude, Oberlin Coll., 1969; J.D., Harvard U., 1974, M.A., 1975, Ph.D. in History, 1977. Bar: Mass. 1974, U.S. Ct. Appeals (3d cir.) 1978. Law clk. U.S. Ct. Appeals (3d cir.), 1977-78; asst. prof. law U. N.C.-Chapel Hill, 1978-81, assoc. prof., 1981-84, prof., 1984—, assoc. dean, 1984—. Mem. Am. Soc. Legal History (dir.), Selden Soc., Conf. Brit. Studies, Orgn. Am. Historians, Soc. Values in Higher Edn., AAUP (pres. chpt.), Order of Coif, Phi Beta Kappa. Author: Combination and Conspiracy: The Legal Status of English Trade Unions, 1799-1871, 1977; contbr. articles to profl. jours. Legal history, Legal education, Real property. Office: U NC Sch Law Van Hecke-Wettach Hall 064A Chapel Hill NC 27514

ORTH, PAUL WILLIAM, lawyer; b. Balt., May 7, 1930; s. Paul W. and Naomi (Howard Bevard) O.; m. Isle Haertle, June 15, 1956; children—Ingrid, Ilse Christine. A.B., Dartmouth Coll., 1951; J.D., Harvard U., 1954. Bar: Mass. 1954, Conn. 1957, U.S. Dist. Ct. Conn. 1958, U.S. Ct. Appeals (2d cir.) 1960, U.S. Ct. Appeals (1st cir.) 1983, U.S. Supreme Ct. 1960. Assoc. Hoppin, Carey & Powell, Hartford, 1957-62, ptnr., 1962—; instr. Sch. Law U. Conn., 1959-81. Chmn., Farmington Conservation Commn., 1982-83; mem. town com. Town of Farmington, 1973-81. Served with AUS, 1954-56. Mem. Hartford County Bar Assn. (pres. 1983-84), Conn. Bar Assn. (chmn. coms.), ABA. Democrat. Club: Farmington Country. Federal civil litigation, Labor, Insurance. Office: 370 Asylum St Hartford CT 06103

ORTIQUE, REVIUS OLIVER, JR., judge; b. New Orleans, June 14, 1924; s. Revius Oliver and Lillie Edith (Long) O.; m. Miriam Marie Victorianne, Dec. 29, 1947; children—Rhesa Marie (Mrs. Alden J. McDonald). AB, Dillard U., 1947, MA, Ind. U., 1949; JD, So. U., 1956; LLD (hon.), Campbell Coll., 1960; L.H.D., Ithaca Coll., 1971; LLD (hon.), Ind. U., 1983. Bar: La. 1956, U.S. Dist. Ct 1956, Eastern Dist. La 1956, U.S. Fifth Circuit Ct. of Appeals 1956, U.S. Supreme Ct 1956. Practiced in New Orleans, 1956-79; judge Civil Dist. Ct. for Orleans Parish, 1979—; lectr. labor law Dillard U., 1950-52, U. West Indies, 1986—; assoc. gen. counsel Community Improvement Agy.; gen. counsel 8th Dist. A.M.E. Ch.; mem. Fed. Hosp. Council, 1966, Pres.'s Commn. on Campus Unrest, 1970, Pres. Bd. Legal Services Corp., 1975-83; chief judge civil cts. Orleans Parish. Former pres. Met. Area Com.; mem. Bd. City Trusts, New Orleans, New Orleans Legal Assistance Corp. Bd., Ad Hoc Com. for Devel. of Central Bus. Dist. City of New Orleans; bd. dirs. Community Relations Council, Am. Lung Assn., Antioch Coll. Law, New Orleans chpt. Operation PUSH, 1981—; bd. dirs., mem. exec. com. Nat. Sr. Citizens Law Ctr., Los Angeles, Criminal Justice Coordinating Com., UN Assn. New Orleans, 1980—; mem. exec. bd. Nat. Bar Found.; mem. exec. com. Econ. Devel. Council Greater New Orleans; past chmn. Health Edn. Authority of La.; trustee, mem. exec. com. Dillard U.; former mem. bd. mgmt. Flint Goodridge Hosp.; mem. adv. bd. League Women Voters Greater New Orleans; mem. men's adv. bd. YWCA; trustee AME Ch., also connectional trustee; chancellor N.O. Fedn. Chs. Served to 1st lt. AUS, 1943-47, ETO, PTO. Recipient Weiss award NCCJ, 1975. Mem. ABA (del.), Nat. Bar Assn. (exec. bd.), La. Bar Assn. (del.), Nat. Legal Aid and Defender Assn. (past pres.), Am. Judicature Soc., Louis A. Martinet Legal Soc., World Peace Through Law Com., Blue Key, Phi Delta Kappa, Alpha Kappa Delta. State civil litigation. Home: 4516 Annette St New Orleans LA 70122 Office: Civil Dist Ct 421 Loyola Ave New Orleans LA 70112

ORTIZ, JAY RICHARD GENTRY, lawyer; b. Washington, Mar. 21, 1945; s. Charles and Catherine Gentry (Candlin) O.; m. Lois Wright Hatcher Greer, June 12, 1982. B.A., Yale U., 1967; postgrad. Stanford U. 1967-68; J.D., U. N.Mex., 1972. Bar: N.Mex. 1973, Mo. 1978, Tenn. 1982, U.S. Dist. Ct. N.Mex. 1973, U.S. Ct. Appeals (10th cir. 1973), U.S. Supreme Ct. 1977, U.S. Dist. Ct. (western dist.) Mo. 1978, U.S. Ct. Appeals (8th cir.) 1978. Assoc. Rodey, Dickason, Sloan, Akin & Robb, Albuquerque, 1972-75; ptnr. Knight, Sullivan, Villella, Skarsgard & Michael, Albuquerque, 1975-77; litigation atty. Monsanto Co., St. Louis, 1977-81; environ. atty. Eastman Kodak Co., Kingsport, Tenn., 1981-84; ops. atty. AT&T, Atlanta, 1984—. Precinct vice chmn. Dem. Party, Albuquerque, 1971-77. Served to lt. (j.g.), USN, 1968-69. Mem. N.Mex. Bar Assn., Mo. Bar Assn., Tenn. Bar Assn., ABA, Order of Coif, Delta Theta Phi (tribune 1972-77). Episcopalian. Federal civil litigation, Environment, General corporate. Home: 1000 Buckingham Circle NW Atlanta GA 30327 Office: AT&T PO Box 7800 Atlanta GA 30357

ORTMAN, WILLIAM ANDREW, SR., lawyer, business executive; b. Detroit, Mar. 22, 1934; s. Frank J. and Marcella Pauline (Gfell) O.; B.A., Wayne State U., 1958; grad. Bus. Sch. U. Mich., 1960; J.D. (regional outstanding student 1962, scholarship cert. and key, jurisprudence awards), U. Detroit, 1963; m. Lavina Mae Ladson, June 29, 1957; children—William A., Nancy Lee, Merrie Jo, Kristy Ann, Keira Therese. Bar: Mich. 1963, Ohio 1963. Radio sta. mgr., 1953-56; para-legal Law Offices Frank J. Ortman, 1956-60, real estate broker, co-partner, 1956—; indsl. relations analyst FoMoCo, 1960-62; pub. info. specialist Dept. Def., Detroit, 1962-63; sr. atty. Ortman & Ortman, Detroit, 1964—; pres. ORT-FAM Inc., 1984—; co-ptnr. The Ortman Co., 1956—; investment counselor, fin. planner, mgmt. cons.; polit. campaign specialist, 1964—; real-estate, mortgage broker, 1956—; gen. counsel, mktg. mgr. Computers Tandem Assocs., CADO of Southeast Mich., Computer Alliance Corp., 1982-83; cons. pub. relations and advt., 1962—, computer systems, 1982—; lectr. St. Joseph Comml. Coll., 1961-62; del. China-U.S. Sci. Exchange, 1984. Bd. govs., past dean Detroit Metro. Alumni Senate; councilman, Farmington Hills area, 1968-75; nominee Mich. Supreme Ct., 1972. Served with U.S. Army, 1953-56. Mem. ABA, Mich., Oakland bar assns., Delta Theta Phi (dean Hosmer Senate 1961, 62), Alpha Kappa Delta. Clubs: Detroit Athletic, German-Am. Cultural Center, Elks. Contbr., author and editor nat., state and local legal jours. Probate, Real property, State civil litigation. Home: 28010 S Harwich Dr Farmington Hills MI 48018 Office: PO Box 42 Franklin MI 48025

ORWOLL, KIMBALL GREGG, lawyer; b. Mpls., July 20, 1954; s. Gregg and Laverne (Flentie) O.; m. Kathleen Jean Bischke, Aug. 4, 1979. BA, St. Olaf Coll., 1976; JD, Hamline U., 1980. Bar: Minn. 1980, U.S. Dist. Ct. Minn. 1980, U.S. Ct. Appeals (8th cir.) 1981. Assoc. Petersen & Stephenson, Rochester, Minn., 1980-85; ptnr. Petersen & Orwoll, Rochester, 1985—. Bd. dirs. Legal Assistance Olmsted County, Rochester, 1983—, Salvation Army, Rochester, 1984—; del., chmn. Olmsted County Ind. Reps., 1982—. Mem. ABA, Minn. Bar Assn., Olmsted County Bar Assn. Lutheran. Lodge: Kiwanis (bd. dirs. Rochester 1984-86). Avocations: mfg. display fireworks, skiing, boating, swimming. General practice, Personal injury, Criminal. Home: 2023 10th Ave NE Rochester MN 55904 Office: Petersen & Orwoll 119 6th St SW Suite B Rochester MN 55902

ORY, CHARLES NATHAN, lawyer; b. Atlanta, Mar 25, 1946; s. Marvin Gilbert and Esther Rose (Levine) O.; m. Carolyn Susan Pruett, June 21, 1976; children: Jebidiah Marlowe, Brett Elizabeth. BA in Econs., George Washington U., 1968; JD, U. Tex.-Austin, 1972. Bar: Tex. 1972, U.S. Dist. Ct. (no. dist.) Tex. 1982, U.S. Dist. Ct. (ea. dist.) Wash. 1981, U.S. Ct. Appeals (5th cir.) 1982. Trial atty. Dept. Justice, Washington, 1973-82; spl. asst. to U.S. Atty., Spokane, 1981; asst. U.S. atty. Dept. Justice, Dallas, 1982-86; dir. litigation, Palmer & Palmer, 1986—; EEO investigator Exec. Offices of U.S. Attys., Dept. Justice, Washington, 1984-86; head litigation sect. Palmer & Palmer, P.C., Dallas, 1986—. Co-founder and mng. editor Am. Jour. Criminal Law, 1971-72. Bd. dirs. Munger Place Hist. Homeowners Assn., Dallas, 1984-86; mem. Clean Dallas East, Inc., 1984-85. Recipient Spl. Achievement award U.S. Dept. Justice civil rights div., 1979, Atty. Gen.'s Spl. Achievement award U.S. Dept. Justice, 1986. Federal civil litigation, Bankruptcy, Labor. Home: 5020 Junius St Dallas TX 75214 Office: Palmer & Palmer PC 1510 One Main Pl Dallas TX 75250

OSAKWE, CHRISTOPHER, legal educator; b. Lagos, Nigeria, May 8, 1942; came to U.S. 1970, naturalized 1979; s. Simon and Hannah (Morgan) O.; m. Maria Elena Amador, Aug. 19, 1982. LL.B., Moscow State U., 1966, LL.M., 1967, Ph.D., 1970; J.S.D., U. Ill., 1974. Prof. law Tulane U. Sch. Law, New Orleans, 1972-81, Eason-Weinmann prof. comparative law, dir. Eason-Weinmann Ctr. for Comparative Law, 1981—; vis. prof. U. Pa., 1978, U. Mich., 1981, Washington and Lee U., 1986; vis. fellow St. Anthony's Coll., Oxford, Eng., U., 1980; cons. U.S. Dept. Commerce, 1980-85. Author: The Participation of the Soviet Union in Universal International Organizations, 1972, The Foundations of Soviet Law, 1981; (with others) Comparative Legal Traditions, 1982; editor Am. Jour. Comparative Law, 1978—, Am. Jour. Legal Edn., 1983-85. Carnegie doctoral fellow Hague Acad. Internat. Law, 1969; Russian research fellow Harvard U., 1972; USSR sr. research exchange fellow, 1982. Mem. ABA, Am. Law Inst., Am. Soc. Internat. Law. Republican. Roman Catholic. Private international, Soviet, Administrative and regulatory. Office: Tulane U Sch Law 6801 Freret St New Orleans LA 70118

OSANN, EDWARD WILLIAM, JR., lawyer; b. Jamaica, N.Y., Oct. 14, 1918; s. Edward William and Anna Bertha (Brandsema) O.; m. Ruth Florence Hamlyn, Sept. 28, 1940; children—Anne Marie, Edward Robert, Ellen Jean. B.M.E., Rensselaer Poly. Inst., 1939; J.D., DePaul U., 1947. Bar: Ill. 1947, U.S. Patent Office 1947, U.S. Dist. Ct. (no. dist.) Ill. 1949, U.S. Dist. Ct. (no. dist.) Ohio 1962, U.S. Dist. Ct. (no. dist.) Ind. 1974, U.S. Ct. Appeals (7th cir.) 1959, U.S. Ct. Appeals (5th cir.) 1981, U.S. Ct. Appeals (11th cir.) 1981, U.S. Ct. Appeals (Fed. cir.) 1982, U.S. Supreme Ct. 1961. Assoc., Leydig, Voit, Osann, Mayer & Holt Ltd., and predecessors, Chgo., 1946-52, ptnr., 1953-85; sole practice, Chgo., 1985—; dir. Ind.-Ky. Electric Co. Chmn. bd. Citizens for a Better Environment, 1977—; pres. trustees Shirley Heinze Environ. Fund, 1981—; chmn. legal com. Save the Dunes Council, 1960—. Served to lt. USNR, 1942-46. Recipient Environ. Quality award Region V EPA, 1975, Environ. Service award Ind. Conservation Council, 1975, Conservation Achievement award Ind. div. Izaak Walton League, 1975. Mem. ABA, Chgo. Bar Assn., Am. Intellectual Property Law Assn., Patent Law Assn. Chgo. Mem. ch. extension bd. Presbytery of Chgo., 1948-56. Clubs: University (Chgo.); Polymathic (Porter County Ind.). Patent, Trademark and copyright, Federal civil litigation. Office: 29 S LaSalle St Suite 420 Chicago IL 60603

OSBORN, DONALD ROBERT, lawyer; b. N.Y.C., Oct. 9, 1929; s. Robert W. and Ruth C. (Compton) O.; m. Marcia Lontz, June 4, 1955; children—David, Judith, Robert; m. Marie A. Johnson, Sept. 11, 1986. B.A., Cornell U., 1951; LL.B., Columbia U., 1957. Bar: N.Y. State 1957, U.S. Tax Ct. 1958, U.S. Ct. Claims 1961, U.S. Ct. Appeals (2d cir.) 1974, U.S. Ct. Appeals (8th cir.) 1974, U.S. Dist. Ct. (so. and ea. dists.) N.Y. 1975, U.S. Supreme Ct. 1975. Assoc. Sullivan & Cromwell, N.Y.C., 1957-64, ptnr., 1964—; Trustee Hamilton Coll., 1978—, Mus. of Broadcasting, 1975-80; trustee, treas. Kirkland Coll., 1969-78; mem. council White Burkett Miller Ctr. Pub. Affairs, 1976-82; bd. dirs., pres. Stevens Kingsley Found., 1967—; sec., treas. Dunlevy Milbank Found., 1974—; pres. bd. dirs. Scarsdale Leasing Corp, 1979—; asst. clerk, bd. dirs. Oyster Harbors Inc. 1969—; dir. CBS, Inc., 1975-80, Mus. Broadcasting, 1975-80. Served with USN, 1951-54. Mem. ABA, N.Y. State Bar Assn., Assn. Bar City N.Y., Am. Bar Found. Presbyterian. Clubs: Scarsdale Golf, Fox Meadow Tennis (Scarsdale, N.Y.), Stratton (Vt.) Mountain Country, Madison Sq. Garden, India House, Board Room, World Trade Ctr. (N.Y.C.). Private international, Probate, Corporate taxation. Home: 1049 Park Ave New York NY 10028 Office: Sullivan & Cromwell 125 Broad St New York NY 10004

OSBORN, JOHN EMORY, lawyer; b. Middletown, N.Y., Sept. 3, 1950; s. Emory Raymond and Dorothy (Williams) O.; m. Christine Beth Charvat; June 30, 1979; children: Stephen, Kathryn. BA in Polit. Sci. and Econs., SUNY, New Paltz, 1972; JD, U. S.C., 1976. Bar: N.Y. 1977, U.S. Dist. Ct. (so. and ea. dists.) N.Y. 1979. Dep. gen. counsel N.Y.C. Comptroller, N.Y.C., 1976-79; assoc. Max E. Greenberg, Cantor & Reiss, N.Y.C., 1979-85; ptnr. Postner & Rubin, N.Y.C., 1985—. Construction. Home: 236 Seeley St Brooklyn NY 11218 Office: Postner & Rubin 17 Battery Pl New York NY 10004

OSBORN, MALCOLM EVERETT, lawyer, educator; b. Bangor, Maine, Apr. 29, 1928; s. Lester Everett and Helen (Clark) O.; m. Claire Anne Franks, Aug. 30, 1953; children—Beverly, Lester, Malcolm, Ernest. B.A., U. Maine, 1952; postgrad. Harvard U. 1952-54; J.D. Boston U. 1956, LL.M., 1961. Bar: Maine 1956, Mass. 1956, U.S. Dist. Ct. 1961, U.S. Tax Ct. 1961, U.S. Claims 1961, N.C. 1965, U.S. Supreme Ct. 1979, U.S. Ct. Appeals (4th cir.) 1980. Tax counsel State Mut. Life Assurance Co., Worcester, Mass., 1956-64; v.p., gen. tax counsel Integon Corp. and other group cos., Winston-Salem, N.C., 1964-81; ptnr. House, Blanco & Osborn, Winston-Salem, 1981—, v.p., gen. counsel, dir. Settlers Life Ins. Co., Bristol, Va., 1984—; lectr. The Booke Seminars, Life Ins. Co., 1985—; adj. prof. Wake Forest U. Sch. Law, Winston-Salem, 1974-82; Disting. guest lectr. Ga. State U., 1965; guest lectr. N.Y.U. Ann. Inst. Fed. Taxation, 1966, 68, 75, 80. Trustee N.C. Council Econ. Edn., 1968-76; bd. dirs. Christian Fellowship Home, 1972-80; co-founder Bereaved Parents Group Winston-Salem, 1978—. Mem. ABA (chmn. com. ins. cos. of taxation sect. 1980-82; chmn. subcom. on continuing legal edn. and publs. 1982—), Am. Bus. Law Assn. (mem. com. fed. taxation 1968—, chmn. 1972-75), Assn. Life Ins. Counsel (com. on co. tax, tax sect. 1965—), N.C. Bar Assn. (com. taxation 1973-78), Fed. Bar Assn. (taxation com. 1973—), Internat. Bar Assn. (com. on taxes of bus. law sect. 1973—), AAUP. Club: Masons (Lincoln, Maine). Com. editor The Tax Lawyer, ABA, 1974-76; author numerous articles in field. Corporate taxation, Personal income taxation, Insurance. Office: 215 Executive Park Blvd Winston-Salem NC 27103

OSBORNE, CAROL ANN, lawyer; b. Erie, Pa., Aug. 26, 1938; d. Clarence Henry and Grace Louise (McLaughlin) Bronson; LL.B., Western State U., 1977, J.D., 1978; m. Dwight E. Osborne, Jr., Jan. 1, 1965 (div. July 1986); children—Dwight E., Joy Louise. Bar: Calif. 1978. Legal sec., Orange County, Calif., 1967-78; individual practice, Orange, Calif., 1978-83; assoc. with Maxine L. Zazzara, Downey, Calif., 1983-85; sole practice, Downey, Calif., 1985—. Active PTA Kraemer Jr. High Sch. and Van Buren Elem. Sch.; treas. Kraemer Parent Booster Club, 1979-80; mem. Valencia High Sch. PTA, others. Mem. ABA, Calif. Bar Assn., Orange County Bar Assn., Calif. Trial Lawyers Assn., Orange County Trial Lawyers Assn., Southeast Bar Assn., Am. Bus. Women's Assn. (chpt. officer), Western State U. Alumni Assn., Nu Beta Epsilon. Republican. Probate, General corporate, Estate planning. Office: 8221 3d St #307 Downey CA 90241

OSBORNE, MICHAEL CLAUDE, lawyer; b. Mexico City, July 18, 1955; came to U.S., 1960; s. Thomas Cramer and Geraldine Merle (Smith) O.; m. Bernadette Marie Morley, Oct. 3, 1982; 1 child, Thomas Cramer II. BA in History, Haverford Coll., 1977; JD, Golden Gate U., 1980. Bar: Calif. 1980, U.S. Dist. Ct. (no. dist.) Calif. 1980, U.S. Ct. Appeals (9th cir.) 1980, U.S. Tax Ct. 1981. Assoc. Anolik Law Offices, San Francisco, 1980-81; dep. dist. atty. El Dorado County, South Lake Tahoe, Calif., 1981-84; asst. dist. atty. City of San Francisco, 1984—; instr. Hastings Coll. Law, San Francisco, 1985—. Mem. ABA, Calif. Dist. Atty.'s Assn. Criminal. Office: Dist Atty's Office 880 Bryant St San Francisco CA 94103

O'SCANNLAIN, DIARMUID FIONNTAIN, circuit judge; b. N.Y.C., Mar. 28, 1937; s. Sean Leo and Moira (Hegarty) O'S.; m. Maura Nolan, Sept. 7, 1963; children: Sean, Jane, Brendan, Kevin, Megan, Christopher, Anne, Kate. AB, St. John's U., 1957; JD, Harvard U., 1963. Bar: Oreg. 1965, N.Y. 1964. Tax atty. Standard Oil Co. (N.J.), N.Y.C., 1963-65; assoc. Davies, Biggs, Strayer, Stoel & Boley, Portland, Oreg., 1965-69; dep. atty. gen. Oreg., 1969-71; public utility commr. of Oreg., 1971-73; dir. Oreg. Dept. Environ. Quality, 1973-74; sr. ptnr. Ragen, Roberts, O'Scannlain, Robertson & Neill, Portland, 1978-86; judge, U.S. Ct. Appeals (9th cir.), San Francisco, 1986—; cons. Office of Pres.-Elect and mem. Dept. Energy Transition Team (Reagan transition), Washington, 1980-81; chmn. com. adminstrv. law Oreg. State Bar, 1980-81. Mem. council of legal advisers Republican Nat. Com., 1981-83; mem. Rep. Nat. Com., 1983-86, chmn. Oreg. Rep. Party, 1983-86; del. Rep. Nat. Convs., 1976, 80, chmn. Oreg. del., 1984; Rep. nominee U.S. Ho. of Reps., First Congl. Dist., 1974; team leader Energy Task Force, Pres.'s Pvt. Sector Survey on Cost Control, 1982-83. Served to maj. USAR, 1955-78. Mem. Fed. Energy Bar Assn., ABA. Roman Catholic. Club: Multnomah (Portland), Nat. Lawyers (Washington). Judicial administration. Home: 2421 SW Arden Rd Portland OR 97201 Office: U S Ct Appeals Pioneer Courthouse 555 SW Yamhill St Portland OR 97204-1396

OSER, RALPH CRANDALL, lawyer; b. Evanston, Ill., May 3, 1946; s. Nelson A. and Virginia R. (Raclin) O.; m. Katherine Treat Ball, Aug. 15, 1969; children: Rebecca Cornell, Nathaniel Treat. BA in History, Trinity Coll., Hartford, Conn., 1968; JD, Vanderbilt U., 1974; MBA, George Washington U., Washington, 1980. Bar: Fla. 1974, D.C. 1975, U.S. Ct. Appeals (5th and D.C. cirs.) 1975, U.S. Dist. Ct. D.C. 1984. Assoc. Ross, Marsh & Foster, Washington, 1974-76; atty. Agy. Internat. Devel., Washington, 1976—; sole practice Washington, 1981—; of counsel Bochet et Associes, Paris, 1984—; lectr. Am. C. of C. of Peru, Lima, 1981; signer official claims U.S. vs. Iran arbitration Dept. State, The Netherlands, 1982. Contbr. articles to profl. jours. Served to 1st lt. U.S. Army, 1968-71, Vietnam. Mem. ABA (co-chmn. publs. internat. law sect. 1980-84), Fed. Bar Assn. (vice chmn. govt. contracts sect. internat. div.), Internat. Bar Assn. Government contracts and claims, Private international, General corporate. Office: 915 15th St NW Suite 300 Washington DC 20005

OSERAN, MELVILLE, lawyer; b. Winnipeg, Man., Can., Oct. 16, 1918; s. Max and Bessie (Wolfe) O.; m. Sylvia S., June 29, 1952; children—Joel, Laura. B.A., U. Wash., 1939, J.D., 1942. Bar: Wash. 1942, U.S. Sup. Ct. 1957. Ptnr., Walthew, Oseran, Warner & Keefe, Seattle, 1950-57, Robbins, Oseran & Robbins, Seattle, 1957-67, Oseran & Hahn, Bellevue, Wash., 1967-72; pres. Oseran, Hahn, Kelley & Spring, P.S., Bellevue, 1972—. Served to capt. U.S. Army, 1943-46. Mem. Wash. State Bar Assn. Jewish. Clubs: Wash. Athletic (Seattle), Bellevue Athletic. General corporate, Probate, Real property. Home: 4817 Lake Washington Blvd NE Apt #7 Kirkland WA 98033 Office: 850 Skyline Tower 10900 NE 4th St Bellevue WA 98004

OSGOOD, ROBERT MANSFIELD, lawyer; b. Elmira, N.Y., Jan. 27, 1942; s. Roland Lorenzo and Isabelle (Mansfield) O.; m. Susanne Mykel, 1963; children: Christopher, Elisabeth, Abigail. BA, Syracuse U., 1963, JD, 1968. Bar: N.Y. 1968, U.S. Dist. Ct. (no. dist.) N.Y. 1969, U.S. Dist. Ct. (so. dist.) N.Y., U.S. Ct. Appeals (2d cir.) 1971, U.S. Dist. Ct. (ea. dist.) N.Y. 1974, U.S. Ct. Appeals (D.C. cir.) 1976, U.S. Supreme Ct. 1977. Ptnr. Sullivan & Cormwell, N.Y.C., 1968—. Fellow Am. Coll. Trial Lawyers; mem. Am. Law Inst. Antitrust, Securities, General corporate. Office: Sullivan & Cromwell 125 Broad St New York NY 10004

OSGOOD, RUSSELL KING, law educator; b. Fairborn, Ohio, Oct. 25, 1947; s. Richard Magee and Mary (Russell) O.; m. Paula Haley, June 6, 1970; children: Mary, Josiah, Micah, Iain. BA, Yale U., 1969, JD, 1974. Bar: Mass. 1974, U.S. Dist. Ct. Mass. 1976. Assoc. Hill & Barlow, Boston, 1974-78; assoc. prof. Boston U., 1978-80; prof. Cornell U., Ithaca, N.Y., 1980—. Served to lt. USNR, 1969-71. Mem. Am. Soc. for Legal History (editor Law and History Rev. 1982—), Osgoode Soc., Stair Soc. Legal history, Corporate taxation, Constitutional law. Office: Cornell Law School Myra Taylor Hall Ithaca NY 14853-4901

O'SHIELDS, JUNE CRUCE, lawyer; b. Atlanta, June 27, 1938; d. Marshel Ember and Anne Beatrice (Cruce) O'S.; m. Joseph Candler Hutchinson, Aug. 12, 1950 (div.); children: June O'Shields, Joseph Candler Jr. BA, Vanderbilt U.; MS, Georgetown U., 1970; JD, Monterey (Calif.) Sch. Law, 1977. Bar: Calif. 1983. Sole practice Salinas, Calif., 1983—. Past election judge State of Va., Fairfax; mem. Dem. Cen. Com., Monterey, 1973-75. Mem. Calif. Bar Assn., Assn. Trial Lawyers Am., Calif. Trial Lawyers Assn., Monterey County Trial Lawyers Assn., Calif. Women Lawyer's Assn., LWV (v.p. Fairfax chpt., chmn. ad hoc com. Monterey chpt.). Family and matrimonial, Personal injury, Labor. Home: 731 Country Club Dr Carmel Valley CA 93924 Office: 325 Cayuga St Salinas CA 93901

OSHIRO, SHARLEEN H., lawyer; b. Honolulu, Feb. 12, 1951; d. Richard C. and Lillian S. (Hieda) O.; m. Allen T. Hagio, Oct. 1969 (div. July 1974); 1 child, Juli Ann; m. Rodney Y. Sato, Nov. 6, 1982; 1 child, Samantha. BA, U. Hawaii, 1973, JD, 1980. Bar: Hawaii 1980, U.S. Dist. Ct. Hawaii 1980, U.S. Ct. Appeals (9th cir.) 1981. Dep. atty. gen. Dept. of Atty. Gen., Honolulu, 1980-85; asst. v.p., legal counsel Servco Pacific Inc., Honolulu, 1985—. Mem. Hawaii Bar Assn. Democrat. Avocations: reading, cooking, dancing, old English sheepdogs. General corporate. Home: 95-155 Waikalani Dr Wahiawa HI 96786 Office: Servco Pacific Inc 900 Fort St Mall Suite 500 Honolulu HI 96813

OSIMITZ, DENNIS VICTOR, lawyer; b. Racine, Wis., May 28, 1951; s. Victor and Julianna (Wiernasz) O.; m. Mary Carol Rindt, June 5, 1976; 1 child, Jeffrey Allen. BA, U. Wis., 1973, JD, 1976. Bar: Wis. 1976, Ill. 1976. U.S. Dist. Ct. (no. dist.) Ill. 1976. Assoc. Sidley & Austin, Chgo., 1976-83, ptnr., 1983—. Mem. ABA, Ill. Bar Assn., Chgo. Bar Assn. Roman Catholic. Club: Union League (Chgo.). General corporate, Securities.

OSIS, DAIGA GUNTRA, lawyer; b. Riga, Lativa, July 24, 1943; d. Voldemars and Sandra (Seja) Amatnieks; m. Aivars Osis, Dec. 2, 1967; 1 child, Andre. BA cum laude, CUNY, Bklyn., 1971; JD, U. (Bridgeport) Conn., 1980. Bar: Conn. 1980, U.S. Dist. Ct. Conn. 1981, U.S. Ct. Appeals (2d cir.) 1982, U.S. Supreme Ct. 1984. Assoc. DePiano & Palmesi, Bridgeport, 1980-85; ptnr. Gans, Leo & Osis, Bridgeport, 1985—; asst. prof. law U. Bridgeport, 1982-83. Research editor U. Bridgeport Law Review, 1979-80. Mem. Bd. Edn., Trumbull, Conn., 1982-84; bd. dirs. Conn. Inst. of Vocal Arts, Southport, Conn., 1984—. Mem. ABA, Conn. Bar Assn., Am. Trial Lawyers Assn., Conn. Trial Lawyers Assn. Democrat. Lutheran. Family and matrimonial, State civil litigation, Personal injury. Home: 175 Middlebrooks Ave Trumbull CT 06611 Office: Gans Leo & Osis 3029 Fairfield Ave Bridgeport CT 06605

OSOFSKY, HERMAN, lawyer; b. Paterson, N.J., July 3, 1940; s. Harry and Rose (Witzel) O.; m. Nancy Ann Newman, Aug. 20, 1972; children—Lara Jane, Dale Ilene, Toby Beth. B.A., Fairleigh Dickinson U., 1962; J.D., Rutgers U., 1964. Bar: N.J. 1965, U.S. Dist. Ct. N.J. 1965, U.S. Ct. Appeals (3d cir.) 1967, U.S. Supreme Ct. 1979, N.Y. 1986. Sole practice, Clifton, N.J., 1965—; asst. counsel Passaic County, N.J., 1973-82. Served with USAR, 1964-67. Bancroft-Whitney scholar Rutgers U., 1964. Fellow Am. Acad. Matrimonial Lawyers; mem. ABA, N.J. Bar Assn., Passaic County Bar Assn. (v.p. 1984, pres. 1985-86). Democrat. Jewish. Family and matrimonial, General practice, Personal injury. Home: 35 Friar Ln Clifton NJ 07013 Office: 408 Clifton Ave Clifton NJ 07011

OSSICK, JOHN JOSEPH, JR., lawyer; b. Charleston, W. Va., Dec. 20, 1951; s. John Joseph and Dorothy (Tezack) O. Student La. State U., 1969-71; B.S., U. Ga., 1973, J.D., 1976. Bar: Ga. 1976. Asst. dist. atty. Brunswick Jud. Cir., Ga., 1976-78; atty. City of Kingsland, 1981—, Camden County Bd. Edn., Kingsland, 1979—, Kingsland Downtown Devel. Authority, 1983—. Mem. Camden County Bar Assn., Brunswick Jud. Cir. Bar Assn., ABA, Ga. Trial Lawyers Assn., Assn. Trial Lawyers Am., Nat. Assn. Criminal Def. Lawyers, Ga. Assn. Criminal Def. Lawyers, Beta Gamma Sigma, Phi Delta Phi. Republican. Roman Catholic. Criminal, Federal civil litigation, General practice. Home: 1305 Downing St Saint Simons Island GA 31522 Office: PO Box 1087 230 S Lee St Kingsland GA 31548

OSSTYN, RANDOLPH BEIER, lawyer; b. Royal Oak, Mich., Apr. 24, 1943; s. Alouis and Doris Helen (Finnie) O.; m. Linda Sue Gregg, Sept. 5, 1970; children: Alicia Anne, Neal Randolph. BA, U. Mich., MA; JD magna cum laude, U. Detroit. Bar: U.S. Supreme Ct. 1980. Tchr., dept. head Detroit Bd. Edn., 1969-76; founding ptnr. Osstyn, Bays, Ferns & Spray, Marquette, Mich., 1979—. Treas. Prince of Peach Luth. Ch., Marquette, 1978-81; founding mem. Save the Janzen Com., Marquette, 1983-85; mem ch. council Messiah Luth. Ch., Marquette, 1984-85; bd. dirs. Marquette Mountain Racing Team, 1982—. Mem. ABA, Wis. Bar Assn., Mich. Bar Assn., Comml. Law League Am. Democrat. Avocations: skiing, running, bridge. Consumer commercial. Home: 264 Timber Ln Marquette MI 49855 Office: Osstyn Bays Ferns & Spray 200 W Washington Suite 500 Marquette MI 49855

OSTAPUK, DAVID R., lawyer; b. Tucson, July 12, 1948; s. John M. and Beverly A. (Armstrong) O.; m. Sandra H. Ewing, Jan. 31, 1981; children: Monica, Benjamin. BA, U. Ariz., 1970, JD, 1973. Bar: Ariz. 1973, U.S. Dist. Ct. Ariz. 1973, U.S. Supreme Ct. 1978. Dep. county atty. Pima County, Tucson, 1973-76; ptnr. Wolfe & Ostapuk, Chartered, Tucson, 1976—; lectr. State Bar Ariz., 1986; judge pro tempore domestic relations div. Pima County Superior Ct., Tucson, 1986—. Bd. dirs. So. Ariz. Legal Aid Soc., 1977-78; legal advisor Kino Learning Ctr., Tucson, 1982; bd. dirs. Las Primeras Lomas, 1982-83. Fellow Ariz. Bar Found., Am. Acad. Matrimonial Lawyers; mem. ABA, Ariz. State Bar (lectr., treas. family law sect. 1980-81). Democrat. Roman Catholic. Club: Old Pueblo (Tucson). Family and matrimonial, State civil litigation, Real property. Home: 5545 N Entrada Quince Tucson AZ 85718 Office: Wolfe & Ostapuk Chartered 160 N Stone Ave 3d Floor Tucson AZ 85701

O'STEEN, VAN, lawyer; b. Sweetwater, Tenn., Jan. 10, 1946; s. Bernard Van and Laura Emelyne (Robinson) O.; m. Deborah Ann Elias, May 18, 1974; children—Jonathan Van, Laura Ann. B.A., Calif. Western U., 1968; J.D. cum laude, Ariz. State U., 1972. Bar: Ariz. 1972, U.S. Dist. Ct. Ariz. 1972, U.S. Ct. Appeals (9th cir.) 1973, U.S. Supreme Ct. 1975. Staff atty. Maricopa Legal Aid Soc., Phoenix, 1972-74; atty. Bates & O'Steen, Legal Clinic, Phoenix, 1974-77; atty. O'Steen Legal Clinic, Phoenix, 1977-80; mng. ptnr. Van O'Steen and Ptnrs., Phoenix, 1980—; pres. Van O'Steen/Lawyer Mktg. Group, Inc., Phoenix, 1985—. Author numerous self-help legal books. Founding dir. Ariz. Ctr. for Law in the Pub. Interest, 1974-80. Served with USNR, 1963-69. Mem. ABA (chmn. spl. com. delivery legal services 1982-85), Am. Legal Clinic Assn. (pres. 1979), Assn. Trial Lawyers Am. Democrat. Administrative and regulatory, Personal injury. Address: 3605 N 7th Ave Phoenix AZ 85013

OSTER, GERALD ARTHUR, lawyer; b. Melrose, Mass., Dec. 27, 1914; s. Abraham and Lillian (Eddlestein) O.; m. Alice Kutz, Mar. 21, 1948; children: Nancy Ann Oster Mullen, Jonathan F., Robert D., Juliann. BS, U. R.I., 1937; JD, U. Md., 1945. Bar: U.S. Dist. Ct. R.I. 1948, U.S. Ct. Appeals (1st cir.) 1949. Ptnr. Oster, Groff & Prescott, Lincoln, R.I., 1945—; clk., solicitor Town of Lincoln, R.I., 1955-59, adminstr., 1959-61. Mem. Pawtucket (R.I.) Area Indsl. Found., 1961—, Lawyer Referral Com.; chmn. Lincoln Indsl. Devel. Com., 1953-61. Served to capt. U.S. Army, 1941-46, PTO. Recipient Appreciation award R.I. Soc. Autistic Children, 1980, Benefactors award Behavioral Devel. Ctr., 1985, Community Recognition award Blackstone Valley C. of C., 1985. Mem. R.I. Bar Assn., Pawtucket Bar Assn. (pres. 1967). Avocations: golf, tennis, sailing. Probate, General corporate. Home: 18 Parker St Lincoln RI 02865 Office: Oster Groff & Prescott 936 Smithfield Ave Lincoln RI 02865

OSTER, ROBERT DANIEL, lawyer; b. Providence, Nov. 19, 1952; s. Gerald A. and Alice (Kutz) O.; m. Lidia Henderson, Mar. 26, 1986. BA magna cum laude, Boston U., 1975; JD, St. Louis U., 1979. Bar: R.I. 1979, U.S. Dist. Ct. R.I. 1979. Ptnr. Oster, Groff & Prescott, Lincoln, R.I., 1979—. Treas. alumni assn. Pawtucket Boys Club, 1984; mem. Lincoln Conservation Com., 1986; bd. dirs. Blackstone Valley Tourism Council, 1985-86. Mem. R.I. Bar Assn. (ho. of dels. 1984-86), Pawtucket Bar Assn. (treas. 1983), R.I. Soc. for Autistic Children. Jewish. Club: Forecourt (Lincoln). Avocations: tennis, running, reading, boating. Family and matrimonial, Bankruptcy, General practice. Office: 936 Smithfield Ave Lincoln RI 02865

OSTERHOUT, RICHARD CADWALLADER, lawyer; b. Abington, Pa., Nov. 16, 1945; s. Robert Edward and Charlotte Leedom (Cadwallader) O.; m. Diane Renee Higgins, Sept. 15, 1982; children: Steven M., Schuyler C. B.A. magna cum laude in History, Pa. State U., 1967; J.D., Temple U., 1974. Bar: Pa. 1974, U.S. Dist. Ct. (ea. dist.) Pa. 1974, U.S. Ct. Appeals (3d cir.) 1984. Assoc. Wood & Floge, Bensalem, Pa., 1974-77; sole practice, Trevose, Pa., 1978-85, Feasterville, Pa., 1985—; solicitor Zoning Hearing Bd., Hulmeville, Pa., 1983—. Contbr. articles to publs. of various hist. socs. Mem. Langhorne Borough Planning Commn. (Pa.), 1974; candidate Republican Nat. Conv., 1984. Served with U.S. Army, 1968-70. Mem. Pa. Bar Assn., Bucks County Bar Assn., Am. Legion, Phi Beta Kappa. Club: Feasterville Businessmen's Assn. (treas. 1985, 86, v.p. 1987—). Lodge: Kiwanis. General practice, State civil litigation, Family and matrimonial. Home: 309 Hemlock Ave Bensalem PA 19020 Office: Richard C Osterhout 1744 Bridgetown Pike Feasterville PA 19047

OSTERMAN, MELVIN HOWARD, JR., lawyer; b. N.Y.C., Sept. 26, 1934; s. Melvin Howard and Selma Elsie (Lenz) O.; m. Norma Grace Meacham, May 29, 1982; children—Lawrence, Edith, Jeffrey, Laura, Andrew. A.B., Cornell U., 1955, LL.B. with distinction, 1957. Bar: N.Y. 1957, U.S. Dist. Ct. (so. dist.) N.Y. 1957, U.S. Dist. Ct. (ea. dist.) N.Y. 1957, U.S. Dist. Ct. (no. dist.) N.Y. 1975, U.S. Ct. Appeals (2d cir.) 1958, U.S. Supreme Ct. 1974. Assoc. White & Case, N.Y.C., 1957-58, 59-62; law clk. to Justice Charles D. Breitel, N.Y. App. Div. 1st Dept., 1958-59; asst. counsel to Gov. Nelson A. Rockefeller, Albany, N.Y., 1962-64, counsel for employee relations, 1968-72; assoc. Graubard Moskowitz McGoldrick Dannett & Horowitz, N.Y.C., 1964-65, mem., 1965-72; dir. employee relations State of N.Y., Albany, 1972-75; mem. Whiteman Osterman & Hanna, Albany, 1975—. Cons. on judiciary Temporary State Commn. on Constl. Conv., 1966; spl. cons. on legal services N.Y.C. Bd. Edn., 1967; mem. Temporary State Commn. on Eminent Domain and Real Property Tax Assessment Rev., 1974-75; mem. faculty Sch. Indsl. and Labor Relations, Cornell U., 1974-76, Empire State Coll., SUNY, 1976-77; cons. N.Y. State Sch. Bds. Assn., 1978—; mem. faculty Grad. Sch. Pub. Affairs, SUNY, Albany, 1979-86 . Pres., Northeastern Living and Learning Center, 1981—. Mem. ABA, N.Y. State Bar Assn. (chmn. com. govt. employee labor relations 1979-82, 84—, mem. exec. com. labor law sect. 1979-82, mem. com. on arbitration 1982-84), Assn. Bar City N.Y., Albany County Bar Assn. Author: Productivity Bargaining in New York State, 1975; contbr. articles to legal publs.; mem. Cornell Law Rev., 1955-57. Labor, State civil litigation, General practice. Home: 32 Darnley Greene Delmar NY 12054 Office: One Commerce Plaza Albany NY 12260

OSTRACH, MICHAEL SHERWOOD, lawyer, business executive; b. Providence, Nov. 7, 1951; s. Morris Louis and Marion Molly Ostrach. AB magna cum laude, Brown U., 1973; JD, Stanford U., 1976. Bar: N.Y. 1977, Calif. 1977, U.S. Dist. Ct. (so. and ea. dists.) N.Y. 1977. Assoc. Debevoise & Plimpton, N.Y.C., 1976-78, Pillsbury, Madison & Sutro, San Francisco, 1978-81; v.p., gen. counsel Cetus Corp., Emeryville, Calif., 1981-86, sr. v.p. legal affairs and gen. counsel, 1986—. Bd. editors Stanford Law Rev., 1976. Mem. ABA, Phi Beta Kappa. General corporate, Securities, Health. Office: Cetus Corp 1400 53d St Emeryville CA 94608

OSTROVSKY, JAN SAMUEL, lawyer; b. Cleve., Aug. 26, 1949; s. Peter and Yetta (Zeidman) O.; m. Deborah Ann Sindelar, June 30, 1972; children: Aaron, Nicholas, Julia. AB, Kenyon Coll., 1971; JD, Ohio State U., 1975. Asst. atty. gen. State of Ohio, Columbus, 1975-76; assoc. Berger & Kirschenbaum, Cleve., 1976-77, Birch, Horton et al, Anchorage, 1977-80; ptnr. Campbell, Ostrovsky & Thwaites, Anchorage, 1980-86; of counsel Bogle & Gates, Anchorage, 1986—. Co-author: Credit Collections and the Law, 1981, Alaska Collection Law, 1983, Alaska Real Estate Foreclosures, 1984, Enforcing Secured Claims in Alaska, 1985. Mem. Alaska Bar Assn. (law examiner's com. 1984, co-founder bankruptcy law com. 1985), Anchorage Bar Assn., Assn. Trial Lawyers Am., Alaska Acad. Trial Lawyers. Bankruptcy, Contracts commercial, Consumer commercial. Home: 6600 Aspen Ridge Anchorage AK 99516 Office: Bogle & Gates 510 L St #600 Anchorage AK 99501

OSTROVSKY, LAWRENCE ZELIG, lawyer; b. Cleve., June 1, 1956; s. Peter and Yetta Ostrovsky. BA, St. John's Coll., Annapolis, Md., 1978; JD, Lewis and Clark Coll., 1982. Bar: Ohio 1982, Alaska 1983. Assoc. Berger & Kirschenbaum, Cleve., 1982, Birch, Horton, Bittner, Pestinger & Anderson, Anchorage, 1983—. Mem. Commonwealth North, Anchorage, 1986. Banking, Bankruptcy, Criminal. Home: 612 M St Anchorage AK 99501 Office: Birch Horton Bittner et al 1127 W 7th Ave Anchorage AK 99501

OSTROWSKI, WILLIAM J., judge; b. Buffalo, Sept. 7, 1925; s. William B. and Anna (Kielich) O.; m. Mary V. Waldron; children: Catherine Ostrowski Amico, Michael, Mary, Susan Ostrowski Beale, James, Julie. BA, Canisius Coll., 1949; LLB, Georgetown U., 1951; LLM, George Washington U., 1952; grad. studies, Heidelberg U. and Nat. Jud. Coll., 1967. Bar: N.Y. 1952. Atty. office of the chief of transp. Dept. of Army, Washington, 1952-53; sole practice Buffalo, 1953—; dep. corp. counsel City of Buffalo, 1956-61, city ct. judge, 1961-75; judge N.Y. Supreme Ct. (8th dist.), 1976—; mem. State Commn. on Jud. Conduct, 1982—; lectr. SUNY Buffalo Sch. Law, 1977-78. Mem. sustaining soc. Mercy Hosp., Albright Knox Art Gallery. Served with U.S. Army, 1943-46, ETO. Mem. ABA (criminal justice com., news reporting and fair trial com. Jud. Adminstrn. div., nat. conf. state trial judges), Am. Law Inst., Fellows of Am. Bar Found., Am. Judicature Soc., Nat. Advocates Soc., N.Y. State Bar Assn. (jud. sect.), Eighth Jud. Dist. Supreme Ct. Assn., Erie County Bar Assn. (criminal law com.). Lodges: The Order of the Alhambra, KC. Office: N Y State Supreme Ct 92 Franklin St Buffalo NY 14202

O'SULLIVAN, JAMES PAUL, lawyer; b. Pitts., Oct. 31, 1938; m. Judith Gallick, Feb. 1, 1964; children: Kathryn, James Jr. AB, John Carroll U., 1961; PhD, U. Conn., 1970; JD, Georgetown U., 1978. Bar: Md. 1978, U.S. Dist. Ct. Md. 1978, U.S. Ct. Appeals (9th and D.C. cirs.) 1981, U.S.

Supreme Ct. 1983. Assoc. Smith, Somerville & Case, Balt., 1978-79; atty. FTC, Washington, 1979-80, FMC, Washington, 1980—. Woodrow Wilson fellow Stanford U., 1961-62. Mem. ABA, AAUP, Md. Bar Assn., Balt. City Bar Assn., Modern Lang. Assn. Am. Antitrust, Administrative and regulatory, Public international. Home: 17-F Ridge Rd Greenbelt MD 20770 Office: FMC 1100 L St NW Washington DC 20573

O'SULLIVAN, THOMAS J., lawyer; b. New Haven, Apr. 7, 1940; s. Thomas J. and Marjorie (Hession) O'S.; m. Anita Brady, Aug. 10, 1968; children: Kathleen, Margaret, Mary Tess, Anne Elizabeth. BA in History, Yale U., 1961; LLB, Harvard U., 1966. Bar: Conn. 1966, U.S. Dist. Ct. Conn. 1967, N.Y. 1967, U.S. Dist. Ct. (so. and ea. dists.) N.Y. 1967, U.S. Ct. Appeals (2d cir.) 1971, U.S. Supreme Ct. 1971, U.S. Dist. Ct. (no. dist.) N.Y. 1976. Assoc. White & Case, N.Y.C., 1966-74, ptnr., 1974—. Served to 1st lt. U.S. Army, 1961-63. Mem. ABA, N.Y. State Bar Assn., Assn. of Bar of City of N.Y. Clubs: Milbrook (Greenwich, Conn.); Yale (N.Y.C.). Federal civil litigation, State civil litigation, Private international. Home: 56 Hillside Rd Greenwich CT 06830 Office: White & Case 1155 Ave of the Americas New York NY 10036

OSWALD, BILLY ROBERTSON, lawyer; b. Columbia, S.C., Feb. 24, 1948; s. James Robertson and Berlie Ruth (Rast) O.; m. Brenda Gale McQuatters, Jan. 31, 1970. B.A. in Polit. Sci., U. S.C., 1971, J.D. 1974. Bar: S.C. 1974, U.S. Ct. Appeals (4th cir.) 1974, U.S. Dist. Ct. S.C. 1975. Sole practice, West Columbia, S.C., 1974-75; ptnr. Sheftman & Oswald, West Columbia, 1975-78, Oswald & Floyd, West Columbia, 1979—. Mem. Lexington County Council, Lexington, S.C., 1979-82, chmn., 1982; mem. Central Midlands Regional Planning Council, 1982, S.C. State Employment and Tng. Council, 1979, Columbia Area Transp. Council; vice chmn. bd. Opportunities Industrialization Ctr. of Midlands, S.C., 1985-86, chmn., 1986—; state campaign dir., State of S.C., Gary Hart for Pres. of U.S., 1984. Served with USAR, 1969-74. Recipient cert. of appreciation Lexington Sch. Dist. 5, 1979, resolution of appreciation Lexington County Council, 1982. Mem. S.C. Trial Lawyers, Assn. Trial Lawyers Am., ABA, S.C. Bar Assn., Lexington and Richland County Bar Assn., Assn. to Advance Ethical Hypnosis. Democrat. Mem. Ch. of Nazarene. Lodges: Woodmen of World, Optimists. Personal injury, Workers' compensation, Insurance. Home: 2124 Raven Trail West Columbia SC 29169 Office: PO Box 4052 1031 Center St W Columbia SC 29169

O'TOOLE, AUSTIN MARTIN, lawyer; b. New Bedford, Mass., Oct. 5, 1935; s. John Brian, Jr. and Helen Veronica O'T.; m. Kay Murphy, Nov. 27, 1982; children: Erin Ann, Austin Martin 2d. B.S. in Bus. Adminstrn., Coll. Holy Cross, 1957; J.D., Georgetown U., 1963. Bar: N.Y. 1965, D.C. 1963, Tex. 1975. Law clk. to judge U.S. Ct. Appeals, Washington, 1962-63; assoc. White & Case, N.Y.C., 1963-74; sr. v.p., dep. gen. counsel, sec. Coastal Corp., Houston, 1974—. Bd. editors Georgetown Law Jour., 1962-63. Bd. dirs. Houston Council on Alcoholism and Drug Abuse, Houston, 1986—. Served as officer USMCR, 1957-60. Mem. Am. Soc. Corporate Secs. (bd. dirs. 1982-85), ABA, Tex. Bar Assn. (com. securities and investment banking), Houston Bar Assn. (past chmn. corp. counsel sect. 1979-80, alt. dispute resolution com. 1986—). Home: 2008 Timberlane Houston TX 77027 Office: White and Case 9 Greenway Plaza Houston TX 77046

O'TOOLE, FRANCIS J., lawyer; b. Dublin, Ireland, Feb. 10, 1944; came to U.S., 1960; s. Francis Herbert and Josephine (McCarthy) O'T.; m. Carole Ann Leland, Apr. 11, 1977; children: Kathleen, Kirra. AB, Harvard U., 1967; JD, U. Maine, 1970. Bar: Maine 1970, U.S. Supreme Ct. 1977, U.S. Dist. Ct. D.C., U.S. Dist. Ct. (ea. dist.) Va., U.S. Ct. Appeals (1st, 2d, 4th, 5th, 7th, 8th, 9th and 10th cirs.). Assoc. Fried, Frank, Harris, Shriver & Jacobsen, Washington, 1971-78, ptnr., 1978—. Editor-in-chief U. Maine Law Rev., 1969-70; contbr. articles to profl. jours. Reginald Heber Smith fellow Calif. Indian Legal Services, 1970-71. Mem. ABA. Avocations: horse breeding and racing. Federal civil litigation, State civil litigation. Home: 1214 Vinita Ln McLean VA 22102 Office: Fried Frank Harris Shriver & Jacobson 600 New Hampshire Ave NW Washington DC 20037

O'TOOLE, JOHN JAMES, lawyer; b. Sommerville, N.J., July 4, 1956; s. John James O'Toole and Gertrude Josephine (Chernesky) O'Toole Hewitt; m. Suzanne Black, Oct. 17, 1981. BA, George Washington U., 1977; JD, Cath. U., 1980. Bar: N.Y. 1981. Assoc. counsel Mfrs. Hanover Bank (Del.), Wilmington, 1980-87, v.p., counsel, 1987—. Bd. dirs. Big Bros. N.Y.C., Inc., 1983—, The Children's Bur. of Del. Inc., 1987—. Clubs: Univ. (N.Y.C.); Siasconset Casino, Sankaty Head Golf (Nantucket, Mass.). Banking, Contracts commercial, General corporate. Home: 915 Overbrook Rd Wilmington DE 19807 Office: Mfrs Hanover Bank 919 Market St Wilmington DE 19801

OTOROWSKI, SHAWN ELIZABETH, lawyer; b. Seattle, Dec. 19, 1952; s. Walter Thomas and Rita Marie (Olsen) McGovern; m. Christopher Lee, Aug. 4, 1978; children: Kirsten Elizabeth, Hilary Marie. BA, U. Wash., 1975; JD, Gonzaga U., 1978. Bar: Wash. 1979, U.S. Dist. Ct. (ea. and we. dists.) Wash. 1979. Law clk. to presiding justice U.S. Dist. Ct., Spokane, 1978-79; assoc. Ferguson & Burdell, Seattle, 1979-86, ptnr., 1986—. Mem. Jr. League of Seattle, 1982; chmn. lawyers div. Variety Club Telethon, Seattle, 1983. Mem. ABA (client security fund com., profl. utilization and career devel. com.), Wash. State Bar Assn., Seattle-King County Bar Assn. (day care com.). Clubs: Seattle Tennis, Seattle Yacht. Avocations: tennis, skiing, sailing. State civil litigation, Federal civil litigation, Contracts commercial. Office: Ferguson & Burdell 2900 One Union Sq Seattle WA 98101

OTT, EMILE CUTRER, lawyer; b. New Orleans, Jan. 18, 1932; s. John Jacob and Kathryn Bingham (Percy) O.; m. Jewell Vegas, June 10, 1960; children—Emile Cutrer, Paul Vegas, Kathryn Ruth. B.A., U. Miss., 1954, LL.B., 1959. Bar: Miss. 1959. Trial atty. NLRB, New Orleans, 1959-66; atty. Auther Sullivan, Jackson, Miss., 1966-69; mem. Fuselier Ott McKee & Walker, P.A., Jackson, Miss., 1969—. Served to 1st lt. USAF, 1954-57. Mem. ABA, Def. Lawyers Assn. Labor. Home: 2315 Irving Pl Jackson MS 39211 Office: 2100 Deposit Guaranty Plaza Jackson MS 39201

OTT, JOHN EDWARD, lawyer; b. Queens, N.Y., June 9, 1955; s. John Joseph and Catherine (McDermott) O.; m. Karen Boynton, Aug. 16, 1980. BA, U. Cen. Fla., 1977; JD, Samford U., 1981. Bar: Fla. 1981, Ala. 1982, U.S. Dist. Ct. (no. dist.) Ala. 1983, U.S. Ct. Appeals (11th cir.) 1983. Law clk. to presiding justice U.S. Magistrate, Birmingham, Ala., 1981-83; asst. U.S. atty. U.S. Atty.'s Office, Birmingham, 1983—. Recipient Spl. Achievement award U.S. Dept. Justice, Washington, 1985; named one of Outstanding Young Men Am., 1985. Mem. ABA, Fla. Bar Assn., Ala. Bar Assn., Birmingham Bar Assn., Young Businessmans' Assn., Order of Barristers. Republican. Baptist. Avocations: canoeing, rock climbing, running. Criminal. Home: 4713 Nottingham Ln Birmingham AL 35223 Office: US Attys Office 200 Fed Courthouse Birmingham AL 35203

OTT, WILLIAM GRIFFITH, law educator, writer; b. Wilmington, Del., Feb. 21, 1909; s. David Lewes and Greta Blauvelt (Griffith) O.; m. Joanna Seyffarth, Dec. 28, 1961; children—Michael, William Griffith Jr., Nancy, David. B.S. in Bus. Adminstrn., U. Del., 1932; LL.B., LaSalle Extension U. Chgo., 1946. Prof. law Goldey Beacom Coll., Wilmington, 1946—, v.p., dir. admissions, 1973-78, pres., 1978; advisor Nat. Assn. Legal Secs. (Del. chpt.); founder W. G. Ott Law Assn. Author: (with others) College Business Law, 6th edit., 1983; Business and the Law, 1979; (series) Business Law, 1980-85; and additional books. Mem. Del. Bus. Tchrs. Assn., Eastern Bus. Tchrs. Assn. (past bd. dirs.). Legal education, Legal history, Business law. Home: 508 Milltown Rd Wilmington DE 19808 Office: Goldey Beacom Coll Limestone Rd Wilmington DE 19808

OTTENHEIMER, EDWIN, lawyer; b. Balt., Sept. 20, 1915; s. Emanuel E. and Bessie (Katzenberg) O.; m. Dorothy Stephany, Mar. 15, 1945; children: Ann Ottenheimer Poltilove, Alan. AB, Johns Hopkins U., 1936; JD, U. Md., 1940. Bar: Md. 1940, U.S. Dist. Ct. Md. 1940.; CPA, Md. Ptnr. Hamburger, Sykes & Ottenheimer, Balt., 1962-69; officer Ottenheimer, Cahn & Patz P.A., Balt., 1972-85; of counsel Weinberg & Green, Balt., 1985—. Author: (with Daniel C. Joseph) Supplementary Proceeding in Maryland, 1955. Mem. ABA, Md. Bar Assn., Balt. City Bar Assn. Avocation: tennis. Home: 7913 Long Meadow Rd Baltimore MD 21208 Office: Weinberg & Green 100 S Charles St Baltimore MD 21201

OTTERMAN, HARVEY BOYD, JR., lawyer; b. Washington, Feb. 18, 1926; s. Harvey Boyd and Pearl Catherine (Hatch) O.; m. Doris Clark Otterman, Oct. 13, 1926; children—Stephen B., David A., Thomas C. A.B., George Washington U., 1948, LL.B., 1950. Bar: D.C. 1950, Vt. 1951. Sole practice, Bradford, Vt., 1951-65; ptnr. Otterman and Allen P.C., Bradford, 1965—; state's atty. State of Vt., 1953-58; mem. Vt. Profl. Conduct Bd., 1973-79, chmn., 1973-77; mem. com. on grievances U.S. Ct. Apls. 2d cir., 1979—. Bd. fellows, vice chmn. Norwich U., Northfield, Vt. Served with U.S. Navy 1943-46. Mem. Orange County Bar Assn. (pres. 1971-74), Vt. Bar Assn. (pres. 1980-81), New Eng. Bar Assn. (pres. 1981-82), Am. Coll. Probate Csl., Am. Bar Found. Probate, State civil litigation, General practice. Home: PO Box 34 West Topsham VT 05086 Office: PO Box 636 Bradford VT 05033

OTTO, BYRON LEONARD, lawyer, state administrator; b. Battle Creek, Mich., Oct. 4, 1940; s. Henry John and Mildred Alice (Wagner) O. B.B.A., St. Edward's U., 1964, M.B.A., 1979; J.D., U. Tex., 1968. Staff atty. State Welfare Dept., Austin, Tex., 1968-75; sole practice, Austin, 1975-77; assoc. with James R. Sloan, Austin, 1978-79; adminstr. State Comptroller, Austin, 1980—. Author articles and monographs. St. Edward's U. scholar, Austin, 1978. Mem. ABA, Tex. Bar. Democrat. Roman Catholic. Administrative and regulatory, General corporate, Real property. Home: PO Box 1435 Austin TX 78767 Office: State Comptroller PO Box 13528 Austin TX 78711

OTTO, JAMES DANIEL, lawyer; b. Long Beach, Calif., June 9, 1949; s. Paul Daniel and Bethal Bertine (Hudspeth) O. B.A. summa cum laude, San Diego State U., 1971; J.D., Northwestern U., 1974. Bar: Calif. 1974, U.S. Dist. Ct. (cen. dist.) Calif. 1974, U.S. Dist. Ct. (so. dist.) Calif. 1981, U.S. Ct. Appeals (9th cir.) 1983. Assoc. firm Cummins & White and predecessor firms, Los Angeles, 1974-78, ptnr., 1978-80, sr. ptnr., 1980—, mng. ptnr., 1982-85; dir., sec. Master Liquidation Co., a N.J. corp., Los Angeles, 1978-87 ; speaker Practicing Law Inst., 1987. Active Big Bros. Am., Los Angeles, 1975-79. Mem. ABA (panelist various seminars), Assn. So. Calif. Def. Counsel, Internat. Assn. Def. Counsel, Los Angeles County Bar Assn., Phi Kappa Phi, Pi Sigma Alpha, Alpha Mu Gamma. Club: Jonathan (Los Angeles), John Henry Wigmore. Insurance, Environment, State civil litigation. Office: Cummins & White 1600 Wilshire Blvd Los Angeles CA 90017

OTTS, LEE MACMILLAN, lawyer; b. Greensboro, Ala., May 21, 1922; s. Archiebald Bruce McEachin and Elizabeth Avery (MacMillan) O.; m. Mary Frances Byrd, Sept. 4, 1948; children: Harriet, Martha Frances, Elizabeth, Mary Lee. AB, U. Ala., 1943, LLB, 1948. Bar: Ala. 1949. Ptnr. Otts & Moore and predecessor firm, Brewton, Ala., 1949—; judge inferior ct. Escambia County, Brewton, Ala., 1951-53; solicitor Escambia County, Brewton, 1953-75, atty., 1958—. Bd. dirs. Brewton Bd. Edn., 1961-76, pres. 1967-76, Ala. Assn. Sch. Bds., 1970-74, 1st v.p. 1973-74; pres. Housing Authority, 1965-72 ; active First Presbyn. Ch., Brewton. Served to capt. U.S. Army, 1943-46, ETO. Decorated Bronze Star, Purple Heart with one oak leaf cluster. Mem. Phi Alpha Delta, Phi Gamma Delta. Club: Brewton Country (bd. dirs. 1978-81). Lodge: Rotary (pres. local chpt. 1953). Oil and gas leasing, Real property. Home: 1515 Poplar Ave Brewton AL 36426 Office: Otts & Moore Box 467 Brewton AL 36426

OUDERKIRK, MASON JAMES, lawyer; b. Des Moines, Feb. 1, 1953; s. Mason George and Florence Astor (Lowe) O.; m. Kari Aune Hormel, May 28, 1983; 1 child, Mason Christopher. BA, Drake U., 1975, JD, 1978. Bar: Iowa 1978, U.S. Dist. Ct. (so. dist.) Iowa 1978. Assoc. M.G. Ouderkirk Law Office, Indianola, Iowa, 1978-79; ptnr. Ouderkirk Law Firm, Indianola, 1979—. Mem. Indianola Police Retirement Bd., 1984—. Mem. ABA, Iowa Bar Assn., Warren County Bar Assn. (sec., treas. 1985—), 5th Jud. Dist. Bar Assn. Episcopalian. Avocations: Tae Kwon Do, fishing, hunting, gardening. Local government, Family and matrimonial, General practice. Home: 307 W Madison Pl Indianola IA 50125 Office: Ouderkirk Law Firm 110 S Howard Box 156 Indianola IA 50125

OULTON, DONALD PAUL, lawyer; b. Kingston, N.Y., July 22, 1930; s. Francis Terrance and Anne Agnes (Carroll) O.; m. Carol Jane Burke; children—David P., Nancy, Sarah, Carol. A.A. in Edn., Boston U., 1955; B.S in Bus. Adminstrn., Boston U., 1958; J.D., Suffolk U., 1969. Bar: Mass. 1970, U.S. Dist. Ct. Mass. 1973, U.S. Supreme Ct. 1978, U.S. Ct. Appeals (1st cir.) 1980, U.S. Ct. Claims 1980, U.S. Tax Ct. 1980, U.S. Ct. Mil. Appeals 1981, U.S. Ct. Internat. Trade 1984, U.S. Ct. Appeals (fed. cir.) 1984. Contract negotiator Raytheon Corp., Bedford, Mass., 1959-65; chief negotiator claims Quincy Shipbldg. Div., Mass., 1965-72; assoc. div. counsel Quincy Shipbldg. 1970-72; asst. dist. atty. Middlesex County, Cambridge, Mass., 1972-75; contract negotiator Electronic Systems div. Office of Staff Judge Adv., U.S. Air Force, Hanscom AFB, Mass., 1974-76, chief atty. fgn. mil. sales, 1976—; trial counsel Natick, Mass., Part-time, 1970—; real estate broker Mass. Realtors Assn., Boston, 1972—. Author: Inquests, 1973, Technology Transfer, 1983, Air Force Trivia, 1985, (with others) In Remembrance of Korea, 1987. Hearing officer Zoning Bd. Appeals, Natick, 1976; lectr. Western New Eng. Coll. Tchr. 9th grade, CCD, St. James Ch., Wellesley, Mass., 1976-83; bd. dirs., co-founder Shamrock Soc., Natick, Mass., 1976—; bd. dirs., counsel Little League, Natick, 1972-75. Served with inf. U.S. Army, 1951-53, Korea. Named Outstanding Civilian Atty. of Yr., U.S. Air Force Systems Command, 1980; Outstanding Civilian Atty. of Yr., U.S. Air Force, Pentagon, 1980, Outstanding Civilian, Air Force Electronic Systems Div., 1983. Mem. Am. Soc. Internat. Law, Air Force Assn., Middlesex Bar Assn., Mass. Bar Assn., Fed. Bar Assn., Mass. Police Chiefs Assn. Democrat. Roman Catholic. Club: Officers. Government contracts and claims, Public international, Criminal. Home: 54 MacArthur Rd Natick MA 01760 Office: Chief Atty Fgn Mil Sales Br Office Staff Judge Adv Contract Law Div Electronic S AFB MA 01731

OUTERBRIDGE, CHERYL, lawyer; b. Monte Vista, Colo., July 11, 1943; d. George Herbert and Gladys Mae (Walker) Hazard; m. J. Robert Outerbridge, June 4, 1961 (div. 1984); 1 child, Grant Hazard; m. Carl F. Nagy, Nov. 16, 1985; B.A., U. Denver, 1968; J.D., U. Colo., 1975. Bar: Colo. 1975, U.S. Dist. Ct. Colo. 1975. Assoc., Gorsuch, Kirgis, Campbell, Walker & Grover, Denver, 1975-79; staff atty. Amax Inc., Golden, Colo., 1979-81; editor-in-chief American Law of Mining, 2d edit., Rocky Mountain Mineral Law Found., Boulder, Colo., 1981-85; sr. atty. AMAX Inc., Golden, Colo., 1985—. Contbr. articles to profl. jours. Mem. ABA, Order of Coif, Colo. Bar Assn., Denver Bar Assn., The Alliance of Profl. Women, Phi Beta Kappa. Mining & Minerals. Office: AMAX Inc 1707 Cole Blvd Golden CO 80401

OVERBY, JON JEFFERSON, lawyer; b. Newport Beach, Calif., June 14, 1953; s. Eber Verell and Jean (Driscoll) O. BA cum laude, Vanderbilt U., 1975; JD, U. Fla., 1978. Bar: Fla. 1979, U.S. Dist. Ct. (so. dist.) Fla. 1980. Sole practice Key West, Fla., 1979—; pub. defender 16th Jud. Cir., Key West, 1983—. Bd. dirs. Festival of the Continents, Key West, 1987—, Tennessee Williams Founders Soc., Key West, 1987—. Mem. ABA, Nat. Assn. Criminal Def. Lawyers. Republican. Avocations: duplicate bridge, scuba diving, classical music, reading, travel. Criminal. Home: P O Box 429 Key West FL 33041 Office: 424 Fleming St Key West FL 33040

OVERBY, LACY RASCO, biotechnology company executive; b. Model, Tenn., July 27, 1920; s. Alious William and Oma Catherine (Thomas) O.; m. Elizabeth Mae Hulette, Oct. 1, 1948; children—Megan Stewart, Ross Vincent, Alison Brooke, Alexander Scott. B.A., Vanderbilt U., 1941, M.S., 1948, Ph.D., 1951. Prodn. supr. DuPont Corp., Barksdale, Wis., 1941-43; teaching asst. Vanderbilt U., Nashville, 1946-49; div. v.p. Abbott Labs., North Chicago, Ill., 1949-83, cons., 1983-84; v.p. Chiron Corp., Emeryville, Calif., 1983—; cons. Children's Meml. Hosp., Chgo., 1970-73; lectr. in molecular biology Northwestern U., Evanston, Ill., 1968-81. Editor: Viral Hepatitis, 1979, rev. edit., 1983; assoc. editor Jour. Med. Virology, 1977—, Asian Jour. Clin. Scis., 1980-84; contbr. articles to profl. jours.; patentee in field. Chmn. bd. dirs. Am. Cancer Soc., Lake County, Ill., 1978-82. Served to comdr. USNR, 1943-46; ETO, PTO. DuPont fellow Vanderbilt U., 1948; vis. scholar U. Ill., Urbana, 1962. Mem. Am. Soc. Biol. Chemists, Am. Soc. Study Liver Diseases, Am. Soc. Microbiology (Pasteur award 1986), Am. Chem. Soc., Sigma Xi. Republican. Episcopalian. Club: Round Hill Country (Alamo, Calif.). Avocations: sports; travel; antique furniture. Home: 28 Cherry Hills Ct Alamo CA 94507 Office: Chiron Corp 4560 Horton St Emeryville CA 94608

OVERGAARD, CORDELL JERSILD, lawyer; b. Chgo., June 1, 1934; s. Kristin and Rose Marie (Jersild) O.; m. Gail A. Gill, Sept. 5, 1959; children: Diane, Karen, Susan. BS with honors, U. Ill., 1957; LLB magna cum laude, Harvard U., 1960. Bar: Ill. 1960. Assoc. Hopkins & Sutter, Chgo., 1960-67, ptnr., 1967—; dir. mem. exec. com. UPI, Inc., 1982-83; pres. Community Cablevision, Inc., 1980-86 ; pres. Gore-Overgaard Broadcasting, Inc., 1986—; pres. bd. trustees NorthCare, 1979-81; sec. Family Weekly, Inc., 1976-80; dir. Prudential Health Care Plan, Inc., 1980—, Cahners Pub. Co., 1970-74, Small Newspaper Group, Inc., 1981—. Mem. Ill. Bd. Ethics, 1973-76, chmn., 1976-80. Mem. ABA, Chgo. Bar Assn. (chmn. corp. law com. 1972-73). Clubs: Law, Mid-Day, Union League, Mid-Am., Legal, Economic (Chgo.). Editor Harvard Law Rev., 1960. General corporate. Home: 2771 Sheridan Rd Evanston IL 60201 Office: 3 First National Plaza Suite 4300 Chicago IL 60602

OVERGAARD, MARY ANN, lawyer; b. Mason City, Iowa, May 29, 1951; d. Gunnar S.M. and Claudia May (Michalek) O.; m. David Earl Cook, Aug. 19, 1972; 1 child, Nels David Overgaard-Cook. BS, U. Nebr., 1972, JD, 1975. Bar: Nebr. 1975, U.S. Dist. Ct. Nebr. 1975, Oreg. 1983, U.S. Dist. Ct. Oreg. 1984, U.S. Supreme Ct. 1985. Counsel Nebr. Regional Med. Program, Lincoln, 1975-76, Nebr. Dept. of Revenue, Lincoln, 1977-78; legal counsel Nebr. Dept. of Edn., Lincoln, 1978-81; legal policy advisor Oreg. Bur. of Labor, Portland, 1981-84; legal advisor Portland Police Bur., 1984—. V.p. Planned Parenthood, Lincoln, 1979; commr. Lincoln/Lancaster Planning Commn., 1980-81; legis. chairperson Oreg. Womens Polit. Caucas, 1986—; v.p., bd. dirs. Portland YMCA, 1985—. Mem. ABA, Multnomah County Bar Assn. Democrat. Unitarian. Clubs: Portland City, Oreg. Road Runners. Avocations: running, bridge. Civil rights, Criminal, Labor. Home: 2772 NE Wiberg Ln Portland OR 97213 Office: Portland Police Bur 1111 SW 2d Ave Room 1526 Portland OR 97204

OVERHOLSER, JOHN W., lawyer; b. Portland, Oreg., June 29, 1937; s. Wayne D. and Evaleth M. (Miller) O.; m. Carol T. Overholser, June 20, 1935; children: Vicki, Stacia, John, Jason. BA, U. Colo., 1959, LLB, 1962. Bar: Colo. 1962, U.S. Dist. Ct. Colo. 1962. Assoc. Brooks and Miller, Montrose, Colo., 1962-64; sole practice Montrose, 1964-68; ptnr. Overholser & Slee, P.C., and predecessors, Montrose, 1968—. Lay speaker Montrose United Meth. Ch.; past chmn. Montrose County Rep. Cen. Com.; past mem., chmn. Regional Library Dist.; past bd. dirs. Montrose C. of C.; active community activities. Mem. ABA, Colo. Bar Assn., 7th Jud. Bar Assn. General practice, Real property, State civil litigation. Office: 333 S Townsend St PO Box 729 Montrose CO 81402

OVERHOLT, HUGH ROBERT, lawyer, army officer; b. Beebe, Ark., Oct. 29, 1933; s. Harold R. and Cuma E. (Hall) O.; m. Laura Annell Arnold, May 5, 1961; children: Sharon, Scott. Student, Coll. of Ozarks, 1951-53; B.A., U. Ark., 1955, LL.B., 1957. Bar: Ark. 1957. Commd. 1st lt. U.S. Army, 1957, advanced through grades to maj. gen., 1981; chief Criminal Law Div., JAG Sch., Charlottesville, Va., 1971-73; chief personnel, plans and tng. Office of JAG, U.S. Army, Washington, 1973-75; staff judge adv. XVIII Airborne Corps, Ft. Bragg, N.C., 1976-78; spl. asst. for legal and selected policy matters Office of Dep. Asst., 1978-79; asst. judge adv. gen. for mil. law Office of JAG, Washington, 1979-81; asst. judge adv. gen. Office of JAG, 1981-85, judge adv. gen, 1985—. Notes and comment editor Ark. Law Rev, 1956-57. Decorated Army Meritorious Service medal with oak leaf cluster, Army Commendation medal with 2 oak leaf clusters., Legion of Merit, Def. Meritorious Service medal. Mem. ABA, Fed. Bar Assn., Ark. Bar Assn., Assn. U.S. Army, Delta Theta Phi, Omicron Delta Kappa, Sigma Pi. Presbyterian. Office: Room 2E432 Pentagon Washington DC 20310

OVERHOLT, MARY ANN, insurance company executive, lawyer; b. Charleston, W. Va., Feb. 15, 1935; d. Francis Alden and Elizabeth Ann (Jones) Clark; m. Marlin Ross Overholt, Dec. 31, 1960 (div. 1980); m. Walter Melvin Redman, Jr., Feb. 14, 1981. B.A., Ohio U., 1956; J.D., Salmon P. Chase Coll. Law, Cin., 1964. Bar: Ohio 1964, U.S. Supreme Ct. 1970, U.S. Ct. Appeals (6th cir.) 1976. Personnel adminstrn. and engring. design staff Gen. Electric Co., Cin., 1956-65; asst. counsel Inter-Ocean Ins. Co., Cin., 1965-68, assoc. counsel, 1968-73, asst. sec., counsel, 1973-77; assoc. counsel Union Central Life Ins. Co., 1977-79; v.p., gen. counsel Union Central Life Ins. Co., Cin., 1979—; sec., dir. Micrographix Data Services Inc., Cin., 1970-74; adj. asst. prof. law Salmon P. Chase Coll. Law, 1973-75. Bd. dirs. Knolls Homeowners Assn., Cin., 1982—, pres., 1983—. Recipient Career Woman of Achievement award Cin. YWCA, 1983. Mem. ABA (vice chmn. life ins. law com. 1979-86, chmn. elect 1986-87), Ohio Bar Assn., Cin. Bar Assn., Assn. Life Ins. Counsel (bd. govs. 1982-84). Club: Lawyers (Cin). Office: Union Central Life Ins Co PO Box 179 Cincinnati OH 45201

OVERTON, BENJAMIN FREDERICK, state justice; b. Green Bay, Wis., Dec. 15, 1926; s. Benjamin H. and Esther M. (Wiese) O.; m. Marilyn Louise Smith, June 9, 1951; children: William Hunter, Robert Murray, Catherine Louise. B.S. in Bus. Adminstrn., U. Fla., 1951, J.D., 1952; LL.D. (hon.), Stetson U., 1975, Nova U., 1977; LL.M., U. Va., 1984. Bar: Fla. 1952. With Office Fla. Atty. Gen., 1952; with firms in St. Petersburg, Fla., 1952-64; city atty. St. Petersburg, 1954-57; circuit judge 6th Jud. Circuit Fla., 1964-74, chief judge, 1968-71; chmn. Fla. Conf. Circuit Judges, 1973; justice Supreme Ct. Fla., Tallahassee, 1974—; chief justice Supreme Ct. Fla., 1976-78; past mem. faculty Stetson U. Coll. Law; mem. faculty, bd. dirs. Nat. Jud. Coll.; mem. Fla. Bar Continuing Legal Edn. Com., 1963-74, chmn., 1971-74; 1st chmn. Fla. Inst. Judiciary, 1972; mem. exec. com. Appellate Judges Conf.; chmn. appellate Structure Commn., 1978-79, Article V Rev. Commn., 1983-84, Matrimonial Law Commn., 1982—, Jud. Council of Fla., 1985—. Contbr. legal publs. Past reader, vestryman, sr. warden St. Albans Episcopal Ch., St. Petersburg, Fla; chmn. U.S. Constn. Bicentennial Commn. Fla., 1986—. Served as E.M., AUS, 1945-47; Served as officer USAR, 1950-74; active duty 1961-62. Fellow Am. Bar Found.; mem. ABA, Fla. Bar Assn., Am. Judicature Soc. (dir., sec.). Democrat. Lodge: Rotary. Office: Supreme Ct Bldg Tallahassee FL 32301

OVERTON, GEORGE WASHINGTON, lawyer; b. Hinsdale, Ill., Jan. 25, 1918; s. George Washington and Florence Mary (Darlington) O.; m. Jane Vincent Harper, Sept. 1, 1941; children—Samuel Harper, Peter Darlington, Ann Vincent. A.B., Harvard U., 1940; J.D., U. Chgo., 1946. Bar: Ill. 1947. Counsel Wildman, Harrold, Allen & Dixon, Chgo. Bd. dirs. Open Lands Project, pres., 1978-81; bd. dirs. Upper Ill. Valley Assn., 1981—, chmn., 1981-84; mem. com. on profl. responsibility of Ill. Supreme Ct., 1986—. Mem. ABA, Ill. Bar Assn., Chgo. Bar Assn. (bd. mgrs. 1981-83), Assn. Bar City N.Y. Real property, Contracts commercial, General corporate. Home: 5648 Dorchester Ave Chicago IL 60637 Office: 1 IBM Plaza Chicago IL 60611

OVERTON, JOHN BLAIR, lawyer; b. Newburgh, N.Y., Dec. 23, 1949; s. Jesse Woodhull and Joan (Blair) O. BA, Columbia U., 1972; JD, Golden Gate U., 1979. Bar: Calif. 1981, U.S. Dist. Ct. (no. dist.) Calif. 1981, U.S. Dist. Ct. (cen. dist.) Calif. 1985, U.S. Ct. Appeals (9th cir.) 1986. Sole practice Sausalito, Calif., 1981—; bd. dirs. Ind. Feature Project of No. Calif. Author: Oregon Clean Water Handbook, 1975. Mem. ABA (chmn. subcom. copyright legis. com. 1985—), Phi Beta Kappa. Avocations: fly fishing, playing music. Trademark and copyright, Entertainment. Office: 2401 Marinship Way Sausalito CA 94965

OVERTON, SHANA L., lawyer, accountant; b. Nashville, July 11, 1951; d. James H. and Faye L. (Taylor) O.; m. Sterling G. Miller, Oct. 23, 1980 (div. Dec. 1985); children: Katherine, Alexandra. BA, Washington U., St. Louis, 1972, MBA, JD, 1976. Bar: Tex. 1977; CPA, Tex. Tax atty. Exxon Co., USA, Houston, 1976-78; sr. tax atty. Tenneco Inc., Houston, 1978-80, tax counsel, 1980-82, sr. tax counsel, 1982—. Mem. Houston Ballet Guild, 1984—. Mem. ABA (tax sect., ins. cos. com.), Houston Bus. Forum, Pi Beta Phi. Episcopalian. Club: Houstonian. Avocations: tennis, skiing. Corporate taxation. Home: 1 Sleepy Oaks Houston TX 77024 Office: Tenneco Inc Tax Dept 1010 Milam Houston TX 77001

OVERTON, WILLIAM RAY, federal judge; b. Malvern, Ark., Sept. 19, 1939; s. Odis Ray and Martha Elizabeth (Ford) O.; m. Susan Linebarger, Jan. 25, 1964; children: William Ford, Warren Webster. B.S. in Bus. Adminstrn, U. Ark., 1962, LL.B., 1964. Bar: Ark. 1964. Assoc., then partner firm Wright, Lindsey & Jennings, Little Rock, 1964-79; U.S. dist. judge Eastern Dist. Ark., Little Rock, 1979—; mem. Ark. Constl. Revision Study Commn., 1967. Hon. fellow Internat. Acad. Trial Lawyers. Mem. Am. Bar Assn., Ark. Bar Assn., Pulaski County Bar Assn. Democrat. Methodist. Club: U. Ark. Alumni. Jurisprudence. Office: U S District Court 600 West Capitol Ave Suite 502 Little Rock AR 72201 *

OWEN, FRANK, III, lawyer, rancher, banker; b. El Paso, Feb. 25, 1926; s. Frank Jr. and Ruth Beatrice (Brown) O.; m. Marianne Farrier, June 14, 1947; children—Catherine Owen Weinstein, Virginia Owen Roberts, Frank IV, William Farrier, Robin Owen Grambling, Lorrie Owen Ballinger. Student Texas Coll. Mines, 1947; J.D., U. Texas., 1951. Bar: Tex. 1951, U.S. Ct. Appeals (5th cir.) 1953. Assoc. Burges, Scott, Raspberry and Hulse, El Paso, 1951-53; ptnr. Owen, Morgan and Niland, El Paso, 1953-60, Owen, Channel, Brewster and Steinberger, El Paso, 1960-75, Owen and Cooper, El Paso, 1975-77, Frank Owen and Assocs. P.C., El Paso, 1977—. Mem. Tex. Legislature, 1951-54; mem. Tex. Senate, 1954-65, pres. pro tem, 1961-65; mem. El Paso Sheriff's Posse. Served with USAF, 1944-46. Recipient Conquistador award city of El Paso, 1961. Mem. El Paso County Bar Assn., Tex. Bar Assn., ABA, El Paso C. of C., VFW, Phi Kappa Tau (Oustanding Alumnus award 1956). Methodist. Clubs: El Paso Country, El Paso, Masons, Shriners (El Maida). General practice, Insurance, State civil litigation. Office: 6040 Surety Dr El Paso TX 79905

OWEN, H. MARTYN, lawyer; b. Decatur, Ill., Oct. 23, 1929; s. Honore Martyn and Virginia (Hunt) O.; m. Candace Catlin Benjamin, June 21, 1952; children—Leslie W., Peter H., Douglas P. A.B., Princeton U., 1951; LL.B., Harvard U., 1954. Bar: Conn. 1954. Assoc. Shipman & Goodwin, Hartford, Conn., 1958-61, ptnr., 1961—. Mem. Simsbury (Conn.) Zoning Bd. Appeals, 1961-67, Simsbury Zoning Commn., 1967-79; sec. Capitol Region Planning Agy., 1965-66; bd. dirs. Symphony Soc. Greater Hartford, 1967-73; trustee Renbrook Sch., West Hartford, Conn., 1963-72, treas., 1964-68, pres., 1968-72, hon. life trustee, 1972—; trustee Simsbury Free Library, 1970-84, Hartford Grammar Sch.; corporator Inst. Living, Hartford. Served to lt. USNR, 1954-57. Mem. ABA, Conn. Bar Assn., Hartford County Bar Assn., Am. Law Inst. Republican. Episcopalian. Clubs: Hartford; Princeton (N.Y.C.); Ivy (Princeton, N.J.); Dauntless (Essex, Conn.). General corporate, Antitrust, Local government. Home: 44 Pinnacle Mountain Rd Simsbury CT 06070 Office: 799 Main St Hartford CT 06103

OWEN, JAMES CHURCHILL, lawyer; b. Cripple Creek, Colo., May 24, 1901; s. James and Winifred (Churchill) O.; m. Alice Wright Mann, Oct. 31, 1925; children: James Churchill, William Mann, Thomas Page. Student, U. Colo., 1919-20; AB, Yale U., 1923; LLB, Harvard U., 1926. Bar: Colo. 1926. Since practiced in Denver; with Holme, Roberts, & Owen (and predecessor firm), 1926—, sr. partner, 1955-86, of counsel, 1986—; legal staff WPB, Washington, 1942-45, asst. gen. counsel, 1944-45. Bd. dirs. Boys' Clubs Am., Boys Clubs Denver. Mem. ABA, Colo. Bar Assn., Denver Bar Assn. Republican. Episcopalian. Clubs: Denver, Denver Country, Cherry Hills Country, Cactus, Mile High (Denver). Lodge: Rotary. Banking, Estate planning. Home: 1201 Williams St Denver CO 80218 Office: Holme Roberts & Owen 1700 Broadway Denver CO 80290

OWEN, JOSEPH G., lawyer, judge; b. Chester, N.Y., Nov. 7, 1933; s. Charles S. and Marie Wolf (Elias) O.; m. Patricia E. Owen, Apr. 28, 1962; children—Elizabeth, Joseph, Ursula, Patrick, Marianne. B.A., CCNY, 1955; J.D., Fordham U., 1959. Bar: N.Y. 1959, U.S. Dist. Ct. (so. and ea. dists.) N.Y. 1959. With firm Galli, Terhune, Gibbons & Mulvihill, N.Y.C., 1959-63, Alfred Schleider, Goshen, N.Y., 1963-65, Schleider & Owen, Goshen, 1965-73; sr. ptnr. Joseph G. Owen, Owen & Grogan, Goshen, 1973-84, surrogate Orange County, Goshen, 1985—. Town justice Town of Wallkill (N.Y.), 1974-84; bd. dirs. Hudson-Delaware council Boy Scouts Am. Served to maj. U.S. Army N.G., to 1970. Mem. ABA, N.Y. State Bar Assn., Orange County Bar Assn., Goshen Bar Assn., Def. Assn. N.Y. Republican. Roman Catholic. Clubs: Kiwanis, KC. Home: PO Box 59 Circleville NY 10919 Office: Orange County Surrogate PO Box 329 Park Pl Goshen NY 10924

OWEN, RICHARD, judge; b. N.Y.C., Dec. 11, 1922; s. Carl Maynard and Shirley (Barnes) O.; m. Lynn Rasmussen, June 6, 1960; children—Carl R., David R., Richard. A.B., Dartmouth Coll., 1947; LL.B., Harvard U., 1950. Bar: N.Y. State bar 1950. Practiced in N.Y.C., 1950-74; assoc. firm Willkie Owen Farr Gallagher & Walton, 1950-53, Willkie Farr Gallagher Walton & Fitzgibbon, 1958-60; individual practice 1960-65; partner Owen & Aarons, 1965-66, Owen & Turchin, 1966-74; asst. U.S. atty. So. Dist. N.Y., 1953-55; trial atty. antitrust div. U.S. Dept. Justice, 1955-58; U.S. dist. judge So. Dist. N.Y., 1974—; Asst. prof. N.Y. Law Sch., 1951-53; assoc. counsel N.Y. State Moreland Com. on Alcoholic Beverage Control Laws, 1963-64. Composer: librettist operas A Moment of War, 1958, A Fisherman Called Peter, 1965, Mary Dyer, 1976, The Death of the Virgin, 1980. Trustee Manhattan Sch. Music, N.Y.C.; founder, bd. dirs. Maine Opera Assn., 1975-85; bd. dirs. N.Y. Lyric Opera Co. Served to 1st lt. USAAF, 1942-45. Decorated D.F.C. with oak leaf cluster, Air medal with 3 oak leaf clusters. Mem. A.S.C.A.P. Republican. Mem. Soc. of Friends. Clubs: Metropolitan Opera, Gipsy Trail, Pine Pond Yacht (commodore 1967-70). Office: US Courthouse Foley Sq New York NY 10007

OWEN, RICHARD KNOWLES, lawyer; b. Pitts., July 16, 1945; s. Douglas James Knowles and Sarah Isabelle (McLaren) O. BA, Franklin & Marshall Coll., 1967; MBA, U. Fla., 1971; JD, John Marshall Law Sch., 1975. Bar: Fla. 1977, N.Y. 1983, U.S. Dist. Ct. (so. dist.) Fla. 1980. Sole practice Coral Gables, Fla., 1975—. Federal civil litigation, State civil litigation, Workers' compensation. Home: 40 Salamanca Ave Apt 9 Coral Gables FL 33134 Office: 156 Almeria Ave Coral Gables FL 33134

OWEN, ROBERTS BISHOP, lawyer; b. Boston, Feb. 11, 1926; s. Roberts Bishop and Monica Benedict (Burrell) O.; m. Kathleen Comstock von Schrader, Aug. 27, 1966; children—David Roberts, Lucy Leffingwell, William Atreus. Student, Dartmouth Coll., 1943-44; A.B. cum laude, Harvard U., 1948, LL.B. cum laude, 1951; Dip.C.L.S., Cambridge U., Eng., 1952. Bar: D.C. 1952, U.S. Ct. Appeals (D.C. cir.) 1953, U.S. Supreme Ct. 1958. Assoc. Covington & Burling, Washington, 1952-60; ptnr. Covington & Burling, 1960-79, 81—; the legal advisor U.S. Dept. State, Washington, 1979-81; mem. Internat. Ct. Arbitration, The Hague, Netherlands. Served to ensign USN, 1943-46. Recipient Disting. Honor award Dept. State, 1981. Fellow Am. Coll. Trial Lawyers; mem. ABA, Council Fgn. Relations, Am. Soc. Internat. Law (exec. council). Clubs: Royal Ocean Racing (London); Metropolitan (Washington). Federal civil litigation, Antitrust, International. Office: PO Box 7566 Washington DC 20044

OWENS, ALETHA RIEDEL, lawyer, university official; b. San Francisco, Dec. 23, 1933; d. George Harold and Aletha Lee (Ellsworth) Riedel; m. Mark Owens, Jr., June 3, 1979. A.B., U. Calif.-Berkeley, 1959; J.D., Golden Gate U., 1963. Bar: Calif. 1964, U.S. Dist. Ct. (no. dist.) Calif. 1964, U.S. Ct. Appeals (9th cir.) 1964, U.S. Supreme Ct. 1971, U.S. Dist. Ct. (ea. dist.) Calif. 1974, Fed. Bd. Contract Appeals 1975, U.S. Ct. Appeals (10th cir.) 1977. Asst. to v.p., gen. counsel U. Calif.-Berkeley, 1964-67, asst. counsel of regents, 1967-75, assoc. counsel of regents, 1975-77; gen. counsel U. Calif. Hastings Coll. of Law, San Francisco, 1977-85; counsel U. Calif. Lawrence Berkeley Lab., 1985—. Contbr. articles, outline, syllabus to profl. jours. Bd. dirs. Children's Hosp. Med. Ctr. of No. Calif., 1975-78, Herrick Hosp., Berkeley, 1978-84, Alta Bates Corp., Berkeley, 1984—, Women's Faculty Club, Berkeley, 1968-72; charter mem. Piedmont Area Republican Women's Club, Calif., 1960—. Recipient art exhibit prize Calif. State Bar, 1970; Newhouse Found. scholar, 1954. Mem. Alameda County Bar Assn. (bd. dirs. 1973-78), Contra Costa Bar Assn., Nat. Assn. Women Lawyers, Calif. Women Lawyers (charter), Nat. Assn. Coll. and Univ. Attys., Queen's Bench. Episcopalian. Contracts commercial, General corporate, Government contracts and claims. Office: U Calif Office of Counsel Lawrence Berkeley Lab One Cyclotron Rd Berkeley CA 94720

OWENS, DENNIS JAMES CAMPBELL, lawyer; b. Kansas City, Mo., Dec. 4, 1945; s. James Charles and Josephine Augusta (Wright) O.; m. Cathy Diane Cambell, Dec. 28, 1968; children: James Campbell, Mollie Kathleeen, Mary Theda, Sean Padraic Washington. BA, Rockhurst Coll., 1967; JD, U. Notre Dame, 1975. Bar: Mo. Supreme Ct. 1975, U.S. Dist. Ct. (we. dist.) Mo. 1975, U.S. Tax Ct. 1976, U.S. Ct. Claims 1976, U.S. Ct. Appeals (8th and D.C. cirs.) 1976, U.S. Supreme Ct. 1978, U.S. Ct. Internat. Trade 1983, U.S. Air Force Ct. of Mil. Rev. 1983, U.S. Ct. Mil. Appeals 1983, U.S. Ct. Appeals (fed. cir.) 1983, U.S. Ct. Appeals (10th cir.) 1984. Law clk. to presiding justice Supreme Ct. of Mo., Jefferson City, 1975-76; sole practice Kansas City, 1976-83; ptnr. Raymond, Raymond and Owens, Kansas City, 1983—. Editor in chief Notre Dame Jour. of Legis., 1974-75; eighth cir. editor ABA Cir. Ct. News Letter, 1983—; author: Missouri Appellate Courts Research Manual, 1976; contbr. articles to law revs. Bd. govs. Citizens Assn. of Kansas City, 1976; trustee (mid-Am. chpt.) Nat. Multiple Sclerosis Soc., Kansas City, 1977; bd. dirs. NCCJ, Kansas City, 1978; ambassador Mo. Colls. Fund, Kansas City, 1982—, chmn. bd. dirs. Coop. Social Services, Kansas City, 1983—; asst. scoutmaster Boy Scouts Am., Kansas City, 1983; pres. Kansas City Pub. Library, 1984-86, gen. chmn. Alliance for Better Libraries, Kansas City, 1986—; hon. consul Repub. of Austria for Mo. and Kans., 1987— . Served to 1st lt. USMC, 1968-71, Vietnam. Recipient Meritorious Achievement award Mo. Library Assn., 1985, Disting. Service award Greater Kansas City Jaycees, 1980; named Outstanding Young Missourian, Mo. Jaycees, 1980, Tchr. of Yr., U. Mo.-Kansas City Dental Sch., 1980. Mem. ABA (Mo. chmn. appellate practice com.), Kansas City Met. Bar assn. (chmn. appellate com. 1984-85), Lawyers Assn. of Kansas City, Mo. Bar Assn., Notre Dame Law Assn. (chmn. Mo. chpt.), Mo. Assn. Trial Attys. Republican. Roman Catholic. Club: Notre Dame (Kansas City) (pres.). Lodge: K.C. Federal civil litigation, State civil litigation, Jurisprudence. Home: 1115 Valentine Rd Kansas City MO 64111 Office: Raymond Raymond & Owens 1820 Commerce Tower 911 Main Kansas City MO 64105

OWENS, HENRY FREEMAN, III, lawyer; b. Cambridge, Mass., June 28, 1943; s. Henry Freeman and Katherine (Derlcotte) O.; m. Cheryl Ellen Doddy, Mar. 15, 1971; children: Christine, Mora, Henry IV. BS, U. So. Conn., 1964; JD, Suffolk U., 1967. Bar: Mass. 1967, U.S. Dist. Ct. Mass. 1968, U.S. Ct. Appeals (1st cir.) 1968, U.S. Supreme Ct. 1978. Asst. dist. atty. Middlesex County, Cambridge, 1967-69; sr. ptnr. Owens & Assocs., Boston, 1969—. Counsellor City of Cambridge, 1971-72; pres. Boston NAACP, 1982-83. Mem. Mass. Black Lawyers Assn. (pres.). Democrat. Avocations: fishing, jogging, home repairs. Federal civil litigation, State civil litigation, Criminal. Home: 283 Prospect St Belmont MA 02178 Office: Owens & Assocs 1 Boston Plaza Boston MA 02108

OWENS, JAMES BENTLEY, III, lawyer; b. Birmingham, Ala., July 23, 1954; s. James Bentley Jr. and Kathleen Ross (Fouche) O.; m. Jennie Jackson, June 6, 1981; 1 child, Jackson Bentley. BS, U. Ala., 1976, JD, 1979. Bar: Ala. 1979, U.S. Dist. Ct. (no. dist.) Ala., U.S. Ct. Appeals (11th cir.). Law clk. to presiding justice U.S. Dist. Ct., Birmingham, 1979-80; assoc. McMillan & Spratling, Birmingham, 1981-83, Starnes & Atchison, Birmingham, 1983—. Mem. ABA (exec. com. young lawyer sect.), Ala. Bar Assn. Baptist. Federal civil litigation, State civil litigation, Insurance. Home: 751 Montgomery Dr Birmingham AL 35213 Office: Starnes & Atchison One Daniel Plaza Birmingham AL 35233

OWENS, JOSEPH FRANCIS, lawyer; b. Chgo., Dec. 13, 1949; s. Joseph Charles and Ellen (Foran) O.; m. Christine Claire Aikens, Oct. 6, 1973; children: Meaghan B., Graham P., Connor T. BA, Loras Coll., 1971; JD, Northwestern U., 1974. Bar: Wis. 1974, U.S. Dist. Ct. (ea. and we. dists.) Wis. 1974, U.S. Dist. Ct. (no. dist.) Ill., U.S. Dist. Ct. Minn., U.S. Ct. Appeals (7th cir.). Assoc. Murphy, Stolper, Brewster & Desmond, Madison, Wis., 1974-78; ptnr. Murphy & Desmond, Madison, 1978—. Bd. of editors Northwestern U. Law Rev., 1973. Chmn. Wiley for Gov. Com., Stoughton, Wis., 1986. Recipient Distinguished Service award U. Wis. Law Sch., 1981. Mem. ABA, Wis. Bar Assn. (bd. govs., gov. 1980-81, exec. com., pres. young lawyers div. 1980-81), Dane Country Bar Assn. (chmn. com. 1985—). Republican. Roman Catholic. Lodge: Lions (pres. Stoughton, Wis. 1986). Avocations: home restoration, music, skiing. Federal civil litigation, State civil litigation, Family and matrimonial. Office: Murphy & Desmond PO Box 2038 Madison WI 53701

OWENS, L(AWRENCE) DALE, lawyer; b. Enterprise, Ala., Jan. 26, 1954; s. Lawrence B. and Helen L. (Daughdrill) O.; m. Irmina Luisa Rivero, Aug. 18, 1979; 1 child, Michael Lawrence. AA, DeKalb Community Coll., 1973; BA, Emory U., 1975, JD, 1978. Bar: Ga. 1978, U.S. Ct. Appeals (5th cir.) 1978, U.S. Ct. Appeals (11th cir.) 1983, U.S. Supreme Ct. 1984. Assoc. Seward & Kissel, Atlanta, 1978-80; assoc. Kilpatrick & Cody, Atlanta, 1980-84, ptnr., 1984—. Mem. ABA, Ga. Bar Assn. (editorial bd. jour. 1985-87, editor-in-chief 1987—), Atlanta Bar Assn., Lawyers Club Atlanta, Order of Coif, Order of Barristers. Republican. Episcopalian. Avocation: golf. Federal civil litigation, Labor, State civil litigation. Home: 747 Yorkshire Rd NE Atlanta GA 30306 Office: Kilpatrick & Cody 100 Peachtree St Suite 3100 Atlanta GA 30043

OWENS, ROBERT FRANKLIN, judge; b. Phoenix, Oct. 6, 1928; s. Franklin Vivian and Velma (Shumway) O.; m. Cheer Henrie, Apr. 11, 1952; children—Guy, Lynn, Kurt, Jed, Liesl. LL.B., U. Ariz., 1954. Bar: Ariz. 1955, Utah 1974. Dept. county atty. County of Maricopa, Phoenix, 1962-64; ptnr. Tanner, Jarvis & Owens, Phoenix, 1964-75; city judge St. George City Ct., Utah, 1975-78; judge 9th Circuit Ct. Utah, St. George, 1978—; lectr. Nat. Jud. Coll., Reno, 1982-83. Vice pres., bd. dirs. Southwest Symphony, St. George, 1983-84; pres. Southwest Civic Chorale, St. George, 1983-84; v.p., bd. dirs. Southwest Concert Series, St. George, 1983-84; mem. Phoenix Environ. Commn., 1972-74. Mem. Utah Circuit Judges Assn. (pres. 1978-80), Utah Jud. Council. Mormon. Criminal. Home: 245 W Hope St Saint George UT 84770 Office: Hall of Justice 9th Circuit Court 200 E 220 N Saint George UT 84770

OWENS, RODNEY JOE, lawyer; b. Dallas, Mar. 7, 1950; s. Hubert L. and Billie Jo (Foust) O.; m. Sherry Lyn Bailey, June 10, 1972; 1 child, Jonathan Rockwell. BBA, So. Meth. U., 1972, JD, 1975. Bar: Tex. 1975, U.S. Dist. Ct. (no. dist.) Tex. 1975, U.S. Tax Ct. 1975, U.S. Ct. Appeals (5th cir.) 1975. Assoc. Durant & Mankoff, Dallas, 1975-78, ptnr., 1978-83; ptnr. David, Meadwos, Owens, Collier & Zachary, Dallas, 1983—. Contbr. articles to profl. jours. Baptist. Probate, Estate taxation, Personal income taxation. Home: 6919 N Janmar Dallas TX 75230 Office: Davis Meadows Owens Collier & Zachary 3700 Interfirst Plaza 901 Main St Dallas TX 75202

OWENS, WILBUR DAWSON, JR., U.S. district judge; b. Albany, Ga., Feb. 1, 1930; s. Wilbur Dawson and Estelle (McKenzie) O.; m. Mary Elizabeth Glenn, June 21, 1958; children: Lindsey, Wilbur Dawson III, Estelle, John. Student, Emory U., 1947-48; J.D., U. Ga., 1952. Bar: Ga. 1952. Mem. firm Smith, Gardner & Owens, Albany, 1954-55; v.p., trust officer Bank of Albany, 1955-59; sec.-treas. Southeastern Mortgage Co., Albany, 1959-65; asst. U.S. atty. Middle Dist. Ga., Macon, 1962-64; asso., then partner Bloch, Hall, Hawkins & Owens, Macon, 1965-72; U.S. dist. judge Middle Dist. Ga., Macon, 1972—, now chief judge. Served to 1st lt., JAG USAF, 1952-54. Mem. Am. Bar Assn., State Bar Ga., Assn. Trial Lawyers Am., Macon Bar Assn., Am. Judicature Soc., Phi Delta Theta, Phi Delta Phi. Republican. Presbyterian. Clubs: Rotarian, Idle Hour Golf and Country. Office: US Dist Ct PO Box 65 Macon GA 31202 *

OWINGS, WILLIAM DONOVAN, lawyer; b. New Orleans, Oct. 17, 1957; s. William Orange and Elizabeth Joyce (Grimsley) O.; m. Carol Olivia Brand, May 23, 1980. BA, U. Ala., 1979, JD, 1982. Bar: Ala. 1982, U.S. Dist. Ct. (no. dist.) Ala. 1982. Sole practice Centreville, Ala., 1982—. Mem. ABA. Lodges: Civitan (treas., sec. Brent, Ala. 1985—), Elks. Avocations: computer sci., legal history. General practice. Office: PO Box 396 105 Court Sq W #208 Centreville AL 35042

OWSLEY, ALVIN MANSFIELD, JR., lawyer; b. Dallas, Feb. 9, 1926; s. Alvin Mansfield and Lucy (Ball) O.; m. Barbara Ann Robinson, June 23, 1950; children: Michael M., Carol Owsley Moreton, Steven A. A.B., Princeton U., 1949; J.D., U. Tex., 1952. Bar: Tex. 1952. Assoc. Baker & Botts, Houston, 1952-63; ptnr. Baker & Botts, Houston, 1964—; dir. Ball Corp.; prin. mgr. Alvin & Lucy Owsley Found. Mem. centennial commn. U. Tex., Austin, 1981-83; assoc. bd. visitors M.D. Anderson Hosp. and Tumor Inst., Houston. Served with arty. AUS, 1944-46, MTO. Fellow Am. Coll. Trial Lawyers; mem. ABA, Houston Bar Assn., Soc. Mayflower Desc. Republican. Presbyterian. Clubs: Houston Country, Tejas; Inns of Court (Houston); Leland Country. Lodges: Order of St. Lazarus; Malta. Home: 65 Briar Hollow Ln Houston TX 77027 Office: Baker & Botts 3000 One Shell Plaza Houston TX 77002

OXMAN, STEPHEN ELIOT, lawyer; b. Denver, July 16, 1947; s. Irving Isadore and Marguerite Frances (Dinner) O.; m. Lynne Marie Caniff, Feb. 3, 1974 (div. 1986); children: Jennifer, Chad. BA, U. Ariz.; JD, John Marshall Law Sch. Bar: Ill. 1974, U.S. Dist. Ct. Colo. 1974. V.p. Oxman & Oxman, P.C., Denver, 1974—. Mem. ABA, Colo. Trial Lawyers Assn., Denver Bar Assn. Democrat. Jewish. State civil litigation, Family and matrimonial, General practice. Home: 658 Steele St Denver CO 80206 Office: 210 Clayton St Suite 1 Denver CO 80206

OYEWOLE, G. GODWIN, lawyer; b. Lagos, Nigeria, Apr. 23, 1942; s. Benjamin Olufayo and Mabel Olubunkunola (Shokoya) O.; m. Saundra Elaine Herndon, Mar. 21, 1970; children: AyodejiBabatunde Olusegun, Kolade Olufayo, Monisola Aramide. BA, SUNY, New Paltz, 1964; MBA, Loyola U., Chgo., 1970; PhD, U. Mass., 1972; JD, Georgetown U., 1980, LLM, 1984. Bar: D.C. 1981, Va. 1982, U.S. Ct. Appeals (4th and D.C. cirs.) 1982. Counsel Nat. Cable TV Assn., Washington, 1980-81; gen. mgr. Sta. WDCU-FM Radio, Washington, 1981-86; mng. atty. Appellate Litigation Assocs., Washington, 1981—. Editor-in-chief Georgetown U. Law Rev., 1979-80. Mem. D.C. Bar Assn., Va. State Bar, Assn. Trial Lawyers Am. Republican. Avocations: jazz, photography, African and Caribbean music. Criminal, Family and matrimonial, Securities. Home: 8206 Riverside Rd Alexandria VA 22308 Office: Appellate Litigation Assocs 450 5th St NW 9th Floor S Washington DC 20001

OYLER, GREGORY KENNETH, lawyer; b. Moses Lake, Wash., Sept. 16, 1953; s. Eugene Milton and Annetta Diane (Williams) O. AB, Princeton U., 1975; JD, Georgetown U., 1978; LLM, NYU, 1981. Bar: Pa. 1978, U.S. Tax Ct. 1978, U.S. Ct. Appeals (D.C. cir.) 1979, D.C. 1981, U.S. Supreme Ct. 1982, U.S. Ct. Claims 1983. Law clk. to judges U.S. Tax Ct., Washington, 1978-80; assoc. Hamel & Park, Washington, 1981-85, ptnr., 1985—. Mem. ABA (tax sect., legis. initiatives com.), D.C. Bar Assn. (tax sect.). Corporate taxation, Personal income taxation, State and local taxation. Office: Hamel & Park 888 16th St NW #700 Washington DC 20006

OZARK, DAMIAN MICHAEL, lawyer, consultant; b. Lackawanna, N.Y., Sept. 3, 1954; s. Norwood Wallace and Theresa Rita (Powers) O.; B.A., U. Miss., 1976; J.D., Miss. Coll., 1980. Bar: Miss. 1981, Fla. 1986. Atty. Chevron U.S.A., Inc., New Orleans, 1981-86; assoc. Conley & Cleary, Bradenton, Fla., 1986—. Precinct capt. Republican Party, New Orleans, 1984; active Rep. Nat. Com., 1984, Nat. Rep. Congl. Com., 1984. Recipient Am. Jurisprudence award, 1980. Mem. ABA, Fla. Bar Assn., Miss. Bar Assn., Am. Assn. Petroleum Landmen, Petroleum Landmen Assn. New Orleans, Denver Assn. Petroleum Landmen, Assn. Trial Lawyers Am., Am. Judicature Soc., Mid-Continent Oil and Gas Assn., Nat. Ocean Industries Assn., New Orleans Bar Assn. (assoc.). Roman Catholic. Oil and gas leasing, Environment, Real property. Home: 3820 Sun Eagle Ln Bradenton FL 33507 Office: Conley & Cleary 2401 Manatee Ave W Bradenton FL 33505

OZER, LISA GOLDBERG, lawyer; b. Kileen, Tex., Feb. 14, 1954; d. Nathaniel and Renee (Slutzky) Goldberg; m. Robert H. Ozer, May 13, 1979. BA, Tufts U., 1976; JD, U. Pa., 1979. Bar: U.S. Dist. Ct. (so. and ea. dists.) N.Y. 1980, U.S. Dist. Ct. N.J. 1985. Assoc. Kronish, Lieb, Weiner & Hellman, N.Y.C., 1979-86. Mem. Phi Beta Kappa. Federal civil litigation, State civil litigation. Home: 187 Great Hills Dr South Orange NJ 07079

OZMON, LAIRD MICHAEL, lawyer; b. Chgo., July 7, 1954; s. Nat Peter and Bette Jean (Rose) O. BA in Polit. Sci. with high honors, Lewis U., 1977; JD, Loyola U., Chgo., 1979. Bar: Ill. 1979, U.S. Dist. Ct. Ill. 1979, U.S. Ct. Appeals (7th cir.) 1979, Fla. 1980, U.S. Supreme Ct. 1983. Assoc. Anesi, Ozmon, Lewin & Assoc., Chgo., 1979-83; sole practice Joliet, Ill., 1983—. Inventor dura file. Mem. ABA, Ill. Bar Assn., Fla. Bar Assn., Chgo. Bar Assn., Assn. Trial Lawyers Am., Ill. Trial Lawyers Assn. (bd. mgrs. 1985—, legis. com.). Democrat. Avocations: skiing, weightlifting, horses. Personal injury, State civil litigation. Office: 54 N Ottawa Joliet IL 60431

OZZELLO, JAN LORRAINE, lawyer; b. Ann Arbor, Mich., May 27, 1953; d. Lawrence Moral and Patricia E. (Anderson) O.; m. John Reed Wilcox, Jan. 30, 1982. BBA, U. Wis., Eau Claire, 1974; JD, U. Wis., Madison, 1977. Bar: Wis. 1977, Mich. 1977, Minn. 1980. Assoc. Warner, Norcross & Judd, Grand Rapids, Mich., 1977-80, Doherty, Rumble & Butler, Mpls., 1980-83; tax cons. Comprehensive Tax Mgmt., Mpls., 1983-84; v.p., corp. counsel Dataserv Fin. Services, Mpls., 1984—; instr. acctg. U. Minn., Mpls., 1983-85; instr. tax Coll. St. Thomas, St. Paul, 1983. Bd. dirs. Brass Tacks Theatre, Mpls., 1981-83. Mem. ABA, Minn. Soc. Attys./CPAs (sec.), Am. Soc. Attys./CPAs, U. Wis. Eau Claire Alumni Assn. (bd. dirs. 1985—). Corporate taxation, Personal income taxation, Securities. Home: 3668 Huntington Saint Louis Park MN 55416 Office: Dataserv Fin Services 12125 Technology Dr Eden Prairie MN 55344

PABIAN, JAY MICHAEL, lawyer; b. Providence, Feb. 11, 1955; s. Harvey and Ruth Pabian; m. Audrey Hope Bigney, Feb. 1, 1979; children: Keith, Jennifer. AB, Brandeis U., 1977; JD, New Eng. Sch. Law, Boston, 1980; MS in Acctg., Northeastern U., 1981; LLM in Taxation, Boston U., 1985. Bar: Mass. 1980, R.I. 1980, U.S. Dist. Ct. Mass. 1980, U.S. Tax Ct. 1980, U.S. Ct. Appeals (1st cir.) 1980. Tax acct. Peat, Marwick & Mitchell, Providence, 1981-83; assoc. Mahoney, Hawkes & Goldings, Boston, 1983—; adj. prof. law New Eng. Sch. Law, Boston, 1980-85; lectr. Lambers Continuing Edn., Boston, 1986—. Mem. Mass. Bar Assn., Boston Bar Assn., Mass. Soc. CPA's, R.I. Bar Assn., Boston Tax Council, Boston Estate Planning Council. Avocations: golf, tennis. Estate taxation, Personal income taxation, Corporate taxation. Home: 10 Osprey Rd Sharon MA 02067 Office: Mahoney Hawkes & Goldings 1 Walnut St Boston MA 02108

PACE, O(LE) B(LY), JR., lawyer; b. Wellington, Ill., Mar. 10, 1915; s. Ole Bly and Ruth A. (Parrish) P.; m. Loey Ann Patterson, Aug. 22, 1937; children: Ole B. III, Steven P., Ann. BS, Ill. Wesleyan U., 1936; LLB, U. Ill., 1939. Bar: Ill. 1939. Asst. state's atty. Marshall County, Ill., 1946-48, 64-68, state's atty., 1948-64; asst. atty. gen. State of Ill., Springfield, 1968-72; sr. ptnr. Pace and Paolucci, Lacon, Ill., 1966-74, Pace and McCuskey, Lacon, 1977-81, Pace, McCuskey & Galley, Lacon, 1981—; bd. dirs. First Nat. Bank Lacon. Adv. bd. St. Francis of Assisi and St. Joseph Nursing Home, Lacon, 1962—, also pres.; trustee Ill. Wesleyan U., 1962-86. Served to lt. USNR, 1942-45. Mem. Am. Legion (comdr. 1946-47), Phi Delta Phi. Republican. Methodist. Lodges: Masons, Rotary (local pres. 1957-58). Personal injury, State civil litigation, Probate. Office: Pace McCuskey & Galley 414 5th St PO Box 279 Lacon IL 61540

PACE, THOMAS, lawyer; b. Teaneck, N.J., July 5, 1951; s. John James and Doris Elizabeth (Ihne) P.; m. Loren Anne Dunn, Sept. 10, 1977; children: Ashley, Ryan, Lindsay. AB with honors, U. N.C., 1973; JD, Washington and Lee U., 1976. Bar: Va. 1976, D.C. 1976, U.S. Ct. Appeals (4th and D.C. cirs.) 1976, U.S. Ct. Appeals (6th cir.) 1978, U.S. Supreme Ct. 1981, N.Y. 1986, U.S. Ct. Appeals (2d cir.) 1986. Assoc. Carr, Jordan, Coyne & Savits, Washington, 1976-79, Arent, Fox, Kintner, Plotkin & Kahn, Washington, 1979-81; communications counsel Dow Jones & Co., Inc., Princeton, N.J., 1981—; chmn. communications steering com. Dow Jones & Co., Inc., Princeton, 1986—. Editor Washington and Lee U. Law Rev., 1975-76. Mem. Am. Newspaper Pubs. Assn. (chmn. telecommunications pub. policy com. 1984—, exec. mem. telecommunications com. 1984—), Info. Industry Assn. (chmn. telecommunications com. 1985—). General corporate, Computer, Commercial law. Office: Dow Jones & Co Inc PO Box 300 Princeton NJ 08540

PACIOUS, SHAUN FRANCIS, lawyer; b. Washington, June 21, 1955; s. Edward John and Anne Theresa (Connolly) P.; m. Patricia Mary Bohlin, Oct. 1, 1983; children: Daniel, Kathleen. BA, Columbia U., 1977; JD, Georgetown U., 1980. Bar: N.Y. 1981, U.S. Dist. Ct. (so dist.) N.Y. 1981.

Assoc. Rogers & Wells, N.Y.C., 1980—. exec. editor Georgetown U. Internat. Law Jour., 1980. Mem. ABA. Roman Catholic. Avocations: skiing, gardening. Contracts commercial, General corporate, Banking. Office: Rogers & Wells 200 Park Ave New York NY 10166

PACK, STUART HARRIS, lawyer; b. N.Y.C., Nov. 2, 1950; s. Irving and Ruth (Blum) P.; m. Robin Carol Levine, Nov. 28, 1976; children: Jennifer, Allison. BA, U. Rochester, 1972; JD, Georgetown U., 1975. Bar: Colo. 1975, U.S. Dist. Ct. Colo. 1975, U.S. Ct. Appeals (10th cir.) 1985. Ptnr. Sherman & Howard, Denver, 1975—. Federal civil litigation, Insurance, Personal injury. Office: Sherman & Howard 4582 Ulster St Pkwy Suite 700 Denver CO 80237

PACKENHAM, RICHARD DANIEL, lawyer; b. Newton, Pa., June 23, 1953; s. John Richard and Mary Margaret (Maroney) P.; m. Susan Patricia Smillie, Aug. 20, 1983. BA, Harvard U., 1975; JD, Boston Coll., 1978; LLM in Taxation, Boston U., 1985. Bar: Mass. 1978, Conn. 1979, U.S. Dist. Ct. Mass. 1979, U.S. Dist. Ct. Mass. 1979, U.S. Ct. Appeals (1st cir.) 1981, U.S. Supreme Ct. 1985. Staff atty. Conn. Superior Ct., 1978-79; assoc. McGrath & Kane, Boston, 1979—. Mem. ABA, Mass. Bar Assn., Conn. Bar Assn., Boston Bar Assn., Mass CLE (faculty). Democrat. Roman Catholic. Club: Harvard (Boston). Family and matrimonial, State civil litigation. Home: 1412 High St Westwood MA 02090 Office: McGrath & Kane 4 Longfellow Place Boston MA 02114

PACKER, MARK BARRY, lawyer, financial consultant; b. Phila., Sept. 18, 1944; s. Samuel and Eve (Devine) P.; A.B. magna cum laude, Harvard U., 1965, LL.B., 1968; m. Donna Elizabeth Ferguson, July 2, 1967; children—Daniel Joshua, Benjamin Dov, David Johannes. Admitted to Wash. bar, 1969, Mass. bar, 1971; assoc. Ziontz, Pirtle & Fulle, Seattle, 1968-70; ptnr. Millhouse Nelle & Packer, Bellingham, Wash., 1972-82, sole practice, Bellingham, 1982—; bd. dirs., corp. sec. No. Sales Co., Inc. Mem. Bellingham Planning and Devel. Commn., 1975-84, chmn., 1977-81, mem. shoreline subcom., 1976-82; pres. Congregation Beth Israel, Bellingham, 1980-82, chmn. rabbi search com., 1986-87; mem. Bellingham Mcpl. Arts Commn., 1986—, landmark rev. bd., 1987—; treas. World Affairs Council N.W. Wash., 1985—; chmn. Bellingham campaign United Jewish Appeal, 1979—. Mem. ABA (sec. urban, state and local govt. law, commn. land use, planning and zoning, sec. real property probate and trust), Wash. State Bar Assn. (sec. environ. and land use law). Republican. Contracts commercial, Real property, Environment. Home: 208 S Forest St Bellingham WA 98225 Office: 1501 Eldridge Ave Bellingham WA 98225

PADDOCK, HAROLD DEWOLF, lawyer; b. Cleve., July 20, 1948; s. Harold Dewolfe Jr. and Marge Alice (Stoneman) P.; m. Barbara Ann Jackson, Mar. 12, 1983; 1 child, David M.D. BBA cum laude, Ohio State U., 1970, JD, 1973. Bar: Ohio 1973, U.S. Dist. Ct. (so. dist.) Ohio 1973, U.S. Supreme Ct. 1977. Referee Franklin County Common Pleas Ct., Columbus, Ohio, 1973-75, 1978-83, chief referee, 1983—; assoc. Wolske & Blue, Columbus, 1975-78; co-devel. and proponent Nat. Settlement Week. Recipient Outstanding Public Employee award Ohio Acad. Trial Lawyers, 1987. Fellow Columbus Bar Found.; mem. ABA, Ohio State Bar Assn., Columbus Bar Assn. (chmn. alternative dispute resolution com. 1984-86, award of merit 1987). Club: Columbus Ski (pres. 1979-81). Avocations: skiing, photography, soccer, softball, jogging. State civil litigation, Judicial administration, Alternative dispute resolution. Office: Franklin County Common Pleas Ct 369 S High St Columbus OH 43215

PADEN, GARY LEWIS, lawyer; b. Wasco, Calif., July 30, 1951; s. Aubrey Lewis and Nedra Maxine (Brown) P.; m. Melinda Reed, Sept. 28, 1982 (div. Jan. 1987). BS, Calif. State U., Fresno, 1973; JD, U. San Diego, 1976; Cert. career prosecutor, U. Houston, 1979. Bar: Calif. 1976. Dep. dist. atty. Tulare County, Visalia, Calif., 1977-79; assoc. Kahn & Soares, Hanford, Calif., 1979-80; sole practice Visalia, 1980-83; ptnr. Simonian, Kalashian & Paden, Visalia, 1984-86, Kalashian & Paden, Visalia, 1986—. Mem. Tulare County Bar Assn., Kings County Bar Assn. (v.p. 1984-85), Calif. Trial Lawyers Assn., Tulare County Trial Lawyers Assn. Republican. Avocations: skin diving, golfing, fishing. Criminal, Personal injury, State civil litigation. Home: 248 N Crenshaw Visalia CA 93291 Office: Kalashian & Paden 225 W Oak Visalia CA 93291

PADEN, LYMAN RUSHTON, lawyer; b. Oklahoma City, Jan. 10, 1954; s. Lyman C. and Wyatt (Rushton) P. BA, Rice U., 1976, M in Acctg., 1977; JD, Stanford U., 1980. Bar: Tex. 1980. Assoc. Liddell, Sapp, Zivley & La Boon, Houston, 1980-85; ptnr. Liddell, Sapp, & Zivley, Houston, 1986—. Articles editor Stanford Law Rev., 1979-80. Mem. ABA. Episcopalian. Clubs: Houston, Texas. Avocation: gardening. Banking, General corporate. Home: 3608 Mulberry Houston TX 77006 Office: Liddell Sapp & Zivley Tex Commerce Tower Houston TX 77002

PADGETT, FRANK DAVID, associate supreme court justice; b. Vincennes, Ind., Mar. 9, 1923. B.A., Harvard U., LL.B., 1948. Bar: Hawaii 1949, U.S. Supreme Ct. 1967. Sole practice Honolulu, 1949-82; propr. Frank D. Padgett law Corp., 1975-82; ptnr. firm Padgett & Rost, Wailuku, Maui, 1975-82; assoc. justice Hawaii Surpeme Ct., Honolulu, 1982—. Mem. ABA, Hawaii Bar Assn., Assn. Trial Lawyers Am., Am. Judicature Soc. (dir. 1977-79). Office: Hawaii Supreme Ct 417 S King St Honolulu HI 96813

PADGETT, GEORGE ARTHUR, lawyer; b. N.Y.C., Feb. 17, 1932; s. Arthur Samuel and Marion Louise (Schramm) P.; m. Ann M. Padgett; children—Ann Linton, James Dunbar. A.B., Hamilton Coll., 1954; LL.B., Georgetown U., 1960. Bar: N.J. 1961, D.C. 1960. Atty. firm Covington & Burling, Washington, 1959-60, Pitney, Hardin & Kipp, Newark, 1961-65; asst. sec., corp. counsel Lionel Corp., N.Y.C., 1965-70; sec., corp. counsel Lionel Corp., 1970-82, sr. v.p., counsel, sec., dir., 1983—; dir. Lionel Leisure, Inc., Phila. Served with U.S. Army, 1954-57. Mem. ABA, N.J. Bar Assn., Am. Soc. Corp. Secs. General corporate. Office: Lionel Corp 441 Lexington Ave New York NY 10017

PADILLA, GERALD VINCENT, lawyer; b. Detroit, July 6, 1949; s. David Joseph and Irene Cecelia (Clos) P.; m. Suzanne Milton, Aug. 30, 1975; children: Rebecca, Michael, Julie. BA in Math., U. Detroit, 1971, JD, 1974. Bar: Mich. 1975, U.S. Dist. Ct. (ea. and we. dists.) Mich. 1975. Asst. atty. gen. Mich. Atty. Gen.'s Office, Lansing, 1975-78; assoc. McCauley & Halpin, Detroit, 1978-80, Plunkett & Cooney, Detroit, 1980-81; ptnr. Siemion, Huckabay & Bodary, Detroit, 1981—. Bd. dirs. Wayne County Neighborhood Legal Services, Detroit, 1985-86. Mem. ABA, Mich. Bar Assn., Detroit Bar Assn., Mackinac Island Horseman's Assn. (bd. dirs. 1983—). Avocations: sailing, flying. Personal injury, Insurance. Office: Siemion Huckabay Bodary Padilla & Morganti 1700 Penobscot Detroit MI 48226

PADILLA, JAMES EARL, lawyer; b. Miami, Dec. 28, 1953; s. Earl George and Patricia (Bauer) P. BA, Northwestern U., 1975; JD, Duke U., 1978. Bar: Ill. 1978, U.S. Ct. Appeals (5th and 7th cirs.) 1978, U.S. Supreme Ct. 1981, Colo. 1982, U.S. Ct. Appeals (10th cir.), D.C. 1985. Assoc. Mayer, Brown & Platt, Chgo. and Denver, 1978-84; ptnr. Mayer, Brown & Platt, Denver, 1985—. Contbg. author: Mineral Financing, 1982. Mem. ABA, Ill. Bar Assn., D.C. Bar Assn., Colo. Bar Assn., Denver Bar Assn. Club: Denver Athletic. Avocation: golf. Banking, Bankruptcy, Contracts commercial. Office: Mayer Brown & Platt 600 17th St Suite 2800S Denver CO 80202

PAGANO, JAMES LAWRENCE, lawyer; b. San Mateo, Calif., July 22, 1955; s. Michelangelo and Patricia E. (Quinlan) P. BA, George Washington U., 1977; JD, U. Santa Clara, 1980. Bar: Calif. 1981, U.S. Dist. Ct. (no. dist.) Calif. 1981, U.S. Dist. Ct. (ea. dist.) Calif. 1984, U.S. Dist. Ct. (cen. dist.) Calif. 1985. Assoc. Campbell, Warburton, Britton, Fitzsimmons & Smith, San Jose, Calif., 1981-86, ptnr., 1986—; jud. arbitrator Santa Clara Ct., 1985—; lectr.moot trial competition Calif. State Bar, Los Angeles, 1985—. Mem. ABA, Santa Clara County Bar Assn. (fee dispute arbitrator 1984—), Assn. Trial Lawyers Am., CAlif. Trial Lawyers Assn. Democrat. Roman Catholic. Avocations: sports, politics. State civil litigation, Real property, General corporate. Office: Campbell Warburton Britton et al 101 Park Ctr Plaza Suite 1200 San Jose CA 95113

PAGANUZZI, ODEN STEPHEN, JR., lawyer; b. Mt. Vernon, N.Y., June 26, 1955; s. Oden S. and Carol E. (Egan) P.; m. Anne Alexis Murges, Nov. 2, 1984. BA, NYU, 1976, JD, 1979. Bar: N.Y. 1980, U.S. Dist. Ct. (so. and ea. dists.) 1980, U.S. Ct. Appeals (2d cir.) 1985, U.S. Supreme Ct. 1985. Assoc. Markfield & Solomon, N.Y.C., 1980-85; ptnr. Markfield, Solomon & Paganuzzi, N.Y.C., 1985—. Mem. ABA, N.Y. State Bar Assn., Nat. Lawyers Guild, N.Y. State Trial Lawyers Assn., Westchester Bar Assn., Assn. of Bar of City of N.Y. Family and matrimonial, Personal injury, Probate. Office: Markfield Solomon & Paganuzzi 158 E 35th St New York NY 10016

PAGE, ALAN CEDRIC, lawyer; b. Canton, Ohio, Aug. 7, 1945; s. Howard F. and Georgianna (Umbles) P.; m. Diane Sims, June 5, 1973; children: Nina, Georgianna, Justin, Khamsin. BA, U. Notre Dame, 1967; JD, U. Minn., 1978. Bar: Minn. 1979, U.S. Dist. Ct. Minn. 1979. Profl. athlete Minn. Vikings, Mpls., 1967-78, Chgo. Bears, 1978-81; assoc. Lindquist & Vennum, Mpls., 1979-85; atty. Minn. Atty. Gen.'s Office, Mpls., 1985—; cons. NFL Players Assn., Washington, 1979-84. Commentator Nat. Pub. Radio, 1982-83. Named NFL's Most Valuable Player, 1971, one of 10 Outstanding Young Men Am., U.S. Jaycees, 1981. Mem. ABA, Minn. Bar Assn., Hennepin County Bar Assn., Minn. Minority Lawyers Assn. Mem. Democratic Farm Labor Party. Avocations: running, biking. Office: Atty Gen's Office 520 Lafayette Rd Saint Paul MN 55155

PAGE, ALFRED EMIL, JR., lawyer; b. N.Y.C., Dec. 28, 1938; s. Alfred Emil and Lillian Marie (Fay) P.; m. Marie Genetta Patane, Sept. 16, 1967; children: Michael, Kenneth, Lianne, Evan. BS in Chemistry, Rensselaer Poly. Inst., 1963; JD cum laude, NYU, 1974. Bar: N.Y. 1975, U.S. Dist. Ct. (so. and ea. dists.) N.Y. 1975, U.S. Ct. Appeals (2d cir.) 1975, U.S. Patent Office 1978, U.S. Supreme Ct. 1980. Analytical research chemist Ciba-Geigy Corp., Ardsley, N.Y., 1963-74; sr. law clk. to judge U.S. Dist. Ct. (so. dist.) N.Y., N.Y.C., 1974-76; assoc. Stephens & Buderwitz, White Plains, N.Y., 1976-81; ptnr. J. Russell Clune P.C., Harrison, N.Y., 1981—; v.p., bd. dirs. High Meadow Coop. Inc., Ossining, N.Y., 1976-81; sec., bd. dirs.B.S.R. (U.S.A.) Ltd., Bardonia, N.Y., 1983. Served to sgt. USMC, 1963-70. Mem. ABA, N.Y. State Bar Assn., Westchester County Bar Assn., Assn. Trial Lawyers Am., Pi Kappa Alpha. Republican. Roman Catholic. Federal civil litigation, State civil litigation, Insurance. Home: 1369 Baldwin Rd Yorktown Heights NY 10598 Office: J Russell Clune PC 480 Mamaroneck Ave Harrison NY 10528

PAGE, CLEMSON NORTH, JR., lawyer; b. Bossier City, La., June 18, 1945; s. Clemson North and Nancy Jean (Strelinger) P.; m. Hollace Esleton Triller, Aug. 29, 1970; children: Janet North, Lindsay Coleman. AB in English Lit., Dartmouth Coll., 1967; JD, Villanova Law Sch., 1977. Bar: Pa. 1977, U.S. Dist. Ct. (ea. dist.) Pa. 1981. Reporter, editor Phila. Bulletin, 1969-74; assoc. Bingaman, Hess, Coblentz & Bell, Reading, Pa., 1977-81, ptnr., 1981—. Vice chmn. Borough Planning Commn., West Reading, 1980-82; mem. Borough Zoning Hearing Bd., Wyomissing Hills, Pa. 1986—; chmn. St. Andrew's Soc. of Phila. Served as lt. USNR. Mem. ABA, Pa. Bar Assn., Berks County Bar Assn. (chmn. profl. edn. com. 1982, chmn. pub. relation com. 1986), Endlich Law Club. Republican. Episcopalian. Club: Wyomissing (Reading). Banking, Consumer commercial, General corporate. Home: 42 Wyomissing Hills Blvd Wyomissing Hills PA 19609 Office: Bingaman Hess Coblentz & Bell 601 Penn St PO Box 61 Reading PA 19603

PAGE, JACK RANDALL, lawyer; b. Waco, Tex., Aug. 1, 1956; s. Jack Bennett and Mary Elizabeth (Cobbs) P.; m. Shirley Jean Hull, Aug. 5, 1978; 1 child, Anna Christine. BBA magna cum laude, Baylor U., 1977, JD, 1980. Bar: Tex. 1980, U.S. Tax Ct. 1985; CPA, Tex. Acct. Allie B. Gates Jr., CPA, Waco, 1975-78; assoc. Pakis, Cherry, Beard & Giotes, Inc., Waco, 1980-86, ptnr., 1986—. Chmn. exploring sales team Heart O'Tex. council Boy Scouts Am., 1983, dist. chmn., 1984-85, v.p., 1986. Recipient Exploring Tng. award, Dist. award of Merit, Heart O'Tex. council Boy Scouts Am., 1985. Mem. ABA, Tex. Bar Assn., Waco-McLennan County Bar Assn., Tex. Young Lawyers Assn., Waco-McLennan County Young Lawyers Assn., Am. Inst. CPA's, Tex. Soc. CPA'S (cen. Tex. chpt.), Tex. Bd. Legal Specialization (cert. tax law 1985). Roman Catholic. Lodge: Order of Demolay (Chevalier 1975). Avocations: hiking, hunting, outdoor activities. Corporate taxation, Personal income taxation, Pension, profit-sharing, and employee benefits. Office: Pakis Cherry Beard & Giotes Inc 800 MBank Tower Waco TX 76701

PAGE, JAMES WILSON, lawyer; b. Pinehurst, N.C., Nov. 2, 1940; s. James Wilson Pierce and Christine (McIntosh) Page; m. Sarah Kathryn Page, Sept. 28, 1968; children: Locke Page, Alexander Page. BS in Indsl. Relations, U. N.C., 1965; JD, Wake Forest U., 1975. Bar: N.C. 1975, U.S. Tax Ct. 1979. Bank examiner Fed. Reserve Bank of Richmond, Va., 1965-67; asst. trust officer Kanawha Valley Bank, Charleston, W.Va., 1967-69; trust officer Wachovia Bank & Trust Co., Winston-Salem, N.C., 1969-72, v.p., 1980-82; v.p. Booke and Co., Winston-Salem, 1975-77; prin. Greeson and Page, P.A., Winston-Salem, 1977-80, 83—. Mem. Winston-Salem Estate Planning Council, 1983—; panel mem. Council for Older Adults, Winston-Salem, 1983—; pres. Penland (N.C.) Sch. of Crafts, 1981-85, trustee, 1981—; v.p. The Crescent Rev., Winston-Salem, 1984-85; bd. dirs. The Jargon Soc., Winston-Salem, 1977-84; legal officer Winston-Salem Power Squadron, 1986—, asst. sec., 1986—. Recipient award for estate planning Am. Jurisprudence, 1975. Mem. ABA, N.C. Bar Assn. (legal services planning com. 1986—), Forsyth County Bar Assn. (chmn. pro bono com. 1985—), N.C. Coll. Advocacy. Republican. Episcopalian. Avocations: hiking, boating, home renovation. Probate, General corporate, Pension, profit-sharing, and employee benefits. Home: 879 Brookleigh Ct Winston-Salem NC 27104 Office: 522 NCNB Plaza Winston-Salem NC 27101

PAGE, LEONARD RONALD, lawyer; b. Dearborn, Mich., Mar. 15, 1944; s. Clyde Harold and Lillian Mary (Fenlon) P.; m. Susan Mary Joseph, May 1, 1965; children: Joseph L., Katherine E. BBA, U. Mich., 1965, MBA, 1968; JD, Detroit Coll. of Law, 1972. Bar: Mich. 1972. Indsl. relations trainee Ford Motor Co., Dearborn, 1968-70; asst. gen. counsel UAW, Detroit, 1970-75, assoc. gen. counsel., 1975—. Mem. ABA (co-chmn. com. on practice and procedure under Nat. Labor Relations Act1986—), Mich. Bar Assn. (chmn. labor law sect. 1984-85). Democrat. Roman Catholic. Avocations: fishing, hunting, sailing, softball. Labor, Pension, profit-sharing, and employee benefits. Home: 1362 Yorkshire Grosse Pointe Park MI 48230

PAGE, LEWIS WENDELL, JR., lawyer; b. Scottsboro, Ala., Nov. 6, 1947; s. Lewis Wendell and Maymie Elizabeth (Parks) P.; m. Dollie Lucretia Roberts, Dec. 24, 1977; children—Margaret Amelia, Katherine Elizabeth. B.A., Auburn U., 1970; J.D., U. Ala., 1973; LL.M., George Washington U., 1975. Bar: Ala. 1973, U.S. Dist. Ct. (no. dist.) Ala. 1974, U.S. Ct. Appeals (5th cir.) 1973, U.S. Ct. Appeals (11th cir.) 1978, U.S. Supreme Ct. 1982. Assoc. firm Sadler, Sadler, Sullivan & Sharp, Birmingham, Ala., 1973-74; assoc. firm Lange, Simpson, Robinson & Somerville, Birmingham, 1975-80, ptnr., 1980—. Served to 2d lt. U.S. Army, 1973. Mem. Ala. State Bar Assn. (chmn. antitrust sect. 1983-84, co-chmn. permanent code commn. 1986-87), Birmingham Bar Assn. (panel chmn. grievance com. 1983-84, chmn. fee arbitration com. 1984-85), ABA (antitrust sect., litigation sect., patent, copyright and trademark sect.), Tau Kappa Epsilon (sec.-treas. 1980-86). Antitrust, Banking, Federal civil litigation. Home: 3905 Jackson Blvd Mountain Brook AL 35213 Office: Lange Simpson Robinson & Somerville 1700 First Ala Bank Bldg Birmingham AL 35203

PAGLIACCETTI, GARY JOHN, lawyer; b. St. Cloud, Minn., Oct. 3, 1954; s. John Joseph and Loretta Patricia (Morelli) P.; m. Mary Ann S. Lanari, Aug. 6, 1977; children: AnnaMarie, Nicole. BA, St. John's U., 1976; JD, Hamline U., 1979. Bar: Minn. 1979, U.S. Dist. Ct. Minn. 1980, U.S. Ct. Appeals (8th cir.) 1980. Asst. atty. St. Louis County, Virginia, Minn., 1980-83; assoc. Cope & Peterson, P.A., Virginia, 1983—. Bd. dirs. Iron Range Rehab. Ctr., Virginia, 1984—, Mt. Iron (Minn.) Area Devel. Assn., 1985. Mem. ABA, Minn. Bar Assn., Minn. Def. Lawyers Assn., Assn. Ins. Attys., Virginia C. of C. (ambassador 1985). Roman Catholic. Club: Virginia Italian/Am. Lodge: Kiwanis. State civil litigation, Insurance, Local government. Office: Cope & Peterson PA 415 S 1st St Virginia MN 55792

PAGLIERANI, RONALD JOSEPH, lawyer; b. Cambridge, Mass., Jan. 27, 1947; s. Joseph and Irene (Woronicz) P.; m. Patricia Ann Sullivan, June 14, 1969; children: Paul J., Stacy E., Claire L. BS in Physics, Boston Coll., 1967; MS in Physics, Northeastern U., 1975; JD, Suffolk U., 1979. Bar: Mass. 1979, U.S. Dist. Ct. Mass. 1980. Assoc. Kenway and Jenney, Boston, 1979-80; patent atty. The Foxboro (Mass.) Co., 1980-83, patent counsel, 1983-84; patent counsel Prime Computer, Inc., Natick, Mass., 1984—. Served to lt. USNR, 1968-71. Mem. Boston Patent Law Assn. (bd. govs. 1985—), Am. Intellectual Property Law Assn., Assn. Corp. Patent Counsel. Roman Catholic. Lodge: KC. Avocations: playing piano, reading, jogging. Patent, Trademark and copyright, Computer. Home: 4 Acorn St Scituate MA 02066 Office: Prime Computer Inc Prime Park Natick MA 02066

PAGNI, ALBERT FRANK, lawyer; b. Reno, Jan. 28, 1935; s. Bruno and Daisy Rose (Recami) P.; m. Nancy Lynne Thomas, Aug. 12, 1961; children: Elisa, Michelle, Melissa, Michael. AB, U. Nev., 1961; JD, U. Calif.-Hastings Coll. Law, 1964. Bar: Nev. 1964. Assoc. Vargas, Dillon, Bartlett & Dixon, Reno, 1965-70; ptnr. Vargas & Bartlett and predecessor firms, Reno, 1970—. Mem. adminstrv. council U. Nev., 1974-81; treas. U. Nev. Legis. Commn., 1973-74, pres., 1975. Served with U.S. Army, 1955-57. Recipient Outstanding Alumni award U. Nev., 1978. Mem. ABA, Washoe County Bar Assn., Nev. Trial Lawyers Assn., Assn. Trial Lawyers Am., Def. Research Inst., Assn. Def. Counsel Calif. and Nev. (no. state chmn. 1983-85), Am. Judicature Assn., State Bar Nev. (bd. govs. 1976—, v.p. 1984-85, pres. elect 1985-86, pres. 1986-87), Order of Coif. Clubs: Wolf, Elks (Reno). State civil litigation, Personal injury, Insurance. Office: 201 W Liberty St Suite 300 PO Box 281 Reno NV 89504

PAHL, STEPHEN DONALD, lawyer; b. Los Angeles, July 23, 1956; s. Donald Alfred and Verlene Virginia Pahl; m. Louise A. Dodd, Feb. 10, 1978. BA cum laude, U. Calif., Santa Barbara, 1977; JD, U. Santa Clara, 1980. Bar: Calif. 1981, U.S. Dist. Ct. (no. and ea. dists.) Calif. 1981, U.S. Ct. Appeals (9th cir.) 1981, U.S. Dist. Ct. (cen. dist.) Calif. 1986. Research atty. Santa Clara County Superior Ct., San Jose, Calif., 1980-81; assoc. Littler, Mendelson, Fastiff & Tichy, San Jose, 1981-82; ptnr. Tarkington, O'Connor & O'Neill, San Jose, 1982—; vice chmn. adv. bd. dirs. Nat. InterCity Bank, Santa Clara, Calif., 1983—. Republican. Baptist. Avocations: pvt. pilot, golf, skiing. Real property, Labor, Contracts commercial. Home: 945 Plaza Dr San Jose CA 95125 Office: Tarkington O'Connor & O'Neill 1611 The Alameda San Jose CA 95126

PAIGE, DAVID ALWIN, lawyer; b. Cambridge, Mass., Dec. 8, 1947; s. Raymond Arthur and Elizabeth (Peterson) P.; m. Mary Jeanne Ronan, July 9, 1976; children: Charles, Maureen, Nicholas. BA in English, Ariz. State U., 1970; JD, U. Ariz., 1975. Bar: Ariz. 1975, U.S. Dist. Ct. Ariz. 1976, U.S. Ct. Appeals (9th cir.) 1983, U.S. Supreme Ct. 1986. Assoc. litigation dept. Bilby & Shoenhair, P.C., Tucson, 1975-79, ptnr. litigation dept., 1980—. Lay adv. Diocese of Tucson, 1977—. Served with USMC, 1966-68. Mem. ABA, Ariz. Bar Assn. (chmn. conv. 1981, disciplinary commn. 1982—), Pima County Bar Assn., Def. Research Inst., Nat. Assn. R.R. Trial Counsel, Am. Bd. Trial Advs. (assoc. 1981—), Tucson Def. Assn. Democrat. Roman Catholic. Club: Old Pueblo (Tucson). State civil litigation, Federal civil litigation, Insurance. Office: Bilby & Shoenhair PC PO Box 871 Tucson AZ 85702

PAINE, JAMES CARRIGER, judge; b. Valdosta, Ga., May 20, 1924; s. Leon Alexander and Josie Carriger (Jones) P.; m. Ruth Ellen Bailey, Sept. 8, 1950; children: James Carriger, Jonathan Jones, JoEllen. B.S., Columbia U., 1947; LL.B., U. Va., 1950, J.D., 1970. Bar: Fla. 1950. Mem. firm Earnest, Lewis, Smith & Jones, West Palm Beach, Fla., 1950-54, Jones Adams Paine & Foster, 1954-60, Jones Paine & Foster, 1960-79; U.S. dist. judge West Palm Beach, 1979—. Bd. dirs., pres. Children's Home Soc. Fla., 1978-80; mem. bd. Episcopal Diocese S.E. Fla. Served to lt. USNR, 1943-47. Mem. Greater West Palm Beach C. of C. (pres. 1973-74), ABA, Fla. Bar Assn., Palm Beach County Bar Assn. Democrat. Club: Lake Toxaway Country. Jurisprudence. Office: 701 Clematis St West Palm Beach FL 33401

PAINTER, CONRAD LEE, law librarian; b. Kalamazoo, May 11, 1950; s. Joseph W. and Lillian A. (Blankenship) P. BA, Wayne State U., 1972; MLS, Sam Houston State U., 1975. Librarian Fla. Dept. Corrections, Homestead, 1975-77, supr. edn., 1977-80; law librarian Dade County, Fla., 1980-83, Thomson, Zeder, Bohrer, Werth & Razook, Miami, Fla., 1983—. Mem. South Fla. Law Library Assn. (pres. 1977-78). Democrat. Librarianship. Office: Thomson Zeder Bohrer et al 4900 Southeast Fin Ctr 200 S Biscayne Blvd Miami FL 33131

PAINTER, JAMES MORGAN, lawyer; b. Huntington, W.Va., Aug. 29, 1952; s. Frederick and Rosalie (Farrow) P.; m. Elizabeth Ann Griffitts, Aug. 19, 1974 (div. 1985); children—Emily Ann, Kathryn Farrow, B.B.A., cum laude, Marshall U., 1976; postgrad. U. Southampton, Eng., 1977-78; J.D., Nova U., 1980. Law clk. to Levy, Plisco, Perry, Shapiro, Kneen & Kindcade, Palm Beach, Fla., 1978-80; assoc. Levy, Shapiro, Kneen & Kingcade, 1980-81, Marchbanks, Bell & Eisen, Boca Raton, Fla., 1981-82, Marchbanks & Eisen, 1982-83; sole practice, Boca Raton, 1983—. Dir. Boca Raton-Delray Beach chpt. Am. Diabetes Assn., 1985. Rotary Internat. fellow, 1977-78. Mem. Fla. Bar Assn., ABA, Palm Beach County Bar Assn., South Palm Beach County Bar Assn., Acad. Trial Lawyers, Nat. Attys. Title Ins. Fund, Attys. Title Ins. Fund. Republican. Presbyterian. Avocations: camping, cabinetry, photography, skiing. State civil litigation, General corporate, Real property. Home: 1100 SW 4th Ave Delray Beach FL 33444

PAINTER, JOHN WOODWARD, lawyer; b. Chgo., June 13, 1953; s. John William and Dorothy (Woodward) P.; m. Donna Biddle, Oct., 1983. BS, Ind. U., 1975; JD, U. Va., 1978. Bar: Ill. 1978, U.S. Dist. Ct. (no. dist.) Ill. 1978. Assoc. Winston & Strawn, Chgo., 1978-86; asst. gen. counsel Farley Industries, Inc., Chgo., 1986-87; sr. counsel, asst. sec. Chgo. Pacific Corp., Chgo., 1987—. General corporate. Home: 871 Burr Ave Winnetka IL 60093 Office: Chgo Pacific Corp 200 S Michigan Ave Chicago IL 60604

PAINTER, MARK PHILIP, judge; b. Cin., Apr. 6, 1947; s. John Philip and Marjorie (West) P.; m. Sue Brunsman Painter. B.A., U. Cin., 1970; J.D., 1973. Bar: Ohio 1973, U.S. Dist. Ct. (so. dist.) Ohio 1973, U.S. Supreme Ct. 1980. Sole practice, Cin., 1973-82; judge Hamilton County Mcpl. Ct., Cin., 1982—. Contbr. articles to profl. jours. Bd. dirs. Citizens Sch. Com., Cin., 1974-76; trustee Freestore Foodbank, Cin., 1984—, Mary Jo Brueggeman Meml. Found., Cin., 1981—; mem. Republican Central Com., Cin., 1972-82. Recipient Superior Jud. Service award Ohio Supreme Ct., 1982, 84, 85. Mem. ABA, Ohio State Bar Assn., Cin. Bar Assn., Am. Judges Assn., Am. Judicature Soc. Club: Bankers (Cin.). Jurisprudence, Judicial administration, Criminal. Home: 2449 Fairview Ave Cincinnati OH 45219 Office: Hamilton County Mcpl Ct 222 E Central Pkwy Cincinnati OH 45202

PAINTER, SAMUEL FRANKLIN, lawyer; b. Lynchburg, Va., Oct. 31, 1946; s. Simon Marcellus and Laura Francis (Lackey) P.; m. Brenda Irene Bogan, Dec. 23, 1972; children: Laura Marcella, Samuel Bogan. BA, U. Va., 1969; JD, Washington and Lee U., 1972. Bar: S.C. 1972, U.S. Dist. Ct. S.C. 1973, U.S. Ct. Appeals (4th cir.) 1974, U.S. Supreme Ct. 1982. Atty Nexsen Pruet Jacobs & Pollard, Columbia, S.C., 1972—; legal advisor S.C. Self-Insurers Assn., Columbia, 1976—. Mem. S.C. Def. Trial Lawyers Assn. Workers' compensation, Insurance. Office: Nexsen Pruet Jacobs & Pollard PO Drawer 2426 Columbia SC 29202

PAINTER, WILLIAM STEENE, lawyer; b. Jackson, Miss., Feb. 28, 1949; s. Lawrence Gilpin and Elizabeth (Steene) P.; m. Patsy Reifers, Nov. 26, 1971; 1 child, Mary Elizabeth. BA, Vanderbilt U., 1971; JD, U. Miss., 1974; LLM in Taxation, NYU, 1975. Bar: Miss. 1974. Ptnr. Gerald, Brand, Watters, Cox & Hemleben, Jackson, 1974-84, Watkins, Ludlam & Stennis, Jackson, 1984—. Author: Mississippi Corporations-Formation and Operation, 1984. Chmn. Miss. Bus. Law Reform Task Force, 1986-87; chmn. bd. of trustees Miss. Mus. of Art, Jackson, 1986-87; bd. dirs. Miss. Law Jour., Inc., Oxford, 1986—; bd. dirs., treas. Miss. Law Jour. Assn., Oxford, 1978—; pres., bd. dirs. Arts Alliance of Jackson/Hinds County, 1984. Mem. ABA (taxation sect., closely held corps. com.), Miss. Bar Assn. Episcopalian. Corporate taxation, General corporate, Estate planning. Office: Watkins Ludlam & Stennis PO Box 427 Jackson MS 39205

PAINTIN, FRANCIS ARTHUR, lawyer; b. Cleve., Feb. 9, 1929; s. Francis Walter and Muriel Alene (Wheeler) P.; m. Carol Margaret Wagner, Jan. 27, 1951; children: David Roderick, Stewart Charles. BS in Chem. Eng., Case Western Res. U., 1951; JD, George Washington U., 1961. Bar: Ohio 1961, D.C. 1962, U.S. Supreme Ct. 1967, Del. 1969, U.S. Ct. Appeals (D.C., 3d and Fed. cirs.). Assoc. Oberlin, Maky & Donnelly, Cleve., 1961-62; atty. patent div. E.I. du Pont de Nemours & Co., Wilmington, Del., 1962—; adj. prof. Del. Law Sch. Widener U., Wilmington, 1975—. Chmn. Del. Harness Racing Commn., 1977—. Served to lt. USCG, 1954-57. Mem. ABA, Del. Bar Assn., Am. Patent Law Assn., Del. Patent Law Assn., ITC Trial Lawyers Assn. (exec. com. 1985—), Order of Coif. Republican. Club: Rodney Sq. (Wilmington). Patent, International trade commission practice. Home: 101 E Pembrey Dr Wilmington DE 19803 Office: EI du Pont de Nemours & Co Legal Dept Wilmington DE 19898

PAINTON, RUSSELL ELLIOTT, lawyer, mechanical engineer; b. Port Arthur, Tex., Dec. 5, 1940; s. Clifford Elliott and Edith Virginia (McCutheon) P.; m. Elizabeth Ann Mullins, Aug. 13, 1969 (div. Dec. 1977); 1 child, Todd Elliott; m. Mary Lynn Weber, May 5, 1981. B.S. in Mech. Engring., U. Tex.-Austin, 1963, J.D., 1972. Bar: Tex. 1972; registered profl. engr., Tex. Engr. Gulf States Utilities, Beaumont, Tex., 1963-66; engr. Tracor, Inc., Austin, 1966-70, corp. counsel, 1973-83, v.p., gen. counsel, 1983—; assoc. firm Brown, Maroney, Rose, Baker & Barber, Austin, 1972, Childs, Fortenbach, Beck and Guyton, Houston, 1972-73. Bd. dirs. ARC, 1976-78, 85—, 2d vice chmn. 1978-80, 1st vice chmn., 1980-82, other offices; gen. counsel Paramount Theatre for Performing Arts, 1977-83; mem. adv. bd. Austin Transp., 1985—,Austin Sci. Acad., 1985—; chmn. Austin council Am. Electronics Assn., 1985-87. Named Boss of Yr., Austin Legal Secs. Assn., 1979-80, one of Outstanding Young Men Am., 1975. Mem. ABA, Tex. Bar Assn. (governing council 1979-80, vice chmn., treas. corp. counsel sect. 1982-83), Travis County Bar Assn., Nat. Chamber Litigation Ctr. , Better Bus. Bur. (arbitrator 1983—), Delta Theta Phi. Republican. Episcopalian. Club: Austin Yacht (race comdr. 1968-69, treas. 1970-71, 87—, sec. 1972-73, 75-76, vice commodore 1980-81, commodore 1981-82, fleet commander 1985-86). Lodge: Internat. Order Blue Gavel. General corporate, Securities, Contracts commercial. Home: 8804 Mountain Ridge Dr Austin TX 78759 Office: Tracor Inc 6500 Tracor Ln Austin TX 78725

PAIRO, PRESTON ABERCROMBIE, JR., lawyer; b. Balt., June 5, 1927; s. Preston Abercrombie and Blossom Winona (Pritchett) P.; m. Carol May Rupprecht, Aug. 12, 1950; 1 child, Preston Abercrombie III. A.A., U. Balt., 1948, J.D., 1951. Bar: Md. 1951. Legal investigator Office of City Solicitor, Balt., 1947-50; mem. Md. Ho. of Dels., 1950-54; asst. states atty. State of Md., Balt., 1954-58; atty. Liquor Bd., City of Balt., 1958-60, Savs. and loan atty., 1960—. Mem. Md. Criminal Def. Bar (bd. dirs.), Assn. Trial Lawyers Am., Md. Bar Assn., Howard County Bar Assn. (chmn. Howard County bench—bar liaison). Democrat. Episcopalian. Club: Ellicott City Optimists (pres. 1968). Lodges: Ben Franklin, Masons, Shriners, Jesters. General practice, Real property. Home: 9032 Overhill Dr Ellicott City MD 21043 Office: Pairo & Pairo 9050 A Frederick Rd Ellicott City MD 21043

PAJDA, THOMAS ALBIN, lawyer; b. East St. Louis, Ill., Apr. 15, 1958; s. Albin Frank and Jane Theresa (Lata) P.; m. Cecilia Eileen Kurtz, Sept. 21, 1985. BA summa cum laude, St. Mary's U., 1979; JD cum laude, So. Ill. U., 1982. Bar: Ill. 1982, Mo. 1983, U.S. Dist. Ct. (so. dist.) Ill. 1982. Asst. state's atty. St. Clair County, Ill., 1982-83; clk. Supreme Ct. Ill., Belleville, 1983-84; atty., asst. sec. Southwestern Bell Telecom, St. Louis, 1984—; part-time faculty Belleville Area Coll., 1983. Named one of Outstanding Young Men in Am. 1981, 83. Mem. ABA, Ill. Bar Assn., Mo. Bar Assn., Bar Assn. Met. St. Louis, St. Clair County Bar Assn. Roman Catholic. Lodge: KC. Avocations: computers, softball, tennis, running, real estate investment. Contracts commercial, General corporate. Home: 1009 Southgate Dr Belleville IL 62223 Office: Southwestern Bell Telecom 1000 Des Peres Rd Suite 104 Saint Louis MO 63131

PAJON, EDUARDO RODRIGUEZ, lawyer; b. Ciego de Avila, Camaquey, Cuba, Nov. 22, 1917; Came to U.S., 1959, naturalized, 1965; s. Francisco Rodriguez Ubals and Maria Luisa Pajon; m. Olga M. Fernandez, Jan. 31, 1942 (div. Apr. 1973); children Olga del Valle, Eduardo R.; m. Maribel Maxwell, Dec. 1973 (div. Jan. 1977); m. Leah Munoz, Sept. 1977; 1 child, Marta M. Munoz Pajon. JD, U. Havana (Cuba), 1941, U. Miami, 1964. Bar: Fla. 1965. Ptnr. firm Helio R. Ecay, Havana, 1941-59, Salley, Barns, Pajon, Guttman & Del Valle (and predecessor firms), Miami, 1967—; head legal dept., sec. Cuban subsidiaries The Cuban Am. Sugar Co. (named changed to N. Am. Sugar Industries, Inc. 1960), N.Y.C., 1952-60; sec., counsel Talisman Sugar Corp., Miami, 1965-72; v.p., dir. Fla. Sugar Corp., Belle Glade, 1960-62, Sunshine Farms, Inc., South Bay, Fla., 1960-72; dir. Intercontinental Bank Miami, Fla. Mem. adv. bd. Fla. Meml. Coll., Miami, 1970—, endowment com. U. Miami, 1969—. Mem. ABA, InterAm. Bar Assn., Fla. Bar Assn., Dade County Bar Assn. Republican. Roman Catholic. Clubs: Miami, Miami City, LaGorce Country (Miami Beach); Coral Gables Country (Fla.); American, Bankers (Miami). Banking, Contracts commercial, General corporate. Office: Suite 700 100 N Biscayne Blvd Miami FL 33132

PALADINO, ROBERT CHRISTOPHER, lawyer; b. Bklyn., Nov. 18, 1950; s. Angelo and Christine (Brunn) P.; m. Lovann Mary Stone, Nov. 17, 1973; children: Jessica, Lauren. B Chem. Engring., Manhattan Coll., 1972, M Environ. Engring., 1974; JD, George Washington U., 1980. Bar: N.Y. 1981. Asst. to pres., dir. fossil fuels, environ. project mgr. Edison Electric Inst., Washington, 1974-80; assoc. Leboeuf, Lamb, Leiby & MacCrae, N.Y.C., 1980; sr. v.p., gen. counsel NPS Techs. Group, Inc., Secaucus, N.J., 1980-87; exec. v.p. York Research Corp., Stamford, Conn., 1987—. Fellow Fed. Water Pollution Control Assn., 1973. Mem. ABA, N.Y. State Bar Assn., Assn. of Bar of City of N.Y. Roman Catholic. Avocation: golf. General corporate, Contracts commercial. Office: York Research Corp 1 Research Dr Stamford CT 06906

PALAHACH, MICHAEL, lawyer; b. N.Y.C., Jan. 30, 1948; s. Michael and Mary Palahach; m. Miriam Ann Boghos, May 10, 1980; 1 child, Michael IV. B.S. in Bus. Adminstrn., U. Fla., 1970, J.D., 1973. Bar: Fla. 1973, U.S. Dist. Ct. (so. dist.) Fla. 1973, U.S. Ct. Appeals (5th cir.) 1973, U.S. Dist. Ct. (mid. dist.) Fla. 1979; cert. trial lawyer, Fla. Ptnr. High, Stack, Lazenby, Palahach & Lacasa, Coral Gables, Fla., 1973—. Mem. Fla. Bar Assn., Dade County Bar Assn., Coral Gables Bar Assn., Fla. Acad. Trial Lawyers, Am. Acad. Trial Lawyers, Nat. Bd. Trial Adv. (cert. trial lawyer). Personal injury, State civil litigation, Federal civil litigation. Home: 6934 Sunrise Pl Coral Gables FL 33134 Office: High Stack Lazenby Palahach & Lacasa 3929 Ponce de Leon Blvd Coral Gables FL 33134

PALAZZO, ROBERT P., lawyer; b. Los Angeles, Apr. 14, 1952; s. Joseph Francis and Muriel Palazzo. BA, UCLA, 1973; MBA, U. So. Calif., 1976, JD, 1976. Bar: Calif. 1976, U.S. Dist. Ct. (so. dist.) Calif. 1977, U.S. Tax Ct. 1977, U.S. Ct. Appeals (9th cir.) 1978, U.S. Supreme Ct. 1980. Assoc. Graham & James, Los Angeles, 1976-78; ptnr. Palazzo & Kessler, Los Angeles, 1978-81; sole practice Los Angeles, 1981—; judge pro tem Los Angeles Mcpl. Ct., 1982—; bd. dirs. Cons. Am. Oil Co., Fin. Systems Internat. Inc. Founder Ohio History Flight Mus.; bd. dirs. Calif. Cancer Found., Los Angeles, 1978—. Mem. Italian Am. Lawyers Assn. (bd. govs. 1980—, 1st v.p. 1984—). Personal income taxation, Corporate taxation, Entertainment. Office: 3002 Midvale Ave #209 Los Angeles CA 90034

PALEOLOGOS, ANITA GUST, lawyer; b. Fresno, Calif., Apr. 5, 1954; d. Maria (Konstantopoulos) Paleologos. BA in Philosophy, Stanford U., 1976, MA in Philosophy, 1977; JD, U. Santa Clara, 1980. Bar: Calif. 1980, U.S. Dist. Ct. (cen. dist.) Calif. 1983, U.S. Tax Ct. 1983. Atty. Sanford, Harmssen & Wilson, San Jose, Calif., 1980-82; assoc. Deering, Walther & Sands, Santa Monica, Calif., 1982-86; assoc. counsel Autoclub of So. Calif., Los Angeles, 1986—. Commr. Santa Monica Fair Election Practice Commn., 1985; appointed by Gov. Deukmejian to Santa Monica Mountains Conservancy Adv. Com., 1986—; mem. Los Angeles Opera League; bd. dirs. Santa Monica Rep. Club, 1984-85. Assoc. editor Santa Clara Law Review, 1979-80. Mem. ABA, Calif. Bar Assn., Santa Monica Bar Assn., Westside Women Lawyers, Los Angeles Profl. Rep. Women (v.p., treas. 1984-85), Stanford Profl. Women. Avocations: piano, travel in Europe and Southeast Asia.

PALERMO, ANTHONY ROBERT, lawyer; b. Rochester, N.Y., Sept. 30, 1929; s. Anthony C. and Mary (Palvino) P.; m. Mary Ann Coyne, Jan. 2, 1960; children: Mark Henry, Christopher Coyne, Peter Stuart, Elisabeth Megan, Julie Coyne, Gregg Anthony. BA, U. Mich., 1951; JD, Georgetown U., 1956. Bar: D.C. 1956, N.Y. 1957. Trial atty. U.S. Dept. Justice, Washington, 1956-58; asst. atty. U.S. Dept. Justice, N.Y.C., 1958-60; asst. atty. in charge U.S. Dept. Justice, Rochester, N.Y., 1960-61; ptnr. Brennan, Centner, Palermo & Blauvelt, Rochester, 1962-81, Harter, Secrest & Emery, Rochester, 1981—. Bd. dirs. McQuaid Jesuit High Sch., Rochester, 1978-84, St. Ann's Home for Aged, Rochester, 1974—; bd. dirs., past pres. Wegman Found., Rochester, 1972—. Fellow Am. Bar Found., N.Y. State Bar Found (bd. dirs.). Am. Coll. Trial Lawyers; mem. ABA (state del. 1980-85, bd. govs. 1985—), N.Y. State Bar Assn. (pres. 1979-80), Monroe County Bar Assn. (pres. 1973). Republican. Roman Catholic. Club: Oak Hill Country (Rochester). Avocation: golf. Federal civil litigation, State civil litigation, General practice. Home: 38 Huntington Meadow Rochester NY 14604 Office: Harter Secrest & Emery 700 Midtown Tower Rochester NY 14604

PALEUDIS, JOHN GEORGE, lawyer; b. Barnesville, Ohio, June 12, 1944; s. George and Hariklia (Fyllas) P.; m. Kathleen Anne Murphy, July 22, 1972; children: Michael John, Anne Marie. BS in Edn., Ohio State U., 1966; postgrad., U. Chgo., 1966-67; JD, U. Cleve., 1973. Bar: Ohio 1973, U.S. Dist. Ct. (so. and no. dists.) Ohio 1981, U.S. Ct. Appeals (6th cir.) 1984, W.Va. 1986, U.S. Ct. Appeals (4th cir.) 1986. Law clk. to presiding judges Cuy County Ohio Common Pleas Ct., Cleve., 1973-77; pub. defender Belmont County, St. Clairsville, Ohio, 1977-81; assoc., ptnr. Kinder, Kinder & Hanlon, St. Clairsville, 1981-84; ptnr. Hanlon, Duff & Paleudis, St. Clairsville, 1984—; prosecutor Juvenile Ct. Belmont County, Ohio, 1987—. Bd. dirs. Belmont County Children's Services, St. Clairsville, 1982-87. Administrative and regulatory, Personal injury, Workers' compensation. Home: 106 Coroline Dr Saint Clairsville OH 43950 Office: Hanlon Duff & Paleudis Co PA 46770 National Rd W Saint Clairsville OH 43950

PALEY, PHILLIP LEWIS, lawyer; b. Richmond, Va., Sept. 17, 1942; s. Ben Alexander and Gertrude (Falk) P.; children—Lizabeth, Sharon. B.S. in Econ., U. Pa., 1964; J.D., Rutgers U., 1967. Bar: N.J. 1967, U.S. Supreme Ct. 1978, U.S. Ct. Claims 1979, U.S. Tax Ct. 1979, U.S. Ct. Internat. Trade 1981, U.S. Dist. Ct. (ea. and so. dists.) N.Y. 1980. Assoc. Daniel L. Golden, South River, N.J., 1969-70, Golden & Shore, 1970-73; ptnr. Golden, Shore & Paley, South River, N.J., 1973-78, Golden, Shore, Paley, Zahn & Richmond, 1978-79; mem. firm Kirsten, Friedman & Cherin, P.A., Newark, 1979-86; mem. firm Kirsten, Simon, Friedman, Allen, Cherin & Linken, Newark, 1987—; adj. instr. bus. law Middlesex County Coll., 1979-81. Councilman-at-large Twp. Council, Twp. of Piscataway (N.J.), 1977-80, pres., 1980, dir. law, 1981—. Served as capt. U.S. Army, 1967-69. Decorated Bronze Star, Army Commendation medal; recipient Bancroft-Whitney award for proficiency in legislation, 1967; Govt. Regulation of Bus. award, 1969. Fellow Am. Acad. Matrimonial Lawyers; mem. ABA, N.J. State Bar Assn., Essex County Bar Assn., Middlesex County Bar Assn., New Brunswick Bar Assn. Democrat. Jewish. Local government, Family and matrimonial, General practice. Home: 133 Berkshire Ct Piscataway NJ 08854 Office: 17 Academy St Newark NJ 07102

PALEY, PIERCE, lawyer; b. N.Y.C., Aug. 25, 1937; s. Morrison P. and Esther (Insel) P.; m. Joan Rosenblum, Oct. 6, 1966; children—Gail E., Jennifer M. B.A., N.Y. U., 1957, LL.B., 1960. Bar: N.Y. 1960. Sole practice, N.Y.C., 1960-76; mem. Pierce Paley, P.C., N.Y.C., 1976-79; ptnr. Hall, Dickler, Lawler, Kent & Friedman, N.Y.C., 1979—. Bd. dirs. Harrison Day Care Ctr., Inc.; sec., trustee Council for Owner Occupied Housing. Mem. N.Y. State Trial Lawyers Assn., Pan Am. Soc. Contbg. editor Real Estate Weekly. Real property. Office: 460 Park Ave New York NY 10022

PALFFY, THOMAS, lawyer; b. Cluj, Rumania, June 30, 1956. BA, U. So. Calif., 1978; JD, Southwestern U., 1980. Bar: Calif. 1982, U.S. Dist. Ct. (cen., ea. and so. dists.) Calif. 1983, U.S. Ct. of Appeals (9th cir.), U.S. Supreme Ct. 1986. Law clk. Calif. Atty. Gen.'s Office, Los Angeles, 1979; sr. adminstrv. aide Jet Propulsion Lab., Pasadena, Calif., 1979-81; assoc. Munns, Kofford, Hoffman, Hunt & Throckmorton, Pasadena, 1982—. Mem. Tournament of Roses Assn., Pasadena, Calif., 1985—. Mem. ABA, Calif. Bar Assn., Los Angeles Bar Assn., Assn. Trial Lawyers Am., Calif. Trial Lawyers Assn. Federal civil litigation, State civil litigation. Office: Munns Kofford Hoffman et al 225 S Lake Ave Penthouse Pasadena CA 91101

PALINCSAR, JOHN ERNEST, lawyer; b. Chgo., Jan. 21, 1949; s. Blanch Catherine (Cerny) P.; m. Annemarie Sullivan, Aug. 2, 1975; 1 child, Danielle. BA, U. Ill., 1970, JD, 1973. Bar: Ill. 1973, Mich. 1983, U.S. Dist. Ct. (so. dist.) Ill. 1974. Mgr. air enforcement services Ill. EPA, Springfield, 1973-77; prof. legal studies Sangamon State U., Springfield, 1977-83; asst. atty. gen. State of Mich., Lansing, 1983-85; gen. atty. Mich. Energy Resources Co., Monroe, 1985—; hearing examiner Ill. Dept. Revenue, 1980-81. Contbr. articles to law jours. Pres. bd. regents Joint U. Adv. Com.; legal counsel Springfield Zool. Soc. Recipient Outstanding Achievement award Illini Union 1969, Medallion award Ill. Am. Revolution Bicentennial, 1976; Edmund James scholar, 1965; Title IX Pub. Adminstrn. grantee, 1980. Mem. Ill. Bar Assn., Mich. Bar Assn. (pub. utilities com.), Task Force on Alternative Forms of Legal Services, Am. Soc. Legal History, Phi Eta Sigma, Omicron Delta Kappa, Mensa. Public utilities, Environment, Legal education. Office: 899 S Telegraph Rd Monroe MI 48161

PALITZ, MURRAY, lawyer; b. N.Y.C., July 16, 1937; s. Nathan and Bettie (Silversmith) P.; m. Linda Stollack, May 22, 1978; children—Jeffrey, Michael, Davin, Adam; m. Rita Liebman, Sept. 4, 1959 (div. 1974). B.S. in Physics/Math., Bklyn. Coll., 1959; M.S. in Systems Mgmt., West Coast U., 1970; J.D., Southwestern U., 1975. Research engr. NASA, Lancaster, Calif., 1959-67; engr. McDonnell Douglas, Santa Monica, Calif., 1968-70, cost/fin. analyst, 1971-75; assoc. Palitz & Assocs. Law Ctr., Westminster, Calif., 1975—. Mem. ABA, Los Angeles County Bar Assn., Assn. Trial Lawyers Am., Calif. Trial Lawyers Assn., Orange County Bar Assn. Republican. Jewish. Club: Toastmasters. Lodges: Kiwanis, Elks, B'nai B'rith. Personal injury, Workers' compensation, Probate. Home: 10551 La Rosa Circle Fountain Valley CA 92708 Office: Palitz & Assocs Law Ctr 8070 Westminster Ave Westminster CA 92683

PALIZZI, ANTHONY N., lawyer; b. Wyandotte, Mich., Oct. 27, 1942; s. Vincenzo and Nunziata (Dagostini) P.; m. Bonnie Marie Kirkwood, Mar. 11, 1966; children—A. Michael, Nicholas A. Ph.B., Wayne State U., 1964, J.D., 1966; LL.M., Yale U., 1967. Bar: Mich. 1967. Prof. law Fla. State U., Tallahassee, 1967-69; prof. law Tex. Tech. U., Lubbock, 1969-71; atty. Kmart Corp., Troy, Mich., 1971-74; asst. sec. Kmart Corp., 1974-77, asst. gen. counsel, 1977-85, v.p., assoc. gen. counsel, 1985—. Editor law rev. Wayne State U., 1964-66. Chmn. Brandon Police and Fire Bd., Mich., 1982—. Mem. ABA, State Bar Assn. Mich., Am. Soc. Corporate Secs. Roman Catholic. General corporate.

PALLAM, JOHN JAMES, lawyer; b. Cleve., May 19, 1940; s. James John and Coralia (Gatsos) P.; married Nov. 29, 1969; 1 child, Alethea. BA, Case Western Res. U., 1962; JD, Ohio State U., 1965. Bar: Ohio 1965, U.S. Ct. Claims 1969, U.S. Ct. Mil. Appeals 1969, U.S. Supreme Ct. 1970. Law clk. to presiding justice Cuyahoga County Ct., Cleve., 1965-66; assoc. Burke, Habor & Berick, Cleve., 1970-73; corp. atty. Midland Ross Corp., Cleve., 1973-80, corp. counsel, 1980—; guest lectr. Nat. Foundry Assn., Chgo., 1986—. Contbr. articles on labor and environ. matters to jours. Legal advisor Am. Hellenic and Prog. Assn., Cleve., 1966—. Served to capt. JAGC U.S. Army, 1966-70, Vietnam. Decorated Bronze Star with oak leaf cluster. Mem. Ohio Bar Assn. (committeeman 1984—), Cleve. Bar Assn. (merit service award 1972), Hellenic Bar Assn., Hellenic Univ. Club. Greek Orthodox. Avocations: history, antiques, golfing, rare books, railroading. Labor, Contracts commercial, Environment. Office: Midland Ross Corp 20600 Chagrin Blvd Cleveland OH 44122

PALLASCH, B. MICHAEL, lawyer; b. Chgo., Mar. 30, 1933; s. Bernhard Michael and Magdalena Helena (Fixari) P.; m. Josephine Catherine O'Leary, Aug. 15, 1981. B.S.S., Georgetown U., 1954; J.D., Harvard U., 1957; postgrad., John Marshall Law Sch., 1974. Bar: Ill. 1957, U.S. Dist. Ct. (no. dist.) Ill. 1958, U.S. Tax Ct. 1961, U.S. Ct. Claims 1961. Assoc. Winston & Strawn, Chgo., 1958-66; resident mgr. br. office Winston & Strawn, Paris, 1963-65; ptnr. Winston & Strawn, Chgo., 1966-70, sr. capital ptnr., 1971—; dir., corp. sec. Tanis Inc., Houghton, Mich., 1972—, Greenbank Engring. Corp., Dover, Del., 1976—, C.B.P. Engring. Corp., Chgo., 1976—, Chgo. Cutting Services Corp., 1977—; corp. sec. Arthur Andersen Assocs. Inc., Chgo., 1976—, L'hotel de France of Ill. Inc., Chgo., 1980—; dir. Bosch Devel. Co., Longview, Tex., Lor Inc., Houghton, Mich., Rana Inc., Madison, Wis., Woodlak Co., Houghton. Bd. dirs. Martin D'Arcy Mus. Medieval and Renaissance Art, Chgo., 1975—; bd. dirs. Katherine M. Bosch Found., 1978—; asst. sec. Hundred Club of Cook County, Chgo., 1966-73, bd. dirs., sec., 1974—. Served with USAFR, 1957-63. Recipient Oustanding Woodland Mgmt. Forestry award Monroe County (Wis.) Soil and Water Conservation Dist., 1975; recipient Youth Mayor of Chgo. award, 1950. Mem. Ill. Bar Assn. (tax lectr. 1961), Advocates Soc., Field Mus. Natural History (life mem.), Max McGraw Wildlife Found. Roman Catholic. Clubs: Travelers (Paris); Saddle and Cycle (Chgo.). General corporate, Private international, Contracts commercial. Home: 3000 N Sheridan Rd Chicago IL 60657 Office: Winston & Strawn One First National Plaza Suite 5000 Chicago IL 60603

PALM, GARY HOWARD, law educator, lawyer; b. Toledo, Sept. 2, 1942; s. Clarence William, Jr. and Emily Marie (Braunschweiger) P. A.B., Wittenberg U., 1964; J.D., U. Chgo., 1967. Bar: Ill. 1967, U.S. Dist. Ct. (no. dist.) Ill. 1967, U.S. Ct. Appeals (7th cir.) 1970, U.S. Supreme Ct. 1974. Assoc. Schiff Hardin & Waite, Chgo., 1967-70; dir. Edwin F. Mandel Legal Aid Clinic, Chgo., 1970—; asst. prof. law U. Chgo. Law Sch., 1970-75, assoc. prof., 1975-83, prof., 1983—; peer rev. reader, clin. edn. grants U.S. Dept. Edn., Washington, 1980, 81, 83, 84, 86; chairperson-elect, chairperson sect. clin. legal edn. Assn. Am. Law Schs., 1985. Mem. Criminal Def. Consortium of Cook County, Inc., Chgo., 1975-77, 86; part-time vol. ACLU, Chgo., 1969-75. Mem. ABA (clin. edn. com. 1974-80, membership com. 1984-85, skills tng. com. 1985), Chgo. Bar Assn., Chgo. Council Lawyers, Ill. State Bar Assn. (legal edn., admission and competance com. 1985—), Am. Trial Lawyers Assn., Assn. Am. Law Schs. (chmn. clin. legal edn. 1986, clin. teaching conferences 1985), Plaintiff Emploees Lawyers Assn. Democrat. Civil rights, Federal civil litigation, Legal education. Home: 1840 N Orleans Ave Chicago IL 60614 Office: Mandel Legal Aid Clinic 6020 S University Ave Chicago IL 60637

PALMA, NICHOLAS JAMES, lawyer; b. Newark, Oct. 28, 1953; s. James Thomas and Venice Maria (Dibenedetto) P.; m. Mary Jo Cugliari, Sept. 1, 1973; children—Nicholas J., Valerie Michele, James Michael. B.S. cum laude, William Paterson U., 1975; J.D., Seton Hall U., 1979. Bar: N.J. 1979, U.S. Dist. Ct. N.J. 1979, U.S. Ct. Appeals (3d cir.) 1985, N.Y. 1986; cert. firearms expert, Hudson County, N.J. Investigator N.J. Pub. Defender's Office, Essex Region, Newark, 1974-75; investigator Hudson County Prosecutor's Office, Jersey City, 1975-79, asst. prosecutor, 1979-81; ptnr. A.J. Fusco, Jr., P.A., Passaic, N.J., 1981—. Recipient Commendation, Dade County Sheriff, Fla., 1976. Mem. Passaic County Bar Assn., N.J. State Bar Assn. Roman Catholic. Criminal, Personal injury, State civil litigation. Home: 59 Frederick St Belleville NJ 07109 Office: A J Fusco Jr PA 40 Passaic Ave PO Box 838 Passaic NJ 07055

PALMBERG, EARL LAVERNE, lawyer; b. Paxton, Ill., Dec. 4, 1918; s. Gustaf Erik and Julia Amanda (Stolle) P.; m. Nida Norene Palmberg, Dec. 12, 1944; children—Gregory E., Joseph E., Teresa M. Palmberg Huff. B.S., U. Ill., 1949, J.D., LL.D., 1949. Bar: Ill. 1949, U.S. Ct. Mil. Appeals 1954, U.S. Supreme Ct. 1954. Corp. atty. U. Ill., Urbana, 1949—; comdr. Legal Flight 9650th Air Res. Squadron, 1952-58, Air Res. Squadron, 1958-69; real estate broker. Served to lt. col., USAAF, 1941-46. Mem. Champaign County Bar Assn., Ill. Bar Assn., Nat. Assn. Coll. and Univ. Attys. (charter), Res. Officers Assn., Air Force Assn. (former pres. Ill. chpt.), Phi Alpha Delta. Clubs: Univ., Exchange (Urbana). Contbr. articles to legal periodicals. General corporate, General practice, Government contracts and claims. Home: 1401 S Grove St Urbana IL 61801 Office: 506 S Wright St Urbana IL 61801

PALMER, ALAN KENNETH, lawyer; b. Bradford, Pa., Feb. 9, 1941; s. James Kenneth and M. Mae (Gore) P.; m. Carole Ellen Mancha, Sept. 14, 1963 (Dec. 1981). AB, Dartmouth Coll., 1963; postgrad., Oxford U., 1963-64; JD, Harvard U., 1967. Bar: D.C. 1970, U.S. Ct. Appeals (D.C., fed. and 10th cirs.), U.S. Supreme Ct. Law clk. to presiding justice U.S. Ct. Appeals (9th cir.), Los Angeles, 1967-68; law clk. to Justice Potter Stewart U.S. Supreme Ct., Washington, 1968-69; assoc. Covington & Burling, Washington, 1969-74; dep. assoc. solicitor Dept. Interior, Washington, 1974-76; bur. competition FTC, Washington, 1976-77, dep. dir. bur. competition, 1977-81, acting dir. bur. competition, 1981; ptnr. Morrison & Foerster, Washington, 1981—; vis. fellow Inst for Social and Policy Studies, Yale U., New Haven, Conn., 1979-80. Contbr. articles to profl. jours. Victor Kramer fellow, 1979. Mem. ABA, Fed. Bar Assn. Administrative and regulatory, Antitrust, Federal civil litigation. Home: 2501 M St NW #718 Washington DC 20037 Office: Morrison & Foerster 2000 Pennsylvania Ave NW Suite 5500 Washington DC 20006

PALMER, ANN THERESE DARIN, lawyer; b. Detroit, Apr. 25, 1951; d. Americo and Theresa (Del Favero) Darin; m. Robert Towne Palmer, Nov. 9, 1974; children: Justin Darin, Christian Darin. BA, U. Notre Dame, 1973, MBA, 1975; JD, Loyola U., Chgo., 1978. Bar: Ill. 1978, U.S. Supreme Ct. 1981. Tax atty. Esmark Inc., 1978; counsel Chgo. United, 1979-81; assoc. Johnson, Cusack & Bell, Ltd., Chgo., 1982-83; sole practice tax law, Chgo., 1983—. Contbr. articles to legal jours. Roman Catholic. Republican. Club: Woman's Athletic (Chgo.). General corporate, Corporate taxation, Pension, profit-sharing, and employee benefits.

PALMER, BRUCE ALEXANDER, lawyer; b. Oskaloosa, Iowa, July 11, 1927; s. Arlo Wheeler and Emma Louise (Swenson) P.; m. Mary Elizabeth Farmer, May 1, 1955; children: Thomas, Eric. BA, William Penn Coll., 1949; JD, U. Iowa, 1954. Bar: Iowa 1954. Ptnr. Palmer & Palmer, Oskaloosa, 1954-63, Charles Stream Assocs., Oskaloosa; sole practice Oskaloosa; assoc. Eric J. Palmer, 1987—. Govt. appeals agent Selective Service, Oskaloosa, 1955—; sch. bd. Oskaloosa Community Sch. Dist., 1984—. Served with USNR, 1945-46, 50-51. Mem. Iowa Bar Assn., Mahaska Bar Assn., 8th Jud. Dist. Bar Assn. Republican. Mem. Christian Ch. Lodges: Kiwanis, Masons. Avocations: philately, coins, reading. General practice, Probate, Personal income taxation. Home: 411 S 1st Oskaloosa IA 52577 Office: Palmer Law Office 111 1/2 High Ave E Oskaloosa IA 52577

PALMER, DAVID GILBERT, lawyer; b. Lakewood, N.J., Jan. 10, 1945; s. Robert Dayton and Lois (Gilbert) P.; m. Susan Edmundson Walsh, Aug. 17, 1968; children: Jonathan, Megan. AB, Johns Hopkins U., 1967; JD, U. Colo., 1970. Bar: Colo. 1970, U.S. Dist. Ct. Colo. 1970, U.S. Ct. Appeals (9th and 10th cirs.) 1970, U.S. Supreme Ct. 1970. Ptnr., chmn. litigation dept. Holland & Hart, Denver, 1970—. Chmn. Northwest region Am. Heart Assn., Dallas, 1986—, bd. dirs., 1986—; pres., bd. dirs. Colo. Heart Assn., Denver, 1974—, C.H. Kempe Nat. Ctr. for Prevention of Child Abuse, Denver, 1984—; bd. dirs. Goodwill Industries, Denver, 1981-84. Mem. ABA, Colo. Bar Assn., Denver Law Club. Presbyterian. Clubs: University, Mile High (Denver). Federal civil litigation, Criminal. Home: 7271 S Pontiac Way Englewood CO 80112 Office: Holland & Hart 555 17th St Denver CO 80202

PALMER, DEBORAH JEAN, lawyer; b. Williston, N.D., Oct. 25, 1947; d. Everett Edwin and Doris Irene (Harberg) P.; m. Kenneth L. Rich, Mar. 29, 1980; children: Andrew, Stephanie. BA, Carleton Coll., 1969; JD, Northwestern U., 1973. Bar: Minn. 1973, U.S. Dist. Ct. Minn. 1973, U.S. Ct. Appeals (8th cir.) 1975, U.S. Supreme Ct. 1978. Econ. analyst Harris Trust & Savs. Bank, Chgo., 1969-70; assoc. Robins, Zelle, Larson & Kaplan, Mpls., 1973-79, ptnr., 1979—. Trustee Carleton Coll., 1984—. Mem. ABA, Minn. Bar Assn., Minn. Women Lawyers Assn. (sec. 1976-78), Hennepin County Bar Assn., Hennepin County Bar Found. (bd. dirs. 1978-81), Carleton Coll. Alumni Assn. (bd. dirs. 1978-82, sec. 1980-82), Women's Assn. of Minn. Orch. (bd. dirs. 1980-85, treas. 1981-83). Federal civil litigation, Antitrust, Securities. Home: 1787 Colfax Ave S Minneapolis MN 55403 Office: Robins Zelle Larson & Kaplan 1800 Internat Ctr 900 Second Ave S Minneapolis MN 55402

PALMER, EDWIN KAYSER, lawyer; b. Selma, Ala., Dec. 14, 1943; s. Seymour and Hannah (Kayser) P.; m. Judy Rephan, Aug. 14, 1966; children: Amanda, Keane, Jill. BA, Tulane U., 1965, JD, 1968. Bar: Ala. 1968, Ga. 1970. Assoc. Cotton, Katz & White, Atlanta, 1969-74; ptnr. Brent, Castellani & Palmer, Atlanta, 1974-78, Palmer, Lamberth, Bonapfel & Cifelli and predecessor firm Cotton, White & Palmer, P.A., Atlanta, 1978—. Past bd. dirs. Ga. Mental Health Inst., Atlanta. Mem. Comml. Law League Am. (chmn. Ga. chpt.). Democrat. Jewish. Avocations: running, camping, writing. Consumer commercial, General corporate, Contracts commercial.

PALMER, HARVARD, lawyer; b. Carlinville, Ill., Sept. 17, 1914; s. Wallace Bister and Caroline Clementine (Crowder) P.; m. Gertrude May Lamping, Aug. 13, 1939; children: Harvard Jr., Gregory Lee. BA, U. Wash., 1934, JD, 1940. Bar: Wash. 1983, U.S. Dist. Ct. (we. dist.) Wash 1938. Sole practice Seattle, 1940-48; head trust dept. Seattle First Nat. Bank, 1948-72; v.p., counsel Clise Cos., Seattle, 1972—. Mem. Seattle Estate Planning Council (past pres., life), U.S. Croquet Assn. Mem. Unitarian Ch. Clubs: College (Seattle), Seattle Yacht. Avocations: sailing, playing croquet. General corporate, Probate, Real property. Home: 9009 View Ave NW Seattle WA 98117 Office: Clise Agy Inc 200 Securities Bldg Seattle WA 98101

PALMER, JOHN MARSHALL, lawyer; b. Fairmont, Minn., June 5, 1906; s. John Earl and Winnifred Ann (Ibertson) P.; m. Mary Louise Arntsen, June 28, 1934 (div.); children: Loring Swift, John Edward, Marsha. B.A., U. Minn., 1928, LL.B., 1931. Bar: Minn. 1931. Assoc. Sweet, Johnson & Sands, Mpls., 1931-32, Stinchfield, Mackall, Crounse, McNally & Moore, Mpls., 1932-42; chief enforcement atty. OPA, St. Paul, 1942-44; ptnr. Stinchfield, Mackall, Crounse & Moore, Mpls., 1944-51, Mackall, Crounse, Moore, Helmey & Palmer, Mpls., 1951-57, Levitt and Palmer, 1957-60, Levitt, Palmer & Bearmon, 1961-65, Levitt, Palmer, Bowen & Bearmon, 1965-68, Levitt, Palmer, Bowen, Bearmon & Rotman, 1968-79; ptnr. Levitt, Palmer, Bowen, Rotman & Share, 1979-82, of counsel, 1982-83; of counsel Briggs & Morgan, 1983—; sec., dir. Triangle Devel. Co. Mem. ABA, Minn. Bar Assn. (pres. 1955-56), Law Alumni Assn. U. Minn. (past pres., dir.), Am. Coll. Trial Lawyers, Phi Gamma Delta, Phi Delta Phi. Episcopalian. Clubs: Minneapolis (Mpls.), University (Mpls.). General practice, Antitrust, Commercial litigation. Home: 10401 S Cedar Lake Rd Apt 219 Minnetonka MN 55343 Office: 2400 IDS Ctr Minneapolis MN 55402

PALMER, JUDITH GRACE, university adminstrator; b. Washington, Ind., Apr. 2, 1948; d. William Thomas and Laura Margaret (Routt) P. BA, Ind. U., 1970; JD cum laude, Ind. U., Indpls., 1973. Bar: Ind. 1974, U.S. Dist. Ct. (so. dist.) Ind. State budget analyst State of Ind., Indpls., 1969-76, exec. asst. to gov., 1976-81, state budget dir., 1981-85; spl. asst. to pres. Ind. U., 1985-86, v.p. for planning, 1986—. Mem. bd. dirs. Columbia Found., 1983—, mem. long range planning com., 1984—, chmn., 1986—, mem. fin. com., 1986—. Named one of Outstanding Young Women in Am., 1978; recipient Sagamore of the Wabash award, 1977, 85, Citation of Merit, Ind. Bar Assn. of Young Lawyers, 1978, Appreciation award, 1980. Mem. ABA, Ind. Bar Assn., Indpls. Bar Assn. Roman Catholic. Club: University. Administrative and regulatory, Legal education, Government contracts and claims. Office: Ind Univ Adminstrn Bldg Rm 120 355 N Lansing St Indianapolis IN 46202

PALMER, MARK JOSEPH, lawyer; b. Columbus, Ohio, June 16, 1957; s. Joseph Russell and Patricia (Weaver) P.; m. Laurie Sue Thompson, June 30, 1984. BA in Bus., Ohio No. U., 1979; postgrad., U. Pa., 1981; JD, Rutgers U., 1982. Bar: Ohio 1982, U.S. Dist. Ct. (so. dist.) Ohio 1983. Assoc. Chester, Hoffman & Willcox, Columbus, 1982—. Mem. adminstrv. bd. Bexley (Ohio) United Meth. Ch., 1986. Postgrad. scholar Nat. Collegiate Athletic Assn., 1979. Mem. Ohio Bar Assn., Columbus Bar Assn. (bus. law com.), Ohio No. U. Alumni Assn. (bd. dirs. 1983—), Bexley Jaycees (v.p. community devel. 1985-86). Republican. Clubs: Athletic (Columbus). Lodge: Sons of Baghdad Investment Club. General corporate, Labor, Real property. Home: 916 S Roosevelt Ave Bexley OH 43209 Office: Chester Hoffman & Willcox 8 E Brood St Columbus OH 43215

PALMER, MICHAEL PAUL, lawyer, educator; b. San Francisco, Mar. 7, 1944; s. Coy Cornelius and Fay Janetta (Conley) P.; m. Gisela Schultz, Jan. 8, 1969; children: Eva Rebecca, Esther Marie. BA, McMurry Coll., Abilene, Tex., 1967; MA, Freie U., Berlin, 1971, PhD, 1976; JD, Georgetown U., 1980. Bar: Ill. 1980, U.S. Dist. Ct. (no. dist.) Ill. 1980, U.S. Ct. Appeals (7th cir.) 1981, U.S. Ct. Appeals (11th cir.) 1981. Research asst. Occupational Safety and Health Rev. Comn., Washington, 1978-79; assoc. Jenner & Block, Chgo., 1980—; adj. prof. Kent Law Sch., Ill. Inst. Tech., Chgo., 1982. Author: Das Problem der Technik, 1976; contbr. articles to profl. jours. Active Lawyers Commn. on Civil Rights, Citizens for a Better Environment, Chgo., John Howard Assn., Chgo. Hon. mention Ammy award Am. Lawyer, 1982. Mem. ABA, Chgo. Council Lawyers, ACLU. Federal civil litigation, State civil litigation, Jurisprudence. Office: Jenner & Block One IBM Plaza Chicago IL 60611

PALMER, PHILIP ISHAM, JR., lawyer; b. Dallas, June 25, 1929; s. Philip I. and Charlene (Bolen) P.; m. Eleanor Hutson, Mar. 7, 1951; children—Stephen Edward, Michael Bolen. B.B.A., So. Methodist U., 1952; LL.B., U. Tex., 1957. Bar: Tex. bar 1957. Since practiced in Dallas; partner firm Palmer, & Palmer P.C. (and predecessor firms), 1957—; chmn. bd. Carolina Mfg. Corp., 1973—, pres., 1969-73; chmn. bd. Commonwealth Nat. Bank, 1967-69; pres. Pennyrich Corp., 1969-72. Co-author: Texas Creditors Rights; Contbr. articles to profl. jours. Vice consul Republic Costa Rica, 1973—. Mem. Am. Bar Assn., Am. Judicature Soc. Club: City. Bankruptcy, Federal civil litigation. Home: 6757 Lake Fair Circle Dallas TX 75214 Office: 1510 One Main Pl Dallas TX 75202

PALMER, R. SCOTT, lawyer; b. Albany, N.Y., Nov. 8, 1944; s. Roger Alan and Alma Jane (Farley) P.; m. Linda Lee Westphal, Sept. 8, 1968 (Dec 1980); children—Mahri Westphal, David Scott, Roger Alan; m. Jane Amerena, Mar. 9, 1981; 1 son, John Robert Winfield. B.A., U. Mich., 1966; J.D. cum laude, U. Miami, 1976. Bar: Fla. 1976, U.S. Dist. Ct. (mid. dist.) Fla. 1977, U.S. Dist. Ct. (no. dist.) Fla. 1981. Asst. state atty. 9th Jud. Circuit, Orlando, Fla., 1976-79; chief field counsel Fla. Dept. Law Enforcement, Tallahassee, 1980-81, dir. exec. investigations, 1981-82; chief prosecutor Statewide Grand Jury of Fla., Exec. Office of Gov., Tallahassee, 1982-86; assoc. Rumberger, Kirk, Caldwell, Cabiness & Burke, Orlando, 1986—; adj. prof. criminal justice Valencia Coll., Orlando, 1977-80; instr. Organized Crime Inst., Orlando, 1980-86, Fla. State U., 1986. Contbr. articles to legal jours. U. Miami Sch. Law Scholar, 1973-76. Mem. ABA. Democrat. Roman Catholic. Criminal. Home: 301 Timbercove Circle Longwood FL 32779 Office: Rumberger Kirk Caldwell Cabiness 101 N Monroe St Suite 900 Tallahassee FL 32301

PALMER, RANDALL BRUCE, lawyer; b. Jefferson City, Mo., Aug. 7, 1952; s. Harry Edward and Jeanetta Jean (Schneider) P. BS in Pub. Adminstrn., U. Mo., 1973, JD, 1980. Bar: Mo. 1980, U.S. Dist. Ct. (we. dist.) Mo. 1980. Staff auditor State of Mo., Jefferson City, 1975-78; atty. Mo. Power & Light Co., Jefferson City, 1980-83, Gas Service Co., Kansas City, Mo., 1983-84; gen. counsel Mo. Pub. Service, Kansas City, 1984—; active Vol. Atty. Project, Kansas City, 1985—. Vol. Big Bros. and Sisters of Kansas City, 1984—; sec., bd. dirs. Hospice Jefferson City, 1981-83. Mem. ABA, Mo. Bar Assn., Kansas City Met. Bar Assn., Midwest Gas Assn. Legal Affairs (3d vice chmn. 1985—). Mem. Christian Ch. (Disciples of Christ). Avocation: photography. Administrative and regulatory, General corporate, Public utilities. Home: 7342 Walnut St Kansas City MO 64114 Office: Mo Pub Service 10700 E 350 Hwy Kansas City MO 64138

PALMER, RANDALL PARHAM, III, lawyer, army officer; b. Birmingham, Ala., Dec. 10, 1944; s. Randall Parham, Jr. and Minnie Palmer; m. Cheryl Ann Jean, Feb. 14, 1970; children—Randall Parham, Brandy Elizabeth. B.A., Langston U., 1968; J.D., Okla. City U., 1976; grad. legal program Judge Adv. Gen.'s Sch., Charlottesville, Va., 1982. Bar: Tex. 1976, U.S. Tax Ct. 1979, U.S. Supreme Ct. 1985. Enlisted U.S. Army, 1969, advanced through grades to maj., 1981; counsel Spl. Rev. Bd., Hdqrs. Dept. Army, Washington, 1979-81; acting clk. of ct., chief spl. actions Army Ct. Mil. Rev., Washington, 1979-81; chief criminal law div. 2d Inf. Div., Korea, 1982; dep. comdr. U.S. Armed Forces Claims Service, Korea, 1983; service sch. instr., Fort Sam Houston, Tex., 1983—; grad. faculty Baylor U., Waco, Tex., Tulane U., New Orleans, Tex. Wesleyan Coll., Fort Worth, 1984; pres. Global Imports, San Antonio. Bd. dirs. United Negro Coll. Fund., San Antonio, 1978-79, Langston U. Devel. Found.; pres. Okla. Intercollegiate Student Assn., 1967-68. Decorated Bronze Star, Meritorious Service medal; recipient Leadership award Okla. Intercollegiate Student Assn. Mem. Nat. Bar Assn. (vice chmn. govt. lawyers div. 1984—), State Bar Tex., Assn. Trial Lawyers Am., ABA, Internat. Legal Soc. Korea, Alpha Phi Alpha (v.p. 1985—, bd. dirs.), Phi Alpha Delta. Lodge: Masons. Personal injury, Legal education, Judicial administration. Office: Global Imports PO Box 8151 San Antonio TX 78208

PALMER, ROBERT ALAN, lawyer, educator; b. Somerville, N.J., June 29, 1948. BA, U. Pitts., 1970; JD, George Washington U., 1976. Bar: Va. 1977. Dir. labor relations Nat. Assn. Mfrs., Washington, 1976-79; assoc. gen. counsel Nat. Restaurant Assn., Washington, 1979-85, gen. counsel, 1985—; adj. assoc. prof. Pa. State U., State College, 1985—. Pres. Arlington Village Condominium Assn., Va., 1983-86. Mem. ABA, Va. State Bar Assn. General corporate, Labor, Legislative. Home: 2600 13th Rd S #397 Arlington VA 22204 Office: Nat Restaurant Assn 311 First St NW Washington DC 20001

PALMER, ROBERT JOSEPH, lawyer; b. Ft. Wayne, Ind., Oct. 23, 1954; s. Herman Joseph and Ruth E. (Hamilton) P.; m. Cynthia Jo Bender, Nov. 6, 1982. AB in Psychology, U. Notre Dame, 1977; JD, Valparaiso U., 1980. Bar: Ind. 1980, U.S. Dist. Ct. (so. dist.) Ind. 1980, U.S. Dist. Ct. (no. dist.) Ind. 1982, U.S. Ct. Appeals (7th cir.) 1985, U.S. Supreme Ct. 1986. Law clk. Ind. Ct. Appeals, Indpls., 1980-82; assoc. May, Oberfell & Lorber, South Bend, Ind., 1982—. Note editor Valparaiso U. Law Rev., 1979-80. Mem. ABA, Ind. Bar Assn., St. Joseph County Bar Assn., 7th Cir. Bar Assn., South Bend-Mishawaka Area C. of C., Notre Dame Club of St. Joseph Valley. Roman Catholic. Federal civil litigation, State civil litigation, Insurance. Home: 1617 Dorwood Dr South Bend IN 46617 Office: May Oberfell Helling & Lorber 300 N Michigan St South Bend IN 46601

PALMER, ROBERT TOWNE, lawyer; b. Chgo., May 25, 1947; s. Adrian Bernhardt and Gladys (Towne) P.; B.A., Colgate U., 1969; J.D., U. Notre Dame, 1974; m. Ann Therese Darin, Nov. 9, 1974; children—Justin Darin, Christian Darin. Bar: Ill. 1974, D.C. 1978, U.S. Supreme Ct. 1978. Law clk. Hon. Walter V. Schaefer, Ill. Supreme Ct., 1974-75; assoc. McDermott, Will & Emery, Chgo., 1975-81, ptnr., 1982-86; ptnr. Chadwell & Kayser, Ltd., 1987—; mem. adj. faculty Chgo. Kent Law Sch., 1975-77, Loyola U., 1976-78. Mem. ABA, Ill. State Bar Assn. (2d place Lincoln Award 1983), Chgo. Bar Assn., D.C. Bar Assn., Internat. Assn. Defense Counsel, Lambda Alpha. Republican. Episcopalian. Clubs: Chgo., Univ. Chgo., Saddle & Cycle; Dairymen's. Contbr. articles to legal jours. and textbooks. Federal civil litigation, State civil litigation, Insurance. Office: Chadwell & Kayser Ltd 8500 Sears Tower Chicago IL 60606-6592

PALMER, RUDOLPH MARTIN, JR., lawyer; b. Washington, Feb. 22, 1944; s. Rudolph Martin and Mossie (Ely) P.; m. Shirley Kay Bloss, Aug. 24, 1969; children—Marty, Andrew, Kathryn, Ruth. B.S., U. Md., 1967; J.D., U. Balt., 1970; postgrad. Nat. Coll. Advocacy, Harvard U., 1983. Bar: Md. 1974, U.S. Ct. Appeals (D.C. cir.) 1974, U.S. Supreme Ct. 1977, U.S. Dist. Ct. Md. 1978. Sole practice, Hagerstown, Md., 1974—. Author: A Symphony of the Preborn, 1984; (with others) Modern Trials-The Second, 1982. Fellow Melvin M. Belli Soc.; mem. Assn. Trial Lawyers Am., ABA, Md. Trial Lawyers Assn., Md. Bar Assn. Republican. Presbyterian. Lodge: Kiwanis. Personal injury, Family and matrimonial, Father's rights in abortion.

PALMER, THOMAS EARL, lawyer; b. Columbus, Ohio, July 21, 1939; s. Dwight Miller and Virginia (Gray) P.; children: Bradley Eames, Richard Thomas; m. Victoria Cochrane, July 6, 1985. BA, Denison U., 1961; JD, U. Mich., 1964. Bar: Ohio 1964, U.S. Dist. Ct. (so. dist.) Ohio 1964, U.S. Ct. Appeals (6th cir.) 1968, U.S. Supreme Ct. 1972, U.S. Ct. Appeals (4th cir.) 1973. Assoc. Knepper, White, Richards & Miller, Columbus, 1964-69, ptnr., 1969-72; ptnr. Moritz, McClure & Palmer, Columbus, 1972-74, Gingery & Palmer, Columbus, 1974-80; mng. ptnr. Squire, Sanders & Dempsey, Columbus, 1980—; lectr. Ohio Legal Ctr. Inst., Columbus. Chmn. Citizens Com. for Progress, Columbus, 1972; troop leader Boy Scouts Am., Columbus, 1977-84. Fellow Am. Coll. Trial Lawyers; mem. ABA, Ohio Bar Assn., Columbus Bar Assn. (community service award 1973), Def. Research Inst. Republican. Presbyterian. Club: Univ., Broadstreet (Columbus). Avocations: camping, boating, gardening, woodworking, bicycling. Federal civil litigation, State civil litigation, Coal Industry. Office: Squire Sanders & Dempsey 155 E Broad St Columbus OH 43215

PALMER, VERNON VALENTINE, law educator; b. New Orleans, Sept. 9, 1940; s. George Joseph and Juliette Marie (Wehrmann) P. B.A., Tulane U., 1962, LL.B., 1965; LL.M., Yale U., 1966; PhD, Pembroke Coll., Oxford U., 1985. Bar: La. 1965, U.S. Supreme Ct. 1981. Asst. prof. law Ind. Sch. Law, Indpls., 1966-70; lectr. law U. Botswana, Lesotho & Swaziland, Roma, Lesotho, 1967-69; prof. Tulane Law Sch., New Orleans, 1970—; Clarence Morrow research prof. law Tulane Law Sch., 1980—; external examiner Nat. U. Lesotho, Roma, 1978-81; reporter for revision of civil code La. Law Inst, 1979; vis. prof. Faculty Law, U. Strasbourg, 1983, The Sorbonne, U. Paris, 1986. Author: The Roman-Dutch and Lesotho Law of Delict, 1970, The Legal System of Lesotho, 1971, The Paths to Privity, 1981, The Law of Lease, 1982; contbr. numerous articles to profl. jours. Pres. French Quarter Residents Assn., 1973-75, Alliance for Good Govt., 1974-75; del. Nat. Democratic Conv., N.Y.C., 1976. Mem. La. Law Inst. Democrat. Roman Catholic. Legal history, Legal education, Civil rights. Home: 547 Jefferson Ave New Orleans LA 70115 Office: 6801 Freret St New Orleans LA 70118

PALMER, WILLIAM RALPH, lawyer; b. South Boston, Va., Jan. 30, 1950; m. Barbara Anne Link, Dec. 25, 1976; children: Alexis Grynell, William Ralph Jr. BA, Lincoln U., 1972; JD, Howard U., 1975. Bar: Va. 1979, U.S. Dist. Ct. (ea. dist.) Va. 1979, U.S. Ct. Appeals (4th cir.) 1979, U.S. Supreme Ct. 1985. Law clk. Bongiovanni & Collins, Denville, N.J., 1975-76; trust asst. Sovran Bank, Richmond, Va., 1977-78; sole practice Richmond, 1979-85; ptnr. Ealey, Palmer & Palmer, Richmond, 1985—; legal counsel Afro Am. Mens Reorgn. Com., Phila., 1981—, Anyabwile Angaza Fraternity, Inc., Concerned Black Men of Richmond, Va., Inc. Appointed escheator for the city of Richmond Gov. of Commonwealth of Va., 1986. Mem. Va. State Bar Assn., Va. Trial Lawyers Assn., Old Dominion Bar Assn., Nat. Bar Assn. Democrat. Baptist. Avocations: reading, running. Personal injury, Bankruptcy, State civil litigation. Home: 104 Larne Ave Richmond VA 23224

PALMETER, N. DAVID, lawyer; b. Elmira, N.Y., Jan. 29, 1938; s. Neal Henry and Elizabeth Jane (McHale) P.; m. Mary Lee Morken, Mar. 14, 1964 (div. 1979); children—Stephen Michael, John David; m. Mary Faith Tanney, Jan. 15, 1983; children: Elizabeth Jane, James Martin. A.B., Syracuse U., 1960; J.D., U. Chgo., 1963. Bar: N.Y. 1963, D.C. 1969. Trial atty. U.S. Dept. Justice, Washington, 1966-68; assoc. Daniels & Houlihan, Washington, 1969-73, ptnr., 1973-75; ptnr. Daniels, Houlihan & Palmeter, Washington, 1975-84, Mudge, Rose, Guthrie, Alexander & Ferdon, Washington, 1984—. Contbr. articles to profl. publs. Mem. ABA, Internat. Bar Assn., Fed. Bar Assn., N.Y. State Bar Assn. Private international, Administrative and regulatory. Home: 2804 29th St NW Washington DC 20008 Office: Mudge Rose Guthrie Alexander & Ferdon 2121 K St Nw Washington DC 20037

PALMIERI, ANGELA, lawyer; b. Detroit, Nov. 28, 1951; d. Idolo and Loretta (Iannucci) P. B.S. in Acctg./Econs., U. Detroit, 1973; J.D., Thomas M. Cooley Law Sch., 1977. Bar: Mich., 1978, U.S. Dist. Ct. (ea. dist.) Mich., 1978, U.S. Ct. Mil. Appeals, 1981, U.S. Supreme Ct., 1981. Student legal asst. to chief dep. atty. gen. State of Mich., Lansing, 1976-77; sole practice, Garden City, Mich., 1978—; cons. attys. Mem. Mich. Bar Assn., Am. Judicature Soc. State civil litigation, Criminal, Jurisprudence. Home: 26545 Ford Rd Dearborn Heights MI 48127 Office: 30905 Ford Rd Garden City MI 48135

PANARO, GERARD PAUL, lawyer; b. Scranton, Pa., July 5, 1949; s. Gerard Anthony and Genivive (Falzett) P.; m. Julie Joyce, Oct. 27, 1979; children: Matthew V., Ryan M. BA, U. Scranton, 1971; PhD, Boston Coll., 1974; JD, Georgetown U., 1977. Bar: D.C. 1977, U.S. Ct. Appeals (D.C. cir.) 1977, Md. 1978, U.S. Dist. Ct. D.C. 1978, U.S. Dist. Ct. Md. 1981. Staff counsel Retail Bakers Am., Washington, 1977-79; assoc. Jenkins, Nystrom & Slerlacci, Washington, 1979-82, Webster, Chamberlain, Bean & McKevitt, Washington, 1982—; gen. counsel Retail Bakers Am., Washington, 1979—, Nat. Candy Brokers Assn., 1982-86, also exec. v.p., 1982-86, Nat. Candy Wholesaler Assn., 1986—. Mem. ABA, D.C. Bar Assn., Md. State Bar Assn. Republican. Roman Catholic. Avocation: reading. Labor, Administrative and regulatory, Legislative. Home: 6117 Highboro Dr Bethesda MD 20817 Office: Webster Chamberlain Bean & McKevitt 1747 Pennsylvania Ave NW Washington DC 20006

PANCHOT, DUDLEY BRADFORD, lawyer; b. Yakima, Wash., Feb. 25, 1930; s. Kenneth Bradford and Marion Roberts (Dudley) P.; m. Anne Louise Swanson, Oct. 28, 1950; children—Yvonne Marie, Jeanne Louise, Marianne Margarite, John Robert. Student U. Puget Sound, 1947-48; B.A. in Econs., U. Wash., 1951, J.D., 1955. Bar: Wash. 1956, U.S. Dist. Ct. (we. dist.) Wash. 1956, U.S. Ct. Appeals (9th cir.) 1957. Assoc. R. Wayne Cyphers, Seattle, 1956, 57, Reaugh, Hart & Allison, Seattle, 1957-62; assoc. Wolfstone & Piehler, Seattle, 1962-63, ptnr., 1964; ptnr. Wolfstone & Panchot, Seattle, 1965-67, Wolfstone, Panchot & Kleist, Seattle, 1968, Wolfstone, Panchot, Kleist & Bloch, Seattle, 1969-70, Wolfstone, Panchot & Bloch, Seattle, 1970-77; ptnr. Wolfstone, Panchot, Bloch & Kelley, Seattle, 1977-81, sr. ptnr., 1981-84; sr. ptnr. Wolfstone, Panchot & Bloch, 1985—; lectr. Bellevue Community Coll., state bar assn. seminars; town counsel Medina (Wash.), 1970-72. Bd. visitors U. Wash. Sch. Law, 1982—; trustee Seattle Central YMCA, 1978—. Mem. ABA, Seattle Bar Assn., King County Bar Assn., Am. Coll. Probate Counsel, Wash. State Bar Assn. (past chmn. tax sect.), Seattle Estate Planning Council, Phi Kappa Delta. Republican. Congregationalist. Club: Harbor (Seattle). Estate planning, Probate, Real property. Home: 1700 90th NE Bellevue WA 98004 Office: Norton Bldg Suite 1117 Seattle WA 98104

PANDOLFE, JOHN THOMAS, JR., lawyer; b. Neptune, N.J., Dec. 15, 1941; s. John T. and Jeannette R. (Pullen) P.; m. Linda Lee Fritzsche, July 12, 1969; 1 child, Leslie. AB, U. Miami, 1965; MS, Monmouth Coll., 1973; JD, U. Miami, 1976. Bar: Fla. 1976, N.J. 1976, U.S. Dist. Ct. N.J. 1976. Sole practice Brielle, N.J., 1976-80; ptnr. Coogan, Pandolfe, Shaw & Rubino (and predecessor firms), Spring Lake, N.J., 1980—; Pres. Avon Hotel Corp., Brielle, N.J., 1984—; lectr. N.J. Inst. Continuing Legal Edn. Mem. ABA, Fla. Bar Assn., N. Bar Assn., Monmouth Bar Assn. Democrat. Roman Catholic. Club: Spring Lake Golf. Real property, General practice. Office: Coogan Pandolfe Shaw & Rubino 215 Morris Ave PO Box 257 Spring Lake NJ 07762

PANE, MICHAEL ANTHONY, IV, lawyer, consultant; b. New Brunswick, N.J., Nov. 1, 1942; S. Remigio Ugo Quirino and Philomena (Pascale) P.; m. Frances Eleanor Heckert, May 7, 1966; children—Michael Anthony V, Natalia Eugenia. A.B., Princeton U., 1964; J.D., Harvard U., 1967. Bar: N.J. 1967, U.S. Dist. Ct. N.J. 1967. Research assoc., then research dir. N.J. County and Mcpl. Govt. Study Commn., 1967-71; exec. v.p. Community Program Assistance, Inc., Trenton, N.J., 1971-75; sr. research analyst Synectics, Trenton, 1971-75; assoc. firm Warren Goldberg and Berman, Trenton and Princeton, N.J., 1975-77; sole practice, Trenton, East Windsor and Hightstown, N.J., 1978—, also cons.; cons. various state and mcpl. govtl. bodies, orgns. and assns.; lectr. numerous legal and local govtl. profl. meetings. Author: Functional Fragmentation and the Traditional Forms of Local Government in New Jersey, 1986; Contbr. numerous articles to profl. publs.; editor N.J. Inst. Mcpl. Attys. Law Rev., 1986—. Campaign chmn. Mercer County unit Am. Cancer Soc., 1975-76; active local and county Dem. Coms., 1967-83. Mem. N.J. Inst. Mcpl. Attys. (trustee 1982—), N.J. Bar Assn., Italy and Colonies Study Circle (U.S.A.) (treas., quar. nat. jour. editor 1981-84). Roman Catholic. Local government, Legislative, Environment. Home: 1 Hidden Springs Ln East Windsor NJ 08520 Office: 307 N Main St Hightstown NJ 08520

PANEC, WILLIAM JOSEPH, lawyer; b. Pawnee City, Nebr., June 22, 1937; s. Albert and Thelma I. (Sebring) P.; m. Carolyn R. McVitty, Aug. 17, 1963. B.S., U. Nebr., 1962, J.D., 1965. Bar: Nebr. 1965, U.S. Dist. Ct. Nebr. 1965. Sole practice, Fairbury, Nebr., 1965—; county judge Jefferson County, Nebr., 1965-70; mem. Nebr. Jud. Qualifications Commn., 1968-70; chmn. Region XIV Crime Commn., 1968-71; cons., 1971-79; cons. for regions VIII, IX, XIV Regional Jail Study, 1972; profl. instr. Nebr. Law Enforcement Adv. Council, 1972; county atty. Jefferson County, 1973-75; village atty. Diller, Nebr., 1975—; atty. Fairbury Airport Authority, 1981—. Bd. dirs. Housing Authority, Fairbury, 1979—, chmn., 1983; bd. dirs. Legal Services of S.E. Nebr., 1984; chmn. Law Day, Jefferson County, 1972, 73. Served with U.S. Army, 1955-56. Mem. Nebr. Assn. Trial Attys., Assn. Trial Lawyers Am., Am. Judicature Soc., Nebr. County Judges Assn. (v.p., pres.), Jefferson County Bar Assn., Internat. Footprinters Assn., U. Nebr. Alumni Assn., Delta Theta Phi. Methodist (trustee), Clubs: Elks, Masons. Author: Probate Procedures and the Uniform Probate Code, 1969; organizer Nebr. Jud. Reform, 1969. State civil litigation, General practice, Probate.

PANEK, MICHAEL JOHN, lawyer; b. Stoke-on-Trent, Eng., Apr. 30, 1946; came to U.S., 1948; s. Walter John and Phyllis Machin (Reid) P.; m. Carol Lynn Cooley, May 22, 1971; children: Sara E., Carrie M., Heather M. BA with highest honors, Mich. State U., 1968; JD, U. Mich., 1973. Ptnr. Farhat, Stony, Panek, Tyler & Kraus, P.C., East Lansing, Mich., 1973-86; sole practice Lansing, Mich., 1986—; adj. prof. Cooley Law Sch., Lansing, 1983; mem. Greater Lansing Estate Planning Council, Lansing, 1973—. Bd. dirs. Greater Lansing Fin. Planning Council. Served to sgt. U.S. Army, 1968-70, Vietnam. Mem. ABA, Mich. Bar Assn., Lansing Cath. Lawyers Guild. Pension, profit-sharing, and employee benefits, Bankruptcy, Estate planning. Home: 1959 Wembley Way East Lansing MI 48823 Office: 217 S Grand Lansing MI 48933

PANELLI, EDWARD ALEXANDER, associate justice; b. Santa Clara, Calif., Nov. 23, 1931; s. Pilade and Natalina (Della Maggiora) P.; m. Lorna Christine Mondora, Oct. 27, 1956; children: Thomas E., Jeffrey J., Michael P. BA cum laude, Santa Clara U., 1953, JD cum laude, 1955, LLD (hon.), 1986. Bar: Calif. 1955. Ptnr. Pasquinelli and Panelli, San Jose, Calif., 1955-72; judge Santa Clara County Superior Ct., 1972-83; assoc. justice 1st Dist. Ct. of Appeals, San Francisco, 1983-84; presiding justice 6th Dist. Ct. of Appeals, San Jose, 1984-85; assoc. justice Calif. Supreme Ct., San Francisco, 1985—; instr. Continuing Legal Edn., Santa Clara, 1976-78. Trustee West Valley Community Coll., 1963-72; trustee Santa Clara U., 1963—, chmn. bd. trustees, 1984—. Recipient Citation, Am. Com. Italian Migration, 1969, Community Legal Services award, 1979, 84, Edwin J. Owens Lawyer of Yr. award Santa Clara Law Sch. Alumni, 1982, Merit award Republic of Italy, 1984. Mem. Nat. Italian ABA (inspiration award 1986), Calif. Trial Lawyers Assn. (Trial Judge of Yr. award Santa Clara County chpt. 1981), Calif. Judges Assn. (bd. dirs. 1982). Republican. Roman Catholic. Avocations: jogging, sailing. Office: Supreme Ct Calif 350 McAllister St San Francisco CA 94102

PANG, PETER CHIUSING, lawyer, business consultant; b. Hong Kong, Dec. 22, 1952; came to U.S., 1964; s. Henry I. and Chun-Kwan (Siu) P.; m. Susan Feltrup, Aug. 4, 1979. AB, U. Calif., Berkeley, 1976; JD, U. Santa Clara, 1979; LLM, U. Houston, 1985. Bar: Tex. 1979, Pa. 1986. Atty. Shell Oil Co., Houston, 1979-86; asst. corp. sec., gen. corp. counsel Triton Bioscis. Inc., Alameda, Calif., 1983-86; counsel Hershey (Pa.) Foods Corp., 1986—. Administrative and regulatory, Private international, Contracts commercial. Home: PO Box 624 Hershey PA 17033 Office: Hershey Foods Corp 14 E Chocolate Ave Hershey PA 17033

PANIAGUAS, JOHN STEVEN, lawyer; b. Gary, Ind., Sept. 7, 1951; s. John and Anne (Mako) P.; m. Kathy Rae Taylor, Apr. 1, 1978; children—Nicole, Joshua, Melissa. B.S.E.E., Purdue U., 1973; J.D., DePaul U., 1982. Bar: Ill. 1982, U.S. Dist. Ct. (no. dist.) Ill. 1982, U.S. Ct. Appeals (7th cir.) 1983, U.S. Patent and Trademark Office, 1983, U.S. Ct. Appeals (fed. cir.) 1984, U.S. Supreme Ct. 1986; registered profl. engr., Ind., Ill. Elec. engr. Sargent & Lundy, Chgo., 1973-76, 79-83, No. Ind. Pub. Service Co., Hammond, 1976-79; patent atty. McGraw Edison Co., Rolling Meadows, Ill., 1983-85, patent atty. Motorola, Inc., Schaumburg, Ill., 1985, assoc. Mason,

Kolehmainen, Rathburn & Wyss, Chgo., 1985—. Mem. Am. Intellectual Property Law Assn., Patent Assn. Chgo., ABA, Ill. State Bar Assn., Chgo. Bar Assn., Am. Jurisprudence Lawyers Co-op, Inst. Electrical and Electronics Engrs., Tau Beta Pi. Roman Catholic. Patent, Trademark and copyright, Unfair competition. Office: Mason Kolehmainen Rathburn & Wyss 20 N Wacker Suite 4200 Chicago IL 60606

PANITZ, LAWRENCE HERBERT, lawyer, health care products company executive; b. N.Y.C., Feb. 3, 1941; s. Abraham Alexander and Anita Rosyln (Zuckerberg) P.; m. Karin Blaschke, May 27, 1965. A.B., Princeton U., 1962; J.D., Columbia U., 1965. Bar: N.Y. 1965. Assoc., Wolf, Haldenstein, Adler, Freeman and Herz, N.Y.C., 1965-69; asst. chief fgn. counsel W.R. Grace & Co., N.Y.C., 1969-74; v.p., asst. gen. counsel Revlon, Inc., N.Y.C., 1974-84; sr. v.p., gen. counsel, chief adminstrv. officer ICN Pharms., Inc., Costa Mesa, Calif., 1985—; arbitrator Am. Arbitration Assn., 1966—. Princeton U. fellow, 1961. Mem. Assn. Bar City N.Y. Republican. Club: Explorers (N.Y.C.). General corporate, Private international. Home: 710 Park Ave New York NY 10021 Office: 710 Park Ave New York NY 10021

PANNELL, JAMES LOUGHRIDGE, lawyer; b. Atlanta, Sept. 12, 1948; s. Charles Adam and Ruth Ann (Loughridge) P.; m. Mary Karen Bedingfield, May 31, 1975; children: Jonathan Bedingfield, Mary Jamison. BBA, U. Ga., 1970, JD, 1974. Bar: Ga. 1974, U.S. Dist. Ct. (so. dist.) Ga. 1974, U.S. Ct. Appeals (11th cir.) 1980, U.S. Supreme Ct. 1980. Assoc. Oliver, Maner & Gray, Savannah, Ga., 1974-79, ptnr., 1980—. Rep. Ga. Ho. of Reps., Atlanta, 1985—. Served to 1st lt. USAR, 1970—; mem. Jud. Nominating Commn., Ga., 1980-81. Mem. ABA, Ga. Bar Assn. (pres. younger lawyers sect. 1979-80, bd. gov. 1978-85, state disciplinary bd. 1979-80), Ga. Bar Found. (trustee 1979-81), Am. Judicature Soc., Nat. Assn. Bond Lawyers, Maritime Law Assn. Democrat. Methodist. Municipal bonds, Federal civil litigation, State civil litigation. Home: 4107 Amsterdam Circle Savannah GA 31405 Office: Oliver Maner & Gray 218 State St W PO Box 10186 Savannah GA 31412

PANNER, OWEN M., United States district judge; b. 1924. Student, U. Okla., 1941-43, LL.B., 1949. Atty. Panner, Johnson, Marceau, Karnopp, Kennedy & Nash, 1950-80; judge U.S. Dist. Ct. Oreg., Portland, 1980—. Office: US Courthouse 602 SW Main St Portland OR 97205 *

PANNILL, WILLIAM PRESLEY, lawyer; b. Houston, Mar. 5, 1940; s. Fitzhugh H. and Mary Ellen (Goodrum) P.; m. Deborah Detering, May 9, 1966 (div. Nov. 1986); children: Shelley, Katherine, Elizabeth. BA, Rice U., 1962; MS, Columbia U., 1963; JD, U. Tex., 1970. Bar: Tex. 1970, U.S. Supreme Ct. 1975, U.S. Ct. Appeals (5th cir.) 1973, U.S. Ct. Appeals (D.C. cir.) 1974, U.S. Ct. Appeals (10th cir.) 1980, U.S. Ct. Appeals (11th cir.) 1981, U.S. Dist. Ct. (so. dist.) Tex. 1975. Assoc. Vinson, Elkins, Searls & Connally, 1970-71; staff asst. Sec. of Treasury, Washington, 1971-72; assoc. Vinson, Elkins, Searls, Connally & Smith, 1972-75; sole practice, 1975-76; ptnr. Pannill and Hooper, Houston, 1977-80; bd. dirs. Reynolds, Allen, Cook, Pannill & Hooper, Inc., Houston, 1980-82; ptnr. Pannill and Reynolds, Houston, 1982-85; sole practice, Houston, 1985—; assoc. editor Litigation Jour. of the Sect. of Litigation, ABA, 1979-81, exec. editor, 1981-82, editor-in-chief, 1982-84, dir. publs., 1984—; lectr. Southwestern Legal Found., 1980, others. Chmn., Legal Found. Am., 1981-82, bd. dirs., 1983—. Served with USMCR, 1963-64. Mem. ABA (council litigation sect. 1986—), Fed. Energy Bar Assn., Houston Bar Assn., Tex. Bar Assn. Episcopalian. Club: Houston. Contbr. articles to profl. jours. FERC practice, Federal civil litigation, State civil litigation. Office: 909 Fannin St Suite 1600 Two Houston Ctr Houston TX 77010-1007

PANTEL, GLENN STEVEN, lawyer; b. Plainfield, N.J., Sept. 25, 1953; s. Donald and Sarah Libby (Pearlman) P.; m. Lisa Pamela Krop, June 28, 1981. AB, Johns Hopkins U., 1975; JD, U. Pa., 1978. Bar: N.J. 1978, U.S. Dist. Ct. N.J. 1978, Pa. 1978, Fla. 1980, U.S. Ct. Appeals (3d cir.) 1982. Law clk. to presiding judge U.S. Dist. Ct. (so. dist.), Miami, Fla., 1978-79; from assoc. to ptnr. Shanley & Fisher P.C., Morristown, N.J., 1979—. Trustee Friday Evening Club Cultural Presenters, Morristown, 1984—. Mem. ABA, Fla. Bar Assn., N.J. Bar Assn., Morris County Bar Assn. Avocations: skiing, sailing. Real property, Environment. Home: 3 Valley View Rd Morristown NJ 07960 Office: Shanley & Fisher PC 80 West End Ave Somerville NJ 08876

PANTZER, KURT FRIEDRICH, JR., lawyer; b. Indpls., May 24, 1928; s. Kurt Friedrich and Katharine Hunter (Ferriday) P.; m. Elizabeth Elliott Kennedy, Aug. 25, 1951; children—Elizabeth E., Katharine H. Pantzer Lange, Kurt Friedrich III, Julia F. B.A., Yale U., 1950; J.D., Harvard U., 1955. Bar: Ind. 1955. Practice law Indpls., 1955—; ptnr. Hendrickson, Travis, Pantzer & Miller, Indpls., 1966—; pres. Ind. Neuromuscular Research Lab., Inc., 1970—; speaker, chmn., author numerous lawyers' insts. on computers and televideo in estate planning and probate, 1979—. Author: Documentary Evidence, 1961, Unauthorized Practice of Law, 1962, Pre-Nuptial Agreements, 1973, Probate Fees, 1976, Orphans' Deduction, 1977; co-editor: Trusts, Wills, Estate Administration and Taxes, Parts 1 and 2, 1963. Pres. Estate Planning Council Indpls., 1977-78; treas. 11th Congl. Dist. Republican Central Com., 1964-66; pres. Marion County Election Bd., 1981-86; bd. dirs. Marion County Muscular Dystrophy Found., 1958-78, pres., 1960-62; bd. dirs. Greater Indpls. chpt. Myasthenia Gravis Found., 1970-77, chmn., 1970-72; bd. dirs. Booth Tarkington Civic Theatre, Indpls., pres., 1977-80; mem. Mayor's Cultural Adv. Council, 1979-83; mem. Mayor's NFL Franchise Com., 1981-83. Served to 1st lt. U.S. Army, 1951-53. Decorated Bronze Star. Fellow Am. Coll. Probate Counsel; mem. ABA, Ind. State Bar Assn., Indpls. Bar Assn., 7th Fed. Circuit Bar Assn., Internat. Acad. Estate and Trust Law (academician), Internat. Wine and Food Soc. (pres. Indpls. br. 1983—). Presbyterian (deacon). Clubs: Columbia, Dramatic (pres. 1980-81), Players, Lambs (dir. 1962—). Probate, General practice, Estate planning. Home: 9401 Spring Mill Rd Indianapolis IN 46260-1462 Office: Suite 240 120 Monument Circle Indianapolis IN 46204-2997

PANZELLA, BERNADETTE, lawyer; b. N.Y.C., Dec. 15, 1947; d. Louis J. and Polly Mary (Gagliardi) P.; divorced; children: Robert G. Schacht Jr., Deborah L. Schacht. AA, S.I. Community Coll., 1973; BA, CUNY, 1975; MA, Columbia U., 1977; JD, Bklyn. Law Sch., 1981. Assoc. Halper & Weinstein, N.Y.C., 1981-82; sole practice S.I., N.Y., 1982—. Mem. ABA, N.Y. State Bar Assn., Assn. Trial Lawyers Am., N.Y. State Women's Bar Assn., Richmond County Bar Assn., N.Y. State Trial Lawyers Assn. Home and Office: 596 Bement Ave Staten Island NY 10310

PANZER, EDWARD S., lawyer; b. N.Y.C., Jan. 3, 1938; s. David Panzer and Paula Tennen; m. Patricia Ann McNamee, Aug. 5, 1973 (div.). BA, CCNY, 1959; LLB, Bklyn. Law Sch., 1962, JD, 1967. Bar: N.Y. 1962, U.S. Dist. Ct. (ea. and so. dist.) N.Y. 1964, U.S. Ct. Appeals (2d cir.) 1973, U.S. Supreme Ct. 1976. With criminal div. Legal Aid Soc., N.Y.C., 1962-64; sr. trial atty. fed. defender Dist. Ct. N.Y., 1964-68; asst. dist. atty. Bronx County, N.Y., 1968-70; sole practice, N.Y.C., 1970—; lectr. law, 1975—; mem. Fed. Criminal Justice Panel So. and Ea. Dists., 1970—, Spl. Homicide Panel, N.Y.C., 1975—, N.Y. State Felony Panel, 1970—. Recipient Human Values award Human Values Com. N.Y.C., 1979-80. Mem. Nat. Assn. Criminal Def. Lawyers, N.Y. State Bar Assn., Calif. Attys. for Criminal Justice, N.Y. State Defenders Assn. Democrat. Criminal. Home: 245 E 93rd St New York NY 10128 Office: 225 Broadway New York NY 10007

PANZER, IRVING RELLER MYRON, lawyer, legal educator; b. East Hampton, N.Y., Nov. 13, 1916; s. Bernhard and Sadie (Reller) P.; m. Sue Burnett, Aug. 31, 1963. BS, NYU; LLB, Harvard U. Bar: N.Y. 1940, U.S. Supreme Ct. 1947, D.C. 1947. Assoc. Pike & Fischer, Washington, 1941; atty. SEC, Washington, 1941-43, U.S. Dept. of Justice, Washington, 1943; ptnr. Fischer, Willis & Panzer, Washington, 1946-60; sole practice Washington, 1960-86; of counsel Paulson, Nace & Norwind, Washington, 1986—; adj. prof. Cath. U. Law Sch., Washington, 1957—. Served to lt. USMC, 1944-46. Mem. ABA, Fed. Bar Assn., D.C. Bar Assn. (bd. dirs. 1985—). Club: Cosmos (Washington) (bd. of mgmt. 1985—). Avocations: tennis, squash, folk songs. Federal civil litigation. Home: 2336 Massachusetts Ave NW Washington DC 20008 Office: Paulson Nace & Norwind 1814 N St NW Washington DC 20036

PANZER, MITCHELL EMANUEL, lawyer; b. Phila., Aug. 2, 1917; s. Max and Cecelia (Kassner) P.; m. Edith Budin, Apr. 13, 1943; children—Marcy C., Leslie S. Katz. A.B. with distinction and 1st honors, Temple U., 1937; J.D. magna cum laude, U. Pa., 1940; LL.D., Gratz Coll., 1972. Bar: Pa. 1942, U.S. Dist. Ct. (ea. dist.) Pa. 1948, U.S. Ct. Appeals (3d cir.) 1949, U.S. Supreme Ct. 1961. Gowen Meml. fellow U. Pa. Law Sch., 1940-41; law clk. Phila. Ct. Common Pleas, No. 7, 1941-42; assoc. Wolf, Block, Schorr and Solis-Cohen, Phila., 1946-54, ptnr., 1954—; spl. adv. counsel Fed. Home Loan Mortgage Corp., Fed. Nat. Mortgage Assn., 1972-82; dir., counsel St. Edmond's Savs. and Loan Assn., Crescent Bldg. and Loan Assn.; dir. State Chartered Group, Pa. Bldg. and Loan Assn. Trustee, Fedn. Jewish Agys. Greater Phila., 1981-82, v.p., 1982-86, trustee, mem. exec. com., 1963-86; bd. overseers Gratz Coll., 1958—, pres., 1962-68. Served to capt. USAF, 1942-46. Decorated Bronze Star medal; recipient Man of Year award Gratz Coll. Alumni Assn., 1964 . Mem. Am. Coll. Real Estate Lawyers, ABA (chmn. spl. com. on residential real estate transactions 1972-73), Pa. Bar Assn. (mem. spl. com. on land titles), Phila. Bar Assn. (chmn. bd. govs. 1971, parliamentarian 1965-67, 71, chmn. charter and by-laws com. 1972), Jewish Publ. Soc. (trustee 1966-81, 85—), Order of Coif (pres. 1961-63, exec. com.). Jewish. Clubs: 21 Jewel Square (Phila.); Masons. Patentee in field. Real property. Home: 505 Oak Terrace Merion Station PA 19066 Office: Wolf Block Schorr & Solis-Cohen 15th & Chestnut Sts SE 12th Floor Packard Bldg Philadelphia PA 19102

PAPE, GLENN MICHAEL, lawyer, accountant, personal financial planner; b. Evergreen Park, Ill., Aug. 20, 1954; s. Gilbert Thomas Pape and Janine Elizabeth (Beheyt) Pape Riveros; m. Nancy Ann Vaske, Apr. 7, 1979; children: Katherine Jo, Courtney Johanna. BA in Classics, U. Chgo., 1978, MBA, 1981; JD, DePaul U., 1979. Bar: Ill. 1979. Cons. tax div. No. Trust Co., Chgo., 1980-81, fin. planner, 1981-82; fin. counselor Continental Ill. Nat. Bank, Chgo., 1982-84; tax mgr. Arthur Andersen & Co., Chgo., 1984—. Active Five Hosp. Homebound Elderly Program, Chgo., 1981; treas. Chamber Music Council Chgo., 1982. Mem. Chgo. Bar Assn. (fed. taxation com.), Ill. State Bar Assn., ABA, Internat. Assn. Fin. Planners, Am. Inst. CPA's, U.S. Chess Fedn., Am. Inst. CPA's. Personal income taxation, Pension, profit-sharing, and employee benefits, Estate planning. Home: 2146 University Dr Naperville IL 60565-3485 Office: Arthur Andersen & Co 33 W Monroe St Chicago IL 60603

PAPERNIK, JOEL IRA, lawyer; b. N.Y.C., May 4, 1944; s. Herman and Ida (Titefsky) P.; m. Barbara Ann Barker, July 28, 1972. BA, Yale U., 1965; JD cum laude, Columbia U., 1968. Bar: N.Y. 1969. Assoc. Shea & Gould, N.Y.C., 1968-76, ptnr., 1976—; lectr. various panels. Author in field. Served with USAR, 1967-73. Mem. ABA, Assn. Bar City N.Y. (chmn. corp. law com., uniform laws com., lectr.), N.Y. State Bar Assn. (lectr. various panels), Tri-Bar Opinion Com. General corporate, Entertainment, Contracts commercial. Office: Shea & Gould 330 Madison Ave New York NY 10017

PAPIANO, NEIL LEO, lawyer; b. Salt Lake City, Nov. 25, 1933; s. Leo and Ruth Ida (Cotten) P. B.A., Stanford, 1956, M.A. in Polit. Sci, 1957; J.D., Vanderbilt U., 1961. Bar: Calif. bar 1961. Partner Iverson, Yoakum, Papiano & Hatch (and predecessor firm), Los Angeles, 1961—; Dir. SCOA Industries, Inc., Ocean Tech., Inc., Pacific United Services Corp., King Nutronics, Inc. Vice pres. Los Angeles County Welfare Planning Council, 1966-71; chmn. Los Angeles Forward, 1970-71; vice chmn. Cal. Com. for Welfare Reform, 1972; mem. Calif. Jud. Selection Com., 1972-74; Co-finance chmn. Republican State Central Com., 1975; Treas. Los Angeles Opera Co., 1964, bd. dirs., 1965; treas. So. Calif. Choral Music Assn., 1964, bd. dirs., 1964-73; bd. dirs. Citizens Adv. Council on Pub. Transp., Mgmt. Council for Research and Tng., Orthopedic Hosp., Stanford U. Athletic Bd., Nat. Athletic Health Inst., Los Angeles Music Center Operating Co.; bd. govs. U. S.O., 1967-71, Performing Arts Council of Los Angeles Music Center, 1981. Mem. Am., Calif. bar assns., Los Angeles Area C. of C. (pres. 1966, dir. 1964-67, 72-75), Phi Delta Theta. Clubs: Rotarian, California, Los Angeles Country. State civil litigation, State and local taxation, Local government. Office: 611 W 6th St Suite 1900 Los Angeles CA 90017

PAPIK, JAMES ELVIN, lawyer; b. Sioux City, Iowa, June 1, 1952; s. Elvin and Gloria (Jacobsen) P.; m. Marta M. Erikson, Mar. 23, 1974; children: Jonathan, Kristin. BA, Doane Coll., 1974; JD, U. Nebr., 1980. Bar: Nebr. 1980, U.S. Dist. Ct. Nebr. 1980. Assoc. Mills Law Office, Osceola, Nebr., 1981-83; ptnr. Mills, Mills & Papik, Osceola, 1983—; bd. dirs. Legal Services of Southeast Nebr., Lincoln. Bd. dirs. Midwest Covenant Home, Stromsburg, Nebr., 1985—. Mem. ABA, Nebr. Bar Assn., Polk County Bar Assn. (pres. 1981—). Avocations: golf, running. General practice, Banking, Real property. Office: Mills Mills & Papik 510 Nebraska Osceola NE 68651

PAPKIN, RACHEL FRIEDBERG, lawyer; b. Balt., June 27, 1939; d. Paul Alvin and Dorothy Theresa (Harris) Friedberg; m. Robert David Papkin, Aug. 29, 1965; children: Steven Caleb, Daniel Mark. BA, Wellesley Coll., 1960; JD, Am. U., 1976. Bar: Md. 1977, D.C. 1977, U.S. Ct. Appeals (4th cir.) 1977, U.S. Dist. Ct. D.C. 1978, U.S. Ct. Appeals (D.C. cir.) 1978, U.S. Dist. Ct. Md. 1979, U.S. Supreme Ct. 1982. Legis. aide to Senator Albert Gore Sr. U.S. Senate, Washington, 1961-65; assoc. Frederick & Jersin, Rockville, Md., 1976-77; sole practice Bethesda, Md., 1978—. Mem. ABA, D.C. Bar Assn., Md. Bar Assn., Women's Bar Assn. Montgomery County (chairperson selections com.), Bar Assn. Montgomery County (ethics com., fee arbitration com., family law sect. council), LWV. Democrat. Jewish. Club: Wellesley (Washington). Avocations: tennis, skiing, cooking. Family and matrimonial. Home: 8200 Lillystone Dr Bethesda MD 20817 Office: 4720 Montgomery Ln Suite 1000 Bethesda MD 20814

PAPKIN, ROBERT DAVID, lawyer; b. New Bedford, Mass., Feb. 26, 1933; s. Barney and Rose (Shuster) P.; m. Rachel Friedberg, Aug. 29, 1965; children—Steven C., Daniel M. A.B., Harvard U., 1954, LL.B., 1957. Bar: Mass. 1957, D.C. 1964. Legal asst. NLRB, Washington, 1958-61; assoc. Cox, Langford & Brown, Washington, 1963-66, ptnr., 1966-73; ptnr. Squire, Sanders & Dempsey, Washington, 1973—. Served with U.S. Army, 1957-58. Fulbright fellow, 1962-63. Mem. ABA, D.C. Bar, Fed. Bar Assn., Inter-Am. Bar Assn. Democrat. Jewish. Clubs: Metropolitan, Cosmos (Washington). Private international, Labor, Administrative and regulatory. Home: 8200 Lilly Stone Dr Bethesda MD 20817

PAPPAS, DAVID CHRISTOPHER, lawyer; b. Kenosha, Wis., Mar. 18, 1936; s. Theros and Marion Lucille (Piperas) P.; m. Laurie Jean Lacaskey, Nov. 26, 1956 (div. 1969); children—Christopher David, Andrea Lynn; m. Nancy Marie Pratt, June 11, 1983. B.S., U. Wis., 1959, S.J.D., 1961. Bar: Wis. 1961, U.S. Dist. Ct. (ea. and we. dists.) Wis. 1965, U.S. Supreme Ct. 1971. Asst. corp. counsel Racine County, Wis., 1961; atty., adviser U.S. Dept. Labor, Washington, 1961-62; staff atty. U.S. Commn. Civil Rights, Washington, 1962-63; asst. city atty. City of Madison, Wis., 1963-65; sole practice, Madison, 1965—. Chmn. Madison Mayor's Citizen Adv. Com., 1964-65; pres. Wis. Cup Assn., Madison, 1965; co-chmn. 2d Congl. Dist. Humphrey for Pres., Madison, 1972. Recipient commendation for Supreme Ct. work Madison City Council, 1965, commendation resolution City of Madison, 1965. Mem. Wis. Bar Assn., Dane County Bar Assn., Wis. Acad. Trial Lawyers, Assn. Trial Lawyers Am., Gt. Lakes Hist. Soc. Republican. Clubs: Madison; South Shore Yacht (Milw.). State civil litigation, Civil rights, Family and matrimonial. Home: Strawberry Hill Deerfield WI 53531 Office: Suite 212 James Wilson Plaza 131 W Wilson St Madison WI 53703

PAPPAS, EDWARD HARVEY, lawyer; b. Midland, Mich., Nov. 24, 1947; s. Charles and Sydell (Sheinberg) P.; m. Laurie Weston, Aug. 6, 1972; children—Gregory Alan, Steven Michael. B.B.A., U. Mich., 1969, J.D., 1973. Bar: Mich. 1973, U.S. Dist. Ct. (ea. dist.) Mich. 1973, U.S. Dist. Ct. (we. dist.) Mich. 1980, U.S. Ct. Appeals (6th cir.) 1983, U.S. Supreme Ct. 1983. Ptnr. firm Dickinson, Wright, Moon, Van Dusen & Freeman, Bloomfield Hills and Detroit, Mich., 1973—; v.p., trustee Oakland-Livingston Legal Aid, 1982-85, pres., trustee, 1985—; mediator Oakland County Cir. Ct., Pontiac, Mich., 1983—; hearing panelist Mich. Atty. Discipline Bd., Detroit, 1983—. Trustee Oakland Community Coll., Mich., 1982-86 ; trustee adv. bd. Mich. Regional Anti-Defamation League of B'nai Brith, Detroit, 1983—. Mem. State Bar Mich. (co-chmn. nat. moot ct. competition com. 1974, 76, com. on atty. discipline, com. on legal aid.), Oakland County Bar Assn. (vice-chmn. continuing legal edn. com., chmn. continuing legal edn. com. 1985-86, editor Laches monthly mag.), ABA, Am. Judicature Soc., Mich. Def. Trial Lawyers, Def. Research and Trial Lawyers Assn., (com. practice and procedure), B'nai B'rith Barristers. Federal civil litigation, State civil litigation. Home: 32223 Scenic Ln Franklin MI 48025 Office: PO Box 509 Dickinson Wright Moon Van Dusen & Freeman 525 N Woodward Ave Bloomfield Hills MI 48013

PAPPAS, GEORGE FRANK, lawyer; b. Washington, Oct. 5, 1950; s. Frank George and Lora Marie (Stauber) P.; m. Susan Elizabeth Bradshaw, Apr. 25, 1980; 1 child, Christine Bradshaw Pappas. B.A., U. Md., 1972, J.D., 1975. Bar: Md. 1976, U.S. Dist. Ct. Md. 1976, U.S. Ct. Appeals (4th cir.) 1976, U.S. Ct. Appeals (D.C. cir.) 1984, U.S. Supreme Ct. 1984, U.S. Dist. Ct. (D.C. cir.) 1986. Assoc. H. Russell Smouse, Balt., 1976-81; assoc. Melnicove, Kaufman, Wiener & Smouse, Balt., 1981-83, ptnr. 1983—; lectr. Wash. Coll. Law, Am. U., Washington, 1980-84; mem. moot ct. bd., 1974-75. Founding editor-in-chief Internat. Trade Law Jour., 1974-75. Served to 1st lt. USAF, 1972-76. Mem. Nat. Assn. R.R. Trial Counsel, Md. Bar Assn. (chmn. internat. coml. law sect., 1980-81), ABA, Omicron Delta Kappa, Phi Kappa Phi, Phi Beta Kappa. Republican. Greek Orthodox. Club: L'Hirondelle. Federal civil litigation, State civil litigation, Construction. Home: 7916 Ruxway Rd Ruxton MD 21204 Office: Melnicove Kaufman Wiener & Smouse 36 S Charles St 6th Fl Baltimore MD 21201

PAPROCKI, THOMAS JOHN, priest, lawyer; b. Chgo., Aug. 5, 1952; s. John Henry and Veronica Mary (Bonat) P. BA, Loyola U., Chgo., 1974; student Spanish lang. study, Middlebury Coll., 1976; M in Divinity, St. Mary of the Lake Sem., 1978; student Spanish lang. study, Instituto Cuannahuac, 1978; Licentiate in Sacred Theology, St. Mary of the Lake Sem., 1979; JD, DePaul U., 1981. Bar: Ill. 1981, U.S. Dist. Ct. (no. dist.) Ill. 1981. Assoc. pastor St. Michael Ch., Chgo., 1978-83; pres. South Chgo. Legal Clinic, 1981—, exec. dir., 1981-85; adminstr. St. Joseph Ch., Chgo., 1983-86; vice-chancellor Archdiocese of Chgo., 1985—; senator Presbyteral senate Archdiocese of Chgo., 1985—; bd. dirs. Cath. Conf. Ill., 1985—. Editorial Adv. Bd. Chicago Catholic Newspaper, 1984-85; contbr. articles to profl. jours. bd. dirs. United Neighborhood Orgn., Chgo., 1982-85, Southeast Community Youth Service Bd., Chgo., 1985, Ctr. for Neighborhood Tech., Chgo., 1986—. Recipient Outstanding Service award Niles Coll. of Loyola U., 1974. Fellow Leadership Greater Chgo.; mem. ABA, Ill. Bar Assn., Chgo. Bar Assn. (Maurice Weigle award 1985), Advocates Soc. Lawyers, Cath. Lawyers Guild, Pi Sigma Alpha, DePaul Alumni Assn. Avocations: hockey, running, reading. Counsel, religious organization, Nonprofit legal clinic, Immigration, naturalization, and customs. Home: 7135 N Harlem Ave Chicago IL 60631 Office: Archdiocese of Chgo 155 E Superior PO Box 1979 Chicago IL 60690

PARAD, BORIS, lawyer, consultant; b. Kiev, Ukraine, USSR, Dec. 25, 1946; came to U.S., 1973; s. Samson and Sara (Wolter) P; m. Yelena Volosevich, Mar. 18, 1983; 1 child, Dennis Joshua. MME, Kiev Civil-Engrs. Inst., 1970; JD, John Marshall Law Sch., 1978. Bar: Ill. 1979, U.S. Dist. Ct. (no. dist.) Ill. 1979, U.S. Patent Office 1980, U.S. Ct. Appeals (D.C. cir.) 1982. Asst. chief mech. dept. State Cons. Inst., Kiev, 1970-73; designer Sargent & Lundy, Engrs., Chgo., 1973-76; law clk. Office of Ill. Atty. Gen., Chgo., 1978-79; atty. Pullman Inc., Chgo., 1979-81, Internat. Harvester, Chgo., 1981-85; assoc. Laff, Whitesel, Conte & Saret, Chgo., 1985-86; sole practice Skokie, Ill., 1986—; cons. proprietary bus. info. Author: Industrial Espionage in the USA: Business Protection Guide, 1986; patentee dispensing container. Mem. Chgo. Bar Assn., Chgo. Patent Law Assn., Internat. Assn. for Protection Indsl. Property, Am. Intellectual Property Law Assn., Am. Soc. Indsl. Security. Patent, Trademark and copyright, Personal injury. Office: 4948 Dempster Skokie IL 60077

PARAN, MARK LLOYD, lawyer; b. Cleve., Feb. 1, 1953; s. Edward Walter and Margaret Gertrude (Ebert) P. AB cum laude in Sociology, Harvard U., 1977, JD, 1980. Bar: Ill. 1980, Mass. 1986. Assoc. Wilson & McIlvaine, Chgo., 1980-83, Lurie Sklar & Simon, Ltd., Chgo., 1983-85, Sullivan & Worcester, Boston, 1985—. Mem. ABA, Mass. Bar Assn. General corporate, Securities, Banking. Home: 84 Gainsborough St #106W Boston MA 02115-4229 Office: Sullivan & Worcester One Post Office Sq Boston MA 02109-2129

PARDIECK, ROGER L., lawyer; b. Seymour, Ind., Mar. 1, 1937; s. Martin W. and Lorna (Wente) P.; m. Margarett Stahl, Sept. 2, 1961; children—Amy, Andrew, Melissa. A.B., Ind. U., 1959, LL.B., 1963. Bar: Ind. 1963, U.S. Dist. Ct. (so. dist.) Ind. 1964, U.S. Ct. Appeals (7th cir.) 1965; diplomate Am. Bd. Trial Advocates. Teaching asst. Ind. U., Bloomington, 1963-64; spl. prosecutor Jackson County, Ind., 1964-65; ptnr. Montgomery, Elsner and Pardieck, 1965-84; prin. Law Offices Roger L. Pardieck, P.C., Seymour, Ind., 1985—; faculty Nat. Inst. Trial Advocacy, Ind.; lectr. in field. Contbr. articles to profl. jours. Bd. dirs. Seymour Girls Club, 1968-72, Seymour C. of C., 1971-75; bd. dirs. Lutheran Community Home, 1964—, pres., 1970; trustee Immanuel Luth. Ch., 1977-80, bd. Immanuel Luth. Sch., 1980-83; adv. bd. Ind. U., Purdue U.-Indpls., 1981-83. Fellow Am. Coll. Trial Lawyers; mem. Assn. Trial Lawyers Am. (bd. govs. 1985—). Ind. State Bar Assn. (bd. govs. 1980-82), Nat. Bd. Trial Advocacy, Am. Judicature Soc., Fed. Bar Assn., Ind. Bar; fellow Ind. Trial Lawyers Assn. (dir. 1969—, pres. 1975). Republican. Lutheran. Club: Seymour Country. Lodge: Elks. Personal injury, Federal civil litigation, State civil litigation. Office: 100 N Chestnut St PO Box 608 Seymour IN 47274

PARENT, LOUISE MARIE, lawyer; b. San Francisco, Aug. 28, 1950; d. Jules D. and Mary Louise (Bartholomew) P.; m. John P. Casaly, Jan. 5, 1980. AB, Smith Coll., 1972; JD, Georgetown U., 1975. Bar: N.Y. 1976, U.S. Dist. Ct. (so. dist.) N.Y. 1976. Assoc. Donovan Leisure, N.Y.C., 1975-77; various positions, then sr. counsel Am. Express Co., N.Y.C., 1977—. Mem. ABA (law and acctg. com. 1986—). Securities, General corporate, Mergers and acquisitions. Home: 800 West End Ave New York NY 10025 Office: Am Express Co Am Express Tower World Fin Ctr New York NY 10285-4900

PARENTE, JAMES JOSEPH, lawyer; b. Chgo., Oct. 6, 1949; s. Salvatore S. and Genevieve (Rooney) P.; m. Barbara Anne Shimkus, Oct. 23, 1971; children—Anne Elizabeth, Jessica Jean, Jeffrey Edward. B.S., Loyola U., Chgo., 1971; J.D., St. Louis U., 1974. Bar: Mo. 1974, U.S. Dist. Ct. (ea. dist.) Mo. 1974, U.S. Ct. Mil. Appeals 1974, Ill. 1978, U.S. Dist. Ct. (cen. dist.) Ill. 1978. Asst. staff judge adv. JAGC, U.S. Army, Fort Knox, Ky., 1974-78; asst. corp. counsel City of Springfield, Ill., 1978-82; asst. dir. Ill. Inst. Continuing Legal Edn., Springfield, 1982—; staff judge adv., justice Ill. Ct. Mil. Appeals, Springfield, 1979—. Bd. dirs. Springfield Deanery Pro-Life Com., 1983-86; mem speakers bur. Springfield Right-to-Life, 1983-85. Served to capt. U.S. Army, 1974-78, major Army N.G., 1978—. Decorated Army Commendation medal, 1978, Army Achievement medal, 1983. Mem. ABA, Mo. Bar Assn., Ill. Bar Assn. (task force on lawyering skills 1983, com. legal edn. and admissions 1984-85), Chgo. Bar Assn., Assn. Continuing Legal Edn. Adminstrs. Roman Catholic. Legal education, State civil litigation, Military. Home: 713 W Vine St Springfield IL 62704 Office: Ill Inst Continuing Legal Edn 2395 W Jefferson St Springfield IL 62702

PARHAM, JAMES ROBERT, lawyer; b. East St. Louis, Ill., June 3, 1921; s. James Elbert and Edith Virginia (May) P.; m. Caroline Short, Nov. 4, 1950 (dec.); m. Elizabeth Joan Rinck, June 29, 1957; children—James R., Jr., Joseph R., John R. A.B., Princeton U., 1943; J.D. with honors, U. Ill., 1948. Bar: Ill. 1948, U.S. Dist. Ct. (so. dist.) Ill. 1948, U.S. Supreme Ct. 1968. Assoc., Pope & Driemeyer, East St. Louis, 1948-59, ptnr., Belleville, Ill., 1960-84, Thompson & Mitchell, 1985—; mem. adv. council Ill. Inst. for Continuing Legal Edn., Springfield, Ill., 1965-74. Contbr. articles to profl. jours. Sec., YMCA of S.W. Ill., Belleville, 1979-84. Served with U.S. Air Corps, 1943-45, USAF, 1950-53. Recipient Man of Yr. award Bicounty YMCA, Belleville, 1973; Disting. Service award Ill. Inst. Continuing Edn., 1974. Fellow Am. Bar Found., Ill. State Bar Found.; mem. Ill. State Bar Assn. (chmn. state tax sect. 1974), ABA, Met. St. Louis Bar Assn., Res. Officers Assn., Order of Coif. Republican. Methodist. Clubs: St. Clair Country (Belleville, v.p. 1955-56); Naples Bath & Tennis (Naples, Fla.); Media (St. Louis). State and local taxation, Labor, General practice. Home: 67 Country Club Pl Belleville IL 62223 Office: Thompson & Mitchell One S Church St PO Box 750 Belleville IL 62222

PARISH, DENNIS MACDONALD, lawyer; b. Norwalk, Ohio, Sept. 21, 1950; s. Neil Burton and Elizabeth Marie (McDonald) P.; m. Catherine Ann Keber, Sept. 1, 1973 (div. Dec. 1975). BE, U. Toledo, 1972, JD, 1981. Bar: Ohio 1982, U.S. Dist. Ct. (no. dist.) Ohio 1983. Asst. credit mgr. City Loan & Savs., Toledo, 1973-74; tchr., athletic dir., football coach Otsego High Sch., Tontogany, Ohio, 1974-77; tchr., football coach Napoleon (Ohio) High Sch., 1977-79; asst. prosecutor Lucas County, Toledo, 1982-84, referee juvenile ct., 1984-86; chief dep. clk., referee probate juvenile ct. Wood County, Bowling Green, Ohio, 1986; sole practice Perrysburg, Ohio, 1986—. Chmn. Selective Service Bd. So. Lucas County, Toledo; trustee Big Bros./Big Sisters N.W. Ohio, Toledo. Recipient Outstanding Community Service award Napoleon Jaycees, 1978, Citizenship award Am. Legion, 1968. Mem. ABA, Ohio Bar Assn., Wood County Bar Assn., Toledo Bar Assn., Assn. Trial Lawyers Am. Republican. Lutheran. Club: Old News Boys (Toledo). Judicial administration, Juvenile, Probate. Home: 22 Terrace Downs Toledo OH 43614 Office: 941 Westbrook Dr #2 Perrysburg OH 43551

PARISH, TAT, lawyer; b. Waupaca, Wis., July 23, 1940; s. Clarence M. and Lucille (Shuda) P.; m. Margaret Holt, July 30, 1965, (div. Apr. 1970); children: Amy, David; m. Angie M., Feb. 22, 1975; Warren, Scott, Brian, John, Tat P., Joseph. BA, Hamline U., 1961; JD, Harvard U., 1965. Bar: Mich. 1965, U.S. Dist. Ct. (we. dist.) Mich. 1966, U.S. Dist. Ct. (no. dist.) Ind. 1968, U.S. Supreme Ct. 1970, U.S. Dist. Ct. (ea. dist.) Mich. 1982, U.S. Ct. Appeals (6th cir.) 1983, U.S. Ct. Appeals (7th cir.) 1985. Sole practice St. Joseph, Mich., 1965—. Served with U.S. Army, 1958, 61-62. Democrat. Federal civil litigation, State civil litigation, Labor. Home: 1508 Fruitwood Dr Saint Joseph MI 49085 Office: 711 Pleasant St PO Box 409 Saint Joseph MI 49805

PARISH, WILLIAM HENRY, lawyer; b. Oakland, Calif., July 28, 1954; s. Harry and Elaine Katherine (Triplett) P.; m. Kathryn Annette, Aug. 14, 1976; children: Michael Erik, Jennifer Christine, Melissa Ann. AA, Hartnell Coll., 1974; BA, Calif. State U., 1977; JD, U. Pacific, 1980. Bar: Calif. 1980, U.S. Dist. Ct. (ea. dist.) Calif. 1980, U.S. Ct. Appeals (9th cir.) 1980. Assoc. Cavalero, Bray, Geiger & Rudquist, Stockton, Calif., 1980-82, ptnr., 1982-87; ptnr. Bray, Geiger, Rudquist, Nuss & Parish, Stockton, Calif., 1987—. Mem. ABA (litigation sect. 1980—), Order of Coif. State civil litigation, Federal civil litigation. Office: Bray Geiger Rudquist Nuss & Parish 311 E Main St Suite 400 Stockton CA 95202

PARISI, FRANK NICHOLAS, lawyer; b. Schenectady, Sept. 13, 1932; s. James P. and Mary (Tomaso) P.; m. Marilyn Campriello; children—Adam, Matthew, Gerard. Student Union Coll., 1951-54; LL.B., Albany U., 1957, J.D., 1968. Bar: N.Y. 1957, U.S. Tax Ct. 1963. Sr. mem. Parisi, DeLorenzo, Gordon, Pasquariello & Weiskopf, P.C., Schenectady, asst. dist. atty., 1962-65; U.S. Govt. appeal agt., 1971; mem. adv. bd. Community State Bank (now First Am. Bank N.Y.), 1977-83. Bd. dirs. Schenectady County YMCA, Tippecanoe br.; past pres. parish council, trustee Our Lady of the Assumption Ch.; mem. Nat. Selective Service Appeal Bd., 1971-76; mem. panel arbitrators Am. Arbitration Assn. Mem. ABA, N.Y. State Bar Assn., Schenectady County Bar Assn. Republican. Roman Catholic. Real property, Probate, Family and matrimonial. Home: 2773 Maida Ln Schnectady NY 12306 Office: 201 Nott Terr Schenectady NY 12307

PARK, J(AMES) WALTER, IV, lawyer; b. Dallas, Sept. 4, 1948; s. J. Walter, III and Babette (Cockerell) P.; m. Mary Anne Garrett, Aug. 4, 1972 (div. 1976); m. Janette Marie Badour, Apr. 29, 1983; children: Nicole Christine, Rachel Suzanne, J. Walter. B.A., So. Meth. U., 1970; J.D., U. Tex., 1974. Bar: Tex. 1974, U.S. Ct. Appeals (5th cir.) 1980, U.S. Ct. Appeals (9th cir.) 1982. Ptnr. Davis & Turlington, Inc., San Antonio, 1974-82; sole practice, San Antonio, 1982—; prin. Park IV Enterprises, San Antonio, 1984—. Active Tobin Hills Neighborhood Assn., 1983—; San Antonio Mus. Assn. Mem. ABA, State Bar Tex., Ducks Unltd., Nature Conservancy. Episcopalian. State civil litigation, General practice, Real property. Home: 504 Garraty San Antonio TX 78209 Office: 1443 One Riverwalk Pl San Antonio TX 78205

PARK, JOSEPH RATHBONE, lawyer; b. Parkersburg, W.Va., Jan. 11, 1949; s. Thomas Hoyt and Rosemary (Rathbone) P.; m. Sue Anne Whitt, Dec. 18, 1971; children—Kelly Marie, Michael Joseph, Laura Christine, Andrew Michael. B.B.A. Marshall U., 1971; J.D., U. Fla., 1973. Bar: Fla. 1974, U.S. Dist. Ct. (mid. dist.) Fla. 1974, U.S. Ct. Appeals (6th cir.), 1974, U.S. Tax Ct. 1975, U.S. Supreme Ct. 1977. Atty. Johnson, Blakely & Pope, P.A., Clearwater, Fla., 1976-77, McMullen & Park, P.A., Clearwater, 1977-78; sr. ptnr. Park & Smith, Clearwater, 1978—. Bd. deacons Calvary Bapt. Ch., Clearwater, 1983—; exec. bd. Pinellas County Right to Life Com., Clearwater, 1984—. Mem. Assn. Trial Lawyers Am., Acad. Fla. Trial Lawyers Assn., Clearwater Bar Assn. (med.-legal liaison com. 1978—), Fla. Bar Assn. (cert. civil trial lawyer), Am. Arbitration Assn., Phi Delta Phi. Republican. State civil litigation, Construction, Personal injury. Home: 104 Annwood Rd Palm Harbor FL 33563 Office: Park Smith Dayton & Bugg PA Barnett Bank Plaza 1150 Clevel St Clearwater FL 33516

PARK, WILLIAM ANTHONY, lawyer; b. Blackfoot, Idaho, June 4, 1934; s. William Clair and Thelma Edelweiss (Shear) P.; m. Elizabeth Taylor, Aug. 26, 1961 (div.); children—Susan E., W. Adam, Patricia A.; m. 2d, Gail Chaloupka, Aug. 6, 1983. A.A., Boise Jr. Coll., 1954; B.A., U. Idaho, 1958, J.D., 1963. Bar: Idaho 1963. Sole practice, Boise, Idaho, 1963-70; atty. gen. State of Idaho, 1971-75; ptnr. Park & Meuleman, Boise, 1975-81, Park & Burkett, Boise, 1983-84, Martin, Chapman, Park & Burkett, 1984—; sole practice, Boise, 1982-83. Chmn. Idaho Bicentennial Commn., 1971-77; bd. dirs. Radio Free Europe/Radio Liberty, Inc., 1977-82, Am. Lung Assn., 1978—. Served with U.S. Army, 1956-58. Recipient Disting. Service award Boise Jaycees, 1971; Disting. Citizen's award Idaho Statesman Newspaper, 1975. Mem. Idaho Bar Assn., Boise Bar Assn., Idaho Trial Lawyers Assn., Am. Trial Lawyers Assn. Democrat. Episcopalian. Club: Crane Creek Country (Boise). Personal injury, General corporate, General civil practice. Home: 706 Warm Springs Ave Boise ID 83702 Office: 775 N 8th St Suite 200 Boise ID 83712

PARKER, ALLAN EDWARD, lawyer; b. Houston, Sept. 21, 1952; s. Allan Edward Sr. and Eleanor Jean (Murray) P.; m. Susan Claire Sommers, Aug. 4, 1973; children: Laura, Christina, Julianna. BS magna cum laude, U. Okla., 1974; JD with honors, U. Tex., 1979. Ptnr. Gary, Thomasson, Hall & Marks, Corpus Christi, Tex., 1979—. Editor: (book) Financing Education, 1974, Issues and Images: Political Selection, 1975. Pres. Parkdale Bapt. Sch. Bd., Corpus Christi, 1985-87; bd. dirs. Christian Conciliation Service of Corpus Christi, 1984-87. Served to 1st lt. U.S. Army, 1974-76. Mem. ABA, Nat. Assn. Sch. Attys., Tex. Assn. Sch. Bds., Council Sch. Attys. Litigation and school law, Civil rights, State civil litigation. Home: 606 Brock Corpus Christi TX 78412 Office: Gary Thomasson Hall & Marks 210 S Carancahua Corpus Christi TX 78412

PARKER, BARRINGTON DANIELS, federal judge; b. Rosalyn, Va., Nov. 17, 1915; s. George A. and Maude (Daniels) P.; m. Marjorie C. Holloman, Sept. 8, 1939; children: Jason Holloman, Barrington D. A.B. cum laude, Lincoln U., 1936; M.A., U. Pa., 1938; J.D., U. Chgo., 1947. Bar: D.C. Practice law 1947-69; judge U.S. Dist. Ct. for Dist. D.C., Washington, 1970—. Mem. ABA, Nat. Bar Assn. Judicial administration. Office: US Courthouse 3d and Constitution Ave NW Washington DC 20001 *

PARKER, CHARLES EDWARD, lawyer; b. Santa Ana, Calif., Sept. 9, 1927; s. George Ainsworth and Dorothy P.; m. Marilyn Esther Perrin, June 23, 1956; children—Mary, Catherine, Helen, George. Student, Santa Ana Coll., U. So. Calif.; J.D., S.W. U.-La. Bar: Calif. 1958, U.S. Dist. Ct. (cen. dist.) Calif. 1958, U.S. Supreme Ct. 1969, D.C. 1971, U.S. Dist. Ct. (no. and so. dists.) Calif. 1981. Prof. law Western State U., Fullerton, Calif., 1973-81; spl. counsel Tidelands, First Am. Title Co., 1980-82; dir. First Am. Fin. Corp., 1981-82. Served to sgt. U.S. Army, 1951-53. Mem. ABA (com. improvement land records, sect. real property), Orange County Bar Assn., Calif. Bar Assn., D.C. Bar Assn. Club: Santa Ana Kiwanis, Lodge: Elks (Santa Ana). Contbr. articles in field to profl. jours. Real property, Legal history. Office: 18101 Charter Rd Villa Park CA 92667

PARKER, CHRISTOPHER WILLIAM, lawyer; b. Evanston, Ill., Oct. 26, 1947; s. Robert H. and Dorothy Boynton P.; m. Mary Ann P., Dec. 28, 1984. BA, Tufts U., 1969; JD, Northeastern U., 1976. Bar: Mass. 1977, U.S. Dist. Ct. Mass. 1977. Law clk. to judge U.S. Bankruptcy Ct. Mass. dist., Boston, 1976-77; assoc. Fletcher, Tilton & Whipple, Worcester, Mass., 1977-79; counsel U.S. Trustee, Boston, 1979-81; assoc. Craig and Macauley P.C., Boston, 1982-84, ptnr., 1984-87; counsel Hinckley, Allen, Tobin & Silverstein, Boston, 1987—. Mem. ABA, Mass. Bar Assn., Boston Bar Assn., Comml. Law League. Club: Union Boat (Boston). Bankruptcy, Consumer commercial, Federal civil litigation. Home: 45 Walnut St Lynnfield MA 01940 Office: Hinckley Allen Tobin & Silverstein 225 Franklin St Suite 2900 Boston MA 02110

PARKER, DALLAS ROBERT, lawyer; b. Houston, Oct. 16, 1947; s. Richard Henry and Rosemary (McMillan) P.; m. Ingrid Elayne Thompson, July 1, 1972; children: Robbie, Nicholas. BA, Vanderbilt U., 1969; JD, U. Tex., 1972. Bar: Tex. 1972. Assoc. Fulbright & Jaworski, Houston, 1972-79, ptnr., 1979-82; ptnr. Baker, Brown, Sharman & Parker, Houston, 1982—; bd. dirs. Butler Drlg. Fluids, Inc., Houston. Editor U. Tex. Law Rev., 1971. Mem. ABA, Tex. Bar Assn., Houston Bar Assn., Order of Coif. General corporate, Securities. Office: Baker Brown Sharman & Parker 3600 Citicorp Ctr Houston TX 77002

PARKER, DANIEL LOUIS, lawyer; b. Smithfield, N.C., Sept. 2, 1924; s. James Daniel and Agnes Augusta (Toussaint) P.; m. Mae Comer Osborne, Aug. 2, 1958. A.B., U.N.C., 1947, LL.B., 1950. Bar: N.C. 1950. With escrow sect. mortgage loan dept. Pilot Life Ins. Co., Greensboro, N.C., 1950-53, with trust dept. N.C. Nat. Bank, Greensboro, 1953-62, investment counsel, 1962-71, counsel 71-77, 2nd v.p., 1977-84; 2nd v.p., asst. gen. counsel Jefferson Standard Life Ins. Co., Greensboro, 1984—. Served with U.S. Army, 1944-46. Mem. N.C. Bar Assn., Assn. Life Ins. Counsel, Greensboro Bar Assn., Greensboro Jr. C. of C., Phi Beta Kappa. Republican. Roman Catholic. Real property, Securities, Investment banking. Home: 308 W Greenway S Greensboro NC 27403 Office: Jefferson Standard Life Ins Co 101 N Elm St Greensboro NC 27401

PARKER, DONA SCOTT, lawyer; b. Hazel Park, Mich., Sept. 30, 1943; d. Donald Scott and Shirley Roth; m. Robert E. Parker, June 27, 1969; children: Robert Scott, Donald Scott. BA, U. Mich., 1961-65; JD, U. Detroit, 1967-70. Sole practice Howell, Mich., 1971-73; sr. ptnr. Parker & Parker, Howell, 1973—; bd. dirs., chmn. audit com. First Nat. Bank, Howell, Citizens Ins. Co. Am; bd. dirs. Hanover Ins. Co., Mass. Bay Ins. Co.; arbitrator Am. Arbitration Assn. Bd. dirs. McPherson Com. Health Ctr., 1973-75; appointed mem. Nat. Adv. Pub. Health Tng. Council HEW, 1975-76; candidate for U. Mich. bd. regents, 1974; bd. dirs. Artrain. Mem. ABA, Assn. Trial Lawyers Am., Mich. Bar Assn. (character and fitness com.), Mich. Trial Lawyers Assn., Mich. Def. Trial Assn., Women Lawyers Assn. of Livingston County (founder 1981), Livingston County Bar Assn. (past sec., pres.). Federal civil litigation, State civil litigation. Office: Parker and Parker 704 E Grand River PO Box 888 Howell MI 48844

PARKER, DOUGLAS MARTIN, lawyer; b. Chgo., Mar. 6, 1935; s. Lewis Wallace and Elaine (Schulz) P.; m. Angela Macintosh, June 5, 1965; children—Heather Louise, Melissa Meredith. A.B., Cornell U., 1956, LL.B., 1958. Bar: N.Y. 1959, U.S. Supreme Ct. 1966, D.C. 1969. Assoc. Mudge Rose Guthrie Alexander & Ferdon, N.Y.C., 1958-59, 62-69, ptnr., 1977—; ptnr. Lankler & Parker, Washington, 1969-73; with Office of Counsel to Pres., 1973; dep. gen. counsel HUD, 1974-77; mem. legal program Ctr. for Pub. Resources, N.Y.C., 1982—. Mem. adv. bd. Protestant Community Ctr., Inc., Newark, 1978—, pres., 1979-80. Served to capt. U.S. Army, 1959-62. Mem. ABA, Fed. Bar Assn., Fed. Bar Council, Am. Arbitration Assn. (comml. arbitration panel), Pilgrims of U.S. Republican. Congregationalist. Clubs: Down Town Assn. (N.Y.C.); Beacon Hill (Summit, N.J.). Federal civil litigation, State civil litigation, Government contracts and claims. Home: 32 Twin Oak Rd Short Hills NJ 07078 Office: Mudge Rose Guthrie Alexander & Ferdon 180 Maiden Ln New York NY 10038

PARKER, DOUGLAS STUART, lawyer; b. Fairbanks, Alaska, Mar. 15, 1953; s. Walter Bruce and Patricia Isabelle (Ertman) P.; m. Janice Ruth Muirhead, June 26, 1976; children: James, Mary. Student, U. Alaska, 1971-72; BA in History, Oreg. State U., 1976; JD, Willamette U., 1981. Bar: Oreg. 1982, Alaska 1983, U.S. Dist. Ct. Alaska 1984, U.S. Claims Ct. 1986. Legis. asst. Oreg. State Senate, Salem, 1975-78; law clk. Oreg. Atty. Gen., Salem, 1980-81; assoc. Bullard, Korshoj et al, Portland, Oreg., 1982-83, Bogle & Gates, Anchorage, 1983—. Staff Willamette Law Rev. 1980-81; author: (manual) Alaska Employment Law, 1985-86, AGC Alaska Wage and Hour Manual for Construction Industry, 1986. Bd. dirs. Neighborhood Assn., Salem, 1981-83. Mem. ABA, Alaska Bar Assn. (employment sec., exec. bd., 1983—), Oreg. Bar, Anchorage Bar Assn. Democrat. Episcopalian. Avocations: skiing, hiking, gardening, home remodeling. Labor, Construction. Home: 13135 Bay Circle Anchorage AK 99515 Office: Bogle & Gates 510 L St Suite 600 Anchorage AK 99515

PARKER, EDNA G., judge; b. Johnston County, N.C., 1930; 1 child, Douglas Benjamin. Student, N.J. Coll. for Women (now Douglass Coll.); B.A. with honors, U. Ariz., 1953; postgrad., U. Ariz. Law Sch.; LL.B., George Washington U., 1957. Law clk. U.S. Ct. Claims, 1957-59; atty.-advisor Office of Gen. Counsel, Dept. Navy, 1959-60; trial atty. civil and tax div. Dept. Justice, 1960-69; adminstrv. judge Contract Appeals Bd., Dept. Transp., 1969-77; spl. trial judge U.S. Tax Ct., 1977-80, judge, 1980—. Mem. ABA, Fed. Bar Assn., D.C. Bar, D.C. Bar Assn., Women's Bar Assn., D.C. Assn. Women Lawyers, Nat. Assn. Women Lawyers, Nat. Assn. Women Judges. Judicial administration. Office: US Tax Ct 400 2d St NW Washington DC 20217 *

PARKER, EMILY ANN, lawyer; b. Winnsboro, Tex., Aug. 17, 1949; d. Roy Denver and Helen Crowder (Connor) P. BA summa cum laude, Stephen F. Austin Coll., 1970; JD cum laude, So. Meth. U., 1973. Bar: U.S. Tax Ct. 1976, U.S. Ct. Appeals (5th cir.) 1977, U.S. Supreme Ct. 1977, U.S. Ct. Claims 1978, U.S. Ct. Appeals (10th and fed. cirs.) 1984. Assoc. Thompson & Knight, Dallas, 1973-79, ptnr., 1979—. Bd. dirs. Child Care Dallas, 1978-83. Mem. ABA (natural resources com., civil and criminal penalties com. tax sect.), Tex. Bar Assn. (chmn. natural resources com. 1982-84, council 1984-87, tax sect.), Dallas Bar Assn. (chmn., council tax sect. 1983), Dallas Women's Found. Democrat. Avocations: tennis, skiing, fishing, reading. Corporate taxation, Environment. Home: 2805 Milton Dallas TX 75205 Office: Thompson & Knight 3300 1st City Ctr Dallas TX 75201

PARKER, GEORGE EARL, lawyer; b. Laurel, Miss., Sept. 12, 1937; s. George Edward and Ruth Lee (Gardner) P.; m. Ruth Nora Holloway, Oct. 23, 1965 (div. 1986); children: Marshall Lee, Allison Victoria, Jonathan Wesley. B.B.A., U. Miss., 1960, LL.B., 1962; postgrad., N.Y. U. Grad. Sch. Law, 1969-70. Bar: Miss. 1962. Mem. firm Satterfield, Shell, Williams and Buford, Jackson, Miss., 1966-67; counsel, asst. sec. Schick Electric, Inc., Lancaster, Pa., 1967-68; atty., asst. sec. Manville Corp., Denver, 1969-71, counsel, asst. v.p., 1971-73, v.p., corp. counsel, 1973-76, v.p., gen. counsel, sec., 1976-80, sr. v.p. law and public affairs, sec., 1980-86, exec. v.p., 1986—, also bd. dirs. Trustee Denver Symphony Assn. Served with JAGC AUS, 1963-66. Mem. Miss., N.Y. State, Colo., D.C. bar assns., Assn. Corp. Secs., Omicron Delta Kappa, Sigma Nu. Republican. Episcopalian. Club: Denver Country. General corporate, Personal injury, Bankruptcy. Office: Manville Corp Ken-Caryl Ranch Denver CO 80217

PARKER, JAMES LEE, lawyer; b. Pitts., Nov. 3, 1938; s. Wallace Mc. and Virginia (Crawford) P.; m. Susan Bruce, July 18, 1962; children—Lee, Heather. B.B.A., U. Pitts., 1963; J.D., Case-Western Res. U., 1967. Bar: Ohio 1967, Pa. 1967, U.S. Supreme Ct. 1972. Gen. counsel, v.p., sec. Matthews Internat. Corp., Pitts., 1967—, also dir.; trustee JHM Ednl. and Charitable Trust, Pitts., 1973—; dir. Fox Chapel Land Trust, Pitts. Author: Pennsylvania Cemetery Law, 1976, 2d edit., 1984. Mem. Borough Environ. Council, Fox Chapel, Pa., 1979—; mem. Fox Chapel Borough Council, 1983—. Mem. Allegheny County Bar Assn. Republican. Episcopalian. Club: Pitts. Field. General corporate. Office: Matthews Internat Corp 6117 Broad St Pittsburgh PA 15206

PARKER, JEFFREY LIONEL, lawyer; b. Feb. 12, 1953; s. Orin Dean and Rita (Clement) P.; m. Dianne Poelman, Aug. 5, 1977; children: Mary Claire, David Orin, Catherine. BA in Polit. Sci. cum laude, Brigham Young U., 1977; JD, Georgetown U., 1980. Bar: Calif. 1980, U.S. Dist. Ct. (cen. dist.) Calif. 1980, U.S. Dist. Ct. (so. dist.) Calif. 1982, U.S. Ct. Appeals (9th and 11th cirs.) 1983. Assoc. Gendel, Raskoff, Shapiro & Quittner, Los Angeles, 1980-81, Smith & Hilbig, Torrance, Calif., 1982-85; ptnr. Smith & Hilbig, Torrance, 1986—. Editor Georgetown U. Law Rev., 1979-80. Mem. ABA, Los Angeles County Bar Assn., Harbor Assn. of Industry and Commerce. Republican. Mormon. Bankruptcy, Federal civil litigation, Environment. Office: Smith & Hilbig 21515 Hawthorne Blvd Union Bank Tower Suite 500 Torrance CA 90503

PARKER, JEFFREY ROBERT, lawyer; b. Indpls., Oct. 3, 1957; s. Milton Duane and Katherine Elizabeth (Sours) P. BS, U. Ariz., 1978, JD, 1981. Bar: Ariz. 1981, U.S. Dist. Ct. Ariz. 1981, U.S. Ct. Appeals (9th cir.) 1981. Ptnr. Carson, Messinger, Elliott, Laughlin & Ragan, Phoenix, 1981—; vol. counsel Vol. Lawyers Program, Phoenix, 1982-85; counsel State Bar Ariz. Phoenix, 1984-85, cons., 1985. Mem. Rep. Nat. Com., 1984—. Mem. ABA, State Bar Ariz., Maricopa County Bar Assn., Beta Gamma Sigma. Club: Plaza (Phoenix). Avocations: Russian and Soviet literature, traveling, bicycling. Federal civil litigation, State civil litigation, Public international. Home: 7791 E Osborn Rd # 92 Scottsdale AZ 85251 Office: Carson Messinger et al 3300 N Central #1900 Phoenix AZ 85012

PARKER, JOHN VICTOR, judge; b. Baton Rouge, Oct. 14, 1928; s. Fred Charles and LaVerne (Sessions) P.; m. Mary Elizabeth Fridge, Sept. 3, 1949; children: John Michael, Robert Fridge, Linda Anne. B.A., La. State U., 1949, J.D., 1952. Bar: La. 1952. Atty. Parker & Parker, Baton Rouge, 1954-66; asst. parish atty. City of Baton Rouge, Parish of East Baton Rouge, 1956-66; atty. Sanders, Downing, Kean & Cazedessus, Baton Rouge, 1966-79; chief judge U.S. Dist. Ct., Middle Dist. La., Baton Rouge, 1979—; vis. lectr. law La. State U. Law Sch. Served with Judge Adv. Gen.'s Corps U.S. Army, 1952-54. Mem. ABA, Am. Judicature Soc., Am. Arbitration Assn., La. State Bar Assn. (past mem. bd. govs.), Baton Rouge Bar Assn. (past pres.), Order of Coif, Phi Delta Phi. Democrat. Club: Baton Rouge Country. Lodges: Masons (32 deg.); Kiwanis (past pres.). Office: Room 228 US Courthouse 707 Florida Ave Baton Rouge LA 70801 *

PARKER, JULIUS FREDERICK, JR., trial atty.; b. Tallahassee, June 24, 1937; s. Julius and Sarah K. (Gold) P.; m. Marie Giddings, Aug. 13, 1960; children—Jennifer M., Julius Frederick, Kelly K. B.A., Fla. State U., 1960; J.D., U. Fla., 1962. Bar: Fla. 1963, U.S. Dist. Ct. (all dists.) Fla. 1965, U.S. Ct. Appeals (5th and 11th cirs.) 1981, U.S. Supreme Ct. 1966. Asso., Parker, Foster & Madigan, Tallahassee, 1963-67; partner, Parker, Skelding, Costigan, McVoy & Labasky, Tallahassee, 1967—. Mem. Fla. Bd. Regents, 1968-76, chmn. Fla. State U. Found., 1982—. Mem. Fla. Bar Assn., ABA. Republican. Episcopalian. Clubs: Governors, Forest Meadows Racquet. Federal civil litigation, State civil litigation, Insurance. Address: PO Box 669 Tallahassee FL 32302

PARKER, KELLIS E., lawyer, educator; b. 1942. J.D., Howard U., 1968. Bar: Colo. 1970. Law clk to presiding judge U.S. Ct. Appeals, 1968-69; acting prof. U. Calif., Davis, 1969-72; assoc. prof. Columbia U., N.Y.C., 1972-75, prof., 1975—. Mem. bd. dirs. Community Action for Legal Services, N.Y.C.; cons. Legal Def. and Edn. Funds, Inc., NAACP, 1972—; mem. exec. com. Nat. Com. Against Discrimination in Housing, 1974—. Author: Modern Judicial Remedies, 1975. Legal education, Constitutional. Office: Columbia U Sch of Law 435 W 116th St New York NY 10027 *

PARKER, LINDA LOUISE, lawyer; b. Kansas City, Mo., Feb. 13, 1950; d. Everett L. and Dorothy C. (Rains) P. BA in History, Biola U., 1972; JD, U. Mo., 1975. Bar: Mo. 1975, U.S. Dist. Ct. (we. dist.) Mo. 1975, U.S. Ct. Appeals (8th cir.) 1975, U.S. Ct. Appeals (10th cir.) 1979, U.S. Tax Ct. 1980, U.S. Supreme Ct. 1980. Assoc. Jackson & Sherman, P.C., Kansas City, 1975-80; asst. U.S. atty. we. dist. Mo., Kansas City, 1980—; lectr. in law various confs. Mem. ABA, Mo. Bar Assn., Christian Legal Soc. (sec. local chpt. 1983-86, pres. 1986—). Republican. Baptist. Avocations: music, Independence (Mo.) symphony and choir. Federal civil litigation, Condemnation, Criminal. Office: US Attys Office 549 US Cthouse 811 Grand Ave Kansas City MO 64106

PARKER, MARK DAVID, lawyer; b. Billings, Mont., Jan. 29, 1955; s. David Joy and Roberta (Stevens) P.; m. Carlene Renee Taubert, Oct. 26, 1985. BA, U. Mont., 1976; JD cum laude, U. San Diego, 1980. Bar: Mont. 1980, Calif. 1980, U.S. Dist. Ct. Mont. 1980. Assoc. Kurth Law Firm, Billings, 1980-83; ptnr. Parker, Sweeney & Healow, Billings, 1983-86; sole practice Billings, 1986—; instr. Rocky Mountain Coll., Billings, 1984-85. Spl. counsel Mont. Commn. on Practice, Helena, 1985-86. Mem. ABA. Republican. Avocations: elk and deer hunting, fishing. State civil litigation, Real property, Personal injury. Home: 58 Shadow Place Billings MT 59102 Office: 401 N 31 Suite 1250 Billings MT 59102

PARKER, MARY ANN, lawyer; b. Pitts., Jan. 6, 1953; d. Harry N. Sr. and Mary (Sperl) P.; m. Nelson Palacios, May 7, 1983. BS cum laude, SUNY, Buffalo, 1975; JD, U. Tenn., 1977. Bar: Tenn. 1978, U.S. Dist. Ct. (mid. dist.) Tenn. 1978, U.S. Ct. Appeals (5th cir.) 1980, U.S. Supreme Ct. 1982. Asst. Dist. Atty. Gen., Ashland City, Tenn., 1977-78; sole practice Nashville, 1978—; instr. Nat. Trial Advocacy Coll., 1983-84. Community Services vol. St. Henry's Women's Club, Nashville, 1984—; mem. Women's Polit. Caucus, Nashville, 1986. Mem. Assn. Trial Lawyers Am. (del. 1983-86, sec. 1985-86, young lawyer's sect. sec. 1982-83, 2d vice chairperson 1983-84, 1st vice chairperson 1984-85, chairperson 1985-86, women's caucus sec. 1981-83, 1st vice chairperson 1983-84, named Del. of Yr. 1986), Tenn. Trial Lawyers Assn. (bd. govs. 1978-86, chairperson consumer and victims coalition com. 1986—), Trial Lawyers Pub. Justice (bd. govs. 1982—), Nashville Bar Assn. (ethics com. 1983—), Tenn. Bar Assn., ABA, Pa. Trial Lawyers Assn. Democrat. Roman Catholic. Avocations: snow and water skiing, tennis. Personal injury, Workers' compensation. Home: 115 Bear Track Nashville TN 37221 Office: Parker & Allen Law Offices 207 3d Ave N 3d Floor Nashville TN 37201

PARKER, MYRNA JEAN, lawyer; b. Lamar, Colo., Aug. 13, 1940; d. Holt K. and Faye Leah (Brite) Beasley; m. Richard Lindley Parker, March 1, 1957; children: Lindley Holt, Ricki Lynn Parker-Scott. AA, Coll. of the Siskiyous, 1972; BA in Social Ecology and Criminal Justice summa cum laude, U. Calif., Irvine, 1974; JD, U. San Diego, 1977. Bar: Ariz. 1977. Cert. legal intern U.S. Dist. Atty.'s office, San Diego, 1967-77; assoc. Maud, Wildermuth & Echeverria, Casa Grande, Ariz., 1978-79; dep. county atty. Maricopa County Atty.'s office, Phoenix, 1979-83; sole practice Phoenix, 1983—. Mem. Maricopa County Bar Assn., ABA (criminal sect.), Ariz. State Bar Assn., U.S. Dist. Ct. (Dist. of Ariz.), Ariz. Trial Lawyers Assn., Ariz. Women Lawyers Assn., Nat. Dist. Atty.'s Assn., Centro Legal Organizing Com., Chicano Legal Systems and Community Advocacy, Nat. Def. Lawyers Assn., Ariz. Def. Lawyers for Criminal Justice (chairperson), AAUW, Phi Beta Kappa. Lodge: Soroptimists. Criminal, Family and matrimonial, State civil litigation. Office: 917 W McDowell Phoenix AZ 85007

PARKER, PATRIC ALLAN, lawyer; b. Flint, Mich., Oct. 13, 1954; s. Allan Lee and Mary Jane (Rodgers) P.; m. Lisa Ann Root, July 24, 1976; children: Katherine McKenzie, Laura Mary. BA, U. Mich., 1976, JD, 1979. Bar: Mich. 1979, U.S. Dist. Ct. (ea. dist.) Mich. 1979. Assoc. Parker & Buckley, Flint, 1979-83; ptnr. Parker, McAra, George, Williams, Parker, Haldy & McCabe P.C., Flint, 1983—; bd. dirs. NBD Mortgage Co., Flint, 1983—; lectr. Inst. Continuing Legal Edn., 1984—. Chmn. bd. appeals City of Fenton, Mich., 1981-85. Mem. Mich. Bar Assn., Genesee County Bar Assn. (chmn. legal services com. 1984—, legal aid com. 1984-85, bd. dirs. 1984—). Avocations: sailing, skiing, running. Real property, General corporate, State civil litigation. Home: 11100 Woodbridge Grand Blanc MI 48439 Office: Parker McAra George et al 1422 W Court St Flint MI 48503

PARKER, RICHARD DAVIES, lawyer, educator; b. 1945. A.B., Swarthmore Coll., 1967; J.D., Harvard U., 1970. Bar: Mass. 1973. Law clk. to presiding judge, U.S. Ct. Appeals, Washington, 1970-71; law clk. to assoc.

justice Potter Stewart, U.S. Supreme Ct., Washington, 1971-72; atty. Children's Def. Fund, Cambridge, Mass., 1973-74; asst. prof. Harvard U., Cambridge, 1974-79, prof., 1979—. Legal education, Constitutional, Criminal. Office: Harvard U Law Sch Langdell Hall Cambridge MA 02138 *

PARKER, RICHARD RALPH, lawyer; b. Auburn, N.Y., May 20, 1948; s. Richard K. and Ann B. Parker; m. Sandra Huddleston, Feb. 14, 1976; children; Leanne, Gregory. BA in Econs., SUNY, Binghamton, 1970; M in Indsl. Labor Relations, Mich. State U., 1971; JD, Fla. State U., 1974. Bar: Fla. 1975, U.S. Ct. Appeals (5th cir.) 1977, S.C. 1978, U.S. Ct. Appeals (4th cir.) 1978, U.S. Ct. Appeals (6th cir.) 1983, U.S. Ct. Appeals (11th cir.) 1984, Tenn. 1986. With Gen. Tire Corp., Akron, Ohio, 1974-75; assoc. Alley & Alley, Tampa, Fla., 1975-77; from assoc. to ptnr. Ogletree, Deakins, Nash, Smoak & Stewart, Greenville, Tenn., 1978-86; mng. ptnr. Ogletree, Deakins, Nash, Smoak & Stewart, Nashville, 1986—. Mem. ABA, Fla. Bar Assn., S.C. Bar Assn., Tenn. Bar Assn. Roman Catholic. Clubs: Poinsett (Greenville); Nashville City. Avocations: tennis, golf. Labor. Office: Ogletree Deakins Nash Smoak & Stewart 500 Church St Nashville TN 37219

PARKER, RICHARD WILSON, lawyer; b. Cleve., June 14, 1943; s. Edgar Gael and Pauline (Wilson) P.; m. Carolyn Edith Kratt, Aug. 9, 1969; children—Brian Jeffrey, Lauren Michelle, Lisa Christine. B.A. cum laude in Econs., U. Redlands, 1965; J.D. cum laude, Northwestern U., 1968. Bar: Ohio 1968, Va. 1974. Assoc. Arter & Hadden, Cleve., 1968-71; asst. gen. atty. Norfolk & Western Ry. Co., Cleve. and Roanoke, Va., 1971-74, asst. gen. solicitor, Roanoke, 1974-78, gen. atty., 1978-84, sr. gen. atty. Norfolk So. Corp., 1984—. Mem. ABA, Ohio Bar Assn., Va. State Bar, Va. Bar Assn., Roanoke Bar Assn. Presbyterian. Real property, Environment, Contracts commercial. Office: 8 N Jefferson St Roanoke VA 24042

PARKER, ROBERT M., judge; b. 1937. B.B.A., U. Tex., 1961, J.D., 1964. Bar: Tex. Ptnr. firm Parish & Parker, Gilmer, Tex., 1964-65; ptnr. firm Kenley & Boyland, Longview, Tex., 1965, firm Roberts, Smith & Parker, Longview, Tex., 1966-71, firm Rutledge & Parker, Ft. Worth, Tex., 1971-72, firm Nichols & Parker, Longview, Tex., 1972-79; judge U.S. Dist. Ct. (ea. dist.) Tex., 1979—. Mem. ABA, Tex. Bar Assn. Judicial administration. Office: US Courthouse P O Box 1499 Marshall TX 75671 *

PARKER, WHILDEN SESSIONS, lawyer, aerospace company executive; b. Baton Rouge, Jan. 27, 1936; s. Fred Charles and Laverne (Sessions) P.; m. Joyce N. Nowak, Mar. 12, 1984; children by previous marriage—Pamela, Elaine, Vance. B.G.S., La. State U., 1960; J.D., George Washington U., 1970. Bar: Va. 1970, D.C. 1971, Fla. 1979. Law clk. U.S. Ct. Claims, Washington, 1970-71; assoc. Sellers, Conner & Cuneo, Washington, 1971-74, Pettit & Martin, Washington, 1974-75; adminstrv. judge Armed Services Bd. of Contract Appeals, Alexandria, Va., 1975-76; v.p., counsel Pratt & Whitney Aircraft Co., West Palm Beach, Fla., 1976—. Served to capt. USMC, 1960-67, Vietnam. Decorated Air medal with 3 stars. Government contracts and claims, Administrative and regulatory, Federal civil litigation. Office: Pratt & Whitney Aircraft Co PO Box 2691 West Palm Beach FL 33402

PARKER, WILLIAM JERRY, lawyer; b. Bowling Green, Ky., Sept. 11, 1931; s. Joseph B. Parker and Rubye Smith; m. Eva Jane Martin, Dec. 19, 1954; children: Jane Beth, William Jerry Jr., Jo Martin, Frederick Smith. BA, Western Ky. U., 1954; JD, Vanderbilt U., 1959. Bar: Ky. 1959, Tenn. 1959, U.S. Dist. Ct. 1960, U.S. Ct. Appeals (6th cir.), U.S. Supreme Ct. 1965. Ptnr. Harlin, Parker & Rudloff, Bowling Green, 1959—. Served to capt. USAF, 1954-57. Mem. Ky. Bar Assn. (gov. 1969-82, pres. 1980). Democrat. Methodist. Lodges: Rotary (pres. 1969), Elks. Federal civil litigation, State civil litigation, Personal injury. Home: 2120 Sycamore Dr Bowling Green KY 42101

PARKER, WILLIAM LAWRENCE, JR., lawyer; b. Pratt, Kans., Feb. 27, 1931; s. William Lawrence and Mabel (Atkinson) P.; m. Donna Lee Smith, Dec. 31, 1981; children—William Lawrence, III, Karen Elaine. B.A., Washburn U., 1955, J.D., 1957. Bar: Kans. 1957, U.S. Supreme Ct. 1963. Ptnr. McCullough, Parker, Wareheim & LaBunker, Topeka, Kans., 1957-71; pres. W.L. Parker, Jr., Chartered, Topeka, 1972—; mgr., house counsel Kans. Constrn. Industry Fringe Benefit Funds, Topeka, 1972—. Editor-in-chief Washburn Law Rev., 1956-57. Trustee Kans. Pub. Employees Retirement System, Topeka, 1972-76; trustee, fin. chmn. Washburn Coll., Topeka, 1973—; tech. dir. Topeka Civic Theatre, Topeka, 1972-74; tech. designer Dance Arts Topeka, 1974-83; pres. Health Care Cost Containment Task Force, Mo. and Kans., 1984—; mem. Gov.'s Task Force on Health Care, 1984—. Recipient Spl. Service award Kans. Bldg. Trades Health and Welfare Fund, 1984. Fellow Fin. Analysts Fedn.; mem. ABA (employee benefit com. 1971—, co.-chmn. subcom. 1971-86), Fringe Benefit Execs. Assn. (pres. 1974-81), Internat. Found. Employee Benefit Plans. Baptist. Lodge: Masons. Avocations: horses, farming, golf. Pension, profit-sharing, and employee benefits, Labor, Insurance. Home: Rural Rt 1 Box 154A Parkerville KS 66872 Office: WL Parker Jr Chartered 4101 Southgate Dr PO Box 5168 Topeka KS 66605

PARKER, WILMER, III, lawyer, educator; b. Ozark, Ala., Oct. 3, 1951; s. Wilmer and Anne Laura (Ragsdale) P.; m. Rebecca Joy Skillern, Aug. 25, 1984; m. Beverly Laura Barnard, Dec. 23, 1972 (div. Dec. 1977). B.S. in Commerce, U. Ala., 1972, M.B.A., 1975; J.D., 1975; LL.M., Emory U., 1976. Bar: Ala. 1975, Ga. 1976, Fla. 1976, U.S. Dist. Ct. (no. dist.) Ga. 1976, U.S. Tax Ct. 1976, U.S. Ct. Appeals (11th cir.) 1986. Assoc. Nall, Miller & Cadenhead, Atlanta, 1975-78; trial atty. tax div. U.S. Dept. Justice, Washington, 1978-83, asst. U.S. atty. Organized Crime Drug Enforcement Task Force, Atlanta, 1983—; lectr. trial advocacy Emory U. Law Sch., Atlanta, 1984—. Named Outstanding Trial Atty., Tax Div., U.S. Dept. Justice, Washington, 1979; recipient Spl. Commendation award U.S. Dept. Justice, 1985, Superior Performance as Asst. U.S. Atty. Dir.'s award, 1986. Mem. ABA (com. on civil and criminal tax penalties of taxation com.). Presbyterian. Criminal, Personal income taxation. Office: Southeastern Drug Task Force 75 Spring St Box 523 Atlanta GA 30303

PARKHURST, BEVERLY SUSLER, lawyer; b. Decatur, Ill., Mar. 20, 1944; d. Sewell and Marion (Appelbaum) Susler; m. Todd S. Parkhust, Aug. 15, 1976. BA, U. Ill., Urbana, 1966; JD, U. Ill., 1969. Bar: Ill. 1969, U.S. Dist. Ct. (no. dist.) Ill. 1969, U.S. Ct. Appeals (7th cir.) 1975, U.S. Supreme Ct. 1980. Assoc. Pope, Ballard, Shepard & Fowle, Chgo., 1969-74; asst. U.S. atty. U.S. Atty.'s Office U.S. Dist. Ct. (no. dist.) Ill., Chgo., 1974-78, exec. asst. U.S. atty., 1978-81; sole practice Chgo., 1982-86; ptnr. Bell, Boyd & Lloyd, Chgo., 1986—; bd. dirs. Internat. Forum of Travel and Tourism Advocates; vice chairperson 2d Internat. Conf. of Travel and Tourism Advocates, Jerusalem, 1986; regional chairperson 3d Internat. Conf. of Travel and Tourism Advocates, San Francisco, 1987; chairperson inquiry bd. Ill. Atty. Registration and Disciplinary Commn., 1985—; guest lectr. legal ethics Wash. U. Law Office, St Louis, 1986; lectr. on travel law, fed. civil procedure and med. malpractice. Contbr. articles to profl. jours. Appointed mem. Ill. State Toll Hwy. Adv. Com., 1985—; mem. steering com. Women in Professions and Trades 1984—, Jewish United Fund, Chgo. James scholar U. Ill., 1962-66; recipient Spl. Achievement award U.S. Dept. Justice, 1978, Dir.'s award, 1981; U.S. Utility Patent grantee 1982. Mem. ABA (chmn. subcom. alternatives to discovery litigation sect. 1984—), Ill. State Bar Assn. (com. profl. responsibility), Women's Bar Assn., Fed. Bar Assn., Nat. Inst. Trial Advocacy (faculty, northeast and midwest regionals). Avocations: scuba diving, swimming, cooking. Travel law, General corporate, Federal civil litigation. Office: Bell Boyd & Lloyd Three First National Plaza 70 W Madison St Suite 3200 Chicago IL 60602

PARKIN, JEFFREY ROBERT, electronics executive, consultant; b. Manchester, N.H., June 20, 1950; s. George Robert and Lillian (St. Angelo) P.; m. Ann Clark, Mar. 18, 1979; children: Todd Jeffrey, Melissa Ann, Scott George. BS, Cornell U., 1972; MSME, U. Tex., 1973; JD, Western New Eng. Coll., 1979. Bar: Conn. 1979. Sr. nuclear engr. Combustion Engring., Inc., Windsor, Conn., 1975-80; atty., engring. mgr. Kero-Sun, Inc., Kent, Conn., 1980-83; pres. Parkin & Assoc., Kent, Conn., 1983-85, Heads-Up Displays, Inc., Kent, Conn., 1986—. Mem. ABA, ASME, Aircraft Owners and Pilots Assn., Conn. Bar Assn. Republican. Avocations: bridge, chess, sports. Administrative and regulatory, Contracts commercial, General corporate. Home: Rt 1 Box 235A Kent CT 06757

PARKINSON, KENNETH WELLS, lawyer; b. Washington, Sept. 13, 1927; s. Kenneth N. and Martha (Wells) P.; m. Pamela Cox, Nov. 16, 1957; children: Anthony, Jeffery, Philip. BA, George Washington U., 1950, BL, 1952. Bar: D.C. 1952, U.S. Dist. Ct. D.C. 1952, U.S. Dist. Ct. Md. 1952, U.S. Ct. Appeals (4th cir.) 1952. Law clk. to presiding justice U.S. Dist. Ct. D.C., Washington, 1952; ptnr. Jackson & Campbell, P.C., Washington, 1953—. Pres. Washington Jr. C. of C., 1958-59; v.p. Legal Aid Soc., Washington, 1964-67, Neighborhood Legal Services Project, Washington, 1964-68; gen. counsel Easter Seal Soc., Washington; bd. dirs. Nat. Easter Seal Soc., 1976—, Salvation Army. Served as cpl. U.S. Army, 1945-46. Named Outstanding Washingtonian, D.C. Jaycees, 1962. Fellow ABA. Republican. Episcopalian. Clubs: Metropolitan, Barristers, Kenwood Country. Lodge: Kiwanis (pres. D.C. 1979-80). General corporate, Federal civil litigation, Contracts commercial. Home: 5417 Duvall Dr Westmoreland Hills MD 20816 Office: Jackson & Campbell PC 1120 20th St NW Suite 300 S Washington DC 20036

PARKIN-SPEER, DIANE, English law educator; b. Salt Lake City, Feb. 19, 1941; d. Lorin David and Thora (Bauer) Parkin; m. Richard L. Speer, June 3, 1963; divorced. B.A. magna cum laude, Lewis & Clark Coll., 1963; M.A., Bowling Green State U., 1965; Ph.D., U. Iowa, 1970. Grad. asst. U. Iowa, Iowa City, 1965-69; assoc. prof. English SW Tex. State U., San Marcos, 1969—; researcher in history English law and rhetoric. Mem. Am. Soc. Legal History, Sixteenth Century Studies Conf., ACLU. Presbyterian. Contbr. articles on English law to profl. jours. Legal history, Jurisprudence, Legal education. Office: SW Tex State U San Marcos TX 78666

PARKS, ALBERT LAURISTON, lawyer; b. Providence, July 18, 1935; s. Albert Lauriston and Dorothy Isabel (Arnold) P.; m. Martha Ann Anderson, Jan. 12, 1961; children: Amy Woodward, George Webster, Reed Anderson. BA, Kent State U., 1958; JD, U. Chgo., 1961. Bar: R.I. 1962, U.S. Dist. R.I. 1963, U.S. Ct. Appeals (1st cir.) 1966, U.S. Supreme Ct. 1980. Assoc. Hanson, Curran & Parks, Providence, 1961-65, ptnr., 1966—; town solicitor, North Kingstown, R.I., 1978-80. Fellow Am. Coll. Trial Lawyers; mem. ABA, R.I. Bar Assn., Maritime Law Assn., Assn. of Ins. Attys., Squantum Assn. Republican. Episcopalian. Clubs: Saunderstown (R.I.) Yacht. Lodge: Masons. State civil litigation, Federal civil litigation, Labor. Home: Hammond Hill Saunderstown RI 02903 Office: Turks Head Bldg Suite 1210 Providence RI 02903

PARKS, ED HORACE, III, lawyer; b. Tulsa, Apr. 11, 1948; s. Ed H. II and Nancy D. (Dickson) P. BS in Philosophy, Okla. State U., 1972; JD, U. Tulsa, 1975. Bar: Okla. 1975, U.S. Dist. Ct. (no. and we. dists.) Okla. 1975, U.S. Ct. Appeals (10th cir.) 1975, U.S. Supreme Ct. 1980. Assoc. Boyd & Parks, Tulsa, 1975-79; ptnr. Parks & Buck, Tulsa, 1980—. Bd. dirs. Okla. Health Systems Agy., Oklahoma City, 1978-86, vice chmn., 1986—. Served with Okla. N.G., 1969-75. Mem. ABA, Okla. Bar Assn., Tulsa County Bar Assn. (grievances com.), Assn. Trial Lawyers Am., Okla. Trial Lawyers Assn., Phi Alph Delta (pres. 1973). Democrat. Baptist. Club: Utica Sq. Lodge: Lions (pres. Tulsa 1976). State civil litigation, Criminal, Family and matrimonial. Home: 1333 E 60th St Tulsa OK 74105 Office: Parks & Buck 1146 E 61st St Tulsa OK 74136

PARKS, GEORGE BROOKS, land development consultant, university dean; b. Lebanon, Ky., Feb. 18, 1925; s. George W. and Eleanor B. (Brooks) P.; children—Paula, William. Student N.C. Central Coll., 1942-44; LL.B., Howard U., 1948; LL.M., George Washington U., 1949. Bar: U.S. Dist. Ct. D.C. 1948, U.S. Ct. Appeals 1949, Ky. 1951, U.S. Supreme Ct. 1952. Assoc. Coleman, Parks & Washington, Washington, 1948-60; sr. title officer Security Title Ins. Co., 1960-63; founder, pres. Mchts. Title Co., Los Angeles, 1963-69; dir. urban affairs Title Ins. & Trust Co., Los Angeles, 1969-70; exec. dir. Housing Opportunity Ctr., Los Angeles, 1970-73; asst. to councilman David Cunningham, Los Angeles, 1973-74; dep. county supr. Los Angeles County, 1974-76; asst. dean South Bay U. Sch., Carson, Calif., 1976-78, Glendale U. Sch. Law, Los Angeles, 1978—; cons. Summa Corp., Los Angeles, 1978-84; pvt. practice cons., Los Angeles, 1978—. Appointed to Productivity Adv. com. City of Los Angeles by Mayor Tom Bradley, 1986. Recipient Cert. of Appreciation, City of Los Angeles, 1979, Outstanding Leadership award Lutheran Housing Corp., 1980; named Disting. Lectr., Nat. Soc. Real Estate Appraisers, 1981, Disting. Alumni, Howard U. Alumni Assn., 1982. Mem. ABA. Democrat. Lutheran. Real property, Legal education. Home: 1149 S Alfred St Los Angeles CA 90035 Office: George B Parks & Assocs 1122 La Crenega Blvd #104 Los Angeles CA 90035

PARKS, KENNETH F., lawyer; b. Lancaster, S.C., Apr. 15, 1951; s. Fred Flowe and Dorothy (Robinson) P.; m. Susan Rogers, Nov. 26, 1975; children: Shelley Rogers, Samuel Steele. BA, Davidson (N.C.) Coll., 1973; JD, Washington and Lee U., 1978; LLM in Taxation, NYU, 1979. Bar: Va. 1978, U.S. Dist. Ct. (ea. and we. dists.) Va., U.S. Tax Ct., U.S. Ct. Appeals (4th cir.). With Hall, Monahan, Engle, Mahan & Mitchell, Leesburg and Winchester, Va., 1979-86; assoc. Law Offices of Woodrow W. Turner Jr., Leesburg, 1986—. Mem. ABA, Va. Bar Assn., Loudoun County Bar Assn. (treas. 1980-81). Probate, Estate taxation, Personal income taxation. Office: Law Offices Woodrow W Turner Jr 604 S King St Leesburg VA 22075

PARKS, WILLIAM ANTHONY, lawyer; b. Boston, Aug. 22, 1947; s. William Anthony and Frances Josephine (Delany) P.; m. Robin Lynn Sweeney, Nov. 17, 1984. BA with distinction, U. Va., 1969, JD, 1972. Bar: Va. 1972, U.S. Dist. Ct. (we. dist.) 1973, U.S. Ct. Appeals (4th cir.) 1977. Resident atty. E.S. Solomon & Assocs., Hot Springs and Corington, Va., 1972-86; commonwealth atty. Bath County, Hot Springs, 1986—; legal advisor Hot Springs Fire and Rescue Assn., Hot Springs, 1980—, Nat. Ski Patrol, Va., W.Va., 1985. chmn. Bath County (Va.) Dem. Com., 1974-85; escheator Commonwealth of Va., Bath County, 1983; vice chmn. Warm Springs (Va.) Sanitation Commn., 1975-79. Mem. Bath County C. of C. (bd. dirs. 1985—), Am. Trial Lawyers Assn., Va. Trial Lawyers Assn. Methodist. Clubs: Nat. Ski Patrol. Lodges: Lions (pres., sec., dep. dist. gov. Bath County club). Avocations: skiing, boating, fishing. Personal injury, Workers' compensation, State civil litigation. Home: PO Box 579 Hot Springs VA 24445 Office: Bath County PO Drawer D Hot Springs VA 24445

PARMENTER, DAVID N., lawyer; b. Salmon, Idaho, Dec. 13, 1951; s. Walter Jack and Shirley Ann (Whitehead) P.; m. Gail Ann Pabst, Aug. 1, 1978; children: Eric, Emily, Jason, Kristina. Grad., Brigham Young U., 1976; JD, U. Idaho, 1979. Bar: Idaho 1979, U.S. Dist. Ct. Idaho 1979, U.S. Tax Ct. 1980. Ptnr. Farnworth, Parmenter & Norton, Moscow, Idaho, 1979-81; sole practice Blackfoot, Idaho, 1982—; profl. river guide, Tour West, Western Rivers, Salt Lake City, 1973-84; lectr. bus. law Wash. State U., Pullman, 1980-82; dep. pros. atty. Bonneville County, Idaho Falls, 1983-84. Missionary Mormon Ch., Venezuela and Colombia, 1971-73. Named one of Outstanding Young Men of Am., 1982. Mem. ABA, Assn. Trial Lawyers Am., Idaho Trial Lawyers Assn., Nat. Fedn. Ind. Businessmen. Republican. Avocations: river running, painting, basketball, writing. Personal injury, Criminal, State civil litigation. Home: 400 E 413 N Blackfoot ID 83221 Office: 99 SW Main Blackfoot ID 83221

PARMET, DONALD JAY, lawyer; b. N.Y.C., Aug. 12, 1931; s. Samuel S. and Bess (Chiet) P.; m. Rhoda Barbara Wohlgemuth, Apr. 10, 1960; children: Debra J., Nancy J. AB, Cornell U., 1952, JD, 1955. Bar: N.Y. 1957, U.S. Dist. Ct. (ea. and so. dists.) N.Y. 1959, U.S. Supreme Ct. 1964. Ptnr. Parmet & Parmet and predecessor firms, Woodbury, N.Y., 1960—. Mem. council Cornell U., Ithaca, N.Y., 1983—. Served to 1st lt. U.S. Army, 1955-57. N.Y. State scholar, 1948-52. Mem. N.Y. State Bar Assn., Nassau County Bar Assn. Clubs: Huntington (N.Y.) Yacht (trustee 1971-83); Cornell (Long Island, N.Y.) (pres. 1982-84). Contracts commercial, General corporate, General practice. Office: Parmet & Parmet 100 Crossways Park Dr W Woodbury NY 11797

PARMLEY, ROBERT JAMES, lawyer, consultant; b. Madison, Wis., Oct. 23, 1950; s. Loren Francis and Dorothy Louise (Turner) P.; m. Debra Paliszewski, Dec. 23, 1982. B.A., U. Va., 1972; J.D., U. S.C., 1975. Bar: S.C. 1975, Tex. 1976, U.S. Dist. Ct. (so. dist.) Tex. 1976, U.S. Tax Ct. 1976, U.S. Ct. Appeals (5th cir.) 1978, U.S. Dist. Ct. (we. and no. dists.) Tex. 1980, U.S. Supreme Ct. 1980. Staff atty., VISTA vol., Tex. Rural Legal Aid, Inc., Alice, 1975-76, mng. atty., Kingsville, 1976-79, sr. staff atty., Kerrville, 1979-81; cons. atty.; sole practice, Kerrville, 1981—. Mem. State Bar Tex., State Bar S.C., Kerr County Bar Assn. Episcopalian. State civil litigation, Federal civil litigation. Office: 222 Sidney Baker S Suite 615 Kerrville TX 78028

PARNELL, WILLIAM BASIL, lawyer; b. Buffalo, Sept. 17, 1949; s. William P. and Patricia (Jones) P.; m. Jeanne E. Lusardi, Aug. 23, 1975; children: William Bradbury, Rory Jordan, Michael Jones. BA, Boston U., 1971; JD, New England Sch. Law, 1976. Bar: Mass. 1977, N.H. 1979, U.S. Dist. Ct. N.H. 1979, U.S. Dist. Ct. Mass. 1980. Adjuster Allstate Ins. Co., Bedford, N.H., 1976-79; sole practice Derry, N.H., 1979-80, Londonderry, N.H., 1985—; ptnr. Dorner and Parnell, Londonderry, 1980-85. Commr. East Derry (N.H.) Fire Dept., 1984-86. Mem. ABA, Assn. Trial Lawyers Am., Am. Soc. Law and Medicine, Mass. Bar Assn., N.H. Bar Assn. (legis. com. 1983-84, pub. info. com. 1984-86, fee dispute resolution com. 1986—), N.H. Trial Lawyers Assn. (gov. 1986—, blue ribbon com. tort reforming legis. 1985-86), Derry Vis. Nurses Assn. (bd. dirs.). Republican. Club: Wentworth Resort Country (Jackson, N.H.). Avocations: golf, skiing. Personal injury, State civil litigation, Health. Home: Partridge Ln East Derry NH 03041 Office: 12 Parmenter Rd Londonderry NH 03053

PARODE, ANN, banker, lawyer; b. Los Angeles, Mar. 3, 1947; d. Lowell Carr and Sabine (Phelps) P. BA, Pomona Coll., 1968; JD, UCLA, 1971. Bar: Calif. 1972, U.S. Dist. Ct. (so. dist.) Calif. 1972, U.S. Ct. Appeals (9th cir.) 1975. Assoc. Luce, Forward et al, San Diego, 1971-75; gen. counsel, sr. v.p., sec. San Diego Trust & Savings, 1975—; judge pro tem San Diego Mcpl. Ct., 1978-84. Mem. ABA, Calif. Bar Assn. (corp. law com. 1980-83, client trust fund commn. 1986—), San Diego County Bar Found. (founder, bd. dirs., pres. 1980-83), San Diego Bar Assn. (bd. dirs. 1977-81, v.p. 1977-78, 80-81, treas. 1979-80), Bank Adminstrn. Inst. (task force on corp. governance), Lawyers Club San Diego. Club: University (San Diego), San Diego Tennis and Racquet. Office: San Diego Trust & Savings Bank 530 Broadway Suite 1208 San Diego CA 92101

PAROFF, PHILIP STEVEN, lawyer; b. Bklyn., June 19, 1948; s. Mannie and Claire (Lacofsky) P.; divorced, 1975; 1 child, Sean. BA, L.I. U., 1970; JD, NYU, 1974. Bar: N.Y. 1975, U.S. Dist. Ct. (ea. dist.) N.Y. 1975, U.S. Dist. Ct. (so. dist.) N.Y. 1976. Sole practice Forest Hills, N.Y., 1975—. Mem. Queens County Housing Ct. Bar Assn. (v.p. 1986—). Landlord-tenant. Home: 45 Willets Pond Path Roslyn NY 11576 Office: 118-35 Queens Blvd Forest Hills NY 11375

PARR, CAROLYN MILLER, judge; b. Palatka, Fla., Apr. 17, 1937; d. Arthur Charles and Audrey Ellen (Dunklin) Miller: m. Jerry Studstill Parr, Dec. 12, 1959; children: Kimberly Susan, Jennifer Parr Turek, Patricia Audrey. BA, Stetson U., 1959; MA, Vanderbilt U., 1960; JD, Georgetown U., 1977; LLD (hon.), Stetson U., 1986. Bar: Md. 1977, U.S. Tax Ct. 1977, D.C. 1979, U.S. Supreme Ct. 1983. Gen. trial atty. IRS, Washington, 1977-81, sr. trial atty. office of chief counsel, 1982; spl. counsel U.S. Dept. Justice, Washington, 1982-85; judge U.S. Tax Ct., Washington, 1985—. Contbr. articles to profl. jours. Mem. ABA, Fed. Bar Assn., Md. Bar Assn., Women's Bar Md., Nat. Assn. Women Judges. Republican. Presbyterian. Corporate taxation, Estate taxation, Personal income taxation. Office: US Tax Ct 400 2nd St NW Washington DC 20217

PARR, JACK RAMSEY, judge; b. Dallas, May 10, 1926; s. Richard Arnold and Mary Lillian (Ramsey) P.; m. Martha Suttle, July 2, 1955; children—Richard Arnold II, Beverly Ann, Geoffrey Alan. B.A., U. Okla., 1949, L.L.B., 1950, J.D., 1970; grad. Nat. Jud. Coll., 1966, Am. Acad. Jud. Edn., 1979, JAG Sch., U.S. Army, 1981. Cert. mil. judge. Bar: Okla. 1950, U.S. Ct. Mil. Appeals 1955, U.S. Supreme Ct. 1955. Sole practice, Edmond, Okla., 1953-58; asst. U.S. atty. Western Dist. Okla., 1958-65; judge 7th Jud. Dist. Okla., 1965—, presiding judge, 1980; vice presiding judge appellate div. Court on the Judiciary; chmn. Okla. Supreme Ct. Commn. Uniform Civil Jury Instrns.; asso. prof. law Oklahoma City U., 1966-67. Served to capt. JAGC, USNR, 1944-46, 51-53; Korea; mem. Naval Res. Trial Judiciary Unit 107, 1980-85. Mem. Okla. Bar Assn. (Outstanding Com. Service award 1969), Oklahoma County Bar Assn. (cert. of merit 1971, Outstanding Service award 1977-78), ABA, Jud. Conf. Okla., Am. Judicature Soc., Navy-Marine Res. Lawyers Assn., Judge Advs. Assn. U.S., Am. Legion, Mil. Order World Wars, Res. Officers Assn. U.S., Ret. Officers Assn., Delta Theta Phi. Clubs: Masons, Elks. Home: 2601 NW 55th Pl Oklahoma City OK 73112 Office: 706 County Courthouse 321 Park Ave Oklahoma City OK 73102

PARRISH, BENJAMIN FRANKLIN, JR., lawyer; b. Griffin, Ga., July 5, 1956; s. Benjamin Franklin Sr. and Betty (Hargraves) P.; m. Donna Ruth Jones, June 5, 1982. BA, Mercer U., 1978, JD, 1982; postgrad., Georgetown U., 1979. Bar: Ga. 1982, U.S. Dist. Ct. (no. dist.) Ga. 1982. Assoc. King & Spalding, Atlanta, 1982-84; atty. Contel Corp., Atlanta, 1984—. Editor in chief Mercer U. Law Rev., 1981-82. Mem. ABA, Ga. Bar Assn., Atlanta Bar Assn. Democrat. Baptist. Avocations: skiing, backpacking. General corporate, Securities. Home: 3 Gilbert Trail Atlanta GA 30308 Office: Contel Corp 245 Perimeter Ctr Pkwy Atlanta GA 30346

PARRISH, JOHN EDWARD, circuit judge; b. Lebanon, Mo., June 10, 1940; s. Folie and Thelma (Osborn) P.; m. Claudia Barbee, Sept. 1, 1962; 1 child, Mark Everett. BBA, U. Mo., 1962, JD, 1965. Acct. Arthur Andersen & Co., St. Louis, 1965-66; ptnr. Phillips & Parrish, Camdenton, Mo., 1968-73; prosecuting atty. Camden County, Camdenton, 1969-73; circuit judge State of Mo., Camdenton, 1973—; mem. State Adv. Group on Juvenile Justice, Jefferson City, Mo., 1981—; vice chmn. Mo. Bd. Cert. Court Reporter Examiners, Jefferson City, 1974—. Bd. dirs. Lake of the Ozarks Gen. Hosp., Osage Beach, Mo., 1977—, pres. 1983-85. Served to capt. U.S. Army, 1966-68. Mem. Mo. Bar Assn., Mo. Council Juvenile Court Judges (pres. 1978-79), Mo. Judicial Conf. (exec. council 1980—), Nat. Council Juvenile and Family Court Judges. Republican. Mem. Christian Ch. (Disciples of Christ). Lodge: Rotary (pres. 1977-78). State civil litigation, Criminal, Juvenile. Home: Route 2 Box 274 Camdenton MO 65020 Office: 26th Jud Cir Ct Camden County Courthouse Camdenton MO 65020

PARRISH, SIDNEY HOWARD, lawyer; b. Orlando, Fla., Mar. 3, 1940; s. Dallis Matthew and Anne (Cashion) P.; m. Faye Olivia Bass, Aug. 12, 1967; children: Sidney Howard Jr., Christine Olivia. BS, Fla. State U., 1963, JD, 1969. Bar: Fla. 1970, U.S. Dist. Ct. (mid. dist.) Fla. 1973, U.S. Ct. Appeals (11th cir.) 1973, U.S. Supreme Ct. 1973. Ptnr. Troutman, Parrish, Williams & Blankenship P.A., Winter Park, Fla., 1970-86, Parrish & Bailey P.A., Orlando, 1986—; asst. atty., prosecutor City of Winter Park, 1970-72; asst. solicitor County of Orange, Fla., 1970-72. Deacon, chmn. bd. of trustees Downtown Bapt. Ch., Orlando, 1986—. Mem. ABA, Orange County Bar Assn. (med./legal com., fed. and state trial practice com.), Assn. Trial Lawyers Am., Acad. Fla. Trial Lawyers, Delta Theta Phi. Federal civil litigation, State civil litigation, Personal injury. Home: 4861 Big Oaks Ln Orlando FL 32806 Office: Parrish & Bailey PA 116 America St Orlando FL 32801

PARRY, WILLIAM DEWITT, lawyer; b. Hartford, Conn., June 4, 1941; s. William Brown and Mary Elizabeth (Caton) p.; m. Andrea Hannah Lewis, June 30, 1973; children: Sara, Jessica. BA, U. Mass., 1963; JD, U. Pa., 1966. Bar: Pa. 1967, U.S. Dist. Ct. (ea. dist.) Pa. 1974, U.S. Ct. Appeals (3d cir.) 1980, U.S. Supreme Ct. 1980. Assoc. Shapiro, Cook & Bressler, Phila., 1966-67; asst. dir. ABA joint com on continuing egal edn. Am. Law Inst., Phila., 1967-73; assoc. Lowenschuss Assocs., Phila., 1973-85; ptnr. Weiss, Golden & Pierson, Phila., 1985—. editor U. Pa. Law Rev., 1964-66, The Practical Lawyer, 1967-73. Founder Phila. area chpt. Nat. Stuttering Project, 1985—; trustee Unitarian Soc. Germantown, Phila., 1983-86. Mem. ABA, Assn. Trial Lawyers Am., Phila. Bar Assn., Pa. Trial Lawyers Assn. Democrat. Avocations: writing, lecturing. Personal injury, Federal civil litigation, State civil litigation. Home: 520 Baird Rd Merion PA 19066 Office: Weiss Golden & Pierson 1822 Spruce St Philadelphia PA 19103

PARRY, WILLIAM HENRY, lawyer, law educator; b. Bklyn., Mar. 25, 1931; s. Edward Joseph and Mary Elizabeth (Devine) P.; m. Barbara Sullivan

Parry, May 17, 1958; children—Marian T., Barbara M., William H., Regina M. B.A. cum laude, St. John's U., 1952, J.D. cum laude, 1955. Bar: N.Y. 1956, U.S. Tax Ct. 1959, U.S. Ct. Clms. 1959, U.S. Ct. Mil. Apls. 1957, U.S. Sup. Ct. 1959. Assoc., S.M. & D.E. Meeker, Bklyn., 1955-56, 60-65, ptnr., 1965-82; gen. counsel Power-Draulics, Inc., 1961-68, P.F.B. Assoc., Inc., 1968—, Eastern Hydraulics, Inc., 1970-74, Q.A. Microfilm, Inc., 1974—, ALAP Nuclear Products, Inc., 1979—; assoc. prof. St. John's U., 1982—; lectr. in field. Committeeman Nassau County (N.Y.) Republican Com., 1965-70. Served to capt. JAGC U.S. Army, 1956-59. Mem. ABA, N.Y. State Bar Assn., Bklyn. Bar Assn., Bklyn. Savs. Bank Atty. Assn., Internat. Assn. Jurists Italy-U.S.A. Roman Catholic. Club: Union League N.Y. Banking, Probate, Real property. Home: 3 Evelyn Ln Syosset NY 11791

PARSKY, GERALD LAWRENCE, lawyer; b. West Hartford, Conn., Oct. 18, 1942; s. Isadore and Nettie (Sanders) P.; m. Susan Haas, June 26, 1966; children: Laura, David; m. Robin Cleary, Jan. 27, 1980. A.B., Princeton U., 1964; J.D., U. Va., 1968. Bar: N.Y. 1969, D.C. 1974, Calif. 1983. Assoc. Mudge Rose Guthrie & Alexander, N.Y.C., 1968-71; spl. asst. to under sec. U.S. Treasury Dept., Washington, 1971-73; exec. asst. to dep. sec. Fed. Energy Office U.S. Treasury Dept., 1973-74, asst. sec. internat. affairs, 1974-77; ptnr. Gibson, Dunn & Cruther, Washington, 1977—; mem. Pres.'s Com. on Productivity, Trilateral Commn. Bd. govs. Performing Arts Council, Los Angeles Music Ctr.; trustee Princeton U. Recipient Alexander Hamilton award U.S. Treasury, 1976. Mem. ABA, Council Fgn. Relations. Clubs: N.Y. Princeton, California. Private international, General corporate. Office: Gibson Dunn & Crutcher Suite 900 1050 Connecticut Ave NW Washington DC 20036

PARSKY, KEITH ALAN, lawyer, video producer; b. Rochester, N.Y., June 12, 1954; s. Jacob and Esther Belle (Mandwelle) P. BA in Theatre cum laude, SUNY, Buffalo, 1975, BA in Environ. Sci. cum laude, 1975; JD magna cum laude, Syracuse U., 1979; ML in Taxation, Georgetown U., 1983. Bar: Md. 1980, D.C. 1981, U.S. Ct. Appeals (4th cir.) 1981. Assoc. Shulman, Rogers, Gandal et al, Washington, 1980-82; asst. pub. defender State of Md., Rockville, 1982-83; ptnr. Kiles & McDermott, P.A., Washington, 1983-84; producer Encore Prodns., Inc., Bethesda, Md., 1985—; sole practice Bethesda, 1986—; of counsel to various law offices, 1985—; cons. Outrage Inc., Washington, 1984. Performer: (videos) An Interview with F. Scott Fitzgerald, 1985, Profl. Integration, 1985; narrator (film) NASA - Post Challenger, 1985; producer, dir. (video) This is Tony Guida, 1985. Mem., performer Adventure Theater, Glen Echo, Md., 1985—; Community producer Montgomery County TV, Rockville, 1985-86. Mem. ABA, Md. Bar Assn., D.C. Bar Assn., Immigration Lawyers Assn., Phi Beta Kappa. Jewish. Avocations: sports, animals. Entertainment, Criminal, Trademark and copyright. Office: Encore Prodns Inc 6601 Pyle Rd Bethesda MD 20817

PARSON, DAVID, lawyer; b. Dubuque, Iowa, Feb. 26, 1924; s. Morris and Lillian (Rotman) P.; m. Barbara Meyers, Dec. 15, 1954; children—Mary, Julie, Ann Morris. A.B. maxima cum laude, Loras Coll., 1944; J.D., U. Chgo., 1947. Bar: Ill. 1947, U.S. Dist. Ct. (no. dist.) Ill. 1948, U.S. Supreme Ct. 1963. Assoc. Kirkland, Ellis, 1947-54, ptnr., 1955-62; dep. gen. counsel USIA, 1962-65; ptnr. Goldberg, Weigle, Gitles, Parson, Chgo., 1965-69; sole practice David Parson, P.C., Chgo., 1970—. Trustee Drexel Home for Aged, 1967-76; trustee Village of Winnetka, 1976-80, bd. police and fire, 1974-76, chmn., 1975-76; caucus vice chmn., 1973; sec. Ill. Commn. on Low Rent Housing, 1967. Mem. ABA, Chgo. Bar Assn. (corp. law chmn. 1986-87). Club: Standard (Chgo.). General corporate, Contracts commercial. Office: 208 S LaSalle Chicago IL 60603

PARSONS, JAMES BOWNE, lawyer; b. Mineola, N.Y., Mar. 21, 1954; s. Edward Finch and Elizabeth (Hubbell) P.; m. Carol Anne Sherfy, Dec. 30, 1977. BA in Polit. Sci., U. Puget Sound, 1976; JD, Lewis and Clark U., 1980. Bar: Oreg. 1980, Wash. 1982, U.S. Tax Ct. 1985, U.S. Dist. Ct. (we. dist.) Wash. 1986. Sole practice Portland, Oreg., 1980-83; assoc. Copenbarger et al, Seattle, 1983-84; mem. Holman & Monahan, Seattle, 1984-86; ptnr. Parsons Law Firm, Seattle, 1986—; bd. dirs. Entertainment Info. Systems, Inc., Seattle, C.J. Parsons, Inc., Seattle, v.p. 1982—. Speaker various non-profit orgns. regarding estate planning and charitable giving. Mem. ABA (sales and fin. transactions com., secured transactions subcoms., taxation sect.), Seattle Bar Assn., King County Bar Assn., Wash. State Bar Assn. (speaker real property, probate and trust sects., corp. and bus. sect.). Democrat. Episcopalian. Club: Magnolia Community. Avocations: traveling, skiing, scuba diving, wine, music. Probate, Corporate taxation, Securities. Home: 4320 30th Ave W Seattle WA 98199 Office: Parsons Law Firm 2121 4th Ave #2300 Seattle WA 98121

PARSONS, RYMN JAMES, lawyer; b. Binghamton, N.Y., Sept. 23, 1955; s. James Edward and Dauna Dee (Robinson) P.; m. Mary Helen Pietro, Apr. 7, 1979. AB, Eisenhower Coll., 1977; JD, Albany Law Sch., 1981. Bar: Conn. 1981, U.S. Dist. Ct. Conn. 1981, U.S. Ct. Mil. Appeals 1986, U.S. Supreme Ct. 1986. Assoc. Ells, Quinlan & Robinson, Canaan, Conn., 1981-83, Cramer & Anderson, New Milford, Conn., 1983-85; commd. lt. USN, Newport, R.I., 1985, judge adv., 1985—. Counsel St. Andrew's Soc. Conn. Inc., 1984-85; scoutmaster Boy Scouts Am., Salisbury, Conn., 1985. Mem. ABA, Conn. Bar Assn., Assn. Trial Lawyers Am., Conn. Trial Lawyers Assn., Am. Judicature Soc. (bd. dirs. 1980-81). Republican. Clubs: Litchfield County (Watertown, Conn.); University, Coasters Navy Yacht. Military, Criminal. Office: Naval Edn Tng Ctr Naval Legal Service Office Newport RI 02841

PARSONS-SALEM, DIANE LORA, lawyer; b. Arlington, Mass., Apr. 17, 1945; d. Hugh Crocker and Tryphena Grace (Reader) Parsons; m. Deeb N. Salem, July 31, 1971 (div. Sept. 1977); 1 child, Nicole D. Salem; m. William R. Fearnley, Apr. 29, 1984. BA, Boston U., 1967; JD, Suffolk U., 1970. Bar: Mass. 1970, U.S. Dist. Ct. Mass. 1972, U.S. Supreme Ct. 1979. Atty. Allstate Ins. Co., Weston, Mass., 1970-72; assoc. Haig Der Manuelian, Boston, 1972-80; sr. assoc. real estate dept. Widett, Slater & Goldman, P.C., Boston, 1980-84; real estate atty. Friendly Ice Cream Corp., Wilbraham, Mass., 1984—. Mem. ABA, Hampden County Bar Assn., Boston Bar Assn., Mass. Assn. Women Lawyers, Mass. Conveyancers Assn., Springfield C. of C., Springfield (Mass.) Bus. and Profl. Women's Club. Roman Catholic. Real property, General corporate, Contracts commercial. Home: 63 Greenwich Rd East Longmeadow MA 01028 Office: Friendly Ice Cream Corp 1855 Boston Rd Wilbraham MA 01095

PARTNOY, RONALD ALLEN, lawyer; b. Norwalk, Conn., Dec. 23, 1933; s. Maurice and Ethel Marguerite (Roselle) P.; m. Diane Catherine Keenan, Sept. 18, 1965. B.A., Yale U., 1956; LL.B., Harvard U., 1961; LL.M., Boston U., 1965. Bar: Mass. 1962, Conn. 1966. Atty. Liberty Mut. Ins. Co., Boston, 1961-65; asso. counsel Remington Arms Co., Bridgeport, Conn., 1965-70; gen. counsel Remington Arms Co., 1970-85, sec., 1983-85; sr. counsel E.I. du Pont de Nemours & Co., Wilmington, Del., 1985—. Served with USN, 1956-58; to capt. USNR (ret.). Mem. Sporting Arms and Ammunition Mfrs. Inst. (chmn. legis. and legal affairs com. 1971-86), ABA, Am. Judicature Soc., U.S. Navy League (pres. Bridgeport council 1975-77, nat. dir., Conn pres. 1977-80, v.p. Empire region 1980-85), Naval Res. Assn. (3d dist. pres., nat. exec. com. 1981-85). Clubs: Chancery, Harvard of Boston, Yale of N.Y.C. General corporate, Antitrust, Personal injury. Home: 616 Bayard Rd Kennett Square PA 19348 Office: 1007 Market St Wilmington DE 19898

PARTON, JAMES, III, lawyer; b. N.Y.C., Oct. 19, 1951; s. James and Jane Audra (Bourne) P.; m. Diane King, Aug. 22, 1976 (dec. Apr. 1980); children: Phillip, Christopher; m. Maureen Ann Brown, Sept. 28, 1985. BA, U. Pa., 1973; JD, U. San Francisco, 1977. Assoc. Erickson, Lynch, Mackenroth, Arbuthnot & Brennan, Inc., San Francisco, 1977-78, Lynch & Loofbourrow, San Francisco, 1978-83; ptnr. Lynch, Loofbourrow, Helmenstine, Gilardi & Grummer, Inc., San Francisco, 1983—. Mem. ABA, Assn. Ins. Attys., San Francisco Bar Assn., Am. Judicature Soc. Personal injury, State civil litigation, Insurance. Office: Lynch Loofbourrow Helmenstine et al 505 Beach St San Francisco CA 94133

PARTRITZ, JOAN ELIZABETH, lawyer, educator; b. Chgo., July 16, 1931; d. Norman John and Florence May (Russell) P. A.B., Ball State U., 1953; M.A., Whittier Coll., 1963; J.D., Loyola U., Los Angeles, 1977. Bar: Calif. 1977, U.S. Dist. Ct. (cen. dist.) Calif. 1981, U.S. Ct. Appeals (9th cir.) 1984, U.S. Supreme Ct. 1985. Copy writer Nelson Advt. Service, Los Angeles, 1953-53; speech, hearing therapist Port Hueneme Sch. Dist., Calif., 1953-54; math. tchr. Montebello Sch. Dist., Calif., 1954-77; comedy writer Foster Prodns., Los Angeles, 1980-83; prof. Calif. State U., Los Angeles, 1978—; assoc. Parker & Dally, Pomona, Calif., 1977—; dir., speaker Inservice Law Seminars, Pomona, 1977—; cons. Foxtail Press, Inc., Whittier, Calif., 1978—. Author: California Modern Mathematics, 1960. Vol. ACLU, Los Angeles, 1981—. NSF grantee, 1965, 66, 69; recipient Nat. Jurisprudence award, 1976. Mem. ABA (tort com. 1978-80, ins. com. 1978—). Assn. Univ. Attys., Calif. Tchrs. Assn. (salary chmn. 1970-71, keynote speaker 1979), La Habra Art Assn. (first prize Water Color Show 1979), AAUW, NOW (speakers bur. 1984—), Women's Political Caucus, Women Trial Lawyers Assn. Democrat. State civil litigation, Workers' compensation, Probate. Home: 10515 S Portada Dr Whittier CA 90603 Office: Parker & Dally 281 S Thomas 5th Floor Pomona CA 91766

PASAHOW, LYNN HAROLD, lawyer; b. Ft. Eutiss, Va., Mar. 13, 1947; s. Samuel and Cecelia (Newman) P.; m. Leslie Aileen Cobb, June 11, 1969; 1 child, Michael Alexander. AB, Stanford U., 1969; JD, U. Calif., Berkeley, 1972. Bar: Calif. 1972, U.S. Ct. Appeals (9th cir.) 1972, U.S. Dist. Ct. (no. dist.) Calif. 1973, U.S. Dist. Ct. (cen. dist.) Calif. 1974, U.S. Dist. Ct. (ea. dist.) Calif. 1977, U.S. Supreme Ct. 1976. Law clk. judge U.S. Dist. Ct. (no. dist.) Calif., San Francisco, 1972-73; assoc. McCutchen, Doyle, Brown & Enersen, San Francisco, 1973-79, ptnr., 1979—. Author: Pretrial and Settlement Conferences in Federal Court, 1983; contbr. articles to profl. jours. Mem. ABA (antitrust sect., com./subcom. chmn. 1981—), Calif. Bar Assn. Democrat. Antitrust, Federal civil litigation, Computer. Office: McCutchen Doyle Brown & Enersen 3 Embarcadero Ctr 28th Floor San Francisco CA 94111

PASCHAL, BEVERLY JO, lawyer; b. Birmingham, Ala., Aug. 21, 1955; d. Arthur Buel and Nellie Jo (Weaver) P. BA with honor, U. North Ala., 1976; JD, Birmingham Sch. Law, 1982. Assoc. St. John & St. John, Cullman, Ala., 1982-84; sole practice Cullman, 1984-85; ptnr. Paschal & Collins, Cullman, 1986—. Mem. Young Dems., Cullman, 1982—. Named one of Outstanding Young Women Am., 1984. Mem. ABA, Cullman County Bar Assn., Ala. Def. Lawyers Assn., Ala. Criminal Def. Lawyers Assn., Pilot Club Internat. (Sweetheart award Cullman 1985), Cullman County Hist. Soc. Baptist. Avocations: horseback riding, rodeos, farming, writing. Criminal, State civil litigation, Family and matrimonial. Home: Rt 10 Box 1675 Cullman AL 35055 Office: Paschal & Collins 422 3d Ave SE Cullman AL 35055

PASCHAL, JOEL FRANCIS, educator; b. Wake Forest, N.C., Jan. 21, 1916; s. George Washington and Laura (Allen) P.; m. Primrose McPherson, Dec. 21, 1949. B.A., Wake Forest Coll., 1935, LL.B., 1938; M.A., Princeton U., 1942, Ph.D., 1948. Bar: N.C. bar 1938. Instr. Wake Forest Coll., 1939-40, Princeton U., 1946-47; research dir. N.C. Commn. for Improvement Adminstrn. Justice, 1947-49; practice law Raleigh, 1949-54; asso. prof. Sch. Law, Duke, 1954-59, prof. law, 1959—, chmn. acad. council, 1966-67. Author: Mr. Justice Sutherland, 1951. Pres. N.C. United World Federalists, 1952; chmn. N.C. adv. com. U.S. Civil Rights Commn., 1962-65. Served with USNR, 1942-46. Mem. Order of Coif. Democrat. Baptist. Club: Carolina Country (Raleigh). Legal education. Home: 1527 Pinecrest Rd Durham NC 27705

PASCOE, CHRISTOPHER JOHN CAMPBELL, lawyer; b. Epsom, Surrey, Eng., Dec. 31, 1934; came to Can., 1974; s. Walter Francis and Mary Lucy (Townsend) P.; m. Sally Ann Svenningson, May 25, 1979 (div. Feb. 1984); children: Miranda Lucy, Guy Robert Francis. BA, Oxford U., 1958, MA, 1961. Bar: London, 1961. Barrister Chancery Div., London, 1961-62; legal advisor Tunnel Cement Ltd., London, 1962-68; sec. Hill Samuel Life Assurance, London, 1968-74; mgr. legal dept. Bank Montreal, Can., 1974-76; v.p., counsel Pratt & Whitney Can. Inc., Montreal, 1976—. Served to lt. Royal Artillery, 1953-55. Mem. Can. Bar Assn. Anglican. Clubs: Mt. Bruno Country, Montreal Rackets. General corporate, Personal injury, Government contracts and claims. Home: 3562 Durocher, Montreal Can H2X 2E5 Office: Pratt & Whitney Canada Inc, 1000 Marie Victorin Blvd E, Longueuil, PQ Canada J4K 4X9

PASEK, JEFFREY IVAN, lawyer; b. Pitts., Apr. 14, 1951; m. Kathryn Ann Hirsh, Aug. 17, 1975; children: Joshua, Benjamin. BA, U. Pitts., 1973; JD, U. Pa., 1976. Bar: Pa. 1976, U.S. Dist. Ct. (ea. dist.) Pa. 1976, U.S. Dist. Ct. (we. dist.) Pa. 1977, U.S. Supreme Ct. 1980, U.S. Dist. Ct. (mid. dist.) Pa. 1984. Assoc. Cohen, Shapiro, Polisher, Shiekman & Cohen, Phila., 1976-84, ptnr., 1984—; lectr. Pa. Bar Inst., Harrisburg, 1980-83, 86—, course planner, 1986—; instr. Inst. for Paralegal Tng., Phila, 1981-82. Mem. nat. governing council Am. Jewish Congress, N.Y.C., 1985; co-chmn. Commn. on Law and Social Action, Phila, 1985—; bd. dirs. Jewish Employment and Vocational Service, Phila., 1982—, asst. treas. 1986—; bd. dirs. Fairmount Geriatric Ctr., 1985—, sec. 1985—; bd. dirs. Pa. Legal Services Ctr., 1987—. Mem. ABA (equal employment opportunity law com. labor law sect.), Pa. Bar Assn., Phila. Bar Assn., Industrial Relations Research Assn., Pa. C. of C. (chmn. industrial relations com. 1984—). Club: Locust. Labor, Civil rights. Office: Cohen Shapiro Polisher et al 12 S 12th St 2400 PSFS Bldg Philadelphia PA 19107

PASKIND, MARTIN BENJAMIN, lawyer; b. Evanston, Ill., Nov. 24, 1936; s. Harry A. and Lenore (Simons) P.; m. Mildred Lynn Chesser, Sept. 5, 1959; children: Leah Adrian Paskind Roff, Rebecca Lynn Paskind Bennett. BA, U. N.Mex., 1962, JD, 1973. Bar: N.Mex. 1973, U.S. Dist. Ct. N.Mex. 1973, U.S. Ct. Appeals (10th cir.) 1978, U.S. Supreme Ct. 1981. Sole practice Albuquerque, 1973-74; from assoc. to sr. ptnr. Paskind, Lynch & Printz P.A., Albuquerque, 1975-86; of counsel Donald D. Becker & Assocs. P.A., Albuquerque, 1986—. Contbr. articles to profl. jours. Pres. First Unitarian Ch., Albuquerque, 1975; bd. dirs. Albuquerque Rehab. Ctr., 1968-71, Planned Parenthood N.Mex., 1974-76, Am. Heart Assn., Albuquerque, 1978-81; sec., bd. dirs. Chamber Orch. Albuquerque. Served to sgt. U.S. Army, 1956-59, Korea. Mem. ABA (bd. editors jour. 1981-84), Am. Judicature Soc., N.Mex. Bar Assn. (publs. com., co-chmn. law office mgmt. com. 1985—), Albuquerque Bar Assn., Albuquerque Lawyers Club, Hist. Soc. U.S. Supreme Ct. Democrat. Avocations: backpacking, cross country skiing. General corporate, General practice, Federal civil litigation. Home: 1605 Morningside NE Albuquerque NM 87110 Office: Donald D Becker & Assocs PA 3601 Carlisle NE Albuquerque NM 87110

PASSANANTE, PAUL JASPER, lawyer; b. St. Louis, Dec. 13, 1951; s. Paul J. and Mary Patricia (Egan) P.; m. Rebecca J. Borntraeger, Feb. 14, 1983; children: Natalie Marie, Joseph Paul. AB, St. Louis U., 1972, JD, 1976. Bar: Mo. 1976, U.S. Dist. Ct. (ea. and we. dists.) Mo. 1976, U.S. Ct. Appeals (8th cir.) 1979, U.S. Supreme Ct. 1979. Ptnr. Wolff, Frankel & Passanante, St. Louis, 1976-79, Gray & Ritter, St. Louis, 1980—; adj. prof. law St. Louis U., 1983-85. Recipient Lon O. Hocker Meml. Trial Lawyer Award Mo. Bar Found., 1980. Mem. St. Louis County Bar Assn. (mem.-at-large 1978, Outstanding Young Lawyer of St. Louis County award 1980), Bar Assn. Met. St. Louis, Lawyers Assn. St. Louis, Mo. Assn. Trial Attys., Assn. Trial Lawyers of Am. Club: Mo. Athletic (St. Louis). Personal injury, Insurance, Criminal. Home: 203 Hawthorne Webster Groves MO 63119 Office: Gray & Ritter 1015 Locust St Suite 900 Saint Louis MO 63101

PASSÉ, JAMES G., lawyer; b. Chgo., Nov. 26, 1951; s. James Joseph and Margaret E. (Bridges) P.; m. Sandra Lea Almond; children: Kathy, Kristin. BS in Pharmacology, U. Ill., 1975; JD, Ill. Inst. Tech., 1979. Bar: Mich. 1979, Ill. 1980. Patent counsel Upjohn & Co., Kalamazoo, 1979-80, G.D. Searle & Co., Skokie, Ill., 1980-83; div. counsel Raychem, Inc., Menlo Park, Calif., 1983-86; gen. counsel Genencor, Inc., South San Francisco, 1986—. Mem. ABA, Am. Intellectual Property Law Assn., San Francisco Patent Law Assn. Republican. Roman Catholic. Avocations: bicycle racing, cooking. Patent, Trademark and copyright, General corporate. Home: 5988 Rainbow San Jose CA 95129 Office: Genencor Inc 180 Kimbal Way South San Francisco CA 94080

PASSIDOMO, JOHN MICHAEL, lawyer; b. White Plains, N.Y., Jan. 11, 1952; s. John Anthony and Gloria (Massaglia) P.; m. Kathleen Cinotti, Sept. 22, 1979; 1 child, Catarina. BA cum laude, Boston Coll., 1974; JD, Stetson U., 1978. Bar: Fla. 1978. Ptnr. Frost & Jacobs, Naples, Fla., 1980—. Pres. Fine Arts Soc. Collier County, Naples, 1987; mem. planning adv. bd. City of Naples, 1986—. Mem. Collier County Bar Assn. (pres. 1987—), Vol. Lawyers Project (pres. 1984-86). Club: Tiger Bay (Naples) (sec., bd. dirs. 1985-86). Lodge: Rotary (bd. dirs. Naples chpt. 1983-84). Real property, General corporate, Local government. Home: 1550 Murex Dr Naples FL 33940 Office: Frost & Jacobs 1300 3d St S Naples FL 33940

PASTERNAK, DAVID JOEL, lawyer; b. N.Y.C., Mar. 5, 1951; s. Rubin and Esther (Fegelman) P.; m. Jacqueline Strull, July 8, 1973. BA in Polit. Sci. cum laude, UCLA, 1973; JD cum laude, Loyola U., Los Angeles, 1976. Bar: Calif. 1976, U.S. Dist. Ct. (cen. dist.) Calif. 1977, U.S. Ct. Appeals (9th cir.) 1977, U.S. Supreme Ct. 1980. Staff counsel enforcement div. Calif. Dept. of Corps., Los Angeles, 1976-79; dep. atty. gen. bus. and tax sect. State of Calif., Los Angeles, 1979-80; assoc. Robinson, Wolas & Diamant, Los Angeles, 1980; assoc. Tyre, Kamins, Katz & Granof, Los Angeles, 1980-84, ptnr., 1984—; judge pro tem Los Angeles Mcpl. Ct.; arbitrator jud. arbitration program Los Angeles Superior Ct. Assoc. editor Loyola U. Law Rev., 1975-76; contbr. articles to profl jours. Chmn. com. on smoking Los Angeles City Council, 1983-84; mem. various coms. Jewish Fedn. Council of Greater Los Angeles. Mem. ABA (exec. com., bd. dirs. 1983-85, pres. Barristers, various sects. and coms., active young lawyers div.), Los Angeles County Bar Assn (various sects. and coms.), Beverly Hills Bar Assn. (various sects. and coms.), Assn. Bus. Trial Lawyers (chmn. membership 1983-84, bd. govs. 1985—), Lawyers Alliance for Nuclear Arms Control, Phi Alpha Delta, UCLA Alumni Assn. Democrat. Avocations: racquetball, bicycling. State civil litigation, Federal civil litigation, Receiverships. Office: Tyre Kamins Katz & Granof 1800 Century Park E 10th Floor Los Angeles CA 90067-1585

PASTORE, RICHARD STEEL, lawyer; b. Bklyn., Sept. 25, 1932; s. Emil M. and Virginia (Steel) P.; m. Joanna Matthews, Aug. 30, 1958; children—Michael M., John A., Anna P., Thomas S., Richard K. B.A., Amherst Coll., 1954, LL.B., Columbia U., 1960. Bar: N.Y. 1960, U.S. Dist. Ct. (so. and ea. dists.) N.Y. 1962, U.S. Tax Ct. 1966, U.S. Supreme Ct. 1967, Conn. 1967, U.S. Dist. Ct. Conn. 1973. Assoc., Mendes & Mount, N.Y.C., 1960-62; ptnr. Sullivan & Pastore, N.Y.C., 1962-65; sole practice, N.Y.C. and Greenwich, Conn., 1965-70; mem. Albert & Pastore, P.C., Greenwich, 1970—, Albert, Pastore & Ward, P.C., N.Y.C., 1973—; dir. New Med. Techniques, Inc., 1973—. Mem. ABA, N.Y. State Bar Assn., Assn. Bar City N.Y., Conn. Bar Assn., Greenwich Bar Assn., Fed. Bar Council, Served to capt. U.S. Army, 1954-57. General practice, General corporate, Private international. Home: 11 Eggleston Ln Old Greenwich CT 06870 Office: 125 Mason St Greenwich CT 06830 also: 275 Madison Ave Suite 2301 New York NY 10016

PASULA, ANGELA MARIE, lawyer; b. Michigan City, Ind., Oct. 2, 1956; d. Edward Joseph Pasula and Theresa Jeanette (Stella) Hack; m. David Mark Prusa, June 19, 1982. BA in Polit. Sci. cum laude, Western Mich. U., 1977; JD, Valparaiso U., 1980. Bar: Mich. 1980. Asst. pros. atty. Kalamazoo (Mich.) Prosecutors Office, 1980-82, Berrien County Prosecutors Office, Niles, Mich., 1982—. Criminal. Office: Berrien County Prosecutors Office 1205 N Front St Niles MI 49120

PATCHAN, JOSEPH, lawyer; b. Bklyn., June 29, 1922; m. Nancy Joy Letaw, Jan. 7, 1952; children: Reed, Judith, David. B.S., Miami U., Oxford, Ohio, 1943; J.D., Cleve. State U., 1952. Bar: Ohio 1952, D.C. 1977. Pvt. practice law 1955-69; judge U.S. Bankruptcy Ct., No. Dist. Ohio, 1969-75; sr. ptnr. Baker & Hostetler, Cleve., 1975—; mem. adj. faculty Cleve. State U. Law Sch., 1959-73; mem. faculty Nat. Bankruptcy Seminar, Fed. Jud. Center, Washington, 1971-77; mem. adv. com. bankruptcy rules U.S. Jud Conf., 1978—. Author: Practice Comments to Rules of Bankruptcy Procedure, 1973—; contbr. articles on bankruptcy law to profl. publs.;. Served with USN, 1943-46. Mem. Ohio Bar Assn., Cleve. Bar Assn. (chmn. bankruptcy and comml. law sect. 1984-86), Nat. Conf. Bankruptcy Judges (assoc.), Assn. Former Bankruptcy Judges, Nat. Conf. Lawyers and Collection Agys. (chmn. 1985—), Millard Filmore Soc. Jewish. Clubs: City (Cleve.); Army and Navy (Washington). Office: 3200 National City Center Cleveland OH 44114

PATE, JOAN SEITZ, judge; b. Islip, N.Y.; d. Anthony and Frances Kowalski; m. Raymond Seitz (div.); children—Laura, Cheryl; m. Howard M. Pate, Dec. 9, 1961; stepchildren—Patricia, Barbara, Marsha, Peggy. B.A., Ariz. State U.; J.D., U. Ariz., 1974. Bar: Ariz. 1974, D.C. 1976, Ky. 1978; C.P.A., Ariz., Ky. Pvt. practice acctg. Phoenix, 1956-69; trial atty. U.S. Dept. Justice, Washington, 1974-78; ptnr. Goldberg & Simpson, Louisville, 1978-83; spl. trial judge U.S. Tax Ct., Washington, 1983—. Contbr. articles to profl. jours. Mem. ABA, Fed. Bar Assn. (bd. dirs. 1983—), Ky. Bar Assn., Ariz. Bar Assn., D.C. Bar Assn., Ky. Soc. C.P.A.s, Order of Coif. Corporate taxation, Estate taxation, Personal income taxation. Home: 1325 18th St NW Apt 304 Washington DC 20036 Office: US Tax Ct 400 2d St NW Washington DC 20217

PATE, MICHAEL LYNN, lawyer; b. Ft. Worth, Tex., July 9, 1951; s. J.B. and Mary Ann (Hable) P.; m. Barbara Ann Linch, May 28, 1977. AA, Schreiner Coll., 1971; BS, Tex. Wesleyan Coll., 1973; JD, U. Tex., 1975. Bar: Tex., D.C. Adminstrv. asst. to Senator Sherman, counsel natural resources com. Tex. Senate, 1976-77; adminstrv. asst. to Lt. Gov. Bill Hobby, Austin, Tex., 1977-79; legis. asst. Senator Bentsen, Washington, 1979-81, legis. dir., 1981-86; ptnr. Bracewell & Patterson, Washington, 1986—. Mem. ABA, Tex. Bar Assn., D.C. Bar Assn. Democrat. Methodist. Avocations: basketball, tennis. Legislative. Office: Bracewell & Patterson 2000 K St NW Suite 500 Washington DC 20006

PATE, WILLIAM AUGUST, lawyer; b. Selma, Ala., Dec. 9, 1942; s. William Herbert and Shirley Rosemary (DeMattie) P.; m. Wanda Arlene Whaley, Feb. 2, 1973. B.A. in Polit. Sci., Citadel, 1964; J.D., U. Miss., 1972. Bar: Miss. 1972, U.S. Dist. Ct. (no. dist.) Miss. 1972, U.S. Dist. Ct. (so. dist.) Miss. 1973. Sole practice, Gulfport, Miss., 1972—. Pres., Saucier (Miss.) Vol. Fire Dept., chmn. Harrison County Park Commn . Served to capt. USAF, 1965-69. Mem. Miss. State Bar, Harrison County Bar Assn., ABA, Miss. Trial Lawyers Assn. Club: Gulfport Yacht. Lodges: Elks, Masons. General practice, Personal injury, Consumer commercial. Home: Rt 3 Box 219 Saucier-Lizana Rd Saucier MS 39574 Office: 2017 20th Ave Gulfport MS 39502

PATEL, AHMED ADAM, lawyer; b. Dashan, Gujarat, India, June 24, 1930; came to U.S., 1973; s. Adam and Huri M. Patel; m. Rabia Patel, May 16, 1956; children: Salim, Shamim, Sajid. MA, Bombay U., 1956, LLB, 1957. Bar: Bombay 1958, Ill. 1976, U.S. Dist. Ct. (no. dist.) Ill. 1976. Asst. pub. defender Cook County, Chgo., 1976—. Democrat. Muslim. Criminal. Office: Pub Defender 2650 S California Chicago IL 60608

PATEL, MARILYN HALL, judge; b. Amsterdam, N.Y., Sept. 2, 1938; d. Lloyd Manning and Nina J. (Thorpe) Hall; m. Magan C. Patel, Sept. 2, 1966; children: Brian, Gian. B.A., Wheaton Coll., 1959; J.D., Fordham U., 1963. Mng. atty. Benson & Morris, N.Y.C., 1963-65; sole practice N.Y.C., 1965-67, San Francisco, 1971-76; atty. Dept. Justice, San Francisco, 1967-71; judge Alameda County Mcpl. Ct., Oakland, Calif., 1976-80, U.S. Dist. Ct. (no. dist.) Calif., San Francisco, 1980—; adj. prof. law Hastings Coll. of Law, San Francisco, 1974-76. Author: Immigration and Nationality Law, 1974; also numerous articles. Mem. bd. of visitors Fordham U. Sch. of Law. Mem. ABA (litigation sect., jud. adminstrn. sect.), ACLU (former bd. dirs.), NOW (former bd. dirs.), Am. Law Inst., Am. Judicature Soc. (bd. dirs.), Calif. Conf. Judges, Nat. Assn. Women Judges (founding mem.), Internat. Inst. (bd. dirs.), Advs. for Women (co-founder). Democrat. Avocations: piano playing; travel. Judicial administration. Office: US District Court 450 Golden Gate Ave PO Box 36060 San Francisco CA 94102

PATEL, PRAVINCHANDRA J., lawyer; b. Jamnagar, India, Jan. 1, 1938; came to U.S. 1977; s. Jamnadas G. and Parvatiben J. Patel; m. Manjula P., May 5, 1960; children: Bimal, Samir. BS, Bombay U., 1958; LLB, Gujarat U., Rajkot, India, 1960; LLM, U. Tex., 1971. Bar: N.Y. 1979, U.S. Dist. Ct. (so. and ea. dists.) N.Y. 1979, U.S. Supreme Ct. 1982. Sole practice N.Y.C., 1979—. Author: Patel's Gujarat High Court Reference Citations, 1978, Patel's Supreme Court Reference Citations, 1978, Patel's Citations of Ad-

ministrative Decisions, 1983, Patel's Immigration Law Digest (3 volumes) 1985. Mem. ABA, Am. Immigration Lawyers Assn., Indo-Am. Lawyers Assn. Immigration, naturalization, and customs, Real property, General corporate. Home: 83-35 116th St #5F Kew Gardens NY 11418

PATERNOSTER, JOHN MILLER, lawyer; b. Cooperstown, N.Y., Aug. 21, 1946; s. Francis Richard and Rebecca Marie (Retz) P. BA, U. N.Mex., 1971; JD, Gonzaga U., 1976. Bar: N.Mex. 1977, U.S. Dist. Ct. N.Mex. 1978. Asst. dist. atty. 9th Jud. Dist., Clovis, N.Mex., 1977-80, 1st Jud. Dist., Santa Fe, 1980-82; asst. atty. gen. State of N.Mex., Santa Fe, 1982—; bd. dirs. Rocky Mountain Info. Network; instr. N.Mex. Law Enforcement Acad., Santa Fe, 1982—. Author: (with others) Grand Jury Manual for New Mexico Prosecutors, 1982, (with others) A Report on the Transfer of State Prisoners and Their Incarceration at the Torrance County Jail, 1982. Mem. ABA, Assn. Trial Lawyers Am. Democrat. Avocations: travel, photography, gardening. Criminal. Office: Atty Gen NMex PO Drawer 1508 Santa Fe NM 87504

PATERSON, KEITH EDWARD, lawyer; b. Jersey City, Feb. 1, 1955; s. Edward Gray and Agnes Brodie (Gray) P.; m. Sharman Hilary Foster, Apr. 26, 1980. BA in English Lit., Susquehanna U., 1976; JD, Fla. State U., 1979; LLM, NYU, 1986. Bar: N.J. 1979, Fla. 1980, U.S. Dist. Ct. N.J. 1979, U.S. Dist. Ct. (no. dist.) Fla. 1980. Assoc. George M. James, Wildwood, N.J., 1979-80, Rosner & Feltman, Hackensack, N.J., 1980-85; sole practice Denville, N.J., 1985—. Mem. ABA, N.J. Bar Assn., Fla. Bar Assn. Mem. Assemblies of God Ch. Avocations: outdoor activities, music. General practice, Probate, Real property. Home: 76 Foxhill Rd Denville NJ 07834

PATIN, SIDNEY L., lawyer; b. Lafayette, La., Dec. 24, 1948; s. Moise M. and Marie (LaGrange) P.; m. Myra Ann LeBoeuf, Jan. 6, 1973; children: Eddie, Shelley, Erin. BA in Acctg., U. Southwest La., 1970; JD, La. State U., 1979. Bar: La. 1979, U.S. Tax Ct. 1979, U.S. Ct. Appeals (5th cir.) 1979; CPA, La. Ptnr. Henderson, Hanemann et al, Houma, La., 1979—. La. State Bd. CPAs. General practice, Consumer commercial, General corporate. Office: Henderson Hanemann et al 300 Lafayette St Houma LA 70360

PATMAN, PHILIP FRANKLIN, lawyer; b. Atlanta, Tex., Nov. 1, 1937; s. Elmer Franklin and Helen Lee (Miller) P.; m. Katherine Sellers, July 1, 1967; children—Philip Franklin, Katherine Lee. B.A., U. Tex., 1959, LL.B., 1964; M.A., Princeton U., 1962. Bar: Tex. 1964, U.S. Dist. Ct. (we. dist.) Tex. 1975, U.S. Dist. Ct. (so. dist.) Tex. 1971, U.S. Supreme Ct. 1970. Atty. office of legal adviser Dept. State, Washington, 1964-67; dep. dir. office internat. affairs HUD, Washington, 1967-69; sole practice, Austin, Tex., 1969—. Ofcl. rep. of Gov. Tex. to Interstate Oil Compact Commn., 1973-83, 87—. Woodrow Wilson fellow 1959. Mem. ABA, Tex. Bar Assn., Tex. Ind. Producers and Royalty Owners Assn., Tex. Law Review Assn., Phi Beta Kappa, Phi Delta Phi. Democrat. Episcopalian. Clubs: Austin, Citadel, Westwood Country, Princeton (N.Y.C.). Contbr. articles to legal jours. Administrative and regulatory, Oil and gas leasing. Office: Perry-Brooks Bldg Suite 312 Austin TX 78701

PATRICK, GARY RAY, lawyer; b. Fayetteville, Tenn., July 8, 1949; s. Harold Shelton and Mary Erlene (England) P.; m. Patricia A. Albright, Dec. 20, 1970; children: Don Garrett, Sally Emily. BS, U. Tenn., 1971, LLS, 1974. Ptnr. Stophel, Caldwell & Heggie, P.C., Chattanooga, 1974-84, Patrick, Beard & Richardson, P.C., Chattanooga, 1984—. Legal counsel Signal Mountain (Tenn.) Welfare Council, 1977; unit leader United Fund, Chattanooga, 1980. Served to 1st lt. U.S. Army, 1974. Mem. ABA, Chattanooga Bar Assn., Chattanooga Jaycees (legal counsel 1975-76). Methodist. Club: Signal Mountain Country. Avocations: gold, tennis, snow skiing, racquetball. Banking, Contracts commercial, Construction. Office: Patrick Beard & Richardson PC 633 Chestnut St Chattanooga TN 37450

PATRICK, H. HUNTER, lawyer, justice; b. Gasville, Ark., Aug. 19, 1939; s. H. Hunter Sr. and Nelle Frances (Robinson) P.; m. Charlotte Anne Wilson, July 9, 1966; children: Michael Hunter, Colleen Annette. BA, U. Wyo., 1961, JD, 1966. Bar: Wyo. 1966, U.S. Dist. Ct. Wyo. 1966, Colo. 1967, U.S. Supreme Ct. 1975. Mcpl. judge City of Powell (Wyo.), 1967-68; sole practice law Powell, 1966—; atty. City of Powell, 1969—; justice of the peace County of Park, Wyo., 1971—; bus. law instr. Northwest Community Coll., Powell, 1968—; bd. dirs. Park County Title Corp., Cody, Wyo. Editor: Bench Book for Judges of Courts of Limited Jurisdiction in the State of Wyoming, 1980—, (rev. annually). Dir. cts. Wyo. Girls State, Powell, 1982-85. Mem. ABA (Wyo. del. judicial adminstrn. div.), Wyo. Bar Assn., Colo. Bar Assn., Park County Bar Assn. (sec. 1969-70, pres. 1970-71), Wyo. Assn. Cts. Ltd. Jurisdiction (pres. 1973-80), Am. Judicature Soc., Am. Judges Assn., Nat. Judges Assn. Democrat. Presbyterian (elder). Lodges: Elks, Rotary (pres. Powell club 1973-74). Avocations: photography, travel, fishing, camping, bicycling. Estate planning, Local government, General practice. Home and Office: PO Box 941 Powell WY 82435

PATRICK, J. VERNON, JR., lawyer; b. Birmingham, Ala., May 7, 1931; s. John Vernon Sr. and Dorothy Gladys (Powell) P.; s. Sylvia Joyce Brown, May 22, 1965; children: Vera Kathryn, Virginia Gladys. AB magna cum laude, Harvard U., 1952, JD magna cum laude, 1955. Bar: Ala. 1955, U.S. Supreme Ct. 1960, D.C. 1962. Clk. to Hugo L. Black U.S. Supreme Ct., Washington, 1955-56; assoc. Bradley & Arant, Birmingham, 1959-61, 63; spl. asst., loan officer Agy. for Internat. Devel., Birmingham, 1962; sr. ptnr. Vann & Patrick, Birmingham, 1963-65, Berkowitz, Lefkovits & Patrick, Birmingham, 1968-83; pres. Patrick & Lacy, P.C. and predecessor firm J. Vernon Patrick, Jr. & Assocs., P.C., Birmingham, 1983—. Contbr. articles to profl. jours. Pres. Jefferson County Mental Health Assn., Birmingham, 1967-68, Jefferson-Blount-St. Clair Mental Health Authority, Birmingham, 1969-72; mem. Independant Presbyn. Ch. Found., Birmingham, 1985-86. Mem. ABA (fed. regulation of securities com., trial practice com.), Am. Law Inst. (study of complex litigation adv. com., project on law of product and process liability adv. com.), Birmingham Bar Assn. Presbyterian. Clubs: The Club, Downtown, Relay Horse (Birmingham). Lodge: Kiwanis. Federal civil litigation, General corporate, Securities. Home: 4140 Old Leeds Ln Birmingham AL 35213 Office: 1201 Financial Ctr Birmingham AL 35203

PATRICK, JAMES DUVALL, JR., lawyer; b. Griffin, Ga., Dec. 28, 1947; s. James Duvall and Marion Wilson (Ragsdale) P.; m. Carol Crosby, June 13, 1970 (div.). BS in Indsl. Mgmt., Ga. Inst. Tech., 1970; JD, U. Ga., 1973. Bar: Ga. 1973, U.S. Dist. Ct. (mid. dist.) Ga. 1973, U.S. Dist. Ct. (so. dist.) Ga. 1983, U.S. Ct. Appeals (5th cir.) 1974, U.S. Supreme Ct., U.S. Ct. Appeals (11th Cir.) 1981, U.S. Tax Ct. 1985. Assoc. Cartledge, Cartledge & Posey, Columbus, Ga., 1973-74; ptnr. Falkenstrom, Hawkins & Patrick, Columbus, 1975, Falkenstrom & Patrick, Columbus, 1975-77; sole practice, Columbus, 1977—; instr. bus. law Chattahoochee Valley Community Coll., Phenix City, Ala., 1975-77; instr. paralegal course Columbus Coll., 1979, 84. Mem. Historic Columbus Found.; local organizer, worker Joe Frank Harris for Gov. Campaign, Columbus, 1982. Mem. State Bar Ga., Ga. Assn. Criminal Def. Lawyers (bd. dirs., v.p.), ABA, Assn. Trial Lawyers Am., Ga. Trial Lawyers Assn., Columbus Young Lawyers Club, Columbus Lawyers Club, Columbus Kappa Alpha Alumni Assn. (sec.), Phi Delta Phi. Methodist. Clubs: Civitan (bd. dirs. 1975-77), Country of Columbus, Georgian (Atlanta). State civil litigation, General practice, Personal injury. Office: 831 2d Ave Columbus GA 31902

PATRICK, KEVIN LAND, lawyer; b. Munich, July 4, 1952; came to U.S., 1954; m. Sean Jackson. BA, Va. Poly. Inst. State U., 1974; JD, U. Tulsa, 1978. Bar: Colo. 1978, U.S. Dist. Ct. Colo. 1978, U.S. Ct. Appeals (10th cir.) 1982. Staff Nat. Energy Law and Policy Inst., Tulsa, 1977-78; assoc. Musick, Williamson et al, Glenwood Springs, Colo., 1978-80; ptnr. Leavenworth, Patrick & Lochhead P.C., Glenwood Springs, 1980-85; sole practice Aspen, Colo., 1985—; spl. counsel First Interstate Bank of Denver, Grand Champions Resort Corp., Town of Gypsum, Shell Oil Co., others. Contbr. articles to profl. jours. Real property, Environment, Local government. Office: 106 S Mill St Suite 200 Aspen CO 81611

PATRICK, PHILIP HOWARD, lawyer; b. Bridsend, Wales, Aug. 12, 1946; s. Frederick Harry and Phyliss Mair (Vaulters) P.; m. Rosalind Elizabeth Davies, Aug. 5, 1969. MusB, U. Wales, 1969; MFA, Princeton U., 1971, PhD, 1973; JD, Washington (D.C.) Coll. Law, 1980. Bar: D.C. 1980, Md. 1981. Sole practice Silver Springs, Md., 1980—; pres. Computing Community Services Corp., Silver Springs, 1981—. Sec. Nat. Welsh-Am. Found., Washington, 1981-84, adv. council, 1984—. Mem. D.C. Computer Law Forum, IEEE. Computer. Home: 7401 Westlake Terr #1202 Bethesda MD 20817 Office: 8607 Second Ave Suite 201 Silver Spring MD 20910

PATRICK, ROBERT JOHN, JR., lawyer; b. San Francisco, July 1, 1934; s. Robert J. and Marie E. (McKinnon) P.; m. Janet Mary Cline, June 13, 1959; children—John, Stewart, William. B.A., Stanford U., 1956, LL.B., 1959; M.Internat. Affairs, Columbia U., 1960. Bar: Calif. 1960, N.Y. 1961, D.C. 1976. Assoc. Cleary, Gottileb, Steen & Hamilton, N.Y.C., 1961-66; assoc. Cleary, Gottileb, Steen & Hamilton, Paris, 1966-69; dep., then internat. tax counsel U.S. Treasury Dept., Washington, 1969-76; ptnr. Delaney & Patrick, Washington, 1976-78; sr. tax counsel Exxon Corp., N.Y.C., 1979-81; ptnr. Jones, Day, Reavis & Pogue, Washington, 1981-83; dir. internat. tax practice Price Waterhouse, Washington, 1983—. Contbr. articles to profl. jours. Recipient Exceptional Service award U.S. Treasury Dept., 1976. Mem. ABA, State Bar Calif., Internat. Fiscal Assn. (v.p. U.S. br. 1978). Corporate taxation, Private international. Address: Price Waterhouse 1801 K St NW Washington DC 20006

PATRICK, ROBERT WINTON, JR., lawyer; b. Tifton, Ga., Jan. 11, 1940; s. Robert Winton and Marguerite (Ryner) P.; m. Celia; children—Celia Dean, Marguerite Elizabeth, Sallie Louise. B.A. with honors, Fla. State U., 1961; J.D. with distinction, Yale U., 1964. Bar: Ga. 1964. Ptnr. Powell, Goldstein, Frazer & Murphy, Atlanta, 1964—; spl. counsel Atlanta Crime Commn., 1967-69; adj. prof. law Emory U., 1968-74. Author: Georgia Appellate Practice Handbook, 1977, The Georgia Lawyers Basic Practice Handbook, 1980; editor-in-chief The Atlanta Lawyer, 1971-73; contbg. editor Litigation, ABA, 1976-80. Woodrow Wilson hon. fellow. Fellow Am. Coll. Trial Lawyers, Internat. Soc. Barristers; mem. Assn. Trial Lawyers Am. (sustaining mem.), N.Y. State Trial Lawyers Assn., Pa. Trial Lawyers Assn., Tex. Trial Lawyers Assn., Sigma Alpha Epsilon. Clubs: Lawyers of Atlanta, The Real Lawyers, The Gov.'s, Commerce, Yale of Ga. General practice. Office: Powell Goldstein Frazer & Murphy Citizens and So Nat Bank Bldg 11th Floor Atlanta GA 30335

PATRICK, WILLIAM BRADSHAW, lawyer, former cemetery executive; b. Indpls., Nov. 29, 1923; s. Fae William and Mary (Bradshaw) P.; m. Ursula Lantzsch, Dec. 28, 1956; children—William Bradshaw, Ursula, Nancy. A.B., The Principia, 1947; LL.B., Harvard U., 1950. Bar: Ind. sup. ct. 1950, U.S. Dist. Ct. (so. dist.) Ind. 1950, U.S. Ct. Apls. (7th cir.) 1961. Ptnr., Patrick & Patrick, Indpls., 1950-53; sole practice, Indpls., 1953—; gen. counsel Met. Planning Commn. Marion County and Indpls., 1955-66; dep. prosecutor Marion County, Ind., 1960-62; past pres., dir. The Cemetery Co., operating Meml. Park Cemetery, Indpls.; sec., dir. Rogers Typesetting Co., Indpls., 1966-85. Pres. Indpls. Legal Aid Soc., 1963. Served to lt. (j.g.) USN, 1942-46. Recipient DeMolay Legion of Honor. Mem. ABA, Ind. Bar Assn., Indpls. Bar Assn., Lawyers Assn. Indpls., Indpls. Estate Planning Council, SAR (sec. Ind. Soc. 1953-59). Clubs: Mason (33 deg.), Shriner. Probate, Estate taxation, General corporate. Address: 1000 King Cole Bldg Indianapolis IN 46204

PATRICOSKI, PAUL THOMAS, lawyer; b. Ft. Rucker, Ala., Mar. 24, 1955; s. Thomas S. and Marie L. (Andruscavage) P.; m. Stephanie M. Galiardi, Aug. 5, 1978; children: Adam Thomas, Matthew Phillip. BS in Biology, St. Vincent Coll., 1977; JD, U. Notre Dame, 1981. Bar: Ill. 1981, U.S. Dist. Ct. (no.dist.) Ill. 1982. Assoc. Dreyer, Foote, Streit, Furgason & Slocum, Aurora, Ill., 1981—. Bd. dirs. Ill. div. South Kane unit Am. Cancer Soc., 1985—, chmn., 1986—. Named one of Outstanding Young Men of Am., Outstanding Ams. Program, 1985. Mem. ABA, Ill. State Bar Assn., Kane County Bar Assn., Notre Dame Alumni Club (bd. dirs. 1982—, pres. 1983). Roman Catholic. Club: Aurora/Fox Valley (sec. 1982). Avocations: hunting, fishing, hockey. General practice, Consumer commercial, Bankruptcy. Home: 770 Gerten Ave Aurora IL 60505 Office: Dreyer Foote Streit et al 900 N Lake St Aurora IL 60506

PATSAVOS, EVELYN CHRISTOU, lawyer; b. Toledo, Sept. 21, 1955; d. Christos C. and Constance (Photos) P. BA in Econs. with highest honors, Wellesley Coll., 1977; JD, Harvard U., 1980. Bar: Fla. 1980, U.S. Ct. Appeals (5th and 11th cirs.) 1981, U.S. Dist. Ct. (so. dist.) Fla. 1981. Assoc. Morgan, Lewis & Bockius, Miami, Fla., 1980-82, Holland & Knight, Miami, 1982-84; atty. legal dept. Eastern Air Lines, Inc., Miami, 1984-86, sr. atty., 1986—. Mem. ABA, Dade County Bar Assn. (Dist. Service award 1984), Nat. Assn. of Women Lawyers, Assn. of Women in Mgmt. Eastern, Miami Wellesley Club. Club: Wellesley; Harvard (Miami). General corporate, Securities, Contracts commercial. Office: Eastern Air Lines Inc Miami International Airport Miami FL 33148

PATTE, GEORGE DAVID, JR., lawyer; b. Batavia, N.Y., Dec. 16, 1945; s. George David and Patricia Elmira (O'Cain) P.; m. Mary Christine Crass, Dec. 28, 1969; children: Chesua Conkling, George David V. BA in Internat. Relations, Ithaca Coll., 1967; JD, U. Louisville, 1974. Bar: N.Y. 1976, U.S. Dist. Ct. (no. dist.) N.Y. 1976. Tchr. spl. studies Dryden (N.Y.) High Sch., 1970-72; sole practice Ithaca, N.Y., 1976-80; ptnr. Greenburg & Patte, Ithaca, 1981—; lectr. bus. law Ithaca Coll., 1985—. Author: (with Greenburg) A Legal View of Your Rights if Injured on the Job, 1986. Pres. Tompkins County Soc. for Prevention Cruelty to Animals, Ithaca, 1980, bd. dirs. 1977-81; mem. Instl. Animal Care and Use Com., Cornell U., Ithaca, 1986-87; bd. dirs. United Way of Tompkins County, 1987—. Mem. ABA, N.Y. State Bar Assn., Tompkins County Bar Assn., N.Y. Trial Lawyers Assn. (pres. so. tier affiliate 1987, bd. dirs. 1987—), Ithaca Coll. Alumni Assn. (bd. dirs. 1982—, chmn. nominations com. 1985). Roman Catholic. Club: Internat. Sunrise (Ithaca). Lodge: Rotary. Avocation: stream fishing for trout. State civil litigation, Construction, Legal education. Home: 1167 Taughannock Blvd Ithaca NY 14850 Office: Greenburg & Patte 121 E Buffalo St Ithaca NY 14850

PATTERSON, CHARLES THOMAS, lawyer; b. Jacksonville, Ill., Aug. 30, 1950; s. Clyde and Helen (Hadden) P.; m. Judith Elaine Lashmett, May 12, 1973; children: Sara, Anne. BS, So. Ill. U., 1972; JD, Drake U., 1975. Bar: Iowa 1975, U.S. Dist. Ct. (no. dist.) Iowa 1975, U.S. Dist. Ct. (so. dist.) Iowa 1985, U.S. Ct. Appeals (8th cir.) 1985, Nebr. 1986. Ptnr. Eidsmoe, Heidman, Redmond, Fredregill, Patterson and Schatz, Sioux City, Iowa, 1975—. Mem. ABA, Iowa State Bar Assn., Iowa Def. Counsel Assn., Woodbury County Bar Assn. (grievance com. 1985-86, arbitration com. 1985-86), Assn. Trial Lawyers Am., Iowa Assn. Workers Compensation Lawyers, Sierra Club. Republican. Methodist. Avocations: hunting, dog tng., environ. work, gardening. Office: Eidsmoe Heidman Redmond et al 200 Home Fed Bldg Sioux City IA 51101

PATTERSON, CHRISTOPHER MALONE, lawyer; b. Lancaster, Pa., July 18, 1952; s. Anthony Russell and Margaret (Simpson) P.; m. Melissa Anne Roman, June 18, 1977; children: Timothy Roman, Elizabeth Christine. BBA in Acctg., U. Notre Dame, 1974; JD, U. Balt., 1978. Bar: Pa. 1978, U.S. Dist. Ct. (ea. dist.) Pa. 1979, U.S. Supreme Ct. 1985, U.S. Supreme Ct. 1986. Assoc. Going & Wiker, Lancaster, 1978-84; sole practice Lancaster, 1984-85; assoc. Windolph, Burkholder, Stainton & Gray, Lancaster, 1985—. Mem. Pa. Bar Assn., Assn. Trial Lawyers Am., Lancaster Radio Transmitting Soc. (bd. dirs. 1984—). Avocations: amateur radio, running. Criminal, State civil litigation, Personal injury. Office: Windolph Burkholder et al 53 N Duke St Suite 420 Lancaster PA 17602

PATTERSON, DENNIS MICHAEL, lawyer, educator; b. N.Y.C., Sept. 29, 1955; s. Patrick Joseph and Mary Theresa (Philbin) P.; m. Barbara Jean Zehler, June 30, 1978; 1 child, Sarah Elspeth. BA in Philosophy, SUNY, Buffalo, 1976, MA in Philosophy, 1978, PhD in Philosophy, 1980, JD, 1980. Bar: Maine 1981, N.Y. 1981, U.S. Dist. Ct. Maine 1981, U.S. Supreme Ct. 1984. Law clk. to presiding justice Supreme Ct. Maine, Portland, 1980-81; assoc. Preti, Flaherty & Beliveau, Portland, 1981-82; lectr. philosophy U. So. Maine, Portland, 1983-84; prof. law U. Maine, Portland, 1985—; ptnr. Loyd, Bumgardner, Field & Patterson, Brunswick, Maine, 1983—. Contbr. articles to profl. jours. Mem. ABA, Maine State Bar Assn., Comml. Law League Am., Am. Trial Lawyers Assn., Am. Philos. Assn., Phi Beta Kappa. Republican. Bankruptcy, Contracts commercial, Jurisprudence. Home: PO Box 337 South Freeport ME 04078 Office: Loyd Bumgardner Field & Patterson 98 Maine St Brunswick ME 04011

PATTERSON, DONALD, lawyer; b. Lincoln, Nebr., Aug. 1, 1924; s. Charles Henry and Ruth Olive (Swingle) P.; m. Mary Louise Verink, Aug. 10, 1947; children: Bruce Donald, Nancy Louise. AB, U. Nebr., 1947; JD, U. Mich., 1950. Bar: Nebr. 1950, Kans. 1950, U.S. Ct. Appeals (10th cir.) 1962, U.S. Supreme Ct. 1980. Assoc. Addington Jones & Davis, Topeka, 1950-54; ptnr. Fisher, Patterson, Sayler & Smith, Topeka, 1955—; Mem. Supreme Ct. Nominating Commn., Kans., 1979—, Kans. Bd. of Discipline, 1980-83. Contbr. articles to profl. jours. Bd. dirs. YMCA of Rockies, Estes Park, Colo., 1971—; deacon, trustee, elder First Presbyn. Ch., Topeka. Mem. ABA, Kans. Bar Assn., Topeka Bar Assn. (pres. 1974-75), Kans. Assn. Def. Counsel (pres. 1973-74), Am. Coll. of Trial Lawyers (fellow), Internat. Assn. Def. Counsel. Republican. Club: Wood Valley Racquet (Topeka). Avocations: tennis, jogging, hiking, choral music. Federal civil litigation, Insurance, Civil rights. Home: 5119 West 25th St Topeka KS 66614 Office: Fisher Patterson Sayler & Smith Bank IV Tower Suite 400 Topeka KS 66603

PATTERSON, DONALD ROSS, lawyer; b. Overton, Tex., Sept. 9, 1939; s. Sam Ashley and Marguerite (Robinson) P.; m. Peggy Ann Schulte, May 1, 1965; children—D. Ross, Jerome Ashley, Gretchen Anne. B.S., Tex. Tech U., 1961; J.D., U. Tex., 1964; LL.M., So. Meth. U., 1972. Bar: Tex. 1964, U.S. Ct. Claims 1970, U.S. Ct. Customs and Patent Appeals 1970, U.S. Ct. Mil. Appeals 1970, U.S. Supreme Ct. 1970, U.S. Dist. Ct. (ea. dist.) Tex. 1982. Commd. lt. (j.g.) U.S. Navy, 1964, advanced through grades to lt. comdr., 1969; asst. officer in charge Naval Petroleum Res., Bakersfield, Calif., 1970-72; staff judge adv., Kenitra, Morocco, 1972-76; officer in charge Naval Legal Service Office, Whidbey Island, Washington, 1976-79; head Mil. Justice Div., Subic Bay, Philippines, 1979-81; ret., 1982; sole practice law, Tyler, Tex., 1982—; instr. U. Md., 1975, Chapman Coll., 1977-79, U. LaVerne, 1980-81. Mem. Tex. Bar Assn., Smith County Bar Assn., Am. Immigration Lawyers Assn., Phi Delta Phi. Republican. Baptist. Club: Toastmasters (Tyler) (past pres.). Lodges: Masons, Rotary, Shriners. Oil and gas leasing, Immigration, naturalization, and customs, Bankruptcy. Home: 703 Wellington St Tyler TX 75703 Office: 777 S Broadway Suite 106 Tyler TX 75701

PATTERSON, GEORGE ANTHONY, lawyer; b. Claremont, N.H., July 15, 1933; s. George Anthony and Irene Katherine (Quigley) P.; m. Miriam Bledsoe, July 3, 1965; children—Stephen, John, Brian. A.B. in Polit. Sci., Citadel, 1955; J.D., Notre Dame U., 1958. Bar: Fla. 1958, U.S. Dist. Ct. (no. dist.) Fla. 1951, U.S. Ct. Mil. Appeals 1962, U.S. Ct. Appeals (5th cir.) 1962, U.S. Supreme Ct. 1962, U.S. Dist. Ct. (so. dist.) Fla. 1963. Law clk. U.S. Dist. Ct. D.C., 1961-62; city atty. Coral Springs (Fla.), 1965-66; asst. mcpl. judge Deerfield Beach (Fla.), 1969-71; town prosecutor Hillsboro Beach (Fla.), 1969-72; ptnr., pres. George A. Patterson, P.A., Deerfield Beach, 1972—. Chmn. Deerfield Beach Charter Revision Com., 1973-74; pres. Notre Dame Alumni Club of Fort Lauderdale, Fla., 1964-65. Served with USAF, 1958-61. Mem. Broward County Bar Assn. (chmn. grievance com. 1969-70, pres. 1975-76), Deerfield Beach C. of C. (pres. 1972-73). Club: Deerfield Beach Rotary (pres. 1970-71). Estate taxation, Probate, Real property. Home: 1528 SE 12th Ct Deerfield Beach FL 33441 Office: 665 SE 10th St Deerfield Beach FL 33441

PATTERSON, ROBERT BRUCE, JR., lawyer; b. Bklyn., Aug. 29, 1946; s. Robert Bruce and Marian (Mitchell) P.; m. Catherine M. Lenz, June 27, 1982. B.A. in Polit. Sci. with distinction, Pa. State U., 1968; J.D. cum laude, Northwestern U., 1971. Bar: Ill. 1971, U.S. Dist. Ct. (no. dist.) Ill. 1971, U.S. Ct. Appeals (7th cir.) 1973, U.S. Supreme Ct. 1978, U.S. Ct. Appeals (8th cir.) 1980. Assoc. Louis G. Davidson & Assocs., Ltd., Chgo., 1971-82; ptnr. Drumke & Patterson, Ltd., Chgo., 1982—; lectr. in field. Served to capt. U.S. Army, 1972; with Army N.G., 1972-77. Russell Sage Found. scholar, 1968-71. Mem. Chgo. Bar Assn., Ill. State Bar Assn., ABA, Ill. Trial Lawyers Assn., Assn. Trial Lawyers Am., Appellate Lawyers Assn., Phi Beta Kappa. Club: Penn State of Chgo. (pres. 1976-77). Contbr. articles to legal jours. Personal injury, Federal civil litigation, State civil litigation. Office: 221 N LaSalle St Suite 1050 Chicago IL 60601

PATTERSON, ROBERT EDWARD, lawyer; b. Los Angeles, Sept. 14, 1942; s. Ellis Elwood and Helen (Hjelte) P.; m. Christina Balboni, Oct. 2, 1971; 1 child, Victor Ellis. BA, UCLA, 1964; JD, Stanford U., 1972, grad. bus. exec. program, 1986. Bar: Calif. 1972. Ptnr. Graham & James, Palo Alto, Calif., 1972—. Served to lt. comdr. USN, 1964-69. Democrat. Club: World Trade. Private international, General corporate, High technology business. Office: Graham & James 2100 Geng Rd Suite 201 Palo Alto CA 94303

PATTERSON, ROBERT HOBSON, JR., lawyer; b. Richmond, Va., Jan. 30, 1927; s. Robert Hobson and Margaret S. (Sargent) P.; m. Luise Franklin Wyatt, June 15, 1952; children—India, Robert Hobson, Margaret. B.A., Va. Mil. Inst., 1949; LL.B., U. Va., 1952. Bar: Va. 1952, U.S. Ct. Appeals (4th cir.) 1953, U.S. Supreme Ct. 1955. Assoc., McGuire, Woods, Battle & Boothe, Richmond, 1952-56, ptnr., 1956—, sr. ptnr., chmn. exec. com., 1978—, chmn., 1984—. Pres. bd. visitors Va. Mil. Inst., 1975; pres. Va. Home for Boys, 1975. Served with USNR, 1945-46. Fellow Am. Coll. Trial Lawyers, Am. Bar Found., Va. Mil. Inst. Alumni Assn. (pres. 1963-65). Republican. Episcopalian. Clubs: Commonwealth, Country of Va., Deep Run Hunt (Richmond). Antitrust, Federal civil litigation, State civil litigation. Office: McGuire Woods Battle & Boothe 1 James Center Richmond VA 23219

PATTERSON, ROBERT SHEPHERD, lawyer; b. Odessa, Tex., May 18, 1953; s. Robert Charles and Ouida Inez (Shepherd) P. BA in Physics, Rice U., 1975; JD, Vanderbilt U., 1978. Bar: Tenn. 1978, U.S. Dist. Ct. (mid. sect.) Tenn. 1978, U.S. Ct. Appeals (6th cir.) 1979. Assoc. atty. Boult, Cummings, Conners & Berry, Nashville, 1978-83, ptnr., atty., 1984—. Bd. dirs. Outlook Nashville, 1985—. Mem. Tenn. Bar Assn., Nashville Bar Assn. Methodist. Clubs: Cumberland, Richland Country (Nashville). Avocations: golf, snow and water skiing, bridge, reading. State civil litigation, Federal civil litigation, Consumer commercial. Office: Boult Cummings Conners & Berry 222 3d Ave N PO Box 198062 Nashville TN 37219

PATTISHALL, BEVERLY WYCKLIFFE, lawyer; b. Atlanta, May 23, 1916; s. Leon Jackson and Margaret Simkins (Woodfin) P.; children by previous marriage: Margaret Ann Arthur, Leslie Hansen, Beverly Wyckliffe, Paige Terhune Pattishall Watt, Woodfin Underwood; m. Dorothy Daniels Mashek, June 24, 1977. BS, Northwestern U., 1938; JD, U. Va., 1941. Bar: Ill. 1941, D.C. 1971. Sole practice Chgo., 1941—; assoc. Pattishall, McAuliffe & Hofstetter and predecessor firms, Chgo., 1950—; dir. Juvenile Protective Assn. Chgo., 1946-79, pres., 1961-63, hon. dir., 1979—; dir. Vol. Intergy. Assn., 1975-78, sec., 1977-78; U.S. del. Diplomatic Confs. on Internat. Trademark Registration Treaty, Geneva, Vienna, 1970-73, Diplomatic Conf. on Revision of Paris Conv., Nairobi, 1981; mem. U.S. del. Geneva Conf. on Indsl. Property and Consumer Protection, 1978; adj. prof. trademark, trade identity and unfair trade practices law Northwestern U. Sch. Law, Evanston, Ill. Author: (with Hilliard) Trademarks, Trade Identity and Unfair Trade Practices, 1974; Unfair Competition and Unfair Trade Practices, 1985; contbr. articles to profl. jours. Served to lt. comdr. USNR, World War II, ETO, PTO; comdr. Res. ret. Fellow Am. Coll. Trial Lawyers (bd. regents 1979-83); mem. Internat. Patent and Trademark Assn. (pres. 1955-57, exec. com. 1955—), Assn. Internationale Pour La Protection De La Propriete Industrielle (mem. of hon.), ABA (chmn. sect. patent, trademark and copyright Law 1963-64), Ill. Bar Assn., Chgo. Bar Assn., D.C. Bar Assn., Chgo. Bar Found. (dir. 1977-83), U.S. Trademark Assn. (dir. 1963-65), Phi Kappa Psi. Clubs: Legal (Chgo.), Law (Chgo.) (pres. 1982-83), Econ. (Chgo.), Mid-Day, Univ. (Chgo.), Mid-America (Chgo.), Selden Soc. London (Ill. rep.), Chikaming Country (Lakeside, Mich.). Trademark and copyright, Federal civil litigation, Private international. Home: 2244 Lincoln Park W Chicago IL 60614 Office: Pattishall McAuliffe & Hofstetter 33 W Monroe St Chicago IL 60603

PATTON, ARTHUR GORDON, lawyer, consultant; b. Herndon, Va., Sept. 19, 1922; s. Arthur Jennings and Lena Ann (Cox) P.; m. Nellie Estelle

Shafer, Dec. 25, 1945; children: Arthur Gordon, James Scott. BA, Yale U., 1946; JD with honors, George Washington U., 1950, LLM, 1954. Bar: D.C. 1951, Fla. 1970, U.S. Dist. Ct. D.C. 1951, U.S. Dist. Ct. (mid. dist.) Fla. 1973, U.S. Tax Ct., U.S. Ct. Mil. Appeals 1957, U.S. Ct. Appeals (D.C. cir.) 1951, U.S. Supreme Ct. 1957. Intelligence analyst Chief Naval Ops., U.S. Navy, 1948-49, spl. agt. Office Naval Intelligence, 1949, counterintelligence analyst, 1949-51, security policy and control officer, 1951-54, security policy office, 1954-55; asst. chief for indsl. security Office of Insp. Gen. U.S. Air Force, 1955-62, asst. to insp. gen., 1962, mem. procurement rev. com., 1963, chief AFETR base procurment office, 1965-66, chief adminstrv. and logistics br. Air Force Range Measurements Lab., 1966-69; sole practice, Melbourne, Fla., 1969-74; assoc. dir. continuing legal edn. The Fla. Bar, Tallahassee, 1974-75; v.p. DBA Systems, Melbourne, 1976-78; sole practice, Indian Harbour Beach, Fla., 1978—; pvt. practice legal and mgmt. consulting, 1970—. Contbr. articles to profl. jours. Served to lt. USMC, 1942-47. Mem. Fed. Bar Assn., Nat. Indsl. Security Assn. (hon.), Delta Theta Phi. Republican. Episcopalian. Real property, General corporate, General practice. Home: 690 Anderson Ct Satellite Beach FL 32937

PATTON, JAMES RICHARD, JR., lawyer; b. Durham, N.C., Oct. 27, 1928; s. James Ralph and Bertha (Moye) P.; m. Mary Margot Maughan, Dec. 29, 1950; children: James Macon, Lindsay Fairfield. A.B. cum laude, U. N.C., 1948; postgrad., Yale U., 1948; J.D., Harvard U., 1951. Bar: D.C. bar 1951, U.S. Supreme Ct. 1963. Attache of Embassy; spl. asst. to Am. ambassador to, Indochina, 1952-54; with Office Nat. Estimates, Washington, 1954-55; atty. Covington & Burling, Washington, 1956-61; sr. partner firm Patton, Boggs & Blow, Washington, 1962—; Lectr. internat. law Cornell Law Sch., 1963-64, U.S. Army Command and Gen. Staff Coll., 1967-68; Mem. Nat. Security Forum, U.S. Air War Coll., 1965, Nat. Strategy Seminar, U.S. Army War Coll., 1967-70, Global Strategy Discussions, U.S. Naval War Coll., 1968, Def. Orientation Conf., 1972; mem. Com. of 100 on Fed. City, Washington; mem. adv. council on nat. security and internat. affairs Nat. Republican Com., 1977-81; bd. dirs. Madeira Sch., Greenway, Va., 1975-81, Lawyers Com. for Civil Rights Under Law, Washington, Legal Aid Soc. Washington, Assn. To Inform Mil.; mem. Industry Policy Adv. Com. for Trade Policy Matters, 1984—. Served with U.S. Army, 1954-55. Mem. ABA (past com. chmn.), Inter-Am. Bar Assn. (past del.), Internat. Law Assn., Am. Soc. Internat. Law (treas., exec. council), Washington Inst. Fgn. Affairs, Phi Beta Kappa, Alpha Epsilon Delta. Clubs: Metropolitan (Washington); Brook (N.Y.C.); Pacific (Honolulu). General corporate. Home: 456 River Bend Rd Great Falls VA 22066 Office: 2550 M St NW Washington DC 20037

PATTON, JOCK, lawyer; b. Elizabeth, N.J., Dec. 11, 1945; s. Robert Ainsworth and Mary Louise (Bergstrom) P.; m. Katherine Jean Stone, Dec. 23, 1968 (div. Nov. 1984); children: Matthew, Morgan; m. Sonchen Carr, Sept. 26, 1986. AB, U. Calif., Berkeley, 1967; JD, U. Calif., Hastings, 1972. Bar: Ariz. 1972, U.S. Dist. Ct. Ariz. 1972, U.S. Ct. Appeals (9th cir.) 1972. Assoc. Streich, Lang, Weeks & Cardon, Phoenix, Ariz., 1972-76; ptnr. Streich, Lang, Weeks & Cardon, Phoenix, 1976—; Bd. dirs. Am. West Airlines, Inc. Contbr. articles on securities law to profl. jours. Served to 1st lt. U.S. Army, 1968-70, Vietnam. Republican. Securities, General corporate. Office: Streich Lang Weeks & Cardon PO Box 471 Phoenix AZ 85001

PATTON, MARTHA JANE, lawyer; b. Richmond, Va., Mar. 24, 1946; d. Samuel Lee and Margaret Lewis (Hines) P.; m. Clifford Harris Pfau, Oct. 30, 1971 (div. Jan. 1979); m. Lynn Burton Daniel, June 28, 1980; children: Jonathan Patton, William Burton. BA, Birmingham So. Coll., 1968; JD, Samford U., 1978. Bar: Ala. 1978, U.S. Dist. Ct. (no. dist) Ala. 1978, US. Dist. Ct. (mid. dist.) Ala. 1985, U.S. Ct. Appeals (11th cir.) 1986. Legal sec. William H. Mills, Birmingham, Ala., 1968-71; adminstr. Selma Project, Tuscaloosa, Ala., 1971-74; atty. Roebuck Legal Clinic, Birmingham, 1978-81; sole practice Birmingham, 1981—. Coordinator West Ala. Planning Devel. Council, Tuscaloosa, 1974-75; pres. Ala. Women's Polit. Caucus, Tuscaloosa, 1973-74; del. candidate Jimmy Carter for Pres., Birmingham, 1980, Jesse Jackson for Pres., Birmingham, 1984; mem. Ala. New S. Coalition, Birmingham, 1986. Mem. ABA, Ala. Bar Assn. (family law sect.), Birmingham Bar Assn., Found. for Women's Health in Ala. (pres. 1986—). Democrat. Episcopalian. Avocations: swimming, jazz listening. General practice, Family and matrimonial, State civil litigation. Office: 2330 Highland Ave Birmingham AL 35205

PATTON, MATTHEW H., lawyer; b. Carrollton, Ga., July 20, 1936; s. Matthew H. and Mary Frances (Alexander) P.; m. Joan Elizabeth Kintz, Jan. 1961 (div.); m. Dianne Campbell, Nov. 24, 1983; children: Melanie Louise, Amanda Elizabeth, John Campbell, Stephen Campbell. AB in History, Duke U., 1958; postgrad., So. Bapt. Theol. Sem., 1960; JD, Emory U., 1963. Assoc. Kilpatrick & Cody, Atlanta, 1963-69, ptnr., 1969—. Chmn. 5th Congl. Dist., Atlanta, 1975-79, Ga. Reps., Atlanta. 1979-81. Mem. Ga. Bar Assn. (bd. govs. 1974—), Atlanta Bar Assn. (chmn. litigation sect. 1981-82), Am. Bd. Trial Advs. (adv.). Federal civil litigation, State civil litigation, Insurance. Home: 4220 Harris Tr NW Atlanta GA 30327 Office: Kilpatrick & Cody 100 Peachtree St 3100 Equitable Bldg Atlanta GA 30043

PATTON, STEPHEN RAY, lawyer; b. Crawfordsville, Ind., Aug. 29, 1953; s. Don C. and Marlene (Miller) P.; m. Linda L. Wilson, Sept. 3, 1977; children: Andrew Caleb, Sean Patrick. BA, Ind. U., 1975; JD magna cum laude, Georgetown U., 1978. Bar: Ill. 1978, U.S. Dist. Ct. (no. dist.) Ill. 1978. Assoc. Kirkland & Ellis, Chgo., 1978-84, ptnr., 1984—; chmn. Lakeview Clinic Chgo.; bd. dirs. Chgo. Vol. Legal Services Found. Mem. ABA (litigation sect.), Am. Judicature Soc. Federal civil litigation, State civil litigation. Office: Kirkland & Ellis 200 E Randolph Dr Chicago IL 60601

PATTON, THOMAS EARL, lawyer; b. Nov. 25, 1940; s. Thomas E. and Alice F. (Rodarmel) P.; m. Patricia Mann, Aug. 12, 1965 (dec.); m. Barbara Wood, Sept. 21, 1974; 1 child, David Earl. A.B., Cath. U. Am., 1962, J.D. summa cum laude, 1965. Bar: N.Y. 1966, D.C. 1966, Va. 1982. Assoc. Sullivan & Cromwell, N.Y.C., 1965-69; mem. Williams Connolly & Califano, Washington, 1970-75; asst. gen. counsel U.S. Dept. Energy, Washington, 1977-78; ptnr. Schnader, Harrison, Segal & Lewis, Washington, 1979—; disting. lectr. Cath. U. Am., 1970-80; dir. Voice Computer Techs. Corp.; nat. arbitrator Am. Arbitration Assn.; bd. dirs. Linus Techs., Inc. Contbr. articles to profl. jours. Mem. Fairfax County Democratic Com., Va., 1976-80; mem. Washington World Affairs Council, 1980—. Mem. ABA. Roman Catholic. Clubs: International (Washington); Washington Golf and Country (Arlington, Va.). Federal civil litigation, Nuclear power, Antitrust. Office: Schnader Harrison Segal & Lewis 1111 19th St NW Washington DC 20036

PATURIS, E(MMANUEL) MICHAEL, lawyer; b. Akron, Ohio, July 12, 1933; s. Michael George and Sophia G. (Manos) P.; m. Mary Ann, Feb. 28, 1965; 1 dau., Sophia E. B.S. in Bus., U. N.C., 1954, J.D. with honors, 1959, postgrad. in acctg., 1959-60. Bar: N.C. 1959, D.C. 1969, Va. 1973; C.P.A., N.C. With acctg. firms, Charlotte and Wilmington, N.C., 1960-63; asso. Poyner, Geraghty, Hartsfield & Townsend, Raleigh, N.C., 1963-64; atty. Chief Counsel's Office, IRS, Richmond, Va. and Washington, 1964-69; ptnr. Reasoner, Davis & Vinson, Washington, 1969-78; sole practice, Alexandria, Va., 1978—; instr. bus. law, econs. and acctg. Bd. editors U. N.C. Law Review. Served with U.S. Army, 1954-56. Recipient Block award U. N.C. Law Sch.; Mem. ABA, D.C. Bar Assn., Va. Bar Assn., Am. Assn. Attys.-C.P.A.s (past pres. Potomac chpt.), Phi Beta Kappa, Beta Gamma Sigma. Republican. Greek Orthodox. Club: Washington Golf and Country (Arlington, Va.). Lodge: Rotary (Tyson's Corner, Va.). Corporate taxation, Estate taxation, General corporate. Home: 2732 N Radford St Arlington VA 22207 Office: 431 N Lee St Alexandria VA 22314

PATZ, EDWARD FRANK, lawyer; b. Balt., Aug. 25, 1932; s. Maurice A. and Violet (Furman) P.; m. Betty Seldner Levi, Nov. 18, 1956; children—Evelyn Anne, Edward Frank, Thomas L. B.S., U. Md., 1954, LL.B., 1959. Bar: Md. 1959. Partner firm Weinberg and Green (and merged predecessors), Balt., 1959—. Bd. dirs. Jewish Family and Children's Service, 1965-71; mem. regional bd. dirs. NCCJ. Mem. ABA, Md., Balt. bar assns. Am. Judicature Soc., Comml. Law League Am. Clubs: Center, Suburban of Baltimore County (bd. govs., pres.). Banking, General corporate, Bankruptcy. Home: 7917 Stevenson Rd Pikesville MD 21208 Office: 100 S Charles St Baltimore MD 21201

PATZKE, JOHN CHARLES, lawyer; b. Milw., Mar. 23, 1954; s. Clifford C. and Valerie S. (Duenow) P.; m. Mary T. Silver, Oct. 2, 1982. B.A. magna cum laude, Marquette U., 1976; J.D., U. Wis., 1979. Bar: Wis. 1979, U.S. Dist. Ct. (ea. dist.) Wis. 1979, U.S. Ct. Appeals (7th cir.) 1980, U.S. Dist. Ct. (ea. dist.) Tex. 1982; U.S. Dist Ct. (we. dist.) Wis., 1984. Law clk. Melli, Shiels, Walker & Pease, Madison, Wis., 1977, Wis. Employment Relations Commn., 1978, NLRB, Milw., 1979; from assoc. to ptnr. Brigden & Petajan, Milw., 1979—. Author (mag.) Milw. Lawyer, 1985, Communications and the Law, 1986; Bus. Age Mag., 1986; Women in Bus. Mag., 1987. Mem. adv. bd. of editors Mid-West Labor and Employment Law Jours., 1983—. Mem. ABA, Milw. Young Lawyers Assn. (com. chmn.), Milw. Bar Assn., Wis. Bar Assn., Am. Soc. Personnel Adminstrn., Personnel and Indsl. Relations Assn. Wis., Alpha Sigma Nu, Pi Sigma Alpha. Lutheran. Labor. Home: 8143 W Winston Way Franklin WI 53132 Office: Brigden & Petajan 600 E Mason St Milwaukee WI 53202

PAUL, BERNARD ARTHUR, lawyer; b. Litchfield, Ill., Oct. 19, 1936; s. Fayette Frederick and Florence Bernadine (Streeb) P.; m. Judy Kay Burrell Paul, July 12, 1959 (div.); m. Rebecca Jane Baker Paul, Dec. 21, 1974; children: Christian Arthur, Clinton Earl. BS, U. Ill., 1958, JD, 1967. Bar: Ill. 1968, U.S. Dist. Ct. (so. dist.) Ill. 1969, U.S. Dist. Ct. (no. dist.) Ill. 1968. Commd. 2d lt. U.S. Air Force 1958, advanced through grades to col., 1985; active duty, 1958-65, Air N.G., 1965—; asst. dir. Ill. Oil Council, Chgo. 1968-69; asst. dir. Williamson-Franklin Legal Aid Bur., Marion, Ill., 1969-70; sole practice, Marion, 1970—. Past deacon United Ch. of Christ. Mem. Williamson County Bar Assn. (pres. 1971-73), U. Ill. Alumni Assn. (life.), Air Force Assn. (life), Nat. Rifle Assn. (life), Vets. of Foreign Wars (life), Aircraft Owners and Pilots Assn. Republican. Lodges: Kiwanis (past pres.), Masons. Criminal, Family and matrimonial, General practice. Home: 514 S Market St Marion IL 62959 Office: 806 W DeYoung St Marion IL 62959

PAUL, CARL FREDERICK, lawyer, former judge; b. N.Y.C., June 10, 1910; s. Carl Frederick and Kate (Wagner) P.; m. Lilian Iris O'Neill, Apr. 18, 1953; children—Julie S., Carl F., Cynthia Marie. A.B. magna cum laude, U. Rochester, 1932; LL.B., Harvard U., 1935. Bar: N.Y. 1935, D.C. 1949, U.S. Supreme Ct. 1941. Assoc., Nixon, Hargrave, Devans & Doyle, Rochester, N.Y., 1935-41, 46-48; atty. Office Gen. Counsel HEW, Washington, 1958-59; commd. officer U.S. Navy, 1941, advanced through grades to capt.; ret., 1958; chief trial counsel NASA, Washington, 1959-74, judge Bd. Contract Appeals, 1974-79; assoc. Burch & Bennett, P.C., Washington, 1979—. Mem. ABA, Fed. Bar Assn. (pres. D.C.), Inter-Am. Bar Assn., D.C. Bar Assn., Monroe County (N.Y.) Bar Assn., Washington Fgn. Law Soc. (pres.), Phi Beta Kappa, Theta Delta Chi. Clubs: University (Rochester, N.Y.); Nat. Aviation (Washington). Government contracts and claims, Administrative and regulatory, Private international. Home: 5702 Warwick Pl Chevy Chase MD 20815

PAUL, DENNIS EDWARD, lawyer; b. Lakewood, Ohio, Sept. 6, 1949; s. Edward and Louise Marie Paul; m. Cheryl Lynn Burnett, Aug. 21, 1976; children—Jennifer Ruth, Molly Anna. B.S. in Journalism, Ohio U., 1971; J.D., Ohio No. U., 1975. Bar: Ohio 1975, U.S. Dist. Ct. (no. dist.) Ohio 1977, U.S. Dist. Ct. (so. dist.) Mich. 1981. Asst. county prosecutor Medina County Prosecutor's Office, Medina, Ohio, 1976; city prosecutor Medina City Prosecutor's Office, 1977; assoc. Gilbert & Parish, Medina, 1978-80; ptnr. Gilbert, Parish & Paul, Medina, 1980; sole practice, Medina, 1981-83; ptnr. Palecek, McIlvaine, Foreman & Paul, Wadsworth, Ohio, 1983—. Chmn. Medina City CSC, 1984—; atty. Medina County Bd. Realtors, 1980. Mem. Ohio Acad. Trial Lawyers, Medina County Bar Assn. (pres. 1984-85), Assn. Trial Lawyers Am., Ohio Bar Assn. Roman Catholic. Personal injury, Criminal, Family and matrimonial. Office: Palecek McIlvaine Foreman & Paul 210 Bank One Bldg Wadsworth OH 44281

PAUL, HERBERT MORTON, lawyer, accountant, taxation educator; b. N.Y.C., July 17, 1931; s. Julius and Gussie Paul; married; children—Leslie Beth, Andrea Lynn. B.B.A., Baruch Coll.; M.B.A., NYU, LL.M.; J.D., Harvard U. Ptnr. Touche Ross & Co., N.Y.C., 1957-82; assoc. dir.-tax Touche Ross & Co., dir. fin counseling; mng. ptnr. Herbert Paul, P.C., N.Y.C., 1982—; dir. N.Y. Estate Planning Council; prof. taxation NYU. Author: Ordinary and Necessary Expenses; editor: Taxation of Banks; adv. tax editor The Practical Accountant; mem. adv. bd. Financial and Estate Planning, Tax Shelter Insider, Financial Planning Strategist, Tax Shelter Litigation Report; bd. dirs. Partnership Strategist, The Business Strategist; cons. Professional Practice Management Mag.; mem. panel The Hot Line; advisor The Partnership Letter, The Wealth Formula; cons. The Insider's Report for Physicians; mem. tax bd. Business Profit Digest; cons. editor physician's Tax Advisor; bd. fin. cons. Tax Strategies for Physicians; tax and bus. advisor Prentice Hall. Mem. bd. overseers Grad. Sch. Bus., NYU; mem. com. on trusts and estates Rockefeller U.; trustee Alvin Ailey Am. Dance Theatre, Associated Y's of N.Y.; bd. dirs. Alumni Fedn. of NYU; co-chmn. accts. div. Fedn. Philantropies. Served with U.S. Army, 1954-56. Mem. Inst. Fed. Taxation (adv. com. chmn.), Internat. Inst. on Tax and Bus. Planning (adv. bd.), Assn. of Bar of City of N.Y., NYU Tax Soc. (pres., chmn. com. on tax shelters), Bur. Nat. Affairs-Tax Mgmt. (adv. com. on exec. compensation), Am. Inst. C.P.A.s (com. on corp. taxation), Tax Study Group, ABA (tax sect.), N.Y. County Lawyer's Assn., N.Y. State Soc. C.P.A.s (chmn. tax div. com. on fed. taxation, gen. tax com., furtherance com., com. on relations with IRS, bd. dirs.), Nat. Assn. Accts., Assn. of Bar of City of N.Y., Accts. Club of Am., Pension Club, Nat. Assn. Estate Planners (bd. dirs.), N.Y. C. of C. (tax com.), Grad. Soc. Bus. of NYU Alumni Assn. (pres.), Pres. Council (NYU). Clubs: Wall St., City Athletic (N.Y.C.); Middle Bay (Oceanside, N.Y.). General corporate, Estate planning, Probate. Office: Herbert Paul PC 805 3rd Ave New York NY 10022

PAUL, JAMES WILLIAM, lawyer; b. Davenport, Iowa, May 3, 1945; s. Walter Henry and Margaret Helene (Hillers) P.; m. Sandra Kay Schmid, June 15, 1968; children: James William, Joseph Hillers. BA, Valparaiso U., 1967; JD, U. Chgo., 1970. Bar: N.Y. 1971, Ind. 1982, U.S. Ct. Appeals (2d cir.) 1971, U.S. Dist. Ct. (so. and ea. dists.) N.Y. 1972, U.S. Supreme Ct. 1977, U.S. Ct. Appeals (6th cir.) 1981, U.S. Ct. Claims 1986. Assoc. Rogers & Wells, N.Y.C., 1970-78, ptnr., 1978—; dir., officer Musica Sacra, Inc., 1972-81. Bd. dirs. Turtle Bay Music Sch., Am. Lutheran Publicity Bur. Mem. ABA (antitrust sect. ins. com.), Assn. Bar City N.Y. (civil ct. com.), N.Y. Law Inst. (life), Fed. Bar Council (young lawyers com.). Democrat. Club: Yale (N.Y.C.). Antitrust, Federal civil litigation, Labor. Home: 50 E 85th St Apt 12-H New York NY 10028 Office: Rogers & Wells 200 Park Ave New York NY 10166

PAUL, JEREMY RALPH, lawyer; b. N.Y.C., July 22, 1956; s. Robert D. and Eve (Weinschenker) P.; m. Laurel Ann Leff, Aug. 29, 1981. AB, Princeton U., 1978; JD, Harvard U., 1981. Bar: N.Y.C. 1982. Law clk. to presiding judge U.S. Ct. Appeals (2d cir.), N.Y.C., 1982-83; instr. U. Miami, Coral Gables, Fla., 1981-82, asst. prof. law, 1983-87, assoc. prof. law, 1987—. Democrat. Jurisprudence, Real property. Office: U Miami Sch Law Po Box 248087 Coral Gables FL 33124

PAUL, JOEL RICHARD, law educator; b. N.Y.C., Oct. 31, 1955; s. Carl William and Natalie Jane (Weissberger) P. BA, Amherst Coll., 1978; JD, Harvard U., 1982; MALD, Fletcher Sch. of Law and Diplomacy, 1982. Bar: Calif. 1982. Assoc. Graham & James, San Francisco, 1982-86; asst. prof. law Am. U., Washington, 1986—. Coordinator Hart presdl. campaign, San Francisco, 1984; alt. Dem. Nat. Conv., San Francisco, 1984; mem. exec. bd. Bay Area Lawyers for Individual Freedom, San Francisco, 1985—. Mem. ABA, Calif. Bar Assn., Am. Soc. Internat. Law, Lawyers Alliance for Nuclear Arms Control, Amherst Alumni Assn. (exec. bd.), Fletcher Alumni Assn. (co-chmn.). Avocations: political activist, fund raising. Private international, Public international, Civil rights.

PAUL, MAURICE M., judge; b. 1932. B.S. in Bus. Adminstrn., U. Fla., 1954, LL.B., 1960. Bar: Fla. Assoc. firm Sanders, McEwan, Mims & MacDonald, Orlando, Fla., 1960-64; ptnr. firm Akerman, Senterfitt, Eidson, Mesmer & Robinson, Orlando, Fla., 1965-66, firm Pitts, Eubanks, Ross & Paul, Orlando, Fla., 1968-69; atty. Orlando, Fla., 1967, 1970-72; judge 9th Fla. Circuit, 1973-82, U.S. Dist. Ct. No. Dist. Fla., 1982—. Judicial administration. Office: US District Court 110 E Park Ave Tallahassee FL 32301 *

PAUL, ROBERT, lawyer; b. N.Y.C., Nov. 22, 1931; s. Gregory and Sonia (Rijock) P.; B.A., N.Y. U., 1953; J.D., Columbia, 1958; m. Christa Holz, Apr. 6, 1975; 1 dau., Gina. Admitted to Fla. bar, 1958, N.Y. bar, 1959; ptnr. Paul, Landy Beiley, Harper & Morrison, P.A., Miami, 1964—; counsel Republic Nat. Bank Miami, 1967—. Past pres. Fla. Philharm., Inc., 1978—; trustee U. Miami. Mem. Am., N.Y., Fla., Inter-Am. bar assns., Greater Miami C. of C. (vice chmn.), French-Am. C. of C. of Miami (pres. 1986—). Private international, Banking, General corporate. Home: 700 Alhambra Circle Coral Gables FL 33134 Office: Paul Landy Beiley & Harper PA 200 SE 1st St Miami FL 33131

PAUL, STEPHEN HOWARD, lawyer; b. Indpls., June 28, 1947; s. Alfred and Sophia (Nahmias) P.; m. Deborah Lynn Dorman, Jan. 22, 1969; children: Gabriel, Jonathan. AB, Ind. U., 1969, JD, 1972. Bar: Ind. 1972, U.S. Dist. Ct. (so. dist.) Ind. 1972. Assoc. Baker & Daniels, Indpls., 1972-78, ptnr., 1979—. Editor in chief Ind. U. Law Jour., 1971. Pres. Belle Meade Neighborhood Assn., Indpls., 1974-78; v.p. counsel Brentwood Neighborhood Assn., Carmel, Ind., 1985—. Mem. ABA (state and local tax com. 1985—), Ind. State Bar Assn., Order of Coif. Republican. Jewish. State and local taxation, General corporate, Municipal bonds. Office: Baker & Daniels 108 N Pennsylvania Indianapolis IN 46204

PAUL, WILLIAM GEORGE, lawyer; b. Pauls Valley, Okla., Nov. 25, 1930; s. Homer and Helen (Lafferty) P.; m. Barbara Elaine Brite, Sept. 27, 1963; children—George Lynn, Alison Elise, Laura Elaine, William Stephen. B.A., U. Okla., 1952, LL.B., 1956. Bar: Okla. bar 1956. Practiced in Norman, 1956, Oklahoma City, 1957—; partner Crowe & Dunlevy, 1962-84; sr. v.p., gen. counsel Phillips Petroleum Co., Bartlesville, Okla., 1985—; assoc. prof. law Oklahoma City U., 1964-68. Author: (with Earl Sneed) Vernon's Oklahoma Practice, 1965. Served to 1st lt. USMCR, 1952-54. Named Outstanding Young Man Oklahoma City, 1965, Outstanding Young Oklahoman, 1966. Fellow Am. Bar Found., Am. Coll. Trial Lawyers; mem. ABA, Okla. Bar Assn. (pres. 1976), Oklahoma County Bar Assn. (past pres.), U. Okla. Alumni Assn. (pres. 1973), Phi Beta Kappa, Order of Coif, Phi Delta Phi, Delta Sigma Rho. Democrat. Presbyn. Federal civil litigation, State civil litigation, General corporate. Home: 1800 Country Club Rd Bartlesville OK 74006 Office: Phillips Bldg 18th Floor Bartlesville OK 74004

PAUL, WILLIAM MCCANN, lawyer; b. Cambridge, Mass., Feb. 9, 1951; s. Kenneth William and Mary Jean (Lamson) P.; m. Janet Anne Forest, Feb. 25, 1984; children: Emily L'Engle, Andrew Angwin. Student, U. Freiburg, Fed. Republic of Germany, 1971-72; BA, Johns Hopkins U., 1973; JD, U. Mich., 1977. Bar: D.C. 1978, U.S. Dist. Ct. D.C. 1978, U.S. Ct. Claims 1984, U.S. Ct. Appeals (4th cir.) 1980, U.S. Ct. Appeals (fed. cir.) 1983. Law clk. to presiding justice U.S. Ct. Appeals (5th cir.), Austin, Tex., 1977-78; assoc. Covington & Burling, Washington, 1978—. Mem. ABA, D.C. Bar Assn., Order of Coif. Presbyterian. Corporate taxation, Personal income taxation. Home: 5604 Chevy Chase Pkwy NW Washington DC 20015 Office: Covington & Burling 1201 Pennsylvania Ave NW Washington DC 20004

PAULSON, CHRISTOPHER ROBERT, lawyer; b. Mpls., June 29, 1947; s. Robert Melvin and Norma (Thorgrimson) P.; m. Judy Karen Hendrix, July 25, 1970; children: Gregory, Karl. BS, U.S. Air Force Acad., 1969; JD, U. Denver, 1976. Bar: Colo. 1977, U.S. Ct. Appeals (10th cir.) 1977. Commd. 2d lt. USAF, 1969, advanced through grades to capt., 1972, res., 1974; ptnr. Saunders, Snyder, Ross & Dickson, Denver, 1981—; asst. majority leader Colo. Ho. of Reps., Denver, 1981-86, majority leader, 1986—. Chmn. water policy com., exec. bd. Western Legis. Conf., San Francisco, 1983—; mem. com. on intergovtl. affairs Council State Govts., Lexington, Ky., 1986—, chmn. toll. fellowship com. 1987; mem. Mountain Bell Futures Com., Denver, 1984-85, 50 for Colo., Denver, 1985-86; adv. bd. Arapahoe County Task Force on Youth and Drugs, Littleton, Colo., 1984; exec. bd. Atlantic Alliance Young Polit. Leaders, Washington, 1985—. Named one of Outstanding Young Men of Am., Jaycees, 1978. Mem. ABA (natural resource sect. 1977—), Colo. Bar Assn. (natural resources sect. 1977—, bd. govs. 1981-82), Denver Bar Assn. (natural resources sect. 1977—), Am. Legis. Exchange Council, Denver Law Club, Denver C. of C. Republican. Presbyterian. Avocations: youth sports, skiing. Real property, Environment. Office: Saunders Snyder Ross & Dickson PC 707 17th St #3500 Denver CO 80202

PAUPORE, JEFFREY GEORGE, lawyer; b. Iron Mountain, Mich., Feb. 22, 1949; s. John Cyril and Marion Maybelle (Plante) P.; m. Patricia Barbara Byzcek, Oct. 26, 1974; children: Kristin Leigh, Eric Jeffrey. BS, No. Mich. U., 1973; JD, Thomas M. Cooley Coll., 1982. Bar: Mich. 1982, Ariz. 1983, U.S. Dist. Ct. Ariz. 1985. Assoc. John Payant Attys., Iron Mountain, 1982, Thomas Sylvester, Tucson, 1983—. Bd. dirs. ARC, Iron Mountain, 1975-77. Mem. Mich. Bar Assn., Ariz. Bar Assn., ABA, Pima County Bar Assn. (vol. radio program 1985—), Iron Mountain Jaycees (v.p. 1974-76). Republican. Roman Catholic. Lodges: Elks (trustee Tucson club 1985—). Avocations: jewelry making, hiking, swimming. Federal civil litigation, Probate, Family and matrimonial. Home: 2051 S Calle Mesa del Oso Tucson AZ 85748 Office: 1605 N Wilmot #106 B Tucson AZ 85712

PAUTSCH, RICHARD JOSEPH, lawyer; b. Omaha, Aug. 11, 1951; s. Lester Ferdinand and Arlene Adelphia (Josephson) P.; m. Nancy Ann Norman, Sept. 22, 1979; children: Catherine Alma, Anna Theressa, Maia Christina. BA in Geology, Carleton Coll., 1973—; MS in Hydrology, U. Nev., 1978; JD with honors, U. Tex., 1980. Bar: Colo. 1981. Assoc. Sherman & Howard, Denver, 1980-81; atty. Diamond Shamrock Corp., Denver, 1981; dist. counsel Tex. Oil & Gas Co., Denver, 1983—. committeeman precinct Lakewood (Colo) Reps., 1986; riverwatch coordinator Trout Unltd., Lakewood, 1986. Alfred P. Sloan scholar Carleton Coll., 1969. Mem. ABA, Colo. Bar Assn., Denver Bar Assn. Avocations: birdwatching, fishing, hiking, genealogy, history. Oil and gas leasing, Real property, General corporate. Home: 2113 S Holland St Lakewood CO 80227 Office: Tex Oil & Gas Corp 1660 Lincoln 18th Floor Denver CO 80264

PAVALON, EUGENE I., lawyer; b. Chgo., Jan. 5, 1933; m. Lois M. Frenzel, Jan. 15, 1961; children—Betsy, Bruce, Lynn. B.S.L., Northwestern U., 1954, J.D., 1956. Bar: Ill. 1956. Sr. ptnr., prin. Asher, Pavalon, Gittler and Greenfield, Ltd., Chgo., 1970—; lectr., mem. faculty various law schs. Former mem. state bd. dirs. Ind. Voters Ill. Served to capt., USAF, 1956-59. Fellow Am. Coll. Trial Lawyers, Internat. Soc. Barristers, Internat. Acad. Trial Lawyers; mem. ABA, Chgo. Bar Assn. (bd. mgrs. 1978-79), Ill. Bar Assn., Ill. Trial Lawyers Assn. (pres. 1980-81), Assn. Trial Lawyers Am. (parlimentarian 1983-84, sec. 1984-85, v.p. 1985-86, pres. elect 1986-87, pres. 1987-88), Am. Bd. Liability Attys. (diplomat). Club: Chgo. Athletic Assn. Author: Human Rights and Health Care Law, 1980; contbr. articles to profl. jours., chpts. in books. Personal injury, Federal civil litigation, State civil litigation. Home: 1540 N Lake Shore Dr Chicago IL 60611 Office: 2 N LaSalle Dr Chicago IL 60602

PAVELA, D. JEAN, lawyer, law association administrator; b. Lawrence, Kans., Jan. 26, 1938; d. Harlan W. and Frances May (McLean) Miller; m. Todd Harold Pavela, Sr., June 2, 1958 (dec. Oct. 1967); children: Linda Kirsten, Todd Harold. BA, Midland Luth. Coll., Fremont, Nebr., 1960; MS, Purdue U., 1962; JD, John Marshall Law Sch., Chgo., 1981. Bar: Ill. 1981, U.S. Dist. Ct. (no. dist.) Ill. 1981, U.S. Ct. Appeals (7th cir.) 1982. Research asst. Chgo. Urban League, 1963-64; exec. dir. Commn. on Human Relations, Kansas City, Kans., 1967-72; dir. Commn. on Human Relations, Maywood, Ill., 1972-82; sole practice Maywood, 1982-84; dir. lawyer referral service Chgo. Bar Assn., 1984—. Bd. dirs. Project Equality of Ill., Chgo., 1982—, Augustana Coll., Rock Island, Ill., 1982—, Delaney Theater Co., Oak Park, Ill., 1985-86; mem. adv. bd. Near West Suburban Housing Ctr., Westchester, Ill., 1982—; mem. council St. John's Luth. Ch., Maywood, Ill., 1977-84, 86—. Recipient Alumni Achievement award Midland Luth. Coll., Fremont, 1982. Mem. ABA, Ill. State Bar Assn., Chgo. Bar Assn., West Suburban Bar Assn., Cook County Legal Assistance Found. (bd. dirs. 1972-74, 82-86, chmn. personnel com. 1984-85), Maywood C. of C. (bd. dirs. 1983-86), Delta Theta Phi. Avocations: reading, piano playing, listening to music, sewing. Lawyer referral, Bar association administration. Home: 2027 S 11th Ave Maywood IL 60153 Office: Chgo Bar Assn Lawyer Referral Service 29 S LaSalle St Chicago IL 60603

PAVETTI, FRANCIS JAMES, lawyer; b. New Haven, Dec. 14, 1931; s. Frank and Ellen (Dawson) P.; m. Sally Thomas, July 5, 1958; 1 child, Leah Thomas. BS, U. Conn., 1953; JD cum laude, Boston coll., 1959. Bar: Conn. 1959, U.S. Dist. Ct. Conn. 1960, U.S. Ct. Appeals (2d cir.) 1966, U.S. Supreme Ct. 1966. Law clk. to presiding justice U.S. Ct. Appeals (2d cir.), Conn., 1959-60; ptnr. Pavetti & Freeman, New London, Conn., 1974—; commr. from Conn. Nat. Conf. Commrs. on Uniform State Laws. Mem. Conn. Dem. State Cen. Commn., 1968-72; trustee, corp. sec. and gen. counsel Eugene O'Neill Meml. Ctr. Found., 1964—; trustee, v.p. Peguot Community Found., 1982—. Mem. ABA (mem. faculty continuing legal edn. 1982), Conn. Bar Assn. (chmn. planning and zoning law sect. 1983-86), Fed. Bar Council (v.p., sec. 1974-80). Democrat. Roman Catholic. Club: Players (N.Y.C.). Real property, State civil litigation, Environment. Home: 18 Strand Rd Goshen Point Waterford CT 06385 Office: Pavetti & Freeman Courthouse Sq Bldg New London CT 06320

PAVIA, GEORGE M., lawyer; b. Genoa, Italy, Feb. 14, 1928; s. Enrico L. and Nelly (Welisch) P.; m. Ellen Salomon, June 15, 1952; children—Andrew, Alison; m. 2d, Antonia Pearse, Dec. 2, 1976; children—Julian, Philippa. B.A., Columbia U., 1948, LL.B., 1951; postgrad. U. Genoa, 1954-55. Bar: N.Y. 1951, U.S. Supreme Ct. 1956, U.S. Dist. Ct. (so. and ea. dists.) N.Y. 1956. Assoc., Fink & Pavia, N.Y.C., 1955-65; sr. ptnr. Pavia & Harcourt, N.Y.C., 1965—. Served to capt. JAGC, U.S. Army, 1951-54. Mem. ABA, Internat. Law Soc., Consular Law Soc. Private international, General corporate. Home: 18 E 73d St New York NY 10021 Office: 600 Madison Ave New York NY 10022

PAVITT, WILLIAM HESSER, JR., lawyer; b. Bklyn., Dec. 9, 1916; s. William Hesser an Elsie (Haring) P.; m. Mary Oden, June 19, 1937; children—William, Howard, Gale, Bruce. A.B., Columbia U., 1937, J.D., 1939. Bar: N.Y. 1939, Philippines 1945, Md. 1946, D.C. 1947, Ohio 1955, Calif. 1958. Law clk. to judge N.Y. Ct. Appeals, 1939-40; assoc. Spence, Windels, Walser, Hotchkiss & Angell, N.Y.C., 1940-44; ptnr. Whiting & Pavitt, Washington, 1948-54; assoc. Toulmin & Toulmin, Dayton, Ohio, 1954-57, Smyth & Roston, Los Angeles, 1957-59; ptnr. Smyth, Roston & Pavitt, Los Angeles, 1960-76, Smyth, Pavitt & Siegemund & Martella, Los Angeles, 1976-82, Beehler, Pavitt, Siegemund, Jagger & Martella, Los Angeles, 1982—. Elder, Pacific Palisades Presbyn. Ch., 1963-65. Served to lt. USN, 1944-46; with USNR, 1946-47. Mem. Los Angeles Patent Law Assn. (pres. 1969-70), State Bar Patent Conf. (chmn. 1970-71), Los Angeles County Bar Assn., Wilshire Bar Assn., Fed. Bar Assn., ABA, Am Patent Law Assn. Republican. Clubs: Rotary of Pacific Palisades (pres. 1976-77), Wilshire Rotary. Contbr. articles on patent law to profl. jours. Patent, Trademark and copyright, Federal civil litigation. Office: 1100 Equitable Plaza 3435 Wilshire Blvd Los Angeles CA 90010

PAWLUC, SONIA M., lawyer; b. Miami, Fla., June 25, 1957; d. Casimer and Genevieve A (Pawelczyk) Pawluc. B.A. magna cum laude, U. Miami, 1977, J.D. magna cum laude, 1981. Bar: Fla. 1981, N.C. 1986, D.C. 1986, U.S. Dist. Ct. (so. dist.) Fla. (gen.) 1981, (trial) 1983, U.S. Ct. Appeals (11th cir.) 1981, U.S. Dist. Ct. (mid. dist.) Fla. 1985, U.S. Ct. Appeals (D.C. cir.) 1986, U.S. Supreme Ct. 1986. Assoc. Holland & Knight, Miami, 1981-83, Morgan, Lewis & Bockius, Miami, 1983—. Mem. ABA, Fla. Bar Assn. (trial lawyers sect., gen. practice sect., media and communications law com.), N.C. Bar Assn. (gen. practice sect.), D.C. Bar Assn., Dade County Bar Assn., Acad. Fla. Trial Lawyers, Assn. Trial Lawyers Am., Soc. Profl. Journalists, Soc. Wig and Robe, Phi Kappa Phi, Kappa Tau Alpha, Delta Theta Mu. Democrat. Roman Catholic. Contbr. articles to profl. jours.; bd. editors So. Dist. Digest, 1981-82. State civil litigation, Federal civil litigation, General practice. Office: Morgan Lewis & Bockius 200 S Biscayne Blvd 5300 Southeast Fin Ctr Miami FL 33131-2339

PAYMENT, KENNETH ARNOLD, lawyer; b. Rochester, N.Y., Aug. 6, 1941; s. Arnold F. and Eleanor J. (Kinsey) P.; m. Heidi F., Aug. 17, 1963; children—Simone, Elise, Ryan. B.S., Union Coll., Schenectady, 1963; LL.B., Cornell U., 1966. Bar: N.Y. 1966, U.S. Dist. Ct. (we. dist.) N.Y. 1967, U.S. Ct. Appeals (2d cir.) 1968. Asso. Wiser, Shaw, Freeman, Van Graafeiland, Harter & Secrest, Rochester, 1966-75, ptnr. Harter, Secrest & Emery, 1975—; instr. Rochester Inst. Tech., 1969, U. Rochester, 1970, Cornell U. Law Sch., Ithaca, N.Y., spring 1971-72. Mem. ABA, N.Y. State Bar Assn. (chmn. constrn. and suretyship div. 1978), Monroe County Bar Assn. (trustee), Rochester C. of C. Presbyterian. Clubs: University (Rochester); Cornell (N.Y.C.). Federal civil litigation, State civil litigation, Antitrust. Home: 4278 Clover St Honeoye Falls NY 14472 Office: Harter Secrest & Emery 700 Midtown Tower Rochester NY 14604

PAYNE, CLARE HUDSON, lawyer; b. Wilmington, Del., Aug. 7, 1952; d. Edward Ellaway and Joan Julie (Poese) Hudson; m. Lewis Hill Payne, Aug. 25, 1973; children: Julia Hill Payne, Edward Lewis. BA, Trinity Coll., 1973; JD, Villanova U., 1979. Bar: Maine 1979, U.S. Dist. Ct. Maine 1979, U.S. Ct. Appeals (1st cir.) 1981. Ptnr. Eaton, Peabody, Bradford & Veague, Bangor, Maine, 1979—, also bd. dirs. Mem. ABA (labor law sect.), Maine Bar Assn., Penobscot County Bar Assn., Eastern Maine Dressage Assn. (chmn. show com.). Republican. Episcopalian. Avocation: riding. Labor. Office: Eaton Peabody Bradford & Veague PO Box 1210 Bangor ME 04401

PAYNE, FREDERICK WARREN, lawyer; b. Washington, Aug. 30, 1949; s. Riner Champ and Madge Larue (Starliper) P.; m. Caroline Wick McCorkle; children: Elizabeth Gilbreath, Sarah Riner. BA, Yale U., 1971; JD, U. Va., 1974. Bar: Va. 1974, U.S. Dist. Ct. (ea. and we. dists.) Va. 1975, U.S. Ct. Appeals (4th cir.) 1976, U.S. Supreme Ct. 1978. Dep. atty. County of Albemarle, Charlottesville, Va., 1974—; asst. commonwealth's atty. County of Albemarle, Charlottesville, 1979; acting commonwealth atty. City of Charlottesville. Candidate for com. atty. Albermarle County Reps., 1982. Mem. ABA, Va. Bar Assn., Charlottesville-Albemarle Bar Assn., Va. Trial Lawyers Assn., Local Govt. Attys. of Va. Republican. Presbyterian. Clubs: Rivanna Rifle and Pistol, Stony Point Sports (pres. 1985-86), Charlottesville Base Ball (Charlottesville) (pres. 1986—). Avocations: hunting, canoeing, baseball, woodworking, calligraphy. Real property, Criminal, State civil litigation. Office: St John Bowling Payne & Lawrence 416 Park St Charlottesville VA 22901

PAYNE, JAMES PARKER, lawyer; b. Kansas City, July 20, 1944; s. Van L. and Vida Leona (Parker) P.; m. Kathryn Marie Shimer, June 11, 1967; children: Melissa Kate, Bradley James. BA in Econs., Washburn U., 1968, JD, 1970. Bar: Kans. 1970, U.S. Dist. Ct. Kans. 1970, U.S. Supreme Ct. 1974, Tex. 1979. Assoc. Goodell, Casey, Briman, Rice & Cogswell, Topeka, 1970-72; asst. atty. gen. Kans. Atty. Gen., Topeka, 1972; counsel Kans. Ins. Dept., Topeka, 1972-75; v.p., gen. counsel, sec. Lone Star Life Ins. Co., Dallas, 1975-83, Res. Life Ins. Co., Dallas, 1983—; bd. dirs. Churchill Life Ins. Co., Phoenix, Ariz., Westland Life Ins. Co., San Francisco. Mem. ABA, Tex. Bar Assn., Kans. Bar Assn., Dallas Bar Assn., Assn. Life Ins. Counsel. Republican. Mem. Christian Ch. Insurance, General corporate, Administrative and regulatory. Office: Res Life Ins Co 403 S Akard St Dallas TX 75202

PAYNE, J(OE) STANLEY, lawyer; b. Rome, Ga., Feb. 18, 1955; s. Joe Stanley Payne and Jeanne Carole (Smith) Klotz. BA, U. Va., 1977; JD, Coll. William and Mary, 1980. Bar: Va. 1980, U.S. Ct. Appeals (D.C. cir.) 1982. Assoc. Sedam & Herge P.C., McLean, Va., 1980-81; gen. counsel, asst. to exec. dir. Va. Port Authority, Norfolk, 1981—; v.p. North Atlantic Ports Assn., 1984—; bd. dirs. Eastern Indsl. Traffic League. Mem. Va. Bar Assn., Norfolk/Portsmouth Bar Assn. Episcopalian. Avocations: tennis, golf. General corporate, Administrative and regulatory, Legislative. Home: 722 Lord Dunmore Dr Virginia Beach VA 23464 Office: Va Port Authority 600 World Trade Ctr Norfolk VA 23510

PAYNE, KENNETH EUGENE, lawyer; b. Kansas City, Kans., Jan. 12, 1936; s. Felton T. and Irene Elizabeth (Snyder) P.; m. Deidre Lee Hood, Aug. 11, 1957; children—Steven Scott, Kendra Ann. B.S., U. Kans., 1959; J.D., Am. U., 1965. Bar: Mo. 1965, D.C. 1967. Assoc., Irons, Birch, Swindler & Mckie, Washington, 1966-69, Irons, Stockman, Sears & Santorelli, 1969-71; asst. gen. counsel U.S. Dept. Commerce, Washington, 1971-73; ptnr. Finnegan, Henderson, Farabow, Garrett & Dunner, Washington, 1973—; del. Inter-Am. Commn. on Sci. and Tech. Transfer, U.S. Dept. State; cons. UN Indsl. Devel. Orgn.; lectr. Practicing Law Inst., Licensing Law and Bus. Inst. Served to capt. U.S. Army, 1960-68. Mem. Licensing Execs. Soc. Internat. (U.S.A. and Can., treas. 1986—) (pres. elect 1982-83, pres. 1983-84), ABA, Am. Patent Law Assn., Assn. Trial Lawyers Am. Republican. Methodist. Contbr. articles to profl. jours. Patent, Trademark and copyright, Antitrust. Home: 3107 N Peary St Arlington VA 22207 Office: Finnegan Henderson Farabow et al 1775 K St NW Suite 600 Washington DC 20006

PAYNE, LESLIE JULIAN, lawyer; b. N.Y.C., Aug. 1, 1945; s. Harry Leslie and Kathryn Louise (Bobel) P.; m. Johanna Ariadne van Nispen, Dec. 28, 1972; children—Chris, Alexander, Theodore, William. B.S. in M.E., Worcester Poly. Inst. (Mass.), 1967; J.D., Catholic U. Am., 1971; LL.M., Georgetown U., 1976. Bar: D.C. 1973, Ill. 1974. Patent examiner U.S. Patent & Trademark Office, Washington, 1967-73; patent atty. Cushman, Darby & Cushman, Washington, 1973-74; patent atty. Pennie & Edmonds, Arlington, Va., 1974-78; patent atty. Polaroid Corp., Cambridge, Mass., 1978—. Author chpt. to book. Mem. ABA, Boston Patent Law Assn. (chmn. pub. relations and activities com. 1981), Am. Intellectual Property Assn. (chmn. subcom. licensing of genetic material 1981-85, univ. industry licensing subcom., 1986—, edn. com. 1986—). Democrat. Roman Catholic. Patent. Office: Polaroid Corp 549 Technology Square Cambridge MA 02139

PAYNE, MARGARET ANNE, lawyer; b. Cin., Aug. 10, 1947; s. John Hilliard and Margaret Mary (Naughton) P. Student Trinity Coll., Washington, 1965-66; B.A., U. Cin. magna cum laude, 1969; J.D., Harvard U., 1972; LL.M. in Taxation, NYU, 1976. Bar: N.Y. 1975, U.S. Dist. Ct. (so. dist.) N.Y. 1975, Calif. 1979, U.S. Dist. Ct. (so. dist.) Calif. 1979. Assoc. Mudge, Rose, Guthrie, and Alexander, N.Y.C., 1972-75, Davis, Polk and Wardwell, N.Y.C., 1976-78, Seltzer, Caplan, Wilkins and McMahon, San Diego, 1978-79, Higgs, Fletcher and Mack, San Diego, 1980—; adj. prof. grad. tax program U. San Diego Sch. Law, 1979—, Calif. Western Sch. Law, San Diego, 1980-82; judge pro tem Mcpl. Ct., San Diego Jud. Dist., 1983—. Bd. dirs. Artist Chamber Ensemble, Inc., San Diego, 1983-85; trustee Library Assn. La Jolla, Calif., 1983-85. Mem. ABA, Calif. State Bar Assn., San Diego County Bar Assn., San Diego Hist. Soc. (bd. dirs. 1983—), Mortar Board, Guidon Soc., Phi Beta Kappa. Republican. Club: Charter 100 (San Diego). Probate, Estate taxation. Home: 3282 Via Alicante La Jolla CA 92037 Office: Higgs Fletcher & Mack 401 W A St 2000 Columbia Centre San Diego CA 92101

PAYNE, NELL, lawyer; b. Hinsdale, Ill., Sept. 2, 1957; d. Henry Berry and Eudora (Young) P. BA, U. Iowa, 1978; JD, George Washington U., 1982. Bar: D.C. 1983, U.S. Dist. Ct. D.C. 1983, U.S. Ct. Appeals (D.C. cir.) 1983, U.S. Supreme Ct. 1986. Mgr. office Wembley Industries, Chgo., 1978-79; legal asst. U.S. Dept. Justice, Washington, 1980-81; staff atty. Senate Budget Com., Washington, 1982-84; chief counsel Senat Beduget Com., Washington, 1984—. Legislative. Office: Senate Budget Com SD-621 Washington DC 20510

PAYNE, RAYMOND LEE, JR., lawyer; b. Kansas City, Mo., Nov. 7, 1927; s. Raymond Lee and Erma Elizabeth (Whitaker) P.; m. Betty Joyce Billingsley, 1948; children—Raymond Lee, Janifer H. Payne Joel, Gregory M.; m. Kathleen Marie Wood, Dec. 14, 1957; m. Patricia Paschall Chancellor, June 17, 1977. B.S., U. Denver, 1959, J.D., 1960. Bar: Colo. 1960; cert. hotel/motel adminstr. Assoc. Harding & Herman, Denver, 1960-62; assoc. Tilly & Skelton, Denver, 1962-66; sole practice, Denver, 1966-67; ptnr. Safran & Payne and predecessors, Denver, 1968-78; sole practice, Denver, 1978—; sec., dir. Commerce Motor Hotel Corp., Adventure Travel Corp., ptnr. Cameron Assocs.; Chmn. bd. S.W. Denver Community Mental Health Services, 1960-74; bd. dirs. Denver Bar Assn. Credit Union, 1979—, chmn. loan com., 1982, pres., 1983-84; chmn. Downtown Dem. Forum. Served with AUS, 1946-47. Mem. Colo. Bar Assn., Denver Bar Assn., Colo.-Wyo. Hotel/Motel Assn. (bd. dirs.). Democrat. Clubs: Over the Hill Gang Ski Team, City of Denver; Toastmasters (Lakewood, Colo.); Masons. Contracts commercial, Probate, Real property. Home: 9200 Cherry Creek South Dr Denver CO 80231 Office: 8000 E Girard Ave South Tower Suite 415 Denver CO 80231

PAYNE, ROBERT WARREN, lawyer; b. Springfield, Mo., Dec. 21, 1950; s. Warren Edwin and Roberta May (Kile) P.; m. Eileen Pack Tremain, Apr. 4, 1947; 1 child, Katherine. AB, Stanford U., 1972; JD, U. Calif., Davis, 1975; LLM, U. London, 1978. Bar: Calif. 1976, Idaho 1976, U.S. Dist. Ct. (no. dist.) Calif. 1976, U.S. Dist. Ct. Idaho 1976. Assoc. Stark, Stewart, Wells & Robinson, Oakland, Calif., 1979-82, Carr, McClellan, Ingersoll, Thompson & Horn, Burlingame, Calif., 1982—. Mem. San Mateo County Trial Lawyers Assn. (bd. dirs. 1984—), San Mateo County Bar Assn. (community affairs com. 1985-87). Club: Peninsula Stanford (Burlingame) (pres. 1986-87). Lodge: Kiwanis. State civil litigation, Trade secrets litigation. Office: Carr McClellan Ingersoll Thompson & Horn 216 Park Rd Burlingame CA 94010

PAYNE, ROY STEVEN, lawyer; b. New Orleans, Aug. 30, 1952; s. Fred J. and Dorothy Julia (Peck) P.; m. Laureen Fuller, Sept. 8, 1973; children: Julie Elizabeth, Kelly Kathryn, Alex Steven. BA with distinction, U. Va., 1974; JD, La. State U., 1977; LLM, Harvard U., 1980. Bar: La. 1977, U.S. Dist. Ct. (we. dist.) La. 1980, U.S. Ct. Appeals (5th cir.) 1980, U.S. Supreme Ct. 1983. Law clk. to judge U.S. Dist. Ct., Shreveport, La., 1977-79; assoc. Blanchard, Walker, O'Quin & Roberts, Shreveport, 1980-83, ptnr., 1984—; instr. New Eng. Sch. Law, Boston, 1979-80. Contbr. articles to profl. jours. Chmn. Northwest La. Legal Services Assn., Shreveport, 1984-85. Mem. ABA, 5th Circuit Bar Assn., La. State Bar Assn. (editorial bd. Forum jour., 1983—, legal aid com.), Shreveport Bar Assn., La. Assn. Def. Counsel, Order of Coif, Phi Kappa Phi, Phi Delta Phi. Democrat. Methodist. Club: Rotary. Federal civil litigation, Insurance, Labor. Home: 406 Brighton Ct Shreveport LA 71115 Office: Blanchard Walker O'Quin & Roberts First Nat Bank Tower 15th Floor Shreveport LA 71101

PAYSON, MARTIN DAVID, entertainment company executive, lawyer; b. N.Y.C., Jan. 4, 1936; s. Joseph J. and Stella (Riemer) P.; m. Doris Leah Greenberg, Mar. 23, 1936; children: Michele, Leslie, Eric. A.B., Cornell U., 1957; LL.B. cum laude, NYU, 1961. Bar: N.Y. 1961. Assoc. Paul Weiss Rifkind Wharton & Garrison, N.Y.C., 1961-67; instr. Law Sch., U. Mich., Ann Arbor, 1963-64; ptnr. Polier Tulin & Payson, N.Y.C., 1967-70; gen. counsel Warner Communications, Inc., N.Y.C., 1970—; also dir. Warner Communications, Inc. Chmn. entertainment div. United Jewish Appeal-Fedn. Joint Campaign, N.Y.C., 1982-84; mem. pres.'s council Tulane U., New Orleans, 1984—; trustee Fedn. Jewish Philanthropies N.Y., N.Y.C., 1983—. Mem. ABA, Assn. Bar City N.Y. Democrat. General corporate. Office: Warner Communications Inc 75 Rockefeller Plaza New York NY 10019 *

PAYTON, DONALD LEE, lawyer; b. Lansing, Mich., Feb. 13, 1949; s. Gerald Lee and Maria (Scurtu) P.; m. Deborah Jean Fox, Mar. 9, 1973; children: Erin Leigh, Kelly Andrea. BA, Mich. State U., 1971; JD, Detroit Coll. law, 1976. Bar: Mich. 1977, U.S. Dist. Ct. (ea. dist.) Mich. 1977. Assoc. Sinelli, Decker & Schmidt, Redford, Mich., 1977-78, Charles F. Decker, Farmington Hills, Mich., 1978-79; from assoc. to ptnr. Kaufman & Payton, Farmington Hills, 1979—. Served to capt. USAR, 1971-79. Mem. ABA, Oakland Bar Assn., Assn. Def. Trial Counsel, Mich. Def. Trial Counsel. Republican. Avocations: reading, tennis, softball, racquetball. State civil litigation, Insurance, Personal injury. Home: 4269 Still Meadow West Bloomfield-Orchard Lake MI 48033 Office: Kaufman & Payton 30833 Northwestern Hwy Farmington Hills MI 48018

PEAKE, DARRYL LEE, lawyer; b. Chgo., Sept. 2, 1952; s. George J. Jr. and Loretta T. (Jadzak) P.; m. Mary M. O'Grady, May 27, 1984. BS in Acctg. and Fin., So. Ill. U., 1974; JD, John Marshall Law Sch., 1980; LLM in Taxation, DePaul U., 1985. Bar: Ill. 1980, U.S. Dist. Ct. (no. dist.) Ill. 1980, U.S. Tax Ct. 1984; CPA, Ill. Various positions leading to adminstr. fed. income taxes Internat. Harvester Co., Chgo., 1974-83; mng. atty. Peake and Pavel, Naperville, Ill., 1980-83; mgr. taxes Household Merchandising Inc., Des Plaines, Ill., 1983-84; appeals officer IRS, Chgo., 1984-85; chief fin. officer, corp. sec. Kilpatrick C Inc., Palos Heights, Ill., 1985—, also bd. dirs.; assoc. Baum, Glick & Wertheimer P.C., Chgo., 1985—. Editor DePaul Tax Law Jour., 1985. Cons. Children's Home & Aid Soc., Chgo., 1984—. Mem. ABA, Am. Inst. CPA's, Ill. State Bar Assn. (fed. taxation sect. 1985—, corp. law sect. 1985—), Chgo. Bar Assn., Ill. CPA Soc. Roman Catholic. Corporate taxation, General corporate, Pension, profit-sharing, and employee benefits. Office: Baum Glick & Wertheimer PC 55 W Monroe Suite 2727 Chicago IL 60603

PEARCE, CARY JACK, lawyer; b. Copeville, Tex., Aug. 28, 1934; s. James Zebulon and Lillian (Graves) P.; m. Joyce Selette Hulsey, Oct. 17, 1959; children—Janet, Joseph, Alissa, Gale. B.A., Baylor U., 1955; LL.B., So. Methodist U., 1962. Bar: Tex. 1962, D.C. 1971. Asst. chief pub. counsel sec. Antitrust div. U.S. Dept. Justice, Washington, 1967-70; dep. gen. counsel White House Office Consumer Affairs, Washington, 1970-71; sole practice, Washington, 1971—; dir. Bankcard Holders Am., W.O.I., Inc. Contbr. articles to profl. jours. Mem. ABA. Unitarian. Club: Lawyers (Washington). Antitrust, Private international, Administrative and regulatory. Home: 3728 Windom Pl NW Washington DC 20016 Office: 1000 Connecticut Ave Suite 1200 Washington DC 20036

PEARCE, LEWIS RICHARD, lawyer; b. Bedford, Ohio, June 20, 1943; s. Lewis Henry and Magdalen (Kane) P.; m. Patricia Ann Breyley, Feb. 22, 1964; children—Kimberly Ann, Jessica Ann. B.B.A., Ohio U., 1965; J.D., Cleve. Marshall Law Sch., 1970. Bar: Ohio 1970, Fla. 1972, U.S. Dist. Ct. (mid. dist.) Fla. 1972, U.S. Ct. Apls. (5th cir.) 1979, U.S. Supreme Ct. 1979. Acct., Sherwin Williams Co., Cleve., 1965-68, tax acct., 1968-70, tax atty., 1970-71; comptroller Cheesem Devel. Corp., Madira Beach, Fla., 1971-72; v.p. adminstrn. Medfield Corp., St. Petersburg, Fla., 1972-74; assoc. Spielvogel & Goldman P.A., Merritt Island, Fla., 1974-76, ptnr., 1976-78; ptnr, Stromire, Westman Lintz, Baugh, McKinley, Antoon & Pearce, P.A., Cocoa, Fla., 1978-82; sole practice, Merritt Island, 1982—; mem. program evaluation com. Fla. Bar, 1980-81, bd. govs. budget com., 1980-82, mem. long range planning com., 1982—. Bd. dirs. Brevard County Legal Aid, Inc., 1980—. Mem. Fla. Bar, ABA, Brevard County Bar Assn. (chmn. atty. realtor relations com.). Real property, General corporate, Probate. Address: 2255 N Courtenay Pkwy PO Box 37 Merritt Island FL 32952

PEARLMAN, ALAN, lawyer; b. Chgo., Aug. 12, 1946; s. Harry and Ethel P.; m. Doreen Desser, Nov. 25, 1972; children—Beth, David. B.Mus.Ed., DePaul U., 1968; J.D., John Marshall Law Sch., 1973. Bar: Ill. 1974, U.S. Tax Ct. 1974, U.S. Ct. Appeals (7th cir.) 1974, U.S. Dist. Ct. (no. dist.) Ill. 1974. Tchr., Chgo. Bd. Edn., 1968-73; asst. state's atty. Cook County (Ill.), 1973-75; ptnr. Stone & Pearlman, 1975-78; sole practice, Skokie, Ill., 1979—. Mem. Ill. Bar Assn., ABA, Chgo. Bar Assn., N.W. Suburban Bar Assn., Nat. Dist. Attys. Assn., Decalogue Soc. Lawyers, Chgo. Fedn. Musicians, Phi Alpha Delta. Club: Moose. Lodge: Masons. Author: Techniques of Rock and Roll Drumming, 1972. Criminal, Personal injury, Family and matrimonial. Office: 8350 Lincoln Ave Skokie IL 60077

PEARLMAN, DAVID HENRY, lawyer; b. White Bear Lake, Minn., June 27, 1943; s. Leon and Charlotte Fern (Blehart) P.; m. Arlyce Lichthardt, June, 1965 (div. July 1970); 1 child, David L.; m. Carol A. Moore, June 7, 1971; children: Gavin E., Adam M. BA, U. Minn., 1965; JD, U. N.Mex., 1969. Bar: N.Mex. 1969, U.S. Dist. Ct. N.Mex. 1969, U.S. Ct. Appeals (10th cir.) 1971, U.S. Dist. Ct. (ea. dist.) Tex. 1977. Ptnr. Duran & Pearlman, Albuquerque, 1969-70; sole practice Albuquerque, 1970-71, 1977—; ptnr. Aldridge & Pearlman, Albuquerque, 1971-73, Aldridge, Baron, Pearlman & Campbell, Albuquerque, 1973-75, Pearlman & Shoobridge, Albuquerque, 1975-77. State rep. N.Mex. Dems., Albuquerque, 1978. Mem. Assn. Trial Lawyers Am., N.Mex. Trial Lawyers Assn., Nat. Bd. of Trial Adv. (cert. trial specialist). Democrat. Jewish. Personal injury, Workers' compensation, State civil litigation. Office: 423 6th St NW Albuquerque NM 87102

PEARLMAN, LISA ANN, lawyer; b. New London, Conn., May 16, 1949; d. Lester S. and Amalia (Rapaport) P.; m. Peter James Benvenutti, May 31, 1974; children: Anna Beyer, Jamie Elizabeth, Amalia. BA magna cum laude, Yale U., 1971; JD, U. Calif., Berkeley, 1974. Bar: Calif. 1974, U.S. Dist Ct. (no. dist.) Calif. 1974, U.S. Ct. Appeals (9th cir.) 1980, U.S. Supreme Ct. 1983. Assoc. Koster, Kohlmeier & Graham, San Francisco, 1974-75; law clk. to presiding justice Calif. Supreme Ct., San Francisco, 1975; teaching fellow Stanford U., Palo Alto, Calif.; assoc. Stark, Stewart, Wells & Robinson, Oakland, Calif., 1976-79, mng. ptnr., 1984-85; ptnr. Stark, Stewart, Wells & Robinson, Oakland, 1980—; Author (with others) California Forms of Jury Instructions. Mem. ABA, State Bar Calif. (litigation sect.), Alameda County Bar Assn. (chmn. law office econ. com.), Order of Coif, Phi Beta Kapppa. Federal civil litigation, State civil litigation. Office: Stark Stewart et al 1999 Harrison St #1300 Oakland CA 94612

PEARLMAN, MICHAEL ALLEN, lawyer; b. Phila., Sept. 22, 1946; s. William and Mary (Stark) P.; m. Ann Gerald, June 1, 1969; children—Benjamin, Amy. B.A., Duke U., 1968, J.D., 1970. Bar: N.C. 1970, D.C. 1971, U.S. Dist. Ct. (mid. dist.) N.C. 1973, N.Y. 1982, Ct. Internat. Trade 1982. Atty. FTC, Washington, 1970-73; assoc. gen. counsel, asst. sec. Fieldcrest Mills, Inc., Eden, N.C., 1973-81; counsel Gen. Electric Co., Syracuse, N.Y., 1981-85; corp. counsel Eastman Kodak Co., Rochester, N.Y., 1985—. Vice pres. Eden YMCA, 1978-79; pres. Rockingham County Arts Council, N.C., 1979-80; mem. Brighton Symphony, 1985—. Recipient Superior Service award FTC, 1972, Gen. Electric Mgmt. award, 1985. Democrat. Jewish. General corporate, Private international, Antitrust. Home: 8 Pin Hook Ln Pittsford NY 14534 Office: Eastman Kodak Co 343 State St Rochester NY 14650

PEARLMAN, PETER STEVEN, lawyer; b. Orange, N.J., June 11, 1946; s. Jack Kitchener and Tiela Josephine (Fine) P.; m. Joan Perlmutter, June 19, 1969; children—Heather, Christopher, Megan. B.A., U. Ill., 1967; J.D., Seton Hall U., 1970. Bar: N.J. 1970, U.S. Dist. Ct. N.J. 1970, U.S. Tax Ct. 1973, U.S. Supreme Ct. 1974, U.S. Ct. Appeals (2d cir.) 1981, U.S. Ct. Appeals (3d cir.) 1983, U.S. Ct. Appeals (7th cir.) 1985. Assoc. Cohn & Lifland, Esquires, Saddle Brook, N.J., 1970-72, ptnr., 1972—; mem. panel arbitrators Am. Arbitration Assn.; lectr. for Inst. Continuing Legal Edn. for State of N.J.; panel mem. for med. malpractice panel hearing N.J. Supreme Ct. Trustee, Temple B'Nai Or, 1981-82. Mem. ABA, N.J. Bar Assn., Assn. Trial Lawyers Am. Federal civil litigation, State civil litigation, General corporate. Home: 9 Harvey Dr Short Hills NJ 07078 Office: Cohn & Lifland Park 80 Plaza West One Saddle Brook NJ 07662

PEARLMAN, SAMUEL SEGEL, lawyer; b. Pitts., May 28, 1942; s. Merle Maurice and Bernice Florence (Segel) P.; m. Cathy Schwartz, Aug. 16, 1964; children—Linda S., Caren E. A.B., U. Pa., 1963, LL.B., 1966. Bar: Pa. 1966, Ohio, 1967, U.S. Ct. Appeals (3d cir.) 1967. Law clk. U.S. Dist. Ct. (Ea. dist.) Pa., 1966-67; assoc. Burke, Haber & Berick, Cleve., 1967-72, prin., 1973-86, ptnr., Berick, Pearlman & Mills, 1986—; lectr. law Case Western Res. U. Sch. Law, 1978-82; mem. registration com. Ohio Div. Securities, 1979—. Mem. ABA, Ohio State Bar Assn., Greater Cleve. Bar Assn. (chmn. securities law sect. 1985-86), Order of Coif. Republican. Jewish. Clubs: Commerce, Clevelander (Cleve.). Author: Cases, Forms and Materials for Modern Real Estate Transactions, 1978, 82. General corporate, Real property. Office: 1111 Superior Ave 1350 Eaton Ctr Cleveland OH 44114

PEARLSTEIN, GERALD, lawyer; b. Winthrop, Mass., Sept. 22, 1947; s. Charles Simon and Rita (Swerling) P.; m. C. Jane Gilfix, Aug. 9, 1969; children: Alex, Abbie. BA in Econs., U. Mass.-Boston, 1969; JD, Suffolk U., 1974. Bar: Mass. 1974, U.S. Dist. Ct. Mass. 1975, U.S. Ct. Appeals (1st cir.) 1979, U.S. Supreme Ct. 1978. Econ. analyst Mass. Dept. Commerce, Boston, 1968-69; budget analyst Northeast Airlines, Boston, 1969-70; asst. controller Nat. Hardgoods, Inc., Newton, Mass., 1970-74; ptnr. firm Pearlstein & Passalacqua, Revere, Mass., 1974-76, Franklin, Pearlstein & Passalacqua, Boston, 1976-83, 86—; sole practice, Boston, 1983-86. Bd. dirs., v.p. North Shore Jewish Community Ctr., Peabody, Mass., 1982-85; cubmaster North Bay council Boy Scouts Am., 1982-85. Served with USAR, 1969-75. Mem. ABA, Mass. Bar Assn., Am. Immigration Lawyers Assn. Republican. Jewish. Lodge: Masons (32 degree, past master). Immigration, naturalization, and customs, Real property, General corporate. Office: 55 Temple Pl Boston MA 02111

PEARMAN, JOEL EDWARD, lawyer; b. Knoxville, Tenn., Jan. 12, 1949; s. Jess Edward and Ozell (Huff) P.; m. Ann Fulmer, Dec. 16, 1972 (div. May 1986); children: Joshua Edward, Paul Jonathan. BA, Bryan Coll., 1971; JD,

U. Tenn., 1973. Bar: Tenn. 1974, U.S. Dist. Ct. (no. dist.) Tenn. 1974. Sole practice Harriman, TN, 1974—. Atty. Foster Care Rev. Com., Kingston, Tenn., 1978-80; commr. Roane County Election Commn., Kingston, 1982—; mem. steering com. Leadership Roane County, Kingston, 1986—. Named one of Outstanding Young Men, 1975-76. Mem. Tenn. Bar Assn., Roane County Bar Assn. (pres. 1983—), Christian Legal Soc. Republican. Baptist. Lodge: Rotary (Harriman pres. 1982-83). State civil litigation, Personal injury, General practice. Office: 431 Devonia St Harriman TN 37748-2087

PEARMAN, ROBERT CHARLES, attorney; b. N.Y.C., Apr. 2, 1953; s. Robert C. and Audrey Joyce (Ketchens) P. B.S. in Econs. cum laude, U. Pa., 1974, J.D., Yale U., 1977. Assoc. Kadison, Pfaelzer, Woodard, Quinn & Rossi, Los Angeles, 1977-81; sole practice law, Los Angeles, 1981-84; ptnr. Burke, Robinson & Pearman, Los Angeles, 1984—. Chmn. Polit. Action Com. Assn. of Minority Real Estate Developers, Los Angeles, 1983; mem. Small Bus. Com., Inglewood C. of C., 1984. Mem. Nat. Bus. League, Bldg. Industry Assn. (home builders council), ABA (real property, probate and trust sect., banking and bus. law sect., forum com. on entertainment and sports), Assn. of Corp. Real Estate Execs., State Bar of Calif. (bus. law sect., real property law sect., ethnic minority relations com.), Los Angeles Urban League, Los Angeles County Bar Assn. (real property sect., bus. and corps. sect., comml. law and bankruptcy sect.), MENSA, Phi Delta Phi. Roman Catholic. Real property, General corporate. Home: 2620 W 84th Place Inglewood CA 90305 Office: Burke Robinson & Pearman 1925 Century Park E Suite 350 Los Angeles CA 90067

PEARSALL, JOHN WESLEY, lawyer; b. Richmond, Va., Aug. 21, 1914. BS, Randolph-Macon Coll., 1935; LLB, U. Richmond, 1941. Bar: Va. 1940. Assoc. McGuire, Riely & Eggleston, Richmond, 1941-50; ptnr. McGuire, Eggleston, Bocock & Woods, Richmond, 1950-53; gen. counsel Va.-Carolina Chem. Corp., Richmond, 1953-56; sole practice, Richmond, 1956-60; ptnr. McCaul, Grigsby & Pearsall, Richmond, 1960-86, Pearsall & Pearsall, 1986—; gen. counsel, dir. Estes Express Lines; Richmond, 1972—. Chpt. chmn. ARC, Chesterfield County, Va., 1944-49, campaign chmn., 1949, campaign chmn. Richmond, Henrico, and Chesterfield, Va., 1950, nat. vice chmn. fund dr., 1956, nat. gov., 1953-55; mem. budget com. Richmond Area Community Chest, 1946-47, mem. exec. com., 1947-55, trustee, 1946-50, campaign chmn., 1951, pres., 1955, United Giver's Fund, 1970; v.p. Children's Aid Soc., Richmond, 1950-55, trustee, 1948-55; active Boy Scouts Am., 1953-56; mem. exec. com. Randolph- Macon Coll., 1958-76, chmn. long range plan com., 1960-76, trustee, 1955-76; mem. Chesterfield County Welfare Bd., 1951-55; trustee Sheltering Arms Hosp., Richmond, 1949-80, Va. Health and Welfare Pension Fund, 1968—; dir. Jr. Achievement, 1975-81; vestryman St. Paul's Episc. Ch., 1967-70, lay reader 1986-87; mem. exec. com. Hist. Richmond Found. (1965-70), Falls of James com., 1979—, exec. com. Chesterfield Hist. Soc., 1985—. Served to lt. j.g. USNR, 1944-46. Mem. ABA, Va. Bar Assn., Richmond Bar Assn., Chesterfield County Bar Assn. (pres. 1963-64), Am. Judicature Soc., Va. State Bar Council (chmn. judicial ethics com. 1970-71), Am. Archaeol. Soc. (pres. 1976), Phi Beta Kappa (pres. Richmond area chpt. 1976-77), Omicron Delta Kappa (Jr. C. of C. Disting. Service award 1948), Lambda Chi Alpha. State civil litigation, General corporate, General practice. Home: 7701 Riverside Dr Richmond VA 23225 Office: Ellen Glasgow House 1 W Main St Richmond VA 23220

PEARSON, CHARLES THOMAS, JR., lawyer; b. Fayetteville, Ark., Oct. 14, 1929; s. Charles Thomas and Doris (Pinkerton) P.; m. Alice Ann Paddock, Mar. 7, 1952; children: Linda Sue, John Paddock. B.S., U. Ark., 1953, J.D., 1954; postgrad., U.S. Naval Postgrad. Sch., 1959; A.M., Boston U., 1963. Bar: Ark. bar 1954. Practice in Fayetteville, 1963—; dir., officer N.W. Communications, Inc., Dixieland Devel., Inc., Jonlin Investments, Inc., World Wide Travel Service, Inc., Okliana Farms, Inc., N.W. Ark. Land & Devel., Inc., Garden Plaza Inns, Inc., Word Data, Inc., M.P.C. Farms, Inc., Fayetteville Enterprises, Inc., NWA Devel. Co., Delta Comm, Inc.; dir., organizer N.W. Nat. Bank. Adviser Explorer Scouts, 1968—; past pres. Washington County Draft Bd.; past pres. bd. Salvation Army. Served to comdr. Judge Adv. Gen. Corps USNR, 1955-63. Mem. Am., Ark., Washington County bar assns., Judge Advs. Assn., N.W. Ark. Ret. Officers Assn. (past pres.), Methodist Men (past pres.), U. Ark. Alumni Assn. (dir.), Sigma Chi (past pres. N.W. Ark. alumni, past chmn. house corp.), Alpha Kappa Psi, Phi Eta Sigma, Delta Theta Phi. Republican. Methodist. Clubs: Mason (32 deg., K.T., Shriner), Moose, Elk, Lion, Metropolitan. Personal injury, Real property, General practice. Office: 36 E Center St Fayetteville AR 72701

PEARSON, CLINTON CHARLES, lawyer; b. Jackson, Tenn., Nov. 1, 1950; s. Seabon Clinton and Loren (Whitnel) P.; m. Sheila Lynn Hollis, May 30, 1970 (div. 1978); m. Carol Ann Tyler, July 14, 1978. BBA in Acctg. magna cum laude, Memphis State U., 1972; JD cum laude, Stetson U., 1977. Bar: Fla. 1977, U.S. Ct. Mil. Appeals 1978, U.S. Supreme Ct. 1981. Commd. 2d lt. USAF, 1972, advanced through grades to maj., 1983; asst. staff judge adv. USAF, Elmendorf AFB, Alaska, 1977-79, area def. counsel, 1979-80; mem. mil. justice div. USAF, Washington, 1980-83, cir. mil. judge, 1983-84; staff judge adv. USAF, Loring AFB, Maine, 1984—; adj. instr. Embry Riddle Aerospace U., Loring AFB, 1985-86, Chapman Coll. Calif., Elmendorf AFB, 1979-80, Anchorage Community Coll., 1978-80, U. Md., 1981. Mem. ABA, Fla. Bar Assn. Republican. Military, Criminal, Government contracts and claims. Home: 17 Wells Dr Loring AFB ME 04751 Office: 42 Combat Support Group Judge Adv Loring AFB ME 04751-5000

PEARSON, HENRY CLYDE, judge; b. Ocoonita, Va., Mar. 12, 1925; s. Henry James and Nancy Elizabeth (Seals) P.; m. Jean Calton, July 26, 1956; children—Elizabeth, Frances, Timothy Clyde. Student Union Coll., 1947-49; LL.B., U. Richmond, 1952. Bar: Va. 1952, U.S. Ct. Appeals (4th cir.) 1957, U.S. Supreme Ct. 1958. Sole practice, Jonesville, Va., 1952-56; asst. U.S. atty. Western Dist. Va., Roanoke, 1956-61; ptnr. Hopkins, Pearson & Engleby, Roanoke, 1961-70; judge U.S. Bankruptcy Ct. Western Dist. Va., Roanoke, 1970—; participant Va. Continuing Edn. Seminars; mem. adv. com. fed. rules bankruptcy procedure. Mem. Va. Ho. of Reps., 1954-56, Va. Senate, 1968-70; Republican nominee Gov. of Va., 1961. Served with USN, 1943-46; PTO. Mem. Va. State Bar, ABA, Va. Trial Lawyers Assn., Assn. Trial Lawyers Am., Am. Judicature Soc., Am. Judges Assn., Fed. Bar Assn., Delta Theta Phi, Tribune Jefferson Senate, Am. Legion, VFW. Methodist. Clubs: Masons, Shriners. Editorial bd. Am. Survey Bankruptcy Law, 1979. Judicial administration, Banking, Bankruptcy. Address: PO Box 2389 Roanoke VA 24010

PEARSON, LINLEY E., state attorney general; b. Long Beach, Calif., Apr. 18, 1946. B.A., The Citadel, 1966; M.B.A., Butler U., 1970; J.D., Ind. U., 1970. Bar: Ind. 1970, U.S. Dist. Ct. (so. dist.) Ind. 1970, U.S. Ct. Appeals (7th cir.) 1977. Law clk. judge Richard Givan Ind. Supreme Ct., 1969-70; pros. atty. Clinton County, 1971-81; atty. gen. State of Ind., Indpls., 1981—; ptnr. Campbell, Hardesty, Pearson & Douglas, Frankfort, Ind., 1971-81. Mem. Ind. Bar Assn., Clinton County Bar Assn. (pres. 1973). Office: Office Atty Gen 219 State House Indianapolis IN 46204 *

PEARSON, NIELS L., lawyer; b. Spokane, Wash., Nov. 2, 1947; s. Weldon G. and Ina (Lipman) Harris P.; m. Gloria Domingo, Aug. 24, 1974; children—Nicole Ann, Leif Gunnar. B.S. in Diplomacy in World Affairs, Occidental Coll., 1970; J.D., NYU, 1973. Bar: Nev. 1973, U.S. Dist. Ct. Nev. 1975, U.S. Supreme Ct. 1977, U.S. Ct. Appeals (9th cir.) 1980. Ptnr. Edwards, Hunt, Pearson & Hale, Las Vegas, Nev., 1975-84, Pearson & Patton, A Profl. Corp., Las Vegas, 1984—; lectr. So. Nev. Claims Assn., 1977, 79, 83. Mem. nat. campaign staff John Lindsey-Pres. Elections, Ariz., Fla., Wis., 1972. Root Tilden fellow NYU, 1970-73. Mem. ABA (fidelity and surety, property law and med. coms. 1977—), Def. Research Inst. (lectr. 1979—), Am. Judica Soc., Nev. Fedn. Defense Counsel (founding, officer 1979—), Phi Beta Kappa, Delta Phi Epsilon. Insurance, Public utilities, State civil litigation. Office: 316 E Bridger St Suite 200 Las Vegas NV 89101

PEARSON, PAUL DAVID, lawyer; b. Boston, Jan. 22, 1940; s. Bernard J. and Ruth (Bayla) Horblit; children—David Todd, Lisa Kari. A.B., Bucknell U., 1961; LL.B., U. Pa., 1964. Bar: Mass. 1966. Staff atty., tech. assoc. lab. of community psychiatry, dept. psychiatry Harvard Med. Sch., Boston, 1966-68; assoc. Snyder Tepper & Berlin, Boston, 1968-71, ptnr., 1971-77; with Hill & Barlow, Boston, 1977—, ptnr., chmn. family law dept.; lectr. Mass. Continuing Legal Edn., New Eng. Law Inst.; instr. law and mental health Boston Psychoanalytic Soc. and Inst., 1975—. Trustee, v.p., legal counsel Boston Ballet Soc.; trustee, chmn., legal counsel Wayland (Mass.) Townhouse; trustee Family Counseling Service (region West); mem., chmn., clk. Wayland Zoning Bd. Appeals; v.p., counsel, Arts Wayland Found., 1982—; vis. fellow Woodrow Wilson Found., 1985—, Mass. Gov.'s Spl. Commn. on Divorce. Served to capt. Mil. Police Corps, USAR. Fellow Am. Acad. Matrimonial Lawyers (pres., bd. mgrs. Mass.); mem. ABA (family law com.), Mass. Bar Assn. (chmn. family law sect.), Boston Bar Assn. (family law com., legis. chmn.). Contbr. articles to profl. jours. Family and matrimonial, Real property, Probate. Home: 31 Jeffrey Rd Wayland MA 01778 Office: 225 Franklin St Boston MA 02110

PEARSON, VERNON R., state supreme court justice; b. 1923. B.A., Jamestown Coll. (S.D.), 1947; LL.B., U. Mich., 1950. Instr. legal research and writing U. Wash.; atty. OPS; ptnr. Davies, Pearson, Anderson & Pearson, Tacoma; judge Ct. Appeals, 1969-82; assoc. justice Wash. Supreme Ct., 1982-87, chief justice, 1987—. Mem. Tacoma-Pierce County Bar Assn. (past pres.), Wash. State Bar Assn. (past gov.). Judicial administration. Office: Supreme Court Wash Temple of Justice Olympia WA 98504 *

PEASLEE, MAURICE KEENAN, lawyer; b. Niskayuna, N.Y., May 3, 1950; s. Lawrence Roswell and Betty Ann (Keenan) P.; m. Darlene Ann McFarland, Apr. 10, 1976. BA, Union U., 1972, JD, 1976. Bar: N.Y. 1977, U.S. Dist. Ct. (no. dist.) N.Y. 1977, U.S. Ct. Appeals (2d cir.) 1982. Law research asst. appellate div. 3d dept. N.Y. State Supreme Ct., Albany, 1976-77; asst. atty. gen. N.Y. State Atty. Gen.'s Office, Albany, 1977-85; asst. counsel N.Y. State Comptrollers Office, Albany, 1985—. Comments editor Union U. Law Rev., 1975-76. Trustee Trinity United Meth. Ch., Albany, 1986—; bd. dirs. 8th Step Coffee House, Albany, 1974-82, chmn. 1977; bd. dirs. Martin Luther King Day Care Ctr., Albany, 1981-83, Neighborhood Resource Ctr., Albany, 1977-80. Mem. ABA, N.Y. State Bar Assn., Justinian Soc. Administrative and regulatory, Municipal bonds, State and local taxation. Home: 392 Hamilton St Albany NY 12210 Office: Office of State Comptroller Alfred E Smith State Office Bldg Albany NY 12236

PECHACEK, FRANK WARREN, JR., lawyer; b. Winona, Minn., May 1, 1944; s. Frank Warren and Gladys (Bjoraker) P.; m. Beth E. Horn, June 4, 1966; children—Jill Ellan, Holly Jo, Frank Warren III. Student Iowa State U., 1963-64; B.A. with honors, U. No. Iowa, 1966; J.D. with honors, U. Iowa, 1969. Bar: Iowa 1969, Nebr. 1983, U.S. Dist. Ct. (so. dist.) Iowa 1969, U.S. Dist. Ct. (no. dist.) Iowa 1970, U.S. Ct. Appeals (8th cir.) 1970, U.S. Ct. Claims 1980, U.S. Tax Ct. 1982. Assoc. Smith, Peterson, Beckman & Willson, Council Bluffs, Iowa, 1969-72, ptnr., 1973—; lectr. Iowa State U., Ames, 1973—; mem. Iowa Supreme Ct. Commn. on Continuing Legal Edn., Des Moines, 1975-82. Contbr. articles to profl. jour. Chmn. Garner Twp. Republican Party, Council Bluffs, 1978—; co-founder, bd. dirs. Pottawattamie County Taxpayers Assn., Council Bluffs, 1979—, pres. 1979-80; bd. dirs. St. John's Luth. Ch., Council Bluffs, 1979-83; co-founder, bd. dirs., pres. Southwest Iowa Ednl. Found., Inc., Council Bluffs, 1984—, pres. 1986—. Mem. Internat. Assn. Assessing Officers, ABA, Nat. Assn. Rev. Appraisers and Mortgage Underwriters (sr. mem., cert. rev. appraiser, cert.), Nat. Assn. Real Estate Appraisers, Nebr. Bar Assn., Iowa Bar Assn. Club: Kiwanis (bd. dirs. 1977-83) (Council Bluffs). Banking, General corporate, Estate planning. Home: 17 Vista Ln Council Bluffs IA 51501 Office: Smith Peterson Beckman & Willson 370 Midlands Mall PO Box 249 Council Bluffs IA 51502

PECK, AARON MARTIN, lawyer; b. Osceola, Iowa, Apr. 26, 1939; s. Stanley and Leah P.; m. Linda Debro, Sept. 4, 1960; children—Anthony, Dena, Jessica. BA, UCLA, 1961, JD, 1964. Bar: Calif. 1965, U.S. Supreme Ct. 1970. Assoc., Pillsbury, Madison & Sutro; assoc. McKenna & Fitting, 1965-69; ptnr. McKenna, Conner & Cuneo, Los Angeles, 1970—. Mem. ABA, Calif. Acad. Appellate Lawyers, Los Angeles County Bar Assn., San Francisco Bar Assn., Wilshire Bar Assn. (mem. bd. govs. 1981-86). Democrat. Federal civil litigation, State civil litigation. Office: McKenna Conner & Cuneo 3435 Wilshire Blvd 28th Floor Los Angeles CA 90010

PECK, BERNARD SIDNEY, lawyer; b. Bridgeport, Conn., July 26, 1915; s. James and Sadie P.; m. Marjorie Eloise Dean, Apr. 10, 1943; children: Daniel Dean, Constance Lynn. B.A., Yale U., 1936, LL.B., 1939. Bar: Conn. 1939, Fla. 1979, N.Y. 1982. Practiced in Bridgeport, 1939-84; ptnr. Goldstein and Peck, 1946-84, Peck & Peck, Naples, Fla., 1983—; judge Mcpl. Ct., Westport, Conn., 1951-55. Moderator town meeting, Westport, 1950-51; mem. Westport Republican Town Com., 1951-79; pres. Westport YMCA, 1957, trustee, 1964-84; pres. endowment bd. YMCA Naples. Served to capt. AUS, 1942-46. Fellow Am. Coll. Trial Lawyers, Internat. Acad. Trial Lawyers; mem. ABA, Collier County Bar Assn., Phi Beta Kappa. Clubs: Linville (N.C.) Ridge Country; Royal Poinciana Golf (dir. 1983—, pres. 1987—), Yale (trustee 1985—) (Naples, Fla.). Estate planning, Personal injury, Probate. Home: 1919 Gulf Shore Blvd N Naples FL 33940 also: 4089 Tamiami Trail N Naples FL 33940

PECK, DAVID HILL, lawyer; b. Lake Forest, Ill., Jan. 26, 1951; s. Claude Jewell and Joan (Hill) P. BA in English, Carleton Coll., 1973; MA in English, Ind. U., 1976; cert. teaching, U. Ill., 1977; JD with honors, Chgo.-Kent Coll. of Law, 1982. Bar: Ill. 1982, U.S. Dist. Ct. (no. dist.) 1982, U.S. Tax Ct. 1984, Tex. 1986, U.S. Dist. Ct. (so. dist.) Tex. 1986. Assoc. Tisher & Wald Ltd., Chgo., 1982-84; trial atty. Office of Chief Counsel, IRS, Houston, 1984—; spl. asst. U.S. Atty., Houston, 1985—. Mem. ABA, Ill. Bar Assn. Episcopalian. Corporate taxation, Personal income taxation, Bankruptcy. Home: 108881 Richmond Ave Apt 716 Houston TX 77042 Office: Dist Counsel IRS 10850 Richmond Ave Suite 350 Houston TX 77042

PECK, DEANA S., lawyer; b. Wichita, Kans., Nov. 6, 1947; d. Richard Rector Williams and Elva Alene (Davis) Williams; m. Frederick Page Peck, June 16, 1967 (div. Nov. 1981); 1 child, Paige. BA, Wichita State U., 1970; JD, U. Kans., 1975. Bar: Ariz. 1975, U.S. Dist. Ct. Ariz. 1981, U.S. Ct. Appeals (9th cir.). Assoc. Streich, Lang, Weeks & Cardon, Phoenix, 1975-80, ptnr., 1980—; vis. lectr. U. Kans. Sch. of Law, Lawrence, 1985. Mem. ABA, Maricopa County Bar Assn., State Bar Ariz. (antitrust sect.), Kans. U. Law Soc. (bd. govs. 1980-82). Antitrust, Federal civil litigation, State civil litigation. Office: Streich Lang Weeks & Cardon 100 W Washington Suite 2100 Phoenix AZ 85003

PECK, JAMES IRVING, IV, lawyer; b. Orange, N.J., Dec. 24, 1948; s. James Irving and Laura (Wagner) P. BA, Franklin and Marshall Coll., 1970; JD, U. Md., 1973. Bar: N.J. 1974, U.S. Dist. Ct. N.J. 1974, U.S. Ct. Appeals (3d cir.) 1976, U.S. Supreme Ct. 1977, N.Y. 1980, U.S. Dist. Ct. (ea. and so. dists.) N.Y. 1982, U.S. Ct. Appeals (2d cir.) 1983. Appellate counsel pub. defender office State of N.J., East Orange, 1973-77; sole practice West Orange, N.J., 1977—. Mem. ABA, Essex County Bar Assn., Assn. Trial Lawyers Am., Phi Alpha Delta. Republican. Methodist. State civil litigation, Personal injury, General practice. Home: 60 Undercliff Rd Montclair NJ 07042-1718 Office: 47 High St West Orange NJ 07052-6101

PECK, JEFFREY JAY, lawyer; b. Rochester, N.Y., Nov. 2, 1957; s. Sidney and Ruth (Baldwin) P.; m. Lisa K. Vigdor, Aug. 8, 1982. AB in Polit. Sci., Duke U., 1979; JD, U. Chgo., 1982. Bar: D.C. 1982, U.S. Dist. Ct. D.C. 1984, U.S. Ct. Appeals (D.C. cir.) 1986. Law clk. to presiding judge U.S. Dist. Ct (no. dist.) Ill., Chgo., 1982-83; assoc. Seifman, Semo, Slevin & Marcus, Washington, 1983-85, Venable, Baetjer, Howard & Civiletti, Washington, 1986—. Mem. ABA, D.C. Bar Assn., Washington Council Lawyers, Nat. Trust for Hist. Preservation, Phi Beta Kappa. Federal civil litigation, State civil litigation, Legislative. Office: Venable Baetjer et al 1301 Pennsylvania Ave NW Washington DC 20004

PECK, JOHN W., federal judge; b. Cin., June 23, 1913; s. Arthur M. and Marguerite (Comstock) P.; m. Barbara Moeser, Mar. 25, 1942 (dec. 1981); children—John Weld, James H., Charles E.; m. Janet Alcorn Wagner; 1 stepchild, Gretchen Wagner. A.B., Miami U., 1935, LL.D., 1966; J.D., U. Cin., 1938, LL.D., 1965; LL.D., Chase Law Sch., 1971. Bar: Ohio bar 1938. Partner Peck, Shaffer & Williams, Cin., 1938-61; judge Ct. Common Pleas, Hamilton County, Ohio, 1950, 54; tax commr. State of Ohio, 1951-54; judge Supreme Ct. of Ohio, 1959-60, U.S. Dist. Ct., So. Dist. Ohio, 1961-66; judge U.S. Ct. Appeals, 6th Circuit, 1966—, sr. judge, 1978—; judge Temporary Emergency Ct. Appeals, 1979—; exec. sec. gov. State of Ohio, 1949; lectr. U. Cin. Coll. Law, 1948-70, Salmon P. Chase Coll. Law, 1949-51; mem. com. on adminstrn. criminal law Jud. Conf. U.S., 1971-79. Trustee Miami U., 1959—, emeritus, 1975—; mem. Princeton City Sch. Dist. Bd. Edn., 1958-63, pres. bd., 1963-69. Served to capt. Judge Adv. Gen. Corps AUS, 1942-46. John Weld Peck Fed. Bldg. dedicated in his honor, 1984. Mem. Cincinnatus Assn., Gyro Club, Beta Theta Phi, Phi Delta Phi. Club: Cin. Literary. Home: 165 Magnolia Ave Glendale OH 45246 Office: U S Ct of Appeal PO and Courthouse Bldg 5th & Walnut Sts Cincinnati OH 45202

PECK, KENNETH ELDON, lawyer; b. Carson City, Nev., June 20, 1950; s. Donald Leon and Thelma Louise (Robinson) P.; m. Katherine Louise Weeks, Oct. 20, 1973; children: Jason Z., Jennifer D., Joy H., Jessica K. BA in Polit. Sci. cum laude, U. Colo., 1971; MA in Pub. Adminstrn., U. Va., 1975; JD, Georgetown U., 1979. Bar: Colo. 1979, U.S. Dist. Ct. Colo. 1979, U.S. Ct. Appeals (10th cir.) 1980, U.S. Supreme Ct. 1983. Research analyst Va. Hwy. Research Council, Charlottesville, 1972-73; budget and mgmt. analyst Prince Georges County Schs., Upper Marlboro, Md., 1974-76; chief legis. asst. U.S. Rep. Paul Trible, Washington, 1977-79; atty. Holland & Hart, Denver, 1979-83, Hopper & Kanouff, Denver, 1983-85, Phelps, Hall, Singer & Dunn, Denver, 1985—; mem. nat., regional and state adv. councils SBA, 1981—; mem. bd. appeals U.S. Dept. Edn., Washington, 1982-84; profl. lobbyist Colo. Legis., Denver, 1983-84; nat. commr. of econ. policy White House Conf. on Small Bus., Denver, 1986. Asst. campaign mgr. Jim Tate for Congress, Fairfax, Va., 1976; bd. dirs. Jefferson County Srs.' Resource Ctr., Wheatridge, Colo., 1982—; pres. Arvada Rep. Club, Colo., 1982; mem. bd. mgrs. Northwest YMCA, Arvada, 1982—. William McIntyre fellow U. Va., 1971-72; law fellow Georgetown U. Law Ctr., 1976-77. Mem. ABA (litigation sect., real property and bus. sect., various coms.), Assn. Trial Lawyers Am., Colo. Bar Assn. (various coms.), Colo. Assn. Comml. Industry (chmn. small bus. legis. com. 1983-85), Denver Bar Assn. (various coms.). Republican. Mem. Ch. of Christ. Avocations: golf, hiking, coaching youth sports. Federal civil litigation, Consumer commercial, Real property. Home: 10935 W 68th Ave Arvada CO 80004 Office: Hopper Kanougg Smith et al 1610 Wynkop St Suite 200 Denver CO 80202

PECK, KERRY REID, lawyer; b. Chgo., Jan. 24, 1952; s. Joseph and Roslyn (Mendell) P.; m. Hillary Weiss; children: Haley, Brandon. BS in Edn., No. Ill. U., 1974; JD with honors, Ill. Inst. Tech., 1978. Bar: Ill. 1978, Fla. 1979, U.S. Dist. Ct. (no. dist.) Ill. 1978, U.S. Dist. Ct. (so. dist.) Fla. 1979, U.S. Tax Ct. 1980, U.S. Ct. Appeals (7th and 11th cirs.) 1980. Ptnr. Peck & Wolf, Chgo., Ft. Lauderdale and Sarasota, Fla., 1978—. Mem. ABA, Fla. Bar Assn., Chgo. Bar Assn. (lectr. 1982—, chmn. young lawyers sect. bench bar speakers and social events, officer, project dir. young lawyers sect. 1986-87, media rep. 1984 Dem. Conv., asst. editor in chief journal 1984-85, editor in chief 1985-86), Decalogue Soc. Lawyers (contbr. articles, lectr., bd. dirs.). State civil litigation, General corporate, Probate. Office: Peck & Wolf 105 W Adams 34th Floor Chicago IL 60603

PECK, LEONARD WARREN, JR., lawyer; b. El Paso, Tex., June 3, 1948; s. Leonard Warren and Perry Elizabeth (Lewis) P.; m. Johanna Lee Blaschke, July 23, 1976; 1 dau., Margaret Elizabeth. A.B., Harvard U., 1970; J.D., U. Tex., 1973. Bar: Tex. 1973, U.S. Dist. Ct. (no. dist.) Tex. 1984, U.S. Dist. Ct. (so. dist.) Tex. 1980, U.S. Dist. Ct. (ea. dist.) Tex. 1980, U.S. Dist. Ct. (we. dist.) Tex. 1980, U.S. Ct. Appeals (5th cir.) 1981, U.S. Ct. Appeals (11th cir.) 1981, U.S. Supreme Ct. 1980. Analyst Tex. Gov.'s Office, Austin, 1974-75; cons. Atty. Gen. Tex. Office, Austin, 1976-80, asst. atty. gen., 1981; dir. research and devel. Tex. Dept. Corrections, Huntsville, 1981-82, legal counsel, 1982—. Mem. ABA, Assn. Computing Machines. Civil rights, Federal civil litigation, State civil litigation. Home: PO Box 1495 Huntsville TX 77340 Office: Tex Dept Corrections PO Box 99 Huntsville TX 77340

PECK, LOUIS PROVOST, state supreme court justice; b. Montpelier, Vt., Dec. 24, 1918; . William Nelson and Mary Alice (Provost) P.; m. Iride Joan Falacci, May 10, 1952; children: Katherine Theresa, Barbara Ellen Leslie, Nancy Elizabeth Jennifer. A.B., U. Notre Dame, 1950, J.D., 1951. Bar: Vt. 1951, U.S. Dist. Ct. Vt., U.S. Ct. Appeals (2d cir.). Sole practice Montpelier, Vt., 1951-57; chief asst. atty. gen. Vt. Atty. Gen. Office, Montpelier, 1957-81; assoc. justice Vt. Supreme Ct., Montpelier, 1981—; chmn. Vt. Statuatory Revision Commn., 1986—. Capt. U.S. Army, 1941-47, ETO. Mem. Inst. Jud. Adminstrn., Vt. Bar Assn. (sec. 1967-80, editor Vt. Bar Jour. 1967-76). Roman Catholic. Club: The Club (Montpelier) (pres. 1970-71). Judicial administration. Office: Vt Supreme Ct 111 State St Montpelier VT 05602

PECK, ROBERT STEPHEN, lawyer, educator; b. Bklyn., Dec. 11, 1953; s. Irwin and Edith Rose (Welt) P.; m. Barbara Bea McDowell, Dec. 19, 1976. BA in Polit. Sci., George Washington U., 1975; postgrad., Cleveland-Marshall Law Sch., 1975-77; JD, NYU, 1978. Bar: N.Y. 1978, U.S. Dist. Ct. (no. and ea. dists.) N.Y. 1979. Congl. aide U.S. Ho. of Reps., Washington, 1972-74; div. dir. Automated Correspondence, Washington, 1974-75; law clk. to presiding justice Cleve. Mcpl. Ct., 1976; editor Matthew Bender & Co., N.Y.C., 1977-78; legal dir. Pub. Edn. Assn., N.Y.C., 1978-82; staff dir. ABA, Chgo., 1982—; legal advisor Freedom to Read Found., Chgo., 1986—; bd. dirs. Citizen Info. Service, Chgo., 1985—; lectr. on constl. law various orgns. Author: We the People, 1987; co-author: Speaking and Writing Truth, 1985; editor: Understanding the Law, 1983, Blessings of Liberty, 1986, To Govern A Changing Society, 1987; contbr. numerous articles on constl. law to law revs. Mem. N.Y. State Edn. Adv. Bd., Albany, N.Y., 1979-81. NEH grantee 1983, 85. Mem. ABA (chmn. pub. election law com. 1983-85, bd. dirs. We the People Constl. Bicentennial project), N.Y. State Bar Assn., Am. Judicature Soc. Democrat. Jewish. Avocations: tennis, music, travel. Constitutional Law, First Amendment Law, Legal history. Office: ABA 750 N Lake Shore Dr Chicago IL 60611

PECKAR, ROBERT S., lawyer; b. N.Y.C., Apr. 30, 1946; s. Paul and Pearl P.; A.B., Rutgers Coll., 1968; J.D., Columbia U., 1972; m. Maxine Zaro, June 29, 1969; children—Marissa, Simara. Admitted to N.J., N.Y. bars, 1972; law clk. firm Greenberg, Trayman, Harris, Cantor, Reiss & Blaskey, N.Y.C., 1969-72; assoc. firm Goetz & Fitzpatrick, 1972-73; individual practice law, 1973-78; mem. firm Peckar & Abramson, P.C., Hackensack, N.J., N.Y.C. and Boca Raton, Fla., 1978—. Mem. adv. council Sch. Constrn. Tech., Fairleigh Dickinson U., 1978—; mem. Village of Pomona (N.Y.) Bd. Zoning and Appeals, 1979-85. Mem. Am. Bar Assn. (chmn. region II pub. contract law sect.), N.J. State Bar Assn. (former chmn. public contract law com.), constrn. Fin. Mgmt. Assn. (bd. dirs.). Construction, State civil litigation, Federal civil litigation. Home: 3 Forest Ridge Upper Saddle River NJ 07458 Office: 223 Moore St Hackensack NJ 07601

PECKHAM, CHARLES ALLEN, lawyer; b. Ottawa, Kans., Nov. 20, 1949; s. James Knoles and Lottie Irene (Northway) P.; m. Connie A. Pitner, Nov. 16, 1984; 1 child, Tionna L. BA summa cum laude, Washburn U., 1971; MA, Ohio State U., 1973; doctoral studies, U. Chgo., 1975-76; JD, Kans. U., 1979. Bar: Kans., U.S. Dist. Ct. Kans. Intern Atty. Gen.'s Office, Topeka, 1979; staff atty. U.S. Dept. of Agr., Washington, 1980-83; assoc. Brown & Creighton, Atwood, Kans., 1983-84; ptnr. Brown & Creighton, Atwood, 1985—; atty. Rawlins County, Atwood, 1985—. Contbr. articles to profl. jours. Fin. chmn. Parkfairfax Condo, Alexandria, Va., 1980-81; pres. Northwest Drifters, Colby, Kans., 1985—. Served to lt. USAF, 1973-74. Mem. ABA, Kans. Bar Assn., Fed. Bar Assn., Kans. Bar Assn., Assn. Trial Lawyers Am. Republican. Methodist. Lodge: Rotary. Avocations: computers, motorcycle riding, long distance running, tennis. Probate, Estate taxation, Personal income taxation. Home: 411 S 6th PO Box 88 Atwood KS 67730 Office: Brown Creighton & Peckham 308 Main PO Box 46 Atwood KS 67730

PECKHAM, EUGENE ELIOT, lawyer, educator; b. Stamford, Conn., Aug. 11, 1940; s. Joseph E. and Margaret (Nabors) P.; m. Judith Alice Chamberlain, Dec. 19, 1964; children—Margaret, Joseph, Elizabeth. B.A. with honors, Wesleyan U., Middletown, Conn., 1962; J.D., Harvard U., 1965. Bar: N.Y. 1965, Fla. 1981, U.S. Tax Ct. 1974, U.S. Ct. Appeals (2d cir) 1975, U.S. Dist. Ct. (no. dist.) N.Y. 1965. Assoc. Hinman, Howard & Kattell, Binghamton, N.Y., 1965-72, ptnr., 1972—; instr. Broome Community Coll., Binghamton, 1968-69, Am. Coll. Life Underwriters, Bryn Mawr, Pa., 1969-70, Am. Coll. Property and Casualty Underwriters, Bryn Mawr, 1970-71; adj. lectr. SUNY-Binghamton, 1972-77, adj. asst. prof.,

1977-81, adj. assoc. prof. acctg., 1981-87, adj. prof., 1987—; vis. lectr. Cornell U., Ithaca, N.Y., 1978, adj. prof., 1984; Peace Corps vol. tchr. Santa Maria U., Arequipa, Peru, 1966-67. Contbr. articles to profl. jours. Pres. Binghamton Girls Club, N.Y., 1974-76, bd. dirs., 1970-77; chmn. bd. Binghamton Boys and Girls Club, 1977; mem. trust fund com. Broome County United Way, N.Y., 1979—; pres. SUNY Found., Binghamton, 1977-79, bd. dirs., 1975-82; bd. dirs. Estate Planning Council So. Tier, 1983—, treas. 1983, sec., 1984, v.p. 1985, pres. 1986—; bd. dirs. Samaritan Counselling Ctr. So. Tier. Inc., 1982—, v.p., 1986, pres. 1987—; co-chmn. sta. WSKG-TV auction, 1983; treas. Roberson Ctr. Arts and Scis., 1980, bd. dirs., 1977-80; chmn. Broome County Community Ambassador Project, 1970-71; mem. Broome Bd. Ethics, 1985—, deacon 1st Presbyn. Ch., Binghamton, 1971-74, moderator, 1974, elder, 1975-78, 87—, trustee, 1980-83; exec. com. Broome County Republican Com., 1980-83, co-chmn. fin. com. 1982-83; pres. Broome County Young Republican Club, 1969-70. Fellow Am. Coll. Probate Counsel; mem. N.Y. State Bar Assn. (exec. com. trusts and estates sect. 1980-84, treas. 1985-86, sec. 1987—, mem. spl. commn. on alt. sources funding legal services 1982-86, action unit 6 1984—), Fedn. Bar Assns. 6th Jud. Dist. (pres. 1984-85), Broome County Bar Assn. (chmn. prepaid legal ins. com. 1976-80, ethics com. 1981—). Probate, Estate taxation, Personal income taxation. Home: 12 Campbell Rd Binghamton NY 13905 Office: Hinman Howard & Kattell 700 Security Mut Bldg Binghamton NY 13901

PECKHAM, ROBERT FRANCIS, chief U.S. district judge; b. San Francisco, Nov. 3, 1920; s. Robert F. and Evelyn (Crowe) P.; m. Harriet M. Behring, Aug. 15, 1953 (dec. Apr. 1970); children: Ann Evelyn, Sara Esther; m. Carol Potter, June 9, 1974. A.B., Stanford U., 1941, LL.B., 1945; postgrad. in law, Yale U., 1941-42; LL.D., U. Santa Clara, 1973. Bar: Calif. 1945. Adminstrv. asst. to regional enforcement atty. OPA, 1942-43; pvt. practice in Palo Alto and Sunnyvale, 1946-48; asst. U.S. atty., 1948-53, chief asst. criminal div., 1952-53; mem. firm Darwin, Peckham & Warren, San Francisco, Palo Alto and Sunnyvale, 1953-59; judge Superior Ct., Santa Clara County, Calif., 1959-66; presiding judge Superior Ct., 1961-63, 65-66; U.S. dist. judge No. Dist. Calif., 1966-76, chief judge, 1976—; trustee Foothill Coll. Dist., 1957-59, pres., 1959; mem. bd. visitors Stanford Law Sch., 1969-75, chmn., 1971-72. State chmn. Adv. Bd. Friends Outside; council mem. Friends of Bancroft Library, 1981—. Recipient Brotherhood award Nat. Conf. Christians and Jews, 1968; recipient award for alt. dispute resolution leadership Ctr. for Pub. Resources, 1984, scholar, 1985. Fellow Am. Bar Found.; mem. ABA (chmn. Nat. Conf. Fed. Trial Judges 1983-84, ho. of dels. 1984—), Fed., San Francisco, Santa Clara County bar assns., Am. Law Inst., Am. Judicature Soc., Soc. Calif. Pioneers (bd. govs. 1984—) Calif. Hist. Soc. (trustee 1974-78), Council Stanford Law Socs. (chmn. 1974-75), U.S. Dist. Ct. for No. Dist. Calif. Hist. Soc. (chmn. 1979—), World Affairs Council (trustee 1979—), Asia Found. (sr. mem. Am.-Asia law del. 1984-85), Phi Beta Kappa, Phi Delta Phi. Office: US Courthouse San Francisco CA 94102

PEDDICORD, ROLAND DALE, lawyer; b. Van Meter, Iowa, Mar. 29, 1936; s. Clifford Elwood and Juanitas Irene (Brittain) P.; children—Erin Sue, Robert Sean. B.S. in Bus. Adminstrn. with honors, Drake U., 1961, J.D. with honors, 1962. Bar: Iowa 1962. Asst. atty. gen. State of Iowa, 1962-63; assoc. Steward, Crouch & Hopkins, Des Moines, 1962-65; ptnr. Peddicord & Sutphin, Des Moines, 1965-82; lectr. in law Drake U., 1962-68; lectr. law Coll. Osteo. Medicine, Des Moines, 1965-72. Editor and chief Drake Law Rev., 1961-62. Nat. bd. dirs., mem. nat. council YMCAs of Am., sec.; bd. dirs., chmn., mem. exec. com. Med-West field com. YMCAs U.S.; bd. dirs. Greater Des Moines YMCA, 1968—, now chmn. bd. dirs., chmn. devel. com. bd. dirs., 1976-85, vice chmn. bd., 1982-86, sec. to nat. bd. Served with USMC, 1954-57. Mem. ABA, Iowa State Bar Assn., Polk County Bar Assn., Assn. Trial Lawyers Am., Iowa Trial Lawyers Assn., Iowa Acad. Trial Lawyers, Iowa Workers' Compensation Attys., Iowa Def. Counsel Assn., Def. Research Inst., Lawyer and Pilots Bar Assn., Aircraft Owners and Pilots Assn., Order of Coif, Delta Sigma Chi, Omicron Delta Kappa, Beta Gamma Sigma. Republican. Methodist. Clubs: Embassy, Hyperion, Pioneer Gun, Chaine Des Rotisseurs (vice chancelier Argentier du Bailliage De Des Moines). Insurance, Personal injury, Federal civil litigation. Office: Peddicord & Wharton 300 Fleming Bldg Des Moines IA 50309

PEDERSEN, C. RICHARD, financial services company executive; b. Havre, Mont., Jan. 10, 1923; s. James G. and Anne (Walsh) P.; m. Muriel Beatrice Jones, Oct. 25, 1951; children—Charles Richard, Arthur Kirk, Lloyd Duncan, Suni, Kari Anne. B.A., U. Mont., 1947; LL.B., Harvard, 1950. Bar: N.Y., Conn. With law firm Dewey, Ballantine, Bushby, Palmer & Wood, N.Y.C., 1950-57; with Primerica Corp., 1957—, asst. sec., 1958-71, asst. gen. counsel, 1960-68, v.p., gen. counsel, 1969—, sec., 1971—, sr. v.p., 1977—. Served to capt. AUS, 1943-46. Decorated Combat Inf. Badge. Mem. ABA, Assn. of Bar of City of N.Y. General corporate. Home: 2 Peaceable Hill Rd Ridgefield CT 06877 Office: Primerica Corp American Ln Greenwich CT 06830

PEDERSEN, LANCE ALDEN, lawyer; b. Billings, Mont., Sept. 7, 1956; s. Alden W. and Lillian K. (Nauman) P.; m. Debra J. Semrow, Aug. 7, 1982. BA, U. Mont., 1978, JD, 1981. Bar: Mont. 1981, U.S. Dist. Ct. Mont. 1981, U.S. Ct. Appeals (9th cir.) 1981. Assoc. Freeman Law Firm, Hardin, Mont., 1981-83; sole practice Hardin, 1983—. Mem. ABA, Am. Judicature Soc., Hardin C. of C. (bd. dirs. 1985), Sports Car Club of Mont. (bd. dirs. 1985), Phi Delta Phi. Lutheran. Banking, Real property, State civil litigation. Home: 1026 Blue Sage Hardin MT 59034 Office: 10 W 4th St Hardin MT 59034

PEDERSEN, NORMAN A., lawyer; b. Modesto, Calif., Dec. 29, 1946; s. Melvin R. and Hilda R. (Akenhead) P. BA, U. Calif., Berkeley, 1970, MA, 1972; JD, UCLA, 1975. Bar: Calif., D.C. Trial atty. Fed. Power Commn., Washington, 1975-77; asst. to commr. Fed. Regulatory Commn., Washington, 1977-79; ptnr. Kadison, Pfaelzer, Woodard, Quinn & Rossi, Washington, 1979—. Administrative and regulatory, FERC practice. Home: 5063 Loughboro Rd NW Washington DC 20016 Office: Kadison Pfaelzer et al 2000 Pennsylvania Ave NW Washington DC 20006

PEDERSON, ROBERT DAVID, lawyer; b. Gallup, N.Mex., Oct. 23, 1953; s. Robert Leo and Alice (Montoya) P.; m. Jamie Gene Jonas, July 8, 1975; children: Jessica, Erik. B of Univ. Studies, U. N.Mex., 1975, JD, 1978; postgrad., Northwestern U., 1983. Bar: N.Mex., 1978, U.S. Dist. Ct. N.Mex. 1978. Assoc. Schuelke, Wolf & Rich, Gallup, 1978-81; v.p. 1st Interstate Bank, Gallup, 1981-84; sole practice Gallup, 1984-85; chief dep. dist. atty. 11th Judicial Dist., McKinley County, N.Mex., 1985—; cons. 1st Interstate Bancorp., Gallup, 1984—; chief children's ct. atty. 11th Judicial Dist., McKinley County, 1985—. State cen. com. N.Mex. Dems., 1984—. Mem. ABA, State Bar Assn. N.Mex.(mock trial judge 1986), McKinley County Bar Assn. (pres. 1982), Northwest Interagency Narcotics Task Force. Democrat. Lutheran. Avocations: coin collecting, target shooting, military history. Criminal, Juvenile, Banking. Office: 11th Jud Dist Dist Atty McKinley County Courthouse Gallup NM 87301

PEDERSON, STEVEN MARC, lawyer; b. Blackduck, Minn., Jan. 5, 1952; s. Erling Lyle and Dorthea Ann (Lindquist) P.; m. Katherine Elaine Shoup, Dec. 29, 1984. BA summa cum laude, Concordia Coll., Moorhead, Minn., 1973; JD with distinction, U. N.D., 1977. Bar: Minn. 1977, U.S. Dist. Ct. Minn. 1978. Assoc. Hull, Robertson, Wohletz & Blahnik, Winona, Minn., 1977-80; ptnr. Hull, Robertson, Wohletz, Blahnik & Pederson, Winona, 1980-81; ptnr. Goldberg, Torgerson, Wohletz, Pflughoeft & Pederson, Winona, 1981—; instr. Winona State U., 1978-84, 86-87. Mem. Def. Research Inst., Minn. Def. Lawyers Assn., Winona County Bar Assn., Minn. Bar Assn., 3d Jud. Dist. Bar Assn., Order of Coif. Roman Catholic. Insurance, State civil litigation, Personal injury. Office: 160 Lafayette PO Box 436 Winona MN 55987

PEDLEY, LAWRENCE LINDSAY, lawyer; b. Hopkinsville, Ky., May 27, 1932; s. Gracean McGoodwin and Elizabeth Lindsay Pedley; m. Ellen Mack, Oct. 9, 1957 (div. 1981); children: Lawrence Lindsay Jr., David M., Joan Elizabeth; m. Jill Flick, Dec. 3, 1981; 1 child, Jill Katharine. BA, The Citadel, Mil. Coll. S.C., 1955; JD, Yale U., 1959. Bar: Ky. 1959, Fla. 1980, U.S. Dist. Ct. Ky. 1959, U.S. Ct. Appeals (6th cir.), U.S. Supreme Ct. V.p. Nat. Industries, Louisville, 1964-66; gen. counsel Life Ins. Co. Ky., Louisville, 1966-69; ptnr. Goldberg & Pedley, Louisville, 1970-80, Pedley, Ross, Zielke & Gordinier, Louisville, 1980—; ptnr. Hardin Properties Group, Louisville, Pedley Ptnrs., Louisville; small bus. owner, Louisville, 1969-70; bd. dirs. Wyland Industries, Inc., Louisville, Profl. Retrieval & Storage, Louisville. Served to capt. JAGC. Mem. ABA, Ky. Bar Assn., Fla. Bar Assn. Clubs: Harmony Landing, Pendennis (Louisville). General corporate, Oil and gas leasing, Securities. Home: 2101 Eastern Pkwy Louisville KY 40204 Office: Pedley Ross Zielke & Gordinier 450 S 3d St Louisville KY 40202

PEDOWITZ, ARNOLD HENRY, lawyer; b. N.Y.C., Nov. 29, 1946; s. Paul and Rose (Winick) P.; m. Wendy Eiseman. BA, U. Wis., 1967; JD, Boston U., 1971; LLM, NYU, 1978. Bar: Mass. 1971, Wash. 1973, N.Y. 1977, N.J. 1977. Sole practice N.Y.C., 1978—. Labor, Real property, State civil litigation. Home: 230 Central Park W New York NY 10024 Office: 380 Madison Ave New York NY 10017

PEDRI, CHARLES RAYMOND, lawyer; b. Hazleton, Pa., Sept. 1, 1951; s. Charles John and Barbara Theresa (Tait) P.; m. Sharon Jones, May 19, 1973; children: Melissa, C. David. BA, Pa. State U., 1973; JD, Temple U., 1976. Bar: 1976, U.S. Dist. Ct. (mid. dist.) Pa. 1980; cert. civil trial adv. Mem. Laputka, Bayless, Ecker & Cohn, P.C., Hazleton, 1976—; instr. Pa. State U., Hazleton, 1978—. Pres. Meals on Wheels, Hazleton, 1985. Mem. ABA, Pa. Trial Lawyers Assn., Pa. Bar Assn., Luzerne County Bar Assn., Phi Beta Kappa, Phi Kappa Phi. Republican. Roman Catholic. Club: Mountain City Lions (pres. 1980). State civil litigation, Federal civil litigation, Personal injury. Home: 1418 Terrace Blvd Hazleton PA 18201 Office: Laputka Bayless Ecker & Cohn PC 6th Floor 1st Valley Bldg Hazleton PA 18201

PEERY, CHARLES EUGENE, lawyer; b. Spring Valley, Minn., Dec. 22, 1933; s. Merle Eugene and Madalyn Clair (McDonough) P.; divorced; children—Laura C. Knechtel, Catherine A. Meade, Suzanna L. B.A., U. Wash., 1959, J.D., 1962. Bar: Wash. 1962, U.S. Dist. Ct. Wash. 1962, U.S. Ct. Appeals (9th cir.) 1963, U.S. Ct. Internat. Trade, 1970, U.S. Supreme Ct., 1971. Trial and corp. atty. legal dept. Safeco Ins. Co., Seattle, 1962-66; ptnr. Preston, Thorgrimson, Ellis & Holman, Seattle, 1966-86, prin., Carney, Stephenson, Badley, Smith, Mueller & Spellman P.S., Seattle, 1986—. Served with USAF, 1954-58. Mem. ABA, Wash. State Bar Assn., Seattle-King County Bar Assn., Wash. Assn. Def. Counsel (pres. 1969-70), Def. Research Inst., Assn. Ski Def. Attys., Fedn. Ins. Counsel, Assn. Trial Lawyers Am., Delta Theta Phi. Republican. Unitarian. Contbr. articles to profl. jours. Insurance, Personal injury, State civil litigation. Office: Carney Stephenson Badley et al 2300 Columbia Ctr Seattle WA 98104

PEET, CHARLES D., JR., lawyer; b. N.Y.C., Sept. 3, 1935; s. Charles D. and Margaret Louise (Sherman) P.; m. Penny Levy, July 29, 1967; children—Alisa, Amanda. B.A., Yale U., 1957; J.D., Harvard U., 1960. Bar: N.Y. 1962. Assoc. Milbank, Tweed, Hadley & McCloy, N.Y.C., 1960-68, ptnr., 1969—. Mem. ABA, N.Y. State Bar Assn., Assn. Bar N.Y.C., Internat. Bar Assn. Banking, Private international. Office: Milbank Tweed Hadley & McCloy 1 Chase Manhattan Plaza New York NY 10005

PEET, JOHN CARLISLE, JR., corporate service company executive; b. N.Y.C., Dec. 14, 1928; s. John Carlisle and Alys Lenore (Sweeley) P.; m. Jane Lauderman, May 26, 1951; children: John Carlisle III, Jeffrey V., Leslie A., Donald N., Sarah J. Grad., The Taft Sch., 1946; B.A., Yale U., 1950; LL.B., U. Va., 1954. Bar: N.Y. bar 1954, Pa. bar 1956. Assoc. White & Case, N.Y.C., 1954-56, Morgan, Lewis & Bockius, Phila., 1956-63; ptnr. Morgan, Lewis & Bockius, 1964-67, Ringe, Peet & Mason, Phila., 1967-69; v.p., gen. counsel, sec. RLC Corp., Wilmington, Del., 1969—; v.p., gen. counsel, sec., dir. Rollins Environ. Services, Inc., 1978—; lectr. Temple U. Law Sch., Am. Trucking Assn., Nat. Tank Truck Assn., Am. Arbitration Assn.; dir. Philanthropic Mut. Life Ins. Co., Jarube, Inc., Talisman, Inc. Exec. editor: Va. Law Rev, 1953-54. Served with CIC U.S. Army, 1950-51. Mem. Am., Pa., Phila., N.Y. bar assns., Raven Soc., Order of Coif, Omicron Delta Kappa. Presbyn. General corporate. Home: 801 Brintons One Bridge Rd West Chester PA 19382 Office: 1 Rollins Plaza Wilmington DE 19803

PEGRAM, JOHN BRAXTON, lawyer; b. Yeadon, Pa., June 29, 1938; A.B. in Physics, Columbia U., 1960; LL.B., NYU, 1965. Bar: N.Y. 1965, U.S. Supreme Ct. 1971. Engr., Fairchild Camera and Instrument Corp., Clifton, N.J., 1960-66; mem. Davis Hoxie Faithfull & Hapgood, N.Y.C., 1966—. Mem. ABA (chmn. patents, trademarks and know-how com. antitrust sect. 1986—; patent, trademark and copyright sect.), N.Y. State Bar Assn., Assn. Bar City N.Y., Am. Intellectual Property Law Assn. (chmn. fed. practice and procedure com. 1974-76, chmn. unauthorized practice com. 1977-79), N.Y. Patent, Trademark and Copyright Law Assn. (sec. 1981-84, v.p. 1986—), Am. Phys. Soc., IEEE, Chartered Inst. Patent Agts. (fgn.), Inst. Trademark Agts. (fgn.) Editor-in-chief The Trademark Reporter, 1984-86; contbr. articles to profl. jours. Patent, Trademark and copyright, Antitrust. Office: 45 Rockefeller Plaza New York NY 10111

PEHRSON, GORDON OSCAR, JR., lawyer; b. San Antonio, Feb. 18, 1943; s. Gordon Oscar and Frances (Burns) P.; m. Janice Sue Hagedorn, May 17, 1969; children: Christopher Wells, Ashley Stewart; m. Sharon Ann McNellage, Jan. 1, 1983. AB, Coll. William and Mary, 1964; JD, U. Mich., 1967; postgrad., U. London, 1967-68. Bar: Ill. 1968, D.C. 1969, U.S. Ct. Claims 1968, U.S. Ct. Mil. Appeals 1968, U.S. Ct. Appeals (D.C. cir.) 1968, U.S. Supreme Ct. 1976, U.S. Ct. Appeals (3d cir.) 1979, U.S. Ct. Appeals (Fed. cir.) 1982. With Sutherland, Asbill & Brennan, Washington, 1970—, ptnr., 1975—; adj. prof. law, Georgetown U., Washington, 1977-81. Contbr. articles on tax law to profl. jours.; editor, The Insurance Tax Rev., 1986—. Served to lt. USN, 1968-70. Fellow in internat. law U. Mich., 1967. Mem. ABA, D.C. Bar Assn., Order of Coif. Episcopalian. Clubs: Met., City Club (Washington). Corporate taxation, Legislative, Administrative and regulatory. Home: 4517 Foxhall Crescent NW Washington DC 20007 Office: Sutherland Asbill & Brennan 1666 K St NW Suite 800 Washington DC 20006

PEIRCE, ELLEN RUST, legal educator; b. Washington, May 5, 1949; d. Wentworth W. and Ethel M. (Byrne) P.; m. Daniel A. Graham, June 10, 1978; 1 child, William. B.A., Bryn Mawr Coll., 1971; J.D., Duke U., 1976. Bar: N.Y. 1977, D.C. 1977, N.C. 1979. Assoc., Mudge Rose Guthrie & Alexander, N.Y.C., 1976-78, Powe Porter Alphin & Whichard, Durham, N.C., 1978-80; assoc. prof. law U. N.C. Sch. Bus. Adminstrn., Chapel Hill, 1980-85, assoc. prof., 1986—; legal cons. IBM, 1983-84, various software cos., N.C.; counsel SSI, Durham, 1978-84. Contbr. articles and chpts. to legal jours.; editor Duke Legal Research and Writing, 1975-76; reviewer legal pub. cos. Mem. ABA, N.Y. State Bar Assn., D.C. Bar Assn., N.C. Bar Assn., Am. Bus. Law Assn., Southeastern Regional Bus. Law Assn. (sec. 1981-82, v.p. 1982-83, pres.-elect 1983-84, pres. 1984-85). Episcopalian. Labor, Personal injury, General corporate. Home: 1 Southampton Pl Durham NC 27705 Office: Univ NC Sch Business Adminstn Chapel Hill NC 27514

PEIRCE, FREDERICK FAIRBANKS, lawyer; b. Torrington, Conn., Jan. 28, 1953; s. Everett L. and Frederica (Fairbanks) P.; m. Calista Joy Landfield, June 21, 1980. BS, Colo. State U., 1975; JD, U. Colo., 1979. Bar: Colo. 1979, U.S. Dist. Ct. Colo. 1979. Assoc. Bratton & Zimmerman, Gunnison, Colo., 1979-80; staff atty. Holland & Hart, Aspen, Colo., 1980-82; assoc. Austin, McGrath & Jordan, Aspen, 1982-84; assoc. Austin & Jordan, Aspen, 1984-87, ptnr., 1987—; bd. dirs. Grassroots Inc., Aspen. Bd. dirs. Aspen Nordic Council Inc., 1985—, Aspen Velo Club Inc., 1986—. NSF grantee, 1975. Mem. ABA, Colo. Bar Assn., Pitkin County Bar Assn. (v.p. 1985-86, pres. 1986—), Phi Kappa Phi. Avocations: skiing, hiking, fishing, cycling, flying. Real property, General corporate, Landlord-tenant. Home: PO Box 269 Aspen CO 81612 Office: Austin & Jordan 600 E Hopkins #205 Aspen CO 81611

PEIRCE, KENNETH B., JR., food products company executive, lawyer; b. Holland, Mich., June 19, 1943; s. Kenneth B. Sr. and Margaret P.; m. Jill Bolhous, June 16, 1978; children: Tracey, Chris, Drew. BA, Notre Dame U., 1965; JD, St. Louis U., 1968. Asst. city counselor City of St. Louis, 1968-72; corp. atty Wolverine World Wide, Rockford, Mich., 1972-74; corp. atty Gerber Products Co., Fremont, Mich., 1974-80, assoc. gen. counsel, 1980-83, sec., gen. counsel, 1983-85, v.p., gen. counsel, 1985-86, exec. v.p., gen. counsel, gen. mgr. apparel group, 1986—; pres. Fremont Area Found., Mich., 1985—; bd. dirs. Old Kent Bank of Fremont, Am. Agrl. Mktg. Assn. Mem. ABA, Mich. Bar Assn., Newaygo County Bar Assn., Am. Mgmt. Assn., Nat. Assn. Mfg., Food and Drug Law Inst. (bd. dirs., trustee 1986). Administrative and regulatory, General corporate. Office: Gerber Products Co 445 State St Fremont MI 49412

PELANDINI, WILLIAM ALBERT, lawyer; b. Vallejo, Calif., Dec. 19, 1946; s. Francis L. and Betty (Tucker) P.; m. Patricia E. Wood, Dec. 20, 1968; children: Matthew, Sarah, Adam. BE, Cen. Washington U., 1969; JD cum laude, U. Puget Sound, 1980. Bar: Wash. 1981, U.S. Dist. Ct. (we. dist.) 1981, U.S. Dist. Ct. (ea. dist.) Wash. 1985., U.S. Ct. Appeals (9th cir.) 1984. Tchr. Kent (Wash.) Sch. Dist., 1969-74, Lake Washington Sch. Dist., Kirkland, Wash., 1974-76; legis. analyst Wash. State Senate, Olympia, 1976-81; assoc. Lane, Powell, Moss & Miller, Seattle, 1981—; sr. analyst fin. inst. and ins. com. Wash. State Senate, Olympia, 1977-81, analyst tort and product liability reform com., 1979-80. Scholarship award for Scholastic Achievement, U. Puget Sound Sch. Law, 1978. Mem. Wash. State Bar Assn. (chmn. product liability update seminar 1984), Assn. Wash. Def. Counsel, Nat. Assn. Railroad Trial Counsel, Seattle/King County Bar Assn. Democrat. Roman Catholic. Banking, Legislative, Personal injury. Home: 4305 Palomino Dr NE Bainbridge Island WA 98110 Office: Lane Powell Moss & Miller 3800 Rainier Bank Tower Seattle WA 98101

PELAVIN, MICHAEL ALLEN, lawyer; b. Flint, Mich., Sept. 5, 1936; s. B. Morris and Betty (Weiss) P.; m. Natalie K. Katz, June 18, 1960; children—Mark, Gordon. Student U. Mich., 1954-55, Wayne State U., 1955-57; J.D., Detroit Coll. Law, 1960. Bar: Mich. 1960, U.S. Tax Ct. 1966, U.S. Ct. Appeals (6th cir.) 1969. Assoc., Pelavin, Pelavin & Powers, P.C., Flint, Mich., 1960-63, ptnr., 1963-71, pres., 1980—; trustee Mut. of Am. Life Ins. Co., 1981—. Chmn. young leadership cabinet United Jewish Appeal, 1973; pres. Flint Jewish Fedn., 1974-77. Mem. ABA, Assn. Trial Lawyers Am., Mich. Bar Assn. Democrat. General corporate, Probate, Personal income taxation. Home: 6168 Sierra Pass Flint MI 48504 Office: Pelavin Pelavin & Powers PC 801 S Saginaw St Flint MI 48502

PELL, WILBUR FRANK, JR., senior U.S. circuit ct. judge; b. Shelbyville, Ind., Dec. 6, 1915; s. Wilbur Frank and Nelle (Dickerson) P.; m. Mary Lane Chase, Sept. 14, 1940; children: Wilbur Frank III, Charles Chase. A.B., Ind. U., 1937, LL.D. (hon.), 1981; LL.B. cum laude, Harvard U., 1940; LL.D., Yonsei U., Seoul, Korea, 1972, John Marshall Sch. Law, 1973. Bar: Ind. 1940. Practice law Shelbyville, 1940-42, 45-70; spl. agt. FBI, 1942-45; sr. ptnr. Pell & Good, 1949-56, Pell & Matchett, 1956-70; judge 7th Circuit, U.S. Ct. Appeals, 1970—, now sr. judge; dep. atty. gen., Ind., 1953-55; dir., chmn. Shelby Nat. Bank, 1947-70. Bd. dirs. Shelbyville Community Chest, 1947-49, Shelby County Fair Assn., 1951-53; dir. Shelby County Tb Assn., 1948-70, pres., 1965-66; dist. chmn. Boy Scouts Am., 1956-57; mem. pres.'s council Nat. Coll. Edn., 1972—; dir. Westminster Found., Ind. U.; hon. dir. Korean Legal Center. Fellow Am. Coll. Probate Counsel, Am. Bar Found.; mem. ABA (Judge Edward R. Finch Law Day U.S.A. Speech award 1973, ho. of dels. 1962-63), Ind. Bar Assn. (pres. 1962-63, chmn. ho. of dels. 1968-69), Fed. Bar Assn., Ill. Bar Assn., Shelby County Bar Assn. (pres. 1957-58), 7th Fed. Circuit Bar Assn., Am. Judicature Soc., Am. Coun. Assn., Shelby County C. of C. (dir. 1947-49), Nat. Conf. Bar Presidents, Riley Meml. Assn., Ind. Soc. Chgo. (pres. 1978-79), Sagamore of Wabash, Blue Key, Kappa Sigma, Alpha Phi Omega, Theta Alpha Phi, Tau Kappa Alpha, Phi Alpha Delta (hon. mem.). Republican. Presbyterian (elder, deacon). Clubs: Evanston (dist. gov. 1952-53, internat. dir. 1959-61), Union League, Legal (pres. 1976-77), Law (Chgo.) (pres. 1984-85). Jurisprudence. Office: 219 S Dearborn St Room 2760 Chicago IL 60604

PELL, WILBUR FRANK, III, lawyer; b. Birmingham, Ala., Sept. 25, 1945; s. Wilbur Frank Jr. and Mary Lane (Chase) P.; m. Carol Ann Channell, Mar. 27, 1971; 1 child, Nathaniel Lane. Student, Union Coll., Schenectady, N.Y., 1963-65; BS, Ind. U., 1967, JD, 1971. Bar: Ind. 1971, Ill. 1971, U.S. Dist. Ct. (no. dist.) Ill. 1971, U.S. Dist. Ct. (no. and so. dists.) Ind. 1971, U.S. Ct. Appeals (7th cir.) 1971, U.S. Supreme Ct. 1979. Assoc. Rooks, Pitts & Poust, Chgo., 1971-72; atty. Internat. Harvester Co., Chgo., 1973-80, sr. atty., 1980-83; sr. counsel Navistar Internat. Corp. (formerly Internat. Harvester Corp.), Chgo., 1984-86, gen. atty., 1986; group counsel Kraft Inc., Glenview, Ill., 1986—. Commr. Wilmette (Ill.) Traffic Commn., 1985—; trustee Kendall Coll., 1980-84; bd. dirs. Wilmette Forum, 1985—, pres. 1987—. Served to 1st lt. USAR, 1968-74. Fellow Am. Bar Found., Fellows Ill. Bar Found. (chmn. 1985-86); mem. ABA, Ill. Bar Assn. (chmn. young lawyers div. 1980-81, chmn. pub. relations com. 1981-82, chmn. fin. com. 1979-81, chmn. election procedures com. 1980-81, assembly 1976—, chmn. rules and by-laws com. 1986—, vice chmn. staff pension com. 1984-86), Ill. Bar Found. (v.p., pres. 1986—), Ind. Bar Assn., Chgo. Bar Assn., Am. Judicature Soc., Legal Club Chgo., Law Club Chgo., 7th Cir. Bar Assn. Presbyterian. Avocations: photography, scuba. General corporate, Contracts commercial, Securities. Home: 714 Greenleaf Ave Wilmette IL 60091 Office: Kraft Inc Law Dept Kraft Ct Glenview IL 60025

PELLICCIOTTI, JOSEPH MICHAEL, lawyer, educator; b. Cortland, N.Y., Jan. 23, 1950; s. Michael Joseph and Mary (Latini) P.; m. M. Beth Hardy, Aug. 4, 1973; 1 child, Michael. BA in Polit. Sci., Alfred U., 1973; M in Pub. Adminstrn., Syracuse U., 1973; JD cum laude, Gonzaga U., 1976. Bar: Ind. 1976, U.S. Dist. Ct. (no. dist.) Ind. 1978, U.S. Ct. Appeals (7th cir.) 1978, U.S. Supreme Ct. 1979. Lectr. polit. sci. Gonzaga U., Spokane, Wash., 1974-76; asst. prof., chmn. polit. sci. dept. St. Joseph's Coll., Rensselaer, Ind., 1976-78; assoc. Law Offices Saul I. Ruman, Hammond, Ind., 1978-80; sole practice Hammond, 1980—; adj. faculty Ind. U. Northwest, Gary, 1980-82, vis. asst. prof., criminal justice coordinator, 1982-84, asst. prof., criminal justice coordinator, 1984—; mem. Saturday morning bar clinic Legal Services Program Greater Gary Inc., 1986. Author: Handbook on Basic Trial Evidence, 1985; contbr. articles to profl. jours. Mem. community affairs adv. bd. Pub. Safety Council Northwest Ind., Gary, 1985—, Lake County Sheriff's Corrections Merit Bd., Crown Point, Ind., 1986—. Mem. ABA, Assn. Trial Lawyers Am., Ind. Bar Assn., Lake County Bar Assn., Am. Judicature Soc., Am. Soc. Pub. Adminstrn. (gov. council Northwest Ind. chpt. 1984—, v.p., pres. elect Northwest Ind. chpt. 1985-86, pres. 1986-87), Am. Arbitration Assn., Justinian Soc. Lawyers Northwest Ind. (sec. 1985—, 1st v.p. 1985—), Midwestern Criminal Justice Assn., Lambda Alpha Epsilon (chpt. advisor 1986). Legal education, General practice, Legal research and writing. Office: 9219 Indianapolis Blvd Highland IN 46322

PELLINO, CHARLES EDWARD, JR., lawyer; b. Chgo., May 2, 1943; s. Charles Edward Sr. and Ella (Didomendico) P.; m. Melinda Poorman, Aug. 20, 1966; children: Charles, Tracy, William. BA, Drake U., 1965; JD, U. Wis., 1968. Bar: Wis. 1968, U.S. Dist. Ct. (we. dist.) Wis. 1972, U.S. Tax Ct. 1984, U.S. Dist. Ct. (ea. dist.) Wis. 1985, U.S. Ct. Appeals (7th cir.) 1985, U.S. Supreme Ct. 1985. Assoc. McAndrews, Fritschler & Huggett, Madison, Wis., 1968-70; ptnr. Fritschler, Ross, Pellino & Protzman, Madison, 1970-73, Fritschler, Pellino & Assocs., Madison, 1973-76, Fritschler, Pellino, Schrank & Rosen, Madison, 1976—; bd. dirs. Frontier Econ. Devel. Corp., N.Y.C., Portman Pharm. Corp., Madison. Contbr. articles to profl. jours. Mem. ABA, Wis. Bar Assn., Nat. Assn. Criminal Def. Lawyers, Wis. Acad. Trial Lawyers, Wis. Assn. Criminal Def. Lawyers (sec.-elect 1987—). Avocations: flying, golf. General corporate, Criminal, Federal tax litigation. Office: Fritschler Pellino Schrank & Rosen 131 W Wilson Suite 601 Madison WI 53703

PELOFSKY, JOEL, judge; b. Kansas City, Mo., June 23, 1937; s. Louis J. and Naomi (Hecht) P.; m. Brenda L. Greenblatt, June 19, 1960; children—Mark, Lisa, Carl. A.B., Harvard U., 1959; LL.B., 1962. Bar: Mo. 1962, U.S. Dist. Ct. (we. dist.) Mo. 1962, U.S. Ct. Appeals (8th cir.) 1968, U.S. Ct. Appeals (10th cir.) 1970. Law clk. to judge U.S. Dist. Ct. (we. dist.) Mo., 1962-63; mem. Miniace & Pelofsky, Kansas City, Mo., 1965-80; asst. pros. atty. Jackson County (Mo.), 1967-71; mem. Kans. City (Mo.) City Council, 1971-79; judge U.S. Bankruptcy Ct., Western Dist. Mo., Kansas City, 1980-85; ptnr. Shughart, Thomson & Kilroy P.C., Kansas City, 1986—; intermittant lectr. in law U. Mo.; mem. Region I, Law Enforcement Assistance Adminstrn. Bd. dirs. Greater Kansas City Mental Health Found.; mem. adv. bd. Urban League, Kansas City, Mo., chmn. human resource

devel. com. Mo. Mcpl. League; bd. dirs., mem. exec. com. Truman Med. Ctr., Kansas City, Mo. Served to lt. U.S. Army, 1963-65. Mem. ABA, Mo. Bar, Kansas City Bar Assn., Comml. Law League. Bankruptcy. Office: Shughart Thomson & Kilroy 120 W 12th Kansas City MO 64105

PELSTER, WILLIAM C., lawyer; b. St. Louis, May 11, 1942; s. William R. and Marie C. (Graefe) P.; m. Terry C. Cuthbertson, Aug. 9, 1969. BA, Oberlin Coll., 1964; JD, U. Mich., 1967. Bar: Mo. 1967, N.Y. 1968, U.S. Dist. Ct. (so. dist.) N.Y. 1968, U.S. Ct. Appeals (2d cir.) 1968, U.S. Supreme Ct. 1972. Law clk. to presiding justice U.S. Ct. Appeals (2d cir.), N.Y.C., 1967-68; assoc. Donovan, Leisure, Newton & Irvine, N.Y.C., 1968-75; ptnr. Skadden, Arps, Slate, Meagher & Flom, N.Y.C., 1976—. Trustee Cancer Care Inc., N.Y.C., 1975—. Mem. ABA, Assn. of Bar of City of N.Y. Antitrust. Office: Skadden Arps Slate Meagher & Flom 919 3d Ave New York NY 10022

PELTIER, LINDA JEANNE, legal educator; b. St. Louis, Nov. 29, 1948; d. Louis Cook and Louisa Harriet (Russell) Peltier; m. James Edward Britain, June 23, 1979. BA in Polit. Sci., Bucknell U., 1970; JD, George Washington U., 1973. Bar: D.C. 1973, Pa. 1975, U.S. Ct. Claims 1974. Assoc. Fried, Frank, Harris et al, Washington, 1973-74; staff atty. Susquehanna Legal Services, Williamsport, Pa., 1974-77; asst. prof. law U. Ky., Lexington, 1977-79; asst., then assoc. prof. law New Eng. Sch. Law, Boston, 1979-82; assoc. prof. law, U. Cin., 1982-86, adj. prof., 1986-87; chmn. univ. jud. council, 1983-86; mem. support group Ctr. for Law and Human Values, N.Y.C., 1983—; coordinator, creator Hunger and Law Conf., Cin., 1983, other confs. Contbr. articles to profl. jours; editor-in-chief Vol. 41, George Washington U. Law Rev., 1972-73. Ending hunger briefing leader The Hunger Project, San Francisco, 1984; mem. mental health/mental retardation adv. bd. Union-Snyder Community Counseling Service, Lewisburg, Pa., 1975-77; advisor Law Explorer Posts 100/830, Williamsport, Pa. and Lexington, Ky., 1975-79. Jr. Year Abroad grantee Inst. Am. Univs., France, 1968-69. Mem. ABA. Democrat. Episcopalian. Banking, Contracts commercial, Legal education. Home: 37 Forest Ave Cincinnati OH 45215 Office: U Cin Coll Law Cincinnati OH 45221

PELTON, GREGORY VERN, lawyer; b. Sterling, Kans., July 11, 1953; s. Elmer L. and Mary L. (Schlagel) P.; m. Christin K. Galloway, Feb. 23, 1985. BS in Sociology, Kans. State U., 1975; JD, Washburn U., 1978. Bar: N. Mex. 1978, U.S. Dist. Ct. N.Mex. 1978. Assoc. Robinson, Stevens & Wainwright, Albuquerque, 1978-81, ptnr., 1982-84; assoc. Beall, Stoker & Clifford, Albuquerque, 1984, Beall & Dawe, Albuquerque, 1985-86; ptnr. Beall, Pelton, O'Brien & Brown, Albuquerque, 1986—. Mem. N.Mex. State Bar Assn., Albuquerque Bar Assn., Def. Lawyers Assn. Republican. Roman Catholic. Lodge: Kiwanis. Avocations: whitewater kayaking, skiing, stained glass. Insurance, Personal injury, Workers' compensation. Office: Beall Pelton O'Brien & Brown 2500 Louisiana NE #400 Albuquerque NM 87110

PELTON, RUSSELL GILBERT, lawyer; b. Monticello, N.Y., July 23, 1914; s. William and May (Morgan) P.; m. Marion Gosart, Dec. 14, 1940; children—William, Marjorie, Marilyn Pelton Barringer. B.S., Syracuse U., 1935; J.D., George Washington U., 1944. Bar: D.C. 1944, N.Y. 1947, U.S. Supreme Ct. 1948, U.S. Dist. Ct. N.Y. 1947; U.S. Ct. Customs and Patent Appeals. Ptnr., Darby & Darby, N.Y.C., 1945-56; sr. v.p. N.Am. Philips Corp., N.Y.C., 1956-75; exec. v.p. U.S. Philips Corp., N.Y.C., 1968-75; of counsel Rogers, Hoge & Hills, N.Y.C., 1976-78; ptnr. Spellman, Joel & Pelton, White Plains, N.Y., 1979-81, Eslinger & Pelton, N.Y.C., 1983—; officer, dir. Tech. Container Corp., N.Y.C., 1977—; former dir. Ferroscube Corp., Savgerties, N.Y., Polyseal Corp., N.Y.C.; lectr. Practising Law Inst., 1953-69; Vice-pres. Siwanoy council Boy Scouts Am., 1948-53; v.p. Rye Neck Bd. Edn., Mamaroneck, N.Y., 1952-62; mem. Zoning Bd. Appeals, 1966-70; town justice, 1970—; trustee Syracuse U., 1968-74. Served with Signal Corps, U.S. Army, 1941-45. Mem. ABA, Am. Patent Law Assn. (past chmn. com. antitrust), N.Y. State Bar Assn. (ethics com., Iolta com.), N.Y. Patent Law Assn. (past bd. govs.), State Magistrates Assn., County Magistrates Assn. (treas., v.p.), Westchester County Bar Assn. (chmn. ethics com.), Assn. Bar City N.Y. (patent com.), IEEE, Am. Radio Relay League, Aircraft Owners and Pilots Assn. Clubs: Wings, Cloud (N.Y.C.); Winged Foot Golf (Mamaroneck, N.Y.); Waccabuc Country (South Salem, N.Y.); Masons, Elks. Patentee in field. Patent, Trademark and copyright, Federal civil litigation. Home: 3 Oxford Rd Larchmont NY 10538 Office: 522 Fifth Ave New York NY 10036

PELTON, RUSSELL MEREDITH, JR., lawyer; b. Chgo., May 14, 1938; s. Russell Meredith and Mildred Helen (Baumrucker) P.; m. Patty Jane Rader, Aug. 12, 1961; children—James, Thomas, Michael, Margaret. B.A., DePauw U., 1960; J.D., U. Chgo., 1963. Bar: Ill. 1963, U.S. Supreme Ct. 1979. Assoc., Peterson, Ross, Schloerb & Seidel and predecessors, Chgo., 1966-72, ptnr., 1972—; co-founder, gen. counsel Chgo. Opportunities Industrialization Ctr., 1969-83; gen. counsel Delta Dental Plan Ill., 1979—; bd. dirs. First United Life Ins. Co., 1979-82. Pres. Wilmette Jaycees, 1970; chmn. Wilmette Sch. Bd. Caucus, 1970-71; Wilmette Dist. 39 Bd. Edn., 1972-80; bd. dirs. Wilmette United Way, 1980-86, campaign chmn., 1983-85, pres., 1985-86. Served to capt. USAF, 1963-66. Mem. Chgo. Bar Assn., Ill. Bar Assn., ABA, Ill. Trial Lawyers Assn., Soc. Trial Lawyers. Federal civil litigation, State civil litigation, Association representation. Home: 607 9th St Wilmette IL 60091 Office: 200 E Randolph Dr Suite 7300 Chicago IL 60601

PELTONEN, JOHN ERNEST, lawyer; b. Manchester, N.H., Dec. 25, 1942; s. Ernest and Anna Frances (McCarthy) P.; m. Katherine Frances Zak, July 29, 1967; children—John Ernest, Laura Katherine Ann, Brian Joseph. B.A., Dartmouth Coll., 1964; J.D., Boston Coll., 1967; M.A., U. Ark., 1972. Bar: N.H. 1967, U.S. Dist. Ct. N.H. 1967, U.S. Ct. Appeals (1st cir.) 1975, U.S. Supreme Ct. 1980. Assoc., Nixon, Christy & Tessier, Manchester, 1972-74; ptnr. Nixon, Christy, Tessier & Peltonen, Manchester, 1974-76; sole practice, Manchester, 1977; ptnr. Stark & Peltonen, Manchester, 1978—. Incorporator, Catholic Med. Ctr., Manchester, 1978—; mem. N.H. Bd. Claims, 1982—; incorporator, bd. dirs. N.H. Lions Sight and Hearing Found., 1978-81. Served to capt. USAF, 1967-72. Mem. N.H. Bar Assn., ABA, Am. Trial Lawyers Assn., N.H. Trial Lawyers Assn., Pi Sigma Alpha. Democrat. Roman Catholic. Lodge: Lions (Goffstown) (pres. 1978-79). Insurance, Personal injury, Environment. Home: RFD #5 Mountain Rd Goffstown NH 03045 Office: Stark & Peltonen PA 121 Middle St Manchester NH 03101

PELUSO, CHARLES JOHN, lawyer; b. Los Banos, Calif., Jan. 5, 1943; s. Frank and Mary E. (Marchese) P.; m. Norma Jean Thorkelson, Aug. 9, 1969. BA, Santa Clara U., 1964; LLD, U. Calif., Berkeley, 1967. Bar: Calif. 1967. Dep. dist. atty. Stanislaus County, Modesto, Calif., 1968-73; assoc. Jensen & Gaarde, Modesto, 1973-75; sole practice Modesto, 1975—. Mem. Calif. Bar Assn., Stanislaus County Bar Assn. General corporate, General practice, Probate. Office: 631 15th St Modesto CA 95350

PELUSO, GINO FRANCIS, lawyer; b. New Kensington, Pa., June 11, 1955; s. Frank M. and Raffaelina (Palumbo) P. BA, St. Vincent Coll., Latrobe, Pa., 1977; JD, Duquesne U., 1980. Bar: Pa. 1981, U.S. Dist. Ct. (we. dist.) Pa. 1981, U.S. Ct. Appeals (3d cir.) 1985. Assoc. Saldamarco & Calaiaro, Pitts., 1980-84; asst. dist. atty. Westmoreland County, Greensburg, 1983—; assoc. Arnold & Lower Burrell, Pitts., 1984—; paralegal instr. Computer Systems Inst., Pitts., 1980-83. Del. candidate Gary Hart for Pres., Arnold, 1984. Mem. ABA, Pa. Bar Assn., Allegheny County Bar Assn., Westmoreland County Bar Assn., Pa. Dist. Attys. Assn., Pa. Domestic Relations Assn., Italian Am. Edn. Soc., Mental Health Assn. (bd. dirs. Reach Ctr. 1986—). Democrat. Roman Catholic. General practice, Family and matrimonial, Bankruptcy. Home: 1806 Ridge Ave Arnold PA 15068 Office: Manor Complex Suite 712 Pittsburgh PA 15219 also: 2768 Leechburg Rd Lower Burrell PA 15068

PELZ, JOEL THOMAS, lawyer; b. Peoria, Ill., Nov. 10, 1955; s. Curtis R. and Georgia Ann (Fitschen) P.; m. Colette Holt, Feb. 15, 1986. BA, Valparaiso U., 1977; JD, Harvard U., 1980. Bar: Ill. 1980, U.S. Dist. Ct. (no. dist.) Ill. 1982, U.S. Ct. Appeals (7th cir.) 1982, U.S. Ct. Appeals (11th cir.) 1986. Assoc. Jenner & Block, Chgo., 1980-86, ptnr., 1987—. Mem. ABA, Chgo. Bar Assn., Chgo. Council Lawyers. Democrat. Lutheran. Federal civil litigation, State civil litigation, Criminal. Home: 1245 W Eddy Chicago IL 60657 Office: Jenner & Block One IBM Plaza 4400 Chicago IL 60611

PENA, RICHARD, lawyer; b. San Antonio, Feb. 13, 1948; s. Merced and Rebecca (Trejo) P.; m. Carolyn Sarah Malley, May 25, 1979; 1 stepchild, Jason Charles Schubert. BA., U. Tex., 1970, J.D., 1976. Bar: Tex. 1976, Colo. 1986. ptnr. Law Offices of Pena & Jones, Austin, 1976—; instr. bus. law St. Edwards U., Austin, 1983, Austin Community Coll., 1981-82; broker Tex. Real Estate Commn., 1980—. Sports editor, Austin Light newspaper, 1982. Bd. dirs. Center for Battered Women, Austin, 1979-82, Austin Assn. Retarded Citizens, 1980-82; chmn. Austin Travis County Mental Health/Mental Retardation Pub. Responsibility Comm., 1979-84; chmn. pvt. facilities monitoring com. Austin Assn. Retarded Citizens, 1981. Named One of Outstanding Young Men Am., Jaycees, 1982. Mem. Travis County Bar Assn. (trustee lawyer referral service 1984-85, bd. dirs. 1986—), Capitol Area Mexican Am. Lawyers (pres. 1985), Legal Aid Soc. Central Tex. (bd. dirs. 1984), Travis County Bar Assn. (bd. dirs. 1986, lawyer referral service com.), Austin Young Lawyers Assn., Tex. Trial Lawyers Assn., State Bar Tex. (fed. judiciary appointments com. 1984), Austin C. of C. (leadership Austin 1985-86), Brotherhood Vietnam Vets. Democrat. Personal injury, Workers' compensation. Home: 312 Golf Crest Austin TX 78734 Office: Pena & Jones 901 Mopac Suite 325 Barton Oaks Plaza Two Austin TX 78743

PENCE, CHRISTOPHER CYRUS, lawyer; b. Spokane, Wash., Feb. 1, 1950; s. Lawrence Cyrus Christine Atrice (Snow) P. BA, Whitman Coll., 1972; JD, Willamette U., 1977. Bar: Wash. 1977, U.S. Dist. Ct. (we. dist.) Wash. 1977. Staff atty. Wash. State Bar Assn., Seattle, 1977-80; assoc. Law Offices of Arthur D. Swanson, Seattle, 1980-81; sole practice Seattle, 1981-85; ptnr. Pence & Dawson, Seattle, 1985—. Mem. Taskforce on Alternative Dispute Resolution, Seattle, 1985-86. Mem. ABA, Am. Trial Lawyers Assn. (law sch. rep.), Wash. State Trial Lawyers Assn., Seattle-King County Bar Assn. Club: Wings Aloft (Seattle). Avocations: flying. Personal injury, Insurance, Professional negligence. Home: 1601 Taylor Ave #503 Seattle WA 98109 Office: Pence & Dawson 3000 Smith Tower Seattle WA 98104

PENDERGAST, JOHN FRANCIS, JR., lawyer; b. Rochester, N.Y., June 7, 1955; s. John Francis Sr.and Jane (Fickenscher) P.; m. Nancy Susan Conrads, May 21, 1977; children: John Francis III, James Conrads, Meghan Lane. BA, Wake Forest U., 1977, JD, 1980. Bar: Ga. 1980, U.S. Dist. Ct. (no. dist.) Ga. 1980, U.S. Ct. Appeals (5th and 11th cirs.) 1980. Assoc. Greenfield, Beltran & Ellis, Atlanta, 1980-82; ptnr. Beltran & Pendergast, Atlanta, 1982-84, Summers, Jones & Pendergast P.C., Atlanta, 1984—; pres. Pro Promotions, Inc. Bd. dirs. Cathedral of Christ the King, Atlanta, 1985—; v.p. Peachtree Park Civic Assn., Atlanta, 1985—. Mem. ABA, Ga. Bar Assn., Atlanta Bar Assn. (bd. dirs. litigation sect.), Lawyers Club Atlanta, Nat. Football League Players Assn. (contract advisor 1983, 86—), Assn. of Reps. of Profl. Athletes, Sierra Club (v.p. 1986—). Democrat. Roman Catholic. Club: Ansley Golf (Atlanta). Avocations: golf, running, music. General corporate, Professional athlete representation, Federal civil litigation. Office: Summers Jones & Pendergast PC 3414 Peachtree Rd NE 710 Monarch Plaza Atlanta GA 30326

PENDERGAST, JOHN JOSEPH, III, lawyer; b. Lewiston, Maine, Jan. 29, 1936; s. John Joseph and Grace (McCarty) P.; m. Joan Cole, June 14, 1958; children—John Joseph, Timothy S., Terrence B., Mary R., Michael C., Joan McCarty. B.A., Yale U., 1957, LL.B., 1960. Bar: R.I. 1960, U.S. dist. ct. R.I. 1960, U.S. Ct. Appeals (1st cir.) 1962. Ptnr. Hinckley, Allen, Tobin & Silverstein, Providence, 1966—; adj. prof. Providence Coll., 1982—. Mem. Cath. Charities panel Diocese of Providence, 1976—, chmn. Human Relations Commn., 1972-76; bd. dirs. Smith Hill Center, 1978—; bd. dirs. R.I. Legal Services, 1969—, chmn. bd., 1979; v.p. Providence Boys Clubs, 1970-72. Mem. ABA, R.I. Bar Assn., Indsl. Relations Research Assn. Clubs: Sakonnet Yacht, University, Yale of R.I. (pres. 1970) (Providence). Labor. Home: 21 Violet St Providence RI 02908 Office: Hinckley Allen Tobin & Silverstein 1500 Fleet Ctr Providence RI 02903

PENDERGRASS, JOHN AMBROSE, lawyer, educator; b. Florence, Ala., Mar. 23, 1953; s. John Ambrose Jr. and Dolly Ruth (Liles) P. BS, Mich. State U., 1976; JD, Case Western Res. U., 1979. Bar: Ohio 1979, Wis. 1983. Atty. Dept. of Interior, Washington, 1979-84; assoc. DeWitt, Sunby, Huggett, Schumacher & Morgan S.C., Madison, Wis., 1984-86; vis. asst. prof. Ill. Inst. Tech.-Kent Coll. Law, Chgo., 1986—. Mem. ABA (natural resources and adminstrv. law sect.), Wis. Bar Assn. Unitarian. Avocations: photography, soccer. Environment, Administrative and regulatory, Legal education.

PENEGOR, ROBERT JOSEPH, lawyer; b. Marquette, Mich., Jan. 23, 1942; s. Clyde Edward and Leona Catherine (Gauthier) P.; m. Patricia Lynne Paynick, June 12, 1967 (div. Jan. 1980); children: Nicole, Joel, Renee; m. Bonnie Lee Krizan, May 23, 1983; 1 child, Peter. BS, U. Mich., 1964; JD, Marquette U., 1967. Bar: Wis. 1967, U.S. Dist. Ct. (ea. dist.) Wis. 1967. Assoc. Peregrine, Marcuvitz, Schimenz & Cameron, Milw., 1976-70; ptnr. Salza & Penegor, Milw., 1970-73, Salza, Penegor & Hauke S.C., Milw., 1973-76; assoc. Peregrine, Schimenz, Marcuvitz, Cameron & Peltin S.C., Milw., 1976-78; sole practice Milw., 1978-82; prin. Penegor Legal Services Ltd. S.C., Brookfield, Wis., 1982—. Mem. Wis. Bar Assn., Assn. Trial Lawyers Am., Wis. Acad. Trial Lawyers. Roman Catholic. Family and matrimonial, Insurance, Personal injury. Home: 250 Joanne Dr Brookfield WI 53005 Office: Penegor Legal Services Ltd 16655 W Bluemound Rd Brookfield WI 53005

PENFOLD, CRAIG A., judge; b. Dallas, Dec. 11, 1942; s. Kenneth Craig and Carlen (Quarnberg) P.; m. Sharon Ann Hasten, Jan. 13, 1974; children: Carlen Tully, Clark Simpson. BA, U. Colo., 1965; JD, U. Tex., 1969. Judge 304th Dist. Ct., Dallas, 1976—. Mem. Foster Child Adv. Service, Tex. Coll. Judiciary, Chem. Awareness Council, Tex. Juvenile Probation Commn., adv. council Tex. Corrections Assn, Dallas County Juvenile Bd., North Cen. Tex. Council of Govts.; chmn. Tex. Task Force on Permanency Planning, adv. com. Tex. Dept. Mental Health and Mental Retardation; bd. dirs. Girls Adventure Trails, Law Foucsed Edn., Inc. Mem. ABA, Dallas Bar Assn. (criminal justice com., family law sect.), Tex. Bar Assn. (family law sect., jud. sect., chmn. juvenile justice com. 1980), Dallas Assn. Young Lawyers, Dallas County Criminal Bar Assn., Nat. Council Juvenile and Family Ct. Judges (cert. com., child support enforcemnt task force, juvenile ct. effectiveness com., chmn. mental retardation com. 1984, chmn. met. cts. com. 1986). Presbyterian. Home: 4505 Beverly Dr Dallas TX 75205 Office: 304th Dist Ct Records Bldg Dallas TX 75202

PENICK, MICHAEL PRESTON, lawyer; b. Covington, Ky., Aug. 9, 1947; s. James Preston and Edith Marie (Smith) P.; m. Christina Sue Lund, June 9, 1979. B.A., Union Coll., 1970; cert. highest proficiency Def. Lang. Inst., 1971; J.D., U. Louisville, 1976. Bar: Ky. 1976, U.S. Dist. Ct. (we. dist.) Ky. 1976, U.S. Ct. Appeals (6th cir.) 1980, U.S. Supreme Ct. 1980. Ptnr. Boehl, Stopher, Graves & Deindoerfer, Paducah, Ky., 1978—. Author: Beginning Bridge Complete, 1983. Served with U.S. Army, 1970-73; ETO. Recipient life master cert. Am. Contract Bridge League, 1976, Judge W.W. Tinsley Meml. award Union Coll., 1970, Faculty Athletic award, 1969, 70. Mem. ABA (products liability com. 1982—), Ky. Bar Assn. (ho. of dels. 1981, 84—), Def. Research Inst. (products liability com. 1979—), Ky. Def. Counsel, Young Lawyers Assn. (pres. 1977). Methodist. Insurance, Workers' compensation, Federal civil litigation. Home: 101 Springwell Ln Paducah KY 42001 Office: Boehl Stopher Graves & Deindoerfer Suite 340 Exec Inn 340 Executive Inn Paducah KY 42001

PENLAND, PAUL STEPHAN, lawyer; b. Dallas, June 30, 1949; s. John Paul and Hortense (Spurger) P.; m. Leslie Ann Derr, Nov. 16, 1968; children: John Walter, Lura Melisa, Christopher Derr. Student, Tex. Tech U., 1967-68, N. Tex. State U., 1968-69, So. Meth. U., 1969-71, Baylor U., 1973-75. Bar: Tex. 1976, Idaho 1976, U.S. Ct. Appeals (9th cir.) 1978, Oreg. 1984, U.S. Supreme Ct. 1985. Police officer City of Colorado Springs, Colo., 1971-73; assoc. Moffatt, Thomas, etc., Boise, Idaho, 1975-79; sole practice Boise, 1979-80; ptnr. Lojek & Penland and predecessor firms Parkinson, Lojek & Penland and Parkinson & Penland, Boise, 1980-85, Penland & Munther, Boise, 1986—. Mem. ABA, Idaho Bar Assn., Oreg. Bar Assn., Tex. Bar Assn., Boise Bar Assn., Internat. Assn. Indsl. Accident Bds. and Commns. (assoc.), Boise Ins. Adjusters Assn. (sec. 1984, v.p. 1985, pres. 1986-87), Idaho Assn. Counties (assoc.), Idaho Def. Council Assn. Republican. Avocations: downhill skiing, soccer. Civil rights, Workers' compensation, Insurance. Home: 3284 Scenic Dr Boise ID 83703 Office: Penland & Munther 711 1/2 W Bannock Boise ID 83701

PENLAND, SAMUEL PERRY, JR., lawyer; b. Jacksonville, Fla., Oct. 13, 1955; s. Samuel Perry Sr. and Sybil Claire (Ramos) P.; m. Dale Redman, Oct. 3, 1981; 1 child, Sarah Michelle. BA, Stetson U., 1978, JD, 1980. Bar: Fla. 1981, U.S. Dist. Ct (mid. dist.) Fla. 1984. Ptnr. Penland, Penland & Pafford P.A., Jacksonville, 1981—. Mem. ABA, Fla. Bar Assn., Assn. Trial Lawyers Am., Wavemasters Soc. Democrat. Avocations: fishing, surfing. Personal injury, Criminal, Family and matrimonial. Home: 2018 Cherokee Dr Neptune Beach FL 32233 Office: Penland Penland & Pafford PA 233 E Bay St 1113 Blackstone Bldg Jacksonville FL 32202

PENMAN, GORDON REESE, lawyer; b. Rochester, Pa., Apr. 26, 1956; s. Robert R. and Jean A. (Gordon) P.; m. Kathleen A. McCarthy, Jan. 14, 1977; children: Andrew G., James I. BA, Coll. William and Mary, 1978; JD, U. Va., 1982. Bar: Mass. 1982, U.S. Dist. Ct. Mass. 1984, U.S. Tax Ct. 1984, U.S. Ct. Appeals (1st cir.) 1984. Editor publications Nat. Ctr. for State Cts., Williamsburg, Va., 1978-79; assoc. Brown, Rudnick, Freed & Gesmer, Boston, 1982—. Mem. ABA, Mass. Bar Assn., Boston Bar Assn. General corporate, Real property, Securities. Home: 9 Atwood St Mansfield MA 02048 Office: Brown Rudnick Freed & Gesmer 1 Federal St Boston MA 02110

PENN, JOHN GARRETT, judge; b. Pittsfield, Mass., Mar. 19, 1932; s. John and Eugenie Gwendolyn (Heyliger) P.; m. Ann Elizabeth Rollison, May 7, 1966; children: John Garrett, Karen Renee, David Brandon. B.A., U. Mass., 1954; LL.B., Boston U., 1957; postgrad., Woodrow Wilson Sch. Public and Internat. Affairs, Princeton U., 1967-68. Bar: Mass 1957, D.C. 1970. Trial atty. tax div. Dept. Justice, from 1961; then reviewer, asst. chief gen. litigation sect.; asso. judge Superior Ct. of D.C., Washington, 1970-79; U.S. dist. judge U.S. Dist. Ct. for D.C., Washington, 1979—. Ex officio dir. D.C. Dept. Recreation Day Care Program, 1978—. Served to 1st lt. Judge Adv. Gen. Corps U.S. Army, 1958-61. Nat. Inst. Public Affairs fellow., 1967. Mem. Am. Fed., Nat., Mass., Washington, D.C. bar assns., Am. Judicature Soc., Boston U. Law Sch. Alumni Assn. Episcopalian. Clubs: Nat. Lawyers (hon.). Jurisprudence. Office: US District Court 6315 US Courthouse 3d and Constitution Ave NW Washington DC 20001 *

PENNEBAKER, SUSAN MCCLIMANS, lawyer; b. Baton Rouge, May 26, 1954; d. James Orr and Carolyn Ruth (Dyson) McClimans; m. Ward G. Pennebaker, May 1, 1976; children: Andrew Dyson, Matthew Orr. BA, LSU, 1976, JD, 1978. Bar: La. 1978, Tex. 1979, U.S. Dist. Ct. (so. dist.) Tex. 1980. Analyst Exxon Co. USA, Houston, 1980; assoc. Stephens & Willey, Houston, 1981-82, of counsel, 1984—; assoc. Stubbeman & McCrae, Houston, 1983-84, Moffett & Davis, Houston, 1982-83; pres., v.p., bd. dirs. Trial Exhibits, Inc., Houston, 1985—. vol. March of Dimes, Houston, 1985—, Easter Seals, 1986—. Mem. Tex. Bar Assn. (legal forms com. 1982-84), La. Bar Assn., Houston Bar Assn., Houston Bus. Forum. Republican. Episcopalian. Oil and gas leasing, General practice. Office: Stephens & Willey 2215 Allied Bank Plaza Houston TX 77002

PENNELL, STEPHEN RICHARD, lawyer; b. Cheyenne, Wyo., Apr. 7, 1952; s. Richard Loren and Glenna Dean (Maple) P.; m. Diana Sue Dirlam, Mar. 9, 1974; children: James Richard, Lauren Michelle. AB summa cum laude, Ind. U., 1973, JD magna cum laude, 1976. Bar: Ind. 1976, U.S. Dist. Ct. (no. and so. dists.) Ind. 1976, U.S. Ct. Appeals (7th cir.) 1978. Assoc. Stuart & Branigin, Lafayette, Ind., 1976—. Editor Ind. U. Law Jour., 1976. Pres. Wesley Found., West Lafayette, Ind., 1980-86. Served to capt. USAR, 1976-84. Mem. ABA, Ind. Bar Assn., Ind. Def. Lawyers Assn., Phi Beta Kappa, Order of Coif. Republican. Methodist. Federal civil litigation, State civil litigation, Personal injury. Home: 3111 Decatur West Lafayette IN 47906 Office: Stuart & Branigin PO Box 1010 Lafayette IN 47902

PENNELL, WILLIAM BROOKE, lawyer; b. Mineral Ridge, Ohio, Oct. 28, 1935; s. George Albert and Katherine Nancy (McMeen) P. AB, Harvard U., 1957; LLB cum laude, U. Pa., 1961; m. Peggy Polsky, June 17, 1958; children: Katherine, Thomas Brooke. Bar: N.Y. 1963, U.S. Dist. Ct. (so. dist.) N.Y. 1964, U.S. Dist. Ct. (ea. dist.) N.Y. 1964, U.S. Ct. Appeals (2d cir.) 1966, U.S. Ct. Claims 1966, U.S. Tax Ct. 1967, U.S. Supreme Ct. 1967. Clk. U.S. Dist. Ct., (so. dist.) N.Y., N.Y.C., 1961-62; assoc. Shearman & Sterling, N.Y.C., 1962-71, ptnr., 1971—. Recent case editor U. Pa. Law Rev., 1960-61. Bd. govs. Bklyn. Heights Assn., 1964-74, pres., 1969-71; chmn. bd. Willoughby House Settlement, 1972—. Served with U.S. Army, 1957. Fellow Salzburg Seminar Am. Studies, 1965. Mem. Fed. Bar Council, ABA, N.Y. State Bar Assn., Assn. Bar City N.Y. Club: Rembrandt. Federal civil litigation, State civil litigation, Private international. Office: Shearman & Sterling 53 Wall St New York NY 10005

PENNEY, FREELAND N.F.T. CHRISTIAN, historical and legal consultant, lawyer; b. St. Joseph, Mo., July 23, 1908; s. John Adams and Laura (Penney) P. A.B., U. Kans., 1928, A.M., 1929, LL.B., 1934; Ph.D., Cornell U., 1931; postgrad. Columbia U. Law Sch., NYU Law Sch. Bar: Kans. 1934, Mo. 1934, N.Y. 1936, U.S. Dist. Ct. (so. dist.) N.Y. 1947, U.S. Supreme Ct. 1945. Law clk. Gwinn & Pell; N.Y.C.; 1934; law clk.; and librarian Scribner & Miller Co., N.Y.C., 1934-36; assoc. atty. and librarian, 1936-39; mem. editorial staff Corpus Juris Secundum, Bklyn., 1939-40; sole practice, N.Y.C., 1941—. Author: Biography of Thomas Hobbes and Compendium of his Jurisprudence, 1939; German Confederation of 1815, Its Structure and Law, 1942; Alexander I of Russia, Biography-His View of International Law, 1942; Law of Wartime Corporations, 1942; The Realizing of Leisure and Its Limits, 1943; Governmental Use of Corporate Device in War and Peace, 1947; Christian General Chiang Kai-Shek of China and His Relations with the United States, 1975; James Penney, Nebr. Muralist, 1984. Mem. exec. com. Men's Class The Riverside Ch., N.Y.C. Mem. N.Y. County Lawyers Assn. (com. on patents, trademarks and copyrights), NYU Alumni Assn., Phi Alpha Delta (treas.). Republican. Federal civil litigation, Trademark and copyright. Home: 342 W 71st St New York NY 10023 Office: 170 Broadway New York NY 10038

PENNIE, DANIEL R., corporate lawyer. BA, Harvard U., 1968; JD, U. Minn., 1972. Ptnr. Oppenheimer, Wolff, Foster, Shepard & Donnelly, Mpls., 1972-80; v.p. gen. counsel, sec. Control Data Corp., Mpls., 1980—. Office: Control Data Corp 8100 34th Ave S Minneapolis MN 55440 *

PENNINGTON, AL, lawyer; b. Birmingham, Ala., Jan. 31, 1949; s. Vader Richards and Johnnie Fae (Hill) P.; m. Andrea Pearson, Aug. 3, 1974; children: Katherine Sigrid, Anna Caroline. BS, U. Ala., 1971, JD, 1974. Bar: Ala. 1974, U.S. Dist. Ct. (so. dist.) Ala. 1976, U.S. Supreme Ct. 1978, U.S. Ct. Appeals (11th cir.) 1983. Trust adminstr. 1st Nat. Bank of Birmingham, 1974; asst. dist. atty. Jefferson County, Birmingham, 1974-76; ptnr. Pennington & Pennington, Mobile, Ala., 1976-80, Pennington, McCleave & Patterson, Mobile, 1982—; sole practice, Mobile, 1980-81; chief asst. dist. atty. Mobile County, 1981; cons. on jail overcrowding Mobile County Commn.-Mobile County Sheriff, 1983—. Com. chmn. Mobile County Wildlife and Conservation Assn., 1976—; mem. Mobile United Way, 1977—; bd. dirs. Hist. Mobile Preservation Soc., 1981; bd. dirs. Old Dauphinway Assn., Mobile, pres., 1985-86; pres. E. Church St. Devel. Assn., Mobile, 1979-81; elected mem. Mobile County Dem. Exec. Com., Ala. Dem. Exec. Com., Ala. Dem. Exec. Bd. Named Outstanding Young Man in Am., U.S. Jaycees, 1980; recipient Community Service award Mobile United, 1980. Mem. ABA, Mobile Bar Assn., Assn. Trial Lawyers Am., Nat. Assn. Criminal Def. Lawyers, Ala. Assn. Criminal Def. Lawyers. Democrat. Methodist. Personal injury, Criminal, Federal civil litigation. Home: 25 S Julia St Mobile AL 36604 Office: Pennington McCleave & Patterson 113 S Dearborn St Mobile AL 36602

PENNINGTON, BROOKS MADDOX, III, lawyer, banker; b. Madison, Ga., Nov. 25, 1954; s. Brooks Maddox Jr. and Jacquelyn (Christian) P.; m. Patricia Chilton, Sept. 22, 1979; 1 child, Christian. BBA, U. Ga., 1976, MBA, JD, 1979. Bar: Ga. 1979. Corp. counsel Pennington Enterprises, Madison, 1979—; chmn., bd. dirs. Bank of Morgan County, Rutledge, Ga.; bd. dirs. Allied Bankshares, Thomson, Ga. Chmn. local Cancer Soc.,

Madison, 1985. Mem. Am. Seed Trade Assn. (chmn. litigation com. 1983—), Ducks Unltd. Democrat. Methodist. Lodge: Kiwanis (pres. Madison chpt. 1986—). General corporate, Banking, Bankruptcy. Home: 1210 Maxey Ln Madison GA 30650 Office: Pennington Enterprises PO Box 290 Madison GA 30650

PENNY, WILLIAM LEWIS, lawyer; b. Memphis, Sept. 4, 1953; s. Charles B. and Dorothy R. (Rivers) P.; m. Linda Brown, Sept. 8, 1979; 1 child, Joseph Martin. BA, U. Tenn., 1975; JD, Nashville YMCA Night Law Sch., 1981. Bar: Tenn. 1981, U.S. Ct. Appeals (6th cir.) 1981. Program evaluator Office of Comptroller, State of Tenn., Nashville, 1975-80; mgr. compliance and audit Tenn. Dept. Edn., Nashville, 1980-82; chief environ. counsel Tenn. Dept. Health and Environment, Nashville, 1982-84, asst. commr., gen. counsel, 1984—. Mem. ABA, Nat. Bar Assn., Tenn. Bar Assn., Assn. Govt. Accts. (editor newsletter, Nashville, 1977-79, sec. Nashville chpt. 1979-80, bd. dirs. Nashville chpt. 1980-84). Methodist. Avocations: music, bluegrass guitar, hiking. Administrative and regulatory, Environment, Health. Home: 6501 Cornwall Dr Nashville TN 37205 Office: Tenn Dept Health and Environment 354 Cordell Hull Bldg Nashville TN 37219

PENSINGER, JOHN LYNN, lawyer; b. Hagerstown, Md., June 5, 1949; s. Linford Snider and Marguerite Joan (McNeal) P.; m. Eileen Sue Howard, Nov. 7, 1972. BA, U.Md., 1971; J.D., U. Balt., 1976. Bar: Md. 1976, D.C. 1977, U.S. Ct. Claims 1977, U.S. Tax Ct. 1977, U.S. Dist. Ct. Md. 1978, U.S. Dist. Ct. D.C. 1978, U.S. Ct. Appeals (4th cir.) 1978, U.S. Ct. Mil. Appeals 1978, U.S. Ct. Appeals (D.C. cir.) 1978, U.S. Customs Ct. 1979, U.S. Supreme Ct. 1980, U.S. Ct. Internat. Trade 1981, U.S. Ct. Appeals (fed. cir.) 1982, U.S. Ct. Appeals (5th cir.) 1986. Mgr., E.M. Willis & Sons, Washington, 1977-79; sole practice, Rockville, Md., 1978-79; atty. Amalgamated Casualty Ins. Co., Washington, 1979-86; asst. gen. counsel Legal Services Corp., Washington, 1986—. Mem. ABA, Md. Bar Assn., Am. Soc. Internat. Law, Fed. Bar Assn. Roman Catholic. Administrative and regulatory, Federal civil litigation, State civil litigation. Home: 11716 Galt Ave Wheaton MD 20902

PENTELOVITCH, WILLIAN ZANE, lawyer; b. Mpls., Sept. 6, 1949; s. Norman Oscar and Esther (Misel) P.; m. Barbara Susan Ziman, Aug. 21, 1971; children: Norman Henry, Tovah Elana. BA summa cum laude, U. Minn., 1971; JD, U. Chgo., 1974. Ptnr. Maslon, Edelman, Borman & Brand, Mpls., 1974—. Federal civil litigation, State civil litigation, Construction. Home: 6 Park Ln Minneapolis MN 55416 Office: Maslon Edelman Borman et al 1800 Midwest Plaza Minneapolis MN 55402

PENTONY, KENNETH RICHARD, lawyer; b. Morristown, N.J., Sept. 21, 1946; s. John Christopher and Rita (Walsh) P.; m. Elaine C. Mahon, Nov. 9, 1969; children: Stephen, Kiersten. BA, Georgetown U., 1968; JD, Seton Hall U., 1974. Bar: N.J. 1974, U.S. Dist. Ct. N.J. 1974, U.S Supreme Ct. 1979. Assoc. Law Office of Seymour Freedman, Freehold, N.J., 1974-77, Shebell & Schibell, Asbury Park, N.J., 1977-79; ptnr. Novins, Farley, York, DeVincens & Pentony, Toms River, N.J., 1979—. Served to sgt. U.S. Army, 1969-71. Mem. ABA, N.J. Bar Assn., Ocean County Bar Assn. (chmn. civil practice com. 1984—), Mercer County Bar Assn., Monmouth County Bar Assn., Am. Arbitration Assn. (arbitrator 1976—, mediator 1986—), Mandatory Arbitration Com. (chmn. 1984—). Republican. Roman Catholic. Federal civil litigation, State civil litigation, Personal injury. Home: 237 Ashlar Way Toms River NJ 08753 Office: Novins Farley York DeVincens & Pentony 202 Main St CN 2032 Toms River NJ 08754

PENZA, JOSEPH FULVIO, JR., lawyer; b. Providence, Sept. 23, 1947; s. Joseph Fulvio Sr. and Ann M. (Barbieri) P. BBA, U. R.I., 1969; JD, Boston U., 1972, LLM in Taxation, 1975. Bar: R.I. 1972, U.S. Dist. Ct. R.I. 1972, U.S. Ct. Appeals (1st cir.) 1975, U.S. Supreme Ct. 1980. Sole practice Providence, 1972-82; ptnr. Olenn & Penza, Providence, 1982—. Mem. R.I. Bar Assn. (chmn. bench/bar com. 1985—), R.I. Trial Lawyers Assn. (v.p. 1986, bd. govs. 1984—), R.I. Amateur Softball Assn. (pres. 1980—), Nat. Amateur Softball Assn. (council mem.). Avocations: softball, racquetball. Federal civil litigation, Personal injury, General practice. Office: Olenn & Penza 1246 Chalkstone Ave Providence RI 02908

PEPE, LOUIS ROBERT, lawyer; b. Derby, Conn., Mar. 7, 1943; s. Louis F. and Mildred R. (Vollaro) P.; m. Carole Anita Roman, June 8, 1969; children—Marissa Lee, Christopher Justin, Alexander Drew. B.Mgmt.Engring., Rensselaer Poly. Inst., 1964, M.S., 1967; J.D. with distinction, Cornell U., 1970. Bar: Conn. 1970, U.S. Dist. Ct. Conn. 1970, U.S. Ct. Appeals (2d cir.) 1971, U.S. Supreme Ct. 1975, U.S. Ct. Claims 1978. Assoc., Alcorn, Bakewell & Smith, Hartford, Conn., 1970-75, ptnr., 1975-82; sr. ptnr. Pepe & Hazard, Hartford, 1983—; adj. assoc. prof. Hartford Grad. Ctr., 1972—. Mem. New Hartford Planning and Zoning Commn., 1973-84, chmn., 1980-84; mem. New Hartford Inland Wetlands Commn., 1975-78, New Hartford Housing Authority, 1971-72. Served to 1st lt., U.S. Army, 1964-66. Decorated Army Commendation Medal; recipient Frazer prize and Robinson Moot Ct. award Cornell U., 1970. Mem. ABA, Conn. Bar Assn., Hartford County Bar Assn., Am. Legion, Cath. War Vets., Phi Kappa Phi. Construction, Federal civil litigation, State civil litigation. Home: 3 Metacom Dr Simsbury CT 06070 Office: One Corporate Center Hartford CT 06103

PEPER, CHRISTIAN BAIRD, lawyer; b. St. Louis, Dec. 5, 1910; s. Clarence F. and Christine (Baird) P.; m. Ethel C. Kingsland, June 5, 1935; children—Catherine K. (Mrs. Kenneth B. Larson), Anne C. (Mrs. John M. Perkins), Christian B. A.B. cum laude, Harvard, 1932; LL.B., Washington U., 1935; LL.M. (Sterling fellow), Yale, 1937. Bar: Mo. bar 1934. Since practiced in St. Louis; partner Peper, Martin, Jensen, Maichel & Hetlage.; Lectr. various subjects Washington U. Law Sch., St. Louis, 1943-61; partner A.G. Edwards & Sons, 1945-67; pres. St. Charles Gas Corp., 1953-72; chmn. St. Louis Steel Casting Inc., Hydraulic Press Brick Co.; pres. Tricor Drilling Co. Editor: An Historian's Conscience: The Correspondence of Arnold J. Toynbee and Columba Cary-Elwes, 1986. Contbr. articles to profl. jours. Mem. vis. com. Harvard Div. Sch., 1964-70; trustee St. Louis Art Mus.; bd. dirs. Chatham House Found. Mem. Am., Mo., St. Louis bar assns., Order of Coif, Phi Delta Phi. Roman Catholic. Clubs: Noonday, University Harvard (St. Louis); East India (London). General corporate, Estate planning, Securities. Home: 1454 Mason Rd Saint Louis MO 63131 Office: 720 Olive St Saint Louis MO 63101

PEPPER, ALLAN MICHAEL, lawyer; b. Bklyn., July 5, 1943; s. Julius and Jeanette (Lasovsky) P.; m. Barbara Benjamin, Aug. 30, 1964; children—Leslie Anne, Joshua Benjamin, Adam Richard, Robert Benjamin. B.A. summa cum laude, Brandeis U., 1964; LL.B. magna cum laude, Harvard U., 1967. Bar: N.Y. 1968, U.S. Dist. Ct. (so. and ea. dists.) N.Y. 1968, U.S. Ct. Appeals (2d cir.) 1968. Law clk. U.S. Ct. Appeals for 2d Circuit, N.Y.C., 1967-68; assoc. Kaye, Scholer, Fierman, Hays & Handler, N.Y.C., 1968-74, ptnr., 1975—; lectr. in field. Mem. exec. com., assoc. nat. chmn. Brandeis U. Alumni Fund, 1979-82, nat. chmn., 1982-85, mem. devel. com. bd. trustees, 1982-85, pres., councillor, 1980—; bd. trustees Brandeis U., 1985—. Recipient Henry Jones-Golda Meier Bnai Brith Youth Services award, 1986; Felix Frankfurter scholar Harvard U. Law Sch., 1964-65; Louis D. Brandeis hon. scholar Brandeis U., 1964. Mem. ABA. Assn. Bar City N.Y. (mem. law firm mgmt. com. 1987—), N.Y. State Bar Assn., Brandeis U. Alumni Assn. (exec. com. 1982-85), Phi Beta Kappa. Democrat. Jewish. Lodge: B'nai B'rith (pres. Henry Jones Lodge 1982-84, mem. Westchester-Putnam council 1982-85, bd. govs. dist. 1, 1985-86). Federal civil litigation, State civil litigation, Antitrust. Address: 425 Park Ave New York NY 10022

PEPPER, JOYCE M., lawyer; b. Chgo., July 23, 1946; d. LaVerne E. and Marian (Hudek) P. B.S. in Journalism, Northwestern U., 1968; M.A. in Journalism, U. Wis., 1970; J.D., DePaul U., 1979. Bar: Ill. 1979, U.S. Dist. Ct. (no. dist.) Ill. 1979. Copywriter, pub. relations staff AT&T, Chgo., 1970-72; editor, speech writer, Sears Roebuck and Co., Chgo., 1973-80, atty., 1980—; asst. sec. Sears Polit. Action Com., Chgo. Mem. ABA, Ill. Bar Assn., Chgo. Bar Assn. Trade practices. Home: 2728 N Hampden Ct Chicago IL 60614 Office: Sears Roebuck and Co Sears Tower Chicago IL 60684

PEPPERMAN, WALTER LEON, II, lawyer; b. Phila., May 8, 1939; s. Maurice Leon and Dorothea Meta (Nendel) P.; m. Susanne Patricia Mahoney, June 17, 1961; children: Richard Carl II, Jennifer Leigh, Victoria Bozeman. BS in Econs., U. Pa., 1961, LLB, 1967. Bar: Del. 1967, U.S. Dist. Ct. Del. 1967, U.S. Ct. Appeals (3d cir.) 1970, U.S. Supreme Ct. 1979, U.S. Ct. Appeals (4th cir.) 1982, U.S. Ct. Appeals (fed. cir.) 1985. Assoc. Morris, Nichols, Arsht & Tunnell, Wilmington, Del., 1967-72, ptnr., 1972—; mem. spl. com. on interest and trust accounts Del. Supreme Ct., vice chmn. commn. on continuing legal edn., 1987—. Profl. div. chmn. United Way Del., 1982-92; treas. Citizens for Bill Quillen, Del., 1983-84. Served to lt. Supply Corps, USN, 1961-63. Recipient Presdl. Sports award in Jogging and Swimming, Sept. 1973. Mem. ABA (tort and ins. practice sect., litigation sect., others), Def. Research Inst., Am. Trial Lawyers Assn., Del. State Bar Assn. (chmn. med. and dental legal relations com. 1972-79, chmn. continuing legal edn. com. 1980-82, others), Del. Trial Lawyers Assn. (pres. 1983-84, chmn. continuing legal edn. com. 1981-84). Clubs: Wilmington Trail, Mason-Dixon Trail Systems Inc., Univ., Whist Rodney Sq. Federal civil litigation, State civil litigation. Home: 4000 Valley Green Rd Greenville DE 19807 Office: Morris Nichols Arsht & Tunnell 12th & Market St PO Box 1347 Wilmington DE 19899

PEPYNE, EDWARD WALTER, lawyer, former educator; b. Springfield, Mass., Dec. 27, 1925; s. Walter Henry and Frances A. (Carroll) P.; m. Carol Jean Dutcher, Aug. 2, 1958; children—Deborah, Edward, Jr., Susan, Byron, Shari, Randy, David, Allison, Jennifer. B.A., Am. Internat. Coll., 1948; M.S., U. Mass., 1951, Ed.D., 1968; postgrad., NYU, 1952-55; prof. diploma, U. Conn., 1964; J.D., Western New Eng. Coll., 1978. Bar: Mass. 1978, U.S. Supreme Ct. 1981. Prin., tchr. Gilbertville Grammar Sch., Hardwick, Mass., 1948-49; sch. counselor West Springfield High Sch., Mass., 1949-53; instr. NYU, 1953-54; supt. schs. New Shoreham, R.I., 1954-56; asst. prof. edn. Mich. State U., 1956-58; sch. psychologist, guidance dir. Pub. Sch. System, East Long, Mass., 1958-62; lectr. Westfield State Coll., 1961-65; dir. pupil services Chicopee Pub. Sch., 1965-68; assoc. prof. counselor edn. U. Hartford, West Hartford, Mass., 1968-71, prof., 1971-85, dir. Inst. Coll. Counselors Minority and Low Income Students, 1971-72, dir. Div. Human Services, 1972-77; cons. Aetna Life & Casualty Co., Hartford, 1962-75; hearing officer Conn. State Bd. Edn., 1980—; exec. dir. Sinapi Assocs., 1959-78; practice law 1978—. Co-author: Better Driving, 1958; assoc. editor: Highway Safety and Driver Education, 1954; chmn. editorial com.: Man and the Motor Car, 5th edit., 1954; contbr. numerous articles to profl. jours. Chief Welfare Services Civil Defense, Levittown, N.Y., 1953-54; chmn. Ashfield Planning Bd., Mass., 1979-83; moderator Town of Ashfield, 1980-81, town counsel, Charlemont, Mass., 1983-84. ; mem. Am. Personnel and Guidance Assn., New Eng. Personnel and Guidance Conf. (dir.), New Eng. Ednl. Research Orgn. (pres. 1971), Am. Assn. Sch. Adminstrs., ABA, Mass. Bar Assn., Mass. Acad. Trial Attys., Am. Psychol. Assn., Am. Ednl. Research Assn., Phi Delta Kappa. Legal education, General practice, Administrative and regulatory. Home: PO Box 31 Suburban Dr Ashfield MA 01330 Office: Suburban Dr PO Box 345 Ashfield MA 01330

PERCELL, MARION, lawyer; b. N.Y.C., June 14, 1953; d. Daniel and Pauline (Friedman) P. BA in Anthropology, Rutgers U., 1975; JD, Seton Hall U., 1980. Bar: N.J. 1980, U.S. Dist. Ct. N.J. 1980, U.S. Ct. Appeals (3d cir.) 1986. Assoc. Lowenstein, Sandler et al, Roseland, N.J., 1980-85; asst. U.S. atty. U.S. Attys. Office, Newark, 1985—. Mem. ABA, N.J. Bar Assn., Essex County Bar Assn., Soc. for Edn. of Am. Sailors. Avocations: sailing, computers, cooking. Appellate-federal criminal appeals. Home: 78 Grove Ave Verona NJ 07044 Office: US Attys Office 970 Broad St Newark NJ 07102

PERCHIK, JERROLD R., lawyer; b. Louisville, Aug. 30, 1957; s. Sidney and Shirley Jeane (Goldberg) P. BA in Acctg., U. Ky., 1979; JD, U. Louisville, 1982. Bar: Ky. 1982, U.S. Dist. Ct. (ea. and we. dists.) Ky. 1982, U.S. Ct. Appeals (6th cir.) 1982. Assoc. Goldberg & Simpson, Louisville, 1982—. Gen. counsel, bd. dirs. Heritage Corp. Louisville, 1984—; bd. dirs., vice chmn. Discover Louisville Orch., 1985—; bd. dirs. Jewish Family and Vocational Service, Louisville, 1986—. Mem. Assn. Trial Lawyers Am., Ky. Acad. Trial Lawyers, Young Lawyers Club. Avocations: golf, tennis, reading. Contracts commercial, Construction, Labor. Office: Goldberg & Simpson PSC 2800 1st Nat Tower Louisville KY 40202

PERER, ALAN HARVEY, lawyer; b. Pitts., Mar. 30, 1948; s. Herbert Leonard and Beatirce (Taper) P.; m. Diane Wilson, Feb. 26, 1977; children: Langley Wilson, Abby Rose. Student, Washington and Jefferson Coll., 1966-69; BA, U. Pitts., 1973, JD, 1976. Bar: Pa. 1976, U.S. Ct. Appeals (3d cir.) 1976. Assoc. Scott, Swensen & Scott, Pitts., 1976-80; ptnr. Swensen & Perer, Pitts., 1980—. Pres., bd. dirs. Pitts. Hearing Speech and Deaf Services Inc., 1979-86. Mem. Pa. Bar Assn. (chmn. person injury com. 1986—), Allegheny County Bar Assn., Pa. Def. Inst. (bd. dirs. 1979-85), U. Pitts. Law Alumni Assn. (bd. dirs. 1984—), Pitts. Athletic Assn. Democrat. Jewish. Personal injury, State civil litigation, Federal civil litigation. Home: 1515 Beechwood Blvd Pittsburgh PA 15217 Office: Swensen & Perer 2201 Lawyers Bldg Pittsburgh PA 15219

PERER, DIANE WILSON, lawyer; b. Rochester, N.Y., Nov. 14, 1946; d. Edward Silvers and Leona (Albright) Wilson; m. Alan H. Perer, Feb. 26, 1977; Langley. AB, Vassar Coll., 1968; JD, U. Pa., 1967. Bar: Pa., U.S. Dist. Ct. (we. dist.) Pa., U.S. Ct. Appeals (3d cir.). Ptnr. Reed, Smith, Shaw & McClay, Pitts., 1976—. Bd. dirs. Pitts. Hearing Speech and Deaf Services, 1980—, Shady Ln. Sch., Pitts., 1984—. Mem. Allegheny County Bar Assn., U. Pa. Law Alumni Assn. (gov. 1981—). Republican. Club: Pitts. Athletic. Assn. Federal civil litigation, State civil litigation, Family and matrimonial. Office: Reed Smith Shaw & McClay 435 6th Ave Pittsburgh PA 15219

PERERA, LAWRENCE THACHER, lawyer; b. Boston, June 23, 1935; s. Guido R. and Faith (Phillips) P.; m. Elizabeth A. Wentworth, July 5, 1961; children: Alice V., Caroline F., Lucy E., Lawrence Thacher. B.A., Harvard U., 1957, LL.B., 1961. Bar: Mass. 1961, U.S. Supreme Ct. 1973. Clk. Judge R. Ammi Cutter, Mass. Supreme Jud. Ct., Boston, 1961-62; asso. firm Palmer & Dodge, Boston, 1962-69; partner Palmer & Dodge, 1969-74; judge Middlesex County Probate Ct., East Cambridge, Mass., 1974-79; partner firm Hemenway & Barnes, Boston, 1979—; faculty Nat. Jud. Coll., Reno; v.p. Mass. Continuing Legal Edn. Inc. Chmn. Boston Fin. Commn., 1969-71; overseer Peter Bent Brigham Hosp., Boston; chmn. Boston Opera Assn.; chmn. Back Bay Archtl. Commn., 1966-72; trustee WGBH Ednl. Found., Boston Athenaeum, The Boston Found. Fellow Am. Acad. Matrimonial Lawyers, Am. Coll. Probate Counsel; mem. Am. Law Inst., ABA, Mass., Boston bar assns., Am. Bar Found., Mass. Bar Found., Met. Opera Assn. Probate, Family and matrimonial, General practice. Home: 18 Marlborough St Boston MA 01116 Office: 60 State St Boston MA 02116

PERESICH, STEPHEN G., lawyer; b. New Orleans, Dec. 27, 1954; s. Giles H. and Beatrice (Bisso) P.; m. Ellen Burton, June 8, 1985; 1 child, Sharon M. BS, Miss. State U., 1977; JD, U. Miss., 1981. Assoc. Page, Mannino & Peresich, Biloxi, Miss., 1981-85, ptnr., 1986—. Mem. ABA, Miss. Bar Assn., Assn. Trial Lawyers Am., Biloxi Jaycees. Lodges: Rotary, Elks. Insurance, Personal injury, General practice. Office: Page Mannino & Peresich 111 W Howard Hall Biloxi MS 39533

PEREYRA-SUAREZ, CHARLES ALBERT, lawyer; b. Paysandu, Uruguay, Sept. 7, 1947; came to U.S., 1954, naturalized, 1962; s. Hector and Esther (Enriquez-Sarano) P.-S.; m. Susan H. Cross, Dec. 30, 1983. BA in History magna cum laude, Pacific Union Coll., 1970; postgrad., UCLA, 1970-71; JD, U. Calif., Berkeley, 1975. Bar: Calif. 1975, D.C. 1980. Staff atty. Western Ctr. Law and Poverty, Inc., Los Angeles, 1976; trial atty. civil rights div. U.S. Dept. Justice, Washington, 1976-79; asst. U.S. atty., criminal div. U.S. Dept. Justice, Los Angeles, 1979-82; sr. litigation assoc. Gibson, Dunn & Crutcher, Los Angeles, 1982-84; sole practice Los Angeles, 1984-86; ptnr. McKenna, Conner & Cuneo, Los Angeles, 1986—. Democrat. Mem. Seventh Day Adventist Ch. Federal civil litigation, State civil litigation, Criminal. Office: McKenna Conner & Cuneo 3435 Wilshire Blvd Suite 2800 Los Angeles CA 90010

PEREZ, DAVID WILLIAM, lawyer; b. Bennington, Vt., July 23, 1956; s. Louis Celestino and Grace Esther (Rogge) P.; m. Haydee Perez, Aug. 12, 1978; children: Christina Lorraine, Robin Gail. BA, Macalester Coll., 1978; JD, U. Minn., 1982. Bar: Wis. 1982, U.S. Dist. Ct. (ea. dist.) Wis. 1982. Atty. Northwestern Mut. Life, Milw., 1982-85, sr. atty., 1985-87, asst. gen. counsel, 1987—. Vol. Mutual Friends, Milw., 1984-86; legal staff Badger Boys State, Ripon, Wis., 1984. Mem. ABA, Wis. Bar Assn., Milw. Young Lawyers Assn. (vol. lawyers project, Outstanding Service by an Individual Atty. award 1985), Am. Corp. Counsel Assn. Avocations: running, racquetball, cross-country skiing. Administrative and regulatory, Insurance. Office: Northwestern Mut Life 720 E Wisconsin Ave Milwaukee WI 53202

PEREZ, LUIS ALBERTO, lawyer; b. Havana, Cuba, Dec. 22, 1956; came to U.S., 1961; s. Alberto and Estela (Hernandez) P. BBA cum laude, Loyola U., New Orleans, 1978, JD, 1981. Bar: La. 1981, U.S. Dist. Ct. (ea. and mid. dists.) La. 1981, U.S. Ct. Appeals (5th and 11th cirs.) 1981, U.S. Dist. Ct. (we. dist.) La. 1983; cert. notary pub., La. Ptnr. Adams and Reese, New Orleans, 1981—. Mem. ABA, La. Bar Assn., Hispanic Lawyers Assn., Beta Gamma Sigma. Avocations: scuba diving, racquetball. Federal civil litigation, Contracts commercial, General corporate. Office: Adams and Reese 4500 One Shell Sq New Orleans LA 70139

PEREZ, RICHARD LEE, lawyer; b. Los Angeles, Nov. 17, 1946; s. Salvador Navarro and Shirley Mae (Selbrede) P.; m. Janice May Smart, July 20, 1970; children: Kristina, Kevin, Ryan. BA, UCLA, 1968; JD, U. Calif., Berkeley, 1971. Bar: U.S. Dist. Ct. (no. dist.) Calif. 1974, U.S. Ct. Appeals (9th cir.) 1974, U.S. Dist. Ct. (ea. dist.) Calif. 1982, U.S. Dist. Ct. (no. dist.) Tex. 1984. Assoc. McCutchen, Doyle, Brown & Enersen, San Francisco, 1972-74, John R. Hetland, Orinda, Calif., 1974-75; ptnr. Lempres & Wulsfberg, Oakland, Calif., 1975-82, Perez, McNabb & Cook, Orinda, 1982—; mem. adv. bd. Computer Litigation Reporter, Washington, 1982-85, Boult Hall High Tech. Law Jour., 1984—. Assoc. editor U. Calif. Law Rev., 1970-71. Served to capt. U.S. Army, 1968-79. Mem. ABA, Alameda County Bar Assn., Contra Costa County Bar Assn. Computer, Federal civil litigation, State civil litigation. Office: Perez McNabb & Cook 140 Brookwood Orinda CA 94563

PEREZ-GIMENEZ, JUAN MANUEL, judge; b. San Juan, P.R., Mar. 28, 1941; s. Francisco and Elisa (Gimenez) P.; m. Carmen R. Ramirez, July 16, 1964; children: Carmen E., Juan C., Jorge E., Jose A., Magdalena. B.B.A., U. P.R., 1963, J.D., 1968; M.B.A., George Washington U., 1965. Bar: P.R. 1968. Mem. firm Goldman, Antonetti & Davila, San Juan, P.R., 1968-71; U.S. atty. San Juan, 1971-75, U.S. magistrate, 1975-79; chief judge U.S. Dist. Ct. P.R., San Juan, 1979—. Mem. Am. Bar Assn., Fed. Bar Assn., Colegio de Abogados. Roman Catholic. Office: US Courthouse PO Box 3671 Old San Juan Station San Juan PR 00904 *

PERGAM, ALBERT STEVEN, lawyer; b. N.Y.C., Dec. 23, 1938; s. Irving and Gertrude (Newman) P.; m. Natalie J. Chaliff, Aug. 14, 1965; children—Ilana N., Elizabeth A. B.A. summa cum laude, Yale U., 1960; postgrad., St. John's Coll., Cambridge, Eng., 1960-61; LL.B. magna cum laude, Harvard U., 1964. Bar: N.Y. 1965. Law clk. to judge U.S. Ct. Appeals (2d cir.), 1964-65; spl. asst., asst. atty. gen. civil rights div. U.S. Dept. Justice, Washington, 1965-66; assoc. firm Cleary, Gottlieb, Steen & Hamilton, N.Y.C., 1966-72; ptnr. Cleary, Gottlieb, Steen & Hamilton, 1973—; resident ptnr Cleary, Gottlieb, Steen & Hamilton, London, 1980-84. Contbr. chpt. on Eurobonds to International Capital Markets and Securities Regulation, 1983, Legal Dimensions of Eurobond Financing, 1983; editorial advisor and contbr. Internat. Fin. Law Review. Mem. ABA, Internat. Bar Assn., N.Y. State Bar Assn., Assn. Bar City N.Y., Phi Beta Kappa. Clubs: Elihu (New Haven); Yale (N.Y.C.); United Oxford and Cambridge (London). General corporate, Private international. Office: Cleary Gottlieb Steen & Hamilton Suite 2700 One State St Plaza New York NY 10004

PERIN, CHARLES HENRY, JR., lawyer; b. Cin., Aug. 15, 1954; s. Charles H. Sr. and Martha H. (Hildenbrand) P.; m. Laurie Koller, June 12, 1982; children: Charles H. III, Edward A. BA, Yale U., 1976; JD, U. Cin., 1980. Bar: Ohio 1980, U.S. Dist. Ct. (so. dist.) Ohio 1980, U.S. Ct. Appeals (6th cir.) 1986. Staff atty. Community Mut. Ins. Co., Cin., 1980-86, mgr., legal advisor corp. appeals dept., 1986—. Mem. ABA, Ohio Bar Assn., Cin. Bar Assn., Nat. Health Lawyers Assn. Republican. Roman Catholic. Insurance, Health, State civil litigation. Home: 3135 Lookout Circle Cincinnati OH 45208 Office: Community Mut Ins Co 1351 William Howard Taft Rd Cincinnati OH 45206

PERKIEL, MITCHEL H., lawyer; b. N.Y.C., Oct. 26, 1949; s. Frank and Ella Perkiel; m. Lois E. Perkiel, June 24, 1984; 1 child, Joshua L. BA, SUNY, Stony Brook, 1971; JD, New York Law Sch., 1974. Bar: N.Y. 1975, U.S. Dist. Ct. (so. and ea. dists.) N.Y. 1975, U.S. Ct. Appeals (2d cir.) 1975. Law clk. to presiding justice N.Y. County Civil Ct., 1975; assoc. Levin & Weintraub & Crames, N.Y.C., 1975-80, ptnr., 1980—. Notes and comments editor New York Law Rev., 1973-74. Served with USAR, 1969-73. Mem. ABA, Assn. of Bar of City of N.Y., N.Y. County Lawyers Assn. Bankruptcy. Office: Levin Weintraub & Crames 225 Broadway New York NY 10007

PERKINS, DONALD W., lawyer; b. Boston, Oct. 2, 1933; s. Eustace Judson and Ruth (Walker) P.; m. Laures Terry, June 19, 1955; children—Donald W. Jr., David J., Terry. A.B. summa cum laude with honors in Econs., Tufts U., 1955; J.D., Harvard U., 1961. Bar: Maine 1961, Mass. 1961, U.S. Dist. Ct. Maine 1961, U.S. Ct. Appeals (1st cir.) 1979, U.S. Supreme Ct. 1980. Law clk. to judge U.S. Dist. Ct. Maine, Portland, 1961-62; ptnr. Pierce, Atwood, Scribner, Allen, Smith & Lancaster, Portland, 1965—. Mem. Gov.'s Task Force on Forest Taxation, 1971-72, Gov.'s Task Force on Indian Claims, 1977-78, Speaker's Select Com. on Workmen's Compensation, 1983-84. Served to capt. USMC, 1955-62. Mem. ABA, Assn. Trial Lawyers Am., Maine State Bar Assn., Cumberland County Bar Assn., Phi Beta Kappa. Natural Resources, administrative, Legislative. Home: 136 Oakhurst Rd Cape Elizabeth ME 04107 Office: 1 Monument Sq Portland ME 04101

PERKINS, EUGENE ORAL, lawyer, oil company executive; b. Washington, Ind., July 2, 1923; s. Charles R. and Gladys (Billings) P.; m. Delores S. Student DePaul U., 1941-42; B.S. in Elec. Engring., U. Iowa, 1946; J.D., U. Colo., 1949. Bar: Colo. 1949. Sole practice, Colorado Springs, 1949-68, 85—; sr. ptnr. Perkins, Goodbee & Martin, Colorado Springs, 1968-85; pres. Perkins Oil Co. Served with U.S. Army, Mem. ABA, Colo. Bar Assn., El Paso County Bar Assn., Colo. Cattlemen's Assn. Oriental Ceramic Soc., Am. Quarter Horse Assn., Am. Gelbrieh Assn., Tau Beta Pi, Phi Alpha Delta. Republican. Clubs: Garden of Gods, El Paso, Broadmoor Golf, Balboa. Author booklets on fin. and Chinese art; contbr. articles on fin., horses, racing and Chinese ceramic art to mags., jours. Real property, Probate. Home: 1900 Mesa Ave Colorado Springs CO 80906 Office: 925 Arcturus Dr Colorado Springs CO 80906

PERKINS, GEORGE FOSTER, lawyer; b. Saratoga Springs, N.Y., June 14, 1917; s. Chester Arthur and Grace Pratt (Schirck) P.; m. Margaret Maude Stoddard, May 7, 1949; children—George Foster, George S. (dec.), Steven Scott, Robert Foster. Student Union Coll., 1935-37, Albany Bus. Coll., 1937-38, Siena Coll., 1947-48, LL.B., Albany Law Sch., 1951. Bar: N.Y. 1951, U.S. Dist. Ct. (no. dist.) N.Y. 1956. Assoc., Butler, Kilmer, Hoey & Butler, Saratoga Springs, N.Y., 1951-53, ptnr., 1953-56; sole practice, Saratoga Springs, 1956-81; ptnr. Perkins and Perkins, Saratoga Springs, 1981—; city judge City of Saratoga Springs, 1961-64. Dir. Literacy Vols. Saratoga, 1983-86; trustee, Dist. 6 Sch. Bd., Saratoga Springs; bd. dirs. YMCA, Saratoga Springs, ARC, Saratoga Springs, Saratoga Springs City Ctr. Authority; pres. Saratoga Pony Baseball League, 1970-72. Served to staff sgt. CIC, USAAF, 1942-45. Decorated Bronze Star. Recipient Citizen award Pop Warner Football, 1972, numerous trophies, medals, awards for age-group victories in long distance running, 1977-86; citations N.Y. State and Nat. Vets. of World War I, 1985. Mem. Saratoga County Bar Assn., N.Y. State Bar Assn., N.Y. State Magistrate's Assn. Democrat. Episcopalian. Clubs: Lions, Am. Legion (life), VFW (life; Community Betterment citation 1984), Saratoga Springs C. of C. (dir. 1974-76), AAU. Lodge: Elks (Old Timer of Yr. award 1985). General corporate, Probate, Real property. Home: 18 Excelsior Spring Ave Saratoga Springs NY 12866 Office: Perkins & Perkins 267 Broadway Saratoga Springs NY 12866

PERKINS, JAMES ALLEN, lawyer; b. Oakland, Calif., May 15, 1952; s. Robert Cone Perkins and Doris Jean (Steinberg) Perkins Goltz; m. Barbara

Carol Bellinghausen, Dec. 19, 1983. B.A. with honors, U. Tex., 1975; J.D., St. Mary's U., 1980. Bar: Tex. 1981, U.S. Dist. Ct. (we. dist.) Tex. 1981, (so. dist.) Tex. 1981, U.S. Ct. Appeals (5th cir.) 1982, U.S. Supreme Ct., 1985. Briefing atty. Fourth Ct. Appeals, San Antonio, 1980-81; assoc. Pat Maloney, San Antonio, 1982-84; sole practice, San Antonio, 1984—; mem. adv. bd. Groos Nat. Bank, 1985—; v.p. Bexar County Health Facilities Corp., San Antonio, 1984—; dir. Bexar County Housing Fin. Authority, 1984—; Commr. Precinct 2 Bexar County Commrs. Ct., San Antonio, 1984—; campaign dir. Com. to Elect Rudy Esquivel Assoc. Justice, San Antonio, 1980, Com. to Elect Paul Elizondo County Judge, San Antonio, 1984. Mem. Tex. Bar Assn., Assn. Trial Lawyers Am., ABA, San Antonio Trial Lawyers Assn., Tex. Trial Lawyers Assn. Democrat. Presbyterian. Federal civil litigation, State civil litigation, Workers' compensation. Office: 314 E Commerce Suite 500 San Antonio TX 78205

PERKINS, JAMES BLENN, JR., lawyer; b. Boothbay Harbor, Maine, June 2, 1912; s. James Blenn Sr. and Fannie (Orne) P.; m. Patricia Anne Irwin, June 7, 1941; children: James, Judith, Sarah, Sandra, Thomas. BA, Bowdoin Coll., 1934; JD, Harvard U., 1937. Bar: Maine 1936, U.S. Supreme Ct. 1946, U.S. Dist. Ct. Maine 1949. Pros. atty. Lincoln County, Wiscasset, Maine, 1939-42, 48-63; ptnr. Perkins and Perkins, Boothbay Harbor, Maine, 1948—; master Maine Chancery, Boothbay Harbor, 1950—; commr. Maine Workers Compensation Commn., Augusta, 1963-80. Moderator town meeting Boothbay Harbor, 1948-82; chmn. planning bd. City of Boothbay Harbor; trustee sch. dist. Boothbay Harbor Region, 1954—. Served to pvt. U.S. Army, 1941-42, to comdr. USN, 1942-47. Fellow Am. Coll. Probate Counsel; mem. ABA, Maine Bar Assn., Lincoln County Bar Assn., Am. Judicature Soc., Assn. Trial Lawyers Am., Am. Legion. Republican. Congregationalist. Lodge: Rotary. Probate, Real property, Estate planning. Home: Townsend Ave Boothbay Harbor ME 04538 Office: Perkins & Perkins 27 School St Boothbay Harbor ME 04538

PERKINS, LLOYD WESLEY, lawyer, judge; b. Port Arthur, Tex., Jan. 2, 1927; s. Erwin Otis and Agnes Mary (Watkeys) P.; m. Dorothy May Oglesby, June 2, 1951; children—David Wesley, John Howard, Daniel Jackson. B.A., So. Meth. U., 1950, LL.M., 1974; J.D., U. Tex., 1953. Bar: Tex. 1953, U.S. Dist. Ct. (ea. dist.) Tex. 1958, U.S. Ct. Appeals (5th cir.) 1959, U.S. Supreme Ct. 1960. Asst. city atty. City of Fort Worth, Tex., 1957-58; asst. U.S. dist. atty. U.S. Dist. Ct. (ea. dist.) Tex., Tyler, 1959-63; city atty. City of Sherman, Tex., 1973-76; judge Grayson County Ct. at Law #2, Sherman, 1976—; bd. dirs. Tex. Ctr. for Judiciary Inc., Austin, 1983—. Pres. Texama Valley council Boy Scouts Am., 1972; bd. dir. Texoma Alcohol and Drug Abuse Council, Sherman, 1982—; bd. of ch. and soc. chmn. interpersonal relations North Tex. Conf. United Methodist Ch., Dallas, 1980—. Served with USAAC, 1945-46. Recipient Silver Beaver award Boy Scouts Am., 1975. Fellow State Bar Tex. (life); mem. U.S. Maritime Law Assn., ABA, Phi Alpha Delta. Democrat. Lodges: Kiwanis (pres. 1981-82), Masons. State civil litigation, Criminal, Probate. Home: 1702 N Ridgeway Dr Sherman TX 75090 Office: Grayson County Justice Ctr Sherman TX 75090

PERKINS, MICHAEL DENNIS, lawyer; b. Pitts., Feb. 16, 1953; s. Norman Clark and Agnes Consilium (Taffee) P. BA, U. Mich., 1976; JD, Thomas M. Cooley Law Sch., 1980. Bar: Mich. 1980, U.S. Dist. Ct. (we. and ea. dists.) Mich. 1980. Staff atty. student legal services Mich. State U., East Lansing, 1980-81; law clk. St. Clair County (Mich.) Cir. Ct., Port Huron, 1981-82; asst. pros. atty Genesee County (Mich.) Prosecutor's Office, Flint, 1982—. Precinct del. Genesee County Dem. Conv., Flint, 1976, Mich. Dem.Conv., Detroit, 1976; active Big Bros./Big Sisters of Flint, 1982—. Mem. ABA, Mich. Bar Assn. (criminal law sect.). Avocation: collection of legal humor. Criminal. Home: 521 S Meade Apt 2 Flint MI 48503 Office: Genesee County Prosecutor's Office 100 Courthouse Flint MI 48502

PERKINS, RANDOLPH M., lawyer; b. Geneva, Ill., Sept. 30, 1956; s. Gerald A. and Janice R. (Keel) P.; m. Lynn M. Wenzel. BS, Ill. State U., 1977; JD, U. Ill., 1982. Bar: Ill. 1982, Wis. 1983, U.S. Dist. Ct. (cen. and no. dists.) Ill. 1983, U.S. Ct. Appeals (7th cir.) 1983. Law clk. to presiding justice Ill. Supreme Ct., Bloomington, 1982-83; assoc. Egan & Laird, subs. of Godfrey & Kahn S.C., Green Bay, Wis., 1983-86, Denissen, Krawzush, Mahoney & Ewald, Green Bay, 1986—. Mem. Nat. Trust for Hist. Preservation, 1986—; pres., bd. dirs. Samaritan House, Green Bay, 1986—. Harno fellow U. Ill., 1977. Mem. ABA, Ill. Bar Assn., Wis. Bar Assn., Brown County Bar Assn., Am. Judicature Soc. Republican. Methodist. Avocations: tennis, golf. Real property, Contracts commercial, General corporate. Home: 225 W Mission Rd Green Bay WI 54301 Office: Denissen Krawzush et al PO Box 10597 Green Bay WI 54307-3067

PERKINS, ROGER ALLAN, lawyer; b. Port Chester, N.Y., Mar. 4, 1943; s. Francis Newton and Winifred Marcella (Smith) P.; m. Katherine Louise Howard, Nov. 10, 1984; children—Marshall, Morgan, Matthew, Justin. B.A., Pa. State U., 1965; postgrad. U. Ill. 1965-66; J.D. with honors, George Washington U. 1969. Bar: Md. 1969, Mass. 1975. Trial atty. Nationwide Ins. Co., Annapolis, Md., 1969-72; assoc. Arnold, Beauchemin & Huber, P.A., Balt., 1973; assoc., then ptnr. Goodman & Bloom, P.A., Annapolis, 1973-76; ptnr. Luff and Perkins, Annapolis, 1976-78; sole practice, Annapolis, 1978—; temp. zoning hearing officer Anne Arundel County, 1984—. asst. city atty. Annapolis, 1980-82; atty. Bd. Appeals of City of Annapolis, 1986—. Coach youth sports. Mem. ABA, Md. State Bar Assn. (bd. govs. 1985-87, exec. com. 1986—, sect. delivery local services, chmn. judicare com. 1981-83, family and juvenile law sect. council 1983—, chmn. 1987), Anne Arundel County Bar Assn. (treas. 1981-83, pres. 1984-85). Republican. Methodist. Family and matrimonial, Local government, State civil litigation. Home: 503 Bay Hills Dr Arnold MD 21012 Office: 105 Forbes St PO Box 665 Annapolis MD 21404

PERKINS, ROSWELL BURCHARD, lawyer; b. Boston, May 21, 1926. A.B. cum laude, Harvard U., 1945, LL.B. cum laude, 1949. Bar: Mass. 1949, N.Y. 1949. Assoc. Debevoise, Plimpton & McLean, N.Y.C., 1949-53; ptnr. Debevoise & Plimpton, and predecessor firms, N.Y.C., 1957—; asst. sec. HEW, 1954-56; counsel to Gov. Nelson A. Rockefeller, State of N.Y., 1959; asst. counsel spl. subcom. Senate Commerce Com. to investigate organized crime in interstate commerce, 1950; chmn. N.Y.C. Mayor's Task Force on Transp. Reorgn., 1966; mem. Pres.'s Adv. Panel on Personnel Interchange, 1968; chmn. adv. com. Medicare Adminstrn. Contracting Subcom. HEW, 1973-74; dir. Fiduciary Trust Co. N.Y., 1963—; trustee Bowery Savs. Bank, 1975-82. Mem. N.Y. Lawyers Com. Civil Rights, 1970-73; mem. nat. exec. com., 1973—, co-chmn., 1973-75; mem. adv. council Woodrow Wilson Sch. Pub. and Internat. Affairs, Princeton U., 1967-69; bd. dirs. The Commonwealth Fund, 1974—; bd. dirs. Sch. Am. Ballet, 1974-85, chmn. bd., 1976-80; dir., sec. N.Y. Urban Coalition, 1967-74; trustee Pomfret Sch., 1961-76; The Brearley Sch., 1969-75; dir. Salzburg Seminar Am. Studies, 1970—; mem. overseers vis. com. Kennedy Sch. Govt., Harvard U., 1971-77, Harvard and Radcliffe Colls., 1958-64, 1971-77. Mem. ABA (commn. on law and economy 1975-79), N.Y. State Bar Assn., Assn. Bar City of N.Y. (chmn. spl. com. on fed. conflict of interest laws 1958-60), Assn. Harvard Alumni (pres. 1970-71), Am. Law Inst. (mem. council 1969, pres. 1980—), Am. Arbitration Assn. (bd. dirs. 1966-71). Author: The New Federal Conflict of Interest Law; editor Harvard Law Rev. Home: 1120 Fifth Ave New York NY 10128 Office: Debevoise & Plimpton 875 3rd Ave New York NY 10022

PERKINS, STEVEN CURTIS, law librarian, law professor; b. Cin., May 1, 1949; s. Denval and Mary Ruth (Ball) P.; m. Carol J. Fritzler-Becker, June 7, 1985; 1 stepchild, Vanessa Becker. BA in Fgn. Affairs magna cum laude, U. Cin., 1976, JD, 1979; LLM, U. Denver, 1983. Bar: Ohio 1979. Reference librarian U. Cin. Coll. of Law, 1979-82, U. Denver Coll. of Law, 1982-83; assoc. librarian U. Cin. Coll. of Law, 1983-84; reference librarian U. Denver Coll. of Law, 1982-83; librarian N.Y. Joint Internat. Law Program, N.Y.C., 1984-85; dir. library, asst. prof. law Western State U. Coll. of Law, Fullerton, Calif., 1985—; librarian collection Urban Morgan Inst. for Human Rights, Cin., 1979-85. Served with M.I. Corps, U.S. Army, 1968-71. Mem. ABA, Am. Assn. Law Libraries, So. Calif. Assn. Law Libraries, Am. Legal Studies Assn. Baptist. Avocations: computers, foreign languages, kayaking, genealogy. Librarianship, Public international, Legal history. Home: 300 Canyon Country Brea CA 92621 Office: Western State U Coll of Law 1111 N State Coll Blvd Fullerton CA 92631

PERKINSON, MAURICE LEON, lawyer; b. Georgetown, Ky., Mar. 18, 1932; s. Ova Dow and Mary (Powers) P.; m. Barbara Jane Zuver, June 12, 1955; children: Sharon Lynn, Sandra Jane Perkinson Brown. BBA, U. Miami, 1958; JD, U. Louisville, 1963. Bar: Ky. 1963, U.S. Dist. Ct. (ea. and we. dists.) Ky., U.S. Supreme Ct. 1972. Sole practice LaGrange, Ky., 1963—; atty. City of LaGrange, 1964-66, Oldham County, Ky., 1972. Mem. Friends of Library, LaGrange; pres. LaGrange PTA, 1967, Oldham County Jr. High Sch. PTA, 1970; chmn. Oldham County ARC, 1965, Oldham County Dem. Party, 1972-75. Served with U.S. Army, 1952-55, Korea. Mem. ABA, Assn. Trial Lawyers Am., Ky. Bar Assn., Ky. Acad. Trial Lawyers, Louisville Bar Assn. Republican. Lodge: Rotary (sec. LaGrange 1966). Federal civil litigation, State civil litigation, General practice. Home: 400 Kentucky St LaGrange KY 40031 Office: 113 E Main St LaGrange KY 40031

PERLAH, PHILIP MICHAEL, lawyer; b. Bklyn., Oct. 16, 1945; s. Arnold B. and Sylvia L. (Zaldin) P.; m. Lois Brandeis, June 15, 1968; children: Steven R., Robin E. BS, Bklyn. Coll., 1966; JD, Fordham U., 1969. Bar: N.Y. 1970. Atty. IBM Corp., Armonk, N.Y., 1969-71; atty. Chesebrough-Pond's Inc., Westport, Conn., 1971-75, st. atty., 1975-83, sr. counsel, 1983—. Mng. editor Fordham U. Law Rev., 1968-69. Mem. Westchester-Fairfield Corp. Counsel Assn. (treas. internat. com. 1985—). General corporate, Private international, Securities. Office: Chesebrough-Ponds Inc Nyala Farm Rd Westport CT 06881-0851

PERLBERG, JULES MARTIN, lawyer; b. Chgo., Jan. 28, 1931; s. Maurice and Louise Mae (Schonberger) P.; m. Dora Ann Morris, Dec. 22, 1968; children: Julia, Michael. B.B.A., U. Mich., 1952, J.D., 1957. Bar: Ill. 1958, D.C. 1964; C.P.A., Ill. Acct. Arthur Andersen & Co., Chgo., 1954-55; faculty U. Mich. Law Sch., Ann Arbor, 1957-58; assoc. Sidley & Austin and predecessor firm, Chgo., 1958-65, ptnr., 1966—. Mem. Glencoe Bd. Edn., (Ill.), 1980—, pres., 1985-86; bd. dirs. Juvenile Diabetes Found., Chgo., 1981—; v.p. Juvenile Diabetes Found, Chgo., 1983-85; exec. bd. Am. Jewish Com., Chgo., 1978—, v.p., 1981-83. Served as 1st lt. U.S. Army, 1952-54. Recipient Gold medal Ill. Soc. C.P.A.s, 1955. Mem. ABA, Chgo. Bar Assn. Clubs: Legal, Law; Mid-Day (Chgo.). Administrative and regulatory, Antitrust, Public utilities. Home: 568 Westley Rd Glencoe IL 60022 Office: Sidley & Austin 1 First Nat Plaza Chicago IL 60603

PERLIN, MARC GERALD, law educator; b. Brookline, Mass., July 15, 1948; s. James J. and Gladys (Goodman) P.; m. Linda S. Karras, Sept. 6, 1970; children: Robyn, Andrea. BA, Boston U., 1970; JD, Northeastern U., 1973. Bar: Mass. 1973. Law clk. to justices Superior Ct. Mass., Boston, 1973-74; legal asst. to chief justice Boston Mcpl. Ct., 1974-75; instr. Suffolk U. Law Sch., Boston, 1975-77, asst. prof., 1977-79, assoc. prof. law, 1979-83, prof. law, 1983—; lectr. Northeastern U. Sch. Law, Boston, 1974-76, Josephson Kluwer Legal Ednl. Ctrs., Culver City, Calif., 1981—; cons. treasury dept. City of Boston; mem. bd. of experts Lawyers Alert, Boston, 1984—. Author: Essential Principles of Family Law, 1984; Co-author: Handbook of Civil Procedure in the Massachusetts District Courts, 1980, Masssachusetts Collection Law, 1984; editor Massachusetts Rules Service, 1980. Mem. Gov.'s Commn. on Child Support, Mass., 1985. Mem. ABA, Am. Arbitration Assn., Mass. Bar Assn., Norfolk County Bar Assn. Legal education. Home: 10 Fawn Circle Randolph MA 02368 Office: Suffolk U Law Sch 41 Temple St Boston MA 02114

PERLIS, MICHAEL FREDRICK, lawyer; b. N.Y.C., June 3, 1947; s. Leo and Betty F. (Gantz) P.; children—Amy Hannah, David Matthew. B.S. in Fgn. Service, Georgetown U., 1968, J.D., 1971. Bar: D.C. 1971, U.S. Dist. Ct. D.C. 1971, U.S. Ct. Appeals 1971, D.C. Ct. Appeals 1971, Calif. 1980, U.S. Dist. Ct. (no. dist.) Calif. 1980, U.S. Ct. Appeals (9th cir.) 1980, U.S. Supreme Ct., 1980. Law clerk D.C. Ct. Appeals, Washington, 1971-72; asst. corp. counsel D.C., Washington, 1972-74; counsel U.S. SEC, div. enforcement, Washington, 1974-75, br. chief, 1975-77, asst. dir., 1977-80; ptnr. Pettit & Martin, San Francisco, 1980—; adj. prof. Cath. U. Am., 1979-80. Mem. ABA (co-chmn. subcom. securities and commodities litigation 1982-83), D.C. Bar Assn., Calif. State Bar Assn., San Francisco Bar Assn. Federal civil litigation, General corporate. Office: Pettit & Martin 101 California St San Francisco CA 94111

PERLMAN, BRUCE MICHAEL, lawyer; b. New Rochelle, N.Y., Nov. 14, 1957; s. Marcel Isaac and Renee Margerie (August) P.; m. Pamela Jane Galis, Aug. 8, 1982. BA cum laude, Brandeis U., 1979; JD, Boston U., 1982. Bar: Conn. 1982, U.S. Dist. Ct. Conn. 1982, U.S. Tax Ct. 1982. Assoc. Bergman, Horowitz, Reynolds & DeSarbo, New Haven, Conn., 1982-84, Slavitt, Connery & Vardamis, Norwalk, Conn., 1984—. Mem. ABA (tax sect.), Conn. Bar Assn., Norwalk/Wilton Bar Assn. , Acad. Model Aeronautics. Jewish. Avocations: bldg. and flying model helicopters, scuba diving. Personal income taxation, Real property, State civil litigation. Office: Slavitt Connery & Vardamis 618 West Ave Norwalk CT 06852

PERLMAN, HARVEY STUART, lawyer, educator; b. Lincoln, Nebr., Jan. 17, 1942; s. Floyd Ted and Rosalyn (Lashinsky) P.; m. Susan G. Unthank, Aug. 27, 1966; children: Anne, Amy. B.A., U. Nebr., 1963, J.D., 1966. Bar: Nebr. 1966, Va. 1980. Teaching fellow U. Chgo. Law Sch., 1966-67; mem. faculty U. Nebr. Sch. Law, 1967-74, prof., 1972-74; prof. law U. Va., Charlottesville, 1974-83; dean law U. Nebr., Lincoln, 1983—; exec. dir. Nebr. Commn. on Law Enforcement. Author: (with Edmund Kitch) Legal Regulation of the Competitive Process, 1972, 79, 86; asso. editor: Jour. Law and Human Behavior, 1974-86. Named Ida Beam Distinguished Vis. Prof. Law, U. Iowa, 1981-86. Mem. Am. Bar Assn., Nebr. Bar Assn., Law-Psychology Assn., Am. Law Inst. Personal injury, Trademark and copyright. Office: U Nebr Coll Law Lincoln NE 68588

PERLMAN, JERALD LEE, lawyer; b. Baton Rouge, Feb. 25, 1947; s. Ralph Robert and Carol Mayer (Herzberg) P.; m. Francine Yvonne McKelvey, May 8, 1984; children: Louise, Lee, Kevin. BA, Washington & Lee U., 1969; JD, La. State U., 1972. Bar: La. 1972, U.S. Dist. Ct. (we. dist.) La. 1972. Assoc. Blanchard, Walker, O'Quin & Roberts, Shreveport, La., 1972-76; ptnr. Blanchard, Walker, O'Quin & Roberts, Shreveport, 1976-83, Walker, Tooke, Perlman & Lyons, Shreveport, 1983—. Assoc. editor La. State U. Law Rev., 1971-72. Bd. dirs. Broadmoor Southside YMCA, Shreveport, 1984-85, vice chmn., 1986, chmn., 1987—; bd. dirs. Shreveport Met. YMCA, 1987—. Served as capt. USAR, 1972. Mem. La. Bar Assn., Shreveport Bar Assn., La. Assn. Def. Counsel (bd. dirs. 1979-81), Order of Coif, Phi Beta Kappa, Omicron Delta Kappa. Democrat. Jewish. Club: Pierremont Oaks Tennis (Shreveport). Avocations: tennis, coaching youth basketball, reading. Personal injury, Insurance. Office: Walker Tooke Perlman & Lyons 1700 Irving Place Shreveport LA 71101

PERLMAN, LAWRENCE, business executive, lawyer; b. St. Paul, Apr. 8, 1938; s. Irving and Ruth (Mirsky) P.; m. Medora Scoll, June 18, 1961; children: David, Sara. B.A., Carleton Coll., 1960; J.D., Harvard U., 1963. Bar: Minn. 1963. Law. clk. for fed. judge 1963; partner firm Fredrikson, Byron, Colborn, Bisbee, Hansen & Perlman, Mpls., 1964-75; gen. counsel, exec. v.p. U.S. pacing ops. Medtronic, Inc., Mpls., 1975-78; sr. partner firm Oppenheimer, Wolff and Donnelly, Mpls., St. Paul, N.Y., Washington, Brussels, 1978-80; sec., gen. counsel, v.p. corp. services Control Data Corp., Mpls., 1980-83; pres., chief operating officer, dir. Comml. Credit Co., 1984-85; pres. Data Storage Products Group, 1985—, pres., exec. v.p., 1986—; bd. dirs. Am. Hoist & Derrick Co., Control Data Corp., Bio-Medicus Corp., Inter-Regional Fin. Group, Inc., The Microelectronics and Computer Tech. Corp.; adj. prof. Law Sch., U. Minn., 1974-76, 79-80. Mem. Mpls. Bd. Estimate and Taxation, 1974-75; chmn. Mpls. Municipal Fin. Commn., 1978-79; bd. dirs. Walker Art Center, 1975-82, Mt. Sinai Hosp., Minn. Orchestral Assn.; trustee Carleton Coll., 1986—; chmn. bd. visitors U. Minn. Law Sch., 1978-80. Mem. Am. Electronics Assn., Phi Beta Kappa. Club: Mpls. General corporate, Private international. Home: 2366 W Lake of the Isles Pkwy Minneapolis MN 55405 Office: Control Data Corp 8100 34th Ave S Minneapolis MN 55440

PERLMAN, RICHARD BRIAN, lawyer; b. N.Y.C., Aug. 19, 1951; s. William H. and Beryl N. (Cohen) P.; m. Virginia Merrill, Aug. 1, 1976; 1 child, Jason Eric. BA, Franklin and Marshall Coll., 1973; JD, Temple U., 1976. Bar: Pa. 1976, U.S. Dist. Ct. (ea. dist.) Pa. 1977, U.S. Supreme Ct. 1982. Assoc. Law Offices of Peter N. Harrison, Doylestown, Pa., 1976-77, Zion & Klein, Bryn Mawr, Pa., 1977-78; founder, owner The Law Ctr., Norristown, Pa., 1978—, West Chester, Pa., 1982—. Pres. Mothers Against Drunk Driving, Chester and Delaware Counties, Pa., 1987—; bd. dirs. Big Bros./Big Sisters, Montgomery County, Pa., 1979-85. Mem. Pa. Bar Assn., Montgomery Bar Assn., Chester County Bar Assn. Avocations: music, classic cars, tennis, travel. Family and matrimonial, Bankruptcy, General practice. Office: The Law Ctr 131 W Market St West Chester PA 19380 also: 528 DeKalb St Norristown PA 19401

PERLMUTH, WILLIAM ALAN, lawyer; b. N.Y.C., Nov. 21, 1929; s. Charles and Roe (Schneider) P.; m. Loretta Kaufman; children: Carolyn, Diane. AB, Wilkes Coll., 1951; LLB, Columbia U., 1953. Bar: N.Y. 1954. Assoc. Cravath, Swaine & Moore, N.Y.C., 1955-61; ptnr. Stroock & Stroock & Lavan, N.Y.C., 1962—; bd. dirs. Knogo Corp., Hicksville, N.Y. Editor Columbia U. Law Rev., 1952-53. Trustee Aeroflex Found., N.Y.C., 1965—, Harkness Ballet Found., N.Y.C., 1975—, Wilkes Coll., Wilkes-Barre, Pa., 1980—, Hosp. for Joint Diseases Orthopaedic Inst., N.Y.C., 1980—, Weininger Found., 1985—. Served to sgt. U.S. Army, 1953-55. Mem. N.Y. State Bar Assn., Assn. of Bar of City of N.Y. Jewish. Clubs: The Downtown Assn., The Wall St. (N.Y.C.). General corporate, Securities, Private international. Home: 880 Fifth Ave New York NY 10021 Office: Stroock & Stroock & Lavan 7 Hanover Sq New York NY 10004-2594

PERLMUTTER, JEROME ALAN, lawyer; b. Montclair, N.J., Apr. 8, 1940; s. William and Anna Florence (Rawitz) P.; m. Vivian Edith Lyons, June 17, 1962; children: Karen, Susan. BS in Econs., U. Pa., 1962; LLB, Columbia U., 1965. Bar: N.Y. 1965. Assoc. Delson & Gordon, N.Y.C., 1965-72; sr. corp. counsel Wickes Cos. Inc., N.Y.C., 1973—. Mem. ABA, Assn. of Bar of City of N.Y. General corporate, Labor. Home: 19 Wood Glen Way Boonton NJ 07005 Office: Wickes Cos Inc 1285 6th Ave New York NY 10019

PERLMUTTER, MARK L., lawyer; b. June 8, 1949; s. Bernard and Adele (Sampson) P.; m. Diane Ireson, June 19, 1971 (div. 1983); children: Eric, Lindsay. BS in Speech, Northwestern U., 1971; JD, U. Tex., 1974. Bar: TEx. 1974, U.S. Ct. Appeals (5th cir.) 1975, U.S. Dist. Ct. (we. dist.) Tex. 1979. Asst. atty. gen. Honors Program, Austin, 1974-75; asst. comptroller field of ops. State Comptroller's Office, Austin, 1975-77; assoc. Hilgers, Watkins & Kazen, Austin, 1977-81, Doggett, Jacks, Marston & Perlmutter P.C., Austin, 1981—. Contbr. articles to profl. jours. Chmn. bd. adjustment, Austin, 1976, John Hill Right for Tex. com., Austin, 1978; mem. adv. bd. Austin Dem. Forum, 1981. Named one of Outstanding Young Men Am., 1979. Mem. Tex. Bar Assn. (Tex. bd. legal specialization, civil trial law sect. 1984), Travis County Bar Assn. (bd. dirs. 1980-81), Tex. Trial Lawyers Assn., Austin Young Lawyers Assn. (pres. 1980-81). Federal civil litigation, State civil litigation, Personal injury. Home: 2202 Woodmont Austin TX 78703 Office: Doggett Jacks Marston & Perlmutter PC 1206 San Antonio Austin TX 78701

PERLOS, ALEXANDER CHARLES, judge; b. Bitola, Yugoslavia, July 15, 1930; came to U.S. 1940, naturalized, 1951; s. Charles G. and Anastasia (Prchevich) P.; m. Ruth Apkarian, 1955; children: Charles A., Mark N., Pamela Honer Perlos, Alexander C. II. BA, Mich. State U., 1953; JD, U. Wis., 1957. Bar: Wis. 1957, Mich. 1957. Sole practice Jackson, Mich., 1957-60, 67-86; ptnr. Rappleye & Perlos, Jackson, 1961-67; judge Mich. Cir. Ct. (4th jud. cir.), Jackson, 1986—. Chmn. Jackson County Dem. Com., 1963; active various dem. causes, 1948—. Mem. ABA, Mich. Bar Assn., Jackson County Bar Assn., Hellenic Bar Assn., Assn. Trial Lawyers Am., Judicature Soc., Ducks Unltd. Mem. Eastern Orthodox Ch. Lodge: Elks. Avocations: farming, gardening, woodworking, boating. Personal injury, Workers' compensation, General practice. Home: 5040 Brookside Dr Jackson MI 49203 Office: Jackson County Courthouse 312 S Jackson St Jackson MI 49201

PERLSTEIN, MITCHELL LESLIE, lawyer; b. N.Y.C., Jan. 4, 1948. BS in Banking and Fin., NYU, 1971; JD, Washington U., St. Louis, 1974. Bar: Fla. 1975. Asst. prof. bus. law Ill. State U., Bloomington, 1972-74; sole practice Miami, Fla., 1974-83; 1st v.p. and gen. counsel I.R.E. Fin. Corp., Miami, 1983-85; ptnr. Spencer, Bernstein, Seemann, Klein & Perlstein, Coral Gables, Fla., 1985-86; sole practice Miami, 1986—. Bd. dirs. Temple Samuel, Miami, 1981-82, Miami Film Festival, 1984—; trustee Coconut Grove Playhouse, Miami, 1982-83. Mem. ABA, Fla. Bar Assn. General corporate, Real property, Securities. Home: 404 Viscaya Ave Coral Gables FL 33134 Office: 4500 Biscayne Blvd Suite 312 Miami FL 33137

PERLSTEIN, PAUL MARK, lawyer; b. Phila., Mar. 23, 1947; s. Max and Rose (Feldman) P.; m. Shirley Ann Herrmann, July 29, 1973 (div. Dec. 1983); children: Michal Adina, Ari David; m. Linda Berman, May 25, 1986. BA, Temple U., 1968; JD, Columbia U., 1971. Bar: Pa. 1972, N.J. 1973, U.S. Dist. Ct. N.J. 1973, U.S. Dist. Ct (ea. dist.) Pa. 1974, U.S. Ct. Appeals (3d cir.) 1974. Law clk. to presiding justice Ct. of Common Pleas, Phila., 1972-74, 75-77; ptnr. Blumfield & Perlstein, Phila., 1973-74; sole practice Phila. and Haddonfield, N.J., 1974-78; ptnr. Perlstein & Segal, Phila. and Haddonfield, N.J., 1978-80, Dranoff-Perlstein Assocs., Phila. and Cherry Hill, N.J., 1980—. Mem. Am. Trial Lawyers Assn., Pa. Trial Lawyers Assn. (bd. dirs. 1981-84), Phila. Trial Lawyers Assn., Phila. Bar Assn. Avocation: trap shooting. Personal injury, Federal civil litigation, State civil litigation. Office: Dranoff-Perlstein Assocs 1604 Spruce St Philadelphia PA 19103

PERLUSS, IRVING HARVEY, lawyer; b. Los Angeles, Nov. 23, 1915; s. Sidney Aaron and Ethel (Simon) P.; m. Panama Kauffman, June 17, 1942; children: Sheldon, Dennis. BS in Bus.Adminstrn. with honors, UCLA, 1937; LLB, U. Calif., Berkeley, 1940. Bar: Calif. 1940, U.S. Dist. Ct. (no. dist.) Calif. 1940; U.S. Supreme Ct.1958. Tax counsel State Bd. of Equalization, Sacramento, 1941-42; dep. asst. atty. gen. State of Calif., Sacramento, 1946-59; dir. Calif. Dept. Employment, Sacramento, 1959-63; judge Calif. Superior Court, Sacramento, 1963-83; of counsel Greve, Clifford, Diepenbrock & Paras, Sacramento, 1983—; justice pro tem Ct. of Appeal, 3rd appellate dist., Sacramento, 1972-82; spl. master Calif. Supreme Ct., Sacramento, 1972. Author: Benefits for Veterans, 1942; editor: Calif. Law Review, 1938-39. Vice chmn. County Mental Health adv. bd., Sacramento, 1967-77; chmn. County Drug Abuse Commn., Sacramento, 1967-77. Served with U.S. Army, 1942-46. Mem. Calif. State Bar Assn., Sacramento County Bar Assn., Calif. Judges Assn. (exec. com. 1975). Democrat. Jewish. Lodges: Masons, Shriners. Administrative and regulatory, State civil litigation, arbitration; private judging. Office: Greve Clifford Diepenbrock & Paras 1000 G St PO Box U2469 Sacramento CA 95811-2469

PERMAN, MARTEY ROBERT, lawyer; b. N.Y.C., May 7, 1939; s. Morris and Ida (Martey) P.; m. Doris Weinstein, Aug. 26, 1967; 1 child, Scott. BS, St. Lawrence U., 1961; JD, NYU, 1966. Bar: N.Y. 1967, D.C. 1968, U.S. Patent Office 1968, Conn. 1985. Patent counsel Xerox Corp., Stamford, Conn., 1966-80; ptnr. Perman & Green, Fairfield, Conn., 1980—. Mem. ABA, Conn. Patent Law Assn. (pres. 1984-85), N.Y. State Patent Trademark & Copyright Assn., Am. Intellectual Property Assn., Westchester-Fairfield Corp. Counsels Assn. Jewish. Patent. Office: Perman & Green 425 Post Rd Fairfield CT 06430

PERNITZ, SCOTT GREGORY, lawyer; b. Milw., Jan. 28, 1953; s. William John and June Mary (Shaw) P.; m. Constance Denise Shefter, Aug. 4, 1979; children—Justin William, Julia Dawn, Jeffrey Scott. B.A. cum laude in Polit. Sci., U. Wis.-Madison, 1975, J.D. cum laude, 1979. Bar: Wis. 1979, U.S. Dist. Ct. (we. dist.) Wis. 1979, U.S. Ct. Appeals (7th cir.) 1979, U.S. Dist. Ct. (ea. dist.) Wis. 1986, U.S. Supreme Ct. 1986. Assoc. Winner, McCallum, Hendee & Wixson, Madison, 1980-82; ptnr. Winner, McCallum, Wixson & Pernitz, Madison, 1983—. Mem. Wis. Acad. Trial Lawyers, ABA, Assn. Trial Lawyers Am., Wis. Bar Assn., Dane County Bar Assn. Club: World Tae Kwon Do. Personal injury, Insurance, State civil litigation. Home: 8019 Shagbark Circle Cross Plains WI 53528 Office: Winner McCallum Wixson & Pernitz 121 E Wilson Madison WI 53703

PERONA, PAUL DOMINIC, JR., lawyer; b. Spring Valley, Ill., Jan. 6, 1939; s. Paul Dominic Sr. and Lena (Guerrini) P.; m. Carole Mae Costa, Dec. 26, 1971; children: Mary, Paul, Mark, Bruce, Michael. BA, U. Notre Dame, 1960; JD, Northwestern U., 1963. Bar: Ill. 1963, U.S. Dist. Ct. (no. and cen. dists.) Ill. 1963, U.S. Ct. Appeals (7th cir.) 1968, U.S. Supreme Ct.

1969. Ptnr. Perona & Perona, Spring Valley, 1963-75, Perona, Perona & Tonozzi, Spring Valley, 1975-84; sole practice Peru, Ill., 1985, 87—; ptnr. Holmstrom & Green, P.C., Peru, 1985-86; atty. City of Spring Valley, 1964-66; chmn., bd. dirs. 1st Nat. Bank Oglesby, Ill., 1977—. Pres. Ill. Valley C. of C., LaSalle, 1969-70; fin. chmn. U.S. Rep. Tom Corcoran, Ottawa, Ill., 1982. Mem. ABA, Ill. Bar Assn., Assn. Trial Lawyers Am., Ill. Trial Lawyers Assn., Starved Rock Notre Dame Alumni Club (pres. 1982-84). Republican. Roman Catholic. Lodge: Holy Name. State civil litigation, General practice, Environment. Home: Rural Rt 1 Peru IL 61354 Office: 4110 Progress Blvd Peru IL 61354

PERONI, ROBERT JOSEPH, legal educator, lawyer; b. Chgo., Feb. 14, 1953; s. Emil Louis and Betty Jean (Del Greco) P. B.S.C., DePaul U., 1973; J.D., Northwestern U., 1976; LL.M. in Taxation, NYU, 1980. Bar: Ill. 1976, U.S. Dist. Ct. (no. dist.) Ill. 1976, U.S. Ct. Appeals (7th cir.) 1977, Calif. 1979, U.S. Dist. Ct. (no. dist.) Calif. 1979, U.S. Ct. Appeals (9th and D.C. cirs.) 1979, U.S. Tax Ct. 1979, U.S. Ct. Claims 1979. Assoc. firm Jenner & Block, Chgo., 1976-78, firm Orrick, Herrington & Sutcliffe, San Francisco, 1978-79; instr. in taxation NYU Sch. Law, N.Y.C., 1980-81; asst. prof. law, Tulane U., New Orleans, 1981-84, assoc. prof., 1984—; prof.-in-residence Office of Chief Counsel, IRS, Washington, 1985-86. Recipient Felix Frankfurter Disting. Teaching award Tulane U. Sch. Law, 1984. Mem. ABA, Ill. State Bar Assn., Calif. Bar Assn., Order of Coif. Articles editor: Jour. of Criminal Law and Criminology, 1975-76, grad. editor, 1979-80, co-mng. editor Tax Law Rev., 1980-81. Personal income taxation, Corporate taxation, General corporate. Home: 3915 Saint Charles Ave Apt 511 New Orleans LA 70115 Office: Tulane U Sch Law 6801 Freret St New Orleans LA 70118

PEROTTI, ROSE NORMA, lawyer; b. St. Louis, Aug. 10, 1930; d. Joseph and Dorothy Mary (Roleski) Perotti. B.A., Fontbonne Coll., St. Louis, 1952; J.D., St. Louis U., 1957. Bar: Mo. 1958. Trademark atty. Sutherland, Polster & Taylor, St. Louis, 1958-63, Sutherland Law Office, 1964-70; trademark atty. Monsanto Co., St. Louis, 1971-85, sr. trademark atty., 1985—. Honored with dedication of faculty office in her name, St. Louis U. Sch. Law, 1980. Mem. Mo. Bar Assn., Bar Assn. Met. St. Louis, ABA, Am. Judicature Soc., Smithsonian Assocs., Friends St. Louis Art Museum, Mo. Bot. Garden. Trademark and copyright. Office: Monsanto Co 800 N Lindbergh Blvd Saint Louis MO 63167

PERRI, AUDREY ANN, lawyer; b. Oxnard, Calif., Feb. 2, 1936; d. Zafon Audry and Francis May (Sandblom) Hartman; m. Frank Perri, Aug. 10, 1958; children—Michael, Michelle. B.A., U. Redlands, 1958; J.D., LaVerne Coll., 1976. Cert. family law specialist State Bar Calif. Tchr. English as fgn. lang., Reykjavic and Akureyre, Iceland, 1962-63; tchr. English and govt. various high schs., Calif., Ill., 1958-76; dep. dist. atty. San Bernardino County, 1976-80; ptnr. law firm Covington & Crowe, Ontario, Calif., 1980—. Articles editor: Jour. Juvenile Justice Law Rev., 1975-76. Mem., host, chmn. Internat. Exchange Program, 1965-84; com. mem. Upland (Calif.) City Council, 1970; mem. Dem. State Central Com., 1981-82; bd. dirs. NCCJ, 1977-82. Mem. Inland Counties Women at Law (founding pres. 1980-81), Calif. Women Lawyers (dir. 1980-84, 1st v.p. 1984), San Bernardino County Bar Assn. (mem. com. 1977-84, dir. 1981-83, 84-86), ABA, Calif. State Bar (conf. del. 1977-86, exec. com. 1985—), AAUW (pres. Ontario-Upland br. 1969-70). Family and matrimonial. Home: 8373 Camino Sur Cucamonga CA 91730 Office: Covington & Crowe PO Box 1515 Ontario CA 91762

PERRIN, GREGORY J., lawyer; b. Bklyn., July 31, 1932; s. Gregory O. and Genevieve C. (Murphy) P.; m. Elizabethann Jesinkey, Aug. 1, 1959; children—Gregory, Annemarie, John, Sean, Thomas, Owen, Justin. B.A. St. John's Coll., 1955, LL.B. 1959. Bar: N.Y. 1953, U.S. Supreme Ct. 1967. Atty criminal div. Legal Aid Soc., N.Y.C., 1959-60; asst. dist. atty. N.Y. County, 1960-64; pvt. practice, N.Y.C., 1964—. Served with U.S. Army, 1951-53. Decorated Bronze Star; recipient Am. Jurisprudence awards in fed. practice, adminstrv. law, admiralty. Mem. ABA; N.Y. State Bar Assn.; N.Y.C. Bar Assn.; N.Y. County Bar Assn. Roman Catholic. Criminal, Federal civil litigation, General practice. Home: 776 Carroll St Brooklyn NY 11215 Office: Gregory J Perrin Atty at Law 233 Broadway New York NY 10007

PERRIS, TERRENCE GEORGE, lawyer; b. Los Angeles, Oct. 18, 1947; s. Theodore John Grivas and Penny (Sfakianos) Perris. BA magna cum laude, U. Toledo, 1969; JD summa cum laude, U. Mich., 1972. Bar: Ohio 1972, U.S. Tax Ct. 1982, U.S. Ct. Claims 1983, U.S. Supreme Ct. 1983. Law clk. to presiding judge U.S. Ct. Appeals (2d cir.), N.Y.C., 1972-73; law clk. to cir. justice Potter Stewart U.S. Supreme Ct., Washington, 1973-74; assoc. Squire, Sanders & Dempsey, Cleve., 1974-80, ptnr., 1980—; v.p., trustee SS&D Found., Cleve., 1984—; lectr. in field; nat. coordinator Taxation Practice Area, 1987—. Mem. Citizens League Greater Cleve., 1976—, com. visitors Cleve. State U. Law Sch., 1986—, Mich. Law Sch. Fund Nat. Com., Ann Arbor, 1986—. Served to capt. U.S. Army, 1974. Mem. ABA (fgn. activities of U.S. taxpayers tax sect.), Ohio Bar Assn., Cleve. Bar Assn. (subchpt. C of internal revenue code task force), Supreme Ct. Hist. Soc., Tax Club Cleve., Order of Coif, Phi Kappa Phi. Republican. Eastern Orthodox. Clubs: U. Mich. (Cleve.); Pres.'s (Ann Arbor, Mich.). Avocation: landscape gardening. Corporate taxation, Personal income taxation. Office: Squire Sanders & Dempsey 1800 Huntington Bldg Cleveland OH 44115

PERRONI, SAMUEL ARNOLD, lawyer; b. Colorado Springs, Colo., July 19, 1948; s. Samuel G. Perroni and Virginia F. (Stoddard) McMullin; m. Patricia A. Watson, Apr. 22, 1969; children—Brian David, Mary Elizabeth. B.S., Ill. Wesleyan U., 1970; J.D. cum laude, U. Ark., 1974. Bar: Ark. 1974, U.S. Dist. Ct. (ea. and we. dists.) Ark., U.S. Ct. Appeals (8th and D.C. cirs.), U.S. Tax Ct., U.S. Supreme Ct. Asst. U.S. atty. Dept. Justice, Little Rock, 1974-79, spl. prosecutor, 1980; sole practice, Little Rock, 1981—; adj. prof. law U. Ark., Little Rock, 1977-79. Pres. Parents and Friends of Children, Little Rock, 1979-85; chmn. Magna Carta in Ark. Com., Little Rock, 1981. Mem. ABA (sect. criminal justice com. legal status of prisoners 1978-79, com. rules of criminal procedure and evidence 1979-83), Am. Judicature Soc., Nat. Health Lawyers Assn., Assn. Trial Lawyers Am., Nat. Assn. Criminal Def. Lawyers, Am. Bar Found. (chmn. pub. awareness com. 1983, Spl. Lawyer Humanitarian award 1981), Ark. Bar Assn. (ho. of dels. 1976-79, co-chmn. law student liaison com. 1977-79, chmn. pub. info. com. 1979-83; Golden Gavel award 1980, editor criminal law handbook), Ark. Trial Lawyers Assn., Pulaski County Bar Assn. (Lawyer Citizen award 1984), Delta Theta Phi. Democrat. Presbyterian. Clubs: Little Rock Civitan (bd. dirs. 1980—, Disting. Citizen award 1984). Lodge: Kiwanis (bd. dirs. 1983-84). Federal civil litigation, Personal injury, Criminal. Office: Perroni Rauls & Looney PA The Koger Ctr 10810 Executive Ctr Dr Suite 215 Little Rock AR 72212

PERRY, ALAN ROGERS, JR., lawyer; b. Bay County, Fla., Dec. 25, 1953; m. Elizabeth Powers, June 11, 1977; children: Kathryn Elizabeth, David Sheldon. BA with honors, U. N.C., Chapel Hill, 1976; JD magna cum laude, U. Mich., 1980. Bar: Ga. 1981; U.S. Dist. Ct. (no. dist.) Ga. 1981; U.S. Ct. Appeals (11th cir.) 1981. Law clk. to presiding justice U.S. Ct. Appeals (D.C. cir.), Washington, 1980-81; assoc. Rogers & Hardin, Atlanta, 1981-82, Kilpatrick & Cody, Atlanta, 1982—. Mem. ABA, Atlanta Bar Assn. Episcopalian. Avocations: basketball, racquet sports, wine. State civil litigation, Federal civil litigation, Personal injury. Office: Kilpatrick & Cody 3100 Equitable Bldg 100 Peachtree St Atlanta GA 30043

PERRY, DAVID LEWIS, lawyer, manufacturing company executive; b. Boston, July 13, 1940; s. George Bangs and Ruth (Gordon) P. B.A., Amherst Coll., 1963; J.D., U. Calif.-Berkeley, 1966. Bar: Calif. 1967, Mass. 1967. Gen. atty. FTC, Washington, 1967-69; atty. Kaiser Aluminum & Chem. Corp., Oakland, Calif., 1969-73; gen. atty. Kaiser Aluminum & Chem. Corp., 1973-83, asst. gen. counsel, 1983-84, v.p., gen. counsel, 1984—. Mem. ABA, San Francisco Bar Assn. General corporate. Office: Kaiser Aluminum & Chem Corp 300 Lakeside Dr Oakland CA 94643

PERRY, EDWARD NEEDHAM, lawyer; b. Cambridge, Mass., Oct. 16, 1946; s. Arthur and Marjorie (Bemis) P.; m. Cynthia Wilson Wood, May 31, 1980. BA, Williams Coll., 1968; JD, Vanderbilt U., 1975. Bar: Mass. 1975, U.S. Supreme Ct. 1980, U.S. Ct. Appeals (9th cir.) 1981, (1st cir.) 1984, (2d cir.) 1984, U.S. Dist. Ct. Mass. 1983. Assoc. cons. Charles Evans & Assocs., Boston, 1971; litigation atty. U.S. Dept. Labor, Washington, 1975-82; ptnr. Perkins, Mecsas, Smith, Arata & Howard, Boston, 1982—. V.p. Alumni Pres.'s Council of Independent Schs., 1987—; trustee Northfield Mount Hermon Sch. (Mass.), 1975-80, 83-86, Trinitarian Congl. Ch., Concord, Mass, 1970—; mem. Town Library Com., Concord, Mass., 1986—; bd. dirs. alumni pres.'s council Ind. Secondary Schs. Served as lt. (j.g.) USN, 1968-70. Recipient Meritorious Achievement award U.S. Dept. Labor, 1979, 80, Spl. Achievement award, 1981. Mem. ABA, Mass. Bar Assn., Alumni Pres.' Council Ind. Schs. (v.p.), Northfield Mount Hermon Sch. Alumni Assn. (pres. 1983-86). Republican. Congregationalist. Labor, Federal civil litigation, State civil litigation. Home: 21 Thoreau St Concord MA 01742 Office: Perkins Mecsas Smith Arata & Howard One Federal St Boston MA 02110

PERRY, GEORGE WILLIAMSON, lawyer; b. Cleve., Dec. 4, 1926; s. George William and Melda Patricia (Arther-Holt) P. B.A. in Econs., Yale U., 1949; J.D., U. Va., 1953. Bar: Ohio 1953, D.C. 1958, U.S. Supreme Ct. 1958, U.S. Ct. Appeals (D.C. cir.) 1959. Atty. U.S. Dept. Justice, Washington, 1954-56; atty. assoc. counsel Com. on Interstate Fgn. Commerce, U.S. Ho. of Reps., Washington, 1960-65; atty., advisor ICC, Washington, 1965-68; assoc. dir. devel. Yale U., New Haven, 1968-70; dir. tax research Pan Am. World Airways, N.Y.C., 1973-75; hearing officer Indsl. Commn. Ohio, Cleve., 1978-81; sole practice, Cleve., 1981—. Served with U.S. Army, 1945-46. Mem. D.C. Bar Assn., Soc. of Cincinnati in State of Conn., Phi Delta Phi. Episcopalian. Administrative and regulatory, General practice. Office: 1801 E 12th St Cleveland OH 44114

PERRY, JAMES B., lawyer; b. Detroit, Nov. 4, 1952; s. Sam amd Mary P. (Cataneo) P.; m. Maryanne Klein, May 21, 1983; 1 child, James Henry. BA, U. Mich., 1974; JD, Emory U., 1977. Bar: Mich. 1977, U.S. Ct. Appeals (6th cir.) 1978, U.S. Dist. Ct. (ea. dist.) Mich. 1981. Assoc. Cox & Youngblood, Troy, Mich., 1977-78, Cox & Hooth, Troy, 1978-83; assoc. Abbott, Nicholson, Quilter, Esshabi & Youngblood P.C., Detroit, 1983-85, ptnr., 1986—. Mem. Grosse Pointe Woods Citizens Block Grant Devel. Commn., Mich., 1984—; pres. bd. govs. Univ.-Ligget Alumni, Grosse Pointe Woods, 1984-86. Mem. ABA, Mich. Bar Assn. (labor law sect.), Industrial Relations Research Assn. (adv. bd. 1983-85). Club: Detroit Athletic. Office: Abbott Nicholson Quilter et al 1840 Buhl Bldg Detroit MI 48226

PERRY, LEE NACE, lawyer, educator; b. Hattiesburg, Miss., Dec. 21, 1949; s. Robert B. and Thelma (Barkley) P.; 1 child from a previous marriage, Robert M.; m. Francine Jackson, Sept. 14, 1984. BS in Engring., U.S. Mil. Acad., 1972; MA in Human Resources Mgmt., Pepperdine U., 1978; JD, U. Miss., 1981. Bar: Miss. 1981, U.S. Dist. Ct. (no. and so. dists.) Miss. 1981, U.S. Ct. Appeals (5th cir.) 1981. Commd. 2d lt. U.S. Army, 1972, advanced through grades to capt., 1976, resigned, 1978; assoc. White & Morse, Gulfport, Miss., 1981-82, ptnr., 1983—. Researcher Appeals Procedure Manual, 1978, Mississippi Model Jury Instructions, 1979. Served to maj. Miss. Air N.G., 1981—. Mem. Harrison County Jr. Bar Assn. (pres. 1985-86). Lodge: Kiwanis (bd. dirs. Gulfport club 1984). Avocations: boating, golf. Federal civil litigation, State civil litigation, Real property. Home: PO Box 1174 Gulfport MS 39502 Office: White & Morse PO Drawer 100 Gulfport MS 39502

PERRY, LINDA SUSAN, lawyer; b. Mobile, Ala., Apr. 5, 1957; d. Ralph John and Susan Mae (Norrell) P.; m. Michael Thomas Ledet, Aug. 31, 1985. BA in English, Journalism, Spring Hill Coll., 1979; JD, U. Ala., 1982. Bar: Ala. 1982, U.S. Dist. Ct. (so. dist.) Ala. 1982, U.S. Ct. Appeals (11th cir.) 1983, Fla. 1986. Sole practice Mobile, 1982—. Mem. ABA (chmn. subcom. gen. practice sect. 1985-86), Mobile Bar Assn. (speakers com.). Democrat. Roman Catholic. Home: 403 Chestnut Dr Tallahassee FL 32301 Office: 503 Govt St Suite 210 Mobile AL 36602

PERRY, MATILDA TONI, lawyer; b. Decatur, Ill.; d. Nathan Otis Perry and Elizabeth May Armstrong; m. Donald Harry Rubin, May 9, 1982; children: Michael, Deborah, Nikki, Brenda, Tom. BA, U. Nev., 1972; JD, U. Calif., Berkeley, 1975. Bar: Calif. 1975, U.S. Supreme Ct. 1980. Atty. State of Calif., Long Beach, 1975-77; dep. county counsel County of Orange, Calif., 1977-83; assoc. Rutan & Tucker, Costa Mesa, Calif., 1983-85; ptnr. Rutan & Tucker, Costa Mesa, 1986—. Mem. ABA, Calif. Bar Assn., Orange County Bar Assn., County Counsel Assn. (sch. law study sect.), Irvine Bus. and Profl. Women Assn. (program chmn. 1985). Municipal bonds, Local government, Administrative and regulatory. Office: Rutan & Tucker 611 Anton Blvd Suite 1400 Costa Mesa CA 92626

PERRY, MICHAEL JOHN, law educator; b. 1945. AB, Georgetown U., 1968; JD, Columbia U., 1973. Law clk. to presiding justice U.S. Dist. Ct. N.Y., N.Y.C., 1973-74, U.S. Ct. Appeals (9th cir.), N.Y., 1974-75; asst. prof. Ohio State U., Columbus, 1975-78, assoc. prof., 1978-79, prof., 1979-83; prof. Northwestern U., Evanston, Ill., 1983—. Office: Northwestern Univ Sch Law 357 East Chgo Ave Chicago IL 60611 *

PERRY, ROBERT HARRY, lawyer, law educator; b. Salem, Oreg., Nov. 18, 1943; s. Howard K. and Mary G. (Neiswender) P. Student, U.S. Naval Acad., 1965-67; BA, U. Kans., 1969, JD, 1973. Bar: Nev. 1974, U.S. Dist. Ct. Nev. 1976, U.S. Ct. Appeals (9th cir.) 1979. Investigator criminal div. Washoe County Dist. Atty.'s Office, Reno, Nev., 1973-74, dep. dist. atty., 1974-76; assoc. Laxalt & Berry, Reno, 1976-80; ptnr. Davenport & Perry, Reno, 1980—; adj. faculty Old Coll. Sch. of Law, Reno, 1985-86; spl. dep. sheriff Carson City (Nev.) County, Neva, 1986—. Served to cpl. USMC, 1962-67. Mem. Washoe County Bar Assn., Assn. Trial Lawyers Am., Nev. Trial Lawyers Assn., Nev. Narcotics Officers Assn., Nev. Med. Legal Screening Panel (panelist), Nat. Bd. Trial Adv. (diplomate). Democrat. Roman Catholic. Avocations: carpentry, racquetball, squash. Federal civil litigation, Insurance, Personal injury. Home: 1481 Genesse Dr Reno NV 89503 Office: Davenport & Perry 200 S Virginia St Suite 500 Reno NV 89501

PERRY, SHERRYL R., lawyer; b. Binghampton, N.Y., Mar. 5, 1941; d. Arthur J.S. and Miriam (Kantor) Rosenbaum; m. David Perry, June 24, 1962. BS in Biochemistry, Drexel U., 1963; MA in English, U. Pa., 1964; JD, Villanova U., 1979. Bar: Pa. 1979, U.S. Dist. Ct. (ea. dist.) Pa. 1979, U.S. Ct. Appeals (3d cir.) 1980. Assoc. Pepper, Hamilton & Scheetz, Phila., 1979-83; ptnr. Perry, Goldstein, Fialkowski & Perry, Phila., 1983—; lectr. ALI-ABA symposiums, 1983-86. Co-author: Planning, Financing and Construction Health Care Facilities, 1983. Mem. ABA, Pa. Bar Assn., Phila. Bar Assn., Def. Research Inst. Republican. Club: Racquet (Phila.). Avocations: photography, skiing,. Products liability, Personal injury, Preventive law, insurance law. Home: 431 Boxwood Rd Rosemont PA 19010 Office: 2 Mellon Bank Ctr Suite 2400 Philadelphia PA 19102

PERRY, VICTOR ALAN, lawyer; b. Yerington, Nev., July 3, 1939; s. Peter John and Regina Barbara (Dini) P.; m. Solveig Maria Haggren, Jan. 12, 1963; children: Lars, Jelaine, Kip. Engr. of Mines, Colo. Sch. Mines, 1961; JD, U. Denver, 1970. Bar: Nev. 1970, U.S. Dist. Ct. (no. dist.) Nev. 1971, U.S. Supreme Ct. 1982. Mining engr. Kennecott Copper, Santa Rita, N.Mex., 1964-66; project engr. REECO, Mercury, Nev., 1966-67; dep. atty. gen. State of Nev., Carson City, 1971-73; ptnr. Cromer, Barker & Michaelson, Reno, Nev., 1975-83, Barker, Gillock & Perry, Reno, 1983—. Served to 1st lt. U.S. Army, 1961-64. Named an Hon. Mexican Counsel, Govt. of Mex., no. Nev., 1973-77. Democrat. Roman Catholic. Lodge: Elks. Avocations: skiing, hiking. Insurance, Personal injury, State civil litigation. Home: 4751 Reds Grade Carson City NV 89701 Office: 620 Humboldt Reno NV 89509

PERRY, WILLIAM SHELBERN, lawyer; b. Abilene, Tex., Jan. 26, 1936; s. Litt Shelbern and Emma Jane (Swanger) P.; children—William Shelbern, Michael M.; m. 2d, Deborah Lynn McCoy, Feb. 11, 1978; 1 child, Lindsay Kate. B.S. in Commerce, Tex. Christian U., 1958; LL.B., Baylor U., 1963, J.D., 1969. Bar: Tex. 1963. Assoc. David L. Hooper, Abilene, 1963-64; ptnr. Hooper and Perry, Abilene, 1964-69, Hooper, Perry and Bradshaw, Abilene, 1969-71; sole practice William S. Perry P.C., Abilene, 1979—. Sec., vice chmn., chmn. Abilene Planning and Zoning Commn., 1976-81; dir., v.p., pres. Abilene Bus. and Estate Planning Council, 1964-70; dir., v.p. Abilene Community Theater; dir. Abilene Met. Ballet Co.; dir., crusade vice chmn., chmn. Abilene chpt. Am. Cancer Soc., 1968-69; mem. Abilene Fine Arts Mus., Abilene Philharmonic Assn. Served with Army N.G., 1954-61. Recipient service awards Am. Cancer Soc., City of Abilene, Abilene Planning and Zoning Commn. Mem. State Bar Tex. (sec., chmn. grievance com. dist. 15D), Abilene Bar Assn. (sec. 1965), Abilene C. of C. Phi Alpha Delta, Phi Delta Thera. Democrat. Mem. Christian Ch. (Disciples of Christ). Clubs: Abilene Country, Fairway Oak Golf and Racquet, Key City Kiwanis (dir., v.p. 1965-69). Real property, Oil and gas leasing, General corporate. Office: 278 S Pioneer St Abilene TX 79605

PERRY, WILSON DAVID, lawyer; b. Wilkes-Barre, Pa., Mar. 30, 1939; s. Robert Clark and Mary Dunlop (Warg) P.; m. Kathryn Senn, June 3, 1969; children: Kathryn Elizabeth, Evelyn Michele. BS in Ceramic Engring., Alfred U., 1961; JD, Duke U., 1969. Bar: Wis. 1969, U.S. Dist. Ct. (ea. dist.) Wis. 1970. Devel. engr. Ferro Corp., Cleve., 1961-66; atty. Northwestern Mut. Life, Milw., 1969-73, asst. gen. counsel, 1973—; counse, sec. Standard of Am. Life, Park Ridge, Ill., 1982—. Mem. bus. and the professions com. Milw. Repertory Theatre; elder, other posts Immanuel Presbyn. Ch., Milw., 1978—; pres., bd. dirs. Friars of St. Michael Hosp., Milw., 1979—; soccer coach Wis. Kickers, Milw., 1981—; cons. JA Applied Econs. and Project Bus., Milw., 1982, 84. Served to 1st lt. U.S. Army, 1962-64, Korea. Mem. Am. Corp. Counsel Assn. (sec., gov., founding gov. Wis. chpt. 1984—). Club: Whitefish Bay Tennis. Avocations: tennis, golf, spectator sports, theatre, church and community service. Insurance, General corporate. Home: 5346 N Hollywood Ave Whitefish Bay WI 53217 Office: Northwestern Mut Life Law Dept 720 E Wisconsin Ave Milwaukee WI 53202

PERSCHETZ, ARTHUR DRIBAN, lawyer; b. Ossining, N.Y., May 17, 1943; s. S. Philip and Rose Lucy (Driban) P.; m. Lois Marsha Winebaum, May 13, 1971; children: Emily Karen, Rachel Carrie. BA, Syracuse U., 1965, JD, 1967. Bar: N.Y. 1969, U.S. Dist. Ct. (so. dist.) N.Y. 1971, U.S. Dist. Ct. (ea. dist.) 1972, U.S. Supreme Ct. 1981. Counsel Royal Indemnity Co., N.Y.C., 1970-73, 1973-83, asst. corp. sec., 1978—, asst. v.p., 1983-86, asst. gen. counsel, 1985—; v.p. legal Royal Indemnity Co., Charlotte, N.C., 1986—; bd. dirs. Royal Indemnity Co., Globe Indemnity Co. Mem. Saltaire Citizens Adv. Com., N.Y, 1976; trustee Inc. Village of Saltaire, 1977-78; bd. dirs. 829 Park Ave Corp., N.Y.C., 1977-86, pres., 1978-86. Served to capt. U.S. Army, 1967-68, Vietnam. Mem. ABA, N.Y. State Bar Assn., N.Y. County Bar Assn., Am. Corp. Counsel Assn., Nat. Assn. Ins. Commrs. (various coms.). Avocations: tennis, music. General corporate, Insurance, Administrative and regulatory. Home: 4516 Belknap Rd Charlotte NC 28211 Office: Royal Ins Co 9300 Arrowpoint Blvd Charlotte NC 28210

PERSKY, SEYMOUR HOWARD, lawyer; b. Chgo., May 22, 1922; s. Joseph E. and Bertha (Solomon) P.; A.A. magna cum laude, City Coll., Chgo., 1949; B.A., Roosevelt U., 1952; J.D., DePaul U., 1952; postgrad. Northwestern U., 1961-62; m. Beverly M. Lipsky, July 8, 1962; children—Jonathen E., Abbe Joan. Admitted to Ill. bar, 1952, U.S. Supreme Ct. bar, 1965; resident counsel Mid-West Loan Co., Chgo., 1953-58; sr. ptnr. firm Persky, Phillips & Berzock, Chgo., 1961-63; practiced in Chgo., 1963—; pub. defender Narcotics Ct., Municipal Ct. of Chgo., 1964—; lectr. Truman Jr. Coll.; mem. Internat. Options Market, Internat. Monetary Market (Chgo. Merc. Exchange). Vice pres. Peoples Rehab. Found., Yiddish Theater Assn.; vice gen. chmn. bd. govs. Israel Bonds of Greater Chgo., chmn. young peoples div., 1970-72, chmn. lawyers div., 1973-74, pres. Prime Minister's Club; bd. govs. Ida Crown Jewish Acad.; bd. dirs. Hillel Torah North Suburban Day Sch., Skokie, Ill. 1973, Arie Crown Day Sch., 1977—, Skokie Valley Synagogue, 1977—, Anti-Defamation League B'nai B'rith, Jewish Nat. Fund, YIVO-Inst. for Jewish Research; ptnr. DePaul U. Coll. Law; mem. endowment bd. DePaul U.; mem. Highland Park Historic Preservation Commn., Ill. Served with USAAF, 1941-44. Recipient Citation City Council of Chgo., 1986. Mem. ABA, Ill. Bar Assn. (chmn. subcom. unauthorized practice law com. 1962), Chgo. Bar Assn. (criminal law com., def. prisoners com.) , Ill. Acad. Criminology, Decalogue Soc., Def. Lawyers Assn., Am. Trial Lawyers Assn., Nat. Trust for Historic Preservation, Lex Legio DePaul U., Soc. Fellows DePaul U., DePaul U. Alumni Assn (mem. exec. bd., chmn. alumni class 1952), Chgo. Assn. Commerce and Industry, Landmarks Preservation Council, Greater N.Mich. Ave. Assn., Mensa, Nu Beta Epsilon. Clubs: City, Covenant of Ill., Execs., Lincoln Park Builders, Cliff Dwellers (Chgo.); Quadrangle (U. Chgo.). Home: 65 Prospect Ave Highland Park IL 60035 Office: 123 W Madison St Chicago IL 60602

PERSONS, JOHN WADE, lawyer; b. Fitchburg, Mass., Dec. 6, 1953; s. Roger W. and Vivian A. (Boudreau) P.; m. Marjorie L. Smith, July 18, 1980; children: Katherine A., Elizabeth W. BA in History magna cum laude, U. Conn., 1975, MA, 1977; JD, Albany Law Sch., 1980. Bar: N.Y. 1981, U.S. Dist. Ct. (no. dist.) N.Y. 1981, U.S. Dist. Ct. (ea. dist.) N.Y. 1985. From law clk. to assoc. Cade & Saunders, Albany, N.Y., 1978-84; legal researcher, writing instr. Albany Law Sch., 1979-80; assoc. Glynn and Mercep, Stony Brook, N.Y., 1984-86; ptnr. Glynn, Mercep and Persons, Stony Brook, 1987—; law guardian Albany County Family Ct., 1984. Mem. The Museums at Stony Brook, 1985—, Three Village Hist. Soc., 1985—. Mem. ABA, N.Y. State Bar Assn. (ins. sect., negligence and compensation law sect.). Democrat. Roman Catholic. Club: Stony Brook Yacht. Personal injury, State civil litigation, Federal civil litigation. Home: 53 Cedar St Stony Brook NY 11790 Office: Glynn Mercep and Persons 111C Main St PO Box 712 Stony Brook NY 11790

PERSYN, MARY GERALDINE, law librarian, law educator; b. Elizabeth, N.J., Feb. 25, 1945; d. Henry Anthony and Geraldine (Sumption) P. AB, Creighton U., 1967; MLS, U. Oreg., 1969; JD, Notre Dame U., 1982. Bar: Ind. 1982, U.S. Dist. Ct. (no. and so. dists.) Ind. 1982. Social scis. librarian Miami U., Oxford, Ohio, 1969-78; staff law librarian Notre Dame (Ind.) Law Sch., 1982-84; dir. law library Valparaiso (Ind.) U., 1984-87, law librarian, assoc. prof. law, 1987—. Editor Journal of Legislation, 1981-82; mng. editor Third World Legal Studies, 1986—. Mem. ABA, Ind. State Bar Assn., Am. Assn. Law Libraries, Ohio Regional Assn. Law Libraries. Roman Catholic. Librarianship, Legal education. Home: 993 Mill Pond Rd Valparaiso IN 46383 Office: Valparaiso U Sch Law Library Valparaiso IN 46383

PERTNOY, LEONARD DAVID, dean; b. Phila., May 19, 1944; s. Irving A. and Vera H. (Horowitz) P.; m. Judith Ann Spilberg, Oct. 14, 1973; children: Mason Andrew, Jarett Alex. AB, Cen. U., 1962; BA, Louisville U., 1966; postgrad., U. Vienna, Australia, 1964-65; JD, U. Miami, 1969. Bar: Fla. 1969, U.S. Dist Ct (so. dist.) Fla. 1976, U.S. Ct. Appeals (5th cir.) 1980, U.S. Ct. Appeals (11th cir.) 1981, U.S. Supreme Ct. 1981. Ptnr. Pertnoy & Spaet, Miami, Fla., 1973-78; pres. Pertnoy, Spaet & Greenburg P.A., Miami, 1978-82, Pertnoy, Greenberg & Sobel P.A., Miami, 1982-84; ptnr. Greenberg & Sobel P.A., Miami, 1984-85; asst. dean St. Thomas Sch. of Law, Miami, 1985—. Mem. Leadership Insight, Miami, 1984—. Mem. Assn. Trial Lawyers Am., Fla. Trial Lawyers Assn., Assn. Continuing Legal Edn. Adminstrs., Phi Delta Phi, Phi Sigma Alpha. Jewish. Avocations: triatholete, adventure treks. State civil litigation, Federal civil litigation, Contracts commercial. Home: 6987 SW 53rd Ln Miami FL 33156 Office: St Thomas Sch of Law 16400 NW 32d Ave Miami FL 33054

PERZLEY, ALAN HARRIS, lawyer; b. Newark, Feb. 9, 1955; s. Irving I. and Charlotte I. (Davidson) P.; m. Janis B. Borodkin, May 28, 1979; 1 child, Jonathan Evan. BA cum laude, U. Va., 1977; JD, Seton Hall U., 1982. Bar: N.J. 1982, U.S. Dist. Ct. N.J. 1982, U.S. Supreme Ct. 1986. Assoc. Crummy, Del Deo, Dolan, Griffinger & Vecchione, Newark, 1982-85, Greenbaum, Rowe, Smith, Ravin, Davis & Bergstein, Woodbridge, N.J., 1985-86, 87—; sr. corp. counsel Bell Atlantic TriCon Leasing Corp., Paramus, N.J., 1986-87. Recipient Eagle Scout award Boy Scouts Am., 1969. Mem. ABA, N.J. Bar Assn., Essex County Bar Assn., Bergen County Bar Assn. Avocations: music, tennis, boating. Real property, Contracts commercial, General corporate. Home: 31-06 Gordon Pl Fair Lawn NJ 07410 Office: Metro Corporate Campus I PO Box 5600 Woodbridge NJ 07095

PESHKIN, SAMUEL DAVID, lawyer; b. Des Moines, Oct. 6, 1925; s. Louis and Mary (Grund) P.; m. Shirley R. Isenberg, Aug. 17, 1947; children—Lawrence Allen, Linda Ann. B.A., State U. Iowa, 1948, J.D., 1951. Bar: Iowa bar 1951. Since practiced in Des Moines; partner firm Bridges & Peshkin, 1953-66, Peshkin & Robinson, 1966—; Mem. Iowa Bd. Law Examiners, 1970—. Bd. dirs. State U. Iowa Found., 1957—, Old Gold Devel. Fund, 1956—, Sch. Religion U. Iowa, 1966—. Fellow Am. Bar Found., Internat. Soc. Barristers; mem. ABA (chmn. standing com. membership 1959—, ho. of dels. 1968—, bd. govs. 1973—), Iowa Bar Assn. (bd. govs. 1958—, pres. jr. bar sect. 1958-59, award of merit 1974), Inter-Am. Bar

Assn., Internat. Bar Assn., Am. Judicature Soc., State U. Iowa Alumni Assn. (dir., pres. 1957). Private international, General corporate, Corporate taxation. Home: 505 36th St Apt 302 Des Moines IA 50312 Office: 1010 Fleming Bldg Des Moines IA 50309

PESIN, EDWARD, lawyer; b. Jersey City, Sept. 23, 1924; s. Samuel and LIbby (Weisman) P.; m. Helene Sylvia Rattner, June 22, 1952; children: EllaMichele, Samuel Richard. AB, Rutgers U., 1947; JD, Harvard U., 1950; LLM, NYU, 1957. Bar: N.J. 1949, N.Y. 1950, U.S. Dist. Ct. N.J. 1949, U.S. Tax Ct. 1951, U.S. Dist. Ct. (so. dist.) N.Y. 1957, U.S. Ct. Claims 1957, Fla. 1982; cert. tax lawyer, 1984. Trial atty. office of chief counsel IRS, 1951-55; atty. J.K. Lasser & Co., N.Y.C., 1955-57; sole practice Newark, 1957-70, N.Y.C., 1957—; ptnr. Greenbaum, Pesin, Rowe & Smith, Newark, 1972-73; lectr. NYU Inst. Fed. Taxation, 1958, 61, 64, N.J. Inst. Continuing Legal Legal Edn., 1961—; chmn. com. on profl. corps. N.J. Supreme Ct., 1981. Editor Jour. Taxation, 1955. Mem. Hudson County Charter Study Commn., 1973-74; bd. dirs. ARC, North Hudson chpt.; bd. dirs. Jewish Hosp. and Rehab. Ctr., 1970-84. Served to lt. AUS, 1943-46. Recipient Loyal Sons of Rutgers award Rutgers U., 1960, SAR award, 1947, Abraham Messler Quick award Rutgers U., 1941. Mem. ABA, N.J. Bar Assn. (chmn. com. fed. taxation 1960-63, rep. Mid-Atlantic Laternal Revenue Regioal Lawyers Liason Com. 1960-75, chmn. com. legal assistance to elderly 1975-80), Fla. Bar Assn., N.Y. State Bar Assn., Hudson County Bar Assn. (chmn. com. taxation 1963-80, 87—), Essex County Bar Assn., N.Y. County Lawyers Assn., Phi Beta Kappa. Corporate taxation, Estate taxation, Personal income taxation. Home: 5 75th St North Bergen NJ 07047 Office: 744 Broad St Newark NJ 07102 also: 8 W 40th St New York NY 10018

PESKIN, STEPHAN HASKEL, lawyer; b. N.Y.C., Oct. 31, 1943; s. Michael and Ruth (Berger) P.; m. Victoria Bond, Jan. 27, 1974. BA, NYU, 1965; JD, Bklyn. Coll., 1968. Bar: N.Y. 1968, U.S. Supreme Ct. 1972, U.S. Dist. Ct. Colo. 1974, Pa. 1979. Assoc. Rothblatt & Rothblatt, N.Y.C., 1968-70; ptnr. Rothblatt, Rothblatt, Scijas & Peskin, N.Y.C., 1970-79, Tolmage, Peskin, Harris & Falick, N.Y.C., 1979—; sr. faculty mem. Nat. Coll. Trial Advocacy, 1978—. Author: Settlement for Top Dollar, 1986; contbr. articles to law jours. Comdg. officer N.Y.C. Aux. Police, Central Park Precinct, 1978—. Mem. ABA, N.Y. County Lawyers Assn., N.Y. Trial Lawyers Assn. (bd. dirs. 1980—, treas. 1982-86, v.p. 1986—), N.Y. Bar Assn., Assn. Trial Lawyers Am. (bd. govs. 1984—). Personal injury, Criminal, Federal civil litigation. Home: 256 W 10th St New York NY 10014 Office: Tolmage Peskin Harris & Falick 20 Vesey St New York NY 10007

PESTLE, JOHN WILLIAM, lawyer; b. Brattleboro, Vt., Feb. 28, 1948; s. Ray Irving and Annette Adelia (Lilley) P.; m. Penelope Mendenhall, Oct. 11, 1969; children: William Joseph, Sara Lilley. BA magna cum laude, Harvard U., 1970; MA magna cum laude, Yale U., 1972; JD magna cum laude, U. Mich., 1975. Bar: Mich. 1975, U.S. Dist. Ct. (we. dist.) Mich. 1975, U.S. Dist. Ct (ea. dist.) Mich. 1978, U.S. Ct. Appeals (6th and D.C. cirs.) 1979, U.S. Supreme Ct. 1980. Assoc. Varnum, Riddering, Wierengo & Christensen, Grand Rapids, Mich., 1975-80; ptnr. Varnum, Riddering, Schmidt & Howlett, Grand Rapids, 1980—, co-chmn. energy and telecommunications practice group, 1986—. Pres. Blodgett Neighborhood Assn., Grand Rapids, 1982—; bd. dirs. Blodgett Mem. Med. Ctr. Community Relations, 1983—, Mich. Trails council Girl Scouts U.S., 1982—; trustee Harvard Glee Club Found., 1987—. Mem. ABA, Fed. Energy Bar Assn. (cogeneration and small power prodn. commn.), Mich. State Bar Assn. (chmn. mcpl. utilities commn., governing council pub. corp. law sect.), State Bar Mich. Found., Grand Rapids Bar Assn., Am. Pub. Power Assn. (vice chmn. legal sect. 1985-86, chmn. 1986-87). Clubs: Harvard of Western Mich. (sec. 1976—, chmn. legal sect. 1986—), Peninsular. Avocations: skiing, skating, photography, gardening. Public utilities, FERC practice, Nuclear power. Home: 515 Plymouth Rd SE Grand Rapids MI 49506

PETERS, AULANA LOUISE, government agency commisioner, lawyer; b. Shreveport, La., Nov. 30, 1941; d. Clyde A. and Eula Mae (Faulkner) Pharis; m. Bruce F. Peters, Oct. 6, 1967. BA in Philosophy, Coll. New Rochelle, 1963; JD, U. So. Calif., 1973. Bar: Calif., 1974. Sec., English corr. Publimondial, Spa, Milan, Italy, 1963-64, Fibramianto, Spa, Milan, 1964-65, Turkish del. to Office for Econ. Cooperation & Devel., Paris, 1965-66; adminstrv. asst. Office for Econ. Cooperation & Devel., Paris, 1966-67; assoc. Gibson, Dunn & Crutcher, Los Angeles, 1973-80, ptnr., 1980-84; commr. SEC, Washington, 1984—; lectr. Rutger Group, Los Angeles Supreme Ct., 1981. Recipient Disting. Alumnus award Econs. Club So. Calif., 1984, Washington Achiever award Nat. Assn. Bank Women, 1986. Mem. ABA, State Bar of Calif. (civil litigation cons. group 1983-84), Los Angeles County Bar Assn., Black Women Lawyers Assn. Los Angeles, Assn. Bus. Trial Lawyers (panelist Los Angeles 1982), Women's Forum, Washington. Office: US SEC Office of the Chairman 450 5th St Washington DC 20549 *

PETERS, DANIEL WAYNE, lawyer; b. Sioux Falls, S.D., June 23, 1956; s. Wayne Henry and Patricia JoAnn (Leiferman) P.; m. Cheryl Keeler, July 28, 1979; 1 child, Christopher Wayne. BS in Acctg. magna cum laude, Ariz. State U., 1978; JD, U. Calif., San Francisco, 1981. Bar: U.S. Dist. Ct. Ariz. 1981, U.S. Ct. Appeals (9th cir.) 1981. Assoc. O'Connor, Cavanagh, Anderson, Westover, Killingsworth & Beshears, Phoenix, 1981—. Mem. ABA (real property sect.), Ariz. State Bar Assn. (sect. corp. banking and bus. law, real property sect., young lawyers sect.), Maricopa County Bar Assn. (young lawyers sect.), U. Calif. Hastings Law Sch. Alumni Assn., Phi Alpha Delta. Republican. Roman Catholic. Avocations: golf, softball, volleyball. Real property, General corporate. Home: 2333 E Christy Dr Phoenix AZ 85028 Office: O'Connor Cavanagh Anderson Westover Killingsworth & Beshears One E Camelback Rd Suite 1100 Phoenix AZ 85012

PETERS, DAVID FRANKMAN, lawyer; b. Hagerstown, Md., Aug. 15, 1941; s. Harold E. and Lois (Frankman) P.; m. Jane Catherine Witherspoon, Aug. 21, 1965; children: Catherine, Elizabeth. BA, Washington and Lee U., 1963; LLB, Duke U., 1966. Bar: Va. 1966, U.S. Dist. Ct. (ea. and we. dists.) Va., U.S. Ct. Appeals (2d, 4th, 7th and D.C. cirs.). Assoc. Hunton & Williams, Richmond, Va., 1966-73, ptnr., 1973—. Pres. Children's Home Soc. Va., Richmond, 1977-78, bd. dirs. 1970—; elder, trustee 1st Presbyn. Ch., Richmond. Mem. ABA, Va. Bar Assn. (chmn. adminstrn. law com. 1985—), Richmond Bar Assn. Lodge: Kiwanis. Avocations: photography, travel. Administrative and regulatory, Antitrust, Legislative. Home: 3 Windsor Way Richmond VA 23221 Office: Hunton & Williams 707 E Main St PO Box 1535 Richmond VA 23219

PETERS, DONALD MULLEN, lawyer; b. Houston, Nov. 23, 1950; s. George Herman and Sarah Elizabeth (Mullen) P.; m. Diane Elaine Womack, Feb. 13, 1982; children: Joshua Michael Robert, Julia Christine. BA, Columbia U., 1973; JD cum laude, U. Tex., 1979. Bar: Ariz. 1979, U.S. Dist. Ct. Ariz 1979, U.S. Ct. Appeals (9th cir.) 1980. Assoc. Snell & Wilmer, Phoenix, 1979-81; ptnr. Meyer, Hendricks, Victor, Osborn & Maledon, Phoenix, 1981—; adj. prof. Ariz. State U., Tempe, 1985-86; judge pro tem Maricopa County Superior Ct., Phoenix, 1986. Bd. dirs. Ariz. Civil Liberties Union, 1984-86. Democrat. Congregationalist. Avocation: music. Federal civil litigation, State civil litigation. Home: 1501 E McLellan Blvd Phoenix AZ 85014 Office: Meyer Hendricks Victor Osborn & Maledon 2700 N 3d St Phoenix AZ 85004

PETERS, ELLEN ASH, state supreme court chief justice; b. Berlin, Mar. 21, 1930; came to U.S., 1939, naturalized, 1947; d. Ernest Edward and Hildegard (Simon) Ash; m. Phillip I. Blumberg; children: David Bryan Peters, James Douglas Peters, Julie Kris Peters. B.A. with honors, Swarthmore Coll., 1951; LL.B. cum laude, Yale U., 1954, M.A. (hon.), 1964, LL.D., 1984; LL.D. (hon.), U. Hartford, 1983, Swarthmore Coll., 1983, Georgetown U., 1984, Conn. Coll., 1984, N.Y. Law Sch., 1984, Colgate U., 1986; HL.D. (hon.), St. Joseph Coll., 1986. Bar: Conn. 1957. Law clk. to judge U.S. Circuit Ct., 1954-55; assoc. in law U. Calif., Berkeley, 1955-56; asst. prof. Yale U. Law Sch., 1956-59, assoc. prof., 1959-64, prof., 1964-75, Southmayd prof., 1975-78, adj. prof., 1978-84; assoc. justice Conn. Supreme Ct., Hartford, 1978-84; chief justice Conn. Supreme Ct., 1984—. Author: Commercial Transactions: Cases, Texts, and Problems, 1971, Negotiable Instruments Primer, 1974; contbr. articles to profl. jours. Bd. mgrs. Swarthmore Coll., 1970-81; trustee Yale New Haven Hosp., 1981-84, Yale Corp., 1986—; mem. Conn. Permanent Commn. on Status of Women, 1973-74, Conn. Bd. Pardons, 1978-81, Conn. Law Revision Commn., 1978-84. Recipient Ella Grasso award, 1982, Jud. award Conn. Trial Lawyers Assn., 1982, citation of merit Yale Law Sch., 1983. Mem. ABA, Conn. Bar Assn., Am. Law Inst. (council). Consumer commercial, Contracts commercial. Office: Connecticut Supreme Ct Drawer N Station A Hartford CT 06106

PETERS, FRANK AUGUST, lawyer; b. Seattle, Aug. 12, 1919; s. Carl A. and Ellen (Fagerquist) P.; m. Gertrude B. Peters, July 20, 1946 (dec. Sept. 1986). BA, U. Wash., 1940, LLB, 1946. Bar: Wash. 1946, U.S. Dist. Ct. (Wash.) 1946, U.S. Ct. Appeals (9th cir.) 1946, U.S. Supreme Ct. 1964. Law clk. to presiding justice U.S. Ct. Appeals (9th cir.), San Francisco, 1946-47; sole practice Tacoma and Puyallup, Wash., 1947—. Contbr. articles to legal and other jours. Pres. Puyallup Rotary Club, 1950. Served to lt. USN, 1942-46, PTO. Mem. Nat. Assn. Criminal Def. Attys., Assn. Trial Lawyers Am., Wash. State Bar Assn. (disciplinary hearing officer Tacoma chpt. 1985—), Wash. State Trial Lawyers Assn. Lodge: Elks. Criminal, Personal injury, Probate. Home: 1722 N James Tacoma WA 98406 Office: 955 Tacoma Ave S Tacoma WA 98402

PETERS, FREDERICK WHITTEN, lawyer; b. Omaha, Aug. 20, 1946; s. Jordan Holt and Elizabeth (O'Bryant) P.; m. Mary Gores Peters, Jan. 2, 1969; children: Mary Irvin, Elizabeth Holt, Margaret Etheridge. BA magna cum laude, Harvard U., 1968; MS with distinction, London Sch. Econs., 1973; JD magna cum laude, Harvard U., 1976. Bar: D.C. 1978, U.S. Dist. Ct. D.C. 1978, U.S. Ct. Appeals (3d and D.C. cirs.) 1979, U.S. Ct. Claims 1981, U.S. Ct. Appeals (11th cir.) 1986. Law clk. to presiding judge U.S. Ct. Appeals (D.C. cir.), Washington, 1976-77; law clk. to justice William J. Brennan U.S. Supreme Ct., Washington, 1977-78; assoc. Williams & Connolly, Washington, 1978-84, ptnr., 1984—. Pres. Harvard Law Rev., 1975-76. Bd. dirs. Cleveland Park Hist. Soc., Washington, 1986—, Washington Area Lawyers for the Arts, 1987—. Served to lt. USNR, 1969-72. Mem. ABA. Democrat. Episcopalian. Avocations: sailing, tennis, computer sci. Criminal, Federal civil litigation, Computer. Home: 3250 Highland Pl NW Washington DC 20008 Office: Williams & Connolly 839 17th St NW Washington DC 20006

PETERS, GEOFFREY WRIGHT, lawyer; b. Wilmington, Del., Oct. 30, 1945; s. William Ernest and Ann (Miller) P.; m. Cecile Felicia Dziekonski, Aug. 26, 1967; children: Gregory Kent, Jessica Mohr. AB, Northwestern U., 1967; MA, JD, U. Denver, 1972. Bar: Colo. 1972, Nebr. 1972, Va. 1978, Minn. 1980, U.S. Supreme Ct. 1980. Sole practice Denver, 1972; prof. law Creighton U., Omaha, 1972-78; dep. dir. Nat. Ctr. State Cts., Williamsburg, Va., 1978-80; pres., dean William Mitchell Coll. of Law, St. Paul, 1980-83; exec. v.p., gen. counsel Minn. Protective Life, Eden Prairie, 1984-86; v.p., chief operating officer Garvey Industries, Wichita, Kans., 1986—; cons. Nat. Wiretap Commn., Washington, 1976-77; bd. dirs. Nat. Assn. Ind. Bus., Mpls. Served with U.S. Army, 1969-71. Fellow CLEAR, Social Sci. Methods In Law; mem. Minn. Bar Assn. (bd. govs. 1980-83). Avocations: flight instructing, commercial piloting. Insurance, General corporate, Contracts commercial. Office: Garvey Industries 301 N Main St Epic Ctr Wichita KS 67202

PETERS, JAMES HENRY, lawyer, accountant; b. Milw., Feb. 23, 1933; s. Henry H. and Blanche (Roney) P.; m. Virginia Bowman, June 14, 1954 (div. July 1974); children: Hudson, William; m. Patricia Ann Kraemer, Jan. 21, 1984. BBA, U. Wis., 1955, LLB, 1956. Bar: Wis. 1956. Tax mgr. Arthur Andersen and Co., Milw., 1958-72; fin. v.p. All Am. Meat Co., Whitehall, Wis., 1972-84; sole practice Whitehall, 1984—; bd. dirs. NFD Inc., Braham, Minn., Chase Panels, Milw. Served to sgt. U.S. Army, 1956-58. Mem. Wis. Bar Assn., Wis. Soc. CPA's, Am. Inst. CPA's. Corporate taxation. Home: 328 McHugh St Holmen WI 54636 Office: All Am Meat Co 1519 Main St Whitehall WI 54773

PETERS, LOREN WALTER, lawyer; b. Midland, S.D., June 5, 1939; s. Walter Theodore and Helen (Buchanan) P.; m. Sandra Lenore Ervin, Aug. 3, 1963; children: Lenore Jean, Tracy Lynn. BS in Mech. Engring., S.D. Sch. of Mines and Tech., 1961; JD, Ohio State U., 1967. Bar: Ohio 1967, U.S. Patent Office 1968, U.S. Dist. Ct. (so. dist.) Ohio 1970, U.S. Supreme Ct. 1971, Tex. 1973, U.S. Dist. Ct. (no. dist.) Tex. 1974, U.S. Dist. Ct. (we. dist.) Tex. 1983. Assoc. Lane, Alton & Horst, Columbus, Ohio, 1970-73, Meyers, Miller & Middleton, Dallas, 1973-79, Glast & Miller, Dallas, 1979-82; sole practice San Antonio, 1982-85; ptnr. Boyd & DuBose, Dallas, 1985-86; assoc. Johnson & Christopher, San Antonio, 1986—. Mem. ABA, Tex. Bar Assn., Am. Arbitration Assn. (panel of arbitrators), Nat. Soc. Profl. Engrs., Tex. Soc. Profl. Engrs. Real property, Construction, General corporate. Home: 2806 Barrel Oak San Antonio TX 78231 Office: Johnson & Christopher 5802 NW Expressway San Antonio TX 78201

PETERS, LOUIS DONALD, lawyer; b. Jacksonville, Fla., Sept. 28, 1932; B.S., in Commerce, U. Notre Dame, 1955; J.D., Southwestern U., 1964. Bar: Calif. 1965. Exec. asst. to exec. officer Los Angeles Superior Ct., 1962-65, probate atty. 1965-66, judge pro tem, 1976-77; ptnr. Lawrence & Peters, Montebello, Calif., 1966-69; sole practice, Montebello, 1970-80, Newport Beach, Calif., 1980—. Bd. dirs. Beverly Hosp., Montebello, 1966—. Personal injury. Home: 1054 Calle Del Cerro No 802 San Clemente CA 92672 Office: 4650 VonKarman Newport Beach CA 92660

PETERS, R. JONATHAN, lawyer, chemical company exec.; b. Janesville, Wis., Sept. 6, 1927; m. Ingrid H. Varvayn, 1953; 1 dau., Christina. B.S. in Chemistry, U. Ill., 1951; J.D., Northwestern U., 1954. Bar: Ill. 1954. Chief patent counsel Englehard Industries, 1972-82, Kimberly-Clark Corp., Neenah, Wis., 1982-85; gen. counsel Lanxide Corp., Newark, Del., 1986—. Served with CIC, U.S. Army, 1955-57. Mem. ABA, Am. Patent Law Assn., Lic. Execs. Soc., Assn. Corp. Patent Counsel. Clubs: North Shore Golf (Menasha, Wis.), Masons. Patent, Trademark and copyright.

PETERS, ROBERT TIMOTHY, lawyer; b. Memphis, Dec. 28, 1946; s. Rhulin Earl and Bertie Nichols (Moore) P.; m. Ruth Audrey Allen, Dec. 11, 1973; children: Lindsay Elizabeth, Christopher Andrew. AA, St. Petersburg Jr. Coll., 1969; BA, U. Fla., 1971, JD, 1973. Bar: Fla. 1973, U.S. Dist. Ct. (mid. dist.) Fla. 1977, U.S. Ct. Appeals (5th cir.) 1981. Ptnr. Goza, Hall & Peters P.A., Clearwater, Fla., 1973-84; sole practice Clearwater, 1984—. Columnist Clearwater Sun newspaper, 1985—. Officer, bd. dirs. Legal Aid Soc. of Clearwater, 1974-78, Gulf Coast Legal Services, Inc., St. Petersburg, 1979-81; founding mem. Clearwater Football Alumni Club, 1978—; bd. dirs. Community Assns. Inst., Clearwater, 1984—. Served to 1st lt. U.S. Army, 1966-68, Vietnam. Decorated Silver Star, Purple Heart, Bronze Star with oak leaf cluster. Mem. Clearwater Bar Assn., Pinellas Real Estate Law Council. Avocations: reading, exercise. Real property, State civil litigation, Probate. Home: 2397 Alligator Creek Rd Clearwater FL 33575 Office: 587 S Duncan Ave Clearwater FL 33518-6316

PETERS, RONALD LLOYD, lawyer; b. N.D., Apr. 20, 1928; s. L.N. and Agatha (Banning) Peters; divorced 1979; 3 children. BS, U. Washington, 1951, LLB, 1953. Bar: Wash. 1953, U.S. Dist. Ct. (we. dist.) Wash. 1953, Hawaii 1982, U.S. Dist. Ct. Hawaii 1982. Ptnr. Peters & Tracy, Tacoma, 1954-75; sole practice Honolulu, 1976—. Served to capt. U.S. Army, 1946-48. Probate, Real property. Office: 7192 Kalanianaole Hwy G240 Honolulu HI 96825

PETERS, SAMUEL ANTHONY, lawyer; b. N.Y.C., Oct. 25, 1934; s. Clyde and Amy (Matterson) P.; m. Ruby M. Mitchell, Apr. 28, 1962; children—Robert, Samuel, Bernard. B.A., N.Y. U.; LL.B., Fordham U. Bar: N.Y. 1961, Calif. 1973, U.S. Supreme Ct. 1967. Law clk. FCC, 1961; trial atty. Dept. Justice, 1961-68; staff atty. Lawyer's Com. for Civil Rights Under Law, 1968-69; atty. legal dept. Atlantic Richfield Co., Los Angeles, 1970, litigation counsel, price and wage control counsel, 1970-73, labor counsel, 1972-79, sr. counsel public affairs, 1980—. instr. Rio Hondo Coll.; bd. dirs. Weingart Enger Assn. Served with U.S. Army, 1955-58. Mem. ABA, Langston Bar Assn., Los Angeles County Bar Assn. Contracts commercial, Legal education, General practice. Home: 11471 Kensington Rd Los Alamitos CA 90720 Office: 515 S Flower St Suite 3031 Los Angeles CA 90071

PETERSEN, A. LEE, lawyer; b. Murray, Utah, June 6, 1930; s. Franklin H. and Myrtle (Jensen) P.; m. Cynthia Z. Dalley, Mar. 4, 1961 (div. Sept. 1974); children—Kirsten Marie, Jared Franklin, Eric John, Adam Lewis, Mark Haydn, Amanda Simone. A.B., Brigham Young U., 1955; J.D., NYU, 1959. Bar: Utah 1960. Law clk., assoc. Monroe J. Paxman, Provo, Utah 1959-60; assoc. Thacher, Proffit, Priser, Crawley & Wood, N.Y.C., 1960-62; sole practice, Fillmore, Utah, 1962-68; asst. U.S. atty. Dist. Alaska, 1968-75; mem. Gregg, Fraties, Petersen, Page & Baxter, 1975-77, Fraties & Petersen, 1977-78; sole practice, Anchorage, 1978-84, ptnr. Law Offices of A. Lee Petersen, P.C., 1987—; of counsel Cummings & Routh, P.C., 1984-86; atty. fin. center br. 1st Nat. Bank, Ketchikan, Alaska, 1976-78; atty. Flowell Electric Assn., 1962-68; city atty. Fillmore, 1964-68, Whittier, Alaska, 1976-77; pres., dir. INI Builders, Inc., 1984—. Republican party legis. dist. chmn., 1965-68, voting dist. chmn., 1966-68; bd. dirs. Fillmore Indsl. Found., 1966-68. Mem. So. Utah Bar Assn. (pres. elect 1967), Fed. Bar Assn., Utah Bar Assn., Assn. Trial Lawyers Am., Alaska Bar Assn., ABA, N.Y. State Bar, Fillmore C. of C. (past dir., sec.). Federal and state civil litigation, Construction, Insurance. Office: 1113 W Fireweed Ln Suite 204 Anchorage AK 99503

PETERSEN, GALE ROY, lawyer; b. Oakland, Nebr., Aug. 12, 1948; s. Roy John and Margaret (Ashley) P.; m. Pauline Adele Matson, Sept. 12, 1970; children: Stephanie Erin, Megan Ashley, Susan Amanda. BEE, U. Nebr., 1970; JD magna cum laude, U. Balt., 1975; LLM in Trade Regulation with highest honor, George Washington U., 1978. Bar: Va. 1975, D.C. 1976, U.S. Ct. Claims 1977, Tex. 1978, U.S. Supreme Ct. 1978, U.S. Dist. Ct. (we. dist.) Tex. 1979, U.S. Ct. Appeals (5th cir.) 1979, U.S. Dist. Ct. (so. dist.) Tex. 1980, U.S. Ct. Appeals (11th cir.) 1981, U.S. Ct. Appeals (fed. cir.) 1982. Law clk. to presiding justice U.S. Patent & Trademark Office, Washington, 1975; tech. advisor, briefing atty. U.S. Ct. Appeals (fed. cir.) 1976-78, Washington, 1976-78; ptnr. Cox & Smith Inc., San Antonio, 1978—, also bd. dirs.; lectr. Patent Resource Group, Inc., Washington, 1980; mem. adv. com. U. Tex. San Antonio, Coll. Scis. and Engring., 1985—; mem. tech. venture subcom. Tex. Research & Tech. Found., San Antonio, 1985—; mem. exec. com. Tech. Adv. Group, San Antonio, 1985—. Mem. Lawyers and Accts. for the Arts, San Antonio, 1982-83, World Affairs Council, San Antonio, 1984; bd. dirs. Christian Edn., San Antonio, 1982-83, Tex. Bus. Hall Fame, 1986—. Mem. ABA, Fed. Bar Assn. (steering subcom., appeals from dist. cts. com.), U.S. Trademark Assn., Am. Intellectual Property Law Assn., Computer Law Assn., Licensing Exec. Soc., Va. Bar Assn., D.C. Bar Assn., Tex. Bar Assn. (council intellectual property law sect. 1985—, chmn. inventor's recognition com. 1985—, chmn. unfair competition and trade secret com.). Republican. Lutheran. Club: Los Amigos Shi (San Antonio) (bd. dirs. 1984—). Avocations: airplane pilot, amateur radio operator, traveling. Patent, Trademark and copyright, Antitrust. Office: Cox & Smith Inc 600 NBC Bldg San Antonio TX 78205

PETERSEN, HOWARD EDWIN, judge; b. Davenport, Iowa, July 21, 1932; s. Harry W. and Edith L. (Speer) P.; m. Mary Catherine Brown, Dec. 27, 1959; children: Holly, Sarah, Meg. AB, Augustana Coll., 1954; postgrad. U. Ill., 1954-55; JD, Northwestern U., 1958. Bar: Iowa 1958, Ill. 1961, Ind. 1962, U.S. Supreme Ct. 1969. Assoc. Kopf & Christiansen, 1958-61, Vail, Mills, Winters & Prince, Decatur, Ill., 1961-62; sole practice, LaGrange and Shipshewana, Ind., 1962-79; atty. LaGrange County, 1972-78; judge 35th Jud. Circuit, LaGrange, 1980—; panel arbitrators Am. Arbitration Assn., 1975; town atty. Shipshewana, 1965-79; atty. Topeka (Ind.), 1968-76, Wolcottville (Ind.), 1970-79, LaGrange, 1973-75; counsel LaGrange County Area Planning Commn., 1969-79, LaGrange County Park and Recreation Bd., 1970-79. Assoc. James Whitcomb Riley Meml. Assn., 1965—; fin. chmn. Girl Scouts of the Singing Sands, 1968-70; trustee Lakeland Sch. Corp., 1970-79, v.p., 1976-79, pres., 1978; alderman City of Davenport, 1959-60; mem. LaGrange County Rep. party; chmn. Young Reps., 1962-64, chmn. fin., 1968-74, precinct committeeman, 1975-79; legis. chmn. LaGrange County Mental Health Assn., 1972—. Served with Iowa Air N.G., 1958-62. Recipient First prize Northwestern U. Nathan Burkan Contest, 1958. Mem. Am. Soc. Law and Medicine, ABA (criminal justice sect., juvenile justice com.),Ind. Bar Found., Ind. Bar Assn. (Ho. of Dels. 1968-84, legal ethics com. 1977—), Ill. Bar Assn., Iowa Bar Assn., Indpls. Bar Assn., Chgo. Bar Assn., LaGrange County Bar Assn. (past pres.), Nat. Conf. Juvenile and Family Ct. Judges (juvenile law reform com.), Ind. Judges Assn. Presbyterian (elder, clk. of session). Judicial administration, Criminal, Family and matrimonial. Home: Route 5 Box 106 Woodland Hills LaGrange IN 46761 Office: Courthouse LaGrange IN 46761

PETERSEN, JACK MARTIN, lawyer; b. Columbia, Mo., Oct. 10, 1956; s. Jack Sterling and Alice Jean (Wright) P.; m. Susan Kay Chantland, June 17, 1978. BA, U. No. Iowa, 1978; JD, Drake U., 1981. Bar: Iowa 1981, U.S. Dist. Ct. (so. dist.) Iowa 1981, U.S. Tax Ct. 1981, U.S. Ct. Appeals (8th cir.) 1981. Assoc. Davis, Hockenberg, Wine, Brown & Koehn, Des Moines, 1981-83; asst. counsel Prin. Mut. Life Ins. Co., Des Moines, 1983-85, Bankers Life Ins. Co., Des Moines, 1985—. Bd. dirs. Iowa Soc. to Prevent Blindness, Des Moines, 1983—. Mem. ABA, Iowa Bar Assn., Polk County Bar Assn. Democrat. Pension, profit-sharing, and employee benefits. Home: 1674 NW 103d Des Moines IA 50322 Office: Prin Mutual Life Ins Co 711 High St Des Moines IA 50309

PETERSEN, JAN FAREL, lawyer; b. Duluth, Minn., Jan. 12, 1949; s. Leonard Henry and Pauline Fredrika (Illgen) P.; m. Linda Marie Sobota, June 21, 1975; children: Alicia, Michele, Janova. BA, U. Minn., 1971; JD, William Mitchell Coll. Law, 1975. Bar: Minn. 1975, U.S. Dist. Ct. Minn. 1975. Asst. city atty. City of St. Cloud, Minn., 1975-79, city atty, 1979—; speaker League of Minn. Cities, St. Paul; bd. dirs. Major Crime Investigation Unit, St. Cloud. Active Atonement Luth. Ch., St. Cloud, 1976—; chmn. dist. camping Boy Scouts Am., St. Cloud, 1980—, advisor law explorer post, 1985—; bd. dirs. Tour of Saints-Bicycle Tour, St. Cloud, 1981—. Mem. ABA, Minn. Bar Assn., Stearns-Benton Bar Assn., Minn. Pub. Employees Labor Relations Assn., Nat. Pub. Employees Labor Relations Assn., Minn. City Attys. Assn. (pres. 1984-85). Avocations: bicycle racing and touring, camping, woodworking, gardening. Local government, Labor, Criminal. Home: 1506 Calvary Hill Ln Saint CLoud MN 56301 Office: City Attys Office 400 2d St S Saint Cloud MN 56301

PETERSEN, LEE, lawyer; b. Akron, Ohio, July 7, 1946. BA in Philosophy, U. Akron, 1966, postgrad., 1966-68; postgrad., Kans. State U., 1968-69; JD, U. Akron, 1981. Bar: Ohio 1981, U.S. Dist. Ct. (no. dist.) Ohio, 1982. Sole practice Akron, 1982—. Mem. ABA, Ohio State Bar Assn., Akron Bar Assn. Democrat. Bankruptcy, Consumer commercial, General practice. Office: 2483 S Main St Akron OH 44319

PETERSEN, O. KEITH, lawyer; b. Grafton, W.Va., July 1, 1928; s. Archie Frederick and Dorothy Lucille (Bort) P.; children—Roger Keith, Kirsten Ruth Shoemaker, Karen Amy, Richard Von; m. 2d Barbara Kathryn Graham, Jan. 3, 1981. B.S. with high honors, Mich. State U., 1952; J.D., U. Mich., 1955. Bar: Mich. 1956, U.S. Dist. Ct. (ea. dist.) Mich., U.S. Dist. Ct. (we. dist.) Mich., U.S. Ct. Appeals (6th cir.). Asst. gen. counsel Consumers Power Co., Jackson, Mich., 1955-56, atty., 1956-70, sr. atty., 1970-75, mng. atty., 1975-86, asst. gen. counsel 1986—. Co-chmn. Jackson Water Study Com.; advisor, Jr. Achievement; fund-raiser Community Chest, Jackson Civitan Club fund for retarded children; active Cub Scouts Am., 1962-64. Mem. ABA (labor, environ., antitrust laws sects.), Mich. Bar Assn. (antitrust, pub. interest law sects., chmn. labor law sect. 1971-72, vice-chmn. environ. law sect. 1980-82, chmn. 1982-83), Jackson County Bar Assn. Clubs: Town, Jackson Racquet, United Conservation, Toastmasters (past pres.). Labor, Environment, Antitrust. Address: 212 W Michigan Ave Jackson MI 49201

PETERSEN, STEVEN FRANK, lawyer; b. Reno, June 4, 1947; s. Frank Raymond and Vera (Novakovich) P.; m. Donna Marie Antracooli, Nov. 19, 1982; children: Lisa Neal, Carly Knight. BS, U. Oreg., 1969; JD, U. San Francisco, 1972. Bar: Nev. 1972, U.S. Dist Ct. Nev. 1972, U.S. Ct. Claims 1973, U.S. Ct. Appeals (9th cir.) 1975, U.S. Supreme Ct. 1972. Ptnr. Petersen & Petersen, Reno, 1972—. Trustee Constance H. Bishop Found. Mem. ABA, Fed. Bar Assn., Am. Judicature Soc., Assn. Trial Lawyers Am., Nev. Trial Lawyers Assn., Nev. Gaming Commn. (state gaming control bd.). Republican. Club: Prospectors (Reno). Office: 1 E Liberty St Suite 611 Reno NV 89501

PETERSILGE, ROBERT, lawyer; b. Cleve., Apr. 4, 1917; s. Arthur Ferdinard Moritz and Esther S., P.; m. Janet Robertson Macdiarmid, June

12, 1948; children—Janet E., Robert J., David A. A.B., Adelbert Coll., 1939; LL.B., Western Res. U., 1941. Staff atty. gen. counsel's office U.S. Treasury Dept., Washington, 1941-42; ptnr. Matz, Petersilge & Weimer, Akron, Ohio, 1946—. Mem. Silver Lake Village Council, Ohio, 1953; pres. Vis. Nurse Service Summit County Ohio, Akron, 1975. Served to lt. USCG, 1942-46. Mem. Akron Bar Assn. (pres. 1962-63), Ohio State Bar Assn. (former mem. probate bd. govs.), ABA. Republican. Congregationalist. Lodge: Rotary, Masons. Avocations: tennis; skiing; playing organ. Probate. Home: 2912 Parkwood Dr Silver Lake Cuyahoga Falls OH 44224 Office: Matz Petersilge & Weimer 411 Wolf Ledges Pkwy Akron OH 44311

PETERSON, BROOKE ALAN, lawyer; b. Omaha, Dec. 6, 1949; s. Lloyd Earl and Priscilla Anne (Bailey) P.; m. Linda Jane Harlem, June 30, 1979 (div. 1980). B.A., Brown U., 1972; J.D., U. Denver, 1975. Bar: Colo. 1975, U.S. Dist. Ct. Colo. 1975. Assoc. Garfield & Hecht, Aspen, Colo., 1975-77, Robert P. Grueter, Aspen, 1977-78; ptnr. Wendt, Grueter & Peterson, Aspen, 1978-79; prin. Brooke A. Peterson, P.C., Aspen, 1979—; mcpl. judge, Aspen, 1980—. Chmn. election commn., Pitkin County, 1979—. Mem. ABA, Colo. Bar Assn. (bd. govs. 1984-86, exec. council 1986—), Pitkin County Bar Assn. (pres. 1981-83), Am. Trial Laywers Assn., Colo. Trial Lawyers Assn. Avocations: skiing, surfing, softball, squash, music. General practice, Real property, General corporate. Home: 0222 Roaring Fork Dr Aspen CO 81611 Office: 315 E Hyman Aspen CO 81611

PETERSON, C(ARL) DONALD, state justice; b. Mpls., Feb. 2, 1918; s. Karl Emil and Emma Marie (Sellin) P.; m. Gretchen Elaine Palen, Dec. 6, 1952; children: Barbara Elaine Peterson Burwell, Craig Donald, Mark Bradley, Polly Suzanne Peterson Bowles, Todd Douglas, Scott Jeffrey. B.A. cum laude, U. Minn., 1939; J.D. with honors (mem. Law Rev.), U. Ill., 1941; grad., Appellate Judges Seminar, N.Y. U., 1967, Nat. Coll. State Trial Judges, 1969. Bar: Minn. 1941, U.S. Supreme Ct 1941. Practice in Mpls., 1941-66; partner firm Howard, Peterson, LeFevere, Lefler, Hamilton & Pearson, 1953-66; justice Supreme Ct. Minn., 1967-86; ret. 1986. Contbr. article to Am. Bar Assn. Jour. Co-chmn. task force study creating Nat. News Council, 20th Century Fund, 1972-73; bd. dirs. state youth in govt. project YMCA, 1968-78; Mem. Minn. Ho. Reps., 1959-62, minority whip, 1961-62, Republican nominee for lt. gov., Minn., 1962. Served to maj. USAAF, 1942-45; Served to maj. USAF, 1951-52. Decorated Bronze Star. Mem. ABA, Minn. Bar Assn., Inst. Jud. Adminstrn., Am. Law Inst., Am. Judicature Soc., Minn. News Council (chmn. 1971-81), Am.-Swedish Inst., Delta Sigma Rho. Presbyn. (elder 1963—, pres. 1964, 79). Clubs: Minnesota (St. Paul); Torske Klubben (Mpls.). Office: Minn Supreme Ct State Capitol Saint Paul MN 55155

PETERSON, CLYDE L., lawyer; b. Phila., Dec. 24, 1924; s. Clyde L. and Avis (Manor) P.; m. Ruth Stimson, Feb. 5, 1949; children—Scott, Stephen, Susan; m. 2d, Carol Peterson, July 2, 1971. B.S., Ind. U., 1949, J.D., 1951. Bar: Ind., U.S. Ct. Appeals (7th cir.), U.S. Ct. Appeals (6th cir.), U.S. Ct. Appeals (D.C. cir.). Assoc. Duck & Neighbours, Indpls., 1952-58, Cadick, Burns, Duck & Neighbours, 1958-75, Cadick, Burns, Duck & Peterson, 1975-80; ptnr. King, Peterson, Haramy & Ebert, Indpls., 1980-83, Peterson, Haramy, Cline & Shoup, 1984—. Pres. 500 Festival, 1971; pres. Community Service Council, 1964; bd. dirs. Children's Bur., Heart Assn., Diabetes Assn., others. Served to 1st. USMC, 1943-46, 50-52. Decorated Bronze Star, Purple Heart, Letter of Commendation; recipient Disting. Service award Indpls. Jaycees, 1961. Mem. ABA, Ind. Bar Assn., Indpls. Bar Assn., Am. Arbitration Assn. Republican. Methodist. Clubs: Columbia, Lawyers, Gyro (Indpls.). Labor, Pension, profit-sharing, and employee benefits. Office: 1530 Market Sq Center Indianapolis IN 46204

PETERSON, DAVID L., judge, educator; b. Long Branch, N.J., Apr. 22, 1943; s. Glen and Doreyn Elizabeth (Latimer) P.; m. Elaine D., June 3, 1968; children—Paul, Kimberly, Shane. B.A., Brigham Young U., 1968; J.D., U. Okla., 1972. Bar: Okla. 1973, U.S. Dist. Ct. (no. dist.) Okla. 1973, U.S. Dist. Ct. (ea. dist.) Okla. 1977, U.S. Ct. Appeals (10th cir.) 1975, U.S. Supreme Ct. 1980. Practice, 1973-81; judge Tulsa County (Okla.) Dist. Ct., 1981—; instr. Tulsa Jr. Coll. Served with M.I., U.S. Army, 1968-70. Mem. ABA, Okla. Bar Assn., Tulsa County Bar Assn., Assn. Trial Lawyers Am., Okla. Trial Lawyers Assn., Phi Alpha Delta. Club: Lions. Criminal, State civil litigation. Home: 8155 E 31st Ct Tulsa OK 74145 Office: Tulsa County Courthouse 340 Tulsa OK 74103

PETERSON, DAVID REID, lawyer; b. Kansas City, Mo., Dec. 1, 1949; s. William Richard and Eleanor Marie (Harper) P.; m. Judy Lee Phillips, Aug. 24, 1979; children: William David, Thomas Reid. Student, U. Freiburg, Fed. Republic of Germany, 1969-70; BA, U. Mich., 1971, JD, 1975. Bar: Mich. 1975, U.S. Dist. Ct. (we. dist.) Mich. 1984, U.S. Dist. Ct. (ea. dist.) Mich. 1985. Researcher for appellate defender State of Mich., Detroit, 1974-75; chief asst. pros. atty. Marquette County, Mich., 1976-82; ptnr. Blakeslee, Chambers & Peterson, Traverse City, Mich., 1982—; vice-chmn. Upper Mich. Legal Services Corp., 1977—. Chmn. Traverse City Zoning Bd. Appeals, 1983—; mem. Grand Traverse County Econ. Devel. Corp., 1985—. Mem. ABA, Mich. Bar Assn., Am. Judicature Soc., Grand Traverse Leelanau-Antrim Bar Assn. Methodist. Lodge: Kiwanis. Avocations: tennis, golf, cross-country ski racing, stamp collecting. General corporate, Oil and gas leasing, General practice. Office: Blakeslee Chambers & Peterson 900 E Front St Traverse City MI 49684

PETERSON, DONALD GEORGE, lawyer; b. Oak Park, Ill., May 20, 1940; s. Otto S. and Catherine E. Peterson. B.A., Miami U., Oxford, Ohio, 1962; J.D., Northwestern U., 1965. Bar: Ill. 1966, U.S. Dist. Ct. (no. dist.) Ill. 1966, U.S. Ct. Appeals (7th cir.) 1982, U.S. Supreme Ct. 1984. Assoc., Garbutt & Jacobson, Chgo., 1967-72; ptnr. Schaffenegger, Watson & Peterson, Ltd., Chgo., 1972—; speaker, instr. Ill. State Bar, Ill. Inst. Continuing Legal Edn., Chgo. Bar, Ill. Trial Lawyers Assn., Casualty Adjusters Assn., Nat. Inst. Mcpl. Law Officers. Bd. dirs. United Way, Clarendon Hills, Ill., 1980-81; legal advisor Community Caucus, Clarendon Hills, 1981. Recipient Hodes Local Govt. award Northwestern U., 1965. Mem. Ill. Bar Assn. (chmn. civil practice council 1983-84, editor newsletter 1980-85, assembly del. 1985—, sec. publs. com. 1986—, mem. fin. com., bar elections supervision com., chmn. assembly spl. com. to propose a program MCLE 1987), Chgo. Bar Assn. (chmn. judiciary com. 1986—, mem. fed. civil procedure com., civil practice com.), Appellate Lawyers Assn., Soc. Trial Lawyers. Ill., Trial Lawyers Club Chgo. Club: East Bank (Chgo.). Federal civil litigation, State civil litigation, Insurance. Office: Schaffenegger Watson & Peterson Ltd Suite 3105 69 W Washington St Chicago IL 60602

PETERSON, DONALD ROY, lawyer; b. Berlin, Wis., Mar. 17, 1933; s. Rueben William and Lucille (Ising) P.; m. Helen Louise Frederick, Aug. 21, 1954; children: John R., Karen L. Peterson Ray, David G., Kathryn L. BBA, U. Wis., 1955, LLB, 1958. Bar: Wis. 1958. Assoc. Borgelt, Powell, Peterson & Frauen, Milw., 1958-64, ptnr., 1964-82; ptnr., pres. Peterson, Johnson & Murray S.C., Milw., 1982—. Mem. ABA, Wis. Trial Lawyers Assn. (past pres.), Am. Coll. Trial Lawyers, Civil Trial Counsel Wis. Republican. Lutheran. Insurance, Personal injury, Federal civil litigation. Office: Peterson Johnson & Murray SC 733 N Van Buren Milwaukee WI 53202

PETERSON, EDWIN J., state supreme court justice; b. Gilmanton, Wis., Mar. 30, 1930; s. Edwin A. and Leora Grace (Kitelinger) P.; m. Anna Chadwick, Feb. 7, 1971; children: Patricia, Andrew, Sherry. B.S., U. Oreg., 1951, LL.B., 1957. Bar: Oreg. 1957. Asso. firm Tooze, Kerr, Peterson, Marshall & Shenker, Portland, 1957-61; mem. firm Tooze, Kerr, Peterson, Marshall & Shenker, 1961-79; assoc. justice Supreme Ct. Oreg., Salem, 1979—, chief justice, 1983—; bd. dirs. Conf. Chief Justices, 1985—. Chmn. Portland Citizens Sch. Com., 1968-70; vice chmn. Young Republican Fedn. Oregon., 1951; bd. visitors U. Oreg. Law Sch., 1978-83, chmn. bd. visitors, 1981-83. Served to 1st lt. USAF, 1952-54. Mem. ABA, Am. Judicature Soc., Internat. Assn. Ins. Counsel, Council State Bar Presidents, Oreg. State Bar (bd. examiners 1963-66, gov. 1973-76, vice chmn. profl. liability fund 1977-78), Multnomah County Bar Assn. (pres. 1972-73), Phi Alpha Delta, Lambda Chi Alpha. Episcopalian. Jurisprudence. Home: 3365 Sunridge Dr S Salem OR 97302 Office: Supreme Ct Bldg Salem OR 97310

PETERSON, FRANKLIN DELANO, lawyer; b. Braham, Minn., Nov. 11, 1932; s. John Erick and Myrtle M. (Anderson) P.; m. Beverly Ann Crabb, Aug. 2, 1958; children: Heidi, Durward, Heather. Student, Augsburg Coll., 1950-51; BA, St. Cloud State Coll., 1955; LLB, William Mitchell Coll. Law, 1961. Bar: Minn. 1961. Field claims adjuster Farmers Mut. Ins. Co., St. Paul, 1955-57; asst. dist. claims mgr. Minn. Farmers Ins. Group, Mpls., 1957-62; sole practice Kenyon, Minn., 1963—; atty. City of Kenyon, 1964-82; v.p. Kenyon Devel. Corp., bd. dirs.; sec. Tri-Valley Constrn. Co., Kenyon, bd. dirs. Chmn. Goldwater for Pres. campaign, Village of Kenyon Reps., 1964, Goodhue County LeVander for Gov., 1966, Goodhue County Reps, 1969-70; sec. Goodhue Selective Service Bd., 1968—; pres. Mineral Springs Chem. Dependency Ctr., 1974-85; mem. Kenyon Pub. Sch. Bd. Edn., 1976-82, treas. 1980-82, Kenyon Booster Club (charter), v.p. 1983; mgr. mgr. Kenyon Legion Baseball, 1979—; bd. dirs. Kenyon Roseview Apts., 1967—, pres. 1985—. Served with USAF, 1950-52. Mem. ABA, Minn. Bar Assn. (jud. dist. del., pres. 1st dist. 1979-80), Goodhue County Bar Assn., Minn. Assn. Plaintiffs Attys., Nat. Assn. Claimants Counsel, Sons of Norway (pres. Kenyon lodge 1969). Lutheran. Clubs: Kenyon Comml., Kenyon Country. Lodge: Masons, Shriners, Lions(pres. Kenyon club). Home: Rural Rt Box B Kenyon MN 55946 Office: 634 2d St Box B Kenyon MN 55946

PETERSON, GALE ROY, lawyer; b. Oakland, Nebr., Aug. 12, 1948; s. Roy John and Margaret (Johnson) P.; m. Pauline Adele Matson, Sept. 12, 1970; children—Stephanie Erin, Megan Ashley, Susan Amanda. B.S. in Elec. Engring., U. Nebr., 1970; J.D. magna cum laude, U. Balt., 1975; LL.M. in Trade Regulation with highest honors, George Washington U., 1978. Bar: Va. 1975, D.C. 1976, Tex. 1978, U.S. Ct. Customs and Patent Appeals 1976, U.S. Patent and Trademark Office 1976, U.S. Ct. Claims 1977, U.S. Supreme Ct. 1978, U.S. Ct. Appeals (5th cir.) 1979, U.S. Dist. Ct. (we. dist.) Tex. 1979, U.S. Dist. Ct. (so. dist.) Tex. 1980, U.S. Ct. Appeals (11th cir.) 1981, U.S. Ct. Appeals (fed. cir.) 1982. Examiner U.S. Patent and Trademark Office, Washington, 1970-76, law clk. to examiner-in-chief Bd. Appeals, 1975; tech. adviser, briefing atty. to chief judge U.S. Ct. Appeals (fed. cir.), Washington, 1976-78; ptnr., dir. firm Cox & Smith, Inc., San Antonio, 1978—; lectr. Patent Resources Group, Washington, 1980, 86. Mem. U. Balt. Law Rev., 1974. Contbr. articles and papers to profl. lit. Mem. bd. Christian edn. Christ Luth. Ch., San Antonio, 1982-83; active Lawyers and Accts. for Arts, San Antonio, 1982-83. Recipient spl. achievement awards U.S. Patent and Trademark Office, 1971-76. Mem. Assn. Former Law Clks. and Tech. Advisors (bd. dirs. 1983—), State Bar Tex. (trade secret and unfair competition com. intellectual property law sect. 1981-82, treas. sect. 1984—), Va. State Bar Assn., D.C. Bar Assn., Tex. State Bar Assn., San Antonio Bar Assn., ABA, Fed. Bar Assn., Am. Intellectual Property Law Assn., San Antonio Intellectual Property Law Assn. (pres. 1984—), U.S. Trademark Assn., Computer Law Assn., Licensing Execs. Soc., San Antonio World Affairs Council. Republican. Lutheran. Clubs: Plaza, Los Amigos Ski (pres. 1983-84, bd. dirs. 1984—) (San Antonio). Patent, Trademark and copyright, Antitrust. Office: Cox & Smith Inc 600 Nat Bank of Commerce San Antonio TX 78205

PETERSON, JAMES CHARLES, lawyer; b. Rochester, Minn., Oct. 23, 1949; s. Charles Allen and Margaret (Hennessey) P.; m. Cynthia Louise Hargesheimer, Apr. 1, 1977. BA in Polit. Sci., U. Minn., 1972; JD, William Mitchell Coll., 1975. Bar: Minn 1976, U.S. Dist. Ct. Minn. 1976, Ohio 1979, U.S. Dist. Ct. (so. and no. dists.) Ohio 1979, W.Va. 1984, U.S. Dist. Ct. (so. dist.) W.Va. 1984, U.S. Ct. Appeals (4th cir.) 1986. Law clk. to chief judge County Ct.of Mpls., 1975-77; assoc. Douglas, Jaycox, Trawick, McManus & Lipport, Mpls., 1977-78; asst. gen counsel The Way Internat., New Knoxville, Ohio, 1978-79, gen. counsel, 1979-83; ptnr. Hill & Wood, Charleston, W.Va., 1983, Hill & Peterson, Charleston, 1984—. Mem. Assn. Trial Lawyers Am., Minn. Bar Assn., Ohio Bar Assn., W.Va. Bar Assn., W.Va. Trial Lawyers Assn. (chmn. budget com. 1985—, bd. govs. 1986—), Kanawha County Bar Assn. Republican. Avocations: jogging, skiing, golf. Personal injury, Federal civil litigation, State civil litigation. Office: One Bridge Pl 10 Hale St Suite 300 Charleston WV 25301

PETERSON, JAMES RICHARD, lawyer, musician; b. St. Paul, May 3, 1950; s. Roger William and Betty Marie (Hall) P.; m. Janice Jean Keenan, May 20, 1978; children: Sarah, Joshua. AB, Harvard U., 1972; JD, U. Mich., 1976. Bar: N.Y. 1977, Alaska 1978, U.S. Dist. Ct. Alaska 1979, U.S. Dist. Ct. (we. dist.) N.Y. 1984. Atty. Broome County Dist. Atty., Binghamton, N.Y., 1977-78; assoc. Burr, Pease & Kurtz, Anchorage, 1979-84, Phillips, Lytle, Hitchcock, Blaine & Huber, Buffalo, 1984-85; counsel Goldome FSB, Buffalo, 1985—. Mem. ABA, N.Y. State Bar Assn., Erie County Bar Assn., Niagara Frontier Corp. Counsels Assn., Am. Fedn. Musicians (Buffalo local 92). Unitarian. Consumer commercial, Banking, General corporate. Home: 155 Roycroft Blvd Snyder NY 14226 Office: Goldome FSB One Fountain Plaza Buffalo NY 14203

PETERSON, JAN ERIC, lawyer; b. Seattle, Apr. 28, 1944; s. Theodore Dare and Dorothy Elizabeth (Spofford) P.; m. Jeanne Elizabeth Clemens, June 25, 1966 (div. Jan. 1984); children: Nels Andrew, Anne Elizabeth; m. Marguerite Victoria Caggiano, Mar. 31, 1984. AB in History, Stanford U., 1966; JD, U. Wash., 1969. Bar: Wash., U.S. Dist. Ct. (we. and ea. dists.) Wash., U.S. Ct. Appeals (9th cir.). Gen. counsel ACLU, Seattle, 1969-71; assoc. Daniel F. Sullivan, Seattle, 1972-73; sr. ptnr. Peterson, Bracelin, Young, Putra, Fletcher and Zeder, Seattle, 1973—. Drafter (state statute) Tap Water Regulation Act, 1983. Mem. ABA (editor assoc. 1976-78), Damages Attys. Round Table (founding), Assn. Trial Lawyers Am. (del. 1985-86), Wash. State Trial Lawyers Assn. (bd. 1973—, pres. 1982-83), Wash. State Bar Assn. (jud. selection 1985—), Am. Bd. Trial Adv. (diplomate), ACLU. Democrat. Avocations: piano, baseball, basketball, golf. Personal injury, Civil rights. Office: Peterson et al 2500 Smith Tower Seattle WA 98104

PETERSON, JOHN CHRISTIAN, lawyer; b. Chgo., Nov. 11, 1951; s. Robert J. and Marian L. (Hickman) P.; m. Martha K. Hemwall, Apr. 6, 1974;; children: Maren Hemwall, Emily Hemwall. BA, Lawrence U., 1973; JD, Washington U., 1976. Bar: R.I. 1976, U.S. Dist Ct. R.I. 1977, U.S. Ct. Appeals (1st cir.) 1977, Wis. 1983, U.S. Dist. Ct. (ea. dist.) Wis. 19823. Assoc. Higgins, Cavanagh & Cooney, Providence, 1976-82; ptnr. Robinson, Robinson, Peterson, Rudolph & Cross, Appleton, Wis., 1982—. Editor R.I. Bar Jour., 1978-82. Bd. dirs. Big Bros./Big Sisters of Fox Valley, Appleton, 1986—; vice chmn. 8th Congl. Dist. Dems., Wis., 1984; chmn. Outagamie County (Wis.) Dems., 1985—. Mem. Assn. Trial Lawyers Am., Wis. Acad. Trial Lawyers (bd. dirs. 1986—), Am. Arbitration Assn. (arbitrator). Democrat. Avocations: camping, canoeing, hiking. State civil litigation, Personal injury, Insurance. Home: 126 S Alton Appleton WI 54911 Office: Robinson Robinson Peterson Rudolph & Cross 103 E College Ave Appleton WI 54911

PETERSON, LAUREL J., lawyer; b. Roseau, Minn., Sept. 22, 1947; s. Leon S. and Leah A. (Finkle) P.; m. Paula A. Peterson, Aug. 14, 1984. BA, Western Colo. U., 1969; JD, Gonzaga U., 1972. Bar: Alaska, Wash. Dist. judge Alaskan Judiciary, Anchorage, 1974-79; ptnr. Houston & Henderson, Anchorage, 1979-81; sole practice Anchorage, 1981—. Personal injury, State civil litigation.

PETERSON, LINDA SUE, lawyer; b. San Francisco, Nov. 18, 1948; d. Harry Adolph and Maxine Maebar (White) P.; m. Alexander Gregory Wesman, Oct. 8, 1978 (div. Dec. 1982). BA, U. Calif., Santa Cruz, 1970; JD, Boston U., 1976. Bar: N.Y. 1977. Staff atty. Allegheny Power Service Corp., N.Y.C., 1977-80; corp. counsel Liggett Group Inc., Montvale, N.J., 1980-81; assoc. Webster & Sheffield, N.Y.C., 1981—. Bd. dirs. Theater by the Blind, N.Y.C., 1983—. Mem. ABA (corp. banking and bus. law sect., subcom. acctg. 1981—), Assn. of Bar of City of N.Y. (lectures and continuing edn. com.). Democrat. General corporate, Securities, Consumer commercial. Home: 45 E Hartsdale Ave #4H Hartsdale NY 10530 Office: Webster & Sheffield 237 Park Ave New York NY 10017

PETERSON, MARK WARREN, lawyer; b. Mpls., Nov. 13, 1947; s. Warren Parker and Muriel Virginia (Lundberg) P.; m. Barbara Ann Jerich, June 28, 1980; 1 child, Jessica Jerich. BA, Northwestern U., 1969; JD cum laude, U. Minn., 1972. Bar: Minn. 1972, U.S. Dist. Ct. Minn. 1972, U.S. Ct. Appeals (8th cir.) 1973, U.S. Supreme Ct. 1976, U.S. Ct. Appeals (6th cir.) 1978, U.S. Ct. Appeals (10th cir.) 1979, U.S. Ct. Appeals (7th cir.) 1981, U.S. Dist. Ct. Iowa 1975, U.S. Dist. Ct. (so. dist) Calif. 1974, U.S. Dist. Ct. (so. dist.) N.Y. 1978, U.S. Dist. Ct. Colo. 1979. Atty. pub. defender's office State of Minn., Mpls., 1972-73; atty. Neighborhood Justice Ctr., St. Paul, 1973-74; ptnr. Thomson, Nordby & Peterson, St. Paul, 1974-77, Friedberg & Peterson, Mpls., 1978-82; sole practice Mpls., 1983—. Author: Misdemeanors and Moving Traffic Violations Manual, 1973, Minnesota Criminal Procedure, 1974, Criminal Pretrial Practice and Procedure, 1986. Mem. Minn. Bar Assn., Assn. Trial Lawyers Am., Acad. Cert. Trial Lawyers (bd. govs. 1983—), Minn. Trial Lawyers Assn. (bd. govs. 1978-86), Nat. Assn. Criminal Def. Lawyers. Democrat. Lutheran. Avocations: watersports, motorcycles, children. Criminal. Home: 6604 Indian Hills Rd Edina MN 55435 Office: 608 2d Ave S Suite 380 Minneapolis MN 55402

PETERSON, NEIL RAYMOND, lawyer; b. Buffalo, N.Y., Apr. 23, 1939; s. Arthur Otto and Esther Regina (Walsh) P.; m. Nancy Lynn Oberdorf, June 15, 1963; children: Michael Neil, Megan Lynn. BA, Georgetown U., 1960, JD, 1963; LLM, George Washington U., 1966. Bar: D.C. 1964, U.S. Dist. Ct. D.C. 1964, U.S. Ct. Appeals (D.C. cir.) 1964, U.S. Supreme Ct. 1968, U.S. Ct. Appeals (10th cir.) 1977, Pa. 1980, U.S. Dist. Ct. (ea. dist.) Pa. 1980, U.S. Ct. Appeals (3d and 4th cirs.) 1980, U.S. Dist. Ct. (mid. dist.) Pa. 1985, U.S. Ct. Appeals (2d cir.) 1985. Trial atty. office of solicitor U.S. Dept. Labor, Washington, 1963-67; trial atty. tort sect. U.S. Dept. Justice Civil Div., Washington, 1967-74, asst. chief tort sect., 1974-77, atty. litigation tng. officer tort sect., 1974-77, chief swine flu counsel tort branch, office of asst. atty. gen., 1977-80; ptnr. Greitzer & Locks, Phila., 1980—; spl. asst. U.S. atty. Dist. of Columbia, 1970; lectr., evaluator Atty. Gen.'s Advocacy Inst., U.S. Dept. Justice, 1973-80, panelist Fed. Rules of Evidence Tapes, U.S. Dept. Justice, 1975; mem. Teton Dam Relief Act Regulations Panel, U.S. Dept. Justice, 1976; witness U.S. Dept. Justice on budgetary and substantive matters, 1975-79; mem. exec. service U.S. Govt., Washington, 1979-80, Plaintiffs' Med. Causation Com. Agent Orange Litigations, U.S. Dist. Ct. (ea. dist.) N.Y. 1980—. Mem. Haverford Citizens Assn., Haverford, Pa., 1984—, League of Voters, Haverford, 1985—. Mem. ABA (lectr. torts and ins. pracitce sect. 1986—), Pa. Bar Assn., Dist. of Pa. Bar Assn., Phila. Bar Assn., Pa. Trial Lawyers Assn, Phila. Trial Lawyers Assn. Roman Catholic. Club: Merion Cricket (Haverford). Avocations: reading, swimming. Federal civil litigation, State civil litigation, Personal injury. Home: 219 Grays Ln Haverford PA 19041 Office: Greitzer & Locks 1500 Walnut St Floor 22 Philadelphia PA 19102

PETERSON, OSLER LEOPOLD, lawyer; b. Mpls., Oct. 19, 1946; s. Osler Luther and Delores (Kealy) P.; m. Sandra Ann Freeto, Jan. 2, 1971 (div. Dec. 1983). BA, Brown U., 1969; JD, Suffolk U., 1976. Bar: Mass. 1976, U.S. Dist. Ct. Mass. 1976. Sole practice Newton, Mass., 1976-84; ptnr. Freeto, Peterson, Scoll & Siciliano, Newton, 1984—; clk. Neww Ctr., Inc., Newton, 1977-84, Lasell Jr. Coll., Newton, 1983-86; pres. Neww Ctr., Inc., Newton, 1984-86, Community Support Systems, Inc., 1986—. Telephone counselor and trainer Contact Boston, Inc., Newton, 1982—. Mem. ABA, Mass. Bar Assn., Assn. Trial Lawyers Am., Mass. Acad. Trial Attys. Personal injury, State civil litigation, General practice. Home: 100 Hull St Newton MA 02160 Office: Freeto Peterson Scoll & Siciliano 2000 Commonwealth Ave PO Box 115 Newton MA 02166

PETERSON, PAUL AMES, lawyer; b. Los Angeles, Feb. 17, 1928; s. Ames and Norma (Brown) P.; div.; children: Daniel C., Andrew G., Mattew A., James E.; m. Barbara J. Henderson, Sept. 12, 1976. BS in Econs., U. Calif., Berkeley, 1953, JD, 1956. Bar: Calif. 1956, U.S. Ct. Appeals (9th cir.) 1956, U.S. Supreme Ct. 1964. Assoc. Law Offices of George W. Phillips, Castro Valley, Calif., 1956-57; ptnr. Peterson, Thelan & Price, San Diego, 1958—; assoc. prof. Calif. Western Coll. Law, San Diego, 1958-60, U. San Diego Law Sch., 1960-63, U. Calif. San Diego, 1984—; bd. overseers U. Calif., San Diego, 1984—; trustee U. Calif. Found., San Diego, 1985—; bd. dirs. Econ. Devel. Corp., San Diego, San Diegans, Inc. Contbr. articles to profl jours. Bd. dirs. San Diego County Water Authority, 1984—, San Diego Conv. Ctr. Corp., 1985—. Served to tech. sgt. U.S. Army, 1946-48, Korea. Mem. Am. Judicature Soc., Fed. Bar Assn., Calif. Bar Assn. Democrat. Avocations: tennis, hiking. Administrative and regulatory, Environment, Real property. Home: 7020 Neptune Pl La Jolla CA 92037

PETERSON, RALPH HENRY, lawyer; b. Hunter, N.D., Aug. 26, 1922; s. Henry R. and Ella C. (Peterson) P.; m. Marjorie C. Youngquist, Sept. 25, 1948; children: Charlotte, Patricia Hareid, Carol Johnson, Anita. BS, U. Minn., 1945, JD, 1947. Bar: Minn. 1947. Ptnr. Peterson, Chesterman, Erickson, Anderson & Hareid and predecessor firms, Albert Lea, Minn., 1947—; bd. dirs. Minn. Vol. Legal Program, Minn. Continuing Legal Edn., Norwest Bank Albert Lea N.A., First State Bank of Emmons; bd. dirs., treas. Jobs Inc., Albert Lea Indsl. Devel. Corp. Pres. Luth. TV Ministries Inc., Albert Lea. Mem. ABA, Minn. State Bar Found. (bd. dirs.), Minn. Bar Assn. (v.p. 1985—), Tenth Dist. Bar Assn. (pres.), Freeborn County Bar Assn. (pres.). Republican. Lodge: Rotary (pres. Albert Lea club), Elks. General corporate, Estate planning, Probate. Home: 929 Lakeview Blvd Albert Lea MN 56007-0169 Office: Peterson Chesterman Erickson Anderson & Hareid 402 S Washington Albert Lea MN 56007-0169

PETERSON, RICHARD THOMAS, lawyer; b. Anaheim, Calif., Apr. 5, 1948; s. Richard Blakeslee and Patsy Ruth (Anderson) P.; 1 dau., Kristina Marie. B.S. cum laude, U. San Francisco, 1970; J.D., UCLA, 1973; LL.M., George Washington U., 1977. Bar: Calif. 1973, U.S. Dist. Ct. (cen. dist.) Calif. 1973, U.S. Ct. Mil. Appeals 1974, U.S. Supreme Ct. 1976. Officer, atty. adv. Adminstrv. Law Div., The Pentagon, U.S. Army, Washington, 1974-77; mem. Hurwitz Remer MacDonald & Meade, Newport Beach, Calif., 1977-83; of counsel Hurwitz, Remer & Di Vincenzo, 1983-86 ; sole practice, 1983-86 ; ptnr. Obrien, Gazin, & Peterson, 1986—; hearing officer Calif. State Bar Ct., 1981—; instr. Pepperdine U. Grad. Bus. Sch., 1983-85, 87. Bd. dirs. Western Diabetes Found., 1980-85, Orange County Legal Aid Soc., 1983—. Served to capt. JAGC, U.S. Army, 1974-77. Decorated Disting. Service medal. Mem. ABA, Orange County Bar Assn. (chmn. legis. com. 1981-82, vice chmn. state bar del. 1982, dir. 1982-87), Calif. Trial Lawyers Assn., UCLA Law Alumni Assn., U.S. Ski Assn., Am. Diabetes Assn., Beta Gamma Sigma, Alpha Sigma Nu. Democrat. Contbr. to Legis. Notes, Orange County Bar Bull., 1981; exec. editor UCLA-Alaska Law Rev., 1972-73. General practice, General corporate, Real property. Home: 50 Columbia St Irvine CA 92715 Office: 611 Anton Blvd Suite 120 Costa Mesa CA 92626

PETERSON, RICHARD WILLIAM, lawyer, magistrate; b. Council Bluffs, Iowa, Sept. 29, 1925; s. Henry K. and Laura May (Robinson) P.; m. Patricia Mae Fox, Aug. 14, 1949; children—Katherine Ilene Peterson Sherbondy, Jon Eric, Timothy Richard. B.A., U. Iowa, 1949, J.D., 1951; postgrad., U. Nebr., Omaha, 1972-80, 86. Bar: Iowa bar 1951. Individual practice law Council Bluffs, 1951—; U.S. commr. U.S. Dist. Ct. So. Dist. Iowa, 1958-70, U.S. magistrate, 1970—; mem. nat. faculty Fed. Jud. Ctr., Washington, 1972—; dir. Western Fed. Savs. and Loan, Council Bluffs; legal advisor, emeritus trustee Christian Home Assn.; verifying ofcl. Internat. Prisoner Transfer Treaties, Mexico City, 1977, La Paz, Bolivia, 1980, 81, Lima, Peru, 1981. Contbr. articles to legal publs. Bd. dirs. Pottawattamie County (Iowa) chpt. ARC, state fund chmn., 1957-58; state chmn. Radio Free Europe, 1960-61; dist. chmn. Trailblazer dist. Boy Scouts Am., 1952-55; mem. exec. council Mid-Am. council, 1976—. Served with inf. U.S. Army, 1943-46. Decorated Purple Heart, Bronze Star; named Outstanding Young Man Council Bluffs C. of C., 1959. Mem. Pottawattamie County Bar Assn. (pres. 1979-80), Iowa Bar Assn. (chmn. com. fed. practice 1978-80), ABA, Fed. Bar Assn., Inter-Am. Bar Assn., Nat. Council U.S. Magistrates (pres. 1978-79), Iowa Conf. Bar Assn. Pres. (pres. 1985-87), Phi Delta Phi, Delta Sigma Rho, Omicron Delta Kappa. Republican. Lutheran. Clubs: Kiwanis (Council Bluffs) (pres. club 1957); Masons. General practice, Probate. Home: 317 Burr Oak Rd Council Bluffs IA 51501 Office: 404-8 First Fed Savs and Loan Bldg Council Bluffs IA 51501

PETERSON, RONALD ARTHUR, emeritus business law educator; b. Valley, Nebr., June 21, 1920; s. Arthur Lawrence and Hazel McClellan (Foster) P.; m. Patricia Marguerite North, Aug. 29, 1942; children—Ronald, Kathleen, Patrick, James, John, Thomas, Mary, Joseph. B.A. in Poly. Sci., U. Omaha, 1943; J.D. in Law, Creighton U., 1948; postgrad. U. Wash., 1963-64. Bar: Nebr. 1948, Wash. 1949. Asst. prof. Seattle U., 1963-76, dir. legal studies, 1973-83, assoc. prof., 1976-84, prof. emeritus dept. bus. law, 1984—; dir., resident agt. Lesan Corp., Seattle. Mem. editorial bd. Introduction to Law and the Legal Process, 1980. Mem. Spl. Task Force on Legislation for Wash. system of pub. libraries, 1971-73; founding mem. Seattle

Archdiocese Sch. Bd., Western Wash., 1969; mem. St. Vincent DePaul Soc., Seattle, 1984. Served to lt. USNR, 1943-46. Recipient Exemplary Tchr. award Alpha Kappa Psi, 1964. Mem. Am. Bus. Law Assn. (del. 1980), Pacific Northwest Bus. Law Assn. (pres. 1984-85), Beta Gamma Sigma. Roman Catholic. Legal education, Contracts commercial. Home: 1625 McGilvra Blvd E Seattle WA 98112

PETERSON, STEVEN A., lawyer; b. Princeton, Minn., Sept. 9, 1953; s. Albin Arthur and Patricia Ann (Samuelson) P.; m. Michelle Behring, Jan. 11, 1980; children: Michael Charles, Stephanie Rose. BA, U. Minn., 1975; JD, Hamline U., 1978. Bar: Minn. 1978, U.S. Dist. Ct. Minn. 1979. Sole practice Milaca, Minn., 1978—. Mem. Minn. Bar Assn. Republican. Lutheran. Lodge: Lions (local bd. dirs.). General practice, Real property, Probate. Home: 8021 Dakota Ave Chanhassen MN 55317 Office: 116 2d Ave SW Milaca MN 56353

PETERSON, WILLIAM GEORGE, lawyer; b. Minn., Sept. 30, 1944; s. Henry Gaufin and Grace Marie (Reker) P.; m. Ann Ophoven. B.A., U. Minn., 1966, J.D., U. Pitts., 1969. Bar: Minn. 1969, U.S. Dist. Ct. Minn. 1970, U.S. Ct. Appeals (8th cir.) 1976, U.S. Supreme Ct. 1976, Wis. 1983. Spl. asst. atty. gen. State of Minn., St. Paul, 1969-78; sole practice, Bloomington, Minn., 1978-80; ptnr. Peterson & Lange, Bloomington, 1980-81; owner Peterson & Assocs., Bloomington, 1981—; instr. hotel and restaurant law Normandale Community Coll., Bloomington, 1981—; referee Hennepin County Conciliation Ct., Mpls., 1982—. Contbr. articles to profl. jours. Bd. dirs. Viking Council Boy Scouts Am., 1981-84, Minn. Valley YMCA; chmn. Hennepin County Ind. Republicans, Mpls., 1984—; mem. Minn. Legislature, 1978-82, Bloomington City Merit Bd., 1983—. Recipient Silver Beaver award Boy Scouts Am., 1981; Legis. Excellence award Minn. Legis. Evaluation Assembly, 1981. Mem. ABA, Minn. State Bar Assn., Minn. Trial Lawyers Assn., Assn. Trial lawyers Am. Roman Catholic. Club: Toastmasters. Lodges: Rotary, K.C. Personal injury, Criminal, State civil litigation. Home: 8835 Penn Lake Circle Bloomington MN 55431 Office: Peterson and Assocs Ltd 8400 Lyndale Ave Bloomington MN 55420

PETITO, BRUCE ANTHONY, lawyer; b. Poughkeepsie, N.Y., Dec. 23, 1947; s. Joseph A. and Corra Dina (Scardacci) P.; m. Suzanne Franke, Nov. 10, 1974; 1 child, Joseph Paul. BA, Syracuse U., 1970, JD, 1973. Bar: N.Y. 1974, U.S. Dist. Ct. (so. and ea. dist.) N.Y. 1974. Sole practice Poughkeepsie, 1974-81; ptnr. Petito & Devorsetz, Poughkeepsie, 1981—; lectr. law St. Francis Coll., Poughkeepsie, 1976-78, Dutchess Community Coll., Poughkeepsie, 1979. Contbr. articles to profl. jours. Mem. Poughkeepsie Jaycees, 1983; bd. dirs. Neighborhood Services Orgn., Poughkeepsie, 1975-79. Mem. Assn. Trial Lawyers Am., N.Y. State Trial Lawyers Assn., N.Y. State Bar Assn., Dutchess County Bar Assn. (chmn. 1979—, exec. com.). Democrat. Roman Catholic. Lodges: KC (bd. dirs. Florentine Council local chpt. 1976-79), Kiwanis (bd. dirs. local chpt. 1984-86). Avocation: golf. State civil litigation, General practice, Landlord-tenant. Office: Petito & Devorsetz 246 Church St Poughkeepsie NY 12603

PETITO, CHRISTOPHER SALVATORE, lawyer; b. Trenton, N.J., Nov. 7, 1955; s. Robert A. and Bebe C. (Chianese) P. BA cum laude, Yale U., 1977, JD, 1981. Bar: N.Y. 1982, U.S. Dist. Ct. (so. dist.) N.Y. 1984, U.S. Ct. Appeals (6th cir.) 1986. Assoc. Rosenman & Colin, N.Y.C, 1981—; asst. counsel Gov.'s Judicial Screening Com. 1st Dept., N.Y.C., 1985. Mem. ABA. Democrat. Roman Catholic. Federal civil litigation, State civil litigation, Antitrust. Office: Rosenman & Colin 575 Madison Ave New York NY 10011

PETOCK, MICHAEL F(RANCES), lawyer; b. Pottsville, Pa., Apr. 6, 1943; s. Michael and Mary Petock; m. Janice, Apr. 27, 1968; children: Michelle, Michael, Douglas. BSEE with high distinction, Pa. State U., 1968; JD with honors, George Washington U., 1971; postgrad., Jefferson Med. Coll., 1980-83. Bar: Pa. 1972, U.S. Patent Office 1972, U.S. Ct. Appeals (3d cir.) 1972, U.S. Ct. Appeals (fed. cir.) 1973, U.S. Supreme Ct. 1976. Patent agt. Gen. Electric Co., Washington, 1968-71; sole practice Phila., 1971—; adj. prof. law Villanova U., 1976-79. Author: Patent Trademarks Copyright and Trade Secrets, 1974; editor: Patent Trademark and Copyright sects. of Pa. Transaction Guide, 1974. V.p. St. Thomas More Soc., 1979. Served with USN, 1961-65. Mem. ABA, Pa. Bar Assn. (chmn. basic legal practice course com. 1972-77, young lawyers sect. 1977-79, bd. govs. 1977-79), Phila. Bar Assn. (chmn. econ. com. 1979), Phila. Patent Law Assn., Engrs. Club Phila. (pres. young engrs. 1976), Order of Coif, Eta Kappa Nu, Phi Kappa Phi, Sigma Taw, Phi Eta Sigma. Club: Waynesboro Country. Avocations: boating, wind surfing, surfing, skiing. Patent, Trademark and copyright, Federal civil litigation. Home: 420 Littlebrook Rd Berwyn PA 19312 Office: 1220 Valley Forge Rd PO Box 856 Valley Forge PA 19481-0856

PETRAITIS, KAREL COLETTE, lawyer; b. Chgo., Apr. 4, 1945; d. Ferdinand John and Dolores (Karroll) P.; B.A., U. Md., 1967, postgrad., 1967-68; J.D., George Washington U., 1971. Bar: Md. 1972, U.S. Supreme Ct. 1977. Law clk. Prince George's County Office of Law (Md.), 1971-72, atty., 1972-80; real estate agt. Harloff & Perkins, Riverdale, Md., 1978-82; individual practice law, College Park, Md., 1980—. Youth coordinator Agnew for Gov., 1966, Mathias for Senate, 1968, Beall for Senate, 1970; nat. committeewoman Md. Young Republicans, 1971-79, dir., 1979-81, legal counsel, 1972-79. Recipient cert. appreciation Prince George County Circuit Ct., 1979; cert. public service Prince George County, 1980; pres. Friends of Md. Summer Inst. for Creative and Performing Arts, 1983-86. Mem. Md. Bar Assn., Prince George County Bar Assn., AAUW, College Park Bd. Trade, past pres., v.p., treas., dir. Elizabeth Seton Alumni Assn., George Washington Law Alumni Assn. (dir. 1979-81, sec. 1982-84, pres. Md. chpt. 1985-87), U. Md. Alumni Assn. (pres. young alumni 1978-80, pres. Prince George's 1986—). Roman Catholic. Family and matrimonial, Personal injury, Probate. Home: 7307 Radcliffe Dr College Park MD 20740 Office: 4321 Hartwick Rd L201 College Park MD 20740

PETRASH, JEFFREY MICHAEL, lawyer; b. Cleve., Dec. 14, 1948; s. Robert Anthony and Naomi Marjorie (Close) P.; m. Patricia Ann Early, May 29, 1971 (div. Mar. 1986); 1 child, Michael Stewart. AB, U. Mich., 1969, JD, 1973. Bar: Mich. 1974, D.C. 1975. Assoc. Dickinson, Wright, McKean, Cudlip & Moon, Detroit, 1973-75, Hamel, Park, McCabe & Saunders, Washington, 1975-78; from assoc. to ptnr. Dickinson, Wright, Moon, Van Dusen & Freeman, Washington, 1978—; v.p., bd. dirs. Counseling Assocs. Inc., Washington, 1977—. Served to capt. U.S. Army, 1973-74. Mem. Soc. Barristers. Democrat. Episcopalian. Avocation: sailing. Administrative and regulatory, FERC practice, Public utilities. Home: 6606 Hillandale Rd Chevy Chase MD 20815 Office: Dickinson Wright Moon Van Dusen & Freeman 1901 L St NW Washington DC 20036

PETREE, WILLIAM HORTON, lawyer; b. Winston-Salem, N.C., Nov. 4, 1920; s. Elbert Heaton and Ethel (Tucker) P.; m. Lena Morris, Dec. 23, 1943; children: William Horton, Mary Jo. BS, U. N.C., 1944, LLB, 1948. Bar: N.C. 1948. Ptnr. Petree, Stockton & Robinson and predecessors, 1956—; bd. dirs. First Fin. Savs. & Loan Corp., First Union Nat. Bank, Winston-Salem, numerous others. Past bd. dirs., mem. exec. com. Old Salem, Inc.; mem. campaign coordinating com. Forsyth County, N.C.; past chmn. found. com. Winston-Salem Found.; past pres. Forsyth County Tb and Health Assn.; bd. dirs. Moravian Home; past chmn. fin. bd. Moravian Ch. in Am., South, trustee, elder; past trustee, exec. com. Salem Coll. Served to 1st lt. USMCR, 1944-46. Mem. Forsyth County Bar Assn. (past pres.), Alpha Tau Omega, Phi Delta Phi. Democrat. Mem. Moravian Ch. Club: Forsyth Country (past dir.). Lodge: Kiwanis (bd. dirs. Winston-Salem chpt., pres. 1976-77). Probate, Personal income taxation, General corporate. Home: 144 Muirfield Dr Winston-Salem NC 27104 Office: 1001 W 4th St Winston-Salem NC 27101

PETREY, KATHERINE GOSSICK, lawyer; b. Oak Ridge, July 27, 1948; d. Ben Roger and Jean Elizabeth (Koehler) Gossick; m. Kenneth Doyle Petrey, Jan. 6, 1973; 1 child, Samuel Harlan. B.A., U. Ky., 1970, J.D., 1974. Bar: Ohio. Assoc. Squire, Sanders & Dempsey, Cleve., 1974-84, ptnr., 1984—. Mem. Nat. Assn. Bond Lawyers, Ohio Bar Assn., Greater Cleve. Bar Assn., Legal Aid Soc. Cleve., Soc. Collectors. Democrat. Clubs: Womens City, Cleve. Garden Ctr. Avocations: gardening, tennis. Municipal bonds, Local government. Office: Squire Sanders & Dempsey 1800 Huntington Bldg Cleveland OH 44115

PETREY, RODERICK NORMAN, lawyer; b. Lakeland, Fla., Sept. 19, 1941; s. Karl Robinson and Lucille (Register) P.; m. Lucy Woodward, Aug. 30, 1969; children: Susan Choate, Sarah Fielden. Student, U. Fla., 1959-60; B.A. magna cum laude, Yale U., 1963; J.D., Harvard U., 1970. Bar: Fla. 1970. Assoc. McKinsey & Co., Inc., Washington, 1970-72; v.p. The Edna McConnell Clark Found., N.Y.C., 1972-77; ptnr. Mahoney Hadlow & Adams, Miami, Fla., 1977-82; pres. Mahoney Hadlow & Adams, 1980-82; mem. firm Valdes-Fauli Cobb & Petrey and predecessor Valdes-Fauli, Richardson & Cobb, P.A., Miami, 1982—; dir. Fla. Legal Services, So. Legal Counsel, Inc. Contbr. Articles to profl. jours. mags. Founder, pres. Fla. Justice Inst., 1979—; chmn. Nat. Rural Center, Assoc. Marine Insts. Fla., 1980-81, 87—; past pres. Fla. Legal Services, Inc.; chmn. Dade Marine Inst., Miami, 1982-86; bd. dirs. Biscayne Bay Marine Inst.; pres., chmn. Mus. Sci., 1984-86. Served to capt. Spl. Forces U.S. Army, 1963-66. Recipient Tobias Simon pro bono award Supreme Ct. Fla., 1986. Fellow Am. Bar Found.; mem. Internat. Bar Assn., ABA (past chmn. standing com. on specialization, mem. consortium on legal services and public 1976-78), Am. Judicature Soc., Fla. Bar Found. (bd. dirs., pres.), Fla. Bar (past mem. exec. council of corp., bus. and banking law sect.), Dade County Bar Assn., Am. Law Inst. Democrat. Banking, Private international, Administrative and regulatory. Office: 3400 One Biscayne Tower 2 S Biscayne Blvd Miami FL 33131

PETRIE, BERNARD, lawyer; b. Detroit, Sept. 9, 1925; s. Milton and Yetta (Schwartz) P. Prep., Culver Mil. Acad., 1943, B.S., U.S. Mil. Acad., 1946; J.D., U. Mich., 1952. Bar: N.Y. 1953, Calif. 1955. Assoc. Cravath Swaine & Moore N.Y.C. 1952-54; assoc. McCutchen, Thomas, Matthew, Griffiths & Greene, San Francisco 1954-56; asst. U.S. atty. No. Dist. Calif. 1957-60; sole practice San Francisco, 1960—; counsel Calif. office Brown & Bain, Phoenix, 1981—. Treas., Actors Workshop, San Francisco, 1961-65. Served to 1st lt. U.S. Army 1946-49; capt. Res. Fellow Am. Coll. Trial Lawyers; mem. ABA, State Bar Calif., Bar Assn. San Francisco, UN Assn. San Francisco (past pres.). Republican. Jewish. Clubs: Calif. Tennis, World Trade, Army and Navy (Washington). General practice, General corporate. Office: 633 Battery St Suite 605 San Francisco CA 94111

PETRIE, GREGORY STEVEN, lawyer; b. Seattle, Feb. 25, 1951; s. George C. and Pauline (Majers) P.; m. Margaret Fuhrman, Oct. 6, 1979; 1 child, Kathryn Jean. AB in Polit. Sci and Econs., UCLA, 1973; JD, Boston U., 1976. Bar: Wash. 1976, U.S. Dist. Ct. (we. dist.) Wash. 1976. Adminstr. Action/Peace Corps, Washington, 1973, Fed. Power Commn., Washington, 1974; assoc. Oles Morrison et al, Seattle, 1976-80; ptnr. Ferguson & Burdell, Seattle, 1981—; bd. dirs. Health Plus (HMO). Mem. ABA, Seattle-King County Bar Assn., Profl. Liability Architects and Engrs. Club: Washington Athletic (Seattle). Avocations: woodworking, skiing. Construction, Health, Pension, profit-sharing, and employee benefits. Office: Ferguson & Burdell 2900 One Union Sq Seattle WA 98101

PETRIE, JOHN THOMAS, lawyer; b. Washington, Mar. 20, 1947; s. Harold John and Joan Barbara (Sullivan) P.; m. Margaret Ann McDonald, Aug. 14, 1971; children: Sarah, Megan, Erin. BA, Seattle U., 1969; JD, U. San Francisco, 1972. Bar: Wash. 1972, U.S. Dist. Ct. (we. dist.) Wash. 1974, U.S. Ct. Appeals (9th cir.) 1975, U.S. Supreme Ct. 1977. Law clk. to presiding justice Wash. Ct. of Appeals, Tacoma, 1972-73; from assoc. to ptnr. Diamond & Sylvester, Seattle, 1973—. Real property. Office: Diamond & Sylvester 2600 Columbia Center Seattle WA 98104

PETRIKIN, JAMES RONALD, lawyer; b. Waynesville, Mo., Dec. 10, 1946; s. John David and Mary Kathryn (Koester) P.; m. Terrie Paulette Bagby, May 1, 1965 (div. 1987); children: Christopher, Timothy, Joshua. BA, U. Mo., St. Louis, 1968; JD, St. Louis U., 1973. Bar: Mo. 1973, Tenn. 1975, U.S. Dist. Ct. (we. dist.) Tenn. 1976, U.S. Ct. Appeals (6th cir.) 1976, Okla. 1982, U.S. Dist. Ct. (no. and we. dists.) Okla. 1982, U.S. Ct. Appeals (10th cir.) 1983. Trial atty. 14th region NLRB, St. Louis, 1973-74; assoc. Young & Perl P.C., Memphis, 1974-77, ptnr., 1977-82; ptnr. Gable & Gotwals P.C., Tulsa, 1982—; bd. dirs. Okla. Bar Profl. Liability Ins. Co., Oklahoma City, 1985—. Coordinator legal div. United Fund, Tulsa, 1985—; pro bono legal services Legal Aid Soc. Eastern Okla., Tulsa, 1985—, bd. dirs., 1987—; bd. dirs. Goodwill Industries, Tulsa, 1987—. Mem. ABA (labor and employment law section), Okla. Bar Assn. (faculty continuing legal edn. program 1983—, chmn. elect labor and employment law sect. 1987—). Democrat. Methodist. Labor, Pension, profit-sharing, and employee benefits, Workers' compensation. Home: 6246 S Yorktown Pl Tulsa OK 74136 Office: Gable & Gotwals 2000 4th Nat Bank Bldg Tulsa OK 74119

PETRO, JAMES MICHAEL, lawyer; b. Cleve., Oct. 25, 1948; s. William John and Lila Helen (Janca) P.; m. Nancy Ellen Bero, Dec. 16, 1972; children: John Bero, Corbin Marie. BA, Denison U., 1970; JD, Case Western Res., 1973. Bar: Ohio 1973, U.S. Dist. Ct. (no. dist.) Ohio 1974, U.S. Ct. Appeals (6th cir.) 1981. Spl. asst. U.S. senator W.B. Saxbe, Cleve., 1972-73; asst. pros. atty. Franklin County, Ohio, 1973-74; asst. dir. law City of Cleve., 1974; ptnr. Petro & Troia, Cleve., 1974-84; dir. govt. affairs Standard Oil Co., Cleve., 1984-86; ptnr. Petro, Rademaker, Matty & McClelland, Cleve., 1986—. Mem. city council Rocky River, Ohio, 1977-79, dir. law, 1980; mem. Ohio Ho. of Reps., Columbus, 1981-84, 86—. Mem. ABA, Ohio State Bar Assn., Cleve. Bar Assn. Republican. Methodist. Federal civil litigation, State civil litigation, General corporate. Home: 315 Falmouth Dr Rocky River OH 44116 Office: Petro Rademaker et al 33 Public Sq Suite 510 Cleveland OH 44113

PETRONE, LOUIS S., lawyer; b. Utica, N.Y., July 6, 1935; s. John Robert and Fortunta (Petrunti) P.; m. Mary Lourdes Palmieri, Aug. 15, 1957; children: John, Beth, Lori, Lisa. BS, Manhattan Coll., 1957; JD, Syracuse U., 1960. Bar: N.Y. 1960, U.S. Dist. Ct. (no. dist.) N.Y. 1961. Sole practice Utica, 1960-62, 72—; ptnr. Clements & Petrone, Utica, 1962-64, Wolfe, Kalil, Brill & Petrone, Utica, 1964-67, Wolfe, Kalil & Petrone, Utica, 1967-72. Mem. bd. visitors Coll. Law Syracuse (N.Y.) U., 1979—, nat. chmn. ann. giving campaign, 1983-84; v.p., bd. dirs. Cen. N.Y. Arts Council, Utica, 1982—; mem. exec. com., trustee St. Elizabeth Hosp., Utica, 1983—. Named Petrone Entrance Gallery, Coll. Law Library Syracuse U., 1985. Mem. ABA, N.Y. State Bar Assn., Assn. of Bar of City of N.Y., Oneida County Bar Assn., Tau Phi Zeta, Utica C. of C. Democrat. Roman Catholic. Clubs: Yahnundasis Golf (New Hartford, N.Y.); Fort Schuyler (Utica). Lodge: Sons of Italy. Avocation: collecting art. Insurance, Personal injury, Consumer commercial. Home: 1600 Parkway E Utica NY 13501 Office: 1624 Genesee St Utica NY 13502

PETRONI, DONALD VICTOR, lawyer; b. Reno, Nev., Apr. 22, 1931; s. Victor and Mary (Cerasola) P.; m. Abby Williams Richmond, June 16, 1956 (div. 1973); children: Victor, Lisa; m. Ann Gelston King, Sept. 7, 1973; stepchildren: Chisholm, Pamela, Samuel, Michael Halle. B.A., U. Nev., 1952; postgrad., Stanford U., 1953, J.D., 1958. Bar: Calif. 1959. Assoc. firm O'Melveny & Myers, Los Angeles, 1958-65; ptnr. O'Melveny & Myers, 1965—. Served with U.S. Army, 1953-55. Mem. ABA, Calif. Bar Assn., Los Angeles County Bar Assn. Democrat. Club: Regency. Home: 10770 Chalon Rd Los Angeles CA 90077 Office: O'Melveny & Myers 1800 Century Park E Los Angeles CA 90067

PETRUCCI, STEPHEN GERARD, lawyer; b. Kalamazoo, Mich., Dec. 2, 1951; s. Gerard S. and Mary (Stouck) P.; m. A. Nannette Nugent, May 28, 1973; children: Angela, Anthony, Matthew. BBA, U. Notre Dame, 1973; MS, Western Mich. U., 1977; JD, U. Denver, 1980. Bar: Colo. 1981, U.S. Dist. Ct. Colo. 1981, U.S. Ct. Appeals (10th cir.) 1983. Strategic and mktg. planning staff Upjohn Co., Kalamazoo, 1973-78; asst. to vice chancellor legal affairs U. Colo. Health Sci. Ctr., Denver, 1979-80; contracts staff Martin-Marietta, Denver, 1981-82; dir. legal affairs, gen. counsel Lear-Siegler, Inc., Denver, 1982-83; shareholder Burg, Aspinwall & Petrucci, P.C., Denver, 1983-85; ptnr. Petrucci & Burk, Denver, 1985—; pres. Pro-Phase, Inc., Denver, 1985—. Mem. ABA, Colo. Bar Assn., Denver Bar Assn., Assn. Trial Lawyers of Am., Colo. Trial Lawyers Assn., Sports Lawyers Assn., Am. Soc. Law and Medicine, Beta Gamma Sigma. Roman Catholic. Medical legal affairs, Sports law, Personal injury. Home: 6227 E Long Pl Englewood CO 80112 Office: Petrucci & Burk Plaza Tower One Suite 1700 6400 S Fiddlers Green Circle Englewood CO 80111

PETRUCELLY, JEFFREY PAUL, lawyer; b. N.Y.C., Feb. 4, 1946; m. Patricia Cantor; 1 child, Michael. BS, CCNY, 1967; JD, Harvard U., 1972. Bar: Mass. 1972, D.C. 1973, U.S. Ct. Appeals (1st cir.) 1981, U.S. Supreme Ct. 1985. Atty. Urban Planning Aid, Cambridge, Mass., 1972-74, Neighborhood Legal Services, Lynn, Mass., 1974-76; ptnr. Petrucelly & Stolzberg, Boston, 1976-80, Schapiro & Petrucelly, Boston, 1980-83, Petrucelly & Nadler P.C., Boston, 1983—; instr. Northeastern U., Boston, 1982-84. Mem. Mass Civil Liberties Union; bd. dirs. Assn. Neighborhood Law Clinics, Cambridge, 1978-81; trustee YMCA, Cambridge, 1982-84. Recipient Thomas Leskes Meml. award CCNY, 1967. Mem. Mass. Bar Assn., Assn. Trial Lawyers Am., Mass. Trial Lawyers Assn., Mass. Lawyers Guild, Am. Arbitration Assn. (arbitrator 1983—). Avocations: tennis, racquetball. Personal injury, General practice, Federal civil litigation. Office: Petrucelly & Nadler PC 6 Beacon St Suite 720 Boston MA 02108

PETRUSH, JOHN JOSEPH, lawyer; b. Rochester, Pa., Oct. 15, 1942; s. Joseph Anthony and Helen Rosemarie (Klucarich) P.; children—John Joseph, Joshua Laurence. A.B. cum laude, Princeton U., 1964; LL.B., Stanford U., 1967. Bar: Calif. 1967, Pa. 1970. Assoc. Bernard Petrie, San Francisco, 1967-68; law clk. to judge Common Pleas Ct. Beaver County (Pa.), 1969; assoc. Buchanan, Ingersoll, Rodewald, Kyle & Buerger, Pitts, 1970-75; sole practice, Beaver, Pa., 1976—. Mem. Beaver Town Council, 1973—; bd. dirs. Beaver County unit Am. Cancer Soc., United Way of Beaver County; trustee Beaver Area Sch. Dist. Edn. Found. Served with USMCR, 1961-63. Mem. ABA, Assn. Trial Lawyers Am., Pa. Bar Assn., Pa. Trial Lawyers Assn. (bd. govs. western chpt.), Allegheny County Bar Assn., Beaver County Bar Assn. Republican. Club: Beaver Valley Country. Personal injury, Workers' compensation, State civil litigation. Home: 331 Wilson Ave Beaver PA 15009 Office: 348 College Ave Beaver PA 15009

PETRY, HERBERT CHARLES, JR., lawyer; b. Carrizo Springs, Tex., Aug. 10, 1917; s. Herbert C. and Florence (Votaw) P.; m. Josephine L. White, July 17, 1947; children: Boothe, John. Diploma, Trinity U., 1936; LL.B., U. Tex., 1947. Bar: Tex. 1940. Since practiced in Carrizo Springs; pres. law firm Petry & Stewart, P.C. real estate and bus. holdings; chmn. bd. Union State Bank, 1975—; bd. dirs. Cen. Power & Light Co. Mem. Tex. Econ. Commn.; regent Inst. Tex. Cultures, 1977—, com. of 100 State on Study of Merit Selection of Judges; bd. dirs. Dimmit County United Way, 1981—, Dimmit County Econ. Found.; pres. Carrizo Springs Indsl. Commn., 1981—; chmn. Tex. Hwy. Commn., 1959-73; adv. regent Inst. Texan Cultures, San Antonio, 1983—. Recipient Bernardo O'Higgins medal Pres. Chile, 1950, Distinguished Alumni award Trinity U., 1968. Mem. ABA, Tex. Bar Assn., Dimmit County Bar Assn. (pres.), Tex. C. of C. (pres. 1967, 72), South Tex. C. of C. (exec. com., Mr. South Tex. 1966, bd. dirs. 1966—), Delta Theta Phi. Methodist (trustee). Club: Lions (dist. gov. 1944-45, internat. dir. 1945-47, v.p. 1947-50, chmn. bd. internat. relations 1946-50, pres. internat. 1950-51). State civil litigation, Probate, Personal injury. Home: Petry Pl Carrizo Springs TX 78834 Office: Petry Law Bldg Carrizo Springs TX 78834

PETTIBONE, PETER JOHN, lawyer; b. Schenectady, N.Y., Dec. 11, 1939; s. George Howard and Caryl Grey (Ketchum) P.; m. Jean Kellogg, Apr. 23, 1966; children: Stephen, Victoria. AB, Princeton U., 1961; JD, Harvard U., 1964; LLM, NYU, 1971. Bar: Pa. 1965, D.C. 1965, N.Y. 1968, U.S. Supreme Ct. 1974. Assoc. Cravath, Swaine & Moore, N.Y.C., 1967-74, Lord, Day & Lord, N.Y.C., 1974-76; ptnr. Lord, Day & Lord, N.Y.C. and Washington, 1976—; bd. dirs., vice chmn. N.Y. State Facilities Devel. Corp., N.Y.C., 1983—. Trustee Civitas, N.Y.C., 1984—. Served to capt. U.S. Army, 1965-67. Mem. ABA, Assn. of Bar of City of N.Y., U.S.- USSR Trade and Econ. Council, Inc., (U.S. co-chmn. legal com. 1980—). Episcopalian. Clubs: Anglers (N.Y.C.), Shelter Island (N.Y.) Yacht, Soc. of Cin. General corporate, Private international, Securities. Home: 1158 Fifth Ave New York NY 10029 Office: Lord Day & Lord 25 Broadway New York NY 10004 also: 1050 Connecticut Ave Suite 300 Washington DC 20036

PETTIETTE, ALISON YVONNE, lawyer; b. Brockton, Mass., Aug. 16, 1952; d. David and Loretta (LeClair) Waters; Student Sorbonne, Paris, 1971-72; B.A., Sophie Newcomb Coll., 1972; M.A., Rice U., 1974; J.D., Bates Coll., 1978. Bar: Tex. 1979, U.S. Dist. Ct. (so. dist.) Tex. 1980, U.S. Ct. Appeals (5th cir.) 1981. Ptnr. Harvill & Hardy, Houston, 1979-83; sole practice, Houston, 1983-84; assoc. O'Quinn & Hagans, Houston, 1984-86, assoc. Jones & Granger, Houston, 1986—; editor Houston Law Rev. U. Houston, 1976-78. Exercise instr. YWCA, Houston, 1976-81, U. St. Thomas, Houston, 1982—. NDEA fellow Rice U., Houston, 1972-74; Woodrow Wilson scholar, Tulane U., New Orleans, 1972. Mem. ABA, Assn. Trial Lawyers Am., Tex. Trial Lawyers Assn., Houston Trial Lawyers Assn., Phi Delta Phi, Phi Beta Kappa. Personal injury, Products liability, Federal civil litigation. Office: Jones & Granger 10000 Memorial 8th Floor Houston TX 77024

PETTIGREW, KAREN BETH, lawyer; b. Lubbock, Tex., July 26, 1948; d. Jim Moore and Wanda Beth (Chastain) Pettigrew. B.A. with honors, Tex. Tech. U., 1970; J.D., So. Meth. U., 1974. Bar: Tex. 1974, U.S. Tax Ct., U.S. Dist. Ct. (so. and no. dists.) Tex. Staff mem. U.S. Senator John G. Tower, Dallas, 1970-71; law clk. U.S. Dept. Justice, Tax Div., Dallas, 1973-74; atty. Andrews & Kurth, Houston, 1974-80, Wyckoff, Russell, Dunn & Frazier, Houston, 1980-82, Morris, Tinsley & Snowden, Houston, 1982-84, Thelen, Marrin, Johnson & Bridges, Houston, 1984—. Bd. dirs. Tex. Tech. U. Century Club, Houston, 1983-86, Bellaire Christian Ch., Houston, 1983; bd. dirs. Houston Red Raider Club, 1981—, v.p., 1986—; mem. Ladies Go-Texan com., 1984—, Skybox com., 1985—, Houston Livestock Show and Rodeo, Houston. Acad. scholar Tex. Tech. U., 1966-70, So. Meth. U. Sch. Law, 1971-74. Mem. Houston Bar Assn., Tex. Bar Assn., ABA, Phi Delta Phi, Phi Kappa Phi, Alpha Lambda Delta, Phi Alpha Theta, Phi Sigma Alpha. Republican (del. state conv. 1984). Mem. Disciples of Christ (deaconess 1983-86, pulpit com. 1986-87). Banking, General corporate, Real property. Home: 3650 Glen Haven Houston TX 77025 Office: Thelen Marrin Johnson & Bridges 1700 Texas American Bank Bldg Houston TX 77002

PETTIT, ROGER LEE, lawyer; b. Winfield, Kans., Dec. 14, 1946; s. Ned Marsten and Roberta (Maxine) P.; m. Rebecca Ann Noltner, Oct. 28, 1968; 1 child, Tristan Roger. BA, Washburn U., 1968; JD, Marquette U., 1974. Bar: Wis. 1974, U.S. Dist. Ct. (ea. and we. dists.) Wis. 1974, U. S. Ct. Appeals (7th cir.) 1977. Sole practice Milw., 1974-75; assoc. Husman, McNaly et al, Milw., 1975-81; ptnr. Petrie, Stocking, Meixner & Zeisig S.C., Milw., 1985—. Mem. Wis. Bar Assn., Wis. Acad. Trial Lawyers. Clubs: South Shore Yacht (Milw.) (vice commodore 1984—), U.S. Power Squadron (sec., law officer 1983—). Avocation: sailing. Personal injury, State civil litigation, Labor. Office: Petrie Stocking Meixner & Zeisig SC 111 E Wisconsin Ave Milwaukee WI 53202

PETTY, KEITH, lawyer; b. Swan Lake, Idaho, June 13, 1920; s. William Dorris and Emma Louise (Johnson) P.; m. Gail Wells, Jan. 11, 1943; children—Kaye Wells Paugh, Jane Wells Taylor, Richard Keith, Scott Robert. B.S., U. Idaho, 1942; J.D., Stanford U., 1948; postgrad. Harvard U., 1943; cert. specialist taxation law Calif. Bd. Legal Specialization. Bar: Calif., 1949, Idaho, 1948. Tax acct. Pacific Telephone Co., San Francisco, 1948-50; acct. John F. Forbes & Co., San Francisco, 1950-54; partner Petty, Andrews, Tufts & Jackson and predecessor firms, San Francisco, San Jose and Palo Alto, Calif., 1954-86; sole practice Palo Alto, 1986—; lectr. in field. Served to lt. USNR, 1942-46. Mem. Calif. Soc. C.P.A.s, San Francisco Bar Assn. Mormon. Clubs: Commonwealth, Univ., Bankers. Probate, Corporate taxation, Real property. Home: 1420 Pitman Ave Palo Alto CA 94301 Office: 755 Page Mill Rd Suite A-240 Palo Alto CA 94304

PETTYJOHN, SHIRLEY ELLIS, lawyer, real estate executive; b. Liberty, Ky., Aug. 16, 1935; d. Wesley Barker and Ada Lou (Bryant) Ellis; m. Flem D. Pettyjohn, Sept. 24, 1955; children: Deena Renee, Ellisa Denise. BS in Commerce, U. Louisville, 1974, JD, 1977. Bar: Ky. 1978. Pres. Universal Devel. Corp., Ky. and Fla., Pettyjohn Inc., Ky. and Ind.; v.p. Continental Investments Corp.; sr. ptnr. Pettyjohn, Grant & Turner, 1987—. Vice-chmn. Louisville and Jefferson County Planning Commn., 1971-75; mem. Gov.'s Conf. on Edn., 1977, jud. nominee, 1981, Met. Louisville Women's Polit. Caucus, Shively Dem. Club; past v.p. Jefferson County Dems. Women's Club. Recipient Mayor's Cert. Recognition, 1974, Mayor's Fleur de lis

award, 1969-73. Mem. ABA, Ky. Bar Assn., Louisville Bar Assn., Women Lawyers Assn., Am. Judicature Soc., Am. Inst. Planners (pres.), Women's C. of C. (past bd. dirs., chmn. legis. com.), Nat. Assn. Female Execs., Am. Legion (aux.), Fraternal Order Police Assn. (award 1982), Louisville Legal Secs. (past pres.), Council of Women Presidents (past pres., Woman of Achievement award 1974), Sigma Delta Kappa, Chi Thi Theta. Clubs: Spirit of 46th, Mose Green, North End, 12th Ward, South End, 3d Ward, Highland Park, Grass Roots, Harry S. Truman, Beargrass, Arts of Louisville. General corporate, Personal injury, Probate. Home: 6924 Norlynn Dr Louisville KY 40228 Office: Ky Home Life Bldg 239 S 5th St Suire 401 Louisville KY 40202

PEVSNER, BEVERLY LIMMER, lawyer; b. Washington, Apr. 2, 1949; d. Ezekiel and Evelyn Geraldine (Ifshin) L.; m. Martin Elliot Gordon, June 21, 1970 (div. Apr. 1979); m. Donald Lawrence Pevsner, Apr. 13, 1980. BA with honors, U. Wis., 1971; postgrad., Nat. Law Ctr., George Washington U., 1978-79; JD cum laude, U. Miami, Fla., 1982. Bar: Fla. 1982, U.S. Dist. Ct. (so. and mid. dists.) Fla. 1983, U.S. Ct. Appeals (fed. cir.) 1983, U.S. Ct. Internat. Trade 1983. Economist CAB, Washington, 1971-77; dir. govt. liaison KLM Royal Dutch Airlines, Washington, 1977-80; assoc. Sandler & Travis, Miami, 1982-84; sole practice Miami, 1984-85; ptnr. Beiley & Pevsner, Miami, 1985—; gen. counsel Miami Fgn. Trade Assn., 1985—. Mem. Citizens Charter Rev. Com., Miami, 1985—. Mem. ABA, Fla. Bar Assn., Fla. Assn. Women Lawyers, LWV (bd. dirs. Dade county chpt. 1985-87). Administrative and regulatory, General corporate. Office: 7600 SW 57th Ave No 125 Miami FL 33143

PEW, JOHN GLENN, JR., lawyer; b. Dallas, Apr. 18, 1932; s. John Glenn and Roberta (Haughton) P. B.A. U. Tex., 1954. LL.B., 1955. Bar: Tex. 1955, U.S. Dist. Ct. (no. dist.) Tex. 1959, U.S. Supreme Ct. 1959, U.S. Ct. Appeals (5th cir.) 1961, U.S. Ct. Appeals (10th cir.) 1982. Ptnr., Jackson, Walker, Winstead, Cantwell & Miller, Dallas, 1964—. Served with USNR, 1955-58. Republican. Presbyterian. Federal civil litigation, State civil litigation. Office: 6000 InterFirst Plaza 901 Main St Dallas TX 75202

PEYTON, GORDON PICKETT, lawyer; b. Washington, Jan. 22, 1941; s. Gordon Pickett and Mary Campbell (Grasty) P.; m. Marjorie G. Parish, June 9, 1962 (div.); children—Janet Porter, William Parish; m. 2d, Jean Nye Groseclose, Oct. 20, 1979. B.A. cum laude, U. of the South, 1962; J.D., Duke U., 1965. Bar: Va. 1965, U.S. Dist. Ct. (ea. dist.) Va. 1966, U.S. Ct. Appeals (4th cir.) 1975, U.S. Ct. Mil. Appeals 1980. Asst. city atty., Alexandria, Va., 1966-69; sole practice, Alexandria, 1966-82; v.p. Peyton, Prendergast and Shapiro, Ltd., Alexandria, 1982-84; pres. Peyton & Shapiro, Ltd., 1985—. Bd. trustees U. of the South, 1972-76, Ch. Schs. in Diocese of Va., 1974-84. Served to 1st. lt. USAF Res. ret. Mem. 4th Cir. Jud. Conf., Va. State Bar, Va. Bar Assn., Va. Trial Lawyers Assn., ABA, Alexandria Bar Assn. (pres. 1982-83), Am. Judicature Soc., Va. Conf. Commrs. of Accts., Alexandria C. of C. (v.p., dir. 1974-77). Episcopalian. Bankruptcy, Family and matrimonial, Probate. Office: Peyton & Shapiro Ltd 117 N Fairfax St Alexandria VA 22314

PFAELZER, MARIANA R., fed. judge; b. 1926. A.B., U. Calif.; LL.B., UCLA Sch. Law. Bar: bar 1958. Judge U.S. Dist. Ct. for Dist. Central Calif. Mem. Am. Bar Assn. Office: US Dist Ct 312 N Spring St Los Angeles CA 90012

PFAFF, ROBERT JAMES, lawyer; b. Pitts., Jan. 12, 1943; s. William Michael and Elizabeth (Ludwig) P.; m. Carol Pillich, June 18, 1977. BS in Edn., Slippery Rock U., 1965; JD, Duquesne U., 1973. Bar: Pa. 1973, U.S. Dist. Ct. (we. dist.) Pa. 1973, U.S. Supreme Ct. 1980. Tchr. secondary schs. Norwin and Jeanette, Pa., 1965-66; suit group supr. Liberty Mut. Ins. Co., Pitts., 1966-70; assoc. Egler, McGregor & Reinstadtler, Pitts., 1973-76; ptnr. Leopold, Eberhardt & Pfaff, Altoona, Pa., 1976-80; sr. ptnr. Meyer, Darragh, Buckler, Bebenek & Eck, Pitts., 1980-84, Pfaff, McIntyre, Dugas & Hartye, Hollidaysburg, Pa., 1984—. Bd. dirs. Blair County Legal Services, Altoona. Mem. ABA, Pa. Bar Assn., Blair County Bar Assn., Allegheny County Bar Assn., Pa. Assn. Mut. Ins. Cos. (claims com.), Pa. Def. Inst., Altoona Area Claims Assn. Republican. Roman Catholic. Avocations: golf, music. Personal injury, State civil litigation, Insurance. Home: 44 Sylvan Heights Dr Hollidaysburg PA 16648 Office: Pfaff McIntyre et al PO Box 533 Hollidaysburg PA 16648

PFALTZ, HUGO MENZEL, JR., lawyer; b. Newark, Sept. 23, 1931; s. Hugo M. and Mary E. (Horr) P.; m. Marilyn M. Muir, Sept. 29, 1956; children—Elizabeth W., William M., Robert L. B.A., Hamilton Coll., 1953; J.D., Harvard U., 1960; LL.M., NYU, 1965. Bar: N.J. 1960, U.S. Dist. Ct. N.J. 1960, U.S. Supreme Ct. 1977. Assoc. McCarter & English, Newark, 1960-61, Bourne & Noll, Summit, N.J., 1961-74; sole practice, Summit, 1974-82; ptnr. Pfaltz & Woller, 1983—; counsel N.J. Council Savs. Instns.; dir. Elizabethtown Water Co.; mem. Battleship N.J. Commn., 1985—, N.J. Law Revision Commn., 1986—. Assoc. editor N.J. Law Jour., 1966—, editor, 1984-86. Chmn. Summit Rep. City Com., 1966, mem. N.J. Constl. Conv., 1966; mem. N.J. Assembly, 1968-72. Served to lt. USNR, 1953-62. Mem. ABA, N.J. Bar Assn., Union County Bar Assn., Summit Bar Assn. Clubs: University (N.Y.C.), Baltusrol (Springfield, N.J.); Essex (Newark); Beacon Hill (Summit, N.J.). Banking, Probate, Estate taxation. Home: 118 Prospect St Summit NJ 07901 Office: 382 Springfield Ave Summit NJ 07901

PFEFFER, DAVID H., lawyer; b. N.Y.C., Mar. 15, 1935. B. Chem. Engring., CCNY, 1956; J.D., NYU, 1961, LL.M. in Trade Regulation, 1967. Bar: N.Y. 1961. With patent dept. U.S. Rubber Co., Wayne, N.J., 1957-61; assoc. Watson, Leavenworth, Kelton & Taggart, N.Y.C., 1961-63; assoc. Morgan & Finnegan, N.Y.C., 1963-70, ptnr., 1971—; village prosecutor Roslyn Harbor, N.Y., 1976-78, village justice, 1979—. Mem. ABA (litigation sect.), N.Y. Bar Assn., N.Y.C. Bar Assn., Am. Intellectual Property Law Assn., N.Y. Patent Trademark and Copyright Law Assn., N.Y. State Magistrates Assn., Nassau County Magistrates Assn., Order of Coif. Patent, Trademark and copyright, Antitrust. Home: 15 Harbor Ln Roslyn Harbor NY 11576 Office: Morgan & Finnegan 345 Park Ave New York NY 10154

PFEFFER, LEO, lawyer, educator; b. Hungary, Dec. 25, 1910; came to U.S., 1912, naturalized, 1917; s. Alter Saul and Hani (Yaeger) P.; m. Freda Plotkin, Sept. 18, 1937; children—Alan Israel, Susan Beth. B.S.S., CCNY, 1930; J.D., NYU, 1933; L.H.D. (h.c.), Hebrew Union Coll.-Jewish Inst. Religion, 1979. Bar: N.Y. 1933. Practice in N.Y.C., 1933—, pvt. tchr. law, 1933-45; lectr. New Sch., 1954-58, Mt. Holyoke Coll., 1958-60; David W. Petergorsky prof. constl. law Yeshivah U., 1962-63; gen. counsel Am. Jewish Congress, 1958-64, spl. counsel, 1964-85; prof. polit. sci. L.I. U., 1964-80, adj. prof., 1981—, chmn. dept., 1964-79; Vis. prof. constl. law Rutgers U., 1965; frequent radio and TV appearances, 1954—. Author: Church, State and Freedom, 1953, rev. edit., 1967, The Liberties of an American, 1956, Creeds in Competition, 1958, (with Anson Phelps Stokes) Church and State in the United States, 1964, This Honorable Court, 1965, God, Caesar and the Constitution, 1975, Religious Freedom, 1977; Religion, State and the Burger Court, 1984; editorial bd.: Jour. Ch. and State, 1958—, Judaism, 1964—; contbr. to various books, encys.; honored by Religion and State: Essays in Honor of Leo Pfeffer, 1985. Pres. Lawyers Constl. Def. Com., 1964-66, counsel, 1967-82, emeritus counsel, 1982—; cons. counsel Religious Coalition for Abortion Rights, 1976—; adv. com. Nat. Project Center for Film and the Humanities, 1974—; mem. religious liberty com. Nat. Council Chs. of Christ in U.S.A.; mem. nat. law com. Anti-Defamation League B'nai B'rith, 1985—, nat. adv. bd. Americans for Religious Liberty, 1985—, nat. legal affairs com. Anti-Defamation League, 1985—. Recipient Religious Freedom award Ams. United for Separation Ch. and State, 1955; citation contbns. to civil rights Minn. Jewish Community Council, 1962; Thomas Jefferson Religious Freedom award Unitarian-Universalist Ch. N.Y., 1967; Bklyn. Civil Liberties award, 1968; citation for contbns. to pub. edn. Horace Mann League, 1972, Lawyers Constl. Def. Com., 1972; award Com. for Pub. Edn. and Religious Liberty, 1972; Townsend Harris medal CCNY, 1974; Rabbi Maurice N. Eisendrath Meml. award Union of Am. Hebrew Congregations, 1977; George Brussel Meml. award Stephen Wise Free Synagogue, 1978; Trustee award for Scholarly Achievement L.I. U., 1978; Ams. United Fund award, 1979; Am. Jewish Congress award, 1980; cert. of merit Council Jewish Fedns., 1984; papers in George Arents Research Library, Syracuse U. Fellow Jewish Acad. Arts and Scis.; Mem. Am. Jewish Congress, Am. Acad. Religion, Am. Acad. Polit. and Social Scis., AAUP (pres. L.I. U. chpt. 1967-68), Jewish Peace Fellowship (exec. com. 1969—, counsel 1979—), ACLU (cons., cooperating atty.), Soc. Sci. Study Religion, N.Y. U. Law Rev. Alumni Assn. (pres. 1964-66), Am. Judicature Soc., Am. Polit. Sci. Assn., Am. Arbitration Assn. (panel arbitrators), Nat. Assn. Intergroup Relations Ofcls., Horace Mann League U.S. (gen. counsel), Am. Soc. for Legal History, Com. for Pub. Edn. and Religious Liberty (founder 1967, gen. counsel 1967-82, counsel emeritus 1982—award). Home: 29 Ridge Terr Central Valley NY 10917

PFEFFER, MILTON B., lawyer; b. N.Y.C., Nov. 24, 1919; s. Ben and Frances (Glasner) P.; m. Ruth Fuchsman, Mar. 8, 1952; children—Carol J., Robert D. BSS, CCNY, 1940; JD, Columbia U., 1943. Bar: N.Y. 1943, U.S. Dist. Ct. (so. dist.) N.Y. 1946, U.S. Dist. Ct. (ea. dist.) N.Y. 1954, U.S. Ct. Appeals (2d cir.) 1947, U.S. Supreme Ct. 1974. Assoc. Scribner & Miller, N.Y.C., 1943-48; ptnr. Gwertman & Pfeffer, N.Y.C., 1970—. Mem. Bronx County Bar Assn. (chmn. com. ins. law). Club: N.Y. Numismatic (past pres.). Author legal monographs in The Insurance Advocate series, 1979-83. Insurance, State civil litigation, Probate. Home: 750 Kappock St New York NY 10463 Office: 115 Broadway New York NY 10006

PFEIFFER, WILLIAM EDWARD, lawyer; b. San Bernadino, July 30, 1946; s. Benedict C. and Doris June (Mehrens) P.; m. Linda Susan Christensen, May 20, 1972; children: Daniell, Christine, Erin Lea. BA, St. Benedict's Coll., 1968; JD, Creighton U., 1973. Bar: Nebr. 1973, U.S. Dist. Ct. Nebr. 1973, U.S. Ct. Appeals (8th cir.) 1975. Ptnr. Speilhagen & Pfeiffer, Omaha, 1973—; lectr. U. Nebr., Omaha, 1977; bd. dirs. Majors Inc., Omaha. Served to sgt. USMC, 1968-70, Vietnam. Mem. ABA, Nebr. Bar Assn., Omaha Bar Assn. Democrat. Roman Catholic. Avocation: coaching youth soccer. Real property, Immigration, naturalization, and customs, State civil litigation. Home: 2407 N 134th St Omaha NE 68164 Office: Speihagen & Pfeiffer Assoc 5010 Dodge St Omaha NE 68132

PFENNIGER, RICHARD CHARLES, JR., lawyer; b. Akron, Ohio, July 26, 1955; s. Richard Charles Pfenniger and Phyllis Irene (Rutan) Gatto. BBA, Fla. Atlantic U., 1977; JD, U. Fla., 1982. Bar: Fla. 1982; CPA, Fla. Acct. Price Waterhouse & Co., Ft. Lauderdale, Fla., 1977-79; assoc. Stearns, Weaver, Miller, Weisller, Alhadeff & Sitterson, P.A., Miami, Fla., 1982-86; ptnr. Greer, Homer, Cope & Bonner P.A., Miami, 1986—. Mem. ABA, Am. Inst. CPA's. General corporate, Securities. Office: Greer Homer Cope & Bonner PA Southeast Fin Ctr Suite 4360 Miami FL 33131

PFENNIGSTORF, WERNER, lawyer; b. Hamburg, Germany, Sept. 28, 1934; s. Walter and Ilse (Schroeter) P.; m. Heika Helene Droenner, Apr. 6, 1963. Habilitation, U. Hamburg, Germany, 1974; J.D., 1960; M.C.L., U. Mich. 1961. Bar: Germany 1962. Wissenschaftl asst. U. Hamburg, 1963-66; staff atty. Ins. Laws Rev. Commn., State Wis., Madison, 1967-70; research fellow U. Hamburg, 1970-72; research atty. Am. Bar Found., Chgo., 1973-86; sole practice, 1986— . Author: Legal Expense Insurance, 1975; editor: (with Spencer L. Kimball) Legal Service Plans, 1977, German Insurance Laws, 2d edit., 1986. Mem. Deutscher Verein für Versicherungswissenschaft, Internat. Assn. Ins. Law., Am. Risk and Ins. Assn. Lutheran. Insurance, Private international, Personal injury. Office: Hermann Pflaume St 6, 5000 Koeln 41, Fed Republic of Germany

PFIFFNER, FRANK ALBERT, lawyer; b. Waukon, Iowa, July 21, 1948; s. Albert Gustave and Wilma (Hirth) P.; m. Mary Michaeline Victor, May 31, 1969; children: Christopher, Amanda, Rebecca. BA magna cum laude, Loras Coll., 1970; MA, U. Iowa, 1974, JD, 1974. Bar: Iowa 1974, Alaska 1975, U.S. Dist. Ct. Alaska 1975, U.S. Ct. Appeals (9th cir.) 1975. Ptnr. Hughes, Thorsness, Gantz, Powell & Brundin, Anchorage, 1974—. Served with U.S. Army, 1970-72. Mem. ABA, Iowa State Bar Assn., Alaska Bar Assn., Am. Arbitration Assn. (nat. panel arbitrators). Roman Catholic. Construction, Federal civil litigation, State civil litigation. Home: PO Box 111642 Anchorage AK 99511 Office: Hughes Thorsness Gantz et al 509 W 3d Ave Anchorage AK 99501

PFUNDER, CURTIS CLARK, lawyer; b. Hartford, Conn., Oct. 8, 1953; s. Elbert Franklin and Helen Eliza (Clark) P. BA, St. Lawrence U., 1975; JD, Suffolk U., 1978. Bar: Mass. 1978, U.S. Ct. Appeals (1st cir.) 1979, Tex. 1983, U.S. Ct. Appeals (5th cir.) 1984. Asst. legal counsel to gov. Commonwealth of Mass., Boston, 1979-81; trial atty. antitrust div. U.S. Dept. Justice, Dallas, 1982-84; trial atty. Gardere & Wynne, Dallas, 1984—; v.p. Nat. Assn. Extradition Officials, 1980-81. Mem. ABA, State Bar of Tex., Dallas Bar Assn., Phi Delta Phi. Republican. Methodist. Federal civil litigation, Antitrust, State civil litigation. Office: Gardere & Wynne 1500 Diamond Shamrock Tower Dallas TX 75201

PHALEN, THOMAS FRANCIS, JR., lawyer; b. Waterbury, Conn., June 27, 1938; s. Thomas Francis and Helen Theresa (Farrell) P.; m. MaryAnne Imwalle, Aug. 31, 1963; children—Thomas Francis III, Timothy J., Helene M., Brian C., Christina V. B.S., Coll. Holy Cross, 1960; J.D., Cath. U. Am., 1967. Bar: Ohio 1967, U.S. Supreme Ct. 1973, U.S. Ct. Appeals (6th cir.) 1972, U.S. Ct. Appeals (D.C. cir.) 1973, U.S. Ct. Appeals (5th cir.) 1980, U.S. Dist. Ct. (so. dist.) Ohio 1969, U.S. Dist. Ct. (no. dist.) Ohio 1972. Law clk. trial exam. div. NLRB, 1966, field atty. region 9, cin., 1967-69; ptnr. Knee, Snyder & Parks, Dayton, Ohio, 1969-73, Latimer & Swing Co., L.P.A., 1973-78; sole practice, Cin., 1978-79; ptnr. Kircher and Phalen, Cin., 1979—; lectr. U. Cin., 1979-83, Xavier U., 1980, Ohio Legal Ctr. Inst., Ohio Labor Seminar, 1983, Ohio Jud. Conf., 1984. Mem: adv. bd. AFL-CIO Lawyers Coordinating Com., 1983—; trustee U. Cin., 1987—; mem. Dem. Cen. Com., chmn. 14th ward Cin. Served to capt. USAF, 1961-64. Mem. Ohio Bar Assn. (chmn. labor law sect. 1980-83). Assoc. editor: The Developing Labor Law, 2d edit., 1983—. Labor. Office: 125 E Court St Suite 1000 Cincinnati OH 45202

PHEBUS, JOSEPH W., lawyer; b. Champaign, Ill., Feb. 13, 1940; s. Darius Edward and Frances (Allen) P.; m. Carolyn Campbell, Apr. 19, 1980; children: D. Michael, John Jeffrey, John Allen, Douglas J. BS in Metallurgy, U. Ill., 1962, JD, 1968. Bar: Ill. 1968, U.S. Dist. Ct. (so. dist.) Ind. 1968, U.S. Dist. Ct. (cen. dist.) Ill. 1970, U.S. Supreme Ct. 1975, U.S. Ct. Appeals (7th cir.) 1981, U.S. Dist. Ct. (no. dist.) Ill. 1984. Engr. Caterpillar Tractor, Peoria, Ill., 1965; assoc. Phillips, Phebus & Tummelson, Urbana, Ill., 1968-71; ptnr. Phebus, Tummelson, Bryan & Knox, Urbana, 1971—; pres., chmn. Western Union Ltd., Urbana, 1982—; v.p., bd. dirs. Cable Communications, Urbana, 1972-82. Alderman City of Urbana, 1968-71; mayor pro-tem, 1971. Served to capt. U.S. Army, 1962-64. Mem. Ill. Bar Assn., Appelate Lawyer Assn. Ill., Assn. Trial Lawyers Am., Ill. Trial Lawyers Assn., Nat. Assn. R.R. Trial Counsel, Order of Coif. Republican. Club: Champaign Country. Personal injury, Federal civil litigation, State civil litigation. Home: 3 Persimmon Circle Urbana IL 61801 Office: Phebus Tummelson Bryan & Knox 136 W Main Urbana IL 61801

PHEILS, DAVID R., JR., lawyer, energy conservation consultant; b. Toledo, Feb. 2, 1934; s. David R. and Selma M. (Pettengil) P.; m. Jo Anne L. Sobecki, Aug. 30, 1958; children—Jon David, Eric Stephen. B.E., U. Toledo, 1960, J.D., 1974. Bar: Ohio 1974, U.S. Dist. Ct. (no. dist.) Ohio 1975, U.S. Ct. Appeals (6th cir.) 1975, U.S. Supreme Ct. 1983. Sole practice, Toledo, 1974-77; ptnr. firm Mako, Pheils & Ray, Perrysburg, Ohio, 1977-79; mng. ptnr. David R. Pheils, Jr. & Assocs., Perrysburg, 1979—; pres. bd. dirs. Forest Hills Utility Co., Newark, Ohio, 1970-79; cons. Design Energy Systems, Perrysburg, 1980—. Patentee solar energy collection device. Valedictorian U. Toledo Coll. Law, 1974. Mem. ABA, Ohio Bar Assn., Assn. Trial Lawyers Am., Perrysburg Hist. Soc. Republican. Civil rights, Federal civil litigation, State civil litigation. Office: David R Pheils Jr & Assocs 410 Louisiana Ave Perrysburg OH 43551

PHELPS, PAUL MICHAEL, lawyer; b. Lake Forest, Ill., Sept. 19, 1933; s. Paul and Elizabeth Anne (Wilson) P.; m. Laura Elaine Pepe, Dec. 26, 1966; stepchildren: Kimberly A. Springer, Wendy L. Field, Gregory L. Field. B.A., Wesleyan U., Middletown, Conn., 1955; LL.B., Harvard U., 1958. Bar: Ill. 1958, U.S. Ct. Mil. Appeals 1959. Asso. atty. Keck Mahin & Cate, Chgo., 1958, 63-65; atty. Ekco Products Co., Chgo., 1965-67, E. J. Brach & Sons, Chgo., 1967-69; asst. corp. sec. R. R. Donnelley & Sons Co., Chgo., 1969-73; asst. counsel Marsh & McLennan, Chgo., 1973-74; corp. sec. Morton-Norwich Products, Inc. (name now Morton Thiokol, Inc.), Chgo., 1974—. Served to capt., JAGC U.S. Army, 1959-63. Mem. ABA, Am. Soc. Corp. Secs. (bd. dirs. 1987—), Phi Beta Kappa, Psi Upsilon. Republican. Episcopalian. Clubs: University, Tower (Chgo.). General corporate, Securities, Corporate secretary. Home: 222 E Chestnut St #10B Chicago IL 60611 Office: 110 N Wacker Dr Chicago IL 60606

PHELPS, RICHARD J., lawyer, state official. Pub. defender State of Wis., Madison. Office: Pub Defender PO Box 7923 Madison WI 53707 *

PHELPS, ROBERT FREDERICK, JR., lawyer; b. Evanston, Ill., Aug. 20, 1956; s. Robert F. and Hanna (Kulej) P.; m. Joan Ann Brisky, Oct. 6, 1984; 1 child, Jennifer Katherine. BA, Trinity Coll., Hartford, Conn., 1978; JD, U. Mich., 1981; LLM, NYU, 1987. Bar: Conn. 1981. Assoc. Cummings & Lockwood, Stamford and Greenwich, Conn., 1981—; cons. Conn. Safe Deposit Assn., 1983—. Bd. dirs. Greenwich Council on Youth and Drugs, Inc., 1985—; vol. Noroton Presbyn. Ch., Darien, Conn. 1986. Mem. ABA (real property, probate and trust sect., tax sect.), Conn. Bar Assn. (estates, tax and real property sects.), Greenwich Bar Assn., Internat. Assn. Fin. Planning (bd. dirs. so. Conn. chpt.), Phi Beta Kappa. Republican. Club: Middlesex. Avocation: tennis. Estate planning, Probate, Personal income taxation. Home: 11 Oakshade Ave Darien CT 06820 Office: Cummings and Lockwood Two Greenwich Plaza Greenwich CT 06830

PHELPS, ROBERT J., lawyer; b. Davenport, Iowa, Apr. 20, 1946; s. Lowell Dean and Helen Berniece (Hall) P.; m. Cheryl Ann O'Brien, Sept. 3, 1966 (div. Nov. 1983); 1 child, Kristin Marie; m. Lauren Gail McNaughton, June 16, 1984; 1 stepson, Randall Lee. BA in History, U. Iowa, 1971; MA in Internat. Relations, U. Ark., 1972; JD, U. Tulsa, 1974. Bar: Okla. 1975, U.S. Dist. Ct. (no. dist.) Okla. 1975. Assoc. Drummond and Raymond, Pawhuska, Okla., 1975; from assoc. to ptnr. Byers and Phelps, Cleve., 1975-83; sole practice Cleve., 1983-87, Davenport, Iowa, 1987—. Mem. Pawnee County Rep. Cen. Com., Cleve., 1986; bd. dirs. Cleve. Area Health Care Found., 1977—. Served as ssgt. USAF, 1968-72. Mem. Okla. Bar Assn., Cleve. C. of C. (chmn. indsl. devel. com. 1986-87). Avocations: reading, swimming, tennis. Consumer commercial, General practice, Probate. Office: Davenport IA 52801

PHIFER, VIRGINIA HUDSON, lawyer, electronics company executive; b. N.Y.C., Dec. 25, 1951; d. Samuel Hudson and Olga Elizabeth (Tridnivka) P. BA, Simmons Coll., 1973; JD, Fordham U., 1981. Bar: N.Y. 1982, U.S. Dist. Ct. (ea. and so. dists.) N.Y. 1982, U.S. Ct. Appeals (2d cir.) 1982. Assoc. Skadden, Arps, Slate, Meagher & Flom, N.Y.C., 1981-84; atty. GTE Service Corp., Stamford, Conn., 1984-86; v.p., gen. counsel, treas. Rapid Power Techs., Inc., Brookfield, Conn., 1986—; also bd. dirs. Rapid Power Techs., Inc., Brookfield. Mem. ABA, N.Y. State Bar Assn., N.Y. County Lawyers Assn. (fed. legis. com.). General corporate, Labor. Home: 13 Brooks Ln Brookfield Center CT 06805 Office: Rapid Power Techs Inc Graysbridge Rd Brookfield CT 06804

PHILIPPS, JOSEPH TIMOTHY, legal educator, lawyer; b. Wheeling, W.Va., Mar. 20, 1940; s. Edwin Emil and Margaret Adelaide (Nesline) P.; m. Sandra Lee Emerson, May 29, 1965; children—Cecelia Marie, Melissa Anne. B.S. in Acctg., Wheeling Coll., 1962; J.D., Georgetown U., 1965; LL.M., Harvard U., 1966. Bar: D.C. 1966, U.S. Dist. Ct. D.C. 1966, U.S. Ct. Appeals (D.C. cir.) 1966, Va. 1983. Prof. law, W.Va. U. Coll. Law, Morgantown, 1966-76; vis. prof. law, Duke U., Durham, N.C., 1976; prof. Loyola Law Sch., Los Angeles, 1977-80, Washington and Lee U., Lexington, Va., 1980-87, prof. in residence Steptoe & Johnson, Washington, 1987—; with Steptoe and Johnson, Washington, 1987—; bd. dirs. W.Va. Tax Inst., 1969-76, No. W.Va. Legal Aid Soc., 1974-76; project dir. study W.Va. tax appeals procedures, ABA Ctr. Adminstrv. Justice, 1974; atty.-advisor implementation Postal Reorgn. Act U.S. Postal Service; spl. asst. atty. gen. W.Va. higher edn. statutes project State of W.Va., 1970; lectr. in field. Ford Found. fellow, Harvard U., 1965; named Outstanding Prof. Coll. Law, W.Va. U. Student Bar Assn., 1969. Mem. ABA (sect. taxation). Democrat. Roman Catholic. Club: Lexington Country. Contbr. articles to law revs. Corporate taxation, Personal income taxation, State and local taxation. Home: 111 Colston Pl Lexington VA 24450 Office: Washington & Lee Sch Law Lexington VA 24450

PHILIPPS, KURT A., lawyer, educator; b. San Antonio, Dec. 26, 1945; m. Heather McDonough. BA, S.W. Tex. U., 1966; MA in Religious Edn., So. Meth. U., 1969, JD, 1972. Bar: Tex. 1972, Ky. 1978, Ohio 1980. Assoc. prof. No. Ky. U., Covington, 1975-77; sole practice Covington, 1977—; assoc. prof. Xavier U., Cin., 1977—. Author: Ky. Practice and Procedure, 1985. Federal civil litigation, Health, Insurance. Home: 8050 Kugler Mill Cincinnati OH 45243 Office: 4th and Madison Covington KY 41011

PHILIPS, JAMES ALBERT, lawyer; b. Alexander City, Ala., June 15, 1950; s. Abram Lewis and Mary (Rice) P.; m. Teri Robison, July 11, 1981. AB with honors, Davidson Coll., 1972; JD, U. Ala., 1975. Bar: Ala. 1975, U.S. Dist. Ct. (so. dist.) Ala. 1975, U.S. Ct. Appeals (5th cir.) 1979, U.S. Ct. Appeals (11th cir.) 1983, U.S. Supreme Ct. 1984. Assoc. Holberg, Tully, Holberg & Danley, Mobile, Ala., 1975-81; sole practice Mobile, 1981—. Counsel Gen. Adminstr. of Mobile County, 1983—; bd. dirs., legal counsel Greater Gulf State Fair, Mobile, 1979-81; bd. dirs., chmn. bldg. com. Florence Crittenton Home, Mobile, 1979—; mem. adminstrv. bd. dirs. Dauphin Way United Meth. Ch., Mobile, 1983—; bd. dirs. Am. Cancer Soc., Mobile, 1978—. Mem. Assn. Trial Lawyers Am., Ala. Trial Lawyers Assn., Mobile Jaycees (v.p., bd. dirs. 1975-80), Omicron Delta Epsilon. Republican. Clubs: Internat. Trade, Exchange (Mobile) (sec., bd. dirs. 1980—). Federal civil litigation, State civil litigation, Real property. Home: 824 Deerfield Dr Mobile AL 36608 Office: 4325 Midmost Dr Mobile AL 36609

PHILLABAUM, STEPHEN DAY, lawyer; b. Spokane, Jan. 3, 1948; s. Donald Earl and Ralda May (Day) P.; m. Sheryl Sue Walinski, Aug. 16, 1969; children: Amanda, Lacy, Ben, Adam. BA, Eastern Wash. U., 1970; MS, Western Wash. U., 1973; JD, U. Puget Sound, 1980. Bar: Wash. 1980, U.S. Dist. Ct. (we. and ea. dists.) Wash. 1980, U.S. Ct. Appeals (9th cir.) 1981. Asst. atty. gen. State of Wash., Spokane, 1980-81; sole practice Spokane, 1981-85; ptnr. Neff, Phillabaum & Harlow, Spokane, 1985—. Author: Employee/Employer Rights in Washington, 1983. V.p., bd. dirs. Crime Check of Spokane County, 1984—; chmn. Secret Witness Program, Spokane, 1985—. Mem. ABA, Wash. State Bar Assn., Spokane County Bar Assn., Associated Engrs. of Spokane County (v.p.). Lodge: Rotary (bd. dirs., pres.-elect 1988—). Clubs: Spokane, Odin. Avocations: skiing, flying. Real property, Workers' compensation, General practice. Office: Neff Phillabaum & Harlow 1201 Washington Mutual Bldg Spokane WA 99201

PHILLIPES, PETER MICHAEL, lawyer; b. N.Y.C., May 21, 1940; s. Arthur Louis and Daisy Lee (Chassin) P.; m. Susan Seidner Bialos, June 16, 1959; children: Debra Lynne, David Alan, Lawrence Fredrick. AB, Columbia Coll., 1960; JD cum laude, NYU, 1967. Bar: N.Y. 1967, D.C. 1968, Calif. 1980. Assoc. Covington & Burling, Washington, 1967-76; gen. atty. Montgomery Ward & Co., N.Y.C., 1976-79; assoc. gen. counsel Levi Strauss & Co., San Francisco, 1979-86; sr. counsel The Stop & Shop Cos., Quincy, Mass., 1986—; pres. San Francisco Fashion Industries, 1984-86; v.p. Internat. AntiCounterfeiting Coalition, 1980-86; bd. dirs. Coalition Apparel Industries Calif., Los Angeles, 1980-86. Trustee, park commr. Village of Kensington, N.Y., Great Neck, N.Y., 1979. Served to lt. USN, 1960-64. Mem. ABA, N.Y. State Bar Assn., Am. Corp. Counsel Assn. (treas. Bay Area chpt. 1985-86), Order of Coif. Antitrust, General corporate, Administrative and regulatory. Office: Stop & Shop Cos Inc PO Box 369 Boston MA 02101

PHILLIPS, ALMARIN, economics educator; b. Port Jervis, N.Y., Mar. 13, 1925; s. Wendell Edgar and Hazel (Billett) P.; m. Dorothy Kathryn Burns, June 14, 1947 (div. 1976); children: Almarin Paul, Frederick Peter, Thomas Rock, David John, Elizabeth Linett, Charles Samuel; m. Carole Cherry Greenberg, Dec. 19, 1976. B.S., U. Pa., 1948, M.A., 1949; Ph.D., Harvard, 1953. Instr. econs. U. Pa. at Phila., 1948-50, 51-53, asst. prof. econs., 1953-56, prof. econs. and law, 1963—; Hower prof. pub. policy U. Pa at Phila., 1983—; chmn. dept. econs. U. Pa. at Phila., 1968-71, 72-73, assoc. dean Wharton Sch., 1973-74, dean Sch. Pub. and Urban Policy, 1974-77; teaching fellow Harvard, 1950-51; assoc. prof. U. Va, 1956-61, prof., 1961-63; vis.

prof. U. Hawaii at Honolulu, summer 1968, U. Warwick, London Grad. Sch. Bus. Studies, 1972, Ohio U., McGill U., 1978, Calif. Inst. Tech, Northwestern U., 1980, Ariz. Coll. Law, 1987; bd. Govs. Fed. Res. System, 1962-73; Bd. Govs. Rand Corp., 1964—; co-dir. Pres.'s Commn. Fin. Structure and Regulation, 1970-71; mem. Nat. Commn. Electronic Fund Transfers, 1976-77; economist mem. Va. Milk Commn., 1958-59. Author: (with R.W. Cabell) Problems in Basic Operations Research Methods for Management, 1961, Market Structure, Organization and Performance, 1962, Technology and Market Structure: A Study of the Aircraft Industry, 1971; Editor: Perspectives on Antitrust Policy, 1965, (with O.E. Williamson) Prices: Issues in Theory, Practice and Policy, 1968, Promoting Competition in Regulated Markets, 1975, The Am. Statistician, 1953-56, assoc. editor, 1965-70, acting editor, 1959-60; editor: Jour. Indsl. Econs., 1974—; Contbr. articles to tech. lit. Served with AUS, 1943-45. Decorated Purple Heart, Bronze Star; Ford Found. faculty research fellow, 1967-68; sr. fellow Brookings Instn., 1970-75. Fellow Am. Statis. Assn., AAAS; mem. Am. Econ. Assn., So. Econ. Assn. (editor jour. 1963-65), Econometric Soc., European Econ. Assn. Administrative and regulatory, Antitrust, Banking. Home: 1115 Remington Rd Wynnewood PA 19096

PHILLIPS, ANTHONY F., lawyer; b. Hartford, Conn., May 18, 1937; s. Frank and Lena Phillips; m. Rosemary Karran McGowan, Jan. 28, 1967; children: Karran, Antonia, Justin. BA, U. Conn., 1959; JD, Cornell U., 1962. Assoc. Willkie, Farr & Gallagher, N.Y.C., 1963-69, ptnr., 1969—. Served as pvt. U.S. Army, 1962-63. Mem. ABA, N.Y. State Bar Assn., N.Y. County Bar Assn., Assn. of Bar of City of N.Y. Federal civil litigation, State civil litigation. Home: 3 Elm Rock Rd Bronxville NY 10708 Office: Willkie Farr & Gallagher One Citicorp Ctr 153 E 53d St New York NY 10022

PHILLIPS, BRIAN REED, lawyer; b. Seattle, June 14, 1951; s. Clifford W. Phillips and Marjorie R. Scripps. BA, Columbia U., 1974; JD, U. Wash., 1979. Bar: Wash. 1979, U.S. Supreme Ct. 1986. Staff atty. Snohomish County Pub. Defender, Everett, Wash., 1979-82; sole practice Everett, 1983—. Bd. dirs. Snohomish County Legal Services Corp., Everett, 1985—. Mem. Wash. Bar Assn., Assn. Trial Lawyers Am., Nat. Assn. Criminal Def. Lawyers, Wash. Trial Lawyers Assn. Avocation: sailing. Criminal, Civil rights, Personal injury. Office: 3113 Rockefeller Ave Everett WA 98201

PHILLIPS, CATHERINE, lawyer; b. Balt., Aug. 28, 1954; s. Ralph West and Dorothy (Miller) P.; m. Mark Lesley Plummer, Sept. 1, 1979; children: Robert Lawrence, Elizabeth Phillips. BS, U. Wash., 1976, JD, 1982. Bar: Wash. 1982. Forest mgr. State of Wash. Dept. Natural Resources, Wauconda, 1976-79; legis. asst. to U.S. Senator Slade Gorton, Wash., 1982-85; chief counsel subcon. on sci., tech. and space Senate Com. on Commerce, Sci. and Transp., Washington, 1985-87; assoc. Perkins, Coie, Seattle, 1987—. Mem. ABA, Wash. State Bar Assn., Soc. Am. Foresters (nat. policy com. 1982-85). Republican. Lutheran. Legislative, Administrative and regulatory, Government contracts and claims. Office: Perkins Coie 1900 Washington Bldg Seattle WA 98101

PHILLIPS, CHARLES PATRICK, lawyer; b. Springfield, Mass., Oct. 9, 1946; s. Charles Patrick and Elizabeth Anne (McNiff) P. AB, Oglethorpe U., 1969; MA in Edn., Ga. State U., 1971; JD cum laude, Woodrow Wilson Coll., 1979. Tchr. Atlanta Pub. Schs., 1971-76; sole practice Atlanta, 1979—; law clk., mediator to presiding judge Fulton County Supreme Ct., Atlanta, 1982-85; dep. dir. Neighborhood Justice Ctr., Atlanta, 1986; mediator, cons. Neighborhood Justice Ctr. of Atlanta, Inc., 1978—. Mem. ABA, Ga. State Bar Assn. Democrat. Roman Catholic. Avocations: tennis, skiing, music, motorcycling. Mediation, Entertainment, Family and matrimonial. Home: 1181 Rennes Ct Atlanta GA 30319 Office: Neighborhood Justice Ctr 976 Edgewood Ave Atlanta GA 30307

PHILLIPS, DENNIS LESLIE, lawyer, army officer; b. Phila., Sept. 2, 1952; s. William Leslie and Margaret Katherine (Wenborne) P.; m. Linda Jane Pogue, June 23, 1974; children—Colleen, Michael, Brian. B.S., U.S. Mil. Acad., 1974; J.D. magna cum laude, Syracuse U., 1981. Bar: N.Y. 1982, U.S. Ct. Mil. Appeals 1982, U.S. Supreme Ct. 1986. Commd. 2d lt. U.S. Army, 1974, advanced through grades to maj., 1986; comdr. 284th M.P. Co., Frankfurt, 1977-78; trial def. counsel Trial Def. Service, Ft. Riley, Kans., 1981-83; dep. staff judge adv. U.S. Army Correctional Activity, Ft. Riley, 1983-85, trial atty. Office Chief Trial Atty. JAGC, Falls Church, Va., 1986—. Instl. rep., com. chmn. Explorer Scouts, Boy Scouts Am., Frankfurt, 1977-78; merit badge counselor Hiawatha council Boy Scouts Am., 1979-81. Decorated Meritorious Service medal with one oak leaf cluster, Army Achievement medal. Mem. ABA, N.Y. State Bar Assn., Fed. Bar Assn., Assn. Trial Lawyers Am., Assn. U.S. Army, Nat. Eagle Scout Assn., Justinian Hon. Law Soc., Order of Coif. Republican. Episcopalian. Government contracts and claims, Military, Criminal. Home: 13215 Pleasant Glen Ct Herndon VA 22071 Office: JAGC Contract Appeals Div Nassif Bldg 5611 Columbia Pike Falls Church VA 22041-5013

PHILLIPS, DOROTHY KAY, lawyer; b. Camden, N.J., Nov. 2, 1945; d. Benjamin L. and Sadye (Levinsky) Phillips; m. Manny D. Pokotilow; children—Bethann P., David M. Schaffzin. B.S. magna cum laude in English Lit., U. Pa., 1964; M.A., Family Life and Marriage Counseling and Edn., NYU, 1975; J.D., Villanova U., 1978. Bar: Pa., N.J., U.S. Dist. Ct. (ea. dist.) Pa., U.S. Dist. Ct. N.J., U.S. Ct. Appeals (3d cir.), U.S. Supreme Ct. Tchr., Haddon Twp. High Sch. (N.J.), and Haddon Heights High Sch. (N.J.), 1964-70; lectr., counselor Marriage Council of Phila., marriage and family life counselor Marriage and Family Life Assocs., Willingboro, N.J., lectr. U. Pa. and Hahnemann Med. Schs., profl. cons., lectr. Lankenau Hosp., Phila., 1970-75; atty. Adler, Barish, Daniels, Levin & Creskoff, Phila., 1978-79, Astor, Weiss & Newman, Phila., 1979-80; ptnr. Romisher & Phillips, P.C., Phila., 1981-86; ptnr., Law Office of Dorothy K. Phillips, 1986—; guest speaker on domestic relations issues on radio and TV shows; featured in newspaper and mag. articles. Mem. Rosenbach Found., Art Alliance, Phila.; bd. dirs. Philadanco; mem. Bus. and Profl. Women's Coalition of Fedn. Jewish Agys. Greater Phila., Bus. Women's Network. Mem. ABA, Assn. Trial Lawyers Am., Pa. Trial Lawyers Assn., Pa. Bar Assn., N.J. Bar Assn., Phila. Bar Assn. (chmn. early settlement program 1983-84, mem. rules drafting com. custody rules, vol. bar diabetes 10K run, 1984-85), Phila. Trial Lawyers Assn., Montgomery County Bar Assn., Camden County Bar Assn., Tau Epsilon Rho Law Soc., Lawyers Club. Family and matrimonial, State civil litigation. Office: 220 S 16th St Suite 600 Philadelphia PA 19102

PHILLIPS, DWIGHT WILBURN, lawyer; b. Detroit, Dec. 19, 1951; s. Wilburn Raymond and Inez Marie (Sims) P. BA, U. San Francisco, 1973; JD, U. Mich., 1976. Bar: Mich. 1976. Assoc. Ronald Crenshaw and Assocs., Detroit, 1976-81; ptnr. Patterson, Phifer & Phillips, Detroit, 1981—. Vice chmn. of bd. dirs. Eastside br. YMCA, Detroit, bd. dirs. 1982—; treas. com. Bradfield for Judge, Detroit, 1984. Mem. Mich. Bar Assn. (workers compensation sect.), Wolverine Bar Assn. (treas. 1979-81), Assn. Trial Lawyers Am., Alpha Phi Alpha. Avocation: model trains. Workers' compensation, Personal injury. Home: 17312 Forrer Detroit MI 48235 Office: Patterson Phifer & Phillips PC 960 Penobscot Bldg Detroit MI 48226

PHILLIPS, ELLIOTT HUNTER, lawyer; b. Birmingham, Mich., Feb. 14, 1919; s. Frank Elliott and Gertrude (Zacharias) P.; m. Gail Carolyn Isbey, Apr. 22, 1950; children—Elliott Hunter, Alexandra. A.B. cum laude, Harvard U., 1940, J.D., 1947. Bar: Mich. 1948. Since practiced in Detroit; ptnr. Hill, Lewis, Adams, Goodrich & Tait, 1953—; chmn. bd. dirs. Detroit & Can. Tunnel Corp.; pres., dir. Detroit and Windsor Subway Co.; mem. Mich. Bd. Accountancy, 1965-73. Contbr. to legal and accounting jours. Chmn. bd. dirs. Detroit chpt. ARC; pres., trustee McGregor Fund; trustee Boys Republic, Detroit Inst. for Children, United Found., Detroit; mem. corp. Cottage Hosp., Grosse Pointe, Mich.; mem. nat. major gifts com. Harvard U., mem. overseers com. to visit Law Sch., also overseers com. univ. resources, Mich. chmn. Harvard Coll. fund; trustee, pres. Ch. Youth Service; mem. Detroit Area Council Boy Scouts Am. Served to lt. comdr. USNR, 1946. Fellow Am. Bar Found.; mem. ABA, Detroit Bar Assn., State Bar Mich., Harvard Law Sch. Assn. (fund chmn. Mich. 1969-72), Asso. Harvard Alumni (v.p., exec. com.), Lincoln's Inn Soc. (Harvard). Episcopalian (vestryman, sr. warden). Clubs: Country, Detroit, Economic, Yondotega; Grosse Pointe; Harvard Eastern Mich. (pres. 1955-56); Harvard (N.Y.C.). Pension, profit-sharing, and employee benefits, General corporate, Non-profit organizations. Home: 193 Ridge Rd Grosse Pointe Farms MI 48236 Office: 32d Floor 100 Renaissance Center Detroit MI 48226

PHILLIPS, GARY STEPHEN, lawyer; b. Far Rockaway, N.Y., June 26, 1957; s. Lawrence and Ilene (Kaufman) P.; m. Debbie J. Kanner, Mar. 27, 1983; 1 child, Joshua Charles. BA with high honors, U. Fla., 1978, JD with honors, 1981. Bar: Fla. 1982, U.S. Dist. Ct. (so. dist.) Fla. 1982, U.S. Ct. Appeals (11th cir.) 1982, U.S. Supreme Ct. 1986. Assoc. Sparber, Shevin, Shapo & Heilbronner, Miami, Fla., 1981—. Contbr. editor U. Fla. Law Rev., 1980-81. Mem. ABA, Am. Judicature Soc., Fla Bar Assn. (litigation, real property, probate and trust law sects.), Dade County Bar Assn., Phi Beta Kappa, Omicron Delta Epsilon, Omicron Delta Kappa. Democrat. Jewish. Lodge: B'nai Brith. State civil litigation, Federal civil litigation, Personal injury. Office: Sparber Shevin et al 1 SE 3d Ave 29th Floor Miami FL 33131

PHILLIPS, GEORGE L., lawyer; b. Fulton, Miss., May 24, 1949; s. Gilbert L. and Grace (Staker) P. B.S., U. So. Miss., 1971; J.D., U. Miss., 1973. Bar: Miss. Assoc. firm Johnson, Pittman & Pittman, Hattiesburg, Miss., 1974-75; partner firm Norris & Phillips, 1975-76; county pros. atty. Forrest County, Miss., 1976-80; U.S. atty. So. Dist. Miss., 1980—; instr. Hattiesburg Police Acad., 1977. Bd. dirs. Forrest County Youth Court; pres. South Central chpt. A.R.C., 1980-81; bd. dirs. Pine Burr area council Boy Scouts Am. Mem. Miss. Prosecutors Assn. (pres.), Fed., Miss. bar assns., Am. Criminal Justice Assn., Nat. Dist. Attys. Assn., Miss. Trial Lawyers. Baptist. Club: Kiwanis. Address: PO Box 2091 Jackson MS 39205

PHILLIPS, JAMES DICKSON, JR., fed. judge; b. Scotland County, N.C., Sept. 23, 1922; s. James Dickson and Helen (Shepherd) P.; m. Jean Duff Nunalee, July 16, 1960; children: Evelyn Phillips Perry, James Dickson, III, Elizabeth Duff, Ida Wills. B.S. cum laude, Davidson Coll., 1943; J.D., U. N.C., 1948. Bar: N.C. bar. Asst. dir. Inst. Govt., Chapel Hill, N.C., 1948-49; partner firm Phillips & McCoy, Laurinburg, N.C., 1949-55, Sanford, Phillips, McCoy & Weaver, Fayetteville, N.C., 1955-60; from asst. prof. to prof. law U. N.C., 1960-78, dean Sch. Law, 1964-74; circuit judge U.S. Ct. Appeals, 4th Circuit, 1978—; Mem. N.C. Wildlife Resources Commn., 1961-63; mem. N.C. Cts. Commn., 1963-75; also vice chmn.; chmn. N.C. Bd. Ethics, 1977-78. Served with parachute inf. U.S. Army, 1943-46. Decorated Bronze Arrowhead, Bronze Star, Purple Heart; recipient John J. Parker Meml. award; Thomas Jefferson award. Mem. Am. Law Inst., N.C. Bar Assn., Am. Bar Assn. Democrat. Presbyterian. Jurisprudence. Office: US Court Appeals PO Box 3617 Durham NC 27702 *

PHILLIPS, JAMES HAROLD, lawyer; b. Bowie, Tex., Dec. 18, 1934; s. Frank Carroll and Mabel Lorraine (James) P.; m. Jean Keir Woodruff, Oct. 2, 1959; children—Susan, John (dec.), Sara, Jamie. B.S.E.E., Rose-Hulman Inst. Tech.-Terre Haute, Ind., 1960; J.D., George Washington U., 1967. Bar: Ariz. 1968, U.S. Dist. Ct. Ariz. 1968, U.S. Patent Office 1968, U.S. Supreme Ct. 1972, U.S. Ct. Customs & Patent Appeals 1974, Tex. 1980, U.S. Ct. Appeals (fed. cir.) 1982. Atty., Gen. Electric, 1967-68; ptnr. Drummond, Cahill & Phillips, Phoenix, 1968-73; asst. patent counsel NCR Corp., Dayton, Ohio, 1973-76; sr. profl. atty. Sun Co. Inc., Dallas, 1976-84; ptnr. Cates & Phillips, Phoenix, 1984—; dir., v.p. Environ. Geotechnics Inc., Dallas, 1982-84; cons. Sun Co. Inc., Dallas, Atlantic-Richfield Co., Plano, Tex., 1984—. Contbr. articles to profl. jours. Charter mem. Phoenix Symphony Council; pres. AMICA-Tex. chpt. Served with USN, 1952-55. Mem. Am. Intellectual Property Law Assn., Am. Arbitration Assn. (arbitrator), Licensing Exec. Soc., Ariz. Bar Assn. (chmn. patent, trademark and copyright sect. 1985-86), Tex. Bar Assn. Republican. Methodist. Patent, Trademark and copyright. Home: 410 E Braeburn Dr Phoenix AZ 85022 Office: Cates & Phillips 3800 N Central Ave # 920 Phoenix AZ 85012

PHILLIPS, JOHN BOMAR, lawyer; b. Murfreesboro, Tenn., Jan. 28, 1947; s. John Bomar Sr. and Betty Blanche (Primm) P.; m. Ellen Elizabeth Ellis, Aug. 9, 1969; children: John Bomar III, Anna Carroll. BS, David Lipscomb Coll., 1969; JD, U. Tenn., 1974. Bar: Tenn. 1974, U.S. Dist. Ct. (ea. dist.) Tenn. 1975, U.S. Tax Ct. 1976, U.S. Ct. Appeals (6th cir.) 1980. Assoc. Caldwell, Heggie & Helton, Chattanooga, 1974-79, ptnr., 1979—. Editor: The Tennessee Employment Law Update, 1986. Sec. Chattanooga State Coll. Found., 1979—; bd. dirs. Council for Alcohol and Drug Abuse, Chattanooga, 1981-83; pres. Boys Club of Chattanooga, 1983-84. Mem. ABA (labor law sect.), Tenn. Bar Assn. (labor law sect.), Chattanooga Bar Assn. (bd. govs. 1978-79), Order of Coif, Phi Kappa Phi. Mem. Disciples of Christ. Clubs: Fairyland Country (Lookout Mountain, Tenn.); Walden (Chattanooga). Lodge: Kiwanis (pres. Chattanooga 1986—). Avocations: tennis, running. Contracts commercial, Labor, Libel. Home: 200 N Hermitage Ave Lookout Mountain TN 37350 Office: Caldwell Heggie & Helton 450 Maclellan Bldg 722 Chestnut St Chattanooga TN 37402

PHILLIPS, JOHN DAVISSON, lawyer; b. Clarksburg, W.Va., Aug. 21, 1906; s. Robert Bruce and Lela (Davisson) P.; m. Virginia Maxwell, Nov. 12, 1932; children: John Davisson, Julia Anne. Student, Washington and Lee U., 1924-25; A.B., W.Va. U., 1928, LL.B., 1930; postgrad., Oxford U., 1930-32. Bar: W.Va. bar 1932. Gen. practice law Wheeling, W.Va., 1932—; mem. firm Phillips, Gardill, Kaiser, Boos & Hartley; asst. pros. atty. Ohio County, 1937-40; city solicitor City of Wheeling, 1942-47; hon. dir. Wheeling Dollar Savs. & Trust Co., M. Marsh & Son, Wesbanco, Inc., Wheeling. Past mem. W.Va. State Bd. Law Examiners. Served as capt. USMCR, World War II. Fellow Am. Bar Founds.; mem. ABA, W.Va. Bar Assn. (pres. 1955-56), Am. Judicature Soc., Phi Kappa Psi, Phi Delta Phi. Episcopalian. Clubs: Wheeling Country, Fort Henry. Banking, General corporate, Probate. Home: 4 Arlington Dr Howard Pl Wheeling WV 26003 Office: 61 14th St Wheeling WV 26003

PHILLIPS, JOHN TAYLOR, judge; b. Greenville, S.C., Aug. 20, 1923; s. Walter Dixon and Mattie Sue (Taylor) P.; m. Elizabeth Parrish, Dec. 18, 1954; children: John Allen, Mary Susan, Linda Lea, Julia. AB, Glenville State Coll., 1952; JD, Mercer U., 1955; LLD, Chapel Hill U., 1980. Bar: Ga., U.S. Dist. Ct. Ga., US. Ct. Appeals, U.S. Supreme Ct. Judge Bibb County State Ct., Macon, Ga. State rep. Ga., 1959-62, senate, 1962-64. Served to capt. USMC, 1950-51. Home: 1735 Winston Dr Macon GA 31206 Office: State Ct Box 5086 Macon GA 31213

PHILLIPS, JOSEPH BRANTLEY, JR., lawyer; b. Greenville, S.C., Dec. 5, 1931. B.S. in Bus. Adminstrn., U. S.C., 1954, J.D., 1955. Bar: S.C. 1955. Assoc. Leatherwood, Walker, Todd & Mann, Greenville, 1958-63, ptnr., 1963—. Chmn. bd. deacons Presbyterian Ch., 1970-71, pres. Men of Ch., 1968-69, chmn. Christian Service Ctr., 1972-73; bd. dirs. Greenville Urban Ministry, 1978. Mem. ABA, S.C. Bar Assn., Greenville Bar Assn., Greenville Young Lawyers Club (pres. 1961-62). Clubs: Greenville Country (pres. 1977), Kiwanis (pres. 1973). Antitrust, General corporate. Home: 1137 Parkins Mill Rd Greenville SC 29607 Office: PO Box 87 Greenville SC 29602

PHILLIPS, KATHLEEN A., lawyer; b. Sumatra, Indonesia, Sept. 19, 1954; Came to U.S., 1959; d. Kenneth Foster and Mary Sybella (Cappel) Tilltson; m. James Steven Phillips, May 24, 1980; children: Erin Leah, Lisa Ellen. BA, U. Akron, 1975, JD, 1979. Bar: Ohio 1979, Tex. 1982, U.S. Ct. Appeals (5th, 11th and D.C. cirs.) 1981. Law clk. Summit County Common Pleas Ct., Akron, Ohio, 1977-80; atty. Shell Oil Co., Houston, 1981—. Mem. ABA, Tex. Bar Assn. Republican. General corporate, Energy, minerals, precious metals, Real property. Office: Shell Oil Co 200 N Dairy Ashford Houston TX 77079

PHILLIPS, LARRY EDWARD, lawyer; b. Pitts., July 5, 1942; s. Jack F. and Jean H. (Houghtelin) P.; m. Karla Ann Hennings, June 5, 1976; 1 son, Andrew H.; 1 stepson, John W. Dean IV. B.A., Hamilton Coll., 1964; J.D., U. Mich., 1967. Bars: Pa. 1967, U.S. Dist. Ct. (we. dist.) Pa. 1967, U.S. Tax Ct. 1969. Assoc. Buchanan, Ingersoll, Rodewald, Kyle & Buerger, P.C. (now Buchanan Ingersoll P.C.), Pitts., 1967-73, mem., 1973—. Bd. dirs. Psychol. Service of Pitts., 1972—, pres., 1985—. Mem. Am. Coll. Tax Counsel, Tax Mgmt. Inc. (adv. bd.), Pitts. Tax Club, ABA (sect. taxation, com. corp. stockholder relationships and sect. real property, probate and trust law), Allegheny County Bar Assn., Pa. Bar Assn. Republican. Presbyterian. Clubs: Duquesne, St. Clair County. Contbr. articles to profl. jours. Corporate taxation, Probate, Personal income taxation. Address: 57th Floor 600 Grant St Pittsburgh PA 15219

PHILLIPS, LAYN R., lawyer. U.S. atty. no. dist. State of Okla., Tulsa. Office: US Courthouse 333 W Fourth St Rm 460 Tulsa OK 74103 *

PHILLIPS, LEO HAROLD, JR., lawyer; b. Detroit, Jan. 10, 1945; s. Leo Harold and Martha C. (Oberg) P.; m. Patricia Margaret Halcomb, Sept. 3, 1983. B.A. summa cum laude, Hillsdale Coll., 1967; M.A., U. Mich., 1968; J.D. cum laude, 1973; LL.M. magna cum laude, Free Univ. of Brussels, 1974. Bar: Mich. 1974, N.Y. 1975, U.S. Supreme Ct. 1977, D.C. 1979. Fgn. lectr. Pusan Nat. U. (Korea), 1969-70; assoc. Alexander & Green, N.Y.C., 1974-77; counsel Overseas Pvt. Investment Corp., Washington, 1977-80, sr. counsel, 1980-82, asst. gen. counsel, 1982-85; asst. gen. counsel Manor Care, Inc., Silver Spring, Md., 1985—; vol. Peace Corps, Pusan, 1968-71; mem. program for sr. mgrs. in govt. Harvard U., Cambridge, Mass., 1982. Contbr. articles to legal jours. Chmn. legal affairs com. Essex Condominium Assn., Washington, 1979-81; deacon Chevy Chase Presbyterian Ch., Washington, 1984—, moderator, 1985-87. Recipient Alumni Achievement award Hillsdale Coll., 1981; Meritorious Honor award Overseas Pvt. Investment Corp., 1981, Superior Achievement award, 1984. Mem. ABA (internat. fin. transactions com., vice chmn. com. internat. ins. law), Am. Soc. Internat. Law (Jessup Internat. Law moot ct. judge semi-final rounds 1978-83), Internat. Law Assn. (Am. br.; com. sec. 1982), D.C. Bar, N.Y. State Bar Assn., Royal Asiatic Soc. (Korea br.), State Bar Mich., Washington Fgn. Law Soc. (sec.-treas. 1980-81, bd. dirs., program coordinator 1981-82, v.p. 1982-83, pres.-elect 1983-84, pres. 1984-85), Washington Internat. Trade Assn. (bd. dirs. 1984—), Assn. Bar City N.Y., Hillsdale Coll. Alumni Assn. (co-chmn. Washington area 1977—). Club: University (N.Y.C.). Private international, General corporate, Contracts commercial. Home: 4740 Connecticut Ave NW Apt 702 Washington DC 20008 Office: Manor Care Inc 10750 Columbia Pike Silver Spring MD 20901

PHILLIPS, MICHAEL JAMES, lawyer; b. Chgo., Aug. 14, 1954; s. Robert Taylor and Mary Alice (McGinnis) P. BA, U. Notre Dame, 1977; JD, DePaul U., 1980. Bar: Ill. 1980, U.S. Dist. Ct. (no. dist.) Ill. 1980, U.S. Ct. Appeals (7th cir.) 1980. Asst. state's atty. Stephenson County, Freeport, Ill., 1981-87, Lake County, Waukegan, Ill., 1987—. V.p. Stephenson County Assn. Prevention of Child Abuse, Freeport, 1984—; bd. dirs. Freeport Big Bros./Big Sisters Inc., 1984—, Freeport Drug Edn. and Prevention Commn., 1985—. Recipient Cert. of Appreciation, Stephenson County Arson Task Force, 1986. Mem. ABA, Ill. Bar Assn. (young lawyers div. com. on child abuse and neglect 1982—), Stephenson County Bar Assn. (Edward N. Pietrucha courtroom decorum award 1982), Ill. State's Attys. Assn. (spl. task force on criminal computer histories 1983). Roman Catholic. Lodge: K.C. (grand knight of initiation com. 1985—). Federal civil litigation, Criminal, Legal advisor to county government. Home: 1870 Delany Rd #118 Gurnee IL 60031 Office: Lake County States Atty 18 N County St Waukegan IL 60085

PHILLIPS, PATRICK PAUL, lawyer; b. Traverse City, Mich., Apr. 28, 1955; s. H. Paul and Florence (Corkwell) P; m. Cynthia Anne Van Straten, Dec. 17, 1983. BA cum laude, U. Richmond, 1977; JD, Capital U., 1980. Bar: Ohio 1980, U.S. Dist. Ct. (so. dist.) Ohio 1981, U.S. Ct. Customs and Patent Appeals 1981, U.S. Ct. Appeals (fed. cir.) 1982. Assoc. Robert E. Stebens, Columbus, Ohio, 1980-86, Schottenstein, Zox & Dunn, Columbus, 1986—; lectr. Capital Law Sch., 1981, 85. Contbr. articles to profl. jours. Deacon East Side Grace Brethern Ch.; jr. council Columbus Mus. Art; bd. dirs. Bexley Celebrations Assn., North Cen. Ohio Dist. Youth Bd. Named one of Outstanding Young Men in Am., 1986. Mem. ABA, Ohio Bar Assn. (bd. govs. patent sect. 1983—), Columbus Bar Assn. (program speaker 1987), Columbus Patent Assn. (pres. 1984-85, program speaker 1981, 83, 85), Bexley Area C. of C. (charter), U. Richmond Alumni Assn. (cen. Ohio rep.), Delta Theta Phi, Omicron Delta Kappa. Republican. Avocations: music, antiques, youth work. Trademark and copyright, Patent, Federal civil litigation. Home: 696 S Roosevelt Ave Bexley OH 43209 Office: Schottenstein Zox & Dunn 41 S High St Columbus OH 43215

PHILLIPS, RANDEL EUGENE, lawyer; b. Winston-Salem, N.C., Nov. 3, 1947; s. Eugene Harold and Mary Barbara (Miller) P.; m. Clora Emily Harmon, Aug. 20, 1970; children: Denise, Catherine, Abigail. BA cum laude, Davidson Coll., 1969; BA, Oxford U., Eng., 1971; JD magna cum laude, Harvard U., 1979. Bar: N.C. 1980, U.S. Dist. Ct. (we. dist.) N.C. 1980, U.S. Dist. Ct. (mid. dist.) N.C. 1981, U.S. Ct. Appeals (4th cir.) 1982, U.S. Dist. Ct. (ea. dist.) N.C. 1985. Law clk. to presiding judge U.S. Dist. Ct., N.C., 1979-80; assoc. Moore & Van Allen, Charlotte, N.C., 1980-85; ptnr. Moore, Van Allen, Allen & Thigpen, Charlotte, 1986—. Deacon First Presbyn. Ch., Charlotte, 1985—; bd. dirs. Community Sch. of Arts, Charlotte, 1981—. Served to capt. U.S. Army, 1971-72. Rhodes scholar, 1968. Mem. ABA, N.C. Bar Assn., N.C. Acad. Trial Lawyers Assn. Democrat. Club: Tower (Charlotte). Avocations: swimming, hiking, reading. Federal civil litigation, State civil litigation. Home: 3201 Cloverfield Rd Charlotte NC 28211 Office: Moore & Van Allen Allen & Thigpen 3000 NCNB Plaza Charlotte NC 28280

PHILLIPS, STEVEN WILLIAM, lawyer, educator; b. Safford, Ariz., May 30, 1946; s. Darrell Sims and Lottie (Stevens) P.; m. Glenda Lee Southard, Nov. 13, 1976; children—Edward Clinton, Staci Lee, Ann Lee. B.S. in Finance, U. Ariz., 1968, J.D. with honors, 1971; postgrad. U. So. Calif., 1971-74. Bar: Ariz. 1971, Calif. 1972, U.S. Tax Ct. 1973, U.S. Ct. Appeals (9th cir.) 1974, U.S. Dist. Ct. Ariz. 1978. Assoc., Willis, Butler, Scheifly, Leydorf and Grant, Los Angeles, 1971-75; assoc. prof. law U. Ariz., 1975-77, adj. prof., 1977—; ptnr. Hecker, Phillips & Hooker, Tucson, 1977—; bd. dirs. Bd. Legal Specialization, State Bar Ariz., 1981—. Recipient U.S. Law Week award U. Ariz., 1971. Mem. State Bar Ariz. (mem. council of tax sect. 1984—), State Bar Calif., ABA, IRS Bar Liaison Com. (chmn. western region 1983-84, chmn. sw region 1987—), Order of Coif. Democrat. Club: Mountain Oyster (Tucson). Contbr. articles to profl. jours. Corporate taxation, Personal income taxation, Securities. Office: Hecker Phillips and Hooker 405 W Franklin St Tucson AZ 85701

PHILLIPS, THOMAS MARION, lawyer; b. Greenville, Tex., Nov. 12, 1916; s. Thomas Moody and Maye Louise (Stallworth) P.; m. Edna Louise Hebert, June 17, 1941; 1 dau., Priscilla Jane. LL.B., U. Tex., 1939. Bar: Tex. 1939, U.S. Dist. Ct. (so. dist.) Tex. 1946, U.S. Ct. Appeals (5th cir.) 1946, U.S. Supreme Ct. 1971. Assoc. Baker & Botts, Houston, 1939-50, ptnr., 1950—, sr. ptnr., 1958—; dir. Tex. Gulf Co., 1967-72, hon. dir., 1972-81; dir. Champion Internat., 1976—. Life mem. U. Tex. Law Sch. Found. Served with M.I., AUS, 1942-46. Mem. Houston Bar Assn. (pres. 1967-68), Tex. Bar Assn. (pres. 1969-70), ABA (ho. dels. 1970-76), Order of Coif, Phi Delta Phi. Episcopalian. Clubs: Houston Country, Houston, Masons. Editor Tex. Law Rev., 1938-39. Federal civil litigation, State civil litigation, General corporate. Office: Suite 3000 One Shell Plaza Houston TX 77002

PHILLIPS, TRAVIS R., lawyer; b. Longview, Tex., Feb. 20, 1948; s. Lowell T. and Alice (Tucker) P.; m. Barbara Shepherd, June 30, 1973 (div. Mar. 1981); m. Mary Diane Bialaszewski, Sept. 10, 1983. B.B.A., Stephen F. Austin State U., 1970; J.D., U. Tex.-Austin, 1972. Bar: Tex. 1972, U.S. Dist. Ct. (we. dist.) Tex. 1974, U.S. Dist. Ct. (so. dist.) Tex. 1981, U.S. Ct. Appeals (5th cir.) 1974. Juvenile pub. defender County of Travis, Austin, 1972-73; ptnr. Phillips & Dorsett, Austin, 1973-76, Phillips, Neals & Woods, Austin, 1976—; gen. counsel Tex. Rental Assn., 1973-81; pres. Tramco Mortgage Co., Austin, 1983—; mayor City of Rollingwood, Tex., 1986—. Author: (manual) Texas Mechanics Lien Laws, 1976. Mem. Travis County Bar Assn. Democrat. Lodges: Masons, Shriners. State civil litigation, Contracts commercial, Real property. Office: Phillips Neal & Woods 1303 San Antonio St Austin TX 78701

PHILO, DUWAYNE ALLEN, lawyer, former educator; b. New Hartford, Iowa, Dec. 11, 1925; s. Claude Allen and Grace Vernette (Mason) P.; m. Rose Shields, June 8, 1950 (dec. 1983); 1 son, Daniel. Student Iowa State Tchrs. Coll., 1946-47; A.B., San Diego State Coll., 1963, M.A. in Edn., 1967; M.A. in History, Chapman Coll., 1973; J.D., Western State U., 1977. Bar: Calif. 1977, U.S. Dist. Ct. (so. dist.) Calif. 1977, U.S. Tax Ct. 1981. Served to sgt. U.S. Marine Corps, 1942-63; tchr., Imperial and San Diego Counties, Calif., 1964-81; sole practice, San Marcos, Calif., 1977—. Dir. North County

Centro; v.p. Oceanside Tchrs. Assn., 1970-71. Decorated Purple Heart, Bronze Star. Mem. Marine Corps Assn., ABA, San Diego County Bar Assn., Profl. Educators Group, NEA. Democrat. Baptist. Bankruptcy, Family and matrimonial, General practice. Home: 6031 Sinton Pl La Mesa CA 92042 Office: 5555 Jackson Dr Suite 204 La Mesa CA 92042

PHILPOTT, ALBERT LEE, state legislator; b. Philpott, Va., July 29, 1919; s. John Elkania and Mary Gertrude (Prillaman) P.; m. Katherine Apperson Spencer, 1941; children—Judy Philpott Marstiller, Albert Lee. B.A., U. Richmond, 1941, J.D., 1947; LL.D., 1978. Atty. Henry County, Commonwealth of Va., 1952-58; mem. Va. Ho. of Dels., 1958—, speaker, 1980—; practice law 1947—. Served to 1st lt. USAAF, 1941-45. Recipient Disting. Service award Am. Legion, 1977; Disting. Alumni award U. Richmond, 1977; Va. Cultural Laureate award for Statesmanship, 1977. Clubs: Elks, Moose, KP. General corporate, Criminal, Personal injury. Office: House of Delegate State Capitol Richmond VA 23219

PHILPOTT, JAMES ALVIN, JR., lawyer; b. Lexington, Va., Apr. 26, 1947; s. James Alvin and Helen (Gibbs) P.; m. Judy Mauze, June 10, 1968; children: John Harman, Jean Cameron, James Hundley. BS in Commerce, Washington & Lee U., 1969, JD summa cum laude, 1972. Bar: N.Y. 1974, Ky. 1980, U.S. Dist. Ct. (so. dist.) N.Y. 1980, U.S. Ct. Appeals (4th cir.) 1980. Law clk. to presiding justice U.S. Ct. Appeals (4th cir.), Ashville, N.C., 1972-73; assoc. Cravath, Swaine & Moore, N.Y.C., 1974-79; exec. v.p., gen. counsel Gainesway Farm, Lexington, Ky., 1980-85; mng. dir. Thoroughbred Adv., Lexington, 1985—; asst. sec. Breeders Cup Ltd., Lexington, 1981—. Editor-in chief Washington & Lee U. Law Rev., 1972. Trustee The Lexington Sch., 1984—. Served to capt. U.S. Army, 1972-73. Mem. ABA (corp., banking and bus. law sect.), Ky. Bar Assn., Ky. Thoroughbred Assn., Washington & Lee U. Sch. Assn. (mem. council 1986—), Omicron Delta Kappa. Presbyterian. Clubs: Idle Hour Country, The Lexington (Lexington). Contracts commercial, General corporate, Securities. Office: Thoroughbred Adv Group Inc 1620 Vine Ctr Lexington KY 40507

PHILPOTT, STEVEN LEE, lawyer; b. Eugene, Oreg., Apr. 14, 1951; s. Lee F. and Rosemary E. (McNutt) P.; m. Katherin Patrice Murphy, June 22, 1974; children: James Justin, Molly Marie. BA in Gen. Arts and Letters, U. Oreg., 1975, JD, 1978. Bar: Oreg. 1978, U.S. Dist. Ct. Oreg. 1979. Assoc. Donald K. Armstrong P.C., Eugene, 1978-80; ptnr. Armstrong & Philpott, Eugene, 1980-82, Armstrong, McCullen & Philpott P.C., Eugene, 1982—. Banking, Contracts commercial, Real property. Home: 3203 Marvin Dr Eugene OR 97404 Office: Armstrong McCullen & Philpott 1420 Green Acres Rd Eugene OR 97401

PHIPPS, BENJAMIN KIMBALL, II, lawyer; b. Boston, Jan. 16, 1933; s. Benjamin Kimball and Bertha Elizabeth (Forsyth) P.; m. Phyllis Jarrett Anderson, Jan. 10, 1962; children—Lisa Jarrett, Christina Caroline. B.S. in Commerce, U. Va., 1955, LL.B., 1958. Bar: Fla. 1964, U.S. Dist. Ct. (no. dist.) Fla., U.S. Claims Ct., U.S. Ct. Appeals (5th and 11th cirs.) U.S. Tax Ct. Editor, Municipal Code Corp., Tallahassee, 1964-65; sole practice, Tallahassee, 1965—; cons. in field. Chmn., Hist. Tallahassee Preservation Bd., 1970—; trustee Maclay Sch.; mem. adv. council WFSU-TV, chmn., 1978—. Served to capt. U.S. Army, 1958-64. Mem. ABA (tax sect. state and local tax com.), Tallahassee Bar Assn., Fla. Bar (vice chmn., treas., chmn. tax sect. 1985-86, editorial bd. Fla. Bar Jour./Fla. Bar News, chmn. 1975-76), Sigma Alpha Epsilon, Phi Alpha Delta, Phi Delta Epsilon. Democrat. Episcopalian. Clubs: Governor's, Cosmos, Exchange, Tiger Bay (dir.), St. Andrews Soc. (pres. 1978-79) (Tallahassee). Contbr. articles to profl. jours.; columnist Tallahassee Democrat. State and local taxation, Federal taxation. Office: PO Box 1351 Tallahassee FL 32302

PHIPPS, JOHN TOM, lawyer; b. Chgo., Sept. 20, 1937; s. J. Oliver and Jean C. (Kirkwood) P.; m. Dorothy B. Barth, Aug. 19, 1961; children—Anne Marie, John B., Karen Louise. B.A., DePauw U., 1959; J.D., U. Ill., 1965. Bar: Ill. 1965, U.S. Dist. Ct. (cen. dist.) Ill. 1966. Practice, Champaign, Ill., 1965—; spl. prosecutor Champaign County, Ill., 1968; bd. dirs. Champaign County Legal Assistance Found., 1966-73, pres., 1971-73; incorporator Land of Lincoln Legal Assistance Found., 1973, bd. dirs., 1972—, chmn., 1981—. Bd. dirs. Clark-Lindsey Village, 1979-80, pres. 1973-75. Served as lt. USAF, 1959-62. Decorated Air Force Commendation medal. Mem. Champaign County Bar Assn. (bd. govs. 1972-74, v.p. 1973-74), ABA (gen. practice sect., vice chmn. solo and small firms com. 1985—), Ill. Bar Assn. (mem. corp. and securities law sect. council 1976-78, chmn. mgmt. and econs. of practice of law sect. council 1980-82, family law sect. 1985—), Assn. Trial Lawyers of Am., Ill. Trial Lawyers Assn. Contbr. articles to profl. jours. and continuing legal edn. books. Family and matrimonial, Personal injury, State civil litigation. Office: 44 Main St PO Box 1866 Champaign IL 61820

PHOLERIC, KAREN JOY, lawyer; b. Phila., Mar. 8, 1947; d. John Francis and Janet Joy (Koepfer) P. Student Pa. State U., 1964-66; B.A., George Washington U., 1968; J.D., Villanova U., 1968-71. Bar: Pa. 1971, U.S. Supreme Ct. 1975. Staff atty. Delaware County Legal Assistance Assn., 1971-73; asst. public defencer, 1973-77; sole practice, 1973-77; ptnr. Borrebach, Pholeric, Tomlinson & Sullivan, 1977-79; sole practice, Media, Pa., 1979—; coadj. instr. Delaware County Community Coll. Bd. dirs. Helen Kate Furness Library, 1979-81, Parent Edn. and Human Relations, 1979-83; chmn. Zoning Hearing Bd., Rose Valley Borough; Republican committee woman Borough of Rose Valley, 1974—. Mem. Pa. Bar Assn. (ho. of dels. 1982—), Delaware County Bar Assn. (com. chmn., dir., past treas., Nicholas D. Vadino Jr. award 1984, Spl. Recognition award 1985, 86). Roman Catholic. General practice, Family and matrimonial, Real property. Office: 201 N Jackson St PO Box 546 Media PA 19063

PIAZZA, ANTHONY ANDREW, lawyer; b. Bridgeport, Conn., July 8, 1942; s. Michael Salvatore and Margaret (Barrett) P.; m. Patricia Jane Cormier, Feb. 18, 1967; children—Anthony, Megan, Richard. Student Seton Hall U., 1964; J.D., Fordham U., 1972. Bar: Conn. 1972, U.S. Dist. Ct. Conn. 1972, U.S. Ct. Appeals (2d cir.) 1974, U.S. Supreme Ct. 1975. Ptnr. Norton & Piazza, Fairfield, Conn., 1972-74, Norton, Piazza & Melmed, Stamford, Conn., 1974-78, Piazza, Melmed & Ackerly, Stamford, 1978—; bd. dirs. Stamford/Norwalk/Danbury Legal Services, Stamford, 1974-75; state trial referee State of Conn., 1984. Contbr. articles to legal jours.; mem. staff Fordham U. Law Jour., 1972. Fellow Am. Acad. Matrimonial Lawyers; mem. Conn. Trial Lawyers Assn. (bd. govs. 1976-77, sec., treas. 1977-79, v.p. 1979-83, pres. 1983-84), Conn. Bar Assn., ABA, Am. Bd. Trial Advs. (assoc.). State civil litigation, Personal injury, Family and matrimonial. Office: Piazza Melmed & Ackerly PC 1318 Bedford St Stamford CT 06905

PIAZZA, ANTHONY MICHAEL, lawyer, legal educator; b. Cleve., July 30, 1951; s. Carl Charles and Betty (Mandanici) P.; m. Deborah Lynn Kiss, Dec. 27, 1974; children: Christopher, Jamie. AA, Cuyahoga Community Coll., 1972; BA, Kent State U., 1974; JD, Ohio Northern U., 1977. Bar: Ohio 1977, U.S. Dist. Ct. (no. dist.) Ohio 1977. Atty. Lichtman Legal Clinic, Cleve., 1977-80; ptnr. Skove & Piazza Co. P.A., Cleve., 1980-82; sole practice Cleve., 1980—; dir. paralegal edn. dept. Dyke Coll., Cleve., asst. prof. 1985—. Mem. ABA (approval com.), Ohio Bar Assn., Cuyahoga Criminal Defenders Assn., Assn. Ind. Colls. and Schs. (accrediting com). Consumer commercial, Family and matrimonial, Personal injury. Home: 4409 Coe Ave North Olmsted OH 44070 Office: 1370 Ontario Suite 950 Cleveland OH 44113

PICARDI, FERDINAND LOUIS, lawyer; b. Syracuse, N.Y., Jan. 28, 1930; s. Anthony S. and Anna Ida (Albolino) P.; m. Aileen Cummiskey, Aug. 9, 1958; children: Matthew, Jane Ann. BSS cum laude, Le Moyne Coll., Syracuse, 1951; JD cum laude, Syracuse U., 1956. Bar: N.Y. 1956, U.S. Dist. Ct. (no. dist.) N.Y. 1957, U.S. Ct. Appeals (2d cir.) 1963, U.S. Supreme Ct. 1980. Assoc. Hiscock Lee Rogers Henley & Barclay, Syracuse, 1956-64, ptnr., 1964-79; mng. ptnr. Hiscock & Barclay, Syracuse, 1978—; instr. mil. justice internat. law and internat. relations Naval Reserve Officers Sch., Liverpool, N.Y., 1956-64; bd. dirs. Key Bank Cen. N.Y.; counsel Town of Manlius, 1969-75; mem. Pres.'s Assocs. LeMoyne Coll., 1966—; chmn. Rep. Jud. Conv. 5th Jud. Dist., N.Y., 1981-82; mem. Bd. of Visitors Syracuse U. Coll. Law, 1964—, chmn. Bd. of Visitors Syracuse U. Coll. Law, 1975-79;. Mem. Pres.'s Assocs. LeMoyne Coll., 1966; alt. del. Rep. Nat. Conv., 1976; pres. Rep. Support Orgn. The Club; state com. man N.Y. Rep. Com.; legal counsel, mem. exec. com. Onondaga County Rep. Com.; vice chmn. Met. Water Bd., Onondaga County, 1980—; bd. dirs. Syracuse Boys Club, 1983—, v.p., 1985, 1987—; chmn. atty.'s sect. Cen. N.Y. United Way, 1980-82; chmn. Syracuse and Onondaga County EEO Rev. Bd. 1980—. Served to lt. USN, 1951-53, lt. comdr. Res. 1953-65. Mem. Syracuse Law Coll. Assn. (exec. sec. 1967-72), LeMoyne Coll. Alumni Assn. (former pres.). Republican. Roman Catholic. Club: Century. General corporate, Local government, Municipal bonds. Home: 7 Wynnridge Rd Fayetteville NY 13066 Office: Hiscock & Barclay 500 Financial Plaza Syracuse NY 13202

PICAVET, ROBERT CLEMENT, lawyer; b. Boston, July 15, 1922; s. Edgar and Jeanne (Gelan) P.; m. Marjorie Catherine McKenney, July 25, 1943; 1 son, Kenneth Robert. A.B., Tufts U., 1944; J.D., Suffolk U., 1959. Bar: Mass. 1959, U.S. Dist. Ct. Mass. 1962, Maine, 1980, U.S. Dist. Ct. Maine 1980, U.S. Supreme Ct. 1981. Claim mgr. Travelers Ins. Co., Danvers, Mass., 1947-82; sole practice, Kennebunkport, Maine, 1982—. Bd. dirs. Plan E Civic Assn., Medford, Mass., 1959-64; chmn. Planning Bd., Medford, 1964-66; rep. Met. Area Planning Council, Boston, 1969-72; mem. Bd. Appeals, Medford, 1976-80; corporator Lawrence Meml. Hosp., Medford, 1976-80. Served with USAAF, 1943-45; MTO, PTO. Mem. Mass. Bar Assn., Maine Bar Assn., Maine Trial Lawyers Assn., York County Bar Assn., Disabled Am. Veterans. Democrat. Lodge: Masons. Workers' compensation, Criminal, Personal injury. Home: Ward Road Extension Kennebunkport ME 04046 Office: PO Box 21 Cape Porpoise ME 04014

PICHA, GEORGE JOHN, lawyer; b. Oak Park, Ill., Jan. 13, 1938; s. George M. and Rosemary (Krivanek) P.; m. Judith L. Eshbaugh, Sept. 14, 1968; children—Michael, Michelle, Thomas. B.A., North Central Coll., 1959; J.D., Northwestern U., 1962. Bar: Ill. 1963, U.S. Dist. Ct. (no. dist.) Ill. 1964. Assoc., Williams, McCarthy & Kinley, 1962-68; ptnr. Williams, McCarthy, Kinley, Rudy & Picha, Rockford, 1968-82; sr. v.p. Williams & McCarthy, P.C., Rockford, 1982—; author, lectr. workers' compensation seminars Ill. Inst. for Continuing Legal Edn., 1972—. Vice pres. United Way Services, Inc., 1981—; bd. dirs. The Janet Wattles Mental Health Ctr., Inc., 1972-82, pres. 1975. Recipient Disting. Service award Rockford (Ill.) Jaycees, 1972. Fellow Ill. Bar Found.; mem. ABA, Ill. Bar Assn., Winnebago (Ill.) Bar Assn., Workers Compensation Lawyers Assn., Ill. Indsl. Commn. Rules Com. Clubs: City of Rockford, Univ. of Rockford. Workers' compensation. Office: PO Box 219 Rockford IL 61105

PICKER, MILLICENT ANN, lawyer; b. Phila., Mar. 17, 1954; d. Edward and Irene (Frailer) P. AB in Sociology, Villanova U., 1975; JD, Ohio Northern U., 1978. Bar: Pa. 1978, U.S. Supreme Ct. 1986. V.p. Worldwide Brokers, Devon, Pa., 1979-81; assoc. counsel Chrysler First, Inc., Allentown, Pa., 1981—. Mem. ABA, Pa. Bar Assn., Lehigh County Bar Assn. Consumer commercial, Banking. Office: Chrysler First Inc 1105 Hamilton St Allentown PA 18101

PICKERING, JOHN HAROLD, lawyer; b. Harrisburg, Ill., Feb. 27, 1916; s. John Leslie and Virginia Lee (Morris) P.; m. Elsa Victoria Mueller, Aug. 23, 1941; children: Leslie Ann, Victoria Lee. A.B., U. Mich., 1938, J.D., 1940. Bar: N.Y. 1941, D.C. 1947. Practiced in N.Y.C. 1941, practiced in Washington, 1946—; asso. Cravath, de Gersdorff, Swaine & Wood, 1941; law clk. to Justice Murphy, Supreme Ct. U.S., 1941-43; asso. Wilmer & Broun, 1946-48, partner, 1949-62; partner Wilmer, Cutler & Pickering, 1962-79, Wilmer & Pickering, 1979-81, Wilmer, Cutler & Pickering, 1981—; vis. lectr. U. Va. Law Sch., 1958; mem. com. visitors U. Mich. Law Sch., 1962-68, chmn. devel. com., 1973-81; chmn. adv. com. on procedures U.S. Ct. Appeals for D.C. Circuit, 1976-82; bd. govs. D.C. Bar, 1975-78, pres., 1979-80. Served to lt. comdr. USNR, 1943-46. Recipient Outstanding Achievement award U. Mich., 1978; Disting. Service award Nat. Ctr. for State Cts., 1985. Mem. ABA (state del. 1984—, chmn. commn. on legal problems of elderly 1985—), D.C. Bar Assn., Am. Law Inst., Barristers Washington, Order of Coif, Phi Beta Kappa, Phi Kappa Phi. Democrat. Mem. United Ch. Christ. Clubs: Lawyers, Metropolitan, Chevy Chase, Internat; Wianno (Mass.). Administrative and regulatory, Federal civil litigation, Libel. Home: 4708 Jamestown Rd Bethesda MD 20816 Office: 2445 M St NW Washington DC 20037-1420

PICKERING, ROBERT GEIN, lawyer; b. Lincoln, Nebr., July 4, 1952; s. William Gein and Alice Victoria (Horton) P.; m. Patricia Lynn Gray, Aug. 14, 1976; children: Kisten Laureen, Julianna Kay. BSBA, U. Denver, 1974; JD, U. San Diego, 1977. Bar: Calif. 1977, U.S. Dist. Ct. (so. dist.) Calif. 1977, Wy. 1978, U.S. Dist. Ct. Wy. 1978, U.S. Ct. Appeals (10th cir.) 1979, U.S. Dist. Ct. (no. dist.) Calif. 1981, U.S. Dist. Ct. (ea. dist.) Calif. 1982, U.S Ct. Appeals (9th cir.) 1983. Law clk. to judge U.S. Ct. Appeals, Cheyenne, Wy., 1978-81; assoc. Lillick, McHose & Charles, San Francisco, 1981-84; ptnr. David & Pickering, Cheyenne, Wyo., 1984-86, Bailey, Pickering, Stock & Welch, Cheyenne, 1986—. Mem. ABA, Calif. Bar Assn., Wyo. Bar Assn., Wyo. Trial Lawyers Assn., Omicron Delta Epsilon, Phi Gamma Mu. Republican. Morman. Federal civil litigation, Personal injury. Office: Bailey Pickering Stock & Welch 1813 Carey Ave Cheyenne WY 82001

PICKERING, WILLIAM HENRY, lawyer; b. Chattanooga, Dec. 14, 1951; s. William H. and Kathryn (Carden) P.; m. Emily Ruth Hudson, May 15, 1976. BA, U. South, 1973; JD, Vanderbilt U., 1976. Bar: Ga. 1976, Ala. 1976, U.S. Dist. Ct. (no. dist.) Ala. 1976, Tenn. 1979, U.S. Dist. Ct. (ea. dist.) Tenn. 1979, U.S. Dist. Ct. (no. dist.) Ga. 1980, U.S. Ct. Appeals (6th cir.) 1984. Assoc. Balch & Bingham, Birmingham, Ala., 1976-79; assoc. Chambliss, Bahner, Crutchfield, Gaston & Irvine, Chatanooga, 1979-80, ptnr., 1981—; atty. City of Lookout Mountain, Ga., 1979—. Assoc. editor Vanderbilt U. Law Rev., 1975-76. Mem. ABA (litigation and labor and employment law sects.), Tenn. Bar Assn., Ga. Bar Assn., Ala. Bar Assn., Chatanooga Bar Assn. (bd. govs. 1986—). Episcopalian. Clubs: Lookout Mountain Golf, Lookout Mountain Fairyland; Walden (Chattanooga). Avocations: golf, tennis. Labor, Federal civil litigation, State civil litigation. Home: 1503 Cinderella Rd Lookout Mountain TN 37350 Office: Chambliss Bahner et al 1000 Tallam Bldg Chattanooga TN 37402

PICKETT, DOUGLAS GENE, lawyer; b. Enid, Okla., Mar. 12, 1953; s. Haskel C. and Gladine (Hutchinson) P. BA, Portland State U., 1975; MA, U. Tex., 1978; JD, U. Oreg., 1981. Bar: Oreg. 1981, U.S. Dist. Ct. Oreg. 1981, Wash. 1986, U.S. Dist. Ct. (we. dist.) Wash. 1986, U.S. Ct. Appeals (9th cir.) 1986. Assoc. Jaqua, Wheatley, Gallagher & Holland, Eugene, Oreg., 1981-83, Niehaus, Hanna, Murphy, Green, Osaka & Dunn, Portland, Oreg., 1984—. Mem. ABA, Assn. Trial Lawyers Am., Wash. State Bar Assn., Oreg. Bar Assn., Oreg. Trial Lawyers Assn., Multnomah County Bar Assn. Republican. Avocations: poetry, music, writing. Federal civil litigation, State civil litigation. Home: 78L Hartwick Terr Banks OR 97106 Office: Niehaus Hanna Murphy Green Osaka & Dunn 1 SW Columbia 11th Floor Portland OR 97258

PICKLE, GEORGE EDWARD, lawyer; b. New Orleans, Nov. 22, 1950; s. George E. Sr. and Virginia (Crowe) P.; m. Karen Lyle, Sept. 18, 1976; children: George E. III, Lauren M. Student, Rhodes Coll., 1968-70; BA, Millsaps Coll., 1972; JD, Georgetown U., 1975. Bar: Miss. 1975, U.S. Ct. Claims 1979, U.S. Tax Ct. 1979, U.S. Ct. Mil. Appeals 1979, U.S. Ct. Appeals (D.C. cir.) 1979, U.S. Supreme Ct. 1979, U.S. Dist. Ct. (so. dist.) Miss. 1980, U.S. Ct. Appeals (5th cir.) 1980, La. 1982, U.S. Dist. Ct. (ea. dist.) La. 1982, U.S. Dist. Ct. (mid. dist.) La. 1985, Tex. 1986. Law clk.to presiding justice U.S. Ct. Appeals (5th cir.), Askerman, Miss., 1975-76; assoc. Upshaw & Ladner, Jackson, Miss., 1980-82, Barham & Churchill, New Orleans, 1982-85; atty. environmental, admiralty and products Shell Oil Co., Houston, 1985—. Co-author, editor: Syllabus on Environmental Law, 1986. Mgr. WYES Public Broadcasting Auction, New Orleans, 1984-85; v.p., counsel Lennox Homeowners' Assn., New Orleans, 1984-85; mem. New Orleans Symphony Guild, 1984-86; legal adv. Ch. of God the Shepherd, Kingwood, Tex., 1984-86. Served to lt. cmdr. (head environ. litigation) USNR, 1976-79. Southwestern Scholar Rhodes Coll., Memphis, 1968. Mem. ABA (vice chmn. young lawyers div. com. on environ. law, award for Profl. Merit, 1976), Def. Research Inst., Miss. Bar Assn. (elections com. 1982), La. Bar Assn., Tex. Bar Assn., Alpha Tau Omega. Republican. Episcopalian. Clubs: Army-Navy Country (Arlington, Va.), Internat. House (New Orleans). Avocations: golf, water skiing. Admiralty, Federal civil litigation, Environment. Home: 3507 Tree Ln Kingwood TX 77339

PICKLE, ROBERT DOUGLAS, lawyer, diversified industry executive; b. Knoxville, Tenn., May 22, 1937; s. Robert Lee and Beatrice Jewel (Douglas) P.; m. Rosemary Elaine Noser, May 9, 1964. AA, Schreiner Mil. Coll., Kerrville, Tex., 1957; BSBA, U. Tenn., Knoxville, 1959, JD, 1961; honor grad. seminar, Nat. Def. U., 1979. Bar: Tenn. 1961, Mo. 1964, U.S. Ct. Mil. Appeals 1962, U.S. Supreme Ct 1970. Atty. Brown Shoe Co., Inc., St. Louis, 1963-69; asst. sec., atty. Brown Shoe Co., Inc., 1969-74; sec., gen. counsel Brown Group, Inc., St. Louis, 1974-85, v.p., gen. counsel, corp. sec., 1985—. Provisional judge Municipal Ct., Clayton, Mo., summer 1972; chmn. Clayton Region attys. sect., profl. div. United Fund Greater St. Louis Campaign, 1972-73, team capt., 1974—; chmn. City of Clayton Parks and Recreation Commn., 1985—; liaison admissions officer, regional and state coordinator U.S. Mil. Acad., 1980—. Served to col. JAG Corps U.S. Army, 1961-63. Fellow Harry S. Truman Meml. Library; mem. ABA, Tenn. Bar Assn., Mo. Bar Assn., St. Louis County Bar Assn., Bar Assn. Met. St. Louis, St. Louis Bar Found. (bd. dirs. 1979—), Am. Corp. Counsel Assn., Am. Soc. Corp. Secs. (treas. St. Louis regional group 1976-77, sec. 1977-78, v.p. 1978-79, pres. 1979-80), U. Tenn. Gen. Alumni Assn. (pres., bd. dirs. St. Louis chpt. 1974-76, 80—, bd. govs. 1982—), U.S. Trademark Assn. (bd. dirs. 1978—), Tenn. Soc. St. Louis (bd. dirs. 1980—, treas., sec., v.p. 1984—, pres. 1987—), Smithsonian Nat. Assocs., Scabbard and Blade, Kappa Sigma, Phi Delta Phi, Phi Theta Kappa, Beta Gamma Sigma, Phi Kappa Phi. Republican. Presbyterian. Clubs: University (St. Louis) (bd. dirs. 1976—, v.p. 1976-77, sec. 1977-79), St. Louis Stadium. Antitrust, General corporate, Trademark and copyright. Home: 214 Topton Way Saint Louis MO 63105 Office: 8400 Maryland Ave Saint Louis MO 63105

PICKUS, ROBERT MARK, lawyer; b. Bklyn., Oct. 29, 1954; s. Leon Carl and Adele Miriam (Ratner) P.; m. Michele Turturro, Nov. 30, 1985. BA, Rutgers U., 1976, JD, 1979. Bar: U.S. Dist. Ct. N.J. 1979, N.J. 1980, N.Y. 1981, Pa. 1981. Sr. assoc. Ribis, McCluskey & Graham, Atlantic City, 1980-84; assoc. gen. counsel Harrah's Marina Hotel Casino, Atlantic City, 1984-85; gen. counsel Trump's Castle Hotel and Casino, Atlantic City, 1985—. Mem. ABA, (gen. practice sect., casino law com., forum com. on entertainment and sports industries), N.J. Bar Assn. (com. casino law, exec. com. young lawyer's div. 1984-86), Atlantic County Bar Assn., Internat. Assn. Gaming Attys. Administrative and regulatory, General corporate, Casino. Home: 663 Weiler's Ln Absecon NJ 08201 Office: Trump's Castle Hotel & Casino Huron Ave and Brigantine Blvd Atlantic City NJ 08401

PIEDMONT, RICHARD STUART, lawyer; b. Niskayuna, N.Y., Mar. 28, 1948; s. Henry Stuart and Lucille (Gagnon) P.; m. Marcia J. Quick, Apr. 11, 1981; m. Denise Nicole Rochette, Michael Norman Rochette, Alexandria Quick. BA, U. Notre Dame, 1971. Bar: N.Y. 1977, U.S. Dist. Ct. (no. dist.) N.Y. 1977. Pres. Phoenix Abstract Corp., Albany, N.Y., 1979-84, v.p., 1984—; ptnr. Piedmont & Rutnik, Albany, 1980-85, Devine, Piedmont & Rutnik, Albany, 1985—. Mem. N.Y. State Bar Assn., N.Y. State Land Title Assn., Eastern N.Y. Land Surveyor's Assn., Schenectady County Bar Assn., Albany County Bar Assn. Democrat. Roman Catholic. Clubs: Mohawk Golf (Niskayuna, N.Y.), Steuben Athletic (Albany). Real property, Probate, Administrative and regulatory. Home: 1144 Wendell Ave Schenectady NY 12308 Office: Devine Piedmont & Rutnik 744-46 Broadway Albany NY 12308

PIEL, ELEANOR JACKSON, lawyer; b. Santa Monica, Calif., Sept. 22, 1920; d. Louis Harris and Blanche Melicent (Virden) Jackson; student U. Calif. at Los Angeles, 1936-39; B.A., U. Calif.-Berkeley, 1940, LL.B., 1943; postgrad. U. So. Calif., 1940-41; m. Gerard Piel, June 24, 1955; 1 dau., Eleanor Jackson. Bar: Calif. 1943, N.Y. 1957. Law clk. U.S. Dist. Ct., San Francisco, 1939, 44; dep. atty. gen. State of Calif., 1944; clk. U.S. Senate Civil Service Com., 1945; legal adviser Supreme Command Allied Powers, Japan, 1945-48; practice law, Los Angeles, 1948-55; atty. Legal Aid. Soc., N.Y.C., 1957-58; practice in N.Y.C., 1957—; mem. com. on bicentennial U.S. cont. U.S. Ct. Appeals (2d cir.). Trustee, NYU, Med. Ctr., 1967—. Fellow ABA (life), Com. Public Justice; mem. Assn. Bar. City N.Y. (mem. spl. com. to revise criminal code 1970-83, com. on penology 1871-76, grievance com. 1973-76) N.Y. Bar Assn., N.Y. County Lawyers Assn., Am. Arbitration Assn. (comml. arbitration com.). Clubs: Cosmopolitan, Women's City (counsel). Federal civil litigation, State civil litigation, Criminal. Home: 1115 5th Ave New York NY 10128 Office: 36 W 44th St New York NY 10036

PIEPLOW, MICHAEL FLINN, lawyer; b. Hutchinson, Kans., June 9, 1945; s. E.C. and Virginia Lee (Perry) P.; m. Kathryn Irene Wagner, Dec. 29, 1973; children: Nathan, Aaron, Sarah. BA cum laude, U. S.D., 1967, JD cum laude, 1970. Bar: S.D. 1970, U.S. Dist. Ct. S.D., U.S. Ct. Appeals (8th cir.), U.S. Supreme Ct. Law clk. to presiding judge U.S. Ct. Appeals (8th cir.), Omaha, 1970-71; from assoc. to ptnr. Davenport, Evans, Hurwitz & Smith, Sioux Falls, S.D., 1971—; bar commr. U. S.D. State Bar, Pierre, 1976-79, mem. disciplinary bd., 1980-86, chmn., 1986—. Editor in chief S.D. Law Rev., 1970. Bd. dirs. ARC, Sioux Falls, Community Concerts, Civic Fine Arts Assn., 1979-85, Pub. Radio, 1985—. Mem. Am. Judicature Soc., Am. Bd. Trial Advs., Assn. Trial Lawyers Am., S.D. Trial Lawyers Assn. (bd. dirs. 1980, 86—), Minnehaha County Bar Assn. (pres. 1986—), Phi Beta Kappa, Omicron Delta Phi, Phi Delta Phi. Republican. Presbyterian. Club: Minnehaha Country (Sioux Falls). Avocations: golf, skiing, sailing, piano, reading. Federal civil litigation, State civil litigation, Insurance. Office: Davenport Evans Hurwitz & Smith 513 S Main Sioux Falls SD 57102

PIERAGOSTINI, ANTHONY JOSEPH, lawyer; b. Mt. Kisco, N.Y., Apr. 19, 1948; s. Egnazio and Concetta (Toto) P.; m. Catherine Rose Cosentino, Aug. 28, 1971; children: A. Justinian, Adam James, Nicole Marie. BCE, Manhattan Coll., 1970, ME in Sanitary, 1971; JD, Union U., 1974. Bar: N.Y. 1975, U.S. Dist. Ct. (so. dist.) N.Y. 1977. Sole practice Mt. Kisco, 1975—; judge Town of Mt. Kisco, 1984—, village atty., 1978-80. Chmn. Rep. Party Town of Mt. Kisco, 1982-83; trustee Town Mt. Kisco, 1976-78. Mem. ABA, N.Y. State Bar Assn., Westchester County Bar Assn., No. Westchester County Bar Assn., N.Y. State Magistrates Assn., Columbian Lawyers Assn. Westchester (bd. dirs. 1986—). Roman Catholic. Clubs: Mt. Kisco Jr. Football (bd. dirs. 1979—), Italian Am. No. Westchester (pres. 1983-84) (Mt. Kisco). Lodges: Elks, Rotary. Home: 310 Spring St Mount Kisco NY 10549 Office: 126 Barker St PO Box 120 Mount Kisco NY 10549

PIERAS, JAIME, JR., federal judge; b. San Juan, P.R., May 19, 1924; s. Jaime Pieras and Ines Lopez-Cepero; m. Elsie Castaner, June 6, 1953; 1 child, Jaime Pieras Castaner. A.B. in Econs., Catholic U. Am., 1945; J.D., Georgetown U., 1948. Bar: P.R. Jr. atty. Luis E. Dubon Law Office, San Juan, 1949-53; jr. atty. Hartzell Law Office, San Juan, 1954-59; sr. ptnr. Pieras & Martin, San Juan, 1960-68, Pieras & Torruella, San Juan, 1968-75; owner Pieras & Esteves, San Juan, 1975-82; judge U.S. Dist. Ct. for P.R., San Juan, 1982—; mem. Com. on the Bicentennial of the Constitution, Judicial Conf. U.S.; mem. Puerto Rico Commn. on the Bicentennial of the U.S. Constituion. Chmn. fin. Statehood Republican Party, San Juan, 1963-64; Rep. nat committeeman for P.R., San Juan, 1967-80. Served to 2d lt. U.S. Army, 1946-47. Mem. ABA, P.R. Bar Assn., D.C. Bar Assn. Lodge: Rotary. Judicial administration. Office: US Dist Ct PO Box 3671 Old San Juan Station San Juan PR 00904 *

PIERCE, DONALD FAY, lawyer; b. Bexley, Miss., Aug. 28, 1930; s. Percy O. and Lavada S. (Stringfellow) P.; m. Norma Faye Scribner, June 5, 1954; children—Kathryn Pierce Peake, D. F., John S., Jeff G. B.S., U. Ala., 1956, J.D., 1958. Bar: Ala. 1958, U.S. Ct. Appeals (5th cir.) 1958, U.S. Dist. Ct. (no. and so. dists.) Ala. 1958, U.S. Ct. Appeals (11th cir.) 1982. Law clk. to presiding judge U.S. Dist. Ct. (so. dist.) Ala., 1958-59; ptnr. Hand, Arendall, Bedsole, Greaves & Johnston, Mobile, Ala., 1964—. Trustee, UMS Prep. Sch., 1980—. Served to 1st lt. U.S. Army, 1951-53. Mem. Ala. Def. Lawyers Assn. (past pres.), Fedn. Ins. Counsel, Am. Acad. Hosp. Attys., Internat. Assn. Def. Counsel, Assn. Ins. Attys., Ins. Counsel Trial Acad. (dir. 1983, 84), Def. Research Inst. (pres. 1987—, chmn. 1987—). Baptist. Contbr. articles to profl. jours. Federal civil litigation, Health, Environment. Home: 4452 Winnie Way Mobile AL 36608 Office: PO Box 123 Mobile AL 36601

PIERCE, DONALD VICTOR JR., lawyer; b. Kansas City, Mo., July 23, 1949; s. Donald Victor and Virginia (Flippin) P.; m. Kathryn Ann Evans, June 23, 1979. AB, U. Mo., 1971; JD, U. Mo., Kansas City, 1975. Bar: Mo. 1975, U.S. Dist. Ct. (we. dist.) Mo. 1975, U.S. Ct. Appeals (8th and

10th cirs.) 1977, U.S. Tax Ct. 1983, U.S. Supreme Ct. 1978. Assoc. Tierney, Pierce & Ernst, Kansas City, 1975-81; mng. ptnr. DeYoung and Pierce, Kansas City, 1981-85; owner Pierce and Assocs., Kansas City, 1985—. Mem. ABA, Assn. Trial Lawyers Am., Mo. Assn. Trial Lawyers, Am. Judicare Soc., Builders Assn. of Mo., Phi Eta Sigma, Sigma Rho Sigma, Omicron Delta Kappa. Club: Blue Hills Country (Kansas City). State civil litigation, Construction, General practice. Home: 9729 Winslow Pl Kansas City MO 64131 Office: Pierce & Assocs 1111 Grand Ave 300 Gate City Bank Bldg Kansas City MO 64106-2447

PIERCE, FRANCIS EDMUND, III, lawyer; b. Gainsville, Fla., Aug. 26, 1954. BA with honors, U. Fla., 1976, JD, 1978. Bar: Fla. 1979, U.S. Dist. Ct. (mid. dist.) Fla. 1979, U.S. Ct. Appeals (5th and 11th cirs.) 1979, U.S. Supreme Ct. 1982. Ptnr. Gurney & Handley P.A., Orlando, Fla., 1978—; mem. 9th cir. med. malpractice arbitration adv. com. Dist. chmn. Boy Scouts Am., Orlando, 1982-84. Mem. ABA, Orange County Bar Assn. (med./legal com.), Fla. Def. Lawyers Assn., Def. Research Inst., Citizen Dispute Settlement Project, Alpha Tau Omega Alumni Assn. (pres. 1981-82, chief province XXXII). Democrat. Roman Catholic. Federal civil litigation, State civil litigation, Insurance. Office: Gurney & Handley PA 225 E Robinson St Landmark Ctr Two Suite 450 Orlando FL 32802-1273

PIERCE, GEORGE CARTER, lawyer, educator; b. Wheeling, W.Va., July 16, 1938; s. George William and Mary (Cupp) P.; m. Frances Rita McCullen, June 13, 1964; 1 son, David Carter. B.A., W.Va. U., 1961, M.A., 1962; postgrad. U. Pa., 1963-67; J.D., Del. Law Sch., 1975. Bar admittee: Pa., 1977. Instr. polit. sci. Temple U. Community Coll., Phila., 1965-67; asso. prof. law and polit. sci. Phila. Coll. Textiles and Sci., 1967—, chmn. dept. humanities and social scis., 1982—. Mem. ABA, Pa. Bar Assn., Bucks County Bar Assn., Phila. Bar Assn., Am. Acad. Polit. and Social Sci., Am. Polit. Sci. Assn., Pa. Polit. Sci. Assn. ACLU, AAUP, Pi Sigma Alpha, Beta Theta Pi. Club: Doylestown (Pa.) Country. Legal education. Home: 790 Triumphe Way Warrington PA 18976 Office: Phila Coll Textiles and Sci Henry Ave and School House Ln Philadelphia PA 19144

PIERCE, HINTON RAINER, lawyer; b. Augusta, Ga., July 16, 1927; s. Benjamine Eugene and Essie (Hankinson) P.; m. Barbara Jean Kline, Mar. 25, 1951; children: Mark Rainer, Virginia. LL.B., U. Ga.-Athens, 1949. Bar: Ga. 1949, Va. 1966. Ins. adjuster Crawford & Co., Chattanooga and Atlanta, 1949-70; br. mgr. Crawford & Co., Waycross, Norfolk, and Honolulu, Ga., Va., 1952-70; U.S. atty for So. Dist. Ga., Savannah, 1981—. Served with USNR, 1945-46. Mem. Augusta Bar Assn. (v.p.), Ga. Bar Assn., Va. Bar Assn. Republican. Presbyterian. Criminal. Home: 3544 Gleneagles Dr Augusta GA 30907 Office: US Atty Box 8999 Savannah GA 31412 *

PIERCE, JAMES WINSTON, JR., lawyer; b. Roanoke Rapids, N.C., Mar. 6, 1953. BA in English, U. N.C., 1975; JD, La. State U., 1979. Bar: La. 1980, U.S. Dist. Ct. (mid. dist.) La. 1982. Staff atty. Sea Grant Legal Program, Baton Rouge, 1980; sole practice Baton Rouge, 1980—; instr. law La. State U., Baton Rouge, 1980-83. Mem. ABA, La. Bar Assn. General practice, Personal injury, Entertainment. Home and Office: 728 Europe St Baton Rouge LA 70802

PIERCE, JOHN G., lawyer; b. Winter Haven, Fla., Jan. 12, 1937; s. Francis E. and Margaret (Butler) P.; children: Kathy, Nancy, John, Mike. B in Chem. Engring., U. Fla., 1959, JD, 1965. Bar: Fla., U.S. Dist. Ct. (mid. dist.) Fla., U.S. Ct. Appeals (11th cir.). Assoc. Anderson & Rush, Orlando, Fla., 1966-68, Arnold & Matheny, Orlando, 1968-70; ptnr. Pierce, Lewis & Dolan, Orlando, 1970-74; sole practice Orlando, 1974—. Served to 1st lt. U.S. Army, 1959-62. Mem. ABA, Fla. Bar Assn. Republican. Roman Catholic. Avocations: golf, boating. General corporate, Real property, Securities. Home: 624 Desoto Dr Casselberry FL 32707 Office: 800 N Fern Creek Ave Orlando FL 32806

PIERCE, JOHN ROBERT, lawyer; b. Boston, Nov. 3, 1949; s. Irving Russell and Mary Elizabeth (Powers) P. BA, Harvard U., 1971; JD, Boston Coll., 1982. Bar: Mass. 1982, U.S. Dist. Ct. Mass. 1983. Assoc. Widett, Slater & Goldman P.C., Boston, 1982-83; sole practice Boston, 1983-86; ptnr. Ross & Pierce, Boston, 1986—. Articles editor Boston Coll. Law Rev., 1981-82. Mem. ABA, Mass. Bar Assn., Boston Bar Assn., Assn. Trial Lawyers Am., New England Hist. Soc., Mass. Soc. Mayflower Descendants. Roman Catholic. Clubs: Old Colony Harvard (southeast Mass.) (exec. com. 1984—); Harvard (Boston). State civil litigation, Probate, General practice. Office: Ross & Pierce 11 Beacon St Boston MA 02108

PIERCE, KEVIN MICHAEL, lawyer; b. Dallas, Sept. 25, 1958; s. Gerald Ray and Marjorie Ann (Sharber) P.; m. Tada Butler, Dec. 13, 1985. BBA, Abilene Christian U., 1979; JD, Tex. Tech U., 1982; LLM in Taxation, So. Meth. U., 1986. Bar: Tex. 1982, U.S. Tax Ct. 1985; CPA, Tex. Tax mgr. Peat, Marwick, Mitchell & Co., Dallas, 1982-84; assoc. Bradford, Snyder & Stevenson, Dallas, 1984-85; atty.-advisor U.S. Tax Ct., Washington, 1986—. Mem. ABA, Tex. Bar Assn., Dallas Bar Assn., Am. Inst. CPA's, Tex. Soc. CPA's, Blue Key, Alpha Chi. Republican. Mem. Ch. Christ. Personal income taxation, Corporate taxation. Office: US Tax Ct 400 2nd St NW Washington DC 20217

PIERCE, LAWRENCE WARREN, federal judge; b. Phila., Dec. 31, 1924; s. Harold Ernest and Leora (Bellinger) P.; m. Wilma Taylor (dec.); m. Cynthia Straker, July 8, 1979; children: Warren Wood, Michael Lawrence, Mark Taylor. B.S. Bus. Adminstrn, St. Joseph's U., Phila., 1948, D.H.L., 1967; J.D., Fordham U., 1951, LL.D., 1982; LL.D., Fairfield U., 1972. Bar: N.Y. State 1951, U.S. Supreme Ct. 1968. Civil law practice N.Y.C., 1952-61; asst. dist. atty. Kings County, N.Y., 1954-61; dep. police commr. N.Y.C., 1961-63; dir. N.Y. State Div. for Youth, Albany, 1963-66; chmn. N.Y. State Narcotic Addiction Control Commn., 1966-70; vis. prof. Grad. Sch. Criminal Justice, State U. N.Y. at, Albany, 1970-71; U.S. dist. judge So. dist. N.Y. 1971-81; judge U.S. Fgn. Intelligence Surveillance Ct., 1979-81; apptd. U.S. circuit judge for 2d Circuit, 1981—; bd. fellows Inst. Jud. Adminstrn.; trustee Practicing Law Inst. Mem. Pres.'s Task Force on Prisoner Rehab., 1969-70; former vice chmn., bd. trustees Fordham U.; vice pres. bd. mgrs. Lincoln Hall for Boys., Havens Relief Fund Soc., bd. dirs. CARE. Served with AUS, 1943-46, MTO. Mem. ABA, 2d Circuit Hist. Soc., Nat. Bar Assn., Fordham Law Alumni Assn. (dir.), SAR (N.Y. chpt.), SR (N.Y. chpt.), Supreme Ct. Hist. Soc. (founding mem.), Inst. Jud. Adminstrn. (bd. fellows), Practising Law Inst. (trustee), Am. Law Inst. Roman Catholic. Home:: Canaan NY 12060 Office:: US Courthouse Foley Square New York NY 10007 *

PIERCE, RICHARD JAMES, JR., legal educator, consultant; b. Norfolk, Va., July 15, 1943; s. Richard James Sr. and Julia Marie (Whitehurst) P.; m. Jill Read B, Aug. 21, 1965; children: Gabriel, Danielle. BS, Lehigh U., 1965; JD, U. of Va., 1972. Bar: D.C. 1972, U.S. Supreme Ct. 1976. Assoc. Sutherland, Asbill & Brennan, Washington, 1972-77; prof. U. Kans., Lawrence, 1977-80; vis. prof. U. of Va., Charlottesville, 1980-81; W. R. Irby prof. Tulane U., New Orleans, 1981-84; prof., dean U. Pitts., 1984-86; George W. Hutchison prof. So. Meth. U., Dallas, 1986—; cons. City of New Orleans, 1982—. Author: Natural Gas Regulation, 1980, Economic Regulation, 1980, Regulated Industries, 1982, Administrative Law and Process, 1985. Served as lt. comdr. USCG, 1966-69. Mem. ABA (adminstrv. sect., pub. utility sect., natural resources sect.), Fed. Energy Bar Assn., Order of Coif. FERC practice, Administrative and regulatory, Oil and gas leasing. Home: 9481 Gate Tr Dallas TX 75238 Office: So Meth U Sch of Law Dallas TX 75275

PIERCE, RICHARD WILLIAM, lawyer; b. Detroit, Sept. 30, 1941; s. Donald Allen and Sarah Elizabeth (Giffen) P.; m. Laura A. Pyle, Aug. 6, 1983; children from previous marriage: Barbara A., Douglas A. BA, Ohio Wesleyan U., 1963; JD, Northwestern U., 1966. Bar: Mich. 1967, U.S. Dist. Ct. (ea. dist.) Mich., U.S. Ct. Appeals (6th cir.). Assoc. Tinkham, Snyder & MacDonald, Wayne, Mich., 1967-68; asst. pros. atty Washtenaw County, Ann Arbor, Mich., 1968-70; ptnr. Ellis, Talcott & Ohlgren, Ann Arbor, 1971-82; sole practice Ann Arbor, 1982—. Mem. Mich. Tech. Council, Ann Arbor, 1983—; bd. dirs. Ann Arbor Area Council for Internat. Bus., 1984—. Mem. Mich. Bar Assn. (chmn. dist. H subcom. character and fitness 1984—), Washtenaw County Bar Assn. (pres. 1976-77), Licensing Execs. Soc., Am. Immigration Lawyers Assn. Presbyterian. Lodge: Kiwanis (local pres. 1978-79). Avocations: tennis, jogging. Immigration, naturalization, and customs, General corporate, Intellectual property transfers. Office: 226 W Liberty Suite 200 Ann Arbor MI 48104

PIERCE, RICKLIN RAY, lawyer; b. Waukegan, Ill., Sept. 16, 1953; s. Forest Ellsworth and Mildred Colleen (Cole) P. B.B.A. in Acctg., Washburn U., 1975; B.A. in Econs., 1978, J.D., 1978. Bar: Kans. 1978, U.S. Dist. Ct. Kans. 1978, U.S. Ct. Appeals (10th cir.) 1981, U.S. Supreme Ct. 1986. Assoc. Law Firm of C. C. Whittaker, Jr., Eureka, Kans., 1978-79; trust officer Smith County State Bank & Trust Co., Smith Center, Kans., 1979-80; staff atty. Northwest Kans. Legal Aid Soc., Goodland, 1980-81; assoc. Jochems, Sargent & Blaes, Wichita, Kans., 1981-82, Garden City, Kans., 1982-83; pres., owner Ricklin R. Pierce, Chartered, Garden City, 1983—. Scoutmaster troop 108 Santa Fe Trail council Boy Scouts Am., Garden City, 1983—; pres., chmn. bd. dirs. Vols., Inc. of Finney County, Garden City, 1984—. Mem. ABA, Assn. Trial Lawyers Am., Kans. Bar Assn., Southwest Kans. Bar Assn., Finney County Bar Assn., Garden City Area C. of C. (legis. com. 1983—). Republican. Methodist. State civil litigation, Probate, Criminal. Home: 1810 E Harding St No 1 Garden City KS 67846 Office: 401 Campus Dr Suite 107 Garden City KS 67846

PIERCE, ROBERT BARTH, lawyer; b. Clarksburg, W.Va., Feb. 14, 1925; s. Everett R. and Phyllis M. (Carder) P.; m. Wilda Morgan (div.); children—Morgan, Mark, Rebecca; m. 2d, Janet Besk, Aug. 28, 1976; 1 child, Hollis. Student Ind. Tech. Coll., 1943-44, Marietta Coll., 1947; LL.B., W.Va. U., 1950. Bar: W.Va. 1950, Mich. 1961, U.S. Dist. Ct. (ea. dist.) Mich. 1961, U.S. Ct. Claims 1976, U.S. Ct. Appeals (6th cir.) 1976. Pres. Pierce and Pierce, P.C., West Bloomfield, Mich., 1974—; asst. regional counsel and sr. trial atty. Office of Chief Counsel, IRS, Detroit, 1953-61; lectr. 4th Ann. Fed. and Mich. Tax Inst., 1976. Served with USN, 1944-46. Mem. Detroit Bar Assn., Fed. Bar Assn. (v.p. Detroit chpt. 1979), State Bar Mich. (mem. probate and trust law sect., council chmn. taxation sect. 1977-78, chmn. IRS-bar assns. meeting 1982), Mich. Bar Assn., Oakland County Bar Assn., ABA, Ohio Bar Assn., W.Va. Bar Assn., Ind. Bar Assn., Ky. Bar Assn., Methodist. Estate taxation, Personal income taxation, Probate. Office: Pierce and Pierce PC 7125 Orchard Lake Rd Suite 303 West Bloomfield MI 48033

PIERCE, RUDOLPH F., lawyer; b. Boston, Aug. 12, 1942; s. Fred D. and Edna M. (Owens) P.; m. Carneice T. Pierce, July 1, 1967; children: Kristen, Khari. BA, Hampton Inst., 1967; JD, Harvard U., 1970. Ptnr. Crane, Inker & Oteri, Boston, 1972-75, Keating, Perretta & Pierce, Boston, 1975-76; magistrate U.S. Dist. Ct. Mass., Boston, 1976-79; justice Mass. Superior Ct., Boston, 1979-85; ptnr. LeBoeuf, Lamb, Leiby & MacRae, Boston, 1985—. Pres. Freedom House, Boston; trustee Children's Hosp., Boston, 1986—; bd. advisors Mass. Mediation Services, Boston, 1985—; bd. dirs. Cath. Charities Bur., Boston; com. head Lawyers for Dukakis, Boston, 1986—. Mem. ABA (fellow), Mass. Bar Assn. (bd. dels. 1985—), Boston Bar Assn. (sec. 1985—). Home: 24 Elmhurst Rd Newton MA 02158 Office: LeBoeuf Lamb Leiby & MacRae 168 Milk St Boston MA 02109

PIERCE, WILLIAM JAMES, educator; b. Flint, Mich., Dec. 4, 1921; s. Francis Scott and Ellen (Pelton) P.; m. Betty Kathren Wise, Nov. 20, 1954; children—Darrell William, Margery Marie, Constance Ellen, Kathren Elizabeth. A.B. in Econs, U. Mich., 1947, J.D., 1949. Faculty U. Mich., 1953—; prof. law, dir. Legislative Research Center, 1958—, asso. dean, 1971-79; exec. sec. Mich. Law Revision Commn., 1966-69; chmn. Citizens Adv. Com. Juvenile Ct., 1964-66; pres. Nat. Conf. Commrs. Uniform State Laws, 1966-69, exec. dir., 1969—. Author: (with Estep, Stason) Atomic Energy and the Law, 1957, (with Lamb, White) Apportionment and Representative Institutions, 1963, (with Read, MacDonald, Fordham) Materials on Legislation, 1973. Mem. Pres.'s Consumer Adv. Council, 1967-69, Mich. Gov.'s Commn. on Mental Health Laws, 1969-72; mem. exec. com. Inst. Continuing Legal Edn., 1964—. Served with AUS, 1943-45. Decorated Bronze Star medal. Mem. Am. Law Inst., Am. Bar Assn. (ho. of dels. 1966-69), State Bar Mich. Legal education, Legislative, Contracts commercial. Home: 1505 Roxbury Rd Ann Arbor MI 48104 Office: U Mich Law Sch Ann Arbor MI 48109-1215

PIERNO, ANTHONY ROBERT, lawyer; b. Uniontown, Pa., Apr. 28, 1932; s. Anthony M. and Mary Jane (Saporita) P.; m. Beverly Jean John, June 20, 1954; children—Kathryn Ann, Robert Lawrence, Linda Jean, Diane Marie. B.A. with highest honors, Whittier Coll., 1954; J.D., Stanford U., 1959. Bar: Calif. 1960, D.C. 1979. Assoc. Bewley, Knoop, Lassleben & Whelan, Whittier, Calif., 1959-61; assoc. Adams, Duque & Hazeltine, Los Angeles, 1961-65; ptnr. Poindexter & Barger, Los Angeles, 1965-67; chief dep. commr. Calif. Dept. Corps, 1967-69, commr., 1969-71; ptnr. Wyman, Bautzer, Rothman & Kuchel, Beverly Hills, Calif., 1971-74; sr. ptnr. DeMarco, Barger, Beral & Pierno, Los Angeles, 1974-75; v.p., gen. counsel Monex Internat., Ltd., Newport Beach, Calif., 1975-76; sr. ptnr. Meml, Jacobs, Pierno & Gersh, Los Angeles, 1976-86; ptnr. Pillsbury, Madison & Sutro, Los Angeles, 1986—; dir. ICAN Assocs. Author: Corporate Disaggregation, 1982. Trustee Whittier Coll., Marymount Palos Verdes Coll. Served with U.S. Army, 1954-56. Mem. Los Angeles County Bar Assn. (recipient Emcalian award 1983), ABA, State Bar Calif. (chmn. com. on corps. 1971-75, advisor to com. on corps. 1975-76, mem. exec. com. Bus. Law Sect. 1976-80, chmn. spl. com. on franchise law 1981-82). Republican. Roman Catholic. Clubs: Regency (Los Angeles); Palos Verdes Breakfast, Palos Verdes Country (Palos Verdes Estates, Calif.). General corporate, Franchising, Securities. Home: 2901 Via Anacapa Palos Verdes Estates CA 90274 Office: 333 S Grand Ave Los Angeles CA 90071

PIERRY, THOMAS JAMES, lawyer; b. Jersey City, Aug. 21, 1937; s. Thomas James and Elizabeth Veronica (Holland) P.; m. Sandra Jean Holtz, Sept. 6, 1958; children—Thomas James, Shawn Elizabeth. B.S., Purdue U., 1959; J.D., U. So. Calif., 1964. Bar: Calif. 1965. Assoc. Magana, Cathcart, McCarthy & Pierry, 1968-70, ptnr., 1970—, mng. ptnr. Wilmington (Calif.) office, 1972—; a founder, dir., sec. Maritime Bank of Calif., 1980—. Mem. Los Angeles County Bar Assn., Assn. Trial Lawyers Am., Calif. Trial Lawyers Assn., Long Beach Bar Assn. Roman Catholic. Club: Bel-Air Country (Los Angeles). Personal injury, Admiralty, State civil litigation. Office: 301 N Avalon Blvd Wilmington CA 90744

PIERSON, GREY, lawyer; b. Abilene, Tex., Dec. 31, 1950; s. Don and Annette (Grubbs) P. Student in history Baylor U., 1971, JD, 1974; student in internat. law Coll. William and Mary, Exeter, Eng., summer 1973. Bar: Tex. 1974, U.S. Dist. Ct. (no. dist.) Tex. 1974, U.S. Ct. Appeals (5th cir.) 1983, U.S. Supreme Ct. 1984. Assoc. Law Office of Tom Sneed, Odessa, Tex., 1974-76, Duke, Duke, & Jelinek, Arlington, Tex., 1976-78; ptnr. Duke & Pierson, Arlington, 1978-79, Pierson, Galyen, & Baker Inc. (formerly Pierson & Galyen, Inc.), Arlington, 1983—; sole practice, Arlington, 1979-83; gen. counsel Mercer Internat. Transp., Ft. Worth, 1979—; sr. legal adviser Dominica Caribbean Freeport Authority, Roseau, W.I., 1979; ptnr. Sta. KVMX-FM, Eastland, Tex., 1981—. Contbr. articles to City Digest mag., 1979-80. Pres. Eastland Youth Council, 1967, Arlington Community Theatre, 1979; mem. state exec. com. Libertarian Party Tex., Austin, 1978; v.p. Mid-Cities Young Republicans, Arlington, 1984, pres., 1985-87. Recipient Disting. Service award Nat. Assn. Disabled Ams., Washington, 1982, Pres.'s award Mid-Cities Young Reps., 1984. Mem. ABA, Tex. Bar Assn., Arlington Bar Assn. Republican. Presbyterian. General corporate, Private international, Real property. Office: Pierson Galyen & Baker Inc 101 E Randol Mill Rd Suite 105 Arlington TX 76011

PIERSON, W. DEVIER, lawyer; b. Pawhuska, Okla., Aug. 12, 1931; s. Welcome D. and Frances (Ratliff) P.; m. Shirley Frost, Feb. 1, 1957; children—Jeffrey, Elizabeth, Stephen. A.B., U. Okla., 1953, LL.B., 1957. Bar: U.S. Dist. Ct. Okla. 1957, U.S. Supreme Ct. 1966, U.S. Ct. Appeals D.C. 1969, U.S. Ct. Appeals (5th cir.) 1972. Assoc., Duval & Head, Oklahoma City, 1957-59; sole practice, Oklahoma City, 1959-65; chief counsel Joint Com. on Orgn. of Congress, 1965-67; assoc. spl. counsel to Pres. and Counselor of White House Office, 1967-68; spl. counsel to Pres. U.S., 1968-69; ptnr. Pierson Semmes & Finley, Washington, 1969—. Served to 1st lt. U.S. Army, 1953-54. Mem. ABA, D.C. Bar Assn., Fed. Bar Assn., Okla. Bar Assn. Federal civil litigation, State civil litigation, FERC practice. Office: 1054 31st St NW Washington DC 20007 *

PIERSON, WILLIAM GEORGE, lawyer; b. Pontiac, Mich., Oct. 13, 1951; s. Robert D. and Elizabeth C. (Brode) P.; m. Dayle M. Eby, May 20, 1972 (div. Mar. 1983); m. Mary K. Grossa, Sept. 25, 1986. BBA, Cen. Mich. U., 1973; JD, Detroit Coll. Law, 1980. Bar: Mich. 1980, U.S. Dist. Ct. (ea. dist.) Mich. 1982, U.S. Supreme Ct. 1985. Sr. assoc. Kohl, Secrest, Wardle, Lynch, Clark & Hampton, Farmington Hills, Mich., 1980—. Mem. Mich. Bar Assn. (mem. negligence sect.), Oakland County Bar Assn. (mem. dist. ct. com. 1983-84, cir. ct. com. 1984-85), Livingston County Bar Assn. (mem. ct. liaison com. 1985-86). Avocations: golf, skiing, boating, camping. Personal injury, Insurance, State civil litigation. Home: 2153 Ridge Rd Highland MI 48031 Office: Kohl Secrest Wardle et al 30903 Northwestern Hwy Farmington Hills MI 48018

PIETROVITO, GUY ROY, lawyer; b. Columbia, S.C., Mar. 25, 1954; s. Jeremiah and Bess (Nahigian) P.; m. Janet Mary Giles, May 12, 1984. BA, Coll. William & Mary, 1976; JD cum laude, Capital U., 1981; LLM in Taxation, Georgetown U., 1982. Bar: Va. 1981, D.C. 1983, U.S. Dist. Ct. D.C. 1984, U.S. Dist. Ct. (ea. dist.) Va. 1985, U.S. Ct. Appeals (4th cir.) 1985. Gen. mgr. Metro Paper Co. Inc., Washington, 1976-78; assoc. Pompan & Murray, Washington, 1982-83, Pompan & Assocs., Alexandria, Va., 1983-84; ptnr. Murray & Pietrovito, Fairfax, Va., 1985—. Editor Capital U. Law Rev., 1979-81. Bd. dirs. St. Stephen's Sch. Alumni Assn., Alexandria, 1982—. Mem. ABA, Fed. Bar Assn., Assn. Trial Lawyers Am., Order of Curia, Order of White Jacket. Episcopalian. Federal civil litigation, State civil litigation, Contracts commercial. Home: 6018 Crown Royal Circle Alexandria VA 22310 Office: Murray & Pietrovito 10482 Armstrong St Fairfax VA 22030

PIETROWSKI, ROBERT FRANK, JR., lawyer; b. Pasadena, Calif., Feb. 7, 1945; s. Robert Frank Sr. and Annabelle (Johnson) P.; m. Barbara Holly Himel, June 25, 1966; children: Robert Frank III, Michael Scott. BS in Petroleum Engring., Stanford U., 1970; JD, U. Va., 1973. Bar: D.C. 1974, U.S. Supreme Ct. 1978. Assoc. Law Offices of Northcutt Ely, Washington, 1973-77, ptnr., 1977-84; ptnr. Bracewell & Patterson, Washington, 1984—; bd. dirs. Environ. Chems., Inc., Chgo., 1982—. Contbr. articles to profl. jours. Served to 1st lt. U.S. Army, 1966-69. Mem. ABA, Am. Soc. Internat. Law, Internat. Bar Assn., Internat. Law Assn., Union Internationale Des Avocats, Sigma Chi. Republican. Episcopalian. Clubs: Metropolitan, Cosmos (Washington); Farmington Country (Charlottesville, Va.); Guards Polo (Windsor, Eng.). Private international, Public international. Office: Bracewell & Patterson 1825 Eye St NW Washington DC 20006

PIETRZAK, ALFRED ROBERT, lawyer; b. Glen Cove, N.Y., June 26, 1949; s. Alfred S. and Wanda M. (Wapniarski) P.; m. Sharon Esther Chizek, July 9, 1978; children—Eric A., Daniel J. B.A., Fordham U., 1971; J.D., Columbia U., 1974. Bar: N.Y. 1975, U.S. Dist. Ct. (so., ea., we. and no. dists.) N.Y. 1975, U.S. Dist. Ct. (no. dist.) Calif. 1983, U.S. Ct. Appeals (2d cir.) 1975, U.S. Ct. Appeals (9th cir.) 1983, U.S. Ct. Appeals (11th cir.) 1985, U.S. Supreme Ct. 1985. Assoc. Brown & Wood (formerly Brown, Wood, Ivey, Mitchell & Petty), N.Y.C., 1974-82, ptnr., 1983—. Mem. ABA, N.Y. State Bar Assn., Assn. Bar City of N.Y. Roman Catholic. Federal civil litigation, State civil litigation, Securities. Home: 525 Monterey Ave Pelham Manor NY 10803 Office: Brown & Wood One World Trade Ctr 58th Floor New York NY 10048

PIETZSCH, MICHAEL EDWARD, lawyer; b. Burlington, Iowa, Aug. 1, 1949; s. Walter E. and Leanna (Moore) P.; m. K. Susan Phillips, June 17, 1978; children: Christine E., Catherine M. AB, Stanford U., 1971; JD, U. Chgo., 1974. Bar: Ill. 1974, Ariz. 1976. Assoc. Schwartz & Freeman, Chgo., 1974-75; ptnr. McCabe, Polese & Pietzsch, Phoenix, 1975—. Contbr. articles to profl. jours. Del. White House Conf. Small Bus., Washington, 1986. Mem. ABA (vice chmn. personal service orgns. com. tax sect. 1986—). Republican. Mem. United Ch. Christ. Club: Stanford Phoenix (pres. 1982-84). Pension, profit-sharing, and employee benefits, Corporate taxation, General corporate. Home: 6339 N 48th Pl Paradise Valley AZ 85253 Office: McCabe Polese & Pietzsch 300 E Osborn Phoenix AZ 85012

PIGA, STEPHEN MULRY, lawyer; b. Bklyn., Apr. 9, 1929; s. Stephen Paul and Ella (Mulry) P.; married, Feb. 23, 1952 (div.); children: Maureen, Stephen, Susan, Elizabeth; m. Emilie Halliday, Aug. 1, 1975; 1 dau., Margaret. A.B., Princeton U., 1950; LL.B., Columbia u., 1955. Bar: N.J. 1955, N.Y. 1956. Assoc. White & Case, N.Y.C., 1955-63; ptnr. White & Case, 1964—. Served to capt. USMCR, 1951-53. Mem. ABA, N.Y. State Bar Assn. (exec. com. tax sect. 1981—, chmn. employee benefits com.), Assn. Bar City N.Y., N.J. Bar Assn., Am. Contract Bridge Assn. (life master), Am. Bowling Congress (300 club). Republican. Clubs: High Mt. Golf, Am. Bowling Congress. Office: White & Case 1155 Avenue of Americas New York NY 10036

PIKE, GEORGE RUSSELL, lawyer, financial executive, investor; b. Reno, Jan. 2, 1938; s. Miles Nelson and Marchand Elise (Newman) P.; m. Eunice Heidi Pike, June 6, 1963 (dec.); m. Mirjana Klaich, Mar. 30, 1974; children: Miles N., Mirjana Elise. BSBA, U. Nev., Reno, 1961; JD, Georgetown U., 1965. Bar: Nev. 1965. U.S. commr. Dist. Nev., Reno, 1968-71, U.S. magistrate, 1971-75; sr. v.p., gen. counsel, exec. asst. to pres. First Fed. Savs. of Nev., Reno, 1970-79; pres. Russell Investment Co., Reno, 1970—, First Fin. Service Corp., Reno, 1976-81, Triad Fin. Corp., San Francisco, 1982-84; v.p. GRZ & A, Walnut Creek, Calif., 1985-86. Bd. dirs. ARC, Reno, 1978-79. Served to capt. U.S. Army, 1965-67. Mem. ABA, State Bar Nev., Washoe County Bar Assn., Calif. Savs. and Loan League. Republican. Episcopalian. Real property, General corporate, Banking. Home: 2680 Spinnaker Dr Reno NV 89509 Office: 121 California Ave Reno NV 89509

PIKE, LAURENCE BRUCE, lawyer; b. Brattleboro, Vt., Sept. 11, 1927; s. Lee Ernest and Alice Louise (Temple) P.; m. Norma I. Ecklund, Sept. 2, 1950; children: Barbara L., William T., Jeffrey O., Alan B. B.A., U. Iowa, 1951; J.D., Columbia U., 1954. Bar: N.Y. 1955. Assoc. firm Simpson Thacher & Bartlett, N.Y.C., 1954-64, ptnr., 1964—. Mem. Scarsdale Town Club, N.Y., 1964-68; mem. capt. Scarsdale Aux. Police, 1960-72. Served with USN, 1945-48. Mem. ABA, Bar Assn. City N.Y., N.Y. State Bar Assn., Phi Beta Kappa. Congregationalist. Clubs: Scarsdale Golf; University (N.Y.C.); Ardsley Curling (N.Y.) (dir., sec. 1974-77). Real property, Banking. Home: 26 Tunstall Rd Scarsdale NY 10583 Office: Simpson Thacher & Bartlett 270 Park Ave New York NY 10017

PIKNA, RAYMOND JOHN, JR., lawyer; b. Akron, Ohio, Sept. 19, 1954; s. Raymond John and Peggy Joan (Musk) P.; m. Christine Marie McDonald, June 30, 1984. BBA in Mgmt., U. Notre Dame, 1976; JD, Case Western Res. U., 1979. Bar: Ohio 1979, U.S. Dist. Ct. (so. dist.) Ohio 1981, U.S. Dist. Ct. (no. dist.) Ohio 1984, U.S. Ct. Appeals (6th cir.) 1985, U.S. Supreme Ct. 1986. Law clk. to chief judge U.S. Bankruptcy Ct., Columbus, Ohio, 1979-81; assoc. Cunningham, Gibbs & Cavalieri Co. L.P.A., Columbus, 1982-83, Knepper, White, Arter & Hadden (successor by merger Cunningham, Gibbs & Cavalieri), Columbus, 1983—; mem. adv. com. on local bankruptcy rules U.S. Dist. Ct. (so. dist.) Ohio, Columbus, 1986—. Coach high sch. boys' basketball team St. Andrew's Cath. Youth Program, Columbus, 1979-86; mem. St. Andrew's Choir, Columbus, 1982—. Mem. ABA (internat. law sect.), Ohio Bar Assn., Columbus Bar Assn. (bankruptcy com., chmn. publs. subcom. 1980-82, chmn. bankruptcy rules com. 1984—). Roman Catholic. Avocations: sports, fgn. langs. Bankruptcy. Office: Arter & Hadden One Columbus Bldg 10 W Broad St Columbus OH 43215

PIKUS, DAVID HELLER, lawyer; b. Newark, Aug. 30, 1955; s. Joseph D. and Lila R. Pikus. AB cum laude, Princeton U., 1977; JD, U. Va., 1980. Bar: N.Y. 1981, N.J. 1982, U.S. Dist. Ct. (so. and ea. dists.) N.Y. 1981, U.S. Dist. Ct. N.J. 1982. Asst. to gov. State of N.J., Trenton, 1977; assoc. Shea & Gould, N.Y.C., 1980—; adj. prof. health law Jersey City State Coll., 1985—. dir. summer youth voter registration Dem. State Com., Trenton, 1977. Mem. ABA, Assn. of Bar of City of N.Y., (mem. nuclear tech. and law com. 1985—). Club: Princeton of N.Y. Federal civil litigation, State civil litigation, Nuclear power. Home: 251 E 51st St #3-B New York NY 10022 Office: Shea & Gould 330 Madison Ave New York NY 10017

PILAT, MICHAEL JOSEPH, civil engineering educator; b. Longview, Wash., Feb. 19, 1938; s. Joseph Michael and Mary Veronica (Lazor) P. B.S. in Chem. Engring., U. Wash., 1960, M.S. in Chem. Engring., 1963, Ph.D. in Civil Engring., 1967. Registered profl. engr., Wash. Engr. Boeing Co., Seattle, 1961-64; mem. faculty U. Wash., Seattle, 1967-71, assoc. prof. civil engring. 1971-78, prof., 1978—. Patentee in field air pollution control. Mem. Am. Chem. Soc., Am. Inst. Chem. Engrs., Air Pollution Control Assn., Am. Assn. for Aerosol Research, Am. Indsl. Hygiene Assn., Fine Particle Soc., TAPPI, Sigma Xi, Tau Beta Pi. Club: Seattle Mountaineers. Legal education, Environment. Home: 7306 57th Ave NE Seattle WA 98115 Office: U Wash Dept Civil Engring FX-10 Seattle WA 98195

PILATO, LOUIS PETER, lawyer; b. Rochester, N.Y., May 6, 1944; s. Patsy and Rose (Pandolfo) P.; m. Marie Matacchiera, Aug. 2, 1969; children—Tristen, Tara. B.A., U. Miami, 1967; J.D., SUNY-Buffalo, 1973. Bar: N.Y. 1973, U.S. Dist. Ct. (we. dist.) N.Y. 1975. Sole practice law, Rochester, N.Y., 1973-74; asst. dist. atty. Monroe County, Rochester, N.Y., 1974-76, spl. asst. dist. atty., 1976-85, chief spl. investigation unit, 1984-85; ptnr. Fero, Collins & Pilato, 1986—; legal counsel Gates Little League, Rochester, 1974-76; instr. Brighton Police Dept., Rochester, N.Y., 1978. Served with AUS, 1969-72. Mem. Monroe County Bar Assn., N.Y. State Dist. Atty.'s Assn., St. Thomas More Lawyers Guild, Italian Am. Bus. Assn. Republican. Roman Catholic. Lodge: Moose (v.p.). Criminal, Family and matrimonial, Real property. Home: 134 Oak Ln Rochester NY 14610 Office: Fero Collins & Pilato 183 E Main St Rochester NY 14604

PILCHER, JAMES BROWNIE, lawyer; b. Shreveport, La., May 19, 1929; s. James Reece and Martha Mae (Brown) P.; m. Maxine Pettit, Jan. 23, 1951; children: Lydia, Martha, Bradley. BA, La. State U., 1952; JD, John Marshall Law Sch., 1955; postgrad. Emory U., 1957. Bar: Ga. 1955. Legal aide to Speaker of Ho. of Reps., 1961-64; assoc. city atty. City of Atlanta, 1964-69; sole practice, Atlanta, 1969—. Exec. committeeman Dem. Exec. Com. of Fulton County, Ga., 1974-87; bd. dirs. Whitehead Boys Club. Mem. State Bar Ga. (vice chmn. gen. practice and trial sect. 1985—, chmn. criminal law sect. 1986-87), Ga. Assn. Criminal Def. Lawyers (pres. 1980-82), Ga. Trial Lawyers (mem. exec. com. 1980—), Ga. Claimants Attys. Assn. (pres. 1983-84), Nat. Assn. Criminal Def. Lawyers (bd. dirs. 1980-85), Ga. Inst. Trial Advocacy (bd. dirs. 1986—), South Fulton Bar Assn. (pres. 1987—). Baptist. Club: Kiwanis (Peachtree, Atlanta pres. 1983-84). Criminal, Personal injury, Workers' compensation. Home: 434 Brentwood Dr NE Atlanta GA 30305 Office: 3355 Lenox Rd NE Atlanta GA 30324

PILECKI, PAUL STEVEN, lawyer; b. Norristown, Pa., Sept. 12, 1950; m. Barbara Derrickson; children: Derek Steven, Christopher Drew. AB, St. Joseph's Coll., Phila., 1972; JD, Temple U., 1978. Bar: Pa. 1978, D.C. 1985. Sr. counsel Fed. Res. Bd., Washington, 1978-84; assoc. Shaw, Pittman, Potts & Trowbridge, Washington, 1984—. Mem. ABA (banking law com.). Banking. Home: 11621 Ayreshire Rd Oakton VA 22124 Office: Shaw Pittman Potts et al 2300 N St NW Washington DC 20037

PILGER, KARL WILLIAM, lawyer; b. Detroit, Nov. 9, 1952; s. Adolphus Christian Pilger and Beulah Ruth (Bressey) Britton; m. Harriet Jenkins McFaul, July 11, 1981. BA with high honors, U. Fla., 1974; JD, Georgetown U., 1977. Bar: D.C. 1977, U.S. Dist. Ct. D.C. 1978, U.S. Ct. Appeals (D.C. cir.) 1978, Va. 1979, U.S. Dist. Ct. (ea. dist.) Va. 1979, U.S. Ct. Appeals (4th cir.) 1979. Assoc. Diuguid, Kennelly & Epstein, Washington, 1977-81; from assoc. to ptnr. Patrick J. Moran, P.C., Washington, 1981-86; ptnr. Moran & Pilger, P.C., Washington, 1986—; faculty Nat. Inst. Trial Adv., Hempstead, N.Y., 1985—. Mem. ABA, D.C. Bar Assn., Fed. Bar Assn., Fairfax County Bar Assn. Federal civil litigation, State civil litigation, General practice. Office: Moran & Pilger PC 1707 L St NW Suite 1050 Washington DC 20036

PILGRIM, GAIL LOUISE, lawyer; b. Elizabeth, N.J., Feb. 1, 1950; d. Frederick John and Meta Louise (Tisch) P; m. Bruce Charles Johnson, Nov. 30, 1985; 1 child, Mark Frederick Charles. AB summa cum laude, Bryn Mawr Coll., 1972, MA, 1974; JD, U. Pa., 1977; LLM, NYU, 1982; Cert., Goethe Inst., Munich, Fed. Republic Germany, 1979, 82. Bar: Pa. 1977, Ohio 1979. Assoc. Obermayer, Rebmann, Phila., 1977-79; corp. atty. Amer-itrust Corp., Cleve., 1979-81; fellow Food & Drug Law Inst., N.Y.C. and Washington, 1981-83; assoc. counsel Rorer Pharm. Corp. and predecessor firm William H. Rorer Inc., Ft. Washington, Pa., 1983—; adj. prof. Temple U., Ambler, Pa., 1985—; translator Quality Patent Translators, Gaithersburg, Md., 1982—. Mem. Legis. Com., Phila. Drug Exchange, 1983—, Internat. Visitors Ctr., Phila., 1986—; soloist local orchs.; bd. dirs. Meetinghouse Strings, Methacton, Pa., 1986—. Mem. ABA (food and drug law com.), Phila. German Soc., Welsh Soc. Avocations: concert pianist, harpsichordist, travel, photography. Food and drug. Home: 367 Roberts Ave Glenside PA 19038 Office: Rorer Pharm Corp 500 Virginia Dr Fort Washington PA 19034

PILIERO, ROBERT DONALD, lawyer; b. N.Y.C., Oct. 6, 1948; s. Joseph Robert and Madelyn (Colantuoni) P.; m. Gloria Fusillo, Apr. 18, 1981. BS in Econs., U. Pa., 1970; JD, Georgetown U., 1974. Bar: N.Y. 1975, D.C. 1983, N.J. 1984, U.S. Dist. Ct. (so. dist.) N.Y. 1975, U.S. Dist. Ct. (ea. dist.) N.Y. 1975, U.S. Dist. Ct. N.J. 1984, U.S. Ct. Internat. Trade 1981, U.S. Ct. Appeals (2d cir.) 1975, U.S. Ct. Appeals (fed. cir.) 1982, U.S. Ct. Appeals (D.C. cir.) 1983. Acct., Haskins & Sells, N.Y.C., 1970-71; assoc. Curtis, Mallet-Prevost, Colt & Mosle, N.Y.C., 1974-78; assoc. Marks, Murase & White (formerly Wender, Murase & White), N.Y.C., 1978-80, ptnr., 1980—. Mem. ABA, Assn. Bar City N.Y., Bar Assn. D.C., N.J. Bar Assn., Fed. Bar Council. Antitrust, Federal civil litigation, Private international. Office: Marks Murase & White 400 Park Ave New York NY 10022

PILLAI, K. G. JAN, law educator, lawyer; b. Quilon, India, Jan. 23, 1936; came to U.S., 1966, naturalized, 1975; s. Raman and Janaky (Amma) P.; m. Sarada J., May 16, 1966; children: Jay J., Jan. BA, U. Kerala, India, 1957, LLB, 1959, LLM, 1965; LLM, Yale U., 1967, JSD, 1969. Bar: D.C. 1975, U.S. Dist. Ct. D.C. 1975, U.S. Ct. Appeals (D.C. cir.) 1975, U.S. Dist. Ct. (ea. dist.) Pa. 1982, U.S. Supreme Ct. 1982. Mgr. Indian affairs Overseas Nat. Airways, N.Y.C., 1970-71; exec. dir. Aviation Consumer Project, Washington, 1971-73; assoc. prof. law Temple U., Phila., 1973-75, prof., 1975-86; dir. office regulatory analysis Fed. Energy Regulatory Commn., 1986—; mem. consumer adv. com. CAB, Washington, 1970-72; bd. dirs., legal adviser India Abroad, N.Y.C., 1982-84; counsel Salween Fin. Services, Phila., 1983-84; pres., bd. dirs. Indian Am. Times Pub. Co., Washington, 1984—. Author: The Air Net, 1969; contbr. articles to legal publs. Treas. Asian Indian Polit. Action Com., Phila., 1982—. Mem. Nat. Assn. Ams. of Asian Indian Descent (nat. chmn. 1980—), Asian Indian C. of C. (nat. chmn. 1983—). Republican. Hindu. General corporate, Securities, Administrative and regulatory. Home: 41 Overbrook Pkwy Overbrook Hills PA 19151 Office: Sch Law Temple U 1719 N Broad St Philadelphia PA 19122

PILLARI, THOMAS, lawyer; b. Lorain, Ohio, May 28, 1947; s. Frank Joseph and Rose (DeMarco) P.; m. Melissa Ann Filbey, July 8, 1972; children: Anthony, Andrew, Timothy, Elizabeth. BS in Engring. Mgmt., USAF Acad., 1969; JD, U. Chgo., 1972. Bar: Mass. 1972, Ohio 1973, Fla. 1982, Colo. 1985. Asst. prof. law USAF Acad., Colo., 1976-78; ptnr. Wickens, Herzer & Panza Co., L.P.A., Cleve., 1978—; lectr. Cleve. Marshall Law Sch., 1981. Mem. ABA, Omicron Delta Epsilon. Roman Catholic. Lodge: Rotary. Avocation: handball. Estate planning, Estate taxation, Probate. Home: 30028 Applewood Dr Bay Village OH 44140 Office: Wickens Herzer & Panza Co LPA 1144 W Erie Ave Lorain OH 44052

PILLING, GEORGE WILLIAM, lawyer; b. Reading, Pa., Mar. 25, 1942; s. Hugh Aiken and Lillian Elenor (Hannah) P.; m. Susan Genung, Sept. 5, 1973 (div. 1975); 1 dau., Jocelyn Kay. B.A., Kalamazoo Coll., 1963; J.D. with distinction, U. Mich., 1966. Bar: Mich. 1968, Calif. 1969, U.S. Dist. Ct. (cen. dist.) Calif. 1969. Clk., Montgomery McCracken, Walker & Rhoads, Phila., summer 1966, Cooper White & Cooper, San Francisco, summer 1968; assoc. Pollock & Palmer, Los Angeles, 1968-70; staff atty. Western Ctr. on Law and Poverty, Los Angeles, 1970-72; ptnr. Shapiro Posell & Pilling, Los Angeles, 1972-73; sole practice, Los Angeles, 1973—; chmn. bd. L.G. & N. Enterprises, Los Angeles, 1978—; dir. Newell Sports Enterprises, Los Angeles. Mem. ACLU (exec. com. So. Calif. div. 1971, 72). Democrat. State civil litigation, Family and matrimonial, General practice. Home: 3453 Coast View Dr Malibu CA 90265 Office: 1107 1/2 Glendon Ave Los Angeles CA 90024

PILLING, JANET KAVANAUGH, lawyer; b. Akron, Ohio, Sept. 5, 1951; d. Paul and Marjorie (Logue) Kavanaugh. B.A., Ohio Wesleyan U., 1973; J.D., U. Mo., 1975; LL.M., Villanova U., 1985. Bar: Pa. 1976, U.S. Tax Ct. 1976, U.S. Dist. Ct. (ea. dist.) Pa. 1976. Atty., Schnader, Harrison, Segal & Lewis, Phila., 1976-83; gen. counsel Kistler-Tiffany Cos., Wayne, Pa., 1983—. Mem. ABA, Phila. Bar Assn., Pa. Bar Assn., Montgomery County Estate Planning Council, Chester County Estate Planning Council, Phi Beta Kappa, Phi Delta Phi. Corporate taxation, Estate planning, Estate taxation. Office: Kistler Tiffany Cos Suite 706 987 Old Eagle School Rd Wayne PA 19087

PINCKNEY, FRANCIS MORRIS, lawyer; b. Columbia, S.C., Mar. 21, 1935; s. Francis Morris and Caroline (Walker) P.; m. Diana Brown, June 20, 1958; children: Elizabeth, Francis, Burton. BS in Mech. Engring., U. S.C., 1957; JD with honors, George Washington U., 1963. Bar: N.C. 1965. Patent examiner U.S. Patent Office, Washington, 1960-63; ptnr. Shefte, Pinckney & Sawyer, Charlotte, N.C., 1963—. Contbr. articles to profl. jours. Chmn. Civil Service Bd., Charlotte, 1980-83; mem. social planning council United Way of Charlotte, 1978-82; bd. dirs. N.C. Hunger Coalition, 1975-78, chmn., 1975-78; chmn. bd. dirs. Charlotte Area Fund Hunger Task Force, 1975-78. Served with USN, 1957-59. Mem. ABA, N.C. Bar Assn. (chmn. patent and trademark com. 1978-81, bd. govs. 1986—), Mecklenburg County Bar Assn. (pres. 1982-83), Patent Office Soc. Democrat. Episcopalian. Lodge: Rotary (pres. 1974-75). Patent. Office: Shefte Pinckney & Sawyer 1208 Cameron Brown Bldg Charlotte NC 28204

PINCKNEY, RONALD ROBERT, lawyer; b. Eugene, Oreg., May 19, 1949; s. Robert B. and Colleen M. (Miller) P.; m. Jill Marie Weir, Mar. 4, 1978; children: Colleen Marie, Cameron Joseph. BA, Willamette U., 1971, JD, 1974. Bar: Washington 1974, U.S. Dist. Ct. (we. dist.) Wash. 1974. Assoc. Walgren, Sexton & McCloskey, Bremerton, Wash., 1974-76; ptnr. McCluskey, Pinckney, Sells, Ryan & Riehl, Bremerton, 1977-84; sole practice Bremerton, 1984—. Fundraiser New YMCA Bldg., Bremerton, 1985. Mem. ABA, Wash. State Bar Assn., Wash. State Trial Lawyers Assn., Kitsap County Bar Assn., Jaycees. Presbyterian. Lodge: Rotary (sec., bd. dirs. Bremerton club 1978-81). Avocations: golf, skiing. Personal injury, Family and matrimonial, General practice. Office: 4040 Wheaton Way Suite 204 Bremerton WA 98310

PINGEL, STEVEN R., lawyer; b. Los Angeles, May 23, 1944; s. G. Albert and Vivian M. (Lyons) P. B.S., Calif. Poly. U., 1968; J.D., UCLA, 1971. Bar: Calif. 1971, U.S. Supreme Ct. 1975. Mem. Lemaire & Faunce, Los Angeles, 1973—; gen. counsel Calif. League of City Employee Assns.; instr. in law Calif. Community Colls. Mem. exec. com. Calif. Republican. Central Com., 1975-77; chmn. legal com. Hacienda Heights (Calif.) Improvement Assn., 1981-82. Mem. ABA, Los Angeles County Bar Assn., Calif. Trial Lawyers Assn., Phi Alpha Delta. Labor, Administrative and regulatory, State civil litigation. Home: 1518 S Folkstone Ave Hacienda Heights CA 91745

PINGREE, BRUCE DOUGLAS, lawyer; b. Salt Lake City, June 6, 1947; s. Howard W. and Lois (Ivie) P.; m. Wendy Wilcox, June 8, 1970 (div. Feb. 1979); children: Christian James, Matthew David, Alexandra Elizabeth, Merideth Gillian, Lauren Ashley. BA in Philosophy, U. Utah, 1970, JD, 1973. Bar: Ariz. 1973. Ptnr. Snell & Wilmer, Phoenix, 1973—; lectr. in field of taxation. Contbr. articles to profl. jours. Trustee Desert Bot. Garden, Phoenix, 1979-84; mem. Men's Art Council of Phoenix Art Mus., 1984—. Served to capt. USAR. Mem. ABA (tax sect., employee benefits com., chmn. task force on retiree med. and other post-retirement welfare benefits, past chmn. task force on flexible benefits, past chmn. task force on fringe benefits; real property, probate and trust sect., employee benefits com.), Order of Coif. Democrat. Episcopalian. Pension, profit-sharing, and employee benefits, Corporate taxation, Personal income taxation. Home: 231 W Morten Ave Phoenix AZ 85021 Office: Snell & Wilmer 3100 Valley Center Phoenix AZ 85073

PINKERTON, ALBERT DUANE, II, lawyer; b. Portland, Oreg., Aug. 28, 1942; s. Albert Duane and Barbra Jean (Payne) P.; 1 child, Albert Duane III. BA, Willamette U., 1964, JD, 1966. Bar: Oreg. 1966, U.S. Dist. Ct. Oreg. 1966, U.S. Ct. Appeals (9th cir.) 1966, Alaska 1985, Calif. 1986. Assoc. Sanders, Lively et al, Springfield, Oreg., 1966-69; ptnr. Spencer & Pinkerton, Burns, Oreg., 1969-70, Cramer, Gronso & Pinkerton, Burns, 1970-74, Cramer & Pinkerton, Burns, 1974-86, Orlebeke, Hutchings & Pinkerton, 1986—. Chmn. diocesen council Episcopal Diocese Eastern Oreg., 1978-83; mem. exec. com. Eastern Oreg. Comprehensive Mental Health Ctr., 1983—. Mem. Oreg. Bar Assn. (sec. com. uniform jury instrns. 1972-73, 82-83, chmn., 1973-74, 83-84, sec. com. proceedures and practices 1985-86, chmn. 1986-87), Assn. Trial Lawyers Am., Oreg. Trial Lawyers Assn., Am. Judicature Soc. Lodges: Lions, Elks, Masons (master 1980-81), Grand Lodge of Oreg. (dist. dep. 1983-86). Contracts commercial, State civil litigation, General practice. Office: Orlebeke Hutchings & Pinkerton PO Box 417 Concord CA 94522

PINKERTON, C(HARLES) FREDERICK, lawyer; b. Salt Lake City, Mar. 7, 1940; s. Charles Frederick II and Margaret L. (McDowell); divorced; children: Charles Frederick, John Dale. BA, Calif. Luth. Coll., 1964; JD, U. Oreg., 1967. Bar: Nev. 1968, U.S. Dist. Ct. Nev. 1968, U.S. Ct. Appeals (9th cir.) 1976. Dep. dist. atty Washoe County Dist. Atty.'s Office, Reno, 1968-71, chief chmn. dep. dist. atty., 1968-71. Served as cpl. USMC, 1959-62. Fellow Am. Coll. Criminal Lawyers; mem. ABA, Am. Trial Lawyers Assn., Nat. Assn. Criminal Def. Lawyers, No. Nev. Trial Lawyers Assn. Criminal, Federal civil litigation, State civil litigation. Office: 543 Plumas St Reno NV 89509

PINKSTON, CALDER FINNEY, lawyer; b. Macon, Ga., Jan. 26, 1957; s. Frank Chapman and Lucille Park (Finney) P.; m. Mary Anne Shouppe, July 28, 1979; 1 child, Alexander Webb. BA, Mercer U., 1978, JD, 1981. Bar: Ga. 1981, U.S. Dist. Ct. (mid. dist.) Ga. 1982, U.S. Ct. Appeals (11th cir.) 1982, U.S. Supreme Ct. 1985. Ptnr. Pinkston & Pinkston, Macon, 1981—; judge protempore civil ct. Bibb County, Macon, 1982—. Mem. fund raising com. Am. Heart Assn., 1984-86; mem. corp. fund com. United Way, 1985; grad. Leadership Macon, 1985, program chmn., 1986, vice chmn. bd. dirs., 1987—; bd. dirs. Macon-Bibb County Humane Soc., 1982—, Harriett Tubman Hist. and Cultural Mus., 1985—, Hay House, 1986—, vice chmn., 1987—; bd. dirs. Macon Arts Alliance. Named one of Outstanding Young Men Am., 1985. Mem. ABA, Ga. Bar Assn. (real property sect.), Macon Bar Assn., Assn. Trial Lawyers Am., Ga. Trial Lawyers Assn., Am. Fin. Services Assn., Macon-Bibb C. ov C. (local govt. com.), Phi Eta Sigma. Democrat. Baptist. Club: Civitan (Macon) (bd. dirs. 1986—). Avocations: reading, politics, hunting, fishing. Real property, Consumer commercial, State civil litigation. Home: 5347 Yorktown Rd Macon GA 31210 Office: Pinkston & Pinkston 165 1st St Macon GA 31201

PINNELL, GARY RAY, lawyer; b. San Antonio, Oct. 2, 1951; s. Raymond A., Jr., and Mary Ruth (Waller) P. B.B.A., U. Tex.-Austin, 1973, postgrad., 1976-77; J.D., St. Mary's U., San Antonio, 1976. Bar: Tex. 1976, U.S. Supreme Ct. 1982, U.S. Ct. Appeals (all cirs.), U.S. Tax Ct. 1976, U.S. Ct. Claims 1977, U.S. Ct. Customs and Patent Appeals 1978. Sole practice, Austin, Tex., 1976-77, San Antonio, 1977—; legis. asst. to Rep. Danny E. Hill, 1977; instr. U. Tex.-Austin, 1976-77. Bd. govs. Soc. Colonial Wars, Tex., 1978—; mem. Tex. Soc. Sons Revolution, 1979—. Decorated officer Order St. John, Queen Elizabeth II, 1977, comdr., 1985; officer Order Polonia Restituta (Poland), 1982, comdr. with star, 1984, grand cross, 1986; knight Teutonic Order (Vatican), 1979, Order Constantine St. George, Italy, 1979, numerous others. Mem. Internat. Bar Assn., State Bar Tex., Mexican Acad. Internat. Law, Omicron Delta Kappa, Delta Sigma Pi, Phi Alpha Delta. Republican. Roman Catholic. Club: St. John's (London). Contbr. articles legal jours. Federal civil litigation, Bankruptcy, Estate planning. Home: 2611 Eisenhower Rd Apt 603 San Antonio TX 78209 Office: La Quinta Plaza 10010 San Pedro Suite 540 San Antonio TX 78216

PINOVER, EUGENE ALFRED, lawyer; b. N.Y.C., Jan. 8, 1948; s. Maurice Alfred and Harriet (Ortner) P.; m. Diana Elzey, Feb. 14, 1974; children: Julia, Benjamin, Hannah. BA cum laude, Dartmouth Coll., 1969; JD cum laude, NYU, 1973. Bar: N.Y. 1974, U.S. Dist. Ct. (so. and ea. dists.) N.Y. 1974. Ptnr. Kaye, Scholer, Fierman, Hays & Handler, N.Y.C., 1974—. Real property. Office: Kaye Scholer Fierman Hays & Handler 425 Park Ave New York NY 10022

PINSKY, IRVING JAY, lawyer; b. New Haven, May 4, 1952; s. Roland Samuel and Jeni (Rohinsky) P. BA, U. Conn., 1976; JD, U. Bridgeport, 1981. Bar: Conn. 1981, U.S. Dist. Ct. Conn. 1981. Sole practice New Haven, 1981—. Mem. ABA, Assn. Trail Lawyers Am., Conn. Bar Assn., New Haven Bar Assn. Democrat. Personal injury, Civil rights, Workers' compensation. Office: 865 Chapel St New Haven CT 06510

PINSKY, MICHELE DOUGHERTY, lawyer; b. Dec. 4, 1955. BA cum laude, U. Pa., 1975, MA, 1976; JD, NYU, 1979. Bar: N.Y. 1980, U.S. Dist. Ct. (so. and ea. dists.) N.Y. 1980, U.S. Ct. Appeals (2d cir.) 1983, U.S. Supreme Ct. 1986. Assoc. Shea & Gould, N.Y.C., 1980-83, Whitman & Ransom, N.Y.C., 1983—. Mem. ABA, N.Y. State Bar Assn. Federal civil litigation, State civil litigation. Office: Whitman & Ransom 200 Park Ave New York NY 10166

PINSON, JERRY D., lawyer; b. Harrison, Ark., Sept. 7, 1942; s. Robert L. and Cleta (Keeter) P.; m. Jane Ellis, Sept. 11, 1964; 1 child, Christopher Clifton. BA, U. Ark., 1964, JD, 1967. Bar: Ark. 1967, U.S. Ct. Appeals (8th cir.) 1967, U.S. Supreme Ct. 1967, U.S. Dist. Ct. Ark. 1968. Dep. atty. gen. State of Ark., Little Rock, 1967-70; ptnr. Pinson & Reeves, Harrison, 1970—. Pres. United Way Boone County, Harrison, 1974. Mem. ABA, Am. Judicature Soc., Assn. Trial Lawyers Am., Ark. Bar Assn., Boone County Bar Assn., Harrison C. of C. (sec. bd. dirs. 1977). Lodge: Rotary (bd. dirs. 1975, v.p. 1976, pres. 1977). State civil litigation, Personal injury, General practice. Home: Rt 2 Harrison AR 72601 Office: Pinson & Reeves Attys at Law PO Box 1111 Harrison AR 72601

PINZLER, WILLIAM MICHAEL, lawyer; b. Bklyn., June 29, 1946; s. Hyman C. and Hannah (Friedman) P.; m. Isabelle Katz, Mar. 29, 1970 (div. Dec. 1985); children: Johanna E., Andrew H. AB, U. Rochester, 1968; JD, Boston U., 1971. Bar: N.Y. 1972, U.S. Dist. Ct. (no., so. and ea. dists.) N.Y. 1974, U.S. Ct. Appeals (2d and 6th cirs.) 1974, U.S. Supreme Ct. 1980. Law clk. to chief judge U.S. Dist. Ct. (no. dist.) Ohio, Cleve., 1971-73; assoc. Phillips, Nizer et al, N.Y.C., 1973-74, Fried, Frank, Harris et al, N.Y.C., 1974-82; ptnr. Pollner, Mezar, Stolzberg et al, N.Y.C., 1982-85, Tenzer, Greenblatt, Fallon & Kaplan, N.Y.C., 1985—. Contbr. articles to profl. jours. Mem. ABA, N.Y. State Bar Assn., Assn. of Bar of City of N.Y. Antitrust, Federal civil litigation, Securities. Office: Tenzer Greenblatt Fallon & Kaplan 405 Lexington Ave New York NY 10174

PIPPEN, JOSEPH FRANKLIN, JR., lawyer, author; b. Richmond, Va., Jan. 11, 1947; s. Joseph Franklin and Selma (Seay) P.; m. Beverly Price, Dec. 20, 1969; children: Joseph F. III, Troy Price. BS in Econs., Va. Tech., 1969; JD, U. Balt., 1975. Bar: Fla. 1981. Mgr. AT&T, Balt., 1969-80; gen. mgr. Micro-Plate, St. Petersburg, Fla., 1980-82; sole practice Largo, Fla., 1982—. Author: Ask an Attorney Florida Law, 1983, 3d Rev. edit., 85, Florida Corporations, 1986. Radio talk host Sta. WPLP, Fla. W. Coast. Served to capt. USNG, 1969-79. Mem. ABA, Fla. Bar Assn., Pinellas Trial Attys. Assn., Pinellas Estate Planning Council, Largo C. of C. Republican. Probate, General corporate, Real property. Home: 8699 Maidstone Ct Largo FL 33543 Office: 655 Ulmerton Rd #11 Largo FL 33540

PIRAINO, THOMAS ANTHONY, lawyer; b. Cleve., July 12, 1949; s. Thomas Anthony and Margaret (Stephens) P.; m. Barbara McWilliams, Sept. 4, 1976; children: Margaret, Ann. BA in History, Allegheny Coll., 1971; JD, Cornell U., 1974. Bar: Ohio 1974. Assoc. counsel Parker-Hannifin Corp., Cleve., 1981-84, asst. gen. counsel, 1984—. Contbr. articles to legal jours. Mem. ABA, Ohio Bar Assn., Am. Corp. Counsel (sec. 1985—), Am. Soc. Corp. Secs. (treas. 1986—). Avocations: tennis, jogging. Antitrust, General corporate, Securities. Office: Parker Hannifin Corp 17325 Euclid Ave Cleveland OH 44112

PIRCHER, LEO JOSEPH, lawyer; b. Berkeley, Calif., Jan. 4, 1933; s. Leo Charles and Christine (Moore) P.; m. Phyllis McConnell, Aug. 4, 1956 (div. April 1981); children—Christopher, David, Eric. B.S., U. Calif.-Berkeley, 1954, J.D., 1957. Bar: Calif. 1958, N.Y. 1985; cert. specialist taxation law Calif. Bd. Legal Specialization. Assoc. Lawler, Felix & Hall, Los Angeles, 1957-62, ptnr., 1962-65, sr. ptnr., 1965-83; sr. ptnr. Pircher, Nichols & Meeks, Los Angeles, 1983—; adj. prof. Loyola U. Law Sch., Los Angeles, 1959-61; corp. sec. Am. Metal Bearing Co., Gardena, Calif., 1975—, dir. Varco Internat. Inc., Orange, Calif., Amex Systems Inc., Los Angeles, 1982—; speaker various law schs. and bar assns. edn. programs. Author: (with others) Definition and Utility of Leases, 1968. Chmn. pub. fin. and taxation sect. Calif. Town Hall, Los Angeles, 1970-71. Mem. Calif. State Bar, N.Y. State Bar, Los Angeles County Bar Assn. (exec. com. comml. law secton), ABA, Nat. Assn. Real Estate Investment Trusts Inc. (cert. specialist taxation law). Republican. Club: California (Los Angeles). Real property, General corporate, Corporate taxation. Office: Pircher Nichols & Meeks 10100 Santa Monica Blvd Los Angeles CA 90067

PISANI, MICHAEL JOSEPH, lawyer, financial services company officer; b. N.Y.C., Mar. 22, 1944; s. Joseph Michael and Agatha Rita (Evaskitis) P.; m. Lynn Patricia Rombach, Dec. 6, 1969; children—Kristen, Tara, Matthew. B.A. in English, Boston Coll., 1965; J.D., NYU, 1968. Bar: N.Y. 1969, U.S. Dist. Ct. (so. dist.) N.Y. 1974, U.S. Ct. Appeals (2d cir.) 1975. Law clk. N.Y.C. Bar Assn., 1966-68; asst. dist. atty. N.Y. County Dist. Atty.'s Office, N.Y.C., 1968-72; assoc. gen. counsel N.Y. Life Ins. Co., N.Y.C., 1972—. Dir. St. Anne's Girls Track Program, Garden City, N.Y., 1980-82; coach Garden City Soccer Programs, 1980—, trustee, 1986—; dir. Kindergarten Boys Soccer Program, 1984-85; others. Named Most Effective Regional Alumni Counsellor, Boston Coll., 1979, others. Mem. N.Y. State Bar Assn. (com. chmn. 1985-86, exec. com. mem. Corp. Counsel sect. 1987—), Securities Industry Assn. Republican. Roman Catholic. Club: Westchester Rugby (trustee 1969-70). Avocations: skiing; platform tennis; softball; reading. General corporate, Insurance, Securities. Address: 93 Roosevelt St Garden City NY 11530

PISANI, ROBERT JOSEPH, lawyer; b. N.Y.C., Oct. 13, 1952; s. Joseph Michael and Agatha Rita (Evaskitis) P. BA, Tulane U., 1974; postgrad., U. Chgo., 1974-75; JD, Am. U., 1978. Bar: D.C. 1979, U.S. Ct. Internat. Trade 1979, Fla. 1981, U.S. Supreme Ct. 1984. Internat. trade analyst U.S. Trade Rep., Washington, 1976-78; atty. treasury dept. U.S. Customs, Washington, 1978—. Mem. ABA. Republican. Roman Catholic. Avocations: running, scuba. Immigration, naturalization, and customs, Public international. Home: 5404 Ridgefield Rd Bethesda MD 20816

PISANI, ROBERT LOUIS, legal association administrator, writer; b. N.Y.C., Feb. 24, 1956; s. Ralph Raymond and Elizabeth (Scholontz) P.; m. Suzanne Petruzel, May 18, 1986. Student U. Calif.-Berkeley, 1974-76. Human rights activist 1978-80; exec. dir. Internat. Legal Def. Counsel, Phila., 1980—. Co-author: The Hassle of Your Life: A Handbook for Families of Americans Jailed Abroad, 1982, Coming Home: A Handbook for Americans Incarcerated in Mexico, 1984, Know the Law: A Handbook for Hispanics Imprisoned in the United States, 1985, Repatriation: A Handbook for Americans Imprisoned in Europe, 1985; contbr. articles to profl. jours. Mem. adv. bd. Fellowship Commn. Phila., 1978-82; mem. Queen Village Neighbors Assn., Phila., 1981-82; Bd. dirs. South St. Neighbors Assn., Phila., 1981—, Washington Sq. West Project Area Com., Phila., 1986—; vol. HELP, Inc., Phila., 1981—. Named one of Outstanding Young Men of Am., U.S. Jaycees, 1983; recipient Cert. of Appreciation, New Eng. and Narcotics Officers Assn., 1983, Acad. Security Edn. and Trainers, 1985. Mem. Amnesty Internat. (urgent action network), Am. Correctional Assn., Am. Soc. Internat. Law, ACLU, Internat. Law Assn., World Future Soc., Internat. Assn. Penal Law, Fgn. Service Assn. (assoc.). Avocations: reading, research, writing. Private international, Criminal, Public international. Office: Internat Legal Def Counsel 111 S 15th St 24th Floor Philadelphia PA 19102

PISAR, SAMUEL, lawyer, author; b. Bialystok, Poland, Mar. 18, 1929; s. David and Helaina (Suchowolski) P.; m. Judith Frehm, Sept. 2, 1971; 1 child, Leah; children by previous marriage—Helaina, Alexandra. LL.B., U. Melbourne, Australia, 1953; LL.M., Harvard U., 1955, D. Juridical Sci., 1959; D.E.S., U. Paris, 1966, LL.D., 1969; L.H.D. (hon.), Dropsie U., 1982, Pepperdine U., 1982. Bar: D.C. 1961, Calif. 1962, N.Y. 1982, Paris Conseil Jurid 1963, London bar Gray's Inn 1966, legal counsel UNESCO 1956-59. Practice internat. law Paris, Washington and London, 1959—; lectr. U. Paris, 1974; mem. President J.F. Kennedy Task Force Fgn. Econ. Policy, 1960; adviser Dept. State, 1961; cons. join econ. com. U.S. Congress, 1962; chmn. conf. East-West Trade Mgmt. Center, Europe, 1969-72; lectr. U. Paris. Author: Coexistence and Commerce, 1970, Les Armes de la Paix, 1970, Of Blood and Hope, 1980, La Ressource Humaine, 1983. Named Citizen of Hon., Aix-en-Provence, France, Disting. Fellow Carnegie Mellon U., Pitts., 1982; recipient Sorbonne medal, Paris, 1983; honored Samuel Pisar Day, Proclamation, Colo. State U., Oct. 13, 1982. Mem. ABA, D.C. Bar Assn., Calif. Bar Assn., Am. Judicature Soc., Association Nationale de Conseils Juridiques, Gray's Inn (London). Made U.S. citizen by spl. act of Congress, 1961. Banking, Contracts commercial, General corporate. Home: 23 Sq de L'ave Foch, Paris 16 France Office: 575 Madison Ave New York NY 10022

PISTILLO, BERNADINO JOSEPH, JR., lawyer; b. Omaha, Nebr., Sept. 22, 1957; s. B.J. and Eleanor Louise (Rohmeyer) P. BA summa cum laude, Creighton U., 1978; JD magna cum laude, Tulane U., 1981. Bar: Nebr. 1981, U.S. Dist. Ct. Nebr. 1981, N.Y. 1985. Assoc. Baird, Holm, McEachen, Pedersen, Hamann & Strasheim, Omaha, 1981-83, Kaye, Scholer, Fierman, Hays & Handler, N.Y.C., 1983-87, Snell & Wilmer, Phoenix, 1987—. Sr. mng. editor Tulane U. Law Rev., 1979-81. Mem. ABA, N.Y. Bar Assn., Nebr. State Bar Assn., Order of the Coif. Corporate taxation, Personal income taxation, Real property.

PITCHER, GRIFFITH FONTAINE, lawyer; b. Balt., Nov. 1, 1937; s. William Henry and Virginia Griffith (Stein) P.; m. Barbara Jean Clarke, Oct. 3, 1945; children—Virginia T., L. Brooke, William T. B., Margaret W. B.A., Johns Hopkins U., 1960; J.D., U. Va., 1963. Bar: Ala. 1963, Fla. 1971. Assoc. Bradley, Arant, Rose & White, Birmingham, Ala., 1963-71; mem. Van den Berg, Gay & Burke, P.A., Orlando, Fla., 1971-76, Mahoney, Hadlow & Adams, P.A., Jacksonville, Fla., 1976-82; ptnr. Squire, Sanders & Dempsey, Miami, Fla., 1982—. Vice-chmn. Winter Park (Fla.) Planning and Zoning Bd., 1974-75. Served with Army N.G., 1961-64. Mem. Nat. Assn. Bond Lawyers, ABA, Fla. Bar, Order of Coif, Delta Phi. Republican. Contbr. articles on law to profl. jours. Municipal bonds.

PITNER, JOSEPH A., lawyer; b. Shreveport, La., Oct. 11, 1941; s. Joseph A. and Patricia Louise (Downs) P.; m. Cissy Cornwell, June 29, 1974 (div. 1985); 1 child, Joseph A. B.B.A., So. Methodist U., 1963, J.D., 1965. Bar: Tex. 1965, U.S. Dist. Ct. (no. dist.) Tex. 1966, U.S. Ct. Mil. Appeals 1966, U.S. Supreme Ct. 1978, U.S. Dist. Ct. (so. dist.) Tex. 1985. Sole practice, Dallas, 1969-77, Houston, 1981—; gen. counsel Gibson Discount Stores, Dallas, 1977-81. Contbr. articles to profl. jours. and mags. Served to lt. USN, 1965-69. Mem. Fed. Bar Assn., Tex. Bar Assn., Houston Bar Assn. Republican. Roman Catholic. Club: Metro. Bus. Assn. (Houston) (v.p. 1983-84). General corporate, Trademark and copyright. Home: 2200 Westfield Blvd Houston TX 77090 Office: 5106 FM 1960 W Suite 359 Houston TX 77069

PITOFSKY, ROBERT, lawyer, educator, university administrator; b. Paterson, N.J., Dec. 27, 1929; s. Morris and Sadye (Katz) P.; m. Sally Levy, June 4, 1961; children—Alexander, David, Elizabeth. B.A., NYU, 1951; LL.B., Columbia U., 1954. Bar: N.Y. 1956, D.C. 1973, U.S. Supreme Ct. 1972. Atty. Dept. Justice, Washington, 1956-57; assoc. Dewey, Ballantine, Bushby, Palmer & Wood, N.Y.C., 1957-63; prof. law NYU, 1963-70; dir. Bur. Consumer Protection, FTC, 1970-73; prof. law Georgetown U. Law Ctr., Washington, 1973-83; dean, exec. v.p. law ctr. affairs 1983—; commr. FTC, 1978-81; of counsel Arnold & Porter, Washington, 1973-78, 81—; vis. prof. law Harvard Law Sch., 1975-76; faculty mem. Salzburg Seminar in Am. Studies (Austria), 1975. Co-author: Cases on Antitrust Law, 1967; Cases on Trade Regulation, 2d edit., 1983; contbr. articles on consumer protection and antitrust to profl. publs. Served with U.S. Army, 1954-56. Recipient Disting. Service award FTC, 1972; named One of Ten Outstanding Mid-Career Law Profs. Time Mag., 1977. Mem. Assn. Am. Law Schs. (anti-trust sect. 1971-72, 82—), Columbia U. Ctr. for Law Econ. Studies (adv. bd. 1975—), ABA (Nat. Insts., antitrust sect. 1982). Democrat. Jewish. Antitrust, Administrative and regulatory, Federal civil litigation. Home: 3809 Blackthorn St Chevy Chase MD 20815 Office: Georgetown U Law Ctr 600 New Jersey Ave NW Washington DC 20001

PITRE, FRANK MARIO, lawyer; b. San Francisco, Jan. 17, 1955; s. Rosario and Rosanna Sarah (Pipia) P. BS cum laude, U. San Francisco, 1977, JD, 1981. Bar: Calif. 1981, U.S. Supreme Ct. 1985. Assoc. Cotchett & Illston, San Mateo, Calif., 1981-85, ptnr., 1986—; panelist, lectr. Calif. Continuing Edn. of Bar, 1986. Coach, vol. St. Dunston's Sch., Millbrae, Calif., 1974-77, Millbrae Lions Youth Orgn., 1974-77. Mem. ABA, Calif. Bar Assn. (commendation 1983, 85), San Francisco Bar Assn., San Mateo County Bar Assn. (cert. merit 1983), Assn. Trial Lawyers Am., Calif. Trial Lawyers Assn. (lectr.), San Mateo Trial Lawyers Assn., San Mateo County Barristers (bd. dirs. 1984-86). Democrat. Roman Catholic. Club: Royal Raquet (Burlingame, Calif.). Avocations: running, weight training. State civil litigation, Personal injury, Insurance. Home: 1335 Magnolia Ave Millbrae CA 94030 Office: Cotchett & Illston San Francisco Airport Office Ctr 840 Malcolm Rd Suite 200 Burlingame CA 94010

PITROF, EUGENE EDWARD, lawyer; b. Oconto, Wis., Aug. 16, 1935; s. Edward Frank and Cecelia Ann (Goebel) P.; m. LeClair L. Powers, Apr. 28, 1962 (div. Jan. 1969); 1 child, Eugenia; m. Nancy Ward, Jan. 25, 1979; children: Sasha, Sonja. BS, Marquette U., 1957, JD, 1959. Bar: Wis. 1959, Md. 1962, U.S. Dist. Ct. Md. 1962, U.S. Supreme Ct. 1973. Ptnr. Pitrof & Starkey, Upper Marlboro and Prince Frederick, Md., 1963—. Served to 1st lt. USAR, 1960-67. Democrat. General practice.

PITT, DOROTHY MOORE, lawyer; b. Rocky Mount, N.C., Mar. 1, 1948; d. Kenneth Edwin and Louise (Ezzell) Moore; m. Ronald C. Pitt, Aug. 26, 1972. BS in Math., East Carolina U., 1970, MEd, 1971; JD, U. Louisville, 1977. Bar: Ky. 1978, U.S. Dist. Ct.) Ind. 1979, U.S. Dist. Ct. (we. and ea. dists.) Ky. 1980, U.S. Ct. Appeals (6th and 7th cirs.) 1980. Personnel mgr. 1st Nat. Bank, Louisville, 1972-73; personnel and labor relations Humana Inc., Louisville, 1973-75; assoc. Greenebaum Doll & McDonald, Louisville, 1978-83, ptnr., 1983—; lectr. U. Louisville Sch. Law, 1979—, mem. steering com. labor law inst., 1985—, mem. curriculum adv. com., 1980-86. Brandeis scholar. Mem. ABA (labor and employment law sect.), Ky. Bar Assn. (co-chmn. labor and employment law sect. 1986—), Louisville Bar Assn. (co-chmn. labor and employment law sect. 1985-86, continuing legal edn. planning com. 1986—), Phi Kappa Phi. Club: Jefferson (Louisville). Avocations: tennis, sailing, racquetball. Civil rights, Federal civil litigation, State civil litigation. Home: 561 Sunnyside Dr Louisville KY 40206 Office: Greenebaum Doll & McDonald 3300 1st Nat Tower Louisville KY 40202

PITT, GEORGE, lawyer; b. Chgo., July 21, 1938; s. Cornelius George and Anastasia (Geocaris) P.; m. Barbara Lynn Goodrich, Dec. 21, 1963; children: Elizabeth Nanette, Margaret Leigh. BA, Northwestern U., 1960, JD, 1963. Bar: Ill. 1963. Assoc. Chapman and Cutler, Chgo., 1963-67; ptnr. Borge and Pitt, and predecessor, 1968—. Served to 1st lt. AUS, 1964. Mem. ABA, Ill. Bar Assn., Chgo. Bar Assn., Phi Delta Phi, Phi Gamma Delta. Municipal Bonds. Home: 600 N McClurg Ct Chicago IL 60611 Office: 120 S LaSalle St Chicago IL 60603 also: 2 Wall St New York NY 10005

PITTARI, STEPHEN JOSEPH, lawyer; b. Bklyn., Nov. 28, 1943; s. John Thomas and Catherine Marie (Paino) P. B.A., Coll. Holy Cross, 1965; J.D., Fordham U., 1968. Bar: N.Y. 1969, U.S. Dist. Ct. (so. and ea. dists.) N.Y. 1976. Assoc. counsel Legal Aid Soc. Westchester County, N.Y., 1969-71, sr. counsel, 1971-73, chief counsel criminal div., 1973-82; chief atty., exec. dir. Legal Aid Soc. Westchester County, 1982—; adj. prof. law Pace U., White Plains, N.Y., 1983—. Mem. Nat. Legal Aid and Defender Assn., ABA, N.Y. Bar Assn., Westchester County Bar Assn. (past chmn. criminal justice sect.), N.Y. State Def. Assn., Mt. Vernon Bar Assn. Roman Catholic. Criminal. Address: 50 Carwall Ave Mount Vernon NY 10552

PITTAS, SYDELLE, lawyer; b. N.Y.C., July 18, 1944; d. Paul Jacob Goldberg and Beatrice (Zam) Rosenberg; m. Michael John Pittas, Sept. 13, 1963 (div. June 1981); children: Pilar Alessandra, Christopher Daniel. BA, Douglass Coll., 1973; JD, Harvard U., 1975. Bar: N.Y. 1976, U.S. Dist. Ct. (so. and ea. dists.) N.Y. 1976, U.S. Ct. Appeals (2d cir.) 1976, Mass. 1977, U.S. Dist. Ct. Mass. 1977, U.S. Ct. Appeals (1st cir.) 1978, U.S. Ct. Appeals (5th and 8th cirs.) 1985, Calif. 1984, U.S. Ct. Appeals (9th cir.). Assoc. Baer & McGoldrick, N.Y.C., 1975-76, Herrick & Smith, Boston, 1976-81, Widett, Slater & Goldman, Boston, 1981-83; ptnr. McCabe/Gordon P.C., Boston, 1983—; adj. faculty trial advocacy workshop, Harvard Law Sch. Actress on legal topics Winchester Players and Needham Players; appeared on tv shows Good Day, Sunday Open House, Sharon King, People Are Talking. Mem. edn. task force NOW, Winchester, Mass., 1977-78, elected Winchester Dem. Com., 1984—; mem. faculty trial adv. workshop Harvard Law Sch. Mem. ABA, Mass. Bar Assn., Women's Bar Assn. (bd. dirs. 1979, speaker's bur., pub. relations). Jewish. Federal civil litigation, Bankruptcy, Entertainment. Home: 30 Mount Pleasant St Winchester MA 01890 Office: McCabe/Gordon PC 200 State St Boston MA 02109

PITTMAN, CRAIG SORRELL, lawyer; b. Enterprise, Ala., Sept. 6, 1956; s. John Edwin and Marjorie (Brunson) P.; children: Craig Jr., Jennifer Leigh. BA, Middlebury Coll., 1978; JD, Samford U., 1981. Bar: Ala. 1981, Fla. 1982. Law clk. to sr. judge U.S. Dist. Ct. (so. dist.) Ala., Mobile, 1981-83; assoc. Hamilton, Butler, Riddick, Tarlton & Sullivan, Mobile, 1983-87; sole practice Mobile, 1987—. Mem. Mobile Bar Assn., Maritime Law Assn., Southeastern Admiralty Law Inst. Club: Houston Mariners. Admiralty, Insurance, Real property. Office: Hamilton Butler & Riddick PO Box 1743 Mobile AL 36633

PITTMAN, EDWIN LLOYD, state official; b. Hattiesburg, Miss., Jan. 2, 1935; s. Lloyd H. and Pauline P.; m. Barbara Peel, Aug. 24, 1957 (dec. Dec. 1984); children: Malanie, Win, Jennifer. B.S., U. So. Miss.; J.D., U. Miss., 1960. Bar: Miss. Practiced law until 1964; mem. Miss. Senate, 1964-72; treas. State of Miss., Jackson, 1976-80, sec. of state, 1980-84; atty. gen. State of Miss., 1984—. Served to 2d lt., Inf. U.S. Army. Mem. U. Miss. Alumni Assn., U. So. Miss. Alumni Assn., Miss. Jaycees (past state dir.), ABA, South Central Miss. Bar Assn. Democrat. Baptist. Clubs: Lions, Masons. Criminal. Office: Attorney Generals Office PO Box 220 Jackson MS 39205 *

PITTMAN, JOSEPH STAFFORD, JR., lawyer; b. Enterprise, Ala., Jan. 11, 1954; s. Joseph Stafford Sr. and Angeline (Hutchison) P. BS in Acctg. cum laude, Birmingham (Ala.) So. Coll., 1979; JD, U. Ala., 1982. Bar: Ala. 1982, U.S. Dist. Ct. (mid. dist.) Ala. 1983, U.S. Ct. Appeals (11th cir.) 1985. Assoc. Pittman & Whittaker, Enterprise, 1982-84; ptnr. Pittman, Whittaker & Pittman, Enterprise, 1984—. Chmn. Am. Heart Assn., Enterprise, 1983; mem. exec. com. Coffee County Dems., Enterprise, 1986. Mem. ABA, Ala. Bar Assn. (internship com.), Coffee County Bar Assn., Assn. Trial Lawyers Am., Ala. Trial Lawyers Assn. (bd. govs. 1985—), Enterprise C. of C. (bd. dirs. 1985). Lodge: Rotary. General practice, State civil litigation, Personal injury. Office: Pittman Whittaker & Pittman 304 S Edwards St Enterprise AL 36331

PITTONI, LUKE M., lawyer; b. Rockville, N.Y., May 14, 1945; s. Mario and Grace (Henjes) P.; m. Mary Jo Rocque, July 8, 1972; children: Elizabeth, Katherine, Ellen. BA in Econs., Holy Cross Coll., 1967; JD, Fordham U., 1971. Bar: N.Y. 1972, U.S. Ct. Appeals (2d. cir.) 1975, U.S. Dist. Ct. (so. and ea. dists.) N.Y. 1975, U.S. Supreme Ct. 1976, U.S. Dist. Ct. Conn. 1977, Conn. 1986. Assoc. Martin, Clearwater & Bell, N.Y.C., 1972-75; trial atty. Anthony L. Schiavetti, N.Y.C., 1975-78; assoc. Alexander & Green, N.Y.C., 1978-79; ptnr. Heidell, Pittoni, Murphy & Bach, P.C., N.Y.C., 1979—; Mem. N.Y. State Com. on Ct. Congestion, N.Y. County Med. Malpractice Mediation Panel; faculty Practicing Law Inst., Law Journal Press; lectr. various profl. orgns. Mem. ABA, Conn. Bar Assn., N.Y. State Bar Assn., Nassau County Bar Assn., Stamford-Darien Bar Assn., Am. Acad. Hosp. Attys., Am. Bd. Profl. Liability Attys., Am. Soc. Law and Medicine, N.Y. State Med. Def. Lawyers Assn., Bklyn.-Manhattan Trial Lawyers Assn., Nassau-Suffolk Trial Lawyers Assn., Maritime Law Assn. Personal injury. Home: 283 Quarry Rd Stamford CT 06903 Office: Heidell Pittoni Murphy & Bach 100 Park Ave New York NY 10017

PITTS, BIRDIA MARIE GREER, lawyer; b. Shreveport, La., Feb. 2, 1952; d. Harry Marshall Jr. and Elessie Versa (Evans) Greer. BA, La. State U., 1974; JD, Southern U., Baton Rouge, 1980. Bar: La. 1981. Asst. dist. atty. State of La., Shreveport, 1980—. Bd. dirs. YMCA, Shreveport, 1981-83, CODAC Drug Rehab. Ctr., Shreveport, 1984-86; sec. Shreveport Women Commn. Recipient Cert. of Achievement, Dept. Health and Human Resources, 1980, Cert. of Recognition, YMCA, 1982, Nat. Council Negro Women, 1982. Mem. ABA (family law sect.), La. Bar Assn., Shreveport Bar Assn. (bd. dirs. young lawyers div.), Assn. Trial Lawyers Am., Shreveport Black Lawyers Assn., Assn. Women Attys., Minority Atty. Assn., Alpha Kappa Alpha. Democrat. Baptist. Avocations: tennis, chess, billards, bass fishing, aerobics. Family and matrimonial, Personal injury, General practice. Office: 509 Marshall St Suite 414 Slattery Bldg Shreveport LA 71101

PIVARNIK, ALFRED J., associate justice state supreme court; b. 1925. LL.B., Valparaiso U. Bar: Ind. 1951. Former Ind. circuit ct. judge Valparaiso; assoc. justice Ind. Supreme Ct., 1977—. Judicial administration. Office: Supreme Court Building 311 State House Indianapolis IN 46204 *

PIVER, SUSAN M., lawyer, insurance manager; b. Phila.; d. David and Rosalind (Nicholas) Myers; m. M. Steven Piver; children: Debra, Carolyn, Kenneth. AB, U. Pa.; postgrad., Temple U.; JD, SUNY, Buffalo, 1976. Bar: N.Y. 1977. Spl. counsel fraud and abuse Erie County (N.Y.) Medicaid, Buffalo, 1976-82, atty., dir. medicaid utilization rev., 1982-85; atty., risk mgr. Children's Hosp. of Buffalo, 1985—; adj. faculty, lectr. financing health care SUNY, Buffalo, 1984. Bd. dirs. Jewish Family Service, Buffalo, 1985—, Regional Perinatal Task Force, Buffalo, 1985—. Mem. Erie County Bar Assn. (med. jurisprudence com. 1978—), Am. Soc. Law and Medicine, Am. Soc. Hosp. Risk Mgrs., Am. Acad. Hosp. Lawyers, Nat. Health Lawyers Assn. Health. Home: 315 Lincoln Pkwy Buffalo NY 14216 Office: Childrens Hosp of Buffalo 219 Bryant St Buffalo NY 14222

PIZIALI, MICHAEL H., lawyer; b. Des Moines, Dec. 10, 1953; s. John James and Stephanie M. (Knezevich) P. BA, U. Iowa, 1976; JD, Creighton U., 1979. Bar: Iowa 1979, U.S. Ct. Appeals (8th cir.) 1981, U.S. Ct. Internat. Trade 1981, U.S. Ct. Claims 1981, U.S. Dist. Ct. (no. and so. dists.) Iowa 1981, U.S. Ct. Appeals (5th and 11th cirs.) 1982, U.S. Dist. Ct. (so. dist.) Tex. 1982, U.S. Supreme Ct. 1983, U.S. Ct. Appeals (3d cir.) 1983, U.S. Ct. Appeals (fed. cir.) 1983, N.Y. 1984, U.S. Dist. Ct. (so. and ea. dists.) N.Y. 1984. Law clk. to presiding justice Iowa Ct. Appeals, Des Moines, 1979-80, U.S. Ct. Appeals (5th cir.), Houston, 1980-81; assoc. Shearman & Sterling, N.Y.C., 1981-83, Morrison Cohen & Singer, N.Y.C., 1985-86, Jones Hirsch Connors & Bull, N.Y.C., 1986—. Editorial staff Creighton Law Rev., 1978-79. Federal civil litigation, State civil litigation. Office: Jones Hirsch Connors & Bull 101 E 52d St New York NY 10022

PIZZI, FRANK ANTHONY, JR., lawyer; b. Newark, Mar. 11, 1939; s. Frank A. and Mafalda B. (Barracano) P.; m. Virginia A. Applegate, June 20, 1964; children—Cynthia Ann, Tracia Ann, Frank A. III. B.S., Villanova U., 1961; J.D., Seton Hall U., 1965. Bar: N.J. 1965, U.S. Dist. Ct. N.J. 1965, U.S. Supreme Ct. 1968. Assoc., ptnr. Frank Pizzi Law Firm, Summit, N.J., 1965-75; sr. mem., prin., pres. Frank A. Pizzi, P.A., Summit, 1979—; judge Mcpl. Ct. Borough of New Providence, 1975—; pres., judge Mcpl. Ct. Twp. Chatham, N.J., 1980-83. Named Outstanding Jaycee of Yr., New Providence-Berkeley Heights Jaycees, 1966, Outstanding Young Man of Yr., 1969; recipient Senatorship award N.J. Jaycees, 1970. Mem. ABA, Assn. Trial Attys. Am., N.J. State Bar, Union County Bar Assn. (pres. 1980), Union County Mcpl. Ct. Judges Assn. (pres. 1981, 82), Summit Bar Assn. Republican. Roman Catholic. Club: Lions. General practice, Family and matrimonial. Office: Frank Pizzi Law Firm 55 Woodland Ave Summit NJ 07901

PIZZULLI, FRANCIS COSMO JOSEPH, lawyer, bioethicist; b. Bklyn., May 16, 1950; s. Dominick Lawrence and Rose Nancy (Ieracitano) P. B.A. in Math. with high honors, U. Calif.-Santa Barbara, 1971; J.D., U. So. Calif., 1974. Bar: Calif. 1975. NEH postdoctoral fellow Inst. of Soc., Ethics and the Life Scis., Hastings Ctr., Hastings-on-Hudson, N.Y., 1974-75; law clk. U.S. Ct. Appeals (9th cir.), 1975-76; assoc. Tuttle & Taylor, Los Angeles, 1977-79, Weissburg & Aronson, Los Angeles, 1979-80, Engel & Engel, Beverly Hills, Calif., 1980-81; sole practice, Santa Monica, Calif., 1981—; speaker, lectr., panelist in bioethics field; bd. dirs. MILA Import Export, Inc., 1985—; pres., dir. Geotermica, Ltd., 1986—. Editor So. Calif. Law Rev., 1973-74. Contbr. articles to profl. publs. Spl. cons. Nat. Commn. for Protection Human Subjects of Biomed. and Behavioral Research, Washington, 1976-77; big brother Cath. Big Bros., Los Angeles, 1979-82. Mem. Los Angeles County Bar Assn. (chmn. and founder biol. and behavioral tech. com. 1977-78, co-chmn. bioethics com. 1981-82), Italian-Am. Lawyers Assn., Order of Coif. Roman Catholic. Lodge: KC. Federal civil litigation, State civil litigation, Entertainment. Office: 1337 Ocean Ave Santa Monica CA 90401

PLACENTI, FRANK MICHAEL, lawyer; b. Columbus, Ohio, Sept. 2, 1953; s. Anthony Joseph and Evelyn (Piteo) P.; m. Barbara McNemar, Aug. 4, 1979. BA cum laude, Ohio State U., 1975, JD summa cum laude, 1979. Bar: Ariz. 1979, U.S. Dist. Ct. Ariz. 1979, U.S. Ct. Appeals (9th cir.) 1979. Ptnr., dir. Streich, Lang, Weeks & Cardon, Phoenix, 1979—; judge pro tem Maricopa County Superior Ct., 1985—. Recorder Phoenix City Hall, 1984, Gov.'s Symposium, Phoenix, 1985, Ariz. Acad., Phoenix, 1984—; chmn. Fed. Practice Program, 1986. James K. Barton Meml. scholar Ohio State U., 1977-79; named one of Outstanding Young Men in Am., 1981. Mem. ABA (litigation, communication law and young lawyers sects.), Ariz. Bar Assn. (lectr. 1985, faculty 1985, civil practice and procedures com.), Maricopa County Bar (chmn. com., lectr. on litigation 1985-86), Phoenix C. of C., Order of Coif, Phi Kappa Theta, Phi Kappa Tau, Phi Eta Sigma. Avocations: golf, photography. State civil litigation, Securities, Federal civil litigation. Office: Streich Lang Weeks & Cardon 100 W Washington Suite 2100 Phoenix AZ 85003

PLAEGER, FREDERICK JOSEPH, II, lawyer; b. New Orleans, Sept. 10, 1953; s. Edgar Leonard and Bernice Virginia (Schiwetz) P.; m. Kathleen Helen Dickson, Nov. 19, 1977; children: Douglas A., Catherine E. BS, La. State U., 1976, JD, 1977. Bar: La. 1978, U.S. Dist. Ct. (ea. dist.) La. 1978, U.S. Ct. Appeals (5th cir.) 1981, U.S. Dist. Ct. (mid. dist.) La. 1985. Law clk. U.S. Dist. Ct. (ea. dist.) La., New Orleans, 1977-79; assoc. Milling, Benson, Woodward, Hillyer, Pierson & Miller, New Orleans, 1979-85, ptnr., 1985—. Treas. St. Vincent DePaul Soc. (St. Clement Conf.), Metairie, La., 1986; bd. dirs. New Orleans Speech and Hearing Ctr., 1985—; selected mem. Met. Area Com. Leadership Forum, 1986—. Mem. ABA, La. Bar Assn., New Orleans Bar Assn. (fed. cts. com.). Republican. Clubs: Bienville (New Orleans), City (New Orleans). Avocations: camping, golf. Labor. Home: 4632 Neyrey Dr Metairie LA 70002 Office: Milling Benson Woodward Hillyer Pierson & Miller 1100 Whitney Bldg New Orleans LA 70130

PLAETZER, ROSS FREDERICK, lawyer; b. Milw., Jan. 24, 1954; s. Heinz H. and Margaret A. (Dickey) P.; m. Laura Keegan, Sept. 12, 1981; 1 child, Kevan B. BS, U. Wis., Milwaukee, 1977; JD, Marquette U., 1980; Diploma in Law, Oxford U., Eng., 1983. Bar: Wis. 1980, U.S. Dist. Ct. (ea. and we. dists.) Wis. 1980, Va. 1984, U.S. Dist. Ct. (ea. and we. dists.) Va. 1984, U.S. Ct. Appeals (4th cir.) 1984. Assoc. Davis & Kuelthau, Milw., 1980-83, Hunton & Williams, Richmond, Va., 1984—. Mem. Whitefish Bay Sch. Bd., Milw., 1976-81. Mem. ABA, Fed. Bar Assn., Va. Bar Assn., Wis. Bar Assn., State Bar Va., Richmond Bar Assn. Episcopalian. Avocations: swimming, tennis, photography, reading. Federal civil litigation, Admiralty, State civil litigation. Home: 4410 Leonard Pkwy Richmond VA 23221 Office: Hunton & Williams 707 E Main St Richmond VA 23219

PLAKAS, LEONIDAS EVANGELOS, lawyer; b. Akron, Ohio, July 18, 1951; s. Evangelos Leonidas and Catherine (Chibis) P.; m. Mary Ann J. Deuri, Sept. 17, 1978; children—Alexander Evangelos, Alyssa Catherine. B.S. cum laude in Bus. Adminstrn., U. Akron, 1973; J.D., 1976. Bar: Ohio 1976, U.S. Dist. Ct. (no. dist.) Ohio 1982, U.S. Ct. Appeals (6th cir.) 1984. Ptnr. firm Tzangas, Plakas & Mannos, Canton, Ohio, 1976—. Contbg. author U. Akron Law Rev., 1976. Trustee, Greek Orthodox Ch. of the Annunciation, Akron, 1973-76, 80-82. Mem. Stark County Acad. Trial Lawyers (trustee, sec., treas. 1982-87, pres. 1987—), Ohio Acad. Trial Lawyers, Am. Trial Lawyers Acad. Democrat. Personal injury, State civil litigation, General corporate. Office: Tzangas Plakas & Mannos 454 Citizens Savs Bldg 110 Central Plaza S Canton OH 44702

PLANTE, PETER PAUL, lawyer; b. Gracefield, Que., Can., Aug. 3, 1920; s. Edgar M. and Georgiana (Monahan) P.; m. Rita Mary Donahue, Sept. 4, 1948; children: Therese, Kathleen, Thaddeus, Maura Ellen, Maryanna, Christina, Stephen, Margaret, Robert, Anthony, Jeanne Marie. B.A., U. Western Ont., Can., 1943; J.D., U. Detroit, 1949. Bar: Vt. 1950, U.S. Dist. Ct. Vt. 1951, U.S. Ct. Appeals (2d cir.) 1961. Ptnr. firm Pierce & Plante, Newport, Vt., 1950-52; assoc. Henry F. Black, White River Junction, Vt., 1952-54; ptnr. firm Black & Plante, White River Junction, 1954-82; pres. firm Plante, Richards, Terino & Hanley, P.C., White River Junction, 1982—; dir. Woodstock Nat. Bank; Town auditor, Norwich, Vt., 1957-60, moderator, 1977—, sch. dir., Norwich, 1957-62, justice of peace, 1960-63; judge Harford Mcpl. Ct., 1962-67; mem. Jud. Selection Bd., 1967-78; chmn. Vt. Parole Bd., 1968-75. Trustee Mary Hitchcock Meml. Hosp., Hanover, N.H., 1968-71; trustee U. Vt., 1975-81, chmn. bd. trustees, 1980-81; trustee Vt. Law Sch., 1980—. Served with AUS, 1943-46. Fellow Am. Bar Found., Am. Coll. Probate Counsel; mem. ABA, Vt. Bar Assn. (pres. 1973-74), Am. Coll. Trial Lawyers, Am. Judicature Soc., Windsor County Bar Assn. Club: K.C. State civil litigation, Local government, Probate. Home: 12 Church St Norwich VT 05055 Office: Plante Richards Hanley & Gevety PO Box 319 219 Christian St White River Junction VT 05001

PLASTARAS, THOMAS EDWARD, lawyer; b. N.Y.C., Aug. 8, 1957; s. Joseph Edward and Lois Jean (Brady) P. BS in Hosp. Adminstrn., Ithaca Coll., 1979; JD cum laude, Calif. Western Sch. Law, 1982. Bar: Calif. 1982, U.S. Dist. Ct. (so. dist.) Calif. 1982, N.Y. State 1983, U.S. Dist. Ct. (ea. and so. dists.) N.Y. 1984, U.S. Tax Ct. 1984, Minn. 1984. Law clk. to presiding justice U.S. Dist. Ct. (so. dist.) Calif., San Diego, 1981-82; assoc. Kelly, Rode, Kelly & Burke, Westbury, N.Y., 1982—. Mem. ABA, Assn. Trial Lawyers Am., N.Y. State Bar Assn., N.Y. State Trial Lawyers Assn., Nassau/Suffolk County Bar Assn. State civil litigation, Personal injury, Federal civil litigation. Home: 7 Swan Ln Hauppauge NY 11788 Office: Kelly Rode Kelly & Burke 900 Ellision Ave Westbury NY 11590

PLASZCZAK, ROMAN THADDEUS, lawyer; b. San Diego, Oct. 3, 1943; s. Thaddeus Roman and Lorrine (Wiedenfelt) P. BA, Western Mich. U., 1965; JD, Detroit Coll., 1968. Bar: Mich. 1968, U.S. Supreme Ct, 1974, U.S. Dist. Ct. (we. dist.) 1979. Asst. pros. atty. Muskegon (Mich.) County, 1970-72; ptnr. Jerkins, Plaszczak, Hurley & Bauhof, Kalamazoo, 1972-79, Plaszczak & Plaszczak, Kalamazoo, 1974—, Plaszczak & Bauhof P.C., Kalamazoo, 1979—. Leader Legal Explorer Scouts, Kalamazoo, 1975-77; vol. Cath. Family Services, Kalamazoo, 1982-83. Served as capt. U.S Army, 1968-70, Vietnam. Decorated Bronze Star; recipient Civil Rights Litigation award ACLU, 1986. Mem. Assn. Trial Lawyers Am., Mich. Bar Assn. (state trial cts. com. 1980—, investigator Mich. atty. grievance com. 1980—), Mich. Trial Lawyers Assn. Republican. Avocations: boating, travel. Personal injury, Federal civil litigation, State civil litigation. Home: 1606 Grove St Kalamazoo MI 49007 Office: Plaszczak & Bauhof PC 137 N Park St Kalamazoo MI 49007

PLATER, FREDERICK OLIVER, lawyer, accountant; b. Oklahoma City, Apr. 1, 1949; s. D. Frank and Eleanor (Kantz) P.; children: Matthew, Rachael. B in Acctg., Oklahoma City U., 1975; JD, Okla. U., 1981. Sole practice Oklahoma City, 1981—; pres. F.O. Plater, P.C., Oklahoma City, 1982—. Mem. ABA, Okla. Bar Assn., Am. Soc. CPA's, Okla. Soc. CPA's (legis. com.). Avocations: tennis, sailing, skiing. Probate, Personal income taxation, Corporate taxation. Home: 1528 NW 38 Oklahoma City OK 73118 Office: 5101 Classen Suite 101 Oklahoma City OK 73118

PLATKIN, LAWRENCE PETER, lawyer; b. Passaic, N.J., June 21, 1956; s. Burton Henry and Annette Rae (Bukaitz) P.; m. Judith Ann Canter, June 24, 1979; children: Alyson Michelle, Matthew Jacob. BA, Rutgers U., 1978, JD, 1981. Bar: N.J. 1981, U.S. Dist. Ct. N.J. 1981, U.S. Ct. Appeals (3d cir.) 1982, U.S. Ct. Appeals (2d cir.) 1984. Assoc. Robinson, Wayne, Levin, Riccio & LaSala, Newark, 1981—. Mem. ABA, N.J. Bar Assn., Essex County Bar Assn., Fed. Bar Assn. of State of N.J., Supreme Ct. N.J. (dist. ethics com.), Omicron Delta Epsilon. Democrat. Jewish. Federal civil litigation, State civil litigation. Office: Robinson Wayne Levin Riccio & LaSala Gateway One Newark NJ 07102

PLATT, HAROLD KIRBY, lawyer; b. Southampton, N.Y., Nov. 7, 1942; s. William Bangs and Edith (Guldi) P.; m. Joan Pritchard, June 20, 1970; 1 child, Timothy Ross. B.S. in Foreign Service, Georgetown U., 1964; J.D., Fordham U., 1971. Bar: N.Y. 1972, U.S. Supreme Ct. 1976. Sole practice, Southampton, 1972-77; ptnr. Platt & Platt, Southampton, 1977-80, Platt, Platt & Platt, Southampton, 1980—. Articles editor Fordham Law Review, N.Y.C., 1970-71. Bd. dirs., sec. Southampton Hosp. Assn., 1979-85. Served with Mil. Police, U.S. Army, 1965-67; Germany. Mem. Suffolk County Bar Assn. (fee disputes com. 1974-82, chmn. 1981-82), N.Y. State Bar Assn., ABA. Real property, Probate, General practice. Home: 9 Dovas Path Southampton NY 11968 Office: Platt Platt & Platt 70 Main St Southampton NY 11968

PLATT, LESLIE A., lawyer; b. Bronx, N.Y., Aug. 7, 1944; s. Harold and Ann (Bienstock) P.; m. Marcia Ellin Berman, Aug. 10, 1969; 1 son, Bill Lawrence. B.A., George Washington U., 1966; J.D., N.Y.U., 1969. Bar: N.Y. 1970, U.S. Dist. Ct. D.C. 1972. Atty. advisor Office Gen. Counsel, HUD, Washington, D.C., 1971-72, legis. atty., 1972-75, asst. gen. counsel for legis. services, 1975-78, assoc. gen. counsel for legis., 1978-80; dep. gen. counsel-legal counsel HEW (HHS 1980), Office Gen. Counsel, Washington, 1980-81, legal counsel and staff dir. White House Agent Orange working group, 1980-81; ptnr. Coan, Couture, Lyons & Moorhead, Washington, D.C., 1981-85, law offices Leslie A. Platt, Washington, 1986—. Patentee in field. Co-chmn. community adv. bd. Fairfax Hosp. Assn. Cameron Glen Facility; chair steering com. Reston/Herndon Bus.-High Schs. partnership. Recipient Disting. Service award HUD, 1978. Mem. ABA, Fed. Bar Assn., Am. Jud. Soc., Fed. Sr. Exec. Service (charter). Real property, Legislative, Administrative and regulatory. Home: 11616 Newbridge Ct Reston VA 22091 Office: 2000 L St NW Suite 200 Washington DC 20036

PLATT, RUTHERFORD HAYES, JR., lawyer, educator, consultant; b. N.Y.C., Nov. 1, 1940; s. Rutherford and Jean (Noyes) P.; m. Constance Adams, Dec. 8, 1966; children: Anne, Stephen. BA, Yale U., 1962; JD, U.Chgo., 1967, PhD, 1971. Bar: Ill. 1968, U.S. Dist. Ct. (no. dist.) Ill. 1968. Staff atty. Open Lands Project, Chgo., 1968-72; prof. U. Mass., Amherst, 1972—; cons. U.S. Water Resources Council, Washington, 1979-81, U.S. Army C.E., Washington, 1977-79. Editor: Beyond the Urban Fringe, 1983. Contbr. articles to profl. jours. Bd. dirs. Conn. River Watershed Council, Easthampton, Mass., 1975-84; mem. Planning Bd., Northampton, Mass., 1974-79. Recipient Nathan Burkan Legal Writing award ASCAP, 1967; HUD urban studies fellow, 1967-69; also NSF grantee. Mem. ABA, Assoc. Am. Geographers, Coastal Soc. Club: Faculty (Mass.); Cosmos (Washington). Legal education, Environment, Local government. Home: 21 Park St Florence MA 01060 Office: U Mass Amherst MA 01003

PLATT, STEVEN IRVING, lawyer, judge; b. Woodstock, Va., Jan. 1, 1947; s. Nathan and Adele (Lober) P.; m. Patricia Lynn Hartlove, Sept. 29, 1973; children: Jason Benjamin, Sarah Edan. BA, U. Va., 1969; JD, Am. U., 1973; cert. of completion, Nat. Jud. Coll., 1980, Nat. Coll. of Probate Judges, 1983. Bar: Md. 1976, U.S. Dist. Ct. Md., 1976. Ptnr. Stern, Platt & Risner, Oxon Hill, Md., 1976-79; judge Orphans Ct., Prince Georges County, Md., 1978-85; ptnr. Platt & Risner, Clinton, Md., 1980—; chief judge Orphans Ct., Prince Georges County, Md., 1985-86; assoc. judge Dist. Ct. Md., Upper Marlboro, Md., 1986—; instr. Paralegal Inst. U. Md. Bd. dirs. United Way, Prince Georges, 1980; bd. mgrs. YMCA, Prince Georges, 1980; mem. Energy Preservation Task Force, Prince Georges, 1980; chmn. Labor Law Revision Task Force, Prince Georges, 1981—; chmn. bd. trustees Henson Valley Montessori Sch., Temple Hills, Md., 1985—. Served with Md. N.G., 1970-76. Mem. ABA, Md. Bar Assn., Prince Georges Bar Assn. (bd. dirs. 1978-85, treas. 1985-86, sec. 1986-87), Am. Trial Lawyers Assn., Nat. Coll. Probate Judges (state rep. 1985-86), Delta Theta Phi. Jewish. Judicial administration. Home: 12302 Asbury Dr Fort Washington MD 20744 Office: 5th Jud Dist Md Dist Ct Judges Chambers Ground Floor Courthouse Upper Marlboro MD 20772

PLATT, THOMAS C., III, lawyer; b. Glen Cove, N.Y., June 18, 1955; s. Thomas C. Jr. and Byrd (Symington) P.; m. Loretta Sullivan, 1979; children: Thomas C. IV, Edward S. AB cum laude, Yale U., 1977; JD, Cornell U., 1980. Bar: N.H. 1980, N.H. Dist. Ct. N.H. 1980. Assoc. Orr and Reno, P.A., Concord, N.H., 1980-85, ptnr., 1985—, also bd. dirs. Vol. United Way, Concord, 1981—, Rudman Re Election Campaign, Concord, 1986—; assoc. dir. Concord Boys Club, 1983—; bd. dirs. Cornell U. Law Rev., 1979-80. Mem. ABA, N.H. Bar Assn. (ethics com. 1986—). Republican. Episcopalian. General corporate, Contracts commercial, Mergers and acquisitions. Office: Orr and Reno PA One Eagle Sq Box 709 Concord NH 03301-0709

PLATT, THOMAS COLLIER, judge; b. N.Y.C., May 29, 1925; s. Thomas Collier and Louise (Lusk) P.; m Ann Byrd Symington, June 25, 1948; children—Ann Byrd, Charles Collier, Thomas Collier, Elizabeth Louise. B.A., Yale U., 1947, LL.B., 1950. Assoc. Root, Ballantine, Harlan, Bushby & Palmer, N.Y.C., 1950-53; asst. U.S. atty. Bklyn., 1953-56; assoc. Bleakley, Platt, Schmidt, Hart & Fritz, N.Y.C., 1956-60, ptnr., 1960-74; judge U.S. Dist. Ct. (ea. dist.) N.Y., Bklyn., 1974—; former dir. Phoenix Mut. Life Ins. Co., RAC Corp., McIntyre Aviation, Inc.; atty. Village of Laurel Hollow, N.Y., 1958-74; acting police justice Village of Lloyd Harbor, N.Y., 1958-63. Alt. del. Republican Nat. Conv., 1964, 68, 72; del. N.Y. State Rep. Conv., 1966; trustee Brooks Sch., North Andover, Mass., 1968-82, pres., 1970-74. Served with USN, 1943-46. Episcopalian. Clubs: Phelps Assn. (New Haven) (bd. govs. 1960—); Cold Spring Harbor Beach (N.Y.) (bd. mgrs. 1964-70); Yale of N.Y.C. Jurisprudence. Office: US Courthouse 225 Cadman Plaza E Brooklyn NY 11201

PLATT, WILLIAM HENRY, lawyer; b. Allentown, Pa., Jan. 25, 1940; s. Henry and Genevieve (McElroy) P.; m. Maureen Hart, Nov. 29, 1969; children—Meredith H., William H., James H. A.B., Dickinson Coll., 1961; J.D., U. Pa., 1964. Bar: Pa. 1967, U.S. Supreme Ct. 1971. Ptnr. Yarus and Platt, Allentown, 1967-77; asst. pub. defender Lehigh County (Pa.), 1972-75, chief pub. defender, 1975-76, dist. atty., 1976—; mem. criminal procedural rules com. Supreme Ct. Pa., 1982—, chmn., 1986—. Mem. Gov.'s Trial Ct. Nominating Commn. Lehigh County, 1984—; mem. Pa. Commn. on Crime and Delinquency Victim Services Adv. Com., 1983—. Served with M.P., U.S. Army, 1964-66. Mem. ABA, Pa. Bar Assn., Lehigh County Bar Assn., Nat. Assn. Dist. Attys. (state dir. 1982-84), Pa. Assn. Dist. Attys. (pres. 1983-84, exec. com. 1980-86, tng. inst. chmn. 1986—), Am. Judicature Soc. Criminal. Home: 435 Iroquois St Emmaus PA 18049 Office: PO Box 1548 Allentown PA 18105

PLATTNER, RICHARD SERBER, lawyer; b. N.Y.C., Aug. 10, 1952; s. Milton and Sallee Sarah (Serber) P.; m. Susan M. Madden, June 4, 1976 (div. June 1979); m. Susan K. Morris, Mar. 30, 1983. BA, Mich. State U., 1973; JD, Ariz. State U., 1977. Bar: Ariz. 1977, U.S. Dist. Ct. Ariz. 1977. Assoc. Wolfe & Harris, Phoenix, 1977-79, Monbleau, Vermeire & Turley, Phoenix, 1979-81; chief of litigation Phillips & Lyon, Phoenix, 1981; sole practice Phoenix, 1982—. Editor: Trial Judges of Maricopa County, 1985; co-editor Jury Verdict Research newsletter, 1982-83. Posse comdr. Maricopa County Sheriff Adj. Posse, 1986; judge pro tem Maricopa County Superior Ct., 1986—. Mem. ABA, Ariz. Trial Lawyers Assn. (editor Ariz. Appellate Highlights), Ariz. Bar. Assn., Maricopa County Bar Assn., Phoenix Trial Lawyers Assn. (bd. dirs. 1983—, pres. 1986-87), Ariz. Profl. Assn. (pres. 1984-86). Insurance, Personal injury.

PLATTO, CHARLES, lawyer; b. Bklyn., Nov. 19, 1945; s. Irving and Mollie Platto; m. Leslie Joan Stoller, Mar. 19, 1969; children: Jamie, Carey, Jody, Terry. BA, U. Pa., 1966; JD, U. Mich., 1969; LLM, NYU, 1974. Bar: N.Y. 1970, U.S. Dist. Ct. (so. and ea. dists.) N.Y. 1972, U.S. Supreme Ct. 1974. Atty. Community Legal Services, Phila., 1969-71; assoc. Cahill, Gordon & Reindel, N.Y.C. and Paris, 1974-76; ptnr. Cahill, Gordon & Reindel, N.Y.C., 1980—. Mem. N.Y. State Bar Assn. (exec. com. banking, bus. corp. law sect., rep. ho. of dels.), Internat. Bar Assn. (vice-chair subcom. on transnat. claims and litigation). Federal civil litigation, State civil litigation, Insurance. Office: Cahill Gordon & Reindel 80 Pine St New York NY 10005

PLATZ, GEORGE ARTHUR, III, lawyer; b. Safford, Ariz., Sept. 12, 1939; s. George Arthur and Dickey Azalea (Slagle) P.; m. Mary Condon, Sept. 20, 1963; m. Andrea Maxwell, Oct. 25, 1979; children—Susan, Stephanie. B.S., Northwestern U., 1960; LL.B., Harvard U., 1963. Bar: Ill. 1964, U.S. Dist. Ct. (no. dist.) Ill. 1964, U.S. Ct. Appeals (7th cir.) 1964, U.S. Tax Ct. 1981, U.S. Supreme Ct. 1981. Assoc. Sidley & Austin, Chgo., 1964-71, ptnr., 1972—. Mem. ABA, Chgo. Bar. Assn. Clubs: Chikaming Country, Monroe. Federal civil litigation, State civil litigation. Office: Sidley & Austin 1 First Nat Plaza Chicago IL 60603

PLATZER, CYNTHIA SIEMEN, lawyer; b. Sarnia, Ont., Can., Aug. 8, 1954; d. Howard John and Gloria Ann (Nugent) Siemen; m. Joel Francis Platzer, May 25, 1979. B.G.S., U. Mich., 1975; J.D., Detroit Coll. Law, 1981. Bar: Mich. 1982, U.S. Dist. Ct. (ea. dist.) Mich. 1982. Paralegal/law clk. St. Clair County Prosecutor's Office, Port Huron, Mich., 1979-82; ptnr. Cleland and Platzer, Port Huron, 1982—; commr., parliamentarian Women's Council Realtors, Port Huron, 1982-84; corp. counsel Goodwill Industries, Port Huron, 1984—, bd. dirs., 1983—, 1st v.p., 1986-87; corp. counsel Child and Family Services, Inc., Port Huron, 1984—. Note and comment editor Detroit Coll. Law Rev., 1980-81. 2d v.p. bd dirs. Goodwill industries of St. Clair County, 1983—; mem. St. Clair County Met. Planning Commn., 1984—, chmn. 1987—. Named Port Huron Young Career Woman, Nat. Assn. Bus. and Profl. Women, 1985, Young Career Woman Region XII, 1985. Mem. St. Clair County Bar Assn., Women Lawyers Assn. Mich., Mich. Trial Lawyers Assn., Eastern Mich. Law Enforcement Assn., U. Mich. Alumni Assn. Clubs: Quota (Port Huron); WLAM (pres. St. Clair, Sanilac, Mich., 1984-85). State civil litigation, Criminal, Local government. Office: Cleland and Platzer 901 Huron Ave Suite 5 Port Huron MI 48060

PLAUT, NATHAN MICHAEL, lawyer; b. Cin., Nov. 25, 1917; s. Jacob Michael and Alice (Sachs) P.; m. Mary Hollis, Aug. 16, 1945; children—Alison P. Palmer, James Hollis. A.B., Harvard U., 1939, spl. student Law Sch., 1946; LL.B., U. Mich., 1941. Bar: Ohio 1941, Mass. 1946, N.H. 1947, U.S. Dist. Ct. N.H. 1947. Assoc. Faulkner, Plaut Hanna Zimmerman & Freund, P.C., and predecessor firms, Keene, NH, 1946-53, ptnr., 1953-82; of counsel FaulknerPlaut Hanna Zimmerman & Freund, P.C., and predecessor firms, Keene, NH, 1983—; mem. visitor's com. U. Mich., 1962-68. Del., N.H. Constl. Conv., 1947—. Served to maj. USMCR, 1942-45. Fellow Am. Coll. Probate Counsel, Am. Bar Found., N.H. Bar Found. (sec., bd. dirs.); mem. Assn. Ins. Attys., ABA (ho. of dels. 1972—, state del. 1979-84, bd. govs. 1984-87, council sr. lawyers div. 1985—), Boston Bar Assn., Cheshire County Bar Assn., N.H. Bar Assn. (pres. 1971-72). Clubs: Harvard (Boston); Keene Country. Lodge: Rotary. Probate. Home: Peg Shop Rd Keene NH 03431 Office: 91 Court St Keene NH 03431

PLAYER, THERESA JOAN, lawyer; b. Great Lakes, Ill., Nov. 17, 1947; d. Heber and Rita Jane (Mulhulland) P. AB, San Diego State U., 1970; JD, UCLA, 1973. Bar: Calif. 1973, U.S. Dist. Ct. (so. dist.) Calif. 1973, U.S. Ct. Appeals (9th cir.) 1978. Staff atty. Legal Aid Soc., San Diego, 1974-78; ptnr. Meaney & Player, San Diego, 1979-80; clin. prof. law U. San Diego, 1980-83, clinic dir., 1983—; faculty mem. Nat. Inst. Trial Advocacy, San Diego, 1982—. Author: California Trial Technique, 1986; contbg. author: Every Woman's Legal Guide, 1980. Recipient Outstanding contribution award San Diego Vol. Lawyers, 1985. Mem. ABA, Criminal Def. Bar Assn., Women's Criminal Def. Bar Assn. (steering com. 1978-84, service award 1982), Calif. Attys. Criminal Justice, Lawyers Club. Democrat. Avocations: triathlons, skiing, golfing. Legal education, State civil litigation. Office: U San Diego Alcala Park San Diego CA 92110

PLEET, JESSE LAWN, lawyer; b. Lebanon, Pa., Dec. 2, 1955; s. David Elihu and Marilyn (David) P. BS, Pa. State U., 1977; JD, Widener U., 1981. Bar: Pa. 1981, U.S. Dist. Ct. (ea. dist.) Pa. 1983. Assoc. Kozloff, Diener, Payne & Fegley, Wyomissing, Pa., 1982-86, ptnr., 1986—. Pres. South Mt. YMCA Alumni Assn., Wernersville, Pa., 1983-85. Mem. ABA, Assn. Trial Lawyers of Am., Pa. Bar Assn., Pa. Trial Lawyers Assn., Berks County Bar Assn. (bd. dirs.), Berks County Young Lawyers Assn. (pres. 1985-86), Sigma Phi Alpha (pres. 1984-86). Avocations: skiing, private pilot. Insurance, Personal injury, Contracts commercial. Home: 1528 Dauphin Ave Wyomissing PA 19610-2118 Office: Kozloff Diener Payne Fegley 2640 Westview Dr PO Box 6286 Wyomissing PA 19610

PLEISS, LARRY THOMAS, lawyer; b. Panama City, Fla., Dec. 28, 1953; s. Kenneth W. and Luise (Lachnit) P.; m. Ann J. Powers, June 25, 1977; children: Candice Ann, Mindy Luise. AA in Bus. Adminstrn., Cypress Coll., 1975; BBA magna cum laude, Calif. State U., Fullerton, 1976; JD cum laude, Pepperdine U., 1979. Bar: Calif. 1979, U.S. Dist. Ct. (cen. dist.) Calif. 1979, U.S. Ct. Appeals (9th cir.) 1984, U.S. Supreme Ct. 1985. Assoc. Kinkle, Rodiger & Spriggs, Santa Ana, Calif., 1979-82; ptnr. Madory, Booth, Zell & Pleiss, Tustin, Calif., 1982—; judge pro tem Orange County Superior Ct., Santa Ana, 1982—. Mem. Pepperdine U. Law Rev., 1977-79. Judge Vincent Dalsimer Moot Ct., Malibu, Calif., 1979—. Mem. ABA, Orange County Bar Assn., Assn. Trial Lawyers Am., Am. Bd. Trial Advs., Am. Arbitration Assn. (arbitrator), Phi Alpha Delta, Alpha Gamma Sigma, Beta Gamma Sigma. Republican. Baptist. Avocations: baseball, basketball, tennis, racquetball, water sports. Federal civil litigation, State civil litigation, Personal injury. Office: Madory Booth Zell & Pleiss 17822 E 17th St Tustin CA 92680-2183

PLESHE, DOROTHY CLARE, lawyer; b. Ishpeming, Mich., Aug. 31, 1953; d. John Frank and Clara Margaret (Lamuth) P. B.A. magna cum laude, U. Utah, 1973, J.D., 1976. Bar: Utah 1976. Ptnr., Greene, Callister & Nebeker (now Callister, Duncan & Nebeker), Salt Lake City, 1976—. Mem. Salt Lake City Bd. Adjustments. Mem. ABA, Utah State Bar, Salt Lake County Bar Assn., Salt Lake City C. of C., Phi Beta Kappa, Phi Kappa Phi. Democrat. Roman Catholic. Articles editor Jour. Contemporary Law, U. Utah, 1974-75. Banking, Consumer commercial, Contracts commercial. Home: 641 6th Ave Salt Lake City UT 84103 Office: 800 Kennecott Bldg Salt Lake City UT 84133

PLESKO, JEFFREY MICHAEL, lawyer; b. Streator, Ill., May 17, 1948; s. Manley and Gladys G. (Berta) P.; m. Megan Kathleen Miller, Oct. 5, 1984. B.A., U. Ill., 1970; J.D., So. Ill. U., 1977. Bar: Ill. 1977, U.S. Dist. Ct. (so. dist.) Ill. 1977, U.S. Ct. Appeals (7th cir.) 1986. Asst. defender Ill. Office of State Appellate Defender, Mt. Vernon, 1977-80; mng. atty. Ill. Guardianship and Advocacy Commn., Carbondale, Ill., 1980—. Adviser pub. affairs com. Mental Health Assn. in Ill., Springfield, 1982—. Served with U.S. Army, 1970-72, Germany. Recipient U.S. Law Week award Bur. Nat. Affairs, Inc., 1977. Mem. Ill. Bar Assn., So. Ill. U. Alumni Assn., Am. Motorcyclist Assn. State civil litigation, Probate, Health. Office: Ill Guardianship and Advocacy Commn 611 E College St Carbondale IL 62901

PLETZ, JOHN STEPHEN, lawyer; b. St. Louis, Mar. 5, 1944; s. John F. and Helen (Fouts) P.; m. Karen Owens, Dec. 26, 1975; children: Brittany Elizabeth, Casey Lee. AB, U. Calif., Berkeley, 1966; JD cum laude, U. Mo., 1975. Bar: Mo. 1976, U.S. Dist. Ct. (we. dist.) Mo. 1976. Counsel, exec. dir. Mo. Elections Com., Jefferson City, 1976-78; dep. sec. state State of Mo., Jefferson City, 1978-81; ptnr. Bartlett, Venters, Pletz & Toppins P.C., Jefferson City, 1981—. Trustee, v.p. Meml. Community Hosp., Jefferson City, 1984—; elder 1st Presbyn. Ch., Jefferson City, 1986—. Mem. ABA, Mo. Bar Assn., Cole County Bar Assn. (pres. 1982), Order of Coif. Lodge: Rotary. General practice, Real property, Government contracts and claims. Home: 330 Sterling Price Rd Jefferson City MO 65101 Office: Bartlett Venters Pletz & Toppins PC 325 Jefferson St Jefferson City MO 65101

PLISHNER, MICHAEL JON, lawyer; b. Rockville Centre, N.Y., Jan. 22, 1948; s. Meyer J. and Lillian (Gold) P.; m. Rosalind F. Schein, Jan. 26, 1969; children: Aaron, Alexander, Elias. BA summa cum laude, Yale U., 1969, JD, 1972. Bar: Calif. 1972, U.S. Dist. Ct. (no. dist.) Calif. 1972, U.S. Ct. Appeals (9th cir.) 1972. Assoc. McCutchen, Doyle, Brown & Enersen, San Francisco, 1972-79, ptnr., 1979—. Mem. ABA (vice chmn. subcom. on alternative dispute resolution, corp. counsel com., litigation sect.), Internat. Assn. Jewish Lawyers and Jurists (bd.govs. 1981—), Phi Beta Kappa. Federal civil litigation, State civil litigation. Home: 114 St Albans Rd Kensington CA 94708 Office: McCutchen Doyle Brown & Enersen 3 Embarcadero Ctr San Francisco CA 94111

PLITT, STEVEN, lawyer, insurance broker; b. N.Y.C., Sept. 15, 1956; s. Fred Walter and Alice (Smerak) P.; m. Kathryn Jo Plitt, Aug. 1, 1980; children: Jordan, Jennifer. BS in Polit. Sci. summa cum laude, with honors, Ariz. State U., 1979; JD with distinction, U. Ariz., 1982. Law clk. to presiding justice Ariz. Ct. Appeals, Phoenix, 1982-83; legis. aide banking and ins. com. Ariz. Ho. of Reps., Phoenix, 1979; assoc. Teilborg, Sanders & Parks P.C., Phoenix, 1983—. Mem. Ariz. Bar Assn., Maricopa County Bar Assn., Phoenix Assn. Def. Counsel, Nat. Order Of Barristers. Personal injury, Insurance, State civil litigation.

PLOTKA, RICHARD F., lawyer; b. Utica, N.Y., Sept. 5, 1935; s. Maxim Jay and Marian (LaPoten) P.; m. Laurinda Jane Hicks, Aug. 24, 1961; children—Richard Mark, Jeffrey Jay. A.B., Hamilton Coll., 1956; LL.B., Harvard U., 1959. Bar: N.Y. 1959, U.S. Dist. Ct. (so. and ea. dists.) N.Y. 1962; U.S. Ct. Appeals (2d cir.) 1962, U.S. Supreme Ct. 1963, Fla. 1981. Assoc. Alfred S. Koffler, Islip, N.Y., 1959-60; sole practice, Bay Shore, N.Y., 1961-63; ptnr. Koffler, Flower & Plotka, Islip, 1963-69, Flower & Plotka, Bay Shore, 1969—. Mem. legal com., adv. bd. Good Samaritan Hosp., West Islip, N.Y., 1978-85, mem. planning com., 1982-85; bd. dirs. Suffolk Hearing and Speech Ctr., Bay Shore, 1974—, L.I. Charities Found., Bay Shore, 1974—; mem. Fire Island Adv. Commn., Islip, 1969-79, chmn., 1973-79. Fellow Am. Acad. Matrimonial Lawyers; mem. Suffolk County Bar Assn. (chmn. civil rights com. 1968-69, chmn. med.-legal com. 1970-75, bd. dirs. 1975-78), N.Y. State Bar Assn. (family law com. 1980), Suffolk County Criminal Bar (v.p. 1969), N.Y. State Trial Lawyers Assn. Clubs: Southward Ho, Bay Shore Yacht, Le Club (N.Y.). State civil litigation, Family and matrimonial, Personal injury. Home: PO Box P-663 Bay Shore NY 11706 Office: Flower & Plotka 120 4th Ave Bay Shore NY 11706

PLOTKIN, LOREN H., lawyer; b. Bklyn., Feb. 8, 1943; s. Arthur and Betty Ann (Strugatz) P. B.A., Harpur Coll., SUNY-Binghamton, 1963; J.D., St. John's U., N.Y.C., 1966. Bar: N.Y. 1966, U.S. Dist. Ct. (so. and ea. dists.) N.Y. 1971, U.S. Tax Ct. 1976. Law asst. appellate div., first dept. N.Y. State Sup. Ct.; ptnr. Lans Feinberg & Cohen, N.Y.C., 1969-81; mem. Levine & Thall, P.C., N.Y.C., 1981-84, Thall and Plotkin, N.Y.C., 1984—; lectr. on entertainment law. Notes and comments editor St. John's U. Law Rev., 1965-66. Entertainment, Real property, General practice. Home: 83 Perry St New York NY 10014 Office: Thall and Plotkin 205 E 31st St New York NY 10016

PLOTNICK, CHARLES KEITH, lawyer, educator, author; b. Phila., Apr. 8, 1931; s. Benjamin and Gertrude (Jacobson) P.; m. Diane M. Needle, June 27, 1954; children—Steven L., Amy B. B.S., Temple U., 1953; LL.B., U. Pa., 1956. Bar: Pa. 1957. Sole practice, Phila., 1957-62; field atty. Office Chief Atty., VA, Phila., 1962-68; ptnr. Miller & Plotnick Norristown, Pa., 1968-73, Hurowitz & Plotnick, King of Prussia, Pa., 1973-83; prin. Charles K. Plotnick, P.C., 1983—; agt., div. mgr. Prudential Ins. Co., 1957-62; lectr. estate planning Grad. Sch. Bus. Adminstrn., now adj. prof. Recipient N.Y. Times award, 1952. Mem. ABA, Pa. Bar Assn., Montgomery County Bar Assn. (chmn. Law Day 1968-78, dir. 1974-77), Montgomery County Estate Planning Council (pres. 1973-74), Nat. Assn. Estate Planning Councils (co-chmn. nat. meeting 1973, regional v.p. 1974-80), C.L.U. Author: The Executor's Manual, 1986; contbr. articles on estate planning to profl. jours.; author: Die Rich, 1983; Get Rich, Stay Rich, 1984. Estate planning, Probate, Estate taxation. Office: Breyer Office Park York and Township Line Elkins Park PA 19117

PLOTNICK, ROBERT NATHAN, law librarian; b. Stamford, Conn., Nov. 21, 1931; s. Samuel and Miriam Bell (Silverman) P.; m. Martha Tieder; children: Seth, Adam, Scot. BA, U Bridgeport, 1953; JD, N.Y. Law Sch., 1956. Law librarian Conn. Library, Bridgeport, Milford and Litchfield, 1958—; librarian Stamford Law Library, 1958-85; asst. clk., dep. clk. Cir. Ct., Stamford, 1960-71; dir. continuing legal edn. U. Bridgeport Sch. Law, 1980-84, paralegal program Sacred Heart U., Bridgeport, 1979-80, Conn. Inst. Legal Studies, Stamford, 1984—; spl. cons. to County, N.Y.C., 1973-74; cons. New London Bar Assn., 1973; adj. prof. Quinnipiac Coll., New Haven, 1975. Author: Equal Employment Opportunity Commission Seminar, 1982. Mem. Am. Assn. Law Librarians (cert. 1969). Librarianship. Home: 40 Caprice Dr Stamford CT 06902 Office: Conn State Library 1061 Main St Bridgeport CT 06601

PLOTTEL, ROLAND, lawyer; b. N.Y.C., Oct. 1, 1934; s. Charles and Frances (Banner) P.; m. Jeanine Parisier, June 3, 1956; children—Claudia, Michael, Philip. B.A., Columbia U., 1955, LL.B., 1958, M.S. in E.E., 1964. Bar: N.Y. 1958, U.S. Patent Office 1962, U.S. Ct. Appeals (D.C. cir.) 1964, U.S. Supreme Ct. 1964. House counsel Radiotronix Communications Labs., N.Y.C., 1958-61; patent atty. Bendix Corp., Teterboro, N.J., 1961-64; internat. patent atty. Western Electric Co., N.Y.C., 1964-70; sole practice, N.Y.C., 1970-87 ; ptnr. Plottel & Roberts, 1987—; of counsel Frishauf, Holtz, Goodman & Woodward, N.Y.C.; lectr. patent law Practising Law Inst.; arbitrator Civil Ct., 1964—. Harlan Fiske Stone fellow. Mem. ABA, N.Y. County Lawyers Assn., Am. Intellectual Property Law Assn., N.Y. Patent Trademark and Copyright Law Assn., IEEE, Internat. Soc. Hybrid Microelectronics, Am. Arbitration Assn. (Service award). Club: City N.Y. Patent, Trademark and copyright, Antitrust. Home: 21 E 79th St New York NY 10021 Office: 30 Rockefeller Plaza New York NY 10112-0025

PLOUFF, THOMAS O'CONNOR, assistant U.S. attorney; b. Milw., Sept. 4, 1953; s. John Fleming and Anna Marie (O'Connor) P.; m. Patricia Lane Tusing, Sept. 11, 1982. BBA, U. Notre Dame, 1976, JD, 1979. Bar: Ind. 1979. Litigation atty. FTC, Washington, 1979-82; trial atty., tax div. U.S. Dept. Justice, Washington, 1982-84; asst. U.S. atty. U.S. Dept. Justice, South Bend, Ind., 1985—. Thomas J. White scholar, U. Notre Dame, 1979; named Outstanding Atty. of Tax Div., U.S. Dept. Justice, Washington, 198. Mem. ABA. Roman Catholic. Federal civil litigation, Criminal. Office: US Attys Office Dept Justice 204 S Main St South Bend IN 46601

PLOWMAN, JACK WESLEY, lawyer; b. Blairsville, Pa., Sept. 12, 1929; s. Ralph Waldo, Sr., and Ethel Beatrice (Nicely) P.; m. Barbara Ellen Brown, Apr. 5, 1952; children—Linda Ellen, Judith Lynn. A.B., U. Pitts., 1951, LL.B. with honors, 1956. Bar: Pa. 1956, U.S. Dist. Ct. (we. dist.) Pa. 1956, U.S. Ct. Appeals 1960, U.S. Supreme Ct. 1978. Assoc. Campbell, Houck & Thomas, Pitts., 1956-57; ptnr. Rose, Houston, Cooper & Schmidt, Pitts., 1957-63, Plowman & Spiegel, Pitts., 1963—; adj. prof. Duquesne U. Sch. Law, 1963-70, 83—. Editor-in-chief Pitts. Legal Jour., 1971-81, U. Pitts. Law Rev., 1955-56. Bd. dirs. Ward Home for Children, United Meth. Ch. Union, 1977-83, Wesley Inst., 1977-81; chancellor Western Pa. Ann. Conf. United Meth. Ch. Served to capt. USAF, 1951-53. Fellow Am. Bar Found., Am. Coll. Trial Lawyers; mem. ABA, Pa. Bar Assn., Allegheny County Bar Assn. (pres. 1982). Republican. Federal civil litigation, State civil litigation. Home: 1025 Lakemont Dr Pittsburgh PA 15243 Office: 925 Grant Bldg Pittsburgh PA 15219

PLUM, STEPHEN HAINES, IV, lawyer; b. N.Y.C., Jan. 31, 1957; s. Stephen Haines III and Elizabeth (Cox) P. BA with honors, U. Sussex, Brighton, Eng., 1978; cert., Coll. Law, London, 1982. Bar: N.Y. 1983, U.S. Dist. Ct. (so., ea. and no. dists.) N.Y. 1983. Assoc. Haight, Gardner, Poor & Havens, N.Y.C., 1982-86, Richards, O'Neil & Allegaert, N.Y.C., 1986—. Mem. ABA, Assn. of Bar of City of N.Y., Maritime Law Assn. Democrat. Banking, Commercial litigation, Contracts commercial. Office: Richards O'Neil & Allegaert 885 Third Ave New York NY 10020

PLUMLY, DANIEL HARP, lawyer; b. Barnesville, Ohio, May 1, 1953; s. Howard Max and Marjorie Ann (Harp) P.; m. Anita Reed, July 04, 1975; children: Kyle, Kathryn Cameron. Ba, Muskingum Coll., 1975; JD, Case

Western Res. Coll., 1978. Bar: U.S. Dist. Ct. (no. dist.) Ohio 1978, U.S. Ct. Appeals (6th cir.) 1979, U.S. Tax Ct. 1983, U.S. Supreme Ct. 1983. Atty. Critchfield, Critchfield & Johnston, Wooster, Ohio, 1978—; bd. dirs. Environ. Brine Services, Inc., Wooster, 1st Fed. Savs. and Loan Assn., Wooster, The Will-Burt Co., Orrville, Ohio, 1986—. Bd. trustees Goodwill Industries Wayne County, Inc., Wooster, 1979—, Just Say No of Wooster, Inc. Mem. ABA, Ohio State Bar Assn., Wayne County Bar Assn., Order of Coif. Republican. Methodist. Avocations: golf, tennis, skiing, bicycling. General corporate, Labor, Securities. Office: Critchfield Critchfield et al PO Box 488 Wooster OH 44691

PLUMP, LESLIE Z., lawyer; b. Bridgeport, Conn., Aug. 6, 1934; s. Meyer Howard and Norma (Terry) P.; m. Ruth S. Shapiro, June 16, 1957; children—Steven, Jennifer, Andrew, Karen, Kathy. A.B., Cornell U., 1955; J.D., Columbia U., 1958. Bar: N.Y. 1959, U.S. Dist. Ct. (ea. dist.) N.Y. 1960, U.S. Dist. Ct. (so. dist.) N.Y. 1960, U.S. Ct. Mil. Appeals 1979, U.S. Ct. Claims 1979, U.S. Supreme Ct. 1979. Real estate csl. Citibank, N.A., N.Y.C., 1962—; sole practice, N.Y.C., 1976—; csl. Glen Cove Community Devel. Agy. and Indsl. Devel. Agy., 1980-83. Mem. Glen Cove (N.Y.) Civil Service Grievance Commn., 1963-64, Glen Cove Capital Budget Planning Commn., 1974-75; mem. Glen Cove Community Devel. Agy., 1984-85; pres. Roxbury (Glen Cove) Civic Assn., 1965; v.p., trustee Sci. Mus. L.I., 1982; mem. secondary sch. com. Cornell U. REal Estate Council; trustee North Country Reform Temple, 1984; active Boy Scouts Am., Glen Cove Jr. Baseball Assn. Mem. Nassau County Bar Assn., Westchester Bar Assn., N.Y. Bar Assn., ABA, Nat. Am. Arbitration Assn. (nat. panel arbitrators). Banking, Real property. Office: 22 E 40th St New York NY 10016

PLUNKETT, ALLEN LEWIN, lawyer; b. Quanah, Tex., Nov. 26, 1941; s. Lewin and Ione (Smith) P.; m. Pam Plunkett, July 10, 1965; children: Jennifer Jan, David Lewin. BA, U. Tex., 1964; LLB, U.Tex., 1965. Bar: Tex. 1965, U.S. Dist. Ct. (we. dist.) Tex. 1966, U.S. Ct. Appeals (5th cir.) 1968. Assoc. Dayton G. Wiley, San Antonio, 1965-67, Wiley, Thornton & Plumb, San Antonio, 1967-69; ptnr. Wiley, Plumb & Plunkett, San Antonio, 1969-70, Wiley, Gibson & Allen, San Antonio, 1970-79, Plunkett, Gibson & Allen, San Antonio, 1979—. Fellow Tex. Bar Found., San Antonio Bar Found.; mem. Am. Bd. Trial Advs. (cert.), Tex. Assn. Def. Counsel (bd. dirs. 1979-80, v.p. 1983-85, 85-86). Republican. Methodist. Lodge: Kiwanis (local pres. 1979-80). Insurance, Federal civil litigation, State civil litigation. Home: Rt 3 Box 3307 Boerne TX 78006 Office: Plunkett Gibson & Allen PO Box BH002 San Antonio TX 78201

PLUNKETT, PAUL EDWARD, judge; b. Boston, July 9, 1935; s. Paul M. and Mary Cecilia (Erbacher) P.; m. Martha Milan, Sept. 30, 1958; children: Paul Scott, Steven, Andrew, Kevin. B.A., Harvard U., 1957, LL.B., 1960. Asst. U.S. atty. U.S. Atty.'s Office, Chgo., 1963-66; ptnr. Plunkett Nisin et al, Chgo., 1966-78, Mayer Brown & Platt, Chgo., 1978-83; judge U.S. Dist. Ct. (no. dist.) Ill., Chgo., 1983—; adj. faculty John Marshall Law Sch., Chgo., 1964-76, 82—, Loyola U. Law Sch., Chgo., 1977-82. Mem. Fed. Bar Assn. Clubs: Legal, Law, Union League (Chgo.). Judicial administration. Office: US Courthouse 219 S Dearborn Chicago IL 60604 *

PLUSS, STEWART JAY, lawyer; b. Denver, Mar. 23, 1951; s. Norman and Barbara (Miller) P. BA, U. Denver, 1974, JD, 1977; postgrad., Northwestern U., 1969-70, 71-72, U. Colo., 1970-71. Bar: Colo., U.S. Dist. Ct. Colo., U.S. Ct. Appeals (10th cir.). Sole practice Denver, 1977-80; sales advisor Longmont (Colo.) Foods Co., 1980-83; investor Denver, 1983-85; assoc. Cogswell & Wheels, Denver, 1985—. Mem. Anti-defamation League. Mem. ABA, Colo. Bar Assn., Denver Bar Assn. Jewish. Club: Green Gables Country. Banking, Contracts commercial, Real property. Home: 2880 S Locust St #700 N Denver CO 80222 Office: Cogswell & Wheels 1700 Lincoln St Suite 3500 Denver CO 80302

PLUYMEN, BERT W., lawyer; b. Hoensbroek, Netherlands, Oct. 3, 1948; s. Harry and Paula Pluymen. BA, Rice U., 1971; JD with honors, U. Tex.-Austin, 1974. Bar: Tex. 1974, U.S. Dist. Ct. (ea. dist.) Tex. 1976, U.S. Dist. Ct. (we. dist.) Tex. 1978, U.S. Supreme Ct. 1978, U.S. Ct. Appeals (5th cir.) 1974, U.S. Ct. Appeals (11th cir.) 1982, U.S. Dist. Ct. (no. dist.) Tex. 1986. Asst. atty. gen. State of Tex., 1974-78; assoc. Byrd, Davis & Eisenberg, Austin, 1978-81, ptnr., 1982; ptnr. Pluymen & Bayer, Austin, 1982—. Bd. dirs., v.p. Austin Dem. Forum, 1987—; bd. dirs. Travis Assn. for the Blind, 1986—, Tex. Consumer Assn. Fellow Tex. Bar Found.; mem. Tex. Young Lawyers Assn. (bd. dirs. 1983-84), Austin Young Lawyers Assn. (pres. 1981-82, named outstanding young lawyer 1985), Travis County Bar Assn. (bd. dirs. 1982-83), Assn. Trial Lawyers Am., Tex. Trial Lawyers Assn. (assoc. bd. dirs. 1980-83), Order of Coif. Personal injury, Workers' compensation. Office: Pluymen & Bayer 8140 Mopac Westpark 2 Suite 150 Austin TX 78759

PLYLER, CRANFORD OLIVER, III, lawyer; b. Thomasville, N.C., Sept. 12, 1957; s. Cranford O. Jr. and Ruth (Hull) P.; m. Pamela Jean Lanning, July 26, 1980. BA, U. N.C., 1979, JD, 1982. Bar: Tex. 1982, N.C. 1984. Assoc. Hinkle, COx, Eaton, Coffield & Hensley, Midland, Tex., 1982-84, Fisher, Fisher & Gayle, High Point, N.C., 1984-85; sole practice Thomasville, 1985—. Republican. Methodist. Lodge: Lions. Real property, State civil litigation, Probate. Office: 50 E Main Suite 107 Thomasville NC 27360

POCHUCHA, LARRY ARTHUR, lawyer; b. Akron, Ohio, Sept. 7, 1949; s. Nicholas Samuel and Lois Jean (Belcher) P.; mm. Margaret O'Brien Boland, Apr. 3, 1971; 1 child, Laurel Alexandra. Student, U. N.C., 1967-69; BA in Polit. Sci., U. Richmond, 1972, JD, 1976. Bar: Va. 1976, U.S. Dist. Ct. (ea. dist.) Va. 1976, U.S. Ct. Appeals (4th cir.) 1977. Ptnr. Collins & Pochucha, Richmond, Va., 1977-85, Smith & Pochucha, Richmond, 1985—; chmn. criminal justice com. young lawyers sect. Va. State Bar, 1978-81, chmn. reducing ct. costs and delays 1984—, mem. family law and criminal law sects. Mem. Richmond Ba Assn., Assn. Trial Lawyers Am., Va. Trial Lawyers Assn., Richmond Criminal Bar Assn. Avocations: golf, snowskiing. State civil litigation, Criminal, Family and matrimonial. Home: 4300 New Kent Ave Richmond VA 23225 Office: Smith & Pochucha 17 W Cary St PO Box 8742 Richmond VA 23220-8792

PODBERESKY, SAMUEL, lawyer; b. Cremona, Italy, Mar. 16, 1946; came to U.S., 1947; s. Noah and Mina (Milikowsky) P.; m. Rosita Brenda Rubinstein, March 8, 1970; children: Daniel J., Michael J. BS in Aeronautical Engrig., U. Md., 1967; JD, U. Md., Balt., 1971. Bar: Md. 1972. Flight test engr. Vertol div. Boeing Co., Phila., 1967-68; regulatory atty. FAA, Washington, 1971-78; dep. asst. gen. counsel U.S. Dept. Transp., Washington, 1978-86, asst. gen. counsel aviation enforcement and proceedings, 1986—. Administrative and regulatory, Antitrust, Aviation. Office: US Dept Transp 400 7th St SW Washington DC 20590

PODELL, ALBERT N., lawyer; b. Bklyn., Feb. 25, 1937; s. Hyman Eli and Dorothy Ruth (Podbersky) P.; m. Stephanie Braxton, Oct. 12, 1969 (div. Dec. 1973). BA, Cornell U., 1958; postgrad., U. Chgo., 1958-60; JD, NYU, 1976. Bar: N.Y. 1978, U.S. Dist. Ct. (so. and ea. dists.) N.Y. 1980, U.S. Ct. Appeals (2d cir.) 1981, U.S. Supreme Ct. 1981, U.S. Ct. Appeals (fed. cir.) 1985. Assoc. Rosenman, Colin, Freund, Lewis & Cohen, N.Y.C., 1976-79, Fried, Frank, Harris, Shriver & Jacobson, N.Y.C., 1979-82, Milgrim, Thomajan, Jacobs & Lee, N.Y.C., 1982-84, Schekter, Rishty & Goldstein, N.Y.C., 1985—. Co-author: Who Needa A Road, 1967; legis. corr. N.Y. Law Jour., 1974-75; contbr. numerous articles to profl. jours. Candidate for N.Y. State Assembly Dems., N.Y.C., 1976; mem. The Nature Conservancy, 1983—; assoc. dir. Citizens Union, N.Y.C., 1972-74; rep. legis. Common Cause, 1974-75; trustee Jean Cocteau Repertory Theatre, 1985—. Served to sgt. U.S. Army, 1960-61. Mem. ABA, N.Y. State Bar Assn., Cornell U. Alumni Assn. (v.p. 1968—). Lodge: B'nai B'rith (v.p. cinema lodge 1969-72). Federal civil litigation, State civil litigation, Contracts commercial. Home: 110 Sullivan St New York NY 10012 Office: Schekter Rishty & Goldstein 10 Columbus Circle New York NY 10019

PODLEWSKI, JOSEPH ROMAN, JR., lawyer; b. Chgo., Jan. 8, 1953; s. Joseph Roman Sr. and Marie Catherine (Fischer) P.; m. Heidi Elizabeth Hanson, May 3, 1986. BA, No. Ill. U., 1975; JD, IIT, 1978. Bar: Ill. 1978, U.S. Dist. Ct. (no. dist.) Ill. 1978. Law clk. to presiding justice Ill. Appellate Ct., Ladd, Ill., 1978-81; atty., tech. advisor Ill. EPA, Springfield, 1981-85, Maywood, 1985—. Mem. ABA, Ill. Bar Assn., Chgo. Bar Assn., Phi Kappa Phi, Delta Theta Phi. Roman Catholic. Environment, Administrative and regulatory, State civil litigation. Home: 4228 Oak Brookfield IL 60513 Office: Ill EPA 1701 S 1st Ave Maywood IL 60153

PODRECCA, ADOLFO AUGUSTO, lawyer; b. Rome, Oct. 6, 1946; came to U.S., 1957; s. Guido Italico and Elsa (Paoloni) P.; m. Kathy Ann Crabbe, June 21, 1969; children: Michel, Mia, Gina. BA, S.W. Mo. State U., 1969; MA, U. Fla., 1971, JD with honors, 1973. Bar: Fla. 1973, U.S. Dist. Ct. (so. dist.) Fla. 1974. Assoc. Pallot, Stern et al, Miami, Fla., 1974-79, Goodhart and Rosner, Miami, 1979-85, Fazio, Dason, DiSalvo and Cannon, and Fazio, Dawson and DiSalvo, Ft. Lauderdale, Fla., 1985—. Author: Italians in Argentina, 1971. Served to 2d. lt. U.S. Army, 1973. Mem. ABA, Fla. Bar Assn., Dante Alighiery Soc. (v.p. 1980-85), Order Sons of Italy (trustee 1980-81), Italian Found., Unity Neighborliness Integrity Charity Opportunity, Italian Am. C. of C. Republican. Roman Catholic. Avocations: gardening, boating, scuba and skin diving. Personal injury, Insurance, State civil litigation. Home: 20530 SW 50 Pl Fort Lauderdale FL 33332 Office: Fazio Dawson DiSalvo & Cannon 633 S Andrews Ave Fort Lauderdale FL 33301

POE, DOUGLAS ALLAN, lawyer; b. Chicago Heights, Ill., Nov. 14, 1942; s. Armand Leslie and Marcella Elizabeth (Grote) P. BA, DePauw U., 1964; JD, Duke U., 1967; LLM, Yale U., 1968. Bar: Ill. 1967, U.S. Ct. Appeals (4th cir.) 1968, U.S. Supreme Ct. 1972, U.S. Ct. Appeals (7th cir.) 1973. Clk. U.S. Ct. Appeals (4th cir.), Balt., 1968-69; law clk. to Chief Justice Warren E. Burger U.S. Supreme Ct., 1969, to Hon. William J. Brennan, Jr., 1970; assoc. Mayer, Brown & Platt, Chgo., 1970-74, ptnr., 1974—. Mem. ABA, Am. Law Inst., Chgo. Council Lawyers, Order of Coif. Federal civil litigation, Antitrust. Office: Mayer Brown and Platt 190 S LaSalle St Chicago IL 60603

POE, FRANKLIN ANDREW, lawyer; b. Flint, Mich., Nov. 27, 1954; s. James Harold and Virginia (Duncan) P.; m. Cynthia Lynn Yeaster, June 19, 1976; 1 child, Katherine. BA, Alma Coll., 1977; JD, Cornell U., 1980. Bar: Maine 1980, U.S. Dist. Ct. Maine 1980. Assoc. Preti, Flaherty & Beliveau, Rumford, Maine, 1980-86, Perkins & Perkins, Boothbay Harbor, Maine, 1986—. Chmn. Rumford Community Ctr., 1980-84; mem. Rumford Fin. Com., 1981-84. Mem. ABA, Maine Bar Assn., Lincoln County Bar Assn., Assn. Trial Lawyers Am., Maine Trial Lawyers Assn. Republican. Methodist. Lodges: Kiwanis (bd. dirs. Rumford), Rotary, Elks. Avocations: sports, history, family. State civil litigation, Probate, Real property. Office: Perkins & Perkins 27 School St Boothbay Harbor ME 04538

POE, LUKE HARVEY, JR., lawyer; b. Richmond, Va., Jan. 29, 1916; s. Luke Harvey and Alice Colburn (Reddy) P. B.S. in Math, U. Va., 1938, J.D., 1941; postgrad. (Rhodes scholar), Oxford (Eng.) U., 1939; D.Phil., Christ Ch., 1957. Bar: Va. bar 1940, D.C. bar and D.C. Ct. Appeals bar 1967, U.S. Supreme Ct. bar 1969, Md. bar 1974. Asso. firm Cravath, Swaine & Moore, N.Y.C., 1941-42; tutor St. John's Coll., Annapolis, Md., 1946-50; asst. dean St. John's Coll., 1947-49, tenure tutor, 1953-60, dir. physics and chemistry lab., 1959-60; asst. chmn. Nat. Citizens Com. for Kennedy and Johnson and chmn. Citizens Com., Pres.'s Inaugural Com., 1960-61; asst. to chmn. bd. Aerojet-Gen. Corp., El Monte, Calif., 1961-63; div. pres. Internat. Tech. Assistance and Devel. Co., Washington, 1963-66; partner firm Howard, Poe & Bastian, Washington, 1966-83; sole practice 1983—; bd. dirs. First Am. Bank of Md.; cons. Dept. Transp., Dept. State; lectr. in field; guest panelist Panel on Sci. and Tech. of Com. on Sci. and Astronautics, U.S. Ho. of Reps., 1970; pres. bd. dirs. Watergate East, Inc., 1976-79. Author: The Combat History of the Battleship U.S.S. Mississippi, 1947; (with others) lab. manuals Einstein's Theory of Relativity, 1957, Electro-Magnetic Theory, 1959; editor: (with others) Va. Mag, 1936-38, U. Va. Law Rev, 1940-41. Chmn. Annapolis Bd. Zoning Appeals, 1966-75; mem. Annapolis Mayor's Task Force, 1967-74, Md. Gov's Commn. on Capital City, 1970-76. Served to lt. comdr. USNR, 1942-46. Mem. Am. Law Inst., AAUP, Raven Soc. (pres.), Soc. Cin., Phi Beta Kappa, Phi Delta Phi. Episcopalian. Clubs: Metropolitan (Washington); Travellers (London); Brook (N.Y.C.); New Providence (Annapolis); Vincent's (Oxford). General corporate, General practice, Private international. Home: 139 Market St Annapolis MD 21401 also: 2500 Virginia Ave NW Washington DC 20037 Office: 1701 Pennsylvania Ave NW Washington DC 20006

POEHNER, GEORGE RICHARD, lawyer; b. Bakersfield, Calif., Oct. 11, 1938; s. George Edwin and Kathryn Elaine (Ray) P.; m. Charlotte Catherine Lindsay, Jan. 28, 1961; children—Laura Louise, Lisa Lynn. B.A., U. Calif.-Berkeley, 1965, J.D., 1968. Bar: D.C. 1969, U.S. Ct. Appeals (D.C. cir.) 1969, U.S. Ct. Appeals (5th and 9th cirs.) 1971, U.S. Ct. Appeals (4th and 10th cirs.) 1972, U.S. Supreme Ct. 1972, U.S. Ct. Appeals (2d cir.) 1974, Tex. 1976, U.S. Ct. Appeals (11th cir.) 1981. Assoc., Covington & Burling, Washington, 1968-75; ptnr. Coke & Coke, Dallas, 1976-82, Moore & Peterson, 1982—. Mem. ABA (antitrust, adminstrv. law, litigation sects.), State Bar Tex. (antitrust, litigation sects.), Dallas Bar Assn. (antitrust sect.), Am. Law Inst. Democrat. Roman Catholic. Antitrust, Federal civil litigation, State civil litigation. Home: 1132 Edith Circle Richardson TX 75080 Office: Moore & Peterson 2800 First City Center Dallas TX 75201

POFF, RICHARD HARDING, justice; b. Radford, Va., Oct. 19, 1923; s. Beecher David and Irene Louise (Nunley) P.; m. Jo Ann R. Topper, June 24, 1945 (dec. Jan. 1978); children: Rebecca, Thomas, Richard Harding; m. Jean Murphy, Oct. 26, 1980. Student, Roanoke Coll., 1941-43; LL.B., U. Va., 1948, LL.D., 1969. Bar: Va. 1947. Partner law firm Dalton, Poff, Turk & Stone, Radford, 1949-70; mem. 83d-92d congresses, 6th Dist. Va.; justice Supreme Ct. Va., 1972—; Vice chmn. Nat. Commn. on Reform Fed. Crime Laws; chmn. Republican Task Force on Crime; sec. Rep. Conf., House Rep. Leadership. Named Va.'s Outstanding Young Man of Year Jr. C. of C., 1954; recipient Nat. Collegiate Athletic Assn. award, 1966, Roanoke Coll. medal, 1967, Distinguished Virginian award Va. Dist. Exchange Clubs, 1970, Presdl. certificate of appreciation for legislative contbn., 1971, legislative citation Assn. Fed. Investigators, 1969, Thomas Jefferson Pub. Sesquicentennial award U. Va., 1969, Japanese Am. Citizens League award, 1972; named to Hall of Fame, Am. Legion Boys State, 1985. Mem. ABA, Va. Bar Assn., Am. Judicature Soc., V.F.W., Am. Legion, Pi Kappa Phi, Sigma Nu Phi. Clubs: Mason, Moose, Lion. Jurisprudence. Office: Supreme Ct Bldg Richmond VA 23210

POFFENBERGER, RICHARD LEE, lawyer; b. Des Moines, June 2, 1935; s. Lee L. and Alice L. (Nelson) P.; m. Virginia Joy, June 27, 1957; children: Elizabeth Ann, Thomas Richard, James Morgan. BBA, Drake U., 1957, JD, 1958. Bar: Iowa 1958, U.S. Dist. Ct. (no. and so. dist.) Iowa 1958, U.S. Ct. Appeals (8th cir.) 1977, U.S. Supreme Ct. 1977. Dir. dept. health ins. State of Iowa, Des Moines, 1958-59; ptnr. Poffenberger & Joy, Perry, Iowa, 1959—; atty. Dallas County, Adel, Iowa, 1970-72; commr. airport City of Perry, Iowa, 1968-76; pres. Perry Industries, Inc., 1985-87. Chmn. zoning commn. City of Perry, 1980—; chmn. adminstrn. United Meth. Ch., Perry, 1980-83. Mem. ABA, Iowa Bar Assn. (chmn. Citizenship award), Dallas County Bar Assn.(sec. 1960-62, pres. 1968), Assn. Trial Lawyers Am., Iowa Trial Lawyers Assn. (founding mem.), Perry C. of C. (bd. dirs. 1963). Club: Perry Golf and Country. Lodge: Kiwanis (pres. 1971), Elks. Avocations: sailing, golf. General practice, Estate taxation, Personal injury. Home: 1816 Willis Ave Perry IA 50220 Office: Poffenberger & Joy 1215 Warford Ave Perry IA 50220

POGREBIN, BERTRAND B., lawyer; b. Bklyn., Apr. 10, 1934; s. Abraham and Esther P.; m. Letty Cottin; children—Abagail, Robin, David. A.B., Rutgers U., 1955; LL.B., Harvard U., 1958. Bar: N.Y. 1959, U.S. Dist. Ct. (ea. dist.) N.Y. 1963, U.S. Dist. Ct. (so. dist.) N.Y. 1963, U.S. Ct. Appeals (2d cir.) 1965, U.S. Ct. Appeals (4th cir.) 1965, U.S. Ct. Appeals (6th cir.) 1970. Mem. Rains & Pogrebin, P.C., N.Y.C., 1959—; adj. prof. law NYU, 1975—, Hofstra Law Sch., 1980-82; vis. lectr. Yale Law Sch., 1983. Bd. dirs. Fund for New Priorities in Am.; exec. bd. Emergency Civil Liberties Com. Mem. ABA, N.Y.C. Bar Assn., Nassau County Bar Assn., Suffolk County Bar Assn., Indsl. Relations Research Assn. Administrative and regulatory, Legal education, Labor. Home: 33 W 67th St New York NY 10023 Office: 210 Old Country Rd Mineola NY 11501 also: 425 Park Ave New York NY 10022

POGUE, RICHARD WELCH, lawyer; b. Cambridge, Mass., Apr. 26, 1928; s. Lloyd Welch and Mary Ellen (Edgerton) P.; m. Patricia Ruth Raney, July 10, 1954; children—Mark, Tracy, David. B.A., Cornell U., 1950; J.D., Mich. Law Sch., 1953. Bar: Mich. 1953, Ohio 1957, U.S. Dist. Ct. (no. dist.) Ohio 1960, U.S. Ct. Appeals (6th cir.) 1972, U.S. Ct. Appeals (D.C. and 9th cirs.) 1979. Assoc. Jones, Day, Reavis & Pogue, Cleve., 1957-60, ptnr., 1961—, mng. ptnr., 1985—; bd. dirs. AmeriTrust Corp., Cleve., Environ. Treatment and Techs. Corp., Findlay, Ohio, Ohio Bell Telephone Co., Cleve., Redland Corp., San Antonio, Rotek Inc., Aurora, Ohio. Chmn. Greater Cleve. Roundtable, 1981-86; mem. Adminstrv. Conf. U.S., 1974-80; chmn. Cleve. Ballet, 1983-85; chmn. United Negro Coll. Fund, Cleve., 1979. Served to capt. U.S. Army, 1954-57. Recipient Outstanding Alumnus award U. Mich. Club, Cleve., 1983. Mem. ABA (chmn. antitrust sect. 1983-84), Ohio State Bar Assn. (chmn. antitrust sect. 1969-73). Chmn. Cleve. Found., 1985—; trustee Univ. Hosps., 1976—. Republican. Mem. United Ch. of Christ. Clubs: Calif. (Los Angeles); Clevelander, Union (Cleve.); Metropolitan (Washington), Links (N.Y.C.). Antitrust. Office: Jones Day Reavis & Pogue North Point 901 Lakeside Ave Cleveland OH 44114

POHL, MARK RONALD, lawyer; b. Buffalo, Aug. 24, 1954; s. Edward Robert and Ruth Louise (Feigensohn) P. BA, SUNY, Fredonia, 1976; JD, George Washington U., 1979. Bar: D.C. 1980, Va. 1980, U.S. Dist. Ct. D.C. 1980, U.S. Ct. Appeals (4th cir.) 1980, U.S. Tax Ct. 1981, U.S. Ct. Appeals (D.C. cir.) 1981, U.S. Ct. Appeals (fed. cir.) 1982, U.S. Dist. Ct. (ea. dist.) Va. 1985, U.S. Dist. Ct. Md. 1985, U.S. Supreme Ct. 1986. Editor tax div. Hoops & Hudson P.C., Washington, 1979-80; atty. contract appeals bd. U.S. Dept. Transp., Washington, 1980-82; sole practice Washington, 1982-83; asst. gen. counsel Washington Met. Area Transit Authority, 1983—; lectr. U. Md., College Park, 1985—. Mem. ABA, Phi Alpha Delta. Republican. Jewish. Lodge: B'nai B'rith. Avocation: bowling. Federal civil litigation, Pension, profit-sharing, and employee benefits, Government contracts and claims. Home: 945 S Buchanan St #77 Arlington VA 22204 Office: Washington Met Transit Authority 600 5th St NW Office Gen Counsel Washington DC 20001

POHORELSKY, VIKTOR VACLAV, lawyer; b. Ludwigsburg, Fed. Republic Germany, Mar. 15, 1949; came to U.S. 1950; s. Evzen and Jana (Pouckova) P.; m. Lillian Louise Bayer, Feb. 26, 1977; children: Nikolai Evzen, Andrei Jan. BA, Tulane U., 1971, JD summa cum laude, 1980. Bar: N.Y. 1982, U.S. Dist. Ct. (so. and ea. dists.) N.Y. 1982, U.S. Ct. Appeals (2d cir.) 1985. Law clk. to presiding justice U.S. Dist. Ct. (we. dist.) La., Lake Charles, 1980, U.S. Ct. Appeals (5th cir.), New Orleans, 1980-81; assoc. Debevoise & Plimpton, N.Y.C., 1981-84; asst. U.S. atty. So. Dist. N.Y., N.Y.C., 1984—. Editor in chief Tulane Law Rev., 1979-80. Mem. Order of Coif. Democrat. Avocations: bicycling, snow skiing, baseball, piano. Criminal, Labor, Federal civil litigation. Office: US Atty's Office One St Andrew's Plaza New York NY 10007

POHREN, EDWARD FRANCIS, lawyer; b. Massapequa, N.Y., Sept. 1, 1954; s. Joseph A. Pohren and Grace M. (Lamb) Wagner; m. Elaine Joyce Schoenberger, July 23, 1977; children: Jessica, Matthew. BA, Seton Hall U., 1976; JD, Creighton U., 1979. Bar: Nebr. 1979, U.S. Dist. Ct. Nebr. 1979, U.S. Ct. Appeals (8th cir.) 1982. Assoc. Dwyer, O'Leary & Martin P.C., Omaha, Nebr., 1979-83; ptnr. Dwyer, Pohren, Wood, Heavey & Grimm, Omaha, 1983—. Bd. dirs. Nebr. Leadership Seminar, Inc., Omaha, 1983—. Named one of Outstanding Young Men in Am., 1982, 84, 86. Mem. ABA, Assn. Trial Lawyers Am., Nebr. Bar Assn., Omaha Bar Assn., Nebr. Assn. Trial Attys., Omaha Jaycees (bd. dirs. 1979-83). Republican. Roman Catholic. Federal civil litigation, State civil litigation, Personal injury. Home: 5104 Lafayette Ave Omaha NE 68132 Office: Dwyer Pohren Wood Heavey & Grimm 1823 Harney St Suite 300 Omaha NE 68102

POINTER, SAM CLYDE, JR., judge; b. Birmingham, Ala., Nov. 15, 1934; s. Sam Clyde and Elizabeth Inzer (Brown) P.; m. Paula Purse, Oct. 18, 1958; children: Minge, Sam Clyde III. A.B., Vanderbilt U., 1955; J.D., U. Ala., 1957; LL.M., NYU, 1958. Bar: Ala. 1957. Partner Brown, Pointer & Pointer, 1958-70; judge U.S. Dist. Ct. No. Dist. Ala., Birmingham, 1970—, (Temp. Emergency Ct. Appeals), 1980—; mem. (Jud. Panel Multi-dist. Litigation), 1980—. Bd. editors: Manual for Complex Litigation, 1979—. Bd. dirs. Ala. Found. Hearing and Speech, 1965-70, Vol. Bur. Greater Birmingham, 1966-72; trustee Crippled Children's Clinic, 1967-72. Mem. Am., Ala., Birmingham bar assns., Am. Law Inst., Farrah Order of Jurisprudence, Phi Beta Kappa. Episcopalian. Jurisprudence. Office: 138 Federal Courthouse Birmingham AL 35203

POIRRIER, MICHAEL JOSEPH, lawyer; b. Lutcher, La., Mar. 6, 1951; s. Ewell Pierre and Georgina (Bourgeois) P.; m. Pamela Ann St. Pierre, Jan. 6, 1973; children: Celeste, Andrea, Kristen. BS in Fin., La. State U., 1973, JD, 1976. Bar: La. 1976, U.S. Dist. Ct. (mid. and ea. dists.) La. 1978. Ptnr. Poirrier & Falterman, Pierre Part, La., 1976—; dir. juvenile probation Assumption Parish Cts., Napoleonville, La., 1977—. Pres. Pierre Part/Belle River Bus. Group, 1980-82, 84. Mem. ABA, La. Bar Assn. (ho. of dels. 1983—), Assumption Bar Assn. (sec., treas. 1985, v.p. 1986, pres. 1987), 23d Jud. Dist. Ct. Bar Assn. (pres. 1986), Jaycees. Democrat. Roman Catholic. Personal injury, Real property, Family and matrimonial. Home: 101 Kirk St Pierre Part LA 70339 Office: Poirrier & Falterman 101 Gerald St Pierre Part LA 70339

POJANOWSKI, JOSEPH A., III, lawyer; b. Paterson, N.J., Oct. 1, 1948; s. Joseph Adolph and Anne (Sulka) P.; m. Mary Alice Glueck, July 8, 1972; children—Allison, Jeffrey, Elizabeth. B.A., St. Michael's Coll., Winooski (Vt.), 1970; J.D., St. Louis U., 1973; student Loyola U., Rome Ctr., 1968. Bar: N.J. 1973, U.S. Dist. Ct. N.J. 1973, U.S. Supreme Ct. 1983. City atty., City of Passaic, N.J., 1977-82; ptnr. Davies, Davies, Pojanowski & Sandberg, Paterson, 1975-84; sole practice, Clifton, N.J., 1984—. Mcpl. chmn. Passaic City Rep. Com., 1973-79; mem. N.J. State Rep. Com., 1981-85. Mem. Passaic County Bar Assn., N.J. State Bar Assn. Roman Catholic. Club: Pennington, Upper Montclair Coutry. Local government, Real property, Contracts commercial. Home: 44 S Parkway Clifton NJ 07014 Office: 871 Allwood Rd Clifton NJ 07012

POKOTILOW, MANNY D., lawyer; b. Paterson, N.J., June 26, 1938; s. Samuel Morris and Ruth (Fuchs) P.; children—Mali, Mona, Charyse, Andrew; m. Dorothy K. Phillips, June 23, 1985. B.E.E., Newark Coll. Engring., 1960; LL.B., Am. U., 1964. Bar: Pa. Examiner U.S. Patent Office, Washington, 1960-64; ptnr. Caesar, Rivise, Bernstein, Cohen & Pokotilow Ltd., Phila., 1965—; lectr., expert witness on protection of computer software, patents, trademarks, trade secrets and copyrights; faculty Temple U. Sch. Law, 1985—. Vol. Support Ctr. for Child Advocates, Phila., 1979—; dir., organizer Phila. Bar-Diabetes 10k Race, Phila., 1980—, Packard Press Road Run Grand Prix, 1986. Recipient Superior Performance award U.S. Patent Office, 1964. Mem. ABA, Assn. Trial Lawyers Am., Phila. Bar Assn. (bd. govs. 1982-84, chmn. sports and recreation com. 1977—), Phila. Patent Law Assn. (bd. govs. 1982-84, chmn. fed. practice and procedure com. 1983—), Phila. Trial Lawyers (chmn. fed. cts. com. 1986—), Lawyers Club Phila. (bd. govs. 1984—), IEEE, Pa. Trial Lawyers, Tau Epsilon Rho (vice chancellor Phila. grad. chpt. 1986—). Patent, Trademark and copyright, Federal civil litigation. Office: Caesar Rivise Bernstein et al 21 S 12th St Philadelphia PA 19107

POLAK, WERNER L., lawyer; b. Bremen, Germany, May 19, 1936; came to U.S., 1946, naturalized, 1955; s. Ludwig and Hilde (Schultz) P.; m. Evelyn F. Ruhmann, June 21, 1959; children—Douglas H., Deborah L. B.A., Columbia U., 1960, LL.B., 1963. Bar: N.Y. 1963. Assoc., Shearman & Sterling, N.Y.C., 1963-72, ptnr., 1972—. Served with U.S. Army, 1954-56. Mem. ABA (standing com. for continuing edn. of the bar). Federal civil litigation, State civil litigation. Office: Shearman & Sterling 53 Wall St New York NY 10005

POLAKAS, JOHN, lawyer; b. Queens, N.Y., Dec. 7, 1954; s. Anthony Joseph and Martha (Rugala) P. BA magna cum laude, CUNY, Queens, 1976; postgrad., Temple U., 1976-77; JD, Bklyn. Law Sch., 1981. Bar: N.Y. 1982, U.S. Dist. Ct. (so. and ea. dists.) N.Y. 1984. Atty. Fgn. Trans. Corp., N.Y.C., 1982-84; assoc. Becker, Goldstein & Graff, N.Y.C., 1984-85; sole practice Bklyn., 1982—; counsel Dickstein & Fabricant, N.Y.C., 1986—; counsel Polakas Fund, Bklyn., 1982—; v.p., producer Victory Internat.

Productions, Inc., N.Y.C., 1985—. Assoc. producer (music film) It's Time, 1985; author: Economic Sanctions. N.Y. State Regents Scholar, 1972. Mem. ABA. Avocations: cinema, racquet sports, music. State civil litigation, Contracts commercial, Entertainment. Home and Office: 218 Berry St Brooklyn NY 11211

POLAN, DAVID JAY, television company executive, lawyer; b. Chgo., Feb. 16, 1951; s. Julius and Jeanne Warsaw (Fox) P.; m. Terri Susan Lapin, Aug. 3, 1980; children—Adam Michael, Daniel Jacob. B.A., U. Ill., 1972; J.D., John Marshall Law Sch., Chgo., 1975. Bar: Ill. 1975, U.S. Dist. Ct. (no. dist.) Ill. 1975, U.S. Ct. Appeals (7th cir.) 1976. Atty., Pritzker & Glass, Ltd., Chgo., 1975-78, Barnett, Ettinger, Glass, Berkson & Braverman, Chgo., 1978-79; gen. mgr. Y.P. Aurora, Ltd., Ill., 1979-83; counsel, corp. sec. JP Communications Co., Tucson, 1981—; sta. mgr. KPOL-TV, Tucson, 1983-86, gen. mgr., 1986—; gen. counsel Northtown Bus Service, Ltd., Lincolnwood, Ill., 1975—; gen. ptnr. THC Ptnrs., Chgo., 1980—; co-owner LV Pictures, Las Vegas, 1984—. Active Orchard Village Assn. for Handicapped, Skokie, Ill., 1981; mem. Soviet Jewry commn. and young leadership commn. Jewish Fedn. So. Ariz., Tucson, 1984, chmn. young leadership commn., 1985, leadership devel. program, 1984—, chmn., 1985—, bd. dirs., 1985—, active various coms.; mem. bd. Congregation Bet Shalom, 1984; assoc. mem. Hadassah, Tucson, 1984; mem. nat. com. for leadership devel. Council Jewish Fedn., 1986—; bd. dirs. Jewish Family Services, 1986—, Tucsonans Say No to Drugs, 1986—, 88-Crime, 1986—. Recipient Community Service Award Jewish Fedn. So. Ariz., 1987. Mem. ABA, Davis-Mountain AFB Council of 50, 1987—. Clubs: Volk Jewish Community Ctr., Diehard Cubs Fan. Communications, Real property, State civil litigation. Office: KPOL-TV Channel 40 2475 N Jack Rabbit Ave Tucson AZ 85745

POLANSKY, LARRY PAUL, court administrator, consultant; b. Blkyn., July 24, 1932; s. Harry and Ida (Gershengoren) P.; m. Eunice Katherine Neun; children: Steven, Harriet, Bruce. BS in Acctg., Temple U., 1958, JD, 1973. Bar: Pa. 1973, U.S. Dist. Ct. (ea. dist.) Pa. 1973, U.S. Ct. Appeals (3d cir.) 1973, D.C. 1978, U.S. Supreme Ct. 1980. Acct., systems analyst City of Phila., 1956-63; data processing mgr. Jefferson Med. Coll. and Hosp., Phila., 1963-65; systems engr. IBM Corp., Phila., 1965-67; dep. ct. adminstr. Common Pleas Cts. of Phila., 1967-76; dep. state ct. adminstr. Pa. Supreme Ct., Phila., 1976-78; exec. officer D.C. Cts., Washington, 1979—; bd. dirs. Search Group Inc.; mem. steering com. D.C. Bar, 1982-85; cons. in field. Author ct. info. systems monograph, 1978; contbr. articles to profl. jour. Served as cpl. U.S. Army, 1951-53, Korea. Fellow Inst. for Ct. Mgmt., Denver, 1984; recipient Reardon award Nat. Ctr. for State Cts., 1982, Distinguished Service award Nat. Ctr. For State Cts., 1986. Mem. ABA (jud. adminstrn. div., chmn. ct. adminstrn. com. 1984-87, bd. of lawyers conf. 1985-86), Conf. State Ct. Adminstrs. (bd. dirs. 1980-86, pres. 1984-85), State Justice Inst. (bd. dirs. 1986—). Republican. Jewish. Club: Counselors (Washington). Avocations: tennis, computers. Computer, Judicial administration. Home: 250 S Reynolds St 1207 Alexandria VA 22304 Office: DC Ct 500 Indiana Ave NW Washington DC 20001

POLANSKY, STEVEN JAY, lawyer; b. Phila., Nov. 21, 1956; s. Larry P. and Eunice K. (Neun) P.; m. Kathleen Diane Spofford, Dec. 4, 1960; children: Michelle, Jeffrey. BBA magna cum laude, Temple U., 1978; JD magna cum laude, Syracuse U., 1981. Bar: Pa. 1981, N.J. 1981, D.C. 1983. Assoc. Cozen, Begier and O'Conner, Phila., 1981-85, LaBrum and Doak, Woodbury, N.J. and Phila., 1985—. Trustee Georgetowne Condo Assn., Lindenwold, N.J., 1982-83. Mem. ABA, N.J. Bar Assn., Pa. Bar Assn., Phila. Bar Assn., Pa. Def. Inst., Camden County Bar Assn., Def. Research Inst. Jewish. Avocations: skiing, carpentry. Personal injury, Insurance, State civil litigation. Office: LaBrum and Doak PO Box 836 66 Euclid St Woodbury NJ 08096

POLASKI, ANNE SPENCER, lawyer; b. Pittsfield, Mass., Nov. 13, 1952; d. John Harold and Marjorie Ruth (Hackett) Spencer; m. James Joseph Polaski, Sept. 14, 1985. BA in Psychology, Allegheny Coll., 1974; MSW, U. Pa., 1976; JD, George Washington U., 1979. Bar: D.C. 1979, U.S. Dist. Ct. (D.C. dist.) 1980, U.S. Ct. Appeals (D.C. cir.) 1980, Ill. 1982, U.S. Dist. Ct. (no. dist.) Ill. 1982, U.S. Ct. Appeals (7th cir.) 1982. Law clk. to assoc. judge D.C. Ct., Washington, 1979-80; trial atty. Commodity Futures Trading Commn., Chgo., 1980-84, sr. trial atty., 1984, dep. regional counsel, 1984—. Mem. ABA, Ill. State Bar Assn., Chgo. Bar Assn. Administrative and regulatory, Federal civil litigation, Commodity futures law. Office: Commodity Futures Trading Commn 233 S Wacker Dr Suite 4600 Chicago IL 60606

POLEBAUM, MARK NEAL, lawyer; b. Lowell, Mass., May 1, 1952; s. Eugene Harvey and Phyllis Diane (Sherman) P.; m. Diane M. Buhl, June 6, 1982; children: Katherine Elizabeth, Jessica Leigh. BA, Middlebury Coll., 1974; JD, NYU, 1978. Bar: Mass. 1979, U.S. Dist. Ct. Mass. 1979. Law clk. to presiding justice U.S. Ct. Appeals (5th cir.), Montgomery, Ala., 1978-79; assoc. Hale and Dorr, Boston, 1979-83, ptnr., 1983—, sr. ptnr., 1986—. Mem. appropriations com., City of Lexington, Mass., 1984—. Watson Found. fellow, 1974-75. Mem ABA (corp., banking and bus. law sects., ad hoc subcom. on scope of uniform comml. code), Mass. Bar Assn., Order of Coif, Phi Beta Kappa. Banking, Bankruptcy, Contracts commercial. Office: Hale and Dorr 60 State St Boston MA 02109

POLIAKOFF, GARY A., lawyer, educator; b. Greenville, S.C., Nov. 25, 1944; s. Herman and Dorothy (Ravitz) P.; m. Sherri D. Dublin, June 24, 1967; children—Ryan, Keith. B.S., U. S.C., 1966; J.D., U. Miami, 1969. Bar: Fla. 1969, D.C. 1971. Sr. ptnr. Becker, Poliakoff & Streitfeld, P.A., Ft. Lauderdale, Miami, Sarasota, West Palm Beach, Clearwater, and Ft. Myers, Fla., 1973—; adj. prof. law Nova U.; panelist Nat. Confs. Community Assns.; lectr. ann. condominium seminars Fla. Bar; participant Fla. Law Revision Council; cons. to White House in drafting Condominium and Coop. Abuse Relief Act, 1980. Mem. exec. com. Anti-Defamation League So. Region. Mem. Fla. Bar (co-chmn. condominium and coop. law sect., chmn. legis. subcom. condominium and coop. law). Author: (with others) Florida Condominium Law and Practice, 1982; contbr. articles to profl. jours. Real property.

POLICY, VINCENT MARK, lawyer; b. Warren, Ohio, Mar. 29, 1948; s. Vincent James and Anna Marie (Berardi) P.; m. Katherine Anne Veazey; children: Nicholas, Katherine Nicole. BA, U. Md., 1970; JD, Georgetown U., 1973. Bar: N.Y. 1974, D.C. 1975, U.S. Supreme Ct. 1977. Assoc. Cahill Gordon & Reindel, Washington and N.Y.C., 1973-78, Hogan & Hartson, Washington, 1978-85; prin. Pohoryles & Greenstein PC, Washington, 1985—. Author: Speedy Trial, A Constitutional Right in Search of Definition, 1973. Mem. D.C. Bar Assn. (chmn. rental housing com. 1985—), D.C. Assn. Realtors (speaker 1984-86), Apt. and Office Bldg. Assn. (lectr. 1985-86), Greater Washington Bd. Trade (subcom. on initiatives), D.C. Builders Assn. (legis. affairs com.), Phi Beta Kappa, Omicron Delta Kappa. Democrat. Roman Catholic. Lodge: KC. Avocation: sailing. Real property, Banking, State civil litigation. Office: Pohoryles & Greenstein PC 1920 N St NW Washington DC 20036

POLING, RICHARD DUANE, lawyer; b. Parkersburg, W.Va., Nov. 4, 1955; s. W. Duane and Willadene (Riggs) P.; m. Debra Ann Holstein, Feb. 23, 1985. AB magna cum laude, W.Va. U., 1978, JD, 1981. Bar: W.Va. 1981, U.S. Dist. Ct. (no. and so. dists.) W.Va. 1981, N.C. 1983, U.S. Dist. Ct. Idaho 1983, U.S. Ct. Appeals (9th cir.) 1983, U.S. Ct. Appeals (4th cir.) 1984, U.S. Dist. Ct. (we.) N.C. 1987, U.S. Dist. Ct. (mid. dist.) N.C. 1987. Assoc. Wilson, Frame & Poling, Morgantown, W.Va., 1981-82, Preiser & Wilson, Charleston, W.Va., 1982-85; ptnr. Karney, Poling & Smith, Charlotte, N.C., 1985—; adj. prof. law W.Va. U., Morgantown, 1981-82. Mem. Advocates for a Safer Vaccine, 1984—, Dissatisfied Parents Together, Vienna, Va., 1985—. Named Outstanding Young Adv. Allegheny County Acad. Trial Lawyers, 1981, One of Outstanding Young Men Am., 1981. Mem. ABA (law and medicine com.), Assn. Trial Lawyers Am. (vice chmn. young lawyers sect. 1985—, exec. com. dept. litigation sect. 1986—), N.C. Bar Assn., W.Va. State Bar (com. on law and medicine 1985-86), Va. Trial Lawyers Assn., W.Va. Trial Lawyers Assn. (pub. relations com.), N.C. Acad. Trial Lawyers (victims rights com.), Phi Beta Kappa, Phi Kappa Phi, Phi Delta Phi. Democrat. Methodist. Avocations: tennis, backpacking, golf. Federal civil litigation, State civil litigation, Personal injury. Home: 1911 S Wendover Rd Charlotte NC 28211 Office: Karney Poling & Smith 1208 S Tryon St Charlotte NC 28202

POLINSKY, A. MITCHELL, law educator; b. 1948. A.B., Harvard U., 1970; Ph.D., MIT, 1973; M.S.L., Yale U., 1976. Asst. prof. econs. Harvard U., Cambridge, Mass., 1973-79, asst. prof. econs. and law, 1977-79; assoc. prof. econs., prof. law Stanford (Calif.) U., 1979-84, Josephine Scott Crocker prof. law and econs., 1984—; mem. exec. com. Internat. Seminar on Pub. Econs., 1979—; research assoc., Nat. Bur. of Economic Reserves, 1978—; mem. Urban Com. on Pub. Econs., 1977—. Legal education. Office: Stanford U Law Sch Stanford CA 94305 *

POLITANO, FRANK LOUIS, lawyer; b. Medford, Mass., June 4, 1949; s. Frank Joseph and Louise (Puma) P.; m. Maria Magliaro, July 19, 1975; 1 child, Frank Domenic. AB summa cum laude, Boston U., 1971; JD, Columbia U., 1974. Bar: N.Y. 1975, U.S. Dist. Ct. (so. and ea. dists.) N.Y. 1975, N.J. 1979, U.S. Dist. Ct. (ea. dist.) N.J. 1979, U.S. Supreme Ct. 1980, U.S. Dist. Ct. Wis. 1985, Wis. 1985. Assoc. Kaye, Scholer, Fierman, Hays & Handler, N.Y.C., 1974-78, Fish & Neave, N.Y.C., 1978-84; trademark counsel S.C. Johnson and Son, Inc., Racine, Wis., 1984—; counsel St. Casimir's Parish, Racine, 1985—. Mem. ABA, Am. Intellectual Property Law Assn. Roman Catholic. Trademark and copyright, Federal civil litigation, Private international. Home: 3528 N Bay Dr Racine WI 53402 Office: SC Johnson and Son Inc 1525 Howe St Racine WI 53403

POLITI, STEPHEN MICHAEL, lawyer, educator; b. Mass., Mar. 30, 1948; s. Selvi J. and Anne (Gargiulo) P.; m. Joan Spignesi, June 29, 1985. AB in Econs. cum laude, U. Mass., 1970; JD, Boston U., 1973, LLM in Taxation, 1974. Bar: Mass. 1973, U.S. Tax Ct. 1977, U.S. Dist. Ct. Mass. 1977. Counsel Joint Legis. Com. on Taxation, Boston, 1973-74; staff atty. Mass. Dept. Revenue, Boston, 1974-79, chief counsel, 1979-83; sole practice Boston, 1983—; prof. Bentley Coll. Grad. Sch. of Taxation, Waltham, Mass., 1977—. Contbr. articles to profl. jours. Former chmn. Lexinton Mass. Bd. of Selectmen. Mem. ABA (chmn. com. on taxes and revenues, urban law sect. 1986—), Mass. Bar Assn. State and local taxation, General practice. Office: 28 State St Suite 2020 Boston MA 02109

POLITO, JOSEPH MICHAEL, lawyer; b. Detroit, Aug. 4, 1950; s. Michael Salvatore and Lucille Florence (O'Gorman) P.; m. Blenda J. Jabalee, Dec. 18, 1971; children: Diona, Jamie, Kimberly, Joseph Jr. BA, Wayne State U., 1972; JD, U. Mich., 1975. Bar: Mich. 1975, U.S. Dist. Ct. (ea. dist.) Mich. 1975, U.S. Ct. Appeals (6th cir.) 1985. Ptnr. Honigman, Miller, Schwartz & Cohn, Detroit, 1975—; adj. prof. Wayne State U. Law Sch., Detroit, 1980-81. Mem. Mich. Bar Assn., Detroit Bar Assn., Mich. Assn. Environ. Profls., Water Pollution Control Fedn., Air Pollution Control Assn. Avocations: boating, music. Environment, Administrative and regulatory, Real property. Office: Honigman Miller Schwartz & Cohn 2290 First National Bldg Detroit MI 48226

POLITZ, HENRY ANTHONY, federal judge; b. Napoleonville, La., May 9, 1932; s. Anthony and Virginia (Russo) P.; m. Jane Marie Simoneaux, Apr. 29, 1952; children: Nyle, Bennett, Mark, Angela, Scott, Jane, Michael, Henry, Alisa, John, Nina. B.A., La. State U., 1958, J.D. (mem. bd. Law Rev. 1958-59), 1959. Bar: La. 1959. Assoc., then partner firm Booth, Lockard, Jack, Pleasant & LeSage, Shreveport, 1959-79; judge U.S. 5th Circuit Ct. Appeals, Shreveport, 1979—; vis. prof. La. State U. Law Center; bd. dirs. Am. Prepaid Legal Services Inst., 1975—; mem. La. Judiciary Commn., 1978-79. Mem. Shreveport Airport Authority, 1973-79, chmn., 1977; bd. dirs. Rutherford House, Shreveport, 1975—, pres., 1978; pres. Caddo Parish Bd. Election Suprs., 1975-79; mem. Electoral Coll., 1976. Served with USAF, 1951-55. Named Outstanding Young Lawyer in La., 1971. Mem. Am. Bar Assn., Am. Judicature Soc., Internat. Soc. Barristers, La. Bar Assn., La. Trial Lawyers Assn., Shreveport Bar Assn., Justinian Soc., Omicron Delta Kappa. Democrat. Roman Catholic. Club: K.C. Jurisprudence. Office: US Court Appeals 500 Fannin St. Shreveport LA 71101 *

POLK, LEE THOMAS, lawyer; b. Chgo., Feb. 25, 1945; s. Lee Anthony and Mary Josephine (Lane) P.; m. Susan Luzader, Mar. 21, 1975. AB, Coe Coll., 1967; JD, U. Chgo., 1970. Bar: Ill. 1970, U.S. Dist. Ct. (no. dist.) Ill. 1970, U.S. Ct. Mil. Appeals 1972, U.S. Dist. Ct. (we. dist.) Mich. 1983, U.S. Claims Ct. 1983, U.S. Ct. Appeals (7th cir.) 1983. Assoc. firm Vedder, Price, Kaufman & Kammholz, Chgo., 1970-72, 75-77, ptnr. 1977-86; ptnr. Murphy, Smith & Polk, 1986—. Contbr. articles on employee benefits and health law to profl. jours. Served to capt. JAGC, U.S. Army, 1972-75. Mem. ABA (sects. on tax, employee benefits, pub. contracts and bus.), Ill. Bar Assn., Chgo. Bar Assn. (vice chmn. employee benefits com. 1986-87), Midwest Pension Conf. (chmn. Chgo. chpt. 1986), Nat. Contract Mgmt. Assn., Nat. Health Lawyers Assn., Phi Beta Kappa, Phi Kappa Phi. Roman Catholic. Club: Union League (Chgo.). Pension, profit-sharing, and employee benefits, Government contracts and claims, Health. Home: 820 Sheridan Rd Evanston IL 60202 Office: Murphy Smith & Polk Two First National Plaza 24th Floor Chicago IL 60603

POLK, ROSS B., lawyer; b. Hattiesburg, Miss., Aug. 25, 1955; s. Frank A. and Martha (Barron) P. BBA, U. Miss., 1976, JD, 1980. Bar: Miss. 1980, U.S. Dist. Ct. (no. dist.) Miss. 1980. Sole practice Hattiesburg, 1980—. Fellow ABA, Miss. Bar Assn., Miss. Assn. Petroleum Landmen, Am. Assn. Petroleum Landmen. Baptist. Avocations: golf, skiing. Oil and gas leasing, Real property. Office: PO Box 16598 Hattiesburg MS 39404

POLK, VICTOR H., JR., lawyer; b. Coral Gables, Fla., July 25, 1955; s. Victor H. Polk and Dorothy (Smith) Hansell; m. Catherine A. Chapman, May 19, 1985. BS, Brown U., 1977; JD, U. Chgo., 1980. Bar: Fla. 1980, Mass. 1985, U.S. Dist. Ct. Mass., U.S. Dist. Ct. (so. dist.) Fla., U.S. Ct. Appeals (11th cir.). Instr. U. Miami Law Sch., Fla., 1980-81; assoc. Greenberg, Traurig, Askew, Hoffman, Lipoff, Quentel & Wolff, Miami, 1981-83, Kenny, Nachwalter & Seymour, Miami, 1983-85, Bingham, Dana & Gould, Boston, 1985—. Democrat. Federal civil litigation, State civil litigation. Home: 25 Euston St #2 Brookline MA 02146 Office: Bingham Dana & Gould 100 Federal St Boston MA 02110

POLLACK, MICHAEL ALAN, lawyer, educator; b. Chgo., Apr. 7, 1953; s. Robert Bernard and Sermata (Shane) P.; m. Patti Dee Gorsky, July 6, 1980; 1 child, Marni Elizabeth. BA, U. Wis., 1974; JD, Tulane U., 1978. Bar: Wis. 1978, Ill. 1979, U.S. Dist. Ct. (no. dist.) Ill. 1979, Fla. 1980, U.S. Ct. Appeals (7th cir.) 1984. Staff atty. Nat. Dist. Atty.'s Assn., Chgo., 1978-80; asst. corp. counsel Mil. County Corp. Counsel, Milw., 1980-83; sole practice Milw., 1983—; adj. prof. Cardinal Stritch Coll., Milw., 1985—. Mem. ABA, Wis. Bar Assn., Fla. Bar Assn., Milw. Bar Assn., Milw. Young Lawyers Assn. (bd. dirs. 1986). Civil rights, State civil litigation, Personal injury. Office: 152 W Wisconsin Ave Suite 634 Milwaukee WI 53203

POLLACK, STANLEY P., lawyer; b. N.Y.C., Apr. 23, 1928; s. Isidor and Anna (Shulman) P.; m. Susan Aronowitz, June 16, 1974; 1 child, Jane. BA, NYU, 1948; JD, Harvard U., 1951; LLM in Taxation, NYU, 1959. Bar: N.Y. 1951, U.S. Dist. Ct. (so. dist.) N.Y. 1955. Sole practice N.Y.C., 1955-61; v.p., gen. counsel James Talcott, Inc., N.Y.C., 1961-73; exec. v.p., gen. counsel Rosenthal & Rosenthal Inc., N.Y.C., 1973—. Served to j.g. lt. USNR, 1951-54. Mem. Bklyn. Bar Assn. (banking com., bankruptcy com.), Fed. Bar Council, Assn. Comml. Fin. Atty.'s (pres. 1968). Club: Harvard (N.Y.C.). Banking, Contracts commercial. Home: 6 Peter Cooper Rd New York NY 10010 Office: Rosenthal & Rosenthal Inc 1451 Broadway New York NY 10036

POLLAK, JEFFREY SAUL, lawyer; b. N.Y.C., Feb. 28, 1953; s. Gerald and Marian (Harris) P. BA, SUNY, Buffalo, 1976; JD, Southwestern U., 1981. Bar: Calif. 1982. Claims supr. Conn. Gen. Life Ins. Co., Santa Monica, Calif., 1977-80; assoc. Hart & Michaelis, Los Angeles, 1981-83; claims dir. Lancer Claim Services, Inc., Anaheim, Calif., 1983—, also bd. dirs.; lectr. ins. cos. and assns. Mem. ABA (subcom. agt. and broker liability, subcom. tort and ins. practice sect.), Am. Mgmt. Assn., Def. Research Inst. (subcom. agt. and broker liability). Insurance, Personal injury. Office: Lancer Claim Services Inc 2331 W Lincoln Blvd Anaheim CA 92803

POLLAK, LOUIS HEILPRIN, judge; b. N.Y.C., Dec. 7, 1922; s. Walter and Marion (Heilprin) P.; m. Katherine Weiss, July 25, 1952; children—Nancy, Elizabeth, Susan, Sarah, Deborah. A.B., Harvard, 1943; LL.B., Yale, 1948. Bar: N.Y. bar 1949, Conn. bar 1956, Pa. bar 1976. Law clk. to U.S. Supreme Ct. Justice Rutledge, 1948-49; with firm Paul, Weiss, Rifkind, Wharton & Garrison, N.Y.C., 1949-51; atty. Dept. State; spl. asst. to ambassador-at-large Dept. State, Jessup, 1951-53; vis. lectr. Howard U. Sch. Law, 1953; asst. counsel Amalgmated Clothing Workers Am., 1954-55; mem. faculty Yale Law Sch., 1955-74, dean, 1965-70; Greenfield prof. U. Pa., 1974-78, dean Law Sch., 1975-78, lectr., 1980—; U.S. dist. judge for Eastern dist. Pa., 1978—; vis. prof. U. Mich. Law Sch., 1961, Columbia Law Sch., 1962. Author: The Constitution and the Supreme Court: A Documentary History, 1966. Mem. New Haven Bd. Edn., 1962-68; chmn. Conn. adv. com. U.S. Civil Rights Commn., 1962-63; mem. bd. NAACP Legal Def. Fund, 1960-78, v.p., 1971-78; chmn. New Haven Human Rights Com., 1963-64. Served with AUS, 1943-46. Mem. Assn. Bar City N.Y., ABA (chmn. sec. individual rights 1970-71), Fed. Bar Assn., Phila. Bar Assn., Am. Law Inst. (council 1978—). Office: 16613 US Courthouse 601 Market St Philadelphia PA 19106

POLLAK, MARK, lawyer; b. Paris, July 16, 1947; came to U.S., 1955; s. Joseph and Zofia (Berkowitz) P.; m. Joanne Elizabeth Harris, Dec. 12, 1976; children: Joshua David, Jonathan Stephen, Benjamin Eric, Rebecca Lynn. BA, Bklyn. Coll., 1968; MA in City Planning, U. Pa., 1972, JD, 1972. Bar: Md. 1972. Assoc. Piper & Marbury, Balt., 1972-81, ptnr., 1981—; pres. Balt. Region Community Devel. Corp., Balt. Corp. Housing Ptnrships. Mem. ABA, Md. Bar Assn. Real property, Municipal bonds. Office: Piper & Marbury 36 S Charles St Baltimore MD 21201

POLLAN, STEPHEN MICHAEL, lawyer, author, lecturer, financial-real estate consultant; b. N.Y.C., May 19, 1929; s. Robert and Harriet (Morganstern) P.; m. Corrine Staller, July 18, 1954; children—Michael, Lori, Tracy, Dana. BBS., L.I. U., 1985; LL.B., Bklyn. Law Sch., 1951. Bar: N.Y. 1951 founder, pres. Country Capital Corp., small bus. investment, N.Y.C., 1960-70; pres. Royal Bus. Funds (AMEX), 1970-76; sr. real estate cons. Nat. Westminster Bank, 1976-78; pres. Stephen M. Pollan & Assocs., Ltd., 1978—; asst. prof. fin. C.W. Post Coll., Sch. Bus. L.I.U.; dir. Credit Inst.; mem. small bus. investment co. adv. council SBA. Vice chmn. UN Com. for UN Day, 1971-72; advisor Pres.'s Commn. Small Bus., 1974; founder Gay Head Taxpayer's Assn., Martha's Vineyard, Mass.; pres. Gay Head Community Council, 1975. Mem. Nat. Assn. Small Bus. Investment Cos. (regional pres. 1975; bd. govs.; cert of appreciation). Co-author: How to Borrow Money, Encyclopedia of Home Buying in Am, How to Get a Loan From a Balky Banker, How to Hire a Pro; guest expert Good Morning Am. TV Show, Miller's Court TV Show. Contracts commercial, General corporate, Banking. Home: 1059 Park Ave #11C New York NY 10128 also: Gay Head Martha's Vineyard MA 02535 Office: 404 E 79th St New York NY 10021

POLLAN, THOMAS MILLER, lawyer; b. San Antonio, Sept. 24, 1945; s. Elbert V. and B. Agnes (Miller) P.; m. Bettie Schoene, May 9, 1974; children: Sarah Catherine, Wilson Thomas. BA, U. Tex., 1968, JD, 1971. Bar: Tex. 1971, U.S. Dist. Ct. (so. dist.) Tex. 1972, U.S. Ct. Appeals (5th cir.) 1972, U.S. Dist. Ct. (we. dist.) Tex. 1973, U.S. Supreme Ct. 1979. Briefing atty. Supreme Ct. Tex., Austin, 1971-72; asst. atty. gen. Tex., Austin, 1972-82, chief ins., banking and securities div., 1976-82; ptnr. Bickerstaff, Heath & Smiley, Austin, 1982—. Mem. adv. com. Tex. Legis. Council Revision Tex. Ins. Code, 1982-83; trustee State Bar of Tex. Ins. Trust, 1985—. Mem. ABA, Tex. Bar Assn., Phi Delta Phi. Administrative and regulatory, Banking, Insurance. Home: 2908 Dover Pl Austin TX 78731 Office: 98 San Jacinto Blvd Suite 1800 Austin TX 78701

POLLARD, BRENDA KREBS, lawyer; b. Pottsville, Pa., Oct. 3, 1954; d. Lewis Milton and Ethel Catherine (Weicker) Krebs; m. Raymond D. Pollard, Dec. 17, 1977 (div. Feb. 1985). BS in Am. Studies magna cum laude, U. Tenn., 1975; JD, U. Ga., 1977. Bar: Ga. 1977, N.C. 1978, U.S. Dist. Ct. (no. dist.) Ga. 1981, U.S. Ct. Appeals (11th cir.) 1981. Assoc. Redmond, Stevens, Loftin and Currie, Asheville, N.C., 1978-80; assoc. counsel II Met. Atlanta Rapid Transit Authority, Atlanta, 1980-82, sr. assoc. counsel, 1982-85; dist. surety counsel Fireman's Fund Ins. Cos., Atlanta, 1985—; mem. panel of constrn. industry arbitrators Am. Arbitration Assn., Atlanta, 1983—. Mem. ABA, State Bar Ga., N.C. State Bar Assn. Republican. Lutheran. Construction, Government contracts and claims, Surety. Home: 709 Glenleaf Dr Norcross GA 30092 Office: Fireman's Fund Ins Cos 302 Perimeter Ctr N Suite 300 Atlanta GA 30346

POLLARD, HENRY, lawyer; b. N.Y.C., Jan. 10, 1931; s. Charles and Sarah (Lanster) P.; m. Adele Ruth Brodie, June 16, 1954; children: Paul A., Lydia S. AB, CCNY, 1953; JD, Columbia U., 1954. Bar: N.Y. 1954, Calif. 1962. Assoc. Sullivan & Cromwell, N.Y.C., 1954, 56-61; ptnr. Pollard, Bauman, Slome & McIntosh, Beverly Hills, Calif., 1961—, Kaplan, LIvingston, Goodwin, Berkowitz & Selvin, Beverly Hills, 1962-81. Editor Columbia U. Law Rev., 1953-54. Served with U.S. Army, 1954-56. Harlan Fiske Stone scholar, 1953-54. Mem. ABA, Calif. Bar Assn., Los Angeles County Bar Assn., Beverly Hills Bar Assn. Securities, General corporate, Real property. Office: Pollard Bauman Slome & McIntosh 450 N Roxbury Dr Beverly Hills CA 90210

POLLARD, MICHAEL ROSS, lawyer, health policy researcher and consultant; b. Flint, Mich., Apr. 14, 1947; s. Gail Winton Pollard and Evelyn Georgeanna (LeMire) Goplen; m. Penelope Brigham, Aug. 22, 1970. AB in Polit. Sci., U. Mich., 1969; JD, Harvard U., 1972, MPH, 1974. Bar: Mass. 1972, D.C. 1975. Profl. assoc. for program devel. Nat. Acad. Scis. Inst. Medicine, Washington, 1974-77, dir. law and ethics div., 1977-78; atty. advisor Office of Policy Planning, FTC, Washington, 1978-81, asst. dir. Bur. Consumer Protection, 1981-83; dir. Office of Policy Analysis, Pharm. Mfrs. Assn., Washington, 1983—; cons. Nat. Ctr. for Health Services Research, Rockville, Md., 1975-80, Office Tech. Assessment U.S. Congress, 1984—. Contbr. articles to profl. jours. James B. Angell scholar U. Mich., 1967, 68, 69. Mem. ABA, Phi Beta Kappa, Pi Sigma Alpha. Democrat. Club: Harvard (Washington). Avocations: running, cycling, gardening, architectural drawing. Antitrust, Health. Home: 7300 Maple Ave Chevy Chase MD 20815 Office: Pharm Mfrs Assn 1100 15th St NW Suite 900 Washington DC 20005

POLLARD, OVERTON PRICE, lawyer; b. Ashland, Va., Mar. 26, 1933; s. James Madison and Annie Elizabeth (Hutchinson) P.; m. Anne Aloysia Meyer, Oct. 1, 1960; children—Mary O., Price, John, Anne, Charles, Andrew, David. A.B. in Econs., Washington and Lee U., 1954, J.D., 1957. Bar: Va. Claims supr. Travelers Ins. Co., Richmond, Va., 1964-67; asst. atty. gen. State of Va., Richmond, 1967, 70-72; spl. asst. Va. Supreme Ct., Richmond, 1968-70; exec. dir. Pub. Defender Commn., Richmond, 1972—; ptnr. Pollard & Boice and predecessor firms, Richmond, 1972—; bd. govs. Va. Criminal Law Sect., Richmond, 1970-72; chmn. prepaid legal services com. Va. State Bar, Richmond, 1982-85; pres. Met. Legal Aid, Richmond, 1978. Del. to State Democratic Conv., Richmond, 1985. Served with USN, 1957-59. Recipient service award Criminal Law Bd. of Govts. for Pub. Defender Study, 1971. Mem. ABA, Va. Bar Assn., Richmond Bar Assn., Nat. Assn. Criminal Def. Lawyers. Democrat. Baptist. Club: Bull and Bear. Lodge: Lions. Avocation: fishing. Criminal, Estate planning. Home: 7726 Sweetbriar Rd Richmond VA 23229 Office: Pub Defender Commn 8550 Mayland Dr Richmond VA 23329

POLLARD, WILLIAM ALBERT, lawyer; b. Nashville, July 7, 1946; s. Thomas Brown and Hilda Alexine (Jolly) P.; m. Karen Elizabeth Momeier, Aug. 31, 1984; 1 child, William A. Jr. B.S., U. S.C., 1968, J.D., 1974. Bar: S.C. 1974, U.S. Dist. Ct. S.C. 1974, U.S. Ct. Appeals (4th cir.) 1974, U.S. Tax Ct. 1977. Assoc. Nexsen, Pruet, Jacobs & Pollard, Columbia, S.C., 1974-78, ptnr., 1978—. Mem. adv. bd. Midlands Tech. Coll., Columbia, 1978-84; endowment chmn., exec. council Indian Rivers Council Boy Scouts Am., 1986—, United Way of the Midlands, 1983, 84. Served to lt. USN, 1968-71. Mem. Am. Soc. Hosp. Attys., Am. Soc. Law and Medicine, Nat. Health Lawyers Assn., S.C. Hosp. Assn., S.C. Hosp. Attys. (bd. govs. 1985—), ABA (forum com. on health law), S.C. Bar Assn. (med., legal affairs com. 1986—), Columbia C. of C. (health care task force). Methodist. Clubs: Summit, Sertoma (pres. 1981-82) (Columbia). Health, Pension, profit-

sharing, and employee benefits, Administrative and regulatory. Home: 416 Princess St Columbia SC 29205 Office: Nexsen Pruet Jacobs & Pollard PO Drawer 2426 Columbia SC 29202

POLLER, JERI, lawyer; b. Tampa, Fla., Nov. 3, 1952; d. Nathan and Lucille (Rosenberg) P. AB, Boston U., 1974; JD, U. Fla., 1976. V.p. real estate counsel Arvida Disney Corp., Boca Raton, Fla., 1977—. Real property, General corporate, Landlord-tenant. Home: 6614 Las Flores Dr Boca Raton FL 33433 Office: Arvida Disney Corp PO Box 100 Boca Raton FL 33432

POLLEY, TERRY LEE, lawyer; b. Long Beach, Calif., June 2, 1947; s. Frederick F. and Geraldine E. (Davis) P.; m. Patricia Yamanoha, Aug. 4, 1973; children: Todd, Matthew. AB, UCLA, 1970; JD, Coll. William and Mary, 1973. Bar: Calif. 1973. Assoc. Loeb & Loeb, Los Angeles, 1973-78; ptnr. Ajalat & Polley, Los Angeles, 1978—; lectr. taxation law U. So. Calif. Mem. editorial bd. William and Mary Law Rev. Elder Grace Brethren Ch., Long Beach. Mem. Calif. Bar Assn. (steering com., property, sales and local tax com. taxation sect.), Los Angeles County Bar Assn. (chmn. and exec. com. taxation sect., chmn. state and local tax com. taxation sect.), Omicron Delta Epsilon. Democrat. State and local taxation. Office: Ajalat & Polley 643 S Olive St Suite 200 Los Angeles CA 90014

POLLEY, VINCENT IRA, lawyer; b. Detroit, Oct. 28, 1954; s. Ira and Margaret Mary (Foley) P.; m. Lynn Marie Zander, Aug. 24, 1979; 1 child, Elizabeth. AB, Harvard U., 1976; JD, U. Mich., 1979. Bar: D.C. 1979, U.S. Ct. Appeals (D.C. cir.) 1980, U.S. Ct. Appeals (4th cir.) 1981, U.S. Supreme Ct. 1983, Mich. 1986. Assoc. Miller & Chevalier, Washington, 1979-84; gen. counsel Applicon-Schlumberger, Ann Arbor, Mich., 1984—, Factron-Schlumberger, Latham, N.Y., 1986—. Author: Operating System Simulation Language Primer, 1975. Assoc. counsel ARC, Washington, 1980-84; pres. Flint Hills Homeowners Assn., Inc, 1982-84; bd. dirs. Boston Premiere Ensemble, Cambridge, 1985. Mem. ABA, AAAS. Computer, Private international, General corporate. Office: Applicon-Schlumberger 4251 Plymouth Rd Ann Arbor MI 48106

POLLIHAN, THOMAS HENRY, lawyer; b. St. Louis, Nov. 15, 1949; s. C.H. and Patricia Ann (O'Brien) P.; m. Donna M. Bickhaus, Aug. 25, 1973; 1 child, Emily Christine. BA in Sociology, Quincy Coll., 1972; JD, U. Notre Dame, 1975. Bar: Mo. 1975, U.S. Dist. Ct. (ea. dist.) Mo. 1975, Ill. 1976, U.S. Dist. (so. dist.) Ill. 1976. Jud. law clk. to presiding justice Mo. Ct. of Appeals, St. Louis, 1975-76; from assoc. to ptnr. Greenfield, Davidson, Mandelstamm & Voorhees, St. Louis, 1976-82; asst. gen. counsel Kellwood Co., St. Louis, 1982—. Pres. Quincy (Ill.) Coll. Alumni Bd., 1986—, Southwest Neighborhood Improvement Assn., St. Louis, 1984. Mem. ABA, Bar Assn. of Met. St. Louis, Mensa. Roman Catholic. Avocations: soccer, scuba diving. General corporate, Contracts commercial, Real property. Home: 4934 Magnolia Saint Louis MO 63139 Office: Kellwood Co 600 Kellwood Pkwy Saint Louis MO 63017

POLLINGER, WILLIAM JOSHUA, lawyer; b. Passaic, N.J., Dec. 14, 1944; s. Irving R. and Ethel (Groudan) P.; m. Helen Rizzo, May 30, 1977; children: Samantha, Zachary. BA, Rutgers U., 1966; JD, Am. U., 1969. Bar: N.J. 1969, U.S. Dist. Ct. N.J. 1969, N.Y. 1981, U.S. Supreme Ct. 1982, U.S. Ct. Appeals (3d cir.) 1986. Assoc. Krieger & Klein, Passaic, 1969-75; ptnr. Delorenzo & Pollinger, Hackensack, N.J., 1975-84; pres. William J. Pollinger, P.A., Hackensack, 1984—; mem. Bergen County Ethics Com., N.J., 1983—. Arbitrator Better Bus. Bur. of Bergen and Rockland Counties, Paramus, N.J., 1983—. Assoc. of Yr. award Builders Assn. No. N.J., Paramus, 1981. Mem. N.J. State Bar Assn., Passaic County Bar Assn., Bergen County Bar Assn., Assn. Trial Lawyers Am., Trial Attys. N.J., Am. Arbitration Assn., Def. Research Inst., Phi Delta Phi. Lodge: Masons (past master). Avocation: stamp and coin collecting. State civil litigation, Personal injury, Insurance. Office: 485 Main St Hackensack NJ 07601

POLLINS, JOHN WILLIAM, III, lawyer; b. Greensburg, Pa., Feb. 19, 1940. AB, U. Mich., 1961, JD, 1964. Bar: Pa. 1964, U.S. Dist. Ct. (we. dist.) Pa. 1976, U.S. Ct. Appeals (3d cir.) 1977, U.S. Supreme Ct. Law clk. to presiding judge Westmoreland County, Pa., 1964-66; ptnr. Pollins & Pollins, Greensburg, 1966-71, Hammer & Pollins, Greensburg, 1972—; spl. asst. atty. gen. Commonwealth of Pa., 1967-72; solicitor Greater Greensburg Indsl. Devel. Corp., Greensburg Parking Authority; mem. civil rules com. Westmoreland County Ct. Common Pleas, 1973—. Contbr. articles to profl. jours. Pres., bd. dirs. Southwestern Pa. Lung Assn., 1976—. Mem. Pa. Bar Assn. (appellate ct. com. 1980-82, civil litigation sect. 1985—), Pa. Trial Lawyers Assn. (amicus curiae com. 1986—), Westmoreland County Bar Assn. (ct. of common pleas rules com. 1972-73, 83, chmn. rules of civil procedure com. 1973-76). State civil litigation, Insurance, Personal injury. Office: 139 S Pennsylvania Ave Greensburg PA 15601

POLLIO, BENEDICT JAMES, b. Bklyn., Mar. 21, 1934; s. Anthony N. and Mildred E. (Golishano) P.; m. Anne L. Ennis, Nov. 24, 1956; children: Kathleen M. Galgano, Nancyanne McAward, Robert J., Susanne McGalley, Ronald A., Christine, Regina G. BBA, St. John's U., 1955, JD, 1961; LLM, N.Y.U., 1967, postgrad. Law Prof. Program, 1970. Bar: N.Y. 1961, Fla. 1977. With Cluett Bros., N.Y.C., 1961-65; founding mem. Redmond & Pollio, P.C. and predecessor firm, Garden City, N.Y.C., 1965—; adj. prof. law, fed. securities regulation St. John's U. Sch. Law; mem. faculty N.Y. State Bar Assn.; lectr. Bar Assn. Nassau County, Advanced Practice Inst. of Hofstra U. Law Sch., Hofstra U. Bus. Sch., other profl. groups. Founding mem. non-profit youth employment agy.; chmn. ch. parish council and fin. com.; various polit. activities. Served to 1st lt. USMC 1954, 55-58. Recipient various acad. and profl. awards. Mem. Assn. Bar of City of N.Y., Bar Assn. Nassau County, N.Y. State Bar Assn., ABA, Fla. Bar Assn., St. John's U. Coll. Bus. Adminstrn. Alumni Assn. (founding dir., officer Nassau chpt.), St. John's U. Law Sch. Alumni Assn. (founding dir., officer Nassau chpt.), Nassau County Bar Assn. (dir., chmn. corp. law com., co-chmn., founder accts. and lawyers com.). Republican. Roman Catholic. Clubs: Garden City Country, Cherry Valley Country (Garden City, N.Y.). Author various research papers. General corporate, Estate planning, Corporate taxation. Home: 119 Whitehall Blvd Garden City NY 11530 Office: 1461 Franklin Ave Garden City NY 11530

POLLOCK, E. KEARS, lawyer, glass manufacturing corporation executive; b. Marion Center, Pa., July 18, 1940; s. Frank M. and Clara B. Pollock; m. Karen L., June 9, 1962; children—Steven, Sean, David, Ann Marie. B.S. in Chem. Engring., Carnegie-Mellon U., 1962, M.S., 1964; J.D., Duquesne U., 1970. Bar: Pa. 1970, U.S. Patent Office 1970, U.S. Supreme Ct. 1973. Patent atty. PPG Industries, Pitts., 1970-77, Patent counsel, 1977-82, dir. research and devel., 1982-86; dir. Auto Products, 1986—; adj. prof. law Duquesne U., Pitts., 1980-86. Bd. dirs. Hampton Sch. Dist., 1977-83, pres., 1979-83. Served to 1st lt. C.E., AUS, 1963-65. Mem. ABA, Am. Patent Law Assn., Allegheny County Bar Assn., Am. Inst. Chem. Engrs. Patentee in field chem. engring. Patent, Trademark and copyright.

POLLOCK, JOHN PHLEGER, lawyer; b. Sacramento, Apr. 28, 1920; s. George Gordon and Irma (Phleger) P.; m. Juanita Irene Gossman, Oct. 26, 1945; children: Linda Pollock Harrison, Madeline Pollock Chiotti, John, Gordon. A.B., Stanford U., 1942; J.D., Harvard U., 1948. Bar: Calif. 1949, U.S. Supreme Ct. 1954. Partner Musick, Peeler & Garrett, Los Angeles, 1953-60, Pollock, Williams & Berwanger, Los Angeles, 1960-80, Rodi, Pollock, Pettker, Galbraith & Phillips, Los Angeles, 1980—. Contbr. articles to profl. publs. Active Boy Scouts Am.; former trustee Pitzer Coll., Claremont, Calif., 1968-76; trustee Jones Found., Good Hope Med. Found., Pacific Legal Found. Served with AUS, 1942-45. Fellow Am. Coll. Trial Lawyers; mem. ABA, Los Angeles County Bar Assn. (trustee 1964-66), Am. Judicature Soc. Federal civil litigation, State civil litigation, Probate. Home: 30602 Paseo del Valle Laguna Niguel CA 92677 Office: 611 W 6th St Los Angeles CA 90017

POLLOCK, STEWART GLASSON, judge; b. East Orange, N.J., Dec. 21, 1932. B.A., Hamilton Coll., 1954; LL.B., N.Y. U., 1957. Bar: N.J. bar 1958. Asso. firm Toner, Crowley, Woelper & Vanderbilt, Newark, 1957-58; asst. U.S. atty. Newark, 1958-60; partner firm Schenck, Price, Smith & King, Morristown, N.J., 1960-74, 76-78; commr. N.J. Dept. Pub. Utilities; counsel to gov. State of N.J., Trenton, 1978-79; asso. justice N.J. Supreme Ct., 1979—; mem. N.J. Commn. of Investigation, 1976-78; bd. dirs. Law Ctr. Found. Asso. editor: N.J. Law Jour; contbr. articles to legal jours. Trustee Coll. Medicine and Dentistry, N.J., 1976. Mem. ABA (exec. com. appellate judge's conf., 1985), N.J. Bar Assn. (trustee 1973-78), Am. Judicature Soc. (dir.), Morris County Bar Assn. (pres. 1973), Inst. for Continuing Legal Edn. (advisory com., dir. Am. Judicates Soc. 1984—). Jurisprudence. Office: Court House Annex Morristown NJ 07960

POLOZOLA, FRANK JOSEPH, federal judge; b. Baton Rouge, Jan. 15, 1942; s. Steve A., Sr. and Caroline C. (Lucito) P.; m. Linda Kay White, June 9, 1962; children: Gregory Dean, Sheri Elizabeth, Gordon Damian. Student Bus. Adminstrn., La. State U., 1959-62, J.D., 1965. Bar: La. 1965. Law clk. to U.S. Dist. Judge E. Gordon West, 1965-66; assoc. firm Seale, Smith & Phelps, Baton Rouge, 1966-68; ptnr. Seale, Smith & Phelps, 1968-73; part-time U.S. magistrate Middle Dist. La., Baton Rouge, 1972-73; U.S. magistrate Middle Dist. La., 1973-80, U.S. dist. judge, 1980—; adj. prof. law Law Center, La. State U., 1977—. Mem. La. Bar Assn., Fed. Bar Assn., Baton Rouge Bar Assn., Fifth Circuit Dist. Judges Assn., Omicron Delta Kappa. Roman Catholic. Clubs: KC, La. State U. Alumni Fedn, La. State U. L Club. Jurisprudence. Office: US District Court 113 US Courthouse Baton Rouge LA 70801 *

POLSKY, HOWARD DAVID, lawyer; b. Phila., Sept. 10, 1951; s. Herman and Meriam (Ternoff) P.; m. Ellyn Rosenthal, Sept. 15, 1984. BA, Lehigh U., 1973; JD, Ind. U., 1976. Bar: Pa. 1976, N.J. 1977, D.C. 1978, U.S. Ct. Appeals (D.C. cir.). Atty. FCC, Washington, 1976-79; assoc. Kirkland & Ellis, Washington, 1979-83; ptnr. Wiley, Rein & Fielding, Washington, 1983—; adj. prof. law Del. Law Sch. Widner U., 1981-84. Mem. ABA, Fed. Bar Assn., Fed. Com. Bar Assn. Administrative and regulatory, Public utilities, Telecommunications. Home: 9836 Faust Dr Vienna VA 22180 Office: Wiley Rein & Fielding 1776 K St NW Washington DC 20006

POLSTER, CARL CONRAD, lawyer; b. East St. Louis, Ill., Nov. 19, 1946; s. Philip B. and Dorothea L. (Baker) P.; m. Ann L. Cunliff, June 8, 1968; children: Melanie, Charles, Caroline. BA, DePauw U., 1968; JD, Washington U., St. Louis, 1971. Bar: Mo. 1971, U.S. Dist. Ct. (ea. dist.) Mo. 1971, U.S. Ct. Appeals (8th cir.) 1971. Sole practice St. Louis, 1971—. Bd. dirs. North Side Team Ministry, St. Louis, 1985—. Mem. Mo. Bar Assn., Met. St. Louis Bar Assn. Republican. Presbyterian. Avocations: tennis, golf. Probate, Estate planning. Home: 1309 W Adams Kirkwood MO 63122 Office: 763 S New Ballas Rd Saint Louis MO 63141

POLSTRA, LARRY JOHN, lawyer; b. Lafayette, Ind., June 28, 1945; s. John Edward and Elizabeth (Vandergraff) P.; m. Joan Marie Blair Rozier, Sept. 2, 1972; 1 stepchild, Shawn M. Rozier. BS in Bus. Mgmt., Bob Jones U., 1968; JD, Atlanta Law Sch., 1976, LLM, 1977. Bar: Ga. 1976, U.S. Dist. Ct. (no. dist.) Ga. 1976, U.S. Ct. Appeals 1976, U.S. Supreme Ct. 1976. Mktg. dir. N.Am. Security, Atlanta, 1972-73; acctg. supr. Allstate Ins. Co., Atlanta, 1973-76; sole practice Atlanta, 1976-77; ptnr. Smith & Polstra, Atlanta, 1977—; arbitrator Fulton County Superior Ct., Atlanta, 1986. Served to 1st lt. USMC, 1968-71, Vietnam. Mem. ABA, Atlanta Bar Assn., Ga. Assn. Trial Lawyers, Ga. Assn. Criminal Def. Lawyers, Marine Corps Assn. Ga. Lawyers. Avocations: golf, softball. State civil litigation, Family and matrimonial, Criminal. Home: 988 Hess Dr Avondale Estates GA 30002 Office: 250 Piedmont Ave NE Suite 1400 Atlanta GA 30308

POLZIN, JOHN THEODORE, lawyer; b. Rock Island, Ill., Dec. 23, 1919; s. Max August and Charlotte Barbara (Trenkenschuh) P.; m. Helen Louise Hosford, Nov. 27, 1969. A.B., U. Ill., 1941, J.D., 1943. Bar: Ill. 1943. Sole practice, Galva, Ill., 1946-55, Chgo., 1975—; city atty., Galva, 1950-54; assoc. Langner, Parry, Card & Langner, Chgo., 1955-75; lectr. Ill. Inst. for Continuing Legal Edn., 1978. Served to lt. USNR, 1943-46. Mem. ABA, Ill. State Bar Assn. (chmn. patent, trademark and copyright law sect. 1981-82), Patent Law Assn. Chgo. (chmn. fgn. trademark com. 1972, 74). Republican. Probate, Trademark and copyright, General practice. Home: 1503 Oak Ave Evanston IL 60201 Office: 122 S Michigan Ave Suite 1452 Chicago IL 60603

POMEROY, GREGG JOSEPH, lawyer; b. Flushing, N.Y., June 22, 1948; s. George Bart and Dianne (Marshall) P.; m. Deborah Christina Pomeroy, Feb. 16, 1985; 1 child, Christopher William. BA, U. Fla., 1971; JD, Samford U., 1974. Bar: Fla. 1974, U.S. Dist. Ct. Fla. 1974, U.S. Ct. Appeals (5th and 11th cirs.) 1974. Asst. pub. defender 17th Jud. Cir., Ft. Lauderdale, Fla., 1974-75; ptnr. Pomeroy, Pomeroy & Pomeroy, Ft. Lauderdale, 1976-86. Served to ensign class 4 USNG, 1970-76. Mem. ABA, Def. Research Inst., Nat. Rifle Assn. Roman Catholic. Clubs: Boat U.S., NRA. Avocation: boating. Personal injury, Insurance. Office: Pomeroy Pomeroy & Pomeroy 1995 E Oakland Park Blvd #300 Fort Lauderdale FL 33306

POMEROY, HARLAN, lawyer; b. Cleve., May 7, 1923; s. Lawrence Alson and Frances (Macdonald) P.; m. Barbara Lesser, Aug. 24, 1962; children: Robert Charles, Caroline Macdonald, Harlan III. B.S., Yale U., 1944; LL.B., Harvard U., 1948. Bar: Conn. 1949, U.S. Supreme Ct. 1954, U.S. Ct. Appeals (fed. cir.) 1954, Ohio 1958, U.S. Dist. Ct. (no. dist.) Ohio 1958, U.S. Claims Ct. 1958, U.S. Ct. Appeals (6th cir.) 1958, U.S. Tax Ct. 1958, D.C. 1975, Md. 1981, U.S. Dist. Ct. (D.C. dist.) 1984, U.S. Ct. Internat. Trade 1984, U.S. Ct. Appeals (D.C. cir.) 1986. Atty. trial sect. tax div. Dept. Justice, Washington, 1952-58; assoc. Baker & Hostetler, Cleve., 1958-62; ptnr. Baker & Hostetler, 1962—, Washington, 1975—; gen. chmn. Cleve. Tax Inst., 1971; lectr. in field. Contbr. articles to profl. jours. Treas. Shaker Heights Democratic Club, Ohio, 1960-62; trustee, mem. exec. com. First Unitarian Ch. of Cleve., 1965-68; gen. counsel, formerly asst. treas. John Glenn Presdl. Com., 1983—; participant Vol. Lawyers Project, Legal Counsel for Elderly, Washington, 1983—. Served to lt. (j.g.) USNR, 1943-46. Mem. ABA, Fed. Bar Assn., D.C. Bar Assn., Ohio Bar Assn., Cleve. Bar Assn., Md. Bar Assn., Montgomery County Bar Assn. Clubs: Nat. Lawyers (Washington); Nat Democratic; Columbia Country (Bethesda); Yale (N.Y.C.). Corporate taxation, Contracts commercial, Federal civil litigation. Home: 4500 Boxwood Rd Bethesda MD 20816 Office: Baker & Hostetler 1050 Conneticut Ave NW Washington DC 20036 also: 3200 National City Ctr Cleveland OH 44414

POMMERVILLE, ROBERT W., corporate lawyer. BA, Occidental Coll., 1965; JD, U. Utah, 1968. Trial atty. Safeco Ins. Co., 1969-70; corp. counsel Beverly Enterprises, Pasadena, Calif., 1970-76, v.p. gen. counsel, 1984—; pres. Currie & Kendall, 1980-84. Office: Beverly Enterprises 873 S Fair Oaks Ave Pasadena CA 91105 *

POMPO, VINCENT MATTHEW, lawyer; b. Phila., Mar. 5, 1957; s. Vincent Carmen and Helen (Passarelli) P. BA, Pa. State U., 1978; JD, Am. U., 1982. Bar: Pa. 1982, N.J. 1983. Asst. counsel, bur. legal services Pa. Dept. Environ. Resources, Harrisburg, 1982-84, asst. counsel, bur. regulatory counsel, 1984-86, asst. counsel, bur. litigation, 1986—. Mem. ABA, Phila. Bar Assn., Phi Alpha Delta (dist. justice 1982-84). Environment, FERC practice, Real property. Office: Dept Environ Resources 1314 Chestnut St Suite 1200 Philadelphia PA 19107

PONADER, WAYNE CARL, lawyer; b. Marshfield, Wis., July 8, 1931; s. Carl Frederick and Alfhild (Anderson) P.; m. Martha Bowen Downs, June 23, 1956; children: Carl W., Erick D., Jonathan W., David W. AB, Ind. U., 1953, JD, 1956. Bar: Ind. 1956, Fla. 1974. Ptnr. Bose McKinney & Evans, Indpls. Pres. Greater Indpls. Housing Devel. Corp., 1976-78, Indpls. Housing Loan Fund, Inc., 1976-78, Episcopal Community Services, Inc., 1976-77. Mem. ABA, Ind. Bar Assn., Fla. Bar Assn., Indpls. Bar Assn., Am. Coll. Mortgage Attys., Am Judicature Soc., Comml. Law League, Order of Coif. Republican. Clubs: Columbia, Skyline (Indpls.). Federal civil litigation, Antitrust, Bankruptcy. Home: 11407 Forest Knoll Circle Noblesville IN 46060 Office: Bose McKinney & Evans 1100 First Ind Bldg Indianapolis IN 46204

PONDER, L(ESLIE) BARBEE, M, lawyer; b. Jan. 8, 1909; s. Leslie Barbee and Catherine Elizabeth (Law) P.; m. Cecelia Spansel, Nov. 2, 1932; children: Leslie B. III, John Lynn, Charles Law. LLB, Tulane U., 1931. Bar: La., U.S. Dist. Ct. La., U.S. Ct. Appeals (5th cir.), U.S. Tax Ct., U.S. Ct. Claims, U.S. Supreme Ct. Ptnr. Ponder and Ponder, Amite, La., 1931—. Mem. ABA, La. Bar Assn., Nat. Skeet Shooting Assn. (La. del.), Phi Alpha Delta. Democrat. Baptist. Lodges: Rotary (past v.p., pres.), Woodmen of World. Criminal, State civil litigation. Home and Office: PO Box 217 123 SE Central Ave Amite LA 70422

PONDER, LESTER MCCONNICO, lawyer, educator; b. Walnut Ridge, Ark., Dec. 10, 1912; s. Harry Lee and Clyde (Gant) P.; m. Sallie Mowry Clover, Nov. 7, 1942; children—Melinda, Constance; m. Phyllis Gretchen Harting, Oct. 14, 1978. B.S. summa cum laude in Commerce, Northwestern U., 1934; J.D. with honors, George Washington U., 1938. Bar: Ark. 1937, Ind. 1948. Atty. Ark. Dept. Revenue, Little Rock, 1939-41; atty. IRS, Chgo. and Indpls., 1941-51; ptnr. Barnes & Thornburg and predecessor Barnes, Hickam, Pantzer & Boyd, Indpls., 1952—; adj. prof. Sch. Law, Ind. U., Bloomington, 1951-54, Sch. Law, Ind. U., Indpls., 1954-63; lectr. polit. sci. Ind. U., Indpls., 1982—. Author: United States Tax Court Practice & Procedure, 1976. Bd. dirs., vice chmn. Ind. chpt. The Nature Conservancy, 1981—; bd. mem. Sigma Chi Found.; mem. adv. bd. Jr. Achievement Indpls., 1982-83. Served with USN, 1942. Fellow Am. Bar Found., Ind. State Bar Found., Ind. Bar Found., Am. Coll. Tax Counsel; mem. ABA, Ind. State Bar Assn., Indpls. Bar Assn., Bar Assn. of Seventh Fed. Cir. Republican. Methodist. Club: Meridian Hills Country (Indpls.). Lodge: Rotary (past bd. dirs.). Corporate taxation, Personal income taxation, Estate taxation. Office: Barnes & Thornburg Merchants Bank Bldg Suite 1313 Indianapolis IN 46204

PONGRACZ, ANN CECILIA, lawyer; b. Phila., Nov. 30, 1953; d. Joseph C. and Dolores M. (De Laurentis) P.; m. Stephen B. Yoken, May 29, 1983; 1 child, Daniel Pongracz. BA, Harvard U., 1975; JD, Temple U., 1980. Bar: Pa. 1980, Calif. 1981, U.S. Dist. Ct. (no. dist.) Calif. 1981. Trial atty. CAB, Washington, 1980-81; assoc. Graham & James, San Francisco, 1981-83; sr. regulatory atty. GTE Sprint Communications Corp., Burlingame, Calif., 1983-87; dir. govt. affairs and industry relations Pacific div. U.S. Sprint Communications Co., Burlingame, 1987—. Mem. ABA, Calif. Bar Assn., Queens Bench. Avocations: scuba diving, canoeing, rafting, hiking, gardening. Telecommunications, Administrative and regulatory. Office: US Sprint Communications Co 700 Airport Blvd B-4 Burlingame CA 94010

PONITZ, JOHN ALLAN, corporate trial lawyer; b. Battle Creek, Mich., Sept. 7, 1949; m. Nancy J. Roberts, Aug. 14, 1971; children: Amy, Matthew, Julie. BA, Albion Coll., 1971; JD, Wayne State U., 1974. Bar: U.S. Dist. Ct. (so. dist.) Mich. 1975, U.S. Ct. Appeals (6th cir.) 1981. Assoc. McMachan & Kaichen, Birmingham, Mich., 1973-75; atty. Grand Trunk Western R.R., Detroit, 1975-80, trial atty., 1980—. V.p. Beverly Hills (Mich.) Jaycees, 1981. Served to capt. USAR, 1974-82. Mem. Mich. Bar Assn., Detroit Bar Assn., Nat. Assn. R.R. Trial Counsel. Lutheran. Avocations: golf, sailing. Federal civil litigation, General corporate, Personal injury. Office: Grand Trunk Western RR Co 131 W Lafayette Blvd Detroit MI 48226

PONOMAREFF, GUYLA WOODWARD, lawyer; b. Charleroi, Pa., May 17, 1932; d. Lloyd Walker and Elizabeth Mary (Carroll) W.; m. George Leonard Ponomareff, June 28, 1959; children—Eleanor, Lisa, Gregory. A.B., Pa. State U., 1953; J.D., U. Pa., 1956; LL.M., Boalt Hall, U. Calif., 1974. Bar: Calif. 1966, D.C. 1956, Pa. 1957; cert. family law specialist. Trial atty., Office Solicitor, U.S. Dept. Labor, Phila., 1956-57; legis. atty., Washington, 1958-59; research atty. Jenks, Kidwell, Goodsill & Anderson, Honolulu, 1959-61; sole practice, Castro Valley, Calif., 1966-70, Lafayette, Calif., 1975—; judge pro tem Mcpl. Ct. Walnut Creek-Danville (Calif.), 1983—; arbitrator Superior Ct. Contra Costa County, 1982—; instr. Armstrong Coll., Berkeley, 1983. Pres. Mt. Diablo chpt. ACLU, 1980-82; bd. dirs. ACLU No. Calif., 1977-80; chmn. legis. com. Contra Costa Child Abuse Prevention, 1982-84, bd. dirs., 1985—; mem. adv. council State Bd. PTA, 1982-83; mem. Contra Costa Battered Women's Alternatives Legal Adv. Com., 1981-83; bd. dirs. Calif. Nat. Womens Polit. , 1984—, co-chmn. Contra Costa, 1976; co-chmn. Contra Costa Com. to Establish a Commn. on Status of Women, 1974-75. Mem. ABA, Contra Costa Bar Assn., Alameda Contra Costa Trial Laywers, Women Laywers of Alameda County, Calif. Women Lawyers. Democrat. Family and matrimonial, Probate. Office: 3687 Mt Diablo Blvd #250 Lafayette CA 94549-3739

PONSOLDT, JAMES FARMER, law educator; b. Jersey City, June 14, 1946; s. Raymond Samuel and Margaret Elizabeth (Farmer) P.; m. Susan Elizabeth Teason, Sept. 5, 1968; children—Katherine, James. A.B., Cornell U., 1968; J.D., Harvard U., 1972. Bar: S.C. 1974, U.S. Dist. Ct. S.C. 1974, U.S. Ct. Appeals (4th cir.) 1975, U.S. Ct. Appeals (7th cir.) 1976, U.S. Ct. Appeals (9th cir.) 1977, U.S. Supreme Ct. 1977, U.S. Ct. Appeals (11th cir.) 1981, U.S. Ct. Appeals (D.C. cir.) 1975. Editorial asst. Atlantic Monthly, Boston, 1968; assoc. firm Paul, Weiss, Rifkind, Wharton & Garrison, N.Y.C., 1972-73; law clk. U.S. Ct. Appeals, 1973-74; sr. trial atty. U.S. Dept. Justice, Washington, 1975-78; vis. prof. law Tulane U., 1982; assoc. prof. law U. Ga. Law Sch., 1978-86, prof., 1986—; lectr. internat. competition law U.U.B., Brussels, Belgium, 1986; witness U.S. Ho. Monopolies Subcom., Washington, 1980-85, Ga. Atty. Gen.'s Office, 1979-80; witness cons. U.S. Senate Judiciary Com., 1983-84. Contbr. articles to profl. jours., editorials to N.Y. Times, Wall St. Jour. Cons., Concerned Water Users of Clarke County, 1983-84; tutor Clarke County Sch. System, 1979-80. Served with USNR, 1969-71. NDEA fellow, 1970-71. Mem. S.C. Bar Assn. Club: Harvard. Antitrust, Federal civil litigation, Criminal. Home: 305 Great Oak Dr Athens GA 30605 Office: U Ga Law Sch Herty Dr Athens GA 30602

PONZINI, JOHN LINO, lawyer; b. N.Y.C., Aug. 29, 1953; s. Lino and Marie (Contino) P. Student U. Nice, France, 1975; B.A., Iona Coll., 1977; J.D., Yeshiva U., 1980. Bar: Conn. 1981, U.S. Dist. Ct. Conn. 1982, U.S. Dist. Ct. (so. dist.) N.Y. 1984. Summer intern N.Y. County Dist. Atty.'s Office, N.Y.C., 1979; sole practice, Stamford, Conn., 1982-87, ptnr. Brandner & Ponzini, 1987—; spl. pub. defender, 1985. Performing arts scholar Catawba Coll., Salisbury, N.C., 1971-72; acad. scholar Iona Coll., 1975-76, Philosophy medal, 1977. Mem. Conn. Bar Assn., ABA, Conn. Trial Lawyers Assn., Assn. Trial Lawyers Am. Federal civil litigation, State civil litigation, Criminal. Office: 5 Hillandale Ave Stamford CT 06902

POOLE, ALBERT HARRISON, lawyer; b. Petersburg, Va., June 2, 1955; s. Albert Prince and Evelyn (McCann) p.; m. Janice Angell, Dec. 30, 1978; children: Henry Harrison, Andrew Dean. BS, Va. Tech., 1977; JD, U. Va., 1980. Bar: Va. 1980, U.S. Dist. Ct. (ea. dist.) Va. 1983, U.S. Ct. Appeals (4th cir.) 1985. Assoc. Kaufman & Canoles, P.C., Norfolk, Va., 1983—. Bd. dirs. VPI German Club Alumni Found., Blacksburg, Va., 1978—. Served to capt. U.S. Army, 1980-83. Mem. ABA (litigation sect.), Am. Trial Lawyers Assn., Va. State Bar (litigation sect.), Norfolk-Portsmouth Bar Assn., Va. Tech. Alumni Assn. (treas. Tidewater chpt. 1984—). Republican. Episcopalian. State civil litigation, Federal civil litigation. Home: 3329 Kings Neck Dr Virginia Beach VA 23452 Office: Kaufman & Canoles PC PO Box 3037 Norfolk VA 23514

POOLE, CECIL F., judge; b. Birmingham, Ala.; children: Gayle, Patricia. LL.B., U. Mich.; LL.M., Harvard U., 1939. Practice of law San Francisco, former asst. dist. atty., 1951-58; clemency sec. to Gov. Brown of Calif., 1958-61; U.S. atty. No. Dist. Calif., 1961-70; Regents prof. Law U. Calif., Berkeley, 1970; counsel firm Jacobs, Sills & Coblentz, San Francisco, 1970-76; judge U.S. Dist. Ct., No. Dist. Calif., 1976-79, U.S. Ct. of Appeals for 9th Circuit, 1979—; adj. prof. Golden Gate U. Sch. Law, 1953-58; mem. adv. com. Nat. Commn. for Reform Fed. Criminal Laws, 1968-70. Served to 2d lt. AUS, World War II. Mem. ABA (chmn. sect. individual rights 1971-72, ho. of dels. 1972-74), San Francisco Bar Assn. (dir. 1975-76). Jurisprudence. Office: PO Box 547 US Ct Appeals and Post Office Bldg San Francisco CA 94101

POOLE, SHARON ALEXANDRA, lawyer; b. Los Angeles, Jan. 31, 1950; d. James Earl and Shirley Lenore (Solo) P.; m. Larry Greenberger, July 4, 1972 (div. Mar. 1983). BS in Communications, Fla. State U., 1977; JD, Stetson U., 1980; LLM in Admiralty, Tulane U., 1982. Bar: Fla. 1981, U.S. Dist. Ct. (mid. dist.) Fla. 1982. Ptnr. Cushman & Poole, St. Augustine, Fla., 1982-83; sole practice St. Augustine, 1983—. Mem. ABA, Nat. Assn. Criminal Def. Lawyers. Admiralty, Family and matrimonial, State civil litigation. Office: 44 Spanish St Saint Augustine FL 32084

POOLE, WILLIAM STITT, JR., lawyer; b. Forrest City, Ark., Nov. 26, 1947; s. William S. Sr. and Mary Jane (Norman) P.; m. Katherine Beadles, Aug. 19, 1972; children: William S. III, Charles Barry, Robert Edward, Mary Katharine. BS, U. Ala., 1971, JD, 1973, LLM in Taxation, 1981. Bar: Ala. 1973, La. 1974, U.S. Dist. Ct. (ea. dist.) La. 1975, U.S. Ct. Appeals (5th cir.) 1979, U.S. Dist. Ct. (so., no. and mid. dists.) Ala. 1980, U.S. Ct. Appeals (11th cir.) 1981, U.S. Dist. Ct. (no. dist.) Ala. 1986. Law clk. to judge U.S. Dist. Ct. (ea. dist.), New Orleans, 1973-75; assoc. Adams & Reese, 1978; sole practice New Orleans, 1979-82, Demopolis, Ala., 1985—; ptnr. Bryant, McNeill & Poole, Demopolis, 1982-85. Author: (with others) How to Administer Estates in Alabama, 1984. Chmn. Christmas on the River, 1980; trustee Dayton (Ala.) Meth. Ch., 1980; trustee, pres. Marengo County Hist. Soc., Demopolis, 1981-83. Served to 1st lt. USAR, 1973-76. Mem. ABA, Ala. Bar Assn., La. Bar Assn., U. Ala. Alumni Assn. (pres. New Orleans chpt. 1977, pres. Demopolis chpt. 1978), Ala. Nat. Alumni Assn. (regional v.p. 1986-87). Corporate taxation, Estate taxation, Personal income taxation. Home: General Delivery Dayton AL 36731 Office: 210 N Strawberry PO Box 118 Demopolis AL 36732

POOLEY, BEVERLEY JOHN, legal educator, librarian; b. London, Eng., Apr. 4, 1934; came to U.S., 1957; s. William Vincent and Christine Beatrice (Coleman) P.; m. Patricia Joan Ray, June 8, 1958; children—Christopher Jonathan, Rachel Vanessa. B.A., Cambridge U., Eng., 1956, LL.B., 1957; LL.M., U. Mich., Ann Arbor, 1958, S.J.D., 1961, M.A.L.S., 1964. Legis. analyst U. Mich. Law Sch., Ann Arbor, 1958-60; lectr. U. Ghana Law Sch., 1960-62; instr. U. Mich. Law Sch., Ann Arbor, 1962-63, asst. prof., 1963-66, assoc. prof., 1966-70, dir. law library, 1966-84, prof., 1970—, assoc. dean law library, 1984—. Author: The Evolution of British Planning Legislation, 1960; Planning and Zoning in the United States, 1961. Scholar, King's Coll., Cambridge, Eng., 1956; Blackstone Scholar, Middle Temple, London, 1957. Democrat. Avocations: Acting; musical comedy; food preparation. Contracts commercial, Librarianship, Legal education.

POOLEY, JAMES HENRY ANDERSON, lawyer, author; b. Dayton, Ohio, Oct. 4, 1948; s. Howard Carl and Daisy Frances (Lindsley) P.; children by previous marriage: Jefferson Douglas, Christopher James; m. Laura Jean Anderson, Oct. 13, 1984. BA, Lafayette Coll., 1970; JD, Columbia U., 1973. Bar: Calif. 1973, U.S. Dist. Ct. (no. dist.) Calif. 1973, U.S. Ct. Appeals (9th cir.) 1974, U.S. Supreme Ct. 1977, U.S. Dist. Ct. (cen. dist.) Calif. 1978. Assoc. Wilson, Mosher & Sonsini, Palo Alto, Calif., 1973-78; ptnr. Mosher, Pooley & Sullivan, Palo Alto, 1978—; lectr. Practicing Law Inst., N.Y.C., 1983, 85-86, Santa Clara U. Sch. Law, 1985—. Author: Trade Secrets, 1982, Protecting Technology, 1983, Trying the High Technology Case, 1984, The Executive's Guide to Protecting Proprietary Business Information and Trade Secrets, 1987; contbr. articles to profl. jours.; editor-in-chief Trade Secret Law Reporter, 1984-85; bd. advisors Santa Clara Computer and High Tech. Law Jour., 1984—. Arbitrator, judge pro tem Santa Clara County Superior Ct., San Jose, 1979—. Mem. ABA, Computer Law Assn., Assn. Bus. Trial Lawyers, Am. Electronics Assn. (chmn. lawyers' com. 1981-82). Republican. Methodist. Federal civil litigation, State civil litigation. Office: Mosher Pooley & Sullivan 525 University Ave Palo Alto CA 94301

POPE, DANIEL JAMES, lawyer; b. Chgo., Nov. 22, 1948. BA, Loyola U., Chgo., 1972; JD cum laude, John Marshall Law Sch., 1975; postgrad., U. Chgo., 1977-78. Bar: Ill. 1975, U.S. Dist. Ct. (no. dist.) Ill. 1982, N.Y. 1983, U.S. Tax Ct. 1985. Corp. trust adminstr. Continental Bank, Chgo., 1972-74; assoc. Haskell & Perrin, Chgo., 1975-77; assoc. Coffield, Ungaretti, Harris & Slavin, Chgo., 1977-81, ptnr., 1981—; instr. John Marshall Law Sch., Chgo., 1978-79; appointed panel atty. Fed. Defender Program, Chgo., 1983. Mem. ABA, Ill. Bar Assn., Chgo. Bar Assn. (chmn. aviation law com. 1979, jud. evaluation com. 1982), Fed. Bar Assn., Chgo. Counsel of Lawyers. Clubs: Tavern (Chgo.), Oak Park Country (Elmwood Park, Ill.). Federal civil litigation, State civil litigation, Criminal. Home: 3000 N Sheridan Rd Apt 17-C Chicago IL 60657 Office: Coffield Ungaretti Harris & Slavin 3500 3 First National Plaza Chicago IL 60602

POPE, DAVID BRUCE, lawyer; b. Lake City, Fla., Nov. 15, 1945; s. Thomas Bass and Nathalie Jane (Estill) P.; m. Martha McEvoy, Aug. 26, 1967; children—John Brandon, Nora Katharine. B.A., Tex. Technol. U., 1968; J.D., U. Houston, 1971. Bar: Tex. 1971, U.S. Ct. Apls. (5th cir., 11th cir.) 1973, 81, U.S. Sup. Ct. 1975. Briefing atty. First Ct. Civil Apls., Houston, 1971-72; assoc. Lynch, Chappel, Allday & Aldridge, Midland, Tex., 1972-76; atty. Texaco, Inc., Houston, 1976-80, Midland, Tex., 1980-82, chief atty., 1982-84, sr. atty., 1985—. Mem. ABA, Tex. Bar Assn., Houston Bar Assn., Midland Bar Assn. Methodist. Club: Greentree Country. Oil and gas leasing, Environment, Administrative and regulatory. Home: 3205 Seaboard Midland TX 79705 Office: Texaco Inc Heritage Ctr 500 N Loraine St PO Box 310 9 Midland TX 79702

POPE, IREE ROSE WILLIAMS, judge; b. Sylvania, Ga., July 26, 1916; d. Hiram Erasmus and Rosie (Bragg) Williams; m. Otto W. Pope, June 19, 1938 (dec. Nov. 26, 1983); 1 child, Otto William (dec.). Grad. high sch., Screven County, Ga.; student Garrett Comml. Sch., Augusta. Dep. clk. Probate Ct., Augusta, 1943-47, clk., 1947-57, judge, 1957—; dir. Ga. Fed. (now Comml. Bank). Past pres. Augusta Area Mental Health Assn.; past bd. dirs. ARC Home Service Com.; past v.p. local orgn. Democratic Party, bd. govs.; past mem. State Dem. exec. com. past mem. adv. com. Half-Way House, Augusta Area Mental Health Assn.; active fund-raising drives; mem. election laws study com. under govs. Griffin and Vandiver, constl. revision com. under Gov. Sanders; bd. dirs. Augusta Richmond County Law Library, also sec., treas.; mem. adv. bd. Parents Without Partners, Inc., Greater Augusta chpt. 131. First Woman elected Judge of any Ct. in Richmond County, Ga. Mem. Internat. Assn. Probate Judges (life), Nat. Assn. Probate Judges (life), Augusta Geneal. Soc. (life), Probate Judges Assn. of Ga. (past sec.-treas.). Roman Catholic. Jurisprudence. Home: 2219 Morningside Dr Augusta GA 30904 Office: Richmond County Probate Ct 401 Municipal Bldg Augusta GA 30911

POPE, JOSEPH RONALD, lawyer; b. La Junta, Colo., Mar. 6, 1951; s. Edward Eugene Pope and Elinor (Jackson) Beaty; m. Katheryn Campbell Tucker, Feb. 5, 1983; 1 child, Alicia Elinor. BA, U. Colo., 1973, JD, 1977. Bar: Colo. 1977, U.S. Dist. Ct. Colo. 1977. Assoc. Law Offices of Robin Crites, Monte Vista, Colo., 1978-79, Law Offices of John Wilder, Monte Vista, 1979; sole practice Boulder, Colo., 1979-80; landman Exxon Co. U.S.A., Midland, Tex., 1980—; supr. title and leasing Exxon Co. U.S.A., Midland, 1985-86, prodn. land coordinator, 1986—. Vol. Midland Community Theatre, 1981—. Mem. ABA, Am. Assn. Petroleum Landmen, Permian Basin Landman's Assn. Presbyterian. Club: Plaza (Midland). Oil and gas leasing, Real property, Administrative and regulatory. Home: 2804 Emerson Ln Midland TX 79705 Office: Exxon Co USA PO Box 1600 Midland TX 79702

POPE, MARK ANDREW, lawyer; b. Munster, Ind., May 22, 1952; s. Thomas A. and Eleanor E. (Miklos) P.; m. Julia Risk Pope, June 15, 1974; children: Brent Andrew, Bradley James. BA, Purdue U., 1974; JD cum laude, Ind. U., 1977. Bar: Ind. 1977, U.S. Dist. Ct. (so. dist.) Ind. 1977, U.S. Ct. Appeals (7th cir.) 1984. Assoc. Johnson & Weaver, Indpls., 1977-79, Rocap, Rocap, Reese & Young, Indpls., 1980-82, Dutton & Overman, Indpls., 1982—. Named Disting. Hoosier, Gov. of Ind., 1974. Fellow Ind. Bar Found., Indpls. Bar Found (disting.); mem. ABA (dist. rep. young lawyers div. 1981-83, exec. council 1981—, cabinet 1982—), Indpls. Bar Assn. (v.p. 1983, chmn. young lawyers div. 1981). Avocations: tennis, golf, running. State civil litigation, Federal civil litigation, Contracts commercial. Home: 5810 White Oak Ct Indianapolis IN 46220 Office: Dutton & Overman PC 710 Century Bldg 36 S Pennsylvania St Indianapolis IN 46204

POPE, MICHAEL ARTHUR, lawyer; b. Chgo., June 27, 1944; s. Arthur Wellington and Phyllis Anne (O'Connor) P.; m. Christine Collins, Nov. 19, 1966; children—Jennifer, Amy, Katherine. B.S., Loyola U., Chgo., 1966; J.D. cum laude, Northwestern U., 1969. Bar: Ill. 1969, U.S. Dist. Ct. (no. dist.) Ill. 1969, U.S. Ct. Appeals (7th cir.) 1970, U.S. Supreme Ct. 1980, N.Y. 1985. Teaching asst. U. Ill. Coll. Law, Champaign, 1969-70; assoc. Isham, Lincoln & Beale, Chgo., 1970-76; ptnr. Phelan & Pope, 1976-80; prin. Phelan, Pope & John, Ltd., 1980—; adj. prof. law Chgo.-Kent Law Sch. Ill. Inst. Tech., 1982-85; treas., bd. dirs. Lawyers Trust Fund Ill. Mem. ABA, Ill. Bar Assn., Chgo. Bar Assn. (editor in chief Chgo. Bar Assn. record), Am. Bd. Profl. Liability Attys. (pres.), Internat. Assn. Defense Counsel (chmn. excess and reinsurance com.) Clubs: Skokie Country (Glencoe, Ill.); East Bank (Chgo.). Insurance, Personal injury, Environment. Office: Phelan Pope & John 180 N Wacker Dr Suite 500 Chicago IL 60606

POPE, PATRICK HARRIS, lawyer, businessman; b. Dunn, N.C., Aug. 27, 1944; s. Claude Efton and Rochelle Olive (Jackson) P.; m. Mary Norfleet Tilghman, Aug. 21, 1965; children—Patrick Tilghman, Wiley Jackson, Caroline Denning. B.S. in Bus. Adminstrn., U. N.C., 1966, J.D. with honors, 1969. Bar: N.C. 1969, U.S. Dist. Ct. (ea. dist.) N.C. 1969. Ptnr. Doffermyre & Pope, Dunn, N.C., 1969-72; sr. ptnr. Pope, Tilghman & Tart, Dunn, 1972—. Research editor N.C. Law Rev., 1969; contbr. articles to profl. jours. Campaign mgr. Harnett County Holshouser for Gov. Com., Dunn, 1972; bd. dirs. Bonders, Inc., Dunn, 1972-80, Gen. William C. Lee Meml. Commn., Inc., Dunn, 1983—; trustee Betsy Johnson Meml. Hosp., Inc., Dunn, 1977-82, vice chmn., 1983-84, chmn., 1984—; chmn. N.C. Heart Assn., 1979. Mem. Harnett County Bar Assn. (pres. 1974-75), 11th Jud. Dist. Bar Assn. (pres. 1974-75, v.p. 1973-74), N.C. Bar Assn., N.C. Acad. Trial Lawyers, N.C. State Bar, Dunn Area C. of C. (bd. dirs. 1982-85), Order of the Coif. Republican. Presbyterian. Club: Chicora Country (bd. dirs. 1982-85). Lodge: Masons. Personal injury, State civil litigation, General practice. Home: 208 W Pearsall St Dunn NC 28334 Office: Pope Tilghman & Tart 100 E Cumberland St Dunn NC 28334

POPE, ROBERT DEAN, lawyer; b. Memphis, Mar. 10, 1945; s. Ben Duncan and Phyllis (Drenner) P.; m. Elizabeth Dante Cohen, June 26, 1971; 1 child, Justin Nicholas Nathanson. AB, Princeton U., 1967; Diploma in Hist. Studies, Cambridge U., 1971; JD, Yale U., 1972, PhD, 1976. Bar: Va. 1974, D.C. 1980. Assoc. Hunton & Williams, Richmond, Va., 1974-80; ptnr. Hunton & Williams, Richmond, 1980—. Mem. Va. Gen. Assembly Continuing Care Task Force, 1985—, adv. council dept. history Princeton U., 1987—. Mem. Va. Bar Assn. (chmn. legal problems of the elderly 1982—), Nat. Assn. Bond Lawyers (treas. 1984-85, sec. 1985-86, pres.-elect 1986—, bd. dirs. 1982—), Am. Acad. Hosp. Attys., Yale Law Sch. Assn. (exec. com. 1985—), Phi Beta Kappa. Republican. Episcopalian. Avocations: history, golf, music. Municipal bonds, Health, Securities. Home: 8707 Ruggles Rd Richmond VA 23229 Office: Hunton & Williams 707 E Main St PO Box 1535 Richmond VA 23219

POPE, WILLIAM ROBERT, lawyer; b. Mt. Mourne, N.C., Feb. 24, 1918; s. James Robert and Mary Elizabeth (Kelly) P.; m. Ina Amelia Barber, Sept. 16, 1945; children—William Robert Jr., James S., Charles V., Elizabeth Pope Gibson, Deborah Pope Webb, Caroline Pope Jarrell; m. Esther Maria Johnson, July 31, 1976. A.A., Brevard (N.C.) Jr. Coll., 1938; B.S., Davidson (N.C.) Coll., 1940; LL.B., U. N.C., 1948. Bar: N.C. 1948, U.S. Dist. Ct. (mid. dist.) N.C. 1956. Assoc. Zeb V. Turlington, Mooresville, N.C., 1948-52; judge Mooresville Recorder's Ct., 1952-63; sr. ptnr. Pope and Brawley, Mooresville, 1963-83, William R. Pope, Mooresville, 1983-84; sole practice, 1984—; pres. Braco, Inc., Rocky River Investment Co.; mem. N.C. Ho. of Reps., 1951-52, 63-64; mem. N.C. Traffic Code Commn., 1963; chmn. adv. com. Iredell County Govt. Complex. Past pres., bd. regents Barum Springs Home for Children. Served to lt. USNR, 1940-45. Decorated D.F.C. Mem. ABA, N.C. Bar Assn., Iredell County Bar Assn. (past pres.), Phi Delta Phi. Democrat. Presbyterian. Clubs: Rotary (Mooresville); Masons (Davidson). General practice, Real property, General corporate. Office: US Hwy 21 S PO Box 1066 Mooresville NC 28115

POPER, MICHAEL CHARLES, lawyer; b. Chgo., Sept. 4, 1943; s. Foster and Esther (Rife) P.; m. Maureen Renee Gore, Sept. 2, 1967; children: Amy Beth, Joshua Benjaman. BSA in Acctg., U. Ill., 1965, JD, 1968. Bar: Ill. 1968, U.S. Dist. Ct. (no. dist.) Ill. 1968. Assoc. Zukowski & Zukowski, Crystal Lake, Ill., 1968-70; ptnr. Zukowski, Poper, Rogers & Flood, Crystal Lake, 1970-84; sole practice Crystal lake, 1984—. Mem. nat. com. Boy Scouts Am., Dallas, 1983—, v.p. Blackhawk Area council Boy Scouts Am., Rockford, Ill., 1983—. Mem. ABA, Ill. Bar Assn., McHenry County Bar Assn., Chgo. Bar Assn., Crystal Lake C. of C. Ambassadors. Club: Ambassador. Lodge: Lions (sec. Crystal Lake 1982-83), Moose. Family and matrimonial, Local government, General corporate. Home: 334 Melrose Ln Crystal Lake IL 60014 Office: 27 N Main St Crystal Lake IL 60014

POPHAM, ARTHUR COBB, JR., lawyer; b. Mar. 31, 1915; s. Arthur C. and Ethel (Estes) P.; m. Mary Corzine, July 6, 1939; children: Carole Popham McKnight, Melinda Popham Benton, Arthur C. III; m. Phoebe T. Kennedy, Nov. 13, 1969. BS, U. Ariz., 1937; JD, U. Mo., 1939. Bar: Mo., 1939, U.S. Dist. Ct. (we. dist.) Mo., 1940. Assoc. Cowgill & Popham, Kansas City, Mo., 1939-40; ptnr. Popham, Conway, Sweeny, Fremont, and Bundschu (and Predecessors) P.C., Kansas City, 1940—, also bd. dirs. Author: Stalking Game From Desert to Tundra, 1986.; contbr. articles on various topics to outdoor mags. Collector, planner Natural History Habitat Groups, Kansas City Mus., 1951-63; pres. bd. dirs. Kansas City Mus. History and Sci., 1952-85. Served to 1st lt. USAAF, 1942-45. Mem. ABA, Mo. Bar Assn., Kansas City Bar Assn. Clubs: Boone and Crockett (Dumfries, Va.) (v.p. 1970-86), Shikar Safari Internat. (Alex, Va.). Avocations: hunting, conservation groups. Insurance, Federal civil litigation, State civil litigation. Home: 5521 Mission Dr Mission Hills KS 66208 Office: Commerce Trust Bldg 922 Walnut Kansas City MO 64106

POPPER, RICHARD J.A., lawyer; b. Leeds, Eng., Apr. 24, 1952; came to U.S., 1964; s. Felix B. and Christina J.A. (Smith) P. BS, Tufts U., 1974; JD, George Washington U., 1977; ML in Taxation, Georgetown U., 1982. Bar: D.C. 1977, U.S. Tax Ct. 1981, Del. 1982. Staff atty. Nat. Rural Utilities Coop. Fin. Corp., Washington, 1978-81; assoc. Murdoch & Walsh, P.A., Wilmington, Del., 1982-84; assoc. Bayard, Handelman & Murdoch, P.A., Wilmington, 1984-86, ptnr., 1986—, also bd. dirs. Mem. ABA, Del. State Bar Assn. Pension, profit-sharing, and employee benefits, Probate, Corporate taxation. Home: 1504 N Lincoln St Wilmington DE 19806 Office: Bayard Handelman & Murdoch PA 1300 Delaware Trust Bldg PO Box 25130 Wilmington DE 19899

POPPER, ROBERT, law school dean; b. N.Y.C., May 22, 1932; s. Walter G. and Dorothy B. (Kluger) P.; m. Mary Ann Schaefer, July 12, 1963; children: Julianne, Robert Gregory. BS, U. Wis., 1953; LLB, Harvard U., 1956; LLM, NYU, 1963. Bar: N.Y. 1957, U.S. Dist. Ct. (so. dist.) N.Y. 1962, U.S. Ct. Appeals (2d cir.) 1962, U.S. Supreme Ct. 1962, U.S. Dist. Ct. (ea. dist.) N.Y. 1969, U.S. Ct. Appeals (7th cir.) 1970, U.S. Ct. Appeals (8th cir.) 1971, Mo. 1971, U.S. Dist. Ct. (we. dist.) Mo. 1973. Trial atty. criminal br. N.Y.C. Legal Aid Soc., 1960-61; asst. dist. atty. N.Y. County, 1961-64; assoc. Seligson & Morris, N.Y.C., 1964-69; mem. faculty School of Law, U. Mo., Kansas City, 1969—, prof., 1973—, acting dean, 1983-84, dean, 1984—, cons. and lectr. in field. Author: Post Conviction Remedies in a Nutshell, 1978, De-Nationalizing the Bill of Rights, 1979; contbr. articles to profl. jours. Mem. Am. Law Inst., N.Y. State Bar Assn., Mo. State Bar Assn., Kansas City Bar Assn., Lawyers Assn. Kansas City. Criminal, Civil rights, Legal education. Office: U Mo Kansas City Sch Law 5100 Rockhill Rd Kansas City MO 64110

POPPETT, MARK ADAMS, lawyer; b. San Bernardino, Calif., Mar. 31, 1944; s. Robert and Winifred Virginia (Adams) P.; m. Elizabeth Theresa McDonald, May 20, 1972. A.A., San Bernardino Valley Coll., 1965; B.A., Calif. State Coll., 1967; J.D., Golden Gate U., 1971. Bar: Calif. 1975, U.S. Dist. Ct. (cen. dist.) Calif. 1976, U.S. Dist. Ct. (no. dist.) Calif. 1977. Claims rep. Travelers Ins. Co., San Francisco and Los Angeles, 1973-75; claims supr., Los Angeles, 1975; trial counsel, Los Angeles and San Jose, 1975-77; mgr.-trial counsel TransAm. Ins. Group, San Francisco, 1977-83; trial counsel Chubb Ins. Group, San Francisco, 1983-84; assoc. Jedeikin, Connor & Green, San Francisco, 1984-87, Law Offices of Patrick E. Catalano, San Diego and San Francisco, 1987—; judge pro tem Mcpl. Ct., San Francisco, 1983—;panel mem. Arbitration Settlement Program San Francisco Superior Ct., 1985—; cert. psychiat. technician Patton State Hosp., San Bernardino, Calif., 1963-66. Mem. ABA (litigation and tort and ins. practice sect.), Calif. State Bar Assn., San Francisco Bar Assn. Democrat. Episcopalian. Club: Commonwealth of Calif. State civil litigation, Insurance, Personal injury. Office: Law Offices of Patrick E Catalano 110 Juniper St San Diego CA 92101-1598

PORACH, RICHARD ANDREW, lawyer; b. Detroit, Sept. 17, 1946; s. Andrew Richard and Esther Josephine (Kessler) P.; m. Melanie Jane Martin, Jan. 3, 1970; 1 child, Erik Andrew. BA, U. Notre Dame, 1968; JD, Dickinson Sch. Law, 1971. Bar: Pa. 1971, U.S. Dist. Ct. (we. dist.) Pa. 1972, U.S. Ct. Appeals (3d cir.) 1985. Atty. Pa. Cen. Transp. Co., Pitts., 1972-76, Consol. Rail Corp., Pitts., 1976-77; atty. Pitts. and Lake Erie R.R. Co., Pitts., 1977-84, asst. sec., 1983—, gen. atty., 1984—; asst. sec. Lake Erie and Eastern R.R. Co., Pitts., 1983-84. Served to capt. U.S. Army, 1972. Mem. ABA, Allegheny County Bar Assn., Nat. Assn. R.R. Trial Counsel, Def. Research Inst., Pa. Def. Assn., Assn. Transp. Practitioners, Ass. Freight Loss and Damage Counsel, Notre Dame Club Pitts. (chmn. scholarship com., alumni schs. com. 1980—). Personal injury, Administrative and regulatory, General corporate. Home: 264 Dutch Ln Pittsburgh PA 15236 Office: Pitts and Lake Erie RR Co Commerce Ct Suite 780 Sta Sq #4 Pittsburgh PA 15219

PORCO, DOMENICK JOSEPH, lawyer; b. Cosenza, Italy, Mar. 16, 1948; came to U.S., 1957; s. Carlo August and Assunta (Chiappetta) P.; m. Marieangela Pasquale, May 5, 1979; children: Jamie Ann, Michael Justin, Alyssa. BA, CCNY, 1972. Bar: N.Y. 1977, U.S. Ct. Appeals (2d cir.) 1978, U.S. Supreme Ct. 1979, U.S. Ct. Appeals (6th cir.) 1981. Assoc. Diller & Schmukler, N.Y.C., 1977-81; sole practice N.Y.C., 1981—; ptnr. Porco & Marino, Eastchester, N.Y., 1983—. Mem. ABA, Westchester County Bar Assn., Eastchester Bar Assn. (treas. 1985—), N.Y. County Lawyers Assn., Columbian Lawyers of Westchester. Republican. Roman Catholic. Lodge: Lions. Criminal, Family and matrimonial, Personal injury. Office: 155 Fisher Ave Eastchester NY 10709

PORETSKY, JOEL A., lawyer; b. Bklyn., Jan. 16, 1946; m. Susan I. Miller, Sept. 6, 1970; children—Lauren, Eric. B.S., Boston U., 1967; J.D. cum laude, Bklyn. Law Sch., 1971; LL.M. in Taxation, NYU, 1972. Bar: N.Y. 1972, U.S. Tax Ct. 1972, U.S. Ct. Appeals (2d cir.) 1975, U.S. Supreme Ct. 1975. Assoc. Fried Frank Harris Shriver & Jacobson, N.Y.C., 1972-77, Baer Marks & Upham, N.Y.C., 1977-78; ptnr. Estroff Waldman & Poretsky, N.Y.C., 1979—; lectr. NAACP Legal Def. Fund. Served with USAR, 1968-74. Mem. N.Y. State Bar Assn., ABA. Co-author: Tax Planning in Financing and Development of Hotels, 1975; contbr. articles to legal jours. Corporate taxation, Personal income taxation. Home: 59 Cambridge Rd Great Neck NY 11023 Office: 666 Fifth Ave New York NY 10103

PORRICELLI, GERALD JOSEPH, lawyer, retail executive; b. Stamford, Conn., Aug. 2, 1948; s. Genaro and Esther (Giordano) P.; m. Marianne Marketta, Sept. 6, 1970; children: Jeanette, Melissa. BS, Fordham U., 1970, JD, 1974. Bar: Conn. 1975, N.Y. 1980. Exec. v.p., counsel Food Mart Inc., Old Greenwich, Conn., 1970—; ptnr. Scherban & Porricelli, Stamford, 1985—; bd. dirs. Associated Foods, Stratford, Conn. Del. rep. meeting Town of Greenwich, 1977-79, 79-81; leader dist. com. Greenwich Reps., 1978-84; Havemeyer Park House Owner's Assn., Greenwich, 1980—. Mem. Full Gospel Businessmens Fellowship, Internat. (pres. 1982—). Lodge: Lions. Avocations: softball, writing, racquetball. Real property, Personal injury, General practice.

PORRO, ALFRED ANTHONY, JR., law educator, consultant; b. Jersey City, Mar. 14, 1935; s. Alfred A. and Nancy Porro. J.D., Rutgers U., 1958; LL.M., Temple U., 1981; postgrad. Immaculate Conception Sem., 1976-79. Bar: N.J. 1958, U.S. Dist. Ct. N.J. 1959, U.S. Supreme Ct. 1965. Sole practice, Lyndhurst, N.J., 1959—; spl. counsel to U.S. Commn. on Marine Sci., Tech. and Engring., 1965-70; prof. U. Balt. Sch. Law, 1981—; cons. water rights and state and local govt. matters; lectr. Rutgers U., Sch. Law, Columbia U., Temple U. Sch. Law, Oklahoma U. Sch. Law, U. Brisbayne Sch. Law, Western Australia Sch. Law, others. Lector, commentator St. Mary's Roman Catholic Ch., Rutherford, N.J.; trustee Bergen County Legal Services Program, Passaic River Coalition; mem. Health and Welfare Council Bergen County; mem. adv. com. Passaic Valley Sewerage Commn. Served to lt. U.S. Army, 1955-59. Recipient Mcpl. Corps. award Lawyers Coop. Pub. Co., 1958, Comml. Law award, 1958, Evidence award, 1958; Outstanding Citizen award Bergen County, 1965; Outstanding Alumnus award Lyndhurst High Sch. Alumni Assn., 1976; Cert. of Merit, Am. Cancer Soc., 1968, Cert. of Merit, Recreation for Exceptional Children, 1972; Nat. award Am. Congress on Surveying and Mapping-Am. Soc. Photogammetry, 1983; First Amendment award, 1983; named Man of Yr., N.J. Soc. Profl. Land Surveyors, 1981; Internat. Acad. Law and Sci. fellow, 1966. Mem. ABA, Fed. Bar Assn., Nat. Inst. Mcpl. Law Officers, Am. Legal Clinic Assn., Scribes, Am. Arbitration Inst., Am. Trial Lawyers Assn., Nat. Assn. Criminal Def. Lawyers, Christina Legal Soc., Nat. Resources Def. Council, Coastal Soc., N.J. Bar Assn. (computer related law com., law day award 1969), Fed. Bar Assn. N.J., Md. State Bar Assn., Pa. Bar Assn., N.J. League Municipalities, N.J. Inst. Mcpl. Attys., Md. Trial Lawyers Assn., N.J. Trial Lawyers Assn., Pa. Trial Lawyers Assn., Bergen County Bar Assn., N.J. State C. of C., Meadowland C. of C. Roman Catholic. Author: (with others) Local Government Law Treatise, 4 vols., 1982; contbr. articles to profl. jours. Real property, Local government. Office: U Balt Sch Law 1420 N Charles St Baltimore MD 21201

PORRO, JAMES EARLE, lawyer; b. Olean, N.Y., Dec. 18, 1946; s. Eugene Woodrow and Audrey Jane (Chew) P.; m. Teresa Ann Castle, Aug. 4, 1970 (Jan. 1976); m. Christine Marie Walsh, Oct. 13, 1978; children: Christopher, Carrie, Heather, Shaelah, Christin. BBA, St. Bonaventure U., 1970; JD, U. Notre Dame, 1975. Bar: Ind. 1975, D.C. 1977, N.Y. 1978, Mich. 1980. Atty.-adviser U.S. State Dept., Washington, 1975-77; assoc. Jaeckle, Fleischmann & Mugel, Buffalo, 1977-79; asst. gen. counsel Rapistan Inc., Grand Rapids, Mich., 1979-82; corp. counsel Kellogg Co., Battle Creek, Mich., 1982—; tech. advisor Internat. Labor Orgn., Geneva, 1984. Served with USN, 1970-72. Mem. ABA, Mich. Bar Assn., Ind. Bar Assn., Erie County Bar Assn., D.C. Bar Assn. Roman Catholic. Avocation: knife throwing. Private international, General corporate, Contracts commercial. Office: Kellogg Co One Kellogg Sq Battle Creek MI 49016

PORTELLI, JOSEPH ANDREW, lawyer; b. Paterson, N.J., Mar. 31, 1955; s. Andrew Peter and Lillian (Mastrogiovanni) Soter; m. Brenda Cosgrove. BA, Villanova U., 1977; JD, Widener U., 1981. Bar: N.Y. 1981, U.S. Dist. Ct. N.J. 1981. Law clk. to presiding justice N.J. State Ct., Paterson, 1981-82; asst. prosecutor Passaic County Prosecutors Office, Paterson, 1982-85; assoc. Barnes & Barnes P.A., Newark, 1985-86; sole practice Totowa, N.J., 1986—. Fundraiser Cooley's Anemia Found., N.J., 1976—. Mem. N.J. Bar Assn., Passaic County Bar Assn. Democrat. Roman Catholic. Avocations: astronomy, reading, golf. Personal injury, Criminal, General practice. Home: 11-B Thornton Place Clifton NJ 07012 Office: 41 Vreeland Ave Totowa NJ 07512

PORTELLI, THOMAS FRANK, lawyer; b. Paterson, N.J., May 29, 1948; s. Andrew P. and Lillian (Mastrogiovanni) Soter. A.B., Seton Hall U., 1970; J.D., N.C. Central U., 1975; LL.M. N.Y.U., 1980. Bar: N.J. 1975. Hearing examiner Bd. Pub. Utilities, State of N.J., 1976-79; sole practice, Totowa, N.J., 1975—; asst. county counsel, labor counsel for Passaic County, N.J., 1981—; counsel T.W.U.A. Funds of Amalgamated Clothing and Textile Workers Union and Local 1733 same union, Local 8-95 Oil, Chemical and Atomic Workers. Police commr. and councilman Borough of Haledon, N.J., 1980-85, pres., 1982-85; mem. adv. bd. Am. Labor Mus. Recipient of Acclamation Pres. Carter, 1979. Recipient Award of Appreciation Haledon Police Dept., 1986. Mem. Passaic County Bar Assn. Democrat. Club: Hamilton (Paterson, N.J.). General practice, Labor, State civil litigation. Home: 9 Lillian Ct Wayne NJ 07470 Office: 205 Route 46 Suite 6A Totowa NJ 07512

PORTER, CHARLES RALEIGH, JR., lawyer; b. Waco, Tex., Sept. 22, 1922; s. Charles Raleigh and Virginia Louise (Bowen) P.; m. Alice Mungall, Sept. 16, 1946; children—Charles Raleigh III, Melissa Ann, Alice Marguerite, Daniel Bowen. B.B.A., U. Tex., 1943, LL.B., 1949. Bar: Tex. 1948, U.S. Dist. Ct. (so. dist.) Tex. 1949, Ct. Appeals (5th cir.) 1955, U.S. Dist. Ct. (we. dist.) Tex. 1972, U.S. Dist. Ct. (no. dist.) Tex. 1977. Asst. Nueces County Attys. Office, Corpus Christi, Tex., 1949-50, Dist. Attys. Office, Corpus Christi, 1950-53; ptnr. Anderson & Porter, Corpus Christi, 1953-63, Sorrell, Anderson & Porter, 1964-68, Porter, Rogers, Dahlman, Gordon & Lee, 1969—; dir. Tex. Commerce Bank-Corpus Christi. Bd. dirs. Meth. Home, Waco; mem. exec. bd. Perkins Sch. Theology, So. Meth. U.

Fellow ABA, Tex. Bar Found.; mem. Nueces County Bar Assn. (pres. 1959-60), U. Tex. Law Sch. Alumni Assn. (bd. dirs.). Served to lt. (j.g.) USNR, 1944-46, PTO. Republican. Methodist. Lodge: Masons (32 degree). State civil litigation, Oil and gas leasing, Banking. Home: 33 Blue Heron St Rockport TX 78382 Office: Porter Rogers Dahlman et al 1800 American Bank Plaza Corpus Christi TX 78475

PORTER, DONALD JAMES, judge; b. Madison, S.D., Mar. 24, 1921; s. Donald Irving and Lela Ann (Slack) P.; m. Harriet J. Whitney, Aug. 22, 1948; children: Donald A., Mary Lela, William W., Carolyn S., Elizabeth C. Student, Eastern Normal Coll., 1938-39; B.S., U. S.D., 1942, LL.B., 1943. Bar: S.D. 1943. Individual practice law Chamberlain, S.D., 1947-59; ptnr. May, Porter, Adam, Gerdes & Thompson, and (predecessor), Pierre, S.D., 1959-77; assoc. justice S.D. Supreme Ct., Pierre, 1977-79; chief judge U.S. Dist. Ct. S.D., 1979—; states atty. Brule County, S.D., 1948-52, 57-59; S.D. commr. Nat. Conf. Commrs. on Uniform State Laws, 1973-76; mem. S.D. Ho. of Reps., 1955-56. Served with U.S. Army, 1943-46, ETO. Mem. Am., S.D. bar assns., Am. Bd. Trial Advocates (charter mem. S.D. chpt.), Am. Judicature Soc. Roman Catholic. Office: US Courthouse 413 Federal Bldg Pierre SD 57501 *

PORTER, HARRY LERICHMOND, lawyer; b. Milan, Mo., Aug. 26, 1912; s. N. Harry and Dorothy Ellen (Booth) P.; m. Wava Vernelle Field, Dec. 22, 1935; children—Alison Porter Thomas, Stephen Douglas. A.B., Park Coll., 1935; LL.B., U. Kansas City, 1941; J.D., U. Mo., 1943; postgrad. MIT, 1944, Washington and Jefferson Coll., 1944. Bar: Mo. 1941, Kans. 1942, U.S. Dist. Ct. (ea. dist.) Mo. 1948. Practiced in Columbus, Kans., 1941-43, Marceline, Mo., 1946—; pros. atty. Cherokee County Kans., 1942-43; city atty. Marceline, Mo., 1946-85; pros. atty. Linn County Mo., 1965-69; com. Mo. Assn. of Social Welfare, 1960-64. Mem. Gov.'s Commn. Commerce and Industry, Mo., 1962-64; chmn. Linn County Democratic Com., 1952-56, vice chmn., 1974—; chmn. 12th Legis. Dist. Dem. Com., 1973—; pres. sch. bd. Marceline Reorganzied Sch. Dist., 1962-63; dir. Linn County Fed. Emergency Relief Program, 1983-84. Served with AUS, 1943-46. Mem. Mo. Bar Assn., 9th Jud. Cir. Bar Assn. (pres. 1962-63, 72-73), Am. Legion, Sigma Phi Sigma, Pi Kappa Delta. Presbyterian. Lodges: Lions, Rotary (pres. 1971). Home: 701 N Missouri Ave Marceline MO 64658 Office: 104 S Kansas Ave Marceline MO 64658

PORTER, JAMES EDUARDO, lawyer; b. Laredo, Tex., May 10, 1948; s. Leo Victor and Beatrice Elia (Leal) P.; m. Virginia Benavidez; children from previous marriage: Sandra Marie, James Eduardo Jr. A.A., San Antonio Coll., 1972; B.A. cum laude, St. Mary's U., 1974, J.D., 1976. Bar: Tex. 1976, U.S. Dist. Ct. (we. dist.) 1978, U.S. Ct. Appeals (5th cir.) 1981. Sole practice, San Antonio, 1976-79; v.p. Botello, Porter & Serna, Inc.; pres. James E. Porter, Atty. at Law, Inc., San Antonio, 1980—. Served to sgt. USMC 1966-70, Vietnam. Mem. ABA, Tex. Bar Assn., Assn. Trial Lawyers Am., San Antonio Bar Assn., San Antonio Trial Lawyers Assn. Roman Catholic. Club: Plaza (San Antonio). Personal injury, Workers' compensation, Family and matrimonial. Office: 301 Fair St San Antonio TX 78223

PORTER, JAMES HARRY, JR., lawyer; b. Balt., Jan. 16, 1956; s. James Harry and Ruth (Parks) P. B.A., Salisbury State Coll., 1977; J.D., U. Balt., 1980. Bar: Md. 1982, U.S. Dist. Ct. Md. 1982, U.S. Bankruptcy Ct. Md. 1982. Law clk., baliff Dist. Ct. Md. for Howard County, Ellicott City, 1980; law clk. Cir. Ct. for Carroll County, Md., 1980-81; assoc. Henry P. Walters, P.A., Pocomoke, Md., 1982—; legal adviser Legal Intern Program for Worcester County, 1983—; instr. Wor-Wic Tech. Community Coll., Salisbury, 1983—. Mem. ABA, Assn. Trial Lawyers Am., Md. Bar Assn., (com. on ethics 1984-85), Worcester County Bar Assn., Md. Trial Lawyers Assn., U. Balt. Alumni Assn. (v.p. Eastern Shore chpt. 1984, pres. 1985-87), Pocomoke City Jaycees. Democrat. Methodist. Lodge: Rotary (bd. dirs., sec. 1986-87). State civil litigation, Criminal, General practice. Home: 147 Pine St Princess Anne MD 21853 Office: Henry P Walters PA 111 Vine St Pocomoke City MD 21851

PORTER, JAMES (LAMAR), lawyer; b. Fayetteville, Ark., Sept. 21, 1953; s. James Skillern and Jo Ann (Wilbourn) P.; m. Debbie Ann Trapp, Sept. 9, 1982; 1 child, Ashley Eileen. BA, Hendrix Coll., 1975; JD, U. Ark., 1978. Bar: Ark. 1978, U.S. Dist. Ct. (ea. and we. dists.) Ark. 1979, U.S. Ct. Appeals (8th cir.) 1979. Dep. prosecutor County of Sebastian, Ft. Smith, Ark., 1978-80; ptnr. Sexton & Porter, Ft. Smith, 1980-82; assoc. Gary Eubanks & Assocs., Little Rock, 1982-84, James Swindoll, Little Rock, 1984-85, Whetstone & Whetstone, Little Rock, 1985—. V.P. Vols. for Children Com., Ft. Smith, 1981-82; pres. bd. dirs. Zion Youth Shelter, Inc., Ft. Smith, 1981-82; active Comprehensive Juvenile Services, Ft. Smith, 1981-82. Mem. Ark. Trial Lawyers Assn., Assn. Trial Lawyers Am., Pulaski County Bar Assn., Ark. Bar Assn. Episcopalian. Personal injury. Home: 5 Sage Grass Ct Little Rock AK 72201 Office: Whetstone & Whetstone 1100 Union Nat Bldg Little Rock AK 72201

PORTER, JAMES MORRIS, lawyer; b. Cleve., Sept. 14, 1931; s. Emmett Thomas and Mary (Connell) P.; m. Helen Marie Adams, May 31, 1952; children: James E., Thomas W., William M., Daniel J. A.B., John Carroll U., 1953; J.D., U. Mich., 1957. Bar: Ohio 1957. Assoc. firm M.B. & H.H. Johnson, Cleve., 1957-62, McAfee, Hanning, Newcomer, Hazlett & Wheeler, Cleve., 1962-67; ptnr. firm Squire, Sanders & Dempsey, Cleve., 1967—, Atty.'s Liability Assurance Soc. Ltd., Hamilton, Bermuda. Served to 1st lt. U.S. Army, 1953-55. Fellow Am. Coll. Trial Lawyers. Republican. Roman Catholic. Clubs: Union, Cleve. Athletic; The Country (Cleve.). Office: Squire Sanders & Dempsey 1800 Huntington Bldg Cleveland OH 44115

PORTER, JAMES WALLACE, II, lawyer; b. Birmingham, Ala., Feb. 7, 1949; s. Irvine Craig and Sarah (Sterrett) P.; m. Kathryn Hicks, Aug. 23, 1974; 1 child, James Wallace III. BA, U. Ala., 1971; JD, Samford U., 1974. Bar: Ala. 1974. Law clk. to presiding justice U.S. Dist. Ct., Mobile, Ala., 1975-77; assoc. Bishop, Sweeney & Colvin, Birmingham, Ala., 1977-78; ptnr. Porter, Porter & Hassinger, Birmingham, 1978—; lectr. Ins. Claims, Birmingham, 1985—. Mem. ABA (litigation sect., tort and ins. sect.), Ala. Bar Assn., Birmingham Bar Assn., Nat. Rifle Assn. (legal com. 1984—), Assn. Transp. Practitioners, Phi Delta Phi, Ala. Hist. Soc. Avocations: shooting, golf, tennis, hunting. Federal civil litigation, Administrative and regulatory, Insurance. Home: 2445 Shades Crest Rd Birmingham AL 35216 Office: Porter Porter & Hassinger 1201 City Federal Bldg Birmingham AL 35203

PORTER, JEFFREY JAMES, lawyer; b. Dallas, Apr. 7, 1955; s. Louis H. and Sara (Collins) P.; m. Susan Wilshusen. BBA, U. Okla., 1977; JD, So. Meth. U., 1980. Bar: Tex. 1980. Assoc. Thompson, Coe, Cousins & Irons, Dallas, 1981-83; atty. Hunt Energy Corp., Dallas, 1983-87; assoc. Page & Addison, Dallas, 1987—. Mem. ABA, Dallas Bar Assn., State Bar Tex. Republican. Methodist. General corporate, Real property, Mergers and acquisitions, secured transactions. Office: Page & Addison 14651 Dallas Pky Suite 700 Dallas TX 75240

PORTER, JOHN ISSAC, lawyer; b. Camden, N.J., Apr. 8, 1949; s. Elwood and Mary Elizabeth (Pitts) P.; m. Linda Joyce McMillan, June 7, 1975; children: Tiffany, John, Joseph, Jeffrey. BS, Rutgers U., 1971, JD, 1978; MBA, Temple U., 1975. Bar: Pa. 1979, N.J. 1979, U.S. Dist. Ct. N.J. 1979, U.S. Dist. Ct (ea. dist.) Pa. 1982, U.S. Supreme Ct. 1983, U.S. Tax Ct. 1985, U.S. Ct. Appeals (3d cir.) 1985. Sales rep. Union Carbide Corp., Cherry Hill, N.J., 1972-73; fin. analyst Ford Motor Co., Dearborn, Mich., 1973-75; fin. research assoc. The Conf. Bd., N.Y.C., 1975-76; atty. Comptroller of the Currency, Washington, 1979-80; assoc. Porter & Jones, East Orange, N.J., 1980-83; sr. atty. Essex-Newark Legal Services, Newark, 1983-84; assoc. counsel Newark Bd. of Edn., 1984-86, Beneficial Mgmt. Corp., Peapack, N.J., 1986—; v.p. Bethany Bapt. Fed. Credit Union, Newark, 1985—. Mem. N.J. Black Rep. Counsel, Newark, 1979. Named one of Outstanding Young Men in Am., U.S. Jaycees, 1979, 81. Mem. ABA, N.J. Bar Assn., Salem County Bar Assn., Assn. Trial Lawyers Am., Assn. of Fed. Bar, Nat. Bankers Assn., N.J. Rep. Lawyers, Nat. Sch. Bds. Assn., NAACP, Phi Alpha Delta. Baptist. General corporate, Personal injury, Administrative and regulatory. Home: 92 Sanford St East Orange NJ 07018

PORTER, LEON EUGENE, JR., lawyer; b. Winston-Salem, N.C., Sept. 22, 1953; s. Leon E. and Ruby H. (Dodson) P.; m. Mary Thompson, June 18, 1977; children: William Markland, Meredith Dodson. BA in Econs. with honors, U. N.C., 1975; JD cum laude, Wake Forest U., 1978. Bar: N.C. 1978, U.S. Dist. Ct. (we., mid. and ea. dists.) N.C., U.S. Ct. Appeals (4th cir.). Law clk. to presiding magistrate U.S. Dist. Ct., Winston-Salem, 1978-79, law clk. to presiding justice, 1978-81; assoc. Petree Stockton, Winston-Salem, 1981—. Bd. dirs., sec. Foxhall Civil Assn., Inc., Winston-Salem, 1984-85; deacon First Presbyn. Ch., Winston-Salem, 1986-87; pres. Teen-Dems. Winston-Salem, 1971. Mem. ABA (forum com. health law, litigation sect.), Nat. Health Lawyers Assn., Forsyth County Bar Assn., Forsyth County Young Lawyers, N.C. Bar Assn. (co-chmn. young lawyers div. com. on lawyers and the arts), Winston-Salem C. of C. (2000 club). Democrat. Lodge: Sertoma (pres. Stratford club 1985, chmn. bd. dirs. 1986—). Avocations: swimming, basketball. Federal civil litigation, State civil litigation, Health. Home: 1200 Green Valley Rd Winston-Salem NC 27106 Office: Petree Stockton & Robinson 1001 W Fourth St Winston-Salem NC 27101

PORTER, MARY HELEN (HOWARD), lawyer; b. Atlanta, Aug. 10, 1957; d. Harry Clay and Mary Helen (Harrison) H.; m. Thomas Tift Porter, June 30, 1979; 1 child, Catherine. BA, U. of the South, Sewanee, Tenn., 1979; JD, Emory U. Bar: Ga. 1982, U.S. Dist. Ct. (no. dist.) Ga. 1983. Sole practice Cartersville, Ga., 1982—. Vol. Human Hospice Cartersville Aux., 1985—. Mem. ABA, Ga. Bar Assn., Assn. Trial Lawyer Am., Ga. Trial Lawyers Assn., Nat. Assn. Criminal Def. Lawyers, Bartow County Cartersville C. of C. Democrat. Presbyterian. Club: Pilot (Cartersville). Avocations: swimming, tennis, horseback riding, waterskiing. Family and matrimonial, Juvenile, General practice. Home: Rt 7 Oakridge Dr Cartersville GA 30120 Office: 16 S Erwin St PO Box 96 Cartersville GA 30120

PORTER, MICHAEL PELL, lawyer; b. Indpls., Mar. 31, 1940; s. Harold Troxel and Mildred Maxine (Pell) P.; m. Alliene Laura Jenkins, Sept. 23, 1967 (div.); 1 child, Genevieve Natalie; m. Janet Kay Smith Hayes, Feb. 13, 1983. Student, DePauw U., 1957-58; BA, Tulane U., 1961, JD, 1963. Bar: La. 1963, U.S. Ct. Mil. Appeals 1964, N.Y. 1969, Hawaii 1971. Clk., U.S. Ct. Appeals (5th cir.), New Orleans, 1963; assoc. Sullivan & Cromwell, N.Y.C., 1968-71; assoc. Cades Schutte Fleming & Wright, Honolulu, 1971-74, ptnr., 1975—; mem. deans council Tulane Law Sch., 1981—; dep. vice chancellor Episcopal Diocese Hawaii, 1980—. Bd. dirs. Jr. Achievement Hawaii, Inc., 1974-84, Inst. Human Services, Inc., 1980—, Hoa Kokua Hospice Vols., Inc., 1984-85. Served with JAGC, U.S. Army, 1963-66, Vietnam. Tulane U. fellow, 1981. Mem. ABA, Assn. Bar City N.Y., Hawaii State Bar Assn. Republican. Episcopalian. Club: Pacific (Honolulu). General corporate, Securities. Office: Cades Schutte Fleming & Wright 1000 Bishop St Honolulu HI 96813

PORTER, ROBERT CARL, JR., lawyer; b. Cin., Sept. 21, 1927; s. Robert Carl and Lavinia (Otte) P.; m. Joanne Patterson, July 5, 1952; children—Robert Carl III, David M., John E. B.A. with distinction, U. Mich., 1949; J.D., Harvard U., 1952. Bar: Ohio 1952, U.S. Dist. Ct. (so. dist.) Ohio 1954, U.S. Ct. Appeals (6th cir.) 1954, U.S. Ct. Mil. Appeals 1956, U.S. Supreme Ct. 1956, U.S. Tax Ct. 1980. Ptnr., Porter & Porter, Cin., 1953-54; sole practice, Cin. 1954-63; sr. ptnr. Porter & McKinney, Cin., 1963—; dir. and officer numerous cos., including Stotts-Friedman Co., Dayton, Corrugated Partitions, Inc., Paul Homes, Inc., Bamber Funeral Home, Inc. Served with JAG Corps, USAF, 1952-53. Mem. ABA, Ohio State Bar Assn., Cin. Bar Assn., Phi Beta Kappa Presbyterian. Clubs: Cin. Country, University, U. Mich., Harvard Law Sch. Assn., Masons (Scottish Rite), Shriners (Cin.). Probate, General corporate, Corporate taxation. Home: 2365 Bedford Ave Cincinnati OH 45208 Office: 2012 Central Trust Tower Cincinnati OH 45202

PORTER, ROBERT WILLIAM, U.S. dist. judge; b. Monmouth, Ill., Aug. 13, 1926; s. William Benson and Vieva Laurel (Drew) P.; m. Lois Virginia Freeman, July 4, 1956; children—Robert William, William Benson, John David. A.B. cum laude, Monmouth Coll., 1949; J.D., U. Mich., 1952. Bar: Tex. bar 1953. Home office counsel Res. Life Ins. Co., Dallas, 1952-54; asso. and partner Thompson, Coe, Cousins, & Irons, Dallas, 1954-74; judge U.S. Dist. Ct., No. Dist., Tex., 1974—; spl. counsel County of Dallas, 1972-74; lectr. Robert A. Taft Inst. of Govt., U. Tex., Arlington, 1972-73. Vice chmn. bd. trustees Lamplighter Sch. Inc., 1967-74, councilman, Richardson, Tex., 1965-66, mayor pro tem., 1966, mayor, 1967; pres. Tex. Assn. Mayors, Councilmen and Commrs., 1965-66, Greater County League of Municipalities, 1966-67; mem. exec. com. N. Central Tex. Council of Govts., 1966-67, 70-72, regional citizen rep., 1967-72; mem. Dallas County Election Bd., 1972-74; original conferee Goals for Dallas, chmn. neighboring communities com., mem. task force com., vice chmn. task force on transp. and communications, chmn. achievement com. for transp. and communications, 1965-74; mem. State Rep. Exec. Com., 1966-68; chmn. Task Force on Modernization of State and Local Govts., 1967; dep. state chmn. Rep. Party of Tex., 1969-71; Dallas County Rep. chmn., 1972-74; mem. adv. council S.W. Center Advanced Study, 1966-69. Served in USN, 1944-46, PTO. Mem. Richardson, Dallas bar assns., State Bar Tex., Barristers Soc., Delta Theta Phi, Alpha Tau Omega. Presbyterian. Jurisprudence. Office: 1100 Commerce St Dallas TX 75242

PORTER, THOMAS WILLIAM, III, lawyer; b. Dallas, Aug. 23, 1941; s. Thomas William and Ruth Mae (Campbell) P.; m. Sally Ann Shell, May 10, 1963 (div. July 1983); children: Elizabeth Elisse, Laura Christina; m. Patty Ann Sanders, Nov. 2, 1985. BBA in Fin., So. Meth. U., 1963; LLB, Duke U., 1966. Bar: Tex. 1966, U.S. Dist. Ct. (no. dist.) Tex. 1967, U.S. Dist. Ct. (so. dist.) Tex. 1975, U.S. Dist. Ct. (we. dist.) Tex. 1977, U.S. Ct. Appeals (5th cir.) 1977. Assoc. Jackson & Walker, Dallas, 1966-72; ptnr. Bracewell & Patterson, Houston, 1972-74, Foreman & Dyess, Houston, 1974-81; sr. ptnr. Porter & Clements, Houston, 1981—; adj. lectr. fin. So. Meth. U., Dallas, 1967; lectr. securities and corp. law State Bar Tex. Continuing Legal Edn. Program, 1977—. Vice chmn. Texans for Rockefeller, Dallas, 1968; bd. dirs. Pub. TV Found. for North Tex., Dallas, 1970-72; trustee St. Paul's United Meth. Ch., Houston, 1974-77; bd. visitors Duke U. Law Sch., 1985—. Mem. ABA (com. on law firms 1981—, fed. regulation of securities com. 1979—), State Bar Tex. (mem. council sect. corp., banking and bus. law 1984-86, securities and investment banking com. 1976—), Houston Bar Assn., Assn. for Corp. Growth (bd. dirs. 1981-83), Phi Delta Phi. Republican. Methodist. Clubs: Houston, Texas (Houston); Seabrook Sailing (Tex.). Securities, General corporate, Private international. Office: Porter & Clements 3500 Republic Bank Ctr Houston TX 77002

PORTER, VERNA LOUISE, lawyer; b. Los Angeles, May 31, 1941. B.A., Calif. State U., 1963; J.D., Southwestern U., 1977. Bar: Calif. 1977, U.S. Dist. Ct. (cen. dist.) Calif. 1978, U.S. Ct. Appeals (9th cir.) 1978. Ptnr. Eisler & Porter, Los Angeles, 1978-79, mng. ptnr., 1979-86, sole practice, 1986—; judge pro-tempore Los Angeles Mcpl. Ct., 1983—; mem. subcom. on landlord tenant law, panelist conv., mem. real property law sect. Calif. State Bar, 1983; speaker on landlord-tenant law to real estate profls., including San Fernando Bd. Realtors. Editorial asst., contbr. Apt. Owner Builder; contbr. to Apt. Bus. Outlook, Real Property News, Apt. Age. Mem. ABA, Los Angeles County Bar Assn., Los Angeles Trial Lawyers Assn., Landlord Trial Lawyers Assn. (founding mem., pres.), da Camera Soc. Republican. Real property, Landlord-tenant, Consumer commercial. Office: 500 S Virgil Ave Suite 360 Los Angeles CA 90020

PORTER, WILLIAM GLOVER, JR., lawyer; b. Columbus, Ohio, Nov. 4, 1923; s. William Glover and Anne (Searight) P.; m. Eve Breslin Peterson, Jan. 12, 1946; children—Cynthia Porter Brown, Marcia Porter Hill. Student Dartmouth Coll., 1941-43, U. Calif.-Berkeley, 1946; L.L.B., Ohio State U., 1949. Bar: Ohio, 1949, U.S. Dist. Ct. (so. and ea. dists.) Ohio 1956, U.S. Dist. Ct. (D.C. dist.) 1982, U.S. Ct. Appeals (D.C. cir.) 1978, U.S. Supreme Ct. 1977. Assoc. Porter, Stanley, Treffinger & Platt, Columbus, Ohio, 1949-56; ptnr. Porter, Wright, Morris & Arthur, Columbus, 1956-81, sr. resident ptnr., Washington, 1981-83, of counsel 1984—. Mem. D.C. Mayor's Internat. Adv. Council, 1983—, Internat. Com. of the Greater Washington Bd. Trade, 1981—; mem. Washington Chamber Orch., 1982—, pres., 1985—. Served to lt. (j.g.) USNR, 1943-45. Fellow Columbus Bar Assn. Found. (charter); mem. ABA, D.C. Bar Assn., Fed. Energy Bar Assn., Ohio State Bar Assn. (chmn. special com. on pub. utilities 1963-70), Edison Elec. Inst. (legal com. 1961-79), Ohio Elec. Utility Inst. (legal com. 1955-79). Republican. Episcopalian. Clubs: Yale (N.Y.C.); Columbia Country (Chevy Chase, Md.), Rocky Fork Hunt and Country (Columbus). Avocations: cabinet making, photography, bird watching, tennis. General corporate, Administrative and regulatory, Public utilities. Home: 4623 Kenmore Dr NW Washington DC 20007 Office: Porter Wright Morris & Arthur 1233 20th St NW Washington DC 20036

PORTERFIELD, JACK BERRY, JR., lawyer; b. Birmingham, Ala., Aug. 27, 1924; s. Jack Berry Porterfield and Laura Lee (Bush) Leonard; m. Laurel Marie Hornsby, June 4, 1948; children: Jack Berry III, Jeffery Alexander, Leslie Hornsby. Student, U. Richmond, 1942, 46-47; LLB, Washington & Lee U., 1949. Bar: Ala. 1949, U.S. Dist. Ct. (no. dist.) Ala., U.S. Ct. Appeals (11th cir.), U.S. Supreme Ct. 1958. Assoc. Lange, Simpson, Robinson & Somerville, Birmingham, 1949-55; pres. Porterfield, Scholl, Bainbridge, Mims & Harper P.A., Birmingham, 1955—. Served to cpl. AC, U.S. Army, 1943-46, PTO. Mem. ABA, Ala. Bar Assn., Birmingham Bar Assn. (pres. 1968). Republican. Episcopalian. Personal injury, Insurance, Workers' compensation. Home: 4209 Antietam Dr Birmingham AL 35213 Office: Porterfield Scholl et al 2 Office Park Circle Birmingham AL 35223

PORTER IV, THOMAS FITZGERALD, lawyer; b. New Iberia, La., Aug. 19, 1952; s. Thomas Fitzgerald III and Vivian Theresa (deBlanc) P.; m. Paula Marie Solomon, Aug. 17, 1974; children: Rachel Renee, Chad Thomas, Kristen Faye. BA, U. S.W. La., 1976; JD, La State U., 1976. Bar: La. 1976, U.S. Dist. Ct. (we. dist.) La. 1977, U.S. Supreme Ct. 1980, U.S. Ct. Appeals (5th cir.) 1981. Law clk. to presiding justice La. Dist. Ct., Lafayette, 1976-77; ptnr. Shelton & Legendre, Lafayette, 1977-80, 1981—. Mem. legal ethics com. Lafayette Parish, 1983—. Mem. ABA, Assn. Trial Lawyers Am., La. Trial Lawyers Assn., U.S. Supreme Ct. Hist. Soc., Lafayette C. of C., U. S.W. La. Alumni Assn., La. State U. Alumni Assn., Lafayette Parish Trial Lawyers Assn., Phi Alpha Delta. Republican. Roman Catholic. Club: Beavers (Lafayette). Avocations: tennis, raquetball, jogging. Personal injury, State civil litigation, General practice. Home: 106 Peck Blvd Lafayette LA 70508 Office: Shelton & Legendre 2448 Johnston St Lafayette LA 70503

PORTMAN, GLENN ARTHUR, lawyer; b. Cleve., Dec. 26, 1949; s. Alvin B. and Lenore (Marsh) P.; m. Katherine Seaborn, Aug. 3, 1974 (div. 1984); m. Susan Newell, Jan. 3, 1987. B.A. in History, Case Western Res. U., 1968; J.D., So. Meth. U., 1975. Bar: Tex. 1975, U.S. Dist. Ct. (no. dist.) Tex. 1975, U.S. Dist. Ct. (so. dist.) Tex. 1983. Assoc. Johnson, Bromberg & Leeds, Dallas, 1975-80, ptnr., 1980—. Asst. editor-in-chief: Southwestren Law Jour., 1974-75; contbr. articles to profl. jours. Mem. ABA, Dallas Bar Assn., So. Meth. U. Law Alumni Assn. (council bd. dirs., v.p. 1980-86, chmn. admissions com.). Republican. Methodist. Clubs: 500 Inc., Assemblage. Real property, Bankruptcy, Contracts commercial. Home: 9503 Winding Ridge Dr Dallas TX 75238 Office: Johnson Bromberg & Leeds 2600 Lincoln Plaza 500 N Akard St Dallas TX 75201

PORTNOY, BARRY MICHAEL, lawyer; b. Everett, Mass., Sept. 10, 1945; s. Samuel and Blanche (Rodofsky) P.; m. Diane Katz, Aug. 20, 1967; children: Adam, Sandra. BA with honors, Harvard U., 1967; JD with honors, Cornell U., 1971. Bar: Mass. 1972, U.S. Dist Ct. Mass. 1972, U.S. Ct. Appeals (1st cir.) 1972. Law clk. to presiding justice U.S. Ct. Appeals (9th cir.), Los Angeles, 1971-72; fellow Inst. Comparative Law U. Florence, Italy, 1973; assoc. Sullivan & Worcester, Boston, 1973-77, ptnr., 1978—, mem. mgmt. com., 1984—. Mem. Zoning Bd. Appeals, Town of Marblehead, Mass., 1976—; trustee Glen Urquhart Sch., Beverly, Mass., 1985—; bd. dir. Greenery Rehab. Group, Inc.; trustee Health and Rehab. Properties Trust, 1986—. Mem. ABA, Mass. Bar Assn., Boston Bar Assn. Health, Bankruptcy, Contracts commercial. Home: 1 Shuman Rd Marblehead MA 01945 Office: Sullivan & Worcester 1 Post Office Sq Boston MA 02109

PORTNOY, IAN KARL, lawyer; b. Phila., Aug. 27, 1943; s. Joseph and Florence Portnoy; m. Judith Kobak; children: Michael, Beth. BA, U. Mich., 1965; JD, Villanova U., 1968. Bar: Pa. 1969, D.C. 1970, U.S. Supreme Ct. 1973. Corp. counsel Villager Industries, Phila.; assoc. Finley, Kumble, Wagner, Heine, Underberg, Manley, Myerson & Casey and predecessor firm, Washington, 1970-75; ptnr. Finley, Kumble, Wagner, Heine, Underberg, Manly, Myerson & Casey and predecessor firm, Washington, 1975—; bd. dirs. The Dial. Sr. editor Nat. Property Law Digest; bd. dirs. The Dial Mag., pub. tv and radio sta. Chmn. bd. dirs. Dumbarton Concert Series, Washington, Live Music Now; devel. bd. Capitol campaign steering and auction com. Georgetown Day Sch.; bd. dirs. Big Brothers, Washington, chmn. annual gourmet dinner. Mem. Am. Arbitration Assn. (comml. com.). Real property, Contracts commercial, Private international. Home: 6010 Onondaga Rd Bethesda MD 20816 Office: Finley Kumble Wagner et al 1120 Conn Ave NW Washington DC 20036

PORTNOY, JEFFREY STEVEN, lawyer; b. Bklyn., July 5, 1947; s. Bernard and Edna (Fure) P.; m. Sandi Edelstein, Mar. 29, 1970; 1 child, Carrie Paige. A.B. in Polit. Sci. cum laude, Syracuse U., 1969; J.D., Duke U., 1972. Bar: Hawaii 1972, U.S. Dist. Ct. Hawaii 1972, U.S. Ct. Appeals (9th cir.) 1973, U.S. Supreme Ct. 1978. Assoc. 1978, U.S. Dist Ct. (no. dist.) No. Mariana Islands 1984. Schutte, Fleming and Wright, Honolulu, 1972-78, ptnr. 1979—; adj. prof. media law Univ. Hawaii dept. journalism, Honolulu, 1986—. Pres., bd. dirs. Hawaii Performing Arts Co., Honolulu, 1980—; mem. Honolulu Community Media Council, 1983—; commr. Honolulu Neighborhood Commn., 1984—; mem. panel of arbitrators Am. Arbitration Assn., 1984—; Democratic State Conv., 1976, 1984; del. Hawaii Judicial Conf., 1985-87; mem. Hawaii Bicentennial Commn; chmn. Honolulu Neighborhood Commn., 1986—. Recipient Freedom of Press award Sigma Delta Chi, 1984. Mem. ABA (forum com. communication, media and law com. 1985-86, chmn. We The People orgn.), Hawaii State Bar Assn. (pub. relations chmn. 1979-84), Hawaii Defense Lawyers Assn. (v.p. 1986—). Jewish. Libel, Insurance, State civil litigation. Home: 5111 Palaole Pl Honolulu HI 96821 Office: Cades Schutte Fleming and Wright PO Box 939 Honolulu HI 96808

PORTO, JOSEPH ANTHONY, lawyer; b. Houston, June 1, 1955; s. Joseph Amodeo and Esther Louise (Spacil) P.; m. Linda Sue Leblanc, Aug. 7, 1982; 1 child, Laurie Marie. BS cum laude, U. Houston, 1977; JD, South Tex. Coll. Law, 1981. Bar: Tex. 1982, U.S. Dist. Ct. (so. dist.) Tex. 1982, U.S. Ct. Appeals (5th cir.) 1982. Law clk. Porto, Trueheart, Houston, 1977-82; briefing atty. Tex. Ct. Crime Appeals, Austin, 1982-83; asst. dist. atty. Harris County Dist. Atty., Houston, 1983—. V.p. U. Houston Young Dems., 1977. Served as ensign USNR. Mem. ABA, Tex. Bar Assn., Tex. Dist. and County Atty. Assn., Assn. Trial Lawyers, Phi Alpha Delta. Roman Catholic. Avocations: hunting, football, basketball, softball, aquatic sports. Criminal, Personal injury, Admiralty. Home: 1515 Apple Park Dr Katy TX 77450 Office: Harris County Dist Atty 201 Fannin Houston TX 77002

PORTO, STEVEN MICHAEL, lawyer, educator; b. Des Moines, Sept. 2, 1952; s. Anthony Francis and Genevieve (Greco) P. Student, Regis Coll., 1970-71, Loyola U., Chgo., 1971-72; BA, Creighton U., 1974, postgrad., 1974-75; JD, Drake U., 1977. Bar: Iowa 1977, U.S. Dist. Ct. (so. dist.) Iowa 1978. Sole practice West Des Moines, 1977—; adj. instr. Des Moines Area Community Coll., Ankeny, Iowa, 1983—. Mem. ABA, Iowa Bar Assn. (com. prepaid legal services), Assn. Trial Lawyers Am. Home: 7509 Madison Urbandale IA 50322 Office: 1200 35th St #403-7 West Des Moines IA 50265

PORZIO, RALPH, lawyer, lecturer, author, editor; b. Bklyn., Aug. 27, 1914; m. Edith Lori, June 6, 1942; 1 child, Ann Lewis. A.B., Drew U., 1938; J.D., Harvard U., 1942. Bar: N.J. 1943, U.S. Supreme Ct. 1943, N.Y. 1981. Of counsel Porzio, Bromberg & Newman, Morristown and N.Y.C.; counsel, bd. of trustees Internat. Coll. Angiology; lectr., London, Vienna, Copenhagen, Dublin, Rome, Lisbon, Geneva, Ghent, Montreal, U.S. Author: The Transplant Age—Reflections on the Legal and Moral Aspects of Organ Transplants, 1969; editor-in-chief: Internat. Jour. Law and Sci., 1975-80; asso. editor, 1969-75; contbr. articles to profl. jours. Mem. Boonton Charter Commn., 1952-53, Bd. Edn., 1953-56; trustee emeritus Drew U., N.J. Conservation Found., Holmes Library, Boonton. Recipient Freedoms Found. citation for writings advancing Am. way of life, 1951, Outstanding Achievements award in arts Drew U., 1956. Fellow Internat. Acad. Law and Sci. (pres., bd. regents), Internat. Soc. Barristers; mem. ABA, N.J. Bar Assn., Morris County Bar Assn. (pres. 1970-71), Fed. Bar Assn.,

Am. Judicature Soc., N.Y. State, N.J. plaintiffs trial lawyers assns., N.J. Soc. Hosp. Attys., World Assn. Med. Law, Law-Sci. Acad. Am., Am. Coll. Legal Medicine, Am. Soc. Law and Medicine, Trial Attys. of N.J. (charter, ann. award for disting. service in cause of justice 1979), Assn. Trial Lawyers Am., N.J. Assn. Sch. Attys., Phi Beta Kappa. Club: Optimist (Morristown) (pres.). Health, State civil litigation. Home: 123 Glover St Boonton NJ 07005 Office: Porzio Bromberg & Newman 163 Madison Ave Morristown NJ 07960 also: 1 Exchange Plaza New York NY 10006

POSNER, DAVID S., lawyer; b. Pitts., Dec. 27, 1945; s. Mortimer B. and Lillian (Smith) P.; m. Marilyn Hope Ackerman, Aug. 14, 1966; children: Morton J., Jennifer L. BS, Carnegie Mellon U., 1969; JD, U. Pitts., 1972. Bar: Pa. 1972, U.S. Supreme Ct. 1981. Ct. adminstr. Washington County, Pa., 1972-76; asst. dist. atty. Washington County, 1976-79; ptnr. Goldfarb & Posner, Washington, Pa., 1979—; pres. Pa. Council of Trial Ct. Adminstrs., 1972-76; solicitor Clk. of Cts., Washington, 1983—. Mem. sect. 85 YMCA, Washington, 1980-85; bd. dirs. United Way, Washington, 1979-85. Served with USAR, 1966-72. Mem. ABA, Pa. Bar Assn., Washington County Bar Assn. (treas. 1982-83). Lodge: B'nai B'rith (past pres.). Avocations: canoeing, photography, outdoors. Real property, Banking, Consumer commercial. Home: 149 S Wade Ave Washington PA 15301 Office: Goldfarb & Posner 50 W Wheeling St Washington PA 15301

POSNER, MICHAEL HOFFMAN, lawyer; b. Chgo., Nov. 19, 1950; s. Harry Randolph and Elizabeth (Hoffman) P. BA with honors, U. Mich., 1972; JD, U. Calif., Berkeley, 1975. Bar: Calif. 1975, Ill. 1976, U.S. Dist Ct. (no. dist.) Ill. 1976. Research asst. Internat. Commn. Jurists, Geneva, 1974; assoc. Sonnenschein, Carlin, Nath & Rosenthal, Chgo., 1975-78; exec. dir. Lawyers Com. for Human Rights, N.Y.C., 1978—; bd. dirs. Amnesty Internat., Americas Watch; vis. lectr. Yale Law Sch., New Haven, 1983—, Columbia Law Sch., N.Y.C., 1984—. Contbr. articles to profl. jours. Term mem. Council Fgn. Relations, N.Y.C., 1980-85. Mem. ABA (chmn. com. on internat. human rights, sect. on individual rights and responsibilities, UN rep.). Democratic. Jewish. Avocations: tennis, skiing, hiking. Civil rights, Public international, Immigration, naturalization, and customs. Office: Lawyers Com for Human Rights 36 W 44th St New York NY 10036

POSNER, RICHARD ALLEN, federal court judge, lecturer; b. N.Y.C., Jan. 11, 1939; s. Max and Blanche Posner; m. Charlene Ruth Horn, Aug. 13, 1962; children: Kenneth A., Eric A. A.B., Yale U., 1959; LL.B., Harvard U., 1962; LL.D. (hon.), Syracuse U., 1986. Bar: N.Y. 1963, U.S. Supreme Ct. 1966. Law clk. Justice William J. Brennan Jr. U.S. Supreme Ct., Washington, 1962-63; asst. to commr. FTC, Washington, 1963-65; asst. to solicitor gen. U.S. Dept. Justice, Washington, 1965-67; gen. counsel Pres.'s Task Force on Communications Policy, Washington, 1967-68; assoc. prof. Stanford U. Law Sch., Calif., 1968-69; prof. U. Chgo. Law Sch., 1969-78, Lee and Brena Freeman prof., 1978-81, sr. lectr., 1981—; circuit judge U.S. Ct. Appeals (7th cir.), Chgo., 1981—; research assoc. Nat. Bur. Econ. Research, Cambridge, Mass., 1971-81; pres. Lexecon Inc., Chgo., 1977-81. Author: Antitrust Law: An Economic Perspective, 1976, Economic Analysis of Law, 3d edit., 1986, The Economics of Justice, 1981, The Federal Courts: Crisis and Reform, 1985; pres.: Harvard Law Rev., 1961-62; editor: Jour. Legal Studies, 1972-81. Fellow AAAS, Am. Law Inst.; mem. ABA, Am. Econ. Assn. Republican. Office: U S Ct of Appeals 219 S Dearborn Chicago IL 60604

POSS, STEPHEN DANIEL, lawyer; b. Buffalo, Jan. 13, 1955; s. Gilbert H. and Bernice L. (Lippman) P. BA magna cum laude, Amherst Coll., 1978; JD, U. Chgo., 1981. Bar: N.Y. 1982, U.S. Tax Ct. 1983, U.S. Dist. Ct. (so. dist.) N.Y. 1984, U.S. Supreme Ct. 1986. Assoc. Cravath, Swaine & Moore, N.Y.C., 1981—. Advisor campaign Quentin Burdick for U.S. Senate, N.D., 1976, Bill Bradley for U.S. Senate, N.J., 1978, Gary Hart for U.S. Senate, Colo., 1980, Jeff Bingaman for U.S. Senate, N.Mex., 1982; bd. dirs. Internat. Forum, N.Y.C., 1984, council N.Y. Law Assocs., N.Y.C., 1985. John Woodruff Simpson fellow, 1978. Mem. ABA. Club: Sierra (life). Federal civil litigation, State civil litigation. Office: Cravath Swaine & Moore 1 Chase Manhattan Plaza New York NY 10005

POST, EARL STOCK, lawyer, accountant; b. Baton Rouge, Feb. 19, 1908; s. Manfred Arthur and Mabel Marie (Stock) P.; m. Doris Charles Kilgore, Nov. 22, 1939; 1 child, Nancy Elizabeth (Mrs. Richard R. Godfrey). LL.B., San Antonio Sch. Law, 1932. Bar: Tex. 1932. Reporter, Sunday editor San Antonio Light newspaper, 1923-31; specialty writer Gulf Pub. Co., Houston, 1928-39; sole practice, San Antonio, 1932-42; revenue officer IRS, San Antonio, 1944-59; atty., pres. Earl S. Post Inc., P.C., San Antonio, 1959—; dir., trustee Good Samaritan Nursing Home, Inc., San Antonio, 1970—. Contbr. articles to profl. jours. Served with M.I., USAAF, 1942-44. Mem. Tex. Bar Assn. (50th Yr. Service award 1982), Tex. Bd. Pub. Accts., Full Gospel Businessmen's Fellowship Internat., San Antonio Bar Assn. Republican. Episcopalian. Club: Optimist (San Antonio). Lodges: Masons, Order Eastern Star. Personal income taxation, Probate, General corporate. Home: 7155 Oakridge San Antonio TX 78229 Office: Atlee B Ayres Bldg Suite 322 San Antonio TX 78205

POST, EDWARD NEAL, lawyer; b. Jersey City, Dec. 27, 1929; s. Edward Randolph and Ethel Elizabeth (Turner) P.; m. Kate Huskins, Dec. 14, 1958; 1 son, Alan Neal. A.B., Guilford Coll., 1951; J.D., U. N.C., 1954. Bar: N.C. 1955. Sr. ptnr. Morgan, Post, Herring & Morgan, High Point, N.C. Named to Outstanding Young Men in Am., U.S. Jaycees, 1962, named Outstanding Local Pres., 1962. Mem. High Point Bar Assn., N.C. Bar Assn., ABA, N.C. Trial Lawyers Assn., High Point Jaycees (life). Democrat. Clubs: Kiwanis, Masons (High Point). General practice, Real property. Home: 1227 Westwood Ave High Point NC 27260 Office: Law Bldg Suite 200 212 E Green Dr High Point NC 27260

POSTER, JEFFREY CHARLES, lawyer; b. N.Y.C., Apr. 25, 1942; s. Irving Carlin and Mae (Zohn) P.; m. Elizabeth Charlotte Boldizar, Nov. 23, 1973. BA, Brandeis U., 1964; MPA, Cornell U., 1967; JD, Suffolk U., 1981. Bar: Mass. 1981, Calif. 1981, U.S. Dist. Ct. (cen. dist.) Calif. 1982, U.S. Ct. Appeals (9th cir.) 1982. Assoc. Hagenbaugh & Murphy, Los Angeles, 1982-83; ptnr. Poster & Sargent, Los Angeles, 1983-85; assoc. Marrone, Robinson, Frederick & Foster, Los Angeles, 1985—. Served to lt. USNR, 1964-73. Mem. ABA, Fed. Bar Assn., Calif. Bar Assn., Los Angeles County Bar Assn. Federal civil litigation, State civil litigation, Insurance. Office: Marrone Robinson Frederick & Foster 3356 Barham Blvd Los Angeles CA 90068

POSTLEWAITE, CHARLES CHAPMAN, lawyer; b. Columbus, Ohio, Feb. 14, 1955; s. William Neal and Margaret Jane (Chapman) P.; m. Molly Jo Thomas, Oct. 5, 1985. BA, Williams Coll., 1977; JD, Ohio No. U., 1981. Bar: Ohio 1982, U.S. Supreme Ct. 1982. Assoc. Postlewaite and O'Brien, Columbus, 1982-83, ptnr., 1984—. Fellow ABA; mem. Am. Judicature Soc., Columbus Bar Assn., Ohio Bar Assn., Franklin County Trial Lawyers Assn., Columbus Jaycees, Charity Newsies. Roman Catholic. Criminal, General corporate, Family and matrimonial. Home: 4229 Haymaker Dublin OH 43017 Office: Postlewaite and O'Brien 150 E Mound St Suite 207 Columbus OH 43215

POSTLEWAITE, PHILIP FREDERICK, law educator. JD, U. Calif., Berkeley, 1970; LLM in Taxation, NYU, 1971. Bar: Wis. 1970, Wash. 1973. Assoc. Foley & Lardner, Milw., 1970-71; instr. in taxation NYU, N.Y.C., 1971-73; assoc. Bogle & Gates, Seattle, 1973-76; assoc. prof. law U. Notre Dame, South Bend, Ind., 1976-81; prof. law Northwestern U., Chgo., 1981—. Author: Policy Readings in Individual Taxation, 1980, International Corporate Taxation, 1980; co-author: Partnership Taxation, 3d ed., vols. I, II and III, 1981, Partnership Taxation Problems and Answers, 1982, International Individual Taxation, 1982, Problems and Materials in Federal Income Taxation, 1986; contbr. articles to profl. jours. Legal education. Home: 417 Abbotsford Rd Kenilworth IL 60043 Office: Northwestern U Sch Law 357 East Chicago Ave Chicago IL 60611

POSTOL, LAWRENCE PHILIP, lawyer; b. Bridgeport, Conn., Oct. 18, 1951; s. Sidney Samual and Eunice Ruth (Schine) P.; m. Ellen Margaret Russell, Mar. 22, 1975; 1 child, Raymond Russell. BS, Cornell U., 1973, JD, 1976. Bar: Conn. 1976, D.C. 1977, U.S. Dist. Ct. D.C. 1977, U.S. Ct. Appeals (D.C. cir.) 1977, U.S. Supreme Ct. 1980, Va. 1982, U.S. Ct. Appeals (4th cir.) 1982, U.S. Dist. Ct. (ea. dist.) Va. 1985. Assoc. Arent, Fox, Kintner & Plotkin, Washington, 1976-80; assoc. Seyfarth, Shaw, Fairweather & Geraldson, Washington, 1980-83, ptnr., 1985—; assoc. Jones, Day, Reavis and Pogue, Washington, 1983-85; lectr. Loyola U., New Orleans, 1983—, Ga. Inst. Tech., Atlanta, 1985—. Contbr. articles to law revs. Mem. ABA. Democrat. Jewish. Avocation: sports. Federal civil litigation, Health, Workers' compensation. Home: 6340 Chowning Pl McLean VA 22101 Office: Seyfarth Shaw Fairweather & Geraldson 1111 19th St Washington DC 20036

POSY, DAVID HOWARD, lawyer; b. Bklyn., Mar. 7, 1948; s. Manuel and Frances (Hendel) P.; m. Mirel Beane, Oct. 24, 1971; children: Yosef, Jonathan, Daniel, Akiva, Ilana, Michael. B in Hebrew Lit., BA, Yeshiva U., 1969; JD, Columbia U., 1972. Bar: N.Y. 1973, U.S. Dist. Ct. (so. and ea. dists.) N.Y. 1974, Pa. 1981. Assoc. Wolf, Haldenstein, Adler, Freeman, Herz & Frank, N.Y.C., 1972-73, Orans, Elson & Polstein, N.Y.C., 1973-75; sr. counsel Westinghouse Electric Corp., Pitts., 1975—. V.p. PTA, Pitts., 1980; bd. dirs. Kollel Bais Yitzchok, Pitts., 1978—. Mem. Pa. Bar Assn. Jewish. Real property, Federal civil litigation, State civil litigation. Office: Westinghouse Bldg 6 Gayeway Ctr Pittsburgh PA 15222

POTASH, M. STEVEN, lawyer; b. Cleve., Dec. 1, 1952; s. Bernard and Helen (Jachimovitz) P.; m. Loree Ellen Green, Mar. 9, 1975; children: Erica Lynn, Karen Lisa, Brian Jacob. BA in Journalism, Ohio State U., 1974; JD, Cleve. State U., 1979. Bar: Ohio 1979, U.S. Dist. Ct. Ohio 1979. Assoc. Law Offices of N.D. Rollins, Cleve., 1979; prin. Potash & Assocs., Beachwood, Ohio, 1979-85; ptnr. Potash & Podor Co. LPA, Beachwood, 1985—; prin. Potash & Nigbor Legal Applications, Beachwood, 1985—; spl. counsel Ohio Atty. Gen., Columbus, 1979—; acting judge South Euclid Mcpl. Ct., 1985—; pres. Turbo Law Labs., Inc., 1985—. Contbr. articles to ABA jour., Nat. Law Jour. Mem. ABA, Cleve. Bar Assn., Assn. Trial Lawyers Am., Am. Coll. Computer Lawyers (chmn.), Fraternal Order of Police. Jewish. Lodge: Masons. Avocations: computers, scuba diving, photography, skiing. Computer, Personal injury, State civil litigation. Home: 1927 Temblethurst Blvd South Euclid OH 44121 Office: 23811 Chagrin Blvd Suite 245 Beachwood OH 44122

POTENZA, JOSEPH MICHAEL, lawyer; b. Stamford, Conn., June 27, 1947; s. Michael Joseph Sr. and Rose Elizabeth (Coppola) P.; m. Wendy Ann David, Dec. 19, 1971 (div. Jan. 1978); m. Karen Louise Yankee, Jan. 28, 1978; children: Wendy Lynn, Chiara Micol. BSEE cum laude, Rochester Inst. Tech., 1970; JD, Georgetown U., 1975. Bar: Va. 1975, D.C. 1976, U.S. Dist. Ct. D.C., U.S. Ct. Appeals (fed. cir.), U.S. Ct. Appeals (6th cir.), U.S. Supreme Ct. Patent examiner U.S. Patent and Trademark Office, Arlington, Va., 1970-74, law clk. bd. appeals, 1974-75, law clk. to presiding judge, 1975-76; assoc. Banner, Birch et al, Washington, 1976-80, ptnr., 1980—; adj. prof. Georgetown U. Law Ctr., Washington, 1985—. Editor (monographs) Sorting Out Ownership Rights in Intellectual Property, 1980, Recent Developments in Licensing, 1981. Recipient Patent and Trademark Office Superior Performance award Dept. Commerce, 1973-75. Mem. IEEE, ABA, (young lawyers div. exec. council 1979—, chmn. legis. action com. 1980—, chmn. patent trademark & copyright com. 1977—), Am. Patent Law Assn. (chmn. unfair compitition com. 1980-81), D.C. Bar Assn. (sec. patent, trademark, copyright sect.), Va. Bar Assn., Phi Sigma Kappa, Alpha Sigma (pres. 1969-70), Tau Beta Pi. Patent, Trademark and copyright, Litigation. Home: 1238 Gilman Ln Herndon VA 22070 Office: Banner Birch Mckie & Becket One Thomas Circle NW Washington DC 20005

POTH, HARRY AUGUSTUS, JR., lawyer; b. Phila., Nov. 5, 1911; s. Harry A. and Mary (Patton) P.; B.S., U. Pa., 1933, LL.B., 1936; m. Eleanor H. Sheils, Apr. 19, 1947; children—Christopher A., Jeremy D. Admitted to N.Y. bar, 1938, D.C. bar, 1948; asso. Reid & Priest, N.Y.C., 1937-48, partner, 1949-81, of counsel, 1982—, mng. partner Washington office, 1949-58; adviser on electric pub. utility matters govts. Greece, 1953-54, Pakistan, 1962-63. Mem. adv. council Nat. Strategy Info. Ctr., 1982—. Served to maj. USAAF, 1942-45. Decorated Bronze Star (U.S.); Cross Merit, Ordine Militario di Malta. Mem. Fgn. Policy Assn. (nat. council), Internat., Fed., Fed. Energy, N.Y. Bar Assn., Am. Bar Assn., Edison Electric Inst., Zeta Psi. Clubs: Wall St., Stanwich, Indian Harbor Yacht (Greenwich, Conn.); Chevy Chase, Metropolitan (Washington). Asso. editor U. Pa. Law Rev., 1935-36; contbr. articles to profl. jours. Public utilities, FERC practice, Antitrust. Home: 28 Ridgebrook Rd Greenwich CT 06830 Office: 40 W 57th St New York NY 10019

POTTER, C. BURTT, lawyer; b. La., Dec. 21, 1908; s. C. C. and Ethel M. (Lewis) P.; m. Marion Judson Jenkins, May 22, 1936; children—C. Burtt, Allan Leslie, John Michael. B.A., Southwestern La. U., 1930; J.D., Baylor U., 1933. Bar: Tex. 1933. Ptnr. Potter & Potter, Corpus Christi, Tex.; county atty. San Patricio County, 1935-43. Mem. Nueces County Bar Assn. (pres. 1949-50), State Bar Tex. (dir. 1950-52). Clubs: Kiwanis, Masons. General practice. Home and Office: 420 Delaine Corpus Christi TX 78411

POTTER, ERNEST LUTHER, lawyer; b. Anniston, Ala., Apr. 30, 1940; s. Ernest Luther and Dorothy (Stamps) P.; m. Gwyn Johnston, June 28, 1958; children—Bradley S., Lauren D. A.B., U. Ala., 1961, LL.B., 1963, LL.M., 1979. Bar: Ala. 1963, U.S. Dist. Ct. (no. dist.) Ala. 1964, U.S. Ct. Appeals (5th cir.) 1965, U.S. Supreme Ct. 1972, U.S. Ct. Appeals (11th cir.) 1982. Assoc. Burnham & Klinefelter, Anniston, Ala., 1963-64; assoc. Bell, Richardson, Cleary, McLain & Tucker, Huntsville, Ala., 1964-66, ptnr., 1967-70; ptnr. Butler & Potter, Huntsville, 1971-82; sole practice Huntsville, 1983—; mem. faculty Inst. Bus. Law and Polit. Sci., U. Ala.-Huntsville, 1965-67. Contbg. author: Marital Law, 1976, 2d edit. 1985. Vice pres. N.Ala. Kidney Found., 1976-77; treas. Madison County Democratic Exec. Com., 1974-78; bd. dirs. United Way Madison County, 1982—; chmn. U. Ala. Huntsville Pub. Ednl. Bldg. Authority, 1976—. Mem. Ala. Law Inst., ABA, Ala. Bar Assn., Madison County Bar Assn., Phi Beta Kappa, Farrah Order of Jurisprudence. Episcopalian. General practice. Address: 221 E Side Sq Suite 2B Huntsville AL 35801

POTTER, FRED LEON, lawyer, insurance company executive; b. Kansas City, Kans., Dec. 15, 1948; s. Donald Warren and Olive Lucile (Ater) P.; m. Mertie Lorraine Scribner, June 13, 1970; children: Mark, Amy, Joy. BA, Harvard U., 1970, MBA, 1972; JD, U. Mich., 1975. Bar: N.H. 1975, U.S. Dist. Ct. N.H. 1975. Assoc. Sulloway, Hollis & Soden, Concord, N.H., 1975-80; pres., gen. counsel Christian Mut. Life Ins. Co., Concord, 1980—; ptnr., mgmt. cons. Potter-Brock Assn., Tucson, 1969-82; trustee Gordon-Conwell Theol. Seminar, South Hamilton, Mass., 1983—; bd. dirs. N.H. Savings Bank, Concord. Clk. Concord Union Sch. Dist., 1978-84; deacon 1st Bapt. Ch., Concord, 1978-85; asst. coach Concord Little League, 1986—. Mem. ABA, N.H. Bar Assn. (treas. 1980-84, v.p. 1984-85, pres. 1986—, Pres. Disting. Service award 1983), Merrimack County Bar Assn. (sec. 1976-80), Christian Legal Soc., Computer Law Assn., Order of Coif. Evangelical. Insurance, Contracts commercial, General corporate. Home: 4 Pond Place Ln Concord NH 03301 Office: Christian Mut Life Ins Co 6 Loudon Rd Concord NH 03301

POTTER, GEORGE ERNEST, lawyer; b. Flint, Mich., Mar. 1, 1937; s. Ernest Davison and Bonnie Jean (Bayley) P.; m. Donna Elizabeth St. John, June 23, 1956; children: Kevin Ernest, Eric Davison, Melissa Elizabeth. AA, Jackson Community Coll., 1956; BA, Albion Coll., 1958; JD, U. Mich., 1960. Bar: Mich. 1960, U.S. Dist. Ct. (ea. dist.) Mich. 1965, U.S. Ct. Appeals (6th cir.) 1967, U.S. Dist. Ct. (we. dist.) Mich. 1969. Assoc. Kleinstiver & Anderson, Jackson, Mich., 1961-65; ptnr. Anderson, Patch, Potter & Patch, Jackson, 1965-71, Patch, Rosenfeld, Potter & Grover, Jackson, 1971-81, Potter & Lefere, Jackson, 1981-85, Potter & Stevens, Jackson, 1986—. Trustee Jackson Community Coll., 1962—. Recipient M. Dale Ensign award Assn. of Community College Trustees, 1964, Disting. Service award Mich. Community Coll. Assn., 1985; named Outstanding Young Man Jackson Jaycees, 1967. Mem. ABA, Def. Research Inst., Mich. Bar Assn., Jasckson County Bar Assn. (sec. 1963-64), Am. Assn. of Community and Jr. Colls. (trustee of yr. award). Republican. Lodge: Rotary (bd. dirs. 1972-75). Avocations: community colleges, travel. Insurance, Personal injury, State civil litigation. Home: 5555 Browns Lake Rd Jackson MI 49203 Office: Potter & Stevens 404 S Jackson St Jackson MI 49201

POTTER, HAMILTON FISH, JR., lawyer; b. Bklyn., Dec. 21, 1928; s. Hamilton Fish and Alma Virginia (Murray) P.; m. Virginia Fox Patterson, Sept. 17, 1953 (div. May 1979); children: Virgnia Patterson, Hamilton Fish, Robert Burnside, Elizabeth Stuyvesant; m. Maureen Ellen Cotter, Nov. 28, 1981; children: Nicholas Fish, Warwick Alonzo. B.A., Harvard U., 1950, LL.B., 1956. Bar: N.Y. Assoc. Sullivan & Cromwell, N.Y.C., 1956-65, ptnr., 1965—; dir. European Am. Bancorp, European Am. Bank. Bd. dirs. Berkshire Farm for Boys, N.Y.C., 1962-71; bd. dirs. Alice and Hamilton Fish Library, Garrison-on-Hudson, N.Y., 1980—; mem. Bd. Correction, N.Y.C., 1963-71; past warden Ch. of Ressurection, 1965-72; trustee Episcopal Sch. of N.Y., 1969-76, Chapin Sch., 1975-81, Knox Sch., 1985—; warden All Saints Episcopal Ch., 1982—; bd. dirs. Dutch Am. West Indies Found., 1984— . Served to lt. (j.g.) USN, 1950-53, korea. Mem. ABA (chmn. banking law com. 1975-80), Am. Bar Found., N.Y. State Bar Assn. (ho. of dels. 1978-80), N.Y. Bar Found., Bar Assn. N.Y. (chmn. banking law com. 1972-74), Am. Law Inst. (3-4-8 com.). Club: India House (N.Y.C.). Banking, Bankruptcy, Commercial financing. Office: Sullivan & Cromwell 125 Broad St 29th Floor New York NY 10004

POTTER, JOHN W., judge; b. Toledo, Ohio, Oct. 25, 1918; s. Charles and Mary Elizabeth (Baker) P.; m. Phyllis May Bihn, Apr. 14, 1944; children: John William, Carolyn Diane, Kathryn Susan. PhB cum laude, U. Toledo, 1940; JD, U. Mich., 1946. Bar: Ohio. Assoc. Zachman, Boxell, Schroeder & Torbet, Toledo, 1946-51; ptnr. Boxell, Bebout, Torbet & Potter, Toledo, 1951-69; mayor City of Toledo, 1961-67; asst. atty. gen. State of Ohio, 1968-69; judge 6th Dist. Ct. Appeals, 1969-82, U.S. Dist. Ct., Toledo, 1982—. Sr. editor U. Mich. Law Rev., 1946; contbr. articles to profl. jours., opinions. Pres. Ohio Mcpl. League, 1965; v.p. Toledo Area C. of C., 1973-74; former assoc. pub. mem. Toledo Labor Mgmt. Commn.; past pres. U. Toledo Alumni Assn.; past pres., former bd. mem. Commn. on Relations with Toledo, Spain; former bd dirs. Toledo Zool. Soc., Cummings Sch., Toledo Opera Assn.; mem., former trustee Epworth United Meth. Ch.; former mem. bd. dirs. Conlon Ctr.; hon. chmn. Toledo Festival Arts, 1980. Served to capt. F.A., U.S. Army, 1942-46. Decorated Bronze Star; recipient Leadership award Toledo Bldg. Congress, 1965, Outstanding Alumnus award U. Toledo, 1967, award of merit Toledo Bd. Realtors, 1967, Resolution of Recognition award Ohio Ho. of Reps., 1982. Fellow Am. Bar Found., Am. Judicature Soc., 6th Jud. Cir. Dist. Judges Assn., Fed. Judges Assn.; mem. ABA, Ohio Bar Assn., Toledo Bar Assn. (exec. com. 1962-64), Lucas County Bar Assn., Nat. Trust for Hist. Preservation, Phi Kappa Phi. Club: Old Newsboys, Toledo. Lodge: Kiwanis. Home: 2418 Middlesex Dr Toledo OH 43606 Office: US Dist Ct 215 US Courthouse Toledo OH 43624

POTTER, RICHARD CLIFFORD, lawyer; b. Providence, Nov. 25, 1946; s. Peter Rex Potter and Helen Louise (McDevitt) St. Onge; m. Anne Algie, Mar. 22, 1975; children: Catherine Anne, David Henry. BA, U. N.C., 1968; JD cum laude, Ind. U., 1973. Bar: Ill. 1973, U.S. Dist. Ct. (no. dist.) Ill. 1973, U.S. Ct. Appeals (8th cir.) 1975, U.S. Ct. Appeals (3d cir.) 1978, U.S. Ct. Appeals (4th and 5th cirs.) 1979, U.S. Ct. Appeals (9th cir.) 1980, U.S. Supreme Ct. 1979. Assoc. Kirkland & Ellis, Chgo., 1973-75; atty. and ptnr. Bell, Boyd & Lloyd, Chgo., 1975—; lobbyist Boise Cascade Corp., Washington, 1981-84. Assoc. editor, exec. officer Ind. Law Jour., 1972-73; author various publs. Bd. dirs. Northbrook (Ill.) Park Dist. adv. council, 1982. Mem. ABA (co-chair litigation subcom. on FTC, vice chmn. internat. law and practice com. on internat. aspects litigation, chmn. internat. law and pracitce subcom. on settlement and ADR), Internat. Bar Assn., Legal Club Chgo., Asia-Pacific Lawyers Assn., Nat. Health Lawyers Assn. Club: University (Chgo.). Antitrust, Federal civil litigation, Health. Home: 2134 Butternut Ln Northbrook IL 60062 Office: Bell Boyd & Lloyd 70 W Madison Chicago IL 60602

POTTER, ROBERT DANIEL, U.S. district judge; b. Wilmington, N.C., Apr. 4, 1923; s. Elisha Lindsey and Emma Louise (McLean) P.; m. Mary Catherine Neilson, Feb. 13, 1954; children—Robert Daniel, Mary Louise, Catherine Ann. A.B. in Chemistry, Duke U., 1947, LL.B., 1950; LL.D., Sacred Heart Coll., Belmont, N.C., 1982. Practice law Charlotte, N.C., 1951-81; judge U.S. Dist. Ct. (we. dist.) N.C., 1981—. Commr. Mecklenburg County, Charlotte, 1966-68. Served to 2d lt. U.S. Army, 1944-47, ETO. Mem. N.C. Bar Assn. Republican. Roman Catholic. Club: Charlotte City. Judicial administration. Home: 2710 Coltsgate Rd Charlotte NC 28211 Office: US Courthouse 268 Charles R Jonas Fed Bldg 401 W Trade St Charlotte NC 28202

POTTER, TANYA JEAN, lawyer; b. Washington, Oct. 30, 1956; d. John Francis and Tanya Agnes (Kristof) P. BA, Georgetown U., 1978, JD, 1981. Bar: D.C. 1981, U.S. Ct. Appeals (Fed. cir.), U.S. Ct. Internat. Trade. Assoc. Ragan and Mason, Washington, 1981—; mediator D.C. Superior Ct., 1986—. Author: Practicing Before the Federal Maritime Commn., 1986. Mem. exec. council Washington Opera's Jr. Com., 1983—, chmn. program com. 1986; mem. internat. com. ARC, Washington, 1986—; auction chmn. Young Friends of ARC, Washington, 1985-86; mem. benefit com. Vincent T. Lombardi Cancer Ctr., Washington, 1985—; del. Georgetown U. Nat. Law Alumni Bd. dirs., 1986—. Recipient Community Service Recognition award ARC, Washington, 1986. Mem. ABA, Bar Assn. of D.C. (exec. council ad law sect. 1985—, moderator adminstrv. law symposium 1986—). Roman Catholic. Clubs: Pisces, Georgetown U. Met. (bd. govs. 1986—) (Washington). Avocations: sports, visiting museums, studying the fine arts. Administrative and regulatory, General corporate, International trade. Office: Ragan and Mason 900 17th St NW Washington DC 20006

POTTER, WILLIAM R., lawyer; b. Springfield, Minn., Jan. 25, 1953; s. Warren R. and DeLoris M. (Mertz) P.; m. Terry B. Bresler, May 31, 1975; children: Michelle Ann, Lisa Marie. BS, Oreg. State U., 1975; JD, U. Oreg., 1978. Bar: Oreg. 1978, U.S. Dist. Ct. Oreg. 1978. Assoc. Hershner, Hunter, Moulton, Andrews & Neill, Eugene, Oreg., 1978-81, ptnr., 1981—. Bd. dirs. Eugene Festival of Musical Theatre, Eugene, 1986—. Mem. Oreg. Bar Assn., Lane County Bar Assn., Order of Coif, Phi Beta Kappa. Democrat. Avocations: reading, running, golf. General corporate, Labor, Real property. Home: 3873 Vine Maple Eugene OR 97405 Office: Hershner Hunter Moulton et al 180 E 11th Eugene OR 97405

POTTICK, FRANCES JEAN, lawyer; b. Manhasset, N.Y., Sept. 22, 1953; d. Edward Wilson Pottick and Margaret Ann (Larsen) Perkel; m. Steven Joseph Varlese, May 10, 1975; children: Benjamin P., Anna K. BA with distinction, U. Rochester, 1974; JD, U. Colo., 1979; postdoctorate, U. Denver, 1983—. Bar: Colo. 1979, U.S. Dist. Ct. Colo. 1979, U.S. Ct. Appeals (10th cir.) 1980, U.S. Tax Ct. 1983, N.Y. 1986. Sole practice Boulder, Colo., 1979-80; assoc. Wegher & Fulton, Denver, 1983-84; prin. Pottick & Assocs., Boulder and Denver, 1984—; bd. dirs. Legal Aid and Defenders Program, Boulder; public speaker in field, 1979—. Staff editor U. Colo. Law Rev., 1978-79. Active Four Mile Canyon Fire Protection Dist, Boulder, 1975-80, Dem. Women Boulder County, 1986—; treas. com. to elect Dorothy Rupert, Boulder, 1986—; mem. hand bell choir 1983—, Trinity Luth. Ch., Boulder, fin. com. 1986—, outreach com. 1986—; mem. hand Bell Choir U. Colo., Boulder, 1986—; bd. dirs. Rocky Mountain Planned Parenthood, Boulder, 1976-78, state bd. dirs. 1978; Boulder County Estate Planning Council. Mem. ABA, Colo. Women's Bar Assn., Boulder Bar Assn. (chmn. tax sect. 1981-82), Nat. Lawyers Guild, NOW (bd. dirs. 1976-77, treas. 1977-78 Boulder chpt.), Greater Denver Tax Counsel Assn., Denver Tax Assn., ACLU, Boulder C. of C., Bus. and Profl. Women, Alliance of Profl. Women, Salesman With a Purpose, Internat. Assn. Fin. Planners. Avocations: voice study, opera, English hand bell choirs. Estate taxation, Personal income taxation, Corporate taxation. Office: Pottick & Assocs 1600 38th St Suite 201 Boulder CO 80301

POTTLE, WILLARD MARSH, JR., lawyer; b. Buffalo, Aug. 18, 1938; s. Willard M. and Frances (Noble) P.; m. Donna Atwill, Aug 24, 1963; children: Willard Marsh III, Deirdre, Louise. AB, Hamilton Coll., 1961; JD, Cornell U., 1964. Bar: N.Y. 1965, U.S. Dist. Ct. (we. dist.) N.Y. 1965. Assoc., ptnr., Pottle, O'Shea, Adamson & Reynolds, Buffalo, 1965-70, Dobozin & Pottle, Buffalo, 1970-82; assoc. practice, Buffalo, 1982-83; sole practice, 1983—; panel chmn. State of N.Y. Arbitration Programs; lectr. N.Y. State Bar Assn. Continuing Legal Edn. Program, U.S. SBA. Common counselman City of Buffalo, 1969. Mem. N.Y. State Bar Assn. (class action com.), Erie County Bar Assn. (mem. unlawful practice com., mem. judiciary com.), Western N.Y. Trial Lawyers Assn., Am. Arbitration Assn., Phi Delta

Phi. Republican. Presbyterian. Club: Rotary. State and federal civil litigation, Insurance, Personal injury. Office: 68 Niagara St Buffalo NY 14202

POTTS, DENNIS WALKER, lawyer; b. Santa Monica, Calif., Dec. 17, 1945; s. James Longworth and Donna (Neely) P.; m. Rebecca Sue Shipley; children—Brandon Earl Woodward, Trevor Shipley. B.A., U. Calif.-Santa Barbara, 1967; J.D., U. Calif.-San Francisco, 1970. Bar: Hawaii 1971, Calif. 1971, U.S. Dist. Ct. Hawaii 1971, U.S. Dist. Ct. (cen. dist.) Calif. 1983, U.S. Ct. Appeals (9th cir.) 1973, U.S. Supreme Ct. 1978. Assoc. Chuck Mau, Honolulu, 1971-74; sole practice, Honolulu, 1974—; mem. litigation com. ACLU, Honolulu, 1977-82. Recipient cert. Coll. of Advocacy Hastings Coll. Law-Loyola U. Sch. Law, San Francisco, 1973. Mem. Assn. Trial Lawyers Am., ACLU of Hawaii (Disting. Service cert. 1974). Clubs: Honolulu; Kailua Racquet. Federal civil litigation, State civil litigation, Personal injury. Office: 333 Queen St Suite 805 Honolulu HI 96813

POTTS, ROBERT LESLIE, lawyer; b. Huntsville, Ala., Jan. 30, 1944; s. Frank Vines and Helen Ruth (Butler) P.; m. Irene Elisabeth Johansson, Aug. 22, 1965; children—Julie Anna, Robert Leslie. Student Newbold Coll., Eng., 1963-64; B.A., So. Missionary Coll., 1966; J.D., U. Ala., 1969; LL.M., Harvard U., 1971. Bar: Ala. 1969, U.S. Dist. Ct. (no. dist.) Ala. 1969, U.S. Dist. Ct. (mid. dist.) Ala. 1973, U.S. Ct. Appeals (5th cir.) 1973, U.S. Dist. Ct. (so. dist.) Ala. 1975, U.S. Supreme Ct. 1976, U.S. Ct. Appeals (11th cir.) 1982, Law clerk to chief judge U.S. Dist. Ct. (no. dist.) Ala., 1969-70; researcher Herrick, Smith, Donald, Farley & Ketchum, Boston, 1970-71; lectr. Boston U., 1971, U. Ala., 1973-75; ptnr. Potts, Young & Blasingame, Florence, Ala., 1971-84; gen. counsel U. Ala. System, 1984—; dir. Bank Ind., Florence, 1975-85; adv. com. Rules Civil Procedure, Ala. Supreme Ct., 1973—; mem. Ala. Bd. Bar Examiners, 1973-79, chmn., 1983-86; mem. bd. mgrs. Nat. Conf. Bar Examiners, 1986—; trustee Ala. State U., 1976-79, Oakwood Coll., 1978-81. Mem. ABA, Ala. Bar Assn. (pres. young lawyers sect. 1979-80), Birmingham Bar Assn., Lauderdale County Bar Assn., Tuscaloosa County Bar Assn. Club: Tuscaloosa Rotary, Masons. Contbr. numerous articles to profl. jours. Federal civil litigation, State civil litigation, General practice. Office: PO Box BT Tuscaloosa AL 35487

POUL, FRANKLIN, lawyer; b. Phila., Nov. 6, 1924; s. Boris and Anna P.; m. Shirley Weissman, June 26, 1949; children—Leslie R., Alan M., Laurie J. Student, U. Pa., 1942-43, Haverford Coll., 1943-44; LL.B. cum laude, U. Pa., 1946. Bar: Pa. bar 1949, U.S. Supreme Ct 1955. Asso. firm Gray, Anderson, Schaffer & Rome, Phila., 1948-56, Wolf, Block, Schorr and Solis-Cohen, Phila., 1956-60; partner Wolf, Block, Schorr and Solis-Cohen, 1960—. Bd. dirs. ACLU, Phila., 1955—, pres., 1975-76. Served with AUS, 1943-46. Mem. Am. Law Inst., Am. Bar Assn., Order of Coif. Antitrust, Securities, Federal civil litigation. Office: 12th Fl Packard Bldg Philadelphia PA 19102

POUND, FRANK R., JR., lawyer; b. Mayo, Fla., Nov. 3, 1933; s. Frank Reese and Elizabeth (Hart) P.; m. Betty Armstrong, Aug. 31, 1957; children: Tamara, Susan, Tracy, Brittain. BS, U. Fla., 1959, JD, 1961. Bar: Fla. 1962, U.S. Dist. Ct. (mid. dist.) Fla. 1962, U.S. Supreme Ct. 1969. Asst. county solicitor Orlando, Fla., 1962-64; trial assoc. Crofton, et.al., Titusville, Fla., 1964-66; assoc. Howell, et.al., Rockledge, Fla., 1966-71; ptnr., pres. Lovering, Pound & Clifton, Cocoa, Fla., 1971—. Chmn. Titusville Airport Authority, 1972, Sheriff's Civil Service Bd., Titusville, 1983-86. Served to col. USMC res., 1952-84. Mem. Acad. Fla. Trial Lawyers, Fla. Bar Assn. (bd. govs. 1979-82), Brevard County Bar Assn. (pres. 1972-73). Lodge: Rotary (Cocoa) (pres. 1982-83). State civil litigation, Personal injury. Office: Lovering Pound & Clifton 1970 Michigan Ave Cocoa FL 32922

POVELL, ROY ALBERT, lawyer; b. Bklyn., Mar. 23, 1929; s. Roy and Antonina (Zebrauskas) P.; m. Ann Wallace MacKinnon, July 20, 1957; children: Roy Dickson, Maryann Wallace, Elizabeth Ona. A.B., Harvard U., 1951, J.D., 1957; LL.M., NYU, 1963. Bar: N.Y. 1958, Fla. 1979. Assoc. Cadwalader, Wickersham & Taft, N.Y.C., 1957-65, ptnr., 1965—; lectr. Practising Law Inst., 1960—, World Trade Inst., 1970—. Author: Practising Law Inst. Handbook Series, 1970—, Foreign Tax Havens, 1973, Foreign Tax Planning, 1983. bd. dirs. Harvard Legal Aid Bur., Cambridge, Mass., 1956-57. Served to commdr. USNR, 1951-54, Korea. Mem. ABA, N.Y. State Bar Assn., Fla. Bar Assn., Internat. Tax Assn. (pres. 1968-69). Clubs: Hasty Pudding (Cambridge); NYU (N.Y.C.). Office: Cadwalader Wickersham & Taft 100 Maiden Ln New York NY 10038 Office: 440 Royal Palm Way Palm Beach FL 33480

POVICH, DAVID, lawyer; b. Washington, June 8, 1935; s. Shirley Lewis and Ethyl (Friedman) P.; m. Constance Enid Tobriner, June 14, 1959; children—Douglas, Johanna, Judith, Andrew. B.A., Yale U., 1958; LL.B., Columbia U., 1962. Bar: D.C. 1962. Law clerk to assoc. judge D.C. Ct. Appeals, Washington, 1962-63; ptnr. Williams & Connolly, Washington, 1963—; speaker Georgetown U. Criminal Practice Inst., mem. exec. com., 1986, 87; speaker Harvard Law Sch. Trial Advocacy Workshop. Bd. dirs., officer Lisner Home for Aged. Mem. D.C. Bar Assn., ABA, Bar Assn. D.C. Barristers. Federal civil litigation, Criminal. Office: 1000 Hill Bldg Washington DC 20006

POWELL, CRAIG STEVEN, lawyer; b. Kansas City, Mo., Sept. 12, 1950; s. James Clarence Powell and Marjorie Marie (Fitzgerald) Bergstrom; m. Cathy Sue Ricketts, June 14, 1975; children: Dustin James, Brett Allen. BS, Kansas State U., 1970; JD, Washburn U., 1974. Bar: Kans. 1974, U.S. Supreme Ct. 1977. Ptnr. McQueary & Powell, Osawatomie, Kans., 1974—; atty. City of Osawatomie, 1974—; atty. Unified Sch. Dist. #367, Miami County, Kans., 1974—; bd. dirs. 1st Nat. Bank and Trust, Osawatomie. Mem. steering com. Osawatomie Pride Program, 1982. Mem. ABA, Kans. Bar Assn., Miami County Bar Assn. Republican. Methodist. Lodges: Lions, Elks, Masons. Avocations: billiards, fishing, golf. General practice, Contracts commercial, Banking. Home: 1816 Parker Osawatomie KS 66064 Office: McQueary & Powell 564 Main Osawatomie KS 66064-0307

POWELL, DAVID WAYNE, lawyer; b. Galveston Island, Tex., Oct. 21, 1957; s. Daniel Benjamin and Anne Marie (Lettermann) P.; m. Emily Stafford Brame. BBA, So. Meth. U., 1979; JD, U. Tex., 1982. Bar: La. 1982, Tex. 1983, D.C. 1986. Assoc. Phelps, Dunbar, Marks, Claverie & Sims, New Orleans, 1982—. Bd. dirs. Inst. for Human Understanding., New Orleans, 1986—. Mem. Am. Inst. CPA's, La. Soc. CPA'S, La. Soc. SAR (sec. 1985), Soc. of 1812, Pilgrams, Loyalists, First Families of Miss. Republican. Episcopalian. Clubs: Essex, Pendennis (bd. dirs. 1986—), Round Table (New Orleans). Corporate taxation, Pension, profit-sharing, and employee benefits, Estate planning. Office: Phelps Dunbar Marks Claverie & Sims 400 Poydras 30th Floor New Orleans LA 70130-3245

POWELL, DOUGLAS RICHARD, lawyer; b. Staton Island, N.Y., Dec. 20, 1953; s. Percy Lloyd and Ruth Martha (Raisch) P.; m. Elizabeth Hammond, Dec. 31, 1977; children: Guyton David, Catherine Hammond. BA, Susquehanna U., 1975; JD, Wake Forest U., 1980. Bar: N.C. 1980, Ga. 1980, U.S. Dist. Ct. (ea. dist.) N.C. 1980, U.S. Dist. Ct. (no. dist.) Ga. 1985, U.S. Ct. Appeals (11th cir.) 1986. Assoc. LeRoy, Wells, Shaw, Hornthal & Riley, Elizabeth, N.C., 1980-81; atty. Fortson and White, Atlanta, 1985—. Served to lt. JAGC, USNR, 1981-85. Mem. ABA, Ga. Bar Assn., Atlanta Bar Assn., N.C. Bar Assn. Republican. Baptist. Avocation: tennis. Federal civil litigation, State civil litigation, Personal injury. Office: Fortson and White 300 Atlanta Fin Ctr 3333 Peachtree Rd NE Atlanta GA 30326

POWELL, JAMES CORBLEY, lawyer; b. Parkersburg, W.Va., Sept. 29, 1955; s. James Milton and Sarah Lou (Gates) P. BS in Mech. Engring., W.Va. U., 1977, JD, 1981. Bar: W.Va. 1981, U.S. Dist. Ct. (no. and so. dists.) W.Va. 1981. Ptnr. Hardman & Powell, Parkersburg, W.Va., 1981—. Commr. Parkersburg Police Civil Service, 1982—. Mem. ABA, W.Va. Bar Assn., Wood County Bar Assn., Assn. Trial Lawyers Am., W.Va. Trial Lawyers Assn. Republican. Presbyterian. Lodge: Elks. State civil litigation, Criminal, General practice. Home: 1521 Liberty St Parkersburg WV 26101 Office: Hardman & Powell 500 Green St Parkersburg WV 26101

POWELL, KAREN ANN PITTS, lawyer; b. Frankfort, Ky., Jan 15, 1958; d. Rex J. and Emily Ann (Watson) Pitts; m. Richard B. Powell, Jr., Dec. 19, 1981; 1 child, Cassandra Jane. BA Transylvania U., 1979; JD, U. Ky., 1982. Bar: Ky. 1982. Assoc. Logan & Gaines, Franfort, Ky., 1982-84; atty. Ky. Dept. Transp., Franfort, 1984, atty. prin.,1984-85, atty. chief, 1985 -. Mem. ABA, Ky. Bar Assn., Ky. Govt. Bar Assn., Am. Soc. for Prevention Cruelty to Animals, , Greenpeace. Democrat. Presbyterian. Club: Bluegrass Striders. Avocations: running, reading. Administrative and regulatory, Civil rights. State civil litigation. Home: 529 Timothy Dr Frankfort KY 40601 Office: Transp Cabinet Office Gen Counsel High St. Frankfort KY 40622

POWELL, LEWIS FRANKLIN, JR., former associate justice U.S. Supreme Court; b. Suffolk, Va., Sept. 19, 1907; s. Lewis Franklin and Mary Lewis (Gwathmey) P.; m. Josephine M. Rucker, May 2, 1936; children: Josephine Powell Smith, Ann Pendleton Powell Carmody, Mary Lewis Gwathmey Powell Sumner, Lewis Franklin, III. B.S., Washington and Lee U., 1929, LL.B., 1931, LL.D., 1960; LL.M., Harvard, 1932. Bar: Va. 1931, U.S. Supreme Ct. 1937. Practiced law in Richmond, 1932-71; mem. firm Hunton, Williams, Gay, Powell and Gibson, 1937-71; assoc. justice U.S. Supreme Ct., 1972-87; chmn. emeritus Colonial Williamsburg Found.; mem. Nat. Commn. on Law Enforcement and Adminstrn. Justice, 1965-67, Blue Ribbon Def. Panel to study Def. Dept., 1969-70. Served to col. USAAF, 1942-46, 32 months, overseas. Decorated Legion of Merit, Bronze Star; Croix de Guerre with palms France).; Trustee emeritus Washington and Lee U.; hon. bencher Lincoln's Inn. Fellow Am. Bar Found. (pres. 1969-71), Am. Coll. Trial Lawyers (pres. 1969-70); mem. ABA (gov., pres. 1964-65), Va. Bar Assn., Richmond Bar Assn. (pres. 1947-48), Bar Assn. City N.Y., Nat. Legal Aid and Defender Assn. (v.p. 1964-65), Am. Law Inst., Soc. Cin., Sons Colonial Wars, Phi Beta Kappa, Phi Delta Phi, Omicron Delta Kappa, Phi Kappa Sigma. Presbyterian. Clubs: Alfalfa; University (N.Y.C.). Judicial administration. Office: US Supreme Court 1 First St NE Washington DC 20543

POWELL, LEWIS FRANKLIN, III, lawyer; b. Richmond, Va., Sept. 14, 1952; s. Lewis F. Jr. and Josephine (Rucker) P.; m. Mims Maynard, June 3, 1978. BA, Washington & Lee U., 1974; JD, U. Va., 1978. Bar: Va. 1978, U.S. Dist. Ct. (ea. and we. dists.) Va. 1979, U.S. Ct. Appeals (4th cir.) 1979, U.S. Ct. Appeals (2d cir.) 1983, U.S. Supreme Ct. 1985. Law clk. to judge U.S. Dist. Ct. (ea. dist.), Richmond, 1978-79; from assoc. to ptnr. Hunton & Williams, Richmond, 1979—; pres. young lawyers conf. Va. State Bar, 1986—. Bd. dirs. William Byrd Community Ho., Richmond, 1982—, Boys Club of Richmond, 1984—. Mem. Richmond Bar Assn. (chmn. improvement justice com. 1982-83), 4th Cir. Jud. Conf. Avocations: skiing, mountaineering, backpacking, duck hunting, tennis. Federal civil litigation, State civil litigation, Environment. Office: Hunton & Williams 707 E Main St Richmond VA 23219

POWELL, MICHAEL CALVIN, lawyer; b. Chesapeake, Va., Mar. 22, 1954; s. William Calvin and Ruth Gertrude (Barnes) P. BA, U. Va., 1976, JD, 1979. Bar: Va. 1979, Md. 1979. Assoc. Piper & Marbury, Balt., 1979-83; asst. atty. gen. State of Md. Atty. Gens. Office, Balt., 1983—. Dupont scholar, 1972. Mem. ABA, Md. Bar Assn., Balt. Bar Assn. Environment, Federal civil litigation, State civil litigation. Home: 8678 Castlemill Circle Baltimore MD 21236 Office: Atty Gens Office 300 W Preston St Baltimore MD 21202

POWELL, OSBORNE EUGENE, JR., judge; b. Columbia, S.C., May 27, 1940; s. Osborne Eugene and Marjorie Davis (Bouknight) P.; m. Kathleen Holloman, June 16, 1963; children—Osborne Eugene III, Jeffrey Scott, John Everett. A.B., Wofford Coll., 1962; LL.B., U. S.C., 1965; grad. Judge Adv. Officers Basic Course, 1965, Judge Adv. Career Course, 1971, JAGC Res. Components Command and Gen. Staff Course, 1975; grad. U.S. Army War Coll., 1984. Bar: S.C. 1965, U.S. Dist. Ct. S.C. 1965, U.S. Ct. Mil. Appeals 1965, U.S. Ct. Appeals (4th cir.) 1974. Personal trust officer First Nat. Bank, Spartanburg, S.C., 1970-71; assoc. Williams & Williams, Spartanburg, 1971-72; asst. city atty. City of Spartanburg, 1971-72; ptnr. Long, Powell, & Whitney, Union, S.C., 1972-77; county atty. Union County (S.C.), 1976-77; assoc. Donelan & Donelan, Columbia, 1977-78; ptnr. Gibbes & Powell, Columbia, 1978-80; fed. adminstrv. law judge Office of Hearings and Appeals, Social Security Adminstrn., Dept. HHS, Macon, Ga. and Columbia, 1980—. Nat. alumni bd. dirs. Wofford Coll., 1972-75; chmn. Union County Democratic Party, 1976-77; bd. dirs. Ft. Jackson Credit Union, 1968-70, Columbia U.S. Employees Credit Union, 1983-86; troop commr. Indian Waters council Boy Scouts Am., 1982-84. Served to col. JAGC, USAR, 1965—, staff judge adv., 1982-86; comdr. 12th JAG Mil. Law Ctr., 1986—. Decorated Meritorious Service medalwith one oak leaf cluster, Army Commendation medal with 2 oak leaf clusters. Mem. ABA, S.C. Bar, Richland and Lexington County Bar Assn., Assn. Adminstrv. Law Judges, Nat. Conf. Adminstrv. Law Judges, Assn. Trial Lawyers Am., Nat. Assn. Social Security Claimants Reps. Episcopalian. Clubs: Ft. Jackson Golf. Administrative and regulatory, Military. Office: Suite 1259 Strom Thurmond Fed Bldg Columbia SC 29201

POWELL, RAMON JESSE, lawyer, government official; b. Macon, Mo., Mar. 1, 1935; s. Robert Evan and Blanche Odella (Dry) P.; A.B. in Econs. with distinction, U. Mo., 1957; postgrad. (Fulbright scholar) U. Brussels, 1957-58; J.D., Harvard U., 1965. Admitted to D.C. bar, 1966, Va. bar, 1975, U.S. Supreme Ct. bar, 1975; atty., advisor Office Gen. Counsel, Office Chief Engrs., Dept. Army, 1965-70; gen. counsel U.S. Water Resources Council, Washington, 1970-74, 80-82; asst. counsel for interagy. relations Office of Chief Counsel, Office of Chief of Engrs., Dept. Army, Washington, 1982—; individual practice law, Washington, 1975-76; pres., gen. counsel Leman Powell Assos., Inc., Alexandria, Va., 1976-80. Served as officer USAF, 1958-62. Mem. ABA, Fed. Bar Assn., D.C. Unified Bar, Bar Assn. D.C., Va. State Bar, Phi Beta Kappa, Omicron Delta Kappa, Delta Sigma Rho, Beta Theta Pi. Club: Nat. Lawyers. Administrative and regulatory. Office: 20 Massachusetts Ave NW Washington DC 20314

POWELL, RICHARD LYNN, lawyer; b. Marietta, Ga., June 10, 1936; s. Guy Arlington and Florine (Dobbins) P.; m. Paula Irene Hosea, Aug. 30, 1959; 1 child, Richele Lynn. Student U. Ga.-Marietta, 1954-59, Ga. State U., 1958-59; LL.B., John Marshall Law Sch., Atlanta, 1963, postgrad., 1963-64. Bar: GA. 1966, U.S. Dist. Ct. (no. dist.) Ga. 1966. Assoc. firm Grubbs, Prosser & Burke, Marietta, 1966-67; sole practice, Marietta, 1967—; lectr. in criminal law and criminal procedure John Marshall Law Sch., 1972-73. Campaign mgr. George W. Darden for Dist. Atty., Cobb County, Ga., 1972; campaign worker George W. Darden for Congress, Cobb County, 1983, 84. Served with U.S. Army, 1955-58. Mem. State Bar Ga. (bd. govs. 1974-78), Ga. Trial Lawyers, Assn. Trial Lawyers Am., Am. Soc. Law and Medicine, Cobb County Bar Assn. (Disting. Service award 1974, pres. 1973-74), Cobb County Trial Lawyers Assn. (pres. 1983-84). Democrat. Club: Marietta Country. Personal injury, Federal civil litigation, Criminal. Office: 142 Forest Ave Marietta GA 30060

POWELL, ROBERT DOMINICK, lawyer; b. Bklyn., Mar. 30, 1942; s. Ralph and Dorothy Piccola; m. Pamela Van Horn, Aug. 19, 1978; 7 sons. BA, U. Pa., 1963; LLB, St. John's Sch. Law, 1966; LLM, Georgetown U., 1978. Bar: N.Y. 1967, D.C. 1968, Md. 1974, U.S. Supreme Ct. 1972, U.S. Circuit Ct. Appeals (1st, 2d, 3d, 4th, 5th, 9th and 11th cirs.). Trial atty. FAA, 1966-68; assoc. Welch & Morgan, 1968-69; ptnr. Smith & Pepper, Washington, 1969-72, Powell & Becker, Washington, 1972-73, Sanders, Schnabel, Joseph & Powell, Washington, 1976-82, Joseph, Powell, McDermott & Reiner, Washington, 1982-86; prin. Law Office of Robert D. Powell, P.C., 1986—; sole practice law, Washington, 1973-76; gen. counsel Nat. Bus. Aircraft Assn., 1970—. Author: (poetry) Faint and Low, Soft and Sweet, 1968. Mem. ABA (forum com. on air and space law), InterAm. Bar Assn., Fed. Bar Assn., N.Y. State Bar Assn., D.C. Bar Assn., Md. Bar Assn., Montgomery County Bar Assn., Internat. Law Soc., Am. Judicature Soc., Assn. Trial Lawyers Am., Civil Aviation Med. Assn., Internat. Aviation Club. Republican. Episcopalian. Clubs: Press, Aero (Washington), Wings. Lodge: Rotary. Air, Private international, Federal civil litigation. Home: 11109 Smokey Quartz Ln Potomac MD 20854 Office: 1750 K St NW Suite 460 Washington DC 20006

POWELL, ROY DURWARD, lawyer; b. Ellisville, Miss., Dec. 14, 1927; s. Leroy and Lena (Cranford) P.; m. Ann Boykin, Feb. 24, 1951; children—Rosemary, Terri Ann, Caroline. A.A., Jones Jr. Coll., 1950; J.D., Miss. Coll., 1962. Bar: Miss. 1962, U.S. Dist. Ct. Miss. 1962, U.S. Ct. Appeals (5th cir.) 1962, U.S. Supreme Ct. 1972. Ptnr., King & Powell, Jackson, Miss., 1962-69, Powell & Sanford, Jackson, 1969-79, Powell & Thrash, Jackson, 1979-82; sole practice, 1982—. Del., Democratic Nat. Conv., 1974; chmn. bd. dirs. McCleur Acad., 1980-82; bd. dirs., chmn. Byram (Miss.) High Sch., 1967-76. Served with U.S. Army, 1952-54. Mem. Hinds County Bar Assn., ABA. Baptist. Clubs: Ducks Unltd.; Lions (pres.) (Bryan). Banking, State civil litigation, Real property. Office: Box 22493 Jackson MS 39225

POWELL, SCOTT ASHLEY, lawyer; b. Jacksonville, Fla., Aug. 29, 1953; s. Harold Leo and Betty Lee (Calhoun) P.; m. Donna Jeanine Peeler, June 8, 1974; children: Burgin, Taylor, Mary Ashley. BS, U. Ala., 1975; JD, Samford U., 1978. Bar: Ala. 1978, U.S. Dist. Ct. (no. dist.) Ala. 1979, U.S. Dist. Ct. (mid. dist.) Ala. 1981. Assoc. Burge & Florie, Birmingham, Ala., 1978-82; ptnr. Burge & Florie, Birmingham, 1982-85, Hare, Wynn, Newell & Newton, Birmingham, 1985—. Mem. ABA, Assn. Trial Lawyers Am., Ala. Trial Lawyers Assn., Am. Judicature Soc. Democrat. Presbyterian. Avocations: golf, running. Personal injury, Federal civil litigation, State civil litigation. Office: Hare Wynn Newell & Newton 700 City Fed Bldg Birmingham AL 35203

POWELL, WILLIAM DON, lawyer; b. Kansas City, Mo., June 7, 1943; s. Earl Ezra and Isabel Francis (Church) P.; m. Dorothy Q. Allemann, June 10, 1967; children—Wesley Brent, Kerri Lynn. B.A., Central Meth. Coll., 1965; postgrad. U. Mo.-Kansas City, 1965-66; J.D., Washburn U., 1969. Bar: Mo. 1970, U.S. Dist. Ct. (we. dist.) Mo. 1970. Assoc., Daniel, Clampett, Ellis, Ritterhouse and Dalton, Springfield, Mo., 1970-75; ptnr. Daniel, Clampett, Ritterhouse, Lilley, Dalton, Powell & Cunningham, Springfield, 1976—. Bd. dirs. Codac Inc., 1973-78, pres., 1975; bd. dirs. Regional Girls Shelter Inc., 1974-80 , sec., 1978 ; bd. dirs., pres. Children's Hearing Sch. SW Mo. Inc., 1978—; bd. dirs. Ozark br., Nat. Multiple Sclerosis Soc., 1981-87 ; Pres. bd. trustees First Unitarian-Universalist Ch. Springfield, 1984-86 . Mem. Def. Research Inst., Mo. Orgn. Def. Lawyers (bd. dirs. 1984—), ABA, Mo. Bar Assn., Greene County Bar Assn. (sec. 1987—). Office: PO Box 10306GS Springfield MO 65808

POWER, JOHN BRUCE, lawyer; b. Glendale, Calif., Nov. 11, 1936; m. Ann Power, June 17, 1961 (div. 1980); children: Grant, Mark, Boyd. AB, Occidental Coll., 1958; JD, N.Y.U., 1961; postdoctoral, Parker Sch. Comparative and Internat. Law, 1972. Bar: Calif. 1962. Assoc. O'Melveny & Myers, Los Angeles, 1961-69, ptnr., 1969—; lectr. in field. Bd. mgrs. Cetral City YMCA; mem. Los Angeles County Rep. Cen. Com., 1962-63. Mem. ABA (vice chmn. internat. fin. subcom. 1984—, comml. fin. services com. corps. banking and bus. law sect.), Calif. Bar Assn. (chmn. partnerships and unincorp. assns. 1981-83, uniform comml. code com. 1984-85, bus. law sect.), Los Angeles Bar Assn., Internat. Bar Assn., Fin. Lawyers Conf. (bd. govs., sec.-treas. 1983-84, v.p. 1984-85, pres. 1985-86), Exec. Service Corps. (sec.), Occidental Coll. Assn. (bd. govs. 1964-67, chmn. 1966-67), Phi Beta Kappa. Club: Calif. (Los Angeles). General corporate, Contracts commercial, Securities. Office: O'Melveny & Myers 400 S Hope St Los Angeles CA 90071-2899

POWERS, ELIZABETH WHITMEL, lawyer; b. Charleston, S.C., Dec. 16, 1949; d. Francis Persse and Jane Coleman (Wham) P. AB, Mt. Holyoke Coll., 1971; JD, U. S.C., 1978. Bar: S.C. 1978, N.Y. 1979. Law clk. to presiding justice S.C. Cir. Ct., Columbia; assoc. Reid & Priest, N.Y.C., 1978-86, ptnr., 1986—. Exec. editor S.C. Law Rev., Columbia, 1977-78. Vol. N.Y. Jr. League, N.Y.C., 1983—. Mem. ABA, DAR, Nat. Soc. Colonial Dames of Am. Republican. Clubs: Tuxedo (Tuxedo Park, N.Y.); Regency Whist (N.Y.C.). Avocations: bridge, tennis, riding, shooting, fly fishing. Public utilities, General corporate. Home: 201 E 69th St Apt 4U New York NY 10021 Office: Reid & Priest 40 W 57th St New York NY 10019

POWERS, GALEN DEAN, lawyer; b. Pleasant Lake, Ind., Sept. 16, 1936; s. Leo and Esther (Huffman) P.; m. Sandra Lee Rickards, May 16, 1970; 1 dau., Kathleen. B.A., U. Mich., 1959, LL.B., 1962. Bar: Mich. 1962, D.C. 1982, Pa. 1985. Chief counsel Health Care Financing Adminstrn., Washington, 1977-79; mng. ptnr. Weissburg and Aronson, Washington, 1979-83; founding ptnr. Powers, Pyles, Sutter & O'Hare, Washington, 1983-86; mng. ptnr. Powers, Pyles, Sutter & Miles, Washington, 1986—. Served to lt. USN, 1963-66. Mem. Nat. Health Lawyers Assn. (dir. exec. com.), Am. Soc. Hosp. Attys. Contbr. articles to profl. jours. Health. Home: 4843 Willett Pkwy Chevy Chase MD 20815 Office: 1015 Eighteenth St NW Washington DC 20036

POWERS, JOHN KIERAN, lawyer; b. Schenectady, Aug. 2, 1947; s. Paul Joseph and Anne Marie (Leahy) P.; m. Eileen Marie Maull, Apr. 4, 1970; children—Erin Kelly, Megan Kerry. B.S., U. Notre Dame, 1969; J.D., Union U., Albany, N.Y., 1972. Bar: N.Y. 1973, U.S. Dist. Ct. (no. dist.) N.Y. 1973, U.S. Dist. Ct. (so. and we. dists.) N.Y. 1982, U.S. Ct. Appeals (2d cir.) 1984, U.S. Supreme Ct. 1985. Assoc. Medwin and McMahon, Albany, 1973-77; sole practice, Albany, 1973-80; pres. John K. Powers, P.C., Albany, 1980-87; ptnr. Powers and Santola, 1987—; trustee N.Y. State Lawyers Polit. Action Com., 1983—; co-counsel N.Y. State Head Injury Assn., 1983-85. Mem. Assn. Trial Lawyers Am., N.Y. State Bar Assn., N.Y. State Trial Lawyers Assn. (bd. dirs. 1983—, exec. com. 1986—), Capitol Dist. Trial Lawyers Assn. (dir. 1979-81, v.p. 1983-85, pres. 1985-86). Democrat. Roman Catholic. Lodge: Lions (pres. 1979-80) (Scotia, N.Y.). Federal civil litigation, State civil litigation. Home: 2021 Salem Rd Schenectady NY 12309 Office: 600 Broadway Albany NY 12207-2205

POWERS, MARCUS EUGENE, lawyer; b. Cedarville, Ohio, Apr. 7, 1929; s. Frederick Armajo and Elizabeth Isabel (Rumbaugh) P. B.A., Ohio Wesleyan U., 1951; J.D. (Root-Tilden scholar), NYU, 1954, LL.M., 1958. Bar: Ohio 1954, N.Y. 1959, Calif. 1964. Asst. prof. law NYU Sch. Law, 1956-60; atty. Am. Brake Shoe Co., N.Y.C., 1959-63; asst. gen. counsel Dart Industries, Inc., Los Angeles, 1963-81; sr. v.p., gen. counsel Nat. Med. Enterprises, Inc., Los Angeles, 1981—; exec. v.p., sec., dir. Health Care Property Investors, Inc., 1985—. Served with U.S. Army, 1954-56. Mem. Los Angeles County Bar Assn. (past chmn. corp. law depts. sect.), Inst. Corp. Counsel (bd. govs., chmn. 1984-86), ABA (mem. Calif. com. on corp. law depts. 1985—, chmn. com. 1985—), Assn. Bar City N.Y., Calif. Coastal Conservancy, Phi Beta Kappa, Omicron Delta Kappa, Phi Delta Theta, Kappa Sigma, Pi Sigma Alpha, Theta Alpha Phi. General corporate, Antitrust, Health. Office: Nat Med Enterprises Inc 11620 Wilshire Blvd Los Angeles CA 90025

POWERS, MARK GREGORY, consultant, lawyer; b. Galveston, Tex., Aug. 14, 1948; s. Robert Kenneth and Ann Joan (Brugliera) P.; m. Kim M. Walker, Aug. 21, 1971; children: Jason Robert, Erin Alison. BBA in Acctg., Georgetown U., 1970; MBA, Gonzaga U., 1972, JD, 1974; CLU, Am. Coll., Bryn Mawr, Pa., 1975, Chartered Fin. Cons., 1982. Bar: Wash. 1974. Prin. Profl. Services Group, Spokane, Wash., 1970-82; sr. v.p. Nat. Assocs., Inc., Spokane, 1982—. Coach, Spokane Youth Soccer, 1982—; pres. Spokane Indoor Soccer Ctr., 1986—. Mem. Wash. State Bar Assn., Nat. Assn. Life Underwriters, Am. Soc. CLU's (pres. 1980-81). Clubs: Spokane; Green Bluff Polo (Mead, Wash.). Pension, profit-sharing, and employee benefits. Home: Route 3 Box 207 Chattaroy WA 99003 Office: National Assocs Inc NW W-600 Riverside Spokane WA 99201

POWERS, TIMOTHY EUGENE, lawyer; b. Waukegan, Ill., Aug. 3, 1955; s. Herman Eugene and Beryl Grace (Weiskittel) P.; m. Joni Grace Helm, Mar. 21, 1987. BA, UCLA, 1977; JD, So. Meth. U., 1980. Bar: Tex. 1980. Assoc. Passman & Jones, Dallas, 1980-82, Haynes and Boone, Dallas, 1982—. Mem. adv. bd. Southwestern Legal Found. Internat. and Comparative Law Ctr., Richardson, Tex., 1982—. Soc. Internat. Bus. fellow, 1987. Mem. ABA (internat. law and practice sect., internat. fin. transactions com., vice chmn. fgn. investment in U.S. real estate com.), Tex. Bar Assn. (council mem. internat. sect.), Dallas Bar Assn. (internat. sect.), Tex. Assn. Bank Counsel, Internat. Tax Assn. Dallas, Dallas Assn. Young Lawyers, Dallas C. of C. (internat. forum), Phi Delta Phi. Republican. Roman Catholic. Private international, Banking. Home: 10911 Aladdin Ln Dallas TX 75229 Office: Haynes and Boone 901 Main St 3100 InterFirst Plaza Dallas TX 75202

POWERS, WILLIAM LEONARD, lawyer; b. Buffalo, Nov. 28, 1952; s. William Daniel and Evelyn Marie (Trenberth) P.; m. Joan April Whiteside, Sept. 25, 1976; children: Keith Kendal, Paul Westmorland, Jane Elizabeth Winefride. BS, USCG Acad., 1974; JD, St. Mary's U., San Antonio, 1981. Bar: Tex. 1982. Commd. lt. USCG, 1974, resigned, 1979; atty. Plunkett, Gibson & Allen, San Antonio, 1982—. George W. Brackenridge scholarship St. Mary's U. Sch. Law, 1980. Mem. ABA, Tex. Assn. Def. Counsel (mem. evidence com. 1986), San Antonio Young Lawyers Assn. Lutheran. Avocations: yachting, sailing. Personal injury, State civil litigation, Insurance. Home: 7351 Hardesty San Antonio TX 78250 Office: Plunkett Gibson & Allen 6243 NW Expressway San Antonio TX 78201

POWLEN, DAVID MICHAEL, lawyer; b. Logansport, Ind., May 28, 1953; s. Daniel Thomas and Bertha Frances (Cappa) P.; m. Karen Lamb Gentleman, Aug. 5, 1978 (div. Jan. 1984); 1 child, Brooks Ryan. AB, Harvard U., 1975, JD, 1978. Bar: Ind. 1978, U.S. Dist. Ct. (so. dist.) Ind. 1978, U.S. Ct. Appeals (7th cir.) 1985. Assoc. Barnes & Thornburg, Indpls., 1978-84, ptnr., 1984—. Mem. ABA (bus. bankruptcy com., secured creditors subcom.), Ind. Bar Assn. (council bankruptcy and creditors rights sect. 1984—), Indpls. Bar Assn. (council comml. law and bankruptcy sect. 1984-86), Am. Bankruptcy Inst., Comml. Law League Am., Nat. Bankruptcy Conf. Republican. Methodist. Clubs: Harvard (Indpls.), Indpls. Sailing. Bankruptcy, Contracts commercial, General corporate. Home: 6463 Bayside S Dr Indianapolis IN 46250 Office: Barnes & Thornburg 1313 Merchants Bank Bldg 11 S Meridian St Indianapolis IN 46204

POWLESS, KENNETH BARNETT, lawyer; b. Marion, Ill., Aug. 11, 1917; s. George Newton and Sarah Maud (Barnett) P.; m. Emily Mary Cygnar, July 17, 1943; children—Linda Carol, James Kenneth, David Griffin, Catherine Celeste. B.S., U. Ill., 1938, J.D., 1940. Bar: Ill. 1940. Ptnr. Powless and Winters, Marion, Ill., 1946-52, Winters, Powless & Morgan, Marion, 1958-63; sole practice, Marion, 1940-41, 52-58, 63-74; ptnr. Powless Law Office, Marion, 1974-82; arbitrator Indsl. Commn. Ill., 1983—; counsel, dir. 1st Bank & Trust Co. of Williamson County. Chmn. bd. Marion Meml. Hosp., 1956-76, bd. dirs. emeritus, 1976—; spl. asst. atty. gen. State of Ill., 1954-58, 73-82; state's atty. Williamson County, 1968-72. Served to capt. U.S. Army, 1941-46; ETO. Mem. Ill. State Bar Assn., Williamson County Bar Assn., Am. Soc. Hosp. Attys. Republican. Methodist. Clubs: Egyptian Illini, Marion Kiwanis (dist. lt. gov. 1971), Elks (exalted ruler 1951), Masons, Shriners. Condemnation, Real property, Local government. Home: 905 N Van Buren St Marion IL 62959 Office: 108 W Jackson St Marion IL 62959

POYOUROW, ROBERT LEE, lawyer; b. Washington, June 30, 1952; s. Marvin J. and Elissa Poyourow; m. Dolores Ann Haluska, Oct. 14, 1978; 1 child, Jonathan Robert. BA, Boston U., 1974, JD, 1977. Bar: N.Y. 1978, U.S. Dist. Ct. (so. and ea. dists.) N.Y. 1978. Assoc. Marshall, Bratter, Greene, Allison & Tucker, N.Y.C., 1977-81; assoc. counsel GAF Corp., N.Y.C., 1981-85; sr. counsel GAF Corp., Wayne, N.J., 1986—. Mem. ABA, Assn. of Bar of City of N.Y. Democrat. Jewish. Avocations: fishing, reading, sports. State civil litigation, Insurance, Antitrust. Home: 404 Passaic Ave West Caldwell NJ 07006 Office: GAF Corp 1361 Alps Rd Wayne NJ 07470

POZYCKI, HARRY STEVEN, JR., lawyer; b. Perth Amboy, N.J., June 9, 1947; s. Harry Stanley and Mary Ann (Vereb) P.; m. Caroline Gibson Bryan, July 9, 1969; children: Caroline, Mary. BA, Brown U., 1969; JD, Fordham U., 1973. Bar: N.J. 1973, U.S. Dist. Ct. N.J. 1973, U.S. Supreme Ct. 1986. Sole practice Sayreville, N.J., 1973; ptnr. Frizell & Pozycki, Metuchen, N.J., 1974—; guest lectr. Woodrow Wilson Sch. Govt. Princeton U., 1983—. Contbr. articles to profl. jours. councilman Metuchen Devel. Commn., 1978—, Borough of Metuchen, 1981-84; chmn. senate race for Bill Bradley, Middlesex County, N.J., 1978; mem. Gov.'s Housing Task Force, 1983—. Mem. N.J. Bar Assn. (founder, bd. dirs. land use sect. 1983—, resolution of commendation 1984), N.J. Fedn. Planning Officials (legis. commn. 1983—), Metuchen C. of C. (Citizen of Yr. 1985). Real property. Home: 72 Hillside Ave Metuchen NJ 08840 Office: Frizell & Pozycki 269 Amboy Ave Metuchen NJ 08840

PRADO, EDWARD CHARLES, U.S. attorney; b. San Antonio, June 7, 1947; s. Edward L. and Bertha (Cadena) P.; m. Maria Anita Jung, Nov. 10, 1973; 1 son, Edward C. A.A., San Antonio Coll., 1967; B.A., U. Tex.-Austin, 1969, J.D., 1972. Bar: Tex. 1972. Asst. dist. atty. Bexar County Dist. Atty.'s Office, San Antonio, 1972-76; asst. pub. defender U.S. Pub. Defender's Office, San Antonio, 1976-80; state dist. judge Tex., San Antonio, 1980; U.S. atty. Dept. Justice, San Antonio, 1980-85; judge U.S. Dist. Ct. (we. dist.) Tex., 1985—. Served to capt. U.S. Army. Named Outstanding Young Lawyer Bexar County (Tex.), 1980. Mem. ABA, Tex. Bar Assn., San Antonio Bar Assn., San Antonio Young Lawyers Assn., Fed. Bar Assn. Republican. Roman Catholic. Judicial administration. Office: US Courthouse 655 E Durango Blvd Suite G-13 San Antonio TX 78206 *

PRAGER, DAVID, chief justice; b. Ft. Scott, Kans., Oct. 30, 1918; s. Walter and Helen (Kishler) P.; m. Dorothy Schroeter, Sept. 8, 1945; children: Diane, David III. AB, U. Kans., 1939, LLB, 1942. Bar: Kans. 1942. Practiced in Topeka, 1946-59; dist. judge Shawnee County (Kans.) Dist. Ct., 1959-71; assoc. justice Kans. Supreme Ct., Topeka, 1971-87, chief justice, 1987—; lectr. Washburn Law Sch., 1948-68. Served to lt. USNR, 1942-46, ETO, PTO. Mem. Kans. Dist. Judges Assn. (past pres.), Order of Coif, Phi Beta Kappa, Phi Delta Theta. Lodge: Lions. Office: Supreme Ct Bldg State Capitol Topeka KS 66612

PRAGER, SUSAN WESTERBERG, law educator; b. Sacramento, Dec. 14, 1942; d. Percy Foster and Aileen M. (McKinley) P.; m. James Martin Prager, Dec. 14, 1973; children: McKinley Ann, Case Mahone. AB, Stanford U., 1964, MA, 1967; JD, UCLA, 1971. Bar: N.C. 1971, Calif. 1972. Atty. Powe, Porter & Alphin, Durham, N.C., 1971-72; acting prof. law UCLA, 1972-77; prof. UCLA Sch. Law, 1977—; assoc. dean law sch. UCLA, 1979-82, dean, 1982—; bd. dirs. Pacific Mutual Life Ins. Co., Newport Beach, Calif. Editor-in-chief, UCLA Law Rev., 1970-71. Trustee Stanford U., 1976-80, 87—. Mem. ABA (council of sect. on legal edn. and admissions to the bar 1983-85), Assn. Am. Law Schs. (pres. 1986), Order of Coif. Legal education, Marital property law. Office: UCLA Sch of Law 405 Hilgard Ave Los Angeles CA 90024

PRATHER, JOHN GIDEON, lawyer; b. Somerset, Ky., Dec. 12, 1919; s. James Frederick and Josephine Linnwood (Collier) P.; m. Marie Jeanette Moore, Oct. 1945; 2 sons, John G., Jerome Moore. B.A., U. Ky., 1940, J.D., 1947. Bar: Ky. 1947, U.S. Dist. Ct. (ea. dist.) Ky. 1950. Pros. atty. Somerset, Ky., 1950-63; commonwealth atty. 28th Jud. Dist., 1963-64; sole practice, Somerset; sr. ptnr. Law Offices of John G. Prather, Somerset; dir. First & Farmers Bank, Somerset. Served to lt. USN, 1942-46; Mem. Pulaski County Bar Assn., Ky. Bar Assn. (ethics com., com. on fees), ABA (probate sect.), Def. Research Inst. Democrat. Mem. Christian Ch. (Disciples of Christ). Clubs: Kiwanis (Somerset), Shriners, Odd Fellows, Masons. General practice, Probate, Estate taxation. Office: Box 106 Somerset KY 42501

PRATHER, JOHN GIDEON, JR., lawyer; b. Lexington, Ky., Sept. 10, 1946; s. John Gideon Sr. and Marie Jeanette (Moore) P.; m. Hilma Elizabeth Skonberg, Aug. 4, 1973; children: John Hunt, Anna Russell. BS in Acctg., U. Ky., 1968, JD, 1970. Bar: Ky. 1971, U.S. Dist. Ct. (ea. dist.) Ky. 1978, U.S. Dist. Ct. (we. dist.) Ky. 1984. Sole practice Somerset, Ky., 1972—. Bd. dirs. United Way, 1978—; mem. state cen. com. Ky. Young. Dems., Frankfort, 1972. Served to 1st lt. USAF, 1971-72, JAG, 1972. Mem. Ky. Bar Assn. (ho. of dels. 1984-85, bd. govs. 1985—, lectr.), Council of Sch. Bd. Attys. (state pres., bd. dirs. 1986—, lectr.), Ky. Def. Council, Pulaski County Indsl. Found. (bd. dirs. 1982—). Mem. Christian Ch. Avocations: boating, flying. State civil litigation, General practice, Personal injury. Home: 510 N Main St Somerset KY 42501 Office: 38 N Public Sq Somerset KY 42501

PRATHER, KENNETH EARL, Lawyer; b. Detroit, May 9, 1933; s. Earl and Agnes (Mesanko) P.; m. Shirley Armstrong, Dec. 26, 1955; children - Eric, Kimberly, Jon, Laura, Lisa; m. 2d Jeanette M. Elder, June 30, 1973; 1 child, Kenneth. Ph. B., Detroit, 1955, J.D. 1960. Bar: Mich. 1960. Assoc. Kenney, Radom, Rockwell & Kenney, Detroit, 1960-66; ptnr. Kenney, Kenney, Chapman & Prather, Detroit, 1966-76; sole practice, Detroit, 1976-82; ptnr. Prather, Hilborn & Harrington P.C., Detroit, 1982, Prather & Harrington, P.C., Detroit, 1982-; adj. prof. law U. Detroit. Fellow Am. Acad. Matrimonial Lawyers; mem. State Bar Mich. (chairperson family law council 1983-84). Club: Detroit Athletic. Contbr. articles to legal jours. Family and matrimonial, Personal injury. Home: 5 Stratford Pl Grosse Pointe MI 48230 Office 3800 Penobscot Bld Detroit MI 48226

PRATHER, LENORE LOVING, state supreme court justice; b. West Point, Miss., Sept. 17, 1931; d. Byron Herald and Hattie Hearn (Morris) Loving; m. Robert Brooks Prather, May 30, 1957; children: Pamela, Valerie Jo, Malinda Wayne. B.S., Miss. State Coll. Women, 1953; LL.B., U. Miss., 1955. Bar: Miss. 1955. Practice with B. H. Loving West Point, 1955-60, sole practice, 1960-62, 65-71, assoc. practice, 1962-65; mcpl. judge City of West Point, 1965-71; chancery ct. judge 14th dist. State of Miss., Columbus, 1971-82; supreme ct. justice State of Miss., Jackson, 1982—; v.p. Conf. Local Bar Assn., 1956-58; sec. Clay County Bar Assn., 1956-71. Mem. Miss. State Bar. Assn., Miss. Conf. Judges, DAR. Episcopalian. Clubs: Pilot, Jr. Aux. Columbus. First woman in Miss. to become chancery judge (1971) and supremecourt justice (1982). Office: Supreme Ct of Miss Gartin Bldg 4th Floor Jackson MS 39201

PRATHER, ROBERT CHARLES, lawyer; b. Kansas City, Mo., Feb. 16, 1945; s. Charles William and Shirley Anne (Kernodle) P.; m. Lana Jo Ball, Jan. 25, 1969; children—Robert Charles, Jr., Lisa Michelle. B.Sc. in Communications, U. Tex., 1967, J.D., 1970; postgrad. U. Tasmania Law Sch., Australia, 1968. Bar: Tex. 1971, U.S. Dist. Ct. (no. dist.) Tex. 1978, U.S. Ct. Appeals (5th and 11th cirs.) 1981, U.S. Supreme Ct. 1978. Staff atty., com. clk. Senator W. T. Moore, State Affairs Com., Tex. Senate, Austin, 1971; asst. dist. atty., Dallas, 1971-74; asst. U.S. atty. No. Dist. Tex., Dallas, 1974-80; econ. crime enforcement specialist U.S. Dept. Justice, Dallas, 1980-81; assoc. trial atty. Turner, Rodgers, Sailers, Jordan & Calloway, Dallas, 1981-83; ptnr., trial atty. Jordan, Dunlap & Prather, Dallas, 1983—; gen. counsel, bd. dirs. Children's Cancer Fund of Dallas, Inc., 1982—. Author: (with others) A Document Numbering System, 1981. Soccer coach YMCA and North Dallas C. of C., 1979-84. Recipient Spl. Achievement award U.S. Dept. Justice, Washington, 1976; Rotary Found. fellow, 1968. Mem. ABA, Tex. Dist. and County Attys. Assn., Dallas Bar Assn., Phi Alpha Delta. Democrat. Baptist. Club: Argyle (pres. 1981)(Dallas), Park City (bd. dirs.). Lodge: Rotary (parliamentarian 1982—). State civil litigation, Federal civil litigation, Contracts commercial. Office: Jordan Dunlap & Prather 8115 Preston Rd Suite 500 Dallas TX 75225

PRATHER, WILLIAM CHALMERS, lawyer, writer; b. Toledo, Ill., Feb. 20, 1921; s. Hollie Cartmill and Effie Fern (Deppen) P. B.A., U. Ill., 1942, J.D., 1947. Bar: Ill. 1947, U.S. Supreme Ct. 1978. Asst. dean U. Ill., 1942-43; atty. First Nat. Bank of Chgo., 1947-51; asst. gen. counsel U.S. Savs. and Loan League, Chgo., 1951-59; gen. counsel U.S. League of Savs. Instns., Chgo., 1959-82, gen. counsel emeritus, 1982—; sole practice, Cumberland County, Ill., 1981—. sem. lectr. in law, banking. Served to lt. Armed Forces, 1943-45. Decorated Bronze Star. Mem. ABA, Internat. Bar Assn., Fed Bar Assn., Ill. Bar. Assn., Chgo. Bar Assn., Nat. Lawyers Club Washington, Phi Delta Phi. Clubs: Cosmos, University, Mattoon Golf and Country, Exeter & County (Eng.); Phi Gamma Delta. Editor: The Legal Bulletin, 1951-81, The Federal Guide, 1954-81; author: Savings Accounts, 1981; contbr. articles to publs. Banking, Contracts commercial, General corporate. Home: Applewood Farm Box 157 Toledo IL 62468 Office: US League of Savs 111 E Wacker Dr Chicago IL 60601 Office: 738 Courthouse Square Toledo IL 62468 also: 738 Courthouse Sq Toledo IL 62468

PRATT, GEORGE CHENEY, judge; b. Corning, N.Y., May 22, 1928; s. George Wollage and Muriel (Cheney) P.; m. Carol June Hoffman, Aug. 16, 1952; children: George W., Lise M., Marcia S., William T. B.A., Yale U., 1950, LL.B., 1953. Bar: N.Y. 1953, U.S. Supreme Ct. 1964, U.S. Ct. Appeals 1974. Law clk. to Charles W. Froessel (Judge of N.Y. Ct. Appeals), 1953-55; assoc. then ptnr. Sprague & Stern, Mineola, N.Y., 1956-60; ptnr. Adromidas, Pratt & Pitcher, Mineola, 1960-65, Pratt, Caemmerer & Cleary, Mineola, 1965-75; partner Farrell, Fritz, Pratt, Caemmerer & Cleary, 1975-76; judge U.S. Dist. Ct. (Eastern Dist. of N.Y.), 1976-82, U.S. Circuit Ct. Appeals for 2d circuit (Uniondale), N.Y., 1982—; disting. vis. prof. Hofstra Law Sch., 1979—; adj. prof. St. John's U. Law Sch., 1978—, Touro Law Sch., 1985—. Mem. N.Y. State Bar Assn., Nassau County bar Assn. Mem. United Ch. of Christ.

PRATT, GREGORY KENT, lawyer; b. Middletown, Ohio, Mar. 26, 1952; s. Loren D. and Ellen Jean (Ewing) P.; m. Christine Delin Richard, Sept. 23, 1978; children: Justinian, Lauren. BA in Econs., Ohio No. U., 1974; JD, Ohio State U., 1977. Bar: Ohio 1977, U.S. Dist. Ct. (so. dist.) Ohio, 1977. Assoc. James D. Ruppert and Assocs., Franklin, Ohio, 1977-78; sole practice Middletown, 1978-87; ptnr. Pratt and Buchert, Middletown, 1987—. Mem. Middletown City Commn., 1981-85; bd. dirs. Big Bros./Big Sisters, Middletown, 1978—, Heart Assn., Butler County, Ohio, 1980-85, YMCA, Middletown, 1986—. Mem. Ohio Bar Assn., Butler County Bar Assn., Middletown Bar assn., Assn. Trial Lawyers Am. Republican. Methodist. Avocations: running, camping, fishing, golf. General practice, State civil litigation, Personal injury. Home: 4802 Sol's Circle Middletown OH 45042 Office: 56 S Main St Middletown OH 45044

PRATT, HAROLD IRVING, lawyer; b. N.Y.C., Apr. 13, 1937; s. H. Irving and Ellen (Hallowell) P.; m. Frances Gillmore, July 2, 1960; children—Frances H., Harold I. Jr., Charles Q.A. B.A. cum laude, Harvard U., 1959, LL.B., 1963. Bar: Mass. 1963. Assoc. Goodwin, Procter & Hoar, Boston, 1963-68; sole practice, Boston, 1968-77; ptnr. firm Nichols & Pratt, Boston, 1977—. Chmn. budget com. Cambridge Republican City Com., 1966-68; dir. Cambridge Civic Assn., 1966-70. Mem. ABA, Boston Bar Assn., Mass. Bar Assn., Episcopalian. Clubs: Union (gov. 1980-86), Harvard (Boston); Country (Brookline, Mass.). Estate planning, Probate, Estate taxation. Home: 157 Coolidge Hill Cambridge MA 02138 Office: Nichols & Pratt 28 State St Suite 1955 Boston MA 02109

PRATT, JOHN EDWARD, law educator, lawyer; b. Key West, Fla., June 29, 1945; s. Lloyd Edward and Marilyn June (Havercamp) P.; m. Sharon Louise Brown, Aug. 31, 1968; 1 child, Randolph Winfield. B.A., So. Meth. U., 1967, J.D., 1974. Bar: Tex. 1974, U.S. Dist. Ct. (no. dist.) Tex. 1975. Ptnr. Schuerenberg, Grimes & Pratt, Mesquite, Tex., 1974-77; asst. city atty. City of Dallas, 1978-80; mem. faculty Cedar Valley Coll., Lancaster, Tex., 1981—. Pres. Friends of Mesquite Pub. Library, Tex., 1975-77; chmn. United Way Fund Drive, Mesquite, 1975; del. Democratic Dist. Conv., Dallas, 1984, 86; alt. del. Dem. State Conv., Houston, 1984; pres. Ponderosa Estates Homeowners Assn., 1986—. Served to lt. USNR, 1967-71. Mem. Am. Bus. Law Assn., Am. Mgmt. Assn., State Bar Tex., Tex. Jr. Coll. Tchrs. Assn., Cedar Valley Coll. Faculty Assn. (pres. 1983-85). Democrat. Mem. Christian Ch. Legal education. Home: 1001 Villa Siete Mesquite TX 75181 Office: Cedar Valley Coll 3030 N Dallas Ave Lancaster TX 75134

PRATT, JOHN HELM, judge; b. Portsmouth, N.H., Nov. 17, 1910; s. Harold Boswell and Marguerite (Rockwell) P.; m. Bernice G. Safford, Oct. 25, 1938; children: Clare, Lucinda (Mrs. Daniel D. Pearlman), John Helm, Jr., Patricia (Mrs. George Moriarty), Mary (Mrs. William DeLong). A.B. cum laude, Harvard U., 1930, LL.B., 1934. Bar: D.C. 1934. Since practiced in Washington; partner firm Morris, Pearce, Gardner & Pratt, 1954-68; asst. counsel Boys Club Greater Washington, 1948-68; U.S. dist. judge, Washington, 1968—. Chmn. Montgomery County (Md.) Housing Authority, 1950-53; Chmn. bd. trustees D.C. Legal Aid Agy., 1967-68; chmn. U.S. Jud. Conf. Com. on Jud. Ethics, 1985—. Served to capt. USMCR, 1942-46, PTO. Decorated Bronze Star, Purple Heart; recipient Army citation for civilian service in field prosthetics, 1948. Mem. Am. Bar Assn. (ho dels. 1963-64), Am. Bar Found., Bar Assn. D.C. (pres. 1963-64), Harvard Law Sch. Assn. (pres. Washington 1952-53), Asso. Harvard Clubs (pres. 1952-53), Marine Corps Res. Officers Assn. (judge adv. gen. 1961-68). Democrat. Roman Catholic. Clubs: Barristers (pres. 1969), Lawyers, Harvard (pres. 1949-51), Chevy Chase. Office: US Courthouse Washington DC 20001

PRATT, PHILIP, judge; b. Pontiac, Mich., July 14, 1924; s. Peter and Helen (Stathis) P.; m. Mary C. Hill, July 26, 1952; children—Peter, Laura, Kathleen. Student (Alumni scholar), U. Mich., 1942-43, LL.B., 1950; student, U. Chgo., 1943-44. Bar: Mich. bar 1951. Title examiner Abstract & Title Co., Pontiac, 1951; asst. pros. atty. Oakland County, Mich., 1952; mem. firm Smith & Pratt, Pontiac, 1953-63; circuit judge 6th Jud. Circuit of Mich., Pontiac, 1963-70; U.S. dist. judge Eastern Dist. Mich., 1970—, chief judge, 1986—. Served with OSS AUS, 1943-46. Decorated Bronze Star medal. Mem. ABA, Oakland County Bar Assn. (pres. 1961), State Bar Mich., Am. Judicature Soc. Jurisprudence. Office: US Courthouse Detroit MI 48226

PRATT, ROBERT WINDSOR, lawyer; b. Findlay, Ohio, Mar. 6, 1950; s. John Windsor and Isabelle (Vance) P.; m. Catherine Camak Baker, Sept. 3, 1977; children: Andrew Windsor, David Camak. AB, Wittenberg U., Springfield, Ohio, 1972; JD, Yale U., 1975. Bar: Ill. 1975, U.S. Dist. Ct. (no. dist.) Ill. 1976, U.S. Ct. Appeals (fed. cir.) 1984. Assoc. Keck, Mahin & Cate, Chgo., 1975-81, ptnr., 1981—. Bd. dirs. Chgo. dist. ARC, 1985—. Mem. ABA, Chgo. Bar Assn. Clubs: River, Yale (Chgo.). Antitrust, Municipal bonds, Contracts commercial. Office: Keck Mahin & Cate 233 S Wacker Dr Suite 8300 Chicago IL 60606

PRATT, STEPHEN MICHAEL, lawyer; b. Los Angeles, Sept. 28, 1945; s. George Lyon and Margaret Louise (Duff) P.; children: Jennifer Victoria, Stephanie Lyon. BA cum laude, Hobart Coll., 1967; JD, U. Va., 1970. Bar: Va. 1970, Md. 1984, U.S. Supreme Ct. 1976. Title officer Titlesearch, Inc., Charlottesville, 1970-71; assoc. John H. Rust, Fairfax, Va., 1971-74; ptnr. Rust, Rust & Pratt, Fairfax, 1974-80, Pratt, Buonassissi & Henning, P.C., Fairfax, 1980-84, of counsel, 1984-85; of counsel Buonassissi, Henning, Campbell & Moffet, 1985—; v.p. RCH Land Sales, Inc., Raymond C. Hawkins Constrn. Co., Inc., Copper Land Co., T & K, Inc., Resource Conservation Mgmt., Inc., 1984—. Pres. Century I Condominium Assn., Ocean City, Md., 1978; treas. Hampton Woods Homes Assn., Inc., 1978-79. Mem. ABA, Va. State Bar Assn. (bd. govs. estates and property sect. 1974-78), Md. State Bar Assn., Fairfax County Bar Assn., Phi Beta Kappa. Episcopalian. Real property, General corporate. Home: 10601 Railroad Ct Fairfax VA 22030 Office: Route 2 Box 985 Catlett VA 22019

PRATTE, DEBORAH MIRIAM, lawyer; b. Providence, Nov. 15, 1952; d. Herbert Arthur and Mildred Theresa (Moseley) P.; m. Timothy Patrick, June 3, 1979; two children. BA, U. R.I., 1974; JD, U. Ariz., 1982. Bar: Ariz. 1982. Sole practice Tucson, 1982-84; ptnr. Pratte & Hayes, Tucson, 1984-86. Bd. dirs. Children's Hospice, Tucson, 1985—. Mem. ABA, Fed. Bar Assn., Ariz. Bar Assn., Pima County Bar Assn., Ariz. Women Lawyers Assn. Family and matrimonial, State civil litigation. Office: Law Office of Deborah Pratte 32 N Stone Ave Suite 502 Tucson AZ 85701

PRAY, DONALD EUGENE, lawyer; b. Tulsa, Jan. 16, 1932; s. Clyde Elmer and Ruth Annette (Frank) P.; m. Margaret Morrow, June 12, 1953; children—Melissa, Susan; m. Lana J. Dobson, Nov. 18, 1985. B.S. in Petroleum Engring., U. Tulsa, 1955; LL.B. with honors, U. Okla., 1963. Bar: Okla. 1963, U.S. Dist. Ct. (no. dist.) Okla. 1965, U.S. Supreme Ct. 1965. Assoc. firm Fuller, Smith, Mosberg, Davis & Bowen, Tulsa, 1963-65; ptnr. firm Schuman, Deese, Pray & Doyle, Tulsa, 1965-68, Pray, Scott & Livingston, and predecessor firm Pray, Scott, Williamson & Marlar, Tulsa, 1968-79; pres., mem. exec. com. firm Pray, Walker, Jackman, Williamson & Marlar (merged with firm Walker & Jackman), Tulsa, 1979—. Bd. dirs. Donald W. Reynolds Found., Grace & Franklin Bernsen Found. Served to capt. USAF, 1955-57. Mem. ABA (econs. com.), Tulsa Estate Planning Forum (pres.), Tulsa Mineral Lawyers Sect. (pres.). Republican. Presbyterian. Clubs: Summit (pres.), Cedar Ridge Country. General corporate, Estate planning, Banking. Office: Pray Walker Jackman Williamson Marlar 900 Oneok Plaza Tulsa OK 74119

PREATE, ERNEST D., lawyer; b. Pescopagano, Italy, Jan. 10, 1909; s. Dominick J. and Theresa B. (Manzo) P.; m. Anne R. Smith, Feb. 11, 1939; children—Ernest D., Donald L., Robert A., Carlon. A.B., Columbia U., 1927; J.D., U. Pa., 1934; L.H.D. (hon.), U. Scranton, 1969. Bar: Pa. 1934, U.S. ct. apls. (3d cir.) 1957. Ptnr. Levy, Mattes, Preate & McNulty, Scranton, Pa., 1958-66, Levy & Preate, Scranton, 1966—; dir., gen. csl. Scranton Lackawanna Indsl. Bldg. Co., Lackawanna Indsl. Fund Enterprises, 1982; chmn. Pocono N.E. Devel. Fund, 1984; dir. First Eastern Bank; chmn. Gov.'s Trial Ct. Nominating Com. Pres., dir. Econ. Devel. Council N.E. Pa. 1977, MetroAction, Inc., 1981; mem. adv. bd., csl. U. Scranton, 1981; trustee Scranton Prep. Sch., 1982; chmn. bd. dirs. Scranton State Gen. Hosp., 1969; bd. dirs., gen. csl. Pa. Devel. Credit Corp., 1963—. chmn. Gov.'s Trial Ct. Nominating Commn., 1986—. Named Disting. Pennsylvanian, William Penn Soc., 1980. Mem. ABA, Pa. Bar Assn., Am. Judicature Soc., Lackawanna County Bar Assn., Community Assn. Inst., Scranton C. of C. (dir.). Republican. Roman Catholic. Clubs: Scranton Country, Scranton. Co-author: Pennsylvania Industrial Development Authority Law, 1956. Contbr. articles to profl. jours. General corporate, Contracts commercial, Banking. Home: 216 E Morton St Old Forge PA 18518 Office: 507 Linden St Suite 400 Scranton PA 18503

PREATE, ROBERT ANTHONY, lawyer; b. Scranton, Pa., July 7, 1944; s. Ernest D. and Anne R. (Smith) P.; m. Jane L. Vitzakovitch, May 22, 1981; children—Michael, Jacquelyn, Allison. B.S., U. Scranton, 1966; J.D., U. N.D., 1969. Bar: Pa. 1969, U.S. Ct. Common Pleas 1969, U.S. Dist. Ct. (mid. dist.) Pa. 1969. Sr. ptnr. Levy & Preate, Scranton, 1973—; dir. Leatherneck Mag., 1972-73. Author: Feasibility Study of a Mine Water Heat Pump Concept-Legal and Environmental Issues and Impacts on System Characteristics, 1980. Bd. dirs. Red Cross of Northeast Pa., Scranton, 1976—, Boy Scouts Am., Scranton, 1976-78; Broadway Theater of Northeast Pa., Scranton, 1979—, Econ. Devel. Council Northeastern Pa., Pittston, 1983. Served to capt. USMC, 1969-73. Recipient Am. Jurisprudence prize for Excellence in Legal Research. Mem. ABA, Pa. Bar Assn., Lackawanna County Bar Assn., Greater Scranton C. of C., VFW, Am. Legion, Phi Delta Phi. Republican. Roman Catholic. Club: Scranton. Contracts commercial, Environment, Pension, profit-sharing, and employee benefits. Office: Levy & Preate 507 Linden St Scranton PA 18503

PREBLE, LAURENCE GEORGE, lawyer; b. Denver, Apr. 24, 1939; s. George Enos and Ruth (Leighton) P.; m. Deborah Joan Horton, Aug. 24, 1963; children—Robin Lee, Randall Laurence. Student, Colo. Sch. Mines, 1961; J.D. cum laude, Loyola U., Los Angeles, 1968. Bar: Calif. 1969, U.S. Dist. Ct. (cen. dist.) Calif. 1969, D.C. 1983. Assoc. firm O'Melveny & Myers, Los Angeles, 1968-76; ptnr. O'Melveny & Myers, 1976—; adj. prof. law Southwestern U., 1970-75; lectr. Loyola U. of Los Angeles Sch. Law, 1984—, Calif. Continuing End. of the Bar, others; lectr., author Practicing Law Inst. Served to capt. U.S. Army, 1962-64. Mem. Los Angeles County Bar Assn. (chmn. real property sect. 1979-80), Calif. Bar Assn. (mem. exec. com. real property sect.), ABA, Am. Coll. Real Estate Lawyers (bd. dirs., bd. govs. 1986—), La Canada-Flintridge C. of C. (pres. 1974-75), Loyola Law Sch. Alumni Assn. (pres. 1978). Republican. Real property, Contracts commercial, Banking. Office: O'Melveny & Myers 400 S Hope St Los Angeles CA 90071

PREGERSON, HARRY, U.S. circuit judge; b. Los Angeles, Oct. 13, 1923; s. Abraham and Bessie (Rubin) P.; m. Bernardine Seyma Chapkis, June 28, 1947; children: Dean Douglas, Kathryn Ann. B.A., UCLA, 1947; LL.B., U. Calif.-Berkeley, 1950. Bar: Calif. 1951. Assoc. Morris D. Coppersmith, 1952; ptnr. William M. Costley, Van Nuys, 1953-65; judge Los Angeles Municipal Ct., 1965-66, Los Angeles Superior Ct., 1966-67, U.S. Dist. Ct. Central Dist. Calif., 1967-79, U.S. Ct. Appeals for 9th Circuit, 1979—; faculty mem., seminar for newly appointed distr. Judges Fed. Jud. Center, Washington, 1970-72; mem. faculty Am. Soc. Pub. Adminstrn., Inst. for Ct. Mgmt., Denver, 1973—. Served to 1st lt. USMCR, 1944-46. Decorated Purple Heart. Mem. ABA (vice-chmn., com. on fed. rules of criminal procedure and evidence sect. of criminal 1972—), Los Angeles County Bar Assn., San Fernando Valley Bar Assn., State Bar Calif., Marines Corps Res. Officers Assn. (pres. San Fernando Valley 1966—). Jurisprudence. Office: US Ct Appeals US Courthouse 312 N Spring St Los Angeles CA 90012 *

PREISER, GODFREY KRAUSE, JR., lawyer; b. Orange, N.J., Jan. 30, 1928; s. Godfrey K. Sr. and Edith (Hammacher) P.; m. Mary Jane DuBois, May 19, 1956; children: Thomas, Andrew, Patricia. AB, Princeton U., 1949; JD, NYU, 1951, MBA, 1959. Bar: N.J. 1951, U.S. Supreme Ct. 1957, N.Y. 1981. Assoc. McCarter & English, Newark, 1951-57; atty. AT&T Bell Labs., Short Hills, N.J., 1957—. Served to capt. USAF, 1951-53. Mem. ABA, N.J. Bar Assn., Essex County Bar Assn. Republican. Methodist. Lodge: Masons. Immigration, naturalization, and customs, Labor, Workers' compensation. Office: AT&T Bell Labs 101 JFK Pkwy Short Hills NJ 07078

PREISER, MONTY L., lawyer; b. Charleston, W.Va., May 2, 1952; s. Stanley Efrom and Joyce (Monfried) P.; m. Sara Louise Thornhill, Sept. 17, 1978; children: Blair, Justin. BA, Tulane U., 1972; JD, W.Va. U., 1976. Assoc. Preiser & Wilson, Charleston, 1976-84, ptnr., 1984-86, mng. ptnr., 1986—. Co-author: Handling Soft Tissue, 1985; contbr. articles to profl. jours. Chmn. Youth for Musky, Charleston, 1972; trustee W.Va. Law/Pac,

Charleston, 1983-86; bd. dirs. W.Va. Conservative Music, Charleston, 1985-86; bd. advs. W.Va. Head Injury Found., Charleston, 1986. Mem. W.Va. Bar Assn. (law and medicine com 1984-86), Assn. Trial Lawyers Am. (bd. govs. 1980-86, chmn. trial tutorial 1985-86, state del. 1976-82, Outstanding state del. 1978), W.Va. Trial Lawyers Assn. (Most Valuable mem. 1982, 86, pres. 1985-86), Melvin Belli Soc. (v.p. 1983-86, founding trustee), MENSA. Democrat. Jewish. Office: Preiser & Wilson 1012 Kanawha Blvd Charleston WV 25301

PREISER, STANLEY EFROM, lawyer; b. Charleston, W.Va., Oct. 16, 1927; s. Joseph and Madeline Minnie (Levy) P.; m. Joyce Monfried, Sept. 6, 1948; children: Monty Lee, Terri Elise. Student, U. Chgo., 1944-45, U. Va., 1945-47; JD cum laude, U. Louisville, 1949; LLM, NYU, 1950. Bar: Ky. 1954, W.Va. 1950, U.S. Ct. Appeals (4th cir.) 1955, U.S. Supreme Ct. 1956. Sr. ptnr. Preiser Law Firm (formerly Preiser & Wilson), Charleston, 1950-85, of counsel, 1985—; of counsel Frank Haddad, Louisville, Baskin, Flaherity Elliot Mannino & Schartz, Fla., Pa. and Washington; bd. dirs. Charleston Nat. Bank. Author: Handling Soft Tissue Injury Cases, rev. edit. 1985; bd. editors: Anatomy of a Personal Injury Lawsuit, 1980. Mem. Assn. Trial Lawyers Am. (exec. com., bd. govs.), W.Va. Trial Lawyers Assn. (past pres.), Internat. Acad. Trial Lawyers, Am. Bd. Trial Advs., Melvin M. Belli Soc. (past pres., chmn.). Republican. Jewish. Office: The Preiser Law Firm Laidley Tower Suite 100 500 Lee St Charleston WV 25301

PREISKEL, ROBERT HOWARD, lawyer; b. Passaic, N.J., Mar. 23, 1922; s. Louis and Lottie (Brown) P.; m. Barbara Scott, Oct. 28, 1950; children—John S., Richard A. B.A., U. Mich., 1943; LL.B., Yale U., 1948. Bar: N.Y. bar 1948. Asso. firm Fried, Frank, Harris, Shiver & Jacobson, N.Y.C., 1948-54; partner firm Fried, Frank, Harris, Shriver & Jacobson, N.Y.C., 1954—; vis. lectr. Yale Law Sch., 1982, 83. Pres. NAACP Legal Def. and Ednl. Fund, Inc., 1984—. Mem. Am. Bar Assn., Assn. Bar City N.Y. (chmn. tax com. 1974-77), N.Y. State Bar Assn. (mem. exec. com. 1977-78), Am. Law Inst. (mem. fed. income tax project), Am. Coll. Tax Counsel. Corporate taxation. Home: 20 E 74th St New York NY 10021 Office: Fried Frank Harris Shriver & Jacobsen 1 New York Plaza New York NY 10004

PREM, F. HERBERT, JR., lawyer; b. N.Y.C., Jan. 14, 1932; s. F. Herbert and Sybil Gertrude (Nichols) P.; m. Patricia Ryan, Nov. 18, 1978; children by previous marriage—Julia Nichols, F. Herbert III. A.B., Yale U., 1953; J.D., Harvard U., 1959. Bar: N.Y. 1960. Assoc. Whitman & Ransom, N.Y.C., 1959-66, ptnr., 1967—; dir. Fuji Photo Film U.S.A., Inc., Fuji Med. Systems USA, Inc., Micro Power Systems, Inc., Noritake Co., Inc., Seiko Instruments U.S.A., Inc., Shimano Am. Corp.; bd. dirs., treas. Community Action for Legal Services Inc., 1967-70; bd. dirs. Legal Aid Soc. N.Y.C., 1969-73. Served to lt. (j.g.) USN, 1953-56. Mem. Assn. Bar City N.Y. (sec. 1967-69), N.Y. State Bar Assn., ABA, Am. Law Inst. Episcopalian. Clubs: University, Yale (N.Y.C.). Private international, General corporate. Office: 200 Park Ave New York NY 10166

PREMACK, PAUL ALLEN, lawyer; b. Aberdeen, S.D., Mar. 15, 1958; s. Herschel David and Bernice (Wintroub) P.; m. Ruthie Stier, Jan. 11, 1981; 1 child, Tiffany Stier, Benjamin. Student, No. State Coll., Aberdeen, 1977; BA, U. Tex., 1979; postgrad., Temple U., 1980; JD, U. Houston, 1982. Bar: Tex. 1982. Sole practice San Antonio, 1982—; v.p. P.J. Ventures Inc., San Antonio, 1983—. Bd. dirs. Capistrano Homeowners Assn. Inc., San Antonio, 1985. Mem. ABA, San Antonio Bar Assn., San Antonio Estate Planners Council. Democrat. Jewish. Lodge: Rotary (founding bd. dirs. San Antonio 1985). Estate planning, General corporate, Computer. Home: 14122 Churchill Estates San Antonio TX 78248 Office: 800 NW Loop 410 San Antonio TX 78216

PRENDERGAST, TERRY NEILL, lawyer; b. Sioux Falls, S.D., May 25, 1953; s. Harry Neill and Dorothy Gretchen (Angerhofer) P.; m. Susan Jane Larson, Aug. 2, 1980; 1 child, Christopher Neill. B.A. cum laude, Augustana Coll., 1975; M.B.A., U. S.D., 1978, J.D. magna cum laude, 1978. Bar: S.D. 1978, U.S. Dist. Ct. S.D. 1978, U.S. Tax Ct. 1981, U.S. Ct. Appeals (8th cir.) 1981. Law clk. U.S. Dist. Ct., Sioux Falls, 1978-79; ptnr. Boyce, Murphy, McDowell & Greenfield, Sioux Falls, 1979—; chmn. continuing legal edn. com. State Bar S.D., Pierre, 1984-87; city atty. Lennox, S.D., 1980-82. Mem. ABA (coms. on corp., banking and bus. law, sci. and tech.), Assn. Trial Lawyers Am., S.D. Trial Lawyers Assn., Comml. Law League Am., Am. Jurisprudence Soc., Assn. Coll. and Univ. Attys. Democrat. Methodist. Lodges: Kiwanis (bd. dirs. 1981-83, v.p. 1986-87), Elks. Federal civil litigation, Banking, Real property. Home: 2904 S 1st Ave Sioux Falls SD 57105 Office: Boyce Murphy McDowell & Greenfield 505 Norwest Bank Bldg Sioux Falls SD 57105

PRENTICE, EUGENE MILES, III, lawyer; b. Glen Ridge, N.J., Aug. 27, 1942; s. Eugene Miles and Anna Margaret (Kiernan) P.; m. Katharine Kirby Culbertson, Sept. 18, 1976; children: Eugene Miles IV, Jessie Kirby. BA, Washington and Jefferson Coll., 1964; JD, U. Mich., 1967. Bar: N.Y. 1973, U.S. Dist. Ct. (so. dist.) N.Y. 1973, U.S. Dist. Ct. (ea. dist.) N.Y. 1974, U.S. Ct. Appeals (2d cir.) 1974. Mgmt. trainee Morgan Guaranty Trust, N.Y.C., 1967-68, 71-73; assoc. White & Case, N.Y.C., 1973-78; assoc. Windels, Marx et al, N.Y.C., 1978-80, ptnr., 1980-84; ptnr. Brown & Wood, N.Y.C., 1984—; bd. dirs. various corps. Trustee Vt. Law Sch., South Royalton, 1984—, Washington and Jefferson Coll., Pa., 1985—. Served to capt. U.S. Army, 1968-70. Mem. ABA, Assn. of Bar of City of N.Y. Republican. Clubs: Links, Union League, N.Y. Athletic Club (N.Y.C.). Banking, General corporate, Private international. Home: 34 W 95th St New York NY 10025 Office: Brown & Wood One World Trade Ctr New York NY 10048

PRENTICE, FREDERICK SHELDON, lawyer; b. Summit, N.J., May 7, 1950; s. Eugene Miles and Anna Margaret (Kiernan) P.; m. Barbara Mary Mayzik, Aug. 13, 1977; children: Hilary Jeanne, Amanda Mary. AB, Dartmouth Coll., 1972; JD, Fordham U., 1977. Bar: N.Y. 1978, U.S. Dist Ct. (ea. and so. dists.) N.Y. 1978, Vt. 1980, U.S. Ct. Appeals (2d dist.) 1980, U.S. Dist. Ct. Vt. 1982, U.S. Supreme Ct. 1986. Assoc. Davis Polk & Wardwell, N.Y.C., 1977-80; asst. counsel Nat. Life Ins., Montpelier, Vt., 1980-85; adj. prof. Vt. Law Sch., S. Royalton, 1982—; v.p., gen. counsel, sec. Chittenden Corp., Burlington, Vt., 1985—. Campaign mgr. Cheney for Atty. Gen., Vt., 1974; chmn. alumni council nominating and trustee search Dartmouth Coll., 1985. Mem. ABA, Vt. Bar Assn., Vt. Bankers Assn., Nat. Assn. Securities Dealers, Inc. (bd. arbitrators). Club: Dartmouth Cen. Vt. (dist. enrollment dir. 1980—). Lodge: Rotary. Avocations: reading, running. Banking, General corporate, Securities. Office: Chittenden Corp 2 Burlington Sq Burlington VT 05401

PRESANT, SANFORD CALVIN, lawyer, educator, author, lecturer; b. Buffalo, Nov. 15, 1952; s. Allen Norman and Reeta (Coplon) P.; m. Ilene Beth Shendell, Dec. 2, 1984; 1 child, Jarrett Matthew. B.A., Cornell U., 1973; J.D. cum laude, SUNY-Buffalo, 1976; LL.M. in Taxation, Georgetown U., 1981. Bar: N.Y. 1977, D.C. 1977, U.S. Ct. Claims 1978, U.S. Tax Ct. 1977, U.S. Supreme Ct. 1982. Staff atty. SEC options task force, Washington, 1976-78; assoc. Barrett Smith Schapiro, N.Y.C., 1978-80, Trubin Sillcocks, N.Y.C., 1980-81; ptnr. Carro, Spanbock, Fass, Geller, Kaster, N.Y.C., 1981-86, Finley, Kumble, Wagner, Heine, Underberg, Manley, Myerson & Casey, N.Y.C., 1987—; adj. assoc. prof. real estate NYU, 1983—; frequent lectr. in tax law; regular TV appearances on Nightly Business Report, Pub. Broadcasting System, 1986—; co-chmn. NYU Conf. Fed. Taxation of Real Estate Transactions, 1987. Author: (with others) Realty Joint Ventures, 1980-86, Tax Sheltered Investments Handbook-Special Update on Tax Reform Act of 1984, Real Estate Syndication Handbook, 1985, Real Estate Syndication Tax Handbook, 1986, The Tax Reform Act of 1986, 1986, The Final Partnership Nonrecourse Debt Allocation Regulations, 1987. Kripke Securities law fellow NYU, 1976. Mem. ABA (nat. chmn. audit subcom. of tax sect. partnership com. 1984-86, partnership tax allocation subcom. chmn. 1986—), N.Y. State Bar Assn. (tax sect. partnership com. 1980—), Assn. of Bar of City of N.Y. Republican. Jewish. Corporate taxation, Personal income taxation, Securities. Office: Finley Kumble Wagner Heine et al 425 Park Ave New York NY 10022

PRESCOTT, RITA ELIZABETH, judge; b. North Tonawanda, N.Y., June 6, 1921; d. William Waldo and Marie Eleanore (Dreyer) P.; B.S., U. Pa., 1943, M.S., 1944; LL.B., Temple U., 1949. Tchr. comml. subjects Prospect Park (Pa.) High Sch., 1945-51; admitted to Pa. bar, 1952; individual practice law, 1952-75; law clk. to James C. Crumlish, Sr., Phila., 1951-58, to Judges Sweeney and Diggins, Ct. Common Pleas Delaware County, Media, Pa., 1958-60; ct. adminstr. County of Delaware, Media, 1961-75; judge Ct. Common Pleas, 32nd Jud. Dist. Commonwealth Pa., 1976—, adminstrv. judge civil div., 1980-84. Bd. overseers Del. Law Sch., Widener U., Brandywine, 1982—. Mem. Am. Bar Assn., Pa. Bar Assn., Delaware County Bar Assn. Donald J. Orlowsky Meml. award 1985), Phila. Bar Assn., Am. Judicature Soc., Inst. Jud. Adminstrs., Nat. Assn. Women Lawyers, Nat. Assn. Trial Ct. Adminstrs., Nat. Fedn. Bus. and Profl. Women, Mortar Bd., Temple U. Law Alumni Assn. (Spl. Achievement award 1983), Med. Coll. Pa. (commonwealth bd.), Pi Lambda Theta, Alpha Xi Delta. Office: Courthouse Media PA 19063

PRESS, CAREN SUE, lawyer; b. Calif., Mar. 15, 1956; d. Burton H. and Rona L. (Page) P.; m. James Wallace Hubbell, Oct. 16, 1983; 1 child, Troy Hubbell. BA, U. Calif., Davis, 1978; JD, Stanford U., 1981. Bar: Colo. 1981, U.S. Dist. Ct. Colo. 1981. Assoc. Parcel, Mayer, Schwartz & Ruttum, Denver, 1981-84; asst. counsel Am. TV and Communications Corp., Englewood, Colo., 1984-87; asst. corp. counsel United Cable TV Corp., Denver, 1987—. Mem. ABA, Colo. Bar Assn., Denver Bar Assn. (chair person young lawyers div. 1985-86, exec. council 1983-86), Colo. Women's Bar Assn. General corporate, Communications. Home: 1539 Monroe st Denver CO 80206 Office: United Cable TV Corp 4700 S Syracuse Pkwy Denver CO 80237

PRESSER, STEPHEN BRUCE, law educator, lawyer; b. Chattanooga, Aug. 10, 1946; s. Sidney and Estelle (Shapiro) P.; children—David Carter, Elisabeth Catherine. A.B., Harvard U., 1968, J.D., 1971. Bar: Mass. 1971, D.C. 1972. Law clk. to judge U.S. Ct. Appeals (D.C. cir.), 1971-72; assoc. Wilmer, Cutler & Pickering, Washington, 1972-74; asst. prof. law Rutgers U., Camden, N.J., 1974-76; vis. assoc. prof. U. Va., 1976-77; prof. Northwestern U., Chgo., 1977—, assoc. dean acad. affairs Sch. Law, 1982-85, bd. dirs. Am. culture program Coll. Arts and Scis., 1979-81; cons. to Bur. Wholesale Sales Reps., Atlanta. Author: (with Jamil S. Zainaldin) Law and American History, 1980; Studies in the History of the United States Courts of the Third Circuit, 1983; assocs. articles editor Guide to American Law, 1985. Recipient summer stipend NEH, 1975; Fulbright Sr. scholar London Sch. Econs. and Polit. Sci., 1983-84. Mem. Am. Soc. Legal History (bd. dirs. 1979-82), Am. Law Inst. Legal history, General corporate, Legal education. Home: 2724 Simpson St Evanston IL 60201 Office: Northwestern U Sch Law 357 E Chicago Ave Chicago IL 60611

PRESSON, WILLIAM RUSSELL, lawyer; b. Memphis, Dec. 10, 1955; s. Russell Barnes and Mary Louise (Ford) P.; m. Rae Nell Hunter, June 28, 1986. BA, Millsaps Coll., 1977; M in Pub. Affairs, JD, U. Tex., 1981. Bar: Miss. 1981, U.S. Dist. Ct. (so. dist.) Miss. 1981, U.S. Ct. Appeals (5th cir.) 1985. Assoc. Gerald, Brand, Watters, Cox & Hemleben, Jackson, Miss., 1981-84, Satterfield & Allred, Jackson, 1984—. Mem. ABA, Miss. State Bar Assn., Hinds County Bar Assn., Miss. Oil and Gas Lawyers Assn. Democrat. Episcopalian. Oil and gas leasing, Probate, Bankruptcy. Home: 1607 Laurel St Jackson MS 39202 Office: Satterfield & Allred 1000 Eastover Bldg PO Drawer 1120 Jackson MS 39205

PRESTON, BRUCE MARSHALL, lawyer, educator; b. Trinidad, Colo., Feb. 24, 1949; s. Marshall Caldwell and Juanita (Killgore) P.; m. Mariannina Erra, Aug. 10, 1974; children: Charles Marshall, Robert Arthur. BS summa cum laude, Ariz. State U., 1971; MA, U. Ariz., 1972, JD, 1975. Bar: Ariz. 1975, U.S. Ct. Appeals (9th cir.) 1976, U.S. Ct. Claims 1983, U.S. Tax Ct. 1983, U.S. Supreme Ct. 1983; cert. fin. planner. Atty. Maricopa County Office of Pub. Defender, Phoenix, 1975-84; ptnr. Simonsen & Preston, Phoenix, 1985-86, Simonsen, Preston, Sargeant & Arbetman, Phoenix, 1986; atty. office of atty. gen. State of Ariz., 1987—; judge pro tem Mcpl. Ct., Phoenix, 1984—; licensee in sales Ariz. Dept. Real Estate, Phoenix, 1981—; adj. faculty Phoenix Coll. for Fin. Planning, Denver, 1984—, Maricopa County Community Coll. Dist., Phoenix, 1985—, Ariz. State U. Coll. of Bus., Tempe, 1986—, Ottawa U., Phoenix, 1986—. Chmn. com., treas., pres. bd. dirs Kachina Country Day Sch., 1982—. Named one of Outstanding Young Men in Am., 1984, 85. Mem. ABA, Ariz. Bar Assn. (cert. specialist criminal law 1982-84), Inst. of Cert. Fin. Planning, Internat. Assn. Fin. Planners, Ariz. State U. Coll. of Liberal Arts Alumni Assn. (chmn. com. 1978-80). Clubs: Economics (Tempe); Variety (Phoenix). Avocations: skiing, boating. Home: 5038 N 35th St Phoenix AZ 85018 Office: Simonson Preston Sargeant & Arbetman 4645 N 32d St Phoenix AZ 85018

PRESTON, CHARLES GEORGE, lawyer, lecturer; b. Fairbanks, Alaska, Nov. 11, 1940; s. Charles William and Gudveig Nicoline (Hoem) P.; m. Hilde Delphine van Stappen, Mar. 12, 1970; children—Charles William, Stephanie Delphine, Christina Nicoline. B.A., U. Wash., 1964, M.P.A., 1968; J.D., Columbia U., 1971. Bar: Wash. 1971, D.C. 1981, U.S. Dist. Ct. D.C. 1981, U.S. Dist. Ct. (we. dist.) Wash. 1971, U.S. Ct. Appeals (9th cir.) 1972, U.S. Ct. Appeals (4th cir.) 1979, U.S. Ct. Appeals (5th cir., D.C. cir.) 1978, U.S. Ct. Appeals (2d cir.) 1980, U.S. Ct. Appeals (11th cir.) 1983, U.S. Supreme Ct. 1977, U.S. Ct. Claims 1982, U.S. Ct. Appeals (fed. cir.) 1982. Assoc. Jones, Grey, Bayley & Olson, Seattle, 1971-72; atty. and asst. csl. for litigation Officer of Solicitor, U.S. Dept. Labor, Seattle, 1972-76, Washington, 1976-81; atty. Air Line Pilots Assn., Washington, 1981-82; ptnr. MacNabb, Preston & Waxman, Washington, 1981—. Lectr. seminars. Mem. ABA, Wash. State Bar, D.C. Bar, Job Planning Inst. (pres. 1985—). Labor, Federal civil litigation, Government contracts and claims. Office: 1112 13th St NW Washington DC 20005

PRESTON, COLLEEN ANN, lawyer; b. Monterey, Calif., Oct. 11, 1955; s. Howard Houston and Catherine (Reid) Harrison; m. Raymond C. Preston Jr., June 12, 1982. B. U. Fla., 1975, JD, 1978; LLM, Georgetown U., 1985. Bar: Fla. 1979, U.S. Ct. Claims 1979, U.S. Ct. Appeals (fed. cir.) 1979. Assoc. Akerman, Senterfitt & Eidson, Orlando, Fla., 1978-79; asst. gen. counsel, com. on armed services U.S. Ho. of Reps., Washington, 1983—. Served to capt. USAF, 1979-83. Avocations: golf, tennis, cross country and downhill skiing. Government contracts and claims, Legislative. Home: 2836 Ft Scott Dr Arlington VA 22202 Office: Armed Services Com Rayburn HOB Room 2120 Washington DC 20515

PRESTON, KEVIN MARK, lawyer; b. Garfield Heights, Ohio, Mar. 19, 1956; s. Kenneth George and RoseMarie (Butala) P.; m. Lenor Ellen Harrison; children: Brooke Lee, Heather Ann. BA cum laude, Bucknell U., 1978; JD cum laude, Cleve.-Marshall Coll. Law, 1980. Bar: Ohio 1981, U.S. Dist. Ct. (no. dist.) Ohio 1981. Assoc., then jr. ptnr. Preston & Preston, Berea, Ohio, 1981—. Recipient Am. Jurisprudence award Lawyers Co-Op Pub. Co., 1979; Cleve.-Marshall Coll. of Law Merit scholar 1978. Mem. ABA, Ohio Bar Assn., Cuyahoga County Bar Assn. (bar admissions com.) Cleve.Bar Assn. (lawyer relations com.), Berea Jaycees (bd. dirs., v.p. community devel.), Omicron Delta Epsilon. Republican. Avocations: skiing, travel, baseball, golf. Family and matrimonial, Personal injury, Probate. Office: Preston & Preston 43 E Bridge St Berea OH 44017

PRESTRIDGE, PAMELA ADAIR, lawyer; b. Delhi, La., Dec. 25, 1945; d. Gerald Wallace Prestridge and Peggy Adair (Arender) Martin. BA, La. Poly. U., 1967; M in Edn., La. State u., 1968, JD, 1973. Bar: U.S. Dist. ct. (mid. dist.) La. 1975, U.S. Dist. Ct. (so. dist.) Tex. 1982, U.S. Ct. Appeals (5th cir.) 1982, U.S. Dist. Ct. (ea. dist.) Tex. 1984. Law clk. to presiding justice La. State Dist. Ct., Baton Rouge, 1973-75; ptnr. Breazeale, Sachse & Wilson, Baton Rouge, 1975-82, Hirsch & Westheimer P.C., Houston, 1982—. Counselor Big Bros., Big Sisters, Baton Rouge, 1968-70; legal cons., bd. dirs. Lupus Found. Am., Houston, 1984—; bd. dirs. Quota Club, Baton Rouge, 1979-82, Speech and Hearing Found., Baton Rouge, 1981-82. Named one of Outstanding Young Women Am., 1980; named Outstanding Profl. Woman Houston, 1984. Mem. ABA, Tex. Bar Assn., Tex. Bar Assn., Houston Bar Assn., Assn. Trial Lawyers Am., Phi Alpha Delta, La. State U. Student Bar Assn. Republican. Episcopalian. Avocations: acting, ultralite flying. Bankruptcy, Federal civil litigation, State civil litigation. Home: 908 Welch Houston TX 77006 Office: Hirsch & Westheimer PC 700 Louisiana #2550 Houston TX 77002

PRESTRIDGE, ROGERS MEREDITH, lawyer; b. Crowville, La., July 31, 1934; s. James Ivy and Vergie (Rogers) P.; m. Kathryn Sinclair, July 3, 1968; children—Dana, Zachary, Kathryn, Bennett. B.A., N.E. La. U., 1961; J.D., La. State U., 1966. Bar: La. 1966. Atty. for Inheritance Collector, Bossier Parish, La., 1966-72; asst. dist. atty. 26th Jud. dist., 1969-72; sole practice, Bossier City, La., 1966—; judge, Bossier City, 1975—; mem. La. Commn. Law Enforcement and Adminstrn. of Criminal Justice, 1973-75. Mem. La. Bd. Regents for Higher Edn., 1975-81; mem. Caddo-Bossier Port Commn., 1976—, pres., 1987—; bd. dirs. River Cities High Tech., Inc. Chmn. Shreveport, Bossier Mil. Affairs Com., 1987; chmn., bd. dirs. Riverside Community Hosp., 1987. Served as capt. USAF, 1954-58, 61-62. Mem. Am. Judges Assn., La. State Bar Assn. (ho. of dels.), Bossier C. of C. (pres. 1986), Nat. Council Juvenile Ct. Judges, Bossier Jaycees (past pres.), Phi Alpha Delta. Democrat. Episcopalian. Club: University (bd. dirs. 1986—). Lodges: Lions, Masons, Shriners. General practice, Personal injury, Probate. Office: 1305 Delhi St PO Box 5262 Bossier City LA 71111

PRESTWOOD, ALVIN TENNYSON, lawyer; b. Roeton, Ala., June 18, 1929; s. Garret Felix and Jimmie (Payne) P.; m. Sue Burleson Lee, Nov. 27, 1974; children: Ann Celeste Prestwood Waller, Alison Bennett, Cynthia Joyce Lee Koplos, William Alvin Lee, Garret Courtney. B.S., U. Ala., 1951, LL.B., 1956, J.D., 1970. Bar: Ala. 1956, U.S. Supreme Ct. 1972, U.S. Ct. Appeals (6th and 11th cirs.) 1981. Law clk. Supreme Ct. Ala., 1956-57; asst. atty. gen. Ala., 1957-59; commr. Ala. Dept. Pensions and Security, 1959-63; pvt. practice Montgomery, Ala., 1963-65, 77-82; partner Volz, Capouano, Wampold, Prestwood & Sansone, 1965-77, Prestwood & Rosser, 1982-85, Capouano, Wampold, Prestwood & Sansone, 1986—; Chmn. Gov.'s Com. on White House Conf. on Aging, 1961; mem. adv. com. Dept. Health, Edn. and Welfare, 1962; sec. Nat. Council State Pub. Welfare Adminstrs., 1962. Editorial bd.: Ala. Law Rev, 1955-56; Contbr. articles to profl. jours. Pres. Morningview Sch. P.T.A., 1970; chmn. Am. Nursing Home Assn. Legal Com., 1972; bd. dirs. Montgomery Bapt. Hosp., 1958-65; chmn. bd. mgmt. East Montgomery YMCA, 1969. Served to 1st lt., inf. AUS, 1951-53. Decorated Combat Inf. Badge.; Recipient Sigma Delta Kappa Scholastic Achievement award U. Ala. Sch. Law, 1956, Law Day Moot Ct. award U. Ala. Sch. Law, 1956. Mem. ABA, Ala. Bar Assn. (chmn. adminstrv. law sect. 1972, 78, 83), Fed. Bar Assn., Montgomery County Bar Assn. (chmn. exec. com. 1971), Farrah Order Jurisprudence, Eleventh Circuit Jud. Conf., Kappa Sigma, Phi Alpha Delta. Club: Exchange Greater Montgomery (pres. 1971). Civil rights, Administrative and regulatory, Federal civil litigation. Home: 1431 Magnolia Curve Montgomery AL 36106 Office: 350 Adams Ave Montgomery AL 36104

PREUSS, RONALD STEPHEN, lawyer, educator; b. Flint, Mich., Dec. 1, 1935; s. Edward Joseph and Harriette Beckwith (Pease) P.; 1 child, William Stephen. AB, U. Mo., 1958, MA, 1963; JD, St. Louis U., 1973; postdoctoral, Worchester Coll., Oxford, Eng., 1979, U. Calif., Berkeley, 1979, U. Paris, 1984. Bar: Mo. 1973, U.S. Dist. Ct. (ea. and we. dists.) Mo. 1973, U.S. Tax Ct. 1979. From instr. to assoc. prof. English St. Louis Jr. Coll. Dist., 1965—; ptnr. Anderson & Preuss, Clayton, Mo., 1973—. Author: Laudamus Te, 1962, The St. Louis Gourmet. 1979, 86, English Elegies, 1983, Melville: A Psychic Biography, 1984; editor St. Louis Gourmet, Newsletter, 1981—; co-editor Criterion mag. 1961-62; columnist Capital Courier newspaper 1962-64. Mem. ABA, Mo. Bar Assn., St. Louis County Bar Assn., Phi Alpha Delta (John L. SUllivan chpt. vice justice 1971-72, justice 1972-73). Probate, Corporate taxation, Personal income taxation. Home: 32 Conway Cove Chesterfield MO 63017 Office: Anderson & Preuss 222 S Meramec Suite 300 Clayton MO 63105

PREVATTE, ELIAS JESSE, lawyer; b. Robeson County, N.C., Sept. 20, 1911; s. James Lawrence and Sarah Margaret (Ausley) P.; m. Flora Clark, May 1, 1938; m. 2d, Amaretta Bennett, July 17, 1954; 1 dau., Donna Prevatte Maynor. B.S., Wake Forest U., 1932, LL.B., 1936. Bar: N.C. 1936, U.S. Dist. Ct. (ea. dist.) N.C. 1942, U.S. Ct. Apls. (4th cir.) 1974. Dist. atty. Brunswick County, N.C., 1945, 50-52; judge Brunswick County Ct., 1944; county atty. Brunswick County, 1942-46, 48-50, 56-72; city atty., Southport, N.C., 1946-48, 73-76; atty. Brunswick County Bd. Edn., 1979—; sr. ptnr. Prevatte, Prevatte, & Peterson, Southport, N.C., 1968—; dir. United Carolina Bank, Southport. Mem. exec. com. N.C. Bapt. State Conv., 1955-65; trustee Bapt. Hosps. Med. Ctr., 1969—; bd. visitors Wake Forest U. Med. Ctr., 1976-78. Mem. ABA, N.C. Bar Assn. Democrat. Baptist. Clubs: Oak Island Golf and Country, Lions, Rotary, Masons, Shriners. General practice, Local government, Probate. Home: 313 E Bay St Southport NC 28461 Office: Prevatte Prevatte & Peterson 122 N Howe St Southport NC 28461

PREVIANT, DAVID, lawyer; b. Milw., Nov. 6, 1910; s. Charles and Anna P.; m. Lois Previant, June 11, 1915; children—Susan Lee, Jonathan. LL.B., U. Wis., 1935. Bar: Wis. 1935, Mich. 1952, D.C. 1961, U.S. Sup. Ct. 1948. Mem. Previant, Goldberg, Uelmen, Gratz, Miller & Brueggeman and predecessors, Milw., 1936—; chief labor counsel Internat. Brotherhood Teamster, 1958—; mem. chmn.'s task force NLRB, 1976-77; mem. Adminstrv. Conf. U.S., 1972-74. Mem. Wis. Arts Bd., 1973-75; bd. dirs. Milw. Repertory Theater, 1969-75. Mem. ABA (chmn. labor law sect. 1974-75, ho. of dels. 1976-77), Wis. Bar Assn., Mich. Bar Assn., D.C. Bar Assn., Fed. Bar Assn., Internat. Soc. Labor Law and Social Legislation (v.p.), Order of Coif. Contbr. articles to profl. jours. Labor. Home: 10105 Charter Mall Mequon WI 53092 Office: 788 N Jefferson St Milwaukee WI 53202

PREVOST, RICHARD JAMES, lawyer; b. Plattsburgh, N.Y., May 5, 1954; s. Herwood Charles and Lauretta Mary (LaBarge) P.; m. Mary Ellen Broderick, Aug. 8, 1981. BS, Norwich U., 1976; JD, Syracuse U., 1978; MS in Bus. Adminstrn., Boston U., 1984. Bar: D.C. 1979, Vt. 1983. Commd. 2d lt. U.S. Army, 1976, advanced through grades to capt., 1979, ret., 1983; def. counsel chief commn. br. JAGC, Schweinfurt, Fed. Republic of Germany, 1979-81; USA claims service Europe JAGC, Mannheim, Fed. Republic of Germany, 1981-82; contract atty. JAGC, Ft. Dix, N.J., 1982-83, Office of Staff Judge Adv., Ft. Sill, Okla., 1983-86; trial counsel European div. U.S. Army Corps. of Engrs., Frankfurt, Fed. Republic of Germany, 1986—. Mem. ABA (pub. contract law sect.), Armed Services Contract Trial Lawyers Assn. (chartered). Government contracts and claims, Construction. Office: USAED EUDOC, Frankfurt APO NY09757, Fed Republic of Germany

PREWITT, DAVID EDWARD, lawyer; b. Phila., Oct. 13, 1939; s. Richard Hickman and Jean (Simpkins) P.; m. Joan Rosella Taylor, June 16, 1939; children: Mary-Alice Graham, Katherine Estill, Elizabeth Bowen. AB, Dartmouth Coll., 1961; JD, Duke U., 1968. Bar: Ky. 1968, Fla. 1970, Pa. 1971, U.S. Dist. Ct. (ea.dist.) Pa. 1971, U.S. Ct. Appeals (3d cir.) 1971; cert. civil trial adv. Nat. Bd. Trial Advocacy. Trial atty. U.S. Dept. Justice, Washington, 1968-69; assoc. Mahoney, Hadlow, Chambers & Adams, Jacksonville, Fla., 1969-70; assoc. White & Williams, Phila., 1971-76, ptnr., 1976-79; ptnr. Prewitt & Oplinger, Phila., 1979-80; pres. David E. Prewitt Assocs., Phila., 1980—. Contbr. articles to profl. jours. Mem. Com. of Seventy, 1977—. Served to col. USAR, 1961—. Decorated Air medal, Vietnam Service medal. Mem. ABA, Ky. Bar Assn., Fla. Bar Assn., Pa. Bar Assn. (lectr. aviation law), Phila. Bar Assn. (chmn. aviation law com., past chmn. mil. affairs com.), Lawyers-Pilots Bar Assn., Assn. Trial Lawyers Am., Phila. Assn. Def. Counsel, Mil. Order of World Wars. Republican. Episcopalian. Club: Merion Cricket (Haverford, Pa.). Aviation litigation, Federal civil litigation, Personal injury. Office: 1411 Walnut St Suite 1225 Philadelphia PA 19102

PREWOZNIK, JEROME FRANK, lawyer; b. Detroit, July 15, 1934; s. Frank Joseph and Loretta Ann (Parzych) P.; m. Marilyn Johnson, 1970; 1 son, Frank Joseph II. AB cum laude, U. Detroit, 1955; JD with distinction, U. Mich., 1958. Bar: Calif. 1959. Sr. ptnr. Memel & Ellsworth, Los Angeles, 1983—. State fin. co-chmn. 1982 campaign Calif. Gov. George Deukmejian; bd. dirs. Calif. Econ. Devel. Corp., 1984—, mem. Pacific Rim Task Force, 1985—; mem. nat. com. U. Mich. Law Sch. Fund, 1969-72, 82-83; mem. com. visitors U. Mich. Law Sch., 1972-75. Served with U.S. Army, 1958-60. Mem. ABA (bus. law sect., law and acctg. com. 1980—, chmn. auditing standards subcom. 1981-86, fed regulation of securities com., proxy solicitations and tender offers subcom. 1978—), State Bar Calif. (bus. law sect., exec. com. 1983-86, corp. governance and takeovers com. 1985—, corps. com. 1980-83), Los Angeles County Bar Assn., Order of Coif.

Republican. General corporate, Securities. Home: 431 Georgina Ave Santa Monica CA 90402 Office: Memel & Ellsworth 6500 Wilshire Blvd Los Angeles CA 90048

PRIBANIC, VICTOR HUNTER, lawyer; b. McKeesport, Pa., Apr. 7, 1954; s. John Edward and Marlene Cecilia (Hunter) P. B.A., Bowling Green State U., 1976; J.D., Duquesne U., 1979. Bar: Pa. 1979, U.S. Dist. Ct. (we. dist.) Pa. 1979, U.S. Ct. Appeals (3d cir.) 1979. Law clk. to presiding justice Pa. Ct. Common Pleas, Pitts., 1982-85; asst. dist. atty. Office of Dist. Atty., Pitts., 1980-82; sole practice, Pitts. and McKeesport, 1982—. Mem. Am. Trial Lawyers Assn., Pa. Trial Lawyers Assn. Democrat. Roman Catholic. Personal injury, State civil litigation, Criminal. Home: 1515 Fawcett Ave White Oak PA 15131 Office: 305 Masonic Bldg McKeesport PA 15132 Address: 513 Court Pl Pittsburgh PA 15219

PRICE, CHARLES STEVEN, lawyer; b. Inglewood, Calif., June 10, 1955; s. Frank Dean Price and Ann (Rounds) Bolling; m. Sandra Helen Laney, Feb. 26, 1983; children: Katherine Laney, Courtney Ann. BA, U. Calif., Santa Barbara, 1976; JD, U. Chgo., 1979. Bar: Ariz. 1980, U.S. Dist. Ariz. 1980, U.S. Ct. Appeals (9th cir.) 1982. Assoc. Brown & Bain P.A., Phoenix, Ariz., 1979-85, ptnr., 1985—. Democrat. Antitrust, Computer, Securities. Office: Brown & Bain PA 222 N Central Ave Phoenix AZ 85004

PRICE, CHARLES U., lawyer; b. Frederick, Md., Feb. 18, 1916; s. Charles Smith and Helen Agnes (Urner) P.; m. Shirlee Walker Schuettinger, Mar. 27, 1969. A.B., Princeton U., 1938; LL.B., Harvard U., 1941. Bar: Md. 1941, U.S. Dist. Ct. Md. 1946. U.S. Ct. Appeals (4th cir.) 1981. Sole practice Frederick, Md., 1946-70, 84—; ptnr. Rollins, Wenner & Price, and successor firm, Frederick, Md., 1971-84; state's atty. Frederick County, Frederick, Md., 1951-54. Served to 1st lt. USAAF, 1941-45. Fellow Am. Bar Found., Md. Bar Found. (chmn. 1979-81); mem. ABA, Md. Bar Assn. (gov. 1974-75), Frederick County Bar Assn. (pres. 1959). Harvard Law Sch. Assn. Md. (pres. 1974-75). Republican. Lutheran. Clubs: Maryland, Frederick Cotillion, Frederick Catoctin. Lodges: Masons, Rotary. General practice, Probate, State civil litigation. Home: 101 E 2d St Frederick MD 21701 Office: 15 N Court St Frederick MD 21701

PRICE, CHRISTIE SPEIR, lawyer; b. Bethel, N.C., Feb. 12, 1954; d. David Ordway and Betty Maude (Smith) Speir; m. H. Craig Price, June 21, 1975; children: David Craig, John Harvey. BS, U. N.C., 1976, JD, 1979. Bar: N.C. 1981. Research asst. N.C. Ct. Appeals, Raleigh, 1979-81; asst. reporter appellate div. N.C. Supreme Ct., Raleigh, 1981-84; assoc. Wyrick, Robbins, Yates, Ponton & Kirby, Raleigh, 1984—. Mem. N.C. Bd. of Corrections, 1977-84; treas. Wake County Dem. Women, 1985-87, pres., 1987—; v.p. N.C. Dem. Women, 1984-86. Mem. ABA, N.C. Bar Assn., Wake County Bar Assn. Methodist. Real property. Home: 1905 Sturbridge Ct Raleigh NC 27612 Office: Wyrick Robbins Yates Ponton & Kirby 4700 Homewood Ct Raleigh NC 27609

PRICE, CLARK ALAN, lawyer, military officer; b. Phoenix, Sept. 8, 1954; s. J. Alan and Cleone (Randall) P.; m. Janet Denise Morgan, Aug. 24, 1977; children: Rebecca Caroline, Benjamin Lloyd. Student, George Mason U., 1972-73; BA, Brigham Young U., 1978, JD, 1981. Bar: Utah 1981, U.S. Dist. Ct. Utah 1981, U.S. Ct. Mil. Appeals 1985. Commd. ensign USNR, 1979, advanced through grades to lt., 1982; atty. legal assistance Naval Legal Service Office, Pensacola, Fla., 1982, head dept. legal assistance, 1982, sr. def. counsel, 1982-83; sr. trial counsel, prosecutor detachment Naval Legal Service Office, Bremerton, Wash., 1985—; judge adv. USS Canopus Naval Base, Charleston, S.C., 1983-85. Mem. ABA, Judge Advs. Assn., Phi Kappa Phi. Republican. Mormon. Avocations: tennis, basketball, piano, choral singing. Military, Family and matrimonial, Probate. Home: 52-C Taffinder Pl Bremerton WA 98312

PRICE, DONALD DOUGLAS, lawyer; b. Maryville, Mo., July 30, 1943; s. Donald LeRoy and Julia Catherine (Aley) P.; m. Jane Davis, Nov. 4, 1967; children—Andrew Douglas, Eric Montgomery. B.S. in Chem. Engring., U. Mo., 1965; J.D., George Washington U., 1968. Bar: D.C. 1968, U.S. Ct. Appeals (D.C. cir.) 1969, Calif. 1970, U.S. Supreme Ct. 1973, U.S. Ct. Appeals (Fed. cir.) 1975. Examiner U.S. Patent and Trademark Office, Washington, 1965-66; patent agt., assoc. Bacon & Thomas, Washington, 1966-69; asst. patent counsel N.Am. Rockwell, Canoga Park, Calif., 1969-71; assoc., then ptnr. Fleit, Jacobson, Cohn & Price, Washington, 1971—. Mem. ABA, Am. Intellectual Property Law Assn., Fedn. Internationale des Conseils en Propriete Industrielle, Assn. Internationale pour la Protection de la Propriete Industrielle, Licensing Execs. Soc. Clubs: Washington Golf and Country (Arlington, Va.); Highlands Swim (McLean, Va.) (pres. 1979-81). Patent. Home: 1423 Highwood Dr McLean VA 22101 Office: Fleit Jacobson Cohn & Price 1217 E St NW Washington DC 20004

PRICE, EDWARD DEAN, U.S. District Court judge; b. Sanger, Calif., Feb. 12, 1919; s. Earl Trousdale and Daisy Shaw (Biggs) P.; m. Katherine S. Merritt, July 18, 1943; children—Katherine Price O'Brien, Edward M., Jane E. B.A., U. Calif., Berkeley, 1947, LL.B., 1949. Bar: Calif. 1949. Assoc. Cleary & Zeff, Modesto, Calif., 1949-51; assoc. Zeff & Halley, Modesto, Calif., 1951-54; ptnr. Zeff, Halley & Price, Modesto, Calif., 1954-63, Zeff & Price, Modesto, Calif., 1963-65, Price & Martin, Modesto, Calif., 1965-69, Price, Martin & Crabtree, Modesto, Calif., 1969-79; judge U.S. Dist. Ct., Fresno, Calif., 1980—; mem. adv. bd. governing com. Continuing Edn. of Bar, San Francisco, 1963-71, governing bd. Calif. State Bar, 1973-76; v.p. Jud. Council, Calif., 1978-79. Contbr. articles to profl. jours. Served with U.S. Army, 1943-46. Mem. ABA, Am. Coll. Trial Lawyers, Am. Bd. Trial Advocates. Democrat. Methodist. State civil litigation. Home: 1012 Wellesley Modesto CA 95350 Office: US Dist Ct 1130 O St Fresno CA 93721

PRICE, GUY BRADLEY, lawyer; b. Gary, Ind., Apr. 17, 1955; s. Howard William Price and Shirley Ann (Elich) Wiginton. BA in Psychology, Ariz. State U., 1977; JD, U. Tulsa, 1980. Bar: Ariz. 1981, U.S. Dist. Ct. Ariz. 1981. Legal intern O'Connor, Cavanagh, Anderson, Westover, Killingsworth & Beshears, Phoenix, 1981; assoc. Cahill, Hanson, Phillips & Mahowald, Phoenix, 1981-86; asst. atty. gen. State of Ariz., Phoenix, 1986—. Parliamentarian Community Orgn. for Drug Abuse, Mental Health and Alcohol Services, Phoenix, 1982; chmn. spl. events Crime Victim Found., 1986—. Named one of Outstanding Young Men in Am., U.S. Jaycees, 1977. Mem. Ariz. Bar Assn., Maricopa County Bar Assn., Assn. Trial Lawyers Am., Ariz. Trial Lawyers Assn., Order of Barrister, Blue Key, Pi Kappa Delta, Pi Kappa Alpha. Democrat. Avocation: sailing. State civil litigation, Real property, Administrative and regulatory. Home: 2609 E Mitchell Phoenix AZ 85016 Office: Office Atty Gen 1275 W Washington Phoenix AZ 85007

PRICE, HOWARD JACK, JR., lawyer; b. Cumberland, Md., Mar. 11, 1955; s. Howard Jack Sr. and Mary Jean (Scott) P.; m. Rebecca Hope Miller, July 22, 1978; children: Jessica Lauren, Joseph Miller. AA, Potomac State Coll., 1975; BA cum laude, West Va. U., 1977; JD with honors, U. Md., 1980. Bar: Md. 1980, U.S. Bankruptcy Ct. 1981, U.S. Dist. Ct. Md. 1982. Counsel Md. Casualty Co., Balt., 1980-82; assoc. Wilson & Wilminson, Cumberland, Md., 1982—; asst. solicitor City of Cumberland, Md., 1982—. Mem. ABa, Md. Bar Assn., Allegheny County Bar Assn. (sec. 1982—). Democrat. Methodist. General practice, Federal civil litigation, Real property. Home: 609 Thompson Ave Cumberland MD 21502 Office: Wilson & Wilkinson 100 S Liberty St Cumberland MD 21502

PRICE, ILENE ROSENBERG, lawyer; b. Jersey City, July 2, 1951; s. Irwin Daniel and Mildred (Riesberg) Rosenberg; m. Jeffrey Paul Price, Feb. 18, 1973. AB, U. Mich., 1972; JD, U. Pa., 1977. Bar: Pa. 1977, D.C. 1978, U.S. Dist. Ct. D.C. 1979, U.S. Ct. Appeals (D.C. cir.) 1979. Assoc. Haley, Bader & Potts, Washington, 1977-80; staff atty. Mut. Broadcasting System Inc., Arlington, Va., 1980-82, asst. gen. counsel, 1982-85; gen. counsel MultiComm Telecommunications Corp., Arlington, 1985—. Mem. ABA, Fed. Communications Bar Assn., Wash. Met. Area Corp. Counsel Assn., Women's Bar Assn. D.C. (bd. dirs. 1984—). Administrative and regulatory, General corporate, Telecommunications. Office: MultiComm Telecommunications Corp 1755 S Jefferson Davis Hwy Arlington VA 22202

PRICE, JAMES LEE, lawyer; b. Austin, Tex., Apr. 22, 1950; s. James Cullen and Marilyn Jean (Bridges) P.; m. Kathleen Newman, Mar. 24, 1973; 1 child, Gregory. BA with distinction, Stanford U., 1972; MA, U. Mich., 1976, JD, 1977. Bar: Mich. 1977. Economist Internat. Union, UAW, Detroit, 1978-85; economist banking com. Ho. of Reps., Washington, 1985-86; staff profl. Dem. policy com. U.S. Senate, Washington, 1986—. Mem. ABA (econ. com.). Democrat. Public international, Personal income taxation. Home: 6511 Elgin Ln Bethesda MD 20817

PRICE, JOHN ALEY, lawyer; b. Maryville, Mo., Oct. 7, 1947; s. Donald Leroy and Julia Catherine (Aley) P.; m. Julie Ann Seipel, Aug. 16, 1969; children—Theodore John, Joseph Andrew. B.S., N.W. Mo. State U., 1969; J.D., U. Kans., 1972. Bar: Kans. 1972, U.S. Dist. Ct. Kans. 1972, U.S. Ct. Appeals (10th cir.) 1972, Tex. 1984, U.S. Ct. Appeals (5th cir.) 1984. Law clk. U.S. Dist. Ct. Kans., Wichita, 1972-74; assoc., then ptnr. firm Weeks, Thomas and Lysaught, Kansas City, Kans., 1974-82; ptnr. firm Winstead, McGuire, Sechrest & Minick, Dallas, 1982—; spl. prosecutor Leavenworth County Dist. Atty., 1970-71, Sedgwick County Dist. Atty., Wichita, Kans., 1971-72. Editor mag. Academic Analyst, 1968-69; assoc. editor U. Kans. Law Rev., 1971-72; author legal publs. Co-dir. Douglas County Legal Aid Soc., Lawrence, Kans., 1971-72; co-pres. Northwood Hills PTA, Dallas, 1984. Mem. ABA, Kans. Bar Assn. (mem. task force for penal reform; Pres.'s Outstanding Service award 1981), Tex. Bar Assn., Blue Key, Order of Coif, Phi Delta Phi, Sigma Tau Gamma (v.p. 1968-69). Democrat. Roman Catholic. Federal civil litigation, Securities, Antitrust. Office: Winstead McGuire Sechrest & Minick 1601 Elm St Suite 700 Dallas TX 75201

PRICE, JOSEPH HUBBARD, lawyer; b. Montgomery, Ala., Jan. 31, 1939; s. Aaron Joseph and Minnie Jule (Reynolds) P.; m. Cynthia Winant Ramsey, Sept. 14, 1963 (div. 1980); children—Victoria Reynolds, Ramsey Winant; m. Courtney McFadden, Apr. 26, 1980. A.B., U. Ala., 1961; LL.B., Harvard U., 1964; postgrad. London Sch. Econs., 1964-65. Bar: Ala. 1964, D.C. 1968. Law clerk to justice Hugo L. Black, U.S. Supreme Ct., Washington, 1967-68; assoc. Leva, Hawes, Symington, Martin & Oppenheimer, Washington, 1968-71; v.p. Overseas Pvt. Investment Corp., Washington, 1971-73; ptnr. Leva, Hawes, et al, Washington, 1973-83, Gibson, Dunn & Crutcher, Washington, 1983—. Mem. CARE Com. Washington; mem. adv. com. Hugo Black Meml. Library, Ashland, Ala.; mem. bd. govs. Opportunity Funding Corp., Washington. Served to capt. U.S. Army, 1966-67; Vietnam. Decorated Bronze Star; Frank Knox Meml. fellow, 1964-67. Mem. ABA, Am. Soc. Internat. Law, Supreme Ct. Hist. Soc., Phi Beta Kappa. Clubs: Metropolitan, Internat. Administrative and regulatory, General corporate, Private international. Home: 3104 Cathedral Ave NW Washington DC 20008 Office: Gibson Dunn & Crutcher 1050 Connecticut Ave NW Washington DC 20036

PRICE, LIONEL FRANKLIN, lawyer; b. New Orleans, Mar. 14, 1940; s. Samuel and Anna Estelle (Harris) P.; m. Cory Jean Smith, Nov. 15, 1974; children: Daniel Saxon, Cassia Amber, Darby Killeen. BA, La. State U., 1963; JD, Tulane U., 1971. Bar: La. 1971, U.S. Dist. Ct. (ea. dist.) La. 1971, U.S. Ct. Appeals (5th cir.) 1971. Assoc. Flanders & Flanders, New Orleans, 1971-74; sole practice, Slidell, La. and New Orleans, 1974—; dir. Gulf Caribe Transport, Inc., New Orleans. Author: Little Gods and Angry Men, 1986; contbr. articles to profl. publs. Bd. dirs. Jefferson Mil. Coll. Found., 1983-84; trustee Bankruptcy Ct. Ea. Dist. La. Served to comdr. USNR, 1963—. Mem. ABA, La. Bar Assn., Naval Res. Assn. (chpt. v.p. 1978-80), Slidell Bar Assn., Internat. Platform Assn., Delta Theta Phi (Outstanding Student award 1971). Admiralty, Entertainment, Personal injury. Home: 1509 Lakewood Dr Slidell LA 70458 Office: PO Box 1236 500 Pontchartrain Dr Slidell LA 70459

PRICE, MONROE EDWIN, legal educator; b. Vienna, Austria, Aug. 18, 1938; came to U.S., 1939; s. Harold Gustav and Alice Mary (Diamant) P.; m. Aimée Bertha Brown, Aug. 15, 1965; children: Joshua, Gabriel, Asher. B.A., Yale U., 1960, LL.B., 1964. Bar: Calif. 1967, N.Y. 1983. Editorial asst. Am. Heritage Pub. Co., N.Y.C., 1960-61; law clk. to assoc. justice Potter Stewart U.S. Supreme Ct., Washington, 1964-65; spl. asst. to Sec. Dept. Labor, Washington, 1965-66; dep. dir. Sloan Commn. Cable Communications, N.Y.C., 1970-72; prof. Sch. Law UCLA, 1967-84; dean Benjamin N. Cardozo Sch. Law Yeshiva U., N.Y.C., 1982—; of counsel Munger Tolles & Rickershauser, Los Angeles, 1980-84; cons. Rand Corp., 1972-73, OEO, 1968-70; dep. dir. Calif. Indian Legal Services, Los Angeles, 1968-77. Author: Law and the American Indian, 1982, (with D. Brenner) Cable Television and Other Non Broadcast Video, 1985. Mem. Internat. Inst. Communications. Democrat. Jewish. Legal education, Indian. Office: Cardozo Sch Law 55 Fifth Ave New York NY 10003

PRICE, PAMELA ODELL, lawyer; b. Balt., Feb. 16, 1945; d. Charles Neepier and Vivian (Kilham) Odell; m. Charles Turner Price, June 24, 1967; children: Travis H., Janet D. BA, Duke U., 1967; JD, U. Fla., 1973. Bar: Fla. 1973. Claims rep. Social Security Adminstrn., Houston, 1967-71; assoc. Watson, Watson & Steadham, Gainesville, Fla., 1973-76, Gray, Harris & Robinson, Orlando, Fla., 1977—. Chmn. adv. bd. Lakemont Elem. Sch., Winter Park, Fla., 1981-85; chmn. fin. com. Asbury Meth. Ch., Maitland, Fla., 1986-87. Mem. Fla. Bar Assn. (exec. council, real property, probate and trust law sects., probate law com.), Cen. Fla. Estate Planning Council. Republican. Clubs: Winter Park Racquet, Interlachen Country (Winter Park), Citrus (Orlando). Estate planning, Probate, Estate taxation. Office: Gray Harris & Robinson PA 201 E Pine St Suite 1200 Orlando FL 32801

PRICE, PHILLIP VINCENT, lawyer; b. Indpls., Jan. 2, 1949; s. Frank A. and Gertrude E. (Maloney) P.; m. Patricia A. Quinn, May 18, 1974; children: William Quinn, Richard Frank. Student, Purdue U., 1967-68; BA in Polit. Sci., U. Wis., 1971; JD, Ind. U., Indpls., 1975. Bar: Ind. 1975, U.S. Ct. Appeals (7th cir.) 1983, U.S. Dist. Ct. (so. dist.) Ind. 1975, U.S. Dist. Ct. (no. dist.) Ind. 1985. Legal advisor Marion County Sheriff Dept., Indpls., 1975-77; assoc. Yarling, Tunnell, Robison & Lamb, Indpls., 1977-78; sole practice Indpls., 1978—. Mem. ABA, Ind. Bar Assn., Indpls. Bar Assn., Nat. Orgn. Social Security Claimants Reps. Democrat. Roman Catholic. Club: U. Wis. Alumni of Indpls. (pres. 1983-84). Pension, profit-sharing, and employee benefits, Administrative and regulatory, Consumer commercial. Home: 2950 W 42d St Indianapolis IN 46208 Office: 1444 Consolidated Bldg 115 N Pennsylvania St Indianapolis IN 46204

PRICE, RICHARD LEE, judge. s. Saul and Claire (Bernstein) P.; m. Carolyn Small; children: Lisa, Howard. BA in Polit. Sci., Roanoke Coll., 1961; LLB, N.Y. Law Sch., 1964; LLD (hon.), Shaw U., 1980. Bar: N.Y. 1965, U.S. Ct. Internat. Trade 1965, U.S. Dist. Ct. (so. and ea. dists.) N.Y. 1966, U.S. Ct. Appeals (2d cir.) 1967, U.S. Supreme Ct. 1974. Assoc. Law Office Harry H. Lipsig, N.Y.C., 1967-69; law sec. to judge Civil Ct., N.Y.C., 1969-76, chief law asst., 1976-80, judge, 1980—; acting justice Bronx (N.Y.) County Supreme Ct.; chmn. com. setting support amount Gov.'s Commn. on Child Support; mem. curriculum devel. com. office of ct. adminstrn. Contbr. articles to profl. jours. Exec. officer Lt. 7th Precinct Auxiliary Police, 1980; chairperson East River Housing Com., 1969, 74-75, 77-81, mem. 1966-69, 71-73, 76; mem. Coordinating Council Coops., 1973—, Citizens Com. ERA, B'nai B'rith Career and Counseling Services (adv. bd.); trustee Bialystoker Synagogue, 1966-79; bd. dirs. East Side Torah Ctr., Grand St. Consumers Soc., 1972—, Fedn. Coops., 1974—, Lower East Side Businessmen's Assn., 1977-80, City Coalition on Child Sexual Abuse, chairperson pub. relations com.; treas. Am. Judges Found. Recipient Pub. Service award Lower East Side Jewish Festival, 1985. Mem. ABA (task force law related edn.), N.Y. State Bar Assn. (chairperson com. on dist. city village and town cts., citizenship edn. and cts. and community coms., chairperson subcom. pub. events and edn.), Assn. of Bar of City of N.Y. (council requirements of cts., lectures, continuing edn. and women in the cts. coms.), Black Bar Assn., N.Y. Women's Bar Assn. (criminal law, children's rights and legal rights of battered women planning coms.), N.Y.C. Criminal and Civil Cts. Bar Assn. (v.p.), Met. Women's Bar Assn. (bd. dirs., chairperson task force on discrimination of women in cts.), N.Y. County Lawyers Assn. (chairperson law related edn. com.), N.Y. State Trial Lawyers Assn. (chairperson jud. adminstrn. and procedure com. 1982), Am. Judges Assn. (asst. treas., bd. govs.), NOW, East Side C. of C. Lodge: B'nai B'rith (pres. lawyers unit). Office: 111 Centre St New York NY 10013

PRICE, ROBERT, investment banker, lawyer, broadcasting executive; b. N.Y.C., Aug. 27, 1932; s. Solomon and Frances (Berger) P.; m. Margery Beth Wiener, Dec. 18, 1955; children: Eileen Marcia, Steven. A.B., NYU, 1953; LL.D., Columbia U., 1958. Bar: N.Y. 1958, U.S. Dist. Ct. 1958, U.S. Ct. Appeals 1958, U.S. Supreme Ct 1958, ICC 1958, FCC 1958, IRS 1958. With R.H. Macy & Co., Inc., 1955-58; practiced in N.Y.C., 1958—; law clk. to judge U.S. Dist. Ct. (so. dist.) N.Y., 1958-59; asst. U.S. atty. So. Dist. N.Y., 1959-60; ptnr. Kupferman & Price, 1960-65; chmn. bd. pres. Atlantic States Ind. Inc., 1963-66; pres. WNVY, Pensacola, Fla., 1965-66, WLOB, Portland, Me., 1965-66; dep. mayor N.Y.C., 1965-66; exec. v.p., dir. Dreyfus Corp., N.Y.C., 1966-69; v.p., investment officer Dreyfus Fund, until 1969; chmn., pres., dir. Price Capital Corp. and Price Mgmt. Corp., N.Y.C., 1969-72; gen. ptnr., spl. counsel Lazard, Freres & Co., 1972-82; pres. N.Y. Law Jour., Nat. Law Jour.; pres., treas., dir. Price Communications Corp., 1979—; chmn., dir. Telemation Inc., 1986—; adv. com. Bankers Trust Co. N.Y.; dir. Transocean Holding Corp., Lane Bryant, Inc.; lectr. National Industrial Conf. Bd.; chmn. N.Y.C. Port Authority Negotiating Com. for World Trade Center, 1965-66; mem. N.Y.C. Policy Planning Council, 1966; spl. counsel N.Y. State Joint Legis. Com. on Ct. Reorgn., 1962-63; asst. counsel N.Y. State Joint Legis. Com. on N.Y. Banking Laws, 1961-62. Author articles. Chmn. govt. and civil service div. United Jewish Appeal Greater N.Y., 1966; co-chmn. Met. N.Y. Red Cross Blood Drive, 1966; mem. nat. exec. com. Columbia Law Sch. 16th Ann. Fund Drive, 1966-67; Vice pres. N.Y. Young Republican Club, 1957-58; campaign mgr. John V. Lindsay campaigns for congressman, N.Y.C., 1958, 60, 62, 64; del. N.Y. Rep. State Conv., 1962, 66; campaign mgr. Nelson A. Rockefeller, Ore. Rep. presdl. primary campaign, 1964, Lindsay campaign for mayor, N.Y.C., 1965; lectr. Rep. Nat. Com., 1966—; bd. dirs. Am. Friends Hebrew U.; past trustee Columbia U. Sch. Pharm. Scis., Birch Wathen Sch. Served with AUS, 1953-55. Recipient Yeshiva U. Heritage award, 1966, Pub. Service award Queens Catholic War Vets., 1966, Pub. Service award Phila. 21 Jewel Sq. Club, 1967. Mem. ABA, FCC Bar Assn., Assn. Bar City N.Y., N.Y. State Dist. Attys. Assn., Council Fgn. Relations, Columbia Law Sch. Alumni Assn. (dir.), Scribes, Tau Kappa Alpha. General corporate, Trademark and copyright. Home: 25 E 86th St New York NY 10028 Office: Price Communications Corp 45 Rockefeller Plaza New York NY 10020

PRICE, ROBERT ALEXANDER, lawyer; b. San Antonio, Feb. 14, 1948; s. Robert A. Jr. and Regina Lee (Stanish) P. BA, U. Tex., 1968, JD, 1971. Bar: Tex. 1971, U.S. Dist. Ct. (we. dist.) Tex. 1973, U.S. Supreme Ct. 1977. Asst. criminal dist. atty. Bexar County, San Antonio, 1972-73; sole practice San Antonio, 1973—. Author, editor: Criminal Law-Nuts and Bolts, 1985. Fellow Tex. Bar Found., San Antonio Bar Assn. (bd. dirs. 1980-82, treas. 1982-83, sec. 1983-84, v.p. 1984-85, pres. 1985-86); mem. Tex. Bar Assn. Criminal, Family and matrimonial, Workers' compensation. Home: 419 Patterson Ave San Antonio TX 78209 Office: 405 S Presa San Antonio TX 78205

PRICE, ROBERT QUENTIN, lawyer; b. Langdon, N.D., Nov. 1, 1911; s. George Milnes and Isabel (McKenty) P.; m. Bernice Greenwood, Mar. 27, 1945; children: Justin R., Philip J. BA, U. N.D., 1933; JD, U. Iowa, 1936. Bar: Iowa 1936, N.D. 1937. Ptnr. Price & Price, Langdon, 1936-49; state atty. Cavalier County, Langdon, 1950-60; atty. City of Langdon, 1960-70; ptnr. Price & LaQua, Langdon, 1970—. Mem. ABA, N.D. Bar Assn. (past pres.). Republican. Roman Catholic. Bankruptcy, Real property, Probate. Home: 1324 8th St Langdon ND 58249 Office: Price & LaQua PO Box 69 Langdon ND 58249

PRICE, RUSSELL EUGENE, lawyer; b. Kenton, Ohio, Dec. 18, 1931; s. Russell Cessna and Hilda E. (Kimmel) P.; m. Margaret Gaynell Atkins, Aug. 20, 1955; children: John Russell, Mary Jo, Brenda. BBA, U. Mich., 1953; JD, Wayne State U., 1958. Bar: Mich. 1958, U.S. dist. ct. (ea. dist.) Mich. 1958. Labor relations supr. Chevrolet Gear & Axle div. Gen. Motors Corp., Detroit, 1959-61; labor atty. NLRB, Detroit, 1961-64, Gerber Products Co., Fremont, Mich., 1964-69; assoc. Landman, Latimer, Clink & Robb, Fremont, 1969-71, ptnr., 1971—; city atty. City of White Cloud (Mich.), 1978—. Trustee Fremont Pub. Schs., 1969-79, bd. attys., 1981—. Served to 1st lt. U.S. Army, 1953-55. Mem. ABA, Mich. Bar Assn., 27th Jud. Cir. Bar Assn., Muskegon County Bar Assn., Newaygo-Oceana County Bar Assn. Republican. Episcopalian. Club: Ramshorn Country. Lodge: Rotary (Fremont pres. 1976). Labor. Home: 503 Lewis Ln Fremont MI 49412 Office: 8 E Main St Fremont MI 49412

PRICE, TERRY, lawyer; b. Birmingham, Ala., Oct. 13, 1953; s. A. C. and Annie (Bush) P.; m. Valerie A. Gilmore, Apr. 5, 1981; 1 child, Aisha Olivia. BA, Columbia U., 1975; JD, U. Calif., Davis, 1978. Bar: Calif. 1978, Ala. 1979, U.S. Dist. Ct. (no. dist.) Ala. 1979, D.C. 1980, U.S. Ct. Appeals (5th and 11th cirs.) 1981, Ga. 1985, U.S. Dist. Ct. (no. dist.) Ga. 1985, U.S. Ct. Appeals (6th cir.) 1985. Trial atty. U.S. Dept. Labor, Birmingham, 1978-84; assoc. Constangy, Brooks & Smith, Atlanta, 1984—. Mem. ABA, Gate City Bar Assn., Forum Com. Sports Law, Nat. Physique Com. Republican. Baptist. Avocations: body building, computer sci., astronomy. Labor, Pension, profit-sharing, and employee benefits, Entertainment. Home: 1685 Fieldgreen Overlook Stone Mountain GA 30088 Office: Constangy Brooks & Smith 230 Peachtree St Suite 2400 NW Atlanta GA 30303-1557

PRICE, TODD ALAN, lawyer; b. Elizabeth, N.J., Sept. 23, 1957; s. Burton Bennett and Naomi (Warhaftig) P.; m. Robin Faith Gutterman, Aug. 7, 1983. BA, Rutgers U., 1979; JD, Tulane U., 1982. Bar: N.Y. 1983. Sole practice N.Y.C., 1982—; instr. Sch. Visual Arts and Entertainment Law. Mem. ABA (entertainment com.), N.Y. County Bar Assn. (chmn. entertainment law com.), N.Y. County Lawyers Assn. (entertainment law com.). Entertainment. Office: 150 Fifth Ave New York NY 10011

PRICE, WALTER JASPER, JR., lawyer; b. Huntsville, Ala., Dec. 8, 1934; s. Walter Jasper and Myra (Milford) P.; m. Margaret Bohning, June 29, 1963; children: Walter J. III, Myra Elissa, Margaret Annan. AB, U. Ala., 1959, LLB, 1961. Bar: Ala. 1961, U.S. Dist. Ct. (no. dist.) Ala. 1961, U.S. Ct. Appeals (5th cir.) 1967, U.S. Supreme Ct. 1970, U.S. Ct. Appeals (11th cir.) 1982. Assoc. Lanier, Price & Shaver, Huntsville, 1961-68; ptnr. Price & Price, Huntsville, 1969-70; sole practice Huntsville, 1969-70, 85—; ptnr. Price & Kempner, Huntsville, 1970-74, Price & Henson, Huntsville, 1979-85; bd. dirs. West Huntsville Land Co.; sec. Token-Link Corp., Huntsville, 1986; lectr. Dept. Econs. and Fin. U. Ala., Huntsville. Bd. editors Ala. Lawyer, 1970-71. Mem. Ala. Bar Assn. (com. on lawyers alcohol and drug abuse 1985-86, task force on alcohol and drugs 1983-85), Southeast Amateur Hockey Assn. (v.p.), So. Youth Hockey League (past pres.), Huntsville Amateur Hockey Assn. (past pres.), Phi Kappa Alpha, Phi Alpha Delta. Presbyterian. Lodge: Kiwanis. Probate, Real property, Bankruptcy. Home: 604 Franklin St Huntsville AL 35801 Office: 221 East Side Sq Huntsville AL 35804

PRICE, WALTER LEE, lawyer; b. Johnson City, Tenn., Mar. 14, 1914; s. Samuel Walter and Nannie Lee (Ratliff) P.; m. Esda Masters, Sept. 25, 1939. Student, Milligan Coll., 1931-33; JD, U. Tenn., 1936. Bar: Tenn. 1936, U.S. Supreme Ct. 1959. Ptnr. Bryant, Price, Cantor, Fox, Booze & Taylor, Johnson City, Tenn., 1959—. Pres. Christian Home for Aged, Inc., Johnson City, 1963-72; bd. dirs. Sister Cities, Internat., Johnson City, 1963—; bd. dirs. Tenn. Higher Edn. Commn., 1973—, vice chmn., 1977-84, chmn. 1984—. Fellow Am. Coll. Probate Counsel; mem. ABA, Am. Assn. Trial Lawyers, Tenn. Bar Assn., Tenn. Trial Lawyers Assn., Washington County Bar Assn., Law Sci. Acad., Am. Arbitration Assn., Am. Coll. Hosp. Attys. Republican. Lodge: Rotary (pres. Johnson City 1973-74). Federal civil litigation, State civil litigation, Probate. Home: 2017 Sherwood Dr Johnson City TN 37601 Office: Bryant Price et al Suite 500 208 Sunset Dr Johnson City TN 37601

PRICE, WARREN, III, state attorney general; b. Washington, June 19, 1943; s. Warren and Frances (Davis) P.; m. Johna Kanoho, Mar. 21, 1967 (div. Mar. 1987); children: Warren Price IV, Brandon Phillip Price. BA in Econs., U. N.C., 1965; JD, U. Calif., San Francisco, 1972. Ptnr. Goodsill, Anderson, Quinn and Stifel, Honolulu, 1972-87; atty. gen. State of Hawaii, Honolulu, 1987—; mem. Jud. Selection Commn., Honolulu, 1985-87. Served to lt. USNR, 1965-69. Mem. Nat. Inst. of Trial Advocacy (faculty 1984-87), Pacific Law Inst. (bd. dirs., faculty 1985—), Order of the Coif, Am. Inns of Ct. Democrat. Episcopalian. Avocations: surfing, tennis. Office: Attorney General's Office 415 S Beretania St RM 405 Honolulu HI 96813

PRICE, WILLIAM CHARLES, JR., lawyer; b. New Castle, Pa., Mar. 16, 1955; s. William Charles and Joanne Louise (Neyman) P.; m. Mary R. Reed, June 10, 1978; children: Sarah, William. B.A. in Polit. Sci., Slippery Rock State U., Pa., 1977; J.D., Duquesne U., Pitts., 1980. Bar: Pa. 1980, U.S. Dist. Ct. (we. dist.) Pa. 1980, U.S. Ct. Appeals (3d cir.) 1982, U.S. Supreme Ct. 1984. Staff atty. So. Allegheny Legal Aid, Johnstown, Pa., 1981; sr. assoc. Lebovitz & Levovitz, P.A., Pitts., 1981-84; prin. Law Office of William C. Price, Jr., Pitts., 1984—. Asst. editor Juris, 1979-80. Merit badge counselor East Valley council Boy Scouts Am., 1983-85. Mem. ABA, Allegheny County Bar Assn., Pa. Bar Assn. (mem. legal services to pub. com. 1983-85), Pa. Trial Lawyers Assn., Assn. Trial Lawyers Am., Nat. Trust Historic Preservation, Swissvale C. of C., Slippery Rock Alumni Assn., Swissvale Jaycees, Mensa. Democrat. Lutheran. Lodges: Rotary, Masons, Shriners. Personal injury, State civil litigation, General practice. Home: 7942 Westmoreland Ave Pittsburgh PA 15218 Office: 2006 Noble St Pittsburgh PA 15218

PRICE, WILLIAM FURLOW, lawyer; b. Huntington Park, Calif., Mar. 28, 1924; s. Lawrence and Pauline (Davis) P. BS, U. So. Calif., 1947, JD, 1949. Bar: Calif. 1949, U.S. Dist. Ct. (cen. dist.) Calif. 1949, U.S. Supreme Ct. 1953. Sole practice Arcadia, Calif., 1949-51, 57-59; spl. counsel to congl. coms., asst. to mem. Congress, Washington, 1951-57; ptnr. Hillings & Price, Pasadena, Calif., 1959; sole practice Pasadena, 1959-70, Newport Beach, Calif., 1970—; ptnr. Hunter & Price, Laguna Hills, Calif., 1967, Newport Beach, 1968-70; judge pro tem Orange County Superior Ct., 1980—. Chmn. hearing panel Panama Canal Tolls, 1976; field rep. v.p. Nixon, 1954, 56; spl. rep. Nixon Presdl. campaign, 1968. Served with USNR, 1941-45. Decorated DFC, Air medal. Mem. ABA, Inter-Am. Bar Assn., Fed. Bar Assn., Orange County Bar Assn., Am. Judicature Soc., Am. Legion, Supreme Ct. Hist. Soc., U.S. Capitol Hist. Soc., Naval Aviation Assn., U.S. Naval Inst. Methodist. General practice. Office: 4650 Von Karman Ave Newport Beach CA 92660

PRICE, WILLIAM SCOTT, lawyer, state official; b. Oklahoma City, Oct. 5, 1948; s. Joel Scott Price and Virginia Allison (Kincheloe) Price Giles; m. Mary Lynn Slattery, Dec. 22, 1970; children: Anne, James, Eileen. B.S.F.S. in Internat. Affairs, Georgetown U., 1970; J.D., Okla. U., 1973. Research asst. Fed. Jud. Ctr., Washington, 1970; legal asst. Judge Alfred P. Murrah, Washington, 1972; legal intern Rhodes, Hieronymus, Holloway & Wilson, Oklahoma City, 1972-73; assoc. Rhodes, Hieronymus, Holloway & Wilson, 1973-74; asst. U.S. atty. Dept. Justice, Oklahoma City, 1975-82; U.S. atty. Dept. Justice, 1982—. Bd. dirs. Children's Med. Research Found., Oklahoma City, 1982—. Recipient Ben Franklin award Sertoma Club, 1984, Outstanding Service in Pub. Interest award Common Cause, 1984, Outstanding Pub. Service award Okla. Polit. Sci. Assn., 1984. Mem. Fed. Bar Assn. (pres. Oklahoma City chpt. 1984-85), Okla. State Bar Assn., Okla. County Bar Assn., Okla. Dist. Attys.' Assn. Lodge: Kiwanis (v.p. 1982-84). Criminal. Home: 1225 Kenilworth St Oklahoma City OK 73114 Office: Dept Justice 4434 US Courthouse 200 NW 4th St Oklahoma City OK 73102 *

PRICHARD, ROBERT INGRAM, III, judge; b. Atlanta, Dec. 4, 1938; s. R.I. and Novello (Mayo) P.; m. Marie Hutchinson, Feb 12, 1981; children: R.I. IV, Jeffery Wayne, Chelye Elizabeth. BS, U. Ala., 1960, JD, 1963. Bar: Miss. 1963, Ala. 1963, U.S. Dist. Ct. (so. dist.) Miss. 1963, U.S. Dist. Ct. (so. dist.) Ala. 1963, U.S. Ct. Appeals (5th cir.) 1965. Ptnr. Stewart & Prichard, Picayune, Miss., 1963-72; judge 15th Jud. Dist. Ct., Miss., 1972—. Office: Cir Ct PO Box 1075 Picaynue MS 39466

PRICHARD, VINCENT MARVIN, lawyer; b. Kirksville, Mo., July 16, 1946; s. George William and Mary Elizabeth (Love) P. B.S., U. Colo., 1969; J.D., U. Denver, 1974. Bar: Colo. 1975, U.S. Dist. Ct. Colo., 1975. Atty. Bur. Hearings and Appeals, Social Security Adminstrn., Denver, 1975-79; asst. regional counsel Dept. Energy, Lakewood, Colo., 1979-82; atty. Fed. Legal Info. Through Electronics, Denver, 1982—. Served with U.S. Army, 1969-71. Mem. Colo. Bar Assn., 1st Jud. Dist. Bar Assn. Administrative and regulatory, Computer, Computer-assisted Legal Research. Home: 30191 Peggy Ln Evergreen CO 80439 Office: HQ USAF/JASL (FLITE) Denver CO 80279-5000

PRIDAVKA, GARY MICHAEL, lawyer; b. Niles, Mich., Jan. 25, 1957; s. Gerald Stephen and Ruth Loraine (Stuchas) P. BA in Econs., Kalamazoo Coll., 1979; JD, Tulane U., 1982. Bar: Tex. 1982, U.S. Dist. Ct. (no. dist.) Tex. 1982. Assoc. Turner, Hitchins, McInerney, Webb, Hartnett & Strother, Dallas, 1982-84, Brice & Barron, Dallas, 1984-85, Brice & Mankoff, P.C., Dallas, 1985—. Acct. vol. profl. div. United Way of Met. Dallas Drive, 1983. Plym Found. scholar, 1975-79, Elk's Nat. Found. scholar, 1975-76, Mich. Merit scholar, 1975-79; named Student of Yr. Niles Rotary Club, 1975. Mem. ABA, Tex. Bar Assn., Dallas Bar Assn. (ethics com., law in changing soc. com., panelist Tex. High Sch. Mock Trial Competition 1984—), Tex. Assn. Young Lawyers, Dallas Assn. Young Lawyers (law explorers post com.). Roman Catholic. Avocation: hist. residence restoration. State civil litigation, Federal civil litigation. Home: 5023 Reiger Dallas TX 75214 Office: Brice & Mankoff PC 300 Crescent Ct Suite 700 Dallas TX 75201

PRIEST, CHARLES RANDALL, lawyer, state legislator; b. Washington, Feb. 7, 1946; s. Charles and Suzanne Marie (Randall) P.; m. Margaret Crotty, June 17, 1967 (div. Feb. 1986); 1 child, Clare Ellen Tuyet. BA in Classics cum laude, Dartmouth Coll., 1967; JD cum laude, U. Maine, 1974. Bar: Maine 1974, U.S. Dist. Ct. Maine 1974. Asst. dir. legis. research Maine Legis., Augusta, 1974-79; from assoc. to ptnr. McTeague, Higbee, Libner, Reitman & Priest, Brunswick, Maine, 1979-84; mem. Maine State Ho. of Reps., 1984—; sole practice Augusta, 1984-86; ptnr. Vafiades & Priest, Augusta, 1986—; instr. U. Maine Sch. Law, Portland, 1980—. Chmn. Augusta Conservation Commn., 1978; mem. Brunswick Dem. Com., 1979—, Cumberland County Dem. Com., Portland, 1982—; bd. dirs. Maine div. Am. Cancer Soc. Served to lt. USN, 1967-71, Vietnam. Decorated Bronze Star. Mem. ABA, Maine Bar Assn., Assn. Trial Lawyers Am., Maine Trial Lawyers Assn., U. Maine Sch. Law Alumni Assn. (pres.). Workers' compensation, Labor, Personal injury. Home: 3 Federal St Brunswick ME 04011-1507 Office: Vafiades and Priest PO Box 1540 31 Grove St Augusta ME 04330

PRIEST, GEORGE L., law educator; b. 1947. BA, Yale U., 1969; JD, U. Chgo., 1973. Assoc. prof. U. Puget Sound, Tacoma, 1973-75; law fellow U. Chgo., 1975-77; prof. U. Buffalo, 1977-80, UCLA, 1980-81, Yale U., New Haven, 1981—. Office: Yale Law Sch Drawer 401A Yale Station New Haven CT 06520 *

PRIEST, GORDON WEBB, JR., lawyer; b. Balt., Feb. 2, 1947; s. Gordon Webb Sr. and Ruth Eloise (Ziehm) P.; m. Cynthia Jean Haslam, May 29, 1971; children: Whitney Bonfield, Blair Maxwell. BA, U. N.C., 1969; JD, U. Balt., 1973. Bar: Md. 1973, U.S. Dist. Ct. Md. 1974, U.S. Ct. Appeals (4th cir.) 1975, U.S. Supreme Ct. 1976. Assoc. White, Page & Lentz, Balt., 1973-78; asst. gen. counsel, asst. sec. PHH Group Inc., Hunt Valley, Md., 1978—; mgr. legal dept. PHH Internat. Ltd., Swindon, Eng., 1985. Contbg. editor U. Balt. Law Rev., 1972-73; editor (jour.) The Grapevine, 1973—. Mem. ABA, Md. Bar Assn., Balt. City Bar Assn., Am. Corp. Counsel Assn., Md. Squash Racquets Assn. (pres. 1984), Wine & Food Soc. Balt. (bd. govs. 1983—). Republican. Episcopalian. Clubs: Maryland (Balt.); L'Hirondelle (Ruxton, Md.). Avocations: squash, tennis, wine, travel, lit. General corporate, Securities, Contracts commercial. Office: PHH Group Inc 11333 McCormick Rd Hunt Valley MD 21031

PRIEST, MAURICE ABNER, JR., lawyer; b. Sacramento, Jan. 31, 1952; s. Maurice Abner Sr. and Gwendolyn Ethel (Spiller) P.; m. Connie Lotspeich, Dec. 29, 1973; children: Cameron Banks, Tyler Cabot. AA with honors, Sacramento City Coll., 1971; BA with honors, U. Calif., Santa Barbara, 1973; JD, Western State U., 1977. Bar: Calif. 1977, U.S. Dist. Ct. (ea. dist.) Calif. 1977. Sole practice Sacramento, 1977-82; ptnr. Priest, Gaffaney & Teal, Sacramento, 1982-85, Priest, Katz & Gaffaney, Sacramento, 1985—; regional atty. Golden State Mobile Homeowners League, Sacramento, 1979-83, exec. dir., 1984-85, legis. adv. 1980—; bd. dirs. Kaplan Found., Sacramento. Contbr. articles to profl. jours. Mem. cen. com. Santa Barbara (Calif.) County Reps., 1972-73, adv. bd. Salvation Army, Sacramento, 1984—, chmn., 1982-84; treas. cen. com. El Dorado County Reps., Placerville, Calif., 1983-85. Mem. Calif. Bar Assn. (founding chmn. mobile home law com. 1981-83, exec. com. real property law sect., vice chmn., treas. 1985), Phi Alpha Delta. Republican. Lodge: Kiwanis. Avocations: travel, photography, sailing. Legislative, Mobile home law, Personal injury. Office: Priest Gaffany & Teal 1112 I St Suite 100 Sacramento CA 95814

PRILLAMAN, FREDERICK CHARLES, lawyer; b. Springfield, Ill., Dec. 29, 1942; s. Karl Richard and Jennie Ann (Ebernau) P.; m. Judy L. Miller, June 26, 1965; children: Fred C. Jr., Theodore S., Katherine E., Jennifer L. BS, Trinity Coll., Hartford, Conn., 1965; JD, Northwestern U., 1968. Bar: Ill. 1968, U.S. Dist. Ct. (so. dist.) Ill. 1968, U.S. Dist. Ct. (no. dist.) Ill. 1974, U.S. Ct. Appeals (7th cir.) 1980. Assoc. Mohan & Bostian, Springfield, 1968-70; atty. Ill. EPA, Springfield, 1970-72; assoc. Mohan Law Offices, Springfield, 1972-74; ptnr. Mohan, Alewelt & Prillaman, Springfield, 1975—. Pres. trustees Springfield YWCA, 1979-81; pres. bd. Springfield High Sch. Boosters, 1982; pres. Ill. State Mus. Soc., 1985—. Mem. Ill. Bar Assn., Sangamon County Bar Assn. Environment, Construction, State civil litigation. Home: 1340 Wiggins Ave Springfield IL 62704 Office: Mohan Alewelt & Prillaman INB Ctr Suite 325 Springfield IL 62701

PRIMPS, WILLIAM G., lawyer; b. Ossining, N.Y., Sept. 8, 1949; s. Richard Byrd and Mary Elizabeth (Guthrie) P.; m. Sophia Elizabeth Beutel, Aug. 25, 1973; children: Emily Ann, Elizabeth Armstrong. BA, Yale U., 1971; JD, Harvard U., 1974. Bar: N.Y. Assoc. LeBoeuf, :amb & MacRae, N.Y.C., 1972-82, ptnr., 1983—. Mem. class council Yale U., New Haven, 1986—; bd. dirs. Community Fund Bronxville Tuckahoe, Eastchester Inc., Bronxville, N.Y., 1986—. Mem. ABA, N.Y. State Bar Assn. (chmn. anti-trust long range policy com.). Republican. Mem. Reformed Ch. Am. Club: Yale (N.Y.C.). Litigation, Antitrust, Product liability litigation. Office: LeBoeuf Lamb Leiby & MacRay 520 Madison Ave New York NY 10022

PRINCE, DAVID CANNON, lawyer; b. Hawkinsville, Ga., July 4, 1950; s. Carl Willis and Carobel (Cannon) P.; m. Mary MacIntyre, June 30, 1973. BA in Econs., Clemson U., 1972; JD, St. John's U., Jamaica, N.Y., 1980. Bar: N.Y. 1981, Ga. 1982, U.S. Dist. Ct. (no. dist.) Ga. 1982. Atty. enforcement SEC, Atlanta, 1981-86; regional counsel E.F. Hutton & Co., Inc., Atlanta, 1986—. Served to capt. USAF, 1972-78. Mem. ABA (co-chairperson young lawyers div. fed. regulation of securities com. 1986—). Democrat. Avocations: sailing, running. Securities, Administrative and regulatory, Federal civil litigation. Home: 653 Park Dr NE Atlanta GA 30306 Office: EF Hutton & Co Inc 3340 Peachtree Rd NE Atlanta GA 30026

PRINCE, KENNETH STEPHEN, lawyer; b. Newton, Mass., Jan. 28, 1950; s. Samuel and Edna L. Prince; m. Patricia Denning, Jan. 15, 1977 (dec. Nov. 1985); 1 child, Kenneth Stephen. BA, U. Pa., 1972; JD, Boston Coll., 1975. Bar: N.Y. 1976, Mass. 1975, U.S. Dist. Ct. (so. and ea. dists.) N.Y. 1978. Assoc. Shearman & Sterling, N.Y.C., 1975-83, ptnr., 1984—. Mem. N.Y. Law Inst. (exec. com. 1984—), Order of Coif. Antitrust. Office: Shearman & Sterling 53 Wall St New York NY 10005

PRINCE, WAYMAN LEE, lawyer; b. Tallulah, La., Apr. 5, 1950; s. Leodie and Julia (Jackson) P.; m. Brenda Lou Clayton, Sept. 20, 1975 (div. July 1983). BS, Bradley U., 1972; JD, Iowa U., 1975. Bar: Iowa 1976, U.S. Dist. Ct. (so. dist.) Iowa 1978, U.S. Supreme Ct. 1979, Tex. 1986, U.S. Dist. Ct. (so. dist.) Tex., 1987. Atty. Rockford (Ill.) City Legal Dept., 1975-77; corp. mgr. Woodward Gov. County, Rockford, 1977-78; asst. counsel Bankers Life Ins. Co., Des Moines, 1978-81; corp. counsel, corp. asst. sec. Guardsman Life Ins. Co., Des Moines, 1981-84; asst. v.p., asst. gen. counsel Am. Gen. Life Ins. Co., Houston, 1984—; bd. dirs. Dollars and Sense, Inc., Houston. Fellow Life Mgmt. Inst. Assn.; mem. Am. Coll. CLU's, Am. Coll. Chartered Fin. Cons. Democrat. Methodist. Lodge: Kiwanis (bd. dirs. 1985-86). Avocations: running, jigsaw puzzles, novels, bowling, swimming. General corporate, Estate planning, Insurance. Home: 4439 Apollo St Houston TX 77018 Office: Am Gen Life Ins Co 2727 Allen Pkwy Houston TX 77019

PRINCE, WILLIAM TALIAFERRO, lawyer; b. Norfolk, Va., Oct. 3, 1929; s. James Edward and Helen Marie (Taliaferro) P.; m. Anne Carroll Hannegan, Apr. 12, 1958; children: Sarah Carroll Prince Pishko, Emily Taliaferro, William Taliaferro, John Hannegan, Anne Martineau, Robert Harrison. Student, Coll. William and Mary, Norfolk, 1947-48, 49-50; A.B., Williamsburg, 1955, B.C.L., 1957, M.L.T., 1959. Bar: Va. bar 1957. Lectr. acctg. Coll. William and Mary, 1955-57; lectr. law Marshall-Wythe Sch. Law, 1957-59; assoc. firm Williams, Worrell, Kelly & Greer, Norfolk, Va., 1959-63; partner Williams, Worrell, Kelly & Greer, 1963—; pres. Am. Inns. of Ct. Marshall-Wythe Sch. Law, 1987—. Bd. editors: The Virginia Lawyer, A Basic Practice Handbook, 1966. Bd. dirs. Madonna Home, Inc., Soc. Alumni of Coll. William and Mary. Served with U.S. Army, 1948-49, 50-52. Fellow Am. Coll. Trial Lawyers, Am. Bar Found., Va. Law Found.; mem. ABA (House of dels. 1984—), Am. Judicature Soc. (bd. dirs. 1984—), Va. State Bar (council 1973-77, exec. com. 1975-80, pres. 1978-79), Va. Bar Assn., ABA, Am. Counsel Assn., Nat. Assn. R.R. Trial Counsel, Va. Assn. Def. Attys., Va. Trial Lawyers Assn., Norfolk and Portsmouth Bar Assn., Am. Inn of Ct. (pres. 1987—). Roman Catholic. Clubs: Harbor, Mallory Country (Norfolk): Lodge: Elks (Norfolk). Federal civil litigation, State civil litigation, Personal injury. Home: 1227 Graydon Ave Norfolk VA 23507 Office: 600 United Va Bank Bldg Norfolk VA 23510

PRINCIPI, ANTHONY JOSEPH, lawyer; b. N.Y.C., Apr. 16, 1944; s. Antonio Joseph and Theresa (Princiotta) P.; m. Elizabeth Ann Ahlering, June 26, 1971; children—Anthony, Ryan, John. B.S., U.S. Naval Acad., 1967; J.D., Seton Hall U., 1975. Commd. 2d lt. U.S. Navy, 1967, advanced through grades to comdr., 1984; line officer U.S. Navy, Washington, 1967-72; atty. JAGC, San Diego, 1975-80; counsel Com. on Armed Service U.S. Senate, Washington, 1980-83, staff dir. Com. on Vet.'s Affairs, 1984—; dep. adminstr. congl. and pub. affairs VA, Washington, 1983-84. Decorated Bronze Star with combat "V", Vietnamese Cross of Gallantry, Navy Commendation medal with combat "V" (3); recipient Meritorious Service medal VA, 1983. Mem. ABA (chmn. subcom. gen. practice sect. 1985—). Republican. Roman Catholic. Avocations: gardening; skiing. Home: 10614 Canterberry Rd Fairfax Station VA 22039 Office: Senate Com on Vet's Affairs 1st and Constitution Aves NE Washington DC 20510

PRINCIPI, ELIZABETH AHLERING, lawyer; b. Whittier, Calif., Apr. 30, 1948; d. Joseph Jerome and Gwendolyn Veronica (Ryan) Ahlering; m. Anthony Joseph Principi, June 26, 1971; children: Anthony, Ryan, John. BS in Nursing, U. San Francisco, 1970; JD, Seton Hall U., 1976; LLM with Highest Honors, George Washington U., 1981. Bar: Iowa 1976, Calif. 1977, U.S. Dist. Ct. (so. dist.) Calif. 1977, U.S. Ct. Mil. Appeals 1978. Commd. ensign nurse corps USN, 1968, advanced through grades to comdr., 1985; trial atty. legal services USN, San Diego, 1977-79, head dept. legal assistance services, 1979-80; sr. atty. med. legal sect. JAGC USN, Washington, 1981-83, spl. asst. med. legal affairs med. commn., 1983-86, counsel inspector gen., 1986—; lectr. Armed Forces Inst. Pathology, Washington, 1980-81, Naval Sch. Health Scis., Washington, 1981—, Naval Med. Command, Washington, 1983—, Contemporary Forums, San Rafael, Calif., 1984—. Cub Scout leader Boy Scouts Am., Springfield, Va., 1980-81. Mem. Calif. Bar Assn., Iowa Bar Assn., Assn. Trial Lawyers Am., Womens Officer Profl. Assn., Nurses in Law and Health. Roman Catholic. Avocations: child devel., jogging, racquetball. Health, Personal injury, Government contracts and claims. Home: 10614 Canterberry Rd Fairfax Station VA 22039 Office: Naval Inspector Gen Bldg 200 Washington Navy Yard Washington DC 20372

PRINGLE, LYNN ALLAN, lawyer; b. Mason City, Iowa, Oct. 16, 1951; s. Lyle Alan and Winnie (Ackley) P. BA with high honors, U. Okla., 1974; JD, Georgetown U., 1977. Bar: Okla. 1977, U.S. Dist. Ct. (we. dist.) Okla. 1978, U.S. Ct. Appeals (10th cir.) 1979, U.S. Dist. Ct. (no dist.) Tex. 1983, U.S. Supreme Ct. 1984. Assoc. Bohanon & Barth, Oklahoma City, 1977-79; assoc. Andrews, Davis, Legg, Bixler, Milsren & Murrah, Oklahoma City, 1979-82, ptnr., 1982-83; ptnr. Jones, Blaney & Pringle, P.C., Oklahoma City, 1983—; adj. prof. Oklahoma City U. Sch. Law, 1984. Contbr. articles to profl. jours. Mem. ABA, Am. Bankruptcy Inst., Okla. Bar Assn. (bankruptcy and reorgn. sects.), Okla. County Bar Assn. Bankruptcy, Banking, Real property. Office: Eagleton Nicholson et al 1300 1st City Pl PO Box 657 Oklahoma City OK 73101

PRINGLE, SAMUEL WILSON, JR., lawyer; b. Pitts., Oct. 14, 1930; s. Samuel W. Sr. and Margaret (Thumm) P.; m. Barbara Borkowski, April 21, 1979; children: Samuel Wilson III, Philip P.; stepchildren: Mary Beth Walley, Robert E. Walley IV. AB, Princeton U., 1952; JD, Harvard U., 1955. Bar: Pa. 1956, U.S. Dist. Ct. (we. dist.) Pa. 1956, U.S. Ct. Appeals (3d cir.) 1957. Assoc. Pringle, Bredin & Martin, Pitts., 1956-59; atty. USX Corp. (formerly U.S. Steel Corp.), Pitts., 1960—. Mem. com. Reps., O'Hara Twp., Pa., 1979-83. Real property, General corporate. Home: 110 Eton Dr Pittsburgh PA 15215 Office: USX Corp 600 Grant St USX Bldg Room 1538 Pittsburgh PA 15230

PRITCHARD, MICHAEL GREGG, legal services director, lawyer; b. Fayetteville, Ark., Feb. 13, 1949; s. Ross Joseph Pritchard and Emily Gregg; m. Deborah Hoffman Jan. 31, 1971 (div. Mar. 1977); 1 child, Kerri-Anne. BA, U. Ark., 1971; JD, Yale U., 1974. Bar: Wis. 1974, U.S. Dist. Ct. (we. dist.) Wis. 1978, Trust Ters. of Pacific Islands 1979, Ark. 1981, U.S. Dist. Ct. (we. dist.) Ark. 1981, S.C. 1986, U.S. Dist. Ct. S.C. 1986. Staff atty. Ctr. for Pub. Representation, Madison, Wis., 1975-77, Wis. Indian Legal Services, Madison, 1977-78, Micronesia Legal Services, Majuro, Marshall Islands, 1979-80; staff atty., dep. dir. Ozark Legal Services, Fayetteville, 1981-85, Palmetto Legal Services, Columbia, S.C., 1985—; adj. prof. U. Wis., Milwaukee, 1977; chmn. Ark. Legal Services Project Dirs. Group, Fayetteville, 1982-84. Mem. Wis. Gov.'s Study Com. on Solar Rights, Madison, 1977; mem. Wis. Legis. Metallic Mining Reclamation Act Revision Com., Madison, 1977; pres. Cen. Madison Housing Corp., 1977-79; mem. Young Dems. of Wash. County, Fayette, Ark., 1982-85; bd. dirs. Southeast Tng. Ctr., Little Rock, 1982-85, ACLU Ark chpt., 1983-85. Mem. ABA, S.C. Bar Assn., Ark. Bar Assn., Wis. Bar Assn., ACLU (bd. dirs. Ark. chpt. 1983-85), Phi Beta Kappa. Lodge: Sertoma. Avocations: archaeology, hiking, film. Management civil legal services program, Federal civil litigation. Home: 1423 Deerwood St Columbia SC 29205 Office: Palmetto Legal Services 2109 Bull St PO Box 2267 Columbia SC 29202

PRITCHARD, TERESA NOREEN, lawyer, law librarian; b. Brackley, Eng., Apr. 2, 1953; d. Boston Forrest and Noreen Phyliss (Taylor) P. BA magna cum laude, Oakland U., 1974; MLS, Wayne State U., 1976, JD cum laude, 1981. Bar: Fla. 1985, Mich. 1981. Law librarian Honigman Miller Schwartz & Cohn, Detroit, 1979-81; assoc. Honigman, Miller, Schwartz & Cohn, Detroit, 1981-83, Rumberger, Kirk et al, Orlando, Fla., 1984-85; dir. research services Gunster, Yoakley, Criser & Stewart, West Palm Beach, Fla., 1985—. Mem. Fla. Bar Assn., Mich. Bar Assn. (judicial and profl. ethics com. 1982-84), Am. Assn. Law Libraries (cert.). Protestant. Avocations: aerobics, gourmet cooking. Environment, Jurisprudence, Librarianship. Office: Gunster Yoakley Criser & Stewart 777 S Flagler Dr West Palm Beach FL 33401

PRITCHARD, THOMAS ALEXANDER, lawyer, paralegal educator; b. Coral Gables, Fla., May 5, 1949; s. John Alexander and Blodwyn Ellen (Lett) P.; m. Maureen M. Rider, Mar. 14, 1979. B.A. in History, U. Fla., 1971; J.D., U. Miss., 1974. Bar: Miss. 1974, U.S. Dist. Ct. (no. dist.) Miss. 1974, U.S. Dist. Ct. (so. dist.) Miss. 1976, U.S. Ct. Appeals (5th and 11th cirs.) 1981. Ptnr. Deen & Pritchard, Gulfport Miss., 1976-77, Joseph, Pritchard, Smith, Biloxi & Gulfport, 1981-83; assoc. C.E. Morris, Jr., Biloxi, 1977-81; sole practice, Biloxi, 1983—; instr. paralegal program Phillips Coll., Gulfport, 1980-82. Editor Jour. Space Law, U. Miss. Sch. Law, 1974. Dir. dependent youth activities Keesler AFB, Harrison County, Miss., 1979-82; mem. membership com. Harrison County Republican Club, 1984. Served to 1st lt. U.S. Army, 1975. Mem. Assn. Trial Lawyers Am., Miss. Trial Lawyers Assn., Delta Theta Phi. Republican. Lutheran. Personal injury, Workers' compensation, General practice. Home: 3507 Courtnay Circle Ocean Springs MS 39564 Office: 1115 W Howard Ave PO Box 958 Biloxi MS 39533

PROBERT, MARK STANLEY, lawyer; b. Los Angeles, Nov. 26, 1946; s. Henry B. and Beatrice (Ganz) P.; m. Sandra Beverly Blum, Mar. 2, 1974; 1 child, Joshua H. B.A. cum laude, L.I. U., 1973; J.D., St. Johns U., 1977. Bar: N.Y. 1978, U.S. Dist. Ct. (ea. dist.) NY. 1982, U.S. Dist. Ct. (so. dist.) N.Y. 1982. Sr. disability claims analyst Office Disability Determinations, N.Y.C., 1973-77; atty., adviser Office Hearings and Appeals, Social Security Adminstrn., Bklyn., 1977-80; assoc. Scheine Fusco & Brandenstein, N.Y.C., 1980-84; sole practice, Merrick, N.Y., 1984—; instr. law Briarcliffe Coll., L.I., N.Y. Mem. editorial adv. com. Social Security Reporting Service, 1982—. Workers' compensation, Personal injury, Pension, profit-sharing, and employee benefits. Home: 1698 Webster Ave Merrick NY 11566

PROBSTEIN, JON MICHAEL, lawyer; b. N.Y.C., June 24, 1953; s. Albert and Lila (Levin) P. B.A. in Psychology, Syracuse U., 1973; J.D., St. John's U., 1976. Bar: N.Y. 1977, U.S. Dist. Ct. (so. dist. and ea. dists.) N.Y. 1982, U.S. Ct. Appeals (2d cir.) 1983. Assoc. Marchi, Jaffe, Cohen, Crystal & Mintz, N.Y.C., 1977-78, Berman & Zivyak, N.Y.C., 1979-80, Graubard, Moskovitz McGoldrick Dannett & Horowitz, N.Y.C., 1981-82; ptnr. Probstein & Napolitano, N.Y.C., 1982—; instr. legal research and writing Benjamin Cardozo Sch. Law, N.Y.C., 1976-77. Mem. ABA, Assn. Trial Lawyers Am., Assn. Bar City N.Y., N.Y. State Bar Assn. Entertainment, Civil litigation, General corporate. Office: Probstein & Napolitano 230 Park Ave Suite 231 New York NY 10169 also: 1925 Century Park E Suite 1260 Los Angeles CA 90067

PROCHNOW, DOUGLAS LEE, lawyer; b. Omaha, Jan. 9, 1952; s. Albert Delmer and Betty Jean (Wood) P. BA with high distinction, U. Nebr., 1974; JD, Northwestern U., 1977. Bar: Ill. 1977, U.S. Dist. Ct. (no. dist.) Ill. 1977. Assoc. Wildman, Harrold, Allen & Dixon, Chgo., 1977-84, ptnr., 1985—. spl. asst. corp. counsel City of Chgo., 1986—. Mem. ABA, Ill. Bar Assn., Chgo. Bar Assn., Assn. Trial Lawyers Am. (assoc.), Ill. Trial Lawyers Assn., Phi Beta Kappa, Phi Eta Sigma. State civil litigation, Insurance, Personal injury. Home: 1230 N State Pkwy Unit 6D Chicago IL 60610 Office: Wildman Harrold Allen & Dixon 1 IBM Plaza Chicago IL 60611

PROCOPIO, JOSEPH GUYDON, corporate executive; b. Paterson, N.J., May 1, 1940; s. Joseph A. and V. Genevieve (Kievitt) P.; m. Joanne Julia Roccato, June 30, 1962 (div. Aug. 1980); children: Jennifer Tehani, Joseph Christian. BS, U.S. Naval Acad., 1962; MS in Ops. Research, Naval Postgrad. Sch., 1971; JD, Cath. U. Am., 1979; LLM, George Washington U., 1984—. Bar: Va. Commd. ensign USN, 1962, served to comdr., 1978, ret., 1983; gen. counsel, sec. Presearch, Inc., Fairfax, Va., 1983-85; v.p. corp. communications ERC Internat., Fairfax, Va., 1985—. Decorated Bronze Star, Meritorious Service medal, Joint Service Commendation awards, Defense Nat. medal (Cambodia), Navy Achievement medal. Mem. Internat. Inst. Strategic Studies, Internat. Bar Assn., ABA, Am. Corp. Counsel. Assn., Va. Bar Assn., World Affairs Council of Washington, U.S. Naval Acad. Alumni Assn., U.S. Naval Acad. Class of 1962 Assn. (bd. dirs. 1978-80, spl. asst. to pres., 1984—). Club: Army/Navy Country (Arlington, Va.). Avocations: golf and tennis, history (legal, military, naval, economic), flying. Securities, Private international, General corporate. Home: 657 S Columbus St Alexandria VA 22314 Office: ERC Internat 3211 Jermantown Rd Fairfax VA 22030

PROCTOR, CHARLES WILLIAM, III, lawyer, title company executive, marketing company executive; b. Evanston, Ill., May 9, 1948; s. Charles William Jr. and Marie Flora (Von Martinitz) P.; m. Maria Olga Listino, Aug. 26, 1972; children—Jennifer Christin, Danielle Alysa, Charles William IV, Justin Vincent. B.A., Temple U., 1973; J.D., Widener U., Wilmington, Del., 1976. Bar: Pa. 1976, U.S. Dist. Ct. (ea. dist.) Pa. 1976, U.S. Ct. Appeals (3d cir.) 1979, U.S. Supreme Ct. 1980, U.S. Tax Ct. 1983, U.S. Claims Ct. 1984, U.S. Dist. Ct. (mid. dist.) Pa. 1984. Sole practice, Newtown Square, Pa., 1976-84; pres. Eagle Enterprises, Broomall, Pa., 1977—; sr. mng. ptnr. Tollen & Proctor, Media, Pa., 1984—; pres., chmn. bd., owner Indsl. Valley Abstract Title Co., 1986—. Contbg. editor Delaware Law Forum, 1975-76. Treas. Young Republicans Delaware County, Media, 1968-71; Bd. dirs., coach Llangollen Hills Swim and Tennis Club, Newtown Square, 1979-80; vestry mem. Christ Episcopal Ch., Media, 1981-83; bd. dirs. and pres. Suburban Swim Club, Newtown Square, 1983—. Mem. Delaware County Bar Assn., ABA, Assn. Trial Lawyers Am., Supreme Ct. Hist. Soc.

Republican. General corporate, General practice, Real property. Office: Tollen & Proctor 15 E Front St Media PA 19063

PROCTOR, DAVID RAY, lawyer; b. Nashville, Apr. 18, 1956; s. Raymond Douglas and Margaret Florence (Coffey) P.; m. Robbin Lynn Fuqua, May 12, 1984; 1 child, Rachael Lynne. AA in Polit. Sci., Cumberland Jr. Coll., 1976; BA in Polit. Sci., Vanderbilt U., 1978; JD, Cumberland Sch. Law, 1981; LLM in Taxation, U. Fla., 1983. Bar: Ala. 1981, Tenn. 1983, U.S. Tax Ct. 1983. Law clk. to presiding justice Ala. Supreme Ct., Montgomery, 1981-82; assoc. Thrailkill & Goodman, Nashville, 1983-84; tax specialist Ala. Farm Bur. Ins. Co., Montgomery, 1984—. Contbg. editor Cumberland Law Rev., 1980-81; contbr. articles to profl. jours. Tchr. Research Bd., Birmingham, Ala., 1980; active Montgomery Area United Way, 1985. Mem. ABA, Ala. Bar Assn., Tenn. Bar Assn., Phi Alpha Delta, Pi Sigma Alpha. Baptist. Avocations: softball, music, sports, charities. Corporate taxation, Personal income taxation, State and local taxation. Home: 10637 N Palomino Dr Montgomery AL 36117 Office: Ala Farm Bur Ins Co 2108 E South Blvd Montgomery AL 36117

PROCTOR, GEORGE EDWIN, JR., lawyer; b. Oklahoma City, Jan. 11, 1951; s. George Edwin and Naomi Francis (Boyington) P.; m. Nancy Dumoff, Jan. 6, 1978. BA, Okla. State U., 1973; postgrad. Oxford U. (Eng.), 1975; JD, Oklahoma City U., 1976; LLM, U. Mo.-Kansas City, 1981. Bar: Okla. 1977, Mo. 1978, U.S. Dist. Ct. (we. dist.) Okla. 1977, U.S. Ct. Appeals (10th cir.) 1977, U.S. Dist. Ct. (we. dist.) Mo. 1978, U.S. Supreme Ct. 1981. Legis. asst. Okla. Senate, Oklahoma City, 1975; research atty. and analyst Midwest Research Inst., Kansas City, Mo., 1976-77; assoc. Paxton, Farrington & Block, Independence, Mo., 1977-78; asst. pros. atty. Jackson County Prosecutor's Office, Kansas City, 1978-81; assoc. Polsinelli, White & Vardeman, Kansas City, 1981-85, Heavner, Jarrett & Kimball, P.C., 1985—. Bd. dirs. Com. for County Progress, 1979—, Citizens Assn., Kansas City, 1983—. Mem. Okla. Bar Assn., Mo. Bar Assn., Assn. Trial Lawyers Am., Am. Judicature Soc., Mo. Trial Lawyers Assn. Democrat. Methodist. Federal civil litigation, State civil litigation, Environment. Home: 303 Sunderland Ct Lee's Summit MO 64063 Office: Heavner Jarrett & Kimball PC 900 Bryant Bldg 1102 Grand Ave Kansas City MO 64106

PROCTOR, KENNETH DONALD, lawyer; b. Balt., Apr. 28, 1944; s. Kenneth Chauncey and Sarah Elizabeth (Kent) P.; m. Judith Danner Harris, Aug. 2, 1969; children—Kenneth Scott, Kent Harris, Janet Cameron. B.S., Lehigh U., 1966; J.D., U. Md., 1969. Bar: Md. 1969, U.S. Dist. Ct. Md. 1970, U.S. Ct. Appeals (4th cir.) 1980, U.S. Supreme Ct. 1974. Law clk. to presiding judge Md. Ct. Appeals, 1969-70; assoc. Miles & Stockbridge, Balt., 1970-73, 74-76, ptnr., Balt., 1976-81, Towson, Md., 1981—; asst. atty. gen. Md., Balt., 1973-74; Trustee, Gilman Sch., Balt., 1982-85. Mem. ABA, Md. State Bar Assn., Balt. County-Balt. City Bar Assn. Democrat. Episcopalian. General practice, State civil litigation, State and local taxation. Office: Miles & Stockbridge 401 Washington Ave Towson MD 21204

PROCTOR, WILLIAM ZINSMASTER, lawyer; b. Des Moines, Nov. 30, 1902; s. Frank and Louise (Zinsmaster) P.; m. Alice S. Bowles, Nov. 24, 1944; children: David J. W., Mary Martha. Student, Drake U., 1920; J.D., U. Mich., 1925. Bar: Iowa 1925. Asso. Bradshaw, Schenk & Fowler, 1925-35; partner Bradshaw, Fowler, Proctor & Fairgrave, Des Moines, 1935—; dir., gen. counsel emeritus Employers Mut. Casualty Co., Employers Modern Life Co., Emcasco Ins. Co., EMC Ins. Group Inc., Dakota Fire Ins. Co., Bismarck, N.D., Am. Liberty Ins. Co., Birmingham, Ala., Union Mut. Ins. Co. Providence; dir. emeritus Norwest Des Moines N.A. Pres. Des Moines Community Chest, 1956, Des Moines United Community Services, 1957; mem. bd. SSS, 1942-55, Iowa appeal bd., 1955-67; Pres. Des Moines Roadside Settlement, 1950-53; Chmn. bd. trustees Hawley Welfare Found., 1968—, Preston Ednl. Trust, 1952—. Mem. ABA, Iowa Bar Assn., Polk County Bar Assn. (pres. 1945), Internat. Bar Assn., Inter-Am. Bar Assn., Am. Judicature Soc., Assn. Bar City N.Y., Fedn. Ins. Counsel. Clubs: Mason (Shriner, Jester), Wakonda, Des Moines (pres. 1953); University (Chgo.). Home: 3401 Lincoln Pl Dr Des Moines IA 50312 Office: Des Moines Bldg Des Moines IA 50307

PROCZKO, TARAS ROMAN, lawyer; b. Frankfurt, Fed. Republic Germany, Aug. 23, 1954; came to U.S., 1956; s. Stefan Peter and Rose (Adieoglu) P.; m. Marta Cristina Durbak, Oct. 11, 1980; children: Daniel Stefan, Paul Bohdan. BA, Ill. Benedictine Coll., Lisle, 1976; JD with distinction, John Marshall Law Sch., Chgo., 1980. Bar: Ill. 1980, U.S. Dist. Ct. (no. dist.) Ill. 1980. Atty. Hart Schaffner & Marx, Chgo., 1980-83, Hartmarx Corp., Chgo., 1983—. Mem. ABA, Ill. Bar Assn., Chgo. Bar Assn., Ukrainian-Am. Bar Assn. Ukrainian Catholic. Avocations: skiing, outdoor sports, reading. Contracts commercial, Labor, General corporate. Office: Hartmarx Corp 101 N Wacker Dr Chicago IL 60606

PRODSKY, EDWARD, lawyer; b. N.Y.C., Oct. 21, 1929. BBA, CCNY, 1950; LLB cum laude, NYU, 1957. Bar: N.Y. 1957, D.C. 1958, Fla. 1975. Ptnr. Spengler, Carlson, Gubar, Brodsky & Frischling, N.Y.C., 1976—; mem. civil div. U.S. Dept. Justice, 1957-58; spl. atty. Atty. Gen.'s Spl. Group Organized Crime, 1958-59; asst. U.S. atty. U.S. Dist. Ct. (so. dist.) N.Y., 1959-62; chief spl. prosecutions div. U.S. Atty.'s Office, 1961-62. Assoc. editor NYU Law Rev., 1956-57; columnist N.Y. Law Jour., 1972—; mem. nat. adv. bd. Profl. Liability Reporter, 1977-78; mem. editorial adv. bd. Securities Regulation Law Jour., 1977—; mem. editorial bd. The Tax Shelter Advisor, 1984—; contbr. articles to profl. jours. Mem. Westchester County Play Land Commn., 1978-81, Westchester Community Mental Health Bd., 1975-78. Fellow Am. Coll. Trial Lawyers, Inter. Acad. Trial Lawyers; mem. ABA, N.Y. State Bar Assn. (civil rights com. 1965-68), Assn. of Bar of City of N.Y. (criminal ct. com. 1963-66, civil rights com. 1966-69), Fed. Bar Council, N.Y. County Lawyers Assn. (fed. legis. com. 1971-73). State civil litigation, Federal civil litigation, General corporate. Office: Spengler Carlson Grebar Prodsky & Frischling 280 Park Ave New York NY 10017

PROFETA, FRED ROBERT, JR., lawyer; b. Flushing, N.Y., Apr. 28, 1939; s. Fred R. and Lynn (Virgilio) P.; m. Susan Burchell, June 12, 1965; children—Katherine Ann, Timothy Howard. B.A., Yale U., 1961; LL.B., Harvard U., 1964, LL.M., 1965. Bar: N.Y. 1966, U.S. Dist. Ct. (so. and ea. dists.) N.Y. 1968, U.S. Ct. Appeals (2d cir.) 1975. Assoc. Cadwalader Wickersham & Taft, N.Y.C., 1965-72; ptnr. Arum Friedman & Katz, N.Y.C., 1972-75; gen. counsel Moran Towing and Transp. Co., Inc., N.Y.C., 1976-79; sole practioner, N.Y.C., 1979—. Mem. ABA, Assn. Trial Lawyers Am., N.Y. State Bar Assn., N.Y. County Lawyers Assn., Maritime Law Assn. Methodist. Club: Maplewood (N.J.). Federal civil litigation, State civil litigation, Personal injury. Office: 100 Maiden Ln Suite 1606 New York NY 10038

PROFFITT, JOHN STEPHEN, III, lawyer; b. Richmond, Va., Mar. 27, 1948; s. J. Stephen Jr. and Lucille Elizabeth (Cornett) P.; m. Deborah Louise Straub, Feb. 17, 1973. B of Commerce, U. Richmond, 1972; JD, U. Va., 1981. Bar: Va. 1981. Ptnr. Stephen Proffitt & Assocs., Richmond, 1981—. Mem. Assn. Trial Lawyers Am., Va. Trial Lawyers Assn. Personal injury, Federal civil litigation, State civil litigation. Home: 221 Sunset Dr Richmond VA 23229 Office: 513 Forest Ave Suite 203 Richmond VA 23229

PROFFITT, ROY FRANKLIN, educator; b. Hastings, Neb., Aug. 6, 1918; s. Harry Louis Franklin and Vera (Roe) P.; m. Jean Malott Humphrey, Mar. 25, 1944. B.S. in Bus. Adminstrn. U. Neb., 1940; J.D., U. Mich., 1948, LL.M., 1956. Bar: Colo. and Neb. bars 1948, Mo. bar 1955. With firm Miller, McKinley & Walsh, Greeley, Colo., 1948; research asso. U. Neb. Coll. Law, 1948-49; from asst. prof. to prof. law U. Mo., 1949-56; Cook fellow U. Mich., 1955-56; mem. faculty U. Mich. (Law Sch.), 1956—; prof. law 1958—, asst. dean, 1956-68, asso. dean, 1968-70; asso. dir. Inst. Continuing Legal Edn., 1970-72, dir. law sch. relations, 1972—, prof. emeritus, 1986—. Editor: (with others) Rules and Cases on Criminal Procedure, 2d edit, 1961. Tech. adviser criminal law revision com. Mo. Senate, 1951-54; member adv. com. drafting rules procedure municipal cts. Mo. Supreme Ct., 1954-55; mem. Spl. Com. Traffic Safety Mich., 1964, Mich. Bail and Criminal Justice Com., 1965-70; mem., sec. Spl. Com. Revision Mich. Criminal Code, 1965-71. Served to lt. comdr. USNR, 1940-45. Mem. Maritime Law Assn. U.S., Order of Coif, Beta Gamma Sigma, Alpha Tau Omega. Club: Mason. Admiralty. Home: 580 Rock Creek Dr Ann Arbor MI 48104

PROFUSEK, ROBERT ALAN, lawyer; b. Cleve., Jan. 14, 1950; s. George John and Geraldine (Hobl) P.; m. Linda Gail Schmidt, May 7, 1972; children—Robert Charles, Kathryn Anne. B.A., Cornell U., 1972; J.D., NYU, 1975. Bar: Ohio 1975, Tex. 1981. Assoc. Jones, Day, Reavis & Pogue, Cleve., 1975-81, Dallas, 1981-82, ptnr., 1982—. Contbr. articles to profl. jours. Trustee Positive Edn. Program, Cleve., 1979-81, Preston Bend Assn., Dallas, 1983-85. Mem. ABA, Tex. Bar Assn., Dallas Bar Assn., Prestonwood C. of C. Democrat. Roman Catholic. Clubs: Exchange, Prestonwood Country, Tower (all Dallas). Securities, General corporate. Home: 16923 Preston Bend Dallas TX 75248 Office: Jones Day Reavis & Pogue 2300 LVT Center Dallas TX 75266

PROM, STEPHEN G., lawyer; b. Jacksonville, Fla., July 8, 1954; s. George W. and Bonnie M. (Porter) P.; m. Leah A. English, Aug. 28, 1976; children: Ashley Brooke, Aaron Jacob. AA in Polit. Sci. with high honors, Fla. Jr. Coll., 1974; BA in Polit. Sci. with high honors, U. Fla., 1977, JD with honors, 1979. Bar: Fla. 1980, U.S. Dist. Ct. (mid. dist.) Fla. 1980, U.S. Dist. Ct. (no. dist.) Fla. 1981, U.S. Tax Ct. 1982, U.S. Ct. Appeals (11th cir.) 1985, U.S. Supreme Ct. 1985. Assoc. Rogers, Towers, Bailey, Jones & Gay, Jacksonville, 1979-83, Foley & Lardner, Jacksonville, 1983-86; ptnr. Christian & Prom, Jacksonville, 1986-87, Christian, Prom & Korn, Jacksonville, 1987—. Sr. mgmt. editor U. Fla. Law Rev., 1978-79. Mem. Leadership Jacksonville, 1984, Jacksonville Community Council Inc., 1985-86; bd. dirs. Mental Health Resource Ctr., Jacksonville, 1984—, Mental Health Resource Found., Jacksonville, 1985—, Youth Crisis Ctr., Jacksonville, 1984-86. Named one of Outstanding Young Men in Am., 1983, 85, one of Outstanding Young Men in Fla., 1986. Mem. ABA (tax, corp. banking and bus. law, health law, mcpl. fin., local gov. law sects.), Fla. Bar Assn. (tax and corp., banking and bus. law sects., health law com., bd. govs. young lawyers sect.), Jacksonville Bar Assn., Am. Acad. Hosp. Attys., Am. Hosp. Assn., Nat. Health Lawyers Assn., Fla. Assn. Hosp. Lawyers, Jacksonville C. of C. (mem. com. of 100 1985—), Jacksonville Jaycees, Order of Coif, Phi Beta Kappa, Phi Theta Kappa, Phi Kappa Phi. Republican. Baptist. Clubs: Wavemasters Soc. (pres. 1984), Downtown Athletic (bd. advisors 1986), Seminole (Jacksonville); Ponte Vedra (Fla.). Avocations: surfing, weightlifting, tennis, jogging, bicycling. Health, Municipal bonds, General corporate. Home: 2802 S 2d St Jacksonville Beach FL 32250 Office: Christian Prom & Korn 6620 Southpoint Dr S Suite 316 PO Box 19276 Jacksonville FL 32245-9276

PROOST, ROBERT LEE, lawyer; b. St. Louis, July 30, 1937; s. Virgil Raymond and Anna Marie (Gaeng) P.; m. Mary Jo McDonald, July 1, 1961; children: Timothy Robert, Mary Elizabeth, Thomas Edward, Daniel Joseph. BS magna cum laude, St. Louis U., 1959; JD, Washington U., St. Louis, 1962. Bar: Mo. 1962, Ill. 1962, Fla. 1979, D.C. 1987. Assoc. Peper, Martin, Jensen, Maichel & Hetlage (and predecessors), St. Louis, 1962-68, ptnr., 1968—; pres., bd. dirs. Silmasco Inc., St. Louis, 1971—, Executype Inc., St. Louis, 1971-78; chmn. bd. St. Louis Fixture Co., 1982-85; chmn. bd. dirs. St. Louis Fixture Co.; lectr. in field. Author: Financing the On-Going Business, 1973, 79, 83, Securities Regulation: Missouri Corporate Law and Practice: Securities Regulation, 1985, 87; contbr. articles to profl. jours. Served to capt. JAGC, USAF, 1962-65. Mem. ABA, Mo. Bar Assn. (bd. govs. 1985—), Ill. Bar Assn., Fla. Bar Assn., Met. St. Louis Bar Assn. (pres. 1978-79), Washington U. Law Alumni Assn. (pres. 1972-73), Am. Judicature Soc., St. Louis U. Arts and Scis. Alumni Assn. (v.p. 1971, bd. of govs. 1987—), Order of Coif, Alpha Sigma Nu, Phi Delta Phi. Roman Catholic. Clubs: Media (St. Louis); Washington U. Faculty (Clayton, Mo.). General corporate, Securities, Banking. Home: 319 Claymont Dr Ballwin MO 63011 Office: Peper Martin Jensen et al 720 Olive St Saint Louis MO 63101

PROPST, ROBERT BRUCE, judge; b. Onatchee, Ala., July 13, 1931; s. Franklin Glenn and Mildred (Moore) P.; m. Elma Jo Griffin, Dec. 29, 1962; children: Stephen, David, Joanne. B.S., U. Ala., 1953, J.D., 1957. Judge U.S. Dist Ct. Ala. Served to 1st lt. U.S. Army, 1953-55. Mem. Jaycees (pres. 1954-60). Methodist. Club: Exchange (Anniston, Ala.). Avocation: golf. Judicial administration. Home: 305 Sky Dr Anniston AL 36201 Office: US Dist Ct Federal Courthouse Birmingham AL 35203 *

PROSPERI, LOUIS ANTHONY, lawyer; b. Altoona, Pa., Jan. 12, 1954; s. Louis Alfred and Ann Francis (DiDimenico) P.; m. Susan Lynn Irwin, Sept. 14, 1985. BS in Bus. Adminstrn. summa cum laude, Georgetown U., 1975; JD cum laude, Harvard U., 1978. Bar: Pa. 1978, U.S. Dist. Ct. (we. dist.) Pa. 1978, U.S. Ct. Appeals (Fed. cir.) 1979, U.S. Ct. Claims 1985, U.S. Tax Ct. 1985. From assoc. to ptnr. Reed, Smith, Shaw & McClay, Pitts., 1978—. Mem. Allegheny County Bar Assn., Pitts. Tax Club. Republican. Roman Catholic. Club: Longue Vue (Verona, Pa.). Avocations: golf, tennis, paddle tennis, softball, cross-country skiing. Corporate taxation, Personal income taxation, State and local taxation. Home: 3036 Grasmere Ave Pittsburgh PA 15216 Office: Reed Smith Shaw & McClay 435 6th Ave Pittsburgh PA 15219

PROTIGAL, STANLEY NATHAN, lawyer; b. Wilmington, Del., June 3, 1950; s. Bernard Protigal. BS in Aircraft Maintenance Engring., Northrop U., 1973; JD, Vt. Law Sch., 1978. Bar: U.S. Patent Office 1977, D.C. 1978. Assoc. Sixbey F. & L., Arlington, Va., 1978-79, atty., 1979-82; staff patent atty. The Bendix Corp., Teterboro, N.J., 1982-83, patent atty., 1983-84; patent atty. Allied-Signal Corp., Morristown, N.J., 1984—. Mem. IEEE, MENSA. Avocations: pvt. pilot, bicycling, skiing. Patent, Legislative, Government contracts and claims. Office: Allied-Signal Corp Park Ave and Columbia Turnpike Morristown NJ 07960-2245

PROTOKOWICZ, STANLEY EDWARD, JR., lawyer, legal educator; b. Balt., Sept. 11, 1954; s. Stanley Edward Sr. and Sally Louise (Carter) P.; m. Leslie Ann Pugh, May 24, 1975; 1 child, Samantha Jean. BA, Franklin & Marshall Coll., 1976; JD, Mercer U., 1979. Bar: Ga. 1979, U.S. Dist. Ct. (no. dist.) Ga. 1979, Md. 1980, U.S. Dist. Ct. Md. 1980, U.S. Ct. Appeals (4th cir.) 1983, U.S. Supreme Ct. 1983. Law clk. to presiding justice Harford County Cir. Ct., Bel Air, Md., 1979-80; sole practice Bel Air, 1980-81; ptnr. Miller, Fry & Protokowicz, Bel Air, 1981—; adj. prof. law Harford Community Coll., Bel Air, 1980—; lectr. various schs. , Harford County, Md., 1983—. Panel mem. Talk Show Sta. WBAL Radio, Owing Mills, Md., 1984-85; contbr. articles to local newspapers, 1984—. Fundraiser Loyola High Sch., Towson, Md., 1985—; vol. lawyer Md. Vol. Lawyer Service, Balt., 1984—; tchr. St. Margarets Roman Cath. Ch., Bel Air, 1985-86; chmn. long range planning com. Harford Day Sch., Bel Air, 1985—, trustee, bd. dirs. 1986—; bd. dirs. The Ballet Co., Churchville, Md., 1986—. Mem. Md. Bar Assn., Harford County Bar Assn. (treas. 1980—), Assn. Trial Lawyers Am., Md. Trial Lawyers Assn., Bel Air Jaycees (sec. 1980—). Democrat. General practice, Family and matrimonial, Personal injury. Home: 319 Catherine Ct Bel Air MD 21014 Office: Miller Fry & Protokowicz 5 S Hickory Ave Bel Air MD 21014

PROUNIS, THEODORE OTHON, lawyer; b. N.Y.C., Feb. 13, 1926; s. Othon D. and Amelia O. (Petrides) P.; m. Lila D. Jentiles, Feb. 22, 1956; children: Othon A., Amelia E. BS, Columbia U., 1949, MS, 1950; JD, Fordham U., 1963. Bar: N.Y. 1964. Sole practice, N.Y.C., 1964—; trustee, pres. Cathedral Archdiocese Greek Orthodox Ch., 1986—. Invested as Archon Deputatos by Ecumenical Patriarch Greek Orthodox Ch., Constantinople, Turkey, 1976; mem. Council Archdiocese N.Am. and S.Am., N.Y.C., 1982—. Served with USAF, 1944-46, PTO. Mem. ABA. Republican. Private international, Corporate taxation, Real property. Office: 777 3d Ave New York NY 10017

PROVANZANO, JOSEPH STEPHEN, lawyer; b. Chelsa, Mass., Apr. 10, 1947; s. Salvatore Dayton and Virginia (Ricciardi) P.; m. Priscilla Diane Chalmers, July 28, 1968; children: Jennifer Diane, Jason Gabriel. BA, Suffolk U., 1970; JD, New England Sch. Law, 1975. Bar: Mass. 1975, U.S. Dist. Ct. Mass. 1976, U.S. Ct. Appeals (1st cir.) 1976, U.S. Supreme Ct. 1982. Sole practice Boston, 1975-79; ptnr. Hayt, Hayt & Landau, Peabody, Mass., 1979-85; ptnr. Rome, George & Vogler, Boston, 1985, of counsel, 1985—; v.p., gen. counsel Healthco Internat. Inc., Boston, 1986—. Author: Massachusetts Colection Law, 1985, rev. edit., 1986, Massachusetts Collection Technique and the Law, 1985, rev. edit., 1986. Legal counsel Lynn (Mass.) Day Activity Ctr., 1979-86, Greater Lynn Friends of Retarded, 1979-86. Served with N.G. USAR, 1967-73. Mem. New England Adjustment Mgrs. Assn. (legal counsel 1979-86). Republican. Roman Catholic. Lodge: Elks. Avocations: skiing, golf, tennis, fishing, hunting. General corporate, Personal injury, General practice. Home: 5 Hampton Ct Lynnfield MA 01940 Office: Healthco Internat Inc 25 Stuart St Boston MA 02116

PROVENZALE, MARYELLEN KIRBY, judge; b. Chgo., Dec. 21, 1938; d. Cornelius A. and Hanora (O'Sullivan) Kirby; children: Donald J. Jr., James P., John G., Patrick L. BA, Mundelein Coll., 1960; JD, DePaul U., 1977. Bar: Ill. 1977, U.S. Dist. Ct. (no. dist.) Ill. 1978. Asst. state's atty. DuPage County, Wheaton, Ill., 1977-85; assoc. judge Ill. 18th jud. cir. DuPage County, Wheaton, 1985—. V.p. Oak Creek Homeowners Assn., Downers Grove, Ill., 1974; mem. criminal justice adv. com., Coll. DuPage, Glen Ellyn, 1984—. Recipient award Glen Ellyn Family Shelter, 1984. Mem. ABA, Ill. Bar Assn., DuPage County Bar Assn., DuPage Assn. Women Lawyers. Roman Catholic. Judicial administration. Home: 1225 Candlewood Dr Downers Grove IL 60515 Office: DuPage County 18th Jud Cir 201 Reber St Wheaton IL 60187

PROVENZANO, VINCENT, lawyer. s. Peter and Lucia (Spagnuolo) P.; m. Gladys Audrey Post, Aug. 2, 1975 (div. July 1982); m. Kay Carpenter, July 6, 1984. BBA, U. Mich., 1974, JD, 1977. Bar: Mich. 1978, U.S. Dist. Ct. (ea. and we. dists.) Mich. 1980, U.S. Ct. Appeals (6th cir.) 1981. Asst. bank mgr. Owosso (Mich.) Savs. Bank, 1974-75; atty. Consumers Power Co., Jackson, Mich., 1978—; sr. v.p., gen. counsel (on leave from Consumers Power) Bandwidth Techs., Inc., Jackson, spring 1985. Del. Dem. Party of Shiawassee County, Mich., 1972. Mem. ABA, Jackson County Bar Assn. Roman Catholic. Lodge: KC. Avocations: golf, bowling, softball, college football and basketball. Personal injury, State civil litigation, General corporate. Home: 2402 Denton Rd Jackson MI 49203 Office: Consumers Power Co 212 W Michigan AVe Jackson MI 49201

PROVENZANO, WILLIAM JOSEPH, lawyer; b. Melrose Park, Ill., Sept. 11, 1949; s. Anthony and Doris Alma (Taylor) P.; m. Jean Ulahogeorge, June 27, 1970; children: Adam Randall, Amanda Taylor. BA, No. Ill. U., 1971; postgrad., U. Ill., 1971-72; JD, John Marshall Law Sch., 1975. Bar: Ill. 1975, U.S. Dist. Ct. (no. dist.) Ill. 1976. Asst. atty. gen. State of Ill., Chgo., 1976-78; sole practice Chgo., 1978-81; atty. Atlantic RIchfield Co., Rolling Meadows, Ill., 1981-86; house counsel Lawson Products Inc., Des Plaines, Ill., 1986—. Mem. ABA, Chgo. Bar Assn., Des Plaines C. of C. and Industry. Avocations: history, golf, raquetball, fishing, travel. General corporate, Pension, profit-sharing, and employee benefits, Labor. Office: Lawson Products Inc 1666 E Touhy Ave Des Plaines IL 60016

PROVORNY, FREDERICK ALAN, lawyer; b. Bklyn., Sept. 7, 1946; s. Daniel and Anna (Wurm) P.; m. Nancy Ileene Wilkins, Nov. 21, 1971; children—Michelle C., Cheryl A., Lisa T., Robert D. B.S. summa cum laude, NYU, 1966; J.D. magna cum laude, Columbia U., 1969. Bar: N.Y. 1970, U.S. Supreme Ct. 1973, D.C. 1975, Mo. 1977; C.P.A., Mo. Law clk. to Judge Harold R. Medina, U.S. Ct. Appeals (2d cir.), N.Y.C., 1969-70; asst. prof. law Syracuse U., 1970-72; assoc. Debevoise, Plimpton, Lyons & Gates, N.Y.C., 1972-75; lectr. Bklyn. Law Sch., Bklyn., 1973-74; assoc. Cole & Groner P.C., Washington, 1975-76; with Monsanto Co., St. Louis, 1976-86, asst. co. counsel, 1978-86; sole practice, Washington, 1986-87, ptnr. Keller & Heckman, 1987—; pres. Sci. and Tech. Assocs., Inc., 1986—. Trustee, Christian Woman's Benevolent Assn. Youth Home, 1979-83. Mem. ABA, Am. Law Inst., Fed. Bar Assn., Assn. Bar City N.Y., Bar Assn. Met. St. Louis (treas. Young Lawyers Sect. 1980-81), Am. Arbitration Assn. (panel comml. arbitrators), Beta Gamma Sigma. Jewish. Clubs: Philo-Mt. Sinai Lodge No. 968, Masons. Contbr. articles to profl. jours. General corporate, Administrative and regulatory, Environment. Home: 11803 Kemp Mill Rd Silver Spring MD 20902 Office: Keller & Heckman 1150 17th St NW Suite 1000 Washington DC 20036

PROVOST, JAMES H(ARRISON), law educator, b. Washington, Oct. 15, 1939; s. Oscar A. and Mary (Howe) P. B.A., Carroll Coll., 1959; S.T.B., U. Louvain (Belgium), 1963, M.A., 1963; J.C.D., Lateran U., Rome, 1967. Chancellor Diocese of Helena, Mont, Roman Catholic Ch. and officialis (presiding judge of Diocesan Tribunal), Helena, 1967-79; assoc. prof. canon law Catholic U. Am., 1979—, also chmn. dept. Canon law; exec. coordinator Canon Law Soc. Am., Washington, 1980-86 . Mem. Cath. Theol. Soc. Am., Canon Law Soc. Am., Can. Canon Law Soc., Canon Law Soc. Gt. Brit. and Ireland, Societe Internationale de droit religieuses et comparees, Consociatio Internationalis. Legal education. Office: Dept of Canon law Am Catholic U Washington DC 20064

PROVOSTY, LEDOUX ROGER, JR., lawyer; b. Alexandria, La., May 24, 1930; s. LeDoux Roger and Miriam Kendall (Baskerville) P.; m. Barbara Anne St. Paul, June 9, 1951; children: Barbara, Jeanne, LeDoux III, Henry, William, Allain, Eugenie. BA, Tulane U., 1951, LLB, 1955. Bar: La. 1955. Assoc. Provosty, Sadler & Scott, Alexandria, 1955-60, ptnr., 1960-65; ptnr. Provosty, Sadler & deLaunay, Alexandria, 1965—; city bd. dirs. Hibernia Nat. Bank, Alexandria. Chmn. Pub. Affairs Research Council, La., 1985—; dean's council Tulane U. Sch. Law. Served to lt. comdr. USNR, 1950-53, Korea. Fellow Am. Bar Found., Am. Coll. Trial Lawyers; mem. La. Bar Assn. (pres. 1986—), La. Bar Found. (life). Democrat. Roman Catholic. Federal civil litigation, State civil litigation. Home: 4503 Willowick Blvd Alexandria LA 71303 Office: Provosty Sadler & deLaunay 934 3d St Alexandria LA 71301

PROZAN, SYLVIA SIMMONS, lawyer, television newscaster; b. Cleve., Apr. 10, 1933; d. James M. and Dora (Shuman) Simmons; m. George B. Prozan, June 24, 1956; children—Michael, Lawrence, Anne, Rebecca. B.A., Barnard Coll., 1955; M.A., Case Western Reserve U., 1959; J.D., U. Calif.-Berkeley, 1975. Bar: Calif. 1976, U.S. Supreme Ct. 1980. Television prodn. staff NBC, N.Y.C.; pub. affairs staff sta. KQED, KPIX, San Francisco, 1963-65; television newscaster, investigative reporter sta. KNTV, San Jose, Calif., 1968-72; adj. prof. J. F. Kennedy Law Sch., Orinda, Calif., 1979-82; sole practice, Burlingame, Calif., 1976—. Mem. State Bar Calif., Calif. Trial Lawyers Assn., Bar of San Francisco, San Mateo County Bar Assn., Union Internationale des Avocats, AAUW. Democrat. Jewish. State civil litigation, Family and matrimonial, Legal education. Home: 2180 Forest View Ave Hillsborough CA 94010

PRUITT, JANA LEE, lawyer; b. Spokane, Wash., Oct. 6, 1955; d. Ben Marvin and Opal Ellen (McGuire) P. B.A. in Polit. Sci., U. Ky., 1977; J.D., U. Louisville, 1980. Bar: Ky. 1981. Assoc. firm Hardy, Logan & Priddy, Louisville, 1979-81; atty. Am. Ins. Assn., N.Y.C., 1982-85; atty. Health Ins. Assn. Am., Washington, 1985—. Mem. ABA, Ky. Bar Assn., Republican. Methodist. Club: Kentuckians of N.Y. Insurance, Legislative. Office: Health Ins Assn Am 1025 Connecticut Ave NW Washington DC 20036

PRUITT, ROBERT GRADY, JR., lawyer; b. Atlanta, Feb. 9, 1930; s. Robert Grady and Ruth (Crockett) P.; m. Ruth Brooks, Sept. 7, 1952; children—Robert Grady III, Bonnie, Sandra, William; B.A., Emory U., 1952, M.S., 1952; J.D., U. Utah, 1962. Bar: Utah 1962. Geologist, AEC, Butte, Mont., 1952-54; geologist, mineral adjudicator U.S. Bur. Land Mgmt., Salt Lake City, 1954-62; assoc. Senior & Senior, Salt Lake City, 1962-66; assoc. Neslen & Mock, Salt Lake City, 1966-70; pres. Pruitt, Gushee & Fletcher, Salt Lake City, 1970—; pres. GeoScout Land & Title Co., Salt Lake City. Mem. Rocky Mountain Mineral Law Found. (trustee, pres. 1978), Utah Assn. Petroleum and Mining Landmen, Utah Geol. Assn. Clubs: University, Elks, Rotary. Oil and gas leasing, Mining and minerals, Real property. Home: 4475 Zarahemla Dr Salt Lake City UT 84117 Office: Pruitt Gushee & Fletcher PC 1850 Beneficial Life Tower Salt Lake City UT 84111

PRUTZMAN, LEWIS DONALD, JR., lawyer; b. Phila., Nov. 1, 1951; s. L. Donald and Caroline (Butler) P.; m. Deborah Sorace, May 24, 1975; children—Sarah, Stephen. A.B., Harvard Coll., 1973; J.D., N.Y.U., 1976. Bar: Pa. 1976, N.Y. 1977, U.S. Dist. Ct. (so. and ea. dists.) N.Y. 1977, U.S. Dist. Ct. (ea. dist.) Pa. 1977, U.S. Ct. Appeals (9th cir.) 1979, U.S. Supreme Ct. 1980, U.S. Ct. Appeals (2d cir.) 1983. Law clerk to judge U.S. Dist. Ct., Phila., 1976-77; assoc. Cravath, Swaine, & Moore, N.Y.C., 1977-84; ptnr. Stecher Jaglom & Prutzman, N.Y.C., 1984—; mem. Fed. Bar Counsel 2nd Cir. Cts. Com., N.Y.C., 1984—. Mem. N.Y. State Bar Assn., ABA, Pa. Bar Assn. Antitrust, Federal civil litigation, State civil litigation. Office: Stecher Jaglom & Prutzman 900 3d Ave New York NY 10022

PRYE, STEVEN MARVELL, lawyer; b. Memphis, Nov. 13, 1952; s. John Allen and Thelma Inez (Buckner) P. BA, Yale U., 1974; JD, Harvard U., 1978; LLM in Taxation, NYU, 1985. Bar: N.Y. 1979, U.S. Dist. Ct. (ea. and so. dists.) N.Y. 1981, U.S. Tax Ct. 1984. Assoc. Stroock, Stroock & Lavan, N.Y.C., 1978-83, DeForest & Duer, N.Y.C., 1983-86, Phillips, Nizer, Benjamin, Krim & Ballon, N.Y.C., 1986—. Sr. editor Harvard Civil Rights and Civil Liberties Law Rev., 1977-78. Named one of Outstanding Young Men of Am., U.S. Jaycees, 1983. Mem. ABA (estate taxation of lifetime transfers com., real property probate and trust law sects.), N.Y. State Bar Assn. (legis., estate planning coms., trust and estates law sect.), Assn. Bar of City of N.Y. (young lawyers com.), NAACP, ACLU, Common Cause Com. Democrat. Avocations: opera, reading, theater, travel. Estate planning, Probate, Estate taxation. Home: 111 Fourth Ave 12 E New York NY 10003 Office: Phillips Nizer Benjamin Krim & Ballon 40 W 57th St New York NY 10019

PRYOR, SHEPHERD GREEN, III, lawyer; b. Fitzgerald, Ga., June 27, 1919; s. Shepherd Green and Jeffie (Moore) P.; m. Lenora Louise Standifer, May 17, 1941 (dec.); m. Ellen Wilder, July 13, 1984; 6 children from previous marriage: Sandra Pryor Clarkson, Shepherd Green, Robert Stephen, Patty Pryor Smith (dec.), Alan Persons, Susan Lenora. BSAE, Ga. Inst. Tech., 1947; JD, Woodrow Wilson Coll. Law, Atlanta, 1974. Bar: Ga. 1974, U.S. Dist. Ct. (no. dist.) Ga. 1974, U.S. Ct. Appeals (5th cir.) 1974, U.S. Ct. Appeals (11th cir.) 1982, U.S. Supreme Ct. 1977. Sole practice, Atlanta, 1974—. Trustee Masonic Children's Home of Ga. Served to capt. U.S. Army, 1941-45. Mem. Ga. Bar Assn., Mensa, Intertel, Sigma Delta Kappa. Republican. Methodist. General practice, General corporate, Real property. Address: 135 Spalding Dr Atlanta GA 30328

PRYOR, WILLIAM BERNARD, lawyer; b. N.Y.C., Apr. 17, 1950; s. Leo and Mary (Rauf) P.; m. Victoria Eugenia Mejia, Apr. 16, 1983; 1 child, Jonathan. BA, SUNY, Albany, 1971; JD, N.Y. Law Sch., 1974. Bar: N.Y. 1975, U.S. Dist. Ct. (so. and ea. dists.) N.Y. 1977, Calif. 1978, U.S. Ct. Appeals (2d cir.) 1978, U.S. Supreme Ct. 1985. Sole practice Law Offices of William Pryor, N.Y.C., 1979—. Mem. Am. Immigration Lawyers Assn. Immigration, naturalization, and customs. Office: 277 Broadway Suite 1208 New York NY 10007

PTASZEK, EDWARD GERALD, JR., lawyer; b. Cleve., Sept. 29, 1950; s. Edward Gerald and Roseanne (Venetta) P.; m. Lucinda Ptaszek, June 20, 1978. JD, Case Western Res. U., 1978. Bar: Ohio, U.S. Dist. Ct. (no. dist.) Ohio, U.S. Tax. Ct. Assoc. Baker & Hostetler, Cleve., 1978-85, ptnr., 1985-86; ptnr. Baker & Hostetler, Columbus, Ohio, 1986—. Mem. ABA, Cleve. Bar Assn., Columbus Bar Assn. Clubs: Hermit (Cleve) (sec. 1985—); Capital (Columbus). Corporate taxation, Personal income taxation, Municipal bonds. Office: Baker & Hostetler 65 E State St Columbus OH 43215

PUCCINELLI, LEO J., lawyer; b. Fagnano, Lucca, Italy, Sept. 8, 1921; came to U.S., 1924; s. Andrea and Gemma (Lemucchi) P.; m. Gertrude Viola Ford; children: Andrew J., Janet P. Basl, Gayle A., Carol A. BA, U. Nev., 1946; JD, U. San Francisco, 1950. Bar: Nev. 1950, U.S. Dist. Ct. Nev. 1950. Ptnr. Castle & Puccinelli, Elko, Nev., 1950-53; sole practice Elko, 1953-78; ptnr. Puccinelli & Puccinelli, Elko, 1978—. Del. Nat. Rep. Conv., Kansas City, Mo., 1976, alt. del., Miami, Fla., 1972; vice chmn. Elko County Reps., 1954; chmn. advisory bd. Nev. Youth Training Ctr., 1967-77; mem. Pub. Defenders Selection Commn., 1971-75, Nev. State Commn. on Crime Delinquency and Corrections, 1975-81, Jud. Discipline Commn., 1982—, Nev. Racing Commn., 1986—. Served with USMC, 1942-45. Mem. Nev. Bar Found. (trustee 1982—), Nev. Bar Assn. (pres. 1976-77, bd. govs. 1966-78), Elko County Bar Assn., Western States Bar Conf. (pres. 1979-80), Nev. Trial Lawyers Assn., Elko Jaycees (life). Roman Catholic. Lodges: Rotary, Elks (exalted ruler 1964-65, 82-84), KC. Family and matrimonial, Personal injury, Probate. Home: 567 14th St Elko NV 89801 Office: Puccinelli & Puccinelli PC 217 1st Interstate Bank Bldg Elko NV 89801

PUCHEU, JOHN HENRI, lawyer; b. Eunice, La., July 2, 1951; s. Jacque B. and Jean (Fontenot) P.; m. Joanne E. Lane, 1977. BS, La. State U., 1973, JD, 1978; LLM, U. Miami, 1979. Bar: La. 1979, U.S. Dist. Ct. (mid. and we. dists.) La. 1979, U.S. Tax. Ct. 1979, U.S. Ct. Appeals 1979. Ptnr. Pucheu & Pucheu, Eunice, 1979—; bd. dirs. Indigent Defender Bd. 27th Jud. Dist., State of La. Participant Liberty Theatre Restoration Project, Eunice, 1986; mem. Eunice Players Theatre. Mem. ABA, La. Bar Assn. (cert. tax atty.), St. Landry Parish Bar Assn., Assn. Trial Lawyers Am., La. Trial Lawyers Assn. Democrat. Roman Catholic. Club: Eunice Country (sec. 1980—). Lodge: Rotary (v.p. Eunice chpt. 1983-85, pres. 1985-86, bd. dirs. 1982—). General practice, Probate, Personal injury. Office: Pucheu & Pucheu PO Box 1109 Eunice LA 70535

PUFFER, LEONARD BRUCE, JR., lawyer; b. Orange, N.J., Dec. 5, 1928; s. Leonard Bruce and Alice (Hartigan) P.; children: Cheryl Ann, Donald Bruce. BS in Bus. Adminstrn., Upsala Coll., 1951; LLB, Seton Hall U., 1957. Bar: N.J. 1957, U.S. Dist. Ct. N.J. 1957, N.Y. 1982, U.S. Ct. Appeals (3d cir.) 1983. Ptnr. Shanley & Fisher P.C., Newark, 1963—; v.p. Shanley & Fisher P.C., Newark and Morristown, N.J., 1981—. Mem. Essex County Ethics Com., Newark, 1970-73; mem. Essex County Dist. Fee Arbitration Com., 1978-83, chmn., 1982-83. Served to sgt. USMC, 1952-54, Korea. Mem. ABA, Fed. Bar Assn., N.J. Bar Assn., Essex County Bar Assn., Morris County Bar Assn., Assn. Trial Lawyers Am., Trial Attys. N.J. Clubs: Morris County Golf, Morristown (N.J.), Essex (Newark). Federal civil litigation, State civil litigation, Personal injury. Home: Schoolhouse Ln Morristown NJ 07960 Office: Shanley & Fisher PC 131 Madison Ave Morristown NJ 07960

PUGH, DAVID EDWARD, lawyer; b. Union, N.Y., July 3, 1950; s. William and Arline (Loudenburg) P.; m. Karin L. Brooks, Sept. 27, 1980; children: Jonathan, Brian, Catherine. Student, Syracuse U., 1968-69; BA, SUNY, Binghamton, 1972; JD, Bklyn. Law Sch., 1975. Bar: N.Y. 1976, U.S. Dist. Ct. (ea. and so. dists.) N.Y. 1977. Sole practice N.Y.C., 1976-81; assoc. Wallman & Kramer, N.Y.C., 1981-83, ptnr., 1984—; lectr. Women's Survival Space, Bklyn., 1978-81; cons. Playcare, Inc., Katonah, N.Y., 1983—. Mem. ABA (family law sect.), N.Y. State Bar Assn. (family law sect.), Assn. Trial Lawyers Am., N.Y. Trial Lawyers Assn. Republican. Presbyterian. Family and matrimonial, State civil litigation. Home: 55 Bedford Rd Katonah NY 10536 Office: Wallman & Kramer 275 Madison Ave New York NY 10016

PUGH, GEORGE WILLARD, legal educator; b. Napoleonville, La., Aug. 17, 1925; s. William Whitmell and Evelyn (Foley) P.; m. Jean Earle Hemphill, Sept. 6, 1952; children: William Whitmell III, George Willard, David Nicholls, James Hemphill. B.A., La. State U., 1947, J.D., 1950; J.S.D., Yale U., 1952; Dr. h.c., U. Aix-Marseille III, France, 1984. Bar: La. 1950. Instr. La. State U. Law Sch., 1950, mem. faculty, 1952—, prof. law, 1959—, Julius B. Nachman prof. law, 1984—; faculty summer session abroad U. Thessaloniki Greece summer 1974, Aix-en-Provence, France, 1985; mem. faculty summer program U. San Diego, Paris, 1977; part-time research cons. La. State Law Inst., 1953-54; 1st jud. adminstr. Jud. Council Supreme Ct. La., 1954-56; vis. prof. U. Tex., summer 1961; vis. Doherty prof. law U. Va., 1966-67; mem. faculty orientation program in Am. law Assn. Am. Law Schs., 1968, law teaching clinic, summer 1969; vis. prof. U. Aix-Marseille (France), 1983; cons. La. State U.S. Vietnam Legal Adminstrn. Project, 1969. Author: Louisiana Evidence Law, 1974, supplement, 1978; Co-author: Cases and Materials on the Administration of Criminal Justice, 2d edit, 1969; coordinator, reporter: Code of Evidence for La. Bd. dirs. Legal Aid Soc. Baton Rouge, 1965—, chmn., 1963-64; adv. bd. St. Alban's Episcopal Student Center, La. State U., 1965-68, 70-72. Served with AUS, World War II. Fellow Comparative Study Adminstrn. Justice, 1962-65. Mem. Am., La., Baton Rouge bar assns., Order of Coif, Omicron Delta Kappa, Lambda Chi Alpha. Democrat. Episcopalian. Criminal, Comparative, Evidence criminal justice law. Home: 167 Sunset Blvd Baton Rouge LA 70808

PUGH, IRBY GENE, lawyer; b. Montgomery, Ala., Jan. 22, 1943; s. Bert O'Neal and Eliza Jordan (Owen) P.; m. Betsy Ann Kerner, June 18, 1961 (div. July 1967); children—Glenn Edward, Eric Norman, Lisa Michelle. B.S., Calif., Poly. Inst., 1966; postgrad. in engring. U. Fla., 1967-69, J.D., 1972. Bar: Fla. 1972, U.S. Ct. Appeals (5th and 11th cirs.) 1973, U.S. Supreme Ct. 1979. Sr. engr. Martin-Marietta Co., Orlando, Fla., 1966-69; mem. staff U. Fla., Gainesville, 1970-72; assoc. Groshorn, Nabors, Miller & McClelland, Titusville, Fla., 1972-73, Fernandez & Scarito, Orlando, 1973-75; ptnr. Barco & Pugh, Orlando, 1975-78; sole practice, Orlando, 1978-86; ptnr., Pugh & Carpenter, 1986—. Coach Little League baseball and football, Orlando, 1973-76; del. Fla. Democratic Conv., 1982; mem. Dem. Exec. Com., Orange County 1984, chmn. 1986—; Dem. candidate Fla. Ho. of Reps., 1984; active Lawton Chiles Re-election Com., 1987—. Recipient several awards Rotary, Kiwanis. Mem. Assn. Trial Lawyers Am., ABA, Nat. Assn. Criminal Def. Lawyers, Fla. Bar Assn, Sierra Club (various awards), League Conservation Voters (bd. dirs. 1982—, awards 1982-83). General practice, Environment, Criminal. Office: 218 Annie St Orlando FL 32806

PUGH, WILLIAM WALLACE, lawyer; b. Flushing, N.Y., Sept. 13, 1941; s. Wallace Raymond and Martha (Greenewald) P.; m. Joyce Curry, Dec. 17, 1977; children: James Thomas, Kristin Anne, Katherine Elizabeth. BS in Physics, Bucknell U., 1963; MS in Ops. Research, NYU, 1966; JD, Cath. U., 1972. Bar: D.C. 1973, U.S. Dist. Ct. D.C. 1976, U.S. Ct. Appeals (D.C. cir.) 1977, U.S. Supreme Ct. 1977. Electronics engr. Grumman Aircraft Engring. Corp., Beth Page, N.Y., 1964-65; mem. tech. staff TRW Systems Group, McLean, Va., 1966-69; advertising examiner FTC, Washington, 1970-72; assoc. Keller & Heckman, Washington, 1972-75; gen. counsel Nat. Motor Freight Traffic Assn., Alexandria, Va., 1975—. Mem. ABA, D.C. Bar Assn., Fed. Bar Assn., Transp. Lawyer Assn., Assn. Transp. Law Practitioners, Delta Theta Phi. Administrative and regulatory, Federal civil litigation, Transportation. Home: 3404 Kimberly Dr Falls Church VA 22042 Office: Nat Motor Freight Traffic Assn 2200 Mill Rd Alexandria VA 22314

PUGLIA, PHYLLIS MARY, lawyer; b. New Orleans, Jan. 5, 1955; d. Francis Anthony and Jane Catherine (Hernandez) P. BA, Southeastern La. U., 1976; JD, La. State U., 1979. Bar: La. 1979, U.S. Dist. Ct. (ea. dist.) La. 1980, U.S. Dist. Ct. (we. dist.) La. 1981. Sole practice Chalmette, La., 1979—. Mem. La. Bar Assn., 34th Jud. Dist. Bar Assn. St. Bernard Parish. Democrat. Roman Catholic. Consumer commercial, Probate, General practice. Home: 417 Doerr Dr Arabi LA 70032 Office: 8301 W Judge Perez Dr 1st Nat Bank Bldg Suite 300 Chalmette LA 70043

PUGLIESE, ROBERT F., corporate executive, lawyer; b. W. Pittston, Pa., Jan. 15, 1933. B.S., U. Scranton, 1954; LL.B., Georgetown U., 1957, LL.M., 1959; grad. advanced mgmt. program Harvard U., 1976. Bar: D.C. 1957, U.S. Dist. Ct. 1957, U.S. Ct. Claims 1958, U.S. Tax Ct. 1957, U.S. Ct. Appeals 1957. Assoc. Hedrick & Lane, Washington, 1957-60; tax counsel Westinghouse Electric Corp., Pitts., 1961-70, gen. tax counsel, 1970-75, v.p., gen. tax counsel, 1975-76, v.p., gen. counsel, sec., 1976—; dir. Westinghouse Credit Corp., Westinghouse Broadcasting, Inc. Trustees La Roche Coll., Pitts.; bd. dirs. St. Francis Health System, Pitts., St. Francis Med. Ctr., Pitts.; mem. exec. com. U. Scranton. Mem. ABA, Assn. Gen. Counsel. General corporate. Office: Westinghouse Bldg Gateway Ctr Pittsburgh PA 15222

PUHALA, JAMES JOSEPH, lawyer; b. Pitts., Sept. 5, 1942; s. Leo Andrew and Agnes (Ruglovsky) P.; m. Linda Sue Lash, Oct. 1, 1977; children: Stephen, Susan, Matthew. BBA, U. Dayton, 1964; MBA, U. Pitts., 1965; JD, Duquesne U., 1974. Bar: Pa. 1974, U.S. Dist. Ct. (we. dist.) Pa. 1974. Mgr. internat. taxes Dravo Corp., Pitts., 1974-79, sr. counsel, 1979-86, group gen. counsel, 1986-87, v.p., assoc. gen. counsel, 1987—. Decorated D.F.C., Bronze Star. Mem. ABA, Allegheny County Bar Assn. Contracts commercial, Construction, General corporate. Home: 149 Inglewood Dr Pittsburgh PA 15228 Office: Dravo Corp 1 Oliver Plaza Pittsburgh PA 15222

PUJADAS, THOMAS EDWARD, lawyer; b. Havana, Cuba, Sept. 20, 1953; s. Guillermo Manuel and Yolanda Ezperanza (de Moya) P.; m. Jeanne Ruth Thigpen, Oct. 28, 1978; children: Kristin Joy, Kari Ann. Student, Emory U., 1971-72; BS, Fla. State U., 1975; JD, U. Fla., 1978. Bar: Fla. 1978, Ga. 1981, U.S. Dist. Ct. (mid. dist.) Ga. 1981, U.S. Dist. Ct. (mid. dist.) Fla. 1981, U.S. Ct. Appeals (5th and 11th cirs.) 1981. Asst. state atty. 4th Jud. Cir. Fla., Jacksonville, 1978-81; ptnr. Walters, Davis, Smith, Meeks & Pittman, Ocilla, Ga., 1981—; atty. Wilcox County, Ga., 1984—. Mem. Fla. Bar Assn., Ga. Bar Assn., Tifton Jud. Cir. Bar Assn. Democrat. Roman Catholic. Avocations: sailing, fishing, hunting, carpentry. General practice, State civil litigation, Contracts commercial. Office: Walters Davis Smith Meeks & Pittman Cherry St Ocilla GA 31774

PULEO, FRANK CHARLES, lawyer; b. Montclair, N.J., Nov. 25, 1945; s. Frank and Kathren (Despenzerie) P.; m. Alice Kathren Leek, June 1, 1968; children—Frank C., Richard James. B.S.E., Princeton U., 1967; J.D., N.Y.U., 1970. Bar: N.Y., 1971. Ptnr., Milbank, Tweed, Hadley & McCloy, N.Y.C., 1970—. Mem. ABA (mem. com. on fed. regulation securities), N.Y. State Bar Assn. Banking, Contracts commercial, General corporate. Office: 1 Chase Manhattan Plaza New York NY 10005

PULIGNANO, NICHOLAS VINCENT, JR., lawyer; b. Jacksonville, Fla., May 20, 1952; s. Nicholas V. Sr. Pulignano and Claire Lee (Garner) Ansley; m. Clara Elizabeth McCarty, Mar. 3, 1984. BS in Math., U. N.C., 1974; JD, U. Fla., 1980. Bar: Fla. 1981, U.S. Dist. Ct. (so., mid. and no. dists.) Fla. 1982, U.S. Ct. Appeals (5th and 11th cirs.) 1982. From assoc. to ptnr. Marks, Gray, Conroy & Gibbs, Jacksonville, 1981—. Served to lt. USN, 1974-78. Mem. Jacksonville Bar Assn., Jacksonville Assn. Def. Counsel, Def. Research Inst., Phi Beta Kappa. Democrat. Episcopalian. Club: Timuquana Country Club. Lodge: Rotary. Avocations: golf, tennis. State civil litigation, Securities, General corporate. Office: Marks Gray Conroy & Gibbs 1200 Gulf Life Dr PO Box 447 Jacksonville FL 32201

PULIS, GREGORY MILTON, lawyer; b. Ridgewood, N.J., Apr. 4, 1952. AB, Dartmouth Coll., 1974; JD, U. Va., 1977. Bar: N.Y. 1978, U.S. Dist. Ct. (so. and ea. dists) N.Y. 1978. Assoc. atty. LeBoeuf Lamb Leiby & MacRae, N.Y.C., 1977-79, Greenbaum, Wolff & Ernst, N.Y.C., 1980-81; bus. affairs exec. William Morris Agy. Inc., N.Y.C., 1981—. Mem. ABA, Assn. Bar of City of N.Y. (entertainment and sports law com.). Entertainment, Securities, General corporate. Home: 3 E 9th St New York NY 10003 Office: William Morris Agy Inc 1350 Ave of the Americas New York NY 10019

PULLEY, LEWIS CARL, lawyer, military officer; b. Okla. City, Aug. 19, 1954; s. George Robert Jr. and Harriet Ruth (Meyers) Pulley. Student, Oxford U., England, 1974; BA with high honors, U. Okla., 1976; JD, Am. U., 1979. Bar: Pa. 1981, U.S. Ct. Mil. Appeals 1982, U.S. Ct. Appeals (D.C. cir.) 1985, U.S. Supreme Ct. 1985, D.C. 1987. Commd. 1st lt. USAF, 1982, advanced through grades to capt., 1982; asst. staff judge adv. Legal Office USAF, Langley AFB, Va., 1982-83; asst. staff judge adv. Legal Office USAF, RAF Upper Heyford, England, 1983-84, area def. counsel Judiciary, 1984-85; asst. staff judge adv. Legal Office USAF, Peterson AFB, Colo., 1985-86, staff judge adv., 1986—. Contbr. over 500 articles to 11 newspapers and mags. (recipient Investigative Reporting award, Okla. City Gridiron Found., 1975, Media award for Econ. Understanding, Dartmouth Bus. Sch., 1980). Ewing Found. fellow, 1975. Mem. ABA, Pa. Bar Assn., Fed. Bar Assn., D.C. Bar Assn., Sigma Delta Chi. Democrat. Jewish. Club: Theodore Roosevelt Assn. (Oyster Bay, N.Y.). Avocations: travel, jogging, collecting polit. paraphernalia, photography. Legislative, Communications. Home: 3586-D Parkmoor Village Dr Colorado Springs CO 80907 Office: 1 Space Wing/JA Peterson AFB CO 80914

PULLIAM, KAREN ANN, lawyer; b. Detroit, Mar. 1, 1950; d. John Benjamen and Caroline G. (Carpenter) P. BS in Spl. Edn., Wayne State U., 1972; MA in Adult Edn., Mich. State U., 1975; JD, U. Detroit, 1981. Bar: Mich. 1981, U.S. Dist. Ct. (ea. dist.) Mich. 1981, U.S. Dist. Ct. (no. dist.) Tex. 1984, Tex. 1985. Dir. Continuation Sch. Lapeer (Mich.) County Intermediate Sch. Dist., 1973-78; assoc. Miller, Canfield, Paddock & Stone, Detroit, 1981-84, Johnson & Swanson, Dallas, 1984-86; ptnr. Pulliam, Hale, Spencer, Goodman, Stanley, Pronske & Trust, P.C., Dallas, 1986—. Mem. ABA, Tex. Bar Assn., Mich. Bar Assn., Fed. Bar Assn., Dallas Bar Assn., Dallas Bankruptcy Bar Assn., Am. Bankruptcy Inst., Comml. Law League., Dallas Bus. and Profl. Women's Club (chmn. women in govt. com. 1986—). Democrat. Roman Catholic. Avocations: reading, traveling, gardening. Bankruptcy, Federal civil litigation, Contracts commercial. Home: 10303 Baronne Circle Dallas TX 75218 Office: Pulliam Hale Spencer et al 2800 InterFirst Plaza LB131 Dallas TX 75250

PULLIAM, MARK STEPHEN, lawyer; b. Bethesda, Md., Nov. 15, 1955; s. Barrett F. and Mary (Reed) P.; m. Jane Anne Kost, May 11, 1985. BS, Am. U., 1977; JD, U. Tex., 1980. Law clk. to judge U.S. Ct. Appeals (9th cir.), Los Angeles, 1980-81; assoc. Latham & Watkins, Los Angeles and San Diego, Calif., 1981—. Contbr. articles to profl. jours. Recipient James Madison award Legal Found. Am., 1983. Mem. ABA, Calif. Bar Assn. Republican. Labor, Federal civil litigation, State civil litigation. Office: Latham & Watkins 701 B St Suite 2100 San Diego CA 92101

PULOS, WILLIAM WHITAKER, lawyer, educator; b. Hornell, N.Y., Aug. 29, 1955; s. William Leroy and Juanita (Whitaker) P. BA in Econs. magna cum laude, Alfred U., 1977; JD, Union U., 1980. Bar: N.Y. 1982, U.S. Bankruptcy Ct. 1982, U.S. Supreme Ct. 1987. Assoc. Degnan and Hotvet, P.C., Canisteo, N.Y., 1981-82; sole practice, Alfred, N.Y., 1982—; prof. bus. adminstrn. Alfred U., 1981—; prof. bus. adminstrn. SUNY-Alfred, 1982-84; tutor Empire State Coll., 1982-86, Alfred State Coll., 1982-86; atty. Town of Alfred, 1982—; atty. Village of Almond, N.Y., 1983—, Allegany County and Steuben County Assigned Counsel Program for Indigent Defendants, 1982-85; spl. prosecutor Allegany County, 1984—; asst. counsel N.Y. State Assembly, 1980; hearing officer N.Y. State Small Claims Assessment Rev., 1983—; dist. tax atty. and appraiser N.Y. State Dept. Taxation and Fin., 1983—. Active Alfred Sta. Vol. Firemen's Assn., Inc., 1985—; treas. Alfred Community Organizers and Renovators, 1985-86. Recipient Outstanding Young Men of Am. award U.S. Jaycees, 1982, 86. Mem. ABA (profl. standards sect.), N.Y. State Bar Assn. (gen. practice sect., ins., negligence and workers compensation sect.), Steuben County Bar Assn., City of Hornell Bar Assn., Canisteo Bar Assn., Allegany County Bar Assn., Assn. Trial Lawyers Am., N.Y. State Trial Lawyers Assn., Am. Arbitration Assn. (comml. panel arbitrators 1983—), Alfred Bus. Assn. Inc., N.Y. State Beef Cattlemen's Assn. (state legislation com. 1982-83, legal counsel state and local divs., so. tier div. treas. 1981-83, asst. sales mgr. 1984, sales mgr. 1985-86), Delta Sigma Phi (local adv. bd., counsel local bd.), N.Y. State Sheriff's Assn. (hon.), U.S. Jaycees. Lodge: Lions. State civil litigation, Federal civil litigation, Personal injury. Office: 44 N Main Box 803 Alfred NY 14802

PUMPHREY, GERALD ROBERT, lawyer; b. Flushing, N.Y., May 31, 1947; s. Fred Paul and Anne (Afferman) P.; m. Joann DeLillo, Oct. 6, 1968; children: Gerald, Christopher, Elena. BBA, St. John's U., 1969, MBA, 1974; JD, Nova U., 1978. Bar: Fla. 1978. Assoc. Walden & Walden, Dania, Fla., 1978; v.p. legal services Golden Bear, Inc., North Palm Beach, Fla., Jack Nicklaus & Assocs., Air Bear, Inc., also bd. dirs., v.p., sec. Triple P, Inc., 1978-83; sole practice, 1983—. Bd. advisors Benjamin Sch. Found. Athletics Assn., 1980-83; coordinator Benjamin Sch. Found., Inc.; mem. golf com. St. Clare's Sch., pres. Home and Sch. Assn., 1983-84. Mem. ABA, Palm Beach County Bar Assn., Palm Beach Gardens C. of C. (co-counsel 1983-86), No. Palm Beach County/Palm Beach Gardens C. of C. (co-counsel), Phi Alpha Delta. Lodge: Kiwanis (charter mem., bd. dirs. Palm Beach Gardens). General corporate, Real property, General practice. Address: 824 US Hwy One Suite 260 North Palm Beach FL 33408

PURCELL, EDWARD ALOYSIUS, JR., lawyer, historian; b. Kansas City, Mo., July 20, 1941; s. Edward A. Sr. and Josephine Marie (O'Neil) P.; m. Rachel Vorspan, Sept. 5, 1982; children: Daniel, Jessica. AB, Rockhurst Coll., 1962; MA, U. Kans., 1964; PhD, U. Wis., 1968; JD, Harvard U., 1979. Asst. prof. U. Calif., Berkeley, 1967-69; assoc. prof. U. Mo., Columbia, 1969-77; vis. assoc. prof. Wellesley (Mass.) Coll., 1974-75; instr. Harvard U., Cambridge, Mass., 1978-79; assoc. Paul, Weiss, Rifkind, Wharton & Garrison, N.Y.C., 1980—. Author: Crisis of Democratic Theory, 1973 (Frederick Jackson Turner prize 1973); also numerous articles (Pelzer prize 1967, Am. Quarterly prize 1983). Fellow Social Sci. Research Council, 1971-72, Harvard Law Sch., 1971-72, 79, Am. Phil. Soc. 1974, Am. Council Learned Socs., 1975, NEH, 1977-78, Ford-Am. Council Learned Socs., 1987-88. Mem. ABA, Assn. of Bar of City of N.Y., NAACP, ACLU, Common Cause. Democrat. Federal civil litigation, State civil litigation, Legal history. Home: 15 W 84th St 4A New York NY 10024 Office: Paul Weiss Rifkind et al 1285 Ave of Americas New York NY 10019

PURCELL, GARY MORGAN, judge; b. Oklahoma City, Dec. 26, 1950; s. Fred Allison and Evelyn (Morgan) P.; m. Chris Aubrey, Aug. 11, 1973; children—Bradley, Michael, Katherine. B.A., U. Okla., 1973; J.D., Oklahoma City U., 1975; grad. Nat. Jud. Coll., Reno, 1980. Bar: Okla. 1976, U.S. Dist. Ct. (we. dist.) Okla. 1976, U.S. Ct. Appeals (10th cir.) 1976. Legal intern Okla. Ct. Criminal Appeals, Oklahoma City, 1975; law clk. U.S. Dist. Ct., Oklahoma City, 1976-79; judge Dist. Ct. Cleveland County, Norman, Okla., 1979—. Dist. vice-chmn. Last Frontier council Boy Scouts Am., Norman, 1980-84. Recipient Am. Jurisprudence awards, 1973-75. Mem. ABA, Okla. Bar Assn., Fed. Bar Assn., Okla. Jud. Conf., Cleve. County Bar Assn., Phi Gamma Delta, Phi Alpha Delta. Democrat. Methodist. Judicial administration, Criminal, State civil litigation. Office: Dist Ct Cleve County 200 S Peters St Norman OK 73069

PURCELL, JAMES EDWARD, lawyer; b. Hempstead, N.Y., July 12, 1945; s. Edward Thomas and Gladys M. P.; m. Margaret M. Kelly, Feb. 1969; children—Ryan, Adam, Kathryn. B.A., Cornell U., 1967; J.D. magna cum laude, Boston U., 1974. Bar: Maine 1974, U.S. Dist. Ct. Maine 1974, U.S. Ct. Appeals (1st cir.) 1978, U.S. Dist. Ct. R.I. 1980, R.I. 1980, Mass. 1985, U.S. Dist. Ct. Conn. 1985. Assoc. Pierce Atwood Scribner Allen Smith & Lancaster, Portland, Maine, 1974-80; assoc., ptnr. Tillinghast, Collins & Graham, Providence, 1980—. Dist. leader Barrington Republican Town Com. (R.I.), 1983-87, chmn., 1987—; mem. Zoning Bd. Rev., Barrington, 1982—. Served to 1st lt. U.S. Army, 1968-71, Vietnam. Mem. ABA (sect. litigation), Am. Trial Lawyers Assn., R.I. Trial Lawyers Assn., Bristol County C. of C. (v.p., dir. 1982—). Republican. Roman Catholic. Federal civil litigation, State civil litigation, Personal injury. Home: 6 Elton Rd Barrington RI 02806 Office: Tillinghast Collins & Graham One Old Stone Sq Providence RI 02903

PURCELL, PAUL M., lawyer; b. Saginaw, Mich., Oct. 22, 1948; s. John Paul and Dorothy R. (Fyle) P.; m. Sally Ann Northway, June 24, 1970; children: Andrew, Amy, Peter. BS, Cen. Mich. U., 1970; JD, Detroit Coll. Law, 1973. Bar: Mich. 1973, U.S. Dist. Ct. (ea. dist.) Mich. 1975. Asst. city atty. City of Saginaw (Mich.), 1973-75; ptnr. Purcell, Tunison & Cline, P.C., Saginaw, 1975—. Bd. dirs. St. Stephen's Sch., Saginaw, 1985—. Mem. ABA, Mich. Bar Assn., Assn. Trial Lawyers Am., Mich. Trial Lawyers Assn. Democrat. Roman Catholic. Avocation: golf. General practice, Insurance, Personal injury. Home: 4470 Seidel Saginaw MI 48603 Office: Purcell Tunison & Cline 5090 State Bldg A Saginaw MI 48603

PURCELL, WILLIAM PAXSON, III, lawyer; b. Phila., Oct. 25, 1953; s. William Paxson Jr. and Mary Lucille (Hamilton) P.; m. Deborah Lee Miller, Aug. 9, 1986. AB, Hamilton Coll., 1976; JD, Vanderbilt U., 1979. Bar: Tenn. 1979, U.S. Dist. Ct. (we. dist.) Tenn. 1980, U.S. Dist. Ct. (mid. dist.) 1985, U.S. Ct. Appeals (6th cir.) 1985, U.S. Supreme Ct. 1986. Staff atty. West Tenn. Legal Services, Jackson, 1979-81; sr. asst. pub. defender Office Pub. Defender Met. Nashville-Davidson County, Nashville, 1981-85; assoc. Lionel R. Barrett, Jr., Nashville, 1985-86; ptnr. Farmer, Berry & Purcell, Nashville, 1986—. Mem. exec. com. 6th dist. Dems., Nashville, 1986—; mem. State Ho. of Reps., Nashville, 1986—; vice chmn. vol. adv. bd. Tenn. Dept. of Corrections, 1986—. Mem. ABA, Nashville Bar Assn., Tenn. Assn. Criminal Def. Lawyers (bd. dirs. 1985-86), Tenn. Bar Assn. Baptist. Criminal, Juvenile, Family and matrimonial. Home: PO Box 60331 Nashville TN 37206 Office: Farmer Berry & Purcell 131 Second Ave N Nashville TN 37201

PURCELL, WILLIAM RIKER, lawyer; b. Richmond, Va., Aug. 22, 1947; s. Thomas Williamson and Martha Converse (Pierce) P.; m. Virginia Harvie Stevens, June 29, 1973; children: Charlotte Brooke, Anne Riker. BA, Va. Mil. Inst., 1970; MEd, U. Va., 1975; JD, Washington and Lee U., 1979. Bar: Ga. 1979, Va. 1981. Assoc. Oliver, Maner & Gray, Savannah, Ga., 1979-81, Glenn, Flippin, Feldmann & Darby, Roanoke, Va., 1981-84; assoc. counsel claims Lawyers Title Ins. Corp., Richmond, 1984—. Bd. dirs. Southwest Va. Opera Soc., Roanoke, 1983-84, Va. Mil. Inst. Library, Lex-

ington, 1987—. Served to capt. USAR, 1977-85. Real property, Insurance. Office: Lawyers Title Ins Corp 6630 W Broad St Richmond VA 23230

PURDOM, WAYNE MILLER, judge; b. Phila., Apr. 14, 1953; s. P. Walton and Bettie (Miller) P.; m. Susan B. Ellis, June 19, 1977; children: Karen, Elizabeth, Catherine. BA in Econs. cum laude, Yale U., 1974; JD, Emory U., 1977, LLM in Taxation, 1980. Bar: Ga. 1977, U.S. Dist. Ct. (no. dist.) Ga. 1977. Ptnr. Purdom & Ellis, Decatur, Ga., 1977-84; assoc. judge Magistrate Ct. DeKalb, Decatur, 1983-84, chief judge, 1985—; cons. in field, Decatur, 1978—. Mem. Ga. Bar Assn., Decatur-DeKalb Bar Assn., Ga. Trial Lawyers Assn. Democrat. Methodist. Judicial administration, State civil litigation, Federal civil litigation. Home: 208 Heatherdown Rd Decatur GA 30030 Office: Magistrate Ct DeKalb County DeKalb Courthouse Room 807 Decatur GA 30030

PURDY, ROGER DANIEL, law educator; b. Sandusky, Ohio, Nov. 12, 1951; s. William Henry and Ann Phoebe (Hamilton) P.; m. Danna Wells Chase, June 24, 1978. AB, Harvard U., 1975; JD, Boston U., 1978. Bar: Mass. 1981, U.S. Dist. Ct. Mass. 1981, U.S. Ct. Appeals (1st cir.) 1981, U.S. Supreme Ct. 1985. Lectr. U. Zambia, Lusaka, 1978-80; staff atty. Ctr. for Criminal Justice Boston U. Law Sch., 1980-81; asst. prof. U. Akron Law Sch., Ohio, 1981-86, assoc. prof, 1986—; cons. Law Devel. Commn., Lusaka, 1979-80; vis. researcher Harvard U. Law Sch., Cambridge, Mass., 1985—; bd dirs. Legis. Research Drafting Service, Akron, 1981—. Contbr. articles to profl. jours. Mem. Lawyers in MENSA. Computer, Legal education, Jurisprudence. Office: U Akron Law Sch Akron OH 44325

PURNELL, CHARLES GILES, lawyer; b. Dallas, Aug. 16, 1921; s. Charles Stewart and Ginevra (Locke) P.; widowed; children—Mimi, Sarah Elizabeth, Charles H., John W. Student Rice Inst., 1938-39; B.A., U. Tex., 1941; student Harvard Bus. Sch., 1942; LL.B., Yale U., 1947. Bar: Tex. 1948. Ptnr., Locke, Purnell, Boren, Laney & Neely, Dallas, 1947—; exec. asst. to Gov. of Tex., Austin, 1973-75. Bd. dirs. Trinity River Authority of Tex., 1975-81; vice chmn. Tex. Energy Adv. Council, 1974. Served to lt. U.S. Navy, 1942-45; PTO. Mem. ABA, Tex. Bar Assn., Tex. Bar Found. Episcopalian. Clubs: Yale, Dallas Country, Dallas (Dallas); Headliners, Town and Gown (Austin); La Jolla (Calif.) Beach and Tennis. General practice, Condemnation, Local government. Home: 4502 Watauga Rd Dallas TX 75209 Office: 3600 Republic Nat Bank Tower Dallas TX 75201

PURSER, DONALD JOSEPH, lawyer; b. Chgo., Apr. 21, 1954; s. Donald Cornelius and Mary Alice (Fashingbauer) P.; m. Dana Lanai Maddy, Nov. 10, 1985. BS, U. Utah, 1975; MS, Reid Coll., 1976; JD, George Mason U., 1980; postdoctoral, Georgetown U., 1981. Bar: Va. 1980, U.S. Tax Ct. 1980, U.S. Ct. Appeals (4th and 10th cirs.) 1980, Utah 1981. Spl. agt. U.S. Dept. of State, Washington, 1976-80; law clk. to judge U.S. Dist. Ct., Alexandria, Va., 1980-81; assoc. Richards, Brandt, Miller & Nelson, Salt Lake City, 1981-83; sole practice Salt Lake City, 1983-85; ptnr. Fowler & Purser, Salt Lake City, 1985—; judge pro tem Salt Lake County Cir. Ct., 1981-85; adj. faculty U. Phoenix, Salt Lake City, 1984—; advance staff office of v.p. of U.S., Washington, 1986—; bd. dirs. Great Am. Get Aways, Inc., Chgo., Am. Western Life Ins. Co., Tarzana, Calif. Mem. ABA (litigation sect., torts and ins. practice sect.), Am. Inn of Ct. II (barrister). Republican. Roman Catholic. Club: Blue Goose (Salt Lake City). Lodge: K.C. Avocations: skiing, stock market, reading. Insurance, State civil litigation, Personal injury. Home: 9850 South 2900 E Sandy City UT 84092 Office: Fowler & Purser 340 E 4th South St Salt Lake City UT 84111

PURSLEY, RICKY ANTHONY, law librarian; b. Wareham, Mass., July 11, 1954; s. Gene Everett and Evelyn May (Silveira) P.; m. Susan Elizabeth Scott, Nov. 27, 1982. BA in Polit. Sci., Boston U., 1976; postgrad., Southwestern U., 1976-78. Law librarian Graham & James, Los Angeles, 1977-79; legal copy editor Arnold & Porter, Washington, 1980-85; law librarian, legal asst. Fisher, Wayland, Cooper & Leader, Washington, 1985—. Named one of Outstanding Young Men in Am. U.S. Jaycees, 1978. Mem. Am. Assn. Law Librarians. Democrat. Roman Catholic. Avocations: music, writing, carpentry. Librarianship, General corporate, Administrative and regulatory. Home: 730 North Abingdon St Arlington VA 22203-2016 Office: Fisher Wayland Cooper & Leader 1255 23d St NW Suite 800 Washington DC 20037-1125

PURTLE, JOHN INGRAM, justice Ark. Supreme Ct.; b. Enola, Ark., Sept. 7, 1923; s. John Wesley and Edna Gertrude (Ingram) P.; m. Marian Ruth White, Dec. 31, 1951; children: Jeffrey, Lisa K. Student, U. Central Ark., 1946-47; LL.B., then J.D., U. Ark., Fayetteville, 1950. Bar: Ark. bar 1950, Fed. bar 1950. Individual practice law Conway, Ark., 1950-53, Little Rock, 1953-78; mem. Ark. State Legislature, 1951-52, 69-70; asso. justice Ark. Supreme Ct., 1979—. Tchr., deacon Baptist Ch. Served with U.S. Army, 1940-45. Mem. Ark. Bar Assn., Am. Judicature Soc., Am. Bar Assn., Ark. Jud. Council. Democrat. Jurisprudence. Office: Supreme Court 3004 Painted Valley Little Rock AR 72212 *

PURVIS, DANIEL BURFORD, lawyer, oil and gas consultant; b. Little Rock, Nov. 19, 1910; s. Walter Moody and Lucy Helen (Burford) P.; m. Susanna Ely, Feb. 1943 (div. Apr. 1949); children—Dana, Robert; m. Elizabeth Harwood Hoskins, Aug. 15, 1950; children—Stephen, Marcia. LL.B., Cumberland U., 1932; J.D., Stamford U., 1939. Bar: Ark. 1932, Tex. 1936, U.S. Dist. Ct. (we. dist.) Tex. 1946. Ptnr. Purvis & Purvis, Hot Springs, Ark., 1932-36; sole practice, San Diego and Alice, Tex., 1936-41; oil producer Dan Purvis and Assocs., San Diego and Alice, 1937-41; pres. Loma Novia Oil Corp., San Diego, Tex., 1937-41; ptnr. Rawlins & Purvis, Monahans, Tex., 1946-47; city atty. City of Monahans, 1947; oil producer Dan Purvis and Assocs., Odessa, Corpus Christi, Tex., 1948-50; sole practice, Odessa and Corpus Christi, 1948-50; pres. Drilcheck Corp., San Antonio, 1957-58; chmn. Fed. Petroleum Bd., Kilgore, Tex., 1961; oil and gas defense cons. Office Sec. Interior, Washington, 1962; oil and gas defense specialist Southeastern U.S. and Panama Canal Zone, Thomasville, Ga., 1962; oil and gas operator, producer Dan Purvis, Marble Falls, Tex., 1964-82; sole practice, Marble Falls, 1965-68; city atty. City of Granite Shoals, Tex., 1968-69; pres. Petrotech Corp., Dallas, 1969-70; oil and gas producer, cons., sole practice law, Austin, Tex., 1982-85; oil cons. RPC Investments, Inc., 1984. Author: Fifty Years in the Texas Oil Patch, 1982. Inventor automatic drilling mud gas analizer, 1954, computer finger, 1982, moth destructor, 1983. Sec. Garland County Young Democrats, Hot Springs, Ark., 1932. Served to capt. USAF, 1942-45. Mem. ABA, Am. Legion, Am. Petroleum Inst., Tex. Bar Assn., Ark. Bar Assn. Methodist. Clubs: Optimist (Marble Falls, Tex.) (pres. 1967); Civitan (Hot Springs, Ark.). Lodges: Masons, Elks, Rotary. Oil and gas leasing. Home: 255 Meadowlakes Dr Marble Falls TX 78654 Office: 1811 W 35th St Austin TX 78703

PURVIS, JOHN ANDERSON, lawyer; b. Greeley, Colo., Aug. 31, 1942; s. Virgil J. and Emma Lou (Anderson) P.; m. Charlotte Johnson, Apr. 3, 1976; 1 child, Whitney; children by previous marriage—Jennifer, Matt. B.A. cum laude, Harvard U., 1965; J.D., U. Colo., 1968. Bar: Colo. 1968, U.S. Dist. Ct. Colo. 1968, U.S. Ct. Appeals (10th cir.) 1978, U.S. Ct. Claims, 1980. Dep. dist. atty. Boulder, Colo., 1968-69; asst. dir. and dir. legal aid U. Colo. Sch. Law, 1969; assoc. Williams, Taussig & Trine, Boulder, 1969; head Boulder office Colo. Pub. Defender System, 1970-72; assoc. and ptnr. Hutchinson, Black, Hill, Buchanan & Cook, Boulder, 1972-85; ptnr. Buchanan, Gray, Purvis and Schuetze, 1985—; acting Colo. State Pub. Defender, 1978; adj. prof. law U. Colo., 1981, 84—, others; lectr. in field. Chmn., Colo. Pub. Defender Commn., 1979—; mem. nominating commn. Colo. Supreme Ct., 1984—; chmn. Boulder County Criminal Justice Com., 1975-81, Boulder County Manpower Council, 1977-78. Recipient Ames award Harvard U., 1964; Outstanding Young Lawyer award Colo. Bar Assn., 1978. Mem. Internat. Soc. Barristers, Colo. Bar Assn., Boulder County Bar Assn., Colo. Trial Lawyers Assn., Am. Trial Lawyers Assn., Trial Lawyers for Pub. Justice. Democrat. Personal injury, State civil litigation, Federal civil litigation. Address: 1050 Walnut St Suite 501 Boulder CO 80302

PUSCH, HERBERT BARRINGER, lawyer; b. Detroit, Feb. 19, 1930; s. Herbert Valentine and Verna Jane (Schumacher) P.; m. Judith Lucille Gustafson, May 20, 1977; children—Hans Barringer, Kurt Gustafson. A.B. in Econs. and Polit. Sci., Cornell U., 1952, M.B.A., 1957, J.D., 1959. Bar: Ill. 1959, U.S. Dist. Ct. (no. dist.) Ill. 1959, U.S. Ct. Appeals (7th cir.) 1978. Assoc. Epton Scott McCarthy & Bohling, Chgo., 1959-60, Schumacher Gilmore, Staub & Payne, Chgo., 1961-70; ptnr. Kelly Olson Pusch Rogan & Siepker and predecessor firm Schumacher Jones Kelly Olson & Pusch, Chgo., 1971—. Author extensive memoranda distributed to U.S. Army officers worldwide, 1981, 83. Sec. Santa Claus Anonymous, Chgo., 1965—; trustee Shattuck-St. Mary's Schs., Faribault, Minn., 1972—. Served with U.S. Army, 1952-54. Decorated Army Commendation medal, Meritorious Service medal. Mem. Chgo. Bar Assn., Ill. Bar Assn., ABA, Ill. Trial Lawyers Assn., Assn. Trial Lawyers Am., Trial Lawyers Club Chgo. Republican. Episcopalian. State civil litigation, Federal civil litigation, Labor. Home: 253 Vine Lake Forest IL 60045 Office: Kelly Olson Pusch Rogan & Siepker Three First Nat Plaza Chicago IL 60602

PUTMAN, LINDA MURRAY, lawyer; b. Greenwich, Conn., June 22, 1953; s. Francis Joseph and Clare Marie (Fassinger) P. AB, Brown U., 1975; JD, U. Conn., 1978. Bar: Conn. 1979, Pa. 1981, U.S. Dist. Ct. (we. dist.) Pa. 1983, U.S. Ct. Appeals (3d cir.) 1983. Assoc. Law Offices of Lawrence E. Larson, Greenwich, 1978-80; law clk. to presiding justice Lawrence County Ct. Common Pleas, New Castle, Pa., 1980-83; assoc. Law Office of Lawrence E. Larson, Greenwich, 1983-86; cons. Consumer Communications Products div. GTE, Stamford, Conn., 1986. Mem. ABA, Conn. Bar Assn. Avocations: endurance and competitive trail riding, running. Private international, Contracts commercial. Home: 36 Ridgeview Ave Greenwich CT 06830 Office: GTE Consumer Communications div 30 Buxton Farms Rd Stamford CT 06905

PUTMAN, (JAMES) MICHAEL, lawyer; b. San Antonio, May 12, 1948; s. Harold David and Elizabeth Finley (Henderson) P. B.B.A., S.W. Tex. State U., 1969; J.D., St. Mary's U., 1972. Bar: Tex. 1972, U.S. Dist. Ct. (we. dist.) Tex. 1980, U.S. Ct. Appeals (5th and 11th cirs.) 1981; cert. personal injury trial law specialist Tex. Bd. Legal Specialization. Ptnr. Putman & Putman (inc. 1981), San Antonio, 1972-81, officer, dir., 1981—. Mem. State Bar Tex. (com. to test qualifications dist. X, 1973—), Assn. Trial Lawyers Am., Tex. Criminal Def. Lawyers Assn., Tex. Trial Lawyers Assn., San Antonio Trial Lawyers Assn. (dir., officer 1975—). Personal injury, Workers' compensation, Labor. Office: Tower Life Bldg 27th Floor San Antonio TX 78205

PUTNAM, PHILIP CONRAD, lawyer; b. Charlottesville, Va., Dec. 7, 1954; s. Gerrie Price and Liane Marie (Seim) P.; m. Lori L. Younger, July 21, 1979; 1 child, Christian Philip. BS in Bus., U. So. Calif., 1977, JD, 1980. Bar: Calif. 1980, U.S. Dist. Ct. (no., cen., ea. and so. dists.) Calif. 1980, U.S. Ct. Appeals (9th cir.) 1980, U.S. Ct. Claims 1984, U.S. Tax Ct. 1984. Assoc. Monteleone & McCrory, Los Angeles, 1980-84, ptnr., 1985—; sec. Rekortan Sports Corp., Seattle, 1982—; bd. dirs. Eby Mine Services Inc., Los Angeles, Kemper Constrn., Los Angeles, Flocrete Mfg. Co., Los Angeles. Elder Faith Luth. Ch., Pasadena, Calif., 1984—; mem. various coms. Calif. Reps., 1980—. Named one of Outstanding Young Men Am., 1983. Mem. ABA, Los Angeles County Bar Assn. (child care com. 1984—), Wilshire Bar Assn. (gov. 1984—), Ill. CPA Soc., Acctg. Circle. Republican. Clubs: Legion Lex, (Los Angeles). Avocations: sailing, skiing, horticulture. General corporate, Corporate taxation, State and local taxation. Home: 2052 Crestlake Ave South Pasadena CA 91030 Office: Monteleone & McCrory 10 Universal City Plaza Suite 2500 Universal City CA 91608

PUTNAM, TERRY MICHAEL, lawyer; b. Albany, Ga., June 7, 1954; s. Thomas Arnold and Betty Lavonia (Taylor) P.; m. Leigh Ann Smith, Aug. 20, 1983. BA, U. Ala., 1976, JD, 1979. Bar: Ala. 1979, U.S. Dist. Ct. (no. dist.) Ala. 1980, U.S. Ct. Appeals (5th cir.) 1980, U.S. Ct. Appeals (11th cir.) 1981, U.S. Supreme Ct. 1985. Assoc. Potts, Young & Blasingame, Florence, Ala., 1979-83; ptnr. Potts, Young, Blasingame & Putnam, Florence, 1983—; univ. atty. U. North Ala., Florence, 1984—. Mem. ABA, Nat. Assn. Coll. and Univ. Attys., Ala Trial Lawyers Assn., Order of Coif, Phi Beta Kappa. Democrat. Avocations: sailing, reading. General practice, Insurance, College & University Law. Home: 513 N Wood Ave Florence AL 35630 Office: Potts Young Blasingame & Putnam 107 E College St Florence AL 35631

PUTTOCK, JOHN LAWRENCE, lawyer; b. Santa Barbara, Calif., Apr. 15, 1949; s. Lawrence Marion and Kathleen (McDonough) P.; m. Erika Sakurai, Oct. 7, 1978. B.A. in Anthropology, U. Calif.-Santa Barbara, 1971; J.D., Golden Gate U., 1976. Bar: Calif. 1977, U.S. Dist. Ct. (cen. dist.) Calif. 1981. Assoc. Law Offices of Fujii & Toda, Tokyo, 1977-81; legal counsel Tokyo Marine Mgmt., Inc., Los Angeles, 1981—. Editor, translator: Products Liability in the U.S., 1983. Alexander Bee scholar, 1973-74, Calif. State scholar, 1967-71. Mem. ABA, Sigma Alpha Epsilon. Insurance, Personal injury, Private international.

PUTZEL, CONSTANCE KELLNER, lawyer; b. Balt., Sept. 5, 1922; d. William Stummer and Corinne (Strauss) Kellner; m. William L. Putzel, Aug. 28, 1945; 1 son, Arthur William. A.B., Goucher Coll., 1942; LL.B., U. Md., 1945, J.D., 1969. Bar: Md. bar 1945. Social worker Balt. Dept. Pub. Welfare, 1945-46; atty. New Amsterdam Casualty Co., Balt., 1947; staff atty. Legal Aid Bur., Balt., 1947-49; with Putzel & Putzel, P.A., Balt., 1950—; pres. Putzel & Putzel, P.A., 1975—; instr. U. Balt. Sch. Law, 1975-77, Goucher Coll., 1976-77; Mem. character com. Ct. Appeals of Md., 1976—. Mem. Md. Com. on Status of Women, 1972-76; mem. Com. to Implement ERA, 1973-76; Pres. U. Md. Law Alumni Assn., 1978; bd. dirs. Legal Aid Bur., 1951-52, 71-73. Fellow Am. Acad. Matrimonial Lawyers; mem. ABA, Md. Bar Assn. (bd. govs. 1972-73, chmn. family law sect. 1978-79), Bar Assn. Balt. City (exec. com. 1970-71), Women's Bar Assn. Balt. (pres. 1951-52), United World Fedn. (vice chmn. nat. exec. council 1968, chmn. Balt. 1967-69). Family and matrimonial. Home: 8207 Spring Bottom Way Pikesville MD 21208 Office: 1700 Reisterstown Rd Pikesville MD 21208

PUYANIC, MAX DANIEL, lawyer; b. Evergreen Park, Ill., Oct. 19, 1947; s. Max F. and Helen B. (Nowicki) P.; children from a previous marriage: Max Jason, David Alexander; m. Jennie E. Puyanic, July, 1986; 1 child, Michael Angelo. BBA, Roosevelt U., 1968; JD, U. Miami, 1972. Bar: Fla. 1972. Sole practice Miami, Fla., 1972—; treas., bd. dirs. Brickell Area Assn., Miami, 1986—. Mem. Dade County Bar Assn. Roman Catholic. Avocations: boating, swimming, fishing, diving. Office: 59 SW 9th St Miami FL 33130

PUZO, MICHAEL JOHN, lawyer; b. N.Y.C., Nov. 2, 1952; s. Henry Joseph and Margaret Cecilia (Murphy) P.; m. Christine Marie Pollock, June 1, 1974; children: Mary Elizabeth, Kathleen, Eileen, James. BA, Boston Coll., 1974, JD, 1977. Bar: Mass. 1977, U.S. Dist. Ct. Mass. 1977. Assoc. Hemenway & Barnes, Boston, 1977-83, ptnr., 1984—. Co-author: Massachusetts Corporations, 1982. Vice chmn. Hingham Bd. Appeals, Mass., 1985—; mem. Hingham Transp. Com., Mass., 1981-85. Mem. ABA, Mass. Bar Assn., Boston Bar Assn., Boston Estate and Bus. Planning Council, Boston Coll. Estate Planning Council (chmn. 1984—), Phi Beta Kappa. Democrat. Roman Catholic. Avocation: singing. Probate, Estate planning, Estate taxation. Home: 83 Cross St Hingham MA 02043 Office: Hemenway & Barnes 60 State St Boston MA 02109

PYFER, JOHN FREDERICK, JR., lawyer; b. Lancaster, Pa., July 25, 1946; s. John Frederick and Myrtle Ann (Greiner) P.; m. Carol Trice, Nov. 25, 1970; children—John Frederick III, Carol Lee. Grad. cum laude, Peddie Sch., 1965; B.A. in Polit. Sci. and Econs., Haverford Coll., 1969; J.D., Vanderbilt U., 1972. Bar: Pa. 1972, U.S. Dist. Ct. (ea. dist.) Pa. 1973, U.S. Tax Ct. 1975, U.S. Supreme Ct. 1975, U.S. Dist. Ct. (mid. dist.) Pa. 1984, U.S. Ct. Appeals (3d cir.) 1986. Law clk. to presiding justice Ct. Common Pleas, Lancaster, Pa., 1972-74; assoc. Xakellis, Perezous & Mongiovi, 1972-76; founding ptnr. Allison & Pyfer, Lancaster, 1976-85, pres. Pyfer & Assocs., 1986—; prof. para-legal tng. Pa. State Extension Service. Council commr., Lancaster-Lebanon Council Boy Scouts Am. Recipient First prize Howard C. Schwab Nat. Essay Contest in Writing, 1972; Eagle Scout with 3 palms, God and Country award, and Order of Arrow, Boy Scouts Am. Mem. Nat. Assn. Criminal Def. Lawyers, Assn. Trial Lawyers Am., Pa. Trial Lawyers Assn., Am. Arbitration Assn., ABA, Pa. Bar Assn., Lancaster Bar Assn., Christian Lawyers Soc., SAR. Republican. United Ch. of Christ (deacon). Clubs: Lions (pres. 1980-82) (Willow Street, Pa.); Masons (Lancaster). Contbr. articles to law revs., law treatises. Criminal, Family and matrimonial, General practice. Home: 1090 Richmond Rd Lancaster PA 17603 Office: Pyfer and Assocs 128 N Lime St Lancaster PA 17603

PYLE, CHARLES VICTOR, JR., judge; b. Greenville, S.C., Dec. 24, 1934; s. Charles Victor and Eugenia (Smith) P.; m. Johanna Douglas Wright, June 8, 1957; children: Louisa Douglas, Sarah Bryson, Charles Victor III. LLB, U. S.C., 1959, JD, 1970; postgrad. Nat. Jud. Coll., 1980. Bar: S.C. 1959, U.S. Dist. Ct. (we. dist.) S.C. 1959, U.S. Ct. Appeals (4th cir.) 1960. Ptnr. Pyle & Pyle Attys., Greenville, S.C., 1959-76; asst. city atty. City of Greenville, 1963-65, mcpl. ct. judge, 1965-68; county judge County of Greenville, 1976-79; resident judge 13th cir. State of S.C., Greenville, 1979—; mem. S.C. Ho. of Reps., 1969-74, 1st vice-chmn. jud. com., 1973-74; chmn. Adv. Com. on Standards Jud. Conduct, 1980—; mem. S.C. Jud. Council, 1984—. Recipient Disting. Service award City of Greenville, 1968, award ABA, 1968. Mem. Am. Judicature Soc. (bd. dirs. 1966-70), S.C. Bar Assn. (cir. v.p. 1966-67, pres. young lawyers conf. 1963-64), S.C. Assn. Circuit Judges (sec.), Phi Delta Phi (pres. 1959). Presbyterian. Judicial administration. Home: 12 Quail Hill Dr Greenville SC 29607 Office: 310 County Courthouse Greenville SC 29601

PYLE, FRANK LEFOREST, SR., lawyer; b. Lewiston, Maine, Aug. 9, 1919; s. Guy LeForest and Marguerite Marie (Chauvin) P.; m. Beatrice DeBacker, Nov. 29, 1968; children: Michael A., Susan B., Patricia M., Frank LeForest, Jr. AB, U. Fla., 1946, JD with honors, 1949. Bar: Fla. 1949, U.S. Dist. Ct. (so. dist.) Fla. 1949. Sr. ptnr. Kinsey, Vincent & Pyle, P.A., Daytona Beach, Fla., 1949—. Chmn. Peabody Auditorium Adv. Bd., Daytona Beach, 1960-70; chmn. County Law Library Trustees, Daytona Beach, 1977—, Jud. Nominating Commn., Fla., 1977-79; treas. Daytona Beach Art League, 1980—. Served to capt. U.S. Army, 1941-46, ETO; col. Res. Decorated 2 Bronze Stars, Purple Heart. Mem. ABA, Fla. Bar Assn., Volusia County Bar Assn. (pres. 1975-76), Judge Advocate's Assn., Fla. Bar (real property, probate and trust sects.), Am. Judicature Soc., U. Fla. Law Rev. Alumni, Res. Officers Assn., Mil. Order World Wars, Phi Delta Phi, Kappa Sigma (v.p. 1941). Democrat. Clubs: Halifax Yacht (commodore 1961), Daytona Playhouse (pres.). Lodge: Kiwanis (pres. Halifax 1962). Estate planning, Probate, Real property. Home: 416 Pelican Bay Dr Daytona Beach FL 32119 Office: Kinsey Vincent & Pyle PA PO Box 3096 Daytona Beach FL 32018

PYLE, LUTHER ARNOLD, lawyer; b. Pontotoc County, Miss., Dec. 5, 1912; s. Thomas Luther and Lillie Dean (Reynolds) P.; m. Elizabeth McWillie Browne, Aug. 9, 1941; children—William A., Robert Bradford, Ben Cameron. LL.B., Cumberland U., 1936, J.D., 1960. Bar: Miss. 1936, D.C. 1974, U.S. Dist. Ct. (no. dist.) Miss. 1936, U.S. Dist. Ct. (so. dist.) Miss. 1946, U.S. Ct. Apls. (5th cir.) 1946, U.S. Ct. Appeals (11th cir.) 1961, U.S. Supreme Ct. 1959. Sole practice, New Albany, Miss., 1936-42; pros. atty. Union County, Miss., 1940-42; assoc. Cameron & Wills, Jackson, Miss., 1946-52; chancellor 5th chancery ct. dist. Miss., 1952-58; ptnr. Watkins, Pyle, Ludlam, Winter & Stennis, Jackson, 1958-80; ptnr. Barnett, Alagia & Pyle, Jackson, 1981-83; sr. ptnr. Pyle, Dreher, Mills & Woods, 1983—; participant World Law Conf., Manila, 1977, Madrid, 1979; bd. dirs. Miss. Bar Commn., 1959-63. Mem. exec. bd. Andrew Jackson council Boy Scouts Am., 1946; bd. govs. Jackson Little Theatre, 1964-67; pres. Jackson Jr. C. of C., 1949; chmn. downtown div. United Givers, Mental Health Assn. Served to lt. col. JAG Corps, U.S. Army, 1942-46. Recipient Silver Beaver award Boy Scouts Am. Fellow Miss. Bar Found.; mem. Fed. Bar Assn., ABA (chmn. continuing legal edn. 1958-74), Am. Judicature Soc. (dir.), Hinds County Bar Assn., Miss. Bar Assn. (chmn. jud. adminstrn. com. 1966-70), U.S. Supreme Ct. Hist. Soc., U.S. C. of C., Jackson C. of C. (dir. 1960-63), Miss. Dept. Res. Officers Assn. (pres. 1950), Am. Legion (past comdr.). Episcopalian. Clubs: University (dir. 1972—), Jackson Country, Annandale Golf, Capital City Petroleum. Contbr. articles to profl. jours. Federal civil litigation, State civil litigation, General practice. Home: 1803 E Northside Dr Jackson MS 39211 Office: Pyle Dreher Mills & Woods 111 E Capitol St Suite 390 Jackson MS 39201

PYLE, ROBERT MILNER, JR., professional association executive; b. Orange, N.J., Oct. 24, 1938; s. Robert M. and Dorothy (Collings) P.; m. C. Page Neville, May 31, 1969; children—Cynthia Neville, Laura Collings. B.A., Williams Coll., 1960; J.D., U. Va., 1963. Bar: N.Y. bar 1964. Assoc. firm Mudge Rose Guthrie & Alexander, N.Y.C., 1963-68; with Studebaker-Worthington, Inc., N.Y.C., 1968-77; sec. Studebaker-Worthington, Inc., 1972-76, assoc. gen. counsel, 1974-77; with Singer Co., N.Y.C., 1977-79; corp. counsel, asst. to sec. Singer Co., 1977-78, sr. corp. counsel, asst to sec., 1979; v.p., counsel Am. Soc. Corp. Secs., Inc., N.Y.C., 1979—; Career counseling rep. for Williams Coll., 1977—. Trustee Pingry Sch., Elizabeth, N.J., 1972-74; trustee Arts Council Suburban Essex Inc., 1979-84, chm. bd., 1981-84; bd. govs. Colonial Dances, Ltd., N.Y.C., 1970-74; bd. dirs., v.p. Millburn-Short Hills Hist. Soc., 1985—; trustee Suburban Community Music Ctr., 1985—. Mem. ABA, Assn. Bar City N.Y., Met. Squash Racquets Assn. (past treas.), Pingry Sch. Alumni Assn. (pres. 1972-74, dir. 1966-78, certificate of merit 1968), Pilgrims U.S., Sigma Phi, Delta Theta Phi, Pi Delta Epsilon. Republican. Episcopalian. Clubs: Racquet and Tennis (N.Y.C.); Bay Head (N.J.) Yacht, Short Hills. General corporate, Securities. Office: 1270 Ave of Americas New York NY 10020

PYLMAN, NORMAN HERBERT, II, lawyer; b. Grand Rapids, Mich., June 6, 1952; s. Norman Herbert and Yvonne Coral (Moelker) P.; m. Janet Lee VandenToorn, Sept. 9, 1977; children—Bradley David, Daniel Jonathan. B.A., Calvin Coll., 1974; J.D. with honors, U. Detroit, 1977. Bar: Mich. 1977, U.S. Dist. Ct. (we. dist.) Mich. 1977. Assoc. Cholette, Perkins & Buchanan, Grand Rapids, 1977-82, ptnr., 1982-85, ptnr. Gruel, Mills, Nims & Pylman, Grand Rapids, 1985—. Bd. dirs. Honey Creek Christian Homes, Lowell, Mich., 1978—. Mem. Grand Rapids Bar Assn., Mich. Bar Assn. (civil procedure com.), ABA. Republican. Christian Reformed. Federal civil litigation, State civil litigation, Personal injury. Home: 134 Holmdene NE Grand Rapids MI 49503 Office: Gruel Mills Nims & Pylman 50 Monroe Pl Suite 700 West Grand Rapids MI 49503

PYSELL, PAUL EDWARD, lawyer; b. Covington, Va., Jan. 20, 1944; s. Charles Glenn and Carrie (Helper) P.; children—Paula Kaye, James Paul; m. Mary Frances Lane, Mar. 1, 1981; 1 child, Paul Edward II. B.A., U. Va., 1971; J.D. cum laude, Washington and Lee U., 1974; student Judge Adv. Gen. Sch., 1975. Bar: Va. 1974, U.S. Dist. Ct. (we. dist.) Va. 1974, U.S. Ct. Mil. Appeals 1975, U.S. Ct. Appeals (4th cir.) 1978, U.S. Supreme Ct. 1986. Lawyer, dir. Legal Aid Soc., Lynchburg, Va., 1974-75; ptnr. Black, Menk, Pysell, Noland & Powers, Staunton, Va., 1978—. Mem. Hist. Stanton Found., Woodrow Wilson Birthplace Found.; bd. dirs. Staunton-Augusta Mental Health Assn., 1983—; campaign chmn. United Way Staunton-West Augusta, 1984—, pres., 1987—; fin. com. chmn. Christ United Meth. Ch., 1985—. Served to capt. U.S. Army, 1975-78; mem. Res. Decorated Meritorious Service medal. Mem. ABA, Va. State Bar, Assn. Trial Lawyers Am., N.G. Assn., Izaak Walton League, Phi Beta Kappa. Club: Parents without partners (legal adviser 1981-83). Lodges: Lions, Moose, Elks. Personal injury, State civil litigation, Federal civil litigation. Home: 480 Mountain View Dr Staunton VA 24401 Office: Black Menk Pysell Noland & Powers PO Box 1206 Staunton VA 24401-0099

PYTYNIA, THOMAS LEE, lawyer; b. Valparaiso, Ind., Mar. 1, 1947; s. Walter Joseph and Irene Elizabeth (Janowski) P.; m. Doris Mae Hirt, May 29, 1976; children: Jonathan Michael, Carolyn Ann. A.B. in History, Ind. U., 1969, J.D., 1973. Bar: Ind. 1973, U.S. Dist. Ct. (no. and so. dists.) Ind. 1973, U.S. Ct. Appeals (7th cir.) 1974, U.S. Supreme Ct. 1978. Law clk. U.S. Dist. Ct. (no. dist.) Ind., Fort Wayne, 1973-74; assoc. Baker & Daniels, Indpls., 1974-77; atty. Eli Lilly & Co., Indpls., 1977-80; gen. counsel, IVAC Corp., San Diego, 1980-85; sr. counsel, Eli Lilly and Co., 1986—. Served with U.S. Army, 1970-72. Mem. Ind. Bar Assn., Phi Beta Kappa. Republican. Roman Catholic. Antitrust, Contracts commercial, General corporate. Home: 4978 Limberlost Trace Carmel IN 46032 Office: Eli Lilly and Co Lilly Corporate Ctr Indianapolis IN 46285

QUACKENBUSH, JUSTIN LOWE, U.S. dist. judge; b. Spokane, Wash., Oct. 3, 1929; s. Carl Clifford and Marian Huldah (Lowe) Q.; m. Marie McAtee; children: Karl Justin, Kathleen Marie, Robert Craig. B.A., U. Idaho, 1951; LL.B., Gonzaga U., Spokane, 1957. Bar: Wash. 1957. Dep. pros. atty. Spokane County, 1957-59; ptnr. Quackenbush, Dean, Bailey & Henderson, Spokane, 1959-80; U.S. dist. judge Eastern Dist. Wash., Spokane, 1980—; part-time instr. Gonzaga U. Law Sch., 1960-67. Chmn. Spokane County Planning Commn., 1969-73. Served with USN, 1951-54.

Mem. ABA, Wash. Bar Assn., Spokane County Bar Assn. (trustee 1976-78), Internat. Footprint Assn. (nat. pres. 1967), Spokane C. of C. (trustee, exec. com. 1978-79). Episcopalian. Club: Spokane Country. Lodge: Shriners. Jurisprudence. Office: US District Court 949 US Courthouse Spokane WA 99201 *

QUADRI, FAZLE RAB, lawyer; b. Dacca, Pakistan, Aug. 5, 1948; came to U.S., 1967; s. Gholam Moula and Jehan (Ara) Q.; children: Ryan F., Tania M. AA, Western Wyo. State, 1969; BA, Calif. State U., 1972; JD, Western State U., 1978. Bar: Calif. 1981. Exec. analyst San Bernardino County, Calif., 1978-82, acting legis. adv., 1982, sr. legis. analyst, 1982—, acting pub. defender, 1984; local gov. rep. State Hazardous Waste Mgmt. Council, Sacramento, Calif., 1982-84; chmn's. rep. County Projects Selection Coms., San Bernardino, 1983—; county rep. S. Coast Air Quality Mgmt. Dist., El Monte, Calif, 1984—. Advisor Mcpl. Adv. Councils, San Bernardino, 1984—; mem. Law Library Bd. Trustees, 1984-85. Named one of Outstanding Young Men of Am., Montgomery, Ala., 1981-82; recipient Presdl. Achievement award Rep. Nat. Com., Washington, 1984. Mem. Calif. Bar Assn., Acad. Polit. Sci.; Calif. State U. Alumni Assn. (bd. dirs.), County Suprs. Assn. of Calif. (bd. liaison). Republican. Islam. Lodges: Kiwanis, Masons, Shriners. Avocations: reading, music, karate, water sports. Legislative, Criminal, Environment. Home: 535 E Mariposa Dr Redlands CA 92373 Office: County San Bernardino Bd Suprs 385 N Arrowhead 5th floor San Bernardino CA 92415

QUAIL, BEVERLY JO, lawyer; b. Glendale, Calif., June 19, 1949; d. John Henry and Dorothy Marie (Sanblom) Q.; m. Timothy D. Roble; children: Benjamin W., Elizabeth L. BA magna cum laude, U. So. Calif., 1971; JD, U. Denver, 1974. Bar: Colo. 1974. Assoc., Conover, McClearn & Heppenstall, P.C., Denver, 1974-75; ptnr. Welborn, Dufford & Brown, Denver, 1975—; broker Colo. Assn. Realtors, 1982-84; lectr. continuing legal edn. Colo.; v.p., bd. mem. Girls Club Denver, 1984—; bd. dirs. Swedish Hosp. Found. Mem. Denver Bar Assn. (com. 1981-84), ABA (chmn. real property litigation com., real property, probate & trust sect. 1986—, comml. leasing com. 1984—), Am. Coll. Real Estate Lawyers, Colo. Real Estate Council, Phi Beta Kappa. Clubs: Denver (coms.), Cherry Hills Country (Denver). Editor newsletter The Colo. Lawyer, 1983-87; contbr. articles to profl. jours. Real property. Home: 19 Random Rd Englewood CO 80110 Office: Welborn Dufford et al 1700 Broadway #1100 Denver CO 80290-1199

QUARLES, JAMES LINWOOD, III, lawyer; b. Huntington, W.Va., Oct. 12, 1946; s. James Linwood Jr. and Beatrice (Hardwick) Q.; m. Sharon Taft, Dec. 20, 1969; children: Jessica, Matthew. BS cum laude, Denison U., 1968; JD cum laude, Harvard U., 1972. Bar: Mass. 1974, U.S. Dist. Ct. Mass. 1975, U.S. Ct. Appeals (D.C. cir.) 1975, U.S. Ct. Appeals (6th cir.) 1979, U.S. Supreme Ct. 1980, D.C. 1981, U.S. Ct. Appeals (2d cir.) 1981, U.S. Ct. Appeals (1st and 4th cirs.) 1983, Md. 1985. Law clk. to presiding justice U.S. Dist. Ct. Md., Balt., 1972-73; with Watergate Spl. Pros. Force, Washington, 1973-75; from assoc. to sr. ptnr. Hale and Dorr, Boston and Washington, 1975—. Democrat. Federal civil litigation, State civil litigation, Securities. Home: 4 Carvel Circle Bethesda MD 20816 Office: Hale and Dorr 1445 Pennsylvania Ave NW The Willard Washington DC 20004

QUARLES, STEVEN PRINCETON, lawyer; b. Kansas City, Mo., May 9, 1942; s. Samuel Princeton and Marianna (Platt) Q.; m. Suzanne Margaret-Mary Cleary, June 2, 1970. AB, Princeton U., 1964; JD, Yale U., 1968. Bar: N.Y. 1980, D.C. 1981. Counsel Senate Com. Energy and Natural Resources, Washington, 1971-78; dir. office coal leasing U.S. Dept. Interior, Washington, 1978-79, dep. under sec., 1979-81; ptnr. Nossaman, Guthner, Knox & Elliott, Washington, 1981-83, Crowell & Moring, Washington, 1983—. Chmn. Sugarloaf Citizens Assn., Dickerson, Md., 1977-81, Md. Hazardous Waste Facilities Siting Bd., Annapolis, 1985—; mem. Md. Sewage Sludge Mgmt. Commn., Annapolis, 1984; mem. adv. com. Montgomery County Solid Waste, Rockville, Md., 1980-85. Fulbright scholar India, 1964-65. Mem. ABA (pub. lands and land use com. natural resources sect.), N.Y. State Bar Assn., D.C. Bar Assn., Nat. Acad. Scis. (energy and mineral resources bd. 1985—, abandoned mine lands com. 1985-86). Democrat. Episcopalian. Avocation: horse breeding. Administrative and regulatory, Environment, Oil and gas leasing. Home: 14001 Mattie Haines Rd Mount Airy MD 21771 Office: Crowell & Moring 1001 Pennsylvania Ave NW Washington DC 20004

QUARLES, WILLIAM DANIEL, lawyer; b. Balt., Jan. 16, 1948; s. William Daniel and Mabel (West) Q.; m. Deborah Ann Grant, Oct. 7, 1969 (div. Aug. 1976); 1 child, Eloise. BS, U. Md., 1976; JD, Cath. U., 1979. Bar: D.C. 1979, U.S. Dist. Ct. Md. 1980, U.S. Ct. Appeals (4th cir.) 1980. Law clk. to presiding judge U.S. Dist. Ct. Md., Balt., 1979-81; assoc. Finley Kumble, Washington, 1981-82; asst. U.S. atty. U.S. Dept. Justice, Balt., 1982-86; sr. assoc. Venable, Baetjer, Howard & Civiletti, Washington, 1986—; Permanent mem. U.S. 4th Cir. Jud. Conf., Richmond, Va., 1986—. Dep. coordinator Presidential Regional Task Force on Organized Crime and Drug Law Enforcement, 1984-85. Mem. ABA, Serjeants Inn. Criminal, Federal civil litigation. Home: 2440 Virginia Ave NW D704 Washington DC 20037 Office: 1301 Pennsylvania Ave NW Suite 1200 Washington DC 20004

QUAST, LARRY WAYNE, lawyer; b. Beulah, N.D., Aug. 13, 1945; s. Clarence and Lorraine (Meske) Q.; m. Linda Mae Borth, June 18, 1971; children: Tiffany, Phillip. BA cum laude, Dickinson Coll., 1968; JD, U. N.D., 1973. Bar: N.D. 1973, U.S. Dist. Ct. N.D. 1973. Small claims ct. referee, magistrate Grand Forks (N.D.) County, 1973-74; justice Mercer County, Stanton, N.D., 1974-78; assoc. Hagen, Quast & Alexander, Beulah, 1974—; atty. City of Stanton, N.D., 1976—. Served to corpsman 4th class USN, 1968-70. Mem. ABA, N.D. Bar Assn. Lutheran. Avocations: raising and racing thoroughbred race horses. State civil litigation, Criminal, Family and matrimonial. Home: 33 W Main Beulah ND 58523 Office: Hagen Quast Alexander 33 W Main Beulah ND 58523

QUAY, THOMAS EMERY, pharmacy company executive, lawyer; b. Cleve., Apr. 3, 1934; s. Harold Emery and Esther Ann (Thomas) Q.; m. Martha Beckham Graham, June 9, 1961 (div.); children: Martha Wyndham, Glynis Cobb, Eliza Emery. A.B. in Humanities magna cum laude (Univ. scholar), Princeton U., 1956; LL.B. (Univ. scholar), U. Pa., 1963. Bar: Pa. 1964. Assoc. firm Pepper, Hamilton & Scheetz, Phila., 1963-65; with William H. Rorer, Inc., Ft. Washington, Pa., 1965—; sec., counsel William H. Rorer, Inc., 1974-79, v.p., gen. counsel, sec., 1979—. Bd. dirs. Main Line YMCA, Ardmore, Pa., 1971-73, chmn. bd., 1972-73; editor 10th Reunion Book Princeton Class of 1956, 1966, 25th Reunion Book, 1981—, class sec., 1976-81, class v.p., 1971-81, pres., 1981-86. Served to lt. (j.g.) USNR, 1957-60. Recipient service commendation Main Line YMCA, 1973. Mem. Am. Bar Assn., Pa. Bar Assn., Phila. Bar Assn., Pharm. Mfrs. Assn. (chmn. law sect. 1983), Phila. Drug Exchange (chmn. legis. com. 1975-78). Democrat. Unitarian. Clubs: Cannon of Princeton U, Sharswood Law of U. Pa. General corporate, Food and drug, Antitrust. Office: 500 Virginia Dr Fort Washington PA 19034

QUELLER, FRED, lawyer; b. N.Y.C., July 10, 1932; s. Victor and Helen (Cenzer) Q.; m. Stephanie Tarler, Aug. 29, 1965; children—Tiffany, Danielle. B.A., CCNY, 1954; J.D., NYU, 1956. Bar: N.Y. 1956, U.S. Dist. Ct. (so. and ea. dists.) N.Y. 1958, U.S. Supreme Ct. 1960, U.S. Ct. Appeals (2d cir.) 1967, Fla. 1980; cert. diplomate civil trial advocacy Nat. Bd. Trial Advocacy, cert. adv. Am. Bd. Trial Advs. Sole practice, N.Y.C., 1956-57, 57-70; ptnr. Queller, Fisher, Block & Wisotsky, N.Y.C., 1970—, now sr. ptnr.; lectr. N.Y. County Lawyers Assn., Practicing Law Inst., Med. Soc. State of N.Y., N.Y. Women's Bar Assn., Victims for Victims, Council of N.Y. Law Assocs., Bklyn. Coll. Inst. for Retired Profls. and Execs., Nassau Acad. Law, Mt. Sinai Med. Ctr., 1975-87; panelist Med. Malpractice Panel of Supreme Ct. State of N.Y., County of N.Y. 1973-87; arbitrator Compulsory Arbitration Service of State of N.Y., 1st Jud. Dept., 1975-87; co-chmn. jud. screening com. of lawyers' com., 1979; adminstrv. sec. ad hoc com. for Preservation of an Elected Judiciary, 1977-80; counsel com. for elected judiciary, 1981-84; mem. coordinating council on lawyer competence of Conf. of Chief Justices, 1983-84; chmn. Big Apple Pothole and Sidewalk Protection Corp., 1982-83, pres. 1984-87. Mem. Assn. Bar City of N.Y., Bronx Bar Assn., N.Y. State Bar Assn. (com. on automobile liability 1981-84), ABA (trial techniques com. 1984), Fla. Bar Assn., Met. Women's Bar Assn. (bd. dirs. 1975-83, lectr. 1975-87, treas. 1978-80, v.p. 1980-81), N.Y. Criminal and Civil Cts. Bar Assn., Bklyn. and Manhattan Trial Counsel Assn., Bklyn. County Lawyers Assn. (com. on Supreme Ct. 1981), N.Y. State Trial Lawyers Assn. (bd. dirs. 1970-80, lectr. 1975-87, v.p. 1980-83, pres. 1984-86,chmn. products liability com. 1980-81, chmn. brief bank com. 1982-84, chmn. expert bank com. 1982-84, Pres.'s award 1986, Disting. Service award 1986). Assn. Trial Lawyers of City N.Y. (bd. dirs. 1975-87), Assn. Trial Lawyers Am., Lawyers Polit. Action Com. (trustee 1984-86), NYU Law Rev. Alumni Assn. Clubs: Downtown Athletic (N.Y.C.). Assoc. editor NYU Law Rev., 1955-56; contbr. articles to Trial Lawyers Quar. Personal injury, State civil litigation. Office: Queller Fisher Bower & Wisotsky 110 Wall St New York NY 10005

QUENNEVILLE, KATHLEEN, lawyer; b. Mt. Clemens, Mich., July 31, 1953; d. Marcel J. and Patricia (Armstrong) Q.;. BA, Mich. State U., 1975; JD, Golden Gate U., 1980. Bar: Calif. 1980. Atty. Wells Fargo Bank, San Francisco, 1980-81; staff counsel Calif. State Banking Dept., San Francisco, 1981-83; assoc. Manatt, Phelps, Ruthenburg & Tunney, Los Angeles, 1983-84; v.p., counsel Bank of Calif., San Francisco, 1984—. Mem. San Francisco Bar Assn. Banking. Office: Bank of Calif 400 California St San Francisco CA 94104

QUIAT, BETTE ELLEN, lawyer; b. Passaic, N.J., Nov. 15, 1952. BA, Boston U., 1974; JD, U. Miami, 1977. Bar: Fla. 1977, N.J. 1978. Assoc. Carey, Dwyer, Cole, Selwood & Bernard, Miami, 1977-81, Law Office Alex Hofrichter, Miami, 1982-83; ptnr. Hofrichter & Quiat, P.A., Miami, 1983-84, Hofrichter, Quiat & Zuckerman, Miami, 1984-86; sole practice Miami, 1986—. Editor (newsletter) Family Law Commentator, 1985. Pres. Big Bros./Big Sisters Greater Miami Inc., 1985-86, bd. dirs., 1981-85. Mem. ABA, Fla. Bar (pres.-elect young lawyers sect. 1986-87, bd. govs. young lawyers sect. 1981-86, family law sect.), Dade County Bar Assn. Family and matrimonial. Office: 8525 SW 92d St Suite B-5 Miami FL 33156

QUIAT, GERALD M., lawyer; b. Denver, Jan. 9, 1924; s. Ira L. and Esther (Greenblatt) Q.; m. Roberta M. Nicholson, Sept. 26, 1962; children: James M., Audrey L., Melinda, Daniel P., Ilana L., Leonard E. A.A., U. Calif., Berkeley, 1942; A.B. and LL.B., U. Denver, 1948, changed to J.D., 1972. Bar: Colo. 1948, Fed. Ct. 1948. Dep. dist. atty. County of Denver, Colo., 1949-52; partner firm Quiat, Seeman & Quiat, Denver, 1952-68, Quiat & Quiat (later changed to Quiat, Bucholtz & Bull, P.C.), 1968; pres. firm Quiat Bucholtz Bull & Laff, P.C. (and predecessors), Denver, 1968-85; sole practice Denver, 1985—. Colo. post comdr. Am. Legion, 1955-56; past judge adv. Colo. dept.; dir., chmn. audit com. Guaranty Bank & Trust Co., Denver.; trustee Rose Health Care Systems, Rose Med. Ctr., Denver, 1967—, pres., chmn. bd. 1976-79; mem. Colo. Civil Rights Com., 1963-71, chmn., 1966-67, 1969-70, chief hearing officer, 1963-71; bd. dirs. AMC Cancer Research Ctr., Denver; chmn. exec. com. Mt. States Region Anti-Defamation League of B'nai B'rith, 1980-82, also bd. dirs., mem. nat. civil rights com., nat. commr.; bd. dirs. Mountain States Region of Anti-Defamation League of B'nai B'rith, also exec. com. mem., chmn. bd. dirs. 1980-82. Served with U.S. Army Inf., 1942-45. Decorated Bronze Star. Mem. Denver Bar Assn., Colo. Bar Assn., ABA, Am. Trial Lawyers Assn., Colo. Trial Lawyers Assn. (pres. 1970-71). Probate, Real property. Home: 8130 Lt Wm Clark Rd Parker CO 80134 Office: 1660 Wynkoop St Suite 850 Denver CO 80202

QUIGGLE, JAMES WILLIAMS, lawyer; b. Washington, Aug. 12, 1924; s. James Williams and Margaret (Cook) Q.; widowed; children: James W., Thomas E. AB, Princeton U., 1948; LLB, U. Va., 1951; LLM, Georgetown U., 1956. Bar: D.C. 1952, Md. 1958. Ptnr. Williams, Myers and Quiggle, Washington, 1951—; adj. prof. fed. tax practice and procedure Georgetown U., 1962-70. Co-author: Procedure Before the Internal Revenue Service, 1984. Mem. ABA (sec. tax sect. 1972-73), Am. Coll. Probate Counsel. Clubs: Metropolitan (Washington); Chevy Chase (Md.). Avocation: tennis. Corporate taxation, Estate taxation, Personal income taxation. Home: 3509 Overlook Ln Washington DC 20016 Office: Williams Myers and Quiggle 888 17th St NW Washington DC 20006

QUIGLEY, LEONARD VINCENT, lawyer; b. Kansas City, Mo., June 21, 1933; s. Joseph Vincent and Rosemary (Cannon) Q.; m. Lynn Mathis Pfohl, May 23, 1964; children: Leonard Matthew, Cannon Louise, Daniel Pfohl, Megan Mathis. A.B., Coll. Holy Cross, 1953; LL.B. magna cum laude, Harvard U., 1959; LL.M. in Internat. Law, NYU, 1962. Bar: N.Y. 1960. Assoc. Cravath, Swaine & Moore, N.Y.C., 1959-67; ptnr. Paul, Weiss, Rifkind, Wharton & Garrison, N.Y.C., 1967—; gen. counsel Archaeol. Inst. Am., Boston. Served to lt. USN, 1953-56. Mem. ABA, Can. Bar Assn., Assn. Bar City N.Y. Clubs: Harvard (N.Y.C.); West Side Tennis (Forest Hill, N.Y.). General corporate, Private international, Oil and gas leasing.

QUIGLEY, THOMAS J., lawyer; b. Mt. Carmel, Pa., July 22, 1923; s. James S. and Helen C. (Laughlin) Q.; m. Joan R. Reifke, Aug. 11, 1956; children—Thomas J., Jr., Joan E., James S. A.B., Bucknell U., 1947; LL.B., Yale U., 1950. Bar: Ohio, U.S. Dist. Ct. Ohio, U.S. Ct. Appeals (6th and D.C. cirs.). With Squire, Sanders & Dempsey, 1950—, adminstr. labor dept., 1971-80, mng. ptnr., Washington, 1980-85; nat. vice chmn., 1985-86; nat. chmn., 1986—. Bd. dirs. Fed. City Council, Washington; trustee Nat. Symphony Orch., Musical Arts Assn. Cleve.; bd. dirs. Served to 1st lt. USAAF, 1942-45. Decorated D.F.C., Air medal with oak leaf cluster. Mem. ABA, Ohio Bar Assn., D.C. Bar Assn., Cleve. Bar Assn., Belgian-Am. C. of C. (bd. dirs.), Democrat. Roman Catholic. Clubs: Union, Kirtland (Cleve.); Yale (N.Y.C.); Potomac Tennis (Md.); Edgartown Yacht (Mass.), Metropolitan (Wash.). Labor. Office: Squire Sanders & Dempsey 1201 Pennsylvania Ave NW PO Box 497 Washington DC 20044

QUILLEN, FORD CARTER, lawyer, state legislator; b. Gate City, Va., Sept. 21, 1938; s. Cecil Dyer and Mary Louise (Carter) Q.; m. Barbara Gail Burdette, Dec. 17, 1961; children—Madre, Carter, Lenoir. B.S., U. Tenn., 1961, J.D., 1966. Bar: Va. 1966. Ptnr. Quillen and Carter, Gate City, 1966-78, sole practice, Gate City, 1978—; now ptnr. Quillen & Fulton, Gate City; mem. Va. Legislature, 1970—, vice chmn. agr. com., mem. privileges and elections com., chmn. mines and minerals resources com., mem. appropriations com.; mem. Joint Legis. and Audit Rev. commn., Coal and Energy Commn. Served with U.S. Army, 1961-63. Recipient Outstanding Legislator award Eagleston Inst., 1975. Mem. ABA, Def. Lawyers Assn., Va. Bar Assn., Va. Trial Lawyers, Va. State Bar, Va. Def. Assn. Democrat. Baptist. Personal injury, Federal civil litigation, Legislative. Office: Quillen & Fulton 111 E Jackson St Gate City VA 24251

QUILLEN, MICHAEL CLAY, lawyer; b. Columbia, Tenn., Aug. 15, 1950; s. Malcolm Patterson and Eva Pearl (Shewmake) Q.; m. Mary James Moore, Aug. 3, 1974; children; Henry, Mary Rodgers, James. BA, Vanderbilt U., 1972; JD, Duke U., 1975. Bar: Ala. 1975, U.S. Dist. Ct. (no. dist.) Ala. 1975, U.S. Ct. Appeals (5th cir.) 1977, U.S. Ct. Appeals (11th cir.) 1981. Ptnr. Cabaniss, Johnston, Gardner, Dumas & O'Neal, Birmingham, Ala., 1975-80, 1981—. Sec. Friends of Red Moutain Mus., Birmingham, 1986—, 1975-80, 1981—. Mem. Red Mountain Mus. Bd., Birmingham, 1980—. Mem. ABA, Ala. State Bar, Birmingham Bar Assn., Nat. Assn. RR Trial Counsel. Presbyterian. Lodge: Rotary. Personal injury, State civil litigation, Federal civil litigation. Home: 4215 Glenwood Ave Birmingham AL 35222 Office: Cabaniss Johnston Gardner et al 1900 1st Nat So Natural Bldg Birmingham AL 35203

QUILLEN, WILLIAM TATEM, lawyer, former state supreme court justice; b. Camden, N.J., Jan. 15, 1935; s. Robert James and Gladys Collings (Tatem) Q.; m. Marcia Everhart Stirling, June 27, 1959; children: Carol Everhart, Tracey Tatem. B.A., Williams Coll., 1956; LL.B., Harvard U., 1959; LL.M., U. Va., 1982. Bar: Del. 1959. Assoc. Richards, Layton & Finger, Wilmington, Del., 1963-64; adminstrv. asst. to Gov. of Del., 1965; assoc. judge Superior Ct. of Del., 1966-73; chancellor State of Del., 1973-76; sr. v.p. Wilmington Trust Co., 1976-78; justice Supreme Ct. of Del., 1978-83; ptnr. Potter Anderson & Corroon, Wilmington, 1983-86; gen. counsel, v.p. Howard Hughes Med. Inst., 1986—; adj. faculty mem. Del. Law Sch., Widener U., 1976-83. Trustee Widener U., 1979—; Democratic candidate for gov. Del., 1984. Served with JAGC, USAF, 1959-62. Mem. Am. Bar Assn., Del. State Bar Assn. Democrat. Presbyterian. Club: Wilmington. General corporate. Office: Howard Hughes Med Inst 6701 Rockledge Dr Bethesda MD 20817

QUINLAN, GUY CHRISTIAN, lawyer; b. Cambridge, Mass., Oct. 28, 1939; s. Guy Thomas and Yvonne (Carver) Q.; m. Mary-Ella Holst, Apr. 18, 1987. A.B., Harvard Coll., 1960, J.D., Harvard U., 1963. Bar: N.Y. 1964, U.S. Dist. Ct. (so. and ea. dists.) N.Y. 1965, U.S. Ct. Appeals (2d cir.) 1967, U.S. Supreme Ct. 1969, U.S. Ct. Appeals (5th and 8th cirs.) 1973, (10th cir.) 1977, U.S. Tax Ct. 1977. Assoc. Rogers & Wells, N.Y.C., 1963-70, ptnr., 1970—. Pres. Unitarian Universalist Service Com.; pres. Yorkville Common Pantry; dir. Yorkville Emergency Alliance; past pres. Unitarian Universalist Dist. of Met. N.Y.; mem. adv. council on ministerial studies Harvard U. Div. Sch. Mem. ABA, N.Y. State Bar Assn., Fed. Bar Council, Am. Assn. Internat. Commn. Jurists, Nat. Council Crime and Delinquency. Democrat. Club: Harvard (N.Y.C.). Antitrust, Federal civil litigation, State civil litigation. Home: 340 E 80th St Apt 12D New York NY 10021 Office: Rogers & Wells Pan Am Building 200 Park Ave New York NY 10166

QUINLAN, JAMES WILLIAM, lawyer; b. Atlanta, Feb. 6, 1958; s. Richard Stephen and Shirley Ann (Jasper) Q.; m. Debra Diane Lewis, Aug. 21, 1982; children: Jessica Anne, Audra Elizabeth, Kathryn Diane. BS in Acctg., Auburn U., 1979; JD, U. Ga., 1982. Bar: Ga. 1982, U.S. Dist. Ct. (no. dist.) Ga. 1984, U.S. Tax Ct. 1984, U.S. Ct. Appeals (11th cir.) 1984. Tax atty. Touche Ross & Co., Atlanta, 1982-84; assoc. Page, Scrantom, Harris & Chapman, P.C., Columbus, Ga., 1984—. First vice chmn. exec. com. Muscogee County Dems., Columbus, 1985, 1st vice chairperson, 1986. Mem. Atlanta Bar Assn., Columbus Lawyers Club. Democrat. Roman Catholic. Avocations: golf, antique cars. Corporate taxation, Pension, profit-sharing, and employee benefits, Personal income taxation. Home: 675 Dogwood Dr Columbus GA 31907 Office: Page Scrantom Harris & Chapman PC 1043 3d Ave Columbus GA 31901

QUINLAN, WILLIAM JOSEPH, JR., lawyer; b. Chgo., Nov. 4, 1939; s. William Joseph and Catherine E. (Bowman) Q.; m. Susan L. Collins, June 16, 1962; children—Kathleen, Michael, Julie, Jennifer. A.B. cum laude, Loyola, U., Chgo., 1961, J.D. cum laude, 1966. Bar: Ill. 1966, U.S. Dist. Ct. (no. dist.) Ill. 1966, U.S. Tax Ct. 1968, U.S. Ct. Appeals (7th cir.) 1972. Assoc. Wilson & McIlvaine, Chgo., 1966-73; ptnr. McDermott, Will & Emery, Chgo., 1973-78, sr. ptnr., 1978—; dir. Wickman Machine Tools, Elk Grove Village, Ill., 1978-81, Eiger Machinery, Inc., Bensenville, Ill., 1981—. Contbr. articles to profl. publs. Mem. St. Athanasius Bd. Edn., Evanston, Ill., 1976, pres., 1978. Mem. ABA (com. on fed. regulation of securities), Chgo. Bar Assn. (chmn. subcom. on securities law), Ill. Bar Assn., Blue Key, Phi Alpha Delta. Roman Catholic. Clubs: Union League, Wilmette Harbor Assn. General corporate, Securities, Municipal bonds. Office: McDermott Will & Emery 111 W Monroe St Chicago IL 60603

QUINN, ANDREW PETER, JR., lawyer, insurance executive; b. Providence, Oct. 22, 1923; s. Andrew Peter and Margaret (Canning) Q.; m. Sara G. Bullard, May 30, 1952; 1 dau., Emily H. A.B., Brown U., 1945; LL.B., Yale U., 1950. Bar: R.I. 1949, Mass. 1960, also U.S. Tax Ct 1960, U.S. Supreme Ct. 1986. Practice in Providence, 1950-59, Springfield, Mass., 1959—; partner Letts & Quinn, 1950-59; with Mass. Mut. Life Ins. Co., 1959—, exec. v.p., gen. counsel, 1971—. Trustee, chmn. bd. MacDuffie Sch.; trustee Baystate Med., Springfield, 1977-80. Served from ensign to lt. (j.g.) USNR, 1944-46. Mem. ABA (co-chmn. nat. conf. lawyers and life ins. cos. 1973), Hampden County (Mass.) Bar Assn., Assn. Life Ins. Counsel (pres. 1983-84), Am. Council Life Ins. (chmn. legal sect. 1971), Life Ins. Assn. Mass. (chmn. exec. com. 1975-77), Asso. Alumni Brown U. (dir. 1969-72). Clubs: New York Yacht, Longmeadow Country; Connecticut Valley Brown University (Springfield) (past pres.). Home: 306 Ellington Rd Longmeadow MA 01106 Office: Mass Mut Life Ins Co 1295 State St Springfield MA 01111

QUINN, JAMES FRANCIS, military lawyer; b. N.Y.C., Feb. 1, 1949; s. James Frederick and Eileen Veronica (Walsh) Q.; m. Victoria Jane Stevens, July 15, 1972. BS in Aerospace Engring., BA in Gen. Arts and Scis., Pa. State U., 1971; JD, St. John's U., 1977; MA in Criminal Justice, John Jay Coll. Criminal Justice, 1986. Bar: N.Y. 1978, U.S. Patent and Trademark Office 1978, U.S. Ct. Mil. Appeals 1978, U.S. Supreme Ct. 1981. Commd. U.S. Army, 1977, advanced through grades to maj., 1985; asst. staff judge adv. U.S. Army, Ft. Huachuca, Ariz., 1978-80; post judge adv. U.S. Army, Ft. Indiantown Gap, Pa., 1980-82; legal advisor intelligence oversight com. European hdqrs. U.S. Army, Heidelberg, Fed. Republic Germany, 1986-87; asst. prof. dept. law U.S. Mil. Acad., West Point, N.Y., 1983-86; judge adv. 1st personnel command U.S. Army, N.Y.C., 1987—; instr. Cochise Community Coll., Sierra Vista, Ariz., 1979-80, Sierra Vista Sch. Real Estate, 1979-80; treas. Huachuca Fed. Credit Union, Ft. Huachuca, 1979-80; bd. dirs. New Cumberland (Pa.) Fed. Credit Union, 1980-82, West Point Fed. Credit Union, 1983-86. Editor: Military Criminal Law and Procedure, 1985, Constitutional Law, 1986. Recipient Pa. Commendation medal Pa. N.G., 1982. Mem. Fed. Bar Assn. (pres. chpt. 788 1979-80), Assn. Trial Lawyers Am., St. John's U. Law Alumni Assn., Pa. State U. Liberal Arts Alumni Soc. (pres. 1984-86), Pa. State Alumni Council (bd. dirs. 1984-86), JAG Assn., Assn. U.S. Army. Republican. Roman Catholic. Club: Pa. State (bd. dirs. Cornwall, N.Y. 1983-86). Avocations: theater, golf. Military. Home: 1266 Fairfax Ave North Tonawanda NY 14120 Office: US Army Command Judge Adv 1st PERSCOM APO New York NY 09081

QUINN, JAMES W., lawyer; b. Bronxville, N.Y., Oct. 1, 1945; s. James Joseph Quinn and Marie Joan (Blossy) Tisi; m. Kathleen Manning, Kellianne, Christopher, Tierney, Kerrin. AB cum laude, U. Notre Dame, 1967; JD, Fordham U., 1971. Bar: N.Y. 1972, U.S. Dist. Ct. (so. and ea. dists.) 1973, U.S. Ct. Appeals (2d cir.) 1976, U.S. Supreme Ct. 1984, U.S. Ct. Appeals (3d, 7th and 9th cirs.) 1985. Assoc. Weil, Gotshal & Manges, N.Y.C., 1971-77, 78-79, ptnr., 1979—; ptnr. Fleisher & Quinn, N.Y.C., 1977-78; adj. assoc. prof. law Fordham U., N.Y.C., 1985—. Editor Fordham U. Law Rev., 1969-71; contbr. articles to legal jours. Mem. ABA (litigation sect., co-chmn. subcom. alternate means of dispute resolution of com. corp. counsel, program chmn. trial practice com., sports and entertainment forum), Assn. of Bar of City of N.Y. (com. on state jurisdiction, com. on entertainment sports). Federal civil litigation, State civil litigation. Home: 1 Maple Way Armonk NY 10504

QUINN, JOHN HARVEY, JR., lawyer; b. Memphis, July 16, 1936; s. John Harvey and Florence Eleanor (Wilson) Q.; m. Joan Corbett, Aug. 26, 1972; 1 child, Caren Joanne. B.A. with honors, Southwestern at Memphis (now Rhodes Coll.), 1958; J.D., U. Va., Charlottesville, 1961. Bar: Va. 1961, Tenn. 1962, D.C. 1963, U.S. Ct. Appeals (D.C. cir.) 1963, U.S. Ct. Appeals (4th cir.) 1962, U.S. Ct. Appeals (2d cir.) 1967, U.S. Ct. Appeals (fed. cir.) 1975, U.S. Supreme Ct. 1964. Law clk. U.S. Ct. Appeals (4th cir.), Parkersburg, W.Va., 1961-62; atty. Howrey, Simon, Baker and Murchison, Washington, 1962-65; exec. dir. Saunders B. Moon Community Action Assn., Alexandria, Va., 1965-66; atty. Zuckert, Scoutt and Rasenberger, Washington, 1966-82; atty., chmn. Quinn, Racusin, Jenkins & Ruttenberg, Chartered (formerly Quinn, Racusin & Ruttenberg, Chartered), Washington, 1982—; instr. law Temple U., Phila., 1968-72, lectr. 1972-82; dir. Nicholson Investment Co., Washington, Richardson, Bellows, Henry and Co., Washington, H.A. Knott Ltd., Silver Spring, Md. Pres. Ctr. for Urban Edn., Inc., Arlington, Va., 1976-78, 80-83, bd. dirs. 1976—. Served in USNR, 1955-63. Mem. ABA. Presbyterian. Club: Nat. Lawyers. Administrative and regulatory, General corporate, Probate. Office: 1730 K St NW Suite 700 Washington DC 20006

QUINN, JOSEPH FRANCIS, lawyer; b. Albany, N.Y., Jan. 29, 1946; s. Joseph Martin and Mary Esther (Badalucco) W.; m. Kirsten Anne Husted, June 29, 1968; children—Patrick Joseph, Eric Thomas. B.A., Union Coll., 1967; J.D., U.Puget Sound, 1976. Bar: Wash. 1976, U.S. Dist. Ct. (we. dist.) Wash. 1976, U.S. Ct. Appeals (9th cir.) 1979, U.S. Supreme Ct., 1985. Assoc., Gordon, Thomas, Honeywell, Malance, Peterson & O'Hern, Tacoma, 1976-79; dep. prosecutor Pierce County Pros. Atty., Tacoma, 1979-83; sole practice, Tacoma, 1983; prin. McCormick, Hoffman, Rees, Faubion, and Quinn, P.S., Tacoma, 1984—; commr. Wash. State Pub. Employment Relations Commn., 1986—; lectr. Wash. Assn. Pros. Attys., 1981-83, Nat. Dist. Attys. Assn., 1985. Mng. editor U. Puget Sound Law Rev., 1975-76. Chmn., Lakewood-University Place Citizens Adv. Bd., Tacoma, 1983-85; bd. dirs. Lakewood United, 1983-84; commr. Wash. State Pub. Employment Relations Commn., 1986—. Served to capt. USAF, 1968-72; ETO. Mem. Tacoma-Pierce County Bar Assn., ABA, Wash. State Bar Assn. Roman Catholic. Local government, State civil litigation, Personal injury.

QUINN, JOSEPH R., state supreme court judge; b. Elizabeth, N.J., Nov. 18, 1932; s. Patrick F. and Claire E. Q.; m. Olga B. Taylor, July 28, 1962; children: Theresa, Lisa, Rita, James, Maria. A.B., St. Peter's Coll., 1957; LL.B., Rutgers U., 1961. Apptd. judge Colo. Dist. Ct., Dist. 2, 1973-80; justice Supreme Ct. of Colo., Denver, 1980—. Office: Supreme Ct of Colo State Capitol Denver CO 80203 *

QUINN, KIRKE CRAVEN, lawyer; b. Grinnell, Iowa, Dec. 31, 1950; s. Carl Smith and Dorothy Beatrice (Craven) Q.; m. Monna Kay Weiland, Feb. 23, 1980; children—Lisa, Kristina, Morgan. B.S., Drake U., 1972, J.D., 1975. Bar: Iowa 1975, U.S. Dist Ct. (no. and so. dists.) Iowa 1976—. Ptnr. firm Doran, Courter and Quinn, Boone, Iowa, 1976—. Pres. Boone County United Way, 1981. Fellow Iowa Acad. Trial Lawyers; mem. Iowa Def. Counsel Assn. Republican. Federal civil litigation, State civil litigation. Home: 2131 McCarthy Rd Ames IA 50010 Office: Doran Courter Quinn & Doran 809 8th St Boone IA 50036

QUINN, STACY SMITH, lawyer; b. DeRidder, La., May 9, 1957; d. William Tousley and Janet Lee (Groth) Smith; m. Patrick Gleason Quinn, June 20, 1981. AB, Dartmouth Coll., 1979; JD, Case Western Reserve U., 1982. Bar: Ohio, 1982, U.S. Dist. Ct. (no. dist.) Ohio 1983. Assoc. Cronquist, Smith, Marshall & Weaver, Cleve., 1982-86, Jones, Day, Reavis & Pogue, N.Y.C. and Cleve., 1986—. Active Jr. League of Cleve., 1982—. Mem. ABA, Ohio Bar Assn., Cleve. Bar Assn., Dartmouth Lawyers Assn. Club: Dartmouth (Cleve.). Avocations: civic vol. work, travel, theatre, skiing, museums. State civil litigation, Personal injury, Federal civil litigation.

QUINN, YVONNE SUSAN, lawyer; b. Spring Valley, Ill., May 13, 1951; s. Robert Leslie and Shirley Eilene (Morse) Q.; m. Ronald S. Rolfe, Sept. 1, 1979. BA, U. Ill., 1973; JD, U. Mich., 1976, MA in Econs., 1977. Bar: N.Y., U.S. Dist. Ct. (ea. and so. dists.) N.Y., U.S. Ct. Appeals (3d, 10th and D.C. cirs.), U.S. Supreme Ct. Assoc. Cravath, Swaine & Moore, N.Y.C., 1977-80; assoc. Sullivan & Cromwell, N.Y.C., 1980-85, ptnr., 1985—. Mem. ABA, Assn. of Bar of City of N.Y. Clubs: Down Town, Broad Street (N.Y.C.). Antitrust, Federal civil litigation, State civil litigation. Office: Sullivan & Cromwell 125 Broad St New York NY 10004

QUINON, JOSE MANUEL, lawyer; b. Camaguey, Cuba, Jan. 15, 1950; came to U.S., 1962, naturalized, 1973; s. Jose Manuel and Gladys Orlinda (Sarduy) Q.; m. Louise Teza, July 9, 1977; children: Samantha, Edward. B.S. in Bus. Adminstrn., Seton Hall U., 1972; J.D., Rutgers U., 1975. Bar: Fla. 1975, U.S. Dist. Ct. (so. dist.) Fla. 1975, U.S. Ct. Appeals (5th and 11th cirs.) 1982, U.S. Dist. Ct. (mid. dist.) Fla. 1986. Assoc., A.M. Schwitalla, Miami, Fla., 1975-77; ptnr. Schwitalla & Quinon, 1977-79; asst. state atty. Major Crimes Div., Dade County, 1979-83; sole practice, Miami, 1983—. Mem. ABA, Fla. Criminal Def. Lawyers Assn. (bd. dirs. 1986-87), Nat. Assn. Criminal Def. Lawyers, Fla. Bar Assn., Dade County Bar Assn. Criminal. Office: 2600 Douglas Rd Penthouse 1 Coral Gables FL 33134

QUINT, ARNOLD HARRIS, lawyer; b. Boston, Jan. 3, 1942; s. Milton and Esther (Kirshen) Q.; m. Susan Arenson, July 23, 1967; children; Ned, Michael. AB, Haverford Coll., 1963; LLB, Yale U., 1966. Bar: D.C. 1967. Supervisory atty. Fed. Power Commn., Washington, 1967-70; from assoc. to ptnr. Hunton & Williams, Washington, 1970—. Mem. ABA, Fed. Energy Bar Assn. (com. chmn. 1979-83). FERC practice, Public utilities. Office: Hunton & Williams 2000 Pennsylvania Ave NW PO Box 19230 Washington DC 20036

QUINTIERE, GARY G., lawyer; b. Passaic, N.J., Nov. 26, 1944; s. Benjamin and Sadie (Riotto) Q.; m. Judy Rosenthal, Aug. 16, 1966; children: Karen, Geoffrey. AB in Govt., Lafayette Coll., 1966; JD, George Washington U., 1969. Law clk. to presiding judge U.S. Ct. Appeals (Fed. cir.), Washington, 1969-70; from assoc. to ptnr. Miller & Chevalier, Washington, 1970-85; ptnr. Morgan, Lewis & Bockius, Washington, 1985—. Mem. ABA, D.C. Bar Assn., Va. Bar Assn. Avocations: tennis, skiing, jogging. Pension, profit-sharing, and employee benefits. Home: 14 Mercy Ct Potomac MD 20854 Office: Morgan Lewis & Bockius 1800 M St NW Washington DC 20036

QUIRK, EDWARD JOHN, lawyer, property developer; b. Yonkers, N.Y., July 21, 1938; s. Edward John and Louise (Rebmann) Q.; m. Maria Elena Blasco, Apr. 7, 1977; children—Maria, Eric. B.Chem. Engring., Cornell U., 1961; J.D., U. San Francisco, 1965. Bar: Calif. 1966, U.S. Ct. Dist. (no. dist.) Calif. 1966, Tex. 1973, Nev. 1974, U.S. Dist. Ct. Nev. 1975, U.S. Patent Office 1966, U.S. Ct. Appeals (9th cir.) 1966, U.S. Ct. Customs and Patent Appeals 1979, U.S. Supreme Ct. 1980, U.S. Ct. Appeals (fed. cir.) 1982. Patent and licensing counsel Shell Oil Co., San Francisco, N.Y.C., Houston, 1965-73; ptnr. Seiler, Quirk & Tratos, Las Vegas, Nev., 1973—; prin. Spanish Tr. Assocs., Las Vegas, 1983—, also dir.; pres., dir. Renaissance Press, Inc., Las Vegas, 1982—. Co-Author, editor: Holy Days, Holidays and Legends, 1983; A Child is Born, 1983. Bd. dirs. Boys and Girls Clubs, Las Vegas, 1978—, mem. exec. bd., 1986—, pres., 1987—. Mem. exec. bd. Discovery Children's Mus., Las Vegas, 1983—; bd. dirs. Young Audiences, Las Vegas, 1982. Recipient Man and Boy award Boys and Girls Clubs Las Vegas, 1984. Mem. Licensing Execs. Soc., Am. Patent Law Assn., N.Y. Patent Law Assn., Los Angeles Patent Law Assoc., San Francisco Patent Law Assn., Nev. Intellectual Property Law Assn. (founder, pres. 1984—). Republican. Clubs: Spanish Tr. Country (founder, bd. dirs.), Las Vegas Country. Patent, Trademark and copyright. Office: Seiler Quirk & Tratos 550 Charleston Suite D Las Vegas NV 89104

QUIRK, LAWRENCE THOMAS, III, lawyer; b. Harrison, N.J., Dec. 5, 1951. BA, Rutgers Coll., New Brunswick, N.J., 1973; JD, Rutgers Coll., Camden, N.J., 1976. Bar: N.J. 1976. Law clk. to judge N.J. Superior Ct., Freehold, 1976-77; assoc. Campbell, Foley, Lee, Murphy & Cernigliaro, Asbury Park, N.J., 1977—. Mem. Monmouth County Bar Assn., N.J. Trial Lawyers Assn. Office: 601 Bangs Ave Asbury Park NJ 07712

QUITMEIER, WILLIAM MICHAEL, lawyer; b. Berwyn, Ill., Nov. 19, 1951; s. William Warren and Em (Zaiden) Q.; m. Nancy Eileen Wessling, Dec. 29, 1973; children: Lesley Michelle, Lindsey Nicole, William Daniel. BA, U. Kans., 1973, JD, 1975. Bar: Mo. 1976, U.S. Dist. Ct. (we. dist.) Mo. 1976. Sole practice Kansas City, Mo., 1976-85; pres. W. M. Quitmeier & Assocs. P.C., Kansas City, 1985—; asst. pros. atty., Kansas City, 1978-80; v.p. Quitmeier/Huck Devel. Co. Alderman, City of Parkville, Mo., 1985—; pres. Christ Ch. Unity, Kansas City, 1985—. Mem. Am. Trial Lawyers Assn., Mo. Bar Assn., Mo. Trial Lawyers Assn., Mo. Real Estate Assn. Lodges: Rotary, Elks. State civil litigation, General corporate, Personal injury. Home: 8804 NW Melody Dr Parkville MO 64152 Office: 4370 N Oak Trafficway Kansas City MO 64116

QUITTMAN, PETER FRANCIS, lawyer; b. Oakland, Calif., Sept. 21, 1946; s. Philip David and Jane (Russell) Q. BS, U. San Francisco, 1968, MA, 1972, JD, 1976. Bar: Calif., U.S. Dist. Ct. Calif., U.S. Ct. Appeals, U.S. Ct. Mil. Appeals. Sole practice Oakland, Calif., 1976—. Served to 1st lt. U.S. Army, 1970-72. Avocations: sports. Probate, State civil litigation. Office: 125 12th St #111 Oakland CA 94607

RAAB, IRA JERRY, lawyer, arbitrator, lecturer; b. N.Y.C., June 20, 1935; s. Benjamin and Fannie (Kirschner) R.; m. Regina Schneider, June 4, 1957 (div.); children: Michael, Shelley; m. Katie Rachel McKeever, June 30, 1979; children—Julie, Jennifer, Joseph. BBA, CCNY, 1955; JD, Bklyn. Law Sch., 1957; MPA, NYU, 1959, postgrad., 1961; MS in Pub. Adminstrn., L.I. U., 1961; postgrad., Adelphi U., 1981—. Bar: N.Y. 1958, U.S. Dist. Ct. (so. and ea. dists.) N.Y. 1960, U.S. Supreme Ct. 1967, U.S. Tax Ct. 1976, U.S. Ct. Appeals (2d cir.) 1977. Sole practice, Woodmere, N.Y., 1958—; agt. Westchester County Soc. Prevention of Cruelty to Children, White Plains, N.Y., 1958; counsel Dept. Correction, City of N.Y., 1959, trial commr., 1976; staff counsel SBA, N.Y.C., 1961-63; asst. corp. counsel Tort Div., City of N.Y., 1963-70; counsel Investigation Com. on Willowbrook State Sch., Boro Hall, S.I., N.Y., 1970; gen. counsel Richmond County Soc. Prevention of Cruelty to Children, Boro Hall, 1970-81; pro bono counsel N.Y.C. Patrolmen's Benevolent Assn., 1974-81; rep. to UN from Internat. Criminal Ct., 1977-78; arbitrator Small Claims Ct., N.Y.C., 1970—, L.I. Better Bus. Bur., 1976—, Nassau County Dist. Ct., 1978—; hearing officer, 1982—; spl. master N.Y. Supreme Ct., 1977—, spl. master, 1977—; lectr. community and ednl. orgns.; instr. paralegal course Lawrence Sch. Dist., N.Y., 1982-84. Chmn. Businessmen's Luncheon Club, Wall St. Synagogue, 1968-79; sec. Community Mediation Ctr., Suffolk County, 1978-80, exec. v.p., 1980-81; vice chmn. Woodmere Incorporation Com., 1980-81; mem. adv. bd. Nassau Expressway Com., 1979-80; bd. dirs. Woodmere Mchts. Assn., 1979-80, v.p., 1979-83, chmn. 1984—; Recipient Consumer Protection award FTC, 1974, 76, 79, Recognition award Pres. Ronald Reagan, 1986, Man of Yr. award L.I. Council of Chambers, 1987; Mem. Am. Judges Assn. (nat. treas. 1978-82, exec. com. 1978-84, gov. dist. II 1974-78, 82—, chmn. civil ct. ops. com. 1975-76, chmn. ednl. film com. 1974-77, editorial bd. Court Rev. mag. 1975-79, 82-86, chmn. speakers' bur. com. 1976-77, chmn. legis. com. 1983—, William H. Burnett award 1983), Am. Judges Found. (pres. 1977-79, chmn. bd. trustees 1979-83, treas. 1974-75, 76-77, trustee 83—), Assn. Arbitrators of Civil Ct. City N.Y. (past pres.), ABA, N.Y. State Bar Assn., Nassau County Lawyers Assn., Nassau County Bar Assn. (mem. criminal cts. com., matrimonial and family ct. com., ct. com., ethics com.), Profl. Group Legal Service Assn. (past pres.), Am. Judicature Soc., Internat. Assn. Jewish Lawyers and Jurists (com. to draft Internat. Bill of Rights of Privacy 1982, council 1981—, bd. govs. 1984—), Am. Arbitration Assn. (arbitrator 1975—, adv. bd. community dispute ctr. 1979-81). Democrat. Hebrew. Lodge: K.P. General practice, State civil litigation, Personal injury. Address: 375 Westwood Rd Woodmere NY 11598

RAAB, SHELDON, lawyer, Bklyn. Nov. 30, 1937; s. Morris and Eva (Shereskevsky) R.; m. Judith Deutsch, Dec. 15, 1963; children—Michael Kenneth, Elisabeth Louise, Andrew John. A.B., Columbia U., 1958; LL.B. cum laude, Harvard U., 1961. Bar: N.Y. 1961, U.S. Ct. Appeals (2d cir.) 1963, U.S. Dist. Ct. (so. and ea. dists.) 1967. Dep. asst. atty. gen. State of N.Y., 1961-63, asst. atty gen., 1963-64; assoc. Fried, Frank, Harris, Shriver & Jacobson and predecessor firm, N.Y.C., 1964-69, ptnr., 1970-81, inc. ptnr., 1981—. Mem. exec. com. lawyers' div. United Jewish Appeal, 1982—. Mem. ABA, N.Y. State Bar Assn. (trial lawyers sect. 1968—), Assn. Bar City N.Y. (adminstrv. law com. 1968-71, spl. com. electric power and environment 1971-73, chmn. energy com. 1974-79, fed. cts. com. 1981-84, state cts. juris. com. 1985—). Democrat. Federal civil litigation, State civil litigation. Office: Fried Frank Harris Shriver & Jacobson 1 New York Plaza New York NY 10004

RAACK, WILLIAM JAMES, lawyer; b. St. Louis, Sept. 29, 1927; s. Raymond Charles and Adelaide (Fahrenhorst) R.; m. Elizabeth E. Croghan, Apr. 7, 1951; children: Carol, David, Mary C., Cynthia, William Jr., Peter. Student, U. Utah, 1945-46, St. Louis U., 1946-48; JD, St. Louis U., 1951. Bar: Mo. 1951, U.S. Dist. Ct. (ea. dist.) Mo. 1956. Ptnr. Wood & Raack, St. Louis, 1956-60, Padberg & Raack, St. Louis, 1961-72, Hearnes, Padberg, Raack et al, St. Louis, 1972-75; sole practice St. Louis, 1975—. Alderman City of Crestwood, Mo., 1957-59, pros. atty. 1959-60; exec. sec. Mo. State Athletic Commn., St. Louis, 1971-74. Mem. Mo. Bar Assn. (bd. govs. 1971-75), St. Louis County Bar Assn., Lawyers Assn. St. Louis (pres. 1967-68), Assn. Trial Lawyers Am., Mo. Trial Lawyers Assn. (bd. govs. 1963-64, 72-76), Legal Aid Soc. (bd. dirs. 1965-68). Democrat. Roman Catholic. Avocations: tennis, fishing. State civil litigation, General practice, Probate. Home: 46 W Glendale Rd Webster Groves MO 63119 Office: 10411 Clayton Rd Suite 305 Saint Louis MO 63131

RAAEN, G(ARY) LEE, lawyer; b. Detroit Lakes, Minn., Jan. 25, 1947; s. Raymond and Viola E. (Lindstrom) R. BA, Pacific Luth.U., 1969; JD, U. Oreg., 1975. Bar: Wash. 1975, U.S. Dist. Ct. (we. dist.) Wash. 1975, U.S. Ct. Claims 1975, U.S. Ct. Appeals (9th cir.) 1975. Assoc. Bonneville, Viert & Morton, Tacoma, 1975-78; sole practice Seattle, 1978—. Chmn. Seattle Vietnam Vets. Leadership Program, 1984.Served with U.S. Army, 1969-71, Vietnam. Mem. ABA, Assn. Trial Lawyers Am., Wash. State Trial Lawyers Assn., Seattle-King County Bar Assn. Personal injury, State civil litigation, General practice. Office: 5700 Columbia Ctr 701 Fifth Ave Seattle WA 98104

RABB, BRUCE, lawyer; b. Cambridge, Mass., Oct. 4, 1941; s. Maxwell M. and Ruth (Cryden) R.; m. Harriet Rachel Schaffer, Jan. 4, 1970; children: Alexander Charles, Katherine Anne. A.B., Harvard U., 1962; C.E.P., Institut d'Etudes Politiques, Paris, 1963; LL.B., Columbia U., 1966. Bar: N.Y. 1966. Clk. to Judge John Minor Wisdom, U.S. 5th Circuit Ct. Appeals, 1966-67; assoc. firm Stroock & Stroock & Lavan, N.Y.C., 1967-68, 71-75; ptnr. Stroock & Stroock & Lavan, 1976—; staff asst. to Pres. U.S., 1969-70; bd. dirs. Internat. League Human Rights, 1971—, gen. counsel, 1977—; vice chmn., bd. dirs. Lawyers Com. Human Rights, 1977—; pub. mem. Adminstrv. Conf. of U.S., 1982-86, spl. counsel, 1986—. Bd. dirs. Citizens Union of N.Y., 1981-87, Ams. Watch, 1982—, Helsinki Watch, 1985—, Fund for Free Expression, 1987—; mem. internat. adv. com. Internat. Parliamentary Group for Human Rights in the Soviet Union, 1984—; sec. Lehrman Inst., 1978—. Mem. Assn. Bar City N.Y., ABA, Am. Law Inst. Clubs: Harvard (N.Y.C.); Met. (Washington). Private international, Banking, General corporate. Office: Strook & Strook & Lavin 7 Hanover Sq New York NY 10004

RABBITT, DANIEL THOMAS, JR., lawyer; b. St. Louis, Sept. 19, 1940; s. Daniel Thomas and Charlotte Ann (Carpenter) R.; m. Susan Lee Scherger, July 26, 1969. B.S. in Commerce, St. Louis U., 1962, J.D. cum laude, 1964. Bar: Mo. 1964, U.S. Supreme Ct. 1970. Assoc. Moser, Marsalek, Carpenter, Cleary, Jaeckel, Keaney & Brown and predecessor, St. Louis, 1964-68, ptnr., 1969-81; mem. Brown, James & Rabbitt, P.C., St. Louis, 1981—. Instr., St. Louis U. Sch. Law, 1968-70; dir. Pub. Service Savs. & Loan Assn. Recipient Lon Hocker Meml. Trial Atty. award Mo. Bar Found., 1975. Fellow Am. Coll. Trial Lawyers; mem. ABA (chmn. young lawyers sect. 1973-74), Mo. Bar, Bar Assn. Met. St. Louis, Internat. Assn. Defense Counsel, Am. Judicature Soc. Democrat. Roman Catholic. Club: Mo. Athletic (gov. 1978-81, v.p. 1980-81). Federal civil litigation, State civil litigation, Personal injury. Office: 705 Olive St Suite 1100 Saint Louis MO 63101

RABIDOUX, MARK KENNETH, lawyer; b. Washington, Oct. 14, 1956; s. Kenneth L. and Phyllis M. (Roberts) R.; m. Karen A. Zaleski, May 30, 1981. B in Gen. Studies, U. Mich., 1978; JD, U. Detroit, 1981. Bar: Mich. 1981, U.S. Dist. Ct. (ea. dist.) 1981. Asst. gen. counsel Advance Mortgage Corp., Southfield, Mich., 1981-84; asst. gen. counsel Regency Savs. Bank FSB, Detroit, 1985-86, gen. counsel, 1986—; instr. real estate law Am. Inst. Paralegal Studies, Detroit, 1985—. Recipient Am. Jurisprudence award Lawyers Co-op Pub. Co., 1980. Mem. ABA, Mich. State Bar Assn. Republican. Roman Catholic. Club: Economic (Detroit). Avocation: golf. Banking, Real property. Home: 1866 Lancaster Grosse Pointe Woods MI 48236 Office: Regency Savs Bank FSB 200 Renaissance Ctr Suite 3060 Detroit MI 48243

RABIN, JANE HURWITZ, lawyer; b. Hartford, Conn., Aug. 7, 1940; d. Joseph Bernard and Ruth (Berman) Hurwitz; m. Edward Harold Rabin, Sept. 9, 1962; children: Daniel J., Rebecca A. BA, Barnard Coll., 1962; MA, U. Calif., Davis, 1970; JD, U. Calif., 1982. Bar: Calif. 1982, U.S. Dist. Ct. (ea. dist.) Calif. 1982, U.S. Dist. Ct. (no. dist.) Calif. 1986. Assoc. Melvin J. CoBen, Sacramento, 1982-84; sole practice Davis, Calif., 1984—. Mem. ABA, Calif. Bar Assn., Sacramento County Bar Assn., Yolo County Bar Assn. Democrat. Jewish. Bankruptcy, Real property, Probate. Home: 619 Barbera Pl Davis CA 95616 Office: 102 E St Davis CA 95616

RABIN, MARY ANN, lawyer; b. St. Louis, June 1, 1934; s. Maurice and Rose M. (Morris) Franklin; m. Erwin R. Rabin, June 15, 1954; children: Julie, Kathy, Michael. Student, Eastman Sch. of Music, 1952-54; BA, Washington U., St. Louis, 1956; postgrad., Washburn U., 1975-76; JD, Case Western Res. U., 1978. Bar: Ohio 1978. Assoc. Sindell, Sindell & Rubenstein, Cleve., 1978-83; sole practice Cleve., 1983—. Trustee Hebrew Free Loan, Cleve., 1982—. Mem. ABA, Ohio Bar Assn., Cleve. Bar Assn. (trustee 1986—), Cuyahoga County Bar Assn. Avocation: music. Bankruptcy, Probate. Home: 1 Bratenahl Pl Bratenahl OH 44108 Office: 800 Standard Bldg #1370 Cleveland OH 44113

RABIN, ROBERT L., lawyer, educator; b. 1939. B.S., Northwestern U., 1960, J.D., 1963, Ph.D., 1967. Bar: Ill. 1963. Asst. prof. U. Wis., Madison, 1966-69, assoc. prof., 1969-70; vis. assoc. prof. Stanford U., Calif., 1970-71, assoc. prof., 1971-73, prof., 1973-84, A. Calder Mackay prof., 1984—; reporter ABA Action Commn. to Improve Tort Liability System. Author: Perspective on the Administrative Process, 1979, Perspectives on Tort Law, 2d edit., 1983, Cases and Materials on Tort Law and Alternatives, 1983, 4th edit., 1987; mem. editorial adv. bd. ABF Research Jour., Jour. Legal Edn., Found. Press. Legal education, Administrative and regulatory, Personal injury. Office: Stanford U Law Sch Stanford CA 94305

RABINOWITZ, ALAN JAMES, lawyer; b. Revere, Mass., Dec. 13, 1949; s. George and Esta (Willis) R. BA in Govt., Norwich U., 1971; JD, New Eng. Sch. Law, 1974. Bar: Mass. 1975, U.S. Dist. Ct. Mass. 1979. Sole practice Boston, 1975-76; asst. property atty. New England Electric System, Westborough, Mass., 1976-81, property atty., 1981—. Mem. ABA, Mass. Bar Assn., Mass. Conveyancers Assn. Real property, Administrative and regulatory, Public utilities. Home: 36 Glenwood Ave Newton MA 02159 Office: New England Electric System 25 Research Dr Westborough MA 01581

RABINOWITZ, DANIEL LAWRENCE, lawyer; b. N.Y.C., Sept. 23, 1950; s. Bernard and Ann Hoch (Kubie) R.; m. Ann F. Thomas, Aug. 18, 1974. AB, Harvard U., 1972; JD, Yale U., 1975. Bar: N.Y. 1976, N.J. 1979, U.S. Supreme Ct., U.S. Ct. Appeals (2d and 3d cirs.), U.S. Dist. Ct. N.J., U.S. Dist. Ct. (so. and ea. dists.) N.Y., U.S. Tax Ct. Law clk. to Judge Herbert J. Stern, U.S. Dist. Ct. N.J., Newark, 1975-77; assoc. Nickerson, Kramer, Lowenstein, Nessen, Kamin & Soll, N.Y.C., 1977-78; asst. U.S. atty. Dist. of N.J., Newark, 1978-81; ptnr. McCarter & English, Newark, 1981—; bd. dirs. Atlantic Industries, Inc., Nutley, N.J.; vis. lectr. Yale Law Sch., 1985-86. Mem. N.J. Bar Assn., Assn. Bar City of N.Y., Assn. Fed. Bar of N.J., Essex County Bar Assn., Hudson County Bar Assn. Clubs: Harvard of N.J. (exec. com., schs. com. 1981—); Essex (Newark); Harvard (N.Y.C.). Criminal, Federal civil litigation, State civil litigation. Office: McCarter & English 550 Broad St Newark NJ 07102

RABINOWITZ, JAY ANDREW, justice Alaska Supreme Ct.; b. Phila., Feb. 25, 1927; s. Milton and Rose (Rittenberg) R.; m. Anne Marie Nesbit, June 14, 1957; children: Judith, Mara, Max, Sara. B.A., Syracuse U., 1949; LL.B., Harvard, 1952. Bar: N.Y. State bar 1952, Alaska bar 1958. Practiced in N.Y.C., 1952-57; law clk. U.S. Dist. Ct. judge, Fairbanks, Alaska, 1957-58; asst. U.S. atty. Fairbanks, 1958-59; dep. atty. gen., chief civil div. State of Alaska, 1959-60; judge Superior Ct. Alaska, 1960-65; justice Alaska Supreme Ct., Juneau, 1965—; chief justice Alaska Supreme Ct., 1972-75, 78—; lectr. U. Alaska. Served with AUS, 1945-46. Mem. N.Y., Alaska bar assns. Club: Harvard (N.Y.C.).

RABINOWITZ, MARK ALLAN, lawyer; b. Chgo., Feb. 9, 1954; s. Marvin Harold and Pauline Betty (Robins) R.; m. Linda Kay Beauseigneur, Feb. 7, 1982. BA summa cum laude, U. Ill., 1975; JD, Harvard U., 1978. Bar: Ill. 1978, U.S. Dist. Ct. (no. dist.) Ill. 1978, U.S. Ct. Appeals (7th cir.) 1979. Ptnr. Levy & Erers, Chgo., 1978-85, McDermott, Will & Emery, Chgo., 1985—. Mem. Phi Beta Kappa. Avocations: history, polit. theory, philosophy. Federal civil litigation, Contracts commercial, Bankruptcy. Office: McDermott Will & Emery 111 W Monroe St Chicago IL 60603

RABINOWITZ, SAMUEL NATHAN, lawyer; b. Hazleton, Pa., Sept. 16, 1932; s. Morris M. and Bodia (Janowitz) R.; m. Barbara G. Cohen, Mar. 27, 1955; children—Fredric E., Mark I., Joshua A. B.A., Pa. State U., 1955; J.D., Temple U., 1959. Bar: D.C. 1959, Pa. 1960. Agt. IRS, Phila., 1956-60; sole practice Phila., 1960-61; ptnr. Blank, Rome, Comisky & McCauley, Phila., 1961—; mem. trust com. Continental Bank, Phila., 1983—; faculty Temple U. Sch. Law. Contbr. articles to profl. jours. Pres. Phila. Friends Boys Town Jerusalem; bd. dirs. Jerusalem Soc. Boys Town; v.p. Jewish Nat. Fund Council, Phila. Fellow Am. Coll. Probate Counsel; mem. ABA, Pa. Bar Assn., Phila. Bar Assn. (chmn. probate and trust sect. 1985—). Clubs: Green Valley Country, Elkview Country, Vesper, Golden Slipper. Lodge: B'nai B'rith. Estate planning, Estate taxation, Probate. Home: 1161 Norsam Rd Gladwyne PA 19035 Office: Blank Rome Comisky & McCauley 1200 Four Penn Ctr Plaza Philadelphia PA 19103

RABOLD, C(HARLES) STEVEN, lawyer; b. Dayton, Ohio, Mar. 29, 1955; s. Don E. and Barbara (Whitacker) R.; m. Tracy Ann Bruscino, Aug. 4, 1979; 1 child, Zachary Steven. BA magna cum laude, Bowling Green (Ohio) State U., 1977; JD, U. Dayton, 1980. Bar: Ohio 1980, U.S. Dist. Ct. (so. dist.) Ohio 1981, U.S. Dist. Ct. (no. dist.) Ohio 1983. Assoc. Cowden, Pfarrer, Crew & Becker, Dayton, 1980-83, Squire, Sanders & Dempsey, Cleve., 1983—, lectr. Worker's Compensation Employer's Resource Council, Cleve. Organizer fund raising Am. Cancer Soc., Cleve., 1986. Mem. ABA, Ohio Bar Assn., Ohio Self-Insurers, Northeast Ohio Self-Insurers, Greater Cleve. Growth Assn. Republican. Methodist. Avocations: running, tennis, fishing, baseball. Workers' compensation. Home: 345 Wagar Rd Rocky River OH 44116 Office: Squire Sanders & Dempsey 1800 Huntington Bldg Cleveland OH 44102

RABUCK, STEVEN KENT, lawyer; b. Aberdeen, S.D., Sept. 29, 1953; s. Glen and Maybelle (Aslesen) R.; m. Catherine Marie Thomas, Apr. 12, 1986. BS, U. S.D., 1976, JD, 1981. Bar: S.D. 1982, U.S. Dist. Ct. S.D., 1982. Social worker Redfield (S.D.) State Hosp. and Sch., 1976-77, S.D. Dept. Social Services, Vermillion, 1977-79; assoc. Andera, Rabuck & Smith, Chamberlain, S.D., 1982—; field instr. social work program U. S.D., Redfield, 1977, 79. Chmn. Brule County Dems., Chamberlain, 1983-86; treas. Brule County Child Protection Team, 1984-85. Mem. ABA, S.D. Bar Assn. (domestic relations com. 1982-83), Brule County Bar Assn. (sec. 1982—), S.D. Trial Lawyers Assn., Mcpl. Attys. Assn., U.S. Jaycees (v.p. 1986—). Lutheran. Lodge: Kiwanis (pres. 1987—). Avocations: history, polit. sci., reading, golf. Family and matrimonial, General practice. Home: 1204 S Main Chamberlain SD 57325 Office: Andera Rabuck & Smith Box 286 Chamberlain SD 57325

RACHANOW, GERALD MARVIN, lawyer; b. Balt., Aug. 7, 1942; s. Louis and Lillyan (Binstock) R.; m. Sally Davis, July 26, 1964; children: Mindy, Shelly, Gary. BS in Pharmacy, U. Md., 1965; JD, U. Balt., 1972. Bar: Md. 1973, U.S. Dist. Ct. Md. 1977, U.S. Supreme Ct. 1977. Consumer safety officer FDA, Rockville, Md., 1973—; ptnr. Rachanow & Wolfson, Randallstown, Md., 1975—; contbr. fed. drug law exam. Nat. Assn. Bds. Pharmacy, 1985. Contbr. articles to profl. jours. Bd. dirs. parent tchr. student orgn. Md. Sch. for Blind, Balt., 1985—; mem. Community Living for Multihandicapped Blind, Balt., 1984—, adv., 1984—, Spina Bifida Assn. Md., Balt., 1985—. Fellow Am. Soc. Pharmacy Law; mem. ABA, Soc. FDA Pharmacists, Heuisler Honor Soc. Avocations: chess, stamp and coin collecting, sports. Administrative and regulatory, Personal income taxation, Probate. Home: 8817 Allenswood Rd Randallstown MD 21133 Office: US FDA 5600 Fishers Ln Rockville MD 20857

RACHLIN, RICHARD STANLEY, lawyer; b. Miami, Fla., Sept. 29, 1947; s. George J. and Rose (Gershon) R.; children—Andrew, Julie. A.B., U. N.C., 1969; J.D., U. Tex., Austin, 1972. Bar: Fla. 1972, Ga. 1973, U.S. Supreme Ct. 1975, U.S. Tax Ct. 1979, U.S. Dist. Ct. (no. dist.) Fla. 1973, U.S. Dist. Ct. (mid. dist.) Fla. 1973, U.S. Dist. Ct. (so. dist.) Fla. 1974, U.S. Dist. Ct. (no. dist.) Ga. 1975, U.S. Ct. Appeals (5th cir.) 1981, U.S. Ct. Appeals (11th cir.) 1981. Clk., U.S. Dist. Ct., Jacksonville, Fla., 1972-73; asst. atty. gen. Fla. Atty. Gen., Tallahassee, 1973-74; atty. Frates, Floyd, Pearson, Miami, 1974-79, Sams, Gerstein & Ward, Miami, 1979-80; ptnr. Payton & Rachlin, P.A., Miami, 1980—. Bd. dirs. Beth David Synagogue, Miami, 1982-84, Boys Club, 1982-84. Research grantee, U. Tex., 1970. Mem. ABA (litigation sect., co-chmn. sub-com. on legal liability), Fla. Bar (cert., chmn. grievance com. 1982-84), Nat. Assn. Trial Lawyers, Acad. Fla. Trial Lawyers, Fed. Bar Assn., Phi Delta Phi. Jewish. Criminal. Office: Payton & Rachlin PA 100 N Biscayne Blvd New World Tower Suite 1810 Miami FL 33132

RACHLIN, ROBERT DAVID, lawyer; b. Hartford, Conn., July 22, 1936; s. John Copeland and Pauline Harriet (Dorenbaum) R.; m. Gertrude Anne Phillips, July 29, 1957; children—Deborah Tamar, Paul Isaac, Rebecca Scott, John Nathan, Julia Bothwell; m. 2d, Catharine Amy Bothwell, July 5, 1980. A.B., Yale U., 1957; J.D., U. Chgo., 1959. Bar: Vt. 1960, U.S. Dist. Ct. Vt. 1960, U.S. Dist. Ct. (no. dist.) Calif. 1982, U.S. Ct. Appeals (2d cir.) 1962, U.S. Supreme Ct. 1982. pres. Downs, Rachlin & Martin and predecessor

firms, Burlington and St. Johnsbury, Vt., 1959—, chief litigation, 1962—; state's atty. Caledonia County, Vt., 1961-64; lectr. Assn. Trial Lawyers Am., 1975-79; mem. Vt. Bd. Bar Examiners, 1972—; mem. Vt. Profl. Conduct Bd., 1976-79. Fellow Internat. Acad. Trial Lawyers; mem. Am. Law Inst., ABA, Lawyer-Pilots Bar Assn., Vt. Bar Assn. Republican. Jewish. Contbr. articles to profl. jours. Federal civil litigation, State civil litigation, Insurance. Office: Downs Rachlin & Martin 100 Dorset St Suite 1 Burlington VT 05401

RACINE, KATHLEEN CELESTE, lawyer, military officer; b. Stanley, N.D., July 13, 1950; d. Milford Leroy Biel and Annie Luella (Lund) Brandt; m. Ronald Leroy Racine, Nov. 22, 1973 (div. May 1983); 1 child, Wade Lee; m. Daniel Francis Bouchard, Jan. 1, 1986. Student, Minot State Coll., 1971-74; BS in Social Work cum laude, U. N.D., 1977, JD, 1980. Bar: N.D. 1980, U.S. Dist. Ct. N.D. 1980, U.S. Ct. Appeals (8th cir.) 1980, U.S. Ct. Mil. Appeals, 1982. Instr. law U. N.D., Grand Forks, 1980; sole practice Grand Forks, 1981-82; commd. 1st lt. USAF, 1982, advanced through grades to capt., 1982; asst. judge adv. USAF, March AFB, Calif., 1982-83, area def. counsel, 1983-84; chief of justice USAF, McGuire AFB, N.J., 1985; asst. judge adv. civil law USAF, Wright Patterson AFB, Ohio, 1986—; legal rep. family advocacy com., Wright Patterson AFB, 1986—. Named one of Outstanding Young Women of Am., 1983. Mem. ABA, Fed. Bar Assn. (Younger Fed. Lawyer award 1985), N.D. Bar Assn. Republican. Lutheran. Avocations: law enforcement agy. tng., juvenile and family crisis intervention, victim-witness support. Criminal, Administrative and regulatory, Military. Home: 412 White Ash Ct Fairborn OH 45324 Office: 2750 Air Base Wing Judge Adv Wright Patterson AFB OH 45433-5000

RACK, THOMAS PAUL, lawyer, educator, actor; b. Bayonne, N.J., Sept. 8, 1953; s. Stephen William and Gladys Susan (Dudowicz) R. BA, Rutgers U., 1975; JD, Potomac Sch. Law, 1979. Bar: Ga. 1979, U.S. Dist. Ct. (no. dist.) Ga. 1979, U.S. Ct. Appeals (5th cir.) 1979, U.S. Ct. Claims, 1979, U.S. Tax Ct. 1979, Md. 1980, U.S. Dist. Ct. Md. 1981, U.S. Ct. Appeals (4th cir.) 1981, Hawaii 1985, D.C. 1985, U.S. Dist. Ct. Hawaii 1986. Transp. mgr. Roadway Express Co., South Kearny, N.J., 1975-76; assoc. Austin & Pahno, Savannah, Ga., 1979-80, Marlow & Peddicord, Towson, Md., 1981-83; v.p. Sentinel Title Corp., Balt., 1983-86; asst. prof. Towson State U., Md., 1983-86; sole practice, Annapolis, Md., 1983-86, Honolulu, 1986—; mem. Atty. Grievance Commn. Md., Annapolis, 1982-86; bd. dirs. J. Finley Ransone & Assocs., Inc., Towson, L.I. Farms, Inc., Phoenix, Md., 1986—; asst. prof. Chaminade MBA program U. Honolulu, 1986—. Com. chmn. voter registration drive, Annapolis, 1981; vice chancellor Trial Ct. Bd. Potomac Sch. Law, 1978-79. Mem. State Bar Ga., Md. State Bar Assn. (mem. com. on unauthorized pracitce of law, 1982-86), D.C. Bar Assn., Hawaii State Bar Assn., Baltimore County Bar Assn., Anne Arundel County Bar Assn, Assn. Trial Lawyers Am. (pres. Potomac chpt. 1978-79), Ga. Trial Lawyers Assn., U.S. Naval Inst., Screen Actor's Guild. Clubs: YMCA (Severna Park, Md.), Propellor. Lodge: Kiwanis (sec. Anne Arundel chpt., citizenship award 1971). Roman Catholic. Real property, State civil litigation, Contracts commercial. Office: 220 S King St Suite 2222 Honolulu HI 96813

RADASKY, DAVID JACOB, lawyer, business executive; b. Fed. Republic Germany, May 13, 1948; came to U.S., 1949; s. Sam and Frieda (Bernstein) R.; m. Sylvia Harding, Jan. 9, 1972; 1 child, Marc H. BS in Econs., U. New Orleans, 1970; JD, Loyola U., New Orleans, 1973. Bar: U.S. Dist. Ct. (ea. dist.) La. 1973. Asst. dist. atty. City of New Orleans, 1973-75; ptnr. Gertler & Gertler, New Orleans, 1975-77; exec. v.p. Columbia Burlap and Bag, Kansas City, Mo., 1977—; v.p. Dallas Bag and Burlap, 1978—, G. & R. Nat., Kansas City, 1978—; pres. Koch Bag and Supply, Kansas City, 1981—. Contbr. articles to profl. jours. Mem. Textile Bag and Packing Assn. (pres. 1985—), World Orgn. Recognized Liquidators and Distbrs. (bd. dirs. 1985—). Republican. Jewish. Lodge: B'nai B'rith (v.p. Kansas City 1979-84). Avocation: tennis. General corporate, Criminal, Contracts commercial. Home: 4605 W 88th Prairie Village KS 66207 Office: Columbia Burlap and Bag 999 Bedford Ave North Kansas City MO 64116

RADCLIFFE, MARK FLOHN, lawyer; b. Dayton, Ohio, Mar. 11, 1952; s. David Laurence and Kathryn Elizabeth (Stoutenburgh) R. Cert. of completion, Sorbonne, Paris, 1972; BS in Chem. magna cum laude, U. Mich., 1974; JD, Harvard U., 1981. Bar: Calif. 1982. Law clk. to chief judge U.S. Dist. Ct. (so. dist.) Calif., San Diego, 1981-82; assoc. Brobeck, Phleger & Harrison, San Francisco, 1982-86, Ware & Freidenrich, San Francisco, 1986—. Contbr. articles (with others) to law reviews. Served to lt. (j.g.) USNR, 1974-77. Mem. ABA (chmn. subcom. 1985—), San Francisco Bar Assn. (chmn. computer law sect. 1985—), Licensing Exec. Soc. Club: Harvard (N.Y.C.). General corporate, Trademark and copyright, Computer. Office: Ware & Freidenrich 400 Hamilton Ave Palo Alto CA 94301

RADCLIFFE, WILLIAM M., III, lawyer; b. Charlottesville, Va., Aug. 1, 1948; s. William M. Jr. Radcliffe and Janet E. (Irvin) Kern; m. Jenny Kathleen Robinson, Aug. 25, 1973; children: Christopher Walker, Eric Martin, Craig Michael. BA, Bucknell U., 1970; JD, Vanderbilt U., 1973. Bar: Pa. 1973, U.S. Supreme Ct. 1977, U.S. Ct. Appeals (3d cir.) 1986. Assoc. Coldren & Coldren, Uniontown, Pa., 1973-78; ptnr. Coldren, DeHaas & Radcliffe, Uniontown, 1978—; vice chmn. Uniontown Health Resources, 1985—; bd. dirs. Uniontown Svgs. and Loan Assn. Mem. Pa. Def. Inst. Democrat. Lodge: Rotary. State civil litigation, Insurance, Personal injury. Office: Coldren DeHaas & Radcliffe 700 Gallatin Bank Bldg PO Box 1327 Uniontown PA 15401

RADDING, ANDREW, lawyer; b. N.Y.C., Nov. 30, 1944; s. Jules and Estelle (Pomerantz) R.; m. Bonnie-Ann Levinson, Oct. 7, 1972; children—Judith Lynne, Joshua David. B.B.A., CCNY Baruch Sch., 1965; J.D., Boston U., 1968. Bar: N.Y. 1968, Md. 1977, D.C. 1977. Grad. fellow Northwestern U. Sch. Law, 1968-69; asst. csl. U.S. Ho. of Reps. Select Com. on Crime, 1969-72; asst. U.S. atty. for Dist. Md., 1972-77; ptnr. Francomano, Radding & Mannes, Balt., 1977-80, Burke, Gerber, Wilen, Francomano & Radding, Balt., 1980-85, Blades & Rosenfeld P.A., Balt., 1985—. Mem. adj. faculty clin. practice skills, criminal law, fed. criminal practice U. Balt. Sch. Law, 1980—; mem. trial experience com. U.S. Dist. Ct., 1986—. Bd. dirs. Copper Hill Condominium, 1979-82, pres., 1981-82; chmn. subcom. Md. Republican Conv., 1981. Mem. ABA, Md. Bar Assn., Balt. City Bar Assn., Fed. Bar Assn. (sec. Balt. chpt. 1981-82, chmn. bd. dirs. 1982, v.p. 1983-84, pres. elect 1985-86, pres. 1986-87), N.Y. State Bar Assn., D.C. Bar Assn., U.S. Atty. Alumni Assn. Md. (pres. 1978—), Md. Inst. Continuing Profl. Edn. for Lawyers (bd. govs.). Jewish. Federal civil litigation, State civil litigation, Criminal. Home: 52 Penny Ln Baltimore MD 21209 Office: Blades & Rosenfeld PA 20 S Charles St Suite 1200 Baltimore MD 21201

RADER, RALPH TERRANCE, lawyer; b. Clarksburg, W.Va., Dec. 5, 1947; s. Ralph Coolidge and Jeanne (Cover) R.; m. Rebecca Jo Vorderman, Mar. 22, 1969; children—Melissa Michelle, Allison Suzanne. B.S. in Mech. Engrng., Va. Poly. Inst., 1970; J.D., Am. U., Washington, 1974. Bar: Va. 1975, U.S. Ct. Customs and Patent Appeals 1977, U.S. Dist. Ct. (ea. dist.) Mich. 1978, Mich. 1979, U.S. Ct. Appeals (6th cir.) 1979, U.S. Dist. Ct. (we. dist.) Mich. 1981, U.S. Ct. Appeals (fed. cir.) 1983. Supervisory patent examiner U.S. Patent Office, Washington, 1970-77; patent atty., ptnr. Cullen, Sloman, Cantor, Grauer, Scott & Rutherford, Detroit, 1977—. Contbr. articles to profl. jours. Mem. adminstrv. bd. First United Methodist Ch., Birmingham, Mich., 1980—. Served with U.S. Army, 1970-76. Recipient Superior Performance award U.S. Patent Office, Washington, 1971-77. Mem. Am. Patent Law Assn., ABA, Mich. Patent Law Assn., Mich. Bar. (mem. governing council patent trademark and copyright law sect. 1981-84), Engrng. Soc. Detroit, Tau Beta Pi, Pi Tau Sigma, Phi Kappa Phi. Methodist. Lodge: Masons. Patent, Trademark and copyright, Federal civil litigation. Home: 4933 Moonglow Dr Troy MI 48098 Office: Cullen Sloman Cantor Grauer et al 2400 Penobscot Bldg Detroit MI 48226

RADER, ROBERT MICHAEL, lawyer; b. Camden, N.J., Sept. 9, 1946; s. Raymond Cornelius and Martha Lou (Freas) R.; m. Eileen Charnesky, June 5, 1976; children: Brennan Matthew, Ashley Marie. BA cum laude, Lafayette Coll., 1968; JD, Cornell U., 1971. Bar: N.J. 1972, D.C. 1977. Law sec. to chief judge U.S. Dist. Ct. N.J., Newark, 1971-73; trial atty. U.S. Justice Dept., Washington, 1973-78; assoc. Conner & Wetterhahn P.C., Washington, 1978-79, ptnr., 1980—. Contbr. articles to profl. jours. Ward chmn. Falls Church Rep. com., Va., 1980-86. Mem. Phi Beta Kappa. Roman Catholic. Club: River Bend Country (Great Falls, Va.). Nuclear power, Administrative and regulatory, Government contracts and claims. Home: 812 Hickory Vale Ln Great Falls VA 22066 Office: Conner & Wetterhahn PC 1747 Pennsylvania Ave NW Suite 1050 Washington DC 20006

RADFORD, MARY FRANCES, law educator; b. Paterson, N.J., May 16, 1952; d. Lewis Candler Jr. and Marguerite Agnes (Sweeney) R.; m. Charles Lee Raudonis, June 27, 1980. BA, Tulane U., 1974; JD, Emory U., 1981. Bar: Ga. 1981, U.S. Dist. Ct. (no. dist.) Ga. 1981, U.S. Ct. Appeals (11th cir.) 1981. Assoc. Hansell & Post, Atlanta, 1981-84; asst. prof. law Ga. State U., Atlanta, 1984—, lectr. continuing legal edn., 1984, 85. Mem. ABA, Ga. Bar Assn. (fiduciary law sect.), Atlanta Bar Assn., Ga. Assn. Women Lawyers. Estate planning, Pension, profit-sharing, and employee benefits, Probate. Home: 44 Lullwater Estate Rd Atlanta GA 30307 Office: Ga State U Coll Law University Plaza Atlanta GA 30303

RADKE, DANIEL LEE, lawyer, legal educator; b. Kansas City, Mo., July 7, 1948; s. Gail Norman and Delores (Laughlin) R.; m. Julie Marie Heskin, Mar. 26, 1977; children—Matthew, Daniel, Sarah. B.A. with highest honors, Mo. Western State Coll., 1972; J.D., U. Mo., 1975. Bar: Mo. 1975, U.S. Supreme Ct. 1979. Staff, then mng. atty. Legal Aid of Western Mo., Kansas City, 1975-79; gen. pvt. practice, asst. pub. defender, 1979-86; mem. part-time faculty Mo. Western State Coll., St. Joseph, 1984—. Bd. dirs. St. Joseph Mental Health Assn., 1979-81, Creative Arts Prodn., St. Joseph, 1984-85, United Cerebral Palsy Buchanan County, 1985—. Served with U.S. Army, 1966-69, Vietnam. Mem. ABA, Mo. Bar Assn., St. Joseph Bar Assn., Mo. Assn. Criminal Def. Lawyers, Am. Trial Lawyers Assn. Criminal, Family and matrimonial, General practice. Home and Office: PO Box 2033 Saint Joseph MO 64501

RADLER, WARREN S., lawyer; b. Mt. Kisco, N.Y., July 6, 1936; s. Hyman J. and Freda (Pomerantz) R.; m. Jill Weber, Aug. 24, 1958; m. Leontine Van Lent, Sept. 1, 1973; children: Jennifer, James. BA, Cornell U., 1957, JD, 1960. Bar: N.Y. 1960, U.S. Dist. Ct. (we. dist.) N.Y. 1961, Ill. 1979, U.S. Dist. Ct. (no. dist.) Ill. 1979. Trial atty. U.S. Dept. Justice, Washington, 1960-61; ptnr. Saperston, Day & Radler, Buffalo, 1961-79; sr. ptnr. Radler & Drucher, Chgo., 1979-81, Rivkin, Radler, Dunne & Bayh, Chgo., 1981—. Fellow Am. Coll. Trial Lawyers; mem. Nat. Inst. Trial Advocacy (faculty), Erie County Trial Lawyers Assn. (bd. dirs. 1974-76). Clubs: Exec. Suite (Buffalo); Mid-Day (Chgo.). Federal civil litigation, Environment. Office: Rivkin Radler Dunne & Bayh 30 N LaSalle St Chicago IL 60602

RADLO, EDWARD JOHN, lawyer, mathematician; b. Pawtucket, R.I., Mar. 7, 1946; s. Edward Zygmund and Sue Mary (Borek) R.; m. Virginia Judith Butts, Nov. 26, 1975; 1 dau., Heather Sue. B.S., MIT, 1967; J.D., Harvard U., 1972. Bar: Calif. 1972, U.S. Dist. Ct. (no. dist.) Calif. 1972, R.I. 1973, U.S. Patent Office 1973, Can. Patent Office 1974. Staff dir. Atty. Gen.'s Adv. Commn. on Juvenile Code Revision, Boston, 1970-72; law clk. R.I. Supreme Ct., 1972-73; patent atty. Honeywell Info. Systems, Waltham, Mass., 1973-74, Varian Assocs., Palo Alto, Calif., 1974-78, Ford Aerospace & Communications Corp., Palo Alto, Calif., 1978-83, patent counsel, 1983—; lectr. law U. Calif., San Jose State U., U. Santa Clara, 1975-78; organizer So. Peninsula Emergency Communications System, 1979—. Mem., Lawyers' Alliance for Nuclear Arms Control, 1982—, Environ. Def. Fund., 1979—. Served with USPHS, 1967-69. Mem. Peninsula Patent Law Assn., San Francisco Patent and Trademark Law Assn., ABA, Internat. Patent and Trademark Assn., Calif. Bar (patent, trademark and copyright sect.), Sigma Xi. Democrat. Clubs: No. Calif. Contest (pres. 1984-85), Assn. Radio Amateurs of So. New England Inc. (sec. 1962-63). General corporate, Private international, Patent. Home: 25811 Estacada Dr Los Altos Hills CA 94022 Office: Ford Aerospace & Communications Corp 3939 Fabian Way Mail Sta A09 Palo Alto CA 94303

RADMER, MICHAEL JOHN, lawyer, educator; b. Wisconsin Rapids, Wis., Apr. 28, 1945; s. Donald Richard and Thelma Loretta (Donahue) R.; children from previous marriage: Christina Nicole, Ryan Michael; m. Laurie J. Anshus, Dec. 22, 1983; 1 child, Michael John. B.S., Northwestern U., Evanston, Ill., 1967; J.D., Harvard U., 1970. Bar: Minn. 1970. Assoc. Dorsey & Whitney, Mpls., 1970-75, ptnr., 1976—; lectr. law Hamline U. Law Sch., St. Paul, 1981-84; gen. counsel, rep., sec. 38 federally registered investment cos., Mpls. and St. Paul, 1977—. Contbr. articles to legal jours. Active legal work Hennepin County Legal Advice Clinic, Mpls., 1971—. Mem. ABA, Minn. Bar Assn., Hennepin County Bar Assn. Club: Mpls. Athletic. General corporate, Securities, Legal education. Home: 4329 E Lake Harriet Pkwy Minneapolis MN 55409 Office: Dorsey & Whitney 2200 First Bank Pl E Minneapolis MN 55402

RADO, PETER THOMAS, lawyer; b. Berlin, Germany, Nov. 12, 1928; came to U.S., 1931, naturalized, 1937; s. Sandor and Emmy (Chrisler) R.; m. Jacqueline Danenberg, Sept. 11, 1977. A.B., Harvard U., 1949, LL.B., 1952, LL.M., 1953. Bar: N.Y. 1952. Assoc., Ide, Haigney & Rado, N.Y.C., 1956-61, ptnr., 1961—. Served as cpl. U.S. Army, 1953-55. Mem. ABA, N.Y. State Bar Assn., Assn. Bar City N.Y., Internat. Bar Assn. Club: Harvard (N.Y.C.). General corporate, Probate, Corporate taxation. Home: 176 E 71st St New York NY 10021 Office: 41 E 42d St New York NY 10017

RADON, JENIK RICHARD, lawyer; b. Berlin, Germany, Jan. 14, 1946; came to U.S., 1951, naturalized, 1956; s. Louis and Irmgard (Hinz) R.; m. Heidi B. Duerbeck, June 10, 1971; 1 child, Kaara H.D. BA, Columbia Coll., 1967; MCP, U. Calif.-Berkeley, 1971; JD, Stanford U., 1971. Bar: Calif. 1972, N.Y. 1975, U.S. Ct. Appeals (2d cir.) 1975, U.S. Dist. Ct. (so. dist.) N.Y. 1975. Assoc. Agnew, Miller & Carlson, Los Angeles, 1971-72, Shearman & Sterling, N.Y.C., 1972-81; ptnr. Radon, Ishizumi and Matar, N.Y.C., Tokyo, Hong Kong, Munich and Bangkok, 1981—; lectr. Polish Acad. Scis., 1980, Tokyo Arbitration Assn., 1983, Japan External Trade Orgn., 1983, 86, Japan Mgmt. Assn., 1983, Japan Inst. Internat. Bus. Law, 1983-84, Va. Ctr. World Trade, 1985. Editor-in-chief Stanford Jour. Internat. Studies, 1970-71; contbr. articles to German bus. and legal pubs. Active Am. Council on Germany, N.Y.C., 1978—, U.S.-Polish Econ. Council, 1987—; mem. exec. com. Afghanistan Relief Com., N.Y.C., 1980—; seminar participant U.S. Polish Trade Commn., Washington, 1981; regional rep. Direct Relief Internat., Santa Barbara, Calif., 1983—; hon. mem. bd. dirs. Freedom Medicine, Honolulu, 1986—. NSF grantee, 1966; Mellon Found. grantee, 1967; Latin Am. Inst. grantee, 1968; Slavic and E. European Inst. grantee, 1968; HUD fellow, 1968-70. Mem. ABA, German-Am. Law Assn., German Forum. Roman Catholic. Club: Deutscher Verein. Private international, General corporate, Banking. Office: Radon Ishizumi & Matar 269 W 71st St New York NY 10023

RADOSEVICH, GEORGE EDWARD, lawyer, educator, cons., researcher, writer; b. Rock Springs, Wyo., Apr. 15, 1942; s. John Thomas and Mary R.; m. Diane Carol Taylor, July 20, 1969 (div.); m. 2d, Cynthia Aline, Aug. 14, 1981; children—Kristi Marie, James Warren Radosevich; 1 stepdau., Teresa Aline Jones. B.A. in Polit. Sci., U. Wyo., 1966, J.D., 1968; M.A. in Agrl. Econs., Colo. State U., 1972. Bar: Wyo. 1969, U.S. Dist. Ct. Wyo. 1969, Colo. 1978, U.S. Dist. Ct. Colo. 1978. Assoc., Vidakovich, Legerski & Radosevich, Lander, Wyo., 1969-76; ptnr. firm Vidakovich, Pappas, Hooper, Radosevich & Rutz, Denver, 1977-80; mng. ptnr. Vidakovich Pappas & Radosevich, Denver, 1980-81; Radosevich & Assos., Denver, 1981-86; Radosevich & Schmitt, P.C., 1987—; research assoc. Colo. State U., Ft. Collins, 1968-72, asst. prof., 1972-76, asso. prof. water law and econs., dept. econs. and acctg., 1976—; prof. water law, agrl. and nat. econ. dept., 1982—; dep. dir. Colo. Irrigation Mgmt., 1986—; affairs officer water law UN, N.Y.C., 1972-73; counsel Eden Valley Irrigation and Drainage Dist., Farson, Wyo., 1971-82; cons., prin. cons. Resources Adminstrn. and Devel., Inc., Denver; cons. nat., internat. water policy, law adminstrn. and water users orgns. U.S. AID, Nigeria, 1972, Afghanistan, 1972-75, Pakistan, 1972-78, Tunisia, 1978, Sri Lanka, 1978-81, Indonesia, 1986, Swaziland, 1984-87; cons. ad hoc com. on water problems, State of Colo., 1975, High Plains Assos., Austin, Tex., 1978-82, Calif. Poly. Inst., 1981, Egypt, 1981, 82, 83, Bangladesh, 1982-86, World Bank, 1980, 83, World Bank in Thailand and Indonesia, 1984-86; organizer, dir. various nat. and internat. water law and mgmt. confs., 1975-85. Co-author: Evolution and Administration of Colorado Water Law, 1966-1976, 1976, Water Policies for Asia, 1987; contbr. chpts. to books in field., articles, book reviews to profl. publs. Served with U.S. Army, 1960-62. Recipient interdisciplinary award Colo. State U., 1949. Mem. ABA (coms. environ. quality and water resources), Am. Assn. Agrl. Law, Am. Immigration Lawyers Assn., Assn. Trial Lawyers Am., Am. Water Resources Assn., Colo. Bar Assn., Colo. River Assn., Colo. River Water Users Assn., Colo. Water Congress, Denver Bar Assn., Fed. Bar Assn., Internat. Assn. Water Law, Internat. Bar Assn., Internat. Commn. on Irrigation Land Drainage, Internat. Law Assn., Internat. Water Resources Assn., Soc. for Internat. Devel., Wyo. Bar Assn., Wyo. Water Devel. Assn. Democrat. Roman Catholic. Participant profl. confs. U.S., Spain, Ecuador, Czechoslovakia, Mex., Argentina, Bangladesh, Morocco, Italy, Egypt, Pakistan. Immigration, naturalization, and customs, Private international, National, international water policy law. Office: Radosevich & Schmitt PC 1050 17th St #330 Denver CO 80265-0301

RADTKE, STEPHEN DAVID, lawyer; b. LaCrosse, Wis., May 18, 1941; s. Gustal Willard and Margaret Elizabeth (Sliter) R.; m. Katherine Naomi Coltvet, Aug. 10, 1963; children: Shawn, Heather, Keith. BS, Winona State Coll., 1963; JD cum laude, William Mitchell Coll. Law, 1973. Bar: Minn. 1973. Instr. math., speech and sci. Addis Ababa, Ethiopia and Minn., 1963-69; group legal asst. Northwestern Nat. Life Ins. Co., Mpls., 1970-73; sole practice Cambridge, Minn., 1973-75, Bloomington, Minn., 1978—; atty. Gelco Corp., Eden Prairie, Minn., 1975-78. Mem. ABA, Minn. Bar Assn., Hennepin County Bar Assn., William Mitchell Coll. Law Alumni Assn. (pres. 1982-84). State civil litigation, Contracts commercial, General corporate. Home: 10781 Hopkins Circle Bloomington MN 55420 Office: 10800 Lyndale Ave S Suite 255 Bloomington MN 55420

RADZILOWSKY, MICHAEL, lawyer; b. Regensberg, Germany, Apr. 5, 1949; came to U.S., 1949; s. Cezary and Tamara (Veremovich) R.; m. Margaret Johnson, Aug. 30, 1970; children: Michael Johnson, William Johnson. BA, Elmhurst Coll., 1970; JD, DePaul U., 1976. Bar: Ill. 1976, U.S. Dist. Ct. (no. dist.) Ill. 1976, U.S. Ct. Appeals (7th cir.) 1976, U.S. Ct. Appeals (5th cir.) 1978, U.S. Supreme Ct. 1980, U.S. Ct. Appeals (4th and 10th cirs.) 1981, U.S. Ct. Appeals (1st, 2d and D.C. cirs.) 1982, U.S. Ct. Appeals (8th cir.) 1984. Tchr. Chgo. Bd. Edn., 1970-73; assoc. Robbins, Schwartz et al, Chgo., 1976-77, DeJong, Poltrock & Giampietro, Chgo., 1978-85; sole practice Chgo., 1985—; counsel Salaried Employees Assn., Chgo., 1980—, Peoria Fedn. Tchrs., 1983—; assoc. counsel Am. Fedn. Tchrs., Washington, 1978-85; cons. Landmarks Preservation Council, Chgo., 1985—; mem. State's Atty.'s Task Force on Womans Issues, Chgo., 1985—. Chmn. adminstrv. bd. Granville Ave. United Meth. Chs., Chgo., 1982—; mem. steering com. Ill. Coalition Against Death Penalty, Chgo., 1978—; pres. 48th ward Dems., Chgo., 1985—; bd. dirs. Edgewater Community Council, Chgo., 1985—. Mem. ABA (labor, gen. practice and econs. sects.), Ill. Bar Assn. (chmn. union legis. sect. 1985—, labor council), Chgo. Bar Assn. (chmn. housing and urban affairs council 1982-84), Assn. Trial Lawyers Am. Labor, Civil rights, Local government. Home: 1412 W Norwood Chicago IL 60660 Office: 35 E Wacker Dr Suite 2150 Chicago IL 60601

RAE, MATTHEW SANDERSON, JR., lawyer; b. Pitts., Sept. 12, 1922; s. Matthew Sanderson and Olive (Waite) R.; m. Janet Hettman, May 2, 1953; children: Mary-Anna, Margaret, Janet. A.B., Duke, 1946, LL.B., 1947; postgrad., Stanford U., 1951. Bar: Md. 1948, Calif. 1951. Asst. to dean Duke Sch. Law, Durham, N.C., 1947-48; assoc. Karl F. Steinmann, Balt., 1948-49; asso. Guthrie, Darling & Shattuck, Los Angeles, 1953-54; nat. field rep. Phi Alpha Delta Frat., Los Angeles, 1949-51; research atty. Calif. Supreme Ct., San Francisco, 1951-52; ptnr. Darling, Hall & Rae and predecessor firms, Los Angeles, 1955—; mem. Calif. Commn. Uniform State Laws, 1985—. Vice pres. Los Angeles County Republican Assembly, 1959-64; mem. Los Angeles County Rep. Central Com., 1960-64, 77—, exec. com., 1977—; vice chmn. 17th Congressional Dist., 1960-62, 28th Congl. Dist., 1962-64; chmn. 46th Assembly Dist., 1962-64, 27th Senatorial Dist., 1977—; mem. Calif. Rep. State Cen. Com., 1966—, exec. com., 1966-67; pres. Calif. Rep. League, 1966-67; trustee Republican Assocs., 1979—, pres., 1983-85, chmn. bd. dirs., 1985—. Served to 2d lt. USAAF, World War II. Fellow Am. Coll. Probate Counsel; academician Internat. Acad. Estate and Trust Law (exec. council 1974-78); mem. ABA, Los Angeles County Bar Assn. (chmn. probate and trust law com. 1964-66, chmn. legislation com. 1980-86, chmn. program com. 1981-82, chmn. membership retention com. 1982-83, trustee 1983-85), South Bay Bar Assn., State Bar Calif. (chmn. state bar jour. com. 1970-71, chmn. probate com. 1974-75, exec. com. estate planning trust and probate law sect. 1977-83, chmn. legislation com. 1977—, probate law cons. group Calif. Bd. Legal Specialization 1977—, chmn. conf. dels. resolutions com. 1987), Lawyers Club of Los Angeles (bd. govs. 1981—, 1st v.p. 1982-83), Am. Legion (comdr. Allied post 1969-70), Legion Lex (dir. 1964—, pres. 1969-71), Air Force Assn., Aircraft Owners and Pilots Assn., Town Hall (gov. 1970-78, pres. 1975), World Affairs Council, Rotary Internat., Internat. Platform Assn., Los Angeles Com. on Fgn. Relations, Phi Beta Kappa (councilor Alpha Assn. 1983—, v.p. 1984-86), Omicron Delta Kappa, Phi Alpha Delta (supreme justice 1972-74, elected to Disting. Service chpt. 1978), Sigma Nu. Presbyterian. Clubs: Commonwealth (San Francisco); Chancery, Stock Exchange (Los Angeles). Probate, Estate taxation, Estate planning. Home: 600 John St Manhattan Beach CA 90266 Office: 606 S Olive St Suite 1900 Los Angeles CA 90014

RAFEEDIE, EDWARD, federal judge; b. Orange, N.J., Jan. 6, 1929; s. Fred and Nabeeha (Hishmeh) R.; m. Ruth Ann Horton, Oct. 8, 1961; children: Fredrick Alexander, Jennifer Ann. BS in Law, U. So. Calif., 1957, JD, 1959; LLD, Pepperdine U., 1978. Bar: Calif. 1960. Sole practice law Santa Monica, Calif., 1960-69; mcpl. ct. judge Santa Monica Jud. Dist., Santa Monica, 1969-71; judge Superior Ct. State of Calif., Los Angeles, 1971-82; dist. judge U.S. Dist. Court for Central Dist. Calif., Los Angeles, 1982—. Trustee Santa Monica Hosp. Med. Ctr., 1979—; bd. dirs. Luth. Hosp. Soc. Corp., Los Angeles, 1985; mem. adv. bd. Greater Western council Boy Scouts Am., Los Angeles, 1980—. Served with U.S. Army, 1950-52, Korea. Judicial administration. Office: US Dist Court 312 N Spring St Los Angeles CA 90012 *

RAFF, DAVID, labor arbitrator, lawyer; b. N.Y.C., Jan. 10, 1945; s. Dan and Helen (Roman) R.; m. Patricia Cooper, Aug. 25, 1968; children—Sherri Michelle, Kenneth Michael. A.B., Syracuse U., 1966; J.D., Bklyn. Law Sch., 1968; LL.M. in Labor Law, N.Y.U., 1970. Bar: N.Y. 1969, U.S. Dist. Cts. (so., ea. dists.) N.Y. 1973, U.S. Ct. Appeals (2d cir.), U.S. Supreme Ct. 1974. Assoc. clin. prof. law N.Y.U. Sch. Law, 1970-79; legal cons. N.Y.C. Bur. Labor Services, 1971-82; legal cons. N.Y. State Fin. Control Bd. and state dep. comptroller for N.Y.C. Affairs, 1976-86; labor arbitrator, 1979—; spl. master for U.S. Dist. Ct. (so. dist.) N.Y. and Dist. Ct. of Colo. Mem. N.Y. State Bar Assn. (chmn. com. on civil rights 1981-85), ABA, Assn. Bar City N.Y., Soc. Profls. in Dispute Resolution. Contbr. articles to legal jours. Labor, Administrative and regulatory, Civil rights. Office: 49-51 Chambers St Suite 220 New York NY 10007

RAFF, DOUGLASS ALAN, lawyer; b. Butte, Mont., Oct. 27, 1938; s. Colin W. and Ruth H. (Brinck) R.; m. Katherine L. Jones, Aug. 19, 1961; children—Colin, Katherine. A.B., Harvard U., 1961, J.D., 1964. Bar: Wash. 1964. Ptnr., Riddell, Williams, Bullitt & Walkinshaw, Seattle, 1964—; chmn. bd., dir. Sasquatch Pub., Inc.; dir. Harbor Properties, Inc., Independent Ale Brewery, Inc. Chmn. Seattle 2000 Commn., 1972-73; trustee World Without War Council; trustee Pilchuck Glass Sch.; mem. bd. visitors U. Wash. Coll. Architecture. Mem. ABA, Wash. State Bar Assn., Seattle-King County Bar Assn. General corporate, Real property. Office: Seattle First Nat Bank Bldg Suite 4400 Seattle WA 98154

RAGAN, CHARLES OLIVER, JR., lawyer; b. Knoxville, Tenn., Dec. 23, 1935; s. Charles Oliver and Jeanette (Butler) R.; m. Pauline Iona Kimsey, Apr. 19, 1958. B.S. in Bus. Adminstrn., U. Tenn., 1958, J.D., 1963. Bar: Tenn. 1964, U.S. Dist. Ct. (ea. dist.) Tenn. 1965. Staff atty. State of Tenn., Chattanooga, 1964-69; atty. Bean & Phillips, Chattanooga, 1969-73; sr. ptnr. Ragan & Schulman, Chattanooga, 1973-75, Ragan & Littleton, Chattanooga, 1975-80, Ragan & Wulforst, Chattanooga, 1980-84; sole practice, Chattanooga, 1984—; Tenn. commnr. Nat. Conf. Commrs. on Uniform State Laws, 1976-80. Campaign treas. for Democratic candidates. Mem. ABA, Assn. Trial Lawyers Am., Tenn. Bar Assn., Tenn. Trial Lawyers Assn. (bd. govs. 1977-81), Chattanooga Trial Lawyers Assn. (pres. 1977), Chattanooga Bar Assn. (bd. govs. 1979-80). Democrat. Methodist. Personal injury, General

practice, Bankruptcy. Home: 185 Woodcliff Circle Signal Mountain TN 37377 Office: Suite 301 Flatiron Bldg 707 Georgia Ave Chattanooga TN 37402

RAGER, KURT THOMAS, lawyer; b. Sioux City, Iowa, Feb. 24, 1952; s. Melvin Leroy and Shirley Ann (Dierking) R.; m. Virginia Lee Slabaugh, Dec. 27, 1974; children: Amy Elizabeth, Kathryn Ann. BS, U. Nebr., 1973, JD, 1977. Bar: Nebr. 1977, U.S. Dist. Ct. Nebr. 1977, Iowa 1984, U.S. Dist. Ct. (no. dist.) Iowa 1984, U.S. Tax Ct. 1986., U.S. Supreme Ct. 1986. Ptnr. Leamer, Rager & Hohenstein, South Sioux City, Nebr., 1978-85, Rager & Hohenstein, P.C., South Sioux City, 1985-86, 86—; bd. dirs. Nebr. Continuing Legal Edn., Lincoln, 1984—; mem. Jud. Nominating Com., 1982—. Sec. Dakota County (Nebr.) Rep. Party, 1984—. Lodge: Kiwanis (pres. South Sioux City club 1983). Contracts commercial, Personal injury, Probate. Home: 212 Wedgewood Dr South Sioux City NE 68776 Office: 101 W 11th St South Sioux City NE 68776-0339

RAGER, R. RUSSELL, lawyer; b. Miles City, Mont., Jan. 15, 1932; s. Harry E. and Esther (Anderson) R.; m. Sharon E. Keeling, Dec. 30, 1959; children: Sean, Kurt, Quita, Elani, Valari, Jordan. BBA, U. N.D., 1956; JD, U. N.Mex., 1958. Bar: N.Mex. 1958, U.S. Dist. Ct. N.Mex. 1959. Sole practice Albuquerque, 1958—; atty. Village of Corrales, 1971-81; bd. dirs. Anderson Devel. Corp., Albuquerque, Anfar Corp., Albuquerque; bd. dirs., sec. J.H. Ryan and Son, Inc., Albuquerque, 1983—. Pres., bd. dirs. Albuquerque Tutoring Assn., 1967; bd. dirs. Luth. Coordinating Council, Albuquerque, 1975; bd. dirs., sec. Maxie L. Anderson Found., Albuquerque, 1984—. Gold Seal scholar, 1949. Mem. ABA, N.Mex. Bar Assn., Albuquerque Bar Assn. Republican. Lutheran. Lodge: Kiwanis (pres. Albuquerque chpt. 1966). Real property, Contracts commercial, General corporate. Home: W Ella Dr Corrales NM 87048 Office: 2500 Louisiana Blvd NE Suite 500 Albuquerque NM 87110

RAGETTÉ-BLAINE, DOROTHEA CONSTANCE, lawyer; b. N.Y.C., Sept. 23, 1930; d. Robert Raymond Ragetté and Dorothea Ottilie (Mettke) Mohan; m. Neale Burnette Blaine, Aug. 3, 1957 (div. Nov. 1965). BA, Barnard Coll., 1952; MA, Calif. State U., Los Angeles, 1968; EdD, UCLA, 1978; JD, Western State U., 1981. Bar: Calif. 1982, U.S. Dist. Ct. (ea., so. and cen. dists.) Calif. 1986. Adminstrv. asst. Reuben Donnelley Corp., Mount Vernon, N.Y., 1955-57, The Nestle Co., White Plains, N.Y., 1957-63; mem. tech. staff Planning Research Corp., Los Angeles, 1964-67; assoc. scientist Holy Cross Hosp., Mission Hills, Calif., 1967-70; sr. adminstrv. analyst County of Orange, Santa Ana, Calif., 1980-83; sole practice Newport Beach, Calif., 1982—; instr. Am. Coll. of Law, Brea, Calif. Pres. bd. dirs. Deerfield Community Assn., Irvine, Calif., 1976. Mem. ABA, Orange County Bar Assn. (del. to Calif. State Bar Conv. 1985, 86, 87), Calif. State Bar Assn., Assn. Trial Lawyers Am., Orange County Trial Lawyers Assn., Calif. Trial Lawyers Assn., Orange County Women Lawyers. Family and matrimonial, Personal injury, Probate. Office: 2121 E Coast Hwy Suite 2000 Corna Del Mar CA 92625

RAGLAND, ALWINE MULHEARN, judge; b. Monroe, La., July 28, 1913; m. LeRoy Smith, 1947 (dec.); children—LeRoy, Caroline Smith Christman; m. 2d, L. Percy Ragland, Mar., 1978. A.A., Principia Coll., St. Louis; J.D., Tulane U., 1935. Bar: La. 1935. Sole practice, Tallulah, La., 1935-74; mem. firm Mulhearn & Smith, 1972-74; judge 6th Jud. Dist. Ct., Lake Prvidence, La., 1974—; atty. for inheritance tax collector Madison Parish, La., 1968-74; former city atty., Delta, La.; temporary judge La. Ct. Appeals (2d cir.), 1976. Charter bd. dirs. Silver Waters council Girl Scouts U.S.A.; past pres. Band Boosters Assn. Tallulah High Sch., Tallulah High Sch. PTA; past dist. dir., past bd. dirs, lay reader 1st Ch. Christ Scientist, Vicksburg, Miss.; past bd. dirs. Delta Christian Sch. Mem. ABA, La. Bar Assn., 6th Jud. Bar Assn., Am. Judges Assn., La. Judges Assn., Am. Judicature Soc., La. Council Juvenile and Family Ct. Ct. Judges (pres.), Nat. Council Juvenile Ct. Judges, So. Juvenile Ct. Judges, Assn. Trial Lawyers Am., La. Trial Lawyers Assn., Family Conciliation Cts. and Services, Nat. Juvenile Ct. Service Assn., La. Conf. Social Welfare, Practicing Law Inst., Nat. Assn. Women Judges, La. Assn. Def. Counsel. Club: Ladies Golf and Tennis Assn. Judicial administration. Home and Office: PO Box 392 Lake Providence LA 71254

RAGLEY, MICHELE ANN GARRICK, lawyer; b. Lincoln, Nebr., Jan. 10, 1948; d. H. Michael and Elizabeth J. (Revale) Garrick; m. Robert L. Ragley, Dec. 24, 1967. BE, Lake Erie Coll., 1970; JD cum laude, Cleveland Marshall Coll., 1982. Bar: Ohio 1982, U.S. Dist. Ct. (no. dist.) Ohio 1983. Law clk. to presiding justice U.S. Appellate Ct. (8th cir.), Cleve., 1982-84; atty. Sherwin-Williams Co., Cleve., 1984—. Fin. chmn. Geauga County LWV, 1985. Mem. ABA, Ohio Bar Assn., Cleve. Bar Assn., Geauga County Bar Assn. Avocations: reading, photography, fishing. General corporate, Contracts commercial, Computer. Home: 7460 Hunters Hollow Trail Russell Township OH 44072 Office: The Sherwin-Williams Co 101 Prospect Ave Cleveland OH 44115

RAGO, DANIEL ANTHONY, lawyer; b. Elizabeth, N.J., July 14, 1935; s. Daniel and Madeline M. (Troiano) R.; m. Alice Louise Blendermann, July 20, 1963 (div.); children: Deborah A., Jennifer L., David G. AB, Seton Hall U., 1960; JD, Fordham U., 1964. Bar: N.Y. 1965, U.S. Dist. Ct. (ea. and so. dists.) N.Y. 1965, U.S. Ct. Appeals (2d cir.) 1966, U.S. Supreme Ct. 1969, U.S. Ct. Customs and Patent Appeals 1980. Workers compensation hearing rep. Liberty Mut. Ins. Co., N.Y.C., 1965; assoc. Schaffner & D'Onofrio, N.Y.C., 1966; asst. U.S. atty. U.S. Dist. Ct. (ea. dist.) N.Y., 1966-69; dep. commr. consumer affairs, Nassau County, N.Y., 1969-70; atty. mktg. and consumer protection J.C. Penney Co., Inc., 1970-72, sr. atty. fed. matters, Washington office, 1972-76, N.E. regional counsel state-local matters, 1976-80, gen. atty.-internat. and intellectual property, N.Y.C., 1980-82, gen. atty. mktg. and consumer protection, N.Y.C., 1982—; mem. Atty. Gen. of Mich. adv. com. on consumer protection rules, 1977-79; mem. adv. com. on EFT rules Ill. Banking Commn., 1979. Trustee Unitarian Ch., Westport, Conn., 1979-81. Served with U.S. Army, 1954-57. Mem. ABA (vice chmn. internat. and comparative adminstrv. law 1981-83, vice chmn. state adminstrv. law 1983-84, chmn. 1984-86, council adminstrv. law sect. 1986—), Fed. Bar Assn. (chmn. adminstrv. practices and procedures com. 1975-77, dep. council chmn. for legis. projects 1977-79, disting. service award 1976), N.Y. State Bar Assn. (vice-chmn. administrv. law com.), Assn. of Bar of City of N.Y. (adminstrv. law com.). Democrat. Lectr. and contbr. articles to legal jours. Administrative and regulatory, Contracts commercial, Private international. Home: 50 Fairview Ave 2-G Norwalk CT 06850 Office: JC Penney Co Inc 1301 Ave of Americas New York NY 10019

RAGONETTI, THOMAS JOHN, lawyer; b. Mt. Vernon, N.Y., June 11, 1949; s. John Louis and Francesalice Miller (Shilton) R.; m. Marcia Lu Lortscher, Dec. 30, 1971; 1 child, Peter Thomas. AB summa cum laude, Cornell U., 1971, M in Regional Planning, 1973; JD cum laude, Harvard U., 1977. Bar: Colo. 1977, U.S. Dist. Ct. Colo. 1977. Zoning cons. pub. fin. and urban planning Econ. Cons. Orgn., Elmira, N.Y., 1973-74, City of Boston, 1975-77; assoc. Davis, Graham & Stubbs, Denver, 1977-82, ptnr., 1982-85; ptnr. Otten, Johnson, Robinson, Neff & Ragonetti, Denver, 1985—. bd. dirs. Cen. City Opera, Denver, 1981-82, Hist. Denver, Inc., 1981-84, Hist. Paramount Found., Denver, 1983—, Metro Denver Arts Alliance, 1983—, Urban Design Forum, Denver, 1984-85, Auraria Found., 1985—, Denver Civic Ventures-Denver Partnership, 1985—. NSF fellow, 1971-73. Mem. ABA, Colo. Bar Assn., Denver Bar Assn., Law Club of Denver, Sports Car Club Am., Rocky Mountain Vintage Racing, Ltd. Club: Cactus. Real property, Land use and planning, General corporate. Home: 636 Monaco Pkwy Denver CO 80202 Office: Otten Johnson et al 950 17th St Suite 1600 Denver CO 80202

RAHL, JAMES ANDREW, lawyer, educator; b. Wooster, Ohio, Oct. 8, 1917; s. James Blaine and Harriet (Munson) R.; m. Jean Mayberry, Sept. 5, 1942; 1 child, James Andrew. B.S., Northwestern U., 1939, J.D., 1942. Bar: Ohio 1942, Ill. 1950, U.S. Supreme Ct. 1962. Atty. OPA, 1942-43; mem. faculty Northwestern U. Law Sch., 1946—, prof. law, 1953—, Owen L. Coon prof., 1974—, dir. research, 1966-72, dean, 1972-77; counsel Chadwell & Kayser, Chgo., 1952—; ptnr. Chadwell & Kayser, Brussels, Belgium, 1963-64; mem. faculty Salzburg Seminar Am. Studies, 1967, 72, 85; Mem. Atty. Gen.'s Nat. Com. to Study Antitrust Laws, 1953-55; mem. White House Task Force Antitrust Policy, 1967-68, UNCTAD Group Experts on Internat. Restrictive Trade Practices, 1973; mem. adv. com. on internat. investment, tech. and devel. Dept. State, 1979—. Author: (with others) Cases on Torts, 1968, 2d edit., 1977, Advanced Torts, 1977, (with Schwerin) Northwestern University School of Law: A Short History, 1960, Common Market and American Antitrust: Overlap and Conflict, 1970; also articles.; Editor-in-chief: Ill. Law Rev., 1941-42. Served to 2d lt. AUS, 1943-46. Mem. ABA (council anti trust sect. 1965-67), Ill., Bar Assn., Chgo. Bar Assn., Chgo. Council Lawyers, Am. Law Inst., Am. Soc. Internat. Law, Law Club Chgo. (pres. 1976-77). Methodist. Legal education, Antitrust. Home: 2426 Marcy Ave Evanston IL 60201 Office: 357 E Chicago Ave Chicago IL 60611

RAHM, DAVID ALAN, lawyer; b. Passaic, N.J., Apr. 18, 1941; s. Hans Emil and Alicia Katherine (Onuf) R.; m. Susan Eileen Berkman, Nov. 23, 1972; children: Katherine Berkman, William David. AB, Princeton U., 1962; JD, Yale U., 1965. Bar: N.Y. 1966, D.C. 1986. Assoc. Paul, Weiss, Rifkind & Wharton, N.Y.C., 1965-66, 1968-69; asst. counsel N.Y. State Urban Devel. Corp., N.Y.C., 1969-72, assoc. counsel, 1972-75; counsel real estate div. Internat. Paper Co., N.Y.C., 1975-80; ptnr. Stroock & Stroock & Lavan, N.Y.C., 1980-83, sr. ptnr., 1984—; lectr. Old Dominion Coll., Norfolk, Va., 1967-68, N.Y.U., 1986—. Contbr. articles to profl. jours. Fund raiser corp. com. N.Y. Philharmonic, N.Y.C., 1980-84. Served with USNR, 1966-68. Mem. ABA (comml. leasing com. real property sect.), N.Y. State Bar Assn. (real property sect.), Assn. of Bar of City of N.Y. (housing and urban devel. com.). Democrat. Presbyterian. Club: Princeton (N.Y.C.). Avocations: music, reading, travel. Real property, Landlord-tenant. Office: Stroock & Stroock & Lavan 7 Hanover Sq New York NY 10004

RAHM, SUSAN BERKMAN, lawyer; b. Pitts., June 25, 1943; d. Allen Hugh and Selma (Wiener) Berkman; m. David Alan Rahm, Nov. 23, 1972; children: Katherine, William. BA with honors, Wellesley Coll., 1965; postgrad., Harvard U., 1966-67; JD, NYU, 1973. Bar: N.Y., U.S. Supreme Ct. 1974. Assoc. Marshall, Bratter, Greene, Allison & Tucker, N.Y.C., 1973-81, ptnr., 1981-82; ptnr. Kaye, Scholer, Fierman, Hays & Handler, N.Y.C., 1982—. Recipient Cert. of Outstanding Service D.C. Redevel. Land Agency, 1969. Mem. ABA, N.Y. State Bar Assn., Assn. of Bar of City of N.Y. Real property. Office: Kaye Scholer Fierman Hays & Handler 425 Park Ave New York NY 10022

RAI, SHAMBHU K., lawyer; b. Hoshangabad, M.P., India, June 22, 1937; s. Shiva C. and Tara M. R.; m. Meera S. Mukerjee, Apr. 13, 1964; children—Leena, Amit. B.S., Sagar U. (India), 1957, LL.B. (Gold medalist), 1959; LL.M., N.Y.U., 1974. Bar: India 1959, Mass. 1975. With Indian Postal Service, 1960-65; sole practice, Bhopal, M.P., India, 1965-71, Boston, 1975-83, also Brighton, Mass., 1975-83, Tustin, Calif., 1983-85, Santa Ana, Calif. 1985—. Pres., India Assn. Greater Boston, 1976-77. Mem. ABA, Mass. Bar Assn., Calif. Bar Assn. Hindu. Real property, Probate, Business law. Office: 1227 W 17th St Santa Ana CA 92706

RAIDEN, MICHAEL E., lawyer; b. Winter Haven, Fla., July 12, 1953; s. Billy Ross and Sylvia (Daniel) R.; m. Sarah Ann Ramsey, Sept. 7, 1974. BA, Fla. State U., 1975; JD, Harvard U., 1978. Bar: Fla. 1978, U.S. Dist. Ct. (mid. dist.) Fla. 1979, U.S. Ct. Appeals (11th cir.) 1984, U.S. Supreme Ct. 1984. Asst. pub. defender City of Bartow (10th Jud. cir.), Fla., 1978-85; sr. law clk. Fla. Ct. Appeals (2d dist.), Lakeland, 1985—. Candidate for Polk County (Fla.) Judge, 1984. Mem. ABA, Winter Haven Bar Assn., Lakeland Bar Assn., Winter Haven Jaycees (sec. 1983-86, community v.p. 1986—, internal v.p. 1984-85). Democrat. Avocations: Fla. history, photography, collector of political memorabilia. State civil litigation, Criminal, Judicial administration. Home: 219 8th St NE Winter Haven FL 33881 Office: Fla Ct Appeals 2d Dist 1005 E Memorial Blvd Lakeland FL 33830

RAIKES, CHARLES FITZGERALD, lawyer; b. Mpls., Oct. 6, 1930; s. Arthur FitzGerald and Margaret (Hawthorne) R.; m. Antonia Raikes, Dec. 20, 1969; children: Jennifer Catherine, Victoria Samantha. B.A., Washington U., 1952; M.A., Harvard U., 1955, LL.B., 1958. Bar: N.Y. State 1959. Assoc. White & Case, N.Y.C., 1958-69; assoc. gen. counsel Dun & Bradstreet, Inc., N.Y.C., 1969-72; v.p., gen. counsel Dun & Bradstreet, Inc., 1972-73, The Dun & Bradstreet Corp., N.Y.C., 1973-76; sr. v.p., gen. counsel The Dun & Bradstreet Corp., 1976—; cons. Bd. Govs. Fed. Reserve System, 1958—. Served with U.S. Army, 1952-54. Woodrow Wilson fellow, 1952. Mem. Assn. Bar City N.Y., Phi Beta Kappa. Clubs: Down Town Assn, Board Room, Harvard. General corporate. Home: 25 Rowayton Woods Drive Norwalk CT 06854 Office: 299 Park Ave New York NY 10171

RAILSBACK, DAVID PHILLIPS, lawyer; b. Newton, Mass., Aug. 21, 1950; s. David and Mary Ann (Phillips) R.; m. Elizabeth Stone, June 7, 1973; 1 child, Meredith. BS summa cum laude, Lehigh U., 1972; JD cum laude, Suffolk U., 1978; LLM, Boston U., 1981. Bar: Mass. 1978, R.I. 1979, U.S. Dist. Ct. R.I. 1979, U.S. Tax Ct. 1979, U.S. Dist. Ct. Mass. 1980. Assoc. Tillinghast, Collins, and Graham, Providence, 1979-81; gen. counsel, treas. New Eng. Rd. Manchinery Co., Fitchburg, Mass., 1981—. General corporate, Personal income taxation. Home: 42 Saw Mill Rd Concord MA 01742 Office: PO Box 1097 Concord MA 01742

RAILTON, WILLIAM SCOTT, lawyer; b. Newark, July 30, 1935; s. William Scott and Carolyn Elizabeth (Guiberson) R.; m. Karen Elizabeth Walsh, Mar. 31, 1979; 1 son, William August; children by previous marriage: William Scott, Anne Greenwood. B.S. in Elec. Engring., U. Wash., 1962; J.D. with honors, George Washington U., 1965. Bar: D.C. 1966, Md. 1966, U.S. Patent Office 1966. Asso., then partner firm Kemon, Palmer & Estabrook, Washington, 1966-70; sr. trial atty. Dept. Labor, 1970-71; asst. counsel OSHA, 1971-72, chief counsel, 1972-77, acting gen. counsel rev. commn., 1975-77; partner firm Reed, Smith, Shaw & McClay, Washington, 1977—; lectr. George Washington U. Law Sch., 1977—, Georgetown U. Law Sch., 1979—. Author legal handbooks. Chmn. Montgomery County (Md.) Republican Party, 1968-70; pres. Montgomery Sq. Citizens Assn., 1970-71; bd. dirs., pres. Foxvale Farms Homeowners Assn., 1979-82. Served with USMC, 1953-58. Recipient Meritorious Achievement medal Dept. Labor, 1972, Outstanding Service award OSHA rev. commn., 1977. Mem. Am. Bar Assn., Md. Bar Assn., Bar Assn. D.C. (vice chmn. young lawyers sect. 1971), Order of Coif, Sigma Phi Epsilon, Phi Delta Phi. Clubs: Oval (U. Wash.); River Bend Country (Gt. Falls). Labor, Patent, Federal civil litigation. Home: 10102 Walker Lake Dr Great Falls VA 22066 Office: 1150 Connecticut Ave NW Washington DC 20036

RAIM, DAVID MATTHEW, lawyer; b. N.Y.C., Mar. 11, 1953; s. Murray S. and Joan D. (Feldman) R.; m. Leslie K. Shedlin, June 12, 1983. BA, Yale U., 1975; JD, U. Pa., 1978. Bar: N.Y. 1979, U.S. Dist. (so. and ea. dist.) N.Y. 1979, U.S. Ct. Appeals (2d cir.) 1981, U.S. Supreme Ct. 1982, D.C. 1985, U.S. Dist. Ct. D.C. 1985. Asst. dir. nat. law dept. Anti-Defamation League of B'nai B'rith, N.Y.C., 1981-82; assoc. Leboeuf, Lamb, Leiby & McRae, N.Y.C. and Washington, 1978-81, 83-86, Hughes Hubbard & Reed PC, Washington, 1986—. Mem. ABA, Def. Research Inst., D.C. Bar Assn. Lodge: B'nai B'rith (chmn. N.Y. civil rights com. Anti Defamation League 1984-85). Insurance, Federal civil litigation, Reinsurance arbitration. Home: 5308 Ventnor Rd Bethesda MD 20816 Office: Hughes Hubbard & Reed 1201 Pennsylvania Ave NW Washington DC 20004

RAIMI, BURTON LOUIS, lawyer; b. Detroit, May 5, 1938; s. Irving and Rae (Abel) R.; m. Judith Morse, Mar. 31, 1963 (div. Mar. 1985); children: Diane L., and Matthew D. BA, Brandeis U., 1960; JD, U. Mich., 1963; LLM, George Washington U., 1964. Bar: Mich. 1963, D.C. 1964, U.S. Ct. Appeals (4th, 7th, 8th, 9th, 10th and D.C. cirs.). Atty. NLRB, Washington, 1964-69; assoc. Morgan, Lewis & Bockius, Washington, 1969-71; dep. gen. counsel FDIC, Washington, 1971-78; ptnr. Rosenman, Colin, Freund, Lewis & Cohen, Washington, 1978-86, Dechert, Price & Rhoads, Washington, 1986—; speaker various insts. Mem. ABA, D.C. Bar Assn. (chmn. bank law com., com. on interest on lawyers trust accounts.). Avocations: sailing, racketball, tennis, travel. Banking, Securities. Home: 4275 Embassy Park Dr NW Washington DC 20016 Office: Dechert Price & Rhoads 1730 Pennsylvania Ave NW Suite 1100 Washington DC 20006

RAINBOLT, JOHN VERNON, II, lawyer; b. Cordell, Okla., May 24, 1939; s. John Vernon (Mike) and Mary Alice (Power) R.; m. Janice Glaub, Oct. 5, 1976; children—John Vernon, III, Sara McLain, Charles Joseph. B.A., Okla. U., 1961, LL.B., 1964; postgrad. George Washington U. 1971-73. Bar: Okla. 1964, D.C. 1971, U.S. Supreme Ct. 1971. Legis. counsel, adminstrv. asst. U.S. Rep. Graham Purcell, Washington, 1967-72; counsel agr. com. U.S. Ho. of Reps., Washington, 1972-75; commr. Commodity Futures Trading Commn., Washington, 1975-78; sole practice, Washington, 1978-82; ptnr. Miles & Stockbridge, Washington, 1982-86; advisor agr. policy Tokyo Roundtable White House, 1978-81; mem. Adminstrn. Conf., U.S., 1976-79. Author and draftsman Commodity Futures Trading Commn. Act, 1974; contbr. articles to legal jours. Served to 1st lt. Inf., U.S. Army, 1964-67. Vice chmn. Commodity Futures Trading Commn., 1975-78. Mem. ABA (chmn. subcom. on fgn. markets and traders 1982-85), U.S. Futures Industry Assn. (assoc.). Clubs: Commodity of Washington, Pisces. Securities, Corporate taxation, Legislative. Office: Miles & Stockbridge 655 15th St NW Washington DC 20005

RAINE, CHARLES MACON, laywer; b. Rockdale, Tex., May 1, 1913; s. John Randolph and Ruby Walton (Woody) R.; m. Susan Starkey, 1938 (div. 1944); 1 child, Thomas Randolph; m. Dorothy Ewing, Sept. 29, 1946; children—William Woody, Patricia Ann. J.D., St. Mary's U., San Antonio, Tex., 1949. Bar: U.S. Dist. Ct. (so. dist.) Tex. 1953, U.S. Dist. Ct. (no. dist.) Tex. 1955. Sole practice, Corpus Christi, Tex., 1950—. Deacon Snyder Presbyn. Ch., Tex., 1956, Parkway Presbyn. Ch., Corpus Christi, 1960. Served to 1st lt. U.S. Army, 1941-46. Mem. Nueces County Bar Assn. Lodge: Masons. Consumer commercial, Personal injury, Workers' compensation. Home: 473 Palmetto St Corpus Christi TX 78412 Office: PO Box 6325 Corpus Christi TX 78411

RAINES, JIM NEAL, lawyer; b. Memphis, Sept. 11, 1943; s. J.E. and Amelia C.R.; m. Julia Walters, Sept. 1, 1979; 1 dau., Lee Pierceson. B.B.A., Memphis State U., 1965, J.D., 1968. Bar: Tenn. 1968, U.S. Dist. ct. (we. dist.) Tenn. 1968, U.S. Ct. Appeals (6th cir.) 1970, U.S. Ct. Appeals (5th cir.) 1975, U.S. Supreme Ct. 1974. Trial atty. antitrust div. U.S. Dept. Justice, Washington, 1968-70; asst. U.S. atty. Western Dist. Tenn., Memphis, 1970-74; ptnr. Burch, Porter & Johnson, 1975-76, Glankler, Brown, Gilliland, Chase, Robinson, Raines, 1976—. Served with USMC, 1960-64. Mem. ABA, Memphis Bar Assn., Shelby County Bar Assn. Presbyterian. Club: Univeristy. Antitrust, Federal civil litigation, Criminal. Office: Glankler Brown Gilliland Chase Robinson & Raines 1 Commerce Sq Suite 1700 Memphis TN 38103

RAINES, KEITH R., lawyer; b. Portland, Oreg., Jan. 5, 1951; s. J. Richard and D. Suzanne (Jonak) R.; m. Paula L. Scully, Aug. 24, 1980; children: Elizabeth, Christopher. DM in French, L'Unv de Pau, France, 1971; BA in Econs., Lewis & Clark Coll., 1972, JD, 1976. Bar: Oreg. 1976, U.S. Dist. Ct. Oreg. 1977, U.S. Ct. Appeals (9th cir.) 1981. Sole practice Portland, 1976-79; assoc. dir. St. Andrew Legal Clinic, Portland, 1979-85, dir., 1985—. Mem. Oreg. Bar Assn. (family law sect.), Multnomah County Bar Assn. (com. delivery legal services to poor), Oreg. Trial Lawyers Assn. Democrat. Roman Catholic. Family and matrimonial, General practice, Public interest law. Office: St Andrew Legal Clinic 807 NE Alberta Portland OR 97211

RAINES, LISA JOY, lawyer; b. N.Y.C., Dec. 30, 1958; d. Arthur and Marilyn Ann (Klein) R.; m. Stephen Peter Push, Nov. 30, 1980. BA, SUNY, Stony Brook, 1979; JD, Georgetown U., 1982. Bar: D.C. 1982, Md. 1983. Atty., policy analyst office tech. assessment U.S. Congress, Washington, 1982-86; dir. govt. relations Indsl. Biotech. Assn., Washington, 1986—. Co-author: Reproductive Health Hazards in the Workplace, 1985, Alternatives to Animal Use in Testing and Research, 1986, Ownership of Human Cells and Tissues, 1987. Speaker D.C. Commn. for Women, Washington, 1986. Mem. ABA. Legislative, Administrative and regulatory. Office: Indsl Biotech Assn 1625 K St NW Washington DC 20006

RAINES, STEPHEN, lawyer; b. N.Y.C., Feb. 4, 1938; s. Louis and Rose (Rosenthal) R.; m. Betsy Kotowitz, Sept. 10, 1960; children: Michael, Jeffrey. BS in Pharmacy, Fordham U., 1959; MS in Pharmacy and Chemistry, U. Mich., 1961, PhD in Pharmacy and Chemistry, 1963, postdoctoral, 1963; JD, Temple U., 1970. Bar: D.C. 1970, Conn. 1971. Research chemist Union Carbide Corp., S. Charleston, W.Va., 1963-65; sr. research chemist Richardson Merrell Co., Phila., 1965-70; patent atty. Am. Cyanamid Co., 1970-72; sr. patent atty. Squibb Corp., Lawrenceville, N.J., 1972-73, Parke, Davis & Co., Detroit, 1973-80; patent counsel Warner-Lambert Co., Morris Plains, N.J., 1980-81, corp. patent counsel, 1981-86, counsel intellectual property, 1986—; instr. chemistry Lawrence Inst. Tech., Southfield, Mich., 1975-78. Contbr. articles to profl. jours.; patentee in field. William S. Merrell research fellow U. Mich., 1959-63; Am. Found. Pharm. Edn. scholar U. Mich., 1962-63. Mem. ABA, N.J. Patent Law Assn., Am. Intellectual Property Law Assn., Rho Chi, Phi Lambda Epsilon. Patent, Trademark and copyright. Office: Warner-Lambert Co 201 Tabor Rd Morris Plains NJ 07950

RAINES, STEPHEN SAMUEL, franchising consulting and development firm executive, lawyer; b. Los Angeles, Aug. 2, 1945; s. Harold Charles and Florence (Pynoos) S.; m. Judith Amanda Masterson, July 18, 1981; children: Jennifer, Jeffrey. BA, UCLA, 1967; JD, Loyola U., Los Angeles, 1971. Bar: Calif. Assoc. Thorpe, Sullivan, Clinnin & Workman, Los Angeles, 1971-75; v.p., gen. counsel United Rent-All, Inc., Los Angeles, 1975-81; pres. Nat. Franchise Assocs., Inc., Atlanta, 1981—; bd. dirs., v.p. Nutrition Med. Ctrs., Hallandale, Fla., 1986—, M & R Advt., Inc., Atlanta; bd. dirs., v.p., sec., treas. Cincy's Franchising, Inc., Atlanta; franchising cons. U.S. SBA, Atlanta, 1984—, Ga. Bus. Devel. Ctrs., Atlanta, 1984—; instr. Loyola U., Los Angeles, 1971-72, U.S. Small Bus. Devel., Atlanta, 1984—, Ga. State U., Atlanta, 1984—; instr. leadership program Ga. Vietnam Vets., Atlanta, 1984—. Bd. dirs., sec. Vets. Resource Bus. Council, Atlanta, 1986. Served with USAR, 1968-74. Loyola U. Sch. Law fellow, Los Angeles, 1971; recipient State of Ga. Bus. Adv. of Yr. award 1987. Mem. ABA, Calif. Bar Assn., Internat. Bar Assn., U.S. Supreme Ct. Bar Assn., Atlanta C. of C., Atlanta Venture Capital Forum (charter), Am. Mgmt. Assn. General corporate. Home: 5759 Albans Way Lithonia GA 30058 Office: Nat Franchise Assocs Inc 1750 Peachtree St Atlanta GA 30309

RAINEY, CHARLES JAMES, lawyer; b. Milw., Jan. 21, 1956; s. James Arthur and Dorothiann Cecelia (Kraftmeyer) R. BS, Marquette U., 1977, JD, 1980, postdoctoral, 1980-81, 84. Bar: Wis. 1980, U.S. Dist. Ct. (ea. and we. dists.) Wis. 1980, U.S. Ct. Appeals (7th cir.) 1985. Assoc. Henry Piano, Milw., 1981-85; sole practice Milw., 1985—. Mem. ABA, Wis. Bar Assn., Milw. Bar Assn., IEEE, Assn. Trial Lawyers Am., Milw. Young Lawyers Assn., 7th Cir. Ct. Appeals Bar Assn., K-9 Obedience Training Club of Menomonee Falls (corp. counsel 1985—, bd. dirs. 1986—). Republican. Roman Catholic. Clubs: Am. Legion Band (Milw.) (corp. counsel 1979-85). Avocations: music, dog training, computer programming. Real property, State civil litigation, Landlord-tenant. Home: 9590 N Range Line Rd River Hills WI 53217 Office: 1139 E Knapp St Milwaukee WI 53202

RAINEY, JOHN DAVID, lawyer; b. Freeport, Tex., Feb. 10, 1945; s. Frank Anson and Jewel Lorene (Hortman) R.; m. Judy Davis, Aug. 17, 1968; children, John David Jr., Jacob Matthew, Craig Thomas. BBA, So. Meth. U., 1967, JD, 1972. Bar: Tex. 1972, U.S. Dist. Ct. (no. dist.) Tex. 1974, U.S. Tax Ct. 1974, U.S. Ct. Appeals (5th cir.) 1981, U.S. Supreme Ct. 1981. Assoc. Taylor, Mizell, Price, Corrigan & Smith, Dallas, 1973-79; ptnr. Gilbert, Gilbert & Rainey, Angleton, Tex., 1979-82, Rainey & LeBoeuf, Angleton, 1982—; bd. dirs. Angleton Bank of Commerce. Mem. City of Angleton Planning and Zoning Commn., 1981-84; mem. Angleton Charter Rev. Commn., 1984, chmn. 1982. Served with U.S. Army, 1969-70. Mem. ABA, State Bar Tex., Brazoria County Bar Assn. (pres. 1983-84). Republican. Methodist. Lodge: Lions (pres. Angleton 1986-87). Avocations: hunting, fishing, woodworking. Banking, Workers' compensation, State civil litigation. Office: PO Box 1316 209 E Mulberry Suite 204 Angleton TX 77515

RAINEY, WILLIAM JOEL, lawyer; b. Flint, Mich., Oct. 11, 1946; s. Ralph Jefferson and Elsie Matilda (Erickson) R.; m. Cynthia Hetsko, June 15, 1968; children—Joel Michael, Allison Elizabeth. A.B., Harvard U., 1968; J.D., U. Mich., 1971. Bar: N.Y. 1973, U.S. Dist. Ct. (so. and ea. dists.) N.Y. 1973, Wash. 1977, U.S. Dist. Ct. (we. dist.) Wash. 1977, U.S. Ct. Appeals (2d cir.) 1973, U.S. Supreme Ct. 1976, U.S. Ct. Appeals (9th cir.)

1978, Ariz. 1987. Assoc. atty. Curtis, Mallet-Prevost, Colt & Mosle, N.Y.C., 1971-76; atty., asst. corp. sec. Weyerhaeuser Co., Tacoma, Wash., 1976-85; v.p., corp. sec., gen. counsel Southwest Forest Industries Inc., Phoenix, 1985—; chmn. taskforce ABA, Chgo., 1984—. Editor U. Mich. Jour. Law Reform, 1970-71. Bd. dirs. Mcpl. League Seattle and King County, 1982-84; bd. dirs. 1st Ave. Service Ctr., Seattle, 1977-85; chmn. Bellevue Planning Commn., Wash., 1984. Served to maj. USAR, 1970—. Mem. ABA, Wash. State Bar Assn. Presbyterian. Lodge: Rotary. Avocations: backpacking, running, fishing. General corporate, Securities, Pension, profit-sharing, and employee benefits. Home: 5478 E Cholla St Scottsdale AZ 85254 Office: Southwest Forest Industries Inc 6225 N 24th St PO Box 7548 Phoenix AZ 85011

RAINONE, MICHAEL CARMINE, lawyer; b. Phila., Mar. 4, 1918; s. Sebastian M. and Mary (Salerno) R.; m. Ledena Tonioni, Apr. 10, 1944; children—Sebastian, Francine. LL.B., U. Pa., 1941. Bar: Pa. 1944, U.S. Dist. Ct. Pa. 1944, U.S. Supreme Ct. 1956. Sr. ptnr. Rainone & Rainone; Phila., 1945—; del. 3d Circuit Jud. Conf., 1984. Bd. dirs., chmn. community relations com. Community Coll. Phila., 1985; past pres., mem. adv. com. Nationalities Service Ctr.; commr. Fellowship Commn., 1973-82; bd. dirs., mem. govt. relations com. Mental Health Assn. Southeastern Pa., 1979-81; pres. Columbia Civic Assn. Pa., Inc., 1984—; chmn. Lawyers Biog. Com. of U.S. Hist. Soc., U.S. Dist. Ct.; trustee Balsh Inst. for Ethnic Studies; regional v.p. Nat. Itailian-Am. Found. Recipient Disting. Service award Nationalities Service Ctr., 1975; Man of Year award Columbus Civic Assn., 1969; Legion of Honor, Chapel of Four Chaplains, 1979, Bronze Medallian award, 1982, Commendation, Senate Pa., 1982. Mem. ABA, Internat. Acad. Law and Sci., Assn. Trial Lawyers Am., Justinian Soc. (bd. govs. 1980-83), Pa. Bar Assn., Pa. Trial Lawyers Assn. (bd. govs. 1982-84), N.Y. Trial Lawyers Assn. (assoc.), Phila. Bar Assn. (asst. sec. 1983, 84), Lawyers Club Phila. (pres. 1982-84), Phila. Trial Lawyers Assn. (pres. 1982-83), Nat. Italian-Am. Bar Assn. (bd. govs.), Am. Arbitration Assn. (arbitrator 1950—), Socialegal Club, St. Thomas Moore Soc. Federal civil litigation, State civil litigation, Consumer commercial. Office: 121 S Broad St 4th Floor Philadelphia PA 19107 Home: 2401 Pennsylvania Ave Philadelphia PA 19130

RAINS, HARRY HANO, lawyer, arbitrator, mediator; b. N.Y.C., Jan. 27, 1909; s. Jackson and Rose (Heller) R.; m. Muriel, June 21, 1942; 1 child, Peggy Jane Rains Goodman. LL.B., St. Lawrence U., 1932; M.P.A., NYU, 1947, LL.M. in Labor Law, 1954. Bar: N.Y. 1933, U.S. Supreme Ct. 1965, U.S. Dist. Ct. (so. and ea. dists.) N.Y. 1947. Referee N.Y. State Dept. Labor, 1936-38, unemployment ins. mgr., 1939-42; sole practice Mineola, N.Y., 1933-42; sr. ptnr. firm Rains & Pogrebin, N.Y.C., 1947-81, of counsel, cons., 1982—; labor arbitrator, mediator, lectr.; prof. labor law CCNY, 1935-37, 46-47; prof. labor law Hofstra U., 1947-52, Harry H. Rains Disting. prof. arbitration and alternative dispute settlement law, 1982—; mem. faculty L.I. U., 1953; dir. Sealectro Corp., John Hassall Co., Inc. Contbr. articles to profl. jours. Mem. Fed. Mediation and Conciliation Service, 1948—; mem. N.Y. State Pub. Employment Relations Bd. Panel Mediators and Fact Finders, 1968—. Served to capt. QMC, AUS, 1942-46. Mem. ABA, Fed. Bar Council, N.Y. State Bar Assn., Nassau County Bar Assn., Nat. Acad. Arbitrators, Indsl. Relations Research Assn., Am. Arbitration Assn. (panel labor arbitrators), L.I. C. of C. (bd. dirs.). Clubs: University (Garden City, N.Y.); Old Westbury Golf and Country (L.I.). Labor, Labor Arbitrator. Home: 31 Frost Creek Dr Locust Valley NY 11560 also: 2685 Coconut Dr Sanibel FL 33957 Office: Rains Bldg 210 Old Country Rd Mineola NY 11501

RAINS, JACK MORRIS, design and management firm executive, lawyer; b. Waco, Tex., Nov. 23, 1937; s. Otis Berlin and Margie (Morris) R.; m. Aileen Blanche Dixon, Dec. 23, 1961; children: Sharon Marie, Anne Michelle, Thomas Kenney Dixon. B.B.A., Tex. A&M U., 1960; J.D., U. Houston, 1967. Bar: Tex. 1967, U.S. Supreme Ct. 1972. Spl. agt. Prudential Ins. Co. Am., 1960-67; asso. firm Childs, Fortenbach, Beck, Guyton (attys.), Houston, 1967-69; mng. partner Neuhaus & Taylor, Architects and Planning Con. (predecessor firm to 3D/International), Houston, 1969-72; founding prin. Diversified Design Disciplines (predecessor firm to 3D/International), Houston, 1972—; pres., dir. 3D/International, Houston, 1972—; chmn. bd. 3D/International, 1982-86; sec. of state State of Tex., Austin, 1987—; founder, dir. Tanglewood Bank, N.A., 1983-86; vis. lectr. U. Houston, Tex. A&M U., U. St. Thomas, Baylor U., U. Tex. Trustee, U. Houston Law Found., 1979—; dir. Houston World Trade Assn., 1979—; mem. Clean Houston Commn., 1980, Internat. Inst. Edn. Adv. Bd., 1979—, Vets. Land Bd. State of Tex., 1983—; dir. U. Houston Law Review Found., 1973—; mem. devel. council Coll. Architecture and Environ. Design, Tex. A&M U., 1981-83, mem. task force internat. bus. Coll. Bus. Adminstrn., 1982-83, mem. exec. com. Council Visual Arts, 1981-83, bd. dirs. Meml. Student Ctr. Enrichment Fund, 1982-84; mem. Dist. Export Council, U.S. Dept. Commerce, 1981-83; mem. adv. bd. Blaffer Gallery, U. Houston, 1983; bd. visitors U. Tex. System Cancer Found., 1983; trustee Ctr. Internat. Bus., 1982-83; bd. govs. Houston Grand Opera, 1982-83; chmn. Tex. Bus. Hall of Fame Found., 1983; sponsoring mem. Asia Soc. Served with USCG, 1960-62. Recipient Pres.'s award U. Houston Law Alumni Assn., 1979, dean's award Coll. of Law, U. Houston, 1978, Outstanding Alumnus award U. Houston Law Alumni Assn., 1983, Outstanding Service award Tex. A&M U. Target 2000 Project, 1983; named Hon. Alumnus, Greys Order, U. Houston, 1982. Mem. ABA, State Bar Tex., Houston Bar Assn., AIA, U. Houston Law Alumni Assn. (v.p., dir. 1967-72), Am. Arbitration Assn., Assn. Former Students Tex. A&M U. (v.p., dir. 1975-78), Houston C. of C. (dir. 1981-82, 83-84), Phi Alpha Delta. Republican. Episcopalian. Clubs: Hawkeye Hunting; Allegro (Houston), River Oaks Country (Houston), University (Houston); Masons, Shriners. Home: 5051 San Felipe 191 West Tower Houston TX 77056 Office: State Capitol 100 E 11th St Austin TX 78701

RAISLER, KENNETH MARK, lawyer; b. New Rochelle, N.Y., May 15, 1951; s. Herbert A. and Norma (Glaubach) R.; m. Sara Ann Kelsey, June 11, 1978; children: Caroline Elisabeth, Katharine Kelsey, David Mark. BSBA, Yale Coll., 1973; JD, NYU, 1976. Bar: N.Y. 1977, D.C. 1977, U.S. Dist. Ct. (so. dist.) N.Y. 1977, U.S. Dist. Ct. D.C. 1977, U.S. Ct. Appeals (2d cir.) 1977, U.S. Ct. Appeals (D.C. cir.) 1977, U.S. Ct. Appeals (7th cir.) 1982, U.S. Ct. Appeals (10th cir.) 1983, U.S. Supreme Ct. 1985. Law clk. U.S. Dist. Ct. (so. dist.) N.Y., N.Y.C., 1976-77; asst. U.S. atty., Washington, 1977-82; dep. gen. counsel Commodity Futures Trading Commn., Washington, 1982-83, gen. counsel, 1983-87; ptnr. Rogers & Wells, N.Y.C., 1987—. Federal civil litigation, Administrative and regulatory, Securities. Office: Rogers & Wells 200 Park Ave New York NY 10166

RAKOFF, JED SAUL, lawyer, author; b. Phila., Aug. 1, 1943; s. Abraham Edward and Doris Tobiah (Michell) R.; m. Ann Rosenberg, Aug. 4, 1974; children—Jena Lynn, Elana Beth, Keira Jan. B.A., Swarthmore Coll., 1964; M. Phil., Balliol Coll., Oxford U., Eng., 1966; J.D., Harvard U., 1969. Bar: N.Y. 1971, D.C. 1983, U.S. Supreme Ct. 1986. Law clk. U.S. Court Appeals (3d cir.), Phila., 1969-70; assoc. Debevoise, Plimpton, Lyons & Gates, N.Y.C., 1970-73; asst. U.S. atty. So. Dist. N.Y., N.Y.C., 1973-80, chief bus. fraud prosecutions U.S. Atty.'s Office, 1978-80; ptnr. Mudge Rose Guthrie Alexander & Ferdon, N.Y.C., 1980—. Author: (with S. Arkin et al) Business Crime, 6 vols., 1981, Criminal Defense Techniques, 6 vols., 1982; contbr. numerous articles to law revs. Mem. exec. bd. N.Y. chpt. Am. Jewish Com., 1971-80, 82—. Mem. ABA, N.Y. State Bar Assn., Assn. of Bar of City of N.Y. (chmn. criminal law com. 1986—), Fed. Bar Council. Democrat. Jewish. Criminal, Federal civil litigation, State civil litigation. Home: 99 W Garden Rd Larchmont NY 10538 Office: Mudge Rose Guthrie Alexander & Ferdon 180 Maiden Ln New York NY 10038

RAKOFF, TODD D., law educator; b. 1946. BA, Harvard U., 1967, JD, 1975; PhB, Oxford U., Eng., 1969; MS in Edn., U. Pa., Phila., 1971. Assoc. Foley, Hong & Eliot, Boston, 1976-79; asst. prof. Harvard U., Cambridge, Mass., 1979-83, prof., 1983—. Office: Harvard Univ Law Sch Cambridge MA 02138 *

RAKOWSKY, CONNIE LEE, lawyer; b. Lima, Ohio, Aug. 13, 1952; s. Rudolph R. and Norma L. (Nott) R.; divorced. AA, Pine Manor Jr. Coll., 1972; BA, Northwestern U., 1974; JD, Ill. Inst. Tech., 1981. Bar: N.H. 1981, U.S. Dist. Ct. N.H. 1981. Ptnr. Orr & Reno, P.A., Concord, N.H., 1981—; bd. dirs. Concord ABC Inc., Bancroft Products, Concord. Mem. ABA, N.H. Bar Assn., Merrimack County Bar Assn., Practising Law Inst., Lawyers Alliance for Nuclear Arms Control, NOW. Jewish. Avocations: cross-country skiing, jogging. Bankruptcy, Contracts commercial, General corporate. Home: PO Box 43 Warner NH 03278 Office: Orr & Reno PA One Eagle Sq PO Box 709 Concord NH 03301

RAKUSIN, STEPHEN BRUCE, lawyer; b. Providence, Dec. 23, 1948; s. James Louis and Beatryce Florence (Sincoff) R.; m. Daryl Roselle Field, June 22, 1970 (div. Mar. 21, 1978); 1 child, Mitchell H.; m. Diane Margaret Smith Clawson, Dec. 23, 1979; children: Michelle, Brian. BJ, U. Fla., 1972, JD, 1974. Bar: Fla. 1978, U.S. Dist. Ct. (mid. dist.) Fla. 1978, U.S. Ct. Appeals (5th and 11th cirs.) 1981, U.S. Dist. Ct. (no. dist.) Fla. 1986. Sole practice Gainesville, Fla., 1974—. Author: Florida Mechanics' Lien Law Manual, 1974, Florida Creditors' Rights Manual, 1977. Excellence in News Writing award William Randolph Hearst Found., 1972. Mem. ABA (forum com. on constrn. industry), Fla. Bar Assn. (chmn. subcom. mechanics' lien law legis., constrn. and pub. contract law com., real property sect.), Assn. Trial Lawyers Am. Democrat. Jewish. Construction, Consumer commercial, State civil litigation. Home: 221 SW 27th St Gainesville FL 32601 Office: 2606 NW 6th St Suite B Gainesville FL 32609

RALABATE, JAMES J(OSEPH), lawyer, marketing company executive; b. Buffalo, Mar. 17, 1928; s. Thomas G. and Lena (Nobile) R.; m. Helen M. Agostinelli, July 29, 1950; children—James, Patti, Sandra, Kathy. B.S. in Chemistry, Canisius Coll., 1950; J.D., Am. U., 1958. Bar: N.Y. 1959, U.S. Patent Office, 1959. Patent atty. Hooker Chem. Co., Niagara Falls, N.Y., 1958-61, Mobay Chem. Corp., Pitts., 1961-63; dir. patents and licensing, gen. patent counsel Xerox Corp., Stamford, Conn., 1963-80; sole practice, Williamsville, N.Y., 1980—; pres. Andral Corp. Served to cpl. U.S. Army, 1952-54. Mem. Conn. Patent Law Assn. (pres. 1980-81), ABA, Am. Patent Law Assn., Niagara Frontier Patent Law Assn., Rochester Patent Law Assn., Licensing Execs. Soc., Conn. Patent Law Assn. (gov. 1981-87), Conn. Patent Counsels Assn. (pres. 1976-80), Erie County Bar Assn. Roman Catholic. Patent, Trademark and copyright. Home: 75 Briarhill Amherst NY 14221 Office: 5792 Main St Williamsville NY 14221

RALLI, CONSTANTINE PANDIA, lawyer; b. Bronxville, N.Y., Apr. 6, 1948; s. Pandia C. and Mary (Motter) R.; m. Alison Rhoads, Aug. 11, 1973; children: Pandia C., Christopher A. BA, Middlebury Coll., 1970; JD, Fordham U., 1973; LLM in Taxation, NYU, 1986. Bar: N.Y. 1974, U.S. Ct. Appeals (2d cir.) 1974, U.S. Dist. Ct. (so. and ea. dists.) N.Y. 1975, U.S. Tax Ct. 1977, Fla. 1985, Conn. 1985. Assoc. Davis Polk & Wardwell, N.Y.C., 1973-81; ptnr. Hall, McNicol, Hamilton & Clark, N.Y.C., 1981—; sec., bd. dirs. A.I. Friedman, Inc., N.Y.C.; sec. Chebeague Corp., Westport, Conn., 1983—. Republican. Presbyterian. Clubs: Union (N.Y.C.); Am. Yacht (Rye, N.Y.). Estate planning, Probate, Estate taxation. Home: 11 Rockridge Rd Rye NY 10580 Office: Hall McNicol Hamilton & Clark 220 E 42d St New York NY 10017 also: 3 Landmark Sq Stamford CT 06904

RALLS, GEOFFREY QUENTIN, lawyer; b. Kansas City, Mo., July 7, 1949; s. James Morrison and Patricia Ann (Dundey) R.; m. April Victoria Facciolo, July 3, 1982; 1 child, Timothy Amadeus. BA, Bensalem Coll., N.Y.C., 1971; JD, Georgetown U., 1980. Bar: N.Y. 1982. Exec. asst. to vice chancellor acad. affairs CUNY, N.Y.C., 1972-76, coordinator spl. programs, 1976-77; law asst. appellate div. 1st Dept., N.Y.C., 1980-83; law sec. Justice John Carro, N.Y.C., 1983-85; exec. asst. to presiding justice appellate div. 1st Dept., N.Y.C., 1985; adminstr. Assigned Counsel Plan, N.Y.C., 1985—; cons. Nat. Ctr. for Productivity and Quality of Working Life, Washington, 1978. Epichayan editor Georgetown U. Law Rev., 1978-80. Commr. Scarborough Fire Dist., Mt. Pleasant, N.Y., 1983—; vol. Archville (N.Y.) Fire Dept. Mem. ABA, Assn. Bar of City of N.Y. (state cts. of superior jurisdiction com. 1986—). Democrat. Avocations: gardening, music, cooking, hiking, painting. Judicial administration, Criminal. Office: Assigned Counsel Plan Appellate Div 1st Dept 27 Madison Ave New York NY 10010

RALLS, RAWLEIGH HAZEN, III, econ. and fin. cons.; b. Oklahoma City, Dec. 14, 1932; s. Rawleigh Hazen and Rosemary Thelma (Sprigg) R.; B.S., U.S. Mil. Acad., 1955; M.S., U.S. Naval Postgrad. Sch., 1964; D.B.A., George Washington U., 1971; m. Barbara Sue Yates, May 24, 1975; children—Creighton Leigh Yates, Rawleigh Hazen Yates; children by previous marriage—Elizabeth Anne, Devon Anne, Rawleigh Hazen IV. Commd. 2d lt. U.S. Army, 1955, advanced through grades to maj., 1966; mem. staff Office Chief of Staff, Pentagon, 1967-68; ret., 1968; asst. prof. U. Ark., Faytteville, 1968-71, assoc. prof., 1971-75; pres. Edn. & Research Assocs., Inc., Little Rock, 1975—; dir. various corps. Fellow AAAS; mem. Okla. Trial Lawyers Assn. (hon.), Ops. Research Soc. Am., Nat. Assn. Bus. Economists, N.Y. Acad. Sci., Personal injury, Admiralty, Federal civil litigation. Office: Edn & Research Assocs Inc 1217 Rebsamen Park Rd Little Rock AR 72202

RALSTON, DAVID THOMAS, JR., Lawyer; b. Balt., Jan. 17, 1954; s. David Thomas Sr. and Dolores Mary (Utermohle) R.; m. Mary Leonard, May 18, 1980; children: Kathleen Keelyn, Mariellen Keelyn, Brian David. BS in Fgn. Service, Georgetown U., 1976, JD, 1979. Bar: N.Y. 1980, D.C. 1985. Assoc. Milbank, Tweed, Hadley & McCloy, N.Y.C., 1979-80, Crowell & Moring, Washington, 1984—. Com. mem. Arlington County (Va.) Reps., 1985-86. Served to capt. JAGC, U.S. Army, 1980-84. Mem. ABA (transp. com. young lawyers div.), N.Y. State Bar Assn., Georgetown U. Law Alumni Assn., Delta Phi Epsilon. Republican. Roman Catholic. Club: Internat. Aviation. Administrative and regulatory, Contracts commercial, Real property. Home: 2105 C N Rolfe St Arlington VA 22209 Office: Crowell & Moring 1100 Connecticutt Ave Washington DC 20036

RAMBO, SYLVIA H., federal judge; b. Royersford, Pa., Apr. 17, 1936; d. Granville A. and Hilda E. (Leonhardt) R.; m. George F. Douglas, Jr., Aug. 1, 1970. B.A., Dickinson Coll., Carlisle, Pa., 1958; J.D., Dickinson Sch. Law, Carlisle, Pa., 1962; LL.D. (hon.), Wilson Coll., Chambersburg, Pa., 1980. Bar: Pa. 1962. Atty. trust dept. Bank of Del., Wilmington, 1962-63; pvt. practice Carlisle, 1963-76; public defender, then chief public defender Cumberland County, Pa., 1976; judge Ct. Common Pleas, Cumberland County, 1976-78, U.S. Dist. Ct. Middle Dist. Pa., Harrisburg, 1979—; asst. adj. prof. law Dickinson Sch. Law, 1973, 76, 77; mem. Gov. Pa. Com. Crime and Delinquency. Mem. Am. Bar Assn., Nat. Assn. Women Lawyers, Nat. Assn. Women Judges, Pa. Bar Assn., Pa. Trial Lawyers Assn., Phi Alpha Delta. Democrat. Presbyterian. Jurisprudence. Office: PO Box 868 Harrisburg PA 17108

RAMEE, THOMAS MARK, lawyer; b. West Point, N.Y., May 28, 1955; s. Paul Wyman and Martha Jean (Schellman). BA, Vanderbilt U., 1977; JD, U. Ga., 1980. Bar: Ga. 1980, S.C. 1981, U.S. Ct. Appeals (5th and 11th cirs.) 1981. Assoc. Brannen, Wessels & Searcy, Savannah, Ga., 1980-83; asst. gen. counsel Gulfstream Aerospace Corp., Savannah, 1983—. Home: Rt 1 Box 77 Clyo GA 31303 Office: Gulfstream Aerospace PO Box 2206 Savannah GA 31402

RAMEKER, WILLIAM JOHN, lawyer; b. Madison, Wis., Sept. 21, 1942; s. Norbert James and Evelyn Marie (McClone) R.; m. Marcia Lu Harryman, June 25, 1966; children: Deborah L., Matthew C., Michael S. BS, Iowa State U., 1965; JD, U. Iowa, 1972. Bar: Iowa 1972, Wis. 1972, U.S. Dist. Ct. (we. dist.) Wis. 1972, U.S. Dist. Ct. (ea. dist.) Wis. 1981. Ptnr. Thompson & Rameker, Madison, 1972-75, Seihr & Rameker, Madison, 1975-78, Rameker & Rudoy S.C., Madison, 1978-81, Murphy & Desmond S.C., Madison, 1981—. Bd. dirs. Wis. Spl. Oylmpics, Inc., Madison, 1977—. Mem. ABA, Wis. Bar Assn. (bd. dirs. bankruptcy, insolvency and creditors rights sect. 1982—, vice chmn. 1983-85, chmn. 1985—), Dane County Bar Assn. Bankruptcy, Consumer commercial, Contracts commercial. Home: 4806 Academy Dr Madison WI 53716 Office: Murphy & Desmond SC 150 E Gilman PO Box 2038 Madsion WI 53701

RAMER, BRUCE M., lawyer; b. Teaneck, N.J., Aug. 2, 1933; s. Sidney and Anne S. (Strassman) R.; m. Ann G. Ramer, Feb. 15, 1965; children—Gregg B., Marc K., Neal I. A.B., Princeton U., 1955; J.D., Harvard U., 1958. Bar: Calif. 1963, N.J. 1958. Assoc., Morrison, Lloyd & Griggs, Hackensack, N.J., 1959-60; ptnr. Gang, Tyre, Ramer & Brown, Inc., Los Angeles, 1963—. Exec. dir. Entertainment Law Inst.; bd. of councilors Law Ctr. U. So. Calif.; past pres. Los Angeles chpt., nat. v.p., bd. govs.; chmn. Nat. Affairs Commn. Am. Jewish Com.; trustee Loyola Marymount U.; mem. corp. bd., mem. agy. task force, discretionary fund distribution United Way; bd. of trustees Los Angeles Children's Mus.; v.p. Fraternity of Friends of Los Angeles Music Ctr. Mem. Los Angeles County Bar Assn., ABA, Calif. Bar Assn., Beverly Hills Bar Assn., Los Angeles Copyright Soc. (pres. 1974-75), Calif. Copyright Conf. (pres. 1973-74). Entertainment. Office: 6400 Sunset Blvd Los Angeles CA 90028

RAMIREZ, DAVID EUGENE, judge; b. Denver, July 10, 1952; s. George and Grace (Sanchez) R.; m. Lydia Alvarez, Nov. 22, 1975; Children: Jude, Marcus. BA, U. Colo., 1975; JD, U. Iowa, 1978. Bar: Colo. 1978, U.S. Dist. Ct. Colo. 1978. Staff atty. Legal Aid, Denver, 1978-80; assoc. counsel Blue Cross- Blue Shield, Denver, 1980-81; asst. atty. City of Denver, 1981-85; judge County of Denver, 1985—; instr. Denver Police Dept., 1982—, Skinner Mid. Sch., Denver, 1983—; lectr. bus. licensing PERA, Salt Lake City, 1985—; speaker Denver Pub. Schs., 1982. Mem. St. Catherine Edn. Bd., Denver, 1985—; v.p. St. Catherine Sch. Council, Denver, 1985—. Recipient Service Colfax on the Hill, 1984—, Recognotion cert. YMCA, 1986. Mem. Colo. Bar Assn., Denver Bar Assn., Hispanic Bar Assn., Assn. Trial Lawyers Am., Iowa Alumni Assn. Roman Catholic. Avocations: running, fishing, hist. reading. Judicial administration, Local government, Business licensing. Home: 4131 Green Ct Denver CO 80211

RAMIREZ, RAUL ANTHONY, U.S. district judge; b. Los Angeles, Mar. 8, 1944; s. Joseph M. and Jessie A. R.; m. Sharon Anne Bush, May 26, 1979; children: John, Suzanne, Joseph. B.A., Los Angeles State Coll., 1967; LL.B., J.D. (Am. Jurisprudence award criminal law 1970), U. Pacific, 1970. Bar: Calif. 1971. Law clk. to presiding judge Sacramento Superior Ct., 1970-71; asso. firm Clarence S. Brown, Sacramento, 1971-74; individual practice Sacramento, 1974-77; judge Sacramento Municipal Ct., 1977-80; U.S. dist. judge Eastern Dist. Calif., Sacramento, 1980—. Recipient various service awards, certs. commendation. Mem. Calif. Judges Assn. Jurisprudence. Address: US Courthouse 650 Capitol Mall Room 2042 Sacramento CA 95814 *

RAMIREZ, WILLIAM EARL, clothing company executive; b. Dalhart, Tex., July 15, 1951; s. Manuel and Isabella Mary (Lindsay) R.; BBA in Acctg., Tex. Tech U., 1973; JD, U. Iowa, 1976; LLM in Taxation, DePaul U., 1980. Bar: Iowa 1976, Ill. 1976. Tax. acct. Price Waterhouse & Co., Chgo., 1976-77; tax research analyst Sunbeam Corp., Chgo., 1977-80; tax atty. Hughes Tool Co., Houston, 1980-85; tax mgr. Levi Strauss & Co., San Francisco, 1985—; speaker Internat. Joint Ventures, 1984. Bd. dirs., treas. Bellerive Homeowners, Houston, 1984-85; vol. Big Bros.-Big Sisters, Houston, 1983-85. Named an Outstanding Young Man, U.S. Jaycees, 1984. Mem. ABA, , Internat. Bar Assn., World Affairs Council. Mensa. Democrat. Methodist. Corporate taxation, Private international, General corporate. Home: 350 Vernon St #2 Oakland CA 94610 Office: Levi Strauss & Co 1155 Battery LS 3 San Francisco CA 94120

RAMSAUR, ALLAN FIELDS, lawyer, lobbyist; b. Rocky Mountain, NC, Dec. 30, 1951; s. Carl Hamilton and Celestine (Fields) R.; m. Jimmie Lynn Brewer, Sept. 2, 1972; 1 child, Katherine Celeste. BS in Polit. Sci., Lambuth Coll., 1974; JD, U. Tenn., 1977. Bar: Tenn. 1977. Staff atty. Tenn. Dept. Mental Health, Nashville, 1977-80; dir. Tenn. Assn. Legal Services, Nashville, 1980-86; campaign dir. Steve Cobb, Nashville, 1986; exec. dir. Nashville Bar Assn., 1986—. Pres. Waverly-Woodland Tenn. Neighborhood Assn., Nashville, 1985; bd. dirs. SAGA, Nashville, 1984—. Mem. ABA (liason to standing com. on legal aid and indigent defendants 1984-86), Tenn. Bar Assn. (pres. young lawyers div. 1985-86), Nat. Legal Aid and Defender Assn. (chmn. legis. com. 1984—), Nashville Bar Assn. (exec. dir. 1986—). Democrat. Methodist. Legislative, Administrative and regulatory, Public benefits. Home: 744 Benton Ave Nashville TN 37204

RAMSEY, BRUCE MITCHELL, lawyer; b. Coral Gables, Fla., Jan. 12, 1956; s. Paul E. and Anna Jean (Piehl) R.; m. Pamela Pratt, May 21, 1983. BA summa cum laude, Fla. State U., 1978; JD with honors, U. Fla., 1981. Bar: Fla. 1981, U.S. Dist. Ct. (so. dist.) Fla. 1982. Ptnr. Jones and Foster, P.A., West Palm Beach, Fla., 1981—; bd. dirs. Fla. Med. Malpractice Claims Council, Inc., Miami, 1985—, pres., 1987—; lectr. Am. Assn. Med. Assistance, Jupiter, Fla., 1986, Jupiter Hosp., Fla., 1987—, Delray Community Hosp., Fla., 1987—. Bd. editors U. Fla. Law Rev., Gainesville, 1978. Mem. ABA, Fla. Bar Assn., Palm Beach County Bar Assn. (Young Lawyers sect.), Fla. Def. Lawyers Assn., Am. Trial Lawyers Assn., Phi Beta Kappa, Phi Sigma Alpha, Fla. Blue Key. Personal injury, Insurance, Products liability. Office: Jones and Foster PA 505 S Flagler Dr West Palm Beach FL 33401

RAMSEY, JOHN ARTHUR, lawyer; b. San Diego, Apr. 1, 1942; s. Wilbert Lewis and Lillian (Anderson) R.; m. Nikki Ann Ramsey, Feb. 9, 1943; children—John William, Bret Anderson, Heather Nichole. A.B., San Diego State U., 1965; J.D., Calif. Western Sch. Law, 1969. Bar: Colo. 1969, Tex. 1978. Assoc., Henry, Cockrell, Quinn & Creighton, 1969-72; atty. Texaco Inc., 1972-80, asst. to pres. Texaco U.S.A., 1980-81, asst. to div. v.p., Houston, 1981-82, div. atty., Denver, 1982—. Bd. dirs. Selective Service, Englewood, Colo., 1972-76; chmn. council Bethany Lutheran Ch., Englewood, 1976. Mem. ABA (vice chmn. oil com. sect. natural resource law 1983—). Republican. Editor in chief: Calif. Western Law Rev., 1969. General corporate, FERC practice. Office: 4601 DTC Blvd Denver CO 80237

RAMSEY, NORMAN PARK, judge; b. Fairchance, Pa., Sept. 1, 1922; s. Joseph L. and Florence (Bennett) R.; m. Margaret Quarngesser, Apr. 15, 1944 (dec. 1979); children: Margaret S. Ramsey Newman, Mary S. Ramsey Gilvarg, Christine M. Ramsey North, Ann L.; m. Tucky Patz, July 10, 1982. Student, Loyola Coll., Balt., 1939-41; LL.B., U. Md., 1947. Bar: Md. 1946. Law clk. to judge U.S. Dist. Ct., 1947-48; asst. U.S. atty. 1948-50; assoc. Semmes, Bowen & Semmes, Balt., 1951-54; partner Semmes, Bowen & Semmes, 1957-80; asst. atty. gen. Md. 1955, dep. atty. gen. Md., 1955-57; lectr. U. Md. Law Sch., 1951-71; judge U.S. Dist. Ct. Md. 1980—. Pres., Balt. CSC, 1963-70; pres. Bd. Sch. Commrs., 1975. Served to 1st lt. USMCR, 1943-46. Mem. Bar Assn. Balt. City, ABA (ho. of dels. 1961-81, bd. govs. 1975-78), Md. Bar Assn. (bd. govs. 1965-75, pres. 1973), Order of Coif, Phi Kappa Sigma. Jurisprudence. Home: 304 Wendover Rd Baltimore MD 21218 Office: 330 US Courthouse Baltimore MD 21201 *

RAMSEY, OWEN JASPER, JR., lawyer; b. La Grande, Oreg., Aug. 21, 1937; s. Owen Jasper Ramsey Sr.; m. Mary Diane Croft, Sept. 4, 1960; children: Jennifer Ramsey Austin, Lisa Ramsey Dion, Samantha, Benjamin. AB, Stanford U., 1959, LLB, 1961. Bar: U.S. Dist. Ct. (ea. and no. dists.) Calif. 1962, U.S. Ct. Appeals (9th cir.) 1962, U.S. Supreme Ct. 1962. Atty. Calif. Atty. Gen. Office, Sacramento, 1962; assoc. Mento, Buchler et al, Sacramento, 1963-72; ptnr. Ramsey, Humphrey & Morrison, Sacramento, 1972, Ramsey, Scott et al, Sacramento, 1973-80, Ramsey, Morrison & keddy, Sacramento, 1980-82, Ramsey, Moore, Morrison & Keddy, Sacramento, 1982—; moderator, lectr. Council Employee Benefits, Sacramento, 1984—. Mem. Calif. Bar Assn., Assn. Def. Counsel, Calif. Trial Lawyers Assn., Am. Arbitration Assn., Am. Bd. Trial Advs., Human Soc. U.S. (bd. dirs.). Avocations: golfing, gardening, reading. Federal civil litigation, State civil litigation, Personal injury. Office: Ramsey Moore Morrison & Keddy 10399 Old Placerville Rd Sacramento CA 95827

RAMSEY, ROBERT LEE, judge, lawyer; b. Glen. Allen, Va., Jan. 9, 1929; s. Hubert Smith and Louise Estelle (Ennis) R.; m. Dorothea Catherine Cherubini, Mar. 28, 1958 (div. 1972); children: Craig John, Matthew Lee, Scott Garrett; m. Lynn Marie Giubbini, July 15, 1978. B.A., Hofstra U., 1954; LL.B., Albany Law Sch., Union U., 1957; J.D., Albany Law Sch. Union U., 1968; M.P.A., SUNY-Albany, 1966; LL.M., So. Meth. U., 1969. Bar: N.Y. 1958, Tex. 1971. Assoc. atty. Kouray & Kouray, Schenectady, 1957-60; spl. agt. FBI, U.S. Dept. Justice, Washington, 1960-64; asst. atty. gen. State of N.Y., Albany, 1964-65; ptnr. Kalteux & Ramsey, Schenectady, 1965-68; chief asst. dist. atty. Schenectady County, N.Y., 1965-68; gen. counsel Internat. Air Transport Assn., Montreal, Que., Can., 1969-70; sr. atty. Air Transport Assn. Am., Washington, 1970; sole practice Dallas, 1970-76; adminstrv. law judge U.S. Dept. Labor, San Francisco, 1976-77; adminstrv. law judge U.S. Dept. Labor, Washington, 1977-81, chmn., chief adminstrv. appeals judge Benefits Rev. Bd., 1981—. Pres. Schenectady

County Republican Citizens Club, 1966-68; atty. Schenectady County Rep. Club, 1964-68. Served with USMC, 1946-48, 50-52. Mem. ABA, State Bar Tex., Fed. Adminstrv. Law Judges Conf. Republican. Presbyterian. Judicial administration, Labor, Aviation. Home: 6114 Pioneer Dr Springfield VA 22150 Office: US Dept Labor Benefits Rev Bd Suite 757 1111 20th St NW Washington DC 20036

RAMSEY, STEPHEN DOUGLAS, lawyer; b. Oklahoma City, Okla., May 10, 1947; s. Oliver F. and Gladys O'Neil (Smith) R.; m. Abigail Havens, June 11, 1977 (div. 1983); 1 child, Andrew Havens. AB, Princeton U., 1969; JD, U. Tex., 1978. Assoc. Coffee, Goldston & Bradshaw, Austin, Tex., 1972-77; atty. U.S. Dept. Justice, Washington, 1978-79, asst. chief pollution control sect., land and nat. resourses div., 1979-80, chief environ. enforcement sect., 1980-85; ptnr. Sidley & Austin, 1985—. Author: Superfund Handbook, 1985. Mem. com. to nominate alumni trustees Princeton U., (N.J.), 1977-80; pub. weigher Travis County, Austin, Tex., 1972-74. Recipient Atty. Gen. Disting. Service award Dept. Justice, 1983. Mem. ABA (nat. resources law sect. com. 1984—, vice chmn. environ. quality com. 1984—), Tex. Bar Assn., D.C. Bar Assn., Travis County Bar Assn. Democrat. Baptist. Environment, Federal civil litigation, Administrative and regulatory. Office: 1722 Eye St NW Washington DC 20912

RAND, RICHARD MALCOLM, lawyer; b. Bellingham, Wash., May 20, 1930; s. Loren B. and Thurza D. (Warren) R.; m. Elise Ann Planchard, July 26, 1952; children—Jeffry W., Gregory L., Eileen E. B.A., U. Wash., 1956, LL.B., 1958. Bar: Wash. 1958, Calif. 1959. Pres. Rand & Ziman, P.C.; lectr. in field. Mem. planned giving com. U. San Diego, former chmn. Served to comdr. USN, 1951-55; USNR, 1955-77. Mem. ABA, Calif. Bar. Estate planning, Probate, Estate taxation. Office: 2120 4th Ave San Diego CA 92101

RANDALL, CAROLYN DINEEN, U.S. judge; b. Syracuse, N.Y., Jan. 30, 1938; d. Robert E. and Carolyn E. (Bareham) Dineen; children: James, Philip, Stephen. A.B. summa cum laude, Smith Coll., 1959; LL.B., Yale U., 1962. Bar: D.C. 1962, Tex. 1963. Practice law Houston, 1962-79; circuit judge U.S. Ct. Appeals 5th Circuit, Houston, 1979—. Trustee, mem. exec. com., treas. Houston Ballet Found., 1967-70; mem. Houston dist. adv. council SBA, 1972-76; mem. Dallas regional panel President's Commn. White House Fellowships, 1972-76, mem. commn., 1977; bd. dirs. Houston chpt. Am. Heart Assn., 1978-79; nat. trustee Palmer Drug Abuse Program, 1978-79; trustee, sec., treas., chmn. audit com., fin. com., mem. mgmt. com. United Way Tex. Gulf Coast, 1979-85. Mem. ABA, Fed. Bar Assn., State Bar Tex., Houston Bar Assn., Phi Beta Kappa. Roman Catholic. Office: US Court Appeals 11020 US Courthouse 515 Rusk Ave Houston TX 77002

RANDALL, MEL SCOTT, lawyer; b. Los Angeles, July 13, 1946; s. Samuel and Florence (Sprintz) Rosenthal. B.A., Calif. State U.-Northridge, 1969; J.D., U. San Fernando Valley Coll., Sepulveda, Calif., 1976. Bar: Calif. 1978, U.S. Dist. Ct. (cen. dist.) Calif. 1978, U.S. Ct. appeals (9th cir.) 1981, U.S. Supreme Ct. 1981. Sole practice, Los Angeles, 1979—, Inglewood, Calif., 1978-79. Advt. editor: U. San Fernando Valley Coll. Law Rev., 1974-75, mng. editor, 1975-76; contbr. articles to profl. jours. Mem. Simon Wiesenthal Ctr. Mem. ABA, Assn. Trial Lawyers Am., Calif. Trial Lawyers Assn., Los Angeles Trial Lawyers Assn., Calif. Bar Assn., Sierra Club, Nat. Resources Def. Council. Democrat. Jewish. Personal injury, Insurance, State civil litigation. Office: 10880 Wilshire Blvd Suite 1900 Los Angeles CA 90024

RANDALL, RICHARD PARKS, lawyer; b. Nov. 15, 1947. BA, U. Va., 1969; MS, George Washington U., 1973; JD, U. Va., 1976. Bar: Pa. 1976, Tex. 1981, Calif. 1985. Sr. counsel Avery Internat., Pasadena, Calif., 1984—. General corporate, Private international, Mergers and acquisitions. Office: Avery Internat Corp 150 N Orange Grove Blvd Pasadena CA 91103

RANDALL, ROGER DARREL, judge; b. Thief River Falls, Minn., Nov. 16, 1941; s. Ross Lee and Ina Belinda (Mikkelson) R.; m. Virginia Mary Redies, May 28, 1966; children—Jennifer, Jocelyn, Jessica, Jeremy, Julie, Joshua, Jill. B.A. cum laude, U. Pacific, 1963; LL.B., Yale U., 1966. Bar: Calif., 1967, U.S. Dist. Ct. (no. dist.) Calif., 1967, U.S. Ct. Appeals, 9th cir., 1967, U.S. dist. cts. (no, eastern, central dists.) Calif. Dep. dist. atty. Kern County Dist. Atty.'s Office, 1969-73; partner Goldberg, Fisher, Randall & Quirk, Bakersfield, Calif., 1973-83; pres. Roger D. Randall, Profl. Corp., 1981-83; preliminary hearing referee State Bar Cts., 1979-82; judge pro-tem Kern County Superior Ct.; judge West Kern Mcpl. Ct., 1983-86; appointed to Kern County Superior Ct., 1986— . Bd. dirs. Estate Planning Council, Bakersfield, 1982—, pres., 1982-83; bd. dirs. Kern County Econ. Opportunity Council, 1970-71. Served to capt., U.S. Army, 1966-69. Nat. Merit scholar, 1959-63. Mem. ABA, Calif. Bar Assn., Kern County Bar Assn. (dir.). Republican. Lutheran.

RANDOLPH, CLYDE CLIFTON, JR., lawyer; b. Elmhurst, Ill., Mar. 11, 1928; s. Clyde Clifton and Madeline (Grady) R.; m. Doris Greene, June 21, 1953 (dec. 1980); children—Rebekah Louise, James Banton; m. Jane Smith, Oct. 8, 1983. LL.B., Wake Forest Coll., 1951. Bar: N.C. 1951, U.S. Dist. Ct. (mid. dist.) N.C. 1951, U.S. Ct. Appeals (4th cir.) 1956, U.S. Supreme Ct., 1958. Practice law, Winston-Salem, N.C., 1951—, ptnr. firm Randolph and Randolph, 1985—; chmn. Contact Teleministries USA, Inc., Harrisburg, Pa., 1973-78, dir., 1971-80. Pres. Forsyth County Legal Aid Soc., Winston-Salem, 1961; chmn. orgn. com. Contact of Winston-Salem, 1969-70. Served with USAR, 1949-56. Mem. Forsyth County Bar Assn. (pres. 1982-83; Disting. Service award 1977), N.C. State Bar Assn., Assn. Trial Lawyers Am., N.C. Acad. Trial Lawyers. Democrat. Episcopalian. Club: Bermuda Run Golf and Country (Advance, N.C.). Avocations: theology, mil. history. Federal civil litigation, Family and matrimonial, Personal injury. Home: 2650 Merry Oaks Trail Winston-Salem NC 27103 Office: Randolph and Randolph 3410 Healy Dr PO Box 24487 Winston-Salem NC 27114-4487

RANDOLPH, ROBERT RAYMOND, lawyer; b. San Antonio, Mar. 19, 1937; s. Ellis C. and Evelyn (Baxter) R.; children: Robert Cean, Grayson Moore; 1 child, Grayson Moore, Justin Ellis Beloff. BSEE, U. Tex., 1960, LLB, 1962. Bar: Tex. 1962. Assoc. Branscomb, Gary, Thomasson & Hall, Corpus Christi, Tex., 1962-63; atty. Tidewater Oil Co., Houston, 1963-64; asst. atty. Harris County, Houston, 1964-65; ptnr. Vinson & Elkins, Houston, 1965—. Mem. ABA, Tex. Bar Assn., Houston Bar Assn. Municipal bonds, Legislative, Real property. Home: 1812 Albans Houston TX 77005 Office: Vinson & Elkins 1001 Fannin 1st City Tower Houston TX 77002-6760

RANDT, CLARK THORP, JR., lawyer; b. Cleve., Nov. 24, 1945; s. Clark Thorp and Mary-Louise (Mitchell) R.; m. Sarah Talcott, Nov. 3, 1979; children: Clark Thorp III, Paull Mitchell. BA, Yale U., 1968; JD, U. Mich., 1975. Bar; N.Y. 1976. Assoc. Milbank, Tweed, Hadley & McCloy, N.Y.C., Hong Kong and Tokyo, 1975-82; first sec., comml. attache U.S. Embassy, Beijing, Peoples Republic of China, 1982-84; ptnr. Heller, Ehrman, White & McAuliffe, San Francisco, 1985; resident ptnr. Heller, Ehrman, White & McAuliffe, Hong Kong, 1986—; cons. Peoples Republic of China ministry of fgn. econ. relations and trade joint legal seminars U.S. Dept. Commerce, 1983-85; legal advisor The Nat. Council U.S.-China Trade, 1984. Contbr. articles to profl. jours. Advisor com. on indsl. competitiveness Calif. State Senate, 1985. Served to staff sgt. USAF, 1968-72. Mem. ABA, Am. Soc. Internat. Law, Am. C. of C. (chmn. Peoples Republic of China comml. relations com. 1987, Disting. Service medal, 1984), Dist. Export Council. Clubs: University (San Francisco); Yale (New York); American (Hong Kong). Private international, Contracts commercial. Home: 22A Branksome, 3 Tregunter Path, Hong Kong Hong Kong Office: Heller Ehrman White & McAuliffe, Caxton House 17/F 1 Duddell St, 1700 Peoples Republic China, Hong Kong Hong Kong

RANEY, DONALD RAYMOND, lawyer; b. Effingham, Ill., Nov. 3, 1954; s. Donald R. and Josephine A. (Scialabba) R.; m. Mary Reed, Oct. 18, 1980. BA, U. Ill., 1976; JD, Wake Forest U., 1979. Bar: Ill. 1979, Mo. 1980, U.S. Dist. Ct. (we. dist.) Mo. 1980, U.S. Dist. Ct. (ea. dist.) Mo. 1981, U.S. Ct. Appeals (8th cir.) 1981, U.S. Dist. Ct. (so. dist.) Ill. 1985. Assoc. Evans & Dixon, St. Louis, 1979-81, Moser, Marsalek, Carpenter, Cleary, Jaeckel & Keaney, St. Louis, 1981-85, Farrell & Long P.C., Godfrey, Ill., 1985—. Mem. ABA, Ill. Bar Assn., Mo. Bar Assn., Bar Assn. Met. St. Louis, Madison County Bar Assn. Roman Catholic. Personal injury, State civil litigation, Federal civil litigation. Office: Farrell & Long PC 1310 W Delmar Godfrey IL 62035

RANIER, NORMAN B., patent agent; b. N.Y.C., May 14, 1928. MS in Physics, U. Chgo., 1950; PhD in Chemistry, U. Del., 1956. Bar: U.S. Ct. Appeals (8th cir.) 1986, U.S. Supreme Ct. 1986; Registered patent agent. Patent chemist E.I. DuPont, Wilmington, Del., 1956-61; dir. research Eltex Research Corp., Providence, R.I., 1961-62; mgr. patent dept. Allied Chem. Co., Richmond, Va., 1962-68; sr. scientist Philip Morris Co., Richmond, 1968-84; prin. profl. Norman Rainer & Assocs., Richmond, 1976—. Inventee in field. Served with U.S. Army, 1952-54. Mem. Va. Bar Assn. Avocation: underwater photography. Office: Norman Rainer & Assocs 2008 Fondulac Rd Richmond VA 23229

RANISZESKI, LAWRENCE FRANK, lawyer; b. Detroit, Oct. 5, 1946; s. Stanley and Frances (Fagasinski) R.; m. Barbara Jean Visbicky, Sept. 29, 1973; children—Veronica Ann, Teresa Michele. B.A., Wayne State U., 1968; J.D. cum laude, Detroit Coll. Law, 1974. Bar: Mich. 1974, U.S. Dist. Ct. (ea. dist.) Mich. 1975, U.S. Ct. Appeals (6th cir.) 1975, U.S. Tax Ct. 1976. Law clk. Mich. Ct. Appeals, Saginaw, 1974-75; assoc., then ptnr. Colombo & Colombo, Birmingham, Mich., 1975—. Served with U.S. Army, 1969-71. Mem. ABA, Mich. Bar Assn., Oakland County Bar Assn., Detroit Bar Assn. Roman Catholic. State civil litigation, General practice, Labor. Office: Colombo & Colombo 1500 N Woodward Ave Suite 100 Birmingham MI 48012

RANK, JOHN THOMAS, lawyer; b. Chgo., Aug. 22, 1947; s. Gerald T. and Estelle M. (Lawler) R.; m. Linda Ann Prasil, July 25, 1970; 1 child, Sean Patrick. BA, U. Notre Dame, 1969; JD, Stanford U., 1972. Bar: Ill. 1972, Calif. 1973, U.S. Ct. Mil. Appeals 1973, U.S. Supreme Ct. 1977, U.S. Dist. Ct. (no. dist.) Ill. 1979. Assoc. Baker & McKenzie, Chgo., 1977-84, ptnr., 1984—. Served as capt. U.S. Army, 1973-77. Mem. ABA, Calif. Bar Assn., Ill. Bar Assn., Chgo. Bar Assn., Am. Arbitration Assn. (arbitrator), Chgo. Trial Lawyers Club. Roman Catholic. Avocation: tennis. State civil litigation, Federal civil litigation, Personal injury. Home: 35 Keswick Ct Lincolnshire IL 60015 Office: Baker & McKenzie 130 E Randolph St Chicago IL 60601

RANKIN, CLYDE EVAN, III, lawyer; b. Phila., July 3, 1950; s. Clyde Evan, Jr. and Mary E. (Peluso) R. A.B., Princeton U., 1972; J.D., Columbia U., 1975; postgrad. Hague Acad. Internat. Law, 1975. Bar: N.Y., N.J., D.C., U.S. Supreme Ct. Law clk. to judge U.S. Dist. Ct. So. Dist. N.Y., 1975-77; assoc. Debevoise, Plimpton, Lyons & Gates, N.Y.C., 1977-79; assoc. Coudert Bros., N.Y.C., 1979-83, ptnr., 1984—. Stone scholar, 1974. Mem. Assn. Bar City N.Y., ABA, N.Y. State Bar Assn., D.C. Bar Assn., N.J. Bar Assn. Roman Catholic. Club: Amateur Comedy (N.Y.C.). Contbr. article to legal jour. General corporate, Private international. Office: 200 Park Ave New York NY 10166

RANKIN, GENE RAYMOND, lawyer; b. Madison, Wis., Sept. 29, 1940; s. Eugene Carleton and Mildred Florence (Blomster) R.; m. Katherine E. Hundt, Aug. 25, 1979. BS, U. Wis., 1966, MS in Planning, 1973, JD, 1980. Bar: Wis. 1980, U.S. Dist. Ct. (we. dist.) Wis. 1980. Systems analyst U. Wis. Primate Research Ctr., Madison, 1967-72; planner Dane County Regional Planning Commn., Madison, 1973-79; with Risser and Risser, Madison, 1980—; dir. land regulation and records dept. Dane County, Madison, 1984—; planning cons., Madison, 1973-77; guest lectr. land use law, admiralty law, U. Wis. Law Sch., 1982-86; guest lectr. land econs. U. Wis. Planning Sch., 1973-81. Author: Historic Preservation Law in Wisconsin, 1982; contbr. articles to profl. psychol. and law jours. Bd. dirs. Madison Trust for Hist. Preservation, 1984-87, Madison Zoning Bd. of Appeals, 1986—; gen. counsel Historic Madison, Inc., 1981—; mem. legis. council Spl. Com. on Condominium Issues, Madison, 1984-85; commr. and vice-chmn. Dane County Housing Authority, 1979-84; chmn. Wis. Chamber Orch. Bd., 1979-81; state chmn. McCarthy 1976 campaign, Madison, 1974-76. Servedwith USCGR, 1958-60. Fellow Nat. Endowment for the Arts and Humanities, 1972. Mem. ABA, Wis. Bar Assn., Dane County Bar Assn. Clubs: U. Wis. Hoofers Sailing (vice commodore 1972), Meml. Union., U.S. Yacht Racing Union. Olympic finalist for Internat. 470 yachting competition, 1976. Avocations: sailing, racquet sports, music, skiing, skating. Environment, Real property, Local government. Home: 2818 Ridge Rd Madison WI 53705 Office: Risser and Risser 140 W Wilson St Madison WI 53703 Office: Dane County Land Regulation 116 City County Bldg Madison WI 53709

RANKIN, JAMES WINTON, lawyer; b. Norfolk, Va., Sept. 9, 1943; s. Winton Blair and Edith (Griffin) R.; m. Donna Lee Carpenter, June 25, 1966 (dec.); children—Thomas James, William Joseph, Elizabeth Jeanne; m. JoAnne Katherine Murray, Feb. 11, 1978. A.B. magna cum laude, Oberlin Coll., 1965; J.D. cum laude, U. Chgo., 1968. Bar: Ill. 1968, U.S. Dist. Ct. (no. dist.) Ill. 1969, U.S. Ct. Appeals (7th cir.) 1971, U.S. Ct. Appeals (5th cir.) 1979, U.S. Supreme Ct. 1975, Calif. 1986. Law clk. U.S. Dist. Ct. (no. dist.) Ill., 1968-69; assoc. Kirkland & Ellis, Chgo., 1969-73, ptnr., 1973—. Mem. ABA, Order of Coif, Phi Beta Kappa. Presbyterian. Clubs: Mid-Am., University (Chgo.); Kenilworth. Antitrust, Federal civil litigation, Health. Address: 633 Kenilworth Ave Kenilworth IL 60043

RANSMEIER, JOSEPH SIRERA, lawyer; b. New Orleans, June 19, 1915; s. John Christian and Viola Denisa (Sirera) R.; m. Margaret Mitchell, Nov. 30, 1940; children: John C., Michael M., Denis S., Margaret Ransmeier Rodgers. AB, Oberlin Coll., 1936; MA, Columbia U., 1937, PhD, 1942; JD, U. Mich., 1952. Bar: N.H. 1952. Instr. econs. Vanderbilt U., Nashville, 1940-41; faculty econs. dept. Dartmouth Coll., Hanover, N.H., 1946-52, prof. econs., 1952; assoc. Sulloway, Hollis & Soden, Concord, N.H., 1952-56, ptnr., 1957-78; ptnr. Ransmeier & Spellman, Concord, 1979—; trustee Concord Savings Bank, 1973—, bd. dirs.; bd. dirs. Concord Electric Co., Community Bankshares Inc., Concord. Author: The Tennessee Valley Authority, 1942; contbr. articles to profl. jours. Mem. Town Hopkinton Sch. Bd., N.H., 1953-59, bd. selectmen, 1960-66, Hopkinton Precint Planning Bd., 1981—; treas. Hopkinton Precint Water Dept., 1955-75; trustee Concord Hosp., 1975-81. Served to capt. U.S. Army, 1942-45. Fellow Am. Coll. Probate Counsel (state chmn. 1980-85); mem. ABA, Merrimack County Bar Assn., Order of Coif, Phi Beta Kappa. Republican. Episcopalian. Probate, Public utilities, General corporate. Home: RFD #3 Briar Hill Rd Box 153 Hopkinton NH 03229 Office: Ransmeier & Spellman 1 Capitol St Concord NH 03301

RANSOM, CLARK TAYLOR, lawyer; b. Phoenix, Mar. 19, 1950; s. Bruce Hickok, Sr. and Miriam (Freridge) R.; m. Susan K. Boxx, Apr. 10, 1978; children: Taylor LeJuene, Zachary Clark, Graham Hickok. BA, U. Wash., 1977; JD, U. Puget Sound, 1980. Bar: Wash. 1980, U.S. Dist. Ct. (we. dist.) Wash. 1980, U.S. Ct. Appeals (9th cir.) 1980. Asst. atty. gen. State of Wash, Olympia, 1980-82; assoc. Ulin, Dann, Elston & Lambe, Seattle, 1982-83; reassumption rules rev. officer Safety div. Wash. State Dept. Labor and Industry, Olympia, 1983-86; asst. dir. Employment Standards Apprenticeship and Crime Div. Wash. State Dept. Labor & Industry, Olympia, 1986—. Labor, Workers' compensation, Administrative and regulatory. Home: 1005 N Lawrence Tacoma WA 98406 Office: ESAC div Dept of Labor and Industries Gen Adminstrn Bldg Olympia WA 98504

RAPAPORT, ROSS SELWITT, lawyer; b. Hartford, Conn., Aug. 9, 1942; s. Milton H. and Dorothy (Zlochiver) R.; m. Susan Grey, Feb. 8, 1964 (div. Feb. 1975); children: Amy E., Rachel H., Donald P.; m. Linda Mulvaney, Sept. 5, 1975. BA, Hobart Coll., 1964; JD, Cornell U., 1967. Bar: Conn. 1967, U.S. Dist. Ct. Conn. 1967, U.S. Supreme Ct. 1982. Assoc. Bernard Glazer, Stamford, Conn., 1967-68, Robert Epstein, Stamford, 1968-69; ptnr. Epstein & Rapaport, Stamford, 1970-77, Rapaport & Benedict, P.C., Stamford, 1977—. Charles Evans Hughes fellow Cornell U., 1964-67. Mem. ABA, Conn. Bar Assn. (bench-bar com. 1974-77, exec. com. family law sect. 1979-82), Stamford Bar Assn., Am. Trial Lawyers Assn., Conn. Trial Lawyers Assn. Clubs: Pine Orchard Yacht and Country (Branford) (bd. of govs. 1985-86); Landmark (Stamford). Office: Rapaport & Benedict PC 750 Summer St Stamford CT 06901

RAPER, WILLIAM CRANFORD, lawyer; b. Ashville, N.C., Aug. 17, 1946; s. James Sidney and Kathryn (Cranford) R.; m. Patricia Dotson, Sept. 28, 1974; children: Kimber-leigh, Heather, James. AB, U. N.C., 1968; JD, Vanderbilt U., 1972. Bar: N.C. 1972, U.S. Ct. Appeals (4th cir.) 1972, U.S. Supreme Ct. 1977, U.S. Ct. Appeals (fed. cir.) 1985. Law clk. to presiding justice U.S. Ct. Appeals (4th cir.), Richmond, Va., 1972-73; ptnr. Womble, Carlyle, Sandridge & Rice, Winston-Salem, N.C., 1974—. Mem. ABA, N.C. Bar Assn., mem. N.C. Assn. of Def. Attys. (charter). Federal civil litigation, State civil litigation, Personal injury. Office: Womble Carlyle Sandridge & Rice PO Drawer 84 Winston-Salem NC 27102

RAPP, GERALD DUANE, lawyer, manufacturing company executive; b. Berwyn, Nebr., July 19, 1933; s. Kenneth P. and Mildred (Price) R.; m. Jane Carol Thomas, Aug. 14, 1954; children—Gerald Duane Jr., Gregory T., Amy Frances. B.S., U. Mo., 1955; J.D., U. Mich., 1958. Bar: Ohio bar 1959. Practice in Dayton, 1960—; partner Smith & Schnacke, 1963-70; asst. gen. counsel Mead Corp., 1970, v.p. human resources and legal affairs, 1973, v.p., corp. sec., 1975, v.p., gen. counsel, corp. sec., 1976, v.p., gen. counsel, 1979, sr. v.p., gen. counsel, 1981—; chmn. Mead Data Cen., Inc., 1971-73. Sr. editor: U. Mich. Law Review, 1957-58. Past chmn. Oakwood Youth Commn.; past v.p., bd. dirs. Big Bros. Greater Dayton; mem. president's visitors com. U. Mich. Law Sch.; past trustee Urbana Coll. ; trustee Ctr. Internat. Mgmt. Studies, Internat. YMCA, Ohio Ctr. Leadership Studies, Robert K. Greenleaf Ctr., Newton Ctr., Dayton and Montgomery County Pub. Library ; bd. dirs. Miami Valley Regional Small Bus. Incubator, Yellow Springs, Ohio. Served to 1st lt. U.S. Army, 1958-60. Mem. Am., Ohio, Dayton bar assns., Phi Kappa Psi, Phi Delta Phi, Beta Gamma Sigma. Presbyterian. Clubs: Rod and Reel, Moraine Country, Dayton Racquet, Dayton Bicycle, Dayton Lawyers, Ye Buz Fuz; Met. (Washington). Antitrust, General corporate. Office: Mead Corp Courthouse Plaza NE Dayton OH 45463

RAPP, JAMES ANTHONY, lawyer, author; b. Williamson, W.Va., Feb. 25, 1949; s. Roy Thomas and Lucille (Middendorf) R.; m. Martha Brune, Dec. 28, 1972; children: Rebecca, Elizabeth Marie, Amy Christine. BS in Communications, U. Ill., Urbana, 1971; JD, Washington U., 1974. Bar: Ill. 1974, Mo. 1975, U.S. Dist. Ct. (we. dist.) Mo. 1975, U.S. Dist. Ct. (so. dist.) Ill. 1975, U.S. Ct. Appeals (7th cir.) 1976, U.S. Ct. Appeals (8th cir.) 1976, U.S. Tax Ct. 1976, U.S. Supreme Ct. 1979, U.S. Dist. Ct. (cen. dist.) Ill. 1980. Prin. Hutmacher, Rapp & Ortbal, P.C. and predecessors, Quincy, Ill., 1974—; asst. corp. counsel City of Quincy, 1976-85. Editorial cons. Illinois Corporations Legal System, 1984; co-author: Illinois Public Community College Act: Tenure Policies and Procedures, 1980; School Crime and Violence: Victims' Rights, 1986; Illinois Domestic Relations Legal System, 1983; editor-in-chief, author: Education Law School Crime and Violence: Victim's Rights, 1986; contbr. chpts. to books, articles to profl. jours. Bd. dirs. United Way Adams County, Inc., Quincy, 1975-81, pres., 1981-82; bd. dirs. Quincy Symphony Orch. Assn., 1976-79, pres., 1979-82. Mem. Adams County Bar Assn., Chgo. Bar Assn., Ill. State Bar Assn., Mo. Bar Assn., ABA, Nat. Assn. Coll. and Univ. Attys., Nat. Orgn. Legal Problems of Edn. General practice, Local government, General corporate. Home: 1223 Scotia Trail Quincy IL 62301 Office: Hutmacher Rapp & Ortbal PC 428 N 6th St Quincy IL 62301

RAPP, ROBERT DAVID, lawyer; b. N.Y.C., Mar. 19, 1950; s. Melville Benjamin and Rachel (Marx) R. BA in Econs., U. Tenn., 1973; JD, Antioch U., 1982. Bar: Tex. 1982, U.S. Dist. Ct. (so. dist.) Tex. 1983, U.S. Ct. Appeals (5th cir.) 1983, U.S. Supreme Ct. 1985. Law clk. to presiding judge U.S. Dist. Ct. (so. dist.) Tex., Houston, 1982-83; ptnr. Mandell & Wright, Houston, 1983—. Contbr. articles to law revs. and profl. jours. Mem. ABA, Fed. Bar Assn. (bd. dirs. Houston chpt. 1985—), Assn. Trial Lawyers Am., Tex. Trial Lawyers Assn., Houston Trial Lawyers Assn. State civil litigation, Federal civil litigation, Personal injury. Home: 2634 Yorktown #367 Houston TX 77056 Office: Mandell & Wright 712 Main Suite 1600 Houston TX 77002

RAPPAPORT, A. JACK, lawyer; b. N.Y.C., Oct. 5, 1912; s. Harry and Eva (Isaacson) R.; married July 11, 1941; children: Mark Lawrence, Ellen. BA, Syracuse U., 1936, JD, 1968. Bar: N.Y. 1946, U.S. Dist. Ct. (no. dist.) N.Y. 1949. Commd. Ordnance U.S. Army, 1941, advanced through grades to maj., ret., 1950; ptnr. Rappaport, Rappaport & Schanz, Binghamton, N.Y. Criminal, Estate planning, Contracts commercial. Office: Rappaport Rappaport & Schanz 11 Congdon Pl Binghamton NY 13901

RAPPAPORT, CHARLES OWEN, lawyer; b. N.Y.C., May 15, 1950; s. Edward and Edith (Novick) R. BA, Columbia U., 1970; JD, NYU, 1975. Assoc. Simpson, Thacher & Bartlett, N.Y.C., 1975-82, ptnr., 1982—. Corporate taxation. Home: 26 N Moore St 4W New York NY 10013 Office: Simpson Thacher & Bartlett One Battery Park Plaza New York NY 10004

RAPPAPORT, EARLE SAMUEL, JR., lawyer; b. Chgo., Jan. 24, 1935; s. Earle Samuel Sr. and Marion (Hendry) R.; m. Nancy Kay, Aug. 4, 1957; children: Tracey, Bret, Leigh, Adam, Kent. BA, U. Ill., 1954, Roosevelt U., 1955; JD, Northwestern U., 1958. Bar: Ill. 1958, U.S. Supreme Ct. 1966. Law clk. to judge U.S. Dist. Ct. (no. dist.) Ill., Chgo., 1958-60; lectr. John Marshall Law Sch., Chgo., 1959-64; ptnr. Edelman & Rappaport, Chgo., 1960-86, Schwartz, Cooper, Kolb & Gaynor, Chgo., 1986—; bd. dirs. Railtrack, Inc., Hinsdale, Ill. Editor Northwestern U. Law Journal, 1957-58. Pres., bd. trustees Fire Protection Dist., Deerfield, Ill., 1975-80. Mem. ABA, Ill. Bar Assn., Chgo. Bar Assn., Assn. Trial Lawyers Am., Niles Jaycees (pres. 1965-66), Order of Coif. Democrat. Jewish. Avocations: golf, boating. State civil litigation, Family and matrimonial, Federal civil litigation. Home: 1247 Deerfield Deerfield IL 60015 Office: Schwartz Cooper Kolb & Gaynor 33 N LaSalle Chicago IL 60602

RAPPAPORT, RICHARD WARREN, lawyer; b. Phila., Sept. 20, 1948; s. Sydney F. and Florence K. (Kail) R. B.S., Boston U., 1970; J.D., U. Miami, 1973; LL.M., Georgetown U., 1974. Bar: Fla. 1974, D.C. 1975, U.S. Dist. Ct. D.C. 1978, U.S. Ct. Appeals (D.C. cir.) 1978, N.Y. 1981, U.S. Dist. Ct. (so. dist.) Fla. 1979, U.S. Supreme Ct. 1981. Sole practice, Washington, N.Y.C. and Pompano Beach, Fla., 1977—. Contbr. articles to profl. jours. Mem. ABA, Assn. Bar N.Y.C., N.Y. State Bar Assn., Fed. Communications Bar Assn. Administrative and regulatory, Private international. Home: 1408 SE Bayshore Dr Miami FL 33131 Office: 3970 Oaks Clubhouse Dr Suite 208 Pompano Beach FL 33069

RAS, ROBERT A., lawyer; b. River Forest, Ill., Oct. 5, 1946; s. Anthony S. and Bernice Ras; m. Susan Payette; 1 child, Kristen. A.B., Georgetown U., 1967, J.D., 1976; M.B.A., U. Chgo., 1973. Bar: D.C. 1976, Ill. 1977, N.Y. 1982. Vice pres. Am. Nat. Bank, Chgo., 1970-75; atty. office of chmn. Arthur Young & Co., N.Y.C. and Chgo., 1976-85; dir. taxes, Deloitte, Haskins & Sells, Oak Brook, Ill., 1985—; congl. liaison Nat. Commn. on Financing of Postsecondary Edn., 1973-74. Assoc. editor The Tax Lawyer, 1974-76. Contbr. articles to profl. jours. Pres., bd. dirs. Oakwood Community Assn., Ill., 1977-80; trustee Fenwick High Sch., Oak Park, Ill., 1984—. Mem. ABA (com. chmn. sect. taxation 1977—), Chgo. Bar Assn., Assn. Bar City of N.Y., Du Page County Bar Assn. Roman Catholic. Clubs: Bath and Tennis, Midwest, Butler Nat. Golf (Oak Brook, Ill.). Federal civil litigation, Banking, Corporate taxation. Home: PO Box 4892 Oak Brook IL 60522 Office: Deloitte Haskins & Sells 2 Mid America Plaza Oakbrook Terrace IL 60181

RASCHE, WILLIAM GRETHER, lawyer; b. Phila., Aug. 4, 1954; s. Herbert Herman and Gertrude Emma (Grether) R.; m. Margaret Ruth Scott, May 30, 1976 (div. Jan. 1984). BA with honors, U. Wis., 1976, JD cum laude, 1980. Bar: Wis. 1980, U.S. Dist. Ct. (we. dist.) Wis. 1980, U.S. Dist. Ct. (ea. dist.) Wis. 1984, U.S. Ct. Appeals (7th cir.) 1984. Assoc. Wendel, Center, Lipman, Peppard & Trachtenberg, Madison, Wis., 1980-87; ptnr. Wendel & Center, Madison, 1987—. Mem. ABA, Wis. Bar Assn., Assn. Trial Lawyers Am., Am. Judicature Soc. Federal civil litigation, State civil litigation, Personal injury. Home: 4208 Morris Park Rd McFarland WI 53558 Office: Wendel & Center 426 S Yellowstone Dr Madison WI 53719

RASCHKE, FRED DAVID, lawyer; b. Houston, Sept. 4, 1954; s. Fred Carl and Maude Mary (Lindsey) R.; m. Susan Kathleen Garrott, June 3,

1978. BBA, U. Tex., 1977; JD, Tex. Tech U., 1980. Bar: Tex. 1981, U.S. Dist. Ct. (ea. and so. dists.) Tex. 1981. Assoc. Mills, Shirley, Eckel & Bassett, Galveston, Tex., 1980-84, ptnr., 1984—. Sponsorship chmn. Boy Scouts Am., Galveston County, 1985-86; bd. dirs. Tex. Tech U. Law Sch. Assn., 1983—. Mem. ABA, Tex. Assn. Def. Counsel, Galveston County Young Lawyers Assn. (pres. 1985-86), Galveston Hist. Soc., Galveston Arts Council, Order of Barristers, Phi Alpha Delta, Omicron Delta Kappa. Methodist. Lodge: Rotary (named one of Outstanding Young Men Am., Galveston club, 1985). Avocation: sports. Insurance, Personal injury, Workers' compensation. Home: 10 Quintana Pl Galveston TX 77551 Office: Mills Shirley et al 400 Washington Bldg 2228 Mechanic Galveston TX 77550

RASHKIND, PAUL MICHAEL, lawyer; b. Jamaica, N.Y., May 21, 1950; s. Murray and Norma (Dorfman) Weinstein; m. Robin Shane, Dec. 20, 1975; children: Adam Charles, Noah Hamilton, Jennifer Elizabeth. AA, Miami-Dade Jr. Coll., 1970; BBA, U. Miami, Coral Gables Fla., 1972, JD, 1975. Bar: Fla. 1975, D.C. 1981, N.Y. 1981, U.S. Dist. Ct. (so. dist.) Fla. 1975, U.S. Ct. Appeals (5th cir.) 1976, U.S. Supreme Ct. 1978, U.S. Dist. Ct. (mid. dist.) Fla. 1979, U.S. Ct. Appeals (2d and 11th cirs.) 1981, U.S. Ct. Appeals (4th and 6th cirs.) 1986, U.S. Dist. Ct. (no. dist.) Fla. 1987; diplomate Nat. Bd. Trial Advocacy-Criminal Law. Asst. state atty. Dade County State Attys. Office, Miami, Fla., 1975-78, chief asst. state atty. in charge of appeals, 1977-78; atty. Sams, Gerstein & Ward, P.A., Miami, 1978-83; ptnr. Bailey, Gerstein, Rashkind & Dresnick, Miami, 1983—; spl. master Ct. Appointment, Miami, 1982-83; arbitrator Dade County Jail Inmates Grievance Program, Miami, 1981—; mem. Fla. Bar Unauthorized Practice of Law Com. C, 11th Jud. Cir., Miami, 1980-84. Contbr. articles on ethics and criminal law to profl. jours. Pres., bd. dirs. Lindgren Homeowners Assn., Miami, Fla., 1981-86. Fellow Am. Bd. Criminal Lawyers (bd. govs. 1980-86; mem. ABA (ethics com. criminal justice sect. 1979—, vice chmn. 1985-87, chmn. 1987—), Fla. Bar Assn., N.Y. Bar Assn., D.C. Bar Assn., Dade County Bar Assn., Assn. Trial Lawyers Am., Acad. Fla. Trial Lawyers (chmn. criminal law sect. 1985-86, diplomate 1986—), Nat. Assn. Criminal Def. Lawyers, Soc. Bar and Gavel, Iron Arrow, Hon. Order Ky. Cols., Omicron Delta Kappa, Delta Sigma Rho-Tau Kappa Alpha, Pi Sigma Alpha, Phi Rho Pi, Delta Theta Phi. Democrat. Jewish. Criminal, State civil litigation. Office: Bailey Gerstein Rashkind & Dresnick 4770 Biscayne Blvd Suite 950 Miami FL 33137

RASICOT, JAMES FREDERICK, law related corporation executive; b. Brainerd, Minn., May 3, 1946; s. Don and Florence (Brick) R. BA, Wayne State Coll., 1969; MS, Mankato State U., 1982; PhD, Century U., 1985. Pres. Affirmative Bus. Communications, Mpls., 1980—. Author: Jury Selection, Body Language and Visual Trial, 1983, Silent Sales, 1986. Mem. Am. Soc. Trial Cons. Legal education, State civil litigation, Personal injury. Home: 6705 Woodedge Rd Minneapolis MN 55364 Office: Affirmative Bus Communications 5100 Eden Ave Suite 201 Minneapolis MN 55436

RASIN, ALEXANDER PARKS, III, lawyer; b. Chestertown, Md., May 21, 1943; s. Alexander Parks Jr. and Henrietta (Bowen) R.; m. Margaret Josephine Baker, June 14, 1969; children: Elizabeth Bowen, Katherine Parks. BA, Washington and Lee U., 1965; LLB, U. Md., 1968. Bar: Md. 1969, U.S. Dist. Ct. Md. 1972, U.S. Supreme Ct. 1974. Ptnr. Rasin & Rasin, Chestertown, 1971-75, Rasin & Sisk, Chestertown, 1976-81; sole practice Chestertown, 1982; ptnr. Rasin & Wright, Chestertown, 1982—. Chmn. United Fund Kent County, Md., 1972; commr. Kent County, 1982—, pres. 1986—; trustee Kent County Pub. Library, 1973-82, pres. 1978-80; trustee Kent Sch. Bd., 1978-86, pres. 1979-81. Served to 1st lt. U.S. Army, 1968-70. Mem. ABA, Md. Bar Assn., Kent County Bar Assn., Kent County Commrs. Assn. (pres. 1986—), Washington and Lee U. Alumni Assn. (pres. Delmarva chpt. 1982-86). Republican. Episcopalian. Real property, Probate, General practice. Home and Office: Rasin & Wright PO Box 228 Chestertown MD 21620

RASKIN, MARTIN ROBERT, lawyer; b. Jersey City, Sept. 29, 1946; s. Bernard and Elsie (Karel) R.; m. Ellen Elizabeth Thompson, Sept. 1, 1968; children: Melissa Beth, Stephanie Lynn. BA, Bloomfield Coll., 1970; JD, Seton Hall U., 1974. Bar: N.J. 1974, U.S. Dist. Ct. N.J. 1974, U.S. Ct. Appeals (3d cir.) 1975, U.S. Ct. Appeals (5th cir.) 1978, U.S. Supreme Ct. 1979, Fla. 1981, U.S. Dist. Ct. (so. dist.) Fla. 1981, U.S. Ct. Appeals (11th cir.) 1982, U.S. Ct. Internat. Trade 1985. Law clk. to presiding chief justice U.S. Dist. Ct. N.J., Newark, 1974-75, asst. U.S. atty., 1975-78; spl. atty. Organized Crime and Racketeering sect. U.S. Dept. Justice, Miami, Fla., 1978-80; chief, criminal div., U.S. Atty.'s Office, so. dist. Fla., Miami, 1980-82; ptnr. Barron, Lehman, Picken & Raskin, Miami, 1982-84, Raskin & Graham, Miami, 1984—. Served to sgt. USAF, 1964-68. Recipient Spl. Achievement awards U.S. Dept. Justice, Washington, 1977, 81, 82; also various awards from FBI, U.S. Secret Service, USCG, U.S. Border Patrol, U.S. Bur. Alcohol, Tobacco and Firearms, U.S. Postal Inspection Service, U.S. Dept. Justice, 1982. Mem. ABA, Assn. Trial Lawyers Am., Acad. Fla. Trial Lawyers, Nat. Assn. Criminal Def. Lawyers, Fed. Bar Assn. Home: 11310 SW 131 Ave Miami FL 33186 Office: Raskin & Graham PA 744 NW 12th Ave Miami FL 33136

RASKOPF, ROBERT LLOYD, lawyer; b. Bklyn., Aug. 3, 1951; s. Lloyd Andrew and Marilyn Frances (Reilly) R.; m. Lisa Nan Fine, July 29, 1978; 1 child, Ryan Allen. BS, Boston Coll., 1973, JD, 1976. Bar: N.Y. 1977, U.S. Dist. Ct. (so. and ea. dists.) N.Y. 1977, U.S. Ct. Appeals (2d cir.) 1982. Assoc. Townley and Updike, N.Y.C., 1976-85, ptnr., 1985—. Editor Trademark Reporter, 1985-86. Mem. ABA (patent, copyright and trademark com.), Assn. Bar of City of N.Y., U.S. Trademark Assn. (assoc.). Avocations: jogging, literature. Home: 301 E 79th St Apt 11E New York NY 10021 Office: Townley and Updike 405 Lexington Ave New York NY 10174

RASMUS, JOHN CHARLES, trade association executive, lawyer; b. Rochester, N.Y., Dec. 27, 1941; s. Harold Charles and Myrtle Leota (Dybevik) R.; m. Elaine Green Reeves, Mar. 19, 1962; children—Kristin, Stuart, Karin. A.B., Cornell U., 1963; J.D., U. Va., 1966. Bar: Va. 1970, U.S. Supreme Ct. 1974. Spl. agt. Def. Dept., Washington, 1966-70; v.p., adminstrv. officer, legis. research counsel U.S. League Savs. Instns., Washington, 1970-83; asst. to exec. v.p. Nat. Assn. Fed. Credit Unions, 1983-84; Fed. adminstrv. counsel Am. Bankers Assn., 1985—. Mem. steering com. legis./fiscal affairs bur. Greater Washington Bd. Trade; vice-chmn. Cornell U. Council's Fed. Govt. Liaison Com., 1981—. Mem. Fed. Bar Assn. (disting. service award 1980, 82, immediate past chmn. long range planning com., past chmn. council fin. instns. and economy), ABA. Clubs: Capitol Hill, Nat. Lawyers, Internat. (Washington), Masons. Legislative, Administrative and regulatory, Banking. Home: 303 Kentucky Ave Alexandria VA 22305

RASMUSSEN, CARL JOHN, lawyer; b. Crandon, Wis., Feb. 27, 1948; s. Carl Frederick and Darina (Moravec) R.; m. Catherine Crow, June 8, 1974; children: Laura Jarmila, Susanna Elizabeth. BA, U. Wis., 1970, MA, 1973, PhD, 1978, JD, 1982. Bar: Wis. 1982, U.S. Dist. Ct. (we. dist.) Wis. 1982. Assoc. Boardman, Suhr, Curry & Field, Madison, Wis., 1982—. Co-author (with Sargent Bush, Jr.): The Library of Emmanuel College Cambridge, 1584-1637, 1986; contbr. articles to profl. jours. Recipient Pro Bono award Dane County Bar Assn., 1985. Mem. ABA (marital deduction subcom. estate planning and drafting com.), Wis. Bar Assn. (inheritance tax subcom. taxation sect.). Mem. United Ch. Christ. Avocation: research and writing on early modern history and culture, 1500-1700. Estate planning, Probate, Jurisprudence. Home: 652 Sprague St Madison WI 53711 Office: Boardman Suhr Curry & Field 1 S Pinckney St Madison WI 53703

RASMUSSEN, FRANK MORRIS, lawyer; b. Modesto, Calif., Sept. 21, 1934; s. Elmer Christian and Mary Evelyn (Bonham) R.; m. Carolyn Anne Humbert, Aug. 22, 1959; children—Kathryn Anne, James Russell, Peter Bonham. A.B., Wabash Coll., 1956; LL.B., Harvard U., 1960. Bar: Ohio 1960, U.S. Dist. Ct. (no. dist.) Ohio, U.S. Mil. Ct. Appeals 1962. Assoc. Squire, Sanders & Dempsey and predecessor firms, Cleve., 1960-70; ptnr. Squire, Sanders & Dempsey, Cleve., 1970—; sec. Madison Equipment Co., Cleve., 1964—, United Screw & Bolt Co., Cleve., 1983—; dir. Weatherchem Corp., Cleve. Trustee, v.p. Cleve. Council on World Affairs, 1970—; trustee, past pres. Greater Cleve. Neighborhood Assn., 1975—; trustee Wabash Coll. Alumni Assn., 1970-83. Mem. ABA, Ohio Bar Assn., Bar Assn. Greater Cleve. Clubs: Cleve. Athletic, Union. General corporate, Securities. Home: 15289 Russell Rd Chagrin Falls OH 44022 Office: Squire Sanders & Dempsey 1800 Huntington Bldg Cleveland OH 44115

RASMUSSEN, RICHARD ROBERT, corporate lawyer; b. Chgo., July 5, 1946; s. Robert Kersten Rasmussen and Marisa Bruna (Batistoni) Brewer; m. Margaret Gay DiUlio, Mar. 24, 1977; children: Kathryn, William. BS, U. Oreg., 1970, JD, 1973. Bar: Oreg. 1973. Atty. U.S. Bancorp, Portland, Oreg., 1973-83, v.p. and mgr., law div., 1983—. Mem. editorial bd. Oreg. Bus. Law Digest, 1979-81, Oreg. Debtor/Creditor newsletter, 1980-84; contbr. articles to profl. jours. Chmn. mgmt. com. YMCA of the Columbia-Willamette, Portland, 1978-79. Mem. Oreg. State Bar Assn. (chmn. corp. counsel com. 1979-81, debtor/creditor sect. 1982-83; sec. com. on sects. 1982-83), ABA, Multnomah County Bar Assn., Beta Gamma Sigma. Club: Founder's (Portland). Avocations: mountaineering, whitewater rafting. Banking, Contracts commercial. Office: US Bancorp Law Div 111 SW 5th Ave Portland OR 97208

RASMUSSEN, THOMAS VAL, JR., lawyer, small business owner; b. Salt Lake City, Aug. 11, 1954; s. Thomas Val and Georgia (Smedley) R.; m. Donita Gubler, Aug. 15, 1978; children: James, Katherine. BA magna cum laude, U. Utah, 1978, JD, 1981. Bar: Utah 1981, U.S.Dist. Ct. Utah 1981, U.S. Supreme Ct. 1985. Atty. Salt Lake Legal Defender Assn., Salt Lake City, 1981-83, Utah Power and Light Co., Salt Lake City, 1983—; co-owner, developer Handi Self-Storage, Kaysville, Utah, 1984—. Adminstrv. editor Jour. Contemporary Law, 1980-81, Jour. Energy Law and Policy, 1980-81. Missionary Ch. of Jesus Christ of Latter-Day Sts., Brazil, 1973-75. Mem. ABA, Utah Bar Assn., Salt Lake County Bar Assn., Phi Eta Sigma, Phi Kappa Phi, Beta Gamma Sigma. Avocations: tennis, softball, skiing, traveling, collecting art. Consumer commercial, Criminal, State civil litigation. Home: 7079 Pine Cone Circle Salt Lake City UT 84121 Office: Utah Power and Light Co 1407 W North Temple Suite 340 Salt Lake City UT 84116

RASOR, CHARLES LEWIS, JR., lawyer; b. Greenwood, S.C., Nov. 9, 1943; s. Charles Lewis and Mary Elspeth (Stewart) R.; m. Barbara Carlton Brothers, June 6, 1966; m. 2d, Marguerite Chapman Manning, Aug. 19, 1977; children—Charles Lewis III, Clark Stewart, Mary Claytor. Cert. specialist in estate planning and probate law. Student U.S. Naval Acad., 1962-64; B.A. cum laude, Furman U., 1966; LL.B., U. Va., 1969. Bar: S.C. 1969, U.S. Dist. Ct. S.C. 1969, U.S. Ct. Appeals (4th cir.) 1974. Assoc. Haynsworth, Perry, Bryant, Marion & Johnstone, Greenville, S.C., 1969-75, ptnr., 1975—; mem. S.C. State Bar Specialization Adv. Bd. Estate Planning and Probate through 1986. Chmn. Meals on Wheels for Sr. Citizens, Inc., Greenville, 1980-82; mem. deferred gifts steering com. Furman U.; bd. dirs. Christ Ch. Endowment Corp. Served with USN, 1962-64. Fellow Am. Coll. Probate Counsel; mem. ABA, S.C. Bar Assn., Greenville County Bar Assn., Greenville Estate Planning Council, Republican. Episcopalian. Clubs: Poinsett, Cotillion (Greenville). Estate planning, Probate, General corporate. Office: PO Box 2048 Greenville SC 29602

RASOR, REBA GRAHAM, lawyer; b. Thorndale, Tex., June 29, 1926; d. Owen D. and Clara W. (Clymore) Graham; m. Mac Roy Rasor, Dec. 24, 1946; children—Graham, Dan, Nancy. B.J. with honors, U. Tex., 1946; J.D. cum laude, So. Meth. U., 1966. Bar: Tex. 1966. With Austin (Tex.) American-Statesman, 1946-51; Tex. Press Assn., 1955-61; ptnr. pub. relations firm, 1955-61; mem. faculty So. Meth. Sch. Law, 1966-70; sole practice, 1970-73; assoc. Raggio & Raggio, Inc., 1973-78; ptnr. Koons, Rasor, Fuller & McCurley, Dallas, 1978—; lectr. in field. Fellow Am. Acad. Matrimonial Lawyers, Tex. Bar Found.; mem. ABA, State Bar Tex., Dallas Bar Assn., Order of Coif. Contbr. articles to profl. jours.; editor: Texas Family Practice Manual, 1976. Family and matrimonial. Home: 5650 Meadowcrest Dr Dallas TX 75230 Office: 2060 1 Main Pl Dallas TX 75250

RASSNER, ALAN CARL, lawyer; b. Long Branch, N.J.; s. Ernest and Reba (Sokol) R.; m. Sandra Harris, Aug. 18, 1956; children: David, Mitchell. BS cum laude, NYU, 1956; LLD, Fordham U., 1960. Bar: N.Y. 1961, U.S. Dist. Ct. (so. and ea. dists.) N.Y. 1962, U.S. Ct. Appeals (2d cir.) 1966, U.S. Supreme Ct. 1970, U.S. Ct. Appeals (5th cir.) 1975. Assoc. Law Office of Jacob Rassner, N.Y.C., 1961-75; ptnr. Rassner & Rassner, N.Y.C., 1975-76, Rassner, Rassner & Olman, N.Y.C., 1976—; chmn. legal com. Kingsbay Housing Co. Inc., Bklyn., 1982—, bd. dirs. Mem. N.Y. State Bar Assn., N.Y. County Lawyers Assn. (admiralty com.), Assn. Trial Lawyers Am., N.Y. State Trial Lawyers Assn. Admiralty, Personal injury. Office: Rassner Rassner & Olman 15 Park Row New York NY 10038

RATCLIFF, JOHN GARRETT, lawyer; b. Laurel, Miss., Mar. 12, 1945; s. Kalford Compton and Mary Claire (Terry) R.; m. Margaret Warner White, Aug. 9, 1980; children—Garrett Bateman, Margaret Lindsley. B.A., Southwestern at Memphis (now Rhodes Coll.), 1966; M.A., U. Va., 1970; J.D., U. Miss., 1973. Bar: Miss. 1973, U.S. Dist. Ct. (no. and so. dists.) Miss. 1973, U.S. Dist. Ct. (so. dist.) Ala., 1973, U.S. Ct. Appeals (5th cir.) 1973, 81, U.S. Dist. Ct. (ea. dist.) La. 1980, U.S. Dist. Ct. (we. dist.) La. 1983, U.S. Supreme Ct., 1983. Founding ptnr. Andalman, Bergmark & Ratcliff, Hattiesburg, Miss., 1973-75; staff atty. North Miss. Rural Legal Services, Oxford, 1977. South Miss. Legal Services, Biloxi and Pascagoula, 1977-78; sole practice, New Orleans, 1980-83, Shreveport, La., 1983—; assoc. Walker, Feazel & Tooke, Shreveport, 1983; atty. Indigent Defender Bd., Shreveport, 1984, 86, 87. Mem. La. Bar Assn., La. Assn. Criminal Def. Lawyers, Nat. Lawyers Guild, Delta Theta Phi, Omicron Delta Kappa, Sigma Alpha Epsilon. Presbyterian. Criminal, Labor, Jurisprudence. Office: Route 1 Box 460 Bossier Parish LA 71112-9710

RATH, DAVID, lawyer; b. Washington, May 13, 1950; s. Frederick Louis Jr. and Ann (Richardson) Rath. AB, Dartmouth Coll., 1972; JD, Franklin Pierce Coll., 1979. Bar: Vt. 1980, U.S. Dist. Ct. Vt. 1980, U.S. Ct. Appeals (2d cir.) 1981. Assoc. Roger E. Kohn & Assocs., Hinesburg, Vt., 1979-81; ptnr. Kohn & Rath, Hinesburg, Vt., 1981—; adj. prof. St. Michael's Coll., Colchester, Vt., 1982—. Bd. dirs. Vt. Judicare Program, Burlington, 1982—; sec. Town of Monkton (Vt.) Planning Commn., 1984—, Town of Monkton Zoning Bd. of Adjustment, 1984—. Mem. Am Trial Lawyers Assn., Vt. Bar Assn. (bd. mgrs. 1984-86, exec. bd. dirs. young lawyers sect. 1980-86), New England Rugby Football Union Referee's Soc. (sr. referee 1982—). Clubs: Dartmouth of Lake Champlain (Burlington) (sec. 1982—). Personal injury, State civil litigation, Legal education. Home: RD #1 Box 195 North Ferrisburg VT 05461 Office: Kohn & Rath PO Box 340 Hinesburg VT 05461

RATH, FRANCIS STEVEN, lawyer; b. N.Y.C., Oct. 10, 1955; s. Steven and Elizabeth (Chorin) R.; m. Denise Stephania Thompson, Aug. 2, 1980. BA cum laude, Wesleyan U., Middletown, Conn., 1977; JD cum laude, Georgetown U., 1980. Bar: D.C. 1980, U.S. Dist. Ct. D.C. 1981, U.S. Ct. Appeals (D.C. cir.), 1981, U.S. Supreme Ct. 1987. Atty., advisor Comptroller of the Currency, Washington, 1980-84; assoc. Verner, Liipfert, Bernhard, McPherson & Hand, Washington, 1984-85; founding ptnr. Wolf, Arnold & Monroig, Washington, 1986—. Editor: Law and Policy in Internat. Bus. 1979-80. Trustee Dunn Loring (Va.) Vol. Fire Dept., 1986. Mem. ABA, D.C. Bar Assn. Private international, General corporate, Banking. Home: Grey Fox Farm 1051 Kelso Rd Great Falls VA 22066 Office: Wolf Arnold & Monroig PC 1850 M St NW Washington DC 20036

RATHGEBER, JOANNE WEIL, lawyer; b. Phila., Oct. 21, 1943; d. Peter and Bruna Argentina (Spada) Pietrangelo; m. Richard Harrison Weil, Oct. 17, 1964 (div. Mar. 1983); children: Jacqueline, Pamela, Karen; m. Michael John Rathgeber, Apr. 30, 1983; stepchildren: Karen, Robin, Eric. BA maxima cum laude, LaSalle U., 1976; JD, Temple U., 1979. Bar: Pa. 1979, U.S. Dist. Ct. (ea. dist.) Pa. 1982. Legal sec. U.S. Atty's Office, Phila., 1961-64; paralegal Crumlish & Kania, Phila., 1965-69; paralegal Connolly & McAndrews, Warminster, Pa., 1970-79, assoc., 1979-83; assoc. Corr, Stevens & Fenningham, Trevose, Pa., 1983-84, ptnr., 1984-85; sole practice Doylestown, Pa., 1986—. Mem. ABA, Pa. Bar Assn., Assn. Trial Lawyers Am., Pa. Trial Lawyers Assn. Republican. Roman Catholic. Lodge: Sons of Italy (author, dir. theater group plays 1975-82). Avocation: piano. State and federal civil litigation, Personal injury, Family and matrimonial. Office: 6 E Court St Doylestown PA 18901

RATHMAN, WILLIAM ERNEST, lawyer, minister; b. Middletown, Ohio, Jan. 10, 1927; s. Ernest Daniel and Marguerite (Sebald) R.; m. Constance Schedler, Nov. 28, 1958; children: Marchie, William E. Jr. BA, Kenyon Coll., 1948; JD, Ohio State U., 1951; United Theol. Seminary, Dayton, Ohio, 1975. Ordained to ministry Episc. Ch. Sole practice Middletown, Ohio, 1952-78; sr. ptnr. Rathman, Elliott & Boyd, Middletown, 1979-84, Rathman, Combs, Schaefer, Valen & Kaup, Middletown, 1985—. Spl. counsel to County of Butler, Middletown, 1956-64, City of Middletown, 1965-66, Ohio Atty. Gen. 1967-69; acting judge mcpl. ct., Middletown, 1969-74; pres. Middletown Community Found., 1972-76, Middletown Chamber Found., 1977-80, Butler County Park Commn., Middletown, 1986—; trustee-at-large Ohio Found. of Ind. Colls., Columbus, 1972—. Served with USN, 1944-46; served to capt. JAGC, USAF, 1958-59. Named Exec. Yr. Middletown chpt. Nat. Secs. Assn., 1969; recipient Outstanding Community Service award Middletown post Am. Legion, 1975, Outstanding Service award Pastoral Counselling Service, 1983. Fellow Am. Coll. Probate Counsel; mem. ABA (mem. estate tax com. 1966-69), Ohio Bar Assn. (council of dels. 1980—), Butler County Bar Assn. (pres. 1980), Middletown Bar Assn. (pres. 1967), Fed. Bar Assn. (pres. Cin. chpt. 1975). Republican. Episcopalian. Clubs: City (Hamilton, Ohio); Moraine Country (Dayton). Lodge: Masons (local treas. 1986—). Home: 501 Thorn Hill Ln Middletown OH 45042 Office: Rathman Combs et al First Nat Bank Bldg 2 N Main St Middletown OH 45042

RATHMELL, ANNE ELIZABETH, lawyer; b. Williamsport, Pa., Nov. 14, 1953; d. John Nicely and Alberta Bernice (Henry) R. BA in Polit. Sci., Denison U., 1975; JD, U. Pitts., 1978. Bar: Pa. 1979. Commd. 2d lt. USMCR, 1975, advanced through grades to maj., 1986; trial def. counsel USMCR, Okinawa, Japan, 1979-80; legal assistance officer USMCR, Washington, 1980-82, spl. counsel, 1982-84, manpower officer, 1984-85, spl. asst. to counsel for commandant, 1985—. Mem. ABA, Pa. Bar Assn., Marine Corps Res. Officers' Assn., VFW Ladies Auxiliary (treas. 1982-83, life mem. nat. home 1983). Republican. Environment, Military, Real property. Office: Office Counsel Commandant USMC Hdqrs Washington DC 20380-0001

RATKOVICH, CYNTHIA, lawyer; b. Chgo., May 22, 1957; d. Steve and Mildred (Evans) Ratkovich. B.S., Purdue U., 1979; J.D., U. Iowa, 1982. Bar: Ill. 1982. Paralegal, sec. Sonnenschein, Carlin, Nath & Rosenthal, Chgo., summer 1978; filing clk. Norus Property Co., Chgo., summer 1979, law clk., summer 1980; sec., asst. mgr. L.J. Sheridan & Co., Chgo., summer 1981; in-house counsel Thomas F. Seay, Chgo., summer 1982, 83, ltd. rep., prin., 1982—; counsel CNA Ins. Co., Chgo., 1983—. Mem. ABA, Ill. State Bar Assn., Chgo. Bar Assn., Alpha Lambda Delta, Phi Kappa Phi, Beta Gamma Sigma, Purdue U. Alumni Assn. Serbian Orthodox. Real property, General corporate. Office: CNA Ins Cos CNA Plaza Law Dept 42S Chicago IL 60685

RATLIFF, WILLIAM D., III, lawyer; b. Ft. Worth, Aug. 25, 1949; s. William D. and Barbara (Warner) R.; m. Julie Martin, Oct. 4, 1980; children—William D., Emily Martin. B.B.A., U. Tex., 1971, J.D., 1974; LL.M., So. Meth. U., 1975. Law clk. U.S. Tax Ct., Washington, 1975-77; mem. Cantey, Hanger, Gooch, Munn & Collins, Ft. Worth, 1977-84, Haynes and Boone, Ft. Worth, 1984—. Fellow Tex. Bar Found.; mem. ABA, State Bar Tex. Republican. Clubs: Ft. Worth, Rivercrest Country. Banking, Probate, Real property. Office: Haynes and Boone 1300 InterFirst Tower Fort Worth TX 76102

RATNER, DAVID LOUIS, legal educator; b. London, Sept. 2, 1931. AB magna cum laude, Harvard U., 1952, LLB magna cum laude, 1955. Bar: N.Y. 1955. Assoc. Sullivan & Cromwell, N.Y.C., 1955-64; assoc. prof. Cornell Law Sch., Ithaca, N.Y., 1964-68, prof., 1968-82; dean, prof. law U. San Francisco Law Sch., 1982—; exec. asst. to chmn. SEC, Washington, 1966-68; chief counsel Securities Industry Study, Senate Banking Com., Washington, 1971-73; vis. prof. Stanford (Calif.) U., 1974, Ariz. State U., Tempe, 1974, U. San Francisco, 1980; Fulbright scholar Monash U., Australia, 1981. Author: Securities Regulation; Materials for a Basic Course, 3d edit., 1986; Securities Regulation in a Nutshell, 2d edit., 1982; Institutional Investors: Teaching Materials, 1978. Administrative and regulatory, General corporate, Legal education. Home: 84 Polhemus Way Larkspur CA 94939 Office: Univ San Francisco Law Sch Kendrick Hall 2130 Fulton St San Francisco CA 94117

RATNER, MICHAEL D., lawyer; b. Cleve., June 13, 1943; s. Harry and Anne (Spott) Ratner. B.A., Brandeis U., 1966; J.D. magna cum laude, Columbia U., 1971. Bar: N.Y. 1971, U.S. Ct. Appeals (2d cir.) 1971, U.S. Ct. Appeals (3d cir.) 1975, U.S. Ct. Appeals (1st cir.) 1976, U.S. Supreme Ct. 1983. Law clk. U.S. Dist. Ct. (so. dist.) N.Y., 1971-72; tchr. NYU Law Sch., N.Y.C., 1973-74; atty. Ctr. for Constl. Rights, N.Y.C., 1978-85; legal dir. Ctr. for Constitutional Rights, 1985—. Contbr. articles to profl. jours. Mem. Nat. Lawyers Guild (pres. 1982-83). Civil rights, Public international. Office: Ctr Constitutional Rights 666 Broadway New York NY 10012

RATTERMAN, DAVID BURGER, lawyer; b. Louisville, Sept. 8, 1946; s. Joseph A. and Esther M. (Burger) R.; m. Mary Miles Sledd, May 31, 1969; children—Andrew August, Sara Chandler. B.S.M.E., U. Ky., 1968; J.D., U. Louisville, 1975, M.B.A., 1980. Bar: Ky. 1976, U.S. Dist. Ct. (we. dist.) Ky. 1976, U.S. Dist. Ct. (so. dist.) Ga. 1979. Design engr. Square D Co., Lexington, Ky., 1968-70; ptnr. Goldberg & Simpson, Louisville, 1975—; tchr. seminars in constrn. law; legal counsel Ky. Council for the Blind, 1975-85. Contbr. articles to profl. jours. Mem. sch. bd. St. Leonard Sch., 1981-84, pres. 1983-84; counsel County Govt. Handicapped Compliance Commn., 1980-85; bd. dirs. United Crescent Hill Ministries, 1974-81, Clifton Neighborhood Devel. Corp., 1974-81. Served with USN, 1970-73, to comdr. Res. Decorated Naval Commendation medal. Fellow Am. Bar Found.; mem. Am. Arbitration Assn., ABA, Ky. Bar Assn. (ho. of dels. 1986—), Louisville Bar Assn., Constrn. Specifications Inst. Roman Catholic. Lodge: Rotary. Federal civil litigation, State civil litigation, Government contracts and claims. Home: 188 Crescent Ave Louisville KY 40206 Office: Goldberg & Simpson 2800 First National Tower Louisville KY 40202

RAU, LEE ARTHUR, lawyer; b. Mpls., July 22, 1940; s. Arthur W. and Selma A. (Lund) R.; m. Janice R. Childress, June 27, 1964; children—Brendan D., Patrick C., Brian T. B.S.B., U. Minn., 1962; J.D., UCLA, 1965. Bar: Calif. 1966, U.S. Ct. Mil. Appeals 1966, U.S. Supreme Ct. 1971, D.C., 1972, U.S. Ct. Appeals (D.C. cir.) 1972, U.S. Dist. Ct. (D.C.) 1973, U.S. Ct. Appeals (3d cir.) 1975, U.S. Ct. Appeals (6th cir.) 1980, Va. 1986. Trial atty. evaluation sect. antitrust div. U.S. Dept. Justice, Washington, 1965-66, appellate sect., 1970-72; assoc. Reed Smith Shaw & McClay, Washington, 1972-74, ptnr., 1975—; mem. constl. and adminstrv. law adv. com. Nat. Chamber Litigation Ctr. Inc.; dir. Communication Specialists Inc.; dir. Telesat Communciations Inc. Contbr. articles to profl. jours. Sec. bd. dirs. Reston Found., 1982—; bd. dirs. Reston Interfaith Inc., 1973, pres., 1984—; mem. Fairfax Com. of 100; mem. Washington Dulles Task Force, 1982—, United Way Social Needs com., 1986—. Served to capt. JAGC, U.S. Army, 1966-70. Decorated Commendation medal with oak leaf cluster. Mem. ABA (antitrust, adminstrv. law, corp. banking and bus. sic. and tech. sects.), D.C. Bar Assn. (past chmn. energy study group), Calif. Bar Assn., Fairfax Bar Assn., U.S. C. of C. (antitrust policy com.), Phi Alpha Delta. Democrat. Lutheran. Antitrust, Administrative and regulatory, General corporate. Home: 1930 Upper Lake Dr Reston VA 22091 Office: 8201 Greensboro Dr Suite 820 McLean VA 22102

RAUL, ALAN CHARLES, lawyer; b. Bronx, N.Y., Sept. 9, 1954; s. Eugene and Eduarda (Muller Mañas) R. AB, Harvard U., 1975, MPA, 1977; JD, Yale U., 1980. Bar: N.Y. 1982, D.C. 1982, U.S. Ct. Appeals (D.C. cir.) 1982, U.S. Dist. Ct. D.C. 1986. Law clk. to judge U.S. Ct. Appeals (D.C. cir.), Washington, 1980-81; assoc. Debevoise & Plimpton, N.Y.C., 1981-86; assoc. counsel Pres. of U.S., Washington, 1986—; cons. Reagan-Bush campaign, N.Y.C., 1984. Mem. Assn. of Bar of City of New York (chmn. subcom. on Cen. Am. issues 1985, mem. com. on inter-Am. affairs 1982—), Federalist Soc. Federal civil litigation, State civil litigation, Private international. Office: Office of Counsel to the Pres The White House Washington DC 20500

RAUNER, VINCENT JOSEPH, lawyer, electronics company executive; b. Kalamazoo, Mich., Apr. 4, 1927. BSE, U. Mich., 1950, JD, 1953. Bar: Ill.

1953. Ptnr. Mueller, Aichele and Rauner, Chgo., 1953-70; dir. patent dept. Motorola, Inc., Franklin Park, Ill., 1970-73, v.p., Schaumburg, Ill., 1973—. Mem. ABA, Assn. Corp. Patent Counsel, Am. Intellectual Property Law Assn., Licensing Execs. Soc., Patent Law Assn. Chgo. Patent, Trademark and copyright, General corporate. Home: 620 Fullerton Pkwy Chicago IL 60614 Office: Motorola Inc 1303 E Algonquin Rd Schaumburg IL 60196

RAUSHENBUSH, WALTER BRANDEIS, educator; b. Madison, Wis., June 13, 1928; s. Paul A. and Elizabeth (Brandeis) R.; m. Marylu de Watteville, May 3, 1956; children: Lorraine Elizabeth, Richard Walter, Carla, Paul Brandeis. AB magna cum laude in Govt., Harvard U., 1950; JD with high honors, U. Wis., 1953. Bar: Wis. 1953. Ptnr. LaFollette, Sinykin & Doyle, Madison, 1956-58; mem. faculty U. Wis.-Madison, 1958—, prof. law, 1966—; project dir. real estate transfer study Am. Bar Found., 1967-72; trustee Nat. Law Sch. Admission Council, 1968-70, 72—, chmn. pre-law com., 1970-74, chmn. services com., 1976-78, pres., 1980-82; legal adviser Madison Citizens Fair Housing, 1961-63, Wis. Citizens Family Planning, 1965-73. Author: Wisconsin Construction Lien Law, 1974, (with others) Wisconsin Real Estate Law, 1984, 2d edit., 1986, Brown on Personal Property, 3d edit, 1975, Real Estate Transactions Cases and Materials, 1985. Served with USAF, 1953-56; col. Res. Mem. ABA, State Bar Wis., Dane County Bar Assn., AAUP, Order of Coif, Phi Beta Kappa, Phi Delta Phi (province pres. 1963-75). Presbyterian (elder). Club: Stage Harbor Yacht (Chatham, Mass.). Legal education, Real property, Landlord-tenant. Home: 3942 Plymouth Circle Madison WI 53705 Office: U Wis Law Sch Madison WI 53706

RAUSS, DENNIS MICHAEL, lawyer; b. Detroit, July 4, 1951; s. Arthur F. and Patricia Ann (O'Keefe) R.; m. Kathleen Dianne Hennessey, Feb. 15, 1974; children: Brendan M., Alison D., Devin T. BA, U. Mich., 1973, JD, 1977. Bar: Mich. 1977, U.S. Dist. Ct. (ea. dist.) Mich. 1977, U.S. Ct. Appeals (6th cir.) 1977, U.S. Dist. Ct. (we. dist.) Mich. 1982. Assoc. Dobson, Hammond, Griffin, Roach, Ziegelman & Sotiroff PC, Detroit, 1977-82, ptnr., 1982—. Mem. ABA, Detroit Bar Assn., Macomb County Bar Assn. Roman Catholic. Club: Detroit Athletic. Federal civil litigation, State civil litigation, Labor. Home: 1352 Blairmoor Ct Grosse Pointe Woods MI 48236 Office: Dobson Hammond Griffin Roach Ziegelman & Sotiroff 400 Renaissance Ctr Suite 1100 Detroit MI 48243 Office: 500 City Ctr Bldg Ann Arbor MI 48104

RAVEN, JONATHAN EZRA, lawyer, optical chain executive; b. Chgo., Jan. 13, 1951; s. Seymour S. and Norma (Blackman) R.; m. Leslie Michelle Shapiro, Dec. 29, 1973; children: Jane Lara, David Louis. BA cum laude, Western Mich. U. 1972; JD, U. Mich., 1975. Bar: Mich. 1975. Assoc., then ptnr., bd. dirs. firm Foster, Swift, Collins & Coey, P.C., Lansing, Mich., 1975-81; sr. v.p., gen. counsel, sec., dir. NuVision, Inc., Flint, Mich., 1981—, also bd. dirs.; v.p., bd. dirs. Bell Optical Inc., Flint. Pres., bd. dirs. Stonelake Condominium Assn., East Lansing, Mich., 1978-81, Flint Jewish Fedn., 1986—, 3d v.p., 1987—; mem. franchise working group Gov.'s Cabinet Council on Jobs and Econ. Devel., Lansing, 1983. Mem. ABA, State Bar Mich., Ingham County Bar Assn., Internat. Franchise Assn. (legis. com.), Am. Arbitration Assn. (panel arbitrators 1980—), Omicron Delta Kappa. Jewish. General corporate, Health, Administrative and regulatory. Office: NuVision Inc 2284 S Ballenger Hwy Flint MI 48501

RAVESON, LOUIS SHEPPARD, lawyer, educator; b. Passaic, N.J., Dec. 14, 1951; s. Irwin Harold and Lorelei Rose (Levine) R.; m. Nancy Goldhill, Oct. 3, 1982. B.A., Antioch Coll., 1972; J.D., Rutgers U., 1976. Bar: N.J. 1976, U.S. Dist. Ct. N.J. 1976, U.S. Ct. Appeals (3d cir.) 1976, N.Y. 1977. Law clk. U.S. Ct. Appeals (3d cir.), Phila., 1976-77; staff atty. Essex-Newark Legal Services, Newark, 1977-79; staff atty. Rutgers Urban Legal Clinic, Newark, 1979-81, co-dir., 1982—; asst. commr. N.J. Dept. Pub. Adv., 1985—; asst. prof. law Rutgers U. Law Sch., Newark, 1982-85, assoc. prof., 1985—; chmn. bd. trustees Essex-Newark Legal Services, Newark, 1982; bd. dirs. Nat. Equal Justice Found., 1984—. Mem. Soc. Am. Law Tchrs., N.J. Bar Assn., N.J. Supreme Ct. Com. (civil litigation and complimentary dispute resolution. Jewish. Civil rights, Federal civil litigation, Legal education. Office: Rutgers U Law Sch 15 Washington St Newark NJ 07102

RAVIOLA, PATRICK RICHARD, lawyer; b. BaYonne, N.J., Sept. 18, 1951; s. Warren Richard and Frances Marie (Sullivan) R.; m. Karen Ann Raviola, Sept. 12, 1981; 1 child, Patrick John. BA in Econs., The State U. of Rutgers, 1973; LLB, Villanova U., 1976. Bar: N.J. 1976, U.S. Dist. Ct. N.J. 1976. Assoc. Zlotkin & Bentley, Hightstown, N.J., 1977-78; asst. pros. atty. Hudson County, Jersey City, N.J., 1978—. Mem. ABA, N.J. Bar Assn. Republican. Roman Catholic. Avocations: golf, reading, music. Criminal. Office: Hudson County Prosecutors Office 595 Newark Ave Jersey City NJ 07306

RAWDON, RICHARD MCLEAN, JR., lawyer; b. Lexington, Ky., Sept. 7, 1943; s. Richard McLean Sr. and Emily (Askew) R.; m. Judy Carol Hatfield, Apr. 8, 1972. BA, Colgate U., 1965; JD, U. Louisville, 1968. Bar: Ky. 1968, U.S. Dist. Ct. (ea. dist.) Ky. 1972, U.S. Ct. Mil. Appeals 1972. Assoc. McKnight & Pryor, Georgetown, Ky., 1968-70; pres. Blue Grass Assocs., Georgetown, 1970-72; sole practice Georgetown, 1972-74; atty. Scott County, Georgetown, 1974-78; ptnr. Rawdon & Brady, Georgetown, 1978—, Neal & Rawdon, Georgetown, 1983—; bd. dirs. G M Taylor Seed Co., Georgetown. Pres. Stamping Ground Ruritan, Georgetown, 1974; bd. dirs. Parks and Recreation Bd., Georgetown. Served as capt. USAR, 1968-74. Mem. ABA, Ky. Bar Assn. (continuing legal edn. recognition award 1980-86), Assn. Trial Lawyers Am. (gov. 1985—), Ky. Acad. Trial Attys. (pres. 1984, gov. 1986—), Nat. Assn. Criminal Def. Lawyers, Cen. Ky. Football Officials Assn. (pres. 1969—), Ky. C. of C. (leadership Ky. award 1985), Scott County C. of C. (pres.), Phi Alpha Delta, Sigma Nu, Boga Doga. Democrat. Episcopalian. Lodge: Optimists (pres. Georgetown club 1984). Personal injury, Criminal, State civil litigation. Home: 847 Duvall Station Rd Georgetown KY 40327 Office: Rawdon & Brady PC PO Box 631 Georgetown KY 40327

RAWLES, EDWARD HUGH, lawyer; b. Chgo., May 7, 1945; s. Fred Wilson and Nancy (Hughes) R.; m. Margaret Mary O'Donoghue, Oct. 20, 1979; children—Lee Kathryn, Jacklyn Ann. B.A., U. Ill., 1967; J.D. summa cum laude, Ill. Inst. Tech., 1970. Bar: Ill., 1970, U.S. Dist. Ct. (cen. dist.) Ill. 1970, U.S. Supreme Ct. 1973, U.S. Ct. Appeals (7th cir.) 1983, Colo. 1984. Assoc. Reno, O'Byrne & Kepley, Champaign, Ill., 1970-73, ptnr., 1973-84; v.p. Reno O'Byrne & Kepley P.C., Champaign, 1984—; mem. student legal service adv. bd. U. Ill., Urbana, 1982—; hearing officer Ill. Fair Employment Practice Commn., Springfield, 1972-74. Diplomate Nat. Bd. Trial Advocacy, 1983. Fellow Ill. State Bar Found., 1984. Mem. Assn. Trial Lawyers Am., Ill. Trial Lawyers Assn., Ill. Bar Assn., Colo. Trial Lawyers Assn., Bar Assn. 7th Fed. Cir., Kent Soc. Honor Men, Phi Delta Theta. Roman Catholic. Federal civil litigation, State civil litigation, Personal injury. Home: Rural Rt 1 Box 137 White Heath IL 61884 Office: Reno O'Byrne & Kepley 501 W Church PO Box 693 Champaign IL 61820

RAWLINGS, SUZANNE CORINNE, lawyer; b. Provo, Utah, Dec. 30, 1955; s. James W. and Joan E. (Berkheimer) R.; m. Richard V. Day, Aug. 19, 1978; 1 child, Jenna Corinne. BA, Grinnell Coll., 1977; JD, U. San Diego, 1980. Bar: Calif. 1980, U.S. Dist. Ct. (so. dist.) Calif., U.S. Dist. Ct. (ea. dist.) Calif. 1981. Dep. counsel County of Imperial, El Centro, Calif., 1981-82; legal counsel Sonoma County Supt. Schs., Santa Rosa, Calif., 1982-83; dep. atty. City of Santa Rosa, 1984—. Mem. ABA, Sonoma County Bar Assn., Sonoma County Women in Law, Phi Delta Phi. Government contracts and claims, Local government. Home: 17371 Buena Vista Ave Sonoma CA 95476 Office: Office of City Atty Santa Rosa PO Box 1678 Santa Rosa CA 95402

RAWLS, EBEN TURNER, III, lawyer; b. Winston-Salem, N.C., Aug. 31, 1949; s. Eben Turner Jr. and Mary Grace (Maus) R.; m. Leslie Ruffin Carter, May 14, 1983. BA cum laude, Duke U., 1972; JD, U. N.C., 1978. Bar: N.C. 1978, U.S. Dist. Ct. (ea. dist.) N.C. 1979, U.S. Dist. Ct. (we. dist.) N.C. 1981, U.S. Ct. Appeals (4th cir.) 1981, U.S. Supreme Ct. 1984. Asst. atty. Office of Pub. Defender, Charlotte, N.C., 1980-83; assoc. Haywood, Carson & Merryman, Charlotte, 1983-85; ptnr. Merryman, Dickinson, Ledford & Rawls, Charlotte, 1985—. Mem. ABA, N.C. Bar Assn., Am. Acad. Trial Lawyers (Lewis F. Powell award 1978), N.C. Acad. Trial Lawyers, Order of Barristers. Democrat. Methodist. Avocations: photography, backpacking. Criminal. Home: 9513 Withers Rd Charlotte NC 28210 Office: Merryman Dickinson Ledford & Rawls 730 E Trade St Suite 523 Charlotte NC 28202

RAWLS, FRANK MACKLIN, lawyer; b. Suffolk, Va., Aug. 24, 1952; s. John Lewis and Mary Helen (Macklin) R.; m. Sally Hallum Blanchard, June 26, 1976; children—Matthew Christopher, John Stephen. B.A. cum laude in History, Hampden Sydney Coll., 1974; J.D., U. Va., 1977. Bar: Va. 1977, U.S. Dist. Ct. (ea. dist.) Va. 1977, U.S. Ct. Appeals (4th cir.) 1977. Assoc. Rawls, Habel & Rawls, Suffolk, 1977-78, ptnr., 1978—. Elder, clk. of session Westminster Presbyn. Ch., Suffolk, 1984—; chmn. bd. dirs. Suffolk Crime Line, 1982—, Suffolk Cheer Fund, 1982—, Covenant Christian Schs., Suffolk, 1982-84; mem. adv. bd. dirs. Salvation Army, Suffolk, 1977-84; treas., bd. dirs. L.T. and Margaret W. Reid Scholarship Fund, 1984—. Mem. Suffolk Bar Assn., Va. Bar Assn., Christian Legal Soc., Va. Trial Lawyers Assn., ABA, Assn. Trial Lawyers Am., Suffolk Bar Assn. Lodge: Rotary. General practice, Personal injury, General corporate. Home: 613 N Broad St Suffolk VA 23434

RAY, CREAD L., JR., state justice; b. Waskom, Tex., Mar. 10, 1931; s. Cread L. and Antonia (Hardesty) R.; m. Janet Watson Keller, Aug. 12, 1977; children—Sue Ann, Robert E., Glenn L., David B., Marcie Lynn, Anne Marie. B.B.A., Tex. A&M U., 1952; J.D., U. Tex., 1957; L.H.D. (hon.), Wiley Coll., Marshall, Tex., 1980. Bar: Tex. bar 1957. Practiced in Marshall, 1957-59; judge Harrison County, 1959-61; justice 6th dist. Ct. Civil Appeals, Texarkana, 1970-80, Supreme Ct. Tex., 1980—. Past pres. Marshall Jaycees, Marshall C. of C.; mem. Tex. Ho. of Reps., 1966-70; active local Boy Scouts Am.; trustees Wiley Coll. Served as officer USAF, 1952-54, Korea. Recipient various Boy Scouts awards. Mem. State Bar Tex., N.E. Tex. Bar Assn. (past pres.), Harrison County Bar Assn. (past pres.), VFW, Am. Legion. Democrat. Methodist. Clubs: Rotary, Elks, Tex. Aggies. State civil litigation, Federal civil litigation, Oil and gas leasing. Home: 4800 Wild Briar Pass Austin TX 78746 Office: PO Box 12248 Capitol Station Austin TX 78711

RAY, DAVID LEWIN, lawyer, accountant; b. Los Angeles, June 17, 1929; s. Herbert and Beatrice (Lewin) R.; m. Arlene Opas, July 15, 1951; children: Stephan, Robyn. BS, UCLA, 1954; JD, U. San Fernando Valley, 1970. Bar: U.S. Dist. Ct. (so., no. and cen. dists.) Calif.; CPA, Calif. Ptnr., acct. Ray & Ray, Los Angeles, 1957-71, Zigmond, Ray & Co., Beverly Hills, Calif., 1971-73; ptnr. Ray, Rolston & Ress, Beverly Hills, 1970-80, Ray & Murray, Beverly Hills, 1973-80, Saltzburg, Ray & Bergman, Los Angeles, 1980—. Served with U.S. Army, 1951-53. Mem. Am. Inst. CPA's, Calif. Soc. CPA's, Am. Assn. Attys.-CPA's, Beverly Hills Bar Assn., Los Angeles County Bar Assn., Los Angeles Trial Lawyers Assn., Am. Arbitration Assn. Club: Brentwood Country. Lodge: Masons. Avocations: sailing, golfing, deep sea diving, photography. Receivership law, State civil litigation, Real property. Office: Saltzburg Ray and Bergman 10960 Wilshire Blvd 1212 Los Angeles CA 90024

RAY, DONALD ARVIN, lawyer; b. Houston, July 29, 1945; s. Haskell E. and Mildred V. (Green) R.; m. Victoria Hendley, Aug. 27, 1965; 1 child, Scott Brandon. BA, Texas A&I U., 1971; JD, Baylor U., 1974. Bar: Tex. 1974, U.S. Dist. Ct. (ea. dist.) Tex. 1978. Ptnr. Manning & Ray, Mabank, Tex., 1974-80; sole practice Gun Barrel City, Tex., 1980-83; prin. Donald A. Ray & Assocs., P.C., Gun Barrell City, 1983—; ptnr. Ray & Gilchrist, Dallas, 1984—, Ray & Terrell, Gun Barrel City, 1985—; v.p. Cedar Creek Title Co., Mabank, Tex., 1979-80; pres. Ray Data Co., Mabank, 1979-80; gen. counsel Security Title Co. of Henderson County, Inc., 1981—; chmn., chief exec. officer Starcross Internat., Inc., Dallas, 1984—; chmn. bd. Service Title Co. of Johnson County, Inc., 1985—; bd. dirs. A.B.O., Inc., Auto Precision Motors, Inc., Lone Star Engine Hard Parts, Inc. Chmn. Mabank-Gun Barrel City Bicentennial Festival U.S.A. Com., 1975-76; founder, lifetime mem. Avanti Soc., pres. 1975-77, stage dir., actor, 1976-83. Served as cpl. USMC, 1966-69. Mem. ABA, Kaufman County Bar Assn., Henderson County Bar Assn., Cedar Creek C. of C. (bd. dirs. 1983-84, Citizen of Yr. award 1983). Democrat. Mem. Ch. of Christ. Club: Cedar Creek Country (Kemp, Tex.). Lodge: Kiwanis (pres., bd. dirs., Mabank 1982). Avocations: painting, drawing. State civil litigation, Contracts commercial, Real property. Home: 138 Randy Circle Mabank TX 75147 Office: Hwy 85 PO Box 307 Mabank TX 75147

RAY, FRANK ALLEN, lawyer; b. Lafayette, Ind., Jan. 30, 1949; s. Dale Allen and Merry Ann (Fleming) R.; m. Carol Ann Olmutz, Oct. 1, 1982; children—Erica Fleming, Robert Allen. B.A., Ohio State U., 1970, J.D., 1973. Bar: Ohio 1973, U.S. Dist. Ct. (so. dist.) Ohio 1975, U.S. Supreme Ct. 1976, U.S. Tax Ct. 1977, U.S. Ct. Appeals (6th cir.) 1977, U.S. Dist Ct. (no. dist.) Ohio 1980, Pa. 1983, U.S. Dist. Ct. (ea. dist.) Mich. 1983; cert. civil trial adv. Nat. Bd. Trial Advocacy. Asst. pros. atty. Franklin County, Ohio, 1973-75, chief civil counsel, 1976-78; dir. econ. crime project Nat. Dist. Attys. Assn., Washington, 1975-76; assoc. Brownfield, Kosydar, Bowen, Bally & Sturtz, Columbus, Ohio, 1978, Michael F. Colley Co., L.P.A., Columbus, 1979-83; pres. Frank A. Ray Co., L.P.A., Columbus, 1983—; mem. seminar faculty Nat. Coll. Dist. Attys., Houston, 1975-77; mem. nat. conf. faculty Fed. Jud. Ctr., Washington, 1976-77. Editor: Economic Crime Digest, 1975-76. Mem. fin. com. Franklin County Republican Orgn., Columbus, 1979-84. Served to 1st lt. inf. U.S. Army, 1973. Named to Ten Outstanding Young Citizens of Columbus, Columbus Jaycees, 1976; recipient Nat. award of Distinctive Service, Nat. Dist. Attys. Assn., 1977. Fellow Columbus Bar Found.; mem. Columbus Bar Assn., Ohio State Bar Assn., ABA, Assn. Trial Lawyers Am., Ohio Acad. Trial Lawyers (trustee 1984-87, sec. 1987—, legis. coordinator 1986—, Pres.' award 1986), Franklin County Trial Lawyers Assn. (trustee 1982-83, treas. 1984-85, chmn. com. negligence law 1983-87, sec. 1985-86, v.p. 1986-87, pres. 1987—). Presbyterian. Personal injury, State civil litigation, Condemnation. Home: 5800 Olentangy Blvd Worthington OH 43085 Office: 330 S High St Columbus OH 43215

RAY, GILBERT T., lawyer; b. Mansfield, Ohio, Sept. 18, 1944; s. Robert Lee Ray and Renatha (Goldie) Washington; m. Valerie J. Reynolds, June 14, 1969; children: Tanika, Tarlin. BA, Ashland Coll., 1966; MBA, U. Toledo, 1968; JD, Howard U., 1972. Assoc. O'Melveny & Myers, Los Angeles, 1972-79, ptnr., 1980—. Mem. Project Restore Pershing Sq., Los Angeles; bd. dirs. Pilgrim Sch., Los Angeles, 1982—, NAACP Legal Def. Fund. Democrat. Club: Riviera (Los Angeles). General corporate. Office: O'Melveny & Myers 400 S Hope St Los Angeles CA 90071-2899

RAY, HUGH MASSEY, JR., lawyer; b. Vicksburg, Miss., Feb. 1, 1943; s. Hugh Massey and Lollie Landon (Powell) R.; m. Florence Hargrove, Sept. 3, 1966; children—Hugh, Hallie. B.A., Vanderbilt U., 1965, J.D., 1967. Bar: Tex. 1967, U.S. Dist. Ct. (so. dist.) Tex. 1967, U.S. Dist. Ct. (we. dist.) La. 1979, U.S. Dist. Ct. (we. dist.) Tex. 1979, U.S. Dist. Ct. (no. dist.) Tex. 1980, U.S. Ct. Appeals (11th cir.) 1982. Asst. U.S. atty. So. Dist. Tex., 1967-68; assoc. Andrews & Kurth, Houston, 1968-77, ptnr., 1977—. Author: Oil and Gas Bankruptcy, A Preventive Approach, Petroleum Management, Vol. 8, No. 6, Oil and Gas Bankruptcy, Editor-in-chief Creditor's Rights in Texas, 1975. Mem. ABA (chmn. real property practice com. 1975-77, chmn. continuing legal edn. com. young lawyers div. 1976-78, vice chmn. 1979, chmn. oil and gas subcom. bus. bankruptcy com.), Fed. Bar Assn., Houston Bar Assn., State Bar Assn. Tex. (chmn. bankruptcy com. 1986—). Episcopalian. Clubs: Houston Country, Texas, Houston. Bankruptcy, Federal civil litigation, State civil litigation. Home: 340 Pinehaven Houston TX 77024 Office: 4200 Texas Commerce Tower Houston TX 77002

RAY, JEANNE CULLINAN, lawyer, insurance company executive; b. N.Y.C., May 5, 1943; d. Thomas Patrick and Agnes Joan (Buckley) C.; m. John Joseph Ray, Jan. 20, 1968; children—Christopher Lawrence, Douglas James. Student Univ. Coll., Dublin, Ireland, 1963; A.B., Coll. Mt. St. Vincent, Riverdale, N.Y., 1964; LL.B., Fordham U., 1967. Bar: N.Y. 1967. Atty., Mut. Life Ins. Co. N.Y. (MONY), N.Y.C., 1967-68, asst. counsel, 1969-72, assoc. counsel, 1972-73, counsel, 1974-75, asst. gen. counsel, 1976-80, assoc. gen counsel, 1981-83, v.p. pension counsel, 1984-85, v.p. area counsel group and pension ops., 1985—; v.p. law, sec. MONY Securities Corp., N.Y.C., 1980-85; v.p. law, sec. MONY Advisers, Inc., N.Y.C., 1980—; sec. MONYCO, Inc., N.Y.C., 1980-85; v.p., counsel MONY Series Fund, Inc., Balt., 1984—. Contbr. articles to legal jours. Cubmaster, Greater N.Y. council Boy Scouts Am., N.Y.C., 1978-84, mem. bd. rev. and scouting com., 1985—. Mem. ABA (chmn employee benefits com. Tort and Ins. Practice sect. 1981-82, v.p. legislation 1983—), Assn. Life Ins. Counsel (chmn. policyholders tax com. Tax sect. 1982—). Pension, profit-sharing, and employee benefits, Securities, General corporate. Office: MONY 1740 Broadway St New York NY 10019

RAY, RODNEY BRUCE, lawyer; b. New Westminster, B.C., Canada, July 23, 1949; s. Bruce Burns and Mildred Joyce (Cantelo) R.; m. Shirley Ann Wakefield, Oct. 10, 1970 (div. May 1982); m. Christine Lioba Berta, Feb. 17, 1984; children: Melinda Joyce, Michael Joseph. BBA, U. Puget Sound, 1973, JD, 1976. Bar: Wash. 1977, U.S. Dist. Ct. (we. dist.) Wash. 1980, U.S. Ct. Appeals (9th cir.) 1982. Assoc. Herrmann, Levenson, Margullis & Finch, Tacoma, 1980-82; ptnr. Herrmann, Levenson, Margullis & Ray, Tacoma, 1982-84, Margullis, Luedtke & Ray, Tacoma, 1984—. Bd. trustees Tacoma Youth Symphony, 1985—, chmn. fund raising com., 1986-87. Served to staff sgt. USAFR, 1970-76. Mem. Wash. Bar Assn., Assn. Trial Lawyers Am., Wash. Trial Lawyers Assn. Democrat. Methodist. Personal injury, Workers' compensation, Pension, profit-sharing, and employee benefits. Home: 3008 112th Ave E Puyallup WA 98372 Office: Margullis Luedtke & Ray 621 Pacific Ave Suite 104 Tacoma WA 98402

RAY, THOMAS MORGAN, lawyer; b. Birmingham, Ala., July 11, 1953; s. Thomas Willard Ray and Margaret Rebecca (Hayden) Hooks. Student, U. Fla., 1978; BS, Jacksonville State U., 1978; JD, Cumberland Law Sch., 1981. Bar: Ala. 1981, U.S. Dist. Ct. (no. dist.) Ala. 1981, U.S. Ct. Appeals (11th cir.) 1981. Law clk. to presiding justice Ala. Cir. Ct.-Criminal (10th jud. cir.), 1980; sole practice Birmingham, 1981-83; assoc. Gordon, Silberman, Wiggins & Childs P.A., Birmingham, 1983—. Bd. dirs. Air Safety Found., Birmingham, 1985—, So. Mus. of Flight, Birmingham, 1985—. Mem. ABA, Ala. Bar Assn. (legis. liaison com. 1985—), Birmingham Bar Assn. (speakers bur. 1982-84), Ala. Trial Lawyers Assn., Brimingham Aero Club (3d v.p. 1985—), Delta Tau Delta (pres. southern div. 1985—), Delta Theta Phi (local pres. 1980). Methodist. Lodge: Kiwanis. Avocations: flying, sailing, scuba diving. Federal civil litigation, Landlord-tenant, Consumer commercial. Home: 119 Moonglow Dr Birmingham AL 35215 Office: Gordon Silberman Wiggins & Childs 1500 Colonial Bank Bldg Birmingham AL 35203

RAYLESBERG, ALAN IRA, lawyer; b. N.Y.C., Dec. 6, 1950; s. Daniel David and Sally Doris (Mantell) R.; m. Caren Thea Coven, Nov. 20, 1983; 1 child, Lisa Maris. BA, NYU, 1972; JD cum laude, Boston U., 1975. Bar: N.Y. 1976, U.S. Dist. Ct. (so. dist.) N.Y. 1976, U.S. Dist. Ct. (ea. dist.) N.Y. 1978, U.S. Tax Ct. 1981, U.S. Ct. Appeals (2d and 5th cirs.) 1982, U.S. Ct. Appeals (1st cir.) 1986. Assoc. Orans, Elsen & Polstein, N.Y.C., 1975-77; assoc. Guggenheimer & Untermyer, N.Y.C., 1977-83, ptnr., 1983-85; ptnr. Rosenman & Colin, N.Y.C., 1985—. Mem. ABA, Fed. Bar Council, Assn. of Bar of City of N.Y., N.Y. County Lawyers Assn. Democrat. Jewish. Federal civil litigation, State civil litigation, Criminal. Office: Rosenman & Colin 575 Madison Ave New York NY 10022

RAYMAN, ROBERT CRAIG, lawyer; b. Somerset, Pa., Sept. 3, 1954; s. Robert George and Doris Irene (Long) R.; m. Laura Lyn Hatch, Aug. 1, 1981. BA, U. Pitts., Johnstown, 1976; JD, U. Pitts., 1979. Bar: Pa. 1979, U.S. Dist. Ct. (we. dist.) Pa. 1979, U.S. Dist. Ct. (mid. dist.) Pa. 1980, U.S. Tax Ct 1985, U.S. Ct. Appeals (3d cir.) 1985. Ptnr. Devecka & Rayman, State College, Pa., 1979—; bd. dirs. Keystone Legal Services, State College. Author numerous poems. Mem. Pa. Bar Assn. (ethics com. 1984—), Centre County Bar Assn., Assn. Trial Lawyers Am. Avocations: backpacking, gardening, reading, collect baseball cards. Bankruptcy, Real property, Personal injury. Home: 108 Pine Tree Ave Boalsburg PA 16827 Office: Devecka & Rayman 111 Sowers St Suite 600 State College PA 16801

RAYMOND, CHARLES MICHAEL, lawyer; b. Chester, Pa., May 22, 1953; s. Charles Anthony and Theresa (Curney) R.; m. Sandra H. Brabham, May 22, 1984. B.A., La. State U., 1975; J.D., Loyola U., New Orleans, 1978. Bar: La. 1979, U.S. Supreme Ct. 1984, U.S. Ct. Appeals (5th cir.) 1979, U.S. Dist. Ct. (mid. dist.) La. 1981, (so. dist.) Tex. 1984, (we. dist.) Mo. 1984, (ea. dist.) La. 1983, D.C. 1987, U.S. Ct. Appeals (11th cir.) 1985, U.S. Ct. Appeals (D.C. cir.) 1987. Asst. city-parish atty. City of Baton Rouge and Parish East Baton Rouge, 1979-84; atty. Gill & Bankston, Baton Rouge, 1982-84, Camp, Carmouche, Barsh, Hunter, Gray Hoffman & Gill, Baton Rouge, 1984-86, E & P litigations Shell Oil Co., 1986—. Exec. v.p. La. Young Democrats, 1977-78; mem.-at-large East Baton Rouge Parish Dem. Exec. Com., 1979-83; coordinator City-Parish Atty.'s Office United Way Campaign, Baton Rouge, 1983. Moot Ct. judge, So. U. Sch. Law, 1983. Mem. Assn. Trial Lawyers Am., ABA, La. Trial Lawyers Assn., La. Bar Assn., Fed. Bar Assn., Pi Sigma Alpha. Democrat. Roman Catholic. Environment, Contracts commercial, Federal civil litigation. Home: 241 10th St New Orleans LA 70124 Office: One Shell Sq Shell Legal Div Suite 4961 701 Poydras St New Orleans LA 70139

RAYMOND, DANA MERRIAM, lawyer; b. Flushing, N.Y., July 28, 1914; s. Charles Merriam and June (Leonard) R.; m. Josephine Sheehan, June 25, 1949; children—Catherine, Peter Dana, John Dana. A.B., U. Calif., 1935; LL.B., Columbia U., 1939. Bar: N.Y. State bar 1939. Since practiced in N.Y.C.; assoc. firm Cravath, Swaine & Moore, 1939-54; mem. firm Brumbaugh, Graves, Donohue & Raymond, 1954—. Bd. dirs. Armstrong Meml. Research Found. Served with AUS, 1940-45. Mem. ABA, N.Y.C. Bar Assn., N.Y. Patent Law Assn., Am. Coll. Trial Lawyers, Am. Bar Found., N.Y. Patent, Trademark & Copyright Law Assn., U.S. Ct. Customs and Patent Appeals. Clubs: Univ. (N.Y.C.); Maidstone (East Hampton, N.Y.). Patent, Federal civil litigation, State civil litigation. Home: 14 E 90th St New York NY 10128 Other: 21 Jeffreys Ln East Hampton NY 11937 Office: 30 Rockefeller Plaza New York NY 10112

RAYMOND, DAVID WALKER, lawyer; b. Chelsea, Mass., Aug. 23, 1945; s. John Walker and Jane (Beck) R.; m. Sandra Sue Broadwater, Aug. 12, 1967 (div.); m. Margaret Byrd Payne, May 25, 1974; children—Pamela Payne, Russell Wyatt. B.A., Gettysburg Coll., 1967; J.D., Temple U., 1970. Bar: Pa. 1970, D.C. 1971, U.S. Supreme Ct. 1974, Ill. 1975, U.S. Dist. Ct. (no. dist.) Ill. 1981. Govtl. affairs atty. Sears, Roebuck and Co., Washington, 1970-74, atty. hdqrs. law dept., Chgo., 1974-80, asst. gen. counsel advt., trademarks and customs, 1981-84, asst. gen. counsel adminstrn., 1984-86, mgr. planning and analysis corp. planning dept., 1986—. Staff Temple Law Quar., 1968-69, editor, 1969-70. Mem. ABA, Fed. Bar Assn., Ill. Bar Assn., Chgo. Bar Assn., Phi Alpha Delta. Presbyterian. General corporate, Administrative and regulatory, Trade Regulation. Office: Sears Roebuck and Co Sears Tower 37th Floor Chicago IL 60684

RAYMOND, DOUGLAS J., lawyer; b. Rapid City, S.D., July 25, 1955; s. Russell D. and Dorothy E. (Spano) R.; m. Joan M. Kuhl, Sept. 20, 1986. BS in Microbiology and Chemistry, U. Md., 1976; JD, U. Denver, 1981. Bar: Colo. 1981, U.S. Dist. Ct. Colo. 1982, U.S. Ct. Appeals (10th cir.) 1982. Ptnr. Borneman & Raymond, Arvada, Colo., 1981-83, Beam, Raymond & Holmes, Denver, 1986; sole practice Denver, 1983-86. Mem. Assn. Trial Lawyers Am. Roman Catholic. Federal civil litigation, State civil litigation, Personal injury. Office: Beam Raymond & Holmes 303 E 17th Ave Suite 660 Denver CO 80203

RAZZANO, FRANK CHARLES, lawyer; b. Bklyn., Feb. 25, 1948; s. Pasquale Anthony and Agnes Mary (Borgia) R.; m. Stephanie Anne Lucas, Jan. 10, 1970; children—Joseph, Francis, Catherine. B.A., St. Louis U., 1969; J.D., Georgetown U., 1972. Bar: N.Y. 1973, U.S. Dist. Ct. (so. dist.) N.Y. 1973, U.S. Dist. Ct. (ea. dist.) N.Y. 1973, N.J. 1976, D.C. 1981, Va. 1984, U.S. Dist. Ct. N.J. 1976, U.S. Dist. Ct. Md. 1977, U.S. Dist. Ct. (no. dist.) Calif. 1981, U.S. Dist. Ct. D.C. 1982, U.S. Ct. Appeals (2d cir.) 1973, U.S. Ct. Appeals (3d cir.) 1975, U.S. Ct. Appeals (D.C. and 5th cirs.) 1983, U.S. Ct. Appeals (4th cir.) 1984, U.S. Supreme Ct. 1976. Assoc. Shea & Gould, N.Y.C., 1972-75; asst. U.S. atty. Dist. of N.J., Newark, 1975-78; asst. chief trial atty. SEC, Washington, 1978-82; ptnr. Shea & Gould, Washington, 1982—; lectr. in field. Scoutmaster Vienna council Boy Scouts Am., 1984. Recipient spl. achievement award Justice Dept., 1977, spl. commendation, 1978. Mem. ABA, Va. Bar Assn., D.C. Bar Assn., Phi Beta Kappa, Eta Sigma Phi. Roman Catholic. Federal civil litigation, State civil litigation,

Securities. Home: 1713 Paisley Blue Ct Vienna VA 22180 Office: Shea & Gould 1627 K St NW Washington DC 20006

RAZZANO, PASQUALE ANGELO, lawyer; b. Bklyn., Apr. 3, 1943; s. Pasquale Anthony and Agnes Mary (Borgia) R.; m. Maryann Walker, Jan. 29, 1966; children—Elizabeth, Pasquale, Susan, ChristyAnn. B.S.C.E., Poly. Inst. Bklyn., 1964; student law, NYU, 1964-66; J.D., Georgetown U., 1969. Bar: Va. 1969, N.Y. 1970, U.S. Ct. Appeals (2d, 3d, 9th and fed. cirs.), U.S. Supreme Ct., U.S. Dist. Ct. (so. and ea. dists.) N.Y., U.S. Dist. Ct. (we. dist.) Tex., U.S. Ct. Customs and Patent Appeals. Examiner U.S. Patent Office, 1966-69; assoc. Curtis, Morris & Safford, P.C., 1969-71, ptnr., 1971—; guest lectr. U.S. Trademark Assn. Bd. editors: Merchandising Reporter, 1986—, Trademark Reporter, 1987—. Republican committeeman Rockland County. Recipient Robert Ridgeway award, 1964. Mem. Fed. Bar Assn., N.Y. Patent Law Assn. (bd. dirs. 1985—), Am. Patent Law Assn., N.Y. Bar Assn., Va. Bar Assn., ABA. Republican. Roman Catholic. Club: N.Y. Athletic. Patent, Trademark and copyright, Federal civil litigation. Address: 15 White Woods Ln Westport CT 06880 also: 14 Deerwood Trail Lake Placid NY 12946

RDUCH, EVITA JOANNE, lawyer; b. Nurenberg, W. Ger., Dec. 9, 1952; came to U.S., 1958; d. Adolf Victor and Lucie (Schroeder) R. B.A., Blackburn Coll., 1974; J.D., John Marshall Law Sch., 1979. Bar: Tex. 1979, U.S. Supreme Ct. 1982, U.S. Ct. Customs and Patents 1982, U.S. Tax Ct. 1982, U.S. Dist. Ct. (no. dist.) Tex. 1982, U.S. Dist. Ct. (so. dist.) Tex. 1980, U.S. Ct. Appeals (3d, 5th, 7th, 9th, 10th and 11th cirs.). Labor relations rep. Employers' Assn. Greater Chgo., 1976-78; pres. Rduch & Whyburn, Inc., Humble, Tex., 1979-81; sole practice, Humble, 1981-83; sr. ptnr. Rduch & Rowney, Humble, 1983-85; pres. Rduch & Rowney, P.C., 1986—; guest lectr. U. Houston, 1979-81. Bd. dirs., asst. sec., v.p. Water Control Improvement Dist. 136, Spring, Tex., 1982-85, v.p., 1986—; textbook adv. com. Spring Ind. Sch. Dist., 1981—; pres., bd. dirs. Birnamwood-Fairfax Homeowners' Assn., Spring, 1980-82; mem. fin. com. St. James Ch., Spring., 1980-86; mem. community bd. Mercer Arboretum Adv. Com., 1981-83. Mem. Assn. Trial Lawyers Am., ABA, Houston Bar Assn. (family law sect. 1983-84). General practice, Family and matrimonial, Personal injury. Office: Rduch & Rowney PC 20713 Aldine-Westfield Humble TX 77338

RE, EDWARD D., federal judge; b. Santa Marina, Italy, Oct. 14, 1920; s. Anthony and Marina (Maetta) R.; m. Margaret A. Corcoran, June 3, 1950; children: Mary Ann, Anthony John, Marina, Edward, Victor, Margaret, Matthew, Joseph, Mary Elizabeth, Mary Joan, Mary Ellen, Nancy Madeleine. B.S. cum laude, St. John's U., 1941, LL.B. summa cum laude, 1943, LL.D. (hon.), 1968; J.S.D., NYU, 1950; Pd.D. (hon.), Aquila, Italy, 1960; LL.D. (hon.), St. Mary's Coll., Notre Dame, Ind., 1968, Maryville Coll., St. Louis, 1969, N.Y. Law Sch., 1976, Bklyn. Coll., CCNY, 1978, Nova U., 1980, Roger Williams Coll., 1982; L.H.D. (hon.), DePaul U., 1980, Coll. S.I., CCNY, 1981. Bar: N.Y. 1943. Appointed faculty St. John's U., N.Y., 1947; prof. law St. John's U., 1951-69, adj. prof. law, 1969-80, Disting. prof., from 1980; vis. prof. Georgetown U. Sch. Law, 1962-67; adj. prof. law N.Y. Law Sch., 1972-82, Martin disting. vis. prof., from 1982; spl. hearing officer U.S. Dept. Justice, 1956-61; chmn. Fgn. Claims Settlement Commn. of U.S., 1961-68; asst. sec. ednl. and cultural affairs U.S. Dept. State, 1968-69; judge U.S. Customs Ct. (now U.S. Ct. Internat. Trade), N.Y.C., 1969—; chief judge U.S. Customs Ct. (now U.S. Ct. Internat. Trade), 1977—; Mem. adv. com. on appellate rules Jud. Conf. U.S., 1976—; chmn. adv. com. on experimentation in the law Fed. Jud. Ctr., 1978-81; Mem. bd. higher edn. City of N.Y., 1958-69, mem. emeritus, 1969—; Jackson lectr. Nat. Coll. State Trial Judges, U. Nev., 1970. Author: Foreign Confiscations in Anglo-American Law, 1951, (with Lester B. Orfield) Cases and Materials on International Law, rev. edit, 1965, Selected Essays on Equity, 1955, Brief Writing and Oral Argument, 4th rev. edit, 1977, (with Zechariah Chafee, Jr.) Cases and Materials on Equity, 1967, Cases and Materials on Equity and Equitable Remedies, 1975; chpt., freedom in internat. soc. Concept of Freedom (edited Rev. Carl W. Grindel), 1955; Cases and Materials on Remedies; Contbr. articles to Legal jours. Served with USAAF, 1943-47; col. JAGC, ret. Decorated Order of Merit Italy; recipient Am. Bill of Rights citation; Morgenstern Found. Interfaith award; USAF commendation medal; Distinguished service award Bklyn. Jr. C. of C., 1956. Mem. ABA (ho. of dels. 1976-78, chmn. sect. internat. and comparative law 1965-67), Bklyn. Bar Assn., Assn. Bar City N.Y., Am. Soc. Internat. Law, Am. Fgn. Law Assn. (pres. 1971-73), Am. Law Inst., Fed. Bar Council (pres. 1973-74), Am. Assn. Comparative Study Law (pres.), Am. Justinian Soc. Jurists (pres. 1974-76), Scribes Am. Soc. Writers on Legal Subjects (pres. 1978). Jurisprudence. Office: US Ct Internat Trade One Federal Plaza New York NY 10007 *

READ, CHARLES ARTHUR, lawyer; b. Washington, Dec. 14, 1919; s. Ernest James and Florence Albertine (Gude) R.; m. Marian Berky, May 23, 1953; children: Susan, Charles, Andrew. B.S. in Commerce, U. Va., 1941, J.D., 1947. Bar: Va. 1947, N.Y. 1948, U.S. Supreme Ct. 1962, D.C. 1965. Biology instr. U. Va., 1938-40; instr. naval scis. Notre Dame U., 1942-43; asst. prof. naval scis. Ga. Inst. Tech., 1946; assoc. Reid & Priest, N.Y.C., 1947-55, ptnr., 1956-86, mng. ptnr., 1981, sr. counsel, 1987—; gen. counsel Pub. Power Corp., Athens, Greece, 1950-52. Chmn. Republican Party, Upper Montclair, N.J., 1960-72; chmn. bd. Perkiomen Sch., 1971-79. Served to lt. USNR, 1942-46. Recipient Raven award U. Va., 1941. Mem. ABA, N.Y. State Bar Assn., Va. Bar Assn., D.C. Bar Assn., U. Va. Alumni Assn. (trustee 1976-82, pres. 1980-81), U. Va. Law Sch. Alumni Assn. (trustee 1982-87), Beta Gamma Sigma. Episcopalian. Clubs: Union League, Down Town Assn., Club at World Trade Center, Wall St., Montclair Golf, Farmington Country. General corporate, Private international, Public utilities. Home: 162 Inwood Ave Upper Montclair NJ 07043 Office: 40 W 57th St New York NY 10019

READ, MICHAEL JOHN, lawyer; b. Pocatello, Idaho, Jan. 25, 1954; s. John Howard and Bonnie Dolores (Poulson) R.; m. LouAnne Barker, Apr. 23, 1976; children: Jennifer, Brandon. BA, Brigham Young U., 1978, JD, 1982. Bar: Idaho 1982, U.S. Dist. Ct. Idaho 1982. Law clk. to presiding justice Idaho 4th Jud. Dist., Boise, 1982-83; assoc. Hamlin & Sasser, Boise, 1983-84; atty. Albertson's Inc., Boise, 1984—. Mem. Boise Master Chorale, 1982—; performer Boise Civic Opera, Boise Music Week, 1984-85, Boise Little Theater, 1986—. Mem. ABA, Idaho Bar Assn., Phi Kappa Phi, Phi Alpha Delta. Mormon. Real property, Federal civil litigation, State civil litigation. Office: Alberstsons Inc 250 Parkcenter Blvd Boise ID 83726

REAGAN, GARY DON, lawyer; b. Amarillo, Tex., Aug. 23, 1941; s. Hester and Lois Irene (Marcum) R.; m. Nedra Ann Nash, Sept. 12, 1964; children—Marc, Kristi, Kari, Brent. A.B., Stanford U., 1963, J.D., 1965. Bar: N.Mex. 1965, U.S. Dist. Ct. N.Mex., 1965. Assoc. Smith & Ransom, Albuquerque, 1965-67; ptnr. Smith, Ransom, Deaton & Reagan, Albuquerque, 1967-68, Williams, Johnson, Houston, Reagan & Porter, Hobbs, N.Mex., 1968-77, Williams, Johnson, Reagan, Porter & Love, Hobbs, 1977-82; sole practice, Hobbs, 1982—; city atty. City of Hobbs, 1978-80; City of Eunice, N.M., 1980—; instr. N.Mex. Jr. Coll. and Coll. of S.W., Hobbs, 1978-84. Mayor, City of Hobbs, 1972-73, 76-77, city commr., 1970-78; pres., dir. Jr. Achievement of Hobbs, 1974-85; pres., trustee Landsun Homes, Inc., Carlsbad, N.Mex., 1972-84; trustee Lydia Patterson Inst., El Paso, Tex., 1972-84, N.Mex. Conf. United Meth. Ch., 1984—; chmn. County Democratic Com., 1983-85. Mem. ABA, State Bar N.Mex. (coms.), Lea County Bar Assn. (pres. 1976-77), Hobbs C. of C. (v.p. 1986-87). Lodge: Rotary (pres. Hobbs 1985-86), Hobbs Tennis (pres. 1974-75). Real property, Banking, Oil and gas leasing. Home: 200 Eagle Dr Hobbs NM 88240 Office: 501 N Linam Hobbs NM 88240

REAGAN, HARRY E., III, lawyer; b. Wichita, Kans., Sept. 9, 1940; s. Harry E. II and Mary Elizabeth (O'Steen) R.; m. Marvene R. Rogers, June 17, 1965; children: Kathleen, Leigh, Mairen. BS, U. Pa., 1962, JD. Bar: Pa. 1965, U.S. Dist. Ct. (ea. dist.) Pa. 1965. From assoc. to ptnr. Morgan, Lewis & Bockius, Phila., 1965—. Chmn. Northampton Twp. Planning Commn., Bucks County, Pa., 1974-79; mem. Warwick Twp. Planning Commn., 1980—. Mem. ABA (labor sect.), Pa. Bar Assn. (labor sect.), Phila. Bar Assn. (labor sect.), Indls. Relations Assn., Indsl. Relations Research Assn. Republican. Presbyterian. Avocations: coaching rugby, skiing, raising horses, bicycling. Labor, Pension, profit-sharing, and employee benefits. Home: 2930 Wilkinson Rd Rushland PA 18956 Office: Morgan Lewis & Bockius 2000 One Logan Sq Philadelphia PA 19103

REAGAN, OWEN WALKER, III, lawyer; b. Belleville, Ill., Jan. 6, 1952; s. Owen Walker Jr. and Alice Bernice (DuBose) R.; m. Janet Lee Mills, Dec. 28, 1974; children: Owen Walker IV, Mills Worthington. BA, Duke U., 1974, MA in Pub. Policy Scis., 1979; JD, U. N.C., 1978. Bar: N.C. 1978. Ptnr. Toms & Reagan and predecessor firm Dimmock, Reagan, Dodd & Toms, Cary, N.C.; sole practice Cary, 1978—. Real property, General corporate, Probate. Home: 1303 Tarbert Dr Cary NC 27511 Office: Toms & Reagan 1125 Kildaire Farm Rd Cary NC 27511

REAGAN, RONALD EVAN, judge; b. Auburn, Nebr., Sept. 13, 1938; s. Charles M. and Dora (O'Dell) R.; m. Jane Ann Harrison, Aug. 1, 1969; 1 child, Sean. BS, U. Nebr., 1960; JD, Creighton Law Sch., 1967. Bar: Nebr. 1967, U.S. Dist. Ct. Nebr. 1967. Sole practice, Bellevue, Nebr., 1967-72; dist. judge Nebr. 2d Jud. Dist., 1972—. Served to capt. USMC, 1960-64. Mem. ABA, Nebr. Bar Assn., Nebr. Dist. Judges Assn. (pres. 1981), Nat. Conf. State Trial Judges (exec. com., del. to JAD council 1985—), VFW. Democrat. Club: Eagles. Jurisprudence. Address: Sarpy County Courthouse Papillion NE 08046

REAGLE, JACK EVAN, lawyer; b. Sharon, Pa., Feb. 26, 1957; s. James Leroy and Barbara (Sarchet) R. BA, Edinboro State Coll., 1979; student, Calif. Western U., 1979-80; JD, U. Akron, 1982. Bar: Pa. 1982, U.S. Dist. Ct. (we. dist.) Pa. 1983. Sole practice Hermitage, Pa., 1981-84; atty. Northwestern Legal Services, Coudersport, Pa., 1984—; pub. defender Potter County, Coudersport, 1984—. Contbr. articles to profl. jours. Mem. ABA, Pa. Bar Assn., Assn. Trail Lawyers Am., Phi Alpha Delta. Republican. Criminal, Family and matrimonial, General practice. Home: Fraker Ln PO Box 674 Coudersport PA 16915-0674

REAL, MANUEL LAWRENCE, U.S. district judge; b. San Pedro, Calif., Jan. 27, 1924; s. Francisco Jose and Maria (Mansano) R.; m. Stella Emilia Michalik, Oct. 15, 1955; children: Michael, Melanie Marie, Timothy, John Robert. B.S., U. So. Calif., 1944, student fgn. trade, 1946-48; LL.B., Loyola Sch. Law, Los Angeles, 1951. Bar: Calif. 1952. Asst. U.S. Atty.'s Office, Los Angeles, 1952-55; pvt. practice law San Pedro, Calif., 1955-64; U.S. atty. So. Dist. Calif., 1964-66; U.S. dist. judge 1966—, now chief judge. Served to ensign USNR, 1943-46. Mem. Am., Fed., Los Angeles County bar assns., State Bar Calif., Am. Judicature Soc., Chief Spl. Agts. Assn., Phi Delta Phi, Sigma Chi. Democrat. Roman Catholic. Club: Anchor (Los Angeles). Office: US Courthouse 312 N Spring St Los Angeles CA 90012 *

REAM, CHRISTOPHER, lawyer; b. Somerville, N.J., Oct. 31, 1942; s. Joseph H. and Anita (Biggs) R.; m. Anne Kelleher, Aug. 10, 1968; children: Jason, Anita. BE, Yale U., 1964; JD, Boalt Hall, Berkeley, Calif., 1971. Bar: Calif. 1971, U.S. Dist. Ct. (no. dist.) Calif. 1971, U.S. Dist. Ct. (cen. dist.) Calif. 1973. Assoc. Wilson, Mosher & Sonsini, Palo Alto, Calif., 1971-76; ptnr. Ream, Roskoph & Busselle, Palo Alto, 1976—. Served to lt. USNR, 1964-68. Mem. ABA, Palo Alto Area Bar Assn. (pres. 1986-87). General corporate, Securities, State civil litigation. Office: Ream Roskoph & Busselle 755 Page Mill Rd Palo Alto CA 94304

REAM, DAVIDSON, writer, law publications manager; b. Ossining, N.Y., May 2, 1937; s. Joseph H. and Anita (Biggs) R.; m. Judith Krampitz, Oct. 1, 1966; children: Michael E., Caitlin D. BA, Yale U., 1961; JD, U. Va., 1964; LLM, U. Calif., Berkeley, 1971. Bar: D.C. 1972. Spl. asst. Supreme Ct. of Pakistan, 1964-65; law program developer The Asia Found., San Francisco and Sri Lanka, 1966-69; research atty. Continuing Edn. of the Bar, Berkeley, 1970-75; publ. dir. ABA, Chgo., 1975-78; publ. mgr. Callaghan & Co., Wilmette, Ill., 1978-83; mng. editor Def. Research Inst., Chgo., 1984—. Editor: Condemnation Practice in California, 1973, Landslide and Subsidence Liability, 1974, Attorney's Guide to Professional Responsibility, 1978. Pres. Ridgeville Assn., Evanston, Ill., 1977-81; alderman City of Evanston, 1983-87; bd. dirs. Dem. Party Evanston, 1978—. Mem. ABA, D.C. Bar Assn. Avocations: hiking, camping, travel, community affairs. Legal publishing, Lawyers' associations, Legal education. Home: 910 Monroe Evanston IL 60202 Office: Defense Research Inst 750 N Lake Shore Dr Chicago IL 60611

REAMEY, GERALD S., lawyer, legal educator, consultant; b. Hot Springs, Ark., Feb. 7, 1948; s. Sanford and Geraldean L. (Sims) R.; m. Kay Lynn Lancaster, Jan. 23, 1970; 1 child, Anne Sanford. BA, Trinity U., 1970; JD cum laude, So. Meth. U., 1976, LLM, 1982. Bar: Tex., U.S. Dist. Ct. (no. dist.) Tex. Ptnr. Kahn & Reamey, Irving, Tex., 1976-77; assoc. Power, Ashley & Kinkeade, Irving, 1977-79; pub. legal advisor Irving Police Dept., Irving, 1979-82; assoc. prof. law St. Mary's U. Sch. of Law, San Antonio, 1982—; instr. So. Meth. U. Law Sch., Dallas, 1977; adj. prof. mgmt. U. of Dallas, Irving, 1977-82; cons. Tex. Mcpl. Cts. Tng. Ctr., Austin, 1985—. Author: A Peace Officer's Guide to Texas Law, 1985. chmn. adv. council Family Life Ctr., San Antonio, 1986—. Served to lt. U.S. Army, 1970-74, ETO. Mem. ABA (criminal justice sect.), Tex. Bar Assn., Tex. Police Assn., Tex. Assn. of Police Atty.'s (chmn. 1981-82), Assn. Am. Law Schs., Order of Coif. Democrat. Avocations: amateur radio operator, sailing. Criminal, Civil rights, Legal education. Home: 2810 Whisper Fawn San Antonio TX 78230 Office: St Marys U Sch of Law One Camino Santa Maria San Antonio TX 78284-0400

REAMS, BERNARD DINSMORE, JR., lawyer, educator; b. Lynchburg, Va., Aug. 17, 1943; s. Bernard Dinsmore and Martha Eloise (Hickman) R.; m. Rosemarie Bridget Boyle, Oct. 26, 1968; children: Andrew Dennet, Adriane Bevin. B.A., Lynchburg Coll., 1965; M.S., Drexel U., Phila., 1966; J.D., U. Kans., 1972; Ph.D., St. Louis U., 1983. Bar: Kans. 1973, Mo. 1986. Instr., asst. librarian Rutgers U., 1966-69; asst. prof. law, librarian U. Kans., Lawrence, 1969-74; mem. faculty law sch. Washington U., St. Louis, 1974—, prof. law, 1976—, librarian, 1974-76, acting dean library services, 1987—. Author: Law For The Businessman, 1974, Reader in Law Librarianship, 1976, Federal Price and Wage Control Programs 1917-1979: Legis. Histories and Laws, 1980, Education of the Handicapped: Laws, Legislative Histories, and Administrative Documents, 1982, Housing and Transportation of the Handicapped: Laws and Legislative Histories, 1983, Internal Revenue Acts of the United States: The Revenue Act of 1954 with Legislative Histories and Congressional Documents, 1983 Congress and the Courts: A Legislative History 1978-1984, 1984, University-Industry Research Partnerships: The Major Issues in Research and Development Agreements, 1986, Deficit Control and the Gramm-Rudman-Hollings Act, 1986, The Semiconductor Chip and the Law: A Legislative History of the Semiconductor Chip Protection Act of 1984, 1986, American International Law Cases, 2d series, 1986, Technology Transfer Law: The Export Administration Acts of the U.S., 1987; co-author: Segregation and the Fourteenth Amendment in the States, 1975, Historic Preservation Law: An Annotated Bibliography, 1976, Congress and the Courts: A Legislative History 1787-1977, 1978, Federal Consumer Protection Laws, Rules and Regulations, 1979, A Guide and Analytical Index to the Internal Revenue Acts of the U.S., 1909-1950, 1979, The Numerical Lists and Schedule of Volumes of the U.S. Congressional Serial Set: 73d Congress through the 96th Congress, 1984, Human Experimentation: Federal Laws, Legislative Histories, Regulations and Related Documents, 1985, American Legal Literature: A Guide to Selected Legal Resources, 1985. Thornton award for Excellence Lynchburg Coll., 1986. Mem. ABA, Am. Assn. Higher Edn., ALA, Spl. Libraries Assn., Internat. Assn. Law Libraries, Am. Assn. Law Librarians, Southwestern Assn. Law Librarians (pres. 1977-78), ABA, Nat. Assn. of Coll. and Univ. Attys., Order of Coif, Phi Beta Kappa, Beta Phi Mu, Phi Delta Phi, Phi Delta Epsilon, Kappa Delta Pi, Pi Lambda Theta. Legal education, Librarianship. Home: 2353 Hollyhead Dr Des Peres MO 63131 Office: Washington U Law Sch Box 1120 Saint Louis MO 63130

REARDON, ANDREW FITZPATRICK, lawyer; b. Cin., Nov. 8, 1945; s. William James and Frances Louise (Blasdel) R.; m. Michele Marie Berard, Dec. 27, 1967; children—Andrew F., Elizabeth B., William J., Mark C. B.A., U. Notre Dame, 1967; J.D., U. Cin., 1974; LL.M. in Taxation, Washington U., St. Louis, 1975. Bar: Ohio 1974, Mo. 1975, Nebr. 1981, Minn. 1981, U.S. Tax Ct. 1981, U.S. Claims Ct. 1981. Assoc. Thompson & Mitchell, St. Louis, 1975-77; gen. tax atty. St. Louis-San Francisco Ry. Co., St. Louis, 1977-79; sr. tax counsel Union Pacific Corp., N.Y.C., 1979-81; asst. gen. counsel Burlington No., St. Paul, 1981-82, asst. v.p. law, 1982-84; gen. counsel, sec. Farm Credit Services, St. Paul, 1984-85; sr. v.p. law and real estate Ill. Cen. Gulf R.R. Co., Chgo., 1985—; lectr. Practicing Law Inst., 1981. Served to lt. USN, 1967-71. Mem. ABA (chmn. com. depreciation and credits tax sect. 1982-84). Roman Catholic. Clubs: St. Paul Athletic; North Oaks Golf; Metropolitan (Washington); Mid-America (Chgo.). Home: 1313 Harlan Ln Lake Forest IL 60045 Office: Ill Cen Gulf RR Co 233 N Michigan Ave Chicago IL 60601

REARDON, GERARD VINCENT, lawyer; b. N.Y.C., Feb. 23, 1951; s. James Joseph and Miriam Elizabeth (Daley) R.; m. Cheryl Lynn O'Brien, May 1, 1976; children: Erin, Shaun, Ryan, Alison, Kevin. BA, Adelphi U., 1973; MA, U. Calgary, Alta., Can., 1977; JD, Hofstra U., 1980. Bar: N.Y. 1981, Colo. 1983, U.S. Dist. Ct. Colo. 1985, U.S. Ct. Appeals (10th cir.) 1986. Landman Dome Petroleum Ltd., Calgary, 1980-81, Axem Resources Inc., Denver, 1981-85; contract adminstr. Martin Marietta Corp., Denver, 1985—. Del. county, state and jud. assemblies, Colo., 1984-86. Mem. ABA (pub. contract law sect.), Delta Tau Alpha. Republican. Mormon. Government contracts and claims, Administrative and regulatory, Jurisprudence. Home: 8665 W Teton Ave Littleton CO 80123 Office: Martin Marietta Corp PO Box 179 Denver CO 80201

REARDON, MARK WILLIAM, lawyer; b. Englewood, N.J., June 7, 1956; s. Matthew Francis and Rose Mary (Snyder) R.; m. Patricia Louise Powers, Apr. 19, 1985. BA, Knox Coll., 1977; JD, Seton Hall U., 1980. Bar: N.J. 1980, U.S. Dist. Ct. N.J. 1980, U.S. Ct. Mil. Appeals 1981. Atty. Boeing Computer Services, Seattle, 1986—. Served to capt. JAGC, U.S. Army, 1981-86. Mem. ABA, Computer Law Assn., Phi Gamma Delta. Republican. Roman Catholic. Government contracts and claims, Computer, Contracts commercial. Office: Boeing Computer Services PO Box 24346 MS 7A-52 Seattle WA 98124

REARDON, MICHAEL EDWARD, lawyer; b. Independence, Mo., Apr. 15, 1948; s. Neil Willison and Marjorie (Winters) R.; m. Gloria Kay Nelson, Jan. 31, 1970; children—Darin Thomas, Laura Michelle. B.A. magna cum laude, William Jewell Coll., 1970; J.D. with distinction, U. Mo.-Kansas City, 1973, LL.M. in Criminal Law, 1978. Bar: Mo. 1973, U.S. Dist. Ct. (we. dist.) Mo. 1974, U.S. Supreme Ct. 1978. Assoc. Morris, Larson, King, Stamper-Bold, Kansas City, Mo., 1973-74, M. Randall Vanet, North Kansas City, Mo., 1974-75; ptnr. Duncan, Russell & Reardon, Kansas City, 1975-82, Michael E. Reardon & Assocs., Kansas City, 1982-86; Clay County Pros. Atty., Liberty, Mo., 1987—. Sec., bd. dirs. Social Rehab. Assn. Clay County, North Kansas City, 1977-86; bd. dirs. Clay County Sheltered Facilities, 1982-84; chmn. Clay County Dem. Com., Kansas City, 1982-84; treas. Mo. 6th Congl. Dist. Dem. Com., 1982—; bd. dirs. Clay County Investigative Squad, Liberty, 1987—. Mem. Mo. Bar Assn., Mo. Assn. Trial Attys., Mo. Assn. Pros. Attys., Clay County Bar Assn., Kansas City Bar Assn., Gladstone C. of C. Lodge: Lions (bd. dirs. Liberty club 1982—). Criminal.

REARDON, TIMOTHY JOSEPH, lawyer; b. Detroit, Aug. 18, 1935; s. Timothy Joseph and Louise (Whelan) R.; m. Joan Maureen Coburn, Aug. 7, 1958; children—Thomas, Michael, Brian, Kathleen. B.B.A., U. Mich., 1957, M.B.A., 1958; J.D., Detroit Coll. Law, 1965. Bar: Mich. 1966, Ill. 1974. Personnel asst. Kroger Co., Ft. Wayne, Ind., 1958-60; mgr. labor relations Allied Products Corp., Detroit, 1960-64; asst. sec., ho. counsel Whitehead & Kales Co., River Rouge, Mich., 1964-69; sole practice law, Muskegon, Mich., 1969-74, Springfield, Ill., 1976—; chief legal counsel Ill. Dept. Personnel, Springfield, 1974-76. Recipient prize for Excellence in Labor Law, Bancroft-Whitney Pub. Co., 1965. Mem. Ill. State Bar Assn. (sec. labor law sect. council 1984—, vice chmn. 1986—), ABA, Sangamon County Bar Assn., Am. Arbitration Assn. (labor arbitration panels 1972—). Roman Catholic. Clubs: Lions, Rotary. Labor, Family and matrimonial. Home: 178 Golf Rd Springfield IL 62704 Office: 2020 Timberbrook Dr Springfield IL 62702

REASER, VERNON NEAL, JR., lawyer; b. Victoria, Tex., Jan. 17, 1942; s. Vernon Neal Sr. and Imogene Clara (Weeks) R.; m. Gail Jean Reaser, Mar. 12, 1970; children: Vernon Neal III, Clayton Neal. BA, U. Houston, 1966; JD, South Tex. Coll., 1969. Bar: Tex., U.S. Dist. Ct. (so. dist.) Tex., U.S. Ct. Appeals (5th and 11th cirs.). Sole practice Victoria, 1970-75; sr. ptnr. Reaser & Wall, Victoria, 1975—; bd. dirs. Tex. Titles, Victoria. Mem. ABA, Tex. Bar Assn., Victoria County Bar Assn. (pres. 1980), Victoria County Jr. Bar Assn. (pres. 1976), Tex. Trial Lawyers Assn. (bd. dirs. 1980-81). Democrat. Avocations: sailing, snow skiing. State civil litigation, General corporate, Oil and gas leasing. Home: 405 Royal Oak Dr Victoria TX 77901 Office: Reaser & Wall 1501 Mockingbird Suite 1 Victoria TX 77904

REASONER, CARROLL JANE, lawyer; b. Washington, Apr. 27, 1951; d. Carroll Dean and Bettie Jane (Edwards) R.; m. Thomas Parker Peffer, Aug. 13, 1977; children: William Thomas, Michael Dean. Student, U. Pa., 1969-70; BA, U. Ia., 1973, JD, 1976. Bar: Ia. 1976, D.C. 1977, U.S. Dist. Ct. (no. dist.) Ia. 1977, U.S. Dist. Ct. (so. dist.) Ia. 1979. Assoc. Shuttleworth & Ingersoll P.C., Cedar Rapids, Ia., 1977-82, ptnr., 1983—, v.p., 1984—; commr. Nat. Conf. of Commrs. on Uniform State Laws, 1983; bd. dirs. Me-Coil Systems Corp. V.p. Cedar Rapids Mus. of Art, 1984—; sec. St. Luke's Meth. Hosp., Cedar Rapids, 1984—; mem. Cedar Rapids/Marion Arts Council; chmn. bd. dirs. STL Health Resources Co., 1986—, STL Care Co., 1986—. Mem. ABA, Ia. State Bar Assn. (bd. govs. 1985-87, pres. young lawyers sect. 1986-87), Linn County Bar Assn., Assn. Women Attys. of Linn County, 6th Jud. Dist. Bar Assn. (pres. 1984—), Order of the Coif. Republican. Methodist. Clubs: Pickwick (Cedar Rapids) (sec. 1984-86); U. Ia. Athletic (Iowa City). Avocations: travel, cooking, tennis, reading. Contracts commercial, Banking, General corporate. Home: 2483 Grande Ave SE Cedar Rapids IA 52403 Office: Shuttleworth and Ingersoll PC 500 MNB Bldg Cedar Rapids IA 52406

REASONER, HARRY MAX, lawyer; b. San Marcos, Tex., July 15, 1939; s. Harry Edward and Joyce Majorie (Barrett) R.; m. Elizabeth Macey Hodges, Apr. 15,1963; children: Barrett Hodges, Elizabeth Macey. B.A. summa cum laude, Rice U., 1960; J.D. with highest honors, U. Tex., 1962; postgrad., U. London, 1962-63. Bar: Tex., D.C., N.Y. Law clk. U.S. Ct. Appeals, 2d Cir., 1963-64; asso. firm Vinson & Elkins, Houston, 1964-69; partner Vinson & Elkins, 1970—, mem. mgmt. com., 1976—; dir. 1st City Nat. Bank of Houston; vis. prof. U. Tex. Sch. Law, 1971, Rice U., 1976, U. Houston Sch. Law, 1977. Author: (with Charles Alan Wright) Procedure: The Handmaid of Justice, 1965. Trustee U. Tex. Law Sch. Found., 1980—, Mus. Fine Arts, Houston, 1982-84. Rotary Found. fellow, 1962-63. Fellow Am. Coll. Trial Lawyers, Internat. Acad. Trial Lawyers, ABA Found., Tex. Bar Found.; mem. Houston Bar Assn. (trustee 1982-83), Assn. of Bar of City of N.Y., ABA (council antitrust sect. 1982—), Am. Law Inst., Chancellors, Houston Com. Fgn. Relations, Internat. Soc. of Barristers, Houston Philos. Soc., Soc. Performing Arts (bd. dirs. 1982—), Order of Coif, Phi Beta Kappa, Delta Phi Alpha, Phi Delta Phi. Democrat. Baptist. Clubs: Houston Country, Rotary, Ramada; Cosmos (Washington). Antitrust, Federal civil litigation, State civil litigation. Home: 2312 Rice Blvd Houston TX 77005 Office: 3000 First City Tower 1001 Fannin Houston TX 77002-6760

REATH, GEORGE, JR., lawyer; b. Phila. Mar. 14, 1939; s. George and Isabel Duer (West) R.; m. Viki Buchsbaum Reath, Feb. 9, 1966; children—Eric, Amanda. B.A., Williams Coll., 1961; LL.B., Harvard U., 1964. Bar: Pa. 1965, U.S. Dist. Ct. (ea. dist.) Pa. 1965. Assoc. Dechert Price & Rhoads, Phila. 1964-70, Brussels 1971-74; atty. Pennwalt Corp., Phila. 1974-78, mgr. legal dept., asst. sec. 1978-87, sr. v.p., legal sec., 1987—. Bd. mgrs. Children's Hosp. Phila. 1974—, sec. 1980-81, vice chmn., 1984—; bd. mgrs. Phila. City Inst. Library 1974—, treas. 1981—. Served with Pa. Army N.G., 1964-70. Mem. ABA, Pa. Bar Assn., Phila. Bar Assn., Am. Soc. Corp. Secs., Phi Beta Kappa. Clubs: Racquet (Phila.); Winter Harbor (Maine) Yacht. General corporate, Contracts commercial. Office: Pennwalt Corporation 3 Parkway Philadelphia PA 19102

REAVES, CRAIG CHARLES, lawyer, educator; b. Pickstown, S.D., May 28, 1952; s. Charles William and Yvonne JoAnn (Ericson) R.; m. Val Gulbranson, Dec. 28, 1971; children: Nathan, Aaron. BA in Bus. and Polit. Sci., U. Kans., 1975, JD, 1978; cert. fin. cons., Am. Coll., Bryn Mawr, Pa., 1984. Bar: Kans. 1978, U.S. Dist. Ct. Kans. 1978, Mo. 1980, U.S. Dist. Ct. (we. dist.) Mo. 1980, U.S. Tax Ct. 1984; CLU. Counsel, agt., mgr., dir. mktg. John Hancock Life Ins. Co., Kansas City, Mo., 1972-80; officer, instr., cons. Creative Cons., Inc., Overland Park, Mo., 1979—; sole practice Kansas City, 1980-84; shareholder, officer, bd. dirs. Crews, Smart, South, Whitehead,

Reaves & Waits P.C., Kansas City, 1984—. Committeeperson Planned Giving, 1980-81; dir. Kansas City Fellowship of Christian Athletes, 1979-86, chmn. bd. dirs., 1982-85; com. chmn. Kansas City Arts Festival, 1985. Mem. CLU Assn. (instr. 1980—, com. chmn. 1985—), Phi Alpha Delta, Delta Sigma Pi (sec. 1974-75). Republican. Presbyterian. Estate planning, Estate taxation, Contracts commercial. Office: Crews Smart South Whitehead et al 401 W 89th St Kansas City MO 64114

REAVLEY, THOMAS MORROW, lawyer, judge; b. Quitman, Tex., June 21, 1921; s. Thomas Mark and Mattie (Morrow) R.; m. Florence Montgomery Wilson, July 24, 1943; children—Thomas Wilson, Marian, Paul Stuart, Margaret. B.A., U. Tex., 1942; J.D., Harvard, 1948; LL.D., Austin Coll., 1974, Southwestern U., 1977, Tex. Wesleyan, 1982; LL.M., U. Va., 1983. Bar: Tex. bar 1948. Asst. dist. atty. Dallas, 1948-49; mem. firm Bell & Reavley, Nacogdoches, Tex., 1949-51; county atty. Nacogdoches, 1951; mem. firm Fisher, Tonahill & Reavley, Jasper, Tex., 1952-55; sec. state Tex. 1955-57; mem. firm Powell, Rauhut, McGinnis & Reavley, Austin, Tex., 1957-64; dist. judge Austin, 1964-68; justice Supreme Ct., Tex., 1968-77; judge U.S. Ct. Appeals, 5th Circuit, Austin, 1979—; pres. Tex. Jud. Council, 1971-76; lectr. Baylor U. Law Sch., 1976—; adj. prof. U. Tex. Law Sch., 1958-59, 78-79. Chancellor Southwest Tex. conf. United Methodist Ch., 1972—; Bd. dirs. Southwestern U., Georgetown, Tex.; pres. Meth. Home, Waco, Tex. Served to lt. USNR, 1943-45. Club: Mason (33 deg.). Jurisprudence. Home: 1312 Meriden Ln Austin TX 78703 Office: Court of Appeals 740 MBank Tower 221 W 6th St Austin TX 78701 *

REBACK, JOYCE ELLEN, lawyer; b. Phila., July 11, 1948; s. William and Sue (Goldstein) R.; m. Itzhak Brook, Aug. 2, 1981; children: Jonathan Zev, Sara Jennie. BA, Brown U., 1970; JD, George Washington U., 1976. Bar: D.C. 1976, U.S. Dist. Ct. D.C. 1976, U.S. Ct. Appeals (D.C. cir.) 1976. Assoc. Fulbright & Jaworski, Washington, 1976-84, ptnr., 1984—. Contbr. articles to profl. jours. Mem. ABA, Women's Bar Assn. D.C. Federal civil litigation, Labor, Education law. Office: Fulbright & Jaworski 1150 Connecticut Ave NW Washington DC 20036

REBACK, RICHARD NEAL, lawyer; b. Knoxville, Tenn., Feb. 9, 1954; s. Theodore and Delores (Robinson) R. BA magna cum laude, Duke U., 1976; JD with honors, U. Tex., 1979. Bar: Tex. 1980, U.S. Ct. Appeals (5th cir.) 1980, D.C. 1981, U.S. Ct. Appeals (D.C. cir.). Law clk. to assoc. judge U.S. Ct. Appeals (5th cir.), Austin, Tex., 1979-80; assoc. Wilmer, Cutler & Pickering, Washington, 1981-83, Swidler & Berlin, Washington, 1984—; Mem. Ballston Ptnrship., Arlington, Va., 1986—. Note editor: Tex. Law Rev., 1978-79. Mem. Ballston-Va. Square Civic Assn., Arlington, 1985—, Am. Israel Pub. Affairs Com., Washington, 1984—; active ACLU; pres. Vernon Sq. Assn., Arlington, 1986. Mem. ABA, D.C. Bar Assn., Tex. Bar Assn., Pi Sigma Alpha, Phi Eta Sigma. Democrat. Jewish. Avocations: athletics, civic and polit. activities. Federal civil litigation, State civil litigation, Administrative and regulatory. Home: 1192 N Vermont St Arlington VA 22201 Office: Swidler & Berlin 1000 Thomas Jefferson St Washington DC 20007

REBANE, JOHN T., lawyer; b. Bamberg, Germany, Oct. 29, 1946; s. Henn and Anna (Inna) R.; m. Linda Kay Morgan, Sept. 22, 1972; children: Alexis Morgan, Morgan James. BA, U. Minn., 1970, JD, 1973. Bar: Minn. 1973. Atty. Land O'Lakes, Inc., Arden Hills, Minn., 1973-80, assoc. gen counsel, 1980-83, v.p., gen. counsel, 1984—. Bd. dirs. Kenwood Isles Area Assn., Mpls., 1982-84, East Calhoun Community Orgn, Mpls., 1976-78. Served with AUS, 1968-70, Vietnam. Mem. Minn. Bar Assn., Hennepin County Bar Assn., Nat. Consel Farm Corp. General corporate, Contracts commercial, Mergers and acquisitions. Office: Land O Lakes Inc 4001 Lexington Ave N Arden Hills MN 55112

REBARCHAK, JAMES, lawyer; b. Pitts., Apr. 24, 1955; s. Thomas John and Faye (Vance) R.; m. Doro Phister, Oct. 8, 1983; 1 child, Louisa Vance. BS in Psychology, Spring Hill Coll., 1977; JD, U. Ala., 1982. Bar: Ala. 1982, U.S. Ct. Appeals (11th cir.) 1982, U.S. Supreme Ct. 1985. Asst. atty. gen. State of Ala., Montgomery, 1982—. Criminal, Personal injury, State civil litigation. Home: 3175 Thomas Ave Montgomery AL 36106 Office: Office of Atty Gen 11 S Union St Montgomery AL 36130

RECORD, RICHARD FRANKLIN, JR., lawyer; b. Mattoon, Ill., Dec. 20, 1937; s. Richard F. and Marian (Rogers) R.; m. Jacqueline C. Cooper, Apr. 2, 1961; children—Alexandra C., Jacqueline R. B.S. in Fgn. Service, Georgetown U., 1959; LL.B., George Washington U., 1963. Bar: Ill. 1963, D.C. 1964. Assoc. Craig & Craig, Mattoon, Ill., 1963-65, ptnr., 1966—. Contbr. writings to legal publs. Precinct committeeman Democratic Party. Fellow Am. Coll. Trial Lawyers; mem. Ill. Bar Assn. (mem. council sect. civil practice and procedure 1971-75, mem. adv. council Ill. Inst. Continuing Legal Edn. 1974-77), Appellate Lawyers Assn. (pres. 1979-80), Ill. Def. Counsel, Soc. Trial Lawyers, Nat. Assn. R.R. Trial Counsel, Coles-Cumberland County Bar Assn. (pres. 1982-83). Episcopalian. Clubs: Mattoon Golf and Country, Chgo. Athletic Assn. State civil litigation, Federal civil litigation. Home: PO Box 333 Mattoon IL 61938 Office: Craig & Craig 1807 Broadway PO Box 689 Mattoon IL 61938

RECTOR, JOEL KIRK, lawyer; b. Moberly, Mo., Nov. 6, 1948; s. Hartman Jr. and Constance (Daniel) R.; m. Jannifer Nielsen, Apr. 3, 1972; children: Molly, Constance, Donna. BA, Brigham Young U., 1974, MBA, 1977, JD, 1978; M in Pub. Adminstrn., Harvard U., 1985. Bar: Utah 1978, U.S. Dist. Ct. Utah 1978. Assoc. Beaslin, Nygaard, Coke & Vincent, Salt Lake City, 1978-79, Walker & Hintze, Salt Lake City, 1979-80; sole practice Salt Lake City, 1980—. State legislator, Utah Ho. Reps., Salt Lake City, 1981-84, chmn. judiciary com. and speaker of 3d House, 1983-84; co-chmn. Utah Rep. Platform Com., 1983; chmn. Utah Rep. Rules Com., 1984. Serves as capt. USAR, 1974—. Mem. Utah Gov.'s Club (bd. govs. 1985—). Mormon. General corporate. Home and Office: 5041 S Boabab Dr Salt Lake City UT 84117

RECTOR, LEO DANIEL, lawyer; b. Colorado Springs, Colo., July 4, 1951; s. Leo Wesley and Dawn Arlene Rector; m. Elizabeth Ann Sirles, Jan. 3, 1970 (div. Dec. 1974); m. Terri Lynn Palmer, Oct. 28, 1978; children—Travis, John, Jennifer. B.S., U. Colo.-Boulder, 1973; J.D., Washburn U., 1975. Bar: Colo. 1976, Kans. 1976, U.S. Dist. Ct. Colo. 1976, U.S. Dist. Ct. Kans. 1976, U.S. Ct. Appeals (10th cir.) 1978, U.S. Supreme Ct. 1980. Ptnr. Rector, Retherford, Mullen & Johnson, Colorado Springs, Colo., 1976—; instr. Pikes Peak Community Coll., Colorado Springs, 1980—. Host: (TV show) Standoff. Quiz master U. Colo. Trivia Bowl, Boulder, 1977—. Mem. Def. Research Inst., Am. Arbitartion Assn. (arbitrator), ABA, Colo. Trial Lawyers. Democrat. Lutheran. Personal injury, Insurance, Federal civil litigation. Home: 1010 Zodiac Dr Colorado Springs CO 80906 Office: Rector Retherford Mullen & Johnson 415 S Sahwatch Ave PO Box 1580 Colorado Springs CO 80903

REDD, CHARLES APPLETON, lawyer; b. Quincy, Ill., Aug. 13, 1954; s. Charles Lambert and Julia (Harrell) R.; m. Susan Backer, June 2, 1978; children: Elizabeth Appleton, Christopher O'Leary, Thomas Charles. BA, St. Louis U., 1976, JD, 1979. Bar: Wis. 1979, U.S. Dist. Ct. (ea. and we. dists.) Wis. 1979, Mo. 1980. Trust adminstr. First Wis. Trust Co., Milw., 1979-80; asst. counsel Centerre Trust Co. of St. Louis, 1980-83; assoc. Armstrong, Teasdale, Kramer, Vaughan & Schlafly, St. Louis, 1983-85, ptnr., 1986—. Mem. ABA, Wis. Bar Assn., Mo. Bar Assn. (council member probate and trust sect.), Bar Assn. Met. St. Louis. Mem. Anglican Ch. Probate, Estate taxation, Estate planning. Home: 7535 Stanford Ave University City MO 63130-3923 Office: Armstrong Teasdale Kramer et al 611 Olive St Suite 1900 Saint Louis MO 63101-1782

REDDEN, JAMES ANTHONY, federal judge; b. Springfield, Mass., Mar. 13, 1929; s. James A. and Alma (Cheek) R.; m. Joan Ida Johnson, July 13, 1950; children: James A., William F. Student, Boston U., 1951; LL.B., Boston Coll., 1954. Bar: Oreg. bar 1955. Since practiced in Medford; mem. firm Collins, Redden, Ferris & Velure, 1957-73; dist. judge pro-tem 1958; treas. State of Oreg., 1973-77; atty. gen. 1977-80, U.S. dist. judge, 1980—. Chmn. Oreg. Pub. Employee Relations Bd.; mem. Oreg. Automobile Ins. Adv. Com.; Mem. Oreg. Ho. of Reps., 1963-69, minority leader, 1967-69. Served with AUS, 1946-48. Mem. Am., Mass. bar assns., Oreg. State Bar, Oreg. Assn. Def. Counsel. Democrat. Lodge: KC. Office: 612 US Courthouse 620 SW Main St Portland OR 97205

REDDEN, JOE WINSTON, JR., lawyer; b. Houston, Jan. 24, 1951; s. Joe Winston and Katherine Louise (Fickessen) R.; m. Kathleen Rae Heap, July 29, 1972; children: Rebecca Kay, Forrest Winston II. BA, Tex. Christian U., 1972; JD, U. Tex., 1975. Bar: U.S. Dist. Ct. (so. and ea. dists.) Tex., U.S. Ct. Appeals (5th cir.). Assoc. Fulbright & Jaworski, Houston, 1975—. Fellow Tex. Bar Found.; mem. ABA, Tex. Bar Assn., Order of Coif, Chancellors, Phi Beta Kappa, Phi Delta Phi. State civil litigation, Federal civil litigation, Personal injury. Home: 5517 Cedar Creek Houston TX 77056 Office: Fulbright & Jaworski 1301 McKinney Houston TX 77010

REDDEN, LAWRENCE DREW, lawyer; b. Tallassee, Ala., Dec. 16, 1922; s. A. Drew and Berta (Baker) R.; m. Christine U. Cunningham, Dec. 20, 1943. A.B., U. Ala., 1943, LL.B., 1949. Bar: Ala. bar 1949. Since practiced in Birmingham; asst. U.S. atty. No. Dist. Ala., 1949-52; partner firm Rogers, Howard, Redden & Mills, 1952-79, Redden, Mills & Clark, 1979—; Civilian aide for Ala. to sec. army 1965-69; Mem. Ala. Democratic Exec. Com., 1966-74. Editor-in-chief: Ala. Law Rev, 1948. Trustee Ala. Law Sch. Found.; adv. council Cumberland Law Sch. Served with AUS, 1943-46; maj. gen. Res. ret. Decorated D.S.M.; recipient Outstanding Civilian Service medal Dept. Army, 1970. Fellow Am. Coll. Trial Lawyers; mem. Internat. Soc. Barristers, Am. Judicature Soc., ABA, Ala. Bar Assn. (pres. 1972-73), Birmingham Bar Assn. (past pres.), Ala. Law Inst. (mem. council), U. Ala. Law Sch. Alumni Assn. (past pres.), Phi Beta Kappa, Alpha Tau Omega, Omicron Delta Kappa. Baptist. Criminal, Federal civil litigation, State civil litigation. Home: 2513 Beaumont Circle Birmingham AL 35216

REDDEN, MICHAEL ALOYSIUS, lawyer; b. Chgo., May 12, 1953; s. John Joseph and Charlette (Schwelm) R.; m. Margi J. Costello, Sept. 18, 1982; 1 child, Katherine. BA, Reed Coll., 1976; JD, Lewis & Clark U., 1980. Bar: Oreg. 1980, U.S. Tax Ct. 1981, U.S. Dist. Ct. Oreg. 1986. Tax cons. Buetelschies and Assocs., Portland, 1980-82; sole practice Portland, 1982-83; ptnr. Redden, McGaughey, Yugler & Jack, Portland, 1983-86; of counsel O'Donnell, Ramis, Elliott & Crew, Portland, 1986—; prof. City University, Portland, 1983-85. Bd. dirs. Keith Martin Ballet, Portland, 1982-86, Storefront Actors Theatre, Portland, 1984-86, Northwest Film Studies Ctr., Portland, 1986—. Mem. ABA, Oreg. Bar Assn., Multnomah Bar Assn., Reed Coll. Alumni Assn. (pres. 1986—), YMCA. Roman Catholic. Avocations: bridge, golf, theatre, literature. Personal income taxation, Entertainment, Corporate taxation. Home: 3435 NE 22d Portland OR 97209 Office: O'Donnell Ramis Elliott & Crew 1727 NW Hoyt Portland OR 97209

REDDEN, ROGER DUFFEY, lawyer; b. Washington, Dec. 19, 1932; s. Layman J. and Elizabeth (Duffey) R.; m. Gretchen Sause, July 14, 1962. A.B., Yale Coll., 1954; LL.B., U. Md., 1957. Bar: Md. 1958, U.S. Dist. Ct. Md. 1958, U.S. Ct. Appeals (4th cir.) 1958, U.S. Supreme Ct. 1965. Law clk. to judge U.S. Ct. Appeals (4th cir.), 1957-58; assoc. Smith, Somerville & Case, Balt., 1959-63, ptnr., 1965-68; asst. atty. gen. State of Md., 1964-65; ptnr. Piper & Marbury, Balt., 1969—; draftsman Md. State Dept. Legis Reference, 1958; counsel Md. Savs. and Loan Study Commn., 1960-61; mem. Gov.'s Commn. to revise testamentary laws of Md., 1965-70; mem. standing com. on rules of practice and procedure Md. Ct. Appeals, 1969-73; mem. Gov.'s Commn. to revise annotated code of Md., 1970—, Appellate Jud. Nominating Commn., 1975-79, Commn. to study Md. Tax Ct., 1978-79; chmn. Task Force on Permits Simplification, 1979-81; dir. Peoples Water Service Co. Editor-in-chief Md. Law Rev., 1956-57; contbr. articles to legal jours. Served with U.S. Army, 1958-59, 61-62. Fellow Am. Bar Found., Md. Bar Found.; mem. Md. State Bar Assn. (chmn. probate and estate law sect. 1966-68, chmn. long range planning com. 1972-73, various coms., council sect. adminstrv. law 1980-82, council sect. corps., banking and bus. law 1978-81), Balt. City Bar Assn. (chmn. com. on continuing legal edn. 1976-77, chmn. com. on judiciary 1978-79, chmn. com. on by-laws 1981-82), ABA, Jud. Conf. U.S. Ct. Appeals for 4th Cir. (conf. study com. 1982-83). Democrat. Episcopalian. General practice, Municipal bonds, Administrative and regulatory. Office: 1100 Charles Center S 36 S Charles St Baltimore MD 21201

REDDER, THOMAS JOSEPH, lawyer, judge; b. Marshall, Minn., June 18, 1955; s. Lester J. and Ardell S. (Hentges) R. BA, Colo. State U., 1978; JD, U. Colo., 1981. Bar: Colo. 1981, U.S. Dist. Ct. Colo. 1981, U.S. Ct. Appeals (10th cir.) 1982, U.S. Supreme Ct. 1985. Sole practice Fort Collins, Colo., 1981—; mcpl. judge Wellington, Colo., 1983—, Timnath, Colo., 1985—. Mem. advance staff White House, Washington, 1977, 78, 80; staff asst. U.S. Senator Daniel Patrick Moynihan, Washington, 1977. Mem. ABA, Colo. Bar Assn., Larimer County Bar Assn. Democrat. Roman Catholic. General practice, State civil litigation, Criminal. Home: PO Box 9626 Fort Collins CO 80525 Office: Savings Bldg 5th Floor 125 S Howes St Fort Collins CO 80521

REDDIEN, CHARLES HENRY, JR., lawyer, business executive, securities financial consultant; b. San Diego, Aug. 27, 1944; s. Charles Henry and Betty Jane (McCormick) R.; m. 2d, Paula Gayle, June 16, 1974; 1 son, Tyler Charles. B.S.E.E., U. Colo.-Boulder, 1966; M.S.E.E., U. So. Calif., 1968; J.D., Loyola U., Los Angeles, 1972. Bar: Calif. 1972, Colo. 1981, U.S. Dist. Ct. 1981. Mgr., Hughes Aircraft Co., 1966-81; sole practice law, 1972—; owner, broker, real estate brokerage firm, 1978—; mem. spl. staff, co-dir. tax advantage group OTC Net Inc., 1981-82; pres., chmn. Heritage Group Inc., investment banking holding co., 1982-84, Plans and Assistance Inc., mgmt. cons., 1982-83, Orchard Group Ltd., investment banking holding co., 1982-84, J.W. Gant & Assocs., Inc., investment bankers, 1983-84; mng. ptnr., chief exec. officer J.W. Gant & Assocs., Ltd., 1984-85; chmn. bd. Kalamath Group Ltd., 1985-86, Heritage group Ltd. Investment Bankers, 1985—; dir. Virtusonics Corp., 1985—; v.p., dir. Heritage Fin. Planners Inc., 1982-83; pres., chmn. PDN Western Region Inc., 1987—; Recipient Teaching Internship award, 1964. Mem. Calif. Bar Assn., Nat. Assn. Securities Dealers, IEEE (chmn. U. Colo. chpt. 1965), Am. Inst. Aero. and Astronautical Engrs., Phi Alpha Delta, Tau Beta Pi, Eta Kappa Nu. Contbr. articles to profl. jours. General corporate. Office: Harlequin Plaza S 7600 E Orchard Rd Suite 160 Englewood CO 80111

REDDIS, FRANCES ELAINE, lawyer; b. Kansas City, Kans., Oct. 19, 1952; d. Frank Ellis and Margaret Elsbeth (Jamieson) Stoker; m. John Joseph Reddis, Aug. 17, 1973. AA, Johnson County Community Coll., 1972; BSBA, Rockhurst Coll., 1974; JD, U. Mo., Kansas City, 1978. Bar: Mo. 1978, U.S. Dist. Ct. (we. dist.) Mo. 1978. Credit analyst Columbia Union Nat. Bank, Kansas City, 1974-75; law clk. to presiding justice Johnson County Dist. Ct., Olathe, Kans., 1977; asst. regional counsel HHS, Kansas City, 1978—. Staff mem. U. Mo. Law Rev. Mem. ABA, Mo. Bar Assn. U.S. Government/Dept. Health and Human Services. Home: 12516 Holmes Rd Kansas City MO 64145 Office: HHS 601 E 12th St Room 535 Kansas City MO 64106

REDISH, MARTIN HARRIS, legal educator; b. Lynbrook, N.Y., Aug. 16, 1945; m. Caren Beverly Redish, June 22, 1969; 1 dau., Jessica. A.B., U. Pa., 1967; J.D. magna cum laude, Harvard U., 1970. Bar: N.Y. 1971, U.S. Dist. Ct. (so. dist.) N.Y. 1971, U.S. Ct. Appeals (2d cir.) 1971, U.S. Ct. Appeals (7th cir.) 1973. Law clk. to presiding justice U.S. Ct. Appeals (2d cir.), 1970-71; assoc. Proskauer, Rose, Goetz & Mendelsohn, N.Y.C., 1971-73; prof. law Northwestern U. Sch. Law, Chgo., 1973—; vis. assoc. prof. law Cornell U., 1977, Stanford U., 1977; mem. 7th Cir. Rules Adv. Com.; cons. U.S. Senate Jud. Com. Mem. Am. Coll. Trial Lawyers (reporter Project on Complex Civil Litigation). Author: Federal Jurisdiction: Tensions in the Allocation of Judicial Power, 1980; Federal Courts: Cases, Comments and Questions, 1983; Freedom of Expression: A Critical Analysis, 1984; contbr. articles to profl. jours. Federal civil litigation. Office: Northwestern U Sch Law 357 E Chicago Ave Chicago IL 60611 *

REDLICH, MARC, lawyer; b. N.Y.C., Nov. 25, 1946; s. Louis and Mollie Redlich; m. Janis Redlich, Jan. 16, 1982; 1 child, Alison. B.A., Queens Coll., 1967; J.D., Harvard U., 1971. Bar: Mass. 1971, U.S. Dist. Ct. 1971, U.S. Ct. Appeals (1st cir.) 1974, U.S. Ct. Appeals (5th cir.) 1984. Assoc. Guterman, Horvitz, Rubin & Rudman, Boston, 1971-75; mem., sr. dir. Widett, Slater & Goldman, Boston, 1975-84; prin. Law Offices of Marc Redlich, Cambridge, Mass., 1984—. Mem. ABA, Mass. Bar Assn., Boston Bar Assn., Assn. Trial Lawyers Am., Nat. Assn. Coll. Univ. Attys., Cambridge C. of C., Phi Beta Kappa. Club: Harvard (Boston). General practice, Federal civil litigation, General corporate. Office: 1000 Massachusetts Ave Cambridge MA 02138

REDLICH, NORMAN, lawyer, university dean; b. N.Y.C., Nov. 12, 1925; s. Milton and Pauline (Durst) R.; m. Evelyn Jane Grobow, June 3, 1951; children: Margaret Bonny-Claire, Carrie Ann, Edward Grobow. A.B., Williams Coll., 1947, LL.D. (hon.), 1976; LL.B., Yale U., 1950; LL.M., NYU, 1955. Bar: N.Y. 1951. Practiced in N.Y.C., 1951-59; assoc. prof. law NYU, 1960-62, prof. law, 1962-74, assoc. dean Sch. Law, 1974-75, dean Sch. Law, 1975—; editor-in-chief Tax Law Rev., 1960-66; mem. adv. com. Inst. Fed. Taxation, 1963-68; exec. asst. corp. counsel, N.Y.C., 1966-68, 1st asst. corp. counsel, 1970-72, corp. counsel, 1972-74; asst. counsel Pres. Commn. on Assassination Pres. Kennedy, 1963-64; chmn. com. on admissions and grievances U.S. 2d Circuit Ct. Appeals, 1978—. Author: Professional Responsibility: A Problem Approach, 1976, Constitutional Law, Cases and Materials, 1981, also articles in field. Chmn. commn. on law and social action Am. Jewish Congress, 1978—; mem. Borough Pres.'s Planning Bd. Number 2, 1959-70, counsel N.Y. Com. to Abolish Capital Punishment, 1958-77; Mem. N.Y.C. Bd. Edn., 1969; Mem. bd. overseers Jewish Theol. Sem., 1973—; trustee Law Center Found. of N.Y. U., 1975—, Freedom House, 1976—, Vt. Law Sch., 1977—, Practising Law Inst., 1980—; trustee Lawyers Com. for Civil Rights Under Law, 1976—, co-chmn., 1979-81; co-chmn. Legal Aid Soc., 1983—. Served with AUS, 1943-45. Decorated Combat Infantryman's Badge. Mem. Assn. Bar City N.Y. (exec. com. 1975-79). Office: NYU School of Law Washington Suare New York NY 10003 *

REDMAN, CLARENCE OWEN, lawyer; b. Joliet, Ill., Nov. 23, 1942; s. Harold F. and Edith L. (Read) R.; m. Barbara Ann Pawlan, Jan. 26, 1964 (div.); children—Scott, Steven; m. 2d, Carla J. Rozycki, Sept. 24, 1983. B.S., U. Ill., 1964, J.D., 1966, M.A., 1967. Bar: Ill. 1966, U.S. Dist. Ct. (ea. dist.) Ill. 1966, U.S. Dist. Ct. (no. dist.) Ill. 1970, U.S. Ct. Appeals (7th cir.), 1973, U.S. Ct. Appeals (4th cir.) 1982, U.S. Supreme Ct. 1975. Assoc., Keck, Mahin & Cate, Chgo., 1969-73, ptnr., 1973—, chief exec. officer, 1986—; spl. asst. atty. gen. Ill., 1975-81. Served to capt. U.S. Army, 1967-69. Decorated Bronze Star. Mem. Ill. State Bar Assn. (chmn. young lawyers sect. 1977-78, del. assembly 1978-81, 84—), Chgo. Bar Assn., ABA, Seventh Cir. Bar Assn. Republican. Clubs: Union League, Met. (Chgo.): Am. Legion (Roselle, Ill.). General corporate, Federal civil litigation, Labor. Office: 8300 Sears Tower 233 S Wacker Dr Chicago IL 60606

REDMAN, ERIC, lawyer; b. Palo Alto, Calif., June 3, 1948; s. M. Chandler and Marjorie Jane (Sachs) R.; m. Anne Mygatt Mueller, June 19, 1971; children: Ian Michael, Graham James. AB, Harvard U., 1970, JD, 1975; BA, Oxford U., 1972, MA, 1980. Bar: Wash. 1975, U.S. Dist. Ct. (we. dist.) Wash. 1975, D.C. 1979, U.S. Ct. Appeals (9th cir.) 1981, U.S. Supreme Ct. 1983. Asst. U.S. senator W.G. Magnuson, Washington and Seattle, 1968-71, 74-75; assoc. Preston, Thorgrimson et al, Seattle, 1975-78, ptnr., 1979-82; ptnr. Heller, Ehrman, White & McAuliffe, Seattle, 1983—. Author: Dance of Legislation, 1973; also book revs., articles. Administrative and regulatory, Public utilities, FERC practice. Office: Heller Ehrman White & McAuliffe 999 3d Ave Seattle WA 98104

REDMOND, DAVID DUDLEY, lawyer; b. Hartford, Conn., May 12, 1944; s. Robert LaVere and Dorothy Iva (Mylchreest) R.; m. Eugenia Blount Scott, Aug. 24, 1968; children—R. Scott, Sarah D. B.A., Washington and Lee U., 1966, LL.B., 1969. Bar: Va. 1970, U.S. Dist. Ct. (ea. dist.) Va. 1972, U.S. Ct. Appeals (4th cir.) 1972. Ptnr. Christian Barton Epps Brent & Chappell, Richmond, Va., 1972—. Served to capt. U.S. Army, 1970-71. Decorated Bronze Star. Mem. ABA, Va. State Bar, Va. Bar Assn., Richmond Bar Assn. (exec. com. 1980), Washington and Lee U. Alumni Assn. (pres. Richmond chpt. 1980-82), Omicron Delta Kappa. Editorial bd. Washington and Lee U. Law Rev., 1968-69. Real property, General corporate. Office: Suite 1200 Mutual Bldg Richmond VA 23219

REDMOND, RICHARD ANTHONY, lawyer; b. Chgo., Oct. 4, 1947; s. Richard Aloysius and Mary Jane (Berger) R.; m. Merrilee Clark, May 5, 1984; 1 child, Richard William. BA, U. Notre Dame, 1969; JD, Cornell U., 1972. Bar: Ill. 1972, U.S. Dist. Ct. (no. dist.) Ill. 1972, U.S. Ct. Appeals (7th cir.) 1975, U.S. Supreme Ct. 1976. Assoc. Freeman & Tingler, Chgo., 1972-75; from assoc. to ptnr. Kennedy, Golan & Morris, Chgo., 1975-81; ptnr. Walsh, Case, Coale & Brown, Chgo., 1981—; mem. com. on profl. responsibility Ill. Supreme Ct., 1983—. Trustee Chgo. Acad. Sci., 1986—. Mem. ABA, Chgo. Bar Assn. (chmn. eminent domain subcom. 1982—). Roman Catholic. Club: Chgo. Athletic. Avocations: mountain climbing, hiking, skiing. Condemnation, Federal civil litigation, State civil litigation. Office: Walsh Case Coale & Brown 2500 Prudential Plaza Chicago IL 60601

REDMOND, ROBERT, lawyer, legal educator; b. Astoria, N.Y., June 18, 1934; s. George and Virginia (Greene) R.; m. Georgine Marie Richardson, May 21, 1966; children—Kelly Anne, Kimberly Marie, Christopher Robert. B.A., Queens Coll., 1955; M.Pub.Adminstrn., CUNY, 1962; J.D., Georgetown U., 1970. Bar: D.C. 1971, Va. 1974, U.S. Supreme Ct. 1974. Commd. 2d lt. U.S. Air Force, 1955, advanced through grades to lt. col., 1972, ret., 1978; served as spl. investigations officer, Korea, Vietnam, W.Ger.; adj. prof. Park Coll., Parkville, Mo., 1977—; sole practice, Vienna, Va., 1980—. Precinct capt. Fairfax County Republican Party (Va.), 1981—; pres. PTO, Falls Church, Va., 1984-86; treas. Fedn. Cath. Schs. PTO, 1986—. Mem. Assn. Trial Lawyers Am., Va. Trial Lawyers Assn., Assn. Former Air Force Office of Spl. Investigations Agts. (chpt. pres. 1984—, nat. membership com. 1986—), Delta Theta Phi. Roman Catholic. Lodge: K.C. (4th deg.). General practice, Personal injury, Consumer commercial. Home: 7802 Antiopi St Annandale VA 22003 Office: 7799 Leesburg Pike Suite 900 Falls Church VA 22043

REDPATH, JOHN S(LONEKER), JR., lawyer, cable television company executive. B.A., Princeton U., 1966; J.D., U. Mich., 1973; LL.M., NYU, 1978. Bar: U.S. Dist. Ct. (so. dist.) N.Y. 1975. Assoc. Dewey, Ballantine, Bushby, Palmer & Wood, N.Y.C., 1974-78; assoc. counsel film programming Home Box Office, Inc., N.Y.C., 1978-79, chief counsel programming, 1979-80, asst. gen. counsel, 1980-81, v.p., gen. counsel, 1981-83, sr. v.p., gen. counsel, 1983—. Served to lt. USNR, 1966-69. Mem. ABA, N.Y. State Bar Assn., Assn. Bar City N.Y. Communications. Office: Home Box Office Inc 1100 Ave of Americas New York NY 10036

REDSTONE, SUMNER MURRAY, theatre executive, lawyer; b. Boston, May 27, 1923; s. Michael and Belle (Ostrovsky) R.; m. Phyllis Gloria Raphael, July 6, 1947; children—Brent Dale, Shari Ellin. B.A., Harvard U., 1944, LL.B., 1947. Bar: Mass. 1947, U.S. Ct. Appeals (1st cir.) 1948, U.S. Ct. Appeals (8th cir.) 1950, U.S. Ct. Appeals (9th cir.) 1948, D.C. 1951, U.S. Supreme Ct. 1952. Law sec. U.S. Ct. Appeals for 9th Circuit, San Francisco, 1947-48; instr. law and labor mgmt. U. San Francisco, 1947; spl. asst. to U.S. atty. gen., Washington, 1948-51; partner firm Ford, Bergson, Adams, Borkland & Redstone, Washington, 1951-54; exec. v.p. NE Drive-In Theatre Corp., Boston, 1954-67; pres. NE Theatre Corp., 1967—; prof. Boston U. Law Sch., 1982, 85-86; bd. dirs. ACE Prodns. Inc. Chmn. met. div. NE Combined Jewish Philanthropies, Boston, 1963; mem. corp. New Eng. Med. Center, 1967—; trustee Children's Cancer Research Found.; chmn. Am. Cancer Crusade, State of Mass., 1984-86; Art Lending Library; sponsor Boston Mus. Sci.; chmn. Jimmy Fund Found., 1960; v.p., mem. exec. com. Will Rogers Meml. Fund; bd. dirs. Boston Arts Festival; bd. overseers Dana Farber Cancer Center, Boston Mus. Fine Arts; mem. presdl. adv. com. on arts John F. Kennedy Center for Performing Arts; bd. dirs. John F. Kennedy Library Found. Served to 1st lt. AUS, 1943-45. Decorated Army Commendation medal; recipient William J. German Human Relations award Am. Jewish Com. Entertainment and Communication Div., 1977, Silver Shingle award Boston U. Law Sch., 1985; named one of ten outstanding young men Greater Boston C. of C., 1958, Communicator of Yr. B'nai B'rith Communications/Cinema Lodge, 1980. Mem. Am. Congress Exhibitors (exec. com. 1961—), Theatre Owners Am. (asst. pres. 1960-63, pres. 1964-65), Nat. Assn. Theatre Owners (chmn. bd. dirs. 1965-66), Motion Picture Pioneers (bd. dirs.), Am., Boston, Mass. bar assns., Harvard Law Sch. Assn., Am. Judicature Soc. Clubs: Mason, University, Variety New Eng., Harvard (Boston). Home: 98 Baldpate Hill Rd Newton Centre MA 02159 Office: 200 Elm St Dedham MA 02026

REED, BRIAN EDWARD, lawyer; b. Sidney, Nebr., Jan. 3, 1955; s. Roy Edward and Allyn Dee (Whitmire) R.; m. Jackie Lynn Jones, July 25, 1976; children: Brianne Lynn, Nicole DeAnne. BA, San Diego State U., 1977; JD, U. San Diego, 1980. Bar: Calif. 1980, U.S. Dist. Ct. (so. dist.) Calif. 1980, U.S. Dist. Ct. (cen. dist.) Calif. 1982, U.S. Dist. Ct. (ea. dist.) Calif. 1986. Assoc. Thacher & Hurst, El Cajon, Calif., 1980, Potter & Eberhardt, Lancaster, Calif., 1981-84; ptnr. Potter & Reed, Lancaster, 1985—; instr. Antelope Valley Coll., Lancaster, 1984-85. Chmn. bd. trustees United Meth. Ch., Lancaster, 1983-85. Named Boss of Yr. Antelope Valley Legal Secs. Assn., 1985. Mem. Assn. Trial Lawyers Am., Calif. Trial Lawyers Assn. (speakers bur. 1981—), Los Angeles Trial Lawyers Assn., Antelope Valley Bar Assn. (sec.). Democrat. Club: Exchange (Lancaster). Avocations: jogging, racquetball. Personal injury, Insurance, State civil litigation. Office: Potter & Reed PO Box 1309 Lancaster CA 93534

REED, BRUCE GILBERT, lawyer; b. New Orleans, Dec. 6, 1947; s. Floyd James and Maureen (Simoneaux) R.; m. Aprill Hotstream, July 18, 1969; Laura, Timothy. JD, Loyola U., 1971. Sole practice New Orleans, La., 1971—. Mem. ABA, La. Bar Assn. (Ho. of Dels.), Assn. Trial Lawyers Am., La. Trial Lawyers Assn., Acad. New Orleans Trial Lawyers (sec., treas.). Democrat. Roman Catholic. Family and matrimonial, Bankruptcy, Personal injury. Home: 3901 Metairie Ct Metairie LA 70002 Office: Colonial Bank Bldg 2714 Canal St New Orleans LA 70119

REED, CHARLES RUFUS, lawyer; b. Garden City, Kans., Aug. 16, 1948; s. Ambers Reed and Estelle (Robinson) Sinclair; m. Paula Marie Weeg; children: Kim Nicole, Alexander Ryan. BS, USAF Acad., 1970; M in Pub. Affairs, Princeton U., 1972; JD, Stanford U., 1978. Bar: Calif. 1978. Assoc. Campbell, Warburton et al, San Jose, Calif., 1978-80; ptnr. Glaspy, Elliott et al, San Jose, 1981-85; mng. ptnr. Reed, Elliott, Creech, Roth & McMahon, San Jose, 1985—. Mem. Berryessa Citizens Adv. Council, 1984—, Friends of the Guadalupe River Park, 1986—, Horizon 2000 Task Force, 1983-84, Sm. Bus. Assn., 1981-83, Enterprise Zone Design Com., 1983, fund raising com. Vinci Park Sch. Site Council, 1981-82, Bay Area Lawyers for the Arts, 1981-82, Urban Services and Constn. and Conveyance Tax Task Force, 1982, Citizens for Park Improvements, 1982, Mayor's Com. on Ballot Measures, 1982, Berryessa Union Sch. Dist. Human Relations Task Force, 1980-81, chmn. community relations subcom., 1981; vice chmn. San Jose Planning Commn., 1985-86, chmn. 1986-87; mem. Mayor's Task Force on Homeless, 1987—; mem. site council Piedmont Mid. Sch., 1986—; bd. dirs. San Jose Repertory Co., 1981-83, bd. counsel, 1982-83. Served to capt. USAF, 1970-75. Mem. ABA, Calif. Bar Assn., Santa Clara County Bar Assn. (mem. exec. com. bus law com., pub. edn. com., San Jose C. of C. (v.p., bd. dirs. 1985—, chmn. high tech. com. 1983-85, praticipant leadership San Jose program, chmn. cen. bus. dist. com. 1981-83), NAACP, Nat. Tooling and Machining Assn. (participant 1984-85), USAF Acad. Assn. of Grads. (founder no. Calif. chpt. 1987). Democrat. Avocations: skiing, racquetball, jogging. Contracts commercial, General corporate, Real property. Home: 1735 Septembersong Court San Jose CA 95131 Office: Reed Eliott Creech Roth Roth & McMahon 100 Park Center Plaza Suite 525 San Jose CA 95113

REED, DAVID Q., lawyer; b. Kansas City, Mo., Sept. 10, 1931; s. James Alexander and Nell (Quinlan) R.; m. Sandra Warrick (div.); m. Astrid M. Henke, Sept. 5, 1959; children: Dupuy W., James A. II, John Erich, Ellen Q. BS, Stanford U., 1957; LLB, U. Mich., 1960. Assoc. Spencer, Fane, Britt & Brown, Kansas City, 1960-66; sole practice Kansas City, 1966-72; ptnr. Kodas, Reed & McFadden, Kansas City, 1972—; bd. dirs. Iowa Electric Power & Light Co., Cedar Rapids. Mem. Mo. Ho. Reps., Jefferson City, 1972-74. Served with U.S. Army, 1952-54. Mem. ABA, Mo. Bar Assn., Kansas City Met. Bar Assn., Assn. Trial Lawyers Am., Mo. Assn. Trial Attys. Clubs: Kansas City, River (Kansas City). State civil litigation, Federal civil litigation, Personal injury. Office: Kodas Reed & McFadden PC 1006 Grand Ave Suite 1350 Kansas City MO 64106

REED, EDWARD CORNELIUS, JR., federal judge; b. Mason, Nev., July 8, 1924; s. Edward Cornelius Sr. and Evelyn (Walker) R.; m. Sally Torrance, July 14, 1952; children: Edward T., William W., John A., Mary E. BA, U. Nev.; JD, Harvard U. Atty. Arthur Andersen & Co., 1952-53; spl. dep. atty. gen. State of Nev., 1967-69; judge U.S. Dist. Ct. Nev., Reno, 1979—. Former vol. atty. Girl Scouts Am., Sierra Nevada Council, U. Nev., Nev. Agrl. Found., Nev. State Sch. Adminstrs. Assn., Nev. Congress of Parents and Teachers; mem. Washoe County Sch. Bd., 1956-72, pres. 1959, 63, 69; chmn. Gov.'s Sch. Survey Com., 1958-61; mem. Washoe County Bd. Tax Equalization, 1957-58, Washoe County Annexation Commn., 1968-72, Washoe County Personnel Com., 1973-77, chmn. 1973; mem. citizens adv. com. Washoe County Sch. Bond Issue, 1977-78, Sun Valley, Nev., Swimming Pool Com., 1978, Washoe County Blue Ribbon Task Force Com. on Growth, Nev. PTA (life); chmn. profl. div. United Way, 1978; bd. dirs. Reno Silver Sox, 1962-65. Served as staff sgt. U.S. Army, 1943-46, ETO, PTO. Mem. ABA (jud. adminstrn. sect.), Nev. State Bar Assn. (adminstrv. com. dist. 5, 1967-79, lien law com. 1965-78, chmn. 1965-72, probate law com. 1963-66, tax law com. 1962-65), Am. Judicature Soc. Democrat. Baptist. Judicial administration. Office: US Dist Ct 5147 Federal Bldg 300 Booth St Reno NV 89509

REED, GLENN EDWARD, lawyer; b. Seattle, Apr. 3, 1944; s. Glenn Walker and Geraldine Ruby (Lyons) R.; m. Anita Constance Mihos, Sep. 28, 1963 (div. Sept. 1980); children: Tina Marie, Trisha Elizabeth; m. Lynn Rae Van Liew, Apr. 18, 1983. BBA, U. Nev., 1964-70; JD, Loyola U., Los Angeles, 1973. Bar: Wash. 1973, U.S. Dist. Ct. (we. dist.) Wash. 1974, Calif. 1979, U.S. Dist. Ct. (ea. dist.) Wash. 1979, U.S. Dist. Ct. (no., cen., so. and ea. dists.) Calif. 1979, U.S. Ct. Claims 1979, U.S. Tax Ct. 1979, U.S. Ct. Mil. Appeals 1979, U.S. Ct. Appeals (9th cir.) 1979, U.S. Supreme. Ct. 1979. Asst. atty. gen. State of Wash., Olympia, 1973-74; assoc. Welts & Welts, Mt. Vernon, Wash., 1974-80; chief civil dep. Skagit County Prosecutor, Mt. Vernon, 1980-81; ptnr. Reed & Wright, Mt. Vernon, 1981-83, McMullen, Reed, Reilly & Weyrich, Mt. Vernon, 1983—. Served with USAF, 1962-66. Mem. ABA, Wash. State Bar Assn., Calif. Bar Assn., Assn. Trial Lawyers Am., Wash. State Trial Lawyers Assn., Calif. Trial Lawyers Assn., Phi Kappa Phi, Alpha Kappa Psi. Personal injury, State civil litigation, Insurance. Home: 4016 Pueblo Heights Mount Vernon WA 98273 Office: McMullen Reed Reilly & Weyrich PO Box 337 Mount Vernon WA 98273

REED, HARRY LOWE, lawyer, educator; b. Houston, Dec. 16, 1923; s. Ira Franklin and Geneva Dewey (Lowe) R.; m. Betty Anne Ghiselin, Dec. 10, 1949; children—Barry, Bruce, Christopher, Shirley. B.A., U. Tex., 1943, J.D., 1948. Bar: Tex. 1948. Atty., Shell Oil Co., 1948-75, gen. atty., 1975-85; adj. prof. South Tex. Coll. Law, 1952-85; prof. law, 1985—. Mem. City Council, Bellaire, Tex., 1953-56, mayor, 1956-57. Served to lt. (j.g.) U.S. Navy, 1943-46. Mem. ABA, Houston Bar Assn., State Bar Tex. Republican. Methodist. Antitrust, Oil and gas leasing, Environment. Home: 5422 Dumfries Houston TX 77096 Office: S Tex Coll Law 1303 San Jacinto Houston TX 77002

REED, JAMES ALEXANDER, JR., lawyer; b. Rochester, N.Y., Feb. 7, 1930; s. James Alexander and Rose Winifred (Nellist) R.; m. Dora Anne DeVries, Feb. 17, 1972 (div. Mar. 1983); children: Geoffrey M., Diane E. BA cum laude, Amherst Coll., 1952; JD, Harvard U., 1955. Bar: N.Y. 1958, U.S. Dist. Ct. (we. dist.) N.Y. 1959, U.S. Dist. Ct. (no. dist.) N.Y. 1960. Assoc. Osborn, Reed, Vande, Vate & Burke and predecessor firms, Rochester, 1958-63; ptnr. Osborn, Reed, Van de Vate & Burke and predecessor firms, Rochester, 1964—; dep. atty. Town of Pittsford, N.Y., 1976-77, atty. 1977—. Served to lt. USNR, 1955-58. Mem. ABA, N.Y. State Bar Assn., Monroe County Bar Assn., Am. Judicature Assn. Republican. Episcopalian. Club: University (Rochester). State civil litigation, Federal civil litigation, Insurance. Home: 11 Washington Ave Pittsford NY 14534 Office: Osborn Reed Van de Vate & Burke 47 S Fitzhugh St Rochester NY 14614

REED, JAMES WILSON, lawyer, gas co. exec.; b. Clay, W.Va., Dec. 19, 1927; s. Edward Ray and Luly Rae (Wilson) R.; m. Helen Lucille Black, June 7, 1952; children—James Wilson, Edward C., Thomas H., Charles D. B.A., W.Va. U., 1951; LL.B., 1952. Bar: W.Va. 1952. Pros. atty. Clay County, W.Va., 1953-56, 68-72, 77-80; gen. counsel Reed Gas Inc., Clay, 1980—, also sec., dir. Served with USAF, 1956-57. Mem. Am. Judicature Soc., ABA. Republican. Methodist. Club: Masons. Estate planning, Oil and gas leasing, Probate. Office: Main St Clay WV 25043

REED, JOHN GRADY, lawyer; b. Peterborough, Ont., Can., Apr. 5, 1929; s. John Theron Sproul and Lilian (Grady) R.; m. Miriam Wilkes Bell, May 1, 1954; children: Christine, Roberta, Karen, Laura, Margaret, Abigail, Elisabeth. A.B., Harvard U., 1951, LL.B., 1957. Bar: N.Y. 1954, D.C. 1957. Assoc. White & Case, N.Y.C., 1957-66; ptnr. White & Case, Washington, 1967—; cons. U.S. Synthetic Fuels Corp., Washington, 1981; dir. Arrangements Abroad, Inc., N.Y.C. Served to lt. (j.g.) USNR, 1951-54; served to capt. Res., 1951-79. Mem. ABA, Assn. Bar City N.Y., D.C. Bar Assn., N.Y. State Bar Assn., Am. Law Inst., Harvard Law Sch. Assn. D.C. (pres. 1982-83, adv. com.). Roman Catholic. Clubs: Met. (Washington); Chevy Chase (Md.). General corporate, Private international. Home: 8221 Burning Tree Rd Bethesda MD 20817 Office: White & Case 1747 Pennsylvania Ave Washington DC 20006

REED, JOHN SQUIRES, II, lawyer; b. Lexington, Ky., Mar. 20, 1949; s. John Squires and Mary Alexander (O'Hara) R.; m. Nancy Claire Battles, Dec. 29, 1973. A.B. in Polit. Sci., U. Ky., 1971; J.D., U. Va., 1974. Bar: Ky. 1974, U.S. Dist. Ct. (ea. dist.) Ky. 1979, U.S. Dist. Ct. (we. dist.) Ky. 1975, U.S. Ct. Appeals (6th cir.) 1975, U.S. Supreme Ct. 1980, U.S. Ct. Appeals (fed. cir.) 1985. Assoc. Greenebaum Doll & McDonald, Louisville, 1974-79, ptnr., 1979—. Mem. Leadership Louisville, 1982, treas., mem. exec. com. Leadership Louisville Alumni Assn., 1984, pres., 1985; bd. dirs. Ky. Council Econ. Edn., 1985—, Nat. Assn. Community Leadership Orgns., 1986—. Served as 1st lt. U.S. Army, 1974. Mem. ABA (antitrust, patent, trademark, copyright and litigation sects.), Ky. Bar Assn., Louisville Bar Assn. (bd. dirs. 1985-86), Phi Beta Kappa. Democrat. Mem. Disciples of Christ. Club: Louisville Boat. Antitrust, Federal civil litigation, Patent. Office: Greenebaum Doll & McDonald 3300 First Nat Tower Louisville KY 40202

REED, JOHN WILSON, lawyer; b. Manchester, Eng., May 31, 1945; came to U.S., 1954; s. Firmin P. and Isabel (Woollam) R.; m. Leslee King, Dec. 27, 1969; children—Ashley King, Cameron King. B.A., Yale U., 1966; J.D., Harvard U., 1969. Bar: La. 1970, U.S. Dist. Ct. (ea. dist.) La. 1970, U.S. Ct. Apls. (5th cir.) 1970, U.S. Ct. Appeals (11th cir.) 1970, N.Y., 1980, U.S. Dist. Ct. (so. dist.) Ala., 1982. Vista vol. New Orleans Legal Assistance Corp., 1969-70, staff atty., 1970-72; sole practice, New Orleans, 1972-78; ptnr. Glass & Reed, New Orleans, 1978—; gen. counsel ACLU of La., New Orleans, 1974-78; mem. faculty New Orleans Bar Rev., 1979—, Nat. Inst. Trial Advocacy, Boulder, Colo., 1984. Mem. Nat. Assn. Criminal Def. Lawyers, Am. Trial Lawyers Assn., La. Trial Lawyers Assn., La. Assn. Criminal Def. Lawyers (v.p. 1985—). Democrat. Criminal. Office: Glass & Reed 338 Lafayette St New Orleans LA 70130

REED, LLOYD H., lawyer; b. Washington, July 31, 1922; s. George W. and Eleanor B. (Newman) R.; m. June E., Sept. 14, 1947; children; Rebecca, Lloyd Allan. BA, Howard U., 1943; LLB, Harvard U., 1949. Bar: D.C. 1949, N.Y. 1950. Atty. to v.p. corp. relations MONY Fin. Services, N.Y.C., 1949—; v.p., sec. MONY Real Estate Investors, N.Y.C., 1985—; bd. dirs. United Mut. Life Ins. Co., N.Y.C., Mortgage Housing Partnership Corp., N.Y.C. Mem. Zoning Bd. of Appeals, Greenburgh, N.Y., 1983—. Mem. ABA, Nat. Bar Assn., Am. Coll. Real Estate Lawyers, N.Y. State Bar Assn. Real property. Office: MONY Fin Services 1740 Broadway New York NY 10019

REED, LOWELL ANDREW, JR., lawyer; b. Westchester, Pa., June 21, 1930; s. Lowell Andrew Sr. and Catherine Elizabeth (Pauly) R.; m. Diane Benson, Jan. 23, 1954; children: Jeffrey Barton, Lowell Andrew III, Diane Susan, Christopher Benson. BBA, U. Wis., 1952; JD, Temple U., 1958. Bar: Pa. 1959, U.S. Dist. Ct. (ea. dist.) Pa. 1961, U.S. Ct. Appeals (3d cir.) 1962, U.S. Supreme Ct. 1970. Corp. trial counsel Pa. Mfrs. Assn. Ins. Co., Phila., 1958-63; assoc. Rawle & Henderson, Phila., 1963-65, gen. ptnr., 1966—; lectr. law Temple U., Pa. Bar Inst. Contbr. articles to profl. jours. Elder Abington (Pa.) Presbyn. Ch.; mem. Pa. Senate Select Com. Med. Malpractice; past pres., bd. dirs. Rydal Meadowbrook Civic Assn.; bd. dirs. Abington Sch. Bd., 1971, World Affairs Council Phila., 1983—; trustee Abington Meml. Hosp., 1983—. Served to lt. comdr. USN, 1952-57. Mem. ABA, Pa. Bar Assn., Phila. Bar Assn. (chmn. medico legal com. 1975, constl. bicentennial com. 1986-87, commn. on jud. selection and retention 1983-87), Phila. Assn. Def. Counsel (pres. 1983-84), Nat. Assn. R.R. Trial Counsel, Temple U. Law Alumni Assn. (exec. com.). Republican. Club: Phila. Racquet. Federal civil litigation, State civil litigation, Insurance. Home: 1056 Huntingdon Rd Abington PA 19001 Office: Rawle & Henderson 211 S Broad St Philadelphia PA 19107

REED, REX HOWARD, foundation executive, lawyer; b. Joliet, Ill., Dec. 7, 1935; s. Howard Odin and Edith Frances (Gray) R.; m. Elizabeth Marie Hvizdos, May 4, 1968; children: Jennifer, Steven, Julia, Roger. BS, U. Ill., 1958; JD, So. Meth. U., 1961. Bar: Tex. 1961, D.C. 1965, U.S. Supreme Ct. 1965. Atty. Fed. Power Co. Commn., Washington, 1965-66, NLRB, Houston, 1966-68; asst. gen. counsel exchange service U.S. Army and USAF, Dallas, 1968-71; exec. v.p., legal dir. Nat. Right to Work Legal Def. Found., Springfield, Va., 1971—. Served to capt. USAF, 1962-65, served to lt. comdr. USNR, 1968-75. Mem. ABA, D.C. Bar Assn., Fed. Bar Assn. Republican. Home: 1819 St Boniface St Vienna VA 22180 Office: Nat Right to Work Legal Def Found 8001 Braddock Rd #600 Springfield VA 22160

REED, ROBERT ALAN, lawyer; b. Pitts., Dec. 1, 1942; s. Thomas Frank and Elizabeth Mary (Kelly) R.; m. Rosemary Alice Werner, Dec. 26, 1967; children: Brian, Kevin. BSE, Purdue U., 1964; LLB, U. Pitts., 1967. Bar: Pa. 1967. Atty. ALCOA, Pitts., 1968-73, gen. atty., 1973-82, asst. gen. counsel, 1982—, asst. sec., 1983-84, sec., 1984—. Vice chair St. Thomas More Cath. Ch. Parish Fin. Council, Bethel Park, Pa., 1987—. Mem. ABA, Allegheny County Bar Assn., Am. Corp. Counsel Assocs., Am. Soc. Corp. Secs. (v.p. Pitts. group 1986—). Club: Duquesne (Pitts.). Avocations: gardening, bridge. General corporate, Pension, profit-sharing, and employee benefits, Securities. Home: 1082 Glen Oak Dr Bethel Park PA 15102 Office: Aluminum Co of Am 1501 Alcoa Bldg Pittsburgh PA 15219

REED, SCOTT, judge; b. Lexington, Ky., July 3, 1921; s. Wilbur Scott and Florence (Young) R.; m. Charlotte Sue Charles, Oct. 12, 1946; 1 child, Geoffrey Scott. J.D., U. Ky., 1945; LL.D., No. Ky. U., 1977. Bar: Ky. 1944. Practice in Lexington, 1944-64; ptnr. Wallace, Turner & Reed, 1954-64; atty. Fayette County, 1952; judge 1st div. Fayette Circuit Ct., 1964-69; justice Ct. Appeals Ky., 1969-75; chief justice Supreme Ct. Ky., 1976-77, justice, 1977-79; judge U.S. Dist. Ct., 1979—; acting asso. prof. U. Ky. Law Sch., 1948-56. Editor-in-chief Ky. Law Jour, 1944; author prefaces. Recipient Algernon Sydney Sullivan medallion U. Ky., 1945; Nat. Coll. Judiciary fellow, 1965. Mem. ABA, Ky. Bar Assn. (citation for outstanding service 1979), Fayette County Bar Assn. (Henry T. Duncan award 1977), Am. Law Inst. (life), Lexington Civil War Roundtable, Order of Coif, Phi Delta Phi. Mem. Disciples of Christ Ch. Office: US Courthouse Fed Bldg PO Box 1910 Lexington KY 40593 *

REED, TYRONE EDWARD, lawyer; b. Cleve., Oct. 13, 1950; s. Eddie and Maxine (Wright) R.; m. Jeanne Kelly, Dec. 13, 1968 (div. Feb. 1983); children: Tammra, Carmen. JD, Cleve. State U., 1976. Bar: Ohio 1976, U.S. Dist. Ct. (no. dist.) Ohio, U.S. Ct. Appeals (6th cir.). Sole practice Cleve., 1976—. Mem. ABA, Ohio Bar Assn., Cleve. Bar Assn. Avocations: weight lifting. Personal injury, Family and matrimonial, Bankruptcy. Home: 3080 York Shire Rd Cleveland Heights OH 44118 Office: 12025 Shaker Blvd #575 Cleveland OH 44120

REED, W. FRANKLIN, lawyer; b. Louisville, Dec. 30, 1946; s. William Ferguson and Stella Elizabeth (Richardson) R.; m. Sharon Ann Coss, June 16, 1973; children: Jonathan Franklin, William Brian, Carrie Ann. BA, Williams Coll., 1968; JD, Columbia U., 1971. Bar: N.Y. 1972, U.S. Dist. Ct. (so. dist.) N.Y. 1975, U.S. Ct. Appeals (2d cir.) 1975, Pa. 1982, U.S. Dist. Ct. (we. dist.) 1983. Assoc. Milbank, Tweed, Hadley & McCloy, N.Y.C., 1971-82; assoc. Reed, Smith, Shaw & McClay, Pitts., 1982-83, ptnr., 1984—. Mem. ABA, Pa. Bar Assn., Allegheny Bar Assn., Carnegie 100, Williams Coll. Alumni Soc. W. Pa. (sec. 1983—), Phi Beta Kappa. Democrat. Presbyterian. Clubs: Rivers (Pitts.), St. Clair Country (Upper St. Clair, Pa.). Avocations: fishing, golf. Real property, General corporate, Public utilities. Home: 525 Miranda Dr Pittsburgh PA 15241 Office: Reed Smith Shaw & McClay 435 6th Ave Pittsburgh PA 15219

REED, WALLACE CALVIN, lawyer; b. Los Angeles, Dec. 11, 1927; s. Fred and Helen Reed; m. Patricia Cameron, June 11, 1949 (div. 1964); children: John, Daniel, Kendall, Tom; m. Anne Bixler, Feb. 14, 1967. BA, U. So. Calif., 1951, JD, 1955. Bar: Calif. 1955, U.S. Dist. Ct. (so. dist.) Calif. 1955. Assoc. Kirtland & Packard, Los Angeles, 1955-65, ptnr., 1965—. Mem. organizing com. Glendale (Calif.) Young Reps., 1955-60. Mem. ABA, Los Angeles County Bar Assn., Calif. Bar Assn., Calif. Medico-Legal Com. (past pres.), Am. Bd. Trial Advs., Assn. So. Calif. Def. Counsel (past exec. bd.), Internat. Assn. Ins. Counsel, Am. Coll. Trial Lawyers, Theta Xi (pres. 1951), Phi Delta Phi (pres. 1955). Clubs: Los Angeles Athletic; Calif. Yacht (Marina Del Rey), Riding and Polo (Burbank, Calif.). Avocations: sailing, skiing, horsemanship. State civil litigation, Insurance, Personal injury. Home: 1524 Alta Park Ln La Cañada CA 91011 Office: Kirtland & Packard 626 Wilshire Blvd Los Angeles CA 90017

REED, WALTER DUDLEY, lawyer, air force officer, university dean; b. Dallas Center, Iowa, June 1, 1924; m. Dorothy Ann Kelly; children—Elizabeth K., William S., Joseph H., Anne T. B.C.S., Drake U., 1948, J.D., 1950; LL.M., McGill U., 1964; postgrad., Hague Acad., Netherlands, 1960. Bar: Iowa 1950, U.S. Supreme Ct. 1964, S.D. 1980. Commd. 2d lt. USAAF, 1944; advanced through grades to maj. gen. USAF, 1977; staff judge adv., asst. staff judge adv. various orgns. 1951-62; mem. internat. law div. Hdqrs. USAF, 1963-67, chief, 1970-73; legal officer Am. embassy, Bangkok, Thailand, 1967-69; dir. civil law Hdqrs. USAF, Washington, 1973; asst. judge adv. gen. Hdqrs. USAF, 1973-77, judge adv. gen., 1977-80; dean Sch. Law, U. S.D., 1980—; mem. U.S. del. Diplomatic Conf. on Reaffirmation and Devel. Internat. Humanitarian Law Applicable to Armed Conflict, 1974-77. Contbr. articles to legal jours. Decorated D.S.M., Legion of Merit with oak leaf cluster, Air Force Commendation medal with two oak leaf clusters, Republic of Korea Presdl. Unit citation. Mem. Am., Fed., Internat. Inst. Space Law, Judge Adv. Assn., Internat. Platform Assn. Public international, Military, Professional responsibility and legal education. Home: 709 Brooks Dr Vermillion SD 57069 Office: Sch Law U SD Vermillion SD 57069

REED, WILLIAM JAMES, lawyer; b. Chgo., Nov. 11, 1943; s. Victor Pritchard and Nora (Catherine) R.; m. Mary Katherine Wasley, Aug. 16, 1969; children: Matthew, Megan, Michael. BA, Seattle U., 1966; JD, U. of the Pacific, 1971. Bar: Calif. 1971. Deputy dist. atty. Monterey County, Calif., 1971-76; ptnr. Knox, Ricksen, Snook, Anthony & Robbins, Oakland, Calif., 1976-82, Archer & McComas, Walnut Creek, Calif., 1982—. Mem. Calif. Bar Assn., Alameda County Bar Assn., Contra Costa County Bar Assn., Assn. of R.R. Trial Lawyers. Republican. Roman Catholic. Club: The Family (San Francisco). Avocations: aviation, wood crafts, golf, tennis, bicycling. State civil litigation, Federal civil litigation. Office: Archer & McComas 1299 Newell Hill Pl Walnut Creek CA 94596

REEDER, F. ROBERT, lawyer; b. Brigham City, Utah, Jan. 23, 1943; s. Frank O. and Helen H. (Heninger) R.; m. Joannie Anderson, May 4, 1974; children—David, Kristina, Adam. J.D., U. Utah, 1967. Bar: Utah 1967, U.S. Ct. Appeals (10th cir.) 1967, U.S. Ct. Mil. Appeals 1968, U.S. Supreme Ct. 1972, U.S. Ct. Appeals (D.C. and 5th cirs.) 1979. Shareholder, dir. Parsons, Behle & Latimer, Salt Lake City, 1968—. Bd. dirs., officer Holy Cross Hosp. Found. Served with U.S. Army, 1967-68. Mem. ABA, Utah State Bar, Salt Lake County Bar. Clubs: University (Salt Lake City), Cottonwood (past pres., bd. dirs.). Public utilities, Contracts commercial, State civil litigation. Office: Parsons Behle & Latimer PO Box 11898 Salt Lake City UT 84147

REEDER, JOE ROBERT, lawyer; b. Tacoma, Nov. 28, 1947; s. William Thomas and Marilyn Ruth (Parker) R.; m. Katharine Randolph Boyce, Jan 1, 1983; children: Rachael Anne, Aubrilyn, Julia. BS, U.S. Mil. Acad., West Point, N.Y., 1970; JD, U. Tex., 1975; LLM, Georgetown U., 1981. Bar: Tex. 1975, U.S. Dist. Ct. (so. dist.) Tex 1975, U.S. Ct. Appeals (5th cir.) 1976, U.S. Ct. Appeals (3rd and 4th cirs.) 1977, U.S. Ct. Claims 1978, U.S. Dist. Ct. D.C. 1979, U.S. Ct. Appeals, U.S. Supreme Ct. 1980, U.S. Ct. Appeals (D.C. cir.) 1983. Commd. 2d lt. U.S. Army, 1970, advanced through grades to maj., 1985; trial atty. litigation div. U.S. Army, Pentagon, D.C., 1976-78; trial atty. contract appeals div. U.S. Army, Pentagon, 1978-79; with adjunct program U.S. Army, 1980—; assoc. Patton, Boggs & Blow, Washington, 1979-82, ptnr., 1983—; law clk. to presiding justice U.S. Dist. Ct. (so. dist.) Tex., 1976. Mem. ABA (assoc. editor pub. contract law jour. 1985—), Assn. Trial Lawyers Am., Fed. Bar Assn., D.C. Bar Assn., Tex. Bar Assn. Episcopalian. Lodge: Rotary. Home: 2301 Ft Scott Dr Arlington VA 22202 Office: Patton Boggs & Blow 2550 M St NW Washington DC 20037

REEDER, ROBERT HARRY, lawyer; b. Topeka, Dec. 3, 1930; s. William Harry and Florence Mae (Cochran) R. A.B. Washburn U., 1952, J.D., 1960. Bar: U.S. Dist. Ct. Kans. 1960, Kans. 1960, U.S. Supreme Ct. 1968. Research asst. Kans. Legis. Council Research Dept., Topeka, 1955-60; asst. counsel Traffic Inst., Northwestern U., Evanston, Ill., 1960-67, gen. counsel, 1967—; exec. dir. Nat. Com. on Uniform Traffic Laws and Ordinances, Evanston, 1982—. Co-author: Vehicle Traffic Law, 1974; The Evidence Handbook, 1980. Author: Interpretation of Implied Consent by the Courts, 1972. Served with U.S. Army, 1952-54. Mem. Com. Alcohol and Other Drugs (chmn. 1973-75). Republican. Methodist. Criminal, Legal education. Office: Nat Com on Uniform Traffic Laws PO Box 1409 405 Church St Evanston IL 60204

REEF, NORMAN SIDNEY, lawyer; b. Portland, Maine, Aug. 13, 1933. BA, Boston U., 1957, LLB, 1960. Bar: Maine 1960, Mass. 1960, U.S. Supreme Ct. 1965. Assoc. Lewis E. Chandler, Cambridge, Mass., 1960-62; sole practice Portland, 1962-63; assoc. Bennett, Schwarz & Reef, Portland, 1964-69; ptnr. Reef & Mooers, Portland, 1969-86, Reef, Jordan & Hrycay, Portland, 1987—; draftsman Jury Reform Bill 1967; mem. Gov.'s Commn. Rehab., 1967, Commn. Revise Ins. Laws, 1967; hearing officer Social Security Adminstrn., 1972—; instr. criminal justice dept. U. Maine, 1973—. Co-chmn. lawyers div. Heart Fund, Portland, 1963; corporator Portland Boys Club, 1968; gen. counsel Maine Dem. Party, 1974—; bd. dirs. Jewish Community Ctr., Portland. Mem. ABA, Assn. Trial Lawyers Am. (chmn. task force home office and budget com., pres. state committeeman 1967-68, assoc. editor jour. 1965), Maine Trial Lawyers Assn. (sec., bd. govs., v.p. 1968-70), Maine Bar Assn., Am. Judicature Soc. State civil litigation, Family and matrimonial, Personal injury. Home: 13 Penny Royal Ct Yarmouth ME 04096 Office: 66 Pearl St Portland ME 04101

REEFER, ELIZABETH DROSS, lawyer; b. Paterson, N.J., Apr. 1, 1951; d. Hartman Harry and Elizabeth (Johns) Dross; m. Thomas Merrick Reefer, June 7, 1975. AB cum laude, Bryn Mawr Coll., 1975; JD, N.Y. Law Sch., 1980. Bar: N.Y. 1980, Mass. 1982, Mo. 1986. Asst. title counsel First Am. Corp., N.Y.C., 1980-81; atty. Shawmut Worcester County Bank N.A., Mass., 1981-82, Shawmut Bank of Boston N.A., 1982-85; assoc. Stinson, Mag & Fizzell, Kansas City, Mo., 1985—. Mem. ABA. Democrat. Episcopalian. Banking, General corporate. Home: 5914 Grand Kansas City MO 64113 Office: Stinson Mag & Fizzell 2100 Boatmen's Ctr Kansas City MO 64141

REEG, KURTIS BRADFORD, lawyer; b. St. Louis, Sept. 1, 1954; s. Jay Flory and Mary Louise (Braun) R.; m. Ruth Miriam Zimmerman, Aug. 22, 1982. BA cum laude, DePauw U., 1976; JD, St. Louis U., 1979. Bar: U.S. Dist. Ct. (ea. dist.) Mo. 1979, U.S. Dist. Ct. (so. dist.) Ill. 1981, U.S. Ct. Appeals (8th cir.) 1984, U.S. Ct. Appeals (7th cir.) 1986. Law clk. to presiding justice Ill. Appellate Ct. (5th dist.), Granite City, 1979-80; assoc. Coburn, Croft & Putzell, St. Louis, Mo. and Belleville, Ill., 1980-86, ptnr., 1986—; instr. legal research and writing St. Louis U., 1979-80. Rep. committeeman 24th ward, St. Louis, 1980. Mem. Ill. Bar Assn., Mo. Bar Assn., Bar Assn. of Met. St. Louis, Phi Alpha Delta, Pi Sigma Alpha. Republican. Avocations: hunting, fishing, softball, astronomy. Federal civil litigation, State civil litigation, Personal injury. Home: 4 Kirken Knoll Dr Saint Louis MO 63131 Office: Coburn Croft & Putzell 1 Mercantile Ctr Suite 2900 Saint Louis MO 63101

REEMSNYDER, RONALD DAVID, lawyer; b. Massillon, Ohio, Aug. 3, 1949; s. Ray Elden and Jean Esther (Hixenbaugh) R.; m. Susan Carol Holschuh, July 25, 1970; children: Carolyn, Andrea, Jill. BA, Mt. Union Coll., 1971; JD, Duke U., 1974. Bar: Ga. 1974, U.S. Dist. Ct. (no. dist.) Ga. 1975, U.S. Dist. Ct. (mid. dist.) Ga. 1979, U.S. Dist. Ct. (so. dist.) Ga., U.S. Ct. Appeals (5th and 11th cirs.). Assoc. Neely, Freeman & Hawkins, Atlanta, 1974-76, Neely & Player, Atlanta, 1976—. Mem. Ga. Bar Assn., Atlanta Bar Assn., Lawyers Club Atlanta, Def. Research Inst., Internat. Assn. Ins. Counsel, Nat. Assn. R.R. Trial Counsel. Club: Druid Hills Golf (Atlanta). Federal civil litigation, State civil litigation, Insurance. Office: Neely & Player PC 75 Poplar St Atlanta GA 30303-2122

REESE, HARRY BROWNE, lawyer, educator; b. 1926. B.A., Ohio State U., 1947; LL.B., Harvard U., 1950. Bar: Ohio 1950, Ill. 1954. Law clk. to presiding judge, U.S. Ct. Appeals (2d cir.) 1950-51; asst. prof., Ohio State U., Columbus, 1951-53; asst. prof. Northwestern U., Chgo., 1953-55, assoc. prof., 1955-57, prof., 1957-75, William Wirt Gurley prof., 1975—. Served with USN, 1943-45. Legal education. Office: Northwestern U Law Sch 350 E Chicago Ave Chicago IL 60611 *

REESE, WILLIAM WILLIS, banker; b. N.Y.C., July 8, 1940; s. Willis Livingston Meiser and Frances Galletin (Stevens) R.; B.A., Trinity Coll., 1963; M.B.A., J.D., Columbia U., 1970. Admitted to N.Y. bar, 1972; research analyst Morgan Guaranty Trust Co., N.Y.C., 1971-73, investment research officer, 1973-77, asst. v.p., 1977-86, v.p., 1986— . Bd. dirs. N.Y.C. Ballet, 1975—, Counseling and Human Devel. Center, 1977—, 3d St. Music Sch. Settlement, 1976—; trustee Millbrook Sch., 1972—. Served with USAF, 1963-67. Mem. Am., Inter-Am., N.Y. State (sec. com. on internat. law 1973-76), Dutchess County bar assns., N.Y. Soc. Security Analysts, Certified Fin. Analysts, Assn. Bar City N.Y. Republican. Episcopalian. Clubs: Union, Racquet and Tennis, Rockaway Hunt, Mt. Holyoke Lodge. Estate planning, Probate, Municipal bonds. Home: 910 Park Ave New York NY 10021

REESE, WILLIS LIVINGSTON MESIER, legal educator; b. Bernardsville, N.J., June 16, 1913; s. William Willis and Augusta (Bliss) R.; m. Frances Gallatin Stevens, June 26, 1937; children: William Willis, Frances Gallatin, John Rathbone, George Bliss, Alexander Stevens. Grad., St. Paul's Sch., N.H., 1931; A.B., Yale U., 1935, LL.B., 1938; LL.D., U. Leuven, Belgium, 1972, Trinity Coll., 1979. Bar: N.Y. 1938. Law clk. Judge Thomas Swan, 1938-39; asso. Winthrop, Stimson, Putnam & Roberts, N.Y.C., 1939-41; from asst. prof. to Charles Evans Hughes prof. law Columbia, 1946—; dir. Parker Sch. Fgn. and Comparative Law, 1955-80; Lectr. Hague Acad. Internat. Law, 1964, 76, mem. curatorium, 1975—; mem. Inst. Internat. Law, 1971—, adv. com. on pvt. internat. law Sec. of State, 1964—; U.S. del. Hague Conf. Pvt. Internat. Law, 1956, 60, 64, 68, 72, 76, 80, 84, 85, ; reporter restatement (2d) conflict laws Am. Law Inst. Author: (with Rosenberg) Cases and Materials on Conflict of Laws, 1984. Bd. dirs. Episc. Ch. Found., 1979—, N.Y. Legal Aid Soc., 1951-71; chmn. Community Action for Legal Services, 1967-70; mem. N.Y. Law Revision Commn., 1973-83; Pres. bd. trustees Millbrook Sch., 1968-77; pres. Five Towns United Fund, 1959, chmn. bd., 1958, 60. Served as capt. AUS, 1941-46. Mem. Am. Assn. Comparative Study Law (sec., dir. 1955-80), Joint Conf. Legal Edn. (1st v.p.), Assn. Bar City of N.Y., Internat. Law Assn. (Am. br.), Am. Bar Assn., Am. Soc. Internat. Law, Am. Fgn. Law Assn. (pres. 1964-67), Am. Assn. UN (pres. Five Towns chpt. 1962-63, 77-81), Acad. Polit. Sci. (life), Inst. Internat. Law, Phi Beta Kappa, Order of Coif. Episcopalian (sr. warden, sec. standing com. Diocese N.Y. 1963-65). Clubs: Century, Rockaway Hunting, Union. Legal. Home: 345 Meadowview Ave Hewlett NY 11557 Office: 345 W 116th St New York NY 10027

REEVES, BARBARA ANN, lawyer; b. Buffalo, Mar. 29, 1949; d. Prentice W. and Doris (S.) Reeves; m. Richard C. Neal; 1 child, Timothy Reeves Neal. Student, Wellesley Coll., 1967-68; B.A. (NSF fellow, Lehman fellow), New Coll., Sarasota, Fla., 1970; J.D. cum laude, Harvard U., 1973. Bar: Calif., D.C. Law clk. U.S. Ct. Appeals, 9th Circuit, Portland, Oreg., 1973-74; assoc. firm Munger, Tolles and Rickershauser, Los Angeles, 1977-78; trial atty. spl. trial sect. Dept. Justice (Antitrust div.), 1974-75; spl. asst. to asst. atty. gen. Antitrust div. Dept. Justice, Washington, 1976-77; chief antitrust div. Los Angeles field office, 1978-81; chief Dept. Justice, 1978-81; ptnr. Morrison & Foerster, Los Angeles, 1981—; del. 9th Cir. Jud. Conf., 1986—; lectr. in field. Contbr. articles to profl. jours. Mem. ABA (litigation sect., antitrust sect., corp., bus. and banking sect.), Los Angeles County Bar Assn. (sect. officer 1980-81, exec. com. trial lawyers 1983-87). Antitrust, Federal civil litigation, Banking. Home: 2649 N Commonwealth Ave Los Angeles CA 90027 Office: Morrison & Foerster 333 S Grand Ave 38th Floor Los Angeles CA 90071

REEVES, GENE, lawyer; b. Meridian, Miss., Feb. 27, 1930; s. Clarence Eugene and May (Philyaw) R.; m. Brenda Wages, Sept. 26, 1980. LL.B., John Marshall U., 1964. Bar: Ga. 1964, U.S. Ct. Appeals (11th cir.) 1965, U.S. Supreme Ct. 1969. Ptnr., Craig & Reeves, Lawrenceville, Ga., 1964-71; sole practice, Lawrenceville, 1971—; judge City Ct., Lawrenceville, 1969-70. Served to sgt. USAF, 1951-54. Mem. Am. Jud. Soc., ABA, Gwinnett County Bar Assn. (pres. 1970-72). Baptist. Criminal, State civil litigation. Home: 221 Pineview Dr Lawrenceville GA 30245 Office: 125 Perry St Lawrenceville GA 32045

REEVES, JEAN BROOKS, lawyer, educator; b. Amarillo, Tex., May 19, 1919; s. Sherman Vester and Letrice (Dixon) R.; m. Lois Julie Johnson, Aug. 10, 1946; children—Stephen, Douglas, Andrew. A.A., North Park Coll., 1939; A.B., Augustana Coll., 1946; J.D., U. Nebr., 1948. Bar: Nebr. 1948, Kans. 1949, U.S. Dist. Ct. Kans. 1949, U.S. Ct. Appeals (10th cir.) 1969, U.S. Supreme Ct. 1971. Atty., A.T. & S.F. Ry. Co., Topeka, Kans., 1948-62, asst. gen. atty., 1962-68, gen. atty., 1968-80; gen. atty. Santa Fe Industries, Topeka, 1980-84; adj. prof. labor and corp. law Washburn U. Contbr. articles to profl. corps., agy. and ptnrs. law; Chmn. Capital Area ARC, Topeka, 1969-71; v.p., fin. chmn. Boys Club, Topeka, 1979-80; trustee Shawnee County Hist. Soc., Topeka, 1968; chmn. legis. com. C. of C., Topeka, 1975-76. Served to maj. U.S. Army, 1941-46; ETO. Decorated Bronze Star medal, Fourragere-Colors of Coix de Guerre; recipient Cert. of Appreciation ARC, 1973; Disting. Service award Boys Clubs, 1982; named Adj. Prof. of Yr., 1987. Mem. Kans. Bar Assn., Topeka Bar Assn. (hon. pres. 1987—), ABA, Nebr. Bar Assn. Republican. Lutheran. Club: Knife and Fork (dir. 1980-83). Lodge: Rotary (dir. 1975-78). Administrative and regulatory, Federal civil litigation, General corporate. Home: 3120 Briarwood Cir Topeka KS 66611 Office: 434 S Topeka Blvd Topeka KS 66603

REEVES, JOHN RAYMOND, lawyer, state legislator; b. Jackson, Miss., Mar. 15, 1957; s. Gordon Robertson and Rae (Robinson) R. B in Pub. Adnministrn., U. Miss., 1979, JD, 1982. Bar: Miss. Sole practice Jackson, 1982—; faculty mem. Miss. Coll., Clinton, 1982—. Mem. Ho. of Reps. from 72d dist. Miss., 1984—; bd. dirs. Citizen's S.W., Inc., Jackson, 1985. Named one of Outstanding Young Men Am., 1983. Mem. Am. Assn. Trial Lawyers, Miss. Bar Assn., Miss. Trial Lawyers Assn., Hinds County Bar Assn. Democrat. Baptist. Avocations: weightlifting, fishing, golfing. Family and matrimonial, Personal injury, General practice. Home: 1880 Camellia Ln Jackson MS 39204 Office: 425 Tombigbee St Jackson MS 39201

REEVES, L. BRIAN, lawyer; b. Bowling Green, Ky., July 7, 1952; s. Lester D. and Dorothy (Ewing) R.; m. Shari Lynn Pederson, Mar. 22, 1975 (divorced); children: Lee, Kelly, Kimberly, Renae. Student, Western Ky. U., 1969-70; BA in Govt., U. Ky., Lexington, 1973; JD, U. Tulsa, 1974. Bar: U.S. Dist. Ct. (ea. dist.) Okla. 1975, U.S. Ct. Appeals (10th cir.) 1975, Ky. 1976, U.S. Dist. Ct. Ky. 1976, U.S. Ct. Appeals (6th cir.) 1979. Sole practice Tulsa, 1975-76, Bowling Green, 1976—. Bd. dirs. Hospice of Bowling Green. Mem. ABA, Ky. Bar Assn. (chmn. law office mgmt. sect. 1981-83, ethics com. 1979—, mem. editorial bd. 1978—), Bowling Green Bar Assn., Christian Legal Soc. (chmn. Ky. chpt. 1980-83). Democrat. General corporate, Probate, Estate planning. Office: PO Box 806 Bowling Green KY 42101

REEVES, MICHAEL C., insurance company executive; b. West Point, Ga., Feb. 11, 1947; s. Charles M. Jr. and Lois (Laney) R.; m. Frances Keith, June 20, 1970; children: Charles, Kathryn, Sarah. BA, Presbyn. Coll., 1969; JD, Wake Forest U., 1973. Bar: N.C. 1973. Assoc. Kellogg, Wheless & White, Manteo, N.C., 1973-74; ptnr. Kellogg, Wheless, White & Reeves, Manteo, 1974-76, Kellogg, White & Reeves, Manteo, 1976-78; v.p. AMI Title Ins. Co., Charlotte, N.C., 1978-83; pres. Safeco Title of N.C. Inc., Charlotte, 1983—. Episcopalian. Real property. Office: Safeco Title of NC Inc 130-D N McDowell St Charlotte NC 28204

REEVES, PHILLIP EARL, lawyer; b. Greenville, S.C., July 2, 1955; s. Earl W. and Gwendolyn LaRue (Moore) R.; m. Laura Player, May 26, 1979; 1 child, Laura Michelle. BA cum laude, Furman U., 1977; JD with distinction, Emory U., 1980. Bar: S.C. 1980, Ga. 1980, U.S. Dist. Ct. S.C. 1982. Staff mem. U.S. Dept. HEW, Atlanta, 1979-80; from assoc. to ptnr. Rainey, Britton, Gibbes & Clarkson, Greenville, 1980—. Co-author: Young Lawyers Handbook on Aging, 1984. Mem. ABA, S.C. Bar Assn., Ga. Bar Assn., Greenville Bar Assn., S.C. Young Lawyers Assn., S.C. Def. Trial Lawyers Assn., Order of Coif. Republican. Baptist. Club: Greenville (S.C.) Country. Lodge: Sertoma (v.p. sponsorship Wade Hampton chpt. 1980—). Avocations: sports, reading, music. State civil litigation, Insurance, Personal injury. Home: Rt 3 Tall Oaks Piedmont SC 29673 Office: Rainey Britton Gibbes & Clarkson PO Box 10589 Greenville SC 29603

REGALADO, ELOISA, lawyer; b. Pinar Del Rio, Cuba, Sept. 9, 1952; came to U.S., 1968; d. Osvaldo Nicanor and Eloisa F. (Tosca) R.; m. William Michael Hess, Oct. 4, 1975; 1 child, Amaris Michelle Hess. AB magna cum laude, Rutgers U., 1975, JD, 1978. Bar: Pa. 1978, N.J. 1978, U.S. Dist. Ct. N.J. 1978, D.C. 1981. Atty. advisor Naval Air Systems Command, Washington, 1978-80; asst. to gen. counsel Office Gen. Counsel Dept. Navy, Washington, 1980-82; assoc. counsel Naval Supply Systems Command, Washington, 1982—; chmn. internat. acquisition com. Defense Acquisition Regulatory Council, Washington, 1984—. Mem. ABA, Phi Beta Kappa. Avocations: reading, running, traveling. Government contracts and claims, Public international. Office: Naval Supply Systems Command Office Counsel Washington DC 20376

REGALIA, EDMUND LOUIS, lawyer; b. Richmond, Calif., Feb. 9, 1931; s. Louis and Constance Mary (Gay) R.; m. Gwendolyn Whiteford, July 1, 1956; children—Douglas, Kenneth, Phillip, Constance. B.A., U. Calif.-Berkeley, 1952, J.D., 1958. Bar: Calif. 1959, U.S. dist. ct. (no., central and ea. dists.) Calif. 1959. Assoc., Thelen, Marrin, Johnson & Bridges, San Francisco, 1959-60; assoc. Orlando J. Bowman, Oakland, Calif., 1960-64; ptnr. Miller, Starr & Regalia, Oakland, 1964—. Bd. dirs. Kennedy-King Meml. Coll. Scholarship Fund. Served to lt. (j.g.) USN 1952-55. Mem. ABA, State Bar Calif., Alameda County Bar Assn., Order of Coif. Democrat. Real property, Federal civil litigation, State civil litigation. Home: 1950 Whitecliff Ct Walnut Creek CA 94596

REGAN, DONALD H., lawyer, educator; b. 1944, A.B., Harvard U., 1963; LL.B., U. Va., 1966; B.Ph. (Rhodes scholar), Oxford (Eng.) U., 1968; Ph.D., U. Mich., 1980. Asst. prof. U. Mich., Ann Arbor, 1968-71, assoc. prof., 1972-73, prof., 1974-83, prof. law and philosophy, 1983—. Guggenheim fellow, 1985; recipient Matchette prize Am. Philos. Assn., 1981. Author: Utilitarianism and Co-operation, 1980; editor U. Va. Law Review, 1966. Legal education, Constitutional. Office: U Mich Law Sch Hutchins Hall Ann Arbor MI 48109

REGAN, MICHAEL PATRICK, lawyer; b. Bklyn., Feb. 22, 1941; s. Cornelius Francis and Marguerite (Cann) R.; m. Susan Ann Light, July 13, 1974; children—Michael Patrick, Brian Christopher, Mark Dennis. B.A. in English, U. Notre Dame, 1963; LL.B., Albany Law Sch., Union U., 1967, J.D., 1968. Bar: N.Y. 1967, Va. 1975. Assoc. Medwin & McMahon, Albany, N.Y., 1967-69; asst. dist. atty. Albany County, N.Y., 1969; corp. atty. Mohasco Corp., Amsterdam, N.Y., 1969-74; asst. gen. csl. Dan River Inc., Danville, Va., 1975-81, assoc. gen. csl., 1981—, asst. sec., 1984—; asst. gen. counsel, asst. sec. Dan River Holding Co., 1984—; asst. sec. Dan River Service Corp. of Va., 1984—. Sec. Dan Pac, polit. action com., Danville; clarinetist, saxophonist Tightsqueeze Philharm. Band; leader: The Dance-Notes. Mem. ABA, N.Y. State Bar Assn., Va. Bar Assn., Danville Bar Assn., Union Internationale des Avocats, Internat. Platform Assn. Republican. Roman Catholic. Club: Rotary (Danville). General corporate, Pension, profit-sharing, and employee benefits, Trademark and copyright. Home: 236 Cambridge Circle Danville VA 24541 Office: 2291 Memorial Dr Danville VA 24541

REGENBOGEN, ELLIS ARNOLD, lawyer; b. N.Y.C., Dec. 6, 1946; s. Harold and Laura Beverly (Hochberger) R.; m. Sally Ann Addlestone, Mar. 28, 1970; children: Scott, Lisa. AB, Dartmouth Coll., 1967; JD, Columbia U., 1970. Bar: N.Y. 1971, U.S. Ct. Appeals (2d cir.) 1974, U.S. Dist. Ct. (so. and ea. dists.) N.Y. 1975. Assoc. Chadbourne, Parke, Whiteside & Wolff, N.Y.C., 1970-79; dep. gen. counsel, sec. Columbia Pictures Industries, Inc., N.Y.C., 1979-86; of counsel Jones, Day, Reavis & Pogue, Dallas, 1986—. Mem. ABA. General corporate, Securities, Entertainment. Office: Jones Day Reavis & Pogue 2300 LTV Ctr 2001 Ross Ave Dallas TX 75230

REGENSTREIF, HERBERT, lawyer; b. N.Y.C., May 13, 1935; s. Max and Jeannette (Hacker) R.; m. Patricia Friedman, Dec. 20, 1967 (div. July 1968); m. Charlotte Lois Levy, Dec. 10, 1980; 1 child, Cara Rachael. BA, Hobart Coll., 1957; JD, N.Y. Law Sch., 1960; MS, Pratt Inst., 1985. Bar: N.Y. 1961, Ky. 1985, U.S. Dist. Ct. (ea. and so. dists.) N.Y. 1962, U.S. Tax Ct. 1967, U.S. Ct. Appeals (2d cir.) 1962, U.S. Supreme Ct. 1967. Ptnr., Fried & Regenstreif, P.C., Mineola, N.Y., 1963—; pres. Manhattan Bagel Co.; controlling ptnr. Sious City Cellular Partnership; cons. in field. Contbr. articles to profl. jours. County committeeman Dem. Com., Queens County, N.Y., 1978-79; arbitrator N.Y. City Civil Ct., 1984-86. Mem. Bar Assn. Nassau County, Phi Delta Phi, Beta Phi Mu. Jewish. Club: Hobart of N.Y. (gov. 1968-69). General practice, Real property, Probate.

REGIRER, WALTER WLODZIMIERZ, lawyer; b. Warsaw, Poland, Dec. 22, 1913. Student Law Sch., Lille, France, 1932; LL.M., U. Warsaw, 1937; J.D., U. Richmond (Va.), 1949. Bar: Va. 1949, U.S. Supreme Ct. 1954. Adminstrv. asst. U.S. Econ. Mission to Monrovia, Liberia, 1945; with export dept. Montgomery Ward, Chgo., 1947; mem. Purcell, Regirer, House & Hall, Richmond, Va., 1949-60; sole practice, Richmond, 1960—; consul. for Mex. in U.S., 1975—; pres., gen. counsel Health of Va., also Plyler's, The Windsor, University Park, 1949—; lectr. internat. law Coll. William and Mary, Richmond, 1955-59; U.S. exhbn. mgr. U.S. Dept. Commerce with embassies Rio de Janeiro, Guatemala, San Salvador, Montevideo and U.S. consulates gen., Zurich and Barcelona, 1963-66; instr. internat. law JAGC Sch., Charlottesville, Va., 1966-70; dir.-gen. Internat. Consular Acad. Served to lt. col. JAGC, USAR, 1949-74. Aide-de-camp to gov. Va., 1958—; col. JAGC Va. Defense Froce. Decorated Brit. Star, 1939-45, Order of Consular Merit, gran official Instituto Consular Interamericano, 1977; recipient Disting. Service award P.R. Consular Corps, 1977. Mem. Nat. Lawyers Club (Washington), ABA (chmn. diplomatic and consular law com.), Fed. Bar Assn. (v.p. 1960-61), Va. State Bar (bar council 1960-64, chmn. internat. health, sr. citizens law sects.), 4th U.S. Circuit Jud. Conf. Editor Consular Rev. (Hardy Cross Dillard Meml. award 1985). Administrative and regulatory, Health. Home: 9 Roslyn Hills Dr Richmond VA 23229 Office: 2420 Pemberton Rd Richmond VA 23233-2099

REGNIER, RICHARD ADRIAN, lawyer; b. Portland, Oreg., Aug. 23, 1931; s. Augustus Jerome and Marietta (Howland) R.; m. Maria Teresa Arguindegui, Oct. 12, 1957; children: Richard Adrian Jr., Lisa Marina, Augustus Jerome II, Teresa Lynn. Student, Harvard U., 1949-50; BS, U.S. Mil. Acad., 1955; LLB, U. Calif., Berkeley, 1962. Bar: Calif. 1963, U.S. Dist. Ct. (so. dist.) Calif. 1963, U.S. Supreme Ct. 1968. Commd. 2d lt. USAF, 1955, advanced through grades to capt., res., 1959; dep. dist. atty. Ventura County, Calif., 1963-65; assoc. Ferguson, Regnier & Paterson, Oxnard, Calif., 1965-68, ptnr., 1968—; instr. criminal law and evidence Ventura County Jr. Coll. and Ventura County Sheriff's Acad., 1963-65; judge pro tem Superior Ct. Ventura County, 1971—. Speaker Right to Life League So. Calif., Ventura County, 1973—; campaign chmn. MacIntyre for Assessor, Ventura County, 1986—. Named Extraordinary Minister of Holy Eucharist, Archbishop of Los Angeles, Ventura, 1971—. Mem. ABA, Calif. Bar Assn. (group ins. com. 1973-76), Ventura County Bar Assn. (Assn. Trial Lawyers Am., Calif. Trial Lawyers Assn. (recognition of experience certs. various areas), Ventura County Trial Lawyers Assn. (pres. 1971, lectr. trial law), Am. Judicature Soc., Ventura County Legal Aid Assn. (pres. 1968), Am. Arbitration Assn. (arbitrator 1967—) Nat. Bd. Trial Adv. (diplomate, cert.). Republican. Lodges: Rotary (pres. 1982-83, Paul Harris fellow 1986), K.C. Avocations: golf, running, weight lifting, skiing. State civil litigation, Personal injury, Federal civil litigation. Home: 4160 N Clubhouse Dr Camarillo CA 93010 Office: Ferguson Regnier & Paterson 315 N A St Oxnard CA 93032

REGO, ALFRED R., JR., lawyer; b. Fall River, Mass., Apr. 3, 1951; s. Alfred R. Sr. and Fernanda (Perreira) R.; m. Lynda J. Gardner, Oct. 8, 1973. BSBA, Bryant Coll., 1973; JD, Franklin Pierce Law Ctr., 1976. Bar: RI. 1976, U.S. Dist. Ct. R.I. 1977. Ptnr. Rego & Rego, Bristol, R.I., 1978—; judge Bristol Probate Ct., R.I., 1978-80, 82-84. Rep. candidate 1st Congl. Dist. R.I., 1984. Named one of Outstanding Young Men in Am., 1979. Mem. ABA, R.I. Bar Assn., Bristol County Bar Assn., Assn. Trial Lawyers Am., R.I. Assn. Trial Lawyers, Immigration and Nationality Lawyers Assn., Nat. Coll. Probate Judges, Am. Judges Assn., Comml. Law League, Bristol C. of C. (rep. econ. devel. com. 1980-84), Bristol Jaycees (treas. 1977). Roman Catholic. Club: Bristol Yacht. Lodge: Rotary (mem. exec. bd. Bristol chpt. 1984-85). Avocations: song writing and recording, musical instruments. Real property, Immigration, naturalization, and customs, Probate. Office: Rego & Rego 557 Hope St Bristol RI 02809

REHBERGER, ROBERT LEE, lawyer; b. St. Louis, Apr. 2, 1949; s. W.R. and Ruth (Grimmer) Schoolfield. BS, Benedictine Coll., Atchison, Kans., 1971; MBA, M in Pub. Adminstrn., U. Puget Sound, 1975; JD, U. Mo., Kansas City, 1980. Bar: Mo. 1981, Ill. 1981, Okla. 1983, D.C. 1985, U.S. Dist. Ct. (we. dist.) Okla., U.S. Dist. Ct. (we. dist.) Mo., U.S. Dist. Ct. (so. dist.) Ill., U.S. Ct. Appeals (10th cir.), U.S. Supreme Ct. Comptroller cir. ct. Madison County, Edwardsville, Ill., 1976-77, law clk. to presiding justice, 1981, asst. states atty., 1981-82; prof. U. Mo., St. Louis, 1982—; instr. Southwestern Okla. State U., Weatherford, 1982—; instr. U. Mo., St. Louis, 1982; faculty advisor Alpha Kappa Psi Southwestern Okla. State U., Weatherford, 1982-86, prof. 1982-86. Served with U.S. Army, 1972-75. Mem. ABA, Okla. Bar Assn., Assn. Trial Lawyers Am., Ill. Bar Assn., Met. Bar Assn., Met. Bar Assn. Kansas City, D.C. Bar Assn., Madison County Bar Assn., Alpha Kappa Psi, Phi Delta Phi. Roman Catholic. Lodge: Kiwanis, Masons, KC. Avocations: water and snow skiing, horse back riding. General practice, Personal injury, Probate. Office: Woodcrest Plaza 1260 Mercantile Dr Highland IL 62249

REHNQUIST, WILLIAM HUBBS, Supreme Ct. justice; b. Milw., Oct. 1, 1924; s. William Benjamin and Margery (Peck) R.; m. Natalie Cornell, Aug. 29, 1953; children: James, Janet, Nancy. BA, MA, Stanford, 1948; MA, Harvard, 1949; LLB, Stanford, 1952. Bar: Ariz. bar. Law clk. to former justice Robert H. Jackson, U.S. Supreme Ct., 1952-53; with Evans, Kitchel & Jenckes, Phoenix, 1953-55; mem. Ragan & Rehnquist, Phoenix, 1956-57; ptnr. Cunningham, Carson & Messenger, Phoenix, 1957-60, Powers & Rehnquist, Phoenix, 1960-69; asst. atty.-gen. office of legal counsel Dept. of Justice, Washington, 1969-71; assoc. justice U.S. Supreme Ct., 1971-1986, chief justice, 1986—; Mem. Nat. Conf. Commrs. Uniform State Laws, 1963-69. Contbr. articles to law jours., nat. mags. Served with USAAF, 1943-46, NATOUSA. Mem. Fed., Am. Maricopa (Ariz.) County bar assns., State Bar Ariz., Nat. Conf. Lawyers and Realtors, Phi Beta Kappa, Order of Coif, Phi Delta Phi. Lutheran. Jurisprudence. Office: Supreme Ct US Washington DC 20543

REIBSTEIN, RICHARD JAY, lawyer; b. Phila., Mar. 12, 1951; s. Albert Simon and Alma (Wilf) R.; m. Susan Barbara Fisch, May 18, 1975. BA with distinction, U. Rochester, 1973; JD with honors, George Washington U., 1976. Bar: Pa. 1976, N.Y. 1979, N.J. 1979, U.S. Dist. Ct. (so. dist.) N.Y. 1979, U.S. Dist. Ct. (ea. dist.) N.Y. 1979, N.J. 1979, U.S. Ct. Appeals (3d cir.) 1980, U.S. Ct. Appeals (2d cir.) 1982, U.S. Supreme Ct. 1983. Staff atty. Dept. Labor, Washington, 1976; counsel NLRB, Washington, 1976-78; assoc. Seham, Klein & Zelman (formerly Surrey, Karasik, Morse & Seham), N.Y.C., 1978-81; assoc. Epstein Becker Borsody & Green, P.C., N.Y.C., 1981-86, ptnr., 1986—; arbitrator Better Bus. Bur. Met. N.Y. Contbr. articles to legal jours. Mem. ABA (devel. of law under NLRA com., sect. labor and employment law 1976—), N.Y. State Bar Assn. (labor arbitration and collective bargaining com., sect. labor and employment law 1980—). Democrat. Labor, Federal civil litigation, State civil litigation. Office: Epstein Becker Borsody & Green PC 250 Park Ave New York NY 10177

REICH, ABRAHAM CHARLES, lawyer; b. Waterbury, Conn., Apr. 17, 1949; s. Samuel and Esther (Gurvitz) R.; m. Sherri Engelman, Aug. 15, 1971; children: Spencer, Alexander. BA, U. Conn., 1971; JD, Temple U., 1974. Bar: Pa. 1974, U.S. Supreme Ct. 1979. Assoc. Fox, Rothschild, O'Brien & Frankel, Phila., 1974-81, ptnr., 1981—. Trustee Phila. Bar Assn. Edn. Found., 1984; v.p., bd. dirs. YM-YWHA, Phila., 1977—. Mem. Phila. Bar Assn. (chairperson profl. responsibility com. 1983-84, chairperson bench-bar com. 1985, chairperson profl. guidance com. 1987—, bd. govs. 1987—). Jewish. Club: Locust (Phila.). Antitrust, Federal civil litigation, Securities. Home: 2224 Mt Vernon St Philadelphia PA 19130 Office: Fox Rothschild O'Brien & Frankel 2000 Market St 10th Floor Philadelphia PA 19103

REICH, LAURENCE, lawyer; b. Jersey City, N.J., Jan. 22, 1931; s. Victor and Miriam (Gross) R.; m. Doris Rita Diamond, Oct. 21, 1965. B.A., U. Chgo., 1951, J.D., 1953. Bar: N.J. 1954, U.S. Dist. Ct. N.J. 1954, U.S. Ct. Appeals, (3d cir.) 1958, U.S. Supreme Ct. 1963, U.S. Tax Ct. 1971, N.Y. 1982, U.S. Dist. Ct. (so. dist.) N.Y. 1982. Mem. firm Carpenter, Bennett & Morrissey, Newark, 1957—, ptnr., 1963—, sr. ptnr., 1970—; mem. Bur. Nat. Affairs Tax Adv. bd., 1972—; lectr. NYU Inst. Fed. Taxation, Tulane Tax Inst., Ark. Tax Inst., Fairleigh Dickinson U. Tax Inst., Seton Hall Tax Inst., N.J. Inst. Continuing Legal Edn., Internat. Bus. Conf., Mid-Atlantic Estate Planing Conf. Served with U.S. Army, 1955-57. Fellow Am. Coll. Tax Counsel; mem. ABA (com. chmn. sect. taxation 1972-74, 85—), N.J. Bar Assn. (chmn. taxation sect. 1975-76), Assn. Fed. Bar State N.J. (v.p.), Essex County Bar Assn. Contbr. articles to profl. jours. Corporate taxation, General corporate, Pension, profit-sharing, and employee benefits. Office: 3 Gateway Ctr Newark NJ 07102

REICH, PERRY SETH, lawyer; b. N.Y.C., Mar. 15, 1949; s. Arnold Anthony and Thelma Ruth (Olensky) R. BA, SUNY, Stony Brook, 1971; JD, Hofstra U., 1974. Bar: N.Y. 1975, U.S. Supreme Ct. 1978, Calif. 1980, Fla. 1981, U.S. Dist. Ct. (ea., so. and no. dists.) N.Y. 1981, U.S. Dist. Ct. (so. dist.) Fla. 1981, U.S. Ct. Appeals (2d, 5th, 9th and 11th cirs.) 1981. Prin. law asst. to Judge Jacob D. Fuchsberg N.Y. State Ct. Appeals, Albany, 1975-78, 81-83; prof. New York Law Sch., N.Y.C., 1978-80; prin. law asst. to Hon. Vito J. Titone appellate div. Supreme Ct. N.Y. Ct. Appeals, Albany, 1983—; adj. prof. Cardozo Law Sch., N.Y.C., 1982, Touro Coll. Sch. Law, Huntington, N.Y., 1982—; lectr. continuing edn. programs various law assns. Author: Guide to Appellate Review in Criminal Cases. Mem. N.Y. State Trial Lawyers Assn., N.Y. County Lawyers Assn. State civil litigation, Criminal, Federal civil litigation. Home: 80-42 Bell Blvd Jamaica NY 11427 Office: 325 E Sunrise Hwy Lindenhurst NY 11757

REICHEL, AARON ISRAEL, lawyer; b. N.Y.C., Jan. 30, 1950; s. Oscar Asher and Josephine Hannah (Goldstein) R. BA, Yeshiva U., 1971, MA, 1974; JD, Fordham U., 1976. Bar: N.J. 1977, N.Y. 1978; ordained rabbi, 1975. Atty. editor securities regulation Prentice-Hall, Englewood Cliffs, N.J., 1977-78; editor, founder govt. disclosure service Prentice-Hall, Paramus, N.J., 1978-82; atty. editor fed. taxation Prentice-Hall, Paramus, 1982—. Author: The Maverick Rabbi, 1st edit., 1984, 2d edit. 1986; co-author (manual) Style and Usage, 1984; contbr. The 1986 Jewish Directory and Almanac, 1986; contbg. editor Complete Guide to the Tax Reform Act of 1986; contbr. articles to profl. jours. Nat. pres. YAVNEH, N.Y.C., 1973-74; mem. youth commn. Am. Jewish Congress, N.Y.C., 1973-76; bd. dirs. Union Orthodox Jewish Congregations Am., N.Y.C., 1973-74, Harry and Jane Fischel Found., N.Y.C., 1977—. Mem. ABA, N.Y. State Bar Assn. (various coms.), Am. Soc. of Access Profls. (founder, 1st chmn. N.Y. chpt.), Nat. Jewish Commn. on Law and Pub. Affairs (family law com.), Yeshiva U. Alumni Assn. (exec. com., editor in chief Bulletin 1974-78). Avocations: writing, baseball, tennis. Personal income taxation, Freedom of information act (government disclosure), General practice. Home: 230 W 79th St New York NY 10024

REICHELDERFER, FRANK A., lawyer; b. Peoria, Ill., May 30, 1919; s. Charles Foster and Edna Maude (Calligan) R.; m. Catherine Evelyn Aaron,

Sept. 28, 1943; children—Mark, Ann, Glen. B.S., U. Ill., 1940, J.D., 1943. Bar: Ill. Assoc., Wilson & McIlvaine, Chgo., 1943-55, ptnr., 1955—; mem. Ill. Bd. Examiners in Accountancy, 1969-72. Mem. exec. council Chgo. council Boy Scouts Am., 1960-62; chmn. bd. govs. Winnetka (Ill.) Community House, 1968-70; chmn. Winnetka Zoning Bd. Apls., 1976-82. Mem. Ill. State Bar Assn. (bd. govs. 1963-67), Chgo. Bar Assn. (bd. mgrs. 1969-71), Am. Coll. Real Estate Lawyers, Law Club Chgo., Legal Club Chgo., Order of Coif, Phi Kappa Phi, Beta Gamma Sigma, Phi Eta Sigma. Republican. Clubs: University (Chgo.) (pres. 1971-73), Attic (pres. 1986-87). Landlord-tenant, Real property. Office: 135 S LaSalle St Chicago IL 60603

REICHERT, ROBERT JOSEPH, lawyer, corporate executive; b. South Bend, Ind., Oct. 2, 1924; s. Joseph S. and Irene (Foley) R.; m. Ruth Winfree, June 10, 1950; children—Joseph, Michael, James, Nancy, Edward. B.S. in Chem. Engring., U. Mich., 1948, J.D., 1952. Bar: N.Y. 1952. Patent atty. Carborundum Corp., Niagara Falls, N.Y., 1952-55; patent atty. DuPont Corp., Wilmington, Del., 1955-70, chief fgn. patent counsel, 1968-71, head environ. div., 1971-80, with legis. environ. affairs dept., 1980-85; with Wilgus Assocs., Realtors, Bethany Beach, Del., 1985—. Served with USN, 1944-46. Mem. Chem. Mfrs. Assn. (environ. quality com. 1978-80, hazard waste com. 1982-85, victims compensation com. 1982-85). Roman Catholic. Environment, Legislative. Home: 4660 Malden Dr Wilmington DE 19803

REICHLER, PAUL STUART, lawyer; b. N.Y.C., Aug. 31, 1947; s. Joseph Lawrence and Rebecca (Cooper) R.; m. Patricia Ann Horton, July 26, 1980; 1 child, Jessica Danielle. BA, Tufts U., 1969; JD, Harvard U., 1973. Bar: D.C. 1973, U.S. Supreme Ct. 1981. Assoc. Arnold & Porter, Washington, 1973-81; ptnr. Powell, Goldstein, Frazer & Murphy, Washington, 1981-84, Reichler & Appelbaum, Washington, 1984—; Mem. Commn. on U.S.-Cen. Am. Relations, Washington, 1982—; dir. Freedom Charter Edn. Fund, Washington, 1986—. Private international, Public international, Federal civil litigation. Office: Reichler & Appelbaum 888 17th St NW Washington DC 20006

REICHMAN, FRED MARSHALL, lawyer; b. St. Louis, Feb. 7, 1931; s. Harry and Florence M. (Korngold) R.; m. Martha M. McAllister, Jan. 30, 1977. AB, JD, Washington U., St. Louis, 1955. Bar: Mo. 1955, U.S. Dist. Ct. (ea. dist.) Mo. 1963, U.S. Ct. Appeals (D.C. cir.) 1975, U.S. Appeals (8th cir.) 1980. Assoc. Karol A. Korngold, St. Louis, 1955-59; ptnr. Reichman & Aguirre, St. Louis, 1960-66, Husch, Eppenberger, Donohue et al, St. Louis, 1967-80, Jackson, Lewis, Schnitzler & Krupman, N.Y.C., 1982-84; sole practice N.Y.C., 1984-86; ptnr. Reichman & Bernstein, St. Louis, 1986; sole practice St. Louis, 1987—. Served to sgt. U.S. Army, 1955-57. Mem. ABA, Mo. Bar Assn., Bar Assn. Met. St. Louis (chmn. continuing legal edn. inst. 1980—). Club: Mo. Athletic (St. Louis). Avocation: sailing. Labor. Office: 1010 Market Suite 1640 Saint Louis MO 63101

REICIN, RONALD IAN, lawyer; b. Chgo., Dec. 11, 1942; s. Frank Edward and Abranita (Rome) R.; m. Alyta Friedland, May 23, 1965; children—Eric, Kael. B.B.A., U. Mich., 1964, M.B.A., 1967, J.D. cum laude, 1967. Bar: Ill. 1967, U.S. Tax Ct. 1967. Mem. staff Price Waterhouse & Co., Chgo., 1966; ptnr. Jenner & Block, Chgo., 1967—. Bd. dirs. Nat. Kidney Found. Ill., 1978—, Scoliosis Assn. Chgo., 1981—, Ruth Page Found. Mem. Chgo. Bar Assn., Internat. Conf. Shopping Ctrs., ABA, Ill. Bar Assn., Chgo. Mortgage Attys. Assn., Phi Kappa Phi, Beta Gamma Sigma, Beta Alpha Psi. Clubs: Executive, Legal (Chgo.). Real property, General practice, General corporate. Home: 1916 Berkeley Rd Highland Park IL 60035 Office: Jenner & Block 1 IBM Plaza 43d Floor Chicago IL 60611

REID, CHARLES ADAMS, III, lawyer; b. Plainfield, N.J., Apr. 21, 1947; s. Charles Adams Jr. and Gertrude C. (Egan) R.; m. Teresa Keenan, May 11, 1974. BA, Colgate U., 1969; JD, Columbia U., 1974. Bar: N.Y. 1974, U.S. Dist. Ct. (ea. and so. dists.) N.Y. 1975, U.S. Dist. Ct. N.J. 1976, U.S. Ct. Appeals (3d cir.) 1983. Law clk. to judge U.S. Dist. Ct. (ea. dist.) N.Y., Bklyn., 1974-75; assoc. Coudert Bros., N.Y.C., 1975-77, Shanley & Fisher, Newark, 1977-82; ptnr. Shanley & Fisher, Newark and Morristown, N.J., 1983—. Mem. planning bd. Peapack-Gladstone, N.J. 1984—, chmn., 1987—; bd. dirs. Morris Ctr. YMCA, Cedar Knolls, N.J., 1986—. Served with U.S. Army, 1970-72, Vietnam. Mem. ABA (litigation sect.), N.J. Bar Assn., Essex County Bar Assn. Clubs: Essex (Newark), Morristown. Federal civil litigation, State civil litigation, Insurance. Home: PO Box 398 Gladstone NJ 07934 Office: Shanley & Fisher PC 131 Madison Ave Morristown NJ 07960-1979

REID, DAVID PAUL, lawyer; b. Tulsa, July 4, 1954; s. David C. Reid and Ann (Bingham) Kelly; m. Charlene McCoy, July 29, 1977; 1 child, Brett David. BBA, Dallas Baptist U., 1976; JD, U. Okla., 1979. Bar: U.S. Dist. Ct. (no. dist.) 1979, U.S. Ct. Appeals (10th cir.) 1982. Jud. intern Okla. Supreme Ct., Oklahoma City, 1978-79; ptnr. Ash, Crews & Reid, Okmulgee and Tulsa, Okla., 1979—. Editor Okla. U. Law Rev., 1977-79. Del. Dem. Nat. Convention, San Francisco, 1984; coordinator 2d dist. campaign Robert Henry for atty. gen., Okmulgee, 1986—; chmn. Okmulgee County Dems., 1985-87. Mem. ABA, Okla. Bar Assn., Assn. Trial Lawyers Am., Okla. Trial Lawyers Assn., Am. Judicature Soc., Order of Coif. Democrat. Lodge: Sertoma (dir. awards and achievement Okmulgee chpt. 1986—). Avocations: tennis, basketball, reading. Personal injury, State civil litigation, Workers' compensation. Home: 2303 Fieldstone Okmulgee OK 74447 Office: Ash Crews & Reid PO Box 727 Okmulgee OK 74447

REID, JOHN EDWARD, lawyer; b. Denver, Sept. 18, 1948; s. Donald Good and Ona Elizabeth (O'Connell) R. BS in MetE, Colo. Sch. of Mines, 1970; JD, U. Colo., 1973. Bar: Colo. 1973, U.S. Dist. Ct. Colo. 1973. Sole practice Ft. Collins, Colo., 1973-78; ptnr. Gross & Reid P.C., Ft. Collins, 1979—. Bd. dirs. Am. Cancer Soc. Larimer County Unit, 1984—. Mem. ABA, Colo. Bar Assn., Larimer County Bar Assn., Ft. Collins Round Table (pres. 1974). Avocations: skiing, handball, sailing. Real property, Probate, Contracts commercial. Home: 2045 Sherell Dr Fort Collins CO 80524 Office: Gross & Reid PC 215 W Oak Suite 720 Fort Collins CO 80521

REID, JOHN JAMES, lawyer; b. Pitts., Mar. 26, 1946; s. Gerald Edward and Mary Catherine (Butler) R.; m. Mary Francis Deane, Oct. 5, 1974; children: Katherine Lynn, Caroline Rose. BA, Cath. U. Am., 1968; JD, Duquesne U., 1972; LLM, Georgetown U., 1975. Bar: Pa. 1972, U.S. Tax Ct. 1972, Fla. 1977, U.S. Ct. Claims 1977. Trial atty. office of chief counsel IRS, Washington, 1972-76; assoc. Giles, Hedrick & Robinson, P.A., Orlando, Fla., 1976-79, ptnr., 1979—. Mem. ABA (taxation sect. 1976—), Fla. Bar Assn. (taxation sect. 1977—), Orange County Bar Assn., Estate Planning Council, Tax Roundtable, Phi Beta Kappa. General corporate, Corporate taxation. Office: Giles Hedrick & Robinson 109 E Church St Suite 301 PO Box 2631 Orlando FL 32802

REID, R(ALPH) BENJAMINE, lawyer; b. Concord, N.C., Jan. 11, 1950; s. Fred Herndon and Frances (Barnhardt) R.; m. Jennie Lou Divine, Dec. 19, 1970; children—Elisabeth Divine, Margaret Hethcox, Benjamine Joseph. A.B., U. N.C., 1971; J.D. cum laude, U. Ga., 1974. Bar: Ga. 1974, Fla. 1974, U.S. Dist. Ct. (so. dist.) Fla. 1974, U.S. Supreme Ct. 1981, U.S. Ct. Appeals (5th cir.) 1974, (11th cir.) 1981. Assoc. Kimbrell & Hamann, P.A., Miami, Fla., 1974-79, mem., 1980—; lectr. Atlanta Bar Product Liability Seminar, Emory U., 1983, U. Miami Law Sch., 1983; mem. products liability com. Def. Research Inst., Chgo., 1984—, program chmn., 1986—. Vestryman, sr. warden St. Philip's Episcopal Ch., Coral Gables, Fla., 1982-85; mem. exec. bd. Episc. Diocese S.E. Fla., Miami, 1982—, standing com., 2986—, sec., 1986—, mem. diocesan obligations and appeals com., 1985; trustee Trinity Episc. Sch., Miami, 1984—; Dade Heritage Trust, Miami, 1984—, treas., 1985, 1st v.p., 1986; bd. dirs. Leadership Miami Alumni Assn., 1984—, exec. com. leadership Miami, 1986—. Mem. Dade County Bar Assn. (bd. dirs. 1982-85), Dade County Def. Bar Assn. (bd. dirs. 1983), ABA (state rep. to regional subcom. 1982-84), Am. Judicature Soc., Am. Assn. for Automotive Medicine, Phi Kappa Phi. Democrat. Federal civil litigation, State civil litigation, Product liability. Home: 905 University Dr Coral Gables FL 33134 Office: Kimbrell & Hamann PA 799 Brickell Plaza Miami FL 33131

REID, RICHARD AYRES, lawyer; b. Balt., Mar. 5, 1931; s. James Wilson and Helen Mae (Ayres) R.; m. Jeanette Foust Fisher, Dec. 19, 1956; children: Helen E. James S., Andrew R. BA, Yale U., 1953; LLB, U. Va., 1956. Bar: Md. 1956, U.S. Dist. Ct. Md. 1960. Ptnr. Royston, Mueller, McLean & Reid, Towson, Md., 1960—. Mem. Jud. Nominating Commn. for. the 3d Jud. Cir. Md., 1976-84. Served to lt. USNR, 1956-59. Mem. ABA, Md. Bar Assn. (bd. govs. 1976-78, 86—), Baltimore County Bar Assn. (pres. 1985), Md. Bar Found., Baltimore County Bar Found. (pres. 1986), Am. Judicature Soc., Am. Coll. Trial Lawyers, St. Andrews Soc. Balt., Disseniers Law Club (pres. 1971). Democrat. Club: Balt. Country. Avocations: hunting, golf, sailing. State civil litigation, Condemnation, Federal civil litigation. Home: 4 Valley Oak Ct Timonium MD 21093 Office: Royson Mueller McLean & Reid 102 W Pennsylvania Ave Towson MD 21204

REID, ROSS, lawyer, retired business executive; b. Spokane, Wash., Mar. 9, 1917; s. William George and Margaret (Gamble) R.; m. Sara Falknor, Dec. 31, 1940 (div.); 1 dau., Heather (Mrs. Edmund A. Schaffzin); m. Marney Sick Meeker, Jan. 19, 1966. A.B., Whitman Coll., 1938; student, U. Wash. Sch. Law, 1938-40; J.D., Northwestern U., 1942. Bar: Ill. 1941, N.Y. 1943, D.C. 1960. Assoc. firm Root, Clark, Buckner & Ballantine, N.Y.C., 1942-53; mem. firm Dewey, Ballantine, Bushby, Palmer & Wood (and predecessors), N.Y.C., 1954-62; v.p., dir., gen. counsel Beechnut Life Savers, Inc., 1962-68; sr. v.p., dir., gen. counsel, exec. com. Squibb Corp., 1968-83, dir. exec. com., 1983-84; dir. Allegheny Power System, Inc.; trustee Emigrant Savs. Bank; mem. N.Y State Lawyers Com. to Support Ct. Reorgn., 1958-60. Chmn. bd. Am. Heart Assn., 1972-74; chmn. N.Y. Heart Assn., 1964-72, exec. com.; bd. dirs. Internat. Cardiology Found.; bd. mem. 1st v.p. Internat. Soc. and Fedn. Cardiology; trustee Whitman Coll., Robert A. Taft Inst. Govt., Food and Drug Law Inst. Served with USAAF, 1945. Recipient Gold Heart award Am. Heart Assn., 1970. Fellow Am. Bar Found.; mem. Am., N.Y., Assn. Bar City N.Y. (chmn. membership com. 1961-64, exec. com. 1962-66), Jud. Conf. Second Circuit (exec. sec. plans com. 1960-64), Am. Judicature Soc., Order of Coif, Beta Theta Pi, Delta Sigma Rho, Delta Theta Phi. Clubs: University (N.Y.C.), West Side Tennis (N.Y.C.); Coral Beach and Tennis (Bermuda); Seattle Tennis. General corporate, Federal civil litigation, Trademark and copyright. Home: 142 E 71st St New York NY 10021 Office: 40 W 57th St New York NY 10019

REID, SUE TITUS, law educator; b. Bryan, Tex., Nov. 13, 1939; d. Andrew Jackson Jr. and Loraine (Wylie) Titus. BS with honors, Tex. Woman's U., 1960; MA, U. Mo., 1962, PhD, 1965; JD, U. Iowa, 1972. Bar: Iowa 1972, U.S. Ct. Appeals (D.C. cir.) 1978, U.S. Supreme Ct. 1978. From instr. to assoc. prof. sociology Cornell Coll., Mt. Vernon, Iowa, 1963-72; assoc. prof., chmn. dept. sociology Coe Coll., Cedar Rapids, Iowa, 1972-74; assoc. prof. law. U. Wash., Seattle, 1974-76; exec. assoc. Am. Sociol. Assn., Washington, 1976-77; prof. law U. Tulsa, 1978—; acting chmn. dept. sociology Cornell Coll., 1965-66; visiting assoc. prof. sociology U. Nebr., Lincoln, 1970; visiting disting. prof. law and sociology U. Tulsa, 1977-78, assoc. dean 1979-81; visiting prof. law U. San Diego, 1981-82; mem. People-to-People Crime Prevention Del. to People's Republic of China, 1982; George Beto Prof. criminal justice Sam Houston U., Huntsville, Tex., 1984-85; lecture/study tour of Criminal Justice systems of 10 European countries, 1985; cons. Evaluation Policy Research Assocs., Inc., Milw., 1976-77, Nat. Inst. Corrections, Idaho Dept. Corrections, 1984. Author: (with others) Bibliographies on Role Methodology and Propositions Volume D - Studies in the Role of the Public School Teacher, 1962, The Correctional System: An Introduction, 1981, Crime and Criminology, 4th ed., 1985, Criminal Justice: Procedure and Issues, 1987, 5th ed., 1987; editor (with David Lyon) Population Crisis: An Interdisciplinary Perspective, 1972; contbr. articles to profl. jours. Recipient Disting. Alumni award Tex. Woman's U., 1979; named One of Okla. Young Leaders of 80's Oklahoma Monthly, 1980. Criminal. Office: U Tulsa Coll Law 3120 E 4th Pl Tulsa OK 74104

REIDENBACH, J. MICHAEL, lawyer; b. San Francisco, Oct. 23, 1944; s. John Clarence and Nancy (Gilliland) R.; m. Claire Gustafson, Sept. 1, 1968; children: Peter, David, Sarah. BA in Internat. Relations, Stanford U., 1967; JD, U. Calif., San Francisco, 1972. Bar: Calif. 1972. Dep. dist. atty. Alameda County, Oakland, Calif., 1972-77; sr. counsel Pacific Gas and Electric Co., San Francisco, 1977-84; gen. counsel Pacific Gas and Transmission Co., San Francisco, 1984—; grader Calif. Bar Exan. Served to maj. USAR, 1969—. Republican. Congregationalist. Office: Pacific Gas Transmission Co 77 Beale St San Francisco CA 94106

REIDENBACH, WILLIAM JOHN, lawyer; b. Columbus, Ohio, July 7, 1930; s. Frederick Atlee and Ruth Higgins (CoVan) R.; m. JoAnn R. Raudebaugh, Mar. 21, 1954; children; Frederick, Faith, Amy, Emily. BSBA, Ohio State U., 1952, JD, 1954. Bar: Ohio 1954, U.S. Dist.Ct. (so. dsit.) Ohio 1959. Assoc. Vorys, Sater, Seymour & Pease, Columbus, 1954-56; atty. Ohio Div. Securities, Columbus, 1956-61; warden Ohio Ins. Dept., Columbus, 1961-63; v.p. gen. counsel, sec. Columbus Mut. Life Ins. Co., 1963—, also bd. dirs. Mem. Columbus Area Leadership Program, 1984; trustee, chmn. ins. depts. com. Griffith Found. for Ins. Edn., Columbus; bd. dirs. Seal Ohio Girl Scouts U.S. Council Inc., Columbus, 1981—. Mem. Assn. Life Ins. Counsel, Am. Council Life Ins. (legal sect.), Phi Delta Phi, Phi Kappa Sigma. Lutheran. General corporate, Insurance. Home: 989 Greenridge Rd Worthington OH 43085 Office: Columbus Mut Life Ins Co 303 E Broad St Columbus OH 43215

REIDL, PAUL WILLIAM, lawyer; b. Cleve., Aug. 20, 1955; s. Ronald William and Dolores (Page) R.B.A., George Washington U., 1977, J.D., 1980. Bar: D.C. 1980. Lectr. speech communication George Washington U., Washington, 1977-80; assoc. Crowell & Moring, Washington, 1980—. Coauthor: Mine Safety and Health Law, 1982, Coal Supply Contracts, 1987. Mem. ABA, D.C. Bar Assn., Order of Coif, Phi Beta Kappa. Republican. Roman Catholic. Avocations: fishing, camping, baseball, gardening, cross country skiing. Antitrust, Federal civil litigation, Mine safety and health. Home: 2710 Hemlock Ave Alexandria VA 22305 Office: Crowell & Moring 1001 Pennsylvania Ave NW Washington DC 20005

REIF, ERIC PETER, lawyer; b. Pitts., Nov. 2, 1942; s. Ernest Carl and Bernice Elizabeth (Thompson) R.; m. Donna Deeter, June 13, 1970; children: Roger Michael, Brian Peter. BA, U. Mich., 1963, JD, 1967. Bar: Mich. 1968, Pa. 1969, U.S. Dist. Ct. (ea., we. and mid. dists.) Pa. 1969. Law clk. to presiding justice Mich. Ct. Appeals, Lansing, 1967-68; trial lawyer Reed, Smith, Shaw & McClay, Pitts., 1968—, ptnr. litigation, 1979—. Mem. ABA, Pa. Bar Assn., Allegheny County Bar Assn., Acad. Trial Lawyers Allegheny County. Democrat. Presbyterian. Club: Longue Vue (Verona, Pa.). Avocations: running, skiing, boating, travel. Federal civil litigation, State civil litigation, Libel. Home: 14 Windsor Rd Pittsburgh PA 15215 Office: Reed Smith Shaw & McClay 435 6th Ave Pittsburgh PA 15219

REIFF, JEFFREY MARC, lawyer; b. Phila., Jan. 24, 1955; s. Morton William and Phyliss (Rubin) R.; m. Dominique F. Edrei, June 3, 1979; children—Justin Alexander, Collin Michael. B.S., B.A. magna cum laude in Mktg. Fin., Am. U., 1976; J.D., Temple U., 1976. Bar: Pa. 1979, U.S. Dist. Ct. Pa. 1975, N.Y. 1985. Ptnr. Sablosky, Wertheimer & Reiff, Phila., 1979-82, Mozenter, Durst & Reiff, Phila., 1982-85; prin., founder Reiff, Haaz and Assocs. and predecessor firms, Phila., 1985—. Mem. young leadership bd. Fedn. Jewish Agys., Phila., 1982—; bd. dirs. Golden Slipper Charities, Phila., 1979—, Solomon Schecker Schs., Phila., 1984. Mem. Phila. Bar Assn. (com. chmn. 1984—), Pa. Bar Assn. (com. chmn., mem. lawyers reference com. young lawyers div. 1980—), Am. Trial Lawyers Assn., Pa. Trial Lawyers Assn., Phila. Trial Lawyers Assn. Clubs: Locust, Golden Slipper (bd. dirs. 1980—), Abington Country (Phila.). Personal injury, Criminal, Entertainment. Home: 229 Holmecrest Rd Jenkintown PA 19046 Office: Jeffrey M Reiff & Assocs 1324 Walnut St Philadelphia PA 19107

REIFSNYDER, DANIEL ALAN, lawyer, foreign affairs officer; b. Washington, Apr. 6, 1950; s. C. Frank and Sally Ann (Evans) R.; m. Bonnie Leigh Shute, Oct. 13, 1984; 1 child, Claire Evans. Student, Institut d' Etudes Politiques, Paris, 1970-71; AB, Trinity Coll., 1972; student, Leningrad (USSR) Gosudarstvenniy Universitet, 1974; MA, Georgetown U., 1976; JD, George Washington U., 1981; postdoctoral, John Hopkins U., 1982-83. Bar: Va. 1981, D.C. 1982, U.S. Ct. Appeals (4th cir.) 1982. Asst. to exec. sec. U.S./Soviet and U.S./Polish conciliation bds. U.S. Dept. of Commerce, Washington, 1974-77, fgn. affairs officer, 1977-84; fgn. affairs officer U.S. Dept. of State, Washington, 1984—. Bd. dirs., v.p. Colonial Village (village I) Unit Owner's Assn., Arlington, Va., 1984-85, bd. dirs., pres., 1985—. Mem. ABA, Va. Bar Assn., D.C. Bar Assn., Arlington Civic Fedn. Episcopalian. Club: Metropolitan. Public international, Administrative and regulatory, Real property. Office: US Dept of State OES/OFA 22d and C Sts NW Washington DC 20520

REIKEN, SAMUEL N., lawyer; b. Jersey City, Jan. 10, 1941; s. Irving and Ruth (Weisman) R.; m. Michelle F. Fishco, Sept. 8, 1962 (div. May 1982); children, Frederick J., Wendy J. AB, Princeton U., 1962; LLB, Columbia U., 1965. Bar: N.J. 1965, U.S. Dist. Ct. N.J. 1965, U.S. Supreme Ct. 1976, N.Y. 1981, U.S. Tax Ct. 1985. Law clerk N.J. Superior Appellate Ct., Newark, 1965-66; assoc. Pitney, Hardin & Kipp, Morristown, N.J., 1966-67, Arthur L. Abrams Law Offices, Newark, 1967-69; ptnr. Abrams & Reiken, Newark, 1969-73, Shapiro, Berson, Hochberg & Reiken, Newark, 1973-76, Wasserman & Reiken, West Orange, N.J., 1976-83, Lampf, Lipkind, Prupis & Petigrow, West Orange, 1983—; incorporator, The Raptor Trust, Millington, N.J., 1983. Trustee Zool. Soc. N.J., West Orange, 1984—. Mem. ABA, N.J. State Bar Assn., Essex County Bar Assn., Fed. Bar Assn. N.J., Princeton Alumni Assn. Essex County. Democrat. Jewish. Club: Princeton (N.Y.C.). Federal civil litigation, State civil litigation, Real property. Home: 390 Melrose Pl South Orange NJ 07079 Office: Lampf Lipkind Prupis & Petigrow 80 Main St West Orange NJ 07052

REILLY, CONOR DESMOND, lawyer; b. Kansas City, Mo., Feb. 12, 1952; s. Desmond M. and Patricia (Carton) R.; m. Margaret M. Cannella, June 8, 1975; children: Katherine C., Michael C. BS, MIT, 1972; JD cum laude, Harvard U., 1975. Bar: N.Y. 1976, U.S. Dist. Ct. (ea. and so. dists.) N.Y. 1976, U.S. Ct. Appeals (2d. cir.) 1977, U.S. Dist. Ct. (D.C. cir.) 1979, U.S. Dist. Ct. (no. dist.) Calif. 1981, U.S. Dist. Ct. (cen. dist.) Calif. 1982. Law clk. to judge U.S. Dist. Ct. (ea. dist.), Bklyn., 1975-76; assoc. Cravath, Swaine & Moore, N.Y.C., 1976-77, Coudert Bros., N.Y.C., 1977-83; assoc. LeBoeuf, Lamb, Leiby & MacRae, N.Y.C., 1983-84, ptnr., 1985—. Editor Harvard U. Law Rev., 1973-74. Hearing officer N.Y.C. Bd. Edn., 1977-79; elected mem. Millburn Twp. Bd. Edn. Mem. ABA, Am. Abitration Assn. (arbitrator). Democrat. Avocation: tennis. General corporate, Securities, Federal civil litigation. Home: 62 Joanna Way Short Hills NJ 07078 Office: LeBeouf Lamb Leiby & MacRae 520 Madison Ave New York NY 10022

REILLY, JOHN ALBERT, lawyer; b. N.Y.C., Dec. 8, 1919; s. John T. and Elizabeth (Pione) R.; m. Mary Veronica Kelly, July 10, 1971; m. Marjorie Jessie Snell, June 28, 1946. B.S., CCNY, 1940; J.D., Harvard U., 1947. Bar: Mass. 1947, N.Y. 1949, Conn. 1977. Patent counsel Kendall Co., Boston, 1947-48; assoc. Kenyon & Kenyon, N.Y.C., 1949-55; ptnr. Kenyon, & Kenyon Reilly Carr & Chapin, N.Y.C., 1955-79; mem. firm Curtis, Morris & Safford, P.C., N.Y.C., 1979—. Chmn. bd. CCNY Fund. Served to 1st lt. C.E., AUS, 1944-46: ETO. Mem. ABA, N.Y. State Bar Assn., Assn. Bar City N.Y., N.Y. Patent Law Assn. (pres. 1979), Am. Patent Law Assn., Fed. Bar Council, CCNY Alumni Assn., Harvard Law Sch. Assn. Club: Harvard (N.Y.C.). Patent, Trademark and copyright. Office: 530 Fifth Ave New York NY 10036

REILLY, JOHN BERNARD, lawyer; b. Bangor, Maine, Sept. 12, 1947; s. Louis J. and Evelyn I. (Lindsay) R.; m. Susan P. Viselli, May 13, 1978; children—Steven, Carolyn, Bridget Jayne. B.A., U. R.I., 1970; J.D. cum laude, Suffolk U., 1976. Bar: R.I. 1976, U.S. Dist. Ct. R.I. 1976, U.S. Claims Ct. 1980, U.S. Supreme Ct. 1983, U.S. Ct. Appeals (1st and 2d cirs.) 1984, Mass. 1985, U.S. Dist. Ct. Mass. 1985, U.S. Ct. Appeals (3rd cir.) 1985. Sole practice, Providence, 1976-81, Warwick, R.I., 1981-83; sr. ptnr. Reilly & Glasson, Warwick, 1984—. Mem. troop council Narragansett council Boy Scouts Am., Warwick, 1982—. Mem. ABA, R.I. Bar Assn., Assn. Trial Lawyers Am., Pi Sigma Alpha, Phi Kappa Psi. Democrat. Roman Catholic. General practice, Criminal, State civil litigation. Home: 24 Superior St Warwick RI 02886 Office: Reilly & Flaherty 65 Jefferson Blvd Warwick RI 02888

REILLY, MICHAEL GERARD, lawyer; b. Fonda, Iowa, July 17, 1957; s. Joseph Daniel and Patricia Kathleen (Mullen) R.; m. Julie Kaye Lamoureux, Aug. 20, 1977; children: Daniel, Tara, Joseph. BBA, Creighton U., 1979, JD, 1981. Bar: Iowa 1981, U.S. Dist. Ct. (no. and so. dists.) Iowa 1981, Nebr. 1982. Assoc. Perkins, Sacks & Hannan, Council Bluffs, Iowa, 1981-84; ptnr. Perkins, Sacks, Hannan & Reilly, Council Bluffs, 1984—. Mem. ABA, Iowa Bar Assn., Nebr. Bar Assn., Assn. Trial Lawyers Am., Iowa Trial Lawyers Assn. Republican. Roman Catholic. Avocations: golf, racquetball, antiques. State civil litigation, Personal injury, Workers' compensation. Home: 113 Sleepy Hollow Council Bluffs IA 51501 Office: Perkins Sacks Hannan & Reilly 215 S Main St Box 1016 Council Bluffs IA 51502

REILLY, SHEILA ANN, lawyer, arbitrator; b. Lake Forest, Ill., Nov. 30, 1943; d. James Dunham and Louise Blossom Reilly; m. L. Bradwish. Student Vassar Coll., 1961-63; B.A., U. Calif.-Berkeley, 1965; J.D., Ill. Inst. Tech., Kent Sch Law, 1978. Bar: Ill. 1978, Calif. 1979. Sole practice, Chgo., 1981—. Mem. Chgo. Bar Assn., Ill. State Bar Assn., ABA. Episcopalian. Clubs: Executives' Chgo.; Soc. Mayflower Desc. Probate. Home: 175 E Delaware Pl Chicago IL 60611 Office: 53 W Jackson Blvd Suite 1231 Chicago IL 60604

REILLY, WILLIAM F(RANCIS), lawyer, state public defender; b. Providence, July 15, 1932; s. Peter P. and Margaret M. (O'Neill) R.; m. Constance P. Hand, June 10, 1961; children—Mary E., Karen A., William F., Michael P. A.B., Providence Coll., 1958; LL.B., Boston U., 1961. Bar: R.I. 1963, U.S. Dist. Ct. R.I. 1966, U.S. Ct. Appeals (1st cir.) 1969, U.S. Supreme Ct. 1973. Assoc., Charles J. Rogers, Quinn & Cuzzone, Providence, R.I., 1963—; ptnr. Breslin, Sweeney, Reilly & McDonald, Warwick, R.I., 1970-71; public defender State of R.I., Providence, 1971—; guest lectr. Roger Williams Coll.; mem. R.I. Gov.'s Justice Commn.; mem. Spl. Legis. Com.; chmn. com. availability of legal services Jud. Planning Council; mem. Bench Bar Adv. Com.; mem. Media Adv. Com.; mem. Spl. Legis. Commn. to Study Bail. Served to sgt. U.S. Army, 1952-54; Korea. Mem. R.I. Bar Assn., Nat. Legal Aid and Defender's Assn., R.I. Def. Attys. Assn. (founder and 1st pres. 1971-72). Club: K.C. Criminal. Office: 250 Benefit St Providence RI 02903

REIMAN, SCOTT A., lawyer; b. Mt. Vernon, Wash., May 6, 1952; s. Paul Gustav Reiman and Marlyn (Bardwell) Barlow. BA, Whitman Coll., 1974; JD, Willamette U., 1979. Bar: Oreg. 1979, U.S. Dist. Ct. Oreg. 1979, Wash. 1980, U.S. Dist. Ct. (we. dist.) Wash. 1984. Tchr. history South Kitsap High Sch., Port Orchard, Wash., 1974-75; ptnr. Vagt, Olsen & Reiman, St. Helens, Oreg., 1979-81; atty. Seattle-King County Pub. Defender Assn., Seattle, 1981—. Mem. judiciary com. Wash. Senate Task Force on child abuse and neglect, Olympia, 1985. Mem. ABA, Wash. State Bar Assn., Oreg. Bar Assn., King County Bar Assn. (criminal law sect.), Nat. Assn. Criminal Def. Lawyers. Democrat. Club: Seattle Mountaineers. Avocations: hiking, photography. Criminal. Office: Seattle-King County Pub Defender Assn 810 3d Ave Suite 800 Seattle WA 98104

REIMER, BILL MONROE, lawyer; b. Kerrville, Tex., Dec. 20, 1947; s. Rudolf Robert and Billie Dove (Coots) R.; m. June Lynn Kovar, Dec. 27, 1969; children—Kristi Lynn, Kendra Lea, Lauren Rae. B.B.A., SW Tex. State U., 1970; J.D., Tex. Tech. U., 1974. Bar: Tex. 1974, U.S. Dist. Ct. (we. dist.) Tex. 1976. Assoc. Bartram, Reagan, Burrus, New Braunfels, Tex., 1974-76; asst. county atty. Comal County, Tex., 1977-79, county atty., 1980—; lectr. bus. law Tex. Luth. Coll., Seguin, 1977; ct. arbitrator U.S. Dist. Ct. (we. dist.) Tex. Founder, bd. dirs. Teen Connection, New Braunfels, 1980—; cons., bd. dirs. New Braunfels, Christian Acad., 1983-84; founder, bd. dirs. Comal County Child Advocacy Assn. Serves as capt. JAGC, Tex. Army N.G. Mem. Tex. Bar Assn., Comal County Bar Assn., Tex. County and Dist. Attys. Assn., South Cen. Bar Assn. Tex. Democrat. Club: Lions (charter mem., pres. 1982-83). Criminal, Juvenile, Military. Home: 805 Encino New Braunfels TX 78130 Office: Comal County Courthouse New Braunfels TX 78130

REIN, ERIC STEVEN, lawyer; b. Chgo., June 16, 1956; s. Huntley J. and Miriam E. (Mesirow) R.; m. Jocelyn L. Farber, Nov. 11, 1984. BA, Washington U., 1978; JD, U. Miami, 1981. Bar: Ill. 1981, Fla., 1982, U.S. Dist. Ct. (no. dist.) Ill. 1982, U.S. Ct. Appeals (7th cir.) 1982. Assoc. Berger, Newmark & Fenchel, Chgo., 1982-85, Schwartz, Cooper, Kolb & Gaynor,

Chgo., 1985—. Mem. Young Bus. Leaders of the JUF, Chgo. Mem. ABA, Ill. Bar Assn., Chgo. Bar Assn. Democrat. Jewish. Avocations: golf, baseball. Federal civil litigation, State civil litigation, Bankruptcy. Office: Schwartz Cooper Kolb & Gaynor 33 N LaSalle St Suite 2222 Chicago IL 60602

REINEN, JEFFREY WILLIAM, probate judge, lawyer; b. Teaneck, N.J., Jan. 20, 1949; s. Joseph A. and E. Bernice (Reuter) R.; m. Daria Marie Gerola, Feb. 12, 1977; 1 child, Jenna Marie. BA in Econs., Fairfield U., 1971; JD, Cath. U. Am., 1974. Bar: Conn. 1974, Fla. 1975, D.C., 1976, U.S. Dist. Ct. Conn. Sole practice, Brookfield, Conn., 1974—; probate judge State of Conn., Brookfield, 1983—. Vice-chmn. Brookfield Dem. Town Com., 1976-79; chmn. Charter Rev. Commn., Brookfield, 1977, Com. on Tax Relief for Elderly, Brookfield, 1977-78; mem. exec. com. Conn. State Probate Assembly. Mem. ABA, Conn. Bar Assn., Fla. Bar, Lawyer-Pilots Bar Assn., Danbury Bar Assn., Omicron Delta Epsilon. Roman Catholic. Lodge: Rotary. Probate, Real property, State civil litigation. Home: 4 Aramon Circle Brookfield Center CT 06805 Office: 536 Federal Rd PO Box 218 Brookfield CT 06804

REINER, JOHN PAUL, lawyer; b. N.Y.C., Sept. 17, 1931; s. Charles Anthony and Jane Cecelia (Walsh) R.; m. Mary Elisabeth Wells, July 27, 1961; children—Mary Elisabeth, Clark Biddle. B.S., Fordham U., 1954; M.S., Columbia U., 1955, J.D., 1960. Bar: N.Y. 1960, U.S. Ct. Appeals (2d cir.) 1961, U.S. Dist. Ct. (so. and ea. dists.) N.Y. 1961. Law clk. U.S. Dist. Ct. (so. dist.) N.Y., 1960-61; asst. U.S. atty. So. Dist. N.Y., 1961-63; assoc. Townley & Updike, N.Y.C., 1964-70, ptnr., 1971—; dir. Evyan Perfumes, Inc., N.Y.C. Bd. dirs., pres. Myasthenia Gravis Found., 1983-85; bd. dirs. Thai Support Found., Fund for UN Decade of Women; mem. del. of Holy See to UN. Served to lt. U.S. Army, 1955-57. Decorated Knight of Malta; Knight Comdr. Order of St. Sylvester, by Pope John Paul II, 1983. Mem. ABA, N.Y. Bar Assn., Assn. Bar City N.Y., U.S. Trademark Assn. Republican. Clubs: Union League, Tuxedo. Trademark and copyright, Federal civil litigation, State civil litigation. Home: 340 E 72d St New York NY 10021 Office: Townley & Updike 405 Lexington Ave New York NY 10174

REINER, SAMUEL THEODORE, lawyer, educator; b. N.Y.C., Dec. 13, 1933; s. Samuel Barclay and Dorothea Mary Reiner; m. Anne Elizabeth Walker, Sept. 3, 1955; children: Samuel Barclay, David Peter, Theodore S.H., Geoffrey F.P. BA, Gettysburg Coll., 1955; JD, Georgetown U., 1957, LLM, 1960; MA, U. Tex., Dallas, 1982. Bar: U.S. Dist. Ct. D.C. 1958, U.S. Tax Ct. 1958, U.S. Ct. Appeals (D.C. cir. 1958), U.S. Supreme Ct. 1965, U.S. Ct. Claims 1968, Tex. 1978, U.S. Ct. Appeals (10th cir.) 1980. Sr. trial atty. IRS, 1957-65; sr. editor Research Inst. Am., 1965-68; prof. taxation, dir. NYU Tax Inst., 1968-76; v.p. Southwestern Legal Found., 1976-77; assoc. dean So. Meth. U., Dallas, 1977-81; ptnr. Reiner & Gregory, Albuquerque and Dallas, 1981-83; dir. client tax communications Ernst & Whinney, Washington, 1983—; trustee Polit. Economy Research Inst.; mem. adv. group to commr. IRS, 1975. Author: Doing Business in Mexico, 1980, Community Property in Estate Planning, 1981, The Effects of the Internal Revenue Code of 1986 on Family Tax Planning. Recipient Hamilton award Dept. Treasury, 1976. Mem. ABA, Nat. Assn. Pub. Accts. Republican. Mem. Soc. of Friends. Estate taxation, Personal income taxation, Estate planning. Office: Ernst & Whinney 1225 Connecticut Ave NW Washington DC 22036

REINHARD, HENRY CORBEN, JR., lawyer, health care management consultant; b. Camden, N.J., Jan. 3, 1937; s. Henry Corben Reinhard Sr. and Naomi (Schmidt) Cattanea; m. Shirley Mae Montgomery, July 13, 1957; children: Robert Dale, Jeffrey Scott, Carolyn Joy, Marni Jean. BBA in Econs. and Fin., U. Houston, 1969; JD, South Tex. Coll. Law, 1972. Bar: Tex. 1972, U.S. Dist. Ct. (no. dist.) Tex. 1986. Assoc. adminstr. St. Luke's Episc. Hosp., Tex. Children's Hosp., Tex. Heart Inst., Houston, 1968-73; chief exec. Ft. Worth Children's Hosp., 1973-78; dir. gen. Hamad Gen. Hosp., Doha, Qatar, 1979-80; exec. v.p., gen. counsel CIGNA Healthplan, Inc., Dallas, 1980-85; asst. to chmn., v.p. INA (later CIGNA) Health Care Group, Inc., Dallas, 1980-85; sole practice Ft. Worth, 1986—; mcpl. judge Azle, Tex., 1976-78; adj. assoc. prof. Tex. Women's U., Denton. Active various planning councils. Mem. ABA, Tex. Bar Assn., Tarrant County Bar Assn., Houston Bar Assn., Am. Coll. Hosp. Adminstrs., Phi Alpha Delta. Mormon. Family and matrimonial, General practice, Health. Office: 675 N Henderson St Suite 300 Fort Worth TX 76107

REINHARDT, DANIEL SARGENT, lawyer; b. Orange, N.J., Jan. 27, 1949; s. Warren Irwin and Winifred Ruth (Sargent) R.; m. Elizabeth Ann Johnson, June 11, 1982; 1 child, Meredith Alexandra. BA, Duke U., 1971; JD, Georgetown U., 1974. Bar: Ga. 1975, U.S. Dist. Ct. (no. dist.) Ga. 1975, U.S. Ct. Appeals (5th and 11th cirs.) 1981, U.S. Dist. Ct. (so. dist.) Ga. 1984, U.S. Dist. Ct. (mid. dist.) Ga. 1985, U.S. Ct. Appeals (4th cir.) 1985. From assoc. to ptnr. Troutman, Sanders, Lockerman & Ashmore, Atlanta, 1974—; dep. asst. atty. gen. State of Ga., 1975-79; instr. trial techniques seminar Emory U., Atlanta, 1984-86, civil practice and procedure seminar Ga. State U., 1986—; arbitrator Fulton County (Ga.) Superior Ct. Named one of Outstanding Young Men of Am. Mem. ABA, Ga. Bar Assn., Atlanta Bar Assn., Atlanta Claims Assn., Ga. Def. Lawyers Assn. Club: Lawyers (Atlanta). Avocation: sports. Federal civil litigation, Personal injury, Insurance. Office: Troutman Sanders Lockerman & Ashmore 127 Peachtree St NE 1400 Candler Bldg Atlanta GA 30043

REINHARDT, ROXANE TOMASI, lawyer; b. Denver, Sept. 4, 1955; d. Gordon Ernest and Georgia Augusta (Schwalls) Tomasi; m. Jeffrey Morgan Reinhardt, May 10, 1981; 1 child, Sarah Kathleen. BS in Criminal Justice, Eastern Ky. U., 1977; JD, U. Ky., 1981. Bar: Ky. 1981, U.S. Dist. Ct. (we. dist.) Ky. 1982, U.S. Dist. Ct. (ea. dist.) Ky. 1983. Assoc. Brown, Todd & Heyburn, Louisville, 1981—. Served to sgt. USAF, 1974-78. State civil litigation, Insurance, Personal injury. Office: Brown Todd & Heyburn 1600 Citizens Plaza Louisville KY 40202

REINHARDT, STEPHEN ROY, judge; b. N.Y.C., Mar. 27, 1931; s. Gottfried and Silvia (Hanlon) R.; children: Mark, Justin, Dana. B.A. cum laude, Pomona Coll., 1951; LL.B., Yale, 1954. Bar: Calif. 1958. Law clk. to U.S. Dist. Judge Luther W. Youngdahl, Washington, 1956-57; atty. O'Melveny & Myers, Los Angeles, 1957-59; partner Fogel Julber Reinhardt Rothschild & Feldman (L.C.), Los Angeles, 1959-80; judge U.S. Ct. Appeals for 9th Circuit, Los Angeles, 1980—; Mem. exec. com. Dem. Nat. Com., 1969-72, nat. Dem. committeeman for Calif., 1976-80; pres. Los Angeles Recreation and Parks Commn., 1974-75; mem. Coliseum Commn., 1974-75, Los Angeles Police Commn., 1975-78, pres., 1978-80; sec., mem. exec. com. Los Angeles Olympic Organizing Com., 1980—; bd. dirs. Amateur Athletic Found. of Los Angeles, 1984—. Served to 1st lt. USAF, 1954-56. Mem. Am. Bar Assn. (labor law council 1975-77). Jurisprudence.

REINHART, RICHARD PAUL, lawyer; b. Cleve., Sept. 1, 1954; s. Richard A. and Carole F. (Kaspar) R.; married; 1 child, Geoffrey. BA with honors, Rollins Coll., 1976; JD with distinction, Emory U., 1979. Bar: Ga. 1979, Fla. 1980. Ptnr. Morris, Manning & Martin, Atlanta, 1979—. Mem. ABA, Fla. Bar Assn., Ga. Bar Assn., Atlanta Bar Assn., Order of Coif, Omicron Delta Kappa. Federal civil litigation, State civil litigation. Office: Morris Manning & Martin 230 Peachtree St Suite 2100 Atlanta GA 30303

REINKE, CECIL EUGENE, lawyer; b. Clinton, Okla., Apr. 5, 1933; s. Christian and Fredreka (Schultz) R.; m. Carol Joyce Roehrich, Sept. 22, 1956; children—Keryl Kris, Alison Dale. Ph.B., N.D. U., 1956, J.D., 1959; M.S., Houston U., 1977; Bar: N.D. 1959, Ark. 1960, Fla. 1963, Tex. 1975, U.S. Supreme Ct. 1979, Oreg. 1981. Asst. dist. counsel C.E., U.S. Army, Little Rock, 1959-61, asst. to gen. counsel Dept. Army, Washington, 1961-63; counsel Orlando office Missile Command, (Fla.), 1963-68; dist. counsel C.E., Galveston, Tex., 1968-79, div. counsel N. Pacific C.E., Portland, Oreg., 1979—. Assoc. editor N.D. Law Rev., 1958-59; contbr. articles to law revs. Pres., chmn. bd. dirs. Galveston Govt. Employees Credit Union, 1972-79. Mem. Fed. Bar Assn. (pres. Houston chpt. 1978, pres. Oreg. chpt. 1983-84, nat. v.p. 9th cir. 1984—), Order of Coif, Phi Kappa Phi. Democrat. Roman Catholic. Club: City (Portland). Construction, Environment, Federal civil litigation. Home: 7805 SW Terwilliger Blvd Portland OR 97219 Office: N Pacific Civ US Army CE PO Box 2870 220 NW 8th Ave Portland OR 82870

REINKE, ROBERT LEE, judge; b. South Bend, Ind., Feb. 28, 1933; s. William A. and Eva M. (Hein) R.; m. Julia J. Blue, Aug. 4, 1956; children: Ann, Kurt, Mark, Karen. BA, Wabash Coll., 1955; JD, U. Chgo., 1958. Bar: Ind. 1958, U.S. Supreme Ct. 1969. Ptnr. Livengood & Reinke, Richmond, Ind., 1958-62; sole practice Richmond, 1962-66; ptnr. Dennis, Reinke & Vertesch, Richmond, 1967-82; judge Wayne Superior Ct. #2, Richmond, 1982—. Mem. ABA, Ind. Bar Assn., Ind. Judges Assn. Republican. Methodist. Home: 433 S 21st St Richmond IN 47374 Office: Wayne Superior Ct #2 Wayne County Cthouse Richmond IN 47374

REINKE, WILLIAM JOHN, lawyer; b. South Bend, Ind., Aug. 7, 1930; s. William August and Eva Marie (Hein) R.; m. Sue Carol Colvin, Jan. 28, 1951; children—Saly Sue Taelman, William A., Andrew J. A.B., Wabash Coll., 1952; J.D., U. Chgo., 1955. Bar: Ind. 1955. Assoc. Barnes & Thornburg and predecessors, South Bend, Ind., 1957-61, ptnr., 1961—. Bd. trustees Stanley Clark Sch., 1970-80, pres., 1977-80; bd. dirs. United Way St. Joseph County, Inc., 1978-81; bd. govs. South Bend Round Table, 1963-65; bd. dirs. Hearing and Speech Center St. Joseph County, 1965-73, pres., 1972-73; mem. adv. bd. Salvation Army, 1973—; bd. dirs. Isaac Walton League, 1970-81; bd. trustees First Meth. Ch., 1967-70; bd. dirs. South Bend Civic Planning Assn., 1965-70. Served with U.S. Army, 1955-57. Mem. ABA, Ind. State Bar Assn., St. Joseph County Bar Assn., Ind. Bar Found., Am. Judicature Soc., Def. Research Inst., Ind. Soc. Chgo. Clubs: Summit (past gov.), Rotary (dir. 1970-73). General corporate, Federal civil litigation, State civil litigation. Home: 1415 E Colfax South Bend IN 46617 Office: 1st Source Bank Bldg South Bend IN 46601

REINSTEIN, JOEL, lawyer; b. N.Y.C., July 23, 1946; s. Louis and Ruth Shukovsky; m. Pearl Sandra Rubin, May 9, 1968; children—Lesli, Louis, Mindy B.S.E., U. Pa., 1968; J.D. cum laude, U. Fla., 1971; LL.M. in Taxation, NYU, 1974. Bar: Fla. 1971, U.S. Tax Ct. 1973, U.S. Dist. Ct. (so. dist.) Fla. 1976. Atty., office of chief counsel IRS, 1971-74; ptnr. Capp, Reinstein, Kopelowitz and Atlas, P.A., Ft. Lauderdale, Fla., 1975-85; dir., Greenberg, Traurig, Askew, Hoffman, Lipoff, Rosen & Quentel, P.A., Ft. Lauderdale, 1985—; lectr. Advanced Pension Planning, Am. Soc. C.L.U.s; lectr. in field. Mem. Fla. Bar Assn. (tax sect.), ABA (tax sect, adj. mem. com. employee benefits), Order of Coif, Phi Kappa Phi, Phi Delta Phi. Mem. editorial bd. U. Fla. Law Rev., 1970-71; contbr. articles to profl. jours. Corporate taxation, General corporate, Estate planning. Office: 500 E Broward Blvd Suite 1350 Fort Lauderdale FL 33394-3076

REINSTEIN, PAUL MICHAEL, lawyer; b. N.Y.C., Jan. 19, 1952; s. Joseph and Edith (Ambaras) R.; m. Gila Ann Moldoff, Apr. 16, 1978; children: Meira, Rachel. BA, Yeshiva Coll., 1973; JD, Yale U., 1976. Bar: N.Y. 1977. Assoc. Fried Frank Harris Shriver & Jacobson, N.Y.C., 1976-83, ptnr., 1983—. Mem. ABA, N.Y. State Bar Assn. General corporate, Securities. Home: 282 Maple St West Hempstead NY 11552 Office: Fried Frank Harris Shriver & Jacobson 1 New York Plaza New York NY 10004

REINSTEIN, RONALD S., judge; b. Camden, N.J., Apr. 13, 1948; s. Alfred Alan and Hilde (Ehrlich) R.; m. Marilyn Ruth Pliskin, Jan 9, 1972; children: Stacy Lynn, Scott Alan. Student, Miami U., 1966-68; BA, Ind. U., 1970, JD, 1973. Bar: Ariz. 1974, U.S. Dist. Ct. Ariz. 1978, U.S. Dist. Ct. Ind. 1978, U.S. Supreme Ct. 1980. Trial supr. Maricopa County Atty's Office, Phoenix, 1974-85; judge Ariz. Superior Ct., Phoenix, 1985—; instr. Nat. Inst. for Trial Advocacy, 1984—, Nat. Coll. Dist. Attys., Houston, 1983—. Com. chmn. PTA, Scottsdale, Ariz., 1985-86. Recipient Cert. of Achievement Victim-Witness Program, 1985, Nat. Inst. for Trial Advocacy, 1984-86, Child Abuse Council, 1985; Award of Excellence Maricopa county Atty's Office, 1985. Mem. ABA (criminal justice and judicial adminstrn. sections), Ariz. Judges Assn., Nat. Inst. for Trial Attys. Democrat. Jewish. Avocations: sports, travel, reading, yard work. Judicial administration. Office: Superior Court Ariz 201 W Jefferson St Phoenix AZ 85003

REINTHALER, RICHARD WALTER, lawyer; b. N.Y.C., Feb. 27, 1949; s. Walter F. and Maureen C. (Tully) R.; m. Mary E. Maloney, Aug. 8, 1970; children: Brian, Scott, Amy. BA in Govt. magna cum laude, U. Notre Dame, 1970, JD summa cum laude, 1973. Bar: N.Y., U.S. Dist. Ct. (so. and ea. dists.) N.Y. 1974, U.S. Ct. Appeals (2d cir.) 1974, U.S. Ct. Appeals (9th cir.) 1976, U.S. Supreme Ct. 1977, U.S. Ct. Appeals (5th cir.) 1978, U.S. Ct. Appeals (11th cir.) 1981. Assoc. White & Case, N.Y.C., 1973-81, ptnr., 1981—. Contbr. articles to profl. jours. Served to 1st lt. U.S. Army, 1974. Mem. ABA (2d cir. chmn. discovery com. 1982—, program coordinator 1986 annual meeting, litigation sect.), N.Y. State Bar Assn. Republican. Roman Catholic. Clubs: Princeton (N.Y.C.), Scarsdale Golf (Hartsdale, N.Y.). Avocations: golf, tennis. Federal civil litigation, Securities, Antitrust. Office: White & Case 1155 Ave of the Americas New York NY 10036

REIS, MURIEL HENLE, lawyer, television executive; b. N.Y.C.; d. Frederick S. and Mary (Meyers) Henle; m. Arthur Reis Jr., Sept. 25, 1953; children: Arthur Henle, Diane Mary, Pamela Robin. BA, Vassar Coll., 1946; LLB, Columbia U., 1949. Bar: N.Y. 1950, U.S. Ct. Appeals (2d cir.) 1959. Asst. gen. counsel ABC, N.Y.C., 1950-52; from asst. gen. counsel to assoc. gen. counsel Metromedia Inc., N.Y.C., 1956-86; v.p. WNEW, N.Y.C., 1974-86; v.p., counsel Fox TV Sta. Inc., N.Y.C., 1986—. Mem. Assn. of Bar of City of N.Y., Internat. Soc. Radio and TV Execs. Entertainment, Libel, Communications, contract litigation. Home: 1136 Fifth Ave New York NY 10128 Office: Fox TV Sta Inc 205 E 67th St New York NY 10021

REIS, ROBERT RICHARD, lawyer; b. Tulsa, Mar. 13, 1939; s. Laurence Donald and Waheta (Larson) R.; m. Linda McLennan, June 2, 1962; children: Karen Ann, R. Richard Jr., Kathryn Bennett. BA in Polit. Sci., Okla. U., 1961, LLB, 1964. Bar: Okla., U.S. Dist. Ct. (no. dist.) Tex., U.S. Ct. Mil. Appeals, U.S. Ct. Appeals (5th and 10th cirs.). Assoc. Farmer, Woolsey, Flippo & Bailey, Tulsa, 1968-69; atty. to sr. atty. Cities Service Oil Co., Tulsa, 1969-79, gen. atty., 1979-83; asst. gen. counsel Cities Service Oil and Gas Corp., Tulsa, 1983—; instr. bus. law Cen. Tex. Jr. Coll., Killeen, 1967-68. Contbr. articles to profl. jours. Mem. law ctr. adv. bd. Okla. U. Law Sch., Norman, 1975-82, Downtown YMCA, Tulsa, 1980-86; elder First Presbyn. Ch., Tulsa, 1984-86. Served to capt. JAGC, U.S. Army, 1964-68, lt. col. Res. Recipient Cert. of Achievement Def. Atomic Support Agy., Sandia Base, N.Mex., 1968. Mem. ABA (natural resources law sect.), Okla. Bar Assn. (mineral law sect.), Tulsa County Bar Assn. (mineral law sect.), Okla. U. Assn. (bd. dirs. 1978-79, Outstanding Service award 1977). Democrat. Presbyterian. Avocations: fishing, golf, running. General corporate, Contracts commercial, Environment. Office: Cities Service Oil & Gas Corp PO Box 300 Tulsa OK 74102

REISMAN, WILLIAM M., lawyer, educator; b. 1939. LL.B., Hebrew U., 1963; LL.M., Yale U., 1964, J.S.D., 1965. Bar: Conn. 1964. Prof. internat. law and jurisprudence Yale U. Law Sch., New Haven, 1969—. Author: Nullity and Revision, Art of the Possible: Diplomatic Alternatives in Middle East, 1971, Puerto Rico and the Foreign Policy Process, 1975, Folded Lies: Bribery, Crusades and Reforms, 1979; (with Weston) Toward World Order and Human Dignity, 1976; (with McDougal) International Law in Contemporary Perspective, 1983. Fulbright grantee, 1966-67. Legal education, Jurisprudence. Office: Yale U Law Sch Drawer 401 A Yale Sta New Haven CT 06520

REISS, ELAINE SERLIN, advertising agency executive; b. N.Y.C., Oct. 27, 1940; d. Morris and Dorothy (Geyer) Serlin; m. Joel A. Reiss, Sept. 1, 1963; children: Joshua Adam, Naomi Lee. B.A., N.Y. U., 1961, LL.M., 1973; LL.B., Columbia U., 1964. Bar: N.Y. 1965. Mgr. legal dept. Doyle Dane Bernbach Advt., 1965-68; mgr. legal clearance dept., then v.p., mgr. legal dept. Ogilvy & Mather, Inc., N.Y.C., 1968-78; sr. v.p., mgr. legal dept. Ogilvy & Mather, Inc., 1978-82, gen. counsel, sec. U.S. bd. dirs., 1982—, exec. v.p., 1985—; industry adv. seminar series on children Georgetown U. Law Sch., 1978-79; mem. part-time faculty NYU Tisch Sch. Arts, 1982—. Recipient Matrix award in advt. N.Y. Women in Communications, 1987. Mem. Am. Assn. Advt. Agencies (chmn. legal com. 1979-81), ABA (com. on corp. law depts.), Assn. Bar City N.Y., Legal Aid Soc. (bd. dirs.). Office: 2 E 48th St New York NY 10017

REISTER, RAYMOND ALEX, lawyer; b. Sioux City, Iowa, Dec. 22, 1929; s. Harold William and Anne (Eberhardt) R.; m. Ruth Elizabeth Alkema, Oct. 7, 1967. AB, Harvard U., 1952, LLB, 1955. Bar: N.Y. 1956, Minn. 1960. Assoc. Paul, Weiss, Rifkind, Wharton & Garrison, N.Y.C., 1955-56; sr. ptnr. Dorsey & Whitney, Mpls., 1959—; instr. U. Minn. Extension Div., 1964-66. Editor (with Larry W. Johnson): Minnesota Probate Administration, 1968. Trustee Mpls. Soc. Fine Arts, 1981-87; treas. Minn. State Hist. Soc., 1986—. Served as 1st lt. U.S. Army, 1956-59. Mem. Am. Coll. Probate Counsel (regent 1980-86), ABA, Minn. Bar Assn., Hennepin County Bar Assn. Clubs: Minneapolis, Harvard of Minn. (pres. 1969-70). Probate, Estate taxation, Estate planning. Home: 93 Groveland Terr Minneapolis MN 55403 Office: Dorsey & Whitney 2100 First Bank Pl E Minneapolis MN 55402

REITE, CHARLES DOUGLAS, lawyer; b. Mpls., June 24, 1942; s. Douglas Eric and Lillian Ellen (Hansen) R.; m. Ann Lorraine Mueller, Dec. 27, 1967; children: Christian, Elizabeth. BA, U. Minn., 1964; JD, U. Mich., 1972. Bar: Minn., U.S. Dist. Ct. Minn., U.S. Ct. Mil. Appeals, U.S. Ct. Appeals (8th cir.), U.S. Supreme Ct. Ptnr. O'Connor & Hannan, Mpls., 1972-80, Frommelt, Eide & Reite, Mpls., 1980-84, Mackall, Crounse & Moore, Mpls., 1984—. Deacon Plymouth Congl. Ch., Mpls., 1983-85; pres. Southwest Activities Council, Mpls., 1983—. Served to capt. USNR, 1960—. Mem. ABA, Minn. Bar Assn., Hennepin County Bar Assn. (ethics com.), Naval and Marine Lawyers Assn. Club: Mpls. Athletic. Federal civil litigation, State civil litigation. Home: 3815 Drew Ave S Minneapolis MN 55410 Office: Mackall Crounse & Moore 1600 TCF Tower Minneapolis MN 55402

REITER, GLENN M., lawyer; b. N.Y.C., Feb. 1, 1951; s. Bernard Leon and Helene (Edson) R.; m. Marilyn Beckhorn, Sept. 5, 1976; children: Benjamin, Diana. BA, Yale U., 1973, JD, 1976. Bar: N.J. 1976, Pa. 1977, D.C. 1978, N.Y. 1979. Law clk. to presiding justice U.S. Ct. Appeals, Phila., 1976-77; assoc. Schnader, Harrison, Segal & Lewis, Phila., 1977-78; assoc. Simpson, Thacher & Bartlett, N.Y.C., 1978-84, ptnr., 1984—; resident ptnr. Simpson, Thacher & Bartlett, London, 1986—. Mem. Phi Beta Kappa. Securities, General corporate. also: 99 Bishopsgate, London EC2M 3XD, England

REITER, JOSEPH HENRY, lawyer; b. Phila., Mar. 21, 1929; s. Nicholas and Barbara (Hellmann) R. A.B., Temple U., 1950, LL.B., 1953. Bar: D.C. 1953, Pa. 1954. Atty. advisor U.S. Army, 1955-61; asst. U.S. atty. Ea. Dist. Pa., 1961-63, asst. U.S. atty. in charge of civil div., 1963-69; chief organized crime and racketeering strike force Western N.Y. State, U.S. Dept. Justice, 1969-70, sr. trial atty. tax div. 1970-72, regional dir. office of drug abuse law enforcement, 1972-73; dep. atty. gen., dir. Drug Law Enforcement Office of Pa., 1973-77; ptnr. Stassen, Kostos and Mason, Phila. 1978-85, Kostos Reiter & Lamer, 1985—; mem. adv. com. Joint State Commn. on Procurement; lectr. in field. Contbr. articles to profl. jours. Mem. Citizens Crime Commn. Pa. Served with U.S. Army, 1953-55. Recipient Meritorious Service award U.S. Atty. Gen. Clark, 1967, Spl. Commendation Asst. U.S. Atty. Gen. Tax Div., 1969, Outstanding Performance award U.S. Atty. Gen. Richardson, 1973. Mem. ABA, Fed. Bar Assn., D.C. Bar Assn., Pa. Bar Assn., Phila. Bar Assn. Democrat. Club: Vesper (Phila.). Federal civil litigation, Criminal, Government contracts and claims. Office: 1608 Walnut St Suite 1300 Philadelphia PA 19103

REITER, JOSEPH JOHN, lawyer; b. Chgo., Feb. 3, 1940; s. Joseph Coleman and Gertrude (O'Malley) R.; m. Janice Sasseen, Aug. 14, 1965; children: Joell, Janea. JD, Stetson Coll. Law, 1968. Bar: Fla. 1968, U.S. Dist. Ct. (so. and mid. dists.) Fla. 1969, U.S. Supreme Ct. 1973, U.S. Ct. Appeals (11th cir.) 1982. Assoc. Howell, Kirby, Montgomery, Levy, Alisen, Perry & Reiter, West Palm Beach, Fla., 1968-73; ptnr. Howell, Kirby, Montgomery, Levy, Alisen, Perry & Reiter, West Palm Beach, 1973-75, Montgomery, Lytal & Reiter, West Palm Beach, 1976-85, Lytal & Reiter, West Palm Beach, 1985—. Pres. YMCA, West Palm Beach, 1983-84; bd. dirs., officer Legal Aid Soc., West Palm Beach; bd. dirs. United Way, West Palm Beach, 1982—. Served to sgt. U.S. Army, 1958-61. Named Man of Yr. YMCA, 1983. Fellow Acad. Fla. Trial. Lawyer, Acad. Matrimony Lawyers; mem. ABA (del. 1985—), Fla. Bar Assn. (bd. of govs. 1981—, pres. 1985-86, chmn. com. 1984-85, vice-chmn. 1984-85), Palm Beach Bar Assn. (pres. 1979-80), Am. Acad. Trial Lawyers,. Lodge: Rotary (pres. West Palm Beach 1980-81). Avocations: running, tennis, flying, skiing. Personal injury, Federal civil litigation, State civil litigation. Home: 7710 S Flagler Dr West Palm Beach FL 33405 Office: Lytal & Reiter 515 N Flagler Dr 10th Floor Northbridge Center West Palm Beach FL 33401

REITH, DANIEL I., lawyer; b. Sacramento, Feb. 28, 1939; s. Mervin Henry and Nancy Elizabeth (Needham) R.; m. Susan Dorothea Totsu, June 16, 1971. AB cum laude, Dartmouth Coll., 1961; LLB, U. Calif., Berkeley, 1964. Bar: Calif. 1965; cert. specialist family law, 1980. Assoc. Thompson & Hubbard, Monterey, Calif., 1965-69; sole practice Monterey, 1969-71; sr. ptnr. Reith, Bebermeyer, Flippo & Wieben, Monterey, 1971—; referee Calif. State Bar Ct., 1973—; instr. Calif. Continuing Edn. of Bar, 1977. Assoc. editor: Calif. Law Rev., 1963-64; contbr. articles to profl. jours. Pres. Monterey County Legal Aid Soc., Calif., 1974; chmn. Monterey Nat. Rugby Tournament, 1971-73. Mem. Monterey County Bar Assn. (pres. 1975), Assn. Trial Lawyers Am., Order of Coif. Republican. Episcopalian. Family and matrimonial, State civil litigation, Personal injury. Office: Reith Bebermeyer Flippo & Wieben 444 Pearl St Monterey CA 93940

REITMAN, JEFFREY B., lawyer; b. Balt., May 19, 1944; s. Albert A. and Selma L. (Lowitz) R.; m. Cheryl Nagelbush, Aug. 20, 1967; children—Kimberly, Glenn. B.S., Ohio State U., 1966; J.D., U. Louisville, 1969. Bar: N.Y. 1970. Assoc. Berg, Becker, Moinester and Dillon, Lynbrook, N.Y., 1969-70; v.p., counsel Chem. Bank, N.Y.C., 1971—; instr. Am. Inst. Banking, 1972-80; chmn. lawyers com. Am. Assn. Equipment Lessors, 1986. Mem. ABA, N.Y. State Bar Assn. Author in field. Banking, Contracts commercial, General corporate. Office: 380 Madison Ave 9th Floor New York NY 10017

REITMAN, SIDNEY, lawyer; b. Bklyn., Mar. 12, 1915; s. Samuel and Celia (Greenman) R.; m. Marian Weil, June 21, 1942; children: Leslie Weil, Jonathan Weil, Marc Weil. Student, Coll. William & Mary, 1932-34; JD, Rutgers U., 1937. Bar: N.J. 1937, N.J. 1953, U.S. Ct. Appeals (3d cir.) 1960, U.S. Supreme Ct. 1960, U.S. Ct. Appeals (D.C. cir.) 1973, U.S. Ct. Appeals (5th cir.) 1975. Sole practice Jersey City, 1937-40; trial atty. NLRB, N.Y.C. and New Orleans, 1940-47; ptnr. Kapelsohn, Lerner, Leuchter & Reitman, Newark, 1947-82; sr. ptnr. Reitman, Parsonnet, Maisel & Duggan, Newark, 1982—. Chmn. N.J. Commn. on Civil Rights, Newark and Trenton, 1960-65; pres. Urban League of Essex County, Newark, 1960-64; counsel United Community Corp. Poverty Agy., Newark, 1965-68; spl. master, U.S. Dist. Ct. Newark and Essex County Jail, 1983—. Served with Signal Corps U.S. Army, 1943-45, ETO. Decorated Bronze Star. Mem. ABA, N.J. Bar Assn. (chmn. labor law sect. 1979-80), Essex County Bar Assn. Jewish. Labor, Federal civil litigation, Civil rights. Home: 8 Club Blvd West Orange NJ 07052 Office: Reitman Parsonnet Maisel & Duggan 744 Broad St Newark NJ 07102

REITZ, CURTIS RANDALL, law educator, lawyer; b. Reading, Pa.; s. Lester S. and Magdalene A. (Crouse) R.; m. Virginia R. Patterson, Dec. 19, 1953 (div.); children—Kevin R., Joanne E., Whitney A.; m. Judith N. Renzulli, Sept. 18, 1983. B.A., U. Pa., 1951, LL.B., 1956. Bar: Pa. 1957, U.S. Supreme Ct. 1959. Law clk. to Chief Justice Earl Warren U.S. Supreme Ct., 1956-57; mem. faculty law U. Pa., Phila., 1957—; asst. prof. law U. Pa., 1957-60, assoc. prof., 1960-63, prof., 1963—, provost, v.p., 1970-71, Algernon Sydney Biddle prof. law, 1985—. Trustee Internat. House Phila.; bd. mgrs. Glen Mills Schs., Pa. Served to 1st lt. U.S. Army, 1951-53. Mem. Am. Law Inst., Nat. Conf. Commrs. on Uniform State Laws, Order of Coif. Construction, Contracts commercial, Professional responsibility. Office: U Pa Law Sch 3400 Chestnut St Philadelphia PA 19104

RELSON, MORRIS, patent lawyer; b. N.Y.C., Apr. 14, 1915; s. Benjamin and Minnie R.; m. Rita L. Rubenstein, Apr. 5, 1941; children—Katherine D., David M., Peter J. B.S., CCNY, 1935; M.A., George Washington U., 1940; J.D., NYU, 1945. Bar: N.Y. 1945, U.S. Supreme Ct. 1950. Elec. engr. Nat. Park Service, 1936-37; patent examiner U.S. Patent Office, 1937-41; patent agt. and atty. Sperry Gyroscope Co., Gt. Neck, N.Y., 1941-48; ptnr. Darby & Darby P.C., and predecessor, N.Y.C., 1948—; vol. spl. master U.S. Dist Ct. for So. Dist N.Y., 1979-80. Author in field. Mem. ABA, Am.

Patent Law Assn., N.Y. Patent Law Assn. (pres. 1976-77), Phi Beta Kappa, Sigma Xi. Patentee in field. Patent, Computer, Trademark and copyright. Home: 27 Tain Dr Great Neck NY 11021 Office: 405 Lexington Ave New York NY 10174

REMBAR, CHARLES (ISAIAH), lawyer, writer; b. Oceanport, N.J., Mar. 12, 1915; s. Louis S. and Rebecca (Schneider) Zaremba; m. Billie Ann Olsson, Feb. 23, 1944; children: Lance Richard, James Carlson. A.B., Harvard U., 1935; LL.B., Columbia U., 1938. Bar: N.Y. 1938. Atty. govt. agencies 1938-42, 45; law sec. N.Y. Supreme Ct., 1946; practice law N.Y.C., 1947—. Author: The End of Obscenity, 1968, Perspective, 1975, The Law of the Land, 1980; Editor: Columbia Law Rev, 1936-38; Contbr. articles to various periodicals. Served with USAAF, 1942-44. Recipient George Polk Meml. award for outstanding book of 1968, 1969. Mem. Assn. Bar City N.Y. (chmn. spl. com. on communications 1972-78), Authors League, P.E.N. Clubs: Century Assn. (N.Y.C.), Harvard (N.Y.C.). Trademark and copyright, Libel, Federal civil litigation. Office: Rembar & Curtis 19 W 44th St New York NY 10036

REMBE, TONI, lawyer; b. Seattle, Apr. 23, 1936; d. Armin and Doris (McVey) R.; m. Arthur Rock, July 19, 1975. Cert. in French Studies, U. Geneva, 1956; LL.B., U. Wash., 1960; LL.M., NYU, 1961. Bar: N.Y., Wash., Calif. Assoc. Chadbourne, Parke, Whiteside & Wolff, N.Y.C., 1961-63; assoc. Pillsbury, Madison & Sutro, San Francisco, 1964-71, ptnr., 1971—; dir. Potlatch Corp., San Francisco, Safeco Corp., Seattle. Bd. dirs. Van Loben Sels Charitable Found., San Francisco; trustee Mills Coll., Oakland. Fellow Am. Bar Found.; mem. ABA, Am. Judicature Soc., State Bar Calif., Bar Assn. San Francisco. Club: Commonwealth of Calif. Office: Pillsbury Madison & Sutro 225 Bush St San Francisco CA 94104

REMELE, LEWIS ALBERT, JR., lawyer; b. Mpls., Nov. 25, 1948; s. Lewis Albert Sr. and Mary Elizabeth (Ryan) R.; m. Constance Ann Bauser, June 26, 1982; 1 child, Lewis Albert III. BA magna cum laude, Harvard U., 1970; JD cum laude, Creighton U., 1975. Bar: Minn. 1975, U.S. Dist. Ct. Minn. 1976, U.S. Ct. Appeals (8th cir.) 1978. Law clk. to presiding judge U.S. Dist. Ct., Mpls., 1975-77, assoc. Simonson & Bartsh, Mpls., 1977-78; ptnr. Rider, Bennett, Egan & Arundel, Mpls., 1978—; bd. dirs. Hennepin County Legal Advice Clinic, Mpls. Mem. ABA, Minn. Bar Assn., Hennepin County Bar Assn. (sec 1986-87), Def. Research Inst., Minn. Def. Lawyers. Club: Harvard (Mpls.) (pres. 1984-85). Federal civil litigation, State civil litigation, Insurance. Office: Rider Bennett Egan & Arundel 2500 First Bank W Minneapolis MN 55402

REMINGER, RICHARD THOMAS, lawyer; b. Cleve., Apr. 3, 1931; s. Edwin Carl and Theresa Henrietta (Bookmyer) R.; m. Billie Carmen Greer, June 26, 1954; children—Susan Greer, Patricia Allison, Richard Thomas. A.B., Case-Western Res. U., 1953; J.D., Cleve.-Marshall Law Sch., 1957. Bar: Ohio 1957, Pa. 1978, U.S. Supreme Ct. 1961. Personnel and safety dir. Motor Express, Inc., Cleve., 1954-58; mng. ptnr. Reminger & Reminger Co., L.P.A., Cleve., 1958—; dir. U.S. Truck Lines, Inc., Del. Cardinal Casualty Co.; mem. nat. claims council adv. bd. Comml. Union Assurance Co., 1980—; lectr. transp. law Fenn Coll., 1960-62, bus. law, Case Western Res. U., 1962-64. Mem. joint com. Cleve. Acad. Medicine-Greater Cleve. Bar Assn.; trustee Cleve. Zool. Soc., exec. com., 1984—, v.p., 1987—; trustee Andrew Sch., Huron Rd. Hosp., Cleve., Cleve. Soc. for Blind, 1987—. Served with AC, USNR, 1950-58. Mem. Fedn. Ins. and Corp. Counsel, Trial Attys. Am. (mem. sect. litigation, also tort and ins. practice), Fed. Bar Assn., ABA (com. on law and medicine, profl. responsibility com. 1977—), Internat. Bar Assn., Ohio Bar Assn. (council dels. 1987—), Pa. Bar Assn., Cleve. Bar Assn. (chmn. med. legal com. 1978-79, profl. liability com. 1977—), Transp. Lawyers Assn., Cleve. Assn. Civil Trial Attys., Am. Soc. Hosp. Attys., Soc. Ohio Hosp. Attys., Ohio Assn. Civil Trial Attys., Am. Judicature Soc., Def. Research Inst., Maritime Law Assn. U.S., Am. Coll. Law and Medicine, 8th Jud. Bar Assn. (life Ohio dist.). Clubs: Mayfield Country (pres. 1980-82), Union, Cleve. Playhouse, Hermit (pres. 1973-75) (Cleve.); Lost Tree (Fla.), Kirtland Country (Cleve.), Rolling Rock (Pa.). Federal civil litigation, State civil litigation, Personal injury. Home: 34000 Hackney Rd Hunting Valley OH 44022 Office: The 113 St Clair Bldg Cleveland OH 44114

REMLEY, DAVID MARK, lawyer; b. Fulton, Mo., June 5, 1955; s. Alvin and Audrey (Wright) R.; m. SuAnne Beth Lorts, June 19, 1976; children: David Michael, Elizabeth Parris. BA, Westminster Coll., 1977; JD, U. Mo., Columbia, 1980. Bar: Mo. 1980, U.S. Dist. Ct. (we. and ea. dists.) Mo. 1980. Law clk. to justice Mo. Supreme Ct., Jefferson City, 1980-81; assoc. Thomosson, Dickerson, Gilbert & Cook, Cape Giardeau, Mo., 1981-85, ptnr., 1986—. Mem. ABA, Mo. Bar Assn., Cape County Bar Assn. Avocations: camping, automobile restoration, woodworking. Federal civil litigation, State civil litigation, Personal injury. Home: 1725 Fremont Cape Girardeau MO 63701 Office: Thomasson Dickerson Gilbert & Cook 715 N Clark Cape Girardeau MO 63701

REMSBURG, F(RANK) RAINE, lawyer; b. Goldsboro, N.C., Apr. 13, 1941; s. Frank H. and Virginia (Raine) R.; m. Jane Slater, Aug. 23, 1967; children: John Raine, Jeffrey Kendall. AB, U. N.C., 1963, MBA, 1964; JD, Duke U., 1967. Bar: N.Y. 1967, N.C. 1967. Assoc. Rogers & Wells, N.Y.C., 1967-73; asst. gen. counsel Hanes Corp., Winston-Salem, N.C., 1973-78, Hanes Group div. Sara Lee Corp., Winston-Salem, 1978—. Bd. dirs. Winston-Salem Urban League, Child Guidance Ctr. Mem. ABA, Assn. Bar City of N.Y., N.C. Bar Assn.. Democrat. Episcopalian. Club: Westwood (Winston-Salem) (pres. 1985-86). General corporate, Federal civil litigation, Antitrust. Home: 1875 Virginia Rd Winston-Salem NC 27104 Office: PO Box 2760 Winston-Salem NC 27102

REMSEN, JOHN LOCKWOOD, lawyer; b. New Brunswick, N.J., Apr. 5, 1928; s. Frank W. and Helen (Lockwood) R.; m. Dorothy Lee Vasser, Sept. 9, 1951; children—John Lockwood, Helen Michelle Remsen Fisher, Stephanie E. Grad. Palm Beach Jr. Coll., 1950; LL.B. cum laude, U. Miami, 1953. Bar: Fla. 1953, U.S. Dist. Ct. Fla. 1953. Ptnr. Cromwell & Remsen, Riviera Beach, Fla., 1955—; past pres. Palm Beach County Legal Aid Soc.; founding dir. Citizens Bank Palm Beach County. Vice chmn. Palm Beach County (Fla.) Area Planning Bd., 1970-72; gen. chmn. PGA Team Championships, 1965, 66, PGA Championship, 1971; chmn. Palm Beach County Bd. Pub. Instrn., 1961-64; trustee Ocean Learning Inst., 1981—; bd. govs. Palm Beach Maritime Mus., 1986—; bd. dirs. Palm Beach County Sports Hall of Fame, 1985—. Served with USMC, 1946-47. Recipient Community Appreciation award, 1984. Mem. Palm Beach County Bar Assn., Fla. Bar Assn. (mem., chmn. grievance com. 1967-70, 75-78, 82—, chmn. unauthorized practice com. 1972-75; mem. profl. ethics com. 1978-82, mem. and chmn. 15th Cir. Fla. Jud. Nominating Commn., 1978-82, 83—), ABA. Democrat. Presbyterian. Clubs: Kiwanis, Jaycees, Elks (North Palm Beach); Govs. of Palm Beaches. Banking, General corporate, Real property. Home: 11960 Lake Shore Pl North Palm Beach FL 33408 Office: 6th Floor Barnett Bank Bldg 2001 Broadway Riviera Beach FL 33404

REMY, WILLIAM EMMETT, lawyer; b. San Marcos, Tex., Aug. 23, 1909; s. William E. and Ora Merle (Peters) R.; m. Martha Caroline Remy, Jan. 7, 1941; children—William E. III, Dorothy Caroline, Martha Caroline; m. 2d, Gloria Anderson Eckert, June 22, 1974; LL.B., U. Tex.-Austin, 1934. Bar: Tex. 1934, U.S. Tax Ct. 1940, U.S. Ct. Customs and Patent Appeals, 1940, U.S. Supreme Ct. 1945. Atty., OPA, 1942-47, div. dir., Washington, 1944-46, dep. adminstr. enforcement, 1946-47; sr. ptnr. Remy, Bayern & Paterson, San Antonio, from 1962; now sole practice, San Antonio; chmn. real property, probate and trust law sect. State Bar Tex. 1974-75; resident rep. Southwestern Legal Found., 1959-72. Mem. vestry St. Mark's Episcopal Ch., also chancellor; trustee, past pres. Boysville Inc.; bd. dirs., past pres. Good Samaritan Ctr.; bd. dirs. Sarah French Home for Aged, Santa Rosa Children's Hosp.; bd. govs. St. Mary's U., San Antonio. Fellow Am. Coll. Probate (past state chmn. Tex.; bd. regents 1981); mem ABA (chmn. com. role and function of estate lawyer com. 1975-77), San Antonio Estate Planners Council (pres. 1961-62), Internat. Acad. Estate and Trust Law, San Antonio Bar Assn. (pres. 1962-63). Club: Kiwanis (pres. 1960). Contbr. articles to profl. jours. Probate, Estate planning. Home: 316 Geneseo Rd San Antonio TX 78209 Office: 1321 Nat Bank of Commerce Bldg San Antonio TX 78205

RENCH, STEPHEN CHARLES, lawyer, lecturer, consultant, educator; b. Coffeyville, Kans., Oct. 11, 1930; s. Stephen and Gladys Mae (Carpenter) R.; m. Loraine Pennock, Oct. 11, 1966. B.A. in Econs., U. Kans., 1952; J.D., Georgetown U., 1959. Bar: Colo. 1959, U.S. Dist. Ct. Colo. 1959, U.S. Ct. Appeals (10th cir.) 1961, U.S. Supreme Ct. 1979. Law clk. to judge U.S. Ct. Appeals (10th cir.), Denver, 1959; law clk. to chief judge U.S. Dist. Ct. Colo., Denver, 1960-61; assoc. Tippit and Haskell, Denver, 1961-63; clk. Probate Ct., Denver, 1964-65; dep. state pub. defender, Denver, 1966-74; tng. dir. Colo. State Pub. Defender System, Denver, 1974-77, tng. dir. as ind. contractor tng. seminars, 1980-82; sole practice, Denver, 1977—; mem. permanent lecturing faculty for summer sessions and seminars Nat. Coll. Criminal Def., Houston, 1974—, course dir., 1977; instr. trial tactics and strategy, evidence courses U. Denver Law Sch., 1979—; lectr. in field throughout U.S. Served to 1st lt. USAF, 1952-56. Mem. Colo. Trial Lawyers Assn., Colo. Criminal Def. Bar, Nat. Assn. Criminal Def. Lawyers, Nat. Legal Aid and Defenders Assn., Nat. Practice Inst., Assn. Trial Lawyers Am., Denver Bar Assn., Colo. Bar Assn., ABA. Author: Fingertip Law for Colorado Public Defenders, 1975; Strategy for Colorado Public Defenders, 1979; The Rench Book, Trial Tactics and Strategy, 1980; Courtbook, 1982; monthly columnist Trade Secrets of a Trial Lawyer, Washington Memo, 1977-78; contbr. articles to profl. publs. State civil litigation, Criminal, Personal injury. Office: 1900 Olive St Denver CO 80220

RENDELL, ROBERT SLOAT, lawyer; b. N.Y.C., Nov. 9, 1940; s. Jesse T. and Emma S. R.; m. Mardi M. Rendell, July 10, 1967; children: Meredith, Lauren. A.B., Princeton U., 1962, LL.B., Harvard U., 1965, LL.M., 1966. Bar: N.Y. 1965. Atty., advisor Office of Internat. Tax Counsel, U.S. Treasury Dept., 1970-72; dep. gen. counsel U.S. Export-Import Bank, 1973-77; ptnr. Rogers & Wells, N.Y.C., 1980—; dir. UMB Bank & Trust Co. Mem. ABA, Bar Assn. City N.Y. Club: Harvard N.Y. Editor: Internat. Fin. Law, 1980. Private international, General corporate, Contracts commercial. Office: 900 Jackson St Dallas TX 75202 *

RENDLEMAN, DENNIS ALAN, lawyer; b. Jerseyville, Ill., Mar. 24, 1956; s. Raymond Nolte and Leota Darlene (Naslund) R.; m. Barbara Lynn Shelow, Jan. 3, 1981; 1 child, Jessica Alexis Shelow. BA in Polit. Sci., U. Ill., 1978, JD, 1981. Bar: Ill. 1981, U.S. Dist. Ct. (cen. dist.) Ill. 1981. Asst. counsel Ill. State Bar Assn., Springfield, 1981—; lectr. Sangamon State U., Springfield, 1985—. Contbr. articles to profl. jours. Pro bono vol. Ill. Vols. for Justice, Springfield, 1982—; performer Springfield Muni Theater, 1985; del. 20th congl. dist. Ill. Nat. Dem. Conv., 1984. Named one of Distinguished Young Men of Am., 1983. Fellow Ill. Bar Found.; mem. ABA (exec. com. legis. action com. young lawyers div. 1986—, lawyers and arts com. 1985—), Ill. Bar Assn., Sangamon County Bar Assn. (v.p. young lawyers div. 1985, pres. 1986, bd. dirs. 1984—). Democrat. Lutheran. Avocations: theater, music, photography. Legal ethics professional responsibility, General corporate, Association law and activities. Home: 401 W Jackson Pkwy Springfield IL 62704 Office: Ill Bar Assn 424 S 2s St Springfield IL 62701

RENDLEN, ALBERT LEWIS, judge; b. Hannibal, Mo., Apr. 7, 1922; s. Charles E. and Norma Lewis R.; m. Dona M. Schwartz; children—Albert Lewis, Susan Virginia. Student, William Jewell Coll., 1939-41; B.A., U. Ill., 1943; J.D., U. Mich., 1948. Bar: Mo. 1948. Mem. firm Rendlen & Renalen, Hannibal, 1948-74; city atty. Alexandria, 1949-52; U.S. commr. Eastern Dist. Mo., 1953-55; judge Mo. Ct. Appeals (St. Louis dist.), 1974-77; chief justice Mo. Supreme Ct., 1982-85, formerly chief justice, now assoc. justice, 1985—. Chmn. Republican State Com., 1973-74, U.S. Constn. Bicentennial Commn. of Mo.; bd. regents NE Mo. State Coll., 1973-75; mem. nat. and dist. adv. council for Small Bus. Adminstrn.; past mem. Marion County Welfare Commn.; past pres. dist. council Boy Scouts Am. Served with U.S. Army, 1943-46; served to comdr. USCG, 1951-70. Mem. Navy League, Res. Officer Assn. NE Mo. (past pres.), Am. Legion, VFW, Am. Judicature Soc. Office: Supreme Ct Bldg Jefferson City MO 65101

RENDON, JOSEFINA MUNIZ, municipal court judge; b. San Juan P.R., June 17, 1949; d. Francisco V. Muniz-Souffront and Gloria (Vazquez de) Muniz; m. Ruben Rendon, June 29, 1974; children—Daniel Ruben, Raquel Ischel. Student U. Tex., 1967-68, Universidad Interamericana, San Juan, P.R., 1968-69; B.A., U. Houston, 1972, J.D., 1976. Bar: Tex. 1977, U.S. Dist. Ct. (so. dist.) Tex. 1979, U.S. Ct. Appeals (5th cir.) 1979. Legal process clk. Pub. Defenders Office, San Francisco, 1977-78; ptnr. firm Rendon & Rendon, Houston, 1978-83; mcpl. ct. judge City of Houston, 1983—; commr., vice-chmn. Civil Service Commn., Houston, 1980-83. Newspaper legal columnist, La Voz de Houston, 1980-83. Bd. dirs. Pub. Interest Advocacy Council, Houston, 1979-81; pres. SER-Jobs for Progress Bd., Houston, 1983—; dist. legal adviser League United Latin Am. Citizens, Houston, 1980-83. Recipient awards League United Latin Am. Citizens; Outstanding Service to Community award City of Houston, 1983; named One of Houston's Most Interesting People, Houston City Mag., 1984. Mem. Am. Judges Assn., Tex. Mcpl. Cts. Assn., ABA, Tex. Bar Assn., Houston Bar Assn., Mex.-Am. Bar Assn., Am. Immigration Lawyers Assn., Puerto Rican Assn. Judicial administration, Administrative and regulatory, Immigration, naturalization, and customs. Office: Mcpl Ct 1400 Lubbock St Houston TX 77002

RENDON, RUBEN, lawyer; b. Edinburg, Tex., Nov. 10, 1948; s. Felipe and Odilia (Molina) R.; m. Josefina Muniz, June 29, 1974; children—Daniel Ruben, Raquel Ischel. Student Pan Am. U., 1967-69; B.A., U. Houston, 1971; J.D., Tex. So. U., 1976. Bar: Tex. 1977, U.S. Dist. Ct. (no. and so. dists.) Tex., U.S. Ct. Appeals (5th cir.). Legal intern Mex.-Am. Legal Def. Fund, San Francisco, 1977-79; ptnr. firm Barrera, Rendon & Rodriguez, Houston, 1979—. State legal adviser League United Latin Am. Citizens, Houston, 1983—. Mem. ABA, Tex. Trial Lawyers Assn., Harris County Criminal Lawyers Assn., Mex. Am. Bar Assn., Order of the Alhambra. Democrat. Roman Catholic. Personal injury, Criminal, Civil rights. Home: 8207 Glenbrae St Houston TX 77061 Office: William T Dearman and Assocs 777 Post Oak Blvd Suite 714 Houston TX 77056

RENFRO, WILLIAM LEONARD, consulting futurist; b. West Palm Beach, Fla., Sept. 9, 1945; s. Ernest Leonard and Oine Warren (McAdams) R. B.S. in Physics, Rensselaer Poly. Inst., 1967, M.S. in Nuclear Engring., 1972; postgrad. Yale U., 1967-68; J.D., U. Conn., 1972. Bar: Conn. 1973. Physicist Combustion Engring., Windsor-Locks, Conn., 1968-69; sole practice, Hartford, Conn., 1973-74; sr. research assoc. The Futures Group, Glastonbury, Conn., 1973-76; analyst futures research Congl. Research Service, U.S. Congress, 1976-80; pres. Policy Analysis Co., Inc., Washington, 1980—; guest lectr. Georgetown U., adj. prof. George Washington U., Indsl. Coll. Armed Forces Nat. Def. U. Mem. Long Range Planning Com. United Way. Mem. Nat. Foresight Network U.S. Congress Mem. Issues Mgmt. Assn. (dir. 1981—, v.p. 1986—), ABA, Conn. Bar Assn., Hartford County Bar Assn., World Futures Soc. Episcopalian. Author: (with others) The Futures Research Handbook, 1977, Anticipatory Democracy, 1978, The Public Affairs Handbook, 1982; Applying Methods and Techniques of Futures Research, 1983; The Legislative Role of Corporations, 1982; Future Research and the Strategic Planning Process, 1985, Non-Extrapolative Forecasting in Business, 1986; editor: Futures Research Quar. World Futures Soc.; issues mgmt. editor The Futurist, 1982—. General corporate, Legislative, Legal education. Office: Policy Analysis Co Inc 1090 Vermont Ave NW Washington DC 20005

RENNER, CLARENCE E., judge, artist; b. Wichita, Kans., Sept. 7, 1922; s. Charles M. and Helen (Hull) R.; m. Dorothy I. Huff, Jan. 24, 1942; children: Diane L. Renner Curtis, Cindy L. Renner Constantino, Charles M., John R., Keith E. AB, Washburn U., Topeka, Kans., 1949, JD, 1950. Bar: Kans. 1950. Sole practice, Pratt, Kans., 1950-75; atty. County of Pratt, Kans., 1957-69; assoc. dist. judge 19th Jud. Dist., 1977-81; adminstrv. judge 30th Jud. Dist., Pratt, 1982—, dist. judge, 1982—; spl. assigned judge Kans. Ct. Appeals, 1986; lectr. Pratt Community Coll.; spl. assigned judge Kans. Ct. Appeals, 1986. Served with USAF, 1942-46. Mem. Kans. Bar Assn., Pratt County Bar Assn., Kans. Dist. Judges Assn., Kans. Dist. and County Attys. Assn. (pres.), Am. Legion, VFW. Democrat. Methodist. Lodge: Elks. Numerous landscape and portrait paintings. Jurisprudence. Home: 415 N Main St Pratt KS 67124 Office: Pratt County Courthouse Pratt KS 67124

RENNER, MICHAEL JOHN, lawyer; b. Tacoma, May 18, 1954; s. William J. and Bernice E. (Bernobich) R. BS, USAF Acad., 1976; JD with honors, U. Tex., 1982. Bar: Tex. 1982, U.S. Ct. Mil. Appeals 1982. Commd. 2d lt. USAF, 1976, advanced through grades to maj., 1986; chief mil. justice USAF, Grissom AFB, Ind., 1982-84; chief info. systems law hdqrs. Communications Command, Scott AFB, Ill., 1984-85, dep. dir. tariff regulatory law hdqrs., 1985-86, dir., 1986—. Editor (newsletter) Telecommunications ADP Crossfeed, 1985—. Mem. ABA, Tex. Bar Assn. Roman Catholic. Military, Government contracts and claims, Public utilities. Office: Hdqrs AFCC/Jay Scott AFB IL 62225

RENNER, ROBERT GEORGE, U.S. district judge; b. Nevis, Minn., Apr. 2, 1923; s. Henry J. and Beatrice M. (Fuller) R.; m. Catherine L. Clark, Nov. 12, 1949; children: Robert, Anne, Richard, David. B.A., St. John's U., Collegeville, Minn., 1947; J.D., Georgetown U., 1949. Bar: Minn. 1949. Pvt. practice Walker, 1949-69; U.S. atty. Dist. of Minn., 1969-77, U.S. magistrate, 1977-80, U.S. dist. judge, 1980—. Mem. Minn. Ho. of Reps., 1957-69. Served with AUS, 1943-46. Mem. ABA, Fed. Bar Assn., Minn. Bar Assn. Roman Catholic. Jurisprudence. Address: US District Court 738 US Courthouse 316 Robert St Saint Paul MN 55101 *

RENNICK, KYME ELIZABETH WALL, lawyer; b. Columbus, Ohio, Dec. 27, 1953; d. Robert Leroy and Julie (Allison) Wall; m. Ian Alexander Rennick, Oct. 15, 1983. BA, Centre Coll., 1975; MA, Ohio State U., 1978; JD, Capital U., 1982. Bar: Ohio 1982, U.S. Dist. Ct. (no. and so. dists.) Ohio 1983. Legal intern Ohio Dept. Natural Resources, Columbus, 1981-83, gen. counsel, 1983-86, chief counsel, 1986—. Editor: Baldwin's Ohio Revised Code Annotated, Title 15 Conservation of Natural Resources, 1984. Mem. ABA, Columbus Bar Assn. Presbyterian. Avocations: running, biking, crafts. Administrative and regulatory, Environment, Government contracts and claims. Office: Ohio Dept Natural Resources Fountain Sq Bldg D-3 Columbus OH 43224

RENO, JANET, lawyer; b. Miami, Fla., July 21, 1938; d. Henry and Jane (Wood) R. A.B. in Chemistry, Cornell U., 1960; LL.B., Harvard U., 1963. Bar: Fla. 1963. Assoc. Brigham & Brigham, 1963-67; ptnr. Lewis & Reno, 1967-71; staff dir. judiciary com. Fla. Ho. of Reps., Tallahassee, 1971-72; cons. Fla. Senate Criminal Justice Com. for Revision Fla.'s Criminal Code, spring 1973; adminstrv. asst. state atty. 11th Jud. Circuit Fla., Miami, 1973-76, state's atty., 1978—; ptnr. Steel Hector and Davis, Miami, 1976-78; mem. jud. nominating commn. 11th Jud. Circuit Fla., 1976-78; chmn. Fla. Gov.'s Council for Prosecution Organized Crime, 1979-80. Bd. dirs. United Way of Dade County, 1979-81. Mem. ABA (Inst. Jud. Adminstrn. Juvenile Justice Standards Commn. 1973-76), Am. Law Inst., Am. Judicature Soc. (Herbert Harley award 1981), Dade County Bar Assn., Fla. Pros. Atty.'s Assn. (pres. 1984-86). Democrat. Criminal, Juvenile. Office: 1351 NW 12th St 6th Floor Miami FL 33125

RENO, OTTIE WAYNE, former judge; b. Pike County, Ohio, Apr. 7, 1929; s. Eli Enos and Arbannah Belle (Jones) R.; Asso. in Bus. Adminstrn., Franklin U., 1949; LL.B., Franklin Law Sch., 1953; J.D., Capital U., 1966; grad. Coll. Juvenile Justice, U. Nev., 1973; m. Janet Gay McCann, May 22, 1947; children—Ottie Wayne II, Jennifer Lynn, Lorna Victoria. Admitted to Ohio bar, 1953; practiced in Pike County; recorder Pike County, 1957-73; common pleas judge Probate and Juvenile divs. Pike County, 1973-79. Mem. adv. bd. Ohio Youth Services, 1972-74. Mem. Democratic Central Com. Camp Creek precinct, 1956-72, 83—; sec. Pike County Central Com., 1960-70; chmn. Pike County Democratic Exec. Com., 1971-72; del. Dem. Nat. Conv., 1972; mem. Ohio Dem. Central Com., 1969-70; Dem. candidate 6th Ohio dist. U.S. Ho. of Reps., 1966; pres. Scioto Valley Local Sch. Dist., 1962-66. Recipient Distinguished Service award Ohio Youth Commn., 1974; 6 Outstanding Jud. Service awards Ohio Supreme Ct.; 15 times Ala. horseshoe pitching champion; named to Nat. Horseshoe Pitchers Hall of Fame, 1978; mem. internat. sports exchange, U.S. and Republic South Africa, 1972, 80, 82. Mem. Ohio, Pike County (pres. 1964) bar assns., Nat. Council Juvenile Ct. Judges, Am. Legion. Mem. Ch. of Christ. Author: Story of Horseshoes, 1963; Pitching Championship Horseshoes, 1971, 2d rev. edit., 1975; Who's Who in Horseshoe Pitching, 1983. General practice, Juvenile, Probate. Home: 148 Reno Rd Lucasville OH 45648

RENSIN, HOWARD M., lawyer; b. Syracuse, N.Y., July 31, 1943; s. Kenneth Coleman and Ethel (Bloom) R.; m. Katherine Kallet, June 13, 1964; children—Joseph, Samuel, David, Deborah. B.A., Syracuse U., 1964; LL.B., George Washington U., 1967, J.D., 1978. Bar: D.C. 1967, Md. 1968, U.S. Supreme Ct. 1971. Law clk. Taylor & Waldron, Washington, 1965-67, assoc., 1967-68; assoc. Schwartzbach & Wortman, Washington, 1968-70; assoc. Lesser & Lesser, Washington, 1970-72; sole practice, Hyattsville, Md., 1972—. Trustee Silver Spring Civic Assn., Md., 1972-79; synagogue trustee, Silver Spring, Md., 1978-80, v.p., 1980-82, chmn. bd., 1982-84. Recipient Amateur Radio Disaster Traffic award, 1982. Mem. Md. Bar Assn., D.C. Bar Assn., Prince George's County Bar Assn., Assn. Trial Lawyers Am., Am. Arbitration Assn. (arbitrator), Am. Radio Relay League, Md. Emergency Traffic Network. State civil litigation. Home: 15221 Centergate Dr Silver Spring MD 20904

RENTZ, JOE HOUSTON, lawyer; b. Port Arthur, Tex.; s. Joe and Odessa (McGee) R.; m. April Lynn Phillips, Sept. 20, 1969; children: Trey, Molly. BA, U.Tex., 1965, JD, 1967. Bar: Tex. 1967. Ptnr. Rentz, Burg & Assocs., Houston, 1967—. Served with USMCR, 1967-69; served to comdr. USNR, 1969—. Family and matrimonial, General corporate, State civil litigation. Home: 11910 Don Caster Houston TX 77024 Office: Rentz Burg & Assoc 6363 Woodway #500 Houston TX 77057

RENZ, WILLIAM TOMLINSON, lawyer; b. Washington, Pa., Feb. 26, 1947; s. William C. and Anna T. (Tomlinson) R.; m. Suellen Gilson, Feb. 3, 1968; children: William T. Jr., Michelle, Michael. BA, Pa. State U., 1969; JD, Dickinson Sch. Law, 1972. Bar: Pa. 1972, U.S. Supreme Ct. 1979, U.S. Ct. Appeals (3d cir.) 1982. From assoc. to ptnr. Power, Bowen & Valimont, Doylestown, Pa., 1972—. Served to capt. U.S. Army, 1969-77. Mem. ABA, Pa. Bar Assn. (treas. young lawyers div.), Bucks County Bar Assn. (bd. dirs. 1984—), Deep Run Sports Assn. (v.p.). Republican. Avocations: racquetball, baseball, chess. Federal civil litigation, State civil litigation. Office: 102 N Main St Doylestown PA 18901

REPETTI, JAMES RANDOLPH, law educator; b. Boston, Nov. 25, 1953; s. Memore A. and Cleo B. (Moon) R.; m. Susan M. Leonard, Aug. 16, 1980; 1 child, Jane. BA magna cum laude, Harvard U., 1975; MBA, JD magna cum laude, Boston Coll., 1980. Bar: Mass. 1980, U.S. Dist. Ct. Mass. 1981. Law clk. to presiding justice U.S. Dist. Ct. Mass., Boston, 1980-81; assoc. Ropes & Gray, Boston, 1981-86; asst. prof.law Boston Coll., Newton, Mass., 1986—. Mem. ABA, Mass. Bar Assn., Boston Bar Assn., Order of Coif. Democrat. Roman Catholic. Club: Hyannisport (Mass.). Avocations: sailing, golf, skiing. General corporate, Federal civil litigation, Corporate taxation. Home: 38 Bonney St Westwood MA 02090 Office: Boston Coll Law Sch 885 Centre St Newton MA 02159

REPETTI, SUSAN LEONARD, lawyer; b. Boston, Jan. 4, 1956; d. Jerome M. and Virginia R. (Curley) Leonard; m. James R. Repetti, Aug. 16, 1980; 1 child, Jane Elizabeth. B.A. in Econs., Wellesley Coll., 1977; student London Sch. Econs., 1975-76; J.D., Boston Coll., 1980; LL.M., Boston U., 1984. Bar: Mass. 1980, U.S. Dist. Ct. Mass. 1981, U.S. Tax Ct. 1982. Assoc. law firm Sullivan & Worcester, Boston, 1980—; lectr. Mass. Continuing Legal Edn., 1985. Editor Boston Coll. Law Rev., 1979-80. Alumnae liaison Wellesley Coll. AC-CESS Assocs., 1981-85; mem. Wellesley Coll. Career Assocs., 1980—. Durant scholar, 1977. Mem. ABA, Mass. Bar Assn., Boston Bar Assn., Order of Coif, Phi Beta Kappa. Roman Catholic. Club: Hyannisport. Corporate taxation, Personal income taxation, Estate taxation. Office: Sullivan & Worcester 1 Post Office Sq Boston MA 02109

REPHAN, JACK, lawyer; b. Little Rock, Mar. 16, 1932; s. Henry and Mildred (Frank) R.; m. Arlene Clark, June 23, 1957; children: Amy Carol, James Clark. B.S. in Commerce, 1954; LL.B., U. Va., 1959. Bar: Va. 1959, D.C. 1961. Asso. Kanter & Kanter, Norfolk, Va., 1959-60; law clk. to Judge Sam E. Whitaker, U.S. Ct. Claims, Washington, 1960-62; asso. Pierson, Ball & Dowd, Washington, 1962-64; partner Danzansky, Dickey, Tydings, Quint

& Gordon, Washington, 1964-77; mem. firm Braude, Margulies, Sacks & Rephan (Chartered), Washington, 1977—; mem. nat. panel arbitrators Am. Arbitration Assn.; lectr. joint com. continuing legal edn. State Bar Va. Contbr. articles to legal jours. Pres. Patrick Henry PTA, Alexandria, Va., 1968-69; treas. John Adams Middle Sch. PTA, Alexandria, 1970-71; pres. Seminary Ridge Citizens Assn., 1976-77; Democratic candidate for Alexandria City Com., 1969. Served to 1st lt. AUS, 1955-57. Mem. ABA (chmn. subcom. procurement jud. remedies, pub. contract sect. 1973-74), Va. Bar Assn. (gov. sect. constrn. law 1979—, vice chmn. 1980-81, chmn. 1981-82), D.C. Bar Assn., Phi Epsilon Pi, Phi Alpha Delta. Jewish. Clubs: Kiwanis (pres. Landmark club, Alexandria 1969), Westwood Country (v.p. 1977-78), Belle Haven Country. Construction, Federal civil litigation, State civil litigation. Home: 7203 Park Terrace Dr Alexandria VA 22307 Office: 1828 L St NW Suite 900 Washington DC 20036

REPPER, GEORGE ROBERT, lawyer; b. Topeka, Dec. 22, 1954; s. George Vincent Jr. and Maria Magdalena (Bullert) R.; m. Helen Linda Zeichner, Aug. 23, 1981; children: Brian Lawrence, Kevin Michael. BS, SUNY, Albany, 1977; JD, Albany Law Sch., 1981. Bar: N.Y. 1982, D.C. 1982, U.S. Patent and Trademark Office 1984. Sole practice Washington, 1982-83; asst. v.p. Bernard, Rothwell & Brown, Washington, 1983—. Mem. ABA (patents, trademarks and copyrights sect.), D.C. Bar Assn. (patents, trademarks and copyrights sect.). Republican. Patent, Trademark and copyright, Federal civil litigation. Office: Bernard Rothwell & Brown PC 1700 K St NW Washington DC 20006

REPPY, WILLIAM ARNEILL, JR., law educator; b. Oxnard, Calif., Mar. 14, 1941; s. William Arneill and Margot Louise Reppy; m. Susan Westerberg, Sept. 30, 1967 (div. 1973); m. Juliann Tenney, Nov. 28, 1975. B.A. with great distinction, Stanford U., 1963, J.D. with great distinction, 1966. Bar: Calif. 1966, N.C. 1971, U.S. Supreme Ct. 1971. Law clk. to Justice William Douglas, U.S. Supreme Ct., Washington, 1967-68; assoc. Tuttle & Taylor, Los Angeles, 1968-71; prof. law Duke U., Durham, N.C. 1971—; cons. Calif. Law Revision Com., Palo Alto, 1979-83; mem. Condominium Statutes Commn., Raleigh, N.C., 1980—. Author: Community Property in California, 1980; Community Property-Gilbert Law Summaries, 1983; co-author: Community Property in U.S., 2d edit., 1982, Texas Matrimonial Property Law, 1983. Mem. editorial bd. Community Property Jour., 1973—. Recipient Nathan Abbot award Stanford U., 1966. Mem. Am. Law Inst., Order of Coif, Phi Beta Kappa. Republican. Family and matrimonial. Office: Duke U Sch Law Durham NC 27706 *

RESER, DON CLAYTON, lawyer; b. San Antonio, Dec. 14, 1950; s. Richard Stair and Mary Luella (Clayton) R.; m. Rebecca Jo Reser, Mar. 30, 1974. A.B. in Econs., Stanford U., 1973; M.B.A., U. Tex., 1976; J.D., U. Houston, 1978. Bar: Tex. 1977, U.S. dist. ct. (we. and so. dists.), U.S. Ct. Appeals (5th and 11th circs.) 1981, U.S. Supreme Ct. 1981, U.S. Tax Ct. 1980. Jr. law clk. to judge U.S. Dist. Ct. Western Dist. Tex., 1977-78, sr. law clk., 1978-79; assoc. Mathis & Bevil, San Antonio, 1979-80, Plunkett, Gibson & Allen, San Antonio, 1980-84, Don C. Reser, P.C., San Antonio, 1984—. Bd. dirs. U. Houston Law Alumni Assn. Mem. ABA, Fed. Bar Assn., Tex. Bar Assn., San Antonio Bar Assn. Republican. Presbyterian. Contbr. article to law jour. Securities. Office: 311 E Ramsey Rd San Antonio TX 78216

RESICH, JOHN JAMES, lawyer; b. San Pedro, Calif., Nov. 17, 1947; s. John James Sr. and Hilda (Morris) R.; m. Shirley Moss, Dec. 19, 1970; children: Melissa, Rebecca, Nicholas. BA, Calif. Poly. U., 1969; JD, U. Calif., Santa Clara, 1972. Bar: Calif. 1972, U.S. Dist. Ct. (cen. dist.) Calif. 1972, U.S. Ct. Appeals (9th cir.) 1972, U.S. Supreme Ct. 1977. Law clk. to presiding justice U.S. Dist. Ct. (cen. dist.) Calif., Los Angeles, 1972; staff atty. Office of U.S. Atty., Los Angeles, 1973-77; assoc. Law Office of John Marin, Wilmington, Calif., 1977; sole practice San Pedro, Calif., 1977—. Bd. dirs. San Pedro Hosp., 1982—, Green Hill Cemetery, San Pedro, 1984—. Mem. Fed. Bar Assn., Los Angeles County Bar Assn., Calif. Bar Assn. Club: Yugoslavia am. (San Pedro) (bd. dirs. 1979-85). General practice, Personal injury, Probate. Office: 840 W 9th St San Pedro CA 90731

RESNECK, WILLIAM ALLAN, lawyer; b. Memphis, Oct. 21, 1945; s. William Saul and Charlotte Helen (Mayer) R.; m. Ellen Diamond, July 27, 1979; 1 child, Joshua. AB, Oberlin Coll., 1967; JD, Ind. U., 1970. Bar: Calif. 1971. Assoc. Steinhart, Goldberg, San Francisco, 1970-75; sole practice San Francisco and Berkeley, Calif., 1975—; adminstrv. law judge State of Calif., Berkeley, 1977—; prof. St. Mary's Paralegal Program, Oakland, Calif., 1979-85; part time dep. atty. City of Berkeley, 1985-87. Mem. Order of Coif. Avocation: whitewater rafting. State civil litigation, Personal injury, Workers' compensation. Office: 2020 Milvia St PO Box 1029 Berkeley CA 94701-1029

RESNICK, CHARLES H., corporate executive, lawyer; b. 1924. A.B., Harvard U., 1948, LL.B., 1950. With Raytheon Co., Lexington, Mass., 1951—, sec., 1963—, gen. counsel, 1964—, v.p., 1968—, Trustee Waltham Hosp., 1962-76; class agt. Harvard Law Sch. Fund, 1978—. Mem. ABA (chmn. com. on corp. law depts. 1971-72, mem. council sect. on bus., banking and corp. law 1977—). General corporate. Office: Raytheon Co 141 Spring St Lexington MA 02173 *

RESNICK, DONALD IRA, lawyer; b. Chgo., July 19, 1950; s. Roland S. and Marilyn B. (Weiss) R.; m. Jill Allison White, July 3, 1977; children: Daniel, Allison. BS with high honors, U. Ill., 1972; JD, Harvard U., 1975. Bar: Ill. 1975, U.S. Dist. Ct. (no. dist.) Ill. 1975. Assoc. Arvey, Hodes, Costello & Burman, Chgo., 1975-80, ptnr., 1981-83; sr. ptnr. Nagelberg & Resnick, Chgo., 1983—. Bd. dirs. Hubbard St. Dance Co., Chgo., 1979—, Ill. chpt. Real Estate Securities and Syndication Inst., Chgo., 1986—. Mem. ABA, Chgo. Bar Assn. Club: Birchwood (Highland Park, Ill.). Real property. Office: Nagelberg & Resnick PC 200 S Wacker Chicago IL 60606

RESNICK, PHILLIP STANLEY, lawyer; b. Mpls., July 19, 1944; s. Sidney L. and Rae J. (Barres) R.; m. Julie Resnick, Aug. 12, 1984; 1 child, Allison. B.A., U. Minn., 1967; J.D., William Mitchell Coll., 1971. Bar: Minn. 1971, U.S. Dist. Ct. Minn. 1972, U.S. Ct. Appeals (8th cir.) 1972, U.S. Supreme Ct. 1977. Ptnr. Resnick and Bartsh, Mpls. Mem. ABA, Nat. Assn. Criminal Def. Lawyers, Minn. Bar Assn., Minn. Trial Lawyers Assn., Hennepin County Bar Assn. Criminal. Office: Resnick and Bartsh 510 Lumber Exchange Bldg Minneapolis MN 55402

RESNICOW, NORMAN JAKOB, lawyer; b. N.Y.C., July 23, 1947; s. Herbert and Melly (Engelberg) R.; m. Barbara Jane Roses, June 14, 1970; children: Daniel Ilan, Joel Ethan. BA summa cum laude, Yale U., 1969, JD, 1972. Bar: N.Y. 1973, U.S. Dist. Ct. (so. and ea. dists.) N.Y. 1973. Assoc. Baker & McKenzie, N.Y.C., 1972-79, ptnr., 1979—. Term mem. Council Fgn. Relations, N.Y.C., 1976-81; exec. com., treas., bd. dirs. Hebrew Immigrant Aid Soc., N.Y.C., 1981—; mem. nat. young leadership cabinet United Jewish Appeal, N.Y.C., 1978-83. Recipient Young Leadership award United Jewish Appeal-Fedn. Jewish Philantrophies, 1978. Mem. ABA (corp. bus. and banking law, internat. law, real estate and probate law sects.), N.Y. State Bar Assn. (internat. law com.), Assn. of Bar of City of N.Y., Phi Beta Kappa. Democrat. Avocation: internat. polit. relations. Private international, Contracts commercial, General corporate. Home: 239 Central Park West Apt 9C New York NY 10024 Office: Baker & McKenzie 805 Third Ave 29th Floor New York NY 10022

RESO, JEROME JOHN, JR., lawyer; b. New Orleans, May 21, 1937; s. Jerome John and Olga (Arsequet) R.; m. Lynne Kelly, June 7, 1958; children—Jerome J., Patrick K., Robert R., Jennifer J. B.B.A., Loyola U., New Orleans, 1961, LL.B., 1961. Bar: La. Ptnr. firm Baldwin & Haspel, New Orleans, 1964—; adj. faculty, lectr. on taxation Loyola U. Sch. Law, 1971-76; dir. Pelican Savs. and Loan Assn., Bryan Chevrolet, Inc., Commonwealth Life Ins. Co. Contbr. articles to law revs., chpts. to books. Bd. dirs. Catholic Found. Archdiocese of New Orleans, Am. Coll. Tax Counsel. Mem. New Orleans Bar Assn., La. Bar Assn., Fed. Bar Assn., ABA, Am. Coll. Probate Counsel, New Orleans Estate Planning Council (past pres., dir.), Tulane Tax Inst. (mem. planning com.). Republican. Roman Catholic. Corporate taxation, General corporate, Estate planning. Office: Baldwin & Haspel 1100 Poydras St Suite 2200 New Orleans LA 70163-2200

RESOR, STANLEY ROGERS, lawyer; b. N.Y.C., Dec. 5, 1917; s. Stanley Burnet and Helen (Lansdowne) R.; m. Jane Lawler Pillsbury, Apr. 4, 1942; children: Stanley R., Charles P., John L., Edmund L., William B., Thomas S., James P. B.A., Yale U., 1939, LL.B., 1946. Bar: N.Y. 1947. Assoc., then ptnr. firm Debevoise & Plimpton, N.Y.C., 1946-65, 71-73, 79—; undersec. Dept. Army, 1965, sec., 1965-71, ambassador negotiations for Mut. and Balanced Force Reductions in Central Europe, 1973-78; undersec. for policy Dept. Def., 1978-79; dir. Sta. WNET-TV. Fellow Yale Corp., 1979-86. Served to maj. AUS, 1942-45. Decorated Silver Star, Bronze Star, Purple Heart; recipient George C. Marshall award Assn. U.S. Army, 1974, Sylvanus Thayer award Assn. Graduates of U.S. Mil. Acad., 1984. Mem. ABA, Assn. Bar City N.Y. (chmn. com. internat. arms control and security affairs 1983-86), Atlantic Council (dir.), Inst. for Def. Analyses (dir.), Arms Control Assn., UN Assn. U.S.A. (dir., mem. arms control panel), Council Fgn. Relations, Com. for Nat. Security (exec. bd.), Am. Council on Germany (bd. dirs.). Republican. Episcopalian. Clubs: Century Assn, Yale; New Canaan Country (Conn.); New Canaan Winter, Metropolitan; Chevy Chase (Md.). General corporate. Home: 809 Weed St New Canaan CT 06840 Office: Debevoise & Plimpton 875 3d Ave New York NY 10022

RESPESS, JAMES WALTER, laywer; b. Pantego, N.C., Apr. 4, 1926; s. James Walter and Mary (Leary) R.; 1 dau., Cheryl Dianne. B.S.B.A., Am. U., 1958, J.D., 1959. Bar: D.C. 1959, Md. 1975, U.S. Dist. Ct. D.C. 1959, U.S. Tax Ct. 1959, U.S. Ct. Appeals (D.C. cir.) 1959, U.S. Ct. Appeals (4th cir.) 1975, U.S. Supreme Ct. 1964. With IRS, 1955-60; chmn. bus. adminstrn. dept. Point Park Coll., Pitts., 1960-62; legis. analyst NEA, Washington, 1962-65; gen. counsel Ams. United for Separation of Ch. and State, Silver Spring, Md., 1976-77; sole practice, Frederick, Md., 1965—. Mem. Nat. Democratic Club, United Dems. of Frederick County; dir., past gen. counsel United Methodist Found. for Balt. Ann. Conf.; deacon SDA Ch.; past pres. Frederick County Battered Spouse Program; co-chair Frederick Commn. on the Bicent. of U.S. Constitution, 1987—. Served in USN, 1943-47, NATOUSA, PTO. Mem. ABA, D.C. Bar Assn., Frederick County Bar Assn., Md. Bar Assn., VFW, Am. Legion. Lodges: Masons (32 deg.), Knight Comdr. Ct. Honor, Shriners, Legion of Honor, Keystone Kopps, Tall Cedars of Lebanon. Legal history, Estate planning, General litigation and corporate. Office: 1317 Orchard Way #A Frederick MD 21701

RESTANI, JANE A., federal judge; b. San Francisco, Feb. 27, 1948; d. Roy J. and Emilia C. Restani. BA, U. Calif., Berkeley, 1969; JD, U. Calif., Davis, 1973. Trial atty. U.S. Dept. Justice, Washington, 1973-76, asst. chief comml. litigation sect., 1976-80, dir. comml. litigation sect., 1980-83; judge U.S. Ct. Internat. Trade, N.Y.C., 1983—. Office: US Ct Internat Trade One Federal Plaza New York NY 10007 *

RESTEINER, HAROLD EDWARD, lawyer; b. Turner, Mich., Oct. 18, 1930; s. Herbert and Agnes (Theiner) R.; children: Eric, Gretchen, Marc. JD, Wayne State U., 1956. Bar: Mich. Ptnr. Somers, Geiger & Resteiner, Flint, Mich., 1955-64; judge probate Genesee County, Flint, 1965-86; ptnr. Mansour, Rizik, Resteiner & Cronin, Flint, 1986-87; sole practice Flint, 1986—; instr. Inst. Continuing Legal Edn.; vis. judge various Mich. Probate Cts. Contbr. articles to profl. jours. Chmn. Region V Crime Commn., treas. Flint Gen. Hosp.; past pres. Genesse Area Mich. Assn. Emotionally Disturbed Children, Tall Pine Council Boy Scouts Am; past v.p. Urban League; active Multiple Sclerosis Soc. Mich., Mich. League for Human Services, Model Cities Fin. Com., Mich. Mental Health Soc., Big Bros. of Greater Flint and Genesse County, bd. mgmt. YMCA Boys Farm; deacon, elder, trustee First Presbyn. Ch.; bd. govs. Goodwill Industries; various other orgns. Served to 1st lt. U.S. Army, 1956-57. Mem. ABA, Mich. Bar Assn. (bd. dirs. jud. conf., probate council), Genesee County Bar Assn., Assn. Trial Lawyers Am., Mich. Trial Lawyers Assn., Nat. Council Juvenile and Family Ct. Judges, Nat. Council Crime and Delinquency, Nat. Coll. Probate Judges (pres. 1986—), Mich. Probate and Juvenile Ct. Judges Assn. (past. pres.). Avocations: travel, sailing, reading, tennis, cross country skiing. Personal injury, Probate, Judicial administration. Office: 1080 Creekwood Trail Burton MI 48509

RESTIVO, JAMES JOHN, JR., lawyer; b. Pitts., Aug. 15, 1946; s. James J. and Dorothy (Ardolino) R.; m. Gail Sharon Hackenburg, July 11, 1970; 4 children. B.A. in History, U. Pa., 1968; J.D., Georgetown U., 1971. Bar: Pa. 1971, U.S. Dist. Ct. (we. and ea. dists.) Pa. 1971, U.S. Ct. Appeals (3d cir.) 1971, U.S. Supreme Ct. 1979. Ptnr. Reed, Smith, Shaw & McClay, Pitts., 1979—, head litigation group, 1986—; dir. Asbestos Claims Facility. Editorial staff Georgetown Law Rev., 1970-71. Mem. ABA, Allegheny County Bar Assn., Nat. Assn. Coll. and Univ. Attys., Def. Research Inst. Federal civil litigation, State civil litigation, Insurance. Office: James H Reed Bldg 435 6th Ave Pittsburgh PA 15230

RESTRICK, JOHN KNIGHT, lawyer; b. Detroit, Nov. 17, 1942; s. Robert Charles and Elizabeth Earle (Knight) R.; m. Marguerite Marie Therese Laviolette, Aug. 13, 1966; children—John, Nicole Louise. B.B.A., U. Mich., 1964, J.D., 1967. Bar: Mich. 1968, Calif. 1974. Atty. Consumers Power Co., Jackson, Mich., 1967-72; dept. counsel Gen. Electric Co., San Jose, Calif., 1972-77, spl. litigation counsel, Fairfield, Conn., 1977-78, div. counsel, Phila., 1979-81, ops. counsel, San Jose, 1981—. Mem. Order of Coif. Nuclear power, Contracts commercial, General corporate. Home: 20534 Sevilla Ln Saratoga CA 95070 Office: Gen Electric Co Nuclear Energy Bus Div 175 Curtner Ave San Jose CA 95125

RETTBERG, CHARLES CLAYLAND, JR., lawyer; b. Balt., Oct. 3, 1930; s. Charles Clayland and Drucilla Bell (Brown) R.; m. Elizabeth Margaret Koessler, June 9, 1956; children—Susan Victoria, Valerie Ann, Charles. A.B., U. Md., 1952, LL.B., 1955. Bar: Md. 1955, Ohio 1969, U.S. Supreme Ct. 1975. Atty. B&O R.R., Balt., 1955-58, asst. gen. atty., 1958-64, asst. gen. solicitor, 1964-68; gen. atty. Chessie System, Cleve., 1968-72, gen. comml. counsel, 1972-79, gen. solicitor, 1980-86; gen. counsel CSX Transp., Balt., 1986—; pres. Rail Transp. Inst., Washington, 1973. Editor-in-chief Md. Law Rev., 1955. Mem. ABA, ICC Practitioners Assn., Eastern R.R. Soc. (chmn. commerce law com. 1978-82), Order of Coif, Delta Theta Phi, Pi Sigma Alpha. Republican. Lutheran. Antitrust, Public utilities. Office: CSX Transp 100 N Charles St Baltimore MD 21201

RETTIG, JAMES MELVIN, lawyer; b. Detroit, Nov. 18, 1943; s. John Wilson and Elma Maria (Sutinen) R.; m. Kaymary Young, June 25, 1966; children: David Jason, Katherine Nicole. BA in Edn., U. Mich., 1965; MA, San Fernando Valley State U. (now known as Calif. State U.), Northridge, 1970; JD, Wayne State U., 1973. Bar: Mich. 1974, U.S. Dist. Ct. (ea. dist.) Mich. 1974, U.S. Dist. Ct. (we. dist.) Mich. 1976. Law clk. to presiding justice Mich. Supreme Ct., Detroit, 1973-75; assoc. Nino E. Green Law Office, Escanaba, Mich., 1975-76; ptnr. Green, Renner, Weisse, Rettig, Rademacher & Clark, P.C., Escanaba, 1976—. Bd. dirs. YMCA Delta County, Escanaba, 1985—; mem. Mich. Dems., 1972—; pres. Bay de Noc Audubon Naturalists, 1986-87. Mem. Mich. Bar Assn. (assemblyman 1978-84), Delta County Bar Assn. (sec. 1985-86, v.p. 1986—), Assn. Trial Lawyers Am., Mich. Trial Lawyers Assn. (bd. dirs. 1985-86), Audubon Soc. Mem. Unitarian Ch. Avocations: aerobics, canoeing, family fun. Workers' compensation. Home: 1205 7th Ave S Escanaba MI 49829 Office: Green Renner Weisse Rettig Rademacher & Clark PC 225 Ludington St Escanaba MI 49829

REUBEN, ALLAN HERBERT, lawyer; b. Pitts., June 24, 1931; s. Monte M. and Miriam (Barthfeld) R.; m. Gladys Winkler, May 25, 1956; children: John David, Patricia Anne, Catherine Ellen. B.A. summa cum laude, U. Pitts., 1953; LL.B. magna cum laude, Harvard U., 1956. Bar: Pa. bar 1957. Law clk. to judge U.S. Ct. Appeals (3d Circuit), 1956-57; asso. firm Wolf, Block, Schorr & Solis-Cohen, Phila., 1957-65; partner Wolf, Block, Schorr & Solis-Cohen, 1965—; lectr. Banking Law Inst., 1969. Mem.: Harvard Law Rev, 1954-56. Trustee Lawyers Com. Civil Rights Under Law, 1976—; chmn., mem. governing bd. employment discrimination referral project Phila. Bar Assn.-Lawyers Com. Civil Rights Under Law, 1971-75; bd. dirs. Pub. Interest Law Center Phila., 1975—; mem. S.E. regional planning council Pa. Gov.'s Justice Commn., 1973-78, exec. com., 1974-78; mem. exec. com. S.E. regional adv. com. Pa. Com. on Crime and Delinquency, 1979-80; trustee Community Legal Services Phila., 1971, 1980-82; bd. dirs. Pa. Legal Services Center, 1978-80, chmn. evaluation com.; bd. commrs. Cheltenham Twp., Pa., 1972—, chmn. health and sanitation com., 1980—; chmn. Shopping Center Task Force, 1981—; vice chmn. Parks and Recreation Com., 1980—; bd. dirs. Phila. Am. Jewish Com., 1965—, v.p., 1973-77; mem. Jewish Community Relations Com., Phila., 1965—, bd. dirs., 1973—, chmn. civil rights com., 1975—; bd. govs. Renal Youth Rehab. Program, 1976-80. Mem. Am. Judicature Soc., ABA, Fed. Bar Assn., Pa. Bar Assn., Phila. Bar Assn. (co-chmn. subcom. riots in N. Phila. 1965, chmn. subcom. invasion of privacy by electronic means 1966-70, 72-78, chmn. speakers Law Day 1966, chmn. speakers bur. 1967, chmn. civil rights com. 1971, 1980-82, chancellor's commn. on abortion 1971-72, public relations com. 1965—, speakers panel 1965—, mem. sect. corp., banking and bus. law 1965—, chmn. com. fin. 1966-67, exec. com. 1969-70, 72, 83, sec. 1973, editor Phila. Lawyer 1969-74, co-chmn. editorial bd. 1974—), Phi Beta Kappa. Securities, Contracts commercial, General corporate. Home: 7914 Ivy Ln Elkins Park PA 19117 Office: 12th Floor Packard Bldg Philadelphia PA 19102

REUBEN, DON H., lawyer; b. Chgo., Sept. 1, 1928; s. Michael B. and Sally (Chapman) R.; m. Evelyn Long, Aug. 27, 1948 (div.); children: Hope Reuben Paul, Michael Barrett, Timothy Don, Jeffrey Long, Howard Ellis; m. Jeannette Hurley Haywood, Dec. 13, 1971; stepchildren: Harris Hurley Haywood, Edward Gregory Haywood. B.S., Northwestern U., 1949, J.D., 1952. Bar: Ill. bar 1952. Practiced with firm Kirkland & Ellis, Chgo., 1952-78; sr. partner Kirkland & Ellis, until 1978, Reuben & Proctor, Chgo., 1978-86; sr. ptnr. Isham, Lincoln & Beale, Chgo., 1986—; gen. counsel for Tribune Co. and subsidiaries, Chgo. Bears Football Club, Inc.; spl. asst. atty. gen. State of Ill., 1963-64, 69, 84; counsel spl. session Ill. Ho. of Reps., 1964, for Ill. treas. for congl., state legis. and jud. reapportionment, 1963; spl. fed. ct. master, 1968-70; Dir. Lake Shore Nat. Bank.; Mem. citizens adv. bd. to Sheriff Cook County, 1962-66; mem. jury instrns. com., 1963-68; com. rules Ill. Supreme Ct., 1963-73; mem. pub. relations com. Nat. Conf. State Trial Judges; mem. Com. Study Caseflow Mgmt. in Law Div., Circuit Ct., Cook County, 1979—; mem. adv. implementation com. U.S. Dist. Ct. for No. Dist. Ill., 1981—; mem. Chgo. Better Schs. Com., 1968—, Chgo. Crime Commn., 1970-80; mem. supervisory panel Fed. Defender Program.; Lectr. on libel, slander, privacy and freedom of press. Mem. nat. legacy com. Multiple Sclerosis Soc., also vice chmn. Central region; bd. dirs. Lincoln Park Zool. Soc., 1972-84, United Cerebral Palsy Assn. Chgo.; mem. citizens bd. Loyola U., Chgo.; trustee Northwestern U., 1977—; mem. vis. com. U. Chgo. Law Sch., 1976-79. Mem. Ill. Bar Assn., Chgo. Bar Assn. (chmn. subcom. on propriety and regulation of contingent fees com. devel. law 1966-69, subcom. on media liaison 80—, mem. com. on profl. info. 1980—), ABA (standing com. on fed. judiciary 1973-79, standing com. on jud. selection, tenure and compensation 1982-85), Am. Law Inst., Am. Judicature Soc., Fellows Am. Bar Found., Bar Assn. 7th Fed Circuit, Am. Coll. Trial Lawyers (Rule 23 com. 1975-82, judiciary com. 1987—), Am. Arbitration Assn. (nat. panel arbitrators), Internat. Acad. Trial Lawyers, Ill. Trial Lawyers Assn., Assn. Trial Lawyers Am., Phi Eta Sigma, Beta Alpha Psi, Beta Gamma Sigma, Order of Coif. Clubs: University, Chicago, Tavern, Mid-America, Chgo. Yacht, Mid-Day, Commercial, Union League of Chgo, Law, Casino (Chgo.); Dunham Woods Riding. Home: 2430 Lakeview Ave Chicago IL 60614 Office: Isham Lincoln & Beale Three First National Plaza Chicago IL 60602

REUBEN, LAWRENCE MARK, lawyer; b. Akron, Ohio, Apr. 5, 1948; s. Albert G. and Sara I. (Rifkin) R. Student, London Sch. Econs., 1969; BS, Ind. U., 1970; JD, Ind. U., Indpls., 1973. Bar: U.S. Dist. Ct. (so. dist.) Ind. 1973, U.S. Dist. Ct. (no. dist.) Ind. 1975, U.S. Ct. Appeals (7th cir.) 1975, U.S. Supreme Ct. 1976, U.S. Ct. Appeals (9th cir.) 1978. Ptnr. Atlas, Hyatt & Reuben, Indpls., 1976—. V.p. Ind. Civil Liberties Union, 1975-84; sec., bd. dirs. Indpls. Humane Soc., 1974-85; fellow Indpls. C. of C.-Lacey Leadership Program, 1982; sec., v.p., bd. dirs. Julian Ctr., Inc., 1983-87; mem. ch.-state commn. Nat. Jewish Community Relations Adv. Council, N.Y.C., 1982-87; bd. dirs. Indpls. Consumer Credit Counseling Bur., 1983-87; pres. Bur. Jewish Edn., 1984-86; parliamentarian Ind. State Dem. Party, 1985-86; mem. Indpls. Police Community Relations Rev. Com., 1983. Recipient Robert Risk award Ind. Civil Liberties Union, 1981, David M. Cook Meml. award Indpls. Jewish Community Relations Council, 1982. Mem. ABA, Fed. Bar Assn., Ind. Bar Assn., Indpls. Bar Assn. Democrat. Jewish. Federal civil litigation, Consumer commercial, General practice. Office: 1444 Consolidated Bldg Indianapolis IN 46204

REUBEN, TIMOTHY D., lawyer; b. Chgo., Apr. 28, 1955; s. Don H. Reuben and Evelyn (Long) Burkhart. BA History magna cum laude, Harvard U., 1977, JD, 1980. Bar: Calif. 1980, U.S. Dist. Ct. (cen. dist.) Calif. 1980, U.S. Dist. Ct. (no. dist.) Calif. 1981, U.S. Ct. Appeals (9th cir.) 1981, U.S. Dist. Ct. (ea. and so. dists.) Calif. 1982, U.S. Supreme Ct. 1984. Assoc. Lillick, McHose & Charles, Los Angeles, 1980-82, Rosenfeld, Meyer & Susman, Beverly Hills, Calif., 1983-87; ptnr. Resch, Polster, Alpert & Berger, Los Angeles, 1987—. Treas. polit. com. Friends of Lindsay Corner, Beverly Hills, 1981—. Mem. ABA, Calif. Bar Assn., Beverly Hills Bar Assn., Santa Monica Bar Assn., Los Angeles Bar Assn., Santa Monica C. of C. (chmn. state and nat. legis. com. 1986). Club: Harvard Los Angeles (area chmn. admissions com. 1984-85). Avocations: tennis, skiing. Libel, Trademark and copyright, Federal civil litigation. Home: 848 Lincoln Blvd #D Santa Monica CA 90403 Office: Resch Polster Alpert & Berger 10821 W Pico Blvd 3d Floor Los Angeles CA 90064

REUM, JAMES MICHAEL, lawyer; b. Oak Park, Ill., Nov. 1, 1946; s. Walter John and Lucy (Bellegay) R. BA cum laude, Harvard U., 1968, JD cum laude, 1972. Bar: N.Y. 1973, D.C. 1974, U.S. Dist. Ct. (so. dist.) N.Y. 1974, Ill. 1979, U.S. Dist. Ct. (no. dist.) Ill. 1982. Assoc. Davis, Polk & Wardwell, N.Y.C., 1973-78; assoc. Minority Counsel Com. on Judiciary U.S. Ho. of Reps., Washington, 1974; ptnr. Hopkins & Sutter, Chgo., 1979—. Intern Senator Charles H. Percy, Washington, 1977; Midwest advance rep. Nat. Regan Bush Com., 1980; mem. Ill. Fin. com. for Reagan Bush '84, Chgo. Served to SP4 USAR, 1969-75. Recipient Harvard U. Honorary Scholarship, 1964-72. Mem. ABA. Republican. Clubs: University, Doubles (N.Y.C.); Lawrence Beach (Atlantic Beach, N.Y.). General corporate, Securities, Banking. Home: 3100 N Sheridan Rd Chicago IL 60657 Office: Hopkins & Sutter 3 First National Bank Chicago IL 60602

REUTER, JAMES WILLIAM, lawyer; b. Bemidji, Minn., Sept. 30, 1948; s. John Renee and Monica (Dugas) R.; m. Patricia Carol Creelman, Mar. 30, 1968; children—Kristine, Suzanne, Natalee. B.A., St. John's U., 1970; J.D., William Mitchell Coll. of Law, 1974. Bar: Minn. 1974, U.S. Dist. Ct. Minn. 1975, U.S. Ct. Appeals (8th cir.) 1985. Editor, West Pub. Co., St. Paul, 1970-73; assoc. Terpstra & Merrill, Mpls., 1974-77; ptnr. Barna, Guzy, Merrill, Hynes & Giancola, Ltd., Mpls., 1977—. Recipient Cert. award Nat. Inst. Trial Advocacy, 1978. Mem. ABA (antitrust and civil litigation com.), Assn. Trial Lawyers Am., Minn. Trial Lawyers Assn. (comml. litigation com.), Minn. Bar Assn. (civil litigation and computer sects.), Hennepin County Bar Assn. (ethics com.), Anoka County Bar Assn. (pres. 1981-82, chmn. jud. selection com. 1982—). Lodge: Kiwanis (Columbia Heights-Fridley) (pres. 1978-79). Avocations: skiing; golf; camping; reading. Federal civil litigation, State civil litigation, Technological litigation. Office: Barna Guzy Merrill Hynes & Giancola Ltd 701 Fourth Ave South Suite 500 Minneapolis MN 55415

REVELEY, WALTER TAYLOR, III, lawyer; b. Churchville, Va., Jan. 6, 1943; s. Walter Taylor and Marie (Eason) R.; m. Helen Bond, Dec. 18, 1971; children—Walter Taylor, George Everett Bond, Nelson Martin Eason. A.B., Princeton U., 1965; J.D., U. Va., 1968. Bar: Va. 1970, D.C. 1976. Asst. prof. law U. Ala., 1968-69; law clk. to Justice Brennan U.S. Supreme Ct., Washington, 1969-70; fellow Woodrow Wilson Internat. Ctr. for Scholars, 1972-73; internat. fellow Council Fgn. Relations, N.Y.C., 1972-73; assoc. Hunton & Williams, Richmond, Va., 1970-76, ptnr., 1976—, mng. ptnr., 1982—; lectr. Coll. William and Mary Law Sch., 1978-80. Author: War Powers of the President and Congress: Who Holds the Arrows and Olive Branch, 1981; mem. editorial bd. Va. Law Rev., 1966-68; contbr. articles to profl. jours. Trustee Princeton U., 1986—; bd. dirs. Fan Dist. Assn., Richmond Inc., 1976-80, pres., 1979-80; bd. dirs. Richmond Symphony, 1980—, v.p., 1984—; bd. dirs. Presbyterian Outlook Found. and Book Service, 1985—; elder Grace Covenant Presbyn. Ch. Mem. Richmond Bar Assn., D.C. Bar Assn., Va. Bar Assn., ABA, Am. Soc. Internat. Law, Am. Judicature Soc., Princeton U. Alumni Assn. Va. (bd. dirs. 1985— pres. 1983-85), Raven Soc., Order of Coif, Phi Beta Kappa, Omicron Delta Kappa. Clubs: Knickerbocker (N.Y.C.); Country of Va., Downtown

(Richmond). Nuclear power, Environment. Home: 2314 Monument Ave Richmond VA 23220 Office: 707 E Main St Richmond VA 23212

REVERCOMB, HORACE AUSTIN, JR., judge, lawyer; b. Richmond, Va., July 4, 1923; s. Horace Austin and Helen Judson (Massie) R.; m. Mary Virginia Kelley, Nov. 20, 1942; children—James A., Elizabeth Revercomb Updegraff, Horace A., Mary Ann Revercomb Early. Student Randolph-Macon Coll., 1940-42; diploma law Smith Deal-Massey Sch. Law, 1952. Bar: Va., U.S. dist. ct. (ea. dist.) Va. Sole practice, King George, Va., 1956-64; judge King George and Stafford County Cts., 1961-73; judge Dist. Cts. 15th Jud. Dist. Va., 1973-81, designated judge, 1981—; ptnr. Revercomb & Revercomb, King George. Served with U.S. Army, 1943-46. Mem. Va. State Bar, Va. Bar Assn., 15th Jud. Cir. Bar Assn. Jurisprudence, General practice. Office: PO Box 133 King George VA 22485

REVERMAN, PHILIP JOHN, JR., lawyer; b. Louisville, May 27, 1946; s. Philip John Sr. and Ruth Marie (Roth) R.; m. Vivian Lee Schmitt, Aug. 10, 1968; children: Melissa Ann, Tiffany Marie. BS in Biology, Bellarmine Coll., 1968; JD, U. Louisville, 1975. Bar: Ky. 1975. Assoc. Boehl, Stopher, Graves & Deindoerfer, Louisville, 1976—. Served to sgt. U.S. Army, 1969-72. Named to Hon. Order Ky. Cols., 1964. Mem. ABA, Ky. Bar Assn., Louisville Bar Assn. Republican. Roman Catholic. Avocations: golf, tennis. Workers' compensation, Federal black lung law. Home: 8713 McKenna Way Louisville KY 40291 Office: Boehl Stopher Graves & Deindoerfer 1 Riverfront Plaza Louisville KY 40202

REVOILE, CHARLES PATRICK, lawyer; b. Newark, Jan. 15, 1934; s. Charles Patrick and Olga Lydia (Zecca) R.; m. Sally Cole Gates, Nov. 8, 1963. B.A., U. Md., 1957, LL.B., 1960. Bar: Md. 1962, U.S. Dist. Ct. Md. 1962, U.S. Supreme Ct. 1970, U.S. Ct. Claims 1976, U.S. Ct. Appeals (fed. cir. cir.) 1982. Legis. counsel Nat. Canners Assn., Washington, 1960-64; asst. counsel Deco Electronics Inc., Washington, 1964-67; div. counsel Westinghouse Electric, Leesburg, Va., 1967-71; v.p., gen. counsel Stanwick Corp., Arlington, Va., 1971-85, sr. v.p., gen. counsel, sec. CACI, Inc., 1985—; lectr., panelist, advisor. Active in Md. Ednl. Found., College Park, 1974—; assoc. Nat. Symphony Orchestra, Washington, 1972—, Smithsonian Instn., 1980—; lawyer, lobbyist various non profit orgns., Washington, 1984. Mem. Md. Bar Assn., Wash. Corp. Counsels Assn., Am. Corp. Counsels Assn. Republican. Roman Catholic. Club: Congl. Country (Bethesda, Md.) (com. chmn. 1966—). General corporate, Government contracts and claims, Private international. Home: 4112 Culver St Kensington MD 20895 Office: CACI Inc 1815 N Fort Myer Dr Arlington VA 22209

REWALD, ROMAN, lawyer; b. Bydgoszcz, Poland, Feb. 6, 1953; came to U.S., 1978; s. Alfons and Regina (Leszczynska) R.; m. Paula Gribbs, Sept. 7, 1985. M in Adminstrn., U. Nicholaus Copernicus, Torun, Poland, 1976, LLM, 1978; JD, U. Detroit, 1982. Bar: Mich. 1983, U.S. Dist. Ct. (ea. dist.) Mich., 1983. Asst. prof. U. Nicholaus Copernicus, 1976-78; assoc. Plunkett, Cooney, Rutt, Watters, Stanczyk & Pedersen, P.C., Detroit, 1983—. Mem. ABA, Detroit Bar Assn., Bar Advs. Assn., Phi Alpha Delta. Roman Catholic. Immigration, naturalization, and customs, Probate, General corporate. Office: Plunkett Cooney Rutt et al 900 Marquette Bldg Detroit MI 48226-3280

REXINGER, ALLAN ROBERT, lawyer, lobbyist; b. Chgo., Aug. 14, 1946; s. Scott Clifton and Eleanor G. (Black) R. B.S., Miami U., Oxford, Ohio, 1968; M.B.A., No. Ill. U., 1970; J.D., Valparaiso U., 1973. Bar: D.C. 1975, U.S. Tax Ct. 1975, U.S. Ct. Mil. Appeals, 1975, U.S. Ct. Appeals (D.C. cir.) 1975, U.S. Dist. Ct. D.C. 1978, U.S. Supreme Ct. 1978. Legis. asst. to Rep. Robert McClory of Ill., Washington, 1973-75; atty., adviser FPC, Washington, 1975-76; legis. rep. Nat. Coal Assn., Washington, 1976-79; asst. gen. counsel, dir. congl. relations Proprietary Assn., Washington, 1979—; counsel Nat. Gas Survey Comm., 1975-76; treas. Proprietary Industry Polit. Action Com., 1979—. Mem. ABA, Am. League Lobbyists, Fed. Bar Assn., Bar Assn. D.C., Am. Soc. Assn. Execs., Phi Delta Theta, Sigma Iota Epsilon, Delta Sigma Pi. Clubs: Dem. National, Capitol Hill, International (Washington). Health, Legislative, FERC practice. Home: 717 A St SE Washington DC 20003 Office: Proprietary Assn 1150 Connecticut Ave NW Washington DC 20036

REXRODE, DAVID STEPHEN, lawyer; b. Bristol, Va., Dec. 7, 1950; s. Thomas Richard and Adelle O'Byne (Hedgecock) R.; m. Sally Ann Matthews, Mar. 24, 1973. AA, Hillsboro Community Coll., 1970; BA, Fla. Atlantic U., 1972; JD, Loyola U., New Orleans, 1978. Bar: Fla. 1980, U.S. Dist. Ct. (mid. dist.) Fla. 1980. Contracts analyst Texaco, Inc., New Orleans, 1974-78; sales rep. Southern Natural Gas, New Orleans, 1978-79; assoc. Barr & Murman P.A., Tampa, Fla., 1979-81; sole practice Tampa, 1981—; bd. dirs. Fla. Legal Assts., Tampa. Mem. Bay Area Vol. Lawyers, Tampa, 1984—, U. South Fla. Legal Aid, 1982—. Served to staff sgt. USAF, 1972-74. Recipient Outstanding Service and Dedication award U. South Fla. Legal Aid, 1983, 84, 85. Mem. ABA, Fla. Bar Assn., La. Bar Assn., Assn. Trial Lawyers Am., Acad. Fla. Trial Lawyers. Democrat. Clubs: Commerce (Tampa) (bd. dirs. 1983-84); Tampa. Lodge: Kiwanis (bd. dirs. Tampa chpt.) 1985—. Avocations: boating, furniture restoration. Personal injury, Family and matrimonial, Probate. Home: 12209 Wood Duck Place Tampa FL 33617 Office: 707 E Kennedy Blvd Tampa FL 33602

REYCRAFT, GEORGE DEWEY, lawyer; b. New Haven, May 2, 1924; s. George Dewey and Katherine Vivien R.; children: George C., Thomas C., Thaddeus J., Ann K., Nancy J., Pamela C., Sheilah M. B.A. with honors and distinction, Wesleyan U., 1947; LL.B., Harvard U., 1950; postgrad., Georgetown U., 1952, Wayne U., 1953. Bar: D.C. 1951, N.Y. 1964. Partner Cadwalader, Wickersham & Taft, N.Y.C., 1963—; vis. prof. George Washington Law Sch., Washington, 1967; atty. Office Gen. Counsel, Dept. Navy, Washington, 1952; trial atty. U.S. Dept. Justice, Washington, 1952-57; asst. chief gen. litigation sect. U.S. Dept. Justice, 1957-58, chief spl. trial sect., 1958-60, chief sect. ops., 1960-63. Served to maj. USAF, 1943-45, 50-52. Mem. Am. Bar Assn., Fed. Bar Assn., Fed. Bar Council, Am. Bar Found., Am. Coll. Trial Lawyers, N.Y. State Bar Assn. (past chmn. antitrust sect.), Assn. Bar City N.Y. (past chmn. com. on trade regulation). Clubs: Harvard (N.Y.C.); Univ. (Washington); Ocean Reef, Shelter Island Yacht. Antitrust, Federal civil litigation, State civil litigation.

REYNOLDS, DANIEL, law educator; b. Duluth, Minn., Aug. 5, 1946; s. Floyd A. and Rosina (Froedel) R. BA, U. Nebr., 1968; JD, Creighton U., 1975. Assoc., then ptnr. Kutak Rock & Campbell, Omaha, 1976-81; from asst. to assoc. prof. law No. Ill U., De Kalb, 1982—; asst. reporter ABA Commn. on Evaluation of Profl. Standards, 1983. Mem. bd. editors ABA/BNA Lawyer's Manual of Profl. Conduct, 1984—. Served to sgt. U.S. Army, 1968-70. Legal Ethics, General corporate, Municipal bonds. Home: 101 Andersen Ct De Kalb IL 60115 Office: No Ill Univ Coll Law De Kalb IL 60115

REYNOLDS, DIXON JACE, lawyer; b. Lubbock, Tex., Aug. 16, 1956; s. John Wiley and Billye Love (Turner) R.; m. Kimberly Ann White, Aug. 7, 1982. BA magna cum laude, Abilene Christian U., 1975; JD, Baylor U., 1982. Bar: Tex. 1982, U.S. Dist. Ct. (no. dist.) Tex. 1982. Assoc. Chris Harris, Arlington, Tex., 1982-83, Chantilis & Morgan, Dallas, 1983-86; ptnr. Chantilis, Morgan & Reynolds, Dallas, 1986—; v.p. J.W.R. Devel., Austin, Tex., 1982-83. Pres., bd. dirs. Bristol on Park, Mesquite, Tex., 1984—; tchr. Garland Rd. Ch. Christ, Dallas, 1982-84; panel leader Highland Oaks "Teaching Teens" Seminar, Abilene, Tex., 1985; bd. dirs. Highland Oaks Huddle Program, Dallas, 1985-86, Cotton Club, Dallas, 1985—. Named one of Outstanding Young Men in Am., Outstanding Ams., 1984-85, Outstanding Tchr., Highland Oaks Ch. Christ, 1984. Mem. ABA, Dallas Young Lawyers Assn. (judge, advisor high sch. mock trial 1984—), Delta Theta Phi (pres. 1980-81, v.p. 1981-82), Omega Rho Alpha, Alpha Chi. Republican. Clubs: Inner Circle (Dallas) (social chmn. 1984—). Lodge: Kinsmen (reporter 1976-79). Avocations: jogging, triathalons, swimming, skiing, working with teenagers. Real property, Family and matrimonial, State civil litigation. Office: Chantilis Morgan & Reynolds 8150 N Central Expressway Suite 1233 Dallas TX 75206

REYNOLDS, FRANK HARRISON, lawyer; b. Adak, Alaska, Apr. 26, 1948; s. Frank Harrison and Patricia Mary (Dowling) R.; m. Patricia Ann Stewart, Mar. 23, 1971. BA, Mich. State U., 1971, MA, 1974; JD, Thomas M. Cooley Law Sch., 1978. Bar: Mich. 1979, U.S. Dist. Ct. (we. dist.) Mich. 1980, U.S. Dist. Ct. (ea. dist.) Mich. 1984. Instr. Lansing (Mich.) Sch. Dist., 1971-80; sole practice Lansing, 1979—; mem. faculty Law and Criminal Justice Ctr. Lansing Community Coll., 1987. Devel. council mem. Ingham Med. Ctr., Lansing, 1981—; mem. Greater Lansing Estate Planning Council; bd. dirs. Moore Living Ctrs., Lansing, 1982-85, Pro Bono Project, Lansing, 1986—. Mem. ABA, Ingham County Bar Assn., Ingham County Felony Appointment Bar Assn. (bd. dirs. 1986—). Republican. Roman Catholic. Club: Civitan (Lansing). General practice, Criminal, Estate planning. Home: 1131 S Genesee Dr Lansing MI 48915 Office: 101 S Washington Sq Suite 706 Lansing MI 48915

REYNOLDS, H. GERALD, lawyer; b. Alexander City, Ala., July 16, 1940; s. James H. and Melba V. (Scott) R.; m. Mary Alice McGiboney, Sept. 3, 1960; children—Cathy, Gerre, Amy, Richie. B.A., Auburn U., 1962; J.D., Cumberland Sch. Law, 1965. Bar: Ala. 1965, Fla. 1977. Ptnr. King and Reynolds, Alexander City, 1965-66; sole practice, Alexander City, 1966-71; corp. counsel U.S. Pipe and Foundry, Birmingham, Ala., 1971-72; environ. counsel Jim Walter Corp., Tampa, Fla., 1972—; judge Ct. Common Pleas, Tallapoosa County, Ala., 1967-68; mem. faculty Alexander City State Jr. Coll., 1966-71. Mem. Ala. Constl. Revision Commn., 1970-75; mem. Ala. Democratic Exec. Com., 1970-72. Mem. Fla. Bar Assn. (chmn. environ. and land use law sect. 1981-82, vice chmn. continuing legal edn. com. 1986—). Democrat. Methodist. Contbr. articles to legal jours. Environment, Health.

REYNOLDS, JERRY LEE, lawyer; b. Springfield, Mo., Oct. 11, 1947; s. Charles Stanley and Helen Elizabeth (Wood) R.; m. Harriet Jane, Dec. 23, 1967; children—Joseph, Betsy, Jacob, James, Allison. J.D., U. Mo., Columbia, 1972. Bar: Mo. 1972, U.S. Supreme Ct. 1976. Pres. Reynolds and Assocs., P.C., Springfield, 1972—. Cubmaster Pack 7, Greater Ozark council Boy Scouts Am., 1977, sentry mem. council, 1980—. Served to capt. USAR, 1970-78. Mem. ABA, Greene County Bar Assn., Mo. Bar Assn., Assn. Trial Lawyers Am., Mo. Assn. Trial Attys. Republican. Methodist. Club: Exchange. (pres. 1978). Personal injury, Federal civil litigation, State civil litigation. Home: 1913 Arcadia Springfield MO 65804 Office: 406 McDaniel Bldg Springfield MO 65806

REYNOLDS, JOSEPH JAY, lawyer; b. New Haven, May 23, 1941; s. Joseph Patrick and Elizabeth Kathryn (Sherin) R.; m. Maxine V. E. Evans, June 23, 1962; children—Bradley, Jay Pat, Janelle. B.A., Stetson U., 1963, J.D., 1966. Bar: Fla. 1966. State's atty. Fla., 1966-69; div. chief, 1968-69; sr. ptnr. Reynolds & Reynolds, 1969—; mcpl. judge City of Boca Raton (Fla.), 1970-72; pub. defender City of Boynton Beach (Fla.), 1970-72; city atty. Boca Raton, 1974-75; mem. Fla. Legislature, 1972-74; tchr. jr. coll. adult edn. course. Bd. dirs. YMCA, Boca Raton, Fla. Mem. ABA, Fla. Bar Assn., Palm Beach County Bar Assn. (sec., treas.), South Palm Beach County Bar Assn. Republican. Lutheran. Clubs: Boca Raton Hotel and Club; King Mount (Scaly, N.C.), Kiwanis. Real property, State civil litigation, General corporate. Office: Reynolds & Reynolds 301 Crawford Blvd Suite 201 Boca Raton FL 33432

REYNOLDS, LOLA SULLIVAN, lawyer; b. New Rochelle, N.Y., Apr. 25, 1955; d. James Francis and Lola Joan (Blank) Sullivan; m. Timothy Gerard Reynolds, Mar. 15, 1980; children: Timothy Gerard Jr., Terence Sullivan, Kieran Patrick. BA, Trinity Coll., Washington, 1977; JD, Fordham U., 1980. Bar: N.Y. 1981, U.S. Dist. Ct. (so. and ea. dists.) N.Y. 1981, U.S. Dist. Ct. N.J. 1981, U.S. Ct. Appeals (2d and 3d cirs.) 1984, U.S. Supreme Ct. 1984. Assoc. gen. counsel Office of Gen. Counsel, The Hearst Corp., N.Y.C., 1980—. Active Friends and Neighbors Club, Mineola, N.Y. Mem. N.Y. State Bar Assn., Assn. of Bar of City of N.Y., Guild of Cath. Lawyers, Phi Beta Kappa. Republican. Roman Catholic. Avocations: swimming, cross country skiing, camping. General corporate, Contracts commercial, General practice. Home: 185 Pomander Rd Mineola NY 11501 Office: The Hearst Corp Office Gen Counsel 959 8th Ave New York NY 10019

REYNOLDS, MARK FLOYD, II, lawyer, management and labor consultant; b. Phila., Apr. 14, 1943; s. Marcus Reuben and Eleanor (Carter) R.; m. Pauline B. Douglass, Sept. 17, 1965; children—Meredith Lynn, Douglass Scott. B.A., Lincoln U., Pa., 1970; J.D., U. Balt., 1975. Bar: Pa. 1975, U.S. Dist. Ct. (ea. dist.) Pa. 1975, U.S. Supreme Ct. 1980, N.C. 1984, U.S. Dist. Ct. (ea. dist.) N.C. 1985, U.S. Ct. Mil. Appeals 1985, U.S. Ct. Appeals (4th cir.) 1986. Atty., Bethelehem Steel Corp., Pa., 1976-84; ptnr. Robert Sheahan & Assocs., High Point, N.C., 1985—; dir. Ready Supply Corp., Johnstown, Pa., 1982—. Vice pres. Penns Woods council Boy Scouts Am., 1981-84; chmn. United Way Greater Johnstown, 1981-84; trustee Slatington Presbyterian Ch., Pa., 1976-81. Served with AUS, 1962-65. Mem. Pa. Bar Assn. (council labor law 1984), ABA (labor law sect. com. on OSHA), N.C. Bar Assn., Lehigh County Bar Assn., Guilford County Bar Assn., Alpha Phi Omega. Republican. Lodge: Masons. Labor, Federal civil litigation, State civil litigation. Home: 151 Wolfetrail Rd Greensboro NC 27406

REYNOLDS, NORMAN EBEN, lawyer; b. Muskogee, Okla., Dec. 1, 1919; s. Norman Eben and Elizabeth (Boyd) R.; m. Margaret Maxey Cooper, Nov. 21, 1953; children: Norman Eben III, Margaret Boyd, Nancy Elizabeth, Robert Cooper. A.B., U. Okla., 1941, LL.B., 1947. Bar: Okla. 1942, U.S. Supreme Ct. 1961. Partner Reynolds, Ridings & Hargis, Oklahoma City, 1947—; dir. Oharco Corp.; mem. Okla. Ho. of Reps., 1949-55; spl. legal cons. Gov. Okla., 1959-63; spl. justice Okla. Supreme Ct., 1961. Pres. trustees Heritage Hall, 1970. Served to capt. AUS, 1942-46. Named Outstanding Young Man in Oklahoma City, 1951. Mem. Comml. Law League Am. (past nat. sec., Pres.'s Cup for disting. service 1980), ABA (co-chmn. nat. conf. lawyers and collection agys. 1979), Okla. Bar Assn., Oklahoma County Bar Assn., Am. Judicature Soc., Mil. Order World Wars, Phi Beta Kappa (past pres. alumni assn.), Sigma Alpha Epsilon (past pres. alumni assn.). Episcopalian (sr. warden 1971, chmn. com. to build Canterbury Living Ctr., pres. Episc. Retirement Community, Inc. 1981—). Club: Sooner Dinner (Oklahoma City) (pres. 1969). Lodge: Kiwanis (Oklahoma City) (pres. 1968). Home: 2212 NW 56th St Oklahoma City OK 73112 Office: 2808 First Nat Bank Bldg Oklahoma City OK 73102

REYNOLDS, RICHARD MORGAN, lawyer; b. Evanston, Ill., Apr. 8, 1937; s. Neil Hilleary and Martha (Morgan) R.; m. Deborah Sloan, July 14, 1962; children—Dolly Sloan, Katherine Sloan. B.A., Yale U., 1959, LL.B., 1962; LL.M., Georgetown U., 1965. Bar: Conn. 1962. Mem. firm Day, Berry & Howard, Hartford, Conn., 1965—, ptnr., 1972—. Trustee Mark Twain Meml., 1967-70, Hartford Rehab. Ctr., 1967-71; chmn. profl. sect. United Way campaign, 1980; bd. dirs. Conn. Easter Seal Soc., 1969-73. Served to capt. JAGC, U.S. Army, 1962-65. Decorated Army Commendation medal. Mem. Hartford County Bar Assn., Conn. Bar Assn., (chmn. antitrust sect. 1983—), ABA, Fed. Bar Assn., Fed. Bar Council, Am. Judicature Soc. Republican. Episcopalian. Clubs: University, Hartford (Conn.); Tennis, Yale of N.Y.C., Hartford Golf. Antitrust. Home: 44 Cherry Brook Rd Canon Center CT 06020 Office: City Place 185 Asylum St Hartford CT 06103

REYNOLDS, WILLIAM BRADFORD, lawyer; b. Bridgeport, Conn., June 21, 1942. B.A., Yale U., 1964; LL.B., Vanderbilt U., 1967. Bar: N.Y. 1968, D.C. 1973, U.S. Supreme Ct. 1971. Assoc. Sullivan and Cromwell, N.Y.C., 1967-70; asst. to Solicitor Gen., Dept. Justice, Washington, 1970-73; ptnr. Shaw, Pittman, Potts & Trowbridge, Washington, 1973-81; asst. atty. gen. Dept. Justice, Washington, 1981—; chmn. Archtl. Transp. Barriers Compliance Bd., 1982-84; counselor to the Attorney General Dept. of Justice, Washington, DC, 1987—. Mem. ABA, Fed. Bar Assn., D.C. Bar Assn., Order of Coif. Civil rights, Federal civil litigation. Office: Main Justice Bldg 10th and Constitution Ave Washington DC 20530 *

REYNOLDSON, WALTER WARD, state supreme court chief justice; b. St. Edward, Nebr., May 17, 1920; s. Walter Scorer and Mabel Matilda (Sallach) R.; m. Janet Aline Mills, Dec. 24, 1942; children: Vicki (Mrs. Gary Kimes), Robert. B.A., State Tchrs. Coll., 1942; J.D., U. Iowa, 1948. Bar: Iowa 1948. Practice in Osceola, 1948-71; justice Iowa Supreme Ct., 1971-78, chief justice, 1978—; lectr. seminar Sch. Law, Drake U., 1968; county atty., Clarke County, Iowa, 1953-57. Contbg.author: Trial Handbook, 1969. Pres. Nat. Ctr. for State Cts., 1984-85. Served with USNR, 1942-46. Recipient Osceola Community Service award, 1968. Mem. Iowa Bar Assn. (chmn. com. on legal edn. and admission to bar 1964-71), ABA, Am. Judicature Soc. (dir. 1983—), Iowa Acad. Trial Lawyers, Conf. Chief Justices (pres. 1984-85), Am. Coll. Trial Lawyers. Office: State Capitol Bldg Des Moines IA 50319

RHEINSTEIN, PETER HOWARD, government official, physician, lawyer; b. Cleve., Sept. 7, 1943; s. Franz Joseph Rheinstein and Hede Henrietta (Neheimer) Rheinstein Lerner; m. Miriam Ruth Weissman, Feb. 22, 1969; 1 child, Jason Edward. B.A. with high honors, Mich. State U., 1963, M.S., 1964; M.D., Johns Hopkins U., 1967; J.D., U. Md., 1973. Bar: Md., D.C.; diplomate Am. Bd. Family Practice. Intern USPHS Hosp., San Francisco, 1967-68; resident in internal medicine USPHS Hosp., Balt., 1968-70; practice medicine specializing in internal medicine Balt., 1970—; instr. medicine U. Md., Balt., 1970-73; med. dir. extended care facilities CHC Corp., Balt., 1972-74; dir. drug advt. and labeling div. FDA, Rockville, Md., 1974-82, acting dep. dir. Office Drugs, 1982-83, acting dir. Office Drugs, 1983-84, dir. Office Drug Standards, 1984—; adj. prof. forensic medicine George Washington U., 1974-76; WHO cons. on drug regulation Nat. Inst. for Control Pharm. and Biol. Products, People's Republic of China, 1981—; advisor on essential drugs WHO, 1985—; FDA del. to U.S. Pharmacopeial Conv., 1985—. Spl. editorial advisor Good Housekeeping Guide to Medicine and Drugs, 1977—; mem. editorial bd. Legal Aspects Med. Practice, 1981—, Drug Info. Jour., 1982—; contbr. articles to Drug Indo. Jour., 1982-86. Recipient Commendable Service award FDA, 1981, group award of merit, 1983. Fellow Am. Coll. Legal Medicine (bd. govs. 1982—, treas., chmn. fin. com. 1985—, Pres.'s award 1985, 86), Am. Acad. Family Physicians (Pres. award 1985-86); mem. Drug Info. Assn. (bd. dirs. 1981—, pres. 1984-85, immediate past pres. 1985-86, v.p. 1986-87, pres. elect 1987—), Fed. Bar Assn. (chmn. food and drug com. 1976-79, Disting. Service award 1977), AMA, ABA, Med. and Chirurgical Faculty Md., Anne Arundel County Med. Soc., Johns Hopkins Med. and Surg. Assn., Md. Bar Assn., Math. Assn. Am., Soc. for Indsl. and Applied Math., Mensa (life), U.S. Power Squadrons, Mich. State U. Alumni Assn. (life), U. Md. Alumni Assn. (life), Johns Hopkins U. Alumni Assn., Delta Theta Phi. Clubs: Chartwell Golf and Country (Severna Park, Md.), Annapolis (Md.) Yacht, Johns Hopkins, Univ. (Balt.). Avocations: boating; electronics; physical fitness. Administrative and regulatory, Health, Personal injury. Home: 621 Holly Ridge Rd Severna Park MD 21146-3520 Office: Dir Office Drug Standards FDA 5600 Fishers Ln Rockville MD 20857

RHEINSTEIN, THOMAS PHILIPP, lawyer; b. N.Y.C., Oct. 13, 1949; s. Ludwig and Clare (Philipp) R.; m. Joy Y. Yagman, July 27, 1975; children: Karen Ilene, Deborah Jill. BA, SUNY, Binghamton, 1972; JD, Bklyn. Law Sch., 1975. Bar: N.Y. 1976, U.S. Dist. Ct. (no. dist.) Ohio 1976, U.S. Tax Ct. 1976, U.S. Supreme Ct. 1979, U.S. Dist. Ct. (we. dist.) N.Y. 1987. Atty. estate tax IRS, Cleve., 1975-80, Rochester, N.Y., 1980—. Served to pvt. 1st class U.S. Army, 1970-71. Mem. N.Y. State Bar Assn. Estate taxation. Home: 130 Parkwood Ave Rochester NY 14620 Office: IRS 100 State St Rochester NY 14614

RHEM, JOHN FITZHUGH, JR., lawyer; b. Wilmington, N.C., Apr. 4, 1949; s. John Fitzhugh and Evelyn (Davis) R.; m. Georgia Heald, Aug. 15, 1972; children: William D.F., Benjamin R.T., Elizabeth F., John C.D. BA, Wofford Coll., 1971; JD, U. S.C., 1975. Bar: S.C. 1975, Tex. 1976. Atty. APCO Oil Corp., Houston, 1976; assoc. Cutrer & Jefferson, Houston, 1976-78; ptnr. Eikenburg & Stiles, Houston, 1978—; bd. dirs. Park 45 Nat. Bank, Houston. Bd. dirs. Tex. Accts. and Lawyers for Arts, 1985—, Houston Young Audiences, 1986—, Pvt. Industry Council Greater Houston, 1984-85, Tex. Chamber Orch., 1982—, exec. com., 1984—. Mem. ABA., S.C. Bar Assn., Tex. Bar Assn., Houston Bar Assn. (chmn. taxation sect. 1985-86, chmn. law and arts com. 1985—), Wofford Coll. Alumni Assn. (bd. dirs. 1985—). Republican. Presbyterian. Club: Briar (Houston). General corporate, Corporate taxation, Legislative. Office: Eikenburg & Stiles 1100 First City Nat Bank Bldg Houston TX 77002

RHIND, JAMES THOMAS, lawyer; b. Chgo., July 21, 1922; s. John Gray and Eleanor (Bradley) R.; m. Laura Haney Campbell, Apr. 19, 1958; children: Anne Constance, James Campbell, David Scott. Student, Hamilton Coll., 1940-42; A.B. cum laude, Ohio State U., 1944; LL.B. cum laude, Harvard U., 1950. Bar: Ill. bar 1950. Japanese translator U.S. War Dept., Tokyo, Japan, 1946-47; congl. liaison Fgn. Operations Adminstrn., Washington, 1954; since practiced in Chgo.; atty. Bell, Boyd & Lloyd, 1950-53, 55—, partner, 1958—; Dir. Kewaunee Equipment Corp., Wilmette, Ill., Lindberg Corp., Chgo., Microseal Corp., Zion, Ill. Commr. Gen. Assembly United Presbyn. Ch., 1963; vice chmn., trustee Hamilton Coll., Clinton, N.Y.; vice chmn., trustee U. Chgo., Northwestern Univ. Assocs.; chmn. Cook County Young Republican Orgn., 1957; Ill. Young Rep. nat. committeeman, 1957-58; v.p., mem. bd. govs. United Rep. Fund Ill., 1965-84; Pres. Ill. Childrens Home and Aid Soc., 1971-73, now life trustee; vice chmn. Ravinia Festival Assn., 1980-84, now life trustee; bd. dirs. E.J. Dalton Youth Center, 1966- 69; governing mem. Orchestral Assn., Chgo.; mem. Ill. Arts Council, 1971-75; mem. exec. com. div. Met. Mission and Ch. Extension Bd., Chgo. Presbytery, 1966-68; trustee Presbyn. Home, W. Clement and Jessie V. Stone Found., U. Chgo. Hosps. Served with M.I. AUS, 1943-46. Mem. ABA, Ill. Bar Assn., Chgo. Bar Assn. (bd. mgrs. 1967-69), Fed. Bar Assns., Chgo. Council on Fgn. Relations, Japan Am. Soc. Chgo., Legal Club Chgo., Law Club Chgo., Phi Beta Kappa, Sigma Phi. Presbyterian (elder). Clubs: Chicago (Chgo.), Glen View (Chgo.), Commercial (Chgo.), Attic (Chgo.), Economic (Chgo.). General corporate. Home: 830 Normandy Ln Glenview IL 60025 Office: Three First Nat Plaza Chicago IL 60602

RHINEHART, R(ICHARD) SCOTT, lawyer; b. Sioux City, Iowa, Aug. 23, 1956; s. Richard Sylvester and Jean (Barber) R.; m. Deborah Catherine Collison, Aug. 4, 1979; children: Rachelle, Melissa, Erika. BA, U. S.D., 1978, JD, 1981. Bar: Iowa 1981, S.D. 1981, U.S. Dist. Ct. S.D. 1981, U.S. Dist. Ct. (no. dist.) Iowa, 1981, U.S. Dist. Ct. (so. dist.) Iowa 1982, U.S. Ct. Appeals (8th cir.) 1985. Assoc. Richard Rhinehart and Assocs., Sioux City, 1981-85, ptnr., 1986—. Pres., bd. dirs. Sioux City Humane Soc. Inc., 1984-85. Mem. Iowa Bar Assn. (young lawyer sect.), Woodbury County Bar Assn., Assn. Trial Lawyers Am., S.D. Trial Lawyers Assn., Sioux City Young Lawyer Club (pres. 1987). Roman Catholic. Avocations: hunting, fishing. Consumer commercial, Contracts commercial, Libel.

RHINERSON, DAVID KEITH, lawyer; b. Owensboro, Ky., Aug. 24, 1956; s. Joseph Pius and Mary Ellen (Gilles) R. BA, Brescia Coll., 1977; JD, U. Louisville, 1980. Bar: Ky. 1980, U.S. dist. Ct. (we. dist.) Ky. 1981. Sole practice Owensboro, 1980—; instr. Am. govt. Owensboro Community Coll., 1984. Pres. Daviess County 4-H Council, Owensboro, 1984; sec. exec. com. Daviess County Reps., 1984—. Mem. ABA, Ky. Bar Assn., Daviess County Bar Assn. (sec., treas. 1986—), Owensboro Jaycees (sec. 1984-85, v.p. 1985-86, named officer of yr. 1984-1985), Owensboro-Daviess County C. of C., Leadership Owensboro Alumni Assn. (bd. dirs. 1985-86). Roman Catholic. Avocations: history, softball. Real property, Consumer commercial, Probate. Home: 4048 Thruston-Dermont Rd Owensboro KY 42303 Office: 233 St Ann St Owensboro KY 42301

RHOADES, JOHN S., federal judge; b. 1925; m. Carmel Rhoades; children: Mark, John, Matthew, Peter, Christopher. AB, Stanford U., 1948, JD, 1951. Pros. atty. City of San Diego, 1955-56, dep. city atty., 1956-57; sole practice San Diego, 1957-60; ptnr. Rhoades, Hollywood & Neil, San Diego, 1960-85; judge U.S. Dist. Ct. (so. dist.) Calif., San Diego, 1985—. Served with USN, 1943-46. Office: US Courthouse 940 Front St San Diego CA 92189 *

RHOADS, GEORGE ROBERT, lawyer; b. Paragould, Ark., Jan. 19, 1953; s. Clarence Robert and Evah Matilda (Treece) R.; m. Sherri Kaye Grimsley, May 13, 1978. BA, U. Ark., Fayetteville, 1975, JD, 1979. Bar: Okla. 1979, U.S. Dist. Ct. (no. dist.) Okla. 1980, Ark. 1981, U.S. Dist. Ct. (we. dist.) Ark. 1984. Assoc. Anderson & Zirkle, Tulsa, 1979; subrogation supr. Farmers Ins. Co., Tulsa, 1980; sole practice Tulsa, 1980-81; corp. counsel Wal-Mart Stores, Bentonville, Ark., 1981-83; assoc. Matthews, Campbell & Stephens, Rogers, Ark., 1983-85; ptnr. Matthews, Campbell & Rhoads, P.A., Rogers, 1985—; atty. City of Lowell, Ark., 1984—, Little Flock, Ark., 1984—; justice of peace Benton County Quorum Ct., Ark., 1983—. Sec. Lowell Planning Commn., 1982-84; mem. Benton County Dem. Club; bd. dirs. Salvation Army, Rogers, 1986—. Mem. ABA, Okla. Bar Assn., Ark. Bar Assn., Benton County Bar Assn. (pres. 1986—), Ark. Trial Lawyers Assn., Lowell C. of C. (pres. 1984—, cert. appreciation 1986). Methodist.

Avocations: golf, antiques. Real property, Contracts commercial, Workers' compensation. Home: 2019 Daisy Dr Rogers AR 72756 Office: Matthews Campbell & Rhoads PA 1st Nat Plaza Suite One Rogers AR 72756

RHODE, SHARI RENÉ, lawyer; b. Valdosta, Ga., July 16, 1951; d. Meyer Jacob and Joan Lois (Frankenstine) R. BS in Criminal Justice, So. Ill. U., 1972, MS in Correctional Adminstrn., 1975, JD, 1976; LLM in Litigation, Emory U., 1987. Bar: Ill. 1976, U.S. Dist. Ct. (so. dist.) Ill. 1976, U.S. Ct. Appeals (7th cir.) 1977, U.S. Supreme Ct. 1979. Assoc. legal counsel So. Ill. U., Carbondale, 1976-80, chief trial atty., 1980—; bd. dirs. So. Ill. U. Credit Union, 1982—. Contbr. articles to profl. jours. Mem. ABA, Ill. Bar Assn. (bd. govs. 1985—), Jackson County Bar Assn., Def. Research Inst., Nat. Inst. Trial Advocacy (adv.), Jackson County Alumni Assn. (bd. dirs. 1977-83). Federal civil litigation, State civil litigation, Civil rights. Home: 352 Lake Dr Rt 6 Murphysboro IL 62966 Office: So Ill U 320 Anthony Hall Carbondale IL 62901

RHODES, ANN MARIE, hospital executive, lawyer; b. Waterloo, Iowa, July 1, 1953; d. John Paul and Kathleen (Kennedy) R.; m. Steven Paul Miller, May 30, 1980; 1 child, Kathleen Kennedy. BS, Coll. St. Teresa, 1975; MA, U. Iowa, 1976, JD, 1982. Bar: Iowa 1982. Instr. Mt. Mercy Coll., Cedar Rapids, Iowa, 1976-77; clin. nursing specialist U. Iowa Hosps. and Clinics, Iowa City, 1977-79, supr. nursing, 1979-82, clin. nursing specialist, 1982-83, asst. to dir., 1983—; adj. asst. prof. mgmt. and adminstrv. law U. Iowa, 1982—. Author: Nursing and the Law, 1984 (named Book of Yr. 1984); contbg. editor Health Care Supr., 1983-85, Topics in Hosp. Law, 1985—; columnist Am. Jour. Maternal Child Nursing, 1985—. Health care advisor to U.S. Senator Tom Harken, 1984—. Mem. ABA, Iowa Bar Assn. (com. on liason with other profls. 1985—), Johnson County Bar Assn., Am. Acad. Hosp. Attys., Am. Soc. Law and Medicine. Democrat. Roman Catholic. Club: Altrusa (Iowa City). Health, Administrative and regulatory, Personal injury. Home: 2238 Bancroft Dr Iowa City IA 52240 Office: U Iowa Hosps and Clinics C-110 gh Iowa City IA 52242

RHODES, KEITH STEWART, lawyer; b. Fargo, N.D., May 13, 1956; s. Harold Alfred and F. Lucille (Ebersole) R.; m. Heidi Leigh Kolberg, Dec. 22, 1978 (div. Feb. 1983); m. Deborah Freedman, Mar. 24, 1984. BA, U. N.D., 1977; student, NYU, 1977-78; JD, U. N.D., 1980. Bar: MD. 1981, U.S. Dist. Ct. Md. 1982. Assoc. Hylyon & Gonzales, Balt., 1980-86, sr. assoc., 1986—. vol. Citizen's Planning and Housing Assn., Balt., 1981—; counsel Md. Women's Orch. Inc., Balt., 1985—, Md. Women's Symphony Inc., Balt., 1985-86. Mem. ABA, Md. Bar Assn., Bar Assn. of Baltimore City, Assn. of Trial Lawyers of Am., Md. Trial Lawyers Assn. Democrat. Federal civil litigation, State civil litigation, Construction. Home: 606 Day St Decorah IA 52101

RHODES, KENNETH ANTHONY, JR., lawyer; b. Scranton, Pa., Aug. 8, 1930; s. Kenneth Anthony Sr. and Martha (Morgan) R.; m. Mary Lammot Belin, Sept. 21, 1958; children: Anthony L.B., Victoria Lammot, William C. AB, Dickinson Coll., 1952; LLD, Harvard U., 1955. Bar: Pa. 1956, U.S. Dist. Ct. (mid. dist.) Pa. 1956. Fgn. service officer U.S. Dept. State, 1958-62; ptnr. Oliver, Price & Rhodes, Scranton, 1962—; lectr. bus. law, Keystone Jr. Coll., 1962-64; bd. dirs. Sauer-France, Melun, Fonderie Musil, Dammerie-les-lys, France. Pres. Mus. Assn. Scranton, 1962-76; pres., bd. dirs. Lackawanna Hist. Soc., Scranton, 1964—. Served with U.S. Army, 1956-58. Republican. Episcopalian. Clubs: Waverly (Pa.) Country. Avocations: collecting classic cars, studying history. Health, Private international, Probate. Office: Oliver Price & Rhodes 220 Penn Ave Suite 300 Scranton PA 18503

RHODES, PAULA RENETTE, legal educator, consultant; b. New Orleans, July 18, 1949; d. Leroy Louis and Marie M. (Richard) R. B.A. cum laude, Am. U., 1971; J.D., Harvard U., 1974. Bar: La. 1975, D.C. 1978, U.S. Supreme Ct. 1980. Law clk. New Orleans Legal Assistance Corp., summer 1972; legal cons. Am. Friends Service Com., St. Louis, 1973; staff atty. La. Dept. Justice, New Orleans, 1974-77; assoc. Dorsey & Marks, New Orleans, 1975-77; atty./demonstration project mgr. Legal Service Corp., Washington, 1977-79, prof. Mid Atlantic Legal Edn. Opportunity Program, Washington, summer 1980; assoc. prof. Howard U. Sch. Law, Washington, 1979—; adj. prof. U. Bridgeport Sch. Law, Conn., 1985; vis. prof. San Diego Sch. Law, 1983-84; legal cons. Inst. Food and Policy Devel., 1982, U.S. Dept. Energy, 1980-81, D.C. Pub. Service Commn., 1979-80, U.S. Adminstrn. on Aging, 1978, Friends World Com. on Consultation, 1981. Assoc. editor The Forum, 1982-83; contbr. articles to legal jours. Bd. dirs. Am. Friends Service Com., 1982—, mem. exec. com. internat. div., 1981-86, mem. nat. women's program com., 1980—, affirmative action rev. com., 1982-84, chairperson peace edn. div., 1984—; co-chmn. Third World coalition, 1983—; bd. dirs. World Hunger Ednl. Service, 1986—; bd. trustees Friends Meeting Washington; mem. Pesticides Action Network Internat., Corp. Haverford Coll., 1986—, Black Women's Agenda, So Others May Eat (SOME), Transafrica; trustee Friends Meeting of Washington; mem. D.C. Solar Task Force, D.C. Commn. on Women, Friends Com. on Nat. Legislation, Debt Crisis Network. Mem. D.C. Bar Assn., La. Bar Assn., Internat. Bar Assn., Fed. Bar Assn. (chpt. dir., treas. continuing legal edn. com.; nat. council 1980-81; participant Bill of Rights program 1980), ABA (subcom. internat. codes and guidelines for multilingual corps.). Quaker. Public international, Private international, Contracts commercial. Office: Howard U Law Sch 2900 Van Ness St NW Washington DC 20008

RHODES, RICHARD RANDOLPH, lawyer; b. Seattle, May 1, 1954; s. James Scott and Patricia (Goss) R.; m. Nancy Luanne Bolin, Nov. 13, 1982; 1 child, Edward Thomas. BA, Williams Coll., 1976; JD, George Washington U., 1981. Bar: D.C. 1981, Va. 1982, U.S. Dist. Ct. D.C. 1982, U.S. Ct. Appeals D.C. 1985. VISTA vol. Sr. Citizens Legal Services, Los Angeles, 1977-78; assoc. Levy & Smith, Washington, 1981-82, Mahoney, Hogan, Heffler & Heald, Washington, 1983—. Mem. ABA. Insurance, Personal injury, State civil litigation. Home: 3308 Peace Valley Ln Falls Church VA 22044 Office: Mahoney Hogan Heffler & Heald 777 14th St NW Washington DC 20005

RHODES, THURMAN HAYWOOD, lawyer; b. Balt., Aug. 18, 1949; s. Thurman Slayton and Iona Foster (Adams) R. B.A., Morgan State Coll., 1972; J.D., Catholic U. Am., 1975. Bar: Md. 1976, U.S. Dist. Ct. Md. 1978, U.S. Supreme Ct. 1980, U.S. Ct. Appeals (4th cir.) 1983, U.S. Ct. Appeals (D.C. cir.) 1985. Legal intern Md. Nat. Capital Park and Planning Commn., Silver Spring, 1975, assoc. gen. counsel, Upper Marlboro, 1975—; mem. inquiry com. Atty. Grievance Commn. of Md., Balt., 1984—. Pres. Hanson Oaks Homeowners Assn., Landover Hills, Md., 1976, Wash. Male Chorale, 1983—; sec. All Souls Unitarian Ch., 1984. Mem. Md. State Bar Assn., Prince George's County Bar Assn., J. Franklin Bourne Bar Assn. Club: Toastmasters (pres. 1983). Administrative and regulatory, Local government, Real property. Home: 6629 23d Pl Hyattsville MD 20782 Office: Md Nat Capital Park and Planning Commn County Admnstrn Bldg Upper Marlboro MD 20772

RHODES, VINCENT ARD, lawyer; b. Detroit, May 11, 1949; s. V.A. and Genevieve Rhodes. BA, Wayne State U., 1975; JD, Thomas Cooley Law Sch., 1979. Bar: Mich. 1979, U.S. Dist. Ct. (ea. dist.) Mich. 1979. Sole practice Detroit, 1979-81; assoc. Kitch & Suhrheinrich, Detroit, 1981-84, Plunkett, Cooney, Rutt et al, Detroit, 1984—. Mem. Mich. Bar Assn., Detroit Bar Assn., Def. Research Inst., Mich. Def. Trial Counsel, Assn. Def. Trial Counsel, Mich. Soc. Hosp. Attys. Republican. Personal injury, State civil litigation, Health. Office: Plunkett Cooney et al 900 Marquette Bldg Detroit MI 48226

RHYNE, CHARLES SYLVANUS, lawyer; b. Charlotte, N.C., June 23, 1912; s. Sydneyham S. and Mary (Wilson) R.; m. Sue Cotton, Sept. 16, 1932 (dec. Mar. 1974); children: Mary Margaret, William Sylvanus; m. Sarah P. Hendon, Oct. 2, 1976; children: Sarah Wilson, Elizabeth Parkhill. B.A., Duke U., 1934, LL.D., 1958; J.D., George Washington U., 1937, D.C.L., 1958; LL.D., Loyola U. of Calif., 1958, Dickinson Law Sch., 1959, Ohio No. U., 1966, De Paul U., 1968, Centre, 1969, U. Richmond, 1970, Howard U., 1975, Belmont Abbey, 1982. Bar: D.C. 1937. Since practiced in Washington; sr. partner Rhyne & Rhyne; gen. counsel Nat. Inst. Municipal Law Officers; professorial lectr. on aviation law George Washington U., 1948-53; gen. counsel Fed. Commn. Jud. and Congl. Salaries, 1953-54; spl. cons. Pres. Eisenhower, 1959-60; Dir. Nat. Savs. & Trust Co.; Mem. Internat Commn. Rules Judicial Procedures, 1959-61, Pres.'s Commn. on UN, 1969-71; spl. ambassador, personal rep. of Pres. U.S. to UN High Commr. for Refugees, 1971. Author: Civil Aeronautics Act, Annotated, 1939, Airports and the Courts, 1944, Aviation Accident Law, 1947, Airport Lease and Concession Agreements, 1948, Cases on Aviation Law, 1950, The Law of Municipal Contracts, 1952, Municipal Law, 1957, International Law, 1971, Renowned Law Givers and Great Law Documents of Humankind, 1975, International Refugee Law, 1976, Law and Judicial Systems of Nations, 1978, Law of Local Government Operations, 1980; editor: Municipal Attorney; Contbr. articles in field. Trustee Geo. Washington U., 1957-67, Duke U., 1961—. Recipient Grotius Peace award, 1958; Freedoms Found. award for creation Law Day-U.S.A., 1959; Alumni Achievement award George Washington U., 1960; Nat. Bar Assn. Stradford award, 1962; gold medal Am. Bar Assn., 1966; 1st Whitney M. Young award, 1972; Harris award Rotary, 1974; U.S. Dept. State appreciation award, 1976; D.C. Bar Assn. Distinguished Service award, 1976; Nansen Ring for refugee work, 1976. Mem. World Peace Through Law Center (pres. 1963—), ABA (pres. 1957-58, chmn. ho. dels. 1956-58, chmn. commn. world peace through law 1958-66, chmn. com. aero. law 1946-48, 51-54, chmn. internat. and comparative law sect. 1948-49, chmn. UN com., chmn. commn. on nat. inst. justice 1972—, nat. chmn. Jr. Bar Conf. 1944-45), D.C. Bar Assn. (pres. 1955-56), Inter-Am. Bar Assn. (v.p. 1957-59), Am. Bar Found. (pres. 1957-58, chmn. fellows 1958-59), Internat. Bar (v.p. 1957-58), Am. Judicature Soc. (dir.), Am. Law Inst., Am. Soc. Internat. Law (life), Nat. Aero. Assn. (dir. 1945-47), Washington Bd. Trade, Duke U. Alumni Assn. (chmn. nat. council 1955-56, pres. 1959-60), Delta Theta Phi, Order of Coif, Omicron Delta Kappa, Scribes. Clubs: Metropolitan, Nat. Press, Barristers, Congressional, Nat. Lawyers, Easton (Md.) Broadcasters. Home: 1404 Langley Pl McLean VA 22101 Office: 1000 Connecticut Ave NW Suite 800 Washington DC 20036

RIBICOFF, IRVING S., lawyer; b. New Britain, Conn., Apr. 16, 1915; s. Samuel and Rose (Sable) R.; m. Belle Krasne, June 27, 1955; 1 child, Dara K. B.A. summa cum laude, Williams Coll., 1936; LL.B., Yale, 1939. Bar: Conn. bar 1939. Since practiced in Hartford; instr. in pub. speaking Williams Coll., 1934-36; atty. reorganization div. SEC, 1939-41; chief price atty. for Conn. OPA, 1942-44; partner Ribicoff & Kotkin (and predecessors), 1941-78; firm Schatz & Schatz, Ribicoff & Kotkin, Hartford, 1978—; Mem. Hartford County Grievance Com., 1957-61, chmn., 1960-61. Bd. dirs. Law Sch. Fund of Yale, Hartford Festival Music, Hartford Jewish Fedn., Symphony Soc. Greater Hartford; exec. com. Yale Law Sch. Assn.; trustee Greater Hartford YMCA; bus. adv. com. N.E. Colls. Fund. Mem. ABA, Conn. Bar Assn. (mem. fed. practice com. 1967—, chmn. 1967-69, mem. specialization com. 1969—, chmn. 1969-74), Hartford County Bar Assn., N.E. Law Inst. (adv. council), Fed. Bar Assn. (Conn. pres. 1964-75), Order of Coif, Phi Beta Kappa. Administrative and regulatory, Federal civil litigation, General practice. Home: 56 Scarborough St Hartford CT 06105 Office: One Financial Plaza Hartford CT 06103

RICCIARDELLI, THOMAS PATRICK, lawyer; b. Winthrop, Mass., Dec. 15, 1948; s. Frederick William and Irma Leonilla (Moran) R.; m. Laurel Ann Patterson, June 21, 1975; 1 child, Anthony Thomas. AB cum laude, Boston Coll., 1970; MBA, Amos Tuck Sch., 1972; JD, Boston Coll., 1979. Bar: Tex. 1979. V.p. planning and legal affairs The Vis. Nurse Assn. of Tex., Dallas, 1980—. Mem. bd. of rev. Nat. League of Nursing, N.Y.C., 1983—, legal affairs com. Nat. Assn. for Home Care, Washington, 1984—, exec. com. Accredited Program for Home Care and Community Health, N.Y.C., 1985—, Goals for Dallas, 1985—; v.p., bd. dirs. Family Care Corp., Dallas, 1981—; sec. Metroplex Health Services, Inc., Dallas, 1981-83, treas., 1981—, bd. dirs., 1981—. Mem. ABA, Tex. Bar Assn., Dallas Estate Planning Council. Club: Toastmasters (sec. 1986—, treas., adminstrv. v.p. 1982-85). Avocation: philology. Administrative and regulatory, Health, Legislative. Home: 845 Warwick Plano TX 75023 Office: The Vis Nurse Assn of Tex 8200 Brookriver Dr #200N Dallas TX 75247-4016

RICCIO, MARIE OLYMPIA, lawyer; b. Bklyn., May 17, 1955; d. William Anthony and Mary (Visco) R. BA, Colgate U., 1977; JD, Duke U., 1980. Bar: La. 1980, U.S. Dist. Ct. (ea. dist.) La. 1980, U.S. Ct. Appeals (5th cir.) 1980. Assoc. Barham & Churchill, New Orleans, 1980-81; law clk. to chief judge U.S. Dist. Ct. (ea. dist.) La., New Orleans, 1981-82; ptnr. Fawer, Brian, Hardy & Zatskis, New Orleans, 1983-86; sole practice New Orleans, 1986—. Mem. Assn. Criminal Def. Lawyers, Assn. Trial Lawyers Am., La. Trial Lawyers Assn., La. Bar Assn. Avocations: ballroom dancing, piano. Personal injury, Criminal, Federal civil litigation. Home and Office: 4476 Music St New Orleans LA 70122

RICCO, EDWARD ROBERT, lawyer; b. Teaneck, N.J., Jan. 17, 1950; s. Leopold Joseph and Rose Mary (Lotito) R.; m. Mary Ann Sweeney, Feb. 2, 1974; children: Alanna Catherine, Susanna Maria. BS, Stevens Inst. Tech., 1971; MA, Columbia U., 1973; JD, U. N. Mex., 1980. Bar: N. Mex. 1980, U.S. Dist. Ct. N. Mex. 1980, U.S. Ct. Appeals (10th cir.) 1981, U.S. Claims Ct. 1983, U.S. Supreme Ct. 1984. Law clk. to chief judge U.S. Dist. Ct., Albuquerque, 1980-81; assoc. Rodey, Dickason, Sloan, Akin & Robb P.A., Albuquerque, 1981-87, also bd. dirs.; mem. com. on uniform jury instructions in civil cases N. Mex. Supreme Ct., Albuquerque, 1986—. Mem. ABA, Albuquerque Bar Assn., Am. Acad. Hosp. Attys., N. Mex. Health Lawyers Assn., Nat. Health Lawyers Assn. Contracts commercial, Health, Federal civil litigation. Home: 1500 Park Ave SW Albuquerque NM 87104 Office: Rodey Dickason Sloan et al 20 First Plaza PO Box 1888 Albuquerque NM 87103

RICE, BEN HERBERT, III, lawyer; b. El Reno, Okla., Sept. 18, 1918. Student, U.S. Naval Acad., 1936-37; B.A., U. Tex., 1941, LL.B., 1942. Bar: Tex. 1942. Ptnr. Carter, Carter & Rice, Marlin, Tex., 1946; asst. atty. gen. State of Tex., 1947-50; assoc. Vinson, Elkins & Weems, Houston, 1951-70; ptnr. Vinson & Elkins, Houston, 1971—. Mem. ABA, State Bar Tex., Houston Bar Assn. Federal civil litigation, State civil litigation, Oil and gas leasing. Office: 32d Floor 1st City Tower Houston TX 77002

RICE, CANICE TIMOTHY, JR., lawyer; b. St. Louis, Apr. 4, 1950; s. Canice Timothy and Elizabeth Jane (Tobin) R. AB, Holy Cross Coll., 1972; JD, U. Mo., 1976. Bar: Mo. 1976, Ill. 1977, U.S. Dist. Ct. (ea. dist.) Mo. 1977, U.S. Dist. Ct. (cen. and so. dists.) Ill. 1977, U.S. Ct. Appeals (7th and 8th cirs.) 1977. Assoc. Cavanagh & Albrecht, St. Louis, 1976-77, Lucas & Murphy, St. Louis, 1977-79; sole practice St. Louis, 1979—; mem. civil practice com. Mo. Bar. Mem. plan commn. University City, Mo., 1984—. Mem. Bar Assn. Met. St. Louis (trial sect., chmn. office econs. com. 1984-87, grievance com., fee dispute com., ad hoc tort law rev. com.), Ill. Bar Assn., Assn. Trial Lawyers Am., Mo. Assn. Trial Attys., Lawyers Assn. Clubs: Racquet, Mo. Athletic, Noonday (St. Louis). Avocations: tennis, squash. Federal civil litigation, State civil litigation, Personal injury. Home: 6624 Kingsbury Blvd Saint Louis MO 63130 Office: 408 Olive #400 Saint Louis MO 63102

RICE, CHARLES MARCUS, II, lawyer; b. St. Louis, June 20, 1946; s. Jay Goldman and Bonna (Lafferty) R.; m. Marian Clifford Jones, June 16, 1979; children: Charles Marcus III, Rebecca Wells. A.B. magna cum laude, Princeton U., 1968; M.Pub. Policy, U. Mich., 1973, J.D. cum laude, 1974. Bar: N.Y. 1975, Mo. 1978. Assoc. Milbank, Tweed, Hadley & McCloy, N.Y.C., 1974-76; ptnr. Lowenhaupt, Chasnoff, Armstrong & Mellitz, St. Louis, 1979—. Mem. adv. council Sch. Forestry, U. Mo., Columbia, 1982—; sec. Anglican Inst., Inc., St. Louis, 1984—, Friends of Cantess/Romess Inc., 1987—. Mem. ABA, Mo. Bar (computer law sect.), Bar Assn. Met. St. Louis (real estate com. 1983—). Real property, Estate planning, General corporate. Home: 8510 Colonial Ln Ladue MO 63124 Office: Lowenhaupt Chasnoff Armstrong & Mellitz 408 Olive St Suite 405 Saint Louis MO 63102

RICE, GEORGE LAWRENCE (LARRY), III, lawyer; b. Jackson, Tenn., Sept. 24, 1951; s. George Lawrence and Judith W. (Pierce) R.; m. Joy Gaia, Sept. 14, 1974; children—George Lawrence, Amy Colleen. B.A. with honors, Southwestern Coll., 1974; J.D., Memphis State U., 1976; student Nat. Coll. Advocacy, Georgetown Law Sch., 1978. Bar: Tenn. 1977, U.S. Supreme Ct. 1980. Assoc. firm Pierce, Rice, Nichols, Stone, Rice & Bursi, Memphis, 1976-81, ptnr., 1981—; lectr. Memphis Cablevision, 1983-84, Sta. WHBQ, Memphis, 1983-85. Author: Divorce Practice in Tennessee. Mem. Memphis Bar Assn. (founding chmn. div. and family law sect.), Tenn. Bar Assn. (chmn. family law sect, litigation sect. council), ABA, Memphis Trial Lawyers Assn., Tenn. Trial Lawyers Assn., Assn. Trial Lawyers Am. Unitarian. State civil litigation, Family and matrimonial, Personal injury. Office: Pierce Rice Nichols Rice et al 147 Jefferson St #600 Memphis TN 38104

RICE, GUY GARNER, lawyer; b. Kansas City, Mo., Mar. 25, 1932; s. Guy William and Elizabeth (Smith) R.; m. Marcia Louise Clines, Dec. 15, 1978; children by previous marriage—Dierk B., Brenda L., Reid R., Sandra L., Student Beloit Coll., 1949-51; A.B., U. Mo., Columbia, 1953; J.D., U. Mo.-Kansas City, 1964. Bar: Mo. 1964, U.S. Dist. Ct. (we. dist.) Mo. 1965. Asst. pros. atty. Jackson County, Mo., 1965, Asst. county counselor, Jackson County, Mo., 1970-71; ptnr. Phillips, Rice & McElligott, Independence, 1968-74; sole practice, Independence, 1978-82; ptnr. Rice & Mouse, Independence, 1983-85, sole practice, 1985—; gen. counsel Med. Info. Service, Inc., 1966-80, Sugar Creek Nat. Bank, 1971-80. Served to 1st lt. U.S. Army, 1953-56. Named Outstanding Young Man, Jaycees, 1958-59; recipient Spoke award Jaycees, 1959. Mem. Estate Planning Assn. Greater Kansas City (pres. 1966-67), Independence Bar Assn. (sec. 1965-66), Eastern Jackson County Bar Assn., Independence C. of C. General corporate. Office: Suite 5 3640 S Noland Rd Independence MO 64055

RICE, JAMES BRIGGS, JR., lawyer; b. Kansas City, Mo., Dec. 31, 1940; s. James Briggs and Oma J. (Smoyer) R.; m. Carolyn Ryan, Aug. 11, 1962 (div.); children: James Briggs III, Cynthia L.; m. Beverly Sue, Oct. 24, 1980. AB, U. Mo., 1962, JD, 1965. Bar: Mo. 1965, U.S. Dist. Ct. (we. dist.) Mo. 1968. Assoc., Rogers, Field & Gentry, Kansas City, 1967-72; ptnr. Wesner, Wesner & Rice, Sedalia, Mo., 1972-75, Rice & Romines, Sedalia, 1975-80; sole practice, Sedalia, 1980—; atty. Sedalia Area Devel. Corp., 1976-79. Chmn., Police Personnel Bd., Sedalia, 1976. Served as capt. U.S. Army, 1965-67; Vietnam. Mem. ABA, Mo. Bar Assn., Pettis County Bar Assn. (pres. 1975), Kansas City Bar Assn., Am. Judicature Soc., Assn. Trial Lawyers Am., Mo. Assn. Trial Atty.'s, VFW, Vietnam Vets. of Pettis County. Republican. Methodist. Lodges: Kiwanis (pres. 1975), Noon-day Optimist, Masons, Shriners. General practice, Personal injury, Workers' compensation. Home: 1610 W 11th Sedalia MO 65301 Office: 701 S Ohio Sedalia MO 65301

RICE, JAMES GORDON, lawyer; b. Flushing, N.Y., Mar. 1, 1948; s. James Joseph and Kathleen (Gordon) R.; m. Jean O'Neil (div. Dec. 1985); 1 child, Melissa; m. Janet D. Filips. BA, U. Dayton, 1973, MA, 1974, JD, 1977. Bar: Ohio 1977, U.S. Dist. Ct. (so. dist.) Ohio 1977, Oreg. 1982, U.S. Ct. Appeals (9th cir.) 1983. Assoc. E.S. Gallon & Assocs., Dayton, Ohio, 1977-82; ptnr. Wolf, Guthrie & Rice, Portland, Oreg., 1982—. Served to sgt. U.S. Army, 1968-70, Vietnam. Mem. ABA, Oreg. Bar Assn., Ohio Bar Assn., Assn. Trial Lawyers Am., Oreg. Trial Lawyers Assn. Democrat. Personal injury, Federal civil litigation, State civil litigation. Home: 1209 SW 6th #406 Portland OR 97204 Office: Wolf Gutherie & Rice 1207 SW 6th Ave Portland OR 97204

RICE, JOHN EDWARD, lawyer; b. Bridgeport, Nebr., Mar. 11, 1927; s. Charles R. and Lyla V. (French) R.; m. Ann M. Yanick, May 9, 1953; children—Mary C., John Michael, Theresa, Joan, Jane, Charles. J.D., Creighton U., 1951. Bar: Nebr. 1951. City atty. City of Bellevue, Nebr., 1955—; ptnr. Rice & Adams, Bellevue, 1951—. Served to sgt. U.S. Army, 1944-46; PTO. Democrat. Roman Catholic. Local government, Real property. Home: 912 Ridgewood Ct Bellevue NE 68005 Office: Rice & Adams 1246 Golden Gate Dr PO Box 397 Papillion NE 68046

RICE, JULIAN CASAVANT, lawyer; b. Miami, Fla., Jan. 1, 1924; s. Sylvan J. and Maybelle (Casavant) R.; m. Dorothy Mae Haynes, Feb. 14, 1958; children—Scott B., Craig M. (dec.), Julianne C., Linda D., Janette M. Student, U. San Francisco, 1941-43; J.D. cum laude, Gonzaga U., 1950. Bar: Wash. 1950, Alaska 1959. Practice law Spokane, 1950-56; practice law Fairbanks, Alaska, 1959—; mem. firm Rice & Ringstad and predecessor firms, Fairbanks, 1959; dir. Alaska Pacific Bank, Anchorage, Alaska Pacific Trust Co., Anchorage; dir., mem. exec. com. Key Bancshares Alaska, Anchorage; mayor Fairbanks, 1970-72; founder, gen. counsel Mt. McKinley Mut. Savs. Bank, Fairbanks, 1965—, chmn. bd., 1979-80; v.p., dir., gen. counsel Skimmers, Inc., Anchorage, 1966-67; gen. counsel Alaska Carriers Assn., Anchorage, 1960-71, Alaska Transp. Conf., 1960-67. Served to 1st lt. AUS, 1943-46. Decorated Bronze Star. Fellow Am. Bar Found.; mem. ABA, Wash. Bar Assn., Alaska Bar Assn., Am. Judicature Soc., Assn. Transp. Practitioners, Transp. Lawyers Assn. Administrative and regulatory, Personal injury, General practice. Office: Rice Bldg 330 Wendell St Fairbanks AK 99701

RICE, MICHAEL DOWNEY, lawyer; b. N.Y.C., Oct. 17, 1938; s. B. Downey Rice and Ellen (Smith) Holmes; m. Dorothy Jones, Mar. 26, 1959; children: Deborah Kelly, Judith Meyer, Karen, Janet, Theresa, Constance. BSE, Princeton U., 1960; JD, Temple U., 1970. Bar: D.C. 1970, N.Y. 1973. Engr. various cos., 1961-68; sr. engr. Booz, Allen & Hamilton, Phila., 1968-71; assoc. Cravath, Swaine & Moore, N.Y.C., 1971-75; atty., advisor U.S. Dept. Transp., Washington, 1976; sole practice Port Washington, N.Y., 1977-85, Old Saybrook, Conn., 1985—. Author: Railroad Equipment Obligations, 1978, Equipment Financing, 1981, Prentice-Hall Dictionary of Business, Finance and Law, 1983. Mem. ABA, Soc. Automotive Engrs., Am. Soc. Testing and Materials. Roman Catholic. Contracts commercial, General corporate, Administrative and regulatory. Home and Office: 515 Main St Old Saybrook CT 06475

RICE, RANDOLF JAMES, lawyer; b. San Jose, Calif., July 1, 1947; s. James Allen and Bette Jean (Welchly) R.; 1 child, James Nicholas. BA, U. Calif., Santa Barbara, 1969; postgrad., Harvard U., 1969-70; MDiv, Grad. Theol. Union, Berkeley, Calif., 1972; JD, U. Calif., San Francisco, 1978. Bar: Calif. 1978, U.S. Dist. Ct. (no. dist.) Calif. 1978, U.S. Dist. Ct. (ea. dist.) Mich. 1981. Assoc. Pillsbury, Madison & Sutro, San Francisco, 1978-85, ptnr., 1986—. Assoc. priest St. philip's Episcop. Ch., 1985—; pres. Bay Area Adoption Service, Sunnyvale, Calif., 1986; bd. dirs. Children's Home Soc. Calif., Los Angeles, 1984-85. Federal civil litigation, State civil litigation, Labor. Home: 3886 Balcom Rd San Jose CA 95148 Office: Pillsbury Madison & Sutro 33 W Santa Clara St San Jose CA 95113

RICE, TERRY AUGUST, lawyer; b. Suffern, N.Y., Aug. 23, 1950; s. James Patrick and Ethyl (Butner) R. BA in Govt., Coll. William and Mary, 1972; JD, Albany Law Sch., 1975. Bar: N.Y. 1976, N.J. 1981, U.S. Dist. Ct. (so. and ea. dists.) N.Y. 1976, U.S. Ct. Appeals (2d cir.) 1980, U.S. Dist. Ct. N.J. 1981. Dep. town atty. Town of Ramapo, N.Y., 1975-77; assoc. Balsamo & Byrne, Suffern, 1977-81; village atty. Village of Suffern, 1977—, Village of Sloatsburg, N.Y., 1982-85; town atty. Town of Tuxedo, N.Y., 1985—; sole practice Suffern, 1981-86; of counsel to Robert E. Blackburn and Assocs., Suffern, 1987—; counsel, coordinator West Ramapo Govt. Reform Com., Suffern, 1982-83; counsel to Village of Chestnut Ridge (N.Y.) Zoning Commn., 1986—; mem. N.Y. State Legis. Com. on State-Local Relations, N.Y. State Conf. of Mayors Adv. Bd., 1983—; speaker at meetings, seminars. Contbr. numerous articles to legal publs. including N.Y. Law Jour. Bd. govs. Good Samaritan Hosp. Found. Mem. Nat. Inst. Mcpl. Law Officers (N.Y. state chmn. 1980-81, 85—, regional v.p. 1981-82, adv. com. of Nat. Mcpl. League Def. Fund, tort liability of municipalities com., zoning and planning com., litigation-trial and appellate practice com., annexation com., civil liberties com., civil rights and voting rights com., legal advocacy com.), ABA (vice chmn. publs. com. urban, state and local govt. law sect., com. govt. liability, com. on land use, planning and zoning), N.Y. State Bar Assn. (legis. com. mcpl. law sect., environ. law sect.), Rockland County Bar Assn. (chmn. mcpl. law com. 1982—), Am. Planning Assn. (chmn. N.Y. Met. chpt. planning and law div., amicus curiae com.). Local government, Personal injury, State civil litigation. Office: 1 Executive Blvd Suffern NY 10901

RICE, V(IRGIL) THOMAS, lawyer; b. La Harpe, Ill., June 29, 1920; s. Vilas E. and Jane N. (Robertson) R.; m. Phyllis Ann Carpenter, Feb. 14, 1969; children: Lesley Jean Rice Luke, Sharon Leilani Rice Routt. BA, U. Ill., 1941, JD, 1948. Bar: Ill. Supreme Ct. 1948, U.S. Dist. Ct. Hawaii 1948, Hawaii Supreme Ct. 1949, U.S. Ct. Mil. Appeals 1960, U.S. Ct. Appeals (9th cir.) 1962, U.S. Customs Ct. 1963, U.S. Supreme Ct. 1971. Assoc. Blaisdell & Moore and predecessor firm, 1948-61; ptnr. Moore, Torkildson & Rice, 1961-64, Rice, Lee & Wong, and predecessor firms, Honolulu, 1964-86; of counsel to Lee, Henderson, Chipchase & Wong, Molokai, Hawaii, 1986—.

Mem. Hawaii Homes Commn., 1960; chmn., sec. Hawaii State Transp. Commn., 1961-63; life mem., bd. dirs. Child and Family Service, 1960-66, 78-79, treas., 1963, pres. 1964-65; bd. dirs. Health and Community Services Council Hawaii, 1967-77, treas. 1968-71, v.p., 1972-74, pres., 1975-77; bd. dirs., chmn. Hawaii Spl. Olympics, 1972-76; mem. State Hawaii Legis. Reapportionment Commn., 1972; hearing officer spl. needs br. Office Instructional Services, State Hawaii Dept. Edn., 1979-81; del. Hawaii Rep. State Conv., 1953-85, chmn. platform com., 1964, 78, party rules com., 1965, mem. Hawaii State Rep. Cen. Com., 1955, 69-73, chmn. Rep. Party Hawaii, 1969-71, chmn. State Rep. Dist. Com., 1955-61, mem. Rep. Nat. Com., 1969-71, del., mem. resolutions com. Nat. Convs., 1972, 76. Served to flying officer RCAF, 1941-43, to capt. USAAF, 1943-45, to maj. JAGC, USAF, 1950-52; lt. col. Res. ret. Decorated D.F.C., Air medal with 3 oak leaf clusters. Fellow Am. Acad. Matrimonial Lawyers; mem. ABA, Hawaii Bar Assn. (chmn. family law com. 1973-85), Ill. Bar Assn., Judge Advs. Assn., Phi Sigma Kappa, Phi Delta Phi. Club: Pacific. Family and matrimonial. Home: PO Box 97 Maunaloa Molokai HI 96770 Office: Lee Henderson Chipchase & Wong 345 Queen St Suite 700 Honolulu HI 96813

RICE, WALTER HERBERT, federal judge; b. Pitts., May 27, 1937; s. Harry D. and Elizabeth L. (Braemer) R.; m. Bonnie Rice; children: Michael, Hilary, Harry. B.A., Northwestern U., 1958; J.D., M.B.A., Columbia U., 1962. Bar: Ohio 1963. Asst. county prosecutor Montgomery County, Ohio, 1964-66; asso. firm Gallon & Miller, Dayton, Ohio, 1966-69; 1st asst. Montgomery County Prosecutor's Office, 1969; judge Dayton Mcpl. Ct., 1970-71, Montgomery County Ct. Common Pleas, 1971-80, U.S. Dist. Ct. So. Dist., Ohio, 1980—; adj. prof. U. Dayton Law Sch., 1976—, bd. visitors, 1976—; chmn. Montgomery County Supervisory Council on Crime and Deliquency, 1972-74; vice chmn. bd. dirs. Pretrial Release, Inc., 1975-79. Author papers in field. Pres. Dayton Area Council Alcoholism on and Drug Abuse, 1971-73; chmn. bd. trustees Stillwater Health Center, Dayton, 1976-79, Family Service Assn. of Dayton, 1978-80. Recipient Excellent Jud. Service award Ohio Supreme Ct., 1976, 77, Outstanding Jud. Service award, 1973, 74, 76; Man of Yr. award Disting. Service Awards Council, Dayton, 1977; Outstanding Jurist in Ohio award Ohio Acad. Trial Lawyers, 1986. Mem. Am. Jud. Soc., Ohio Bar Assn., Dayton Bar Assn.

RICE, ZELOTES SYLVESTER, lawyer; b. Sparta, Wis., July 4, 1923; s. Zelotus Sylvester and Vena Rae (Hemstock) R.; m. Babette Lasker, Sept. 18, 1971; 1 child, David Zelotes. BS, U. Wis., 1948, JD, 1950. Bar: Wis. 1950, U.S. Dist. Ct. (we. dist.) Wis. 1950, N.Y. 1954, U.S. Ct. Appeals (7th cir.) 1959, U.S. Supreme Ct. 1969. Ptnr. Rice & Abbott S.C., Sparta, Wis., 1950—; atty. U.S. Dept. of Justice, Washington, 1951-53; assoc. McCanliss & Early, N.Y.C., 1953-54. Commr. Wis. Employment Relations Commn., Madison, 1963-75; sec. Wis. Dept. of Transp., Madison, 1975-77, Wis. Dept. of Labor, Industry and Human Relations, Madison, 1977-79. Recipient Dist. Service Citation Assn. Labor Relations Agys., 1979. Mem. Wis. Bar Assn., Indsl. Research Assn., Am. Arbitration Assn., Nat. Acad. Arbitrators. Democrat. Roman Catholic. Club: University (Milw.). Labor, Probate, General practice. Home: 603 N Water St Sparta WI 54656 Office: Rice & Abbott SC 112 W Oak St Sparta WI 54656

RICH, BRADLEY POPE, lawyer; b. Montpelier, Idaho, June 28, 1949; s. William J. and Dixie (Pope) R. BA magna cum laude, U. Utah, 1971, JD, 1974. Bar: Utah 1974, U.S. Dist. Ct. Utah 1974, U.S. Ct. Appeals (10th cir.) 1982. Legal counsel Legal Defenders Assn., Salt Lake City, 1974-80; assoc. O'Connell & Yengich, Salt Lake City, 1981-82; ptnr. Yengich, Rich, Xaiz & Metos, Salt Lake City, 1983—. Mem. com. Salt Lake City Landmarks, 1980—; chmn. 1983. Democrat. Avocations: windsurfing, travel, languages, literature, music. Criminal. Office: Yengich Rich Xaiz & Metos 72 E 400 S Suite 355 Salt Lake City UT 84111

RICH, CHRISTOPHER CHARLES, state ofcl., lawyer; b. Brookline, Mass., June 8, 1952; s. Francis Patrick and Catherine Louise (Lochiatto) R. B.S., Boston Coll., 1974; J.D., Suffolk U., 1978. Bar: Mass. 1978, U.S. dist. ct. Mass. 1979, U.S. Ct. Appeals (1st cir.) 1979, U.S. Supreme Ct. 1984. Br. mgr. Logan Equipment Corp., Boston, 1972; spl. police officer Dennis (Mass.) Police Dept., 1973-75, Harwich (Mass.) Police Dept., 1974-75, Suffolk County (Mass.) Dist. Atty.'s Office, 1974-78, asst. dist. atty. maj. violations div. Suffolk Ct., Suffolk County Dist. Atty., 1979; asst. chief legal counsel Mass. Dept. Pub. Works, 1979; dep. sec. Mass. Dept. Pub. Utilities, Boston, 1979—; spl. police officer Saugus (Mass.) Police Dept., 1982—; sole practice, Boston, 1982-83; sr. assoc. atty. Mass. office Hayt, Hayt & Landau, 1983-84; ptnr., 1984—; bus. cons. Mem. Saugus Town Meeting, 1975-78; keyperson United Way Fund Drive, 1982-83. Recipient John B. Atkinson award Boston Coll., 1974. Mem. Mass. Bar Assn., ABA, Justinial Law Soc., New Eng. Narcotic Enforcement Officers Assn. (dir., gen. counsel), Internat. Narcotic Enforcement Officers Assn., Phi Delta Phi. Roman Catholic. Club: Saugus Italian Am. (gen. counsel 1983—). Public utilities, Administrative and regulatory, State civil litigation. Home: 94 Saugus Ave Saugus MA 01906 Office: 187 Condor St East Boston MA 02128 also: 200 Corporate Pl Peabody MA 01961-6027

RICH, EDWARD WILLIAM, lawyer; b. Lockport, N.Y., May 24, 1950; s. Edward and Betty Jane (Pahl) R.; m. Ann Marie Mathieu, July 5, 1980; 1 child, Ashley. BSME, MIT, 1972, MS, 1972; JD, Stanford U., 1976. Bar: Mass. 1977, N.Y. 1977, Idaho 1977, U.S. Dist. Ct. Idaho 1977, U.S. Ct. Appeals (9th cir.) 1978, Mich. 1980, U.S. Dist. Ct. (ea. dist.) Mich. 1980, U.S. Supreme Ct. 1980. Asst. dist. atty. Niagara County Dist. Atty.'s Office, Lockport, N.Y., 1976; assoc. Elam & Burke, Boise, Idaho, 1977-79; atty. Dow Chem., Midland, Mich., 1979—. Mem. Mich. Bar Assn., Mass. Bar Assn., Tau Beta Pi, Pi Tau Sigma. General corporate, Financial law. Home: PO Box 2236 Midland MI 48641-2236 Office: Dow Chem Corp 2030 Dow Ctr Midland MI 48674

RICH, GILES SUTHERLAND, judge; b. Rochester, N.Y., May 30, 1904; s. Giles Willard and Sarah Thompson (Sutherland) R.; m. Gertrude Verity Braun, Jan. 10, 1931 (dec.); 1 child, Verity Sutherland Grinnell (Mrs. John M. Hallinan); m. Helen Gill Field, Oct. 10, 1953. S.B., Harvard, 1926; LL.B., Columbia, 1929; LL.D. (hon.), John Marshall Law Sch., Chgo., 1981. Bar: N.Y. bar 1929; registered to practice U.S. Patent Office, 1934. Practice of law N.Y.C., 1929-56; specializing patent and trademark law; partner Williams, Rich & Morse, 1937-52, Churchill, Rich, Weymouth & Engel, 1952-56; assoc. judge U.S. Ct. Customs and Patent Appeals, 1956-82; circuit judge U.S. Ct. Appeals (Fed. cir.), 1982—; lectr. patent law Columbia, 1942-56, N.Y. Law Sch., 1952; adj. prof. Georgetown U. Law Sch., 1963-69. Author articles in field. Recipient Jefferson medal N.J. Patent Law Assn., 1955; Kettering award Patent Trademark and Copyright Inst. George Washington U., 1963; Founders Day award for distinguished govt. service, 1970; Freedman Found. award Am. Inst. Chemists, 1967; Eli Whitney award Conn. Patent Law Assn., 1972. Mem. Assn. Bar City, N.Y., Am. Bar Assn., Am. Patent Law Assn., N.Y. Patent Law Assn. (pres. 1950-51), Rochester Patent Law Assn. (hon. life), Los Angeles Patent Law Assn. (hon.), San Francisco Patent Law Assn. (hon. life), Nat. Lawyers Club (hon.). Clubs: Harvard (Washington), Cosmos (Washington). Office: US Ct Appeals Fed Circuit 717 Madison Pl NW Washington DC 20439

RICH, MARCIA R., lawyer; b. N.Y.C., Dec. 29, 1948; d. Jack and Beatrice (Fishman) R. B.A., Bard Coll., 1970; J.D., Bklyn. Law Sch., 1973. Bar: N.Y. 1974, U.S. Dist. Ct. (ea. dist.) N.Y., 1976. Staff atty. juvenile rights div. Legal Aid Soc. N.Y.C., 1973-77; assoc. law asst. to justices Supreme Ct. 1st Jud. Dist., N.Y.C., 1977-87; mng. atty. Howard, Darby & Levin, 1987—. Vol. Am. Heart Assn., N.Y.C., 1979—. Mem. New York County Lawyers Assn. (com. law reform 1983—), ABA, N.Y. State Bar Assn., Assn. Law Assts. City N.Y. (exec. bd. 1980-81), N.Y. Women's Bar Assn. State civil litigation, Family and matrimonial, Juvenile. Office: Howard Darby & Levin 10 E 53d St New York NY 10022

RICH, MARVIN LEWIS, lawyer; b. Kansas City, Mo., Nov. 21, 1933; s. Isadore and Allene Ethel (Levy) R.; m. Patricia Carol Uhlmann, Aug. 31, 1963; children: Helen Alison, Meredith Lynne. BA in History with distinction, U. Mo., 1956; LLB, Harvard U., 1959. Bar: Mo. 1959. Ptnr. Rich, Granoff, Levy & Gee, Kansas City, 1959—; bd. dirs. H & R Block Inc., Kansas City. Mem. ABA, Kansas City Bar Assn., Phi Beta Kappa. Republican. Jewish. Clubs: Kansas City, Carriage (Kansas City). Lodge: B'nai B'rith. Avocations: tennis, swimming. General corporate, Securities, Corporate taxation. Home: 6632 Wenonga Rd Mission KS 66208 Office: Rich Granoff Levy & Gee 1100 Main Suite 2300 Kansas City MO 64105

RICH, MICHAEL JOSEPH, lawyer; b. N.Y.C., June 19, 1945; s. Jesse and Phyllis (Sternfeld) R.; m. Linda Christine Kubis, July 19, 1969; children—David Lawrence, Lisa Diane. B.A., Gettysburg Coll., 1967; J.D., Am. U., 1972. Bar: Del. 1973, U.S. Dist. Ct. Del. 1973, U.S. Supreme Ct. 1976, Pa. 1981. Law clk. Del. Supreme Ct., Georgetown, 1972-73; assoc. Tunnell & Raysor, Georgetown, 1973-76; ptnr. Morris, Nichols, Arsht & Tunnell, Georgetown, 1983—; ptnr. Dunlap, Holland & Rich, Georgetown, 1976-80; gen. counsel Pearlette Fashions Inc., Lebanon, Pa., 1981-83; minority counsel Del. Ho. of Reps., Dover, 1977-79; mem. Del. Gov's Magistrate Commn., 1980, 1983-86; sec. Del. Gov's. Jud. Nominating Commn., 1986—. Bd. dirs. People's Place II, Inc., Milford, Del., 1973-77; pres. Bi-County United Way, Inc., Milford, 1977-78. Served to 1st lt. U.S. Army, 1967-69, Vietnam. Dean's fellow Am. U., 1971-72. Mem. ABA, Del. Bd. of Bar Examinees, Del. Bar Assn. (exec. com. 1986—), Sussex County Bar Assn. (v.p. 1986—). General practice, State civil litigation. Office: Morris Nichols Arsht & Tunnell PO Box 231 Georgetown DE 19927

RICH, R(OBERT) BRUCE, lawyer; b. N.Y.C., Oct. 28, 1949; s. John J. and Sylvia (Berkenblit) R.; m. Melissa Jo Saxe; children—Megan, Alexander. A.B., Dartmouth Coll., 1970; J.D., U. Pa., 1973. Bar: N.Y. 1974, U.S. Dist. Ct. (so. and ea. dists.) N.Y. 1974, U.S. Ct. Appeals (2d cir.) 1980, U.S. Supreme Ct. 1980, U.S. Ct. Appeals (D.C. cir.) 1985. Assoc. firm Weil, Gotshal & Manges, N.Y.C., 1973-81, ptnr., 1981—; adj. prof. law N.Y. Law Sch. Contbg. author: Cultivating the Wasteland: Can Cable Put the Vision Back in TV'9, 1983. Contbr. articles to profl. jours. Bd. advisers Communications and the Law, Westport, Conn., 1983—. Mem. ABA (antitrust law sect., forum com. on communications law), Assn. Bar City N.Y. (com. on trade regulation 1982-85, communications law com. 1985—), Phi Beta Kappa. Antitrust, Federal civil litigation, Trademark and copyright. Office: Weil Gotshal & Manges 767 Fifth Ave New York NY 10153

RICH, ROBERT STEPHEN, lawyer; b. N.Y.C., Apr. 30, 1938; s. Maurice H. and Natalie (Priess) R.; m. Myra N. Lakoff, May 31, 1964; children: David, Rebecca, Sarah. A.B., Cornell U., 1959; J.D., Yale U., 1963. Bar: N.Y. 1964, Colo. 1973, U.S. Tax Ct. 1966, U.S. Sup. Ct. 1967, U.S. Ct. Clms. 1968, U.S. Dist. Ct. (so. dist.) N.Y. 1965, U.S. Dist. Ct. (ea. dist.) N.Y. 1965, U.S. Dist. Ct. Colo. 1980, U.S. Ct. Apls. (2d cir.) 1964, U.S. Ct. Apls. (10th cir.) 1978; conseil juridique, Paris, 1968. Assoc., Shearman & Sterling, N.Y.C., Paris, London, 1963-72; ptnr. Davis, Graham & Stubbs, Denver, 1973—; adj. faculty U. Denver Law Sch., 1977—; dir. Clos du Val Wine Co. Ltd., 1972—, several corps.; mem. Colo. Internat. Trade Adv. Council, 1985—. Bd. dirs. Denver Internat. Film Festival, 1978-79, Alliance Française, 1977—; actor, musician N.Y. Shakespeare Festival, 1960; trustee, sec. Denver Art Mus., 1982—. Served to capt., arty. AUS, 1959-60. Mem. ABA, Union Internationale des Avocats, Internat. Fiscal Assn., Internat. Bar Assn., Colo. Bar Assn., N.Y. State Bar Assn., Assn. of Bar City of N.Y. Clubs: Denver, Yale (N.Y.C.). Author treatises on internat. taxation. Contbr. articles in field to profl. jours. Corporate taxation, Private international. Office: Davis Graham & Stubbs PO Box 185 Denver CO 80201

RICH, STEVEN EUGENE, lawyer; b. Hanford, Calif., Oct. 6, 1953; s. Myrle Eugene and Eula Mae (Pierson) R.; m. Robin René LaJoie, Mar. 19, 1978; children: Jason Eron, Stefani Rene, Kimberly Nicole. Student, U. Calif., Riverside, 1975; BA with honors, Loma Linda U., 1976; JD, Willamette U., 1979. Bar: Oreg. 1980, U.S. Dist. Ct. Oreg. 1981, U.S. Ct. Appeals (9th cir.) 1981, U.S. Supreme Ct. 1983. Asst. atty. gen. Oreg. Dept. Justice, Salem, 1980-81; ptnr. Ingram, Rich & Jeske, Grants Pass, Oreg., 1981—; mem. Josephine County Realtor/Atty. Joint Com., Grants Pass, Oreg., 1986—. Exec. dir. So. Oreg. Resources Alliance, Grants Pass, 1983-85; bd. dirs. Family Friends, Grants Pass, 1985—. Mem. ABA, Oreg. State Bar Assn., Josephine County Bar Assn., Oreg. Criminal Def. Lawyers Assn., Josephine County Def. Lawyers (pres. 1985—, bench/bar com. 1985—). Republican. Adventist. Avocations: racquetball, bicycling. Real property, Probate, Criminal. Office: Ingram Rich & Jeske 505 NE 7th St Grants Pass OR 97526

RICH, WAYNE ADRIAN, JR., lawyer; b. Cin., Dec. 27, 1941; s. Wayne Adrian Sr. and Ellen Fern (Peters) R.; m. Charlotte Jean Pritt, July 28, 1968 (div. Aug. 1977); m. Regina Ann Gillooly, Oct. 4, 1980. BA, Colgate U., 1964; JD, Duke U., 1967. Bar: W.Va. 1967, U.S. Dist. Ct. (so. dist.) W.Va. 1967, U.S. Ct. Appeals (4th cir.) 1971. Asst. U.S. atty. so. dist., State of W.Va., 1971-79; 1st. asst. U.S. atty., chief crime div. State of W.Va., 1979-81, U.S. atty., 1981-82; 1st asst. U.S. atty., chief criminal div. U.S. Dist. Ct. (so. dist.), W.Va., 1982—. Served as capt. USMC, 1968-71, col. Res., 1971—. Mem. W.Va. Bar Assn. Democrat. Presbyt. Criminal, Military, Government attorney. Office: US Attys Office PO Box 3234 Charleston WV 25332

RICHARD, DOUGLAS WAYNE, lawyer; b. Harvey, Ill., Jan. 13, 1955; s. Lloyd N. and Myrtle (Rost) R. B.S. in Ops. Mgmt., No. Ill. U., 1977; J.D., John Marshall Law Sch., 1980. Bar: Ill. 1980, U.S. Dist. Ct. (no. dist.) Ill. 1980, U.S. Dist. Ct. (cen. dist.) Ill. 1984. Assoc. Tate & Assocs., Chgo., 1980-81; asst. state's atty. Vermilion County State's Atty.'s Office, Danville, Ill., 1981-84; assoc. Satter, Ewing & Beyer, Pontiac, Ill., 1985—. Mem. Ill. State Bar Assn., ABA. Republican. Methodist. Insurance, State civil litigation, General practice. Home: 812 1/2 W North St Pontiac IL 61764 Office: Satter Ewing & Beyer 402 N Plum PO Box 440 Pontiac IL 61764

RICHARD, JOHN MARSTON, JR., lawyer; b. Russellville, Ky., May 26, 1950; s. John Marston Sr. and Virginia Adelaide (Wood) R.; m. Maurice Rose McClure, Aug. 12, 1977. BA, Western Ky. U., 1974; JD, No. Ky. U., 1979. Bar: Ky. 1979, U.S. Dist. Ct. (ea. dist.) Ky. 1980, U.S. Ct. Appeals (9th cir.) 1980, Alaska 1981, U.S. Dist. Ct. Alaska 1981, U.S. Supreme Ct. 1984. Assoc. Drathman & Weidner, Anchorage, 1980-82, Settles, Kalamarides and Assocs., Anchorage, 1982; ptnr. Kalamarides, MacMillan & Richard, Anchorage, 1983; sole practice Anchorage, 1984-86; supervising atty. welfare fraud sect. Office of Atty. Gen. State of Alaska, Anchorage, 1986—. Mem. Assn. Trial Lawyers Am., Nat. Assn. Criminal Def. Lawyers. Episcopalian. Avocation: mountaineering. Criminal. Office: Office of Atty Gen 1031 W 4th Ave Suite 110 Anchorage AK 99501

RICHARD, MONTE DWIGHT, lawyer; b. Oklahoma City, Feb. 27, 1945; s. Clayton Walter and Vera Pearl (Peebles) R.; m. Patricia Ann Richard, Dec. 29, 1966; children: Christopher, Sarah, Jennifer. BS cum laude, Calif. State U., Northridge, 1968; MS, U. Ill., 1969; JD cum laude, Loyola U., Los Angeles, 1973. Bar: Calif. 1973, U.S. Dist. Ct. (cen. dist.) Calif. 1973, U.S. Dist. Ct. (so. dist.) Calif. 1975, U.S. Supreme Ct. 1977, U.S. Ct. Appeals (9th cir.) 1978. Assoc. Hosp, Lytle, Richard & Granieri, Pasadena, Calif., 1973—. Mem. Blue Key, Tau Beta Pi, Sigma Alpha Epsilon. Republican. Avocations: computers, fishing. Banking, Insurance, State civil litigation. Home: 1139 Flintridge Ave LaCanada CA 91011 Office: Hosp Lytle Richard & Granieri 1100 E Green St Pasadena CA 91106

RICHARDS, ALAN EDWARD, lawyer; b. Chgo., Mar. 7, 1949; s. Robert E. and Ann R. (Ekhart) R.; m. Meridee G. Johnson, June 13, 1970; children: Kate Elizabeth, Zachary Stephen. B.A., Carthage Coll., Kenosha, Wis., 1970; J.D., Marquette U., 1976. Bar: Wis. 1976, Ill. 1977, U.S. Dist. Ct. (no. dist.) Ill. 1977. Ptnr. Richards & Ralph, Chartered, Libertyville, Ill., 1977-87, Richards Ralph & Eiden, Chartered, Vernon Hills, Ill., 1987—. Editor Marquette U. Law Rev., 1975-76. Mem. ABA, Ill. Bar Assn., Lake County Bar Assn. State civil litigation, Contracts commercial. Office: Richards Ralph & Eiden Chartered 175 Hawthorne Pkwy Vernon Hills IL 60061

RICHARDS, ARTHUR V., lawyer, corporate executive; b. 1939; married. B.B.A., St. John's U., 1963, LL.B., 1966. With Melville Corp., Harrison, N.Y., 1969—, asst. sec., 1970-77, sec., gen. atty., 1977—. General corporate. Office: Melville Corp 3000 Westchester Ave Harrison NY 10528 *

RICHARDS, DAVID ALAN, lawyer; b. Dayton, Ohio, Sept. 21, 1945; s. Charles Vernon and Betty Ann (Macher) R.; m. Marianne Catherine Del Monaco, June 26, 1971; children—Christopher, Courtney. B.A. summa cum laude, Yale U., 1967, J.D., 1972; M.A., Cambridge U., 1969. Bar: N.Y., 1973. Assoc. Paul, Weiss, Rifkind, Wharton & Garrison, N.Y.C., 1972-77, Coudert Bros., N.Y.C., 1977-80, ptnr., 1981-82; ptnr., head real estate group Sidley & Austin, N.Y.C., 1983—; gov. Anglo-Am. Real Property Inst. U.S./U.K., 1983—, sec., 1987—. Contbr. articles to profl. jours. Trustee Scarsdale Pub. Library, 1984—, v.p., 1987—. Mem. ABA (real property, probate and trust sect., council 1982—, Am. Coll. Real Estate Lawyers (chmn. amicus curiae brief com. 1985—, gov. 1987—), Internat. Bar Assn., Assn. Bar City N.Y. (real property com. 1978-80, 84—). Democrat. United Ch. of Christ. Club: Shenorock Shore (Rye, N.Y.). Real property. Home: 18 Forest Ln Scarsdale NY 10583 Office: Sidley & Austin 520 Madison Ave New York NY 10022

RICHARDS, GERALD THOMAS, lawyer, consultant; b. Monrovia, Calif., Mar. 17, 1933; s. Louis Jacquelyn Richards and Inez Vivian (Richardson) Hall; children: Patricia M. Richards Grauf, Laura J., Dag Hammarskjold; m. Mary Lou Richards, Dec. 27, 1986. BS magna cum laude, Lafayette Coll., 1957; MS, Purdue U., 1963; JD, Golden Gate U., 1976. Bar: Calif. 1976, U.S. Dist. Ct. (no. dist.) Calif. 1977, U.S. Patent Office 1981, U.S. Ct. Appeals (9th cir.) 1984, U.S. Supreme Ct. 1984. Computational physicist Lawrence Livermore (Calif.) Nat. Lab., 1967-73., planning staff lawyer, 1979, mgr. tech. transfer office, 1980-83, asst. lab. counsel, 1984—; sole practice, Livermore, 1976-78; mem. exec. com., policy advisor Fed. Lab. Consortium for Tech. Transfer, 1980—; panelist, del. White House Conf. on Productivity, Washington, 1983; del. Nat. Conf. on Tech. and Aging, Wingspread, Wis., 1981. Commr. Housing Authority, City of Livermore, 1977, vice chairperson, 1978, chairperson, 1979; pres. Housing Choices, Inc., Livermore, 1980-84; bd. dirs. Valley Vol. Ctr., Pleasanton, Calif., 1983, pres., 1984-86. Recipient Engring. award Gen. Electric Co., 1956. Served to maj. U.S. Army, 1959-67, Korea. Korea. Mem. ABA, Alameda County Bar Assn., Livermore-Amador Valley Bar Assn. (sec. 1978), Phi Beta Kappa, Tau Beta Pi, Sigma Pi Sigma. Club: Commonwealth Calif. Government contracts and claims, Construction, General practice. Home: PO Box 9001-129 Pleasanton CA 94566 Office: Lawrence Livermore Nat Lab PO Box 808 L-701 Livermore CA 94550

RICHARDS, JANET LEACH, lawyer, educator; b. Somerville, Tenn., Jan. 19, 1948; d. Wilmer Homer and Loraine Lottie (Robertson) Leach; m. William Michael Richards, Mar. 6, 1976; children—Jamie, Robert. B.S., Memphis State U., 1969, J.D., 1976. Bar: Tenn. 1976, U.S. Dist. Ct. (we. dist.) Tenn. 1976. Stewardess, methods analyst Delta Airlines, Atlanta, 1969-74; assoc. J.B. Cobb & Assocs., Memphis, 1976-78; asst. prof., asst. dean students affairs Memphis State Law Sch., 1978-1980, assoc. prof., 1981—, assoc. dean, 1986—. Recipient Sam A. Myar, Jr. Meml. award for Outstanding Young Lawyer in Memphis. Mem. Memphis and Shelby County Bar Assn. (pres. Young Lawyers' 1981, bd. dirs. 1980-81, 83-84), Memphis State Law Alumni Assn. Home: 1605 Vinton Memphis TN 38104 Office: Memphis State U Sch Law Memphis TN 38152

RICHARDS, MARTA ALISON, lawyer; b. Memphis, Mar. 15, 1952; d. Howard Jay and Mary Dean (Nix) Richards; m. Jon Michael Hobson, May 5, 1973 (div. Jan. 1976); m. 2d, Richard Peter Massony, June 16, 1979; 1 child, Richard Peter Massony, Jr. Student Vassar Coll., 1969-70; A.B. cum laude, Princeton U., 1973; J.D., George Washington U., 1976. Bar: Assoc., Phelps, Dunbar, Marks, Claverie & Sims, New Orleans, 1976-77; assoc. counsel Hibernia Nat. Bank, New Orleans, 1978; assoc. Singer, Hutner, Levine, Seeman & Stuart, New Orleans, 1978-80, Jones, Walker, Waechter, Poitevent, Carrere & Denegre, New Orleans, 1980-84; ptnr. Mmahat Duffy & Richards, 1984, Montgomery, Barnett, Brown, Read, Hammond & Mintz, 1984-86, Montgomery & Richards, 1986—; lectr. paralegal inst. U. New Orleans, 1984—. Contbr. articles to legal jours. Treas. alumni council Princeton U., 1979-81. Mem. ABA, La. Bar Assn., Fed. Bar Assn., New Orleans Bar Assn., Princeton Alumni Assn. New Orleans (pres. 1982—). Episcopalian. Banking, Contracts commercial, Consumer commercial. Home: 1133 8th St New Orleans LA 70115 Office: Montgomery and Richards 707 1st Nat Bank Commerce Bldg New Orleans LA 70112

RICHARDS, PAMELA MOTTER, lawyer; b. Columbus, Ohio, Feb. 24, 1950; d. L. Clair and Mildred Jo (Williams) Motter; m. John W. Richards, II, Mar. 1, 1975 (div. 1984); children—Christine Elizabeth, Teresa Jo. B.A., DePauw U., 1972; J.D., Ohio No. U., 1975. Bar: Ga. 1975. Assoc., Cowart, Varner & Harrington, Warner Robins, Ga., 1977-82; ptnr. Cowart, Varner, Harrington & Richards, Warner Robins, 1982-83, Cowart, Varner & Richards, 1983-84; sole practice, Robins, 1984—. Bd. dirs., sec. Kids Stuff Learning Ctrs. of Am., Warner Robins, 1983—, Warner Robins Day Care Ctr., 1976-80, Am. Cancer Soc., 1981—; v.p. Warner Robins C. of C., 1981-82, dir., 1980-82; vice chmn. Hospice of Houston County, 1986—. Mem. State Bar of Ga., Houston County Bar Assn., ABA, Houston County Assn. for Exceptional Children (bd. dirs. 1985—, pres. 1986—). Club: Civitan. Contracts commercial, Probate, State and local taxation. Office: PO Box 818 Warner Robins GA 31099

RICHARDS, PAUL A., lawyer; b. Oakland, Calif., May 27, 1927; s. Donnell C. and Theresa (Pasquale) R.; m. Ann Morgans, May 20, 1948 (dec. 1984); 1 child, Paul M.; m. Janet Flyge, Aug. 12, 1982. BA, U. Pacific, 1950; JD, U. San Francisco, 1953. Bar: Nev. 1953, U.S. Dist. Ct. Nev. 1953, U.S. Supreme Ct. 1964, U.S. Ct. Claims 1976, U.S. Ct. Appeals (9th cir.) 1982. Sole practice, Reno, 1953—, prin. Paul A. Richards, Ltd.; prof. environ. law Sierra Nevada Coll., 1970-80. Mem. Washoe Dem. Central Com., 1959-74, chmn., 1964-66, vice chmn., 1966-68; trustee Sierra Nevada Coll., 1970-82, Ducks Unltd., 1964-72; trustee emeritus, 1974—; mem. Fed. Land Law Commn., Nev., 1973-80; bd. dirs. Reno Rodeo Assn., 1963, pres., 1979. Served with U.S. Navy, 1945-46. Recipient Pres.'s Buckle and award Reno Rodeo Assn., 1979. Mem. Nev. Bar Assn., Washoe County Bar Assn. Democrat. Roman Catholic. Club: Press. Lodge: Elks. Bankruptcy, General corporate, Federal civil litigation. Office: 248 S Sierra St Richards Bldg Suite 1 Reno NV 89501

RICHARDS, ROBERT BYAM, lawyer, insurance company executive; b. Glen Ridge, N.J., Jan. 18, 1942; s. Kenneth Watson and Helen Leola (Wile) R.; m. Diana Lee Gibbs, Jan. 4, 1964 (separated); children—Jennifer Lynn, Robert Thomson. B.S. in Bus. Adminstrn., Lehigh U., 1963; J.D., Duquesne U., 1973. Bar: Pa. 1973, U.S. Dist. Ct. (we. dist.) Pa. 1973, U.S. Supreme Ct. 1987. Exec. trainee Mfrs. Hanover Trust Co., N.Y.C., 1963-66; real estate staff asst. PPG Industries, Inc., Pitts., 1966-72; assoc. Goldman & Unatin P.A., Pitts., 1972-74; asst. title officer Commonwealth Land Title Ins. Co., Pitts., 1974-77, v.p., 1977—, assoc. counsel, 1977-83, counsel, 1983— ; regional staff, 1985—, cons. mineral titles U.S. Steel Corp., Pitts., 1981; cons. real estate condemnation and mineral titles to dir. dept. aviation Allegheny County, 1981—; cons. real estate ins. litigation Rose, Schmidt, Dixon & Hasley, Pitts., 1981—; panelist Law 4 You, Sta. WTAE-TV, 1984-85; Law 2 You, Sta. KDKA-TV 1986; instr. in field Elder, trustee Southminster Presbyterian Ch., Mount Lebanon, Pa., 1980-84. Mem. Allegheny County Bar Assn. (council mem. real estate sec. 1979-81, asst. sec., sec. 1982-83, vice chmn. 1984, chmn. 1985, chmn. nominating com. 1986; mem. bankruptcy and comml. law sect. 1983—; mem. spl. fee determination com., 1986—). Republican. Real property, Probate, Contracts commercial. Office: Commonwealth Land Title Ins Co Frick Bldg Mezzanine Level 437 Grant St Pittsburgh PA 15219

RICHARDS, ROBERT MAYO, judge advocate U.S. Air Force; b. New Orleans, May 12, 1940; s. Clarence Mayo and Nina Pearl (Russell) R.; m. Shelba Dean Easley, Aug. 22, 1964 (div. 1974); 1 child: Rebecca Jane; m. Sandra Jean Tucker, June 13, 1981; 1 stepdau., Kimberly Dawn Daly. B.A., U. Tex., 1962, LL.B., 1964. Bar: Tex. 1964, U.S. Ct. Mil. Appeals 1981. Judge advocate 354th Tactical Fighting Wing, Myrtle Beach, AFB, S.C., 1965-67, staff judge advocate 6931st Security Group, Greece, 1967-69, 307th Bomb Wing, McCoy, AFB, Fla., 1969-71; mil. judge USAF Judiciary, Fla., 1971-72, Tex., 1972-74; asst. judge advocate Hdqrs. USAF, Germany, 1974-76, staff judge advocate, 35th Tactical Fighter Wing, Calif., 1976-79, 4th Tactical Fighter Wing, N.C., 1979-82; chief cir. mil. judge USAF Judiciary 7th Cir., Yokota AB, Japan, 1982-85; staff judge advocate 23d Air Force, 1985-86; dep. staff judge adv. Hdqrs. Mil. Airlift Command, Scott AFB, Ill., 1986—. Decorated Legion of Merit, meritorious service and commendation medals USAF. Mem. ABA, Tex. Bar Assn., Arnold Air Soc. (region comdr. 1961-62). Democrat. Presbyterian. Club: Toastmasters (v.p. McCoy AFB

1970-71). Military, Judicial administration, Criminal. Office: Hdqrs MAC/JA Scott AFB IL 62225

RICHARDS, ROBERT WILLIAM, lawyer; b. Pasadena, Tex., Nov. 26, 1956; s. James Polk Sr. and Doris Genelle (Holcomb) R.; m. Cynthia Ann Thrash, Aug. 9, 1975. BA, Baylor U., 1978, JD, 1980. Bar: Tex. 1980, U.S. Dist. Ct. (ea. dist.) Tex. 1982, U.S. Ct. Appeals (5th cir.) 1982, U.S. Supreme Ct. 1984. Ptnr. Ament, Dixon & Richards, Jacksonville, Tex., 1980-84, Adamson, Phifer & Richards, Jacksonville, 1985—; v.p. Richards Food Mart, Inc., Rusk, Tex., 1982—. Mem. Cherokee County Child Protective Service Bd., Rusk, 1983—, chmn., 1985—. Named one of Outstanding Young Men of Am. U.S. Jaycees, 1981. Mem. ABA, Assn. Trial Lawyers Am., Tex. Trial Lawyers Assn., Cherokee County Bar Assn. (pres. 1982-83), Phi Delta Phi, Alpha Chi Honor Soc., Gamma Beta Phi Soc. Avocations: scuba diving, golf. Personal injury, State civil litigation, General practice. Home: 2404 O'Keefe Rd Jacksonville TX 75766 Office: Adamson Phifer & Richards 516 E Commerce PO Drawer 1309 Jacksonville TX 75766

RICHARDS, SUZANNE V., lawyer; b. Columbia, S.C., Sept. 7, 1927; s. Raymond E. and Elise C. (Gray) R. A.B., George Washington U., 1948, J.D. with distinction, 1957, LL.M., 1959. Bar: D.C., 1958. Sole practice, Washington, 1974—; lectr. in family law. Recipient John Bell Larner award George Washington U., 1958; named Woman Lawyer of the Yr., Women's Bar Assn. D.C., 1977. Mem. Bar Assn. D.C. (treas. 1979-80, 80-81, sec. 1981-82, dir. 1982-87), Women's Bar Assn. (pres. 1977-78), Trial Lawyers Assn. of D.C. (bd. govs. 1978-82, 85—, treas. 1982-85), D.C. Bar Assn., Fed. Bar Assn., Nat. Assn. Women Lawyers, ABA (D.C. Ct. Appeals com. on unauthorized practice 1986—). General practice. Office: 1701 K St NW Washington DC 20006

RICHARDSON, ANDREW JAMES, lawyer; b. Toronto, Ont., Can., Oct. 14, 1943; came to U.S., 1948; s. Andrew and Winnifred Maud (Stewart) R.; m. Gail Hastings McKeague, June 7, 1969; children: Katherine S., Andrew G., Elizabeth B. AB in Physics, Colo. State Coll., 1964, MA in Sci. Edn., 1968; MA in Physics, Ind. State U., 1969; JD, George Washington U., 1974. Bar: Va. 1974, Ind. 1981, U.S. Ct. Appeals (fed. cir.) 1975, U.S. Ct. Appeals (4th cir.) 1979. Assoc. Littlepage, Quaintance, Arlington, Va., 1974-76, ptnr., 1977-81; of counsel Jenkins, Coffey et al, Indpls., 1981-82, Barnes & Thornburg, Indpls., 1982—; of counsel Cyr & Dupont, Arlington, 1980-82. Mem. ABA, Am. Intellectual Property Law Assn., Ind. Bar Assn., Va. Bar Assn. Patent, Trademark and copyright, Private international. Office: Barnes & Thornburg 11 S Meridian Indianapolis IN 46204

RICHARDSON, DENNIS MICHAEL, lawyer, educator; b. Los Angeles, July 30, 1949; s. Ralph Lee and Eva Catherine (McGuire) R.; 1 child, from previous marriage, Scott Randol; m. Catherine Jean Coyl, July 27, 1973; children: Jennifer Eve, Valerie Jean, Rachel Catherine, Nicole Marie, Marie Christina, Laura Michelle. BA, Brigham Young U., 1976, JD, 1979. Bar: Oreg. 1979. Ptnr. Richardson and Andersen, P.C., Central Point, Oreg., 1979—; bd. dirs. Pacific Coll. Art and Design; guest lectr. in field; Contbr. articles to profl. jours. Scoutmaster Boy Scouts Am., Central Point, 1981—; dist. chmn. Citizens for Am., Oreg. 2d Congl. Dist.; bd. dirs. Oreg. Lung Assn., 1980, Oreg. Shakespearean Festival, Ashland, 1981, Jackson County Legal Services, 1982. Served as helicopter pilot U.S. Army, 1969-71, Vietnam. Decorated Vietnamese Cross Gallantry. Republican. Personal injury. Office: 55 S 5th St Central Point OR 97502

RICHARDSON, DOUGLAS FIELDING, lawyer; b. Glendale, Calif., Mar. 17, 1929; s. James D. and Dorothy (Huskins) R.; m. Leni Tempelaar-Lietz, June 26, 1959; children—Arthur Wilhelm, John Douglas. A.B., UCLA, 1950; J.D., Harvard U., 1953. Bar: Calif. 1953. Assoc. O'Melveny & Myers, Los Angeles, 1953-68, ptnr., 1968-86, of counsel, 1986—. Author: (with others) Drafting Agreements for the Sale of Businesses, 1971, Term Loan Handbook, 1983. Bd. govs. Town Hall of Calif., Los Angeles, 1974—, sec., 1977, v.p., 1978-79, pres., 1984, chmn. sect. on legis. and adminstrn. of justice, 1968-70, pres. Town Hall West, 1975, mem. adv. bd. 1973—; bd. dirs. Hist. Soc. So. Calif., 1976-82, pres., 1980-81. Mem. ABA (com. on devels. in bus. financing, com. state regulation of securities, com. corp. law and acctg., com. employee benefits and exec. compensation of sect corp. banking and bus. law.), Calif. Bar Assn., Los Angeles County Bar Assn. (chmn. com. Law Day 1968, exec. com. comml. law sect. 1974-78, exec. com. corp. law sect. 1975-86), Nat. Assn. Bond Lawyers, Phi Beta Kappa. Presbyterian (elder). General corporate, Municipal bonds. Home: 1637 Valley View Rd Glendale CA 91202 Office: O'Melveny & Myers 400 S Hope St Los Angeles CA 90071

RICHARDSON, ELLIOT LEE, lawyer; b. Boston, July 20, 1920; s. Edward P. and Clara (Shattuck) R.; m. Anne F. Hazard, Aug. 2, 1952; children: Henry, Nancy, Michael. A.B. cum laude, Harvard U., 1941, LL.B. cum laude, 1947, LL.D., 1971; also other hon. degrees. Bar: Mass. 1949, D.C. 1980. Law clk. to Judge Learned Hand, U.S. Ct. Appeals, 2d Circuit, N.Y., 1947-48, Supreme Ct. Justice Felix Frankfurter, 1948-49; asso. firm Ropes, Gray, Best, Coolidge & Rugg, Boston, 1949-53, 55-56; asst. to Mass. Senator Leverett Saltonstall, 1953-54; acting counsel to Mass. Gov. Christian A. Herter, 1956; asst. sec. legislation HEW, 1957-59; U.S. atty. for Mass. 1959-61, spl. asst. to atty. gen. U.S., 1961; ptnr. firm Ropes & Gray, Boston, 1961-64; lt. gov. Mass. 1965-67, atty. gen. Mass., 1967-69, under sec. state, 1969-70; sec. HEW, 1970-73; sec. def. 1973, atty. gen. U.S., 1973; fellow Woodrow Wilson Internat. Center for Scholars, Washington, 1974-75; ambassador to Ct. of St. James's, London, 1975-76; sec. commerce 1976-77; ambassador-at-large, spl. rep. of pres. to Law of the Sea Conf., Washington, 1977-80; sr. resident partner Milbank, Tweed, Hadley & McCloy, Washington, 1980—; Bd. dirs. John Hancock Mutual Life Ins. Co., Furia, Samuels Co.; mem. adv. bd. Ctr. for Oceans Law and Policy; former mem. adv. com. Mass. Council for Pub. Schs.; mem. environ. adv. bd. Riedel Environ. Tech. Active Work in Am. Inst., Am. Friends Univ. Edinburgh; chmn. Hitachi Found; bd. dirs. Am. Ditchley Found.; trustee Roger Tory Peterson Inst., Urban Inst., U.S. Council on Internat. Bus.; mem. environ. adv. bd. Riedel Environ. Tech., Comptroller Gen.'s Cons. Panel; former trustee Radcliffe Coll., Mass. Gen. Hosp.; former pres. World Affairs Council, Boston; former bd. dirs. Salzburg Seminar in Am. Studies, Mass. Bay United Fund, United Community Services of Met. Boston. Served to 1st lt. inf. U.S. Army, 1942-45, ETO. Decorated Bronze Star, Purple Heart with oak leaf cluster; recipient Jefferson award Am. Inst. Public Service, 1974; Thomas Hart Benton award Kansas City Art Inst., 1976; Emory R. Buckner medal Fed. Bar Council, 1977; Penn Club award, 1977; Albert Lasker Spl. Public Service award, 1978, Neptune award, 1984. Mem. UN Assn. of U.S. (chmn.), Am. Acad. Diplomacy (bd. dirs.). Office: Milbank Tweed Hadley & McCloy 1825 Eye St NW Washington DC 20006

RICHARDSON, GREG DREXEL, lawyer; b. Edgerton, Wis., Dec. 22, 1955; s. Hubert Drexel and Kathryn Elizabeth (Kobs) R.; m. Judy Lee Gross, May 21, 1983. BA in Polit. Sci., U. Wis., Whitewater, 1978; JD, U. Wis., Madison, 1981, MA in Pub. Policy and Adminstrn., 1985. Bar: Wis. 1981, U.S. Dist. Ct. (we. dist.) Wis. 1981. Asst. dist. atty. Grant County, Lancaster, Wis., 1981-83, Winnebago County, Oshkosh, Wis., 1983-84; assoc. legal counsel InterVarsity Christian Fellowship, Madison, 1986-87; regional dir. Justice Fellowship, Washington, 1987—. Mem. Evangelicals for Social Action, Amnesty Internat. Mem. ABA, Wis. Bar Assn., Christian Legal Soc., Am. Soc. Pub. Adminstrn., Assn. Pub. Justice, Western Govtl. Research Assn., Phi Kappa Phi, Phi Alpha Theta. Democrat. Baptist. Avocations: reading, history, films, walking, board games. Criminal, Administrative and regulatory, Legislative. Office: Justice Fellowship PO Box 17181 Washington DC 20041

RICHARDSON, JOHN CARROLL, lawyer; b. Mobile, Ala., May 3, 1932; s. Robert Felder and Louise (Simmons) R.; m. Cicely Tomlinson, July 27, 1961; children—Nancy Louise, Robert Felder III, Leslie. B.A., Tulane U., 1954; LL.B. cum laude, Harvard U., 1960. Bar: Colo. 1960, N.Y. 1965, D.C. 1972. Assoc. Holland & Hart, Denver, 1960-64; legal v.p. Hoover Worldwide Corp., N.Y.C., 1964-69; v.p., gen. counsel Continental Investment Corp., Boston, 1969-70; dep. tax legis. counsel U.S. Treasury Dept., Washington, 1970-71, tax legis. counsel, 1972-73; ptnr. Brown, Wood, Ivey, Mitchell & Petty, N.Y.C., 1973-79, LeBoeuf, Lamb, Leiby & MacRae, N.Y.C., 1979—. Served to lt. comdr. USN, 1954-57. Mem. ABA (vice chmn. com. adminstrv. practice 1982-84, chmn. 1984-86), N.Y. State Bar Assn. (exec. com. tax sect. 1975-84), D.C. Bar Assn. Club: N.Y. Athletic. Corporate taxation. Office: LeBoeuf Lamb Leiby & MacRae 520 Madison Ave New York NY 10022

RICHARDSON, JOSEPH ABLETT, JR., banker; b. Pitts., May 23, 1928; s. Joseph A. and Genevieve (Loveless) R.; m. Sally Straessley, June 23, 1950; children—Dean F., Amy Richardson Howcroft, Christopher J. B.E., Yale U., 1948; J.D., U. Pitts., 1952. Bar: Pa. 1953, U.S. Supreme Ct., 1966. Vice pres. Pitts. Nat. Bank, 1961-77, v.p., resident atty., asst. sec., 1976-77, sr. v.p., gen. counsel, sec., 1977—; sr. v.p., gen. counsel, sec. PNC Fin. Corp., Pitts., 1983—, Pitts. Nat. Corp., 1977-82. Mem. Am. Soc. Corp. Secs. Administrative and regulatory, Banking, General corporate. Office: PNC Fin Corp Pittsburgh Nat Bldg 5th Ave and Wood St Pittsburgh PA 15265

RICHARDSON, KAREN LEROHL, lawyer; b. Albuquerque, Sept. 15, 1950; d. John Kenneth and Ann (Castleman) Lawrence Lerohl; B.A., Coll. William and Mary, 1972; J.D., Am. U., 1978; postgrad. George Washington U., 1980-82. Admitted to Va. bar, 1979, U.S. Ct. Claims bar, 1980, U.S. Supreme Ct., 1982, U.S. Ct. Appeals (4th cir.) 1982, Calif., 1984; supr. law dept. Prudential Ins. Co., Washington, 1972-74; law clk. Arnold and Porter, Washington, 1975-78; atty. Def. Logistics Agy., Alexandria, Va., 1978-80; atty. Office Sec. Def., Washington, 1980-84; counsel TRW Inc., 1984—. V.p. William and Mary Alumni Soc., Los Angeles chpt. Recipient Presidential Sports award, 1980; Disting. Youth award Dept. Army, 1976. Mem. Am. Bar Assn. (dep. chmn., mem. subcom. 1980—), Fed. Bar Assn., Va. Bar Assn., ACLU, Am. Corp. Counsel Assn., Nat. Contract Mgmt. Assn., Calif. Bar Assn., Los Angeles County Bar Assn., William and Mary Alumni Assn. (v.p. greater Los Angeles chpt.) Nat. Women's Polit. Caucus , others. Club: Cameron Station Tennis (pres. 1980). General corporate, Government contracts and claims. Office: TRW Inc One Space Park Redondo Beach CA 90278

RICHARDSON, RANDOLF EMRYS, lawyer; b. Wheeling, W.Va., Aug. 12, 1951; s. Dolf Birkenhauer and Judy (Rose) R.; m. Cynthia Kaye Rhodes, July 15, 1972; children: Briana Rachelle, Hilary Nicole, Zachary Dolf, Thaddeus Emrys. AA in Biology, Potomac State Coll., 1971; BA in Biology, W.Va. U., 1973, BS in Psychology, 1974, JD, 1980. Bar: W.Va. 1980, U.S. Dist. Ct. (no. dist.) W.Va. 1980, U.S. Ct. Appeals 1980. Assoc. Galbraith, Seibert & Kasserman, Wheeling, 1980-83; ptnr. Seibert, Kasserman, Farnsworth, Gillenwater, Glauser & Richardson, Wheeling, 1983—; bankruptcy trustee No. Dist. W.Va., Wheeling, 1983-85. Mem. counsel Christ Luth. Ch., Wheeling, 1980—, trustee Mozart Improvement Assn., Wheeling, 1980—; ch. organist, Wheeling, 1983-85. Mem. ABA, W.Va. State Bar Assn. (exec. bd. mem. Young Lawyers sect. 1980-86), Assn. Trial Lawyers Am., W.Va. Trial Lawyers Assn., Civitans (bd. dirs. 1986—). Democrat. Avocations: wood carving, music. Bankruptcy, Federal civil litigation, State civil litigation. Home: 64 E Frazier Ave Wheeling WV 26003 Office: Seibert Kasserman et al PO Box 311 1217 Chapline St Wheeling WV 26003

RICHARDSON, ROBERT OWEN, lawyer; b. Gallatin, Mo., Sept. 7, 1922; s. Denver Oscar and Opal (Wellman) R.; m. Carroll Sparks, July 7, 1951 (div.); children—Robert Steven, Linda Colleen; m. 2d, Viola Kapantais Wempe, Dec. 22, 1977. B.S. in Physics, Drury Coll., 1946; LL.B., George Washington U., 1954, J.D., 1968; M.S., Fla. Inst. Tech., 1977. Bar: U.S. Dist. Ct. (D.C.) 1954, U.S. Patent Office 1954, U.S. Ct. Customs and Patent Appeals 1958, Calif. 1958, N.H. 1961, Iowa 1976, U.S. Supreme Ct. 1961, Can. Patent Office, 1962, U.S. Ct. Appeals (fed. cir.) 1982. Patent examiner U.S. Patent Office, Washington, 1949-54; patent atty. Navy Electronics Lab., San Diego, 1954-56, Gen. Dynamics, San Diego, 1956-60; chief patent counsel Sanders Assocs., Nashua, N.H., 1960-62; patent atty. TRW, Canoga Park, Calif., 1963-64, McDonnell Douglas, Santa Monica, Calif., 1964-75; patent counsel U.S. Army Armament Munitions Chem. Command, Rock Island, Ill., 1975-85; patent arbitrator Am. Arbitration Assn., 1984—; judge pro tem Los Angeles Mcpl. Ct., 1967-68. Author: How To Get Your Own Patent, 1981. Democratic nominee for Congress from Mo. 6th Dist., 1951. Served to lt. comdr. USNR, 1942-73. Mem. Govt. Patent Lawyer's Assn., Am. Patent Law Assn., Patent Law Assn. San Diego, Patent Law Assn. Los Angeles, Patent Law Assn. Boston, Patent Law Assn. Iowa. Lodges: Masons, Shriners. Patent, Trademark and copyright, Patent Arbitration.

RICHARDSON, ROBERT WOODROW, lawyer; b. Evart, Mich., May 3, 1917; s. Judson E. and Laura M. (McConnel) R.; m. Elizabeth Janet O'Hara, July 1, 1944; children: Robert, Scott, Thomas. AB, Mich. State U., 1940; JD, U. Mich., 1946. Bar: Mich. 1946, U.S. Dist. Ct. (we. dist.) Mich. 1947. Ptnr. Law, Weathers & Richardson, Grand Rapids, 1951—. Mayor City of East Grand Rapids, Mich., 1957-63, city atty., 1963-86; airport atty. Kent County, Grand Rapids, Mich., 1960—. Served to 1st lt. USAF, 1941-45, NATOUSA. Decorated Air medal with six oak leaf clusters. Mem. Mich. Bar Assn., Grand Rapids Bar Assn. (pres. 1974-75). Republican. Episcopalian. Clubs: University, Kent Country (Grand Rapids). Lodge: Masons (32 degree). Avocation: sports. Real property, Local government, Estate planning. Home: 2136 Wilshire S E Grand Rapids MI 49506 Office: Law Weathers & Richardson 500 Union Bank Bldg Grand Rapids MI 49503

RICHARDSON, SALLY M., lawyer; b. Houston, June 10, 1947; s. Marion Byrne and Willie Grace (Dugas) R. BBA in Fin., U. Houston, 1970, MBA in Fin., 1974; MA in Econs., Rice U., 1978; JD, U. Miami, 1981. Bar: Fla. 1981, U.S. Dist. Ct. (so. dist.) Fla. 1981, U.S. Ct. Appeals (11th cir.) 1981, U.S. Dist. Ct. (mid. dist.) Fla. 1982. Research analyst Fayez Sarofim & Co., Houston, 1970-71; portfolio mgr. Am. Gen., Houston, 1971-74; instr U. Houston and Rice U., 1974-78; assoc. Shutts & Bowen, Miami, Fla., 1980—. Agy. relations panel United Way, 1984—. John M. Olin fellow, 1978-81. Mem. ABA, Fla. Bar Assn., Dade County Bar Assn. (bd. dirs. 1984—). Avocations: sailing, tennis. Federal civil litigation, State civil litigation, Construction. Office: Shutts & Bowen 1500 Edward Ball Bldg Miami FL 33133

RICHARDSON, SCHUYLER HARRIS, III, lawyer; b. Birmingham, Ala., June 9, 1952; s. Patrick William Richardson and Martha Alice (Holliman) Simms; m. Cynthia Otwell Bagby, Aug. 16, 1974; children: Patrick William II, Frances Celeste. BA, Davidson Coll., 1974; JD, U. Ala., Tuscaloosa, 1977. Bar: Ala., 1977, U.S. Dist. Ct. (no. dist.) Ala. 1977, U.S. Ct. Appeals (5th cir.) 1979, U.S. Supreme Ct. 1980, U.S. Ct. Appeals (11th cir.) 1981. Law clerk to judge U.S. Dist. Ct. (no. dist.) Ala., Birmingham, 1977-78; ptnr. Bell, Richardson, Herrington, Sparkman & Shepard, P.A., Huntsville, Ala., 1978—. Profl. div. chmn. Madison County United Way, Huntsville, 1982; fundraiser Huntsville Hosp. Found., 1984. Mem. ABA, Nat. Assn. R.R. Trial Counsel, Ala. Bar Assn., Ala. Def. Lawyers Assn., Madison County Bar Assn. Democrat. Methodist. Lodge: Rotary. Federal civil litigation, State civil litigation, Insurance. Home: 4026 Dunsmore St Huntsville AL 35802 Office: Bell Richardson et al PO Box 2008 116 S Jefferson St Huntsville AL 35804

RICHARDSON, SCOTT NEIL, lawyer; b. Trenton, N.J., June 2, 1953; s. Donald Wilfred and Jane Alger (Jardine) R.; m. Leslie Ann Uberman, Dec. 23, 1978; children: Adam Jeffrey and Brendan Paul (twins). BA, U. Fla., 1975, JD, 1978. Bar: Fla. 1978, U.D. Dist. Ct. (so. dist.) Fla. 1981, U.S. Ct. Appeals (5th and 11th cirs.) 1981. Asst. state atty. West Palm Beach, Fla., 1978-82; assoc. Reid & Ricca P.A., West Palm Beach, 1982-85; ptnr. Atterbury, Goldberger & Richardson P.A., West Palm Beach, 1986—. Mem. Palm Beach County Bar Assn., Assn. Trial Lawyers Am., Nat. Assn. Criminal Def. Lawyers. Criminal, Personal injury, State civil litigation. Office: Atterbury Goldberger & Richardson 1655 Palm Beach Lakes Blvd Suite 802 West Palm Beach FL 33401

RICHARDSON, WILLIAM F., lawyer; b. Ill., Apr. 20, 1948; s. Donald Richardson and Dorothy Warren; m. Barbara A. Szot (div. 1983). BS, U. Ill., 1970, JD, 1973. Bar: Ill. 1973. Ptnr. Peterson, Ross, Schloerb & Seidel, Chgo., 1973—. Mem. ABA. Construction, Insurance, Bankruptcy. Office: Peterson Ross Schloerb & Seidel 200 E Randolph Dr Chicago IL 60601

RICHER, ALAN BRIAN, lawyer; b. Newark, Feb. 15, 1954; s. Harvey H. and Ethel L. (Lazarowitz) R.; m. Jessica Ellen Locke, Sept. 1, 1985. BS in Mgmt. summa cum laude, Syracuse U., 1976, JD magna cum laude, 1979. Bar: Tex. 1979, U.S. Tax Ct. 1980, U.S. Dist. Ct. (so. dist.) Tex. 1980, U.S. Ct. Appeals (5th cir.) 1980, N.J. 1981, U.S. Dist. Ct. N.J. 1981, U.S. Ct. Claims 1981, U.S. Ct. Appeals (Fed. cir.) 1982, U.S. Supreme Ct. 1982. Tax atty. Exxon Co. USA, Houston, Tex., 1979-81, Exxon Chem. Co., Darien, Conn., 1981-84; tax counsel Data Gen. Corp., Westboro, Mass., 1984—. Superior Academic scholar N.Y. State Soc. CPA's,1976. Mem. ABA, N.J. Bar Assn., Tex. Bar Assn., Order of Coif, Justinian Honor Soc., Beta Alpha Psi. Jewish. Avocations: antiques, jazz, popular music, sports. Corporate taxation, Estate taxation, Personal income taxation. Office: Data Gen Corp 4400 Computer Dr Westboro MA 01580

RICHERT, JOHN LOUIS, judge; b. Kankakee, Ill., May 5, 1931; s. Joseph John and Janet (Wimmer) R.; m. Barbara Blake Richert, Nov. 13, 1954; children: James, Ann, Mary, Barbara, Jane, Jacqueline, John, Celeste, Kathleen, Susan, Heather. AB, St. Josephs Coll., Rensselaer, Ind., 1953; JD, Valparaiso U., 1960. Bar: Ind., U.S. Dist. Ct. (no. dist.) 1960, U.S. Dist. Ct. (so. dist.) 1960. Justice of the peace County of Pulaski, Ind., 1958-60; sole practice Winamac, Ind., 1960-82; judge 59th Jud. Cir. Ind., 1983—; instr. bus. law St. Joseph's Coll., 1960-63; pros. atty. 59th Judicial Circuit Ind., 1963-66; govt. appeal agent, advisor of registrants Selective Service System, 1969-75; atty. County of Pulaski, 1977-80; local counsel Pinto case Ford Motor Co. Served with U.S. Army, 1953-55. Mem. Winamac C. of C., Ind. Bar Assn., Starke-Pulaski County Bar Assn., Ind. State Judges Assn. Roman Catholic. Lodge: K.C. Judicial administration. Home: RR #1 Winamac IN 46996 Office: Courthouse Winamac IN 46996

RICHESON, HUGH ANTHONY, JR., lawyer; b. Aberdeen, Md., Apr. 22, 1947; s. Hugh Anthony Sr. and Mary Evelyn (Burford) R.; m. Melissa Anne Baum, Apr. 4, 1970; children: Hugh Anthony III, Heidi E., Holly K., Hagin G., Herald Joshua. BBA, U. Richmond, 1969; JD, U. Fla., 1973. Bar: Fla. 1974, U.S. Dist. Ct. (mid. dist.) Fla. 1975. Assoc. Bryant, Dickens, Rumph, Franson & Miller, Jacksonville, Fla., 1974-76, ptnr., 1977; sole practice Orange Park, Fla., 1977-82; ptnr. Smith, Hallowes & Richeson, Orange Park, 1982-83; sole practice Palm Harbor, Fla., 1984—. Pres. Full Gospel Bus. Men's Fellowship Internat., Orange Park, 1983-84, Palm Harbor, 1985—; chmn. North Pinellas (Fla.) Pregnancy Ctr., Palm Harbor, 1986. Mem. Clay County Bar Assn. (pres. 1981-82), Clearwater Bar Assn., Assn. Trial Lawyers Am., Acad. Fla. Trial Lawyers, Fla. Council Bar Assn. Pres.'s (life), Christian Legal Soc., Phi Delta Phi. Republican. Mem. Christian Ch. Personal injury, State civil litigation, General corporate. Home: 2463 Indian Trail E Palm Harbor FL 33563 Office: 1209 US Hwy 19 N Suite 251 PO Box 99 Palm Harbor FL 34682

RICHEY, CHARLES ROBERT, U.S. judge; b. Logan County, Ohio, Oct. 16, 1923; s. Paul Dorrence and Mariam (Blaine) R.; m. Agnes Mardelle White, Mar. 25, 1950; children: Charles Robert Jr., William Paul. A.B., Ohio Wesleyan U., 1945; LL.B., Case-Western Res. U., 1948. Bar: Ohio 1949, D.C. 1951, U.S. Supreme Ct. 1952, Md. 1964. Legis. counsel former Congresswoman Frances P. Bolton, Ohio, 1948-49; practice in Washington and Chevy Chase, Md., 1950-71; founding partner firm Richey & Clancy, Chevy Chase, 1964-71; gen. counsel Md. Pub. Service Commn., 1967-71; judge U.S. Dist. Ct. D.C., 1971—; sat by designation as mem. U.S. Ct. Appeals for D.C., 1972-75, 77-85; mem. Temporary Emergency Ct. Appeals, 1983-84, Commn. on Adminstrn. Probation System, Jud. Conf. U.S., 1984—; lectr. speech, debate coach Am. U., 1954-55; adj. prof. trial practice Georgetown Law Center, 1976; mem. adv. bd. CLE Program, from 1979; mem. faculty Nat. Coll. State Judiciary, 1973-75, Fed. Jud. Center, from 1977, U.S. Atty. Gen.'s Advocacy Inst., Washington, 1974—; spl. counsel, councilmanic redistricting Montgomery County Govt., 1965-66; vice chmn. Charter Revision Commn., 1967-68; frequent lectr. ABA, ALI-ABA, PLI, ATLA ann. meeting, confs., CLE and civic groups throughout U.S. Contbr. articles to profl. jours. Gen. counsel Boys' Clubs Greater Washington, 1969-71, bd. dirs., 1957-71; affiliate mem. D.C. Urban Renewal Council and Citizens Housing Commn., 1961-64; chmn. parents assn. Sidwell Friends Sch., Washington, 1968-70; mem. Montgomery County Bd. Appeals, 1965-67, chmn., 1966-67; trustee Immaculata Coll., Washington, 1970-73, Suburban Hosp., Bethesda, Md., 1967-71. Recipient Outstanding and Dedicated Public Service award Montgomery County, Md., 1966, 68; Disting. Citizenship award Gov. Md., 1971; Annual award of merit Adminstrv. Law Judges of U.S., 1979; Dedicated Pub. Service Citation Montgomery County, 1966-68. Fellow Am. Bar Found.; mem. ABA (chmn. com. on alcohol and drug abuse 1973-76, chmn. com. on sentencing probation and parole 1976-77, mem. council criminal justice sect. 1976-80, chmn. nat. adv. com. Project ADVOCATE 1976-80, chmn. nat. conf. fed. trial judges 1980-81, council jud. adminstrv. div. 1980-81, ho. of dels. 1981-85), D.C. Bar Assn., Md. Bar Assn., Am. Judicature Soc., Assn. Trial Lawyers Am. (faculty Nat. Coll. Advocacy 1975-77, Outstanding Fed. Trial Judge award 1979), Nat. Conf. Fed. Trial Judges (chmn. 1980-81, officer, mem. exec. com. from 1975), Supreme Ct. Hist. Soc. (founding mem.), Soc. of Benchers of Case Western Res. U. Sch. Law, Omicron Delta Kappa, Delta Sigma Rho, Pi Delta Epsilon, Phi Delta Phi, Phi Gamma Delta (gen. counsel 1960-63). Methodist. Clubs: Masons (Washington) (33 deg.), Nat. Lawyers (Washington), Univ. (Washington). Office: US Dist Court 3d and Constitution Ave Washington DC 20001 •

RICHMAN, ALAN ELLIOTT, lawyer; b. Norwalk, Conn., Sept. 28, 1949; s. Daniel Powell and Louise (Woolf) R.; m. Kathryn Louise Hawks, July 15, 1978; children: Aaron Powell, Anne Ballinger. BA with distinction, U. Wis., 1971; JD, U. Denver, 1974. Bar: Colo. 1975, U.S. Dist. Ct. Colo. 1975, U.S. Ct. Appeals (10th cir.) 1982. Assoc. Hoffman, McDermott & Hoffman, Denver, 1975-78; sole practice Denver, 1978-79; assoc. legal counsel Regional Transp. Dist., Denver, 1979-83; assoc. Hansen & Breit P.C., Denver, 1983-84, ptnr., 1984; ptnr. Breit, Best, Richman & Bosch P.C., Denver, 1985—; lectr., instr. various colls., seminars and assns., 1976-85. Mem. Colo. Bar Assn. (chmn. interprofl. com. 1985—), Denver Bar Assn. (jud. adminstrn. com.). Personal injury, Construction, State civil litigation. Home: 5240 Lakeshore Dr Littleton CO 80123 Office: Breit Best Richman & Bosch 1512 Larimer St Suite 900 Denver CO 80202

RICHMAN, FREDERICK ALEXANDER, lawyer; b. Pasadena, Calif., Oct. 18, 1945; s. Matthew and Ruth (Beckman) R.; m. Judith R., Oct. 24, 1971; children—Robert, David. A.B. cum laude, Harvard U., 1967; J.D. cum laude, NYU, 1970. Bar: Calif. 1971. Assoc. firm O'Melveny & Myers, Los Angeles, 1970-77; ptnr. O'Melveny & Myers, 1978—. Mem. ABA, Calif. Bar Assn., Los Angeles County Bar Assn. Corporate taxation, State and local taxation, Personal income taxation. Office: O'Melveny & Myers Suite 600 1800 Century Park E Los Angeles CA 90067

RICHMAN, MARC HERSH, lawyer; b. Dallas, Apr. 17, 1945; s. Victor William and Maryon W. (Weinberger) R.; m. Ann Bornstein, July 13, 1975; children—Alisa, Jennifer, Mollie. B.A., So. Meth. U., 1967, J.D., 1970. Bar: Tex. 1970, U.S. Dist. Ct. (no. and so. dists.) Tex. 1970, U.S. Ct. Appeals (5th cir.) 1975, U.S. Dist. Ct. (we. dist.) Tex. 1978, U.S. Tax Ct. 1980, U.S. Ct. Appeals (11th cir.) 1981, U.S. Dist. Ct. (we. dist.) Ark. 1983, U.S. Supreme Ct. 1986; cert. peace officer, Tex. Prin., owner Marc Hersh Richman, Dallas, 1974—; instr. Dallas Sheriff Acad.; lectr. jr. colls., schs. on law enforcement, and the law; Atty. Dallas County Sheriff's Assn., 1974—, Constables and Sheriff of Dallas County, 1975—, Balch Springs Police Assn., 1980—, Waxahachie Police Assn., 1986—; city atty., Segoville, Tex., 1981—. Mem. Nat. Assn. Criminal Def. Attys., Tex. Criminal Def. Atty. Assn., Tex. Trial Lawyers Assn., ABA, Tex. Bar Assn., Dallas Bar Assn., Tex. Assn. City Attys. Clubs: Sports Car Club Am., Nat. Hot Rod Assn., Am. Hot Rod Assn. Federal civil litigation, State civil litigation, Criminal. Office: 306 Record St Dallas TX 75202

RICHMAN, SHELDON BARNETT, lawyer, author; b. N.Y.C., Mar. 1, 1944; s. Harry L. and Jean B. (Weinstein) R.; m. Arleen B. Friedel, May 26, 1970. B.A., CUNY, 1965, J.D., Bklyn. Law Sch., 1968. Bar: N.Y. 1968. Ptnr. Zik & Richman, N.Y.C., 1969-70; adminstrv. asst. Empresa Falconi, Quito, Ecuador, S.Am., 1970-71; legal editor Securities Regulation & Law Report, Bur. Nat. Affairs, Inc., Washington, 1972-75, mng. editor Antitrust & Trade Regulation Report, 1975—; lectr. on continuing legal edn.; pres. dir. River Farms Conservancy, 1982—; Mem. ABA (antitrust law, litigation and corp., banking and bus. law sects.), Internat. Bar Assn. (sect. bus. law), Nat. Health Lawyers Assn., D.C. Bar Assn., Anti-Trust Inst. (bd. dirs. 1976—). Lodges: F&AM (master 1987—), Tall Cedars of Lebanon. Antitrust, Ad-

ministrative and regulatory, Private international. Home: 2741 Carter Farm Ct Alexandria VA 22306 Office: 1231 25th St NW Washington DC 20037

RICHMAN, STEPHEN CHARLES, lawyer; b. Newark, Nov. 13, 1943; s. Abraham and Sylvia (Weissman) R.; m. Dinah Ellenberg, Aug. 25, 1968; children—Alex, Marni. B.S. in Bus. Adminstrn., SUNY-Buffalo, 1965; J.D., George Washington U., 1968. Bar: D.C. 1968, Pa. 1972, N.Y. 1983. Field atty. NLRB, 1969-72; assoc. Wilderman, Markowitz & Kirschner, 1972-73; assoc., then ptnr. Markowitz & Kirschner, 1973-79; ptnr. Markowitz & Richman, Phila., 1979—; former instr. Pa. State U. Mem. ABA, Pa. Bar Assn., Phila. Bar Assn. Labor.

RICHMAN, STEPHEN IAN, lawyer; b. Washington, Pa., Mar. 26, 1933; m. Audrey May Gefsky. B.S., Northwestern U., 1954; J.D., U. Pa., 1957. Bar: Pa. 1958. ptnr. Ceisler, Richman, Sweet Law Firm, P.A., Washington. lectr. W.Va. U. Med. Ctr., Grand Rounds, 1984. Mem. Am. Coll. Chest Physicians, Pa. Thoracic Soc., Am. Thoracic Soc., The Energy Bur., Coll. of Pathologists, Allegheny County Health Dept., Am. Pub. Health Assn., Indsl. Health Assn., Self-Insurers Assn., Am. Iron and Steel Inst., Can. Thoracic Soc., . Author: Meaning of Impairment and Disability, Chest, 1980, Legal Aspects for the Pathologist, in Pathology of Occupational and Environmental Lung Disease, 1987.f Labor and the Congress, 1986, Medicolegal Aspects of Asbestos for Pathologists, Arch. Pathology and Laboratory Medicine, 1983, Legal Aspects for the Pathologist, In Pathology of Occupational and Environmental Lung Disease, 1987. Mem. legal com. Indsl. Health Found., Pitts. Mem. ABA (workers compensation and employers liability law com.), Pa. Bar Assn. (governing council worker's compensation sect.), Washington County (Pa.) Bar Assn., Assn. Trial Lawyers Am., Pa. Chamber Bus. and Industry (compensation com.). Workers' compensation, Personal injury, Federal civil litigation. Home: 820 E Beau St Washington PA 15301 Office: Suite 200 Washington Trust Bldg Washington PA 15301

RICHMOND, DIANA, lawyer; b. Milw., July 5, 1946; d. William Lee and Laurel Jean (Bohlmann) Schultz; m. Gerald E. Ragan, Jan. 17, 1981; 1 child, Kavana. B.A., U. Chgo., 1967; J.D. with highest honors, Golden Gate U., 1973. Bar: Calif. 1973, U.S. Dist. Ct. (no. dist.) Calif. 1973. Assoc. Stern, Stotter & O'Brien, San Francisco, 1973-77; sole practice, San Francisco, 1977-80, 83—; ptnr. Richmond & Kadushin, San Francisco, 1981-82; chmn. exec. com. family law sect. Calif. State Bar, 1984-85. Author: Marital Termination Settlements, supplements, 1978-85. Editorial cons. Calif. Family Law Practice, 1984-86. Recipient Outstanding Alumna award Golden Gate U. Sch. of Law, 1985. Fellow Am. Acad. Matrimonial Lawyers (sec. no. Calif. chpt. 1983-85), Barrister Club San Francisco (pres. 1979), Bar Assn. San Francisco (bd. dirs. 1983-84, cert. of merit 1977). Democrat. Family and matrimonial. Office: 100 The Embarcadero San Francisco CA 94105

RICHMOND, JAMES G., lawyer; b. 1944. BA, JD, Ind. U. Bar: Ind. 1969. U.S. atty. no. dist. State of Ind., Hammond. Office: 312 Fed Bldg 507 State St Hammond IN 46320 *

RICHMOND, ROBERT LAWRENCE, lawyer; b. St. Petersburg, Fla., Sept. 30, 1943; s. Chester A. and Barbara (O'Connell) R.; children—Kristen, Meghan, Alyson. A.B., Georgetown U., 1965; J.D., U. Oreg., 1970. Bar: Oreg. 1970, Alaska 1970, U.S. Dist. Ct. Alaska 1970, U.S. Ct. Appeals (9th cir.) 1971. Ptnr. Richmond, Willoughby, & Willard, Anchorage, 1975-81; sr. ptnr. Richmond & Quinn, 1981-84, Richmond & Quinn, Anchorage, 1984—. Bd. dirs. Alaska Treatment Ctr., Anchorage, Girl's Club Alaska, Anchorage. Served to capt. U.S. Army, 1965-67. Speak Up winner Alaska Jaycees, 1971. Mem. Alaska Bar Assn., Oreg. Bar Assn., ABA, U.S. Maritime Law Assn. (proctor in admiralty). Republican. Roman Catholic. Club: Commonwealth North (Anchorage). State civil litigation, Admiralty, Federal civil litigation. Address: 135 Christensen Dr Anchorage AK 99501

RICHMOND, WILLIAM FREDERICK, JR., lawyer; b. Albany, Oreg., June 7, 1943; s. William Frederick and Mary Jane (McQuilkin) R.; m. Carolyn Jean Wheatley, Mar. 3, 1973; children: Frederick Scott, Christina Jean. BBA, Marshall U., 1967; JD, U. Tenn., 1972. Bar: W.Va. 1972. Sole practice Beckley, W.Va., 1972-73; assoc. Bowers, Hodson, Henderson, Beckley, W.Va., 1974-76; ptnr. Bowers, Hodson, Henderson & Richmond, Beckley, W.Va., 1976-84, Abriams, Byron, Henderson & Richmond, Beckley, W.Va., 1984—. Counsel Beckley Human Rights Commn., 1972-80, chmn. 1979-80; founding counsel Beckley Contact Teleministries Inc., 1976-78; founding counsel, sec. Beckley-Raleigh County Policeman-Fireman Relief Fund, 1982—. Mem. ABA, Am. Judicature Soc., Raleigh County Bar Assn., W.Va. State Bar Assn., W.Va. Def. Lawyers Assn., Def. Research Inst., Woodrow Wilson High Sch. Alumni Assn. Inc. (pres. 1982—). Republican. Presbyterian. Club: Black Knight Country (bd. dirs. 1983—, pres. 1985—). Lodges: Moose, Elks. Avocations: swimming, tennis, photography, hiking. Workers' compensation, Insurance, General practice. Home: 117 Lee St Beckley WV 25801 Office: Abrams Byron Henderson & Richmond PO Drawer W Beckley WV 25802

RICHMOND, WILLIAM PATRICK, lawyer; b. Cicero, Ill., Apr. 5, 1932; s. Edwin and Mary (Allgier) R.; m. Elizabeth A., Jan. 9, 1954 (div.); children: Stephen, Janet, Timothy. A.B., Albion Coll., 1954; J.D., U. Chgo., 1959. Bar: Ill. 1959, N.Y. 1985. Assoc. Sidley & Austin, Chgo., 1960-67, ptnr., 1967—. Served with U.S. Army, 1954-56. Fellow Am. Coll. Trial Lawyers; mem. Soc. Trial Lawyers, Chgo. Bar. Assn., Ill. State Bar Assn., ABA. Republican. Methodist. Clubs: Legal, Union League (Chgo.); Ruth Lake Country (Hinsdale, Ill.). Federal civil litigation, State civil litigation, Personal injury. Home: 1310 N Ritchie Ct Chicago IL 60610 Office: Sidley & Austin One First Nat Plaza Chicago IL 60603

RICHNER, ROBERT ANDREW, lawyer; b. Bedford, Ohio, May 19, 1951; s. Robert D. and Virginia R. (Stewart) R.; m. Lynn C. Spivey, Aug. 25, 1973; 1 child, R. Evan. BSBA, U. Akron, 1970-73; JD, Case Western Res. U., 1976. Bar: Ohio 1976, U.S. Dist. Ct. (no. dist.) Ohio 1980, U.S. Ct. Appeals (6th cir.) 1984. Ptnr. Law Offices Richner & Zahniser, Twinsburg, Ohio, 1977-84, prin., 1985—. Bd. dirs. No. Summit County Multi-Service Ctr., Macedonia, Ohio, 1980-83. Mem. ABA, Akron Bar Assn. Republican. Lutheran. Lodge: Rotary (pres. Twinsburg 1982, bd. dirs.). Avocations: jogging, antique collecting and restoring. Real property, Probate, Contracts commercial. Home: 9063 Charles Ct Twinsburg OH 44087 Office: Richner & Zahniser 2771 E Aurora Rd PO Box 104 Twinsburg OH 44087

RICHSTEIN, ABRAHAM RICHARD, lawyer; b. N.Y.C., Apr. 18, 1919; s. Morris and Ida (Stupp) R.; m. Rosalind Bauman; children: Eric, Jonathan. B.S., CCNY, 1939; J.D., Fordham U., 1942; LL.M. in Internat. Law, NYU, 1956; M.S. in Internat. Affairs, George Washington U., 1966; diploma, Command and Gen. Staff Coll., 1958, Nat. War Coll., 1966. Bar: N.Y. 1942, U.S. Supreme Ct 1956, D.C. 1977. Enlisted as pvt. U.S. Army, 1942, advanced through grades to col., 1966; served with Mil. Intelligence, U.S. 9th Army U.S. Army, Europe, 1944; legal staff U.S. War Crimes Commn. U.S. Army, Ger., 1946; staff officer UN Command (U.S. Army), Far East, 1951-53; mil. law judge (Hdqrs. First Army), 1954-57; chief internat. affairs Office Judge Adv., Hdqrs. US Army Europe U.S. Army, 1960-63; chief plans office Office Judge Adv. Gen., Washington, 1963-64; judge adv. Hdqtrs. U.S. Army Combat Devels. Command, 1964-66; ret. 1969; asst. gen. counsel AID, State Dept., 1969-81; gen. counsel ACDA, Washington, 1981-83; mem. faculty Nat. War Coll., 1966-68; joint staff planner, policy and planning directorate Joint Chiefs Staff, Washington, 1968-69. Editorial bd.: Mil. Law and Law of War Rev, 1960-63; Book rev. editor: Fordham Law Rev, 1941-42. Decorated Bronze Star.; recipient AID Superior Honor award, 1980, ACDA Meritorious Honor award, 1983. Mem. Am. Soc. Internat. Law. Home: 8713 Mary Lee Ln Annandale VA 22003

RICHTER, ALFRED GRAMMAR, JR., lawyer; b. Webster Groves, Mo., Oct. 9, 1950; s. Alfred G. and Olivia (Holton) R.; m. Elizabeth Morrow, Aug. 15, 1975; children: Whitney Elizabeth, Damon Michael. BA in History, St. Louis U., 1972; JD, Washington U., 1976. Bar: Mo. 1976, U.S. Dist. Ct. (ea. dist.) Mo. 1977, U.S. Ct. Appeals (8th cir.) 1977, Tex. 1986. Atty. Southwestern Bell Telephone, St. Louis, 1976-84; v.p., gen. atty. Southwestern Bell Telecom, St. Louis, 1984-86; gen. atty. Southwestern Bell Telephone, Austin, Tex., 1986—. Mem. ABA, Mo. Bar Assn., Tex. Bar Assn., Travis County Bar Assn., St. Louis Metro Bar Assn., Am. Assn. of Ind. Investors, Order of Coif, Phi Beta Kappa, Phi Alpha Theta, Etma Sigma Phi. General corporate, Public utilities, Administrative and regulatory. Office: Southwestern Bell Telephone 1616 Gundalupe Austin TX 78746

RICHTER, GARY STEPHEN, lawyer; b. N.Y.C., June 30, 1937; s. Maxwell and Estelle (Weiss) R.; m. Judith L. Hilton, Oct. 27, 1963. BS, NYU, 1957, JD, 1960. Bar: N.Y. 1961, U.S. Dist. Ct. (so. dist.) N.Y. 1961. Assoc. Groban & Rava, N.Y.C., 1961-65; ptnr. Novack & Richter, N.Y.C., 1965-68; assoc. counsel, asst. sec. Ward Foods Inc., N.Y.C., 1968-72; sr. staff counsel The Hertz Corp., N.Y.C., 1972-73; asst. gen. counsel Estee Lauder Inc., N.Y.C., 1973—. Research editor NYU Law Rev. 1958-60. Served with U.S. Army, 1961-62. Mem. N.Y. State Bar Assn., Beta Gamma Sigma. Democrat. Avocations: golf, painting, tennis, stand-up comedy. General corporate, Contracts commercial, Private international. Office: Estee Lauder Inc 767 Fifth Ave New York NY 10153

RICHTER, MARTIN EDWARD, lawyer, law educator; b. Baker, Oreg., June 3, 1947; s. Forrest Edward and Pauline (Hudgens) R.; m. Pamela Ann Mollenhauer, Oct. 28, 1967; children—Sean Martin, Shannon Michelle. B.B.A. in Mktg., North Tex. State U., 1973; J.D., St. Mary's Sch. Law, San Antonio, 1975. Bar: Tex. 1976, U.S. Ct. Appeals (5th and 11th cirs.) 1977, U.S. Dist. Ct. (no. and ea. dists.) Tex. 1985. Assoc. Rivera & Ritter, San Antonio, 1976-77, Rivera, Ritter & Richter, San Antonio, 1977-78, Law Office Martin E. Richter P.C. San Antonio, 1978-84; asst. gen. counsel State Bar Tex., Dallas, 1984—. Served with USMC, 1966-70. Mem. ABA, Assn. Trial Lawyers Am., Tex. Bar Assn. (state bar coll. 1986), Tex. Trial Lawyers Assn. Jurisprudence, Judicial administration, Administrative and regulatory. Office: Office Gen Counsel State Bar Tex 714 Jackson St Suite 850 Dallas TX 75202

RICHTER, TOBIN MARAIS, lawyer; b. Washington, Dec. 31, 1944; s. Vivian Craig and Leora Chapelle (Aultman) R.; m. Elizabeth Mills Dunlop, July 11, 1970; children: Ian, Lauren. B in City Planning, U. Va., 1967, JD, 1973. Bar: Ill. 1973, U.S. Dist. Ct. (no. dist.) Ill. 1973, U.S. Ct. Appeals (7th cir.) 1977, U.S. Supreme Ct. 1979. Assoc. Ross & Hardies, Chgo., 1973-80, ptnr., 1981-84; ptnr. Spindell, Kemp, Kimmons & Kimball, Chgo., 1984—; adj. instr. U. Wis., Osh Kosh, 1976. Co-author: Federal Land Use Regulation, 1977; contbr. articles to profl. jours. Legal counsel 44th Ward Community Zoning Bd., Chgo., 1980; v.p., Aux. Bd. Chgo. Architecture Found., 1983; pres., bd. dirs. Landmarks Preservation Council Ill., Chgo., 1986, Nat. Ctr. for Preservation Law, Washington, 1986—. Served to 1st lt. U.S. Army, 1968-70, Vietnam. Mem. ABA, Ill. Bar Assn. (judge Lincoln Writing awards contest 1982), Chgo. Bar Assn., Soc. Am. Mil. Engrs. (v.p. 1980, 84, 86), Am. Planning Assn. Clubs: Econ. (Chgo.); Dunham Woods (Wayne, Ill.). Avocations: tennis, pottery. Federal civil litigation, State civil litigation, Real property. Office: Spindell Kemp Kimmons & Kimball 135 S La Salle #1040 Chicago IL 60603

RICKER, WILLIAM HOWARD, lawyer; b. Galion, Ohio, July 26, 1955; s. Howard Leroy and Mary Margaret (McKenzie) R.; m. Sandra Sue Fischer, May 19, 1979; 1 child, Andrew Spence. BS, Miami U., 1977; postgrad., Pepperdine U., 1978-79; JD, U. Ariz., 1981. Bar: Ariz. 1981, U.S. Dist. Ct. Ariz. 1982, U.S. Ct. Appeals (9th cir.) 1982. Assoc. Haralson, Kinerk & Morey, P.C., Tucson, 1981—. Deacon St. Andrew's Presbyn. Ch., Tucson, 1985—. Mem. Assn. Trial Lawyers Am., So. Ariz. Trial Lawyers (bd. dirs. 1985—), Ariz. Trial Lawyers Assn., Am. Judicature Soc. Democrat. Avocations: golf, softball, reading. Personal injury, Insurance, State civil litigation. Home: 5160 N Grey Mountain Trail Tucson AZ 85715 Office: Haralson Kinerk & Morey PC 82 S Stone Ave Tucson AZ 85701

RICKERT, JEANNE MARTIN, lawyer; b. Cambridge, Mass., May 13, 1953; d. Robert Torrence and Margaret (Mutchler) Martin; m. Scott Edwin Rickert, Aug. 19, 1978. BA, Cornell U., 1975; JD, Case Western U., 1978. Bar: Ohio 1980, U.S. Dist. Ct. (no. dist.) Ohio 1980. Law clk. to presiding justice U.S. Dist. Ct. Ohio, Akron, 1978-80; assoc. Jones, Day, Reavis & Pogue, Cleve., 1980—. Mem. Ohio State Bar Assn. (corp. law com. 1985—). General corporate, Contracts commercial. Office: Jones Day Reavis & Pogue 1700 Huntington Bldg Cleveland OH 44115

RICKETTS, MICHAEL EDWARD, lawyer; b. Seattle, Aug. 10, 1954; s. Robert Neville and Hannah Mathilda (Peltola) R.; m. Kimberlee Don Bachman, Sept. 24, 1983; children: Whitney Catherine, Samuel Tyler. BA in Econs., Whitman Coll., 1976; JD, U. Wash., 1979. Bar: Wash. 1979, U.S. Dist. Ct. (we. dist.) Wash. 1979, U.S. Dist. Ct. (ea. dist.) Wash. 1980, U.S. Ct. Appeals (9th cir.) 1980, U.S. Dist. Ct. (so. dist.) Ala. 1980. Assoc. Foulds, Felker, Johnson & McHugh PS, Seattle, 1979-82; ptnr. Burns & Ricketts, Seattle, 1982-85; assoc. Foulds, Felker, Pierson & Ryder PS, Seattle, 1986—. Mem. ABA, Wash. Bar Assn., Seattle-King County Bar Assn. Unitarian. State civil litigation, Insurance. Home: 7007 36th Ave NE Seattle WA 98115 Office: Foulds Felker Pierson et al 505 Madison St Suite 300 Seattle WA 98104

RICKHOFF, THOMAS EMMET, judge; b. Farragut, Idaho, July 13, 1944; s. John and Lela Rickhoff; m. Carol Norene Mumford, Sept. 5, 1970; children: Hans, Erika, Franz, Fritz. BA, St. Mary's U., San Antonio; JD, St. Mary's U., 1969. Bar: Tex., U.S. Dist. Ct. (we. dist.) Tex. Spl. trial atty. Crime and Racketeering Strike Force, U.S. Dept. Justice, New Orleans, 1974-76; chief spl. crimes U.S. Atty.'s Office (we. dist.) Tex., 1976-77; ptnr. Strother, Johnson & Rickhoff, San Antonio, 1977-78; dist. clk. Bexar County, San Antonio, 1978-81, judge 289th dist., 1982—; advisor Ch. Community Drug Task Force, San Antonio, 1984—; assoc. prof. law St. Mary's U., San Antonio, 1985—; bd. dirs. local police and fire depts., schs. Served to capt. U.S. Army, 1970-74, Vietnam, lt. col. Res. Named Politician Yr. Light newspaper, San Antonio, 1979. Republican. Roman Catholic. Criminal, Juvenile, Military. Home: 525 Moss Mt San Antonio TX 78528 Office: 289th Dist Ct Bexar County Courthouse Main Plaza San Antonio TX 78205

RICO, JULIEANN, lawyer; b. Buffalo, July 19, 1957; d. Concetta Gerace Rico. BS, Fla. State U., 1977; JD, Cath. U., 1980. Bar: Fla. 1981, U.S. Dist. Ct. (so. and mid.) dists. Fla. 1981, U.S. Ct. Appeals (5th and 11th cirs.) 1981. Assoc. Walton, Lantaff & Schroeder, West Palm Beach, Fla., 1980-82; sole practice West Palm Beach, 1982-83; assoc. counsel facilities and operations Palm Beach Sch. Bd., West Palm Beach, 1983-86; assoc. Boose, Casey, Ciklin, Lubitz, Martens, McBane & O'Connell, West Palm Beach, 1986—; adj. prof. Nova U., Ft. Lauderdale, Fla., 1981-85. Bd. dirs. adv. commn. on status of women, Palm Beach County, 1981, 45th St. Mental Health Ctr., West Palm Beach, 1983-84. Mem. ABA, Fla. Bar Assn. (bd. govs. young lawyer sect. 1984-85), Palm Beach County Bar Assn. (pres. young lawyers sect. 1986-87, sec. young lawyers sect. 1984, treas. young lawyers sect. 1983, bd. dirs. 1987—), Assn. Trial Lawyers Am., Am. Arbitration Assn. (arbitrator). Republican. Roman Catholic. Club: Palm Beach Sailing (social chmn. 1985-86). Avocations: sailing, cooking, golf. Construction, State civil litigation, Government contracts and claims. Office: 515 N Flagler Dr 19th Floor West Palm Beach FL 33406

RIDDELL, RICHARD HARRY, lawyer; b. Seattle, Nov. 29, 1916; s. Charles F. and Kathryn (Wykoff) R.; m. Dolores Gloyd, Feb. 10, 1970; children by previous marriage—Dorothea Riddell Parry, Wendy, Kathryn, Mark W. A.B., Stanford, 1938; LL.B., Harvard, 1941. Bar: Wash. 1941. Partner Riddell, Williams, Bullitt and Walkinshaw (and predecessors), Seattle, 1941—; dir. King Broadcasting Co., Seattle. Chmn. Seattle Transit Commn., 1971. Served with USAAF, 1941-45. Fellow Am. Coll. Trial Lawyers; mem. ABA, County Bar Assn. (pres. 1963-64), Wash. State Bar Assn. (pres. 1976-77). Clubs: Seattle Tennis, Rainier (Seattle); Broadmoor Golf. Home: 1620 43d E Seattle WA 98112 Office: Riddell Williams Bullit & Walkinshaw 4400 Sea 1st Bank Bldg Seattle WA 98154

RIDDICK, WINSTON WADE, SR., lawyer; b. Baton Rouge, Feb. 11, 1941; s. Hebert Hobson and Elizabeth (Wade) R.; m. Patricia Ann Turner, Dec. 25, 1961;1 child, Winston Wade. BA, U. Southwestern La., 1962; MA, U. N.C., 1963; PhD, Columbia U., 1965; JD, La. State U., 1973. Bar: La. 1974, U.S. Dist. Ct. (so., mid. and we. dists.) La., U.S. Ct. Appeals (5th cir.). Asst. prof. gov., dir. Inst. Gov. Research, La. State U., Baton Rouge, 1966-67; dir. La. Higher Edn. Facilities Commn., Baton Rouge, 1967-72; exec. asst. state supt. La. Dept. Edn., Baton Rouge, 1972-73; ptnr. Riddick, Riddick & Riddick, Baton Rouge, 1973—; asst. commnr., gen. counsel La. Dept. Agr., Baton Rouge, 1981—; cons. Riddick & Assoc., Baton Rouge, 1973—; part-time faculty mem. So. U., Baton Rouge, 1974—; pres., bd. dirs. 535 Investment Co. Inc., Baton Rouge, 1983—, Riddick Investment Ltd., Baton Rouge, 1981—. Spl. asst. to Gov. John J. McKeithen on Nat. Ctr. for Edn. in Politics Fellowship, 1966—; state campaign mgr. Gillis W. Long for Gov., Baton Rouge, 1971; mem. East Baton Rouge Parish Dem. Exec. Com., 1981-84. Mem. La. Trial Lawyers Assn. (bd. govs. 1978-80). Presbyterian. Administrative and regulatory, General practice, Real property. Home: 1563 Oakley Dr Baton Rouge LA 70816 Office: 10065 Old Hammond Hwy Baton Rouge LA 70816

RIDDLE, DAVID ANDREW, lawyer, educator; b. Ft. Belvoir Va., Aug. 5, 1952; s. Howard Dean and Joan Helena (Carroll) R.; m. Linda Wilkinson, June 2, 1979. BA with high honors, U. Hawaii, 1974; JD, Calif. Western Law Sch., 1977; LLM cum laude in internat. and comparative law U. Brussels, 1985. Bar: Hawaii 1978, U.S. Dist. Ct. Hawaii 1978, U.S. Ct. Appeals (9th cir.). Commd. officer U.S. Army JAG, advanced through grades to capt., 1978; prosecutor, Fed. Magistrate Ct., Honolulu, 1977-78; chief prosecutor Ft. Shafter, Hawaii, 1978-79, def. counsel chief, legal assistance, 1979, chief legal asst., Seoul, Korea, 1979-80, chief fgn. claims div., Seoul, 1980-82; chief fgn. claims commns., Mannheim, W.Ger., 1982-84, officer-in-charge U.S. Claims Office, Brussels, 1984-86, civilian govt. atty., advisor Nuremberg (Fed. Republic Germany) Law Ctr., 1986—; instr. bus. law U. Md., Seoul, 1980-81; lectr. internat. law Boston U. Grad. Internat. Relations Program, Brussels, 1985-86. Mem. Korean Am. Friendship Assn., 1981-82. Recipient Arthur Lyman Dean prize U. Hawaii, 1973-74. Mem. ABA (fgn. claims com. sect. internat. law), Fed. Bar Assn., Internat. Bar Assn., Am. Soc. Internat. Law. Club: Mid Pacific Road Runners. Public international, Military. Office: US Army HQS 1st Armored Div Nuremberg Law Ctr APO New York NY 09696

RIDDLE, MICHAEL LEE, lawyer; b. Abilene, Tex., Oct. 7, 1946; s. Joy Lee and Francis Irene (Brandes) R.; m. Suzan Ellen Shaw, May 25, 1969 (div.); m. 2d, Carol Jackson, Aug. 13, 1977; 1 son, Robert Andrew. B.A., Tex. Tech U., 1969, J.D. with honors, 1972. Bar: Tex. 1972. Assoc. Geary Brice Barron & Stahl, Dallas, 1972-75; ptnr. Baker Glast Riddle Tuttle & Elliott, Dallas, 1975-80; ptnr. Riddle & Brown, Dallas, 1980—, sr. ptnr., 1980—; chmn. bd. Provident Bancorp Tex. ; bd. dirs. U.S.A. Film Festival, pres., 1984-86. Mem. ABA, Tex. Bar Assn., Dallas Bar Assn. Democrat. Lutheran. Clubs: University, Lakewood Country, Lincoln City (Dallas). Banking, Real property. Office: 4004 Belt Line Rd Suite 200 Dallas TX 75244

RIDDLE, ROBERT EDWARD, lawyer; b. Hagerstown, Md., Jan. 27, 1936; s. Robert Roscoe and Euliah (Price) R.; m. Nyra Boyd, June, 1959 (div. 1967); m. Kathleen Keenan, May 27, 1972; children: Jennifer Marie, Miegan Elizabeth. BS, Wake Forest U., 1957, JD, 1958; MPA, Western Carolina U., 1985. Bar: N.C. 1959, U.S. Dist. Ct. (we. dist.) N.C. 1959, U.S. Ct. Appeals (3d cir.) 1959. Ptnr. Wilson & Riddle, Asheville, N.C., 1960-67, Riddle, Shackleford & Hyler, Asheville, 1970-84, Riddle, Kelly & Cagle, Asheville, 1984—. Contbr. articles to profl. jours. Mem. bd. commrs. Buncombe County, Asheville, N.C., 1980-84. Served with U.S. Army, 1958-60. Mem. N.C. Bar Assn. (chmn. family law sect. 1984), Buncombe County Bar Assn. (pres. 1979-80), Am. Acad. Trial Lawyers, N.C. Acad. Trial Lawyers (bd. dirs. 1984—), Am. Acad. Matrimonial Lawyers. Democrat. Presbyterian. Family and matrimonial, Federal civil litigation, General practice. Home: Rt 1 Brooks Branch Rd Leicester NC 28748 Office: 35 N Market St Asheville NC 28807

RIDDLES, AMIS JOE, lawyer; b. Honey Grove, Tex., June 26, 1941; s. Amis Edward and Margaret Marie (Pinson) R.; m. Elizabeth Grant, Aug. 26, 1960; children—A.J. Riddles, Patrick Riddles; m. Sallie Rae Green, Sept. 27, 1977. B.A., Austin Coll., 1963; LL.B., U. Houston, 1966. Bar: Tex. 1966, U.S. Dist. Ct. (no. dist.) Tex. 1967, U.S. Dist. Ct. (ea. dist.) Tex. 1981, U.S. Ct. Appeals (5th and 11th cirs.) 1981, U.S. Supreme Ct. 1984. Sole practice, Dallas County, Tex., 1966—. Author: (novel) The Dragon Prince, 1977; The Feathered Serpent, 1980. Mem. ABA, Dallas Bar Assn., Tex. Bar Assn., State Bar Tex. (hon. mem. Coll. of State Bar), Richardson Bar Assn. (past pres.), Order of Barons, Phi Delta Phi. Episcopalian. Insurance, Personal injury, State civil litigation. Office: Joe Riddles & Assocs 1050 Plaza of the Americas Dallas TX 75201

RIDENOUR, RONALD H., lawyer; b. Knox, Tenn., June 1, 1946; s. J. Carson and Alice R. (Dockery) R.; m. Linda L. Higginbotham, June 1, 1968; children: Kara, Amy. BS, Cumberland Coll., 1968; JD, Nashville Evening Law Sch., 1976. Bar: Tenn. 1977, U.S. Dist. Ct. (ea. dist.) Tenn. 1977, U.S. Ct. Appeals (6th cir.) 1982, U.S. Supreme Ct. 1982. Ptnr. Ridenour & Ridenour, Clinton, Tenn., 1977—; chmn. East Tenn. Med. Malpractice Rev. Bd., 1980-82. Mem. ABA, Tenn. Bar Assn., Tenn. Assn. Criminal Def. Lawyers, Anderson County Bar Assn., Anderson County Jaycees (sec. 1978, v.p. 1979, pres. 1980). Republican. Avocation: sports. Criminal, Family and matrimonial, Personal injury. Home: 206 Orchard Knob Rt 3 Clinton TN 37716 Office: Ridenour & Ridenour 108 S Main St Clinton TN 37716

RIDEOUT, RICHARD SCOTT, lawyer; b. Batavia, N.Y., Dec. 7, 1950; s. Elmer William and Theresa Mae (Maloney) R.; m. Anne Marie Rideout, Nov. 1, 1954; children: Elizabeth Anne, Erin Marie. B.A. with honors, U. Wyo., 1973; J.D. cum laude, U. San Francisco, 1976. Bar: Calif. 1976, Wyo. 1977, U.S. Supreme Ct. 1980, U.S. Ct. Appeals (9th and 10th cirs.), U.S. Ct. Claims 1985. Law clk. presiding justice Wyo. Supreme Ct., 1978-79; asst. atty. gen. Wyo. State Atty. Gen.'s Office, 1979-80; ptnr. Vines, Rideout, Gusea & White, P.C., Cheyenne, Wyo., 1980-85, ptnr. Freudenthal, Salzburg, Bonds & Rideout, P.C., 1986—; asst. pub. defender State of Wyo., part-time, 1982-83; counsel Wyo. State Dems., 1985—. Mem. Am. Trial Lawyers Assn., ABA (vice chmn. tort and ins. practice sect., nat. joint project on appellate practice), San Francisco Bar Assn., Wyo. Trial Lawyers Assn. (amicus curiae com. 1982—), Wyo. State Dems. (counsel 1985—), U. San Francisco Law Soc. (McAuliffe Honor Soc.), Phi Beta Kappa, Phi Kappa Phi. Democrat. Roman Catholic. Author: Wyoming Appellate Practice Handbook, 1985. Contbr. articles to legal jours. Federal civil litigation, State civil litigation, Criminal. Home: 2720 Capitol Ave Cheyenne WY 82001 Office: Freudenthal Salzburg et al 314 E 21st St PO Box 387 Cheyenne WY 82003-0387

RIDER, JAMES LINCOLN, lawyer; b. Newburgh, N.Y., Feb. 11, 1942; s. Meyer J. Rider and Marion (Weinberg) Levin; m. Eleanor Yazbeck, Nov. 5, 1977; children—Jordan E., Michael J. B.A., Lafayette Coll., Easton, Pa., 1963; J.D., Fordham U., 1966. Bar: N.Y. 1966, D.C. 1971, Va. 1972, U.S. Dist. Ct. D.C. 1971, U.S. Dist. Ct. (ea. dist.) Va. 1972, U.S. Dist. Ct. Md. 1973, U.S. Ct. Appeals (D.C. cir.) 1971, U.S. Ct. Appeals (4th cir.) 1972, U.S. Ct. Appeals (8th cir.) 1976, U.S. Supreme Ct. 1975. Ptnr., Margolius, Davis, Finkelstein & Rider, Washington, 1971—. Advisor Parents Without Ptnrs., No. Va., 1979—; trustee Somerset Sch., Washington, 1983—. Served to capt. U.S. Army, 1967-71. Decorated Disting. Service medal. Mem. D.C. Bar, Va. Bar Assn., Assn. Trial Lawyers Am. State civil litigation, Family and matrimonial, Real property. Office: Margolius Davis Finkelstein & Rider 1503 21st St NW Washington DC 20036

RIDGELY, HENRY JOHNSON, lawyer; b. Camden, Del., Nov. 17, 1913; s. Charles duPont and Helene Marjorie (Rudolph) R.; A.B., U. Del., 1935; J.D., George Washington U., 1939; m. Mary Lille Berry, Dec. 3, 1938 (dec.); children—Nicholas, Henry duPont; m. 2d, Gloria J. Rogers, Sept. 9, 1967 (div.); 1 son, John Henry; m. 3d, Sandra M. Maybee, Mar. 16, 1974. Bar: D.C. 1939, Del. 1940, U.S. Supreme Ct. 1943. now Henry J. Ridgely, P.A. and Assocs., Dover and Georgetown, Del. dep. atty. gen. of Del. for Kent County, 1947-54; atty. Kent County Levy Court, 1947-49; revised Code Commn., 1949-53; dir. Legislative Reference Bur. (chief counsel to gov. and Gen. Assembly), 1957-61; dir. Del. R.R. Co. Spl. atty. to Del. ins. commr., 1964-67, 69; personnel commr. Kent County, 1967-68; mem. preliminary investigatory com. Ct. of Judiciary, 1984-86; mem. adv. com. on litigation ethical problems Del. Supreme Ct., 1983—, apptd. mem. evaluation com. Judges of Family Ct. Del. Supreme Ct., 1986—. Mem. Del. Commn. Shell Fish, 1943, Commn. for Feebleminded, 1955-56; mem. Del. Code Revision

Commn., 1957-61, Superior Ct. Jury Study Com., 1963-64; 1st chmn. Del. Pension Fund Trustees, 1970-74; vice chmn. econ. devel. com. Gov.'s Del. Tomorrow Project, 1974-77. Del. Republican Nat. Conv., 1952, 56; asst. gen. counsel Del. State Rep. Com., 1972-74. Bd. dirs. Del. State Ballett, Kent County Arts Council Served as lt. USNR, 1943-46. Mem. Am., Del. (v.p. 1961-64, 79-80, 1787 Bicentennial Com. 1986—), D.C., Fed., Inter Am., Kent County (pres. 1967-68) bar assns., Am. Judicature Soc., Assn. Trial Lawyers Am., Nat. Assn. Criminal Def. Lawyers, Nat. Assn. R.R. Trial Counsel, English-Speaking Union, hist. socs. Del., Md., and Pa., S.A.R. (Silver Citizenship award 1978), Magna Charter Barons, Air Force Assn., VFW (life), Am. Legion (life), Sigma Nu. Episcopalian. Republican. Clubs: Masons (32 deg., Shriner, K.T.), Odd Fellows. Clubs: Church of Del. (pres. 1961-62), Tred Avon Yacht., Chesapeake Bay Yacht Racing Assn., Capitol Hill (D.C.), U. Del. Blue and Gold, Amateur Radio (W3ZEU). General practice, Personal injury, Family and matrimonial. Home: Spruce Haven RD 2 Box 194A Camden DE 19934 also: 1 Cape Henhopen Dr Apt 37 Lewes DE 19958 Office: 307 S State St PO Drawer C Dover DE 19901

RIDGEWAY, HENRY DORMAN, lawyer; b. San Antonio, Oct. 31, 1952; s. Woodrow and Lois (Lawrence) R.; m. Gwendolyn Diaz, Oct. 1, 1976. BA in English, U. Tex., 1977, JD, 1981. Bar: Tex. 1982. Adminstrv. asst. Tex. Senate, Austin, 1981-82, gen. counsel agr. subcom., 1982; assoc. Stanley Eisenberg, P.C., San Antonio, 1983—. Mem. ABA, Coll. State Bar Tex. (bd. dirs. 1987—), San Antonio Trial Lawyers Assn., San Antonio Young Lawyers Assn. Lodge: Masons (chaplain Harlandale chpt. 1986). Personal injury, Workers' compensation, Insurance. Home: 7050 Forest Meadow San Antonio TX 78240 Office: Stanley Eisenberg PC 10000 1H 10 W #213 San Antonio TX 78230

RIDINGS, MARCIA MILBY, lawyer; b. Lexington, Ky., Sept. 3, 1949; d. Robert Lee and Gladys Ruth (Kitrell) Milby; m. James A. Ridings, Dec. 26, 1970 (div. July 1985); 1 child, James Stefan. BA magna cum laude, Georgetown U., 1970; MA, U. Ky., 1973, JD with honors, 1976. Bar: Ky. 1976, U.S. Dist. Ct. (ea. dist.) Ky. 1977. High sch. tchr. Frankfort, Ky., 1972-73; sr. law clk. to presiding justice U.S. Dist. Ct., Lexington, 1976-79; ptnr. Hamm, Milby & Ridings, London, Ky., 1979—; bd. dirs. London/Laurel Co. Ch./Commerce. Bd. dirs. Gov.'s Council Vol. Services, Frankfort, 1983—, Wilderness Rd. council, Girl Scouts U.S., 1984—; mem. Younger Womans Circle 1st Christian Ch., London, deaconess, 1987—; mem. steering com. citizens for sports equity Eastern Ky. U., 1987—. Named one of Outstanding Young Women in Am., 1985. Mem. Ky Bar Assn. (bd. govs. 1986—), Ky. Acad. Trial Attys. (bd. govs. 1983-86), U. Ky. Coll. of Law Alumni Assn. (bd. dirs. 1986—). Republican. Avocation: tennis. State civil litigation, Insurance, Personal injury. Home: S Main St London KY 40741 Office: Hamm Milby & Ridings 120 N Main St London KY 40741

RIDLOFF, RICHARD, real estate executive lawyer, consultant; b. N.Y.C., July 18, 1948; s. Sol and Daisey (Metz) R.; m. Caren Sara Berger, Mar. 27, 1977; children: Michael Joshua, Daniel Joseph. B.A. cum laude, Queens Coll., 1969; J.D., Cornell U., 1972. Bar: N.Y. 1973. Assoc. counsel Mut. of N.Y., N.Y.C., 1972-79; sr. v.p., gen. counsel, sec. MONY Real Estate Investors, N.Y.C., 1979-85; v.p. investments MONY Fin. Services, N.Y.C., 1985—; pres. MONY Realty Ptnrs. Inc., Purchase, N.Y., 1985—; bd. advisors Internat. Tele-Mgmt. Systems, 1985—; mem. adv. commn. on real property ins. to Calif. Sen. Com. on Ins. Claims and Corps., 1986—. Author: A Practical Guide to Construction Lending, 1985. Editor: Real Estate Financing Newsletter, 1980-85 ; contbr. articles to profl. jours. Mem. secondary sch. interviewing com. Cornell U., Ithaca, N.Y., 1981—; chmn. fed. legislation com. Nat. Assn. Real Estate Investment Trusts, Washington, 1981-82. Mem. ABA (mem. real property com., fin. sect. real property, probate and trustlaw 1979—), N.Y. Bar Assn., Am. Land Title Assn. (assoc.), Oakwood-Princeton Park Civic Assn., Omicron Delta Epsilon, Pi Sigma Alpha, Alpha Epsilon Pi. Republican. Real property, Construction, Contracts commercial. Office: MONY Fin Services 1740 Broadway New York NY 10019

RIEBESEHL, E. ALLAN, lawyer; b. N.Y.C., July 7, 1938; s. Harold J. and Phyllis R.; m. Suzanne C. Moore, July 28, 1963; children—Gregory, Christopher. B.A., CCNY, 1961; J.D., Fordham Law Sch., 1966; LL.M., NYU, 1972. Bar: N.Y. 1966, U.S. Tax Ct. 1968, U.S. Supreme Ct. 1970, U.S. Ct. Appeals (2d cir.) 1971, U.S. Dist. Ct. (ea. dist.) N.Y. 1973, U.S. Dist. Ct. (so. dist.) N.Y., 1974. Tax atty. Kennecott Copper Corp., N.Y.C., 1966-69, Celanese Corp., 1969-70, Pan Am. World Airways, N.Y.C., 1970-71; sole practice, Mineola, N.Y., 1971—. adj. prof. Touro Law Sch. Past pres. Woodbury-Syosset Republican Club; past v.p. Syosset Hosp. Community Adv. Bd. Served with USMC, 1961-66. Fellow Am. Acad. Matrimonial Lawyers; mem. ABA, Am. Judicature Soc., C.W. Post Tax Inst., Am. Arbitration Assn., Cath. Lawyers Guild, N.Y. State Bar Assn., Nassau County Bar Assn., Suffolk County Bar Assn., Nassau Lawyers Assn., Lawyers in Mensa. Club: Kiwanis (past pres.) (Mineola, N.Y.). Contbr. articles to profl. jours. Family and matrimonial, Personal income taxation. Office: 999 Brush Hollow Rd Westbury NY 11590

RIECKER, JOHN E(RNEST), lawyer, banker; b. Ann Arbor, Mich., Nov. 25, 1930; s. Herman H. and Elizabeth (Wertz) R.; A.B. with distinction, U. Mich., 1952, J.D. with distinction, 1954; m. Margaret Ann Towsley, July 30, 1955; children—John Towsley, Margaret Elizabeth. Admitted to Mich. bar, 1954, Calif. bar, 1955, bar U.S. Tax Ct., U.S. Supreme Ct. Bar, U.S. Treasury Bar; asso. law firm Bonisteel & Bonisteel, Ann Arbor, 1954-55; partner firm Francis, Wetmore & Riecker. Midland, Mich., 1958-65; partner firm Gillespie Riecker & George, Midland, 1966-85; sr. ptnr. Riecker, George, Hartley & Van Dam and Camp, P.C., 1985—; chmn. bd., dir. First Midland Bank & Trust Co., 1970-78; dir. Comerica Bank-Midland; sec., dir. numerous Mich. corps. Mem. NAM trade mission to EEC, 1964. Trustee, treas. Delta Coll., 1965-68; mem. bd. mgrs. United Fund Midland 1960-64, chmn., 1980—; sec. Midland City Charter Rev. Com., 1964, mem. Spl. Charter Commn., 1972; bd. dirs. Midland Found., 1974; mem. Bd. Ethics State of Mich., 1976—; sec. Dow Found., Towsley Found. Ann Arbor; mem. exec. com. Mich. United Fund, 1970-72; bd. govs. Northwood Inst., 1969-71; benefactor U. Mich.; vice chmn. bd. dirs. U. Mich. Devel. Council, 1982—; chmn. bd. dirs. Central Mich. U. Devel. Council, 1983-86; bd. govs. Cranbrook Acad. Art, 1980-84; chmn. Matrix: Midland, 1981-83; bd. dirs. steering com. U. Mich. Grad. Sch. Bus., 1982—; mem. com. visitors U. Mich. Law Sch., 1981—; vice chmn. Campaign for Mich., 1984; bd. dirs. Hillsdale Coll., 1985—; exec. com., trustee Mich. Hist. Soc., 1985—. Served as 1st lt., Judge Adv. Gens. Corps, AUS, 1955-58 now capt. Res. Recipient U. Mich. Outstanding Alumni award, 1984. Mem. Midland County (pres. 1962-63), Am., Calif., Mich. (tax council) bar assns., Midland C. of C. (pres. 1971), Phi Beta Kappa, Phi Kappa Phi, Phi Eta Sigma, Sigma Iota Epsilon, Alpha Delta Phi, Phi Delta Phi. Republican. Episcopalian. Clubs: Benmark, Midland Country, Saginaw, Saginaw Valley Torch; Detroit Athletic, Renaissance; President's, Benefactors (U. Mich). Mem. bd. editors Mich. Law Rev., 1953-54. Contbr. articles to profl. jours. Estate taxation, Estate planning, Probate. Home: 3211 Valley Dr Midland MI 48640 Office: 414 Townsend St Midland MI 48640

RIEGER, MITCHELL SHERIDAN, lawyer; b. Chgo., Sept. 5, 1922; s. Louis and Evelyn (Sampson) R.; m. Rena White Abelmann, May 17, 1949 (div. 1957); 1 child, Karen Gross Cooper; m. Nancy Horner, May 30, 1961 (div. 1972); step-children—Jill Levi, Linda Hanan, Susan Felsenthal, James Geoffrey Felsenthal; m. Pearl Handelsman, June 10, 1973; step-children—Steven Newman, Mary Ann Malarkey, Nancy Newman. A.B., Northwestern U., 1944; J.D., Harvard U., 1949. Bar: Ill. 1950, U.S. Dist. Ct. (no. dist.) Ill. 1950, U.S. Supreme Ct. 1953, U.S. Ct. Mil. Appeals 1953, U.S. Ct. Appeals (7th cir.) 1954. Legal asst. Rieger & Rieger, Chgo., 1949-50, assoc., 1950-54; asst. U.S. atty. No. Dist Ill., Chgo., 1954-60; 1st asst. No. Dist Ill., 1958-60; assoc. gen. counsel SEC, Washington, 1960-61; ptnr. Schiff Hardin and Waite, Chgo., 1961—; instr. John Marshall Law Sch. Chgo., 1952-54. Contbr. articles to profl. jours. Mem. Chgo. Crime Commn., 1965—; pres. Park View Home for Aged, 1969-71; Rep. precinct committeeman, Highland Park, Ill., 1964-68; bd. dirs. Spertus Mus. Judaica. Served to lt. (j.g.) USNR, 1943-46, PTO. Fellow Am. Coll. Trial Lawyers; ABA, Chgo. Bar Assn., Ill. State Bar Assn., Am. Judicature Soc., 7th Circuit Bar Assn., Fed. Bar Assn. (pres. Chgo. chpt. 1959-60, nat. v.p. 1960-61), Phi Beta Kappa. Jewish. Clubs: Standard, Metropolitan, Lake Shore Country, Law of Chgo., Cliff Dwellers. Avocations: photography; skiing; sailing. Federal civil litigation. Home: 4950 Chicago Beach Dr Chicago IL 60615 Office: Schiff Hardin & Waite 7200 Sears Tower 233 S Wacker Dr Chicago IL 60606

RIEGERT, ROBERT ADOLF, legal educator, consultant; b. Cin., Apr. 21, 1923; s. Adolf and Hulda (Basler) R.; m. Roswitha Victoria Bigalke, Oct. 28, 1966; children—Christine Rose, Douglas Louis. B.S., U. Cin., 1948; LL.B. cum laude, Harvard U., 1953; J.U.D. magna cum laude, U. Heidelberg, Fed. Republic Germany, 1966; postgrad., U. Mich., Harvard U., Yale U., MIT. Bar: D.C. 1953, Cts. Allied High Commn. Germany 1954. Mem. Harvard Legal Aid Bur., 1952; sole practice Heidelberg, 1954-63; vis. assoc. prof. So. Methodist U. Law Sch., Dallas, 1967-71; prof. law Cumberland Law Sch., Samford U., Birmingham, Ala., 1971—; dir. Cumberland Summer Law Program, Heidelberg; disting. vis. prof. Salmon P. Chase Coll. Law, 1983-84; mem. pattern jury instrn. com. State of Ala. Author: (With Robert Braucher) Introduction to Commercial Transactions, 1977, Documents of Title, 1978; contbr. articles to profl. jours. Chmn. subcom. on com. law Ala. Pattern Jury Instruction Com. Served to 1st lt. USAAF, 1943-46. Grantee Dana Fund for Internat. and Comparative Law, 1979; grantee Am. Bar Found., 1966-67; German Acad. Exchange, 1953-55, mem. Harvard Legal Aid Bur., Salmon P. Chase Coll. law scholar, 1950; Pres.'s scholar U. Cin., 1941. Mem. Internat. Acad. Comml. and Consumer Law (v.p.), ABA (com. on new payment systems), Am. Law Inst., Assn. Am. Law Schs. (chmn. sect. internat. exchanges), Ala, Pattern Jury Instructions Com., German Comparative Law Assn., Acad. Soc. German Supreme Cts. Club: Army-Navy (Washington). Contracts commercial, Banking, Private international. Office: Cumberland Law Sch Birmingham AL 35229

RIEKE, FORREST NEILL, lawyer; b. Portland, Oreg., May 26, 1942; s. Forrest Eugene and Mary Neill (Whitelaw) R.; m. Madonna Bernardi, Apr. 2, 1966; children: Mary Jane, Forrest Ermelindo. AB in Polit. Sci., Stanford U., 1968; JD, Willamette U., 1971. Bar: Oreg. 1971, U.S. Dist. Ct. Oreg. 1974, U.S. Ct. Appeals (9th cir.) 1975, U.S. Supreme Ct. 1977. Sr. dep. dist. atty. Multnomah County, Portland, 1971-76; ptnr. Rieke, Geil & Savage P.C., Portland, 1977—. Contbr. editor Williamette U. Law Rev., 1971. Chmn. legis. com. Council Great Schs., Washington, 1985—; bd. dirs. Portland Pub. Schs., 1978—, Columbia Willamette United Way, Portland, 1983—. Mem. ABA, Oreg. Bar Assn. (indigent accused def. com., chmn. law related edn. com. 1985, bd. dirs. criminal law sect. 1979-84), Multnomah County Bar Assn., Oreg. Criminal Def. Lawyers Assn. Republican. Presbyterian. Club: Multnomah Athletic. Lodge: Rotary. Federal civil litigation, Personal injury, Criminal. Home: 2758 NW Calumet Terr Portland OR 97210 Office: Rieke Geil & Savage PC 820 SW 2d Ave Portland OR 97204

RIEMANN, FREDERICK ALOYSIUS, law librarian; b. Valley Twp., Pa., Dec. 17, 1947; s. Frederick Aloysius and Mary Frances (Gray) R.; m. Sharon MacElroy, Feb. 7, 1970; children: Frederick Jr., Gretchen, Frances, Clare, Elizabeth, Timothy, Michael, Daniel. AB, Temple U., 1972; MLS, U. Tex., 1974. Librarian reference and documents Tex. State Law Library, Austin, 1977-80; asst. librarian Gulf Cos. Law Library, Houston, 1980-82, sr. librarian, 1982-85; chief law librarian Chevron USA Inc., Houston, 1985—. Served to sgt. U.S. Army, 1966-69. Mem. Am. Assn. Law Libraries, Southwestern Assn. Law Libraries, Houston Assn. Law Librarians (exec. bd. 1983). Roman Catholic. Librarianship. Home: 29330 Brookchase Dr Spring TX 77386 Office: Chevron USA Inc 1301 McKinney Room 2150 Houston TX 77210

RIEMER, GEORGE ARTHUR, lawyer; b. Milw., May 12, 1950; s. Oskar and Leopoldine (Stadler) R. BA, Pacific Luth. U., 1971; JD, Valparaiso U., 1974. Bar: Wash. 1975, U.S. Dist. Ct. (we. dist.) Wash. 1975, Oreg. 1980, U.S. Supreme Ct. 1986. Staff atty. Wash. State Bar Assn., Seattle, 1975-77; asst. and sr. asst. atty. City of Vancouver, Wash., 1977-80; gen. counsel Oreg. State Bar, Portland, 1981-84, assoc. exec. dir., gen. counsel, 1984—. Mem. Multnomah County Cir. Ct. Arbitration Panel, 1985—, Beaverton Planning Commn., Oreg. 1985-86. Mem. ABA, Oreg. State Bar Assn., Wash. State Bar Assn., Multnomah Bar Assn., Nat. Orgn. Bar Counsel. Democrat. Avocation: distance running. Administrative and regulatory, Jurisprudence. Office: Oreg State Bar 5200 SW Meadows Rd PO Box 1689 Lake Oswego OR 97035-0889

RIEMERSMA, JEFFREY KURT, lawyer; b. Alma, Mich., Aug. 30, 1954; s. Clifford Henry and Helen Dorothy (Wolgast) R.; m. Elizabeth Ann Shooks, Sept. 1, 1979; children: Jamie Lynn, Kristen Ann. BA, Hope Coll., 1976; JD, Thomas Cooley Law Sch., 1979. Bar: Mich. 1979, U.S. Dist. Ct. (ea. dist.) Mich. 1985, U.S. Dist. Ct. (we. dist.) Mich. 1986. Assoc. Weringa & Sevensma, Grand Rapids, Mich., 1979-80; chief asst. pros. Gratiot County, Ithaca, Mich., 1980-85; v.p., legal counsel Bank of Alma, 1985—; adj. prof. bus. law Alma Coll., 1983—. Cons. Gratiot Multidisciplinary Team, Alma, 1982-85;l treas. Gratiot County Child Adv., Alma, 1986—. Mem. ABA, Mich. Bar Assn., Gratiot County Bar Assn. (pres. 1982-83). Republican. Presbyterian. Club: Pine River Country (Alma). Lodge: Elks. Avocations: sports, literature. Consumer commercial, Criminal, Bankruptcy. Home: 1002 N State Alma MI 48801 Office: Bank of Alma 311 Woodworth Alma MI 48801

RIESENFELD, STEFAN ALBRECHT, law educator, cons.; b. Breslau, Ger., June 8, 1908; came to U.S., 1934, naturalized, 1940; s. Conrad Ernst and Margarethe (Landecker) R.; m. Phyllis B. Thogrimson, Dec. 23, 1943; children—Peter William, Stefan Conrad. J.U.D., U. Breslau, 1932, U. Milan, 1934; LL.B., U. Calif.-Berkeley, 1937; S.J.D., Harvard U., 1940; B.S., U. Minn., 1943; D.h.c., U. Cologne (Ger.), 1970. Bar: Minn. 1939, U.S. Supreme Ct. 1978. Prof. law U. Minn., Mpls., 1938-52; prof. law U. Calif.-Berkeley, 1952—, Emanuel S. Heller prof., 1954-75, prof. emeritus, 1975—; prof. law U. Calif., Hastings Coll. Law, San Francisco, 1975—; cons. to U.S. Bd. Econ. Warfare, 1942, UN ad hoc com., 1952; counselor on internat. law Dept. Def., 1955, Dept. State, 1977-82; mem. Adv. Com. on Bankruptcy Rules, 1961-72; vis. prof. various U.S. and fgn. univs.; cons. Calif. law revision commn., 1970-81, Legal Ref. Bur. of Hawaii, 1968-74. Served with USN, 1943-46. Recipient Silver medal Dept. State, 1979, 84; Verdienstkreuz, Fed. Republic of Germany, 1975. Mem. ABA, Nat. Bankruptcy Conf., Am. Acad. Arts and Scis., Am. Soc. Internat. Law, Internat. Law Assn. (Am. br.), Soc. Legal History. Lutheran. Author: Protection of Fisheries Under International Law, 1943, Modern Social Legislation, 1950, (with Hetland, Maxwell and Warren) California Secured Land Transactions, 3d edit., 1984, Creditors' Remedies and Debtors' Protection, 4th edit., 1986. Public international, Bankruptcy, Real property. Home: 1129 Amador Ave Berkeley CA 94707 Office: U Calif Berkeley Law Sch Boalt Hall Berkeley CA 94720

RIESER, JOHN PAUL, lawyer; b. Homestead, PA, Sept. 24, 1956. BA with distinction, Northwestern U., 1978; cert., Pushkin Inst., Moscow, 1978; JD cum laude, Harvard U., 1981. Bar: Ohio 1981, U.S. Dist. Ct. (so. dist.) Ohio 1981, U.S. Ct. Appeals (6th cir.) 1982. Assoc. Estabrook, Finn & McKee, Dayton, Ohio, 1981-83; sole practice Dayton, 1983-85; ptnr. Rieser & Marx, Dayton, 1985—; Lectr. bus. law Sinclair Community Coll., Dayton, 1984-85; bd. dirs. Subler Systems USA, Inc., Versailles, Ohio, Vantage Transport, Inc., Versailles, Shenandoah Motor Express, Inc., Versailles, Eastgate Ford, Inc., John Meyer Buick-Pontiac-GMC, Dayton and Xenia, 1984—. Editor: Harvard Internat. Law Jour., 1979-81; also contbr. articles to newspapers and profl. jours. Arbitrator Montgomery County (Ohio) Med. Malpractice Arbitration Panels, 1983—. Mem. ABA, Assn. Trial Lawyers Am., Ohio Bar Assn., Dayton Bar Assn., Harvard U. Alumni Assn. (fund raiser 1985). Democrat. Roman Catholic. General corporate, Federal civil litigation, Contracts commercial. Office: Rieser & Marx 40 W 4th St Dayton OH 45402

RIFE, GARY ALAN, lawyer; b. Anadarko, Okla., Sept. 10, 1953; s. Johnny Killian and Sharon Sage (Franklin) R.; m. Jonella Jean Frank, Feb. 8, 1980. BBA in Acctg., U. Okla., 1975, JD, 1978. Bar: Okla. 1978, U.S. Dist. Ct. (we. dist.) Okla. 1979, U.S. Ct. Appeals (10th cir.) 1979, U.S. Supreme Ct. 1983. Assoc. McKenzie Law Office, Norman, Okla., 1978-81; gen. counsel Okla. Bar Assn., Norman, 1981-83; ptnr. English, Patten & Rife, Norman, 1983—. Contbr. articles to profl. jours. Bd. dirs. Juvenile Services, Inc., Norman, 1985—. Bar: ABA, Assn. Trial Lawyers Am., Okla. Bar Found., Okla. Trial Lawyers Assn., Okla. Bar Assn. (named Outstanding Young Lawyer 1984, house del. 1980-86, bd. govs. 1986—, chmn. legal ethics com. 1985-86, adminstrn. of justice com. 1984—), Cleveland County Bar Assn. (pres. 1982), Oklahoma County Bar Assn., Am. Inn of Ct. (barrister). Democrat. Methodist. Lodge: Rotary. General practice, Bankruptcy, Professional responsibility, lawyer discipline. Home: 515 Shawnee St Norman OK 73071 Office: English Patten & Rife 210 E Main St Suite 200 Norman OK 73071

RIFE, O(SCAR) JENNINGS, lawyer; b. Wayne, W.Va., Aug. 23, 1915; s. O. Jennings and Mamie (Wellman) R.; m. Bernice Poindexter, Mar. 28, 1970; m. Elizabeth Scherr Harrison, Aug. 16, 1952; 1 son, John J. Student Marshall U., 1933-35, U. Ky., 1935-36; A.B., George Washington U., 1938; J.D. with honors, 1941. Bar: W.Va. 1946, U.S. Tax Ct. 1947. Clk. to Senator M.M. Neely, Washington, 1937-41; sole practice, Huntington, W.Va., 1946—; sr. ptnr. Rife & Daugherty; dir. 1st Huntington Nat. Bank; instr., lectr. Marshall U., 1948-52. Served to lt. USNR, 1942-46. Mem. ABA, W.Va. Bar Assn., W.Va. Tax Inst. (dir. 1967-72, pres. 1972), Phi Delta Phi. Democrat. Episcopalian. Club: Guyan Country. Lodge: Kiwanis. Corporate taxation, Estate taxation, Personal income taxation. Home: 162 Woodland Dr Huntington WV 25705 Office: 421 10th St Suite 900 Huntington WV 25701

RIFFER, JEFFREY KENT, lawyer, educator; b. Gary, Ind., Sept. 8, 1953; s. Howard and Jeanne (Fischer) R.; m. Catherine Anne Conway, Oct. 22, 1985. BS, Ind. U., 1975, JD, 1978. Bar: Ind. 1978, Calif. 1979, U.S. Ct. Appeals (7th cir.) 1979, U.S. Ct. Appeals (9th cir.) 1981. From assoc. to ptnr. Kadison, Pfaelzer, Woodard, Quinn & Rossi, Los Angeles, 1979—; adj. prof. Pepperdine U., Malibu, Calif., 1979—. Author: Sports and Recreational Injuries, 1985, (jour.) An Overview of Sex Discrimination in Amateur Athletics, 1983. Mem. ABA, Los Angeles County Bar Assn., Order of Coif, Beta Gamma Sigma, Beta Alpha Psi. Republican. Jewish. Federal civil litigation, State civil litigation, Family and matrimonial. Office: Kadison Pfaelzer et al 707 Wilshire Blvd 40th Floor Los Angeles CA 90017

RIFFKIN, MITCHELL SANFORD, lawyer; b. Providence, Dec. 30, 1944; s. Ira and Rose (Kirshenbaum) R. BA, U. R.I., 1966; JD, Boston U., 1969. Bar: R.I. 1969, U.S. Dist. Ct. R.I. 1970, U.S. Ct. Appeals (1st cir.) 1980. Pros. atty. City of Warwick, R.I., 1971-72; mcpl. judge City of Warwick, 1980—; magistrate bail commr. Kent County, R.I., 1973—. Chmn. Fed. Block Grant Allocation Subcom., Warwick, 1976—; chmn. Group Home Placement for Mentally Retarded, Warwick, 1976—; chmn. Mayor's Fin. Adv. Commn., Warwick, 1985—. Named One of Outstanding Young Men of Yr., U.S. Jaycees, 1976. Fellow Pi Sigma Alpha (past pres.); Mem. ABA (arbitrator), R.I. Bar Assn. (ho. of dels., chmn. ethics com. 1982—), R.I. Audubon Soc., U.S. Power Squadron. Democrat. Jewish. Lodges: B'nai B'rith (bd. govs. 1978), Masons. Personal injury, Family and matrimonial, State civil litigation. Home: 95 Cedar Bay Dr Warwick RI 02888 Office: 615 Jefferson Blvd Warwick RI 02886

RIFKIND, ROBERT SINGER, lawyer; b. N.Y.C., Aug. 31, 1936; s. Simon H. and Adele (Singer) R.; m. Arleen Brenner, Dec. 24, 1961; children—Amy, Nina. B.A., Yale U., 1958; LL.B., Harvard U., 1961. Bar: N.Y. bar 1961, U.S. Supreme Ct. bar 1965. Asst. to solicitor gen. Dept. Justice, 1965-68; asso. firm Cravath, Swaine & Moore, N.Y.C., 1962-65, 68-70; partner Cravath, Swaine & Moore, 1971—. Trustee Dalton Sch., N.Y.C., 1975-83, hon. trustee, 1983—, pres., 1977-79; trustee, bd. dirs. The Loomis Inst., 1987—; bd. govs. Am. Jewish Com., 1977—; trustee Jewish Publ. Soc. Am., 1973—; bd. dirs., exec. com. Jewish Theol. Sem. Am., 1983—; bd. dirs. Benjamin N. Cardozo Sch. Law, 1984—. Recipient Stanley M. Isaacs Human Relations award Am. Jewish Com., 1983. Fellow Am. Coll. Trial Lawyers, N.Y. Bar Found.; mem. ABA, Am. Law Inst., Assn. Bar City N.Y., Phi Beta Kappa. Democrat. Antitrust, Federal civil litigation, State civil litigation. Office: 1 Chase Manhattan Plaza New York NY 10005

RIFKIND, SIMON HIRSCH, lawyer; b. Meretz, Russia, June 5, 1901; came to U.S., 1910, naturalized, 1924; s. Jacob and Celia (Bluestone) R.; m. Adele Singer, June 12, 1927; children—Richard Allen, Robert Singer. B.S., CCNY, 1922; LL.B., Columbia U., 1925; Litt.D., Jewish Theol. Sem., 1950; LL.D., Hofstra Coll., 1962, Brandeis U., 1977, CCNY, 1978; J.D., Hebrew U. of Jerusalem, 1980. Bar: N.Y. bar 1926, Ill. bar 1957. Legislative sec. to U.S. senator Robert F. Wagner, 1927-33; partner firm Wagner, Quillinan and Rifkind, N.Y.C., 1930-41; fed. judge So. N.Y. Dist., 1941-50; mem. firm Stevenson, Rifkind & Wirtz, Chgo., 1957-61; partner Paul, Weiss, Rifkind, Wharton & Garrison, 1950—; Dir. Sterling Nat. Bank & Trust Co. N.Y.; Herman Phleger vis. prof. law Stanford, 1975; Spl. master Colo. River litigation U.S. Supreme Ct.; chmn. Presdl. R.R. Commn., 1961-62; mem. State Commn. Govtl. Operations City N.Y., 1959-61; co-chmn. President's Commn. on Patent System, 1966-67; mem. mayors mediation panel N.Y. City teachers strike, 1963. Mem. Bd. Higher Edn. City N.Y., 1954-66; Chmn. adminstrv. bd. Am. Jewish Com., 1953-56, chmn. exec. bd., 1956-59; former chmn. bd., now hon. chmn. exec. com. Jewish Theol. Sem.; bd. dirs. Beth Israel Med. Center, N.Y.C., 1972-86, now emeritus; chmn. bd. Charles H. Revson Found., Inc., 1975-87, bd. dirs., 1987—, Tudor Found., Inc.; bd. dirs., pres. Norman and Rosita Winston Found., Inc., 1975-87, bd. dirs., 1987—. Recipient Medal of Freedom, 1946. Mem. Assn. Bar City N.Y., Am. Coll. Trial Lawyers (regent 1967-71, pres. 1976-77), Phi Beta Kappa. Democrat. Jewish. Club: Harmonie (N.Y.C.). Adviser to Gen. Eisenhower on Jewish matters in Am. occupation zone, 1945. Office: Paul Weiss Rifkind et al 1285 Ave of the Americas New York NY 10019

RIFMAN, AVRUM KATZ, lawyer; b. Balt., Oct. 19, 1905; s. Hyman Shemon and Zeesla Baile (Katz) R.; m. Ruth Pell, May 4, 1935; children—Samuel Sholom, Melvin Sadler. LL.B., U. Md., 1926. Bar: Md. 1926, U.S. Dist. Ct. Md. 1927, U.S. Ct. Appeals (4th cir.) 1946, U.S. Supreme Ct. 1950. 1st asst., chief, trial div. City of Balt., 1943-45; trial magistrate So. Dist. Balt., 1951-53; Md. mem. Nat. Conf. Commrs. of Uniform State Laws, 1957-61; judge Mcpl. Ct. of Balt., 1968-70; master-in-chancery Supreme Bench of Balt., 1971-75; judge Archdiocesan Ct. Balt., 1977—; panel chmn. malpractice claims Md. Health Claims Arbitration Act, 1977—. Mem. ABA, Md. Bar Assn., Baltimore City Bar Assn., Jewish Hist. Soc. Md. Jewish. Clubs: Mason, Allied, B'nai B'rith. Contbr. articles of legal jours. General practice, General corporate, Legal history.

RIGBY, KENNETH, lawyer; b. Shreveport, La., Oct. 20, 1925; s. Samuel and Mary Elizabeth (Fearnhead) R.; m. Jacqueline Carol Brandon, June 10, 1951; children—Brenda, Wayne, Glen. B.S. magna cum laude, La. State U., 1950, J.D., 1951. Bar: La. 1951, U.S. Ct. Appeals (5th cir.) 1966, U.S. Supreme Ct. 1971, U.S. Tax Ct. 1981, U.S. Ct. Appeals (11th cir.) 1982. Ptnr. Love, Rigby, Dehan, Love & McDaniel, 1951—; mem. Marriage-Persons Com. La. Law Inst., 1981—. Sec. madatory continuing legal edn. com. La. Supreme Ct., 1987—. Served with USAAF, 1943-46. Fellow Am. Acad. Matrimonial Lawyers; mem. ABA, Assn. Trial Lawyers Am., La. Trial Lawyers Assn., Shreveport Bar Assn. (pres. 1973-74), La. State Bar Assn. (chmn. com. on continuing legal edn. 1974-75, chmn. family law sect. 1981-82, bd. of govs. 1986—). Methodist. Contbr. articles to profl. jours. Family and matrimonial, State civil litigation, Personal injury. Office: Johnson Bldg 6th Floor 412 Milam St Shreveport LA 71101

RIGBY, RAY WENDELL, lawyer; b. Rexburg, Idaho, Apr. 16, 1923; s. J. Lester and Hattie L. Rigby; m. Lola Cook, Dec. 8, 1944; children—Laura Jean, Beverly, Joyce, Jerry R., Blair J., Beth, Natalie. B.S., U. Idaho, 1948, J.D., 1950. Bar: Idaho 1950, U.S. Dist. Ct. Idaho 1950, U.S. Sup. Ct. 1980. Mem. Rigby, Thatcher, Andrus, Rigby & Perkes, Rexburg, 1958—; pros. atty. Madison County (Idaho), 1950-64; mem. Idaho Senate, 1965-72; dir. Valley Bank, Valley Bancorp. and Banco, Inc., Idaho Falls, and North Fork Reservoir Co., St. Anthony, Idaho. Idaho rep. Western States Water Council, 1972—, chmn., 1982; del. world conf. on water U.S. State Dept. to U.N., 1977; chmn. Interstate Conf. on Water Problems, 1979-81, Idaho Legis. Compensation Commn., 1982-86; chmn. Gov.'s Task Force on Swan Falls, 1983-85; mem. Idaho Commn. on Bicentennial of U.S. Constn. Served with USAAF, 1943-44. Named Outstanding Young Man of Yr., Madison County Jr. C. of C., 1952, Most Outstanding Freshman Senator-38th Session Idaho Legislature, Idaho Press Club, 1965, Man of Yr., Sta.-KRXK, 1967, Outstanding Legislator in Idaho, VFW, 1971, Outstanding Citizen, Rexburg C. of C., 1977. Mem. ABA, Idaho Bar Assn., 7th Jud. Dist. Bar Assn. (pres. 1979), Am. Judicature Soc. Democrat. Mormon. Club: Rotary (Rexburg)

(dist. gov. 1986-87). General practice. Home: 2131 N 3000 W9 Rexburg ID 83440 Office: 25 N 2d St E PO Box 250 Rexburg ID 83440

RIGGS, ARTHUR JORDY, lawyer; b. Nyack, N.Y., Apr. 3, 1916; s. Oscar H. and Adele (Jordy) R.; m. Virginia Holloway, Oct. 15, 1942; children—Arthur James (dec.), Emily Adele Riggs Freeman, Keith Holloway, George Bennett. A.B., Princeton U., 1937; LL.B., Harvard U., 1940. Bar: Mass. 1940, Tex. 1943; cert. specialist in labor law. Assoc., Warner, Stackpole, Stetson & Bradlee, Boston, 1940-41; staff mem. Solicitors Office U.S. Dept. Labor, Washington and Dallas, 1941-42; mem. Johnson, Bromberg, Leeds & Riggs, Dallas, 1949-81; of counsel Geary, Stahl & Spencer, Dallas, 1981—. Mem. ABA, State Bar Tex., Dallas Bar Assn., Southwest Legal Found., Phi Beta Kappa. Labor, Pension, profit-sharing, and employee benefits. Office: 16479 Dallas Pkwy Suite 800 Dallas TX 75248

RIGGS, CHARLES EARLE, lawyer; b. Louisville, Mar. 9, 1941; s. Charles Edmond Jr. and Mary Ann (Madeira) R.; m. Norma Jean Crispin, Jan. 16, 1960. BA in Pre Law, U. West Los Angeles, 1976, JD, 1976. Bar: Calif. 1976, U.S. Dist. Ct. (cen. dist.) Calif. 1977. Agt. titles Comml. Standard Title Co., Painesville, Ohio, 1963-68; title officer Title Ins. and Trust Co., Los Angeles, 1968-71; closing officer Alison Mortgage Trust Co., Los Angeles, 1971-75; counsel br. Lawyers Title Ins. Co., Los Angeles, 1975-78; sr. rep. Ticor Title Ins Co., Los Angeles and San Francisco, 1978-81; v.p., counsel Umet Properties Corp., Beverly Hills, Calif., 1981-83; v.p., assoc. regional counsel Chgo. Title Ins. Co., Pasadena, Calif., 1983—. Mem. editorial staff U. West Los Angeles Law Rev., 1976. Served with U.S. Army, 1959-62. Mem. ABA, Calif. Bar Assn., Los Angeles County Bar Assn., Am. Land Title Assn., Calif. Land Title Assn. Republican. Avocations: collecting stamps, World War II history. Real property, Insurance. Office: Chgo Title Ins Co 3280 E Foothill Blvd Pasadena CA 91107

RIGGS, DAN BRITT, lawyer; b. Oklahoma City, Dec. 26, 1949; s. Carroll A. and Mayme B. (Britt) R.; m. Kathryn Ann Elliott, Aug. 17, 1975. BA with honors, U. Wyo., 1972, LLB with honors, 1975. Bar: Wyo. 1975, U.S. Dist. Ct. Wyo. 1975, U.S. Ct. Appeals (10th cir.) 1975. Assoc. Lonabaugh & Vanderhoof, Sheridan, Wyo., 1975-76, ptnr., 1976-81; ptnr. Lonabaugh & Riggs, Sheridan, 1981—. Articles editor Land & Water Law Rev., 1974-75. Mem. Sheridan Planning Commn., 1977-84. Mem. ABA, Wyo. State Bar Assn., Am. Trial Lawyers Assn., Wyo. Trial Lawyers Assn., Sheridan County Bar Assn. (pres. 1985-86). Republican. Avocation: tennis. Insurance, Oil and gas leasing, Personal injury. Home: 55 Hillcrest Ct Sheridan WY 82801

RIGGS, DOUGLAS A., lawyer; b. Rigby, Idaho, Aug. 20, 1944; s. Ursel and Elsie Riggs; m. Heidi Bankart Eddy, Dec. 27, 1985. BS, Brigham Young U., 1966; MS, W.Va. U., 1967; JD, Cornell U., 1973. Bar: Alaska 1974, D.C. 1985. Assoc. Johnson, Christensen & Schamberg Inc., Anchorage, 1974-75; gen. counsel Alaska State Housing Authority, Anchorage, 1975-76, exec. dir., 1976-77; spl. counsel to the gov. State of Alaska, Washington, 1977-79; counsel Citizens for Mgmt. for Alaska Lands Inc., Washington, 1979; sole practice Anchorage, 1979-80; ptnr. Bogle & Gates, Anchorage, 1980-83; spl. asst. to pres. for pub. liaison The White House, Washington, 1983-85; gen. counsel U.S. Dept. Commerce, Washington, 1985—. Counsel Senator Frank H. Murkowski campaign, Anchorage, 1980; mem. exec. com. Senator Ted Stevens re-election campaign, Anchorage, 1982-83. Served to sgt. U.S. Army, 1967-70. Mem. Alaska Bar Assn., D.C. Bar Assn. Republican. General practice. Home: 5206 Massachusetts Ave Bethesda MD 20816 Office: Dept Commerce 14th & Constitution Ave NW Washington DC 20230

RIGGS, GREGORY LYNN, lawyer; b. Columbus, Ohio, Apr. 21, 1948; s. Roy Albert and Edith Myrtle (Riggins) R.; m. Janet Kaye Adams, June 26, 1982; 1 child, Caroline Ashley. BA, U. NC., 1970, Oxford U., 1976; JD, Emory U., 1979. Atty. Delta Air Lines, Atlanta, 1979-84, sr. atty., 1984—. Labor, Federal civil litigation, Aviation. Home: 907 Beaverbrook Dr Atlanta GA 30318 Office: Law Dept Delta Air Lines Inc Hartsfield Internat Airport Atlanta GA 30320

RIGGS, JOHN HUTTON, JR., lawyer; b. Plainfield, N.J., Nov. 21, 1936; s. John Hutton and Helen Virginia (Butler) R.; m. Dominique Lacoste, Dec. 28, 1965; children: Emilie L., Francis L., Jennifer C. BA, Yale U., 1958; JD, U. Va., 1964. Bar: N.Y. 1965, U.S. Dist. Ct. (so. and ea. dists.) N.Y. 1976, Conseil Juridique France 1976. Assoc. Haight, Gardener, Poor & Havens, N.Y.C., 1964-67; assoc. White & Case, N.Y.C., 1967-68, Paris, 1968-71; ptnr. White & Case, N.Y.C., 1972-75, Paris, 1976—. Trustee Am. Library Paris; bd. dirs., chmn. legal com. Am. C. of C. France Inc.; bd. dirs. Am. Hosp. Paris. Served to lt. USN, 1958-61. Mem. ABA, Internat. Bar Assn., Assn. of Bar of City of N.Y., Am. Soc. Internat. Law, Union Internat. des Avocats. Episcopalian. Clubs: Cercle Interallie, Polo, American (Paris) (pres. 1982-84). Banking, General corporate, Private international. Home: 8 Ave Frederic Le Play, Paris 75007, France Office: White & Case, 20 Pl Vendome, Paris 75001, France

RIGGS, ROBIN L., lawyer, educator; b. Salt Lake City, May 10, 1953; s. Elvin Loy and Cleo (Judd) R. BA with honors, U. Utah, 1977; M in Pub. Adminstrn., Brigham Young U., 1982, JD, 1982. Assoc. gen. counsel Legis. Research and Gen. Counsel, Salt Lake City, 1982—; sr. counsel Tax Recodification Commn., Salt Lake City, 1984—; exec. dir. Utah Constl. Revision Commn., Salt Lake City, 1985—. Author: Legislation Bill Drafting Manual for Utah, 1985. Mem. Utah State Bar Assn. (exec. council young lawyers sect., sec. 1986-87, exec. council, chmn. community services com. 1985-86). Mormon. Legislative, Municipal bonds, State and local taxation. Home: 274 E 2300 S Bountiful UT 84010

RIGGS, ROGER D., lawyer; b. Mt. Sterling, Ky., Aug. 18, 1946; s. Raymond Donald and Estelle (Stephens) R.; m. Ann Riggs, Dec. 27, 1968; children: Martin, Melissa. BA, Georgetown U., 1968; JD, U. Ky., 1973. Bar: Ky. 1974. Ptnr. Bryan, Fogle & Riggs, Mt. Sterling, Ky., 1974-81, Maxey, Riggs & Moore, Mt. Sterling, 1981—; atty. City of Mt. Sterling, 1975—. Chmn. Montgomery County Dem. Com. Mem. Ky. Acad. Trial Lawyers (chmn.), Ky. Mcpl. Attys. Assn. (treas. 1985-86, sec. 1986-87). Baptist. Lodges: Kiwanis (bd. dirs.), Odd Fellows. Personal injury, Workers' compensation, Medical negligence. Home: PO Box 53 Mount Sterling KY 40353 Office: Maxey Riggs Moore & Cowden 20 Court St Mount Sterling KY 40353

RIGHEIMER, FRANK S., JR., lawyer; b. Chgo., Feb. 28, 1909; s. Frank Stahl Sr. and Helen Elizabeth (Maddock) R.; m. Karen Gardner, 1948 (dec. 1978); m. Dena Frasier, 1979. BA, Yale U., 1929; BBL, Harvard U., 1932. Bar: Ill. 1933, U.S. Supreme Ct. 1937, Fla. 1973. Asst. state's atty. State of Ill., 1932-34; asst. gen. counsel SEC, Washington, 1934-37; ptnr. Righeimer, Martin, Bridewell & Cin Quino, Chgo. and Palm Beach, Fla., 1937—; spl. asst. U.S. atty. gen., 1936-37; spl. asst. Ill. Atty. Gen., 1950-84; master in chancery Ill. Superior Ct., 1949-55. Served to lt. col. U.S. Air Corps., 1942-45, ETO. Decorated Legion of Merit. Fellow Internat. Acad. Trial Lawyers; mem. ABA, Ill. Bar Assn., Fla. Bar Assn., Chgo. Bar Assn., Law Club Chgo., Legal Club Chgo. Condemnation, State civil litigation. Home: 389 S Lake Dr Palm Beach FL 33480 Office: Righeimer Martin Bridewell & Cinquino 1355 S LaSalle St Chicago IL 60603 Also: 205 Worth Ave Palm Beach FL 33480

RIGHTNOUR, DONALD, lawyer; b. Johnstown, Pa., Feb. 2, 1957; s. Harry M. and Joann (Gunselman) R.; m. Susan Rene Dallapé, Aug. 12, 1978. BS in Acctg., Pa. State U., 1979; JD, U. Denver, 1981; LLM in Taxation, Georgetown U., 1986. Bar: D.C. 1982, U.S. Tax Ct. 1982. Atty. to Office of Chief Counsel IRS, Washington, 1982-86; asst. tax counsel Fairchild Industries, Inc., Chantilly, Va., 1986—. Mem. ABA, Phi Alpha Delta, Phi Eta Sigma, Beta Gamma Sigma, Beta Alpha Psi. Roman Catholic. Avocations: golf, reading. Corporate taxation, State and local taxation, Personal income taxation. Home: 9731 Ironmaster Dr Burke VA 22015 Office: Fairchild Industries Inc 300 W Service Rd Chantilly VA 22021-9998

RIKLEEN, LAUREN STILLER, lawyer; b. Winthrop, Mass., Apr. 29, 1953; d. Joseph Stiller and Elaine Lillian (Brodie) Stiller; m. Sander A. Rikleen, May 25, 1975. Student Clark U., 1971-73; BA, magna cum laude, Brandeis U., 1975; JD, Boston Coll., 1979. Bar: Mass. 1979, U.S. Dist. Ct. Mass. 1980, U.S. Ct. Appeals (1st cir.) 1980, U.S. Supreme Ct. 1985. Asst. dir. Flaschner Jud. Inst., Boston, 1979-81; atty. enforcement div. EPA, Boston, 1981-82, Office Regional Counsel, 1982-84; asst. v.p. for negotiations Clean Sites, Inc., Alexandria, Va., 1984-87; asst. atty. gen. Mass. Dept. of the Atty. Gen., 1987—. Contbr. articles to legal publs. Mem. Wayland Planning Bd., Mass., 1980-83; mem. Met. Area Planning Council, Boston, 1980-84 . Recipient Merit award EPA, 1982. Mem. ABA (natural resources com.), Boston Bar Assn. (environment com.), Soc. Profls. in Dispute Resolution. Democrat. Environment. Office: Mass Dept of Atty Gen One Ashburton Pl Boston MA 02108

RIKLI, DONALD CARL, lawyer; b. Highland, Ill., June 16, 1927; s. Carl and Gertrude Louise (Stoecklin) R.; m. Joan Tate, Oct. 10, 1953; children: Kristine, David. AB, Ill. Coll., 1951; JD, U. Ill., 1953. Bar: Ill. 1953, U.S. Dist. Ct. (so. dist.) Ill. 1961, U.S. Ct. Appeals (7th cir.) 1968, U.S. Supreme Ct. 1974. Sole practice Highland, 1953—; atty. City of Highland, 1956-59. Author: The Illinois Probate System, 1974, 75, 77; bd. editors Illinois Real Property I, 1966, 71, Lawyers World, 1970-72, Law Notes, 1981-83, The Compleat Lawyer, 1985—. Served with U.S. Army, 1945-47. Fellow Am. Coll. Probate Counsel, Ill. Bar Found.; mem. ABA (council gen. practice sect. 1981—, chmn. sole practitioners and small firms com. 1981-84, coordinator com. 1984—, dir. law practice mgmt. div. econs. law practice sect. 1981-83), Ill. Bar Assn. (chmn. Bill of Rights com. 1967-68, council gen. practice sect. 1982-83, vice chmn. 1982-83, council estate planning probate and trust sect. 1976-81, sec. 1980-81), Madison County Bar Assn. (pres. 1966-67). Mem. United Ch. of Christ. Probate, Real property, Estate planning. Home: 1312 Old Trenton Rd Highland IL 62249 Office: 914 Broadway Highland IL 62249

RIKON, MICHAEL, lawyer; b. Bklyn., Feb. 2, 1945; s. Charles and Ruth (Shapiro) R.; m. Leslie Sharon Rein, Feb. 11, 1968; children—Carrie Rachel, Joshua Howard. B.S., N.Y. Inst. Tech., 1966; J.D., Bklyn. Law Sch., 1969; LL.M., NYU, 1974. Bar: N.Y. 1970, U.S. Dist. Ct. (so. and ea. dists.) N.Y. 1971, U.S. Ct. Appeals (2d cir.) 1972, U.S. Supreme Ct. 1973, U.S. Ct. Appeals (5th and 11th cirs.) 1981. Asst. corp. counsel City of N.Y., 1969-73; law clk. N.Y. State Ct. Claims, 1973-80; ptnr. Rudick and Rikon, P.C., N.Y.C., 1980—. Contbr. articles to profl. jours. Pres. Village Greens Residents Assn., 1978-79; chmn. bd. Arden Heights Jewish Ctr., Staten Island, N.Y., 1976-77; pres. North Shore Republican Club, 1977; mem. community bd. Staten Island Borough Pres., 1977. Mem. ABA, Assn. Trial Lawyers Am., N.Y. State Bar Assn. (spl. com. of condemnation law), N.Y. County Bar Assn., N.Y. County Lawyers Assn. Republican. Jewish. Avocations: collecting stamps, photography, collecting miniature soldiers. Condemnation, State civil litigation, Real property. Home: 133 Avondale Rd Ridgewood NJ 07450 Office: Rudick & Rikon PC 150 Broadway New York NY 10038

RILEY, ARCH WILSON, JR., lawyer; b. Wheeling, W.Va., Jan. 15, 1957; s. Arch W. Sr. and Mary List (Paull) R.; m. Sally Ann Goodspeed, Aug. 9, 1980; 1 child, Ann Jerome. BA in French and Econs., Tufts U., 1979; JD, W.Va. U., 1982. Bar: W.Va. 1982, U.S. Dist. Ct. (no. and so. dists.) W.Va. 1982. Assoc. Riley & Yahn, Wheeling, 1982, Riley & Broadwater, Wheeling, 1982-83; ptnr. Riley & Riley, Wheeling, 1983—; bd. dirs., Upper Ohio Valley Crisis Hotline Inc., Wheeling, 1983—, v.p. 1983-87, pres., 1987—. Chmn. Human Rights Commn., Wheeling, 1985; committeeman Ohio County Dem. Execs., Wheeling, 1984—; bd. dirs., treas. No. Panhandle Behavioral Health Ctr., Wheeling, 1984—. Mem. W.Va. Bar Assn., Ohio County Bar Assn. (sec. 1983-84), Assn. Trial Lawyers Am. Presbyterian. Clubs: Wheeling Country, Ft. Henry (Wheeling). General practice, Contracts commercial, General corporate. Office: Riley & Riley 27 Haddale Ave Suite 200 Riley Bldg Wheeling WV 26003

RILEY, DAVID EDWARD, lawyer; b. Ann Arbor, Mich., July 7, 1953; s. Edward Joseph and Mary Jane (Hunt) R.; m. Janine Lynn Rodman, July 30, 1982. B.A. in Econs., Wayne State U., 1976, J.D., 1979; LL.M. in Corp. Law, NYU, 1985. Bar: Mich. 1979, U.S. Dist. Ct. (ea. dist.) Mich. 1979, U.S. Ct. Appeals (6th cir.) 1984, N.Y. 1986. Assoc. Martin S. Baum, PC, Detroit, 1979-82, Miller, Cohen, Martens & Ice, PC, Detroit, 1982-84, Kramer, Levin, Nessen Kamin & Frankel, 1985—. Recipient Moot Ct. Achievement award Wayne State U., 1979. Mem. Mich. Bar Assn., NY. State Bar Assn., Detroit Bar Assn., Young Lawyers Assn., Order of Barrister, Mensa (No. N.J. chpt.). Roman Catholic. General corporate, Securities. Office: Kramer Levin Nessen Kamin & Frankel 919 Third Ave 40th Floor New York NY 10022

RILEY, DENNIS JAMES, lawyer; b. N.Y.C., Aug. 7, 1948. BA, BS, LaSalle Coll., 1970; JD, Cornell U., 1973. Bar: N.Y. 1974, U.S. Ct. Claims 1974, U.S. Tax Ct. 1974, U.S. Ct. Customs and Patent Appeals, 1974, 82, U.S. Ct. Mil. Appeals 1975, D.C. 1977, U.S. Ct. Appeals (D.C. cir.) 1982. Of counsel Fried Frank Shriver et al, N.Y.C., Washington, 1976-80; ptnr. Spriggs, Bode & Hollingsworth, Washington, 1981—. Author: Federal Contracts Grants and Assistance, 1985; editor: Contract Appeal Manual, 1985. Served to capt. U.S. Army, 1970-76. Mem. ABA (chmn. patent, trademark and data rights com.), Fed. Bar Assn. (contract appeals com.). Government contracts and claims, Computer, Construction. Office: Spriggs Bode & Hollingsworth 1015 15th St NW Suite 1100 Washington DC 20005

RILEY, DOROTHY COMSTOCK, state justice; b. Detroit, Dec. 6, 1924; d. Charles Austin and Josephine (Grima) Comstock; m. Wallace Don Riley, Sept. 13, 1963; 1 child, Peter Comstock. B.A. in Polit. Sci., Wayne State U., 1946, LL.B., 1949. Bar: Mich. 1950, U.S. Dist. Court (ea. dist.) Mich. 1950, U.S. Supreme Court 1957. Atty. Wayne County Friend of Court, Detroit, 1956-68; ptnr. Riley & Roumell, Detroit, 1968-72; judge Wayne County Circuit, Detroit, 1972, Mich. Ct. Appeals, Detroit, 1976-82; justice Mich. Supreme Court, Detroit, 1982-83, 85—; mem. U.S. Jud. Conf. Commn. on State-Fed. Court Relations. Co-author manuals, articles in field. Mem. adv. com. Citizenship Edn. Study, 1946-50. Recipient Disting. Alumni award Wayne U. Law Sch., 1977; Headliner award Women of Wayne, 1977; Donnelly award, 1946. Mem. ABA (family law sect. 1965—; vice chmn. gen. practice sect. com. on juvenile justice 1975-80; mem. jud. adminstrn. sect. 1973—, standing com. on fed. ct. improvements), Am. Judicature Soc., Fellows Am. Bar Found., Mich. State Bar Found., State Bar Mich. (civil liberties com. 1954-58, young lawyers sect. 1956-60, family law sect. 1966—), Detroit Bar Assn. (pub. relations com. 1955-56, author Com. in Action column, Detroit Lawyers 1955, chmn. friend of ct. and family law com. 1974-75), Nat. Women Judges Assn., Nat. Women Lawyers Assn., Women Lawyers Assn. Mich. (pres. 1957-58), Karyatides, Pi Sigma Alpha. Republican. Roman Catholic. Club: Women's Econ. Avocations: reading; gardening. Judicial administration. Office: Michigan Supreme Court 1425 Lafayette Bldg Detroit MI 48226

RILEY, JOE GLENARD, judge; b. Memphis, Oct. 13, 1947; s. Glenard and Charlotte (Curry) R.; m. Connie Donnell Riley, Nov. 28, 1969; children: John, David, Scott. BS, U. Tenn., 1969, JD, 1972. Bar: Tenn. 1972, U.S. Ct. Appeals (5th cir.) 1974, U.S. Dist. Ct. (we. dist.) Tenn. 1974. Sole practice Ridgely, Tenn., 1972-78; cir. judge State of Tenn., Ridgely, 1978—; chmn. ethics com. Tenn. Jud. Conf., 1984-86, exec. com., 1983-86. Trustee Lambuth Coll., Jackson, Tenn., 1984—. Served with N.G., 1969-75. Named Lake County Citizen or Yr., Tiptonville (Tenn.) Civitan Club, 1985; recipient Liberty Through Law award, Tenn. Young Lawyers Conf., 1983. Mem. ABA, Tenn. Bar Assn., Tenn. Jud. Conf. Methodist. Avocations: hunting, fishing, golf. Judicial administration, State civil litigation, Criminal. Home: 560 Headden Dr Ridgely TN 38080 Office: 115 Lake St Ridgely TN 38080

RILEY, JOHN FREDERICK, lawyer; b. Salisbury, N.C., Oct. 18, 1938; s. John Horace and Beatrice (Williams) R.; m. Jan Colby, June 20, 1965; children: John Michael, Jennifer Lynn, Julia Grace. BA, Wake Forest U., 1960; JD, U. N.C., 1967. Bar: N.C. 1967. Law clk. to presiding justice N.C. Supreme Ct., Raleigh, 1967-68; assoc. Leroy, Wells, Shaw & Hornthal, Elizabeth City, N.C., 1968-70; ptnr. Leroy, Wells, Shaw, Hornthal & Riley, Elizabeth City, N.C., 1970-85, Hornthal, Riley, Ellis & Maland, Elizabeth City, N.C., 1985—. Chmn. adv. bd. Salvation Army, Elizabeth City, 1976-77; trustee Elizabeth City State U., 1981—. Hankins scholar Wake Forest U., Winston-Salem, N.C., 1956. Mem. ABA, N.C. Bar Assn. (bd. dirs. real property sect. 1979-83), N.C. Land Title Assn., Elizabeth City Bar Assn. (pres. 1973-74), 1st Jud. Dist. Bar Assn. (pres. 1985-86). Democrat. Methodist. Club: Town Point (Norfolk, Va.). Lodge: Kiwanis (pres. 1974-75). Avocations: golf, tennis, boating. Real property, General corporate, Probate. Home: 101 Inlet Dr Elizabeth City NC 27909 Office: Hornthal Riley Ellis & Maland 301 E Main St PO Box 220 Elizabeth City NC 27909

RILEY, KIRK HOLDEN, lawyer; b. San Diego, Sept. 5, 1950; s. Richard Ross and Jerrine Rhae (Dennis) R.; m. Cheryl Ann Wilde, Aug. 5, 1972; children: Brooke, Kevin, Matthew, Rebecca, Conor. BA, U.S. Internat. U., San Diego, 1972; JD, Calif. Western Sch. Law, San Diego, 1975; LLM, Boston U., 1978. Bar: Calif. 1975. Assoc. Brian D. Monaghan, San Diego, 1976; tax cons. Touche Ross & Co., San Francisco, 1979-80, mgr. tax dept., San Diego, 1980, 82-83, supr. tax dept., Washington, 1980-81; assoc., mem. Branton Wilson & Armstrong, A.P.C., San Diego, 1983—; instr. U. Calif.-San Diego, 1983. Mem. ABA, San Diego County Bar Assn., Greater San Diego Sports Assn. Republican. Mormon. Personal income taxation, Corporate taxation, Real property. Home: 9249 Dillon Dr Ln Mesa CA 92041 Office: Branton & Wilson APC 701 B St Suite 1255 San Diego CA 92101

RILEY, MARK LOUIS, lawyer; b. Lafayette, La., June 24, 1955; s. Louis Ellsworth and Catherine Marie (Bauer) R.; m. Cynthia Neal Brasselle, May 24, 1980; children: David Brasselle, Catherine Elizabeth. BA, La. State U., 1977, JD, 1980. Bar: La. 1980, U.S. Dist. Ct. (ea., mid. and we. dists.) La. 1980, U.S. Ct. Appeals (5th cir.) 1980. From assco. to ptnr. Onebaye, Donohue et al, Lafayette, 1980—. Mem. ABA, La. Bar Assn., La. Assn. Def. Counsel, Order of Coif, Phi Delta Phi. Roman Catholic. Lodge: Rotary. Avocation: military history. State civil litigation, Workers' compensation, General practice. Office: Onebare Donohoe et al PO Box 3507 Lafayette LA 70502

RILEY, MICHAEL HYLAN, lawyer; b. Ardmore, Okla., Oct. 26, 1951; s. Paul Emerson and Anne (Hylan) R. AB cum laude, Harvard U., 1973; JD, Northeastern U., 1978. Bar: Mass. 1978, U.S. Dist. Ct. Mass. 1980, U.S. Ct. Appeals (1st cir.) 1980. Assoc. White, Inker, Aronson, Boston, 1979-83, Chaplin & Milstein, Boston, 1984-86, Goldstein & Manello, Boston, 1986—; lectr. Met. Coll. Boston U., 1986—. Author: Estate Administration, 1985. Mem. ABA, Mass. Bar Assn., Boston Bar Assn. Democrat. Avocations: books, music, food, wine, backpacking. Estate planning, Probate, Estate taxation. Home: 13 Ellery St #4 Cambridge MA 02138 Office: Goldstein & Manello 265 Franklin St Boston MA 02110

RILEY, PAUL E., judge; b. Wilmington, Ohio, Dec. 19, 1925; s. Lewis E. and Ethel M. (Moore) R.; m. Jean B. Riley, May 21, 1948; children—Michael T., Kathryn Riley Dupuis, Julia Ann. A.B. cum laude, Wilmington Coll., 1954; J.D., Chase Coll. Law, 1958; postgrad. Miami U., 1964. Bar: Ohio 1958, D.C. 1971, U.S. Supreme Ct. 1971. Sole practice, 1958-64; ptnr. Pusateri & Riley, 1964-67; judge probate Juvenile Div., C. Common Pleas, 1967-77, judge Civil and Criminal Divs., 1977—; lectr. in history Wilmington Coll., 1960; lectr. Advocacy Inst., U. Cin., 1977; lectr. Ohio Coll. Trial Judges, 1982. Mem. Ohio Ho. of Reps., 1964-66. Served as sgt. USMC, 1944-46; PTO. Decorated Purple Heart with cluster, Bronze Star; recipient 12 awards for superior jud. service Ohio Supreme Ct., 1975-81. Mem. Clinton County Bar, Ohio Common Pleas Judges Assn., Am. Judicature Soc., Am. Legion, Phi Alpha Delta. Republican. Roman Catholic. State civil litigation, Legal history, Legal education. Home: 297 N Spring St Wilmington OH 45177 Office: 3 South St 3d Floor Wilmington OH 45177

RILEY, PETER JAMES, lawyer; b. Teaneck, N.J., June 7, 1956; s. John Bernard and Mary Ann (Lannig) R.; m. Laura Willson Latham, June 12, 1982. BBA, U. Tex., 1978; JD, So. Meth. U., 1981. Bar: Tex. 1981, U.S. Dist. Ct. (no. dist.) Tex. 1981. Ptnr. Thompson & Knight, Dallas, 1981—. Mem. ABA, Dallas Bar Assn. Republican. Methodist. Avocation: golf. Real property, Contracts commercial, Landlord-tenant. Home: 6705 Aberdeen Dallas TX 75230 Office: Thompson & Knight 3300 1st City Ctr Dallas TX 75201

RILEY, ROBERT HENRY, lawyer; b. Dayton, Ohio, Mar. 20, 1931; s. Harry R. and Lucille N. Riley; m. Dacie R. Linfield, Aug. 29, 1957; children: Ruth, Dacie. BA, U. Va., 1954; cert. Mandarin Chinese, Def. Lang. Inst., 1955; MBA, U. Pa., 1959; JD, Seton Hall U., 1979. Bar: N.Y. 1980. V.p. Chase Manhattan, N.Y.C., 1959-80; ptnr. R. H. Riley & Assocs., Middletown, N.J., 1980—; counsel Meyers, Tersigni, Kaufmann, Lurie, Feldman & Gray, N.Y.C., 1980—; chmn. bd. dirs. US Digital Disc Corp., N.Y.C., 1986—. Served with U.S. Army, 1954-57. Mem. ABA, N.Y. State Bar Assn., Info. Industry Assn. (bd. dirs. 1966-76, treas.), Beta Gamma Sigma, Phi Alpha Theta. Avocations: golf, comml. art. Computer, Trademark and copyright, General corporate. Home: 14 Holland Rd Middletown NJ 07448

RILEY, STEVEN ALLEN, lawyer; b. Nashville, Tenn., Oct. 2, 1952; s. Harris DeWitt Jr. and Margaret (Barry) R.; m. Laura Anne Trickett, Mar. 15, 1980; children: Mary Louise, Margaret Reed. BA, Vanderbilt U., 1974, JD, 1978. Bar: Tenn. 1978, U.S. Dist. Ct. (mid. dist.) Tenn., U.S. Ct. Appeals (6th cir.), U.S. Supreme Ct. Ptnr. Bass, Berry & Sims, Nashville, 1978—. Mem. ABA (litigation and antitrust sects.), Assn. Trial Lawyers Am., Tenn. Bar Assn., Nashville Bar Assn. Presbyterian. Federal civil litigation, Personal injury, Antitrust. Office: Bass Berry & Sims 2700 First Am Ctr Nashville TN 37238

RILL, JAMES FRANKLIN, lawyer; b. Evanston, Ill., Mar. 4, 1933; s. John Columbus and Frances Eleanor (Hill) R.; m. Mary Elizabeth Laws, June 14, 1957; children: James Franklin, Roderick M. AB cum laude, Dartmouth Coll., 1954; LLB, Harvard, 1959. Bar: D.C. bar 1959. Legis. asst. Congressman James P. S. Devereux, Washington, 1952; sole practice Washington, 1953—; assoc. Steadman, Collier & Shannon, 1959-63; ptnr. Collier, Shannon & Rill, 1963-69, Collier, Shannon, Rill & Scott, 1969—; bd. dirs. The Winston Group, Inc., Washington, Marshall Durbin Food Corp., Birmingham, Ala. Contbr. articles to profl. jours. Trustee Bullis Sch., Potomac, Md. Served to 1st lt. arty. AUS, 1954-56. Mem. ABA (past chmn. legis. com., mem. council, chmn. elect, sect. of antitrust law, vice chmn. com. agy. adjudication sect. adminstrv. law), D.C. Bar Assn., Phi Delta Theta. Clubs: Met., Loudon Valley. Home: 7305 Masters Dr Potomac MD 20854 Office: Suite 308 1055 Thomas Jefferson St NW Washington DC 20007

RINALDI, FRANK ROBERT, lawyer; b. Mt. Vernon, N.Y., May 19, 1927; s. Frank Joseph and Fulvia (Ferranti) R.; m. Jean Murphy, May 31, 1952; children: Kirk, Stephen (dec.). BA magna cum laude, Harvard U., 1947, JD, 1950. Bar: N.Y. 1951, U.S. Dist. Ct. (so. dist.) N.Y., U.S. Ct. Appeals (2nd circuit). Atty. Donovan Leisure Newton & Levine, N.Y.C., 1950-53; gen. atty. CBS Inc., N.Y.C., 1953-57, ABC, N.Y.C., 1957-64; atty. MGM Studios, N.Y.C., 1964-70; v.p., asst. gen. counsel James Talcott Inc., N.Y.C., 1970-76, gen. counsel, 1976-79; v.p., counsel Irving Trust Co., N.Y.C., 1979-86, sr. counsel, 1986—. Served to lt. (j.g.) USN, 1945-46. Mem. N.Y. Bar Assn., Phi Beta Kappa. Democrat. Roman Catholic. Avocations: writing, jogging. Banking, Contracts commercial. Home: 4 Peter Cooper Rd New York NY 10010 Office: Irving Trust Co 1290 Ave of Americas 3d Floor New York NY 10010

RINALDI, KEITH STEPHEN, lawyer, accountant; b. Poughkeepsie, N.Y., Aug. 3, 1952; s. John Kevin and Corinne Frances (McCagg) R.; m. Debra Jean Knapp, Sept. 4, 1983; 1 child, Gabrielle P. BS in Acctg., Fordham U., 1974; JD, N.Y. Law Sch., 1977; LLM in Taxation, NYU, 1978. Bar: N.Y. 1978, U.S. Tax Ct. 1978, U.S. Dist. Ct. (so. and ea. dists.) N.Y. 1979, U.S. Dist. Ct. (no. dist.) N.Y. 1982. Acct., atty. Rinaldi Tax, Inc., Poughkeepsie, 1975—; prin. Keith S. Rinaldi, P.C., Poughkeepsie, 1984—; ptnr. Vasti & Rinaldi, P.C., Pleasant Valley, N.Y., 1980-84; propr., broker Arlington Assocs. Realty Co., Poughkeepsie, N.Y., 1985—. Counsel Police Athletic League of Poughkeepsie, 1982—, Mid. Hudson Italian Am. Cultural Fedn., Inc., Poughkeepsie, 1983—, Dutchess County War Casualty Com., Poughkeepsie, 1985—. Mem. ABA, N.Y. Bar Assn., Dutchess County Bar Assn., Poughkeepsie Area C. of C., Fordham U. Alumni Assn., N.Y. Law Sch. Alumni Assn., NYU Alumni Assn., Mus. Natural History (assoc.),

Smithsonian Inst. (assoc.), Town and City Poughkeepsie Police Benevolent Assn. (hon.). Avocations: skiing, hunting, deep sea fishing, tennis. Personal injury, Personal income taxation, Probate. Home: 111 Fox Run Poughkeepsie NY 12603 Office: 10 Arlington Ave Poughkeepsie NY 12603

RINCK, GARY M., lawyer; b. Chgo., Feb. 28, 1952; s. H. Carl Rinck; m. Virginia L. Flower, Sept. 8, 1984. BA cum laude, Yale U., 1974; JD, Harvard U., 1977; diploma in law, Oxford (Eng.) U., 1978. Bar: Calif. 1977. Clk. to presiding justice U.S. Dist. Ct. (cen. dist.) Calif., Los Angeles, 1978-79; assoc. Morrison & Foerster, San Francisco, 1979-84, ptnr., 1984—. Mem. ABA (litigation sect.), Calif. Bar Assn. (ligigation sect.), San Francisco Bar Assn. (litigation sect.). Democrat. Federal civil litigation, State civil litigation, Private international. Office: Morrison & Foerster 1 Market Plaza San Francisco CA 94105

RINDAL, ELLEN JOAN, ., lawyer, educator; b. Kyushu, Japan, Dec. 31, 1950; came to U.S., 1952; d. Palmer M. and Hatsue W. (Watabe) R.; m. Larry N. Wahlquist, Dec. 28, 1977 (div. July 1978). BA in Polit. Sci. with honors, U. Iowa, 1973; JD with honors, Chgo. Kent Coll. of Law, 1976. Bar: Ill. 1976, U.S. Dist. Ct. (no. dist.) Ill. 1976. Ptnr. Rindal & Walder, Hanover Park, Ill., 1976-78; assoc. Travis, Tucker & Assocs., Schaumburg, Ill., 1978-79; sole practice Schaumburg, 1979-80; assoc. W.A. Pietrasik & Assocs., Chgo., 1980; sole practice Ellen J. Rindal P.C., Elgin, Ill., 1980—; instr. Coll. of DuPage, Glen Ellyn, Ill., 1977—, MacCormac Jr. Coll., Elmhurst, Ill., 1985—, instr. Am. Inst. Paralegal Studies, Chgo., 1985—. Mem. ABA, Ill. Bar Assn., Chgo. Bar Assn., Northwest Suburban Bar Assn., Nat. Assn. Female Execs. Avocations: reading, hiking, learning to fly. Real property, State civil litigation, General corporate. Home: 344 Ventura Club Dr Roselle IL 60172 Office: 318 E Division St Elgin IL 60120

RINDEN, GERRY MUNDT, lawyer; b. Alvord, Iowa, Mar. 23, 1939; s. Gunder and Florence Elizabeth (Mundt) R.; m. Sherrill Lee Hansen, Dec. 21, 1963; children: Jennifer E., Allison L. Grad., U. Iowa, 1957-61, LLB, 1965. Bar: Iowa 1965, Ill. 1965. Assoc. Cook, Blair, Balluff & Nagle, Davenport, Iowa, 1965-66; ptnr. Klockau, McCarthy, Ellison & Rinden, Rock Island, Ill., 1967-85, Wintroub & Rinden, Des Moines, Iowa, 1986—. Mem. ABA, Am. Judicature Soc., Am. Trial Lawyers Assn., Iowa Bar Assn., Iowa Trial Lawyers Assn., Ill. Bar Assn. (chmn. com. on ins. program 1973-76, vice chair com. on profl. responsibility 1983-86, chmn. 1986—), Ill. Trial Lawyers Assn., Def. Research Inst. Republican. Pesbyterian. Club: Chgo. Athletic Assn. Avocations: reading, golf. Insurance, Personal injury. Home: 5208 Boulder West Des Moines IA 50265 Office: Wintroub & Rinden 404 Hubbell Bldg Des Moines IA 50309

RINER, JAMES WILLIAM, lawyer; b. Jefferson City, Mo., Dec. 25, 1936; s. John Woodrow and Virginia Loraine (Jackson) R.; m. Carolyn Ruth Hicke, May 14, 1976; children—Alicia Gayle, Angela Gayle, Amity Gayle. B.A., U. Mo., 1957, LL.B., 1960. Bar: Mo. 1960, U.S. Dist. Ct. (we. dist.) Mo. 1982. Asst. atty. gen. Atty. Gen.'s Office Mo., Jefferson City, 1960; commd. 1st lt. U.S. Air Force, 1960, advanced through grades to lt. col., 1974; ret., 1981; ptnr. Inglish, Monaco, Riner & Lockenvitz, P.C., 1985—, Jefferson City; city pros. Jefferson City, 1983—; city atty. California, Mo., 1985—. Contbg. author: Mo. Ins. Practice Manual, 1986. Decorated Bronze Star, Meritorious service medal. Mem. ABA, Mo. Bar Assn. Democrat. Lodge: Masons. Insurance, Workers' compensation, Real property. Home: 1106 Cimmaron Jefferson City MO 65101 Office: Inglish Monaco Riner & Lockenvitz 237 E High St Jefferson City MO 65101

RINEY, THOMAS CHARLES, lawyer; b. Bartlesville, Okla., Aug. 13, 1951; s. John Charles and Lila (Fullhart) R.; m. Sandra Candice Walker, Aug. 21, 1971; children: James P., Kenneth C. BA, U. Okla., 1972, JD, 1976. Bar: Tex. 1976, U.S. Dist. Ct. (no. dist.) Tex. 1977, U.S. Ct. Appeals (5th cir.) 1977, U.S. Ct. Appeals (11th cir.) 1981, U.S. Supreme Ct. 1984. Assoc. Gibson, Ochsner & Adkins, Amarillo, Tex., 1976-80; ptnr. Gibson, Ochsner & Adkins, Amarillo, 1980—. Bd. dirs., sec. Amarillo Speech, Hearing and Language Ctr., 1983—. Mem. ABA (dist. rep., mem. exec. council young lawyers div. 1986—), State Bar Tex. (bd.dirs. state bar coll. 1985—), Amarillo Bar Assn. (mem. exec. council 1985—), Tex. Young Lawyers Assn. (bd. dirs. 1982-84, treas. 1983-84), Tex. Assn. Def. Counsel (v.p., pres. 1984-85, bd. dirs. 1985—), Phi Delta Phi. Republican. Roman Catholic. Club: Amarillo. Lodge: Kiwanis (pres. Downtown club 1981-83, 86—). State civil litigation, Federal civil litigation, Personal injury. Office: Gibson Ochsner & Adkins 500 1st National Bank Bldg Amarillo TX 79101

RING, DOUGLAS RALPH, lawyer; b. Rochester, N.Y., July 24, 1944; s. Selden and Norma Ring. BA, La Verne Coll., 1973; JD, U. West Los Angeles, 1977. Dep. supv. Los Angeles County, 1975-81; assoc. Buchalter & Nemer, Los Angeles, 1981-84; ptnr. MacDonald & Halsted, Los Angeles, 1984-85, Howard, Ring & Chizever, Los Angeles, 1985-87, Shea & Gould, Los Angeles, 1987—; judge pro-tem Mcpl. Ct., Downey and Alhambra; v.p. Calif. Adminstrv. Law Coll., 1980-82. Author newspaper column on law and real estate, 1981—. Chmn. Neighborhood Justice Ctr., 1981-83, Western Cen. Los Angeles, bd. dirs. 1982—; pres. Los Angeles Theatre Ctr., 1983-85; mem. govt. affairs com. Bldg. Industry Assn., Los Angeles, 1986—; bd. dirs. Alternative Living for the Aging, Los Angeles, 1986—, Cen. Theatre Group, Los Angeles, 1986—. Mem. Calif. Bar Assn. (bd. editors Calif. Bar Journal 1978-80), Los Angeles County Bar Assn. (pub. affairs com., bench-bar media com., justice coordinating com., bd. editors 1979-82). Office: Howard Ring & Chizever 10960 Wilshire Blvd Los Angeles CA 90024

RING, LEONARD M., lawyer; b. Taurage, Lithuania, May 11, 1923; came to U.S., 1930, naturalized, 1930; s. Abe and Rose (Kahn) R.; m. Donna R. Cecrle, June 29, 1959; children—Robert Steven, Susan Ruth. Student, N.Mex. Sch. Mines, 1943-44; LL.D., DePaul U., 1949, J.D., 1971. Bar Ill. 1949. Spl. asst. atty. gen. State Ill., Chgo., 1967-72; spl. atty. Ill. Dept. Ins., Chgo., 1967-73; spl. trial atty. Met. San. Dist. Greater Chgo., Chgo., 1967-77; lectr. civil trial, appellate practice, tort law Nat. Coll. Advocacy, San Francisco, 1971, 72; mem. com. jury instrns. Ill. Supreme Ct., 1967-71, 73—; nat. chmn. Attys. Congl. Campaign Trust, Washington, 1975-79. Author: (with Harold A. Baker) July Instructions and Forms of Verdict, 1972. Editorial bd. Belli Law Jour., 1983—; adv. bd. So. Ill. U. Law Jour., 1983—. Contbr. chpts. to books, numerous articles to profl. jours. Trustee, Roscoe Pound-Am. Trial Lawyers Found., Washington, 1978-80; chmn. bd. trustees Avery Coonley Sch., Downers Grove, Ill., 1974-75. Served with U.S. Army, 1943-46. Decorated Purple Heart. Fellow Am. Coll. Trial Lawyers, Internat. Acad. Trial Lawyers, Internat. Soc. Barristers; mem. Soc. Trial Lawyers, Am. Judicature Soc., Appellate Lawyers Assn. (pres. 1974-75), Assn. Trial Lawyers Am. (nat. pres. 1973-74), Ill. Trial Lawyers Assn. (pres. 1966-68), Trial Lawyers for Pub. Justice (founder), Chgo. Bar Assn. (bd. mgrs. 1971-73), ABA (sect. council 1983—), Ill. Bar Assn., Kans. Bar Assn. (hon. life), Lex Legio Bar Assn. (pres. 1976-78), Inner Circle Advs. Clubs: Metropolitan, Plaza, Meadow, River; Monroe (Chgo.). State civil litigation, Personal injury, Federal civil litigation. Home: 6 Royal Vale Dr Ginger Creek Oak Brook IL 60521 Office: 111 W Washington St Chicago IL 60602

RING, LUCILE WILEY, lawyer; b. Kearney, Nebr., Jan. 2, 1920; d. Myrtie Mercer and Alice (Cowell) W.; m. John Robert Ring, Mar. 28, 1948; children—John Raymond, James Wiley, Thomas Eric. A.B., Kearney State Coll., 1944; J.D., Washington U., 1946. Bar: Mo. 1946, U.S. Dist. Ct. (ea. dist.) Mo. 1947, U.S. Ct. Appeals (8th cir.) 1972. Atty.-adviser, chief legal group adjudications br. Army Fin. Ctr., St. Louis, 1946-52; exec. dir. lawyer referral service St. Louis Bar, 1960-70; sole practice, St. Louis, 1960—; staff law clk. U.S. Ct. Appeals (8th cir.), St. Louis, 1970-72; exec. dir. St. Louis Com. on Cts., 1972—; legal advisor Mo. State Anat. Bd., 1965—; adj. prof. adminstrv. law Webster Coll., Webster Groves, Mo., 1977-78; mem. Mo. Profl. Liability Rev. Bd., State of Mo., 1977-79. Author, editor: Guide to Community Services - Who Do I Talk To, 1974, 75, 1976-79; St. Louis Court Directories, 1972, 73, 74, 75; Felony Procedures in St. Louis Courts, 1975; contbr. articles to profl. jours. Mem. Mo. Mental Health Authority, 1964-65; bd. dirs., v.p. Drug and Substance Abuse Council, met. St. Louis, 1976-83; mem. adv. council St. Louis Agy. on Tng. and Employment, 1976-83; mem. Mayor's Jud. Reform Subcom., St. Louis, 1974-76. Washington U. Sch. Law scholar, 1944-46; 1st Mo. woman nominated for St. Louis Ct. Appeals, Mo. Appellate Commn., 1972; recipient letter of commendation Office of Chief of Fin., U.S. Army, 1952. Mem. Bar Assn. Met. St. Louis (v.p. 1975-76), Legal Services of Eastern Mo., Inc. (v.p. 1978-79, dir.), Legal Aid Soc. of St. Louis City and County (bd. dirs. 1977-78), HUD Women and Housing Commn. (commr. 1975), Mo. Assn. Women Lawyers (treas. 1959-60, pres. 1960-61), Pi Kappa Delta, Sigma Tau Delta, Xi Phi. Methodist. Club: Washington U. Dental Faculty Wives (pres. 1972-74). General practice. Home: 755 Catalpa Ave Webster Groves MO 63119 Office: Suite 1002 Syndicate Trust Bldg 915 Olive St Saint Louis MO 63101

RING, RONALD HERMAN, lawyer; b. Flint, Mich., Nov. 30, 1938; s. Herman and Lydia (Miller) R.; m. Joan Kay Whitener, Aug. 5, 1966. AB, U. Mich., 1961, LLB, 1964. Bar: Mich. 1964, U.S. Dist. Ct. (ea. dist.) Mich. 1966. Assoc. Beagle, Benton & Hicks, Flint, 1964-69; ptnr. Beagle & Ring, Flint, 1970-80, Beagle, Ring & Beagle, Flint, 1980-85, Ring, Beagle & Busch, Flint, 1985—. Mem. meml. com. Crossroads Village, Flint, 1981; pres. Family Service Agy., Genesee County, Mich., 1986. Mem. ABA, Assn. Trial Lawyers Am., Mich. Bar Assn. (delivery of legal service com. 1986, med. malpractice panel 1986), Genesee County Bar Assn. (pres. 1980-81, bd. dirs. 1979-82, cir. ct. mediation panel 1986). Club: Ostego Ski (Gaylord, Mich.). Avocations: skiing, sailing. State civil litigation, Personal injury, General practice. Home: 1022 Western Hills Flint MI 48504 Office: Ring Beagle & Busch 700 Mott Found Bldg Flint MI 48502

RINGEL, DEAN (L), lawyer; b. N.Y.C., Dec. 12, 1947; m. Ronnie Sussman, Aug. 24, 1969; children: Marion, Alicia. BA, Columbia Coll., 1967; JD, Yale U., 1971. Bar: N.Y. 1972, U.S. Ct. Appeals (6th cir.) 1972, U.S. Ct. Appeals (2d and D.C. cirs.) 1974, U.S. Supreme Ct. 1976, U.S. Ct. Appeals (10th cir.) 1982. Law clk. to presiding justice U.S. Ct. Appeals (6th cir.), 1971-72; assoc. Cahill Gordon & Reindel, N.Y.C., 1972-79; ptnr. Cahill, Gordon & Reindel, N.Y.C., 1979—. Mem. ABA (vice chmn. com. on freedom of speech and press 1978-79), Assn. of Bar of City of N.Y. (communications com., fed. legis. com.). Federal civil litigation, State civil litigation, Libel. Office: Cahill Gordon & Reindel 80 Pine St New York NY 10005

RINGEL, FRED MORTON, lawyer; b. Brunswick, Ga., July 19, 1929; s. Phil S. and Louise (Pfeiffer) R.; m. Toby Markowitz, Mar. 18, 1962; children: Andrew Franklin, Douglas Eric, Michael Stanley, Edrea Janet Piper. A.B., U. Ga., 1950; LL.B. magna cum laude, Harvard U. (mem. bd. Law Rev. 1954-55), 1955. Bar: Ga. 1951, Fla. 1955, N.Y. 1956. Research asst. Am. Law Inst., N.Y.C., 1955-56; asso. firm Cravath, Swaine & Moore, N.Y.C., 1956-59; atty. W.R. Grace & Co., N.Y.C., 1959-60; mem. firm Rogers, Towers, Bailey, Jones & Gay, Jacksonville, Fla., 1961—; also treas. Rogers, Towers, Bailey, Jones & Gay. Contbr. articles to legal jours. Bd. govs. Fla. Nature Conservancy, 1962-69. Served with USAF, 1951-53; 1t. Col. Res. Recipient Oak Leaf award Nature Conservancy, 1974. Mem. Am. Bar Assn., Am. Law Inst., Phi Beta Kappa. General corporate, Probate, State and local taxation. Home: 4478 Craven Rd W Jacksonville FL 32217 Office: 1300 Gulflife Dr Jacksonville FL 32207

RINGER, DARRELL WAYNE, lawyer; b. Elizabeth, N.J., Apr. 14, 1948; s. Darrell Wayne and Elva (Brown) R.; m. Mary Kay Williamson, Mar. 6, 1970 (div. May 1977); 1 child, Daniel Benjamin; m. Rebecca Ruth Bonner, Feb. 23 1979; 1 child, Darren Wayne. BS in Physics, W.Va. U., 1971; MBA, U. N.D., 1975; JD, W.Va. U., 1978. Bar: W.Va. 1978, U.S. Dist. Ct. (no. and so. dists.) W.Va. 1978. Assoc. Jones, Williams, West & Jones, Clarksburg, W.Va., 1978-80, Moreland & Ringer, Morgantown, W.Va., 1980-83, Reeder, Shuman, Ringer & Wiley, Morgantown, 1983—; 1st asst. prosecutor Monongalia County, W.Va., 1985—. Bd. dirs. Monongalia County (W.Va.) Mental Health Assn., Morgantown, 1981-83; mem. W.Va. U. Animal Care and Use Com., 1985—. Served to capt. USAF, 1971-75. Mem. ABA, W.Va. Bar Assn. (com. on admissions to the bar 1986—), Monongalia County Bar Assn. (sec. 1980—), Assn. Trial Lawyers Am., W.Va. Trial Lawyers Assn. (bd. govs. 1982—). Democrat. Avocation: amateur radio. General corporate, Criminal, Personal injury. Home: 249 Park St Morgantown WV 26505 Office: Reeder Shuman et al 256 High St Morgantown WV 26507

RINGER, JAMES MILTON, lawyer; b. Orlando, Fla., July 9, 1943; s. Robert T. and Jessie M. (Rowe) R.; m. Jaquelyn Hope, Apr. 10, 1965; children—Carolyn Hope, James Matthew. A.B., Ohio U., 1965; J.D., Cornell U., 1968. Bar: N.Y. 1968, U.S. Dist. Ct. (no. dist.) N.Y. 1968, U.S. Dist. Ct. (so. and ea. dists.) N.Y. 1972, U.S. Ct. Appeals (2d cir.) 1972, U.S. Ct. Claims 1976, U.S. Dist. Ct. (we. dist.) N.Y. 1978, U.S. Ct. Appeals (4th cir.) 1981, U.S. Ct. Appeals (9th cir.) 1983. Assoc. Rogers & Wells, N.Y.C., 1968-78, ptnr., 1978—; instr. bus. law U. Alaska, 1970-71. Editor Cornell Law Rev., 1967-68. Served to lt. JAGC, USNR, 1969-72. Mem. ABA. Republican. Episcopalian. Federal civil litigation, Contracts commercial, Securities. Office: Rogers & Wells 200 Park Ave New York NY 10166

RINGER, JOHN WILLIAM, associate judge; b. Dexter, Mo., July 18, 1936; s. John Lee and Helen (Boyd) R.; m. Carolyn Irvin, July 18, 1954 (div. 1967); 1 dau., Lisa Denise; m. Debra Lou Calhoun, Dec. 4, 1976; 1 child, James Michael; 1 stepchild, Lora Brooke Bailey. A.B., William Jewell Coll., 1958; J.D., U. Mo., 1960. Bar: Mo. 1960, U.S. Dist. Ct. (ea. dist.) Mo. 1964, U.S. Tax Ct. 1974. Assoc. Powell, Ringer & Bischof (and predecessor firms), Dexter, 1960-63, ptnr., 1963-79, sr. ptnr., 1979-86; assoc. judge juvenile and criminal div, Mo. 35th Jud. Cir., 1986—. Contbr. Mo. Law Rev. Pres., Dexter Meml. Hosp., 1964—; campaign dir. Stoddard County March of Dimes, 1960-64, campaign treas. 1964-67; co-chmn. Community Betterment Com., 1971-73. Mem. Mo. Assn. Trial Attys., Am. Trial Lawyers Assn., ABA, Mo. Bar Assn., Am. Judicature Soc., Stoddard County Bar Assn., Mo. Soc. Hosp. Attys., Am. Acad. Hosp. Attys., Dexter C. of C. (past dir., Community Leadership award 1964). Democrat. Baptist (pres., bd. dirs. 1968-77, music dir. 1960-80). Club: Kiwanis (past pres.). Avocations: yard work, model airplanes. Contracts commercial, Juvenile, Criminal. Home: 405 N Walnut PO Box 337 Dexter MO 63841 Office: Cir Ct Div II PO Box 339 Bloomfield MO 63825

RINGKAMP, STEPHEN H., lawyer; b. St. Louis, Nov. 14, 1949; s. Aloysius G. and Melba Ann (Finke) R.; m. Patricia Sue Fuse, July 5, 1971; children—Christa, Angela, Laura. B.S.E.E., St. Louis U., 1971, J.D. cum laude, 1974. Bar: Mo. 1974, U.S. Dist. Ct. (ea. dist.) Mo. 1974, U.S. Ct. Appeals (8th cir.) 1974. Law clk. 22d Jud. Circuit Mo., St. Louis, 1974-75; assoc. Hullverson, Hullverson & Frank, Inc., St. Louis, 1976—; reporter, mem. com. on civil instrns. Mo. Supreme Ct., 1981—; adj. prof. law St. Louis U., 1983—; mem. faculty Nat. Practice Inst. Products Liability Conf., 1984; lectr. legal seminars. Contbr. articles to legal jours. Recipient Trial Lawyer award Mo. Bar Found., 1983. Mem. ABA, Mo. Bar (vice chmn. civil practice com. 1983-84), Mo. Assn. Trial Attys. (bd. govs. 1980—), Assn. Trial Lawyers Am., Bar Assn. Met. St. Louis, Lawyers Assn. St. Louis. Personal injury. Office: Hullverson Hullverson & Frank Inc 1010 Market St Saint Louis MO 63101

RINGLAND, ROBERT PAUL, judge; b. Cin., Oct. 6, 1945; s. James Wilson and Dorothy (Sandel) R.; 1 child, Adam Lyle. BA, Ohio State U., 1963; JD, U. Cin., 1970. Bar: Ohio 1971, US Dist. Ct. (so. dist.) Ohio 1971, US Supreme Ct. 1978. Atty. John Gehrig & Co., Cin., 1971-73; asst. pros. atty. Clermont County, Batavia, Ohio, 1973-77; sole practice, Batavia, 1973-83; judge Clermont County Ct., Batavia, 1977-83; judge Common Pleas Ct., Batavia, 1983—. Author: Child Sex Abuse Evidence Problems, 1986, Child Abuse Evidence Outline for Ohio Judges Resource Manual, 1986. Atty. Legal Aid Soc., Batavia, 1969-70. Served to 1st lt. JAG, US Army, 1970-71. Recipient Superior Jud. Service award Supreme Ct., Ohio, 1977-83, Dist. Award of Merit, Boy Scouts Am., Cin., 1984. Mem. 648 Bd. (chmn. 1973-74). Methodist. Lodges: Rotary (bd. dirs. 1979-80), Masons. Avocations: golf, fishing, racquetball, paleontology. Judicial administration. Office: Common Pleas Ct 270 Main St Batavia OH 45103

RINGLE, BRETT ADELBERT, lawyer; b. Berkeley, Calif., Mar. 17, 1951; s. Forrest A. and Elizabeth V. (Darnall) R.; m. Sue Kinslow, May 26, 1973. B.A., U. Tex., 1973, J.D., 1976. Bar: Tex. 1976, U.S. Dist. Ct. (no. dist.) Tex. 1976, U.S. Supreme Ct. 1980, U.S. Ct. Appeals (5th cir.) 1984. Ptnr., Shank, Irwin & Conant, Dallas, 1976-86, Jones, Day, Reavis & Pogue, Dallas, 1986—; adj. prof. law So. Meth. U., Dallas, 1983. Author: (with J. W. Moore and H. I. Bendix) Moore's Federal Practice, Vol. 12, 1980, Vol. 13, 1981, (with J. W. Moore) Vol. 1A, 1982. Mem. Dallas Bar Assn. Federal civil litigation, State civil litigation, General practice. Home: 6423 Malcolm Dr Dallas TX 75214 Office: Jones Day Reavis & Pogue 2300 LTV Ctr PO Box 660623 Dallas TX 75266

RINGLE, PHILIP HAMILTON, JR., lawyer; b. Portland, Oreg., Mar. 23, 1931; s. Philip Hamilton and Audrey Louise (Smallhouse) R.; m. Reba Nan Burris, Aug. 22, 1959; children—James B., Sara Louise. B.A., Willamette U., 1953, J.D., 1956. Bar: Oreg. 1957. Assoc. Green, Richardson, Green & Griswold, Portland, Oreg., 1958-63, Hibbard, Jacobs, Caldwell & Kincart, Oregon City, Oreg., 1963-65, Misko, Njust & Ringle, Oregon City, 1965-67; ptnr. Ringle & Herndon, Gladstone, Oreg., 1968-76; pres. Ringle, Herndon & Beck, P.C., Gladstone, Oreg., 1976-85; pres. Ringle & Herndon, P.C., 1985-86; sole practice, Gladstone, 1986—; mcpl. ct. judge City of Gladstone, 1965—. Mem. ABA, Oreg. Trial Lawyers Assn., Oreg. State Bar Assn., Clackamas County Bar Assn., Multnomah Bar Assn., Oreg. Mcpl. Judges Assn. (pres. 1975-77). Republican. Presbyterian (elder). Clubs: The Court (Portland), Schnee Vöeli Ski (Portland) (pres. 1960-61). Lodges: Elks (Milwaukie, Oreg.), Rotary (pres. Oregon City club 1970-71). Co-editor: Oregon Special Court Bench Book, 1978. Family and matrimonial, Personal injury, Workers' compensation. Office: 405 W Arlington Gladstone OR 97027

RINKEL, MICHAEL JOSEPH, lawyer; b. Detroit, July 6, 1950; s. Robert William Rinkel and Jeanne Isabelle (Wilkinson) Butler; m. Georgia Lynne Grovesteen, Sept. 8, 1979. BA, U. Mich., 1972; JD, U. Detroit, 1977; LLM in Labor, Wayne State U., 1983. Bar: Mich. 1978, U.S. Supreme Ct. 1983. Assoc. Raymond L. Krell, P.C., Detroit, 1978, Brian M. Smith & Assocs., Troy, Mich., 1979-81, Sloan, Benefiel & Farrer, P.C., Kalamazoo, 1981-82; ptnr. Siemion, Huckabay, Bodary, Padilla & Morganti, Detroit, 1982—. Mem. ABA, Mich. Bar Assn., Oakland County Bar Assn., Assn. Def. Trial Counsel. Avocations: racquetball, cycling, running, reading, music. Personal injury, Workers' compensation, Insurance. Office: Siemion Huckabay et al 1700 Penobscot Detroit MI 48226

RINKER, ANDREW, JR., lawyer; b. New Orleans, Jan. 6, 1957; s. Andrew and Frances Marion (Fitzpatrick) R. BS, La. State U., 1978, MBA, 1981; JD, Tulane U., 1982. Bar: La. 1982, U.S. Ct. Appeals (5th cir.) 1982, U.S. Dist. Ct. (ea. and we. dists.) La., U.S. Supreme Ct. 1986. Ptnr. Chaffe, McCall, Phillips, Toler & Sarpy, New Orleans, 1982—; editor in chief Tulane Law Rev., New Orleans, 1981-82. Contbr. articles to profl. jours. Mem. ABA, La. State Bar Assn., New Orleans Bar Assn., La. Law Inst., Phi Kappa Phi, Beta Gamma Sigma, Omicron Delta Kappa. Republican. Roman Catholic. Club: So. Yacht (New Orleans). Avocations: sailing, golf, tennis, hunting. General corporate, Municipal bonds, Probate. Home: 2115 Palmer Ave New Orleans LA 70118 Office: Chaffe McCall Phillips et al 210 Baronne St 1500 FNBC Bldg New Orleans LA 70112

RINN, LOUISE ANNE, lawyer; b. Sangley Point, Philippines, Apr. 28, 1955; (parents Am. citizens); d. John Patrick Jr. and Patricia Eileen (Moylan) R.; m. Gregory Boyd Davies, Oct. 9, 1982. BA in Polit. Sci. and Econs. magna cum laude, U. Nebr., 1977; JD, Columbia U., 1980. Bar: Nebr. 1980, U.S. Dist. Ct. Nebr. 1980, U.S. Ct. Appeals (D.C. cir.) 1985. Sole practice Omaha, 1980-81; atty. Union Pacific R.R., Omaha, 1981-82, asst. gen. atty., 1982—; chmn. Western Transp., San Francisco, 1985-86. Class mem. Leadership Omaha, 1984. Mem. ABA (antitrust div., pub. utilities sect.), Nebr. Bar Assn., Assn. Transp. Practitioners (vice chmn. law sem. 1984-85), Phi Kappa Phi, Pi Upsilon Delta. Democrat. Avocations: dance, walking. Antitrust, Administrative and regulatory. Home: 2119 S 61st St Omaha NE 68106 Office: Union Pacific RR 1416 Dodge St Room 830 Omaha NE 68179

RINSKY, JOEL CHARLES, lawyer; b. Bklyn., Jan. 29, 1938; s. Irving C. and Elsie (Millman) R.; m. Judith L. Lynn, Jan. 26, 1963; children: Heidi M., Heather S., Jason W. BS, Rutgers U., 1961, LLB, 1962, JD, 1968. Bar: N.J. 1963, U.S. Dist. Ct. N.J. 1963, U.S. Supreme Ct. 1967, U.S. Ct. Appeals (3d cir.) 1986. Sole practice Livingston, N.J., 1964-77, 82—; ptnr. Rinsky & Del Plato, P.A., N.J., 1977-82. Mem. exec. com. Essex County (N.J.) Dems., 1983—; Dem. com. person Millburn-Short Hills, N.J., 1982—, vice chmn. 1983—; bd. govs. Lake Naomi Assn. Pocono Pines, Pa., 1983—; trustee Student Loan Fund, Millburn, 1983—. Fellow Am. Acad. Matrimonial Lawyers; mem. N.J. Bar Assn., Essex County Bar Assn., N.J. Automobile Arbitration Program (arbitrator). Jewish. Avocations: tennis, running, chess, golf, piano. Family and matrimonial, Personal injury, Real property. Home: 23 Winthrop Rd Short Hills NJ 07078 Office: 600 South Livingston Ave Livingston NJ 07039

RIORDAN, JOHN, lawyer; b. Bakersfield, Calif., Nov. 14, 1932; s. John and Genevieve (McNulty) R.; m. Geraldine O'Boyle, June 16, 1960 (div. 1969); children—Liam, Sean. B.S., U. San Francisco, 1954, J.D., 1959. Bar: Calif. 1959, D.C. 1964. Adminstrv. asst. U.S. Congressman, Washington, 1960-64; sole practice, San Francisco, 1965—. Commr. Dept. Welfare, City of San Francisco, 1964-68; trustee San Francisco Community Coll., 1972—; bd. dirs. Council Civic Unity, Irish Lit. and Hist. Soc. Workers' compensation, Social security disabilities claims. Home: 507 Polk St #330 San Francisco CA 94102 Office: 507 Polk St Suite 330 San Francisco CA 94102

RIORDAN, RAY JOSEPH, JR., lawyer; b. Oklahoma City, Sept. 25, 1943; s. Ray Joseph and Eileen (Kelley) R.; m. Phyllis Laubmeier, Aug. 10, 1968; children: R.J., Maria, Phyl. BS, Marquette U., 1965; JD, U. Wis., 1968. Bar: Wis. 1968, U.S. Supreme Ct. 1976. Asst. dist. atty. Green Lake County, Berlin, Wis., 1968-69; sr. ptnr. Riordan & Sorenson, Ripon, Wis., 1969-79; exec. v.p., gen. counsel Wis. State Telephone Assn., Madison, Wis., 1979—; sec., treas. Wis. State Telephone Assn., Madison, 1981—; bd. dirs. Bank of Middleton, Wis., 1983—. Mem. ABA, Wis. Bar Assn., Am. Acad. Trial Lawyers, Wis. Acad. Trial Lawyers, Ripon C. of C. (pres. 1973-75), Ripon Jaycees (pres. 1971-72). Lodges: Kiwanis, Optimists. Avocations: water sports, bridge. Public utilities. Office: Wis State Telephone Assn 4610 University Ave Suite 640 Madison WI 53705

RIPPE, JOHN HENRY, lawyer; b. Brownsville, Minn., June 12, 1907; s. Herman and Lisa Wilhelmina (Kuecker) R.; m. Alice Miriam Sprague, Sept. 12, 1933; children: Jonette Fitzgerald, Susan Haugstad, Alison Brenna. BA, Upper Iowa U., 1928; JD, Wis. U., 1937. Bar: Wis. 1938, U.S. Dist. Ct. Wis. 1938, Minn. 1944, U.S. Dist. Ct. Minn. 1944. Ptnr. Flynn Rippe & Flynn, Caledonia, Minn., 1938-60, Roerkohl, Rippe & Lee, Caledonia, 1960-77, Rippe, Hammell & Murphy, Caledonia, 1977—; bd. dirs. Sprague Nat. Bank, Caledonia. Bd. of trustees Upper Iowa U., Fayette, 1980—, Caledonia Meth. Ch.; past chmn. 1st Dist. Minn., Rochester, Houston County Reps., Caledonia; bd. dirs. Camp Winnebago; past bd. of trustees Crippled Children and Adults of Minn. Named to Football Hall of Fame Upper Iowa U., 1984. Mem. ABA, Wis. Bar Assn., Minn. Bar Assn. (past chmn.), Am. Judicature Soc., 3d Dist. Bar Assn. (past chmn.), Houston County Bar Assn. (past chmn.). Methodist. Lodge: Elks. Avocations: golf, fishing. Probate, General practice, Real property. Office: Rippe Hammel & Murphy Sprague Profl Bldg Caledonia MN 55921

RIPPLINGER, GEORGE RAYMOND, JR., lawyer; b. East St. Louis, Ill., Apr. 19, 1945; s. George Raymond and Virginia Lee (Toupnot) R. A.B., U. Ill., 1967, J.D., 1970. Bar: Ill. 1970, U.S. Dist. Ct. (so. dist.) Ill. 1970, U.S. Ct. Appeals (7th cir.) 1970, U.S. Dist. Ct. (ea. dist.) Ill. 1972, U.S. Supreme Ct. 1973, U.S. Dist. Ct. (ea. dist.) Mo. 1977, U.S. Ct. Appeals (8th cir.) 1977. Assoc. Meyer & Meyer, Belleville and Greenville, Ill., 1970-72; assoc. Meyer & Kaucher, Belleville and Highland, Ill., 1972-73; sole practice Belleville, 1974; ptnr. Ripplinger & Walsh, Clayton, Mo., 1974-76, Ripplinger, Dixon & Hoffman and predecessors, now Ripplinger, Dixon & Ver Steegh, Belleville and Clayton, 1976—. Bd. visitors U. Ill. Coll. Law, 1979-86, pres. 1983-84; chmn. Southwestern Ill. chpt. ACLU, 1971-74, 76—; mem. exec. com. Sierra Club, 1981-85. Served to maj., USAR, 1970—. Fellow Am. Bar Found., Ill. Bar Found.; mem. ABA (chmn. workers compensation com., gen. practice sec. 1985—), Ill. Bar Assn., East St. Louis Bar Assn., St. Clair County Bar Assn., Met. St. Louis Bar Assn., Mo. Bar Assn., Assn. Trial Lawyers Am., Ill. Trial Lawyers Assn., Res. Officers Assn. Democrat. Personal injury, Workers' compensation, Criminal. Office: 2215 W Main Belleville IL 62223 Office: 319 N Fourth St Saint Louis MO 63102

RIS, WILLIAM KRAKOW, JR., lawyer; b. Denver, Oct. 27, 1947; s. William K. and Patty (Nash) R.; m. Adrienne Wolf, June 14, 1970; children:

Dylan, Ethan. BA, Northwestern U., 1969; MA, Johns Hopkins U., 1971; JD, U. Denver, 1974; LLM, Georgetown U., 1978. Bar: Colo., 1975, D.C., 1977, U.S. Supreme Ct., 1978. Trial atty. Civil Aeronautics Bd., Washington, 1975-78; counsel Senate Commerce Commn., Washington, 1978-83; ptnr., gen. counsel Wexler, Reynolds, Harrison & Schule, Washington, 1983—. Contbr. articles to profl. jours. Legislative, Administrative and regulatory. Home: 9507 Kingsley Ave Bethesda MD 20814 Office: Wexler Reynolds Harrison & Schule 1317 F ST NW Washington DC 20004

RISACHER, MARTIN EUGENE, judge, educator; b. Washington, Ind., Apr. 23, 1947; s. Leo Eugene and Catherine Phoebe (Summers) R.; m. Katherine Anne Klueh, June 4, 1971; 1 dau., Shannon Leigh. B.A. magna cum laude, Ind. State U., 1972; J.D., Ind. U., 1975; grad. Ind. Jud. Coll., Indpls., 1982. Bar: Ind., U.S. Dist. Ct. (so. dist.) Ind. 1975. Investigator, pros. atty. Dubois County (Ind.), Jasper, 1975-76; judge Dubois County Ct., Jasper, 1976-80, Dubois Superior Ct., Jasper, 1980—; faculty mem. Nat. Jud. Coll., Reno, 1980—. Project dir. Dubois County Boys and Girls Homes, 1976—; pres. Alcohol Countermeasure Program, Jasper, 1976—; chmn. fin. com. St. Joseph Hosp. Found., Huntingburg, Ind., 1982—; mem. exec. com. Dubois County Substance Abuse Taskforce, 1983—. Served to 1st lt. U.S. Army, 1966-69. Mem. Nat. Council Juvenile and Family Ct. Judges, Ind. Council Juvenile and Family Ct. Judges, Ind. Judges Assn. Democrat. Roman Catholic. Jurisprudence, Legal education, Criminal. Home: RD 1 Box 136B Dubois IN 47546 Office: Dubois Superior Ct Courthouse Jasper IN 47546

RISCH, JAMES E., state senator, lawyer; b. Milw., May 3, 1943; s. Elroy A. and Helen B. (Levi) R.; m. Vicki L. Choborda, June 8, 1968; children—James E., Jason S., Jordan D. B.S. in Forestry, U. Idaho, 1965, J.D., 1968. Dep. pros. atty. Ada County, Idaho, 1968-69, chief dep. pros. atty., 1969-70, pros. atty., 1971-75; mem. Idaho Senate, 1974—, majority leader, 1977-82, pres. pro tem, 1983—; ptnr. Risch Goss, Insinger & Salladay, Boise, Idaho, 1975—; prof. law Boise State U., 1972-75. Mem. ABA, Idaho Bar Assn., Boise Bar Assn., Am. Judicature Soc., Nat. Dist. Attys. Assn. (bd. dirs. 1977), Idaho Pros. Attys. Assn. (pres. 1976), Phi Delta Theta, Xi Sigma Pi. Republican. Roman Catholic. Avocations: hunting; fishing; skiing; horseback riding; tennis. State civil litigation, General corporate, Federal civil litigation. Home: 5400 S Cole Rd Boise ID 83709 Office: Risch Goss Insinger & Salladay 407 W Jefferson Boise ID 83702

RISIK, PHILIP MAURICE, lawyer; b. N.Y.C., Jan. 18, 1914; s. Isidor Morton and Celia (Merken) R.; m. Natalie Wynn, Nov. 5, 1948; children—David, Stephen, Elizabeth. B.Sc., NYU, 1932, J.D., 1936. Bar: N.Y. 1937, Md. 1975, U.S. Dist. Ct. (so. dist.) N.Y. 1940, U.S. Dist. Ct. (D.C. dist.) 1970, U.S. Dist. Ct. Md. 1982, U.S. Ct. Claims 1975, U.S. Ct. Appeals (D.C. cir.) 1975, U.S. Ct. Appeals (8th cir.) 1979, U.S. Supreme Ct. 1975, U.S. Ct. Appeals (4th and 5th cirs.) 1986. Practice, N.Y.C., 1937-41, 46-49; counsel N.Y. QM Procurement Agy., N.Y.C., 1949-51; procurement specialist Office Sec. Def., Washington, 1953-62; adminstrv. judge Armed Services Bd. Contract Appeals, Washington, 1962-74; of counsel Wachtel Ross & Matzkin, Chevy Chase, Md., 1974—; Contbr. articles to George Washington U. Law Rev., Fed. Bar Jour. Area v.p. Montgomery County PTAs, Rockville, Md., 1969; trustee sch. dist., Kemp Mill, Md., 1967. Served to col. U.S. Army, 1941-46, 51-53; ETO. Decorated Bronze Star; recipient Conspicuous Service Cross, State of N.Y., 1947, Meritorious Civilian Service medal Sec. Def., 1974. Mem. ABA (council) pub. contract law sect. 1969), Am. Arbitration Assn. (nat. panel arbitrators). Jewish. Lodges: Masons (sr. steward 1949). Government contracts and claims, Contracts commercial, Federal civil litigation. Home: 10224 Windsor View Dr Potomac MD 20854 Office: Wachtel Ross & Matzkin 5530 Wisconsin Ave Chevy Chase MD 20815

RISINGER, D. MICHAEL, lawyer, educator; b. Kansas City, Mo., Mar. 31, 1945; s. Homer D. and Madeline F. Risinger; m. Celia A. Defensor, Oct. 17, 1977; children: Ariel Michelle, Michael R. Defensor, Jonathan Marshall. B.A. magna cum laude in Polit. Sci, Yale U., 1966; J.D. cum laude, Harvard U., 1969. Bar: Pa. 1973, N.J. 1978, N.Y. 1983. Asst. counsel Mass. Joint Legis. Com. on Drugs and Drug Abuse, 1969; tchr. N.Y.C. Public Schs., 1969-71; law clk. to judge U.S. Dist. Ct. Eastern Dist. Pa., 1972-73; asst. prof. law Seton Hall U., Newark, 1973-76; asso. prof. Seton Hall U., 1976-79, prof., 1979—; vis. sr. fellow U. Singapore, 1985-86; lectr. on evidence N.J. Inst. Continuing Legal Edn., N.J. Jud. Coll., N.J. Adminstrv. Law Inst., Practising Law Inst., N.Y.C.; trial adv. trainer Nat. Legal Services Corp.; mem. N.J. Supreme Ct. Com. on Evidence. Author: (with Mark P. Denbeaux) Trial Evidence, 1978; contbr. articles to profl. jours. Mem. Am. Bar Assn., Am. Law Inst. Club: Essex (Newark). Legal education, Federal civil litigation, State civil litigation. Home: 251 Washington St Jersey City NJ 07302 Office: Seton Hall U 1111 Raymond Blvd Newark NJ 07102

RISMAN, MARC DALE, lawyer; b. Cleve., Nov. 30, 1954; s. Robert Richard and Joan (Lieberman) R. BS in Polit. Sci. and Econs., Claremont Men's Coll., 1975; JD, U. Utah, 1978. Bar: Calif. 1978, Nev. 1979, U.S. Dist. Ct. Nev. 1979. Assoc. Anolik et al, San Francisco, 1978-79, Graziadei et al, Las Vegas, Nev., 1979-80; sole practice Las Vegas, 1980—. Bd. dirs. Rep. Men's Club, Clark County, Nev., 1980—; candidate Nev. atty. gen., 1982. Mem. ABA, Assn. Trial Lawyers Am., Nev. Bar Assn., Calif. Bar Assn., Sports Lawyers Assn. Avocations: skiing, boating, boxing, traveling, flying. Sports and entertainment law, Airline and travel industry law, Personal injury. Home: 1074 Tam O'Shanter Las Vegas NV 89109 Office: 330 S 3d St Suite 810 Las Vegas NV 89101

RISNER, PAUL EDWARD, lawyer; b. Detroit, Dec. 3, 1957. BA in English, BA in History, Jacksonville U., 1978; JD, U. Fla., 1982. Bar: Fla. 1982, U.S. Dist. Ct. (mid. dist.) Fla. 1983, U.S. Ct. Appeals (11th cir.) 1983. Sole practice Gainesville, Fla., 1982-83; atty. Fla. East Coast Ry., St. Augustine, Fla., 1984—. Mem. ABA, St. John's County Bar Assn. General corporate, Real property, Environment. Office: Fla East Coast Ry 1 Malaga St Saint Augustine FL 32084

RISSMAN, EMANUEL A., judge; b. Chgo., Dec. 28, 1910; s. Sidney and Anna (Rosin) R.; m. Edie Levitt, June 6, 1937; children—Arthur, Susan. J.D., DePaul U., 1934. Bar: Ill. 1935, Calif. 1949. Sole practice, Chgo., 1935-69; judge Cir. Ct. Cook County, 1969—; lectr. Nat. Jud. Coll.; speaker jud. seminars, Tuscaloosa, Ala., 1982, Vancouver, B.C., Can., 1982; speaker Consumers Conf., Washington, 1983. Bd. dirs. Portes Cancer Clinic. Mem. ABA (chmn. small claims cts. com., exec. com. spl. judges 1984—, Franklin Flashner award 1983-84), Chgo. Bar Assn., Los Angeles County Bar Assn., Calif. Bar Assn., Jud. Assn. Ill., Am. Judicature Soc., Phi Beta Epsilon. Club: Covenant (Chgo.) Author: Small Claim Forms Guidebook, 1981; How to Use the Pro Se Court. Jurisprudence. Home: Apt 7C 3470 Lake Shore Dr Chicago IL 60657

RISTAU, MARK MOODY, lawyer, petroleum consultant; b. Warren, Pa., Mar. 21, 1944; s. Harold J. and Eleanor K. (Moody) R. B.A., Pa. Mil. Coll., 1966; B.A., Widner Coll., 1966; J.D., Case Western Res. U., 1969. Bar: Pa. 1970, D.C. 1972, U.S. Supreme Ct. 1973, N.Y. 1982. Sole practice, Warren, 1970-85, Warren and Vancouver, B.C., Can., 1976-85, Jamestown, N.Y., 1982-85, sr. ptnr. Ristau & McKeirnan, Warren, 1986—; sr. dir. Pa. Allied Oil Producers, 1972-78, atty. for Pa. Field Producers, 1981-85; ptnr. SAR Devel., 1984—, Slagle Almendinger & Ristau, 1983—; dir. Try-M Fin. Co., 1978-81; counsel United Refining Co., Pennbank, Enchanced Oil Recovery, Consol. Services, 1982-84; chmn. bd. Comml. Service Corp., U.S. interim trustee, 1979—; U.S. counsel Brazilian Promotions, Inc. of Brazilian Govt., 1981-85; v.p. Daytona Apts., Inc., Daytona Beach, Fla.; sec. Daytona Devel. League. Mem. Warren County Bd. Pub. Assistance, 1970-71, chmn., 1971-72; mem. Broward County (Fla.) Devel. League, 1981-83; mem. Fla. Profl. Recruitment Assn., 1980-83. Recipient Tate Meml. award, 1981; Sambas award, 1981. Mem. Warren County Bar Assn. (sec.), Assn. Trial Lawyers Am., Am. Arbitration Assn. Clubs: Eagles (hon. life); Ipanema (Brazil); Conewango (Warren). Contbr. articles on law to profl. jours.; case reporter Legal Intelligencer, 1972-79. Bankruptcy, Bankruptcy, Criminal. Home: 208 Kinzua Rd Warren PA 16365 Office: 410-411 Marine Bank Bldg Warren PA 16365

RITCH, JAMES EARLE, JR., lawyer; b. Charlotte, N.C., Apr. 27, 1931; s. James Earle and Nena Fay (Williams) R.; m. Maria de Lourdes Grande-Ampudia, Apr. 27, 1963; children—James, Alejandro, Lourdes. B.A., Duke U., 1953; LL.B., Yale U., 1956; Licenciate in Law, Nat. U. Mex., 1964. Bar: D.C. 1958, N.C. 1958, Tex. 1959, Republic of Mex. 1965. Assoc. firm Baker & Botts, Houston, 1958-59; assoc., then ptnr. firm Santamarina & Steta, Mexico City, 1959-75; ptnr. firm Ritch y Rovzar, Mexico City, 1975—. Contbr. articles to legal publs. Angier B. Duke scholar, 1949-53; Fulbright scholar, Santiago, Chile, 1956; Rotary Found. fellow, Lima, Peru, 1957. Mem. ABA, Ilustre y Nacional Colegio de Abogados, Am. C. of C. of Mex. (dir. 1978-79), Academia Mexicana de Derecho Internacional Privado, Am. Soc. Internat. Law. Club: University (Mexico). Banking, Private international, Contracts commercial. Home: Fresnos 28, Lomas Palo Alto, Mexico City 05110, Mexico Office: Ritch y Rovzar, Amberes 5 PH, Mexico City 06600, Mexico

RITCHEY, JOSEPH THOMAS, lawyer; b. Birmingham, Ala., Sept. 22, 1955; s. Joseph and Elaine (Adams) R.; m. Ann Martin, July 14, 1984; 1 child, Sarah Beth. BS, U. Ala., 1977; JD, Samford U., 1981; LLM, NYU, 1983. Bar: Ala. 1981, Tex. 1983. Law clk. to presiding justice Ala. Supreme Ct., Montgomery, 1981-82; assoc. Locke, Purnell, Boren, Laney & Neely, Dallas, 1983-85, Sirote, Permutt, Friend, Friedman, Held & Apolinsky, Birmingham, Ala., 1985—. Editor-in-chief Samford U. Law Rev., 1980-81. Mem. ABA, Tex. Bar Assn., Ala. Bar Assn., Birmingham Bar Assn. Melkite Catholic. Personal income taxation, General corporate, Securities. Home: 2828 Cahawba Trail Birmingham AL 35243 Office: 2222 Arlington Ave PO Box 55727 Birmingham AL 35255

RITCHIE, ALBERT, lawyer; b. Charlottesville, Va., Sept. 29, 1939; s. John and Sarah Dunlop (Wallace) R.; m. Jennie Wayland, Apr. 29, 1967; children—John, Mary. B.A., Yale U., 1961; LL.B., U. Va., 1964. Bar: Ill. 1964. Assoc. Sidley & Austin, Chgo., 1964-71, ptnr., 1972—. Bd. dirs. Erie Neighborhood House, Chgo., 1978—; bd. dirs. United Charities of Chgo., 1979—, v.p., 1982-83. Served to capt. U.S. Army, 1965-67. Mem. Chgo. Legal Aid Bur., Ill. Bar Assn., ABA, Legal Club Chgo. (pres. 1986—). Episcopalian. Clubs: LaSalle (Chgo.); Indian Hill (Winnetka, Ill.). Real property, Landlord-tenant. Office: One First Nat Plaza Suite 4600 Chicago IL 60603

RITCHIE, JOHN, lawyer; b. Norfolk, Va., Mar. 19, 1904; s. John and Edith (Kensett) R., Jr; m. Sarah Dunlap Wallace, Apr. 20, 1929; children: John, Albert. B.S., U. Va., 1925, LL.B., 1927; J.S.D., Yale U., 1931; LL.D. (hon.), Coll. William and Mary, 1979. Bar: Nebr. 1927, Ill. 1957, Va. 1942, Mo. 1952, Wis. 1953. With Ritchie, Chase, Canaday & Swenson, Omaha, 1927-28; asst. prof. law Furman U., 1928-30, U. Wash., 1931-36; Sterling fellow Yale U., 1930-31; prof. law U. Md., 1936-37; prof. law U. Va., 1937-52, asst. dean, 1941-49; dean law sch., Kirby prof. law Washington U., 1952-53; prof., dean Sch. Law, U. Wis., 1953-57, Law Sch., Northwestern U., Chgo., 1957-72; John Henry Wigmore prof. Law Sch., Northwestern U., 1966—, emeritus prof. and dean, 1972—; prof. law U. Va., 1972-74, now scholar-in-residence; vis. distinguished prof. U. Tenn., 1974, U. Okla., 1975, Coll. William and Mary, 1976; Tucker lectr. Washington and Lee U.; Detocqueville lectr. Marquette U.; bd. dirs. First Nat. Bank and Trust Co., Evanston, 1963-72. Co-author: Decedent's Estates and Trusts, 1955, 6th edit., 1982; author: The First Hundred Years: A Short History of the School of Law of the University of Virginia for the Period 1826-1926, 1978; Editorial bd., Found. Press.; Contbr. various legal publs. Mem. Ill. Jud. Adv. Council, 1964-68; bd. dirs. Am. Council on Edn., 1965-68, First Nat. Bank and Trust Co., Evanston, Ill., 1963-72, United Charities Chgo., 1966-72. Served to col. U.S. Army, 1942-45. Decorated Bronze Star, Army Commendation medal. Fellow Am. Bar Found.; mem. ABA (ho. of dels. 1957-71), Va. Bar Assn., Ill. Bar Assn., Chgo. Bar Assn., Assn. Am. Law Schs. (pres. 1964), Law Club Chgo., Judge Advs. Assn. (pres. 1951-52), Order of Coif (nat. pres. 1952-55), Raven Soc., Phi Beta Kappa, Omicron Delta Kappa, Phi Kappa Psi, Phi Delta Phi. Episcopalian. Clubs: Wayfarers, Colonnade, Greencroft, Law Club of Chgo. Probate. Home: 1848 Westview Rd Charlottesville VA 22903 Office: Sch Law U Va Charlottesville VA 22903

RITCHIE, ROBERT FIELD, lawyer; b. Dallas, July 9, 1917; s. Robert Allan and Sallie Bowen (Field) R.; m. Catherine Canfield, Sept. 14, 1949; children—Allan, Lee, Ann, Kate, Sara, Beth. B.S., So. Meth. U., 1939, LL.B., 1941; LL.M., U. Mich., 1942, S.J.D., 1953. Bar: Tex. 1941. Ptnr. Ritchie Ritchie & Crosland, Dallas, 1946-66; ptnr. Ritchie Crosland & Egan, Dallas, 1966-82, Andrews & Kurth, Dallas, 1982—. Author: Integration of Public Utility Holding Companies, 1954. Bd. govs. So. Meth. U., 1970-87; mem. exec. bd. Circle Ten council Boy Scouts Am., 1964—; elder Presbyterian Ch., Dallas, 1976—. Served to 1st lt. USAF, 1942-46; PTO. Recipient Silver Beaver award Boy Scouts Am., 1970, Disting. Eagle Scout award, 1975, Order of San Jacinto, Sons Republic of Tex., 1979. Mem. ABA, Dallas Bar Assn., Tex. Bar Found., Kappa Alpha (Court of Honor 1974). Clubs: Dallas, Dallas Country and Tower. Avocation: photography. General corporate, Probate, Estate taxation. Home: 3939 Marquette Dallas TX 75225 Office: Andrews & Kurth 4400 Thanksgiving Tower Dallas TX 75201

RITCHIE, THOMAS BROWN, lawyer; b. Muncie, Ind., Sept. 29, 1947. BS, U. Redlands, 1969; JD, U. LaVerne, 1977. Bar: Calif. 1977, U.S. Dist. Ct. (cen. dist.) Calif. 1979, U.S. Ct. Appeals (4th cir.) 1979, U.S. Supreme Ct. 1982. Ptnr. Banks & Ritchie, Upland, Calif., 1979—; bd. dirs. Inland Mediation Bd. Mem. State Bar Calif. (real estate commn. 1984—), Western San Bernadino County Bar Assn. (past pres., bd. dirs. 1980—). Real property, Construction, State civil litigation. Office: Banks & Ritchie Civic Ctr Law Offices 10788 Civic Center Dr Rancho Cucamonga CA 91730

RITCHIE, WILLIAM PAUL, lawyer; b. Columbus, Ohio, June 3, 1946; s. Austin Everett and Helen (Drake) R.; m. Diane Smith, Aug. 2, 1969; 1 child, Elizabeth Drake. BS in Bus. Adminstrn., Ohio State U., 1968, LLD, U. Va., 1971. Bar: Ohio 1971, Calif. 1973, Ill. 1987. Assoc. Jones, Day, Reavis & Pogue, Cleve., 1971-77, ptnr., 1977—, ptnr.-in-charge, Chgo., 1987—. Served to lt. USAR, 1972. Mem. ABA, Ohio Bar Assn., Calif. Bar Assn., Cleve. Bar Assn. Republican. Club: Mayfield Country (Cleve.). General corporate, Banking, Private international. Home: 55 W Goethe St #1252 Chicago IL 60610 Office: 225 W Washington Chicago IL 60606

RITER, BRUCE DOUGLAS, lawyer; b. Harvey, Ill., Dec. 20, 1949; s. Russell and Kathryn (Boller) R.; m. Gudrun Weinheimer, May 11, 1978; children: Christina, Andreas. BEE, So. Ill. U., 1972; JD, Northwestern U., 1975. Bar: U.S. Patent Office 1974, Md. 1975, U.S. Ct. Appeals (D.C. cir.) 1977, Va. 1979, U.S. Supreme Ct. 1980. Assoc. Beall & Jeffery, Washington, 1975-79, Schwartz, Jeffery, Schwaab et al, Alexandria, Va., 1979; ptnr. Schwartz, Jeffery, Schwartz et al, Alexandria, Va., 1980; patent counsel Schlumberger Drilling and Prodn. Services N.Am., Sugarland, Tex., 1980-82, Schlumberger Wireline Atlantic, Clamart, France, 1982-85, Schlumberger Computer Aided Systems, Sunnyvale, Calif., 1985—. Recipient stipend Max Planck Inst. Mem. ABA, IEEE. Computer, General corporate, Patent. Office: Schlumberger-Computer Aided Systems 1259 Oakmead Pkwy Sunnyvale CA 94086

RITTENHOUSE, SUSAN MERRICK, lawyer; b. Balt., Feb. 25, 1948; d. Frank Cook and Evelyn (Merrick) R.; m. Michael S. Libowitz, Oct. 12, 1985. BS in Journalism, Syracuse U., 1970; JD, U. Md., 1976. Bar: Md. 1976, U.S. Dist. Ct. Md. 1977. Fin. analyst Mercantile Bank, Balt., 1976-77; assoc. Frank, Bernstein, Conaway & Goldman, Balt., 1977-80; asst. div. securities Md. Atty. Gen., Balt., 1981-87, commr. securities, 1983—; tchr. U. Md. Sch. of Law, Balt., 1977-84. Mem. ABA, Md. Bar Assn., Balt. City Bar Assn., Womens Bar Assn. Avocations: sculpting, writing, gardening. Securities. Office: Md Div Securities 7 N Calvert St 4th Fl Baltimore MD 21202

RITTER, ANN L., lawyer; b. N.Y.C., May 20, 1933; d. Joseph and Grace (Goodman) R. B.A., Hunter Coll., 1954; J.D., N.Y. Law Sch., 1970; postgrad. Law Sch., NYU, 1971-72. Bar: N.Y. 1971, U.S. Ct. Appeals (2d cir.) 1975, U.S. Supreme Ct. 1975. Writer, 1954-70; editor, 1955-66; tchr., 1966-70; atty. Am. Soc. Composers, Authors and Pubs., N.Y.C., 1971-72, Greater N.Y. Ins. Co., N.Y.C., 1973-74; sr. ptnr. Brenhouse & Ritter, N.Y.C., 1974-78; sole practice, N.Y.C., 1978—. Editor N.Y. Immigration News, 1975-76. Mem. ABA, Am. Immigration Lawyers Assn. (treas. 1983-84, sec. 1984-85, vice chair 1985-86, chair 1986-87), N.Y. State Bar Assn., N.Y. County Lawyers Assn., Assn. Trial Lawyers Am., N.Y. State Trial Lawyers Assn., N.Y.C. Bar Assn. Democrat. Jewish. Immigration, naturalization, and customs, Family and matrimonial, Personal injury. Home: 47 E 87th St New York NY 10128 Office: 420 Madison Ave New York NY 10017

RITTER, DEBORAH BRADFORD, lawyer; b. Boston, Nov. 4, 1953; d. Edmund Underwood and Priscilla (Rich) R. BA, Yale U., 1974; JD, Boston Coll., 1980. Bar: N.H. 1980, Mass. 1981. Assoc. McLane, Graf, Raulerson & Middleton, P.A., Manchester, N.H., 1980-82, Singer, Stoneman, Kunian & Kurland, P.C., Boston, 1983—; dir. N.H. Legal Assistance Corp., Concord, 1982-84. Sec. N.H. Performing Arts Ctr., 1980-85; bd. dirs. Yale Alumni Schs. Com., Boston, 1982—. Mem. ABA, Mass. Bar Assn., N.H. Bar Assn. Real property, Contracts commercial, General corporate. Home: 413 Hammond St Chesnut Hill MA 02167 Office: Singer Stoneman Kunian & Kurland PC 100 Charles River Plaza Boston MA 02114

RITTER, G. CHRISTOPHER, lawyer; b. Columbia, Mo., Apr. 3, 1956; s. E. Gene and Constance A. (Nishimiya) R.; m. Jill A. Stevenson, June 22, 1985; 1 child, C. Andrew. BA, Ind. U., 1978; JD, U. Chgo., 1981. Bar: Calif. 1981, U.S. Dist. Ct. (no. dist.) Calif., U.S. Dist. Ct. (ea. dist.) Calif., U.S. Dist. Ct. (we. dist.) Okla., U.S. Ct. Appeals (9th and 7th cirs.). Atty. Pettit & Martin, San Francisco, 1981—; asst. prof. U. Calif., San Francisco, 1982—. Mem. Bar Assn. of San Francisco (co. chair litigation com. 1984-85, chair legis. com. Barristers Club 1985). Federal civil litigation, State civil litigation, Legal education. Home: 231 Divisadero St San Francisco CA 94117 Office: Pettit & Martin 101 California St 35th Fl San Francisco CA 94111

RITTER, ROBERT FORCIER, lawyer; b. St. Louis, Apr. 7, 1943; s. Tom Marshall and Jane Elizabeth (Forcier) R.; m. Karen Gray, Dec. 28, 1966; children: Allison Gray, Laura Thompson, Elisabeth Forcier. BA, U. Kans., 1965; JD, St. Louis U., 1968. Bar: Mo. 1968, U.S. Dist. Ct. (ea. and we. dists.) Mo. 1968, U.S. Ct. Mil. Appeals 1972, U.S. Supreme Ct. 1972, U.S. Ct. Appeals (8th cir.) 1980, U.S. Dist. Ct. (so. dist.) Ill. 1982. Assoc. Gray & Sommers, St. Louis, 1968-71; ptnr. Gray & Ritter, 1974—; bd. dirs. United Mo. Bank of St. Louis; adv. com. 22d cir. Supreme Ct., 1985—; lectr in field. Served to capt. USAR, 1968-74. Recipient Law Week award Bur. Nat. Affairs, 1968. Fellow Internat. Soc. Barristers, Am. Coll. Trial Lawyers, Internat. Acad. Trial Lawyers; mem. Bar Assn. Met. St. Louis (chmn. trial sect., 1978-79, exec. com. 1980-82, award of merit 1976, award of achievement 1982, chmn. bench bar conf. 1983), Mo. Bar Assn. (council practice and procedure com. 1972—, council tort law com. 1982—, bd. govs. 1984—), Mo. Bar Found. (outstanding trial lawyer award, 1978), ABA, Lawyers Assn. St. Louis (exec. com. 1976-81, pres. 1977-78), Mo. Assn. Trial Attys. (bd. govs. 1984—), Assn. Trial Lawyers Am. Presbyterian. Clubs: Media, Mo. Athletic, Bellerive Country, John's Island; Racquet of Ladue. Contbr. articles to law jours. Personal injury, Federal civil litigation, State civil litigation. Office: 1015 Locust St Suite 900 Saint Louis MO 63101

RITTER, ROBERT JOSEPH, lawyer; b. N.Y.C., Aug. 11, 1925; s. Robert Reinhart and Mary (Mandracchia) R.; m. Barbara Willis Foust, Oct. 1, 1955 (div. May 1977); children—Robert Thornton, Jan Willis, Nancy Carol. Student Bklyn. Poly. Inst., 1943; B.A. cum laude, Queens Coll., 1949; J.D., NYU, 1953, LL.M. in Internat. Law, 1955. Bar: N.Y. 1953. Acct. UN Secretariat, N.Y.C., 1949-54; asst. counsel RCA Corp., N.Y.C., 1955-58; atty. CIBA-GEIGY Corp., Ardsley, N.Y., 1958-60; atty. Bell Telephone Labs., Inc., Murray Hill, N.J., 1960-70; tax atty. AT&T Technologies, Inc., N.Y.C., 1970-85; mgr. fin. AT&T Corp. Hdqrs., Parsippany, N.J., 1985—; asst. sec. 14 AT&T subs. telephone cos. Contbr. articles to legal jours. Pres. Harry B. Thayer chpt., Telephone Pioneers of Am., N.Y.C., 1983-84; bd. dirs. Somerset Hills YMCA, Bernardsville, N.J., 1971-73; candidate (Democratic) N.Y. State Assembly, Westchester County, N.Y., 1965; chmn. Am. Cancer Soc. Fund Drive, Bronxville, N.Y., 1964. Served with USAAF, 1943-46; ATO. Recipient Crusade award Am. Cancer Soc., 1965, Masonic Service award, 1947, Am. Legion Citizenship award, 1943, Eagle Scout award Boy Scouts Am., 1941. Mem. Nat. Tax Assn.-Tax Inst. Am. (chmn., advisor state sales and use taxation com. 1984—, chmn. prodn. exemption subcom. 1978-84), Council of State C. of C. (com. on state taxation 1982—), NYU Law Alumni Assn. Democrat. Episcopalian. Clubs: City of N.Y., Rossmoor Tennis (pres. 1987—), Church of N.Y. Lodge: Kiwanis (1st v.p. 1970-71). Corporate taxation, General corporate, Public international. Home: 3-N Village Mall Jamesburg NJ 08831 Office: AT&T Corp Hdqrs 5 Wood Hollow Rd Parsippany NJ 07054

RITTNER, KATHLEEN ARDELL, lawyer; b. Harrisburg, Pa., Jan. 20, 1949; d. William Frederick and Frances Marie (Zlogar) R.; m. Frank Morgan Taber, June 30, 1984. BA, Pa. State U., 1969, MEd, 1972; JD with honors, DePaul U., 1980. Bar: Ill. 1980, U.S. Dist. Ct. (no. dist.) Ill. 1980, U.S. Ct. Appeals (7th cir.) 1981, U.S. Dist. Ct. (mid. dist.) Pa. 1983, U.S. Ct. Appeals (3d cir.) 1983, Ind. 1987, U.S. Dist. Ct. (no. dist.) Ind. 1987. Assoc. Coffield, Ungaretti, Harris & Slavin, Chgo., 1980-82; dep. atty. gen. organized crime and pub. corruption sect. State of Pa., Harrisburg, 1982-84, dep. atty. gen., asst. to dir. criminal law div., 1984-85, dep. atty. gen. exec. office, 1985-86, dep. atty. gen., dir. bur. consumer protection, 1986-87; assoc. Barnes and Thornburg, Ft. Wayne, Ind., 1987—. Coordinator outside activities Greater Harrisburg Arts Festival 1986, 1985-86; press spokesperson, state vol. info. coordinator com. to re-elect atty. gen. Zimmerman, Pa., 1984. Mem. ABA, Pa. Bar Assn., Chgo. Bar Assn. (co-chmn. law day clinics 1981-82), Women's Bar Assn. (conf. co-chmn. women in law conf. 1980-81), Allen County Bar Assn., Harrisburg Area Women Lawyers Assn. (chmn. constn. by laws com. 1983-84, mem. exec. bd. 1985-87, treas. 1985-87), Pa. State U. Alumni Assn. (bd. dirs. liberal arts 1983—, alumni council 1986—), Kappa Alpha Theta (adv. bd. Harrisburg Alumni chpt. 1982-86, sec. 1984-85, v.p. 1985-86, pres. 1986-87). Roman Catholic. Clubs: Pa. State (Chgo.) (pres.); Pa. State (Harrisburg). Avocations: gourmet cooking, travel, reading, skiing, golf. Federal civil litigation, State civil litigation. Home: 13310 Timbercrest Trail Fort Wayne IN 46804 Office: Barnes and Thornburg 600 One Summit Sq Fort Wayne IN 46801

RIVERA, ARMANDO, lawyer; b. Zacatecas, Mex., Jan. 30, 1952; s. Jose and Aurelia (Jimenez) R.; m. Anna Lydia Fisher, Dec. 28, 1974; children: Armando Diego, Ana Marisea. BA in Psychology, Stanford U., 1973; JD, U. Ariz., 1977. Bar: Ariz. 1977, U.S. Dist. Ct. Ariz. 1978. Law clk. to presiding justice U.S. Dist. Ct., Tucson, 1977-79; assoc. Davis & Epstein, Tucson, 1979-82; assoc. dean law sch. U. Ariz., Tucson, 1982-85; assoc. Miller & Pitt, P.C., Tucson, 1985—; mem. bd. examiners State Bar Ariz., 1985—. Mem. Ariz. Acad., Phoenix, 1981—. Workers' compensation, Personal injury. Office: Miller & Pitt PC 111 S Church Tucson AZ 85701

RIVERA, HENRY MICHAEL, lawyer; b. Albuquerque, Sept. 25, 1946; s. Henry Eugene and Mary (Vela) R.; m. Catherine Kil, Mar. 1, 1969; 1 son, Henry Eugene. B.A., U. N.Mex., 1968, J.D., 1973; B.B.A., U. Albuquerque, 1981. Bar: N.Mex. 1973, D.C. 1981. Ptnr. firm Sutin, Thayer & Browne, Albuquerque, 1973-81; commr. FCC, Washington, 1981-85; ptnr. Dow, Lohnes & Albertson, Washington, 1985—; sr. adv. to several U.S. telecom delegations including ITU Plenipotentiary Conf. (Nairobi), Kenya, 1982; bd. dirs. Telecommunications-Computer Applications Agy. of Nat. Research Council; advisor telecommunications panel internat. law U.S. Dept. State. Editor: Pollution and Political Boundaries: U.S.-Mexican Environmental Problems, 1973; mem. bd. editors Telematics, 1986; contbr. articles to legal jours. Chmn. bd. N.Mex. affiliate Am. Diabetes Assn., 1978-80, D.C. affiliate, 84-85, bd. dirs., vice chmn. com. govt. relations nat. orgn., chmn. bd. nat. orgn., 1985-86. Served with U.S. Army, 1968-70. Named Outstanding Young Lawyer, State Bar N.Mex., 1981; award for outstanding leadership in govt. Nat. Assn. Black Owned Broadcasters, 1985, Charles H. Best award of Outstanding Service in the Cause of Diabetes, Am. Diabetes Assn., 1986; decorated Bronze Star. Mem. Albuquerque Bar Assn., D.C. Bar Assn., ABA(vice chmn. broadcast commn. for Sci. and Tech. sect. 1986). Administrative and regulatory, Public international, Public utilities. Home: 1505 Natalie Joy Ln McLean VA 22101 Office: 1255 23rd St NW Suite 600 Washington DC 20037

RIVERA, JUAN, lawyer; b. Bklyn., Aug. 2, 1954; s. Jacobo and Maxima (Diaz) R.; m. Iris Aldea, Oct. 23, 1983; 1 child, Jazmyn. BA, Colombia U., 1976; JD, Hofstra U., 1980. Bar: N.Y. 1981. Assoc. Barst & Mukamal, N.Y.C., 1984; gen. ptnr. Rivera & Walker, Bklyn., 1984-86; sole practice Bklyn., 1986—. Mem. advance com. V.P. Walter Mondale, N.Y.C., 1977. Served to sgt. U.S. Marines, 1974-75. Mem. N.Y. State Bar Assn., P.R. Bar Assn., Hispanic Bar Assn. Democrat. Roman Catholic. Immigration, naturalization, and customs, Real property, Family and matrimonial. Office: 26 Court St Suite 2610 Brooklyn NY 11242

RIVERA, LUIS ERNESTO, lawyer; b. San Juan, P.R., Aug. 29, 1950; s. Luis Ramon and Aurea (Montalvo) R.; m. Martha Macia, Feb. 3, 1974; children: Luis E. II, Alejandro L., Cristina M. BA in Liberal Arts, U. P.R., 1970, JD, 1973; LLM, Georgetown U., 1976. Bar: P.R. 1974, D.C. 1975, U.S. Ct. Mil. Appeals 1975, U.S. Ct. Appeals (D.C. cir.) 1975, Fla. 1980, U.S. Supreme Ct. 1984. Legal advisor Bd. of Vets. Appeals, Washington, 1973-75, 80; gen. counsel Am. Assurance Assn., Miami, 1980-83; gen. counsel, v.p., sec. Fla. Life Ins. Co., Miami, 1980—; research cons. U. P.R., Rio Piedras, 1971-73. Bd. dirs., sec. Fellowship Ho., Miami, 1983—. Served to maj. USAF, 1975-80. Mem. ABA, Air Force Assn. (life). Republican. Roman Catholic. Lodges: Kiwanis (bd. dirs. 1983-84, 87—). Insurance, Military, Criminal. Home: 12240 SW 2d St Miami FL 33184 Office: Fla Life Ins Co 6600 SW 57th Ave Miami FL 33143

RIVERA, OSCAR R., lawyer, corporate executive; b. Habana, Cuba, Dec. 8, 1956; s. Alcibiades R. and Marian (Fernandez) R. BBA, U. Miami, 1978; JD, Georgetown U., 1981. Bar: Fla. 1981, U.S. Dist. Ct. (so. dist.) Fla. 1982, U.S. Tax Ct. 1982. Assoc. Corrigan, Zelman & Bander P.A., Miami, Fla., 1978-83; ptnr. Siegfried, Kipnis & Rivera P.A., Miami, 1984—; bd. dirs. Miami Benetton Corp., Dadeven Corp., Miami, Capital Property and Casualty Co., Miami. Asst. mgr. campaign to elect Michael O'Donovan, Miami, 1976; mem. youth adv. bd., Miami, 1975-78, youth planning council Dade County, Miami, 1975-78. Mem. ABA, Dade County Bar Assn., Cuban Am. Bar Assn., Inter-Am. Bar Assn., Omicron Delta Kappa, Phi Kappa Phi, Orange Key, Greater Miami C. of C. Club: Little Havana. Lodge: Kiwanis. Avocations: photography, skiing. Real property, Landlord-tenant, General corporate.

RIVERA, WALTER, lawyer; b. N.Y.C., Jan. 18, 1955; s. Marcelino and Ana Maria (Reyes) R. BA, Columbia U., 1976; JD, U. Pa., 1979. Bar: N.Y. Law clk. to cen. legal research staff N.Y. State Ct. Appeals, Albany, 1979-81; asst. atty. gen. State of N.Y., N.Y.C., 1981-85; sole practice N.Y.C., 1985—; chairperson Third World Lawyers Caucus, N.Y. State Atty. Gen.'s Office, N.Y.C., 1984; arbitrator Civil Ct. of City of N.Y., 1985—; panel mem. N.Y. Metro Legal Services Plan, N.Y., 1986—. Mem. ABA, Puerto Rican Bar Assn., Nat. Hispanic Bar Assn., N.Y. State Bar Assn. Avocations: camping, travel. State civil litigation, General practice. Home: 3225 Decatur Ave Bronx NY 10467 Office: 2710 Broadway New York NY 10025

RIVES, JAMES DAVIDSON, JR., lawyer; b. New Orleans, July 30, 1925; s. James Davidson and Marion Mosley (Smith) R.; m. Mary Elizabeth Thibaut, June 22, 1948; children—James Davidson III, Katherine Jane, Frank W., Bronier T. B.A., Tulane U., 1948, J.D., 1950. Bar: La. 1950, U.S. Dist. Ct. (ea. dist.) La. 1950, U.S. Ct. Appeals (5th cir.) 1955. Titleman, Humble Oil & Refining Co., New Orleans, 1951-55; atty. for La., Continental Oil Co., Houston, 1955-59; ptnr. Ogden, Woods & Rives, 1959-62, Ogden, Woods, Henriques & Rives, 1962-65, Ogden, Rives & Ogden, 1965-70; sole practice, New Orleans, 1970-82, Metairie, La., 1982-84, Many, Lococo, Kimble & Rives, 1984—. Served with USMCR, 1943-44. Mem. La. State Bar Assn., New Orleans Bar Assn., ABA, Am. Judicature Soc. Republican. Methodist. Clubs: Petroleum, Tchefuncta, Beau Chene (New Orleans). General practice, General corporate, Oil and gas leasing. Office: Suite 1304 First National Bank of Commerce Bldg New Orleans LA 70112

RIVET, DIANA WITTMER, lawyer, economic developer; b. Auburn, N.Y., Apr. 28, 1931; d. George Wittmer and Anne (Jenkins) Wittmer Hauswirth; m. Paul Henry Rivet, Oct. 24, 1952; children: Gail, Robin, Leslie, Heather, Clayton, Eric. BA, Keuka Coll., 1951; JD, Bklyn. Law Sch., 1956. Bar: N.Y. 1956, U.S. Dist. Ct. (ea. and so. dists.) N.Y. 1975. Sole practice, Orangeburg, N.Y., 1957—; county atty. Rockland County (N.Y.), 1974-77; asst. to legis. chmn. Rockland County, 1978-79; counsel, adminstr. Indsl. Devel. Agy., Rockland County, 1980—, Greater Rockland Local Devel. Corp., 1981—; counsel, exec. dir. Pvt. Industry Council Rockland County, 1980—; pres. Environ. Mgmt. Ltd., Orangeburg, 1980—; mem. air mgmt. adv. com. N.Y. State Dept. Environ. Conservation 1984. Pres. Rockland County council Girl Scouts U.S., 1981-84; chmn. Rockland County United Way campaign, 1983-84; bd. dirs. Rockland County Assn., West Nyack, 1981—. Recipient Community Service award Keuka Coll., 1965; Disting. Service award Town of Orangetown, 1970; named Businessperson of Yr., Jour. News, Rockland County, 1982. Mem. N.Y. State Bar Assn. (mcpl. law sect. exec. com. 1976-83, environ. law sect. exec. com. 1974-86). Democrat. Mem. Religious Soc. of Friends. Environment, Real property, Municipal bonds. Address: 1 Lester Dr 35 Orangeburg Rd Orangeburg NY 10962

RIVETTE, FRANCIS ROBERT, lawyer; b. Syracuse, N.Y., May 1, 1952; s. Francis Patrick and Barbara Parker (Smith) R. BA, Allegheny Coll., 1974; JD, Syracuse U., 1977. Bar: N.Y. 1978, U.S. Dist. Ct. (no. dist.) N.Y. 1978, D.C. 1980. Sole practice Syracuse, 1978—; corporate counsel Fangand Enterprises Ltd., 1976—. Mem. ABA, Onondaga County Bar Assn., Phi Delta Phi, Phi Gamma Mu. Republican. Clubs: Syracuse Corvette (pres. 1985, 86), Nat. Corvette Restorers Soc. (nat. judge 1985). General practice, Personal injury, General corporate. Home: 200 Old Liverpool Rd Liverpool NY 13088 Office: 1501 Milton Ave Solvay NY 13209

RIVIERE, CHRISTOPHER HENRY, lawyer; b. Thibodaux, La., Dec. 17, 1956; s. Clarence Joseph and Jane Louise (McCulla) R. BS in Econs., Nicholls State U., 1978; JD, Tulane U., 1981. Bar: La. 1981. Assoc. Porteous, Hainkel, Johnson & Sarpy, Thibodaux, 1981-86, ptnr., 1986—; v.p. Riviere Ins. Agy., Thibodaux, 1975—. Mem. Thibodaux Vol. Fire Dept.; bd. dirs. Bayou Lafourche Arts Counsel, Lafourche Parish, 1983—, Thibodaux Vol. Fire Bd., 1987—. Mem. ABA, La. Bar Assn. (ho. of dels. 1986—), Lafourche Parish Bar Assn. (pres. 1985, v.p. 1984, sec., treas. 1983), La. Trial Lawyers Assn., La. Assn. Def. Counsel, New Orleans Def. Counsel Assn. Democrat. Roman Catholic. Avocations: arts, fishing, hunting. Home: 310 Bayou Ln Thibodaux LA 70301 Office: Porteous Hainkel Johnson & Sarpy 211 W 5th St Thibodaux LA 70301

RIVOIR, WILLIAM HENRY, III, lawyer; b. Phila., Jan. 19, 1951; s. William H. Jr. and Sarah E. (Stiner) R.; m. Linda F. Reed, Oct. 6, 1984; 1 child, Steven Henry. BA, Dickinson Coll., 1972; JD, George Washington U., 1975. Bar: Pa. 1975, Fla. 1976, D.C. 1980, U.S. Supreme Ct. 1980, Ariz. 1985. Atty. Pa. Dist. Attys. Office, West Chester, 1976-84; regional counsel, sr. atty. Office of the Comptroller of the Currency, Washington and Memphis, 1976-84; ptnr. Storey & Ross, P.C., Phoenix, 1985—. Contbr. articles to profl. jours. Mem. ABA, Ariz. Bar Assn., Pa. Bar Assn., D.C. Bar Assn., Maricopa Bar Assn., SAR (Pa. soc.). Banking, General corporate. Office: Storey & Ross PC 4742 N 24th St Court 1 4th Floor Phoenix AZ 85016

RIZZO, PAUL ROBERT, lawyer; b. Pittsfield, Mass., Mar. 16, 1955; s. Paul Michael and Mary Rose (Imbriani) R. BS in Acctg., U. Scranton, 1977; JD, Cath. U., 1980. Bar: N.J. 1980. Law clk. to presiding justice Somerville, N.J., 1980-81; assoc. Franchino, Lenahan & Cross, Raritan, N.J., 1981-83, Fuerst, Yusem & Boehmer, Raritan, 1983-84; sole practice Somerville, 1984—; legal counsel Raritan Bd. Adjustment, 1985—. Bd. dirs., legal counsel YMCA, Somerville, 1984—. Mem. ABA, N.J. Bar Assn., Assn. Trial Lawyers Am., Somerset County Bar Assn. Democrat. Roman Catholic. Personal injury, Insurance, Real property. Home: 98 Bluebird Dr Somerville NJ 08876 Office: 195 E High St Somerville NJ 08876

ROACH, ARVID EDWARD, II, lawyer; b. Detroit, Sept. 6, 1951; s. Arvid Edward and Alda Elizabeth (Buckley) R. B.A. summa cum laude, Yale U., 1972; J.D. cum laude, Harvard U., 1977. Bar: D.C. 1978, N.Y. 1978, U.S. dist. ct. D.C. 1978, U.S. dist. ct. (so. dist.) N.Y. 1978, U.S. Ct. Appeals (10th cir.) 1980, U.S. Ct. Appeals (2d cir.) 1981, U.S. Ct. Appeals (D.C. cir.) 1981, U.S. Ct. Appeals (7th and 9th cirs.) 1982, U.S. Supreme Ct. 1983, U.S. Dist. Ct. Md., 1985. Law clk. to judge U.S. Dist. Ct., 1977-78; assoc. Covington & Burling, Washington, 1978-85, ptnr., 1985—. Mem. ABA, ACLU. Contbr. articles to legal jours. Administrative and regulatory, Federal civil litigation, Pension, profit-sharing, and employee benefits. Office: 1201 Pennsylvania Ave NW Washington DC 20044

ROACH, EDGAR MAYO, JR., lawyer; b. Pinehurst, N.C., June 2, 1948; s. Edgar Mayo Sr. and Rhuamer (Richardson) R.; m. Deborah Day, Oct. 10, 1970; children: Edgar Mayo III, John Clifton. BA, Wake Forest U., 1969; JD with honors, U. N.C., 1974. Bar: N.C. 1974, Va. 1976, U.S. Ct. Appeals (4th cir.) 1976. Law clk. to judge U.S. Ct. Appeals (4th cir.), Abingdon, Va., 1974-75; assoc. Hunton & Williams, Richmond, Va., 1975-80; ptnr. Hunton & Williams, Raleigh, N.C., 1981—. Public utilities, Nuclear power. Home: 6115 Louisburg Rd Raleigh NC 27604 Office: Hunton & Williams PO Box 109 Raleigh NC 27602

ROACH, JON GILBERT, lawyer; b. Knoxville, June 17, 1944; s. Walter Davis and Lena Rose (Chapman) R.; m. Mintha Marie Evans, Oct. 22, 1977; 1 child, Jon G. III. B.S., U. Tenn., 1967, J.D., 1969. Bar: Tenn. 1970, D.C. 1981, U.S. Ct. Appeals (6th cir.). Assoc. Stone & Bozeman, Knoxville, 1970-71; sole practice, Knoxville, 1971-83; city atty., dir. of law, Knoxville, 1976-83; resident ptnr. Peck Shaffer & Williams, Knoxville, 1983—; mem. faculty Knoxville Bus. Coll., 1973-74. Active Big Bros., Big Sisters of Knoxville, Am. Cancer Soc., Jr. Achievement. Mem. ABA, Tenn. Bar Assn., Knoxville Bar Assn., D.C. Bar Assn., Assn. Trial Lawyers Am., Tenn. Trial Lawyers Assn., Nat. Inst. Mcpl. Law Officers, Nat. Assn. Bond Lawyers. Democrat. Baptist. Club: Kiwanis (East Knoxville). Municipal bonds, General practice, Probate. Home: 1701 River Shore Dr Knoxville TN 37914 Office: Peck Shaffer Williams 2410 Plaza Tower Knoxville TN 37929

ROACH, PATRICK JOSEPH, lawyer; b. West Union, Iowa, July 6, 1952; s. Mark F. and Ann M. (Mihm) R.; m. Susan Mary Sarcone, June 25, 1975; children: Julia Sarcone, Michael Sarcone. BA, U. Notre Dame, 1974; JD, Georgetown U., 1977. Bar: Ill. 1977, U.S. Dist. Ct. (no. dist.) Ill. 1977, D.C. 1982, U.S. Dist. Ct. D.C. 1982. Assoc. Bell, Boyd, Lloyd, Haddad & Burns, Chgo., 1977-81; assoc. Bell, Boyd & Lloyd, Washington, 1981-84, ptnr., 1985—. Mem. ABA, D.C. Bar Assn. Antitrust, Federal civil litigation, Private international. Office: Bell Boyd & Lloyd 1615 L St NW Washington DC 20036

ROACH, PETER TATIAN, lawyer; b. Jamaica, N.Y., Oct. 19, 1952; s. John Tatian Roach and Martha (Fried) Nadler; m. Susan Destacy, June 5, 1976 (div. July 1986); children: Nicole, Erin, Kimberly. BA in Math., SUNY, Binghamton, 1973; JD, St. John's U., Jamaica, 1978. Bar: N.Y. 1979. License investigator N.Y. State Dept., Mineola, 1973-75; asst. to v.p. Lynric Assocs., Franklin Sq., N.Y., 1975-78; gen. counsel Case Capital Corp., Garden City, N.Y., 1978-84, pres., 1984—; gen. counsel, chief operating officer Metrofund, Ltd., Garden City, 1984—; sr. ptnr. Roach & Bergman, Garden City, 1984—; lectr. real estate, finance C.W. Post U., Greenvale, N.Y. Arbitrator Better Bus. Bur. Mem. ABA, N.Y. State Bar Assn., Nassau County Bar Assn. (panel mem. real estate seminar). Banking. Office: Roach & Bergman 600 Old Country Rd Garden City NY 11530

ROACH, RICHARD R., JR., lawyer; b El Paso, Tex., July 1, 1943; s. Richard R. and Idalena (Myers) R.; m. Mary Elizabeth Roehrig, June 15, 1979; children: Kristen Elizabeth, Clifton Philip. BA in Journalism and Mass Communication with honors, N.Mex. State U., 1971; JD, Stetson U., 1976. Bar: Fla. 1976, U.S. Dist. Ct. (mid. dist.) Fla. 1976, U.S. Ct. Appeals (5th and 11th cirs.) 1981. Staff counsel Travelers Ins. Co., Tampa, Fla., 1976-77; assoc. Marvin B. Woods P.A., Lakeland, Fla., 1977-79, Woods & Roach P.A., Lakeland, 1979-81; ptnr. Woods, Murray & Roach P.A., Lakeland, 1981-86, Woods & Roach, Lakeland, 1987—. Leader Boy Scouts Am., St. Petersburg, 1976-77. Served to sgt. U.S. Army, 1965-68, Vietnam. Mem. Fla. Bar Assn. (chmn. bd. editors), Lakeland Bar Assn., Acad. Fla. Trial Lawyers (various coms.), Polk County Trial Lawyers Assn., Assn. Trial Lawyers Am., Phi Delta Phi, Am. Legion. Democrat. Lodges: Elks, Lions (pres. Lakeland 1979—). Avocations: camping, fishing, woodworking. Personal injury, Workers' compensation. Home: 2612 Coventry Ave Lakeland FL 33803 Office: Woods & Roach 106 Paffen Heights Ave PO Drawer AR Lakeland FL 33802

ROACHELL, RICHARD WILSON, lawyer; b. Little Rock, Ark., May 14, 1946; s. Woodrow Wilson and Juanita Mary (Holland) R.; m. Beverly Anne Bone, July 20, 1951. BA, U. Ark., Little Rock, 1973, JD, 1978. Bar: Ark. 1978, U.S. Supreme Ct. 1983. Ptnr. Cearley, Mitchell & Roachell, Little Rock, 1978-86, Mitchell & Roachell, Little Rock, 1986—. Contbr. articles to profl. jours. Served to staff sgt. USAF, 1965-69, Vietnam. Bar: ABA, Am Trial Lawyers Assn., Ark. Bar Assn., Ark. Bar Found., Ark. Trial Lawyers Assn., Pulaski County Bar Assn., Nat. Orgn. Lawyers Representing Edn. Assns. Democrat. Baptist. Avocations: collecting polit. Americana, landscaping, gardening. Civil rights, Legal education, Federal civil litigation. Home: 1421 N University Little Rock AR 72207 Office: Mitchell & Roachell 1014 W 3d PO Box 1510 Little Rock AR 72203

ROADY, CELIA ALLMAN, lawyer; b. Bat Cave, N.C., Dec. 6, 1951; d. C. Edwin and Jo (Pryor) Allman; m. Stephen E. Roady, June 26, 1976; children: Laura Pryor, Peter Elder. AB in Psychology, Duke U., 1973, JD, 1976; LLM in Taxation, Georgetown U., 1979. Bar: D.C. Ptnr. Ginsburg, Feldman & Bress, Washington, 1976—. Mem. ABA (chmn. exempt orgns. com. legis. devels. task force). Democrat. Baptist. Office: Ginsburg Feldman & Bress 1250 Connecticut Ave NW Washington DC 20036

ROAN, FORREST CALVIN, JR., lawyer, title company executive; b. Waco, Tex., Dec. 18, 1944; s. Forrest Calvin and Lucille Elizabeth (McKinney) R.; m. Vickie Joan Howard, Feb. 15, 1969 (div. Dec. 1983); children: Amy Katherine, Jennifer Louise. BBA, U.Tex., Austin, 1973, JD, 1976. Bar: Tex. 1976, U.S. Dist. Ct. (we. dist.) Tex. 1977, U.S. Ct. Appeals (5th cir.) 1977, U.S. Ct. Appeals (11th cir.) 1981, U.S. Supreme Ct. 1979. Prin. Roan & Assocs., Austin, 1969-71; counsel/com. dir. Tex. Ho. of Reps., 1972-75; assoc. Heath, Davis & McCalla, Austin, 1975-78; prin. Roan & Gullahorn, P.C., Austin, 1978-85, Roan & Simpson, P.C., 1986—; bd. dirs. Pioneer Title Co., 1980—; bd. dirs. Waterloo Fin. Services, Inc., Capital Nat. Corp., Capital Nat. Life Ins. Co., Natesco Underwriters, Tex. Lawyers Credit Union, chmn., 1982, 83; dir. pub. law sect. State Bar Tex., 1980-84. Served with U.S. Air N.G., 1966-74. Mem. Travis County Bar Assn., ABA, Heritage Soc. Austin, Knights of the Symphony, Tex. Lyceum Assn. (v.p., bd. dirs. 1983-87), Austin C. of C. Methodist. Clubs: Citadel, Austin, Headliners, Capital. Lodges: Masons, Shriners (grand lodge, Parsons Masonic Master 1976-77). Administrative and regulatory, Insurance, Public utilities. Office: Roan & Simpson PC 1950 One American Ctr Austin TX 78701

ROARK, JIMMY LEE, lawyer; b. Hazard, Ky., Dec. 5, 1948; s. John and Emma Lou (Fowler) R.; m. Deborah Louise McIntyre, July 6, 1983. BBA, Morehead State U., 1973; JD, U. Ky., 1977. Bar: Ky. 1977, U.S. Dist. Ct. (ea. and we. dists.) Ky. 1979, U.S. Ct. Appeals (6th cir.) 1979. Ptnr. Cook & Roark, Whitesburg, Ky., 1977-80; asst. county atty. Letcher County, 1978-80; ptnr. Barret, Haynes, May, Carter & Roark P.S.C., Hazard, 1980—. Served with U.S. Army, 1970-72. Mem. ABA, Assn. Trial Lawyers Am., Ky. Bar Assn., Ky. Acad. Trial Attys., Perry County Bar Assn. Federal civil litigation, State civil litigation, Insurance. Office: Barret Haynes May et al 113 Lovern St Hazard KY 41701

ROARK, JOHN OLEN, lawyer; b. Bug Tussle, Tex., Nov. 1, 1940; s. Walter Allen Roark and Gladys Pauline (Whitt) Trotter; m. Kathleen Doyle Harris, June 13, 1964; children: Wayne, Allen, Sharon. BA, Southwestern U., 1962; JD, S. Tex. Coll. Law, 1966. Bar: Tex. 1967. Assoc. Morgan & Dudensing, Houston, 1967-72, Musslewhite & Roark, Houston, 1972-74; sole practice Temple, Tex., 1974-81; ptnr. Roark & Fernandez, Temple, 1982-86. Fellow Tex. Bar Found., Tex. Bar Assn.; mem. Assn. Trial Lawyers Am. (sustaining), Tex. Trial Lawyers Assn. (bd. dirs. 1982—). Democrat. Methodist. Insurance, Personal injury, Workers' compensation. Office: 503 N Main Temple TX 76501

ROBB, DEAN ALLAN, lawyer, farmer; b. Coulterville, Ill., Feb. 26, 1924; s. Zenas Allan and Mary Dorothy (Cunningham) R.; m. Barbara Gulley, Aug. 24, 1947 (div.); children—Laura Robb Knott, Dean Allan, Blair M; m. Cindy Mathais, 1983; 1 stepson, Matthew Zenas. B.S., U. Ill., 1946; J.D., Wayne State U., 1949. Bar. Mich. 1949, U.S. Dist. Ct. (ea. dist.) Mich. 1950, U.S. Dist. Ct. (we. dist.) Mich. 1960, U.S. Ct. Appeals (6th cir.) 1960, U.S. Dist. Ct. (no. dist.) Ind. 1962, U.S. Dist. Ct. (no. dist.) Ohio 1968, U.S. Supreme Ct. Sr. ptnr. Goodman, Crockett, Eden & Robb, Detroit, 1950-71; sole practice, owner Dean A. Robb, P.C., Traverse City, Mich., 1971-76; pres. Robb, Dettmer & Phillips, Traverse City, 1976-81, Robb, Dettmer, Messing & Thompson, P.C., Traverse City, 1983-86, Robb, Messing & Palmer, 1986—; lectr. various state, nat. and local bar assns.; guest lectr. Detroit Coll. Law, Thomas Cooley Law Sch., U. Detroit Law Sch., U. Mich., U. Miss.; mem. faculty Bat. Coll. Advocacy Assn. Trial Lawyers Am., Practicing Law Inst., N.Y.C., Inst. Continuing Legal Edn., Ann Arbor, Mich. Apptd. to jud. selection com. Western Dist. U.S. Dist. Ct. Mich., 1986—; nat. pres. Citizens Legal Clinic-Trial Lawyers for Pub. Justice; instr. seminar Inst. for Continuing Legal Edn. Bd. dirs. NW Mich. br. ACLU; mem. Traverse City and Leelanau Players; exec. sec. Met. Detroit Fair Employment Practices Council, Dodge Community House; bd. dirs. Rehab. Inst. Detroit; vol. atty. Penrickton Nursery Sch. for Visually Handicapped Children, Taylor, Mich.; mem. Traverse City Light and Power Bd., 1984-85, citizens' adv. com. to the Grand Traverse Bd. for new detention facilities, 1986; pres. Grand Traverse Hist. Soc., 1987—; contbr., trustee and fundraiser Traverse City Civic Players, 1973-78; active supporter Traverse Area Found., 3d level Crisis Intervention Ctr.; served on Pres. Jimmy Carter's selection com. for Western Dist. Fed. Judges; intern Presbyn. Ch., 1946-47. Served with USN, 1942-44. Recipient Lawyer of Yr. award Wayne State U., 1975-76, Outstanding Lawyer Alum award Wayne State U., 1975. Fellow Am. Coll. Trial Lawyers; mem. Assn. Trial Lawyers Am. (past nat. co-chmn. nat. com. on civil rights, past chmn. R.R. law sect.), Mich. Trial Lawyers Assn. (past pres.) , Nat. Lawyers Guild (mem.-at-large), ABA, Grand-Traverse-Leelanau-Antrim County Bar Assn., Mich. Bar Assn., Nat. Assn. Criminal Def. Lawyers, Actors Equity, Wayne State U. Alumni Assn. (exec. bd.), DAV, NOW, NAACP (life), Sierra Club, Friends of the Earth. Coauthor: Lawyers Desk Reference, 1964-75; co-editor Rights of Railroad Workers, 1973; contbr. articles to legal publs. Civil rights, Federal civil litigation, State civil litigation. Office: Robb Messing & Palmer PC 420 E Front St Box 1132 Traverse City MI 49685

ROBB, ELIZABETH ANN, lawyer; b. Macomb, Ill., Dec. 10, 1955; d. Robert Walker and Mary Ellen (Herndon) R.; m. Alan Lee Sender, Aug. 8, 1982. Student, Albion Coll., 1974; BA magna cum laude, Wesleyan U., Bloomington, Ill., 1978; JD, Loyola U., Chgo., 1981. Bar: Ill. 1981, U.S. Dist. Ct. (cen. dist.) Ill. 1981. Asst. prof. law Ill. State u., Normal, 1978-79; assoc. Reynard Law Offices, Bloomington, 1982; asst. pub. defender McLean County, Bloomington, 1982—; ptnr. Reynard & Robb, Bloomington, 1983—; mem. Mediation Task Force, Bloomington, 1984—. Chmn. adv. panel Countering Domestic and Sexual Violence, Bloomington, 1986—; pres. bd. dirs. Bloomington Day Care Ctr., 1985—; bd. dirs. Ill. Wesleyan Assocs., 1985—. Mem. ABA, Ill. State Bar Assn., McLean County Bar Assn. (sec. 1982-83), Assn. Trial Lawyers Am., Sigma Kappa Alumnae Assn. (bd. dirs. 1982—). Jewish. Avocations: traveling, gardening, reading. Family and matrimonial, Juvenile, Real property. Home: 410 Marian Ave Normal IL 61761 Office: Reynard & Robb 109 W Jefferson Bloomington IL 61701

ROBB, JOHN ANTHONY, JR., lawyer; b. Pitts., Mar. 26, 1947; s. John Anthony and Angela Virginia (Boccella) R.; m. Jacqueline Fiester, June 23, 1973; children: Christopher Jonathon, Jessica Fiester. BA, Denison U., 1969; JD, Duquesne U., 1972. Bar: Pa. 1972, U.S. Dist. Ct. (we. dist.) Pa. 1972, U.S. Ct. Appeals (3d cir.) 1974, U.S. Supreme Ct. 1982. Legal advisor, law clk. to presiding justice U.S. Dist. Ct. (we. dist.) Pa., Pitts., 1972-73; legal advisor, law clk. to presiding judge U.S. Ct. Appeals (3d cir.), Phila., 1973-74; assoc. Royston, Robb & Leonard, Pitts., 1974-77; ptnr. Robb, Leonard & Mulvihill, Pitts., 1977—. Chmn. Sewickley (Pa.) Civil Service Commn., 1976-86. Mem. ABA, Allegheny County Bar Assn., Assn. Trial Lawyers Am., Pa. Trial Lawyers Assn., Order of Barristers. Club: Rivers (Pitts.). Federal civil litigation, State civil litigation, Insurance. Home: 94 Merriman Rd Sewickley PA 15143 Office: Robb Leonard & Mulvihill 2300 One Mellon Bank Ctr Pittsburgh PA 15219

ROBB, SCOTT HALL, lawyer, communications executive; b. White Plains, N.Y., Mar. 1, 1944; s. Arch Howard and Eleanore Dorothy (Sullivan) R. BA, Yale U.; JD, Georgetown U.; LLM, NYU. Bar: N.Y. 1969, D.C. 1971. Assoc. Javits & Javits, N.Y.C., 1970-71; sr. atty. NBC, Inc., Washington, 1972-76; sr. ptnr. Robb & Kuhns, N.Y.C., 1977-84, Robb & Henning, N.Y.C., 1984—; founder, v.p., gen. counsel, sec. United Satellite TV, 1981-82; v.p., sec., dir. Citicom Corp., World Com Inc., Orbita Technologies Corp.; v.p., dir. Interlog Publishing; pres. Communications Research Inst.; dir. In Touch Networks, Inc., Devine Communications Corp., Howard Communications Corp.; pres., dir. Arch Robb Found. for Edn. in Telecommunications; adj. prof. communications Iona Coll., New Rochelle, N.Y.; chmn., sec., gen. counsel Shipboard Satellite Network, Inc.; sec., gen. counsel Independence Broadcasting Corp.; gen. counsel Urban Satellite Cable Corp. Author: Television/Radio Age Communications Cousebook, 1978-82, (with Arthur Belenduik) Broadcasting Via Satellite, 1978; editor: (with Michael Botein) Competition Regulation: The Case of the Mass Media, 1977; exec. producer, host Spectrum Ednl. Video Cassettes. Pres., bd. dirs. Alzheimers Disease Communications Found.; bd. dirs., gen. counsel Am. Soc. Hypertension. Mem. ABA, Fed. Communications Bar Assn. (mem. exec. com. 1975-78), N.Y. State Bar Assn., D.C. Bar Assn., Assn. Bar City N.Y. Clubs: Yale, Players (N.Y.C.); Univ. (Washington); Yale Golf (New Haven, Conn.); Scarsdale (N.Y.) Golf. Entertainment, General corporate, Health. Home: 171 Brite Ave Scarsdale NY 10583 Other: 2122 Massachusetts Ave Washington DC 20008 Office: 515 Madison Ave Suite 3600 New York NY 10022

ROBBINS, ARCHIE LEW, lawyer; b. Meade, Kans., Apr. 10, 1934; s. Elijah Nelson and Carrie Dillie (Stout) R.; m. Mary Frances Eidson, May 25, 1956; 1 child, Mark Bryan. BA in Chemistry, SW Mo. State, 1956; JD, Tulsa U., 1966. Bar: Okla. 1966, U.S. Dist. Ct. (no. dist.) Okla. 1971. Tchr. Ozark (Mo.) High Sch., 1955-56; research chemist Phillips Petroleum, Bartlesville, Okla., 1956-66, patent atty., 1966—; mayor City of Bartlesville, 1981—. Named one of Outstanding Young Men Am., Outstanding Americans Found., 1970. Mem. Washington County Bar, Okla. Bar Assn. (past pres. patent and trademark sects.), Fed. Bar Assn., Bartlesville C. of C. Republican. Presbyterian. Lodge: Lions (Bartlesville) (past pres.). Avocation: tennis. Patent. Home: 130 Forrest Park Rd Bartlesville OK 74003 Office: Phillips Petroleum Co 218 PLB Bartlesville OK 74004

ROBBINS, DONALD MICHAEL, lawyer; b. Woonsocket, R.I., Oct. 2, 1935; s. Robert Sidney and Nancy Ruth (Medoff) R.; m. Esther Sharp, Aug. 30, 1959; children: Jeffrey, Benjamin. Student, Brandeis U., 1953-55; A.B., U. Mich., 1957; LL.B., Boston U., 1960. Bar: Mass. 1961, R.I. 1962. Individual practice law 1961-68; v.p., sec., gen. counsel Hasbro, Inc., Pawtucket, R.I., 1968—. Bd. dirs., former chmn. Big Bros. R.I.; bd. dirs. Miriam Hosp.; former pres. Temple Emanu-El; chmn. Israel Bonds State of R.I. Mem. Am. Soc. Corp. Secs., Mass. Bar Assn., R.I. Bar Assn. Home: 93 Pratt St Providence RI 02906 Office: 1027 Newport Ave Pawtucket RI 02861

ROBBINS, IRA PAUL, law educator; b. Bklyn., Jan. 2, 1949; s. Martin M. and Seena (Seidman) R.; m. Joyce Adrienne Flinker, Aug. 16, 1970; children: Alexandra, Andrew, Melissa. AB, U. Pa., 1970; JD, Harvard U., 1973. Bar: N.Y. 1974, U.S. Ct. Appeals (2d cir.) 1975, D.C. 1984. Law clk. to presiding justice U.S. Ct. Appeals (2d cir.), N.Y.C., 1973-75; assoc. prof. law, dir. Kans. Defender Project U. Kans., Lawrence, 1975-79; prof. law and justice Am. U., Washington, 1979—; visiting prof. law Georgetown U. Law Ctr., Washington, 1982; cons. Nat. Inst. Corrections, Washington, 1983—, Fed. Jud. Ctr., Washington, 1983—, also acting dir. Continuing Edn. and Tng. Div. Fed. Jud. Ctr., 1986. Author: Comparative Postconviction Remedies, 1980; editor, contbr. Prisoners' Rights Sourcebook, 1980, The Law and Processes of Post Conviction Remedies, 1982, Prisoners and the Law, 1985; contbr. articles to profl. jours. Ethel and Raymond F. Rice scholar, 1978, Pauline Ruyle Moore scholar, 1980, Barnard T. Welsh scholar, 1982—; Jud. fellow, 1985-86; named one of Outstanding Young Men Am.,

U.S. Jaycees, 1982. Mem. ABA (reporter study on pvt. prisons 1984—), Am. Law Inst., Assn. Am. Law Schs. (exec. council criminal justice sect. 1983—), Internat. Assn. Penal Law, Phi Beta Kappa. Criminal, Legal education. Office: Am U Washington Coll Law 4400 Massachusetts Ave NW Washington DC 20016

ROBBINS, JOHN BOYD, judge; b. Malvern, Ark., Dec. 13, 1942; s. Hershel David and Clara Opal (Buck) R.; m. Shara Diane Thornton, Aug. 31, 1962; children: John Kelly, Emma Caroline. Student, Henderson U., 1960, S.W. Grad. Sch. Banking, Dallas, 1965-67, U. Tenn., 1971-72; postgrad., Ouachita Bapt. U., 1972; JD, Vanderbilt U., 1973. Bar: Ark. 1973, U.S. Dist. Ct. (we. and ea. dists.) Ark. 1974. Bank examiner Comptroller of Currency, Washington, 1962-64, State Bank Dept., Little Rock, Ark., 1964-65; v.p., trust officer First Nat. Bank, Hot Springs, Ark., 1965-70; law clk. to chief judge U.S. Ct. Appeals (8th cir.), Little Rock, 1973-74; ptnr. Wooton, Slagle & Robbins, Hot Springs, 1974-84; chancellor, probate judge State of Ark., Hot Springs, 1985—. Bd. dirs. Ark. Jail Ministries, 1986—, Garland County Council on Aging, 1979—, Salvation Army of Garland County, 1982—, Red Cross of Garland County, 1975-81. Mem. ABA, Ark. Bar Assn., Garland Bar Assn., Order of the Coif. Democrat. Baptist. Lodge: Mid-Am. Lions. Home: 109 Camelot Ln Hot Springs AR 71913 Office: Chancery Ct 303 Garland County Courthouse Hot Springs AR 71901

ROBBINS, LYNDA JEAN, lawyer; b. Boston, Dec. 21, 1954; d. Melvin and Miriam Diane (Ephross) Edelstein; m. David L. Robbins, Spet. 4, 1977; 1 child, Melissa Rachel. BA, Suffolk U., 1977, JD, 1979. Bar: Mass. 1979, U.S. Dist. Ct. Mass. 1980. Sole practice Chelmsford, Mass., 1980—. Mem. ABA, Mass. Bar Assn., Greater Lowell Bar Assn., Mass. Assn. Women Lawyers. Family and matrimonial, Probate. Office: 3 Summer St Chelsford MA 01824

ROBBINS, ROBERT JOSEPH, JR., lawyer; b. Lenoir, N.C., June 20, 1950; s. Robert Joseph Sr. and Patricia (Hart) R.; m. Linda Gail Knotts, Aug. 19, 1972; 1 child, Kimberly Caroline. AB in Polit. Sci., U. N.C., 1972, cert. in tax law, 1974; cert. in real estate law, Duke U., 1975; JD, U. N.C., Durham, 1976. Bar: N.C. 1976, U.S. Dist. Ct. (we. and mid. dists.) N.C. 1976. Cons. Planned Estate Services, Durham, N.C., 1976-78; sole practice Lenoir, 1978, 1980-82; assoc. Beal & Beal, Lenoir, 1979-80; ptnr. Robbins & Flaherty, Lenoir, 1982—. Research editor N.C.C.U. Law Rev., 1975. Treas. Miss Caldwell County Scholarship Pageant, Inc., Lenoir. Mem. ABA, N.C. Bar Assn., N.C. Trial Lawyers Assn., Lenoir Jaycees (legal advisor 1981-86, external v.p. 1979-80). Democrat. Methodist. Lodge: Kiwanis (past pres., Most Outstanding Mem. N.C. chpt. 1984). Avocations: tennis, golf. Personal injury, Real property, Consumer commercial. Office: Robbins & Flaherty 204 Main St NW PO Box 2307 Lenoir NC 28645

ROBBINS, SARA ELLEN, law librarian; b. Balt., Mar. 3, 1952; d. Malcolm Lee and Norma (Corman) R. BA, U. Cin., 1974; MLS, Pratt Inst., 1977; JD, Ohio State U., 1985. Bar: Ohio 1985. Cataloger Bklyn. Law Sch. Library, 1977-79, assoc. librarian, 1984-85, acting dir., 1985-86, dir., 1986—; head tech. services Cardozo Law Sch. Library, N.Y.C., 1979-81; research editorial asst. Yale Law Sch. Library, New Haven, 1982-83. Author: Surrogate Parenting: Annotated Review of the Literature, 1984; (with others) Library Automation: A Systems and Software Sampler, 1985. Recipient Am. Jurisprudence award Lawyer's Coop. Pub. Co., 1984. Mem. ABA, Ohio Bar Assn., Am. Assn. Law Libraries, Law Library Assn. Greater N.Y., Spl. Libraries Assn. Librarianship, Legal education, Legal history. Office: Bklyn Law Sch Library 250 Joralemon St Brooklyn NY 11201

ROBBINS, VERNON EARL, lawyer, accountant; b. Balt., Aug. 16, 1921; s. Alexander Goldborough and Anne Jeanette (Bubb) R.; m. Ruth Adele Holland, Oct. 21, 1941; m. 2d, Alice Sherman Meredith, Feb. 17, 1961; 1 dau., Sharon Holland; 1 stepdau., Susan Victoria Causey. A.B.A., Md. Sch. Acctg., 1941; J.D., U. Balt., 1952. Bar: Md. 1952. Internal revenue agt. IRS, Balt., 1942-52; ptnr. Robbins, Adam & Co., C.P.A. firm, Cambridge, Md., 1952—; sole practice law, Cambridge, 1952—; mem. adv. bd. Cambridge Balt. Fed. Savs. & Loan Assn.; bd. dirs. Bank of Eastern Shore. Served with U.S. Maritime Service, 1941-42. Named Boss of Yr., Tidewater chpt. Nat. Secs. Assn., 1978. Mem. ABA, Md. bar Assn., Am. Inst. C.P.A.s., Md. Assn. C.P.A.s., Am. Assn. Atty.-C.P.A.s., Am. Judicature Soc., Navy League, Dorchester County Hist. Soc., Dorchester Art Center. Democrat. Methodist. Club: Cambridge Yacht. Lodges: Elks, Masons, Shriners. Corporate taxation, Estate taxation, Personal income taxation. Office: PO Box 236 118 Cedar St Cambridge MD 21613

ROBE, EDWARD SCOTT, lawyer; b. Cumberland, Ohio, July 9, 1936; s. Thurlow Scott and Mary Alice (McKibben) R.; m. Sally Ann Allen, June 19, 1960; children: Lisa Kathleen Robe Clay, Scott McKibben, Jennifer Allen Robe Meyer. AB, Ohio U., 1959; JD, Duke U., 1963. Bar: Ohio 1963, U.S. Supreme Ct. 1968. Ptnr. Robe & Keifer, Athens, Ohio, 1963—; pres. Law Abstract Pub. Co., 1973-74; bd. commrs. grievances and discipline Ohio Supreme Ct., Columbus, 1975-80. Trustee Sheltering Arms Hosp. Found., 1973-80, chmn. bd. trustees, 1979-80; mem. Athens County Bd. Elections, 1969-81, chmn., 1980-81; chmn. Athens County Rep. Exec. Com., 1970-72, mem. Ohio bd. Psychology, 1981-87, sec., 1985-86. Served to capt. USNG, 1965-70. Fellow Ohio State Bar Found.; mem. Ohio Bar Assn. (exec. com. 1971-74), Ohio Acad. Trial Lawyers, Athens County Bar Assn. (pres. 1969-70), Am. Judicature Soc., State Ohio Bd. Psychology (sec. bd. 1985-86). Methodist. Club: Symposiarchs. Lodge: Rotary (pres. 1981-82). Avocation: reading. General practice, Probate, Real property. Office: Robe & Keifer 14 W Washington St Athens OH 45701

ROBERSON, CLIFFORD EUGENE, law educator, lawyer; b. Iola, Tex., Feb. 24, 1937; s. Burrel Allen and Sue (Crouch) R.; children—Clif, Marshall, Kenneth, Dwayne; m. Mariam Daniels, Nov. 21, 1981. B.A., U. Mo., 1961; J.D., Am. U., 1967; LL.M., George Washington U., 1976; Ph.D., U.S. Internat. U., 1974. Bar: Tex. 1967, U.S. Tax Ct. 1969, U.S. Supreme Ct. 1970, Calif. 1978, U.S. Dist. Ct. (we. dist.) Tex. 1984. Prof. St. Edward's U., Austin, Tex., 1979-83; dir. Nat. Dist. Attys. Coll., Houston, 1983-84; prof. Calif. State U.-Fresno, 1984—, dir. Justice Ctr., 1984—. Author: Legal Guide for Pilots, 1972; Law of Employment, 1985. Contbr. articles on criminal justice to profl. jours. Served to maj. USMC, 1961-79. Mem. Nat. Assn. Dist. Attys., ABA, Tex. Bar Assn. Criminal, Labor, Legal education. Home: PO Box 3893 Pinedale CA 93650 Office: Calif State U Fresno CA 93740

ROBERSON, LINDA, lawyer; b. Omaha, Nebr., July 15, 1947; d. Harlan Oliver and Elizabeth Aileen (Good) R.; m. Gary M. Young, Aug. 20, 1970; children: Elizabeth, Katherine, Christopher. BA, Oberlin Coll., 1969; MS, U. Wis., 1970, JD, 1974. Bar: Wis. 1974, U.S. Dist. Ct. (we. dist.) Wis. 1974. Legis. atty. Wis. Legis. Reference Bur., Madison, 1974-76, sr. legis. atty., 1976-78; assoc. Rikkers, Koritzinsky & Rikkers, Madison, 1978-79; ptnr. Koritzinsky, Neider, Langer & Roberson, Madison, 1979-85, Stolper, Koritzinsky, Brewster & Neider, Madison, 1985—; lectr. U. Wis. Law Sch., Madison, 1978—. Co-author: Real Women, Real Lives, 1978, Marital and Non-Marital Agreements, 1981, Wisconsin's Marital Property Reform Act, 1984, Understanding Wisconsin's Marital Property Law, 1985, A Guide to Property Classification Under Wisconsin's Marital Property Act, 1986. Mem. ABA, Wis. Bar Assn., Dane County Bar Assn., Legal Assn. of Women. Estate planning, Probate, Family and matrimonial. Office: Stolper Koritzinsky Brewster & Neider 7617 Mineral Point Rd Madison WI 53717

ROBERSON, LYNN MARIE, lawyer; b. San Antonio, Jan. 23, 1951; d. Rupert P. and Rosemary E. (Kramer) R.; m. Henry M. Newkirk, April 21, 1984. BA, U. Md., 1973; JD, U. Minn., 1979. Bar: Minn. 1979, U.S. Dist. Ct. Minn. 1979, U.S. Ct. Appeals (8th cir.) 1980, Ga. 1983, U.S. Dist. Ct. (no. and mid. dists.) Ga. 1983, U.S. Ct. Appeals (11th cir.) 1983. Assoc. Robins, Zelle, Larson & Kaplan, Mpls., 1979-83, Atlanta, 1983-84; assoc. Swift, Currie, McGhee & Hiers, Atlanta, 1984—; instr. law U. Minn., Mpls., 1977-79. Mem. ABA, Ga. Bar Assn., Atlanta Bar Assn., Decatur-Dekalb Bar Assn., Atlanta Women's Network. Personal injury, Insurance, Federal civil litigation. Office: Swift Currie McGhee & Hiers 771 Spring St NW Atlanta GA 30379

ROBERTS, ALLEN B., lawyer; b. Phila., Apr. 27, 1945; s. Thomas and Jeanne (Smolen) R. BS, U. Pa., 1966; JD, Temple U., 1971. mem. bd. Fund for Aging Services Inc., N.Y.C., 1984—. Club: New York Athletic. Labor. Home: 480 Park Ave New York NY 10022 Office: Roberts & Finger 767 Third Ave New York NY 10017

ROBERTS, B. K., lawyer, former judge; b. Sopchoppy, Fla., Feb. 5, 1907; s. Thomas and Florida (Morrison) R.; m. Mary Newman, Aug. 20, 1937; children: Mary Jane, Thomas Frederick. J.D., U. Fla., 1928; LL.D., U. Miami, 1954; D.H.L., Fla. State U., 1980. Bar: Fla. 1928. Practiced in Tallahassee, 1928-49; justice Supreme Ct. of Fla., 1949-77, chief justice, 1953-54, 61-63, 71-72, ret., 1977; sr. partner firm Roberts, Baggett, LaFace & Richard, and predecessor, 1977—; v.p., dir. Tallahassee Bank & Trust Co. (now Barnett Bank), 1948-49; Mem. awards jury Freedoms Found. at Valley Forge, 1962; mem. Fla. Constl. Revision Commn., 1966, 77; chmn. subcom. on human rights; chmn. Jud. Council Fla., 1962-77; mem. exec. com. Nat. Conf. Chief Justices, 1966, dep. chmn., 1972-73. Chmn. trustees Fla. State U. Found.; bd. counselors Fla. Presbyn. Coll. Served as lt. comdr. USCG; Served as lt. comdr. 1942-45; shipping commr. 1943-45, Port Jacksonville, Fla. Recipient Distinguished Citizen award Stetson U. Coll. Law (2). Mem. Internat. Bar Assn. (patron), Inter-Am., ABA (UN com., world order under law com.; ofcl. ct. rep. London meeting 1957), Fla. Bar Assn. (past v.p.), Tallahassee Bar Assn. (past pres.), Am. Judicature Soc., Am. Law Inst., Newcomen Soc. Eng., Am. Legion (mem. nat. distinguished guests com.), Alpha Kappa Psi, Fla. Blue Key, Fla State U. Gold Key, Soc. of Wig and Robe, Phi Alpha Delta, Delta Chi. Democrat. Presbyterian. Clubs: Governor's, Killearn Golf and Country, Hendersonville (N.C.) Country. Lodges: Masons; Shriners; Elks; Odd Fellows; Kiwanis. General corporate, State civil litigation, Municipal bonds. Home: MSS Box 3005 Tallahassee FL 32303 Office: PO Drawer 1838 Tallahassee FL 32302 Address: 101 E College Ave Tallahassee FL 32302

ROBERTS, BONITA KOEHLER, lawyer; b. Elmhurst, Ill., Aug. 12, 1947; d. Earl August and Marian Edith (Wilson) Koehler. BA, U. New Orleans, 1973, MA, 1975; JD, Loyola U., New Orleans, 1980. Bar: La. 1980. Law librarian Sessions, Fishman, New Orleans, 1978-81; prof. St. Mary's Law Sch., San Antonio, 1981—. Author: Legal Research Guide: Patterns and Practices, 1986. English Speaking Union scholar, 1974. Mem. ABA, La. Bar Assn., Bexar County Women's Bar Assn. (coordinator 1986—), Assn. Am. Law Schs., World Affairs Council. Legal education, Librarianship, Labor. Office: St Mary's Law Sch 1 Camino Santa Maria San Antonio TX 78284

ROBERTS, BRIAN MICHAEL, lawyer; b. Cin., May 28, 1957; s. Shearl Joseph and Mary Ruth (Christian) R.; m. Carol Denise Zimmerman, July 28, 1979; children: Nicholas Brian, Mary Katelin. BS in Bus., Miami U., Oxford, Ohio, 1979; JD, U. Dayton, 1982. Bar: Ohio 1982, U.S. Dist. Ct. (so. dist.) Ohio 1983, U.S. Ct. Appeals (6th cir.) 1984. Assoc. Jablinski, Folino & Roberts Co. LPA, Dayton, Ohio, 1979-82, Jablinski, Folino, Roberts, Schultz & Martin Co. LPA, Dayton, 1982—. Organizer, scheduler legal presentations to engaged couples Family Life Office, Archdiocese of Cin., Dayton 1982—. Mem. Ohio State Bar Assn., Ohio Acad. Trial Lawyers, Dayton Bar Assn., Montgomery County Trial Lawyers Assn. Republican. Roman Catholic. Workers' compensation, Personal injury, State civil litigation. Home: 3830 Gardenview Pl Kettering OH 45429 Office: Jablinski Folino Roberts et al 214 W Monument Ave Dayton OH 45402

ROBERTS, DAVID GLENDENNING, justice Supreme Court Maine; b. Fort Fairfield, Maine, July 17, 1928; s. Melvin Philip and Ethel (Chamberlain) R.; m. Rose Marie Downie, Feb. 9, 1952; children: Michael, Mary, Dorothy, Catherine, Sarah, Joseph, Susan. A.B., Bowdoin Coll., 1950; LL.B., Boston U., 1956. Bar: Maine 1956, U.S. Dist. Ct. Maine 1959, U.S. Ct. Appeals (1st cir.) 1964. Ptnr. Pendleton and Roberts, Caribou, Maine, 1956-61; asst. U.S. atty. U.S. Dept. Justice, Bangor, Maine, 1961-66; sole practice Bangor, 1966-67; justice Maine Superior Ct., Bangor, 1967-80; assoc. justice Supreme Jud. Ct., Bangor, 1980—; mem. Maine Jud. Council, Augusta, 1969-77, 80-86. Served to lt. U.S. Army, 1951-53. Democrat. Roman Catholic. Judicial administration. Office: Supreme Jud Ct Penobscot County Courthouse PO Box 1068 Bangor ME 04401 *

ROBERTS, E. F., lawyer, educator; b. 1930. B.A., Northeastern U., Boston, 1952; LL.B., Boston Coll., 1954. Bar: Mass. 1954. Asst. prof. law Villanova U., Pa., 1957-59, assoc. prof. law, 1959-60, prof. law, 1960-64; prof. law Cornell U., Ithaca, N.Y., 1964—, Edwin H. Woodruff prof. law; vis. prof. Nottingham U., Eng., 1962-63, Harvard U., 1983; mem. edn. panel Environ. Law Reporter, 1971-80; cons. in field. Author: Public Regulation on Title Insurance, 1960, Land Use Planning, 2d edit., 1975, Law and the Preservation of Agricultural Land, 1982, (with Cleary et al.) McCormick on Evidence, 3d edit., 1984. Mem. Am. Law Inst., Internat. Council of Environ. Law. Legal education, Environment, Real property. Office: Cornell U Sch Law Ithaca NY 14853 *

ROBERTS, EDWARD CALHOUN, lawyer; b. Columbia, S.C., Oct. 17, 1937; s. John Cornelius and Cecilia (Allen) R.; m. Margaret C. Roberts, Sept. 1967 (dec. July 1978); children: Kathryn A., John G.; m. Beverly Means, July 10, 1980; 1 child, Beverly M. AB, U. S.C., 1959, JD, 1962; LLM, Georgetown U., 1963. Bar: S.C. 1962, U.S. Ct. Appeals (4th cir.) 1965, U.S. Supreme Ct 1973, U.S. Ct. Appeals (D.C. cir.) 1974. Atty. S.C. Electric and Gas Co., Columbia, 1967-72, sr. atty., 1972-80, gen. counsel, 1980-82, v.p. legal counsel, 1982—. Co-author: Freedom from Federal Establishment, 1965. Pres. Columbia Urban League, 1977-79, Columbia Lyric Opera Co., 1983-85, Columbia Music Festival Assn., 1986—. Served to sgt. USMCR, 1963-69. Mem. S.C. Bar Assn. (chmn. com. to revise corp. laws 1976-81), Am. Law Inst., S.C. Law Inst. (treas.), Edison Electric Inst. (legal com.). Public utilities, Securities, General corporate. Home: 8 Woodhill Circle Columbia SC 29209 Office: SC Electric and Gas Co Legal Dept (106) Columbia SC 29218

ROBERTS, EDWARD THOMAS, lawyer; b. Washington, Oct. 3, 1949; s. Richard Brooke Titus and Irena Zuzanna (Eiger) R.; m. Theresa Yvonne Binczyk, Nov. 26, 1977; children—Emily Brooke, Jonathan Chambers. A.B., Princeton U., 1971; J.D., George Washington U., 1974. Bar: Md. 1974, D.C. 1975, U.S. Ct. Appeals (D.C. cir.) 1976, U.S. Dist. Ct. D.C. 1982, U.S. Dist. Ct. Md. 1982, U.S. Supreme Ct. 1982, U.S. Ct. Appeals (4th cir.) 1986. Asst. state's atty. Prince George's County State's Atty.'s Office, Upper Marlboro, Md., 1975; asst. U.S. atty. U.S. Atty.'s Office, Washington, 1975-86, Md., 1986—; U.S. Atty's Office Organized Crime and Drug Enforcement Task Force, Balt., 1986—. Mem. Md. Bar Assn., D.C. Bar Assn., Nat. Dist. Attys. Assn., Md. State's Attys. Assn. Democrat. Episcopalian. Club: Columbia Country (Chevy Chase, Md.). Office: U S Atty Office U S Courthouse 101 W Lombard St Baltimore MD 21201

ROBERTS, HARRY MORRIS, JR., lawyer; b. Dallas, June 10, 1938; s. Harry Morris and La Frances (Reilly) R.; m. Nancy Beth Johnson, Mar. 7, 1964; children: Richard Whitfield, Elizabeth Lee. BBA, So. Meth. U., 1960; LLB, Harvard U., 1963. Bar: Tex. 1963, U.S. Dist. Ct. (no. dist.) Tex. 1964, U.S. Ct. Appeals (5th cir.), 1972, U.S. Supreme Ct. 1971. Sr. ptnr. Thompson & Knight, Dallas, 1963—; chmn. real estate, probate and trust law sect. State Bar Tex., 1984-85; vis. scholar U. Tex. Law Sch., 1986. Contbr. articles to legal jours. Trustee, sec. Shelter Ministries of Dallas, 1982—. Mem. ABA, Tex. Bar Found., Dallas Bar Assn. (chmn. real estate sect. 1981), Am. Coll. Real Estate Lawyers. Episcopalian. Clubs: Salesmanship (Dallas), Dallas, Dallas Country. Real property, Landlord-tenant, Purchase and development. Office: Thompson & Knight 3300 First City Ctr Dallas TX 75201

ROBERTS, J. WILLIAM, lawyer; b. 1942. BA, Ill. Wesleyan U.; JD, Washington U. Bar: Ill. 1968. U.S. atty. cen. dist. State of Ill., Springfield. Office: PO Box 375 Springfield IL 62705 *

ROBERTS, JAMES HAROLD, III, lawyer; b. Omaha, Aug. 11, 1949; s. James Harold Jr. and Evelyn Doris (Young) R.; m. Marilyn Novak, June 29, 1974; children: Jessica Noël, Meredith Caitlin. BA, U. Notre Dame, 1971; JD, St. Louis U., 1974. Bar: Iowa 1974, U.S. Ct. Mil. Appeals 1974, U.S. Supreme Ct. 1979, D.C. 1981. Govt. contract atty. U.S. Gen. Acctg. Office, Washington, 1978-83, U.S. Dept. Treasury, Washington, 1983—. Editor St. Louis U. law rev., 1973-74. Served to capt. JAGC, U.S. Army, 1974-78, maj. USAR/NG, 1978—. Mem. ABA (pub. contract law sect.), D.C. Bar Assn., Fed. Bar Assn. Roman Catholic. Government contracts and claims. Home: 308 N Monroe St Arlington VA 22201 Office: IRS Office of Chief Counsel 1111 Constitution Ave NW Washington DC 20224

ROBERTS, JAMES ISAAC, SR., lawyer; b. Sumter, S.C., Apr. 8, 1947; s. James Richardson and Kate Goodwyn (Appelt) R.; m. Barbara Camille Hogan, Oct. 10, 1969; children: James Isaac, Kathryn Camille, Philip Louis. BA, Presbyn. Coll., 1969; JD, Woodrow Wilson Coll. Law, 1975, LLM, 1978; MEd Clemson U., 1978. Bar: Ga. 1975. Sole practice, Elberton, Ga., 1976, 77-80; ptnr. Shurling & Roberts, Elberton, 1976-77, Roberts & Hodges, Elberton, 1980—; county atty., 1978-82; judge Elberton Mcpl. Ct.; lectr. seminars. Vol rep. Am. Bible Soc., 1976—; deacon First Presbyn. Ch. of Elberton, 1978-80, 81-82; chmn. steering com. Trinity Presbyn. Ch., 1982-85; mem. adv. bd. Elberton service unit Salvation Army, 1985—; chmn. crusade Elbert County Unit, Am. Cancer Soc., 1979-80, v.p., 1980-81, pres., 1981-82. Served with U.S. Army, 1970-72. Recipient Cert. of Merit, Am. Cancer Soc., 1980. Mem. Ga. Bar Assn., No. Cir. Bar Assn., Elberton Bar Assn. (sec.-treas., 1984-85, v.p. 1985-86, pres. 1986-87), Assn. Trial Lawyers Am., Ga. Trial Lawyers Assn. Club: NE Ga. Clemson. Lodges: Rotary (bd. dirs. Elberton chpt. 1978-79), Iptay, Elks (corp. dir. Elberton 1979-81). Avocation: collecting baseball cards. Personal injury, Workers' compensation, General practice. Home: 139 Myrtl St Elberton GA 30635 Office: Roberts & Hodges 23 N Public Sq Elberton GA 30635

ROBERTS, JARED INGERSOLL, lawyer; b. Phila., Mar. 20, 1946; s. Brooke and Anna (Ingersoll) R.; m. Katherine Marx Sherwood, May 17, 1986. BA, Princeton U., 1968; JD, U. Va., 1974. Bar: Pa. 1974, U.S. Dist. Ct. (ea. dist.) Pa. 1975, U.S. Ct. Appeals (3d cir.) 1978, U.S. Supreme Ct. 1978, D.C. 1985. Assoc. Duane, Morris & Heckscher, Phila., 1974-82; spl. counsel U.S. Dept. Transp., Washington, 1982-84; assoc. gen. counsel Nat. R.R. Passenger Corp., Washington, 1984—. Served to lt (j.g.) USN, 1968-70. Mem. ABA, Pa. Bar Assn., D.C. Bar Assn. Republican. Episcopalian. Avocations: sailing, ice hockey, railroads. Contracts commercial, Environment, Real property. Home: 4631 N 15th St Arlington VA 22207 Office: Amtrak Law Dept 400 N Capitol St NW Washington DC 20001

ROBERTS, JAYNE KELLY, lawyer; b. N.Y.C., Sept. 30, 1948; d. William Frederick and Kathleen (Kelly) Mueller; m. Malcolm Jerome Roberts, Oct. 10, 1972; children—Chris, Karyn, Paul, Mark, Michael, Seth. B.A., U. Calif.-Berkeley, 1977; J.D., U. San Francisco, 1980. Bar: Calif. 1981, U.S. Dist. Ct. 1981. Assoc., Sandvick & Martin, Oakland, 1981; sole practice, San Francisco, 1981—. Bd. govs. Bard Coll., Annandale on Hudson, N.Y., 1982. Mem. Am. Assn. Trial Lawyers, Calif. Assn. Trial Lawyers, San Francisco Trial Lawyers (bd. dirs. 1986—). Democrat. Personal injury, Family and matrimonial, Real property. Office: 601 Montgomery St 19th Floor San Francisco CA 94111

ROBERTS, KEITH EDWARD, SR., lawyer; b. White Hall, Ill., Apr. 27, 1928; s. Victor Harold and Ruby Harriet (Kelsey) R.; m. Marthan Dusch, Sept. 4, 1954; 1 son, Keith Edward. Student, Western Ill. U., 1946-47, George Washington U., 1947-48; B.S., U. Ill., 1951, J.D., 1953. Bar: Ill. 1953, U.S. Dist. Ct. (no. dist.) Ill. 1957, U.S. Dist. Ct. (so. dist.) Ill. 1961, U.S. Dist. Ct. (no. dist.) Ohio 1960, U.S. Ct. Mil. Appeals 1954, U.S. Ct. Appeals (7th cir.) 1968. Assoc. J.D. Quarant, Elizabethtown, Ill., 1953-56; staff atty. Pa. R.R. Co., Chgo., 1957-60; assoc. Henslee, Monek & Henslee, Chgo., 1960-67; sole practice, Naperville, Ill., 1967-68; ptnr. Donovan, Atten, Mountcastle, Roberts & DaRosa, Wheaton, Ill., 1968-77; pres. Donovan & Roberts, P.C., Wheaton, 1977—. Served to capt. U.S. Army, 1954-57. Mem. ABA, Assn. Trial Lawyers Am., Ill. Bar Assn., DuPage County Bar Assn. (gen. counsel 1976-86). Democrat. Presbyterian. State civil litigation, Family and matrimonial, Criminal. Office: PO Box 417 Wheaton IL 60187

ROBERTS, LARRY F., lawyer, consultant; b. San Bernardino, Calif., Dec. 8, 1946; s. Bob F. and Catherine E. (Hughes) R.; m. Kathryn Louise Thomas, Oct. 25, 1966; four children. BA, U. Calif., Santa Barbara, 1972; JD, Pepperdine U., 1976. Bar: Calif. 1976. Sole practice Running Springs, Calif., 1976—; corp. counsel Dedo Moldings Inc., San Bernardino, 1976-82. Served with USN, 1966-70. Mem. ABA. Republican. Lodge: Lions. Real property, Bankruptcy.

ROBERTS, PATRICIA SUSAN, lawyer; b. Hammond, Ind., Sept. 1, 1953; d. Wayne Thomas and Lois (Schurgers) R.; m. James Stanley Kowalik, July 27, 1985. BA, Ind. U., 1975, JD, 1978. Bar: Ind. 1978, U.S. Dist. Ct. (so. dist.) Ind. 1978. Rep. State Farm Ins. Co., Indpls., 1978-79; atty. United Farm Bur. Mut. Ins. Co., Indpls., 1979-85, corp. counsel, 1985—. Insurance, General corporate, Pension, profit-sharing, and employee benefits. Home: 1523 E Lawrence Ave Indianapolis IN 46227 Office: United Farm Bur Mut Ins Co 130 E Washington St Indianapolis IN 46204

ROBERTS, PATRICK KENT, lawyer; b. Waynesville, Mo., Feb. 9, 1948; s. J. Kent and Winona (Clark) R.; m. Jeanne Billings, April 17, 1976; children: Christopher, Kimberly, Courtney. Student, U. Ill., Urbana, 1970; AB, U. Mo., 1970, JD, 1973. Bar: Mo. 1974, U.S. Dist. Ct. (we. dist.) Mo. 1974, U.S. Ct. Appeals (8th cir.) 1979. Ptnr. Daniel, Clampett, Lilley, Dalton, Powell & Cunningham, Springfield, Mo., 1976—. Mem. com. Greene County Dems., Springfield, 1982-84. Mem. ABA, Mo. Orgn. Def. Lawyers, Springfield Claims Assn. Democrat. Methodist. Lodge: Rotary. Federal civil litigation, State civil litigation, Insurance. Home: 3561 Eastwood Blvd Springfield MO 65804 Office: Daniel Clampett Lilley et al 3171 E Sunshine PO Box 10306 Springfield MO 65808

ROBERTS, RICHARD JACK, law educator, labor arbitrator, consultant; b. London, Ont., Can., July 5, 1942; s. Arthur George and Alice Isobel (Mitchell) R.; m. Rochelle Elanor Roy, Sept. 4, 1965; children—Jeannine, Maria-Lise. B.Sc., U. Western Ont., 1965; J.D., Georgetown U., 1970. Bar: D.C. 1971, U.S. Ct. Appeals (D.C. cir.) 1972, Law Soc. Upper Can. 1975. Law clerk to presiding judge U.S. Ct. Appeals, D.C., 1970-71; assoc. Steptoe & Johnson, D.C., 1971-73; from asst. prof. to assoc. prof. law U. Western Ont., London, 1973-80, prof., 1981—; counsel, Peter Steinmetz & Assoc., Toronto, 1986—; vis. prof. law U. San Diego, 1980-81; dir. Can.-U.S. Law Inst., London, Ont. and Cleve., 1975-80, 86-87; cons. Bur. Competition Policy, Govt. Can., 1975—, Bur. Indsl. Property, Govt. Can., 1976-79; counsel Royal Commn. Pharms., Toronto and Ottawa, Can., 1984-85. Contbr. articles to profl. jours. Editor Intellectual Property Jour., 1983—. Active Republican Party Va., 1971-73, Liberal Party, London, 1981—. Grantee Law Found. Ont., 1975—, Ivey Found., 1976, Govt. U.S. Bicentennial, 1976. Mem. Am. Arbitration Assn., Ont. Arbitration Assn., Ont. Grievance Settlement Bd. (vice chmn. 1979—). Presbyterian. Antitrust, Entertainment, Labor. Home: 1058 The Parkway, London, ON Canada Office: U Western Ont, Faculty Law, London, ON Canada

ROBERTS, ROSS T., federal judge; b. 1938. B.A., DePauw U., 1960; J.D., U. Mo., 1963. Ptnr. Roberts & Fleischaker, Joplin, Mo., 1963; ptnr. Shook, Hardy, Ottman, Mitchell & Bacon, Kansas City, Mo., 1968-70, Roberts & Fleischaker, Joplin, 1970-82; pros. atty. Jasper County, Joplin, 1971-77; judge U.S. Dist. Ct. (we. dist.) Mo., Kansas City, 1982—. Judicial administration. Office: U S Dist Ct US Courthouse 811 Grand Ave Room 716 Kansas City MO 64106 *

ROBERTS, RUSSELL HILL, lawyer; b. Frankfort, Ky., Dec. 7, 1937; s. Clark Blackwell and Mary Alice (May) R.; m. Martha Franklin Young, June 11, 1960; children: Victoria Hill, Mary Ashton. BA, U. Va., 1960, LLB, 1963. Bar: Va. 1963. Ptnr. Ashby & Roberts, Fredericksburg, Va., 1963-72, Roberts & Crosley, Fredericksburg, 1972-80, Roberts & Ashby, Fredericksburg, 1980—; bd. dirs. 1st Va. Bank, Falls Ch. Chmn. Rappahannock Juvenile Detention Com., Fredericksburg, 1972-79. Mem. ABA, Va. State Bar (council 1971-80), Am. Coll. Trial Lawyers, Def. Research Inst., Va. Assn. Def. Attys. (pres. 1979-80), Assn. Ins. Attys., Fredericksburg Area C. of C. (bd. dirs. 1984—). Club: Fredericksburg Country (bd. dirs. 1968-71). Avocations: hunting, fishing, tennis, travel. State civil litigation, Probate,

Federal civil litigation. Home: 1218 Sophia St Fredericksburg VA 22401 Office: Roberts & Ashby 1014 Prince Edward St Fredericksburg VA 22404

ROBERTS, SIDNEY I., lawyer; b. Bklyn., Nov. 29, 1913; s. David I. and Ray (Bleicher) Robinovitz; m. Arlene Lee Aron, June 4, 1961; 1 son, Russell Lewis. B.B.A., CCNY, 1935; LL.B. magna cum laude, Harvard U., 1938. Bar: N.Y. 1938; C.P.A., N.Y. With Michael Schimmel & Co. (C.P.A.s), N.Y.C., 1938-39, S.D. Leidesdorf & Co. (C.P.A.s), N.Y.C., 1939-49; with firm Roosevelt, Freidin & Littauer, N.Y.C., 1950-56, Anderson & Roberts, N.Y.C., 1956-57, Roberts & Holland, N.Y.C., 1957—; adj. prof. law Columbia U., 1971-78; mem. adv. council Internat. Bur. Fiscal Documentation. Author: (with William C. Warren) United States Tax Income Taxation of Foreign Corporations and Nonresident Aliens, 1966, (with others) Annotated Tax Forms: Practice and Procedure, 1970; contbr. articles to profl. jours. Mem. Internat. Bar Assn., ABA (sect. on taxation, council dir. 1970-73, chmn. com. on cooperation with state and local bar assns. 1968-70, chmn. com. on taxation of fgn. income 1963-64), N.Y. State Bar Assn. (tax sect. exec. com. 1967-87, chmn. com. on tax sect. planning 1968-70, chmn. com. on tax policy 1970-72), Assn. of Bar of City of N.Y., N.Y. State Soc. CPA's, Internat. Fiscal Assn. (mem. exec. com. 1972-77, pres. U.S.A. br. 1972-73). Jewish. Corporate taxation, Personal income taxation. Office: Roberts & Holland 30 Rockefeller Plaza New York NY 10112

ROBERTS, TED BLAKE, lawyer, state representative; b. Des Moines, May 17, 1952; s. Howard Leslie and Beverly (Routt) R.; m. Suzanne Garrett, May 22, 1976; 1 child, Elizabeth Catherine. BBA with highest distinction, U. Iowa, 1974; JD with honors, U. Tex., 1977. Bar: Tex. 1977, D.C. Bar Assn., 1978, U.S. Ct. Appeals (5th cir.) 1981. Briefing atty. Tex. Ct. Appeals (13th cir.), Corpus Christi, 1977-79; mng. atty. Meredith, Donnell & Abernethy, Corpus Christi, 1979—; rep. 36th dist. Tex. Legislature, Corpus Christi and Rockport, 1985—. Legal counsel Nueces County Reps., Tex., 1983, Pastoral Counseling Ctr., Corpus Christi, 1983; bd. dirs., parliamentarian Money Mgmt. Counseling & Services, Corpus Christi, 1980-84. Murray scholar U. Iowa, 1973. Mem. ABA, Tex. Bar Assn., D.C. Bar Assn., Nueces County Bar Assn. (bd. dirs. 1980-82), Christian Businessmen's Com. (co-founder 1978). Presbyterian. Club: Toastmasters (pres. Corpus Christi 1980-81). Avocation: fishing. State civil litigation, Insurance, Legislative. Home: 433 Parade Corpus Christi TX 78412 Office: Meredith Donnell & Abernethy 1515 1st City Bank Tower Corpus Christi TX 78477

ROBERTS, THOMAS ALBA, lawyer; b. Ft. Wayne, Ind., Sept. 7, 1946; s. Jack and Elizabeth (Wallace) R.; m. Mary Alice Buckley, Aug. 11, 1973; children: Kaitrin M., John A., Kara B. BA, Georgetown U., 1969, JD, 1972. Bar: N.Y. 1973, U.S. Dist. Ct. (so. dist.) N.Y. 1973, U.S. Ct. Appeals (2d cir.) 1973, Tex. 1976, U.S. Supreme Ct. 1977, U.S. Dist. Ct. (so. dist.) Tex. 1978, U.S. Ct. Appeals (5th and 11th cirs.) 1982. Assoc. Winthrop, Stimson, Putnam & Roberts, N.Y.C., 1972-75; ptnr. Moore & Peterson, Dallas, 1975-80; mng. ptnr. Moore and Peterson, Dallas, 1980—; adj. prof. law So. Meth. U., Dallas, 1977-78. Mem. fin. com. St. Rita Ch., Dallas, 1983—. Mem. ABA, Tex. Bar Assn., Dallas Bar Assn., Bar Assn. of City of N.Y., Dallas C. of C. Roman Catholic. Avocations: horse breeding, skiing, fishing, golf. General corporate, Securities, Mergers and acquisitions. Home: 7523 Overdale Dr Dallas TX 75240 Office: Moore & Peterson 2800 First City Ctr Dallas TX 75201

ROBERTS, VIRGIL PATRICK, lawyer, business executive; b. Ventura, Calif., Jan. 4, 1947; s. Julius and Emma D. (Haley) R.; m. Eleanor Green, Aug. 28, 1973; m. 2d, Brenda Cecilia Banks, Nov. 10, 1979; children—Gisele Simone, Hayley Tasha. A.A., Ventura Coll., 1966; B.A., UCLA, 1968; J.D., Harvard U., 1972. Bar: Calif. 1972. Assoc. Pacht, Ross, Warne Bernhardt & Sears, Los Angeles, 1972-76; ptnr. Manning, Reynolds & Roberts, Los Angeles, 1976-79, Manning & Roberts, 1980-81; exec. v.p., gen. counsel Solar Records, Los Angeles, 1981—; pres. Dick Griffey Prodns., Los Angeles, 1982—; judge pro tem Los Angeles, Beverly Hills Mcpl. Cts., 1975—; past bd. dirs. Los Angeles Black Leadership Coalition, Beverly Hills Bar Assn., Los Angeles Legal Aid Found., others. Bd. dirs. Coro Found., 1984—; commr. Calif. Commn. for Tchr. Credentialing, 1980-83; v.p. Los Angeles Ednl. Partnership, 1983—. Mem. Black Entertainment and Sports Lawyers (treas., bd. dirs. 1982—). Lead atty. for NAACP in Crawford vs. Bd. Edn. desegregation case, Los Angeles, 1979-80. Entertainment. Address: 4151 Charlene Dr Los Angeles CA 90043

ROBERTS, WILLIAM B., lawyer; b. Detroit, Aug. 23, 1939; s. Edwin Stuart and Marjorie Jean (Wardle) R.; m. Cathleen Anne Thompson, Sept. 1, 1962; children: Bradford William, Brent William, Katrina Marjorie. B.A., Mich. State U., 1961; J.D. with distinction, U. Mich., 1963. Bar: Mo. 1964, Fla. 1983. Mem. firm Thompson & Mitchell, St. Louis, 1963-67; atty. Monsanto Co., 1967-70; exec. v.p., sec., gen. counsel Chromalloy Am. Corp., Clayton, Mo., 1970-78; exec. v.p.-adminstrn., gen. counsel, sec. Chromalloy Am. Corp., 1978-82; sole practice law 1983—; owner SpiralCool Co., Bellevue, Ohio; mem. exam. com. of policyowners Northwestern Mut. Life Ins. Co., Milw., 1978; del. to U.S./China Joint Session on Trade, Investment and Econ. Law, Beijing, Peoples Republic of China, 1987. Bd. dirs., assoc. mem. Internat. Comparative Law Ctr., Southwestern Legal Found. Mem. ABA, Mo. Bar Assn., St. Louis Bar Assn. (chmn. antitrust sect. 1973), Fla. Bar Assn., Collier County Bar Assn., Delta Theta Phi. Methodist. Club: Forest Hills Country (St. Louis). Home: 27 Chesterfield Lakes Rd Chesterfield MO 63017 also: 2294 Royal Ln Naples FL 33962 Office: 150 Long Rd Suite 200 Chesterfield MO 63107

ROBERTSHAW, JAMES, lawyer, pilot; b. Greenville, Miss., May 19, 1916; s. Frank Newell and Hannah Mary (Aldridge) R.; m. Sylvia Schively, Apr. 26, 1956; children: Mary Nicholson, Sylvia Yale, Frank Paxton. SB, Miss. State U., 1937; JD, Harvard U., 1940, Vet.'s Cert., Harvard Bus. Sch., 1946; postgrad. Command and Gen. Staff Sch., 1943. Bar: Miss. 1940, U.S. Dist. Ct. (no. dist.) Miss. 1951, U.S. Ct. Appeals (5th cir.) 1954, U.S. Supreme Ct. 1967, U.S. Dist. Ct. (so. dist.) Miss. 1984. Sole practice, Greenville, Miss., 1940, 46-62; ptnr. Robertshaw & Merideth, 1962-84; ptnr. Robertshaw, Terney & Noble, Greenville, 1984—. Chmn. Community and County Devel. Com., Miss. Econ. Council, 1968-70; mem. Miss. Ho. of Reps., 1953-56; chmn. Greenville Airport Commn., 1967-73, Indsl. Found., 1974; mem. Miss. Supreme Ct. com. Technology in the Courts, 1987—. Served to col. U.S. Army, 1941-46. Decorated Legion of Merit, Croix de Guerre (France). Mem. Am. Judicature Soc., Miss. Bar Found. Episcopalian. Clubs: Univ. (Washington), Greenville Golf and Country. State civil litigation, Condemnation, State and local taxation. Home: PO Box 99 Greenville MS 38702 Office: Robertshaw Terney & Noble 128 South Poplar St Greenville MS 38702

ROBERTSON, ALICE OTA, patent attorney; b. San Francisco; d. Uhei and Aye (Morihara) Ota; m. Dale N. Robertson; 1 child, Scott Clark. BS, U. Tex., 1944; MS, U. Minn., 1946; PhD, U. Wis., 1953; JD, U. Colo., 1967. Bar: Colo. 1968, U.S. Dist. Ct. Colo. 1968. Patent atty. Dow Chem. Co., Midland, Mich., 1956-60; pvt. practice patent agt. and cons. Boulder, Colo., 1960-68; sole practice patent atty., cons. Boulder, 1968-72; patent atty., cons. Johnson & Johnson, New Brunswick, N.J., 1973-83; patent atty. Merck & Co. Inc., Rahway, N.J., 1983-86, sr. patent assoc., 1986—; lectr. Regis Coll., Denver, 1970-71. Inventor chem. compound, 1957. Alt. del. Rep. State Conv., Mich., 1959. Mem. Am. Chem. Soc. (sec. Colo. chpt. 1963-65, chmn. 1967, Colo. councilor 1969-71; mem. patent com. 1970-85, 86—), N.J. Patent Law Assn., Sigma Xi, Iota Sigma Pi. Avocations: skiing, golf. Home: 5 Tempe Ct Scotch Plains NJ 07076 Office: Merck & Co Inc 127 E Lincoln Ave Rahway NJ 07065-0907

ROBERTSON, DAVID GOVAN, lawyer; b. Chgo., May 3, 1947. AB, Stanford U., 1969; JD, Yale U., 1973. Bar: Calif., U.S. Dist. Ct. (no., cen., ea. and we. dists.) Calif. Law clk. to presiding judge U.S. Dist. Ct.; assoc. Morrison & Foerster, San Francisco, 1974-79, ptnr., 1979—. Danforth Found. Grad. fellow Yale, 1970-72. Mem. Phi Beta Kappa. Securities, Federal civil litigation, Private international. Office: Morrison & Foerster 345 California St San Francisco CA 94104

ROBERTSON, DAVID HASWELL, JR., lawyer; b. Evanston, Ill., Sept. 30, 1952; s. David Haswell and Barbara Ann (Hinners) R. A.B., Dartmouth Coll., 1971; J.D., Ill. Inst. Tech./Chgo.-Kent Coll., 1981. Bar: Ill. 1981, U.S. Dist. Ct. (no. dist.) Ill. 1981. Assoc. Leavitt & Schneider, Chgo., 1981-82; A.P. Herman & Assocs., Chgo., 1983—. Mem. Chgo. Bar Assn., Ill. State Bar Assn., ABA, Assn. Trial Lawyers Am. Congregationalist. Clubs: University, Lincoln Park Lacrosse (pres. 1982—). Personal injury, Family and matrimonial, Real property. Office: AP Herman & Assocs 134 N LaSalle #416 Chicago IL 60602

ROBERTSON, DOUGLAS STUART, lawyer; b. Portland, Oreg., Jan. 9, 1947; s. Stuart Neil and Mary Katherine (Gates) R.; m. Nan Reinhorn, Dec. 27, 1970; 1 child, Lauren Amanda. B.S., Oreg. State U., 1969, M.A. in Bus. Adminstrn., 1970; J.D. U. Denver, 1973. Bar: Oreg. 1973, U.S. Dist. Ct. Oreg. 1974, U.S. Ct. Appeal (9th cir.) 1977, U.S. Supreme Ct. 1977. Staff atty. Multnomah County Bar Assn. Legal Aid, Portland, 1973-75; ptnr. Bouneff, Chally & Marshall, Portland, 1975-80; asst. gen. counsel Orbanco Fin. Services, Portland, 1980-83; gen. counsel Hyster Credit Corp., Portland, 1983-86; v.p., gen. counsel PacifiCorp Credit Inc., 1986—; chmn. bd., chief exec. officer Deschutes River Preserve, Inc., Portland, 1982—. Mem. editorial bd. Denver Jour. of Internat. Law and Policy, 1971. Served with U.S. Army 1968-70. Mem. ABA, Comml. Law League, Multnomah County Bar Assn., Republican. Club: Flyfisher's of Oreg., Oreg. Trout. Contracts commercial, General corporate. Home: 2972 Vale Ct Lake Oswego OR 97034 Office: Pacific Credit Inc PO Box 1531 Portland OR 97207

ROBERTSON, EDWIN DAVID, lawyer; b. Roanoke, Va., July 5, 1946; s. Edwin Traylor and Norma Burns (Bowles) R.; m. Anne Littelle Ferratt, Sept. 7, 1968. BA with honors, U. Va., 1968, LLB, 1971. Bar: N.Y. 1972, U.S. Ct. Appeals (2d cir.) 1972, U.S. Dist. Ct. (ea. and so. dists.) N.Y. 1973, U.S. Supreme Ct. 1975, U.S. Dist. Ct. (ea. dist.) Mich. 1986. Assoc. Cadwalader, Wickershaft & Taft, N.Y.C., 1972-80, ptnr., 1980—. Bd. dirs. Early Music Found. N.Y., N.Y.C., 1983—. Served to 1st lt. USAF, 1972. Mem. ABA, Fed. Bar Council, N.Y. County Lawyers Assn. (chmn. bankruptcy com. 1983-87, bd. dirs. 1985—), Jefferson Soc., Order of Coif, Phi Beta Kappa, Phi Kappa Psi. Republican. Episcopalian. Club: Down Town (N.Y.C.). Federal civil litigation, Computer, Libel. Home: 311 E 71st St New York NY 10021 Office: Cadwalader Wickersham & Taft 100 Maiden Ln New York NY 10038

ROBERTSON, HORACE BASCOMB, JR., educator; b. Charlotte, N.C., Nov. 13, 1923; s. Horace Bascomb and Ruth (Montgomery) R.; m. Patricia Lavell, Aug. 11, 1947; children—Mark L., James D. B.S., U.S. Naval Acad., 1945; J.D., Georgetown U., 1953; M.S., George Washington U., 1968. Commd. ensign U.S. Navy, 1945, advanced through grades to rear adm., 1972; line officer 1945-55, law specialist, 1955-68; spl. counsel to sec. Navy, Washington, 1964-67; judge adv. Navy, 1968-76; spl. counsel to chief naval ops. Washington, 1970-72; dep. judge adv. gen. Navy Dept., Washington, 1972-75; judge adv. gen. Navy Dept., 1975-76; prof. law Duke, 1976—. Decorated D.S.M. Mem. Am. Bar Assn., Fed. Bar Assn. (nat. council), Am. Soc. Internat. Law. Methodist. Public international, Legal education, Personal injury. Home: 5 Stoneridge Circle Durham NC 27705 Office: Duke U Sch Law Durham NC 27706

ROBERTSON, JAMES ALLEN, risk mgmt. consultant, writer, lecturer; b. Burlington, Iowa, Jan. 24, 1948; s. George Allen and Betty Irene (Beck) R.; student Knox Coll., 1965-66; B.A., U. Iowa, 1969; postgrad. San Francisco Theol. Sem./Grad. Theol. Union, 1969-70; M.S.A., Pepperdine U., 1976; m. Stephanie Peacock. Casualty underwriter Hartford Ins. Group, San Francisco, 1970-72, supervising underwriter, 1972-73, Los Angeles, 1973-74; asst. v.p. Tausch Ins. Brokers, Santa Ana, Calif., 1974-75; cons. Warren, McVeigh, Griffin & Huntington, 1975-76; sr. v.p. Reed Risk Mgmt., San Francisco, 1976-78; pres. James A. Robertson & Assoc., Inc., 1978-87; prin. cons., Warren, McVeigh & Griffin, Newport Beach, Calif., 1979-83; pres. Ins. Litigation Cons., 1984-87; sr. cons., nat. dir. profl. ins. publs. Coopers & Lybrand, Newport Beach, 1987—; assoc. in risk mgmt. C.P.C.U. Mem. Soc. Chartered Property Casualty Underwriters (pres. Orange Empire chpt. 1985-86, nat. publs. com. 1984-87), Soc. Risk Mgmt. Cons. (chmn. profl. practices com. 1986-87), Omicron Delta Kappa. Republican. Author: The Umbrella Book, 1976, 2d edit., 1979-83; Key Financial Ratios, 1978; ISO Commercial Liability Forms, 1984, 4th edit., 1986; It's Time to Take the Mystery Out of Umbrellas, 1984; editor Risk Mgmt. Letter, 1981-83. Insurance, Personal injury, Workers' compensation. Office: Coopers & Lybrand One Newport Place 1301 Dove St Newport Beach CA 92660

ROBERTSON, JAMES L., Mississippi supreme court justice; b. Greenwood, Miss., July 30, 1940; s. Lawrence Devall R. and Susie Lawton R.; m. Lilliam Janette Humber, Aug. 30, 1963; children—Kenneth Carter, John Lamar, Christopher Lawton. B.A., U. Miss., 1962; J.D., Harvard U., 1965. Atty. Greenville, Miss., 1965-79; atty. Oxford, Miss., 1979-83; justice Miss. Supreme Ct., Jackson, 1983—; instr. U. Miss. Law Sch., 1977—. Mem. Am. Judicature Soc., ABA. Judicial administration. Office: Office of Supreme Ct Jackson MS 39205

ROBERTSON, JOSEPH DAVID, lawyer; b. Pitts., Dec. 24, 1944; s. Sinon Joseph and Marie Catherine (Nold) R.; m. Susan Louise Lyon, Apr. 10, 1968; children—Brian, Mark. Student Coll. Steubenville, 1962, U. Md., 1968-69; B.A., Willamette U., 1971, J.D. cum laude, 1974. Bar: Oreg. 1974, U.S. Dist. Ct. Oreg. 1974, U.S. Ct. Appeals (9th cir.) 1976. Shareholder Garrett, Seideman, Hemann, Robertson & De Muniz, P.C., Salem, Oreg., 1974—; mem. Oreg. State Bd. Bar Examiners, Portland, 1983-86; adj. prof. law for trial practice Willamette U. Coll. Law, 1976-78. Contbr. articles to profl. publs. Mem., chmn. Faye Wright local Adv. Com., Salem, 1978-83; mem. Judson local sch. adv. com., Salem, 1984-85; cubmaster Willamette Council Boy Scouts Am., 1979—, mem. troop com., 1983—; mem. workers' compensation com. Associated Oreg. Industries, Salem, 1982—; coach Salem Parks & Recreation soccer program, 1979-85; coach Judson Little League, Salem, 1981; mem. disciplinary rev. com. Faye Wright Sch., Salem, 1982. Served with USMC, 1963-67. Recipient Advocacy award Internat. Acad. Trial Lawyers, 1974. Mem. ABA, Workers' Compensation Def. Lawyers Assn., Am. Soc. Law and Medicine, Marion County Bar Assn., Oreg. State Bar (mem. exec. com. litigation sect. 1983-84), Oreg. Trial Lawyers Assn. (bd. govs. 1976-78), Oreg. Assn. Def. Counsel. Republican. Club: Salem Tennis and Swim. Workers' compensation, State civil litigation, Insurance. Office: 1011 Commercial St NE Box 749 Salem OR 97308

ROBERTSON, JOSEPH MARTIN, lawyer; b. Danville, Ill., Apr. 30, 1952; s. Calloway Middleton and Barbara (Holland) R. AB in Polit. Sci., Miami U., Oxford, Ohio, 1974; JD, U. Cin., 1978; postgrad., Ohio State U., 1978-79, U. Md., 1984. Bar: Ohio 1978, U.S. Dist. Ct. (so. dist.) Ohio 1980, U.S. Dist. Ct. (no. dist.) Calif. 1984. Atty. Southeastern Ohio Legal Services, Chillicothe and Steubenville, 1979-80, Dept. of the Army, C.E. Office of Counsel, Huntington, W.Va. and Jacksonville, Fla., 1980-83; asst. atty. gen. State of Ohio, Columbus, 1983-84; trial atty. Dept. of Navy Office of Gen. Counsel, Washington, 1984—. Recipient Spl. Service award Dept. of the Army, 1983. Mem. ABA (natural resources law sect.). Environment, Administrative and regulatory, Federal civil litigation. Office: Dept of Navy Office of Gen Counsel Litigation Office Washington DC 20360

ROBERTSON, MARK ALEXANDER, lawyer; b. Vallejo, Calif., Jan. 22, 1950; s. Philip Owen Robertson and Susan (Taylor) Briscoe; m. Susan Jennings, Apr. 22, 1978. BA with honors, DePauw U., 1972; JD, U. Okla., 1975. Bar: Okla. 1975, U.S. Dist. Ct. (we. dist.) Okla. 1975, U.S. Ct. Appeals (10th cirs.) 1975, U.S. Ct. Appeals (8th cir.) 1976. Assoc. Linn, Helms, Kirk & Brikett, Oklahoma City, 1975-77, Kornfeld, McMillin, Phillips & Upp, Oklahoma City, 1978-81; ptnr. Kornfeld, Franklin & Phillips, Oklahoma City, 1981—, pres., 1984—. Mem. Okla. Symphony Orchestra Assoc. Bd., Oklahoma City, 1981—. Mem. ABA (vice chmn. marketing of legal services com., econs. of law sect. 1984—), Young Pres. Orgn. (western Okla. chpt., membership chmn. 1986—). Democrat. Episcopalian. Avocations: skiing, golf. Securities, General corporate. Office: Kornfeld Franklin & Phillips 301 NW 63d St Suite 600 Oklahoma City OK 73116

ROBERTSON, RONALD E., lawyer; b. Long Beach, Calif., Nov. 8, 1935; married; two children. B.S., Calif. State U.-Los Angeles, 1961; J.D., UCLA, 1964. Vice pres., gen. counsel Amcord, Inc., 1971-75; prof. law Mississippi Coll., 1975-78, Pepperdine U., 1978-81; ptnr. Musick, Peeler & Garret, 1981-84; chief counsel Reagan-Bush '84 Com., 1984; gen. counsel HHS, Washington, 1985—. Office: HHS Room 722A 200 Independence Ave SW Washington DC 20201 *

ROBERTSON, TED ZANDERSON, judge; b. San Antonio, Sept. 28, 1921; s. Irion Randolf and Aurelia (Zanderson) R.; m. Avis Cole, Dec. 29, 1955. Student, Tex. A&I, 1940-42; LL.B., St. Mary's U., San Antonio, 1949. Bar: Tex. 1949. Chief civil dept. Dist. Atty.'s Office, Dallas County, Tex., 1960-65; judge Probate Ct. 2, Dallas County, 1965-69, Juvenile Ct. 2, Dallas County, 1969-75, 95th Dist. Ct., Dallas County, 1975-76, Ct. Civil Appeals, 5th Supreme Jud. Dist., Dallas, 1976-82, Supreme Ct. Tex., Austin, 1982—; guest lectr. So. Meth. U., Dallas, Dallas County Juvenile Bd., Tex. Coll. of the Judiciary, 1970-82. Active Dallas Assn. for Retarded Children; active Dallas County Commn. on Alcoholism, Dallas County Mental Health Assn. Served as yeoman USCG, 1942-46. Recipient Golden Gavel St. Mary's U., San Antonio, 1979; named Outstanding Alumnus St. Mary's U., 1981. Mem. Am. Judicature Soc., Tex. Bar Assn., Dallas Bar Assn., Dallas County Juvenile Bd. Democrat. Methodist. Lodges: Masons; Lions. Home: 6233 Highgate Ln Dallas TX 75214 Office: Supreme Ct Tex Capitol Sta PO Box 12248 Austin TX 78711 *

ROBERTSON, WILLIAM SHORE, judge; b. Richmond, Va., June 20, 1939; s. Alexander Cralle and Eugenia (Bailey) R.; m. Barbara Brewster Williams, June 26, 1966; 1 son, Stuart Alexander. A.B., Coll. William and Mary, 1961; J.D., U. Va., 1964. Bar: Va. 1964. Assoc., Martin & Alexander, Warrenton, Va., 1966-67; ptnr. Martin, Alexander & Robertson, Warrenton, 1967-78; asst. commonwealth's atty. Fauquier County, Warrenton, Va., 1968-74; mem. Martin, Walker & Lawrence P.C., Warrenton, 1978-80; circuit judge 20th Jud. Circuit Va., Warrenton, 1980—; mem. Jud. Conf. Va., 1980—; mem. Jud. Inquiry and Rev. Commn. of Va., 1985—. Sec. Warrenton Bd. Zoning Appeals, 1967-70, town council and vice mayor, 1973-80; pres. Fauquier chpt. Va. Mus. 1968-69; Faruquier County chmn. Nat. Capital Area Fund Drive, Boy Scouts Am., 1968-69, 1975; chmn. Fauquier County Schs. Study and Adv. Com, 1970; bd. dirs. Fauquier County Mental Health Assn., 1970-74; chmn. Warrenton United Meth. Ch., 1970-72, lay leader, 1973-75, 1982-83; bd. dirs. Fauquier Hosp. Maternity Clinic, 1971-74; v.p. Highland Sch. Bd., 1975-76, chmn., 1978; mem. Fauquier County Library Bd., 1974-77, Welfare Bd., 1975-80; mem. adv. bd. Family Guidance Ctr., 1974-76. Served to capt. U.S. Army, 1964-66. Mem. ABA, Va. State Bar (council 1969-73, bd. govs. criminal law sect. 1982-86), Va. Bar Assn., Warrenton-Fauquier C. of C. (v.p. 1978-79), Fauquier County Bar Assn. (pres. 1976-77), Jaycees (external v.p. 1968-69; Outstanding Young Man of Yr. local chpt. 1969), Phi Alpha Delta, Omicron Delta Kappa, Lambda Chi Alpha. Clubs: Rotary (hon. Warrenton-Fauquier), Fauquier, Chestnut Forks Tennis, Vint Hill Officer's (hon.). Lodge: Optimists. Judicial administration. Address: PO Box 985 Warrenton VA 22186

ROBERTSON, WILLIAM WITHERS, lawyer; b. Morristown, N.J., Nov. 3, 1941; s. Thomas Withers and Jessie (Swain) R.; m. Barbara C. Zimmerman, Aug. 14, 1965; children: Barbara Ellen, William Withers, Jessie Swain. B.A., Rutgers U., 1964, LL.B., 1967. Bar: N.J. bar. Law sec. to judge Superior Ct. N.J., 1967-68; asst. U.S. atty. 1972-76, 1st asst. U.S. atty., 1978-80; U.S. atty. Dist. N.J., 1980-81; chief Newark Organized Crime Strike Force, 1976-78; ptnr. firm Hannoch & Weisman, Roseland, N.J., 1981—. Mng. editor Rutgers Law Rev., 1966-67. Trustee Rutgers U., 1984—. Served to capt. JAGC USAR, 1968-72. Mem. Rutgers U. Law Sch. Alumni Assn. (officer, council 1986—), Rutgers U. Alumni Fedn. (pres. 1981-83). Criminal, Federal civil litigation, State civil litigation. Office: Hannoch and Weisman 4 Becker Farm Rd Roseland NJ 07068

ROBICHAUX, JAMES HALL, lawyer; b. Houston, June 20, 1955; s. Thomas Joseph and Jane (Hall) R.; m. Kathi Anne FitzSimmons, Feb. 26, 1983; children: Kandice Anne, Lindsey Hall. BBA, U. Tex., 1977, JD, 1979. Bar: U.S. Dist. Ct. (so. dist.) Tex. 1980, U.S. Ct. Appeals (5th cir.) 1980, U.S. Dist. Ct. (ea. dist.) Tex. 1984. Assoc. Meredith & Donnell, Corpus Christi, Tex., 1980-82, Harris, Cook & Browning, Corpus Christi, 1982-85; mem. Harris, Cook, Browning, Jordan & Hyden, Corpus Christi, 1986—. Mem. State Bar Tex., Nueces County Bar Assn. Episcopalian. Avocations: scuba, tennis, swimming, jogging. Federal civil litigation, State civil litigation, Contracts commercial. Home: 6625 Whitewing Corpus Christi TX 78413 Office: Harris Cook Browning Jordan & Hyden 1700 First City Bank Tower Corpus Christi TX 78401

ROBIE, WILLIAM RANDOLPH, lawyer, govt. ofcl.; b. Balt., Sept. 15, 1944; s. Fred Smith and Mary Louise (Kent) R. B.A., Northwestern U., 1966, J.D., 1969. Bar: Ill. 1969, D.C. 1975, U.S. Ct. Mil. Appeals 1971, U.S. Supreme Ct. 1973. Assoc. Hubachek, Kelly, Rauch & Kirby, Chgo., 1969-70; commd. officer U.S. Army JAGC, 1970, advanced through grades to capt.; with res., 1974-81; asst. gen. counsel, Office Consumer Affairs, HEW, 1974-75; assoc. dir. legal edn. inst. Civil Service Commn., 1975-78; counsel to assoc. atty. gen. for atty. personnel, 1978-79, dep. assoc. atty. gen., 1979-81, assoc. dep. atty. gen. U.S. Dept. Justice, 1981; dir. Office Atty. Personnel Mgmt., Office Dep. Atty. Gen., U.S. Dept. Justice, Washington, 1981-83; chief immigration judge Exec. Office for Immigration Rev., U.S. Dept. of Justice, Falls Church, Va., 1983—; instr., chmn. adv. bd. Paralegal Studies Project, U. Md., 1976—. Richard Weaver fellow, 1966-67. Mem. ABA (chmn. spl. com. delivery of legal services 1979-82), Fed. Bar Assn. (chmn. council on the fed. lawyer 1978-82, nat. dep. sec. 1984-85, nat. sec. 1985-86, nat. 2d v.p. 1986-87), Judge Advocates Assn. (dir. 1975-82, chmn. field organization com. 1981-85, 2d v.p. 1986-87), Ill. Bar Assn., Chgo. Bar Assn., D.C. Bar. Republican. Presbyterian. Club: Nat. Lawyers Contbr. articles to profl. jours. Administrative and regulatory, Judicial administration, Immigration, naturalization, and customs. Home: 111 Roberts Ct Alexandria VA 22314 Office: US Dept Justice 5201 Leesburg Pike Suite 1501 Falls Church VA 22041

ROBILLARD, WALTER GEORGE, lawyer, surveyor; b. Glens Falls, N.Y., June 9, 1930; s. George Walter and Edith Elba (LaFontaine) R.; m. Sarah Reedy, Dec. 28, 1952; children: Charlotte Nora, Therese Nan. BS in Forestry cum laude, N.Y.S. Coll. Forestry, 1952; MA in Pub. Adminstrn., U. Okla., 1972; JD with honors, Atlanta Law Sch., 1982, LLM, 1983. Bar: Ga. 1982, U.S. Dist. Ct. (no. dist.) Ga. 1982. Instr. Miss. State U., State College, 1952-53; asst. project engr. Michael Baker Jr. Inc., Jackson, Miss., 1953-57; surveyor U.S. Forest Service, Atlanta, 1957—; sole practice Atlanta, 1982—. Co-author: Evidence and Procedures for Boundary Location, 2d ed., 1961, Boundary Control and Legal Principles, 3d ed., 1986, Clark on Surveying and Boundaries, 5th ed., 1987. Recipient Award of Honor, U.S. Dept. Agr., 1986, Cert. of Appreciation, State of Ark., State of Okla. Fellow Am. Congress on Surveying: Mapping (pres. 1983-84, bd. dirs.). Republican. Roman Catholic. Avocation: teaching. Real property, Boundary law-riparian. Home: 1601 Berkeley Ln NE Atlanta GA 30329

ROBINETT, MARK WEBSTER, lawyer; b. Kansas City, Kans., Mar. 24, 1950; s. Marion Webster and Mary Elizabeth (Dixon) R.; m. Carolyn Jane Evans, May 10, 1971; children: Kellis Wayne, Travis Lawrence. BS in Edn., U. Kans., 1972, MA in English, 1977; JD with honors, U. Tex., 1979. Tchr. Kans. City Pub. Schs., 1972-75; assoc. Bawcom & Assocs., Austin, 1980-81; briefing atty. Tex. State Ct. Appeals, Amarillo, 1981-82; dir. hearing and appeals Tex. Edn. Agy., Austin, 1982-86; assoc. Brim & Arnett, Austin, 1986—. Mem. ABA, Tex. Bar Assn., Travis County Bar Assn., Tex. Trial Lawyers Assn. Democrat. Administrative and regulatory, School law. Home: 4002 Beaconsdale Dr Austin TX 78727 Office: Brim & Arnett 1012 Mopac Circle #102 Austin TX 78746

ROBINOWITZ, STUART, lawyer; b. Port Chester, N.Y., Apr. 6, 1929; s. Sam and Rose (Goldstein) R.; m. Anne, July 15, 1952; children: Cathy, Susan, Richard, Robert, Jane. B.A., Williams Coll.; LL.B., Yale U. Bar: N.Y. 1953. Ptnr. Rosenman, Colin, Kaye, Petscheck & Freund, N.Y.C., 1961-70, Paul Weiss, Rifkind, Wharton & Garrison, N.Y.C., 1970—; vis. lectr. Yale U. Law Sch., 1981-83. Mem. Assn. Bar City N.Y. (sec. 1963-64), ABA, N.Y. State Bar Assn., N.Y. County Lawyers Assn., Phi Beta Kappa. Antitrust, Federal civil litigation, Trademark and copyright. Office: Paul Weiss Rifkind Wharton & Garrison 1285 Ave of Americas New York NY 10019

ROBINS, LAWRENCE RICHARD, lawyer; b. Chgo., Mar. 18, 1957; s. Norman Alan and Sandra (Ross) R.; m. Vivian Katsaros, July 14, 1984; 1 child, Gregory Norman. BA in Polit. Sci., Emory U., 1979; JD, Loyola U., Chgo., 1982. Bar: Ill. 1982, U.S. Dist. Ct. (no. dist.) Ill. 1982, U.S. Dist. Ct. (ea. dist.) Mich. 1985, U.S. Ct. Appeals (7th and D.C. cirs.) 1985. Assoc.

Laff, Whitesel, Conte & Saret, Chgo., 1982—. Adminstr. Nat. Novice Hockey Assn., Chgo; bd. dirs. No. Ill. Chpt. Cystic Fibrosis Found. Mem. ABA, Ill. Bar Assn., Chgo. Bar Assn., 7th Cir. Bar Assn., Patent Law Assn. Chgo. Federal civil litigation, Trademark and copyright, State civil litigation. Office: Laff Whitesel Conte & Saret 401 N Michigan Ave Suite 2000 Chicago IL 60611

ROBINSON, ADELBERT CARL, lawyer, justice; b. Shawnee, Okla., Dec. 13, 1926; s. William H. and Mayme (Forston) R.; m. Marilyn Ruth Stubbs, Dec. 28, 1963 (div.); children: William, James, Schuyler, Donald, David, Nancy, Lauri. Student Okla. Baptist U., 1944-47; JD, Okla. U., 1950. Bar: Okla. 1950. Practice, Muskogee, Okla., 1956—; with legal dept. Phillips Petroleum Co., 1950-51; adjuster U.S. Fidelity & Guaranty Co., 1951-54, atty., adjuster-in-charge, 1954-56; ptnr. Fite & Robinson, 1956-62, Fite, Robinson & Summers, 1963-70, Robinson & Summers, 1970-72, Robinson, Summers & Locke, 1972-76, Robinson, Locke & Gage, 1976-80, Robinson, Locke, Gage & Fite, 1980-83, Robinson, Locke, Gage, Fite & Williams, Muskogee, 1983—; police judge, 1963-64; mcpl. judge, 1964-70; prin. justice Temp. Div. 36 Okla. Ct. Appeals, 1981—; pres., dir. Wall St. Bldg Corp., 1969-78, Three Forks Devel. Corp., 1968-77, Rolo Leasing, Inc., 1971—, Suroya II, Inc., 1977—; sec., dir. Weddles Food Stores, Muskogee Tom's Inc., Blue Ridge Corp., Harborcliff Corp.; bd. dirs. First Bancshares of Muskogee, Inc., First of Muskogee Corp., First City Bank, Tulsa; adv. dir. First Nat. Bank & Trust Co. of Muskogee; mng. ptnr. RLG Ritz, 1980—; ptnr. First City Real Estate Partnership, 1985—. Chmn. Muskogee County (Okla.) Law Day, 1963; chmn. Muskogee Area Redevel. Authority, 1963; chmn. Muskogee County chpt. Am. Cancer Soc., 1956; pres. bd. dirs. Muskogee Community Council; bd. dirs. United Way of Muskogee, Inc., 1980—, v.p., 1982, pres. 1983; bd. dirs. Muskogee Community Concert Assn., Muskogee Tourist Info. Bur., 1964-68; bd. dirs., gen. counsel United Cerebral Palsy Eastern Okla., 1964-68; trustee Connors Devel. Found., Connors Coll., 1981—. Served with if. AUS, 1945-46. Mem. ABA, Okla. Bar Assn. (chmn. uniform laws com. 1970-72, chmn. profl. coop. com. 1965-69, past regional chmn. grievance com.), Muskogee County Bar Assn. (pres. 1971, mem. exec. council 1971-74), Okla. Assn. Def. Counsel (dir.), Okla. Assn. Mcpl. Judges (dir.), Muskogee C. of C., Delta Theta Phi. Methodist. Club: Rotary (pres. 1971-72). Banking, Estate planning, Real property. Home: 2800 Robin Ln Muskogee OK 74403 Office: 530 Court St PO Box 87 Muskogee OK 74401

ROBINSON, ARCHIE STIRLING, lawyer; b. Long Beach, Calif., May 28, 1939; s. Wendell Stirling and Bonnie Mae (Noble) R.; m. Susan Kay Hunter, Aug. 19, 1962; children—Jennifer, Christopher, Matthew, Benjamin. A.B., Columbia U., 1960; J.D., Stanford U., 1963. Bar: Calif. 1964, U.S. Dist. Ct. (no. dist.) Calif. 1964, U.S. Ct. Appeals (9th cir.) 1964; cert. specialist in civil litigation Nat. Bd. Trial Advocacy. Mng. ptnr. Robinson & Wood, Inc. and predecessors, San Jose, Calif., 1964—; bd. dirs. Def. Research Inst. Chmn., bd. dirs. City Team Ministries; bd. dirs. Good Samaritan Hosp.; trustee Saratoga Federated Ch. Mem. ABA, Calif. State Bar Assn., Santa Clara County Bar Assn., Assn. Def. Counsel (past pres.), Am. Coll. Trial Lawyers, Calif. Def. Counsel (pres.), Assn. Ins. Attys., Am. Bd. Trial Advs., Internat. Assn. Ins. Counsel, Fedn. Ins. Counsel, San Jose C. of C., Assn. Calif. Tort Reform (bd. dirs.). Republican. Clubs: Stanford Golf (past pres.), Saint Claire (San Jose), San Jose Athletic. Contbr. numerous articles to profl. jours. State civil litigation, Insurance, Personal injury. Office: 227 N 1st St Suite 300 San Jose CA 95113

ROBINSON, AUBREY EUGENE, JR., federal judge; b. Madison, N.J., Mar. 30, 1922; s. Aubrey Eugene and Mabel (Jackson) R.; m. Sara E. Payne, Dec. 31, 1946 (dec.); children: Paula Elaine Robinson Collins, Sheryl Louise; m. Doris A. Washington, Mar. 17, 1973. B.A., Cornell U., 1943, LL.B., 1947. Bar: N.Y. and D.C. 1948. Practice with law firms Washington, 1948-65; assoc. judge Juvenile Ct. D.C., 1965-66; assoc. judge U.S. Dist. Ct. D.C., 1966—, chief judge, 1982—; gen. counsel Am. Council Human Rights, 1953-55, dir., 1955; mem. D.C. Commrs.'s Com. Child Placement Regulations, 1954-62; adj. prof. Am. U., 1975-84. Mem. D.C. Pub. Welfare Adv. Council, 1963-65; mem. Washington Urban League Adoption Project, 1959; mem. membership steering com. Health and Welfare Council D.C., 1961-66, Jud. Council of USA, 1982—; mem. budget steering com. Health and Welfare Council Nat. Capital Area, 1963-66; mem. exec. com. Interreligious Com. Race Relations, 1966-67; exec. com., bd. dirs. D.C. Citizens for Better Pub. Edn., 1964-66; trustee United Planning Orgn. D.C., 1963-66, Washington Center Met. Studies, 1967-74, Cornell U., 1982—; bd. dirs. Family and Child Services Washington, 1954-63, v.p., 1958-61; bd. dirs. Family Service Assn. Am., 1958-68, Washington Action for Youth, 1962-64, Barney Neighborhood Settlement House, 1962-64, Eugene and Agnes E. Meyer Found., 1969-85, Consortium Univs. Washington Met. Area, 1969-74, Fed. Jud. Ctr., 1978-82; mem. adv. council Cornell Law Sch., 1974-80; bd. trustees Cornell U., 1982—. Served with AUS, 1943-46. Mem. ABA (mem. com. cts. and community 1972—, mem. adv. com. judges function 1970-72), Nat. Conf. Fed. Trial Judges (chmn. 1973). Jurisprudence. Office: US Court House 3d and Constitution Ave NW Washington DC 20001

ROBINSON, BARBARA PAUL, lawyer; b. Oct. 19, 1941; d. Leo and Pauline G. Paul; m. Charles Raskob Robinson, June 11, 1965; children—Charles Paul, Torrance Webster. A.B. magna cum laude, Bryn Mawr Coll., 1962; LL.B., Yale U., 1965. Bar: N.Y. State 1966, U.S. Tax Ct. 1972, U.S. Ct. Appeals (2d cir.) 1974, U.S. Dist. Ct. (so. and ea. dists.) N.Y. 1975. Assoc. Debevoise & Plimpton (formerly Debevoise, Plimpton, Lyons & Gates), N.Y.C., 1966-75; ptnr. Debevoise & Plimpton (formerly Debevoise, Plimpton, Lyons & Gates), 1976—; mem. adv. bd., lectr. Practising Law Inst.; arbitrator Am. Arbitration Assn., 1987—. Contbr. articles to profl. jours. Pres. bd. trustees Trinity Sch. Fellow Am. Coll. Probate Counsel, N.Y. Bar Found. (pres.); mem. ABA, N.Y. State Bar Assn. (vice chmn. com. on trust adminstrn., trusts and estates law sect. 1977-81), Assn. Bar City N.Y. (chmn. com. on trusts, estates and surrogates cts. 1981-84, judiciary com. 1981-84, council on jud. adminstrn. 1982-84, nominating com. 1984-85, mem. exec. com. 1986—). Clubs: Yale, Washington. Estate planning, Probate, Estate taxation. Office: Debevoise & Plimpton 875 3d Ave New York NY 10022

ROBINSON, BERNARD LEO, lawyer; b. Kalamazoo, Feb. 13, 1924; s. Louis Harvey and Sue Mary (Starr) R.; B.S., U. Ill., 1947, M.S., 1958, postgrad. in structural dynamics, 1959; J.D., U. N.Mex., 1973; m. Betsy Nadell, May 30, 1947; children—Robert Bruce, Patricia Anne, Jean Carol. Research engr. Assn. Am. Railroads, 1947-49; instr. architecture Rensselaer Poly. Inst., 1949-51; commd. 2d lt. Corps Engrs., U.S. Army, 1945, advanced through grades to lt. col., 1965, ret., 1968; engr. Nuclear Def. Research Corp., Albuquerque, 1968-71; admitted to N.Mex. bar, 1973, U.S. Supreme Ct. bar, 1976; practiced in Albuquerque, 1973-85, Silver City, N.Mex., 1985—; lectr. bus. adminstrn. Western N.Mex. U., Silver City, 1986—. Dist. commr. Boy Scouts Am., 1960-62. Vice chmn. Republican Dist. Com., 1968-70. Decorated Air medal, Combat Infantryman's Badge, Joint Services Commendation medal. Mem. ASCE, Soc. Am. Mil. Engrs., ABA, N.Mex. Bar Assn., Grant County Bar Assn., Ret. Officers Assn., DAV, Assn. U.S. Army. General corporate, Corporate taxation, Consumer commercial. Home: 3306 Royal Dr Silver City NM 88061 Office: PO Box 4070 Silver City NM 88062

ROBINSON, CALVIN STANFORD, lawyer; b. Kalispell, Mont., Mar. 31, 1920; s. Calvin A. and Berta Ella (Green) R.; m. Nancy Hanna, Dec. 13, 1945; children—Terrill S., Calvin D., Robert B., Barbara E. B.A., U. Mont., 1944; postgrad. U. Wash., U. Calif.; J.D., U. Mich., 1949. Bar: Ill. 1949, Mont. 1949. Ptnr. Murphy, Robinson, Heckathorn & Phillips and predecessors, Kalispell, Mont., 1950—; mem. Mont. Gov.'s Com. Bus. Corp. Laws. Mem. Mont. Environ. Quality Council, Gov.'s Revenue Estimating Council; vice chmn. Mont. Bd. Housing; past mem. Mont. Bd. Edn., Mont. U. Bd. Regents. Served to lt. USNR, 1942-46. Fellow Am. Coll. Probate Counsel; mem. Mont. Bar Assn., N.W. Mont. Bar Assn., Ill. Bar Assn., ABA. Democrat. Episcopalian. Banking, General corporate, Probate. Home: 315 Crestview Dr Kalispell MT 59901 Office: One Main Bldg PO Box 759 Kalispell MT 59901

ROBINSON, DAVID HOWARD, lawyer; b. Hampton, Va., Nov. 24, 1948; s. Bernard Harris and Phyllis (Canter) R.; m. Nina Jane Briscoe, Aug. 20, 1979. B.A., Calif. State U., Northridge, 1970; J.D., Cabrillo Pacific U., 1975. Bar admittee: Calif., 1977, U.S. Dist Ct. (so. dist.) Calif., 1977, U.S. Ct. Claims, 1979, U.S. Supreme Ct., 1980. adminstr.Cabrillo Pacific U. Coll. Law, 1977; asso. Gerald D. Egan, San Bernardino, Calif., 1977-78, Duke & Gerstel, San Diego, 1978-80, Rand, Day & Ziman, San Diego, 1980-81; sole practice, San Diego, 1981—. Mem. San Diego County Bar Assn., San Diego Trial Lawyers Assn. State civil litigation, Personal injury, Family and matrimonial.

ROBINSON, DAVID WALLACE, lawyer; b. Lincolnton, N.C., Nov. 22, 1899; s. David W. and Edith (Childs) R.; m. Elizabeth Gibbes, Jan. 21, 1933; children: Caroline Robinson Ellerbe, David W.; m. Susan Gibbes, Sept. 17, 1955; 1 child, Heyward Gibbes. AB, Roanoke Coll., 1919; AM, LLB, U. S.C., 1921, LLD (hon.) 1963; spl. student Harvard Law Sch., 1921-22; LLD (hon.) Presbyn. Coll., 1941. Bar: S.C. 1921, U.S. Ct. Appeals (4th cir.) 1923, U.S. Supreme Ct. 1933. Adj. prof. Law Sch. U. S.C., Columbia, 1926-32; ptnr. Robinson, McFadden, Moore, Pope, Williams, Taylor & Brailsford and predecessors, Columbia, 1922—; legal cons. Pub. Works Adminstrn., 1939; gen. counsel Fed. Power Commn., 1939-40; legal cons. Bur. Econ. Warfare, 1941-42; ptnr. Gibbes Machinery Co. Trustee Presbyn. Coll., 1960-70; elder Eastminster Presbyn. Ch., Columbia; chmn. bequest com. Presbyn. Ch. U.S.; mem. Columbia Art Mus. Commn., 1956-69; bd. dirs. Carolina Children's Home, Community Chest, Columbia YMCA; state chmn. United Fund; mem. S.C. Edn. Fin. Com., 1950-55; chmn. com. to draft and adopt city mgr. govt., Columbia, 1949-50, Mcpl.-County Consolidation, 1962-63, S.C. legis. com. to study election laws, 1952-54; mem. U. S.C. Chair Endowment Found.; vice chmn. Capitol City Found. Served with U.S. Army, 1918, USAAF, 1942-46. Recipient Disting. Alumnus award U. S.C., 1976. Fellow Am. Coll. Trial Lawyers (regent 1969-73); mem. ABA, S.C. Bar Assn. (pres. 1956). Richland County Bar Assn. (pres. 1947), S.C. State Bar (pres. 1968, recipient DuRant award 1980), Am. Law Inst. (life), Am. Bar Found. (life), Jud. Council S.C. Clubs: Palmetto, Summit, Forest Lake. Lodge: Kiwanis. Antitrust, Federal civil litigation, State civil litigation. Office: Robinson McFadden Moore Pope Williams Taylor & Brailsford Columbia SC 29202

ROBINSON, DAVIS ROWLAND, lawyer; b. N.Y.C., July 11, 1940. B.A. magna cum laude, Yale U., 1961; LL.B. cum laude, Harvard U., 1967. Bar: N.Y. 1968, D.C. 1971, U.S. Supreme Ct. 1972. Fgn. service officer Dept. State, Washington, 1961-69; assoc. firm Sullivan & Cromwell, N.Y.C., 1969-71; assoc. and ptnr. firm Leva, Hawes, Symington, Martin and Oppenheimer, Washington, 1971-81; legal adviser Dept. State, Washington, 1981-85; ptnr. Pillsbury, Madison & Sutro, Washington, 1985—. Pres. Harvard Legal Aid Bur., 1966-67. Mem. Assn. Bar City of N.Y., Am. Law Inst., Fed. Bar Assn., ABA, Am. Soc. Internat. Law, Phi Beta Kappa. Private international, Public international, General corporate. Office: Pillsbury Madison & Sutro 1667 K St NW Suite 1100 Washington DC 20006

ROBINSON, EDWARD T., III, lawyer; b. Glen Cove, N.Y., May 23, 1932; s. Edward Jr. and Helen (Rahilly) R.; m. Lynn Simmons; children: Edward IV, Wendy, Christopher, Jeffrey, Lesley, Michael. AB, Holy Cross Coll., 1954; JD, Georgetown U., 1960. Bar: N.Y. 1961, U.S. Dist. Ct. (ea. dist.) N.Y. 1961. Counsel Royal-Globe ins. Co., Mineola, N.Y., 1960-64; sole practice Oyster Bay, 1964-70; ptnr. Robinson & Cincotta, Oyster Bay, 1970-85, Robinson & Lynch, Oyster Bay, 1985—; mem. adv. bd. Chgo. Title Ins. Co., N.Y.C., 1982—; trustee Theodore Roosevelt Assn., 1985—; mem. exec. council N.Y. State Conf. Bar Leaders; counsel Oyster Bay-East Norwich Cen. Sch. Dist., Manhasset Union Free Sch. Dist. Troop chmn. Boy Scouts Am., Oyster Bay; chmn. Forget-Me-Not ball United Cerebral Palsy. Named Man of Yr., 1979, United Cerebral Palsy, Nassau County. Mem. N.Y. State Bar Assn. (nominating com.), Nassau County Bar Assn. (pres. 1986-87), C. of C. (past pres.). Republican. Roman Catholic. Club: Nassau Country. Avocations: golf, tennis, jazz music. Real property, Probate, State civil litigation. Home: 60 Calvin Ave Syosset NY 11791 Office: Robinson & Lynch 34 Audrey Ave Oyster Bay NY 11771

ROBINSON, GREGORY CHARLES, lawyer, manufacturing company executive; b. Chgo., Sept. 26, 1946; s. John Charles and Shirley Jane (Arneson) R.; B.S. in Indsl. Mgmt., Purdue U., 1969; M.B.A., Ind. U., 1972, J.D., 1972; m. Christy True Evans, June 17, 1967; children—Hillary True, Taylor Davis. Admitted to Ind. bar, 1972; comml. banking officer Central Nat. Bank, Cleve., 1972-75; pres., sec., treas. Custom Materials Inc., Chagrin Falls, Ohio, 1975—; pres. CMI Leasing Inc., Chagrin Falls, 1979—; gen. partner CMI Properties Ltd., Chagrin Falls, 1977—; sec., treas. Mfg. Machines Systems Inc., Chagrin Falls, 1980—; pres. Custom-Pac Extrusions Inc, Chagrin Falls, 1984—. Mem. Am. Bar Assn., Assn. Profl. M.B.A.'s, Chagrin Falls Jaycees (pres. 1977-78, dir. 1976-79, Outstanding Jaycee award 1980, Distinguished Service award, 1983), Phi Kappa Psi, Phi Delta Phi. Office: 16865 Park Circle Chagrin Falls OH 44022

ROBINSON, HARLO LYLE, lawyer; b. Shelley, Idaho, Mar. 10, 1925; s. Clarence and Vilate (Hainey) R.; m. Janet Allen Alderson, Dec. 28, 1969; children—Thomas Allen, Harlo Todd. B.S., U. Utah, 1949; J.D., U. Calif.-Berkeley, 1952. Bar: Calif. 1953, Hawaii 1970. Gen. counsel Dillingham Corp., Honolulu, 1968-76; assoc. Ikazaki, Lo, Youth & Nakano, 1976-77; of legal counsel Bob Pomery Cons., Tehran, Iran, 1977-79, Saudi Arabia Parsons, Yanbu, Saudi Arabia, 1979—. Assoc. editor Calif. Law Rev., 1951-52. Adv. bd. Southwestern Legal Found., Dallas, 1971-82. Republican. Mem. Christian Ch. Construction, Private international, Securities. Home: 696 Kalanipuu St Honolulu HI 96825

ROBINSON, HERBERT, lawyer; b. N.Y.C., Feb. 21, 1916; s. Louis Michael and Mary (Goldberg) R.; widowed; children: Walter Bruce, Philippa, Stella. BSS, CCNY, 1937; LLB, Harvard U., 1940. Bar: N.Y. 1941, Mass. 1941, U.S. Supreme Ct. 1958. Assoc. Liebman & Eulau, N.Y.C., 1942-43; ptnr. Liebman, Eulau & Robinson, N.Y.C., 1949-77; pres. Robinson & Perlman, P.C., N.Y.C., 1977—; of counsel Summit Rovins & Feldesman, N.Y.C., 1987—; bd. dirs. UBZ Corp., Fairview, N.J. Life fellow Pierpont Morgan Library, N.Y.C.; chmn. Friends of City Coll. Library; bd. dirs. The Eyebank for Sight Restoration, Inc., N.Y.C., Jewish Bd. Family and Children's Services, Inc., N.Y.C. Served as sgt. U.S. Army, 1943-46, CBI. Mem. ABA, N.Y. State Bar Assn., Assn. of Bar of City of N.Y., Fed. Bar Council, Selden Soc. Democrat. Club: Friars (N.Y.C.). Conflict of interest in business, Fidelity bond litigation. Home: 211 E 70th St New York NY 10021 Office: Robinson & Perlman PC 32 E 57th St New York NY 10022 also: Summit Rovins & Feldesman 445 Park Ave New York NY 10021

ROBINSON, IRWIN JAY, lawyer; b. Bay City, Mich., Oct. 8, 1928; s. Robert R. and Anne (Kaplan) R.; m. Janet Binder, July 7, 1957; children: Elizabeth Binder Robinson Schubiner, Jonathan Meyer, Eve Kimberly. AB, U. Mich., 1950; JD, Columbia U., 1953. Bar: N.Y. 1955. Assoc. Breed Abbott & Morgan, N.Y.C., 1955-58; asst. to ptnrs. Dreyfus & Co., N.Y.C., 1958-59; assoc. Greenbaum Wolff & Ernst, N.Y.C., 1959-65; ptnr. Greenbaum Wolff & Ernst, 1966-76; sr. ptnr. Rosenman & Colin, N.Y.C., 1976—; bd. dirs. Bernard Chaus, Inc., N.Y.C.; treas. Saarsteel, Inc., White Plains, N.Y., 1970—; sec. Takara Toy Corp., N.Y.C., 1983—. Bd. dirs. Henry St. Settlement, N.Y.C., 1960-85, Nat. Jewish Welfare Bd., N.Y.C., 1967—, Philippine-Am. C. of C., 1970—, Am.-Asean Trade Council, Inc., N.Y.C., 1978—. Served as sgt. U.S. Army, 1953-55. Mem. ABA, N.Y. State Bar Assn., Assn. Bar City N.Y., Internat. Bar Assn. Republican. Jewish. Club: Sunningdale Country (Scarsdale, N.Y.). Banking, General corporate, Real property. Home: 4622 Grosvenor Ave Riverdale NY 10471 Office: Rosenman & Colin 575 Madison Ave New York NY 10022

ROBINSON, JEFFREY ALAN, lawyer; b. Bklyn., July 15, 1950; s. Robert and Francis (Kane) R.; m. Mary E. Dicke, July 8, 1979; 1 child, Emily Louise Dicke Robinson. BA, Brandeis U., 1972; MA in Internat. Law and Diplomacy, Tufts U., 1974; JD, Hofstra U., 1977. Bar: Wash. 1978, U.S. Dist. Ct. (we. dist.) Wash., 1978. Staff atty. Puget Sound Legal Services, Tacoma, 1977-80; ptnr. Jackson & Robinson, Gig Harbor, Wash., 1980-82; sole practice Gig Harbor, 1982-85; ptnr. Gordon, Misner & Robinson, Gig Harbor, 1985—; assoc. prof. real estate law Tacoma Community Coll., 1980-84. Chmn. Penisula Adv. Commn., Gig Harbor, 1983—; vice chmn. Pierce County Citizens Adv. Bd., 1984—. Mem. ABA, Wash. State Bar Assn., Tacoma-Pierce County Bar Assn. (chmn. labor law com., com. for concerns of children, mandatory arbitration com.), Gig Harbor-Penisula C. of C. (trustee 1983-85). Jewish. Lodge: Lions (trustee Gig Harbor 1982-84). Real property, Contracts commercial, Family and matrimonial. Office: Gordon Misner & Robinson PO Box 710 Gig Harbor WA 98335

ROBINSON, JOHN HARVEY, lawyer; b. Cleve., Jan. 23, 1919; s. George Gallup and Ada Jane (Riebennacht) R.; m. Vula Cinderella McCoy, June 7, 1942; children: Mary Margaret, Jane Louise, John Harvey Jr. BA, Ohio U., 1941; JD, Case Western Res. U., 1948; postdoctoral, U. Hawaii, 1950. Bar: Ohio 1948, Hawaii 1951, U.S. Dist. Ct. Hawaii 1951, U.S. Ct. Appeals (9th cir.) 1951. Dir. research Hawaiian Econ. Found., Honolulu, 1948-49; regional atty. U.S. VA, Honolulu, 1949-55, chief atty. Pacific region, 1955-61; sr. ptnr. Robinson & Englehart, Honolulu, 1961—. Adminstrv. asst. Dem. majority floor leader Hawaii Legislature, Honolulu, 1961, to Rep. Tom Gill U.S. Congress, Hawaii, 1962-64; sec. Oahu Dems., Honolulu, 1965. Served as spl. agt. CIC, 1942-45, PTO. Mem. ABA, Fed. Bar Assn., Hawaii Bar Assn., Assn. Trial Lawyers Am., Nat. CIC Assn. (life), Am. Arbitration Assn. (nat. arbitrators panel 1958). Lutheran. Avocation: writing historical novels. State civil litigation, Probate, Personal injury. Home: 1182 Akuila Pl Kailua HI 96734 Office: Robinson & Englehart 820 Mililani St Suite 711 Honolulu HI 96813

ROBINSON, JOHN ROWLAND, lawyer; b. N.Y.C., June 11, 1935; m. Barbara Gahan, Jan. 31, 1959; children—Christopher, Abigail, Perry, John. A.B. in History, Boston U., 1961, J.D., 1964; P.M.D., Harvard U. Bus. Sch., 1973. Bar: N.Y., U.S. Dist. Ct. (so. dist.) N.Y., U.S. Ct. Appeals (2d cir.), U.S. Supreme Ct. Formerly assoc. Simpson, Thacher & Bartlett, N.Y.C., then, U.S. atty.'s rep. spl. task force Dept. Justice, then asst. U.S. atty. So. Dist. N.Y., then ptnr. Rooney & Robinson, N.Y.C., then sr. exec. v.p. and chmn. fin. com. Sperry & Hutchinson Co., N.Y.C., also dir.; then practice, N.Y.C.; now sole practice, Rye, N.Y.; counsel Conn. Bank & Trust Co., Hartford; dir. Ashford Capital Mgmt. Co., Wilmington, Del.; pres., chief exec. officer Robash, Inc., N.Y.C.; chmn. Edwin J. Beinecke Trust, N.Y.C.; pres. Kerry Found., N.Y.C., Skerryvore, Found., N.Y.C.; trustee, founder, mem. legal and fin. coms. Natural Resources Def. Council, Inc., environ. law firm, N.Y.C.; lectr. Practising Law Inst.; vis. prof. U. R.I. Sch. Urban Planning. Trustee, mem. exec. com., sec. bd. trustees, mem. acad. affairs tenure com. Boston U.; bd. visitors Boston U. Sch. Law; hon. nat. trustee Ducks Unltd.; trustee Greenwich (Conn.) Country Day Sch., Foxcroft Sch., Middleburg, Va. Served 2 yrs. active duty inf. U.S. Army. Recipient Young Lawyers Chair award Boston U. Sch. Law; named to Collegium of 100 Disting. Alumni, Boston U. Mem. Assn. Bar City of N.Y., ABA (vice chmn. com. environ. law), N.Y. State Bar Assn., Fed. Bar Assn. Clubs: Am. Yacht (Rye); Harvard, N.Y. Yacht (N.Y.C.); Dunes (former bd. dirs.), Point Judith Country (Narragansett, R.I.); Northeast Harbor Fleet, Northeast Harbor Tennis and Beach Clubs (Northeast Harbor, Maine). Author R.I. Bar Assn. publ.: A Perspective on Some Rhode Island Decisions—1828 and 1885, 1976; author Guide to the Natural Areas of the Lower Hudson Chapter of The Nature Conservancy, 1977. Office: 14-16 Elm Pl Rye NY 10580

ROBINSON, JULIA ORMES, lawyer; b. N.Y.C., Sept. 10, 1953; d. Robert Verner and Mary Ann (Otto) Ormes; m. Derrick Wait Robinson, June 6, 1981; children: Jeffrey Ormes, Lindsay Howell. BA, Colo. Coll., 1975; JD, U. Colo., 1981. Bar: Colo. 1981, U.S. Dist. Ct. Colo. 1981, U.S. Ct. Appeals (10th cir.) 1982, U.S. Tax Ct. 1983. Editorial asst. Science Mag., Washington, 1975-76; writer, editor Nat. Ctr. Atmospheric Research, Boulder, Colo., 1976-78; assoc. Grant, McHendrie, Haines & Crouse, P.C., Denver, 1981-87, ptnr., 1987—. Mem. exec. com. Met. Denver Water Authority, 1985—, v.p. 1987—, adv. com. Met. Water Providers, Denver, 1984—. Mem. ABA, Colo. Bar Assn., Denver Bar Assn., Colo. Women's Bar Assn., Colo. Coll. Alumni Assn. (admission coordinator 1982-86). Democrat. Local government, Probate, Real property. Home: 103 Mineola Ct Boulder CO 80303 Office: Grant McHendrie Haines & Crouse PC 1700 Lincoln St Suite 3000 Denver CO 80203-1086

ROBINSON, KENNETH PATRICK, lawyer, electronics company executive; b. Hackensack, N.J., Dec. 12, 1933; s. William Casper and Margaret Agnes (McGuire) R.; m. Catherine Esther Lund, Aug. 26, 1961; children—James, Susan. B.S. in Elec. Engring., Rutgers U., 1955; J.D., NYU, 1962. Bar: N.Y. 1962. With Hazeltine Corp., Commack, N.Y., 1955—, patent counsel, 1966-69, gen. counsel, 1969-78, sr. counsel, 1978-80, gen. counsel, 1980—, sec., 1971—, v.p., 1984—; v.p. Hazeltine Research Inc., Chgo., 1966—, dir. Hazeltine Ltd., London, 1973-80; dir. Imlac Corp., Needham, Mass., 1978-83. Served to 1st lt. USAF, 1955-57. Mem. ABA, N.Y. State Bar Assn., Am. Patent Law Assn., IEEE, Licensing Execs. Soc. Roman Catholic. General corporate, Patent. Home: 137 Darrow Ln Greenlawn NY 11740 Office: Hazeltine Corp Commack NY 11725

ROBINSON, LEE HARRIS, lawyer; b. N.Y.C., Aug. 2, 1939; s. Bernard and Bess (Polotnick) R.; m. Marilyn Yudien, June 13, 1963; children—Shari, Brett; m. Susan Stroble, June 22, 1985. B.A., Cornell U., 1961; LL.B. cum laude, Columbia U., 1964. Bar: N.Y. 1965, U.S. Dist. Ct. (so. dist.) N.Y., U.S. Ct. Appeals (2d cir.). Assoc. Rosenman Colin Kaye Petschek Freund & Emil, N.Y.C., 1964-73; ptnr. Rosenman & Colin, N.Y.C., 1973—; dir. Columbia Artists Mgmt. Inc., N.Y.C. Contbr. articles to profl. jours. Mem. exec. com. young men's div. Albert Einstein Coll. Medicine, N.Y.C., 1979—, Cornell Assn. Class Officers, 1981—. Mem. ABA (benefits sub-com. of sect. on taxation). Republican. Jewish. Club: Old Oaks (Purchase, N.Y.). Avocations: golf, tennis. Pension, profit-sharing, and employee benefits, General corporate. Home: 437 Orienta Ave Mamaroneck NY 10543 Office: Rosenman & Colin 575 Madison Ave New York NY 10022

ROBINSON, LOGAN GILMORE, lawyer; b. Cin., Dec. 26, 1949; s. Landon Graves and Alis (Rule) R.; m. Edrie Baker Sowell, Sept. 22, 1983; children: Leyland G., Linden G. BA, Cornell U., 1972; JD, Harvard U., 1976; Cert. Competence in German, Goethe Inst., Freiburg, Fed. Republic Germany, 1978. Bar: Ohio 1977, N.Y. 1979, U.S. Ct. Internat. Trade 1983. Research faculty Leningrad (USSR) State U., 1976-77; research officer U. Leiden, The Netherlands, 1977-78; assoc. Wender, Murase & White, N.Y.C., 1978-81, Coudert Bros., N.Y.C., 1981-83; sr. counsel TRW Inc., Cleve., 1983-87; asst. gen. counsel Chrysler Corp., Detroit, 1987—. Author: An American in Leningrad, 1982, paperback, 1984, Evil Star, 1986, paperback, 1987. Mem. Am. Fgn. Law Assn. (past sec.), Am. Soc. Internat. Law, German-Am. Law Assn., Phi Beta Kappa. Private international, General corporate, Contracts commercial. Office: Chrysler Corp 12000 Chrysler Dr Highland Park MI 48288-1919

ROBINSON, MARY LOU, U.S. district judge; b. Dodge City, Kans., Aug. 25, 1926; d. Gerald J. and Frances Strueber; m. A.J. Robinson, Aug. 28, 1949; children: Rebecca Aynn Gruhlkey, Diana Ceil, Matthew Douglas. B.A., U. Tex., 1948, LL.B., 1950. Bar: Tex. 1949. Practice law Amarillo, 1950-55; judge County Ct. Potter County, Tex., 1955-59; judge (108th Dist. Ct.), Amarillo, 1961-73; assoc. justice Ct. of Civil Appeals for 7th Supreme Jud. Dist. of Tex., Amarillo, 1973-77; chief justice Ct. of Civil Appeals for 7th Supreme Jud. Dist. of Tex., 1977-79; U.S. dist. judge No. Dist. Tex., Amarillo, 1979—. Named Woman of Year Tex. Fedn. Bus. and Profl. Women, 1973. Mem. Nat. Assn. Women Lawyers, ABA, Tex. Bar Assn., Amarillo Bar Assn., Delta Kappa Gamma. Presbyterian. Jurisprudence. Office: PO Box 13248 Amarillo TX 79189

ROBINSON, MICHAEL, lawyer; b. Nacogdoches, Tex., Jan. 23, 1956; s. Rutherford and Ruth Helen (Kees) R.; m. Susan Lois Stagg, Mar. 21, 1981; children: Caroline Rebecca, John Michael. BS, Northwestern State U. La., 1978; JD, La. State U., 1981. Bar: La. 1981, U.S. Dist. Ct. (ea. dist.) La. 1981, U.S. Ct. Appeals (5th cir.) 1982. Law clk. to presiding justice La. Supreme Ct., New Orleans, 1981-82; assoc. Barham & Churchill, New Orleans, 1982-85, Martzell & Thomas, New Orleans, 1985-86, Pucheu & Pucheu, Eunice, La., 1986—. Mem. editorial panel Longshore Newsletter, 1985—. Mem. ABA, Am. Trial Lawyers Assn., La. Bar Assn., Miss. Trial Lawyers Assn. (hon.), La. Trial Lawyers Assn., Order of Coif. Avocations: reading, writing, sports. Admiralty, Federal civil litigation, General practice. Office: Pucheu & Pucheu 106 W Park Ave Eunice LA 70535

ROBINSON, NICHOLAS ADAMS, lawyer, law educator; b. N.Y.C., Jan. 20, 1945; s. Albert Lewis and Agnes Claflin (Adams) R.; m. Shelley Miner, Jan. 5, 1969; children: Cynthia M., Lucy A. BA cum laude, Brown U., 1967; JD cum laude, Columbia U., 1970. Bar: N.Y. 1971, U.S. Dist. Ct. (so. and ea. dists.) N.Y. 1972, U.S. Supreme Ct. 1974, U.S. Ct. Appeals (2d and

7th cirs.) 1972. Law clk. to U.S. dist. judge, so. dist. N.Y., 1970-72; assoc. Marshall, Bratter, Greene, Allison & Tucker, N.Y.C., 1972-78, counsel, 1978-82; assoc. prof. law Pace U. Sch. Law, White Plains, N.Y., 1978-81, prof., 1981—, dir. Ctr. for Environ. Legal Studies, 1982—; counsel Winer, Neuburger & Sive, N.Y.C., 1982-83; dep. commr., gen. counsel N.Y. State Dept. Environ. Conservation, Albany, 1983-85; counsel Sive, Paget & Reisel, 1985—; del. U.S.A. environ. law meetings with USSR, 1974-87; chmn. Environ. Adv. Bd. to Gov. Mario Cuomo, 1985—. Contbr. articles to profl. jours. Nat. bd. dirs. UN Assn. of U.S.A., 1966-76, 79—, U.S. Com. for UNICEF, 1970-80, World Environment Ctr., 1981—; bd. dirs. Westchester County Soil and Water Conservation Dist., 1976-83; chmn. N.Y. State Freshwater Wetlands Appeals Bd., 1976-83; mem. bd. edn. Union Free Sch. Dist. of Tarrytown, 1981-83, 85. Recipient N.Y. State Gov.'s Citation for Hist. Preservation, 1983. Mem. Internat. Council Environ. Law, Am. Soc. Internat. Law, ABA, N.Y. State Bar Assn. (chmn. environ. law sect. 1979-80, environ. law award 1981), Assn. Bar City N.Y. (chmn. environ. law com. 1977-78, mem. internat. law com. 1985—), Westchester County Bar Assn., Sierra Club (nat. bd. dirs. 1979-83), Phi Beta Kappa. Democrat. Unitarian. Legal education, Environment, Private international. Home: 258 Kelburne Ave North Tarrytown NY 10591 Office: Pace U Sch Law 78 N Broadway White Plains NY 10603

ROBINSON, PATRICIA DOUGHERTY, judge; b. Rorchester, Pa., Sept. 8, 1939; d. Clifford Clark and Sarah Jessie (McChain) Dougherty; m. James McKee Robinson III, June 1, 1965; children—Sarah Elizabeth, James McKee IV. B.S., U. Okla., 1965; J.D. with distinction, Oklahoma City U., 1974; LL.M., U. Va., 1985. Bar: Okla. 1975, U.S. Ct. Appeals (D.C. cir.) 1975, U.S. Ct. Appeals (10th and 5th cirs.) 1976. Tchr. history and English, Analy High Sch., Sebastopol, Calif., 1966; head librarian NE br. Oklahoma City Pub. Library, 1970-71; corp. atty. Kerr-McGee Corp., Oklahoma City, 1974-77; asst. dist. atty. Oklahoma County, Oklahoma City, 1977-80; referee, jud. asst. Okla. Supreme Ct., Oklahoma City, 1980-81; judge Okla. Ct. of Appeals, Oklahoma City, 1982—. Chmn. com. Lyric Theater, Oklahoma City, 1982; judge Okla. Girls State, 1982-84; active March of Dimes, 1982-84. Phi Delta Phi scholar, 1973; named Woman of Yr., Okla. Pub. Co., Oklahoma City, 1982. Fellow Okla. County Bar; mem. Nat. Assn. Women Judges, Woman Lawyer Assn. (merit award 1982), Okla. County Bar Assn., Bus. and Profl. Women's Assn. (Woman of Yr. 1983), Phi Delta Phi (historian 1972-73, exchequer 1973-74). Presbyterian. State civil litigation. Home: 400 NW 39th St Oklahoma City OK 73118 Office: Okla Ct of Appeals State Capitol Room 104 Oklahoma City OK 73105

ROBINSON, RANDALL PHILIP, lawyer; b. McAlester, Okla., Oct. 22, 1956; s. Joseph Edgar Jr. and Kathryn (Philippi) R.; m. Carolyn Ranae Phillips, Jan. 2, 1986. BA, Okla. State U., 1978; JD, U. Okla., 1982. Bar: Okla. 1982, U.S. Dist. Ct. (we. dist.) Okla. 1983. Assoc. Gary B. Homsey & Assocs., Oklahoma City, 1982—. Mem. Okla. Trial Lawyers Assn. Workers' compensation, Personal injury. Home: 517 NW 41st St Oklahoma City OK 73118 Office: Gary B Homsey & Assocs 4816 N Classen Oklahoma City OK 73118

ROBINSON, RICHARD RUSSELL, lawyer; b. Cedar Falls, Iowa, July 3, 1925; s. George Clarence and Juanita Louise (Thiede) R.; m. Carolyn Elizabeth Sage, Sept. 5, 1954; children—Timothy Todd, Elizabeth Ann Robinson Schneider, Edward William. A.B., Harvard U., 1949; M.A., U. Chgo., 1950; LL.B., U. Wis., 1956. Bar: Wis. 1956, U.S. Dist. Ct. (ea. dist.) Wis. 1956, U.S. Ct. Appeals (7th cir.) 1957, U.S. Supreme Ct. 1964, U.S. Dist. Ct. (we. dist.) Wis. 1982. Law clk. Fed. Dist. Ct. Milw., 1956-58; ptnr. Godfrey, Trump & Hayes, Milw., 1970—. Served with AUS, 1943-46. Decorated Combat Infantryman's Badge. Mem. State Bar Wis., Milw. Bar Assn., Am. Judicature Soc., Def. Research Inst., Nat. Assn. R.R. Trial Counsel. Methodist. Lodges: Rotary (Milw.); Masons (Whitefish Bay). State civil litigation, Federal civil litigation. Home: 535 W Manor Circle Bayside WI 53217 Office: Godfrey Trump & Hayes 700 N Water St Suite 700 Milwaukee WI 53202

ROBINSON, ROBERT GEORGE, lawyer; b. Lakewood, Ohio, July 5, 1956; s. John Haines and Barbara Jean (Bauer) R.; m. Shannon L. Rupp, Nov. 25, 1978; children: Lindsay, John. BS in Bus. with high honors, Western Ill. U., 1977; JD, Loyola U., Chgo., 1982; LLM in Taxation, DePaul U., 1987. Bar: Ill. 1982, U.S. Dist. Ct. (no. dist.) Ill. 1983. With Peat, Marwick & Mitchell, Chgo., 1977-79, Price Waterhouse, Chgo., 1979-81; tax atty. Gleason & Assocs. Inc., Oak Brook, Ill., 1981-83; supr. Grant Thorton, Chgo., 1983-86, Harris, Milott & Robinson, Oakbrook Terr., 1986—; sec. Eatery Concepts, Inc., Elmhurst, Ill., 1985—, Joe's Liquor Cabinet, Inc., Carol Stream, Ill., 1986—. Mem. ABA, Ill. Bar Assn., Chgo. Bar Assn., Am. Inst. CPA, Ill. Inst. CPA. Republican. Roman Catholic. Avocations: softball, tennis, skiing, basketball, chess. Probate, Real property, Personal income taxation. Home: 543 Woodbine Oak Park IL 60302 Office: Harris Milott & Robinson 1634 Ardmore Suite 106 Oakbrook Terrace IL 60181

ROBINSON, RUSSELL MARABLE, II, lawyer; b. Charlotte, N.C., Mar. 13, 1932; s. John Moseley and Camilla Croom (Rodman) R.; m. Sally Gossett Dalton, Sept. 4, 1953; children: Camilla, Russell III, Sally. Student, Princeton U., 1950-52; LLB, Duke U., 1956. Bar: N.C. 1956, U.S. Dist. Ct. (ea., mid. and we. dists.) N.C., U.S. Ct. Appeals (4th cir.). From assoc. to ptnr. Lassiter, Moore & Van Allen, Charlotte, 1956-60; ptnr. Robinson, Bradshaw & Hinson P.A., Charlotte, 1960—. Author: North Carolina Corporate Law and Practice, 3d edit., 1982. Gen. Counsel Morehead Found., Chapel Hill, N.C., 1965—; chmn. United Way Mecklenburg County, Charlotte, 1976, pres., 1978. Fellow Am. Bar Found.; mem. ABA, N.C. Bar Assn., Order of Coif, Phi Beta Kappa. Republican. Episcopalian. General corporate, Securities. Home: 3829 Bonwood Dr Charlotte NC 28211 Office: Robinson Bradshaw & Hinson PA 1900 Independence Ctr Charlotte NC 28246

ROBINSON, SAMUEL FRANCIS, JR., lawyer, county ofcl.; b. Chattanooga, July 23, 1942; s. Samuel Francis and Ruth Elizabeth (Cates) R.; m. Sally Elizabeth Lindsay Robinson, Mar. 25, 1967; children—Rob, Elizabeth, Susannah, Samuel Francis. B.A. in Polit. sci., U. N.C., 1967; postgrad. Emory U., 1967-68; J.D., U. Tenn., Knoxville, 1970. Bar: Tenn. 1970. Assoc., Hall, Haynes, Lusk and Foster, Chattanooga, 1970-74; partner Robinson, Stanley & Burnette and predecessors, Chattanooga, 1974-82, Robinson & Crutchfield, Chattanooga, 1982—; commr. County of Hamilton, Tenn., 1978-82; mem. Hamilton County Indsl. Devel. Bd., 1982-84, Hamilton County Tourist Devel. Agy., 1982-84; trustee Chattanooga-Hamilton County Hosp. Authority, 1984—. V.p. Chattanooga Riverbend Festival, 1982-86, competitive events and exhbns., 1983-86, sec., 1986—. Served with U.S. Army, 1962-65. Mem. ABA, Fed. Bar Assn., Tenn. Bar Assn., Chattanooga Bar Assn., Tenn. Trial Lawyers Assn., Chattanooga Trial Lawyers Assn., Assn. Trial Lawyers Am. Democrat. Episcopalian. Clubs: Golf & Country (Signal Mt., Tenn.). Personal injury, Federal civil litigation, State civil litigation. Office: 424 Georgia Ave Chattanooga TN 37403

ROBINSON, SANDRA ANN, lawyer; b. Hackensack, N.J.; d. John Henry and Martha Carrington (Toliver) R. B.A., Howard U., 1969; J.D., 1972. Bar: Pa. 1979, U.S. Dist. Ct. N.J. 1981, N.J. 1981, U.S. Supreme Ct. 1983. Legal intern Ctr. Clin. Legal Studies, Washington, 1970-72; clk. to presiding justice Superior Ct. N.J., Passaic County, 1972-73; litigational appeals atty. Essex-Newark Legal Services Corp., Newark, 1973-78, assoc. exec. dir., 1979-84, acting exec. dir., 1984-85, exec. dir., 1985—; county adjuster County of Bergen, Hackensack, 1984; planning bd. atty. City of Hackensack, 1982-84. Legal rep. Mary McLeod Bethune Scholarship Fund, Hackensack, 1978—; active Hackensack Mcpl. Com., 1975—, Rent Stabilization Bd., Hackensack, 1973-77, Urban League Bergen County Inc., 1980—; sec. Hackensack Citizens Adv. Com., 1972—; bd. govs. Hackensack Med. Ctr., 1984—; v.p. N.J. Assn. Correction, Trenton, 1978—; bd. dirs. Bergen County Family Services, 1986—. Named Woman of Yr., Hackensack Day Care Ctr. 1983, one of Outstanding Young Women Am., 1981. Mem. ABA, Am. Judicature Soc., Bergen County Bar Assn., Bergen County Women Lawyers, Fed. Bar Assn., N.J. Inst. Mcpl. Attys., N.J. State Bar Assn., Pa. Bar Assn., Assn. Trial Lawyers Am., Howard U. Alumni Assn. (Bergen County sec., region II rep. 1972—, Disting. Daughter 1982) Kappa Beta Pi. Democrat. Clubs: Bergen County Links Inc. (parliamentarian 1983—), Nat. Bus. and Profl. Womens Nat. Sojourner Truth Meritorious Service award 1984). General practice, Family and matrimonial, Bankruptcy. Home: 287 Central Ave Hackensack NJ 07601

ROBINSON, SARA MOORE, lawyer; b. Chgo.; d. Herbert Jackson and Emma (Roberts) Moore; m. Donald Louis Robinson; children: Marshall Jackson, Margaret Moore. BA, Beloit Coll., 1959; JD, Cath. U. Am., 1965. Bar: D.C. 1966, U.S. Dist. Ct. D.C. 1966, U.S. Ct. Appeals (D.C. cir.) 1966, U.S. Supreme Ct. 1969. Counsel to Hon. Henry S. Reuss, Washington, 1966-76; cons. Robinson Assocs., Washington, 1977—; ptnr. Solomon, Tinkham & Robinson, Washington, 1985—; adj. assoc. prof. Boston U., 1976—. Bd. dirs. United Way, Washington, 1976-84, social planning com., 1984—; mem. Choral Arts Soc. Washington, 1982—. Mem. Fed. Bar Assn., Women's Bar Assn., Assn. Trial Lawyers Am., D.C. Bar Assn. (co-chmn. steering com. sect. 17), Am. Immigration Lawyers Assn. Episcopalian. Avocations: singing, reading, dancing. Probate, Real property, Immigration, naturalization, and customs. Office: Solomon Tinkham & Robinson 1629 K St NW Suite 801 Washington DC 20006

ROBINSON, SPOTTSWOOD WILLIAM, III, judge, lawyer; b. Richmond, Va., July 26, 1916; s. Spottswood William, Jr. and Inez (Clements) R.; m. Marian Bernice Wilkerson, Mar. 5, 1936; children—Spottswood William IV, Nina Cecelia (Mrs. Oswald G. Govan). Student, Va. Union U., Richmond, 1932-34, 35-36, LLD (hon.), 1955; LLB magna cum laude, Howard U., 1939, LLD (hon.), 1981; LLD (hon.), Georgetown U., 1983, N.Y. Law Sch., 1986. Bar: Va. bar 1943, U.S. Supreme Ct 1948. Teaching fellow law Howard U., 1939-48, instr. law, 1941-43, asst. prof. law, 1943-46, asso. prof. law, 1946-48, on leave, 1947-48; prof., dean Howard U. (Law Sch.), 1960-63; ptnr. Hill & Robinson, Richmond, 1943-44, Hill, Martin & Robinson, Richmond, 1944-55; sole practitioner Richmond, 1955-60; legal rep. Va. NAACP Legal Def. and Ednl. Fund Inc., 1948-50, legal rep. for SW regional counsel, 1951-60; v.p., gen. counsel Consol. Bank and Trust Co., Richmond, 1963-64; judge U.S. Dist. Ct. D.C., 1964-66, U.S. Ct. Appeals D.C., 1966—. Mem. U.S. Commn. on Civil Rights, 1961-63. Recipient Annual Alumni award in law Howard U., 1951, award Old Dominion Bar Assn., 1964, Charles Hamilton Houston Medallion Merit Washington Bar Assn., 1976; citation Sigma Delta Tau, 1962, Va. Union U. Alumni Assn., 1964, Howard Law Alumni Assn., 1968, Nat. Bar Assn., 1975. Mem. ABA, Va. Bar Assn., Bar Assn. City of Richmond (hon.), Assn., Bar Assn. D.C. (hon.), Nat. Lawyers Club (hon.), Nat. Bar Assn. (citation 1975). Episcopalian. Office: US Courthouse 3d and Constitution Ave NW Washington DC 20001

ROBINSON, STANLEY DANIEL, lawyer; b. N.Y.C., July 29, 1926; s. David H. and Anna R. R.; m. Janet M. Wolff, July 1, 1951; children—Nancy Lyn, Susan Terry, James Alan. B.A., Columbia U., 1947, LL.B., 1949. Bar: N.Y. bar 1949, U.S. Supreme Ct. bar 1968. Law clk. to judge U.S. Dist. Ct. for So. Dist. N.Y., 1949-50; asst. U.S. atty. So. Dist. of N.Y., 1950-52; asso. firm Kaye, Scholer, Fierman, Hays & Handler, N.Y.C., 1952-59; partner firm Kaye, Scholer, Fierman, Hays & Handler, 1959—; mem. adv. bd. Bur. of Nat. Affairs antitrust sect. Served with USNR, 1944-46. Mem. Am. Coll. Trial Lawyers, Am. Bar Found., Am. Bar Assn., N.Y. State Bar Assn., Assn. Bar City of N.Y., Phi Beta Kappa. Jewish. Home: 214 Hillair Circle White Plains NY 10605 Office: 425 Park Ave New York NY 10022

ROBINSON, STUART JAY, lawyer; b. Balt., Nov. 7, 1948; s. Malvin Albert and Beverly (Jolson) R.; m. Audrey Gail Gibson, Dec. 11, 1982. B.A., U. Md., 1971; J.D., U. Balt., 1974; student Columbia U., 1966-67, Jewish Theol. Sem., 1966-67; postgrad. Georgetown U., 1977-78. Bar: Md. 1974, U.S. Supreme Ct. 1977, U.S. Ct. Appeals (4th cir.) 1975, (D.C. cir.) 1977, U.S. Dist. Ct. 1974, U.S. Ct. Appeals for D.C. 1975, for Md. 1974. Sole practice law, Bel Air, Md., 1981—; asst. prof. U. Balt., 1975-77; adj. faculty Nova U., Ft. Lauderdale, 1977-79, Towson State U., 1981-82; legal counsel Anti-Smokers Group, 1977; legal panel Balt. Neighborhoods Inc., 1976—; counsel Balt. City Food Stamp Com., 1975; spl. asst., law clk. Legal Counsel to Minister of Interior, Jerusalem, Israel, summer 1973; law clk., intern Balt. City Pub. Defenders Office, 1973-74, panel atty., 1974—, others; spl. econ. devel. rep. to Italy for State of Md. and Harford County, Md. Chmn. personnel adv. bd. Harford County, 1983-84; bd. dirs. Harford Center, 1983-84; mem. adv. bd. Addict Referral and Counseling, 1979-82; legal cons. Oak Grove Bapt. Ch., Churchville, Md., 1974, Highland Community Assn. of Street, Md., 1983—, others. Recipient Harry C. Byrd male citizenship award U. Md., 1970-71. Mem. Balt. City Bar Assn., Md. Bar Assn., Harford County Bar Assn., Balt. County Bar Assn., ABA, Washington Bar Assn., Md. Trial Lawyers Assn. (bd. govs. 1985-86), Phi Alpha Theta, Eta Beta Rho, Omicron Delta Kappa, Zeta Beta Tau, Phi Sigma Delta. Democrat. Jewish. General practice, Personal injury, Criminal. Home: 3975 Street Rd Street MD 21154 Office: Stuart Jay Robinson Esquire 8 N Main St Bel Air MD 21014

ROBINSON, THOMAS HART, lawyer, educator; b. Richmond, Va., Feb. 3, 1948; s. Carey Hart and Rose (Strauss) R. B.S. in Econs., Va. Commonwealth U., 1970, postgrad., 1978; J.D., Coll. William and Mary, 1973. Bar: Va. 1973, U.S. Dist. Ct. 1974. Clk., Richmond Legal Aid, 1972-73; asst. prof. Va. Commonwealth U., 1973-78; ptnr. Deal Felts & Robinson, Richmond, 1976-86; Felts and Robinson, 1986— ; guest lectr. various univs., 1973—; dir. Va. Ski Inc., Richmond; gen. counsel Lowrey Organ Ctr., Inc., Fairmont, W. Va., 1977-83. Author: Handbook for Name Changes, 1972; contbr. articles to profl. jours. Del., Democratic Com., Henrico County, Va., 1980; chmn. Credit Consumers Counsil, Richmond, 1981; spl. commr. Henrico County Cir. Ct., 1982; mem. spl. com. Supreme Ct. of Va. for Edn. of Newly Appointed Cir. Ct. Judges, 1986—. Recipient B.E. Major award R.P.I. of Richmond; Man of Yr. award Va. Ski Inc. Mem. Va. State Bar (mem. pres.'s council), Henrico Bar Assn. (pres. 1982-83), Richmond Criminal Bar Assn., Am. Trial Lawyers Assn., Phi Delta Phi (v.p.). Personal injury, Criminal, General practice. Office: 4799 S Laburnum Ave Richmond VA 23231

ROBINSON, WAYNE E., lawyer; b. Grant, Mich., Mar. 17, 1928; s. Clarence Allen and Gladys (Brown) R.; m. Lillian Fernandez, June 26, 1954; children—Liliana Robinson Graham, Wayne E. B.A. in Econs., Mich. State U., 1949, M.A. in Econs., 1951; J.D., Suffolk U., 1968. Bar: Mass. 1968, Colo. 1978. Commd. 1st lt. U.S. Air Force, 1954, advanced through grades to lt. col., 1971; asst. prof. air sci. U. P.R., 1960-64; adv. to Vietnam Air Force, 1969-70; staff judge adv. Air Force Acctg. and Fin. Ctr., Denver, 1974-78, ret., 1978; sole practice Aurora, Colo., 1978—. Decorated Bronze Star medal, Meritorious Service medal, Legion of Merit; recipient Disting. Fed. Atty. award Denver Fed. Exec. Bd., 1977. Mem. Fed. Bar Assn. (v.p. 1975-76, Earl W. Kintner award 1976), Colo. Bar Assn., Aurora Bar Assn. (pres. 1981-82), ABA, Am. Soc. Mil. Comptrollers, Air Force Assn. Republican. Roman Catholic. Lodge: Rotary. Bankruptcy, Family and matrimonial, Probate. Home: 4835 Durham St Boulder CO 80301 Office: 1450 S Havana St Suite 404 Aurora CO 80012

ROBINSON, WILLIAM ADAMS, lawyer; b. Flushing, N.Y., Sept. 7, 1936; s. William E. and Marjorie Robinson. B.A., in Internat. Econs., Stanford U., 1958, postgrad. Law Sch., 1960-62; J.D., Golden Gate U., 1964. Bar: Calif. 1965, U.S. Supreme Ct. 1984. Assoc. Barfield, Barfield & Dryden, San Francisco, 1965-66; ptnr. Goldeen, Goldeen & Robinson, Lafayette, Calif., 1966-70; assoc. Miller, Van Dorn & Bowen, San Francisco, 1970-71; sr. trial counsel Calif. State Automobile Assn., San Francisco, 1971—; dep. sheriff Santa Clara County, Calif., 1962; claims authorizer Social Security Adminstrn., San Francisco, 1963-64; lectr. C.E.B., Golden Gate U. Law Sch., San Francisco Law Sch., 1978—; referee State Bar Ct. state and fed. jud. arbitrator. Pres. Easter Seal Soc., Marin County, Calif., 1978-79. Served to capt. USNR (politico-mil. affairs 1980—). Mem. Am. Arbitration Assn. (arbitrator), Bar Assn. San Francisco (chmn. arbitration com.), U.S. Navy League. Republican. Episcopalian. Clubs: Naval Air Sta. Aero (Alameda, Calif.); Tiburon Yacht (commodore 1983). Author: Practicing California Judicial Arbitration, CEB, 1983. Insurance, State civil litigation, Arbitration. Home: 257 Cleveland Ave Mill Valley CA 94941 Office: 100 Van Ness Ave San Francisco CA 94102

ROBINSON, WILLIAM T., III, lawyer; b. Covington, Ky., Jan. 6, 1945; s. William T. Jr. and Hilda C. (Tatermann) R.; m. Joan Mary Wernersbach, Aug. 2, 1969; children: William Taylor IV, Todd Arthur. AB, Thomas More Coll., 1967; JD, U. Ky., 1971. Bar: Ky., Ohio, U.S. Dist. Ct. (ea. dist.) Ky., U.S. Dist. Ct. (so. dist.) Ohio, U.S. Ct. Appealsl (6th cir.), U.S. Supreme Ct. Ptnr. Robinson, Arnzen, Parry & Wentz, P.S.C., Covington, Ky., 1971—; adj. prof. No. Ky. U., 1977—; lectr. numerous seminars. Mem. legal edn. planning com. Ky. Council on Higher Edn., 1984-85, adv. com. paralegal program Eastern Ky. U., 1983-85; cathn. nat. fund drive U. Ky., 1982-83; bd. of trustees Redwood Sch. and Rehabilitation Ctr., 1971-81, 83—, sec., 1972-73, 1st v.p., 1973-75, pres., 1975-78, bd. of overseers, 1981-83; bd. of trustees, chmn. Dorothy Wood Found., 1980—; bd. dirs. Cin. chpt. ARC, 1979-85; chmn. alumni fund drive Thomas More Coll., 1986—. Mem. ABA, Ohio Bar Assn., Fed. Bar Assn., Ky. Bar Assn.(specialization com., dist. co-chmn. jud. amendment 1975, ethics com., chmn. Ho. of Dels. 1981-82, Recognition award for continuing legal edn. 1982, 83, 84, 85), Am. Bar Found. (lifetime fellow), Ky. Bar Found. (bd. dirs. 1981—, sec., treas. 1983-84), No. Ky. Bar Assn., Cincinnatio Bar Assn., Kenton County Bar Assn. (mem. exec. com. 1973-75, chmn. legal-med. com. 1978-83, Ann. Merit award 1973), Ky. Def. Counsel Assn., Internat. Assn. Ins. Counsel, Acad. Trial Lawyers Am., So. Conf. Bar Pres.s', Nat. Conf. Bar Pres.s', U. Ky. Alumni Assn. (bd. dirs. 1981—), No. Ky. C. of C. (vice chmn. 1985-86, bd. dirs. 1980—, Profl. of Yr. 1980), Thomas More Coll. Alumni Assn. (bd. dirs. 1972—, pres. 1974-75, chmn. alumni fund drive 1974-75), Phi Alpha Theta, Alpha Delta GAmma, Phi Delta Phi. Personal injury, Federal civil litigation, State civil litigation. Home: 3783 Narrows Rd Erlanger KY 41018 Office: Robinson Arnzen Parry & Wentz 600 Greenup St PO Box 472 Covington KY 41012

ROBISCH, ROBERT KARL, lawyer; b. Indpls., Aug. 4, 1953; s. Robert C. and Margaret H. (Higgins) R. AB cum laude, Xavier U., 1975; M Pub. Affairs, Ind. U., 1977, JD, 1980. Bar: Ind. 1981, U.S. Dist. Ct. (so. dist.) Ind. 1981. Dep. atty. gen. State of Ind., Indpls., 1981—. Mem. ABA, Ind. State Bar Assn., Indpls. Bar Assn., Am. Soc. Pub. Adminstrn., Ind. Soc. Pub. Adminstrn. Roman Catholic. Administrative and regulatory, Federal civil litigation, Government contracts and claims. Home: 4410 Ingleside Ln Indianapolis IN 46227 Office: Atty Gen Ind 219 State House Indianapolis IN 46204

ROBISON, CHARLES BENNETT, legal consultant; b. Lewistown, Ill., Jan. 6, 1913; s. Marvin Thomas and Minnie Dell (White) R.; m. Katherine Louise Parkins, Sept. 23, 1939; children—Kenneth P., Peter C., Dianne R. Marcell, Alice R. Berntson. A.B. cum laude, Knox Coll., 1934; J.D., Northwestern U., 1937. Bar: Ill. 1937. Assoc., Meyers & Matthias and predecessors, Chgo., 1938-73; v.p., gen. counsel Protection Mut. Ins. Co., Park Ridge, Ill., 1973-78; cons., counsel Meyers & Matthias, Matthias & Matthias, Chgo., 1978-83; legal cons. Luth. Brotherhood, Mpls., Nat. Fraternal Congress of Am., Chgo., 1983—. Mem. adv. bd. Northwest Suburban council Boy Scouts Am., 1959-84. Served to maj. AUS, 1941-45. Recipient Northwest Suburban Council Silver Beaver award, Boy Scouts Am., 1959. Mem. Ill. State Bar Assn., ABA, Fedn. Ins. and Corp. Counsel (past pres.), Fedn. Ins. and Corp. Counsel Found. (pres. 1975—), Assn. Fraternal Benefit Counsel. Republican. Congregationalist. Insurance. Home: 1639 Campbell Ave Des Plaines IL 60016 Office: 1300 Iroquois Dr Room 260 Naperville IL 60540

ROBISON, JOSEPH ALBERT, lawyer; b. Newark, Dec. 8, 1948; s. Frank A. and Helen K. (Kasserman) R.; m. Nancy Ann Bish, June 15, 1977 (div. Aug. 1982); m. Marcie Lou Fulk, Oct. 6, 1984; 1 child, Emily Arin. BS, Case Western Res. U., 1971; JD, Cleve. State U., 1975. Bar: Ohio 1975, U.S. Dist. Ct. (so. dist.) Ohio 1980. Assoc. McDonald, Robison & Koehler, Newark, Ohio, 1975-84, Jones, Norpell, List, Miller & Howarth, Newark, 1984—. Treas. Big Bros./Big Sisters, Licking County, 1977—, Am. Diabetes Assn., Licking, County, 1981—, bd. dirs., Ohio, 1981—. Democrat. Methodist. Lodge: Lions. Avocations: tennis, softball, painting. Juvenile, Probate, Real property. Home: 596 King Ave Newark OH 43055 Office: Jones Norpell List Miller & Howarth 2 N First St PO Box 4010 Newark OH 43055

ROBISON, WILLIAM ROBERT, lawyer; b. Memphis, May 5, 1947; s. Andrew Cliffe and Elfrieda (Barnes) R.; m. Antoinette Dello Iacono, Sept. 8, 1973 (div. Dec. 1979); m. Hye Sook Park, Dec. 17, 1982. AB, Boston U., 1970; JD, Northeastern U., 1974. Bar: Mass. 1974, D.C. 1975, U.S. Dist. Ct. Mass. 1975, U.S. Ct. Appeals (1st cir.) 1975, U.S. Dist. Ct. Conn. 1977, U.S. Supreme Ct. 1977, Calif. 1978, U.S. Dist. Ct. (cen. dist.) Calif. 1979, U.S. Ct. Appeals (9th cir.) 1979. Assoc. Meyers, Goldstein, et al, Boston, 1975-76, Cooley, Shrair, et al, Springfield, Mass., 1976-78, Hertzberg, et al, Los Angeles, 1978-79, Marcus & Lewi, Santa Monica, Calif., 1980-81; sole practice Santa Monica, 1981—; lectr. Northeastern U., Boston, 1975-76; judge pro-tem., Mcpl. Ct., Los Angeles, 1984—, Los Angeles Superior Ct., 1987—. Co-author: Commercial Transactions, 1976. Bd. dirs. Boston Legal Asst. Project, 1972-75, Action for Boston Community Devel., Inc., 1971-75. Mem. ABA, Los Angeles County Bar Assn., Santa Monica Bar Assn. (Cert. of Appreciation 1987). Democrat. Unitarian. State civil litigation, Construction, Real property. Home: 2546 Amherst Ave Los Angeles CA 90064 Office: 3250 Ocean Park Blvd Suite 100 Santa Monica CA 90405

ROBOL, RICHARD THOMAS, lawyer; b. Norfolk, Va., Feb. 8, 1952; s. Harry James and Lucy Henley (Johnson) R.; m. Melissa Janet Sengstack, June 3, 1978; children: Thomas Coke, Robert Talbot. BA, U. Va., 1974; JD, Harvard U., 1978. Bar: Va. 1979, U.S. Dist. Ct. (ea. dist.) 1979, U.S. Ct. Appeals (4th cir.) 1979, U.S. Dist. Ct. (we. dist.) Va. 1981, U.S. Supreme Ct. 1982. Law clk. to presiding justice U.S. Dist. Ct. (ea. dist.) Va., 1978-79; ptnr. Seawell, Dalton, Hughes & Timms, Norfolk, 1979—; pro bono counsel Nat. Commn. for Prevention Child Abuse, Norfolk, 1983, Tidewater Profl. Assn. on Child Abuse, 1983, Parents United Va., 1981-82, Sexual Abuse Help Line, 1983-86. Contbr. articles to law revs.; contbg. editor: International Law for General Practitioners, 1981. Bd. dirs. Va. Opera Assn. Guild, Norfolk, 1983—; deacon Cen. Bapt. Ch., Norfolk, 1980-83; mem. Boyd-Graves Conf. on Civil Procedure in Va., 1981—. Fulbright scholar, 1974. Mem. Va. State Bar Assn. (bd. dirs. internat. law sect. 1984—, chmn. 1982-83), Va. Young Lawyers Assn. (cir. rep. 1984—), Va. Assn. Def. Attys., Norfolk-Portsmouth Bar Assn. (chmn. speakers bur. 1979—), Assn. Ins. Attys., Def. Research Inst. Democrat. Avocations: camping, rowing, fishing, gardening. Contracts commercial, Federal civil litigation, Private international. Home: 221 Sir Oliver Rd Norfolk VA 23505 Office: Seawell Dalton Hughes & Timms 900 Wainwright Bldg Bute and Duke Sts Norfolk VA 23510

ROBY, DANIEL ARTHUR, lawyer; b. Anderson, Ind., Aug. 16, 1941; s. Virgil A. and Frances E. R.; m. Carolyn Sue Eaton, June 14, 1964; 1 dau., Kerilynn. A.B. with honors, Ind. U., 1963, J.D., 1966. Bar: Ind. 1966, U.S. Dist. Ct. (no. dist.) Ind. 1967, U.S. Dist. Ct. (so. dist.) Ind. 1966, U.S. Ct. Appeals (7th cir.) 1968. Practice law, Anderson, and Ft. Wayne, Ind.; faculty lectr. Ind. U. Past pres. Allen County (Ind.) Heart Assn., Northeastern Ind. Heart Assn.; chmn. bd. Ind. affiliate Am. Heart Assn.; past pres. bd. mgrs. Faith Baptist Ch.; past pres. Interagy. Drug and Alcohol Council. Mem. Ind. State Bar Assn., Allen County Bar Assn. (bd. dirs. 1983), Assn. Trial Lawyers Am., Ind. Trial Lawyers Assn. (exec. com., bd. dirs. 1980—, named Lawyer of Yr. 1986), Am. Arbitration Assn. (bd. arbitrators). Club: Shriners. Contbr. articles to legal jours. Federal civil litigation, State civil litigation, Personal injury. Home: 6224 Cordava Ct Fort Wayne IN 46815 Office: 127 W Berry St Fort Wayne IN 46802 also: 420 E 8th St Anderson IN 46015

ROBY, RICHARD ERIC, lawyer; b. Oakland, Calif., Aug. 19, 1945; s. Eric Richard and Gloria Jean (Heinze) R.; m. June Lee David, Aug. 4, 1984; 1 child, Erika Nicole. AB, U. Calif., Berkeley, 1968; JD, U. Calif., San Francisco, 1978. Bar: Calif. 1978, U.S. Dist. Ct. (no. dist.) Calif. 1978. Adminstr., tchr. Marin Head Start, San Rafael, Calif., 1968-75; assoc. Law Office W. McFadden, San Mateo, Calif., 1978-79, Lynch & Loofbourrow, San Francisco, 1979-80; asst. sec., asst. gen. counsel Am. Forest Products Co., San Francisco, 1980—; gen. ptnr. Gelato Vero Caffe, San Diego, 1982—. Mem. ABA, San Francisco Bar Assn. Contracts commercial, General corporate, Real property. Office: Am Forest Products Co 2740 Hyde St San Francisco CA 94109

ROCCOGRANDI, ANTHONY JOSEPH, lawyer; b. N.Y.C., Apr. 2, 1935; s. Joseph Anthony and Mary (Cannella) R.; m. Paulette Bolinskey, Apr. 25,

1973; children—Jacqueline Marie, John Michael. B.S., CCNY, 1956; J.D., NYU, 1965. Bar: N.Y. 1968, D.C. 1969, U.S. Dist. Ct. (so. dist.) N.Y. 1969, U.S. Dist. Ct. D.C. 1969, U.S. Ct. Appeals (D.C. cir.) 1969. Atty., Bur. Drug Abuse Control, Washington, 1965-67; asst. chief counsel Bur. Narcotics and Dangerous Drugs, Dept. Justice, Washington, 1968-71; spl. asst. U.S. atty. Dept. Justice, Washington, 1969; gen. counsel Nat. Commn. on Marihuana and Drug Abuse, Washington, 1971-73; assoc., ptnr. Chayet & Sonnenreich, Washington, 1974-81; ptnr. Sonnenreich & Roccograndi, Washington, 1982—; cons. Med. Device Consultants, Inc., Attleboro, Mass., 1981—; dir. Genetic Research Labs., Inc. Author: The 1970 Federal Drug Act, 1973; also articles. Mem. Brent Soc., N.Y. State Bar Assn., D.C. Bar Assn., Fed. Bar Assn., ABA. Health, Administrative and regulatory, General corporate. Home: 201 Longview Dr Alexandria VA 22314 Office: Sonnenreich & Roccograndi 600 New Hampshire Ave NW Suite 720 Washington DC 20037

ROCHE, BYRON ATHERTON, lawyer, corporate professional; b. East St. Louis, Ill., Aug. 8, 1921; s. Francis D. and Freda L. (Pace) R.; m. Elizabeth Miller, Mar. 5, 1948; children: Byron A. Jr., Linda R., Bradford M., Dorothy L. Roche Auble. JD, Washington U., 1947. Bar: Mo. Assoc. Carter, Bull & Baer, St. Louis; ptnr. Murphy & Roche, St. Louis, 1948-69; v.p., gen. counsel, sec. Hussmann Corp., Bridgeton, Mo., 1969-85, v.p. law, sec., 1985-86, ret., 1986; bd. dirs. Hussmann Corp. and subs. Served to maj. USAAF, WWII. Republican. Lutheran. Home: 36 Raven's Pointe Dr Lake Saint Louis MO 63367

ROCHE, JOHN JEFFERSON, lawyer; b. N.Y.C., Apr. 12, 1934; s. William and Florence E. (Garvey) R.; m. Judith J. Stackpole, Sept. 4, 1980; 1 child from previous marriage, Forrest B. A.B., Brown U., 1957; LL.B., Boston U., 1964. Bar: Mass. 1964, U.S. Tax Ct. 1976. Asst. atty. gen. Dept. Atty. Gen., Boston, 1964-67; assoc. Hale & Dorr, Boston, 1967-72, jr. ptnr., 1972-80, sr. ptnr., 1980—. trustee The Hotchkiss Sch.; bd. dirs. Big Bros. Assn. Boston, Indian Soc., Norm Conway Inst. Served with U.S. Army, 1959-62. Fellow Am. Coll. Probate Counsel, Internat. Acad. Estate and Trust Law; mem. ABA, Mass. Bar Assn., Boston Bar Assn. Republican. Congregationalist. Club: Wig and Penn (London); Winchester Country. Lodge: Masons. Estate planning, Probate, Estate taxation. Office: Hale & Dorr 60 State St Boston MA 02109

ROCHE, THOMAS GARRETT, lawyer; b. Pitts., Oct. 22, 1953; s. Gerald Dennis and Marian Alice (McGraw) R.; m. Carolyn Lee Berkey, Aug. 13, 1983. B.A., W.Va. U., 1976; J.D., Western State U. Coll. Law, 1979. Bar: Calif. 1982, U.S. Dist. Ct. (so. and cen. dists.) Calif. 1982. Asst. law librarian Nat. U. Sch. Law, San Diego, 1980-84; sole practice, San Diego, 1982—. Recipient Corpus Juris Secundum award Bancroft-Whitney Pub. Co., 1976-77. Mem. ABA, Calif. State Bar Assn., San Diego Trial Lawyers Assn., Delta Theta Phi (treas. 1977-78, Wm. H. Thomas Nat. Oral Advocacy award 1977). Federal civil litigation, State civil litigation, Criminal. Office: 1200 Third Ave Suite 1100 San Diego CA 92101

ROCHELLE, VICTOR CLEANTHUS, lawyer, consultant; b. El Reno, Okla., Nov. 4, 1918; s. Floyd Emerson and Goldie Opal (Dunbar) R.; m. Marjorie Armitage, Dec. 20, 1946 (div. 1956); children—Vickie Adrianne, Margo Renee; m. Patricia Ann Leary, Mar. 20, 1964; children—Elizabeth Ann, Linda Raquel. B.A., U. Tex., 1940; LL.B., Columbia U., 1947. Bar: Tex. 1948, U.S. Dist. Ct. Ill. 1953. Assoc. Tom Hartley, Atty., Pharr, Tex., 1947-49; assoc. Kelly, Looney, McLean & Littleton, Edinburg, Tex., 1949-52; personal injury supr. Country Mut. Ins. Co., Chgo., 1952-57, claims mgr., 1957-61, Bloomington, Ill., 1961-69; cons., dir. litigation Country Mut., Country Casualty, Mid-Am., 1969-84; ins. law cons., 1984—; lectr. in field; arbitrator Mut. Casualty, 1965-70. Served to lt. comdr., USN, 1941-45. Mem. ABA, Tex. Bar Assn., Ill. Bar Assn., McLean County Bar Assn., Internat. Assn. Ins. Counsel, Property Loss Bur., Def. Research Inst., Am. Judicature Soc. Republican. Insurance, Personal injury, State civil litigation. Address: 27 LaTeer Dr Normal IL 61761

ROCHELLE, WILLIAMS JENNINGS, JR., lawyer; b. Corsicana, Tex., Aug. 9, 1917. A.B., George Washington U., 1938, J.D., 1940. Bar: D.C. bar 1940, Tex. bar 1941. Partner firm Rochelle & Balzersen (and predecessors), Dallas, 1947—. Contbr. articles to legal jours.; contbg. editor: Collier on Bankruptcy. Mem. Am. Bar Assn., Nat. Bankruptcy Conf., State Bar Tex. Bankruptcy, Oil and gas leasing. Office: Rochelle & Balzersen 1st City Ctr Dallas TX 75201

ROCHKIND, LOUIS PHILIPP, lawyer; b. Miami, Fla., June 25, 1948; m. Rosalind H. Rochkind, July 4, 1971. BA in Psychology cum laude, U. Mich., 1970, JD cum laude, 1974. Bar: Mich. 1974, U.S. Dist. Ct. (ea. dist.) Mich. 1974. Ptnr. Jaffe, Snider, Raitt & Heuer, Detroit, 1974—; adj. prof. law Wayne St. U. Law Sch.; lectr. various profl. assns. and orgns. Assoc. editor U. Mich. Law Rev.; contbr. articles to profl. jours. publs. Mem. adv. bd. Fin. Trans. Inst. of U. Detroit. Mem. Am. Bankruptcy Inst. (bd. dirs.), Comml. Law League (bankruptcy sect. 1981—), Mich. Bar Assn. (chmn. bankruptcy law com. real property law sect. 1982—, governing council real property law sect. 1980—, creditor-debtor law com. of corp., fin. and bus. law sect. 1980—), Detroit Bar Assn. (local rules in bankruptcy subcom. creditor-debtor law sect. 1980—), Phi Kappa Phi. Bankruptcy, Contracts commercial, Consumer commercial. Office: Jaffe Snider Raitt & Heuer 1800 First Nat Bldg Detroit MI 48226

ROCHKIND, MARK HOWARD, lawyer; b. N.Y.C., Aug. 11, 1943; s. Louis Philip and Shirley Freda (Lipkowitz) R.; m. Janet Gay Morris, Apr. 19, 1969; children—Eric Bradley, Keith Ryan. B.S., N.Y.U., 1965; J.D., Rutgers U., 1968. Bar: N.Y. 1969, N.J. 1972. Mem. staff tax dept. Arthur Anderson, N.Y.C., 1968-70; corp. counsel Prel Corp., Saddlebrook, N.J., 1970-73; sole practice, Caldwell, N.J., 1973—. Served to 2d lt. U.S. Army, 1967-75. Mem. N.J. Bar Assn., Essex County Bar Assn., Caldwell C. of C. Club: Rotary. Family and matrimonial, Probate, Real property. Office: 7 Cleveland St Caldwell NJ 07006

ROCHLIN, PAUL R., lawyer; b. Balt., Dec. 14, 1934; s. Jack Ellis and Sara (Levin) R.; m. Lois David, Oct. 25, 1962 (div. 1969); children—Greg, Jennifer; m. Joyce Tretick, July 12, 1973; children—Keith Sopher, Maura Sopher. LL.B., U. Balt., 1958. Bar: Md. 1959, U.S. Dist. Ct. Md. 1959. Assoc. firm Milton Talkin, Balt., 1959-61; assoc. firm Rochlin & Settleman, Balt., 1961-63, ptnr., 1963-78, pres., sr. ptnr. Rochlin & Settleman, P.A., Balt., 1978—. Bd. dirs. Balt. Jewish Council, 1979. Mem. Assn. Trial Lawyers Am., Md. State Bar Assn., Balt. City Bar Assn., Md. Trial Lawyers Assn. Jewish. Clubs: The Suburban, The Center. Personal injury, Workers' compensation, State civil litigation. Office: Rochlin and Settleman PA 110 E Lexington St Baltimore MD 21202

ROCKEFELLER, REGINA STRAZZULLA, lawyer; b. Boston, Mar. 31, 1951; d. Philip and Anne Lenore (Silvestro) Strazzulla; m. Godfrey Anderson Rockefeller Jr., Aug. 3, 1974; children: Victoria Hamilton, Lisa Anderson. Lang. cert., U. Dijon, France, 1970; BA in Polit. Sci. magna cum laude, Tufts U., 1973; JD cum laude, Boston Coll., 1976. Bar: Mass. 1977, Fla. 1977, U.S. Dist. Ct. Mass. 1977. Ptnr. Hutchins & Wheeler, Boston, 1976—; bd. dirs. Strazzulla Bros. Co., Inc., Fort Pierce, Fla. Trustee Waltham (Mass.) Weston Hosp. and Med. Ctr., 1980—; bd. dirs. Hospice West, Inc., Waltham, 1984—. Mem. ABA, Mass. Bar Assn. (chmn. health law sect. 1986—), Fla. Bar Assn., Nat. Health Lawyers Assn. Club: Prouts Neck Country (Maine); Tufts (Boston). Health, General corporate, Administrative and regulatory. Office: Hutchins & Wheeler 1 Boston Pl Boston MA 02108

ROCKEL, JOHN EDWARD, lawyer; b. Cin., Sept. 30, 1944; s. Edwin Louis and Cecilia (Lasita) R.; m. Rita Martinelli, Oct. 10, 1970; children: Brian Louis, Jason Edward, Jennifer Lillian. BS, U. Cin., 1970; JD, No. Ky. State U., 1975. Bar: Ohio 1975, U.S. Dist. Ct. (so. dist.) Ohio 1975, U.S. Ct. Appeals (6th cir.) 1975, U.S. Supreme Ct. 1980. Sole practice Cin., 1980—. Served with USN, 1962-64. Federal civil litigation, State civil litigation, Personal injury. Home: 5851 Rapid Run Cincinnati OH 45238 Office: 5 W 4th Suite 2300 Cincinnati OH 45275

ROCKLEN, KATHY HELLENBRAND, lawyer, banker; b. N.Y.C., June 30, 1951; d. Samuel Henry and Sheila (Kurzrok) Hellenbrand; m. R. Michael Rocklen, Aug. 26, 1972 (div. June 1978). BA, Barnard Coll., 1973; JD magna cum laude, New England Sch. Law, 1977. Bar: N.Y. 1978, U.S. Dist. Ct. (so. and ea. dists.) N.Y. 1982, U.S. Dist. Ct. (no. dist.) Calif. 1985. Assoc. Weiss, Rosenthal, N.Y.C., 1977-79; interpretive counsel N.Y. Stock Exchange, N.Y.C., 1979-81; asst. counsel Bradford Nat. Corp., N.Y.C., 1981-84; asst. v.p. E.F. Hutton & Co. Inc., N.Y.C., 1984, v.p., 1985, 1st v.p., 1986; v.p., gen. counsel S.G Warburg (U.S.A.) Inc., N.Y.C., 1986—. Office mgr. Com. to elect Charles D. Breitel Chief Judge, N.Y., 1973. Named one of Outstanding Young Women in Am., 1976. Mem. ABA, N.Y. Women's Bar Assn., Assn. of Bar of City of N.Y. (second century com. 1982-85, sec. second century com. 1985-86, sex and law com. 1982-85, young lawyers com. 1979-82, corp. law com. 1986—, spl. com. on drugs and law 1986—). Club: Downtown Athletic (N.Y.C.). Avocation: running. General corporate, Securities, Banking. Home: 153-29 82d St Howard Beach NY 11414 Office: SG Warburg (USA) Inc 787 7th Ave New York NY 10019

ROCKWELL, DAVID HOSMER, lawyer; b. Hartford, Conn., Jan. 8, 1944; s. Ford A. and Barbara (Hosmer) R.; m. Nancy Louise Byrd, June 11, 1966; children: Lori Elizabeth, Brian David. BA with honors, U. Kans., 1966; JD cum laude, U. Mich., 1972. Bar: Mo. 1972, Wash. 1977. Assoc. Stinson, Mag & Fizzell, Kansas City, Mo., 1972-77; ptnr. Jones, Grey & Bayley P.S., Seattle, 1977—. Editor notes U. Mich. Law Rev., 1971-72. Served to lt. (j.g.) USN, 1966-69. Mem. Wash. State Bar Assn. (exec. com. real property, probate and trust sect. 1983—, lectr. 1983—, dir. real property council 1985—). Real property, Contracts commercial. Office: Jones Grey & Bayley PS 3600 One Union Sq 600 University Seattle WA 98101

ROCKWELL, MARK PAUL, lawyer; b. Riverside, N.J., Nov. 5, 1957; s. Paul Martin and Catherine Ann (King) R. AB, Lafayette Coll., 1979; JD, Del. Law Sch., 1982. Bar: N.J. 1982, Pa. 1982, U.S. Dist. Ct. N.J. 1982, U.S. Ct. Appeals (3d cir.) 1983. Jud. law clk. Del. Superior Ct., Wilmington, 1982; assoc. Heuser & McDonald, Matawan, N.J., 1983, Rappaport & Rosenberg, Trenton, N.J., 1984-85, Franchino & Lenahan, Somerville, N.J., 1986—. Grantee Ruby Vale found., 1981. Mem. N.J. Def. Assn. Episcopalian. Avocations: saltwater surf fishing, fresh water trout fishing. State civil litigation, Administrative and regulatory, Pension, profit-sharing, and employee benefits. Home: 1506 Jonathan Ct Princeton NJ 08540 Office: Franchino & Lenahan PO Box 977 Somerville NJ 08876

RODDENBERRY, BONNIE LINDQUIST, lawyer; b. Lafayette, Ind., June 26, 1948; d. John Theodore and Evelyn May Lindquist; m. Stephen Keith Roddenberry, June 12, 1971; children: Thomas, David, Samuel. BA, Wellesley Coll., 1970; JD cum laude, Harvard U., 1973. Bar: Fla. 1974, N.Y. 1974, U.S. Ct. Appeals (2d cir., 5th cir., 11th cir.), U.S. Dist. Ct. (so. dist.) Fla., U.S. Dist. Ct. (so. dist.) N.Y. Assoc. Cravath, Swaine & Moore, N.Y.C., 1973-78, Morgan, Lewis & Bockius, Miami, Fla., 1978-80; sole practice Miami, 1980—; co-chmn. corps. com. of Fla. bar., 1981-86. Contbr. chpt. to Florida Corporations, 1985. Mem. Bar of City of N.Y., Dade County Bar Assn., Harvard Law Sch. Assn. Fla. (prs.-elect). Republican. Presbyterian. Clubs: Wellesley of Miami (treas. 1985—); Harvard of Miami (bd. dirs. 1980-86). Avocations: reading, tennis, water skiing. General corporate, Real property, Probate. Office: 14140 SW 69 Ave Miami FL 33158

RODDEWIG, RICHARD JOHN, lawyer; b. Evergreen Park, Ill., May 1, 1948; s. Clair Matthew and Geraldine (Hendrick) R.; m. Noreen Jordan, Aug. 13, 1971; children: Claire, Jordan, Andrew. BA summa cum laude, U. Notre Dame, 1970; JD, U. Chgo., 1974, MA, 1976. Bar: Ill. 1974, U.S. Dist. Ct. (no. dist.) Ill. 1974. Assoc. Ross & Hardies, Chgo., 1973-76; research atty. Northeastern Ill. Planning Commn., Chgo., 1977-78; prin. Roddewig & Assocs., Chgo., 1978—; atty.-cons. Australia, Internat. Comparative Land Use Project, The Conservation Found., Washington, 1974-75; cons. real estate Shlaes & Co., Chgo., 1978—; adj. prof. Governor's State U., Park Forest S., Ill., 1978, Northeastern Ill. U., Chgo., 1979, U. Ill. Sch. Urban Scis., Chgo., 1979-82; lectr. in field. Author: Green Bans: The Birth of Australian Environmental Politics, 1978; co-author: Rehab for Profit: New Opportunities in Real Estate, 1984; contbr. articles to profl. jours. Bd. govs. Landmarks Preservation Council Ill., 1976-79, 82-85, v.p. 1978-79, 83-84, Ill. Hist. Sites Adv. Council, 1979-82, Ill. Gov.'s Adv. Task Force Hist. Preservation, 1984; bd. trustees Ill. Hist. Preservation Agy., 1985—; mem. Gov.'s Task Force on Tourism, Springfield, Ill., 1986—. Recipient Profl. Preservationist of Yr. Chgo. Coordinating Com. on Landmarks, 1985. Mem. ABA (vice-chmn. land use com. 1985-86, chmn. hist. preservation law subcom.), Ill. Bar Assn., Chgo. Bar Assn., Lambda Alpha Internat. (Ely chpt.), Frederick Law Olmsted Soc. Riverside (bd. dirs. 1986—), Phi Beta Kappa. Roman Catholic. Club: Monroe (Chgo.). Avocations: backpacking, skiing. Local government, Real property, Personal income taxation. Home: 118 Scottswood Riverside IL 60546 Office: Shlaes & Co 20 N Michigan Ave Chicago IL 60602

RODDY, VIRGINIA NIEHAUS, lawyer; b. El Paso, Tex., Feb. 3, 1939; d. Frank Henry and Lyla (Kirkpatrick) Niehaus; m. James Charles; children: James Charles Jr., Frank Hardy. BA, Tulane U., JD; student, U. Birmingham, Eng. Bar: La. 1979, U.S. Dist. Ct. (ea., we. and mid. dists.) La., U.S. Ct. Appeals (5th cir.). Ptnr. Phelps, Dunbar, Marks, Claverie and Sims, New Orleans, 1979—. Advisor Jr. League of New Orleans, 1985-87; mem. Tulane Assocs., New Orleans, 1985-87; bd. dirs. La. Nature and Sci. Ctr., 1986—. Recipient Achiever's award Godchaux's, New Orleans, 1985; named Homecoming Chmn. Tulane U., 1985. Mem. La. Bar Assn. (ho. of dels. Orleans Parish), Assn. Women Attys., Counsel for Profl. Women, Fed. Bar Assn. (bd. dirs. New Orleans chpt. 1983-86, sec. 1984-85, treas. 1985-86, chmn. fed. bar seminar 1983-84, 2d v.p. 1986). Episcopalian. Insurance, Federal civil litigation, State civil litigation. Home: 5508 Hurst St New Orleans LA 70115 Office: Phelps Dunbar et al 400 Poydras 30th Floor New Orleans LA 70130

RODENBERG, GEORGE WILLIAM, JR., business law educator; b. Chgo., Dec. 17, 1946; s. George W. Sr. and Rita Ann (Waleske) R.; m. Pok Hui Chong, Sept. 27-1972; 1 child, George W. IV. BA in History, U. Tex., El Paso, 1969; MA in Mus. Sci., Tex. Tech U., 1977, MBA in Internat. Bus., JD, 1981. Bar: Tex. 1981. Researcher Tex. Tech U. Sch. of Medicine, Lubbock, 1977-78; prof. bus. law Ill. Wesleyan U., Bloomington, 1981—. Contbr. articles to profl. jours. Vol. arbitrator Better Bus. Bur. of Cen. Ill., Peoria, 1985—. Served to maj. U.S. Army, 1969-75, Korea. Seminar scholar Southwestern Legal Found., Tex., 1983. Mem. ABA (legal edn. com. 1981-83, uniform comml. code com. 1986—), Am. Bus. Law Assn., Acad. Internat. Bus., Midwest Bus. Law Assn., Midwest Assn of Pre Law Advisors, Am. Legion, Nat. Rifle Assn. (life). Republican. Episcopalian. Avocations: collecting mil. insignia, Lionel trains. Legal education, Private international. Office: Ill Wesleyan U Bloomington IL 61701

RODENBURG, CLIFTON GLENN, lawyer; b. Jamestown, N.D., Apr. 5, 1949; s. Clarence and Dorothy Irene (Peterman) R.; m. Donna Michele Stockman, Mar. 1, 1980. B.S., N.D. State U., 1971; J.D., U. N.D., 1974; M.L.I.R., Mich. State U., 1976. Bar: N.D. 1974, U.S. Dist. Ct. (N.D.) 1974, U.S. Ct. Appeals (8th cir.) 1974, Minn. 1980, U.S. Supreme Ct. 1980, S.D. 1983, Nebr. 1984, U.S. Dist. Ct. (Minn.) 1984, U.S. Dist. Ct. (Nebr.) 1984, Wis. 1985, U.S. Dist. Ct. Wis. 1985, Mont. 1986, U.S. Dist. Ct. (Mont.) 1986. Ptnr., Gackle, Johnson & Rodenburg, Fargo, N.D., 1976—; pres., gen. counsel On The Run, Inc., Fargo, 1980—. Contbg. editor: The Developing Labor Law, 1976-80; drafter N.D. garnishment statutes, 1982. Labor, Consumer commercial.

RODGERS, FREDERIC BARKER, judge, lawyer; b. Albany, N.Y., Sept. 29, 1940; s. Prentice Johnson and Jane (Weed) R.; m. Judy Reed, Feb. 24, 1973. AB, Amherst Coll., 1963; JD, Union U., 1966. Bar: N.Y. 1966, U.S. Ct. Mil. Appeals 1968, Colo. 1972, U.S. Supreme Ct. 1974, U.S. Ct. Appeals (10th cir.) 1981. Chief dep. dist. atty., Denver, 1972-73; commr. Denver Juvenile Ct., 1973-79; mem. Mulligan Reeves Teasley & Joyce, P.C., Denver, 1979-80; pres. Frederic B. Rodgers, P.C., Breckenridge, Colo., 1980—; county judge County of Gilpin, 1987—; presiding mcpl. judge cities of Breckenridge, Blue River, Black Hawk, Central City, Empire, Idaho Springs and Westminster, Colo., 1979—; chmn. com. on mcpl. ct. rules of procedure Colo. Supreme Ct., 1984—. Mem. Colo. Commn. on Children, 1982-85. Served with JAGC, U.S. Army, 1967-72; to maj. USAR, 1972—. Decorated Bronze Star with oak leaf cluster, Air medal. Recipient Spl. Community Service award Colo. Am. Legion, 1979. Mem. ABA, Colo. Bar Assn. (bd. govs. 1986—), Denver Bar Assn. (bd. trustees 1979-82), Continental Divide Bar Assn., First Judicial Dist. Bar Assn., Colo. Mcpl. Judges Assn. (pres. 1986-87), Denver Law Club (pres. 1981-82), Am. Judicature Soc., Marines Meml. Club. Episcopalian. Club: University (Denver). Contbr. articles to profl. jours.. Contracts commercial, Real property, Juvenile. Home: 210 E 4th High St Central City CO 80427-0398 Office: Bank of Breckenridge Bldg 106 N French St Suite 220 Breckenridge CO 80424-0567

RODGERS, JOHN HUNTER, lawyer; b. Lubbock, Tex., Jan. 18, 1944; s. James O'Donnell Rodgers and Dorothy (Ulin) Carpenter; m. Anne C. Smith, Nov. 29, 1969; children; Anne Elizabeth, Catherine Hunter. BA, Tex. A&M, 1966; JD, U. Tex., 1969. Bar: Tex. 1969, U.S. Supreme Ct. 1973. Atty. Southland Corp., Dallas, 1973-79, v.p., gen. counsel, 1979—. Mem. visual arts com. Tex. A&M U., 1985—; bd. dirs. student fund enrichment bd Tex. A&M U., 1986—. Served to capt. U.S. Army, 1969-73, Vietnam. Mem. ABA, Tex. Bar Assn., Dallas Bar Assn., Southwestern Legal Found. (adv. bd. internat. and comparitive law ctr. 1986). Roman Catholic. General corporate, Real property. Office: Southland Corp 2828 N Haskell Ave Dallas TX 75221

RODGERS, PAUL BAXTER, III, lawyer; b. Columbia, S.C., Nov. 7, 1952; s. Paul Baxter Jr. and Marianne (Guerry) R.; m. Fredanel Miller Strickland, Nov. 17, 1978; children: Miriam Guerry, Paul Baxter II. BS in Fin. magna cum laude, U. S.C., 1975; JD, Washington & Lee U., 1978. Bar: S.C. 1978, U.S. Dist. Ct. S.C. 1978, U.S. Ct. Appeals (4th cir.) 1980. Assoc. Robinson, McFadden, Moore and Pope, Columbia, 1978-82; ptnr. Robinson, McFadden, Moore, Pope, Williams, Taylor and Brailsford, Columbia, 1982—. Served to 1st lt. USAR, 1975-77. Mem. ABA, S.C. Bar Assn., Richland County Bar Assn., S.C. Def. Trial Attys. Assn., Phi Beta Kappa, Omicron Delta Kappa. Episcopalian. Clubs: Forest Lake, Tarantella (Columbia). Lodge: Rotary (bd. dirs. Capital club 1987—). Avocations: tennis, golf, jogging. Insurance, Personal injury, Workers' compensation. Home: 739 Hampton Hill Rd Columbia SC 24209 Office: Robinson McFadden Moore et al 1801 Main St Columbia SC 29202

RODGERS, RALPH EMERSON, lawyer; b. Tyler, Tex., July 1, 1954; s. John Wilbur and Margaret Ann (Bray) R.; m. Bonita Marie Groom, Dec. 1, 1975; children: Donna Jo, William Thomas. BA with honors, U. Fla., 1975; JD magna cum laude, U. Miami, 1979. Bar: Tenn. 1979, U.S. Dist. Ct. (ea. dist.) Tenn. 1979, U.S. Ct. Appeals (6th cir.) 1980, U.S. Ct. Appeals (11th cir.) 1981, U.S. Ct. Appeals (5th cir.) 1984, Colo. 1986, U.S. Dist. Colo. 1986. Trial atty. TVA, Knoxville, 1979-86; assoc. Wells, Love & Scoby, Boulder, Colo., 1986—. Mem. editorial bd. U. Miami Law Rev., 1978. Recipient Am. Jurisprudence Book award 1978. Mem. ABA, Am. Corp. Counsel Assn., Colo. Bar Assn., Soc. of Wig and Robe, Tenn. Bar Assn. Republican. Avocations: writing, running, skiing, fishing. Construction, Federal civil litigation, State civil litigation. Home: PO Box 13892 Boulder CO 80308-3892 Office: Wells Love & Scoby 225 Canyon Blvd Boulder CO 80302

RODGERS, RICARDO JUAN (RICK), lawyer; b. Ardmore, Okla., Sept. 25, 1934; s. John Bush and Gladys Louise (James) R.; 1 child, Michelle Xan. B.B.A., U. Okla., 1963, J.D., 1965. Bar: Okla. 1965, U.S. Dist. Ct. (we. dist.) Okla. 1965, U.S. Supreme Ct. 1974. Asst. county atty. Stephens County Duncan, Okla., 1965-66; ptnr. Bennett & Rodgers, Duncan, 1966-74; sr. ptnr., pres. Rodgers & Link, P.C., Duncan, 1974—. Chmn. Duncan United Fund, 1969; trustee Okla. Christian Coll., 1968. Served with USN, 1955-57. Recipient Leadership award Sooner council Girl Scouts U.S., 1979, Disting. Service award Jaycees, 1969. Fellow Okla. Bar Found. (bd. dirs. 1978-83); mem. Okla. Bar Corp. Ins. Co. (trustee), Okla. Bar Assn. (bd. govs. 1977-79), Okla. Trial Lawyers Assn. (bd. dirs.), ABA, Okla. U. Law Sch. Alumni Assn. (bd. dirs. 1973). Mem. Ch. of Christ. Lodge: Elks. Personal injury, Federal civil litigation, State civil litigation. Home: 2206 Carolin Dr Duncan OK 73533 Office: Rodgers & Link Inc PO Box 1228 Duncan OK 73533

RODGERS, SHARON LYNETTE, lawyer; b. Charleston, S.C., July 15, 1956; d. James Alonzo and Gloria Mae (Amsler) R.; m. Frampton Wyman Toole III, Aug. 4, 1979; 1 child, Frampton Wyman IV. BA summa cum laude, U. S.C., 1977, JD cum laude, 1980. Bar: S.C. 1980, U.S. Dist. Ct. S.C. 1981, U.S. Ct. Appeals (4th cir.) 1982. Assoc. Toole & Toole, Aiken, S.C., 1980; in house counsel Graniteville (S.C.) Co., 1980-85, asst. sec., 1985—. mem. bd. trustees HCA Aiken Regional Med. Ctrs., 1982-84, vice chmn. 1984—; sec. Gregg-Graniteville Found., Inc., 1983-85. Mem. ABA, S.C. Bar Assn., Order of the Coif, Order of Wig & Robe, Phi Beta Kappa. Democrat. Presbyterian. Avocations: gardening, reading. General corporate, Pension, profit-sharing, and employee benefits, Labor. Office: Graniteville Co Marshall St Graniteville SC 29829

RODGERS, THOMAS PAUL, lawyer; b. Midland, Tex., May 8, 1950; s. Joseph Paul and Lola Catherine (Thomas) R. BA in English Lit., La. State U., 1971; JD, Rutgers U., 1974. Bar: Pa. 1974, Calif. 1981, U.S. Dist. Ct. (no. dist.) Calif. 1981. Asst. legal officer Internat. Union for Conservation of Nature and Natural Resources, Bonn, Fed. Republic Germany, 1974-75; atty. enforcement div. N.J. Dept. of Environ. Protection, Trenton, 1976-77, U.S. EPA, Phila., 1978-79; sole practice San Francisco, 1981—; cons. U.S. Govt., San Francisco, 1985-86. Author poetry; contbr. articles to profl. jours. Bd. dirs. Golden Gate Performing Arts, Inc., San Francisco, 1980-82. Mem. ABA, Calif. Bar Assn. (outstanding pro bono atty. 1984, 85), San Francisco Bar Assn. (outstanding pro bono atty. 1984, 85), Bay Area Lawyers for Individual Freedom, Internat. Counsel of Environ. Law. Democrat. Lodge: Lions (bd. dirs. Castro chpt.). Avocations: weight lifting, exercise, piano, travel, gardening. General practice, Probate, Landlord-tenant. Office: 460 Noe St San Francisco CA 94114

RODKEY, FREDERICK STANLEY, JR., lawyer; b. Urbana, Ill., Oct. 25, 1930; s. Frederick Stanley and Temple (Ryan) R.; m. Suzanne Ooms, June 15, 1963; children—Gretchen, Geoffrey. B.A., Stanford U., 1953; postgrad. Boalt Hall Sch. Law, U. Calif., 1954; J.D., Chgo.-Kent Coll. Law, 1956. Bar: Ill. 1957. Atty., Chgo. Title & Trust, 1956-57; assoc. Newton, Wilhelm & Kennedy, Chgo., 1957-59; atty. Household Fin. Corp., Chgo., 1959-64; counsel Res. Ins. Co., Chgo., 1964-66; ptnr. Crandall & Rodkey, Evanston, Ill., 1966-67; sole practice, Freeport and Lena, Ill., 1967—; atty. Village of German Valley, Ill., 1973—, Village of Ridott, Ill., 1974—, Village of Lena, 1977—, Village of Cedarville, Ill., 1979—; spl. asst. atty. gen. State of Ill., 1973-76; asst. pub. defender Stephenson County, Ill., 1971—; atty. Lena Park Dist., 1977—. Chmn. Central com. Stephenson County Republican Party, 1972-74. Mem. Ill. Bar Assn., Chgo. Bar Assn., Stephenson County Bar Assn., Chgo.-Kent Alumni Assn., (past treas.), Stephenson County Hist. Soc., Stanford Alumni Assn., Alpha Sigma Phi, Pi Sigma Alpha, Nu Beta Epsilon. Mem. United Ch. of Christ. Clubs: Lions (past pres.), Men's Garden Club of Freeport (past pres.), Elks. Probate, Consumer commercial, Criminal. Home: 1126 S Benson Blvd Freeport IL 61043 Office: 200 Post Office Bldg Freeport IL 61032

RODOWSKY, LAWRENCE FRANCIS, state justice; b. Balt., Nov. 10, 1930; s. Lawrence Anthony and Frances (Gardner) R.; m. Colby Fossett, Aug. 7, 1954; children—Laura Rodowsky Ramos, Alice Rodowsky-Seegers, Emily, Sarah, Gregory, Katherine. A.B., Loyola Coll., Balt., 1952; LL.B., U. Md., 1956. Bar: Md. 1956. Ct. crier, law clk. U.S. Dist. Ct. Md., 1954-56; asst. atty. gen. State of Md., 1960-61; asso., partner firm Frank, Bernstein, Conaway & Goldman, Balt., 1956-79; assoc. judge Ct. Appeals Md., Annapolis, 1980—; mem. rules com. Ct. Appeals Md., 1969-80; lectr., asst. instr. U. Md. Law Sch., 1958-68, 87—; reporter jud. dept. Md. Constl. Conv. Commn., 1966-67. Chmn. Gov. Md. Commn. Racing Reform, 1979. Fellow Am. Coll. Trial Lawyers; mem. ABA, Md. Bar Assn., Balt. Bar Assn. Roman Catholic. Jurisprudence. Home: 4306 Norwood Rd Baltimore MD 21218 Office: Clarence M Mitchell Jr Courthouse Room 620 Baltimore MD 21202

RODRIGUEZ, ARIEL ANTONIO, judge; b. Havana, Cuba, Nov. 8, 1947; came to U.S., 1960; s. Laurentino C. and Josefina Maria Rodriguez; m. Lourdes Valdes-Munoz, Nov. 20, 1983; 1 child, Gabriel Antonio. B.A., Rutgers Coll., 1970, J.D., 1973. Bar: N.J. 1973, U.S. Dist. Ct. N.J. 1973,

U.S. Supreme Ct. 1977. Asst. prosecutor Hudson County, Jersey City, 1973-76; ptnr. Iglesias & Rodriguez, Union City, N.J., 1976-84; sr. trial counsel, Firemans Fund Ins. Co., 1984-85; judge, Superior Ct. N.J., 1985—; mem. ethics com. N.J., 1980-82, mem. model civil charges com., 1982-83. Author: Constitutional Study of Equatorial Guinea, 1973. Mem. Assn. Trial Lawyers Am., N.J. Bar Assn., Hispanic Bar Assn. N.J. (trustee 1983-84), North Hudson Lawyers Club (pres. 1984-85), Hudson County Bar Assn. Republican. Methodist. State civil litigation, Personal injury, Family and matrimonial. Home: 317-77 St North Bergen NJ 07047 Office: Superior Ct of NJ 595 Newark Ave Jersey City NJ 07306

RODRIGUEZ, JOSE GABRIEL, lawyer; b. Havana, Cuba, June 14, 1945; came to U.S., 1949; s. Jose Gabriel and Ada Carmen Rodriguez; m. Donna K. Winters, Sept. 10, 1965 (div. Apr. 1983); children: Tracy Anne, Kerry Aileen. BA, Fla. Atlantic U., 1971; JD, U. Fla., 1976. Bar: Fla. 1976, U.S. Dist. Ct. (so. dist.) 1977, U.S. Ct. Appeals (5th cir.) 1977, U.S. Ct. Appeals (11th cir.) 1981. Assoc. Adams & Coogler, West Palm Beach, Fla., 1976-77, Montgomery & Lytal, West Palm Beach, 1977-79, Johnson & Bakst, West Palm Beach, 1979-81; sole practice West Palm Beach, 1981—. Chmn. Hispanic Human Resources Council, West Palm Beach, 1978-81; v.p. Community Action Council, West Palm Beach, 1980-84. Mem. ABA, Acad. Fla. Trial Lawyers, Assn. Trial Lawyers Am., Nat. Assn. Criminal Def. Lawyers. Republican. Methodist. Avocations: fishing, scuba diving. Personal injury, Criminal. Home: 115 Tacoma Ln Palm Beach Shores FL 33405 Office: 1801 Australian Ave S West Palm Beach FL 33409

RODRIGUEZ, JOSEPH H., federal judge; b. 1930; m. Barbara Marriner. AB, La Salle Coll., 1955; JD, Rutgers U., 1958. Assoc. Brown, Connery et al, Camden, N.J., 1959-82; judge U.S. Dist. Ct. N.J., Camden, 1985—; instr. law Rutgers U., N.J., 1972-82; chmn. State Commn. of Investigation, N.J., 1974-79. Chmn. State Bd. of Higher Edn., N.J., 1971-73. Office: 201 U S Courthouse 401 Market St Camden NJ 08101 *

RODRIGUEZ-DIAZ, JUAN E., lawyer; b. Ponce, P.R., Dec. 27, 1941; s. Juan and Auristela (Diaz-Alvarado) Rodriguez de Jesus; m. Sonia de Hostos-Anca, Aug. 10, 1966; children: Juan Eugenio, Jorge Eduardo, Ingrid Marie Rodriguez. BA, Yale U., 1963; LLB, Harvard U., 1966; LLM in Taxation, N.Y.U., 1969. Bar: N.Y. 1968, P.R. 1970. Assoc. Baker & McKenzie, N.Y.C., 1966-68; assoc. McConnell, Valdes, Kelley, Griggs, Sifre & Ruiz-Suria, San Juan, P.R.; undersec. Dept. Treasury P.R., 1971-73; mem. Sweeting, Pons, Gonzalez & Rodriguez, 1973-81; sole practice, Hato Rey, P.R., 1981—; dir. Ochoa Indsl. Sales Corp., Camaleglo Corp., Ochoa Telecom, Inc., Las Americas Trust Co., Ital/Americas Foods Corp., Paramount Foods Corp. Bd. govs. Acqueduct and Sewer Authority P.R., 1979-84; mem. adv. com. collective bargaining negotiation of P.R. Elec. Power Authority to Gov. P.R., 1977-78; bd. govs. P.R. council Boy Scouts Am., mem. transition com., 1984-85. Mem. ABA, N.Y. State Bar Assn., P.R. Bar Assn. Roman Catholic. Clubs: AFDA, San Juan Yacht. General corporate, Corporate taxation, Banking. Home: Calle Fresno #1 Urb San Patricio Caparra Heights PR 00921 Office: Suite 920 Chase Bldg 416 Ponce de Leon Ave Hato Rey PR 00918

RODRIQUEZ, JANET LOIS, lawyer; b. Trinidad, Colo., Mar. 19, 1954; d. Philemon and Louisa Eleanor (Gonzales) R. BA, Colo. State U., 1976; JD, U. Colo., 1980. Bar: Colo. 1981, U.S. Dist. Ct. Colo. 1981. Staff atty. Legal Aid, Ft. Collins, Colo., 1981-84; sole practice Ft. Collins, 1984—. Precinct committeeman Dems., Ft. Collins, 1984—; bd. dirs. Multiple Sclerosis, Ft. Collins, 1983. Mem. ABA, Colo. Bar Assn., Larimer County Bar Assn. (chmn. young lawyers sect. 1984-85, bd. dirs. young lawyers sect. 1984—, chmn. continuing legal edn. com. 1985—, bench/bar com. 1985-86), Larimer County Women's Bar Assn. (sec. 1986—). Roman Catholic. Avocations: gardening, fishing, classical ballet. State civil litigation, Family and matrimonial, General practice. Office: 116 N College Suite 1 Fort Collins CO 80524

ROE, RAMONA JERALDEAN, lawyer, state official; b. Gassville, Ark., May 27, 1942; d. Roy A. and Wanda J. (Finley) R. B.A., U. Ark., 1964; J.D., U.Ark.-Little Rock, 1976. Bar: Ark. 1976, U.S. Dist. Ct. (ea. and we. dists.) Ark. 1979. Mng. ptnr. Roe & Hunt, Rogers, Ark., 1977-78; sole practice, Rogers, Ark., 1978-81, Little Rock, 1982-84; assoc. Richardson & Richardson, Little Rock, 1981-82; dep. exec. dir. Ark. Workers' Compensation Commn., Little Rock, 1984—. Contbr. articles to profl. jours. Recipient Am. Jurisprudence awards U. Ark. Sch. Law, 1971-72, Corpus Juris Secundum award, 1971, Hornbook award, 1971, Am. Judicature award, 1972. Mem. AAUW (treas. 1980), Bus. and Profl. Women (chpt. treas.-v.p. 1978-80), Delta Theta Phi (clk. of rolls 1973-74, tribune 1974-75), Mensa, Lambda Tau, Internat. Platform Assn. Methodist. Workers' compensation. Office: Ark Workers' Compensation Commn Justice Bldg Little Rock AR 72201

ROEDEL, JOHN KENNEDY, JR., lawyer; b. Denver, Aug. 5, 1937; s. John Kennedy and Teresa (Morrow) R.; m. Carolyn Virginia Miller, June 19, 1965 (div. Oct. 1986); children—Kevin, Edward, Thomas. B.S. in Chem. Engring. cum laude, U. Notre Dame, 1959; J.D. cum laude, St. Louis U., 1969. Bar: Mo. 1969, U.S. Dist. Ct. (we. dist.) Mo. 1969, U.S. Dist. Ct. (ea. dist.) Mo. 1972, U.S. Ct. Appeals (8th cir.) 1973, U.S. Ct. Appeals (7th cir.) 1976, U.S. Supreme Ct. 1977, U.S. Ct. Customs and Patent Appeals 1982. Chem. Engr. Monsanto Co., Sauget, Ill., 1959-69; assoc. Koenig, Senniger, Powers & Leavitt, St. Louis, 1969-74, ptnr., 1974-79; ptnr. Senniger, Powers, Leavitt & Roedel, St. Louis, 1979—; instr. patent law St. Louis U. Law Sch., 1975. Trustee St. Louis Community Coll., 1977-83, pres., 1981-82. Mem. ABA (patent sect., chmn. environ. law com. 1981-82, chmn. small bus. com. 1982-84, amicus briefs com. 1984-85, resolution com. 1986—), Bar Assn. Met. St. Louis (chmn. environ. projects com. 1972-74, chmn. patent sect. 1978-79), Am. Inst. Chem. Engrs. Republican. Roman Catholic. Club: Mo. Athletic (St. Louis). Patent, Trademark and copyright, Antitrust. Office: 611 Olive St Saint Louis MO 63101

ROEGER, WILLIAM COLEY, JR., lawyer; b. Doylestown, Pa., Apr. 15, 1947; s. William Coley and Alice Virginia (McKeown) R.; m. Ellen R. Ball, Apr. 4, 1970; children: William C. III, Matthew Barton. BS in Physics, Muhlenberg Coll., 1969; JD, Dickinson U., 1973. Bar: Pa. 1973, U.S. Dist. Ct. (ea. dist.) Pa. 1981. Assoc. Pa. Power and Light Co., Allentown, 1973-75; assoc., pres. Donald B. Smith and Assoc., Perkasie, Pa., 1975-86; pres. Roeger & Walker, Perkasie, 1986, Roeger, Walker & Bahls, Perkasie, 1986—. Contbr. articles to profl. jours. Mem. council Peace Luth. Ch., Perkasie, 1977-83; exec. com. Bucks County Rep. Com., Pa., 1978—. Served to capt. Pa. Air N. G., 1970-83. Mem. ABA, Pa. Bar Assn., Bucks County Bar Assn., Pa. Trial Lawyers Assn. (bd. govs. 1980—, exec. com. 1984—), Jaycees (named one of Outstanding Young Men in Am.), Porsche Club Am., Tau Kappa Epsilon. Lutheran. Avocations: tennis, woodworking. State civil litigation, Family and matrimonial, Personal injury. Home: 239 Evergreen Dr Perkasie PA 18944 Office: Roeger Walker & Bahls 210 W Walnut St PO Box 218 Perkasie PA 18944

ROEGNER, HAROLD EDWARD, lawyer; b. Paterson, N.J., Sept. 25, 1901; s. Edward W. and Mary Ella (Stewart) R.; m. Doris Trautman, Nov. 1933 (dec. Nov. 1955). BA, Columbia U., 1928; LLB, N.Y. Law Sch., 1931. Bar: N.Y. 1933. Sole practice Goshen, N.Y., 1931—; asst. dist. atty. County of Orange, N.J., 1944-46; atty. Village of Goshen, N.Y., 1948-62; justice Town of Goshen, 1958-68. Republican. Presbyterian. Lodge: Masons (master 1942-44). General practice. Home: 317 Main St Goshen NY 10924 Office: 138 Main St Goshen NY 10924

ROEHL, JERRALD J(OSEPH), lawyer; b. Austin, Tex., Dec. 6, 1945; s. Joseph E. and Jeanne Foster (Scott) R.; m. Nancy J. Meyers, Jan. 15, 1977; children: Daniel J., Katherine C., J. Ryan, J. Taylor. BA, U. N.Mex., 1968; JD, Washington and Lee U., 1971. Bar: N.Mex. 1972, U.S. Ct. Appeals (10th cir.) 1972, U.S. Supreme Ct. 1977. Practice of Law, Albuquerque, 1972—; pres. Jerrald J. Roehl & Assocs., 1976-84, Roehl & Henkel, P.C., 1984—. lectr. to profl. groups; real estate developer, Albuquerque. Bd. dirs. Rehab. Ctr. of Albuquerque, 1974-78; mem. assocs. Presbyn. Hosp. Ctr., Albuquerque, 1974-82. Recipient award of recognition State Bar N.Mex., 1975, 76, 77. Mem. ABA (award of achievement Young Lawyers div. 1975, council econs. of law practice sect. 1978-80, exec. council Young Lawyers div. 1979-81, fellow div. 1984—, council tort and ins. practice sect. 1981-83), N.Mex. Bar Assn. (pres. young lawyers sect. 1975-76), Albuquerque Bar Assn. (bd. dirs. 1976-79), N.Mex. Def. Lawyers Assn. (pres. 1983-84), Sigma Alpha Epsilon, Sigma Delta Chi, Phi Delta Phi. Roman Catholic. Clubs: Albuquerque Country, Albuquerque Petroleum. Bd. advs. ABA Jour., 1981-83; bd. editors Washington and Lee Law Rev., 1970-71. Insurance, Federal civil litigation, General corporate. Home: 4000 Aspen Ave NE Albuquerque NM 87110 Office: Roehl & Henkel 300 Central Ave SW 3d Central Plaza Suite 2500 E Albuquerque NM 87102

ROESS, MARTIN JOHN, lawyer, banker; b. Ocala, Fla., Dec. 18, 1907; s. Martin John and Mary (Anderson) R.; m. Alice Guion, Nov. 21, 1981; children—Diane Celeste, Robert Thornton, Martin John, Mary Susan, Morgen Leslie, Sherry Allison, Lori. A.B., Cornell U., 1930, LL.D., 1931. Bar: Fla. 1932, D.C. 1938, U.S. Supreme Ct. 1935. Assoc. Rogers & Towers, Jacksonville, Fla., 1931-34; chief counsel Large Scale Housing div. FHA, Washington, 1934-37, dist. dir., Jacksonville, 1947-48; assoc. gen. counsel Internat. Paper & Power Co., N.Y.C., 1937-38; practice, St. Petersburg, Fla., 1938—; gen. counsel A. Lloyd Goode Contracting Co., Washington, 1938-43; pres., gen. counsel Builders Mortgage Corp., St. Petersburg, 1948-51; assoc. atty. Holland & Runyon, St. Petersburg, 1948-51; acting dir. Shelter div. Fed. CD Authority, Washington, 1951-52; owner, operator Martin Roess Co., Jacksonville, 1952-55; judge Fla. 6th Jud. Cir., 1967-68; owner, chmn. Am. Nat. Bank, South Pasadena, St. Petersburg, 1963-74; organizer, chmn. Am. Nat. Bank, Tyrone, St. Petersburg, 1972-74; chmn. Am. Nat. Bank, Clearwater, Fla., 1955-74; organizer, chmn. N.Am. Mortgage Corp., St. Petersburg, 1955-74; chmn., pres. N. Am. Ins. Agy., Inc., St. Petersburg, 1955-84; owner, dir. Lawyers Land Title Corp., St. Petersburg, 1958-85; founder, chmn., pres. Guaranty Savs. and Loan Assn., St. Petersburg, 1960-82; founder, pres. Internat. Travel Assoc., Inc., St. Peterburg, 1976—, Tour Hosts of Fla., Inc., 1977—; of counsel Jacobs, Robbins-Gaynor, P.A. Past bd. dirs. Fla. Council of 100; past chmn. Oceanography Com. Fla., Mem. ABA, St. Petersburg Bar Assn., Fla. Bar Assn., Fla. Bankers Assn., Am. Bankers Assn., Mortgage Bankers Assn., St. Petersburg Bd. Realtors, Fla. Savs. and Loan League, U.S. League Savs. Assns., U.S. C. of C., St. Petersburg C. of C., Ind. Bankers Fla. (past dir.), Cornell Law Assn., Phi Beta Kappa, Phi Delta Phi. Clubs: University (Washington); Cornell (N.Y.C.); River (Jacksonville); Yacht (St. Petersburg); Centre (Tampa). Banking, Legislative. Office: PO Box 40070 Saint Petersburg FL 33743

ROESSLER, P. DEE, lawyer, municipal judge; b. McKinney, Tex., Nov. 4, 1941; d. W.D. and Eunice Marie (Medcalf) Powell; m. George L. Roessler, Jr., Nov. 16, 1963; (div. Dec. 1977); children—Laura Diane, Trey. Student Austin Coll., 1960-61, 62-64, Wayland Bapt. Coll., 1961-62; B.A., U. West Fla., 1968; postgrad. East Tex. State U., 1975, U. Tex.-Dallas, 1977; J.D., So. Meth. U., 1982. Bar: Tex. 1982, U.S. Dist. Ct. (ea. dist.) Tex. 1983, U.S. Dist. Ct. (no. dist.) Tex. 1983. Tchr., Van Alstyne Ind. Sch. Dist., Tex., 1968-69; social worker Dept. Social Services, Fayetteville, N.C., 1971-73, Dept. Human Services, Sherman and McKinney, Tex., 1973-79, 81; mem. firm Abernathy & Roeder, McKinney, Tex., 1982-85, Ronald W. Uselton, Sherman, 1985-86, program coordinator Collin County Community Coll., McKinney, 1986—; judge City of McKinney Mcpl. Ct., 1986—; mem. Collin County Shelter for Battered Women, 1984-86, chmn., 1984-85; v.p. Collin County Child Welfare Bd., 1985—, pres. 1986 ; Republican jud. candidate Collin County, 1986; chmn. bd. Tri County Consortium Mental Health Mental Retardation, 1984-85; mem. Tex. Area 5 Health System Agy., 1979; mem. Collin County Mental Health Adv. Bd., 1978-79. Mem. Collin County Bar Assn., Collin County Women's Bar (chmn. 1984-85). Baptist. Avocations: dancing, tennis, golf, reading, writing. Family and matrimonial, Criminal, State civil litigation. Home: 2118 Chippendale St McKinney TX 75069 Office: Collin County Community Coll 2200 University McKinney TX 75069

ROETHE, JAMES NORTON, lawyer; b. Milw., Jan. 27, 1942; s. Arthur Frantz and Bess Irma (Norton) R.; m. Nita May Dorris, July 15, 1967; children—Melissa Dorris, Sarah Rebecca. B.B.A., U. Wis.-Madison, 1964, J.D., 1967. Bar: Wis. 1967, Calif. 1968, U.S. Dist. Ct. (No. dist.) Calif. 1971, U.S. Ct. Claims 1977, U.S. Ct. Appeals (9th cir.) 1971. Assoc., Pillsbury, Madison & Sutro, San Francisco, 1971-77, ptnr., 1978—; staff atty. Commn. on CIA Activities within U.S., Washington, 1975. Editor: Africa, 1967; editor-in-chief Wis. Law Rev., 1966-67. Bd. dirs. Orinda Assn. (Calif.), 1984-85, pres. 1986. Served to lt. USNR, 1967-71. Mem. Wis. Bar Assn., Calif. Bar Assn., Bar Assn. San Francisco, Phi Kappa Phi, Order of Coif. Republican. Clubs: Orinda Country; Stock Exchange (San Francisco). Federal civil litigation, State civil litigation, Public utilities. Home: 36 Fallen Leaf Terr Orinda CA 94563 Office: Pillsbury Madison & Sutro PO Box 7880 225 Bush St San Francisco CA 94104

ROETHER, ROBERT HENRY, II, lawyer; b. Urbana, Ill., May 11, 1944; s. Robert H. and Eleanor E. (Edwards) R.; m. Barbara Sharon Yellen, Aug. 11, 1968; children: Geoffrey Alan, Andrew Winston, Matthew Brant. BS, Mich. State U., 1966; JD, Wayne State U., 1969. Bar: Mich. 1969, U.S. Dist. Ct. (ea. dist.) Mich. 1971, U.S. Ct. Appeals (6th cir.) 1975, U.S. Supreme Ct. 1983. Sole practice Birmingham, Mich. Personal injury.

ROETTGER, CLYDE EDWARD, JR., lawyer; b. Richmond, Va., Jan. 13, 1950; s. Clyde Edward and Rose Marie (Sullivan) R.; m. Barbara Henrietta Anneliese Banze, June 2, 1979; 1 child, David William Schaefer. B.A., U. Va., 1971; J.D., U. Richmond, 1975, M.A., 1981. Bar: Va. 1976. Adminstrv. asst. Va. Gen. Assembly, Richmond, 1973-76, Va. Ho. Appropriations Com., 1976-77; legal counsel, research Ed Lane for Atty. Gen., 1977; enrolling clk. Va. Ho. of Delegates, 1978; city atty. City of Colonial Heights, Va., 1978—; legal counsel Dist. 19 Mental Health Bd., 1986—; cons. in field. Chmn. Chesterfield County Democratic Com., 1976-78; mem. Va. Dem. State Central Com., 1975; co-chmn. Chesterfield County Bicentennial Commn., 1975-76; active Colonial Heights Hist. Soc. Mem. ABA, Nat. Inst. Mcpl. Law Officers, Local Govt. Attys. Va., Petersburg Bar Assn., Colonial Heights Bar Assn. (sec. 1986—), Chesterfield Bar Assn., U. Va. Alumni Assn. Episcopalian. Lodge: Masons. Local government. Home: 140 Carroll Ave Colonial Heights VA 23834 Office: City of Colonial Heights 1507 Boulevard Colonial Heights VA 23834

ROETTGER, NORMAN CHARLES, JR., federal judge; b. Lucasville, Ohio., Nov. 3, 1930; s. Norman Charles and Emma Eleanora R.; children: Virginia, Peggy. B.A., Ohio State U., 1952; LL.B. magna cum laude, Washington and Lee U., 1958. Bar: Ohio 1958, Fla. 1958. Assoc. Frost & Jacobs, Cin., 1958-59; asso. firm Fleming, O'Bryan & Fleming, Ft. Lauderdale, Fla., 1959-63; partner Fleming, O'Bryan & Fleming, 1963-69, 71-72; dep. gen. counsel HUD, Washington, 1969-71; judge U.S. Dist. Ct., So. Dist. Fla., Ft. Lauderdale, 1972—. Served to lt. (j.g.) USN, 1952-55; to capt. Res. 1972. Mem. ABA, Fed., Fla., Broward County bar assns., Am. Judicature Soc., Order of Coif, Omicron Delta Kappa, Kappa Delta Rho. Presbyterian. Clubs: Masons; Coral Ridge Yacht (Ft. Lauderdale). Office: US Courthouse 299 E Broward Blvd Fort Lauderdale FL 33301 *

ROFF, ALAN LEE, lawyer; b. Winfield, Kans., July 2, 1936; s. Roy Darlus and Mildred Marie (Goodale) R.; m. Molly Gek Neo Tan, July 21, 1980: 1 child: Cynthia Lee Edwards. BA with honors and distinction, U. Kans., 1964, JD with distinction, 1966. Bar: Okla. 1967. Staff atty. Phillips Petroleum Co., Bartlesville, Okla., 1966-75, sr. atty., 1976-85, sr. counsel, 1986—; bd. dirs. Singapore Chems. Phillips Petroleum, Singapore. Editorial bd. Kans. Law Rev., 1965-66. Precinct com. man Rep. Party, Lawrence, Kans., 1963-64; assoc. justice Kans. U. Chancery Club; mem. Kans. U. Young Reps. Elizabeth Reeder scholar U. Kans., 1965-66, Eldon Wallingford award, 1964-66. Mem. ABA, Okla. Bar Assn., Washington County Bar Assn., Order of Coif, Phi Alpha Delta, Pi Sigma Alpha. Mem. First Christian Ch. Club: Phoenix (Bartlesville) (bd. dirs. 1985-86, gen. counsel 1986—). Lodge: Masons. Avocation: travel. Private international, General corporate, Contracts commercial. Office: 1209 Adams Bldg 4th and Keeler Bartlesville OK 74004

ROGAN, PATRICK GOODE, lawyer; b. New Haven, May 4, 1944; s. Richard Robert and Mary (Goode) R.; m. Rilla L. Rothwell, Dec. 20, 1967; children: Kevin, Megan, Brendan. BA, Claremont McKenna Coll., 1966; JD, Loyola U., Los Angeles, 1972. Bar: Calif. 1972, U.S. Dist. Ct. (cen. dist.) Calif. 1972, U.S. Dist. Ct. (so. dist.) Calif. 1984, U.S. Dist. Ct. (no. dist.) Calif. 1986. Trial atty. pub. defender's office Los Angeles County, 1972-78; assoc. Lillick, McHope & Charles, Los Angeles, 1979-80, ptnr., 1980—. Served with U.S. Army, 1967-69, Vietnam. Mem. ABA (torts and ins. practice sect.), Assn. Trial Lawyers Am., Calif. Bar Assn. (disciplinary examiner 1974—), Assn. So. Calif. Def. Counsel, Los Angeles County Bar Assn. (conf. del. exec. com. 1985—, trial lawyer sect. 1978—, pub. affairs com. 1979—, legis. rev. com. 1984, lectr. 1979—). Democrat. Roman Catholic. Club: Los Angeles Athletic, University (Los Angeles). Avocations: snow skiing, surfing, windsurfing. Criminal, Federal civil litigation, Personal injury. Office: Lillick McHose & Charles 725 S Figueroa Los Angeles CA 90017-2513

ROGEL, TODD STEPHEN, lawyer; b. Newark, Nov. 11, 1952; s. Max and Terese Rich (Grosman) R.; m. Mary Bryan Hurst, June 17, 1978. B.A. with honors, U. N.C., 1975; J.D. cum laude, Georgetown U., 1978. Bar: Va. 1978, Fla. 1979, U.S. Dist. Ct. (so. dist.) Fla. 1982, N.C. 1982, U.S. Ct. Appeals (5th cir.) 1981, U.S. Ct. Appeals (11th cir.) 1982. Law clerk to presiding justice U.S. Ct. Appeals (5th cir.), 1978-79; assoc. Greenberg, Traurig et al, Miami, Fla., 1979-80; assoc. Fromberg, Fromberg, Gross, Shore, Lewis & Rogel, P.A., Miami, 1980-82, ptnr., 1982—; ptnr. Clark & Rogel, Sylva, N.C., 1982. Contbr. articles to profl. jours. Mem. Dade County Bar Assn. (mem. gen. jurisdiction com. 1981—, med. profession liaison com. 1982—), N.C. Bar Assn. (mem. litigation sect. 1982-83), ABA (mem. litigation sect., tort and ins. practice sect., civil practice rules com. 1983, automobile law com. 1985), Fla. Bar (mem. civil procedure rules com. 1983—, health law com. 1983—, trial lawyers sect. 1983—), Va. Bar Assn., N.C. State Bar Assn., N.C. Acad. Trial Lawyers Assn. (mem. litigation sect.), Assn. Trial Lawyers Am., Acad. Fla. Trial Lawyers, Am. Judicature Soc., Internat. Assn. Jewish Lawyers and Jurists. Democrat. Jewish. Lodges: Rotary (South Miami); Optimists (Sylva, N.C.); Lions (Ackerman, Miss.). Personal injury, State civil litigation, Insurance. Home: 13611 SW 110th Terr Miami FL 33188 Office: Fromberg Fromberg Gross et al 420 S Dixie Hwy 3d Floor Coral Gables FL 33143

ROGERS, DAVID H., lawyer; b. Hempstead, N.Y., May 2, 1929; s. Ralph Ashdown and Gladys Dorothy (Hollister) R.; m. Constance Noel Decker, Aug. 15, 1953; children: Barry, Bruce, Carol. BA, Harvard U., 1951, LLB, 1954. Bar: N.Y. 1956, Calif. 1957, U.S. Dist. Ct. (no. dist.) Calif., U.S. Ct. Appeals (9th cir.). Law clk. to presiding justice U.S. Ct. Appeals (9th cir.), San Francisco, 1957-58; ptnr. Hardin & Fletcher, Oakland, Calif., 1958-68; dir. India Peace Corps., New Delhi, 1968-73; chmn. Micronesian Claims Commn., Siapan, Mariana Islands, 1974-76; gen. counsel Fgn. Claims Settlement Commn., Washington, 1976—. Served with U.S. Army, 1954-56. Public international. Office: Foreign Claims Settlement Commn 111 20th NW Washington DC 20579

ROGERS, EDWARD LEE, lawyer; b. Portland, Oreg., Dec. 11, 1931; s. John Carlos and Ruth Viola (Jorgenson) R.; m. Ailene Chartier Kane, Nov. 17, 1961; children: Ruth Anne, John Edward, Helen Chartier, Daniel Lee. BS, U. Oreg., 1954, LLB, 1956; LLM in Taxation, NYU, 1959. Bar: Oreg. 1956, D.C. 1960, U.S. Dist. Ct. D.C. 1960, U.S. Ct. Appeals (D.C. cir.) 1960, U.S. Ct. Appeals (4th cir.) 1961, U.S. Ct. Claims 1967, U.S. Ct. Appeals (1st and 10th cirs.) 1967, U.S. Supreme Ct. 1967, U.S. Ct. Appeals (9th cir.) 1968, U.S. Ct. Appeals (7th cir.) 1969, Maine 1973, N.Y. 1973, U.S. Ct. Appeals (8th cir.) 1973, U.S. Ct. Appeals (11th cir.) 1986. Atty., advisor U.S. Tax Ct., Washington, 1957-61; atty. appellate sect., tax div. U.S. Dept. Justice, Washington, 1961-69; gen. counsel Environ. Def. Fund, East Setauket, N.Y., 1969-73; asst. atty. gen. EPA, Maine, 1973-76; counsel Natural Resources Council, Augusta, Maine, 1976-79; prin. dep. asst. sec. U.S. Army, Washington, 1979-81, acting asst. sec., 1981; sole practice Washington, 1981—; adj. prof. law Bowdoin Coll., Brunswick, Maine, 1974-75, 79, Antioch Sch. Law, Washington, 1983. Author: (with others) Environmental Litigation, 1972; also articles. Pres. Profl. Tenants Assn. Inc., Washington, 1982—, McLean (Va.) High Sch. Student-Parents Tchrs. Assn., 1982-83; trustee United Meth. Ch., East Pittston, Maine, 1977-79. Mem. Environ. Law Assocs., Environ. Law Inst. Democrat. Avocations: camping, canoeing, swimming, chess, ping-pong. Administrative and regulatory, Federal civil litigation, Environment. Home: 6601 Jerry Pl McLean VA 22101 Office: 1765 P St Suite 2 Washington DC 20036

ROGERS, ERNEST MABRY, lawyer; b. Demopolis, Ala., Sept. 22, 1947; s. James B. and Ernestine B. (Brewer) R.; m. Jeanne Edwards, Dec. 15, 1979; children—Gilbert B., Katherine B., Mary C. B.A., Yale U., 1969; J.D., Harvard U., 1974. Bar: Ala. 1974, U.S. Dist. Ct. (no. dist.) Ala. 1975, U.S. Ct. Appeals (5th cir.) 1975, U.S. Ct. Appeals (11th cir.) 1981, U.S. Supreme Ct. 1981, U.S. Ct. Claims 1983. Law clk. to presiding justice U.S. Dist. Ct. no. dist. Ala., 1974-75; ptnr. Bradley, Arant, Rose & White, Birmingham, Ala., 1981—. Contbr. articles to profl. jours. Episcopalian. Lodge: Kiwanis. Construction, Federal civil litigation, State civil litigation. Office: Bradley Arant Rose & White 1400 Park Pl Tower Birmingham AL 35203

ROGERS, GORDON DEAN, lawyer; b. Rochester, N.Y., Jan. 19, 1952; s. Elmer G. and Ruby H. (Hamrick) R.; m. Mary E. Moroney, Sept. 24, 1983. BA, SUNY-Oswego, 1973; JD, U. Miami, Fla., 1977. Bar: Fla. 1977, U.S. Dist. Ct. (so. dist.) Fla. 1977, U.S. Ct. Appeals (5th cir.) 1978, U.S. Ct. Appeals (11th cir.) 1981, U.S. Supreme Ct. 1984. Ptnr. Muller, Mintz, Kornreich, Caldwell, Casey, Crosland & Bramnick, P.A., Miami, 1977—. Baptist. Civil rights, Labor, Local government. Office: Muller Mintz Kornreich et al 200 S Biscayne Blvd Suite 3600 Miami FL 33131

ROGERS, HARVEY D., lawyer; b. Krosniewice, Poland, Jan. 2, 1946; s. Bernard and Rose (Zaltztrager) R.; m. Maria C. Rogers, Dec. 22, 1978; children: Daniel, Randall, Rachel, Amanda. BA, CCNY, 1968, MA, 1970; JD, U. Miami, 1974. Bar: Fla., U.S. Dist. Ct. (no. and so. dists.) Fla., U.S. Ct. Appeals (5th and 11th cirs.), U.S. Supreme Ct. Sole practice Miami, Fla., 1974—; arbitrator Am. Arbitration, Miami, 1975—. Fellow Fla. Criminal Defense Attys.; mem. ABA, Lawyers Title, Fla. Trial Lawyers Assn., Phi Alpha Delta. Avocations: history, sports, fishing. General practice, Criminal, State civil litigation. Home: 13104 SW 108th Ave Miami FL 33176

ROGERS, HELEN SFIKAS, lawyer; b. Wheeling, W.Va., Sept. 25, 1953; d. John Simon and Stella (Theodore) S.; m. Charles Edward Rogers, Oct. 30, 1976; 1 child, Sara Anastasia. BA, Vanderbilt U., Nashville, 1974; JD, YMCA Night Sch., Nashville, 1980. Bar: Tenn. 1980, U.S. Dist. Ct. (mid. dist.) Tenn. 1980, U.S. Tax Ct. 1981, U.S. Ct. Appeals (6th cir.) 1982, U.S. Supreme Ct. 1983. Ptnr. Watts, Lewis, Jones & Rogers, Nashville, 1980-84, Link, Porter, Jones & Rogers, Nashville, 1984—. Vol. atty. YWCA Legal Clinic, Nashville, 1981—. Democrat. Greek Orthodox. State civil litigation, Federal civil litigation, Personal injury. Home: 5504 Deer Way Dr Nashville TN 37211 Office: 401 Church St Nashville TN 37219

ROGERS, JAMES DEVITT, judge; b. Mpls., May 5, 1929; s. Harold Neil and Dorothy (Devitt) R.; m. Leanna Morrison, Oct. 18, 1968. AB, Dartmouth Coll., 1951; JD, U. Minn., 1954. Bar: Minn. 1954. Assoc. Johnson & Sands, Mpls., 1956-60; sole practice Mpls., 1960-62; judge Mpls. Municipal and Dist. Ct., 1959—; mem. faculty Nat. Judicial Coll. Bd. dirs. Mpls. chpt. Am. Red Cross, chmn. service to mil. families and vets. com. Served to sgt. U.S. Army, 1954-56. Mem. ABA (chmn. nat. conf. spl. ct. judge, spl. com. housing and urban devel. law, traffic ct. program com., chmn. criminal justice sect., jud. adminstrn. div.). Club: Mpls. Athletic. Office: 1856-C Govt Ctr Minneapolis MN 55487

ROGERS, JAMES THOMAS, lawyer; b. Denver, Oct. 3, 1941; s. John Thomas and Elizabeth (Milligan) R. J.D., U. Wis., 1966. Bar: Wis. 1966, U.S. Tax Ct. 1976, U.S. Ct. Claims, 1975, U.S. Ct. Customs and Patent Appeals, 1975, U.S. Supreme Ct. 1973. Chmn., Madison (Wis.) Legal Aid Soc., 1965-66; dist. atty. Lincoln County (Wis.), 1967, 69-73; spl. dist. atty. pro tem Oneida County (Wis.), 1972, Price County (Wis.), 1972-76, Lincoln County (Wis.), 1976-84; spl. city atty. City of Wausau (Wis.), 1973, 74, 77; ptnr. Rogers & Bremer, Merrill, Wis., 1973—. Chmn. Judiciary Com., N.E. Crime Control Commn., 1971-72. Chmn., Lincoln County Republican Com., 1971-73. Mem. State Bar Wis. (spl. com. on prosecutorial improvements 1983—), Lincoln County Bar Assn. (pres. 1969-70), Wis. Dist. Attys. Assn. (life), ABA (drunk driving com. of criminal justice sect., vice chmn. asset and investment mgmt. com. sec. econs. of law practice, marriage and cohabitation com. family law sect., def. services commn. criminal law sect.), Nat. Assn.

Criminal Def. Lawyers, Assn. Trial Lawyers Am., Wis. Acad. Trial Lawyers (bd. dirs. 1985—), Tex. Trial Lawyers Assn., N.Y. State Trial Lawyers Assn., Personal Injury Lawyers Assn., Wis. Assn. Criminal Def. Lawyers (sec. 1986-87, pres.-elect 1987—, bd. dirs. 1986—). Club: Wausau. Criminal, Personal injury, Labor. Home: 1408 E 8th St Merrill WI 54452 Office: Rogers & Bremer 120 S Mill St Merrill WI 54452-0438

ROGERS, JEFFREY LANGSTON, lawyer, educator; b. Washington, July 26, 1944; s. William Pierce and Adele (Langston) R.; m. Kristine Olson, Sept. 18, 1971; children: Karin, Tyler. AB, Dartmouth Coll., 1966; student, Harvard U., 1966-67; JD, Yale U., 1973. Bar: Oreg. 1973, U.S. Dist. Ct. Oreg. 1975, U.S. Ct. Appeals (9th cir.) 1975. Trial atty. Pub. Defender's Office, Portland, Oreg., 1973-75; asst. atty. U.S. Dept. Justice, Portland, 1975-77, 81-85; ptnr. Ransom, Rogers & Blackman, Portland, 1978-80; atty. City of Portland, 1985—; part-time faculty Lewis and Clark Law Sch., Portland, 1977—; pro-tempore judge county dist. Ct., Portland, 1979-80; chmn. Oreg. Psychiat. Security Rev. Bd., Portland, 1979-81; asst. prof. to assoc. prof. dept. psychiatry Oreg. Health U., Portland, 1981—. Contbr. articles on law, psychiatry and medicine to profl. jours. Chmn. Sudden Infant Death Project Adv. Bd., Portland, 1980-82; bd. dirs. Hospice House, Portland, 1982-83. Served to lt. JAGC USNR, 1968-70, Vietnam. Mem. Multnomah Bar Assn., ACLU of Oreg. (lawyer's com.). Avocations: photography, camping, hiking, skiing. Local government, Health, Criminal. Home: 356 SW Kingston Ave Portland OR 97201 Office: City Atty's Office 315 City Hall Portland OR 97204

ROGERS, JOHN ELLSWORTH, lawyer; b. Shamrock, Tex., Sept. 17, 1942; s. Theodore R. and Virginia (Harvey) R.; children: Jennifer Leah, Daniel Gordon; m. Ma Luisa Gutierrez Zamora, Jan. 3, 1987. AB, Harvard U., 1965; MIA, Columbia U., 1968, JD, 1969. Bar: N.Y. 1971. Assoc. Milbank, Tweed, Hadley & McCloy, N.Y.C., 1969-82; sr. counsel Bank of Am. Nat. Trust and Savs. Assn., N.Y.C., 1982-86, Bank of Am. Inc., Mexico City, 1986—. bd. dirs. N.Y. chpt. Soc. for Internat. Devel. Mem. ABA, Assn. of the Bar of the City of N.Y. (chmn. com. on Inter-Am. Affairs 1984-86). Clubs: Harvard (N.Y.C. and Mexico City). Avocations: tennis, theater, cinema, photography. Banking, Private international, General corporate. Home: Calle Pirineos 615, 11000 Colonia Lomas de Chapultepec Mexico Office: Bank of Am Nat Trust & Savs Assn, Paseo de la Reforma 116, 06600 Mexico DF Mexico

ROGERS, JOHN T. MILBURN, lawyer; b. Chattanooga, May 31, 1949; s. John W. and Tina (Williams) R.; m. Donna Crosby, Feb. 15, 1969; children—Trenny, Jenny, Emily, Shelley. B.S., U. Tenn., 1971, J.D., 1974. Bar: Tenn. 1974, U.S. Dist. Ct. (ea. dist.) Tenn. 1975, U.S. Ct. Appeals (6th cir.) 1984; diplomate Civil Trial Advocate Nat. Bd. Trial Advocacy, Washington, 1983, Criminal trial advocate, 1985. Founder, sr. ptnr. Rogers, Laughlin, Nunnally & Hood, Greeneville, Tenn., 1974—. Vice chmn. Greene County Dems., Greeneville, 1982; county fin. chmn. Gore for Senate, 1984. Named Outstanding Young Man of Greene County, Greeneville Jaycees, 1979; mem. Tenn. Trial Lawyers Assn. (life, pres. 1984-85), Tenn. Assn. Criminal Def. Lawyers (bd. dirs. 1981-85), Tenn. Bar Assn. (ho. dels. 1979-85), Upper Eastern Tenn. Trial Lawyers Assn. (pres. 1981-82), Nat. Assn. of Criminal Def. Lawyers, Am. Trial Lawyers Assn., ABA, Greene County Bar Assn. (pres. 1978-79), Lawyers Involved For Tenn. (founder). Baptist. Club: Gold Star (founder). Lodges: Elks, Moose, Exchange Club. Personal injury, Criminal, General practice. Home: 1211 Upland Ave Greeneville TN 37743 Office: Rogers Laughlin Nunnally & Hood 100 S Main St Greeneville TN 37743

ROGERS, JUDITH W., state judge. Judge U.S. Ct. Appeals (D.C. cir.), Washington. Office: US Ct Appeals DC cir 500 Indiana Ave NW Washington DC 20001 *

ROGERS, LAURENCE STEVEN, lawyer; b. N.Y.C., Jan. 19, 1950; s. Henry and Frances (Kanarek) R.; m. Iris S. Rosen, July 2, 1977; 1 child, Matthew Benjamin. BSEE with distinction, Cornell U., 1972; JD, NYU, 1975. Bar: N.Y. 1976, U.S. Dist. Ct. (ea. and so. dists.) N.Y. 1976, U.S. Ct. Appeals (Fed. cir.) 1983, U.S. Patent and Trademark Office. Ptnr. Fish & Neave, N.Y.C., 1986—. Mem. ABA, N.Y.C. Bar Assn., N.Y. Patent, Trademark and Copyright Law Assn., Fed. Cir. Bar Assn., Phi Kappa Phi, Eta Kappa Nu, Tau Beta Pi. Patent, Trademark and copyright, Federal civil litigation. Home: 15 Aspen Rd Scarsdale NY 10583 Office: Fish & Neave 875 3d Ave New York NY 10022

ROGERS, MATTHEW STEPHEN, lawyer; b. N.Y.C., Dec. 4, 1952; s. James Andrew and Kathleen Winifred (Murphy) R. BA, Marist Coll., 1974; JD, U. Bridgeport, 1980. Bar: N.J. 1980, U.S. Dist. Ct. N.J. 1980. Asst. prosecutor Bergen County, Hackensack, N.J., 1981-84; assoc. Contant, Contant, Schuber, Scherby & Atkins, Hackensack, 1984; atty. Bd. Adjustment, Ramsey, N.J., 1985—. Mem. exec. com. Bergen County Dem., Hackensack, 1985-86. Mem. ABA, Bergen County Bar Assn., Assn. Trial Lawyers Am., N.J. Fedn. Planning Ofcls. Roman Catholic. State civil litigation, Criminal, Local government. Office: Contant Contant Schuber Scherby & Atkins 33 Hudson St Hackensack NJ 07601

ROGERS, RICHARD DEAN, judge; b. Oberlin, Kans., Dec. 29, 1921; s. William Clark and Evelyn May (Christian) R.; m. Helen Elizabeth Stewart, June 6, 1947; children—Letitia Ann, Cappi Christian, Richard Kurt. B.S., Kans. State U., 1943; J.D., Kans. U., 1947. Bar: Kans. bar 1947. Partner firm Springer and Rogers (Attys.), Manhattan, Kans., 1947-58; instr. bus. law Kans. State U., 1948-52; partner firm Rogers, Stites & Hill, Manhattan, 1959-75; gen. counsel Kans. Farm Bur. & Service Cos., Manhattan, 1960-75; judge U.S. Dist. Ct., Topeka, Kans., 1975—. City commnr., Manhattan, 1950-52, 60-64, mayor, 1952, 64, county atty., Riley County, Kans., 1954-58, state rep., 1964-68, state senator, 1968-75; pres. Kans. Senate, 1975. Served with USAAF, 1943-45. Decorated Air medal, Dfc. Mem. Kans., Am. bar assns., Beta Theta Pi. Republican. Presbyterian. Club: Masons. Jurisprudence. Office: 410 Federal Bldg 444 S E Quincy St Topeka KS 66683

ROGERS, RICHARD MICHAEL, judge; b. Lorain, Ohio, Dec. 8, 1944; s. Paul M. and Lillie (Morris) R.; m. Sophia Lydia Wagner, Dec. 23, 1967; children: L. Danielle, David K., Marisa D., Matthew D. BA, Ohio No. U., 1966, JD, 1972. Bar: Ohio 1972, U.S. Dist. Ct. (no. dist.) Ohio 1973. Assoc. Martin, Hall & Rogers, Marion, Ohio, 1972-76; ptnr. Rogers & Rogers, Marion, 1976-81; asst. law dir., police prosecutor City of Marion, 1973-74, pub. defender, 1975; asst. county prosecutor Marion County, 1976-81; village solicitor, La Rue, Ohio, 1976-81; judge Marion Mcpl. Ct., 1982—. Mem. Marion Active 20/40 Service Club, 1973-84, treas., 1976-80, bd. dirs., 1976-84, pres., 1980-81; chmn. bd. dirs., pres. and co-founder Marion Area Driver Re-edn. Project, 1974-81; pres. Big Bros./Big Sisters Marion County, 1986-87, bd. dirs., 1984—; mem. sch. bd. St. Mary's Elem. Sch., 1985—, v.p., 1986; bd. dirs. Marion Cath. High Sch. Endowment Fund, 1986—. Served with U.S. Army, 1968-69. Recipient Superior Jud. Service award Ohio Supreme Ct., 1982-85. Mem. Ohio State Bar Assn. (jud. adminstrn. and legal reform com. 1982—, modern cts. com. 1982-85), Marion County Bar Assn. (pres. 1985-86), Mcpl. Judges Assn. (jury instrn. com. 1982-85, legis. com. 1985—, bd. dirs. 1987—), Ohio Jud. Conf. (gen. adminstrn. legal reform com. 1984—), Ohio Bar Coll., Delta Theta Phi, Sigma Pi. Republican. Methodist. Avocations: golf, scuba diving. Criminal, General practice, Judicial administration. Home: 310 Edgefield Blvd Marion OH 43302 Office: Marion Mcpl Ct 233 W Center St Marion OH 43302

ROGERS, SHARYN GAIL, lawyer; b. DuBois, Pa., Aug. 5, 1948; d. John and Betty (Heberling) Rogers; 1 dau., Kristyn Leigh. B.A., SUNY-Buffalo, 1970, M.A., 1972, J.D., 1977. Bar: N.Y. 1978. Law clk. to county atty. Erie County, Buffalo, N.Y., 1977, asst. dist. atty., 1978-79; assoc. firm Damon & Morey, Buffalo, 1979—. Mem. ABA, N.Y. State Bar Assn., Erie County Bar Assn. Methodist. Personal injury, State civil litigation, Insurance. Office: Damon & Morey 1600 Main Pl Tower Buffalo NY 14202

ROGERS, TERRY LEE, lawyer; b. Colby, Kans., June 4, 1954; s. Wendell Arthur and Tressie Margaret (Bailey) R.; m. m. Paula Jane Fisher, Nov. 25, 1972 (div. Jan. 1979); m. Sheri Everts, Aug. 14, 1982; children: Justin Everts, Elizabeth Everts. BA magna cum laude, Washburn U., 1976, JD, 1979. Bar: Kans. 1979, U.S. Dist. Ct. Kans. 1979, U.S. Ct. Appeals (5th cir.) 1983. Ptnr. Morgan and Rogers, Oberlin, Kans., 1979-84; sole practice Oberlin, 1984—; atty. City of Oberlin, 1980—, County of Decatur, Oberlin, 1985—, Unified Sch. Dist. #316, Rexford, Kans., 1982—. Elected county atty. Decatur County, 1985. Mem. Kans. Bar Assn., Phi Kappa Phi. Avocations: baseball, basketball, tennis, biking. State civil litigation, Federal civil litigation, Personal injury. Office: 612 East Ash Oberlin KS 67749

ROGERS, THOMAS CHARLES, lawyer; b. Bryn Mawr, Pa., Oct. 26, 1952; s. Thomas James and Regina Alice (Conroy) R.; m. Maura-Ellen Kelly, Jan. 15, 1983; 1 child, Megan Kelly. BS with distinction, Pa. State U., 1975; MA, Villanova U., 1978, JD cum laude, 1982. Bar: Pa. 1982, U.S. Dist. Ct. (ea. dist.) Pa. 1982, U.S. Ct. Appeals (3d cir.) 1982, N.J. 1983, U.S. Dist. Ct. N.J. 1983. Assoc. White & Williams, Phila., 1982—. Mem. Pa. Bar Assn. (real property probate and trust sect.), N.J. Bar Assn. (real property probate and trust sect.), Phila. Bar Assn. (real property com., sales conveyancing and title ins. sect.). Democrat. Roman Catholic. Real property, Banking. Office: White & Williams 1234 Market St Philadelphia PA 19107

ROGERS, THOMAS SYDNEY, lawyer; b. New Rochelle, N.Y., Aug. 19, 1954; s. Sydney Michael Rogers Jr. and Alice (Meier) Steinhardt; m. Sylvia Texon, Oct. 9, 1983; 1 child, Robert Samuel. BA, Wesleyan U., 1975; JD, Columbia U., 1979. Bar: N.Y. 1980, U.S. Dist. Ct. (so. and ea. dists.) N.Y. 1980, U.S. Ct. Appeals (D.C. cir.) 1981. Legis. asst. to Congressman Richard Ottinger U.S. Ho. Reps., Washington, 1975-76, sr. counsel subcom. telecommunications, 1981-86; assoc. Lord, Day & Lord, N.Y.C., 1979-81; v.p. policy planning and bus. devel. Nat. Broadcasting Co., Inc., N.Y.C., 1987—; mem. Arlington (Va.) County Cable TV Pub. Access Corp., 1984—; lectr. in field. Judge Nat. Competition on Cable TV Pub. Access programming, 1986. Named one of Outstanding Young Men in Am., 1985. Mem. N.Y. State Bar Assn. Legislative, Communications. Home: 17 Pine Ridge Rd Larchmont NY 10538 Office: NBC Inc 30 Rockefeller Plaza Room 626 New York NY 10112

ROGERS, W. SHERMAN, lawyer, legal educator; b. Washington, Aug. 2, 1951. BA summa cum laude, Oakwood Coll., 1973; JD, Howard U., 1976; LLM in Labor Law, George Washington U., 1981. Bar: D.C. 1977, Ala. 1977, U.S. Dist. Ct. D.C. 1979, U.S. Ct. Appeals (D.C. cir.) 1979, U.S. Ct. Appeals (2d, 4th and 10th cirs.) 1980, U.S. Ct. Appeals (5th and 11th cirs.) 1981, U.S. Supreme Ct. 1986, U.S. Dist. Ct. (no. dist.) Ala. 1987. Research asst. internat. affairs div. Communication Satellite Corp., 1975; Reginald Heber Smith fellow Legal Aid Soc. of Birmingham (Ala.), Inc., 1976-77; vis. lectr. in law Miles Coll. Sch. of Law, Birmingham; staff atty. Birmingham (Ala.) Area Legal Services Corp., 1977-78; sole practice Washington, 1979; atty., advisor EEOC, Washington, 1979-83; assoc. prof. law Thurgood Marshall Sch. of Law, 1983—; vis. assoc. prof. law Howard U., 1986—. Named one of Outstanding Young Men in Am.,1983, 85. Mem. ABA, Fed. Bar Assn., Nat. Bar Assn., Ala. Trial Lawyers Assn., Nat. Assn. Securities Dealers, Thurgood Marshall Sch. of Law Alumni Assn. (lectr. 1985), Phi Delta Phi. Home: 503 Foxglove Dr Missouri City TX 77489 Office: Thurgood Marshall Sch of Law PO Box 11453 Washington DC 20008

ROGERS, WILLIAM BRITTON, lawyer; b. Carlsbad, N.Mex., Sept. 18, 1930; s. William B. and Mabel (Patrick) R.; m. Joanne Harper, Aug. 31, 1955 (div. Jan. 1958). B.A., U. Okla., 1952, LL.B., 1955. Bar: U.S. Ct. Appeals (10th cir.) 1957, Okla. 1960, U.S. Dist. Ct. (no., ea. and we. dist.) Okla. 1960, U.S. Supreme Ct. 1978. Assoc. Ames, Daugherty, Bynum & Black, Oklahoma City, 1958-60; ptnr., Ames, Daugherty, Bynum, Black & Rogers, Oklahoma City, 1960-84, William B. Rogers & Assocs., 1984—; gen. counsel ACLU of Okla., 1982, pres., 1983. Served to capt. USAF, 1955-57. Mem. ABA, Okla. Bar Assn., Oklahoma County Bar Assn., Assn. Trial Lawyers Am., Okla. Assn. Def. Counsel. Democrat. Federal civil litigation, State civil litigation, Civil rights. Home: 7004 N Roff Oklahoma City OK 73116

ROGOFF, MARC JEFFREY, lawyer; b. Rahway, N.J., Sept. 2, 1953; s. Martin and Ivy (Winn) R. BS, Monmouth Coll., 1975; JD, George Mason U., 1981. Bar: N.J. 1981, U.S. Dist. Ct. N.J. 1985, U.S. Supreme Ct. 1985. Assoc. Dato, Kracht & Gill, Woodbridge, N.J., 1981-85; ptnr. Gill & Rogoff, Woodbridge, 1985—. Bd. dirs. Jewish Community Ctr., Edison, N.J., 1982—; vol. atty. Middlesex County Legal Services Corp., 1984—; pres. bd. trustees Wyndmoor Condominium Assn., Woodbridge, 1985-86. Mem. ABA, N.J. Bar Assn., Middlesex County Bar Assn., Am. Trial Lawyers Assn., Middlesex County Trial Lawyers Assn., Tau Kappa Epsilon (bd. dirs. 1985-86), Delta Theta Phi. Democrat. Jewish. Avocations: skiing, basketball, softball. Personal injury, Family and matrimonial, Criminal. Office: Gill & Rogoff 100 W Pond Rd Woodbridge NJ 07095

ROGOVIN, LAWRENCE H., lawyer; b. N.Y.C., June 10, 1932; s. Abraham and Laura (Kohn) R.; m. Saundra Schwartz, Aug. 11, 1957; children—Jayne Lina, Wendy Renee, Evan Lewis. B.S. in Econs., U. Pa., 1953; LL.B. cum laude, NYU, 1956. Bar: N.Y. 1956, Fla. 1971. Dep. asst. atty. gen State of N.Y., 1956-57, asst. atty. gen., 1960-61; assoc. Fields, Zimmerman, Klopper, Skodnick & Segall, Queens, N.Y., 1961-62; assoc. Squadron, Gartenberg, Ellenoff & Plesent and predecessors, N.Y.C., 1962-67, ptnr., 1967-72; sole practice, Miami, Fla., 1972-74; ptnr. Squadron, Ellenoff, Plesent & Lehrer, N.Y.C., 1974-75; assoc. Cohen, Angel & Feinberg, North Miami, Fla., 1975-78; ptnr. Cohen, Angel & Rogovin, North Miami, 1978-82; ptnr. Cohen, Rogovin, Reed & Ivans, Miami, 1982-83. Served to 1st lt. JAGC USAFR, 1957-60. Recipient NYU Founders Day award, 1956. Mem. ABA, Fla. Bar Assn., Assn. Trial Lawyers Am., Acad. Fla. Trial Lawyers, Fed. Bar Assn., North Dade Bar Assn. Real property, Federal civil litigation, General practice. Home: 19160 NE 19th Pl North Miami Beach FL 33179 Office: 1799 NE 164th St Beach FL 33162

ROGOVIN, MITCHELL, lawyer; b. N.Y.C., Dec. 3, 1930; s. Max Shea and Sayde (Epstein) R.; m. Sheila Ann Ender, Jan, 31, 1954; children: Lisa Shea, Wendy Meryl, John Andrew. AB, Syracuse U., 1951; LLB, U. Va., 1954; LLM, Georgetown U., 1959. Bar: Va. 1953, D.C. 1968, U.S. Tax Ct., U.S. Ct. Appeals (1st, 2d, 4th, 5th, 9th, D.C. and fed. cirs.), U.S. Supreme Ct. Chief counsel IRS, Washington, 1964-66; asst. atty. gen. U.S. Dept. Justice, Washington, 1966-69; ptnr. Arnold & Porter, Washington, 1964-76, Rogovin, Huge & Lenzner, Washington, 1976—; spl. counsel CIA, 1975-76; bd. dirs. nuclear regulation com. Spl. Inquiry into 3 Mile Island, 1979-80. Gen. counsel John Anderson Pres. Campaign, 1980. Served to capt. USMC, 1954-58. Mem. Ctr. for Law and Social Policy (chmn. bd. dirs.), Council on Fgn. Relations, The Wilderness Soc. (governing bd.). Federal civil litigation, Personal income taxation, Criminal. Home: 3226 Volta Pl Washington DC 20007 Office: Rogovin Huge & Lenzner 1730 Rhode Island Ave Washington DC 20036

ROHM, BENITA JILL, lawyer; b. Altoona, Pa., Aug. 28, 1953; s. Clayton Benson and Betty Jean (Shaffer) R. BS, Carnegie-Mellon U., 1975, MS, 1976; JD, Seton Hall U., 1979. Bar: N.J. 1979, U.S. Ct. Appeals (3d cir.) 1979; U.S. Patent and Trademark Office. Patent atty. legal staff Bell Telephone Labs., Murray Hill, N.J., 1975-79; litigation atty. Hopgood, Calimafde, Kalil, Blaustein & Judlowe, N.Y.C., 1979-82; sole practice N.Y.C., 1982-84; ptnr. Rohm & Monsanto, Cranford, N.J., 1984—. Mem. ABA, Am. Intellectual Property Law Assn. Club: Cranford Coll. Women's. Avocation: music. Patent, Trademark and copyright. Office: Rohm & Monsanto 512 Springfield Ave Cranford NJ 07016

RÖHM, EBERHARD HEINRICH, lawyer; b. Munich, Germany, Nov. 16, 1940; came to U.S., 1970, naturalized, 1977. JD, U. Heidelberg-U. Bonn, Fed. Republic Germany, 1968, Fordham U., 1976. Bar: Fed. Republic Germany 1973, N.Y. 1975; U.S. Dist. Ct. (so. dist.) N.Y. 1975, U.S. Ct. Appeals (2d cir.) 1975, U.S. Tax Ct. 1976, U.S. Supreme Ct. 1982. Prin. Law Offices Röhm Internat., P.C., N.Y.C., 1975—. Contbr. many articles and lectures on internat. pvt. and Am. corp. law to profl. jours. Founding dir., sec. German Forum, N.Y., German Sch. N.Y. Mem. ABA, N.Y. State Bar Assn., Westchester County Bar Assn., Assn. Bar City N.Y., Internat. Bar Assn., Am. Arbitration Assn. (arbitrator 1976—), N.Y. Fgn. Lawyers Assn. (chmn. 1974-83), German Am. Law Assn. (bd. dirs. 1977-81), Am. Soc. Internat. Law, Am. Fgn. Law Assn., Consular Law Soc., Explorers Club, Deutscher Verein (bd. dirs. N.Y.C. 1981-84). Private international, General corporate, Real property. Home: 485 Park Ave New York NY 10022 Office: Law Offices Röhm Internat PC 767 Fifth Ave New York NY 10153

ROHRBACH, WILLIAM JOHN, JR., lawyer; b. Milw., Aug. 27, 1946; s. William John and Mary Ellen (Shutzman) R.; m. Kathy M. Cherek, Jan. 27, 1968; children—Jennifer, Anne, Ryan. Student St. Norberts Coll., 1964-67; B.A., Marquette U., 1968; J.D., Baylor U., 1973. Bar: Tex. 1973, U.S. Dist. Ct. (so. dist.) Tex. 1974, U.S. Ct. Appeals (5th and 11th cirs.) 1981. Ptnr. Sullins, Johnston Rohrbach & Magers, Houston, 1976—. State civil litigation, Contracts commercial, Real property.

ROHRER, DEAN COUGILL, lawyer; b. Indpls., Jan. 25, 1940; s. William Jay and Frances (Cougill) R.; m. Christina Marie Scheele, Dec. 20, 1969; children—Jonathan William, Mary Kirstin, Jay Andrew. Student U. Edinburgh (Scotland), 1960-61, U. South Australia, 1964; A.B., Union Coll., 1962; LL.B., U. Va., 1966. Bar: N.Y. 1966, U.S. Dist. Ct. (so. dist.) N.Y. 1969, U.S. Ct. Appeals (2d cir.) 1968, Conn. 1974, U.S. Dist. Ct. (ea. dist.) N.Y. 1975, U.S. Dist. Ct. Conn. 1975. Assoc. Winthrop, Stimson, Putnam & Roberts, N.Y.C., 1966-68, Simpson Thacher & Bartlett, N.Y.C., 1969-71; asst. U.S. atty. U.S. Atty.'s Office, N.Y.C., 1971-73; sr. atty. GTE Corp., Stamford, Conn., 1973-76, asst. gen. counsel, 1976-84, v.p., assoc. gen. counsel telephone operating group, 1984—. Trustee Pound Ridge Land Conservancy, N.Y., 1986—; coach Bedford Youth Soccer Club, N.Y., 1982-86; pres. Pound Ridge Elem. Sch. Assn., N.Y., 1983-84; mem. council on ministries Pound Ridge Community Ch., 1984. Mem. ABA, N.Y. State Bar Assn., Conn. Bar Assn., Westchester Fairfield Corp. Counsel Assn., Stamford Darien Bar Assn. Clubs: Royal Ocean Racing (London), Storm Trysail, Larchmont Yacht. Federal civil litigation, General corporate, Public utilities. Home: Woodland Rd Pound Ridge NY 10576 Office: GTE Corp One Stamford Forum Stamford CT 06904

ROHRMAN, DOUGLASS FREDERICK, lawyer; b. Chgo., Aug. 10, 1941; s. Frederick Alvin and Velma Elizabeth (Birdwell) R.; m. Susan Vitullo; children—Kathryn Anne, Elizabeth Clelia. A.B., Duke U., 1963; J.D., Northwestern U., 1966. Bar: Ill. 1966. Legal coordinator Nat. Communicable Disease Center, Altanta, 1966-68; assoc. Keck, Mahin & Cate, Chgo., 1968-73, ptnr., 1973—; exec. v.p., dir. Kerogen Oil Co., 1967—. Vice chmn., commr. Ill. Food and Drug Commn., 1970-72. Served as lt. USPHS, 1966-68. Mem. Am., Chgo. (chmn. com. on food and drug law 1972-73), 7th Circuit bar assns., Am. Soc. Law and Medicine, Selden Soc. Democrat. Episcopalian. Clubs: Legal, Metropolitan; River; Wigmore; Washington Duke. Co-author: Commercial Liability Risk Management and Insurance, 2 vols., 1978, 1986. Contbr. articles on law to profl. jours. Contracts commercial, Food and drug, Insurance. Home: 520 Brier St Kenilworth IL 60043 Office: 8300 Sears Tower Chicago IL 60606

ROJ, WILLIAM HENRY, lawyer; b. Phila., Mar. 29, 1949; s. Joseph S. and Mary B. (Schmidt) R.; m. Mary Lynn Durham, Dec. 20, 1969; children: Wesley Durham, Douglas Durham. BA, Western Md. Coll., 1970; MA in Econs., Duke U., 1971; JD, U. Va., 1975. Bar: Ohio 1975. Assoc. Jones, Day, Reavis & Pogue, Cleve., 1975-82, ptnr., 1983—; sec. Austin Powder Corp., Cleve., 1984—, WJD Corp, Coeburn, Va., 1985—, bd. dirs. Trustee Austin Powder Found., Cleve., 1984—. Served to 1st lt. U.S. Army, 1970-71. Nat. Def. Fellow Duke U., 1970. General corporate, Private international, Banking. Office: Jones Day Reavis & Pogue 1700 Huntington Bldg Cleveland OH 44115

ROJAS, JOSE IGNACIO, lawyer; b. La Habana, Cuba, Jan. 14, 1957; s. Fred A. and Teresa de Jesus (Hernandez) R.; m. Diane Virginia Perry, Sept. 5, 1981. Student, U. Miami, 1974-76; BA, U. Fla., 1978; JD, U. Miami, 1981. Bar: Fla. 1981, U.S. Dist. Ct. (so. dist.) Fla. 1981. Assoc. Cuadrado & Sosby, Miami, Fla., 1981-83, Fromberg, Fromberg, Gross, Shore, Lewis & Rogel, P.A., Miami, 1983—. Speaker (TV program) Legal Vision, 1985; articles and comments editor jour. Lawyer of Ams., 1981. Mem. Spanish Am. League Against Discrimination, Miami, 1985—; pres. Kendale Homeowners Assn., Miami, 1986-87, bd. dirs., 1985—. Mem. Acad. Fla. Trial Lawyers (civil rules com. 1985—), Assn. Trial Lawyers Am., Dade County Trial Lawyers Assn., Dade County Bar Assn., Cuban Am. Bar Assn., Fla. Bar (chmn. subcom. info. exchange computer law com. 1985—, editor newsletter 1986, 87), Order of Barristers. Republican. Roman Catholic. Avocations: snow skiing, racquetball. Personal injury, Computer, State civil litigation. Office: Fromberg Fromberg Gross Shore Lewis & Rogel PA 420 S Dixie Hwy 3rd Floor Coral Gables FL 33146

ROLF, RAMON FREDERICK, JR., lawyer; b. Bloomington, Ind., Oct. 17, 1950; s. Ramon F. and Dorothy L. (Connor) R.; m. Carolee Trapp, Aug. 18, 1979; 1 child, Christopher C. BBA, Western Mich. U., 1973; JD, Detroit Coll. of Law, 1977. Bar: Mich. 1977, U.S. Dist. Ct. (so. dist.) Mich. 1977. Revenue agt. IRS, Detroit, 1973-75; tax staff Arthur Young and Co., Detroit, 1977-79; ptnr. Bower, Rogers & Rolf, Midland, Mich., 1979-82, Currie & Kendall, Midland, 1982—; pres., bd. dirs Northeastern Mich. Estate Planning Council, Saginaw, 1985. Treas., bd. dirs. Midland Gladwin Mental Health Bd., Midland, 1981-85; pres. bd trustees. Meml. Presbyn. Ch., Midland, 1985. Mem. ABA, State Bar of Mich., Midland County Bar Assn., Midland County C. of C. (bd. dirs. 1984—). Presbyterian. Banking, Probate, Personal income taxation. Office: Currie & Kendall PC 6024 Eastman Rd Midland MI 48640

ROLFE, ROBERT MARTIN, lawyer; b. Richmond, Va., May 16, 1951; s. Norman and Bertha (Cohen) R.; m. Catherine Dennis Stone, July 14, 1973; children: P. Alexander, Asher B., Joel A. BA, U. Va., 1973, JD, 1976. Bar: Va. 1976, N.Y. 1985, U.S. Dist. Ct. (ea. and we. dists.) Va. 1976, U.S. Supreme Ct. 1979, U.S. Ct. Appeals (4th cir.) 1976, U.S. Ct. Appeals (2d cir.) 1979, U.S. Dist. Ct. (ea. dist.) Mich. 1985, U.S. Ct. Appeals (D.C. cir.) 1985, U.S. Dist. Ct. (so. dist.) N.Y. 1985. Assoc. Hunton & Williams, Richmond, 1976-83, ptnr., 1983—. Contbr. articles to profl. jours. Mem. bd. dirs. Jewish Family Services, Richmond. Mem. ABA (litigation sect., torts and ins. practice sect.), Va. Bar Assn., Va. State Bar, Richmond Bar Assn., Va. Trial Lawyers Assn., Order of Coif. Federal civil litigation, Nuclear power, Condemnation. Home: 18 Greenway Ln Richmond VA 23226 Office: Hunton & Williams PO Box 1535 Richmond VA 23212

ROLFE, RONALD STUART, lawyer; b. N.Y.C., Sept. 5, 1945; s. Nat and Florence I. (Roth) R.; m. Yvonne Susan Quinn, Sept. 1, 1979. A.B., Harvard U., 1966; J.D., Columbia U., 1969. Bar: N.Y. 1969, U.S. Ct. Appeals (2d cir.) 1970, U.S. Dist. Ct. (so. and ea. dists.) N.Y. 1971, U.S. Supreme Ct. 1973, U.S. Ct. Appeals (9th cir.) 1977, U.S. Dist. Ct. (no. dist.) Calif. 1982, U.S. Ct. Appeals (5th cir.) 1982, U.S. Ct. Appeals (6th cir.) 1984, U.S. Dist. Ct. (ea. dist.) Ky. 1984. Law clk. to judge U.S. Dist. Ct. (so. dist.) N.Y., 1969-70; assoc. Cravath, Swaine & Moore, 1970-77, ptnr., 1977—. Sec. bd. trustees Allen-Stevenson Sch., 1981—. Kent and Stone scholar, 1969. Mem. ABA, N.Y. State Bar Assn., Assn. Bar City N.Y., Fed. Bar Council, Am. Law Inst. Clubs: Harvard, Wall St., University, Down Town Assn. (N.Y.C.); Stanwich (Greenwich, Conn.). General practice, Federal civil litigation, State civil litigation. Office: 1 Chase Manhattan Plaza New York NY 10005

ROLICH, FRANK ALVIN, insurance company executive, lawyer; b. Hudson, Wyo., Apr. 3, 1926; s. Frank Joseph and Mary Frances (Tekavec) R.; m. Margaret Geraldine Evans, Dec. 29, 1951; children—Zannifer Gail, Zinna Rae, Reef Kirby. B.A., U. Wyo., 1951, J.D., 1953. Bar: Wyo. 1953, U.S. Dist. Ct. Wyo. 1956. Claim rep. State Farm Ins. Co., Rock Springs, Wyo., 1953—, office adminstr., 1971—. Served with U.S. Army, 1944-46. Democrat. Roman Catholic. Lodge: Lions (pres. 1967-68). Personal injury, Insurance. Home: 712 B St Rock Springs WY 82901 Office: State Farm Ins Co 1695 Sunset Dr Suite 102 Rock Springs WY 82901

ROLLINSON, MARK, lawyer; b. Chattanooga, Dec. 8, 1935; s. Turner Earl and Josephine (Orput) R.; m. Barbara Crain, Sept. 7, 1957; children—Barbara Louis, Alice Orput, Marjorie Ann, Amy Claire; m. 2d, Carole Seliger, Oct. 30, 1971. A.B. in Econs., Duke U., 1958; LL.B., George Washington U., 1962. Bar: D.C. 1964, Md. 1975, Va. 1982, U.S. Dist. Ct. Md. 1976, U.S. Dist. Ct. (ea. dist.) Va. 1982, U.S. Ct. Appeals (D.C. cir.) 1963, U.S. Ct. Appeals (4th cir.) 1984. Asst. trust officer Nation Savs. and Trust Co., 1958; staff economist Foster Assoc., 1959; treas., exec. com. Human

Scis. Research, Inc., 1960-62; v.p. Greater Washington Investors, Inc., 1963-71; ptnr. Rollinson & Schaumberg, Washington, 1972-77; resident ptnr. Dykema, Gossett, Spencer, Goodnow & Trigg, Washington, 1978-81; ptnr. Smith Rollinson, Alexandria, Va., 1982—; mem. task force on inflation White House Conf. on Small Bus., 1979-80, exptl. research and devel. incentives program NSF, 1974-75. Mem. ABA (taxation sect., corp., banking and bus. law sect., internat. law sect., standing com. on law and tech., 1980-81, governing com. of forum com. on franchising, 1976-81, planning coms. confs.), D.C. Bar Assn. (chmn. com. on computer-assisted legal research), Internat. Bar Assn. (sect. bus. law). Republican. Episcopalian. Clubs: Belle Haven Country, Lawyers, Alexandria Businessmen's. Contbr. writings to legal publs.; speaker in field seminars and schs. General corporate, Federal civil litigation. Office: 603 King St Alexandria VA 22314

ROLLS, JOHN MARLAND, JR., lawyer, law educator; b. San Francisco, Nov. 18, 1937; s. Jack M. and Margaret Rita (Tracy) R.; m. Dorothy K. Higa, Oct. 2, 1976; children: Dana Kimiko, Jennifer Mariko. BA, Stanford U., 1959, LLB, 1962. Bar: Hawaii 1965, U.S. Dist. Ct. Hawaii 1965, U.S. Ct. Appeals (9th cir.) 1967, U.S. Supreme Ct. 1970. Asst. prof. dept. social scis. U.S. Mil. Acad., West Point, N.Y., 1962-65; assoc. Ashford & Wriston, Honolulu, 1965-68, ptnr. 1970—; instr. Grad. Realtors Inst., Hawaii Assn. Realtors, Honolulu, 1976-84; adj. prof. U. Hawaii Sch. Law, Honolulu, 1980-84; mem. adv. com. to commr. fin. instns., State of Hawaii, 1985—. Co-editor: Hawaii Conveyance Manual, 1979, 2d edit. 1983. Served to maj. U.S. Army, 1962-65, 68-69, Vietnam, col. Res. Decorated Bronze Star. Mem. ABA, Hawaii Bar Assn. (bd. dirs. real property and fin. services sect. 1983—, vice-chmn. 1986, chmn. 1987). Republican. Episcopalian. Real property, Contracts commercial, Consumer commercial. Office: Ashford & Wriston 235 Queen St Honolulu HI 96813

ROLSTON, GEORGE DREW, lawyer; b. Wheeling, W.Va., Mar. 3, 1947; s. George Henry and Beulah (Morgan) R.; m. E. Ann Auldridge, May 24, 1969; 1 child, Kevin Lee. BS, W.Va. U., 1969; LLD, Ohio State U., 1972. Bar: U.S. Dist. Ct. (so. dist.) Ohio 1977. Assoc. Johnston, Stilwell & Oberlin, Logan, Ohio, 1974-77, L.Jackson Henniger, Logan, Ohio, 1977; sole practice Logan, Ohio, 1977—. Served to 1st lt. U.S. Army, 1972-74. Mem. ABA, Ohio Bar Assn., Hocking County (Ohio) Bar Assn. Republican. Lodge: Rotary. Avocation: reading. General practice, Real property, Criminal. Home: 978 Louise Ave Logan OH 43138 Office: 61 N Market St Logan OH 43138-1291

ROMAINE, DOUGLAS PATTESON, lawyer; b. Jacksonville, Fla., Jan. 17, 1952; s. Mason III and Anne Corbin (Parker) R.; m. Jane Williams Collins, Jan. 24, 1976; children: Jane Hundley, Anne Mason, Holly, Douglas Randolph. BA, U. Va., 1970; JD, U. Richmond, 1978; LLM in Taxation, NYU, 1979. Bar: Va. 1978, Fla. 1980, U.S. Ct. Claims 1980, U.S. Tax Ct. 1980, Ky. 1983, U.S. Dist. Ct. (ea. dist.) Ky. 1985. Assoc. Mahoney, Hadlows & Adams, Jacksonville, 1979-81, Smith & Hulsey, Jacksonville, 1981-82; assoc. Stoll, Keenon & Park, Lexington, Ky., 1983-84, ptnr., 1985—. Mem. ABA (taxation sect.), Keeneland Assn. Republican. Episcopalian. Corporate taxation, Personal income taxation, Estate taxation. Office: Stoll Keenon & Park 1000 1st Security Plaza Lexington KY 40507

ROMAN, DAVID JOHN, lawyer; b. Rome, N.Y., Feb. 15, 1951; s. John P. and Betty L. (Lauri) R. BS, Cornell U., 1973; JD, Union U., 1976. Bar: N.Y. 1977, U.S. Dist. Ct. (no. dist.) N.Y. 1977,. Law clk. to presiding justice N.Y. Supreme Ct., Oswego, 1976-77; ptnr. Shanley, Sullivan & Roman, P.C., Oswego, 1976-83, Sullivan & Roman, Oswego, 1983—; dist. tax atty. N.Y. Dept. Taxation and Fin., Albany, 1983—; atty. Town of Minetto, N.Y., 1979—; mem. N.Y. Law Guardian's Adv. Com., 4th Dept. Appellate div., Rochester, 1985—; law clk. to presiding justice Oswego County Family Ct., 1986—. Bd. dirs. Oswego YMCA, 1986; pres. bd. dirs. Farnham Youth Devel. Ctr., Inc., Oswego, 1980—. Mem. ABA, N.Y. State Bar Assn., Oswego County Bar Assn. (treas. 1982-83, 2d v.p. 1983-84, 1st v.p. 1984-85, pres. 1985—), Sigma Phi Epsilon. Democrat. Roman Catholic. Club: Oswego Country. Lodge: Elks. Avocations: skiing, racquetball, golf, nautilus tng. Family and matrimonial, Real property, Estate taxation. Home: RD5 Box 130 Oswego NY 13126 Office: Sullivan & Roman 34 E Bridge St Oswego NY 13126

ROMAN, DAVID WILLIAM, lawyer; b. Bklyn., July 3, 1950; s. Isauro Roman Delgado and Sylvia Rodriguez Irizarry; m. Eva Melendez, Aug. 10, 1985; 1 child, Gabriel David. B.A., Houghton (N.Y.) Coll., 1972; M.B.A., Harvard U., 1973; postgrad. Hague (Netherlands) Acad. Internat. Law, 1977; J.D., U. Ga., 1978. Bar: Ga. 1978, P.R. 1979, U.S. Dist. Ct. (no. dist.) Ga. 1978, U.S. Dist. Ct. P.R. 1979, U.S. Ct. Appeals (1st cir) 1980, U.S. Ct. Internat. Trade 1981, U.S. Ct. Appeals (5th and 11th cirs.) 1981, U.S. Supreme Ct 1983. Market analyst Coca-Cola U.S.A., Atlanta, 1973-75; practice law, San Juan, P.R., 1978-80, Atlanta, 1980-82; asst. fed. pub. defender Dist. P.R., 1982—, chief appellate div. Office of Fed. Pub. Defender, 1983—. Mem. P.R. Bar Assn., Ga. Bar Assn., Nat. Assn. Criminal Def. Lawyers, Fed. Bar Assn. (treas. P.R. chpt. 1986-87, lectr. fed. bar rev. course). Club: Kiwanis (San Juan). Criminal, Civil rights, Public international. Address: PO Box 861 San Juan PR 00902

ROMAN, RONALD PETER, lawyer; b. N.Y.C., Apr. 8, 1945; s. Charles Philip and Dorothy C. (Raphael) R.; m. Deborah Lynn, Dec. 21, 1969; children—Lindsay Rachel, Ryan Alan. B.S. in Bus., Pa. State U., 1968; M.B.A., Pace U., 1973; J.D., Fordham U., 1976. Bar: N.J. 1976, N.Y. 1985, U.S. Dist. Ct. N.J. 1976, U.S. Tax Ct. 1978, U.S. Ct. Appeals (3d cir.) 1979, Fla. 1980, U.S. Dist. Ct. (so. dist.) Fla. 1980, U.S. Supreme Ct. 1980, U.S. Ct. Appeals (11th cir.) 1981. Assoc., Eichler & Forgosh, Irvington, N.J., 1976-78; gen. counsel Flower World of Am., West Deptford, N.J., 1979; staff counsel Arthur Murray Internat., Coral Gables, Fla., 1979-80; gen. counsel, v.p. Wuv's Internat. Inc., Ft. Lauderdale, Fla., 1980; sr. ptnr. Ronald Peter Roman, P.A., Miami, Fla., 1980—; pres. Franchise Resources Inc., Miami, 1981—. Co-author: (manual) Franchise Law: A Primer, 1982; Franchise Law, 1985. Contbr. articles to profl. jours. Mem. ABA. Franchise Law, General corporate, Probate. Office: Goldberg Semet Lickstein Et Al 201 Alhambra Circle Coral Gables FL 33134

ROMANO, HENRY SCHUBERTH, JR., lawyer; b. Chgo., Oct. 2, 1948; s. Henry S. and Patricia M. (Paisley) R.; m. Virginia E. Copp, Aug. 13, 1976; children: Henry S. III, Emily C., Anthony R. BA, U. Notre Dame, 1970, JD, 1977; LLM, DePaul U., 1984. Bar: Ill. 1977, U.S. Dist. Ct. (no. dist.) Ill. 1977, Fla. 1978. Assoc. Romano & Romano, Skokie, Ill., 1977—; instr. Mallinckrodt Coll., Wilmette, Ill., 1982—. Served to lt. USN, 1970-74. Mem. Fed. Trial Bar, Fla. Bar Assn., Ill. Bar Assn., Chgo. Bar Assn. Roman Catholic. General practice, Probate, Real property. Home: 1916 Keeney Evanston IL 60202 Office: Romano & Romano 4711 Golf Rd Suite 408 Skokie IL 60076

ROMANO, JANET BOCCHINO, lawyer; b. Newark, N.J., June 26, 1947; d. John Giacomo and Connie (Zoppi) B.; m. Mario Giovanni, July 25, 1970; children: Gabriella, Franca. BA, Montclair (N.J.) State Coll., 1969; JD, Seton Hall Law Sch., Newark, 1975. Bar: N.J. 1975, U.S. Dist. Ct. N.J. 1975. Ptnr. Romano & Romano, Verona, N.J., 1975—. Pres. Essex Fells (N.J.) PTA, 1981; v.p. Essex Fells Bd. Edn., 1985, pres. 1986. Mem. Assn. Trial Lawyers Am., N.J. State Bar Assn., Essex County Bar Assn., U.S. Dist. Ct. Hist. Soc. Club: Fells Brook. Consumer commercial, Real property, Personal injury. Home: 110 Devon Rd Essex Fells NJ 07044 Office: Romano & Romano 573 Bloomfield Ave Verona NJ 07044

ROMANOW, RICHARD BRIAN, lawyer; b. Portland, Maine, Oct. 14, 1953; s. Harold Morris and Florence (Levine) R.; m. Anita Sturman, June, 19, 1976; children: Bryan Curtis, Daniel Eric. BA, U. Maine, 1976; JD, Suffolk U., 1979. Bar: Mass. 1980, Maine 1980, U.S. Dist. Ct. Maine 1980. Ptnr. Brunette, Shumway, Romanow & Ryer, Portland, 1980—. Chmn. Portland Dems., 1982-84; mem. Portland Charter Commn., 1984—, Portland Civil Service Commn., 1986—; bd. dirs. Maine Ctr. for Blind, Portland, 1980—. Mem. ABA, Maine Bar Assn. Jewish. Avocations: golf, reading, politics. State civil litigation, Criminal, Family and matrimonial. Home: 44 Sunset Ln Portland ME 04102 Office: Brunette Shumway Romanow & Ryer 465 Congress St Portland ME 04101

ROMANYAK, JAMES ANDREW, lawyer; b. Chgo., July 21, 1944; s. James Basil and Helen Marie (Piorkowski) R.; m. Joan Beverly Culkin, Oct. 13, 1973 (div. 1980). B.A., U. Ill., 1966, J.D., 1969. Bar: Ill. 1969, U.S. Dist. Ct. (no. dist.) Ill. 1972, U.S. Ct. Appeals (7th cir.) 1972, U.S. Supreme Ct. 1984. Staff atty. Chgo. Bar Assn., 1970-71; exec. sec. Young Lawyers sect., 1971-72; gen. atty. Chgo., Milw., St. Paul & Pacific R.R., Chgo., 1972-79; pvt. practice, Chgo., 1979—. Democratic candidate for U.S. Ho. of Reps. from 14th Dist. Ill., 1978. Mem. ABA, Ill. State Bar Assn., Chgo. Bar Assn., Nat. Assn. R.R. Trial Counsel. Democrat. Roman Catholic. Federal civil litigation, State civil litigation. Office: Romanyak & Miller 111 W Washington St Suite 1611 Chicago IL 60602

ROMBS, VINCENT JOSEPH, accountant, lawyer; b. Newport, Ky., Mar. 8, 1918; s. John Thomas and Mathilda (Fromhold) R.; m. Ruth Burns, Aug. 15, 1942; 1 child, Ellen (Mrs. James P. Herman). Student Xavier U., 1936-37; BS with honors, Southeastern U., 1941; JD, Loyola U., Chgo., 1952. Bar: Ill. 1952; CPA, Ill. Tax ptnr. with local and nat. pub. acctg. firms, Chgo., 1952—; assoc. Laventhol & Horwath, Chgo., 1970-75; of counsel Edelman Chartered, 1975—; Ostrow Reisin Berk & Abrams, Ltd., 1977—; pres. Vincent J. Rombs, Ltd., 1982—. Bd. dirs. Miller Found. Served to lt. comdr., USNR, 1941-46. Recipient Scholarship Key award Delta Theta Phi, 1953. Mem. Am. Inst. CPA's, Ill. Soc. CPA's, Ill. Bar Assn. Pension, profit-sharing, and employee benefits, Corporate taxation, Personal income taxation. Home: 915 E Golf Rd Apt 3 Arlington Heights IL 60005 Office: 1 N LaSalle St Suite 1714 Chicago IL 60602 Address: 676 Saint Clair St Suite 2100 Chicago IL 60611

ROME, DONALD LEE, lawyer; b. West Hartford, Conn., May 17, 1929; s. Herman Isaac and Juliette (Stern) R.; m. Sheila Ward, Apr. 20, 1958; children: Adam Ward, Lisa, Ethan Stern. SB, Trinity Coll., 1951; LLB, Harvard U., 1954. Bar: Conn. 1954, U.S. Dist. Ct. 1955, U.S. Cir. Ct. Appeals 1965, U.S. Supreme Ct. 1965. Assoc. Ribicoff and Kotkin, Hartford, Conn., 1954-58, ptnr., 1958-67; ptnr. Rosenberg, Rome, Barnett, Sattin & Santos, and predecessor, Hartford, 1967-83, Robinson & Cole, Hartford, 1983—; mem. Conn. Gov.'s Study Commn. on Uniform Consumer Credit Code, 1969-70; chmn. Conn. bar advisory com. of attys. to make recommendations to U.S. dist. ct. for proposed changes of bankruptcy rules in dist. Conn., 1975-77; mem. Bankruptcy Merit Screening Com. for Dist. Ct., 1980-81; lectr. in law U. Conn., 1965-74, 81-83; mem. faculty Sch. Banking of the South, La. State U., 1982-84; lectr. continuing legal edn. on secured creditors' rights, comml. fin., bankruptcy and uniform comml. code, 1958—; corp. adv. bd. dirs. Conn. Nat. Bank. Co-author: A Comparative Analysis and Study of the Uniform Consumer Credit Code in Relation to the Existing Consumer Credit Law in Connecticut, 1970; author: Business Workouts Manual, 1985; contbg. author: Connecticut Practice Book, 1978, Collier Bankruptcy Practice Guide, 1981, Asset-Based Financing: A Transactional Guide, 1984; contbr. articles to profl. jours. Past mem. bd. dirs. New Eng. region Am. Jewish Com., also Hartford chpt., Hebrew Home for Aged, Hartford; past mem. bd. trustees Temple Beth Israel, West Hartford. Mem. ABA (bus. bankruptcy com. and comml. fin. services com., sect. on corp., banking and bus. law), Fed. Bar Assn. (bankruptcy law com.), Conn. Bar Assn. (chmn. sect. comml. law and bankruptcy 1977-80, chmn. spl. com. scope and correlation 1983-84), Hartford County Bar Assn. (continuing legal edn. com.), Conn. Bar Found., Assn. Comml. Fin. Attys. (pres. 1978-80), Am. Arbitration Assn. (mem. panel comml. arbitrators), Am. Bankruptcy Inst., Comml. Law League Am., Harvard Law Sch. Assn. Conn. (pres. 1970-71). Clubs: Hartford, Harvard of N.Y.C, Trinity. Lodge: Masons (32 deg., trial commn. Conn. grand lodge 1970-82). Contracts commercial, Bankruptcy, Banking. Home: 46 Belknap Rd West Hartford CT 06117 Office: Robinson & Cole 1 Commercial Plaza Hartford CT 06103-3597

ROME, EDWIN PHILLIPS, lawyer; b. Phila., Oct. 7, 1915; s. John Jacob and Etta (Phillips) R.; m. Chloe Denham, Oct. 30, 1946 (div. 1969); m. Rita Joseph, Aug. 19, 1969. B.A., Swarthmore Coll., 1937; LL.B., U. Pa., 1940. Bar: Pa. Law clk. Pa. Supreme Ct., Phila., 1940-42; assoc. William A. Gray, Phila., 1942-47; ptnr. Gray, Anderson, Schaffer & Rome, Phila., 1947-54, Blank, Rome, Comisky & McCauley, Phila., 1954—. Author: Arizona Annotations to the Restatement of the Law of Agency, The Child and the Law in Pennsylvania, Corporate and Commercial Free Speech; contbr. articles to profl. jours. Trustee William Penn Found., 1973-79, Phila. Mus. Art; bd. dirs. Phila. Opera Co.; pres. bd. Walnut Street Theatre, 1983-86; bd. overseers U. Pa. Law Sch. Fellow Am. Bar Found., Internat. Acad. Trial Lawyers; mem. ABA, Phila. Bar Assn., Pa. Bar Assn., Lawyers' Club Phila., Am. Coll. Trial Lawyers, Soc. Archtl. Historians (hon. counsel), Phi Beta Kappa. Democrat. Jewish. Club: Down Town (Phila.). Antitrust, Federal civil litigation, State civil litigation. Office: Blank Rome Comisky & McCauley 4 Penn Center Plaza Philadelphia PA 19103

ROME, LEWIS B., lawyer; b. Hartford, Conn., Sept. 12, 1933; s. Albert H. Rome and Celia M. (Sabol) R.; m. Ann Nicolle, Nov. 24, 1957; children: Thomas, Richard, Deborah, David. BA, U. Conn., 1954; JD, U. Conn., Hartford, 1957. Bar: Conn. 1957. Ptnr. Rome Case, Kennelly and Klebanoff, P.C., Conn., 1957—; corporator Winsted Meml. Hosp., 1975—, St. Francis Hosp., 1976—, Hartford Hosp., 1978—; mem. exec. com. Nat. Conf. State Legis., 1975-79. Advisor OEO, 1973-74; chmn. bd. Greater Hartford Visitors and Conv. Bur., 1980-81; bd. dir. Coordinating Council for Founds., Inc., 1973—; mem. Town Council of Bloomfield, Conn., 1961-69; mem. Futures Task Force Bd. Govs. for Higher Edn., 1985—; mayor Bloomfield, 1965-69; chmn. Greater Hartford Transit Dist., 1965-66, Capitol Regional Council of Elected Ofcl., 1967-69; senator State of Conn., 1970-79, senate majority leader, 1973-75, senate minority leader, 1975-79; Rep. candidate for lt. gov., 1978, cndidate for gov., 1982; bd. dirs. Mt. Sinai Hosp., 1975—; trustee exec. com. Conn. Pub. TV, 1975-82, U. Conn. Law Sch. Found., Inc., 1975—, pres. 1980. Mem. ABA, Conn. Bar Assn., Hartford County Bar Assn., Am. Judicature Soc., U.Conn. Sch. Law Alumni Assn. (recipient Outstanding Alumnus award 1981). Avocations: flying, sports. Real property. Home: 443 Simsons Rd Bloomfield CT 06002 Office: Rome Case Kennelly & Klebanoff PC 693 Bloomfield Ave Bloomfield CT 06002

ROME, MORTON EUGENE, lawyer; b. Balt., Sept. 9, 1913; s. Morris Albert and Charlotte (Beckman) R.; m. Frances Rotter, Dec. 31, 1952; 1 dau., Nancy Randolph Hester. A.B., Johns Hopkins U., 1933; J.D., Harvard U., 1936. Bar: Md. 1936, U.S. Supreme Ct. 1942. Asst. state's atty. Baltimore City, 1939-42; asst. prosecutor to justice Robert H. Jackson, U.S. Supreme Ct. at Nuremberg Trial of Goering, Hess, Keitel, Von Ribbentrop, others; counsel White, Mindel, Clarke & Hill; dir. numerous cos. Served as lt. comdr. U.S. Navy, 1942-46. Mem. Bar Assn. Balt. City (past v.p.), Md. Bar Assn. (past v.p.), Baltimore County Bar Assn. Republican. Episcopalian. Probate. Home: 6401 Murray Hill Rd Baltimore MD 21212 Office: Susquehanna Bldg 6th Floor 29 W Susquehanna Ave Towson MD 21204

ROMERO, FREDERICK ARMAND, lawyer; b. Los Angeles, Aug. 17, 1948; s. Armand and Esther (Nuanes) R.; m. Gloria Tenorio, June 14, 1969; children: Yvette, Yvonne, Jenny, Michelle. BA, Calif. State U., Los Angeles, 1975; JD, UCLA, 1979. Bar: Calif. 1980, U.S. Dist. Ct. (cen. dist.) Calif. 1982, U.S. Tax Ct. 1982. Atty. tax law specialist IRS, Washington and Los Angeles, 1979-81; atty. tax and employee benefits Antin, Stern, Litz & Grebow, Los Angeles, 1981—; lectr. numerous orgns., 1980—. Contbg. author Mich. State Bar Jour., 1984, The Pension Actuary Jour., 1985, Plan Horizons, 1985. Served with USMC, 1967-69, Vietnam. Mem. ABA, Los Angeles County Bar Assn., Beverly Hills Bar Assn., Century City Bar Assn., The Group Inc. Roman Catholic. Avocations: tennis, cars, continuing edn. Pension, profit-sharing, and employee benefits, Corporate taxation. Office: Antin Stern Litz & Grebow 10900 Wilshire Blvd Suite 600 Los Angeles CA 90024

ROMMEL, JOHN MARSHALL, lawyer; b. Washington, Aug. 14, 1925; s. Royal Rupert and Ethel Lorraine (Masey) R.; m. Barbara Wingate Fenderson, May 14, 1949; children—John Marshall, Jan L., W. Brett, Brian A., Jeffrey B. B.A., George Washington U. and Am. U., 1954; J.D., Am. U., 1954. Bar: D.C. 1954. Assoc., Lancaster, Allwine & Rommel, 1954-57; ptnr. Rommel, Allwine & Rommel, 1958-67; ptnr. Rommel & Rommel, 1968-72; ptnr. Beveridge, DeGrandi & Kline, Washington, 1972-84, Kline, Rommel & Colbert, 1985—. Mem. D.C. Bar Assn., ABA, Assn. Trial Lawyers Am., U.S. Trademark Assn., Patent and Trademark Inst. Can., Am. Intellectual Property Law Assn., Md. Patent Law Assn., Am. Arbitration Assn. (panel). Club: Lakewood Country (Rockville, Md.). Federal civil litigation, Patent, Trademark and copyright. Home: 9040 Rouen Ln Potomac MD 20854 Office: 1 Farragut Sq S 7th Floor Washington DC 20006

ROMNEY, RICHARD BRUCE, lawyer; b. Kingston, Jamaica, Dec. 29, 1942; came to U.S., 1945, naturalized, 1956; s. Frank Oswald and Mary Ellen (Burton) R.; m. Beverly Cochran, Sept. 11, 1965 (dec. 1984); children—Richard Bruce, Jr., Stephanie Cochran. B.A., U. Pa., 1964; J.D., U. Va., 1972. Bar: N.Y. 1973, U.S. Ct. Appeals (2d cir.) 1975. Assoc. Dewey, Ballantine, Bushby Palmer & Wood, N.Y.C., 1972-80, ptnr., 1981—. Mem. editorial bd. U. Va. Law Rev., 1970-72. Served to lt. USN, 1964-68. Mem. ABA, N.Y. State Bar Assn., Assn. Bar City N.Y., Order of Coif. Republican. General corporate, Securities. Home: 6 Kevin Dr Suffern NY 10901 Office: Dewey Ballantine Bushby et al 140 Broadway New York NY 10005

RONCA, JAMES ALEXANDER, lawyer; b. Trenton, N.J., May 2, 1953; s. Alexander Fulvio and Mary Theresa (Comford) R.; m. Bernadette Maureen Lynn, Apr. 9, 1983; 1 child, Jacqueline Maureen. AB in History, St. Joseph's Coll., 1975; JD, Coll. William & Mary, 1978. Bar: N.J. 1978, U.S. Dist. Ct. N.J. 1978. Law clk. to judge N.J. Superior Ct., Trenton, 1978-79; asst. prosecutor Burlington County, Mt. Holly, N.J., 1979-83, 85—; assoc. Lewis, Siegel & Wood, Trenton, 1984; dep. atty. gen. div. criminal justice State of N.J., Trenton, 1984-85; Mem. com. on pretrial intervention N.J. Supreme Ct., Trenton, 1981; instr. Burlington County Police Acad., 1979-83, 85—. Mem. Kings Grant Civic Assn., Marlton, N.J., 1983—. Mem. ABA, Nat. Dist. Attys. Assn., N.J. Bar Assn., N.J. Asst. Prosecutors Assn., Burlington County Bar Assn., Mercer County Bar Assn. Democrat. Roman Catholic. Club: 71 Athletic Assn. (Marlton) (pres. 1985—). Avocations: Am. history (civil war), photography, sports. Criminal, Environment, Legal history. Office: Burlington County Prosecutors Office 49 Rancocas Rd Mount Holly NJ 08060

RONDEPIERRE, EDMOND FRANCOIS, insurance company executive; b. N.Y.C., Jan. 15, 1930; s. Jules Gilberte and Margaret Murray (Moore) R.; m. M. Anne Lerch, July 5, 1952; children—Aimee S., Stephen C., Peter E., Anne W. B.S., U.S. Mcht. Marine Acad., 1952; J.D., Temple U., 1959. Bar: D.C. 1959. Third mate Nat. Bulk Carriers, 1952-53; field rep. Ins. Co. N.Am., 1955-59, br. mgr., 1959-61, underwriting officer, 1961-67, asst. gen. counsel, 1967-70, gen. counsel, 1970-76; v.p., dep. chief legal affairs INA Corp., 1976-77; v.p., gen. counsel Gen. Reinsurance Corp., Stamford, Conn., 1977-79, sr. v.p., corp. sec., gen. counsel, 1979-80, corp. v.p., gen. counsel, sec., 1980—, also bd. dirs.; bd. dirs. Gen. Reassurance Corp., Gen. Star Mgmt. Co., Gen. Star Indemnity Co., Gen. Star Nat. Ins. Co., Gen. Reservices Corp., N. Star Reinsurance Corp., Herbert Clough, Inc., NYIE Security Fund. Bd. dirs. Stamford Mus. Served to lt. USN, 1953-55. Mem. ABA, D.C. Bar Assn., Inter Am. Bar Assn., Soc. CPCU, Internat. Assn. Ins. Counsel (past dir.), Reins. Assn. Am. Roman Catholic. Club: Stamford Yacht. General corporate, Insurance. Home: 8 Linda Ln Darien CT 06820 Office: Gen Reinsurance Corp Fin Ctr PO Box 10350 Stamford CT 06904-2350

RONEY, PAUL H., federal judge; b. Olney, Ill., Sept. 5, 1921; m. Sarah E. Roney; children: Susan Roney Lohe, Paul Hitch Jr., Timothy Eustis. Student, St. Petersburg Jr. Coll., 1938-40; B.S. in Econs, U. Pa., 1942; LL.B., Harvard U., 1948; LL.D., Stetson U., 1977; LL.M., U. Va., 1984. Bar: N.Y. 1949, Fla. 1950. Assoc. Root, Ballantine, Harlan, Bushby & Palmer, N.Y.C., 1948-50; ptnr. Mann, Harrison, Roney, Mann & Masterson (and predecessors), St. Petersburg, Fla., 1950-57; sole practice 1957-63; ptnr. Roney & Beach, St. Petersburg, 1963-69, Roney, Ulmer, Woodworth & Jacobs, St. Petersburg, 1969-70; judge U.S. Circuit Ct. 5th Circuit, St. Petersburg, 1970-81; judge U.S. Circuit Ct. 11th Circuit, St. Petersburg, 1981-86, chief judge, 1986—; mem. adv. com. on adminstrv. law judges U.S. CSC, 1976-77. Served in U.S. Army, 1943-46. Fellow Am. Bar Found.; mem. Am. Bar Assn. (chmn. legal adv. com. Fair Trial-Free Press 1973-76, mem. task force on cts. and public 1973-76, jud. adminstrn. div., chmn. appellate judges conf. 1978-79, mem. Gavel Awards com. 1980-83), Am. Judicature Soc. (dir. 1972-76), Am. Law Inst., Fla. Bar Assn., St. Petersburg Bar Assn. (pres. 1964-65), Nat. Jud. Coll. (faculty 1974, 75), Jud. Conf. U.S. (subcom. on jud. improvements 1978-84). Jurisprudence. Home: One Beach Dr SE Bayfront Tower Saint Petersburg FL 33701 Office: US Court Appeals 601 Federal Bldg 144 1st Ave S Saint Petersburg FL 33701

RONQUILLO, ALLAN LOUIS, automotive financial corporation executive, lawyer; b. New Orleans, July 31, 1941; s. Louis and Rita Henrietta (O'Brien) R.; m. Karen Marie Munster, June 6, 1964; children—Robin, Lesley, Allan Louis. Student La. State U., 1959-62; J.D., Tulane U., 1965. Bar: La. 1965, Mich. 1968. Atty., def. div. Chrysler Corp., New Orleans, 1965-67, staff atty. legal dept., Detroit, 1967-72, sr. atty. internat., legal dept. Chrysler Fin. Corp., Troy, Mich., 1972-78, internat. dir. Europe, Paris, 1978-79, asst. counsel legal dept., Troy, 1979-80, asso. gen. counsel, 1980-85, v.p. and gen. counsel, 1985—; chmn. law forum Am. Fin. Services Assn., 1987—. Mem. ABA, Mich. State Bar Assn., La. Bar Assn., Am. Fin. Services Assn. (law com.). Antitrust, Consumer commercial, Contracts commercial. Office: Chrysler Fin Corp 901 Wilshire Dr Troy MI 48084

ROOD, RALPH EDWARD, lawyer; b. Washington, Ga., Nov. 7, 1943; s. Arthur Edward Rood, Jr. and Amelia (Golucke) Brooks; m. Cynthia Merriman Hooper, June 9, 1966; children: Virginia Hooper, Amelia Gordon. BBA, U. Ga., 1966; JD, U. Miss., 1972. Bar: Miss. 1972, U.S. Dist. Ct. (no. dist.) Miss. 1972, U.S. Ct. Appeals (5th cir.) 1972, U.S. Supreme Ct. 1977, U.S. Ct. Appeals (6th cir.) 1980. From assoc. to ptnr. Gholson, Hicis & Nichols, Columbus, Miss., 1971—. Research editor Miss. Law Jour., Oxford, 1971-72. Mem. exec. com. Lowndes County Rep. Party, Columbus; vestry St. Paul's Episcopal Ch., Columbus, 1978-82. Served to lt. USN, 1966-69. Mem. ABA, Miss. Bar Assn., Maritime Law Assn. of U.S. (proctor in admiralty), Miss. Def. Lawyers (com. chmn. 1983), Def. Research Inst., Ducks Unltd. (outstanding sponsor com. 1983, outstanding dist. dir. 1985, sec. Miss. council). Republican. Episcopalian. Clubs: Magowah Gun and Country (Columbus) (bd. dirs. 1976-79, 82-85); Bossom Bayou Hunt (Tallahatchie County, Miss.) (pres. 1986). Avocations: reading, hunting, fishing, retriever field trials, running. Insurance, Admiralty, General practice. Home: 2801 Niles Rd Columbus MS 39701 Office: Gholson Hicks & Nichols 605 2d Ave N Columbus MS 39703

ROOF, VERNON DONALD, lawyer; b. Ridgway, Pa., Oct. 11, 1950; s. George Franklin and Anne Marie (Paolella) R.; m. Frances Ann Cenni, Mar. 25, 1972; children: Megen Rae, Brittany Ann. BA cum laude, Indiana (Pa.) U, 1972; M Pub. Adminstrn., U. Pitts., 1974; JD with distinction, Ohio No. U., 1976. Bar: Pa. 1976, U.S. Dist. Ct. (we. dist.) Pa. 1982. Sole practice Ridgway, 1976; ptnr. Pontzer and Roof, Ridgway, 1986—; instr. continuing legal edn. program Indiana (Pa.) U., 1978-82; asst. dist. atty. Elk County, Ridgway, 1978-86, dist. atty., 1986—. Mem. ABA, Pa. Bar Assn., Elk County Bar Assn. (treas. 1978—), Phi Kappa Phi, Phi Alpha Delta. Democrat. Roman Catholic. Lodges: Elks, Sons of Italy. General practice. Office: Pontzer and Roof 235 Main St Po Box 431 Ridgway PA 15853

ROOKS, JOHN NEWTON, lawyer; b. Evanston, Ill., Jan. 7, 1948; s. R. Newton and Ruth Dunlop (Darling) R.; m. Mary Preston Noell, Sept. 15, 1973; children—John Newton, Thomas N. B.A., DePauw U., 1970; J.D., Washington U., 1973. Bar: Ill. 1973, U.S. Dist. Ct. (no. dist.) Ill. 1973. Corp. atty. No. Trust Co., Chgo., 1973-76; ptnr. Hynds, Rooks & Yohnka and predecessor firms, Morris, Ill., 1976—. Chmn. bd. ARC, Morris, 1980-82; mem. adminstrv. council 1st United Meth. Ch., Morris, 1985-86; trustee, 1982-84; mem. citizen's adv. com. Morris Community High Sch., 1984-87. Mem. ABA, Ill. Bar Assn., Chgo. Bar Assn., Grundy County Bar Assn. (pres. 1983-84), Grundy County C. of C. (chmn. bd. 1982). Republican. Methodist. General practice, Estate taxation, General corporate. Home: 102 Briar Ln Morris IL 60450 Office: Hynds Rooks & Yohnka PO Box 685 Morris IL 60450

ROONEY, GEORGE WILLARD, lawyer; b. Appleton, Wis., Nov. 16, 1915; s. Francis John and Margaret Ellen (O'Connell) R.; m. Doris I. Maxon, Sept. 20, 1941; children—Catherine Ann, Thomas Dudley, George Willard. B.S., U. Wis., 1938; J.D., Ohio State U., 1948. Bar: Ohio 1949. Assoc. Wise, Roetzel, Maxon, Kelly & Andress, Akron, Ohio, 1949-54; ptnr.

Roetzel & Andress, and predecessor, Akron, 1954—; dir. Bank One of Akron, Duracote Corp. Nat. bd. govs. ARC, 1972-78; v.p. Akron council Boy Scouts Am., 1975-86; pres. Akron Automobile Assn., 1980, trustee, 1986—; chmn. bd. Akron Gen. Med. Center, 1981-86; trustee Mobile Meals Found., Bluecoats, Inc.. Served to maj. USAAF, 1942-46. Decorated D.F.C. with 2 oak leaf clusters, Air medal with 3 oak leaf clusters; recipient Disting. Community Service award Akron Labor Council, 1973; Disting. Service award Summit County chpt. ARC, 1978. Mem. ABA, Ohio Bar Assn. Akron Bar Assn. Am. Judicature Soc. Republican. Roman Catholic. Clubs: Rotary (past pres.), Portage Country (past pres.), Cascade (bd. govs.) (Akron), KC. Labor, General corporate. Home: 2863 Walnut Ridge Rd Akron OH 44313 Office: 75 E Market St Akron OH 44308

ROONEY, MATTHEW A., lawyer; b. Jersey City, May 19, 1949; s. Charles John and Eileen (Dunphy) R.; m. Jean M. Alletag, June 20, 1973 (div. Dec. 1979); 1 child, Jessica Margaret; m. Diane S. Kaplan, July 6, 1981; 1 child; Kathryn Olivia. AB magna cum laude, Georgetown U., 1971; JD cum laude, U. Chgo., 1974. Bar: Ill. 1975, U.S. Dist. Ct. (no. dist.) Ill. 1975. Law clk. to presiding justice U.S. Ct. Appeals (7th cir.), Chgo., 1974-75; assoc. Mayer, Brown & Platt, Chgo., 1975-80, ptnr., 1981—. Assoc. editor U. Chgo. Law Rev., 1973. Mem. ABA, 7th Cir. Bar Assn., Order of Coif, Phi Beta Kappa. Democrat. Roman Catholic. Avocations: jogging, gardening. Federal civil litigation, Securities, Nuclear power. Home: 2718 Sheridan Rd Evanston IL 60201 Office: Mayer Brown & Platt 190 S LaSalle St Chicago IL 60603

ROONEY, MICHAEL JAMES, lawyer, educator, insurance executive; b. Bloomington, Ill., Dec. 18, 1947; s. James Patrick and Nellie Mae (Schaefer) R.; m. Melody Ann Rowe, Aug. 23, 1969 (div. May 1972); m. Pamela Sue Harrison, Feb. 1, 1974; children: Dawn Susanne, Donald Edward, Joseph Michael. BS in Edn., Ill. State U., 1971; JD, U. Ill., 1976. Bar: Ill. 1976, U.S. Ct. Appeals (7th cir.) 1978. Atty. Atty.'s Title Guaranty Fund, Inc., Champaign, Ill., 1976-81, v.p., corp. counsel, 1981-83; exec. v.p. Attys.' Title Guaranty Fund, Inc., Champaign, Ill., 1983—; also bd. dirs. Attys.' Title Guaranty Fund, Inc., Colo.; bd. dirs. Ill. Inst. Continuing Legal Edn., Springfield, lectr. 1978—; vis. asst. prof. Coll. Commerce U. Ill., Champaign, 1982—. Author: Searching Illinois Real Estate Titles, 1978, Attorney's Guide to Title Insurance, 1980, rev. edit., 1984; also articles. Pres. Mahomet (Ill.)-Seymour Boosters, 1983-84. Fellow Am. Bar Found., Ill. Bar Found. (charter); mem. ABA (chmn. real property com. gen. practice sect. 1983—, real property probate and trust law), Ill. Bar Assn. (sec. real estate sect. council 1984-85, vice chmn. 1985-86, chmn. 1986—), Internat. Right of Way Assn. (instr. 1983—), Champaign County Bar Assn., Chgo. Bar Assn. Real property, General corporate, Legal education. Home: 12 Woodridge Ct Mahomet IL 61853 Office: Attys Title Guaranty Fund Inc 2408 Windsor Pl Champaign IL 61820

ROONEY, PAUL C., JR., lawyer; b. Winnetka, Ill., Oct. 23, 1943; s. Paul C. and Mary K. (Brennan) R.; m. Maria Elena Del Canto, Sept. 6, 1980. BA, Harvard U., 1963, LLB, 1966. Bar: Mass. 1968, N.Y. 1972, Fla. 1980, Tex. 1980, U.S. Dist. Ct. (ea. and so. dists.) N.Y., U.S. Ct. Appeals (2d cir.). Ptnr. White & Case, N.Y.C., 1983—. Served to lt. USNR, 1966-69. Mem. ABA, N.Y. State Bar Assn., Fla. Bar Assn., Tex. Bar Assn., Dallas Bar Assn. Clubs: Union League, Harvard (N.Y.C.). Corporate taxation, Personal income taxation, Municipal bonds. Home: 417 Park Ave New York NY 10022 Office: White & Case 1155 Ave of the Americas New York NY 10036

ROOS, ROBERT CARL, JR., lawyer; b. Oak Park, Ill., Oct. 1, 1941; s. Robert Carl Sr. and Persis Etta (Warren) R.; m. Barbara Elizabeth Swanson, Sept. 12, 1970; children: Amy Elisabeth, Alison Katherine. AB, Wabash Coll., 1963; LLB, Duke U., 1966. Bar: Ill. 1966, U.S. Dist. Ct. (no. dist.) Ill. 1967, N.C. 1976. Assoc. Winston & Strawn, Chgo., 1966-70; atty. Teletype Corp., Skokie, Ill., 1970-75, Western Electric, Greensboro, N.C., 1975-78, Teletype Corp., Skokie, 1978-84; gen. atty. AT&T Teletype Corp., Skokie, 1984-85; atty. AT&T Info. Systems, Lisle, Ill., 1986—. Mem. mission fin. com. Wheaton (Ill.) Bible Ch., 1984—. Mem. ABA, Ill. Bar Assn., Chgo. Bar Assn. Avocations: genealogy, reading, cooking. Antitrust, Contracts commercial, General corporate. Home: 1641 Woodlawn St Wheaton IL 60187

ROOT, LAWRENCE CHARLES, lawyer; b. Hinsdale, Ill., Dec. 26, 1947; s. Earnest Calvin and Martha Rowena (Kissinger) R.; m. Judy Lynn Dudick, Mar. 23, 1968; children: Robyn Lyn, Colleen Deanne. BBA, Ferris State Coll., 1970; JD, U. Detroit, 1975. Bar: Mich. 1975. Assoc. Plunkett, Cooney, Rott, Watters & Stanzwk, Detroit, 1975; sole practice Big Rapids, Mich., 1975-76; judge 49th Jud. Cir. Ct., Big Rapids and Reed City, Mich., 1977—. Mem. council St. Peter's Luth. Ch., Big Rapids, 1976—, congregation pres., 1985—; treas. bd. edn., St. Peters Luth. Christian Day Sch., Big Rapids, 1977-85; mem. council Pere Marquette Watershed Council, 1976—. Mem. ABA, Mich. Bar Assn., Mich. Judges Assn., Am. Judicature Assn., Safari Club Internat., Nat. Rifle Assn. Avocations: fishing, hunting, reading, shooting, sports. Judicial administration. Office: 49th Jud Cir Ct 400 Elm PO Box 822 Big Rapids MI 49307

ROOT, STUART DOWLING, lawyer; b. Chagrin Falls, Ohio, Oct. 14, 1932; s. Elton Albert and Virginia Saxton (Dowling) R.; m. Jean D. Youse, Dec. 28, 1957 (div. Jan. 1972); children: Bryan, Kathleen, Timothy, Todd; m. Patricia Stoneman Graff, Apr. 26, 1976. BA, Ohio Wesleyan U., 1955; JD, Columbia U., 1960. Bar: N.Y. 1960. Assoc. Cadwalader, Wickersham & Taft, N.Y.C., 1960-68, ptnr., 1969-81, 84—; pres. Bowery Savs. Bank, N.Y.C., 1981-82, vice chmn., 1982-83; lectr. Practising Law Inst., Am. Law Inst.; bd. dirs. Fed. Home Loan Bank of N.Y. Chmn. bd. Harlem Sch. Arts, N.Y.C., 1974-83, trustee emeritus, 1984—; bd. dirs. Open Space Inst., 1976-80, 84—. Served with AUS, 1955-57. Mem. Am. Bar Assn., N.Y. Geneal. and Biol. Soc., Down Town Assn., Century Assn. Clubs: Pelham Country, Econ. Banking, Real property. Home: 190 Boulevard Pelham NY 10803 Office: Cadwalader Wickersham & Taft 100 Maiden Ln New York NY 10038

ROPER, HARRY JOSEPH, lawyer; b. Bridgeport, Conn., Apr. 15, 1940; s. Harold Joseph and Madeline (Sullivan) R.; m. Helen L. Marlborough, Oct. 1, 1976; children—Kendall, Timothy, Melissa, Elizabeth. B.E.E., Rensselaer Poly. Inst., 1962; LL.B., NYU, 1966. Bar: Ill. 1966, U.S. Dist. Ct. (no. dist.) Ill. 1966, U.S. Ct. Appeals (7th cir.) 1966, U.S. Ct. Appeals (fed. cir.) 1982. Assoc. Neuman, Williams, Anderson & Olson, Chgo., 1966-70, ptnr., 1970—. Mem. ABA (chmn. intellectual properties com. litigation sect. 1982-85), Chgo. Bar Assn., Bar Assn. 7th Fed. Cir., Patent Law Assn. Chgo., Am. Patent Law Assn., Chgo. Council Lawyers. Club: Union League (Chgo.). Federal civil litigation, Patent, Trademark and copyright. Home: 611 Fullerton Pkwy Chicago IL 60614 Office: Neuman Williams Anderson & Olson 77 W Washington St Chicago IL 60602

ROPER, MILARD KING, JR., lawyer; b. Queens, N.Y., May 22, 1948; s. Milard King Sr. and Betty Marshall (Ramsey) R.; m. Diana Sherwood, Nov. 3, 1983; children: Amy Kathleen, Milard King III, Regina Sherwood. BA cum laude, SUNY, New Paltz, 1970; JD, U. Akron, 1972. Bar: N.Y. 1973, U.S. Dist. Ct. (so. and ea. dists.) 1973, U.S. Ct. Appeals (2d cir.) 1973. Assoc. Roper & Neary, Huntington, N.Y., 1973-75; sole practice Floral Park, N.Y., 1975-83; ptnr. Roper & Sherwood, Floral Park, 1983—. Editor case and comments U. Akron Law Rev., 1972. Mem. ABA, N.Y. State Bar Assn., Nassau County Bar Assn., Queens County Bar Assn., State Trial Lawyers Am., N.Y. State Trial Lawyers Assn. Office: Roper & Sherwood 22 N Tyson Ave Floral Park NY 11001

ROPER, PETER P., bar association executive; b. Akron, Ohio, Apr. 8, 1924; s. Boro and Ann M. (Ropar) Petrovich; m. Mary P. Volkar, Sept. 2, 1949; 1 son, Mark E. B.A. cum laude, Western Res. U., 1949, M.A., 1950; J.D., Cleve. State U., 1961. Bar: Ohio 1961, U.S. Dist. Ct. (no. dist.) Ohio 1962. Teaching fellow Am. history and deptl. asst. history dept. Cleve. Coll., 1949-50; informational writer, chief pub. relations dept. Ohio Dept. Hwys., 1950-53; pub. relations dir. Ohio Advt. Agy., Cleve., 1953-56; publicity and promotion mgr. Sta. WERE, Cleve., 1956-61; sole practice, Cleve. and Richfield, Ohio, 1961-68; asst. atty. gen. Ohio, 1961-62; labor-mgmt. arbitrator Am. Arbitration Assn., 1966-70; exec. dir. and sec. Bar Assn. Greater Cleve., 1968-78; exec. dir. Pa. Bar Assn., 1978—. Mem. Pa. Legal Services Corp.; sec. Pa. Bar Trust; capt. CAP. Served with USAAF, 1943-45. Mem. Pa. Bar Assn., ABA, Cleve. Bar Assn. (hon.), Nat. Assn. Bar Execs. Episcopalian. Contbr. articles to legal jours.; editor: Directory of Bar Activities ABA, 1976. State civil litigation, Jurisprudence, Legal history. Office: PA Bar Assn PO Box 186 Harrisburg PA 17108 *

ROPER, ROBERT ST. JOHN, lawyer; b. N.Y.C., Oct. 12, 1944; s. Anton John Roper and Angela Joan (Senatore) Berger; m. Libby Jane Colen, Jan. 23, 1982; Children: Adam, Eric. BS, Boston U., 1966; JD, Georgetown U., 1969; LLM, George Washington U., 1981. Bar: D.C. 1969, Mass. 1971, Calif. 1976. Ptnr. Liotta & Roper, Washington, 1970-72; project dir. Georgetown Clinic, Washington, 1972; dep. dir. Law Students in Ct., Washington, 1972-76; asst. atty. U.S. Dept. Justice, Washington, 1976-80; assoc. gen. counsel Nat. Cable TV Assn., Washington, 1981-84; ptnr. LeBoeuf, Lamb, Leiby & MacRae, Washington, 1985—. Mem. Fed. Communications Bar Assn. Communications. Office: LeBoeuf Lamb Leiby & MacRae 1333 New Hampshire Ave NW Suite 1100 Washington DC 20036

ROPIEQUET, JOHN L., lawyer; b. Highland Park, Ill., Apr. 16, 1947; s. Arthur C. and Jeanne (Prior) R. BA, Johns Hopkins U., 1969; JD, Northwestern U., 1972. Bar: Ill. 1972, U.S. Dist. Ct. (no. dist.) Ill. 1973, U.S. Ct. Appeals (3d cir.) 1981, U.S. Ct. Claims 1984, U.S. Ct. Appeals (5th cir.) 1984. Assoc. Arnstein, Gluck, Lehr & Milligan and predecessor firms, Chgo., 1973-76, ptnr., 1977—. Contbr. articles to profl. jours. V.p., bd. dirs. Family Counseling Service of Evanston (Ill.) and Skokie Valley, 1984—. Mem. ABA, Ill. Bar Assn., Chgo. Bar Assn., Nat. Health Lawyers Assn., Ill. Assn. Hosp. Attys., Def. Research Inst., Johns Hopkins U. Alumni Assn., Northwestern U. Law Sch. Alumni Assn. Republican. Methodist. Club: Metropolitan (Chgo.). Federal civil litigation, Health, Environment. Office: Arnstein Gluck Lehr Barron & Milligan 7500 Sears Tower Chicago IL 60606

ROPSKI, GARY MELCHIOR, lawyer; b. Erie, Pa., Apr. 19, 1952; s. Joseph Albert and Irene Stefania (Mszanowski) R.; m. Barbara Mary Schleck, May 15, 1982. B.S. in Physics, Carnegie-Mellon U., 1972; J.D. cum laude, Northwestern U. Sch. Law, 1976. Bar: Ill. 1976, U.S. Patent and Trademark Office 1976, U.S. Dist. Ct. (no. dist.) Ill. 1976, U.S. Ct. Appeals (7th cir.) 1977, U.S. Dist. Ct. (ea. dist.) Wis. 1977, U.S. Ct. Appeals (3d cir.) 1981, U.S. Ct. Claims 1982, Pa. 1982, U.S. Ct. Appeals (Fed. cir.) 1982, U.S. Supreme Ct. 1982, U.S. Dist. Ct. (ea. dist.) Mich. 1984, U.S. Dist. Ct. (no. dist.) Calif. 1986. Assoc. Willian Brinks Olds Hofer Gilson & Lione Ltd., Chgo., 1976-81, shareholder, 1981—; adj. prof. patents and copyrights Northwestern U. Sch. Law, Chgo., 1982—. Contbr. numerous articles to profl. jours. Mem. ABA, Am. Intellectual Property Law Assn., Patent Law Assn. Chgo., Chgo. Bar Assn. Roman Catholic. Clubs: University, Columbia Yacht (Chgo.). Patent, Trademark and copyright, Federal civil litigation. Home: 1169 S Plymouth Ct #311 Chicago IL 60605 Office: One IBM Plaza Suite 4100 Chicago IL 60611

RORICK, ALAN GREEN, lawyer; b. Seneca, Mich., Oct. 22, 1918; s. John Porter and Bertha (Green) R.; m. Evelyn Edwards, May 10, 1941; children—Emily, Stephen, Josephine, Mark. B.S., U.S. Military Acad., 1940; LL.D., Case Western Res. U., 1947. Bar: Ohio bar 1948. Asso. firm Baker & Hostetler, Cleve., 1947-57; partner firm Baker & Hostetler, 1957-83, mng. partner, 1974-79. Mem. Bd. Edn., Brecksville, Ohio, 1962-67, pres., 1966, councilman, Village of Waite Hill, Ohio, 1978—. Served to maj. U.S. Army, 1940-45. Mem. Am. Bar Assn., Ohio Bar Assn., Cleve. Bar Assn., Am. Law Inst. Republican. Mem. United Ch. of Christ. General practice, Probate, Real property. Home: 7610 Eagle Rd Waite Hill OH 44094 Office: 3200 National City Tower Cleveland OH 44114

RORIMER, LOUIS, lawyer; b. N.Y.C., Feb. 17, 1947; s. James J. and Katherine (Serrell) R.; m. H. Savery Fitz-Gerald, July 1, 1978; children: Sarah, James. Student, Phillips Acad., 1965; BA, Harvard U., 1969; JD, Case Western Res. U., 1975. Bar: Ohio 1975. Assoc. Jones, Day, Reavis & Pogue, Cleve., 1975-83, ptnr., 1984—. Served to lt. (j.g.) USNR, 1969-71, PTO. Mem. ABA, Greater Cleve. Bar Assn. General corporate, Securities. Home: 2880 Woodbury Rd Shaker Heights OH 44120 Office: Jones Day Reavis & Pogue 1700 Huntington Bldg Cleveland OH 44115

RORSCHACH, JACK L., lawyer; b. Muskogee, Okla., Sept. 20, 1909; s. Emil E. and Emma Elnora (Roush) R.; m. Gertie L. Carroll, Sept. 23, 1935; 1 child, Don J. LLB, U. Okla., 1931. Bar: Okla. 1931, U.S. Supreme Ct. 1938. Sole practice Pryor, Okla., 1931-32, Vinita, Okla.; ptnr. Rorschach, Pitcher, Castor & Hartley, Vinita; spl. justice Okla. Supreme Ct., 1948; gen. counsel Grand River Dam Authority, Vinita, 1937-38, KAMO Electric Cooperative, 1948—; bd. dirs. Colonial Royalties, Tulsa, Cathey's Inc., Tulsa. Chmn. bd. control Craig Gen. Hosp., Vinita, 1962-83; state rep. and senator, Oklahoma City, 1934-41; pres. Vinita C. of C., 1964. Served to maj. arty. U.S. Army, 1942-45, ETO. Elected to Okla. Rural Electrification Adminstrn. Hall of Fame, 1985. Mem. Craig County Bar Assn. (pres. 1970-81). Democrat. Methodist. Lodge: Lions (pres. Vinita 1946-47, dist. gov. Okla. 1948-49). Avocations: tennis, swimming. Condemnation, Probate, Real property. Office: Rorschach Pitcher Castor & Hartley 244 S Scraper Vinita OK 74301

ROSBE, WILLIAM LOUIS, lawyer; b. Evanston, Ill., Feb. 17, 1944; s. Robert L. and Margaret H. (Black) R.; m. Marta Nordenholz, Aug. 27, 1967; 1 child, Kimberly. BA, Yale U., 1966; JD, Cornell U., 1975. Bar: Va. 1975, U.S. Ct. Appeals (4th cir.) 1977, U.S. Supreme Ct. 1979, U.S. Ct. Appeals (D.C. cir.) 1980. Assoc. Hunton & Williams, Richmond, Va., 1975—. Asst. gen. counsel Robert E. Lee council Boy Scouts Am., Richmond, Va. Served to col. USMCR, 1986. Mem. ABA (vice chmn. electric power commn. natural resources sect.), Va. Bar Assn. (chmn. environ. law sect. 1985-85), Richmond Bar Assn. Environment. Office: Hunton & Williams 707 E Main St PO Box 1535 Richmond VA 23212

ROSCOE, GEORGE DENNIS, lawyer; b. Highland Park, Mich., Oct. 4, 1951; s. George L. and Lukrecia (Turkus) Roscoe. B in Music Edn., Youngstown State U., 1975; M Music Edn., W.Va. U., 1976; JD, Cleveland Marshall Coll. Law, 1981, LLM, 1983. Bar: Ohio 1981, U.S. Dist. Ct. (no. dist.) Ohio 1983. Atty., advisor social security adminstrn. HHS, Cleve., 1982-86, 87—; supervisory atty. HHS, Chgo., 1986. Editor Cleve. State U. Law Rev., 1981. Mem. ABA, Fed. Bar Assn. Administrative and regulatory, Social security, Federal civil litigation. Office: Office Hearings and Appeals Statler Office Tower Suite 1150 1127 Euclid Ave Cleveland OH 44115

ROSDEITCHER, SIDNEY S., lawyer; b. Bayonne, N.J., June 2, 1936; s. Morris and Lee (Rosenbluth) R.; m. Linda Latter, Aug. 28, 1960; children: Elizabeth, David, Emily. AB, Columbia U., 1958; LLB magna cum laude, Harvard U., 1961. Bar: N.Y., D.C., U.S. Dist. Ct. (so. and ea. dists.) N.Y., U.S. Tax Ct., U.S. Ct. Appeals (1st, 2d, 3d, 4th, 8th, 9th, and 10th cirs.), U.S. Supreme Ct. Atty. office of legal counsel U.S. Dept. Justice, Washington, 1961-62; advisor to commr. FTC, Washington, 1965-66; assoc. Paul, Weiss, Rifkind, Wharton & Garrison, N.Y.C., 1962-65, 66-72, ptnr., 1972—; adj. prof. civil liberties law Bklyn. Law Sch., 1974-76. Article editor Harvard U. Law Rev., 1960-61; contbr. articles to legal jours. Mem. D.C. Bar Assn. (model rules spl. com. 1982-85), Assn. of Bar of City of N.Y. (chmn. profl. and jud. ethics com. 1979-82, fed. cts. com. 1982—). Antitrust, Civil litigation. Home: 90 Riverside Dr New York NY 10024 Office: Paul Weiss Rifkind Wharton & Garrison 1285 Ave of the Americas New York NY 10019

ROSE, ANDREW JAMES EVANS, lawyer; b. Sewickley, Pa., June 29, 1946; s. John Evans Sr. and Esme Joceyln (Pattison) R. BA, Colgate U., 1968; JD, U. Pitts., 1973. Bar: Pa. 1973, U.S. Supreme Ct. 1979, U.S. Tax Ct. 1981. Assoc. Rose, Schmidt, Chapman, Duff & Haslay and predecessor firms, Pitts., 1973-79, ptnr., 1979-86; mng. atty. Hyatt Legal Services, Pitts., 1986—. Served with U.S. Army, 1968-70. Republican. Clubs: Duquesne (Pitts.); Allegheny Country (Sewickley). Administrative and regulatory, General practice. Home: 512 Sewickley Heights Dr Sewickley PA 15143

ROSE, CAROL MARGUERITE, law educator; b. Washington, Apr. 12, 1940; d. J. Hugh and Marie (Meenehan) R. BA, Antioch Coll., 1962; MA, U. Chgo., 1963, JD, 1977; PhD, Cornell U., 1970. Bar: Ill. 1977, Calif. 1978, D.C. 1978. Instr. history Ohio St. U., Columbus, 1969-73; assoc. dir. So. Govtl. Monitor Project, Atlanta, 1975-76; law clk. to judge U.S. Ct. Appeals (5th cir.), Austin, Tex., 1977-78; asst. prof. law Stanford (Calif.) U., 1978-80; acting prof. law U. Calif., Berkeley, 1980-82; prof. law Northwestern U., Chgo., 1982—. Bd. editors Foundation Press, Minneola, N.Y., 1986—. Mem. Am. Assn. Law Schs. (vice-chariperson local govt. sect.), Am. Hist. Assn., Order of Coif. Environment, Real property, Legal education. Home: 2153 N Seminary Chicago IL 60614 Office: Northwestern U Sch Law 357 E Chicago Ave Chicago IL 60611

ROSE, CHARLES ALEXANDER, lawyer; b. Louisville, Ky., June 14, 1932; s. Hector Edward and Mary (Shepard) R.; m. Katherine Claire Adams, Aug. 2, 1973; children—Marc, Craig, Lorna, Gordon, Alex, Sara. B.A., U. Louisville, 1954, J.D., 1960. Bar: Ky. 1960. U.S. Ct. Appeals (6th cir.) 1970, Ind. 1978, U.S. Supreme Ct. 1978. Sole practice, Louisville, Ky., 1960-63; assoc. Jones, Ewen & McKenzie, Louisville, 1963-65; ptnr. Curtis & Rose, Louisville, 1965-81, Weber & Rose, Louisville, 1981—. Served to lt. USAF, 1954-56. Mem. ABA, Ky. Bar Assn., Ind. Bar Assn., Louisville Bar Assn., Am. Soc. Hosp. Attys., Brandeis Soc., Fedn. Ins. Counsel. Republican. Episcopalian. Clubs: River Road Country, Pendennis (Louisville), Jefferson. Personal injury. Office: 2300 Citizens Plaza Louisville KY 40202

ROSE, CHARLES JON, lawyer; b. Boston, Nov. 2, 1952; s. Herbert Phillip Rose and Paula C. (Stein) Weissman; m. Sandra Lee Glenn, Aug. 7, 1977 (div. July 1983); 1 child, Jason Samuel. BA, Rutgers U., 1974; JD, U. Miami, 1977. Bar: Fla. 1977, U.S. Dist. Ct. (so. dist.) Fla. 1978, Colo. 1979, D.C. 1979, U.S. Dist. Ct. Colo. 1982. Assoc. Jay Dermer Law Offices, Miami Beach, Fla., 1978-79, Richard A. Anderson, P.C., Lakewood, Colo., 1979-80, Stitt, Wittenbrink & Nieman, P.C., Westminster, Colo., 1980-84; sole practice Denver, 1984—; asst. city atty. Georgetown, Colo., Erie, Colo., and Westminster, 1980-84, City of Lafayette, Colo., 1985—; mcpl. relief judge Erie County, 1986—; bd. dirs. Met. Lawyers Referral Service, Denver. Treas. campaign Com. to elect Teddi Jo Samano to State Legislature, Denver, 1984; mem. exec. Com. to elect Romer for Gov., Adams County, 1986; floor leader Com. to elect Baca for Congress, Adams County, 1986; bd. dirs. Crimestoppers Inc., Westminster, 1983—. Mem. ABA, D.C. Bar Assn., Fla. Bar Assn., Colo. Bar Assn. (family law sect.), Adams County Bar Assn., Soc. Bar and Gavel, MetroNorth C. of C. (steering com. for leadership program 1984—, chmn. 1986—). Democrat. Avocations: sports, politics, music. Family and matrimonial, Criminal, Municipal prosecution. Office: 6800 Broadway Suite 102 Denver CO 80221

ROSE, DENNIS EDWARD, lawyer; b. East St. Louis, Ill., Apr. 24, 1947; s. William Edward and Bertha Beatrice (Oliver) R. BA in Social Studies, U. Ill., 1969, JD, 1972. Bar: Ill. 1972, Mo. 1983. Ptnr. Donovan, Hatch & Constance, P.C., Belleville, Ill., 1973—; bd. dirs. Ill. Continuing Legal Edn., Chgo., 1977, Ill. State Bar Assn., Springfield, 1983-84. V.p., bd. dirs. Belleville YMCA, Ill., 1984—; mem. exec. com., bd. dirs. St. Louis chpt. March of Dimes, 1986. Served to capt. U.S. Army, 1972. Insurance, Personal injury, State civil litigation. Home: 4954 Lindell #5E Saint Louis MO 63108 Office: Donovan Hatch & Constance 8 E Washington Belleville IL 62220

ROSE, EDITH SPRUNG, lawyer; b. N.Y.C., Jan. 7, 1924; d. David L. and Anna (Storch) Sprung; m. David J. Rose, Feb. 15, 1948; children—Elizabeth Rose Stanton, Lawrence, Michael. B.A., Barnard Coll., 1944; LL.B., Columbia U., 1946. Bar: N.Y. 1947, N.J. 1973. Adminstr., Practising Law Inst., N.Y.C., 1947-48; ptnr. Smith, Lambert, Hicks & Miller, Princeton, N.J., 1974—. Mem. ABA, N.J. Bar Assn., Princeton Bar Assn., Women's Law Caucus of Mercer County. Club: Princeton (N.Y.C.). Estate planning, Family and matrimonial, General practice. Home: 201 Lambert Dr Princeton NJ 08540 Office: PO Box 627 1 Palmer Square Princeton NJ 08540

ROSE, ELIHU ISAAC, lawyer; b. Bklyn., Nov. 27, 1941; s. Aaron Henry and Frances (Klinger) R.; A.B., Columbia U., 1963, M.B.A., 1965; J.D., St. John's U., Bklyn., 1968; m. Gail Roberta Cohen, Aug. 22, 1964; children—Melissa Kaye, Heidi Jill. CPA, N.Y.; bar: N.Y. 1969. Sr. tax acct. Price Waterhouse & Co., N.Y.C., 1967-71; dir. taxes Exec. Monetary Mgmt., Inc., N.Y.C., 1971-79; pres. Elihu I. Rose, P.C., Roslyn, N.Y., 1979—. Mem. ABA, Am. Inst. CPAs, N.Y. State Bar Assn., N.Y. State Soc. CPAs, Bar Assn. Nassau County, Pension Counsel L.I. (pres. 1981). Personal income taxation, Pension, profit-sharing, and employee benefits, Corporate taxation. Office: 1044 Northern Blvd Roslyn NY 11576

ROSE, I. NELSON, law educator; b. Los Angeles, May 23, 1950; s. Bernard and Helen Mae (Nelson) R.; m. Audree Dee Agbayani, Sept. 25, 1982. B.A., UCLA, 1973; J.D., Harvard U., 1979. Bar: Hawaii 1979, Calif. 1980, U.S. Dist. Ct. Hawaii 1979, U.S. Ct. Appeals (9th cir.) 1980. Pvt. practice, Honolulu, 1979-82; asst. prof. law Whittier Coll., Los Angeles, 1982-85, assoc. prof. 1985—; cons. legal gaming. Author: Gambling and the Law, 1986; also articles in profl. jours. Founder, counsel Hawaii Lions Eye Bank, Honolulu, 1979-82; v.p., counsel Calif. Council on Compulsive Gambling. Mem. ABA, Calif. State Bar Assn., Hawaii Bar Assn., Internat. Assn. Gaming Attys. Democrat. Jewish. Gambling law, Legal education. Home: 1839 Colby Ave #1 Los Angeles CA 90025 Office: Whittier Coll Sch Law 5353 W 3d St Los Angeles CA 90020

ROSE, JOHN T., II, lawyer; b. N.Y.C., Feb. 24, 1947; s. John and Susan (Brown) R.; m. Myrtis McKnight, Aug. 23, 1970; children: Rhonda, Keryn. AB, Hunter Coll., 1968; JD, Harvard U., 1971. Bar: N.Y. 1973, Calif. 1973, U.S. Dist. Ct. (so. dist.) N.Y. 1973, U.S. Dist. Ct. (cen. dist.) Calif. 1986. Law clk. to judge U.S. Dist. Ct. (so. dist.) Calif., Los Angeles, 1971-72; assoc. Polettie, Freidin, Prashker, Feldman & Gartner, N.Y.C., 1972-74; atty., v.p. law staff NBC, Inc., N.Y.C., 1974—; arbitrator White Plains City Ct., N.Y., 1981—. Mem. ad hoc adv. com. White Plains Bd. of Edn., N.Y., 1981-86; bd. dirs. White Plains Housing Information Soc., 1984-86. Named one of Black Achievers in Industry Harlem YMCA, 1983. Mem. Assn. of Bar of City of N.Y. (entertainment and sports law com.), Am. Arbitration Assn. (arbitrator comml. panel 1974—). Methodist. Labor, Real property, Entertainment. Home: 88 Midchester Ave White Plains NY 10606 Office: NBC Inc 30 Rockefeller Plaza New York NY 10112

ROSE, JONATHAN CHAPMAN, lawyer; b. Cleve., June 8, 1941; s. Horace Chapman and Katherine Virginia (Cast) R.; m. Susan Anne Porter, Jan. 26, 1980; 1 son, Benjamin Chapman. A.B., Yale U., 1963; LL.B. cum laude, Harvard U., 1967. Bar: Mass. 1968, D.C. 1972, U.S. Supreme Ct. 1976, Circuit Ct. Appeals 1977, Ohio 1978. Law clk. Justice R. Ammi Cutter, Mass. Supreme Jud. Ct., 1967-68; spl. asst. to U.S. pres., 1971-73; gen. counsel Council on Internat. Econ. Policy, 1973-74; assoc. dept. atty. gen. U.S. Dept. Justice, 1974-75; dept. asst. atty. gen. U.S. Dept. Justice (Antitrust Div.), 1975-77; asst. atty. gen. Office of Legal Policy, 1981-84; ptnr. firm Jones, Day, Reavis & Pogue, Washington, 1977-81, 84—. Served to 1st lt. U.S. Army, 1969-71. Mem. Adminstrv. Conf. of U.S., Am. Bar Assn., D.C. Bar Assn., Mass. Bar Assn., Ohio Bar Assn., Fed. Bar Assn., Am. Law Inst. Republican. Episcopalian. Clubs: Met, Chevy Chase, Union, Yale, Harvard. Administrative and regulatory, Antitrust, Private international. Office: Metropolitan Sq 655 15th St NW Washington DC 20005

ROSE, LEONARD, lawyer; b. Boston, Mar. 19, 1927; s. Morris and Sylvia (Kahn) R.; m. Joan Bennett, Aug. 11, 1971; children from previous marriage—Jennifer Susan, Edward Daniel, Marcie Ann; stepchildren—Linda Goldstein Selig, Michael Howard Goldstein. A.B., Harvard U., 1950; J.D., Boston U., 1952; LL.M., John Marshall Law Sch., 1961; postgrad. Harvard Law Sch., 1973-74. Bar: Mass. 1953, Ill. 1957, D.C. 1966, N.H., 1971, U.S. Supreme Ct. 1959, U.S. Ct. Appeals (1st cir.) 1954, (7th cir.) 1958, U.S. Ct. Internat. Trade 1962, U.S. Dist. Ct. Mass. 1954, U.S. Dist. Ct. (no. dist.) Ill. 1958, U.S. Dist. Ct. R.I. 1980, U.S. Dist. Ct. Conn. 1985. Sole practice law, Boston, 1953-57, Chgo., 1957-64; ptnr. firm Rose & Stansbury (name later changed to Mason, Albright, Stansbury & Rose), Chgo. and Washington, 1965- 71; asst. gen. counsel Hampshire Designers, Inc., Manchester, N.H., 1971-72; sole practice law Falmouth, Mass., 1975-86, ptnr. Rose & Kahrl, Falmouth, 1986—; permanent master Trial Ct. Mass., 1974—; mem. nat. panel arbitrators Am. Arbitration Assn., 1965—; exec. com. bd. dirs. Mass. Bay Marine Studies Consortium, Inc.; faculty John Marshall Law Sch.,

Chgo., 1969-70; admiralty counsel Am. Sail Tng. Assn., Council of Ednl. Ship Owners, 1976-79. Contbr. articles to profl. jours. Patentee in field. Served to comdr. JAGC, USNR 1944-46, 46-79. Mem. ABA, Maritime Law Assn. U.S., Mass. Bar Assn., N.H. Bar Assn., D.C. Bar Assn., Chgo. Bar Assn. Jewish. Clubs: Harvard of Boston, N.Y.C., Cape Cod, Waquoit Bay Yacht (commodore 1977-78). Admiralty, Private international, Federal civil litigation. Home: 184 Seapit Rd Waquoit East Falmouth MA 02536 Office: 157 Locust St Falmouth MA 02540

ROSE, LOIS ANN, lawyer; b. Lemmon, S.D., July 24, 1947; d. Clifford Glenn and Alta Mae (Davison) Schnell; m. Charles R. Rose, Aug. 12, 1967. BS with honors, U. S.D., 1970, JD with honors, 1979. Bar: S.D. 1979, U.S. Dist. Ct. S.D. 1979. Assoc., ptnr. Davenport, Evans, Hurwitz & Smith, Sioux Falls, S.D., 1979-84; sole practice Sioux Falls, 1984—; continuing legal edn. com. State Bar of S.D., Pierre, 1980-83, legislation com. 1982—; bar examiner S.D. Bd. of Bar Exams., Pierre, 1984—. Trustee Sioux Falls Pub. Library, 1983—. Probate, Pension, profit-sharing, and employee benefits, General corporate. Office: Suite 200 Law Ctr Bldg 505 W 9th St Sioux Falls SD 57104

ROSE, MICHAEL EDWARD, lawyer; b. N.Y.C., Dec. 12, 1943. BE, City Coll. of N.Y., 1966; MS, EE, U. So. Calif., 1971; JD magna cum laude, Loyola U., Los Angeles, 1974. Bar: N.Y. 1974, Calif. 1974. Mem. tech. staff Hughes Aircraft, Los Angeles, 1966-71; atty. U.S. Dept. of Justice, Washington, 1974-75, Atlantic Richfield Corp., Los Angeles, 1975-76; counsel broadcast CBS Inc., N.Y.C., 1976—. Mem. Fed. Communications Bar Assn., Assn. of Bar of City of N.Y. Avocation: photography. Administrative and regulatory, Contracts commercial, Entertainment. Home: 415 W 24th St New York NY 10011 Office: CBS Inc 51 W 52d St New York NY 10011

ROSE, MICHAEL I., lawyer; b. Oakland, Calif., Apr. 7, 1945; s. Murray L. and Elaine F. Rose; children: Ryan, Darren. BS, U. Miami, 1967; JD, Samford U., 1970. Bar: Fla. 1971, U.S. Supreme Ct. 1975, U.S. Ct. Appeals (D.C. cir.) 1978. Sole practice Miami, 1971—. State civil litigation, Family and matrimonial, Immigration, naturalization, and customs. Office: 28 W Flagier St #303 Miami FL 33130

ROSE, NORMAN, lawyer; b. N.Y.C., July 7, 1923; s. Edward J. and Frances (Ludwig) R.; div.; children—Ellen Rose Scharf, Michael. B.B.A., CCNY, 1947; J.D., N.Y. Law Sch. 1953. Bar: Fla. 1979, N.Y. 1954, U.S. Dist. Ct. (ea. dist.) N.Y. 1956, U.S. Dist. Ct. (so. dist.) N.Y. 1960, U.S. Dist. Ct. (so. dist.) Fla. 1981, U.S. Ct. Appeals (2d cir.) 1967, U.S. Tax Ct. 1956, U.S. Supreme Ct. 1961. Sole practice, N.Y.C., 1954-69, Garden City, N.Y., 1969-79, Ft. Lauderdale, Fla., 1979—; ptnr. Dean, Falanga & Rose, Carle Pl., N.Y., 1979—; referee Small Claims Ct., N.Y.C., 1959-69; arbitrator Accident Claims Tribunal, Am. Arbitration Assn., 1960-65; C.P.A., N.Y.C., 1951-57; lectr. in field. Author law note Liability of Golfer to Person Struck by Ball, 1959 (Hon. mention 1960). Pres. Nassau S. Shore Little League, Lawrence, N.Y., 1966-68; treas. 5 Towns Democratic Club, Woodmere, N.Y., 1966-67; chmn. United Fund, Village of Lawrence, 1967. Served to cpt. USAF, 1943-45, ETO. Decorated Disting. Flying Cross (ETO), Air medal, Silver star, Purple Heart, Presdl. Unit citation. Mem. Assn. Trial Lawyers Am. (sustaining), Acad. Fla. Trial Lawyers (sustaining), Broward County Trial Lawyers Assn., N.Y. State Assn. Plantiffs Trial Lawyers, N.Y. State Bar Assn., Fla. Bar Assn., Nassau County Bar Assn. (chmn. med.-legal com. 1975-77), Lawyer/Pilots Bar Assn. Democrat. Jewish. Club: Lawrence Country (bd. govs. 1966-68); Old Westbury Country (bd. govs. 1975), Lodges: Masons, Shriners. Personal injury, Insurance, State civil litigation. Home: 3200 Port Royale Dr N Fort Lauderdale FL 33308 Office: Radice Corporate Ctr 800 Corporate Dr Fort Lauderdale FL 33334

ROSE, RICHARD LOOMIS, lawyer; b. Long Branch, N.J., Oct. 21, 1936; s. Charles Frederick Perrott and Jane Mary (Crotta) R.; m. Marian Frances Irons, Apr. 1, 1960; children: Linda, Cynthia, Bonnie. B.A., Cornell U., 1958; J.D., Washington and Lee U., 1963. Mem. firm Townsend & Lewis, N.Y.C., 1963-65; partner Cummings & Lockwood, Stamford, Conn., 1965—; dir. Vitam Center, Inc.; Mem. spl. adv. com. to Conn. banking commr. Editor: Washington and Lee Law Rev. Served as 1st lt. AUS, 1958-60. Mem. Am. Bar Assn., Conn. Bar Assn. (exec. com. corp. sect., exec. com. banking sect.), Assn. Bar City N.Y., Phi Delta Phi, Omicron Delta Kappa, Phi Delta Theta. Republican. Episcopalian. Club: New Canaan Country. Banking, Administrative and regulatory, Contracts commercial. Office: 10 Stamford Forum PO Box 120 Stamford CT 06904

ROSE, ROBERT STANTER, lawyer; b. Bronxville, N.Y., Sept. 11, 1943; s. Walter Clair and Betty Jane (Stanter) R.; m. Sandra Wallace Killough, Sept. 29, 1969; children: Christian Killough, Robert Stanter Jr. BA, St. Lawrence U., 1965; JD, Union U., 1968. Bar: N.Y. 1973, U.S. Dist. Ct. (no. dist.) N.Y. 1973, U.S. Supreme Ct. 1978. Confidential law clk. N.Y. State Supreme Ct., Binghamtom, 1974-76; asst. dist. atty. Broome County, Binghamtom, 1976-78; ptnr. Twining, Nemia, Hill & Steflik, Binghamtom, 1984—; atty. Town of Sanford, N.Y., 1984—, Town of Dickinson, N.Y., 1983—; commr. elections Broome County, N.Y., 1985—. Vestryman Christ Episcopal Ch., Binghamton, 1982-84; chmn. Broome County Rep. Com., Binghamton, 1983—; bd. dirs. Broome County Hist. Soc., Binghamton, 1981-86. Served to capt. U.S. Army, 1969-72, Vietnam. Mem. ABA, N.Y. State Bar Assn. (trial lawyers sect., ins., negligence and compensation law sect., mcpl. law sect., com. on civil practice law and rules), Broome County Bar Assn. (bd. dirs. 1986—), N.Y. State Trial Lawyers Assn. (legis. com., bd. dirs. 1987—). Clubs: Binghamton, Live Wire. Lodge: Rotary. State civil litigation, Local government, Personal injury. Home: 8 Chapin St Binghamton NY 13905 Office: Twining Nemia Hill & Steflik 53 Front St PO Box 1750 Binghamton NY 13902

ROSE, STEVEN MARC, lawyer; b. Pitts., Apr. 28, 1949; s. Alex J. Rose and Bertha Gertrude (Lubet) Steinberg; m. Elizabeth Helen Yeats, Dec. 18, 1975; children: Eliot Yeats, Rachel Anna Yeats. Bar: Oreg. 1974, U.S. Dist. Ct. Oreg. 1974, U.S. Ct. Appeals (9th cir.) 1977. Sole practice Portland, Oreg., 1975-77; ptnr. Rose & Senders, Portland, 1977—; judge pro tem Multnomah County Dist. Ct., Portland, 1979—, domestic relations Multnomah County Cir. Ct., Portland, 1984—. Mem. Oreg. State Bar Assn. (disciplinary trial panel), Multnomah Bar Assn. (com. on sole practicioners and small firms 1984-85). Democrat. Jewish. Avocations: outdoor activities, athletics. Real property, State civil litigation, General practice. Office: Rose & Senders 400 SW 6th Ave #907 Portland OR 97204

ROSE, WILLIAM, corporate lawyer; b. 1928. BA, Emerson Coll.; LLB, Fordham U. Assoc. Levin, Rosmarin & Schwartz, 1955-65; with Callaway Mills Inc., 1965-68, Indian Head Inc., 1968-74; v.p. Beaunit Inc., 1974-79; with Avnet Inc., N.Y.C., 1979-80, v.p. gen. counsel, 1980—. Office: Avnet Inc 767 Fifth Ave New York NY 10153 *

ROSE, WILLIAM SHEPARD, JR., lawyer; b. Columbia, S.C., Mar. 9, 1948; s. William Shepard and Meta Cantey (Boykin) R.; m. Frances John Hobbs, Aug. 11, 1973; children—Katherine Cummings, William Shepard, III, Whitaker Boykin. B.A. in English, U. South, 1970; J.D., U. S.C., 1973; LL.M. in Taxation, Georgetown U., 1976. Bar: S.C. 1973, Ohio 1970, D.C. 1974, U.S. Dist. Ct. D.C. 1976, U.S. Tax Ct. 1976, U.S. Supreme Ct. 1976. Trial atty. Office of Chief Counsel IRS, Washington, 1973-77; assoc. Frost & Jacobs, Cin., 1977-80, McNair Glenn et al., Hilton Head Island, S.C., 1980-83, ptnr., 1983—; chmn. and dir. Sea Pines Montessori Sch., Hilton Head Broadcasting, Hilton Head Planned Parenthood, MBR Corp., Adwell Corp., Hilton Head Prep. Sch., Contbr. articles to profl. jours. Asst. to chmn. of bus. fund raising Beaufort County United Way, Hilton Head Island, 1984; coordinator for Republican Sen. Thurmond Campaign, 1984. Mem. ABA (past chmn. subcom. tax sect.), Ohio Bar Assn., D.C. Bar Assn., S.C. Bar Assn., Beaufort County Bar Assn., Hilton Head Bar Assn. Republican. Episcopalian. Clubs: Hilton Head Cotillion, Ducks Unltd., Caroliniana Ball. Corporate taxation, Probate, General corporate. Home: 11 Jessamine Pl Hilton Head Island SC 29928 Office: McNair Law Firm PA PO Box 5914 Hilton Head Island SC 29938

ROSE-ACKERMAN, SUSAN, law and political economy educator; b. Mineola, N.Y., Apr. 23, 1942; d. R. William and Rosalie (Gould) Rose; m. Bruce A. Ackerman, May 29, 1967; children—Sybil, John. B.A., Wellesley Coll, 1964; Ph.D., Yale U., 1970. Asst. prof. U. Pa., Phila, 1970-74; lectr. Yale U., New Haven, 1974-75, asst. prof., 1975-78, assoc. prof., 1978-82; prof. law and polit. economy Columbia U., N.Y.C., 1982-87; dir. Ctr. for Law and Econ. Studies Columbia U., 1983-87; Ely prof. of Law and Polit. Econ. Yale U., New Haven, Conn., 1987—; Mem. rev. panel Program on Regulation and Policy Analysis, NSF, Washington, 1982-84; vis. prof. U. Rome, 1984. Author: (with Ackerman, Sawyer and Henderson) Uncertain Search for Environmental Quality, 1974 (Henderson prize 1982); Corruption: A Study in Political Economy, 1978; (with E. James) The Nonprofit Enterprise in Market Economies, 1986; editor book, The Economics of Nonprofit Institutions, 1986; contbr. articles to profl. jours.; bd. editors: Jour. Law, Econs. and Orgn., 1984—. Mem. Assn. Pub. Policy and Mgmt. (mem. policy council 1984—), Law and Soc. Assn. (trustee 1984-86), Am. Econ. Assn., Assn. Am. Law Schs. Democrat. Legal education, Administrative and regulatory, Environment. Office: Yale U Law Sch 401A Yale Sta New Haven CT 06520

ROSEMAN, ARNOLD DAVID, lawyer; b. N.Y.C., Apr. 10, 1917; s. Samuel Victor and Pauline (Kaplan) R.; m. Rose L. Mirkin, June 20, 1948; children—Paula Saler, Robert L. B.S., CCNY, 1938; J.D., Harvard U., 1941. Bar: N.Y. 1941, U.S. Dist. Ct. (so. and ea. dists.) N.Y. 1946, U.S. Ct. Appeals (2d cir.) 1946, U.S. Supreme Ct. 1960. Sole practice, N.Y.C., 1941—; N.Y. State commr. of investigation, 1974-75; acting city judge New Rochelle (N.Y.), 1972; spl. dist. atty. Westchester County, N.Y., 1977-78; lectr. N.Y. State Bar, 1979-82. Whip and minority leader Westchester Bd. Suprs., 1957-67; chmn. Community Chest, 1956-57. Served to capt. USAAF, 1941-46; PTO. Mem. ABA, N.Y. State Bar Assn., Westchester County and New Rochelle Bar Assn. Democrat. Clubs: Lions (pres. 1974), VFW, Am. Legion, Elks. Author: (with others) Basic Criminal Practice, 1979-83. Criminal, Legal education, General practice. Address: 38th Floor 122 E 42d St New York NY 10168

ROSEMAN, CHARLES SANFORD, lawyer; b. Jersey City, Feb. 26, 1945; s. Leon and Edith (Neidorf) R.; m. Jodyne Florence Snyder, July 3, 1967; children—Rochelle Lynn, Loren Scott. B.A., Calif. State U., 1968; J.D., U. San Diego, 1971. Bar: Calif. 1972, U.S. Dist. Ct. (so. dist.) Calif. 1972, U.S. Dist. Ct. (cen. dist.) Calif. 1975, U.S. Supreme Ct. 1980. Assoc. Greer, Popko, Nickoloff & Miller, San Diego, 1972-73; ptnr. Roseman & Roseman, San Diego, 1973-78, Roseman & Small, San Diego, 1978-82, Frank, Roseman, Freedus & Mann, San Diego, 1982-86 ; Roseman and Mann, 1986—; judge pro tem San Diego County Mcpl. Ct., 1975—; San Diego County Superior Ct., 1977—; also arbitrator. Pres. Tifereth Israel Synagogue, San Diego, 1981-83; bd. dirs. Glenn Aire Community Devel. Assn., San Diego, 1972-73, Big Bros. San Diego County, 1973-81; bd. dirs. San Diego County Anti-Defamation League, 1981-83, chmn. exec. com., 1984-85. Mem. Assn. Trial Lawyers Am., ABA, Calif. Trial Lawyers Assn. (Recognition of Experience award 1984), Calif. Bar Assn., Am. Arbitration Assn. (arbitrator, panel 1980—), San Diego Bar Assn., San Diego Trial Lawyers Assn. (bd. dirs. 1982-84), U. San Diego Sch. Law Alumni Assn. (bd. dirs. 1972-73). Democrat. Lodge: B'nai B'rith (pres. 1978). State civil litigation, Insurance, Personal injury. Office: Roseman & Mann 101 W Broadway Suite 1100 San Diego CA 92101

ROSEMAN, MARK ALAN, lawyer; b. Akron, Ohio, Nov. 6, 1942; s. H.A. and Sylvia (Reaven) R.; children: Seth Robert, Nathan. AB, Dartmouth Coll., 1964; JD, Boston U., 1967; postdoctoral, Wharton Coll., 1967-68. Bar: Pa. 1968, Fla. 1980. Sole practice Hollywood, Fla., 1968—. Author: Legal Protection for the Computer Programmer, 1986. Mem. ABA (sci. and tech. sect.), Fla. Bar Assn. (computer law com.), Broward County Bar Assn., Computer Law Assn. Democrat. Jewish. Computer. Home: PO Box 1973 Hollywood FL 33022 Office: 733 N Southlake Dr Hollywood FL 33019

ROSEMARIN, CAREY STEPHEN, lawyer; b. Englewood, N.J., Aug. 19, 1950; s. Jack L. and Muriel Ruth (Gordon) R.; m. Joan Maxine Lafer, June 17, 1973; 1 child, Benjamin Joseph. BS, U. Mich., 1972; MS, Pa. State U., 1974; JD, U. Tenn., 1978. Bar: Tenn. 1978, Ill. 1982, U.S. Dist. Ct. (ea. dist.) Tenn. 1978, U.S. Dist. Ct. (no. dist.) Ill. 1982. Research assoc. Union Carbide Corp., Oak Ridge, Tenn., 1974-80; asst. regional counsel U.S. EPA, Chgo., 1980-86; sr. assoc. Katten, Muchin, Zavis, Pearl, Greenberger & Galler, Chgo., 1986—. Mem. ABA, Tenn. Bar Assn., Chgo. Bar Assn. (chmn. environ. law com. 1985-86), Environ. Law Inst. (assoc.). Jewish. Avocations: licensed glider pilot, bicycling. Environment, Civil rights. Office: Katten Muchin Zavis Pearl et al 525 W Monroe St Chicago IL 60606-3693

ROSEN, ALEX L., lawyer, consultant; b. Vienna, Austria, Feb. 17, 1906; s. Moses and Lisa (Locker) R.; m. Anne Frances Auslander, June 29, 1930; children—Marvin, Leslie, Roberta. B.A., Columbia U., 1927; LL.B., Bklyn. Law Sch., 1931. Bar: N.Y. 1932, U.S. Dist. Ct. (so. dist.) N.Y. 1935, U.S. Ct. Appeals (2d cir.) 1951, U.S. Supreme Ct. 1959, U.S. Tax Ct. 1971. Sole practice, N.Y.C., now, Palm Beach, Fla.; lectr. Contbr. articles to profl. jours. Mem. Palm Beach (Fla.) Democratic Club. Mem. N.Y. Trial Lawyers Assn., U.S. County Lawyers Assn. Democrat. Jewish. Lodges: Masons, B'nai B'rith. Bankruptcy, Contracts commercial, Estate planning.

ROSEN, ARTHUR R., lawyer; b. Biloxi, Miss., Mar. 15, 1950; s. Harry H. and Rose (Hechler) R.; m. Barbara Dreyfuss, Aug. 21, 1981 (div. June 1985). BA, NYU, 1971; JD, St. John's U., N.Y.C., 1974; APC, NYU, 1975; MBA, Rensselaer Poly Inst., 1977. Bar: N.Y. 1974, U.S. Dist. Ct. (no., so. and ea. dists.) N.Y. 1975, U.S. Ct. Appeals (2d cir.) 1975, U.S. Tax Ct., U.S. Ct. Appeals (4th cir.) 1978, U.S. Supreme Ct. 1978. Tax specialist Coopers & Lybrand, N.Y.C., 1974-75; dep. counsel N.Y. Dept. Taxation, N.Y.C., 1976-79; mgr. tax policy programs Xerox Corp., Rochester, N.Y., 1979-83; div. mgr. taxes AT&T, Morristown, N.J., 1983—. Contbr. articles to profl. jours. Mem. ABA (chmn. state and local tax com. 1985—), N.Y. State Bar Assn. (co-chmn. N.Y. tax matters com. 1984—), Inst. Property Taxation, Internat. Assn. Assessing Others, Nat. Assn. State Bar Tax Sects. (mem. exec. com. 1985—). State and local taxation, Corporate taxation. Office: AT&T 412 Mt Kemble Ave Morristown NJ 07960

ROSEN, CATHRYN JO, legal educator; b. Bradford, Pa., Nov. 11, 1952; d. Arthur Arnold and Alyse (Hample) R.; m. Stephen Franklyn Ritner, May 16, 1982; 1 child, Scott Benjamin. BA, Case Western Reserve U., 1974; JD, Temple U., 1978, LLM, 1987. Bar: Pa. 1978, U.S. Dist. Ct. (ea. dist.) Pa. 1979. Law clk. Pa. Supreme Ct., Erie, 1978-79; assoc. Schnader, Harrison, Segal & Lewis, Phila., 1979-82; lectr. law Temple U., Phila., 1982-84, asst. prof. criminal justice, 1984—; cons. Pa. Dep. Sheriff's Tng. Curriculum Devel. Project, Phila., 1985-86, Pa. Mcpl. Police Officers Basic Tng. Curriculum Devel. Project, 1986-87. Mem. ABA, Am. Soc. Criminology, Phila. Bar Assn., Acad. Criminal Justice Scis., Law and Soc. Assn. Avocations: skiing, tennis. Criminal, Legal education. Office: Temple U Dept Criminal Justice Philadelphia PA 19122

ROSEN, GARY ALAN, lawyer; b. N.Y.C., June 13, 1955; s. Harry and Arline (Kreiswirth) R.; m. Lisa Suzanne Alpert, Aug. 21, 1983. BA in Econs., Hofstra U., 1979; JD, Emory U., 1982. Bar: Ga. 1982, Md. 1983, U.S. Dist. Ct. Md. 1983, U.S. Ct. Appeals (4th cir.) 1983, D.C. 1984, U.S. Dist. Ct. D.C. 1984. Law clk. to presiding justice U.S. Bankruptcy Ct., Rockville, Md., 1982-83; assoc. Lerch, Early, Roseman & Frankel, Bethesda, Md., 1983-85, Zuckerman, Spaeder, Goldstein, Taylor & Kolker, Washington, 1985-86; prin. Gary A. Rosen, chartered, Washington, 1987—. Mem. ABA (corps., banking and bus. law sect.), Montgomery County Bankruptcy Bar Assn. (chmn.). Democrat. Jewish. Bankruptcy. Home: 4980 Cloister Dr Bethesda MD 20852 Office: 7315 Wisconsin Ave Suite 901N Bethesda MD 20814

ROSEN, GARY MITCHELL, lawyer; b. Akron, Ohio, Mar. 26, 1953; s. Bernard I. and Ruth Bernice (Stan) R.; m. Toby Lynn Schneiderman, May 20, 1984; 1 child, Adam Herschel. BA, Tufts U., 1975; JD, George Washington U., 1978. Bar: Ohio 1978, U.S. Dist. Ct. (no. dist.) Ohio 1979, U.S. Ct. Appeals (6th cir.) 1980. Assoc. Blakemore, Rosen, Meeker & Varian Co., Akron, Ohio, 1978—; chief city prosecutor City of Akron, 1984—; mem. editorial adv. bd. Mental and Physical Disability Law Reporter, Washington, 1983-84. Sec. Akron Jewish Community Fedn., 1986 (young leadership award 1984); bd. dirs. Akron Jewish Ctr., 1984; mem. adv. bd. Massillon (Ohio) State Hosp., 1981-84. Recipient Outstanding Service award Summit County Mental Health Assn., Akron, 1984, 85, 86. Mem. ABA (chmn. young lawyers div. 1983-84, com. delivery of services to disabled, commn. of mentally disabled 1984-85), Ohio Bar Assn., Akron Bar Assn. Democrat. Jewish. Criminal, Local government, Mental health. Home: 369 Sand Run Rd Akron OH 44313 Office: City of Akron 161 S High St Akron OH 44313

ROSEN, HOWARD THEODORE, lawyer; b. Newark, Mar. 8, 1928; s. Jacob Irving and Fae Evelyn (Mandelbaum) R.; m. Selma Margulis, June 17, 1951; children: James Eliot, Amy Maude Rosen Carden, Jonathan. BS, Syracuse U., 1948; LLB, Harvard U., 1951. Bar: N.J. 1952, U.S. Supreme Ct. 1968. Law sec. to presiding justice N.J. Supreme Ct., Newark, 1951-52; sole practice Newark, 1953-61; ptnr. Clapp & Eisenberg, Newark, 1961-69, 86—, Rosen, Weiss, McCarthy & Burstein, Newark, 1969-86. N.J. commr. Nat. Conf. Uniform State Laws, Chgo., 1976—; commr. N.J. Law Revision Commn., Trenton, 1987—; mem. U.S. del. UN Gen. Assembly, N.Y.C., 1979. Served to capt. USAF, 1952-53. Mem. ABA, N.J. Bar Assn. (chmn. pub. utilities sect. 1983-84), Essex COunty Bar Assn. Democrat. Jewish. Clubs: Orange Lawn Tennis (South Orange, N.J.); Essex (Newark). Avocations: fgn. relations, tennis. Public utilities, State civil litigation, General corporate. Home: 99 Sagamore Rd Millburn NJ 07041 Office: Clapp & Eisenberg 80 Park Plaza Newark NJ 07102

ROSEN, JEFFREY J., lawyer; b. N.Y.C., May 13, 1949; s. Fred and Jane (Krieger) R.; m. Jeanine Matte, Oct. 18, 1985. BA, Harvard U., 1971, JD, 1978. Bar: D.C. 1980. Reporter, columnist Rocky Mountain News, Denver, 1971-75; law clk. to presiding justice U.S. Ct. Appeals, Washington, 1978-79; law clk. to justice William J. Brennan U.S. Supreme Ct., Washington, 1979-80; spl. asst. to sec. U.S. Treasury, Washington, 1980-81; assoc. Paul, Weiss et al, Washington, 1981-85; assoc. O'Melveny & Myers, Washington, 1985-87, ptnr., 1987—. Supreme Ct. editor Harvard Law Rev. Mem. ABA (tax sect., tech. rev. com.), D.C. Bar Assn. Corporate taxation, General corporate. Home: 10221 Forest Lake Dr Great Falls VA 22066 Office: O'Melveny & Myers 1800 M St NW Washington DC 20036

ROSEN, JON HOWARD, lawyer; b. Bklyn., May 20, 1943; s. Eli and Vera (Horowitz) R.; m. Norma Jane Crist, Feb. 15, 1976; children: Jason Marc, Hope Terry. BA, Hobart Coll., 1965; JD, St. John's U., 1968; postgrad. Bernard Baruch Sch. Bus., CCNY, 1969-71. Bar: N.Y. 1969, Calif. 1975, Wash. 1977. Atty. FAA, N.Y.C., 1968-71; regional atty., contract adminstr. Air Line Pilots Assn., N.Y.C., Chgo., Los Angeles, San Francisco, 1971-77; sole practice Seattle, 1977-80; ptnr. Frank and Rosen, Seattle, 1981—; instr. labor studies Shoreline Community Coll., 1978—. Mem. ABA (union co-chmn. sub-com. on pub. sector arbitration), Seattle-King County Bar Assn. (past chmn. aviation and space law sect., chmn. Pacific Coast Labor Law Conf., past chmn. labor law sect.), AFT. Administrative and regulatory, Labor. Home: 2216 13th Ave E Seattle WA 98102 Office: 705 2d Ave Suite 1201 Seattle WA 98104

ROSEN, MARTIN JAY, lawyer; b. N.Y.C., Nov. 15, 1942; s. Herman S. and Ida (Ginsberg) R.; m. Bonnie C., Dec. 24, 1964; children—Scott F., Brian M. B.A., Hobart Coll., 1964; LL.B., NYU, 1967. Bar: N.Y. 1967, U.S. Supreme Ct. 1976. Law asst. Appellate Div. First Dept., N.Y.C., 1967-68; assoc. Battle, Fowler, Stokes & Kheel, N.Y.C., 1968-69; confdl. law sec. to justice Supreme Ct. Westchester County (N.Y.), 1969-71; ptnr. Kahn, Goldman & Rosen, Westchester County, 1971-74; sole practice, White Plains, N.Y., 1975—; lectr. in field. Fellow Am. Acad. Matrimonial Lawyers; mem. ABA, N.Y. State Bar Assn., Westchester County Bar Assn. (chmn. family law), Rockland County Bar Assn., White Plains Bar Assn. Contbr. articles to legal jours. Family and matrimonial. Home: 4 Aberdeen Dr West Nyack NY 10994 Office: 175 Main St Suite 415 White Plains NY 10601

ROSEN, MICHAEL JAMES, attorney; b. Miami, Fla., Oct. 25, 1949; s. E. David and Muriel G. (Gerstein) R.; m. Barbara Yagman, Aug. 8, 1971; children—Jason, Lauren. B.A., U. South Fla., 1971; J.D., U. Miami, 1974. Bar: Fla. 1974, U.S. Dist. Ct. (so. dist.) Fla. 1974, U.S. Ct. Appeals (5th cir.), 1975, U.S. Ct. Appeals (6th cir.) 1979, U.S. Dist. Ct. (mid. dist.) Fla. 1980, U.S. Ct. Appeals (11th cir.) 1981, U.S. Ct. Appeals (2d cir.) 1983, U.S. Tax Ct., U.S. Supreme Ct. 1979. Asst. fed. pub. defender Fed. Pub. Defender, Miami, 1974-76; ptnr. Rosen & Rosen, P.A., Miami, 1976—. Mem. ABA, Fed. Bar Assn. (chmn. criminal discovery com. 1983), Nat. Assn. of Criminal Defense Lawyers, ACLU. Criminal, Federal civil litigation. Home: 8023 SW 103rd St Miami FL 33156 Office: Rosen Law Offices PA New World Tower 100 N Biscayne Blvd Suite 2910 Miami FL 33132-2305

ROSEN, NATHAN AARON, law librarian, lawyer, consultant; b. Kansas City, Mo., Sept. 12, 1955; s. Emanuel and Golda (Singer) R.; m. Priva Hannah Simon, Oct. 27, 1985. BA, U. Mo., 1977, JD, 1979; MLS, Columbia U., 1985. Bar: Mo. 1980, U.S. Dist. Ct. (we. dist.) Mo. 1980, U.S. Ct. Appeals (8th cir.) 1980. Assoc. Martin, Gorin & Assocs., Kansas City, 1980-82, Charles, House & Assocs., Kansas City, 1982-85; law librarian Proskauer, Rose, Goetz & Mendelsohn, Kansas City, 1984—; cons. Law Research Inst., N.Y.C. and Kansas City, 1980—. Author: Real Estate Syndication, 1985, Corporate Social Responsibility, 1986; contbr. articles to profl. jours. Mem. ALA, Am. Assn. Law Libraries, Am. Soc. for Info. Sci., Law Library Assn. Greater N.Y., Spl. Library Assn. Avocations: racquetball, sci. fiction, judo. Librarianship, Computer.

ROSEN, NORMAN EDWARD, lawyer; b. Providence, July 2, 1938; s. Albert and Lillian (Korb) R.; m. Estelle Cutler, Sept. 5, 1966; children—James, Vanessa. A.B., Harvard U., 1959; LL.B., Columbia U., 1962; M.A., George Washington U., 1965. Bar: N.Y. 1962, D.C. 1963, U.S. Supreme Ct. 1966. Trial atty. FTC, Washington, 1962-67; assoc. Paskus, Gordon & Hyman, N.Y.C., 1967-69; ptnr. Levin, Kreis, Ruskin & Gyory, N.Y.C., 1970-72; staff v.p., sr. counsel trade regulation and licensing RCA, N.Y.C., 1972-82, Princeton, N.J., 1982-86; sr. v.p., gen. counsel Gen. Electric and RCA Licensing Mgmt. Operation, Inc., Princeton, 1986—. Contbr. articles to profl. jours. Mem. ABA (chmn. antitrust sect. patent trademark and know-how com. 1983-86, mem. antitrust sect. council 1986—), Assn. Bar City N.Y., Am. Intellectual Property Law Assn. Clubs: Harvard (N.Y.C.); Surf (Quogue). Antitrust, Private international, Patent. Home: 333 E 23d St Apt 8D New York NY 10010 Office: RCA Two Independence Way PO Box 2023 Princeton NJ 08540

ROSEN, SIDNEY MARVIN, lawyer; b. Detroit, June 27, 1939; s. Fred A. and Gertrude (Cole) R.; m. Babette Van Praag, July 3, 1971; children: Jordan, Aviva. BS, U. Ariz., 1961, JD, 1964. Bar: Ariz. 1964, U.S. Dist. Ct. Ariz. 1964, Calif. 1965, U.S. Dist. Ct. Calif. 1965, U.S. Supreme Ct. 1971. Asst. atty. gen. State of Ariz., Phoenix, 1964-66, spl. asst. atty. gen., 1968-69; assoc. Kirkwood, Kaplan, Russin & Vechi, Bangcock, Thailand and Saigon, Vietnam, 1967-68; ptnr. Rosen, Waters & Enriquez and predecessor firm, Phoenix, 1970—; co-founder, law instr. Ariz. Bar Rev. Course, 1965-73; prof. internat. law Grad. Sch. Phoenix, 1975-76; former gen. counsel Nat. Speakers Assn., 1973-85. Candidate Dem. nomination for atty. gen. State of Ariz., 1974, U.S. Congress, 1976; mem. Ariz.-Mex. Gov.'s Commn., 1974—, counsel commerce and industry sect., 1974—; chmn. campaign Bonds for Israel, Ariz., 1980-85. Mem. Ariz. Bar Assn. (latin Am. relations com.), Calif. Bar Assn., Maricopa County Bar Assn., World Assn. Lawyers, Nat. Speakers Assn. (founder, former gen. counsel 1973-85), World Affairs Council, Hospitality Internat. (host), FIABCI (Internat. Real Estate Fedn., gen. counsel Ariz. chpt. 1985—), Ariz. World Trade Assn. (former bd. dirs.), Jaycees (treas. Ariz. chpt. 1969-70, ambassador to Philippine Islands 1969-70), Phi Alpha Delta. Democrat. Jewish. Lodge: Kiwanis. Avocations: stamp collecting, phoptography, world traveling, camping, scuba diving. Home: 119 E Alvarado Rd Phoenix AZ 85004 Office: Rosen Waters & Enriquez 4323 N 12th St Suite 104 Phoenix AZ 85014

ROSEN, TED MANUS, lawyer; b. N.Y.C., Dec. 29, 1946; s. Michael and Harriet (Skolnick) R.; m. Nancy J. Berger, June 25, 1972; 1 child, Melissa Ann. BA, Queens Coll., 1967; JD, NYU, 1971. Bar: N.Y. 1971, U.S. Dist. Ct. (so. and ea. dists.) N.Y. 1973, U.S. Ct. Appeals (2d cir.) 1973, U.S. Supreme Ct. 1978, U.S. Ct. Internat. Trade 1981, U.S. Ct. Claims 1985. Assoc. Fried, Frank, Harris, Shriver & Jacobson, N.Y.C., 1973-75, Robinson, Perlman, Kirschner & Leffler, N.Y.C., 1975-79; sole practice

N.Y.C., Great Neck, N.Y., 1979—; arbitrator N.Y. Stock Exchange, N.Y.C., 1981—, Am. Stock Exchange, N.Y.C., 1979—, Nat. Assn. Securities Dealers, N.Y.C., 1980—; judge adminstrv. law N.Y.C. Environ. Control Bd., 1980—. Candidate Dems. N.Y. State Senate, 1984; chief Great Neck (N.Y.) Cen. Aux. Police, 1982—; trustee Incorporated Village of Great Neck Plaza, 1985—. Mem. N.Y. State Bar Assn., Great Neck Lawyers Assn., Phi Beta Kappa, Psi Chi. Democrat. Jewish. Avocations: reading, sports, movies. State civil litigation, Consumer commercial, Federal civil litigation. Office: Station Plaza E Great Neck NY 11021

ROSEN, WILLIAM WARREN, lawyer; b. New Orleans, La., July 22, 1936; s. Warren Leucht and Erma (Stich) R.; m. Eddy Kahn, Nov. 26, 1965; children: Elizabeth K., Victoria A. BA, Tulane U., 1958, JD, 1964. Bar: La. 1964, U.S. Dist. Ct. (ea. dist.) La. 1965, U.S. Ct. Appeals (5th cir.) 1965, U.S. Dist. Ct. (we. dist.) La. 1984, U.S. Supreme Ct. 1984, U.S. Dist. Ct. (mid. dist.) La. 1985. Assoc. Dodge & Friend, New Orleans, 1965-68, Law Office of J.R. Martzell, New Orleans, 1968-70; sole practice New Orleans, 1970-79; ptnr. Lucas & Rosen (and predecessor firms), New Orleans, 1979—; mem. adv. com. paralegal studies program Tulane U., 1977-86; instr. legal interviewing and legal investigation U. New Orleans Paralegal Inst., 1986—, Tulane U., 1980-81, paralegal studies program bus. orgns., 1978. Mem. budget and planning com. Jewish Welfare Fedn., 1970-73, adv. council for drug edn. La. Dept. of Edn., 1973, profl. adv. com. Jewish Endowment Found., 1982—, exec. com. U.S. Olympic Com., La., 1982-84; treas. Dad's Club Isidore Newman Sch., 1981-82, v.p., 1982-84, pres., 1984-85; pres. Uptown Flood Assn., 1982-85; bd. dirs. Jewish Children's Home Service, 1967-73, Jewish Family and Children's Service, 1973-76, Met. Crime Commn. of New Orleans, 1976-82. Served as spl. agt. USAF, 1958-61. Fellow, Inst. of Politics. Loyola U. Mem. ABA (vice chmn. pub. relations com. 1974-76), Fed. Bar Assn. (bd. dirs. 1970-75, chmn. continuing legal edn. com. 1970-71, recording sec. 1971, 72, 2d v.p. 1973-75), La. Bar Assn. (chmn. state youth drug abuse edn. program 1970-73), New Orleans Bar Assn., Bankruptcy Bar Assn. of La. (mem. exec. com. 1974-76), Assn. Trial Lawyers Am., Comml. Law League of Am., La. Trial Lawyers Assn. (bd. of govs. 1982-85, pres.'s adv. council 1980-82, 85—), Met. Young Lawyers Assn. (bd. dirs. 1971-72), New Orleans Estate Planning Council, Am. Arbitration Assn. (arbitrator). State civil litigation, Federal civil litigation, General practice. Office: Lucas & Rosen 722 First NBC Bldg New Orleans LA 70112

ROSENAU, KENNETH H., lawyer; b. Phila., June 13, 1955; s. Hugo and Carol (Wissbrun) R. BA, George Washington U., 1977; JD, Am. U., 1980. Bar: D.C. 1980. Sr. ptnr. Stern, Rosenau and Rosenthal, Washington, 1981—; adj. prof. Northern Va. Law Sch., Arlington, 1983-87. Active Vol. Atty.'s Office, Washington, 1981-83. Criminal, Family and matrimonial, State civil litigation. Office: Stern Rosenau and Rosenthal 2141 P St NW Washington DC 20037

ROSENBAUM, ELI M., lawyer; b. N.Y.C., May 9, 1955; s. Irving M. and Hanni S. (Schein) R. Student, London Grad. Sch. Bus. Studies, 1976; BS in Econs., U. Pa., 1976, MBA, 1977; JD, Harvard U., 1980. Bar: N.Y. 1981, U.S. Ct. Appeals (D.C. cir.) 1981, D.C. 1985, U.S. Dist. Ct. (so. and ea. dists.) N.Y. 1985, U.S. Supreme Ct. 1987. Trial atty. office of spl. investigations, criminal div. U.S. Dept. Justice, Washington, 1980-83; assoc. litigation dept. Simpson Thacher & Bartlett, N.Y.C., 1984-85; gen. counsel World Jewish Congress, N.Y.C., 1985—. Speaker fund raising events United Jewish Appeal, Fedn. Jewish Philanthropies, N.Y.C., 1984—; mem. adv. bd. Holocaust/Human Rights Research Project, Boston Coll. Law Sch., Newton, Mass., 1985—. Mem. ABA, D.C. Bar Assn., Assn. of Bar of City of N.Y., Am. Fin. Assn. Federal civil litigation, Public international, Prosecution of Nazi war criminals. Office: World Jewish Congress 1 Park Ave New York NY 10016

ROSENBAUM, JAMES MICHAEL, judge; b. Fort Snelling, Minn., Oct. 12, 1944; s. Sam. H. and Ilene D. (Bernstein) R.; m. Marilyn Brown, July 30, 1972; children—Alexandra, Victoria and Catherine (twins). B.A., U. Minn., 1966, J.D., 1969. Bar: Minn. 1969, Ill. 1970, U.S. Supreme Ct. 1979. VISTA staff atty. Leadership Council for Met. Open Communities, Chgo., 1969-72; assoc. Katz, Taube, Lange & Frommelt, Mpls., 1972-77; ptnr. Rosenbaum & Rosenbaum, Mpls., 1977-79, Gainsley, Squier & Korsh, Mpls., 1979-81; U.S. dist. atty. U.S. Dept. Justice, Mpls., 1981-85; judge U.S. Dist. Ct., 1985—. Author booklet: Guide to Practice Civil Rights Housing, 1972. Campaign chmn. People for Boschwitz, Minn., 1978. Mem. Hennepin County Bar Assn. (ethics com. 1980—), Minn. State Bar Assn., ABA Fed. Bar Assn. (bd. dirs., v.p. 1981—). Republican. Jewish. Civil rights. Office: U S Dist Ct 669 U S Courthouse 110 S 4th St Minneapolis MN 55401

ROSENBAUM, MARTIN MICHAEL, insurance company executive; b. Hannover, Germany, Aug. 8, 1923; s. Emil Elias and Pauline (Latte) R.; came to U.S., 1939, naturalized, 1944; m. Hanna Lore Serog, July 6, 1952; children—Thomas F., Evelyn J. B.S. in Bus. Adminstrn., Boston U., 1948; J.D., N.Y.U., 1952; LL.M. in Taxation, 1956. Bar: N.Y. 1953, U.S. Supreme Ct. 1968. With Chubb & Son Inc., 1948—; with Chubb Corp., N.Y.C., 1967—, v.p., tax dir., sr. tax counsel, 1972—; v.p. taxes subs. Chubb & Son Inc., 1968—, Fed. Ins. Co., 1968—, Vigilant Ins. Co., 1979—, Pacific Indemnity Co., 1979—, Gan-Anglo Am. Ins. Co., 1981—; dir., pres. subs. DHC Corp. 1982—; dir. Am. Ins. Co.; lectr. in taxation field. Served in AUS, 1943-46; ETO. Mem. ABA (mem., chmn. fgn. ins. subcom., past chmn. Non-Life Ins. Subcom.), N.Y. State Bar Assn., Assn. Bar City of N.Y., N.Y. County Lawyers Assn., Am. Ins. Assn. (mem., past chmn. tax com.), Soc. Ins. Accts. (mem., past chmn. tax com.) Jewish. Corporate taxation, Estate taxation, Personal income taxation. Address: 100 William St New York NY 10038

ROSENBERG, ARNOLD STEVEN, lawyer; b. Rochester, N.Y., June 22, 1951; s. Martin and Carol B. (Golden) R.; m. Mary Nelly Reyes, Nov. 15, 1981; 1 child, Julian. BA, Cornell U., 1972; JD, Harvard U., 1976. Bar: Ill. 1976, Calif. 1979, N.Y. 1982, U.S. Tax Ct. 1985. Staff atty. Legal Assistance Found., Chgo., 1976-79; assoc. Cornfield & Feldman, Chgo., 1979-81; labor and regulatory atty. N.Y. Telephone Co. div., AT&T, N.Y.C., 1981-83; assoc. Marron, Reid & Sheehy, San Francisco, 1983-85, Bancroft, Avery & McAlister, San Francisco, 1985—. Bd. dirs. Congregation Ner Tamid, San Francisco, 1985—. Ford Found. fellow, 1972-73. Mem. ABA, Bar Assn. San Francisco, Barristers Club San Francisco (chmn. antitrust com. 1983—). Democrat. Avocations: piano, French horn, liturgical cantillation. Federal civil litigation, State civil litigation, Labor. Office: Bancroft Avery & McAlister 601 Montgomery St San Francisco CA 94111

ROSENBERG, ARTHUR HARRISON, lawyer; b. Bklyn., Dec. 15, 1952; s. Erwin I. and Estelle (Seitzman) R.; m. Joan T. Lippman, Feb. 12, 1983; children: Matthew J., Jaclyn D. BS cum laude, Dowling Coll., 1974; JD, NYU, 1982. Bar: N.Y. 1982, U.S. Dist. Ct. (so., ea. and we. dists.) N.Y., U.S. Ct. Appeals (3d cir.), U.S. Supreme Ct. Engr. Grumman Aerospace Corp., Bethpage, N.Y., 1979-82; assoc. Kreindler & Kreindler, N.Y.C., 1982—. Inventor superplastic forming titanium structures. Mem. ABA, Assn. Trial Lawyers Am., N.Y. Bar Assn. Republican. Avocation: comml. pilot. Personal injury, Aviation litigation, State civil litigation.

ROSENBERG, BURTON STUART, lawyer; b. New Haven, Nov. 15, 1949; s. Herbert T. and Frances Rosenberg; m. Patricia Anderson, Oct. 7, 1984; children: Mark Daniel, David Matthew, Jeffrey Barrett. BA, Lehigh U., 1971; JD, NYU, 1974. Bar: Conn. 1975, U.S. Dist. Ct. Conn. 1975, U.S. Ct. Appeals (2d cir.) 1982. Assoc. Law Office Norman Zolot, New Haven, 1974-79; atty. Gen. Telephone & Electronics, Stamford, Conn., 1980-82; sole practice Hamden, Conn., 1983—. Contbg. editor: The Developing Labor Law, 1979. Mem. ABA (labor law sect.), Conn. Bar Assn. (co-chmn. arbitration sect. 1982, labor and employment law sect.), Assn. Trial Lawyers Am. Democrat. Jewish. Labor, Pension, profit-sharing, and employee benefits, Federal civil litigation. Office: PO Box 5278 Hamden CT 06518

ROSENBERG, GARY MARC, lawyer; b. N.Y.C., June 4, 1950; s. David and Edna (Goldberg) R.; m. I. Denise Estes, July 3, 1971; children: Dena Elyse, Janna Beth, Adam Ilan. BA, Queens Coll., 1971; JD, Bklyn. Law Sch., 1974. Bar: N.Y. 1975, U.S. Dist. Ct. (so. dist.) N.Y. 1976, U.S. Supreme Ct. 1985. Pres. Rosenberg & Estis, P.C., N.Y.C., 1976—. Author: Rent Stabilization Digest, 1983, (pamphlet) Complete Guide to Sublets and Assignments, 1983. Real property, Landlord-tenant. Office: Rosenberg & Estis PC 228 E 45 St New York NY 10017

ROSENBERG, GERALD ALAN, lawyer; b. N.Y.C., Aug. 5, 1944; s. Irwin H. and Doris (Lowinger) R.; m. Rosalind Navin, Aug. 13, 1971; children: Clifford D., Nicholas D. BA cum laude, Yale U., 1966; JD, Harvard U., 1969. Bar: N.Y .1970, Calif. 1971, U.S. Dist. Ct. (so. dist.) N.Y. 1971, U.S. Ct. Appeals (2d cir.) 1974, U.S. Dist. Ct. (we. dist.) N.Y. 1977, U.S. Dist. Ct. (cen. dist.) Calif. 1978, U.S. Supreme Ct. 1979, U.S. Dist. Ct. (ea. dist.) N.Y. 1981, U.S. Tax Ct. 1984. Atty. Legal Aid Soc. San Mateo/VISTA, Redwood, Calif., 1969-70; asst. atty. U.S. Dept. Justice, N.Y.C., 1971-75; assoc. Rosenman, Colin, Freund, Lewis & Cohen, N.Y.C., 1975-77, ptnr., 1978—; arbitrator U.S. Dist. Ct. (ea. dist.) N.Y. Bd. dirs. Non Profit Coordinator Com. Inc., N.Y.C., 1983—. Mem. Am. Law Inst., Nat. Assn. Securities Dealers (arbitrator). Assn. Yale Alumni (del. at large 1986—). Club: Yale (N.Y.C.). Federal civil litigation, State civil litigation, Real estate valuation and taxation. Office: Rosenman & Colin 575 Madison Ave New York NY 10022

ROSENBERG, H. N., lawyer, educator; b. Pitts., July 13, 1926; s. A.H. and Elizabeth (Cohen) R.; m. Harriet, June 18, 1950 (dec. Aug. 1978); children: Mark, Marjorie, Ted, Larry, Jim; m. Susan Marks, Dec. 18, 1980. BA, U. Mich., 1948; LLB, U. Pitts., 1951. Bar: Pa., U.S. Dist. Ct. (we. dist.) Pa., U.S. Ct. Appeals (3d cir.). Ptnr. Rosenberg and Rosenberg, Pitts., 1952-63; pres. Rosenberg, Kirshner, Pitts., 1963—; adj. prof. law U. Pitts., 1977—. Editor U. Pitts. Law Rev., 1949. Served to lt. U.S. Army, 1944-46. Mem. Acad. Trial Lawyers (bd. govs.), Pa. Def. Inst., Allegheny County Bar Assn. (exec. v.p., treas., bd. govs.), Order of Coif. Democrat. Jewish. Avocations: tennis, bridge. Federal civil litigation, State civil litigation, Probate. Office: 1500 Grant Bldg Pittsburgh PA 15219

ROSENBERG, JEROME ROY, lawyer, accountant; b. N.Y.C., Oct. 5, 1926; s. Louis and May (Schack) R.; m. Julia Daniels, Apr. 21, 1968; children—Louise I., Daniel M. B.S., NYU, 1949, J.D., 1953, LL.M. in Taxation, 1972; postgrad. Oxford U., 1949. Bar: N.Y. 1956, U.S. Tax Ct. 1965, U.S. Supreme Ct. 1968, U.S. Ct. Claims 1977, U.S. Dist. Ct. (so. dist.) N.Y. 1985, U.S. Dist. Ct. (ea. dist.) N.Y. 1985. Acct., Apfel & Englander, C.P.A.s, N.Y.C., 1950-52; with Abraham J. Briloff, C.P.A., N.Y.C., 1952-54; with Samuel Aronowitz & Co., C.P.A.s, N.Y.C., 1955-57; with David Berdon & Co., C.P.A.s, N.Y.C., 1957-63; sole practice, N.Y.C., 1964—; lectr. NYU, 1972. Served with USAF, 1943-45. Mem. ABA, Bar Assn. N.Y.C., Am. Inst. C.P.A.s, N.Y. Soc. C.P.A.s. (mem. exec. tax com. 1983—). Jewish. Author: Managing Your Own Money, 1979; asst. tech. editor Jour. Taxation, 1964; mem. editorial bd. Practical Acct., 1968-85; sr. tech. editor Income Tax Workbook, 1970-75. Personal income taxation, State and local taxation, Probate. Home: 50 Park Ave New York NY 10016

ROSENBERG, JOHN EDWARD, lawyer, software company executive; b. Cin., Feb. 12, 1953; s. Richard Harvey and Janice Ellin (Sargoy) R.; m. Rebecca Voltz, June 10, 1979. AB, Brown U., 1975; JD, U. Pa., 1978. Bar: Pa. 1978. Ptnr. Rosenberg & Kavjian, 1978-80, Rosenberg & Juechter, 1980; mng. ptnr. Rosenberg, Jakobi & Voltz, West Chester, Pa., 1981-82; mng. ptnr. Rosenberg, Manzone & Voltz, 1983-85; pres., chief exec. officer Echo Data Services, Inc., Lionville, Pa., 1983—. Mem. ABA, Pa. Bar Assn., Assn. Trial Lawyers Am., Chester County Bar Assn. General corporate, Real property, Computer. Office: Marsh Creek Corp Ctr Lionville PA 19353

ROSENBERG, MAURICE, lawyer, educator; b. Oswego, N.Y., Sept. 3, 1919; s. Samuel and Diana (Lishansky) R.; m. Ruth Myers, Dec. 7, 1941 (dec. Nov. 1945); 1 child, David Lee; m. Gloria Jacobson, Dec. 19, 1948; children: Joan Myra, Richard Sam. A.B., Syracuse U., 1940; LL.B. (editor-in-chief Law Rev.), Columbia, 1947. Bar: N.Y. bar 1947. Law sec. to judge N.Y. Ct. Appeals, 1947-49; assoc. firm Cravath, Swaine & Moore, N.Y.C., 1949-53, Austrian, Lance & Stewart, N.Y.C., 1953-56; prof. Columbia U. Law Sch., 1956, Nash prof., Harold R. Medina prof. procedural jurisprudence, 1973—; on leave 1979-81; dir. Project Effective Justice, 1956-64, Walter E. Meyer Research Inst. Law, 1965-71; spl. asst. to atty. gen. U.S., 1976; vis. prof. Harvard U., 1969-70; cons. U.S. Dept. Justice, 1977-79, asst. atty. gen. U.S., 1979-81; lectr., U.S., Asia and Europe; mem. faculty Nat. Coll. State Trial Judges.; mem. Mayor N.Y.C. Com. on Judiciary, 1962-77; chmn. Adv. Council Appellate Justice, 1970-75, Council on Role of Cts., 1978-80. Author: (with Harold Korn and Hans Smit) Elements of Civil Procedure, 1962, 4th edit., 1985, (with Willis Reese) Conflict of Laws, 8th edit, 1984, The Pretrial Conference and Effective Justice, 1964, (with Paul Carrington and Daniel Meador) Justice on Appeal, 1976, (with James D. Hopkins and Robert MacCrate) Appellate Justice in New York, 1982; Editor: Dollars, Delay and the Automobile Victim, 1968, (with Lloyd Ohlin) Law and Social Research, 1977. Trustee Practising Law Inst., 1979—. Served with AUS, 1941-45, ETO. Fellow Am. Acad. Arts and Scis., Inst. Jud. Adminstrn.; mem. ABA (commn. to reduce ct. delay and expenses 1979-84, adv. com. on rules of civil procedure to U.S. Supreme Ct. 1980—), Assn. Bar City N.Y., Assn. Am. Law Schs. (pres. 1972-73), Am. Judicature Soc. (bd. dirs.). Clubs: Century (N.Y.C.); Cosmos (Washington). Federal civil litigation, Legal education, Private international. Home: 10 Hunting Ridge Rd White Plains NY 10605 Office: Columbia U Law Sch 435 W 116 St New York NY 10027

ROSENBERG, MICHAEL, corporate lawyer; b. N.Y.C., Oct. 13, 1937; s. Walter and Eva (Bernstein) R.; m. Jacqueline Raymonde Combe, Apr. 29, 1966; children: Andrew James, Suzanne Jennifer. AB in Econs. with honors, Ind. U., 1959; LLB, Columbia U., 1962. Bar: N.Y. 1963, U.S. Dist. Ct. (so. and ea. dists.) N.Y. 1966. From. dep. asst. atty. gen. to asst. atty. gen. N.Y. State Dept. Law, N.Y.C., 1963-66; assoc. Hellerstein, Rosier & Rembar, N.Y.C., 1966-73; assoc. gen. counsel Gen. Instrument Corp., N.Y.C., 1973-78; from assoc. gen. counsel to dep. gen. counsel U.S. Filter Corp., N.Y.C., 1978-82; v.p., gen. counsel, sec. Alfa-Laval Inc., Ft. Lee, N.J., 1982—. Mem. ABA, N.Y. State Bar Assn., N.Y.C. Bar Assn. General corporate. Office: Alfa-Laval Inc 2115 Linwood Ave Fort Lee NJ 07024

ROSENBERG, MYER (MIKE), lawyer; b. Beaver Falls, Pa., Oct. 25, 1913; s. Eli and Ethel R.; m. Nadine L. Miller, Mar. 1, 1942; children—Michael, Linda, Mary Ann. B.A., U. Kans., 1935; J.D., U. Mich., 1939. Bar: N.Mex. 1940, U.S. Supreme Ct. 1967. Gen. practice law, Carlsbad, N.Mex., 1940—. Mem. N.Mex. Adv. Com. to U.S. Commn. on Civil Rights, 1958-61; mem. adv. council N.Mex. Hosp., 1955-70; mem. N.Mex. State Bd. Bar Commrs., 1963-72. Recipient Cert. of Appreciation N.Mex. Supreme Ct., 1983. Fellow Am. Coll. Probate Counsel; mem. State Bar N.Mex. (pres. 1971-72, mem. med.-legal panel 1979—), ABA, N.Mex. Trial Lawyers Assn. (dir. 1979-81), Assn. Trial Lawyers Am., Am. Judicature Soc., Internat. Assn. Jewish Lawyers and Jurists. Probate, Personal injury, Estate planning. Home: 1302 W Riverside Dr Carlsbad NM 88220 Office: PO Box 1597 Carlsbad NM 88220

ROSENBERG, PAUL HERSCHEL, lawyer; b. Des Moines, July 14, 1951; s. Raymond and Gene Louise (Bowman) R. BA, Drake U., 1975, JD, 1978. Bar: Iowa 1978, U.S. Dist. Ct. (so. dist.) Iowa 1978, U.S. Ct. Appeals (8th cir.) 1978. Assoc. Rosenberg, Rosenberg & Reade, Des Moines, 1978-82; ptnr. Rosenberg Law Firm and predecessor firm Rosenberg, Rosenberg & Reade, Des Moines, 1982—. Mem. ABA, Iowa Bar Assn. (criminal law com.), Polk County Bar Assn., Assn. Trial Lawyers Am., Iowa Trial Lawyers Assn. Democrat. Jewish. Federal civil litigation, Criminal, General practice. Office: Rosenberg Law Firm 505 5th Ave Suite 1010 Des Moines IA 50309

ROSENBERG, PETER DAVID, lawyer, patent examiner, educator; b. N.Y.C., Aug. 2, 1942; s. Frederick and Martha (Grossman) R. B.A., NYU, 1962, B. Chem. Engring., 1963; J.D., N.Y. Law Sch., 1968; LL.M., George Washington U., 1971. Bar: N.Y. 1970, U.S. Ct. Appeals (2d cir.) 1970, U.S. Dist. Ct. (so. and ea. dists.) N.Y. 1971, U.S. Supreme Ct. 1973, U.S. Dist Ct. (no. and we. dists.) N.Y. 1979, U.S. Ct. Appeals D.C. 1982, U.S. Ct. Internat. Trade 1982, U.S. Ct. Mil. Appeals 1982. Examiner U.S. Patent and Trademark Office, Washington, 1968—; assoc. professorial lectr. George Washington U.; Recipient Silver Medal award U.S. Dept. Commerce, 1981. Mem. U.S. Supreme Ct. Hist. Soc., ABA (antitrust sect.). Author: Patent Law Fundamentals, 1975, 2d edit. 1980, revised 1986; assoc. editor Jour. Patent and Trademark Office Soc.; contbr. articles to profl. jours. Patent, Trademark and copyright, Private international. Home: 1400 S Joyce St Arlington VA 22202

ROSENBERG, PRISCILLA ELLIOTT, lawyer; b. Rochester, NY, Feb. 17, 1952; d. Clarence Roy and Mary M. (Mascle) Elliott; m. Alan Mark Rosenberg, May 7, 1983; children: Anne Marian, Tracy Jean. Student, U. Rochester, 1973, Rochester Inst. Tech., 1973-74; BA, SUNY, Stony Brook, 1975; JD, Bklyn. Law Sch., 1978. Bar: N.Y. 1979, U.S. Dist. Ct. (ea. and so. dists.) N.Y. 1979. Assoc. Shearman & Sterling, N.Y.C., 1978-84; asst. counsel Siemens Capital Corp., N.Y.C., 1985-86, assoc. counsel, 1986—. Contbr. articles to profl. jours. Mem. ABA, N.Y. State Bar Assn. Jewish. General corporate. Home: 87-80 98th St Woodhaven NY 11421 Office: Siemens Capital Corp 767 Fifth Ave New York NY 10153

ROSENBERG, RUTH HELEN BORSUK, lawyer; b. Plainfield, N.J., Feb. 23, 1935; d. Irwin and Pauline (Rudich) Borsuk; children—Joshua Cohen, Sarah, Rebecca, Daniel, Miriam, Tziporah, Isaac. A.B., Douglass Coll., 1956; J.D., U. Pa., 1963. Bar: Pa. 1964, N.Y. 1967, U.S. Supreme Ct. 1969, U.S. Ct. Appeals (D.C. cir.) 1969, D.C. 1986, Md. 1987. Law clk. Ct. Common Pleas, Phila., 1963-64; assoc. Blank, Rudenko, Klaus & Rome, Phila., 1964-67; atty. Office Corp. Counsel, City of Rochester, 1967-68; assoc. Nixon, Hargrave, Devans & Doyle, Rochester, 1968-74, ptnr., 1975—; vice chairperson character and fitness com. Appellate div. 4th dept. 7th Jud. Dist. N.Y. Supreme Ct., 1976-80, mem. grievance, 1981-84. Bd. dirs. Soc. Prevention Cruelty to Children, 1976-77; bd. dirs. N.Y. Civil Liberties Union, 1972-85, v.p., 1976-85; bd. dirs. Jewish Home and Infirmary, 1978-83, pres., 1980-83, v.p., 1983; bd. dirs. Hillel Sch., Jewish Fedn. Rochester. Mem. ABA, D.C. Bar Assn., Md. Bar Assn., Monroe County Bar Assn., Phi Beta Kappa. Real property. Office: One Thomas Circle Suite 800 Washington DC 20005

ROSENBERG, SAMUEL IRVING, lawyer; b. New Orleans, Sept. 3, 1915; s. Nathan and Rae (Marks) R.; m. Claire Ruth Frehling, Nov. 1, 1945; children: Ann, Robert M. BA, Tulane U., 1935, LLB, 1937. Bar: La. 1937, U.S. Dist. Ct. (ea. dist.) La. 1937, U.S. Supreme Ct. 1960, U.S. Ct. Appeals (5th cir.) 1981. Ptnr. Mintz & Rosenberg, New Orleans, 1937-41; sole practice New Orleans, 1945-52; ptnr. Polack, Rosenberg, Rittenberg & Endom and predecessor firm, New Orleans, 1952—. Bd. editors Tulane U. Law Rev., 1935-37. Atty. Orleans Parish Sch. Bd, 1952—; past pres. Children's Bur., New Orleans; chmn. trustees of trust funds Jewish Children's Home Service, New Orleans. Recipient Monte M. Lemann award La. Civil Service, 1971. Mem. Am. Judicature Soc., Nat. Council Sch. Attys., Nat. Orgn. Legal Problems in Edn., World Trade Ctr., New Orleans C. of C., Sigma Alpha Mu. Democrat. Club: Lakewood Country (New Orleans) (v.p. 1979-80, bd. dirs. 1980—). Avocations: golf, bridge. School litigation, Probate, General practice. Home: 4915 Bancroft Dr New Orleans LA 70122 Office: Polack Rosenberg Rittenberg & Endom 938 Lafayette St Suite 100 New Orleans LA 70113-1067

ROSENBERG, SHELDON, lawyer; b. Bklyn., July 18, 1934; s. Harry and Sadie R.; children: Shari Glover, Marc, Ellen, David. BA, City Coll. N.Y., 1961; JD, Harvard U., 1964. Bar: Fla. 1964, U.S. Dist. Ct. (so. dist.) Fla. 1965, U.S. Supreme Ct. 1975, U.S. Tax Ct. 1976. Ptnr. Ress, Gomez, Rosenberg and Howland, P.A., North Miami, Fla., 1964—. Contbr. articles to profl. jours. Bd. dirs. Miami Chamber Symphony. Served with U.S. Army, 1956-58. Mem. ABA, Fla. Bar Assn. (chmn. corp. banking and bus. law sect. 1973-74), Dade County Bar Assn., North Dade Bar Assn. Jewish. Club: F. Avocations: photography. Contracts commercial, Probate, General practice. Office: Ress Gomez Rosenberg Howland & Mintz 11755 Biscayne Blvd North Miami FL 33181

ROSENBLATT, EDWARD MILTON, lawyer; b. N.Y.C., Apr. 30, 1952; s. Mark and Bronia (Ratzenstein) R.; m. Deborah S. Klein, June 21, 1975; children: Robert Oren, Benjamin Michael. BA, SUNY, Binghamton, 1974; MA, U. Hartford, 1976; JD, U. Conn., 1981. Bar: Conn. 1981, U.S. Dist. Ct. Conn. 1984. Assoc. Murtha, Cullina, Richter & Pinney, Hartford, Conn., 1981-84, Hebb & Gitlin, Hartford, 1984-85, Gager, Henry & Narkis, Waterbury, Conn., 1985—. Author series of articles exploring the Arab Israeli conflict 1984-85. Pres. Greater Southington (Conn.) Jewish Cong., 1984-85; mem. exec. bd. community relations com. Greater Hartford Jewish Fedn., 1984—. Recipient Excellence award Lawyers Co-op, 1981; named Young Leader of Yr., Greater Hartford Jewish Fedn., 1984. Mem. ABA, Conn. Bar Assn., Assn. Trial Lawyers Am., Conn. Trial Lawyers Assn. Democrat. Avocations: musical composition and performance, coaching softball. Real property, Landlord-tenant, Contracts commercial. Home: 17 Rustic Oak Dr Southington CT 06489 Office: Gager Henry & Narkis One Exchange Pl Waterbury CT 06722

ROSENBLATT, JOEL I., lawyer; b. Bklyn., July 31, 1939; s. Harry and Fay (Winter) R.; m. Lynn Burton, Mar. 10, 1966; children: Deborah, Michael, Lauren. BEE, N.Y. Poly. U., 1960; MBA, U. Pa., 1962; JD, Cath. U., 1972. Bar: U.S. Patent Office 1970, D.C. 1973, N.Y. 1976, Ohio 1978, U.S. Ct. Appeals (fed. cir.) 1979, U.S. Dist. Ct. (no. dist.) Ohio 1983, Fla. 1985. Atty. Xerox Corp., Rochester, N.Y., 1973-78; sr. atty. intellectual property Allied Corp., Morristown, N.J., 1979-84, Harris Corp., Melbourne, Fla., 1984—. Mem. Am. Intellectual Property Assn., Fla. Bar Assn. (computer law com. 1985—). Club: Melbourne Yacht. Avocation: sailing. Computer, Patent, Trademark and copyright. Home: 445 11th Ave Indialantic FL 32903

ROSENBLATT, PETER RONALD, lawyer, former ambassador; b. N.Y.C., Sept. 4, 1933; s. William and Therese Amalia (Steinhardt) R.; m. Naomi Henriette Harris, July 1, 1952; children: Therese Sarah Sonenshine, Daniel Harris, David Steinhardt. B.A., Yale U., 1954, LL.B., 1957; postgrad. fellow, Tel-Aviv U., 1971. Bar: N.Y. 1959, D.C. 1969. Teaching asst. history Yale U., New Haven, 1954-55; asst. dist. atty. N.Y. County, 1959-62; asso. Stroock & Stroock & Lavan, N.Y.C., 1962-66; dep. asst. gen. counsel AID, Washington, 1966; mem. White House staff, Washington, 1966-68; jud. officer, chmn. bd. contract appeals U.S. Post Office Dept., Washington, 1968-69; v.p., dir. EDP Technology, Inc., Washington, 1969-71; chmn. bd. Internat. Devel. Services, Washington, 1969-71; spl. cons. to Senator Edmund S. Muskie, 1970-72; practice law Washington, N.Y.C., 1972-77, 81—; personal rep. of Pres. (with rank ambassador) to conduct negotiations on future polit. status of Trust Ter. of Pacific Islands, Washington, 1977-81; mem. Mid. East study group Dem. Adv. Council of Elected Officials, 1974-76. Sec., chmn. exec. com. Coalition for a Dem. Majority, 1973-77, pres., 1983—; bd. dirs. Com. on Present Danger, 1976-77, 82—. Served to 2d lt. Q.M.C., AUS, 1957-58. Mem. ABA, Assn. Bar City N.Y., N.Y. County Lawyers Assn. Jewish. Government relations, Public international, Private international. Office: 1001 Connecticut Ave NW Suite 707 Washington DC 20036

ROSENBLATT, STEPHEN WOODBURN, lawyer; b. Atlanta, Dec. 20, 1948; s. William F. and Nancy E. (Gosser) R.; m. Elisabeth M. Gernert, Mar. 22, 1975; children: Kathrine, Emily, Nancy. BA, Vanderbilt U., 1970; JD with honors, U. Miss., 1975. Bar: U.S. Dist. Ct. (no. and so. dists.) Miss. 1975, U.S. Ct. Appeals (5th cir.) 1977. Mem. Butler, Snow, O'Mara, Stevens & Cannada, Jackson, Miss., 1975—; pres. Miss. Young Lawyers Sec., Jackson, 1984-85; mem. Miss. Bd. of Bar Commn., Jackson, 1983-86. Chmn. bd. deacons 1st Presbyn. Ch., Jackson, 1984, elder, 1986. Served with U.S. Army, 1980-82. Mem. ABA, Miss. Bar Assn. (2d v.p. 1985-86), Hinds County Bar Assn., Miss. Bankruptcy Conf., Jackson Young Lawyers Assn. (pres. 1982), Jackson Vanderbilt Club (pres. 1979). Republican. Presbyterian. Avocations: tennis, jogging, camping, skiing. Bankruptcy, Contracts commercial, Consumer commercial. Office: Butler Snow O'Mara Stevens & Cannada 200 E Capitol St PO Box 22567 Jackson MS 39225

ROSENBLITH, ROBERT MANUEL, lawyer; b. N.Y.C., May 22, 1943. BA, Hunter Coll., 1965; JD, Bklyn. Coll., 1968. Bar: N.Y. 1968, U.S. Dist. Ct. (so. and ea. dists.) N.Y. 1970, U.S. Ct. Appeals (2d cir.) 1975. Asst. dist. atty. Kings County, N.Y.C., 1969; assoc. Shearman & Sterling, N.Y.C., 1972-78; ptnr. Riposanu, Joyce, Ahearn, Aballi & Diaz-Cruz, N.Y.C., 1978; assoc. Mfrs. Hanover Trust Co., N.Y.C., 1969-72, v.p., assoc. gen. counsel, 1978—; speaker Uniform Comml. Code Inst., Banking Law Inst. Contbg. editor, author Letter of Credit Report newsletter, 1986; contbr. articles to profl. jours. Trustee Temple Emanuel of North Jersey,

1972. Mem. N.Y. Bar Assn. Avocations: pinball, bowling, golf. Banking, Federal civil litigation, State civil litigation. Home: 2 Danebury Downs Upper Saddle River NJ 07458 Office: Mfrs Hanover Trust Co 270 Park Ave New York NY 10017

ROSENBLUM, GLENN FREDRICK, lawyer, editor; b. Phila., Dec. 31, 1952; s. Edwin Irwin and Roberta (Brodsky) R.; m. Sherrie Joan Greenberg, Sept. 18, 1983. B.A. summa cum laude, Temple U., 1973; J.D., U. Pa., 1976. Bar: Pa. 1976, U.S. Dist. Ct. (ea. dist.) Pa. 1976, N.J. 1979, U.S. Dist. Ct. N.J. 1979, U.S. Dist. Ct. (mid. dist.) Pa. 1986, U.S. Ct. Appeals (3d cir.) 1986. Law clk. Phila. Ct. Common Pleas, Phila., 1976-81; opinion editor Legal Intelligencer and Pa. Law Jour. Reporter, Phila., 1977-83; editor-in-chief Pa. Dist. and County Reports, Phila., 1981-83; assoc. Korn, Kline & Kutner, Phila., 1983—; vis. instr. Community Coll. Phila., 1980; lectr. Multistate Legal Studies, Phila., 1978-84; founder law clk. seminar series Phila. Ct. Common Pleas, 1978-81. Developer, editor Packard's Law Reports, 1981-83. Research asst. to book: The Law of Sales and Sales Financing, 1975. Vol atty. Phila. Com. Seventy, 1977-82. Mem. ABA, Pa. Bar Assn., Phila. Bar Assn., Pa. Def. Inst., Phi Beta Kappa, Pi Sigma Alpha. Jewish. Club: Lawyers of Phila. Federal civil litigation, Insurance, Legal education. Home: 2401 Pennsylvania Ave Apt 11-B-23 Philadelphia PA 19130 Office: Korn Kline & Kutner 1845 Walnut St Suite 2100 Philadelphia PA 19103

ROSENBLUM, VICTOR GREGORY, educator; b. N.Y.C., June 2, 1925; s. George and Vera (Minster) R.; m. Louise Rann, Feb. 21, 1946; children: Susan, Ellen, Laura, Keith, Jonathan, Peter, Warren, Joshua. A.B., Columbia U., 1945, LL.B., 1948; Ph.D., U. Calif.-Berkeley, 1953; D.H.L., Hebrew Union Coll., 1970; D.L., Siena Heights Coll., 1982. Bar: Ill., N.Y., U.S. Supreme Ct. Lectr. polit. sci. U. Calif.-Berkeley, 1949-52, asst. prof. polit. sci., 1953-57; assoc. prof. polit. sci. Northwestern U., 1958-63, prof. polit. sci. and law, 1963-68, 70—; pres. Reed Coll., Portland, Oreg., 1968-70; sr. legal cons. project on bankruptcy govtl. studies div. Brookings Instn., 1964-69; vis. Fulbright lectr. Sch. Law U. Louvain, Belgium, 1966-67, vis. prof., 1978-79; mem. Adminstrv. Conf. U.S., 1982-86. Editor-in-chief: Adminstrv. Law Rev., 1958-62; author: Law As A Political Instrument, 1955, (with A.D. Castberg) Cases on Constitutional Law: Political Roles of the Supreme Court, 1973, (with Frances Zemans) The Making of a Public Profession, 1981; contbr. to law revs., also law and polit. sci. books. Staff assoc. Govtl. Affairs Inst., Washington, 1952-53; cons., assoc. counsel Subcom. on Exec. and Legis. Reorgn., Com. on Govt. Ops., U.S. Ho. of Reps., 1956-57; bd. dirs. Center for Adminstrv. Justice, 1972-78. Mem. ABA (council sect. adminstrv. law 1962-65, 72-75, chmn. 1977-78), Fed. Bar Assn., Am. Polit. Sci. Assn., Law and Soc. Assn. (pres. 1970-72), Am. Judicature Soc. (dir. 1982—, chmn. bd. 1985-86), Assn. Am. Law Schs. (exec. com. 1984—, pres. 1987), Phi Beta Kappa, Pi Sigma Alpha. Democrat. Jewish. Legal education. Home: 2030 Orrington Ave Evanston IL 60201 Office: 357 E Chicago Ave Chicago IL 60611

ROSENFELD, ALEXANDER M., lawyer; b. Bklyn., May 4, 1941. BA, CUNY, Bklyn., 1962; JD, NYU, 1965. Bar: N.Y. 1966, U.S. Supreme Ct. 1970, U.S. Customs Ct., U.S. Tax Ct., U.S. Dist. Ct. (ea. and so. dists.) N.Y., U.S. Ct. Appeals (2d, 5th and 11th cirs.), Fla. 1973, U.S. Dist. Ct. (so. dist.) Fla. 1973. Ptnr. Rosenfeld & Stein, Miami, Fla., 1966—. Mem. North Dade Bar Assn. (pres. 1984-85). Consumer commercial, Bankruptcy, Contracts commercial. Office: Rosenfeld & Stein 18260 NE 19th Ave North Miami Beach FL 33162

ROSENFELD, ARNOLD R., lawyer, state official. Pub. defender State of Mass., Boston. Office: Pub Counsel Services Com 80 Boylston St Suite 600 Boston MA 02116 *

ROSENFELD, MICHEL, lawyer, educator; b. Neuilly, France, July 5, 1948; came to U.S., 1966; s. Ernest and Ildiko (Rosenbaum) R.; m. Evelyn Korngold, June 1, 1969; children: Nicole Maia, Alexis Gideon. BA, Columbia U., 1969, MA, 1971, M in Philosophy, 1978; JD, Northwestern U., 1974. Bar: N.Y. 1976, U.S. Dist. Ct. (so. and ea. dists.) N.Y. 1979. Assoc. Skadden, Arps, Slate, Meagher & Flom, N.Y.C., 1977-80, Rosenman, Colin, Freund, Lewis & Cohen, N.Y.C., 1980-82; assoc. prof. N.Y. Law Sch., N.Y.C., 1982-85, prof., 1985—. Contbr. articles to profl. jours. Mem. ABA, Am. Assn. Law Schs. Jewish. Legal education, Jurisprudence. Office: NY Law Sch 57 Worth St New York NY 10013

ROSENFELD, ROBERT THOMAS, lawyer; b. Cleve., July 2, 1933; s. William Henry and Rose B. (Gold) R.; m. Patricia A. Smith, Mar. 21, 1959 (div. 1975); children—Alison B., Abby S.; m. Vivian L. Smith, Apr. 6, 1975. A.B., Brown U., 1954; LL.B., Case Western Res. U., 1958. Bar: Ohio 1958, U.S. Supreme Ct. 1966. Field atty. Nat. Labor Relations Bd., Seattle and Cleve., 1958-62; ptnr. Rosenfeld & Palay, Cleve., 1962-70; sole practice, Cleve., 1970-72; ptnr. Rosenfeld & Gross, Cleve., 1972-83, Walter, Haverfield, Buescher & Chockley, Cleve., 1983—; instr. collective bargaining Cleve. State U. Indsl. Relations Ctr. Bd. dirs. Friends of Crawford Mus., Cleve., 1983-84; pres. Suburban Temple. Served to comdr. USCGR, 1956-57. Mem. ABA (labor law sect.), Ohio Bar Assn., Cleve. Bar Assn., Am. Arbitration Assn. (labor panel). Republican. Jewish. Club: Classic Car Rolls Royce Owners. Avocation: car collecting. Labor. Home: 2675 Fairmount Blvd Cleveland Heights OH 44106 Office: Walter Haverfield Buescher et al 1215 Terminal Tower Cleveland OH 44113

ROSENFIELD, ANDREW M., lawyer; b. Chgo., Sept. 20, 1951; s. Maurice and Lois (Fried) R.; m. Betsy Bergman, Sept. 10, 1978; children: Zachary William, Edwin Alexander. BA with honors, Kenyon Coll., 1973; MA, Harvard U., 1976; JD cum laude, U. Chgo., 1978. Bar: Ill. 1978. Pres., founder Lexecon Inc., Chgo., 1977—; adj. prof. Northwestern U. Law Sch., Chgo., 1985-86; lectr. in law U. Chgo., 1986—; lectr. numerous law and bus. seminars. Mem. vis. com. U. Chgo. Law Sch., 1982-85; council mem. U. Chgo. Grad. Sch. Bus., 1983—; mem. auxiliary bd. Art Inst. Chgo., 1982—; mem. mng. bd. Ct. Theatre, U. Chgo., 1982—; bd. dirs. Steppenwolf Theatre, 1982—, mem. exec. com., 1983—; bd. dirs. Family Focus, Inc., 1982—, mem. exec. com., chmn. fin. com., 1983—; bd. dirs. Chgo. Opera Theatre, 1982—. Mem. Order of Coif. Jewish. Clubs: Arts, Chicago, Standard (bd. dirs.1985—). Antitrust, Regulated industries, Securities. Home: 209 E Lake Shore Dr Chicago IL 60611 Office: Lexecon Inc 332 S Michigan Ave Chicago IL 60604

ROSENFIELD, HARRY NATHAN, lawyer; b. N.Y.C., Aug. 17, 1911; s. Max and Anna (Kutchai) R.; 1 child, Marianne Rosenfield Smigelskis. BA, City Coll. of N.Y., 1931; LLB, Columbia U., 1934; JD, NYU, 1942; DHL, Los Angeles Coll. Chiropractic, 1981. Bar: N.Y. 1934, U.S. Supreme Ct. 1945, U.S. Ct. Appeals (D.C. cir.) 1954. Asst. to Mayor LaGuardia City of N.Y., 1933-34, asst. to commr. bd. of edn., 1934-42; asst. adminstr. Fed. Security Adminstrn., Washington, 1942-48; commr. DP Commn., Washington, 1948-52; exec. dir. Com. on I & N, Washington, 1952-53; sole practice Washington, 1953—; gen. counsel Nat. Safety Council, Chgo., 1952-87. Contbg editor Nat. Safety News, Chgo., 1953-87. Mem. exec. com. Interreligious Commn. Racial Matters, Washington; del. UN Econ. and Social Council, Geneva, 1948; bd. dirs., sec. Greater Washington Ednl. TV Assn., Washington. Recipient Appreciation award Nat. Safety Council, 1970, Humanitarian award Am. Chiropractic Assn., 1984. Mem. ABA (chmn. immigration and copyright com.), Fed. Bar Assn. (ethics com.), D.C. Bar Assn. (ethics com.), U.S. Copyright Soc. (bd. trustees), Assn. Immigration and Naturalization Lawyers, Nat. Lawyers Club, Nat. Dem. Club, Phi Beta Kappa. Avocations: writing legal articles, mountain climbing, poetry. Administrative and regulatory, Health, Legislative. Office: 1050 17th St NW Washington DC 20036

ROSENHAN, DAVID L., psychologist, educator; b. 1929. A.B., Yeshiva U., 1951, M.A., 1953; Ph.D., Columbia U., 1958. Prof., Haverford (Pa.) Coll., 1960-62; psychologist Ednl. Testing Service, 1962-68; assoc. prof. Princeton (N.J.) U., 1963-68; prof. Swarthmore (Pa.) Coll., 1968-70, Stanford (Calif.) U., 1970—; mem. NIMH, 1970-74; cons. trial tactics, juries, forensic psychology. Vis. fellow Wolfson Coll., Oxford, Eng., 1977-78. Fellow AAAS, Am. Psychol. Assn. (pres. div. psychology and law); mem. Am. Psychology Law Soc. (trustee 1978-79), Am. Bd. Forensic Psychology. Author: (with London) Foundations of Abnormal Psychology, 1968; Theory and Research in Abnormal Psychology, 2d edit., 1975; (with Gergen, Nisbett, Clarr) Social Psychology, 1975; (with Selgman) Abnormal Psychology, 1984; adv. editor Holt, Rinehart & Winston, 1965-76. Legal education, Constitutional. Office: Stanford U Sch of Law Stanford CA 94305 *

ROSENHOUSE, NATHAN, lawyer; b. Bklyn., Aug. 24, 1930; s. Barnet and Sonia (Diamond) R.; m. Phyllis Berman, June 21, 1955 (div. 1971); children: Lisa, Barry, Bonnie. BA, Bklyn. Coll., 1951; JD, NYU, 1954. Bar: N.Y. 1954, U.S. Dist. Ct. (so. and ea. dists.) N.Y. 1955, N.J. 1959, U.S. Dist. Ct. N.J. 1959, U.S. Supreme Ct. 1961. Ptnr. Rosenhouse, Cutler & Zuckerman, 1968-79; sole practice Somerset County, N.J., 1980—; atty. bd. edn. Twp. of Franklin, Somerset County, N.J., 1962-70; mcpl. prosecutor Twp. of Franklin, 1963-66; atty. bd. adjustment Twp. of Franklin, 1964-65; atty. bd. edn., Borough of South Bound Brook, Somerset County, 1973-75; atty. bd. edn. Twp. of Hillsborough, Somerset County, 1973-76; talk show moderator WCTC-AM, Somerset, 1975—. Lectr. law civic orgns. Mem. ABA, N.J. Bar Assn., Somerset County Bar Assn., Assn. Trial Lawyers Am. Democrat. Jewish. General corporate, State civil litigation, Probate. Office: 600 Franklin Blvd Somerset NJ 08873

ROSENN, HAROLD, lawyer; b. Plains, Pa., Nov. 4, 1917; s. Joseph and Jennie (Wohl) R.; m. Sallyanne Frank, Sept. 19, 1948; 1 child, Frank Scott. BA, U. Mich., 1939, JD, 1941. Bar: Pa. 1942, U.S. Supreme Ct. 1957. Ptnr. Rosenn & Rosenn, Wilkes Barre, Pa., 1948-54, Rosenn, Jenkins & Greenwald, Wilkes Barre, 1954—; asst. dist. atty Luzerne County, Pa., 1952-54; mem. Gov.'s. Justice Commn., Pa., 1968-73, Crime Commn., Pa., 1968-73, Fed. Judicial Nominating Com., Pa., 1977-79, Appellate Ct. Nominating Com., Pa., 1979-81. Chmn. ARC, Wilkes Barre, 1958-60; pres. Pa. Council on Crime and Delinquency, Harrisburg, 1969-71; bd. dirs. Coll. Misericordia, Dallas, Pa., 1976-86, Hoyt Library, Kingston, Pa., 1971-78, Nat. Council on Crime and Delinquency, N.Y.C., 1969-71; chmn. United Way Campaign of Wyoming Valley, 1975; pres. United Way, Wyoming Valley, 1978-80. Served to capt. USAAF, 1942-45, ETO. Named Honoree, Wyo. Vally Interfaith Council, 1986. Mem. ABA, Pa. Bar Assn., Am. Judicature Soc., Pa. State Bd. Law Examiners. Republican. Jewish. Clubs: U. Mich. (N.E. Pa.) (pres. 1946-76), Westmoreland (Wilkes Barre). Lodge: B'nai Brith (pres. Wilkes Barre 1952-53, Community Service award 1976). Avocations: travel, antique Wedgewood. General corporate, Family and matrimonial, General practice. Home: 29 Hedge Pl Kingston PA 18704 Office: Rosenn Jenkins & Greenwald 15 S Franklin St Wilkes Barre PA 18711

ROSENSAFT, LESTER JAY, management consultant, reorganization lawyer, business executive; b. Leominster, Mass., Jan. 11, 1958; s. Melvin and Beatrice (Golombek) R. B.S. in Econs., Wharton Sch., U. Pa., 1978; J.D., Case Western Res. U., 1981, M.B.A., 1981; LL.M. in Corporate Law, NYU, 1983. Bar: Ohio 1981, U.S. dist. ct. (no. dist.) Ohio 1982, U.S. dist cts. (ea., we., no., so. dists.) N.Y. 1982. Practice corp. and comml. law, Ohio, 1981—, reorgn. law fed. cts. Ohio, N.Y., 1982—; mem. firm Hall, Rosensaft & Yen, Cleve. and Singapore, 1981—; with Cons. to Mgmt., Inc., Cleve., N.Y.C., Boston, Hong Kong, 1977—, v.p., 1977-80, pres. and chief exec. officer, 1980-83, chmn., 1983—; pres. and chief exec. officer Eljay Devel. Corp., 1985-86; chmn. and chief exec., vice chmn. bd. officer Logistix Ltd., 1987—; vice chmn. bd. Paramount Systems Design Group, Inc., N.Y.C., 1982—; v.p. corp. devel., mem. bd. dirs. Ameritec Corp., N.Y.C., 1983—; v.p., chief fin. officer, mem. bd. dirs. Chipurnoi Inc., L.I. City, N.Y., 1983—; v.p., chief fin. officer Kinnerton Industries, N.Y.C. and London, 1983—; vice chmn., gen. counsel, mem. bd. dirs. GIOIA Couture, Inc., Akron, Ohio, 1984—; dir. Honeybee Robotics Ltd., Taiwan and N.Y.C., dir. Pelletier Brothers, Inc., 1986— , Advanced RAdiator Techs., Inc., Fitchburg, Mass., 1987—; ednl. cons.; advisor indsl. devel. and strategic urbanism; cons. federally funded biomed. research projects. Co-author (with Melvin Rosensaft): Industrial Development Survey for City of Leominster, 1978. Contbr. articles to profl. jours. Mem. exec. adv. council Keene State Coll., 1984—. Mem. ABA, Greater Cleve. Bar Assn., Ohio State Bar Assn., Assn. Bar City N.Y., Assn. Trial Lawyers Am., Am. Mgmt. Assn., Am. Mktg. Assn. Wharton Club Cleve. (exec. com.), Wharton Club N.Y., U. Pa. Clubs Cleve., U. Pa. Club N.Y., Bankruptcy Lawyers Bar Assn., N.Y.C. Reorgn. Roundtable, Internat. Soc. Strategic Planning Cons., Soc. Profl. Mgmt. Cons., Inst. of Mgmt. Cons. (cert. mgmt. cons.), North Cen. Mass. C. of C. (indsl. devel. com. 1984—), Phi Alpha Delta (vice justice). Clubs: Boca Beach, Boca Pointe Golf and Racquet, Boca West, Boca Raton Hotel and Club (Boca Raton, Fla.). Bankruptcy, General corporate, Real property. Home: 59 Crescent Rd Leominster MA 01453

ROSENSAFT, MENACHEM ZWI, lawyer, author, community leader; b. Bergen-Belsen, Germany, May 1, 1948; came to U.S., 1958, naturalized, 1962; s. Josef and Hadassah (Bimko) R.; m. Jean Bloch, Jan. 13, 1974; 1 child, Joana Deborah. B.A., M.A., Johns Hopkins U., 1971; M.A., Columbia U., 1975, J.D., 1979. Bar: N.Y. 1980. Adj. lectr. dept. Jewish studies CCNY, 1972-74, professorial fellow, 1974-75; research fellow Am. Law Inst., 1977-78; law clk. to judge U.S. Dist. Ct. (so. dist.) N.Y., N.Y.C., 1979-81; assoc. Proskauer, Rose, Goetz & Mendelsohn, N.Y.C., 1981-82, Kaye, Scholer, Fierman, Hays & Handler, N.Y.C., 1982—. Author: Moshe Sharett, Statesman of Israel, 1966, Fragments, Past and Future (poetry), 1968, Not Backward to Belligerency, 1969; editor Bergen Belsen Youth Mag., 1965; book rev. editor Columbia Jour. Transnat. Law, 1978-79; contbr. to various publs. including The New York Times, The New York Post, Columbia Human Rights Law Rev., Jewish Social Studies, Leo Baeck Inst. Year Book XXI, Columbia Jour. Environ. Law, Reform Judaism, Letzte Nayes, Tel Aviv, Asahi Evening News, Tokyo, Midstream. Chmn. Internat. Network of Children of Jewish Holocaust Survivors, 1981-84, founding chmn., 1984—, chmn. 2d Generation Com. Am. Gathering of Jewish Holocaust Survivors, 1982-85, chmn. action com., 1985—; chmn. commn. on human rights World Jewish Congress, 1986—, chmn. exec. com. Am. sect., 1986—; mem. exec. com. Am. Jewish Congress, 1986—; chmn. 2d Generation Adv. Com. to U.S. Holocaust Meml. Council, 1983—; mem. N.Y.C. Holocaust Meml. Commn., 1982-87, chmn. collections com., 1987—; organizer, leader demonstration against President Reagan's visit to Bitburg cemetary, Bergen-Belsen, 1985. Recipient Parker Sch. recognition of achievement with honors in internat. and fgn. law, 1979; Harlan Fiske Stone scholar, 1977-79. Mem. ABA, Assn. Bar City N.Y., Phi Beta Kappa. Federal civil litigation, Private international. Home: 179 E 70th St New York NY 10021 Office: Kaye Scholer Fierman Hays & Handler 425 Park Ave New York NY 10022

ROSENSTEIN, ROBERT BRYCE, lawyer; b. Santa Monica, Calif., Feb. 26, 1954; s. Franklin Lee and Queen Esther (Shall) R.; m. Resa Shanee Brookler, Nov. 30, 1980; children: Shaun Franklin, Jessica Laney. BA, Calif. State U., Northridge, 1976; JD, Southwestern U., 1979. Bar: Calif. 1979, U.S. Dist. Ct. (cen. dist. Calif.) 1980, U.S. Tax Ct. 1981. Service rep. Social Security Adminstrn., Los Angeles, 1974-77; tax cons. Am. Tax Assocs., Los Angeles, 1970-78, ptnr., 1978; prin., pres. Robert B. Rosenstein, PC, Los Angeles, 1979-84; ptnr. Rosenstein and Werlin, Los Angeles, 1984—; corp. counsel, bd. dirs. Security Control Systems, Inc., Canoga Park, Calif., Sirius Computer Corp.; corp. counsel Spartan Computer, Unicomp, Inc., Palmadale Investment, Inc., 1986—, Bldg. Systems Evaluation, Inc., Diagnostic Engring., Inc., 1986—; pres. Will Find, Inc., 1986—. Recipient Am. Jurisprudence award Bancroft Whitney. Mem. ABA (taxation com.), Assn. Trial Lawyers Am., Los Angeles Bar Assn. Republican. Jewish. Lodges: Masons, Ionic, Composite. Avications: sports, reading, golf. General corporate, Personal income taxation, Probate. Office: Rosenstein and Werlin PC La Cienega Blvd Suite 815 PO Box 92971 Los Angeles CA 90009-2971

ROSENSTOCK, LOUIS ANTHONY, III, lawyer; b. Petersburg, Va., July 27, 1941. BA, Washington and Lee U., 1963; JD, LLB, U. Richmond, 1966. Judge 11th Jud. Dist., Petersburg, 1973-75; sole practice Petersburg. Served to Capt. JAGC, U.S. Army, 1966-71. Mem. ABA, Petersburg Bar Assn. (pres. 1984-85), Nat. Assn. Criminal Def. Lawyers, Va. Trial Lawyers Assn. Criminal, Family and matrimonial, Personal injury. Office: 224 N Sycamore St Petersburg VA 23803

ROSENTHAL, ALAN DAVID, lawyer; b. Dallas, Apr. 28, 1949; s. Harry and Esther (Moskowitz) R.; m. Sondra Elise Aron, May 19, 1985; children: Adam, Kenneth, Jennifer. BSEE summa cum laude, Princeton U., 1971; JD, U. Tex., 1974. Bar: Tex. 1974, U.S. Dist. Ct. (so. dist.) Tex. 1975, U.S. Ct. Appeals (5th cir.) 1975, U.S. Ct. Appeals (fed. cir.) 1982, U.S. Ct. Claims 1986. Assoc. Baker & Botts, Houston, 1974-81, ptnr., 1982—. Mem. ABA, Tex. Bar Assn., Am. Intellectual Property Law Assn., Houston Patent Law Assn. Jewish. Avocations: gardening, fishing. Patent, Trademark and copyright. Home: 6614 Wakeforest Houston TX 77005 Office: Baker & Botts One Shell Plaza Houston TX 77002

ROSENTHAL, ALBERT JOSEPH, university dean, law educator, lawyer; b. N.Y.C., Mar. 5, 1919; m. Barbara Snowden, June 30, 1953; children: Edward H., Thomas S., William I. B.A., U. Pa., 1938; LL.B., Harvard U., 1941. Bar: N.Y. 1942, U.S. Supreme Ct. 1947. Law clk. to judge U.S. Ct. Appeals 1st Circuit, Boston, 1941-42; spl. appellate atty. OPA, Washington, 1946-47; law clk. to Justice Frankfurter U.S. Supreme Ct., Washington, 1947-48; asst. loan officer IBRD, Washington, 1948-50; atty. Dept. Justice, Washington, 1950-52; gen. counsel Small Def. Plants Adminstrn., Washington, 1952-53; ptnr. Golden Wienshienk & Rosenthal, N.Y.C., 1953-64; prof. law Columbia U., N.Y.C., 1964—, Maurice T. Moore prof., 1974—, dean Sch. Law, 1979-84; hearing officer N.Y. State Dept. Environ. Conservation, 1975, 77; mem. N.Y. State Law Revision Commn., 1987—. Author: (with H. Korn and S. Lubman) Catastrophic Accidents in Government Programs, 1963, (with F. Grad and G. Rathjens) Environmental Control: Priorities, Policies and the Law, 1971, Federal Regulations of Campaign Finance, 1972, (with F. Grad. and others) The Automobile and the Regulation of Its Impact on the Environment, 1975; contbr. articles to profl. jours. Mem. Logan Airport Master Plan Study Team, 1975. Served to capt. USAAC, 1942-45. Fellow Am. Acad. Arts and Scis., Am. law Inst. Legal education, Constitutional, Environment. Home: 15 Oakway Scarsdale NY 10583 Office: Columbia U Law Sch 435 W 116th St New York NY 10027

ROSENTHAL, GARY L., lawyer; b. Tulsa, Okla., July 19, 1949; s. Charles Orkin and Sylvia (Falk) R.; m. Lee Hyman, Mar. 30, 1982; 1 child, Rebecca Falk. AB, Harvard U., 1971, JD, 1975. Law clk. to presiding justice U.S. Ct. Appeals (5th cir.), Dallas, 1975-76; ptnr. Vinson & Elkins, Houston, 1976—. Home: 2519 Glenhaven Houston TX 77030 Office: Vinson & Elkins 3300 First City Tower 1001 Fannin Houston TX 77001-6760

ROSENTHAL, GERALD ALLEN, lawyer; b. Balt., Oct. 7, 1950; s. Eric S. and Ilse (Prahl) R. BA, Elmira (N.Y.) Coll., 1972; MBA, NYU, 1974; JD, Boston U., 1977. Staff analyst Chase Manhattan Bank, N.Y.C., 1972-74; assoc. Gadsby & Hannah, Boston, 1977—. Contbr. articles to profl. jours. Mem. ABA, Mass. Bar Assn., Boston Bar Assn. (co-chmn. profl. ethics com., fee com., steering com. profl. services sect., bicentennial of U.S. Constn. com.), Am. Arbitration Assn. (comml. panel). Federal civil litigation, State civil litigation, Banking. Home: 770 Boylston St Boston MA 02199 Office: Gadsby & Hannah 1 Post Office Square Boston MA 02109

ROSENTHAL, JONATHAN, transportation executive; b. Hollywood, Calif., Sept. 20, 1955; s. Isadore and Fay M. (Chazen) R. BA cum laude, Calif. State U., Northridge, 1977; postgrad., U. Calif., Santa Barbara, 1976-77, Uppsala (Sweden) U., 1977-78; JD, Southwestern Sch. Law, Los Angeles, 1980. Bar: Colo. Assoc. Gorsuch Kirgis Campbell Walker & Grover, Denver, 1980-82, Brownstein, Hyatt, Farber & Madden, Denver, 1982-84; pres., founder NetAir Internat., Denver, 1983—, also bd. dirs.; clk. U.S. Ct. Appeals, Washington, 1980; nationwide competitor Philip Jessup Moot Court Team, 1979-80. Bd. dirs. Calif. Jazz Festival, 1976; patron Denver Symphony, 1982—, Denver Art Mus., 1982—; bd. dirs. Am. Israel Pub. Affairs Com., Denver, 1984—; chmn. Re-Election of Atty. Gen., Denver, 1980. Statewide debate champion Calif. State U., 1976; named one of Outstanding Young Men Am. U.S. Jaycees, 1980. Mem. ABA, Colo. Bar Assn., Denver Bar Assn. Democrat. Office: NetAir Internat 1250 14th St Denver CO 80202

ROSENTHAL, KENNETH WOLFGANG, lawyer; b. Frankfurt, Fed. Republic Germany, Nov. 2, 1929; came to U.S., 1944; s. Ludwig and Florence (Koenigsberger) R.; m. Joan Finkelstein, Apr. 10, 1960; children: Jeffrey, David. BA, Syracuse U., 1951; LLB, U. San Francisco, 1958. Bar: Calif. 1959, U.S. Dist. Ct. (no. dist.) Calif. 1959, U.S. Ct. Appeals (9th cir.) 1959, U.S. Supreme Ct. 1972. Assoc. Jay A. Darwin, San Francisco, 1959-61; ptnr. Darwin, Rosenthal & Leff, San Francisco, 1961-69; pres. Rosenthal & Leff Inc., San Francisco, 1969—; del. 9th Cir. Jud. Conf. Contbr. numerous articles to profl. jours. Served as cpl. AUS, 1953-55. Mem. Nat. Bd. Trial Advocacy (cert.), Am. Bd. Trial Advs. (cert.), Calif. Bar. Assn. (legal specialization sect., civic trial advocacy com.), San Francisco Bar Assn., San Francisco Trial Lawyers Assn. (bd. dirs. 1976-84, pres. 1984). Democrat. Jewish. Avocations: photography, jogging. Admiralty, Personal injury, Federal civil litigation. Office: Rosenthal & Leff Inc 100 Bush San Francisco CA 94104

ROSENTHAL, LAWRENCE GERALD, lawyer, assistant attorney general; b. N.Y.C., May 19, 1956; s. David Rosenthal and Rose (Zider) Gorman; m. Kristin Bumiller, Aug. 19, 1985. BA, U. Tex., 1978; JD, U. Houston, 1981. Bar: Tex. 1982, U.S. Ct. Appeals (5th and 11th cirs.) 1982, D.C. 1985, Md. 1985, U.S. Ct. Appeals (3d cir.) 1986. Assoc. Royston, Rayzor, Vickery & Williams, Houston, 1981-85, Hill, Betts & Nash, Washington, 1985-86; asst. atty. gen. State of Md., Balt., 1986—. Mem. ABA, Southeastern Admiralty Law Inst. Admiralty, Private international, Construction. Office: State of Md Contract Litigation Unit 15 Charles Plaza Suite 102 Baltimore MD 21201

ROSENTHAL, MARTIN RICHARD, lawyer; b. Boston, May 10, 1947; s. Alfred Hertz and Anne (Kaplan) R.; m. Margaret Harwood Van Deusen, June 12, 1983. BA, Harvard U., 1968; MA, JD, Stanford U., 1972. Bar: Mass. 1973, U.S. Dist. Ct. Mass. 1978. Legal asst. dist. attys. office Suffolk County, Boston, 1972-73; staff atty. Mass. Defenders Com., Boston, 1973-78; supervising atty. Mass. defenders com. State of Mass., Boston, 1978-84; tng. dir. Pub. Counsel Services Com., Boston, 1984—. Mem. town meeting Town of Brookline, Mass., 1979-85, mem. fin. adv. com., 1983-85, selectman, 1985—; mem. adv. com. Citizens Against Death Penalty, Boston, 1982—; bd. dirs. Mass. Council for Pub. Justice, Boston, 1984—, Civil Liberties Union of Mass., 1985—. Mem. ABA, Nat. Assn. Criminal Def. Lawyers, Nat. Lawyers Guild (exec. com. Mass. chpt. 1978-85), Nat. Legal Aid and Defender Assn., Mass. Assn. Criminal Def. Lawyers (exec. com. 1979-85), Mass. Bar Assn., Boston Bar Assn. (council mem. 1983-86, co-chmn. criminal law steering com. 1985—). Democrat. Jewish. Avocations: local politics, Boston Celtics. Criminal. Home: 62 Columbia St Brookline MA 02146 Office: Com for Pub Counsel Services 80 Boylston St Boston MA 02146

ROSENTHAL, ROBERT MICHAEL, lawyer; b. N.Y.C., Dec. 28, 1936; s. David and Anna R.; m. Nina Silver, July 3, 1983. BSBA, U. Pa., 1960; JD, Southwestern U., Los Angeles, 1976. Bar: Calif. 1976. Motion picture producer Paramount Pictures Corp., N.Y.C., 1970-73; sole practice Los Angeles, 1976—; pres. Bel Air Broadcasting Corp., 1985—. Trustee Lawrence Acad., Mass., 1980—; bd. dirs. Legal Aid Found., 1984-86, Los Angeles, U.S. com. Sports for Israel, Phila., 1985—. Served to capt. USAR. Mem. ABA, Los Angeles Bar Assn., Beverly Hills Bar Assn. (bd. dirs. 1983-85), Century City Bar Assn. Club: Beach Point (Mamaroneck, N.Y.). State civil litigation, Federal civil litigation. Office: 10100 Santa Monica Blvd Suite 2600 Los Angeles CA 90067

ROSENTHAL, STEVEN S., lawyer; b. Washington, Aug. 26, 1952; s. Jacob Wolfe and Muriel Hanna (Brenner) R. BA magna cum laude, Clark U., 1975; JD, U. Calif., San Francisco, 1978. Bar: Calif. 1978, U.S. Dist. Ct. (no. dist.) Calif. 1978, U.S. Ct. Appeals (D.C. cir.) 1979, U.S. Supreme Ct. 1984. Sole practice San Francisco, 1979—. Mem. edn. com. Jewish Community Fedn., San Francisco; bd. dirs. Coalition for Better Housing, San Francisco, 1983—. Mem. Assn. Trial Lawyers Am., Calif. Trial Lawyers Assn., Lawyers' Club San Francisco (gov. 1985—), Calif. State Bar Conf. (del. 1982—), Phi Beta Kappa, Hebrew Free Loan Assn. Democrat. Club: Concordia-Argonaut (San Francisco). Avocations: skiing, photography, golf. State civil litigation, Landlord-tenant, General practice. Office: 1255 Post St #935 San Francisco CA 94109

ROSENTHAL, STEVEN SIEGMUND, lawyer; b. Cleve., May 22, 1949; s. Fred Siegel and Natalie Josephine Rosenthal; m. Ilene Edwina Goldstein, Oct. 1, 1983. AB, Dartmouth Coll., 1971; JD, Harvard U., 1974. Bar: Fla. 1974, D.C. 1975, U.S. Supreme Ct. 1978, Calif. 1983. Law clk. to presiding justice U.S. Ct. Appeals (D.C. cir.), 1974-75; assoc. Covington & Burling, Washington, 1975-80; assoc. Morrison & Foerster, Washington, 1980-81, ptnr., 1981—; lawyer rep. Jud. Conf. D.C. Cir., 1981-83. Contbr. articles on environ. law to profl. jours. Pres. Family and Child Services Washington, 1986—, trustee, 1978—. Mem. ABA (chmn. environ. values com. adminstrv. law sect. 1981-84), Phi Beta Kappa. Republican. Environment, Federal civil litigation, Administrative and regulatory. Office: Morrison & Foerster 2000 Pennsylvania Ave NW Suite 5500 Washington DC 20005

ROSENZWEIG, CHARLES LEONARD, lawyer; b. N.Y.C., Apr. 12, 1952; s. William and Frieda (Dechner) R.; m. Rya R. Mehler, June 14, 1975; children: Jessica Sara, Erica Danielle. AB cum laude, Princeton U., 1974; JD, NYU, 1977. Bar: N.Y. 1978, U.S. Dist. Ct. (ea. and so. dists.) N.Y. 1978, U.S. Ct. Appeals (7th cir.) 1980, U.S. Ct. Internat. Trade 1981, U.S. Ct. Appeals (2d cir.) 1985. Assoc. Graubard, Moskovitz et al, N.Y.C., 1977-85; ptnr. Shaw & Reed, N.Y.C., 1985-87, Rand, Rosenzweig, Smith & Radley, N.Y.C., 1987—. Mem. ABA (internat. law sect.), N.Y. State Bar Assn., Assn. of Bar of City of N.Y., NYU Alumni Assn. (chmn. jour. internat. law and politics alumni 1985—). Democrat. Jewish. Club: Princeton (N.Y.C.). Avocations: skiing, tennis. Private international, Federal civil litigation, General corporate. Home: 37 Franklin Rd Scarsdale NY 10583 Office: Rand Rosenzweig Smith & Radley 335 Madison Ave New York NY 10017

ROSENZWEIG, THEODORE B., lawyer; b. N.Y.C., Apr. 14, 1948; s. Joseph and Elsa Ruth (Davis) R.; m. Barbara Conviser, Jan. 23, 1977; 1 child, Brian Eliott. BA, NYU, 1969; JD, Fordham U., 1973. Bar: N.Y. 1974, U.S. Dist. Ct. (ea. dist.) N.Y. 1976, U.S. Dist. Ct. (so. dist.) N.Y. 1976, U.S. Ct. Appeals (2d cir.) 1977. Asst. dist. atty. Kings County Dist. Atty.'s Office, Bklyn., 1973-79, sr. trial atty. homicide bur., 1978-79; assoc. McAloon, Friedman & Mandell, P.C., N.Y.C., 1979-82, ptnr., 1983—; mem. faculty Nat. Inst. for Trial Advocacy Program, Benjamin N. Cardozo Sch. of Law, N.Y.C., 1984. Mem. N.Y. State Bar Assn. (trial lawyers sect.). Democrat. Jewish. State civil litigation, Personal injury, Medical malpractice. Home: 230 Garth Rd Scarsdale NY 10583 Office: McAloon Friedman & Mandell PC 116 John St New York NY 10038

ROSER, MICHAEL R., lawyer; b. Camden, N.J., Oct. 20, 1948; s. John William and Lucille Dorris (Lang) R.; m. Linda Kay Bryan, Dec. 28, 1972; children: Nathan, Zachary. BA, Bates Coll., 1971; JD, Dickinson Sch. of Law, 1975. Bar: Mo. 1975, U.S. Dist. Ct. (we. dist.) Mo. 1975, U.S. Ct. Appeals (10th cir.) 1982, U.S. Ct. Appeals (8th cir.) 1984. From assoc. to ptnr. Berman, DeLeve, Kuchan & Chapman, Kansas City, Mo., 1975—; lectr. U. Mo., Columbia, 1977—, U. Mo. Kansas City, 1977—, Nat. Assn. Credit Mgmt., Kansas City, 1977—. Mem. ABA, Mo. Bar Assn., Kansas City Bar Assn. (lectr.), Phi Beta Kappa. Episcopalian. Club: Vanguard II (Kansas City, Mo.). Bankruptcy, Contracts commercial. Office: Berman DeLeve Kuchan & Chapman 1006 Grand Suite 600 Kansas City MO 64106

ROSETT, ARTHUR IRWIN, lawyer, educator; b. N.Y.C., July 5, 1934; s. Milton B. and Bertha (Werner) R.; children: David Benjamin, Martha Jean, Daniel Joseph; m. Lucie Cheng, 1983. A.B., Columbia U., 1955, LL.B., 1959. Bar: Calif. 1968, N.Y. State 1960, U.S. Supreme Ct. 1963. Law clk. U.S. Supreme Ct., 1959-60; asst. U.S. atty. So. Dist. N.Y., 1960-63; practice law N.Y.C., 1963-65; assoc. dir. Pres.'s Commn. on Law Enforcement and Adminstrn. Justice, 1965-67; acting prof. law UCLA, 1967-70, prof., 1970—. Author: (with A. Mueller) Contract Law and Its Application, 1971, 3d, rev. edit., 1983, (with D. Cressey) Justice by Consent, 1976. Served with USN, 1956-58. Mem. Am. Law Inst. Legal education, Contracts commercial, Private international. Home: 641 S Saltair Ave Los Angeles CA 90049 Office: UCLA Law Sch Los Angeles CA 90024

ROSI, PHILIP RINALDO, lawyer; b. Chgo., Apr. 9, 1938; s. Alcide Louis and Barbara (Shambaugh) R.; m. Joann Duff, Nov. 2, 1968; children: Rachele Duff, Philip R. II, Emma Josephine, Jenny Shambaugh. BSME, Carnegie Inst. Tech., Pitts., 1959; postgrad., U. Ill., 1960; JD, U. Chgo., 1963; postgrad., John Marshall Law Sch., 1964. Bar: Ill. 1963, Vt. 1970, Mich. 1980. Design engr. Lockhead Aircraft Co., Burbank, Calif., 1959; assoc. McDougall, Hersh et al, Chgo., 1963-66; legis. atty., budget examiner U.S. Bur. Budget, Washington, 1966-68; asst. to comptroller Fed. Power Commn., Washington, 1968-70; ptnr. Kristensen, Cummings, et al, Brattleboro, Vt., 1970-80, Thompson, Zirnhelt, Bowron & Rosi, P.C., Traverse City, Mich., 1980-86; sole practice Traverse City, 1987—. Mem. ABA, Vt. Bar Assn., Ill. Bar Assn., Mich. Bar Assn. Republican. Lodge: Rotary. General corporate, Oil and gas leasing, State civil litigation. Home: 1223 Randolph Traverse City MI 49684 Office: 160 E State Suite II Traverse City MI 49685-1826

ROSINEK, JEFFREY, judge; b. N.Y.C., Sept. 13, 1941; s. Isidore and Etta (Kramer) R.; m. Sandra Gwen Rosen, Aug. 7, 1977; 1 child, Ian David. B.A. in History, U. Miami, 1963, postgrad. in Polit. Sci., J.D., 1974. Bar: Fla., 1974. Tchr., Coral Gables (Fla.) High Sch., 1963-78; sole practice, Miami, Fla., 1974-76; assoc. Tendrich and Todd, Miami, 1976-77; ptnr. Rosinek & Blake, Miami, 1977-86; judge Dade County Court, Miami, 1986—; instr. Boston U., 1975. Chmn. Miami Environ. Research Adv. Com., 1969-73; mem. Dade County Youth Adv. Bd., 1973-75; bd. dirs. U. Miami Law Sch., treas. alumni; past pres. Dade County Young Democrats; mem. Congl. Civilian Rev. Bd., 1975—, chmn., 1976-78; bd. dirs., treas. Fla. Congl. Com., Legal Services Greater Miami; Fla. chmn. Project Concern Internat.; v.p. Beth David Congregation, 1976-85; bd. trustees Haven Ctr.; bd. dirs., treas., organizer South Miami-Kendall pro bono project Legal Service of Greater Miami, 1983-86. Recipient award Jewish Theol. Sem., 1978. Mem. ABA, Dade County Bar Assn., South Miami-Kendall Bar Assn. (past pres.), Coral Gables Bar Assn., Wig and Robe (chancellor 1973-74), Bar and Gavel Soc. Clubs: Biscayne Bay Kiwanis (past pres., lt. gov. Fla. Dist., Maj. Emphasis chmn.), Key Internat. (counselor Fla. dist., Key of Honor 1979, Key Club honoree 1984). Family and matrimonial, General practice, Judicial administration. Home: 535 Bird Rd Coral Gables FL 33146 Office: 100 Meridian Ave Miami Beach FL 33139

ROSINI, NEIL JUSTIN, lawyer; b. N.Y.C., Sept. 23, 1951; s. Edward A. and Eva (Nardelli) R.; m. Elizabeth Freije Rosini, May 22, 1982. BA, U. Notre Dame, 1973; JD, Yale U., 1976. Bar: N.J. 1976, U.S. Dist. Ct. N.J. 1976, N.Y. 1977, U.S. Dist. Ct. (so. and ea. dist.) N.Y. 1977, U.S. Ct. Appeals (2d cir.) 1982. Atty. Townley & Updike, N.Y.C., 1976-81; assoc. Franklin, Weinrib, Rudell & Vassallo P.C., N.Y.C., 1981-85, ptnr., 1985—. Contbr. articles to profl. pubs.; author: (comic strip) Trials of Ledbetter, 1978-83. Mem. ABA, Assn. Bar of City of N.Y. Libel, Entertainment, Trademark and copyright. Office: Franklin Weinrib Rudell & Vassallo 950 Third Ave New York NY 10022

ROSINY, FRANK RICHARD, lawyer; educator; b. N.Y.C. Mar. 3, 1940. Student Duke U., 1958-59; A.B. with highest honors, U. N.C., 1961; J.D., Columbia U., 1964. Bar: N.Y. 1964, U.S. Supreme Ct. 1968, Fla. 1982, N.J. 1984. Assoc. Berman & Frost, N.Y.C., 1964-65; sole practice, N.Y.C., 1966-72; ptnr. Rosenman, Colin, Freund, Lewis & Cohen, N.Y.C., 1973-79, Rosiny & Rosiny, N.Y.C., 1979—; adj. prof. N.Y. Law Sch., 1977—, Bklyn. Law Sch., 1984—; mem. departmental disciplinary com. 1st dept. N.Y. State Supreme Ct., 1986—. Mem. Assn. Bar City of N.Y. (com. on state legislation 1967-70, com. on profl. jud. ethics 1977-80, com. on profl. discipline, 1980-82), N.Y. County Lawyers Assn. (dir. 1977-81), ABA (vice chmn. com. on advocacy, gen. practice sect. 1976-78, chmn. com. comm. law 1981-83), N.Y. State Bar Assn. (chmn. com. profl. ethics 1976-81, chmn. spl. com. to rev. rules of profl. conduct 1979-83), Phi Beta Kappa. Contbg. author: New York Civil Practice, vols. 10 and 10A, 1970. Home: 240 Central Park S New York NY 10019 Office: Rosiny & Rosiny 61 Broadway New York NY 10006

ROSKIN, PRESTON EUGENE, lawyer; b. St. Louis, Feb. 20, 1946; s. Chester F. and Evelyn (Kogan) R.; m. Linda Mc Girl, Nov. 28, 1980; children—Eric, Brian, David. B.S. in Civil Engring., U. Mo., 1970, J.D., 1971. Bar: Mo. 1971, Ill. 1972, U.S. Dist. Ct. (ea. dist.) Mo. 1971, U.S. Ct. Appeals (8th cir.) 1972, U.S. Supreme Ct. 1972. Sole practice, Clayton, Mo., 1971-76, 80-83, 85—; ptnr. Floyd & Roskin, Clayton, 1976-80, Phelps, Coffin, Roskin, Andreatta & Lorenz, Clayton 1983-85. Mem. Assn. Trial Lawyers Am., ABA, Mo. Bar, Mo. Assn. Trial Attys. (bd. govs., exec. com.), St. Louis Met. Bar Assn., St. Louis County Bar Assn., Ill. Bar Assn., Attys. Motivated for Mo. Jewish. Personal injury, State civil litigation, Workers' compensation. Home: 9 Woodbridge Park Rd DesPeres MO 63131 Office: 100 S Brentwood Blvd 5th Floor Clayton MO 63105

ROSKOVENSKY, VINCENT JOSEPH, II, lawyer; b. Uniontown, Pa., Mar. 15, 1950; s. Vincent S. and Gertrude F. Roskovensky; m. Christine D. Bruni, July 16, 1977; 1 child, Vincent M. B.A., U. Pitts., 1971; J.D., Duquesne U., 1974. Bar: Pa. 1974, U.S. Dist. Ct. (we. dist.) Pa. 1975. Sole practice, Uniontown, 1974—; asst. dist. atty. Fayette County (Pa.), 1975-77; solicitor Smithfield Borough, Smithfield, Pa., 1981—, Albert Gallatin Mcpl. Authority, Lake Lynn, Pa., 1980—; pres. Poca Coal Land Co., Uniontown. Treas., past pres. Fayette County Children and Youth Adv. Com., Uniontown. Mem. Pa. Bar Assn., Fayette County Bar Assn., Assn. Trial Lawyers Am., ABA. Democrat. Roman Catholic. Club: Exchange. State civil litigation, General practice, Criminal. Home: Heritage Hills Rd Uniontown PA 15401 Office: 9 Court St Uniontown PA 15401

ROSKY, BURTON SEYMOUR, lawyer; b. Chgo., May 28, 1927; s. David T. and Mary W. (Zelkin) R.; m. Leatrice J. Darrow, June 16, 1951; children: David Scott, Bruce Alan. Student, Ill. Inst. Tech., 1944-45; B.S., UCLA, 1948; J.D., Loyola U., Los Angeles, 1953. Bar: Calif. 1954, U.S. Supreme Ct 1964, U.S. Tax Ct 1964; C.P.A., Calif. Auditor City Los Angeles, 1948- 51; with Beidner, Temkin & Ziskin (C.P.A.s), Los Angeles, 1951-52; supervising auditor Army Audit Agy., 1952-53; practiced law Los Angeles, Beverly Hills, 1954—; partner Duskin & Rosky, 1972-82, Rosky, Landau & Fox, 1982—; lectr. on tax and bus. problems. Judge pro tem Beverly Hills Mcpl. Ct.; mem. Los Angeles Mayor's Community Adv. Council. Contbr. profl. publs. Charter sponsor Los Angeles County Mus. Arts; contbg. mem. Assocs. of Smithsonian Instn.; charter mem. Air and Space Mus; mem. Am. Mus. Natural History, Los Angeles Zoo; sustaining mem. Los Angeles Mus. Natural History; mem. exec. bd. So. Calif. council Nat. Fedn. Temple Brotherhoods, mem. nat. exec. bd. Served with USNR, 1945-46. Walter Henry Cook fellow Loyola Law Sch. Fellow Jewish Chautauqua Soc. (life mem.); mem. Am. Arbitration Assn. (nat. panel arbitrators), Am. Assn. Attys.-C.P.A.s (charter mem. pres. 1968), Calif. Assn. Attys.-C.P.A.s (charter mem., pres. 1963), Calif. Soc. C.P.A.s, Calif., Beverly Hills, Century City, Los Angeles County bar assns., Am. Judicature Soc., Chancellors Assocs. UCLA, Tau Delta Phi, Phi Alpha Delta.; mem. B'nai B'rith. Jewish (mem. exec. bd., pres. temple, pres. brotherhood). Club: Mason. Corporate taxation, Estate taxation, Probate. Office: 8383 Wilshire Blvd Beverly Hills CA 90211

ROSNER, JONATHAN LEVI, lawyer; b. N.Y.C., Sept. 4, 1932; s. Oscar S. and Miriam (Reinhardt) R.; m. Lydia Sokol, Dec. 23, 1956; children: Beth, Marianne, Josh. BA, Wesleyan U., Middletown, Conn., 1954; JD, NYU, 1959. Bar: N.Y. 1959, U.S. Dist. Ct. (so. dist.) N.Y. 1962, U.S. Dist. Ct. (ea. dist.) N.Y. 1964, U.S. Ct. Appeals (2d cir.) 1964, U.S. Supreme Ct. 1964, U.S. Dist. Ct. Md. 1969, U.S. Dist. Ct. P.R. 1972, U.S. Ct. Appeals (D.C. cir.) 1976, U.S. Dist. Ct. (ea. dist.) Mich. 1984, U.S. Ct. Appeals (11th cir.) 1984. Law clk. to judge U.S. Dist. Ct. (so. dist.) N.Y., N.Y.C., 1959-60, asst. U.S. atty., 1960-63; ptnr. Rosner, Rosner & McEvoy, N.Y.C., 1963-79; sole practice N.Y.C., 1979-85; ptnr. Rosner & Goodman, N.Y.C., 1985—; adj. prof. law NYU, 1970-83, Pace U., White Plains, N.Y., 1984—; chief counsel N.Y.C. Spl. Commn. on Power Failure, 1977, criminal justice and force N.Y. State Commn., N.Y.C., 1985—. Co-author: How to Prepare Witnesses for Trial, 1985. Bd. dirs. Westchester Jewish Community Services, 1970-73; trustee Woodlands Community Temple, 1971-76; mem. Wesleyan U. Alumni Assn. (adv. council 1972-79, schs. com. 1964-78). Served with U.S. Army, 1954-56. Mem. ABA, N.Y. State Bar Assn. (com. on grievances 1974-76), Assn. Bar of City of N.Y. (coms. on profl. discipline 1983—, grievances 1970-74, entertainment 1964-68, 78, 82, panelist 1976-78), N.Y. County Lawyers Assn., NYU Law Alumni Assn. (bd. dirs. 1969-73, 75-79), N.Y. Univ. Law Rev. Alumni Assn. (bd. dirs. 1965-69, 84—), N.Y. County Dist. Attys. Ann. Trial Advocacy Program (faculty 1978-83). Federal civil litigation, State civil litigation, Criminal. Home: 33 High Ridge Rd Hartsdale NY 10530 Office: Rosner & Goodman 342 Madison Ave New York NY 10573

ROSOFF, WILLIAM A., lawyer; b. Phila., June 21, 1943; s. Herbert and Estelle (Finkel) R.; m. Beverly Rae Rifkin, Feb. 7, 1970; children: Catherine D., Andrew M. BS with honors, Temple U., 1964; LLB magna cum laude, U. Pa., 1967. Bar: Pa. 1968, U.S. Dist. Ct. (ea. dist.) Pa. 1968. Law clk. U.S. Ct. Appeals (3d cir.), 1967-68; instr. U. Pa. Law Sch., Phila., 1968-69; assoc. Wolf, Block, Schorr & Solis-Cohen, Phila., 1969-75, ptnr., 1975—, chmn. exec. com., 1987—; bd. dirs. Korman Co.; guest lectr. confs. and seminars on tax law; mem. Commerce Clearing House Tax. Trans. Adv. Bd., 1983—; mem. legal activities policy bd. Tax Analysts, 1978—. Editor U. Pa. Law Rev., 1965-67; mem. bd. contbg. editors and advisors Jour. Partnership Taxation, 1983—; author reports and papers on tax law. Bd. dirs. Phila. chpt. Am. Soc. for Technion; dir., mem. com. on law and social action Phila. council Am. Jewish Congress. Fellow Am. Coll. Tax Counsel; mem. Am. Law Inst. (cons. taxation of partnerships 1976-78, assoc. reporter taxation of partnerships, 1978-82, mem. adv. group, adv. group on fed. income tax project 1982—), Order of Coif, Beta Gamma Sigma, Beta Alpha Psi. Club: Locust. Corporate taxation, Personal income taxation. Office: 12th Floor and Packard Bldg 15th and Chestnut Sts Philadelphia PA 19102

ROSOW, MALCOLM BERTRAM, lawyer; b. N.Y.C., Mar. 19, 1922; s. Nelson and Irene (Steiner) R.; m. Carol Joy Sherman, Mar. 9, 1944; children—Michael, Kenneth, Wendy, Heidi. Student CCNY, 1938-40, U. Wis., 1940-43; LL.B., NYU, 1948. Bar: N.Y. 1949, U.S. Dist. Ct. (so. dist.) N.Y. 1949, (ea. dist.) N.Y. 1954, U.S. Dist. Ct. (ea. dist.) Wis. 1982, U.S. Cts. Appeals (2d cir.) 1956, (5th cir.) 1979, (6th cir.) 1980, (1st cir.) 1982, (D.C. cir.) 1981, U.S. Supreme Ct. 1958. Assoc., William L. Standard, N.Y.C., 1949-57, Standard, Weisberg, Harolds & Malament, N.Y.C., 1957-61, Standard, Weisberg & Harolds, 1961-67; ptnr. Standard, Weisberg Heckerling & Rosow, N.Y.C., 1967-81; pres. Standard Weisberg Heckerling & Rosow, P.C., 1981—. Contbr. articles to legal jours. Served to 1st lt. Signal Corps, U.S. Army, 1944-46; ETO. Mem. NYU Law Rev. Alumni Assn. (v.p. 1960-62), N.Y. State Bar Assn., ABA, N.Y. County Lawyers Assn., Internat. Assn. Ins. Lawyers, Def. Research Inst., Maritime Law Assn. U.S., Def. Assn. N.Y. Club: World Trade (World Trade Ctr. N.Y.) (founding mem.). Admiralty, Insurance. Home: 430 Roslyn Rd Roslyn Heights NY 11577 Office: Standard Weisberg Heckerling & Rosow PC 61 Broadway New York NY 10006

ROSOW, STUART L., lawyer; b. N.Y.C., Mar. 28, 1950; s. Bernard and Lillian (Bonime) R.; widowed. AB cum laude, Yale U.; JD cum laude, Harvard U. Law clk. to presiding justice U.S. Ct. Appeals (7th cir.), Chgo., 1975-76; assoc. Paul, Weiss et al, N.Y.C., 1976-79; assoc. Kaye, Scholer, Fierman, Hays & Handler, N.Y.C., 1979-84, ptnr., 1984—. Mem. ABA, N.Y. State Bar Assn., Assn. of Bar of City of N.Y. Corporate taxation, Personal income taxation. Office: Kaye Scholer Fierman Hays & Handler 425 Park Ave New York NY 10022

ROSS, ALAN HAROLD, lawyer, insurance company executive; b. Lowell, Mass., May 22, 1945; s. Harold G. and Ursula (Donahue) R.; m. Patricia M. Rusnak, June 19, 1976. BA, U. Notre Dame, 1967; MBA, Boston Coll., 1969; JD, Villanova U., 1974. Bar: Pa. 1974, U.S. Dist. Ct. (ea. dist.) Pa. 1975, U.S. Ct. Appeals (3d cir.) 1978, U.S. Supreme Ct. 1984. Market analyst Penn Cen. Co., Phila., 1969-70; atty. Liberty Mut. Ins. Co., Phila., 1974-86; mng. atty. Hartford Ins. Group, Phila., 1986—. Mem. ABA, Pa. Bar Assn., Phila. Bar Assn., Phila. Assn. Def. Counsel, Lawyers Club Phila., Paoli-Malvern Jaycees (v.p. 1979, bd. dirs. 1980, dir. of yr. award 1980). Republican. Roman Catholic. Club: Downtown (Phila.). Avocations: sailing, photography, golf. Federal civil litigation, State civil litigation, Personal injury. Office: Hartford Ins Group 1515 Market St Suite 606 Philadelphia PA 19102

ROSS, BOBBIE JEAN, lawyer; b. Mound, La., Jan. 14, 1955; d. Robert Honer and Rosie Lee (Harrison) Gray; 1 child Derrick. BA in Interior Design, So. U. A&M, 1977, JD, 1980. Bar: La. 1981, U.S. Dist. Ct. (we. dist.) La. 1981, U.S. Dist. Ct. (ea. dist.) La. 1983, U.S. Ct. Appeals (5th cir.) 1983, U.S. Supreme Ct. 1986. Staff atty. North La. Legal Service Corp., Monroe, 1980-83; exec. dir., gen. counsel S.W. La. Legal Services, Lake Charles, 1983—; lectr. So. U., Baton Rouge, 1984; instr. McNeese State U., Lake Charles, 1985—. Mem. Nat. Bar Assn., Am. Trial Lawyers Assn., La. Trial Lawyers Assn., Lake Charles C. of C. Democrat. Baptist. Administrative and regulatory, Family and matrimonial, Landlord-tenant. Home: 736 Cleveland St Lake Charles LA 70602 Office: SW La Legal Services Soc Inc 1011 Lake Shore Dr Suite 402 Lake Charles LA 70602

ROSS, BRUCE SHIELDS, lawyer; b. Los Angeles, Feb. 1, 1947; s. Floyd and Mary Louise (Shields) R.; m. Janet G. Ross, Jan 27, 1968 (div. Jan. 1977); 1 child, Stephanie; m. Carol Burlingame, Apr. 2, 1977; children: Andrew, Tiffany. AB cum laude, Oberlin Coll., 1968; JD, U. Calif., Berkeley, 1971. Bar: Calif. 1971, U.S. Tax Ct. 1973, U.S. Dist. Ct. (cen. dist.) Calif. 1977. Assoc. Nossman and Krueger, Los Angeles, 1971-73; from assoc. to ptnr. Poindexter & Doutre, Los Angeles, 1973-78; assoc. Alschuler & Grossman, Los Angeles, 1978, ptnr., 1979-84; ptnr. Morrison & Foerster, Los Angeles, 1984—. Note and comments editor U. Calif. Law Rev., 1970-71; author: Calif. Practice Guide: Probate, 1986; contbr. articles to profl. jours. Fin. chmn. Boy Scouts Am., Glendale, Calif., 1984-85; trustee Pacific Asia Mus., Pasadena, Calif., 1983—; gov. The Webb Schs. of Calif., Claremont, 1987—. Mem. ABA, Los Angeles County Bar Assn. (exec. com. tax. sect. 1984-85), Am. Coll. Probate Counsel, Order of Coif. Democrat. Unitarian. Avocations: racquetball, running, music, opera. Pension, profit-sharing, and employee benefits, Probate, Estate taxation. Home: 430 Coutin Ln Glendale CA 91206 Office: Morrison & Foerster 333 S Grand Ave 38th Floor Los Angeles CA 90071

ROSS, CHRISTOPHER THEODORE WILLIAM, lawyer; b. Denver, Oct. 19, 1925; s. Michael Peter and Martha (Stockhausen) R.; m. Luise Maria Reile, June 11, 1952 (div.); children—Mark Alexander, Katherine Luise, Sonya Catherine (dec.). LL.B. U. Buffalo, 1950; J.D., SUNY-Buffalo, 1968. Bar: N.Y. 1951, U.S. Dist. Ct. (we. dist.) N.Y. 1952, U.S. Ct. Mil. Appeals 1953, U.S. Supreme Ct. 1970, U.S. Ct. Appeals (2d cir.) 1971. Assoc. Lutwak, Parrino & Maurin, Buffalo, 1959-63; sole practice, Buffalo, 1963—. Pres. N.Y. State Assn. Bds. Visitors Dept. Mental Hygiene, 1974-78; pres. West Seneca (N.Y.) Devel. Ctr., 1968-70, 72-74; trustee Buffalo Boy's & Girls Clubs. Served as aviator USN, 1943-46, 52-59; comdr. USNR, ret. Mem. N.Y. Bar Assn., Erie County Bar Assn., N.Y. Trial Lawyers Assn., Erie County Trial Lawyers Assn., Lawyer-Pilots Bar Assn., Naval Res. Assn. (v.p. legis.). Republican. Roman Catholic. Clubs: Buffalo Athletic, Quiet Birdmen, Saints and Sinners, Silver Wings. Criminal, Personal injury, Aviation negligence. Office: 330 Statler Towers Buffalo NY 14202

ROSS, DONALD ROE, U.S. judge; b. Orleans, Nebr., June 8, 1922; s. Roe M. and Leila H. (Reed) R.; m. Janice S. Cook, Aug. 29, 1943; children—Susan Jane, Sharon Kay, Rebecca Lynn, Joan Christine, Donald Dean. LL.B., U. Nebr., 1948. Bar: Nebr. bar 1948. Practice law Lexington, Nebr., 1948-53; mem. firm Swarr, May, Royce, Smith, Andersen & Ross, 1956-70; U.S. atty. Dist. Nebr., 1953-56; gen. counsel Republican party, Nebr., 1956-58; mem. Rep. Exec. Com. for Nebr., 1952-53; nat. com. mem. Rep. Exec. Com. for Nebr., Nebr., 1958-70; vice chmn. Republican Nat. Com., 1965-70; U.S. circuit judge 8th Circuit, U.S. Ct. Appeals, 1971—; Mayor City of Lexington, 1953. Home: 9936 Essex Dr Omaha NE 68114 Office: Federal Bldg Omaha NE 68101

ROSS, EUNICE LATSHAW, judge; b. Bellevue, Pa., Oct. 13, 1923; d. Richard Kelly and Eunice (Weidner) Latshaw; m. John Anthony Ross, May 29, 1943 (dec. Jan. 1978); 1 child, Geraldine Ross Coleman. B.S., U. Pitts., 1945, LL.B., 1951. Bar: Pa. 1952. Atty., Pub. Health Law Research Project, Pitts., 1951-52; atty. jud. asst., law clk. Ct. Common Pleas, Pitts., 1952-70; adjunct law prof. U. Pitts., 1967-73; dir. family div. Ct. Common Pleas, Pitts., 1970-72; judge Ct. Common Pleas of Allegheny County, Pitts., 1972—; mem. Bd. Jud. Inquiry and Rev., Commonwealth of Pa. Author: (with others) Survey of Pa. Public Health Laws, 1952. Contbr. articles to legal publs. Com. person for 14th ward, vice chmn. Democratic Com., Pitts., 1972; exec. com. bd. trustees U. Pitts., 1980—; adv. bd. Animal Friends, Pitts., 1973—; bd. mem. The Program, Pitts., 1983—, Pitts. History and Landmarks Fedn., West Pa. Hist. Soc., West Pa. Conservancy. Recipient Disting. Amumna award U. Pitts., 1973, Medal of Recognition, 1987; named Girl Scout Woman of Yr., Pitts. council Girl Scouts U.S., 1975; cert. of Achievement Pa. Fedn. Women's Clubs, 1975, 77. Mem. Allegheny County Bar Assn. (vice chmn., exec. com. young lawyers sect. 1956-59), Pitts. Bus. and Profl. Women's Club, Pa. State Trial Judges Conf. Club: Monday Luncheon. State civil litigation, Probate, Estate taxation. Home: 1204 Denniston Ave Pittsburgh PA 15217 Office: 802 City-County Bldg Pittsburgh PA 15219

ROSS, GERALD ELLIOTT, lawyer; b. Chatham, Ont., Can., Aug. 9, 1941; s. Sanford Finlay and Helen Letitia Violet (Russell) R.; m. E. Sue Goetz, Dec. 29, 1963 (div. July 1975); m. Diana Guadalupe, Nov. 23, 1975; children—James Russell, Margaret Emily. B.B.A., U. Mich., 1962, M.B.A., 1963, J.D. cum laude, 1967. Bar: N.Y. 1968, U.S. Dist. Ct. (so. and ea. dists.) N.Y. 1969, U.S. Ct. Appeals (2d cir.) 1973, U.S. Ct. Appeals (8th cir.) 1973, U.S. Supreme Ct. 1973, U.S. Ct. Appeals (1st cir.) 1983. Assoc. Dewey Ballantine Bushby Palmer & Wood, N.Y.C., 1967-74, Dunnington, Bartholow & Miller, N.Y.C., 1974-77; sr. atty. J.C. Penney Co., N.Y.C., 1977-81; sole practice Law Offices Gerald Ross, N.Y.C., 1981-85; founding ptnr. Fryer, Ross & Gowen, 1986—. Vestryman Christ and St. Stephen's Ch., N.Y.C., 1981-86, treas., 1983-86; mem. stewardship, budget and adminstrv. coms. Episcopal Diocese of N.Y., 1982-86 . Served to 1st lt. U.S. Army, 1963-65. Mem. N.Y. State Bar Assn., Assn. Bar City of N.Y., Am. Arbitration Assn. (panel constrn. arbitrators). Clubs: N.Y. Yacht (N.Y.C.); Am. Yacht (Rye, N.Y.). Federal civil litigation, General corporate, General practice. Home: 160 West End Ave New York NY 10023 Office: 551 Fifth Ave New York NY 10176

ROSS, HOWARD PHILIP, lawyer; b. Chgo., May 10, 1939; s. Bernard and Estelle (Maremont) R.; m. Loretta Teresa Benquil, 1962 (div.); children: Glen Joseph, Cynthia Ann; m. Jennifer Kay Shirley, 1984. BS, U. Ill., 1961; JD, Stetson Coll. Law, 1964. Bar: Fla. 1964, U.S. Ct. Appeals (5th cir.) 1965, U.S. Ct. Appeals (11th cir.) 1981, U.S. Supreme Ct. 1969; cert. civil trial lawyer. Assoc. Parker & Battaglia and predecessor firm, St. Petersburg, Fla., 1964-67; ptnr. Battaglia, Ross, Hastings, Dicus & Andrews and predecessor firms, St. Petersburg, 1967—; lectr. Stetson Coll. Law, St. Petersburg, 1971-72, adj. prof., 1987—. Author: Florida Corporations; contbr. articles to profl. jours. Recipient Woman's Service League Best Groomed award, 1979, Fla. Bar merit citation, 1974. Mem ABA, Fla. Bar Assn., St. Petersburg Bar Assn., Am. Soc. Writers on Legal Subjects, Assn. Trial Lawyers Am., Assn. Fla. Trial Lawyers, Smithsonian Assocs. Republican. Jewish. Club:Treasure Island Tennis and Yacht (bd. govs.). State civil litigation, General corporate, Commercial. Address: PO Box 41100 980 Tyrone Blvd Saint Petersburg FL 33743

ROSS, JAMES ANDREW, lawyer; b. Pitts., Nov. 5, 1946; s. Andrew and Jean Rodgers (Burford) R.; m. Mary Ann Mongillo, Dec. 16, 1983; children: Nathan, Benjamin. BS in Engring., U. Pitts., 1968, MBA, 1969; JD, Duquesne U., 1977. Bar: U.S. Dist. Ct. (we. dist.) Pa. 1977, Pa. 1985. Constrn. engr. Ross & Kennedy, Pitts., 1972-77, v.p., counsel, 1977—. Ski instr., guide West Pa. Blind Leisure Opportunities, Pitts. and Boyce Park, Pa., 1984-85. Served to capt. USAF, 1969-72. Mem. ABA, NSPE, Pa. Bar Assn., Allegheny County Bar Assn., Lawyer Pilots Bar Assn., Profl. Ski Instrs. Am. (assoc. cert.). Republican. Presbyterian. Clubs: Mountain, County Line Bldg. and Ski (Somerset, Pa.); Condor Aero (Zelienople, Pa.). Avocations: snow skiing, water skiing, cycling, flying, boating. Construction, General corporate, Labor. Home: 2355 West Gate Dr Pittsburgh PA 15237 Office: Ross & Kennedy Corp 1610 Babcock Blvd Pittsburgh PA 15209

ROSS, JAMES ULRIC, lawyer, accountant, educator; b. Del Rio, Tex., Sept. 14, 1941; s. Stephen Mabrey and Beatrice Jessie (Hyslop) R. BA, U. Tex., 1963, JD, 1965. Bar: Tex. 1965, U.S. Tax Ct. 1969; CPA, Tex. Estate tax examiner IRS, Houston, 1965-66; tax acct. Holmes, Raquet, Harris & Shaw, San Antonio, 1966-67; sole practice law and acctg., Del Rio and San Antonio, 1968—; instr. St. Mary's U., San Antonio, 1973-75; assoc. prof. U. Tex., San Antonio, 1975—. Active San Antonio Symphony Assn., United

Fund, Am. Heart Assn. Mem. ABA, Tex. Bar Assn., San Antonio Bar Assn., Am. Assn. Atty.-CPAs, Am. Acctg. Assn., Am. Bus. Law Assn., San Antonio Estate Planners Council. Contbr. articles to legal jours. Probate, Corporate taxation, Personal income taxation. Home: 8000 Denore #68 San Antonio TX 78229 Office: 760 Texas Commerce Bank Bldg 7550 IH 10 West San Antonio TX 78229

ROSS, JOHN BOWEN, JR., lawyer; b. Raleigh, N.C., Mar. 19, 1938; s. John Bowen and Margaret Ameliz (Ellison) R.; m. Wanda Allene West, Sept. 21, 1960; children: Polly Ellison, John Bowen III, Ameliz West. BME, Duke U., 1960, LLB, 1963. Bar: N.C. 1964, U.S. Patent Office 1964, U.S. Ct. Customs and Patent Appeals 1973. Patent trainee Chemstrand Co., Decatur, Ala., 1963-65; law assoc. B.B. Olive, Durham, N.C., 1965-67; patent atty. Monsato Co., Research Triangle Park, N.C., 1967-74; patent and trademark counsel Grand Met USA, Inc. (formerly Liggett Group Inc., Montvale, N.J., 1974—. Patentee in field. Named Hon. Col. Commonwealth of Ky., 1985—. Mem. Licensing Exec. Soc., Am. Patent Law Assn., U.S. Trademark Assn. Republican. Episcopalian. Club: Hope Valley Country (Durham, N.C.). Avocation: golf, sailing, photography. Patent, Private international, Technology transfer. Home: 415 Tar Landing Villas Rt 4 Morehead City NC 28557 Office: PO Box 295 Morehead City NC 28557

ROSS, MATTHEW, lawyer; b. N.Y.C., Dec. 28, 1953; s. Harvey and Cecile (Shelsky) R.; m. Susan Ruth Goldfarb, Apr. 20, 1986. BS in Econs., U. Pa., 1975; JD, U. Va., 1978. Bar: N.Y. 1979, U.S. Dist. Ct. (so. dist.) N.Y. 1979. Assoc. Cravath, Swaine & Moore, N.Y.C., 1978-84; prin., assoc. gen. counsel Peat Marwick Main & Co., N.Y.C., 1984—. Mem. ABA (corp. law sect.), N.Y. State Bar Assn. (corp. banking and bus. law sect.), Assn. of Bar of City of N.Y., Beta Gamma Sigma. Avocations: basketball, tennis, skiing, travel. General corporate, Securities, Accountants' Liability. Home: 17 Carthage Ln Scarsdale NY 10583-7507 Office: Peat Marwick Main & Co 345 Park Ave New York NY 10154

ROSS, MATTHEW H., lawyer; b. N.Y.C., Aug. 17, 1913; s. Julius and Lena Ross; m. Mildred Berger; children: Jane, Allen. BS in Econs., St. John's U., 1934; LLB, U. Va., 1937; LHD (hon.), Hebrew Union Coll., 1977, DHO (hon.), 1979. Bar: N.Y. 1937, U.S. Dist. Ct. (so. dist.) N.Y. 1937, U.S. Tax Ct. 1937. Atty. various firms; ptnr. Warshaw, Burstein, Cohen, Schlesinger et al, N.Y.C., of counsel. Pres. Cen. Synagogue, N.Y.C., 1959-64; chmn. bd. dirs. Union Am. Congregation, N.Y.C., 1971-77; chmn. exec. com. World Union Progressive Judaism, 1984—. Mem. ABA, Assn. of Bar of City of N.Y. Club: Birchwood Country (pres. 1971-73). General practice. Home: 16 Sutton Pl New York NY 10022 Office: Warshaw Burstein Cohen Schlesinger et al 555 Fifth Ave New York NY 10017

ROSS, MICHAEL AARON, lawyer; b. Newark, Sept. 15, 1941; s. Alexander Ash and Matilda (Blumenthal) R.; m. Leslie Gordon, June 26, 1976; children—Christopher Gordon, Alan Gordon. B.A., Franklin and Marshall Coll., 1963; J.D., Columbia U., 1966; M.S. in Econs., U. London, 1967. Bar: N.Y. 1968. Assoc., then ptnr. Shearman & Sterling, N.Y.C., 1967—; dir. MFY Legal Services Inc. Mem. ABA, New York County Lawyers Assn., Bar City N.Y. Club: University. Banking, General corporate, Energy financing. Office: 153 E 53d St New York NY 10022

ROSS, MICHAEL FREDERICK, lawyer; b. Coral Gables, Fla., Sept. 20, 1950; s. George Thomas and Frances (Brown) Skaro. BA, Yale U., 1973; JD, U. Conn., 1979; MLS, So. Conn. State U., 1981. Bar: Conn. 1979, U.S. Dist. Ct. Conn. 1979, Fla. 1979, U.S. Ct. Claims 1980, U.S. Tax Ct. 1980, U.S. Ct. Customs and Patent Appeals 1980, U.S. Ct. Mil. Appeals 1980, U.S. Ct. Appeals (1st, 2d and D.C. cirs.) 1980, U.S. Ct. Appeals (5th, 9th and 11th cirs.) 1981, U.S. Ct. Appeals (Fed. cir.) 1982, U.S. Supreme Ct. 1982, N.J. 1983, U.S. Dist. Ct. N.J. 1983, U.S. Ct. Appeals (3d, 4th, 6th, 7th, 8th and 10th cirs.) 1983, Mass. 1984, U.S. Dist. Ct. Vt. 1984, V.I. 1985, U.S. Dist. Ct. V.I. 1985, Temp. Emergency Ct. Appeals 1985. Sole practice New Haven, Conn., 1979-82, 85—; chief of adjudications Conn. Motor Vehicle Dept., Wethersfield, 1980-82; adminstrv. law judge State of Conn. Motor Vehicle Dept., Wethersfield, 1985—; asst. atty. gen. State of Conn., Hartford, 1982-84, Dept. of Law, St. Croix, V.I., 1984-85. Chmn. selective service system Conn. Local Bd. 11, 1982—. Mem. ABA, Conn. Bar Assn., Mass. Bar Assn., Boston Bar Assn., Mensa. Democrat. Jewish. Club: Fence, Morys Assn. (New Haven). Family and matrimonial, Personal injury, Probate. Home: 6 Dogwood Hill Mount Carmel CT 06518-2706 Office: 91 Wall St Madison CT 06443

ROSS, MURRAY LOUIS, lawyer, corporate professional; b. Rochester, N.Y., Apr. 26, 1947; s. Charles Allen and Florence L. (Falk) R.; m. Linda Marie Wabschall, Dec. 26, 1970. AB in History, Lycoming Coll., 1969; JD, U. Toledo, 1972. Bar: Pa. 1976. Asst. to exec. v.p. Falk Machinery Inc., Rochester, 1972-74; corp. sec. Phila. Stock Exchange Inc., 1975—; corp. sec. Fin. Automation Corp. Phila. Inc., 1982—, Phila. Bd. Trade Inc., 1984—. Mem. ABA, Phila. Bar Assn., Securities Assn. Phila., Fin. Analysts Phila. Avocations: collecting wines, golf, ice hockey, skating. Securities, Computer. Home: 1126 Woodstock Ln West Chester PA 19382 Office: Phila Stock Exchange Inc 1900 Market St Philadelphia PA 19103

ROSS, OTHO B., III, lawyer; b. Charlotte, N.C., July 23, 1951; s. Otho B. and Dorothy (Lowe) R. B.S.E. magna cum laude with distinction, Duke U., 1974; J.D., U. N.C., 1977. Bar: N.Y. 1978, U.S. dist. ct. (so. and ea. dists.) N.Y. 1978. Assoc. Gaston Snow Beekman & Bogue, N.Y.C., 1978-83; sr. atty. Sony Corp. Am., Park Ridge, N.J., 1983-87; assoc. Stiefel, Gross, Kurland & Pavane, P.C., N.Y.C., 1987—. Recipient Bd. Editors award, 1977. Mem. Assn. Bar City N.Y., ABA, Eta Kappa Nu. Club: N.Y. Athletic. Contbr. articles to N.C. Law Rev., Jour. Patent Office Soc.; research editor N.C. Law Rev., 1976-77. Contracts commercial, Federal civil litigation, Trademark and copyright. Address: 30 Waterside Plaza #30-G New York NY 10010

ROSS, ROBERT DWAIN, lawyer; b. Hope, Ark., Dec. 3, 1932; s. George Raymond and Alma Lillian (Putman) R.; m. Frances Roots Mitchell, June 15, 1963; children—Robert Mitchell, Virginia Frances, Mary Starr. Student So. State Coll., 1951-53; B.S.L., U. Ark., 1962, J.D., 1962. Bar: Ark. 1961, U.S. Dist. Ct. (ea. dist.) Ark. 1962, U.S. Supreme Ct. 1966. Law clk. Ark. Supreme Ct., 1961-62, 63; assoc. Pope, Shamburger, Buffalo & Ross, Little Rock, 1963-65, ptnr., 1965—; sec., exec. dir. Ark. Constl. Conv., 1980. Bd. dirs. Elizabeth Mitchell Children's Ctr., 1972-78, 83—, treas., 1974, pres., 1978, 84-85, v.p. and treas., 1983; bd. dirs. Quapaw Quarter Assn., 1977-80, pres., 1979. Served with U.S. Army, 1956-58. Fellow Ark. Bar Found. (bd. dirs. 1982-85); mem. ABA, Ark. Bar Assn. (sec.-treas. 1969-72, ho. of dels. 1973-76, 78-81, mem. exec. council 1973, 75-78, chmn. 1981-82), Pulaski County Bar Assn. (dir. 1978-79), Assn. Trial Lawyers Am. Democrat. Episcopalian. General practice, State civil litigation, Federal civil litigation. Office: 300 Spring Bldg Suite 400 Little Rock AR 72201

ROSS, ROBERT JOHN, lawyer; b. Chgo., May 12, 1956; s. Francis Joseph and Ann Susan (McGovern) R.; m. Debra Sue Nelson, June 23, 1979; children: Patrick, William. AD, Triton Coll., 1975; BA in Econs. with highest honor, U. Ill., Chgo., 1977; JD with honor, DePaul U., 1980. Bar: Ill. 1980, U.S. Dist. Ct. (no. dist.) Ill. 1980. Assoc. Schwartz & Freeman, Chgo., 1980-82, Law Offices of J.A. Macaluso, Chgo., 1982-84, Nisen, Elliott & Meier, Chgo., 1984-86; sole practice Chgo., 1986—; vol. atty. free legal clinic, Oak Park, 1982—. Active Oak Park Dems., 1980—. Mem. ABA, Christian Legal Soc., Ill. Bar Assn., Chgo. Bar Assn (various coms.), West Suburban Bar Assn., Phi Alpha Delta Law Fraternity, Phi Kappa Phi. Democrat. Roman Catholic. Avocations: books, walking, camping. Personal injury, Probate, Contracts commercial. Office: 1 N LaSalle St Suite 2717 Chicago IL 60602

ROSS, ROBERT T., lawyer; b. Washington, Mar. 30, 1957; s. Bradford and Dorothy (Hardy) R.; m. Laurie Hughes, June 25, 1983. BA, Hampden-Sydney Coll., 1979; JD, Mercer U., 1982. Bar: Ga. 1982, D.C. 1983, U.S. Ct. Appeals (D.C. cir.) 1983, U.S. Dist. Ct. (no. dist.) Ga. 1984, U.S. Ct. Appeals (11th cir.) 1984. Law clk. to presiding justice U.S. Dist. Ct. (no. dist.) Ga., Atlanta, 1982-84, asst. U.S. atty. U.S. Dept. Justice, 1984-86; assoc. Hicks, Maloof and Campbell, Atlanta, 1986—. Mem. ABA, Ga. Bar Assn. (mem. intrastate moot ct. com. 1985-86), Atlanta Bar Assn., D.C. Bar Assn., Fed. Bar Assn. (treas. Atlanta chpt. 1986-87). Club: Ansley Golf (Atlanta). Avocations: sailing, softball, tennis, swimming, motorboating. Federal civil litigation, State civil litigation, Contracts commercial. Office: Hicks Maloof and Campbell 101 Marietta Tower Suite 3401 Atlanta GA 30335

ROSS, SUSAN KOHN, lawyer; b. Plymouth, Eng., Nov. 10, 1945; came to U.S., 1949; d. Fritz and Blanka (Fleischmann) Kohn; m. James Wilson Ross, July 24, 1976. BA in History, UCLA, 1967; JD, Southwestern U., 1977. Bar: Calif. 1978, U.S. Dist. Ct. Calif. 1986; cert. custom house broker. Sole practice Huntington Beach & Manhattan Beach, Calif., 1978-80, San Francisco, 1980-81; assoc. Yanello & Flippen, Oakland, Calif., 1981-82; sole practice Beverly Hills, Calif., 1982; assoc. Grayson, Maxwell & Sugarman, Los Angeles, 1982-83; sole practice Los Angeles, 1983—; ptnr. Herrick & Ross, 1986—; judge pro tem panel Los Angeles Mcpl. Ct., 1985—, judge pro tem panel Santa Monica Bar; past instr. Transp. Training Inst., Los Angeles, Transp. Edn. Ctr., Oakland; mediator Van Nuys Superior Ct., Santa Monica Superior Ct.; mem. panel Los Angeles Juvenile Ct., 1986—, superior ct. com., 1984—. Mem. ABA (litigation and family law sects.), Calif. Bar Assn. (chmn. subcom. child custody and visitation family law sect. 1983-85, del. state conv. 1984—), Los Angeles County Bar Assn. (vice chmn. atty.-client relations com. 1984—), Silver Key. Construction, State civil litigation, Customs and international trade law. Office: 13101 Washington Blvd Suite 234 Los Angeles CA 90066

ROSS, THOMAS WARREN, judge; b. Greensboro, N.C., June 5, 1950; s. Charles Burdette and Mary Brownie (Franklin) R.; m. Susan Donaldson, June 17, 1972; children: Thomas Warren Jr., Mary Kathryn. BA in Polit. Sci., Davidson Coll., 1972; JD with honors, U. N.C., 1975; grad., Nat. Jud. Coll., 1985. Bar: N.C. 1975, U.S. Ct. Appeals (4th cir.) 1979, U.S. Supreme Ct. 1979. Asst. prof. pub. law Inst. Govt., U. N.C., Chapel Hill, 1975-76; ptnr. Smith, Patterson, Follin, Curtis, James & Harkavy, 1976-82; adminstrv. asst. to congressman Robin Britt N.C., 1983-84; judge N.C. Superior Ct, 1984—; pres. Cen. Carolina Legal Services, Inc., 1981-82; mem. com. on sentencing and corrections Nat. Conf. of State Trial Judges. Deacon First Presbyn. Ch., Greensboro; dem. precinct chmn., Guilford County, 1979-81; chmn. Guilford County Dems., 1981-83, Guilford County Substance Abuse Study Commn., Guilford County Correctional Coalition; active United Way Campaign, 1979-81, Greensboro Heart Fund Campaign, 1980-82, Gov.'s N.C. Statewide Comphrensive Recreation Plan Policy, 1982-83; mem. exec. counsel Gen. Green council Boy Scouts Am., steering com. Greensboro Coalition Substance Abuse, 1986—; bd. dirs. Women's Residential Ctr. Named Boss of Yr., Greensboro Legal Secs. Assn., 1981, Outstanding Young Man Am. in Greensboro, Jaycees, 1984. Mem. ABA (jud. adminstrn. sect.), N.C. Bar Assn., Greensboro Bar Assn. Home: 12 Wedgewood Ct Greensboro NC 27403 Office: Guilford County Courthouse PO Drawer T-5 Greensboro NC 27402

ROSS, WAYNE ANTHONY, lawyer; b. Milw., Feb. 25, 1943; s. Ray E. and Lillian (Steiner) R.; m. Barbara L. Ross, June 22, 1968; children: Gregory, Brian, Timothy, Amy. BA, Marquette U., 1965, JD, 1968. Bar: Wis. 1968, Alaska 1969. Asst. atty. gen. State Alaska, 1968-69; trustee, standing master Superior Ct. Alaska, 1969-73; assoc. Edward J. Reasor & Assocs., Anchorage, 1973-77; prin. Wayne Anthony Ross & Assocs., 1977-83; ptnr. Ross, Gingras & Frenz, Anchorage and Cordova, Alaska, 1983-84, Ross & Gingras, Anchorage and Cordova, 1985; ptnr. Ross, Gingras, Bailey and Miner, P.C., Anchorage and Cordova, 1986—; lt. col. Alaska State Guard, comdg. officer profl. and tech. detachment; pres. Tyone Mountain Syndicate, Inc.; instr. Anchorage Community Coll. Columnist Anchorage Times; outdoor editor Alaska Bar Rag. Parliamentarian, chmn. Dist. 8 Rep. Com.; alt. del. Rep. Nat. Conv., 1984; bd. dirs. Nat. Firearms Mus. Devel. Fund, Inc.; chmn. advisors commn. Alaska Land Use Council. Mem. ABA, Alaska Bar Assn. (Stanley award), Wis. Bar Assn., Anchorage Bar Assn., Spenard Bar Assn., Nat. Rifle Assn. (bd. dirs. 1980—), Alaska Gun Collectors Assn. (pres.), Ohio Gun Collectors Assn., Smith and Wesson Collectors Assn., Alaska Rifle Club (legis. office), Alaska Rifle and Pistol Assn. (v.p.), Alaska Peace Officers Assn. Roman Catholic. Family and matrimonial, Criminal, Personal injury. Home: PO Box 101522 Anchorage AK 99510 Office: 1007 W 3rd Ave Suite 204 Anchorage AK 99501

ROSS, WILLIAM JARBOE, lawyer; b. Oklahoma City, May 9, 1930; s. Walter John and Bertha (Jarboe) R.; m. Mary Lillian Ryan, May 19, 1962; children: Rebecca Anne, Robert Joseph, Molly Kathleen. B.B.A., U. Okla., 1952, LL.B., 1954. Bar: Okla. 1954. Since practiced in Oklahoma City; asst. municipal counselor Oklahoma City, 1955-60; mem. firm Rainey, Ross, Rice & Binns, 1960—, partner, 1965—; Dir. Petrounited Terminals, Inc., PetroUnited Holdings, Inc. Bd. dirs. St. Anthony's Hosp. Found. Mem. Okla. Bar Assn., Okla. Heritage Assn. (chmn. edn. com.), The Newcomen Soc., Phi Alpha Delta, Beta Theta Pi. Clubs: Oklahoma City Golf and Country, Econ. (Okla.). Lodges: Rotary, K.C. General practice, Estate planning, Probate. Home: 6923 Avondale Ct Oklahoma City OK 73116 Office: Rainey Ross Rice & Binns 735 First National Ctr W Oklahoma City OK 73102

ROSS, YAN MICHAEL, lawyer; b. N.Y.C., Dec. 2, 1942; s. Herman J. and Pauline (Chodeck) R.; m. Deedee Corradini, Mar. 21, 1981; children—Matthew Kennett, Elizabeth Feiga. A.B., Princeton U., 1964; J.D., Yale U., 1967. Bar: D.C. 1969, U.S. Supreme Ct. 1973, U.S. Ct. Appeals (10th cir.) 1980, Utah 1982. Counsel to Republican mems. banking com. U.S. Ho. of Reps., Washington, 1970-75; alt. U.S. exec. dir. Inter-Am. Devel. Bank, Washington, 1975-77; ptnr. Metzger, Shadyac & Schwarz, Washington, 1977-82; ptnr. Parsons, Behle & Latimer, Salt Lake City/Washington, 1982—; adj. prof. grad. sch. bus. U. Utah, 1986—. Trustee, Utah Heritage Found., 1982—, Utah Air Travel Commn., 1983—, chmn., 1986—. trustee Internat. Vis. Utah Council, 1986—, chmn., 1986—; chmn. nat. adv. council Ballet West, 1984—. Served to 1st lt. USAF, 1968-70. Mem. ABA, Fed. Bar Assn., Inter-Am. Bar Assn., Salt Lake Area C. of C. (chmn. fed. issues com. 1983—). Episcopalian. Clubs: Ft. Douglas (Salt Lake City), Capitol Hill (Washington). Banking, Mergers and acquisitions, Contracts commercial. Office: Parsons Behle & Latimer 185 S State St Salt Lake City UT 84111

ROSSEN, JORDAN, lawyer; b. Detroit, June 13, 1934; s. Nathan Paul and Rebecca (Rizy) R.; m. Susan Friebert, Mar. 24, 1963 (div. June 1972); 1 child, Rebecca; m. M. Elizabeth Bunn, Jan. 3, 1981; children—N. Paul, Jordan David. B.A., U. Mich., 1956; J.D., Harvard U., 1959. Assoc. Sullivan, Elmer, Eames Moody, Detroit, 1960-62; assoc. Sugar & Schwartz, Detroit, 1962-64; asst. gen. counsel UAW, Detroit, 1964-74, assoc. gen. counsel, 1974-83, gen. counsel, 1983—; vice pres. N.P. Rossen Agy., Inc., Detroit, 1960-83; gen. counsel Mich. Health & Social Security Research Inst., Inc., Detroit, 1965-83; dir. UAW Job Devel. & Tng. Corp., Detroit, 1984—. Editor: Mich. Bar Labor Section Publication, 1961-64. Contbr. articles to profl. jours. Pres. Young Democrats, Mich., 1963-65; chmn. Americans for Democratic Action, Mich., 1966-68; chmn. Voter Registration Dem. Party, Mich., 1967. Recipient Human Rights award City of Detroit, 1978. Mem. ABA, Mich. Bar Assn., Nat. Bar Assn., Wolverine Bar Assn., Women Lawyers Assn., Lawyers Guild. Jewish. Labor, Administrative and regulatory, Civil rights. Office: Legal Dept UAW 8000 E Jefferson St Detroit MI 48214

ROSSI, ALAN DAVID, lawyer; b. Danbury, Conn., Apr. 23, 1956; s. Sydney Anthony and Theresa Virginia (DelMonte) R.; m. Tamara Luce, June 21, 1986. BA in History, U. Conn., 1978; JD, Gonzaga U., 1981. Bar: Wash. 1982, U.S. Dist. Ct. (ea. dist.) Wash. 1982. Sole practice Spokane, Wash., 1982-83; asst. pub. defender Spokane County Pub. Defender, Spokane, 1983—. Vol. Spokane Crisis Services, 1981-86. Mem. Wash. State Bar Assn., Nat. Assn. Criminal Def. Lawyers, Wash. Assn. Criminal Def. Lawyers. Roman Catholic. Criminal.

ROSSI, FAUST F., lawyer, educator; b. 1932. B.A., U. Toronto, 1953; J.D., Cornell U., 1960. Bar: N.Y. 1960. Tax trial atty., Dept. Justice, Washington, 1960-61; sole practice, Rochester, N.Y., 1961-66; assoc. prof. Cornell U., Ithaca, N.Y., 1966-69; prof. 1970—, Samuel S. Leibowitz prof. trial techniques, 1982—; cons. report of fed. class actions Am. Coll. of Trial Lawyers, 1971-72; cons. com. on proposed fed. rules of evidence N.Y. Trial Lawyers Assn., 1970; cons., instr. annual seminar N.Y. State Trial Judges, 1970-78; cons., instr. Nat. Inst. for Trial Advocacy, 1974-75, 80-84; cons. N.Y. Law Revision Commn. Project for N.Y. Code of Evidence, 1978-80. Served to lt. j.g. USN. Mem. Order of Coif. Author: Study of the Proposed Federal Rules of Evidence, 1979; Report on Rule 23 Class Actions, 1972; The Federal Rules of Evidence, 1970. Legal education. Office: Cornell U Law Sch Ithaca NY 14853

ROSSI, MARY ANN, lawyer; b. Pittston, Pa., June 7, 1951; d. Felix John and Regina Joan (Shannon) R.; m. Jeffrey Patterson Lewis, Aug. 19, 1978. BA in English, Marywood Coll., 1973; MA in French, Ind. State U., 1974; JD, Dickinson Sch. Law, 1979. Bar: Pa. 1979, U.S. Dist. Ct. (ea. dist.) Pa. 1981, U.S. Ct. Appeals (3d cir.) 1982. Law clk. to presiding justice Pa. Commonwealth Ct., Harrisburg, 1979-81; assoc. MacElree, Harvey et al, West Chester, Pa., 1981-86, Riley Law Assocs. Ltd., Paoli, Pa., 1986—; speaker career day Kennett High Sch., Kennett Sq., Pa., 1983, Am. Cancer Soc., West Chester, 1983-84, Marywood Coll., Scranton, Pa., 1984. Mem. Pa. Bar Assn., Chester County Bar Assn. (bd. dirs. 1986—), Assn. Trial Lawyers Am., Pa. Trial Lawyers Assn. Republican. Roman Catholic. Avocations: needlework, furniture refinishing, gardening. State civil litigation, Personal injury, Real property. Home: 918 Paoli Pike West Chester PA 19380

ROSSI, MICHAEL DUDLEY, lawyer; b. Warren, Ohio, Apr. 12, 1950; s. Eugene E. and Virginia L. (Porter) R.; m. Roseanne Bernard, Aug. 20, 1971; children: Amy, John, Benjamin, Abby. BA, U. Notre Dame, 1972; JD, Cath. U. Am., 1975. Bar: Ohio 1975, U.S. Dist. Ct. (no. dist.) Ohio 1976, U.S. Supreme Ct. 1982, Pa. 1984. Assoc. Guarnieri & Secrest, Warren, 1975-80, ptnr., 1980—. Bd. dirs. Birthright of Trumbull County, Inc., Warren, (chmn. 1980—), Residential Horizons, Inc., Girard, Ohio, 1977-81; Warren YMCA (mem. com. 1976-85). Mem. ABA, Ohio Bar Assn., Trumbull County Bar Assn., ACLU. Roman Catholic. Avocations: reading, running. State civil litigation, Federal civil litigation, Civil rights. Office: Guarnieri & Secrest 151 E Market St PO Box 4270 Warren OH 44482

ROSSI, RAYMOND ERNEST, lawyer; b. Chicago Heights, Ill., Aug. 1, 1953; s. Arnold P. and Elsie S. (Nardoni) R.; m. Terri L. Wilson, June 25, 1972; children: Amanda M., Brandon M., Carmen A., Drake A. BA, N. Cen. Coll., Naperville, Ill., 1975; MBA, DePaul U., 1977; JD, John Marshall Law Sch., 1980. Bar: Ill. 1980, U.S. Dist. Ct. (no. dist.) Ill. 1980, U.S. Ct. Appeals (7th cir.) 1984. Atty. S. Suburban Law Clinic, Richton Park, Ill., 1980, Scarborough & Co., Chgo., 1980-82, Bishop & Crawford, Ltd., Oak Brook, Ill., 1982—; instr. Joliet (Ill.) Jr. Coll., 1981-82. Assoc. editor Young Lawyer's Jour., 1982. Mem. Frankfort Twp. Planning Commn., Frankfort, Ill., 1987—; area chmn. Rich Twp. Reps., Inc., Park Forest, Ill., 1982-86; v.p., treas. Prestwick Home Owner's Assn., Frankfort, 1985-86, pres., 1987—. Named one of Outstanding Young Men Am., Jaycees, 1982; recipient award Frankfort Mokena Star Pubs., 1987. Mem. ABA (gen. practice sect. 1980—, comml. law sect. 1980—), Ill. Bar Assn. (ins. sect. 1980—, civil practice sect. 1980—), Chgo. Bar Assn. (comml. law sect. 1980—, trial techniques sect. 1980—), Will County Bar Assn., Cath. Lawyers Guild, Oak Brook Execs. Roman Catholic. Club: Prestwick Country (Frankfort). Lodges: KC, Lions. Avocation: tennis. Home: 938 Shetland Dr Frankfort IL 60423 Office: Bishop & Crawford Ltd 1315 W 22d St Suite 300 Oak Brook IL 60521

ROSSI, RONALD GREGORY, lawyer; b. San Benito, Tex., Oct. 3, 1952; s. Louis P. Rossi and Violet (Nelson) Kennedy; m. Margaret L. Toal, Aug. 21, 1976; children: Damon, Megan, Erin. BA with honors, U. Mich., 1974, JD, 1977. Bar: Colo. 1980, U.S. Dist. Ct. Colo. 1980, U.S. Ct. Appeals (10th cir.) 1980. Assoc. Cogswell & Wehrle, Denver, 1979-82, Mayer, Brown & Platt, Denver, 1982-84; ptnr. Rossi & Stone P.C., Denver, 1984—. Chmn. legal panel, fund raising ACLU, Denver, 1980-84. Mem. ABA, Colo. Bar Assn., Denver Bar Assn. Avocations: woodworking, painting, squash, reading. Oil and gas leasing, Securities, Public international. Home: 4343 Montview Blvd Denver CO 80207 Office: Rossi & Stone PC 370 17th St Suite 4250 Denver CO 80202

ROSSI, WILLIAM MATTHEW, lawyer; b. Coldwater, Ohio, June 11, 1954; s. Hugh Dominic and Patricia Jean (Putts) R.; m. Constance Sue Streacker, July 21, 1973; children: Bryan Thomas, Lauren Michelle. BA cum laude, Miami U., Oxford, Ohio, 1977; JD magna cum laude, U. Dayton, 1981. Bar: Ohio 1981, U.S. Dist. Ct. (so. dist.) Ohio 1982, U.S. Supreme Ct. 1986. Assoc. Milliken & Fitton, Hamilton, Ohio, 1981-83; dep. law dir., chief city negotiator City of Middletown, Ohio, 1984—; bd. dirs. Columbia Inst. Bus., Middletown, 1977-78; lectr. Sawyer Coll., Dayton, 1982-83. Asst. coach Knothole Baseball, Middletown, 1981; bd. dirs. Butler County Mental Health Ctr., Hamilton, 1983—, Summer Youth Theatre, Middletown, 1985—; mem. bd. rev. Troop 20, Boy Scouts Am., 1986—. Recipient Am. Jurisprudence award Lawyers Coop. Pub. Co., 1979, 81, Internat. Youth Achievement award Internat. Biog. Ctr. and Am. Biog. Inst., 1982. Mem. ABA, Ohio Bar Assn., Ohio Pub. Employer Labor Relations Assn., Nat. Pub. Employer Labor Relations Assn., Ohio Mcpl. Attys. Assn., Phi Beta Kappa, Phi Delta Phi (bd. dirs., historian 1979-80). Republican. Roman Catholic. Avocations: golf, travel, writing. Labor, Local government, State civil litigation. Home: 2807 Central Ave Middletown OH 45044 Office: City of Middletown One City Centre Plaza Middletown OH 45042

ROSSINI, RAYMOND DOMINIC, lawyer; b. St. Paul, Apr. 16, 1948; s. Reno Dominic and Rosemary (Vanderah) R.; 1 child, Elizabeth. BA in Math., English, St. John's U., Collegeville, Minn., 1970; JD, U. Minn., 1973. Bar: Minn. 1973, U.S. Tax Ct. 1975, U.S. Ct. Appeals (8th cir.) 1975. Acct. Arthur Andersen & Co., Mpls., 1973-75; assoc. Thompson, Hessian, Fleicher, McKasy & Soderberg, Mpls., 1975-77; ptnr. Rossini & Assocs. P.A. and predecessor firms, Mpls., 1977—. Mem. various coms. Citizen's League, Mpls. and St. Paul, 1974-79. Mem. ABA, Minn. Bar Assn., Hennepin County Bar Assn. Lodge: Kiwanis (bd. dirs. Mpls. club). Avocations: volleyball, handball, racquetball, tennis, chess. General corporate, Estate planning, Real property. Home: 4225 Lynn Ave S Edina MN 55416 Office: 5353 Gamble Dr Suite 150 Minneapolis MN 55416

ROSSITER, ROBERT FRANCIS, JR., lawyer; b. Camp LeJeune, N.C., July 16, 1956; s. Robert Francis Sr. and Mary Jane (Paden) R.; m. Mary Beth Frankman, June 9, 1984; 1 child, Robert III. BS in Mgmt., Purdue U., 1978; JD cum laude, Creighton U., 1981. Bar: Nebr., U.S. Dist. Ct. Nebr., U.S. Ct. Appeals (8th cir.). Law clk. to presiding judge U.S. Dist. Ct. Nebr., Omaha, 1981-83; assoc. Fraser, Stryker, Veach, Vaughn, Meusey, Olsen, Boyer & Bloch, Omaha, Nebr., 1983—; instr. Creighton U. Law Sch., Omaha, 1982—. Mem. ABA, Nebr. Bar Assn. (exec. com. young lawyers sect.), Omaha Bar Assn. (chmn. lawyers in the Schs. 1986-87), Nebr. Assn. Trial Attys., Alpha Sigma Nu, Pi Kappa Alpha. Roman Catholic. State civil litigation, Labor. Office: Fraser Stryker Veach Vaughn et al 500 Electric Bldg Omaha NE 68101

ROSSMANN, ANTONIO, lawyer, educator; b. San Francisco, Apr. 25, 1941; s. Herbert Edward and Yolanda (Sonsini) R. Grad. Harvard U., 1963; J.D., 1971. Bar: Calif. 1972, D.C. 1979, U.S. Supreme Ct. 1979, N.Y. 1980. Law clk., Calif. Supreme Ct., 1971-72; assoc. Tuttle & Taylor, Los Angeles, 1972-75; pub. advisor Calif. Energy Commn., 1975-76; sole practice, San Francisco, 1976-82, 85—; exec. dir. Nat. Center for Preservation Law, 1979-80; mem. McCutchen, Doyle, Brown & Enersen, San Francisco, 1982-85; adj. prof. law Hastings Coll. Law, 1981-84; vis. prof. UCLA Sch. Law, 1985—. Bd. dirs. Planning and Conservation League, 1984—, Calif. Water Protection Council, 1982-83, San Francisco Marathon, 1982—, Western State Endurance Run, 1986—; pres., bd. dirs. Toward Utility Rate Normalization, 1976-79. Served to lt. comdr. USN, 1963-68. Fulbright lectr., U. Tokyo, 1987. Mem. Calif. State Bar (chmn. com. on environment 1978-82), Assn. Bar City of N.Y. Clubs: Harvard of San Francisco and N.Y.C. Contbr. articles to legal jours.; editor Harvard U. Law Rev., 1969-71. Environment, Natural Resources. Office: 380 Hayes St San Francisco CA 94102

ROSSO, CHRISTINE HEHMEYER, lawyer; b. N.Y.C., Apr. 7, 1947; d. Alexander and Florence I. (Millar) Hehmeyer; m. David John Rosso, Mar. 18, 1978; children—Christine, Mark. B.A., Pitzer Coll., 1969; J.D., Northwestern U., 1972. Bar: Ill. 1972. Assoc., Isham, Lincoln & Beale, Chgo., 1972-78; participating ptnr. Chapman and Cutler, Chgo., 1978-83;

chief charitable trusts and solicitations div. Office of Ill. Atty. Gen., Chgo., 1983—. Sec. bd. dirs. Chgo. Hearing Soc., 1984—; mem. women's bd. Goodman Theatre, Chgo. Mem. ABA, Womens Bar Assn. Ill., Chgo. Bar Assn. (vice chmn. pub. utility law com. 1979, chmn. 1980), Nat. Assn. State Charity Ofcls. (v.p. 1985—, pres. 1986—). Episcopalian. Club: Economic (Chgo.). Administrative and regulatory, Probate. Home: 520 W Fullerton Pkwy Chicago IL 60614 Office: Atty Gen Ill 100 W Randolph St 12th floor Chicago IL 60601

ROSSO, DAVID JOHN, lawyer; b. Yonkers, N.Y., Mar. 30, 1938; s. Virginio and Florence (Pedrazzo) R.; m. Christine Hehmeyer, Mar. 18, 1978; children—Marilyn-Jayne G., David J., Matthew C., Christine H., Mark H. B.M.E., U. Detroit, 1961; J.D., U. Mich., 1963; cert. comparative law U. Rome, 1964. Bar: Ill. 1964, U.S. Dist. Ct. (no. dist.) Ill. 1965, U.S. Ct. Appeals (7th cir.) 1981. Assoc. Isham, Lincoln & Beale, Chgo., 1964-70, ptnr., 1971—; U.S. del. Atlantic Conf., 1974, 78; mem. Chgo. Crime Commn., 1975—; assoc. Adlai Stevenson Inst., 1969-74. Ford Found. fellow, 1963-64; Fulbright fellow, 1963-64. Mem. Council on Fgn. Relations, Chgo. Council Fgn. Relations (bd. dirs. 1969—, treas., 1971-82, exec. com., 1971-85, chmn. fin. com. 1970-82), Chgo. Com., Com. on Fgn. Affairs, Com. on Fgn. and Domestic Affairs (co-founder, co-chmn. exec. com. 1969-75), ABA, Chgo. Bar Assn., UN Assn. (bd. dirs. Chgo. 1970-73), Order Coif. Clubs: Mid-Day, Econ. (Chgo.), Legal. Administrative and regulatory, Banking, Private international. Office: Isham Lincoln et al 3 1st Nat Plaza Chicago IL 60602

ROSTER, MICHAEL, lawyer; b. Chgo., May 7, 1945. AB, Stanford U., 1967, JD, 1973. Bar: Calif. 1973, D.C. 1980. Reporter UPI, Chgo., 1965; writer Time-Life, San Francisco, 1966-67; ptnr. McKenna, Conner & Cuneo, Los Angeles and Washington, 1973-87, Morrison & Foerster, Los Angeles, 1987—. Contbr. articles to profl. jours. Bd. dirs. Stanford Alumni Assn., 1987—; Chmn. Cityscape Panel of Strategic Planning Commn., Pasadena, Calif., 1985—; trustee Pasadena Heritage, 1986—. Served to lt. (j.g.) USN, 1969-71. Mem. ABA (chmn. com. on savings insts. 1985—, fin. services com. 1981—), Calif. Bar Assn. (chmn. banking com. 1978-79), Am. Coll. Mortgage Attys. Ckubs: Univ. (Washington), Los Angeles Athletic. Banking. Office: Morrison & Foerster 333 S Hope St Los Angeles CA 90071

ROSZKOWSKI, JOSEPH JOHN, lawyer; b. Pawtucket, R.I., Aug. 11, 1938; s. Joseph J. and Anna T. Roszkowski; m. Geraldine J. Szpila, July 2, 1966. BA, Alliance Coll., 1960; JD, Marquette U., 1964. Bar: Wis. 1964, U.S. Dist. Ct. (ea. dist.) Wis. 1964, R.I. 1965. Ptnr. Zimmerman, Roszkowski & Brenner, Woonsocket, R.I., 1965—; corporator Fogarty Hosp., North Smithfield, R.I., 1976—. Mem. Nat. Ski Patrol, R.I., 1974—; legal counsel R.I. Tuna Tournament, 1975—; bd. dirs. R.I. Legal Services, Providence, 1974—, Legal Aid Soc., Providence, 1985—. Mem. R.I. Bar Assn. (pres. 1985-86), Am. Law Inst., AM. Judicature Sic., Fed. Tax Inst. New England (adv. com. 1985-86), R.I. Med. Examiners, U.S. Jaycees (nat. dir. 1968). Lodge: Rotary (v.p. Cumberland, R.I. 1986). Avocations: skiing, sailing, gardening, tennis. Health, Real property, Probate. Home: 1 Cook Rd Cumberland RI 02864 Office: Zimmerman Roszkowski & Brenner 1625 Diamond Hill Rd Woonsocket RI 02895

ROSZKOWSKI, STANLEY JULIAN, judge; b. Booneville, N.Y., Jan. 27, 1923; s. Joseph and Anna (Christkowski) R.; m. Catherine Mary Claeys, June 19, 1948; children: Mark, Gregory, Dan, John. B.S., U. Ill., 1949, LL.D., 1954. Bar: Ill. 1954. Sales mgr. Warren Petroleum Co., Rockford, Ill., 1954; mem. firm Roszkowski, Paddock, McGreevy & Johnson, Rockford, from 1955; now dist. judge U.S. Dist. Ct., Rockford; pres. First State Bank, Rockford, 1963-75; chmn. bd. First State Bank, 1977—. Chmn. Fire and Police Commn., Rockford, 1967-74, commr., 1974—; chmn. Paul Simon Com., 1972; active Adlai Stevenson III campaign, 1968-71, Winnebago County Citizens for John F. Kennedy, 1962, Winnebago County Democratic Central Com., 1962-64; bd. dirs. Sch. of Hope, 1960—; mem. Ill. Capital Devel. Bd., 1974—. Served with USAAF, 1943-45. Decorated Air medal with 2 oak leaf clusters.; recipient Pulaski Nat. Heritage award Polish Am. Congress, Chgo., 1982. Mem. Am., Ill., Fla., Winnebago County bar assns., Am. Coll. Trial Lawyers, Am. Judicature Soc., Am., Ill. trial lawyers assns., Am. Arbitration Assn. (arbitrator). Club: Forest Hills Country (Rockford). Office: US Dist Ct 211 S Court St Rockford IL 61101

ROTGIN, PHILIP NORMAN, lawyer; b. Long Beach, N.Y., Mar. 29, 1942; s. Louis and Rheba (Lipman) R.; m. Rochelle Marilyn Schneeweis, July 3, 1965; children—Karen Ann, Michael Alan. B.S. in Econs., Wharton Sch. Fin. and Commerce, U. Pa., 1963; LL.B., Columbia U., 1966. Bar: N.Y. 1967, U.S. Tax Ct. 1973, U.S. Dist. Ct. (so. dist.) N.Y. 1979, U.S. Dist. Ct. (ea. dist.) N.Y. 1979. Atty. Home Life Ins. Co., N.Y.C., 1966-70; sole practice, N.Y.C., 1970—; mem. faculty Paralegal Inst., L.I.U., N.Y.C., 1977. Contbr. numerous articles to legal, dental, bus. publs. Mem. Estate Planning Council N.Y.C., Profl. Planners Forum (pres. 1980), N.Y. State Bar Assn., Assn. Bar City N.Y. Pension, profit-sharing, and employee benefits, Estate planning, General corporate. Home: 2277 Halyard Dr Merrick NY 11566 Office: Philip N Rotgin PC 622 3d Ave New York NY 10017

ROTH, ALEXANDER DUNBAR, lawyer; b. New Orleans. BA, Stanford U., 1968; JD, U. Mich., 1975. Bar: Ill. 1975, Va. 1979. Atty. Swift & Co., Chgo., 1975-78; dir. Washington office Am. Fedn. Info. Processing Socs., Arlington, Va., 1978-82; sole practice Fairfax, Va., 1982—; bd. dirs. Novasoft, Inc., Fairfax, Zimcre Ltd., Annandale, Va. Author: (with others) Toward a Law of Global Communication Networks, 1986. Mem. ABA (chmn. com. law electronic mail and teleconferencing 1984—), Assn. for Computing Machinery (program chmn. annual conf. 1984). Computer, General corporate. Office: 8230 Boone Blvd Suite 400 Vienna VA 22180

ROTH, HADDEN WING, lawyer; b. Oakland, Calif., Feb. 10, 1930; s. Mark and Jane (Haley) R.; married 1959 (div. 1972); 1 child, Elizabeth Wing. AA, Coll. Marin, 1949; BA, U. Calif., Berkeley, 1951; JD, U. Calif., San Francisco, 1957. Bar: Calif. 1958, U.S. Dist. Ct. (no. dist.) Calif. 1958, U.S. Ct. Appeals (9th cir.) 1958, U.S. Supreme Ct. 1966. Ptnr. Roth & Thorner, San Rafael, Calif., 1957-63; sole practice San Rafael, 1963—; dep. atty. City of San Rafael, 1958-60, City of Sausalito and Mill Valley, Calif., 1964-66; dep. dist. atty. County of Marin, 1960-63; judge Marin County Mcpl. Ct., 1966-70; cons. Marin Muni Water Dist., Corte Madera, Calif.; atty. Town of Ross and San Anselmo, Calif.; lectr. law Golden Gate Coll. Law, San Francisco, 1971-73. Chmn. Marin Coll. Bond Campaign, 1971, Prison Task Force, 1973; bd. dirs. Marin Gen. Hosp., 1964-66. Served to corp. U.S. Army, 1952-54. Named Outstanding Citizen of Yr., Coll. Marin, 1972. Mem. Marin County Bar Assn. Avocations: Running, racquetball, reading. Local government, State civil litigation, Real property. Home: 343 Fairhills Dr San Rafael CA 94901 Office: Roth & Thorner 1050 Northgate Dr San Rafael CA 94903

ROTH, JANE RICHARDS, judge; b. Phila., June 16, 1935; d. Robert Henry Jr. and Harriett (Kellond) Richards; m. William V. Roth Jr., Oct. 9, 1965; children: William V. III, Katherine K. BA, Smith Coll., 1956; LLB, Harvard U., 1965. Adminstrv. asst. various fgn. service posts U.S. State Dept., 1956-62; assoc. Richards, Layton & Finger, Wilmington, Del., 1965-73, ptnr., 1973-85; judge U.S. Dist. Ct. Del., Wilmington, 1985—. Trustee Hist. Soc. Del., Wilmington; mem. Chesapeake Bay Girl Scouts Council, Wilmington; hon. chmn. Del. chpt. Arthritis Found., Wilmington; bd. dirs. U. Del Library Assocs., Newark, Del. Recipient Nat. Vol. Service citiation Athritis Found., 1982. Mem. Fed. Judges Assn., Del. State Bar Assn. Republican. Episcopalian. Home: 2206 Old Kennett Rd Wilmington DE 19807 Office: US Courthouse 844 King St Lock Box 12 Wilmington DE 19801 *

ROTH, JEFFREY STUART, lawyer, judge, educator; b. Lakewood, N.J., Feb. 16, 1955; s. Nathaniel Harold and Harriette (Schiff); m. Patti Ellen Sacks, Aug. 20, 1983. AB, Rutgers U., 1977; JD, Del. Law Sch., 1980. Bar: N.J. 1980, U.S. Dist. Ct. N.J. 1980, U.S. Supreme Ct. 1985. Ptnr. Roth & Roth, P.A., Lakewood, 1980—; mcpl. ct. judge Jackson Twp., N.J., 1985-87, Eaglewood Twp., N.J., 1987—; adj. prof. Brookdale Coll., Lincroft, N.J., 1981-82, Ocean County Coll., Toms River, N.J., 1982—; legal asst. Office of Gov., Newark, Del., 1979-80. Mgr. Jackson Little League, N.J., 1981—, sec., 1982-83, advisor, 1983-84, treas., 1985—; legis. aide N.J. State Assemblyman John. T. Hendrickson, 10th Dist., 1983-85. Henry Rutgers scholar, 1977. Mem. ABA (cert. of meritt 1979), N.J. State Bar Assn. (mem. com. sports related law 1980—), Assn. Trial Lawyers Am., Ocean County Bar Assn. (membership com. chmn. 1984-85), Jackson C. of C. (pres. 1987—), Jackson Jaycees, Pi Sigma Alpha, Phi Delta Phi. Republican. Personal injury, General practice, Family and matrimonial. Office: Roth & Roth PA 241 1st St Lakewood NJ 08701

ROTH, KENNETH DAVID, lawyer; b. Bklyn., Feb. 12, 1948; s. Ben A. and Sally T. (Dancik) R.; m. Sharon G. Kipness, Aug. 15, 1970; children—Sari Alissa, Scott Aaron. Student Hunter Coll., 1965-67; B.A. in Polit. Sci., L.I. U., 1970; J.D. cum laude, Rutgers U., Camden, 1973. Bar; N.J. 1973, U.S. Dist. Ct. N.J. 1973, U.S. Ct. Appeals (3d cir.) 1978, U.S. Supreme Ct. 1977. Assoc. Davis & Reberkenny, P.A., Cherry Hill, N.J., 1973-79, ptnr., 1980—, v.p., also dir. Assoc. editor Rutgers-Camden Law Jour., 1972-73; mem. GEMS Landfill Litigation-Generators Steering Com. Mem. ABA, N.J. Bar Assn. (environ. law sect. del. to gen. council), Camden and Burlington County Bar Assn., Ednl. Negotiators Assn. N.J., N.J. Sch. Bds. Assn. Democrat. Jewish. Environment, Federal civil litigation, Real property. Office: Davis Reberkenny & Abramowitz PA 499 Cooper Landing Rd PO Box 5459 Cherry Hill NJ 08002

ROTH, MICHAEL DUNDON, lawyer; b. N.Y.C., Feb. 16, 1952; s. Harry Abraham and Lillian (Dundon) R.; m. Sharon Felder. BA, U. Mass., 1977; JD, Boston Coll., 1977. Bar: Tex. 1976, Mass. 1977, D.C. 1978, Calif. 1984. Assoc. Carr, Jordan, Coyne & Savits, Washington, 1979-82, Memel, Jacobs, Pierno & Gersch, Los Angeles, 1982-84, McDermott & Traynor, Pasadena, Calif., 1984-86; sole practice Los Angeles, Calif., 1986—. Contbr. articles on health care law to profl. jours. Bd. dirs. St. Francis Ctr., Washington, 1981-84, Jewish Social Service Agy., Washington, 1983-84. Mem. ABA (chmn. health care law com. 1983-85, vice chmn. medicine and law com. 1984—), Nat. Health Lawyers Assn. (bd. dirs.). Health, General corporate.

ROTH, MICHAEL JOSEPH, lawyer, anesthetist; b. Dayton, Ohio, Feb. 24, 1951; s. Jerome C. and Helen E. R.; m. Donna M. Brandstetter, Aug. 25, 1973; children—Christopher, Matthew, Kimberly. B.S. in Health Sci., Anesthesiology, Case Western Res. U., 1973, J.D., 1978. Bar: Ohio 1978, U.S. Patent and Trademark Office 1979, U.S. Ct. Customs and Patent Appeals 1979, U.S. Ct. Appeals (fed. cir.) 1982, Ill. 1985. Anesthesiologist's asst. Cleve. Metropolitan Gen. Hosp., 1976-78; patent atty. Procter & Gamble, Cin., 1978-84; patent and trademark atty. Abbott Labs., Abbott Park, Ill., 1984-86, sr. atty., 1986—; instr. Met. Anesthesia Instrumentation Course, Cleve., 1977-78. Author copyrighted med. software for evaluation of cardiac function, 1977. Parish council rep. St. Bartholomew Ch., Cin., 1982-84; Deanery rep. Archdiocese of Cin., 1982-84. Nat. Merit Scholar 1969-73. Mem. Cin. Bar Assn. (mem. com. on admissions), Cin. Patent Law Assn., Phi Delta Phi (magister 1976-77, vice magister 1977-78; Officer's cert. of merit 1977, 78). Democrat. Roman Catholic. Home: 9 Altoona Ct Vernon Hills IL 60611 Office: Abbott Labs D-377 AP6C Abbott Park IL 60064

ROTH, PHILLIP JOSEPH, judge; b. Portland, Oreg., Feb. 29, 1920; s. Harry William and Minnie Alice (Segel) R.; m. Ida Lorraine Thomas, Feb. 22, 1957 (div. 1977); children: Phillip J. Jr., David William; m. Allison Blake Ramsey, Feb. 14, 1978. BA cum laude, U. Portland, 1943; JD, Lewis & Clark U., 1948. Bar: Oreg. 1948, U.S. Dist. Ct. Oreg. 1949, U.S. Ct. Appeals (9th cir.) 1959, U.S. Supreme Ct. 1962. Dep. atty. City of Portland, 1948-50; dep. dist. atty. Multnomah County, Portland, 1950-52; sole practice Portland, 1952-64; cir. judge Multnomah County State of Oreg., Portland, 1964—, presiding cir. judge, 1970-71, 76-78; adj. prof. Lewis & Clark U. Law Sch., Portland, 1978-80, mem. standing com., 1972—; mem. exec. com. Nat. Conf. State Trial Judges, 1980-83, 86—. Author: Sentencing: A View From the Bench, 1973; co-author: The Judicial Immunity Doctrine Today: Between the Bench and a Hard Place, 1984. Rep. Oreg. Legislature, 1952-54; Rep. nominee for Congress, 1956; chmn. Oreg. Rep. Cen. Com., 1962-64; mem. adv. bd. Portland Salvation Army, 1976—; bd. overseers Lewis & Clark Coll., 1972—. Named Alumnus of Yr. U. Portland, 1963; named Alumnus of Yr. Lewis & Clark Law Sch., 1973. Mem. ABA (chmn. jud. immunity com. jud. adminstrn. div. 1982—, commn. on standards of jud. adminstrn. 1973-77), Oreg. Bar Assn. (bd. govs. 1961-64), Multnomah County Bar Assn. (pres. 1959), Am. Judicature Soc., U. Portland Alumni Assn. (pres. 1976), Lewis & Clark U. Alumni Assn. (pres. 1974-76, 80-81), Delta Theta Phi. Jewish. Clubs: City, University (Portland). Lodges: Masons, Shriners, B'nai B'rith. Judicial administration. Home: 3615 SW Dosch Ct Portland OR 97221

ROTH, ROBERT CHARLES, lawyer; b. Racine, Wis., Feb. 6, 1945; s. Robert Charles and Lucille (Holy) R.; m. Karen Trombley, May 18, 1974; children: David, Michael. BBA, St. Nobert Coll., 1967; JD, Marquette U., 1970; postgrad. course in law, George Washington U., 1972. Bar: Wis. 1970, U.S. Dist. Ct. (ea. dist.) Wis. 1970, U.S. CT. Mil. Appeals 1970, U.S. Army Ct. Mil Rev. 1971, Colo. 1974, U.S. Dist. Ct. Colo. 1974, U.S. Ct. Appeals (10th cir.) 1974, U.S. Ct. Appeals (5th cir.) 1979, U.S. Ct. Claims 1980. Atty. Shaw & Coghill, Denver, 1974-76; ptnr. Shaw, Spangler & Roth, Denver, 1976—; bd. dirs. Love Oil Co., Denver. Served as capt. U.S. Army, 1970-74. Mem. ABA, Colo. Bar Assn., Denver Bar Assn., Wis. Bar Assn., Fed. Bar Assn., Assn. Trial Lawyers Am., Colo. Trial Lawyers Assn. Clubs: University, Athletic (Denver). Avocations: basketball, golf. Federal civil litigation, State civil litigation, Oil and gas. Office: Shaw Spangler & Roth 1700 Broadway Suite 1400 Denver CO 80290

ROTH, ROBERT LLOYD, lawyer, educator; b. New Rochelle, N.Y., Dec. 27, 1954; s. Albert Noah and Fay (Levine) R.; m. Jacqueline Carolyn Cohen, May 29, 1983; 1 child, Lindsay Anne. BA in History and Latin, Lehigh U., 1976; JD, Syracuse U., 1982. Bar: Md. 1982. Counsel com. constl. and adminstrv. law Md. Ho. of Dels., Annapolis, 1982-83; revisor Commn. to Revise Annotated Code Md., Annapolis, 1983-85; staff atty., asst. atty. gen. State of Md., Balt., 1986—; revision cons., 1984—; adj. prof. U. Balt. Sch. Law, 1984—. Pres. Oakland Hills Condominium Assn., Arnold, Md., 1983-85; asst. campaign dir. Citizens for Esce, Fayetteville, N.Y., 1981; asst. press sec. Citizens for Senator Sarbanes, Balt., 1982. Mem. ABA (tax sect.), Md. State Bar Assn. (tax sect.). Democrat. E. Coast champion U.S. Masters Swimming, Md., 1984. Legislative, Health, State and local taxation. Home and Office: PO Box 6311 Annapolis MD 21401

ROTH, RONALD ANTHONY, lawyer; b. Danville, Ill., Jan. 5, 1953; s. Daniel Anthony and Josephine Louise (Spoden) R.; m. Christie Ellen Roberts, Mar. 15, 1980; 1 child, Shannon. BA, DePauw U., 1975; JD, Washington U., St. Louis, 1978. Bar: Ill. 1978, U.S. Dist. Ct. (so. and cen. dists.) Ill. 1978. Assoc. Young, Welsch, Young & Hall, Danville, 1978-79; assoc. Bernard & Davidson, Granite City, Ill., 1979-85, ptnr., 1986—. Mem. ABA, Ill. Bar Assn., Madison County Bar Assn. Democrat. Roman Catholic. Avocations: hist., music. Personal injury, Insurance, Federal civil litigation. Home: 19 Meadowlark Ct Granite City IL 62040 Office: Bernard & Davidson 3600 Nameoki Rd Granite City IL 62040

ROTHBLATT, EMMA ALDEN, lawyer; b. N.Y.C., Apr. 26, 1918; d. Milton and Mary Alden; 1 dau., Henrietta R. Santo. B.A. cum laude, Hunter Coll., 1938; M.A., Columbia U., 1939; J.D., Fordham U., 1948. Bar: Calif. 1949, N.Y. 1949, Fla. 1976, U.S. Supreme Ct. 1960. First dep. commr. N.Y.C. Dept. Commerce and Pub. Events, 1954-66; asst. to dir. policewomen N.Y.C. Police Dept.; formerly mgr. Darrow Investigative Service, N.Y.C.; organizer, supr. UN and Consular Corps coms. Recipient Medals of Honor, Austria, Brazil, Republic China, W.Ger., Italy, Philippines, French Legion Honor, Personal award Queen Elizabeth, Govt. Tokyo award, award Fedn. Hispanic Socs., 1957; designated godmother Puerto Rican Parades. Regional v.p. Pres. Eisenhower's Civic People to People Com. Mem. Fla. Assn. Women Lawyers, Internat. Fedn. Women Lawyers, Inter-Am. Bar Assn., Am. Acad. Profl. Law Enforcement. Democrat. General practice. Office: 36 Sevilla Ave Coral Gables FL 33134

ROTHENBERG, PETER JAY, lawyer; b. N.Y.C., Apr. 3, 1941; s. Max and Judith (Berkowitz) R.; m. Laraine H. Silver, Aug. 29, 1970; children: Daniel, Jason. AB, Harvard U., 1961, LLB, 1964. Bar: N.Y. 1965, U.S. Tax Ct. 1969. Dep. counsel judiciary sub. com. on jud. machinery U.S. Senate Com., Washington, 1965-66; assoc. Paul, Weiss, Rifkind, Wharton & Garrison, N.Y.C., 1969-73, ptnr., 1974—. Served to capt. U.S. Army, 1966-69. Mem. N.Y. State Bar Assn. (exec. com. tax sect. 1979-87), Assn. of Bar of City of N.Y. (tax com. 1977-79), Internat. Fiscal Assn. Democrat. Jewish. Corporate taxation, Personal income taxation. Home: 895 Park Ave New York NY 10021 Office: Paul Weiss Rifkind Wharton & Garrison 1285 Ave of the Americas New York NY 10019

ROTHENBERG, STEVEN ALAN, lawyer; b. Miami Beach, Fla., May 25, 1952; s. David and Shirley (Dooley) R.; m. Margaretta McFarland, Oct. 15, 1983. AA, U. Fla., 1972; BS, U. Pa., 1974; JD, U. Chgo., 1977. Bar: Ill. 1977, D.C. 1978, Fla. 1978, U.S. Dist. Ct. D.C. 1979, U.S. Ct. Appeals (D.C. cir.) 1979, U.S. Supreme Ct. 1982. Atty. CAB, Washington, 1977-84, Pension Benefit Guaranty Corp., Washington, 1984-86. Chmn. profl. programs com. Wharton Sch. Club of Washington, 1984-85, sec., 1985-86, v.p. 1986—. Mem. ABA. Avocations: tennis, bridge, photography. Pension, profit-sharing, and employee benefits, Administrative and regulatory, Federal civil litigation. Home: 3200 Jocelyn St NW Washington DC 20015 Office: Pension Benefit Guaranty Corp 2020 K St NW Washington DC 20006

ROTHERMEL, JOAN EBERT, lawyer; b. N.Y.C., Feb. 22, 1948; d. Edmund Francis and Lathelia Marie (Keesey) Ebert; m. Timothy Simes Rothermel, Aug. 11, 1974; children—Sara Ebert, David Edmund. B.A. cum laude, Goucher Coll., 1970; postgrad. Law Ctr. George Washington U., 1971-72; J.D. cum laude, Fordham U., 1976. Bar: N.Y. 1977, U.S. Dist. Ct. (so, ea. dists.) N.Y. 1977, D.C. 1980, U.S. Ct. Appeals D.C. 1981. Legis. asst. Congressman Bradford Morse, Washington, 1970-72; spl. asst. to Undersec. Gen. Polit. and Gen. Assembly Affairs, UN, N.Y.C., 1972-76; law clk. Surrey, Karasik, Morse & Seham, N.Y.C., 1976-77; assoc. Surrey, Karasik, Morse & Seham, N.Y.C., 1977-79; assoc. Seham, Klein & Zelman, N.Y.C., 1979-83, ptnr., 1983—. Recipient Thaddeus Stevens award Fordham U., 1976, West Pub. Co. award in constl. law, 1976. Mem. ABA, Assn. Bar City of N.Y., D.C. Bar Assn., Phi Beta Kappa. Episcopalian. Labor, Pension, profit-sharing, and employee benefits. Home: 245 E 40th St New York NY 10016 Office: Seham Klein & Zelman 485 Madison New York NY 10022

ROTHERMEL, JOHN FISHER, III, title insurance executive, lawyer; b. Birmingham, Ala., Mar. 27, 1949; s. John F. and Minnie (Monk) R.; m. Jaquie Newton; children—Joel, Jeremy, Jason, Christopher, Adrienne. A.A., Tyler Jr. Coll., 1969; B.A., So. Meth. U., 1971; J.D., 1975. Bar: Tex. 1974. Atty., Chgo. Title Ins. Co., Dallas, 1976-78; counsel Equitable Gen. Ins. Co., Fort Worth, 1978-79; atty. Hunt Properties, Inc., Dallas 1979-80; asst. regional counsel Lawyers Title Ins. Corp., Dallas, 1980-83; pres. Title Resources Guaranty Co., Plano, Tex., 1983-84; v.p., gen. counsel Title Resources Corp., Plano, 1983-87; adv. dir. Title Resources Guaranty Co., Plano, 1983-87; pres. Title Underwriters of Tex., Austin, 1981-83; mem. title ins. com. State Bar Tex. 1980—; lectr. in field. Bd. dirs. Dallas Children's Choir, 1983. Mem. Tex. Land Title Assn. (ex officio bd. dirs. 1981-83, chmn. judiciary com. 1984—, chmn. rates, rules and forms com. 1980—, case editor news), Dallas Bar Assn., Plano Bar Assn. Democrat. Roman Catholic. Real property, Insurance, Administrative and regulatory. Home: 4303 Camden Dallas TX 75206 Office: Hardin Rothermel & Hardin Dallas Title Co 886 Tex Commerce Bank Bldg Plaza of the Ams LB150 Dallas TX 75201

ROTHMAN, BERNARD, lawyer; b. N.Y.C., Aug. 11, 1932; s. Harry and Rebecca (Fritz) R.; m. Barbara Joan Schaeffer, Aug. 1953; children—Brian, Adam, Helene. B.A. cum laude, CCNY, 1953; LL.B., NYU, 1959. Bar: N.Y. 1959, U.S Dist. Ct. (ea. and so. dists.) N.Y. 1962, U.S. Ct. Apls. (2d cir.) 1965, U.S. Supreme Ct. 1966, U.S. Tax Ct. 1971. Assoc. Held, Telchin & Held, 1961-62; asst. U.S. atty. U.S. Dept. Justice, 1962-66; assoc. Edward Gettinger & Peter Gettinger, 1966-68; ptnr. Schwartz, Rothman & Abrams, P.C., 1968-78; ptnr. Finkelstein, Bruckman, Wohl, Most & Rothman, N.Y.C., 1978—; acting judge Village of Larchmont, 1981-87, dep. Village atty., 1974-81, former arbitrator Civil Ct. N.Y.C., family disputes panel Am. Arbitration Assn. Exec., guest lectr. domestic relations and family law Cardozo Law Sch. and Albert Einstein Coll. Med.; mem. exec. bd., past v.p. Westchester Putnam council Boy Scouts Am., past mem. nat. council, 1977-81, recipient Silver Beaver award, Wood Badge award; past pres. Congregation B'Nai Israel, 1961-63; pres. B'Nai B'rith, Larchmont chpt., 1981-83. Fellow Am. Acad. Matrimonial Lawyers (co-chmn. interdisciplinary com. on mental health and family law 1986—, bd. govs. N.Y. chpt. 1986—); mem. ABA (family law sect.), N.Y. State Bar Assn. (exec. com. family law sect. 1982, co-chmn. com. on mediation and arbitration 1982, com. on legis. 1978-86, com. on child custody 1985), Assn. of Bar of City of N.Y., N.Y. State Magistrates Assn., Westchester Magistrates Assn. Democrat. Clubs: N.Y. Road Runners, Limousine 6 Track. Family and matrimonial, State civil litigation. Office: Finkelstein Bruckman Wohl Most & Rothman 801 2d Ave New York NY 10017

ROTHMAN, DAVID BILL, lawyer; b. N.Y.C., Apr. 25, 1952; s. Julius and Lillian (Halpern) R.; m. Jeanne Marie Hickey, July 7, 1974; children: Jessica Suzanne, Gregory Kozak. BA, U. Fla., 1974, JD, 1977. Bar: Fla. 1977, U.S. Dist. Ct. (so. dist.) Fla. 1980, U.S. Ct. Appeals (5th cir.) 1980, U.S. Supreme Ct. 1981, U.S. Ct. Appeals (11th cir.) 1982, U.S. Dist. Ct. (ea. dist.) Ky. 1985, U.S. Dist. Ct. (mid. dist.) Fla. 1986. Asst. state atty. Dade County States Atty., Miami, Fla., 1977-80; ptnr. Thornton & Rothman, Miami, 1980—. Mem. ABA, Fla. Bar Assn., Dade County Bar Assn. (criminal ct. com. 1984—), Nat. Assn. Criminal Def. Lawyers, Fla. Criminal Def. Attys. Assn. Democrat. Jewish. Avocations: running, racquetball, weightlifting, reading. Criminal. Home: 9941 SW 129 St Miami FL 33176 Office: Thornton & Rothman PA SE Financial Ctr Suite 2860 200 S Biscayne Blvd Miami FL 33131

ROTHMAN, HENRY ISAAC, lawyer; b. Rochester, N.Y., Mar. 29, 1943; s. Maurice M. and Golde (Nusbaum) R.; m. Golda R. Shatz, July 13, 1966; children: Alan, Miriam, Cheryl, Suri. BA, Yeshiva U., 1964; JD, Cornell U., 1967. Bar: N.Y. 1967. Trial atty. SEC, N.Y.C., 1967-69; ptnr. Booth, Lipton & Lipton, N.Y.C., 1969-87, Parker, Chapin, Flattau & Klimpl, N.Y.C., 1987—. V.p. Manhattan Day Sch., N.Y.C., 1985—; bd. dirs. Camp Morasha, Lake Como, Pa., 1982—, Yeshiva U. High Schs., N.Y.C., 1984—, Assn. of Jewish Sponsored Camps, Inc., 1986—. Mem. ABA (com. on fed. regulation of securities), N.Y. State Bar Assn., Assn. of Bar of City of N.Y., Nat. Assn. Hebrew Day Schs. (exec. com. 1980—), Yeshiva U. Alumni Assn. (pres. 1986—). General corporate, Securities. Office: Parker Chapin Flattau & Klimpl 1211 Avenue of the Americas New York NY 10036

ROTHMAN, HOWARD JOEL, lawyer; b. N.Y.C., July 10, 1945; s. Samuel and Avy (Avrutin) R.; m. Joan Andrea Solomon, July 2, 1967; children: Samantha, Rodney. BA, CCNY, 1967; JD, Bklyn. Law Sch., 1971; LLM, NYU, 1972. Bar: N.Y. 1972. From assoc. to ptnr. Marshall, Bratter, Greene, Allison & Tucker, N.Y.C., 1972-82; ptnr. Rosenman & Colin, N.Y.C., 1982—; mem. adv. panel Commr. Fin. of City of N.Y., 1981-83. Contbr. articles to profl. jours. Mem. ABA (closely held corps. com. 1977—, real estate probs. com. 1980—), N.Y. State Bar Assn. (corps. com. 1979—, partnerships com. 1979—, N.Y.C. tax matters com.), Bur. Nat. Affairs (real estate jour. 1984—, tax. mgmt. adv. bd. 1979—). Corporate taxation, State and local taxation, Personal income taxation. Office: Rosenman & Colin 575 Madison Ave New York NY 10022

ROTHMAN, ROBERT PIERSON, lawyer; b. Syracuse, N.Y., May 2, 1946; s. R. Raymond and Arlene (Pierson) R.; m. Tovah Guttenplan Rothman, Mar. 26, 1972; children—Arlene Rachel, Aaron Jeffrey, Sarah Michelle. B.A., Pa. State U., 1967; J.D., Syracuse U., 1972. Bar: N.Y. 1973, U.S. Dist. Ct. (no. dist.) N.Y. 1973. Ptnr., Menter, Rudin & Trivelpiece, Syracuse, 1972-78; assoc. Samuel H. Greene, 1978-79; owner, pres. Robert P. Rothman, P.C., Syracuse, 1979—. Officer Syracuse Jewish Fedn., 1980—. Mem. Syracuse Assn. Credit Mgmt. (dir., officer), Mid-York Med. Accts. Mgmt. (dir., officer), Consumer Credit Assn. City of N.Y. Lodges: Syracuse Rotary (found. officer), Temple Soc. of Concord (trustee). Jewish. Consumer commercial, Bankruptcy. Home: 104 Cammot Ln Fayetteville NY 13066 Office: Robert P Rothman PC 107 University Bldg Syracuse NY 13202

ROTHSCHILD, DONALD PHILLIP, legal educator, arbitrator; b. Dayton, Ohio, Mar. 31, 1927; s. Leo and Anne (Office) R.; m. Ruth Eckstein, July 7, 1950; children—Nancy Lee, Judy Lynn Hoffman, James Alex. A.B., U. Mich., 1950; J.D. summa cum laude, U. Toledo, 1965; LL.M., Harvard U., 1966. Bar: Ohio 1966, D.C. 1970, U.S. Supreme Ct. 1975.

Teaching fellow Harvard U. Law Sch., Cambridge, Mass., 1965-66; instr. solicitor's office U.S. Dept. Labor, Washington, 1966-67; vis. prof. U. Mich. Law Sch., Ann Arbor, 1976; prof. law George Washington U. Nat. Law Ctr., Washington, 1966—, dir. Consumer Protection Ctr., 1971—; dir. Inst. Law and Aging, Washington, 1973—, Ctr. for Community Justice, Washington, 1974—, Nat. Consumers League, Washington, 1981—; v.p. Regulatory Alternatives Devel. Corp., Washington, 1982—; cons. Washington Met. Council Govt., 1979-82; mayoral appointee Adv. Com. on Consumer Protection, Washington, 1979-80; chmn. bd. dirs. D.C. Citizens Complaint Ctr., Washington, 1980. Co-author: Consumer Protection Text and Materials, 1973; Collective Bargaining and Labor Arbitration, 1979; Fundamentals of Administrative Practice and Procedure, 1981. Contbr. numerous articles to profl. publs. Mem. FTC Adv. Council, Washington, 1970. Recipient Community Service award Television Acad., Washington, 1981. Mem. Nat. Acad. Arbitrators, Fed. Mediation and Conciliation Service, Am. Arbitration Assn., ABA, D.C. Bar Assn., Phi Kappa Phi. Jewish. Labor, Administrative and regulatory, Contracts commercial. Home: 2450 Virginia Ave NW Washington DC 20037 also: Shadow Farm Unit #4 Wakefield RI 02879 Office: George Washington U Nat Law Ctr Washington DC 20052

ROTHSCHILD, EDGAR MEYER, III, lawyer; b. Memphis, June 8, 1951; s. Joseph Adler and Peggy (Goodman) R.; m. Gina Levine, Aug. 14, 1977 (div. May 1985); children: Alan Meyer, Rebecca Levine. AB, Bowdoin Coll., 1973; JD, Memphis State U., 1976. Bar: Tenn. 1976, U.S. Dist. Ct. (mid. dist.) Tenn. 1978, U.S. Ct. Appeals (6th cir.) 1982. Legis. coordinator office Urban and Fed. Affairs State of Tenn., Nashville, 1976-77; assoc. editor Lawyers Coop. Pub. Co., Rochester, N.Y., 1977-78; assoc. Levine, Levine & Rothschild, Nashville, 1978-83; ptnr. Rothschild & Lefkovitz, Nashville, 1983—. Mem. ABA, Tenn. Bar Assn., Nashville Bar Assn., Comml. Law League, Nat. Assn. of Chpt. 13 Trustees. Democrat. Jewish. Lodge: B'nai B'rith. Bankruptcy. Home: 239 Cherokee Rd Nashville TN 37205 Office: Rothschild & Lefkovitz 500 Church St 2d Floor Nashville TN 37219

ROTHSCHILD, STEVEN BRUCE, lawyer; b. Jackson, Mich., Oct. 23, 1953; s. Max and Anne Portia (Fox) R.; m. Gloria Schwartz, Aug. 14, 1956, children: Chaim, Shmuel, Zev, Yosef. BA, U. Mich., 1974; JD, Harvard U., 1978. Bar: N.Y. 1979. Assoc. Spengler, Carlson, Gubar & Brodsky, N.Y.C., 1978-79, Moser & Singer, N.Y.C., 1979-80, Feit & Ahrens, N.Y.C., 1980-86; ptnr. Sheps & Rothschild, N.Y.C., 1986—; mng. trustee TAT Found., Monsey, N.Y. Dem. committeeman, Rockland County, N.Y., 1979—. James Angell scholar U. Mich., 1971-74. Mem. ABA (corp. banking and bus. law, natural resources law and econs. of law practice sects.), N.Y. State Bar Assn., Assn. of Bar of City of N.Y. Jewish. General corporate, Securities, Venture capital. Home: 6 Pinewood Dr Monsey NY 10952 Office: Sheps & Rothschild 1180 Ave of Americas New York NY 10036

ROTHSCHILD, STEVEN JAMES, lawyer; b. Worcester, Mass., Mar. 23, 1944; s. Alfred and Ilse (Blumenfeld) R. B.A., U. Vt., 1965; J.D., Georgetown U., 1968. Bar: D.C. 1968, Del. 1969. Law clk. to chancellor Del. Ct. Chancery, 1968-69; asso. firm Prickett Ward Burt & Sanders, Wilmington, Del., 1969-72; partner Prickett Ward Burt & Sanders, 1972-79; partner firm Skadden Arps Slate Meagher & Flom, Wilmington, 1979—; mem. Del. Bd. Bar Examiners, 1979-83. Campaign chmn. United Way Del., 1980, bd. dirs., 1978-85, v.p., 1981-84; bd. dirs. Milton & Hattie Kutz Home, 1972—, pres., 1982-84; bd. dirs. Del. region NCCJ, 1981—; trustee Del. Art Mus., 1986—; chmn. Del. Citizens Conf. on Adminstrn. of Justice, 1982; bd. dirs. Hebrew Immigrant Aid Soc., 1986—. Mem. ABA, Bar Assn. D.C., Assn. Bar City N.Y. (corp. law com.), Del. Bar Assn. (chmn. program com. 1978-79, chmn. bench and bar conf. com. 1979-80, mem. corp. law com. 1973—, exec. com. 1973). General corporate, Federal civil litigation, State civil litigation. Office: One Rodney Sq PO Box 636 Wilmington DE 19899

ROTHSTEIN, BARBARA JACOBS, federal judge; b. Bklyn., Feb. 3, 1939; d. Solomon and Pauline Jacobs; m. Ted L. Rothstein, Dec. 28, 1968; 1 child, Daniel. B.A., Cornell U., 1960; LL.B., Harvard U., 1966. Bar: Mass. bar 1966, Wash. bar 1969. Individual practice law Boston, 1966-68; asst. atty. gen. State of Wash., 1968-77; judge Superior Ct., Seattle, 1977-80, Fed. Dist. Ct. Western Wash., Seattle, 1980—; faculty Law Sch. U. Wash., 1975-77, Hastings Inst. Trial Advocacy, 1977, N.W. Inst. Trial Advocacy, 1979—. Recipient Matrix Table Woman of Year award, 1980. Mem. Am. Judicature Soc., Am. Bar Assn. (judicial sect.), Phi Beta Kappa, Phi Kappa Phi. Jurisprudence. Office: US District Court 411 US Courthouse 1010 Fift Ave Seattle WA 98104

ROTHSTEIN, ROBERT RICHARD, lawyer, educator; b. Bklyn., Nov. 19, 1944; s, Jerome Harold and Dorothy (Levine) R.; m. Sarah Bennett, June 30, 1979. AB, U. Calif., Berkeley, 1966, JD, 1974; MA, UCLA, 1967, postgrad., 1970. Bar: N.Mex. 1974, U.S. Dist. Ct. N.Mex. 1974, U.S. Ct. Appeals (10th cir.) 1979, U.S. Supreme Ct. 1979. Asst. pub. defender N.Mex. Pub. Defender Dept., Santa Fe, 1974-76; ptnr. Rothstein, Bailey, Bennett, Daly & Donatelli, Santa Fe, 1976—; instr. Nat. Inst. Trial Advocacy, Dallas, 1982—; mem. N.Mex. Supreme Ct. Rules of Evidence Comn., 1985—. Mem. State Bar N.Mex. (bd. dirs. trial practice sect. 1983—, chmn. criminal law sect. 1983-84), N.Mex. Trial Layers Assn. (bd. dirs. 1982—), Nat. Assn. Criminal Def. Lawyers, Assn. Trial Lawyers Am. Democrat. Jewish. Civil rights, Criminal, Libel. Home: Rt 9 Box 76 Santa Fe NM 87505 Office: Rothstein Bailey Bennett et al PO Box 8180 Santa Fe NM 87504-8180

ROTHWELL, THOMAS HENRY, law educator, retired magistrate; b. San Diego, Sept. 21, 1923; s. Thomas Albert and Louise (Klots) R.; m. Anne Duggan, Jan. 3, 1950; 1 son, Bradford. Student, Calif. State U.-San Diego, 1943; B.S.B.A., U. Calif.-Berkeley, 1948; J.D., U. Calif.-San Francisco, 1951. Bar: Calif. 1952, U.S. Dist. Ct. (no. dist.) Calif. 1952, U.S. Ct. Appeals (9th cir.) 1952, U.S. Supreme Ct. 1967. Assoc. firm Scofield, Hanson & Jenkins, San Francisco, 1952-53; staff atty. Legal Aid Soc., San Francisco, 1953-58; exec. atty. Legal Aid Soc., Alameda County, Calif., 1958-63; chief counsel Legal Aid Soc., San Francisco, 1963-71; adj. instr. Hastings Coll. Law, U. Calif.-San Francisco, 1964-70, adj. asst. prof. law, 1970-71, assoc. prof., 1971-72, prof. law, 1972—; magistrate U.S. Dist. Ct. (no. dist.) Calif., 1975-83; atty. for formation City of Kensington, Calif., 1955-56; gen. counsel, sec. formation com. Fed. Criminal Def. Office, U.S. Dist. Ct. (no. dist.) Calif., 1964-68; pres. Calif. Pub. Defenders and Legal Aid Assn., 1966-67. Author books including: How to Avoid Losing a Good Case for Appellate Reversal, 1978; Opinions, Orders and Other Matters, 1979, 2d edit., 1981, Credibility of Counsel, 1986; cons. editor: The California Family Lawyer, vol. I, 1962, vol. II, 1963. Trustee United Bay Area Crusade, 1968-72; founding mem., gen. counsel Kensington Property Owners Assn., 1971-75. Served to maj. USAFR, 1943-63. Mem. State Bar Calif., ABA, Nat. Conf. Spl. Ct. Judges, San Francisco Bar Assn., Order of Coif, Order of Daedalians. Republican. Episcopalian. Federal civil litigation, State civil litigation, Criminal. Office: 200 McAllister St San Francisco CA 94102

ROTI, THOMAS DAVID, lawyer, supermarket exec.; b. Evanston, Ill., Jan. 20, 1945; s. Sam N. and Theresa S. (Salerno) R.; m. Donna Sumichrast, July 22, 1972; children—Thomas S., Kyle D., Rebecca D., Gregory J. B.S., Loyola U., Chgo., 1967, J.D. cum laude, 1970. Bar: Ill. 1970, U.S. Dist. Ct. (no. dist.) Ill. 1971, U.S. Ct. Appeals (7th cir.) 1971. Sr. law clk. to chief judge U.S. Dist. Ct. No. Dist. Ill., 1971-72; assoc. Arnstein, Gluck & Lehr, Chgo., 1972-73, Boodell, Sears et al., Chgo., 1973-75; asst. gen. counsel Dominick's Finer Foods, Inc., Northlake, Ill., 1975-77, v.p., gen. counsel, 1977—. Served to maj. U.S. Army, 1967—. Recipient Am. Jurisprudence award, 1970; Alumni Assn. award Loyola U., 1970. Mem. ABA, Ill. Bar Assn., Chgo. Bar Assn., Res. Officers Assn., Am. Corp. Counsel Assn., Chgo. Zool. Soc., U.S. Golf Assn., Loyola Alumni Assn., Art Inst. Chgo., Phi Alpha Delta, Alpha Sigma Nu. Roman Catholic. General corporate, Antitrust, Contracts commercial. Office: 333 Northwest Ave Northlake IL 60164

ROTTER, EMANUEL NORMAN, lawyer; b. Milw., Jan. 11, 1928; s. Louis H. and Sara (Manhoff) R.; m. Sandra Schulner, July 5, 1952; children: Margie S., Barbara A., Steven M. BBA, U. Wis., 1949; JD, Marquette U., 1952. Bar: Wis. 1952, U.S. Dist. Ct. (ea. dist.) Wis. 1952. Sole practice, Milw., 1952—; lic. real estate broker, Wis., 1953-63; ct. commr. Milwaukee County (Wis.), 1982—; life ins. agt. (lic.), Wis. Mem. ABA (gen. practice sect., sub-com. sole practitioners and small firms), Wis. Bar Assn., (family law, bankruptcy, and creditor's rights, gen. practice sects.), Milwaukee County Bar Assn. (arbitration com., jud. selection com.), Am. Arbitration Assn. (panel), Wis. Acad. Trial Lawyers, Nat. Audubon Soc., U.S. Tennis Assn., Am. Assn. Ret. Persons. Jewish. Lodges: B'nai B'rith, Beth El Ner Tamid Men's (Milw.). Probate, Family and matrimonial, General corporate. Office: 4353 W Fond Du Lac Ave Milwaukee WI 53216

ROTTLER, TERRY ROBERT, lawyer; b. Taylorville, Ill., Nov. 11, 1951; s. Robert Raymond and Norma Jean (Samples) R.; m. Charlene Ann Chamberlin, July 24, 1981; children: Jeffrey, Karen, Lisa. BA, Cen. Meth. Coll., 1974; JD, U. Mo., Kansas City, 1976. Bar: Mo. 1977, U.S. Dist. Ct. (ea. dist.) Mo. 1978. Assoc. Roberts & Roberts, Farmington, Mo., 1976-84; ptnr. Elpers & Rottler P.C., St. Genevieve, Mo., 1984—; sec. Silvanus Products, St. Genevieve, Mo., 1984—, bd. dirs.; bd. dirs. Landmark Title and Abstract, St. Genevieve. Mem. Landmarks and Urban Design Commn., St. Genevieve, 1979-81, St. Genevieve County Cen. Dem. Com., 1980—; chmn. 20th Senatorial Dist. Dem. Com., Mo., 1982—; treas. 10th Congl. Dist. Dem. Com., Mo., 1985—. Named one of OUtstanding Young Men Am., 1980. Mem. ABA, Mo. Bar Assn., 24th Cir. Bar Assn., St. Genevieve County Bar Assn., Jaycees. Presbyterian. Lodge: Elks. Avocations: politics, music, sports. Construction, General practice, Real property. Home: Rt 2 Saint Genevieve MO 63670 Office: Elpers & Rottler PC 296 Market St Saint Genevieve MO 63670

ROUBICEK, CHRISTOPHER JOHN, lawyer; b. Lincoln, Nebr., Oct. 8, 1951; s. Frank John and Janet Kolb (Smith) R.; m. Karen Diane Foulk, Jan. 7, 1973; children: Ben Josef, Sarah Louise, Nathan Foulk. BE, U. Nebr., 1972, MEd, 1978; JD, Gonzaga U., 1981. Bar: Wash. 1981. Auditor U.S. Army, Ft. Belvoir, Va., 1976-77; ptnr. Hallett & Roubicek, Castle Rock, Wash., 1981—; atty. City of Castle Rock, 1981-85. Exec. bd. dirs. Health Care Found, Castle Rock, 1985—; pres. MOnticello Med. Ctr., Longview, Wash., 1984. Served with U.S. Army, 1973-76. Mem. ABA, Wash. State Bar Assn., Wash. State Trial Lawyers, Nat. Assn. Hospital Devel. Probate, Real property, General practice. Office: Hallett & Roubicek 701 Front Box 600 Castle Rock WA 98611

ROUGE, CHERYL ANNE, lawyer; b. Syracuse, N.Y., Jan. 7, 1952; d. Robert George and Ruth Frances (Klein) R. BA, Duke U., 1974; JD, Georgetown U., 1980. Bar: Pa. 1980, U.S. Dist. Ct. (ea. dist.) Pa. 1980, U.S. Ct. Appeals (3d. cir.) 1983. Assoc. White & Williams, Phila., 1980—. Mem. ABA, Pa. Bar Assn., Phila. Bar Assn. Real property, General corporate, Contracts commercial. Office: White & Williams 1234 Market St Philadelphia PA 19107

ROUGEUX, DONNA RISELLI, lawyer; b. Teaneck, N.J., Feb. 8, 1951; d. G. James and Josephine Mary (Massaro) Riselli; children: Jennifer Carol, James Daniel. Bar: Fla. 1981, U.S. Dist. Ct. (so. dist.) Fla. 1983. In ho. counsel Dublin Engring. Co., North Miami Beach, Fla., 1981-82; sole practice Miami, Fla., 1982-83, 85—; asst. fed. pub. defender So. Dist. Fla., Miami, 1983-85. Mem. ABA, Fla. Bar Assn., Assn. Trial Lawyers Am., Fla. Assn. Criminal Def. Lawyers, Nat. Assn. Criminal Def. Lawyers. Avocations: sailing, water sports, bicycling, needle craft. Criminal, Private international, Construction. Office: 1149 SW 27th Ave Suite 205 Miami FL 33135

ROULAND, JAY THOMAS, bar association executive; b. Detroit, Aug. 17, 1935; s. John Edward and Esther (Failor) R.; m. Suzanne Freeman Rowell, Apr. 18, 1970; children: Christopher Jay, Carolyn Elizabeth, Michael Russell. B.A. magna cum laude with high honors in Econs, Kenyon Coll., 1957; J.D., Duke, 1960. Bar: Mich. bar 1961, also U.S. Supreme Ct 1961; Cert. assn. exec. Atty. FTC, 1960-62; div. gen. trade restraints FTC, Washington, 1963-67; exec. dir. Fed. Bar Assn., Washington, 1967-86; del. to Am. Bar Assn. Ho. of Dels., Honolulu, 1967; dist. v.p. for D.C. dist. Am. Bar Assn. Ho. of Dels., 1966-67; nat. chmn. Younger Lawyers, 1965-66; sec. Suzanne Rouland Assocs. Ltd., Reston, Va.; mem. adv. com. Hotel Mgmt./Restaurant Mgmt. Sch. Montgomery (Md.) Coll., No. Va. Hotel and Restaurant Mgmt. Sch. Editor: Fed. Bar News, 1966-67; mng. editor, 1965-66. Class agt. Kenyon Coll., 1957-82; pres. D.C. Area Alumni Assn., 1980-83; Commn. Reston Soccer Assn., 1981-83, treas., 1983-84. Recipient meritorious service award FTC, 1962; spl. commendation for distinguished service Fed. Bar Assn., 1970. Mem. Am. Soc. Assn. Execs. (govt. relations com. 1973-77, 80-81, chmn. profl. assns. council 1977-79, membership com. 1979-81, long-range planning com. 1978-79), Washington Soc. Assn. Execs. (chmn. survey and research com. 1978-79, chmn., chief exec. officer Round Table 1980-81, dir. 1983—), Restaurant Assn. of Met. Washington (exec. v.p. 1986—), Internat. Soc. Restaurant Assn. Execs. Episcopalian (vestryman 1966-70, del. Va. Diocesan Council 1967-71, Sunday Sch. tchr. 1980-81). Legal association executive. Home: 12126 Basset Ln Reston VA 22091 Office: 2112-D Gallows Rd Vienna VA 22180

ROUNICK, JACK ABRAHAM, lawyer; b. Phila., June 5, 1935; s. Philip and Nettie (Brownstein) R.; B.B.A., U. Mich., 1956; J.D., U. Pa., 1959; m. Noreen A. Garrigan, Sept. 4, 1970; children—Ellen, Eric, Amy, Michelle. Admitted to Pa. bar, 1960, U.S. Dist. Ct. (ea. dist.) Pa., 1960; spl. asst. atty. gen., 1963-71; ptnr. Israelit & Rounick, 1960-67, Moss & Rounick, 1968-69, Moss, Rounick & Hurowitz, Norristown, Pa., 1969-72, Moss & Rounick, Norristown, 1972-73; co-mng. ptnr. Pechner, Dorfman, Wolffe, Rounick and Cabot, Norristown, 1973—; v.p. Martin Lawrence Enterprises, Inc. Pa. Young Republican fin. chmn., 1964-66, treas., 1966-68, chmn., 1968-70. Recipient Boss of Yr. award Montgomery County Legal Secs. Assn., 1970, cert. of appreciation Pa. Bar Inst., 1980. Fellow Am. Acad. Matrimonial Lawyers (pres. Pa. chpt. 1982-84, gov. 1983-85, v.p. 1985—); mem. ABA, (council family law sect. 1982-87, chmn. scope and correlation com. family law sect. 1984-86, fin. officer 1987—), Pa. Bar Assn. (past chmn. family law sect.; Spl. Achievement award 1979-80), Montgomery Bar Assn. Republican. Jewish. Club: Meadowlands Country (Blue Bell, Pa.). Author: Pennsylvania Matrimonial Practice, 3 vols., 1982. Editor, Pa. Family Lawyer, 1980. Contbr. articles to profl. jours. Family and matrimonial. Office: 68 E Penn St Norristown PA 19401

ROUNTREE, ASA, lawyer; b. Birmingham, Ala., Aug. 9, 1927; s. John Asa and Cherokee Jemison (Van de Graaff) R.; m. Elizabeth Rhodes Blue, Aug. 11, 1951; children—Robert B., John A. A.B., U. Ala., 1949; LL.B., Harvard U., 1954. Bar: Ala. 1954, U.S. Dist. Ct. (no. dist.) Ala. 1954, U.S. Ct. Appeals (5th cir.) 1955, N.Y. 1962, U.S. Dist. Ct. (so. dist.) N.Y. 1963, U.S. Ct. Appeals (2d cir.) 1963, U.S. Supreme Ct. 1972. Assoc. Cabaniss & Johnston, Birmingham, Ala., 1954-60, ptnr., 1960-62; assoc. Debevoise & Plimpton, N.Y.C., 1962-63, ptnr., 1963—. Served with U.S. Army, 1945-46, to lt., 1951-53. Mem. ABA (chmn. litigation sect. 1980-81), Ala. Bar Assn., N.Y. State Bar Assn., Assn. Bar City N.Y., Am. Law Inst., Am. Coll. Trial Lawyers, Am. Bar Found. Episcopalian. Clubs: River (N.Y.C.); Mountain Brook (Birmingham). Federal civil litigation, State civil litigation. Office: Debevoise & Plimpton 875 3d Ave New York NY 10022

ROUSE, LEGRAND A., II, lawyer, educator; b. Spartanburg, S.C., June 11, 1933; s. LeGrand and Hilda Virginia (Ariail) R.; m. Patricia Adelle White, Aug. 23, 1958; children—LeGrand A. III, Laurie Adelle, Daniel Morris. A.B. in History and Polit. Sci., Wofford Coll., 1954; LL.B., U. S.C.; 1959, J.D., 1970; M.A. in Govt., Am. U., 1969. Bar: S.C. 1959, U.S. Dist. Ct. S.C. 1959, U.S. Ct. Appeals (4th cir.) 1964, U.S. Supreme Ct. 1963. Sole practice, Spartanburg S.C., 1959-63, 68-69; assoc. counsel, jud. improvements subcom. U.S. Senate Judiciary Com., Washington, 1963; profl. staff mem. U.S. Senate P.O. and Civil Service Com., Washington, 1964-68; instructional specialist Office of Instructional TV, S.C. Dept. Edn., Columbia, 1970-73; social studies cons. curriculum devel. S.C. Dept. Edn., 1973-79; spl. asst. legal and legis. affairs to State Supt. Edn., Columbia, 1979—; cons. S.C. Council for Social Studies, Columbia, 1973-78; dir. S.C. Council Econ. Edn., Columbia. Author: Government-Politics-Citizenship, tchr. lesson guide, 1971-72; creator, on-camera instr. Government-Politics-Citizenship TV series, 1970-72; project dir. econs. edn. kit for tchrs. grades 1-12: People, Production, Profits, 1977. Mem. S.C. Ho. of Reps., Columbia, 1961-64; alt. del. Nat. Democratic Conv., 1964. Served to 1st lt. USAF, 1955-57. Recipient Schoolmens' medal Freedoms Found. at Valley Forge, 1974. Mem. S.C. Bar Assn., S.C. State Employees' Assn. (pres. 1980-82). Methodist. Lodge: Masons. Legislative. Home: 1021 Milton Ln Columbia SC 29209 Office: Office of Supt Edn 1429 Senate St Columbia SC 29201

ROUSH, BRADLEY CRAIG, lawyer; b. Lima, Ohio, Dec. 27, 1953; s. Walter J. and Eleanor L. (Casey) R.; m. Judith A. Rigali, Oct. 3, 1981; 1 child, Walter Dane. BA, Ohio No. U., 1976, JD, 1979. Bar: Ohio 1979, U.S. Dist. Ct. (no. dist.) Ohio 1983. Asst. prosecutor Allen County Prosecutor, Lima, 1979-84; ptnr. Kill, Shaw & Roush, Lima, 1979-84; gen. counsel Health Care REIT Inc., Lima, 1984-86; gen. counsel, sec. Arbor Health Care Co., Lima, 1986—. Bd. dirs. Child & Family Service, Lima, 1984, Victim & Offender Group, Lima, 1983. Mem. ABA, Nat. Dist. Attys. Assn., Ohio State Bar Assn., Allen County Bar Assn. Republican. Lodge: Elks. Avocations: golf, tennis. General corporate, Federal civil litigation, State civil litigation. Home: 619 Atalan Trail Lima OH 45805 Office: Arbor Health Care Co 1100 Shawnee Rd Lima OH 45805

ROUSH, GEORGE EDGAR, lawyer; b. Tuolumne, Calif., Feb. 29, 1916; s. George Edgar and Ethyl Ruth (Gaskill) R.; m. Sarah Catherine Kragness, Mar. 29, 1944; children—Jane Margaret Roush Melicker, George Edgar III. B.S., U. Calif.-Berkeley, 1940; J.D., N.Y. Law Sch., 1951; life certs. Calif. Community Coll., Sacramento, 1979. Bar: N.Y. 1953, U.S. Ct. Customs and Patent Appeals, 1954, U.S. Supreme Ct. 1970, U.S. Ct. Appeals (fed. cir.) 1982. Patent agt. Philips Labs. Inc., Irvington-on-Hudson, N.Y., 1946-48; patent atty. RCA Labs., Princeton, N.J., 1948-56; div. atty. CBS-Hytran, Danvers, Mass., 1956-57; patent atty. Marchant Calculators, Oakland, Calif., 1957-60, IBM, San Jose, Calif., 1960-82; instr. West Valley Community Coll., Saratoga, Calif., part-time 1979—. Inventor automatic phasing for synchronous radio telegraph systems. Served to lt. col. Signal Corps, U.S. Army, 1940-46. Fellow Internat. Acad. Law and Sci.; mem. IEEE (sr. life mem.), Soc. Wireless Pioneers (life Pioneer mem.), Patent Office Soc. (assoc.), Patent Trademark and Copyright Law Assn. San Francisco. Republican. Episcopalian. Lodge: Kiwanis (pres. Cambrian Park, San Jose 1967). Patent, Trademark and copyright. Home: 16250 Jacaranda Way Los Gatos CA 95030

ROUSTAN, YVON D., lawyer; b. Managua, Nicaragua, June 22, 1944; came to U.S., 1962; s. Pierre Dominique and Concepcion (Reyes) R.; m. Estela Maria Fiol, Apr. 2, 1967; children: Estela, Pierre, Paul. BA, St. Mary's Coll., Winona, Minn., 1966; MBA, U. Chgo., 1969; JD, DePaul U., 1976. Chief chemist Bird and Son Inc., Chgo., 1967-69; mgr. Grasas S.A., Chinandega, Nicaragua, 1969-72; assoc. Vincent Lopez, Chgo., 1976-77; sole practice Chgo., 1977—. Mem. ABA, Ill. Bar Assn., Chgo. Bar Assn., Latin Am. Bar Assn., Council of Trial Lawyers, ACLU. Lodge: Lions (Chgo.) (v.p. 1983, pres.). Avocations: computers, reading. Federal civil litigation, State civil litigation, Criminal. Office: 2911 N Cicero Chicago IL 60641

ROUT, ROBERT HOWARD, lawyer; b. N.Y.C., Apr. 14, 1927; s. David S. and Shirley (Rosenthal) R.; m. Valerie Marrow, Jan. 27, 1958; children—Robert Howard, W. Christopher, Romanie Marrow. Grad., N.Y. State Maritime Acad., 1947; BA, U. Wis.-Madison, 1949; JD, Harvard U., 1952. Bar: N.Y. 1953, U.S. Ct. Mil. Appeals 1953, P.R. 1958, U.S. Dist. Ct. P.R. 1958, Conn. 1976, U.S. Ct. Appeals (1st cir.) 1983, U.S. Supreme Ct. 1983. Practice law, N.Y.C., 1955-58; sole practice, San Juan, P.R., 1958-75; ptnr. Aller & Rout, Lakeville, Conn., 1975—. Chmn. Zoning Bd. Appeals, Salisbury, Conn., 1984—. Served to lt. USNR, 1953-55. Mem. Assn. Bar City N.Y., Colegio de Abogados de P.R., Conn. Bar Assn. Club: Harvard (N.Y.). Lodge: Rotary (sec. 1982-84). General practice, Probate, Real property. Home: Wells Hill Lakeville CT 06039 Office: Aller & Rout Lakeville CT 06039

ROUVELAS, EMANUEL LARRY, lawyer; b. Seattle, Sept. 10, 1944; s. Larry E. and Mary (Derezes) R.; m. Marilyn S. Edmunds, Jan. 23, 1967; children: Eleftherios, Mary. BA, U. Wash., 1965; JD, Harvard U., 1968. Bar: Ill. 1968, D.C. 1973. Assoc. Kirkland & Ellis, Chgo., 1968-69; of counsel U.S. Senate Com. on Commerce, Washington, 1969-73; chief counsel U.S. Senate Mcht. Marine and Fgn. Commerce Subcoms., Washington, 1973—; Mem. adv. bd. Congl. Maritime Caucus, Washington, 1985-87, Fed. Maritime Commn. Transition Adv. Com., 1980-81. Mem. ABA, Fed. Bar. Assn., Maritime Adminstrn. Bar Assn., Propeller Club U.S. (bd. govs. 1983—), Nat. Lawyers Club. Club: Georgetown (Washington). Legislative, Administrative and regulatory, Transportation law. Office: Preston Thorgrimson Ellis & Holman 1735 New York Ave NW Suite 500 Washington DC 20006

ROVER, EDWARD FRANK, lawyer; b. N.Y.C., Oct. 4, 1938; s. Frederick James and Wanda (Charkowski) R.; m. Maureen Wyer, June 15, 1968; children—Elizabeth, Emily, William. A.B., Fordham U., 1961; J.D., Harvard U., 1964. Bar: N.Y. 1964, U.S. Tax Ct. 1968, U.S. Dist. Ct. (so. dist.) N.Y. 1975. Assoc. White & Case, N.Y.C., 1964-71, ptnr., 1972—; bd. dirs. Churchill Trust Co., N.Y.C., Cranshaw Corp., N.Y.C., Stage #, N.Y.C. Bd. dirs., v.p. Tune In Inc., N.Y.C., 1978-85. Mem. ABA, N.Y. Bar Assn., Assn. Bar City N.Y. Clubs: Larchmont Yacht, Harvard, The Board Room. Avocations: sailing; skiing. Corporate taxation, Estate taxation, Pension, profit-sharing, and employee benefits. Home: 1111 Park Ave New York NY 10128 Office: White and Case 1155 Ave of the Americas New York NY 10036

ROVINE, ARTHUR WILLIAM, lawyer; b. Phila., Apr. 29, 1937; s. George Isaac and Rosanna (Lipsitz) R.; m. Phyllis Ellen Hamburger, Apr. 7, 1963; children: Joshua, Deborah. AB, U. Pa., 1958; LLB, Harvard U., 1961; PhD, Columbia U., 1966. Bar: D.C. 1964, N.Y. 1984. Assoc. Curtis, Mallet-Prevostt, Colt & Mosle, N.Y.C., 1964-66; asst. prof. Cornell U., Ithaca, N.Y., 1966-72; editor Digest of U.S. Practice in International Law U.S. Dept. State, Washington, 1972-75, asst. legal adviser, 1975-81; agt. U.S. Govt. to Iran-U.S. Claims Tribunal U.S. Dept. State, The Hague, Netherlands, 1981-83; of counsel Baker & McKenzie, N.Y.C., 1983-85, ptnr., 1985—; adj. prof. law Georgetown U., Washington, 1977-81. Author: The First Fifty Years: The Secretary-General in World Politics, 1920-1970, 1970; editor: Digest of U.S. Practice in International Law, 1973, 74; co-editor: The Case Law of the International Court of Justice, 1968, 1972, 1974, 1976; bd. editors Am. Jour. Internat. Law, 1977-87; also articles. Mem. ABA (chmn. internat. law sect. 1985-86), Am. Soc. Internat. Law (cert. of merit 1974, exec. council 1975-77), Hebrew Immigrant Aid Soc. (bd. dirs. 1987—). Private international, Federal civil litigation, State civil litigation. Home: 150 E 61st St New York NY 10021 Office: Baker & McKenzie 805 3rd Ave New York NY 10022

ROVINS, JEFFREY SETH, lawyer; b. N.Y.C., Mar. 20, 1943; s. Louis and Rachel (Rauch) R.; m. Julie Lynn McMurray, May 15, 1983; 1 child, Jessica. B.A., St. Lawrence U., 1963; M.A., Columbia U., 1966; J.D., U. Va., 1970. Bar: N.Y. 1970, U.S. Dist. Ct. (so. dist.) N.Y. 1976, U.S. Dist. Ct. (ea. dist.) N.Y. 1981. Asst. dist. atty. N.Y. County Dist. Atty., N.Y.C., 1970-77; assoc. Bower & Gardner, 1977-78; ptnr. Rovins & Miller, 1979-80, Jeffrey S. Rovins, Esq., N.Y.C., 1981—; judge NYU Moot Ct., 1981—. Served to capt. U.S. Army, 1967-69, Vietnam. Recipient Bronze Star. Mem. Mayors Task Force on Rape, N.Y.C., 1975—. Mem. N.Y. County Lawyers Assn. Jewish. Federal civil litigation, State civil litigation, Insurance. Office: 170 Broadway New York NY 10038

ROVIRA, LUIS DARIO, state justice; b. San Juan, P.R., Sept. 8, 1923; s. Peter S. and Mae (Morris) R.; m. Lois Ann Thau, June 25, 1966; children—Douglas, Merilyn. B.A., U. Colo., 1948, LL.B., 1950. Bar: Colo. bar 1950. Now justice Colo. Supreme Ct., Denver.; Mem. Pres.'s Com. on Mental Retardation, 1970-71; chmn. State Health Facilities Council, 1967-76. Bd. dirs. YMCA, 1969-78; pres. Lowe Found. Served with AUS, 1943-46. Mem. Colo. Assn. Retarded Children (pres. 1968-70), ABA, Colo. Bar Assn., Denver Bar Assn. (pres. 1970-71), Alpha Tau Omega, Phi Alpha Delta. Republican. Clubs: Athletic (Denver), Country (Denver). Jurisprudence. Home: 4810 E 6th Ave Denver CO 80220 Office: Colo Judicial Bldg Denver CO 80203

ROVNER, DAVID PATRICK RYAN, lawyer; b. Phila., Aug. 6, 1952; s. Edward Isadore and Cecilia C (Ryan) R. AB, St. Joseph's U., 1974; JD, Villanova U., 1977. Bar: Pa. 1977, U.S. Ct. Claims 1978, U.S. Dist. Ct. (ea. dist.) Pa. 1977, U.S. Ct. Appeals (3rd cir.) 1978, U.S. Supreme Ct. 1982. Assoc. Krusen, Evans & Byrne, Phila., 1977-80; ptnr. German, Gallagher &

Murtagh, Phila., 1980—. Editor: Pennsylvania Insurance Law, 1980. Chmn. Lower Merion-Narberth Dem. Com., Ardmore, Pa., 1979; solicitor, past pres. The Neighborhood Club of Bala-Cynwyd, Pa., 1978—. Mem. ABA, Pa. Bar Assn., Phila. Bar Assn., Phila. Trial Lawyers Assn., Phila. Lawyers Club. Democrat. Roman Catholic. Club: Peale. Federal civil litigation, State civil litigation, Workers' compensation. Home: 303 Bryn Mawr Ave Bala-Cynwyd PA 19004 Office: German Gallagher & Murtagh 1818 Market St Philadelphia PA 19103

ROVNER, JACK ALAN, lawyer; b. Boston, May 6, 1946; s. Abraham George and Sarah Rebecca (Miller) R.; m. Sheila Marie Boyle, June 24, 1979; children—Joseph Conahan, Edward Witty, Benjamin Flanagan. B.A., Brandeis U., 1968; J.D. cum laude, Boston U., 1976. Bar: Ill. 1976, U.S. Dist. Ct. (no. dist.) Ill. 1976, U.S. Ct. Appeals (7th and 9th cir.) 1979, U.S. Supreme Ct. 1979. Admin. asst. U.S. EPA, Boston, 1971-73; assoc. Kirkland & Ellis, Chgo., 1976-81, ptnr. 1982—. Served to lt. jr. grade USCG, 1968-71. Article editor Boston U. Law Rev., 1974-76. Mem. ABA (litigation sect.), Nat. Health Lawyers Assn. Club: Mid-Am. Federal civil litigation, Antitrust, Health. Office: Kirkland & Ellis 200 E Randolph Dr Chicago IL 60601

ROWAN, BEVERLY ADELE, lawyer; b. Rochester, N.Y., Aug. 27, 1935; d. Earle Vincent and Helen Ernestine (Bastian) Jamroz. A.B., U. Miami (Fla.), 1961, J.D., 1970. Bar: Fla. 1970, U.S. Ct. Appeals (5th cir.) 1970, U.S. Dist. Ct. (so. dist.) Fla. 1970, U.S. Supreme Ct. 1975, U.S. Ct. Appeals (11th cir.) 1983, U.S. Dist. Ct. (mid. dist.) Fla. 1983. Research prof. U. Miami Law Sch., Coral Gables, Fla., 1970-74; assoc. prof. U. Fla. Law Sch., Gainesville, 1972-73; dir. advocacy Joseph P. Kennedy Jr. Found., Washington, 1974-75, legal and legis. cons., 1975—; cons. and lectr. in field, Washington, 1978—; sole practice, Ocala, Fla., 1981—. Author, editor: The Law and the Retarded, 1972; contbr. chpts. to books and articles to profl. jours. Bd. dirs. Fla. Inst. NeuroDynamics, Ft. Lauderdale, 1978—, Children's Home Soc. of Fla., Ocala, 1982—; charter mem. Zonta Internat., Ocala div., Chgo., 1984—; active numerous other civic orgns. Recipient Letter of Appreciation, Fla. Ho. of Reps., 1970; Cert. of Appreciation, Fla. Assn. for Retarded Citizens, 1972, Spl. Olympics Program, 1975. Mem. ABA, Nat. Council Juvenile and Family Ct. Judges, Council for Exceptional Children, Nat. Council Orgns. for Children and Youth, Nat. Assn. Retarded Citizens, Am. Assn. Mental Deficiency, Consortium Concerned with Devel. Disabilities, Am. Psychology-Law Soc., Nat. Coalition for Children's Justice, Emotionally-Behaviorally Disturbed Children Task Force, Fla. Bar Assn., Dade County Bar Assn. (chmn. youth com. 1971-72), Marion County Bar Assn. Family and matrimonial, Probate, Real property. Home: 8141 S Magnolia Ave Ocala FL 32676 Office: 11 N Magnolia Ave Ocala FL 32670

ROWAN, JUSTIN MICHAEL, lawyer; b. Murchison, Tex., June 15, 1920; s. Samuel Nuell and Stella (Hobbs) R. m. Maurine Duncan, May 26, 1945; children: Justin Michael Jr., Martha Rowan Stafford. BS, N. Tex. State U., Denton, 1940; JD, U. Tex., 1949. Bar: Tex. 1949, U.S. Dist. Ct. (no. dist.) Tex. 1954, U.S. Dist. Ct. (ea. dist.) Tex. 1964, U.S. Supreme Ct. 1972, U.S. Ct. Appeals (5th cir.) 1975. Exec. dir. Veterans Land Bd., Austin, Tex., 1949-51; atty. Tex. Gen. Land Office, Austin, 1951-52; ptnr. Rowan, George, Parker & Whitehurst and predecessor firms Loftis, Rowan, Files et al and Justice, Justice & Rowan, Tyler, Tex., 1952—; judge 321st Dist. Ct., Tyler. Pres. Mother Frances Hosp. Bd., Tyler; mem. Tyler City Plan Comm. Served to maj. U.S. Air Force, 1942-47. Fellow Tex. Bar Found. (life); mem. Tex. Bar Assn., Smith County Bar Assn. (pres. 1972-73). Democrat. Baptist. Lodge: Kiwanis (local pres., Tex.-Okla. dist. chmn.). Avocations: golf, training and showing quarter horses. Real property, Oil and gas leasing, Family and matrimonial. Home: 3615 Wynnwood Dr Tyler TX 75701 Office: Rowan George Parker & Whitehurst 912 1st Pl Tyler TX 75702

ROWAN, MICHAEL JOHN, lawyer; b. Dansville, N.Y., July 25, 1951; s. John W. and Patricia A. (Wheeler) R. BA, Hamilton Coll., 1973; JD, Washington and Lee U., 1977. Bar: Tex. 1978. Assoc. Johnson, Bromberg & Leeds, Dallas, 1977-83; ptnr. Stutzman & Bromberg, Dallas, 1984—. Mem. ABA, Dallas Bar Assn. Republican. Roman Catholic. Club: Verandah (Dallas). Avocations: running, tennis. Real property. Office: Stutzman & Bromberg 2323 Bryan St Suite 2200 Dallas TX 75201

ROWAN, RONALD THOMAS, lawyer; b. Bozeman, Mont., Nov. 6, 1941; s. Lawrence Eugene and Florence M.; m. Katherine Terrell Sponenberg, Sept. 4, 1964; children—Heather, Nicholaus, Matthew. B.A., Wichita U., 1964; J.D., U. Denver, 1969. Bar: Colo. 1969, U.S. Dist. Ct. Colo. 1969. Asst. city atty. City of Colorado Springs, Colo., 1969-71; asst. dist. atty. 4th Jud. Dist., Colorado Springs, 1971-79; gen. counsel U.S. Olympic Com., Colorado Springs, 1979—. Chmn. CSC, Colorado Springs, 1975—; v.p. Criminal Justice Adv. Bd., 1983—; chmn. El Paso Crimnal Justice Adv. Com.; bd. dirs. Crimestoppers, 1982—, pres. 1987—; chmn. Community Corrections Bd., 1981. Mem. ABA, Colo. Bar Assn., El Paso County Trial Lawyers (pres. 1972), El Paso County Bar Assn., U. Denver Law Alumni (chmn.). Republican. Roman Catholic. General corporate, Sports and entertainment. Home: 2915 Nevermind Ln Colorado Springs CO 80917 Office: US Olympic Com 1750 E Boulder St Colorado Springs CO 80909-5760

ROWDEN, MARCUS AUBREY, lawyer, former government official; b. Detroit, Mar. 13, 1928; s. Louis and Gertrude (Lifsitz) Rosenzweig; m. Justine Leslie Bessman, July 21, 1950; children: Gwen, Stephanie. B.A. in Econs, U. Mich., Ann Arbor, 1950, J.D. with distinction, 1953. Bar: Mich. 1953, D.C. 1978. Trial atty. Dept. Justice, 1953-58; legal advisor U.S. Mission to European Communities, 1959-62; solicitor, assoc. gen. counsel, gen. counsel AEC, 1965-74; commr., chmn. U.S. NRC, Washington, 1975-77; ptnr. Fried, Frank, Harris, Shriver and Jacobson, Washington, 1977—. Served with AUS, 1946-47. Decorated officer Order Legion of Honor Republic of France; Recipient Disting. Service award AEC, 1972. Mem. Am., Fed., Mich., D.C. bar assns., Internat. Nuclear Law Assn., Order of Coif. Home: 7937 Deepwell Dr Bethesda MD 20817 Office: Fried Frank Harris Shriver & Jacobson 1001 Pennsylvania Ave NW Washington DC 20004

ROWE, HELEN ROBERTA, lawyer; b. Milw., Oct. 9, 1939; d. Robert Karl and Winifred Grace (Sheaffer) Hofem; m. Charles Emerson Rowe, Aug. 11, 1978; children—Patricia, Katherine, Douglas, Rebecca, Michael. B.S., Western State U., 1978, J.D., 1980. Bar: Calif. 1980. Reporter Daily Transcript, San Diego, legal adminstr. Rowe & McEwen, San Diego, 1969-76, assoc., 1980-83; ptnr. Rowe, McEwen, Konold & Rowe, 1982—. Mem. San Diego Small Bus. Adv. Bd. Mem. ABA (vice chairperson lawyers pub. relations com.), Calif. Bar Assn. (Conf. of Dels., corp. com.), San Diego County Bar Assn. (historian, pub. relations chmn.), Calif. Women Lawyers Assn., Lawyers Club of San Diego (pres. 1986-87), Continuing Edn. of Bar (bus. law adv. com.), So. Calif. Women for Bus. Ownership (pres.), Western State University Alumni Assn. (pres. 1986-87). General corporate. Office: Rowe McEwen Konold & Rowe 110 W C St Suite 2100 San Diego CA 92101

ROWE, JACK DOUGLAS, lawyer; b. Coldwater, Mich., Nov. 14, 1930; s. Herschel Harold and Ellen Moore (Preston) R.; m. Amy Lou Lytle, Aug. 11, 1956; children: Andrew, Todd, Scott, Michael. BA, DePauw U., 1952; JD, U. Mich., 1955. Bar: Mich. 1955, U.S. Dist. Ct. (ea. and we. dists.) Mich. 1956, U.S. Ct. Appeals (6th cir.) 1967. Assoc. Erickson, Dyll, Marentay & Slocum, Detroit, 1956, 60-62, Cary, Begole & Martin, Detroit, 1962-68; v.p. successor firm Joselyn, Rowe, Grinnan, Hayes & Feldman P.C., Detroit, 1968—; law instr. U. Ga., 1958-60; mem. ct. adminstrn. com. Mich. Bar, 1967-73, cir. cit. adminstrn. com., 1974—, ct. adminstrn. com. Detroit Bar, 1981—. Pres. Grosse Pointe Little League, 1974; active YMCA Indian Guides; deacon, trustee, elder Presbyn. Ch. Served to capt. U.S. Army, 1956-60. Mem. ABA, Mich. Bar Assn., Oakland County Bar Assn., Detroit Bar Assn. (adminstrn. com. negligency law 1981—, cir. ct. com. 1985—), Assn. Def. Trial Counsel (pres. 1975-76), Mich. Def. Trial Counsel, Phi Alpha Delta. Republican. Lodge: Elks. Personal injury, State civil litigation, Federal civil litigation. Office: 1805 Ford Bldg Detroit MI 48226

ROWE, JAMES HENRY, III, lawyer; b. Washington, June 6, 1951; s. James Henry Jr. and Elizabeth (Ulman) R.; m. Lucy Smith Adams, June 20, 1981. BA, LLB cum laude, Harvard U., 1973; JD, Georgetown U., 1979. Bar: U.S. Dist. Ct. (so. and ea. dists.) N.Y. 1980, U.S. Dist. Ct. D.C. 1985, U.S. Ct. Appeals (D.C. cir.) 1985. Assoc. Curtis, Mallet-Prevost, Colt & Mosle, N.Y.C., 1979-83, Washington, 1983-86; ptnr. Corcoran, Youngman & Rowe, Washington, 1986—; trustee Legal Aid Soc., Washington, 1985—. mem. presdl. campaign activities Senate Select Com., Washington, 1973-74, Senate intelligence com., 1975, campaign Carter for Pres., Atlanta, 1976; counsel campaign Hollings for Pres., Washington, 1984—, Hollings for U.S. Senate, Washington, 1985-86, com. Tim Wirth for Senate, Washington, 1986—; trustee com. of 100 on Fed. City, Washington, 1985—. Democrat. Clubs: Federal City, Harvard (Washington). Federal civil litigation, Legislative, Administrative and regulatory. Home: 3539 Edmunds St NW Washington DC 20007 Office: Corcoran Youngman & Rowe 1511 K St NW Suite 1100 Washington DC 20005

ROWE, PAUL ANDREW, lawyer; b. Budapest, Hungary, June 9, 1936; came to U.S., 1939; s. Bela and Mary (Laszlo) Rosenberg; children—Jacqueline, Douglas. A.B., Tufts U., 1958; LL.B., Columbia U., 1961. Bar: N.Y. 1961, U.S. Dist. Ct. (so. dist.) N.Y. 1961, N.J. 1962, U.S. Dist. Ct. N.J. 1962, U.S. Ct. Appeals (3d cir.) 1979, U.S. Dist. Ct. (ea. dist.) N.Y. 1981; cert. civil trial atty. Ptnr., Greenbaum, Rowe, Smith, Ravin, Davis & Bergstein, and predecessors firms, Newark, 1962—; lectr. Inst. Continuing Legal Edn. Served with USAR, 1961-67. Mem. ABA, N.J. State Bar Assn., Essex County Bar Assn. (trustee 1981-85, sec. 1985—, treas. 1986), Assn. Trial Lawyers Am. State civil litigation, Federal civil litigation, Family and matrimonial. Office: Gateway One Newark NJ 07102 also: Engelhard Bldg PO Box 5600 Woodbridge NJ 07095

ROWE, ROBERT GAMMELL, III, lawyer; b. Ft. Meade, Md., July 9, 1954; s. Robert Gammell Jr. and Ann-Marie Elizabeth (Johnson) R. AB summa cum laude, Bowdoin Coll., 1976; JD cum laude, Boston U., 1979; LLM, Georgetown U., 1983. Bar: Pa. 1979, Mass. 1979, U.S. Dist. Ct. (ea. dist.) Pa. 1979, D.C. 1980. Officer regulatory compliance Riggs Nat. Bank, Washington, 1980-82, asst. v.p., 1982-85; asst. v.p. Nat. Bank Washington, 1985—. Sec. Arlington Players, Va., 1984; treas. MSII Homeowners Assn., Alexandria, 1984-85. SURDNA Found. fellow, 1975; recipient Sylvia Robinson award Boston U., 1979. Mem. ABA, D.C. Bar Assn., Phi Beta Kappa. Republican. Lutheran. Avocations: community theater, running, scuba diving. Banking, Administrative and regulatory, Contracts commercial. Office: Nat Bank Washington 4340 Connecticut Ave NW Washington DC 20008

ROWE, RUSSELL PAUL, lawyer, utility company official; b. Denver, Nov. 7, 1946; s. Russell W. and Letitia A. (Smith) R.; m. Daviana Oliphant, Dec. 20, 1964; children—Russell W., Jordan M. B.A. with distinction, U. Colo., 1967, J.D., 1970. Bar: Colo. 1970, U.S. Dist. Ct. Colo. 1970, U.S. Ct. Appeals (l0th cir.) 1972, U.S. Supreme Ct. 1976. Clk. to judge U.S. Dist. Ct. Colo., 1970-71; assoc. DeMuth, Eiberger, Kemp & Backus, and predecessors, Denver, 1971-75, ptnr., 1976-78; atty. Mountain Bell Telephone Co., Denver, 1978-84, Colo. gen. atty., 1984—; gen. counsel, dir. NCS, Inc., Englewood, Colo., 1983-84; dir. Vesta Group, Inc., 1986-87; sec., dir. Video Alert, 1985— v.p., gen. counsel El Paso Telephone Co., 1985—; counsel, mem. Gov.'s Com. Personnel Mgmt., 1980-81; guest lectr. Hastings Coll. Law, 1982. Mem. adv. bd. Colo. Assn. Occupational Nurses, 1982-83. Colo. U. Regents scholar, 1964-68; Flatirons Found. scholar, 1967-70. Mem. ABA, Colo. Bar Assn., Denver Bar Assn., Colo. Assn. Corp. Counsel, Phi Beta Kappa. Republican. Lutheran. Editor/revisor: King's Colorado Practice, 1976-77. Labor, Public utilities, Consumer commercial. Home: 8460 E Jamison Circle S Englewood CO 80112 Office: 931 14th St #1300 Denver CO 80202

ROWE, THOMAS DUDLEY, JR., legal educator; b. Richmond, Va., Feb. 26, 1942; s. Thomas Dudley and Georgia Rosamond (Stripp) R. B.A., Yale U., 1964; M.Phil., Oxford U., Eng., 1967; J.D., Harvard U., 1970. Bar: D.C. 1971, N.C. 1976. Law clk. to assoc. justice Potter Stewart U.S. Supreme Ct., 1970-71; asst. counsel adminstrv. practice subcom. U.S. Senate, 1971-73; assoc. Miller, Cassidy, Larroca & Lewin, Washington, 1973-75; assoc. prof. Duke U. Sch. Law, Durham, N.C., 1975-79, prof., 1979—, assoc. dean for research, 1981-84; vis. prof. Georgetown U. Law Ctr., Washington, 1980-81, U. Mich. Law Sch., Ann Arbor, fall 1985; fellow U.S. Dept. Justice, Washington, 1980-81. Contbr. articles to profl. jours. Bd. dirs. Pvt. Adjud. Ctr. Recipient Disting. Teaching award Duke Bar Assn., 1985; Rhodes scholar, 1964-67. Mem. ABA, Am. Law Inst. (adviser preliminary study of complex litigation 1985-86, project dir. Better Way Study 1986—). Democrat. Legal education, Federal civil litigation, Civil rights. Office: Duke U Sch Law Durham NC 27706-2580

ROWLAND, GILFORD GLENN, lawyer; b. Chariton, Iowa, Oct. 25, 1899; s. Charles A. and Eliza Maria (Vinsel) R.; m. Mary Elizabeth Schmalhorst, Oct. 18, 1930; 1 son, Gilford G. B.A. with gt. distinction, Stanford U., 1923, J.D., 1925. Bar: Calif. 1925, U.S. Dist Ct. (no. dist.) Calif. 1925, U.S. Ct. Appeals (9th cir.) 1925, U.S. Supreme Ct. 1956. Assoc. Butler, Van Dyke & Desmond, Sacramento, 1925-28; atty. Calif. State Automobile Assn., Sacramento, 1928-32; sole practice, Sacramento, 1932-34; ptnr. Rowland & Parker, and predecessor firms Rowland & Craven and Rowland & Paras, Sacramento, 1936—; dean McGeorge Sch. Law, 1929-37. Served with U.S. Army, 1918. Mem. Sacramento County Bar Assn. (judiciary com. 1959-69), State Bar Calif. (bd. govs. 1934-38, pres. 1937-38, jud. selection com. 1960-65, revision rules of profl. conduct com. 1971-72, history of law of Calif. com. 1979-81), ABA; life mem. Am. Bar Found., Am. Law Inst., Am Judicature Soc.; mem. Sacramento Met. C. of C. (dir. 1946-48), Phi Beta Kappa. Republican. Clubs: Sutter, Del Paso Country (Sacramento). General practice, Labor, Legislative. Office: 1151 Robertson Way Sacramento CA 95818

ROWLAND, RICHARD ARTHUR, lawyer; b. Tracy, Minn., Nov. 29, 1923; s. Richard Harlan and Elfrieda C. (Bendixen) R.; m. Lorraine M. Wandling, June 12, 1945; 1 child, Leslie Ann. BS in Chem. Engring., S.D. Sch. Mines, 1949; JD, U. Nebr., 1981. Bar: Nebr. 1982, U.S. Dist. Ct. Nebr. 1982, U.S. Ct. Appeals (8th cir.) 1982, U.S. Supreme Ct. 1986. Commd. 2d lt. U.S. Army, 1943, advanced through grades to capt., 1954; asst. chief water resource planning div. C.E. U.S. Army, Omaha, to 1979; ret. U.S. Army, 1984; sole practice Omaha, 1982—. Mem. Am. Trial Lawyers Assn., Nebr. Bar Assn. (chmn. gen. practice sect. 1984-86), Omaha Bar Assn., Delta Theta Phi. Family and matrimonial, Probate, Real property. Home: 645 Beverly Dr Omaha NE 68114 Office: 1613 Farnam St Suite 517 Omaha NE 68102

ROWLAND, SAM E., lawyer; b. New Blaine, Ark., Feb. 9, 1934; s. Ray D. and Wordna (Reed) R.; m. Betsy Kay Leach, June 4, 1982; children—Melinda, Michelle, Stuart. B.B.A., Tex. A&M U., 1955; J.D., So. Meth. U., 1960. Bar: Tex. 1960, U.S. Dist. Ct. (so. dist.) Tex. 1973, U.S. Ct. Appeals (5th cir.) 1977, (11th cir.) 1982, U.S. Supreme Ct. 1976. Contract adminstr. Tex. Instruments, Dallas, 1955-60; v.p., dir. Internat. Data Systems, Dallas, 1960-64, Tex. Aluminum Co., Dallas, 1964-67; pres. Rowland Corp., Dallas, 1967-69; pres. ADS Corp., Mpls., 1969-72; sr. ptnr. Rowland & Keim, Houston, 1972—. Served to 2d lt. U.S. Army, 1957. Mem. ABA, Tex. Bar Assn., Houston Bar Assn. Clubs: Exchange (pres. 1974-76 (Houston); Aggie (bd. dirs. 1980—), Tex. A&M Lettermans Assn. (bd. dirs. 1981—) (College Station, Tex.). General corporate, Securities, Oil and gas leasing. Office: Rowland & Keim 1360 Post Oak Blvd Suite 1700 Houston TX 77056

ROWLETTE, ROGER LEE, lawyer; b. Mpls., July 31, 1952; s. Joseph Rowlette and Mona Clarice (Hintz) Krone; m. Virginia Ann Sacco, Aug. 18, 1973. B in Applied Studies, U. Minn., 1975; JD cum laude, William Mitchell Coll. Law, 1982. Bar: Minn. 1982, U.S. Dist. Ct. Minn. 1982. Assoc. Johnson & Lindberg, P.A., Mpls., 1983—; arbitrator no-fault system Minn. Ct., Mpls., 1986. Editor William Mitchell Law Rev., 1980-82. Recipient award of merit William Mitchell Alumni Assn., 1982. Mem. ABA, Minn. Bar Assn., Hennepin County Bar Assn., Phi Alpha Delta. Republican. Lutheran. Avocations: golfing, running. Insurance, Federal civil litigation, State civil litigation. Home: 1653 Bohland Saint Paul MN 55116 Office: Johnson & Lindberg PA One Appletree Sq Suite 900 Minneapolis MN 55420

ROWLEY, HORACE PEREZ, III, lawyer; b. Houston, Dec. 7, 1940; s. Horace Perez Jr. and Monita (Hohenstein) R.; m. Wendy B. Kornegay, Oct. 20, 1979; 1 child, Hardin Parisher. B.B.A., Tulane U., 1962, LL.B., 1967. Bar: La. 1967, U.S. Ct. Appeals (5th cir.) 1967, U.S. Dist. Ct. (ea. dist.) La. 1967, D.C. 1970, U.S. Supreme Ct. 1970, N.Y. 1971, U.S. Tax Ct. 1971, U.S. Ct. Mil. Appeals 1971, U.S. Ct. Claims 1971, U.S. Ct. Custom and Patent Appeals 1971, U.S. Dist. Ct. (mid. dist.) La. 1973, U.S. Dist. Ct. (we. dist.) La. 1983. Asst. U.S. atty. Dept. Justice, New Orleans, 1967-70; sole practice law, N.Y.C., 1971-75, New Orleans, 1976—. Founder Suburban Rural Rights Coalition, N.Y., N.J. and Conn., 1972, editor, pub. newsletter, 1972-75. Served to lt. (j.g.) USN, 1962-64. Mem. La. State Bar Assn., Assn. Trial Lawyers Am., N.Y. State Trial Lawyers Assn., New Orleans Bd. Trade. Roman Catholic. Federal civil litigation, Construction, Consumer commercial. Home and Office: 116 Fairway Dr Covington LA 70433

ROY, ELSIJANE TRIMBLE, U.S. dist. judge; b. Lonoke, Ark., Apr. 2, 1916; d. Thomas Clark and Elsie Jane (Walls) Trimble; m. James M. Roy, Nov. 23, 1943; 1 son, James Morrison. J.D., U. Ark., Fayetteville, 1939; LL.D. (hon.), U. Ark., Little Rock, 1978. Bar: Ark. 1939. Atty. Ark. Revenue Dept., Little Rock, 1939-44; mem. firm Reid, Evrard & Roy, Blytheville, Ark., 1945-54, Roy & Roy, Blytheville, 1954-63; law clk. Ark. Supreme Ct., Little Rock, 1963-65; asso. justice Ark. Supreme Ct., 1975-77; U.S. dist. judge for Eastern and Western Dists. Ark., Little Rock, 1977—; judge Pulaski County (Ark.) Circuit Ct., Little Rock, 1966; asst. atty. gen. Ark., Little Rock, 1967; sr. law clk. U.S. Dist. Ct., Little Rock and Ft. Smith, 1967-75; Mem. med. adv. com. U. Ark. Med. Center, 1952-54; Committeewoman Democratic Party 16th Jud. Dist., 1940-42; vice chmn. Ark. Dem. State Com., 1946-48; mem. chmn. com. Ark. Constnl. Commn., 1967-68. Recipient Disting. Alumna citation U. Ark., 1978, Gayle Pettus Pontz award, 1986; named Ark. Woman of Yr. Bus. and Profl. Women's Club, 1969, 76, Outstanding Appellate Judge Ark. Trial Lawyers Assn., 1976-77. Mem. Nat. Assn. Women Lawyers, Am. Bar Assn., Ark. Bar Assn., AAUW, Little Rock Women Lawyers (pres. 1939, 42), Ark. Women Lawyers (pres. 1940-41), Mortar Bd., P.E.O., Delta Theta Phi., Chi Omega. Club: Altrusa. Jurisprudence. Office: US Post Office and Courthouse PO Box 3255 Little Rock AR 72203

ROY, JAMES ROBERT, lawyer; b. Lewiston, Maine, Aug. 11, 1945; s. Robert P. and Margaret (Donahue) R. Student, Nasson Coll., 1965; BA in History, U. Maine, 1968; JD, U. Conn., 1973. Bar: Conn. 1975. Pension and tax counsel Nat. Planning & Service Orgn., Southbury, Conn., 1976-78; tax atty., advisor IRS, Washington, 1978—; adj. prof. tax Morse Sch. Bus., Hartford, Conn., 1975; photographer chpt. 65 Nat. Treasury Employees Union, Washington, 1982—. Freelance photographer (recipient various awards 1978—, copyrighted photos 1982-84) 1978—. Served with USN, 1968-70, Vietnam. Mem. Conn. Bar Assn. (prepaid legal com.), Potomac Soc. Stereo Photographers (treas. 1984—), Hartford Sports Car Club (pres. 1973-74), Phi Kappa Phi. Roman Catholic. Club: Greater Washington Council of Camera (chmn. competition 1985—). Corporate taxation, Personal income taxation, Pension, profit-sharing, and employee benefits. Home: 1021 Arlington Blvd E-706 Arlington VA 22209 Office: IRS 1111 Constitution Ave NW Room 5409 Washington DC 20224

ROY, RICHARD E., lawyer; b. Portland, Oreg., July 7, 1939; s. Leighton Eugene and Dorris Mary (Scott) R.; m. Jeanne Beverly Hawley, June 9, 1962; children: Bradley Scott, Jeffrey Alan, Melinda Louise. BS in Engring., Oreg. State U., 1961; MS in Engring., Stanford State U., 1966; JD, Harvard U., 1970. Bar: Oreg. 1970, U.S. Dist. Ct. Oreg. 1970. Assoc. Stoel, Rives, Boley, Fraser & Wyse, Portland, 1970-76, ptnr., 1976—; mem. corp. commrs. task force corp. law, chmn. 1985; mem. model bus. corp. Act Task Force, 1986-87. Editor: Advising Oregon Businesses, 5 Vols., 1985. Chmn. Oreg. Water Policy Rev. Bd., Salem, 1975-77; mem. fin. com. Representative Les Aucoin, Portland, 1985-86; pres., bd. dirs. Oreg. Scholastic Chess Found., Portland, 1983-87. Served to lt. USN, 1961-65. Mem. Oreg. State Bar Assn. (chmn. bus. and corp. sect. 1982-83), Profl. Engrs. Soc. of Oreg. Democrat. Club: City (Portland). Avocations: music, backpacking. Home: 2420 SW Boundary Portland OR 97201 Office: Stoel Rives Boley Fraser Wyse 900 SW 5th Ave Portland OR 97204

ROY, WILLIAM ALAN, lawyer; b. Detroit, Mar. 24, 1949; s. Vincent Odell and Mary Rita (Sullivan) R.; m. Sharon Ann Wilson, July 2, 1971; children: Robin Christine, Susannah Christine. BA, U. Mich., 1971, JD, 1974. Bar: Mich. 1974, U.S. Dist. Ct. (ea. dist.) Mich. 1975, U.S. Ct. Appeals (6th cir.) 1977. Ptnr. Bushnell, Gage, Doctoroff & Reizen, Southfield, Mich., 1974-83, Roy, Shecter & Vocht, PC, Birmingham, Mich., 1983—. Mem. Mich. Bar Assn. (chmn. gen practice sect. 1985—, treas. 1983-85, arbitration com. 1983—), Oakland County Bar Assn. (treas. gen. practice sect. 1983-85), Southfield Bar Assn., Am. Trial Lawyers Assn., Mich. Trial Lawyers Assn. Republican. Roman Catholic. Avocations: sports participation, golf hockey, baseball, art appreciation, reading. Federal civil litigation, State civil litigation, General practice. Home: 1601 Sheffield Birmingham MI 48008 Office: Roy Shecter & Vocht PC 877 S Adams Rd Suite 302 Birmingham MI 48011

ROYCE, RAYMOND WATSON, lawyer, rancher, citrus grower; b. West Palm Beach, Fla., Mar. 5, 1936; s. Wilbur E. and Veda (Watson) R.; m. Catherine L. Setzer, Apr. 21, 1979; children—Raymond, Steven, Nancy, Kathryn. B.C.E., U. Fla., 1958, J.D., 1961. Bar: Fla. 1961, U.S. Dist. Ct. (so. dist.) Fla. 1961, U.S. Ct. Appeals (5th cir.) 1961, U.S. Ct. Appeals (11th cir.) 1981. Assoc. William W. Blakeslee, Palm Beach, Fla., 1961-62; pres. Scott, Royce, Harris & Bryan P.A., Palm Beach, 1962—, pres. 1982—; chmn. Palm Beach County Zoning Task Force; bd. dirs. Econ. Council. Mem. Fla. Bar (gov. 1974-78), Palm Beach County Bar Assn. (pres. 1973-74), Am. Judicature Soc., Fla. Trial Lawyers Assn., Fla. Citrus Mut., Fla. Cattleman's Assn., Insternat. Brangus Breeders Assn., Phi Delta Phi, Fla. Blue Key. Democrat. Presbyterian. Real property, Administrative and regulatory, General corporate. Home: 5550 Whirlaway Rd Palm Beach Gardens FL 33418 Office: 450 Royal Palm Way Palm Beach FL 33480

ROYER, DONALD E., corporate lawyer, financial holding company executive; b. 1949. Grad., Ariz. State U.; JD, Western State U., 1977. V.p. Am. Savs. and Loan Assn., Irvine, Calif., 1983-85, exec. v.p., acting gen. counsel, 1985, sr. exec. v.p., gen. counsel, 1985—; v.p., asst. gen. counsel Fin. Corp. of Am. (parent), Irvine, Calif., 1983-84, sr. v.p., acting gen. counsel, 1984-85; exec. v.p. Fin. Corp. of Am. (parent), Irvine, 1985—. Office: Fin Corp of Am 18401 Von Karman Ave Irvine CA 92715 *

ROYLANCE, D. C., lawyer; b. Bismarck, N.D., June 18, 1920; s. William G. and Freda (Zender) R.; m. Joan Stieber, 1954 (dec. 1973); children—Stephen Michael, Kathleen Moore; m. Mary Lou Wagner, 1978. LL.B., George Washington U., 1952. Bar: D.C. bar 1952, U.S. Supreme Ct. bar 1960. Now mem. firm Roylance, Abrams, Berdo & Goodman, Washington. Mem. ABA, Bar Assn. D.C., Am. Intellectual Property Law Assn., Soc. Plastics Engrs., Order of Coif, Phi Alpha Delta. Home: 12210 Glen Mill Rd Potomac MD 20854 Office: 1225 Connecticut Ave Washington DC 20036

ROYSTON, CHRISTOPHER MICHAEL, lawyer; b. Tokyo, Feb. 16, 1950; s. John Peter and Elizabeth Mylod (McNamara) R.; m. Rebecca Lukens Young, June 9, 1973; children: Brendan Thomas, Martha McNamara. BA, U. Pa., 1972; JD, Boston U., 1976. Bar: Conn. 1976, U.S. Dist. Ct. Conn. 1976. Staff atty. legal services State of Conn., Bridgeport, 1976-80; assoc. Cohn & Birnbaum, Hartford, Conn., 1980-81; ptnr. Coan, Lewendon & Royston, New Haven, 1981—. Mem. ABA, Conn. Bar Assn., Comml. Law League. Bankruptcy, Contracts commercial, Personal injury. Home: 280 McKinley Ave New Haven CT 06515 Office: Coan Lewendon & Royston 18 Trumbull St New Haven CT 06511

ROZANSKI, STANLEY HOWARD, lawyer; b. N.Y.C., July 19, 1952; s. Israel and Frida (Huber) R.; m. Ilene Newman, Dec. 31, 1975; 1 child, Justin. BA, Hunter Coll., 1974; JD, San Fernando Coll. Law, 1977. Bar: Calif. 1978, U.S. Dist. Ct. (cen. dist.) Calif. 1978, U.S. Ct. Appeals (9th cir.) 1982. Ptnr. Mackey & Rozanski, Los Angeles, 1980—, Mackey, Rozanski & Friedland, San Jose, Calif., 1983—; judge pro tem Los Angeles County Cts., 1985—. Recipient Outstanding Contributions award State Bar Calif., 1985. Mem. Calif. Bar Assn., Assn. Trial Lawyers Am., Calif. Trial Lawyers Assn., Los Angeles Trial Lawyers Assn., ABA, Los Angeles County Bar Assn., Beverly Hills Bar Assn. Jewish. Avocations: skiing, swimming, golf. Criminal, Personal injury, Insurance. Office: Mackey & Rozanski 11330 Santa Monica Blvd Los Angeles CA 90025

RUANE, JAMES JOSEPH, lawyer; b. Jersey City, June 29, 1949; s. William J. and Margaret (Moran) R.; m. Patricia O'Neill, Dec. 18, 1971; children: James, Genevieve, Brendan. BA, Fairfield U., 1971; JD, U. Conn., 1977. Bar: Conn. 1977, U.S. Dist. Ct. Conn. 1978, U.S. Ct. Appeals (2d cir.) 1984. Asst. pub. defender State of Conn., Bridgeport, 1977-84; assoc. Meehan & Meehan, Bridgeport, 1984—. Mem. Bridgeport Bar Assn. (chmn. criminal law com. 1986—), St. Thomas More Soc. (chmn. 1985-86). Democrat. Roman Catholic. Criminal. Office: Meehan & Meehan 76 Lyon Terr Bridgeport CT 06604

RUANO, WILLIAM J., patent atty.; b. Pitts., Apr. 20, 1908; s. Urbano and Maria (De Nardo) R.; m. Adelaide Maffei, Sept. 24, 1930 (dec. 1976); children—William J., Joy, Mary Elaine, Robert. B.S. in Elec. Engring., Carnegie Mellon U., 1929; LL.B., George Washington U., 1933; M.Patent Law, Washington Coll. Law, 1934. Bar: D.C. 1933, Ill. 1945, U.S. Supreme Ct. 1940. Patent atty. Westinghouse Electric Co., Pitts., 1938-42, Christy, Parmelee & Strickland, Pitts., 1946-49; sole practice, Pitts., 1949—. Sch. dir. Upper St. Clair Twp.; mem. bd. commrs. Upper St. Clair Twp., 1964-78, pres., 1974-77, dist. justice, 1977-78. Served as lt. col. Signal Corps and C.E., U.S. Army, 1942-46; PTO. Named Outstanding Citizen of Upper St. Clair, Republican Party, 1974. Mem. ABA, Am. Patent Law Assn., Pitts. Patent Law Assn. (pres. 1975). Republican. Roman Catholic. Clubs: Bethel-St. Clair Rotary (pres. 1974), Elks (Bethel Park, Pa.). Patentee nuclear reactor control. Patent, Trademark and copyright. Home: 102 Wiltshire Dr Pittsburgh PA 15241 Office: 402 St Clair Bldg Pittsburgh PA 15241

RUARK, DAVIS RUTHERFORD, lawyer; b. Salisbury, Md., July 29, 1955; s. Elmer Francis and Eunice (Hayes) R.; m. Jayne Gray Lindeke, Apr. 1, 1978 (div. Apr. 1981); m. Sara Susan Donny, July 28, 1984; 1 child, Davis Lee. BA, Wake Forest U., 1977; JD, U. Balt., 1981. Bar: Md. 1981, U.S. Dist. Ct. Md. 1982. Law clk. to presiding justice Md. Cir. Ct., Salisbury, 1981-82; dep. state's atty. State of Md., Salisbury, 1982-87, state's atty., 1987—; lectr. in criminal justice U. Md. Eastern Shore, Princess Anne, 1984—; guest lectr. Salisbury State Coll., 1986. Bd. dirs. Am. Cancer Soc., Salisbury, 1983, Newtown Neighborhood Assn., Salisbury, 1986. Recipient Disting. Service award Salisbury Police Dept., 1985; Fred E. Inbau scholar, 1985. Mem. ABA, Md. Bar Assn., Wicomico County Bar Assn., Nat. Dist. Attys. Assn., Md. State's Attys. Assn., Wicomico County Hist. Soc. (bd. dirs. 1985—). Democrat. Baptist. Lodges: Masons, Lions. Criminal, Legal education. Home: 310 Park Ave PO Box 934 Salisbury MD 21801 Office: State's Attys Office Courthouse PO Box 1006 Salisbury MD 21801

RUBAGUMYA, GEORGE WILLIAM, lawyer; b. Ft. Portal, Toro, Uganda, Oct. 9, 1955; came to U.S., 1973; s. Gabriel and Veredianne (Kigennye) Rwabutogo. BA in Econs., U. Nebr.; JD, Creighton U.; LLM, London Sch. Econs. Bar: Tex. 1982, U.S. Dist. Ct. (no. dist.) Tex. 1982, U.S. Ct. Internat. Trade 1982, U.S. Ct. Appeals (5th cir.) 1982. Assoc. Orr & Orr, Ft. Worth, 1982-84; asst. atty. gen. State of Tex., Austin, 1984-86; assoc. Gray & Becker, Austin, 1986—; cons. internat. trade. Federal civil litigation, State civil litigation, Private international. Office: Gray & Becker 323 Congress Ave McKean-Eilers Bldg Austin TX 78701

RUBENDALL, CHARLES WESLEY, II, lawyer; b. Harrisburg, Pa., Sept. 14, 1950; s. Robert Lee and Pauline Marie (April) R. BA, Yale U., 1972; JD cum laude, Dickinson Sch. Law, 1976. Bar: Pa. 1976, U.S. Dist. Ct. (mid. dist.) Pa. 1977, U.S. Tax Ct. 1978, U.S. Ct. Appeals (3d cir.) 1981, U.S. Dist. Ct. (ea. dist.) Pa. 1982, U.S. Claims Ct. 1984. Assoc. Keefer, Wood, Allen & Rahal, Harrisburg, Pa., 1976-81, ptnr., 1981—; mem. lawyers adv. com. U.S. Dist. Ct. (mid. dist.) Pa., 1986—; lectr. on trial advocacy Dickinson Sch. of Law, Carlisle, Pa., 1985-87. Editor in chief Dickinson Law Rev., 1975-76. Alumni trustee Dickinson Sch. Law, 1977-80. Mem. ABA, Def. Research Inst., Pa. Def. Inst., Pa. Bar Assn., Dauphin County Bar Assn., York County Bar Assn. Federal civil litigation, State civil litigation, Personal injury. Office: Keefer Wood Allen & Rahal 210 Walnut St PO Box 11963 Harrisburg PA 17108-1963

RUBENFELD, STANLEY IRWIN, lawyer; b. N.Y.C., Dec. 7, 1930; s. George and Mildred (Rose) R.; m. Caryl P. Ellner, June 8, 1952; children: Leslie Ann, Lise Susan, Kenneth Michael. B.A., Columbia U., 1952, J.D., 1956. Bar: N.Y. 1956. Practice law N.Y.C., 1956-65, 68—, 1965-68; assoc. Shearman & Sterling, 1956-65; ptnr. Shearman & Sterling, Paris, 1965-68, N.Y.C., 1968—; sec. Dowell Schlumberger; bd. dirs. Orbisphere Corp., Orbisphere Labs. Editor-in-chief: Columbia Law Rev., 1955-56; contbr. articles to profl. jours. Chmn. task force Columbia U. Law Sch., N.Y.C., 1982—; bd. dirs., past pres. Port Washington (N.Y.) Community Chest; former bd. dirs. Residents for a More Beautiful Port Washington. Served to lt. (j.g.) USNR, 1952-54. Stone scholar, 1951-52, 54-55, 55-56; Rockefeller Found. grantee, 1955. Mem. ABA, N.Y. State Bar Assn. (exec. com. tax sect.), Assn. of Bar of City of N.Y. (tax com., past chmn. com. recruitment lawyers), Nat. Assn. Law Placement (past dir., exec. com.), Columbia Law Sch. Alumni Assn. (chmn. placement com., past dir.), Columbia Coll. Alumni Assn. (pres.), Tax Club (past chmn.), Phi Delta Phi, Tau Epsilon Phi. Clubs: Downtown Assn; Broad St. (N.Y.C.). Corporate taxation, Personal income taxation, General corporate. Home: 41 Longview Rd Port Washington NY 11050 Office: Shearman & Sterling 53 Wall St New York NY 10005

RUBENS, JAMES I., lawyer; b. Rochester, N.Y., Jan. 16, 1954; s. Leonard I. and Jane (Waldman) R.; m. Jami Rosenblum, June 6, 1982. BS in Engring., U. Pa., 1976; JD cum laude, U. Miami, 1979. Bar: Fla. 1980, N.Y. 1980, Mass. 1983. Assoc. Mousaw, Vigdor, Reeves, Heilbronner & Kroll, Rochester, 1979-83; ptnr. Craig & Macauley P.C., Boston, 1983—. Banking, Securities, General corporate. Office: Craig & Macauley 600 Atlantic Ave Boston MA 02210

RUBENS, JANE CORA, lawyer, law librarian; b. Richmond, Va., June 5, 1945; s. Joseph M. and Majorie C. (Ostreweis) R. AB, Vassar Coll., 1967; MS in Library Sci., Columbia U., 1968; JD, Fordham U., 1979. Bar: N.Y. 1980, U.S. Dist. Ct. (so. and ea. dists.) N.Y. 1980, U.S. Supreme Ct. 1986. Librarian Fordham U., N.Y.C., 1968-70; head librarian Coudert Bros., N.Y.C., 1970-80, assoc., 1980—. Mem. ABA, Assn. of Bar of City of N.Y., Consular Law Soc. (asst. treas. 1984—), Am. Assn. Law Librarians, Am. Immigration Lawyers Assn. General corporate. Home: 220 E 63rd St New York NY 10021 Office: Coudert Bros 200 Park Ave New York NY 10166

RUBENSTEIN, ALLEN IRA, lawyer; b. N.Y.C., Apr. 1, 1942; s. Nathan and Ida (Yankowitz) R.; m. Carole Toby Ballin, Aug. 24, 1963; children—Daniel Stuart, Samuel Philip. B.S. in Physics, CCNY, 1962; Ph.D. in Physics, MIT, 1967; J.D., Boston U., 1974. Bar: U.S. Dist. Ct. (so. and ea. dists.) N.Y. 1975, U.S. Ct. Appeals (2d cir.) 1975, U.S. Ct. Appeals (1st and fed. cir.) 1982. Physicist Stanford U., Calif., 1967-69; fellow Weizmann Inst., Rehovoth, Israel, 1969-71; assoc. Kenyon & Kenyon, N.Y.C., 1974-82; ptnr. Gottlieb, Rackman & Reisman, P.C., N.Y.C., 1982—; adj. prof. Boston U., 1971-74. Trustee Beth Israel Anshei Emet, Bklyn., 1981—. Recipient Ward medal CCNY, N.Y.C., 1962. Mem. Am. Phys. Soc., ABA, Phi Beta Kappa. Patent, Trademark and copyright, Federal civil litigation. Home: 59 Livingston St Brooklyn NY 11201 Office: Gottlieb Rackman & Reisman PC 1430 Broadway New York NY 10018

RUBENSTEIN, HERBERT R., lawyer; b. Shreveport, La., Apr. 22, 1953; s. Nathan A. and Yetta (Rosenberg) R.; m. Laurie J. Bassi, June 8, 1980; children: Jason Bassi, Kathleen Bassi. BA in Politics, Washington and Lee U., 1974; diploma, U. Bristol, Briston, Eng., 1975; M in Pub. Affairs, U. Tex., 1977; JD, Georgetown U., 1982. Bar: D.C. 1982, Md. 1983, U.S. Dist. Ct. D.C. 1983, Va. 1984, U.S. Dist. Ct. (ea. dist.) Va. 1985, U.S. Ct. Appeals (fed. cir.) 1985, U.S. Ct. Appeals (4th cir.) 1986. Sr. research assoc. Am. Insts. Research, Washington, 1977-80; policy analyst U.S. Dept. Health and Human Services, Washington, 1980-83; assoc. Kuder, Temple & Smollar, Washington, 1983, Margolius, Davis, Finkelstein & Rider, Washington, 1984-85; prin. Herbert Rubenstein and Assocs., P.C., Washington, Md. and Va., 1985—. Co-precinct chmn. Jim Nathanson for City Council, Washington, 1986; mem. adv. bd. D.C. Hotline, Washington, 1984—; mem. dem. com. Ward III, 1986—. Recipient Internat. Study award Rotary Found. Internat., 1975; Lyndon B. Johnson merit fellowship Lyndon B. Johnson Sch. Pub. Affairs, 1976. Mem. ABA, D.C. Bar Assn., Md. Bar Assn., Va. Bar Assn., Assn. Trial Lawyers Am., Phi Beta Kappa. Democrat. Jewish. Avocations: golf, snow and water skiing, running. General practice, Legislative, Family and matrimonial. Home: 3820 Calvert St NW Washington DC 20007 Office: Herbert Rubenstein and Assocs PC 1818 North St SW West Lobby Washington DC 20036

RUBENSTEIN, HY DAVID, county attorney; b. Bklyn., Aug. 9, 1956; s. Morton and Maureen (Herman) R.; m. Margo Reva Brooks, June 10, 1979; children: Benyamin Yosef, Shoshana Nehama, Sara Etel, Atara Gitel. BA in Am. Studies, John Jay Coll. Criminal Justice, N.Y.C., 1977; JD, Bklyn. Law Sch., 1980. Bar: N.Y. 1980, U.S. Ct. Mil. Appeals 1981, Ariz. 1984, U.S. Dist. Ct. Ariz. 1984, U.S. Supreme Ct. 1984. Assoc. Harold Hyams & Assocs., Tucson, 1984-85; dep. county atty. Pima County, Tucson, 1985—; lectr. Sierra Vista (Ariz.) Sch. Real Estate, 1981-83; legal counsel Va'ad HaKashruth, Tucson, 1986—. V.p. Congregation Chofetz Chayim, Tucson, 1985—; mem. Nat. Council Synogogue Youth. Served to capt. JAGC, U.S. Army, 1980-84. Named one of Outstanding Young Men in Am., U.S. Jaycees, 1984. Mem. ABA, Ariz. Bar Assn., Pima County Bar Assn., Am. Trial Lawyers Assn., Orthodox Union N.Y. Jewish. Avocations: camping, off-road driving, ghost town hunting. Criminal, Personal injury, Probate. Home: 5720 E 5th St Tucson AZ 85711 Office: Pima County Atty 110 W Congress Tucson AZ 85701

RUBENSTEIN, MARK A., lawyer; b. Bridgeport, Conn., Apr. 12, 1946; s. Joseph and Ruth (Kaufman) R.; m. Jane N. Milberg, June 18, 1981; 1 dau., Michele I. Milberg. B.A., Boston U., 1968, J.D., 1971. Bar: Conn. 1971. Assoc. Goldman & Rosen, Bridgeport, 1973-77; ptnr. Rubenstein & Cederbaum, Westport, Conn., 1977-83; mng. ptnr. Rutkin, Rubenstein Effron & Ury, Westport, 1983—; Mem. internat. bd. dirs., internat. treas. Juvenile Diabetes Found. Internat., 1981-85; pres. Merritt Pkwy. adv. com. Mem. ABA (family law sect., child custody com.), Conn. Bar Assn. (exec. com. family law sect., real estate com.), Westport Bar Assn., Downtown Merchants Assn. (v.p.). Jewish. Family and matrimonial, Real property, General corporate. Home: 30 North Ave Westport CT 06880 Office: 121 Post Rd E PO Box 5143 Westport CT 06881

RUBENSTEIN, MARTIN JEFFREY, lawyer; b. Staten Island, N.Y., Dec. 14, 1947; s. Isidore and Sylvia (Grossman) R.; m. Billa Reiss, Aug. 18, 1973; children: Daniel, Arie. BA, Wagner Coll., 1970; JD, St. John's U., Jamaica, N.Y., 1973. Bar: N.Y. 1974, U.S. Dist. Ct. (so. and ea. dists.) N.Y. 1976. Atty. State of N.Y., N.Y.C., 1973-74; assoc. Kelner & Kelner, N.Y.C., 1974-86; sole practice N.Y.C., 1986—; Pres. Advanced Biotechmics Inc., N.Y.C., 1985—; prin. Telephoto Co. Contbr. articles to various newspapers. Mem. N.Y. State Bar Assn., N.Y. County Lawyers Assn. Personal injury, State civil litigation. Home: 20 Uxbridge St Staten Island NY 10314 Office: Kelmer & Kelmer 225 Broadway New York NY 10314

RUBENSTEIN, RICHARD EDWARD, legal educator; b. N.Y.C., Feb. 24, 1938; s. Harold Simon and Josephine (Feldman) R.; m. Elizabeth Marsh, Aug. 26, 1962 (div. Mar. 1975); children—Alec Louis, Matthew Robert; m. Brenda Libman, Sept. 21, 1975; children: Nicole Hana, Shana Elise. B.A. magna cum laude, Harvard U., 1959; J.D., 1963; M.A., Oxford U. (Eng.), 1961. Bar: D.C. 1964. Assoc. Steptoe & Johnson, Washington, 1963-67; asst. dir. Adlai Stevenson Inst. Internat. Affairs, Chgo., 1967-70; prof. polit. sci. Roosevelt U., Chgo., 1970-79; prof. law Antioch Sch. Law, Washington, 1979—; adv. cons. Nat. Commn. on Causes and Prevention Violence, Washington, 1968-69; lectr. Ctr. for Legal Studies, Washington, 1980—. Author: Rebels in Eden, 1970, Left Turn, 1973, Alchemisrs of Revolution, 1987; Editor: Mass Violence in America series, 1968, Great Courtroom Battles, 1974. Coordinator Chgo. Peace Action Coalition, 1970-72. Rhodes scholar Oxford U., 1959-61; Fulbright prof., Aix-en-Provence, France, 1976. Mem. Am. Assn. Polit. Sci., Am. Assn. Rhodes Scholars, Soc. Am. Law Tchrs., Conf. on Critical Legal Studies. Jewish. Legal education, Jurisprudence. Home: 5300 Ventnor Rd Bethesda MD 20816 Office: Antioch Sch of Law 2633 16th St NW Washington DC 20009

RUBENSTEIN, ROBERT MAYER, lawyer; b. Windsor, Ont., Can., May 18, 1951; s. Alfred Ian and Lilyan (Cherniak) R.; m. Theresa Ann Godek, June 29, 1976; children: Nicole, Andrea. Student, Oakland U., 1968-71; AB, U. Mich., 1971; postgrad., U. B.C., 1975-76; JD, U. Fla., 1978. Bar: Fla. 1978, U.S. Dist. Ct. (so. dist.) Fla. 1979, U.S. Ct. Claims 1979, U.S. Tax Ct. 1979, U.S. Ct. Appeals (5th cir.) 1979. Assoc. Greenberg, Traurig et al, Miami, Fla., 1978-83; ptnr. Finley, Kumble, Wagner, Heine, Underberg, Manley & Casey, Miami, 1984—. Mem. ABA, Fla. Bar Assn., Dade County Bar Assn., Order of Coif, Phi Beta Kappa. Jewish. Avocations: chess, sports. Corporate taxation. Office: Finley Kumble Wagner et al 777 Brickell Ave Miami FL 33131

RUBENSTEIN-KURSH, NAN, lawyer; b. Pitts., June 17, 1955; d. Erwin and Faye (Rosenfeld) Rubenstein; m. Steven R. Kursh, June 8, 1980; 1 child, Eliza Ashton. AB, Smith Coll., 1977; MA, U. Pa., 1979; JD, Northeastern U., 1982. Bar: Mass. 1982, Pa. 1983, U.S. Dist. Ct. Mass. 1983. Sole practice Sherborn, Mass., 1982-83; v.p. and counsel Blackacre Fin. Software, Inc., Framingham, Mass., 1983—, also bd. dirs. Contbr. articles to profl. jours. Mem. computer study com. Town of Sherborn, 1984-85. Mem. ABA (legal tech. adv. counsel, working group on real estate software), Mass. Bar Assn., Pa. Bar Assn. Jewish. Avocation: gardening. Computer, Real property, Trademark and copyright. Office: Blackacre Fin Software Inc Point West Pl 111 Speen St Framingham MA 01701

RUBERTO, ANTHONY JAMES, JR., district attorney; b. Pittsfield, Mass., Nov. 18, 1942; s. Anthony J. and Edith (Sonsini) R.; m. Linda M. Becerra, Feb. 14, 1970; 1 child, James A. B.A. in Econ., Boston Coll., 1965; J.D., Boston U., 1969. Bar: Mass. 1969, U.S. Dist. Ct. Mass. 1971, U.S. Supreme Ct. 1976. Ptnr., Ruberto & Ruberto, 1969-79; dist. ct. prosecutor Western Dist. Mass., Pittsfield, 1972-78; dist. atty. Berkshire County, Pittsfield, 1979—. Mem. Gov.'s Anti-Crime Council, 1983—, Victim Assistance Bd., 1983—. Named an Outstanding Young Man of Am., 1972, Dist. Atty. of Yr. State of Mass., 1986. Mem. Gov.'s Anti-Crime Council, Victim Assistance Bd. Mem. Nat. Dist. Atty.'s Assn. (bd. dirs.), Mass. Dist. Attys. Assn. (past pres.), Pittsfield Jaycees (pres. 1972). Democrat. Roman Catholic. Club: ITAM. Home: 257 Holmes Rd Pittsfield MA 01201 Office: Berkshire Dist Attys Office 44 Bank Row PO Box 1969 Pittsfield MA 01202

RUBIN, ALVIN BENJAMIN, judge; b. Alexandria, La., Mar. 13, 1920; s. Simon and Frances (Prussack) R.; m. Janice Ginsberg, Feb. 19, 1946; children: Michael H., David S. B.S. in Bus. Adminstrn, La. State U., 1941, LL.B., 1942. Bar: La. 1942. Sole practice Baton Rouge, 1946-66; ptnr. Sanders, Miller, Downing, Rubin & Kean, 1946-66; U.S. dist. judge Eastern Dist. La., 1966-77; U.S. circuit judge 5th Circuit Ct. Appeals, 1977—; adj. prof. law La. State U. Law Sch., 1946—; lectr. taxation Am. Law Inst., Tulane U. Tax Inst., Ga. Tax Inst., La. State U. Mineral Law Inst., vis. lectr. Law Sch. So. U., 1985—, Law Sch. Duke U., 1985—; arbitrator Fed. Mediation and Conciliation Service, 1964-66; vis. lectr. Duke U. Law Sch., 1986—, So. La. Law Sch., 1986—; bd. dirs. Fed. Jud. Ctr. Author: (with McMahon) Louisiana Pleadings and Judicial Forms Annotated, (with Janice G. Rubin) Louisiana Trust Handbook, (with Gerald LeVan) Louisiana Wills and Trusts, (with Anthony D. Leo) Law Clerk's Handbook; bd. editors: Manual for Complex Litigation, 1983—. Chmn. Baton Rouge Zoning Study Com.; mem. La. Legislative Adminstrv. Procedure Com. Sec. Baton Rouge United Givers Fund, 1954-66; bd. dirs. C.L.E.P.R., 1970-80, 86, Cornell U., 1980-86, New Orleans Jewish Welfare Fedn., 1972-76; mem. vis. com. Law Sch., U. Chgo., 1972-75, U. Miami, 1974-80, Harvard U., 1975-82, disting. jud. visitor U. Notre Dame, 1980, U. Iowa, 1983, U. Conn., 1984; past bd. dirs. Baton Rouge chpt. Girl Scouts Am., Mental Health Guidance Center, Community Chest, Community Services Council, Nat. Assn. Crippled Children and Adults; past adv. bd. local Salvation Army, YWCA, Blundon Orphanage; trustee Temple B'nai Israel, 1966-74, Temple Sinai, 1973-76. Served to capt. AUS, 1942-46, ETO. Recipient Golden Deeds award for civic service, 1964; Brotherhood award NCCJ, 1968; named Disting. Alumnus La. State U., 1982. Mem. ABA (bd. editors jour. 1976-82, mem. task force competency in legal edn. 1978-80, chmn. estate and gift tax com. 1964, chmn. sect. bar activities 1963, chmn. lawyer referral com. 1969-72), La. Bar Assn. (chmn. sect. trust estates, probate and immovable property law 1961, chmn. labor law sect. 1957, jr. bar sect. 1955, com. on ct. adminstrn. Jud. Conf.), Nat. Acad. Arbitrators, Am. Arbitration Assn., La. Law Inst., Order of Coif, Phi Beta Kappa, Phi Delta Phi, Omicron Delta Kappa, Blue Key (hon.). Lodge: Mason (32 deg.). Jurisprudence. Office: US Court Appeals 2440 One American Pl Baton Rouge LA 70825

RUBIN, BARRY, lawyer, state official. Pub. defender State of Hawaii, Honolulu. Office: Pub Defender Office 200 N Vineyard Blvd Suite 200 Honolulu HI 96817 *

RUBIN, BURTON JAY, lawyer, editor; b. Bklyn., Jan. 23, 1946; s. Samuel and Sidell (Greenfield) R.; m. Janice Ann Edelstein, Feb. 17, 1974; 1 dau., Jennifer Sidell. A.B. in Biology, Guilford Coll., Greensboro, N.C., 1966; J.D., U. N.C., 1969. Bar: Va. 1971; U.S. Ct. Customs and Patent Appeals 1975. Legal editor Labor Relations Reporter, Bur. Nat. Affairs, Inc., Washington, 1970; asst. editor U.S. Law Week, 1970-74, asst. mng. editor Patent, Trademark and Copyright Jour., 1974-75, mng. editor U.S. Patents Quar., 1975-85; sr. atty., dir. legal dept. Am. Soc. Travel Agts., 1985—; cons. Roundhouse Sq. Psychiat. Ctr., Alexandria, Ctr. Behavioral Med., Ctr. Behavioral Medicine, Rockville, Md. Mem. Fairfax County Water Authority, Va.; mem. Fairfax County Police-Citizens Adv. Council, 1982-83, alt. mem., 1984-85; mem. West Springfield Police-Citizens Adv. Com., 1979—, chmn., 1981; bd. dirs. Bur. Nat. Affairs, 1984-85; mem. Fairfax County Rep. Com., 1982-85. Mem. ABA. Contbr. articles to profl. jours. Patent, Trademark and copyright. Office: 4400 MacArthur Blvd NW Washington DC 20007

RUBIN, CARL BERNARD, U.S. district judge; b. Cin., Mar. 27, 1920; s. John I. and Ethel (Friedman) R.; m. Gloria Weiland, Sept. 23, 1945; children: Marc W., C. Barry, Pam G., Robert S. B.A., U. Cin., 1942, J.D., 1944. Bar: Ohio 1944. Practiced in Cin., 1944-71; asst. pros. atty. Hamilton County (Ohio), Cin., 1950-60; judge U.S. Dist. Ct. So. Dist. Ohio, 1971—, chief judge, 1979—; Instr. criminal law Chase Coll. Law, Cin., 1965-67; mem. com. on ct. adminstrn. fed. cts. U.S. Jud. Conf., 1975-83; mem. Jud. Council 6th Circuit, 1985—; adj. prof. law U. Dayton Coll. Law, 1976. Mem. Cin. Civil Service Commn., 1960-66, chmn., 1965-66; pres. S.W. Ohio Regional Transit Authority, 1971. Mem. Am. Contract Bridge League (dir. 1966-73, pres. 1970-71), 6th Circuit Dist. Judges Assn. (pres. 1977-78). Office: US Courthouse 5th and Walnut Sts Cincinnati OH 45202 *

RUBIN, DALE MICHAEL, lawyer; b. Los Angeles, July 1, 1950; s. Bernie and Phyllis Lila (Hirschberg) R.; m. Lydia Peraza, Mar. 30, 1985. BA in Polit. Sci., Calif. State U., Northridge, 1972; JD, U. San Fernando Valley, 1975. Bar: Calif. 1976, U.S. Dist. Ct. (cen. dist.) Calif. 1976. Trial assoc. Lehrer & Medill, Beverly Hills, Calif., 1976-78; sole practice Beverly Hills, 1978-80; ptnr. Rubin & Rubin, Van Nuys and Oxnard, Calif., 1980—; guest lectr. seminars Calif. Trial Advocacy, 1983; judge pro tem Los Angeles Mcpl. Ct., Van Nuys, 1984—. Recipient Cert. Appreciation Los Angeles Jud. Dist. Mcpl. Ct. Calif., 1984-85. Mem. Los Angeles County Bar Assn., Calif. Trial Lawyers Assn. (guest lectr. 1979—), Los Angeles Criminal Bar Assn., San Fernando Valley Criminal Bar Assn. Republican. Criminal, State civil litigation, Personal injury. Home: 3720 Ocean Dr Oxnard CA 93030 Office: Rubin & Rubin 14253 Delano St Van Nuys CA 91401

RUBIN, DAVID SAMUEL, lawyer; b. Baton Rouge, Feb. 17, 1952; s. Alvin Benjamin and Janice (Ginsberg) R.; m. Rosalind Miller, June 11, 1974; children: Sarah, Joel, Lindi. BS, La. State U., 1974, JD, 1978. Bar: La. 1978, U.S. Dist. Ct. (ea., mid. and we. dists.) 1978, U.S. Ct. Appeals (5th and 11th cirs.) 1981, U.S. Supreme Ct. 1983. Ptnr. Kantrow, Spaht, Weaver & Blitzer, Baton Rouge, 1978—. Assoc. editor La. State U. Law Rev., 1977-78; contbr. articles to profl. jours. Mem. ABA (ho. of dels. 1986—), Am. Bankruptcy Inst., La. Bar Assn. (continuing legal edn. com.), Baton Rouge Bank Counsel Group (bd. dirs. 1986—), Order of Coif, Phi Kappa Phi. Banking, Bankruptcy, Consumer commercial. Office: Kantrow Spaht Weaver & Blitzer PO Box 2997 Baton Rouge LA 70821-2997

RUBIN, JANET BETH, lawyer; b. Bklyn., Apr. 8, 1952; s. Frank Leon and Evelyn Bernice (Tumin) R.; m. Thomas Joseph Corcoran, Feb. 19, 1984 (div. Dec. 1985). BA, U. Va., 1974; JD, Coll. of William and Mary, 1977. Bar: Va. 1977, U.S. Dist. Ct. (ea. dist.) Va. 1981, D.C. 1982, U.S. Ct. Appeals (4th cir.) 1982, U.S. Ct. Appeals (D.C. cir.) 1983, U.S. Dist. Ct. Md. 1983, U.S. Dist. Ct. D.C. 1983. Atty. Wash. Met. Area Transit Authority, 1980—. Served to capt. U.S. Army, 1977-80. Mem. ABA, D.C. Women's Bar Assn., D.C. Bar Assn., Va. Women's Atty. Assn. Democrat. Jewish. Avocations: swimming, reading. Personal injury, Federal civil litigation, State civil litigation. Home: 2643B S Walter Reed Dr Arlington VA 22206 Office: Wash Met Area Transit Authority 600 5th St NW Washington DC 20001

RUBIN, JOSEPH, lawyer; b. N.Y.C., May 4, 1927; s. Charles and Frieda (Herbst) R.; m. Marjorie Topper; children—Lawrence S., David E. B.A., CCNY, 1948; LL.B., Bklyn. Law Sch., 1950. Bar: N.Y. 1950, U.S. Supreme Ct. 1973, U.S. Dist. Ct. (ea. and so. dists.) N.Y. 1973. Sole practice, Smithtown, N.Y., 1970-83; ptnr. Rubin & Rothman, Smithtown, 1983—; lectr. Suffolk Acad. Law, 1982—. Author: New York Collections, 1982. Served with USN. Mem. N.Y. State Bar Assn., Suffolk County Bar Assn. Consumer commercial, State civil litigation, General practice. Office: Rubin & Rothman 496 Smithtown By-Pass Smithtown NY 11787

RUBIN, KENNETH ALLEN, lawyer; b. Rockville Centre, N.Y., Nov. 24, 1947; s. Albert Alton and Marion (Osterweis) R.; m. Susan Kurman, Sept. 14, 1980; 1 child, Jennifer. BS, Cornell U., 1969, MS, 1971, JD, 1973. Bar: D.C. 1974, N.Y. 1974, U.S. Ct. Appeals (D.C. cir.) 1974, U.S. Ct. Appeals (5th cir.) 1975, U.S. Ct. Appeals (4th, 9th and 10th cir.) 1976, U.S. Ct. Appeals (3d, 8th and 11th cirs.) 1986. Trial atty. Dept. Justice, Washington, 1973-74; ptnr. Morgan, Lewis & Bockius, Washington, 1974—; adj. prof. USDA Grad. Sch., Washington, 1977—, U. Ala., Huntsville, 1978—, Antioch U., Washington, 1978; lectr. Cornell U., Ithaca, N.Y., 1979—. Environment, Legal education, Administrative and regulatory. Office: Morgan Lewis & Bockius 1800 M St NW Washington DC 20036

RUBIN, ROBERT SAMUEL, lawyer; b. Cin.; s. Carl B. and Gloria (Weiland) R.; m. Virginia K. Carson, May 14, 1983; children: John C., Claire W. LLB, U. Wales, Aberystwyth, Eng., 1976; JD, U. Cin., 1979. Bar: Ohio 1979, U.S. Dist. Ct. (so. dist.) Ohio 1979. Assoc. Brown, Cummins & Brown, Cin., 1979-82, Hartsock, Harris & Schneider, Cin., 1982-83, Porter, Wright, Morris & Arthur, Cin., 1983—; mem. arbitration rules com. U.S. Dist. Ct. (so. dist.) Ohio 1984. Trustee Smith Tyler Meml. Trust, Cin., 1982—. Mem. ABA, Ohio Bar Assn., Cin. Bar Assn. Republican. Club: Cin. Racquet. Banking, General corporate, State civil litigation. Home: 2207 E Hill Ave Cincinnati OH 45208 Office: Porter Wright Morris & Arthur 2200 Columbia Plaza 250 E 5th St Cincinnati OH 45202

RUBIN, SCOTT JEFFREY, lawyer; b. Syracuse, N.Y., Oct. 2, 1957; s. Leonard Charles Rubin and Irma Lucille (Wolicki) Golfin; m. Cynthia Ann Surmacz, May 31, 1981. BA with distinction, Pa. State U., 1978; JD with honors, George Washington U., 1981. Bar: Pa. 1981, U.S. Dist. Ct. (mid. dist.) Pa. 1982. Assoc. Laws & Staruch, Harrisburg, Pa., 1981-83; asst. consumer adv. Commonwealth of Pa., Harrisburg, 1983—. Membership coordinator Common Cause of Pa., Harrisburg, 1976-77, counsel, 1982-83. Trustee scholar, George Washington U., 1979-81. Mem. ABA. Avocation: photography. Public utilities, Environment. Home: 3 Lost Creek Dr Selinsgrove PA 17870 Office: Office of Consumer Adv 1425 Strawberry Sq Harrisburg PA 17120

RUBIN, STEPHEN, lawyer; b. Bklyn., May 17, 1944; s. Aaron and Mary (Pehr) R.; m. Barbara Lehman, Sept. 17, 1968; children: Jason, Canaan. BA, U. Pa., 1966; JD, Columbia U., 1969. Bar: N.Y. 1969, U.S. Supreme Ct. 1973, U.S. Ct. Appeals (7th cir.) 1981, D.C. 1982, U.S. Dist. Ct. D.C. 1982, U.S. Ct. Appeals (D.C. cir.) 1982, U.S. Ct. Appeals (fed. cir.) 1983, U.S. Ct. Appeals (11th. cir.) 1984, U.S. Dist. Ct. (so. and ea. dists.) N.Y. 1985, U.S. Ct. Appeals (2d cir.) 1985. Law clk. to presiding justice U.S. Ct. Appeals (3d cir.), Phila., 1969-70; atty. antitrust div. U.S. Dept. Justice, Washington, 1970-72; prof. law U. Fla., Gainsville, 1972-82; ptnr. Holland & Knight, Washington, 1982-87, Shea & Gould, Washington, 1987—; adminstrv. law judge Fla. Dept. Legal Affairs, Tallahassee, 1973-75; cons. Fla. Pub. Service Commn., Tallahassee, 1978-82. Author: Regulating the Professions, 1979. German Marshall fellow, 1976. Mem. ABA (com. chmn. 1976—), Am. Law Inst., D.C. Bar Assn., N.Y. State Bar Assn., Fed. Communications Bar Assn. Avocation: urban architecture and planning.

Antitrust, Banking, Trademark and copyright. Home: 7804 Buckboard Ct Potomac MD 20854 Office: Holland & Knight 888 17th St NW Washington DC 20006

RUBIN, STEPHEN WAYNE, lawyer; b. N.Y.C., Mar. 29, 1951; s. Oscar R. and Irene J. (Widelok) R.; m. Eileen Grossman, Sept. 23, 1978; children: Ashley G., Camner G. BS, Cornell U., 1973; JD, Columbia U., 1976. Bar: N.Y. 1977, U.S. Dist. Ct. (so. dist.) N.Y. 1977. Assoc. Gordon, Hurwitz & Butowsky, N.Y.C., 1976-79; assoc. Feit & Ahrens, N.Y.C., 1979-84, ptnr., 1984—; lectr. grad. sch. bus., NYU, 1985—; bd. dirs. Lanson Industries, Cullman, Ala. Co-contbr. law articles to profl. jours. Bd. dirs., sec. Friends of Israel Def. Forces, N.Y.C., 1985—. Mem. ABA, N.Y. State Bar Assn., Assn. of Bar of City of N.Y. General corporate, Securities, Mergers and acquisitions. Office: Feit & Ahrens 488 Madison Ave New York NY 10022

RUBINFELD, DANIEL L., law educator, consultant; b. Newark, May 3, 1945; s. William A. and Ann (Weinstein) R.; m. Gail N. Soon, Aug. 25, 1973; children: Sarah, Rachel. BA in Math. magna cum laude, Princeton U., 1967; MS in Econs., MIT, 1968, PhD, 1972. Instr. Suffolk U., Boston, 1968-70, Wellesley (Mass.) Coll., 1970-71; asst. prof. U. Mich., Ann Arbor, 1972-77, assoc. prof., 1977-82, prof. econs. and law, 1982-83; prof. econs. and law U. Calif., Berkeley, 1983—; cons. MIT/Harvard, 1972, Urban Inst., 1973, Nat. Acad. Sciences, 1974, 85—, U.S. Treasury, 1984-85; economist Staff of Pres. Council Econ. Advisors, 1969; mem. adv. panel NSF program law and social sci., 1982-84. Author: Statistical Analysis of Economic and Financial Data, rev. ed., 1974, Essays on the Law and Economics of Local Governments, 1979, Econometric Models and Economic Forecasts, 2d ed., 1981; co-editor: American Domestic Priorities: An Economic Appraisal, 1985; editorial bd. Pub. Fin. Quarterly, 1980—, Law and Soc. Rev., 1982—, Evaluation Rev., 1985—; also articles. Mem. Ann Arbor Rent Control Study Commn. 1973, faculty adv. bd. U. Calif. Ctr. Real Estate and Urban Econs., Berkeley, 1983. NSF grantee; Woodrew Wilson fellow, 1967, NSF fellow, 1968-69, Nat. Bur. Econ. Research fellow, 1975-76. Mem. Am. Econ. Assn., Nat. Tax Assn., Econometric Soc., Law and Soc. Assn., Phi Beta Kappa. Legal education. Office: U Calif Berkeley Sch Law 360 Boalt Hall Berkeley CA 94720

RUBINKOWSKI, CONRAD SIGMUND, lawyer, film critic; b. Chgo., July 15, 1951; s. Sigmund Felix and Lee (Zak) R.; m. Kathryn I. Friedli, July 3, 1982; 1 child, Leo Joseph. B.S., Ill. Inst. Tech., 1973; J.D., U. Ill., 1976. Bar: Ill. 1976, U.S. Dist. Ct. (no. dist.) Ill. 1976, U.S. Dist. Ct. (ea. dist.) 1978. Asst. states atty. States Atty.'s Office, Danville, Ill. 1977-80; atty. Joint Com. on Adminstrv. Rules, Springfield, Ill., 1981-83; atty. Ill. Commerce Commn., Springfield, 1983—. Mem. ABA, Chili Appreciation Soc. Internat., Amnesty Internat., Phi Delta Phi. Roman Catholic. Lodges: Raccoons, Mystic Knights of Sea (exalted piscator 1986). Administrative and regulatory, Public utilities.

RUBINOWITZ, LEONARD S., lawyer, educator; b. 1943. B.A., U. Wis.-Madison, 1965; LL.B., Yale U., 1968. Bar: Conn. 1968. Spl. asst. to adminstr. HUD, Chgo., 1969-72; research assoc. Ctr. for Urban Affairs, Northwestern U., Chgo., 1972-75, assoc. prof. law and urban affairs, 1975-80; prof., 1980—; Field assoc. Brookings Inst., 1975—. Author: Low Income Housing: Suburban Strategies, 1974. Legal education, Administrative and regulatory. Office: Northwestern U Law Sch 357 E Chicago Ave Chicago IL 60611 *

RUBINSTEIN, AARON, lawyer; b. N.Y.C., Nov. 15, 1950; s. Jacob and Golda Rubinstein; m. Carri Sue Zogan, Mar. 3, 1974; children: David Michael, Jennifer Lauren. BA magna cum laude, Cornell U., 1972; JD, NYU, 1975. Bar: N.Y. 1976, U.S. Dist. Ct. (so. and ea. dists.) 1976, U.S. Supreme Ct. 1986. Assoc. Kaye, Scholer, Fierman, Hays & Handler, N.Y.C., 1975-84, ptnr., 1985—. Mem. ABA, Order of Coif. Federal civil litigation, State civil litigation, Securities. Home: 62 Stratton Rd Scarsdale NY 10583 Office: Kaye Scholer Fierman Hays & Handler 425 Park Ave New York NY 10022

RUBINSTEIN, LOUIS BARUCH, lawyer, consultant; b. Providence, Dec. 5, 1908; s. Israel Sessel and Fannie Rebecca (Rubin) R.; m. Lillian Berger, Dec. 20, 1950; children—Louis H., Michael L.; m. 2d, Dorothy L. Gottlieb, June 6, 1982. B.A., Yale U., 1931, J.D., 1934. Bar: D.C. 1936, R.I. 1938, U.S. Supreme Ct. 1974. Counsel, advisor on internat. law U.S. Dept. State, 1934-38; chief legal officer Dept. Employment Security State of R.I., 1965-76; counsel Zietz, Mittleman & Webster, 1950-82; mem. Gates, Mellion & Rubinstein, Providence, 1982—; master in chancery Superior Ct. R.I.; lectr. in field. Hon. dir. Temple Emanuel Jewish Community Ctr.; hon. pres. R.I. Region Jewish Nat. Fund; hon. sec. Jewish Fedn. of R.I., 1982—. Served with USAF, 1942-45. Mem. R.I. Bar Assn. (award of merit 1977, 82, 85, mem. exec. com. 1977-81, editor in chief Jour. 1977-81), Am. Arbitration Assn. (arbitrator labor-mgmt. panel). Democrat. Clubs: Kirkbrae Country (Lincoln, R.I.); Boca Teeca Country (Boca Raton, Fla.), Yale of R.I., Masons (past master), Shriners. Contbr. articles to profl. jours. Administrative and regulatory, Nuclear power, Labor. Address: 299 NW 52d Terrace #417 Boca Raton FL 33431

RUBIO, HERMAN FRANK, lawyer; b. Miami, Fla., Aug. 11, 1952; s. Herman Frank and Carmen S. Rubio. B.A., U. Miami, 1973, J.D., 1976. Bar: Fla. 1976, D.C. 1981, N.Y. 1982. Asst. pub. defender Dade County Pub. Defender's Office, Miami, 1975-77; ptnr. Flynn Rubio & Tarkoff, Miami, 1977-83; prin. H. Frank Rubio, P.A., Miami, 1983—. U. Miami Honor scholar, 1973; recipient Am. Jurisprudence award Bancroft-Whitney Co., 1975. Mem. ABA, Nat. Assn. Criminal Def. Lawyers, Fed. Bar Assn., Assn. Trial Lawyers Am., Acad. Fla. Trial Lawyers. Democrat. Roman Catholic. Office: 1481 NW North River Dr Miami FL 33125

RUBOCK, DANIEL BENJAMIN, lawyer; b. Bklyn., Oct. 9, 1954; Samuel and Sylvia Rubock. BA, Yale U., 1976; JD, Columbia U., 1979. Bar: N.Y. 1980, U.S. Dist. Ct. (so. and ea. dists.) N.Y. 1981, U.S. Ct. Appeals (2d cir.) 1983, U.S. Supreme Ct. 1984. Assoc. Finley, Kumble & Wagner, N.Y.C., 1979-80, Proskauer & Rose, N.Y.C., 1980-81, White & Case, N.Y.C., 1981—. Committeeman N.Y. County Dem. Com., 1983. Mem. N.Y. State Bar Assn. (profl. discipline com.). Real property. Home: 333 E 43rd St Apt 804 New York NY 10017 Office: White & Case 1155 Ave of the Americas New York NY 10036

RUBRIGHT, CHARLES RUSSELL, lawyer; b. South Bend, Ind., Jan. 29, 1947; s. Charles E. and Evelyn (Morris) R. B.S., Ind. State U., 1969; J.D., Ind. U., 1973. Bar: Ind. 1974. Hearing officer Ind. Edn. Employment Relations Bd., Indpls., 1973-75; ptnr. Bose Mc Kinney & Evans, Indpls., 1975—. Mem. ABA (subcom. on state and local govt. collective bargaining), Ind. Bar Assn., Ind. Mcpl. Lawyers Assn. Republican. Methodist. Club: Indpls. Sailing. Labor, Administrative and regulatory. Home: 3422 Alsuda Ct Indianapolis IN 46205 Office: Bose McKinney & Evans 1100 First Indiana Bldg Indianapolis IN 46204

RUCK, ANDREW JOSEPH, lawyer; b. Phila., Feb. 22, 1930; s. Andrew F. and Helen (Fodderingham) R.; m. Mary Scott, May 11, 1957; children: Helen, Andrew S., Marianne, Christopher, Mark. BA, LaSalle U., 1952; JD, Temple U., 1955. Bar: Pa. 1982, U.S. Dist. Ct. 1987, U.S. Ct. Appeals 1987. Atty. bond claims Fireman's Fund Inc., Phila., 1960-69; v.p. Reliance Ins. Co., Phila., 1970-86; assoc. Duane, Morris & Heckscher, Phila., 1986—. Mem. ABA, Pa. Bar Assn., Phila. Bar Assn. Republican. Roman Catholic. Construction, Government contracts and claims. Home: 344 Stenton Ave Plymouth Meeting PA 19462 Office: Duane Morris & Heckscher 1500 One Franklin Plaza Philadelphia PA 19102

RUCKER, JERRY DON, lawyer; b. Dallas, Jan. 10, 1942; s. J.R. and Lola Dean (Pierce) R.; m. Andria Neal, Apr. 3, 1982; children: William Kurt, Austin Neal. BA, So. Meth. U., 1964, LLB, 1967; grad., Universidad Nacional Autonoma, Mexico City, 1966. Bar: Tex. 1967, U.S. Supreme Ct. 1970. Trial atty. Akin, Gump, Strauss, Hauer & Feld, Dallas, 1970-72, Braniff Airways, Tex. and S.Am., 1972-75; sole practice Dallas, 1976-85; pntr. Dooley, Rucker, Maris & Foxman, Dallas, 1986—; chmn. bd. Gen. Am. Fidelity & Guaranty Corp., Dallas. Editor Jour. Air Law Commerce, 1966-67. City councilman, Dallas, 1983—; pres. N. Cen. Tex. Council Govts., Dallas, 1984-85; mem. Fin. Adminstrn. and Intergovtl. Relation steering com. Nat. League of Cities, Washington, 1984-87; del. White House Conf. on Small Bus., Washington, 1986. Served to lt. comdr. JAGC, USNR, 1968-70. Arthur S. Hanson scholar, Dallas, 1966; recipient El Sombrero award Tex. LULAC, Dallas, 1986. Mem. Am. Arbitration Assn. (constrn. claims panel arbitrator 1980—), Tex. Bar Assn., Dallas Bar Assn., North Dallas C. of C. (bd. dirs. 1985—), Tex. Atlantic Alliance, N. Tex. Commn. Construction, Private international, Government contracts and claims. Home: 5807 Glen Falls Ln Dallas TX 75209

RUCKER, WILLIAM BROWNING, lawyer; b. Bedford, Va., Apr. 13, 1944; s. Ambrose Alexander and Helen (Wingfield) R.; m. Johanna Irene Zimmerman, Aug. 5, 1972; children: William B. Jr., Andrew Harper, Stuart Alexander. BS, U. Va., 1966; MS in Real Estate Devel., Am. U., 1971, MBA, 1971; studied law, Va. Bd. Bar Examiners, 1981. Bar: Va. 1981. Urban planner Fairfax County, Va., 1970-76, exec. asst. to county exec., 1976-81, dep. dir. bldg. dept., 1981-85; sole practice Fairfax, 1981—; v.p. West*Group, McLean, Va., 1985—. Contbr. articles to profl. jours. Served as lt. USNR, 1966-69. Mem. ABA, Am. Inst. Cert. Planners (Urban Planning Achievement award 1975), Am. Planning Assn., No. Va. Bd. Realtors, Fairfax County, C. of C. (land use com.). Avocations: aviation, camping, hunting, fishing. Construction, Real property, Local government. Home: 10811 Glen Mist Ln Fairfax VA 22030 Office: West Group Inc 1600 Anderson Rd McLean VA 22102

RUDA, HOWARD, finance company executive; b. N.Y.C., Sept. 7, 1932; s. Menahem and Lucy (Gillenson) R.; B.A., Coll. City N.Y., 1954; J.D., Columbia, 1959; m. Leah E. Zeliger, Sept. 22, 1963; 1 child, Amy. Bar: N.Y. 1959, U.S. Dist. Ct. (so. and ea. dists.) N.Y. 1959. Assoc., then ptnr. Laporte & Meyers, N.Y.C., 1959-63; staff atty., then gen. counsel Meinhard Comml. Corp., N.Y.C., 1963-68; with C.I.T. Group Holdings, Inc., N.Y.C., 1968—, asst. gen. counsel, 1968—, gen. counsel, v.p., dir. C.I.T. Corp., C.I.T. Leasing Corp., 1973-84; lectr. Practicing Law Inst., Banking Law Inst.; dir. Am. Bankruptcy Inst. Editor: Asset Based Financing. Served with U.S. Army, 1954-56. Mem. ABA (chmn. equipment financing com. 1982-85), Am. Law Inst., Phi Beta Kappa. Jewish. Contracts commercial, Banking, Bankruptcy. Home: 8 Mirrielees Rd Great Neck NY 11021 Office: CIT Group 135 W 50th St New York NY 10020

RUDA, JACQUES SERGE, lawyer; b. Brussels, Oct. 17, 1952; came to U.S., 1954; s. Srul and Sylvia Sara (Altmejdt) R.; m. Lisa Jan Flaxer, July 5, 1981; m. Emily Melissa, Charles Mayer. BA, U. Colo., 1974; postgrad., Tel Aviv U., 1972; JD, U. Colo., 1977. Bar: Colo. 1977, U.S. Dist. Ct. Colo. 1982, U.S. Ct. Appeals (10th cir.) 1982. Bailiff, law clk. to presiding justice 2d Jud. Dist. Colo., Denver, 1976; assoc. Mosley, Wells & Johnson, Denver, 1979-86; sole practice Denver, 1986—. Mem. ABA, Colo. Bar Assn., Denver Bar Assn. Democrat. Jewish. Real property, Consumer commercial, General practice. Home: 696 Dexter Denver CO 80220 Office: 1331 17th St Suite 510 Denver CO 80207

RUDD, DONNIE, lawyer, educator; b. Winnie, Tex., Feb. 28, 1942; s. Eddie and Veta Mae (Bales) R.; m. Dianne Marks, Apr. 3, 1974; children—Lori, Cindy, Jack, Glory, Louisa, Donisa, Terisa, Donald. B.S. in Chem. Engring., Tex. A&M U., 1964; J.D., Chgo.-Kent Coll. Law, 1969. Bar: Ill., 1969, Can. Patent Office, 1968, U.S. Patent Office, 1967, U.S. Tax Ct., 1971, U.S. Dist. Ct. (no. dist.) Ill., 1969, U.S. Ct. Mil. Appeals, 1971, U.S. Ct. Appeals (7th cir.), 1971, U.S. Ct. Customs and Patent Appeals, 1971, U.S. Ct. Claims, 1973, U.S. Cts. Appeals (5th and 11th cirs.), 1981. Patent atty. Quaker Oats Co., 1965-72; dir. litigation U.S. Gypsum Co., 1972-75; sr. ptnr. Rudd & Assos., Schaumburg, Ill., 1975—; instr. condominium law Harper Coll., Coll. DuPage, Oakton Coll. Pres. Bd. Edn. Sch. Dist. 54, 1972-76; mem. Hoffman Estates (Ill.) Plan Commn., 1972-76. Named one of Five Most Outstanding Condominium Attys. in Am. Condominium Council, Chgo., 1983. Mem. ABA, Ill. State Bar Assn., NW Suburban Bar Assn., Lawyer-Pilots Bar Assn. Republican. Baptist. Author: The Everything Book on Condominiums, 1982, 1984 Amendments to the Illinois Condominium Act, 1984, The 100 Most Commonly Asked Questions About Condominiums, 1985; contbr. articles on condominium law to profl. jours. Condominium law, Federal civil litigation, State civil litigation. Office: 1030 W Higgins Schaumburg IL 60195

RUDER, DAVID STURTEVANT, lawyer, educator; b. Wausau, Wis., May 25, 1929; s. George Louis and Josephine (Sturtevant) R.; m. Susan M. Small; children: Victoria Chesley, Julia Larson, David Sturtevant II, John Coulter; stepchildren: Elizabeth Frankel, Rebecca Frankel. B.A. cum laude, Williams Coll., 1951; J.D. with honors, U. Wis., 1957. Bar: Wis. 1957, Ill. 1962. Of counsel Schiff Hardin & Waite, Chgo., 1971-76; assoc. Quarles & Brady, Milw., 1957-61; asst. prof. law Northwestern U., Chgo., 1961-63, assoc. prof., 1963-65, prof., 1965—, assoc. dean Law Sch., 1965-66, dean Law Sch., , 1977-85; cons. Am. Law Inst. Fed. Securities Code, parts XVI and XVII; planning dir. Corporate Counsel Inst., 1962-66, 76-77 (com. mem. 1977—); vis. prof. law U. Pa., Phila., 1971; C.R.B. vis. lectr. Universite de Liege, 1967; faculty Salzburg Seminar, 1976; mem. legal adv. com. to bd. dirs. N.Y. Stock Exchange, 1978-82; mem. com. on profl. responsibility Ill. Supreme Ct.; mem. adv. bd. Securities Regulation Inst. Editor-in-chief: Williams Coll. Record, 1950-51, U. Wis. Law Rev, 1957; editor: Proc. Corp. Counsel Inst, 1962-66; contbr. articles to legal periodicals. Served to 1st lt. AUS, 1951-54. Fellow Am. Bar Found. (bd. dirs. 1984-86), Ill. Bar Found.; mem. ABA (council sect. on corp., banking and bus. law 1970-74), Chgo. Bar Assn. (com. chmn.), Ill. Bar Assn., Wis. Bar Assn., Am. Law Inst., Order of Coif, Gargoyle Soc., Phi Beta Kappa, Phi Delta Phi, Zeta Psi. General corporate, Securities. Home: 325 Orchard Ln Highland Park IL 60035 Office: 357 E Chicago Ave Chicago IL 60611

RUDER, JAY STANLEY, lawyer; b. Phila., July 27, 1955; s. Martin and June (Miller) R.; m. Sharon Becker, June 28, 1981; children: Benjamin Stephen, Andrew Frank. BA cum laude, Harvard U., 1976; JD cum laude, Temple U., 1979. Bar: Pa. 1979, U.S. Dist. Ct. (ea. dist.) Pa. 1979, U.S. Ct. Appeals (3d cir.) 1980, N.J. 1984, U.S. Dist. Ct. N.J. 1984. Assoc. Meltzer & Schiffrin, Phila., 1979-86, ptnr., 1986-87; pres. Fox, Rothschild, O'Brien & Frankel, Phila., 1987—. Corresponding sec. Congregation Beth El Young Assocs., Cherry Hill, N.J., 1986. Mem. ABA, Pa. Bar Assn., Phila. Bar Assn. Democrat. Jewish. Avocations: reading, writing, drawing. Real property, Landlord-tenant, Contracts commercial. Home: 1817 Russet Dr Cherry Hill NJ 08003 Office: Fox Rothschild O'Brien & Frankel 2000 Market St Philadelphia PA 19103

RUDLIN, DAVID ALAN, lawyer; b. Richmond, Va., Nov. 4, 1947; s. Herbert and Dorothy Jean (Durham) R.; m. Judith Bond Faulkner, Oct. 4, 1975; 1 child, Sara Elizabeth. B.A. with high distinction, U. Va., 1969, J.D. with honors, 1973. Bar: Va. 1973, U.S. Dist. Ct. (ea. dist.) Va. 1975, U.S. Ct. Appeals (4th cir.) 1975, U.S. Ct. Appeals (10th cir.) 1980, U.S. Ct. Appeals (2d cir.) 1983, U.S. Supreme Ct. 1979. Assoc. gen. counsel U.S. Commn. on Orgn. of Govt. for Conduct of Fgn. Policy, Washington, 1973-75; assoc. Hunton & Williams, Richmond, 1975-82, ptnr., 1982—; adj. faculty William and Mary Coll., Marshall-Wythe Sch. Law, Williamsburg, Va., 1982—; vis. lectr. U. Va. Sch. Law, Charlottesville, 1980—. Bd. dirs., v.p. Cystic Fibrosis Found., Richmond; coordinator annual fund raising campaign U. Va. Law Sch., Richmond. Mem. ABA, Va. Bar Assn., Va. Trial Lawyers Assn., Richmond Bar Assn. Federal civil litigation, Environment, Libel. Office: Hunton & Williams PO Box 1535 Richmond VA 23212

RUDLOFF, WILLIAM J., lawyer; b. Bonne Terre, Mo., Feb. 19, 1941; s. Leslie W. and Alta M. (Hogenmiller) R.; m. Rita Howton, Aug. 5, 1965; children: Daniel, Andrea, Leslie, Susan. AB, Western Ky. U., 1961; JD, Vanderbilt U., 1965. Bar: Ky. 1965, Tenn. 1965, U.S. Supreme Ct. 1975; cert. civil trial specialist Nat. Bd. Trial Advocacy. Mem. Harlin, Parker & Rudloff and predecessors, Bowling Green, Ky., 1965—; U.S. magistrate Western Dist. Ky., 1971-75. NDEA fellow U. Nebr. 1961-62. Fellow U. Ky., Charter Life; mem. Ky. Bar Found., Assn. Ins. Attys., Am. Bd. Trial Advocates, Am. Counsel Assn., Def. Research Inst., Ky. Def. Counsel, Assn. Trial Lawyers Am., ABA, Ky. Bar Assn., Bowling Green Bar Assn., Am. Coll. Forensic Psychiatry, Trial Attys. Am., Internat. Assn. Ins. Counsel. State civil litigation, Federal civil litigation, Insurance. Home: 517 Ashmoor Dr Bowling Green KY 42101 Office: 519 E 10th St Bowling Green KY 42101

RUDNICK, MARVIN JACK, lawyer; b. St. Joseph, Mich., Mar. 9, 1948; s. Milton P. and Edna O.R.; m. Cynthia Jane Vanhooser, Sept. 4, 1982; children: Matthew, Andrew. BA, Middlebury Coll., 1970; JD, Syracuse U., 1973. Bar: N.Y. 1973. Corp. atty. Oneida Ltd., N.Y., 1973-76, assoc. counsel, 1976-84, asst. gen. counsel, 1985-86, v.p., sec., gen. counsel, 1986—; mem. adj. faculty Utica Coll., Syracuse U., Utica, N.Y., 1982-84; bd. dirs. Oneida Silversmith's Div. Pres. Sherrill-Kenwood Community Chest, Sherrill, N.Y., 1979-81. Served as 1st lt. U.S. Army, 1974, maj. res. Mem. ABA, N.Y. State Bar Assn., Madison County Bar Assn., Justinian Soc. Republican. General corporate, Environment, Trademark and copyright. Office: Oneida Ltd Kenwood Station Oneida NY 13421

RUDOFF, SURIE, lawyer; b. Bklyn., Feb. 8, 1954; d. Stanley and Judith (Feder) R.; m. Robert Gary Sugarman, June 16, 1985. BS in Econs., Barnard Coll., 1975; JD, Columbia U., 1979. Bar: N.Y. 1980, U.S Dist. Ct. (so. dist.) N.Y. 1980. Assoc. Weil, Gotshal & Manges, N.Y.C., 1979-83; assoc. counsel Tri-Star Pictures Inc., N.Y.C., 1983-86, v.p. legal affairs, 1986—. Contbr. articles to profl. jours. Democrat. Jewish. Avocation: running. Entertainment, Trademark and copyright, Antitrust. Home: 55 E 87th St #12E New York NY 10128 Office: Tri-Star Pictures Inc 711 Fifth Ave New York NY 10022

RUDOLPH, GEORGE COOPER, lawyer; b. Butte, Mont., June 29, 1951; s. Newton Nathaniel and Delores (Losk) R.; Student Mont. Coll. Mineral, Sci. and Tech., 1969-71; B.A. magna cum laude in Psychology, U. S.C., 1973; J.D., U. Calif.-San Francisco, 1976. Bar: Calif. 1976, U.S. Dist. Ct. (cen. dist.) Calif. 1977, U.S. Dist. Ct. (no. dist.) Calif. 1977, U.S. Dist. Ct. (so. dist.) Calif. 1983, U.S. Ct. Appeals (9th cir.) 1977, U.S. Supreme Ct., 1985. Assoc. Fulop, Rolston, Burns & McKittrick, Beverly Hills and Newport Beach, Calif., 1976-81, Fulop & Hardee, Newport Beach, 1981-82; ptnr. Fulop & Hardee, Newport Beach, 1982, McKittrick, Jackson, DeMarco & Peckenpaugh, Newport Beach, 1983—; lectr. Calif. Continuing Edn. of The Bar, 1985—; Univ. Calif., Irvine, Los Angeles San Diego, Santa Barbara, 1985—. Mem. ABA, Assn. Trial Lawyers Am., Orange County Bar Assn. Democrat. Jewish. Lodge: B'nai B'rith. Federal civil litigation, State civil litigation, Insurance. Office: McKittrick Jackson McKittrick & Peckenpaugh 4041 MacArthur Blvd Newport Beach CA 92660

RUDOLPH, JAMES LEONARD, lawyer; b. Beverly, Mass., Sept. 26, 1950; s. Robert P. and Joyce B. (Yoffa) R.; m. Susan B. Gouchberg, Oct. 31, 1981. B.A., U. Denver, 1972; J.D., Boston Coll., 1975. Bar: Mass. 1975, U.S. Dist. Ct. Mass. 1976, U.S. Ct. Appeals (1st cir.) 1978, U.S. Supreme Ct. 1984. Ptnr. Gargill, Sassoon & Rudolph, Boston, 1976— Chmn. Swampscott Zoning Bd. Appeals (Mass.), 1984—, mem., 1983—; v.p. Jewish Rehab. Ctr., Swampscott, 1984—; v.p Camp Kingswood, Bridgton, Maine, 1983—; bd. dirs. Camp Bauercrest, Amesbury, Mass. Mem. Boston Bar Assn., Mass. Bar Assn., ABA, Assn. Trial Lawyers Am., Mass. Conveyancers Assn. Jewish. Clubs: Belmont Country (Mass.); Boston Yacht (Marblehead, Mass.). Lodge: Mt. Scopus (Malden, Mass.). Real property, Contracts commercial, General corporate. Office: Gargill Sassoon & Rudolph 92 State St Boston MA 02109

RUDOLPH, RICHARD, lawyer; b. Birmingham, Ala., Apr. 28, 1948; s. Carvin and Willie Lee (Harvey) R.; m. Doris Sheppard, Aug. 12, 1978. BA with honors, Ala. A&M U., 1970; JD, So. U., 1974. Bar: La. 1975, D.C. 1978, U.S. Supreme Ct. 1982. Specialist tax law Regional Counsels Office, Chgo., 1974-75; asst. atty. gen. La. Dept. Justice, Baton Rouge, 1975-82; sole practice Baton Rouge, 1982—. Mem. Community Assn. for the Welfare of Sch. Children, Baton Rouge, 1986—. Research fellow U. Fla., 1969; named one of Outstanding Young Am., U.S. Jaycees, 1979. Mem. ABA, Nat. Bar Assn., Assn. Trial Lawyers Am., Baton Rouge C. of C., Delta Theta Phi (founder, pres. 1978—, western dist. chancellor 1982—), Omega Psi Phi (chmn. community liaison com. 1978—), Beta Kappa Chi. (pres. 1969—),. Avocation: writing poetry. Environment, Legal education. Home: 4123 Raleigh Dr Baton Rouge LA 70814 Office: 200 Government St Suite 150 Baton Rouge LA 70802

RUDY, MARK STUART, lawyer; b. New Britain, Conn., Aug. 6, 1944; s. Isadore and Mary (Blumenthal) R.; m. Beverly M. Manber, Mar. 15, 1975 (div. Oct. 1977); m. M. Victoria Cochran, Oct. 18, 1980; 1 child, Sherry. BA, U. Conn., 1966; JD, Georgetown U., 1969. Bar: Va. 1970, D.C. 1971, Calif. 1975. Mng. atty. Legal Services Program, Washington, 1971-74; trial atty. EEOC, San Francisco, 1974-76; sole practice San Francisco, 1976-80; ptnr. Bushnell, Caplan, Fielding & Rudy, San Francisco, 1981-84, Law Offices of Mark Stuart Rudy, San Francisco, 1984—. Co-author: Wrongful Termination Practice, 1986. Mem. Calif. Bar Assn., Va. Bar Assn., Calif. Trial Lawyers Assn., San Francisco Trial Lawyers Assn. Labor. Home: 7084 Westmoorland Berkeley CA 94705-1755 Office: 530 Bush St 5th Floor San Francisco CA 94108-3623

RUDY, PETER HARRIS, lawyer; b. Hartford, Conn., Feb. 6, 1952; s. Burton Macy and Sylvia (Harris) R. BS in Journalism, Boston U., 1974; MPA, U. Hartford, 1979; JD, William and Mary Coll. of Law, 1982. Bar: Va. 1982, U.S. Ct. Appeals (4th cir.) 1982, U.S. Dist. Ct. (ea. and we. dists.) Va. 1983, U.S. Supreme Ct. 1985, Conn. 1986, Colo. 1986, U.S. Dist. Ct. Colo. 1986, U.S. Ct. Appeals (10th cir.) 1986. Asst. atty. gen. State of Vt., Richmond, 1982-85; assoc. Holland & Hart, Denver, 1985—. Cons. campaign Humphrey for Pres., Washington, 1972, campaign Carter for Pres., 1976, campaign Robb for Gov., 1981. Woodrow research grantee, 1978. Mem. ABA, Va. Bar Assn., Colo. Bar Assn. Labor, Federal civil litigation, Civil rights. Home: PO Box 8749 Denver CO 80201 Office: Holland & Hart 555 17th St Denver CO 80202

RUEGGER, PHILIP THEOPHIL, III, lawyer; b. Plainfield, N.J., Oct. 14, 1949; s. Philip T. Jr. and Gloria Marie (McLaughlin) R.; m. Rebecca Lee Huffman, Aug. 3, 1974; children: Sarah, Brittain, Michael. AB, Dartmouth Coll., 1971; JD, U. Va., 1974. Bar: N.Y. 1975. Assoc. Simpson, Thatcher & Bartlett, N.Y.C., 1974-81, ptnr., 1981—. Mem. Phi Beta Kappa. Presbyterian. Clubs: Manursing Island (Rye, N.Y.); Broadstreet (N.Y.C.). Avocation: sports. General corporate. Home: 275 Grace Church St Rye NY 10580 Office: Simpson Thacher & Bartlett One Battery Park Plaza New York NY 10004

RUEGSEGGER, MARTIN CRAIG, lawyer; b. Salina, Kans., Jan. 15, 1950; s. Lester I. and Dorothy Inez (Gibbs) R.; m. Nancy Diane Garrelts, May 22, 1971; children: Christopher, Carissa, Tasha. BS in Chemistry, Kans. State U., 1972; JD, So. Meth. U., 1975. Bar: Tex. 1976, Mo. 1981, D.C. 1985, U.S. Dist. Ct. (no., we., so. and ea. dists.) Tex., U.S. Dist. Ct. (ea. dist.) Mo., U.S. Dist. Ct. (ea. and we. dists.) Ark., U.S. Ct. Customs and Patent Appeals, U.S. Ct. Appeals (5th, 8th, D.C. and fed. cirs.), U.S. Supreme Ct. Atty. Southwestern Bell Telephone, Dallas, 1977-81, St. Louis, 1981-82; atty. Advanced Mobile Phone Service, Basking Ridge, N.J., 1982-83; gen. counsel BellSouth Mobility, Atlanta, 1983-86; gen. atty. BellSouth Services, Birmingham, Ala., 1986—. Contbr. articles to profl. jours. Mem. ABA, Dallas Bar Assn. Methodist. Avocations: running, oenophile, bibliophile. Public utilities, General corporate, Antitrust. Home: 2312 Tanglewood Brook Ln Birmingham AL 35243 Office: BellSouth Services Inc Birmingham AL 35203

RUEN, LOWELL VERNON, lawyer; b. Spokane, Wash., July 6, 1954; s. Vernon P. Ruen and Leitoi Isabelle (Pratt) Ruen; m. Kathleen Mary Butler, Mar. 30, 1984. AS, North Idaho Coll., 1974; BBA, Gonzaga U., 1976, JD, 1980; LLM in Taxation, NYU, 1981. Bar: Wash. 1980; CPA, Wash. With McFarland & Alton, P.S., Spokane, 1977-85, ptnr., 1985—. Mem. City of Spokane Zoning Bd., Spokane Estate Planning Council. Mem. Wash. State Bar Assn., Spokane Bar Assn., Am. Inst. CPA's, Wash. Soc. CPA's (program chmn. Spokane chpt. 1985-86, sec., treas. Spokane chpt. 1986—, fed. taxation com. 1982—). Republican. Avocations: golf, gardening. State and local taxation, Estate taxation, Personal income taxation. Home: S 3605 Jefferson Dr Spokane WA 99203 Office: McFarland & Alton PS 1800 Seafirst Fin Ctr Spokane WA 99201

RUF, H(AROLD) WILLIAM, JR., corporation executive, lawyer; b. Madison, Wis., July 1, 1934; s. Harold W. and Margaret (Dottridge) R.; m. Suzanne Williams, Aug. 25, 1962 (div. Jan. 1978); m. Jocelyn C. Ruf, Nov.

21, 1981; children: David W., Margaret E., Katharine S. BS, U. Wis., 1960, JD, 1962. Bar: Wis. 1962, Ohio 1963. Field atty. N.L.R.B., Cleve., 1962-65; counsel Oglebay Norton Co., Cleve., 1965-74, dir. indsl. relations, 1974-78, v.p., 1978—. Trustee Shaker Lakes Nature Ctr., Cleve. 1985, Hill House, Cleve., 1986. Served to cpl. U.S. Army, 1954-56. Clubs: Cleve. Skating, Cleve. Athletic. Labor, Pension, profit-sharing, and employee benefits, Workers' compensation. Home: 13415 Shaker Blvd Cleveland OH 44120 Office: Oglebay Norton Co 1100 Superior Ave Cleveland OH 44114

RUFF, CHARLES F.C., lawyer; b. Cleve., Aug. 1, 1939; s. Carl Ruff and Margaret (Klein) Carson; m. Susan R. Willis, June 9, 1962; children: Carin, Christina. AB, Swarthmore Coll., 1960; LLB, Columbia U., 1963. Bar: N.Y. 1963, D.C. 1973, U.S. Supreme Ct. 1969, U.S. Ct. Appeals (2d, 3d, 4th, 5th, 6th, 9th, 10th and D.C. cirs.). Instr. law U. Liberia., 1963-65; research assoc. African law ctr. Columbia U., 1966; instr. legal methods U. Pa., 1966-67; trial atty. organized crime and racketeering sect., criminal div. U.S. Dept. Justice, 1967-70, chief mgmt. and labor sect. criminal div., 1970-72; prof. Antioch Law Sch., 1972-73; assoc. prof. law Georgetown U., 1973-79; U.S. atty. Dist. of Columbia, 1979-82; ptnr. Covington & Burling, 1982—; asst. spl. prosecutor Watergate Spl. Prosecution Force, 1973-75, spl. prosecutor, 1975-77; chief insp. Drug Enforcement Adminstrn., 1975; dep. insp. gen. HEW, 1977-78; assoc. dep. atty. gen. U.S. Dept. Justice, 1978-79, acting. dep. atty. gen. 1979. Fellow Am. Bar Found.; mem. ABA (rep., vice chmn. bd. regents Nat. Coll. Dist. Attys. 1985—, D.C. Bar Assn. (bd. govs. 1983-86, exec. com. 1985-86). Federal civil litigation, Criminal. Home: 3521 Ordway St NW Washington DC 20044 Office: Covington & Burling 1201 Pennsylvania Ave NW PO Box 7566 Washington DC 20044

RUFFNER, CHARLES LOUIS, lawyer; b. Cin., Nov. 7, 1936; s. Joseph H. and Edith (Solomon) R.; m. Mary Ann Kaufman, Jan. 30, 1966; children: Robin Sue, David Robert. BSBA in Acctg., U. Fla., 1958; JD cum laude, U. Miami, 1964. Bar: Fla. 1964, U.S. Dist. Ct. (so. and mid. dists.) Fla. 1964, U.S. Ct. Appeals (5th cir.) 1964, U.S. Claims Ct. 1966, U.S. Tax Ct. 1966, U.S. Supreme Ct. 1968; cert. in taxation Fla. Bd. Tax Certification. Trial atty. tax div. Dept. Justice, Washington, 1964-67; pres. Forrest, Ruffner, Traum & Hagen, P.A., Miami, Fla., 1967-78; pres. Ruffner, Hagen & Rifkin, P.A., Miami, 1978-81; tax ptnr. Myers, Kenin, Levinson, Ruffner, Frank & Richard, Miami, 1982-84; pres. Charles L. Ruffner, P.A., 1984—; lectr. Fla. Internat. U., Miami. Mem. Dade County Bar Assn., Fed. Bar Assn., ABA, Fla. Bar (exec. council tax sect. 1967-83), South Fla. Tax Litigation Assn. (chmn. 1986-87), Phi Alpha Delta, Phi Kappa Phi. Author: A Practical Approach to Professional Corporations and Associations, 4 edits., 1970, Tax Talk column Miami Law Rev.; editor Miami Law Rev., 1963-64; amicus curiae Fla. Bar in test case of validity of profl. corps.; contbr. numerous articles on taxation to law jours. Corporate taxation, Personal income taxation, State and local taxation. Office: 3001 SW 3d Ave Suite 100 Miami FL 33129

RUGGERI, ROBERT EDWARD, lawyer; b. N.Y.C., Sept. 16, 1952; s. Mario Philip and Margaret Gloria (Pascale) R.; m. Mary Beth Thackeray, June 6, 1981. BA, Union Coll., 1974; JD, Antioch U., 1980. Bar: D.C. 1981, U.S. Dist. Ct. D.C. 1982, U.S. Ct. Internat. Trade 1982, U.S. Ct. Appeals (fed. and D.C. cirs.) 1982, U.S. Supreme Ct. 1984. Young profl. Commn. European Communities, Brussels, Belgium, 1980-81; legal cons. Secretariat, OECD, Paris, France, 1981-82; assoc. Stewart & Stewart, Washington, 1982-83, Graham and James, Washington, 1984-85, Rogers & Wells, Washington, 1985—. Editor comments Antioch Law Jour., 1979-80. Fulbright scholar U.S. Info. Agy., 1980-81. Mem. ABA, D.C. Bar Assn., Washington Fgn. Law Soc. (sec., treas. 1985—). Democrat. Roman Catholic. Private international, Federal civil litigation, Legislative. Home: 8707 62d Ave College Park MD 20740 Office: Rogers & Wells 1737 H St NW Washington DC 20006

RUGGIERO, THOMAS W., lawyer; b. Glen Cove, N.Y., Dec. 2, 1946; s. Philip P. and Virginia M. Ruggiero; m. Patricia W. Ruggiero, Aug. 7, 1971; 2 children. AB in Hist., St. Michael's Coll.; JD, Boston Coll. Bar: N.Y. 1972. From assoc. to ptnr. LeBoeuf, Lamb, Leiby and MacRae, N.Y.C. Mem. ABA. Municipal bonds. Office: LeBoeuf Lamb Leiby & MacRae 520 Madison Ave New York NY 10022

RUGGLES, RUDY LAMONT, lawyer; b. Phila., Jan. 10, 1909; s. Daniel Emery and A. Leona (Rudy) R.; m. Ruth Cain, Dec. 14, 1935; children: Rudy Lamont, Mrs. Jean Ruggles Romoser. Student, U. Cin., 1926-27, Harvard U., 1927-31; Harvard scholar, Geneva (Switzerland) Sch. Internat. Studies, 1929; J.D., Boston U., 1934. Bar: Ill. 1935, U.S. Supreme Ct 1960. Asso. Isham, Lincoln & Beale, Chgo., 1935-42; regional atty. OPA, 1942-43; mem. firm Chadwell, Kayser, Ruggles, McGee & Hastings, Chgo., 1946-75; of counsel Chadwell, Kayser, Ruggles, McGee & Hastings, 1976-82. Mem. vis. com. humanities div. U. Chgo., 1959-74, mem. citizens bd., 1963—; mem. Chgo. Crime Commn.; mem. nat. bd. Nat. Book Com.; bd. dirs., chmn. legal aid bur. com. United Charities Chgo.; bd. overseers vis. com. to Harvard Coll., 1964-70; bd. overseers vis. com. to Harvard Div. Sch., 1969-75, also mem. standing com. univ. resources; bd. dirs., exec. com. Evanston Hosp., 1965-75; mem. Northwestern U. Assocs.; past chmn. lawyers div. Chgo. Crusade of Mercy; trustee Newberry Library, 1964-79, life trustee, 1979—; mem. The Chgo. Com., The Hundred Club of Cook County. Served to lt. USNR, 1944-46. Recipient award disting. service to profession, community and youth of Am. Monticello Coll., 1959. Fellow Am. Bar Found.; mem. Fellows of Ill. Bar Found. (charter), Am., Ill. (named sr. counselor), Chgo., 7th Fed. Circuit bar assns., Am. Soc. Internat. Law, Am. Judicature Soc., Law Club Chgo., Legal Club Chgo., Harvard Alumni Assn. (dir.), Beta Theta Pi, Phi Delta Phi. Clubs: Comml. (Chgo.), Econ. (Chgo.) (dir., past pres.), Harvard (Chgo.) (past pres.), Caxton (Chgo.) (past pres.), Chgo. Literary (Chgo.), Chicago (Chgo.) (past pres., dir.), Mid-America (Chgo.), Mid-Day (Chgo.) (trustee, past pres.), Wayfarers (Chgo.); Glen View (Golf, Ill.); Indian Hill (Winnetka); Grolier (N.Y.C.); Everglades (Palm Beach, Fla.), Lost Tree (Palm Beach, Fla.), Old Port Yacht (Palm Beach, Fla.). Antitrust, General corporate, Government contracts and claims. Home: 11975 Turtle Beach Rd Lost Tree Village North Palm Beach FL 33408

RUHL, JOHN BENJAMIN, lawyer; b. N.Y.C., Nov. 26, 1957; s. Harold John and Margaret (O'Keeffe) R.; m. Lisa M. LeMaster, Apr. 23, 1983. BA, U. Va., 1979, JD, 1982; LLM, George Washington U., 1986. Bar: D.C. 1982, Va. 1984, U.S. Dist. Ct. D.C., U.S. Ct. Appeals (D.C. cir.), U.S. Supreme Ct. 1986. Assoc. Fulbright & Jaworski, Washington, 1982-86, Austin, Tex., 1986—. Mem. ABA (natural resources law sect.), Va. Bar Assn., D.C. Bar Assn. Environment, Administrative and regulatory, Federal civil litigation. Office: Fulbright & Jaworski 600 Congress Ave Suite 2400 Austin TX 78701

RUIZ-SURIA, FERNANDO, lawyer; b. San Juan, P.R., May 18, 1916; s. Abelardo and Teresa (Suria) R.; m. Irma Bosch, Aug. 18, 1946; children—Fernando, Vanessa, Ivan, Mimi. B.A., U. P.R., 1938, LL.B., 1940. Bar: P.R. 1941, U.S. Dist. Ct. P.R. 1941, U.S. Ct. Appeals (1st cir.) 1959, U.S. Supreme Ct. 1963, U.S. Ct. Appeals D.C. 1977, Temporary Emergency Ct. Appeals 1980. House counsel Shell Co. Ltd., San Juan, 1942-53; sr. ptnr. Sifre & Ruiz-Suria, San Juan, 1953-67, McConnell Valdes Kelley Sifre Griggs & Ruiz-Suria, San Juan, 1967-81; of counsel McConnell Valdes et al; dir. corps.; mem. jud. confs.; former mem. P.R. Bar Examiners; former mem. Evidence Rules Com. Fellow Am. Coll. Trial Lawyers; mem. ABA, Colegio de Abogados de P.R., Sara Bay C. of C., Meadows C. of C. Roman Catholic. Clubs: Bird Key Yacht (Sarasota, Fla.); Bankers (San Juan, P.R.). Federal civil litigation, State civil litigation, Real property. Office: McConnell Valdes et al Pan American Bldg 10th Floor San Juan PR 00918

RUMA, RONALD EDWARD, lawyer; b. Great Lakes, Ill., Nov. 18, 1953; s. Francis Thomas and Laura Rose (Leible) R.; m. Susan Stamps, July 16, 1978; 1 child, Dominic Francis. BCE, Mich. State U., 1975, MCE, 1976, JD, 1981. Bar: Calif. 1981, U.S. Dist. Ct. (no. dist.) Calif. 1981; registered profl. engr., Calif. Engr. Bechtel Power Corp., Ann Arbor, Mich., 1976-78; assoc. Hancock, Rothert & Bunshoft, San Francisco, 1981—. Mem. San Francisco Bar Assn., Am. Soc. Civil Engrs., Lawyers Club of San Francisco, Barristers of San Francisco. Construction, Insurance, State civil litigation. Office: Hancock Rothert & Bunshoft 4 Embarcadero Ctr 10th Fl San Francisco CA 94111

RUMAN, SAUL I., lawyer; b. Chgo., May 12, 1925; s. James A. and Pauline (Scharfer) R.; m. Beverlee Mahan, June 17; children—Conrad Ruman Conrad, Melissa Ruman Stewart, Elizabeth. B.S., Ind. U., 1949, J.D. with distinction, 1952. Bar: Ind. 1952, U.S. Supreme Ct. 1963, U.S. Dist. Ct. Ind. 1952, U.S. Ct. Appeals (7th cir.) 1962. Sole practice, Hammond, Ind., 1952—; mng. ptnr. Saul I. Ruman and Assocs.; former lectr. bus. law Ind. U. N.W.; mem. faculty numerous insts. on law; mem. com. on rules of practice and procedure Supreme Ct. Ind., 1983—; mem. Ind. Supreme Ct. character and fitness com., 1975—. Bd. visitors Ind. U. Sch. Law, 1973—; bd. advisors N.W. Campus Ind. U., 1973-85; faculty Nat. Inst. Trial Advocacy, 1984-86. Trustee Ind. Legal Services Fund, 1978, 84. Served with USN, 1942-45. Fellow Internat. Acad. Trial Lawyers (dir. 1980—); mem. Ill. Trial Assn., Ind. Bar Assn. (chmn. trial lawyers sect. 1970-71), Ind. Trial Lawyers Assn. (dir. 1971-80, pres. 1980-81), Coll. Fellows, Assn. Trial Lawyers Am., Am. Bd. Trial Advocates, Order of Coif. Club: Tennis. Personal injury, Federal civil litigation, State civil litigation. Office: 5261 Hohman Ave Hammond IN 46320

RUMMAGE, STEPHEN MICHAEL, lawyer; b. Massillon, Ohio, Dec. 27, 1955; s. Robert Everett and Kathleen Patricia (Newman) R.; m. Elizabeth Anne Seivert, Mar. 24, 1979; 1 child, Everett Martin. BA in History and English, Stanford U., 1977; JD, U. Calif., Berkeley, 1980. Bar: Wash. 1980, U.S. Dist. Ct. (we. dist.) 1980, U.S. Ct. Appeals (9th cir.) 1983, U.S. Supreme Ct. 1985. Assoc. Davis, Wright et al, Seattle, 1980-85; ptnr. Davis Wright and Jones, Seattle, 1986—. Co-author: Employer's Guide to Strike Planning and Prevention, 1985. Mem. ABA, Fed. Bar Assn., Wash. State Bar Assn. (trustee young lawyers sect. 1981-83), Seattle-King County Bar Assn., Order of the Coif, Phi Beta Kappa. Democrat. Roman Catholic. Club: Seattle. Federal civil litigation, Labor, Securities. Office: Davis Wright and Jones 1501 4th Ave Suite 2600 Seattle WA 98101

RUMMEL, EDGAR FERRAND, lawyer; b. New Bern, N.C., June 29, 1929; s. Robert French and Reba Jeanette (Burgess) R.; m. Lillian Hildebrandt, Dec. 28, 1954. B.A., Ohio State U., 1955; J.D., DePaul U., 1965; LL.B., U. London, Eng., 1973; LL.M., George Washington U., 1978. Bar: U.S. Dist. Ct. D.C. 1967, U.S. Ct. Appeals (D.C. cir.) 1968, U.S. Supreme Ct. 1971, Md. 1980. Atty.-adviser Dept. Army, Washington, 1971-74, 78, counsel U.S. Army Real Estate Agy., Frankfurt, W.Ger., 1975-77, supervisory atty.-adviser, asst. div. chief Office of Chief of Engrs., Dept. Army, Washington, 1977-83; sr. atty. advisor Office of Judge Advocate Gen., Dept. Army, Washington, 1983-85, trial atty., 1987—; spl. asst. U.S. Atty. Dist. Colo., 1985-87; chmn. mineral leasing com. Dept. Def., 1981-84; mem. Oreg. Nat. Trial Adv. Council, 1983-84. Served with AUS, 1947-51. Mem. ABA, Md. State Bar Assn., Am. Soc. Legal History. Democrat. Episcopalian (vestryman 1981-84). Clubs: Nat. Lawyers, Md. Univ. Lodge: Rotary. Real property, Environment, Legal history. Home: 7812 Adelphi Ct Adelphi MD 20783 Office: 20 Massachusetts Ave Room 5138 Washington DC 20314

RUMMONDS, JAMES SCOTT, lawyer; b. Pomona, Calif., Oct. 10, 1942; s. Raymond R. and Ruth (Waits) R.; m. Sue Ann (Clause) R., Dec. 21, 1962; children: Jerald Scott, James Raymond, Joshua A.C. BA, Stanford U., 1968, JD, 1973. Bar: Calif. 1974, U.S. Dist. Ct. (no. dist.) Calif. 1985. Ptnr. Germino et al, Los Banos, Calif., 1974-82, Rummonds, Clause & Mair, Santa Cruz, Calif., 1983—; faculty mem. Hastings Inst. Trial and Appellate Advocacy, San Francisco, 1983—, Fed. Practice Program, U.S. Dist. Ct. (no. dist.) Calif., San Jose, 1985—, Nat. Inst. of Trial Advocacy, N.W. Regional; chief exec. officer, chmn. bd. dirs. Bowox Corp., Santa Cruz, Legal Aid, Inc., Santa Cruz. Contbr. articles to profl. jours. Mem. Pres.' Commn. Population Growth and the Am. Future, Washington, 1970-72; pres. Los Barrancos Homeowners Assn., La Selva Beach, Calif, 1985. Served with USN, 1960-63. Mem. Santa Cruz County Bar Assn., Assn. Trial Lawyers Am., Calif. Trial Lawyers Assn., Nat. Environ. Law Soc. (founder 1970), Stanford Environ. Law Soc. (founder 1969). Republican. Club: Tired Iron Team Surfing (Santa Cruz) (founder). Personal injury, State civil litigation. Office: Rummonds Clause & Mair 331 Soquel Ave Santa Cruz CA 95062

RUMRELL, RICHARD GARY, lawyer; b. Tampa, Fla., Nov. 30, 1945; s. Clarence J. and Arline M. Rumrell; m. Jo Van Rooy, Dec. 20, 1969; children: Jason S., Dylan A. Ba, U. S. Fla., 1967; JD with honors, Fla. State U., 1970. Bar: Fla. 1971, D.C. 1976. Adminstrv. asst. senator Law Chiles, Tallahassee, Fla., 1967; legis. intern Fla. Legislature Dept., Tallahassee, 1968-69; staff dir. elections Fla. Ho. of Reps., Tallahassee, 1971; asst. states atty. 4th Jud. Cir. Fla., Jacksonville, Fla., 1971-74; assoc. Smathers & Thompson, Jacksonville, 1975-82; ptnr. Smathers & Rumrell, Jacksonville, 1982—, Rumrell & Vlcek, Jacksonville, 1985—. Author: (with others) Florida: Historical and Contemporary Life in the Sunshine State, 1974. Past pres. port com. Econ. Devel. Council, Jacksonville; pres. Mental Health Clinic of Jacksonville, 1981; chmn. Pvt. Industry Council, Jacksonville, 1985-86. Mem. ABA, Am. Judicature Soc., Maritime Law Assn., Southeastern Admiralty Law Assn., Fla. Bar Assn., Jacksonville Bar Assn. Clubs: River, Propeller. Avocation: fishing. Federal civil litigation, State civil litigation, Admiralty. Office: Rumrell & Vlcek PA 12-14 E Bay St Jacksonville FL 32202

RUND, WILLIAM DRAKE, lawyer; b. St. Louis, Feb. 14, 1927; s. Emmet Henry and Emily Lee (Taylor) R.; m. Lois Ruth Darr, May 20, 1950; children—William Drake, Christine Eldarrat, Mark, Mary Ann, James, Kathryn, Thomas, Margaret, Robert. B.S., St. Louis U., 1948; J.D., Wash. U., 1954. Bar: Mo. 1954, U.S. Dist. Ct. (ea. dist.) Mo. 1955. Law clk. Judge Roy W. Harper, St. Louis, 1954-55; sole practice, 1954-57; asst. cir. atty. City of St. Louis, 1957-58; v.p., sec., gen. counsel Gen. Contract Fin. Corp. and Securities Investment Co., St. Louis, 1958-68; ptnr. Fordyce & Mayne, 1968-72; clk. U.S. Dist. Ct. (ea. dist.) Mo., 1972-79, U.S. magistrate, 1972-76, clk. of ct. U.S. Bankruptcy Ct., 1979—. Served with USAAC, 1945-46. Mem. ABA, Mo. Bar Assn., Met. St. Louis Bar Assn., Nat. Conf. Bankruptcy Clks., Soc. for Preservation and Encouragement of Barber Shop Quartet Singing in Am., Phi Delta Phi. Roman Catholic. Bankruptcy, Consumer commercial, General corporate. Office: 1114 Market St Room 730 St Louis MO 63101

RUNDEL, KENNETH MARTIN, lawyer; b. Lansing, Mich., Jan. 25, 1947; s. Harold Fowler and Evelyn Louise (Poruba) R.; m. Emily Caroline Eads, June 21, 1980; children: Lauren Emily Eads-Rundell, Jessica Evelyn Eads-Rundell. BS in Psychology, Cen. Mich. U., 1969; JD, So. Meth. U., 1979. Bar: Tex. 1979, U.S. Dist. Ct. (no. dist.) Tex. 1980. Sole practice Dallas, 1979-81, 84—; ptnr. Rundel & Whaley, Dallas, 1981-82; program dir. Sta. KRBE radio, Houston, 1982-84; pres. Owners Listing Service Inc., Dallas, 1984—; also bd. dirs. Owners Listing Service Inc., Irving, Tex.; voice talent Jackie Townsend Agy., Dallas, 1984—. Announcer Sta. KZEW radio, Dallas, 1986—. Bd. dirs. Montessori Acad. North Tex. Sch. Bd., Flower Mound, 1985—. Mem. ABA, Tex. Bar Assn., Dallas C. of C., Better Bus. Bur. Avocations: radio announcing, softball. General corporate, Entertainment, Trademark and copyright. Home: 1625 Solway Lewisville TX 75067 Office: Owners Listing Service Inc 1425 Greenway Suite 600 Irving TX 75038

RUNDIO, LOUIS MICHAEL, JR., lawyer; b. Chgo., Sept. 13, 1943; s. Louis Michael Sr. and Germaine Matilda (Pasternack) R.; m. Ann Marie Bartlett, July 10, 1971; children: Matthew, Melissa. BS in Physics, Loyola U., Chgo., 1965, JD, 1972. Bar: Ill. 1972, U.S. Dist. Ct. (no. dist.) Ill. 1972, U.S. Ct. Appeals (7th cir.) 1974, U.S. Dist. Ct. (ea. dist.) Mich. 1983. Assoc. McDermott, Will & Emery, Chgo., 1972-77, ptnr., 1978—. Served to 1st lt. U.S. Army, 1965-68, Vietnam. Mem. ABA, Chgo. Bar Assn. Environment, Federal civil litigation, State civil litigation. Home: 676 Skye Ln Inverness IL 60010 Office: McDermott Will & Emery 111 W Monroe St Chicago IL 60603-4067

RUNDLETT, ELLSWORTH TURNER, III, lawyer; b. Portland, Maine, Jan. 12, 1946; s. Ellsworth Turner II and Esther (Stevens) R.; m. Lisa Warren, Oct. 25, 1964 (div. June 1967); 1 child, Ellsworth Turner IV; m. Jamie Donnelly, June 7, 1982. A.B. cum laude, Bowdoin Coll., 1968; J.D., U. Maine, 1973. Bar: Maine 1973, U.S. Dist. Ct. Maine 1973, U.S. Ct. Appeals (1st cir.) 1973. Bowdoin Coll. intern U.S. Senate, Washington, 1967; law clk. Superior Ct. Maine, Portland, 1972-73; asst. corp. counsel City of Portland, 1973-76; ptnr. Childs, Emerson, Rundlett, Fifield & Childs, Portland, 1980—; Contbr. legal articles to Maine Bus. Digest, 1978-84. Pres. Pine Tree Alcohol Treatment Ctr., Windham, Maine, 1978-80; trustee Portland Players, Inc., South Portland, Maine, 1977-84, pres., 1985—. Mem. Cumberland County Bar (trustee 1983-84, 86-87), Maine Bar Assn., Am. Trial Lawyers Assn., Maine Trial Lawyers Assn., U. Maine Law Alumni (bd. dirs. 1984-87). Clubs: Cumberland, Portland (gov. 1983-86), Bowdoin of Portland (pres. 1978) (Portland). Personal injury, General practice, State civil litigation. Office: Emerson Rundlett & Fifield 257 Deering Ave Portland ME 04103

RUNFOLA, ROSS THOMAS, lawyer, educator; b. Buffalo, Aug. 30, 1943; s. Joseph Paul and Isabelle Louise (Santi) R.; m. Sheila Kuch, Dec. 26, 1982; children: Jennifer, Ross Thomas. BA summa cum laude, SUNY, Buffalo, 1965, MA, 1968, PhD, 1973, JD, 1981. Bar: N.Y. 1982. Prof. social scis. Medaille Coll., Buffalo, 1969—; asst. prof. SUNY, Buffalo, 1970-73; sports columnist Buffalo New Times, Buffalo, 1973-74; co-anchor Sta. WUTV, Buffalo, 1974; reporter Buffalo Courier Express, Buffalo, 1975-76; columnist Spree mag., Buffalo, 1979-82; legal asst. Erie County Pub. Adminstr., Buffalo, 1981; ptnr. Fiorella, Leiter & Runfola, Buffalo, 1982-86, Matusick, Spadafora & Verrastro, Buffalo, 1986-87; spl. matrimonial council Siegel, Kelleher & Kahn, Buffalo, 1987—. Author: Jock: Sports and Male Identity, 1980; contbr. numerous articles to profl. jours.; writer: Organized Sports: Are They Good for Young People, 1975. Active Mayor's Energy Task Force City of Buffalo, 1973, Attica Prison Task Force, N.Y., 1973, Western N.Y. Consortium on Higher Edn., 1974, Erie County (N.Y.) Task Force on Physical Edn. and Recreation for Meeting the needs of the Handicapped, 1974, Instl. Task Force Pvt. Colls. Western N.Y., 1974, Western N.Y. Higher Edn. Task Force, 1975, Legis. Adv. Com. N.Y. State Assembly, 1976, Children's Hosp. Adolescence Program, 1978, Western N.Y. Heart Assn., 1978, Southern Poverty Law Ctr., 1978—, Erie County Dem. Com., 1978—, Step Family Assn. Western N.Y., 1983—, Frontier Dem. Club, 1983—. Named one of Outstanding Young Men of Am. by Outstanding Young Men Am., 1980; numerous others. Mem. ABA, N.Y. State Bar Assn., Erie County Bar Assn. Roman Catholic. Avocations: writing, reading, bicycling, cross country skiing. Family and matrimonial. Home: 96 Cleveland Ave Buffalo NY 14222 Office: Siegel Kelleher & Kahn 426 Franklin St Buffalo NY 14202

RUNSTAD, JUDITH MANVILLE, lawyer; b. Ontario, Oreg., July 15, 1944; d. Gerry Wright and Jean (Thurston) Manville; m. H. Jon Runstad, Dec. 3, 1977. BS, U. Idaho, 1966, MS, 1967; JD, U. Wash., 1974. Bar: Wash. 1974. Tchr. Shorecrest High Sch., Seattle, 1967-71; assoc. Foster, Pepper & Riviera, Seattle, 1974-79, ptnr., 1979—; bd. dirs. Safeco Mut. Funds, Seattle. Exec. editor U. Wash. Law Rev. Bd. govs. Griffin Coll., Seattle, 1982—; trustee Downtown Seattle Assn., 1982—, v.p. 1985-86, pres. 1986-87; trustee Seattle Art Mus., 1984—, Seattle Repertory Theatre, 1985—; bd. dirs. ACT Theater, Seattle, 1979-84. Mem. ABA, Wash. State Bar Assn. (bd. dirs. land use sect.), Urban Land Inst., Seattle C. of C. (gen. counsel 1985-86), Lamda Alpha, Phi Beta Kappa. Clubs: Seattle Tennis, Seattle Yacht, Wash. Athletic.

RUPERT, DONALD WILLIAM, lawyer; b. Clearfield, Pa., Oct. 15, 1946; s. Donald Lee and Dorothy Mae (Bonsall) R.; m. Patricia A. Rupert, June 21, 1969. BS in Chemistry, Miami U., Ohio, 1968; JD, Washburn U., Topeka, 1976. Bar: Tex. 1976, Ill. 1978, U.S. Ct. Appeals (Fed. cir.) 1978, U.S. Dist. Ct. (so. dist.) Tex. 1977, U.S. Ct. Appeals (7th cir.) 1981, U.S. Dist. Ct. (no. dist.) Ill. 1979. Assoc. Arnold, White & Durkee, Houston, 1976-78, Kirkland & Ellis, Chgo., 1978-83, ptnr., 1983-86; ptnr. Neuman, Williams, Anderson & Olson, Chgo., 1986—; cons. USAF, Dayton, Ohio, 1974-81. Contbr. articles to profl. jours. Served to capt. USAF, 1968-74. Miami U. Research fellow, 1967, Grad. Research fellow, 1968. Mem. ABA, Am. Intellectual Property Law Assn., Tex. Bar Assn., Ill. Bar Assn., Phi Kappa Phi. Democrat. Presbyterian. Federal civil litigation, Environment. Home: 2519 Park Pl Evanston IL 60201 Office: Neuman Williams Anderson & Olson 77 W Washington Chicago IL 60602

RUPORT, SCOTT HENDRICKS, lawyer; b. Paterson, N.J., Nov. 22, 1949; s. Fred Hendricks and Juyne (Kennedy) R.; m. Linda Darlene Smith, Sept. 12, 1970; children—Brittany Lyle, Courtney Kennedy. B.S. in Bus. Adminstrn., Bowling Green State U., 1971; J.D., U. Akron, 1974. Bar: Ohio 1974, Pa. 1984, U.S. Dist. Ct. for no. dist. Ohio 1974, U.S. Ct. Appeals for 6th circuit, 1975, U.S. Supreme Ct. 1978. Assoc. firm Schwab, Sager, Grosenbaugh, Rothal, Fort, Skidmore & Nukes Co., L.P.A., Akron, Ohio, 1974-76, Skidmore & George Co., L.P.A., Akron, 1976-79, Skidmore, Ruport & Haskings, Akron, 1979-83; ptnr. firm Roderick, Myers & Linton, Akron, 1983-85; sole practice,Akron, 1985—; instr. real estate law U. Akron, 1976-77, adj. asst. prof. constrn. tech. Coll. Engring., 1983—. Served as capt., Fin. Corps, USAR, 1971-79. Mem. ABA, Akron Bar Assn., Ohio Bar Assn., Ohio Acad. Trial Lawyers, Assn. Trial Lawyers Am., Beta Gamma Sigma, Sigma Chi. Republican. Presbyterian. State civil litigation, Construction, Real property. Office: CitiCenter Bldg 6th Floor 146 S High St Akron OH 44308-1344

RUPP, JOHN PETER, lawyer; b. Westerly, R.I., Dec. 30, 1944; s. Paul P. and Doris T. (Savin) R.; m. Maureen E. O'Bryon, June 30, 1968; children—Megan E., Erin O. B.A., U. Iowa, 1967; J.D., Yale U., 1971. Bar: Maine 1971, D.C. 1971, U.S. Ct. Appeals (1st cir.) 1971. U.S. Ct. Appeals (9th and 4th cirs.) 1975. U.S. Supreme Ct. 1976, U.S. Ct. Appeals (10th cir.) 1977. Law clk. to chief judge First Cir. Ct. Appeals, 1971-72; assoc. Covington & Burling, Washington, 1972-74, ptnr., 1977—; asst. to solicitor gen. Dept. Justice, Washington, 1974-77; chmn. lawyers com. Children's Def. Fund, Washington, 1983-84. Author: (with others) The Rights of Gays, 1974, 83. Mem. steering com. Americans for Democratic Action, Washington, 1973; credentials judge Democratic Party, 1984. Democrat. Roman Catholic. Mem. ACLU. Administrative and regulatory, Antitrust, Federal civil litigation. Office: Covington & Burling 1201 Pennsylvania Ave NW Washington DC 20044

RUPPE, ARTHUR MAXWELL, lawyer; b. Boone, N.C., Dec. 15, 1928; s. Arthur Monroe and Floye (Robinson) R.; m. Ruth Marie Ledford; children: Ruth Carol, Sharon Marie, Arthur Maxwell Jr., Susan Lunette. AA, Gardner Webb Coll., 1947; AB, U. N.C., 1950, JD, 1952. Bar: N.C. 1952, U.S. Dist. Ct. (ea. dist.) N.C. 1955, U.S. Ct. Mil. Appeals 1968. Asst. staff, judge advocate U.S. Army, Ft. Bragg, N.C., 1952-55; sole practice Fayetteville, N.C., 1955—. Served to 1st lt. U.S. Army, 1952-55. Mem. ABA, Assn. Trial Lawyers Am., N.C. Bar Assn. (sustaining), 12th Jud. Dist. Bar Assn., Cumberland County Bar Assn. (pres. 1982-83), N.C. Acad. Trial lawyers (patron). Democrat. Baptist. Lodge: K.P. Avocations: snow ski, tennis. State civil litigation, Personal injury, Workers' compensation. Home: 336 Summertime Rd Fayetteville NC 28303 Office: 115 S Cool Spring St Fayetteville NC 28301

RUPPERSBERGER, CHARLES ALBERT, III, lawyer; b. Balt., Jan. 31, 1946; s. Charles Albert Jr. and Margaret (Wilson) R.; m. Kay Murphy, Dec. 28, 1968; children: Charles Albert, Jill Ann. BA, U. Md., 1967; JD, U. Balt., 1970. Bar: Md. 1972, U.S. Supreme Ct. 1977. Social worker Balt. City Schs., 1967-69; claims adjuster U.S. Fidelity and Guaranty Co., Balt., 1969-70; law clk. to presiding justice Balt. County Cir. Ct., Towson, 1970-72; asst. state's atty. Balt. County State's Atty., Towson, 1972-80; ptnr. Ruppersberger, Winter, Clark & Mister, Timonium, Md., 1980—; chief of investigation div. State's Atty.'s Office, Towson, 1972-80; liaison Balt. County Police Dept. and Md. State Police, 1973-80. Coach, v.p. Cockeysville (Md.) Recreation Council, 1978—; campaign mgr. for senator Francis X. Kelly, Annapolis, Md., 1980-85; councilman Balt. County Council, 1985—; legal council Balt. County Athletic League; pres. Topfield condominium Assn., Cockeysville, 1975-78, Greater Timonium Community Council, 1980—, co-chmn. fundraising U. Hosp.; bd. dirs. Timonium (Md.) Meth. Ch., 1984—. Recipient Appreciation award Balt. County Order of Fraternal Police, 1977, Cert. of Appreciation Balt. County Police, 1979; named one of Outstanding Young Marylanders Jaycees, 1979. Mem. Md. Bar Assn. (grievance com.), Balt. County Bar Assn. (chmn. bench-bar com.), Nat. Coll. Dist. Attys. (advisor 1974-80), U. Md. Alumni Assn. (v.p.), U.S. LaCrosse Team. Democrat. Methodist. Lodge: Masons. Personal injury, State civil litigation, Consumer commercial. Office: Ruppersberger Winter & Clark 30 E Padonia Rd Suite 404 Timonium MD 21093

RUPPERT, JAMES DELANO, II, lawyer; b. Franklin, Ohio, Jan. 16, 1936; s. Paul Edward and Sarah Elizabeth (Morgan) R.; m. Paula Ann Riley, June 10, 1960; children—Todd Riley, James D. III. B.S., U.S. Mil. Acad., 1960; J.D., U. Cin., 1966. Bar: Ohio 1966, U.S. Dist. Ct. (so. dist.) Ohio 1966, U.S. Ct. Appeals (6th cir.) 1971, U.S. Ct. Appeals (5th cir.) 1981, U.S. Supreme Ct. 1981. Ptnr. Riley & Ruppert, Franklin, Ohio, 1966-69; ptnr. Ruppert, Kirby & Powers, Franklin, 1969-71; sr. ptnr. James D. Ruppert & Assocs., Franklin, 1971—; lectr. in field; dir. Miami Valley (Ohio) Bldg. & Loan, Miami Valley Bank of SW Ohio; spl. counsel to atty. gen. Ohio, 1971—, to Wright State U., 1981—, to Ohio Bd. Edn., 1982—. Mem. Dirs. Club Pub. T.V. Ch. 14, 16, Dayton, 1983—. Served with U.S. Army, 1960-63. Mem. Warren County Bar Assn., Assn. Trial Lawyers Am., ABA, Ohio State Bar Assn., Melvin M. Belli Soc. (trustee), Am. Soc. Legal Medicine. Democrat. Presbyterian. Clubs: Elks, Eagles. Personal injury, State civil litigation, Criminal. Office: PO Box 369 Franklin OH 45005

RUPPERT, JOHN LAWRENCE, lawyer; b. Chgo., Oct. 7, 1953; s. Merle Arvin and Loretta Marie (Ford) R.; m. Katharine Marie Tarbox, June 5, 1976. BA, Northwestern U., 1975; JD, U. Denver, 1978; LLM in Taxation, NYU, 1979. Bar: Colo. 1978, U.S. Dist. Ct. Colo. 1978, Ill. 1979, U.S. Tax Ct. 1981. Assoc. Kirkland & Ellis, Denver, 1979084, ptnr., 1984—; lectr. in field. Contbr. articles to profl. jours. Mem. Colo. Bar Assn. (exec. council tax sect. 1985—), Denver Bar Assn. Corporate taxation, Personal income taxation, State and local taxation. Office: Kirkland & Ellis 1999 Broadway Suite 4000 Denver CO 80202

RUPPERT, MARK RICHARD, lawyer, military officer; b. Cin., Feb. 3, 1956; s. Richard Joseph and Eva (Harmon) R.; m. Cary Beth Brooks, Aug. 4, 1979 (div. May 1986). BA in Polit. Sci. with honors, U. Cin., 1978; JD with honors, Ohio State U., 1981. Bar: Mich. 1981, U.S. Dist. Ct. (ea. and we. dists.) Mich. 1982, U.S. Ct. Mil. Appeals 1984. Assoc. Foster, Swift, Collins & Coey PC, Lansing, Mich., 1981-83; judge adv. USAF, FE Warren AFB, Mich., 1983—. Mem. Mich. Arthritis Found., Lansing, 1983. Mem. ABA, Mich. Bar Assn., Air Force Assn., Internat. Plastic Modelers Soc., Phi Beta Kappa. Republican. Roman Catholic. Avocations: skiing, sailing, golf, hunting, studying military history. Military, Criminal, Labor. Home: 4108 N 1st St FE Warren AFB WY 82001 Office: USAF Trial Judiciary 4th Cir Lowry AFB CO 80230-5802

RUSCH, JONATHAN JAY, lawyer; b. Nyack, N.Y., Oct. 16, 1952; s. Thaddeus David and Alice Marjorie (Lewis) R.; m. Doreen Evelyn Lacovara, Aug. 10, 1974; children: Rachel Madeline, Catherine Elizabeth. AB in Pub. Affairs with honors, Princeton U., 1974; MA, U. Va., 1978, JD, 1980. Bar: D.C. 1981, U.S. Dist. Ct. D.C. 1981, U.S. Ct. Appeals (D.C. cir.) 1981, U.S. Ct. Appeals (7th cir.) 1985. Assoc. Cleary, Gottlieb, Steen & Hamilton, Washington, 1980-83; spl. asst. to atty. gen. U.S. Dept. Justice, Washington, 1983-84; counsel Pres. Commn. on Organized Crime, Washington, 1984-86; dir. office of fin. enforcement U.S. Dept. Treasury, Washington, 1986—. Mem. ABA (chmn. antitrust, competition and trade regulation com. 1986—). Republican. Roman Catholic. Club: Tower (Princeton, N.J.). Avocations: racewalking, writing. Administrative and regulatory, Criminal. Home: 4600 Connecticut Ave NW #206 Washington DC 20008 Office: US Dept Treasury 1500 Pennsylvania Ave NW Washington DC 20220

RUSCITELLA, MARIA MARTHA, lawyer; b. Phila., May 9, 1954; d. Ulysses Thomas and Joan Marie (Hagner) Ruscitella. B.A., Elmira Coll., 1975; J.D., Delaware Law Sch., Wilmington, 1978. Bar: Pa. 1979. Sole practice, Wayne, Pa., 1979-80; corp. counsel C.D.M. Inc., Hatboro, Pa., 1980-82; sole practice, Paoli, Pa., 1982-83; gen. counsel Theriault's Inc., Annapolis, Md., 1983-85, corp. counsel Devel. Resources, Inc., Alex, Va., 1985—. Contbr. monthly newsletter The Dollmasters, 1983; contbr. The Law Forum, 1976—. Mem. Annapolis Law Ctr., 1983—; treas. Women's Law Ctr. Anne Arundel County. Mem. ABA, Pa. Bar Assn., Md. Bar Assn., Women's Bar Assn. Md., Delta Theta Phi. Republican. Roman Catholic. Home: 313 E Mason Ave Alexandria VA 22301 Office: Devel Resources Inc 1600 Duke St Alexandria VA 22314

RUSE, STEVEN DOUGLAS, lawyer; b. Wichita, Kans., Mar. 8, 1950; B.A., U. Kans., 1972; J.D., Creighton U., 1975. Bar: Mo. 1975, U.S. Dist. Ct. (we. dist.) Mo. 1975, Kans. 1982, U.S. Dist. Ct. Kans. 1982. Law clk. to dist. justice U.S. Dist. Ct. Mo., Kansas City, 1975-77; assoc. Shughart, Thomson & Kilroy, Kansas City, 1977-81, ptnr., 1981—. Mem. ABA, Mo. Bar Assn., Kans. Bar Assn. Federal civil litigation, State civil litigation, Insurance. Office: Shughart Thomson & Kilroy PO Box 25670 Overland Park KS 66225

RUSH, DOUGLAS KEVIN, lawyer; b. Paterson, N.J., Oct. 11, 1950; s. H.J. and Grace (Cronce) R.; m. Janette Massie Lohman, Feb. 14, 1983. BS, U.S. Naval Acad., 1972; JD cum laude, St. Louis U., 1981. Bar: Mo. 1981, U.S. Dist. Ct. Mo. 1981, U.S. Ct. Appeals (8th cir.) 1981, U.S. Supreme Ct. 1986. Instr. St. Louis (Mo.) U. Sch. of Law, 1980-81; assoc. Armstrong, Teasdale, Kramer & Vaughan, St. Louis, 1981—. Mem. St. Louis Bd. of Edn., 1985—. Served to lt. USN, 1968-78, Vietnam; lt. comdr. USNR, 1978—. Mem. Mo. Bar Assn., Bar Assn. of Met. St. Louis, St. Louis Ambassadors, Order of Woolsack. Democrat. Lutheran. Clubs: Media, Glen Echo Country Club. Admiralty, Federal civil litigation, State civil litigation. Office: Armstrong Teasdale Kramer & Vaughan 611 Olive St Saint Louis MO 63101

RUSH, FLETCHER GREY, JR., lawyer; b. Orlando, Fla., Dec. 28, 1917; s. Fletcher Grey and Elizabeth (Knox) R.; m. Lena Mae Willis, June 6, 1942; children: Margaret Patricia Rush White, Richard Fletcher. B.S. in Bus. Adminstrn. with honors; L.L.B. with honors, U. Fla., 1942; LL.D. (hon.), Fla. So. Coll., 1975. Bar: Fla. 1942. Practice in Orlando, 1946—; pres. firm Rush, Marshall, Bergstrom, Reber, Gabrielson & Jones, P.A., 1957—; Trustee Lawyers Title Guaranty Fund, 1953-65, chmn. bd., 1962-63, gen. counsel, 1968—; v.p., dir., gen. counsel Orlando Fed. Savs. & Loan Assn., 1955-75; dir. Trust Co. Fla., 1974-82; mem. jud. nominating council Supreme Ct. Fla., 1972-73, jud. nominating commn., 1983—. Conbr. articles to legal jours. Mem. Orlando Municipal Planning Bd., 1961-63; mem. Orlando Loch Haven Park Bd., 1973-81, vice chmn., 1978-81; bd. regents State Fla. Colls. and Univs., 1965; trustee Coll. Orlando, 1960-71, Fla. House, Inc., Washington, 1974-76; mem. president's council U. Fla., 1970—; v.p., exec. com. U. Fla. Found., 1973-75, bd. dirs., 1971-75; bd. dirs. Inst. for Study of Trial, Central Fla. U., 1978-80; mem. president's council Nat. Meth. Found., 1977-82. Served as officer F.A. AUS, 1942-46, ETO. Recipient Distinguished Service award Stetson U., 1967; Outstanding Alumnus award John Marshall Bar Assn. U. Fla. Coll. Law, 1971; Distinguished Alumnus award U. Fla., 1976. Fellow Am. Coll. Probate Counsel, Am. Coll. Mortgage Attys. (regent 1974-77), Am. Bar Found.; mem. Am. Law Inst., ABA (ho. of dels. 1967-85, adv. bd. jour. 1968-71, chmn. standing com. on legislation 1973-75, on lawyers title guaranty funds 1979-83), Fla. Bar (bd. govs. 1959-67, pres. 1966-67), Am. Judicature Soc. (dir. 1968—, exec. com. 1972, treas. 1973-75, v.p. 1975-77, pres. 1977-79), U. Fla. Law Center Assn. (trustee, exec. com., chmn. bd. trustees 1973-75), Nat. Legal Aid and Defender Assn., Blue Key (pres. Fla. 1941), Phi Kappa Phi, Alpha Tau Omega, Phi Delta Phi. Republican. Methodist (chmn. ch. adminstrv. bd. 1961-63, 75-76, trustee 1968-74, 77-80, trustee Fla. Conf., 1973-76). Clubs: Country, Univ. (Orlando) Orange County Old Timers (pres. 1986-87). Lodge: Kiwanis (pres. North Orlando club 1954). General corporate, Probate, Real property. Home: 1105 Edgewater Dr Orlando FL 32804 Office: 55 E Livingston St Orlando FL 32802

RUSH, STEPHEN KENNETH, lawyer; b. Columbus, Ind., Mar. 16, 1942; s. Kenneth E. and Jane (Boyle) R.; m. Nancy Burns, June 19, 1965; children—Jeffrey, Stephanie. B.S.M.E., Stanford U., 1965, M.S.M.E., 1967; J.D., Vanderbilt U., 1976. Bar: Tenn. 1976, U.S. Dist. Ct. (mid. dist.) Tenn. 1977, U.S. Ct. Appeals (6th cir.) 1977. Trustee in bankruptcy U.S. Bankruptcy Ct., Nashville, 1974-75; assoc. Farris, Warfield & Kanady, Nashville, 1976-79, ptnr., 1980—. Patentee propulsion system for diver. Served to comdr. USN, 1967-73. Mem. ABA, Assn. Trial Lawyers Am., Tenn. Bar Assn., Nashville Bar Assn., Internat. Bar Assn., Internat. Assn. Entertainment Lawyers, Nat. Trust for Hist. Preservation. Federal civil litigation, Entertainment, Libel. Home: Route 5 Wilson Pike Franklin TN 37064 Office: Farris Warfield & Kanady Third Nat Bank Bldg 17th Floor Nashville TN 37219

RUSHER, DERWOOD H., II, lawyer; b. Roanoke, Va., Dec. 23, 1954; s. Derwood H. and Edith (McFadden) R. BS, Va. Poly. Inst. and State U., 1977; JD, U. Richmond, 1980. Bar: Va. 1980, U.S. Ct. Appeals (4th cir.) 1980, U.S. Ct. Appeals (7th cir.) 1981, U.S. Ct. Appeals (5th, 6th, 10th, 11th, D.C. cirs.) 1987. Assoc. Street, Street, Street, Scott & Bowman, Grundy, Va., 1980-81; atty. Standard Oil Co., Chgo., 1981-84, Lexington, Ky., 1984-86; assoc. Womble, Carlyle, Sandridge & Rice, Winston-Salem, N.C., 1986—. Named one of Outstanding Young Men of Am., 1984, 86. Mem. ABA, Phi Kappa Phi, Phi Delta Phi, Beta Gamma Sigma, Sigma Chi. Baptist. Federal civil litigation, General corporate, Administrative and regulatory. Home: 150 Charlestowne Circle Winston-Salem NC 27103 Office: Womble Carlyle Sandridge & Rice PO Drawer 84 Winston-Salem NC 27102

RUSING, MICHAEL JOHN, lawyer; b. Fairbanks, Alaska, Mar. 27, 1957; s. Russell William and Rosemary (Burke) R.; m. Elizabeth Frances Djokovich, May 30, 1982. BA magna cum laude, U. San Francisco, 1977; JD, Stanford U., 1980. Bar: Ariz. 1980, U.S. Dist. Ct. Ariz. 1980, U.S. Ct. Appeals (9th cir.) 1983, U.S. Ct. Appeals (Fed. cir.) 1984, U.S. Supreme Ct. 1985. Assoc. Bilby & Shoenhair P.C., Tucson, 1980-85, ptnr., 1986—. Exec. com. mem. so. Ariz. chpt. March of Dimes, Tucson, 1984—, Barr for Ariz., Tucson, 1986—; asst. chmn. legal div. United Way, Tucson, 1985; bd. dirs. Active 20-30 Club, Tucson, 1983-84. Fellow St. Ives Law Soc.; mem. ABA (litigation sect.), Ariz. Bar Assn. Tucson Def. Bar Assn. (program dir. 1985-86, treas. 1986—), Def. Research Inst., Tucson Fiesta Bowl Com., Leadership of Tucson, Pi Sigma Alpha. Republican. Roman Catholic. Clubs: Stanford of So. Ariz. (pres. 1985—), Mountain Oyster, (Tucson). Avocations: hunting, tennis, wines. State civil litigation, Federal civil litigation, Personal injury. Office: Bilby & Shoenhair PC 2 E Congress Tucson AZ 85701

RUSK, L. GILES, lawyer; b. Wingate, Tex., Dec. 31, 1932; s. L.G. and Louise (Jenkins) R.; m. Ruth Russell, Mar. 6, 1954; children—Blake W., Byron W. B.S., U. Houston, 1959, postgrad., 1960; J.D., S. Tex. Coll. Law, Houston, 1966. Bar: Tex. 1966, U.S. Dist. Ct. (so. dist.) Tex. 1969, U.S. Dist. Ct. (we. dist.) Tex. 1970, U.S. Ct. Appeals (5th cir.) 1970, U.S. Supreme Ct. 1971, U.S. Dist. Ct. (ea. dist.) Tex. 1975. Ptnr., Werner & Rusk, Houston, 1974-84; sole practice L. Giles Rusk, P.C., Houston, 1984—. Pres., bd. dirs. Unity Ch. Christianity, 1969-72. Mem. ABA, Am. Trial Lawyers Assn., Houston Bar Assn., Houston Trial Lawyers Assn., Tex. Trial Lawyers Assn., N.Y. Trial Lawyers Assn., East Tex. Trial Lawyers Assn., Houston Ednl. Found. (bd. dirs. 1970), Delta Theta Phi. Served with USAF, 1953-54. Federal civil litigation, State civil litigation, Personal injury. Office: 3636 San Jacinto St Houston TX 77004 also: 4002 North St Nacogdoches TX 75961

RUSS, CHARLES PAUL, III, lawyer, corporation executive; b. N.Y.C., Aug. 24, 1944; s. Charles Paul Jr. and Dorothea (von Frieling) R.; m. Dianne P. McLaughlin, June 24, 1969; children: Alexander Peter, Andrew William. B.A., Amherst Coll., 1966; J.D., Columbia U., 1969. Bar: N.Y. 1970, Ga. 1973. Assoc. Sullivan & Cromwell, N.Y.C., 1969-72; assoc. Gambrell & Mobley, Atlanta, 1972-74, ptnr., 1974; sr. atty. Stauffer Chem. Co., Westport, Conn., 1975-78; asst. gen. counsel Geo Internat. Corp., Stamford, Conn., 1978-80, v.p., gen. counsel, 1980-84; v.p., sec., gen. counsel NCR Corp., Dayton, Ohio, 1984—. Harlan Fiske Stone scholar Columbia U., 1969. Mem. ABA, Am. Corp. Counsel Assn., Ohio State Bar Assn., Assn. Gen. Counsel. Clubs: Dayton Country, Miami Valley Hunt and Polo, NCR Country, Seabrook Island Ocean. Home: 745 Oakwood Ave Dayton OH 45419 Office: NCR Corp 1700 S Patterson Blvd Dayton OH 45479

RUSS, LAWRENCE, lawyer; b. Detroit, Aug. 18, 1950; m. Marion Long. BA, U. Mich., 1972, JD, 1977; MFA in Writing, U. Mass., 1974. Bar: Ill. 1977, U.S. Dist. Ct. (no. dist.) Ill. 1977, Conn. 1981, U.S. Dist. Ct. Conn. 1981. Assoc. Sonnenschein, Carlin, Nath & Rosenthal, Chgo., 1977-81; ptnr. Trager & Trager P.C., Fairfield, Conn., 1981-86; asst. atty. gen. State of Conn., Hartford, 1986—. Author: (poetry) The Burning Ground, 1981; also articles. Vol. atty. Lawyers for Creative Arts, Chgo., 1978-80, ALCU, Chgo., 1979-81, Conn. Vol. Lawyers for Arts, 1983—. Mem. Conn. Bar Assn. (chmn. arts and law com.), Poetry Soc. Am., ACLU. Federal civil litigation, Trademark and copyright, Entertainment. Home: 245-49 Unquowa Rd Fairfield CT 06430 Office: Atty Gens Office 90 Brainard Rd Hartford CT 06114

RUSSELL, ALLAN DAVID, lawyer; b. Cleve., May 6, 1924; s. Allan MacGillivray and Marvel (Codling) R.; m. Lois Anne Robinson, June 12, 1947; children: Lisa Anne, Robinson David, Martha Leslie. B.A., Yale U., 1945, LL.B., 1951. Bar: N.Y. 1952, Conn. 1956, Mass. 1969, U.S. Supreme Ct. 1977. Atty. Sylvania Electric Products, Inc., N.Y.C., 1951-56; div. counsel Sylvania Electric Products, Inc., Batavia, N.Y., 1956-65; sr. counsel Sylvania Electric Products, Inc., 1965-71; sec., sr. counsel GTE Sylvania Inc., Stamford, Conn., 1971-76; asst. gen. counsel GTE Service Corp., 1976-80, v.p., assoc. gen. counsel staff, 1980-83; sole practice law Redding, Conn., 1983—; sec., dir. mktg. subs. Sylvania Entertainment Products Corp., 1961-67; sec. Wilbur B. Driver Co. Dist. leader Republican party, New Canaan, Conn., 1955-56; sec. bd. dirs. Youth Found., Inc., 1982-83, bd. dirs., 1985—; v.p. Collie Club Am. Found., Inc., 1986—, also bd. dirs.; planning commn. Redding, Conn., 1987—; warden Christ Ch. Parish, Redding, 1987—. Served with USAAF, 1943-46. Mem. Bar Assn. City N.Y., Conn. Bar Assn. (exec. com. corp. counsel sect.), Am. Soc. Corp. Secs., St. Nicholas Soc., Westchester-Fairfield Corp. Counsel Assn., SAR, Collie Club of Am. Found., Inc. (v.p., dir. 1986—), Soc. Colonial Wars, Yale Alumni Assn. (sec. local chpt. 1953-56), Phi Delta Phi. Antitrust, General corporate, Administrative and regulatory. Home: 9 Little River Lane Redding CT 06896

RUSSELL, CHARLES STEVENS, justice, educator; b. Richmond, Va., Feb. 23, 1926; s. Charles Herbert and Nita M. (Stevens) R.; m. Carolyn Elizabeth Abrams, Mar. 18, 1951; children: Charles Stevens, David Tyler. B.A., U. Va., 1946, LL.B., 1948. Bar: Va. 1949, U.S. Dist. Ct. (ea. dist.) Va. 1952, U.S. Ct. Appeals (4th cir.) 1955, U.S. Supreme Ct. 1958. Assoc. firm Jesse, Phillips, Klinge & Kendrick, Arlington, Va., 1951-57; ptnr. Jesse, Phillips, Klinge & Kendrick, 1957-60, Phillips, Kendrick, Gearheart and Aylor, Arlington, 1960-67; judge 17th Jud. Ct. Va., Arlington, 1967-82, Supreme Ct. Va., Richmond, 1982—; mem. jud. council Va., 1977-82; adj. prof. law George Mason U., Arlington, 1977-86, T.C. Williams Sch. Law U. Richmond, 1987—; mem. exec. com. Va. State Bar, Richmond, 1964-67; mem. faculty Nat. Jud. Coll., Reno, 1980—. Mem. Adv. Com. on Youth, Arlington; mem. nat. council of trustees Freedoms Found., Valley Forge, Pa., 1986—. Served to lt. comdr. USNR, 1944-51. Fellow Am. Bar Found.; mem. ABA, Arlington County Bar Assn., Va. Bar Assn., Va. Trial Lawyers Assn., Am. Judicature Soc. Episcopalian. Club: Downtown (Richmond). Jurisprudence. Home: 11 James Falls Dr Richmond VA 23221 Office: 100 N 9th St Richmond VA 23219

RUSSELL, CHERYL ANNE, lawyer; b. Tooele, Utah, Aug. 19, 1952; s. Melvin Reed and Barbara Jean (Weyland) R. BS in Pre Law Studies magna cum laude, Utah State U., 1973; JD, Brigham Young U., 1976. Bar: Utah 1976, U.S. Dist. Ct. Utah 1976. Sole practice Logan, Utah, 1976—; pub. defender Rich County, Randolph, Utah, 1981-83, atty., 1984-86; pub. defender Cache County, Logan, 1977-83, 87—. Mem. admission com. United Way, Logan, 1978, 82, exec. com. Parents Against Drug Abuse, Logan, 1981-84; bd. advisors Teenage Pregnancy Com., Logan, 1986. Mem. ABA, Utah Bar Assn. (legal services com.), Cache County Bar Assn., Prosecutors Assn. Utah, Nat. Dist. Attys. Assn. Mormon. Lodge: Soroptimists (pres. Logan 1983-85). Avocations: skiing, scuba diving, basketball, wind surfing, arts and crafts. Criminal, Family and matrimonial, General practice. Office: 256 N 1st W Logan UT 84231

RUSSELL, DAVID BRENT, lawyer; b. Portage, Wis., Aug. 13, 1948; s. Donald Eugene and Jean (Cuff) R.; m. Nancy Jean Senior, June 7, 1975; children: Angela, Christopher. BBA, U. Wis., 1974, JD, 1979. Bar: Wis. 1979, U.S. Dist. Ct. (we. dist.) Wis. 1979. Assoc. Hale, Skemp, Hanson & Skemp, LaCrosse, Wis., 1979-83, ptnr., 1983—. Dir. Discovery Child Care Ctrs., LaCrosse, 1980-83; deacon 1st Bapt. Ch., LaCrosse, 1986—. Mem. State Bar of Wis., LaCrosse County Bar Assn. (sec., treas. 1986—), U.S. Curling Assn. (bd. dirs. 1986—), Wis. State Curling Assn. (bd. dirs. 1977—, v.p. 1982-84, pres. 1984-86). Avocations: curling, golf, tennis, running. Bankruptcy, General practice. Office: Hale Skemp Hanson & Skemp 515 State Bank Bldg LaCrosse WI 54601

RUSSELL, DAVID L., U.S. district judge; b. Sapulpa, Okla., July 7, 1942; s. Lynn and Florence E. (Brown) R.; m. Dana J. Wilson, Apr. 16, 1971; 1 child, Sarah Elizabeth. B.A., Okla. Bapt. U., 1963; J.D., Okla. U., 1965. Bar: Okla. 1965. Asst. atty. gen. State of Okla., Oklahoma City, 1968-69, legal adviser to gov., 1969-70; legal adviser Senator Dewey Bartlett, Washington, 1973-75; U.S. atty. for Western dist. Okla. Dept. Justice, 1975-77, 81-82; ptnr. Benefield & Russell, Oklahoma City, 1977-81; judge U.S. Dist. Ct. (east, no., west dists.) Okla., Oklahoma City, 1982—. Mem. ABA, Okla. Bar Assn., Fed. Bar Assn. (pres. Oklahoma City chpt. 1981). Republican. Methodist. Club: Men's Dinner (bd. dirs.). Lodge: Rotary. Jurisprudence. Home: 2309 NW 119th Terr Oklahoma City OK 73120 Office: US Dist Ct 3321 US Courthouse 200 NW 4th St Oklahoma City OK 73102

RUSSELL, DAVID WILLIAMS, lawyer; b. Lockport, N.Y., Apr. 5, 1945; s. David Lawson and Jean Graves (Williams) R.; A.B. (Army ROTC scholar, Daniel Webster scholar), Dartmouth Coll., 1967, M.B.A., 1969; J.D. cum laude, Northwestern U., 1976; m. Frances Yung Chung Chen, May 23, 1970; children—Bayard Chen, Ming Rennick. English tchr. Talledega (Ala.) Coll., summer 1967; math. tchr. Lyndon Inst., Lyndonville, Vt., 1967-68; instr. econs. Royalton Coll., South Royalton, Vt., part-time 1968-69; asst. to pres. for planning Tougaloo (Miss.) Coll., 1969-71, bus. mgr., 1971-73; mgr. will and trust rev. project Continental Ill. Nat. Bank & Trust Co. Chgo., summer 1974; law clk. Montgomery, McCracken, Walker & Rhoads, Phila., summer 1975; admitted to Ill. bar, 1976, Ind. bar, 1983; Winston & Strawn, Chgo., 1976-83; ptnr. Klineman, Rose, Wolf & Wallack, Indpls., 1983-87, Johnson, Smith, Densborn Wright & Heath, 1987—; cons. Alfred P. Sloan Found., 1972-73; dir., sec. Forum for Internat. Profl. Services, 1985—; lectr. Ind. Law, Gov's Ind. Trade Mission to Japan, 1986, internat. law Ind. Continuing Legal Edn. Forum, 1986. Mem. nat. selection com. Woodrow Wilson Found. Adminstrv. Fellowship Program, 1973-76; vol. Lawyers for Creative Arts, Chgo., 1977-83. Woodrow Wilson Found. Adminstrv. fellow, 1969-72. Mem. Am., Ill., Ind., Indpls., bar assns., Dartmouth Lawyers Assn., Indpls. Assn. Chinese Ams., ACLU, Chinese Music Soc., Zeta Psi. Presbyterian. Securities, Real property, Private international. Home: 10926 Lakeview Dr Carmel IN 46032 Office: 1000 Market Sq Center 151 N Deleware Indianapolis IN 46204

RUSSELL, DONALD STUART, judge; b. Lafayette Springs, Miss., Feb. 22, 1906; s. Jesse and Lula (Russell) R.; m. Virginia Utsey, June 15, 1929; children: Donald, Mildred, Scott, John. A.B., U. S.C., 1925, LL.B., 1928; postgrad., U. Mich., 1929; LL.D., Wofford Coll., Lander Coll., The Citadel, U.S.C., Emory U., Clemson U., C.W. Post Coll. Bar: S.C. 1928. Practiced law Spartanburg, 1930-42; with Nicholls, Wyche & Byrnes, Nicholls, Wyche & Russell, and Nicholls & Russell, 1930-42; pvt. practice 1938-42, 47-51, 57-63; mem. Price Adjustment Bd., War Dept., Washington, 1942; asst. to dir. econ. stablzn. 1942, asst. to dir. war moblzn., 1943; dep. dir. Office War Moblzn. Reconversion, 1945; asst. sec. state 1945-47; pres. U. S.C., 1951-57; gov. S.C. 1963-65, mem. U.S. Senate from S.C., 1965-66, U.S. Dist. Ct. judge, 1967-71, U.S. Ct. Appeals judge, 1971—. Mem. Wriston Com. on Reorgn. Fgn. Service, 1954; trustee emeritus Emory U., Atlanta; trustee Converse Coll., Spartanburg, S.C., Benedict Coll., Columbia, S.C. Served as maj. AUS, 1944, SHAEF, France. Mem. ABA, Am. Law Inst., S.C. Bar Assn., Spartanburg County Bar Assn., Phi Beta Kappa. Methodist. Jurisprudence. Office: US Court Appeals Spartanburg SC 29301 *

RUSSELL, EDWIN FORTUNE, lawyer; b. Rochester, N.Y., Aug. 27, 1910; s. Herman and Nell Amelia (Fortune) R.; m. Betty Louise Larson, Aug. 8, 1942; children—Edwin Larson, Sarah Russell Etchart. B.S. in Chem. Engring., U. Mich., 1933, M.S. Chem. Engring., 1933; J.D., N.Y.U., 1938. Bar: N.Y. 1939, U.S. Dist. Ct. (ea. dist.) N.Y., U.S. Ct. Appeals (5th cir.), U.S. Supreme Ct. Assoc. Cullen and Dykman, Bklyn., 1938-52, ptnr., 1952—; counsel Village of Bronxville (N.Y.), 1961-65, mayor, 1965-67, chmn. zoning bd. appeals, 1968-83, justice, 4-yr. term. Chmn. Bronxville Republican Village Com., 1979-81. Served to lt. comdr. USNR, 1942-46. Fellow Am. Bar Found.; mem. N.Y. State Bar Assn. (chmn. ho. of dels. 1975-76, pres. 1976-77), ABA (ho. of dels. 1976-82, N.Y. State interim del. 1981-82), Bklyn. Bar Assn., Westchester Bar Assn., Fed. Energy Bar Assn. (pres. 1954), N.Y. State Bar Found. Episcopalian. Clubs: Siwanoy Country (pres. 1973-75, Bronxville); Bklyn., Masons, U. Mich. Pres.'s; Nat. Lawyers (Washington). General corporate, Public utilities, FERC practice. Home: 39 Park Ave Bronxville NY 10708 Office: 177 Montague St Brooklyn NY 11201

RUSSELL, GLOVER ALCORN, JR., lawyer; b. Clarksdale, Miss., July 10, 1955; s. Glover Alcorn and Ann Garland (Weaver) R.; m. Mary Lou Love, Aug. 6, 1977; children: Frances Ann, Glover Alcorn III. BBA, Delta State U., 1977; JD, U. Miss., 1981; LLM in Taxation, NYU, 1982. Accnt. Miss. State Dept. Edn., Jackson, 1977-78; assoc. Magruder, Montgomery, Brocato and Hosemann, Jackson, 1982—. Treas. Miss. chpt. Nat. Multiple Sclerosis Soc., Jackson, 1983-85, chmn., 1985—. Mem. ABA, Am. Inst. CPA's, Miss. Bar Assn., Miss. Soc. CPA's. Episcopalian. Lodge: Kiwanis. Avocations: hunting, camping, jogging. Pension, profit-sharing, and employee benefits, General corporate, Corporate taxation. Office: Magruder Montgomery Brocato Hosemann 1800 Deposit guaranty Plaza Jackson MS 39201

RUSSELL, HAROLD LOUIS, lawyer; b. Abingdon, Va., July 1, 1916; s. Harold L. and Bess N. (Kinzel) R.; m. Katherine C. (Thompson) May 19, 1939; 1 child, Katherine T. Russell Prophet; m. Mildred Baggett Roach, Sept. 5, 1970. AB, Hendrix Coll., 1937; JD, Columbia U., 1940. Bar: N.Y. 1941, Ga. 1942, U.S. Ct. Appeals (1st, 2d, 3d, 5th, 11th and D.C. cirs.), U.S. Supreme Ct. 1950, D.C. 1972. Assoc. Gambrell & Russell and predecessors, Atlanta and N.Y.C., 1941-47, ptnr., 1947-84; ptnr. Smith, Gambrell & Russell, 1984—. Bd. dirs. Atlanta Fed. Defender Program, 1973-80, pres. 1978-79; bd. visitors, Columbia Law Sch., 1959—, mem. exec. com., 1978—; mem. council Adminstrv. Conf. of U.S., 1968-76; bd. legal advisers Southeastern Legal Found., 1976—. Recipient Alumni Fedn. medal Columbia U., 1965; Disting. Alumnus award, Hendrix Coll., 1969. Fellow Am. Coll. Trial Lawyers, Am. Bar Found.; mem. ABA (past chmn. pub. utilities law sect., past chmn. spl. com. on legal service procedure, past chmn. adminstrv. law sect., ho. of dels. 1983—), D.C. Bar Assn., Fed. Bar Assn., Atlanta Bar Assn., Atlanta Lawyers Club, Assn. Bar City of N.Y., Columbia Law Sch. Alumni Assn. (nat. pres. 1973-75), Atlanta C. of C., Phi Delta Phi. Democrat. Episcopalian. Clubs: Capital City, Piedmont Driving. Administrative and regulatory, Antitrust, Federal civil litigation. Home: 3999 Parian Ridge Rd NW Atlanta GA 30327 Office: Smith Gambrell & Russell 2400 First Atlanta Tower Atlanta GA 30383

RUSSELL, HAROLD SWIFT, lawyer, manufacturing company executive; b. Chgo., Jan. 3, 1935; s. Paul S. and Carroll Russell; m. Margo Stratford, June 10, 1961; children—Nathan W., Nina D., Peter L. B.A., Yale U., 1957, J.D., U. Chgo., 1962, M.C.L., 1964. Bar: Ill. 1962, N.Y. 1964, Pa. 1983. Assoc., White & Case, N.Y.C., 1964-66, Sidley & Austin, Chgo., 1966-71; asst. legal adviser for European affairs U.S. Dept. State, Washington, 1971-76; assoc. gen. counsel FMC Corp., Chgo. and Phila., 1976-87, v.p. govt. affairs, 1987—. General corporate, Private international, Environment. Home: 7307 Elbow Ln Philadelphia PA 19119 Office: 1627 K St Washington DC 20007

RUSSELL, JOHN DRINKER, legal educator and administrator, consultant; b. Portland, Oreg., Sept. 19, 1911; s. Charles Bert and Alice Eleanor (Drinker) R.; m. Lucille Erica Umbreit, July 11, 1953. B.A., Stanford U., 1931, M.A., 1941; LL.B., Northwestern Sch. Law, Lewis and Clark Coll., 1935. Bar: Oreg. 1935, U.S. Dist. Ct. Oreg. 1936. Ptnr. Berg, Jones & Russell, Portland, 1935-38; counselor, instr. Menlo Coll., Menlo Park, Calif., 1938-42, dir. admissions, registrar, 1946-55, prof. domestic and internat. comml. law, 1946-77, dir. top acad. adminstr., 1955-77, part time prof. law and internat. bus., 1977-81, prof. emeritus, 1981—. Active Menlo Park Master Plan Com., 1955-56. Served to comdr. USNR, 1942-63. Mem. ABA, Inter-Am. Bar Assn., Internat. Bar Assn., Am. Bus. Law Assn., Am. Soc. Internat. Law, Law Assn. for Asia and Western Pacific, Oreg. State Bar, Union Internationale des Avocats, Internat. Law Assn., Am. Legion, Am. Assn. Ret. Persons, Res. Officers Assn., Ret. Officers Assn., Delta Sigma Pi, Delta Theta Phi, Phi Delta Kappa. Republican. Presbyterian. Club: Rotary (pres. Menlo Park 1952-53, chmn. Rotary Found. scholarships com. Dist.

513 1981—). General corporate, Contracts commercial, Legal education. Home: Channing House 850 Webster St #714 Palo Alto CA 94301 Office: Menlo Coll Menlo Park CA 94025

RUSSELL, JOHN WILSON, circuit judge; b. Carlinville, Ill., Dec. 7, 1920; s. John Harvey and Julia Clare (Wilson) R.; m. Joie Day Landon, Nov. 25, 1961; children: Mary, J.C., Mik, Peter, Sarah, Cindy, J.P. BA, Lake Forest Coll., 1942; JD, Northwestern U., 1950. Bar: Ill. 1950. Sole practice Carlinville, 1950-77; cir. justice 7th Jud. Cir. of Ill., Carlinville, 1977—. Served to lt. USN, 1942-46, PTO. Home: 630 E Main Carlinville IL 62626

RUSSELL, ROBERT BERNARD, lawyer; b. Iowa City, Iowa, June 4, 1918; s. William Fletcher R. AB, Harvard U., 1941, JD, 1948. Bar: Mass. 1948, U.S. Ct. Custom and Patent Appeals 1960, U.S. Supreme Ct. 1963, U.S. Ct. Claims 1964. Ptnr. Kenway, Jenney Witter & Hildreth, Boston, 1950-55, Porter, Chithick & Russell, Boston, 1955-60; sr. ptnr. Russell, Chithick & Pfund, Boston, 1960-68, Russell & Nields, Boston, 1968-82, Russell & Tucker, Boston, 1982—; mem. faculty Northeastern U. Law Sch., 1954-55, Suffolk U. Law Sch., 1959-62; lectr. Harvard U. Bus. Sch., 1954-78; metall. cons. Served with USN, World War II. Decorated Bronze Star. Mem. ABA, Am. Patent Law Assn., Boston Patent Law Assn. Clubs: Union (Boston); The Country (Brookline, Mass.). Patent, Antitrust, Trademark and copyright. Home: 288 Heath St Chestnut Hill MA 02167 Office: 99 Chauncy St Suite 608 Boston MA 02111

RUSSELL, ROBIE GEORGE, lawyer; b. Moscow, Idaho, July 7, 1948; s. George Robie Russell and Jean Ray (Atkinson) O'Reilly; m. Nancy Kay Olson, May 31, 1975; children: George Robie, Erin Kay. BS in Polit. Sci., Pub. Adminstrn., U. Idaho, 1972, cert. in Pub. Adminstrn., 1974, JD, 1978. Bar: Idaho 1979, U.S. Dist. Ct. Idaho 1979, U.S. Ct. Claims 1980, U.S. Ct. Appeals (9th cir.) 1980, U.S. Tax Ct. 1981, U.S. Ct. Appeals (fed. cir.) 1985, U.S. Supreme Ct. 1985. Dep. atty. gen. State of Idaho, Boise, 1979-81, sr. dep. atty. gen., div. chief, 1981—; counsel Idaho Sec. of State, Boise, 1982—. Contbg. author: Idaho Media Law Handbook, 1986; editor: Idaho Cities Mag., 1974-75, (newsletter) Local Govt. Legal News, 1981—; contbr. articles to profl. jours. Pres., treas. Lincoln Day Assn., Boise, 1979—; vice chmn. Selective Service Bd., Boise, 1983—; chmn., vice chmn. Ada County Reps., Boise, 1984—. Named one of Outstanding Young Men in Am., 1980—. Mem. ABA, Idaho State Bar Assn., Boise Bar Assn., Nat. Inst. Mcpl. Law Officers, Assn. Idaho City Attys. (sec., treas 1981—, founder), Assn. Idaho Cities (advisor 1981—, Boyd Martin award 1985), Phi Alpha Delta, U. Idaho Alumni Assn. (bd. dirs. 1973-74), Sons and Daus. of Idaho Pioneers. Republican. Club: U. Idaho Vandal Boosters (Moscow, Idaho) (chpt. pres., bd. dirs. 1975—). Lodge: Elks. Avocations: stamp collecting, fishing, gardening, music, lit. Local government, Environment, Administrative and regulatory. Home: PO Box 894 Boise ID 83701 Office: Office of Atty Gen Statehouse Boise ID 83720

RUSSELL, STEVEN TURNER, lawyer; b. Palo Alto, Calif., Apr. 11, 1950; s. Dell Jayne Russell and Patricia Nancy (Robinson) Williams; m. Crisca Bierwert, Aug. 14, 1976; children: Robin Wilderness, Lars Conan, Morgan Shahan. Student, UCLA, 1968-69; BA with distinction, Stanford U., 1972; JD cum laude, Boston Coll., 1976. Bar: Wash. 1976, U.S. Dist. Ct. (we. dist.) Wash. 1976. Staff counsel Boston Coll. L.A.B., Waltham, Mass., 1974; legal intern Anderson, Hunter, Everett, Wash., 1975; assoc. Helsell, Fetterman, Seattle, 1976-78; sole practice Seattle, 1979-83; assoc. Detels, Madden, Crockett & McGee, Seattle, 1984-86, Bradbury, Bliss & Riordan (successor firm), Seattle, 1986—. Mem. ABA, Wash. State Bar Assn., Seattle-King County Bar Assn. Avocations: downhill skiing, running, rowing, drawing, carving. Admiralty, Federal civil litigation, Workers' compensation. Office: Bradbury Bliss & Riordan 1310 IBM Bldg Seattle WA 98101

RUSSELL, THOMAS HUNTER, lawyer; b. Ventura, Calif., Sept. 6, 1940; s. Leo Hunter and Gwendolyn Bernice (Jones) R. B.S.L., U. So. Calif., 1962, J.D., 1965. Bar: Calif. 1965, U.S. Dist. Ct. (cen. dist.) Calif. 1965. Mem. firm Kinkle, Rodiger & Spriggs, Los Angeles, 1965-67; sole practice law, Los Angeles, 1967—. Mem. City-County Consolidation Commn., Los Angeles, 1982—, Republican State Central Com., Calif., 1983—; treas., dir. Community Services Ctr., Los Angeles, 1979—; chmn. Bach Festival Found., Los Angeles, 1984. Mem. Criminal Cts. Bar Assn., State Bar of Calif., Calif. Atty. for Criminal Justice, Lawyers for Human Rights, Calif. Trial Lawyers Assn.; Am. Guild Organists. Republican. Congregationalist. Lodge: Masons. Criminal, Personal injury, State civil litigation. Home: 2421 Glendower Ave Hollywood CA 90027 Office: 6290 Sunset Blvd #1000 Hollywood CA 90028

RUSSELL, TOMAS MORGAN, lawyer; b. Kankakee, Ill., Feb. 27, 1934; s. Allie Tomas and Marieta A. (Kieffer); children—Heather, Hilary. B.S., U. Wis., 1963, J.D., 1967. Bar: Ill. 1967, Wis. 1967. Ptnr. Hopkins & Sutter, Chgo., 1973—; dir., mem. exec. com. Ill. Inst. for Continuing Legal Edn., 1981—, chmn. task force on continuing legal edn., 1982—. Co-founder, chmn. U. Wis. Law Sch. Civil Rights Research Council, 1965-66. Served with USN, 1953-57. Life fellow Chgo. Bar Found.; mem. ABA (chmn. com. on product safety 1975—), Ill. Bar Assn. (chmn. jud. adminstrn. sect. 1981-82, long range planning commn. 1985—), Chgo. Bar Assn. (chmn. standing com. on trial bar rules 1981—, long range planning comm. 1986—), Am. Judicature Soc., Law Club Chgo., ACLU, Wis. Bar Assn., Bar Assn. 7th Cir., U. Wis. Benchers Soc., Urban League Chgo., Better Govt. Assn., Businessmen in Pub. Interest, U. Wis. Law Alumni Assn. (pres.). Clubs: University, Chgo. Yacht (Chgo.). Contbr. articles in field. Insurance, Federal civil litigation, Administrative and regulatory. Home: 3600 N Lake Shore Dr Chicago IL 60613

RUSSELL, WILLIAM OLIVER, lawyer; b. Mineral, Kans., July 12, 1922; s. William and Anna (Oliver) R.; m. Betty Joan Hoffmeier, Mar. 4, 1596; 1 child, Barbara Jo. JD, U. Mo., 1949. Bar: Mo. 1949, U.S. Dist. Ct. (we. dist.) 1950. Asst. U.S. atty. U.S. Dist. Ct. (we. dist.) Mo., 1953-57; city atty. City of Joplin, Mo., 1960-62; sole practice Joplin, 1963—. Pres. bd. regents S.W. Mo. State U., 1966-67. Served to capt. inf., U.S. Army, 1943-46, ETO. Mem. ABA, Mo. Bar Assn., Jasper County Bar Assn. (past pres.). Republican. Presbyterian. Lodge: Kiwanis. Avocation: tennis. General practice, Probate, Family and matrimonial. Home: 2031 Ozark Joplin MO 64801 Office: 416 Commerce Executive Ctr Joplin MO 64801

RUSSIN, JONATHAN, lawyer, consultant; b. Wilkes-Barre, Pa., Oct. 30, 1937; s. Jacob S. and Anne (Wartella) R.; m. Antoinette Stackpole, Oct. 6, 1962; children—Alexander, Andrew, Benjamin, Jacob. B.A., Yale U., 1959, LL.B., 1963. Bar: D.C. 1963. Research asst. Law Faculty, U. East Africa, Dar es Salaam, Tanganyika, 1961-62; regional legal adviser for Caribbean, AID, 1967-69; ptnr. Kirkwood, Kaplan, Russin & Vecchi, Santo Domingo, Dominican Republic, 1969-74, Washington, 1974-78; ptnr. Kaplan Russin & Vecchi, Madrid, 1978-81, Washington, 1981—; cons. on financing worker's housing in less developed countries of Latin Am.; Washington rep. Dominican Am. C. of C. Trustee St. Nicholas Cathedral, Washington, St. Vladimir's Orthodox Theol. Sem., Crestwood, N.Y.; legal adviser Orthodox Ch. in America, Diocese of Washington; bd. dirs. Delphi Research Assocs., Washington. Mem. Latin Am. Studies Assn., Caribbean Studies Assn., ABA, Inter-Am. Bar Assn. Republican. Clubs: Yale of N.Y., Yale of Washington. Contbr. articles to profl. jours. Private international, General corporate, Latin America transactions. Office: 1215 17th St NW Washington DC 20036

RUSSO, ANTHONY JOSEPH, JR., lawyer; b. N.Y.C., Feb. 4, 1950; s. Anthony Joseph and Marie (Cardone) R.; m. Lorraine Valerie Ferrigno, Aug. 25, 1974; children: Joseph Jonathan, Jonathan Anthony. BA, St. John's U., 1971, JD, 1974. Bar: N.Y. 1975. Assoc. Ahearn, Damanti & Carlson, N.Y.C., 1975-81; dir. retirement planning, assoc. counsel Lord, Abbett & Co., N.Y.C., 1982—; active pension and tax coms. Investment Co. Inst., Washington, 1983—. Pension, profit-sharing, and employee benefits, Probate, Securities. Home: 73-63 189th St Fresh Meadows NY 11366 Office: Lord Abbett and Co 63 Wall St 17th Fl New York NY 10005

RUSSO, NANCY MARGARET, lawyer; b. Cleve., Oct. 6, 1956; d. Humbert and Maureen Helen (McCaffery) R.; m. Joel F. Sacco. A.B. in Polit. Sci., W. Liberty State Coll., 1977; J.D., Cleveland-Marshall Law Sch., 1981. Bar: Ohio 1982, U.S. Dist. Ct. (northeastern dist.) Ohio 1982. Investigator Lake County Narcotics, Painesville, Ohio, 1977-78; with Marriott Inn, Cleve., 1978-79; legal sec. Bartunek, Garofoli, Cleve., 1979-81; paralegal/litigation asst. Calfee, Halter & Griswold, Cleve., 1981-84; atty., fin. and fraud investigator Blue Cross/Blue Shield of Ohio, 1984—, media rep. 1987—. Contbg. author ref. book: Ohio Family Law, 1984. Vol. atty. Cleve. Attys. Seeking Equity, 1983—; participant legal clinic staff Law Day, Cleve., 1980-86. Mem. ABA, Am. Trial Lawyers Assn., Greater Cleve. Bar Assn., Ohio Bar Assn., Nat. Health Lawyers Assn., Met. Crime Bur., Fraud Investigators Assn., W. Liberty State Coll. Alumni Assn., Chi Omega. Roman Catholic. Avocations: theatre, lit., skiing. Criminal, Insurance, Health. Office: Blue Cross/Blue Shield of No Ohio 2060 E 9th St Cleveland OH 44115

RUSSO, ROY R., lawyer; b. Utica, N.Y., July 26, 1936; s. Chester F. and Helen L. (Gacek) R.; m. Ann M. Obernesser, Sept. 19, 1959; children: Andrew F., Susan Elizabeth. BA, Columbia U., 1956; LLB, Syracuse U., 1959. Bar: N.Y. 1959, D.C. 1967, U.S. Supreme Ct. 1969. Sole practice, Washington, 1959—; atty. FCC, 1959-66; mem. Cohn & Marks, 1966—. V.p., bd. dirs. St. Mary's Housing Corp., Annandale and Manassas, Va., 1971—; pres. Cath. Charities Bd. Arlington (Va.) Diocese, 1980-84; pres. Cath. for Housing, Inc., 1979-84. Served with USAFR, 1960-66. Mem. ABA, Fed. Communications Bar Assn., Computer Lawyers Assn., Internat. Inst. Communications, John Jay Assocs., Soc. Columbia Grads., Order of Coif, Phi Alpha Delta. Administrative and regulatory. Home: 6528 Bowie Dr Springfield VA 22150 Office: 1333 New Hampshire Ave NW Suite 600 Washington DC 20036

RUSTON, DONALD ALLEN, lawyer; b. Globe, Ariz., Nov. 28, 1929; s. Ira Edwin and Evelyn P. (Mills) R.; m. Gloria I. Hendershot, Apr. 15, 1950 (div. Jan. 1975); children: Jeane, Donald, Terri; m. Joyce Helene Fager Nance, Feb. 11, 1979; 1 child, Karen. BA, Pepperdine Coll., 1951; JD, UCLA, 1954. Bar: Calif. 1955, U.S. Dist. Ct. (cen. and so. dists.) Calif. 1955, U.S. Ct. Appeals (9th cir.) 1983, U.S. Dist. Ct. (ea. dist.) Tex. 1983. Atty. Liberty Mut. Ins. Co., Los Angeles, 1954-56; assoc. Jarrett & Morgan, Los Angeles, 1956-60; ptnr. Tuller Ruston & Perez, Fullerton, Calif., 1961-65, Ruston & Nance, Santa Ana, Calif., 1965—; mem. exec. com. Am. Bd. Trial Advocates, 1959-62, 79—; trustee Nat. Inst. Trial Advocacy, 1985. Chair Calif. Senate Com. on No Fault Ins., 1976-77. Diplomate Am. Bd. Trial Advocates (nat. pres. 1981, chpt. pres. 1970, Lawyer of Yr. award 1982). Fellow Am. Coll. Trial Lawyers, Internat. Soc. Barristers, Internat. Acad. Trial Lawyers, Am. Bar Found.; mem. Assn. So. Calif. Def. Counsel (pres. 1971-72), ABA, Orange County Bar Assn. (dir. 1964-72), Am. Arbitration Assn., Def. Research Inst., UCLA Sch. Law Founders, Pepperdine U. Assocs., Phi Alpha Delta (chpt. justice 1953-54). Republican. Federal civil litigation, State civil litigation, Personal injury. Office: Ruston & Nance 902 N Grand Ave Suite 202 Santa Ana CA 92701

RUTHERFORD, GLEN BIBEE, lawyer; b. Knoxville, Tenn., July 25, 1948; s. William Carl and Mary Gertrude (Bibee) R. AA, Hiwassee Jr. Coll., 1968; BS, U. Tenn., 1970, JD, 1975. Bar: Tenn. 1975, U.S. Dist. Ct. (ea. dist.) Tenn. 1976, U.S. Ct. Appeals (6th cir.) 1985. Assoc. Lockett, Slovis & Weaver, Knoxville, 1976—. Deacon, tchr. Woodlawn Christian Ch., Knoxville, 1972—; pres. Knoxville Community Service Ctr., 1984—, Vols. of Am., Knoxville, 1984—. Mem. ABA, Tenn. Bar Assn., Knoxville Bar Assn. Republican. Lodge: Masons, Kiwanis (pres. South Knoxville chpt. 1981-82). Personal injury, Workers' compensation, Criminal. Home: 128 Gilbert Ln Knoxville TN 37920 Office: Lockett Slovis & Weaver PO Box 1670 Knoxville TN 37901

RUTKOFF, ALAN STUART, lawyer; b. Chgo., May 31, 1952; s. Roy and Harriet (Ruskin) R.; m. Mally Zoberman, Dec. 22, 1974; children: Aaron Samuel, Jordana Michal, Robert Nathaniel. BA with high distinction, U. Mich., 1973; JD magna cum laude, Northwestern U., 1976. Bar: Ill. 1976, U.S. Dist. Ct. (no. dist.) Ill. 1979, U.S. Ct. Appeals (7th cir.) 1977, U.S. Ct. Appeals (3d cir.) 1979, U.S. Ct. Appeals (5th cir.) 1983, U.S. Supreme Ct. 1983. Assoc. Altheimer & Gray, Chgo., 1976-80; ptnr. Kastel & Rutkoff, Chgo., 1980-83, Holleb & Coff Ltd., Chgo., 1983-84, McDermott, Will & Emery, Chgo., 1984—. Mem. ABA, Chgo. Bar Assn., Order of Coif. Federal civil litigation, Labor, Professional liability--accountants, lawyers. Home: 801 Timber Hill Rd Highland Park IL 60035 Office: McDermott Will & Emery 111 W Monroe St Chicago IL 60603

RUTLAND, JOHN DUDLEY, lawyer; b. Austin, Tex., Jan. 4, 1931; s. Jesse Blake and Myrtle Estelle (Miller) R.; m. Eva Lou Smith, Jan. 1, 1953 (div.); 1 child, Joseph Blake; m. Beryl Ann Beebe, Apr. 25, 1985. B Bus., U. Tex., 1956; JD, U. Houston, 1961. Bar: Tex. 1961, U.S. Supreme Ct. 1971. With Gibraltar Savs. Assn., Houston, 1956-64, Southwestern Life Ins. Co., Dallas, 1964-67; sole practice, Beaumont, Tex., 1967—; cons. oil mktg. Mem. ABA, Tex. Bar Assn., Jefferson County Bar Assn., Port Arthur Bar Assn., Photog. Soc. Am. Episcopalian. Club: Port Arthur Camera. Lodge: Rotary (past pres. Beaumont). Pension, profit-sharing, and employee benefits, Family and matrimonial, Oil and gas leasing.

RUTLEDGE, GARY RAY, state official, lawyer; b. Asheville, N.C., Nov. 13, 1950; s. Robert Earl and Mary Elizabeth (Rogers) R.; m. Danna Louise Depew, Aug. 7, 1976. Student Fla. Jr. Coll., 1969-70; B.A., U. Fla., 1972, J.D., 1976. Bar: Fla. 1976. Assoc., Bolton-Margulies Law Firm, Miami, Fla., 1976-79; ptnr. Margulies-Rutledge, P.A., Miami, 1979; dir. div. pari-mutuel wagering Miami Dept. Bus. Regulation, State of Fla., 1979-81, sec. Dept. of Bus. regulation, State of Fla., 1981-84; ptnr. Sparber, Shevin, Shapo & Heilbronner, P.A., 1984—. Mem. Fla. Bar Assn., Dade County Bar Assn., ABA, Nat. Assn. State Racing Commrs. (former mem. exec. com.). Democrat. Congregationalist. Club: U. Fla. Blue Key Alumni. Administrative and regulatory, Legislative, State civil litigation. Home: 6449 Count Turf Trail Tallahassee FL 32308 Office: Sparber Shevin Shapo & Heilbronner PA 315 S Calhoun St Tallahassee FL 32301

RUTLEDGE, IVAN CATE, legal educator; b. White Pine, Tenn., Dec. 24, 1915; s. Wiley B. and Tamsey (Cate) R.; m. Carroll Burrage, July 24, 1951; children: Ann Elaine, Thomas Carroll. B.A., Carson Newman Coll., 1934; M.A., Duke U., 1940, LL.B., 1946; LL.M., Columbia U., 1952. Bar: Ga. 1946, Wash. 1951, Ohio 1966. Tchr. pub. schs. Cleveland, Tenn., 1934-37, Cuthbert, Ga., 1937-39; high sch. prin. 1938-39; jr. examiner Bur. Budget, Washington, 1942-43; asst. prof. law Mercer U., 1946-47; asst. prof. law U. Wash., 1947-51, assoc. prof., 1951-53, prof., 1953-54; prof. law Ind. U., 1954-63, Ohio State U., Columbus, 1963-79; prof. emeritus Ohio State U., 1979—; dean Ohio State U. (Law Sch.), 1965-70; Walter F. George disting. prof. law Mercer U., Macon, Ga., 1979—; Vis. prof. law U. Ark., George Washington U., U. N.C., U. Queensland. Bd. dirs. Nat. Consumers League, 1958-79. Mem. ABA, Am. Law Inst., Nat. Acad. Arbitrators, Order of Coif, Pi Gamma Mu. Administrative and regulatory, Labor, State civil litigation. Home: 3188 Vista Circle Macon GA 31204 Office: Walter F George Law Sch Mercer U Macon GA 31207

RUTLEDGE, ROGER KEITH, lawyer; b. Knoxville, Tenn., Dec. 27, 1946; s. Joseph P. and Jean Mae (Karnes) R.; m. Lily Mee Kin Hee, June 6, 1970; children: Amelia Leilani, Sarah Elizabeth. BA in History with honors, U. N.C., 1968; JD cum laude, Am. U., 1977. Bar: Tenn. 1977, U.S. Dist. Ct. (we. dist.) Tenn. 1978, U.S. Supreme Ct. 1982. With agrl. extension U.S. Peace Corps, Nepal, 1968-70; fgn. service officer U.S. Dept. State, Washington and Italy, 1971-76; ptnr. Rutledge & Rutledge, Memphis, 1977—. Editor fiction Carolina Quar., 1967-68; assoc. editor Am. U. Law Rev., 1976-77. Mem. campaign com. Jim Sasser U.S. Senate, Shelby County, Tenn., 1980, 86, Albert Gore Jr. U.S. Senate, Shelby County, 1984; mem. Tenn. Conservation Council, Nashville, 1983, ACLU. Mem. ABA, Tenn. Bar Assn. (pub. relations com., author pamphlet Going Into Bus. 1985), Memphis/Shelby County Bar Assn. (spl. publs. com., editor-in-chief Bar Forum 1986—), Am. Judicature Soc., Phi Alpha Theta. Democrat. Methodist. General practice, General corporate, Immigration, naturalization, and customs. Office: Rutledge & Rutledge 1000 Brookfield Rd Memphis TN 38119

RUTTEN, RAND JOHN, lawyer; b. San Diego, Oct. 21, 1954; s. Reuben John and Laura Mae (Crockett) R.; m. Kathleen Lynn Simpson, Nov. 10, 1984; children: Kiana Lynn, Aaron Lee. BS in Environ. Sci., U. Calif., Riverside, 1977; JD, Western States U., 1981. Bar: Calif. 1981. Sole practice Santa Barbara, Calif., 1981-82; assoc. Sutherland & Gerber, El Centro, Calif., 1982—. Mem. Calif. Bar Assn., Imperial County Bar Assn., Calif. Trial Lawyers Assn., Assn. Trial Lawyers Am. Personal injury, General practice, State civil litigation. Office: Sutherland & Gerber 300 S Imperial Ave Suite 7 El Centro CA 92243

RUTTENBERG, HAROLD SEYMOUR, lawyer; b. Chgo., Oct. 27, 1941; s. Irving Norman and Marge Harriet (Roth) R.; children from previous marriage: Adam, Michael, Leslie; m. Marcia Patsy Pritikin, Jan. 3, 1983; children: Sheronna, Aaron. BBA, U Wis., 1962; JD, Northwestern U., 1965; LLM, Georgetown U., 1968. Bar: Ill. 1965, Minn. 1970, Iowa 1972, U.S. Dist. Ct. (no. dist.) Ill. 1965, U.S. Tax Ct. 1969, U.S. Claims Ct. 1969, U.S. Supreme Ct. 1969. Atty. Office of Chief Counsel, Interpretive div. IRS, Washington, 1965-69; assoc. Mullin, Galison, Swirnoff & Weinberg, Mpls., 1969-71, Doherty, Rumble & Butler, St. Paul, 1971-72; assoc. gen. counsel Meredith Corp., Des Moines, 1972-83, v.p., gen. counsel Meredith/Burda, Des Moines, 1983—. Bd. dirs. Goodwill Industries, Des Moines, 1973-75, Iowa Taxpayers Assn., Des Moines, 1972—, Bur. for Jewish Living, Des Moines, 1981—, chairperson fin. com., 1986—; v.p. tax com. Iowa Assn. Bus. and Industry, 1986; mem. action council Des Moines Ctr. Sci. and Industry, 1975-79, 84—; sec. Greenwood Elem. Sch. PTA, Des Moines, 1982-83; mem. adv. bd. Blank Park Zoo, 1985—. Mem. ABA, Iowa Bar Assn., Polk County Bar Assn., Iowa Assn. Bus. and Industry (vice chmn. tax com. 1986—), Internat. Platform Assn., Am. Corp. Counsel Assn., Am. Immigration Lawyers Assn., Polk-Des Moines Taxpayers Assn. (dir., mem. exec. com. 1985), Greater Des Moines C. of C. Republican. Club: Des Moines Golf and Country. General corporate, Immigration, naturalization, and customs, Pension, profit-sharing, and employee benefits. Home: 16 34th St Des Moines IA 50312 Office: Meredith/Burda 1716 Locust St Des Moines IA 50336

RUTTER, THOMAS BELL, lawyer; b. Clayton, N.J., Nov. 15, 1935; s. Raymond Hahn and Charlotte Anne (Guerin) R.; m. Bertha La Rue Geiger, June 25, 1955; children—Kristine Anne, Kimberly, Thomas Bell; m. 2d, Nancy Marie Suszenski, Sept. 8, 1981; 1 dau., Amy. A.B., U. Chgo., 1959, J.D., 1962. Bar: Pa. 1962, U.S. dist. ct. (ea. dist.) Pa. 1962, U.S. Tax Ct. 1965, U.S. Ct. Apls. (1st cir.) 1982, U.S. Ct. Apls. (5th cir.) 1982, U.S. Ct. Apls. (3d cir.) 1962, U.S. Sup. Ct. 1965. Assoc. Schnader, Harrison, Segal & Lewis, Phila., 1962-68; ptnr. Litvin & Rutter, Phila., 1969-72; sole practice, Phila., 1972-78; sr. ptnr. Rutter, Turner & Stein, 1978—. Instr. trial advocacy Emory U. Law Sch., Hastings Coll. Law, U. Calif., San Francisco, Hofstra U. Law Sch., Nat. Inst. for Trial Advocacy, 1972—. Served with M.I., USAF, 1954-58; Korea. Mem. ABA, Pa. Bar Assn., Phila. Bar Assn., Pa. Trial Lawyers Assn., Order of Coif. Democrat. Mem. United Ch. of Christ. Club: Vesper (Phila.). Contbr. articles to legal publs. Federal civil litigation, Criminal, Personal injury. Home: 129 Pine St Philadelphia PA 19106 Office: Suite 872 Public Ledger Bldg Philadelphia PA 19106

RUTZICK, MARK CHARLES, lawyer; b. St. Paul, Sept. 6, 1948; s. Max Arthur and Bertha (Ward) R.; m. Penny Kay Roberts, July 15, 1979; children—Elizabeth Leslie, Karen Deborah. B.A., U. Mich., 1970; J.D., Harvard U., 1973. Bar: N.Y. 1974, U.S. Ct. Appeals (2d cir.) 1975, U.S. Supreme Ct. 1977, U.S. Ct. Appeals (9th cir.) 1982, Oreg. 1984. Spl. asst. corp. counsel N.Y.C. Housing Adminstrn., 1973-75; assoc. Alexander Hammond P.C., N.Y.C., 1975-76; asst. atty. gen. N.Y. State Atty. Gen., N.Y.C., 1976-78; atty. Dept. Justice, Washington, 1978-82, spl. litigation counsel, 1982-83, atty.-in-charge field office, Portland, Oreg., 1983-86; counsel Preston, Thorgrimson, Ellis & Holman, Portland, 1986—. Mem. Lake Oswego Energy Conservation Adv. Com. Mem. ABA, Oreg. State Bar Assn. Administrative and regulatory, Federal civil litigation. Home: 18700 Wood Duck Way Lake Oswego OR 97034 Office: Preston Thorgrimson et al 3200 US Bancorp Tower 111 SW Fifth Ave Portland OR 97204

RUUD, GLENN F., lawyer; b. Davenport, Iowa, Dec. 14, 1945; s. Robert M. and Betty J. (Kelly) R.; m. Mary Jean Hill, Dec. 22, 1966; children: Eric J., Ryan N. BA, U. Iowa, 1972; JD with high distinction, John Marshall Law Sch., 1975. Bar: Ill. 1975, Iowa 1975, U.S. Dist. Ct. (cen. dist.) Ill. 1976. Staff atty. U.S. Army Weapons Command, Rock Island, Ill., 1975-76; assoc. Winstein et al, Rock Island, 1976-79, ptnr., 1979-83; ptnr. Ruud & Scovil, Rock Island, 1983—. Mem. editorial bd. John Marshall Jour., Chgo., 1974-75. Treas., bd. dirs. Quint Cities Drug Abuse Council, Davenport, 1975-76; bd. dirs. Safer Found., Rock Island, 1985-86. Mem. ABA, Ill. Bar Assn., Iowa Bar Assn., Scott County Bar Assn., Rock Island County Bar Assn. (chmn. continuing legal edn. com. 1986—), Assn. Trial Lawyers Am., Ill. Trial Lawyers Assn., Assn. Trial Lawyers Iowa. Democrat. Methodist. State civil litigation, Family and matrimonial, Personal injury. Home: 402 Bruce Ave Milan IL 61264 Office: Ruud & Scovil 2009 9th Ave Rock Island IL 61201

RUUD, MILLARD HARRINGTON, legal association administrator, emeritus educator; b. Ostrander, Minn., Jan. 7, 1917; s. Mentor L. and Helma M. (Olson) R.; m. Barbara W. Dailey, Aug. 28, 1943; children: Stephen D., Christopher O., Michael L. B.S. in Law, U. Minn., 1942, LL.B., 1947; LL.D., Georgetown U., 1980, U. Pacific, 1981, New Eng. Sch. Law, 1981, Southwestern U., 1983, Widener U., 1987, John Marshall Law Sch., 1987. Bar: Minn. 1947, Tex. 1956. Asst. prof. law U. Kans., 1947-48; assoc. prof. U. Tex., 1948-52, prof., 1952-78, 80-83, prof. emeritus, 1983—; asst. exec. dir. Tex. Legis. Council, 1950-52; exec. dir. Assn. Am. Law Schs., Washington, 1973-80, 83-87; mem. Tex. Commn. Uniform State Laws, 1967—; cons. legal edn. Am. Bar Assn., 1968-73; chmn. Law Sch. Admission Council, 1966-69, Council on Legal Edn. Opportunity, 1968. Mem. Tex., Am. bar assns., Am. Law Inst., Order of Coif (sec.-treas. 1981-83). Club: Cosmos. Legislative, Contracts commercial. Home: 3416 Foothill Terr Austin TX 78731 Office: Assn Am Law Schs One Dupont Circle NW Washington DC 20036

RUWART, DAVID PETER, lawyer; b. Balt.; s. William M. and Inez W. (Wilder) R.; m. Susan J. Collins, Oct. 15, 1960; children—Carole, Sharon, Peter, Denise. B.A., Xavier U., Cin., 1954; J.D., U. Detroit, 1957; LL.M. in Taxation, NYU, 1957. Bar: Mich. 1957, U.S. Dist. Ct. (ea. dist.) Mich. 1957. Sole practice, Detroit, 1957-81; prin. in charge bus. law sect. Plunkett, Cooney, Rutt, Watters, Stanczyk & Pedersen, P.C., Detroit, 1982—; mem. faculty U. Detroit Law Sch., 1969-74, Wayne State U., 1966-69, U. Mich., 1964-66. Mem. ABA, Mich. State Bar Assn., Detroit Bar Assn., Fed. Bar Assn., Am. Judicature Soc. Roman Catholic. Corporate taxation, General corporate, Probate. Home: 43 Deming Ln Grosse Pointe MI 48236

RUXIN, PAUL THEODORE, lawyer; b. Cleve., Apr. 14, 1943; s. Charles and Olyn Judith (Koller) R.; m. Joanne Camy, May 25, 1965; children—Marc J., Sarah. B.A., Amherst Coll., 1965; LL.B., U. Va., 1968. Bar: Ill. 1968, Ohio 1977, U.S. Dist. Ct. (no. dist.) Ill. 1968, U.S. Ct. Appeals D.C. 1972. Assoc. Isham, Lincoln & Beale, Chgo., 1968-73, ptnr., 1974-77; ptnr., chmn. energy utilities sect. Jones, Day, Reavis & Pogue, Cleve., 1977—. Chmn. Hudson Archtl. and Hist. Bd. Rev., 1981—; exec. bd. Greater Cleve. Boy Scouts Am., 1978—; treas. Amherst Alumni Assn., Cleve., 1977; Mem. ABA, Ohio State Bar Assn. (pub. utilities sect.), Bar Assn. Greater Cleve., Fed. Energy Bar Assn. (com. chmn. 1981). Clubs: Country of Hudson; Rowfant (Cleve.) Public utilities, FERC practice, Administrative and regulatory. Home: 40 Wellgate Dr Hudson OH 44236 Office: Jones Day Reavis & Pogue 1700 Huntington Bldg Cleveland OH 44115

RUZOW, DANIEL ARTHUR, lawyer; b. Bronx, N.Y., Apr. 27, 1951; s. Theodore Morton and Renee Rhoda (Braunstein) R.; m. Meris Francie Entin, June 16, 1974; children: Jenny, Benjamin. BA, Franklin & Marshall Coll., 1973; JD, Fordham U., 1976. Bar: N.Y. 1977, U.S. Ct. Appeals (2d cir.) 1977, U.S. Dist. Ct. (so. and ea. dists.) N.Y. 1977, U.S. Dist. Ct. (no. and we. dists.) N.Y. 1985. Assoc. Arum, Friedman & Katz, N.Y.C., 1976-79; asst. counsel N.Y. State Dept. Environ. Conservation, Albany, 1979-80, hearings counsel, 1980-84, asst. commr., commr.'s counsel, 1984-85; assoc. Whiteman, Osterman & Hanna, Albany, 1985-86, ptnr., 1986—. Mem. Town. of Clifton Park (N.Y.) Democratic Com., 1985—, bioethics com. St. Margaret's House & Hosp. for Babies, Albany, 1984—; co-chmn. Clifton Park Nursery Sch., 1986. Mem. ABA, N.Y. State Bar Assn. (co-chmn. environ. impact assessment com. of environ. law sect. 1983—, mem. bd. of

editors, editor environ. jour. 1984—), Assn. Bar City N.Y., Albany Bar Assn. Democrat. Jewish. Environment, Administrative and regulatory, State civil litigation. Home: 38 Acorn Ave Clifton Park NY 12065 Office: Whiteman Osterman & Hanna One Commerce Plaza Albany NY 12260

RYALS, KENT, lawyer, songleader; b. Oklahoma City, Mar. 11, 1944; s. Marlin Dewey and Juanita Opal (Bettes) R.; m. Susan Walters, May 20, 1978; children: Katherine Beckett, David Andrew, Mary Bernice. BA, Okla. City U., 1966; postgrad., George Washington U., 1967-68, U. Okla., 1970; JD, Okla. City U., 1974. Bar: Okla. 1975, U.S. Dist. Ct. (no. dist.) Okla. 1975. Atty. Eastern State Hosp., Vinita, Okla., 1975-78; sole practice Vinita, 1978—. Committeeman Craig County Rep. Party, Vinita, 1977-79, vice chmn. 1984, chmn. 1985—; chmn. deacons, songleader Trinity Bapt. Ch., 1978-85; choir dir. Pilgrim Presbyn. Ch., 1986—. Great Plan scholar Okla. City U., 1962-66. Mem. ABA, Assn. Trial Lawyers Am., Okla. Bar Assn. (del. 1983), Okla. Trial Lawyers Assn. (bd. dirs. 1980-81, 82-86, Cert. Meritorius Achievement 1972), Craig County Bar Assn., Christian Legal Soc., Soc. for Preservation and Encouragement of Barber Shop Quartet Singing in Am. (novice champion cen. state dist. 1982). Club: Lions (songleader, 1984-85), Kiwanis (pres. 1979-80) (Vinita). Avocations: barber shop quartets, Am. sign lang., French, German. General practice, State civil litigation, Family and matrimonial. Home: 529 N Brewer Vinita OK 74301 Office: 217 S Wilson PO Box 114 Vinita OK 74301-0114

RYAN, ALLAN ANDREW, JR., lawyer, author, lecturer; b. Cambridge, Mass., July 3, 1945; s. Allan Andrew and Anne (Conway) R.; m. Nancy Foote, June 30, 1978; children: Elisabeth, Andrew. A.B., Dartmouth Coll., 1966; J.D. magna cum laude, U. Minn., 1970. Bar: D.C. 1972, Mass. 1985. Law clk. U.S. Supreme Ct. Justice Byron R. White, 1970-71; asso. Williams, Connolly & Califano, Washington, 1974-77; asst. to Solicitor Gen. U.S., Washington, 1977-80; dir. Office of Spl. Investigations, Dept. Justice, Washington, 1980-83, spl. asst. to atty. gen., 1983; pvt. practice 1983-85; asst. gen. counsel Harvard U., 1985—. Author: Quiet Neighbors: Prosecuting Nazi War Criminals in America, 1984. pres., editor-in-chief: Minn. Law Rev., 1969-70. Bd. dirs. Facing History and Ourselves Nat. Found., 1985—. Served to capt. USMC, 1971-74. Recipient Internat. Human Rights award Anti-Defamation League of B'nai B'rith, 1986. Mem. ABA, D.C. Bar Assn., Boston Bar Assn. Federal civil litigation, Public international. Office: Harvard U Office Gen Counsel 1350 Massachusetts Ave Suite 980 Cambridge MA 02138

RYAN, ATHERTON BEAL, lawyer; b. Norwood, Mass., Mar. 23, 1934; s. Francis A. and Evangeline A. (Atherton) R.; m. Alice Blowen, June 15, 1957; children: Daryl Ann, Linda, Kenneth, Janet, Martha. BA, U. Conn., 1956, LLB, 1959. Bar: Conn. 1959, U.S. Dist. Ct. Conn. 1960, U.S. Ct. Appeals (2d cir.) 1967, U.S. Tax Ct. 1980. Staff atty. Liberty Mut. Ins., Manchester, Conn., 1960-64; ptnr. DuBeau & Ryan P.C., Rockville, Conn., 1964—; chmn. grievance com. Tolland County, Conn., 1975-85; trial referee Conn. Jud. Dept., Tolland County, 1984—; bar counsel grievance com. Tolland and Hartford Counties, 1985—. Chmn. Planning and Zoning Commn., Ellington, Conn., 1962-78, town counsel, 1978-82, 86—. Served with Conn. N.G., 1959-65. Mem. Conn. Bar Assn., Tolland County Bar Assn. (pres.). Republican. Congregationalist. Lodge: Rotary (pres. 1978-79). General practice, State civil litigation, Real property. Office: DeBeau & Ryan PC 38 Park St Rockville CT 06066

RYAN, D. JAY, lawyer; b. N.Y.C., May 19, 1943; s. Dudley F. and Maud D. (Delaney) R.; m. Janeen L. Bausch, Aug. 12, 1979; 1 child, Erin. AB in Am. Govt., Georgetown U., 1965; JD, U. Ariz., 1968. Bar: Ariz. 1968, U.S. Dist. Ct. Ariz. 1968, U.S. Ct. Appeals (9th cir.), U.S. Supreme Ct. 1972. Sole practice Phoenix, 1968-69, 72—; asst. atty. gen. State of Ariz., Phoenix, 1970-72; lay mem. Ariz. State Bd. Accountancy, 1974-79, pres. 1979. Contbr. articles to porfl. jours. V.p., bd. dirs. Ariz. Recreational Ctr. for Handicapped, 1981-86; pres., bd. dirs. Cen. Ariz. Regional Epilepsy Soc., 1973-78. Mem. Ariz. Bar Assn. (law com.), Maricopa County Bar Assn. (pub. relations), Jaguar Club. Republican. Roman Catholic. Avocations: water skiing, scuba, jogging, weight lifting. Administrative and regulatory, Consumer commercial, State civil litigation. Home: 1602 W Vernon Phoenix AZ 85007 Office: 2627 N 3d St Phoenix AZ 85004

RYAN, DAVID CHARLES, lawyer; b. Wheeling, W.Va., Sept. 5, 1949; s. Charles Christian and Virginia Rose (Gostyla) R.; m. Susan Rex Ryan, July 17, 1976. BA in Sociology, Wheeling Coll., 1971; cert. Russian lang., Def. Lang. Inst., 1972; cert. in internat. law, Oxford U., 1978; JD, U. Balt., 1982. Bar: Md. 1982, U.S. Dist. Ct. Md. 1983. Linguist Nat. Security Agy., Ft. George Meade, Md., 1975-78, staff officer, 1981-83, atty., 1983—; staff officer Dept. Def., 1978-81. Mem. East African Wildlife Soc., Nairobi, Kenya, 1986—, Nat. Trust for Hist. Preservation, Washington, 1985—, Friends of Nat. Zoo, Washington, 1984—. Served to sgt. USAF, 1971-75. Mem. ABA, Fed. Bar Assn., Md. Bar Assn. Democrat. Roman Catholic. Avocations: travel, animal welfare. Intelligence Law, Administrative and regulatory, Public international. Office: Gen Counsel Nat Security Agy 9800 Savage Rd Fort George G Meade MD 20755-6000

RYAN, DONALD KEVIN, lawyer; b. Louisville, Oct. 17, 1952; s. James Edward and Dorothy Gwendolyn (McNeil) R. BS in Acctg., U. Ky., 1974; JD, U. Louisville, 1977; LLM in Taxation, Emory U., 1978. Bar: Ky. 1977, U.S. Dist. Ct. (we. dist.) Ky. 1979, U.S. Tax Ct. 1979, U.S. Ct. Appeals (6th cir.) 1982. Assoc. Washer, Kaplan, Rothschild, Aberson & Miller, Louisville, 1978-79, Borowitz & Goldsmith, Louisville, 1979—. Mem. Louisville Estate Planning Council, 1978—. Mem. ABA, Ky. Bar Assn. (CLE recognition award 1981, 82), Louisville Bar Assn. Republican. Roman Catholic. Louisville Ski. Avocations: basketball, water & snow skiing. Personal income taxation, Estate taxation, Corporate taxation. Home: 822 Huntington Rd Louisville KY 40207 Office: Borowitz & Goldsmith 1825 Meidinger Tower Louisville KY 40202

RYAN, FRANK JAMES, lawyer; b. Evergreen Park, Ill., Aug. 27, 1956; s. Frank James and Lucille Louise (Bort) R.; m. Lynn Marie Mucha, Oct. 26, 1985. BA in Speech Communications, No. Ill. U, 1978; JD, John Marshall Sch. of Law, 1981. Bar: Ill. 1981, U.S. Dist. Ct. (no. dist.) Ill. 1981. Ptnr. Vandenberg & Ryan, Midlothian, Ill., 1982, Creswell, Fares & Ryan, Chicago Heights, Ill., 1982—; mem. Cable Com., Palos Heights, Ill., 1982, rules com. Sports and Pasttime, Palos Heights, 1986—. Mem. Ill. Bar Assn., Chgo. Bar Assn., South Suburban Bar Assn., No. Ill. U. Alumni Assn. (bd. dirs. 1982-85). Roman Catholic. Avocations: golf, softball. Personal injury, Family and matrimonial, Criminal. Home: 7713 Golf Dr Palos Heights IL 60463 Office: Creswell Fares & Ryan 233 Joe Orr Rd Chicago Heights IL 60411

RYAN, GARY LEE, lawyer, corporate counsel; b. Binghamton, N.Y., June 14, 1946; s. Harold A. and Augusta E. (Hahn) R.; m. Mildred Anne Soldo, June 12, 1971; children: Gretchen Lindsay, Jonathan Bradley. BS cum laude, Duquesne U., 1968; JD with honors, George Washington U., 1974. Bar: Va. 1974, U.S. Dist. Ct. (no. dist.) Okla. 1977, U.S. Supreme Ct. 1978, U.S. Ct. Claims 1978, U.S. Ct. Appeals (7th cir.) 1978, U.S. Ct. Appeals (D.C. cir.) 1978, D.C. 1979, U.S. Dist. Ct. D.C. 1979, U.S. Ct. Internat. Trade 1982, La. 1986, U.S. Ct. Appeals (5th cir.) 1987. Trial atty. Comptroller of the Currency, Washington, 1974-78; ptnr. McDermott, Will & Emery, Washington, 1979-84; v.p. and assoc. counsel Hibernia Nat. Bank, New Orleans, 1984—. Served with U.S. Army, 1968-73. Mem. ABA (banking law com. of corp., banking and bus. law sect.), Fed. Bar Assn. Banking, Administrative and regulatory, General corporate. Home: 127 Longwood Dr Mandeville LA 70448 Office: Hibernia Nat Bank Legal div 313 Carondelet St New Orleans LA 70130

RYAN, HAROLD L., federal judge; b. Weiser, Idaho, June 17, 1923; s. Frank D.R. and Luella Neibling R.; m. Ann Dagres, Feb. 17, 1961; children: Michael C., Timothy F., Thomas P. Student, U. Idaho, 1941-43, U. Wash., 1943-44, U. Notre Dame, 1944; LL.B., U. Idaho, 1950. Bar: Idaho. Atty. 1950—; pros. atty. Washington County, Idaho, 1951-52; mem. Idaho State Senate, 1962-66; judge U.S. Dist Ct. Idaho, 1981—. mem. Idaho State Senate 1962-66. Mem. Am. Bd. Trial Advocates. Judicial administration. Office: US Courthouse PO Box 040 Federal Bldg Boise ID 83724 *

RYAN, HOWARD CHRIS, state chief justice; b. Tonica, Ill., June 17, 1916; s. John F. and Sarah (Egger) R.; m. Helen Cizek, Oct. 16, 1943; children: John F., Elizabeth Ellen, Howard Chris. B.A., U. Ill., 1940, LL.B., J.D., 1942; LL.D. (hon.), John Marshall Law Sch., 1978. Bar: Ill. 1942. Practice in Decatur, 1946-47, Peru, 1947-57; asst. state's atty. LaSalle County, 1952-54, county judge, 1954-57, circuit judge, 1957-68; chief judge 1964-68; judge appellate ct. 3d Jud. Dist. Ill., 1968-70; justice Ill. Supreme Ct., 1970—, chief justice, 1981-84. Served with USAAF, 1942-45. Mem. Am., Ill., LaSalle County bar assns., Am. Judicature Soc., Am. Legion, Phi Alpha Delta. Republican. Methodist. Lodges: Masons; Elks; Odd Fellows. Home: Box 397 Tonica IL 61370 Office: 111 E Jefferson St Ottawa IL 61350

RYAN, HUGH HARVEY, lawyer; b. Kansas City, Mo., Feb. 3, 1949; s. Walter H. and Evelyn O. (Wright) R.; m. Margie L. Hastings, Sept. 9, 1969; children: Hugh H. II, Timothy W. B in Adminstrv. Justice, U. Mo., Kansas City, 1974, M in Pub. Adminstrn., 1978, JD, 1981. Bar: Mo. 1982, U.S. Dist. Ct. (we. dist.) Mo. 1982. State trooper Mo. State Hwy. Patrol, Lee's Summit, 1971-78; assoc. Paden, Welch, Martin, Albano & Graeff P.C., Independence, Mo., 1981—; asst. pros. atty. City of Blue Springs, Mo., 1982—, City of Sugar Creek, Mo., 1982—. Mem. Met. Kansas City Bar Assn. (workers compensation med. legal com., adv. 1986—, vice chmn. 1987), Eastern Jackson County Bar Assn., Am. Assn. Trial Attys., Mo. Assn. Trial Attys. Methodist. Personal injury, Workers' compensation. Home: 3610 Basswood Dr Lee's Summit MO 64063 Office: Paden Welch Martin Albano & Graeff 311 W Kansas Law Bldg Independence MO 64050

RYAN, J. RICHARD, lawyer; b. N.Y.C., Oct. 23, 1929; s. Peter Leon and Mary Martha (Franklin) R.; m. Diana Louise Gambarelli, Nov. 6, 1954; children—Christopher, Claudia. B.A., Georgetown U., 1951, J.D., Fordham U., 1954. Bar: N.Y. 1956, U.S. Dist. Ct. (so. dist.) N.Y., 1957, U.S. Supreme Ct., 1987. Assoc. Engel, Judge, Miller, Sterling & Reddy, N.Y.C., 1956-63, ptnr., 1963-66; ptnr. Kantor, Shaw & Ryan, N.Y.C., 1966-71; ptnr. Ryan & Silberberg, N.Y.C., 1971-84, Ryan & Fogerty, 1984—. Bd. dirs. Guiding Eyes for the Blind, Inc., pres., 1973-77. Mem. Bar Assn. City N.Y. (Young Lawyers Com. 1957-60), N.Y. State Bar Assn., ABA, Copyright Soc. Candidate for mayor, Pelham, N.Y., 1963. Served with AUS, 1954-56. Clubs: Pelham Country (past pres.), N.Y. Athletic, Union League. General practice, Contracts commercial, Trademark and copyright. Home: 211 The Boulevard Pelham NY 10803 Office: 90 Park Ave Suite 902 New York NY 10016

RYAN, JAMES, III, lawyer; b. New Orleans, Nov. 1, 1941; s. James Coogan and Sarah (Turner) R.; m. Elizabeth H. Woodward, July 15, 1967; children: Marie-Louise D., Elizabeth C. BS, Tulane U., 1963, JD, 1973. Bar: La. 1973, U.S. Dist. Ct. (ea. dist.) La. 1973, U.S. Supreme Ct. 1979. Ptnr. Session, Fishman, Rosenson, Boisfontain, Nathan & Winn, New Orleans, 1973—. Served to maj. USAF, 1964-70, with Res. 1970-84. Decorated Silver Star. Mem. Fed. Bar Assn. La. (sec. 1985-86, treas. 1986-87), La. State Bar Assn. (Ho. of Dels. 1983—). Democrat. Admiralty, Federal civil litigation, State civil litigation. Home: 1305 7th St New Orleans LA 70115 Office: Sessions Fishman et al 35th Floor Place St Charles 201 St Charles Ave New Orleans LA 70170

RYAN, JAMES FRANCIS, university administrator; b. Milw., Sept. 2, 1928; s. Francis Joseph and Olive (Fuller) R.; m. Betty Aspinwall, Jan. 31, 1953 (dec. Jan. 1986); children—Francis, Timothy, Susan, Cynthia. B.S., Marquette U., 1950. Supr. research Wash. State Tax Commn., Olympia, 1953-60; exec. sec. Govn's. Tax Adv. Council, Olympia, 1957-59; chief budget analyst Wash. State Central Budget Agy., Olympia, 1960-65, acting budget dir., 1965; asst. to v.p. for bus. and fin. U. Wash., Seattle, 1965-66; budget dir. Wash. State Central Budget Agy., Olympia, 1966-67; asst. v.p. for bus. and fin. and dir. fin. U. Wash., Seattle, 1967-69, v.p. for planning and budget, 1969-74, v.p. for bus. and fin., 1974-85; mem. bd. trustees Fred Hutchinson Cancer Research Ctr., Seattle, 1972—; vice chmn. Wash. State Data Processing Authority, Olympia, 1977-85; mem. adv. bd. Washington State Supply Mgmt. Adv. Bd., Olympia 1982-85. Mem. bd. trustees Seattle Book Store, 1977-85. Served to lt. USN, 1950-53. Roman Catholic. Avocations: woodworking. Land use and planning, Personal injury, Real property. Home: PO Box 1237 Vashon Island WA 98070

RYAN, JAMES FREDERICK, lawyer, educator; b. Boston, Mar. 11, 1928; s. James Denvir and Harriet Chenery (Bonney) R.; m. Dorothea Elizabeth Dydek, Sept. 1, 1958. A.B., Harvard U., 1949, LL.B., 1952. Bar: Mass. 1952, U.S. Dist. Ct. Mass. 1959, U.S. Ct. Mil. Appeals 1957, U.S. Ct. Appeals (1st cir.) 1979, U.S. Supreme Ct. 1957. Teaching fellow in law Harvard U. Law Sch., 1956-57; sole practice, Boston, 1958—; lectr. Suffolk Law Sch., 1958—; atty. Mass. Crime Commn., 1963-64; asst. corp. counsel City of Boston, 1968-73. Pres. alumni council Roxbury Latin Sch., 1976-78. Served with JAG Corps, USAF, 1953-56; Korea. Recipient Wellington prize for disting. service Roxbury Latin Sch., 1970. Mem. ABA, Mass. Bar Assn., Boston Bar Assn. Club: Harvard (Boston). Author: Massachusetts Bar Examination—Questions, Answers, Comments, 1973; contbr. articles to legal jours. Legal education, Local government, State and local taxation. Office: 15 Court Sq Suite 710 Boston MA 02108

RYAN, JAMES LEO, federal judge; b. Detroit, Nov. 19, 1932; s. Leo Francis and Irene Agnes Ryan; m. Mary Elizabeth Rogers, Oct. 12, 1957; children: Daniel P., James R., Colleen M., Kathleen A. LL.B., U. Detroit, 1956; LL.D. (hon.), Madonna Coll., 1976, Detroit Coll. Law, 1978, Thomas M. Cooley Law Sch., Lansing, Mich., 1986, U. Detroit Sch. Law, 1986. Justice of peace Redford Twp., Mich., 1963-66; cir. judge 3d Jud. Circuit Mich., 1966-75; justice Mich. Supreme Ct., 1975-86; judge U.S. Ct. Appeals (6th cir.), 1986—; faculty U. Detroit Sch. Law, Nat. Jud. Coll., Reno, Am. Acad. Jud. Edn., Washington. Contbr. article to legal jour. Served with JAGC, USNR, 1957-60; to capt. JAGC, Res. 1960—. Mem. Am. Judicature Soc., ABA, Detroit Bar Assn., Naval Res. Lawyers Assn., Nat. Conf. Appellate Ct. Judges, Fed. Judges Assn., State Bar Mich. Roman Catholic. Club: KC. Jurisprudence. Office: U S Ct of Appeals 20793 Farmington Rd Suite 24 Farmington Hills MI 48024

RYAN, JAMES VINCENT, lawyer; b. N.Y.C., Apr. 7, 1927; s. John James and Harriette (Clarke) R.; m. Anne Marie Murray, Aug. 29, 1951; children: James, Maureen, Emmett, Kevin, Deirdre. BS, Purdue U., 1948; LLB, Fordham U., 1951. Bar: N.Y. 1951. Atty. U.S. Dept. Justice, Washington, 1951; asst. U.S. atty. U.S. Dist. Ct. (so. dist.) N.Y., N.Y.C., 1951-54; assoc. Paul, Weiss, Rifkind, Wharton & Garrison, N.Y.C., 1954-55; from assoc. to ptnr. Lundgren, Lincoln & McDaniel, N.Y.C., 1955-65; ptnr. Webster & Sheffield, N.Y.C., 1965-76, Rogers & Wells, N.Y.C., 1977—. Served to lt. (j.g.) USNR, 1945-50. Fellow Am. Coll. Trial Lawyers. Republican. Roman Catholic. Clubs: Winged Foot Country (Mamaroneck, N.Y.) (sec. 1983—), Sky (N.Y.C.). Federal civil litigation, Securities, Admiralty. Office: Rogers & Wells Pan Am Building 200 Park Ave New York NY 10166

RYAN, JOHN JOSEPH, lawyer; b. New Haven, Dec. 14, 1951; s. John J. and Mary (Reinhard) R. BA in English with honors, U. Notre Dame, 1973; JD, Boston Coll., 1976. Bar: Conn. 1976, U.S. Dist. Ct. Conn. 1977, U.S. Ct. Claims 1979, U.S. Tax Ct. 1979, U.S. Ct. Appeals (2d cir.) 1979, U.S. Supreme Ct. 1979, U.S. Dist. Ct. (so. and ea. dists.) N.Y. 1980. Sole practice Norwalk, Conn., 1976-78; asst. clk. to presiding judge Conn. Superior Ct., Stamford, 1977-78; assoc. Keene & Milici, Norwalk, 1978-83; ptnr. Lyons & Ryan, Norwalk, 1983—; corp. counsel City of Norwalk, Conn., 1981-83. Mem. Darien (Conn.) Rep. Town Com., 1984—, Conn. Rep. Cen. Com., Hartford, 1985—; del. to White House Conf. on Small Bus., Washington, 1986; bd. dirs. Friends of Norwalk Clean and Green Inc., 1983—. Mem. ABA, Conn. Bar Assn., Norwalk Bar Assn., Assn. Trial Lawyers Am., Conn. Trial Lawyers Assn., Am. Arbitration Assn. (panel of arbitrators 1980—), Greater Norwalk C. of C. (bd. dirs., exec. bd. 1983—, Small Business Advocate of Yr. award 1986). Club: Notre Dame Alumni of Fairfield County (sec. 1980-83, v.p. 1983-85, pres. 1986—). State civil litigation, Criminal, Real property. Office: Lyons & Ryan PO Box 1085 71 East Ave Norwalk CT 06856

RYAN, JOSEPH, lawyer; b. Seattle, Feb. 11, 1942; s. John Joseph and Jane (Wing) R.; m. Mary Katherine Gavin, Aug. 20, 1963; children: Michael Gavin, Kathleen Ann, Jennifer Jo. BA, U. Washington, 1964; JD, Columbia U., 1967. Ptnr. O'Melveny & Myers, Los Angeles, 1976—; teacher, lecturer N.Y. Law Jour. Author: Stating Your Case--How To Interview for a Job as a Lawyer, 1982. Bd. dirs. Pasadena Playhouse, Los Angeles, 1981, Planetary Soc., Pasadena, 1981, Westridge Sch., Los Angeles, 1982. Served to capt. U.S. Army, 1968-70. Mem. ABA, N.Y. Bar Assn., D.C. Bar Assn., Calif. Bar Assn., Los Angeles County Bar Assn. (teacher, lectr.), Nat. Assn. Bond Lawyers (legis. com.), Bond Club Los Angeles, Practicing Law Inst. (teacher, lectr.), CEB (teacher, lectr.), Pub. Securities Assn. (treas. regional com.), Nat. Assn., Rehab. and Housing Officials, N.Am. Securities Adminstrn. Assn. Republican. Roman Catholic. Clubs: Valley Hunt (Pasadena), Men's Garden (Los Angeles), Pacific Union (San Francisco). Avocations: marathon running, hiking, camping. Municipal bonds, Securities, General corporate. Home: 1900 Midlothian Dr Altadena CA 91001 Office: O'Melveny & Myers 400 S Hope St Los Angeles CA 90071

RYAN, L(AWRENCE) THOMAS, JR., lawyer; b. Binghamton, N.Y., Feb. 10, 1952; s. Lawrence Thomas Sr. and Rita Marie (Burns) R.; m. Pamela Mae Gant, Apr. 30, 1983; 1 child, Lawrence Thomas III. BS, U. Ala., 1975, JD, 1978. Bar: Ala. 1979, U.S. Dist. Ct. (no. dist.) Ala. 1979, U.S. Ct. Appeals (11th cir.) 1985. Assoc. Lammons, Bell & Sneed, Huntsville, Ala., 1978-80; sole practice Huntsville, 1980-84; ptnr. Ryan & Robins, Huntsville, Ala., 1980-84, Simpson, Hamilton & Ryan, Huntsville, Ala., 1984—. Bd. dirs. Children's Adv. Ctr., Huntsville, 1985—. Named one of Outstanding Young Men Am., 1983, 84. Mem. Assn. Trial Lawyers Am., Ala. Trial Lawyers Assn., Comml. Law League. Democrat. Roman Catholic. Lodge: Kiwanis. Avocations: boating, water sports, fishing, bowling. State civil litigation, Contracts commercial, General practice. Home: 8447 Hogan Dr SE Huntsville AL 35802 Office: Simpson Hamilton & Ryan PO Box 5 Huntsville AL 35802

RYAN, LEONARD EAMES, lawyer, public affairs consultant; b. Albion, N.Y., July 8, 1930; s. Bernard and Harriet Earle (Fitts) R.; m. Ann Allen, June 18, 1973; 1 child, Thomas Eames Allen-Ryan. Grad., Kent Sch., 1948; A.B., U. Pa., 1954; J.D., N.Y. U., 1962. Bar: D.C., N.Y. bars 1963, U.S. Ct. of Appeals, D.C 1963, U.S. Dist. Ct. for So. and Eastern Dists. of N.Y 1965, U.S. Ct. of Appeals for the Second Circuit 1966, U.S. Supreme Ct. bar 1967. Reporter Upper Darby (Pa.) News, 1954; newsman AP, Pitts., Phila., Harrisburg, N.Y.C., 1955-62; reporter, spl. writer on law N.Y. Times, 1962-63; info. adviser corp. hdqrs. IBM, N.Y.C., 1963; atty. firm Perrell, Nielsen & Stephens, N.Y.C., 1964-66; trial atty. Civil Rights Div. Dept. Justice, Washington, 1966-68; asst. to dir. bus. affairs CBS News, N.Y.C., 1968; program officer Office Govt. and Law, Ford Found., N.Y.C., 1968-74; individual practice law and pub. affairs cons. N.Y.C., 1974—; adminstrv. law judge N.Y. State Div. Human Rights, 1976—, N.Y. State Dept. Health, 1982—, N.Y. State Dept. Agr. and Mkts., 1987—; impartial hearing officer Office for Handicapped, N.Y.C. Bd. Edn., 1976—; hearing examiner Family Ct. of State of N.Y., N.Y. County, 1981-82; arbitrator Small Claims Ct., N.Y.C., 1974-84; bd. dirs. Community Action for Legal Services Inc., N.Y.C., 1971-77, vice-chmn., 1975-77; co-chmn. Citizens Com. to Save Legal Services, N.Y.C., 1975-76; bd. dirs. Lower East Side Service Center, N.Y.C., 1977—. Author: So You Want to Go Into Journalism, 1963; Contbr. articles to profl. jours. Served with USAR, 1950-57. Mem. Am. Judicature Soc., Nat. Legal Aid and Defender Assn., Assn. Bar City of N.Y., N.Y. State Bar Assn. Democrat. Clubs: St. Elmo, Phila. Federal civil litigation, State civil litigation, Criminal. Office: 32 Orange St Brooklyn NY 11201

RYAN, MARIAN TERESA, lawyer, educator; b. Cambridge, Mass., Sept. 12, 1954; d. Robert Leo and Teresa Barbara (O'Neil) R. BA, Emmanuel Coll., 1976; JD, Boston Coll., 1979. Bar: Mass. 1980, U.S. Dist. Ct. Mass. 1980. Asst. dist. atty. Middlesex County, Cambridge, 1979—; instr. bus. law Emmanuel Coll., Boston, 1985—. Trustee Mt. St. Joseph Acad., Brighton, Mass., 1984—, Notre Dame Acad., Hingham, Mass., 1985—. Democrat. Roman Catholic. Criminal. Home: 1 Prescott St Somerville MA 02143 Office: Middlesex Dist Attys Office 40 Thorndike St Cambridge MA 02140

RYAN, MICHAEL EDMOND, communications company executive, lawyer; b. N.Y.C., May 30, 1938; s. John J. and Mary K. (Mulligan) R.; m. Ellen Todaro, Feb. 10, 1962; children: Michael, Patrick, MaryEllen. B.B.A., St. John's U., Jamaica, N.Y., 1963; J.D., Fordham U., 1967; grad. Advanced Mgmt. Program., Harvard U. 1983. Bar: N.Y. 1967, U.S. Supreme Ct. 1972. With N.Y. Times Co., 1956—, prodn. mgr., 1960-63, asst. controller, 1963-67, corp. atty., 1967-70, asst. sec., 1970-74, sec., corp. counsel, 1974-79, v.p. law, fin., adminstrn., 1979-80, sr. v.p. corp. devel., broadcasting, cable-TV and forest products, 1980—. Bd. dirs. Fordham U. Law Sch. Served with U.S. Army, 1961-62. Recipient Am. Jurisprudence Corps. award Lawyers Coop. Pub. Co., 1967. Mem. ABA, Fed. Bar Assn., Assn. Bar City N.Y. Clubs: Sands Point Golf, Forest Hills, West Side Tennis. General corporate, Antitrust. Office: NY Times Co 229 W 43d St New York NY 10036

RYAN, PETER JOHN, lawyer; b. N.Y.C., Sept. 13, 1922. B.S., U.S. Mil. Acad., 1943; LL.B., NYU, 1950, LL.M., 1963. Bar: N.Y. 1953, U.S. Dist. Ct. (so. dist.) N.Y. 1953. Commd. 2d lt. U.S. Army, 1943, advanced through grades to lt. col., 1951; ret. 1953; assoc. Fried, Frank, Harris, Shriver & Jacobson, N.Y.C., 1953-60, ptnr., 1960-87; pres. Alfred Harcourt Found., White Plains, N.Y., 1985—; bd. dirs. Harcourt Jovanovich, Inc. Mem. Assn. Bar City N.Y., N.Y. State Bar Assn., ABA. Democrat. Home: 79 Kerry Ln Chappaqua NY 10514 Office: Alfred Harcourt Found 20 Haarlem Ave White Plains NY 10603

RYAN, READE HAINES, JR., lawyer; b. Plainfield, N.J., Jan. 4, 1937; s. Reade Haines and Anne Mary (Moment) R.; m. Joan Louise Larson, June 16, 1966; children—Reade Haines III, Rebecca Marie. A.B., Princeton U., 1959; LL.B., Harvard U., 1965. Bar: N.Y. 1966, Calif. 1985. Assoc. firm Shearman & Sterling, N.Y.C., 1965-73; ptnr. Shearman & Sterling, 1973—; lectr. Practicing Law Inst., 1977-87, Am. Law Inst.-ABA, 1979-87. Served to lt. USN, 1959-62. Mem. Internat. Bar Assn., ABA, Calif. State Bar, N.Y. State Bar Assn., Assn. Bar City N.Y., Los Angeles County Bar Assn., Beverly Hills Bar Assn. Republican. Clubs: Montauk (Bklyn.); Los Angeles Athletic. Banking, Contracts commercial, General corporate. Home: 201 Homewood Rd Los Angeles CA 90049 Office: Shearman and Sterling 21st Floor 725 S Figueroa St Los Angeles CA 90017

RYAN, THOMAS JOSEPH, lawyer; b. Waltham, Mass., Sept. 10, 1945; s. Joseph H. and Mary (Murphy) R.; m. Margaret Atkins, June 21, 1969. B.A., St. Lawrence U., 1968; J.D. with honors, Suffolk U., 1974; LL.M. in Trade Regulation, NYU, 1977; P.M.D., Harvard U. Grad. Sch. Bus. Adminstrn., 1982. Bar: Mass. 1974, N.Y 1975, Wis. 1984. Sales rep. Gen. Foods Corp., New Haven, 1969-71, atty., White Plains, N.Y., 1974-76, sr. atty., 1976-77, counsel, 1977-80, sr. counsel, 1980-83; dir. legal services Oscar Mayer Foods Corp., Madison, Wis., 1983-84, v.p., chief legal counsel, 1984—; bd. dirs. Oscar Mayer Found., Madison, 1984-86; mem. allocations com. Dane County United Way, 1984—; chmn. legal com. Pet Food Inst., 1978-80; chmn. legal com. Am. Meat Inst., 1987—. Trustee Suffolk U. Law Alumni, 1982—; alumni rep., admissions office St. Lawrence U., Canton, N.Y., 1983—. Mem. ABA (anti-trust and corp. sects., corp. counseling com. 1986—), N.Y. State Bar Assn. (anti-trust and bus. law sects.), Sigma Chi (chpt. trustee 1970—). Lodge: Kiwanis (chmn. maj. emphasis com. Madison 1986—). Administrative and regulatory, Private international, General corporate. Office: Oscar Mayer Foods Corp PO Box 7188 Madison WI 53707

RYAN, THOMAS TIMOTHY, JR., lawyer, government official; b. Washington, June 13, 1945; s. Thomas Timothy and Elizabeth (Ockershausen) R.; m. Judith Rush, June 13, 1970. A.B., Villanova (Pa.) U., 1967; J.D., Am. U., 1973. Bar: D.C. 1973. Fellow Urban Transp. Inst., Washington, 1972-73; atty. NLRB, Washington, 1973-74, Balt. and Washington, 1974-75, 76-80; dep. gen. counsel Pres. Ford Com., 1975-76; solicitor Dept. Labor, 1981-83; ptnr. Pierson, Ball & Dowd, Washington, 1983—; adj. prof. Georgetown U. Law Sch., 1979-83; mem. bd. Overseas Pvt. Investment Corp., 1981-83, Am. Council Young Polit. Leaders, 1983—; mem. bd. Program for Advancement of Tech. in India. Served to 1st lt. USAR, 1965-70. Mem. ABA, Fed. Bar Assn., D.C. Bar Assn. Republican. Roman Catholic. Jurisprudence.

RYAN, TIMOTHY LEO, lawyer, educator; b. Tucson, Mar. 9, 1943; s. Martin Ray and Blancle H. Ryan; children: Todd M., Heather S. BA, Oreg.

State U., 1969; JD, U. Ariz., 1972. Bar: Oreg. 1972, U.S. Dist. Ct. Oreg. 1972, Ariz. 1976, U.S. Dist. Ct. Ariz. 1976. Assoc. Goode, Goode et al, Albany, Oreg., 1972-76, Lesher & Kimble, Tucson, 1976-82, Kimble, Gouthrie & Ryan, Tucson, 1982-83, Simmil Hill, Tucson, 1983-85, Lesher & Borodkin, Tucson, 1985-86, Simmil Hill, Phoenix, 1986—; instr. Oreg. State U., Corvallis, 1974-75; spl. counsel Atty. Gen.'s Office of Ariz., Phoenix, 1977—. Mem. Oreg. State Bar Assn., Ariz. Bar Assn., Pima County Bar Assn. (chmn. Bridge the Gap 1979-85), Am. Arbitration Assn. (arbitrator 1976—), Order of the Coif. Avocations: woodworking, traveling. Federal civil litigation, State civil litigation, Personal injury. Home: 5211 N 24th St #101 Phoenix AZ 85016 Office: Simmil Hill et al 3700 N 24th St Phoenix AZ 85016

RYAN, TOMAS FINNEGAN, lawyer; b. Portland, Oreg., June 24, 1949; s. Thomas Hadley and Madeline (Finnegan) R.; m. Connemara McNicholas, Dec. 29, 1979; Bridget Hadley, Tomas Ouane, Paul Finnegan. BA in Polit. Sci., U. Portland, 1971; JD, Lewis and Clark Coll., 1974. Bar: Oreg. 1976, U.S. Dist. Ct. Oreg. 1977, U.S. Ct. Appeals (9th cir.) 1977. Law clk. Oreg. Cir. Ct., Portland, 1975-76; sole practice Portland, 1976—. Immigration, naturalization, and customs, Personal injury, Probate. Office: 621 SW Morrison 415 Am Bank Bldg Portland OR 97205

RYAN, WILLIAM J., lawyer; b. Niagra Falls, N.Y., Feb. 20, 1934; m. Mary Kelly, 1960; children: William J. Jr., Peter M., Joseph A., Patricia R., John T. AB, Hobart Coll., 1956; LLB, Fordham U., 1959. Bar: N.Y. 1960, U.S. Dist. Ct. (so. and ea. dists.) N.Y. 1961, U.S. Ct. Appeals (2d cir.) 1961. Assoc. Rogers & Wells, N.Y.C., 1960-68; from gen. atty. to internat. v.p. Johnson & Johnson, New Brunswick, N.J., 1968-85; chief counsel U.S. Senate Labor Com., Washington, 1985-86; v.p., gen. counsel Cytoga Corp., Princeton, N.J., 1987—. Served with USNG, 1959-66. Mem. ABA, N.Y. Bar Assn. Republican. Roman Catholic. Contracts commercial, Legislative, Pharmaceutical drug and medical devices.

RYAN, WILLIAM JOSEPH, JR., lawyer; b. Derby, Conn., Mar. 20, 1951; s. William Joseph and Eleanor (Koon) R.; m. Ann Shirley Wilkinson, June 16, 1973; children—Melissa Ann, William III, Matthew J. B.A. in Psychology cum laude, Fairfield U., 1973; J.D., U. Conn., 1977. Bar: Conn. 1977, U.S. Dist. Ct. Conn. 1977. Sole practice, Derby, 1977-82; ptnr. firm Ryan & Tyma, Derby, 1983-86, Wetmore, Ryan & Tyma, 1986—; bd. dirs. New Haven Legal Assistance, 1981-83. Mem. Oxford Planning and Zoning Commn., Conn., 1981-82, Oxford Bd. Edn., 1983—; v.p. Oxford Republican Town Com., 1984. Mem. Valley Bar Assn. (treas. 1981-82, sec. 1982-83, pres. 1983-84), ABA, Conn. Bar Assn., Assn. Trial Lawyers Am. Roman Catholic. Lodge: Lions (pres. 1984). State civil litigation, General practice, Real property. Home: 10 Crest Rd Oxford CT 06483 Office: Wetmore Ryan & Tyma 231 Coram Ave Shelton CT 06484

RYBAK, MICHAEL DENNIS, lawyer; b. Torrington, Conn., July 17, 1951; s. Frank J. and Elizabeth M. (Wanklin) R.; m. Diane J. Winters, Nov. 20, 1981; children: Michael D. Jr., Matthew P. Student, U. Fribourg, Switzerland, 1971-72; AB, Georgetown U., 1973, JD, 1976. Bar: Conn. 1976, U.S. Dist. Ct. Conn. 1976. Counsel Cigna Corp., Hartford, Conn., 1976-85; ptnr. Guion & Stevens, Litchfield, Conn., 1985—; sec. Harwinton Land Trust, Inc., 1985—. Mem. Harwinton (Conn.) Hist. Soc.; selectman Town Harwinton, 1977-81; legis. Conn. Ho. of Reps., Hartford, 1979-87. Mem. ABA, Conn. Bar Assn., Litchfield County Bar Assn. Democrat. Roman Catholic. Lodges: Lions, Elks. General practice, State civil litigation, Real property. Home: 100 Litchfield Rd Harwinton CT 06791 Office: Guion & Stevens PO Box 338 Litchfield CT 06759

RYDBERG, MARSHA GRIFFIN, lawyer; b. Tampa, Fla., Dec. 11, 1946; d. Jack and Nibia (Santana) Griffin; m. Thomas Henry Rydberg; children—Kristen Elizabeth, Nancy Marshall. B.A., Emory U., 1968; J.D. cum laude, Stetson U., 1976. Bar: Fla. 1976, U.S. Dist. Ct. (mid. dist.) Fla. 1977, U.S. Dist. Ct. (so. dist.) Fla. 1984, U.S. Ct. Appeals (11th cir.) 1977, U.S. Supreme Ct. 1983. Christian youth worker Young Life Campaign, 1968-70; youth dir. First Presbyterian Ch., Tampa, 1970-73; assoc. Gibbons, Tucker, McEwen, Smith, Cofer & Taub. Tampa, 1976-79; assoc. Taub & Williams, Tampa, 1979-83, ptnr., 1983—. Chmn. news editorial bd. Fla. Bar Jour., 1984-85. Contbr. articles to profl. jours. Bd. dirs. Jr. League Tampa, 1979-80, atty., 1983-85; elder Temple Terrace Presbyn. Ch., Fla., 1982-85. Recipient Bob Sikes Incentive award, Judge Joe Morris award, Am. Jurisprudence awards for excellence in law. Mem. Internat. Acad. Trial Lawyers, ABA (com. on commendation zoning and property use), Fla. Bar Assn. (pub. relations com.), Hillsborough County Bar Assn. (chmn. fed. ct. liaison com. 1982, chmn. Law Day com. 1984-85, sec. 1985-86, editor bulletin 1986—), Phi Alpha Delta (outstanding scholastic achievement award). Democrat. Federal civil litigation, State civil litigation, Local government. Home: 2410 Prospect Rd Tampa FL 33629 Office: Taub & Williams 100 S Ashley Dr Suite 2100 Tampa FL 33602

RYDER, BRUCE DAVID, lawyer; b. Independence, Mo., July 22, 1955; s. Donald Eugene and Winona Elaine (McClure) R.; m. Linda Louise Kinnard, Oct. 12, 1985. BA, U. Kans., 1976; JD, Harvard U., 1979. Bar: Mo. 1979, U.S. Dist. Ct. (ea. dist.) Mo. 1979, Ill. 1980, U.S. Ct. Appeals (8th cir.) 1981. Assoc. Coburn, Croft & Putzell, St. Louis, 1979-85, ptnr., 1985—. Mem. ABA, Ill. Bar Assn. State civil litigation, Federal civil litigation, Personal injury. Home: 430 Holmes Pl Webster Groves MO 63119 Office: Coburn Croft & Putzell 1 Mercantile Ctr Suite 2900 Saint Louis MO 63101

RYMER, PAMELA ANN, federal judge; b. Knoxville, Tenn., Jan. 6, 1941. A.B., Vassar Coll., 1961; LL.B., Stanford U., 1964. Bar: Calif. 1966, U.S. Ct. Appeals (9th cir.) 1966, U.S. Ct. Appeals (10th cir.), U.S. Supreme Ct. Assoc. Lillick McHose & Charles, Los Angeles, 1966-72, ptnr., 1973-75; ptnr. Toy and Rymer, Los Angeles, 1975-83; judge U.S. Dist. Ct. (cen. dist.) Calif., Los Angeles, 1983—; faculty The Nat. Jud. Coll., 1986. Mem. Calif. Postsecondary Edn. Commn., 1974—, chmn., 1980-84; mem. Los Angeles Olympic Citizens Adv. Commn.; bd. visitors Stanford Law Sch., 1986—; bd. dirs. Constl. Rights Found., 1985—. Mem. ABA, Los Angeles County Bar Assn. (chmn. antitrust sect. 1981-82), Assn. of Bus. Trial Lawyers. Judicial administration. Office: US District Court cen dist Calif 312 N Spring St Los Angeles CA 90012

RYMER, TERRIE ADRIENNE, lawyer; b. Chgo., May 23, 1946; d. David Maurice and Myrna (Zaremsky) Rymer; m. Frank R. Vozak. B.A. with distinction, U. Mich., 1968; J.D., Northwestern U., 1981. Bar: Ill. 1981, U.S. Dist. Ct. (no. dist.) Ill. 1981. Social services worker various locations, Chgo. and N.Y.C., 1968-78; tutor Stanley Kaplan Ednl. Ctr., Chgo., 1978-79; assoc. Fischel & Kahn, Chgo., 1981-83; staff atty. AMA, Chgo., 1983—. Author: Physician-Hospital Contracts, 1983, Physician-Hospital Joint Ventures, 1987; also articles. Bd. dirs. Protection & Advocacy, Inc., Chgo., 1985—. Mem. ABA (mem. sect. individual rights and responsibilities 1981—, health law forum 1983—), Ill. Bar Assn., Chgo. Bar Assn. (hosp. and health law com. 1983—). Jewish Health. Office: Office of Gen Counsel AMA 535 N Dearborn Chicago IL 60610

SABA, JOSEPH PHILIP, lawyer; b. Phila., July 25, 1947; s. Joseph M. and Sadie (Hassy) S.; m. Mary M. Ellis, Aug. 9, 1969; children: Joseph M., Colin. BA, King's Coll., 1969; MA, Harvard U., 1971; JD, Yale U., 1976. Officer Fgn. Services, Dept. State, Washington, 1971-76; ptnr. Surrey & Morse, Washington, 1976-86, Jones, Day, Reavis & Pogue, Washington, 1986—; counsel Am. Businessmen's Group, Riyadh, Saudi Arabia, 1981-84. Sr. editor and pub. Exec. Reports, 1978—; contbr. articles to profl. jours. Mem. ABA, Washington Fgn. Affairs Soc. Democrat. Roman Catholic. Private international, Administrative and regulatory, Contracts commercial. Home: 7709 Laurel Leaf Dr Potomac MD 20854 Office: Jones Day Reavis & Pogue 1250 Eye St NW Washington DC 20005

SABATH, KENNETH MICHAEL, lawyer; b. Newark, Sept. 12, 1956; s. Vincent Frank and Nellie (Barauskis) S.; m. Lanko Shoji, Mar. 21, 1985. BA, Bates Coll., 1977; JD, Suffolk U., 1980. Bar: Hawaii 1980, U.S. Dist Ct. Hawaii 1980, U.S. Ct. Appeals (9th cir.) 1980, U.S. Ct. Mil. Appeals 1984. Sole practice Honolulu, 1984—; cons. Honolulu Legal Secretaries Assn., 1986—; ct. observer Ambassador Mike Mansfield, Am. embassy, Tokyo, 1982-84. Cons. Sexual Problems Information and Referal Services, 1985-86; mem. U.S. Armed Services Com., Honolulu, 1986—. Served to lt. (judge adv.) USN, 1980-84. Recipient certs. appreciation ARC, U.S. Navy Family Advocacy, 1982-84. Mem. Internat. Legal Soc., ABA (cert. of appreciation 1986), Assn. Trial Lawyers Am., Judge Advs. Assn., Hawaii State Bar Assn., Hawaii C. of C., Soc. Chinese Profls., Honolulu Acad. Arts, Japanese Culture Study. Republican. Roman Catholic. Family and matrimonial, Military, Personal injury. Home: 2452 Tusitala St #806 Honolulu HI 96815 Office: 1188 Bishop St #3210 Honolulu HI 96813

SABERS, RICHARD WAYNE, justice; b. Salem, S.D., Feb. 12, 1938; s. Emil William and Elrena Veronica (Godfrey) S.; m. Colleen D. Kelley, Aug. 28, 1965; children: Steven Richard, Susan Michelle, Michael Kelley. BA in English, St. John's U., Collegeville, Minn., 1960; JD, U. S.D., 1966. Bar: S.D. 1966, U.S. Dist. Ct. S.D. 1966, U.S. Ct. Appeals (8th cir.) 1983. From assoc. to ptnr. Dana, Golden, Moore & Rasmussen, Sioux Falls, S.D., 1966-86; justice Supreme Ct. S.D., Pierre and Sioux Falls, 1986—. Mem. editorial bd. U. S.D. Law Rev., 1965-66. State rep. March of Dimes, Bismarck, N.D., 1963; bd. dirs. St. Joseph Cathedral, Sioux Falls, 1971-86; trustee, bd. dirs. O'Gorman Found., Sioux Falls, 1978-86; mem. sch. bd. O'Gorman High Sch., Sioux Falls, 1985-86. Served as 1st lt. U.S. Army, 1960-63. Named Outstanding Young Religious Leader, Jaycees, Sioux Falls, 1971. Mem. ABA, S.D. Bar Assn., Inst. Jud. Adminstrn., St. John's Alumni Assn. (pres. Sioux Falls chpt. 1975-86). Republican. Roman Catholic. Lodge: Elks. Avocations: tennis, water skiing, snow skiing, sailing, sports. Judicial administration, State civil litigation, Personal injury. Home: 401 N DuLuth Ave Sioux Falls SD 57104 Office: SD Supreme Ct 415 N Dakota PO Box 84726 Sioux Falls SD 57118

SABIN, JOHN MERRILL, lawyer; b. Glendale, Calif., Dec. 21, 1954; s. Merrill Rex and Marie Elizabeth (Huber) S.; m. Terry Lynne Pitts, June 21, 1979; children: Tiffany, John, Rachel. M in Acctg., Brigham Young U., 1981, MBA, JD, 1982. Bar: Calif. 1982, Mo. 1983, Ariz. 1983, U.S. Dist. Ct. (we. and ea. dists.) Mo. 1983, U.S. Dist. Ct. Ariz. 1984, U.S. Dist. Ct. (cen. dist.) Calif. 1984, U.S. Ct. Appeals (9th cir.) 1985. Instr. Brigham Young U., Provo, Utah, 1979-82; assoc. Bryan Cave, McPheeters & McRogerts, St. Louis, 1982-84; gen. counsel ValEquity Inc., Tucson, 1984—; bd. dirs. Tucson Savings and Loan Assn.; instr. U. Phoenix, Tucson, 1986—; adj. prof. Eller Ctr. U. Ariz., Tucson, 1986—; cons. bus. and legal, 1984—; pres., bd. dirs. JD & JD Enterprise Inc., Orem, Utah, 1979—. Chmn. voting dist. Utah Reps., Provo, 1981-82, county and state del., 1978-80; bd. dirs. Tanque Verde Valley Assn., Tucson, 1986. Mem. ABA, Am. Inst. CPA's, Am. Assn. Atty.-CPA's, Ariz. Soc. CPA's, Phi Kappa Phi, Beta Gamma Sigma, Beta Alpha Psi. Republican. Mormon. Avocations: sports officiating, golf, camping. General corporate, Real property, Legal education. Office: ValEquity Inc 5210 E Williams Circle #114 Tucson AZ 85711-4477

SABLEMAN, MARK STEPHEN, lawyer; b. St. Louis, Sept. 13, 1951; s. Chester L. and Lillian E. (Pape) S.; m. Lynn Oden Melby, Jan. 26, 1985; 1 child, Paul Edward. BA, Grinnell Coll., 1972; MS in Journalism, Northwestern U., 1973; JD, Georgetown U., 1979. Bar: Ill. 1979, Fla. 1980, Mo. 1986, U.S. Ct. Appeals (7th cir.) 1981, U.S. Ct. Appeals (8th cir.) 1983. Assoc. Reuben & Proctor, Chgo., 1979-86, Thompson & Mitchell, St. Louis, 1986—. Mem. ABA (forum com. on communications law, subcom. on gavel awards). Democrat. Presbyterian. Avocation: proprietor of private printing press. Libel, Federal civil litigation, State civil litigation. Home: 21 Chaminade Creve Coeur MO 63141 Office: Thompson & Mitchell 1 Mercantile Ctr Saint Louis MO 63101

SABO, WILLIAM DENES, lawyer; b. East Chicago, Ind., Sept. 24, 1948; s. Gazle James and Carolyn Dorothy (Sikich) S.; m. Nancy Lynne Poppendeck, June 15, 1975. B.S. in Chem. Engring., U. Wis.-Madison, 1971, J.D. 1974. Bar: Wis. 1974, U.S. Dist. Ct. (ea. dist.) Wis. 1974, U.S. Patent Office 1974, Trust Ter. of Pacific Islands 1977, Commonwealth of No. Mariana Islands 1978, U.S. Dist. Ct. No. Mariana Islands 1978. Assoc. Quarles & Brady, Milw., 1974-77; asst. pub. defender Trust Ter. of Pacific Islands, Saipan, No. Mariana Islands, 1977-78; chief pub. defender Commonwealth of No. Mariana Islands, Saipan, 1978-79; assoc. patent counsel Olin Corp., Cheshire, Conn., 1980-85 ; fgn. legal cons. Cen. Internat. Law Firm, Seoul, Korea, 1985—; mem. council, mem. exec. com. No. Marianas Commonwealth Council Improvement of Criminal Justice System, 1978-79. Fund raiser YMCA, Milw., 1974, United Fund, Milw., 1975, United Performing Arts Fund, Milw., 1976; disaster vol. Tropical Storm Saipan, ARC, 1978. Mem. ABA, Am. Intellectual Property Law Assn., Conn. Patent Law Assn., Asia Pacific Lawyers Assn., Northern Marianas Bar Assn., Am. C. of C. in Korea, Royal Asiatic Soc., East African Wildlife Soc., Nat. Audubon Soc. Patent, Trademark and copyright, Technology related law. Home: Chongro Ku Dangju Dong, Sejong Apt 904, Seoul Korea Office: Cen Internat Law Firm, Kwanghwamoon PO Box 356, Seoul Korea

SABOUNGHI, JOSEPH M., lawyer. s. Raymond F. and Fernande (Ayac) S. BA, St. John's U., 1976; JD, Yeshiva U., 1979. Bar: N.Y. 1981, U.S. Tax Ct. 1981, U.S. Claims Ct. 1981, U.S. Ct. Appeals (2d cir.) 1981. Tax counsel N.Y. Life Ins., N.Y.C., 1980-85; sr. dir., tax counsel Wolper Ross & Co., N.Y.C., 1985-86; v.p., tax counsel 1st Annuity Corp., West Orange, N.J., 1986—; sole practice Queens, N.Y., 1980—; bd. dirs. Melt Corp., N.Y.C. Mem. ABA, N.Y. State Bar Assn., N.Y. County Lawyers Assn., N.Y. Estate Planning Council. Republican. Roman Catholic. Avocations: running, weightlifting, scuba diving, photography. Pension, profit-sharing, and employee benefits, Estate taxation, Corporate taxation.

SACASAS, RENE, lawyer; b. N.Y.C., July 10, 1947; s. Anselmo and Orlanda (Soto) S.; m. Cathy Lee Van Natta, Jan. 24, 1970. BA, Am. U., 1969; JD, Emory U., 1975. Bar: Fla. 1976, U.S. Dist. Ct. (so. dist.) Fla. 1976, U.S. Ct. Appeals (5th cir.) 1976, U.S. Supreme Ct. 1980, U.S. Ct. Appeals (11th cir.) 1983. Law clk. McLarty and Aiken, Atlanta, 1974-76; assoc. Welbaum, Zook, Jones, Williams, Miami, Fla., 1976-79; ptnr. Darrach, Merkin and Sacasas, Miami, 1979-83, Merkin & Sacasas, Miami, 1984-86; of counsel Welbaum, Zook, Jones & Williams, Miami, 1986—; asst. prof. bus. law U. Miami, 1985—. Mem. ABA, Fla. Bar Assn. (vice chmn. grievance com. 1981-84), Dade County Bar Assn., Latin Am. C. of C., U.S. Jaycees, Cuban Am. Bar Assn., Phi Sigma Kappa (ET chpt. pres. 1968). Author: Comfort Letters, 1987. Banking, Real property, Private international. Home: 12715 SW 102d Terr Miami FL 33186 Office: Welbaum Zook Jones & Williams 2701 S Bayshore Dr PH Suite Miami FL 33133

SACHS, HOWARD F(REDERIC), U.S. judge; b. Kansas City, Mo., Sept. 13, 1925; s. Alex F. and Rose (Lyon) S.; m. Susanne Wilson, 1960; children—Alex Wilson, Adam Phinney. B.A. summa cum laude, Williams Coll., 1947; J.D., Harvard U., 1950. Bar: Mo. bar 1950. Law clk. U.S. Dist. Ct., Kansas City, Mo., 1950-51; pvt. practice Kansas City, 1951-79; U.S. dist. judge Western Dist. Mo., Kansas City, 1979—. Contbr. articles to various publs. Mem. Kansas City Commn. Human Relations, 1967-73; chmn. Jewish Community Relations Bur., 1968-71, Kansas City chpt. Am. Jewish Com., 1963-65; mem. exec. com. Nat. Jewish Community Relations Adv. Council, 1968-71; pres. Urban League Kansas City, 1957-58, Kansas City chpt. Am. Jewish Congress, 1974-77; co-chmn. Kansas City chpt. NCCJ, 1958-60; mem. Kansas City Sch. Dist. Desegregation Task Force, 1976-77; pres. Jackson County Young Democrats, 1959-60; treas. Kennedy-Johnson Club, Jackson County, 1960. Served with USNR, 1944-46. Mem. Am. Bar Assn., Am. Judicature Soc., Mo. Bar, Kansas City Bar Assn., Lawyers Assn. Kansas City, Phi Beta Kappa. Jurisprudence. Home: 816 W 68th Terr Kansas City MO 64113 Office: US Dist Ct US Courthouse 811 Grand Ave Room 443 Kansas City MO 64106

SACHS, IRVING JOSEPH, lawyer, accountant, pension consultant; b. Chgo., Sept. 12, 1922; s. Philip and Ida (Camras) S.; m. Bettie Taub, June 8, 1947 (dec. Jan. 1964); children—Richard, Melissa, Ilene, Philip; m. 2d Francine Lee Rodbard, Aug. 15, 1965; children—Marc, Jan, Wayne, Jason. B.S. in Acctg., DePaul U., 1948, J.D., 1951. Bar: Ill. 1951; C.P.A., Ill. Sr. ptnr. Sachs, Shapiro & Silver, Chgo. and Skokie, Ill., 1954-65, Sachs, Rosenberg & Kosin, Chgo., 1954-62; sole practice, Chgo. and Highland Park, Ill., 1962-76; pres. Nat. Pension Consultants, Inc., Chgo., 1978-79, Alliance Pension Consultants, Inc., Skokie, 1979—. Served with Signal Corps, U.S. Army, 1943-46, ETO, PTO. Jewish. Pension, profit-sharing, and employee benefits. Office: Alliance Pension Cons Inc 9933 Lawler Ave Suite 505 Skokie IL 60077

SACHS, JEFFREY MICHAEL, lawyer; b. New Haven, Dec. 17, 1957; s. Kalman A. and Edith K. Sachs. BA, Colby Coll., 1979; JD, Emory U., 1982. Bar: Conn. 1982, Ga. 1982, U.S. Dist. Ct. Conn. 1982. Spl. asst. corp. counsel City of West Haven, 1983-84; ptnr. Sachs, Delaney, Maretz & Zemetis, New Haven, 1982—; bd. dirs., v.p. Resortworks of Newport (R.I.) Inc., 1985—, Resortworks of Aspen (Colo.) Inc., 1985—. Writing editor Emory Law Jour., Atlanta, 1981-82. Mem. ABA, Ga. Bar Assn., Conn. Bar Assn. Real property, Contracts commercial, General corporate. Home: 765 Quinniplac Ave New Haven CT 06513 Office: Sachs Delaney Maretz & Zemetis 388 Orange St New Haven CT 06515

SACHS, PHILIP DAVID, lawyer; b. St. Louis, July 30, 1947; s. Ben and Nellie (Newmark) S.; m. Patricia Ann Burt, Oct. 29, 1980; children: Matthew Donald, Jonathan Edward. BJ, U. Mo., 1975; JD, U. Idaho, 1980. Bar: Idaho 1980, U.S. Dist. Ct. Idaho 1980, Wyo. 1982, U.S. Dist. Ct. Wyo. 1982. Atty. Idaho Legal Aid, Lewiston, 1981-82, Lincoln County Atty.'s Office, Kemmerer, Wyo., 1982-86; sole practice Kemmerer, 1982—. Served with USN, 1968-72. Mem. ABA, Idaho Bar Assn., Wyo. Bar Assn. Avocation: photography. Consumer commercial, General corporate, General practice. Home: PO Drawer 232 Kemmerer WY 83101 Office: 1100 Pine Ave Suite 1f Kemmerer WY 83101

SACHS, SIDNEY STANLEY, lawyer; b. Washington, Dec. 25, 1916; s. William Michael and Rebecca (Krupsaw) S.; m. Betty Kossow, Nov. 20, 1941; children: Ellen (Mrs. Richard Rodin), Susan (Mrs. Richard W. Goldman), Jane, John. B.A., Am. U., 1937; LL.B., Georgetown U., 1941. Bar: D.C. 1942, Md. 1949, U.S. Supreme Ct 1949. Law clk. to judge U.S. Emergency Ct. Appeals, 1943-45; asst. U.S. atty. D.C., 1945-49; practice law D.C., and Md., 1949—; instr. Washington Coll. Law, Am. U., 1947-52; mem. bd. Inst. Criminal Law and Procedure, Georgetown U., 1955—, chmn. continuing legal edn. adv. bd., 1979—, adv. com. legal intern program, 1965—; mem. Jud. Conf. for, D.C., 1958—; mem. com. on admissions and grievances U.S. Ct. Appeals for D.C. circuit, 1978, chmn. com., 1979-83. Bd. govs. Citizens Communications Center (merged into Inst. Public Representation, Georgetown U. Law Center); bd. dirs. D.C. Assn. Mental Health, 1964-66, Regional Ctr. for Infants and Young Children; trustee Public Defender Service, 1965-75, Washington Sch. Psychiatry, 1973—; chmn. bd. Hearing, Ednl. Aid and Research Found., 1976-85. Fellow Am. Bar Found., Am. Coll. Trial Lawyers; mem. ABA (ho. of dels. 1970-84, state del. 1972-81, bd. govs. 1981-84, chmn. standing com. on alternate dispute resolution 1984—, council sr. lawyers div. 1985—, chmn. internat. law and practice sect. com. on internat. property, estate and trust law 1984-87), Fed. Bar Assn. (sec. com. atomic energy 1950-52), Am. Law Inst., Inter-Am. Bar Assn., Bar Assn. D.C. (pres. research found. 1959, pres. assn. 1966-67), D.C. bar (gov. 1972-75), ACLU. Jewish. Clubs: University, Burning Tree (Md.). General practice, Family and matrimonial, Estate planning. Home: 2717 Daniel Rd Chevy Chase MD 20815 Office: 1140 Connecticut Ave NW Washington DC 20036

SACHS, WILLIAM, lawyer; b. Bayonne, N.J., July 25, 1906; s. Max and Annie Dora (Zimmerman) S.; m. Alice E. Levine, Nov. 3, 1945; 1 child, Martin H. BA, NYU, 1926; JD, Rutgers U., 1927; LLM cum laude, John Marshall Law Sch., Jersey City, 1947. Bar: N.J. 1928, U.S. Dist. Ct. N.J. 1928, U.S. Supreme Ct.1969. Ptnr. Sachs & Sachs, Bayonne, N.J., 1928-62; sole practice Bayonne, 1963—; prof. law John Marshall Law Sch., 1946-49. Judge advocate AMVETS, N.J., 1964-70, comdr., Hudson County, 1946; pres. Bayonne Aid Progressive Assn., 1940, 46. Served to sgt. AUS, 1941-45. Recipient Cert. Appreciation, AMVETS, 1968, Cert. Merit, AMVETS, 1966. Mem. N.J. Bar Assn., Hudson County Bar Assn., Bayonne Bar Assn. Jewish. Lodges: Masons (master 1941), B'nai B'rith. Avocations: baseball, basketball, boxing, tennis. General practice, Personal injury, Probate. Home: 729 Suburban Rd Union NJ 07083 Office: 5 W 22d St Suite 201 Bayonne NJ 07002

SACK, EDWARD J., lawyer; b. N.Y.C., Apr. 7, 1930; s. Isidor and Rose (Barash) S.; m. Susanne Pletman, Sept. 6, 1953. A.B., Harvard U., 1951, LL.B., 1954; LL.M., NYU, 1959. Bar: N.Y. 1954, U.S. Dist. Ct. (so. dist.) N.Y. 1959, U.S. Ct. Appeals (4th cir.) 1975, U.S. Ct. Appeals (2nd cir.) 1979, U.S. Supreme Ct. 1982. Assoc. Simpson Thacher & Bartlett, N.Y.C., 1954-66; atty. Am. Electric Power Service Corp., N.Y.C., 1966-69; sr. atty. Consol. Edison Co., N.Y.C., 1969-79; gen. counsel Internat. Council Shopping Ctrs., N.Y.C., 1979—. Bd. regents L.I. Coll. Hosp., Bklyn., 1977—. Mem. Bar Assn. City of N.Y. Administrative and regulatory, Legislative. Office: 665 Fifth Ave New York NY 10022

SACK, SYLVAN HANAN, lawyer; b. Phila., Dec. 26, 1932; s. Isidore F. and Mollye (Bellmore) S.; m. Ellen L. Foreman, Aug. 13, 1972; children: Reuben H., Sara I. M.S. in Bus. Adminstrn, Pa. State U., 1956; J.D., U. Balt., 1964. Bar: Md. 1964, U.S. Tax Ct. 1967, U.S. Supreme Ct. 1970; C.P.A., Md. Agt. IRS, Balt., 1956-67; practice in Balt., 1967—; asso. counsel Safety First Club of Md., 1975-78, counsel, 1979—; gov. Md. chpt. Retinitis Pigmentosa Found., 1974-75. Contbr. articles to profl. jours. Chmn. Indsl. Toxicology NIOSH Function, 1977, Occupational Disease Forum, 1979, OSHA and Diseases in Workplace Seminar, 1981. Mem. Fed. Bar Assn. (gov. chpt. 1968—, chmn. bd. govs. 1969-70, chmn. environ. law program 1984), ABA (chmn. subcom. sect. taxation 1972-75), Md. Bar Assn., Am. Trial Lawyers Assn.; mem. Md. Trial Lawyers Assn. (lectr. toxic torts 1983 conv.). Toxic chemical exposure torts, Personal injury, Environment. Home: 27 Brightside Baltimore MD 21208 Office: 2404 St Paul St Baltimore MD 21218

SACKLER, ARTHUR BRIAN, lawyer; b. Utica, N.Y., June 9, 1950; s. Joseph Leon and Leonore (Guttman) S.; m. Linda J. Cimarusti, May 27, 1979; 1 child, Joshua Michael. B.A., Syracuse U., 1970, J.D., 1973; LL.M., Georgetown U., 1979. Bar: N.Y. 1974, D.C. 1975, U.S. Dist. Ct. D.C. 1979, U.S. Supreme Ct. 1979, U.S. Ct. Appeals (D.C. cir.) 1981. Appeals examiner U.S. Civil Service Commn., Washington, 1973-75, atty. advisor, 1975-76, trial atty., 1976-79; gen. counsel Nat. Newspaper Assn., Washington, 1979-82; dir. pub. policy devel. Time Inc., Washington, 1982—; mem. Joint Washington Media Com., 1979—, Am. Copyright Council, Washington, 1984-86; faculty communications law Practicing Law Inst., 1980, forum com. on communications law seminar, 1980; instr. Am. Press Inst., 1980-82. Editor and contbr.: Federal Laws Affecting Newspapers, 1981; founder, editor newsletter News Media Update, 1979-82; contbr. articles to profl. jours., newspapers. Pres. Birnam Wood Community Assn., Potomac, Md., 1983-84; sec., treas. Potomac Springs Community Assn., Potomac, Md., 1986-87. Mem. ABA (vice chair postal matters subcom., adminstrv. law sect.), D.C. Bar Assn., Fed. Communications Bar Assn., Fed. Bar Assn., Mag. Pubs. Assn. (govt. relations com. N.Y.C. 1982-85), Am. Advt. Fedn. (govt. relations com. Washington 1984—), Direct Mktg. Assn. (govt. relations com. 1986—), Am. Tort Reform Assn. (corp. steering com. 1986—), Assn. Am. Pubs. (postal com. N.Y.C. 1983—). Jewish. Clubs: Nat. Press, Bethesda Country. Legislative, Administrative and regulatory. Office: Time Inc 1050 Connecticut Ave NW Washington DC 20036

SACKS, BARRY HOWARD, lawyer; b. Boston, Aug. 21, 1939; s. Louis and Edith Leah (Sax) S. BS, MIT, 1961, MS, 1964, PhD, 1967; JD, Harvard U., 1973. Bar: Calif. 1973, U.S. Dist. Ct. (no. dist.) Calif. 1973, U.S. Tax Ct. 1973, U.S. Ct. Appeals (9th cir.) 1973. Postdoctoral fellow U. Paris, 1967-68; asst. prof. U. Calif., Berkeley, 1969-70; assoc. Winokur, Maier & Zang, San Francisco, 1973-83, Shartsis, Friese & Ginsburg, San Francisco, 1983—. Inventee electron pulse oscillator; contbr. articles to profl. jours. Fellow NSF. Mem. ABA, Calif. Bar Assn. (cert. specialist in taxation law), Sigma Xi. Democrat. Jewish. Corporate taxation, Pension, profit-sharing, and employee benefits. Home: 2557 Clay St San Francisco CA 94115 Office: Shartsis Friese & Ginsburg One Maritime Plaza San Francisco CA 94111

SACKS, IRA STEPHEN, lawyer; b. N.Y.C., Dec. 6, 1948; s. Marvin Leonard and Mildred (Finkelstein) S.; m. Lois Berk, Aug. 15, 1970; children: Jennifer, Allison. BS, MIT, 1970; JD, Georgetown U., 1974. Bar: N.Y. 1975, U.S. Dist. Ct. (so. and ea. dists.) N.Y. 1975, U.S. Ct. Appeals (2d cir.) 1975, U.S. Ct. Appeals (3d cir.) 1984, U.S. Supreme Ct. 1985, U.S. Ct. Appeals (9th cir.) 1986. Assoc. Kaye, Scholer, Fierman, Hays & Handler, N.Y.C., 1974-82, ptnr., 1983—. Contbr. articles to profl. jours. NSF fellow, 1970. Mem. ABA (com. on pvt. antitrust litigation antitrust sect.), N.Y. State Bar Assn., Assn. of Bar of City of N.Y. Democrat. Jewish. Avoca-

tions: tennis, softball. Antitrust, Securities, Federal civil litigation. Home: 303 E 83rd St New York NY 10028 Office: Kaye Scholer Fierman Hays & Handler 425 Park Ave New York NY 10583

SADLER, BRUCE PHILLIP, lawyer; utility company executive; b. Berkeley, Calif., Aug. 11, 1928; s. Clarence Theodore and Dorris Reba (Smoak) S.; m. Ruby Vidich, June 24, 1961; children: Stephen Paul, Susan Elaine. AA, U. Calif.-Berkeley, 1947, BS, 1949, MBA, 1955; JD, Hastings Coll. Law, U. Calif.-San Francisco, 1954. Bar: Calif. 1955, U.S. Dist. Ct. (no. dist.) Calif. 1955, U.S. Ct. Appeals (9th cir.) 1955, U.S. Dist. Ct. (ea. dist.) Calif. 1967. Reader, U. Calif.-Berkeley, 1948-51, 53-55; expediter Gilmore Steel and Supply Co., San Francisco, 1944-50; adjuster, claims investigator, atty. Indsl. Indemnity Co., San Francisco, 1955-58; atty., supr. workers compensation sect. Pacific Gas & Electric Co., San Francisco, 1958-79, mgr. safety, health and claims dept., 1979—; lectr. Calif. Continuing Edn. of Bar, 1962. Mem. labor and store bds. Associated Students U. Calif., 1945-48; mem. troop com. San Mateo County council Boy Scouts Am., 1975-77; trustee Carlmont United Meth. Ch., 1967-70. Served to 1st lt. Q.C., U.S. Army, 1951-53, to capt. USAR, 1953-64. Recipient Gold medal Pacific Coast Gas Assn., 1960. Mem. Pacific Coast Gas Assn., Pacific Coast Elec. Assn., Calif. State Bar Assn., No. Calif. Council Self-Insurers (past-chmn.), San Francisco Barristers Club (past chmn. workers' compensation com.), Am. Gas Assn. (claims com.), Calif. C. of C. (workers compensation com.), Calif. Self-Insurers Assn. (past chmn. legis. com., past mem. bd. mgrs., past mem. exec. com., self-insurer's adv. com.). Workers' compensation, Personal injury. Office: 123 Mission St Room H521 San Francisco CA 94106

SADLER, PAUL LINDSEY, lawyer; b. Freer, Tex., Apr. 29, 1955; s. Harold and Pete (Mix) S.; m. Ronda Walker, Aug. 3, 1974; children: Erin, Brandon. BBA, Baylor U., 1978, JD, 1979. Bar: Tex. 1979, La. 1980, U.S. Dist. Ct. (ea. and so. dists.) Tex. 1984, U.S. Ct. Appeals (5th cir.). Assoc. Haley, Fulbright, Winniford, Bice & Davis, Waco, Tex., 1979-80, Luffey, Price, Dunn & Sadler, Monroe, La., 1980, Ramey, Flock, Hutchins, Jeffus, McClendon & Crawford, Tyler, Tex., 1981-82; ptnr. Wellborn, Houston, Adkison, Mann, Sadler & Colley, Henderson, Tex., 1982—. Named one of Outstanding Young Men Am., 1982. Mem. Assn. Trial Lawyers Am., Tex. Trial Lawyers Assn., Delta Theta Phi. Baptist. Lodge: Optomists. Personal injury, Federal civil litigation, State civil litigation. Office: Wellborn Houston et al 110 N Main St PO Box 1109 Henderson TX 75653-1109

SADOWSKI, WILLIAM EDWARD, lawyer, state legislator; b. Springfield, Mass., Mar. 17, 1944; s. Stanley Edward and Mary Wanda (Trzasko) S.; m. Jean Marie Garcia, Nov. 15, 1969; children—Jill, Ryan. B.A., U. Fla., 1966, J.D. 1969. Bar: Fla. 1969, U.S. Dist. Ct. (so. dist.) Fla. 1969, U.S. Supreme Ct. 1972, U.S. Ct. Appeals (11th and 5th cirs.) 1981, U.S. Dist. Ct. (middle dist.) Fla. 1984. Assoc. Helliwell, Melrose & DeWolf, Miami, 1969-73, ptnr., 1973-80; of counsel Steel Hector & Davis, Miami, 1980-83; ptnr. Akerman, Senterfitt & Eidson, Miami, 1984—; spl. counsel on water issues to Fla. Ho. of Reps., 1982-84; dir. Legal Services of Greater Miami, Inc.; bd. govs. Ins. Exchange Americas, Inc.; mem. Fla. Ho. of Reps., 1976-82, chmn. com. on ins., 1978-80, com. on regulatory reform, 1980-82; mem. commn. on Fla. appellate ct. structure; joint legis.-exec. commn. on post-secondary edn., chmn. task force on water; vice chmn. governing bd. South Fla. Water Mgmt. Dist., 1984-86, chmn., 1986—; mem. governing bd. Fla. Keys Acqueduct Authority, 1984-85; chmn. Gov.'s Fla. Rivers Study Com., 1984-85; mem. Speaker's Adv. Com. on the Future, 1985—. Named Most Valuable Legislator St. Petersburg (Fla.) Times, 1979; recipient Nelson Poynter Civil Liberties award Fla. chpt. ACLU, 1980, Outstanding Pub. Leadership award Greater Miami C. of C. Mem. Dade County Bar Assn., Fla. Bar, ABA, Am. Judicature Soc., Hist. Assn. So. Fla. (trustee). Democrat. Contbr. articles to profl. jours. Federal civil litigation, Insurance, General corporate. Office: 801 Brickell Ave 24th floor Miami FL 33131

SAEKS, ALLEN IRVING, lawyer; b. Bemidji, Minn., July 14, 1932; m. Linda J. Levin; 1 child, Adam Charles. B.S. in Law, U. Minn., 1954, LL.B., 1956. Bar: Minn. 1956, U.S. Dist. Ct. Minn. 1956, U.S. Ct. Appeals (8th cir.) 1957, U.S. Ct. Appeals (fed. cir.) 1959, U.S. Supreme Ct. 1959. Asst. U.S. atty. Dept. Justice, St. Paul, 1956-57; assoc. Leonard Street & Deinard, Mpls., 1960-63, ptnr., 1964—; adj. prof. law U. Minn. Law Sch., 1960-65; mem. adv. com. Nat. Interest on Lawyers Trust Accounts Clearinghouse, 1983-86; chmn. Lawyer Trust Account Bd., Interest on Lawyers Trust Accounts., 1984—. Chmn. Property Tax Com., 1986-87; bd. dirs. Citizens League, Mpls., 1984—. Served to 1st lt. JAGC, U.S. Army, 1957-60. Fellow Am. Bar Found.; mem. Hennepin County Bar Assn. (pres. 1983-84), ABA, Minn. State Bar Assn., Order of Coif, Phi Delta Phi. Federal civil litigation, State civil litigation, Bankruptcy. Office: Leonard Street and Deinard 100 S 5th St Minneapolis MN 55402

SAFER, JAY GERALD, lawyer; b. Jacksonville, Fla., Oct. 11, 1946; s. Moe B. and Rubye (Lipsitz) S.; m. Annette Fashing, Nov. 26, 1970; children: Michelle Laurie, Ellie Renee. BA, Vanderbilt U., 1968; JD, Columbia U., 1971. Bar: N.Y. 1972, U.S. Dist. Ct. (so. and ea. dists.) N.Y. 1973, U.S. Ct. Appeals (2d cir.) 1974, U.S. Dist. Ct. Conn. 1984. Assoc. Paul, Weiss, Rifkind, Wharton & Garrison, N.Y.C., 1971-75, Hardee, Barovick, Konecky & Braun, N.Y.C., 1975; assoc. LeBoeuf, Lamb, Leiby & MacRae, N.Y.C., 1975-80, ptnr., 1980—. Served to capt. U.S. Army, 1972. Harlan Fiske Stone scholar, Columbia U., 1971. Mem. ABA. Federal civil litigation, State civil litigation, Antitrust. Office: LeBoeuf Lamb Leiby & MacRae 520 Madison Ave New York NY 10022

SAFFELS, DALE EMERSON, federal judge; b. Moline, Kans., Aug. 13, 1921; s. Edwin Clayton and Lillian May (Cook) S.; m. Margaret Elaine Nieman, Apr. 2, 1976; children by previous marriage: Suzanne Saffels Gravitt, Deborah Saffels Knorr, James B.; stepchildren: Lynda Cowger Harris, Christopher Cowger. A.B., Emporia State U., 1947; LL.B., J.D. cum laude, Washburn U., 1949. Bar: Kans. 1949. Individual practice law Garden City, Kans., 1949-71, Topeka, 1971-75, Wichita, Kans., 1975-79; U.S. dist. judge Dist. of Kans., Kansas City, 1979—; chmn. bd. Fed. Home Loan Bank of Topeka, 1978-79. Bd. govs. Sch. Law Washburn U.; pres. Kans. Dem. Club, 1957; Dem. nominee Gov. of Kans., 1962; county atty., Finney County, Kans., 1951-55; mem. Kans. Ho. of Reps., 1955-63, minority leader, 1961-63; mem. Kans. Corp. Commn., 1967-75, chmn., 1968-75; mem. Kans. Legis. Council, 1957-63; Kans. rep. Interstate Oil Compact Commn., 1967-75, 1st vice chmn., 1971-72; pres. Midwest Assn. Regulatory Commn., 1972-73, Midwest Assn. R.R. and Utilities Commrs., 1972-73; bd. dirs. Nat. Assn. Regulatory Utility Commrs., 1972-75. Served to maj. Signal Corps U.S. Army, 1942-46. Recipient Disting. Alumnus award Emporia State U., 1974, Disting. Alumnus award Washburn U., 1983. Mem. ABA, Kans. Bar Assn., Sedgwick County Bar Assn., Am. Judicature Soc. Lutheran. Jurisprudence. Home: 8901 Maple Dr Overland Park KS 66207 Office: 118 US Courthouse PO Box 1278 Kansas City KS 66117

SAFFER, JUDITH M., lawyer; b. N.Y.C., June 10, 1942; d. Gilbert and Rose (Elizer) Mack; m. Brian H. Saffer, June 13, 1965; children—Amy, Ian. B.A., NYU, 1965, LL.B., 1967. Bar: N.Y. 1968, U.S. Dist. Ct. (so. and ea. dists.) N.Y. 1968, U.S. Ct. Appeals (2d cir.) 1975. Sr. counsel ASCAP, N.Y.C., 1981-86, asst. gen. counsel, BMI, 1986—. Bd. dirs. Symphony Space. Mem. ABA. Copyright Soc. U.S.A. Trademark and copyright, Federal civil litigation, Labor. Home: 77 Winchip Rd Summit NJ 07901

SAFI, DEBORAH CAVAZOS, lawyer; b. Dallas, Feb. 8, 1953; d. Arnaldo Nelson and Ila Mae (Rinn) Cavazos; m. Hazim Jawad Safi, July 28, 1979; 1 child, Jawad Joseph. BA, Baylor U., 1975, JD, 1977. Bar: Tex. 1977. Assoc. Andrew & Kurth, Houston, 1977-81; corp. atty. Transco Energy Co., Houston, 1981-83; sole practice Houston, 1983-85; of counsel Anderson, Boone & Harrell, Houston, 1985—. Served on fund raising com. Children's Mus., Houston, 1986; co-leader Blue Bird/Camp Fire Girls, Waco, Tex., 1972-73. Named one of Transco Outstanding Women of 1982, Transco Energy Co. and YWCA, Houston 1982; recipient Am. Jur. award in conflicts of law The Lawyers Coop. Publ. Co., 1977. Fellow Tex. Bar Found., Houston Bar Found.; mem. ABA, Houston Bar Assn., Houston Young Lawyers Assn. (v.p. 1986-87, treas. 1984-86, bd. dirs. 1982-84, com. chmn. 1980-82, named Outstanding Com. Leader, 1982), Tex. Young Lawyers Assn. (bd. dirs. 1986-88, co-editor newsletter 1986-87), Fed. Energy Bar Assn., Delta Delta Delta, Phi Delta Phi. Oil and gas leasing.

SAFT, STUART MARK, lawyer; b. N.Y.C., Feb. 17, 1947; s. Stanley and Dorothy (Ligerman) S.; m. Stephanie C. Optekman, June 6, 1970; children: Bradley S., Gordon D. BA, Hofstra U., 1968; JD, Columbia U., 1971. Bar: N.Y. 1972, Fla. 1975, U.S. Dist. Ct. (so. dist.) N.Y. 1975. Asst. gen. counsel Joseph Bancroft & Son Co., N.Y.C., 1972-74; ptnr. Brauner, Baron, Rosenzwerz, Kligler & Sparber, N.Y.C., 1974-81, Powsner, Saft & Powsner, N.Y.C., 1981-84, Goldschmidt, Oshatz & Saft, N.Y.C., 1984—; v.p., bd. dirs. Council of N.Y. Coops., N.Y.C., 1981—. Contbr. articles to profl. jours. Served to capt. USAR, 1968-76. Mem. ABA, N.Y. Bar Assn., Fla. Bar Assn. Real property, General corporate. Office: Goldschmidt Oshatz & Saft 825 3d Ave New York NY 10017

SAGEHORN, THOMAS JOHN, lawyer; b. Long Beach, Calif., June 30, 1952; s. Eldor George Sagehorn and Alberta Lorraine (Salisbury) Bursen; m. Cheryl Lynn Dickinson, Aug. 13, 1977; children: Kathryn Louise, Scott John, Anne Christy. BA in Pol. Scis., Stanford U., 1974; JD, So. Meth. U., 1978. Assoc. counsel Bonanza Internat., Inc., Dallas, 1977-79; legal counsel Ponderosa, Inc., Dayton, Ohio, 1979, mgr. real estate property, 1980, area dir., franchise adminstr., 1981-82; sr. corp. atty., asst. sec. La Quinta Motor Inns, Inc., San Antonio, 1982-83, dir. devel. adminstrn., 1983-84; assoc. Law Offices Polunsky and Beitel, San Antonio, 1984-86; sole practice San Antonio, 1986—; pres., chmn. bd. Chainvision Corp., San Antonio; bd. dirs. Hemisphere Distbg., Inc., San Antonio. Author articles on franchising. Trustee San Antonio Local Devel. Co., 1985—; bd. dirs. Encino Pk. Mcpl. Utility Dist. No. 1, San Antonio, 1984. Named one of Outstanding Young Men Am., Jaycees, 1984. Mem. ABA. Franchise law, Landlord-tenant, Real property. Home: 13274 Hunter's Lark San Antonio TX 78230 Office: 14607 San Pedro Suite #170 San Antonio TX 78232

SAGER, JONATHAN WARD, lawyer; b. Syracuse, N.Y., Apr. 10, 1954; s. Roderick Cooper and Ruth (Ross) S.; m. Karen Wisherath, Oct. 26, 1979; children: Sarah Elizabeth, Rebecca Claire. BA, Colgate U., 1975; JD, Washington and Lee U., 1978. Bar: N.Y. 1979, U.S. Dist. Ct. (no. dist.) N.Y. 1979, Fla. 1980. Assoc. Williams, Micale & Wells, Syracuse, 1978-82, Edward W. Dietrich P.C., Syracuse, 1982-84; ptnr. Dietrich & Sager, Syracuse, 1984-85; assoc. counsel The Mut. Life Ins. Co. of N.Y., Syracuse, 1985-87, also bd. dirs. fed. credit union, counsel, 1987—. Counsel Dewitt Community Ch. and Dewitt Community Ch. Found., 1981—. Mem. N.Y. State Bar Assn. (com. assn. ins. programs), Fla. State Bar, Onondaga County Bar Assn. (grievance com.). Republican. Avocation: golf. Insurance, Contracts commercial, Individual life insurance operations in a mutual company. Home: 5127 Shiraz Ln Fayetteville NY 13066 Office: The Mutual Life Ins Co NY One Mony Plaza PO Box 4830 Syracuse NY 13221

SAGER, SHELDON MORRIS, lawyer; b. Miami, Fla., July 27, 1953; s. Louis and Eleanor (Quartin) S.; m. Colleen Cort, Dec. 26, 1976; children: Jeremy John, Robin Anne. BSBA, U. Fla., 1975; JD, Case Western Res. U., 1978. Bar: Ohio 1978, U.S. Dist. Ct. (no. dist.) Ohio 1978, U.S. Ct. Claims 1978, U.S. Tax Ct. 1978, U.S. Ct. Appeals (6th cir.) 1985. Assoc. McCarthy, Lebit, Crystal & Haiman L.P.A., Cleve., 1978-83, ptnr., 1984—; law dir. City of Lyndhurst, Ohio, 1983-84. Mem. ABA, Ohio Bar Assn., Cleve. Bar Assn., Cuyahoga County Law Dirs. Assn. Democrat. Unitarian. Corporate taxation, Personal income taxation, General corporate. Home: 20120 Scottsdale Blvd Shaker Heights OH 44122 Office: McCarthy Lebit Crystal & Haiman 900 Illuminating Blvd Cleveland OH 44113

SAGETT, JAN JEFFREY, lawyer, former government official; b. Chgo., Dec. 12, 1943; s. Leonard Henry and Carolyn (Zilberman) S.; B.S. with honors, U. Ill.-Urbana, 1965; J.D., U. Chgo., 1968. Bar: Ill. 1969, D.C. 1969, U.S. Supreme Ct. 1972; C.P.A., Ill. Assoc., McDermott, Will, and Emery, Chgo., 1968-69; spl. asst. to dir. Office of Minority Bus. Enterprise, Washington, 1969; spl. counsel, asst. gen. counsel Office Econ. Opportunity, Washington, 1969-73; legis. counsel Small Bus. Adminstrn., Washington, 1973-74; dep. assoc. commr., legal counsel Social Security Adminstrn., Washington, 1974-81; asst. gen. counsel legis. affairs Edison Electric Inst., Washington, 1981—. Contbg. author: Federal Regulatory Process: Agency Practices and Procedures, 1981-84. Pres., dir. Embassy Park Homeowners' Assn., Washington, 1981-82. Served with USAR, 1968. Recipient Tuition scholarship U. Chgo. Law Sch., 1965-68; Performance award Office of Econ. Opportunity, 1972; selected for Sr. Mgrs. in Govt. program Harvard U., 1978. Mem. ABA, Washington Met. Area Corp. Counsel Assn., Am. Corp. Counsel Assn., Beta Gamma Sigma, Phi Eta Sigma, Pi Lambda Phi (exec. council 1963-64), Phi Kappa Phi, Beta Alpha Psi. Jewish. Legislative, Administrative and regulatory, Public utilities. Office: Edison Electric Inst 1111 19th St NW Washington DC 20036

SAGSTUEN, WARREN RICHARD, lawyer; b. Thief River Falls, Minn., Aug. 24, 1945; s. Louis Richard and Vivian Adeline (Larson) S.; m. Nancy Jo Wolf, Aug. 25, 1973 (div. Aug. 1979); m. Coleen Mary Brady, Jan. 26, 1985; 1 child, Margaret Brady. BA, U. Minn., 1967, JD, 1972. Bar: Minn. 1972, U.S. Dist. Ct. Minn. 1974, U.S. Ct. Appeals (8th cir.) 1978, U.S. Supreme Ct. 1979. Law clk. to presiding justice U.S. Dist. Ct., Faribault, Minn., 1972-73; assoc. Le Fevere, Lefler, Hamilton & Pearson, Mpls., 1973-76; asst. pub. defender Hennepin County Pub. Defender's Office, Minn., 1976—. Active Am. Cancer Soc., Mpls., 1976, 77, United Fund, Mpls., 1984. Served with U.S. Army, 1968-70, Vietnam. Decorated Bronze Star. Mem. ABA, Minn. State Bar Assn., Am. Judicature Soc., Nat. Assn. Criminal Def. Lawyers, Aircraft Owners and Pilots Assn. Democrat. Lutheran. Avocations: photography, amateur aviation. Criminal. Home: 9848 65th St N Stillwater MN 55082 Office: Hennepin County Pub Defender C-2300 Government Ctr Minneapolis MN 55487

SAHA, SUNIL KUMAR, lawyer; b. Calcutta, India, Dec. 14, 1939; came to U.S., 1970; s. Gopi and Priya Saha; m. Minati Saha, Jan. 17, 1977; 1 child, Dalia. BA, Calcutta U., 1960, MA, 1963, LLB, 1970; LLB, Boston U., 1970; LLM, Suffolk U., 1973. Bar: Calcutta High Ct. 1975, R.I. 1979, U.S. Dist. Ct. R.I. 1979. Sr. faculty mem. South Suburban, Calcutta, 1964-67; mgr. Morse Shoe Co., Canton, Mass., 1970-71; legal analyst Stavisky & Greeley, Boston, 1974-76; legal asst. R.I. Atty. Gen., Providence, 1977-80; sole practice Providence, 1980—; counsel legal and labor relations, personnel officer Steel-O-Craft Engring. and Mfg. Co., Calcutta, 1974-80. Mem. ABA, Fed. Bar Assn., R.I. Bar Assn. Immigration, naturalization, and customs, Labor, Landlord-tenant. Home: 75 Raymond St Providence RI 02908

SAHL, JOHN PATRICK, law educator; b. N.Y.C., July 26, 1951; s. George John and Geraldine Ann (Hennigan) S. Student, Monmouth Coll., West Long Branch, N.J., 1969-72; BA, Boston Coll., 1974; JD, Vermont Law Sch., 1979. Bar: Conn. 1982, U.S. Dist. Ct. Conn 1982. Gen. counsel Ambience, Inc., Sharon, Vt., 1979-80; instr. law U. Bridgeport, Conn., 1980-82, asst. dean, asst. prof. law, 1982—; pres. Negril, Inc., Westport, Conn., 1984-86; host cable TV talk show Face to Face, 1983-85. Bd. dirs. Due Diligence Inc., 1986—. Mem. ABA, Conn. Bar Assn. (profl. ethics com. 1983—, task force to promote minority participation), ACLU, Nat. Assn. Law Placement (Fair Employment Practices com.), Am. Assn. Law Schs. (bd. dirs. sports com.). Club: Darien (Conn.) County. Entertainment, Trademark and copyright, Sports. Home: 8 North Gate Rd Westport CT 06880 Office: U Bridgeport Sch Law 303 University Ave Bridgeport CT 06601

SAHLSTROM, E(LMER) B(ERNARD), lawyer; b. Seattle, Feb. 25, 1918; s. August Waldimer and Alma Carolyn (Ostrom) S.; m. Phyllis May Horstman, June 18, 1946; children—Gary Bernard, Sherry Lynn Sahlstrom Monohan, Gregory Lane. B.S., U. Oreg., 1945, J.D., 1947. Bar: Oreg. 1947, U.S. Dist. Ct. Oreg. 1977, U.S. Dist. Ct. Hawaii, 1977, U.S. Ct. Appeals (9th cir.), 1977, U.S. Supreme Ct. 1977; CPA, Oreg. Acct. Haskins & Sells, N.Y.C., 1941-44; mem. Thompson & Sahlstrom, Eugene, Oreg., 1947-57, Sahlstrom, Lombard, Starr & Vinson, and predecessor, Eugene, 1957-76, Sahlstrom & Lombard, Eugene, 1976-78; sole practice Eugene, 1978-80; ptnr. Sahlstrom & Dugdale, Eugene, 1980—. Bd. visitors U. Oreg. Law Sch., 1977-79. Mem. Oreg. State Bar, ABA, Assn. Trial Lawyers Am. (1st v.p. western regional conf. 1954, 4th v.p. conf. 1956, dir. 1955-56, v.p. Oreg. chpt. 1970-71, pres. So. Oreg. chpt. 1972-74), Am. Judicature Soc., Assn. Attys. and CPA's, Oreg. State Bar (com. taxations, unauthorized practice of law, procedure and practice, continuing legal edn., council on ct. procedures), U. Oreg. Sch. Law Alumni Assn. (bd. dirs., pres., bd. vis.), Phi Alpha Delta, Beta Alpha Psi. Clubs: Country, Town (dir. 1970-71, pres. 1978) (Eugene). Lodge: Elks. Family and matrimonial, Personal injury, State civil litigation. Home: 715 Fair Oaks Dr Eugene OR 97401 Office: Sahlstrom & Dugdale 915 Oak St Eugene OR 97401

SAIDMAN, GARY K., lawyer; b. Washington, July 29, 1952; s. Harry and Rose K. (Kruger) S.; m. Suzan R. Kinbar, Mar. 25, 1984; 1 child, Benjamin A. BS, SUNY, Stony Brook, 1974; JD, Emory U., 1978. Bar: Ga. 1978, D.C. 1983, U.S. Dist. Ct. (no. dist.) Ga. 1978, U.S. Ct. Appeals (5th cir.) 1978, U.S. Ct. Appeals (11th cir.) 1981. Assoc. Seward & Kissel, Atlanta, 1978-80; assoc. Kilpatrick & Cody, Atlanta, 1980-86, ptnr., 1986—. Mem. Lawyers Club Atlanta. Avocation: sailing. Computer, Private international, General corporate. Office: Kilpatrick & Cody 100 Peachtree St Suite 3100 Atlanta GA 30043

SAILER, HENRY POWERS, lawyer; b. Peking, China, Jan. 7, 1929; s. Randolph Clothier and Louise (Egbert) S.; divorced; children: Anne, Katherine, Henry Powers, Randolph, Elizabeth. A.B., Princeton U., 1951; LL.B., Harvard U., 1956. Bar: D.C. bar 1957. Law clk. Justice John Marshall Harlan, U.S. Supreme Ct., 1958; asso. Covington & Burling, Washington, 1956-58, 59-62; partner Covington & Burling, 1962—; Dir. Nat. Com. on U.S.-China Relations, 1973-78, vice-chmn., 1978—. Democrat. Club: Metropolitan. Office: 1201 Pennsylvania Ave NW Washington DC 20004

SAIMAN, MARTIN S., lawyer; b. N.Y.C., Jan. 27, 1932; s. Adolph and Mary (Kaplan) S.; m. Rita C. Chernick, Apr. 10, 1955; children: Lisa, Richard, Gwen. A.B., Columbia Coll., 1953, LL.B., 1955. Bar: N.Y. 1956. Ptnr. firm Kaye, Scholer, Fierman, Hays & Handler, N.Y.C., 1971—; bd. dirs. Ticor Title Guarantee Co., N.Y.C. Bd. dirs. Smalley Found., 1966—. Mem. ABA, Assn. Bar City N.Y. Club: City Athletic. Real property. Address: 425 Park Ave New York NY 10022

SAINT, ROBERT EDWARDS, lawyer; b. New Castle, Ind., Aug. 17, 1953; s. William Kirklin and Nancy (Pfohl) S. B.A., Ball State U., 1976; J.D., Ind. U., 1979. Bar: Ind. 1979, U.S. Dist. Ct. (so. and no. dists.) Ind. 1979, U.S. Ct. Appeals (7th cir.) 1981. Prosecutor Ind. Securities Commn., Indpls., 1979-80; ptnr. Coons & Saint, Indpls., 1980—; dir. Leviticus Project Multi-State Strike Force, Indpls., 1981-84. Mem. Am. Trial Lawyers Assn., Ind. Trial Lawyers Assn., Ind. Bar Assn., Indpls. Bar Assn. Republican. Personal injury, Securities, Criminal. Office: Coons & Saint 440 N East St Indianapolis IN 46204

ST. ANTOINE, THEODORE JOSEPH, legal educator, lawyer; b. St. Albans, Vt., May 29, 1929; s. Arthur Joseph and Mary Beatrice (Callery) S.; m. Elizabeth Lloyd Frier, Jan. 2, 1960; children: Arthur, Claire, Paul, Sara. AB, Fordham Coll., 1951; JD U. Mich., 1954; postgrad. (Fulbright grantee), U. London (Eng.), 1957-58. Bar: Mich. 1954, Ohio 1954, D.C. 1959. Assoc., Squire, Sanders & Dempsey, Cleve., 1954; assoc., ptnr. Woll, Mayer & St. Antoine, Washington, D.C., 1958-65; assoc. prof. law U. Mich. Law Sch., Ann Arbor, 1965-69, prof. 1969—; dean, 1971-78; pres. Nat. Resource Ctr. for Consumers of Legal Services, 1974-78; labor arbitrator; mem. Pub. Rev. Bd., UAW, 1973—; chmn. UAW-GM Legal Services Plan, 1983—; Mich. Gov.'s spl. counselor on workers' compensation, 1983-85. Served to 1st lt. JAGC, U.S. Army, 1955-57. Mem. ABA (past sec. labor law sect., council 1985—), Am. Bar Found., State Bar Mich. (past chmn. labor relations law sect.), Nat. Acad. Arbitrators (bd. govs. 1985—), Internat. Soc. Labor Law and Social Security (U.S. br., exec. com. 1985—), Indsl. Relations Research Assn., Order of Coif. Democrat. Roman Catholic. Author (with R. Smith, L. Merrifield and C. Craver) Labor Relations Law: Cases and Materials, 4th edit., 1968, 7th edit., 1984; contbr. numerous articles to various profl. jours. Contracts, Labor, Real property. Home: 1421 Roxbury Road Ann Arbor MI 48104 Office: U Mich Law Sch Ann Arbor MI 48109-1215

ST. CLAIR, SCOTT ANDREW, lawyer; b. Lafayette, Ind., Aug. 1, 1951; s. Charles Raymond and Jeanette Evelyn (Simonson) St. C.; m. Judith Ann Krause, July 1, 1979; children: Gregory, Kevin. BA, U. Mich., 1973; JD, U. Colo., 1976. Bar: Colo. 1976, U.S. Dist. Ct. Colo. 1976. Ptnr. Balis, St. Clair & Frieling, Boulder, Colo., 1976-80; sole practice Boulder, 1980-84; ptnr. Holder & St. Clair, Boulder, 1985—. Mem. Assn. Trial Lawyers Am. Avocation: golf. Personal injury, Insurance, Automobile law. Office: 1919-14th St 614 Boulder CO 80302

ST. JOHN, JAMES BERRY, JR., lawyer; b. Sanford, Fla., Dec. 14, 1940; s. James Berry and Marion Kistler (Appleby) St. J.; m. Mary Ann Newman, Dec. 28, 1963; children: James, Matthew. AB, U.S.C., 1962; JD, Tulane U., 1970. Bar: La. 1971, U.S. Dist. Ct. (ea. dist.) La. 1971, Fla. 1971, U.S. Dist. Ct. (ea., we., and mid. dists.) La. 1971, U.S. Ct. Appeals (5th cir.) 1971, U.S. Ct. Appeals (1st cir.) 1978, U.S. Ct. Appeals (4th cir.) 1980, U.S. Ct. Appeals (11th cir.) 1981, U.S. Ct. Appeals (9th and D.C. cirs.) 1986. Assoc. Liskow & Lewis, New Orleans, 1970-73, ptnr., 1973—. Served to lt. comdr. USN, 1962-67. Mem. ABA (chmn. natural resources law 1985—). Republican. Episcopalian. Club: Pickwick (New Orleans). Environment, Oil and gas leasing, Federal civil litigation. Office: Liskow & Lewis One Shell Square 50th Fl New Orleans LA 70139

ST. JOHN, THOMAS WILLIAM, lawyer; b. Appleton, Wis., July 27, 1944; s. William Sylvester and Helen Marie (Schuster) St. J.; m. Micaela Helen Levine; children: Jessica Helen, Benjamin William, Saul Aaron, Jacob Henry. BBA, U. Wis., 1966, MBA, 1967; JD summa cum laude, Marquette U., 1972. Bar: Wis. 1972, U.S. Dist. Ct. (ea. and we. dists.) Wis. 1972, U.S. Ct. Appeals (7th cir.) 1972, U.S. Ct. Appeals (9th cir.) 1976, U.S. Supreme Ct. 1975. Law clk. U.S. Dist. Ct., Milw., 1972-74; atty. Friebert & Finerty, Milw., 1974-78, ptnr., 1978-82; ptnr. Friebert, Finerty & St. John, Milw., 1982—; mem. Wis. 7th Circuit Jury Com., Chgo., 1976-80; spl. master jail visitation and desegregation cases U.S. Dist. Ct., Milw., 1977—; ct. commr. Milwaukee County Circuit Ct., 1978—; atty., chmn. Milw. Pub. Housing Rev. Bd., City of Milw., 1975; atty. Counseling Ctr. Milw., 1976-82. Served with U.S. Army, 1969-71. Vilas fellow, Fonteine-McCurdy scholar U. Wis. Grad. Sch., 1967, Swietlik scholar Marquette U. Law Sch., Milw., 1971-72. Diplomate Nat. Bd. Trial Advocacy. Mem. Am. Trial Lawyers Assn., Am. Judicature Soc., Wis. Acad. Trial Lawyers (bd. dirs.), Wis. Bar Assn., Milw. Bar Assn., 7th Circuit Bar Assn., Alpha Sigma Nu. Democrat. Clubs: Wisconsin, Le Club (Milw.). Federal civil litigation, State civil litigation. Home: 2608 E Wood Pl Shorewood WI 53211 Office: Friebert Finerty and St John Two Plaza E Suite 1250 330 E Kilbourn Ave Milwaukee WI 53202

ST. LANDAU, NORMAN, lawyer; b. Vienna, Austria, Apr. 14, 1920; s. Henry M. and Anka (Nemirovska) St. L.; m. Maisie Dennis, July 18, 1942; children—Lorraine, Jon L., Norman D. B.S., A.B. with honors, U. Ill., 1941; LL.B., Rutgers U., 1948; LL.M., NYU, 1951. Bar: D.C. 1948, U.S. Supreme Ct. 1952, N.J. 1958. With Pitts. Plate Glass Co., Ohio, 1941-42; with Johnson & Johnson, New Brunswick, N.J., 1942-84, internat. counsel, 1957-84, chief trademark counsel, 1961-84; dir. Johnson & Johnson Internat.; of counsel Lalos, Leeds, Keegan, Lett & Marsh, Washington, 1983-85, Durand, Gorman, Heher, Imbriaco & Morrice, Princeton, N.J., 1984-86, Imbriaco & Morrice, Princeton, 1984-86, Brylawski, Cleary & Leeds, 1985—; ptnr. Heher, Clarke & St. Landau, Princeton, 1987—; chmn. bd. Action Law Systems, Inc., 1987—; dir., officer numerous affiliates; mem. adv. com. U.S. Sec. State and Commr. Patents, 1975—; div. chmn. N.J. State Bar. Fgn. editor Les Nouvelles, 1965—. Mem. Nat. Fgn. Trade Council (chmn. indsl. property com.), N.J. Patent Law Assn. (past pres.), Nat. Council Patent Law Assns. (sec.-gen.), Nat. Panel Arbitrators, Am. Arbitration Assn., ABA, Am. Chem. Soc. (nat. councillor), Am. Patent Law Assn. (bd. mgrs.), Am. Immigration Lawyers Assn., Inter-Am. Assn. Indsl. Property (exec. com.), Internat. Patent and Trademark Assn., Lic. Execs. Lawyers, Nassau Soc. Club: Nat. Lawyers Nassau. Lodge: Rotary. Immigration, naturalization, and customs, Trademark and copyright, Administrative and regulatory. Home: 822 E Meadow Dr Bound Brook NJ 08805 Office: 105 College Rd E Forrestal Ctr Princeton NJ 08540

ST. PE, PHILIPPI PIERRE, lawyer; b. New Orleans, Oct. 2, 1939; s. Oliver William and Lucie Marie (Philippi) St P.; b. Margaret Ursula Maher, Aug. 7, 1965; children—Kenneth, Simonne, Philippi. LL.B., Loyola U., New Orleans, 1963. Bar: La. 1964. Assoc. Stringer, Manning, Metairie, La., 1961-68; ptnr. Stringer, Manning & St. Pé, Metairie, 1968-71, Francipane, Regan & St. Pé, Metairie, 1971—; judge ad hoc First Parish Ct., 1973. Bd. govs.

Cystic Fibrosis Found., 1972; mem. Jefferson Parish Personnel Bd., 1974-82; mem. exec. com. Loyola U. Sch. Law, 1976-78. Recipient Monte Lemann award La. Civl Service League, 1981. Mem. Jefferson Parish Bar Assn. (sec. 1971, v.p. 1972, pres. 1973), La. Trial Lawyers Assn. (bd. govs. 1980-81), La. State Bar (ho. of dels. 1975—, bd. govs. 1979-80, ethics and grievance com. 1981—), Christian Bros. Found. (New Orleans). Club: St. Matthew Action (St. Matthew Ch., River Ridge, La.). Personal injury, Insurance. Home: 9421 Calvary Ct River Ridge LA 70123 Office: 3324 N Causeway Blvd Metairie LA 70002

ST. ROSE, EDWINA LOSEY, lawyer; b. Charlottesville, Va., Aug. 25, 1952; d. Edward Lee and Emma Jane (Brown) Losey; m. Dennis Anthony St. Rose, Oct. 6, 1979; 1 child, Dennis Anthony II. BA, Barnard Coll., 1973; JD, George Washington U., 1976. Bar: Pa. 1978, U.S. Ct. Appeals (D.C. cir.) 1984. Legal editor Bur. Nat. Affairs, Washington, 1977-80; atty., advisor Social Security Adminstrn., Arlington, Va., 1980-83; employee relations, devel. specialist Naval Intelligence Command, Washington, 1983-85; sole practice Ft. Washington, 1985—; investigator EEO, 1985—. Named One of Outstanding Young Women of America, 1984. Mem. ABA, Pa. Bar Assn., D.C. Bar Assn., Prince Georges County Bd. of Realtors, Md. Bd. Realtors, D.C. Bd. of Realtors. Baptist. Avocations: tennis, traveling. Labor. Home: 209 E Tantallon Dr Fort Washington MD 20744

SAJOVEC, FRANK MICHAEL, JR., lawyer; b. Cleve., Aug. 14, 1936; s. Frank M. and Pauline (Tolar) S.; m. Patricia A. Brozak, Sept. 27, 1958; children: Michael, Carol, Joan. BSME, Carnegie-Mellon U., 1958; JD, Cleve. State U., 1966. Bar: Ohio 1967. Patent atty. Libbey-Owens-Ford Co., Toledo, 1966-69; assoc. patent counsel Eaton Corp., Cleve., 1969—. Mem. ABA, Ohio Bar Assn., Cleve. Bar Assn., Cleve. Patent Law Assn., Am. Intellectual Property Assn. Patent, Trademark and copyright. Office: Eaton Corp Eaton Ctr Cleveland OH 44114

SALACUSE, JESWALD WILLIAM, lawyer, educator; b. Niagara Falls, N.Y., Jan. 28, 1938; s. William L. and Bessie B. (Buzzelli) S.; m. Donna Booth, Oct. 1, 1966; children: William, Maria. Diploma U. Paris, 1959; AB, Hamilton Coll., 1960; JD, Harvard U., 1963. Bar: N.Y. 1965, Tex. 1980. Lectr. in law Ahmadu Bello U., Nigeria, 1963-65; assoc. Conboy, Hewitt, O'Brien & Boardman, N.Y.C., 1965-67; assoc. dir. African Law Ctr., Columbia U., 1967-68; prof., dir. Research Ctr., Nat. Sch. Adminstrn., Zaire, 1968-71; Middle East regional advisor on law and devel. Ford Found., Beirut, 1971-74, rep. in Sudan, 1974-77; vis. prof. U. Khartoum (Sudan), 1974-77; vis. scholar Harvard Law Sch., 1977-78; prof. law So. Meth U., Dallas, 1978-80, dean, prof. law, 1980-86; dean, prof. internat. law The Fletcher Sch. Law and Diplomacy Tufts Univ., Boston, 1986—; cons. Ford Found., 1978-82, U.S. Dept. State, 1978-80; lectr. Georgetown U. Internat. Law Inst., 1978-84, Universidad Panamericana, Mexico City, 1981; chmn. com. on Middle Eastern law Social Sci. Research Council, 1978-84; bd. dirs. Dallas Bar Found., Council for Internat. Exchange of Scholars, Dispute Mediation Service of Dallas, Inc. Author: (with Kasunmu) Nigerian Family Law, 1966, An Introduction to Law in French-Speaking Africa, vol. I, 1969, vol. II, 1976, (with Steng) International Business Planning, 1982; contbr. articles to profl. jours. Mem. ABA, Am. Law Inst., Am. Soc. Internat. Law. Legal education, Private international, Public international. Home: 20 Professors Row Medford MA 02155 Office: Tufts U Fletcher Sch Law and Diplomacy Office of Dean Medford MA 02155

SALADINO, JOSEPH CHARLES, lawyer; b. South Beloit, Ill., Mar. 4, 1920; s. Agostino and Josephine (DiGiovanni) S.; m. Lois Marie Guidotti, Aug. 25, 1951; children—Jo-Ann, LeAnn, Mark J. B.S., U. Ill., 1947, J.D., 1950. Bar: Ill. 1950. Practice, South Beloit, 1950—; ptnr. Saladino & Saladino. Served to capt. AUS, 1942-46. Decorated Bronze Star. Mem. ABA, Ill. Bar Assn., Winnebago County Bar Assn. Republican. Roman Catholic. General practice. Home: 12272 N Ledges Dr Roscoe IL 61073 Office: 634 Blackhawk Blvd South Beloit IL 61080

SALAN, JOHN FRANCIS, lawyer; b. Washington, Jan. 24, 1942; s. Lacy John and Marie Cecilia (Rowan) S.; m. Helen Ann Zolkosky, Nov. 24, 1967; children—Sara, Anne Marie, Elizabeth. Student U. Mich., 1960-61; B.A., Eastern Mich. U., 1965; J.D., Wayne State U., 1968. Bar: Mich. 1969, U.S. Dist. Ct. (ea. dist.) Mich. 1969, U.S. Dist. Ct. (we. dist.) Mich. 1976. Supervising atty. Neighborhood Legal Services, Detroit, 1968-69; asst. prosecutor Washtenew County (Mich.), Ann Arbor, 1969-72, sr. asst. prosecutor, 1973-74; pros. atty. Emmet County (Mich.), Petoskey, 1974—; dir. Pros. Attys. Coordinating Council, Lansing, Mich., 1978-83. Chmn. United Way campaign, Petoskey, 1983; gen. chmn. Parents In Action, Petoskey, 1983—; mem. Emmet County Republican Exec. Com., 1975—. Mem. Mich. Bar Assn., Nat. Dist. Attys. Assn., Pros. Attys. Assn. Mich. (bd. dirs. 1975—, pres. 1982-83), Charlevoix-Emmet County Bar Assn., Nat. Sheriffs Assn. Roman Catholic. Lodge: Rotary (bd. dirs. 1983—). Criminal, Juvenile, Local government. Office: Emmet County Pros Attys Office City-County Bldg Petoskey MI 49770

SALAS, CAMILO KOSSY, III, lawyer; b. Guayaquil, Guayas, Ecuador, Oct. 2, 1952; s. Camilo Reinaldo Salas Jr. and Norma Piedad (Mena) Carlin. Student, La. State U., 1971-74; BA, U. New Orleans, 1977; JD, Tulane U., 1981. Bar: La. 1981, U.S. Dist. Ct. (ea. dist.) La. 1981, U.S. Ct. Appeals (5th cir.) 1981, U.S. Dist. Ct. (we. dist.) La. 1983. Assoc. Sessions, Fishman, Rosenson, Boisfontaine, Nathan & Winn, New Orleans, 1981—. Mem. ABA (com. on admiralty and maritime litigation), Fed. Bar Assn., InterAm. Bar Assn. (com. on pvt. internat. law), Internat. Bar Assn. (com. on maritime and transp. law), Hispanic Bar Assn. New Orleans, La. Hispanic C. of C. Republican. Roman Catholic. Admiralty, Insurance, Private international. Home: 1131 Arabella St New Orleans LA 70115 Office: Sessions Fishman Rosenson Boisfontaine Nathan & Winn 201 St Charles Ave New Orleans LA 70170

SALAZAR, JOHN PAUL, lawyer; b. Albuquerque, Feb. 6, 1943; s. Henry Houghton and Anita (Chavez) S.; m. Terri J. Bestgen, June 12, 1967; children—Monique Michelle, John Paul, Stephen Houghton. B.A. in Econs., U. N.Mex., 1965; J.D., Stanford U., 1968. Bar: N.Mex. 1968, U.S. Dist. Ct. N.Mex. 1968, U.S. Ct. Appeals (10th cir.) 1968, U.S. Supreme Ct. 1979. Assoc., Rodey, Dickason, Sloan, Akin & Robb, P.A., Albuquerque, 1968—, dir., 1974—. Bd. visitors Stanford U. Law Sch., 1973-76; state campaign chmn. Jeff Bingaman for Atty. Gen., 1978, Jeff Bingaman for U.S. Senate, 1982; campaign treas. Ronald A. Ginsburg for Dist. Judge, 1980; mem. U. N.Mex. Search com. for assoc. provost for community edn., 1978-79, Albuquerque Econ. Forum, chmn. govtl. affairs com.; former bd. dirs. N.Mex. Symphony Orch., N.Mex. Easter Seal Soc.; vice chmn. City of Albuquerque Charter Revision Com., 1970-71, Albuquerque Unity, 1971-73; Chmn. N.Mex. Disting. Pub. Service Awards Councils, 1986; former mem. N.Mex. Democratic State Central Com. Mem. ABA (condemnation zoning and property use litigation com. Litigation sect., land use com. Urban, State and Local Govt. sect.), N.Mex. State Bar (jud. selection com.). Albuquerque Bar Assn. (former mem. jud. selection com., former dir.), N.Mex. State Bar Assn. (former sec.-treas. Young Lawyers sect., mem. Real Property, Probate and Trust sect., mem. Pub. Adv. sect.), Greater Albuquerque C. of C. (chmn. city affairs com. 1972, v.p. govtl. affairs 1973, pres.-elect 1974, pres. 1975, chmn. nominating com. 1977), U. N.Mex. Alumni Assn. (pres. 1983-84, exec. com., bd. dirs.), Albuquerque Armed Forces Adv. Assn., Presbyn. Hosp. Ctr. Assocs. Roman Catholic. Clubs: Albuquerque Country, Lawyers. Administrative and regulatory, Real property, State civil litigation. Office: PO Box 1888 Albuquerque NM 87103

SALCH, STEVEN CHARLES, lawyer; b. Palm Beach, Fla., Oct. 25, 1943; s. Charles Henry and Helen Louise (Alverson) S.; m. Mary Ann Prim, Oct. 7, 1967; children—Susan Elizabeth, Stuart Trenton. B.B.A., So. Meth. U., 1965, J.D., 1968. Bar: Tex. 1968, U.S. Tax Ct. 1969, U.S. Dist. Ct. (so. dist.) Tex. 1969, U.S. Dist. Ct. (ea. dist.) Tex. 1972, U.S. Ct. Appeals (5th cir.) 1969, U.S. Ct. Appeals (fed. cir.) 1982, U.S. Claims Ct. 1982. Assoc. Fulbright & Jaworski, Houston, 1968-71, participating assoc., 1971-75, ptnr., 1975—. Contbr. articles to legal jours. Pres. Tealwood Owners Assn., 1982-83, Meml. High Sch. PTA, 1985-86; mem. Tex. PTA (Hon. Life Member award 1986). Mem. State Bar Tex., Houston Bar Assn., ABA (council dir., tax. sect. 1985—), Am. Law Inst., Nat. Tax Assn., Tax Inst. Am., Am. Coll. Tax Counsel, Internat. Fiscal Assn., Harris County Heritage Soc., Galveston Hist. Found., Smithsonian Assocs., Mus. Fine Arts Soc., Colonial Williamsburg Found., Am. Bar Found., Houston Bar Found., Beta Alpha Psi, Phi Eta Sigma, Order Coif, Phi Delta Phi. Presbyterian. Clubs: Houston, Cotillion, Lakeside Country, Houston Center, Governor's, Galveston Country, R.L. Smith Yacht. Corporate taxation, Private international, Administrative and regulatory. Home: 342 Tamerlaine Houston TX 77024 Office: Fulbright & Jaworski 51st Floor 1301 McKinney St Houston TX 77010

SALCITO, DONALD, lawyer; b. Waterbury, Conn., Jan. 22, 1953; s. Daniel Richard and Jenny (Rosa) S.; m. Catherine Ruth Claassen, July 1977; children: Jordan Catherine, Kendyl Ruth, Anne-Marie Cresenza. BA, U. Conn., 1975; JD, U. Ariz., 1979. Bar: U.S. Dist. Ct. Colo. 1980, U.S. Ct. Appeals (9th cir.) 1980, U.S. Supreme Ct. 1985, U.S. Ct. Appeals (10th cir.) 1986. Assoc. Head, Moye, Carver & Ray, Denver, 1979-80; assoc. Roath & Brega, P.C., Denver, 1980-86, ptnr., 1986-87; assoc. Ballard, Spahr, Andrews & Iangersoll, Denver, 1987—. Symposium editor U. Ariz. Law Rev., 1978. Mem. ABA (fed. regulation securities corp. banking and bus. law sect.), Colo. Bar Assn., Denver Bar Assn., 32d Rocky Mountain Mineral Law Inst. (mining sect. com.), Phi Beta Kappa, Phi Alpha Theta. Democrat. Avocations: swimming, hiking, biking. Securities, Federal civil litigation, General corporate. Office: Roath & Brega PC 1700 Lincoln St Suite 2222 Denver CO 80203

SALDIN, THOMAS R., corporate lawyer; b. 1929. BA, Carleton Coll., 1968; JD, Cin. Coll. Law, 1974. Law clk. to presiding justice U.S. Dist. Ct. (so. dist.) Okla., 1974-76; assoc. Benjamin, Faulkner, Tepe & Sach, Cin., 1976-78; asst. gen. counsel Albertson's Inc., Boise, Idaho, 1978-81, v.p., gen. counsel, 1981-83, sr. v.p. gen. counsel, 1983—. Office: Albertsons Inc 250 Parkcenter Blvd Boise ID 83726 *

SALE, EDWIN WELLS, lawyer; b. Fisher, Ill., June 29, 1912; s. Leslie Oscar and Margaret Laurinda (Moore) S.; m. Esther E. Sale, Aug. 1, 1936; 1 dau., Margaret Sale Hubbard. B.S., Northwestern U., 1934; J.D., U. Ill., 1937. Bar: Ill. 1937, U.S. Supreme Ct. 1944, U.S. Dist. Ct. (ea. dist.) Ill. 1959, U.S. Ct. Appeals (7th cir.) 1960. Legal researcher Claims dept. Lumbermen's Mut. Ins. Co., Chgo., 1937-38; sole practice, Champaign, Ill., 1938-42, Kankakee, Ill., 1946—. Served with U.S. Army, 1942-46. Decorated Army Commendation medal. Mem. Kankakee Bar Assn. (pres.), C.of C., Am. Arbitration Assn., Ill. Bar Assn., Chgo. Bar Assn., ABA, Judge Advocates Assn., Am. Coll. Probate Counsel, Appellate Lawyers Assn., Am. Judicature Soc., Am. Legion, Delta Upsilon, Phi Delta Phi. Republican. Methodist. Clubs: Kankakee Country. Lodge: Rotary. Contbr. articles to profl. jours. Federal civil litigation, State civil litigation, Probate. Home: 22 Chatham Circle N Kankakee IL 60901 Office: Suite 440 1 Dearborn Sq Kankakee IL 60901

SALEM, ALBERT MCCALL, JR., lawyer; b. Washington, Apr. 3, 1939; s. Vivian (Zaytoun) S.; married; 4 children. AB, U. N.C., 1960, JD, 1963. Bar: N.C. 1963, Fla. 1965. Ptnr. Yado, Salem, Keel, Nelson and Bergmann, P.A., Tampa, Fla., 1966-85. Served to capt. USAF, 1963-66. State civil litigation, Estate planning, General practice. Office: Yado Salem et al 4830 W Kennedy Blvd PO Box 18607 Tampa FL 33679

SALEM, MICHEAL CHARLES, lawyer; b. Cushing, Okla., June 29, 1949; s. Joseph A. and Adele A. (Joseph) S. BSEE, U. Okla., 1971, M in Pub. Adminstrn., JD, 1975. Bar: Okla. 1975, U.S. Dist. Ct. (we. dist.) Okla. 1975, U.S. Ct. Appeals (10th cir.) 1976, U.S. Supreme Ct. 1978. Ptnr. Rawdon & Salem, Norman, Okla., 1975-84; sole practice Norman, 1985—. Recipient Meritorious Vol. Service award ACLU Okla., 1982, Angie Debo Civil Liberties award ACLU Okla., 1983. Mem. ABA, Okla. Bar Assn. (Courageous Advocacy award 1984), Okla. Trial Lawyers Assn., Okla. Criminal Def. Lawyers Assn., Am. Radio Relay League (Cert. Appreciation 1981), Cen. Okla. Radio Amateurs Club (contbg. editor monthly publ.). Avocations: amateur radio, pvt. pilot. Civil rights, Personal injury, Criminal. Office: 101 E Gray Norman OK 73069

SALEM, RICHARD JOSEPH, lawyer; b. New Bern, N.C., Mar. 31, 1947; s. Albert McCall Sr. and Vivian (Zaytoun) S.; m. Eileen Monley, Nov. 24, 1977; 1 child, Susan McCall. AB cum laude, Belmont Abbey Coll., 1969; JD with distinction, Duke U., 1972. Bar: Fla. 1972, U.S. Dist. Ct. (mid. dist.) Fla., U.S. Tax Ct., U.S. Ct. Appeals (5th and 11th cirs.), U.S. Supreme Ct. Ptnr. Salem, Salem, Musial & Morse, P.A., Tampa, Fla., 1972-81, Salem, Saxon & Nielsen P.A., Tampa, 1981—. Mem. Tampa Urban League, 1976—, citizens adv. council Hillsborough County Bd. Commrs., Mayor's Ybor City Devel. Adv. Com.; candidate Dem. nomination U.S. Ho. of Reps., 1978; exec. committeeman, adv. council Gulf Coast Scouting USA, 1974—; chmn. First Fla. Regional Scouting for Handicapped Program, 1974, Dem. exec. com. Hillsborough County 1976-78, chmn. 1st Hillsborough County Dem. Conv.; mem. Fla. Dems. Cen. Com., Fla. Dems. Appeals Com., Hillsborough County Carter/Mondale Steering Com.; chmn. bd. trustees Fla. Sch. Deaf and Blind, St. Augustine, 1978; bd. dirs. Playmakers, 1981—, Tampa Lighthouse for Blind, 1978—; gen. counsel, bd. dirs. Tampa Econ. Devel. Corp. Named one of Outstanding Young Men of Am., 1975; named one of The Best of the New Generation, Men and Women Under Forty Who Are Changing Am., Esquire mag., 1984. Mem. ABA (bd. of govs. law student div.), Fla. Bar Assn., Am. Blind Lawyers Assn., Hillsborough County Bar Assn., Internat. Bar Assn., Ybor City C. of C. (bd. dirs. 1977—), Greater Tampa C. of C. (com. of 100 1979—), Town N Country Jaycees (Outstanding Young Man of Yr. award 1974), Brandon Jaycees (Dist. Service award 1976), Phi Alpha Delta, Delta Epsilon Sigma, Phi Kappa Theta. Roman Catholic. Club: Tiger Bay. Avocations: reading, swimming, music, cycling. Administrative and regulatory, Federal civil litigation, General corporate. Office: Salem Saxon & Nielsen PO Box 3399 Tampa FL 33601

SALERNO, TERRENCE JOSEPH, lawyer; b. Omaha, Nov. 22, 1952; s. Sebastian Anthony and Norita Alice (Kelley) S.; m. Kim Renee Meyer, July 22, 1983. BA, U. Nebr., 1975; JD, Creighton U., 1979. Bar: Nebr. 1979, U.S. Dist. Ct. Nebr. 1979, U.S. Ct. Appeals (8th cir.) 1986. Assoc. Kelley, Kelley & Lehan, Omaha, 1979-81; dep. pub. defender Douglas County, Omaha, 1981-85; ptnr. Schrempp, Hoagland, Gerdes & Salerno, Omaha, 1985-86, Schrempp. Gross & Salerno, Omaha, 1986—. Vol. com. to elect Robert Kerrey for Gov. Nebr., 1982, com. to elect Mike Kelley for Douglas County commr., 1984. Mem. Nebr. Bar Assn., Assn. Trial Lawyers Am., N.Y. State Trial Lawyers Assn., Nebr. Assn. Trial Lawyers, Sierra Club. Democrat. Roman Catholic. Lodge: Sons of Italy. Avocations: skiing, canoeing. Personal injury, Criminal, Workers' compensation. Home: 3524 State St Omaha NE 68112 Office: Schrempp Gross & Salerno 617 N 90th St Omaha NE 68114

SALERNO, THOMAS JAMES, lawyer; b. Jersey City, Aug. 30, 1957; s. Thomas E. and Imelda (Gyurik) S.; m. Tricia Joan Neary, Feb. 14, 1982; 1 child, Alissa Lee. BA summa cum laude, Rutgers U., 1979; JD cum laude, U. Notre Dame, 1982. Bar: Ariz. 1982, U.S. Dist. Ct. Ariz. 1982, U.S. Ct. Appeals (9th cir.) 1982. Ptnr. Streich, Lang, Weeks & Cardon, Phoenix, Ariz., 1982—; lectr. Am. Inst. Banking, Phoenix, 1983—, Nat. Assn. Credit Mgmt., 1983—, Profl. Edn. Systems, Inc., Eau Claire, Wis., 1984—, Robert Morris Assn., Phoenix, 1984—. Author: Appellate Structure and Procedure Under the New Bankruptcy Rules, 1984, Bankruptcy Litigation and Practice: A Practitioner's Guide, 1986, Bankruptcy Practice in Arizona, 1986, The Bankruptcy Code: A Practitioner's Primer, 1985, Arizona's New Exemtion Statute, 1983; co-author: Bankruptcy: The Ultimate Intrusion Upon Creditor's Rights, 1984, A New Way to Pay Old Debts: An Advanced Chapter 11 Manual, 1987. Mem. Vol. Legal Services Program. Mem. ABA (bankruptcy com.), Ariz. Bar Assn. (bankruptcy sect.), Assn. Trial Lawyers Am., Am. Bankruptcy Inst., Comml. Law League, Phi Beta Kappa, Pi Sigma Alpha. Avocations: tennis, racquetball, travel. Bankruptcy, Federal civil litigation. Home: 9638 N 33d St Phoenix AZ 85028 Office: Streich Lang Weeks & Cardon 100 W Washington Phoenix AZ 85001

SALES, JAMES BOHUS, lawyer; b. Weimar, Tex., Aug. 24, 1934; s. Henry B. and Agnes Mary (Pesek) S.; m. Beuna M. Vornsand, June 3, 1956; children: Mark Keith, Debra Lynn, Travis James. B.S., U. Tex., 1956, LL.B. with honors, 1960. Bar: Tex. 1960. Practiced in Houston, 1960—; sr. ptnr. firm Fulbright & Jaworski, 1960—; advocate, Am. Bd. Trial Advocates; pres.-elect State Bar of Tex., 1987-88. Contbr. articles legal publns. Trustee South Tex. Coll. Law, 1982—. Served with USMCR, 1956-58. Fellow Internat. Acad. Trial Lawyers, Am. Coll. Trial Lawyers, Am. Bar Found., Tex. Bar Found., Houston Bar Found. (chmn. bd.); mem. Internat. Assn. Ins. Counsel, ABA (ho. of dels. 1984-88), Def. Research Inst., So. Tex. Coll. Trial Advocacy (dir. 1983—), Fed. Bar Assn., State Bar Tex. (pres.-elect 1986—, bd. dirs. 1983-86, chmn. bd. 1985-86), Tex. Assn. Def. Counsel (v.p. 1977-79, 83-84), Houston Bar Assn. (pres. 1980-81, Outstanding Service award 1977, 78, Pres.'s and Bd. Dirs. award 1983), Gulf Coast Legal Found. (dir. 1982-85), Houston C. of C., The Forum. Roman Catholic. Clubs: Westlake (bd. govs.), Houston Athletic, Inns of Ct. State civil litigation, Federal civil litigation, Personal injury. Home: 10803 Oak Creek Houston TX 77024 Office: 1301 McKinney St Houston TX 77010

SALIBELLO, SALVATORE JOSEPH, lawyer; b. Bklyn., Jan. 29, 1936; s. Joseph and Maria Loretta (Patalano) S.; m. Anna Josephine Galante, May 30, 1958; children: Kristen, Mia, Philip. AB, Columbia U., 1957, BS in Industrial Engring., 1962; MBA, Rutgers U., 1965; JD, Seton Hall U., 1976. Bar: N.J. 1977, U.S. Supreme Ct. 1981, U.S. Ct. Appeals (3d cir.) 1982, U.S. Dist. Ct. (ea. dist.) N.Y. 1983, U.S. Ct. Appeals (2d cir.) 1984. Pilot Pan Am World Airways, N.Y.C., 1966—; sole practice Morristown, N.J., 1977—; arbitrator U.S. Dist. Ct. N.J., Newark, 1985—. Served to lt. comdr. USNR, 1957-71. Mem. ABA, N.J. Bar Assn., Morris County Bar Assn., Assn. Trial Lawyers Am., Lawyer-Pilot Bar Assn. Avocations: skiing, travel, theatre. Aviation tort litigation, Administrative and regulatory, Personal injury. Home: 211 Jockey Hollow Rd Bernardsville NJ 07924 Office: 10 Park Pl Suite 307 Morristown NJ 07960

SALIM, ABDULLAH (REGINALD ARMISTICE HAWKINS), JR., lawyer, consultant; b. Charlotte, N.C., May 18, 1948; s. Reginald Armistice and Catherine Elizabeth (Richardson) H.; m. Umme Salma, June 2, 1972; children: Salah, Abdullah, Salma. B.A., U. N.C., 1970; postgrad. Howard U., 1970-71, U. Md., 1976; J.D., George Mason U., 1981. Bar: Md. 1983, U.S. Ct. Appeals Md. 1983. Library asst. Smithsonian Inst. Mus. Natural History, Washington, 1966; writer, researcher Pride Inc., Washington, 1970; temp. tchr. D.C. Pub. Schs., 1970-71; sr. appraiser, claim rep. Aetna Life & Casualty Co., McLean, Va., 1971-78; mgr. Assocs. IV Theaters, Oxon Hill, Md., 1974-75; pub. transport mgr. D.C. Barwood Cabs, Washington, 1977-78; mgr. E & S Cons., Washington, 1981-82; material damage cons. Crawford & Co., Fairfax, Va., 1982-84; sole practice law, Silver Spring, Md., 1983—; hist. cons. Abdullah Salim & Assocs., Silver Spring, 1983—. Mem. Md. Black Reps. council, 1984; coach Little League Baseball, Rockville, Md. and Silver Spring, 1984; nat. assoc. Smithsonian Inst., Washington, 1984; trustee A.L. Richardson scholarship fund, 1984—. Hurbert Lehman scholor, 1966; recipient Immigration Law award Ayuda Neighborhood Services, 1981. Mem. Am. Soc. Internat. Law, Nat. Bar Assn., ABA, Am. Trial Lawyers Assn., Md. Trial Lawyers Assn., George Mason U. Internat. Law Soc. (v.p. 1980-81), George Mason U. Black Law Students Assn. (chmn. 1980-81), U. N.C. Alumni Assn., George Mason U. Alumni Assn., Phi Delta Phi. Republican. Muslim. Immigration, naturalization, and customs, General practice, Personal injury. Home: 1016 Merrimac Dr Silver Spring MD 20903 Office: 4500 College Ave Suite 201 College Park MD 20740

SALISBURY, JOHN FRANCIS, chems., distillery and chemical company executive, lawyer; b. Limon, Costa Rica, Dec. 15, 1930; s. Edward I. and Kathleen (O'Sullivan) S.; m. Nancy Furlong, Aug. 20, 1960; children: Adrienne, Philippa, Anne, Eugenia. A.B., Villanova U., 1952; J.D., U. Pa., 1958. Bar: N.Y. 1959. Assoc. firm Breed, Abbott & Morgan, N.Y.C., 1958-66; sec. Nat. Distillers & Chem. Corp., N.Y.C., 1966-74; v.p., sec., gen. counsel Nat. Distillers & Chem. Corp., 1974—. Chmn. bd. Am. Found. for Tropical Medicine, Liberian Inst. Tropical Medicine.; bd. dirs. Brazilian Am. C. of C., Brazilian Cultural Found.; trustee Pop Warner Found. Served with USNR, 1952-55. Decorated Rhee Battle Commendation medal Korean, U.S. Commendation medal. Mem. N.Y. Bar Assn. Clubs: Union League (N.Y.C.), Sky (N.Y.C.). Home: 484 Old Long Ridge Rd North Stamford CT 06903 Office: National Distillers & Chem Corp 99 Park Ave New York NY 10016 *

SALITERMAN, RICHARD ARLEN, lawyer, educator; b. Mpls., Aug. 3, 1946; s. Leonard Slitz and Dorothy (Sloan) S.; m. Laura Shrager, June 15, 1975; 1 son, Robert Warren. B.A. summa cum laude, U. Minn., 1968; J.D., Columbia U., 1971; LL.M., N.Y.U., 1974. Bar: Minn. 1972, D.C. 1974. Mem. legal staff U.S. Senate Subcom. on Antitrust and Monopoly, 1971-72; acting dir., dep. dir. Compliance and Enforcement div. Fed. Energy Office, N.Y.C., 1974; mil. atty. Presdl. Clemency Bd., White House, Washington, 1975; sole practice, Mpls., 1975—; adj. prof. law Hamline U., 1976-81. Vice chmn. Hennepin County Bar Jour., 1983—. Bd. dirs. Mpls. Urban League, 1987—. Served with USN, 1972-75. Mem. ABA, Minn. State Bar Assn., Hennepin County Bar Assn. (sec., mem. editoral bd. Hennepin Lawyer, governing council). Clubs: Oakridge Country (Hopkins, Minn.); Mpls. General corporate, General practice, State civil litigation.

SALIWANCHIK, ROMAN, lawyer, consultant; b. Michigan City, Ind., Nov. 12, 1926; s. John Reuben and Mary Alice (Kuta) S.; m. Doris Mae Colligan, May 30, 1954; children—Doris, Michael, David. B.S., Purdue U., 1952; J.D., Ind. U., 1961. Bar: U.S. Dist. Ct. (so. dist.) Ind. 1961, U.S. Dist. Ct. (we. dist.) Mich. 1963, U.S. Patent and Trademark Office 1963, U.S. Ct. Customs and Patent Appeals 1968, U.S. Supreme Ct. 1978, U.S. Ct. Appeals (Fed. cir.) 1982. Chemist, microbiologist Eli Lilly & Co., Indpls., 1952-61; patent Lawyer Upjohn Co., Kalamazoo, Mich., 1961-84; sole practice, Richland, Mich., 1984—, Gainesville, Fla., 1984—. Author: Legal Protection for Microbiological and Genetic Engineering Inventions, 1982. Editor Ind. U. Law Jour., 1959-61. Contbr. articles to profl. jours. Served with USCG, 1944-46, PTO. Mem. Mich. Bar Assn. (mem. council 1974-77, com. chmn. 1977-78), Am. Intellectual Property Law Assn., Soc. Indsl. Microbiology (chmn. com. 1977—), Am. Soc. Microbiology, Am. Chem. Soc., U.S. Fedn. for Culture Collections (mem. exec. bd. 1984—), Phi Alpha Delta. Patent, Trademark and copyright. Office: 529 NW 60th St Suite B Gainesville FL 32607

SALLEN, DAVID URBAN, lawyer; b. Ft. Madison, Iowa, June 23, 1952; s. Urban Frank and Lillian Virginia (Ashby) S.; m. Sheila Marie Strang, Jan. 5, 1985. B.A. in Sociology and Philosophy, St. Ambrose Coll., 1974; J.D., U. Iowa, 1977. Bar: Iowa 1977, U.S. Dist. Ct. (no. and so. dists.) Iowa 1977, U.S. Ct. Appeals (8th cir.) 1978, U.S. Supreme Ct. 1980. Assoc., Morr & Shelton, Chariton, Iowa, 1977-79; asst. county atty. Lucas County (Iowa), 1977-79; pub. defender Lee County, Ft. Madison, 1979—; sole practice, Ft. Madison, 1982—. Chairperson Ft. Madison Human Rights Commn., 1980—, Lee County Community Action Agy., 1982—; mem. jud. coordinating com. Iowa Supreme Ct., Des Moines, 1981—, mem. commn. indigent def. transition com., 1985-87; council mem. St. Marys Parish, Ft. Madison, 1982-84; pres. Iowa Pub. Defenders Assn., 1982-83; sec. Community Services Council, 1983—; mem. com. drinking drivers Iowa State Legislature, Des Moines, 1984-85. Recipient Cert. of Appreciation, Southeast Iowa Community Action Agy., 1983, Friends Reach Out, Inc., 1982. Mem. Nat. Assn. Crim. Def. Lawyers, Nat. Legal Aid and Defender Assn., Iowa State Bar Assn., ABA, Lucas County Bar Assn. (pres. 1978-79), Am. Judicature Soc., Lee County Bar Assn. Club: Dominic. Lodge: K.C. Criminal, Juvenile, General practice. Home: 309 6th St Fort Madison IA 52627 Office: 707 1/2 Ave G Fort Madison IA 52627

SALLET, JONATHAN BRUCE, lawyer; b. Abington, Pa., Apr. 10, 1952; s. Maynard Nathan and Shirley Edith (Lechtman) S. BA, Brown U., 1974; JD, U. Va., 1978. Bar: D.C. 1980, U.S. Dist. Ct. D.C. 1981, U.S. Ct. Appeals (D.C. cir.) 1981, U.S. Ct. Appeals (5th cir.) 1982, U.S. Ct. Appeals (4th and 6th cirs.) 1984, U.S. Supreme Ct. 1985. Law clk. to presiding judge U.S. Ct. Appeals (D.C. cir.), 1978-79; law clk. to Justice Lewis F. Powell Jr. U.S. Supreme Ct., Washington, 1979-80; assoc. Miller, Cassidy, Larroca & Lewin, Washington, 1980-85, ptnr., 1985—. Co-author: Representing Small Business, 1985; editor in chief U. Va. Law Rev., 1977-78; contbr. articles to profl. jours. Mem. Am. Judicature Soc., Supreme Ct. Hist. Soc., Raven Soc., Order of Coif. Federal civil litigation, State civil litigation, Criminal. Office: Miller Cassidy Larroca & Lewin 2555 M St NW Suite 500 Washington DC 20037

SALLUS, MARC LEONARD, lawyer; b. Washington, Sept. 14, 1954; s. Gerald M. and Bette R. (Rosenthal) S.; m. Julianne Wagner, Aug. 11, 1979. BA, Claremont Men's Coll., 1976; JD, U. Calif., Hastings, 1979. Bar: Calif. 1979, U.S. Dist. Ct. (cen., so. and ea. dists.) Calif. 1980, U.S. Ct.

Appeals (9th cir.) 1980. Assoc. Long & Levit, Los Angeles, 1979-80, Overton, Lyman & Prince, Los Angeles, 1980-87, Brobeck, Phleger & Harrison, Los Angeles, 1987—. Chmn. adv. bd. Nat. Resource Ctr. for Child Advocacy and Protection, Washington, 1985-86. Mem. ABA (chmn. com. for child abvocacy and protection young lawyers sect. 1985—), Los Angeles County Bar Assn. (bd. trustees 1986—, exec. com. 1986—, asst. v.p. 1986—), Los Angeles County Barristers (pres. 1987—, pres.-elect 1986-87, v.p. 1985-86, exec. com., 1984—, chmn. child abuse com. 1983-85). Democrat. Jewish. Probate, State civil litigation, Bankruptcy. Office: Brobeck Phleger & Harrison 444 S Flower St 43d Floor Los Angeles CA 90017

SALOMON, BARBARA, lawyer; b. San Francisco, Nov. 17, 1950; d. Maurice Sidney Salomon and Louise (Barkan) Klein. BA in Anthropology with distinction, Stanford U., 1972; JD, U. Calif., San Francisco, 1977. Bar: Colo. 1978, U.S. Dist. Ct. Colo. 1979, U.S. Ct. Appeals (10th cir.) 1979. Assoc. Holland & Hart, Denver, 1977-79, Kelly, Haglund, Garnsey & Kahn, Denver, 1979-81; ptnr. Donnell, Davis & Salomon, Denver, 1981-85; assoc. Feder, Morris & Tamblyn P.C., Denver, 1985—. Pres., bd. dirs. Project Safeguard, Denver, 1984—; bd. dirs. Legal Aid Soc. Met. Denver, 1983—. Named one of Outstanding Young Women Am., 1983, 85. Mem. ABA (real estate probate and tax sect., family law sect.), Colo. Bar Assn. (probate and trust sect., Pro Bono award 1986), Denver Bar Assn. (named vol. lawyer of yr. 1982), Colo. Women's Bar Assn. (sec. 1980-81, treas. 1985-86), Colo. Trial Lawyers Assn., Colo. Whitewater Assn., Sierra Club. Democrat. Episcopalian. Avocations: whitewater boating, skiing. State civil litigation, Family and matrimonial, Estate planning.

SALOMON, DARRELL JOSEPH, lawyer, educator; b. San Francisco, Feb. 16, 1939; s. Joseph and Rosalie Rita (Poole) S.; m. Patty Marie Fitzimons, Sept. 21, 1969 (div.). Student Georgetown U., 1957-59; student U. San Francisco, 1960-62, J.D., 1966. Bar: Calif. 1970, U.S. Dist. Ct. (no. dist.) Calif. 1970, U.S. Supreme Ct. 1971. Assoc., Offices of Joseph L. Alioto, San Francisco, 1970, 73, Demanes & Sanders, Burlingame, Calif., 1972; dep. city atty. City of San Francisco, 1972; with Salomon & Costello, 1981; practice specializing in antitrust law and trade regulation, San Francisco, 1977-84; ptnr. Hill, Farrer & Burrill, Los Angeles, 1984-87, Lawler, Felix & Hall, 1987—; lectr. law Santa Clara U. Mem. Human Rights Commn. City and County of San Francisco, 1975, mem., past pres. CSC, 1976-84; trustee San Francisco War Meml. and Performing Arts Ctr., 1984—; bd. dirs. Los Angeles Symphony Master Chorale, 1985—. D'alton-Power scholar, 1957; recipient Disting. Service citation United Negro Coll. Fund, 1975. Mem. ABA, San Francisco Bar Assn., Calif. Trial Lawyers Assn. (bd. govs. 1977), Service Employees Internat. Union (hon. life), Soc. Calif. Pioneers. Democrat. Club: Chit Chat. Contbr. articles to profl. jours. Antitrust, State civil litigation, Legal education. Office: Lawler Felix & Hall Hill Farrer & Burrill 34th Floor 445 S Figueroa St Los Angeles CA 90071

SALOMON, RICHARD ADLEY, lawyer; b. Chgo., Nov. 3, 1953; s. Bernard S. Salomon and Marian (Schwarz) Elkan. Student, U. Chgo., 1973-74; BA magna cum laude, Carleton Coll., 1975; JD magna cum laude, Harvard U., 1979. Bar: Ill. 1980, U.S. Dist. Ct. (no. dist.) Ill. 1980, U.S. Ct. Appeals (7th cir.) 1983, U.S. Dist. Ct. (no. dist.) Ga. 1986, U.S. Dist. Ct. (so. dist.) N.Y. 1986. Assoc. Jones, Day, Reavis & Pogue, Cleve., 1979; law clk. U.S. Dist. Ct. (no. dist.) Ill., Chgo., 1980; assoc. Mayer, Brown & Platt, Chgo., 1981-86, ptnr., 1986—; asst. atty. gen. State of Ill., Chgo., 1981-83; cons., spl. commn. to Study Cook County Cts., Chgo., 1985—; Senate Select Com. on Secret Mil. Assistance to Iran and Nicaraguan Opposition, 1987—; program chmn. Columbia U. media and soc. seminars, 1986—; lectr. on litigation abuse, ethics, white collar crime and racketeering litigation, 1984—. Author: Analysis of Executive Impoundment Reports, 1975; contbg. author Dombroff on Unfair Litigation Tactics, 1985; also numerous tech. and newspaper articles. Alumni rep., speaker Carleton Coll., 1980—; mem. Chgo. Council. Fgn. Relations, 1981—; legal adv. LaRabida Children's Hosp., Chgo., 1983. Am. Legion scholar 1967; Thomas J. Watson fellow 1975-76; recipient Harold Goettler Pol. Insts. Prize 1974. Mem. ABA (litigation sect., individual rights and liberties sect., spl. asst. to chmn. commn. on professionalism 1985-86), Ill. Bar Assn., Chgo. Bar Assn., Lawyers' Alliance for Nuclear Arms Control, Aspen Inst. for Humanistic Studies (seminar on justice and soc.), Carleton Coll. Athletic Soc., U.S. Tennis Assn. Jewish. Club: Harvard (Chgo.). Avocations: philately, tennis, photography, piano. Federal civil litigation, State civil litigation, Legislative. Office: Mayer Brown & Platt 190 S LaSalle St Chicago IL 60603

SALOOM, KALISTE JOSEPH, JR., judge, lawyer; b. Lafayette, La., May 15, 1918; s. Kaliste and Asma Ann (Boustany) S.; m. Yvonne Adelle Nassar, Oct. 19, 1958; children—Kaliste, Douglas James, Leanne Isabelle, Gregory John. B.A. with high distinction, U. Southwestern La., 1939; J.D., Tulane U., 1942. Bar: La. 1942. Atty. City of Lafayette (La.), 1948-52; judge City and Juvenile Ct., Lafayette, 1952—; tech. adviser Jud. Adminstrn. of Traffic Cts.; mem. jud. council La. Supreme Ct., 1960-64; bd. dirs. Nat. Ctr. for State Cts., Williamsburg, Va., 1978-84; mem. Nat. Hwy. Traffic Safety Adminstrn. Adv. Com., U.S. Dept. Transp., 1977-80, Nat. Com. on Uniform Traffic Laws, 1986. Served with U.S. Army, 1942-45. Recipient Civic Cup, City of Lafayette, 1965, Pub. Service award U.S. Dept. Transp., 1980; Disting. Jurist award Miss. State U. Pre-Law Soc., 1987. Mem. ABA (Benjamin Flaschner award 1981), Am. Judges Assn. (William H. Burnett award 1982), Nat. Council Juvenile Ct. Judges, La. City Judges Assn. (past pres.), La. Juvenile Ct. Judges Assn. (past pres.), Am. Judicature Soc., Order of Coif. Democrat. Roman Catholic. Clubs: Oakbourne Country (Lafayette); KC. Bd. editors Tulane Law Rev., 1941; contbr. articles to profl. jours. Juvenile, State civil litigation, Traffic Laws. Home: 502 Marguerite Blvd Lafayette LA 70503 Office: 211 W Main St Lafayette LA 70501

SALTER, LEONARD MELVIN, lawyer; b. Chelsea, Mass., Aug. 30, 1912; s. Albert and Charlotte (Kulvin) S.; m. Charlotte Berns, Sept. 27, 1941; children: Charles, Richard, William. AB cum laude, Harvard U., 1933, JD, 1936. Bar: Mass. 1936, U.S. Dist. Ct. Mass. 1937, U.S. Supreme Ct. 1962. Ptnr. Wasserman & Salter, Boston, 1939—. Author 6 books on world and internat. law. V.p. Speech and Hearing Found., Boston, 1975-80. Served with U.S. Army, 1943-46. Mem. Mass. Bar Assn., Boston Bar Assn., Comml. Law League Am. (bd. govs. Chgo. 1968-70, pres. 1970-71). Democrat. Lodge: Masons. Avocations: writing, travelling, lecturing. Bankruptcy, Contracts commercial. Home: 40 Old Colony Rd Chestnut Hill MA 02167 Office: Wasserman & Salter 31 Milk St Boston MA 02109

SALTER, LESTER HERBERT, lawyer; b. Waterbury, Conn., Apr. 26, 1918; s. Nathan M. and Eva G. (Levy) S.; m. Nina P. Scheftel, Sept. 15, 1951; 1 child, Ellen Lee. B.S. in Econs, U. Pa., 1940, LL.B., 1948. Bar: R.I. bar 1948. Trial atty. Office of Chief Counsel, IRS, Newark and Boston, 1949-53; individual practice law Providence, 1953-57; partner firm Salter & McGowan, Providence, 1957-70, Salter, McGowan, Arcaro & Swartz, 1970-74; pres. firm Salter, McGowan, Swartz & Holden, Inc., Providence, 1974—; lectr. Northeastern U., 1955-56; chmn. U. R.I. Fed. Tax Inst., 1972-77; chmn. disciplinary bd. Supreme Ct., R.I., 1975-81; mem. R.I. Adv. Commn. Jud. Appts., 1978-82. Assoc. editor: R.I. Bar Jour, 1961-68. Served with F.A. AUS, 1941-46. Decorated Bronze Star. Mem. ABA, R.I. Bar Assn. (pres. 1986-87), Am. Judicature Soc., Am. Law Inst. Club: Metacomet Country of East Providence (pres. 1980-82). Corporate taxation, Personal income taxation, Estate taxation. Home: 75 Blackstone Blvd Providence RI 02906 Office: 1500 Fleet Nat Bank Bldg Providence RI 02903

SALTIEL, DAVID MICHAEL, lawyer; b. Chgo., June 14, 1954; s. Robert David and Libby Esther (Miller) S.; m. Sandra Pomerantz, Mar. 17, 1985. BBA with distinction, U. Mich., 1975; JD, U. Ill., 1979. Bar: Ill. 1980. Ptnr. Greenberg, Keele, Lunn & Aronberg, Chgo., 1979—. Treas. Lawyers for Creative Arts, 1984-85, sec., 1985-86, v.p., 1987—, bd. dirs. 1982—; commr. Village of Lincolnshire Plan Commn., Ill., 1986—. Mem. ABA, Ill. Bar Assn., Chgo. Bar Assn. General corporate, Real property, Entertainment. Home: 26 Regents Ln Lincolnshire IL 60015 Office: Greenberg Keele Lunn & Aronberg One IBM Plaza Suite 4500 Chicago IL 60611

SALTMAN, STUART IVAN, lawyer; b. Holyoke, Mass., Mar. 16, 1940; s. Abraham and Sidel Esther (Schultz) S.; m. Sandra Lee, Sept. 19, 1964; children—Jason, Michael, Laura. B.S. in Polit. Sci., U. Mass., 1961; J.D., Case Western Res. U., 1964. Bar: Mass. 1965, Ohio 1965, Pa. 1975. Assoc. gen. counsel Internat. Chem. Workers, Akron, Ohio, 1965; assoc. Metzenbaum, Gaines, Krupansky, Finley & Stern, Cleve., 1965-67; staff U.S. Dept. Labor, Cleve., 1967-69; staff NLRB, Cleve., 1969-70; regional atty. EEOC, Cleve., Phila. and Washington, 1970-75; chief labor counsel Westinghouse Electric Corp., Pitts., 1975—. Recipient hon. award excellence in labor law Case Western Res. U. 1965. Mem. ABA, Allegheny County Bar Assn. (chmn. 1986—). Club: Masons (Holyoke). Labor. Home: 1467 Old Meadow Rd Upper St Clair PA 15241 Office: Rm 1209 11 Stanwix St Pittsburgh PA 15222

SALTONSTALL, STEPHEN LEE, lawyer; b. N.Y.C., Apr. 14, 1944; s. John Lee Jr. and Margaret (Bonnell) S.; Ellen Claire Bosinoff, Jan. 1, 1984; 1 child, Shannon. AB magna cum laude, Harvard U., 1967; JD, Northeastern U., 1976. Bar: Mass. 1976, U.S. Dist. Ct. Mass. 1977, U.S. Ct. Appeals (1st cir.) 1979, U.S. Supreme Ct. 1980, Vt. 1982, U.S. Dist. Ct. Vt. 1983. Sole practice Boston, 1976-78; gen. counsel Mass. Correctional Legal Services, Boston, 1978-80; counsel for Berkshire County, Mass. Dept. Social Services, Pittsfield, 1980-82; ptnr. Witten & Carter, P.C., Bennington, Vt., 1982—. Town Counsel, Sandgate, Vt., 1982-86. Mem. ABA, Vt. Bar Assn., Bennington County Bar Assn. (v.p. 1983-86, pres. 1986—), Nat. Assn. Criminal Def. Lawyers, Phi Beta Kappa. Democrat. Criminal, State civil litigation, Federal civil litigation. Home: RFD #1 Box 2570 Sandgate VT 05250 Office: Witten & Carter PC 109 Silver St PO Box 620 Bennington VT 05201

SALTOUN, ANDRE M., lawyer; b. Baghdad, Iraq, Jan. 21, 1929; came to U.S., 1947; s. Meir and Synthia (Noury) S.; m. Beverly Melnik, 1947 (div. 1959); children: Myra, Cynthia, Julie; m. Francine Klein, Aug. 17, 1960; children: Diane, Josiane, Carol. BA, U. N.C., 1950; JD, U. Wis., 1960. Bar: Calif., Ill., Wis., U.S. Dist. Ct. (no. dist.) Ill., U.S. Ct. Claims, U.S. Tax Ct., U.S. Ct. Appeals (6th, 7th, and 10th cirs.), U.S. Supreme Ct. Ptnr. Baker & McKenzie, Chgo., 1964—. Contbr. articles to profl. jours. Mem. ABA, Ill. Bar Assn., Calif. Bar Assn., Wis. Bar Assn., Chgo. Bar Assn., Chgo. Assn. Commerce and Industry. (bd. dirs.). Clubs: Bankers (San Francisco); Mid-Am., Plaza (Chgo.). Corporate taxation, Private international. Office: Baker & McKenzie Prudential Plaza Suite 2800 Chicago IL 60601

SALTZBERG, EDWARD CHARLES, lawyer; b. Cambridge, Mass., Dec. 23, 1947; s. Harry M. and Anne (Arnold) S.; m. Carol Lerman, Jan. 18, 1975; children: Michele, Jill. BA, Boston U., 1969, MBA, 1973; JD, Suffolk U., 1976. Bar: Mass. 1977. Assoc. Hennessy and Kilburn, Boston, 1976-78, Robert Bigelow, Woburn, Mass., 1978-79; ptnr. Bigelow and Saltzberg, Woburn, 1980-86, Warner and Stackpole, Boston, 1986. Author law rev. articles; co-editor: Computer Law Newsletter, 1979—. Mem. ABA, Mass. Bar Assn., Computer Law Assn., Boston Patent Law Assn., Boston Computer Soc. Computer, Federal civil litigation, Contracts commercial. Office: Warner and Stackpole 28 State St Boston MA 02109

SALTZMAN, BARRY NEAL, lawyer; b. Bklyn., Mar. 29, 1954; married; one daughter, one son. BA (valedictorian), Yeshiva U., 1976; JD, Harvard U., 1979. Bar: N.Y. 1980, U.S. Dist. Ct. (so. and ea. dists.) N.Y. 1981. Assoc. Baer, Marks, Upham, N.Y.C., 1979-87, Shea & Gould, N.Y.C., 1987—. Mem. ABA. Labor, Federal civil litigation, State civil litigation. Office: Shea & Gould 330 Madison Ave New York NY 10017

SALTZMAN, JOAN, lawyer; b. Phila., Sept. 9, 1947; d. Samuel and Rose (Litvin) S. B.A. in English Philosophy, U. Pitts., 1969; M.A. in English, U. Pa., 1970; J.D., Rutgers U., 1973. Bar: Pa. 1973, U.S. Dist. Ct. (ea. dist.) Pa. 1974, U.S. Ct. Appeals (3d cir.) 1979, U.S. Supreme Ct. 1979. Law clk. Ct. Common Pleas, Phila., 1973-74; staff atty. Defender Assn. Phila., 1974-77; assoc. Klovsky Kuby & Harris, Phila., 1978-82; clin. supr. U. Pa. Law Sch., 1982-84; sole practice specializing in med. malpractice, Phila., 1984—; co-regional dir., team leader, asst. team leader Nat. Inst. Trial Advocacy, Notre Dame, Ind., 1976—. Mem. ABA, Phila. Bar Assn., Community Services Inst. (pres. 1982-84). Personal injury, Federal civil litigation, State civil litigation. Home: 406 S 7th St Philadelphia PA 19147 Office: 1608 Walnut St 18th Floor Philadelphia PA 19102

SALTZMAN, MICHAEL I., lawyer, educator, author; b. Paterson, N.J., Mar. 1940; s. Edward H. and Frances C. (Bornstein) S.; m. Sandra Leslie Gabrilove, May 20, 1973. A.B., Colgate U., 1961; J.D. Bar: N.Y. 1971, D.C. 1965, Calif. 1974. Trial atty. tax div. U.S. Dept. of Justice, Washington, 1964-69; assoc. Roberts & Holland, N.Y., 1969-70; chief tax unit U.S. Atty's. Office, (so. dist.) N.Y., 1970-72; ptnr. Kaplan, Livingston, Goodwin, Berkowitz & Sellvin, Beverly Hills, Calif., 1972-75; sole practice, N.Y.C., 1975-82; ptnr. Saltzman & Holloran, 1982—; adj. prof. law NYU. Author: IRS Practice and Procedure, 1981. Mem. ABA, N.Y. State Bar Assn., Assn. Bar City New York, Am. Coll. Tax Counsel. Club: Univ. (N.Y.C.). Criminal, Federal civil litigation, State civil litigation. Office: One Rockefeller Plaza New York NY 10020

SALUP, STEPHEN, lawyer, educator; b. N.Y.C., s. Mannie and Gladys (Friedman) S.; m. Rebecca Scharfmann, June 27, 1983; children—Dana, Stacey, Brett. B.A., U. Md., 1962; LL.B., NYU, 1965. Bar: N.Y. 1965, Fla. 1976, U.S. Dist. Ct. (so. and ea. dists.) N.Y. 1966. Assoc. Shatzkin and Cooper, N.Y.C., 1965-67; real estate counsel Swift and Co., N.Y.C., 1967-69; gen. counsel, dep. adminstr. N.Y.C. Econ. Devel. Adminstrn, 1969-73; assoc. Weisman, Celler, Spett and Madlin, N.Y.C., 1973-74; real estate counsel Nat. Kinney Corp., N.Y.C., 1974-84; gen. counsel Starrett Housing Corp., 1984—; assoc. prof. St. John's U., N.Y.C., 1976-79, Adelphi U., N.Y.C., 1980. Editor casebook Legal Aspects of Athletic Administration, 1976-78. Mem. Local Planning Bd., Queens County, N.Y., 1972-76; Cable TV Commn., Lawrence, N.Y., 1979-81; del. Republican Jud. Conv., 1968; committeeman Rep. County Com. Mem. ABA, Assn. Bar City of N.Y., Lindsay Civic Assn. (v.p. 1970-74). Democrat. Jewish. Construction, Real property, Labor. Home: 25 Wimbledon Dr North Hills NY 11576 Office: Starrett Housing Corp 909 3d Ave New York NY 10022

SALUS, HERBERT WIEDER, JR., lawyer; b. Phila., Sept. 15, 1922; s. Herbert W. and Therese (Born) S. B.A., U. Pa., 1943, LL.B., 1948. Bar: Pa. 1949, U.S. Supreme Ct. 1974. Sole practice, Phila., 1948-62, 80-84; spl. asst. atty. gen. State of Pa., Phila., 1963-70; judge Common Pleas Ct., Phila., 1970-73; assoc. Kramer & Salus, Phila., 1973-80; ptnr. Salus and Orlowitz, Phila., 1984—. Trustee Chapel Four Chaplins, Phila., 1970-83. Served as capt. U.S. Army, 1942-43. Mem. ABA, Pa. Bar Assn., Phila. Bar Assn. Republican. Jewish. Club: Locust (Phila.). General practice, State civil litigation, Pension, profit-sharing, and employee benefits. Home: P-4 Touraine Apts 1520 Spruce St Philadelphia PA 19102 Office: Penn Ctr Suite 1000 Philadelphia PA 19102

SALVAN, SHERWOOD ALLEN, lawyer; b. N.Y.C., Dec. 2, 1942; s. Harry and Marie Ann (Deranio) s. BBA, St. Francis Coll., N.Y.C.; MBA, Pace U.; JD, N.Y. Law Sch.; postdoctoral, NYU. Tax specialist Haskins & Sells, N.Y.C., 1969-71; sole practice N.Y.C., 1972—; mem. cen. screening com. first dept. N.Y. Appellate Div., 1977-82; spl. master N.Y. County Supreme Ct., 1977-85. Contbr. articles to profl. jours. V.p. N.Y. County Dem. Club, 1980—; jud. del. N.Y. County dems., 1983—. Mem. N.Y. County Lawyers Assn. (chairperson com. word processing 1978-86), Am. Judge Assn. Federal civil litigation, Criminal, State civil litigation. Home: 526 E 83d St New York NY 10028

SALZBERG, ARTHUR JONATHAN, lawyer; b. Washington, Mar. 21, 1951; s. Samuel Solomon and Rebbeca Ruth (Schechter) S. B.A. cum laude, NYU, 1973; J.D. cum laude, Northwestern U., 1976. Bar: Calif. 1977, D.C. 1979, U.S. Dist. Ct. (cen. dist.) Calif. 1982, U.S. Dist. Ct. (so. dist.) Calif. 1984. Trial atty. Bur. Competition, FTC, Washington, 1976-78; assoc. Brownstein Ziedman & Schomer, Washington, 1978-80; sr. trial atty. Commodity Futures Trading Commn., Washington, 1980-82, br. chief div. of enforcement Western region, Los Angeles, 1982-84, regional counsel Western region, 1984—. Mem. ABA, Calif. Bar Assn., D.C. Bar Assn., Bar Assn. D.C., D.C. Fed Bar Assn. Jewish. Administrative and regulatory, Federal civil litigation, Commodities. Office: Commodity Futures Trading Commn 10850 Wilshire Blvd Suite 370 Los Angeles CA 90024

SALZMAN, RICHARD STEPHEN, judge; b. N.Y.C., Apr. 6, 1933; s. Leonard and Jeannette (Levy) S.; m. Lois Ann Wallace, July 18, 1959; children—John Marx, Andrew Henry. A.B., Columbia U., 1954, LL.B., 1959. Bar: N.Y. 1960, U.S. Supreme Ct. 1963, D.C. 1970, U.S. Ct. Appeals (1st, 2d, 3d, 4th, 5th, 7th, 9th and D.C. cirs.), U.S. Ct. Claims 1970, U.S. Dist. Ct. (so. dist.) N.Y. 1961, D.C. 1970. Law clk. U.S. Ct. Appeals (D.C. cir.), Washington, 1959-60; assoc. Botein, Hays, Sklar & Herzberg, N.Y.C., 1960-62; trial atty. Dept. Justice, Washington, 1962-67; asst. chief counsel Dept. Transp., Washington, 1967-70; practice, Washington, 1970-74; adminstrv. judge U.S. Nuclear Regulatory Commn., Washington, 1974-81; judge D.C. Superior Ct., 1981—. Bd. dirs. Forest Hills Citizens Assn., Washington, 1972. Served to lt. USN, 1954-57. Recipient Adminstrv. award Superior Service Dept. Transp., 1968. Mem. D.C. Bar Assn., ABA. Democrat. Jewish. Clubs: Nat. Lawyers (Washington), Palisades (Potomac, Md.). Office: Superior Ct of DC 500 Indiana Ave NW Washington DC 20001

SALZMAN, STANLEY P., lawyer; b. N.Y.C., Jan. 30, 1931; s. George D. and Fanny M. (Pugach) S.; m. Leona Schames, June 18, 1958 (dec. Nov. 1967); m. Marilyn J. Bzura, Feb. 3, 1974; children: Ira J., Mark B., Debra G., Jeffrey M. David, Steven B. David. BA, Bklyn. Coll., 1952; JD, Bklyn. Law Sch., 1955. Bar: N.Y. 1956, U.S. Dist. Ct. (so. and ea. dists.) N.Y. 1960, U.S. Supreme Ct. 1964, U.S. Ct. Appeals (2d cir.) 1966. Assoc. Otterbourg, Steindler, Houston & Rosen, N.Y.C., 1957; ptnr. Venitt, Adler & Salzman, N.Y.C., 1958-66, Friesner & Salzman, Great Neck, N.Y., 1966—; bd. dirs. Colora Printing Inks Inc., Linden, N.J. Consumer commercial, State civil litigation. Office: Friesner & Salzman 1000 Northern Blvd PO Box 700 Great Neck NY 11022

SAM, DAVID, judge; b. Hobart, Ind., Aug. 12, 1933; s. Andrew and Flora (Toma) S.; m. Betty Jean Brennan, Feb. 1, 1957; children: Betty Jean, David Dwight, Daniel Scott, Tamara Lynn, Pamela Rac, Daryl Paul, Angie, Sheyla. BS, Brigham Young U., 1957; JD, Utah U., 1960. Bar: Utah 1960, U.S. Dist. Ct. Utah 1966. Sole practice Duchesne, Utah, 1963-76; dist. judge State of Utah, 1976-85; judge U.S. Dist. Ct. Utah, Salt Lake City, 1985—; atty. City of Duchesne, 1963-72, Duchesne County, 1966-72; commr. Duchesne County, 1972-74. Chmn. Jud. Nomination Com. for Cir. Ct. Judge, Prove, Utah, 1983; bd. dirs. Water Resources, Salt Lake City, 1973-76. Served to capt. JAGC, USAF, 1961-63. Mem. ABA (ct. delayreduction com. 1972—), Utah Bar Assn. , Am. Judicature Soc., Am. Inns of Ct. VII (counseler 1986—), Utah Jud. Conf. (chmn. 1982—), Utah Dist. Judges Assn. (pres. 1982-83). Mormon. Avocations: beekeeping, reading, sports, cooking chinese food. Criminal, General practice, Judicial administration. Home: 1171 E 300 North Springville UT 84663 Office: US Dist Ct 350 S Main St Room 110 Salt Lake City UT 84101

SAMALIN, EDWIN, lawyer, educator; b. N.Y.C., Sept. 19, 1935; s. Harry Louis and Sydell (Fisher) S.; m. Sheila Karen Samalin, Oct. 12, 1961; children—David Seth, Andrew Evan, Jonathan Daniel. B.S., U. R.I., 1957; J.D., N.Y. Law Sch., 1962. Bar: N.Y. 1963, U.S. Supreme Ct. 1976. Tax atty. Electric Bond & Share Co., N.Y.C., 1963; ptnr. Samalin & Sklaver, Yorktown Heights, N.Y., 1969-78; sole practice, Yorktown Heights, 1963-69, 78-84; ptnr. Samalin & Bock, Yorktown Heights, 1984—; adj. faculty Mercy Coll., Dobbs Ferry, N.Y., 1974—; commodity cons. Murlas Commodities, Yorktown Heights, 1982-83; ptnr. Patterson (N.Y.) Realty Assn., 1983—; pres. Sammark Realty Corp., Westchester, N.Y., 1984—; commodity cons. Dem. candidate for County Legislature, 1973. Served to capt. U.S. Army, 1957-59. Mem. N.Y. State Bar Assn., Westchester County Bar Assn., Yorktown Bar Assn. (pres. 1982, Man of Yr. 1983), Am. Arbitration Assn. (arbitrator 1974—), Phi Delta Phi. Family and matrimonial, State civil litigation, Real property. Home: 951A Heritage Hills Somers NY 10589 Office: Samalin & Bock PC 2000 Maple Hill St Yorktown Heights NY 10598

SAMANSKY, J. LEONARD, lawyer; b. Bklyn., Dec. 12, 1936; s. Frank S. and Edna R. Samansky; m. Shirley J. Farber, Feb. 28, 1977; 1 son, Adam; children by previous marriage—Debra Rosenzweig, Janet Lord, Linda Weinstein. B.A., Bklyn. Coll., 1958; J.D., Bklyn. Law Sch., 1961. Bar: N.Y. 1961, U.S. Supreme Ct. 1973. Assoc. Lipkowitz & Plaut, N.Y.C., 1961-70, ptnr., 1970-83; sole practice, N.Y.C., 1983—; Mem. nat. personnel com., N.Y. regional bd. Anti-Defamation League of B'nai B'rith, 1973—; chmn., trustee, mem. exec. com. Kingsbrook Jewish Med. Ctr.; mem. bd. Appeals, Village of Saddle Rock (N.Y.), 1980-84, trustee, 1984—; pres. Isaac Albert Research Inst.; pres. Saddle Rock Civic Assn., 1981-83. Mem. ABA, Assn. Bar City N.Y., Bklyn. Bar Assn., Am. Immigration Lawyers Assn., U.S. Coast Guard Aux., U.S. Power Squadrons (comdr. Great Neck chpt.). Democrat. Jewish. Club: Masons. Labor, Immigration, naturalization, and customs, Environment. Home: 20 Greenleaf Hill Great Neck NY 11023 Office: 36 W 44th St New York NY 10036

SAMAY, Z. LANCE, lawyer; b. Janoshaza, Hungary, Dec. 2, 1944; B.A., Rutgers U., 1967; J.D., Seton Hall U., 1970. Bar: N.J. 1970, U.S. Ct. Appeals (3d cir.) 1974, U.S. Supreme Ct. 1976, N.Y. 1987. Law sec. Appellate div. Superior Ct. N.J., 1970-71; asst. U.S. Atty. Dist. N.J., 1971-76; chief Environ. Protection Div., Office of U.S. Atty. Fed. Dist. N.J., 1972-74, chief Civil Div., 1974-76; now pres. Z. Lance Samay, P.C., Morristown, N.J.; adj. prof. environ. law Seton Hall U. Sch. Law, 1973, 74, 76; trial instr. Atty. Gen.'s Advocacy Inst., 1975, 76; vice chmn. consumer affairs com. Fed. Exec. Bd., 1973-74, chmn. human resources com., 1974-75, chmn. relations with academia com., 1975-76. Recipient U.S. Atty. Gen's spl. commendation for outstanding service, 1973; U.S. Dept. Justice spl. achievement award for sustained superior performance, 1972, 76. Mem. ABA, N.J. Bar Assn., Fed. Bar Assn., Morris County Bar Assn., Am. Judicature Soc., Seton Hall Law Alumni Assn. (adv. com. to dean 1971-72, trustee 1975-80, treas. 1975-76, pres. 1976-79, mem. deans search com. for Seton Hall Law Ctr. 1977-78). Co-founder, notes and rewrite editor Seton Hall Law Rev., 1969-70, case notes editor Seton Hall Law Jour., 1969. General practice, Federal civil litigation, State civil litigation. Home: Mountain Lakes and Bernardsville NJ 07046 Office: One Washington St Morristown NJ 07960

SAMEK, JEFFREY WAYNE, lawyer; b. N.Y.C., Dec. 16, 1952; s. Joseph Norton Samek and Dolores (Makemnos) Rudin; m. Fern Douek, June 9, 1974; children: Joshua, Allison. BA in Polit. Sci., SUNY, Buffalo, 1974; JD, U. Miami, 1977. Bar: Fla. 1978, U.S. Dist. Ct. (so. dist.) Fla., U.S. Ct. Appeals (5th and 11th cirs.). Ptnr. Samek & Besser, Miami, Fla. Mem. Dade County Bar Assn. (cert. of honor 1983-86), Fla. Criminal Def. Lawyers Assn. (sec. 1985—, Liberty's Last Champion award 1985). Democrat. Jewish. Lodge: B'nai B'rith (pres. bd. dirs. Miami 1982-84, bd. dirs. 1978—). Avocation: youth baseball. Criminal, Juvenile. Office: Samek & Besser 1925 Brickell Ave Miami FL 33129

SAMEL, JEFFREY, lawyer; b. N.Y.C., Dec. 29, 1952; s. Shirley (Buchbinder) Samel. BA, NYU, 1973, JD, 1976. Bar: N.Y. 1977, U.S. Dist. Ct. (ea. and so. dists.) N.Y. 1979. Asst. dist. atty. Queens County, N.Y.C., 1977-82; asst. corp. counsel N.Y.C. Law Dept., 1982-83; ptnr. Armienti & Samel, Mineola, N.Y., 1983-84, McCarthy, Armienti & Samel, N.Y.C., 1984-86, Armienti & Samel, N.Y.C., 1987—. State civil litigation, Insurance, Personal injury. Office: Armienti & Samel 40 Exchange Pl New York NY 10005

SAMELS, STEPHEN COOPER, lawyer; b. Duluth, Minn., Feb. 13, 1932; s. Frederick Arthur and Marion Alice (Lowe) S.; m. Karen Ruth Thrana, Jan. 17, 1959; children: Cynthia Anne, Elisabeth Marie, Scott Cooper. BSL, U. Minn., 1957, JD, 1959. Bar: Minn. 1959, N.Y. 1964, U.S. Dist. Ct. (no. dist.) N.Y. 1963, U.S. Dist. Ct. D.C. 1965, U.S. Ct. Appeals (D.C. cir.) 1966, U.S. Supreme Ct. 1965. Ptnr. Swan, Mattson, Pougiales & Samels, Rochester, Minn., 1960-63; asst. county atty. Olmsted County (Minn.), 1962-63; atty. Gen. Products div. IBM Corp., Endicott, N.Y., 1963-64, staff atty. Fed. Systems div., Gaithersburg, Md., 1965-66, area counsel Systems Mfg. div., Rochester, Minn., 1967-72, staff counsel European Labs., Boeblingen, W.Ger., 1973-76; sr. staff counsel IBM Europe, Paris, 1977-79, counsel System Products div., White Plains, N.Y., 1980-82, sr. counsel Office of Sr. Vice Pres. and Gen. Counsel, Armonk, N.Y., 1982—; instr. in negotiable instruments Am. Banking Assn., 1961-63. Pres. Rochester Young Rep. Club, 1961. Served with U.S. Army, 1952-55. Mem. ABA, D.C. Bar Assn., Minn. Bar Assn., N.Y. State Bar Assn., Am. Arbitration Assn., La Confrerie des Chevaliers du Tastevin, Delta Tau Delta. General corporate, Federal civil litigation, Securities. Office: IBM Corp Armonk NY 10504

SAMET, ANDREW BENJAMIN, lawyer; b. N.Y.C., Dec. 23, 1941; s. Leon and Clara (Belfar) S.; m. Susan McAnalley, Sept. 24, 1965; 1 dau., Vanessa. B.A., Cornell U., 1962; J.D., NYU, 1965. Bar: N.Y. 1966, Mich. 1971. Assoc. atty. Hughes Hubbard & Reed, N.Y.C., 1968-71; with Bendix Corp., Southfield, Mich., 1971-83, assoc. gen. counsel, 1981-83; assoc. gen. counsel Allied Corp., Morristown, N.J., 1983—, sec., 1985-86; staff v.p., assoc. gen. counsel Allied-Signal, Inc., 1985—. Served to capt. U.S. Army, 1966-68. Decorated Army Commendation medal. Mem. ABA, Mich. State Bar. General corporate. Office: Allied-Signal Inc. PO Box 2245R Morristown NJ 07960

SAMET, JOSEPH, lawyer; b. N.Y.C., July 6, 1949; s. Morris M. and Evelyn (Goldberg) S.; m. Jeanne Friedberg, July 16, 1978; 1 child, Lara. BA, Queens Coll., 1971; JD, Bklyn. Law Sch., 1974. Bar: N.Y. 1975, U.S. Dist. Ct. (so. and ea. dists.) N.Y. 1975, U.S. Ct. Appeals (2d cir.) 1977, U.S. Supreme Ct. 1978. Law clk. to presiding justice U.S. Bankruptcy Ct., N.Y.C., 1974-75; assoc. Stroock, Stroock & Lavan, N.Y.C., 1975-81, Moses & Singer, N.Y.C., 1981-83, Paul, Weiss, Rifkind, Wharton & Garrison, N.Y.C., 1983—; lectr. Practising Law Inst., N.Y.C., 1981-86; adj. prof. law Bklyn. Law Sch., 1986—. Author: Collier Bankruptcy Practice Guide, 1981, Collier on Bankruptcy, 1982. Mem. ABA, N.Y. State Bar Assn., Assn. of Bar of City of N.Y., Nat. Bankruptcy Conf. (assoc.), Comml. Law League (chmn. continuing legal edn. 1982-86, lectr., bd. dirs. bankruptcy and insolvency sect. 1985—, pres. fund for pub. edn. 1986—). Democrat. Jewish. Avocations: long distance running, softball. Bankruptcy, Contracts commercial, Federal civil litigation. Home: 501 Highland Ave Upper Montclair NJ 07043 Office: Paul Weiss Rifkind Wharton & Garrison 1285 Avenue of the Americas New York NY 10019

SAMOLE, MYRON MICHAEL, lawyer, management consultant; b. Chgo., Nov. 29, 1943; s. Harry Lionel and Bess Miriam (Siegel) S.; m. Sandra Rita Port, Feb. 2, 1967; children—Stacey Ann, Karen Lynn, Rena Mara, David Aaron. Student U. Ill., 1962-65; J.D., DePaul U., 1967; postgrad. John Marshall Lawyers Inst., 1967-69. Bar: Ill. 1967, U.S. Dist. Ct. (no. dist.) Ill. 1968, U.S. Ct. Appeals (7th cir.) 1968, Fla. 1981. Sole practice, Chgo., 1967-79, Miami, Fla., 1981—; chmn. bd. Fidelity Electronics and subs., Miami, 1969-83; pres. Fidelity Hearing Instruments, Miami, 1984—, Samole Enterprises, Inc., Miami, 1986—, Fla. Citrus Tower, Inc., Clermont, 1986—; bd. dirs. Enterprise Bank Fla., Miami; Bd. dirs. South Dade Greater MiamiJewish Fedn., Jewish Fedn. TV, Miami, Cen. Agy. for Jewish Edn., Congregation Beth David, Miami. Jewish Vocat. Service scholar U. Ill., Champaign, 1962-65. Mem. ABA, Chgo. Bar Assn., Ill. State Bar Assn., Fla. Bar Assn., Dade County Bar Assn., Ill. Trial Lawyers Assn., Miami C. of C., Phi Alpha Delta. Democrat. Lodges: Masons, Shriners. Family and matrimonial, Negligence, Real property. Office: Samole Enterprises Inc 11270 SW 59th Ave PO Box 1123 Miami FL 33156

SAMPATH, ELIZABETH MARGARET DEBORAH, lawyer; b. Englewood, N.J., Oct. 29, 1951; d. Roy and Gloria Merle (Latchman) S.; m. John Robert Suter, Aug. 9, 1976. BA in Internat. Affairs, George Washington U., 1973; JD, Rutgers U., 1976. Bar: Pa. 1976, U.S. Dist. Ct. (ea dist.) Pa. 1978. Atty. U.S. Dept. Energy, Phila., 1976-81, The Bell Telephone Co., Phila., 1982-81. Mem. ABA, Phila. Bar Assn. Labor, Public utilities. Office: The Bell Telephone Co One Parkway 16th Floor Philadelphia PA 19102

SAMPLES, STEPHEN SHAY, lawyer; b. Tuscaloosa, Ala., Sept. 18, 1951; s. John W. and Avie Lee (Lovelace) S.; m. Colleen M. Samples, June 19, 1982. BA, U. Ala., 1973; JD, Cumberland Law Sch., 1976. Ptnr. Hogan, Smith, Alspough, Samples & Pratt, Birmingham, Ala., 1976—. Mem. ABA, Birmingham Bar Assn. (mem. grievance com. 1985—, officer young lawyers com. 1983-85), Assn. Trial Lawyers Am., Ala. Trial Lawyers Assn. (mem. exec. com. 1985—, bd. govs. 1981-85). Democrat. Presbyterian. Personal injury, Federal civil litigation, Insurance.

SAMPSON, MICHAEL PAUL, tax educator, lecturer, writer; b. Balt., May 22, 1940; s. Paul Jennings and Lola Delella (Hardegen) S. B.S., Cornell U., 1962, M.B.A., 1965, J.D., 1966; LL.M. in Taxation, Georgetown U., 1973. Bar: D.C. 1967. Audit staff internat. services div. Coopers & Lybrand, C.P.A.s, N.Y.C., 1966-68; pres. Pinata Party, Inc., N.Y.C., 1968-70; asst. prof. acctg. George Mason U., Fairfax, Va., 1970-73; assoc. prof. acctg. U. Balt., 1973-75, prof., chmn. dept. taxation, dir. grad. program in taxation, 1976-83; prof., dir. grad. program in taxation Am. U., Washington, 1983—; vis. prof. taxation U. Oreg., Eugene, 1975-76; cons. SBA, 1978; cons. editor Tax Reduction Inst., Washington; mem. faculties Grad. Realtors Insts., Va., Del., Ky.; profl. lectr. various legal and realtors assns.; C.P.A., N.Y. Author: The Impact of Taxation on Small Business-A Proposal for Reform, 1978; 1031 Casebook, 1978; Impact of 1980-1981 Tax Changes on Real Estate, 1981; Residential Real Estate Tax Handbook, 1980, supplement, 1981; contbr. articles to publs. in fields. Served with USAR, 1962-68. Mem. ABA (com. on real estate tax problems tax sect. 1976-79), Am. Inst. C.P.A.s, Am. Acctg. Assn., N.Y. Soc. C.P.A.s, Am. Taxation Assn. Democrat. Methodist. Corporate taxation, Estate taxation, Personal income taxation. Home: 614 G St SW Washington DC 20024

SAMSON, ANTHONY DONALD, lawyer; b. Huntington Park, Calif., Nov. 27, 1933; s. Nick and Alice Marguerite (Livingston) Hulbert S.; m. Betty White, May 1, 1957 (div. June 1964); 1 child, Nickie Michelle; m. Gloria Perez, Jan. 30, 1965; children—Ixchel Alyssa, Kyra Marina. A.A., Riverside City Coll., 1958; A.B., U. Calif.-Riverside, 1963; J.D., UCLA, 1968. Bar: Calif. 1969, U.S. Dist. Ct. (so. dist.) Calif. 1969. Asst. credit mgr. Sears Roebuck & Co., Riverside, Calif., 1957-65; sole practice, Riverside, 1968-70; chief fraud div. San Diego Dist. Atty.'s Office, 1983—; lectr. Fla. Gov.'s Conf., Orlando, 1975, Nat. Coll. Dist. Attys., Houston, 1978; lectr., cons. Tng. Ctr., Dept. Justice, Sacramento, 1978—. Treas. Democratic Profl. Club, San Diego, 1978—; del. State Dem. Conv., Sacramento, 1983, Conf. Dels. to State Bar, 1985-86; bd. dirs. Utility Consumer Action Network, San Diego, 1983. Served with U.S. Army, 1953-55, Korea, Japan. Recipient Cert. of Appreciation, So. Calif. Fraud Investigators, Ventura, 1982, 83, Disting. Service award Calif. Dist. Atty. Investigators Santa Barbara, 1983. Mem. Consumer Protection Council (sec. 1980-83), State Bar Calif. (exec. com. real property sect. 1986-87, consumer fin. subcom. bus. law sect. 1986-87, del. conf. of dels. 1984-86), Calif. Dist. Attys. Assn., San Diego County Bar Assn., San Diego Lawyer's Club. Democrat. Episcopalian. Criminal, State civil litigation, Antitrust. Office: San Diego Dist Atty 220 W Broadway San Diego CA 92103

SAMSON, PETER, lawyer; b. Princeton, N.J., Oct. 26, 1951; s. Hugh and Edith (Willett) S.; m. H. Bannard Porter, Dec. 22, 1973; children: David, Brian, Catherine. BA, U. Pa., 1973; JD, New Eng. Sch. Law, 1976. Bar: Pa. 1976, U.S. Dist. Ct. Pa. 1980, U.S. Ct. Appeals (3d cir.) 1981, U.S. Supreme Ct. 1983. Staff atty. Defender Assn. of Phila., 1976-80; assoc. White & Williams, Phila., 1980-86, ptnr., 1986—. Mem. ABA, Pa. Bar Assn., Phila. Bar Assn., Pa. Def. Inst., Assn. of Def. Counsel. Democrat. Avocations: skiing, sailing, wind surfing. Personal injury, State civil litigation, Federal civil litigation. Home: 241 Atlee Rd Wayne PA 19087 Office: White & Williams 1234 Market St 17th floor Philadelphia PA 19107

SAMUEL, RAPHAEL, lawyer; b. N.Y.C., Oct. 11, 1946; s. Sam and Sarah R. (Hollenberg) S. BS in Math. magna cum laude, L.I. U., 1968; JD, NYU, 1971. Bar: N.Y. 1972, U.S. Dist. Ct. (so. and ea. dists.) N.Y. 1973, U.S. Ct. Appeals (2d cir.) 1973. Staff atty. N.Y.C. Housing Authority, 1972-78, asst. chief litigation, 1978-83, chief research, opinions and spl. assignments, 1983—; agy. rep. Nat. Leased Housing Assn., Washington, 1981, 84, 85. Sec. Waterside Tenants Assn., N.Y.C., 1976-78; pres. 130 Water St. Tenants Assn., N.Y.C., 1978-80; sec. 50 8th Ave. Tenants Corp., Bklyn., 1980-83. Served with USNG, 1969-75. Mem. ABA, Fed. Bar Council, N.Y. County Lawyers Assn., Nat. Assn. Housing and Redevel. Ofcls. Democrat. Jewish. Lodge: KP. Avocations: computer databases, opera, sporting events. Federal civil litigation, State civil litigation, Government contracts and claims. Office: NYC Housing Authority 250 Broadway Room 614 New York NY 10007

SAMUEL, REUBEN, lawyer; b. Sarid, Israel, Oct. 8, 1942; came to U.S., 1947; s. Frederick Alexander and Esther Else (Tanowitski) S.; m. Kay Schwartz, June 17, 1973 (div. Dec. 1976); m. Janet Evelyn Bartucci, Oct. 18, 1981; 1 child, Alexandra Elizabeth. Student, Pratt Inst., Bklyn., 1960-62; BBA, CCNY, 1970; JD, Bklyn. Law Sch., 1975. Bar: N.Y. 1976, U.S. Dist Ct. (so. and ea. dists.) N.Y. 1976, U.S. Supreme Ct. 1980. V.p. Fred Samuel Co. Inc., Long Island City, N.Y., 1967-76; pvt. practice N.Y.C., 1976—; lectr. real property CUNY, Bklyn., 1985; mem. state-fed. jud. council's subcom. on trial delays and adjournments Appellate Div. 1st Dept., 1982, sec. inter-departmental com. marriage counseling and alcoholism programs in family cts. of City of N.Y. 1984-85, mem. adv. com. family ct. , 1984—, mem. steering com. Fordham Law Sch/ct. seminar on child sexual abuse, 1984-85, chmn. appellate div. 1st dept. cen. screening and oversight com. 18B family ct. panel, 1985—. Co-pub. (legal newsletters) Family Court Newsfront, 1982-84, Comment & Counsel, 1985—. sec., v.p. Temple Shaaray Tefila, N.Y.C., 1979—; pres. Gramercy Park Residence Corp., N.Y.C. Mem. ABA (young lawyers com., gen. practice com., family law com.), N.Y. State Bar Assn. (family law sect., gen. practice sect.), Assn. Bar of City of N.Y., N.Y. County Lawyers' Assn. (chmn. com. on family ct. 1981-84). Republican. Jewish. Avocations: jogging, opera, chamber music. Real property, Family and matrimonial, Contracts commercial. Home: 60 Gramercy Park N New York NY 10010 Office: Leffler & Samuel PC 360 Lexington Ave New York NY 10017

SAMUELS, JANET LEE, lawyer; b. Pitts., July 18, 1953; d. Emerson and Jeanne (Kalish) S.; m. David Arthur Kalow, June 18, 1978; children—Margaret Emily Samuels-Kalow, Jacob Richard Samuels-Kalow. B.A. with honors, Beloit Coll., 1974; J.D., NYU, 1977. Bar: N.Y. 1978, D.C. 1980. Staff atty. SCM Corp., N.Y.C., 1977-80, corp. atty., 1980-83, sr. corp. atty., 1983-85, assoc. gen. counsel Allied Paper div., 1983-86, Holtzmann, Wise & Shepard, 1986—. Adviser student adviser program NYU Law Sch., 1982—. Mem. ABA, Assn. Bar City N.Y., Assn. Trial Lawyers Am., N.Y. State Bar Assn., Mortar Board, Phi Beta Kappa. General corporate, Securities, Contracts commercial. Office: Holtzmann Wise & Shepard 745 Fifth Ave New York NY 10151

SAMUELS, SEYMOUR, JR., lawyer; b. Nashville, Oct. 23, 1912; s. Seymour and Maud Stella (Rosenfeld) S.; m. Essie Wenar, July 7, 1937; children—Seymour Samuels, Charles W. B.A., Vanderbilt U., 1933, J.D. 1935. Bar: Tenn. 1935, U.S. Dist. Ct. (mid. dist.) Tenn. 1937, U.S. Ct. Appeals (6th cir.) 1943, U.S. Tax Ct. 1940, U.S. Supreme Ct. Sole practice Nashville, 1935-40; ptnr. Samuels & Allen, Nashville, 1940-42; area rent atty., dep. rent dir. OPA, Nashville, 1942-43; ptnr. Nashville Bag & Burlap Co., 1946-59; dep. dir. law Nashville Met. Govt., 1963-67; ptnr. Hooker & Willis, Nashville, 1967, Hooker, Hooker, Willis & Samuels, Nashville, 1968; assoc. Farris, Evans & Evans, Nashville, 1969-71; ptnr. Farris, Warfield & Samuels, Nashville, 1972-74, Schulman, Leroy & Bennett, Nashville, 1975—. Mem. Nashville Met. Traffic and Parking Commn., 1967-70, Met. Govt. Charter Revision Com., 1970-73, Met. Govt. Transit Authority, 1973-74; chmn. Davidson county Democratic Campaign Com., 1968. Served with USN, 1943-46. Mem. ABA, Tenn. Bar Assn., Nashville Bar Assn., Am. Judicature Soc., Order of Coif, Phi Beta Kappa. Club: Nashville City. General corporate, General practice, Administrative and regulatory. Home: 4487 Post Pl Apt 68 Nashville TN 37205 Office: 501 Union St Suite 701 PO Box 2707 Nashville TN 37219

SAMUELSON, JACQUELINE K., lawyer; b. Detroit, Aug. 8, 1953; d. Edwin Luther and Wanda (Frye) S.; m. Paul Worth Prueitt, Oct. 3, 1980; 1 child, Rachel Leigh Prueitt. BA summa cum laude, Bradley U., 1975; JD with honors, U. Iowa, 1979. Bar: Iowa 1980, U.S. Dist. Ct. (no. and so. dists.) Iowa 1980, U.S. Ct. Appeals (8th cir.) 1986. Law clk. to presiding justice U.S. Dist. Ct. (so. dist.) Iowa, Des Moines, 1979-80; ptnr. Whitfield, Musgrave, Selvy, Kelly & Eddy, Des Moines, 1980—. Editor Iowa Law Rev., 1979. Mem. ABA, Def. Research Inst., Iowa Def. Counsel, Iowa Bar Assn. (chmn. young lawyers sect., corp. law com., trade regulation com.), Iowa Orgn. Women Attys. (pres. 1984-85, exec. bd. 1985—), Polk County Women Attys. (sec. 1983-84, chmn. profl. action com. 1982-83), Order of Coif, Phi Kappa Phi. Federal civil litigation, State civil litigation. Home: 696 48th St Des Moines IA 50312 Office: Whitfield Musgrave et al 1300 First Interstate Bank Bldg Des Moines IA 50309

SAMUELSON, KENNETH LEE, lawyer; b. Natrona Heights, Pa., Aug. 22, 1946; s. Sam Abraham and Frances Bernice (Robbins) S.; m. Marlene Ina Rabinowitz, Jan. 1, 1980; children: Heather, Cheryl. BA magna cum laude, U. Pitts., 1968; JD, U. Mich., 1971. Bar: Md. 1972, D.C. 1980, U.S. Dist. Ct. Md. Trial Bar 1984. Assoc. Weinberg & Green, Balt., 1971-73; assoc. Dickerson, Nice, Sokol & Horn, Balt., 1973; asst. atty. gen. State of Md., 1973-77; sole practice, Balt., 1978; ptnr. Linowes and Blocher, Silver Spring, Md., and Washington, 1979—. Author in field. Bd. dirs. D.C. Assn. for Retarded Citizens, Inc., 1981—. Served to capt. U.S. Army, to 1976. Mem. ABA (chmn. subcom. on subletting and assignment provisions, comml. leasing com., sect. real property, probate and trust law 1985—), D.C. Bar (comml. real estate com.), Md. State Bar Assn. (real property, planning and zoning sect., spl. com. on lawyers opinions in comml. transactions, chmn. comml. transactions com., litigation sect. 1982-84), Montgomery County Bar Assn., Phi Beta Kappa. Contracts commercial, Real property. Address: 8720 Georgia Ave PO Box 8728 Silver Spring MD 20910

SAMUELSON, WAYNE PAUL, lawyer; b. Pitts., Nov. 12, 1950; s. Paul John and Anne Caroline (Takacs) S.; m. Patricia Diann Lytle, July 14, 1973; children: Anita Elaine, Laura Suzanne. BA, Pa. State U., 1972; JD, U. Pitts., 1975; student, U.S. Army JAG Sch., 1978-79. Bar: Pa. 1975, U.S. Ct. Mil. Appeals 1976, U.S. Supreme Ct. 1979. Commd. 2d lt. USMC, 1975, advanced through grades to major, 1982; pros. and defense counsel USMC, Camp Pendleton, Calif., 1976-78; pros. atty. USMC, On Sta. Judge Adv. Iwakuni, Japan, 1979-80; pros., rev. officer USMC, On Sta. Judge Adv. Parris Island, S.C., 1980-84; mil. judge spl. cts. USMC, Quantico, Va., 1984-86; resigned USMC, 1986; asst. Atty. U.S. Dist. Ct. (middle dist.) Pa., 1986—. Mem. ABA, Fed. Bar Assn., Allegheny County Bar Assn. Methodist. Avocations: golf, collecting 1950's rock and roll music. Military, Criminal. Home: 90 Fairview Dr Lewisburg PA 17837 Office: US Dist Ct mid dist Pa Post Office Bldg Lewisburg PA 17837

SANBORN, ALBERT BECKWITH, II, lawyer; b. Pasadena, Calif., May 26, 1950; s. Albert Whittemore II and Gayle (Corgiat) S.; m. Sammye Jo Sanborn, Aug. 11, 1985; 1 child, Albert Whittemore Sanborn III. BA, U. Calif., San Diego, 1972; MPH, U. Tex., 1973; JD, Lewis and Clark Coll., 1977. Bar: Oreg. 1978, Tex. 1985, Ind. 1986, U.S. Supreme Ct. 1986. Counsel Healthlink Corp., Portland, Oreg., 1981-84; gen. counsel Harris Meth. Health System, Ft. Worth, 1984-85; legal counsel Holy Cross Health Systems, South Bend, Ind., 1985—. Vol. Spl. Olympics, South Bend, 1985. Mem. ABA, Am. Corp. Counsel Assn., Nat. Health Lawyers Assn., Hosp. Fin. Mgmt. Assn. Republican. Episcopalian. Lodge: Rotary. Avocation: sailing. General corporate, Health, Corporate taxation. Home: 16585 Barryknoll Way Granger IN 46530 Office: Holy Cross Health System 3606 E Jefferson South Bend IN 46615

SANBORN, RICHARD JOHN JAY, lawyer; b. Wichita, Kans., Feb. 27, 1954; s. Keith and Wanda Katherine (Szymborsky) S. BA, Wichita State U., 1976; JD, Washburn U., 1981. Bar: Kans. 1981, U.S. Dist. Ct. Kans. 1981, U.S. Ct. Appeals (10th cir.) 1981, U.S. Supreme Ct. 1984. Ptnr. Cranmer & Sanborn, Wichita, 1981-83; sole practice Wichita, 1983-84; ptnr. Sanborn, Sadowsky & Mills, Wichita, 1985—; cons. Sedgwick County Dist. Atty., Wichita, 1974-76, Great Bend, Kans. Police Dept., 1976-77; legal counsel Sedgwick County Clk., Wichita, 1981-84; gen. counsel Kans. Bldg. and Constrn. Trades Council, AFL-CIO, 1983—; atty. City of Mulvane, Kans., 1984—. Mem. Sedgwick County Dem. Cen. Com., Wichita, 1985—; correspondent Western Conf. on Criminal and Civil Problems, Wichita, 1975—; commr. Ark. River Interstate Commn., Kans., Colo., Okla., 1983—; bd. dirs. Wichita (Kans.) Police Social Service Ctr., 1975-76. Mem. ABA, Kans. Bar Assn., Wichita Bar Assn., Assn. Trial Lawyers Am., Kans. Trial Lawyers Assn. (bd. govs. 1986—), Nat. Assn. Criminal Def. Lawyers, Kans. Assn. of City Attys. (Cert. of Appreciation 1980), Wichita Labor Fedn., Phi Alpha Delta, Lambda-Alpha. Democrat. Avocations: riding, shooting, stamp collecting, swimming, skiing. Labor, Federal civil litigation, Municpal corporations. Home: 3805 Longview Ln Wichita KS 67218-2013 Office: Sanborn Sadowsky & Mills 434 N Market Suite 200 Wichita KS 67202-2012

SANCHELIMA, JESUS, patent lawyer; b. Havana, Cuba, May 28, 1949; came to U.S. 1967; s. Juan Sanchelima and Victoria Wedemeyer; m. Flor Angel, Jan. 4, 1986. AA, Miami Dade Jr. Coll.; BSEE, U. Fla., 1970; JD, U. Miami, 1976. Bar: Fla. 1977, D.C. 1981. Product engr. ITT, W. Palm Beach, Fla., 1971; quality control mngr. Coulter Electronics, Hidleoh, Fla., 1972-74; sales engr. Cartwright & Bean, Ft. Lauderdale, Fla., 1974-80; pres. Jesus Sanchelima, P.A., Miami, 1977—. Chmn. Latin Am. Com. for City of N. Miami Beach (Fla.), 1984. Am. Intellectual Property Law Assn., U.S. Trademark Assn., ABA. Patent, Trademark and copyright. Office: 235 SW Le Jeune Rd Miami FL 33134

SANCHEZ, ERNESTO, lawyer; b. Havana, Cuba, June 29, 1935; s. Ernesto and Maria J. (Jerez) S.; m. Maria del Carmen Gonzalez-Parra, June 10, 1967; 1 child, Ernesto Javier. BA, Champagnat Coll., Havana, 1952 summa cum laude; LLD summa cum laude, U. St. Thomas of Villanova, Havana, 1957; grad., NYU Law Sch., 1959; JD, U. Miami, 1982. Bar: Fla. 1982. Assoc. Moran Valdes Forcade, Havana, 1957-61; atty. Equitable Life, N.Y.C., 1961-69; div. counsel Latin Am. Pepsico Inc., N.Y.C., 1969-78; v.p., counsel Bacardi & Co. Ltd., Nassau, Bahamas, 1978-80; sole practice Miami, 1982—. Mem. ABA, Fla. Bar Assn., Inter Am. Bar Assn., Licensing Exec. Soc., Internat. Ctr. Fla. Republican. Roman Catholic. General corporate, Contracts commercial, International franchising, trademark licensing. Home: 1530 Catalonia Ave Coral Gables FL 33134 Office: 814 Ponce de Leon Blvd Suite 505 Coral Gables FL 33134

SANCHEZ, MANUEL, lawyer; b. Chgo., Dec. 1, 1947; s. Salomon and Margaret (Flores) S.; m. Mary Eileen Wilson; children: Annette, Manny. BA, No. Ill. U., 1970; JD, U. Pa., 1974. Assoc. Hinshaw, Culbertson, Moelmann, Hoban & Fuller, Chgo., 1974-80, ptnr., 1980-86; ptnr. Sanchez & Daniels, Chgo., 1987—. Mem. ABA, Ill. Bar Assn., Chgo. Bar Assn., Trial Lawyers Club of Chgo. (bd. dirs.), Soc. Trial Lawyers, Ill. Trial Lawyers Assn. Personal injury, State civil litigation, Insurance. Office: Sanchez & Daniles 333 W Wacker Dr Suite 810 Chicago IL 60606

SAND, DAVID BYRON, lawyer; b. Mpls., Jan. 28, 1946; s. William James and Lois E. (Crane) S.; m. June Ann Striffler, Sept. 14, 1969; children—Kristin, Maren, Brandon. B.A. cum laude, St. Olaf Coll., 1968; J.D. cum laude, Duke U., 1975. Bar: Minn. 1975, U.S. Dist. Ct. Minn. 1976, U.S. Ct. Appeals (8th cir.) 1978. Assoc. Briggs and Morgan, St. Paul, 1975-80, ptnr., Mpls., 1980—; mem. panel of constrn. industry arbitrators Am. Arbitration Assn., Mpls., 1981—. Chmn. Arden Hills Park & Recreation (Minn.), 1983—; bd. trustees Hamline Methodist Ch., St. Paul, 1984—. Served to lt. (j.g.) USNR, 1969-72. Recipient Service award Minn. Bd. Archtl. Engring. and Land Surveying, 1983. Mem. ABA (litigation sect. and forum com. constrn. industry), Internat. Bar Assn. (internat. constrn. contracts). Construction, State civil litigation. Office: Briggs and Morgan 2400 IDS Ctr Minneapolis MN 55402

SAND, LEONARD B., judge; b. N.Y.C., May 24, 1928. B.S., NYU, 1947; LL.B., Harvard, 1951. Bar: N.Y. 1953, U.S. Supreme Ct. 1956, D.C. 1969. Clk. to dist. ct. judge N.Y., 1952-53; asst. U.S. atty. So. Dist. N.Y., 1953-54; asst. to U.S. Solictor Gen., 1956-59; mem. firm Robinson, Silverman, Pearce, Aronsohn Sand and Berman, N.Y.C., 1960-78; judge U.S. Dist. Ct. So. Dist. N.Y., 1978—; adj. prof. law NYU. Note editor: Harvard Law Rev, 1950-51. Del. N.Y. State Constl. Conv., 1967; v.p., treas. Legal Aid Soc. Fellow Am. Coll. Trial Lawyers; mem. Assn. Bar City N.Y., N.Y. State, Am. bar assns., Fed. Bar Council. Jurisprudence. Office: US Dist Ct Foley Sq New York NY 10007

SANDAGE, DOUGLAS S., lawyer; b. Corpus Christi, Tex., July 15, 1951; s. Loren and Doris (Staley) S. BA cum laude, Vanderbilt U., 1973; JD, U. Tex., 1976. Bar: Tex. 1976, U.S. Dist. Ct. (so. dist.) Tex., U.S. Ct. Appeals (5th cir.). Trial atty. Baker & Botts, Houston, 1976-80, Funderburk & Funderburk, Houston, 1980-81, Lorance & Thompson, Houston, 1981-84, Sandage, Heath & Elskes, Houston, 1984—; mem. alumni council Tex. Mil. Inst., San Antonio, 1984—. Chief legis. asst. U.S. Senator Paula Hawkins, Washington, 1981; active Big Bros. and Big Sisters, Inc., Houston, 1979-85. Mem. Tex. Trial Lawyers Assn. Democrat. Baptist. State civil litigation, Contracts commercial. Office: Sandage Heath & Elskes 2701 Fannin St Houston TX 77002

SANDALOW, TERRANCE, lawyer, university dean; b. Chgo., Sept. 8, 1934; s. Nathan and Evelyn (Hoffing) S.; m. Ina Davis, Sept. 4, 1955; children: David Blake, Marc Alan, Judith Ann. A.B., U. Chgo., 1954, J.D., 1957. Bar: Ill. 1958, Mich. 1978. Law clk. presiding justice U.S. Ct. Appeals (2d cir.), 1957-58; law clk. to justice Potter Stewart U.S. Supreme Ct., Washington, 1958-59; assoc. Ross, McGowan & O'Keefe, Chgo., 1959-61; assoc. prof. law U. Minn., Mpls., 1961-64, prof., 1964-66; prof. law U. Mich., Ann Arbor, 1966—; dean Law Sch. U. Mich., 1978-87. Author: (with F.I. Michelman) Government in Urban Areas, 1970, (with E. Stein) Courts and Free Markets, 1982; contbr. to legal jours., periodicals. Mem. Mpls. Commn. Human Relations, 1965-66. Fellow Ctr. Advanced Study in Behavioral Scis., U. Mich. Law Sch., 1972-73. Mem. ABA. Legal education, Constitutional. Office: U Michigan Law Sch 301 Hutchins Hall Ann Arbor MI 48109-1215

SANDER, FRANK ERNEST ARNOLD, law educator; b. Stuttgart, Germany, July 22, 1927; came to U.S., 1940, naturalized, 1946; s. Rudolf and Alice (Epstein) S.; m. Emily Bishop Jones, Apr. 26, 1958; children: Alison Bishop, Thomas Harvey, Ernest Ridgway Sander. A.B. in Math. magna cum laude, Harvard U., 1949, LL.B. magna cum laude, 1952. Bar: Mass. 1952, U.S. Supreme Ct 1952. Law clk. to Chief Judge Magruder U.S. Ct. Appeals, 1952-53; law clk. to Justice Frankfurter, U.S. Supreme Ct., 1953-54; atty. tax div. Dept. Justice, 1954-56; with firm Hill & Barlow, Boston, 1956-59; mem. faculty Harvard Law Sch., 1959—, prof. law, 1962—, Bussey prof., 1981—; spl. fields fed. taxation, family law, welfare law, dispute resolution; chmn. Council on Role of Cts.; mem. panels Am. Arbitration Assn., Fed. Mediation and Conciliation Service; mem. Gov.'s Commn. on Probate and Family Ct.; chmn. Council on Legal Edn. Opportunity, 1968-70; cons. Dept. Treasury, 1968; treas. Harvard Law Rev., 1951-52. Author: (with Foote and Levy) Cases and Materials on Family Law, 3d edit., 1985; (with Gutman) 4th edit. Tax Aspects of Divorce and Separation, 1985; (with Westfall and McIntyre) 2d edit. Readings in Federal Taxation, 1983; (with Goldberg, Green) Dispute Resolution, 1985. Chmn., Mass. Welfare Adv. Bd., 1975-79; mem. com. civil and polit. rights Pres.'s Commn. Status Women, 1962-63; mem. tax mission Internat. Program Taxation to Republic of Colombia, 1959; trustee Buckingham Browne and Nichols Sch., 1969-75. Served with AUS, 1946-47. Mem. ABA (chmn. standing com. dispute resolution 1986—), Boston Bar Assn., Phi Beta Kappa. Legal education, Family and matrimonial, Dispute resolution. Home: 74 Buckingham St Cambridge MA 02138

SANDER, MALVIN GUSTAV, lawyer; b. Pitts., Feb. 7, 1946; s. Malvin Gustav and LaVerta Carol (Martin) S.; m. Carol Jean Kribel, Nov. 12, 1966; children—Paul Malvin, Amy Lynne, Elizabeth Leigh, Mark Gustav. B.S. in Edn., Bucknell U., 1967; J.D. in Law, Duquesne U., 1972. Bar: Pa. 1972, U.S. Dist. Ct. (we. dist.) Pa. 1972. Assoc. Houston, Cooper, Speer & German, Pitts., 1972-73; corporate counsel Sharon Steel Corp., Pa., 1973-78; vp., sec. NVF Co., Sharon Steel Corp., Miami Beach, Fla., 1979-81; v.p. law and adminstrn. Pa. Engring. Corp., Pitts., 1981—; v.p., gen. counsel Sharon Steel Corp., Sharon, Pa., 1984—. Dist. chmn. Keystone dist. Boy Scouts Am., 1975-77; mem. Coalition for Employment through Exports, Washington, 1982—. Mem. Am. Trial Lawyers Assn., ABA, Pa. Bar Assn., Delta Theta Phi. Republican. Roman Catholic. Contracts commercial, General corporate, Private international. Home: 2412 Mill Grove Rd Pittsburgh PA 15241 Office: Pennsylvania Engring Corp 32d St Pittsburgh PA 15201

SANDERS, BARRETT, lawyer; b. Chgo., Mar. 31, 1937; s. Robert and Marie (Hiebl) S.; m. Barbara L., Nov. 25, 1968 (dec. May 1983); children: Amy Marie, Robert. Bar: Fla. 1970. Sole practice Miami, Fla., 1970-73; counsel Southeast Mortgage Co., Miami, 1973—; legis. chmn. Mortgage Bankers of Fla. 1977-79, legis. editor 1979-84. Columnist real estate law Miami and Broward Rev., 1980-87. Recipient: Brown L. Whatley Disting. Service award Mortgage Bankers of Fla., 1979; Disting. Service award Fla. Assn. Realtors, 1984. Mem. ABA, Fla. Bar Assn. (chmn. editorial bd. Fla.

Bar Jour. 1985-86). Real property, General corporate. Home: 7430 SW 172d St Miami FL 33157

SANDERS, CARLTON EDWARD, lawyer; b. Millwood, Ky., Apr. 14, 1937; s. Earl H. and Mae (Farris) S.; m. Sue Eisenmenger, Feb. 16, 1974. B.S. in Bus. Adminstrn., Ind.U.-Jeffersonville, 1972; J.D., U. Louisville, 1976. Bar: Ind. 1977, U.S. Dist. Ct. (so. dist.) Ind. 1977. Office mgr. Burroughs Corp., West Palm Beach, Fla., 1962-70; supr. scheduling Capitol Holding Corp., Louisville, 1970-74; bench clk. Jefferson County Circuit Ct., Louisville, 1974-75; parole officer Ky. Dept. Corrections, Louisville, 1975-77; sole practice, Lanesville, Ind., 1977—; dep. prosecutor Harrison-Crawford County, Corydon, Ind., 1979; judge Harrison-Crawford County Ct., 1984—. Mem. council St. Peter's Lutheran Ch., Corydon, 1983-85; bd. dirs. Louisville Luth. Home, 1979-84. Served with U.S. Army, 1956-59. Mem. ABA, Ind. Bar Assn., Corydon C. of C. Democrat. Lodge: Masons. Criminal, State civil litigation, General practice. Home: Rural Route 1 PO Box 417 Lanesville IN 47136 Office: PO Box 147 W Main St Lanesville IN 47136

SANDERS, DOYLE DEE, lawyer; b. Vinton, Iowa, May 27, 1947; s. Verle H. and Culah O. (Evens) S.; m. Margaret D. Doty, Sept. 1, 1969; children: Robin D., Betsy D. BA, Drake U., 1969, MBA, 1972, JD with honors, 1972. Bar: Iowa 1972, U.S. Dist. Ct. (so. and no. dist.) Iowa 1972, U.S. Ct. Mil. Appeals 1973, U.S. Supreme Ct. 1976, Nebr. 1977, U.S. Tax Ct. 1980, U.S. Ct. Appeals (8th cir.) 1986. Assoc. Peddicord, Simpson & Sutphin, Des Moines, 1970-73, 77-83, Peddicord & Sutphin, Des Moines, 1983-84, Peddicord & Wharton, Des Moines, 1984—. Pres. Des Moines Urban Mission Council, 1984-85, Jobless United, Des Moines, 1984—; bd. dirs. Johnston (Iowa) Community Sch. Dist., 1985—. Served to capt. JAGC, USAF, 1973-77. Mem. ABA, Iowa Bar Assn., Polk County Bar Assn., Fed. Bar Assn. (chpt. pres. 1983-85, Nat. Outstanding Chpt. award 1985, chpt. sec. 1985—, nat. del. 1984—), Johnston C. of C. Republican. Methodist. Club: Westside Breakfast (pres. 1984-85) (West Des Moines, Iowa). Lodge: Rotary. Federal civil litigation, State civil litigation, Contracts commercial. Home: 5325 NW 90th Ct Johnston IA 50131 Office: Peddicord & Wharton 218 6th Ave Suite 300 Des Moines IA 50309 also Office: 5785 Merle Hay Rd PO Box 253 Johnston IA 50131

SANDERS, EDWIN PERRY BARTLEY, judge; b. Madisonville, Ky., July 12, 1940; s. Virgil Perry and Eunice Jane (Denton) S.; m. Kathryn Walker, Jan. 28, 1967; children—Christopher Charles, Carroll Denton. B.S. in Bus., Stetson U., 1965, J.D., 1968. Bar: Fla. Ptnr. Ford, Wren and Sanders, 1968-69; mem. Landis, Graham, French, Husfeld and Ford, P.A., DeLand, Fla., 1970-83; prof. real estate Stetson U. Sch. Bus. Adminstrn., 1980-83; judge 7th Jud. Cir. Ct., Volusia County, Fla., 1983—. Served with U.S. Army. Mem. Fla. Bar Assn., Volusia County Bar Assn. Democrat. Episcopalian. Clubs: Lake Beresford Yacht, Rotary (DeLand). Home: 340 Washington Oaks Dr DeLand FL 32720 Office: Volusia County Courthouse Suite 206 DeLand FL 32720 also: PO Box 611 DeLand FL 32721

SANDERS, GARY WAYNE, lawyer; b. Wilmington, Del., Dec. 29, 1949; s. Harland Wesley and Anna Marie (Hermanal) S.; m. Cheryl Ann Clark, Aug. 22, 1980. BS, Cal. State Poly. U., 1972; JD, Western State U., 1977. Bar: Calif. 1977. Corp. planner Cert. Grocers, Los Angeles, 1969-74; asst. character coordinator Walt Disney Prodns., Anaheim, Calif., 1968-78; sole practice Seal Beach, Calif., 1978-79; v.p., sec., gen. counsel Care Enterprises, Laguna Hills, Calif., 1979—. Mem. ABA, Calif. Bar Assn., Orange County Bar Assn., Nat. Health Lawyers Assn. Republican. Lutheran. Lodges: Elks, Masons. Health, General corporate. Office: Care Enterprises 23046 Avenida De La Carlota #700 Laguna Hills CA 92653

SANDERS, HAROLD BAREFOOT, JR., judge; b. Dallas, Feb. 5, 1925; s. Harold Barefoot and May Elizabeth (Forrester) S.; m. Jan Scurlock, June 6, 1952; children—Janet Lea, Martha Kay, Mary Frances, Harold Barefoot III. B.A., U. Tex., 1949, LL.B., 1950. Bar: Tex. bar 1950. U.S. atty. No. Dist. Tex., 1961-65; asst. dep. atty. gen. U.S., 1965-66; asst. atty. gen. 1966-67; legis. counsel to President U.S., 1967-69; partner firm Clark, West, Keller, Sanders & Butler, Dallas, 1969-79; U.S. dist. judge for No. Dist. Tex., Dallas, 1979—. Mem. Tex. Ho. of Reps., 1952-58; Democratic nominee for Congress, 1958, for, U.S. Senate, 1972. Served to lt. (j.g.) USNR, World War II. Mem. ABA, Fed. Bar Assn. (dir. nat. council 1963-66, Distinguished Service award Dallas 1964), Dallas Bar Assn. (dir.), State Bar Tex., Tex. Ex-Students Assn. (pres. Dallas 1955-56, pres. Washington chpt. 1968-69), Blue Key, Phi Delta Phi, Phi Delta Theta. Methodist. Clubs: Mason. (Dallas), Chaparral (Dallas). Office: US Courthouse 1100 Commerce St Dallas TX 75242

SANDERS, JAMES WORTHINGTON, lawyer; b. Scranton, Pa., Sept. 30, 1946; s. John H. and Kathryn (Ellis) S.; m. Barbara H., Dec. 18, 1971; children: John H. II, Susan E., Robert H. BA, Baldwin-Wallace Coll., 1968; JD, Cleve. State U., 1973. Bar: Ohio 1973, U.S. Dist. Ct. (no. dist.) Ohio 1974, U.S. Supreme Ct. 1976. Asst. gen. counsel Cleve. Regional Sewer Dist., 1973-76; asst. sec. and counsel Oglebay Norton Co., Cleve., 1976—. Contbg. author: The Encyclopedia of Cleveland History, 1987. Mem. Greater Cleve. Growth Assn. Pub. Affairs Com., 1976—, Citizens League of Cleve., 1983—, bd. edn. St. Thomas Sch., Rocky River, Ohio, 1984—. Mem. Greater Cleve. Bar Assn., Ohio Bar Assn., Jaycees (pres. 1979-80), Rocky River Hist. Soc. (historian), Phi Kappa Tau (Key award 1976). Republican. Lutheran. General corporate, State civil litigation, Public utilities. Home: 21060 Aberdeen Rd Rocky River OH 44116 Office: Oglebay Norton Co 1100 Superior Ave Cleveland OH 44114

SANDERS, JOEL S., lawyer; b. Mpls., Mar. 25, 1955; s. David M. and Miriam (Gelfand) S.; m. Carol G. Bieri, May 25, 1984; 1 child, Daniel. BA, Antioch Coll., 1976; JD, U. Calif., Berkeley, 1982. Bar: Calif. 1982, U.S. Dist. Ct. (no. dist.) Calif. 1982, U.S. Ct. Appeals (9th cir.) 1983, U.S. Dist. Ct. (cen. dist.) Calif. 1984. Law clk. to presiding judge U.S. Ct. Appeals (9th cir.), 1982-83; atty. antitrust div. U.S. Dept. Justice, San Francisco, 1983—. Mem. ABA, Order of Coif. Antitrust, Federal civil litigation. Office: US Dept Justice 450 Golden Gate PO Box 36046 San Francisco CA 94102

SANDERS, JOHN MONCRIEF, lawyer; b. Houston, Feb. 22, 1936; s. John Austin and Elizabeth (Moncrief) S.; m. Ann Clark, Aug. 13, 1960; children—Julie, Scott. A.B. cum laude, Baylor U., 1957, J.D. cum laude, 1960. Bar: Tex. 1960. Ptnr. Fulbright & Jaworski, Houston, 1973—. Trustee Baylor U., 1981—. Mem. ABA, Houston Bar Assn., State Bar Tex., Tex. Assn. Bank Counsel (dir., pres. 1982), Phi Alpha Delta. Banking, Contracts commercial. Office: Fulbright & Jaworski 1301 McKinney Houston TX 77010

SANDERS, MICHAEL LEO, lawyer; b. Salzburg, Austria, Aug. 28, 1954; came to U.S., 1955; s. Leo Francis and Elizabeth Jane (Crowe) S.; m. Susan Linda Kramer, Aug. 16, 1980. BBA, Western Ill. U., 1976; JD, U. Ill., 1980. Bar: Ill. 1980, Colo. 1981, U.S. Dist. Ct. Colo. 1981; CPA, Ill., Colo. Treas. Stelle (Ill.) Industries Inc., 1976-77; tax atty. Deloitte, Haskins & Sells, Denver, 1980-81; corp. counsel Wood Bros. Homes Inc., Golden, Colo., 1981-84; v.p. Custom Aluminum Products Inc., South Elgin, Ill., 1984—; bd. dirs. Sky Hi-Tech Inc., St. Charles, Ill.; pres. Aerovision Corp., St. Charles, Ill. Mem. ABA, Ill. Bar Assn. Democrat. Computer, Legislative, Real property. Home: 38 Lakewood Circle Saint Charles IL 60174 Office: Custom Aluminum Products Inc 414 W Division South Elgin IL 60177

SANDERS, MIKE CHARLES, lawyer; b. Sledge, Miss., Sept. 29, 1953; s. Joe B. and Claudine (Cofer) S.; m. Susan Craig, Aug. 13, 1976; children: James Mitchell, Mary Rachel. BA, Northeast La. U., 1978; JD, La. State U., 1981. Bar: La. 1981, U.S. Dist. Ct. (we. dist.) La. 1982, U.S. Ct. Appeals (5th cir.) 1985. Assoc. Davenport, Files & Kelly, Monroe, La., 1981-85, ptnr., 1986—. Served with U.S. Army, 1973-76. Mem. La. Assn. Def. Counsel. Republican. Baptist. Avocations: hunting, dog breeding, racquetball, chess. Insurance, Personal injury. Office: Davenport Files & Kelly 1509 Lamy Ln Monroe LA 71201

SANDERS, RUSSELL RONALD, lawyer; b. Pitts., May 20, 1956; m. Janice M. Ioli, Aug. 16, 1975; 1 child, Craig D. BA in History, U. Pitts., 1978, JD, 1982. Bar: Pa. 1982, U.S. Dist. Ct. (we. dist.) Pa. 1982, U.S. Ct. Appeals (3d cir.). Assoc. May & Long, P.C., Pitts., 1982—. Mem. ABA, Pa. Bar Assn., Allegheny County Bar Assn. Democrat. Roman Catholic. Avocations: hunting, fishing, camping, softball. Bankruptcy, Consumer commercial, General practice. Office: May & Long PC 600 Grant St Suite 670 Pittsburgh PA 15219

SANDERS, THELMA E., lawyer; b. Okemah, Okla., Jan. 11, 1955; d. Hobart Curtis and Maurine (Lee) S.; m. James Clardy, June 28, 1980 (div. Feb. 1986). BS in Polit. Sci., Tenn. State U., 1975; JD, Tex. So. U., 1979. Bar: Tex. 1979, U.S. Dist. Ct. (no. dist.) Tex. 1980, U.S. Ct. Appeals (5th cir.) 1987. Staff atty. U.S. Dept. Edn., Dallas, 1979—; bd. dirs. North Cen. Tex. Legal Services Found., Dallas. Bd. dirs. Dallas Area Women's Polit. Caucus, 1983-84, Dallas Cable TV Adv. Bd., 1985-86. Mem. ABA, Nat. Bar Assn., Dallas Bar Assn. (com. chairperson 1985), Dallas Assn. Black Women Attys. (pres. 1982-83, treas. 1986-87). Administrative and regulatory, Family and matrimonial, Civil rights. Office: Law Offices of Earl Luna 1525 Elm St Dallas TX 75201

SANDERS, WILLIAM HENRY, lawyer; b. Princeton, W.Va., Feb. 24, 1917; s. Hartley and Ina (Hylton) S.; m. Katherine Grizzard Little, June 6, 1946; children: David, Mary, Katherine, Henry. AB, Randolph-Macon Coll., 1940; LLB, U. Va., 1942, LLM in Internat. Law, 1946. Bar: Va. 1942, W.Va. 1948. Asst. staff sec. Office of Mil. Gov. Gen. Lucius Clay, Berlin, 1946-47; ptnr. Sanders, Austin & Swope, Princeton. Author: Legacy of Homes and Families. Served to major USMC, 1942-45, PTO. Decorated Navy Cross, Bronze Star, Purple Heart. Mem. ABA, Assn. Trial Lawyers Am., W.Va. Bar Assn. Republican. Episcopalian. State civil litigation, Personal injury, Condemnation. Office: Sanders Austin & Swope 320 Courthouse Rd Princeton WV 24740

SANDERSON, WILLIAM WOODROW, JR., lawyer; b. Huntsville, Ala., Apr. 29, 1954; s. William Woodrow and Glenn Iris (Rowe) S.; m. Myra Ann Monk, July 19, 1980. BA, U. Ala., 1976, MPA, JD, 1979. Bar: Ala. 1979, U.S. Ct. Appeals (5th cir.) 1979, U.S. Dist. Ct. (no. dist.) Ala. 1980, U.S. Ct. Appeals (11th cir.) 1981. Law clk. to presiding justice U.S. Ct. Appeals (5th cir.), Tuscaloosa, Ala., 1979-80; assoc. Lanier, Shaver & Herring, Huntsville, Ala., 1980-85, ptnr., 1986—. Bd. dirs. Harris Home for Children, Huntsville, 1982—, chmn., 1987—. Mem. ABA, Huntsville-Madison County Bar Assn. (pres. young lawyers div. 1985-86). Democrat. Methodist. Lodge: Optimists (pres. Huntsville 1983-84). Avocations: golf, tennis. State civil litigation, General practice. Home: 806 Wells Ave Huntsville AL 35801 Office: Lanier Shaver & Herring 404 Madison St Huntsville AL 35801

SANDLER, GILBERT LEE, lawyer; b. Jacksonville, Fla., Jan. 9, 1944; s. Theodore Tobias and Laurette (Simons) S.; m. Diane Fass, Mar. 18, 1946; children—Scott Duchon, Julie Duchon. A.B., Dartmouth Coll., 1966; J.D., N.Y. U., 1969. Bar: Fla. 1969, N.Y. 1975. Trial atty. Customs Sect., U.S. Dept. Justice, N.Y.C., 1969-75; assoc. Freeman, Meade, Wasserman, Sharfman & Schneider, N.Y.C., 1975-77; ptnr. Sandler & Travis, Miami, Fla., N.Y.C., Los Angeles and Washington, 1977—; nat. com. chmn. Am. Assn. Exporters and Importers. Mem. ABA, Fla. Bar Assn. (chmn.-elect internat. law sect., editor internat. sect. quar.), Customs and Internat. Trade Bar Assn. (bd. dirs. 1978—, treas. 1980—). Immigration, naturalization, and customs, Private international, Administrative and regulatory. Office: Rivergate Plaza 444 Brickell Ave Suite 500 Miami FL 33131

SANDLER, LEWIS HERBSMAN, lawyer, real estate executive; b. N.Y.C., July 2, 1936; s. Samuel Herbsman and Celia (Rubin) S.; m. Viveca M. Lindahl, Sept. 30, 1967 (div. Oct. 1971); 1 child, Stephanie J.; m. Willy Klinkhamer, Oct. 27, 1973; 1 child, Derek J. A.B., Hamilton Coll., 1958; LL.B., Columbia U., 1961. Bar: N.Y. 1962, Tex. 1981. Atty. Port of N.Y., 1961-65, Equitable Life Assurance Co., N.Y.C., 1965-68; assoc. Finley, Kumble, Underberg, Persky & Roth, N.Y.C., 1968-71, ptnr., 1971-73; ptnr. Cohen & Sandler, N.Y.C., 1973-74, Poletti, Freidin, Prasker, Feldman & Gartner, N.Y.C., 1975-77; gen. counsel, gen. ptnr. Southwest Realty, Ltd., Dallas, 1977—; gen. ptnr. real estate ltd. partnerships; dir. SRL, Inc., Dallas. Bd. govs. Boys Athletic League, N.Y.C., 1976-79. Mem. N.Y. State Bar Assn., Tex. Bar Assn. Real property, Securities. Home: 9718 Estate Ln Dallas TX 75238 Office: Southwest Realty Ltd 7424 Greenville Ave Suite 201 Dallas TX 75231

SANDLER, MICHAEL DAVID, lawyer; b. Los Angeles, Feb. 27, 1946. AB, Stanford U., 1967; JD, Yale U., 1972. Assoc. Steptoe & Johnson, Washington, 1972-75, 77-79, ptnr., 1980-85; spl. asst. to legal adviser Dept. of State, Washington, 1975-77; ptnr. Foster, Pepper & Riviera, Seattle, 1985—; adj. prof. law Georgetown U., Washington, 1979, 81-82, U. Wash., Seattle, 1985—. Vol. Peace Corps, Ethiopia and Ghana, 1968-70. Antitrust, Private international, Federal civil litigation. Office: Foster Pepper & Riviera 1111 3d Ave Seattle WA 98101

SANDMAN, IRVIN WILLIS, lawyer; b. Seattle, Mar. 19, 1954. BA summa cum laude, U. Wash., 1976; JD summa cum laude, UCLA, 1980. Bar: U.S. Dist. Ct. (we. dist.) Wash. 1980. Assoc. Graham & Dunn, Seattle, 1980—. Staff mem. UCLA Law Review. Mem. ABA, Wash. State Bar Assn. (exec. com. creditor/debtor sect., editor newsletter 1984—, speaker continuing legal edn.). Bankruptcy, Contracts commercial, General corporate. Office: Graham & Dunn 3400 Rainer Bank Tower Seattle WA 98101-2653

SANDMAN, JAMES JOSEPH, lawyer; b. Albany, N.Y., June 16, 1951; s. Edgar A. and Margaret M. (Dugan) S.; m. Elizabeth D. Mullin, June 2, 1985. AB summa cum laude, Boston Coll., 1973; JD cum laude, U. Pa., 1976. Bar: Pa. 1976, D.C. 1977, U.S. Supreme Ct. 1980, Colo. 1982. Law clk. to judge U.S. Ct. Appeals (3d cir.), Wilkes-Barre, Pa., 1976-77; assoc. Arnold & Porter, Washington, 1977-82; assoc. Arnold & Porter, Denver, 1982-83, ptnr., 1984—; bd. dirs. Colo. Lawyers Com., Denver. Exec. editor U. Pa. Law Rev., 1975-76. Mem. ABA, Colo. Bar Assn., Denver Bar Assn., D.C. Bar Assn., Order of Coif, Phi Beta Kappa. Democrat. Roman Catholic. Federal civil litigation, State civil litigation. Home: 460 S Marion Pkwy Denver CO 80209 Office: Arnold & Porter 1700 Lincoln St Denver CO 80203

SANDROCK, SCOTT PAUL, lawyer; b. Massillon, Ohio, Apr. 11, 1953; s. H. Paul and Alvina (Huber) S.; m. Marianne Griffin, Aug. 28, 1976; children: Paul, Christopher. BA, U. Notre Dame, 1975; JD, Ohio State U., 1978. Bar: Ohio 1978, U.S. Dist. Ct. (no. dist.) Ohio, U.S. Ct. Claims, U.S. Ct. Internat. Trade, U.S. Tax Ct., U.S. Ct. Customs and Patent Appeals, U.S. Ct. Mil. Appeals, U.S. Ct. Appeals (6th cir.). From assoc. to ptnr. Black, McCuskey, Souers & Arbaugh, Canton, Ohio, 1978—; lectr. Vis. Nurse Soc., 1978—. Author, editor: History of the Canton Jaycees 1934-1984, 1984; also articles. Campaign captain United Way, 1978—, Walsh Coll., 1978—, Malone Coll., 1978—, YMCA, 1978—; merit badge counselor Buckeye council Boy Scouts Am., 1978—, active numerous coms., 1978—; councilman Village of Navarre, Ohio, 1984-85, chmn. bldgs. and land com., 1984-85; mem. Stark County Regional Planning Commn., 1984-85; coach Jackson Baseball Assn., 1986—; trustee Neighborhood Inc., 1980-81, Vis. Care Inc., 1982—, Canton Ctr. Inc., 1984-85; trustee Stark County Parents Anonymous Inc., 1984—, pres., 1985—. Recipient Mayor's citation City of Canton, 1985. Mem. ABA (corp., banking and bus. law sect., antitrust sect., franchise forum), Ohio Bar Assn. (computer law com.), Stark County Bar Assn. (bar admissions com., corp. law com., lectr. 1979, 82, 85), Jaycees (bd. dirs. 1983-85). Republican. Roman Catholic. Club: Notre Dame (Canton) (sec., treas. 1979—). General corporate, Antitrust, State civil litigation. Home: 5443 Echodell Ave NW North Canton OH 44720 Office: Black McCuskey Souers & Arbaugh 220 Market Ave S Canton OH 44702

SANDS, DARRY GENE, lawyer; b. Charleston, Ark., Jan. 4, 1947; s. Anthony Wayne and Marjorie (Elkins) S.; m. Charlotte Moore, Dec. 28, 1968; 1 child, Spencer Justin. B.S., U. Ark., 1969; J.D., U. Kans., 1974. Bar: Mo. 1974, U.S. Dist. Ct. (we. dist.) Mo. 1974. Ptnr. Dietrich, Davis, Dicus, Rowlands, Schmitt & Gorman, Kansas City, Mo., 1980. Mem. ABA, Mo. Bar, Kansas City Bar Assn., Order of Coif. Democrat. Club: Lake Quivira Country (Kansas City). General corporate, State civil litigation, Local government. Home: 5341 Canterbury St Fairway KS 66205 Office: Dietrich Davis Dicus Rowlands Schmitt & Gorman 1100 Main St 1700 City Center Sq Kansas City MO 64105

SANDS, JON F(REDERICK), lawyer; b. Denver, Mar. 6, 1954; s. LeRoy Leon and Annabelle Mae (Lebsock) S.; m. Sheri Marie Buffington, Dec. 21, 1985. BS in Journalism, U. Colo., 1976, JD, 1980. Bar: Colo. 1980, U.S. Dist. Ct. Denver 1980. Assoc. Heyl, Bostrom and Musyl, Denver, 1980-81; assoc. Haligman, Zall and Lottner, Denver, 1981-86, ptnr., 1986—. Bd. dirs. Denver Dumb Friends League, 1986. Mem. Colo. Bar Assn., Denver Bar Assn., Assn. Trial Lawyers Am., Colo. Trial Lawyers Assn. Avocations: cross-country skiing, wilderness exploration. Federal civil litigation, State civil litigation, Construction. Office: Haligman All and Lottner 7887 E Belleview Englewood CO 80111

SANDS, JUDITH DAVIES, lawyer; b. Ely, Eng., May 5, 1939; came to U.S., 1953; s. Hugh Sykes Davies and Joyce Cynthia (Hume) Raymo; m. Robert James, Dec. 27, 1979. BA, Radcliffe Coll., 1959; LLD, Columbia U., 1962; LLM, NYU, 1973. Bar: N.Y. 1963. Legal officer Chem. Bank, N.Y.C., 1964-69; atty. CBS, Inc., N.Y.C., 1969-72; assoc. Shearman & Sterling, N.Y.C., 1972-73; sr. atty. Bristol-Myers Co., N.Y.C., 1973-76, Pfizer Inc., N.Y.C., 1976-79; atty. Am. Home Products Corp., N.Y.C., 1980—. Private international, Contracts commercial, Health. Home: 20 E 9th St New York NY 10003 Office: Am Home Products Corp 685 3d Ave New York NY 10017-4049

SANDSTROM, DALE VERNON, commissioner; b. Grand Forks, N.D., Mar. 9, 1950; s. Ellis Vernon and Hilde Geneva (Williams) S. BA, N.D. State U., 1972; JD, U. N.D., 1975. Bar: N.D. 1975, U.S. Dist. Ct. N.D. 1975, U.S. Ct. Appeals (8th cir.) 1976. Asst. atty. gen., chief consumer fraud and antitrust div. State of N.D., Bismarck, 1975-81, securities commr., 1981-83, pub. service commr., 1983—; mem. Gov.'s com. on Security and Privacy, Bismarck, 1975-76, Gov.'s com. on Refugees, Bismarck, 1976; chmn. Gov.'s com. on Comml. Air Transp., Bismarck, 1983-84. Mem. platform com. N.D. Reps., 1972, 76, exec. com. 1972-73, 1982—, dist. chmn. 1981-82; rep. candidate for State of N.D. Pub. Service Commn., 1984. Mem. ABA, N.D. Bar Assn., Burleigh County Bar Assn., Nat. Assn. Regulatory Utility Commrs. (energy conservation com.), N.A. Assn. Securities Adminstrs., Order of De Molay (Legion of Honor award). Lutheran. Lodges: Shriners, Elks, Masons (chmn. grand youth com. 1979—, Youth Leadership award 1986). Administrative and regulatory, Public utilities, FERC practice. Home: 310 W Reno Ave Bismarck ND 58501 Office: Pub Service Commn State Capitol Bismarck ND 58505

SANDWEG, WILLIAM HENRY, III, lawyer; b. Houston, July 3, 1944; s. William Henry Jr. and Rose Marie (Jackson) S.; m. Jean Hine, Aug. 8, 1970; children: William, John, Kathryn, Anne. BS in Fgn. Service, Georgetown U., 1966; JD, Ariz. State U., 1974. Bar: Ariz. 1974, U.S. Dist. Ct. Ariz. 1974, U.S. Ct. Appeals (9th cir.) 1981. Assoc. Evans & Kunz Ltd., Phoenix, 1974-75, Robbins & Green, P.A., Phoenix, 1975—; judge pro tem Maricopa County (Ariz.) Superior Ct., 1985—. Editor sr. comment Ariz. State Law Jour., 1973-74. Served to capt. USAF, 1966-71. Mem. Am. Bd. Trial Advocates (assoc.), Phoenix Assn. Def. Counsel (bd. dirs. 1975—, treas. 1986—). Democrat. Roman Catholic. Personal injury, Insurance, State civil litigation. Home: 2211 E North Ln Phoenix AZ 85028 Office: Robbins & Green PA 3300 N Central Ave Suite 1800 Phoenix AZ 85012

SANETTI, STEPHEN LOUIS, lawyer; b. Flushing, N.Y., June 25, 1949; s. Alfred Julius Sanetti and Yolanda Marie (DiGioia) Boyes; m. Carole Leighton Koller, Sept. 21, 1974; children—Christopher Edward, Dana Harrison. B.A. in History with honors, Va. Mil. Inst., 1971; J.D., Washington and Lee U., 1974. Bar: Conn. 1975, U.S. Ct. Mil. Appeals 1975, U.S. Dist. Ct. Conn. 1978, U.S. Ct. Appeals (2d cir.) 1979, U.S. Supreme Ct. 1980. Litigation atty. Marsh, Day & Calhoun, Bridgeport, Conn., 1978-80; gen. counsel Sturm, Ruger & Co., Southport, Conn., 1980—; Served to capt., chief criminal law 1st Cavalry Div. Staff Judge Advocate, U.S. Army, 1975-78. Mem. ABA (litigation sect.), Def. Research Inst. (dir. product liability adv. council), Conn. Bar Assn., Phi Delta Phi. Republican. Roman Catholic. General corporate, Federal civil litigation, Product liability. Office: Sturm Ruger and Co Inc 1 Lacey Pl Southport CT 06490

SANFORD, KENDALL THAINE, lawyer; b. Joplin, Mo., May 18, 1943; s. Thaine F. and Maxine T. (Chase) S.; m. Norma Jeanne Catlett, Oct. 16, 1964; children: John, James (twins), Jeffrey, Jeremy. Student, Stanford U., 1961-64; BA, U. Denver, 1970, JD, 1974. Bar: Colo. 1974, U.S. Dist. Ct. Colo. 1974, U.S. Ct. Appeals (10th cir.) 1974, U.S. Supreme Ct. 1978, U.S. Ct. Appeals (D.C. cir.) 1981. Assoc. Holland & Hart, Denver, 1974-77; atty. Denver & Rio Grande Western R.R. Co., Denver, 1977-78, asst. gen. atty., 1978-79, gen. atty., 1979-84, commerce counsel, 1984—. Mem. Colo. R.R. Assn. (chmn. 1983—), Order of St. Ives, Denver Bulldog Club (pres. 1985—). Avocations: raising and showing bulldogs. Administrative and regulatory, Antitrust, Transportation. Home: 3175 S Xanthia Denver CO 80231 Office: Denver & Rio Grande Western RR Co Box 5482 Denver CO 80217

SANG, PETER BENNETT, lawyer; b. N.Y.C., July 28, 1941; m. Barbara Jean Cargo, Aug. 23, 1983. BA in Econs., Bucknell U., 1962; LLB, Boston U., 1965, LLM in Taxation, 1967. Bar: Mass. 1965, U.S. Ct. Claims 1970, U.S. Tax Ct. 1970, Maine 1971. Tax acct. Coopers & Lybrand, Boston, 1965-68; assoc. Gadsby & Hannah, Boston, 1968-71; sole practice Portland, Maine, 1971—; bd. dirs. Harris Baking Co., Waterville, Maine. Commr. Maine Lottery, Augusta, 1973-77. Mem. Maine Bar Assn. (chmn. IRS tax liaison com. 1984—). Personal income taxation, Corporate taxation, Estate taxation. Office: 95 Exchange St Portland ME 04101

SANGALIS, GREGORY THEODORE, lawyer; b. Bloomington, Ind., Sept. 8, 1955; s. Nicholas Theodore and Evelyn Jean (Halas) S.; m. Jane Elizabeth Ahlbrand, Sept. 2, 1978; children: Theodore Russell, Anna Jane. Student, St. Cloud State U., 1973-74; BS in Bus., Ind. U., 1977; MBA, U. Minn., 1981, JD, 1980. Bar: Minn. 1980, U.S. Dist. Ct. Minn. 1980. Assoc. Wiese & Cox Ltd., Mpls., 1981-84; gen. counsel Peavey Co., Mpls., 1984-86; assoc. gen. counsel Waste Mgmt. Inc., Oak Brook, Ill., 1986—. Mem. ABA, Minn. Bar Assn., Hennepin County Bar Assn., Beta Gamma Sigma. Republican. Methodist. Avocations: golf, tennis, racquetball. General corporate.

SANGER, HERBERT SHELTON, JR., lawyer, former government official; b. Oak Hill, W.Va., Aug. 6, 1936; s. Herbert Shelton and Ethel Dean (Layne) S.; m. Rita Adele Baumgartner, Aug. 20, 1958; children: Charles, Carole, Warren, George. A.B. in English and Polit. Sci, Concord Coll., Athens, W.Va., 1958; LL.B., W.Va. U., Morgantown, 1961. Bar: W.Va. 1961, U.S. Supreme Ct. 1976, U.S. Ct. Appeals 5th and 6th cirs. 1973, 10th cir. 1978, 11th cir. 1981, 4th cir. 1982. Lifetime del. 6th Cir. Jud. Conf.; staff atty. Office of Gen. Counsel, TVA, Knoxville, 1961-69; asst. gen. counsel power Office of Gen. Counsel, TVA, 1969-72, assoc. gen. counsel litigation and power, 1972-73, dep. gen. counsel, 1973-75, gen. counsel, 1975-86; ptnr. Wagner, Myers & Sanger, P.C., Knoxville, 1986—; asst. prof. law U. Tenn.; Arthur B. Hodges prof. law W.Va. U.; chmn. bd. dirs. TVA Retirement System, 1975-86; bd. dirs. Paribas Concorde Trust, Ltd. Recipient Lawyers Coop award, 1961, Lawyers Title Ins. Co. award, 1961. Mem. ABA, Fed. Bar Assn., W.Va. Bar Assn., Am. Corp. Counsel Assn. (bd. dirs.), Internat. Nuclear Law Assn. Baptist. General corporate, Federal civil litigation, Government contracts and claims. Home: 5100 Malibu Dr Knoxville TN 37918 Office: 1801 Plaza Tower PO Box 1308 Knoxville TN 37901-1308

SANGER, SCOTT HOWARD, lawyer; b. Chgo., Nov. 8, 1948; s. Alvin Beryl and Elaine June (Elman) S.; m. Betty Jane Gordon, June 27, 1971; children—Aaron Lee, Abby Gordon. B.A., Tulane, U., 1970; J.D., Northwestern U., 1973. Bar: Ill. 1973, N.Mex. 1980, U.S. Dist. Ct. (no. dist.) Ill. 1973. Assoc. Altman, Kurlander & Weiss, Chgo., 1973-75; assoc. Newman, Stahl & Shadur, Chgo., 1975-80; sole practice, Taos, N.Mex., 1980—; gen. ptnr. Taos Inn Assocs., Taos, 1981—. Mem. Taos Hist. Commn., 1983—. Mem. Chgo. Bar Assn., Ill. Bar Assn., ABA, N.Mex. Bar Assn. Real property, Contracts commercial, Probate.

SANNA, RICHARD JEFFREY, lawyer; b. N.Y.C., July 20, 1949; s. Francis and Ann (Bryant) S.; m. Rosemarie A. Lagnena, Nov. 21, 1971;

children: John, Kristen, Michele, Elisabeth, Kelly. BA, St. Johns U., Jamaica, N.Y., 1971; JD, Del. Law Sch., 1975. Bar: N.Y. 1977, U.S. Dist. Ct. (so. dist.) N.Y. 1978, U.S. Dist. Ct. (ea. dist.) N.Y. 1979, U.S. Ct. Appeals (2d cir.) 1979, U.S. Supreme Ct. 1980. Assoc. McKay, King, Castricone & Piazza, Queens, N.Y., 1978-80; sr. ptnr. Sarisohn, Sarisohn, Thierman, Carner & LeBow, Commack, N.Y., 1980-82; ptnr. Migliore, Sanna & Infranco P.C., Commack, 1982-85; sole practice Hauppauge, N.Y., 1985-86, Commack, 1986—. Cubmaster Cub Scouts Am., Bethpage, 1982-84; mem. adv. council St. Martins of Tours Ch., Bethpage, N.Y., 1983—; atty. Bethpage Civic Assn., 1985—. Mem. N.Y. State Bar Assn., Suffolk County Bar Assn. (chmn. fee dispute com. 1984-86), Assn. Trial Lawyers Am., N.Y. Trial Lawyers Assn., Columbian Lawyers Assn. Republican. Roman Catholic. Lodge: K.C. Real property, Personal injury, General practice. Home: 91 Sycamore Ave Bethpage NY 11714 Office: 320 Verterans Memorial Hwy Commack NY 11725

SANNER, ROYCE NORMAN, corporation executive; b. Lancaster, Minn., Mar. 9, 1931; s. Oscar N. and Clara (Hermanson) S.; m. Janice L. Sterne, Dec. 27, 1972; children—Michelle Joy, Craig Allen. B.S., Moorhead State Coll., 1953; LL.B. cum laude, U. Minn., 1961. Tchr. English Karlstad (Minn.) High Sch., 1955-57; counsel IDS Life Ins. Co., Mpls., 1961-68; v.p., gen. counsel IDS Life Ins. Co., 1969-72, exec. v.p., gen. counsel, 1972-77; dir. corporate devel. Investors Diversified Services, Inc., Mpls., 1968-69; v.p., gen. counsel Investors Diversified Services, Inc., 1975-78; v.p. Investors Diversified Services, Inc. (Benefit Plans Service Group), 1978-80, v.p., gen. counsel, 1980-82; v.p. law Northwestern Nat. Life Ins. Co., 1982-83, sr. v.p., gen. counsel, sec., 1983—. Mem. Citizens League; trustee Fairview Hosp., bd. dirs. Midwest Corp. Counsel Ctr. Served with arty. U.S. Army, 1953-55. Mem. Am., Minn., Hennepin County, Fed. bar assns., Assn. Life Ins. Counsel, Corp. Counsel Assn. Minn. (bd. dirs.), Minn. C.of C. and Industry (bd. dirs.). Club: Mpls., Mpls. Rotary. General corporate, Insurance, Securities. Office: 20 Washington Ave S Minneapolis MN 55440

SANSEVERINO, RAYMOND ANTHONY, lawyer; b. Bklyn., Feb. 16, 1947; s. Raphael and Alice Ann (Camerano) S.; m. Karen Marie Mooney, Aug. 24, 1968 (dec. 1980); children—Deirdre Ann, Stacy Lee; m. Victoria Vent, June 6, 1982. A.B. in English Lit., Franklin & Marshall Coll., 1968; J.D. cum laude, Fordham U., 1972. Bar: N.Y. 1973, U.S. Dist. Ct. (so. dist. and ea. dist.) N.Y. 1973, U.S. Ct. Appeals (2d cir.) 1974, U.S. Supreme Ct. 1986. Assoc. Rogers & Wells, N.Y.C., 1972-75, Corbin & Gordon, N.Y.C., 1975-77; ptnr. Corbin Silverman & Sanseverino, N.Y.C., 1978—. Contbr. articles to profl. jours. Articles editor Fordham Law Review, 1971-72. Recipient West Pub. Co. prize, 1972. Mem. ABA, Assn. of Bar of City of N.Y., N.Y. State Bar Assn. Republican. Roman Catholic. Clubs: Twin Oaks Swim and Tennis (Chappaqua, N.Y.) (bd. dirs. 1981—). Real property, Landlord-tenant. Office: Corbin Silverman & Sanseverino 805 3d Ave New York NY 10022

SANSON, BARBARA ELIZABETH, lawyer; b. Wiesbaben, Fed. Republic of Germany, Jan. 25, 1955; came to U.S., 1973; d. Allan David and Gertrude Maria (Trendl) S. Student, U. London, 1975-76; AB, Bryn Mawr Coll., 1977; JD, Dickinson Sch. Law, 1980. Bar: Pa. 1980, U.S. Dist. Ct. (ea. dist.) Pa. 1981. Law clk. Lehigh County Ct., Allentown, Pa., 1980-82; assoc. Duane Morris & Heckscher, Phila., 1982-84; atty. ICI Americas Inc., Wilmington, Del., 1984—. Mem. ABA, Pa. Bar Assn., Phila. Bar Assn. Avocation: ice skating. General corporate, Antitrust. Home: 1510 Naudain St Philadelphia PA 19146 Office: ICI Americas Inc Concord Pike & New Murphy Rd Wilmington DE 19897

SANT, JOHN TALBOT, lawyer; b. Ann Arbor, Mich., Oct. 7, 1932; s. John Francis and Josephine (Williams) S.; m. Almira Baldwin, Jan. 31, 1959; children—John Talbot, Richard Baldwin, Frank Williams. A.B., Princeton U., 1954; LL.B., Harvard U., 1957. Bar: Mo. 1957. Assoc. Thompson, Mitchell, Douglas & Neill, St. Louis, 1958-60; with McDonnell Douglas Corp., St. Louis, 1960—, sec., 1962-69, sec., asst. gen. counsel, 1969-75, corp. v.p., gen. counsel, 1975—. Mem. St. Louis Bar Assn., Mo. Bar Assn., ABA. Club: St. Louis Country. General corporate. Home: 9 Ridgewood Rd Saint Louis MO 63124 Office: McDonnell Douglas Corp Dept H008 PO Box 516 Saint Louis MO 63166

SANTA MARIA, PHILIP JOSEPH, III, lawyer; b. Ft. Lauderdale, Fla., Oct. 10, 1945; s. Philip Joseph Jr. and Margaret Elizabeth (Hillard) S.; m. Gail Suzanne Claussen, Aug. 23, 1969; children: Todd, Carly. AB, Gettysburg (Pa.) Coll., 1967; JD, Am. U., 1970. Bar: Md. 1970, U.S. Ct. Mil. Appeals 1971, U.S. Supreme Ct. 1975, D.C. 1976, Calif. 1976, U.S. Dist. Ct. Md. 1977, U.S. Ct. Appeals (4th cir.) 1977. Assoc. Simpson & Simpson, Rockville, Md., 1974-75; sole practice Gaithersburg, Md., 1975-79; ptnr. Haight, Rosfeld, Noble & Santa Maria, Gaithersburg, 1980-81, Santa Maria & Greenberg, Gaithersburg, 1981—. Mem. editorial bd. Am. U. Law Rev., 1969; author pamphlet What To Do. Mem. Standby Selective Service Local Bd. 69, Montgomery County, Md., 1981-83, Standby Selective Service Bd. of Appeals, Md., 1983—. Served to capt. USAF, 1970-74. Named one of Outstanding Young Men in Am., 1971. Mem. ABA, Calif. Bar Assn., D.C. Bar Assn., Montgomery County Bar Assn., Md. Trial Lawyers Assn. Clubs: Montgomery Soccer, Inc. (league commr. 1985); Gaithersburg Tennis Assn. (pres. 1976); Snowbird Youth Ski (Md.) (pres. 1975-76). Personal injury, State civil litigation, Family and matrimonial. Home: 19001 S Pike Creek Place Gaithersburg MD 20879 Office: Santa Maria & Greenberg Six Montgomery Village Ave Suite 330 Gaithersburg MD 20879

SANTANDREA, MARY FRANCES, lawyer; b. Melrose Park, Ill., Apr. 14, 1952; d. Francis Paul and Agnes Rose (Franch) S. B.A. (James scholar), U. Ill.-Urbana, 1974, M.A., 1976; J.D. cum laude, Santa Barbara Coll. Law, 1982. Bar: Calif. 1982, U.S. Dist. Ct. (cen. dist.) Calif. 1982, U.S. Ct. Appeals (9th cir.) 1982. Legal researcher Cavalletto, Webster, Mullen & McCaughey, Santa Barbara, Calif., 1979-80; legal researcher M.J. Treman, Santa Barbara, 1980-81; legal researcher Bargiel & Carlson, Santa Barbara, 1981-82; research atty. Halde, Thomas, Kallman & Hulse, Santa Barbara, 1982-83; litigation atty. Anderson & Geller, Santa Ana, Calif., 1983-85, Ambrosi & Lavoie 1985-86, Smith & Smith, Costa Mesa, Calif., 1986—. Mem. ABA, Calif. Bar Assn., Los Angeles County Bar Assn., Orange County Bar Assn. Democrat. Roman Catholic. Banking, Consumer commercial, State civil litigation. Office: Smith & Smith 888 S Figueroa St Los Angeles CA 90017

SANTANGELO, BETTY J., lawyer; b. N.Y.C., Sept. 5, 1950; d. Alfred E. and Betty L. Santangelo; m. Thomas Egan, Oct. 11, 1981. BA, Trinity Coll., 1971; JD, Fordham U., 1974. Bar: N.Y. 1975, Fla. 1975, U.S. Dist. Ct. (so. and ea. dists.) N.Y. 1975, U.S. Ct. Appeals (2d cir.) 1975. Assoc. Martin, Obermaier & Morvillo, N.Y.C., 1974-76; law clk. to presiding justice U.S. Dist. Ct. (so. dist.) N.Y., N.Y.C., 1976-77; asst. U.S. atty. So. Dist. N.Y., N.Y.C., 1977-83; asst. gen. counsel Merrill Lynch, Pierce, Fenner & Smith, N.Y.C., 1983—; adj. prof. law Fordham U., N.Y.C., 1982-84. Mem: N.Y. State Bar Assn., N.Y. Women's Bar Assn., Assn. of Bar of City of New York. Criminal, Securities. Office: Merrill Lynch 165 Broadway New York NY 10080

SANTANIELLO, ANGELO GARY, judge; b. New London, Conn., May 28, 1924; s. Samuel C. and Katie Santaniello; m. Catherine A. Driscoll, June 1948 (dec.); children—Samuel Gary, Lisa Mary; m. Catherine M. Cooper, Sept. 27, 1968; 1 child, Maria Roberta. B.A., Coll. Holy Cross, 1945; JD, Georgetown U., 1950. Bar: Conn. 1950, U.S. Dist. Ct. Conn. Sole practice, New London, 1950-65; judge Conn. Cir. Ct., 1966-71, Conn. Ct. Common Pleas, 1971-73; judge Conn. Superior Ct., 1973-85, adminstrv. judge, 1978-85, chief adminstrv. judge, 1979-85; now justice Conn. Supreme Ct., Hartford; asst. prosecuting atty. New London Police Ct., 1951-55. Trustee, New London Pub. Library, Mitchell Coll., Lawrence and Meml. Hosp.; bd. dirs. Holy Cross Alumni, Am. Cancer Soc., New London Fed. Savs. and Loan; chmn. New London Republican Party, 1956-65; nat. committeeman Conn. State Young Reps., 1959-61; legal counsel Conn. State Senate Rep. Minority, 1961-65; campaign mgr. to gubernatorial candidate, 1962; mem. athletic council Holy Cross Coll., 1971-77; vice chmn. bd. of trustees Mitchell Coll., 1976-86. Served to lt. (j.g.) USNR, 1942-46. Recipient Columbus award Italian-Am. Civic Assn., 1964; In Hoc Signo award Holy Cross Coll., 1976; 1st Humanitarian award Eastern Conn. chpt. March of Dimes, 1983. Mem. Am. Justinian Soc., New London Bar Assn., Conn. Bar Assn. Office: Supreme Ct Drawer N Sta A Hartford CT 06106

SANTEMMA, JON NOEL, lawyer; b. Oceanside, N.Y., Dec. 24, 1937; s. Esterino E. and Emilie E. (Davis) S.; m. Lynne Maurer, Dec. 27, 1960; children—Suzanne, Deborah, Jon E., Christopher Jon. B.A., Cornell U., 1960; J.D., Fordham U., 1963. Bar: N.Y. 1963, U.S. Ct. Mil. Appeals 1969, U.S. Ct. Claims 1969, U.S. Supreme Ct. 1969, U.S. Dist. Ct. (ea. dist.) N.Y. 1977. Assoc. Parnell Callahan, N.Y.C., 1963-64; assoc. Warburton, Hyman, Deeley & Connolly, Mineola, N.Y., 1964-66; law sec. to adminstrv. judge of Nassau County, Mineola, 1966-71; sole practice, Mineola, 1971-74; ptnr. Santemma & Murphy, P.C., Mineola, 1974—; lectr. in field. Trustee Inc. Village of Laurel Hollow (N.Y.), 1979—; mem. Nassau County Republican Law Com., 1979—. Recipient Outstanding Man of Yr. in Law award L.I. U., 1976. Mem. Am. Bar Found., N.Y. Bar Found., N.Y. State Bar Assn. (ho. of dels. 1980—, mem. exec. com. 1984—), Nassau County Bar Assn. (pres. 1979-80, pres.'s award for outstanding service 1981), N.Y. State Trial Lawyers Assn., Suffolk County Bar Assn., Assn. Bar City N.Y. Clubs: Huntington Country, Winter, Elks (Huntington); Cold Spring Harbor (N.Y.) Beach; Garden City Golf. Contbr. articles to profl. jours. Condemnation, State and local taxation, Federal practice. Address: 170 Old Country Rd Mineola NY 11501

SANTINI, GEORGE, lawyer; b. Cheyenne, Wyo., Oct. 19, 1955; s. Bruno and Margherita (Simeoni) S. BS, U. Wyo., 1978, JD, 1981. Bar: Wyo. 1981, U.S. Dist. Ct. Wyo. 1981, U.S. Ct. Appeals (9th cir.) 1984, U.S. Ct. Appeals (10th cir.) 1985. Law clk. Wyo. Supreme Ct., Cheyenne, 1981-84; assoc. Charles E. Graves & Assocs., Cheyenne, 1984—. Sr. editor Land and Water Law Rev., 1980-81. Thurman Arnold Meml. scholar U. Wyo., 1978-81. Phi Beta Kappa. Democrat. Roman Catholic. Federal civil litigation, State civil litigation, Personal injury. Home: 3302 Frontier #204 Cheyenne WY 82001 Office: Charles E Graves & Assocs 408 W 23rd St Cheyenne WY 82001

SANTIRE, STANLEY PAUL, lawyer; b. Houston, Oct. 21, 1943; s. Paul Sam and Beulah Marie (Fress) S.; m. Helen Athena Garabedian, June 25, 1967; children—Heather Santire. B.B.A., U. Houston, 1966; J.D., U. Tex-Austin, 1972; postgrad. Hague Acad. Internat. Law (Netherlands), 1979, Columbia U., 1979. Bar: Tex. 1972, D.C. 1979. Ptnr. firm Phipps, Smith & Herz, Galveston, Tex., 1972-77; pres. S & S Venture Co., Galveston, 1976-79; chmn. Proto Tex., Houston, 1978—; legal counsel Lockheed Internat., Geneva, Switzerland, 1979-82; pres. Stanley Santire, P.C., Houston, 1982—; exec. v.p. Envex Corp., Houston, 1984—; cons. Mawarid Investments, London, 1980-82, Saudi Arabian Devel. Co., 1981-82; lectr. Internat. Trade Adminstrn., 1983. Contbr. articles to profl. jours. Chmn. Polit. Action Com., Galveston, 1975-77. Served to lt. USN, 1966-69. Named Outstanding Exec., Lockheed Corp., 1980-82. Environment, Private international. Office: Stanley Santire PC PO Box 42539 Houston TX 77042

SANTOLI, JOSEPH RALPH, lawyer; b. Hackensack, N.J., Mar. 14, 1957; s. Joseph Anthony and Concettina (Fontana)S.; m. Margaret Cyrilla Lamie, Oct. 3, 1982. AB cum laude, Rutgers U., 1979, JD, 1982. Bar: N.J. 1982, U.S. Dist. Ct. N.J. 1982, U.S. Ct. Appeals (3d cir.) 1986, U.S. Supreme Ct. 1986. Law clk. to presiding justice chancery div., matrimonial N.J. State Superior Ct. of Bergen County, Hackensack, 1982-83; ptnr. Ferro & Ferro, Ridgewood, N.J., 1983-86, Santoli and Larsen, Ridgewood, N.J., 1986—; lectr. Bergen County Bar Assn., Hackensack, 1985—, Paramus (N.J.) sch. system, 1985—, Waldwick (N.J.) and Midland Pk. (N.J.) sch. systems, 1986—. Mem. ABA, N.J. State Bar Assn., Bergen County Bar Assn. (civil litigation com.), Assn. Trial Lawyers Am. Avocations: antiques, languages. Personal injury, State civil litigation, Federal civil litigation. Home: 435 Fairfield Ave Ridgewood NJ 07450 Office: Santoli and Larsen 615 Franklin Turnpike Ridgewood NJ 07450

SANTONA, GLORIA, lawyer; b. Gary, Ind., June 10, 1950; d. Ray and Elvira (Cambeses) S.; m. Douglas Lee Frazier, Apr. 12, 1980. BS in Biochemistry, Mich. State U., 1971; JD, U. Mich., 1977. Bar: Ill. 1977. Atty. McDonald's Corp., Oak Brook, Ill., 1977-82, dir. staff, 1982-86, dir. home office, 1986—, sr. corp. atty., 1982—. Mem. ABA, Ill. Bar Assn., Chgo. Bar Assn., Am. Corp. Counsel Assn. General corporate, Securities, Financial law. Office: McDonalds Corp 1 McDonald Plaza Oak Brook IL 60521

SANTOPIETRO, ALBERT ROBERT, lawyer; b. Providence, R.I., Oct. 18, 1948; s. Alfred and Marie (Epifanio) S.; m. Linda Williams Standridge, Nov. 22, 1974; children: Hope, Spencer, Anna. BA, Brown U., 1969; JD, U. Va., 1972. Bar: R.I. 1973, U.S. Dist. Ct. R.I. 1973, Ill. 1974, Conn. 1983. Atty. Met. Life Ins. Co., Oak Brook, Ill., 1974-75, Seligman Group, N.Y.C., 1975-76; atty. Mut. Benefit Life Ins. Co., Newark, 1976-78, asst. counsel, 1978-81; atty. Aetna Life and Casualty, Hartford, Conn., 1981-82, counsel, 1982—. Mem. Am. Corp. Counsel Assn., ABA, Conn. Bar Assn. Real property, General corporate, Contracts commercial. Home: Talcott Forest Rd Farmington CT 06032 Office: Aetna Life and Casualty City Place Hartford CT 06156

SANTORO, MICHAEL ANTHONY, lawyer; b. Montreal, Que., Can., Dec. 10, 1954; came to U.S., 1958; s. Gaetano Orazio and Maria (Tati) S. AB, Oberlin Coll., 1976; JD, NYU, 1981. Bar: N.Y. 1982. Assoc. Webster & Sheffield, N.Y.C., 1981-85; gen. counsel BioTechnica Internat. Inc., Cambridge, Mass., 1985-87, Finevest Services, Inc., Greenwich, Conn., 1987—; panelist, mem. forum on minority hiring in legal profession NYU Law Sch., 1983-84. Mem. Phi Beta Kappa. General corporate, Contracts commercial, Administrative and regulatory. Home: 39 Connecticut Ave Greenwich CT 06830 Office: Finevest Services Inc 191 Mason St Greenwich CT 06830

SANTUCCI, JOHN J., district attorney; b. N.Y.C., Apr. 2, 1931; m. Edna Ann Hayes, 1954; children—Mary Santucci Scantlebury, Thomas, John, Carol, Robert, Edna. LL.B., St. John's U. Bar: N.Y. 1953, U.S. Supreme Ct. 1968. Asst. dist. atty. Queens County, N.Y., 1958-64, dist. atty., 1977—; mem. N.Y.C. Council, 1964-68, N.Y. State Senate, 1968-76. Bd. dirs. Boy Scouts Am.; legis. advisor Muscular Dystrophy Assn.; trustee Soc. for Prevention Cruelty to Children; hon. dir. Multiple Sclerosis Soc., trustee Jamaica Hosp.; bd. dirs. Friends of Iris Hill Nursery Sch.; mem. 1st N.Y. State Gov.'s Law Enforcement Forum. Recipient numerous awards for pub. service, including: Mayor's Activist award, Prime Minister's medal State of Israel, Disting. Service award Cath. War Vets., Queens County Bar Assn. plaque, Nat. Orgn. for Victims' Assistance award. Mem. New York State Dist. Attys.' Assn. (exec. com.), Nat. Dist Attys.' Assn., Queens County Bar Assn., ABA, N.Y. State Bar Assn. Criminal, Federal civil litigation, State civil litigation. Office: Dist Atty 125-01 Queens Blvd Kew Gardens NY 11415

SAPIR, MICHAEL LYNN, lawyer; b. Miami, Fla., May 19, 1958; s. Leon and Florence (Douglas) S. BA, U. Miami, 1978, MBA, 1981; JD, Georgetown U., 1982. Bar: Fla. 1982, D.C. 1983. Assoc. Jorden, Melrose & Schuette, Miami, 1982-84, Finley, Kumble, Wagner, Heine, Underberg, Manley, Myerson & Casey, Washington, 1984—. Recipient Disting. Service award Dade County Bar Assn., 1984. Mem. ABA (corp., banking and bus. law sect., individual and human rights sect.). General corporate, Securities, Insurance. Office: Finley Kumble Wagner et al 1120 Connecticut Ave NW Washington DC 20036

SAPP, ERNESTINE S., lawyer; b. Huntsville, Tex., Jan. 31, 1941; d. Ernest Stubblefield and Ira Lee (Vaughn) Thomas; m. Walter James Sapp, Aug. 18, 1962; children: Van Benedict, Erik Martin, Elizabeth Ann. BS, Wiley Coll., 1962; student, U. Del. Cultural Exchange Seminar, 1971; JD, Jones Law Inst., 1976; postgrad., U. Ala., others, 1977—. Affirmative action officer Tuskegee (Ala.) Inst., 1975-77; staff atty. legal service div. U. Ala., Montgomery, 1977, Gray, Seay and Langford, Montgomery and Tuskegee, 1977-83; ptnr. Gray, Langford, Sapp, Davis and McGowan, Montgomery and Tuskegee, 1983—; mem. Rules Adv. Com. on Juvenile Procedures, 1985-87. Mng. editor Tuskegee Progressive Times Ala. Press Assn. (Best Thing We've Done All Year award 1971). Mem. comparative law delegation People to People Internat., People's Republic of China, 1986; vol. chmn. ARC of Macon County, Tuskegee, 1969-73; candidate Ala. House of Reps. Dist. 67, Bullock and Macon Counties, 1978; women's coordinator Ala. Dem. Conf., 1983—, mem. rules com. 1984. Mem. ABA, Ala. Bar Assn., Ala. State Bar Assn. (trustee lawyer reference bd. 1984-85), Ala. Trial Lawyers Assn. (bd. govs.), Nat. Bar Assn. (sect. chmn. 1984-86, bd. govs., Outstanding Law Sect. award 1985), Nat. Bar Assn. (chmn. civil rights sect. 1984—), AAUW (legal adv. fund advisory com. 1984—), Iota Phi Lambda, Delta Sigma Theta. Democrat. Roman Catholic. Clubs: Links, Inc. (v.p. 1985-87), 100 Black Women (bd. dirs. 1983—) (Tuskegee). Federal civil litigation, Family and matrimonial, Tort. Home: 908 Neal St Tuskegee Institute tuskegee AL 36088 Office: Gray Langford Sapp Davis and McGowan PO Box 239 Tuskegee AL 36083

SAPP, WALTER WILLIAM, lawyer, energy company executive; b. Linton, Ind., Apr. 21, 1930; s. Walter J. and Nona (Stalcup) S.; m. Eva Kaschner, July 10, 1957; children: Karen Elisabeth, Christoph Walter. A.B. magna cum laude, Harvard, 1951; J.D. summa cum laude, Ind. U., 1957. Bar: Ind. 1957, N.Y. 1959, Colo. 1966, U.S. Supreme Ct. 1972, Tex. 1977. Practice in N.Y.C., 1957-60, Paris, France, 1960-63, Colorado Springs, 1966-76; assoc. atty. Cahill, Gordon, Reindel & Ohl, N.Y.C., 1957-60, Paris, 1960-63, N.Y.C., 1963-65; partner Cahill, Gordon, Reindel & Ohl, 1966; gen. counsel Colo. Interstate Corp., 1966-76, v.p., 1968-76, sec., 1971-76, sr. v.p., dir., exec. com., 1973-75, exec. v.p., 1975-76; v.p. Coastal States Gas Corp., 1973-76; sr. v.p., gen. counsel Tenneco, Inc., Houston, 1976—, sec., 1984-86; Editor-in-chief Ind. U. Law Jour., 1956-57. Trustee Houston Ballet, 1982-85; bd. dirs. Harris County Met. Transit Authority, 1982-84. Served to lt. USNR, 1951-54. Mem. ABA, N.Y. State Bar Assn., Tex. Bar Assn., Assn. Bar City N.Y., Order of Coif. Mem. United Ch. of Christ. Clubs: Coronado, Houston Racquet. General corporate, Private international, Securities. Office: Tenneco Bldg PO Box 2511 Houston TX 77001

SARABIA, ANTONIO ROSAS, lawyer; b. Chihuahua, Mex., June 29, 1913; s. Rafael Rosas and Maria S.; children—Antonio Rosas II, Sean Rosas. B.S. in Chem. Engring., Ind. Tech. Coll., 1942; J.D., U. Chgo., 1949. Bar: Ill. 1950. Assoc. Baker, McKenzie & Hightower, Chgo., 1949-52, ptnr., 1952-62; sole practice, Chgo., 1962-64; sr. assoc. Lord, Bissell & Brook, Chgo., 1964-65, ptnr., 1966-83; faculty mem. Lawyers Inst. John Marshall Law Sch., Chgo., 1962-73. Mem. legis. com. Chgo. Crime Commn., 1971—; bd. dirs. Geographic Soc. of Chgo., 1970-78, 3d v.p., 1978—. Mem. ABA (internat. law sect. 1970—, council 1971-75, budget officer 1972-78), Inter-Am. (membership com.), Ill. State Bar Assn. (internat. law sect. chmn. 1965-66, council 1974-75), Chgo. Bar Assn. (charter flight com. 1961-82, internat. and fgn. law com. 1982—, internat. human rights 1978—, chmn. 1980—), Am. Fgn. Law Assn. (pres. Chgo. br. 1952-59), Am. Arbitration Assn., Mexican Am. Lawyers Assn. Clubs: Univ., Mid-Am. Contbr. articles to profl. jours. Contracts commercial, General corporate, Private international. Home: 175 E Delaware Pl Apt 7805 Chicago IL 60611 Office: 79 W Monroe St Suite 1320 Chicago IL 60603

SARACINO, SAMUEL FRANCIS, lawyer; b. Denver, May 7, 1951; s. Samuel and Therese Marie (Muto) S.; m. M. Victoria Ries, June 21, 1975; children: Daniel J., Martha E. Student, Lake Forest Coll., 1969-71; BA, Wesleyan U., 1973; JD, U. Chgo., 1977. Bar: Colo. 1978, U.S. Tax Ct. 1978, Wash. 1979, U.S. Dist Ct. (we. dist.) Wash. 1979. Lectr. U. Chgo. Law Sch., 1976-77; assoc. Davis, Graham & Stubbs, Denver, 1978-79, Davis, Wright, Todd, Riese & Jones, Seattle, 1979-83; ptnr. Davis, Wright & Jones, Seattle, 1984—. Bigelow Teaching fellow U. Chgo., 1976-77. Mem. ABA, Wash. Bar Assn., Seattle-King County Bar Assn. Corporate taxation, General corporate, State and local taxation. Office: Davis Wright & Jones 2600 Century Sq 1501 4th Ave Seattle WA 98101-1688

SARADJIAN, MARTIN LUTHER, lawyer, educator; b. Stamford, Conn., Apr. 20, 1936; s. Nerses and Zarouhi (Morjikian) S.; m. Margaret Eleanor Ludloff, Oct. 13, 1945; children—Peter, Matthew. A.B., U. Conn., 1958, M.A., 1960; J.D., New Eng. Sch. Law, 1964; cert. Lee Inst., 1964; postgrad. Henry George Sch. Econs., 1963-64. Bar: Mass. 1964, U.S. Supreme Ct. 1969. Assoc., Hayes & Creney, Hyannis, Mass., also counsel Bass River Savs. Bank, 1965-66; assoc. Simeone, Simeone & Tanzi, Walpole, Mass., 1967-69, Joseph Alekshun, Boston, 1967-72, Twohig, Rcade & Shimon, Boston, 1972-73; sole practice, Lexington, Mass., 1974—; asst. prof. law Bentley Coll., Waltham, Mass., 1973-77, assoc. prof., 1977—, chmn. library com.; student advisor Newbury Jr. Coll., 1970-74, dean of students, 1969-71, dir. placement, 1969-71, chmn. curriculum devel., 1972-74, chmn. acad. standards com., 1972-73; lectr. Babson Coll., Wellesley, Mass., 1972-73, Newbury Jr. Coll., Boston, 1967-68, Bay State Jr. Coll., Boston, Fed. Savs. and Loan Inst., 1970-74, Am. Inst. Banking, 1970-72; cons. ACLU, Harvard Law Sch., Small Bus. Mgmt. Program for Black Businessmen of Town of Brookline, SBA; notary pub.; gen. counsel Mass. Guidance Assn.; pre-law sch. advisor Ednl. Testing Service, Princeton, N.J., 1974—; guest lectr. chs., univs., law clubs; lectr. on environ. law New Eng. Environ. Conf. Tufts U., Medford, Mass.; participant seminars, panels in field; participant projects with city mgr. of Hartford, 1960-61. Asst. treas. Beacon Hill Friends House, Inc., Boston; mem. ACLU, Burn Inst., Boston; chmn. investment com. Pilgrim Congl. Ch., Lexington, 1984—. Mem. ABA, Mass. Bar Assn., Boston Bar Assn., Middlesex Bar Assn., Supreme Ct. Hist. Soc., Assn. Trial Lawyers Am., Mass. Assn. Trial Lawyers, North Atlantic Regional Bus. Law Assn. (dir., treas. 1970—), Eastern Bus. Tchrs. Assn., Mass. Assn. Conservation Commn., Nat. Wildlife Fedn., Conservation Law Found., Nature Conservancy, Nat. Hist. Preservation Trust, Farmland Trust, Conn. Fund for Environment, Conn. Conservation Commn., Kappa Delta Pi, Phi Sigma Alpha, Phi Alpha Theta, Phi Sigma Kappa. Clubs: Bentley Coll. Law (advisor), Bentley Coll. Armenian (advisor). Lodges: Masons, Shriners. Contbr. articles to real estate publs. Real property, Legal education, Environment. Home: 259 Bedford St Lexington MA 02173 Office: Bentley Coll Waltham MA 02254

SARAKIN, LLOYD BRADLEY, lawyer; b. N.Y.C., May 30, 1955; m. Leslie F. Leonard, Aug. 29, 1982; 1 child, David Lowell. BA, Lehigh U., 1977; JD, U. Miami, 1980. Bar: Fla. 1981, N.Y. 1982, N.J. 1985, U.S. Dist. Ct. (so. and ea. dists.) N.Y. 1982, U.S. Dist. Ct. (so. dist.) Fla.1981. Assoc. Ruben, Schwartz & Schnall, N.Y.C., 1980-84; counsel The Belcher Co. N.Y., Inc., Hasbrouck Heights, N.J., 1984—. Mem. ABA, N.J. State Bar Assn., Am. Corp. Counsel Assn. Contracts commercial. Office: The Belcher Co NY 611 Rt 46 W Hasbrouck Heights NJ 07604

SARB, THOMAS PATRICK, lawyer; b. Detroit, Oct. 14, 1951; s. Gerard Francis Sr. and Patricia Margaret (Hickey) S.; m. Ruth Ann Brevitz, May 26, 1979; children: Anna Katherine, Elizabeth Anne. AB, U. Notre Dame, 1973; JD, U. Mich., 1976. Bar: Mich., 1977, U.S. Dist. Ct. (we. dist.) Mich. 1977. Law clk. to chief judge U.S. Dist. Ct. (we. dist.), Grand Rapids, Mich., 1976-78; assoc. Miller, Johnson, Snell & Cummiskey, Grand Rapids, 1978-83, ptnr., 1983—; lectr. on bankruptcy matters Inst. for Continuing Legal Edn., Ann Arbor, Mich., 1985—, Nat. Bus. Inst., Eau Claire, Wis., 1986—. Dir. fin. St. Andrew's Cathedral, Grand Rapids, 1983—; bd. dirs. Urban Inst. Contemporary Arts, Grand Rapids, 1985—. Mem. ABA, Mich. Bar Assn., Grand Rapids Bar Assn. Bankruptcy, corporate reorganization, Contracts commercial. Office: Miller Johnson Snell & Cummiskey 800 Calder Plaza Bldg Grand Rapids MI 49506

SARGEANT, ROBERT WALTON, lawyer; b. Cleve., Sept. 1, 1957; s. Charles Robert and Charlotte Anne (Walton) S. BA, Macalester Coll., 1979; JD, Ind. U., 1982. Bar: Wash. 1982, U.S. Dist. Ct. (we. dist.) Wash. 1982, U.S. Ct. Appeals (9th cir.) 1982. Law clk. to presiding justice, bailiff King County Superior Ct., 1983-84; assoc. Law Office Eric L. Freise, Seattle, 1984—. Mem. ABA, Wash. State Bar Assn., Seattle-King County Bar Assn., Wash. Assn. Def. Counsel. Republican. Presbyterian. Avocations: skiing, tennis, cooking, soccer, fiction. Insurance, State civil litigation, Federal civil litigation. Office: Law Offices Eric L Freise 108 S Washington St Suite 400 Seattle WA 98104

SARGEANT, WILLIAM LESLIE, lawyer; b. Cleve., Sept. 15, 1944; s. William Walden and Edith (Lyne) S.; m. Susan Leslie Hadley, June 22, 1968; children: Kimberly Lyne, Victoria Jean, Julia Grace, William Hadley. BA, Kent State U., 1966; JD, Boston U., 1969. Bar: Ohio 1969, Calif. 1974, D.C. 1974, Va. 1986. Trial atty. USAF, Wright Patterson AFB, Ohio, 1969-73; assoc. Schramm, Raddue & Seed, Santa Barbara, Calif., 1973-75; chief counsel Gen. Research Corp., Santa Barbara, 1975-77, Flow Gen., Inc., McLean, Va., 1977-83; sec., gen. counsel Evaluation Research Corp., Vienna, Va., 1983-85; v.p., sec., gen. counsel ERC Internat. Inc., Vienna, 1985—.

Mem. ABA, Fed. Bar Assn., Am. Corp. Counsel's Assn., Am. Soc. Corp. Secs. Methodist. General corporate, Government contracts and claims, Private international. Office: ERC Internat Inc 3211 Jermantown Rd Fairfax VA 22030

SARGENTICH, LEWIS D., legal educator; b. 1944. A.B., Occidental Coll., 1965; B.A., U. Sussex, Eng., 1967; J.D., Harvard U., 1970. Bar: D.C. 1972. Law clk. to assoc. justice Thurgood Marshall, U.S. Supreme Ct., Washington, 1970-71; staff counsel Washington Residential Project, 1971-72; assoc. gen counsel, United Mine Workers, Washington, 1973-74; asst. prof. Harvard U., Cambridge, Mass., 1975-79, prof., 1979—. Legal education, Jurisprudence. Office: Harvard U Law Sch Cambridge MA 02138 *

SARGENTICH, THOMAS OLIVER, legal educator, researcher; b. Los Angeles, May 9, 1950; s. Daniel Milo and Margaret Amelia (Lientz) S.; m. Susan Hazard Farnsworth, Jan. 2, 1981. A.B. magna cum laude, Harvard U., 1972, J.D. cum laude, 1977; M.Phil. in Politics, Magdalen Coll., Oxford U., 1974. Bar: D.C. 1978, U.S. Supreme Ct. 1981. Law clk. to presiding judge U.S. Ct. Appeals, Phila., 1977-78; atty.-advisor Office of Legal Counsel, U.S. Dept. Justice, Washington, 1978-83; lectr. Am. U., Washington, 1981, assoc. prof. law, 1983-86, prof. law, 1986— ; adj. prof. law Georgetown U., Washington, 1982; lectr. on adminstrv. and constl. law to various orgs., 1981—. Contbr. articles in field to legal jours. Mem. Am. U. Fulbright scholarship com., Washington, 1984—, Am. U. Inst. Rev. Bd., Washington, 1984, admissions com. Washington Coll. Law, Am. U., 1983-86. Recipient Eliot medal Harvard U., 1972, Detur prize Harvard U., 1970, Mallinckrodt prize Harvard U., 1972, Mark De Wolfe Howe award Harvard Law Sch., 1977, Outstanding Performance award U.S. Dept. Justice, 1981; John H. Finley fellow Harvard U., 1972, English-Speaking Union fellow, 1973. Mem. Phi Beta Kappa. Administrative and regulatory, Legal education, Jurisprudence. Office: Am U Washington Coll Law 4400 Massachusetts Ave NW Washington DC 20016

SARKIS, FREDERICK DERR, lawyer, educator; b. Jan. 25, 1912; s. E.D. and Anna Sarkis; m. Margaret Travis, Mar. 12, 1938; children—Edwin, Sally. B.S.C., Temple U., 1936, J.D., 1942. Bar: Pa. 1948, U.S. Dist. Ct. (ea. dist.) Pa. 1958, U.S. Supreme Ct. 1959, U.S. Ct. Appeals (fed. cir.) 1982. Chief contract adminstrn. U.S. Army, Phila., 1940-46; asst. treas. B-L-H Corp., Phila., 1946-52; counsel Vertol-Boeing, Phila., 1952-57; sr. ptnr. Stassen, Kephart, Sarkis & Kostos, Phila., 1959-70; now ptnr. Murphy and Sarkis, Melbourne, Fla.; lectr. industry groups, Fla. and Pa., 1960—, U. Central Fla., Orlando, 1979-83, Rollins Coll., Winter Park, Fla., 1983—. Trustee Wyoming Sem., Kingston, Pa., 1970-84; gen. counsel Pa. Sports Hall of Fame, Phila., 1960-70; pres. Fla. Sports Hall of Fame, Inc., Maitland, 1978—; active community civic assns. Mem. Fed. Bar Assn. (pres. Orlando chpt. 1978-80, del. nat. council 1978—, bd. dirs. Phila. chpt. 1960-78). Methodist. Club: Union League. Lodges: Masons, Shriners. Government contracts and claims, Legal education, Federal civil litigation. Home: 2569 Newfound Harbor Dr Merritt Island FL 32952 Office: Murphy and Sarkis 1811 S Riverview Dr Melbourne FL 32901

SARKO, LYNN LINCOLN, lawyer; b. Elgin, Ill., June 27, 1956; s. James Andrew and Yvette Irene (Sallesse) S.; m. Rachel A. Nugent, June 3, 1978; 1 child, Max. BBA, U. Wis., 1977, MBA, 1978, JD, 1981. Bar: Wis. 1981, U.S. Dist. Ct. (we. dist.) Wis. 1981, U.S. Ct. Appeals (9th cir.) 1982, D.C. 1983, U.S. Dist. Ct. D.C. 1983, U.S. Ct. Appeals (10th and D.C. cirs.) 1983, U.S. Ct. Appeals (4th and 7th cirs.) 1984, U.S. Supreme Ct. 1984, Wash. 1986. Law clk. to presiding justice U.S. Ct. Appeals (9th cir.), Seattle, 1981-82; assoc. Arnold and Porter, Washington, 1982-84; asst. U.S. atty. U.S. Dept. Justice, Washington, 1984-86; counsel Keller Rohrback, Seattle, 1986—. Editor-in-chief Wis. Law Rev., 1980-81. Legal cons. Dem. Nat. Com., Washington, 1984. Mem. ABA (com. on complex crimes sect. of litigation 1982—), Washington Council Lawyers, Asst. U.S. Atty.'s Assn. Avocations: mountain climbing, ice climbing, alpine skiing. Criminal, Judicial administration. Home: 550 Aloha St Boat #304 Seattle WA 98101 Office: US Atty US Dist Courthouse Washington DC 20001

SARNO, DANIEL ANTHONY, federal administrative law judge; b. Boston, Apr. 29, 1943; s. Daniel A. and Susan Alice (Moran) S.; m. Brenda Margaret Fenton, June 29, 1968; children: Dana Marie, John Eric, Amy Elizabeth. BS, Tufts U., 1965; JD, Suffolk Law Sch., 1974. Bar: Mass. 1974, U.S. Dist. Ct. Mass. 1977, U.S. Supreme Ct. 1980, Pa. 1985. Asst. dist. atty. Suffolk County Dist. Atty., Boston, 1975-78; trial atty. FCC, Washington, 1978-83; adminstrv. law judge U.S. Dept. Labor, Pitts., 1983—. Served to lt. USN, 1965-69. Mem. ABA (jud. adminstrn. div., conf. of adminstrv. law judges), Fed. Adminstrv. Law Judges Conf., Am. Legion, DAV (life). Administrative and regulatory. Home: 140 Woodhaven Dr Mount Lebanon PA 15228 Office: US Dept Labor Office Adminstrv Law Judges Office Adminstrv Law Judges 7 Parkway Ctr Suite 200 Pittsburgh PA 15220

SARNOWSKI, DAVID FRANCIS, lawyer; b. Hawthorne, Nev., Dec. 31, 1952; s. Herbert Justin and Elaine Catherine (Conelly) S.; m. Rebecca Jan Pleasants, Aug. 9, 1977; children: Adrienne Marie, Justin Andrew. BA in History, U. Santa Clara, 1974, JD, 1981. Bar: Nev. 1981, U.S. Dist. Ct. Nev. 1982, U.S. Ct. Appeals (9th cir.) 1984, U.S. Supreme Ct. 1986. Assoc. gen. counsel State Indsl. Ins. System, Carson City, 1981-84; dep. atty. gen. State of Nev., Carson City, 1984—. Mem. cen. com. Carson City Reps., 1984—. Served to 1st lt. U.S. Army, 1974-78. Mem. ABA, Nev. Bar Assn., Washoe County Bar Assn., First Jud. Dist. Bar Assn., Assn. Govt. Attys. in Capital Litigation. Roman Catholic. Avocations: running, gardening, camping. Criminal, Civil rights, Workers' compensation. Office: Nev Atty Gen Office Heroes Meml Bldg Capitol Complex Carson City NV 89710

SAROKIN, H. LEE, judge; b. Perth Amboy, N.J., Nov. 25, 1928; s. Samuel O. and Reebe (Weinblatt) S.; m. Marjorie Lang, Apr. 23, 1971; children: James Todd, Jeffrey Scott, Abby Jane. A.B., Dartmouth Coll., 1950; J.D., Harvard U., 1953. Bar: N.J. 1954. Assoc. Lasser, Lasser, Sarokin & Hochman, Newark, 1955-58; partner Lasser, Lasser, Sarokin & Hochman, 1958-79; asst. county counsel Union County, N.J., 1959-65; U.S. dist. judge Dist. of N.J., Newark, 1979—. Fellow Am. Bar Assn.; mem. Am. Law Inst.; Mem. N.J. Bar Assn., Essex County Bar Assn., Fed. Bar Assn. Office: Post Office and Courthouse Newark NJ 07102

SAROSDY, JANE GRAFFEO, lawyer; b. Dallas, June 22, 1953; d. Joseph Victor Graffeo and Margaret Jane (Dunn) Graffeo Uchman; m. Randall Louis Sarosdy, Oct. 29, 1983; 1 child, William Randall. BA summa cum laude with honors, Newcomb U. of Tulane U., 1975, postgrad., 1977-78; JD, Stanford U., 1980. Bar: D.C. 1981. Law clerk to presiding justice U.S. Ct. Appeals, D.C., Washington, 1980-81; assoc. Covington & Burling, Washington, 1981-84; atty.-adviser Office Internat. Tax Counsel, U.S. Dept. Treasury, Washington, 1984-86, cons., 1986—. Sr. articles editor Stanford Law Rev., 1979-80. Active NOW, Washington, 1980—, Women's Legal Def. Fund, Washington, 1980—. Recipient Pierce Butler prize Tulane U., 1975, alumni medal, 1978, Belcher Evidence award Stanford U., 1980. Mem. ABA, Women's Bar Assn. D.C., Fed. Bar Assn., Phi Beta Kappa. Democrat. Corporate taxation, Personal income taxation, Pension, profit-sharing, and employee benefits. Home and Office: 2008 Rhode Island Ave McLean VA 22101-4921

SAROYAN, SUREN MICHAEL, lawyer; b. Fresno, Calif., Aug. 14, 1905; s. Michael and Pepron (Nishkian) S.; m. Neoma Saroyan, July 13, 1932; children—Doris Rodrigo, Bette Laird. B.A., Stanford U., 1926, J.D., 1929. Bar: Calif. 1929, U.S. Ct. Appeals (9th cir.). Pres. ANCHA, San Francisco, 1947—; of counsel Cartwright & Slobodin, Inc., San Francisco, 1945—(now Cartwright, Slobodin, Bokelman, Borowsky, Wartnick, Moore & Harris, Inc. Del. Democratic Nat. Conv., 1948, alt. del., 1952, 56; trustee U. La Verne. Mem. San Francisco Bar Assn., San Francisco Lawyers Club, Calif. Trial Lawyers Assn., Assn. Trial Lawyers Am. Mem. Armenian Orthodox Ch. Clubs: Olympic, San Francisco Press. Banking, Personal injury. Home: 67 San Andreas Way San Francisco CA 94127 Office: Cartwright Slobodin Borowsky et al 101 California St Suite 2600 San Francisco CA 94111

SARTER, ALVIN JAY, lawyer; b. N.Y.C., May 30, 1956; s. Nathan and Betty (Cohen) S.; m. Kathi A. Adler, July 30, 1978; 1 child, Brynne L. BA in Polit. Sci. summa cum laude, SUNY, Binghamton, 1977; JD, U. Pa., 1980. Bar: D.C. 1981, U.S. Dist. Ct. D.C. 1981, U.S. Ct. Appeals (D.C. cir.) 1981, N.Y. 1983. Law clk. to presiding justice U.S. Ct. Appeals (Fed. cir.), Washington, 1980-81; assoc. Covington & Burling, Washington, 1981-83, Aronoff & David, Washington, 1983-85, Battle & Fowler, N.Y.C., 1985—. Mem. Phi Beta Kappa. Real property. Home: 26 Berrian Rd New Rochelle NY 10804 Office: Battle & Fowler 280 Park Ave New York NY 10017

SASSER, DONALD JULIAN, lawyer; b. West Palm Beach, Fla., Apr. 13, 1943; s. G. Julian and Colombe C. (Couture) S.; m. Diane Alinda, Aug. 12, 1967; children—Thomas J., Susanne A. A.B., Loyola U., New Orleans, 1965; J.D., U. Fla. 1967. Bar: Fla. 1967, D.C. 1968. Assoc. A.F. O'Connell, West Palm Beach, 1968-70, Ronald Sales, Palm Beach, Fla., 1970-73; ptnr. Johnston, Sasser, Randolph & Weaver, West Palm Beach, 1973—; lectr. Fla. Bar. State of Fla. area pres. Panama C.Z. Boy Scouts Am., also regional bd. dirs., v.p. Gulf Stream council. Recipient Silver Beaver award Boy Scouts Am., 1975, also Silver Antelope award Boy Scouts Am. Fellow Am. Acad. Matrimonial Lawyers; mem. Internat. Acad. Matrimonial Lawyers (charter), Fla. Bar (exec. council family law sect.), ABA, Fla. Bar Assn., Palm Beach County Bar Assn. Democrat. Roman Catholic. Club: Optimist (pres. West Palm Beach). Contbr. articles on continuing legal edn. to profl. jours. State civil litigation, Family and matrimonial, General practice. Home: 264 N Country Club Dr Atlantis FL 33462 Office: Johnston Sasser Randolph & Weaver 310 Okeechobee Blvd West Palm Beach FL 33401 Office: PO Drawer M West Palm Beach FL 33402

SASSER, JONATHAN DREW, lawyer; b. Monroe, N.C., Mar. 1, 1956; s. Herman Wallace and Faith Belzora (Harrington) S. BA with honors, U. N.C., 1978, JD with honors, 1981. Bar: N.C. 1981, N.Y. 1983, U.S. Dist. Ct. (so. and ea. dists.) N.Y. 1983, U.S. Dist. Ct. (no. dist.) Tex. 1983, U.S. Dist. Ct. (ea. dist.) N.C. 1986, U.S. Ct. Appeals (4th cir.) 1987. Law clk. to presiding justice N.C. Supreme Ct., Raleigh, N.C., 1981-82; assoc. Paul, Weiss, Rifkind, Wharton & Garrison, N.Y.C., 1982-86, Moore & Van Allen and predecessor firm Powe, Porter & Alphin P.A., Durham, N.C., 1986—. Editor: Cellar Door, 1977-78. Dem. precinct chmn., Chapel Hill, N.C., 1976-82. John Motley Morehead Found. fellow, Chapel Hill, 1974; John Motley Morehead Found. scholar, Chapel Hill, 1978. Mem. ABA, N.C. State Bar Assn., N.C. Bar Assn., N.Y. State Bar Assn. Baptist. Avocation: running. Federal civil litigation, State civil litigation, Civil rights. Home: 414 Carolina Circle Durham NC 27707 Office: Moore & Van Allen 301 W Main St PO Box 3843 Durham NC 27702

SATCHER, JAMES ALTON, JR., lawyer; b. Rome, Ga., Mar. 7, 1950; s. James Alton and June (Knight) S.; m. Jennifer Paris, Nov. 25, 1970; children: Kimberly, James, Jason. BA, Berry Coll., 1971; JD, U. Ga., 1975. Bar: Ga. 1975, U.S. Dist. Ct. (no. dist.) Ga. 1975, U.S. Ct. Appeals (5th and 11th cirs.) 1975. Law clk. to presiding justice Superior Ct., Cartersville, Ga., 1975-76; sole practice Rome, 1976—. Mem. ABA, Ga. Trial Lawyers Assn., Berry Coll. Alumni Assn.. Democrat. Baptist. Club: YMCA. Lodge: Masons. State civil litigation, Federal civil litigation, Civil rights. Home: Kingston Rd Rome GA 30161 Office: 520 Broad St Rome GA 30161

SATINSKY, BARNETT, lawyer; b. Phila., June 17, 1947; s. Alex and Florence (Talsky) S.; m. Fredda Andrea Wagner, June 17, 1973; children: Meagen, Sara Beth, Jonathan. AB, Brown U., 1969; JD, Villanova U., 1972. Bar: Pa. 1972, U.S. Dist. Ct. (ea. dist) Pa. 1975, U.S. Dist. Ct. (mid. dist.) Pa. 1975, U.S. Ct. Appeals (3d cir.) 1981. Law clk. Phila. Ct. Common Pleas, 1972-73; dep. atty. gen. Pa. Dept. Justice, Harrisburg, 1973-75; 1st asst. counsel Pa. Pub. Utility Commn., Harrisburg, 1975-77, chief counsel, 1977; assoc. Fox, Rothschild, O'Brien & Frankel, Phila., 1978-81, ptnr., 1981—. Children Services Rev. com., United Way Southeast Pa., 1984-86; bd. dirs. ACLU, Harrisburg, 1973-74. Mem. ABA (pub. utility, labor and employment law sects., employee benefits com. 1984—), Pa. Bar Assn. (labor relations, pub. utility law sects. 1980—), Phila. Bar Assn. (labor law, pub. utility law coms. 1980—), Nat. Assn. Coll. and Univs. Attys., Nat. Assn. Regulatory Commrs. (staff subcom. law 1977), Indsl. Relations Assn. Phila. Democrat. Jewish. Labor, Public utilities. Office: Fox Rothschild O'Brien & Frankel 2000 Market St Philadelphia PA 19103

SATO, SHO, lawyer, educator; b. 1923. A.B., Denver U., 1944; LL.B., Harvard U., 1951. Bar: Calif. 1952. Dep. atty. gen. Calif. State's Atty. Gen.'s Office, 1952-55; acting assoc. prof. U. Calif.-Berkeley, 1955-57, assoc. prof., 1957-59, prof. law, 1959—; Fulbright lectr. U. Tokyo, 1966, Fulbright researcher, 1981; Fulbright resident U. Kobe, Japan, 1970; vis. scholar Nihon U., Japan, 1977; mem. Gov.'s Commn. on Law of Preemption, 1966-67; mem. Calif. Law Rev. Commn., 1960-69, vice-chmn., 1965-67, chmn., 1967-69. Author: (with Van Alstyne) State and Local Government Law, 2d edit., 1977. Legal education, Local government. Office: U Calif Law Sch Boalt Hall Berkeley CA 94720 *

SATROM, ROBERT CHARLES, lawyer; b. Cleve., Sept. 16, 1955; s. LeRoy Martin and Grace Emma (Reinhardt) S.; m. Susan Mary Noble, Dec. 9, 1977 (div. Oct. 1980); m. Martha Jeanne Pearsall, June 28, 1986. BA, Kent State U., 1976; JD, MS in Fgn. Service, Georgetown U., 1981. Bar: Calif. 1981, D.C. 1982, N.Y. 1984, U.S. Supreme Ct. 1986. Atty. Office of Comptroller of the Currency, Washington, 1981-84; assoc. Rogers & Wells, N.Y.C., 1984—. Mem. ABA, Inter-Am. Bar Assn., Fed. Bar Assn., Phi Beta Kappa, Pi Sigma Alpha. Avocations: jogging, racquetball. Banking, Securities, Public international. Office: Rogers & Wells 200 Park Ave New York NY 10166

SATTER, RAYMOND NATHAN, lawyer; b. Denver, Oct. 19, 1948; s. Charles Herbert and Muriel Vera (Tuller); m. Suzanne Elizabeth Ehlers, May 28, 1977. BA, U. Denver, 1970; JD, Cath. U., 1973. Bar: Colo. 1973, U.S. Dist. Ct. Colo. 1973, U.S. Ct. Appeals (10th cir.) 1973, U.S. Supreme Ct. 1976, U.S. Tax Ct. 1981. Assoc. Wallace & Armatas, Denver, 1973-75; ptnr. Tallmadge, Wallace & Hahn, Denver, 1975-77; sole practice Denver, 1978—; gen. counsel Satter Dist., Denver, 1977-78; assoc. mcpl. judge City of Englewood, Colo., 1985-86. Pres. Young Artists Orch. Denver, 1985-87; sec. Denver Symphony Assn., 1985-86. Mem. Am. Arbitration Assn., Colo. Bar Assn. (ethics com.), Arapahoe Bar Assn., Denver Bar Assn. Democrat. Sailing, opera, classical music, fishing. Federal civil litigation, State civil litigation, Civil rights. Office: 910 16th St #1125 Denver CO 80202-2910

SATTLER, JAMES MICHAEL, lawyer; b. Salt Lake City, Feb. 6, 1940; s. Walter P. Sattler and Olive S. (Davis) Dahn; m. Kathleen Cloward, Sept. 6, 1962; children: James Michael II, Ralph Douglas. BS, U. Utah, 1962, JD, 1966. Bar: Hawaii 1966, Calif. 1971. Assoc. Anderson, Wrenn & Jenks, Honolulu, 1966-72; ptnr. Jenks, Kidwell, Goodsill & Anderson, Honolulu, 1972-74, Sattler, Spradlin & Brandt, Honolulu, 1974-75; sole practice Honolulu, 1975—; pres., bd. dirs. Honolulu Trains and Hobbies, Inc., Vintage Cars of Hawaii, Inc., Honolulu. Editor U. Utah Law Rev., 1965-66, Jour. Hawaii Bar, 1967-68. V.p., bd. dirs. Cloward Found. Med. Research, Honolulu, 1965—. Mormon. Clubs: Honolulu, Oahu Country (Honolulu). Avocations: collecting Lionel trains and cars. Federal civil litigation, State civil litigation, Real property. Home: 1588 Hoaaina St Honolulu HI 96821 Office: 841 Bishop St Suite 2020 Honolulu HI 96813

SATZ, PERRY, lawyer; b. Bklyn., Feb. 5, 1931; s. Michael and Rose Elsie (Abramowitz) S.; m. Linda Frances Goebel, Jan. 21, 1962; children: Michael A., Michelle L. BA, U. Ill., 1953; LLB, Cornell U., 1958. Bar: N.Y. 1958. Ptnr. Satz & Kirshon P.C., Poughkeepsie, N.Y., 1959—; lectr. family law Marist Coll., Poughkeepsie, 1976-81. Bd. dirs. paralegal adv. bd. Marist Coll., 1976—, Dutchess County Family Services, Poughkeepsie, 1986—. Served to 1st lt. U.S. Army, 1953-55, Korea. Fellow Am. Acad. Matrimonial Lawyers (panelist 1985); mem. ABA (arbitrator 1975—), N.Y. State Bar Assn. (speaker family law 1983, 86), Dutchess County Bar Assn. (speaker 1986). Republican. Jewish. Club: Dutchess Golf and Country. Avocations: golf, swimming, music. Family and matrimonial. Office: Satz & Kirshon PC 309 Mill St Poughkeepsie NY 12601

SAUER, DAVID ALLEN, lawyer; b. Terre Haute, Ind., Mar. 26, 1957; s. Frederick and Claire Tews (Essig) S.; m. Priscilla Harnesk, Mar. 13, 1982. BA, St. Lawrence U., 1979; JD, U. Conn., 1982. Bar: Conn. 1982, U.S. Dist. Ct. Conn. 1983. Assoc. James M. Marinelli P.C., New Britain, Conn., 1982—. Mem. ABA, Conn. Bar Assn., Conn. Trial Lawyers Am. Personal injury, State civil litigation, Criminal. Home: 98 Acorn Dr Middletown CT 06457 Office: James M Marinelli PC 65 S High St New Britain CT 06050

SAUER, WILLIAM JACOB, lawyer; b. La Crosse, Wis., July 18, 1917; s. Samuel Jacob and Kathryn M. (Hartje) S.; m. Helen Jean Sauer, Aug. 30, 1947; children: Mary Sauer Smolek, Kay Sauer Garcia, Jan, Sam J., Beth Kiela. BA, Beloit Coll., 1938; LL.B, U. Wis., 1941. Bar: Wis. 1941, U.S. Dist. Ct. (we. dist.) Wis. 1941, U.S. Ct. Appeals (8th cir.) 1974, U.S. Ct. Appeals (7th cir.) 1976, U.S. Supreme Ct. 1964. Sole practice La Crosse, 1946-81; sr. mem. Sauer, Becker, Flanagan & Lynch Ltd., La Crosse, 1981—; lectr. U. Wis., 1968, 70. Bd. editors Wisbar Taxnews; contbr. articles to profl. jours. Pres. La Crosse Symphony Orch., 1947-49. Served to lt. (j.g.) USCG, 1943-46. Mem. ABA, Wis. State Bar Assn. (bd. dirs. taxation sect.), La Crosse County Bar Assn. (sec. 1947-49, pres. 1968-69), Am. Judicature Soc., Benchers Soc. of U. Wis. Law Sch., Order of Coif, Phi Beta Kappa, Delta Sigma Rho. General corporate, Probate, Real property. Home: 2121 Main St La Crosse WI 54601 Office: 421 Main St Suite 400 La Crosse WI 54601

SAUL, IRA STEPHEN, lawyer; b. West Reading, Pa., Apr. 2, 1949; s. Charles Ryweck and Florence Rebecca (Sussman) S.; m. Elizabeth Claire Barclay, Nov. 30, 1974; children—Barclay Charles, Amanda Emerson. B.A., Dickinson Coll., 1971; J.D., Am. U., 1975. Bar: Va. 1975, U.S. Dist. Ct. (ea. dist.) Va. 1976, U.S. Ct. Appeals (4th cir.) 1977, D.C. 1978, U.S. Dist. Ct. D.C. 1978, U.S. Ct. Appeals (D.C. Cir.) 1985. Assoc. Miller, Gattsek, Tavenner, Rosenfeld & Schultz, Bailey's Crossroads, Va., 1975-77; ptnr. Saul & Barclay, Fairfax, Va., 1978—. Mem. No. Va. Apt. Assn. Recipient cert. of Appreciation Inst. Real Estate Mgmt., 1982, 83. Mem. ABA, Assn. Trial Lawyers Am., Fairfax Bar Assn., Va. Trial Lawyers Assn. Republican. State civil litigation, Real property, Personal injury. Office: Saul & Barclay 4055 Chain Bridge Rd Fairfax VA 22030

SAUL, IRVING ISAAC, lawyer; b. Washington, Pa., July 9, 1929; s. Israel Jacob and Jennie (Green) S.; m. Lita Brown, Dec. 29, 1950; children: Joanne Ilene, Sandra Lynn. BA, Washington and Jefferson Coll., 1949; LLB, U. Pitts., 1952; postgrad. Georgetown U., 1949, Ohio State U., 1951. Bar: Ohio 1952, U.S. Supreme Ct. 1961, U.S. Ct. Appeals (6th cir.) 1966, U.S. Ct. Appeals (7th cir.) 1978, U.S. Ct. Appeals (4th cir.) 1978, U.S. Dist. Ct. (so. dist.) Ohio 1954, U.S. Dist. Ct. (no. dist.) Ohio 1967, U.S. Dist. Ct. (ea. dist.) Wis. 1973. Sole practice, Dayton, Ohio, 1952—; spl. counsel Coolidge, Wall, Womsley & Lombard Co., L.P.A., Dayton, 1986—; cons. in antitrust litigation; bd. advs. Fed. Civil Practice Abstracts, 1986—; lectr. in field. James Gillespie Blaine scholar, 1948. Mem. ABA, Ohio Bar Assn. (chmn. fed. cts. and practice com. 1977-79, chmn. pvt. enforcement com. 1979—, bd. govs. antitrust sect. 1982—), Dayton Bar Assn. (chmn. fed. ct. practice com. 1976-77, 78-80), Am. Judicature Soc., Phi Beta Kappa. Jewish. Clubs: Cin., Masons (Shriner). Contbr. articles to profl. jours. Antitrust, Federal civil litigation, State civil litigation. Office: 113 Bethpolamy Ct Dayton OH 45415

SAUL, ROLAND DALE, lawyer, district attorney; b. Plainview, Tex., Mar. 7, 1948; s. Doyle Randolph and Dorothy Nell (Miller) S.; m. Sandra Rae Story, Mar. 25, 1973; 1 child, Dusty Brooke. B.S., Wayland Baptist Coll., 1970; J.D. Tex. Tech. U., 1973. Bar: Tex. 1973, U.S. Supreme Ct. 1980, U.S. Dist. Ct. (no. dist.) Tex. Asst. criminal dist. atty. Deaf Smith County, Hereford, Tex., 1973-76, criminal dist. atty., 1978—; ptnr. Tubb, Easterwood & Saul, Hereford, 1976-79, Saul, Smith & Davis, 1979-83. Chmn. Am. Heart Assn., Hereford, 1978, Cystic Fibrosis Assn., Hereford, 1982—. Mem. State Bar Tex., Tex. Dist. and County Attys. Assn., Nat. Dist. Attys. Assn. Democrat. Methodist. Lodge: Rotary. Criminal, General practice. Home: Route 4 Hereford TX 79045 Office: Box 1816 Hereford TX 79045

SAULSBERRY, CHARLES R., lawyer; b. Goshen, Ala., Sept. 4, 1957; s. Asia W. and Ruby (Jones) S.; m. Dana R. Scott. AB, Harvard U., 1979; JD, Northwestern U., 1982. Bar: Ill. 1982, U.S. Dist. Ct. (no. dist.) Ill. 1982. Assoc. Winston & Strawn, Chgo.; bd. dirs. Investors Ednl. Services, Chgo., Investors Cons. Services, Chgo. Vol. Lawyers Com. for Mayor Harold Washington, Chgo., 1982, 86—; v.p. New Chgo. Com., Chgo., 1984—; bd. mem. Cabrini Green Legal Aid, Chgo., 1985—. Mem. ABA, Chgo. Bar Assn., Young Exec. in Politics, Chgo. Council Lawyers (sec., bd. dirs. 1985—). Avocations: tennis. General corporate, Municipal bonds. Home: 1700 E 56th St Chicago IL 60637 Office: Winston & Strawn 1 First Nat Plaza Chicago IL 60603

SAUNDERS, CHARLES ALBERT, lawyer; b. Boulder, Colo., Jan. 18, 1922; s. Charles and Anna (Crouse) S.; m. Betti Friedel, Oct. 18, 1946; children—Melanie, Stephen, Cynthia, Shelley. B.A., U. Houston, 1942; LL.B., U. Tex., 1945. Bar: Tex. bar 1945. Since practiced in Houston; partner firm Fulbright & Jaworski, 1959—; dir. Brookside Corp. Editor: How to Live—and Die—With Probate, 8 vols, 1968, Texas Estate Administration, 1975. Bd. dirs. Houston Symphony Soc., 1964—; bd. dirs. San Jacinto Lung Assn., 1965—, pres., 1972-73. Mem. Am. Bar Assn., State Bar Tex., Houston Bar Assn. Republican. Presbyterian. Home: 19 Willowron Dr Houston TX 77024 Office: 1301 McKinney Ave Houston TX 77010

SAUNDERS, DAVID LIVINGSTON, lawyer; b. Huntington, W.Va., Dec. 30, 1939; s. Henry Rosemond and Clover Pauline (Morrison) S.; m. JoAnn Kay Coil, July 29, 1961; children: Kaye Anne, Liesl Maria. BA, U. Notre Dame, 1969, JD, 1973. Bar: Ind. 1973, U.S. Dist. Ct. (no. dist.) Ind. 1974, U.S. Supreme Ct. 1979. Ptnr. Hartzog, Barker, Hepler & Saunders, Goshen, Ind., 1974—. Producer videotape The Trouble with Sarah, 1983. Panelist Ind. Juvenile Judges Conf., Brown County, 1985; mem. Community Child Protection Team, Elkhart County, Ind., 1979—, Ind. Permanent Families Task Force, 1984—; judge adminstrv. law Ind. Emergency Med. Services, Indpls., 1985—. Mem. ABA, Ind. Bar Assn., Ind. Trial Lawyers Assn., Ind. Mcpl. Lawyers Assn., Nat. Council Juvenile and Family Ct. Judges. Republican. Mem. Nazarene Ch. Avocations: golf, bicycling, reading, singing with family. Juvenile, Local government, General practice. Home: 65648 State Rd 15 Rd Goshen IN 46526 Office: Hartzog Barker Hepler & Saunders 118 N Main St Goshen IN 46526

SAUNDERS, GEORGE LAWTON, JR., lawyer; b. Mulga, Ala., Nov. 8, 1931; s. George Lawton and Ethel Estell (York) S.; m. Joanne Rosa Helperin, Dec. 4, 1959 (div.); children: Kenneth, Ralph, Victoria; m. Terry M. Rose, Sept. 21, 1975. B.A., U. Ala., 1956; J.D., U. Chgo., 1959. Bar: Ill. 1960. Law clk. to chief judge U.S. Ct. Appeals (5th cir.), Montgomery, Ala., 1959-60; law clk Justice Hugo L. Black, U.S. Supreme Ct., Washington, 1960-62; assoc. Sidley & Austin, Chgo., 1962-67, ptnr., 1967—. Served with USAF, 1951-54. Mem. ABA, Ill. State Bar Assn., Chgo. Bar Assn., Chgo. Council Lawyers, Order of Coif, Phi Beta Kappa. Democrat. Baptist. Clubs: Chicago, Saddle and Cycle, Mid-Am., Quadrangle, Law, Legal (Chgo.). General practice, Antitrust, Administrative and regulatory. Home: 179 E Lake Shore Dr Chicago IL 60611 Office: Sidley & Austin 1 First National Plaza Chicago IL 60603

SAUNDERS, LONNA JEANNE, lawyer, newscaster; b. Cleve., Nov. 26, 1952; d. Jack Glenn and Lillian Frances (Newman) Slaby. Student, Dartmouth Coll., 1972-73; AB, Vassar Coll., 1974; JD, Northwestern U., 1981. Bar: Ill. 1981. News dir., morning news anchor Sta. WKBK, Keene, N.H., 1974-75; reporter Sta. KDKA, Pitts., 1975; pub. affairs dir., news anchor Sta. WJW, Cleve., 1975-77; morning news anchor Sta. WBBG, Cleve., 1978; talk host, news anchor Sta. WIND-AM, Chgo., 1978-82; atty. Arvey, Hodes, Costello & Burman, Chgo., 1981-82; host, news anchor WCIU-TV, Chgo., 1982-85; staff atty. Better Govt. Assn., Chgo., 1983-84; news anchor, reporter Sta. WBMX-FM, Chgo., 1984-86; sole practice Chgo., 1985—; news anchor Sta. WKQX-FM, Chgo., 1987—; guest talk host sta. WMCA, N.Y.C., 1983; host, producer "The Lively Arts" Cablevision Chgo., 1986; atty. Lawyers for Creative Arts, Chgo., 1985—. Contbg. editor Chgo. Life mag., 1986—; contbr. articles to profl. jours.; creator (pub. affairs program) "Ask The Schools" WBBM-AM. Recipient Akron Press Club award (best pub. affairs presentation); Scripps Howard found. grantee, 1978-79, 79-80; AFTRA George Heller Meml. scholar, 1980-81. Mem. Dartmouth Lawyers Assn., Women's Bar Assn. Ill., Investigative Reporters and Editors, Nat. Acad. TV Arts and Scis., ABA (exec. coms. Lawyers and

the Arts, Law and Media), Sigma Delta Chi. Roman Catholic. Clubs: Chgo. Vassar, Vassar (N.Y.C.), Chgo. Dartmouth. Avocations: theater, piano. Entertainment, Libel. Home: 1212 S Michigan Ave #2206 Chicago IL 60605 Office: 134 N LaSalle St Suite 1220 Chicago IL 60602

SAUNDERS, PAUL CHRISTOPHER, lawyer; b. N.Y.C., May 21, 1941; s. John Richard and Agnes Grace (Kelly) S.; m. Patricia Newman, Sept. 14, 1968; children—Paul Christopher, Michael Eagan. A.B., Fordham Coll., 1963; J.D., Georgetown U., 1966; Certificat d'Études Politiques, Institut d'Études Politiques,, Paris, 1962. Bar: N.Y. 1966, D.C. 1967, U.S. Supreme Ct. 1969, U.S. Ct. Appeals (2d cir.) 1971, U.S. Ct. Appeals (5th cir.) 1980, U.S. Ct. Appeals (11th cir.) 1981, U.S. Ct. Appeals (6th cir.) 1982, U.S. Ct. Appeals (9th cir.) 1985. Assoc. Cravath, Swaine & Moore, N.Y.C., 1971-77, ptnr., 1977—. bd. editors Georgetown Law Jour. Trustee Fordham prep. sch.; v.p., dir. Legal Aid Soc. Served to capt. JAGC, U.S. Army, 1967-71. Decorated Knight of Malta, 1982. Fellow Am. Bar Found.; mem. ABA, N.Y.C. Bar Assn., Cardinal's Com. of Laity. Democrat. Roman Catholic. Clubs: Apawamis, Westchester Country (Rye, N.Y.). Federal civil litigation, State civil litigation, Antitrust. Home: 1220 Park Ave New York NY 10128 also: Polly Park Rd Rye NY 10580

SAUNDERS, ROBERT LEONARD, lawyer; b. Altus, Okla., July 28, 1948; s. Raymond D. and Mary Jo (Long) S.; m. Duane Christine Ray, July 28, 1973; children: Ryan Robert, Blake Leonard. BA, Okla. U., 1970; JD, Okla. City U., 1974. Bar: Pa. 1975, U.S. Dist. Ct. (we. dist.) Pa. 1977. Ptnr. Mutzabaugh, Mutzabaugh, Saunders & Mattie, Bradford, Pa., 1976—; asst. dist. atty. McKean County, Pa., 1977—; mem. hearing com. Disciplinary Bd., Supreme Ct. of Pa., 1979-85. Bd. dirs. McKean County Water & Sewer Authority, 1986—; pres. Children's Home of Bradford, Pa., 1983-86, Ramsbottom Ctr. for Retarded Children, Bradford, Pa., 1983-86; treas. Allegany Highland council Boy Scouts Am., 1982-85; bd. dirs. The Learning Ctr., Bradford. Mem. ABA, Pa. Bar Assn., McKean County Bar Assn. (treas. 1980-82, pres. 1986—), Pa. Trial Lawyers Assn, Bradford C. of C. (bd. dirs.), Exchange Club. Republican. Lodge: Rotary. State civil litigation, Personal injury, Workers' compensation. Home: Taintor Rd Lewis Run PA 16738 Office: 52 Boylston St Bradford PA 16701-0342

SAUNTRY, SUSAN SCHAEFER, lawyer; b. Bangor, Maine, May 7, 1943; d. William Joseph and Emily Joan (Guenter) Schaefer; m. John Philip Sauntry, Jr., Aug. 18, 1968; 1 child, Mary Katherine. BS in Foreign Service, Georgetown U., 1965, JD, 1975. Bar: D.C. 1975, U.S. Dist. Ct. D.C. 1975, U.S. Ct. Appeals (D.C. cir.) 1975, (4th cir.) 1977, (6th cir.) 1978, (10th cir.) 1983, U.S. Supreme Ct. 1983. Program analyst EEO Com., Washington, 1968-70, U.S. Dept. Army, Okinawa, 1970-72; assoc. Morgan, Lewis & Bockius, Washington, 1975-83, ptnr., 1983—. Co-author: Employee Dismissal Law: Forms and Procedures, 1986; contbr. articles to profl. jours. Mem. ABA, D.C. Bar Assn., D.C. Women's Bar Assn., Am. Assn. Univ. Women, Nat. Women's Party, Nat. Fed. Bus. & Profl. Women, USA, Phi Beta Kappa, Pi Sigma Alpha. Democrat. Labor. Office: Morgan Lewis & Bockius 1800 M St NW Washington DC 20036

SAVAGE, BARRY EMERY, lawyer; b. Jackson, Mich., Apr. 19, 1940; s. Herbert E. and Marva V. (Schultz) S.; B.A. in Econ., U. Mich., 1962, J.D., 1965; m. Joyce A. Diaz, Oct. 6, 1977; 1 son by previous marriage, Steven Vincent. Admitted to Ohio bar, 1965, Mich. bar, 1966; practice in Toledo, 1965—; with firm Savage & Lindsley, P.A., Toledo; engaged in real estate investment, 1968—. Mem. Mich. Bar Assn., Toledo Bar Assn. (chmn. unauthorized practice com. 1970-72), ABA. Club: Toledo Yacht. Banking, Bankruptcy, Contracts commercial. Home: 1663 Organdette Maumee OH 43537 Office: Savage & Lindsley Co 405 Madison 1850 OH Citizens B Toledo OH 43604-1294

SAVAGE, EDWARD TURNEY, lawyer; b. Boston, Feb. 14, 1946; s. Arthur Turney and Katrine (Tuttle) S. B.A., Amherst Coll., 1968; M.B.A., J.D., Harvard U. Bar: Calif. 1975, N.Y. 1975, U.S. Dist. Ct. (no. dist.) Calif. 1975, U.S. Dist. Ct. (so. dist.) N.Y. 1975. Law clk. to presiding justice U.S. Dist. Ct. (no. dist.) Calif., San Francisco, 1974-75; assoc. Cadwalader, Wickersham & Taft, N.Y.C., 1975-77; ptnr. Rosenman Colin Freund Lewis & Cohen, N.Y.C., 1977—. Pres. Friends of Amherst Athletics, 1979-82. Served to lt. (j.g.) USN, 1968-70; lt. comdr. Res. Recipient Disting. Service award Harvard Bus. Sch., 1974; Amherst Meml. scholar, 1970; Woodroff Simpson fellow, 1971. Mem. Westfield Jaycees. Republican. Presbyterian. General corporate, Securities, Computer. Home: 401 E 88th St #16A New York NY 10128 Office: Rosenman & Colin 575 Madison Ave New York NY 10022

SAVAGE, HAROLD MICHAEL, lawyer; b. Bloomfield, N.J., Apr. 21, 1921; s. Vincent F. and Jennie P. (Post) S.; m. Marguerite A. James, June 26, 1948; 1 child, Harold M. Jr. BS, Fordham U., 1942; postgrad., Georgetown U., 1950; LLB, St. John's U., 1950; postgrad., NYU, 1950. Bar: N.J. 1950. Instr. continuing legal edn., matrimonial law Newark, 1974—; now ptnr. Savage & Savage, Bloomfield. Mem. bd. edn., North Caldwell, N.J., 1960-67, pres. 1966-67. Fellow Am. Acad. Matrimonial Lawyers (N.J. chpt. fellow, bd. mgrs. 1981—), Essex County Bar Assn. (chmn. family law sect. 1972-73); mem. ABA (editor family law newsletter 1972-75, council mem. family law sect. 1975-76), N.J. Bar Assn. (chmn., trustee family law sect. 1972-73, 76-79), Bloomfield Lawyers Club (pres. 1957-58), Fordham U. Club N.J. (pres. 1956-57). Republican. Roman Catholic. Club: Seaview Country (Absecon, N.J.). Avocation: golf. Family and matrimonial. Home: 12 Deer Trail Rd North Caldwell NJ 07006

SAVAGE, JOHN WILLIAM, lawyer; b. Seattle, Oct. 11, 1951; s. Stanley and Jennie Sabina (Siggstedt) S.; m. Rebecca Lee Abraham, Oct. 1, 1983. Student Lewis and Clark Coll., 1969-71; B.A., U. Wash., 1973; J.D., Northwestern Sch. Law, Lewis and Clark Coll., 1977. Bar: Oreg. 1977, U.S. Dist. Ct. Oreg. 1977, U.S. Ct. Appeals (9th cir.) 1977, U.S. Supreme Ct. 1985. Sole practice, Portland, Oreg., 1977-79; ptnr. Bailey, Olstad, Rieke, Geil & Savage, P.C., Portland, 1979-80; ptnr., shareholder Rieke, Geil & Savage, P.C. Portland, 1980—; mem. Oreg. Literacy Inc., Portland, 1979-85. Mem. standing com. City Club, Portland, 1984—, chmn. law and pub. safety standing com. 1985— . Mem. Multnomah Bar Assn. (v.p. young Lawyers sect. 1980, pres.-elect 1981, pres. 1982, Dist. Service award), ABA (chairperson Young Lawyers sect. Nat. Community Law Week 1983-84, Inmate Grievance Com. 1984—), Oreg. Bar Assn. (def. of indigent accused com. 1985—), Oreg. Criminal Def. Lawyers Assn. (bd. dirs. 1984-86). Personal injury, State civil litigation, Criminal. Home: 397 Furnace Lake Oswego OR 97034 Office: Rieke Geil & Savage PC 820 SW 2d Ave Suite 200 Portland OR 97204

SAVAGE, JOHN WILLIAM, JR., lawyer; b. DeBeque, Colo., Apr. 25, 1951; s. John William and Joan Nan (Leonhardt) S.; m. Sally Maria Brands, June 10, 1978; children: Catherine Brands Savage, Maria Brands Savage, Louis Brands Savage, John Brands Savage. Student, U. Colo., 1970-73; BA in History, U. So. Calif., 1976; JD, U. Denver, 1979. Bar: Colo. 1979, U.S. Dist. Ct. Colo. 1979, U.S. Ct. Appeals (10th cir.) 1985. Assoc. Donald M. Lesher P.C., Denver, 1979-80; sole practice Rifle, Colo., 1980—; sec. Shale Inc., Rifle, 1981—; bd. dirs. West Anvil Water and Power, Rifle, Rifle Ski Corp. V.p. Holistic Health Found., Denver, 1980—; chief Rifle Fire Dept., 1985-87, Rifle Ambulance Dept., 1984; co-vice chmn. Garfield County Reps., Rifle, 1984-87. Mem. 9th Jud, Dist. Bar Assn. (sec., treas. 1983-85), Upper Colo. Bd. Realtors. Lodge: Elks. Avocations: hunting, fishing, golf, sports, travel. General practice, Real property, Water law and oil shale claims patent litigation. Office: PO Box 1926 Rifle CO 81650

SAVAGE, THOMAS YATES, lawyer; b. Fredericksburg, Va., Apr. 13, 1956; s. Joseph L. and Marie (Radolinski) S.; m. Julia Savino, Sept. 1, 1984. BS in Mass Communications, Va. Commonwealth U., 1978; JD, Washington and Lee U., 1982. Bar: Va. 1982. Sole practice Fredericksburg, 1982—. Dist. chmn. Fauquier County Dem. Com., Va., 1985; treas. Jonathon S. Lynn Campaign Com. for Commonwealth Atty., Fauquier, 1986; mem. Friends of the Rappahannock, Fredericksburg. Named one of Outstanding Young Men of Am., 1984. Mem. ABA, Fredericksburg Area Bar Assn. (sec. 1982-83), Va. Trial Lawyers Assn., Fredericksburg Jaycees (Outstanding 1st Yr., 1983). Roman Catholic. Lodge: Elks. Avocations: canoeing, survival games, jogging, skiing. Family and matrimonial, Criminal, Real property. Office: 210 Wolfe St Fredericksburg VA 22401

SAVELKOUL, DONALD CHARLES, lawyer; b. Mpls., July 29, 1917; s. Theodore Charles and Edith (Lindgren) S.; m. Mary Joan Holland, May 17, 1941; children: Jeffrey Charles, Jean Marie, Edward Joseph. BA magna cum laude, U. Minn., 1939; JD cum laude, William Mitchell Coll. Law, 1951. Bar: Minn. 1951, U.S. Dist. Ct. Minn. 1952, U.S. Ct. Appeals (8th cir.) 1960, U.S. Supreme Ct. 1971. Adminstrv. work various U.S. govt. depts., including Commerce, War, Labor, Wage Stblzn. Bd., 1940-51; mcpl. judge Fridley, Minn., 1952-53; law practice Mpls. and Fridley, 1951—; chmn. bd. Fridley State Bank, 1962—, Blaine State Bank, 1972—; pres. Banrein, Inc., Blaine Bldg. Corp., Babbscha Co.; mem. faculty William Mitchell Coll. Law, 1952-59, corp. mem., 1956—; sec. Fridley Recreation and Service Co., 1955—; me. Minn. Legislature, 1967-69. Mem. Gov.'s Com. Workers Compensation, 1965-67, Gov.'s Adv. Council on Employment Security, 1957-60; chmn. Fridley Police Civil Service Commn., 1962-63. Served to 1st lt. AUS, 1943-46. Decorated Bronze Star. Mem. ABA, Minn. Bar Assn., Hennepin County Bar Assn., Justice William Mitchell Soc., Am. Legion, Phi Beta Kappa. Roman Catholic. Clubs: Midland Hills Country, U. Minn., Pres.'s, Alexandria Country. Banking, General corporate, Personal injury. Home: 916 W Moore Lake Dr Fridley MN 55432 Office: Fridley State Bank Bldg 6315 University Ave NE Fridley MN 55432

SAVELL, EDWARD LUPO, lawyer; b. Atlanta, Apr. 29, 1921; s. Leon M. and Lillian (Lupo) S.; m. Bettie Patterson Hoyt, Oct. 11, 1944; 1 dau., Mary Lillian Savell Clarke. B.B.A., Emory U., 1947, LL.B., 1949. Bar: Ga. 1948. Practiced law Atlanta, 1948—; partner Savell & Williams, Atlanta, 1953—; instr. John Marshall Law Sch., 1952-56. Contbr. articles to legal jours. Served with USAF, 1942-45, CBI. Fellow Internat. Acad. Trial Lawyers (pres. 1978—, dean of acad. 1976); mem. Atlanta Bar Assn. (sec.-treas. 1953-54), ABA, State Bar Ga., Ga. Def. Lawyers Assn. (founder, v.p.), Internat. Assn. Ins. Counsel, Atlanta Claims Assn., Lawyers Club Atlanta, Chi Phi, Phi Delta Phi. Presbyterian. Clubs: Cherokee Town and Country, Commerce, Univ. Yacht (past commodore). Federal civil litigation, Business torts, Personal injury. Home: 4350 E Conway Dr Atlanta GA 30327 Office: 2300 Equitable Bldg 100 Peachtree St Atlanta GA 30303

SAVIANO, EDWARD STEVEN, lawyer; b. N.Y.C., Sept. 16, 1953; s. Edward Anthony and Alda Mary (Giorgi) S. BS in Bus. and Econs. with honors, Lehigh U., 1975; JD with honors, Villanova U., 1978; LLM in Tax, NYU, 1980. Bar: Fla. 1978, Pa. 1978, N.Y. 1979, N.J. 1981. Tax acct. Ernst & Whinney, N.Y.C., 1978-79; assoc. Wormser, Kiely, Alessandroni, Hyde & McCann, N.Y.C., 1980-86; gen. counsel Lilly, Sullivan et al, N.Y.C., 1986—; adj. prof. Iona Coll., New Rochelle, N.Y., 1983-84. Mem. ABA (tax sect.), N.Y. State Bar Assn. (tax sect.), Fla. Bar Assn. Corporate taxation, Personal income taxation, Private international. Home: 201 E 17th St Apt 12-F New York NY 10003 Office: Lilly Sullivan et al 17 Battery Pl New York NY 10004

SAVILLE, ROYCE BLAIR, lawyer; b. Cumberland, Md., Aug. 5, 1948; s. E. Blair and Audrey (Cosner) S.; m. Sharon Ann Brinkman, Apr. 3, 1981; children—Melissa Ann, Lauren Ashley, Meagan Elizabeth. B.A., W.Va. U., 1970; J.D., W.Va. Coll. Law, 1974. Bar: W.Va. 1974, U.S. Dist. Ct. (so. and no. dists.) W.Va. 1974. Assoc., William J. Oates, Jr. Atty. at Law, Romney, W.Va., 1974-75; ptnr. Oates and Saville Attys. at Law, Romney, 1975-77; sole practice, Romney, 1978—; pres. Potomac Land Co., 1975—; mental hygiene commr. Hampshire County, Romney, 1976—; mcpl. judge City of Romney, 1980—. Mem., Hampshire County Devel. Authority, Romney, Hampshire County Farm Bur.; dir. Potomac Highlands Travel Council, Elkins, W.Va., 1984—; del. W.Va. Democratic Conv., Charleston, 1984; vestryman St. Stephen's Episcopal Ch., Romney, 1984-86. Mem. ABA, W.Va. Bar Assn., Assn. Trial Lawyers Am., W.Va. Trial Lawyers Assn., W. Va. Law Sch. Assn. (life), W.Va. U. Alumni Assn. (life), Phi Alpha Delta (life). Lodges: Rotary, Masons. Real property, State civil litigation, General practice. Home: Liberty Hall 276 E Main St Romney WV 26757 also: Mill Island Moorefield WV 26836 Office: 95 W Main St PO Box 2000 Romney WV 26757

SAVIT, JOEL B., lawyer; b. N.Y.C., Nov. 17, 1947; s. Sam and Ada (Hirshson) S.; m. Sarah Anne Prus; children: Robert, Marissa. BS, Bklyn. Coll., 1969; JD, St. John's U., Jamaica, N.Y., 1975. Bar: N.Y. 1976, U.S. Dist. Ct. (ea. and so. dists) N.Y. 1976. Assoc. Larry H. Lipsig, P.C., N.Y.C., 1976-77, Schneider, Kleinick & Weitz, N.Y.C., 1977-80; sole practice N.Y.C., 1980-84; assoc. Philip M. Damashek, P.C., N.Y.C., 1984—. Coach North Bellmore Soccer League, 1985; committeeman 45th A.D. Rep. Club, 1977-81. Mem. Am. Trial Lawyers Assn., N.Y. Trial Lawyers Assn. Federal civil litigation, State civil litigation, Personal injury. Home: 2648 Rachel St South Bellmore NY 11710 Office: Philip M Damashek PC 35 Worth St New York NY 10013

SAVITT, SUSAN SCHENKEL, lawyer; b. Bklyn., Aug. 21, 1943; d. Edward Charles and Sylvia (Dlugatch) S.; m. Harvey Savitt, July 2, 1969 (div. 1978); children: Andrew Todd, Daniel Cory. BA magna cum laude, Pa. State U., 1964; JD, Columbia U., 1968. Bar: N.Y. 1968, U.S. Dist. Ct. (so. and ea. dists.) N.Y. 1973, U.S. Tax Ct. 1973, U.S. Ct. Appeals (2d cir.) 1981, U.S. Supreme Ct. 1980. Atty. Nassau County Legal Services, Freeport, N.Y., 1973-74; assoc. Bernardo & Farrauto, Yonkers, N.Y., 1975-77; asst. corp. counsel City of Yonkers, 1977-78; adj. prof. Elizabeth Seton Coll., Yonkers, 1982-83; from assoc. to ptnr. Epstein, Becker, Borsody & Green, P.C., N.Y.C., 1978—. Mem. Hastings-on-Hudson (N.Y.) Sch. Bd., 1984—, v.p., 1986—; trustee Westchester County Civil Liberties Union, White Plains, N.Y., 1976-77; v.p. PTSA, 1974-76. Mem. ABA, N.Y. State Bar Assn., N.Y. State Women's Assn., N.Y. State Sch. Bd. Attys. Assn., N.Y. State Pub. Employer Labor Relations Assn., Pa. State Alumni Club (v.p. Westchester County 1985—), Westchester County C. of C., N.Y. C. of C. (mem. small bus. com.), Phi Beta Kappa, Alpha Kappa Delta, Phi Gamma Mu, Pi Kappa Phi. Local government, Labor, Federal civil litigation. Office: Epstein Becker Borsody & Green PC 250 Park Ave New York NY 10177-0077

SAVRANN, RICHARD ALLEN, lawyer; b. Boston, July 29, 1935; s. Abraham B. and Doris (Curhan) S.; m. Diane Barbara Kleven, Dec. 22, 1957; children: Stephen Keith, Russell Carl. BA, Harvard U., 1956, JD, 1959. Bar: Mass. 1959, U.S. Dist. Ct. Mass. 1963, U.S. Ct. Appeals (1st cir.) 1965. Assoc. Law Office of Jerome Rappaport, Boston, 1963-69; asst. atty. gen. Commonwealth of Mass., Boston, 1969-70; ptnr. Newell, Savrann & Miller, Boston, 1969-76; sr. ptnr. Kunian, Savrann & Miller, Boston, 1976-81, Singer, Stoneman, Kunian & Kurland, P.C., Boston, 1981—. Chmn. Andover (Mass.) Housing Authority, 1972—; pres. Hospice of Greater Lawrence, North Andover, Mass., 1984; bd. dirs. Boston Latin Sch. Found., 1986—. Mem. ABA, Mass. Bar Assn., Boston Bar Assn. Club: Indian Ridge Country (Andover). Avocations: golf, opera. State civil litigation, Personal injury, General corporate. Home: 11 Sheridan Rd Andover MA 01810 Office: Singer Stoneman Kunian & Kurland PC 100 Charles River Plaza Boston MA 02114

SAWYER, JAMES, lawyer; b. N.Y.C., Feb. 18, 1946; s. Jules and Florence Barbara (Wishnew) S.; m. Dianne Gelfand, June 27, 1965; children—Kim, Caryn. B.A., Adelphi U., 1967; J.D., St. John's U., 1969. Bar: N.Y. 1970, U.S. Dist. Ct. (so. and ea. dists.) N.Y. 1971, U.S. Tax Ct. 1972, U.S. Ct. Appeals (2d cir.) 1972, U.S. Ct. Appeals (1st cir.) 1975, Fla. 1981, U.S. Supreme Ct. 1981. Ptnr. Martin, Van De Walle & Sawyer, Great Neck, N.Y., 1970-81, Hession, Halpern, Bekoff & Sawyer, Mineola, N.Y., 1982-87, Sawyer & Davis, Garden City, N.Y., 1987—. Exec. v.p. Temple Or-Elohim, Jericho, N.Y., 1983—. Mem. ABA, N.Y. State Bar Assn., Nassau County Bar Assn. Jewish. Federal civil litigation, Personal injury, Probate. Office: Sawyer & Davis 200 Garden City Plaza Garden City NY 11530

SAWYER, ROBERT KENDAL, JR., lawyer; b. Boston, Dec. 14, 1947; s. Robert K. and Eleanor Grace (Rideout) S.; m. Nancy Scola, Aug. 24, 1969; children: David, Elizabeth. BA, U. Mass., 1969; JD, Suffolk U., 1980. Bar: Mass. 1980, U.S. Dist. Ct. Mass. 1981, U. Supreme Ct. 1984. Counsel devel. div. Dunkin Donuts, Inc., Randolph, Mass., 1980—. Chmn. Community Cable Access Commn., Medfield, Mass., 1985—. Mem. ABA (forum sub-com. on franchising 1980—, mem. sect. real property div., com. on coml. leasing), Mass. Bar Assn., Internat. Bar Assn., Internat. Franchise Assn. Real property, Landlord-tenant, Franchising. Office: Dunkin Donuts Inc 5 Pacella Park Dr PO Box 317 Randolph MA 02368

SAWYER, THEODORE D(ANIEL), lawyer; b. Columbus, Ohio, May 2, 1938; s. Theodore Daniel and Elizabeth (Morgan) S.; m. Barbara L. Jones, Aug. 27, 1964; children—Chad, Bret, Andrew. B.A., Ohio State U., 1960; postgrad. Ohio U., 1961-62; J.D., Ohio NO. U., 1965. Bar: Ohio 1966, U.S. Dist. Ct. (so. dist.) Ohio 1967, U.S. Ct. Appeals (6th cir.) 1981, U.S. Supreme Ct. 1982. Asst. law dir. City of Springfield (Ohio), 1966; assoc. Potts, Schmidt & Lewis, Columbus, 1966-69; ptnr. Crabbe, brown, Jones, Potts & Schmidt, after 1970, now Crabbe, Brown et al. Pres. Forest Park Civic Assn., Columbus, 1972-73. Mem. Ohio Assn. Civil Trial Attys. (pres. 1977-78), exec. com. 1973-81), Lawyers Club Columbus (pres. 1979-80), Barristers Club, Columbus Def. Assn. (pres. 1974-75), Def. Research Inst. (regional v.p. 1979-81, dir. 1982—), Columbus Bar Assn., Ohio State Bar Assn., ABA, Internat. Assn. Ins. Counsel (chmn. med. malpractice com.), Am. Judicature Soc., Am. Arbitration Assn. Lutheran. Club: Creighton. Author monograph: (with Mary Picken): Defending the Hospital Emergency Room, 1981. Federal civil litigation, State civil litigation, Personal injury. Home: 2026 Guilford Rd Columbus OH 43221 Office: Crabbe Brown et al One Nationwide Plaza 2500 PO Box 15039 Columbus OH 43215

SAWYIER, MICHAEL TOD, lawyer; b. Boston, Jan. 6, 1948; s. Calvin Parker and Fay (Horton) S.; m. Judith Puistonen, June 6, 1968; children: Julianne Patricia, Justine Fay, Alexandra Lee. BA, Harvard U., 1969; JD, U. Chgo., 1972; LLM, Yale U., 1973. Bar: Ill. 1972, D.C. 1974, N.Y. 1974, Calif. 1976, Ind. 1983, U.S. Dist. Ct. (no. dist.) Ill. 1979, U.S. Ct. Appeals (7th cir.) 1981, U.S. Dist. Ct. (no. and so. dists.) Ind. 1983, U.S. Supreme Ct. 1984. Atty.-adviser Office of Legal Adviser U.S. Dept. State, Washington, 1974-75; assoc. Pillsbury, Madison and Sutro, San Francisco, 1975-77, Baker and McKenzie, Chgo., 1977-79, Foss, Schuman, Drake & Barnard, Chgo., 1979-87; ptnr. Mathewson, Hamblet & Casey, Chgo., 1987—; v.p., bd. dirs. Columbiad Devels., Inc., Chgo., Columbiad Services Inc.; bd. dirs. Beverly Bank Chgo. Bd. dirs. Music of Baroque, Chgo., 1977—; mem. guarantors' bd. Goodman Theatre, Chgo., 1984—. Recipient Paul Cornell prize Hyde Park Hist. Soc., Chgo., 1982. Mem. ABA, Ill. Bar Assn., Chgo. Bar Assn., Ind. Bar Assn., Am. Soc. Internat. Law. Clubs: Chgo. Literary, Saddle and Cycle, Cliffdwellers (Chgo.). Antitrust, Real property, Securities. Home: 4939 S Greenwood Ave Chicago IL 60615 Office: Mathewson Hamblet & Casey 36 W Randolph St Chicago IL 60601

SAX, JOSEPH LAWRENCE, lawyer, educator; b. Chgo., Feb. 3, 1936; s. Benjamin Harry and Mary (Silverman) S.; m. Eleanor Charlotte Gettes, June 17, 1958; children—Katherine Elaine, Valerie Beth, Anne-Marie. A.B., Harvard, 1957; J.D., U. Chgo., 1959. Bar: D.C. 1960, U.S. Supreme Ct. 1966. Atty. Dept. Justice, Washington, 1959-60; pvt. practice Washington, 1960-62; prof. U. Colo. Law Sch., 1962-65, U. Mich. Law Sch., Ann Arbor, 1966-86, U. Calif., Berkeley, 1987—; vis. prof. U. Calif. Law Sch., Berkeley, 1965-66, 86, Stanford Law Sch., 1985; fellow Ctr. Advanced Study in Behavioral Scis., 1977-78; cons. U.S. Senate Com. on Pub. Works, 1970-71; mem. cons. council Conservation Found., 1969-73; mem. legal adv. com. Pres.'s Council on Environ. Quality, 1970-72; mem. environ. studies bd. Nat. Acad. Sci., 1970-73; mem. Mich. Environ. Rev. Bd., 1973-74. Author: Waters and Water Rights, 1967, Water Law, Planning and Policy, 1968, Defending the Environment, 1971, Mountains Without Handrails, 1980, Legal Control of Water Resources, 1986. Bd. dirs. Environ. Law Inst., Washington, 1970-75; trustee Center for Law and Social Policy, 1970-76; regional gov. Internat. Council Environmental Law; gov.'s rep. Gt. Lakes Task Force, 1984-85. Served with USAF, 1960. Environment, Real property. Home: 850 Powell St #106 San Francisco CA 94108

SAX, SPENCER MERIDITH, lawyer; b. Passaic, N.J., June 7, 1955; s. Sander and Sylvia (Manelis) S.; m. Carie Dale Casper, Nov. 4, 1984. BA, Columbia U., 1977; JD, Vanderbilt U., 1980. Bar: Fla. 1980, U.S. Dist. Ct. (so. dist.) Fla. 1980, U.S. Ct. Appeals (5th and 11th cirs.) 1981, U.S. Supreme Ct. 1984. Assoc. Sales & Weissman, P.A., West Palm Beach, Fla., 1980-81, Sachs & Weiss, P.A., Boca Raton, Fla., 1981-85; ptnr. Sachs & Sax, Boca Raton, 1985—. Mem. Palm Beach County Bar Assn. (vice chmn. condominium com. 1985—), South Palm Beach County Bar Assn. State civil litigation, Construction, Condominium. Office: Sachs & Sax PA 1499 W Palmetto Park Rd Boca Raton FL 33432

SAXON, JANET D., federal government official. Chief adminstrv. law judge U.S. Internat. Trade Commn., Washington. Office: US Internat Trade Com Chief Adminstrv Law Judge 701 E St NW Washington DC 20436 *

SAXON, JOHN DAVID, lawyer, policy analyst, educator; b. Anniston, Ala., July 21, 1950; s. J.Z. and Sarah Elizabeth (Steadham) S.; m. Elizabeth Lord, Mar. 10, 1973. B.A with honors, U. Ala., 1972, J.D., 1977; grad. Exec. Program Stanford U., 1986; M.A., U. N.C., 1973. Bar: Ala. 1977, U.S. Dist. Ct. (no. dist.) Ala. 1977, U.S. Supreme Ct. 1983. Adminstrv. asst. to acting chief exec. officer U. Ala.-University, 1976-77; assoc. Sirote, Permutt, Friend, Friedman, Held & Apolinsky, P.A., Birmingham, Ala., 1977-78; spl. asst. to Vice Pres. U.S., Washington, 1978-79; counsel subcom. on jurisprudence and govt. relations Com. on Judiciary, U.S. Senate, Washington, 1979-80, counsel Select Com. on Ethics, 1980-83; dir. corp. issues RCA, Washington, 1983-86; Washington rep., 1986-87, Gen. Electric Co., 1986-87; assoc. counsel U.S. Senate Selecte com. on secret mil. assistance to Iran and the Nicaraguan Opposition, 1987—; adj. instr. polit. communication U. Md., 1982-83 ; instr. speech communication U. Ala.-University, 1973; instr. speech communication and mgmt. Brewer Jr. Coll., Tuscaloosa, 1975-77; adj. instr. civil litigation Samford U., Birmingham, 1977-78; vis. scholar The Hastings Ctr., 1983; mem. Am. Observer Delegation, Kettering Found., U.S.-China Task Force, 1986—; bd. dirs. White House Fellows Found., 1981-84 , pres., 1983-84; mem. bd. advisers Center for Publ. Law and Service, U. Ala. Sch. Law, 1976-83; mem. Pres.'s Commn. White House Fellowships, 1983-84; mem. Washington Local Devel. Corp, 1986—. Served to 2d lt. U.S. Army, 1974, capt. Res. White House fellow, 1978-79; named Disting. Mil. Grad., U. Ala., 1972, recipient Bench and Bar Outstanding Sr. award, 1977. Mem. ABA (spl. com. litigation sect.), Ala. Bar Assn., Fed. Bar Assn., Am. Judicature Soc., White House Fellows Assn. (pres. 1983-84), Omicron Delta Kappa, Omicron Delta Epsilon, Phi Alpha Theta, Pi Sigma Alpha. Democrat. Methodist. Contbr. articles to newspapers and legal publs., chpts. to books. Legislative, Jurisprudence.

SAYAD, PAMELA MIRIAM, lawyer; b. San Francisco, Apr. 13, 1949; d. Samuel Daniel and Charlotte (Yonan) S.; A.B. in Polit. Sci., U. Calif.-Berkeley, 1970; J.D., U. Notre Dame Sch. Law, 1973; Bar: D.C. 1974, U.S. Dist. Ct. D.C. 1974, Mass. 1980, U.S. Dist Ct. (no. dist.) Calif. 1981, Calif. 1982, U.S. Dist. Ct. (no. dist.) Calif., 1981, U.S. Ct. Appeals (9th cir.) 1981, U.S. Dist. Ct. D.C. 1974, U.S. Ct. Appeals (D.C. cir.) 1974, U.S. Dist. Ct. Mass. 1980, U.S. Dist. Ct. (ea. dist.) Calif. 1986. Atty. U.S. HEW, Washington, 1973-74; atty. solicitor's office Div. Indian Affairs, U.S. Dept. Interior, Washington, 1974-77; asst. U.S. atty. for D.C., Washington, 1977-80; assoc. Swartz & Swartz, Boston, 1980-81; assoc. Archer, Rosenak & Hanson, San Francisco, 1981-82, Bourhis, Lawless & Harvey, San Francisco, 1982-83; ptnr. Sayad & Trigero, San Francisco, 1983—; bd. of trustees Calif. Indian Legal Services, 1984—; bd. dirs. Found. Study Electorial Reform. Author: (with others) Criminal Practice Inst. Manual, 1980; Litigating for Profit, 1983; also articles. Mem. Jr. League San Francisco, 1981—. Mem. ABA, Assn. Trial Lawyers Am., Calif. Trial Lawyers Assn., Bar Assn. San Francisco, Calif. Women Lawyers, Gamma Phi Beta. Democrat. Presbyterian. Federal civil litigation, State civil litigation, Personal injury. Office: Sayad & Trigero 444 Market St Suite 930 San Francisco CA 94111

SAYERS, RANDALL WILLIAM, lawyer; b. South Bend, Ind., Sept. 27, 1952; s. Richard A. and Mary K. (Bybee) S.; m. Jeanne W. Walters, Apr. 30, 1983; 1 child, Justin R. BA, U. Notre Dame, 1974; MA, Ind. U., 1975; JD, William Mitchell Coll. Law, 1981. Bar: Minn. 1981, U.S. Dist. Ct. Minn. 1981. Asst. dir. corps. Minn. Sec. of State, St. Paul, 1976-78, dir. corps., 1979-81; assoc. Hansen, Dordell, Bradt, Odlaug & Bradt, St. Paul, 1981—; rep. Minn. Adv. Task Force on Corp. Law, St. Paul, 1980-81. Vol. atty. So. Minn. Regional Legal Services, St. Paul, 1986; arbitrator Better Business Bur., Mpls., 1986. Mem. ABA, Minn. Bar Assn., Ramsey County Bar Assn. (co-chmn. bus. banking and corp. sect. 1986), Minn. Def. Lawyers Assn. General corporate, Probate, State civil litigation. Office: Hansen Dordell et al 444 Cedar St 1200 Conwell Tower Saint Paul MN 55101

SAYLER, JOHN LISTON, lawyer; b. Cleve., Oct. 8, 1956; s. Paul T. Jr. and Patricia (Merry) S.; m. Beth Woike, July 7, 1979. BA, Ohio No. U., 1978; JD, Cleveland Marshall Coll. Law, 1981. Bar: Ohio 1981, U.S. Dist. Ct. (no. and ea. dists.) 1983. Sole practice Cleve., 1982—. Mem. ABA, Ohio Bar Assn., Cleve. Bar Assn. Republican. United Methodist. Avocations: antiques, fishing, outdoor recreation. Bankruptcy, Consumer commercial, Family and matrimonial. Home: 1296 W 106 St Cleveland OH 44102 Office: 745 Leader Bldg Cleveland OH 44114

SAYLER, ROBERT NELSON, lawyer; b. Kansas City, Mo., June 1, 1940; s. John William and Roberta (Nelson) S.; m. Martha Leith, Aug. 1962; children: Christina, Bentley. BA, Stanford U.; JD, Harvard U. Bar: U.S. Dist. Ct. D.C. 1966, U.S. Ct. Appeals (D.C. cir.) 1966, U.S. Supreme Ct. 1971, D.C. 1972, U.S. Ct. Appeals (2d cir.) 1977. From assoc. to ptnr. Covington & Burling, Washington, 1965—. V.p. Neighborhood Legal Services, Washington, 1980-82; pres. Legal Aid Soc., Washington, 1983-84. Fellow Am. Bar Found.; mem. ABA (dir. programs, program chmn. 1981, 85, council, chmn. litigation sect.). Democrat. Federal civil litigation, General corporate, Insurance. Office: Covington & Burling 1201 Pennsylvania Ave NW PO Box 7566 Washington DC 20044

SAYLOR, LARRY JAMES, lawyer; b. Biloxi, Miss., Nov. 7, 1948; s. Rufus Don and Alice Julia (Kidd) S.; m. Mary L. Mullendore, Dec. 27, 1975; children: David James, Stephen Michael. AB in Political Sci., Miami U., Oxford, Ohio, 1970; M in City and Regional Planning, Ohio State U., 1976; JD, U. Mich., 1976. Bar: D.C. 1976, Mich. 1977, U.S. Ct. Appeals (D.C. cir.) 1977, U.S. Ct. Appeals (6th cir.) 1978, U.S. Supreme Ct. 1981, U.S. Ct. Appeals (10th cir.) 1982. Law clk. to presiding judge U.S. Ct. Appeals (D.C. cir.), Washington, 1976-77; ptnr. Miller, Canfield, Paddock and Stone, Detroit, 1977—. Article editor Mich. Law Rev., 1975-76; contbr. articles to profl. jours. Served to 1st lt. USAF, 1970-72. Mem. ABA (antitrust and litigation sects.), Mich. Bar Assn., D.C. Bar Assn., World Trade Club. Club: Detroit Econ. Avocations: skiing, woodworking. Antitrust, Federal civil litigation, State civil litigation. Home: 424 Lincoln Rd Grosse Pointe MI 48230 Office: Miller Canfield Paddock & Stone 2500 Comerica Bldg Detroit MI 48230

SAYRE, CHARLES MICHAEL, lawyer; b. Waterloo, Iowa, July 26, 1945; s. Charles Dowd Sayre and Kathleen Louise (Riebe) Hoenig. BSBA, U. Nebr., 1967, JD, 1978. Bar: N.Mex. 1978, Colo. 1979, U.S. Dist. Ct. Colo. 1979. Broker 1st Mid Am. Inc., Lincoln, Neb., 1971-73; realtor Austin and Co., Lincoln, 1973-75; ptnr. Calkins, Kramer et al, Denver, 1978-83; sole practice Denver, 1983-86; ptnr. Sayre, Ankele & Icenogle, Englewood, Colo., 1986—. Served to lt. USNR, 1967-70, Vietnam. Mem. ABA, Colo. Bar Assn., Denver Bar Assn., N.Mex. Bar Assn. Local government, Municipal bonds, Real property. Home: 3602 S Grape Denver CO 80237 Office: 7720 E Belleview Ave Suite 250 Englewood CO 80111

SAYRE, JOHN MARSHALL, lawyer; b. Boulder, Colo., Nov. 9, 1921; s. Henry Marshall and Lulu M. (Cooper) S.; m. Jean Miller, Aug. 22, 1943; children—Henry M., Charles Franklin, John Marshall, Ann Elizabeth Sayre Taggart (dec.). B.A., U. Colo., 1943, J.D., 1948. Bar: Colo. 1948, U.S. Dist. Ct. Colo. 1952, U.S. Ct. Appeals (10th cir.) 1964. Law clk. trust dept. Denver Nat. Bank, 1948-49; asst. cashier, trust officer Nat. State Bank of Boulder, 1949-50; ptnr. Ryan, Sayre, Martin, Brotzman, Boulder, 1950-66, Davis, Graham & Stubbs, Denver, 1966—. Bd. dirs. Boulder Sch. Dist. 3, 1951-57; city atty. City of Boulder, 1952-55; gen. counsel Colo. Mcpl. League, 1956-63; counsel No. Colo. Water Conservancy Dist. and mcpl. subdist., 1964-87, spl. counsel, 1987—, bd. dirs. dist., 1960-64; legal counsel Colo. Assn. Commerce and Industry. Served to lt. (j.g.) USNR, 1943-46. Decorated Purple Heart. Fellow Am. Bar. Found.; mem. ABA, Colo. Bar Assn., Boulder County Bar Assn., Denver Bar Assn., Nat. Water Resources Assn. (Colo. dir. 1980—, pres. 1984-86). Republican. Episcopalian. Clubs: Denver Country, Denver, Petroleum. Real property, Local government. Office: PO Box 185 Denver CO 80201

SAYRE, MATT MELVIN MATHIAS, lawyer; b. Seattle, Sept. 5, 1934; s. Melvin Edward and Ethyl Elizabeth (Mathias) S.; m. Sheri Teagle, Oct. 21, 1956; children—Jeffrey Mathias, Steven Michael, David Matthew. B.A., U. Wash., 1956; J.D., Gonzaga U., 1964. Bar: Wash. 1964, D.C. 1981, U.S. Dist. Ct. (we. dist.) Wash. 1964, U.S. Ct. Appeals (9th cir.) 1972, U.S. Supreme Ct. 1980. Law clk. Justice Robert T. Hunter, Olympia, Wash., 1964-65; asst. counsel Pacific Car & Foundry Co. Renton, Wash., 1965-66; ptnr. Mullavey, Hageman, Treece & Sayre, Seattle, 1966-69, McBride & Sayre, 1969-71; sole practice Seattle, 1971—; judge pro tem King County Superior Ct., 1973-83. Served to 1st lt. USAF, 1957-60. Mem. ABA, Wash. Bar Assn. (spl. dist. counsel 1982—, editorial adv. bd. 1986—), Seattle-King County Bar Assn. (treas. 1982-85, trustee 1985—), South King County Bar Assn., Wash. Trial Lawyers Assn., Beta Theta Pi, Phi Delta Phi. Clubs: Wash. Athletic, Rainier Golf and Country, Lions. General practice, Probate, State civil litigation. Office: Boren & Jefferson Bldg 1016 Jefferson St Seattle WA 98104

SBARATTA, RICHARD MARK, lawyer; b. Jersey City, July 1, 1948; s. Philip and Carmela (Dono) S.; m. Corinne MacMahon, June 11, 1977; children—Brianne, Ryan, Kyle. B.A., Montclair State Coll., 1970; M.A. in Econs., Pa. State U., 1974; J.D., N.Y. Law Sch., 1978. Bar: N.Y. 1979. Econ. analyst Nat. Econ. Research Assocs., N.Y.C., 1974-78; regulatory atty. AT&T, N.Y.C., 1978-83; v.p., gen. counsel Nat. Exchange Carrier Assn., Whippany, N.J., 1983-85; solicitor Bell South, Atlanta, 1985—. Served with U.S. Army, 1971-72. Mem. ABA, N.Y. State Bar Assn., Am. Econ. Assn., Omicron Delta Epsilon. Administrative and regulatory. Home: 1504 Ballard St Silver Spring MD 20910 Office: So Bell Ctr 675 W Peachtree St NE Atlanta GA 30375

SCAGNELLI, JOHN MARK, lawyer; b. N.Y.C., Feb. 5, 1951; s. John Paul and Bernice (Aparo) S.; m. Marilyn Joyce Lehmann, July 24, 1950; 1 son, Jeffrey Mark. B.A., Yale U., 1972, J.D., 1975. Bar: N.Y. 1976, U.S. Dist. Ct. (ea. and so. dists.) N.Y. 1976, N.J. 1984. Assoc. Townley & Updike, N.Y.C., 1975-77; house counsel Chesebrough-Pond's Inc., Greenwich, Conn., 1977-79; assoc. Milgrim, Thomajan, Jacobs & Lee, N.Y.C., 1979-82; v.p., gen. counsel Allied Maintenance Corp., N.Y.C., 1982-86, counsel Clapp& Eisenberg, Newark, 1986—. Contbr. articles to profl. jours.; mem. editorial bd. Trademark Reporter, 1978—. Mem. ABA, N.Y. State Bar Assn. (environ., labor, employment, trade regulation), Assn. Bar City N.Y., N.Y. County Lawyers Assn., N.J. State Bar Assn. Labor, Environment, Trademark and copyright. Home: 84 Candace Ln Chatham NJ 07928 Office: Clapp & Eisenberg 80 Park Plaza Newark NJ 07102

SCALES, JOHN K., federal government official; b. Oct. 19, 1937; s. Richard Davies and Constance (Kent) S. BA, Williams Coll., 1959; postgrad., Cornell Law Sch. Assoc. Sullivan & Worcester, Boston, 1962-67; mem. Pres.'s Commn. on Civil Disorder, Washington, 1967-68; Rep. counsel mem. U.S. Senate, Washington, 1969-75; atty., adviser office of gen. counsel Agy. for Internat. Devel., Washington, 1982-85; gen. counsel Peace Corps, Washington, 1985—. Office: Peace Corps Office of the Director 806 Connecticut Ave NW Washington DC 20525 *

SCALETTA, PHILLIP JASPER, lawyer, educator; b. Sioux City, Iowa, Aug. 20, 1925; s. Phillip and Louise (Pelmulder) S.; m. Helen M. Scaletta; children—Phillip R., Cherl D. Kesler. B.S., Morningside Coll., Sioux City, 1948; J.D., U. Iowa, 1950. Bar: Iowa 1950, U.S. Dist. Ct. Iowa 1950, Ind. 1966, U.S. Supreme Ct. 1968. Ptnr. McKnight and Scaletta, Sioux City, 1950-51; field rep. Farmers Ins. Group, Sioux City, 1951-54, sr. liability examiner, Aurora, Ill., 1954-60; br. claims mgr., Ft. Wayne, Ind., 1960-66; prof. law Purdue U., West Lafayette, Ind., 1966—, prof. bus. law Krannert Grad Sch. Mgmt. Mem. Ind. Gov's Commn. Individual Privacy, 1975. Recipient Best Tchr. of Yr. award Standard Oil Ind. Found., 1972; Outstanding Tchr. award Purdue U. Alumni Assn., 1974. Mem. Am. Arbitration Assn., Am. Bus. Law Assn. (pres.), Am. Judicature Soc., ABA, Ind. Bar Assn., Tippecanoe County Bar Assn., Tri State Bus Law Assn., Midwest Bus. Adminstrn. Assn., Ind. Acad. Social Scis., Internat. Bar Assn., Computer Law Assn., Inc., Beta Gamma Sigma (bd. govs.). Author: Business Law, Principles and Cases, 1st edit., 1982, 2d edit., 1985; co-author workbook, 1982; contbr. numerous articles to profl. jours. Labor, Personal injury, Legal education. Office: Purdue U 511 Krannert Bldg West Lafayette IN 47906

SCALIA, ANTONIN, justice; b. Trenton, N.J., Mar. 11, 1936; s. S. Eugene and Catherine Louise (Panaro) S.; m. Maureen McCarthy, Sept. 10, 1960; children—Ann Forrest, Eugene, John Francis, Catherine Elisabeth, Mary Clare, Paul David, Matthew, Christopher James, Margaret Jane. A.B., Georgetown U., 1957; student, U. Fribourg, Switzerland, 1955-56; LL.B., Harvard, 1960. Bar: Ohio 1962, Va. 1970. Assoc. Jones, Day, Cockley & Reavis, Cleve., 1961-67; assoc. prof. U. Va. Law Sch., 1967-70, prof., 1970-74; gen. counsel Office Telecommunications Policy, Exec. Office of Pres., 1971-72; chmn. Adminstrv. Conf. U.S., Washington, 1972-74; asst. atty. gen. U.S. Office Legal Counsel, Justice Dept., 1974-77; vis. prof. Georgetown Law Center, 1977, Stanford Law Sch., 1980-81; vis. scholar Am. Enterprise Inst., 1977; prof. Law Sch., U. Chgo., 1977-82; judge U.S. Ct. Appeals (D.C. Cir.), 1982-86; justice U.S. Supreme Ct., Washington, 1986—; cons. CSC, 1969, 77, FCC, 1977, FTC, 1978, 80; Bd. dirs. Nat. Inst. for Consumer Justice, 1972-73, Center for Adminstrv. Justice, 1972-74; adv. council for legal policy studies Am. Enterprise Inst., 1978—. Editor: Regulation mag, 1979-82. Sheldon fellow Harvard, 1960-61. Mem. ABA (council, sect. adminstrv. law 1974-77, chmn. sect. adminstrv. law 1981-82, chmn. conf. sect. chmn. 1982-83). Office: US Supreme Ct Washington DC 20543

SCALLY, JOHN JOSEPH, JR., lawyer; b. Glen Ridge, N.J., Feb. 3, 1951; s. John Joseph and Emelia (Passudette) S.; m. Karen Elizabeth Scofield, Aug. 29, 1981; 1 child, Courtney. A.B., Muhlenberg Coll., 1973; J.D. Cath. U. Am., 1976. Bar: N.Y. 1977, N.J. 1977, D.C. 1977, U.S. Dist. Ct. N.J. 1977. Assoc. firm Mudge Rose Guthrie & Alexander, N.Y.C., 1976-82; ptnr. firm McCarter & English, Newark, 1982—. Mem. debt mgmt. adv. com. N.J. Local Fin. Bd., Trenton, 1983—. Mem. Nat. Assn. Bond Lawyers, N.J. Mcpl. Attys., Mcpl. Fin. Officers Am., Mcpl. Fin. Officers N.J. Roman Catholic. Clubs: Fiddler's Elbow Country (Bedminster, N.J.); Essex (Newark); World Trade Ctr. (N.Y.C.); N.J. Bond. Municipal bonds. Home: 10 Highland Ave Short Hills NJ 07078 Office: McCarter & English 550 Broad St Newark NJ 07102

SCAMMEL, HARRY GLENN, lawyer; b. Dallas, Aug. 28, 1948; s. Byrt Curtis and Leah Glenda (Baker) S.; m. Van Thi Tran, Sept. 14, 1986. BA, Yale U., 1970; JD, Harvard U., 1973. Bar: Tex. 1973, Calif. 1980. Assoc. Kilgore & Kilgore, Dallas, 1973-74, 77-78; trial atty. Interstate Commerce Commn., Washington, 1978-87; minority counsel Energy and Commerce Com. U.S. Ho. of Reps., Washington, 1987—. Served to lt. (JAGC) USNR, 1974-77. Mem. ABA (adminstrv. law sect., antitrust sect., rev. of rulemaking com.), Tex. Bar Assn., Calif. Bar Assn. Avocation: aviation and naval history. Administrative and regulatory, Federal civil litigation, Antitrust. Home: 3005 Torrey Place Alexandria VA 22302-3914 Office: House Annex II Room H2564 Washington DC 20515

SCANLON, LAWRENCE JOSEPH, lawyer; b. Akron, Ohio, May 22, 1951; s. Charles F. and Elizabeth Lawrence (Powell) S. BA, U. Akron, 1974, JD, 1978. Bar: Ohio 1978, U.S. Dist. Ct. (no. dist.) Ohio 1979, U.S. Ct. Appeals (6th cir.) 1983, U.S. Supreme Ct. 1986. Ptnr. Scanlon & Henretta, L.P.A., Akron, 1978—. Mem. ABA, Ohio Bar Assn., Akron Bar Assn., Assn. Trial Lawyers Am., Ohio Acad. Trial Lawyers, Nat. Inst. Trial Adv., Am. Soc. Law and Medicine, Aquatic Safety Injury Group. Personal injury, Professional negligence. Home: 176 N Portage Path Akron OH 44308 Office: Scanlon & Henretta LPA 76 S Main St 1515 Ohio Edison Bldg Akron OH 44308

SCANNELL, DAVID GEORGE, lawyer; b. Worcester, Mass., Apr. 24, 1939; s. Joseph Emmett and Mary Sylvester (Jollymore) S.; m. Susan Man Lloyd, July 6, 1968; children: Christopher, Anik, Kirsten. AB, Georgetown U., 1961; LLB, MBA, Columbia U., 1964. Bar: N.Y. 1965, U.S. Dist. Ct. (so. dist.) N.Y. 1968. Assoc. Donovan, Leisure, Newton & Irvine, N.Y.C., Paris and London, 1965-74; atty. Bangor Punta Corp., Greenwich, Conn., 1974-76, sr. atty., 1976-81, assoc. gen. counsel, 1981-86; sole practice Conn. and N.Y., 1986—. Mem. Westchester Fairfield Corp. Counsel Assn. (bd. dirs. 1984-86). Democrat. Roman Catholic. Contracts commercial, General corporate, General practice. Home and Office: 110 Turtleback Rd S New Canaan CT 06840

SCANTLEBURY, HILARY THOMAS, lawyer; b. N.Y.C., Apr. 13, 1944; s. Terence Patrick and Tatiana Scantlebury; 1 child, Colin David. BS, Fordham U., 1965, JD, 1975. Bar: Calif. 1976, Ill. 1978, U.S. Dist. Ct. (no. dist.) Ill. 1979. Claims atty. U.S. Aviation Underwriters, N.Y.C., 1976-79; assoc. Haskell & Perrin, Chgo., 1980-83; sole practice Chgo., 1984—. Served to capt. USMC, 1966-72. Personal injury, Insurance. Home: 4412 Capstan Dr Hoffman Estates IL 60195 Office: 20 N Wacker Dr Suite 3710 Chicago IL 60606

SCARBOROUGH, TONY, state supreme court judge. Former presiding judge 6th Jud. Dist., N. Mex. Dist. Ct.; judge New Mexico Supreme Court, Santa Fe, NM, 1987—. Office: NMex Supreme Ct PO Box 848 Santa Fe NM 87504

SCARDILLI, FRANK JOSEPH, lawyer; b. Newark, July 19, 1920; s. Joseph and Julia Scardilli; B.A. Montclair State Coll., 1942; LL.B., Yale U., 1949; postgrad. (Fulbright scholar) U. Rome (Italy), 1949-50, Cambridge (Eng.) U., summer 1950; LL.M., NYU, 1968. Bar: N.J. 1950, D.C. 1952, N.Y. 1954, U.S. Ct. Appeals (2d cir.) 1977, U.S. Dist. Ct. N.J., U.S. Dist. Ct. (so. and ea. dists.) N.Y. With Nat. Prodn. Authority, U.S. Dept. Commerce, Washington, 1951-53; with Garfield, Salomon & Mainzer, N.Y.C., 1954-70, White & Case, N.Y.C., 1970-75; with U.S. Atty's Office, Newark, 1975-77; vis. prof. Harvard Bus. Sch., Cambridge, Mass., 1959-60; staff counsel U.S. Ct. Appeals (2d cir.) N.Y., 1977—; TV lectr on law for nonlawyers. Trustee Inst. for Gen. Semantics. Served with USAAF, 1942-46. Mem. N.Y. Soc. for Gen. Semantics (pres.), ABA, Columbian Lawyers, Inst. for Jud. Adminstrn., Fed. Bar Council. Club: Harvard Bus. Sch. (N.Y.C.). Federal civil litigation. Home: 33 Greenwich Ave New York NY 10014 Office: Room 2803 US Courthouse Foley Sq New York NY 10007

SCARMINACH, CHARLES ANTHONY, lawyer; b. Syracuse, N.Y., Feb. 19, 1944; s. John Louis and Lucy (Egnoto) S.; children: John, Catherine, Karen. BA, U. Buffalo, 1965; JD, Syracuse U., 1968. Bar: N.Y. 1968, S.C. 1974. Gen. counsel Sea Pines Co., Hilton Head Island, S.C., 1973-78; sole practice, Hilton Head Island, 1978-83; ptnr. Novit & Scarminach, P.A., Hilton Head Island, 1983—. Chmn. bd. Sea Pines Montessori Sch., Hilton Head Island, 1979-83; bd. dirs. Hilton Head Preparatory Sch., 1984—, chmn. bd. trustees 1986—. Served to maj. U.S. Army, 1968-73. Mem. ABA, S.C. Bar Assn., N.Y. State Bar Assn. Democrat. Roman Catholic. Club: Sea Pines. General corporate, General practice, Real property. Home: 4 Spanish Moss Hilton Head Island SC 29928 Office: Novit & Scarminach PA PO Drawer 14 Hilton Head Island SC 29938

SCAROLA, JOHN, lawyer; b. Bklyn., July 24, 1947; s. John Anthony and Grace Ellen (Turnbull) S.; m. Anita Helene Kargauer, Jan. 4, 1969; children: Kristen, John Michael, Janna, David, Cara. BA, Georgetown U., 1969, JD, 1973. Bar: Fla. 1973, U.S. Dist. Ct. (so. dist.) Fla. 1974, U.S. Ct. Appeals (5th cir.) 1976. Chief felony prosecutor State Atty.'s Office, 15th Jud. Cir., West Palm Beach, Fla., 1973-78; ptnr., dir. Montgomery, Searcy & Denney P.A., West Palm Beach, 1978—; spl. counsel Fla. Jud. Qualifications Commn., Tallahassee, 1981—; asst. spl. prosecutor Statewide Grand Jury, Fla., 1977-78; instr. Palm Beach Jr. Coll., Lake Worth, Fla., 1974-78. Candidate Fla. State Senate, Dist. 84, 1978; chmn. bd. The Lord's Place Inc., West Palm Beach, 1981—; bd. dirs. Children's Genetic Disease Found., Miami, Fla., 1982—, Serra Club of the Palm Beaches, West Palm Beach, 1980—. Served with USAR, 1966-72. Mem. ABA, Fla. Bar (bd. cert. civil litigation 1984, pres.'s pro bono award 1984), Acad. Fla. Trial Lawyers, Palm Beach County Bar Assn., Palm Beach County Trial Lawyers Assn., West Palm Beach Jaycees. (bd. dirs.). Roman Catholic. State civil litigation, Federal civil litigation. Home: 2719 Embassy Dr West Palm Beach FL 33401 Office: Montgomery Searcy & Denney PA 2139 Palm Beach Lakes Blvd West Palm Beach FL 33409

SCARZAFAVA, JOHN FRANCIS, lawyer; b. Oneonta, N.Y., Apr. 4, 1947; s. Francis R. and Nettie (Ho Talen) S.; m. Nettie Jean Chambers; 1 child, Robert Francis; stepchildren: Angela Atkinson, Amber Atkinson, Amy Atkinson. BA, St. Bonaventure U., 1973; JD, St. Mary's U., San Antonio, 1975. Bar: Tex. 1975, U.S. Ct. Appeals (5th cir.) 1976, U.S. Dist. Ct. (we. dist.) Tex. 1978, U.S. Supreme Ct. 1979, N.Y. 1981, U.S. Dist. Ct. (no. dist.) N.Y. 1982. Assoc. Gochman & Weir, San Antonio, 1975-77, ptnr., 1977-78; ptnr. Scarzafava & Davis, San Antonio, 1978-82; sole practice Oneonta, 1982—. Contbr. numerous articles to profl. law jours. Chmn. Dem. Com., Oneonta, 1982-85; Dem. committeeman, Otsego County, N.Y., 1982-85; bd. dirs. St. Bonaventure U. Nat. Alumni, v.p. 1986—; bd. dirs. St. Mary's U. Sch. Law Alumni, 1979; mem. Citizen's Bd., Hartwick Coll., 1984—. Served to sgt. USAF, 1967-70. Mem. Assn. Trial Lawyers Am. (nat. sec. Labor law Sect. 1980, lectr. nat. conv. 1982, 86, instr. various Nat. Coll. of Adv. 1979—), Tex. Trial Lawyers Assn., N.Y. State Trial Lawyers Assn., San Antonio Trial Lawyers Assn., Delta Theta Phi (Dean Bickett Senate 1977). Roman Catholic. Club: 6th Ward Athletic (bd. dirs. 1984-85), President's (St. Mary's U.). Personal injury, Federal civil litigation, State civil litigation. Home: RD 1 Box 70D Oneonta NY 13820 Office: 48 Dietz St Suite C Oneonta NY 13820

SCARZAFAVA, NETTIE JEAN, lawyer; b. Bee Branch, Ark., Mar. 22, 1946; d. Robert Harry and Sylvia Yetive (Linn) Chambers; m. Robbie Ray Atkinson, Dec. 22, 1967 (div. 1976); children—Angela Linn, Amy Raye, Amber Jean; m. John Francis Scarzafava, Nov. 16, 1978. B.S., U. Central Ark., 1968; J.D., St. Mary's U., 1975. Bar: Tex. 1976, N.Y. 1981, U.S. Dist. Ct. (no. dist.) N.Y. 1981. Tchr. West Memphis Jr. High Sch., Ark., 1968-70, Alfred Beech Jr. High Sch., Savannah, Ga., 1970-71; sole practice, San Antonio, 1975-76, Oneonta, N.Y., 1981—; adminstrv. law judge Tex. Employment Commn., San Antonio, 1976-81; asst. gen. counsel Govt. Employees Credit Union, San Antonio, 1981; town justice Town of Oneonta, 1981—. Bd. dirs. Otsego County Family Services, 1982-84, OURS Assocs., Oneonta Youth Bur. Mem. AAUW, LWV, Assn. Trial Lawyers Am., N.Y. State Trial Lawyers Assn., Otsego County Magistrates Assn. (v.p. 1983-84), N.Y. State Magistrates Assn., Delta Theta Pi, Alpha Chi. Democrat. Methodist. Judicial administration, General practice. Office: 48 Dietz St Suite C Oneonta NY 13820

SCAVO, JAMES J., lawyer; b. Bklyn., Nov. 27, 1951; m. Dana K. Scavo. BA, SUNY, 1973; JD, St. John's U., 1976. Bar: Ga. 1976, Calif. 1985. Ptnr. Weinstock, Scavo & Montalto, Atlanta; cons. drafting Ga. Time Share Act, 1982. Contbr. articles to profl. jours. Chmn. Atlanta Clean City Commn., 1978-80; legal liaison Neighborhood Planning Units, Atlanta, 1976-80; trustee Community Assns. Inst. (nat. bd. 1981—). Mem. Ga. Bar Assn., Calif. Bar Assn., Atlanta Bar Assn. (chmn. real estate sect. 1986—). Real property, Administrative and regulatory, General corporate. Office: Weinstock Scavo & Montalto 3405 Piedmont Rd NE Suite 300 Atlanta GA 30305

SCEPER, DUANE HAROLD, lawyer; b. Norfolk, Va., Nov. 16, 1946; s. Robert George and Marion Eudora (Hynes) S.; m. Sharon Diane Cramer, July 4, 1981; stepchildren: Karin Stevenson, Diane Stevenson. BS in Law, Western State U., 1979, JD, 1980. Bar: Calif. 1982, U.S. Dist. Ct. (so. dist.) Calif. 1982. Field engr. Memorex/Tex. Instruments, San Diego, 1968-70; computer programmer San Diego, 1970-81; atty. Allied Ins. Group, San Diego, 1981-85; sole practice San Diego, 1985—; cons. computers 1980—; lectr. estate planning various orgns. Patentee in field. Active Com. to Elect King Golden to Congress, San Diego, 1978. Served with USAF, 1965-68. Recipient Am. Jurisprudence award, 1979. Mem. ABA, San Diego County Bar Assn., Assn. Trial Lawyers of Am., Calif. Trial Lawyers Assn., San Diego Trial Lawyers Assn., Delta Theta Phi. Democrat. State civil litigation, Estate planning, Insurance. Home: 2641 Massachusetts Ave Lemon Grove CA 92045 Office: 707 Broadway Suite 1100 San Diego CA 92101

SCHAAF, DOUGLAS ALLAN, lawyer; b. Green Bay, Wis., Nov. 18, 1955; s. Carlton Otto and Fern (Brunette) S.; m. Deborah L. Thomas, June 6, 1981 (div. Sept. 1985). BBA in Internat. Bus., St. Norbert Coll., DePere, Wis., 1978; JD, U. Notre Dame, 1981. Bar: Ill. 1981. Assoc. McDermott, Will & Emery, Chgo., 1981-84, Skadden, Arps, Slate, Meagher & Flom, Chgo., 1984—. Atty. Chgo. Vol. Legal Services, 1982—. Roman Catholic. Corporate taxation, General corporate, Personal income taxation. Home: 10 E Ontario #4301 Chicago IL 60611 Office: Skadden Arps Slate Meagher & Flom 333 W Wacker Dr #2100 Chicago IL 60606

SCHACHERL, ANNE WASHECHEK, lawyer, educator; b. Milw., July 6, 1954; d. Robert H. and Lorraine D. (Ulrich) Washechek; m. John A. Schacherl, July 9, 1977; 1 child, Katherine Cutler. BS, Carroll Coll., 1974; JD, U. Wis., 1979. Bar: Wis. 1979, U.S. Dist. Ct. (we. dist.) Wis. 1979, U.S. Dist. Ct. (ea. dist.) Wis. 1980. Assoc. DeWitt, Sundby, Huggett, Schumacher & Morgan, Madison, Wis., 1979-81; ptnr. Smith & Merg, Madison, 1981—; law instr. Madison Area Tech. Coll., 1981—; lectr. on probate and estate planning U. Wis. Law Sch., Madison, 1983, 86. Mem. Madison Art League, 1984—, Madison Symphony Orch. League, 1986—. Mem. ABA, Wis. Bar Assn., Wis. Bar Found. (vol. pub. access atty. 1979—), Wis. Fedn. Tchrs., Wis. Vocat. Bus. Edn. Assn., Delta Sigma Nu, Kappa Delta Pi, Alpha Kappa Delta. Avocations: sailing, cross country skiing. Probate, Legal education. Home: 9018 Colby Rd Mount Horeb WI 53572 Office: Smith & Merg 131 W Wilson St Suite 203 Madison WI 53703

SCHACHNER, MARK J., lawyer; b. N.Y.C., Dec. 19, 1954. BA, Brown U., 1978; JD, Boston U., 1982. Bar: Mass. 1982, N.Y. 1983. Paralegal R.I. Conservation Law Found., Providence, 1977-79; assoc. Miller, Mannix, Lemery & Kafin P.C., Glens Falls, N.Y., 1982-85, ptnr., 1985—. Mem. ABA, N.Y. State Bar Assn. (environ. law sect.), Warren County Bar Assn., Saratoga County Bar Assn., Sierra Club, Friends of Animals. Avocations: tennis, skiing, outdoor sports. Environment. Home: Rural Rt 5 Box 186 Glens Falls NY 12801 Office: Miller Mannix Lemery & Pratt PC 1 Broad St Plaza Glens Falls NY 12801

SCHACHTER, ALESA ROSE, lawyer; b. Hollywood, Calif., Jan. 23, 1955; d. Al S. Schachter and Donna (Wolfe) Rozella; m. Bruce R. Madewell, Mar. 9, 1985. BA cum laude, UCLA, 1978; JD, U. Calif., Davis, 1981. Bar: Calif. 1982, U.S. Dist. Ct. (ea. dist.) Calif. 1983, U.S. Ct. Appeals (9th cir.) 1985. Assoc. Johnson & Hoffman, P.C., Sacramento, Calif., 1982—. Mem. Equal Rights Advs., San Francisco, 1980—. Mem. ABA, Sacramento County Bar Assn., Women Lawyers Sacramento. Avocations: running, photography, aerobics instruction, poetry. Civil rights, Federal civil litigation, State civil litigation. Office: Johnson & Hoffman PC 2143 Hurley Way Suite 122 Sacramento CA 95825

SCHACHTER, OSCAR, lawyer, educator; b. N.Y.C., June 19, 1915; s. Max and Fannie (Javits) S.; m. Mollie Miller, Aug. 9, 1936 (dec. July 1980); children: Judith (Mrs. John Modell), Ellen (Mrs. John P. Leventhal); m. Muriel L. Sackler, June 14, 1982. BSS, Coll. City N.Y., 1936; JD, Columbia, 1939. Bar: N.Y. bar 1939. Editor-in-chief Columbia Law Rev., 1938-39; sole practice N.Y.C., 1939-40; atty. U.S. Dept. of Labor, Washington, 1940; chief nat. defense sect. in law dept. FCC, 1941; sect. of law com. and adviser on internat. communications Bd. of War Communications, 1941-42; prin., divisional asst., adviser on wartime econ. controls and on European liberated areas U.S. Dept. State, 1942-43; asst. gen. counsel UNRRA, 1944-46; drafting officer UNRRA council sessions, 1944-45; legal adv. UNRRA del. to USSR and Poland, 1945; legal counselor UN, 1946-52, dir. gen. legal div., 1952-66; dep. exec. dir., dir. studies UN Inst. for Tng. and Research, 1966-75; lectr. law Yale U. Law Sch., 1955-71; Carnegie lectr. Hague Acad. Internat. Law, 1963-82; Rosenthal lectr. Northwestern U. Law Sch., 1974; prof. law Columbia U. Law Sch. and Faculty Internat. Affairs, 1975—, Hamilton Fish prof. internat. law and diplomacy, 1980-85, prof. emeritus, 1985—; chmn. legal com. UN Maritime Conf., 1948; legal cons. UNESCO, 1948; past dir. Gen. Legal Div. of UN; served as legal adviser various internat. confs. and UN councils and coms.; sec. legal adv. com. UN Atomic Energy Commn., 1946-47; vice chmn. Internat. Investment Law Conf., 1958; exec. sec. Internat. Arbitration Conf., 1958; mem. panel arbitrators Internat. Ctr. for Settlement of Investment Disputes, 1980—. Author: Relation of Law, Politics and Action in the U.N, 1964, Sharing the World's Resources, 1977, International Law in Theory and Practice, 1985; co-author: Across the Space Frontier, 1952, Toward Wider Acceptance of

UN Treaties, 1971, International Law Cases and Materials, 1980; contbr. articles and monographs on internat. law, internat. instns., legal philosophy, human rights, internat. peace and security, internat. resources to legal jours.; editor-in-chief Am. Jour. Internat. Law, 1978-84, hon. editor, 1985—; co-editor: Competition in International Business, 1981; editorial bd. Marine Policy. Bd. dirs. Internat. Peace Acad., 1970-82. Fellow Am. Acad. Arts and Scis., World Acad. Art and Sci.; mem. Am. Soc. Internat. Law (pres. 1968-70, hon. v.p., mem. exec. council, Manley Hudson medal 1981), Council on Fgn. Relations, Inst. de Droit Internat., Internat. Law Assn., Internat. Astronautical Acad., Phi Beta Kappa. Club: Chaos (N.Y.). Legal education. Home: 11 E 86th St New York NY 10028 Office: Columbia U Law Sch New York NY 10027

SCHACHTER, RICHARD J., lawyer; b. Bklyn., Mar. 30, 1934; s. Bruno and Anna (Sklar) S.; m. Judith N. Naidorff, June 21, 1937; children: Karen D., Linda B. BS, NYU, 1955, LLB, 1961. Bar: N.Y. 1961, N.J. 1964, U.S. Dist. Ct. N.J. 1964, U.S. Dist. Ct. (so. dist.) N.Y. 1964, U.S. Ct. Appeals (3d cir.) 1967, U.S. Supreme Ct. 1969. Trade mark agt. Langner, Parry, Card & Langner, N.Y.C., 1961-62, Hasseltine, Lake & Co., N.Y.C., 1962-63; assoc. Abrams, Kestenbauh & Hendricks, Plainfield, N.J., 1963; ptnr. Schachter & Wohl, Somerville, N.J., 1964, Halpern, Schachter & Wohl, Somerville, 1964-71, Schachter, Wohl, Cohn & Trombadore P.A., Somerville, 1971-85, Schachter, Cohn, Trombadore & Offen P.A., Somerville, 1985—; atty. Twp. of Branchburg, Somerville, 1977; bd. dirs. U.S. Bronze Powders Inc., Flemington. Chmn. Plainfield Heart Drive, 1963; treas. Somerset County Legal Services, Somerville, 1968-72; county chmn. N.J. Lawyers for Bill Bradley, Roseland, 1984; trustee Temple Beth El, Somerville, 1964-73. Mem. ABA, N.J. Bar Assn., Somerset County Bar Assn., Assn. Trial Lawyers Am., N.J. Trial Lawyers Assn. Democrat. State civil litigation. Office: Schachter Cohn Trombadore & Offen PA 45 E High St Somerville NJ 08876

SCHACK, DAVID PAUL, lawyer; b. Huntsville, Ala., Dec. 21, 1957; s. Ronald Henry and Felicia Joan (Petluck) S.; m. Sue Louise Heyler, Aug. 14, 1982; children: Alexandra, Trevor. BA, Stanford U., 1979; JD, UCLA, 1982. Bar: Calif. 1982, U.S. Dist. Ct. (cen. dist.) Calif. 1983, U.S. Ct. Appeals (9th cir.) 1983, U.S. Dist. Ct. (ea. dist.) Mich. 1985. Extern U.S. Ct. Appeals (9th cir.), 1981; assoc. Nossaman, Guthner, Knox & Elliott, Los Angeles, 1982-84, Mitchell, Silberberg & Knupp, Los Angeles, 1984—. Article editor UCLA Law Rev., 1981-82. Mem. ABA, Calif. Bar Assn., Los Angeles Bar Assn., Assn. Bus. Trial Lawyers, Phi Beta Kappa. Democrat. Federal civil litigation, State civil litigation, Insurance. Home: 3626 Seahorn Dr Malibu CA 90265 Office: Mitchell Silberberg & Knupp 11377 W Olympic Blvd Los Angeles CA 90064

SCHACK, ROBERT J., lawyer; b. N.Y.C., Jan. 8, 1944; s. Jerome Arthur and Elizabeth (Thompson) S. Cert. in Spanish U. Internacional Menendez-Pelayo, Santander, Spain, 1964; B.A. with honors, Haverford Coll., 1965; J.D., NYU, 1974. Bar: N.Y. 1975, U.S. Dist. Ct. (so. and ea. dists.) N.Y. 1978, U.S. Ct. Appeals (2d cir.) 1978, U.S. Supreme Ct. 1978. Staff counsel Citizens Com. for Children, N.Y.C., 1974-76; sr. atty. N.Y. State Mental Hygiene, N.Y.C., 1976-77; asst. atty. gen. State of N.Y., N.Y.C., 1977—; adj. prof. Baruch Coll., N.Y.C., 1984; vice-chmn. profl. conduct com. div. cen. screening for Family Ct. Panel, 1985—. Co-author: Undelivered Care: The Incapacitated and the Mentally Ill New York City Defendant, 1972. Contbr. articles to law and computer jours. Drafter social service legislation. Bd. editors, editor-in-chief law sch. and coll. newspapers. Trustee Inst. of Child Mental Health, N.Y.C.; co-founder, bd. dirs., past pres., co-counsel WNCN Listeners' Guild, N.Y.C., 1974-82; co-founder, bd. dirs. Saving Families for Children, 1976-81; Woodrow Wilson fellow 1965; recipient Kroner Meml. award NYU, 1974, Commendation award WNCN Listeners' Guild, 1976; cert. Liberty Through Law Program, 1984. Mem. N.Y. State Bar Assn. (chmn. subcoms. on juvenile justice and child welfare 1978—), N.Y. County Lawyers Assn. (chmn. subcom. family ct. com. 1986—, chmn. com. medicine and mental health 1983-85), Assn. Bar City of N.Y. (chmn. subcom. family ct. and family law com. 1982-83). Nat. Council Juvenile and Family Ct. Judges, ABA. Democrat. Jewish. State civil litigation, Juvenile, Family and matrimonial. Home: 330 E 71st St Apt 2F New York NY 10021 Office: New York State Dept Law 120 Broadway New York NY 10271

SCHADE, ALOHA LEE, lawyer; b. Hobbs, N.Mex., June 16, 1944; d. Benjamin Charles Marshall and Aloha L. Gillian; children: Kelly Elizabeth Stapleton, Jennifer Lynn Stapleton. BA, Goucher Coll., 1976; JD, Lewis & Clark Coll., 1980. Bar: Oreg. 1980. Law clk. to judge Multnomah County Cir. Ct., Portland, Oreg., 1980-82; sole practice Portland, 1982—; chmn. com. for protection of human subjects Northwest Kaiser Permanente, Portland, 1981—; instr. Health Scis. Ctr. U. Oreg., Portland, 1981—. Mem. life and death decisions com. ACLU, Portland, 1984, adv. bd. Jefferson Meeting on Constn. in Oreg., adv. panel Oreg. Health Decisions. Mem. Multnomah County Bar Assn. (med. soc. bioethics com. 1984—), Oreg. Assn. Ry. Passengers (pres. 1982—), Cornelius Hon. Soc. Democrat. Mem. Soc. of Friends. State civil litigation, Family and matrimonial, Personal injury. Home: 2147 N E 13th Portland OR 97212 Office: 1001 SW 5th St Orbanco Bldg Suite 1001 Portland OR 97204

SCHAECHER, SUSAN MARIE, lawyer; b. Columbus, Nebr., Feb. 12, 1957; d. Ivan John and Gloria Dorothy (Fischer) S. BA in Journalism, U. Nebr., 1979, JD, 1982. Bar: Nebr. 1982, U.S. Dist. Ct. Nebr. 1982, Colo. 1985, U.S. Dist. Ct. Colo. 1985. Atty. Western Nebr. Legal Services, North Platte, 1982-83, Legal Services of Southeast Nebr., Beatrice, 1983-84; assoc. Nelson & Harding, Denver, 1984—. Mem. vol. staffing com., Artreach, Denver, 1985—. Mem. ABA (labor law sect.), Colo. Bar Assn. (labor law com.), Nebr. Bar Assn., Denver Bar Assn., Colo. Assn. Commerce and Industry, Alliance Profl. Women (co-chmn fund raising com.). Republican. Roman Catholic. Avocations: swimming, skiing, biking. Labor. Office: Nelson & Harding 717 17th St Suite 2600 Denver CO 80202

SCHAEFER, CHARLES HAROLD, lawyer; b. Margaretville, N.Y., Nov. 15, 1951; s. Harold Charles and Theresa (Huetter) S.; m. Lorraine Mary Ferrara, Mar. 5, 1983; 1 child, Catherine Elyse. BA, SUNY, Albany, 1973; JD, Union U., 1976. Bar: N.Y. 1977, U.S. Dist. Ct. (no. dist.) N.Y. 1977, U.S. Supreme Ct. 1980. Assoc. Moon & Clay, Catskill, N.Y., 1977-80; ptnr. Clay, Deily & Schaefer, Catskill, 1980-85, Deily & Schaefer, Catskill, 1985—; atty. Town of Prattsville, N.Y., 1978—. Trustee Zadock Pratt Mus. Inc., Prattsville, 1979—; coordinator com. to elect Ed Cloke for Dist. Atty., 1985. Mem. ABA, N.Y. State Bar Assn., Greene County Bar Assn. Republican. Lodges: Rotary (sec. Windham club 1981-82, pres. Catskill club 1986—), Elks. State civil litigation, Contracts commercial, Real property. Office: Deily & Schaefer One Bridge St Catskill NY 12414

SCHAEFER, DANIEL ROBERT, lawyer, state official; b. Hartford, Conn., Apr. 1, 1939; s. Abraham Maurice and Alice (Leavitt) S. AB, Yale U., 1961; LLB, U. Conn., 1964. Bar: Conn. 1964, U.S. Dist. Ct. Conn. 1970, U.S. Dist. Ct. Vt. 1973, U.S. Ct. Appeals (2d cir.) 1970, U.S. Ct. Appeals (3d cir.) 1973, U.S. Supreme Ct. 1972. Reporter Hartford Courant, summers, 1960-62; asst. clk. Hartford County Superior Ct., 1968; asst. atty. gen. State of Conn., Hartford, 1968—. Mem. Gov.'s Consumers Adv. Council Conn., 1975-79; pres. West End Civic Assn., Hartford, 1984-85. Served with USNR; lt. comdr. Res. Mem. ABA, Conn. Bar Assn., Hartford County Bar Assn., Hartford County Fed. Bar Assn., Naval Res. Assn., Res. Officers Assn. Democrat. Jewish. Club: Yale. Lodge: B'nai B'rith. Federal civil litigation, State civil litigation. Home: 126 Tremont St Hartford CT 06105

SCHAEFER, DAVID STUART, lawyer; b. Bklyn., Nov. 27, 1955; s. Martin Schaefer and Ruth (Shefts) Tilton; m. Ilyse D. Glass, Nov. 14, 1982; 1 child, Jason. BS, MIT, 1978; JD, NYU, 1981. Bar: N.Y. 1982. Assoc. Cole & Deitz, N.Y.C., 1981-82, Shea & Gould, N.Y.C., 1982—. mem. ABA, N.Y. State Bar Assn. Avocarions: fishing, sailing, skiing. Banking, General corporate, Securities. Office: Shea & Gould 330 Madison Ave New York NY 10017

SCHAEFER, NANCY, lawyer; b. Chgo., Aug. 10, 1941; d. Walter Vincent and Marguerite (Moreland) S.; m. Chester T. Kamin, Sept. 8, 1962; children: Stacey, Scott. BA cum laude, Radcliffe Coll., 1962; JD, U. Chgo., 1974. Bar: Ill. 1974, U.S. Dist. Ct. (no. dist.) Ill. 1974, U.S. Ct. Appeals (7th cir.) 1978, U.S. Supreme Ct. 1978, U.S. Ct. Appeals (fed. cir.) 1984. Reporter Chgo. Tribune, 1963; assoc. Pope, Ballard, Shepard & Fowle, Chgo., 1974-79; assoc. Karon, Morrison & Savikas, Ltd., Chgo., 1979-81, ptnr., 1981—; Mem. admissions com. U.S. Dist. Ct. (no. dist.) Ill., Chgo., 1982—; mem. adv. com. U.S. Ct. Appeals (fed. cir.), 1984—. Fellow ABA (chmn. appellate practice com. litigation sect. 1982—); mem. Am. Law Inst., Fed. Cir. Bar Assn. (pres. 1985-86), Ill. Bar Assn., Chgo. Bar Assn. (chmn. fed. civil procedure com. 1983-84). Club: Legal (Chgo.). Avocations: reading, tennis, hiking. Federal civil litigation, State civil litigation. Office: Karon Morrison & Savikas 233 S Wacker Dr Suite 5700 Chicago IL 60606

SCHAEFER, PATRICK MARK, bank executive; b. Omaha, June 6, 1957; s. Nicholas J. and Colleen Z. (Dulac) S.; m. Diane Marie Wages, Apr. 30, 1983; 1 child, Katherine. BBA, U. Colo., 1979; JD, Creighton U., 1982. Bar: Nebr. 1982, U.S. Dist. Ct. Nebr. 1982, N.Mex. 1987. Tax lawyer Touche Ross & Co., Omaha, 1982-83; asst. v.p., trust officer State Bank & Trust, Council Bluffs, Iowa, 1983-85; trust officer Sunwest Bank, Albuquerque, 1985-86. Probate. Home: 3901 Montgomery Blvd Apt 1308 Albuquerque NM 87109 Office: Sunwest Bank Trust Dept PO Box 26900 Albuquerque NM 87125

SCHAEFER, WILLIAM GOERMAN, JR., lawyer; b. Kansas City, Mo., June 16, 1941; m. Sharon Saylor, Dec. 21, 1963; children: James, Kristen. B.A., U. Kans., 1963; J.D., Harvard U., 1966. Bar: Ill. 1966, D.C. 1978. Partner firm Sidley & Austin, Chgo. and Washington, 1966-74, 78—; v.p., gen. counsel DeKalb Corp., Ill., 1974-77. Mem. Am., D.C., Chgo. bar assns. Environment, Federal civil litigation, General corporate. Office: Sidley & Austin 1722 Eye St NW Washington DC 20006

SCHAEFFER, EDWIN FRANK, JR., lawyer, finance company executive; b. N.Y.C., Nov. 29, 1930; s. Edwin Frank and Rachel Townsend (Bouchier) S.; m. Joan Cameron Sherwood, Apr. 7, 1956; children: Edwin Frank III, Cameron, Donald. AB, Washington and Lee U., 1952; JD, Harvard U., 1955. Bar: Ky, 1955, U.S. Dist. Ct. (ea. and we. dists.) Ky. 1957, U.S. Ct. Appeals (6th cir.) 1957. Assoc., Bullitt, Dawson & Tarrant, Louisville, 1955-60, ptnr., 1960-63; ptnr. Kincaid, Wilson, Schaeffer & Hembree, P.S.C., Lexington, Ky., 1963-79, bd. dirs., chmn. bd. dirs., 1979—; vice chmn., bd. dirs. Ky. Fin. Co., Inc., 1976-84, chmn., 1984—; bd. dirs. Ky. Central Life Ins. Co., Lexington, Central Bank & Trust Co., Lexington. Bd. dirs. Lexington Philharm., 1970-80, United Way, 1976-80, 84—, Lexington Civic Ctr., 1982—, Hospice of Bluegrass. Served with JAGC, AUS, 1955-57. Fellow Am. Bar Found.; mem. ABA, Ky. State Bar Assn., Fayette County Bar Assn., Louisville Bar Assn., Greater Lexington C. of C. (bd. dirs. 1986—). Democrat. Presbyterian. Club: Lexington Country. General corporate, Banking. Address: 500 Kincaid Towers Lexington KY 40508

SCHAEFFER, FORREST GRIM, JR., judge; b. Allentown, Pa., Sept. 9, 1927; s. Forrest Grim and Mary Elizabeth (Gitt) S.; m. Dorothea Lee, June 25, 1959; children: Andrew Lee, Katherine Lee, Dorothea Elizabeth, Phillip Christ, Forrest Grim III. BA with high honors, Lehigh U., 1950; LLB, Harvard U., 1953. Bar: Pa. 1954, U.S. Dist. Ct. (ea. dist.) Pa. 1954, U.S. Supreme Ct. 1967. Ptnr. Edelman & Schaeffer, Reading, Pa., 1954-76; judge ct. common pleas Berks County, Reading, 1976-83, pres. judge ct. common pleas, 1983—. Mayor Borough of Kutztown, Pa., 1966-70; nat. committeeman Young Dems. Pa., Harrisburg, 1962-66. Served with USAAF, 1946-47. Mem. ABA, Pa. Bar Assn., Pa. Trial Lawyers Assn., Phi Beta Kappa. Democrat. Mem. United Ch. of Christ. Avocations: history, chess, antique automobiles. Judicial administration, Jurisprudence. Office: Berks County Courthouse 6th and Court Sts Reading PA 19601

SCHAEFFER, MARGARET GROEFSEMA, judge; b. Detroit, Nov. 21, 1920; d. Elmer H. and M. Blanche (Gibbons) Groefsema; m. Marvin G. Schaeffer, Aug. 28, 1948; children: Christine, Paul, William, Virginia. AB, U. Mich., 1943, JD with distinction, 1945. Bar: Mich. 1945, U.S. Ct. Appeals (6th cir.) 1945, U.S. Dist. Ct. (ea. dist) Mich. 1948, Calif. 1949. Law clk. to presiding justice U.S. Ct. Appeals (6th cir.), Cin., 1945-46; assoc. E.H. Grofsema Law Office, Detroit, 1946-48, 49-55, Markle & Markle, Detroit, 1955-73; atty. Workers Compensation Appeals Bd., Lansing, Mich., 1973-74; judge 47th Dist. Ct., Farmington, Mich., 1975—. Council mem. City of Farmington Hills, Mich., 1973-74; trustee Farmington Twp., 1969-73. Mem. Am. Assn. U. Women, Oakland County Dist. Judges (pres. 1979), Nat. Assn. Women Lawyers. Home: 26900 Drake Farmington Hills MI 48018 Office: 47th Dist Ct 32795 W Ten Mile Farmington MI 48018

SCHAEFFER, SHIRLEY ANN, lawyer; b. Chgo., Sept. 5, 1955; d. Peter and Susan Schaeffer. BS, U. Ill., 1977; JD, Ill. Inst. Tech., Chgo., 1980. Bar: Ill. 1980. Atty. SEC, Chgo., 1980—; adj. instr. legal writing and appellate advocacy Loyola U., Chgo., 1983—. Mem. ABA, Chgo. Bar Assn. Securities, Legal education. Office: SEC 219 S Dearborn Room 1204 Chicago IL 60604

SCHAEFFER, SUSAN FAY, judge; b. Kittanning, Pa., June 29, 1942; d. Edwin and Orvetta (Barr) S. A.A., St. Petersburg Jr. Coll., 1962; B.S., Fla. State U., 1964; J.D. cum laude, Stetson U., 1971. Bar: Fla. 1971, U.S. Ct. Appeals (5th cir.) 1975, U.S. Supreme Ct. 1975. Asst. prof. Stetson U., 1971-73; sole practice law, St. Petersburg, Fla., 1974-75, 77-82; asst. pub. defender State of Fla., 1975-78, cir. judge 6th Jud. Cir., Clearwater, 1982—. Bd. dirs. Pinellas Emergency Mental Health Services, 1984—; bd. of overseers Stetson U. Coll. of Law, 1986. Named Outstanding Grad. Fla. Bar, 1971; Outstanding Participant, State Moot Ct., 1971. Mem. St. Petersburg Bar Assn., ABA, Fla. Bar Assn., Pinellas County Trial Lawyers, Criminal Def. Lawyers Pinellas County (pres. 1982), Assn. Trial Lawyers Am., Am. Judicature Soc., Fla. Conf. Cir. Judges, Nat. Assn. Women Judges, Nat. Assn. Criminal Def. Lawyers. Lodge: Soroptimists (Women Honoring Women award 1985). Office: Circuit Ct Judge 5100 144th Ave N Clearwater FL 33520

SCHAFER, STEVEN HARRIS, lawyer; b. Woonsocket, R.I., Apr. 19, 1954. BA in Econs. magna cum laude, U. Mass., 1976; JD, Boston Coll., 1979. Bar: Conn. 1979, U.S. Dist. Ct. Conn. 1979, Mass. 1980, U.S. Dist. Ct. Mass. 1981, U.S. Ct. Appeals (1st cir.) 1981. Assoc. O'Brien, Shafner et al, Groton, Conn., 1979-81, Parker, Coulter, Daley & White, Boston, 1981-84, Meehan, Boyle & Cohen, Boston, 1985; sole practice Boston, 1985—. Mem. ABA, Mass. Bar Assn., Boston Bar Assn., Assn. Trial Lawyers Am., Mass. Acad. Trial Lawyers, Phi Kappa Phi. Personal injury, State civil litigation, Federal civil litigation. Home: 9 Hawthorne Pl Boston MA 02114 Office: 44 Bromfield St Suite 700 Boston MA 02108

SCHAFFER, GEORGE JOHN, lawyer; b. Pitts., July 1, 1907; s. George August and Philomena (Reese) S.; m. Winifred Mahen, 1933; children—Winifred, Marylyn F.; m. 2d, Mildred Annette Gerberding, Sept. 1, 1966. Ph.B., Northwestern U., 1959; J.D., Chgo.-Kent Coll. Law, 1954. Bar: Ill. 1955. With Bell Telephone of Pa., 1926-46, Ill. Bell Telephone Co., 1946-59; instr. Chgo.-Kent Coll. Law, 1959, prof., 1959-63; sole practice, Elmhurst, Ill., 1963-65, 82—; agt. estate and gift taxes, Chgo., 1965-72, regional analyst, 1972-74; tchr. comml. law Coll. of Du Page, Glen Allyn, Ill., 1969-70; tax. cons. Served with AUS, 1943-45. Mem. Ill. State Bar Assn., Fed. Bar Assn., Du Page County Bar Assn., Am. Legion. Republican. Presbyterian. Clubs: Medinah Temple, Mason, Shriners. Probate, Estate taxation, Estate planning. Home and Office: 381 Ferndale Ave Elmhurst IL 60126

SCHAFFER, KENT ALAN, lawyer; b. Houston, Aug. 22, 1954; s. Randolph Lee and Myrna (Bregman) S.; m. Nancy Louise Antunez, Oct. 13, 1984; children: Max Christiana, Zachary Randolph. BA, U. Tex., 1978; JD, U. Houston, 1981. Bar: Tex. 1981, U.S. Dist. Ct. (so. dist.) Tex. 1982, U.S. Dist. Ct. (ea. and we. dists.) Tex. 1983, U.S. Ct. Appeals (5th cir.) 1983. Sole practice Houston. Mem. Houston Bar Assn., Nat. Assn. Criminal Def. Lawyers (fed. ct. adv. council), Tex. Criminal Def. Lawyers Assn. (bd. dirs. 1986-87, Outstanding Service award 1984), Harris County Criminal Lawyers Assn., Nat. Orgn. for Reform of Marijuana Laws (legal com.). Democrat. Jewish. Criminal. Home: 4015 Drummond Houston TX 77025 Office: 3401 Louisiana Suite 270 Houston TX 77002

SCHAFFER, THOMAS ALAN, lawyer; b. Cleve., June 28, 1947; s. Wilbur Eugene and Dorothy Jane (Kershaw) S.; m. Gail Helen Scarborough, Aug. 23, 1970 (div. 1975); m. Susan Elizabeth Most, Sept. 24, 1977; children: Griffin Thomas, Andrew Michael. B.A. in History, U. Mich., 1969; J.D., U. Cin., 1972. Bar: Ohio. Assoc. Graham, Schaffer & West, Cin., 1972-76; pub. defender Dayton, Ohio, 1976-78; sole practice law, Dayton, 1978-83; mem. firm Sutton, Overholser & Schaffer, Dayton, 1983—. Served to capt. USAF, 1969-73. Mem. Nat. Assn. Criminal Def. Lawyers (bd. dirs. 1986—), Ohio Bar Assn., Dayton Bar Assn. (chmn. criminal law com. 1980-82), Ohio Acad. Trial Lawyers, Assn. Trial Lawyers Am. Avocations: Skiing; music; golf; tennis. Personal injury, Criminal. Home: 641 Ridgedale Rd Dayton OH 45406 Office: Sutton Overholser & Schaffer 1700 First Nat Plaza Dayton OH 45402

SCHAFFNER, THEODORE W., lawyer; b. Faribault, Minn., May 18, 1946; s. C.W. and Grace Lorraine (Magnussen) S.; m. Kathleen Burns, June 24, 1981; children: Jessica Leigh, Meredith Alison. BA, Ohio State U., 1968; JD, Harvard U., 1971. Bar: Ohio 1971, Ill. 1977. Assoc. Porter, Stanley, Platt & Arthur, Columbus, Ohio, 1971-75; counsel A.E. Staley Mfg. Co., Decatur, Ill., 1975-79, TRW Inc., Cleve., 1979-87; sr. corp. counsel Motorola, Inc., Schaumburg, Ill., 1987—. Mem. ABA, Cleve. Bar Assn. (trustee securities law sect. 1985—, speaker securities law seminar 1983-86). Securities, General corporate. Home: 2102 Shetland Rd Inverness IL 60067 Office: Motorola Inc 1303 E Algonquin Rd Schaumburg IL 60196

SCHAGER, RICHARD JOSEPH, JR., lawyer; b. Cleve., Mar. 5, 1950; s. Richard J. Sr. and Eunice A. (Shevlin) S. BS, Bowling Green U., 1972; JD, Case Western Res. U., 1978. Bar: Ohio 1978, N.Y. 1979. Assoc. Barret, Smith, Schapiro, Simon & Armstrong, N.Y.C., 1979-80, Wender, Murase & White, N.Y.C., 1980—; fgn. law expert, vis. lectr. in corp., comml. and internat. trade law Shanghai (China) Inst. Fgn. Trade, 1985—. Assoc. editor Case Western Res. U., 1976-77, mng. editor, 1977-78. Mem. ABA, Assn. of Bar of City of N.Y., N.Y. County Lawyers Assn. General corporate, Private international, Public international.

SCHAIBLE, GRACE BERG, state attorney general. BA in History and Polit. Sci., U. Alaska; MA in History, George Washington U.; JD, Yale U., 1959. Mem. Alaska Legis. Council, 1953-56, acting dir., 1956; assoc. McNealy and Merdes, 1959-66; ptnr. Schaible, Staley, DeLisio and Cook (formerly Merdes, Schaible, Staley and DeLisio), from 1966; also past gen. counsel U. Alaska; past city atty. Cities of Fairbanks, Barrow, Kotzebue and North Pole; past gen. corp. counsel Arctic Slope Regional Corp.; now atty. gen. State of Alaska, 1987—. Mem. Fairbanks Estate Planning Council; bd. dirs. United Way of Tanana Valley; past bd. dirs., treas. Fairbanks Devel. Authority; mem. bd. regents U. Alaska, 1985—. Fellow U. Alaska Found. (past bd. dirs.); mem. ABA, Alaska Bar Assn., Tanana Valley Bar Assn., Fairbanks C. of C. (past bd. dirs.), U. Alaska Alumni Assn., (past bd. dirs., officer). Office: Office of Atty Gen PO Box K State Capitol Juneau AK 99811

SCHANCK, PETER CARR, law educator; b. Chgo., May 9, 1938; s. Francis Raber and Kathryn (Short) S.; m. Sally Cessna, Aug. 10, 1960 (div. 1974); children—Christine, Brett, Derick, Julia; m. Karen Ushman, July 10, 1974. B.A., Dartmouth Coll., 1960; J.D., Yale U., 1963; M.L.S., U. Md., 1972. Bar: Conn. 1963. Legal specialist Library of Congress, Washington, 1965-71; head reference dept. law library U. Mich., Ann Arbor, 1974-78; assoc. prof. law, dir. law library U. Detroit, 1978-82; prof. law, dir. law library U. Kans., Lawrence, 1982—; mem. adv. bd. Law Library Jour., 1984-86, Legal Reference Services Quar., 1981-84. Author: A Guide to Legal Research, 1976, 2d edit., 1978; contbr. articles to profl. publs. Mem. Mich. Assn. Law Libraries (pres. 1979-80), Am. Assn. Law Libraries, Mid.-Am. Assn. Law Libraries (pres. elect 1987-89, pres. 1989—). Legal education, Legislative, Librarianship. Home: 1731 Indiana St Lawrence KS 66044 Office: U Kans Law Sch Green Hall Lawrence KS 66045

SCHANZ, STEPHEN JOHN, lawyer, educator; b. Kalamazoo, Nov. 28, 1952; s. Albert J. and Colleen M. (Haley) S.; m. Jennifer L. Carrington, Aug. 6, 1982. BBA, Western Mich. U., 1974; JD, Pepperdine U., 1979. Bar: Mich. 1979, U.S. Dist. Ct. (we dist.) Mich. 1979. Staff atty. Kalamazoo Legal Aid, 1979-80; sole practice Kalamazoo, 1981-84; ptnr. Lilly, Domeny, Durant, Byrne & Schanz P.C., Kalamazoo, 1984—; asst. prof. bus. Western Mich. U., Kalamazoo, 1985—; seminar speaker Upjohn Healthcare Services, Kalamazoo, 1983—. Mem. ABA, Mich. Bar Assn., Kalamazoo County Bar Assn., Mich. Trial Lawyers Assn., Am. Soc. Law and Medicine, Nat. Health Lawyers Assn., Mich. Health Care Lawyers Assn. General corporate, Health, Real property. Office: Lilly Domeny Durant Byrne & Schanz 505 S Park St Kalamazoo MI 49007

SCHAPIRO, RUTH GOLDMAN, lawyer; b. N.Y.C., Oct. 31, 1926; d. Louis Albert and Sarah (Shapiro) Goldman; m. Donald Schapiro, June 29, 1952; children: Jane Goldman, Robert Andrew. A.B., Wellesley Coll., 1947; LL.B., Columbia U., 1950. Bar: N.Y. 1950, D.C. 1978. Asst. to reporters Am. Law Inst. Fed. Income Tax Statute, N.Y.C., 1950-51; assoc., then ptnr. Proskauer Rose Goetz & Mendelsohn, N.Y.C., 1955—; mem. nominating commn. U.S. Tax Ct., 1978-81. Notes editor: Columbia Law Rev., 1949-50; editor: Tax Shelters, Practising Law Inst., 1983; contbr. articles to legal jours. Vice-chmn. adv. com. NYU Inst. Fed. Taxation, 1979-85; mem. adv. com. NYU-IRS Continuing Legal Edn. Project. Fellow Am. Bar Found., N.Y. Bar Found.; mem. ABA, N.Y. State Bar Assn. (chmn. tax sect. 1981-82, exec. com. 1982-84, ho. of dels. 1981-84, chmn. fin. com. 1984-87, chmn. spl. com. on Women in the Cts. 1986—), Assn. Bar City N.Y. (taxation com. 1972-75, 78-79), N.Y. County Lawyers Assn., Am. Judicature Soc. Jewish. Club: N.Y. Wellesley (N.Y.C.). Corporate taxation, Personal income taxation, Estate taxation. Home: 1035 Fifth Ave New York NY 10028 Office: Proskauer Rose Goetz & Mendelsohn 300 Park Ave New York NY 10022 *

SCHAPLOW, TERRY FREDERICK, lawyer; b. Bozemen, Mont., Dec. 26, 1952; s. Milton F. and Peggy W. (Westlake) S.; m. Peggy C. Gander, June 18, 1977; children: Jesse, Jay. BA, Mont. State U., 1975; JD, Willamette U., 1980. Bar: Mont. 1981, U.S. Dist. Ct. Mont. 1985, U.S. Ct. Appeals 1985, U.S. Supreme Ct. 1985. Law clk. to presiding justice Mont. Supreme Ct., Helena, 1982-83; assoc. Morrow, Sedivy & Bennett P.C., Bozeman, Mont., 1983—. Mem. ABA (signifigant decisions and title ins com.), Mont. Bar Assn. Presbyterian. Avocations: magic, mech. inventions, swimming. Real property, Banking. Home: 723 S 5th Bozeman MT 59715 Office: Morrow Sedivy & Bennett PC 208 E Main Suite 202 Bozeman MT 59715

SCHARF, JARED J., lawyer; b. N.Y.C., June 8, 1947; s. Seymour L. and Eve M. (Silberman) S.; m. Barbara Gale Lawrence, Aug. 12, 1971; children—Adam, Jonathan. B.A., NYU, 1969; J.D., George Washington U., 1973; LL.M. in Taxation, NYU, 1978. Bar: N.Y. 1974, U.S. Supreme Ct. 1980, U.S. Ct. Appeals (2d cir.) 1975, U.S. Ct. Appeals (9th cir.) 1981, U.S. Dist. Ct. (so. and ea. dists.) N.Y. 1974, U.S. Tax Ct. 1985. Asst. dist. atty. Bronx Dist. Atty.'s Office, 1973-77; supervisory trial atty., criminal sect., tax div. U.S. Dept. Justice, Washington, 1977-84; sole practice, White Plains, N.Y., also N.Y.C., 1984—. Recipient Outstanding Atty. award, tax div. U.S. Dept. Justice, 1979, Spl. commendation U.S. Dept. Justice, 1981. Criminal, Personal income taxation, Federal civil litigation. Home: 55 Avon Circle Rye Brook NY 10573 Office: One N Broadway White Plains NY 10601

SCHARF, ROBERT LEE, lawyer; b. Chgo., May 13, 1920; s. Charles A. and Ethel Virginia (McNabb) S.; m. Jacqueline B. Scharf, Nov. 2, 1940; children—Bonnie Scharf Heald, Mary Ellen Pinero, Robert L. J.D., Loyola U., 1948. Bar: Ill. 1949, Calif. 1972. With FBI, 1940-73; dep. atty. City of Los Angeles, 1973-84; atty Mitsui Mfrs. Bank, Los Angeles, 1984-85; former tchr. Santa Monica Community Coll.; real estate broker. Mem. arbitrators panel Los Angeles County Superior Ct. Served to 2d lt. U.S. Army, 1944-46. Mem. Los Angeles County Bar Assn., Soc. Former FBI Agts. Club: Lawyers (bd. govs., 2d v.p.) (Los Angeles). Workers' compensation, Criminal, Condemnation. Office: PO Box 702 Tarzana CA 91356

SCHATZ, ARTHUR HERSCHEL, lawyer; b. Hartford, Conn., Dec. 31, 1918; s. Nathan A. and Dora (Goldberg) S.; m. Cecil Ruskay, Feb. 11, 1945; children: Ellen Levine, Robert F., Daniel N. A.B., Cornell U., 1940, J.D., 1942. Bar: Conn. 1942, Fed. Ct 1946. Sr. partner Schatz & Schatz, Hartford, 1945-78, Schatz & Schatz, Ribicoff & Kotkin, Hartford, 1978-87; trial counsel, cons. in forensic sci.; lectr. Cornell Law Sch., 1959-72, U. Conn., 1959-72, New Eng. Law Inst., 1960-76; faculty Law Sci. Inst., U.

Tex.; del. Internat. Congress on Forensic Sci., 1960, 63, 66, 69, 72, 75, 78; v.p., gen. counsel, 1975-78; del. Congress Internat. Assn. Traffic Accident Medicine, 1963, 66, 69, 72, 75; mem. Conn. Commn. on Medicolegal Investigations, 1969-85, vice chmn., 1972-79. Mem. council Cornell U., 1970-77; trustee Forensic Sci. Found., 1969-72, Law-Sci. Found Am.; trustee, v.p., gen. counsel Internat. Reference Orgn. in Forensic Medicine, 1969-87. Fellow Am. Acad. Forensic Scis. (chmn. jurisprudence sect., mem. exec. council 1959-71, sec.-treas. 1969-71); mem. Brit. Acad. Forensic Scis., Am. Assn. Automotive Medicine, Cornell Law Assn. (exec. com. 1958-62), Am., Conn., Hartford County bar assns., New Eng. Law Inst. (exec. com. 1960-76), Soc. Med. Jurisprudence. State civil litigation, General corporate, Personal injury. Home: 6183 Finsbury Ct Palm Beach Gardens FL 33418 Office: 1 Financial Plaza Hartford CT 06103 Address: 3 Landmark Sq Stamford CT 06901

SCHATZ, JAMES EDWARD, lawyer; b. St. Paul, Minn., Mar. 19, 1946; s. Walter Carl and Muriel Anne (Muckleston) S.; m. Louise Katherine Gillham, Jan. 25, 1969; children: Brendan James, Brian Carl. BA, MacAlaster Coll., 1968; JD magna cum laude, U. Minn., 1972. Bar: Minn. 1972, U.S. Dist. Ct. Minn. 1973, U.S. Ct. Appeals (8th cir.) 1973, U.S. Supreme Ct. 1976. Law clk. to presiding justice U.S. Dist. Ct., Mpls., 1972-73; assoc., then ptnr. Doherty, Rumble & Butler, St. Paul, 1974-78; ptnr. Opperman & Paquin, Mpls., 1979—. Bd. dirs. Minn. Higher Edn. Facilities Authority, St. Paul, 1973-79, Minn. Job Skills Ptnrship., St. Paul, 1983—. Mem. ABA, Fed. Bar Assn., Minn. Bar Assn., Order of Coif, Pi Sigma Alpha. Club: Pool and Yacht (Lilydale, Minn.). Avocations: skiing, golf, racquetball, canoeing, travel. General corporate, Contracts commercial, Trademark and copyright. Home: 2120 Charlton Rd Saint Paul MN 55118 Office: Opperman & Paquin 100 Washington Ave S Minneapolis MN 55401

SCHATZ, RICHARD ANSELL, assistant states attorney; b. Hartford, Conn., Oct. 24, 1929; s. Julius Berger and Madeline (Ansell) S.; m. Susan Trombley, Sept. 24, 1972 (dec. Mar. 1986); 1 child, Russell Henry. B.A., Amherst Coll., 1951; J.D., Yale Law Sch., 1954. Bar: Conn. 1954, U.S. Dist. Ct. Conn. 1962, U.S. Ct. Mil. Appeals 1955. Asst. states atty. County of Hartford, Conn., 1965-82, County of New London, Conn., 1983-86; sole practice, Conn., 1957-82. Bd. dirs. Mt. Sinai Hosp., Hartford, 1970-75. Served to 1st lt. JAGC, U.S. Army, 1955-57. Mem. ABA, Conn. Bar Assn., Nat. Dist. Attys. Assn. State civil litigation, Criminal, Personal injury. Home: 12 Water St Apt 306 Mystic CT 06355 Office: Suisman Shapiro Wool Brennan & Gray PO Box 1591 Mariner Sq Suite 240 New London CT 06320

SCHATZ, WILLIAM BONSALL, lawyer; b. McKeesport, Pa., Jan. 18, 1946; s. Carl Frederick and Florence Raye (Hopkins) S.; m. Betty Hurley, Aug. 2, 1970; children: Amanda Raye, Megan Hurley, Michael Hoyt. BBA, Case Western Reserve U., 1968, JD, 1973. Bar: Ohio 1973, U.S. Dist. Ct. (no. dist.) Ohio 1973, U.S. Supreme Ct. 1977, U.S. Ct. Appeals (6th cir.) 1984. Asst. dir. law City of Cleve., 1973-77; asst. gen. counsel Northeast Ohio Regional Sewer Dist., Cleve., 1977-78, gen. counsel, 1978—; speaker on constrn. and liability ins. Contbr. articles on constrn. and liability ins. to profl. jours. Mem. ABA, Ohio Bar Assn., Water Pollution Control Fedn., Assn. Met. Sewerage Agys. (chmn. ins. com. 1985-87, attys. com.), Cuyahoga County Law Dirs. Assn., Am. Mgmt. Assn. Club: Chagrin Valley Athletic (Chagrin Falls, Ohio). Construction, Environment, Government contracts and claims. Home: 40 Park Ln Moreland Hills OH 44022 Office: NE Ohio Regional Sewer Dist 3826 Euclid Ave Cleveland OH 44115

SCHATZKI, GEORGE, legal educator; b. 1933. A.B., Harvard U., 1955, LL.B., 1958, LL.M., 1965. Teaching fellow Harvard U., Cambridge, Mass., 1963-65; prof. law U. Tex.-Austin, 1965-79; dean U. Wash. Sch. Law, Seattle, 1979-82, prof., 1979-84; dean U. Conn. Sch. Law, Hartford, 1984—, prof., 1984—; vis. prof. law U. Pa., Phila., 1973-74, Harvard U., Cambridge, Mass., 1977-78. Co-author: Labor Relations and Social Problems: Collective Bargaining in Private Employment, 1978. Legal education. Office: Univ Conn Law School 55 Elizabeth St Hartford CT 06105

SCHATZOW, MICHAEL, lawyer; b. Washington, Apr. 22, 1949; s. Arthur Schatzow and Clara (Schwalb) Ravner; m. Amy Rizika, Sept. 10, 1977; children: Adam, Margaret. AB, Case Western Res., 1970; JD, U. Chgo., 1973; LLM, Georgetown U., 1978. Bar: D.C. 1973, U.S. Ct. Appeals (D.C. cir.) 1974, U.S. Dist. Ct. Md. 1975, U.S. Ct. Appeals (4th cir.) 1976, U.S. Supreme Ct. 1977, U.S. Ct. Appeals (5th cir.) 1979, U.S. Ct. Appeals (11th cir.) 1981, U.S. Ct. Appeals (9th cir.) 1983. Asst. fed. pub. defender Md. Dist. Ct., Balt., 1975-78; asst. U.S. atty. La. Dist. Ct. (ea.), New Orleans, 1978-81, Md. Dist. Ct., Balt., 1982-86; assoc. Melnicove, Kaufman, Weiner, Smouse & Garbis P.A., Balt., 1986—. Mem. ABA, Md. Bar Assn., Balt. City Bar Assn. Criminal, Federal civil litigation, State civil litigation. Home: 109 Taplow Rd Baltimore MD 21212 Office: Melnicove Kaufman Weiner Smouse & Garbis 36 S Charles St Baltimore MD 21201-3060

SCHAUB, CLARENCE ROBERT, lawyer, realtor; b. Huntington, W.Va., Feb. 14, 1932; s. Clarence and Mae Howell (Jordan) S.; m. Patricia Martin Halseth, Oct. 24, 1984; 1 son, Robert Andrew. Student Vanderbilt U., 1949-50, U.S. Mil. Acad. Prep. Sch., 1952, Marshall U., 1953-56; J.D., W.Va. U., 1959. Bar: W.Va. 1959, various U.S. Dist. Cts. and U.S. Cts. of Appeals. Law clk. to U.S. Dist. Judge, 1959-60; assoc. Jenkins & Jenkins, later ptnr. Jenkins, Schaub, Fenstermaker & Wood, 1960-76; sole practice, Huntington, 1976-85; ptnr. Schaub & Bryant, L.C., 1985—; instr. labor law Marshall Community Coll.; officer, dir. various corps.; pres., broker Practical Concepts, Inc., 1978—. Charter mem. Huntington Human Relations Commn., 1973-75, chmn., 1975; founding mem. Family Life Resource Ctr., pres., 1979. Served with USAF, 1951-53. Mem. ABA (forum com. title constrn. industry), Fed. Bar Assn., Lawyer-Pilots Bar Assn., W.Va. Bar Assn., Cabell County Bar Assn. (pres. 1978-79), Am. Judicature Soc., Def. Research Inst., Am. Arbitration Assn. (nat. panel arbitrators), Mensa. Democrat. Presbyterian. Club: Guyan Golf and Country (Huntington). Labor, Construction, Federal civil litigation. Office: 1111 WVa Bldg Huntington WV 25701

SCHAUFFLER, HARVEY ELLIOTT, JR., lawyer; b. Glassport, Pa., June 29, 1918; s. Harvey E. and Ada (Barlow) S. BA, U. Pitts., 1938, JD, 1942. Bar: Pa. 1943. sole practice, Pitts., 1946—; solicitor State Capital Savs. & Loan Assn., Harrisburg, Pa.; co-counsel Pitts. chpt. DAV. Chmn. Pa. Employ the Physically Handicapped Com., 1956, mem., 1979—; owner Sandybrook Egyptian Arabian Horse Industry, Beaver, Pa., 1986—; owner Salaheldin Farms, Beaver, 1986—; owner, developer Cascades Golf and Townhouse Complex, 1986—. Fellow Acad. Trial Lawyers Allegheny County; mem. Am. Arbitration Assn., Pa. Trial Lawyers Assn., Assn. Trial Lawyers Am., Allegheny County Bar Assn., Pa. Bar Assn. Internat. Platform Assn., Am. Legion, Pyramid Soc. Assn. Republican. Methodist. Clubs: Indian Creek Country, Surf, Palm Bay (Miami, Fla.); Youghiogheny Country. Personal injury, Probate, Family and matrimonial. Home: 506 Marie St Glassport PA 15045 Office: 803 Frick Bldg Pittsburgh PA 15219

SCHECHNER, DAVID, lawyer; b. Newark, Feb. 25, 1929; s. Sheridan and Selma Sophia (Schwarz) S.; m. Norma Myra Nurkin, Oct. 18, 1953; children: Sara Jane Schechner Genuth, Paul S., David S. AB, Lafayette Coll., 1950; JD, Harvard U., 1953. Bar: N.J. 1953, D.C. 1953, U.S. Dist. Ct. N.J. 1953, U.S. Ct. Mil. Appeals 1954, U.S. Ct. Appeals (3d cir.) 1958, U.S. Supreme Ct. 1958. Law clk. to post judge advocate U.S. Army, Ft. Meade, Md., 1953-55; assoc. Schapira & Farkas, Newark, 1955-58; sole practice Newark, 1958-65; ptnr. Schechner & Targan, West Orange, N.J., 1965—; counsel Village of South Orange (N.J.), 1978—; Barton Svgs. and Loan, Newark, 1963-84. Contbr. articles to profl. jours. Counsel South Orange (N.J.) Planning Bd., 1968-78; pres. South Orange Citizens Party League, 1970. Served with U.S. Army, 1953-55. Mem. ABA, N.J. Bar Assn., Essex county Bar Assn. Democrat. Jewish. Avocation: fishing. Local government, Contracts commercial, Real property. Home: 400 Woodland Place South Orange NJ 07079 Office: Schechner & Targan 80 Main St West Orange NJ 07052

SCHECHTER, ARTHUR LOUIS, lawyer; b. Rosenberg, Tex., Dec. 6, 1939; s. Morris and Helen (Brilling) S.; m. Joyce Proler, Aug. 28, 1964; children—Leslie, Jennifer. B.A., U. Tex., 1962, J.D. 1964; postgrad. U. Houston, 1964-65. Bar: Tex. 1964, U.S. Dist. Ct. (ea. and so. dists.) Tex. 1966, U.S. Ct. Appeals (5th cir.), U.S. Supreme Ct. 1976, cert. Tex. Bd. Legal Specialization to Personal Injury Trial Law. Pres. firm Dowman, Jones & Schechter, Houston, 1964-76, Schechter, Eisenman & Solar, Houston, 1976—; dir. Bank of Harris County, Houston; speaker Marine Law Seminar, 1983. Contbr. to Law Rev., 1984. Bd. dirs. Theatre Under the Stars, Houston, 1972-78, Congregation Beth Israel, Houston, 1972-84, Am. Jewish Com., Houston, 1982-84; mem. fin. council Nat. Dem. Orgn., 1979; mem. Deans Council, U. Tex. Law Sch. Found., Austin, 1981-84; v.p. Beth Israel Congregation; chmn. fgn. relations commn. Am. Jewish Com. Recipient Service award Congregation Beth Israel, 1976. Mem. Tex. Trial Lawyers Assn. (chmn. admiralty sect.), Am. Jewish Com. (exec. com.), Houston Trial Lawyers Assn., Houston Bar Assn., Assn. Trial Lawyers Am. Democrat. Jewish. Clubs: Westwood Country (bd. dirs., sec.), Houston Racquet (Houston). Admiralty, Personal injury. Home: 519 Hunterwood Dr Houston TX 77024

SCHECHTER, DANIEL PHILIP, lawyer; b. N.Y.C., Nov. 29, 1942; s. Isadore and Jenny (Waldman) S.; m. Sara P. Howell (div. 1977); children: Matthew, Ellen; m. Elizabeth Coolse, Oct. 1, 1983. BA, Columbia U., 1964, LLB, 1967. Bar: N.Y. 1968. Law clk. to judge U.S. Dist. Ct. (so. dist.) N.Y., N.Y.C., 1967-68; assoc. Fried, Frank, Harris, Shriver & Jacobson, N.Y.C., 1968-75, ptnr., 1975—. Mem. ABA, N.Y. State Bar Assn. Club: India House (N.Y.C.). Banking, General corporate. Office: Fried Frank Harris Shriver & Jacobson 1 New York Plaza New York NY 10004

SCHECHTER, DAVID ALAN, corporate lawyer; b. 1939. BA, U. Mich., 1959, JD, 1962; LLM, NYU, 1963. With Commerce Clearing House, 1963-65, Arthur Anderson & Co., 1965-67, Brown & Williamson Tobacco Corp., Louisville, 1967-78; v.p. Batus Inc., Louisville, 1978-79, v.p., gen. counsel, 1979—. Office: Batus Inc 2000 Citizens Plaza Louisville KY 40202 *

SCHECHTER, DONALD ROBERT, lawyer; b. N.Y.C., Feb. 24, 1946; s. Joseph and Katherine (Beer) S.; m. Roberta Sharon Horowitz, July 3, 1968; children: Elizabeth Anne, Sarah Marilyn. BA, Queens Coll., 1967; JD, Bklyn Law Sch., 1971. Asst. dist. atty. Queens County, Kew Gardens, N.Y., 1971-73; asst. atty. gen. organized crime task force City of N.Y., 1973-74; sole practice Forest Hills, N.Y., 1974—; legal counsel Centro Civico Colombiano, Jackson Heights, N.Y., 1978—, Fedn. of Merchants and Profls. of Queens, Spanish Orgn., Jackson Heights, 1978—; hearing officer Family Ct., Queens County, Jamaica, N.Y., 1977; consumer counsel Civil Ct., Queens County, 1980. Mem. ABA, N.Y. State Bar Assn., Queens County Bar Assn. (chmn. lawyer placement), Nassau County Bar Assn., Audobon Soc., Sierra Club. Democrat. Jewish. Clubs: Glass Soc. Corvette, N.Y. Mets Dream Week. Lodge: KP. Avocations: antique automobiles, baseball, history, antiques. Criminal, Consumer commercial, Family and matrimonial. Office: 118-21 Queens Blvd Forest Hills NY 11375

SCHECHTER, STUART, lawyer; b. N.Y.C., Feb. 8, 1958; s. William and Pauline (Jaret) S. BA, San Diego State U., 1977; JD, U. San Diego, 1981. Bar: Calif. 1982, U.S. Dist. Ct. (so. and no. dists.) Calif. 1982, U. Ct. Appeals (9th cir.) 1982. Sole practice San Diego, 1982—. Cons. Am. Cancer Soc., San Diego County, 1985, 86. Mem. Internat. Am. Bar Assn., San Diego Trial Lawyers Assn, Assn. Trial Lawyers, Societe Internationale Des Advocats., Phi Beta Kappa. Avocations: pvt. pilot, computers. Estate planning, Probate, General corporate. Home: 3638 Mount Abbey Ave San Diego CA 92111-4004 Office: 1380 Garnet Ave Suite E-288 San Diego CA 92109

SCHECHTERMAN, LAWRENCE, lawyer; b. Elizabeth, N.J., June 23, 1943; s. Josef and Sylvia (Berger) S.; m. Suzanne Lois Hilzenradt, May 31, 1981; children: Jill Laura, Danielle Sara, Danielle Beth, Nicole Corin, Gregory Jared. B.A., U. Miami, Fla., 1966; J.D., Suffolk U., 1969; LL.M., NYU, 1973. Bar: N.J. 1969, U.S. Dist. Ct. N.J. 1969, U.S. Ct. Appeals (D.C. cir.) 1970, U.S. Tax Ct. 1970, U.S. Supreme Ct. 1972, N.Y. 1980, U.S. Ct. Appeals (11th cir.) 1982, Fla. 1983, U.S. Dist. Ct. (so. dist.) Fla. 1983, U.S. Dist. Ct. (mid. dist.) Fla. 1984. Tax assoc. Coopers & Lybrand, N.Y.C., 1969-70; assoc. Bendit, Weinstock & Sharbaugh, Newark, 1970-72; sole practice, East Brunswick, N.J., 1972; gen. counsel Equinox Solar, Inc., Miami, Fla., 1981-83; mem. Lawrence Schechterman, P.A., Boca Raton, Fla., 1983—. Author: (poetry) New Dimensions: An Anthology of American Poetry, 1967. Contbr. articles to legal jours. Councilman, Twp. of East Brunswick, 1976-80. Mem. N.J. State Bar Assn., Fla. Bar, Palm Beach County Bar Assn., Middlesex County Bar Assn. (trustee 1977-80, sec. 1980-81), ABA. Securities, General corporate, Taxation. Home: 11937 Sandlake Dr Boca Raton FL 33428 Office: One Lincoln Pl 1900 Glades Rd Suite 301 Boca Raton FL 33431

SCHECK, DONALD GORDON, lawyer; b. Hackensack, N.J., Jan. 9, 1949; s. Harold Gordon and Elise Roger (Weir) S.; m. Rosanne A. Leone, July 30, 1972; children: Anne Catherine, Caitlin Ashley. BA, Lafayette Coll., 1971; JD, Vermont Law Sch., 1977. Bar: Pa. 1978, U.S. Ct. Appeals (3d cir) 1982, U.S. Dist. Ct. (mid. dist.) Pa. 1983, U.S. Ct. Appeals (fed. cir.) 1984. Sole practice Stroudsburg, Pa., 1978-85; pub. defender Monroe County, Stroudsburg, 1978-79; asst. dist. atty. Monroe County, Stroudsburg, 1979-80; mem. Scanlon, Lewis and Williamson, East Stroudsburg, 1985—; arbitration panelist Monroe County Ct. Common Pleas, Stroudsburg, 1978—, divorce master, 1979-83, 84—. Bd. mgrs. Barrett Twp. YMCA, Mountainhome, Pa., 1980-84. Mem. ABA, Pa. Bar Assn. (family law sect.), Monroe County Bar Assn. (family law sect. 1984—). Avocation: running. Real property, Family and matrimonial, State civil litigation. Home: E Dogwood Ln Mountainhome PA 18342 Office: Scanlon Lewis and Williamson 190 Washington St East Stroudsburg PA 18301

SCHECK, FRANK FOETISCH, lawyer; b. Albuquerque, Apr. 9, 1923; s. Frank Henry and Ethel Jane (Garrett) S.; m. Jane Leonore Rembowski, Aug. 17, 1946; children—Christopher G., Jennifer J., Carl P. B.S., Calif. Inst. Tech., 1948; LL.B., Columbia U., 1951. Bar: N.Y. 1951, U.S. Dist. Ct. (so. dist.) N.Y. 1953, U.S. Ct. Appeals (2d cir.) 1959, U.S. Supreme Ct. 1959, U.S. Ct. Appeals (7th cir.) 1966, U.S. Ct. Appeals (D.C. cir.) 1983. Assoc. Pennie, Edmonds, Morton, Barrows & Taylor, N.Y.C., 1951-60; ptnr., Pennie, Edmonds, Morton, Taylor & Adams, N.Y.C., 1961-69, sr. ptnr., 1970—. Served with U.S. Army, 1942-45. Decorated Purple Heart. Mem. ABA, Am. Patent Law Assn., N.Y. Patent Law Assn. (dir. 1982-85), Assn. Bar City N.Y., Am. Radio Relay League. Conservative. Presbyterian. Club: Princeton U. (N.Y.C.). Patent, Trademark and copyright, Federal civil litigation. Office: Pennie & Edmonds 1155 Ave of Americas New York NY 10036

SCHECTER, SANDRA JAN, lawyer; b. Dec. 14, 1949. BA magna cum laude, NYU, 1972, JD cum laude, 1975. Bar: U.S. Dist. Ct. (so. dist.) N.Y. 1976. Assoc. White & Case, N.Y.C., 1975-84, ptnr., 1984—. Mem. ABA, Am. Inst. Investment Council, Nat. Assn. Bond Lawyers, Order of Coif, Phi Beta Kappa. Banking, Project finance, Public finance. Office: White & Case 1155 Ave of Americas New York NY 10036

SCHECTMAN, HERBERT A., executive lawyer; b. N.Y.C., Aug. 8, 1930; s. Leon and Ethel (Brown) S.; m. Evelyn P. DePalma, Apr. 15, 1956 (div. 1974); children: Bart T., Robert; m. Lois Regent Driscoll, Apr. 11, 1974. A.B., Syracuse U., 1952; M.A., Columbia U., 1958, J.D., 1958. Bar: N.Y. 1959. Atty. U.S. Govt., Bklyn., 1958-60; atty. The Lummus Co., N.Y.C., 1960-62; assoc. gen. counsel Gen. Electric Credit Co., N.Y.C. and Chgo., 1962-67; div. counsel General Electric Co., N.Y.C., 1967-69; atty.-ptnr. Belfer, Bogart & Schectman, N.Y.C., 1969-74; sr. v.p. adminstrn., gen. counsel, sec. Chrysler Capital Corp. (formerly E.F. Hutton Credit Corp.), Greenwich, Conn., 1974—; also dir. Chrysler Capital Corp. (formerly E.F. Hutton Credit Corp.); arbitrator N.Y.C. Civil Ct. Small Claims, N.Y.C., 1974-85, sr. v.p. ops. and adminstrn., 1986—. Served with USAF, 1951-54; ETO. Mem. Am. Judges Assn., N.Y. State Bar Assn. Office: Chrysler Capital Corp Greenwich Office Park I Greenwich CT 06830 *

SCHEER, ALAN I., lawyer; b. Yonkers, N.Y., Mar. 3, 1942; s. Harold and Malvene E. (Balkind) S. Student, Cornell U., 1960-61; BS, NYU, 1964; JD, Bklyn. Law Sch., 1967. Bar: Conn. 1967, U.S. Ct. Appeals (2d cir.) 1970, U.S. Supreme Ct., 1974. Sole practice, 1967-72; sec., gen. counsel Dunham-Bush, Inc., West Hartford, Conn., 1973-80; resident ptnr. Widett, Slater & Goldman, Hartford, Conn., 1980-83; prin. Updike, Kelly & Spellacy, P.C., Hartford, 1984—. Exec. v.p. bd. dirs. Hartford Chamber Orch., 1984—; trustee Long Wharf Theatre, New Haven, 1987—. Labor. Home: One Gold St Hartford CT 06103

SCHEER, PETER EDWARD, lawyer; b. Boston, Feb. 26, 1951; s. Justin and Deborah Lee (Satz) S.; m. Libby Morrow Cater, Sept. 8, 1984. BA, Amherst Coll., 1973; JD, Harvard U., 1978. Bar: D.C. 1978, U.S. Ct. Appeals (1st, 2d, 5th and 9th cirs.) 1980, U.S. Ct. Appeals (D.C. cir.) 1982, U.S. Supreme Ct. 1986. Newspaper reporter Berkshire Eagle, Pittsfield, Mass., 1973-75; assoc. Hughes, Hubbard & Reed, Washington, 1978-79; spl. asst. to asst. atty. gen. criminal div. U.S. Dept. Justice, Washington, 1979-80; ptnr. Onek, Klein & Farr, Washington, 1981—; adj. prof. constl. law George Mason U., Alexandria, Va., 1984-85; gen. counsel, bd. dirs. Nat. Security Archive, Washington. Editor Harvard Law Rev., 1977-78. Fundraiser Amherst (Mass.) Coll.; pro bono counsel ACLU, others. Mem. ABA (health law, internat. law, law and nat. security coms.), D.C. Barr Assn. (communications law com.), Phi Beta Kappa. Avocations: tennis, movies. Federal civil litigation, Health, National security. Home: 4604 30th St NW Washington DC 20008 Office: Onek Klein & Farr 2550 M St NW Washington DC 20037

SCHEER, ROBERT J., lawyer, paper company executive; b. Lima, Ohio, Apr. 12, 1944; s. S.W. and Mary E. Scheer; m. Judith, Mar. 13, 1971. B.S., Manchester Coll., 1966; J.D., U. Toledo, 1969. Bar: Ohio 1969, U.S. Supreme Ct. 1981. Asst. dean of students U. Toledo, 1969; assoc. Fuller & Henry, Toledo, 1970-77; with Owens-Ill., Inc., 1977-82; mgr. labor relations and labor law Crown Zellerbach Corp., San Francisco, 1982—. Mem. ABA. Labor. Home: 249 Dantley Way Walnut Creek CA 94598 Office: One Bush St Suite 803 San Francisco CA 94104

SCHEFFLER, STUART JAY, lawyer; b. Phila., Oct. 9, 1950; s. Walter and Fritzy (Salkoff) S.; m. Barbara Jane Green, July 3, 1975. BA cum laude, Pa. State U., 1972, MPA, 1973; JD, Temple U., 1980. Bar: Pa. 1980, U.S. Dist. Ct. (ea. dist.) Pa. 1981, U.S. Ct. Appeals (3d cir.) 1983, U.S. Supreme Ct. 1986. Tchr. Sch. Dist. of Phila., 1974-75; claims authorizer Social Security Adminstrn., HEW, Phila., 1975-76, equal opportunity specialist Office of Civil Rights, 1976-77; paraprofessional Law Offices of Ronald A. Bell., Bala Cynwyd, Pa., 1978-80; assoc. Law Office of Robert B. Mozenter, Phila., 1980-81, Gekoski & Bogdanoff, Phila., 1981-82; ptnr. Rubin & Scheffler, Phila., 1982-84; sole practice, Phila., 1984—. Councilman Bakers Bay Condominium Assn., Phila., 1982. Mem. ABA, Pa. Bar Assn., Phila. Bar Assn., Am. Trial Lawyers Assn., Phila. Trial Lawyers Assn., Pa. Trial Lawyers Assn., Drug Info. Assn., Phi Beta Kappa, Delta Sigma Rho, Tau Kappa Alpha, Zeta Beta Tau. Democrat. Club: Hartikvah Basketball Assn. (Phila.) (v.p. 1974—). Personal injury, State civil litigation, Insurance. Office: 1712 Locust St Philadelphia PA 19103

SCHEFMAN, LESLIE CRAIG, lawyer; b. Detroit, Nov. 7, 1949; s. Myron and Theda (Bankle) S.; m. Carol Ruth Garfield, Apr. 12, 1973; children—Lauren Elyse, Alyssa Brooke, Jamie Reed. B.A., U. Mich., 1971; J.D., Wayne State U., 1974. Bar: Mich. 1974. Assoc. firm Lippitt, Harrison, Friedman & Zack, Southfield, Mich., 1974-77; sole practice, Detroit, 1978-80; ptnr. firm Schefman & Fenton, Detroit, 1980-81, firm Schefman & Miller, P.C., Birmingham, Mich., 1982—. Alpert Found. scholar, 1971. Mem. State Bar Mich. (standing com. medico-legal problems 1982-83, standing com. on mentally disabled 1984-87), Assn. Trial Lawyers Am., Mich. Trial Lawyers Assn. (legis. com. 1984), Am. Soc. Law and Medicine, Oakland County Bar Assn. Jewish. Personal injury, Federal civil litigation, State civil litigation. Office: Schefman & Miller PC 255 E Brown St Suite 440 Birmingham MI 48011

SCHEIBE, ROBERT HENRY, lawyer; b. N.Y.C., Nov. 12, 1946; s. Erich and Kaete (Loebhardt) S.; m. Judith F. Rose, Aug. 15, 1970; children—Alexandra, Gabrielle. B.A., Hobart Coll., 1967; J.D., Georgetown U., 1970. Bar: N.Y. 1971, U.S. Dist. Ct. (so. dist.) N.Y. 1975. Assoc. White & Case, N.Y.C., 1970-78; mem. Zalkin, Rodin & Goodman, 1978—. Mem. ABA, Assn. Bar City N.Y. Banking, Bankruptcy, Contracts commercial. Office: Zalkin Rodin & Goodman 750 3d Ave New York NY 10017

SCHEIBER, HARRY N., legal educator; b. N.Y.C., 1935. B.A. Columbia U., 1955; M.A., Cornell U., 1957, Ph.D., 1961; M.A. (hon.), Dartmouth Coll., 1965. instr. history Dartmouth Coll., 1960-68, prof., 1968-71; prof. Am. history U. Calif.-San Diego, 1971-80; prof. law Boalt Hall, U. Calif.-Berkeley, 1980—, chmn. jurisprudence and social policy program, 1982-84; Fulbright disting. sr. lectr., Australia, 1983. Chmn. Littleton Griswold Prize Legal History; pres. N. H. Civil Liberties Union, 1969-70; chmn. Project '87 Task Force on Pub. Programs, Washington, 1982-85; dir. Berkeley Seminar on Federalism, 1986; cons. judiciary study U.S. Adv. Commn. Intergovernmental Relations, 1985—. Recipient Sea Grant Colls. award, 1981-83, 84-85, 86—; fellow Ctr. Advanced Study in Behavioral Scis., Stanford Calif., 1967; Guggenheim fellow, 1971; Rockefeller Found. humanities fellow, 1979, NEH fellow, 1985-86; NSF grantee, 1979, 80. Mem. Am. Hist. Assn., Orgn. Am. Historians, Agrl. History Soc. (pres. 1978), Econ. History Assn. (trustee 1978-80), Law and Soc. Assn. (trustee 1979-81), Am. Soc. Legal History (dir. 1982-86), Am. Bar Found. (legal history fellowship com.), Nat. Assessment History and Citizenship Edn. (chmn. com. 1986-87). Author books, the most recent being: (with L. Friedman) American Law and the Constitutional Order, 1978; contbr. articles to law revs., 1963—. Legal history, Environment, Legal education. Office: U Calif Berkeley Law Sch Boalt Hall Berkeley CA 94720

SCHEIDEGGER, KENT STEPHEN, lawyer; b. Arlington, Va., Dec. 31, 1953; s. Paul Francis and Elizabeth (Walker) S.; m. Lada Phasook, April 11, 1981. BS with honors, N.Mex. State U., 1976; JD with distinction, McGeorge Sch. Law, Sacramento, 1982. Bar: Calif. 1982, U.S. Ct. Appeals (9th cir.) 1985. Commd. nuclear research officer USAF, Sacramento, 1976, advanced through grades to capt., 1982; resigned USAF, 1982; assoc. Neumiller & Beardslee, Stockton, Calif., 1983-84; gen. counsel Calif. Cooler Co., Stockton, 1984—. Mem. ABA, San Joaquin County Bar Assn., McGeorge Alumni Assn. (Amicus lex scholar 1981), Order of the Coif. Republican. Unitarian. General corporate, Contracts commercial. Office: Calif Cooler Co PO Box 55329 Stockton CA 95205

SCHEIDER, JAMES PRINGLE, JR., lawyer; b. Savannah, Ga., Jan. 9, 1943; s. James Pringle Sr. and Mary Roberta (Bythewood) S.; m. Taffy Garner, Dec. 1, 1984. BA, U. S.C., 1970; JD, George Mason U., 1980. Bar: S.C. 1981. Asst. minority counsel U.S. Senate Judiciary Com., Washington, 1980; assoc. Dowling, Sanders, Dukes, Hilton Head Island, S.C., 1980-84; ptnr. Jones, Scheider & Patterson, Hilton Head Island, 1984—. Commnr. Hilton Head Med. Commn., 1984—; trustee Hilton Head Mus., 1985—. Served with USMC, 1962-63. Named one of Outstanding Young Men in Am.; named Realtor of Yr., Hilton Head Bd. Realtors, 1975. Mem. ABA, S.C. Bar Assn. (mem. house of dels. 1985—), Beaufort County Bar Assn. (sec. 1986-87), Hilton Head Bar Assn. (pres. 1984-85). Republican. Avocations: running, flying, farming. Real property, Contracts commercial, General corporate. Office: Jones Scheider & Patterson PA PO Drawer 7049 Hilton Head Island SC 29938

SCHEIFLY, JOHN EDWARD, tax lawyer; b. Mexico, Mo., Aug. 25, 1925; s. Luke Clauser and Isabella (Sprankle) S.; m. Patricia Ann Lenhart, Dec. 27, 1947; children: John Edward, Jan Ellen. Sc.B., Brown U., 1945; J.D., Washington and Lee U., 1948. Bar: Calif., W.Va. Practice law Los Angeles, 1953—; mem. firm Baker, Scheifly & Porter, Huntington, W.Va., 1949-53, McClean, Salisbury, Petty & McClean, Los Angeles, 1953-57, Willis, Butler, Scheifly, Leydorf & Grant (and predecessors), Los Angeles, 1958-81, Bryan, Cave, McPheeters & McRoberts, Los Angeles, 1981-84, Morgan, Lewis & Bockius, Los Angeles, 1984—; lectr. tax law U. So. Calif., 1960-74. Author lectr. fed. tax matters profl. publs., insts. Served to lt. USNR, 1943-46, 51-53. Mem. Los Angeles County Bar Assn. (chmn. tax. sect. 1965-66), ABA (mem. council sect. taxation 1974-77), State Bar Calif. Clubs: Jonathan (Los Angeles); Hacienda Golf (LaHabra, Calif.); Monterey Country (Palm Desert, Calif.). Home: 9441 Friendly Woods Ln Whittier CA 90605 Office: Morgan Lewis and Bockius 801 S Grand Ave Los Angeles CA 90017

SCHEIGE, STEVEN SHELDON, lawyer; b. N.Y.C., Mar. 15, 1950; s. Manfred Herman and Liba (Miller) S.; m. Fortuna Faye Gorelick, July 8, 1973; children—Robert, Susan-Lisa. B.A., Rutgers U., 1972; J.D., Georgetown U., 1975. Bar: Md. 1975. Atty.-advisor Occupational Safety and Health Rev. Commn., Washington, 1975-78, supervisory atty., 1978-80, asst. chief counsel, 1980—. Spl. project coordinator PTA, Montgomery County, Md., 1984. Mem. ABA, Md. State Bar Assn., Phi Beta Kappa. Jewish. Labor, Administrative and regulatory. Office: Occupational Safety and Health Rev Commn 1825 K St NW Suite 400 Washington DC 20006

SCHEINHOLTZ, LEONARD LOUIS, lawyer; b. Pitts., June 2, 1927; s. Bernard A. and Marie (Getzel) S.; m. Joan R. Libenson, Aug. 16, 1953; children: Stuart, Nancy, Barry. B.A., U. Pa., 1948, M.A., 1949; LL.B., Columbia U., 1953. Bar: Pa. 1954, U.S. Ct. Appeals (3d cir.) 1959, U.S. Supreme Ct. 1972, U.S. Ct Appeals (6th Cir.) 1968, (4th cir.) 1973. Assoc. Reed, Smith, Shaw & McClay, Pitts., 1953-62, spl. ptnr., 1962-64, gen. ptnr., 1964—, head labor dept., 1980-86; dir. Am. Arbitration Assn., N.Y.C., 1980—. Author: Exemption Under the Anti-Trust Laws for Joint Employer Activity, 1982, The Arbitrator as Judge and Jury: Another Look at Statutory Law in Arbitration, 1985. Vice chmn. Pa. AAA Fedn., Harrisburg, 1982-85 ; chmn. W. Pa. AAA Motor Club, 1979-82; trustee Montefiore Hosp., Pitts., 1976-79. Served with USN, 1945-46. Mem. ABA, Pa. Bar Assn., Allegheny County Bar Assn. Republican. Jewish. Club: Duquesne. Labor, Pension, profit-sharing, and employee benefits. Home: 746 Pinoak Rd Pittsburgh PA 15243 Office: 435 6th Ave Mellon Sq Pittsburgh PA 15219

SCHEINKMAN, ALAN DAVID, legal educator, lawyer; b. Newark, May 1, 1950; s. Henry R. and Gertrude (Einhorn) S.; m. Deborah Steinberg, July 1, 1978; children—Michael, Rebecca. B.A., George Washington U., 1972; J.D., St. John's U., Jamaica, N.Y., 1975. Bar: N.Y. 1976, U.S. Dist. Ct. (so. and ea. dists.) N.Y. 1977. Law clk. N.Y. Ct. Appeals, Albany, 1975-77; assoc. firm Marshall, Bratter, Greene, Allison & Tucker, N.Y.C., 1977-79, Golenbock & Barell, N.Y.C., 1979-82; assoc. prof. law St. John's U., Jamaica, N.Y., 1983—; assoc. counsel N.Y. State Temporary Commn. to Recodify Family Ct. Act, Albany, 1982; lectr. N.Y. State Annual Jud. Seminar. Author: Practice Commentaries to McKinney's N.Y. Domestic Relations Law, 1981—; reporter N.Y. Pattern Jury Instructions; directing editor McKinney's Texts and Forms. Mem. N.Y. State Bar Assn. (com. on appellate ct., co-editor One on One), N.Y. State Trial Lawyers Assn. (vice chmn. matrimonial com.), ABA, Assn. Bar City of N.Y (state cts. of superior jurisdiction com.). Legal education, Family and matrimonial, State civil litigation. Home: 2385 Bunney Ct Yorktown Heights NY 10598 Office: St John's U School of Law Grand Central and Utopia Pkwys Jamaica NY 11439

SCHELER, BRAD ERIC, lawyer; b. Bklyn., Oct. 11, 1953; s. Bernard and Rita Regina (Miller) S.; m. Amy Ruth Frolick, Mar. 30, 1980; children: Ali M., Maddie H. BA magna cum laude, Lehigh U., 1974; JD, Hofstra U., 1977. Bar: N.Y. 1978, U.S. Dist. Ct. (so. and ea. dists.) N.Y. 1978. Assoc. Weil, Gotshal & Manges, N.Y.C., 1977-81; ptnr. Fried, Frank, Harris, Shriver & Jacobson, N.Y.C., 1981—. Research editor Hofstra U. Law Rev., 1975-77. Treas., bus. mgr. Trustees of Gramercy Park, N.Y.C., 1979—. Named one of Outstanding Young Men Am., 1980. Mem. ABA (bus. bankruptcy com. corp. banking and bus. law sect., creditors' rights com. litigation sect.), N.Y. State Bar Assn., Assn. of Bar of City of N.Y., Sigma Alpha Mu (v.p. 1973). Jewish. Bankruptcy, Contracts commercial, Corporate finance and business reorganizations. Home: 32 Maple Hill Dr Larchmont NY 10538-1614 Office: Fried Frank Harris Shriver & Jacobson One New York Plaza New York NY 10004

SCHELLER, ARTHUR MARTIN, JR., law educator; b. Berlin, Wis., Oct. 7, 1927; s. Arthur M. and Ruth M. (Keehn) S.; m. Ann M. Palisin, June 19, 1954; children—Mary, Helen, Arthur, Stephen, Suzanne, Fritz, John, Raissa. B.A., St. Norbert Coll., 1949; J.D., Marquette U., 1954. Bar: Wis. 1954; U.S. Dist. Ct. (ea. dist.) Wis., U.S. Dist. Ct. (no. dist.) Ill. 1960, U.S. Tax Ct. 1983, U.S. Ct. Appeals (7th cir.) 1967. Asst. prof. Loyola U., Chgo., 1958-60; prof. DePaul U., Chgo., 1960-75; prof. John Marshall Law Sch., Chgo., 1975—; cons. N.E. Ill. Planning Commn., Chgo., 1964-66, Corp. Engrs., 1962-63; lectr. in field, 1979-83. Editor: (with others) Law Manual for Community Organizers, 1970-84. Contbr. articles to profl. publs. Nat. v.p. Cath. Civil Rights League, Milw., 1975-79. Served with USN, 1945-46. Recipient numerous Outstanding Teacher awards. Mem. Wis. Bar Assn., Ill. Bar Assn. Roman Catholic. Club: Union League (Chgo.). Probate, Real property, Legal education. Home: 300 Meacham Park Ridge IL 60068 Office: John Marshall Law Sch 315 S Plymouth Ct Chicago IL 60604

SCHEMAHORN, CLYDE E., lawyer; b. LaGrange County, Ind., Aug. 27, 1906; s. Matthias R. and Lillian M. (Shoup) S.; m. Edith Irene, Oct. 28, 1924; children—Virginia D., Merlin L., Keith E., Phillip R. Bar: Ind. 1939. Sole practice, LaGrange, Ind., 1940—. Founding mem. U.S. Senatorial Club, 1977—; mem. Republican Nat. Com., 1976—; charter mem. Rep. Presdl. Task Force, 1982, Presdl. Trust, 1987—; sponsor Victory Fund, Nat. Rep. Congl. Com., 1972—; mem. Ind. State Rep. Party. Mem. Ind. Bar Assn. (gen. practice sect.), Ind. Sheriffs Assn. Methodist. Probate, Estate taxation, Personal income taxation. Office: Rural Route 5 LaGrange IN 46761

SCHEMBER, STEVEN GEORGE, lawyer; b. Dayton, Ohio, July 7, 1945; s. George Henry and Doris (McCrea) S.; m. Cynthia Marie Waltman, Aug. 16, 1969; children: Meredith McCrea, Andrew Hinsdill. BS, USCG Acad., 1967; JD, U. Mich., 1970. Bar: Mich. 1970, U.S. Dist. Ct. (we. dist.) Mich. 1970, U.S. Ct. Appeals (6th cir.) 1974, Fla. 1979, U.S. Dist. Ct. (mid. dist.) Fla. 1979, U.S. Ct. Appeals (5th cir.) 1979, U.S. Ct. Appeals (11th cir.) 1981. Ptnr. Parmenter, Forsythe & Rude, Muskegon, Mich., 1970-78, Dykema, Gossett, Spencer, Goodnow & Trigg and predecessor firm Kirk, Pinkerton, Savary, Carr & Strode, P.A., Sarasota, Fla., 1978—; vis. prof. law U. So. Fla., 1984-85. Pres. Sarasota County Heart Assn., 1986—; bd. dirs. Midnight Cove II Condominium Assn., Sarasota, 1980-86. Mem. ABA (rules revision subcom. 1984—), Acad. Fla. Trial Lawyers Assn. (legis. liason 1984—, bd. dirs. comml. sect. 1984—, speakers bur. chmn. 1984—), Sarasota County Bar Assn., Sarasota C. of C. (bd. dirs. growth mgmt. com. 1984—). Clubs: Bath and Raquet, University (Sarasota). Avocations: tennis, boating, jogging. Federal civil litigation, State civil litigation, Personal injury. Office: Dykema Gossett Spencer et al 720 S Orange Ave Box 3798 Sarasota FL 33578

SCHENKEIN, PAMELA EPHRAIM, lawyer; b. N.Y.C., Jan. 17, 1936; d. Jerome W. and Muriel (Abrahams) Ephraim; m. William F. Schenkein, Jan. 28, 1954; children: Suzanne, Edward. BSBA, U. Denver, 1957, JD, 1980. Bar: Colo. 1981, U.S. Dist Ct. Colo. 1981, U.S. Ct. Appeals (10th cir.) 1981, U.S. Supreme Ct. 1986. Assoc. Wiegand & Assocs., Englewood, Colo., 1981-82; asst. atty. gen. Colo. Dept. Law, Denver, 1983; sole practice Englewood, 1983—; instr. bus. law U. Colo., Denver, 1981. Bus. editor U. Denver Law Rev., 1979-80. Committeewoman Englewood Reps., 1976; mem. Cherry Creek Rep. Women's Club; mem. benefit com. Rocky Mountain chpt. Arthritis Found.; mem. bylaws com. Arap County Reps., 1987—. Recipient Nathan Burkan Meml. award ASCAP, 1980, Am. Jurisprudence award in Ins., 1980, Linn Labor Law award 1980; Sherman and Howard Fellow, 1980. Mem. Colo. Bar Assn. (bd. govs. 1985—, budget policy task force 1986—, budget com. 1987—), Douglas-Elbert County Bar Assn. (officer 1985—). Republican. Avocations: reading, opera, concerts, plays, gourmet cooking. Probate, Real property, Family and matrimonial. Home and Office: 5906 E Briarwood Circle Englewood CO 80112

SCHENKKAN, PIETER (PETE) MEADE, lawyer; b. Durham, N.C., Nov. 5, 1947; s. Robert Frederic and Jean Gregory (McKenzie) S.; m. Mary Frances Victory, June 20, 1970; children: Benjamin McKenzie, Nathaniel Victory, Zachary Alexander. BA with highest honors, U. Va., 1969; BA with 1st class honors, Oxford U., 1972, MA, 1972; JD with high honors, U. Tex., 1975. Bar: Tex. 1975, U.S. Dist. Ct. D.C. 1975, U.S. Dist. Ct. (so. dist.) Tex. 1976, U.S. Dist. Ct. (we. dist.) Tex. 1980, U.S. Ct. Appeals (10th cir.) 1983, U.S. Ct. Appeals (5th cir.) 1983. Assoc. Vinson & Elkins, Houston, 1975-77, 79-82; ptnr. Vinson & Elkins, Austin, 1982—; spl. asst. atty gen. State of Tex., Austin, 1977-78. Note and comment editor Tex. Law Rev. Mem. Atlantic Council, Washington, 1985—; bd. dirs. Tex. Assn. of Atlantic Council, 1986—; chmn. Travis County (Tex.) Carter-Mondale Campaign, 1980; vice chancellor Epis. Diocese of Tex., 1984—. Rhodes scholar Oxford U., 1968. Fellow Tex. Bar Found.; mem. ABA, Fed. Bar Assn., Fed. Energy Bar Assn., Travis County Bar Assn., Order of Coif. Democrat. Episcopalian. Administrative and regulatory, Federal civil litigation, State civil litigation. Office: Vinson & Elkins 1800 First City Ctr 816 Congress Ave Austin TX 78701-2496

SCHENKLER, BERNARD, lawyer; b. Trani, Italy, Aug. 25, 1948; s. Wolf and Nettie Schenkler; m. Ellen Haberman, Sept. 25, 1977; children: Alan, Sarah. BA, U. Pa., 1970; JD, Columbia U., 1973. Bar: N.Y. 1974, N.J. 1977, D.C. 1979, U.S. Ct. Appeals (2d cir.) 1975, U.S. Dist. Ct. (so. and ea. dists.) N.Y. 1975, U.S. Tax Ct. 1978, U.S. Ct. Mil. Appeals 1978, U.S. Supreme Ct. 1980, U.S. Ct. Appeals (3rd cir.), U.S. Dist. Ct. (no. and we. dists.) N.Y. 1980, U.S. Ct. Claims 1985, U.S. Ct. Internat. Trade 1985. Atty bus. law unit N.Y.C. Human Resources Adminstrn., 1973-76, exec. asst. to gen. counsel, 1977; assoc. Ravin, Sarasohn, Cook, Baumgarten & Fisch, West Orange, N.J., 1978-85; ptnr. Ravin, Sarasohn, Cook, Baumgarten, Fisch & Baime, Roseland, N.J., 1986. Mem. Randolph Twp. (N.J.) Bd. of Ethics, 1978-80. Mem. ABA, N.Y. State Bar Assn., N.J. State Bar Assn., Essex County Bar Assn., D.C. Bar. Jewish. Club: White Meadow Temple Men's Club (Rockaway, N.J.). Avocations: photography, stamp collecting, model railroading. Bankruptcy, Contracts commercial, State civil litigation. Office: Ravin Sarasohn et al 103 Eisenhower Pkwy Roseland NJ 07068

SCHEPPS, VICTORIA HAYWARD, lawyer; b. Brockton, Mass., June 11, 1956; d. William George and Lucy Victoria (Mitcheroney) Hayward; m. Frank Schepps, Sept. 18, 1982. B.A., Suffolk U., 1977; J.D., U. San Diego, 1981. Instr., Northeastern U., Boston, 1981-83; assoc. Hoffman & Hoffman, Boston, 1983-85, Mark J. Gladstone, P.C., 1985—; mem. adv. bd. Northeastern U. Paralegal Program, Boston, 1982—. Mem. Mass. Bar Assn., ABA, Mass. Conveyancing Assn., Forum Com. Entertainment and Sports Law. Democrat. Roman Catholic. Real property. Home: 11 Overlook Rd Randolph MA 02368 Office: Mark J Gladstone PC 402 N Main St PO Box 788 Randolph MA 02368

SCHER, HOWARD DENNIS, lawyer; b. Ft. Monmouth, N.J., Apr. 23, 1945; s. George Scher and Rita (Eitches) Zar; m. Eileen Sue Sklaroff, Sept. 15, 1968; children; Seth Micah, Eli David. BA, Brandeis U., 1967; JD, Rutgers U., 1971. Bar: Pa. 1971, U.S. Dist. Ct. (ea. dist.) Pa. 1971, U.S. Ct. Appeals (3rd cir.) 1971, U.S. Supreme Ct. 1975. Asst. city solicitor City of Phila., 1971-73; assoc. Goodis, Greenfield, Henry & Edelstein, Phila., 1973-74; assoc. Montgomery, McCracken, Walker & Rhoads, Phila., 1977-80, ptnr., 1980—. Zoning chmn. Logan Sq. Neighborhood Assn., Phila., 1982—; assoc. sec. Jewish Employment Vocational Services, Phila., 1985—; asst. sec. Temple Beth Zion Beth Israel, Phila., 1984—. Mem. Phila. Bar Assn., Pa. Bar Assn., ABA, Brandeis U. Alumni Assn. (v.p. 1983—). Federal civil litigation, State civil litigation. Home: 2112 Spring St Philadelphia PA 19103 Office: Montgomery McCracken Walker & Rhoads 3 Parkway Suite 2000 Philadelphia PA 19102

SCHER, MARK WACLAW, lawyer; b. Warsaw, Poland, Oct. 6, 1946; came to U.S., 1969; s. Seweryn and Alicja Stefania (Brokman) Szer; m. Ilona S. Wiener, July 31, 1971 (div. Nov. 1979); Ecaterina Weiszmann, Nov. 13, 1979; 1 child, Daniel J. LLM, U. Warsaw, Poland, 1969, NYU, 1983; JD, Cleve. State U., 1973. Bar: Pa. 1974, N.Y. 1976, U.S. Dist. Ct. (so. dist.) N.Y. 1979. Gen. atty. Dept. of Justice, N.Y.C., 1976-79; adminstrv. law judge State of N.Y., N.Y.C., 1979-82; sole practice N.Y.C., 1982—; lectr. Polish Bar Assn., Warsaw, 1986; legal cons. Polish Consulate, N.Y.C., 1982—. Mem. ABA, N.Y. State Bar Assn., Am. Immigration Lawyers Assn., Fgn. Law Assn., N.Y. County Lawyers Assn. Republican. Avocations: classical music, theatre, literature. Immigration, naturalization, and customs, Private international.

SCHER, STANLEY JULES, lawyer; b. Bklyn., Dec. 19, 1929; s. Leo A. and Frances (Goldman) S.; m. Susan Goldman, June 16, 1957; children—William Goldman, Peter Lawrence, Alison Hope. LL.B., Bklyn. Law Sch., 1952. Bar: N.Y. 1954, U.S. Dist. Ct. (so. and ea. dists.) N.Y. 1960, U.S. Supreme Ct. 1970. Ptnr. Tullman, Fisher & Scher, N.Y.C., 1954-62; founder, sr. ptnr. Garbarini, Scher & DeCicco, P.C., N.Y.C., 1962—; med.-legal lectr. physicians, hosps., health-related facilities, 1970—; mem. faculty N.Y. State Trial Lawyers Assn., 1975—; lectr. Nassau Acad. Law, 1984, N.Y. State Bar Assn., 1983. Pres. Baker Hill Civic Assn., Great Neck, N.Y., past zone leader Great Neck Democratic Com., mem. Nat. CIC Orgn., Great Neck. Served with U.S. Army, 1952-54. Mem. ABA, Assn. Trial Lawyers Am., Soc. Med. Jurisprudence, N.Y. State Bar Assn., N.Y. County Lawyers Assn., Queens County Bar Assn., Nassau County Bar Assn. Jewish. Club: Temple Israel Couples (Great Neck, N.Y.) (past pres.). Lodge: B'nai B'rith. Health, Insurance, Personal injury. Home: 59 Essex Rd Great Neck NY 11023 Office: Garbarini & Scher PC 500 Fifth Ave New York NY 10110

SCHERER, RICHARD SIGMUND, lawyer; b. Mpls., Aug. 13, 1946; s. Carl Sigmund and Laura (McDaniel) S.; m. Nancy Nyrop; 1 child, Matthew Donald. BA, Gustavus Adolphus U., 1968; JD, U. Minn., 1975. Bar: Minn. 1975, U.S. Dist. Ct. Minn. 1975, U.S. Ct. Appeals (8th cir.) 1975. Ptnr. Castor, Ditzler, Klukas & Scherer, Mpls., 1975—. Served with U.S. Army, 1970-72, Vietnam. Mem. ABA, Minn. Bar Assn. Republican. Congregationalist. Avocations: fishing, gardening. State civil litigation, Insurance, Personal injury. Home: 6508 Cherokee Trail Edina MN 55435 Office: Castor Ditzler Klukas & Scherer 247 3d Ave S Minneapolis MN 55415

SCHERMER, MARSHA ROCKEY, lawyer; b. Chgo., July 23, 1940; d. Theodore Franklin and Clarys Wilhelmina (Smith) Rockey; m. Harry Angus Schermer, Jan. 3, 1971 (div. Sept. 1982). BA in Psychology, Antioch Coll., 1963; MA in Design, Ohio State U., 1965, PhD in Philosophy, 1974, JD, 1980. Bar: 1980, U.S. Dist. Ct. (so. dist.) Ohio 1981, U.S. Ct. Appeals (4th cir.) 1985. Asst. atty. gen. State of Ohio, Columbus, 1980-84; rate counsel Am. Electric Power, Columbus, 1984-86; legal dir. Pub. Utilities Commn. Ohio, Columbus, 1986—. Mem. ABA, Ohio Bar Assn., Columbus Bar Assn. Public utilities, Administrative and regulatory. Home: 2791 Kensington Pl E Columbus OH 43202 Office: Pub Utilities Commn Ohio Legal Dept 180 E Broad St Columbus OH 43215

SCHERMER, OSCAR SELIG, lawyer; b. Phila., Nov. 28, 1933; s. Charles Samuel and Stella (Caplan) S.; m. Karen Kooperman, June 8, 1968; children: Stephanie, Jamie, Cathie. BS in Acctg., U. Pa., 1955; JD, Temple U., 1960. Bar: Pa. 1960, U.S. Dist. Ct. (so. dist.) Pa., U.S. Dist. Ct. (so. dist.) N.J., U.S. Dist. Ct. Del., U.S. Ct. Appeals (3d cir.) 1960. Law clk. to presiding justice Ct. Common Pleas, Phila., 1960-62; ptnr. Schermer & Schermer, Phila., 1962-77, Boardman & Schermer, Phila., 1978-86; sole practice Phila., 1986—. Served to 1st lt. QMC USN, 1955-57. Mem. ABA, Pa. Bar Assn., Phila. Bar Assn., Assn. Trial Lawyers Am., Pa. Trial Lawyers Assn., Phila. Trial Lawyers Assn., Lawyers Club. Club: Urban (Phila.). Lodges: Shriners (dir. equity 1964-70), Masons. Avocations: fishing, computers. State civil litigation, Personal injury, Probate. Office: 1234 Market St Suite 2050 Philadelphia PA 19107

SCHERMERHORN, SANDRA LEIGH, lawyer; b. Easton, Pa., July 7, 1944; d. George Lewis and Martha Claire (Cunningham) S. BA in Polit. Sci., Beaver Coll., 1966; JD, U. Mo., Kansas City, 1969. Bar: Mo. 1970, U.S. Dist. Ct. (we. dist.) Mo. 1970, U.S. Ct. Appeals (10th cir.) 1976, U.S. Ct. Appeals (8th cir.) 1978. Law clk. to presiding justice U.S. Dist. Ct. (we. dist.) Mo., Kansas City, 1970-73; ptnr. Spencer, Fane, Britt & Browne, Kansas City, 1973—. Trustee Legal Aid Western Mo., Kansas City, 1984—. Named Woman of Yr. Dimensions Unltd. Inc., 1985. Mem. ABA, Kansas City Met. Bar Assn. (pres. 1985), Kansas City Bar Found., Lawyers Assn. Kansas City, Nat. Caucus Met. Bar Leaders (pres. 1985—). Presbyterian. Club: Cen. Exchange (Kansas City). Avocations: golf, softball, swimming, reading. Federal civil litigation, State civil litigation, Civil rights. Home: 6410 Summit Kansas City MO 64113 Office: Spencer Fane Britt & Browne 1000 Power & Light Bldg Kansas City MO 64105

SCHEWE, BRUCE VICTOR, lawyer, educator; b. Ft. Polk, La., Oct. 5, 1955; s. M. William and M. Delois (Jones) S.; m. Robin Lynn May, Aug. 5, 1979 (div. Aug. 1983). BS, La State U., 1977, JD, 1981. Bar: La. 1981, U.S. Dist. Ct. (we., ea. and mid. dists.) La. 1982, U.S. Ct. Appeals (5th and 11th cirs.) 1981. Law clk. to presiding judge U.S. Ct. Appeals (5th cir.), New Orleans, 1981-82; assoc. Liskow & Lewis, New Orleans, 1982-87, ptnr., 1987—; lectr. law Loyola U., New Orleans, 1983—. Exec. editor La. State U. Law Rev., 1981; contbr. articles to profl. jours. Served to 1st lt. USAR, 1977-82. Mem. ABA, La. Bar Assn., Fed. Bar Assn., La. Assn. Def. Counsel, Order of Coif, Assn. Henri Capitant (v.p. 1986—). Democrat. Episcopalian. Club: Metairie (La.) Country. Federal civil litigation, Consumer commercial, Banking. Home: 1436 Toledano St New Orleans LA 70115 Office: Liskow & Lewis 1 Shell Sq 50th Floor New Orleans LA 70139

SCHIAVETTI, ANTHONY LOUIS, lawyer; b. N.Y.C., Oct. 24, 1929; s. Francis Xavier and Carmela (Colucci) S.; m. Geraldine L. Cioffi, Nov. 29, 1953; children: Francis Xavier, Donna Marie Schiavetti Devaney. BS, Fordham U., 1951, JD, 1959. Bar: N.Y. Patrolman police dept. City of N.Y., 1953-57; assoc. Martin, Clearwater & Bell, N.Y.C., 1960-74; atty. Wausau (Wis.) Ins. Co., 1974-82; sr. ptnr. Schiavetti, Begos & Nicholson, N.Y.C., 1982—. Bd. dirs. Am. Fedn. for Aging Research, N.Y.C.; mem. Columbus Citizens Found., Inc. Served to 1st lt. U.S. Army, 1951-53, Korea. Mem. ABA, N.Y. State Bar Assn. Roman Catholic. Club: Wykagyl Country (New Rochelle, N.Y.). Avocations: golf, bridge. State civil litigation, Personal injury, Insurance. Office: Schiavetti Begos & Nicholson 1633 Broadway New York NY 10019

SCHIEFELBEIN, LESTER WILLIS, JR., lawyer; b. Berwyn, Ill., Feb. 17, 1946; s. Lester Willis and Mary Kathryn (Kelly) S.; m. Linda Ann Boyle, Aug. 15, 1970; children—Tracy, Christy, Lesley, Bryan. B.S., Ariz. State U., 1968, J.D., 1971; LL.M., George Washington U., 1975. Bar: Calif. 1972, Ariz. 1971, U.S. Supreme Ct. 1976, D.C. 1982. Atty., U.S. Dept. Energy, Washington, 1978-82; co. counsel Lockheed Electronics Co., Inc., Plainfield, N.J., 1982—, mem. office of pres., 1986—. Trustee Round Top Club, Warren, N.J., 1983—. Served to capt. JAGC, USAF, 1971-78, to maj. USAFR, 1979—. Recipient Exceptional Service citation U.S. Dept. Energy, 1981, 82. Mem. Fed. Bar Assn. (chmn. research and devel. com. 1982—, Disting. Service award 1982, 83, 86, vice chmn. internat. procurement com. 1979-81), ABA. General corporate, Government contracts and claims. Office: Lockheed Electronics Co Inc 1501 US Hwy 22 CS 1 Plainfield NJ 07061

SCHIEFFER, JOSEPH H., lawyer; b. Stamford, Conn., May 17, 1951; s. Joseph H. and Shirley A. (Winant) S.; m. Catherine A. McDonald, Mar. 24, 1979; 1 child, Patrick. BA, U. San Francisco, 1973; JD, U. Calif., San Francisco, 1976. Bar: Calif. 1976. Atty. Livingston, Grant, Stone & Kay, San Francisco, 1976-79; assoc. Zimmerman & Kalkstein, Oakland, Calif., 1979-81, Stark, Wells, Rahl, Field & Schwartz and predecessor firm Stark, Stewart, Wells & Robinson, Oakland, 1981—. Democrat. Roman Catholic. State civil litigation, Landlord-tenant. Office: Stark Stewart Wells & Robinson 1999 Harrison St #1300 Oakland CA 94618

SCHIESSWOHL, CYNTHIA RAE SCHLEGEL, lawyer; b. Colorado Springs, July 7, 1955; d. Leslie H. and Maime (Kascak) Schlegel; m. Scott Jay Schiesswohl, Aug. 6, 1977; 1 child, Leslie Michelle. BA cum laude, So. Meth. U., 1976; JD, U. Colo., Boulder, 1978; postgrad. U. Denver, 1984. Bar: Colo. 1979, U.S. Dist. Ct. (Colo.) 1979, U.S. Ct. Appeals (10th cir.) 1984, Wyo. 1986. Research clk. City Atty.'s Office, Colorado Springs, 1976; investigator Pub. Defender's Office, Colorado Springs, 1976; dep. dist. atty., 4th Jud. Dist. Colo., 1979-81; sole practice law, Grand Junction, Colo., 1981-82, Denver, 1983-84; assoc. Law Offices of John G. Salmon P.C., 1984-85; sole practice, Laramie, Wyo., 1985—; guest lectr. Pikes Peak Community Coll., 1980. Staff U. Colo. Law Rev., 1977. Advisor, Explorer Law Post, Boy Scouts Am., 1980-81; ex officio mem. ch. devel. com. Cen. Rocky Mt. region Christian Ch. (Disciples of Christ), 1986—; vol. Project Motivation, Dallas, 1974. Mem. ABA, Wyo. Bar Assn., Colo. Bar Assn. (ethics com. 1984-85, long range planning com. 1985—, chairperson 1986—), Pi Sigma Alpha, Alpha Lambda Delta, Alpha Delta Pi. Republican. United Methodist (mem. evangelism commn. 1987—, mem. fin. com. youth and music depts. 1979-81, lay del. to Rocky Mountain Ann. Conf. 1986-88). General practice, General corporate, Church law.

SCHIFF, ALAN LEWIS, lawyer; b. Hempstead, N.Y., Dec. 16, 1935; s. Morris Joseph Schiff and Eillas Bertha (Rundback) Feinberg; children: Debora, Dina, Jeremy, Ari. BSBA, U. Fla., 1957; LLB, Yale U., 1960. Ptnr. Siegel, O'Connor, Schiff, Zangari & Kainen P.C. and predecessor firms, New Haven, 1960—; adj. prof. New Haven U., 1982-84, U. Bridgeport Sch. Law, 1984—. Pres. New Haven Jewish Community Council Housing Corp., 1978-80, So. Conn. State U. Found., New Haven, 1980-85; trustee Yale-New Haven Hosp., 1984—. Mem. ABA, Conn. Bar Assn., New Haven County Bar Assn. Club: Quinnipiack (New Haven). Personal income taxation, Corporate taxation, Estate planning. Home: 66 N Lake Dr Unit B-2 Hamden CT 06517 Office: Siegel O'Connor Schiff et al 171 Orange St New Haven CT 06510

SCHIFF, GARY STEVEN, lawyer; b. South Bend, Ind., May 8, 1956; s. Philip and Charlotte (Gilbert) S.; m. Donna Cohen, July 6, 1980; 1 child, Caren Rachel. BS, Ind. U., JD; LLM, NYU. Bar: Ind. 1981, ALa. 1983, U.S. Dist. Ct. (no. dist.) Ind., U.S. Dist. Ct. (no. dist.) Ala., U.S. Tax Ct., U.S. Ct. Appeals (11th cir.). Assoc. Garelick, Cohen et al, Indpls., 1980-81; assoc. Najjar, Denaburg et al, Birmingham, Ala., 1983-87, ptnr., 1987—. Author: Alabama Corporation, 1985. Mem. ABA, Ala. Bar Assn., Birmingham Bar Assn. Corporate taxation, Probate, Estate taxation. Home: 3564 Hampshire Dr Birmingham AL 35223 Office: Najjar Denaburg et al Birmingham AL 35203

SCHIFF, GUNTHER HANS, lawyer; b. Cologne, Fed. Republic of Germany, Aug. 19, 1927; came to U.S., 1936; s. Hans and Alice (Goldstein) S.; m. Katharine MacMillan, Jan. 27, 1950 (div. 1957); children—Eric Alan, Mary Alice; m. JoAnn R. Schiff. B.S.F.S., Georgetown U., 1949, J.D., 1952. Bar: D.C. 1952, Calif. 1953. Assoc., ptnr. various firms, Los Angeles, 1954—; now sr. ptnr. Finley, Kumble, Wagner, Heine, Underberg, Manley, Myerson & Casey, Beverly Hills, Calif.; sec. Los Angeles Copyright Soc., Beverly Hills, 1975-76. Contbr. articles to profl. jours. Pres. Beverly Hills Civil Service Commn., 1984-85; chmn. Rent Control Rev. Bd., Beverly Hills, 1980-84. Served with USNR, 1944-45. Mem. Beverly Hills Bar Assn. (chmn. Resolutions Com. 1977-78), Los Angeles County Bar Assn., ABA, Judicature Soc., U.S. Copyright Soc. Democrat. Clubs: Lake Arrowhead Country, Calif. Yacht. Avocations: sailing; skiing; golfing. Entertainment, Real property, General corporate. Home: 612 N Foothill St Beverly Hills CA 90210 Office: Finley Kumble Wagner et al 9100 Wilshire Blvd Beverly Hills CA 90212

SCHIFF, LOUIS HOWARD, lawyer; b. Bklyn., June 3, 1955; s. Melvin and Sally (Brandes) S.; m. Leslee Lindahl, Sept. 3, 1983. BS in Journalism, U. Fla., 1977; JD, Hamline U., 1980. Bar: Fla. 1981. Assoc. Barton, Cox & Davis, Gainesville, Fla., 1981-82, Mark S. Schector, P.A., Ft. Lauderdale, Fla., 1982; sole practice Tamarac, Fla., 1983-85; ptnr. Schiff & Schlissel, Tamarac, 1985—; instr. bus. law Santa Fe Community Coll., Gainesville, 1981-82; mem. adv. bd. Ambassador Savs. & Loan, Tamarac, 1985-86. Talk show host Sta. WNWS-Radio (formerly Sta. WGBS-Radio), Miami, Fla., 1985—. Mem. econ. devel. bd. Broward County, Ft. Lauderdale, 1984—; bd. dirs. Broward County Council of Chambers, 1984—; mem. salary rev. bd. City of Tamarac, 1986; chmn. econ. devel. bd., Tamarac, 1986—. Mem. ABA, Am. Arbitration Assn., Acad. Fla. Trial Lawyers, Tamarac C. of C. (v.p. 1984-85, pres. 1985-87). Democrat. Jewish. Lodges: Kiwanis (sec. Tamarac 1983-85), Masons. Personal injury, State civil litigation, General practice. Office: Schiff & Schlissel 7300 W McNab Rd Tamarac FL 33319

SCHIFF, MATTHEW BART, lawyer; b. Harvey, Ill., May 18, 1957; s. Lawrence Robert Schiff and Ivy (Graber) Berchuck; m. Patricia Foisie, Sept. 5, 1982; 1 child, Anne Felice. BA, Cornell U., 1979; JD, Boston U., 1982. Bar: Ill. 1982, U.S. Dist. Ct. (no. dist.) Ill. 1982, U.S. Ct. Appeals (7th cir.) 1983. Assoc. Clausen, Miller, et al., Chgo., 1982-85, Schulman, Silverman & Eaton, Chgo., 1985-86, Katten, Muchin, Zavis, Pearl, Greenberger & Galler, Chgo., 1986—. Articles editor Am. Jour. of Law and Medicine, 1981-82. State civil litigation, Contracts commercial, Insurance. Home: 2233 Birchwood Ave Wilmette IL 60091 Office: Katten Muchin et al 525 W Monroe Chicago IL 60606

SCHIFF, SCOTT W., lawyer; b. Columbus, Ohio, Apr. 30, 1957; s. Robert Lee Schiff and Shirlie (Wilson) Levitin. BA, Ohio State U.; JD, Capital U. Bar: Ohio 1982, U.S. Dist. Ct. (no. dist.) Ohio, U.S. Ct. Appeals (6th cir.). Sole practice law Columbus, 1982—; Mem. Columbus Criminal Law Com., 1982—. Basketball chmn. Columbus Jewish Ctr. Mem. ABA, Columbus Bar Assn., Am. Trial Lawyers Assn. Avocations: sports, real estate, music, travel. Criminal, Personal injury. Office: 1243 S High St Columbus OH 43206

SCHIFF, STEVEN HARVEY, lawyer; b. Chgo., Mar. 18, 1947; s. Alan Jerome and Helen M. (Ripper) S.; m. Marcia Lewis, Nov. 8, 1968; children—Jaimi, Daniel. B.A., U. Ill.-Chgo., 1968; J.D., U. N.Mex., 1972. Bar: N.Mex. 1972, U.S. Dist. Ct. N.Mex. 1972, U.S. Ct. Appeals (10th cir.) 1980. Asst. dist. atty. Dist. Atty.'s Office, Albuquerque, 1972-77; sole practice, Albuquerque, 1977-79; asst. city atty., Albuquerque, 1979-81; dist. atty. State of N.Mex., Albuquerque, 1981—; lectr. U. N.Mex., Albuquerque, 1981—. Chmn. Bernalillo County Republican Party Conv., Albuquerque, 1984, 87. Served to lt. col. and staff judge advocate N.Mex. Air N.G. Recipient Law Enforcement Commendation medal SR, 1984. Mem. Albuquerque Bar Assn., N.Mex. Bar Assn., ABA, N.Mex. Dist. Atty.'s Assn., Nat. Dist. Atty.'s Assn. Republican. Jewish. Club: Civitan. Lodge: B'nai Brith (pres. 1976-78). Criminal. Home: 804 Summit NE Albuquerque NM 87106 Office: Dist Atty's Office 415 Tijeras NW Albuquerque NM 87102

SCHIFFBAUER, WILLIAM G., lawyer; b. Columbia, S.C., Feb. 17, 1954; s. John R. and Jean A. Schiffbauer; m. Sarah L. Powers; 1 child, J. William. BS, U. Nebr., 1976; JD, Creighton U., 1979; LLM, George Washington U., 1987. Bar: Nebr. 1979, U.S. Dist. Ct. Nebr. 1979, U.S. Ct. Claims 1982, U.S. Tax Ct. 1982. Counsel U.S. Senator J.J. Exon, Washington, 1979-85; assoc. Groom & Nordberg, Washington, 1985—. Mem. ABA, Nebr. Bar Assn., Environ. Law Inst., Omicron Delta Kappa. Democrat. Roman Catholic. Legislative, Corporate taxation, Environment. Office: Groom & Nordberg 1701 Pennsylvania Ave NW Washington DC 20008

SCHIFFMAN, DANIEL, lawyer; b. N.Y.C., Nov. 7, 1932; s. Jacob and Eva (Katzin) S.; m. P.G. Galex, June 26, 1955 (div.). BBA, CCNY, 1959; JD, NYU, 1962. Bar: N.Y. 1962, U.S. Sup. Ct. 1975, U.S. Ct. Appeals (2d cir.) 1980 (3d cir.) 1966, U.S. Dist. Ct. (so. dist.) 1966 (ea. dist.) 1979. Musician, 1950-55; public acct. Meyerson & Levine, CPA, N.Y.C., 1959-61; legal sec. to Chief City Magistrate, N.Y.C., 1961-62; assoc. Maxwell & Diamond, N.Y.C., 1962-66; sole practice, N.Y.C., 1966-74, 78—; mem. Schiffman & Ellenbogen, N.Y.C., 1975-78; counsel to adminstr. Commonwealth of P.R. Econ. Devel. Adminstrn., 1971-73; counsel, migration div. Commonwealth of P.R. Labor Dept., 1970-72; dir. MAESTRO Found., London; cons., lectr. Practising Law Inst., N.Y.C., 1963-68, 82; advisor U.S. GSA, 1979; treas. Citizens for a Responsive Congress, 1978-80. Recipient Bancroft Whitney prize, 1959. Mem. ABA, Assn. of Bar of City of N.Y., Internat. Bar Assn., Fed. Bar Council, Nat. Assn. Gaming Attys., N.Y.C. Jr. C. of C. (legal advisor). Clubs: Nat. Arts (chmn. music com., bd. govs.), NYU (N.Y.C.). Mem. staff NYU Law Rev., 1961-62. General practice, Entertainment, Federal civil litigation. Home: 903 Park Ave New York NY 10021 Office: 380 Lexington Ave Suite 4900 New York NY 10168

SCHIFFMAN, STEVEN MITCHELL, lawyer, journalist; b. Forest Hills, N.Y., Apr. 14, 1949; s. Murray Moshe and Myra (Speigler) S.; m. Judith Sarah Markovitch, Nov. 22, 1977; 1 child, Myra Ida Gladys Miriam. BA, U. Miami, Coral Gables, 1972; MA, U. Denver, 1973; JD, Touro Law Sch., 1983; LLM, London Sch. of Econs. and Polit. Sci., 1984. Bar: N.J. 1975, U.S. Dist. Ct. N.J. 1975, U.S. Dist. Ct. (ea. and so. dists.) N.Y. 1975, U.S. Ct. Internat. Trade 1975, U.S. Ct. Appeals (2d cir.) 1975. Producer, reporter Kol Israel/Voice of Israel, Jerusalem, 1976-78; journalist internat. affairs WBAI-FM Radio, N.Y.C., 1978—; press officer UN Hdqrs., N.Y.C., 1979-80; dir. bus. affairs Studio I TV Network, N.Y.C., 1980-83; UN Corr. newspaper The (London) Daily Express, 1980-83; legal, media cons. SMS Assocs., London, 1982-84; gen. counsel Caribbean TV Network, N.Y.C., 1984—; mng. dir. Internat. TV Barter Ltd., N.Y.C., 1985—; bd. dirs. Paradise Ventures Ltd., Aruba, West Indies. Charter mem. com. N.Y. Dems. for Reagan, N.Y.C., 1979-80; founder com. Internat. Dems. for Reagan, 1983-84; vol. mcpl. and legal affairs Peace Corps. Charles Edison Meml. Youth Found. scholar, 1972-73, Internat. Radio/TV Soc., 1972-74; grantee U. Denver, 1972-73. Mem. ABA, Assn. Trial Lawyers Am., N.Y. State Trial Lawyers Assn., Friends of London Sch. of Econs. Jewish. Avocations: public speaking, journalism, broadcasting, traveling. Entertainment, Private international, Legislative. Home: 22 Tehama St Brooklyn NY 11218-7184 Office: Caribbean TV Network Ltd 505 Fifth Ave Suite 1602 New York NY 10036

SCHILDHAUSE, SOL, lawyer; b. N.Y.C., Sept. 5, 1917; s. Jacob and Fannie (Gerber) S.; m. Phyllis Sydell, May 23, 1943 (divorced); children: Susan Schildhause Tash, Peter, Richard. BS, CCNY, 1937; JD, Harvard U., 1940. Bar: N.Y. 1941, D.C. 1972, U.S. Ct. Claims 1975, U.S. Supreme Ct. 1978. Mng. ptnr. Sta. KOMA-AM, Oklahoma City, 1956-57; adminstrv. law judge FCC, Washington, 1963-66, chief cable TV bur., 1966-73; ptnr. D.C. office Farrow, Schildhause & Wilson, 1973—; lectr. Practicing Law Inst., 1985. Mem. ABA (asst. chmn. cable TV com. 1986), FCC Bar Assn. Democrat. Jewish. Telecommunications, Cable TV and Broadcast. Office: Farrow Schildhause & Wilson 1730 M St NW Suite 708 Washington DC 20036

SCHILLER, DONALD CHARLES, lawyer; b. Chgo., Dec. 8, 1942; s. Sidney S. and Edith (Lastick) S.; m. Eileen Fagin, June 14, 1964; children—Eric, Jonathan. Student, Lake Forest Coll., 1960-63; J.D., DePaul U., 1966. Bar: Ill. 1966, U.S. Dist. Ct. (no. dist.) Ill. 1966, U.S. Supreme Ct. 1972. Ptnr. Schiller & Schiller, Chgo., 1966-81; firm merged with Joseph N. DuCanto, became Schiller & DuCanto, Ltd., Chgo., 1981-82; became Schiller, DuCanto and Fleck, Family Law, Chgo., 1982—; speaker profl. confs. Contbr. chpts. and articles to profl. publs. Mem. steering com. on juvenile ct. watching LWV, 1980-81. Recipient Maurice Weigle award Chgo. Bar Found., 1978, various certs. of appreciation profl. groups; named One of Am.'s best divorce lawyers, Town and Country, 1985, One of Chgo.'s best divorce lawyers, Crain's Chgo. Bus., 1981. Fellow Am. Bar Found.; mem. ABA (chmn. council family law sect. 1985-86, mem. House of Dels., 1984—, editor-in-chief Family Law Newsletter 1977-79, editorial bd., vice chmn. Family Advocate Mag. 1979-84, mem., chmn., co-chmn. coms., speaker confs.), Ill. Bar Assn. (treas. 1981-84, v.p. 1984-86, pres. 1987—, bd. govs. 1977-83, chmn. family law sect. 1976-77, editor Family Law Bull. 1976-77, mem., chmn. coms., lectr.), Chgo. Bar Assn. (exec. com. young lawyers sect. 1972-73, mem., chmn., vice chmn. coms., lectr.), Am. Acad. Matrimonial Lawyers (v.p. Ill. chpt. 1981-84, bd. mgrs. 1975-81, co-counsel, co-author Amicus Curiae Brief, mem., co-chmn. coms., lectr.), Ill. Inst. Continuing Legal Edn. (faculty, lectr.), Ill. Trial Lawyers Assn. (chmn. family law sect. 1979-81, lectr.), Am. Arbitration Assn., Internat. Soc. Family Law. Family and matrimonial. Office: 200 N LaSalle St Suite 2700 Chicago IL 60601

SCHILLER, ROBERT JAMES, lawyer, educator; b. Cambridge, Mass., Feb. 28, 1922; s. Abraham I. and Jennie Schiller; m. Phyllis Mamber, July 21, 1946; children: Robert J. Jr., Heidi A. BS, U. Mass., 1943; JD, Boston Coll., 1951. Bar: Mass. 1952, U.S. Ct. Customs and Patent Appeals 1964, U.S. Ct. Appeals (D.C. cir.) 1979, U.S. Ct. Appeals (Fed. cir.) 1982, U.S. Supreme Ct. 1982. Assoc. Kaplan & Linsky, Boston, 1952-55; asst. patent atty. Polaroid Corp., Cambridge, 1955-58; chief patent counsel Epsco Inc., Cambridge, 1958-60; ptnr. Rosen & Schiller, Newton, Mass., 1960-63, Schiller & Pandiscio, Waltham, Mass., 1963-86, Schiller, Pandiscio & Kusmer, Cambridge, Mass., 1986—; instr. law Boston Coll., Newton, 1971-85. Served to lt. USNR, 1943-46, PTO. Mem. ABA, Boston Patent Law Assn. Patent, Trademark and copyright, Federal civil litigation. Office: Schiller Pandiscio & Kusmer 125 Cambridge Park Dr Cambridge MA 02140

SCHIMBERG, A. BRUCE, lawyer; b. Chgo., Aug. 26, 1927; s. Archie and Helen (Isay) S.; m. Barbara Zisook; children: Geoffrey, Kate. Ph.B., U. Chgo., 1949, J.D., 1952. Bar: Ohio 1952, Ill. 1955. Assoc. Paxton & Seasongood, Cin., 1952-55; ptnr. Schimberg, Greenberger, Kraus & Jacobs, Chgo., 1955-65, Leibman, Williams, Bennett, Baird & Minow, Chgo., 1965-72, Sidley & Austin, Chgo., 1972—; lectr. U. Chgo., 1961-62. Contbr. articles to legal jours. Bd. dirs. U. Chgo. Law Sch. Alumni Assn., 1969-72; dir. vis. com. U. Chgo. Law Sch., 1980-83. Served to 2d lt. U.S. Army, 1945-47. Mem. ABA, Ill. State Bar Assn., Chgo. Bar Assn., 7th Cir. Bar Assn. Clubs: Mid-Day; Lake Shore Country (Chgo.). Bankruptcy, Contracts commercial. Home: 209 E Lake Shore Dr Chicago IL 60611

SCHIMMENTI, JOHN JOSEPH, lawyer; b. N.Y.C., Mar. 21, 1938; s. John Marcus and Mae M. (Miranti) S.; m. Mary Elizabeth Sleep, Apr. 18, 1964. B.A., Columbia Coll., 1959; J.D., Georgetown U., 1962, LL.M., 1964. Bar: D.C. 1962, N.Y. 1964, Calif. 1965, U.S. Dist. Ct. (cen. dist.) Calif. 1965, U.S. Ct. Appeals (9th cir.) 1966, U.S. Supreme Ct. 1971. Trial atty. Anti-trust div. U.S. Dept. Justice, Washington, 1962-64, Lands div., Los Angeles, 1965-67; trial atty. Santa Fe R.R., Los Angeles, 1968-70; ptnr. Schimmenti, Mullins & Berberian, El Segundo, Calif., 1971—. Mem. S.W. Dist. Bar Assn. (pres. 1983), Los Angeles Bar Assn. (condemnation com. 1983), Columbia U. Alumni of So. Calif. (pres. 1978). Republican. Roman Catholic. Club: El Segundo Rotary (pres. 1977). Condemnation. Office: 426 Main St El Segundo CA 90245

SCHINK, JAMES HARVEY, lawyer; b. Oak Park, Ill., Oct. 2, 1943; s. Norbert F. and Gwendolyn H. (Hummel) S.; m. Lisa Wilder Haskell, Jan. 1, 1972 (div. 1980); children—David, Caroline; m. April Townley, Aug. 14, 1982. B.A., Yale U., 1965, J.D., 1968. Bar: Ill. 1968, Colo. 1982. Assoc. Sidley & Austin, Chgo., 1968; law clk. to judge U.S. Ct. Appeals, Chgo., 1968-69; assoc. Kirkland & Ellis, Chgo., 1969-72, ptnr., 1972—. Sustaining fellow Art Inst. Chgo. Mem. ABA, Ill. Bar Assn., Chgo. Bar Assn. Republican. Presbyterian. Clubs: Chicago, University, Saddle and Cycle (gov.), Mid-American (Chgo.); Denver Athletic; Yale of N.Y.C. Antitrust, Environment, Federal civil litigation. Home: 1836 N Sedgwick St Chicago IL 60614 Office: Suite 5800 200 E Randolph Dr Chicago IL 60601

SCHIRALDI, RICHARD JOHN, lawyer, CPA; b. Youngstown, Ohio, Dec. 26, 1954; s. John George and Theresa Marie (Ambrosia) S. BA, Youngstown State U., 1976; JD, U. Akron, 1980. Bar: Ohio 1981, U.S. Dist. Ct. (no. dist.) Ohio 1981, U.S. Tax Ct. 1981. Franchise income tax agt. Ohio Dept. Taxation, Youngstown, 1977-80; staff acct. Touche Ross & Co., Youngstown, 1980-81; tax cons. DeNicholas, Leicht, Masters & Sakony, Youngstown, 1981-83; tax mgr. Cohen & Co., Youngstown, 1983—. Mem. ABA, Am. Inst. CPA's, Ohio State Bar Assn., Ohio Soc. CPA's, Estate Planning Council of Mahoning-Shenango Valley. Personal income taxation, Corporate taxation, Estate taxation. Home: 2129 Buckeye Circle Youngstown OH 44502 Office: Cohen & Co 1000 Wick Bldg Youngstown OH 44503

SCHIRMEISTER, CHARLES F., lawyer; b. Jersey City, June 18, 1929; s. Charles F. and Louise S. (Schneider) S.; m. Barbara J. Fredericks, Feb. 9, 1952; children—Pamela, Charles Bradford. B.A., U. Mich., 1951; LL.B., Fordham U., 1956. Bar: N.Y. 1956. Asst. dist. atty. N.Y. County (N.Y.), 1956-61; assoc. Reid & Priest, N.Y.C., 1961-71, ptnr., 1971—. Deacon, Community Congregational Ch., Short Hills, N.J.; trustee Daytop Village, N.Y.C., Ocean Grove (N.J.) Camp Meeting Assn., 118 E 60th Corp., N.Y.C. Served to capt. USMC, 1951-53. Mem. ABA, N.Y. County Lawyers Assn., Sigma Alpha Epsilon. Republican. Clubs: University (N.Y.C.); Channel (Monmouth Beach, N.J.). Antitrust, General corporate, Federal civil litigation. Home: 15 Beechcroft Rd Short Hills NJ 07078 Office: 40 W 57th St New York NY 10019

SCHISLER, GEORGE MILFORD, JR., lawyer; b. Corpus Christi, Tex., Sept. 25, 1957; s. George Milford Sr. and Rose Virginia (Stamper) S.; m. Yvonne Jean Pendleton, Feb. 11, 1983. BS in Econs., U. Pa., 1979; JD, U. Mich., 1982. Bar: Calif. 1982, U.S. Dist. Ct. (no. dist.) Calif. 1982, U.S. Dist. Ct. (cen. dist.) Calif. 1986. Assoc. Chickering & Gregory, San Francisco, 1982-84, Jackson, Tufts, Cole & Black, San Jose, Calif., 1984—. Mem. ABA, San Francisco Bar Assn., Santa Clara County Bar Assn. Democrat. Methodist. Avocation: sports. Securities, Federal civil litigation, State civil litigation. Office: Jackson Tufts Cole & Black 60 S Market St 10th Floor San Jose CA 95113

SCHLAU, PHILIP, lawyer; b. N.Y.C., Sept. 25, 1922; s. Joseph and Bella (Brown) S.; m. Florence Schlau, Jan. 31, 1947; children—Stacey, Bethel. B.B.A. cum laude, CCNY, 1943; J.D., Harvard U., 1949. Bar: N.Y. 1949, U.S. Dist. Ct. (so. dist.) N.Y. 1950, U.S. Dist. Ct. (ea. dist.) N.Y. 1950, U.S. Ct. Appeals (2d cir.) 1951, U.S. Supreme Ct. 1959. Sr. trial atty. U.S. Fidelity & Guaranty Co., 1950-57; ptnr. Schlau & Nadelson and predecessors, N.Y.C., 1959-70; sr. ptnr. Newman & Schlau P.C., N.Y.C., 1970-84, Newman, Schlau, Fitch & Burns, P.C., 1984—. Served to capt. AUS, 1943-46. Mem. ABA, N.Y. State Bar Assn., N.Y. County Lawyers Assn., Def. Research Inst. Federal civil litigation, State civil litigation, Insurance. Home: 214-04 27th Ave Bayside NY 11360 Office: 305 Broadway St New York NY 10007

SCHLECHT, WILLIAM ROGERS, lawyer; b. Carthage, Mo., Nov. 20, 1955; s. Walter Putnam and Mary Katharine (Molloy) S.; m. Kimberly Diane Bosley, June 2, 1979; 1 child, Katharine Elizabeth. AB, Drury Coll., 1978; JD, U. Mo., 1981. Bar: Mo. 1981, U.S. Dist. Ct. (we. dist.) Mo. 1981. Law clk. to presiding judge U.S. Ct. Appeals (8th cir.), Kansas City, Mo., 1981-83; assoc. Morrison, Hecker, Curtis, Kuder & Parrish, Kansas City, 1983—; bd. dirs. Ward Pkwy. Homes Assn., Kansas City, 1985—. Mem. ABA (ad hoc com. on new payments code), Lawyers Assn. Kansas City. Republican. Contracts commercial, Banking. Home: 7325 Mercier Kansas City MO 64114 Office: Morrison Hecker Curtis Kuder & Parrish 1700 Bryant Bldg Kansas City MO 64106

SCHLECHTY, JOHN L., lawyer; b. Lincoln Park, Mich., Sept. 26, 1955; s. Howard Thomas and Ellen Marie (Fischer) S.; m. Cynthia M. Odle, Dec. 8, 1979. BA, U. Dayton, 1977; JD, U. Tenn., 1980. Bar: Tenn. 1980, U.S. Dist. Ct. (cen. dist.) Tenn. 1981, U.S. Ct. Appeals (6th cir.) 1986. Assoc. Glasgow & Assocs., P.C., Nashville, 1980-83, Morton, Lewis, King & Krieg, Nashville, 1983-86; sole practice Nashville, 1986—. Mem. ABA, Tenn. Bar Assn. (com. on civil procedure 1984), Tenn. Trial Lawyers Assn., Nashville Bar Assn.; Court Practice Inst. (diplomate). General practice, Insurance, Labor. Office: The Pilcher Bldg Suite 312 144 2d Ave N Nashville TN 37201

SCHLEICHER, ESTELLE ANN, lawyer; b. Buffalo, Sept. 28, 1947; d. Martin Edward and Peggy (Lewin) S. B.A., SUNY-Brockport, 1969; J.D., U. Pacific, 1979. Research asst. SRI Internat., Menlo Park, Calif., 1969-72; clk. Wallace J. Smith Inc., Sacramento 1976-78; assoc., 1980-81; sole practice, Sacramento, 1981—; judge pro tem Sacramento County Claims Ct.; instr., Pacific Coll. Legal Careers, Sacramento, 1982-85. Bd. dirs. Sacramento County Law Library Found. Judge, coach high sch. Law-related Ednl. Conf., Sacramento, 1982—. Soroptimist scholar, 1978; McGeorge scholar, 1977-79. Mem. ABA, Calif. State Bar Assn. (com. on appellate cts. 1986—, sec.), Sacramento County Bar Assn. (dir. small law practice sect. 1986—), Calif. Trial Lawyers Assn. (assoc. editor CTLA Forum), Capitol City Trial Lawyers Assn. (dir. 1986—), McGeorge Sch. Law Alumni Assn. (bd. dirs. 1987—). Jewish. State civil litigation, Federal civil litigation, Criminal. Office: 2201 21st St Sacramento CA 95818

SCHLEIFER, RICHARD WAYNE, lawyer; b. N.Y.C., Feb. 28, 1953. BA, CUNY, 1974; JD, Hofstra U., 1977. Bar: N.Y. 1978, U.S. Dist. Ct. (ea. and so. dists.) 1978, Fla. 1982, U.S. Ct. Appeals (2d cir.) 1984, U.S. Supreme Ct. 1984. Assoc. Zimmer, Fishbach & Hertan, N.Y.C., 1980-82; sole practice N.Y.C., 1982-86; ptnr. Sulkow, Birnbach, Jasilli & Schleifer, N.Y.C., 1986—. Recipient 2d Nat. prize ASCAP, 1976. Mem. ABA, N.Y. State Bar Assn., N.Y. County Lawyers Assn. General corporate, Consumer commercial, State civil litigation. Office: 230 Park Ave Suite 951 New York NY 10007

SCHLENDER, E. LEE, lawyer; b. El Centra, Calif., Jan. 2, 1942; s. Edwin C. and Linda (Tafoya) S.; m. Judith L. Jewell, Dec. 7, 1969; 1 child, Jennifer L. BA, Idaho State U., 1964; JD, U. Idaho, 1967. Bar: Idaho 1967, U.S. Dist. Ct. Idaho 1967, U.S. Ct. Appeals (9th cir.) 1974. Sole practice, Ketchum, Idaho, 1967—. Mem. Idaho State Bar Assn., Idaho Trial Lawyers Assn., Assn. Trial Lawyers Am., Nat. Bd. Trial Advocacy (diplomate), Am. Judicature Soc. (bd. dirs. 1978-81). Democrat. Roman Catholic. Personal injury, State civil litigation, Federal civil litigation. Home: Deerfield Subdiv Hailey ID 83333 Office: PO Box 2910 220 2d Ave S Hailey ID 83333

SCHLESINGER, EDWARD SAMUEL, lawyer; b. N.Y.C., Nov. 29, 1929; s. Milton H. and Anna K. (Mirkin) S.; m. Renee L. Chasalow, Feb. 23, 1958 (div. 1981); children: Sarah S. Frankel, Nancy S. Izenson; m. Ann S. Kliman, Dec. 30, 1981. BS in Psychology with Honors, Tulane U., 1950; JD, Harvard U., 1957. Bar: D.C. 1957, Ill. 1959, N.Y. 1961. Tax law specialist IRS, Washington, 1957-58; assoc. Law Office David Altman, Chgo., 1958-60, Greenbaum, Wolff & Ernst, N.Y.C., 1960-65; sole practice N.Y.C., 1965—; adj. prof. NYU Law Sch., 1980—; vis. adj. prof. U. Miami Law Sch., Coral Gables, Fla., 1977—; lectr. various orgns. Contbr. articles to profl. jours. Served to lt. USN, 1951-54. Fellow Am. Coll. Probate Counsel; mem. ABA, Am. Law Inst. (Am. Law Inst./ABA Rawle award 1983), Assn. of Bar of City of N.Y., N.Y. State Bar Assn. Republican. Jewish. Avocations: biking, shooting. Estate planning, Probate, Estate taxation. Home: 73 Brewster Rd Scarsdale NY 10583 Office: 630 3d Ave New York NY 10017

SCHLESINGER, RUDOLF BERTHOLD, lawyer, educator; b. Munich, Germany, Oct. 11, 1909; s. Morris and Emma (Aufhauser) S.; m. Ruth Hirschland, Sept. 4, 1942; children: Steven, June, Fay. Dr.Jur. summa cum laude, U. Munich, 1933; LL.B., Columbia, 1942. Law sec. to Chief Judge Irving Lehman, N.Y. Ct. Appeals, 1942-43; confidential law sec. Judges N.Y. Ct. Appeals, 1943- 44; asso. Milbank, Tweed, Hope & Hadley, N.Y.C., 1944-48; asso. prof. Cornell U., 1948-51, prof., 1951-75, William N. Cromwell prof. internat. and comparative law, 1956-75; prof. Hastings Coll. Law, U. Calif., 1975—, vis. prof., 1974; Cons. N.Y. State Law Rev. Commn., 1949—; mem. adv. com. internat. rules of jud. procedure, 1959-66; vis. prof. Columbia, 1952, Salzburg Seminar, 1964; Charles Inglis Thomson distinguished vis. prof. U. Colo., summer 1976. Author: Cases, Text and Materials on Comparative Law, 2d edit, 1959, 3d edit., 1970, 4th edit., 1980, 5th edit., 1987/88 (with Baade, Damaska & Herzog), Formation of Contracts: A Study of the Common Core of Legal Systems, 2 vols, 1968; others.; Editor-in-chief: Columbia Law Rev, 1941-42; bd. editors: Am. Jour. Comparative Law; Author articles legal topics. Trustee Cornell U., 1961-66. Carnegie Corp. Reflective year fellowship, 1962-63. Mem. Am. Law Inst. (life), Am. Bar Assn., Internat. Acad. Comparative Law, Phi Beta Kappa, Order of Coif. Private international, Comparative. Home: 2601 Vallejo St San Francisco CA 94123

SCHLEY, MICHAEL D., lawyer; b. Calif., Jan. 4, 1955; m. Donna L. Greene, Jan. 4, 1974; children: Nathaniel, Erica. BA, Westmont Coll.; JD, U. Calif., San Francisco. Bar: Calif., D.C., U.S. Supreme Ct. Atty. Fed. Home Loan Bank Bd., Washington, 1980-83; assoc., gen. counsel Fried, Frank et al, Washington, 1983-85; sr. v.p., gen. counsel Fin. Corp. of Santa Barbara, Calif., 1985—; gen. counsel Fed. Credit Unions Bur., Fed. Home Loan Bank Bd., 1981-82; mem. adv. bd. Money and Real Estate. Mem. ABA (com. on savings insts.), Calif. League Atty. Commn., Santa Barbara C. of C. (govt. rev. com.). Republican. Banking.

SCHLINGER, ALEXANDER PETER, lawyer; b. N.Y.C., Mar. 17, 1948; s. William and Rudolfine (Laster) S. BA, CUNY, Flushing, 1969; MA, Pa. State U., 1970; JD, Bklyn. Law Sch., 1975. Bar: N.Y. 1976, U.S. Dist. Ct. (ea. and so. dists.) N.Y. 1977, U.S. Ct. Appeals (2d cir.) 1979, U.S. Supreme Ct. 1979. Staff atty. HHS, Cin., 1976-77, Social Security Adminstrn. Office Hearings and Appeals, N.Y.C., 1977-81; asst. dist. atty. Queens County, Kew Gardens, N.Y., 1981—. Mem. ABA. Democrat. Avocations: book collecting, tennis, travel. Criminal, Administrative and regulatory. Office: Office of Queens Dist Atty 125-01 Queens Blvd Kew Gardens NY 11415

SCHLINKERT, WILLIAM JOSEPH, lawyer; b. Bronxville, N.Y., Feb. 18, 1954; s. William Joseph Schlinkert and Ann Frances (Schilling) S.; m. Meggin Ann Gemmill, Aug. 6, 1978; children: Brian, Kyle. BA, U. Dallas, 1975; JD, U. Calif., Berkeley, 1978; LLM in Taxation, Georgetown U., 1981. Bar: Calif. 1978, U.S. Tax Ct. 1981. Atty. office of chief counsel IRS, Washington, 1978-81; assoc. Farella, Braun & Martel, San Francisco, 1981-85, ptnr., 1986—. Mem. ABA, Bar Assn. San Francisco. Avocations: golf, tennis. Corporate taxation, General corporate, State and local taxation. Office: Farella Braun & Martel 235 Montgomery St San Francisco CA 94104

SCHLOSS, LAWRENCE JAMES, lawyer; b. Greenville, Mich., Oct. 17, 1947; s. Leo James and Margaret Ann (Sims) S.; m. Trudee Lee Elder, Sept. 15, 1973; children: Lawrence John, Meredith Katherine. BA in Econs., Xavier U., 1970; JD, Detroit Coll. Law, 1973. Bar: Mich. 1973, U.S. Ct. Appeals (6th cir.) 1978. Assoc. Dickinson, Brandt, Hanlon, Becker & Lanctot, Detroit, 1973-77; ptnr. Glime, Daoust, Wilds, Rusing & LeDuc, Mt. Clemens, Mich., 1977—. Bd. dirs. Rochester Little League Football, 1986, 87. Mem. ABA, Mich. Bar Assn., Oakland County Bar Assn., Macomb County Bar Assn., Rochester Bar Assn., Am. Arbitration Assn., Mich. Def. Trial Council, Detroit Adjusters Assn. (pres. 1984-85). Club: Oakland U. (pres.), Xavier U. (pres.), Detroit. Avocations: golf, skiing, caoching YMCA baseball and soccer. State civil litigation, Insurance, General corporate. Home: 2851 Current Dr Rochester Hills MI 48063 Office: Glime Daoust et al 25 N Gratiot Ave Mount Clemens MI 48046

SCHLOTT, MARY CAMILLE, lawyer; b. Keokuk, Iowa, Sept. 29, 1932; d. Roy A. and Marjorie Louise (Dadant) Grout; m. Richard J. Schlott, Aug. 23, 1953 (div. May 1977); children: David, Susan, Nicholas; m. Harry A. Repenning, Oct. 21, 1977. BS, Iowa State U., 1955; MS, Purdue U., 1959; JD, John Marshall Law Sch., 1974. Bar: Ill. 1974, U.S. Dist. Ct. (no. dist.) Ill. 1974, U.S. Supreme Ct. 1979. Asst. atty. gen. State of Ill., Chgo., 1974-76; sole practice Arlington Heights, Ill., 1976-78, 1982—; ptnr. Schlott & Wolf, Ltd., Arlington Heights, 1978-82; gen. counsel Wheeling Twp. Rep. Orgn., Arlington Heights, 1983—; bd. dirs. Cook County Legal Assistance Found., Chgo., 1983-85. Commr. Arlington Heights Environ. Control Commn., 1971-74, Arlington Heights Planning Commn., 1982—; parliamentarian Community and Econ. Devel. Assn. of Cook County, Chgo., 1984-87; pres. LWV, Arlington Heights, 1968-69, Friends Arlington Heights Library, 1968-69. Recipient Outstanding Service award Vol. Service Bur., 1983, Disting. Service award Community and Econ. Devel. Assn. Cook County, 1984. Mem. ABA, Ill. Bar Assn., Chgo. Bar Assn., Women's Bar Assn. Ill., Northwest Suburban Bar Assn., Nat. Assn. Social Security Claimants' Reps. (sustaining). Republican. Presbyterian. Family and matrimonial, Pension, profit-sharing, and employee benefits. Office: 2045 S Arlington Heights Rd Suite 113 Arlington Heights IL 60005

SCHLOTTERBECK, WALTER ALBERT, mfg. co. lawyer; b. N.Y.C., Dec. 22, 1926; s. Albert Gottlob and Maria Louise (Fritz) S.; m. Pauline Elizabeth Hoerz, Sept. 2, 1951; children—Susan, Thomas, Paul. A.B., Columbia U., 1949, LL.B., 1952. Bar: N.Y. bar 1953. Counsel Gen. Electric Co. (various locations), 1952—; v.p., corp. counsel Gen. Electric Co. (various locations), N.Y.C., 1970—; sec. Gen. Electric Co. (various locations), 1975-76, gen. counsel, 1976—, sr. v.p., 1977—. Served with USNR, 1944-46. General corporate. Home: 752 Town House Rd Fairfield CT 06430 Office: Fairfield CT 06431

SCHLUETER, DAVID ARNOLD, law educator; b. Sioux City, Iowa, Apr. 29, 1946; s. Arnold E. and Helen A. (Dettmann) S.; m. Linda L. Boston, Apr. 22, 1972; children—Jennifer, Jonathan. B.A., Tex. A&M U., 1969; J.D., Baylor U., 1971, LL.M., U. Va., 1981. Bar: Tex. 1971, D.C. 1973, U.S. Ct. Mil. Appeals 1972, U.S. Supreme Ct. 1976. Legal counsel U.S. Supreme Ct., Washington, 1981-83; assoc. dean, prof. law St. Mary's U., San Antonio, 1983-86, prof., 1986—; chmn. JAG adv. council, 1974-75. Author: Military Criminal Justice: Practice and Procedure, 1982, 2d edit., 1987; (with others) Military Rules of Evidence Manual, 1981, 2d. edit., 1986, Texas Rules of Evidence Manual, 1983; contbr. articles to legal pubs. Served to maj. JAGC, U.S. Army, 1972-81. Decorated Nat. Def. Service Medal, Army Commendation medal, Meritorious Service medal with oak leaf cluster, Joint Services medal. Mem. ABA (vice chmn. com. on criminal justice and mil. 1983-84), Tex. Bar Assn. Republican. Lutheran. Criminal, Legal education, Military. Office: St Marys U Sch Law One Camino Santa Maria San Antonio TX 78284

SCHMAL, TIMOTHY JAMES, lawyer, legal educator; b. Hammond, Ind., Dec. 17, 1956; s. Robert George and Patricia Clare (Beggs) S; m. Judy Aiko

Shibata, Jan. 19, 1985. BA magna cum laude, Calif. State U., Fresno, 1979; JD cum laude, Santa Clara U., 1982. Bar: Calif. 1982, U.S. Dist. Ct. (no. dist.) Calif. 1982. Instr., legal research, writing Santa Clara (Calif.) U. Sch. Law, 1982-83; assoc. Gassett, Perry & Frank, San Jose, Calif., 1983—; adj. prof. San Francisco Law Sch., 1985—. Mem. ABA, Santa Clara County Bar Assn., Santa Clara Law Alumni Assn. (bd. dirs. 1984—), Phi Alpha Delta. Democrat. Roman Catholic. Club: San Jose Athletic. Avocations: running, golf, backpacking. State civil litigation, Construction, Legal education. Home: 5683 Hollyleaf Ln San Jose CA 95118 Office: Gassett Perry & Frank 210 N 4th St San Jose CA 95112

SCHMALBECK, RICHARD LOUIS, law educator; b. Chgo., Dec. 31, 1947; s. George Louis and Betty Jeanne (Strecker) S.; m. Ann E. Salitsky, Aug. 25, 1973. AB in Econs. with honors, U. Chgo., 1970, JD, 1975. Bar: Ohio 1975, D.C. 1977. Asst. to dir. and economist Ill. Housing Devel. Authority, Chgo., 1971-73; assoc. Vorys, Sater, Seymour & Pease, Columbus, Ohio, 1974-76; spl. asst. to assoc. dir. for econs. and govt. Office of Mgmt. and Budget, Washington, 1976-77; assoc. Caplin & Drysdale, Washington, 1977-80; assoc. prof. law Duke U., Durham, N.C., 1980-84, prof. law, 1984—; chmn. hearing com. Duke U., 1985—, vice chmn. acad. council, 1984-85. Assoc. editor U. Chgo. Law Rev., 1974-75; contbr. articles to profl. jours. Mem. ABA (articles editor jour. 1977-80), Phi Beta Kappa. Legal education, Personal income taxation, Corporate taxation. Office: Duke U Sch Law Durham NC 27706

SCHMERER, SUSAN ANN, lawyer; b. N.Y.C., July 21, 1946; d. William and Florence Hermine (Grossberger) S. BA, Chatham Coll., Pitts., 1968; JD, U. Oreg., 1977. Bar: Oreg. 1977, U.S. Dist. Ct. Oreg. 1977. Ptnr. Schmerer & Mehringer, Eugene, Oreg., 1977—. V.p. Temple Beth Israel, Eugene, 1984-85, sec. 1985-86. Mem. Oreg. State Bar Assn., Oreg. Criminal Def. Lawyers Assn., Lane County Lawyers Assn., Lane County Women Lawyers Assn. Democrat. Juvenile, General practice. Office: Schmerer & Mehringer 1001 W First Ave Eugene OR 97402

SCHMERTZ, ERIC JOSEPH, lawyer, labor management-arbitrator; b. N.Y.C., Dec. 24, 1925; married; 4 children. A.B., Union Coll., 1948, LL.D. (hon.), 1978; cert., Alliance Francaise, Paris, 1948; J.D., NYU, 1954. Bar: N.Y. 1955. Internat. rep. Am. Fedn. State, County and Mcpl. Employees, AFL-CIO, N.Y.C., 1950-52; asst. v.p., dir. labor tribunals Am. Arbitration Assn., N.Y.C., 1952-57, 59-60; indsl. relations dir. Metal Textile Corp. subs. Gen. Cable Corp., Roselle, N.J., 1957-59; exec. dir. N.Y. State Bd. Mediation, 1960-62, corp. dir., 1962-68; labor-mgmt. arbitrator N.Y.C., 1962—; mem. faculty Hofstra U. Sch. Bus., 1962-70; prof. Hofstra U. Sch. Law, 1970—, Edward F. Carlough disting. prof. labor law, 1981—, dean Sch. Law, 1982—; 1st Beckley lectr. in bus. U. Vt., 1981; dir. Wilshire Oil Co. cons. and lectr. in field. Co-author: (with R.L. Greenman) Personnel Administration and the Law, 1978; contbr. chpts. to books, articles to profl. jours., to profl. law confs., seminars and workshops. Mem. numerous civic orgns. Served to lt. USN, 1943-46. Recipient Testimonial award Southeast Republican Club, 1969; Alexander Hamilton award Rep. Law Students Assn. Mem. Nat. Acad. Arbitrators, Am. Arbitration Assn. (law com.; Whitney North Seymour Sr. medal 1984), Fed. Mediation and Conciliation Service, N.Y. Mediation Bd., N.J. Mediation Bd., N.J. Pub. Employment Relations Bd., N.J. Pub. Employment Relations Bd. Clubs: NYU (bd. govs.); Hofstra U. Address: 685 W 247th St Riverdale New York NY 10471

SCHMIDT, BENNO CHARLES, JR., lawyer; b. Washington, Mar. 20, 1942; s. Benno Charles and Martha (Chastain) S.; children by previous marriage—Elizabeth, Benno II; m. Helen Cutting Whitney, 1980; 1 child, Christina. B.A., Yale U., 1963, LL.B., 1966; LLB, Princeton U., 1986. Bar: D.C. 1967. Law clk. Chief Justice Earl Warren, U.S. Supreme Ct, Washington, 1966-67; spl. asst., asst. atty. gen. Office Legal Counsel U.S. Dept. Justice, Washington, 1967-69; Harlan Fiske Stone prof. law Columbia U., N.Y.C., 1973-86, dean Law Sch., 1969-86; pres., prof. law Yale U., New Haven, 1986—; dir. Nat. Humanities Ctr., Chapel Hills, N.C., 1985. Author: Freedom of the Press versus Public Access, 1974; (with A.M. Bickel) The Judiciary and Responsible Government 1910-1921, 1985. Office: Yale Univ Office of Pres New Haven CT 06520 *

SCHMIDT, C. JEFFERS, JR., lawyer; b. Hartford, Conn., Feb. 26, 1946; s. Carlton J. and Mary Anne (Smith) S.; m. Louise Seyffer, Nov. 23, 1973; children: Lolita K., C.J. III. BA, U. Va., 1968; JD, U. Richmond, 1972. Bar: Va. 1972, U.S. Dist. Ct. (ea. dist.) Va. 1972, U.S. Ct. Appeals (4th cir.) 1974, U.S. Supreme Ct. 1977. Law clk. to presiding justice Va. Supreme Ct., Richmond, 1972-74; assoc. Woodward, Wood & Street, Richmond, 1974-76; ptnr. Wood & Schmidt, Richmond, 1976-80; sole practice Richmond, 1980-83; commonwealth atty. County of Lancaster, Va., 1984—; trustee U.S. Bankruptcy Ct., Richmond, Va., 1976-84; atty. County of Lancaster, 1984—. Editor U. Richmond Law Rev., 1970-72. Sec. Citizens Against Crime, Lancaster, Va.; bd. dirs. Crime Solvers, Inc. Served with USCGR, 1969-75. Mem. ABA, Va. Bar Assn., Richmond Bar Assn. (pres. young lawyers sect. 1981-82), Northern Neck Bar Assn., U.S. Dist. Attys. Assn., Va. Assn. Commonwealth Attys. Episcopalian. Lodge: FOP, Lions. Criminal, Local government, General practice. Home: PO Box 428 Irvington VA 22480 Office: Commonwealth Attys Office Lancaster Courthouse PO Box 204 Lancaster VA 22503

SCHMIDT, CHARLES EDWARD, lawyer; b. N.Y.C., Oct. 6, 1951. A.B. cum laude, Boston Coll., 1972; J.D., Fordham U., 1975; Bar: N.Y. 1976, U.S. Supreme Ct. 1982. Law clk. Lilly Sullivan & Purcell, P.C., N.Y.C., 1973-76, assoc., 1976-84; assoc. Donovan Maloof Walsh & Kennedy, N.Y.C., 1984-86; ptnr. Kennedy & Lillis, N.Y.C., 1986—. Mem. ABA, N.Y. State Bar Assn., N.Y. County Lawyers Assn., Maritime Law Assn., Assn. Average Adjusters U.S. (assoc.). Admiralty, Insurance, Federal civil litigation. Home: 444 E 86th St New York NY 10028 Office: Kennedy & Lillis 100 Maiden Ln New York NY 10038

SCHMIDT, DALE RUSSELL, lawyer; b. Berea, Ohio, Aug. 8, 1948; s. Russell A. and Dorothy D. Schmidt; m. Donna L. Van Stone, May 30, 1970; children: Ian Fletcher, Inge Brooke. BA, Yale U., 1970; JD, Am. U., 1976. Bar: Va. 1976, U.S. Ct. Appeals (4th cir.) 1978, D.C. 1980, U.S. Ct. Appeals (D.C. cir.) 1980. Systems dir. Hon. Robert W. Kasten, Jr., Washington, 1977-78; mgr. legal services Nat. Elec. Mfrs. Assn., Washington, 1978—. Served with U.S. Army, 1970-71. Mem. ABA (chmn. Greater Washington Soc. Assn. Execs. law and legis. com. 1982-84, vice chmn. internat. and comparative adminstrn. law 1984—). Avocations: music, reading. Administrative and regulatory, Personal income taxation, General practice. Office: National Electrical Mfrs Assn 2101 L St NW Washington DC 20037 also: PO Box 2534 Alexandria VA 22301

SCHMIDT, EDWARD CRAIG, lawyer; b. Pitts., Nov. 26, 1947; s. Harold Robert and Bernice (Williams) S.; m. Elizabeth Lowry Rial, Aug. 18, 1973; children—Harold Robert II, Robert Rial. B.A., U. Mich., 1969; J.D., U. Pitts., 1972. Bar: Pa. 1972, N.Y. 1982, U.S. Dist. Ct. (we. dist.) Pa. 1972, U.S. Ct. Appeals (3d. cir.) 1972, U.S. Ct. Appeals (D.C. cir.) 1975, U.S. Ct. Appeals (9th cir.) 1982, U.S. Supreme Ct. 1981. Assoc. Rose, Schmidt, Chapman, Duff & Hasley, Pitts., 1972-77, ptnr., 1977—; mem. adv. com. Superior Ct. Pa., 1978—. Co-editor; Antitrust Discovery Handbook-Supplement, 1982. Asst. editor: Antitrust Discovery Handbook, 1980. Contbr. articles to profl. jours. Bd. dirs. Urban League, Pitts., 1974-77. Mem. ABA (mem. civil practice and procedures com. antitrust sect. 1974—), Supreme Ct. Hist. Soc., Pa. Bar Assn., D.C. Bar Assn., Allegheny County Bar Assn. (pub. relations com. council civil litigation sect. 1977-80), Acad. Trial Lawyers Allegheny County (bd. govs. 1985—), Am. Counsel Assn., Assn. Ins. Attys., U. Pitts. Law Alumni Assn. (bd. govs. 1980). Clubs: Rolling Rock (Ligonier, Pa.); Duquesne (Pitts.). Republican. Antitrust, Personal injury, Federal civil litigation. Home: 5432 Northumberland St Pittsburgh PA 15217 Office: Rose Schmidt Chapman Duff & Hasley 900 Oliver Bldg Pittsburgh PA 15222

SCHMIDT, GORDON WILLIAMS, lawyer; b. Pitts., July 15, 1950; s. Harold Robert and Bernice (Williams) S.; m. Debra DuPont, May 26, 1973; children: Gregory William, Katherine McKinstry. BA, Syracuse U., 1972; JD, U. Pitts., 1975. Assoc. Rose, Schmidt & Dixon, Pitts., 1975-80; ptnr. Rose, Schmidt, Chapman, Duff & Hasley, Pitts., 1980—. Antitrust, Labor, Federal civil litigation. Home: 112 Buckingham Rd Pittsburgh PA 15215 Office: Rose Schmidt Chapman Duff & Hasley Oliver Bldg 9th Floor Pittsburgh PA 15222

SCHMIDT, HAROLD ROBERT, lawyer; b. Braddock, Pa., Sept. 4, 1913; s. Abraham I. and Gustella (Frankle) S.; m. Bernice V. Williams, June 24, 1941; children: Barbara N. Schmidt Wickwire, Edward C., Gordon W. AB, U. Mich., 1934; LLB, U. Pitts., 1937. Bar: Pa. 1937, D.C. 1976. Sr. ptnr. in charge litigation Rose, Schmidt, Chapman, Duff & Hasley and predecessors, Pitts., Washington, Harrisburg, Pa., Washington, Pa., 1946—; co-chmn. Lawyers Non-Partisan Com. to Secure Additional Judges for Ct. Common Pleas, Allegheny County, 1963; chmn. Com. to Modernize Jury Selection Procedures, Allegheny County, 1965; permanent mem. Jud. Conf. 3d Circuit; former govt. appeal agt. local bd. 19, SSS, Pitts.; panel participant 1st Internat. Med.-Legal Seminar Pitts. Inst. Legal Medicine, U. Rome, 1965; lectr. 3d seminar U. London Med. Coll., 1967; lectr. short course on antitrust law So. Meth. U., 1979, 80, 82-83. Author: Handbook and Guide to the Federal Coal Mine Health and Safety Act of 1969 and Related State Statutes, 1970; contbg. author: Antitrust Law and the Coal Industry, 1983; editor-in-chief: U. Pitts. Law Rev., 1936-37. Chmn. exec. com. Pitts. chpt. Am. Jewish Com.; emeritus bd. dirs. ann. giving fund U. Pitts.; bd. visitors Sch. Law, 1978—; mem. Ft. Pitt Mus. Assocs.; ann. fund leadership com. U. Mich.; mem. Gov.'s Trial Ct. Nominating Commn. of Allegheny County, Pa., 1979; chmn. 1985— Appellate Ct. Nominating Commn. Pa., 1985; bd. visitors So. Meth. U. Sch. Law, 1984—. Served to capt. AUS, World War II. Fellow Internat. Acad. Trial Lawyers (bd. dirs., dean acad. 1983, pres.-elect 1986, pres. 1987); mem. World Assn. Lawyers (founder, life mem.), ABA (mem. council sect. antitrust law 1984-85, vice chmn. civil practice and procedure com. sect. antitrust law 1980-82), Pa. Bar Assn., Allegheny County Bar Assn., Supreme Ct. Hist. Soc., Nat. Assn. R.R. Trial Counsel, JAG Assn., Acad. Trial Lawyers Allegheny County (past pres.), U. Pitts. Law Sch. Alumni Assn. (past pres.), Am. Law Inst., World Peace through Law Ctr., Am. Judicature Soc., Internat. Soc. Barristers (past gov.), Soc. Mining Law Antiquarians, Pa. Inst. Legal Medicine, Pa. Def. Inst., Def. Research Inst., Res. Officers Assn. U.S., Pa. Soc., Order of Coif, Phi Beta Kappa, Phi Kappa Psi, Phi Eta Sigma. Clubs: Duquesne, Concordia, University Michigan (past pres.), Downtown (past pres.). Lodge: Masons. Federal civil litigation, Antitrust, State civil litigation. Home: 154 N Bellefield Ave The Bristol Apt #20 Pittsburgh PA 15213 Office: Oliver Bldg Pittsburgh PA 15222

SCHMIDT, JOHN ALDIN, lawyer, accountant; b. Galveston, Tex., Sept. 15, 1949; s. J.B. III and Mary Jane (Mills) S.; m. Germaine E. Llewellyn; children: Tara, Lauren. BBA with honors, U. Tex., 1971, JD, 1976. Bar: Tex. 1978, U.S. Dist. Ct. (so. dist.) Tex. 1978, U.S. Tax Ct. 1979, U.S. Supreme Ct. 1984, U.S. Ct. Appeals (5th cir.) 1986. Sr. auditor Pub. Accts., Houston, 1971-73; hearing examiner Tex. R.R. Commn., Austin, 1977; assoc. Smith & Herz, Galveston, 1977-80, Dibrell, Greer & Brown, Galveston, 1980-81; sole practice Galveston, 1981-86; assoc. McLeod, Alexander, Powel & Apffel, P.C., Galveston, 1986—. Trustee Galveston County Parks Bd., 1984-86; bd. dirs. Hist. Preservation, Washington, 1985. Roman Catholic. Real property, Personal income taxation, Securities. Home: 68 Campeche Circle Galveston TX 77551 Office: McLeod Alexander Powel & Apffel 802 Rosenberg PO Box 629 Galveston TX 77553

SCHMIDT, LYNNE DIANNE, lawyer; b. Phila., Sept. 6, 1955; d. Lester John and Bernice Marie (Grady) S. BS, Bowling Green State U., 1977; JD, U. Pitts., 1980. Bar: Pa., 1981, U.S. Dist. Ct. (we. dist.) Pa., 1985. Atty. Nat. Labor Relations Bd., Cin., 1980-84, PPG Industries, Inc., Pitts., 1984—. Exec. topics editor U. Pitts. Law Rev., 1979-80. Avocations: skiing. Labor, Pension, profit-sharing, and employee benefits. Office: PPG Industries Inc One PPG Pl 39E Pittsburgh PA 15272

SCHMIDT, MICHAEL BRUCE, energy corporation executive, lawyer; b. Corpus Christi, Tex., Sept. 22, 1948; s. James E. and Ella (Ilse) S.; m. Terria Lee Brown, May 26, 1973; children—Lindsey Elliott and Michael James. B.B.A., U. Tex., 1970; J.D., South Tex. Coll., 1973. Bar: Tex. 1973, U.S. Dist. Ct. (so. dist.) Tex. 1974, U.S. Ct. Appeals (5th cir.) 1975. Assoc., Pratt & Shuart, Corpus Christi, Tex., 1974-75; v.p., legal counsel CRC Corp., Corpus Christi, 1975-76; sec., land mgr. Peninsula Resources, Corpus Christi, 1976-79; pres. Risa Energy Corp., Corpus Christi, 1979—. Pres. sch. bd. St. Patrick's Parochial Sch., Corpus Christi, 1983—. Mem. Tex. Bar Assn., Nueces County Bar Assn., Am. Assn. Petroleum Landmen, Corpus Christi Assn. Petroleum Landmen (treas. 1978-79, exec. com. 1979-80). Roman Catholic. Oil and gas leasing. Home: 315 Louise Corpus Christi TX 78404 Office: Risa Energy Corp 750 Tex Commerce Plaza PO Box 2791 Corpus Christi TX 78403

SCHMIDT, PAUL WICKHAM, lawyer; b. Milw., June 25, 1948; s. Edmund Julian and Barbara (Wickham) S.; m. Cathryn Ann Piehl, June 27, 1970; children: Thomas Wickham, William Piehl, Anna Patchin. BA cum laude, Lawrence U., 1970; JD cum laude, U. Wis., 1973. Bar: Wis. 1973, U.S. Dist. Ct. (we. dist.) Wis. 1973, U.S. Supreme Ct. 1982. Atty. advisor Bd. Immigration Appeals, Washington, 1973-76; gen. atty. office of gen. counsel Immigration and Naturalization Service, Washington, 1976-78, acting gen. counsel, 1979-81, 86—, dep. gen. counsel, 1978—. Mem. ABA, Wis. Bar Assn., Fed. Bar Assn. Avocations: soccer coaching, gardening, camping, history. Immigration, naturalization, and customs, Administrative and regulatory, Legislative. Home: 711 South View Terr Alexandria VA 22314 Office: Immigration and Naturalization Service 425 I St NW Washington DC 20536

SCHMIDT, RICHARD MARTEN, JR., lawyer; b. Winfield, Kans., Aug. 2, 1924; s. Richard M. and Ida (Marten) S.; m. Ann Downing, Jan. 2, 1948; children—Eric, Gregory, Rolf (dec.), Heidi. A.B., U. Denver, 1945, J.D., 1948. Bar: Colo. bar 1948, D.C. bar 1968. Dep. dist. atty. City and County of Denver, 1949-50; mem. firm McComb, Zarlengo, Mott & Schmidt, Denver, 1950-54; partner firm Schmidt & Van Cise (and predecessor), Denver, 1954-65; gen. counsel USIA, 1965-68; partner firm Cohn and Marks, Washington, 1969—; counsel spl. agrl. investing subcom. U.S. Senate, 1959-60; Mem. Gov.'s Council Local Govt., Colo., 1963-64; chmn. Mayor's Jud. Adv. Com., Denver, 1963-64, Gov.'s Supreme Ct. Nominating Com., 1964-65; mem. Gov.'s Oil Shale Adv. Com., 1963-65, Colo. Commn. on Higher Edn., 1965; chmn. Washington Journalism Center, 1979-81. Trustee U. Denver. Mem. ABA (chmn. standing com. on assn. communications 1969-73, chmn. forum com. on communications 1979-81, co-chmn. nat. conf. lawyers and reps. of media 1984—), Colo. Bar Assn. (gov.), Denver Bar Assn. (pres. 1963-64), D.C. Bar Assn. Episcopalian. Clubs: Denver Law (pres. 1955-56), Denver Press; Federal City (Washington), International (Washington), Nat. Press (Washington). Administrative and regulatory, Libel, Legislative. Home: 115 5th St SE Washington DC 20003 Office: Cohn and Marks 1333 New Hampshire Ave NW Washington DC 20036

SCHMIDT, WAYNE WALTER, association executive; b. St. Louis, Feb. 8, 1941; s. Warren W. and Geneva N. (Walker) S.; children: Andrew M., Nancy K. BA, U. N.Mex., 1964; JD, Oklahoma City U., 1966; LLM, Northwestern U., 1974. Bar: N.Mex. 1966, Ill. 1968, D.C. 1970, N.Y. 1982. Dir. police legal advisor program Northwestern U., 1968-70; counsel Internat. Assn. Chiefs of Police, 1970-73; exec. dir. Am. for Effective Law Enforcement, Inc., Chgo., 1973—; pres. Pub. Safety Personnel Research Inst., 1974—, Govt. Employment Research Inst., Inc., 1986—; cons. Uniform Code of Criminal Procedure. Served with U.S. Army, 1966-67. Co-author: Legal Aspects of Criminal Evidence, 1978, Introduction to Criminal Evidence, 1982; editor Fire and Police Personnel reporter, 1975—, Pub. Employment Health reporter, 1986—. Mem. ABA (liaison to criminal justice council 1973—). Republican. Club: Rotary. Civil rights, Criminal, Local government. Office: 5519 N Cumberland Ave Suite 1008 Chicago IL 60656

SCHMIDT, WHITNEY LAWRENCE, lawyer; b. N.Y.C., Feb. 1, 1955; s. Lawrence William and Esther B. (Mathews) S.; m. Caroline Ann Bassette, Nov. 13, 1982. BA cum laude, Harvard U., 1977; JD, Vanderbilt U., 1980. Bar: N.J. 1980, U.S. Dist. Ct. N.J. 1980, U.S. Dist. Ct. (ea. and so. dists.) N.Y. 1981, D.C. 1981, N.Y 1982, U.S. Dist. Ct. D.C. 1982, U.S. Dist. Ct. (cen. dist.) Fla. 1982, U.S. Ct. Appeals (3d and D.C. cirs.) 1982, Md. 1983, Calif. 1983, U.S. Ct. Appeals (6th and 11th cirs.) 1983, U.S. Ct. Appeals (9th cir.) 1984, U.S. Supreme Ct. 1984. Law clk. to judge N.J. Supreme Ct., Trenton, 1980-81, U.S. Dist. Ct. D.C., 1981-82; assoc. Davis, Polk & Wardwell, N.Y.C., 1982-86; asst. U.S. atty. Mid. Dist. Fla., Tampa, 1986—; mem. faculty BAR/BRI Bar Rev., Chgo., 1982—. Assoc. articles editor Vanderbilt Law Rev. 1980. Mem. ABA, Assn. Trial Lawyers Am., Order of Coif. Republican. Avocations: beekeeping, auto mechanics, antique auto restoration. Federal civil litigation, State civil litigation, Criminal. Office: US Atty's Office 500 Zack St Room 410 Tampa FL 33602

SCHMIDT, WILLIAM LESNETT, lawyer; b. Pitts., May 31, 1946; s. William Chamberlain and Mary Jane (Lesnett) S.; m. Patricia Anne Shortle, Apr. 12, 1975; children—William Michael, Sheri Lynn. B.A., Am. U., 1969, J.D., 1972. Bar: Va. 1973, U.S. Dist. Ct. (ea. dist.) Va. 1974, U.S. Supreme Ct. 1976, U.S. Ct. Appeals (4th cir.) 1979. Assoc. Shomette, Stanhagen & Durrette, Falls Church, Va., 1973-74; assoc., ptnr. Lesh, Brown & Schmidt, Fairfax, Va., 1974-77; sr. ptnr. Schmidt & Busman, Springfield, Va., 1977-84; sole practice, Springfield, 1984—. Trustee Valley Forge Mil. Acad., Wayne, Pa., 1980-82, bd. dirs., 1974—, vice chmn. bd. visitors, 1984; pres., bd. dirs. Valley Forge Mil. Acad. Alumni Assn., 1980; v.p., fund raiser Fort Hunt Crew Boosters, Alexandria, 1980-83; co-chmn. Lawyers for Ford, Va., 1976; mem. Nixon for Pres. Campaign Com., 1968. Recipient Distang. Service award Valley Forge Mil. Acad., 1983; Province XIX Thomas Arkle Clark award Alpha Tau Omega, 1969. Mem. ABA, Va. State Bar, Va. Trial Lawyers Assn., Assn. Trial Lawyers Am., Fairfax Bar Assn., Internat. Platform Assn., Phi Alpha Delta, Omicron Delta Kappa. Republican. Presbyterian. General corporate, Family and matrimonial, General practice. Home: 8202 Treebrooke Ln Alexandria VA 22308 Office: 6564 Loisdale Ct Springfield VA 22150

SCHMITT, JOHN FRANCIS, lawyer; b. Indpls., Dec. 27, 1950; s. Herman Louis and Amelia Agnes (Sustarsich) S.; m. Regina Ann Louden, Jan. 15, 1969 (div. Feb. 1975); 1 child, Michael Joseph; m. Julie Ann Zellers, Aug. 11, 1979 (div. May 14, 1986). AB in Polit. Sci. with distinction, Ind. U., 1976, JD, 1979. Bar: Ind. 1979, U.S. Dist. Ct. (so. dist.) Ind. 1979, U.S. Ct. Appeals (7th cir.) 1982. Dep. auditor of state State of Ind., Indpls., 1976-78; assoc. Lewis, Bowman, St. Clair & Wagner, Indpls., 1979-83, ptnr., 1984—. Pres. Ind. Young Dems., 1975-76. Mem. ABA, Ind. State Bar Assn., Indpls. Bar Assn., Assn. Trial Lawyers Am., Ind. Trial Lawyers Am., AFL-CIO Lawyers Coordinating Com. Avocations: guitar, bicycling, golf, tennis, fishing. Labor, Personal injury, Workers' compensation. Home: 604 N Tibbs Ave Indianapolis IN 46222 Office: Lewis Bowman St Clair & Wagner 5101 Madison Ave Indianapolis IN 46227

SCHMITT, JOSEPH FRANCIS, lawyer; b. Madison, Wis., Oct. 3, 1940; s. Al B. and Loretta Christine (Marx) S.; m. Rosine Lieu, Apr. 22, 1970; 1 child, Lillian Kim. Student, St. Mary's Coll., 1958-60, Loras Coll., 1961; J.D., U. Wis., 1965. Bar: Wis. 1965, U.S. Dist. Ct. (we. dist.) Wis. 1965, U.S. Dist. Ct. (ea. dist.) Wis. 1981, U.S. Supreme Ct. 1983. Asst. gen. counsel CMI Investment Co., Madison, Wis., 1972-76; assoc. gen. counsel Miller Brewing Co., Milw., 1976-81; prin. Joseph F. Schmitt & Assocs., S.C., Cedarburg, Wis., 1981—. Bd. dirs. COPE Hotline, 1982; mem. Madison Area Bus. Advisory Council, 1975-76. Served to capt. USAF; 1965-72; Vietnam. Decorated Bronze Star; Vietnam Honor medal (1st class). Mem. ABA, Wis. State Bar Assn., Ozaukee Bar Assn., Milw. Bar Assn. Roman Catholic. Federal civil litigation, State civil litigation, General corporate. Office: W52 N687 Highland Dr Cedarburg WI 53012

SCHMITZ, THOMAS MATHIAS, lawyer; b. Cleve., June 1, 1938; s. Augustine A. and Lenora C. (Gerhart) S.; m. Gloria E. Sabo, June 6, 1964; children: Christopher T., Susan T. BS in Chem. Engrng., Case Inst. Tech., 1961; JD, Cleve.-Marshall Law Sch., 1967; MBA in Internat. Mgmt., Baldwin-Wallace Coll., 1985. Bar: Ohio 1967, U.S. Patent Office 1968; registered profl. engr., Ohio. Sr. engr. E.F. Hauserman Co., Cleve., 1964-67; patent atty. B.F. Goodrich Co., Akron, Ohio, 1967-69; assoc. Slough & Slough, Cleve., 1969-72; sr. patent atty. SCM Corp., Cleve., 1972-84, gen. patent counsel, 1984-86; gen. patent counsel, asst. gen. counsel The Glidden Co. (formerly SCM Corp.), Cleveland, 1986—. Contbr. articles to profl. jours. Bd. dirs. Fontbonne Home, Lakewood, Ohio, 1981—. Mem. ABA, Cleve. Patent Law Assn. (bd. dirs. 1975-83, 85—, pres. 1985-86), Am. Patent Law Assn. Avocation: golf. Patent, Public international, Environment. Home: 17228 Ernadale Ave Cleveland OH 44111 Office: The Glidden Co 900 Huntington Bldg 925 Euclid Ave Cleveland OH 44111

SCHMOLL, HARRY F., JR., educator, lawyer; b. Somers Point, N.J., Jan. 20, 1939. B.S., Rider Coll., 1960; J.D., Temple U., 1967. Bar: Pa., D.C. 1969, N.J. 1975. With claims dept. Social Security Adminstrn., Phila., 1960-67; staff atty. Pa. State U., State College, 1968-69; regional dir. Pa. Crime Commn., State College, 1969-70; campaign aide U.S. Senator Hugh Scott, Harrisburg, Pa., 1970; sole practice, State College, 1970-74, Manahwkin, N.J., 1975—; instr. criminal justice Pa. State U., University Park, 1969-74, assoc. prof. criminal justice Burlington County Coll., Pemberton, N.J., 1974—; judge mcpl. ct., Stafford Twp., 1982-85. Gen. counsel German Heritage Council of N.J., Inc. Mem. Pa. Bar Assn., N.J. Bar Assn., Ocean County Bar Assn. Mem. Stafford Twp. Com., 1979-81, dep. mayor, 1979. Club: German-Am. Club of So. Ocean County (pres.). Author: New Jersey Criminal Law Workbook, 1976, 2d edit. 1979. Legal education. Office: 37 Rona Ln Manahawkin NJ 08050

SCHMUHL, THOMAS ROEGER, lawyer; b. Phila., Oct. 4, 1946; s. Norman George and Ethel Sandt (Roeger) S.; m. Jean Giannone, Aug. 3, 1974; children—Andrew, Deborah. A.B., Johns Hopkins U., 1968, M.A., 1968; J.D., U. Pa., 1971. Bar: Pa. 1971, U.S. Dist. Ct. (ea. dist.) Pa. 1971, U.S. Supreme Ct. 1980. Assoc. Schnader, Harrison, Segal & Lewis, Phila., 1971-78, ptnr., 1979—, chmn. bus. dept., 1984—. Served to capt., USAR, 1968-75. Mem. Internat. Bar Assn., ABA, Phila. Bar Assn., Pa. Bar Assn., Nat. Assn. Bond Lawyers, Com. of Seventy, Internat. Bar Assn. Club: Racquet of Phila. General corporate. Office: 1600 Market St Philadelphia PA 19103

SCHMULTS, EDWARD CHARLES, lawyer, corporate executive; b. Paterson, N.J., Feb. 6, 1931; s. Edward M. and Mildred (Moore) S.; m. Diane E. Beers, Apr. 23, 1960; children: Alison C., Edward M., Robert C. B.S., Yale U., 1953; J.D., Harvard U., 1958. Bar: N.Y. State 1959, D.C. 1974. Assoc. White & Case, N.Y.C., 1958-65; ptnr. White & Case, 1965-73, 77-81; gen. counsel Treasury Dept., Washington, 1973-74; undersec. Treasury Dept., 1974-75; dep. counsel to Pres. U.S., 1975-76; dep. atty. gen. U.S. Dept. Justice, Washington, 1981-84; sr. v.p. external relations, gen. counsel GTE Corp., Stamford, Conn., 1984—; lectr. securities laws. Bd. dirs. Germany Fund, USA-Republic of China Econ. Council; trustee Refugee Policy Group, Trinity Sch., N.Y.C., 1977-81. Served with USMCR, 1953-55. Mem. Am., N.Y. State, Fed. bar assns., Assn. Bar City N.Y., Adminstrv. Conf. U.S. (council 1977-84). Clubs: Sakonnet Golf (Little Compton, R.I.); Metropolitan (Washington). Office: GTE Corp One Stamford Forum Stamford CT 06904

SCHMUTZ, ARTHUR WALTER, lawyer; b. Akron, Aug. 2, 1921; s. Paul Edward and Elizabeth (Williams) S.; m. Elizabeth Moore, June 17, 1951; children: David H., Stuart R., Jonathan M., Anne Marie. A.B. summa cum laude, Johns Hopkins U., 1949; LL.B. cum laude, Harvard U., 1952. Bar: Calif. 1953. Asso. Gibson, Dunn & Crutcher, Los Angeles, 1952-59; ptnr. Gibson, Dunn & Crutcher, 1960-69, sr. ptnr., 1969-86, adv. ptnr., 1987—; bd. dirs. Calif. Fed., Inc., Los Angeles, Calif. Fed. Savings and Loan, Los Angeles, Ducommun Inc., Los Angeles. Trustee Orthopedic Hosp., Los Angeles. Served with USAAF, 1942-45. Decorated Bronze Star. Fellow Am. Bar Found.; mem. ABA, Los Angeles County Bar Assn., Phi Beta Kappa. Clubs: Calif., La Jolla Beach and Tennis, Lakeside Golf. General corporate. Office: 333 S Grand Ave Los Angeles CA 90071

SCHMUTZ, JOHN FRANCIS, lawyer; b. Oneida, N.Y., July 24, 1947; s. William L. and Rosemary S.; m. H. Marie Roney, June 7, 1969; children—Gretchen, Jonathan, Nathan. B.A. cum laude, Canisius Coll., 1969; J.D. cum laude, Notre Dame U., 1972; LL.M., George Washington U., 1975. Bar: Ind. 1972, U.S. Ct. Mil. Appeals 1972, U.S. Tax Ct. 1973, D.C. 1975, U.S. Supreme Ct. 1975. Legislation and major projects officer Office Judge Adv. Gen., 1972-74; appellate atty. U.S. Army Legal Services Agy., 1974-75; assoc. Ice, Miller, Donadio & Ryan, Indpls., 1976-77; staff atty. Burger Chef Systems, Inc., Indpls., 1977-78, sr. atty., 1979, asst. chief legal counsel, 1978-

70, chief legal counsel, 1980, v.p., gen. counsel, sec., 1981—; v.p. legal Hardee's Food Systems, Inc., 1983—; dir., v.p. Bursan Credit Union; dir. Food Service and Lodging Inst.; dir., v.p. Blahs, Inc., RIX Systems, Inc., Burger Chef Distributive Corp.; v.p. Hardee's Food Systems, Inc. Mem. ABA, Fed. Bar Assn., Ind. Bar Assn., D.C. Bar Assn., Indpls. Bar Assn., Am. Assn. Corp. Counsel, Nat. Restaurant Assn. Republican. Roman Catholic. Lodge: K.C. Exec. editor Notre Dame Law Rev., 1971-72. General corporate, Contracts commercial, Franchising. Home: 305 Old Coach Rd Rocky Mount NC 27801 Office: 1233 N Church St Rocky Mount NC 27801

SCHNACK, KENT RICHARD, lawyer; b. Quincy, Ill., June 8, 1953; s. Loren Edward and Sarama Schnack; m. Salli A. Merkel, July 12, 1980 (div. Sept. 1983); children: Ryan, Christopher. BA, Valparaiso U., 1975, JD, 1978. Bar: Ill. 1978, U.S. Dist. Ct. (cen. dist.) Ill. 1979. Law clk. to presiding justice Ind. Appellate Ct., Indpls., 1978-79; assoc. Loos, Schnack & Siebers, Quincy, 1979-80, ptnr., 1980—. Mem. ABA, Ill. Bar Assn., Adams County Bar Assn. (sec. 1985-86), Assn. Trial Lawyers Am., Ill. Trial Lawyers Assn. Avocations: tennis, jogging. State civil litigation. Office: Loos Schnack & Siebers 510 Vermont St Quincy IL 62301

SCHNALL, FLORA, lawyer; b. Bklyn., Oct. 7, 1935; d. Benjamin and Jean (Heilweil) S. B.A. magna cum laude, Smith Coll., 1956; J.D., Harvard U., 1959. Asst. counsel to Gov. Nelson A. Rockefeller State of N.Y., Albany, 1959-60; assoc. Milbank, Tweed, Hadley & McCloy, N.Y.C., 1960-69; ptnr. Milbank, Tweed, Hadley & McCloy, 1984—; from assoc. to sr. ptnr. Rosenman Colin Freund Lewis & Cohen, N.Y.C., 1969-84. Contbg. author: Real Estate Titles. Bd. dirs. Northside Ctr. Child Devel., Inc., N.Y.C., 1980—, Citizens Housing and Planning Council, N.Y.C., 1982—. Mem. Am. Coll. Real Estate Lawyers (bd. govs. 1984—), ABA (real property probate sect., council 1987), N.Y. State Bar Assn. (editor real property law sect. of newsletter 1980—, chmn. 1987, mem. ho. of dels. 1986—). Club: India House. Banking, Contracts commercial, Landlord-tenant. Office: Milbank Tweed Hadley & McCloy 1 Chase Manhattan Plaza New York NY 10005

SCHNAPP, ROGER HERBERT, lawyer; b. N.Y.C., Mar. 17, 1946; s. Michael Jay and Beatrice Joan (Becker) S.; m. Candice Jacqueline Larson, Sept. 15, 1979. BS, Cornell U., 1966; JD, Harvard U., 1969; grad. Pub. Utility Mgmt. Program, U. Mich., 1978. Bar: N.Y. 1970, Calif. 1982, U.S. Dist. Ct. (so. dist.) N.Y. 1975, U.S. Dist. Ct. (no. dist.) Calif. 1980, U.S. Dist. Ct. (cen. dist.) Calif. 1982, U.S. Dist. Ct. (ea. dist.) Calif. 1984), U.S. Ct. Appeals (2d cir.) 1970, U.S. Ct. Appeals (4th and 6th cirs.) 1976, U.S. Ct. Appeals (7th cir.) 1977, U.S. Ct. Appeals (8th cir.) 1980, U.S. Supreme Ct. 1974. Atty. CAB, Washington, 1969-70; labor atty. Western Electric Co., N.Y.C., 1970-71; mgr. employee relations Am. Airlines, N.Y.C., 1971-74; labor counsel Am. Electric Power Service Corp., N.Y.C., 1974-78, sr. labor counsel, 1978-80; indsl. relations counsel Trans World Airlines, N.Y.C., 1980-81; sr. assoc. Parker, Milliken, Clark & O'Hara, Los Angeles, 1981-82; ptnr. Rutan & Tucker, Costa Mesa, Calif., 1983-84; ptnr. Memel, Jacobs, Pierno, Gersh & Ellsworth, Newport Beach, Calif., 1985-86; ptnr. Memel, Jacobs & Ellsworth, Newport Beach, 1986-87; sole practice, Newport Beach, 1987—; cons. collective bargaining Am. Arbitration Assn.; commentator labor relations Fin. News Network; lectr. Calif. Western Law Sch., Calif. State U.-Fullerton, Calif. State Conf. Small Bus., Indsl. League Orange County; lectr. collective bargaining Pace U., N.Y.C. N.E. regional coordinator Pressler for Pres., 1979-80. Mem. ABA (R.R. and airline labor law com., internat. labor law com.), Internat. Bar Assn., N.Y. State Bar Assn., Calif. Bar Assn., Conf. R.R. and Airline Labor Lawyers, Newport Harbor Area C. of C., Orange County C. of C. Republican. Jewish. Clubs: Balboa Bay, Lincoln of Orange County, Center. Lodge: Masons. Author: Arbitration Issues for the 1980s, 1981; A Look at Three Companies, 1982; editor-in-chief Industrial and Labor Relations Forum, 1964-66; contbr. articles to profl. publs. Labor, Legislative. Office: PO Box 9049 Newport Beach CA 92658

SCHNEEBAUM, STEVEN MARC, lawyer; b. N.Y.C., Oct. 29, 1948; s. Harry and Nathalie (Maharam) S.; m. Karen McGovern, Aug. 20, 1972; children: Megan A., Rachel C. BA, Yale U., 1969; MA, Oberlin Coll., 1970; BA, Oxford U., Eng., 1976; MCL, George Washington U., 1978. Bar: D.C. 1978, U.S. Dist. Ct. D.C. 1978, U.S. Ct. Appeals (D.C. cir.) 1980, U.S. Ct. Internat. Trade 1981, U.S. Ct. Appeals (10th cir.) 1981, U.S. Ct. Appeals (7th cir.) 1982, U.S. Ct. Claims 1983, U.S. Ct. Appeals (fed. cir.) 1984, U.S. Ct. Appeals (4th cir.) 1985, U.S. Ct. Appeals (9th cir.) 1987. Assoc. Patton, Boggs & Blow, Washington, 1978-83, ptnr., 1983—; adj. lectr. law Cath. U., Washington, 1979-82. Contbr. articles to profl. jours. Bd. dirs., vice chmn. Legal Counsel For the Elderly, Washington, 1982-87, chmn., 1987—; bd. dirs., vice chmn. Internat. Human Rights Law Group, Washington, 1982—. Recipient Cert. Appreciation D.C. Bar, 1984, Pro Bono award Internat. Human Rights Law Group, 1986. Mem. ABA, Fed. Bar Assn., Am. Soc. Internat. Law, Washington Fgn. Law Soc. Federal civil litigation, Private international, Public international. Office: Patton Boggs & Blow 2550 M St NW Washington DC 20037

SCHNEIDER, DANIEL MAX, legal educator; b. Cin., Sept. 13, 1948; s. Meyer R. and Berenice R. (Hecht) S.; m. Elizabeth G. Schulman, July 15, 1978; children: Anna, Claire. AB, Washington U., St. Louis, 1970; JD, U. Cin., 1973; LLM, NYU, 1976. Bar: Ohio 1973, N.Y. 1978. Law clk. to presiding judge U.S. Dist. Ct. (so. dist.) Ohio, Columbus, Ohio, 1973-75; assoc. LeBoeuf, Lamb, Leiby & MacRae, N.Y.C., 1978-81, Murphey, Young & Smith, Columbus, 1981-84; assoc. prof. No. Ill. U., DeKalb, 1984—. Contbr. articles to profl. jours. Yale U. Law Sch. research fellow, 1976-77. Corporate taxation, Estate taxation, Personal income taxation. Office: No Ill Univ Coll Law DeKalb IL 60115

SCHNEIDER, EARL GARY, lawyer; b. Chgo., Apr. 6, 1933; s. Isadore and Doris (Shiffman) S.; m. Enid R. Levy, Aug. 29, 1954; children—Keith, Gene. J.D., Ill. Inst. Tech.-Chgo. Kent Coll. Law, 1955. Bar: Ill. 1955. Ptnr. Miller, Schneider & Galasso and predecessor, Chgo., 1957-78, Schneider & Morrison Ltd., Chgo., 1978-87, Schneider & Schneider, P.C., 1987—. Served with U.S. Army, 1955-57. Mem. ABA, Ill. Trial Lawyers Assn. Personal injury, State civil litigation. Home: 3745 Bordeaux Northbrook IL 60062 Office: Schneider & Schneider PO Box 14828 Chicago IL 60614

SCHNEIDER, ELIZABETH KELLEY, law librarian; b. Bloomington, Ill., July 10, 1946; d. George Raymond and Lucille Genvieve (Sutter) Kelley; m. John James Schneider, Aug. 21, 1982. BA in History, Wesleyan U., Ill., 1968; MLS, U. Minn., 1969; JD, William Mitchell Coll. of Law, 1973. Bar: Minn. 1974, U.S. Dist. Ct. Minn. Librarian Ramsy County Law Library, St. Paul, 1971-73; asst. law librarian U. of Akron (Ohio) Coll. of Law, 1973-74; prof. law, librarian Hamline U. Sch. Law, St. Paul, 1974-81; dir. Maricopa County Law Library, Phoenix, 1981—; instr. legal research Ariz. Legal Secs. Assn., 1982, Phoenix Coll., 1982-85, Ariz. State Library Assn., 1984. Mem. ABA, Am. Assn. Law Libraries, Phoenix Area Assn. Law Libraries (pres. 1985-86), Ariz. Women Lawyers Assn., Desert Sun Aux., Nat. Assistance League (sec. 1985—), Alpha Gamma Delta (pres. 1985-86). Librarianship, Law office administration, Professional responsibility. Office: Maricopa County Law Library 101 W Jefferson 2d Floor Phoenix AZ 85003

SCHNEIDER, FREDERICK RICHARD, law educator; b. Milw., July 11, 1939; s. Clifford R. and Eunice R. (Druse) S.; m. Karen M. Andersen, Dec. 21, 1963; children: Kari, Richard, Carl. BA, Luther Coll., 1961; JD, U. Chgo., 1964. Bar: Wis. 1964, U.S. Dist. Ct. (we. dist) Wis. 1964, U.S. Tax Ct. 1967. Assoc. Steele, Smyth, Klos & Smyth, La Crosse, Wis., 1964-69; asst. prof. law Chase Coll. Law, Cin., 1969-1972; assoc. prof. Chase Coll. Law, No. Ky. U., Highland Heights, 1972-73, prof., 1973—, asst. dean, 1974-76. Contbr. articles to profl. jours. Cons. Ohio dist. Am. Lutheran Ch., Columbus, 1977—. Mem. ABA, Cin. Bar Assn. (profl. ethics com. 1975—). Probate, Legal education, Estate taxation. Home: 8643 Empire Ct Cincinnati OH 45231 Office: No Ky U Chase Coll Law Highland Heights KY 41076

SCHNEIDER, GARY BRUCE, lawyer; b. Beatrice, Nebr., Oct. 20, 1947; s. Wilferd F. and Norma L. (Tegtmeier) S.; m. Mary Lynne Nelson, Apr. 13, 1968; 1 child, Christopher Paul. BS, U. Nebr., 1969, JD, 1974; LLM, NYU, 1979. Bar: Nebr. 1974, Colo. 1974, U.S. Supreme Ct. 1977, U.S. Tax Ct. 1980. Dep. county atty. Lancaster County, Lincoln, Nebr., 1974-75; asst. atty. gen. State of Nebr., Lincoln, 1975-78; assoc. Woods, Aitken et al, Lincoln, 1979-82, ptnr., 1983—. Served with U.S. Army, 1969-71. Mem. ABA (tech. and econs. in planning com. of real property, probate and trust sect., taxation sect., legal econs. sect.), Nebr. Bar Assn. Lutheran. Avocations: woodworking, hunting, outdoor activities, dancing. Probate, General corporate, Estate taxation. Office: Woods Aitken et al 206 S 13th St 1500 American Charter Lincoln NE 68508

SCHNEIDER, HARVEY ROBERT, lawyer; b. N.Y.C., May 3, 1952; s. Sandy and Dorothy (Seisser) S.; m. Barbara Karen Blattman; children: Rachel, Scott, Bradley. AA, Dean Jr. Coll., 1972; BA, Alfred U., 1974; JD, Nova U., 1977. Bar: Fla. 1977, U.S. Dist. Ct. (so. dist.) Fla. 1978, U.S. Ct. Appeals (5th and 11th cirs.) 1981, U.S. Supreme Ct. 1984. Staff trial atty. Pub. Defenders Office, Palm Beach, Fla., 1978-80; ptnr. Kind & Schneider, Boca Raton, Fla., 1980-84; sole practice Boca Raton, 1984-85; ptnr. Rhoads & Sinon, Boca Raton, 1986—. Mem. ABA, South Palm Beach County Bar Assn., Nat. Assn. Criminal Def. Lawyers. Democrat. Jewish. State civil litigation, Criminal, Family and matrimonial. Office: Rhoads & Sinon 1200 N Federal Hwy Suite 308 Boca Raton FL 33432

SCHNEIDER, HOWARD, lawyer; b. N.Y.C., Mar. 21, 1935; s. Abraham and Lena (Pincus) S.; m. Anne Evelyn Gorfinkle; children—Andrea Rose, Jeffrey Winston. A.B., Cornell U., 1956, J.D., 1959. Bar: N.Y. 1959, D.C. 1976. Assoc., then ptnr. Stroock & Stroock, N.Y.C., 1959-75; gen. counsel Commodity Futures Trading Commn., Washington, 1975-77; ptnr. Rosenman & Colin, N.Y.C., 1977—. Contbr. articles to profl. jours. Served to capt. USAR, 1956-66. Mem. Assn. Bar City of N.Y. (chmn. com. 1982—). Republican. Jewish. Club: Harmonie (N.Y.C.). Home: 830 Park Ave New York NY 10021 Office: Rosenman & Colin 575 Madison Ave New York NY 10022

SCHNEIDER, JAMES FREDERICK, judge; b. Balt., Nov. 18, 1947; s. Joseph F. and Mary L. S. B.A., U. Balt., 1969, J.D., 1972. Bar: U.S. Dist. Ct. Md. 1973, U.S. Ct. Appeals 1972. Law clk. to judge Supreme Bench Balt., 1972-73; asst. state's atty. for Balt., 1973-78; gen. equity master to Supreme Bench Balt., 1978-82; judge U.S. Bankruptcy Ct. for Dist. Md., 1982—; historian, archivist Supreme Bench Balt. Recipient Silver Key award Law Student div. Am. Bar Assn., U. Balt., 1972. Mem. Bar Assn. Balt. City, Md. State Bar Assn., Heuisler Honor Soc. Author: The Story of the Library Company of the Baltimore Bar, 1979; The Centennial of the Bar Association of Baltimore City, 1980. Bankruptcy, Criminal, Legal history. Office: 909 US Courthouse 101 W Lombard St Baltimore MD 21201

SCHNEIDER, KAREN BUSH, lawyer, educator; b. Lansing, Mich., Mar. 17, 1951; d. Gerard Joseph and Emily Virginia (Szoka) Bush; m. Lawrence Patrick Schneider, May 8, 1976. BA, U. Notre Dame, 1973, JD, 1976. Bar: Mich. 1976, U.S. Dist. Ct. (we. dist.) Mich. 1976, U.S. Dist. Ct. (ea. dist.) Mich. 1981. From assoc. to ptnr. Foster, Swift, Collins & Coey, P.C., Lansing, 1976—; adj. prof. Thomas M. Cooley Law Sch., Lansing, 1985—; mem. jud. qualifications com. State Bar Mich., 1987—. Contbr. legal briefs to profl jours. Mem. ABA, Am. Arbitration Assn. (labor arbitrator 1985—), Mich. Bar Assn., Ingham County Bar Assn. (bd. dirs., sec. 1982-83, pubs. com. 1983-85, chm. pubs. com. 1984-85), Am. Lung Assn. of Mich. (bd. dirs. 1985—, chmn. personnel com. 1986—), Assn. of Career Women, Notre Dame Alumni Assn. of Lansing (sec. 1979-80, pres. 1980-81, pub. relations officer 1981-82, v.p. 1983-85), Ingham County Humane Soc. (bd. dirs. 1984—, corresponding sec. 1984, recording sec. 1985, fund-raising chmn. 1985—, pres. 1986—). Roman Catholic. Avocation: sailing. Labor, Civil rights. Home: 2543 Kodiak Dr East Lansing MI 48823 Office: Foster Swift Collins & Coey PC 313 S Washington Sq Lansing MI 48933

SCHNEIDER, KARL HERBERT, lawyer; b. Columbus, Ohio, May 10, 1957; s. Herbert Henry and Betty Ramona (List) S.; m. Jennifer Furash, Mar. 27, 1982; 1 child, Jason Edward. BA, Denison U., 1979; JD, Capital U., 1982. Bar: Ohio 1982, U.S. Dist. Ct. (so. dist.) Ohio 1983. Exec. v.p. W. Saxbe Enterprises, Columbus, 1980-82; sole practice Columbus, 1982—; gen. counsel HER Inc., Columbus, 1984—; lectr. real estate groups, Columbus, 1980—, Columbus Tech. Inst., 1985—. Bd. dirs. Franklin County Forum, Columbus, 1983-85. Mem. Pi Sigma Alpha, Omicron Delta Epsilon. Republican. Presbyterian. Clubs: Columbus Athletic, Agonis. Avocations: marathon running, triatholon. Real property, State civil litigation, Administrative and regulatory. Office: 4656 Executive Dr Columbus OH 43220

SCHNEIDER, KENNETH PAUL, lawyer; b. Newton, Mass., Dec. 12, 1948; s. Robert and Charlotte (Grass) S. AB magna cum laude, Columbia U., 1973; JD, Cornell U., 1978. Bar: N.Y. 1979, U.S. Dist. Ct. (no., so. and ea. dists.) N.Y. 1979. Law clk. to justice N.Y. State Ct. System, N.Y.C., 1979-80; assoc. Schwartz, Klink & Schreiber P.C., N.Y.C., 1980—. Mem. ABA, N.Y. State Bar Assn., N.Y. County Lawyers Assn., Am. Judicature Soc., Phi Beta Kappa. Federal civil litigation, State civil litigation. Home: 363 E 76th St Apt 8K New York NY 10021 Office: Schwartz Klink & Schreiber PC 666 3d Ave New York NY 10017

SCHNEIDER, LAZ LEVKOFF, lawyer; b. Columbia, S.C., Mar. 15, 1939; s. Philip L. and Dorothy Harriet (Levkoff) S.; m. Ellen Linda Shiffrin, Dec. 12, 1968; 1 son, David Allen. B.A., Yale U., 1961, LL.B., 1964; LL.M., NYU, 1965. Bar: D.C. 1965, N.Y. 1965, Fla. 1970. Assoc. Fulton, Walter & Duncombe, N.Y.C., 1965-67, Rosenman, Colin Kaye Petschek Freund & Emil, N.Y.C., 1967-69; assoc. Kronish, Lieb, Weiner, Shainswit & Hellman, N.Y.C., 1969-70; ptnr. Ruden Barnett McClosky & Schuster, Ft. Lauderdale, Fla., 1970-80; sole practice, Ft. Lauderdale, 1980-86; ptnr. Sherr, Tiballi, Fayne & Schneider, Ft. Lauderdale, Fla., 1987—. Mem. exec. com. Fla. regional bd. Anti Defamation League, 1972-82. Mem. ABA, Fla. Bar Assn., Broward County Bar Assn. (chmn. sect. corp. bus. and banking law 1978-80). Jewish. Club: Yale (pres. 1977-79). Grad. editor Tax Law Rev., 1964-65. General corporate, Securities. Office: 600 Corporate Dr Fort Lauderdale FL 33334

SCHNEIDER, MICHAEL LOUIS, lawyer; b. Evanston, Ill., Jan. 16, 1954; s. Olin M. and Dorothy (Frady) S.; m. Sidney Carlson Roesch, Sept. 4, 1976; 1 child, Martha Elisabeth. BA, Auburn U., 1976; JD, U. Tenn., 1979. Bar: Tenn. 1979, U.S. Dist. Ct. (ea. dist.) Tenn. 1980, U.S. Ct. Appeals (6th cir.) 1984, Fla. 1986. Assoc. Bell & Assocs., Cleve., 1979-81; ptnr. Banks & Schneider, Cleve., 1981-84; law clk. to presiding judge U.S. Ct. Appeals (1st cir.), Tallahassee, 1985; asst. pub. defender 2d jud. cir. State of Fla., Tallahassee, 1986—. Mem. ABA, Fla. Bar Assn., Tenn. Bar Assn. General practice, Criminal, Bankruptcy. Home: 4475 Bayshore Circle Tallahassee FL 32308 Office: Pub Defenders Office Barnett Bank Bldg Suite 480 PO Box 671 Tallahassee FL 32302

SCHNEIDERMAN, IRWIN, lawyer; b. N.Y.C., May 28, 1923; s. Meyer and Bessie (Klein) S.; m. Roberta Haig, Nov. 28, 1966; 1 child, Eric T. B.A., Bklyn. Coll., 1943; LL.B. cum laude, Harvard U., 1948. Bar: N.Y. bar 1949, D.C. bar 1952. Since practiced in N.Y.C.; assoc. Cahill Gordon & Reindel, 1948-59, partner, 1959—; bd. dir. Contel Corp.; spl. cons. to chmn. SEC, 1981-82, mem. adv. com. on tender offers, 1983. Trustee Bklyn. Coll. Found., 1983—; bd. dirs. N.Y.C. Opera. Served to lt. (j.g.) USNR, 1943-46. Mem. N.Y. State Bar Assn., ABA, Assn. Bar City N.Y. Clubs: Harvard, Wall St. General corporate, Securities. Home: 203 E 72d St New York NY 10021 Office: 80 Pine St New York NY 10005

SCHNEIDERMAN, TED, lawyer; b. Akron, Ohio, Apr. 3, 1932; s. Sam and Eva (Shapiro) S.; m. Rolinda Barnett, Nov. 29, 1954; children: Toby Rosen, Karen, Nancy Levin, Amy. BBA, Kent State U., 1955; JD summa cum laude, Ohio State U., 1956. Bar: U.S. Dist. Ct. (no. dist.) Ohio 1958, U.S. Supreme Ct. 1963, U.S. Ct. Appeals (6th cir.) 1975. Sole practice Akron, 1956-81; judge Akron Mcpl. Ct., 1981—; asst. prosecutor Summit County, 1959-63; spl. counsel State of Ohio, 1963-70, City of Akron, 1966-69, City of Cuyahoga Falls, 1971-74; presiding adminstrv. judge Akron Mcpl. Ct., 1983-84. Gen. counsel Akron Civic Theatre, 1975-76; pres. adv. bd. Oriana House, Inc., regional bd. ADL, 1966—, bd. dirs. Akron Jewish Community Fedn., Community Hall Found., Akron Jewish Family Service; mem. exec. com. Summit County Reps., 1974-82; mem. Akron Health Commn., 1977-82, v.p., 1981-82; moderator Akron Civic Forum of Air; bd. dirs. Akron Jewish Ctr. 1973-80, v.p., 1977-78, past chmn. steering com.). Recipient Founders award B'nai B'rith, 1975, Superior Jud. Service award Ohio Supreme Ct., 1981-85. Mem. ABA (criminal justice sect.), Ohio Bar Assn., Akron Bar Assn. (jud. adminstrn. and legal reform com., criminal law com., law day com.), Assn. Trial Lawyers Am., Ohio Trial Lawyers Assn., Am. Judicature Soc., Akron Metro Judges Assn. (pres.), Ohio State Alumni Assn. (life, past pres.). Avocations: politics, sailing, football, children, dogs. Home: 100 Schocalog Rd Akron OH 44313 Office: Akron Mcpl Ct 217 S High St Room 924 Akron OH 44308

SCHNEIER, MARC MALVIN, legal editor; b. New Haven, Feb. 18, 1955; s. Bernard and Rehla (Freilich) S. AB, U. Calif., Berkeley, 1977; JD, U. Calif., Davis, 1981. Bar: Calif. 1981, U.S. Dist. Ct. (no. dist.) Calif. 1981. Assoc. David Gold P.L.C., San Francisco, 1981-83; editor Litigation Research Group, San Francisco, 1983—. Editor: Construction Litigation Reporter, Litigation Research Group, San Francisco, 1983—; contbr. articles to profl. jours. Treas. Royal Scottish Country Dance Soc., San Francisco, 1984-86, chmn., 1986—. Recipient Bur. Nat. Affairs award, 1981. Mem. ABA, Phi Beta Kappa. Democrat. Jewish. Avocations: dancing, reading. Construction, Government contracts and claims. Home: 1235 Peralta Ave Berkeley CA 94706 Office: Litigation Research Group 500 Howard St San Francisco CA 94105

SCHNELL, RONALD HANS, lawyer; b. Jersey City, Dec. 1, 1941; s. Hans Anthony and Martha (Thomasberger) S.; m. Lucyann Hobson, Apr. 10, 1965 (div. Mar. 1984); children: Cary Miller, Connie Raissi, T. Gardner Bayless, Ron Jr. AAS, Rockland Community Coll., 1961; LLB, Stetson U., 1965. Bar: Fla., U.S. Ct. Appeals. Dep. ct. clk. Clearwater, Fla., 1963-65; asst. atty. Pinellas County Commn., Clearwater, 1965-69; ptnr. Carr & Schnell, St. Petersburg, Fla., 1969—. Mgr., umpire Pasadena Little League, St. Petersburg, 1968-76; candidate, state rep., county judge Boy Scouts Am., Gulfport, Tallahassee, 1970, cubmaster, 1972-76; pres. Stetson Young Reps. Club, Gulfport, 1965; bd. dirs. Boy Scouts Am., 1972-76. Mem. ABA, St. Petersburg Bar Assn. (mem. numerous coms. 1970—), Assn. Trial Lawyers Am., Pinellas County Trial Lawyers Assn., Acad. Fla. Trial Lawyers (key man 1978—). Lodges: Mid County Optimists (bd. dirs. Clearwater club 1965-67), Bayview Optimists Club (bd. dirs., v.p., pres. St. Petersburg club 1969-77), Breakfast Optimists (bd. dirs., pres. 1978—). Avocations: softball, swimming, fishing, boating. Personal injury, Family and matrimonial, General practice. Home: 7015 Grevilla Ave S Saint Petersburg FL 33707 Office: Carr & Schnell 1325 Arlington Ave N Saint Petersburg FL 33705

SCHNIPPER, DON MARTIN, lawyer; b. Little Rock, Jan. 17, 1939; m. Mary Ann Evans, June 3, 1961; children: Caroline, Elizabeth. AB, U. Ark., 1963, JD, 1964. Bar: Ark. 1964, U.S. Supreme Ct. 1971. Ptnr. Wood, Smith, Schnipper & Clay, Hot Springs, Ark., 1964—; spl. assoc. justice Ark. Supreme Ct., 1976—. V.p. 1st United Meth. Ch., 1976-77, pres. 1977, vice chmn. bd. dirs. 1975-76; chmn. Ouachita Regional Counseling and Mental Health Ctr., 1977, pres. bd. dirs. 1970l bd. dirs. Hot Springs Childrens Home. Fellow Am. Bar Found.; mem. ABA, Ark. Bar Assn. (chmn. young lawyers sect. 1969-70, ho. of dels. 1973-76, exec. council 1976-79, chmn. exec. council 1980-81, pres. 1985-86), Garland County Bar Assn. (pres.), Ark. Trial Lawyers Assn., Hot Springs C. of C. (bd. dirs. 1966—, pres. 1977, Distinguished Service award 1970), U. Ark. Alumni Assn. (bd. dirs. 1978-84, nat. pres. 1982-83). Home: 850 Quapaw St Hot Springs AR 71901 Office: Wood Smith Schnipper & Clay 123 Market St Hot Springs AR 71901

SCHNUCK, TERRY EDWARD, lawyer; b. St. Louis, Oct. 10, 1952; s. Donald Otto and Doris Irene (Letson) S.; m. Sally Barrows Braxton, May 24, 1980; children: Hadley Braxton, Terry Edward Jr. BA in Econs., Tulane U., 1975; MBA, Washington U., St. Louis, 1980; JD, St. Louis U., 1980. Bar: Mo. 1980. Assoc. Greensfelder, Hemker, Wiese, Gale & Chappelow, St. Louis, 1980-84; chief legal counsel, sec. Schnuck Markets Inc., Bridgeton, Mo., 1984—, also bd. dirs.; bd. dirs. Creative Data Services Inc., St. Louis. Bd. dirs. St. Louis Charitable Found., St. Louis, 1984—, Urban League of Met. St. Louis, 1987—. Mem. ABA, Mo. Bar Assn., Bar Assn. of Met. St. Louis, Beta Theta Pi. Republican. Presbyterian. Club: Bellerive Country (St. Louis). General corporate, Legislative. Office: Schnuck Markets Inc 12921 Enterprise Way Bridgeton MO 63044

SCHNURMAN, ALAN JOSEPH, lawyer; b. N.Y.C., July 1, 1945; s. Albert and Ruth (Sirota) S.; m. Judith Bernstein, Mar. 31, 1974; children—Michele, David. B.S. in Acctg., Bklyn. Coll., 1967; J.D., N.Y. Law Sch., 1971. Bar: N.Y. 1972, U.S. Ct. Appeals (2d cir.) 1973, U.S. Dist. Ct. (ea. and so. dists.) N.Y. 1974, U.S. Supreme Ct. 1976. Acct. tax dept. Arthur Andersen & Co., N.Y.C., 1971-72; sole practice, N.Y.C., 1972-80; ptnr. Zalman & Schnurman, N.Y.C., 1980—. Host Lawline cable TV program; assoc. editor N.Y. State Trial Lawyers Quar., 1981. Mem. ABA, Am. Judges Assn., N.Y. State Bar Assn., Am. Trial Lawyers Assn., N.Y. State Trial Lawyers Assn., Assn. Trial Lawyers N.Y.C. (bd. dirs. 1986—), N.Y. County Lawyers Assn., N.Y. Law Sch. Alumni Assn. (bd. dirs. 1983—). Democrat. Jewish. State civil litigation, Personal injury, Insurance. Home: 623 3d St Brooklyn NY 11215 Office: Zalman & Schnurman 63 Wall St New York NY 10005

SCHOBER, GARY MICHAEL, lawyer; b. N.Y.C., May 17, 1953; s. Louis Joseph and Lena (Fiore) S.; m. Barbara Mary Sweeney, Nov. 12, 1982. BS magna cum laude, St. Bonaventure U., 1975; JD cum laude, Georgetown U., 1980. Bar: N.Y. 1980, U.S. Dist. Ct. (we. dist.) N.Y. 1980. Ptnr. Hodgson, Russ, Andrews, Woods & Goodyear, Buffalo, 1979—; bd. dirs. Empire Nat. Leasing, Inc., Buffalo, Oasis Systems, Inc., Buffalo, MBMS, Inc., Buffalo. Editor Law and Policy in Internat. Bus., Georgetown U., 1978. Mem. exec. com. Buffalo 2000, 1985—; firm chmn. United Way, Buffalo, 1985—. N.Y. State Regents Scholar, 1971. Mem. ABA, N.Y. State Bar Assn. (lectr.), Erie County Bar Assn.(lectr.), Nat. Honor Soc. Cath. Univs. and Colls. Republican. Avocations: jogging, racquetball. Computer, General corporate, Contracts commercial. Home: 12 Jasmine Ct East Amherst NY 14051 Office: Hodgson Russ Andrews et al One M&T Plaza Buffalo NY 14203

SCHOBER, THOMAS LEONARD, lawyer; b. Green Bay, Wis., Jan. 5, 1946; s. Leonard M. and Ruth (Christoh) S.; m. Suzan C. Murray, Sept. 5, 1981. BA, Northwestern U., 1968; JD, U. Wis., 1973. Bar: Wis. 1973. Assoc. Trowbridge Law Firm, Green Bay, 1973-81; ptnr. Schober & Ulatowski, Green Bay, 1981-86, Schober, Ulatowski & Hinchey S.C., Green Bay, 1984-86; sole practice Green Bay, 1986—; chmn. bd. atty.'s profl. responsibility com. Dist. 14, Supreme Ct. Wis., 1985—. Pres. YMCA, Green Bay, 1984-85. Served as sgt. U.S. Army, 1968-70, Vietnam. Mem. ABA, Wis. Bar Assn., Def. Research Inst., Nat. Assn. R.R. Trial Counsel. State civil litigation, Insurance, Transportation rail. Office: 1825 S Webster Ave Green Bay WI 54301-2253

SCHOCHOR, JONATHAN, lawyer; b. Suffern, N.Y., Sept. 9, 1946; s. Abraham and Betty (Hechtor) S.; m. Joan Elaine Brown, May 31, 1970; children—Lauren Aimee, Daniel Ross. B.A., Pa. State U., 1968; J.D., Am. U., 1971. Bar: D.C. 1971, Md. 1974 U.S. Dist. Ct. D.C. 1971, U.S. Ct. Appeals (D.C. cir.) 1971, U.S. Dist. Ct. Md. 1974, U.S. Ct. Appeals (4th cir.) 1974, U.S. Supreme Ct. 1986. Assoc., McKenna, Wilkinson & Kittner, Washington, 1970-74; assoc. Ellin & Baker, Balt., 1974-84; ptnr. Schochor, Federico & Staton, Balt., 1984—; lectr. in law; expert witness to state legis. Assoc. editor-in-chief American U. Law Rev., 1970-71. Mem. ABA, Assn. Trial Lawyers Am., Am. Judicature Soc., Md. State Bar Assn. (spl. com. on health claims arbitration 1983), Md. Trial Lawyers Assn. (bd. govs. 1986-87, mem. legis. com., 1985-86, chmn. legis. com. 1986-87), Balt. City Bar Assn. (legis. com. 1986), Bar Assn. D.C., Internat. Platform Assn., Phi Alpha Delta. Personal injury, Federal civil litigation, State civil litigation. Office: Schochor Federico & Staton PA 1211 St Paul St Baltimore MD 21202

SCHODER, WENDELL LOUIS, lawyer; b. Battle Creek, Mich., July 11, 1926; s. Harold Maurice and Hildred Angeline (Baird) S.; m. Helen Marie Bauman, Feb. 3, 1951; children—Patrice Schoder Emmerson, Robert, Gerald, Martha Schroeder Terry, Mary, David. Student Georgetown U., 1946-47; J.D., U. Detroit, 1951. Bar: Mich. 1951, U.S. Dist. Ct. (we. dist.) Mich. 1953. Sole practice, Battle Creek, 1951-64; cir. ct. commr. Calhoun County, Marshall, Mich., 1954-60, asst. pros. atty., 1960-64, probate judge, 1965-84; of counsel Holmes, Mumford, Schubel, Norlander & Macfarlane, Battle Creek, 1984—; instr. law Kellogg Community Coll., Battle Creek, 1974-79; lectr. in field. Contbr. in field. Apptd. Mich. Mental Health Adv.

Council, Lansing, 1975-77; chmn. Mich. Mental Health Research, Lansing, 1975-77; pres. Goodwill Industries/Family Services, Battle Creek, 1969-70. Served with U.S. Army, 1944-46. Recipient Mental Health Services award VA, 1981, Commendation Chief Atty. VA, 1984; Snyder-Kok award Mental Health Assn. for Mich., 1983. Mem. ABA, Mich. Bar Assn. (chmn. probate and estate planning council), Calhoun County Bar Assn. (pres. 1963-64), Mich. Assn. Probate Judges. Republican. Roman Catholic. Club: Exchange (pres. 1973-74) (Battle Creek). Lodges: K.C. (4 degree). Probate. Home: 251 Martha Dr Battle Creek MI 49015 Office: Holmes Mumford Schubel et al 66-68 E Michigan Mall Battle Creek MI 49017

SCHOEMANN, RUDOLPH ROBERT, lawyer; b. Chgo., Nov. 2, 1930; s. Rudolph and Anna Elise (Claus) S.; m. Florence Margaret Olivier, May 17, 1952 (div.); children—Peggy Ann Schoemann Salathe, Rudolph Robert III, Richard Randolph (dec.), Rodney Ryan; m. Marie Louise Gandolfo Webb, Dec. 2, 1983. Student, Wabash Coll., Crawfordsville, Ind., 1946-47; B.C.S., Loyola U. of South, New Orleans, 1959, J.D., 1952; B.A., Tulane U., 1966, LL.M. in Admiralty Law, 1981; postgrad. U. New Orleans, 1981-82. Bar: La. 1952, U.S. Supreme Ct. 1959, U.S. Ct. Appeals (5th cir.) 1952, U.S. Ct. Appeals (11th cir.) 1981, U.S. Ct. Appeals (D.C. cir.) 1982, U.S. Dist. Ct. Md. 1957, U.S. Dist. Ct. (ea. dist.) La. 1952, U.S. Dist. Ct. (we. dist.) La. 1960, U.S. Dist. Ct. (mid. dist.) La. 1952, U.S. Ct. Mil. Appeals, 1953, U.S. Ct. Customs and Patent Appeals 1953, U.S. Ct. Claims 1953. Assoc. James J. Morrison, New Orleans, 1952-54; ptnr. Smith & Schoemann, New Orleans, 1955-60, Schoemann & Gomes, 1961-63, Schoemann, Gomes, Ducote & Collins, 1963-67, Schoemann, Gomes & Ducote, 1968-74, Rudolph R. Schoemann, 1974-77, Schoemann & Golden, 1978-79, Schoemann, Swaim, Morrison & Cockfield, 1979-80, Schoemann & Assocs., 1980—(all New Orleans). Served with La. N.G., 1949-52, to 1st lt. JAGC, U.S. Army, 1952-53; capt. Res. ret. Mem. ABA, La. Bar Assn., New Orleans Bar Assn., La. Def. Assn., New Orleans Def. Assn., Def. Research Inst., Soc. Naval Architects and Marine Engrs., Fed. Bar Assn. Republican. Lutheran. Insurance, Admiralty, Personal injury. Address: 3670 Gentilly Blvd New Orleans LA 70122

SCHOEN, PAUL GERALD, lawyer; b. St. Louis, June 30, 1945; s. Sidney R. and Marian (Krout) S.; m. Janice Sirles, June 11, 1967 (div. Jan. 1984); 1 child, Suzanne K.; m. Bobbie S. Winner, May 25, 1985. B.S., So. Ill. U., 1967; J.D., U. Ill., 1970. Bar: Ill. 1970, U.S. Dist. Ct. (ea. dist.) Ill. 1970, U.S. Supreme Ct. 1980, U.S. Ct. Appeals (7th cir.) 1982. Assoc., Medlin, Zimmer & South, Carbondale, Ill., 1970-71, Don Mitchell Law Office, Carbondale, 1971-77; ptnr. Feirich, Schoen, Mager & Green (formerly Feirich, Schoen, Mager, Green & Assocs.), Carbondale, 1977—; dir. Mid Am. Bank & Trust Co. of Carbondale. Co-author: Legal Publication, Ch. 9, Pleadings Illinois Civil Practice Before Trial, 1978. Mem. bd. commrs. So. Ill. Airport Authority, Carbondale, 1971-80, chmn. 1972-73; chmn. Jackson County chpt. ARC, Carbondale, 1979. Mem. ABA, Ill. State Bar Assn., Jackson County Bar Assn., So. Ill. U. Alumni Assn. (pres. 1975). Jewish. Office: Feirich Schoen Mager Green & Assocs 2001 W Main St Carbondale IL 62901

SCHOEN, STEVAN JAY, lawyer; b. N.Y.C., May 19, 1944; s. Al and Ann (Spevack) S.; m. Noelle L'Hommedieu, Sept. 2, 1972. B.S., U. Pa., 1966; J.D., Cornell U., 1969; M.Phil. in Internat. Law, Cambridge U. (Eng.), 1979. Bar: N.Mex. 1970, N.Y. 1970, U.S. Dist. Ct. N.Mex. 1973, U.S. Ct. Appeals (10th cir.) 1973, U.S. Supreme Ct. 1976, U.S. Tax Ct. 1973, U.S. Ct. Internat. Trade 1982. Atty., Brennan, Schoen & Eisenstadt, Albuquerque, 1976—; nat. dir. Vista law recruitment U.S. OEO and Gen. Electric Co., Washington, 1970-71; atty. U.S. OEO, Albuquerque, 1971-73; chief atty. N.Mex. Dept. Health and Social Services, Albuquerque, 1975-76. Bd. dirs. Sandoval County Human Services (N.Mex.), 1983—; bd. dirs., v.p. Placitas Vol. Fire Dept., 1975—; mem. Albuquerque Com. on Fgn. Relations, 1982—. Recipient cert. of Appreciation, N.Mex. Supreme Ct., 1982, N.Mex. Sec. of State, 1980, U.S. OEO, 1971; European Ct. Justice grantee, 1979; Gerald Bailey Found. awardee, 1979. Mem. State Bar N.Mex., State Bar N.Y., Oxford-Cambridge Soc. N.Mex. (sec.). Club: Oxford-Cambridge. Private international, Probate, General corporate. Home: Star Route Box 327 Placitas NM 87043 Office: 4316 Carlisle NE Albuquerque NM 87107

SCHOENBAECHLER, EDWARD LEWIS, lawyer; b. Louisville, May 9, 1951; m. Mary Ellen Schoenbaechler, July 28, 1973; children: Kerry, Katie, Danny, Timmy. Student, U. Detroit, 1969-71; BA, Bellarmine Coll., 1973; JD, U. Louisville, 1976. Bar: Ky. 1976, U.S. Dist. Ct. (we. dist.) Ky. 1976, U.S. Ct. Appeals (6th cir.) 1979. Asst. county atty. Jefferson County, Ky., 1976-81; assoc. Goldberg & Simpson, Louisville, 1981—. Mem. ABA (forum com. health law, litigation sect.), Ky. Bar Assn., Louisville Bar Assn. Democrat. Roman Catholic. Avocation: music. Health, Probate, State civil litigation. Home: 18 Eastover Ct Louisville KY 40206-2705 Office: Goldberg & Simpson 2800 First Nat Tower Louisville KY 40202

SCHOENBLUM, JEFFREY A., law educator; b. 1948. AB, John Hopkins U., 1970; JD, Harvard U., 1973. Law clk. to presiding justice U.S. Ct. Appeals (2d cir.), N.Y.C., 1973-74; assoc. Wilkie, Farr & Gallagher, N.Y.C., 1974-77; asst. prof. Vanderbilt U., Nashville, 1977-80, assoc. prof., 1980-83, prof., 1983—. Office: Vanderbilt U Sch Law Nashville TN 37240 *

SCHOENECK, CHARLES A., JR., lawyer; b. Syracuse, N.Y., Feb. 3, 1912; s. Charles A. and Louise E. (Kappesser) S.; m. Elizabeth Ellen Brandt, Oct. 11, 1946; children—Charles A., Elisabeth S. A.B., Syracuse U., 1933; LL.B., Harvard U., 1936. Bar: N.Y. 1936, U.S. Dist. Ct. (no. dist.) N.Y. 1953. Assoc. Bond Schoeneck & King, Syracuse, N.Y., 1936-41, mem., 1941-42, ptnr., 1946—; mem. N.Y. Assembly, Albany, 1955-60, majority leader, 1959-60. N.Y. State Republican chmn., 1967-69; del. Nat. Rep. Conv., 1968, chmn. N.Y. del., mem. electoral coll., 1972. Served to capt. U.S. Army, 1942-46. Decorated Bronze Star; recipient Alumni award Syracuse U., 1982. Fellow Am. Bar Found.; mem. Onondaga County Bar Assn., ABA, Sigma Alpha Epsilon. Episcopalian. Clubs: Century, Onondaga Golf and Country, Bellevue Country. Administrative and regulatory, General practice, Legislative. Office: Bond Schoeneck & King 1 Lincoln Center Syracuse NY 13202

SCHOENER, GEORGE FRANCIS, JR., lawyer; b. Phila., Oct. 17, 1954; s. George Francis Sr. and Irene Louise (Nocito) S.; m. Patrice Irene Cipressi, Nov. 24, 1984. BS, Rensselaer Poly. Inst., 1975; JD, Villanova U., 1978. Bar: Pa. 1978, U.S. Dist. Ct. (ea. dist.) Pa. 1978, U.S. Ct. Appeals (3d cir.) 1983. Assoc. Kessler & Sorin, Phila., 1978-81; ptnr. M. Mark Mendel Ltd., Phila., 1981—. Mem. ABA, Pa. Bar Assn., Phila. Bar Assn. (medico-legal and state civil jud. procedures coms. 1978—), Pa. Trial Lawyers Assn., Phila. Trial Lawyers Assn., Fed. Bar Assn., Justinian Soc. Lodge: KC. Avocation: long distance running. Personal injury, State civil litigation, Criminal. Home: 6116 N Fairhill St Philadelphia PA 19120 Office: M Mark Mendel Ltd 1620 Locust St Philadelphia PA 19103

SCHOENEWOLF, WALTER WAYNE, lawyer; b. Newark, July 10, 1941; s. Louis Daniel and Alice Marion (Hildebrand) S.; m. Martha Jane, June 6, 1964; children—Barbara Jane, W. Scott, Brenda J. B.A., Colgate U., 1963; J.D., Rutgers U., 1966. Bar: N.J. 1967, U.S. Dist. Ct. N.J., 1967, U.S. Supreme Ct. 1972. Assoc. Porzio, Bromberg & Newman, Morristown, N.J., 1967-68, Haines, Schman & Butz, Toms River, N.J., 1968-71; asst. prosecutor Ocean County, N.J., 1971-73; sole practice Brick, N.J., 1971-79, 86—; ptnr. Schoenewolf & Cunningham, Brick, N.J., 1979-85; prosecutor Brick Twp., 1971-78; atty. Brick Twp. Planning Bd., 1976-80, Lakehurst (N.J.) Planning Bd., 1971—. Served to 1st lt. USAFR, 1966-73. Mem. ABA, N.J. Bar Assn., N.J. Inst. Mcpl. Attys., Ocean County Bar Assn. Presbyterian. General practice, Probate, Family and matrimonial. Home: 402 Brighton Ave Spring Lake NJ 07762 Office: 263 Drum Point Rd Brick NJ 08723

SCHOENFELD, BARBARA BRAUN, lawyer; b. Phila., Apr. 17, 1953; d. Irving Leon Braun and Virginia (Parker) Sand; m. Larry Jay Schoenfeld, June 29, 1975; children: Alexander, Gordon. BA cum laude, U. Pa., 1974, M in City Planning, Social Work, 1977; JD, Boston U., 1982. Bar: R.I. 1982, U.S. Dist. Ct. R.I. 1982. Assoc. planner Del. Valley Hosp. Council, Phila., 1978-79; assoc. Tillinghast, Collins & Graham, Providence, 1980, 81, Edwards & Angell, Providence, 1982-86, Ropes & Gray, Providence, 1986—. Chmn., bd. dirs. Com. Women's Health Concerns, Phila., 1978-79; bd. dirs. Jewish Family Service, Providence, 1982—; co-chmn. admissions com. U. Pa. Alumni Club, Providence, 1982—. Mem. ABA, R.I. Bar Assn., Nat. Women's Health Network, Am. Pub. Health Assn. (steering com., womens caucus). Democrat. Jewish. Club: Ledgemont Country Club (Seekonk, Mass.). Avocations: skiing, travel, french. Banking, General corporate, Health. Office: Ropes & Gray 30 Kennedy Plaza Providence RI 02903

SCHOENFIELD, RICK MERRILL, lawyer; b. Chgo., July 21, 1951; s. Herbert and Bernice (Krichilsky) S. B.A., Northwestern U., 1973, J.D. cum laude, 1976; cert. Nat. Inst. Trial Advocacy, Chgo., 1979. Bar: Ill. 1976, U.S. Dist. Ct. (no. dist.) Ill. 1977, U.S. Ct. Appeals (7th cir.) 1979, U.S. Ct. Appeals (4th cir.) 1984, U.S. Supreme Ct. 1984. Assoc. Ettinger & Lake, Chgo., 1976-79, Ettinger & Assocs., Ltd., Chgo., 1979-81; ptnr. Ettinger & Schoenfield, Ltd., Chgo., 1981—; instr. De Paul Law Sch., Chgo., 1977-78. Recipient Award for Pro Bono Litigation, Operation Lakewatch, Chgo., 1983. Mem. Assn. Trial Lawyers of Am., Ill. Trial Lawyers Assn., Bus. and Profl. People for the Pub. Interest, Am. Jewish Congress, Nat. Resources Def. Council, Sierra Club. Personal injury, Civil rights, Criminal. Office: Ettinger & Schoenfield Ltd 180 N LaSalle Suite 1020 Chicago IL 60601

SCHOENI, KENNETH ROGER, lawyer; b. Alliance, Ohio, July 17, 1955; s. Kenneth Delmar and Rita Mae (Edgerton) S.; m. Marcia Dianne White, Aug. 20, 1977; children: John Kenneth, Lindsay Elisabeth. Student, Heidelberg Coll., 1973-74; BS, Bowling Green State U., 1977; JD, U. Minn., 1982. Bar: Minn. 1982, U.S. Dist. Ct. Minn. 1982, U.S. Ct. Appeals (8th cir.) 1982, Ohio 1983, U.S. Dist. Ct. (so. dist.) Ohio 1985, U.S. Ct. Appeals (6th cir.) 1985. Assoc. Gill & Brinkman, St. Paul, 1982-84; atty. litigation Minn. Mut. Lfe Ins. Co., St. Paul, 1984; assoc. Kohnen & Kohnen, Cin., 1985—. Mem. ABA, Ohio Bar Assn., Cin. Bar Assn., Assn. Reps. Profl. Athletes. Republican. Methodist. Avocations: golf, softball. Personal injury, Insurance, Sports law. Home: 7412 Euclid Ave Cincinnati OH 45243 Office: Kohnen & Kohnen 441 Vine St 1400 Carew Tower Cincinnati OH 45202

SCHOLES, MYRON S., law and finance educator; b. 1941. BA, McMaster U., 1962, MBA, 1964; PhD, U. Chgo., 1969. Instr. U. Chgo. Bus. Sch., 1967-68; assoc. prof. U. Chgo., 1974-75, prof., 1976-83; asst. prof. MIT Mgmt. Sch., Cambridge, 1968-72, assoc. prof., 1972-73; prof. Stanford (Calif.) U., 1983—. Office: Stanford U Grad Sch of Bus Stanford CA 94305 *

SCHOLLENBERGER, DAVID KENNON, lawyer; b. Akron, Ohio, Sept. 14, 1955; s. Charles Sundy and Rosanne (Kennon) S.; m. Mel Ann Robinson, Aug. 8, 1981. BA, Colo. Coll., 1977; MBA, JD, U. Denver, 1982. Bar: Colo. 1982. Assoc. Holiday Inns, Inc., London, 1982-83, Memphis, 1983-84; assoc. NCR Corp., Dayton, Ohio, 1984—. Contbr. articles to profl. jours. Alpert scholar Alpert Found., Denver, 1981-82; U. Denver Coll. Bus. scholar, 1979-82. Avocations: tennis, squash, jogging, skiing. Private international. Home: 78 E Dixon Ave Oakwood OH 45419 Office: NCR Corp Law Dept 1700 S Patterson Blvd Dayton OH 45419

SCHONBERGER, ARNE CARL, lawyer; b. Tamaqua, Pa., Dec. 23, 1949; s. Joseph M. and Dorothy Schonberger; m. Olivia Chavez, Feb. 19, 1984; 1 child, Lyle. BBA, U. Tex., El Paso, 1971; JD, Tex. Tech U., 1974. Bar: Tex. 1974, U.S. Dist. Ct. (we. dist.) Tex. 1974. Atty. State of Tex., El Paso, 1974-76; sole practice El Paso, 1976—. Mem. adv. com. to City Bldg. Inspector, El Paso, 1986—; pres. bd. dirs. Jewish Family Service, El Paso, 1984-86; bd. dirs., v.p. West Tex. Assn. for Handicapped, El Paso, 1983—; bd. dirs. Am. Council of The Blind for Tex., El Paso, 1984-86. Mem. Tex. Bar Assn. (family law sect.). Democrat. Family and matrimonial, Personal injury. Office: 521 Texas El Paso TX 79901

SCHOONOVER, RANDALL CHARLES, lawyer; b. Canton, Ill., Apr. 12, 1951; s. Albert Charles and Narka Leona (Gardner) S. BB in Acctg., Western Ill. U., 1973; JD, John Marshall Law Sch., 1978. Bar: Colo. 1978, U.S. Dist. Ct. Colo. 1978, U.S. Ct. Appeals (10th cir.) 1979; CPA, Ill., Colo.; lic. real estate broker, Colo. Acct. Clifton, Gunderson & Co., Springfield, Ill., 1973-75; assoc. Tilly & Graves, Denver, 1978-82, Burns, Wall, Smith & Mueller, Denver, 1982-83; in-house counsel Tele-Communications, Inc., Denver, 1983-85; mng. atty. legal dept. Western Tele-Communications, Inc., Denver, 1985—. Mem. Ill. Big Brother Program, Springfield, 1973-75, Colo. Big Brother Program, Denver, 1983-84; vol. Colo. Spl. Olympics, Denver, 1980—. Named one of Outstanding Young Men Am., 1985. Mem. ABA, Colo. Bar Assn., Denver Bar Assn., Springfield Jaycees. Baptist. Avocations: flying, music, woodworking, outdoor sports. General corporate, Real property, Securities. Home: 710 Grape St Denver CO 80220 Office: Western Telecommunications Inc 5690 DTC Blvd #500 Englewood CO 80111

SCHOR, EDWARD NEIL, lawyer; b. N.Y.C., Aug. 22, 1947; s. Irving S. and Aida Libby (Neiman) S.; m. Abby Zukerman, Apr. 11, 1976; children: Katharine, Emily. BA, Franklin & Marshall Coll., 1969; JD, NYU, 1972. Bar: N.Y. 1973. Atty. U.S. Dept. HEW, Washington, 1973-74, ABC, Inc., N.Y.C., 1974-76; counsel Meredith Corp., N.Y.C., 1976-81; counsel broadcasting Viacom Internat. Inc., N.Y.C., 1981—. Broadcasting and cable. Office: Viacom Internat Inc 1211 Ave of the Americas New York NY 10036

SCHORLING, WILLIAM HARRISON, lawyer; b. Ann Arbor, Mich., Jan. 7, 1949; s. Otis William Schorling and Ruthann (Bales) Schorling Moorehead; m. Lynne Ann Newcomb, June 1, 1974; children—Katherine Pearce, Ann Oury, John Roberts. B.A. cum laude, Denison U., 1971; J.D. cum laude, U. Mich., 1975. Bar: Pa. 1975, U.S. Ct. Appeals (3d cir.) 1977. Ptnr. Eckert, Seamans, Cherin & Mellott, Pitts., 1984—; lectr. Pa. Bar Inst., Harrisburg, 1983—, Pa. Bar Assn., Harrisburg, 1983—, Comml. Law League, N.Y.C., 1984—. Contbr. articles to profl. jours. Active Golden Triangle YMCA Bd. Mgmt., Pitts., 1985—, Profl. Edn. Systems, Inc., Eau Claire, Wis. Mem. ABA (bus. bankruptcy com., chmn. bus. lawyer task force), Pa. Bar Assn., Allegheny County Bar Assn. (mem. govtl. council bankruptcy sect., chmn. local bankruptcy rules subcom., mem. ethics com.). Presbyterian. Club: Longue Vue (Verona, Pa.). Bankruptcy, Contracts commercial. Home: 7525 Tuscarora St Pittsburgh PA 15208 Office: Eckert Seamans Cherin & Mellott 600 Grant St 42d Floor Pittsburgh PA 15219

SCHORNER, JAMES ALAN, lawyer, accountant; b. Plainfield, N.J., Aug. 21, 1951; s. Alfred W. and Jeanne B. (Bamford) S.; m. Judith A. Earlywine, Sept. 1, 1984. BA, Westminster Coll., 1973; JD, U. Pitts., 1979. Bar: Pa. 1979, Fla. 1980, U.S. Tax Ct. 1983. Acct. Touche Ross and Co., Miami, Fla., 1973-82; sole practice Vero Beach, Fla., 1982—. Mem. ABA, Fla. Bar Assn., Fla. Inst. CPA's. Avocations: weight lifting, bridge. Personal income taxation, Probate, Estate taxation. Office: PO Box 3838 Vero Beach FL 32964-3841

SCHORR, KENNETH L., lawyer, legal association administrator; b. Hazleton, Pa., Feb. 28, 1952; s. Alvin L. and Ann (Girson) S. Student, NYU, 1972; BA, Brandeis U., 1973; JD, U. Mich., 1975; postgrad. in law, George Wash. U., 1974; postgrad. in bus., So. Meth. U., 1985-86. Bar: Va. 1975, Ark. 1976, Ariz. 1980, D.C. 1980, Tex. 1983, U.S. Dist. Ct. (ea. dist.) Va., U.S. Dist. Ct. (ea. and we. dists.) Ark., U.S. Dist. Ct. (no. dist.) Tex., U.S. Dist. Ct. (we. dist.) Pa., U.S. Dist. Ct. (we. dist.) La., Colo., Ariz., U.S. Ct. Appeals (5th, 8th, 9th cirs.), U.S. Supreme Ct. Atty. Schorr & Bachmann P.A., Little Rock, 1975-77, Youngdahl & Larrison, Little Rock, 1977-79; litigation dir. Community Legal Services, Phoenix, 1979-83; exec. dir. North Cen. Tex. Legal Services Found., Inc., Dallas, 1983—; adj. prof. So. Meth. U. Law Sch., Dallas, 1985—; mem. Tex. Bd. Optometry, Austin, 1986—; bd. dirs. Tex. Legal Services Ctr., Austin; vice-chmn. Dallas Bar Assn. Ethics Com., 1986. Contbr. articles to legal manuals. Fellow Tex. Bar Found., Murphy Ctr. for Codification of Human and Organizational Law; mem. ABA, Tex. Bar Assn., Ariz. Bar Assn., Ark. Bar Assn., Va. Bar Assn., D.C. Bar Assn., Nat. Lawyers Guild. Democrat. Jewish. Civil rights, Labor. Office: North Cen Tex Legal Services Found Inc 3108 Live Oak Dallas TX 75204

SCHOUMACHER, BRUCE HERBERT, lawyer; b. Chgo., May 23, 1940; s. Herbert Edward and Mildred Helen (Wagner) S.; m. Alicia Wesley Sanchez, Nov. 4, 1967; children: Liana Cristina, Janina Maria. BS, Northwestern U., 1961; MBA, U. Chgo., 1963, JD, 1966. Bar: Nebr. 1966, U.S. Dist. Ct. Nebr. 1966, Ill. 1971, U.S. Ct. Appeals (7th cir.) 1979, U.S. Dist. Ct. (no. dist.) Ill. 1982, U.S. Supreme Ct. 1982, U.S. Claims Ct. 1986. Assoc. Luebs, Tracy & Huebner, Grand Island, Nebr., 1966-67; assoc. McDermott, Will & Emery, Chgo., 1971-76, ptnr., 1976—; instr. bus. adminstrn. Bellevue Coll., Nebr., 1967-70; lectr. U. Md., Overseas Prodram, 1970. Author: Engineers and the Law: an Overview, 1986; contbg. author: Construction Law; contbr. articles to profl. jours. Served to capt. USAF, 1967-71, Vietnam. Decorated Bronze Star, 1971. Mem. ABA, Nebr. Bar Assn., Ill. Bar Assn. (sec. membership and bar activities com. 1986-87, council ins. law sect. 1986—), Chgo. Bar Assn. (chmn. fed. civil procedure com. 1982-83), Def. Research Inst., Ill. Assn. Def. Trial Counsel, Chgo. Bldg. Congress (bd. dirs. 1985—), The Legal Club, The Law Club, Pi Kappa Alpha, Phi Delta Phi. Republican. Methodist. Club: Tower (Chgo). State civil litigation, Federal civil litigation, Construction. Office: McDermott Will & Emery 111 W Monroe St Chicago IL 60603

SCHOUWEILER, BART MCCLAIN, lawyer; b. Wnedell, Idaho, Aug. 11, 1934; s. Leroy and Dora Lucille (Murphy) S.; m. LaVonne Douthit, Jan. 30, 1981. AA, Menlo Coll., 1954; BA, Stanford U., 1956; LLB, Georgetown U., 1959. Bar: Nev. 1959, U.S. Dist. Ct. Nev. 1959, U.S. Ct. Appeals (9th cir.) 1969. Asst. atty. City of Reno, 1963-64; U.S. atty. U.S. Dept. Justice, Las Vegas, Nev., 1969-72; sole practice Reno, 1972—. Pres. Reno Young Reps., 1965. Served to capt. JAGC, USAF, 1960-63. Mem. ABA, Washoe County Bar Assn. Republican. Episcopalian. Probate, Estate planning, General corporate. Office: 1 E 1st St Suite 904 Reno NV 89501

SCHOYER, DAVID KENNEDY, lawyer, bank executive; b. Pitts., Oct. 21, 1946; s. Edward Holyoke and Elizabeth (Foster) S.; m. Nancy Larson, Feb. 1, 1969 (div. Sept. 30, 1977; children: William Sill, Elizabeth Wadsworth; m. Linda Walker, Sept. 6, 1981; 1 child, Claire Pomeroy. BA, Harvard U., 1966; cert. Theological Studies, Pacific Sch. Religion, 1973; MA, Western Ky. U., 1970; JD, U. Denver, 1975. Bar: Colo. 1975, U.S. Dist. Ct. Colo. 1979, Pa. 1981, U.S. Dist. Ct. (we. dist.) Pa. 1981. Sole practice Denver, 1975-81; law clk. to presiding justice U.S. Bankruptcy Ct., Pitts., 1981-82; house counsel, corp. sec. Landmark Savings Assn., Pitts., 1982—. Mem. ABA, Pa. Bar Assn., Allegheny County Bar Assn., Am. Corp. Counsel Assn. Clubs: H-Y-P, Pitts. Golf. Banking, General corporate. Home: 7425 Richland Ave Pittsburgh PA 15208 Office: Landmark Savings Assn 335 Fifth Ave Pittsburgh PA 15222

SCHRADER, ALFRED EUGENE, lawyer; b. Akron, Ohio, Nov. 1, 1953; s. Louis Clement and Helen Maye (Eberz) S.; m. Cathy Diane Fincher, Apr. 17, 1982; children—Eric Brian, Angela Diane. B.A. in Polit. Sci. magna cum laude, Kent State U., 1975; J.D., Ohio State U., 1978. Bar: Ohio 1978, U.S. Dist. Ct. (no. dist.) Ohio 1978, U.S. Ct. Appeals (6th cir.) 1985, U.S. Supreme Ct. 1985. Dep. clk. Summit County Clk. of Cts., Akron, 1972-74; sole practice, Akron, 1978—; spl. counsel Bath Twp., Ohio, 1980—; law dir. Northampton Twp., Ohio, 1983-86, Franklin Twp., Ohio, 1984—, Twinsburg Twp., Ohio, 1981—; spl. counsel Richfield Twp., Ohio, 1983-85; consulting counsel law dept. City of Cuyanoga Falls, 1986; spl. annexation counsel Bath, Perry and Shawnee Twps., Allen County, Ohio, 1986—; spl. counsel Carlisle Twp., Lorain County, 1986-87; spl. annexation counsel Brimfield Twp., Portage County, 1986—. Trustee Springfield Twp., Ohio, 1973—, pres., 1975, 79, 82; mem. adv. com. Community Devel. Block, Summit County, 1985—, Summit County Annexation Com., Ohio, 1981-85; mem. Summit County Jail Study Commn., 1983, 84; mem. adv. bd. Springfield Schs., 1975. Mem. Akron Bar Assn. (v.p. legis. com. 1981-82), Ohio Acad. Trial Lawyers, Assn. Trial Lawyers Am., Ohio Bar Assn., Summit County Twp. assn. (exec. com. 1983—), Ohio Twp. Assn. (exec. com. 1983—). Democrat. Roman Catholic. Local government, Personal injury, General practice. Home: 3344 Brunk Rd Akron OH 44312 Office: Dalessio Shapiro Manes et al 441 Wolf Ledges Pkwy Suite 400 Akron OH 44311-1054

SCHRADER, CHARLES RAYMOND, lawyer; b. Portland, Oreg., Feb. 18, 1947; s. Raymond Augustus and Pauline Louise (Poulsen) S.; m. Mary Louise Sievers, Aug. 12, 1970; children: Tiffany Louise, Elizabeth Brooke. BCE, Stanford U., 1969, MCE in Constrn. Mgmt., 1970; JD, U. Oreg., 1977. Bar: Oreg. 1977, Wash. 1978, U.S. Dist. Ct. (we. dist.) Wash. 1978, U.S. Ct. Claims 1981, U.S. Supreme Ct. 1985. Constrn. engr., mgr. Procter & Gamble Co., U.S. and Can., 1970-74; gen. counsel, gen. mgr. Wildish Group Cos., Eugene, Oreg., 1978-83; assoc. Harrang, Swanson, Long & Watkinson, P.C., Eugene, 1983-85; mng. ptnr. Allen, Kilmer, Schrader, Yazbeck & Chenoweth, P.C., Portland and Eugene, 1985—. Author: Construction Law: Changes, Claims and Negotiations, 1979, Avoidance and Defense of Construction Claims, 1984, Oregon Construction Lien and Bond Claim Handbook, 1986; (column) Pacific Builder and Engineer, 1983—; contbr. articles to profl. jours. V.p., bd. dirs. Oreg. State U. Constrn. Edn. Found., Corvallis, 1983—. Mem. ASCE (editor newsletter), Associated Gen. Contractors Am. (bd. dirs., exec. com. Oreg.-Columbia chpt. 1983—, contract documents coordinating com.). Clubs: Eugene Country, Town, Downtown Athletic (Eugene). Avocation: tennis. Construction, General corporate. Office: Allen Kilmer Schrader Yazbeck & Chenoweth PC 1001 SW 5th Ave Suite 1600 Portland OR 97204

SCHRAFF, PAUL ALBERT, lawyer; b. Cleve., July 2, 1949; s. Albert G. and Patricia M. (McCarty) S.; m. Deborah L. DuVall, June 17, 1978; children: Christopher L., Devin P. BS in Computer Sci., U. Dayton, 1971; MBA, Cleve. State U., 1973, JD summa cum laude, 1977. Bar: Ohio 1977, U.S. Dist. Ct. (no. dist.) Ohio 1978, Fla. 1978, Hawaii 1981, U.S. Dist. Ct. Hawaii 1981, U.S. Ct. Appeals (9th cir.) 1985. Assoc. Ford, Whitney, Crump & Schulz, Cleve., 1977-81, Carlsmith & Dwyer, Honolulu, 1981-83; cons. Coopers & Lybrand, Honolulu, 1983-84; assoc. Dwyer, Imanaka, Neeley & Peterson, Honolulu, 1985—, dir., 1987—. Mem. ABA, Hawaii Bar Assn., Fla. Bar Assn., Data Processing Mgmt. Assn. (legis. liaison 1985—), Am. Arbitration Assn. Federal civil litigation, State civil litigation, Computer. Office: Dwyer Imanaka Neeley & Peterson 900 Fort St Mall Suite 1800 Honolulu HI 96813

SCHRAM, STEVEN H., lawyer; b. Teaneck, N.J., Feb. 3, 1953; s. Louis and Lucy (Jedlinsky) S.; m. Suzanne J. Weiss, June 20, 1976 (div. Dec. 1983); m. Marla Anne Glickfield, Nov. 26, 1984; 1 child, Lauren Jamie. BS in Econs. magna cum laude, U. Pa., 1975; JD cum laude, Georgetown U., 1978. Bar: D.C. 1978, U.S. Tax Ct. 1978. Assoc. Danzansky & Dickey, Washington, 1978-84; ptnr. Finley, Kumble, Wagner, Heine, Underberg, Manley, Myerson & Casey, Washington, 1984—. Mem. ABA (tax sect.). Jewish. Club: Woodmont (Rockville, Md.). Avocations: golf, tennis, skiing. Personal income taxation, Contracts commercial, Corporate taxation. Home: 7831 Whiterim Terr Potomac MD 20854 Office: Finley Kumble Wagner Heine et al 1120 Connecticut Ave NW Washington DC 20036

SCHRAMM, BERNARD HALL, lawyer, packaging co. exec.; b. Richwood, W.Va., June 21, 1932; s. Bartley and Lenore Arlene (Simmons) S.; m. Barbara Ann Baer, July 11, 1955; children—Elizabeth Dawn, Robert Bartley Schramm. B.S. in Bus. Administrn., W.Va. U., 1955, LL.B., 1961. Bar: W.Va. 1961, Ohio 1974. Mem. law dept. Monongahela Power Co., Fairmont, W.Va., 1961-66, Top Value Enterprises Inc. Dayton, Ohio, 1966-74, Mead Corp., Dayton, 1974-77; sec., gen. counsel Green Bay (Wis.) Packaging Inc. 1977—; instr. bus. law Miami Jacobs Jr. Coll. Dayton. Bd. dirs. Green Bay Symphony; bd. dirs. Nat. R.R. Museum, Bay Lakes council Boy Scouts Am. Served to 1st lt. U.S. Army, 1955-58. Mem. Green Bay C. of C., ABA, W.Va. Bar Assn., Ohio State Bar Assn., Brown County Bar Assn., Wis. Paper Council (chmn. govt. relations), Assn. Corp. Counsel Am. (bd. dirs. Wis. chpt.), U.S. C. of C. (council on antitrust policy). Antitrust, General corporate. Office: PO Box 19017 Green Bay WI 54307-9017

SCHRAMM, FREDERIC BERNARD, lawyer; b. Cleve., June 3, 1903; s. A. Bernard and Flora Frederica (Leutz) S. B.S., Case Inst. Tech., 1925; J.D., George Washington U., 1931; LL.M., Western Res. U., 1955. Bar: U.S. Patent Office 1930, D.C. 1931, Ohio 1944, N.Y. 1933, Calif. 1957. Patent atty. Gen. Electric Co., Schenectady, 1925-42; ptnr. Richey & Watts, Cleve., 1942-54, Kendrick, Schramm & Stolzy, Los Angeles, 1954-60, Schramm, Kramer & Sturges, Cleve., 1960-72, Schramm & Knowles, Cleve., 1972-80; instr. Fenn Coll., 1973-74, Cleve. Marshal Law Sch., Cleve. State U., 1974-75. Mem. ABA, Cleve. Bar Assn., Am. Patent Law Assn., Cleve. Patent Law Assn., IEEE, Sigma Xi, Eta Kappa Nu, Tau Beta Pi. Clubs: Kiwanis (Shaker Heights, Ohio); Univ., Torch (Cleve.). Author: Handbook on Patent Dis-

putes, 1974; contbr. articles to law jours. Patent, Trademark and copyright. Office: 3570 Warrensville Center Rd Suite 201 Cleveland OH 44122

SCHRAMM, MARILYN JEAN, lawyer; b. Chgo., Nov. 14, 1951; d. Robert and Dorothy (Wood) S. BA, DePaul U., 1977; MA, Northwestern U., 1981, JD, 1981. Bar: Ill. 1981, U.S. Dist. Ct. (no. dist.) Ill. 1981. Assoc. Sidley & Austin, Chgo., 1981-85; atty. Quaker Oats Co., Chgo., 1985—. Mem. ABA, Ill. Bar Assn., Chgo. Bar Assn., Women's Bar Assn. Ill., Pi Gamma Mu. Avocation: team sports. General corporate, Trademark and copyright, Antitrust. Home: 6166 N Sheridan Rd #2K Chicago IL 60660 Office: The Quaker Oats Co Merchandise Mart Plaza Chicago IL 60654

SCHRAMM, PAUL HOWARD, lawyer; b. St. Louis, Oct. 6, 1933; s. Benjamin Jacob and Frieda Sylvia (Goruch) S.; m. Susan Ann Susman, June 6, 1959; children: Scott Lyon, Dean Andrew, Thomas Edward. AB, U. Mo., 1955, JD, 1958. Bar: Mo. 1958, U.S. Dist. Ct. (ea. dist.) Mo. 1963, U.S. Ct. Appeals (8th cir.) 1967, U.S. Tax Ct. 1970, U.S. Supreme Ct. 1972. Ptnr. Schramm & Schramm, St. Louis, 1959-61, Schramm & Morganstern, St. Louis, 1970-76, Schramm, Pines & Marshall, St. Louis, 1977-79, Schramm, Newman, Pines & Freyman, St. Louis, 1979-82, Schramm, Pines & Spewak, St. Louis, 1983-85, Schramm & Pines, St. Louis, 1985—; pros. atty. City of Ellisville, Mo., 1973-77; judge Ellisville mcpl. div. St. Louis County Cir. Ct., 1977-83. Mem. Bar Assn. Met. St. Louis (exec. com. 1976-77, chmn. county sect. 1976-77), St. Louis County Bar Assn. (chmn. lawyers reference service 1971, cir. ct. jud. com. 1970), Phi Delta Phi. Club: University (St. Louis). Avocations: music, sports, reading. General civil trial and appellate practice, federal and state, General corporate, Family and matrimonial. Home: 2 Cedar Crest Ladue MO 63132 Office: Schramm & Pines 120 S Central Ave Saint Louis MO 63105

SCHRANK, RAYMOND EDWARD, II, lawyer; b. Fond du Lac, Wis., Aug. 1, 1944; s. Raymond Edward and Bertha (Schorer) S.; m. Pamela Sue Abramson, Aug. 12, 1967 (div.); children—Kenneth, Scott, Brian; m. Barbara A. Potter, 1984; children: Kristin, Curtis, Jenifer Wilson (stepdau.). BS with honors, U. Wis.-Oshkosh, 1967, JD, 1970. Bar: Wis. 1970, U.S. Dist. Ct. (ea. dist.) Wis. 1974, U.S. Dist. Ct. (we. dist.) Wis. 1970, U.S. Ct. Appeals (7th cir.) 1976; cert. civil trial advocate Nat. Bd. Trial Advocacy 1984. Asst. dist. atty. Sheboygan County (Wis.), 1970-71; Dane County Legal Services, 1971-72; ptnr. Graff & Schrank, Madison, Wis., 1972-75, Fritschler, Pellino, Schrank & Rosen, 1976—. Mem. ABA, Wis. Bar Assn., Dane County Bar Assn., Am. Trial Lawyers Assn. (chmn. People's Law Sch.), Wis. Acad. Trial Lawyers (dir. 1982—). Lutheran. Contbr. articles to law jours. Federal civil litigation, State civil litigation, Personal injury. Office: Fritschler Pellino Schrank & Rosen 131 W Wilson St Suite 601 Madison WI 53703

SCHRECK, ROBERT A., JR., lawyer; b. Buffalo, July 22, 1952; s. Robert A. and Dorothy M. Schreck. BS in Bus. Adminstrn., Georgetown U., 1974; MBA, Northwestern U., 1975, JD, 1978. Bar: Ill. 1978. Ptnr. McDermott, Will & Emery, Chgo., 1978—. Mem. ABA, Chgo. Bar Assn. Clubs: Monroe (Chgo.). Securities, Contracts commercial, General corporate. Office: McDermott Will & Emery 111 W Monroe St Chicago IL 60603

SCHRECKENGAST, WILLIAM O., lawyer; b. Greenwood, Ind., Oct. 14, 1926; s. Vernon Edward and Marthena O. (Mullinex) S.; m. Helen Margaret Sheppard, Nov. 11, 1949; children: Pamela, Sandra, James, John. LLB, Ind. U., 1956. Ptnr. Kitley, Pontius & Schreckengast, Beech Grove, Ind., 1957-59, Kitley & Schreckengast, Beech Grove, 1959-63, 78-82, Kitley, Schreckengast & Davis, Beech Grove, 1963-78, Schreckengast & Lovern, Indpls., 1982—. Chmn. Ind. campaign John Walsh for Sec. of State, Indls., 1958; chmn. ward Beech Grove Dems., 1958-60. Served to 1st sgt. U.S. Army, 1944-46, PTO. Mem. ABA, Ind. Bar Assn. (bd. mgrs. 1973-74, pres. citation 1974, pres. trial lawyer sect. 1977-78), Am. Judicature Soc., Nat. Inst. Trial Advocacy (teaching faculty 1980-85), Platform Soc. Republican. Club: Hillview Country (Franklin, Ind.). Lodge: Masons. Avocations: golf, flying. State civil litigation, Insurance, Personal injury. Home: 3780 Fairview Rd Greenwood IN 46142 Office: Schreckengast & Lovern 7743 S Meridian Indianapolis IN 46217

SCHREIBER, ALAN HICKMAN, lawyer; b. Muncie, Ind., Apr. 4, 1944; s. Ephriam and Clarrisa (Hickman) S.; m. Phyllis Jean Chamberlain, Dec. 22, 1972; children—Jennifer Aline, Brett Justin. Student DePauw U., 1962-64; B.S. in Bus., Ind. U., 1966, J.D., 1969. Bar: Fla. 1971, U.S. Dist. Ct. (so. dist.) Fla. Asst., State Atty.'s Office, Ft. Lauderdale, Fla., 1971-76; pub. defender 17th Jud. Circuit, Ft. Lauderdale, 1976—; cons. Fla. Bar News on Criminal Law, 1982; lobbyist for indigent funding, Fla., 1980—. Contbr. articles to profl. jours. Mem. Democratic Exec. Com., Ft. Lauderdale, 1980; mem. Plantation Democratic Club, 1983; campaign chmn. Goldstein for Atty. Gen. Fla., 1982. Named Young Dem. of Yr., Broward County Young Dems., 1980; Man of Yr., Jewish War Vets., 1982. Mem. Fla. Bar Assn., Broward County Bar Assn., ABA, Nat. Legal Aid Defenders Assn., Phi Alpha Delta. Criminal. Home: 885 Orchid Dr Plantation FL 33317 Office: Broward County Adminstrn County Govt Ctr 115 S Andrews Ave Fort Lauderdale FL 33301

SCHREIBER, ELIOT BRUCE, lawyer; b. N.Y.C., May 6, 1956; s. Sidney Peter and Hazel Ellen (Sukoff) S.; m. Jayne Cross, May 19, 1985. BA magna cum laude, Brown U., 1978; JD, Northwestern U., 1981. Bar: Ill. 1981, U.S. Dist. Ct. (no. dist.) Ill. 1981. Assoc. Sonnenschein et al., Chgo., 1981-83; v.p., chief operating officer, gen. counsel Internat. Beverages Inc., Ogden, Utah, 1983—. Contbr. articles to N.Y. newspapers. Mem. ABA, Ill. State Bar Assn., Chgo. Bar Assn., Phi Beta Kappa. Avocations: music, squash, travel. General corporate, Private international.

SCHREIBER, JAMES PHILLIP, lawyer; b. Cleve., Jan. 7, 1942; s. Harry H. and Toby G. (Sigman) S.; m. Marilyn E. Phillips, Nov. 29, 1981; children: Sarah B., Nicholas H. B.A. cum laude, UCLA, 1963; LL.B., Boalt Hall, U. Calif.-Berkeley, 1966. Bar: Calif. 1966, U.S. Dist. Ct. (cen. dist.) Calif. 1966. Dep. pub. defender Los Angeles County (Calif.), 1967-68; assoc. Zagon Schiff Hirsch & Levine, Beverly Hills, Calif., 1968-71, ptnr. Schiff Hirsch & Schreiber, 1971-80, Schreiber & Feller, 1980-86, Levine & Schreiber, 1986—. Mem. Los Angeles County Bar Assn., Calif. State Bar, Beverly Hills Bar Assn. Federal civil litigation, Family and matrimonial, Entertainment. Office: Levine & Schreiber 415 N Camden Dr Beverly Hills CA 90210

SCHREIBER, KURT GILBERT, lawyer; b. Milw., Aug. 22, 1946; s. Raymond R. and Mildred L. (Kleist) S.; m. Nelda Beth Van Buren, May 3, 1974; children—Katharine Anne, Matthew Edward. A.B. in Econs., Cornell U., 1968; J.D., U. Mich., 1971. Bar: Wis. 1971, Tex. 1979. Internat. atty. Tenneco Internat. Holdings Co., London, 1974-78; atty. Tenneco Inc., Houston, 1978-80; 2d v.p., asst. gen. counsel Am. Gen. Corp., Houston, 1980-83, v.p., gen. counsel, 1983-84, sr. v.p., gen. counsel, 1984-85, exec. v.p., gen. counsel, 1985—. Mem. ABA. Clubs: Heritage, Forum. Home: 4023 Essex Ln Houston TX 77027 Office: Am Gen Corp 2929 Allen Pkwy Houston TX 77019

SCHREIBER, RONALD, lawyer; b. Bronx, Nov. 7, 1953. BA magna cum laude, CUNY, Queens, 1974; JD, U. Chgo., 1977. Bar: Ill. 1977. Assoc. Tenney & Bentley, Chgo., 1977-80, Aaron, Schimberg & Hess, Chgo., 1980-84, D'Ancona & Pflaum, Chgo., 1985—. Mem. ABA, Ill. Bar Assn., Chgo. Bar Assn. (trust law, probate practice coms.), Chgo. Estate Planning Council. Estate planning, Probate, Estate taxation. Office: D'Ancona & Pflaum 30 N LaSalle St Suite 3100 Chicago IL 60602

SCHREIBER, SALLY ANN, lawyer; b. El Paso, Tex., July 23, 1951; d. Warren Thomas Jr. and Joyce (Honey) S.; m. David Gaston Luther, Jr., Apr. 2, 1977; children: Amanda Honey, Ryan Thorp Luther. BBA, U. N.Mex., 1973; JD, Stanford U., 1976. Bar: Calif. 1976, Tex. 1977. Assoc. Johnson & Swanson, Dallas, 1976-81, ptnr., 1981—; speaker seminar on leveraged buyouts Advanced Mgmt. Research Internat., Dallas, 1984, current devel. in ptnrship. law U. Tex., Austin, 1984. Editor Stanford Law Rev., 1975-76. Bd. dirs. The Lyric Opera of Dallas, 1982-86, bd. trustees, 1986—; mem. Stanford (Calif.) Law Sch. Bd. Vis., 1981-84; sponser The 500 Inc., Dallas, 1980—. Mem. ABA, Dallas Bar Assn., Tex. Bar Assn. (revision corp. law com. Copr., Banking and Bus. sect. 1981—, ptnrship law com. 1985—), Calif. Bar Assn., Theatre 3 Guild, Dallas Mus. Art, Dallas Mus. Art Collectors Forum, Shakespeare Festival of Dallas, Lyric Opera of Dallas Guild. General corporate, Securities. Home: 2737 Purdue Dallas TX 75225 Office: Johnson & Swanson 900 Jackson St Dallas TX 75202-4499

SCHREIBER, WILLIAM MARK, lawyer; b. Passaic, N.J., Mar. 29, 1948; s. Morris and Beatrice (Ramer) S.; m. Elaine Deborah Rothberg, Aug. 17, 1972; children: Marc Howard, Rachel Susan. AB, Franklin & Marshall Coll., 1970; JD, Syracuse U., 1973. Bar: N.J. 1974, U.S. Dist. Ct. N.J. 1973, U.S. Ct. Appeals (2d cir.) 1974. Law clk. to judge N.J. Superior Ct., Paterson, 1973-74; assoc. Claudat & Kealy, Jersey City, N.J., 1974-76; ptnr. Hoffman & Schreiber P.A., Red Bank, N.J., 1976—. Mem. ABA, N.J. Bar Assn. (exec. com. family law sect.), Monmouth Bar Assn. (Early settlement program), Red Bank Jaycees. Jewish. Lodge: B'nai B'rith. Avocations: sports cars, gardening, reading. Family and matrimonial. Home: 19 Marshall Rd Wayside NJ 07712 Office: Hoffman & Schreiber 199 Broad St Red Bank NJ 07701

SCHROEDER, CARL FREDERICK, JR., lawyer; b. Chgo., Nov. 21, 1948; s. Carl Frederick Sr. and Margaret Elizabeth (Schroeder) S.; m. Diane Elizabeth Nielson, Aug. 9, 1969; children: Michael, Elizabeth, Paul. BA, Valparaiso U., 1970; JD, Loyola U., Chgo., 1973. Bar. Ill. 1973, U.S. Dist. Ct. (no. dist.) Ill. 1973; diplomate Nat. Bd. Trial Advocacy. Assoc. atty. Querrey, Harrow, Gulanick and Kennedy, Chgo., 1973-76, James Thomas Demos, Ltd., Chgo., 1976-78; sole practice, Wheaton, Ill., 1978-79; ptnr. Nelson, Jerz, Pietsch, O'Leary, Walters and Schroeder, Wheaton, 1979-82; pres. Carl F. Schroeder, Ltd., Wheaton, 1982—; lectr. Ill. Inst. for Continued Legal Edn., Springfield, Ill., 1978-85. Contbr. articles to profl. jours. Mem. commn. on adjudication Luth. Church Mo. Synod No. Ill. Dist., Chgo., 1980—; pres. Trinity Luth. Ch., Lombard, Ill. Mem. ABA, Ill. Bar Assn., DuPage County Bar Assn., Am. Trial Lawyers Assn., Ill. Trial Lawyers Assn. Republican. Personal injury, State civil litigation, Federal civil litigation. Office: 2100 Manchester Wheaton IL 60189

SCHROEDER, JAMES WHITE, lawyer; b. Elmhurst, Ill., Apr. 19, 1936; s. Paul W. and Thelma C. (White) S.; m. Patricia N. Scott, Aug. 18, 1962; children—Scott W., Jamie C. B.A., Princeton U., 1958; J.D., Harvard U., 1964. Bar: Colo. 1964, U.S. Dist. Ct. Colo. 1964, U.S. Ct. Appeals (10th cir.) 1965, U.S. Supreme Ct. 1972, U.S. Dist. Ct. D.C. 1973, U.S. Ct. Appeals (D.C. cir.) 1974, U.S. Ct. Appeals (8th cir.) 1977, U.S. Ct. Appeals (3d cir.) 1981, U.S. Claims Ct. 1983, U.S. Ct. Appeals (fed. cir.) 1983. Ptnr., Moseley, Wells & Schroeder, Denver, 1965-72; adminstrv. ptnr., mgmt. com. Kaplan, Russin & Vecchi, Washington, 1973—; arbitrator Am. Arbitration Assn. Active ACLU, Ams. for Democratic Action, Smithsonian Instn., Denver Symphony Orch., Denver Art Mus. Served to lt., USNR, 1958-64. Am. Field Service scholar, 1953; NROTC scholar, 1954. Mem. Denver Bar Assn., Colo. Bar Assn., D.C. Bar Assn., ABA, Assn. Trial Lawyers Am. Democrat. Clubs: University, Sierra, Princeton (pres. 1982-84) (Washington); Princeton (N.Y.C.), Cap and Gown (Princeton); Lincoln's Inn (Harvard). Private international, Federal civil litigation, Government contracts and claims. Home: 4102 Lester Ct Alexandria VA 22311

SCHROEDER, JOHN, lawyer; b. Montebello, Calif., Aug. 29, 1954; s. Albert Ernest and Sarah Ann (McGarry) S.; m. Sherri Lynn Captor, Apr. 27, 1985. BA cum laude, Calif. Poly., Pomona, 1977; JD, U. S.D., 1980. Bar: Calif. 1981, N.Y. 1981, U.S. Dist. Ct. (cen. dist.) Calif. 1985, U.S. Supreme Ct. 1986. Assoc. Richard Jon Weisman, Inc., N.Y.C., 1981-82, Carter, Monkman, Sanborn & Mills, Los Angeles, 1982-83; ptnr. Robert Parker Mills, Inc., Pasadena, Calif., 1983—. Mem. ABA, Los Angeles County Bar Assn., Pasadena Bar Assn. (chmn. pub. and client relations com.), So. Calif. Def. Counsel. Roman Catholic. Avocations: golf, volleyball. State civil litigation, Construction, Insurance. Home: 5959 Birdie Dr La Verne CA 91750 Office: Robert Parker Mills 911 E Colorado Blvd 3rd Fl Pasadena CA 91106

SCHROEDER, JOHN WALTER, lawyer; b. Charlotte, Mich., Jan. 3, 1953; s. Walter Phelps and Leora (Coleman) S. AB, UCLA, 1976; JD, U. Calif., Berkeley, 1980. Bar: Calif. 1981. Assoc. Shenas, Robbins, et al, San Diego, 1980-82; corp. counsel San Francisco Pension Corp., 1982-84, Advanced Micro Devices, Sunnyvale, Calif., 1984-87; assoc. Graham & James, 1987—. Pension, profit-sharing, and employee benefits, Securities, General corporate.

SCHROEDER, MARY MURPHY, judge; b. Boulder, Colo., Dec. 4, 1940; d. Richard and Theresa (Kahn) Murphy; m. Milton R. Schroeder, Oct. 15, 1965; children: Caroline Theresa, Katherine Emily. B.A., Swarthmore Coll., 1962; J.D., U. Chgo., 1965. Bar: Ill. 1966, D.C. 1966, Ariz. 1970. Trial atty. Dept. Justice, Washington, 1965-69; law clk. Hon. Jesse Udall, Ariz. Supreme Ct., 1970; mem. firm Lewis and Roca, Phoenix, 1971-75; judge Ariz. Ct. Appeals, Phoenix, 1975-79, U.S. Ct. Appeals (9th Cir.), Phoenix, 1979—; vis. instr. Ariz. State U. Coll. Law, 1976, 77, 78. Contbr. articles to profl. jours. Mem. Am. Bar Assn., Ariz. Bar Assn., Fed. Bar Assn., Am. Law Inst., Am. Judicature Soc. Democrat. Club: Soroptimists. Jurisprudence. Office: US Ct Appeals (9th cir) 6421 US Courthouse& Fed Bldg 230 N 1st Ave Phoenix AZ 85025

SCHROEDER, STUART R., lawyer; b. Milw., Aug. 13, 1948; s. Leroy A. and Nina J. (Henschen) S.; m. Pamela Ellen Bach, Mar. 3, 1973; children: Casey, Elizabeth, Andrew. BA, U. Wis., Milw., 1971; JD with distinction, Oklahoma City U., 1976; LLM in Taxation, Boston U., 1977. Bar: Wis. 1977, U.S. Dist. Ct. (ea. and we. dists.) Wis. 1979, U.S. Supreme Ct. 1985. Assoc. Isaksen, Lathrop et al, Madison, Wis., 1977-78, Sletteland & Nye, Milw., 1978-79, Cook & Franke, Milw., 1979-81; ptnr. von Briesen & Purtell, Milw., 1981—. Contbg. editor Milwaukee Lawyer mag., 1986. Bd. dirs. Midwest Athletes Against Childhood Cancer Fund, Milw., 1982—. Mem. ABA, Wis. Bar Assn., Waukesha County Bar Assn., Milw. County Bar Assn., Milw. Estate Planning Council. Club: Milw. Athletic. Avocations: outdoor activities, vol. work. General corporate, Private international, Corporate taxation. Home: N31 W29005 Hillcrest Dr Pewaukee WI 53029 Office: von Briesen & Redmond 411 E Wisconsin Ave Suite 700 Milwaukee WI 53202

SCHROEDER, WALTER ALLEN, lawyer; b. San Francisco, July 29, 1954; s. Carl Walter and Mary (Lee) S.; m. Lee Walthall, Jan. 1, 1982; B.S. in Bus. Adminstrn., Georgetown U., 1976; J.D., U. Houston, 1979. Bar: Tex. 1979, D.C. 1984, U.S. Dist. Ct. (we., no. and so. dists.) Tex., U.S. Ct. Appeals (5th and 11th cirs.), U.S. Supreme Ct. Asst. treas. G.U. Fed. Credit Union, Washington, 1976-77; asst. to pres. U.S.E. Credit Union, Houston, 1977-79; analyst Banc Systems, Inc., Houston, 1979; briefing atty. Tex. Ct. Civil Appeals, Ft. Worth, 1979-80; asst. counsel Am. Ins. Assn., Houston, 1980-81; atty. Rolston & Hausler, Houston, 1981-85, Chamberlain, Hrdlicka, White, Johnson & Williams, 1985-86, Hollrah, Lange & Thoma, 1986—; pres., bd. dirs., Park Regency Council Co-owners. Trustee Found. Amateur Radio, Inc. Washington, 1972-76, chmn. audit com., 1975-76; treas. Houston Echo Soc., 1979. Recipient Indsl. Peace award Georgetown U., 1976. Mem. Am. Bar Assn., D.C. Bar Assn., Houston Bar Assn., Houston Young Lawyers Assn., State Bar Tex., Tex. Assn. Bank Counsel. Republican. Lutheran. Clubs: University (Houston). Author articles in field. Home: 2333 Bering Dr #104 Houston TX 77057 Office: Hollrah Lange & Thoma Four Houston Ctr 1331 Lamar Suite 1570 Houston TX 77010

SCHROEDER, WILLIAM FRANCIS, lawyer; b. Trenton, N.J., July 13, 1947; s. Francis Bernard and Anne Marie (Lodge) S.; m. Rebecca Mae Noble, May 30, 1970; 1 child, Jonathan. BA, LaSalle U., 1969; JD, Temple U., 1974. Bar: Pa. 1974, U.S. Dist. Ct. (ea. dist.) Pa. 1978, U.S. Ct. Appeals (3d cir.) 1985. From assoc. to ptnr. Stuckert & Yates, Newtown, Pa., 1974—. Mem. ABA, Pa. Bar Assn., Bucks County Bar Assn. Democrat. Avocations: astronomy, bicycling, sports. Banking, State civil litigation, Local government. Home: 1956 Buckingham Dr Jamison PA 18929 Office: Stuckert & Yates 1 S State St Newtown PA 18940

SCHROER, GENE ELDON, lawyer; b. Randolph, Kans., Aug. 29, 1927; s. Harry Edward and Florence Lillian (Schwartz) S.; m. Edith Grace Kintner, Apr. 7, 1956; children: Kenneth G., Rebecca J., Sonya J., Connie J. BA, Washburn U., 1957. Bar: Kans. 1957, U.S. Dist. Ct. Kans., U.S. Ct. Appeals (10th cir.), U.S. SupremeCt. Sole practice Topeka, 1957-68; ptnr. Schroer & Rice, P.A., Topeka, 1968—. Contbr. articles to profl. jours. Supr. Shawnee County Soil Conservation Dist., Topeka, 1968-84. Mem. ABA, Kans. Bar Assn., Assn. Trial Lawyers Am. (gov. 1976-79, seminar lectr. 1973—, chmn. tort sect. 1974-75), Kans. Trial Lawyers Assn. (gov. 1972—, seminar lectr. 1974—, pres. 1974-75), Trial Lawyers for Pub. Justice (bd. dirs.), Nat. Bd. of Trial Advocacy (sustaining founder, instr. and lectr. 1978, 81—), Nat. Coll. Adv. (instr.), Advanced Coll. Adv. (instr.), N.Y. Acad. Sci., Civil Justice Found. (founding sponsor). Democrat. Presbyterian. Personal injury, Federal civil litigation, State civil litigation. Office: Schroer & Rice PA 115 E 7th St Topeka KS 66603

SCHROER, J. MICHAEL, lawyer; b. Celina, Ohio, June 19, 1942; s. John Henry and Rose Agnes (Dorian) S.; m. Mary B. White, Oct. 28, 1967; children—Amy, Jenni, Rebecca. B.S., Ohio State U., 1964; J.D., Ohio No. U., 1968. Bar: Mich. 1968, U.S. Dist. Ct. (we. dist.) Mich. 1969, U.S. Dist. Ct. (ea. dist.) Mich. 1976. Research clk. Circuit Ct., Lansing, Mich., 1968-69; assoc. firm Sinas, Dramis, Brake & Turner, Lansing, 1969-70; chief asst. Ingham County Friend of Ct., Lansing, 1970-71; referee Washtenaw County Friend of Ct., Ann Arbor, Mich., 1971-76; sole practice, Ann Arbor, 1976-77; ptnr. Malley and Schroer, Ann Arbor, 1977-86, Ellis, Talcott, Ohlgren & Ferguson, P.C., 1986—; pres. Mich. Bd. Law Examiners, 1982-86. Host Legaline Sta. WAAM, Ann Arbor, 1984-85 . Mem., chmn. Pittsfield Charter Twp. Bd. Appeals, Ann Arbor, 1976-84 chmn., mem. Pittsfield Charter Twp. Planning Commn., 1982-84; bd. dirs. Washtenaw Devel. Council, 1985—. Mem. Washtenaw County Bar Assn., Mich. Bar Assn. Democrat. Roman Catholic. Club: Chippewa Hills Swim and Tennis (pres. 1980-81). State civil litigation, Federal civil litigation, Contracts commercial. Office: Ellis Talcott Ohlgren & Ferguson PC 320 N Main Suite 300 Ann Arbor MI 48104

SCHROPP, JAMES HOWARD, lawyer; b. Lebanon, Pa., June 20, 1943; s. Howard J. and Maud E. (Parker) S.; m. Jo Ann Simpson, Sept. 4, 1965; children: James A., John C., Jeffrey M., Jeremy M. BA, U. Richmond, 1965; JD, Georgetown U., 1973. Bar: D.C. 1973, U.S. Supreme Ct. 1980. Asst. gen. counsel SEC, Washington, 1973-79; ptnr. Fried, Frank, Harris, Shriver & Jacobson, Washington, 1979—; adj. prof. Georgetown U., Washington, 1982—. Mem. ABA (discovery com. litigation sect. 1984—, tender offer litigation subcom. corp. banking and bus. law sect. 1985—). Securities, General corporate, Federal civil litigation. Office: Fried Frank Harris Shriver & Jacobson 1001 Pennsylvania Ave Washington DC 20004

SCHROT, JOHN JOSEPH, JR., lawyer; b. South Bend, Ind., July 20, 1950; s. John Joseph and Mary Eileen (O'Keefe) S.; m. Deborah Lynne Brown, Aug. 14, 1976; children: Lisa, Erica, Jacquelyn. BS, Wayne State U., 1972; MBA, U. Toronto, Ont., Can., 1974; JD, Detroit Coll. of Law, 1977. Bar: Mich. 1977, U.S. Dist. Ct. (ea. dist.) Mich. 1977, U.S. Ct. Appeals (6th cir.) 1982, U.S. Tax Ct. 1983. Law clk. U.S. Bankruptcy Ct., Flint, Mich., 1977-78; assoc. Tyler & Canham P.C., Detroit, 1978-79, Alan R. Miller P.C., Birmingham, Mich., 1979—; instr. Marygrove Coll., Detroit, 1974, Detroit Coll. of Bus., Pontiac, Mich., 1975, Walsh Coll. of Acctg. and Bus. Adminstrn., Troy, Mich., 1975-76. Editor: Detroit Coll. of Law Rev., 1976. Mem. City Commn. Adj. Parking Com., Birmingham, 1984, transp. com. Birmingham Bd. Edn., 1985. Edward Rakow scholar Fed. Bar Found., 1976. Mem. ABA, State Bar Mich., Oakland County Bar Assn., Def. Counsel Assn. Roman Catholic. State civil litigation, Personal injury, Family and matrimonial. Office: 300 E Maple Rd Suite 200 Birmingham MI 48011

SCHROTH, PETER W(ILLIAM), lawyer, educator; b. Camden, N.J., July 24, 1946; s. Walter and Patricia Anne (Page) S.; m. Keven Anne Murphy, Jan. 2, 1986; children: Laura Salome Erickson-Schroth, Julia James. A.B., Shimer Coll., 1966; J.D., U.Chgo., 1969, M.Comp.L., 1971; S.J.D., U. Mich., 1979; postgrad. U. Freiburg (W.Ger.), Faculté Internationale pour l'Enseignement de Droit Comparé. Bar: Ill. 1969, N.Y. 1979, Conn. 1985. Asst. prof. So. Meth. U., 1973-77; fellow in law and humanities Harvard U., 1976-77, vis. scholar, 1980-81; assoc. prof. N.Y. Law Sch., 1977-81; prof. law Hamline U., St. Paul, 1981-83; dep. gen. counsel Equator Bank Ltd., 1984—; adj. prof. law U. Conn., 1985—. Mem. ABA, Am. Fgn. Law Assn. (dir.), Am. Assn. Comparative Study of Law (dir.), Internat. Bar Assn., Assn. Trial Lawyers Am., Conn. Civil Liberties Union (dir.), Environ. Law Inst. (assoc.), Columbia U Peace Seminar (assoc.). Author: Foreign Investment in the United States, 2d edit., 1977; (with Stiefel) Products Liability: European Proposals and American Experience, 1981; Handbook for Practice of Comparative Law, 1983; bd. editors Am. Jour. Comparative Law; editor in chief ABA Environ. Law Symposium, 1980-83; contbr. articles to profl. jours. Banking, Environment, Private international. Office: Equator House 111 Charter Oak Ave Hartford CT 06106

SCHUCK, CARL J., lawyer; b. Phila., Nov. 21, 1915; s. Joseph and Christina (Schadl) S.; m. Mary Elizabeth Box, June 7, 1941; children: Mary Ann, John, James, Catherine, Christopher. B.S., St. Mary's Coll., 1937; postgrad., U. So. Calif.; J.D., Georgetown U., 1941. Bar: D.C. 1940, Calif. 1943, U.S. Supreme Ct. 1952. Atty. Dept. Justice, Washington, 1940-42, Alien Property Custodian, San Francisco, 1942-44; mem. firm Overton, Lyman & Prince, Los Angeles, 1947-79, profl. corp. mem. firm, 1979-85; lectr. Practising Law Inst., 1973; Del. 9th Circuit Jud. Conf., 1963-80, chmn. lawyer-dels. com., 1972, mem. exec. com., 1976-80, chmn. exec. com., 1977-78; mem. disciplinary bd. State Bar Calif., 1970-71. Fellow Am. Coll. Trial Lawyers (chmn. com. on complex litigation 1979-81, regent 1981-85), Los Angeles County Bar Assn. (trustee 1974-76), Phi Alpha Delta. Club: Chancery (pres. 1984-85). Antitrust, Federal civil litigation, State civil litigation. Home and Office: 4723 Cordoba Way Oceanside CA 92056 Office: 550 S Flower St 6th Floor Los Angeles CA 90071

SCHUCK, PETER H., lawyer, educator; b. N.Y.C., Apr. 26, 1940; s. Samuel H. and Lucille (Horner) S.; m. Marcy Cantor, June 26, 1966; children: Christopher, Julie. B.A. with honors, Cornell U., 1962; J.D. cum laude, Harvard U., 1965, M.A., 1969; LL.M., NYU, 1966; M.A. (hon.), Yale U., 1982. Bar: N.Y. State 1966, D.C. 1972. Practiced law N.Y.C., 1965-68; teaching fellow in govt. Harvard U., 1969-71; cons. (Center for Study of Responsive Law), Washington, 1971-72; dir. Washington office Consumers Union, 1972-77; dep. asst. sec. for planning and evaluation HEW, Washington, 1977-79; vis. scholar Am. Enterprise Inst. for Public Policy Research, Washington, 1979; assoc. prof. law Yale U., 1979-81, prof., 1981-86, Simeon E. Baldwin prof. law, 1986—; vis. prof. Georgetown U. Law Ctr., 1986-87; lectr. profl., acad., bus., univ., govt. and citizen groups. Author: The Judiciary Committees, 1975, Suing Government, 1983; Citizenship without Consent, 1985; Agent Orange on Trial, 1986; contbr. articles, revs. to profl. and popular publs. Guggenheim fellow, 1984-85. Jewish. Home: 1056 Whitney Ave Hamden CT 06517 Office: Yale Law Sch 401 A Yale Sta New Haven CT 06520

SCHUCKIT, ROBERT JAY, lawyer; b. Milw., Aug. 14, 1957; s. Rubin and Dollie (Altschuler) S. BS cum laude, Brandeis U., 1979; JD, U. Wis., 1982. Bar: Wis. 1982, Ill. 1982, U.S. Dist. Ct. (we. dist.) Wis. 1982, U.S. Dist. Ct. (no. dist.) Ill. 1982. Assoc. Keck, Mahin & Cate, Chgo., 1982—; guest lectr. dept. engring. U. Wis., Madison, 1986—. Assoc. counsel Chgo. Vol. Legal Services, 1985—. Mem. Wis. Bar Assn., Assn. Trial Lawyers Am. Democrat. Jewish. Avocations: competitive ice hocky, roller skating. Federal civil litigation, State civil litigation, Insurance. Home: 2910 N Pine Grove #3 Chicago IL 60657 Office: Keck Mahin & Cate 233 S Wacker Dr Chicago IL 60606

SCHUH, STEPHEN JOSEPH, lawyer; b. Cin., Aug. 10, 1952; s. Arthur J. and Mary M. (List) S.; m. Debra Ann Sybo, July 26, 1976; children: Matthew, David. BA in Acctg. cum laude, Ohio U., 1974; JD, No. Ky. U., 1978. Bar: Ohio 1978, U.S. Dist. Ct. (so. dist.) Ohio 1978, U.S. Ct. Appeals (6th cir.). Constable Hamilton County Ct. Common Pleas, Cin., 1974-78; asst. pub. defender, trial atty. Hamilton County, Cin., 1978-80; ptnr. Schuh & Goldberg, Cin., 1980—. Precinct exec. Hamilton County Rep. Cen. Com., Cin., 1975—; mem. Hamilton County Reps., Cin.; trustee No. Am. Aircraft Mus., Cin., 1985—; bd. dirs. Christ Child Day Nursery, Cin., 1981—. Mem. ABA, Ohio Bar Assn., Cin. Bar Assn. Roman Catholic. Club: Greater Cin. Airmans. Avocations: aviation, golf, swimming, jogging. Personal injury, Consumer commercial, Criminal. Office: Schuh & Goldberg 2662 Madison Ave Cincinnati OH 45208

SCHUIT, STEVEN REINER, lawyer; b. Haarlem, The Netherlands, Oct. 9, 1942; came to U.S., 1980; s. Jan Willem and Frances Mathilde (Tromp) S.; m. Marjolaine Williams, Oct. 28, 1982; 1 child, Solco Willem Paul. Lyceum, Rijnlands Lyceum, Wassenaar, Netherlands, 1961; masters, Groningen (Netherlands) U., 1969. Assoc. Vos & Seidel, Groningen, 1970-71, Loeff & van der Ploeg, Rotterdam, Netherlands, 1972-74; ptnr. Loeff & van der Ploeg, Amsterdam, Netherlands, 1974-80; sr. resident ptnr. Loeff & van der Ploeg, N.Y.C., 1980—. Author, editor: Dutch Business Law, 1978; author: Dutch Works Council Act, 1981. Mem. ABA, Internat. Bar Assn., Internat. Fiscal Assn., Assn. Bar City of N.Y. (com. fgn. and comparative law 1982—), Grotius Academie (gov.), The Netherlands Club. Avocations: tennis, music. Private international, Public international. Home: 92 Barrow St New York NY 10014 Office: Loeff & van der Ploeg 1270 Ave of Americas New York NY 10020

SCHUKOSKE, JANE ELLEN, lawyer; b. Middletown, Conn., July 23, 1951; d. John Albert and Mary Ann (Jelinek) S. BA, Boston U., 1973; JD, Vanderbilt U., 1977. Bar: Va. 1978, U.S. Dist. Ct. (ea. dist.) Va. 1978, U.S. Ct. Appeals (4th cir.) 1982, D.C. 1987. Staff atty. Tidewater Legal Aid Soc., Norfolk, Va., 1977-79; mng. atty. Tidewater Legal Aid Soc., Norfolk, 1980, Legal Services of No. Va., Alexandria, 1980-82; exec. dir. Va. Poverty Law Ctr., Richmond, Va., 1983-86; fellow Harrison Inst Pub. Law Georgetown U. Law Ctr., Washington, D.C., 1986—; cons. Legal Services Corp., Washington, 1981-83. Bd. dirs. Mental Health Assn. Tidewater, Norfolk, 1979-80. Mem. ABA, Va. Trial Lawyers Assn., Va. Women Atty.'s Assn. (treas. 1984-86, bd. dirs. 1983-86, editor Lex Claudia newsletter 1983-84). Consumer commercial, Contracts commercial. Office: Harrison Inst for Pub Law 25 E St NW #514 Washington DC 20001

SCHULER, ALISON KAY, lawyer; b. West Point, N.Y., Oct. 1, 1948; d. Richard Hamilton and Irma (Sanken) S.; m. Lyman Gage Sandy, Mar. 30, 1974; 1 child, Theodore. A.B. cum laude, Radcliffe Coll., 1969; J.D. Harvard U., 1972. Bar: Va. 1973, D.C. 1974, N.M. 1975. Assoc., Hunton & Williams, Richmond, Va., 1972-75; asst. U.S. atty. U.S. Atty.'s Office, Albuquerque, 1975-78; adj. prof. law U. N.Mex., 1983-85; ptnr. Sutin, Thayer & Browne, Albuquerque, 1978-85, Montgomery & Andrews, P.A., Albuquerque, 1985—. Bd. dirs. Am. Diabetes Assn., Albuquerque, 1980-85, chmn. bd. dirs., 1984-85; bd. dirs. June Music Festival, 1980—, pres., 1983-85; chairperson Albuquerque Com. Foreign Relations, 1984-85; mem. N.Mex. Internat. Trade and Investment Council, Inc., 1986—. Mem. Fed. Bar Assn. (coordinator), ABA, Va. Bar Assn., N.Mex. State Bar Assn. (chmn. corp., banking and bus. law 1982-83), Nat. Assn. Women Lawyers, Am. Jud. Soc., Harvard Alumni Assn. (mem. fund campaign, regional dir. 1984-86, v.p. 1986—, chmn. clubs com. 1985—), Radcliffe Coll. Alumnae Assn. Bd. Mgmt. (regional dir. 1984—). Club: Harvard-Radcliffe (pres. 1980-84). Securities, Contracts commercial, Private international. Home: 632 Cougar Loop NE Albuquerque NM 87122 Office: Montgomery & Andrews PA 707 Broadway NE PO Box 26927 Albuquerque NM 87125

SCHULHOFER, STEPHEN JOSEPH, law educator, consultant; b. N.Y.C., Aug. 20, 1942; s. Joseph and Myrelle (Schonceit) S.; m. Laurie Wohl, May 28, 1975; children—Samuel, Jonah. A.B., Princeton U., 1964; LL.B., Harvard U., 1967. Bar: D.C. 1968, U.S. Dist. Ct. (ea. dist.) Pa. 1973, U.S. Supreme Ct. 1973. Law clk. U.S. Supreme Ct., Washington, 1967-69; assoc. Coudert Freres, Paris, 1969-72; prof. law U. Pa., Phila., 1972—; vis. prof. University of Chicago, 1985—. speedy trial reporter U.S. Dist. Ct., Wilmington, Del., 1975-80; cons. U.S. EPA, Washington, 1977-78. Author: Prosecutorial Discretion and Federal Sentencing Reform, 1979. Editor: Criminal Law and its Processes, 1983. Contbr. articles to profl. jours. Trustee, Community Legal Services, Inc., Phila., 1981—. Walter Meyer grantee Am. Bar Found., 1984. Mem. Am. Law Inst., Law and Soc. Assn., Am. Soc. Polit. and Legal Philosophy. Criminal, Civil rights, Judicial administration. Office: University of Chicago 1111 East 60th Street Chicago IL 60637 *

SCHULLER, STEPHEN ARTHUR, lawyer; b. Wilmington, N.C., Jan. 18, 1951. BA, Northwestern U., 1973; JD, U. Tulsa, 1976. Bar: Okla. 1976, U.S. Dist. Ct. (no. dist.) Okla. 1976, Ill. 1977. Corp. atty. Roper Corp., Kankakee, Ill., 1977; assoc. Prichard, Norman, Reed & Wohlgemuth, Tulsa, 1977-82; ptnr. Prichard, Norman & Wohlgemuth, Tulsa, 1982-83, Barrow, Gaddis, Griffith & Grimm, Tulsa, 1983—. Mem. Ill. Bar Assn., Okla. Bar Assn. (chmn. bd. dirs. real property sect. 1986), Tulsa Title and Probate Lawyers Assn. Clubs: The Tulsa. Lodge: Rotary. Real property, Contracts commercial, State civil litigation. Office: Barrow Gaddis Griffith & Grimm 610 S Main St Suite 300 Tulsa OK 74119-1224

SCHULMAN, JOANNE, lawyer; b. Los Angeles, Aug. 6, 1952; d. Seymour and Florence (Simon) S. BA, U. Calif., Berkeley, 1974; JD, Golden Gate U., 1978. Bar: Calif. 1978, U.S. Supreme Ct. 1983. Staff atty. Alameda County Legal Aid Soc., Oakland, Calif., 1977-80; ptnr. Gerber & Schulman, San Francisco; staff atty. Nat. Ctr. Women and Family Law, N.Y.C., 1980-86, Calif. Senate Task Force on Family Equity, 1986—; bd. dirs. Rape Crisis Ctr., San Pablo, Calif., Womens History Research Ctr., Berkeley, Calif. Author: (with others) Interstate Child Custody Law, 1982, Legal Advocacy for Battered Women, 1982, Child Custody Litigation, Women and the Law, 1984; contbr. numerous articles to profl. jours. Commr. N.Y. State Child Support Commn., 1984—. Mem. ABA (exec. com. custody and child support coms.), N.Y. State Bar Assn. (custody com.), N.Y. Womens Bar Assn. (matrimonial com.). Avocations: crossword puzzles, travel, reading, swimming. Family and matrimonial, Civil rights, Poverty law.

SCHULMAN, MICHAEL ROBERT, lawyer; b. Washington, Sept. 10, 1946; s. James H. and Doris (Greenfield) S.; m. Joan M. Camperlino, Feb. 18, 1978; children: Douglas James, Jacie Lauren. BA, Carnegie-Mellon U., 1968; MA in Teaching, Duquesne U., 1971, JD cum laude, 1977. Bar: Pa. 1977, Tex. 1980. Math. tchr. Allderdice High Sch., Pitts., 1968-76; legal asst. Wheeling-Pittsburgh Steel Corp., Pitts., 1976-77; law clk. to judge U.S. Dist. Ct. (we. dist.) Pa., Pitts., 1977-79; assoc. Vinson & Elkins, Houston, 1980-83; assoc. Johnson & Swanson, Dallas, 1983-84, ptnr., 1984—. Mem. Nat. Assn. Bond Lawyers (panelist 1985), Tex. Bar Assn. Avocations: tennis, skiing, running. Municipal and public finance. Office: Johnson & Swanson 900 Jackson St Dallas TX 75202-4499

SCHULMAN, STEVEN GARY, lawyer; b. Gloversville, N.Y., June 10, 1951; s. Jacob and Selma Pearl (Shapiro) S. BA, Williams Coll., 1973; MA, Fletcher U., 1975, MALD, 1976; JD, U. Chgo., 1980. Bar: N.Y. 1981, D.C. 1981, U.S. Dist. Ct. (so. dist.) N.Y. 1981, U.S. Ct. Internat. Trade 1982. Law clk. to assoc. judge U.S. Ct. Claims, Washington, 1980-81; assoc. Cravath, Swaine & Moore, N.Y.C., 1981-86, Milberg, Weiss, Bershad, Specthrie & Lerach, N.Y.C., 1986—. Mem. ABA, N.Y. State Bar Assn., D.C. Bar Assn., Assn. Bar of City of N.Y. Federal civil litigation, Securities. Office: Milberg Weiss Bershad Specthrie & Lerach 1 Pennsylvania Plaza New York NY 10119

SCHULNER, LAWRENCE MAYER, lawyer; b. Chgo., Aug. 14, 1938; s. Harry and Ethel (Greenberg) S.; m. Diane Banchik, Sept. 1, 1962 (div. June 1970) children—Sherri Ellen, Keith Allen; m. 2d Sharalynn Stein, Aug. 15, 1970; 1 son, Matthew Loren. B.S. in Bus. Adminstrn., Roosevelt U., 1959; J.D., UCLA, 1963. Bar: Calif. 1964, U.S. Dist. Cts. (so. and cen. dists.) Calif. 1964, U.S. Ct. Appeals (9th cir.) 1964, U.S. Ct. Appeals (4th cir.) 1969. Tax acct. Pritkin, Finkel & Co., Beverly Hills, Calif., 1963-65; ptnr. Rudoff & Schulner, Los Angeles, 1965-67; pres. Fin. Concepts Inc., Los Angeles, 1967-73, Capital Concepts, Corp., Los Angeles, 1969—, L & L Distbrs., Inc., Los Angeles; v.p. Med.-Dental Bus. Service, Inc., Los Angeles, 1964-67; pres., dir. Complan Inc., Los Angeles, 1969—; chmn. bd. Nightwatch Corp., Los Angeles; pres. L.M. Schulner, Law Corp., Camarillo, Calif., 1977—; ptnr. Schulner & Camarena, Camarillo, 1983—; faculty mem. Hastings Coll. Advocacy, 1986-87; chmn. bd. Nat. Computer Car Network, Camarillo, 1982-85; judge pro tem Ventura Superior Ct., 1981-84, Ventura Mcpl. Ct., 1981-84. Democratic candidate for mayor Los Angeles, 1969, for U.S. Ho. Reps., 1969, chmn. Congressman Tom Rees campaign, 26th Dist., 1970; bd. dirs. Los Angeles West Side br. ARC; organizer Van DeKamp for Atty. Gen., Calif., 1983; chmn. com. United Jewish Fund, Los Angeles, 1980-82; Named to Outstanding Young Men Am., 1970. Mem. Ventura Bar Assn., Los Angeles Trial Lawyers Assn., Ventura Trial Lawyers Assn., Calif. Bar Assn. Democrat. Personal injury, Insurance, Bankruptcy. Office: L M Schulner Law Corp 360 Mobile Ave Camarillo CA 93010

SCHULT, THOMAS PETER, lawyer; b. Great Falls, Mont., Sept. 12, 1954; s. Peter Henry and Louise (de Russy) S.; m. Margo C. Soulé, Sept. 18, 1982. BS in Russian History, U. Va., 1976, JD, 1979. Bar: U.S. Dist. Ct. (we. dist.) Mo. 1979, U.S. Ct. Appeals (10th cir.) 1983, U.S. Ct. Appeals (7th, 8th and 11th cirs.) 1984, U.S. Ct. Appeals (5th cir.) 1985. Ptnr. Lathrop, Koontz & Norquist, Kansas City, Mo., 1979—. Committeeman Jackson County Reps., Kansas City, 1984—. Mem. ABA (products liability com.), Mo. Bar Assn. (lectr. continguing legal edn.), Def. Research Inst. Episcopalian. Federal civil litigation, State civil litigation, Personal injury. Office: Lathrop Koontz & Norquist 2345 Grand Ave Suite 2600 Kansas City MO 64108

SCHULTE, JEFFREY LEWIS, lawyer; b. N.Y.C., July 24, 1949; s. Irving and Ruth (Stein) S.; m. Elizabeth Ewan Kaiser, Aug. 13, 1977; children: Andrew Riggs, Ian Garretson. BA, Williams Coll., 1971; postgrad., Harvard U., 1971-72; JD, Yale U., 1976. Bar: Pa. 1978. Law clk. to judge U.S. Ct. Appeals (3d cir.), Newark, 1976-77; assoc. Schnader, Harrison, Segal & Lewis, Phila., 1977-84, ptnr., 1985—. Mem. ABA, Pa. Bar Assn., Phila. Bar Assn., Phi Beta Kappa. Clubs: Yale (Phila.), Phila. Racquet. Resource recovery, Securities, General corporate. Office: Schnader Harrison Segal & Lewis 1600 Market St Suite 3600 Philadelphia PA 19103

SCHULTESS, LEROY KENNETH, lawyer, consultant; b. Garrett, Ind., May 7, 1907; s. George Mathias and Elizabeth (Lehmbeck) S.; m. Sarah Mildred Atwater, Apr. 28, 1942. A.B., Mich. U., 1929; J.D., Northwestern U., 1932. Bar: Ind. 1933. Practice law, LaGrange, Ind.; pres. Creek Chub Bait Co., Garrett, Lure, Inc., Garrett; hon. dir. Farmers State Bank, LaGrange. Recipient Meritorious awards Farmers State Bank, VFW, Boy Scouts Am., Am. Lung Assn. Mem. U. Mich. Alumni Assn., LaGrange C. of C., ABA, Ind. Bar Assn. (Golden Anniversary award), LaGrange County Bar Assn. (Outstanding and Dedicated Service awards), Sigma Chi, Phi Delta Phi. Clubs: Rotary (LaGrange) (pres. 1956-7), LaGrange Country. Lodges: Shriners, Masons. Banking, General corporate, Criminal. Home: 414 W Michigan St LaGrange IN 46761 Office: Farmers State Bank Bldg 220 S Detroit St LaGrange IN 46761

SCHULTZ, ALLEN H., lawyer; b. Chgo., Mar. 15, 1911; s. Kalman and Minnie (Goldman) S.; m. Ida G. Greenberg, Oct. 13, 1940; children—Jay L., Edward A. J.D., DePaul U., 1932. Bar: U.S. Ct. Appeals (7th cir.) 1945, U.S. Dist. Ct. (no. dist.) Ill. 1932. Legal adv. Ill. Liquor Control Commn., 1934; sole practice, Chgo., 1934-71; ptnr. Schultz & Schultz, Chgo., 1972—. Mem. ABA, Ill. State Bar Assn., Chgo. Bar Assn., Bar Assn. of 7th Fed. Cir., Decalogue Soc. Lawyers, Am. Judicature Soc., Pi Gamma Mu. Jewish. Antitrust, Federal civil litigation, State civil litigation. Office: 221 N LaSalle St Suite 1826 Chicago IL 60601

SCHULTZ, LOUIS WILLIAM, justice Supreme Ct. Iowa; b. Deep River, Iowa, Mar. 24, 1927; s. M. Louis and Esther Louise (Behrens) S.; m. D. Jean Stephen, Nov. 6, 1949; children—Marcia, Mark, Paul. Student, Central Coll., Pella, Iowa, 1944-45, 46-47; LL.B., Drake U., Des Moines, 1949. Bar: Iowa. Claims supr. Iowa Farm Mut. Ins. Co., Des Moines, 1949-55; partner firm Harned, Schultz & McMeen, Marengo, Iowa, 1955-71; judge Iowa Dist. Ct. (6th dist.), 1971-80; justice Iowa Supreme Ct., 1980—; county atty. Iowa Couty, 1960-68. Served with USNR, 1945-46. Mem. Am. Bar Assn., Iowa Bar Assn. (bd. govs.), Iowa Judges Assn. (pres.). Republican. Lutheran. Jurisprudence. Office: Univ Iowa Coll of Law Iowa City IA 52242

SCHULTZ, MANUEL, lawyer, business executive; b. Detroit, May 20, 1928; s. William and Jeanette (Marder) S.; m. Nadine Friedman, Apr. 19, 1959; children—William, Janine. Student UCLA, 1947-50; B.A., N.Y. U., 1951; LL.B., Columbia U., 1956. Bar: N.Y. 1957. Assoc. Conboy, Hewitt, O'Brien & Boardman, N.Y.C., 1956-59; sole practice, 1959-63; mem. Schultz, Frank & Sussman, 1963-64; atty. Celanese Corp., N.Y.C., 1964-67, sr. atty., 1967-73, asst. sec., gen. atty., 1973-76, v.p., sec., asst. gen. counsel, 1976-84; v.p., gen. counsel, sec. Triangle Industries, Inc., New Brunswick, N.J., 1984—. Trustee Youth Symphony Orch. N.Y., N.Y.C. Served to tech. sgt. USAF, 1951-52; Korea. Mem. Assn. Bar City N.Y., Am. Soc. Corp. Secs. (dir.). Club: Princeton of N.Y. Author portfolio: The Board of Directors, 1978. General corporate. Home: 33 Burr Farms Rd Westport CT 06880

SCHULTZ, RICHARD ALLEN, administrator, lawyer, farmer; b. Emporia, Kans., Jan. 3, 1939; s. Ebur Samuel and Opal Mae (Porter) S.; m. Esther Marie Strafuss, May 8, 1971; children—William Allen, Bryan Lee. B.S. in Indsl. Mgmt., U. Kans., 1961; J.D., Washburn U. of Topeka, 1970. Bar: Kans. 1971. Sole practice, Topeka, 1970-71; dep. dir. Kans. Govs. Com. Criminal Adminstrn., 1971-73; asst. jud. adminstr. Kans. Supreme Ct., 1973-76; ct. adminstr. 3rd Jud. Dist., Kans., 1976-83; dep. sec. Dept. Corrections State of Kans., Topeka, 1983—. Exec. bd. Topeka YMCA; dist. officer Jayhawk Area council Boy Scouts Am., Nat. Eagle Scout Assn. Served to lt. USN, 1961-67. Decorated Navy Commendation award; recipient Topeka Bar Assn. Liberty Bell award, 1983. Mem. Topeka Bar Assn., Kans. Bar Assn., ABA, Nat. Trial Ct. Adminstrs., Phi Alpha Delta, Alpha Tau Omega. Democrat. Methodist. Clubs: Knife and Fork, KU Williams Fund Outland. Lodge: Elks. Criminal, Jurisprudence, Legislative. Office: 900 Jackson Suite 400 Topeka KS 66603

SCHULTZ, STEPHEN OTTO, lawyer; b. Adrian, Mich., Oct. 27, 1951; s. Kenneth Otto and Jeannette Cora (Christmas) S.; m. Jane Ellen Nietert, June 22, 1985. BA, Oakland U., 1973; MA, Mich. State U., 1975; JD, Wayne State U., 1978. Bar: Mich. 1978, U.S. Dist. Ct. (we. dist.) Mich. 1979, U.S. Ct. Appeals (6th cir.) 1980, U.S. Dist. Ct. (ea. dist.) Mich. 1985. Ptnr. Foster, Swift, Collins & Coey, Lansing, Mich., 1978—. Mem. ABA (labor law sect., urban state local govt. law sect.), Mich. Bar Assn. (pub. corp. law sect.). Democrat. Episcopalian. Avocations: skiing, camping, golf. Administrative and regulatory, Local government, Labor. Office: Foster Swift Collins & Coey 313 S Washington Sq Lansing MI 48933

SCHULZ, DAVID ALAN, lawyer, educator; b. Blue Island, Ill., Mar. 30, 1952; s. Edmund Leonard and Marjorie Ann (Johnson) S. BA, Knox Coll., 1974; MA in Econs., Yale U., 1976, JD, 1978. Bar: N.Y. 1979, U.S. Dist. Ct. (so., no. and ea. dists.) N.Y., U.S. Ct. Appeals (2d and D.C. cirs.), U.S. Supreme Ct. Assoc. Rogers & Wells, N.Y.C., 1978-86, ptnr., 1986—; staff counsel Nat. Unity Campaign for John Anderson, Washington, 1980; adj. prof. Fordham U. Law Sch., N.Y.C., 1983—. Assoc. counsel N.Y. State Dem. Com., 1982-85; counsel N.Y. Del. to Nat. Conv., San Francisco, 1984; asst. counsel Jud. Screening Com., N.Y.C., 1985—. Mem. ABA (forum com. on communications law), Assn. Bar of City of N.Y. (communications law com.), ACLU. Libel, Federal civil litigation, Civil rights. Home: 752 W End Ave New York NY 10025 Office: Rogers & Wells 200 Park Ave New York NY 10166

SCHULZ, KEITH DONALD, corporate lawyer; b. Burlington, Iowa, Dec. 20, 1938; s. Henry Carl and Laura Iral (Bowlin) S.; m. Emily Brooks Roane, Apr. 19, 1985; children: Keith Jr., Sarah, Christine, Stefan. BA, U. Iowa, 1960, JD, 1963. Bar: Iowa 1963, Ill. 1966. Dep. Sec. of State, State of Iowa, Des Moines, 1965-66; atty. AT&T, Chgo., 1966-67; sec., gen. counsel Borg-Warner Acceptance Corp., Chgo., 1967-74; asst. gen. counsel Borg-Warner Corp., Chgo., 1974-84, v.p., gen. counsel, 1984—. Contbr. articles to profl. jours. Chmn., bd. dirs. Performance Community, Chgo. Vol. Legal Services Found., Chgo. Fellow Am. Bar Found.; mem. ABA (co-chmn. pro bono project, com. on corp. law depts. 1985-86), Ill. Bar Assn., Iowa Bar Assn., Chgo. Bar Assn., Assn. Gen. Counsel, Am. Corp. Counsel Assn., Am. Soc. Corp. Secs., Law Club of Chgo. Clubs: University, Economic (Chgo.). Avocations: tennis, bicycling. Office: Borg-Warner Corp 200 S Michigan Ave Chicago IL 60604

SCHULZ, WILLIAM FREDERICK, JR., lawyer, educator; b. Urbana, Ill., Feb. 18, 1912; s. William Frederick and Christene (Beeuwkes) S.; m. Jean H. Smith, Aug. 9, 1936 (dec. 1974); 1 son, William Frederick III; m. Rose Mary Pease, June 25, 1976. AB, U. Ill., 1932, MA in History, 1934, JD, 1937. Bar: Ill. 1937, Pa. 1962. Asst. atty. gen. Ill., 1937-41; asst. public utilities counsel OPA, 1946; assoc. prof. law Stetson U., 1946-48; vis. asso. prof. law Ind. U., 1948-49; prof. law U. Pitts., 1949—. Author: Conservation Law and Administration, 1953, also articles and revs.; Editor: Adminstrv. Law Rev, 1962-74, Transp. Law Jour, 1968-75. Mem. Pa. Forest Commn. Served from 1st lt. to maj. JAGC AUS, 1941-46. Mem. Fed., Am., Ill., Pa., Allegheny County bar assns., Am. Law Inst., Am. Judicature Soc., Am. Acad. Polit. and Social Sci., Am. Soc. Legal History, Selden Soc., Order of Coif, Zeta Psi, Phi Delta Phi. Democrat. Unitarian. Administrative and regulatory, Criminal, Health. Home: Apt 904 220 N Dithridge St Pittsburgh PA 15213

SCHUMACHER, BARRY LEE, lawyer; b. Akron, Ohio, May 19, 1952; s. Lee Richard and Jane (Barry) S.; m. Judy Martha Sedlak, Dec. 7, 1974; children: John Barry, Jennifer Martha. BS in Biology, Allegheny Coll., 1974; JD, U. Denver, 1979, LLM in Taxation, 1980. Bar: Colo. 1979, U.S. Dist. Ct. Colo. 1979, U.S. Tax Ct. 1980, U.S. Ct. Appeals (10th cir.) 1982, U.S. Ct. Claims 1985. Law clk. to judge U.S. Dept. Interior, Denver, 1978; assoc. Oates, Austin, McGrath & Jordan, Aspen, Colo., 1980-82; ptnr. Wright & Schumacher, Aspen, 1982—; instr. law Colo. Mountain Coll., Aspen, Colo., 1985. Mem. ABA (staff editor of taxation jour. 1983—), Colo. Bar Assn., Denver Bar Assn., Pitkin County Bar Assn., Phi Alpha Delta. Republican. Corporate taxation, Personal income taxation, Securities. Home: 0115 Glen Eagles Dr Aspen CO 81611 Office: Wright & Schumacher 201 N Mill St Suite 106 Aspen CO 81611

SCHUMACHER, HARRY RICHARD, lawyer; b. Bklyn., June 21, 1930; s. Henry Richard and Martha (Hagenbucher) S.; m. Mary Channing Stokes, Nov. 23, 1963 (dec. Feb. 1980); children—Richard, Garry. B.A., Yale U., 1951; J.D. magna cum laude, Harvard U., 1958. Bar: N.Y. 1959, U.S. Supreme Ct. 1964. Assoc. firm Cahill Gordon & Reindel and predecessor firms, N.Y.C., 1958-67, ptnr., 1968—. Bd. dirs. N.Y. Lawyers for the Pub. Interest, Inc., 1980-83. Mem. Manhattan Borough Pres.'s Community Planning Bd. 6, 1962-66; Democratic candidate for N.Y. State Assembly, 1962, 63; bd. dirs. Incarnation Camp, Ivoryton, Conn., 1961-72. Served to lt. (j.g.), USNR, 1951-54. Mem. ABA, N.Y. Bar Assn., Assn. Bar City of N.Y., Fed. Communications Bar Assn., N.Y. County Lawyers Assn. (bd. dirs. 1987—), U.S. Trademark Assn., Am. Judicature Soc. Episcopalian (vestryman). Clubs: Union, Downtown, Yale, N.Y.C., Narragansett (R.I.) Dunes. Administrative and regulatory, Federal civil litigation, State and local taxation. Home: 1133 Park Ave New York NY 10128 Office: 80 Pine St New York NY 10005

SCHUMACHER, PAUL MAYNARD, lawyer; b. Columbus, Nebr., Apr. 4, 1951; s. Maynard Mathew and Rita Bell (Jarosz) S.; m. Michele Suzanne Gassé, June 26, 1976; children: Nicole Suzanne, Kristen Paulette. AA, Platte Coll., 1971; BS, Fort Hays U., 1973; JD, Georgetown U., 1976. Bar: Fla. 1976, Nebr. 1977, U.S. Dist. Ct. Nebr. 1977. Mem. staff U.S. Senate, Washington, 1974-76; sole practice Miami, Fla. and Columbus, 1976—; v.p. Megavision Corp., Columbus, 1976—. Treas. prin. Rep. campaign com. U.S. Senate candiate, Lincoln, Nebr., 1978-79; atty. Platte County, Columbus, 1979-87. Mem. Nebr. Bar Assn., Fla. Bar Assn., Nat. Dist. Attys. Assn. Republican. Roman Catholic. Lodge: Rotary, Elks. Avocation: physics. Local government, General corporate, General practice. Home: 6255 Meyer Rd Columbus NE 68601 Office: 1765 26th Ave Columbus NE 68601

SCHUMACHER, ROD M., lawyer; b. Dumas, Tex., June 15, 1950; s. Ernest J. and Billie F. Schumacher; m. Jeri J. Ashcraft, June 6, 1975; 1 child, Casey. BS, Midwestern U., 1972; MS, Trinity U., 1974; JD, U. Tex., 1979. Bar: Tex. 1980, N.Mex. 1980, U.S Dist. Ct. N.Mex. 1980, U.S. Ct. Appeals (10th cir.) 1980, U.S. Dist. Ct. (we. dist.) Tex. 1984. Hosp. adminstr. Humana, Inc., Andrews, Tex. and Denver, 1973-77; assoc. Atwood & Malone, Roswell, N.Mex., 1980—, ptnr., 1983—; instr. Eastern N.Mex. U., Roswell, 1980—. Trustee Eastern N.Mex. Med. Ctr., Roswell, 1981—, First United Meth. Ch., Roswell, 1981-83. Mem. ABA, Am. Acad. Hosp. Attys., Tex. Bar Assn., N.Mex Bar Assn. Republican. Methodist. Avocations: sports, travel. Consumer commercial, Health. Home: 703 La Jolla Roswell NM 88201 Office: Atwood Malone Mann & Turner 500 N Main 9th Floor Roswell NM 88201

SCHUMACHER, STEPHEN JOSEPH, lawyer; b. Los Angeles, Feb. 5, 1942; s. Joseph Charles and Theresa Isabel (Flynn) S.; children by previous marriage—William Scott, Stacey Elizabeth. A.B., U. So. Calif., 1963; J.D., Hastings Coll. Law, U. Calif., 1967; LL.M. in Taxation, N.Y.U., 1969. Bar: Calif. 1968. Assoc. Stephens, Jones, LaFever & Smith, Los Angeles, 1967-68; assoc. Wenke, Taylor, Schumacher & Evans, Santa Ana, Calif., 1970-79, ptnr., 1979; ptnr. Schumacher & Evans, Costa Mesa, Calif., 1979—; instr. real estate taxation U. Calif.-Irvine, 1980-83. Bd. dirs. Orange County Opportunities Industrialization Center, 1973-75. Mem. ABA, Calif. Bar Assn., Orange County Bar Assn., Newport Beach Realtors Assn., Calif. Realtors Assn., Am. Realtors Assn. Club: Balboa Bay. Real property, Corporate taxation, Personal income taxation. Office: 3151 Airway Ave Suite A-1 Costa Mesa CA 92626

SCHUMAIER, STEVEN GEORGE, lawyer; b. St. Louis, July 24, 1946; s. Irwin Jacob and Dorothy Grace (Reno) S.; m. Cassandra Jill Willoughby, Jan. 13, 1974; children: Sally, Lisa. BA, U. Mo., 1968, JD, 1971. Bar: Mo. 1971, U.S. Dist. Ct. (ea. dist.) Mo. 1972, U.S. Tax Ct. 1978, U.S. Ct. Appeals (8th cir.) 1985. Assoc. Carter, Brinker & Doyen, Clayton, Mo., 1971-78; ptnr. Taylor, Schumaier & Sluggett, Clayton, 1978-84; sr. ptnr. Schumaier, Roberts & McKinsey, Clayton, 1984—; bd. dirs. Bus. Interiors, St. Louis. Mem. ABA, St. Louis County Bar Assn., St. Louis Met. Bar Assn., Assn. Trial Lawyers Am., Mo. Assn. Trial Lawyers. Lutheran. Club: Algonquin Golf (Glendale, Mo.). Avocations: golf, tennis. Insurance, Personal injury. Home: 601 E Monroe St Kirkwood MO 63122 Office: Schumaier Roberts & McKinsey 8000 Maryland Ave Suite 620 Clayton MO 63105

SCHUMAN, CLIFFORD RICHARD, lawyer; b. N.Y.C., June 11, 1913. s. Samuel and Bertha (Schiff) S.; m. Charlotte Suchman; 1 child, Bonnie. B.A., N.Y. U., 1932; J.D., Columbia U. Law Sch., 1935. Bar: N.Y. 1935, U.S. Dist. Ct. (so. dist.) N.Y. 1938, U.S. Dist. Ct. (ea. dist.) N.Y. 1938, U.S. Tax Ct. 1940, U.S. Ct. Appeals (2d cir.) 1960, U.S. Supreme Ct. 1939. Sole practice, N.Y.C., 1980—; dir. Bolivia R.R. Co., 1938-42; adj. prof. Law Baruch Coll., City U. N.Y., 1971—; mem. law faculty Adelphi U. 1977-78; cons. revision ins. law N.Y. State Law Revision Commn., 1980-81; legal adv. N.Y.C. Selective Service Bd., Harlem Area, 1939-42. Served with JAGC, AUS, 1942-44. Recipient Alumni Meritorious Service award N.Y. U., 1972, Sesquicentennial Crystal award, 1982. Mem. ABA, N.Y. State Bar Assn., Assn. Bar City N.Y. (mem. com. on uniform state laws 1966-84, chmn. 1981-84), N.Y. County Lawyers Assn., N.Y. U. Alumni Assn.-Heights Coll. (pres. 1967-69, dir. 1965—), Alumni Fedn. N.Y. U. (dir. 1967—), Phi Beta Kappa, Pi Lambda Phi. Lodges: B'nai B'rith, Masons (N.Y. state grand dir. ceremonies 1966-67). Editor Columbia Law Rev., 1933-35; contbr. articles to profl. jours. General practice, State civil litigation, General corporate. Home: 40 W 77th St New York NY 10024 Office: 747 3d Ave New York NY 10017

SCHUMAN, WILLIAM PAUL, lawyer; b. Chgo., May 6, 1954; s. Alvin W. and Gloria (Kayner) S.; m. Caryn Gutmann, Dec. 20, 1980; 1 child, Lindsey J. BBA, U. Mich., 1976; JD, Harvard U., 1979. Bar: U.S. Dist. Ct. (no. dist.) Ill. 1979. Assoc. McDermott, Will & Emery, Chgo., 1979-84, ptnr., 1985—. Mem. ABA, Ill. Bar Assn., Chgo. Bar Assn. Avocations: softball, golf, basketball. Securities, Federal civil litigation. Home: 1863 Clavey Rd Highland Park IL 60035 Office: McDermott Will & Emery 111 W Monroe St Chicago IL 60603

SCHUR, JEROME, lawyer; b. Milw., May 20, 1927; s. Ben and Bertha (Stein) S.; married; children: Ellen, Cynthia. BA, U. Wis., 1948; JD, Yale U., 1951. Bar: Wis. 1951, Ill. 1952. Ptnr. Katz, Friedman, Schur & Eagle, Chicago, 1951—; asst. to chief judge Cook County Cir. Ct., Chgo., 1967. Served with USN, 1944-45. Mem. ABA, Ill. Bar Assn. (chmn. indsl. sect.), Chgo. Bar Assn. (chmn. labor law com. 1984-85), Assn. Trial Lawyers Am. (chmn. workers compensation sect.), Chgo. Council of Lawyers. Labor, Workers' compensation. Office: Katz Friedman Schur & Eagle 7 S Dearborn Chicago IL 60603

SCHURR, M. RANDOLPH, lawyer; b. Evanston, Ill., Dec. 25, 1952; s. George M. and Rosamaude Jean (Burgess) S. BA in History, Colo. Coll., 1975; JD, U. Ariz., 1980. Bar: Ariz. 1980, U.S. Dist. Ct. Ariz. 1980, U.S. Ct. Appeals (9th cir.) 1982. Dep. county atty. Yavapai County, Prescott, Ariz., 1981-85, supr. civil div., 1985—. Local government, Government contracts and claims, Land use and planning. Office: Yavapai County Courthouse Prescott AZ 86301

SCHUSTER, PHILIP FREDERICK, II, lawyer; b. Denver, Aug. 26, 1945; s. Philip Frederick and Ruth Elizabeth (Robar) S.; m. Barbara Lynn Nordquist, June 7, 1975; children: Philip Christian, Matthew Dale. BA, U. Wash., 1967; JD, Willamette U., 1972. Bar: Oreg. 1972, U.S. Dist. Ct. Oreg. 1974, U.S. Ct. Appeals (9th cir.) 1986, U.S. Supreme Ct. 1986. Dep. dist. atty. Multnomah County, Portland, Oreg., 1972; title examiner Pioneer Nat. Title Co., Portland, 1973-74; assoc. Buss, Leichner et al, Portland, 1975-76; from assoc. to ptnr. Kitson & Bond, Portland, 1976-77; sole practice Portland, 1977—. Contbr. articles to profl. jours. Organizer Legal Aid Services for Community Clinics, Salem, Oreg. and Seattle, 1969-73; dem. committeeman, Seattle, 1965-70. Mem. ABA, NAACP (exec. bd. 1979—). Lodges: Sertoma, Elks. Avocations: river drifting, camping, swimming, jogging, writing. Personal injury, Probate, Real property. Office: 1500 NE Irving Suite 540 Portland OR 97232

SCHUSTER, ROBERT PARKS, lawyer; b. St. Louis, Oct. 25, 1945; s. William Thomas Schuster and Carolyn Cornforth (Daugherty) Hathaway; 1 child, Susan Michele. A.B., Yale U., 1967; J.D. with honors, U. of Wyo., 1970; LL.M., Harvard U., 1971. Bar: Wyo. 1971, U.S. Ct. Appeals (10th cir.) 1979, U.S. Supreme Ct. 1984. Dep. county atty. County of Natrona, Casper, Wyo., 1971-73; sole practice, Casper, 1973-76; assoc. Spence & Moriarity, Casper, 1976-78; ptnr. Spence, Moriarity & Schuster, Jackson, Wyo., 1978—. Trustee U. Wyo., 1985—. Ford Found. Urban Law fellow, 1970-71; pres. United Way of Natrona County, 1974; bd. dirs. Dancers Workshop, 1981-83. Mem. ABA, Assn. Trial Lawyers Am., Nat. Assn. of Criminal Defense Lawyers. Wyo. Trial Lawyers Assn. Federal civil litigation, State civil litigation. Home: PO Box 548 Jackson WY 83001 Office: Spence Moriarity & Schuster 265 W Pearl Jackson WY 83001

SCHUSTER, STEVEN VINCENT, lawyer; b. Englewood, N.J., Mar. 27, 1952; s. Vincent Theodore and Eliane (Danis) S. B.A., Gettysburg Coll., 1974; J.D., U. Richmond, 1977. Bar: Va. 1977, N.J. 1977, U.S. Dist. Ct. N.J. 1977. Assoc. firm Bruce K. Byers, Esquire, Ridgewood, N.J., 1977-78, Margolis & Gordon, Union, N.J., 1978-80, R.J. Inglima, P.A., Paramus, N.J., 1980-83; sole practice, Cresskill, N.J., 1983—; corp. counsel Agfa Gevaert, Inc., Teterboro, N.J., 1983—, atty. zoning bd. Borough of Dumont; mcpl. prosecutor Borough of Bergen; trustee Bergen County Task Force Crimes Against Children Inc., Agfa Gevaert Rex, White Plains, N.Y., 1983-85; dir. Metacomet Inc. Mem. county com. Bergen County Rep. Orgn., N.J., 1978-82, 85—; aide to state senator Gerald Cardinale, Cresskill, 1979—; councilman Borough of Cresskill, 1982-84; prosecutor Borough of Cresskill, 1985—. Recipient Presdl. Achievement award, Washington, 1981. Mem. ABA, N.J. Bar Assn., Va. Bar Assn., Bergen County Bar Assn. Roman Catholic. General corporate, Legislative, Local government. Address: 170 Palisade Ave Cresskill NJ 07626 Office: 65B W Madison Ave Dumont NJ 07628

SCHUTT, WILLIAM ELDON, lawyer; b. Oakland, Calif., Aug. 10, 1941. BSME, Calif. Maritime Acad., 1964; JD, U. San Francisco, 1974. Bar: Calif. 1975, U.S. Dist. Ct. (no. dist.) Calif. 1975. Chief engr. Delta Steam Ship Co., San Francisco, 1975-84, Am. Pres. Lines, Oakland, Calif., 1984-86; sole practice Boulder City, Nev., 1986—. Mem. Soc. Naval Architects and Marine Engrs., Marine Engrs. Beneficial Assn., ABA, Calif. Bar Assn., Am. Immigration and Lawyers Assn. Immigration, naturalization, and customs, Admiralty, Private international. Office: 557 California St Suite 20 Boulder City NV 89005

SCHUTZER, GEORGE JEFFREY, lawyer; b. San Antonio, Feb. 8, 1955; s. Saul Samuel and Judith (Weiner) S.; m. Carolyn Milliman Bausch, Sept. 4, 1983. BA, Williams Coll., 1977; JD, Yale U., 1980. Bar: D.C. 1980, U.S. Dist. Ct. D.C. 1981, U.S. Ct. Claims 1981, U.S. Tax Ct. 1981, U.S. Ct. Appeals (D.C. cir.) 1981. From assoc. to ptnr. Patton, Boggs & Blow, Washington, 1980—. Contbr. articles to Constructor mag. Bd. dirs. Windgate Homeowners Assn., Arlington, Va., 1986. Mem. ABA (taxation com. 1981—), Phi Beta Kappa. Democrat. Jewish. Avocations: softball, bicycling, spectator sports. Corporate taxation, Personal income taxation, Legislative. Home: 2508E S Arlington Mill Dr Arlington VA 22206-3302 Office: Patton Boggs & Blow 2550 M St NW Washington DC 20037

SCHUUR, ROBERT GEORGE, lawyer; b. Kalamazoo, Dec. 5, 1931; s. George Garrett and Louise Margaret (DeVries) S.; m. Susan Elizabeth White, Sept. 28, 1968; children—Arah Louise Adele, Jeremiah Donald Garrett. A.B., U. Mich., 1953, LL.B., 1955. Bar: Mich. 1955, N.Y. 1956. Assoc. Reid & Priest, N.Y.C., 1955-65, ptnr., 1966—. Served with USN, 1956-58. Mem. Assn. Bar City of N.Y., N.Y. State Bar Assn., ABA, Phi Beta Kappa. Club: University (N.Y.C.). General corporate, Public utilities, Securities. Office: 40 W 57th St New York NY 10019

SCHUURMAN, WILLEM GERHARD, patent lawyer; b. Wakkerstroom, Transvaal, Republic of South Africa, June 21, 1940; came to U.S., 1979; s. William B. and Rina (Du Preez) S.; m. Fiona J. Barnetson, Nov. 19, 1969; children—Greg W., Bruce J., Angus D., D. Geordie. B.S., U. Cape Town, Republic of South Africa, 1962, LL.B., 1964; J.D. with honors, S. Tex. Coll. Law, Houston, 1981. Bar: Tex. 1981, U.S. Dist. Ct. (so. dist.) Tex. 1982, U.S. Dist. Ct. (we. dist.) Tex. 1985. Ptnr. Adams & Adams, Pretoria, Republic of South Africa, 1967-79; assoc. Arnold, White & Durkee, Houston, 1979-83, ptnr., 1983—. Mem. Am. Intellectual Property Law Assn., ABA, Internat. Fedn. Indsl. Property Attys. U.S. (council 1982—), Travis County Bar Assn., Licensing Exec. Soc., Internat. Assn. for the Protection of Indsl. Property. Republican. Clubs: Westwood Country, Pretoria Country. Patent, Federal civil litigation. Home: 1203 Constant Springs Austin TX 78746 Office: Arnold White & Durkee 2300 One American Ctr 600 Congress Austin TX 78701 also: Box 4433 Houston TX 77210

SCHUWERK, ROBERT PAUL, law educator; b. Evanston, Ill., Sept. 12, 1942; s. Paul Paul Edward and Helene Romaine (Rogers) S.; m. Mary Suzanne Hair, Aug. 24, 1974; children: Robert Charles, Michael Deering, Mary Evelyn. BS, U. Chgo., 1964, MA in Teaching of Mathematics, 1966, JD, 1972. Bar: Ill. 1972, Tex. 1984. Law clk. to judge U.S. Dist. Ct. La., New Orleans, 1972-73; staff counsel Ill. Law Enforcement Commn., Chgo., 1973-77; assoc. Plotkin & Jacobs, Chgo., 1977-81; assoc. prof. U. Houston Law Ctr., 1981—. Mem. ABA, State Bar Tex. (co-reporter model rules of profl. conduct com. 1984-86, grievance com. 4-F 1986—), Harris County Criminal Def. Lawyers. Presbyterian. Legal education, Jurisprudence, Federal civil litigation. Home: 16379 Larkfield Dr Houston TX 77059 Office: U Houston Law Ctr 4800 Calhoun St Houston TX 77004

SCHUYLER, DANIEL MERRICK, lawyer, educator; b. Oconomowoc, Wis., July 26, 1912; s. Daniel J. and Fannie Sybil (Moorhouse) S.; m. Claribel Seaman, June 15, 1935; children: Daniel M., Sheila Gordon. A.B. summa cum laude, Dartmouth Coll., 1934; J.D., Northwestern U., 1937. Bar: Ill. 1937, U.S. Supreme Ct. 1942, Wis. 1943. Tchr. constl. history Chgo. Latin Sch., 1935-37; asso. Schuyler & Hennessy (attys.), 1937-42, partner, 1948; partner Schuyler, Richert & Stough, 1948-58, Schuyler, Stough & Morris, Chgo., 1958-76, Schuyler, Ballard & Cowen, 1976-83, Schuyler, Roche & Zwirner, P.C., 1983—; treas., sec. and controller B-W Superchargers, Inc. div. Borg-Warner Corp., Milw., 1942-46; lectr. trusts, real property, future interests Northwestern U. Sch. Law, 1946-50, asso. prof. law, 1950-52, prof., 1952-80, prof. emeritus, 1980—. Author: (with Homer F. Carey) Illinois Law of Future Interests, 1941; supplement, 1954; (with William M. McGovern, Jr.) Illinois Trust and Will Manual, 1970; supplements, 1972, 74, 76, 77, 79, 80, 81, 82, 83, 84; contbr. to profl. jours. Republican nominee for judge Cook County Circuit Ct., 1958; bd. dirs. United Cerebral Palsy Greater Chgo.; bd. mgrs. Bartelme Homes and Services. Fellow Am. Bar Found.; mem. Chgo. Estate Planning Council (past pres., Disting. Service award 1977), Am. Coll. Probate Counsel (past pres.), Internat. Acad. Estate and Trust Law, ABA (past mem. ho. dels., past chmn. sect. real property, probate trust law), Chgo. Bar Assn. (past chmn. coms. on trust law and post-admission edn., past bd. mgrs.), Ill. Bar Assn. (past chmn. real estate and legal edn. sects., past bd. govs.), Wis. Bar Assn., Phi Beta Kappa, Order of Coif, Phi Kappa Psi. Clubs: Legal (Chgo.), Law (Chgo.), Chicago (Chgo.), University (Chgo.). Estate planning, Health, General practice. Home: 324 Cumnor Rd Kenilworth IL 60043 Office: 3100 Prudential Plaza Chicago IL 60601

SCHWAAB, RICHARD LEWIS, lawyer, educator; b. Oconomowoc, Wis., Nov. 15, 1945. B.S. in Chem. Engring., U. Wis., 1967; J.D. with honors, George Washington U., 1971, LL.M. in Internat. Law with highest honors, 1979. Bar: Va. 1971, U.S. Dist. Ct. (ea. dist.) Va. 1979, U.S. Supreme Ct. 1980, U.S. Ct. Appeals (fed. cir.) 1982. Ptnr., Stepno, Schwaab & Linn, Arlington, 1972-74, Bacon & Thomas, Arlington, 1974-78, Schwartz, Jeffery, Schwaab, Mack, Blumenthal & Evans, P.C., Alexandria, 1978—; lectr. law George Washington U., 1978—. Max Planck Inst. Fgn. and Internat. Patent, Copyright and Competition Law fellow, 1971-72. Mem. ABA, Am. Patent Law Assn., Va. State Bar (gov. 1974-78), Am. Soc. Internat. Law, Internat. Patent and Trademark Assn., Internat. Fedn. Indsl. Property Attys., Phi Kappa Phi, Tau Beta Pi. Co-author Patent Practice, 6 vols., 1985; International Patent Law: EPC & PCT, 3 vols., 1978; Intellectual Property Protection for Biotechnology Worldwide, 1987. Contbr. articles to profl. jours. Patent, Antitrust, Trademark and copyright. Office: King St Sta 1800 Diagonal Rd Alexandria VA 22313

SCHWAB, CAROL ANN, lawyer; b. Washington, Mo., Mar. 2, 1953; d. Calvin George and Edith Emma (Starke) Schermann; m. Steven Joseph Schwab, May 31, 1975. BA, Southeast Mo. State U., 1975; JD, U. Mo., 1978; LLM, Washington U., St. Louis, 1985. Bar: Mo. 1979, N.C. 1986. Law clk. to presiding justice U.S. Dist. Ct. (we. dist.) Kansas City, Mo., 1979-82; assoc. Bryan, Cave, McPheeters & Roberts, St. Louis, 1982-84, Smith, Anderson, Blount, Dorsett, Mitchell & Jernigan, Raleigh, N.C., 1985-87, Poyner & Spruill, Raleigh, 1987—; instr. legal writing St. Louis U. Sch. Law, 1984. Contbr. articles to profl. jours. Recipient John S. Divilbiss award U. Mo., 1977. Mem. ABA, N.C. Bar Assn., Mo. Bar Assn. Republican. Roman Catholic. Corporate taxation, Estate taxation, Personal income taxation. Office: PO Box 10096 Raleigh NC 27605-0096

SCHWAB, DAVID E., II, lawyer; b. N.Y.C., May 8, 1931; s. Auguste and Dorothy L. (Stern) S.; m. Ruth Schwartz, June 23, 1953; children: Wendy S. Schnall, Peter D. BA, Bard Coll., 1952; LLB, Yale U., 1955. Bar: N.Y. 1955, U.S. Dist. Ct. (so. and ea. dists.) N.Y. 1956, U.S. Ct. Appeals (2d cir.) 1956, U.S. Supreme Ct. 1967, Fla. 1981. Law clk. to judge U.S. Dist. Ct. (so. dist.) N.Y., N.Y.C., 1955-56; assoc. Benjamin, Galton & Robbins, N.Y.C., 1956-59; ptnr. Schwab Goldberg Price & Dannay and predecessor firms, N.Y.C., 1959—; bd. dirs. CJI Industries Inc., N.Y.C., La. and N.W. R.R., Homer, La., H.E. Salzberg Co. Inc., N.Y.C., Avery Inc., N.Y.C. Trustee Bard Coll., Annandale-on-Hudson, N.Y., 1963—, chmn. 1984—; pres. Temple Israel of No. Westchester, Croton-on-Hudson, N.Y., 1976-78. Mem. ABA, Assn. Bar of City of N.Y. Democrat. Jewish. Club: Yale (N.Y.C.). Lodge: B'nai B'rith. General corporate, Probate, Transportation. Home: 68 Cedar Dr Briarcliff Manor NY 10510 Office: Schwab Goldberg Price & Dannay 1185 Ave of Americas New York NY 10036

SCHWAB, ELMO, lawyer; b. Gonzales, Tex., Jan. 17, 1937; s. Elmo and Mary Doris (Riemenschneider) S.; m. Claudette Taylor, Sept. 19, 1960; children: Mary Suzanne, Taylor Townsend. BA with honors, U. Tex., Austin, 1959, JD, 1962; MA, U. Houston, 1980. Bar: Tex., 1962, U.S. Supreme Ct., 1968. Assoc. Barker & Barker, 1962-66, McLeod, Alexander, Powel & Apffel, 1967-68; ptnr. Barker, Lain, Schwab, Tulloch & Allen and predecessors, 1969-82; sole practice, Galveston, Tex., 1982—; adj. prof. legal medicine U. Tex. Med. Br.; researcher, writer in law and humanities. Mem. Galveston Cultural Arts Council, Galveston Hist. Found.; pres. Family Service Galveston, 1971-72. Nat. Endowment Humanities fellow, 1976-77. Mem. Am. Trial Lawyers Assn., World Peace Through Law Soc., Am. Philos. Assn., Am. Soc. Law and Medicine. Democrat. Episcopalian. Club: Rotary. General practice, Family and matrimonial, Jurisprudence. Home: 2618 Gerol Ct Havre LaFitte Galveston TX 77551 Office: 600 US Nat Bank 2201 Market Galveston TX 77550

SCHWAB, STEPHEN WAYNE, lawyer; b. Washington, Jan. 25, 1956; s. A. Wayne and Elizabeth (Parsons) S.; m. Debora Zellner, May 26, 1979; 1 child, Benjamin Earl. BA, Northwestern U., 1979; JD, Dickinson Sch. Law, 1982. Bar: Ill. 1982, U.S. Dist. Ct. (no. dist.) Ill. 1983, U.S. Ct. Appeals (7th cir.) 1985, U.S. Ct. Claims 1986. Assoc. Pretzel & Stouffer, Chgo., 1982-85, Rudnick & Wolfe, Chgo., 1985—. Mem. ABA, Ill. Bar Assn., Chgo. Bar Assn., Phi Eta Sigma. Democrat. Episcopalian. Labor, Federal civil litigation, State civil litigation. Office: Rudnick & Wolfe 30 N LaSalle St 28th Floor Chicago IL 60602

SCHWABE, JOHN BENNETT, II, lawyer; b. Columbia, Mo., June 14, 1946; s. Leonard Wesley and Hazel Fern (Crouch) S. A.B., U. Mo.-Columbia, 1967, J.D., 1970. Bar: Mo. 1970, U.S. Dist. Ct. (we. dist.) Mo. 1970, U.S. Ct. Mil. Appeals 1971, U.S. Supreme Ct. 1973. Owner, prin. John B. Schwabe, II & Assocs., Columbia, 1974—, St. Louis, 1984—. Trustee, lay leader, mem. adminstrv. bd. Wilkes Blvd. United Meth. Ch., 1974-79, chmn. pastor-parish relations com., 1984-85 ; mem. Friends of Music, Columbia, 1979—, bd. dirs., 1979-81; bd. dirs. Mo. Symphony Soc., 1984-85 . Served to capt. JAGC, USAF, 1970-74. Mem. ABA, Boone County Bar Assn. (sec. 1977-79), Bar Assn. Met. St. Louis, Assn. Trial Lawyers Am., Mo. Assn. Trial Attys., Personal Injury Lawyers Assn., Lawyers Assn. St. Louis, Columbia C. of C., Am. Legion, Phi Delta Phi. Methodist. Club: Wilkes Men's (pres. 1977-79) (Columbia). Personal injury, State civil litigation, Workers' compensation. Office: 314 N Broadway Marquette Bldg Suite 830 Saint Louis MO 63102

SCHWABENLAND, EDWARD JOHN, lawyer; b. Phila., May 9, 1950; s. Conrad J. and Frances C. (Kenny) S.; m. Paula D. Funk, May 19, 1979; 1 child, Mark. BA, Albright Coll., Reading, Pa., 1972; JD, Widener U., Villanova, Pa., 1976. Bar: Pa. 1976, U.S. Dist. Ct. (we. dist.) Pa. 1977, U.S. Ct. Appeals (3d. cir.) 1977, U.S. SupremeCt. 1980, U.S. Dist. Ct. (ea. dist.) Pa. 1981. Asst. U.S. atty. U.S. Atty.'s Office, Pitts., 1977-81; assoc. Griffith & Burr, Phila., 1981—. Federal civil litigation, State civil litigation, Criminal. Home: Maple Ave and Woodmere Ct Paoli PA 19301 Office: Griffith & Burr 1608 Walnut St Philadelphia PA 19103

SCHWARCZ, STEVEN LANCE, lawyer, adjunct law educator; b. N.Y.C., Nov. 10, 1949; s. Charles and Elinor Schwarcz; m. Susan Beth Kolodny, Aug. 24, 1975; children—Daniel Benjamin, Rebekah Mara. B.S. summa cum laude, in Engring., New York U., 1971; J.D., Columbia U., 1974. Bar: N.Y. 1975, U.S. Dist. Ct. (so. dist.) N.Y. 1975. Assoc. Shearman & Sterling, N.Y.C., 1974-82, ptnr., 1983—; adj. prof. law Yeshiva U., Benjamin N. Cardozo Sch. Law, N.Y.C., 1983—. Contbr. articles to profl. jours. Chmn. Friends of the Eldridge St. Synagogue, N.Y.C., 1979—, Legis. Drafting Research Fund. Recipient First Prize award Pub. Speaking Contest, N.Y. U., 1971; George Granger Brown scholar, 1971; NSF grantee in Math., 1969. Mem. Assn. Bar City of New York (environ. law com. 1975-78, nuclear tech. com. 1979-81, sci. and law com. 1985—, chmn. 1987—). Tau Beta Pi. Jewish. Banking, Bankruptcy, Legal education. Office: Shearman & Sterling 53 Wall St New York NY 10005

SCHWARTZ, AARON ROBERT, lawyer, former state legistator; b. Galveston, Tex., July 17, 1926; s. Joseph and Clara (Bulbe) S.; m. Marilyn Cohn, July 14, 1951; children: Richard Austin, Robert Allen, John Reed, Thomas Lee. Pre-law student, Tex. A&M U., 1948; J.D., U. Tex., 1951. Bar: Tex. 1951. Mem. Tex. Ho. of Reps., 1955-59; Mem. Tex. Senate, 1960-81, past chmn. rules, jurisprudence and natural resources coms.; chmn. Tex. Coastal & Marine Council, U.S. Coastal States Orgn.; bd. dirs. Ins. Corp. of Am., Houston, Columbia Savings and Loan, Clear Lake, Tex. Contbr. articles to profl. jours. Mem. U. Tex. Med. Br. Devel. Found. Served with USN, 1944-46; to 2d lt. USAFR, 1948-53. Recipient conservation and legis. awards, Outstanding Citizen award Galveston Jr. C. of C., 1981, Man of Yr., People of Vision award Galveston chpt. Soc. for Prevention of Blindness, 1986, Disting. Service award Nat. Hurricane Conf., 1987. Mem. Tex. State Bar Assn., Tex. Trial Lawyers Assn., Galveston County Bar Assn. Democrat. Jewish. State civil litigation, Legislative, Local government. Home: 10 South Shore Dr Galveston TX 77550 Office: 1331 Lamar Suite 560 Houston TX 77010

SCHWARTZ, ALAN URIEL, lawyer; b. Mt. Vernon, N.Y., Feb. 13, 1933; s. Milton and Gertrude A. (Scheinbart) S.; m. Paula Dunaway, Aug. 29, 1959 (div. 1982); children—Matthew Carlos, John Burnham; m. H. Louise Nussbaum, Nov. 2, 1985. B.A. with honors in Govt., Cornell U.; LL.B., Yale U. Bar: N.Y. 1957, Calif. 1985. Fellow Assn. Bar of City of N.Y., N.Y.C., 1956-57; assoc., ptnr. Greenbaum Wolff & Ernst, N.Y.C., 1957-62, ptnr., 1962-79; ptnr. Barovick, Konecky, Schwartz, Kay & Schiff, N.Y.C., 1979-81, Fulop & Hardee, Beverly Hills, Calif., 1981-83, Finley Kumble Wagner Heine, Underberg, Manley, Myerson & Casey, Beverly Hills, Calif., 1983—; dir. Brooksfilms, Beverly Hills, Mcht. Bank Calif. Author: Privacy, 1961, Censorship, 1962, Lawyers and What They Do, 1963; contbr. articles to Pubs. Weekly, Atlantic Monthly, Saturday Rev., others. Bd. dirs. Fund for Free Expression; mem. Helsinki Watch. Mem. Assn. Bar City of N.Y., Century Assn. Democrat. Avocations: sailing; skiing; tennis. Entertainment. Office: Finley Kumble Wagner et al 9100 Wilshire Blvd 10 E Beverly Hills CA 90212

SCHWARTZ, ALLEN G., lawyer; b. Bklyn., Aug. 23, 1934; s. Herbert and Florence (Safier) S.; m. Joan Ruth Teitel, Jan. 17, 1965; children: David Aaron, Rachel Ann, Deborah Eve. B.B.A., CCNY, 1955; LL.B., U. Pa., 1958. Bar: N.Y. bar 1958. Asst. dist. atty. Office of Dist. Atty., N.Y. County, 1959-62; assoc. firm Paskus Gordon & Hyman, N.Y.C., 1962-65; ptnr. firm Koch Lankenau Schwartz & Kovner, N.Y.C., 1965-69, Dornbush Mensch Mandelstam & Schwartz, N.Y.C., 1969-75, Schwartz & Schreiber (P.C.), N.Y.C., 1975-77; corp. counsel City of N.Y., 1978-81; ptnr. Schwartz Klink & Schreiber P.C., 1982-87, Proskaver, Rose, Goetz & Mendelsohn, N.Y.C., 1987—; mem. N.Y.C. Criminal Justice Coordinating Council, 1978-81; mem. N.Y.C. Pub. Devel. Corp., 1978-81, N.Y.C. Bd. Revision of Awards, 1978-81, Mayor's Concessions Rev. Com.; mem. ex officio N.Y.C. Bd. Ethics; pro bono sports commr. City of N.Y., 1982-83. Research editor: U. Pa. Law Rev, 1957-58. Mem. ABA, Assn. Bar City of N.Y., N.Y. State Bar Assn. Home: 100 Kirby Ln Rye NY 10580 Office: Proskauer Rose Goetz & Mendelsohn 666 3d Ave New York NY 10017

SCHWARTZ, ARTHUR EDWARD, lawyer; b. N.Y.C., Feb. 19, 1955; s. Isadore and Bella (Sussman) S.; m. Marsha Ann Lederman, June 15, 1980; 1 child, Zachary Ian. BA in History summa cum laude, SUNY, Bufflo, 1977; JD, Am. U., Washington, 1980. Bar; Fla. 1982, D.C. 1984. Law clk. U.S. Dept. Labor, Washington, 1980-81; asst. gen. counsel NSPE, Washington, 1982-86, gen. counsel, 1986—. Mem. ABA, Am. Corp. Counsel Assn., Phi Beta Kappa. Jewish. Construction, Government contracts and claims, General corporate. Home: 107 N Columbus St Arlington VA 22203 Office: NSPE 1420 King St Alexandra VA 22314

SCHWARTZ, ARTHUR JAY, lawyer; b. Atlanta, May 28, 1947; s. William B. Jr. and Sonia (Weinberg) S.; m. Joyce Straus, Aug. 12, 1972; children: Tracy Jill, Allison Jaye. BA, U. N.C., 1969; JD, Emory U., 1972. Bar: Ga. 1972, U.S. Dist. Ct. (no. dist.) Ga. 1972, U.S. Ct. Appeals (11th cir.) 1972. Ptnr. Smith, Gambrell & Russell, Atlanta, 1972—; sec., bd. dirs. Lamin Art, Inc., Chgo., 1984—. Bd. dirs. Am. Jewish Com., Atlanta, 1982-84, The Temple, Atlanta, 1983-85. Served with USAR, 1970-72. Mem. Am. Technion Soc. Atlanta (v.p., bd. dirs. 1980—). Avocations: tennis, running, boating. General corporate, Securities, Contracts commercial. Office: Smith Gambrell & Russell 3333 Peachtree Rd NE Atlanta GA 30326

SCHWARTZ, BRUCE S., lawyer; b. Phila., Feb. 6, 1939; s. Sidney and Betty Rudin (Taub) S.; m. Marilyn Brownstein, Feb. 28, 1976; children—Cydney, Billie Samantha. B.S., Phila. Coll. Textiles & Scis., 1960; J.D., U. Miami, Fla., 1963. Bar: Fla. 1963, U.S. Supreme Ct. 1971; cert. civil trial practice lawyer. Ptnr. Linet, Schwartz & Klein, North Miami Beach, Fla., 1963-70, Schwartz, Steinhardt, Weiss & Weinstein, P.A., North Miami Beach, 1970—; mcpl. judge City of North Miami Beach, 1971-75; rep. to Fla. Patient's Compensation Fund, Fla. Bar. Mem. Assn. Trial Lawyers Am., Acad. Fla. Trial Lawyers (bd. dirs. 1973-75, Coll. Diplomates 1979—), Def. Research Inst., North Dade Bar Assn. (pres. 1970-71). Personal injury. Home: 11111 Biscayne Blvd Miami FL 33161 Office: Schwartz Steinhardt Weiss & Weinstein PA 2750 NE 187th St North Miami Beach FL 33180

SCHWARTZ, CHARLES WALTER, lawyer; b. Brenham, Tex., Dec. 27, 1953; s. Walter C. and Annie (Kuehn) S.; m. Trisha Bradway, Sept. 2, 1983. B.S., U. Tex.-Austin, 1975, M.A., 1980, J.D., 1977; LL.M., Harvard U., 1980. Bar: Tex. 1977. Law clk. to presiding judge U.S. Ct. Appeals (5th cir.), Austin, Tex., 1977-79; assoc. Vinson & Elkins, Houston, 1980-86, ptnr., 1986—. Contbr. articles to law revs. Mem. ABA, Houston Bar Assn., Houston Young Lawyers Assn., Tex. Law Rev. Assn., Bar Assn. 5th Circuit. Federal civil litigation, Antitrust, Securities. Home: 2829 Timmons Ln #116 Houston TX 77027 Office: Vinson & Elkins 2906 First City Tower 1001 Fannin Houston TX 77002-6760

SCHWARTZ, DAVID, lawyer, arbitrator, mediator; b. N.Y.C., July 7, 1916; s. Hyman and Nettie (Strauss) S.; m. Louisa Van Wezel, June 15, 1968; children by previous marriage: Jonathan, Joanna M. AB cum laude, NYU, 1936; LLB magna cum laude, Harvard U., 1939. Bar: N.Y. 1940, D.C. 1965, U.S. Supreme Ct. 1946, U.S. Ct. Claims 1954. Assoc. Karelsen & Karelsen, N.Y.C., 1939-40; spl. asst. to atty. gen. Dept. Justice, Washington, 1941-42, chief trial atty. antitrust and enemy property div., 1945-56; law clk. to Justice Stanley F. Reed, 1942-43; legal adviser Greece and Balkan missions UNRRA and predecessor State Dept., 1943-45; gen. counsel Devel. & Resources Corp., N.Y.C., 1956-57; ptnr. Stroock & Stroock & Lavan, N.Y.C., 1957-68; trial judge U.S. Ct. Claims Washington, 1968-82; sole practice law, Washington, 1982—; adj. prof. law Georgetown U., 1981—; adj. asst. prof. NYU law sch., 1957-68; adj. prof. U. Pa. Law Sch., 1984; vis. prof. U. Wis. at Madison Law Sch., summers 1976, 78, U. San Diego Law Sch., summers 1977, 79-81, Inst. Internat. and Comparative Law, London, summers 1983, 85. Co-author: Government Litigation-Cases and Notes, 1963, Litigation with the Federal Government, 2d edit., 1983. Recipient John D. Rockefeller III Pub. Service award, 1955. Mem. ABA, Fed. Bar Assn., D.C. Bar Assn., Assn. Bar City N.Y., Am. Law Inst. (bd. advisers restatement of contracts second). Democrat. Jewish. Government contracts and claims, Federal civil litigation, Administrative and regulatory. Office: 1417 33d St NW Washington DC 20007

SCHWARTZ, DAVID ELVING, lawyer; b. Newark, Oct. 5, 1954; s. Joseph and Eleanor Juliber (Elving) S. BA, Drew U., 1976; JD, Seton Hall U., 1979. Bar: N.J. 1980, U.S. Dist. Ct. N.J. 1980, U.S. Ct. Internat. Trade 1986, U.S. Ct. Appeals (3d cir.) 1986. Law clk. to mcpl. judge N.J. State Ct., Elizabeth, 1979-80; sole practice Springfield, N.J., 1980—, Montclair, N.J., 1985—; cons. Internat. Ctr. for Ednl. Advancement, Newark, 1985—; bd. dirs. Barataria Corp., Inc., Montclair, Ingesco, Ltd., Newark, Met. Fantasy, Wargaming and Sci. Fiction Assn., Inc., Denville. Contbr. articles to profl. jours. Mem. ABA, N.J. Bar Assn., Union County Bar Assn. Club: Royal (Springfield, N.J.) (bd. dirs. 1980—). Avocations: military history, game designing. Federal civil litigation, State civil litigation, Contracts commercial. Home: 569 S Springfield Ave Springfield NJ 07081 Office: 460 Bloomfield Ave Montclair NJ 07081

SCHWARTZ, DAVID HAROLD, lawyer; b. N.Y.C., Nov. 14, 1939; s. Herman M. and Blanche S.; m. Carol Joan Levitt, Aug. 2, 1966; children—Stephanie, Hilary, Douglas. A.B., N.Y. U., 1960; J.D., Columbia U., 1963. Bar: N.Y. 1964, D.C. 1964. Assoc. Arent, Fox, Kintner, Plotkin & Kahn, Washington, 1964-70; sec. D.C. City Council, 1970-72; ptnr. Melrod, Redman & Gartlan and predecessor, Washington, 1972-81; ptnr. Willkie Farr & Gallagher, Washington, 1981—; adj. prof. law Georgetown U. Law Center, 1970-71, 85—. Bd. dirs. Washington Polit. Action Com. Harlan Fisk Stone scholar Columbia U. Sch. Law, 1962, 63, Nat. scholar, 1963. Mem. D.C. Bar Assn., ABA, N.Y. State Bar Assn. Republican. Jewish. Club: University (Washington). Real property, Contracts commercial, Local government. Home: 3555 Springland Ln NW Washington DC 20008 Office: Willkie Farr & Gallagher 1155 21st St NW Washington DC 20036

SCHWARTZ, DAVID LOUIS, lawyer; b. N.Y.C., Dec. 22, 1936; s. Abraham and Anne (Wasserman) S.; m. Nancy Ruth Schnitzer, Sept. 21, 1963; children: Sally Jean, Anne Judith, Daniel Adam. B.A., Columbia U., 1957; LL.B., U. Va., 1960. Bar: Va. 1960, N.Y. 1961. Assoc. Cravath Swaine & Moore, N.Y.C., 1960-68, ptnr., 1969—; mem. real estate adv. com. SEC, 1972. Served with AUS, 1960-61. Mem. Assn. Bar City N.Y., ABA, N.Y. State Bar Assn., Va. State Bar. Home: 1021 Park Ave New York NY 10028 Office: One Chase Manhattan Plaza New York NY 10005

SCHWARTZ, DONALD LEE, lawyer; b. Milw., Dec. 8, 1948; s. Bernard L. and Ruth M. (Marshall) S.; m. Susan J. Dunst, June 5, 1971; children: Stephanie Jane, Cheryl Ruth. BA, Macalester Coll., 1971; JD, U. Chgo., 1974. Bar: Ill. 1974. Assoc. Sidley & Austin, Chgo., 1974-80, ptnr., 1980—. Chmn. Ill. Conservative Union, 1979-81, bd. dirs. 1977-85. Served with U.S. Army, 1971-77. Mem. ABA (uniform comml. code com., comml. fin. services commn.), Ill. Bar Assn. (sec. council banking and bankruptcy sect. 1982-83), Chgo. Bar Assn. (chmn. comml. law com. 1980-81, fin. insts. com. 1982-83). Republican. Episcopalian. Clubs: Thorngate Country (Deerfield, Ill.); Monroe (Chgo.). Avocation: golf. Banking, Bankruptcy, Contracts commercial. Home: 1140 Oakley Ave Winnetka IL 60093 Office: Sidley & Austin One First National Plaza Chicago IL 60603

SCHWARTZ, EDWARD ARTHUR, digital equipment manufacturer; b. Boston, Sept. 27, 1937; s. Abe and Sophie (Gottheim) S.; children: Eric Allen, Jeffrey Michael. A.B., Oberlin Coll., 1959; LL.B., Boston Coll., 1962; postgrad., Am. U., 1958-59, Northeastern U., 1970; student Exec. Program, Stanford U., 1979. Bar: Conn. 1962, Mass. 1965. Legal intern Office Atty. Gen., Commonwealth of Mass., 1961; assoc. Schatz & Schatz, Hartford, Conn., 1962-65, Cohn, Reimer & Pollack, Boston, 1965-67; v.p., gen. counsel, sec. Digital Equipment Corp., Maynard, Mass., 1967—; vis. prof. law Boston Coll., 1987; dir. Stanmar, Inc., N.E. Legal Found. Editor Boston Coll. Indsl. and Comml. Law Rev, 1960-62, Ann. Survey Mass. Law, 1960-62. Bd. dirs. The Computer Mus. Mem. ABA, Mass. Bar Assn., Boston Bar Assn., Am. Corp. Counsel Assn. (bd. dirs.). General corporate. Home: 62 Todd Pond Rd Lincoln MA 01773 Office: 111 Powdermill Rd Maynard MA 01754

SCHWARTZ, EDWARD RICHARD, lawyer; b. Paterson, N.J., Dec. 29, 1934; s. Meyer and Marion (Gross) S.; m. Leah Fay Blackman, Dec. 23, 1967; children—Marla Jo, Sandra V. A.B. cum laude, Williams Coll., 1956; LL.B., Harvard U., 1959. Bar: D.C. 1959, N.J. 1963; cert. civil trial atty., N.J. Assoc. Toner, Crowley, Woelper & Vanderbilt, Newark, 1963-68; jr. ptnr. Toner, Vanderbilt, Michaels & Light, Newark, 1968, Michels, Schwartz, & Maher, Newark, 1969-72; sr. ptnr. Schwartz & Andolino, Newark, 1972-77; pres. Schwartz & Andolino, P.A., Livingston, N.J., 1977—. Served to capt. JAGC, USAR, 1960-63. Mem. Essex County Bar Assn., N.J. Bar Assn., ABA, Trial Attys. of N.J., Assn. Fed. Bar N.J., Maritime Law Assn. U.S., Fedn. Ins. Counsel, Fedn. Ins. Attys., Def. Research Inst., N.J. Trial Lawyers Assn. Republican. Jewish. Contbr. articles to profl. jours. Personal injury, Insurance, State civil litigation. Home: 3 Birchwood Dr Livingston NJ 07039 Office: 354 Eisenhower Pkwy Livingston NJ 07039

SCHWARTZ, GARY T., law educator; b. 1940. BA, Oberlin (Ohio) Coll., 1962; JD, Harvard U., 1966. Legal asst. Undersecretary Transp., Washington, 1968-69; prof. UCLA, 1969—. Office: U Calif Sch Law 405 Hilgard Ave Los Angeles CA 90024 *

SCHWARTZ, IRWIN H., lawyer; b. Bklyn., Mar. 25, 1948; s. Julius and Sylvia (Holzman) S.; m. Barbara T. Granett, July 3, 1971; 1 child, Matthew Lane. BA, Bklyn. Coll., 1968; JD, Stanford U., 1971. Bar: Calif. 1972, Washington 1972, U.S. Ct. Appeals (9th cir.) 1972, U.S. Supreme Ct. 1977. Asst. U.S. atty. U.S. Dist. Ct. (we. dist.) Wash., Seattle, 1972-74, exec. asst. U.S. atty., 1974-75, fed. pub. defender, 1975-81; sole practice Seattle, 1981—. Mem. Nat. Assn. Criminal Def. Lawyers (bd. dirs. 1985—). Club: Wash. Athletic (Seattle). Avocations: photography, woodworking. Federal civil litigation, Criminal. Office: 710 Cherry St Seattle WA 98104

SCHWARTZ, JAMES WILLIAM, lawyer; b. Pitts., Aug. 4, 1934; s. James S. and Dorothy (Spitzner) S.; m. Elizabeth Ann Kahn, Aug. 2, 1958; children—Elizabeth, Kathleen, James, Dorothy. A.B., Duquesne U., 1956; J.D., Villanova U., 1959. Bar: Pa. 1960, U.S. Dist. Ct. (ea. dist.) Pa. 1960. Ptnr., Saul, Ewing, Remick & Saul, Phila.; dir. Boekel Industries, Inc., ECTA Corp.; lectr. securities regulation Villanova U. Law Sch. 1969-72, U. Pa. Law Sch. 1982; lectr. Pa. Bar Inst. Bd. dirs. Penn Valley Civic Assn. Mem. ABA, Pa. Bar Assn., Phila. Bar Assn. (lectr.), Order of Coif. Republican. Roman Catholic. Clubs: Union League, Germantown Cricket (Phila.). Editor-in-chief: Villanova Law Rev. 1958-59; author: Formation of a Pennsylvania Business Corporation 1969-81. General corporate, Securities. Office: 3800 Centre Square West Philadelphia PA 19102

SCHWARTZ, JEFFREY BYRON, lawyer; b. Phila., Dec. 3, 1940; s. Carl Sidney and Tessie Claire (Cohen) S.; m. Joan S. Weinman, Aug. 4, 1963; children—Kevin, Jill. B.S., Pa. State U., 1962; J.D., U. Pa., 1965; M.B.A., Am. U., 1967. Bar: Pa. 1965, D.C. 1968, La. 1969. Staff acct. Price Waterhouse & Co., Washington, 1962; trial atty. SEC, Washington, 1965-68; sr. atty. New Orleans Legal Assistance, 1968-70; gen. counsel Nat. Tenants Orgn., Washington, 1970-73; litigation atty. Nat. Health and Environ. Law Project, Washington, 1971-74; chief counsel Pa. Dept. Health, Harrisburg, 1974-79; ptnr. Berriman & Schwartz, King of Prussia, Pa., 1979-85; sr. ptnr. Wolf, Block, Schorr & Solis-Cohen, Phila., 1985—; guest lectr. on welfare and health law U. Pa. Sch. Law, Tulane U. Law Sch., Wayne State U. Law Sch. and Georgetown U. Law Sch.; instr. Catholic U. Am. Law Sch., 1972-73; course planner Pa. Bar Inst., 1980—. Reginald Heber Smith fellow, 1968-70. Mem. Am. Soc. Hosp. Attys., Nat. Health Lawyers Assn. (dir.), Pa. Soc. Hosp. Attys. (pres., bd. dirs. 1983-85), Hosp. Attys. Southeastern Pa., Am. Pub. Health Assn. (chmn. health law com. 1978-81), Pa. Bar Assn., D.C. Bar Assn. Democrat. Jewish. Contbr. articles to profl. jours. Health, Federal civil litigation, State civil litigation. Home: 10 Radcliffe Rd Bala Cynwyd PA 19004 Office: Wolf Block Schorr & Solis-Cohen 15th and Chestnut Sts 12th Floor Philadelphia PA 19102

SCHWARTZ, JOSEPH ANTHONY, III, lawyer; b. Washington, Nov. 6, 1946; s. Joseph A. Jr. and Rita (Decker) S.; m. Maureen Margaret Walsh, June 17, 1967; children: Megan, Molly, Michael. BA, U. Notre Dame, 1968, MA, 1970; JD, U. Va., 1973. Bar: Md. 1973, U.S. Dist. Ct. Md. 1973, U.S. Ct. Appeals (4th cir.) 1975. Assoc. Semmes, Bowen & Semmes, Balt., 1973-77; sole paractice Balt., 1978-79, 1985—; ptnr. Brocato & Schwartz, Balt., 1980-82, Brocato, Schwartz & Keelty, Balt., 1983-85; sole practice Balt., 1985—; lectr. Villa Julie Coll. of Constl. Law, Balt., 1975-79. Bd. dirs. Md. Am. Auto Assn. Mem. ABA, Md. Bar Assn., Balt. City Bar, Serjeants Inn Law Club, Nat. Assn. Coll. and Univ. Attys. (panelist profl. symposium, 1986). Roman Catholic. Legislative, Administrative and regulatory, Federal civil litigation. Home: 605A W Joppa Rd Baltimore MD 21204 Office: 6 W Madison St Baltimore MD 21201

SCHWARTZ, KOVE JEROME, lawyer, podiatrist; b. Hartford, Conn., Sept. 1, 1938; s. Maurice and Mollie (Hurwitz) S.; m. Kathleen Rossi, Apr. 26, 1972; children: Jeffrey Michael, Andrew Eric. DPM, Ohio Coll. Podiatric Medicine, 1961; BA, Cen. Conn. State U., 1972; JD, U. Conn., 1976. Bar: Conn. 1977. Practice medicine specializing in podiatrics Newington, Conn., 1961—; sole practice Newington, 1977—. Contbr. articles on med. malpractice risk mgmt. to profl. jours. Named Podiatrist of Yr. Conn. Podiatric Med. Assn., 1977. Mem. ABA, Am. Podiatric Med. Assn. (spl. editor jour. 1979, pres. 1986-87). Republican. Jewish. Health, Personal injury. Home: 45 Reverknolls Avon CT 06111 Office: 1247 Main St Newington CT 06111

SCHWARTZ, LAURENS R., lawyer, author, computer consultant; b. East Orange, N.J., Sept. 3, 1951. BA in Polit. Philosophy magna cum laude, Yale U., 1973; MA in Creative Writing, Boston U., 1975; JD, NYU, 1981. Bar: N.Y. 1982, U.S. Dist. Ct. (ea. and so. dists.) N.Y. 1982. Assoc. Botein, Hays, Sklar & Herzberg, N.Y.C., 1981-82, Kramer, Levin, Nessen, Kamin & Frankel, N.Y.C., 1983-84; sole practice N.Y.C., 1984—; guest speaker on computerizing pub. houses, Internat. Assn. Ind. Pubs. Conf. 1985. Author: (screenplays) Poet of His People, 1978 (best screenwriter award San Antonio), Carthage, 1981 (Emmy nominee); (books) Jews and the American Revolution, 1987, Computer Law Forms Handbook, 1986—, computer law editor Lindey on Entertainment, Publishing and the Arts, 1985—; co-producer TV program Mayan, 1974; bd. rev. editors Computer Graphics World Mag., 1986—; contbr. articles to profl. jours. Recipient Goethe Inst. award, 1970. Mem. Am. Arbitration Assn. (panel of computer arbitrators). Avocation: German. Computer, Entertainment, Trademark and copyright. Office: 5 E 22d St Suite 15D New York NY 10010

SCHWARTZ, LAWRENCE B., lawyer, accountant, banker; b. Bridgeport, Conn., May 17, 1929; s. Joseph A. and Augusta J. (Josephson) S.; m. Valerie Markman, July 13, 1972; children—David, Roberta, Richard. B.S. in Econs., Wharton Sch., U. Pa. 1951; J.D., U. Conn. 1954. Bar: Conn. 1954, U.S. Dist. Ct. Conn. 1955, U.S. Tax Ct. 1956. Ptnr. Gladstone, Schwartz, Baroff & Blum, Bridgeport, 1962; chmn. bd., chmn. exec. com. Lafayette Bank and Trust Co., Bridgeport, 1965—, also dir.; treas. Town of Trumbull, Conn., 1958, Trumbull Sch. Lunch Program, 1958-60; sec. Conn. Bd. Pardons, Hartford, 1972-78; dir. Frigitronics, Inc., Shelton, Conn. Recipient Gold medal Conn. Soc. C.P.A.s, 1954. Mem. Conn. Bar Assn., ABA, Assn. Trial Lawyers Am., Profl. Orgn. Attys. and C.P.A.s. Jewish. Clubs: Algonquin (Bridgeport); Rolling Hills Country (Wilton, Conn.). Lodge: Odd Fellows. Banking, Real property, Corporate taxation. Home: 93 Old Hickory Rd Fairfield CT 06430 Office: Gladstone Schwartz Baroff & Blum 1087 Broad St Bridgeport CT 06604

SCHWARTZ, LEONARD JAY, lawyer; b. San Antonio, Sept. 23, 1943; s. Oscar S. and Ethel (Eastman) S.; m. Sandra E. Eichelbaum, July 4, 1965; 1 dau., Michele Fay. B.B.A., U. Tex. 1965, J.D., 1968. Bar: Tex. 1968, Ohio 1971, U.S. Dist. Ct. (no., ea., we., so. dists.) Tex., U.S. Dist. Ct. (no., so. dists.) Ohio, U.S. Dist. Ct. Nebr., U.S. Ct. Appeals (5th, 6th, 7th, 11th cirs.), U.S. Supreme Ct. 1971. Assoc. Roberts & Holland, N.Y.C., 1968-70; ptnr. Rigely, Schwartz & Fagan, San Antonio 1970-71; staff counsel ACLU of Ohio, Columbus, 1971-73; ptnr. Schwartz, Fisher, Spater, McNamara & Marshall, Columbus, 1973-77, Schwartz & Fishman, Columbus, 1977-79; elections counsel to sec. of state of Ohio, Columbus 1979-80; ptnr. Waterman & Schwartz, Austin, Tex., 1981-84; mng. dir. Schwartz, Waterman, Fickman & Van Os, P.C., Austin and Houston, 1984-85, sole practice, Austin, 1985-86; mng. dir. Schwartz & Eichelbaum, P.C., Austin, 1986—. lectr. in field. Contbr. articles to profl. jours. Recipient Outstanding Teaching Quizmaster award U. Tex. Sch. Law, 1968. Mem. ABA, Tex. Bar Assn., Travis County Bar Assn., Am. Trial Lawyers Assn., Tex. Trial Lawyers Assn., Phi Delta Phi. Jewish. Labor, Federal civil litigation, Administrative and regulatory. Home and Office: 5800 Back Ct Austin TX 78731

SCHWARTZ, MARTIN WEBER, lawyer, investment advisory company executive, business consultant, author; b. N.Y.C., Sept. 30, 1944; s. Robert R. and Rose Weber (Caesar) S.; B.A., NYU, 1965; J.D., Bklyn. Law Sch., 1968. Bar: N.Y. 1971, U.S. Supreme Ct. 1975. Spl. agt. Customs Agy. Service U.S. Dept. Treasury, 1970-71; spl. agt. security, 1973-76; asst. dist. atty. Bronx County, City N.Y., 1971-73; sole practice, Yonkers, N.Y., 1976—; chief welfare frauds unit Dist. Atty.'s Office, N.Y.C., 1972-73; pres. Wall St. Research Corp., N.Y.C., 1982-85, MRM Corp., 1985—; Recipient Commendation Govt. Can., 1971; Commendation U.S. Atty. So. Dist. N.Y. 1971; Commendation Bronx County N.Y.C. Dist. Atty., 1972; Commendation Police Commr. City N.Y. 1973; cert. award U.S. Dept. Treasury, 1976. Mem. ABA, N.Y. State Bar Assn., Assn. Bar City N.Y., N.Y. Acad. Sci. Jewish. Contbr. in field. Labor, Criminal, Workers' compensation. Office: 23 Centuck Station Yonkers NY 10710

SCHWARTZ, MARVIN, lawyer; b. Phila., Nov. 3, 1922; s. Abe and Freda (Newman) S.; m. Joyce Ellen Sidner, Sept. 7, 1947; children: John Burkhart, Daniel Bruce, Pamela Louise. LL.B., U. Pa., 1949. Bar: Pa. bar 1950, N.Y. bar 1951, D.C. bar 1955. Law sec. to judge U.S. Ct. Appeals, 3d Circuit, Phila., 1949-50; law sec. to Mr. Justice Burton of Supreme Ct. U.S., Washington, 1950-51; asso. firm Sullivan & Cromwell, N.Y.C., 1951-60; partner Sullivan & Cromwell, 1960—. Chmn. Zoning Bd. of Adjustment, Alpine, N.J., 1966-74; mem. Planning Bd., Alpine, 1966-67; bd. overseers U. Pa. Law Sch. Served with Signal Corps U.S. Army, 1943-46. Mem. Am. Coll. Trial Lawyers (sec., bd. regents, gation 1978-81, chmn. Downstate N.Y. com. 1976-78), Am. Law Inst., Am. Bar Assn. (coordinating group on impact big case on litigation costs and delay), N.Y. Bar Assn., Pa. Bar Assn., D.C. Bar Assn. Democrat. Jewish. Clubs: Univ. (N.Y.C.), Downtown Assn. (N.Y.C.), City Midday (N.Y.C.). Administrative and regulatory, Federal civil litigation, State civil litigation. Office: Sullivan & Cromwell 125 Broad St New York NY 10004

SCHWARTZ, MICHAEL ADAM, lawyer; b. N.Y.C., Aug. 21, 1953; s. William and Ruth (Efron) S. BA in English cum laude, Brandeis U., 1975; MA in Theater Arts, Northwestern U., 1976; JD, NYU, 1981. Bar: N.Y. 1982, U.S. Dist. Ct. (so. and ea. dist.) N.Y. 1983, U.S. Ct. Appeals (2d cir.) 1984. Actor Nat. Theater for Deaf, Chester, Conn., 1977-78; law clk. to judge U.S. Dist. Ct. (so. dist.) N.Y., N.Y.C., 1981-82; asst. dist. atty. N.Y. County Dist. Atty.'s Office., N.Y.C., 1983—. Author: Gallaudet College Encylopedia on Deafness, 1986. Trustee N.Y. Soc. for Deaf, N.Y.C., 1984—. Recipient Honarary award Ruth Kirzon Group, N.Y.C., 1980, Honarary award N.Y. Soc. for Deaf, 1984. Mem. ABA, Union League of Deaf. Democrat. Jewish. Avocations: reading, swimming, photography. Criminal. Home: 101 MacDougal St 4A New York NY 10012 Office: NY County Dist Atty's Office One Hogan Pl New York NY 10013

SCHWARTZ, MICHAEL STEVEN, lawyer; b. Providence, Dec. 17, 1953; s. Harold and Lillian (Newman) S.; m. Cynthia Resnick, Sept. 8, 1985. BA, Am. U., 1975; JD, SUNY, Buffalo, 1978. Bar: R.I. 1978, U.S. Dist. Ct. R.I. 1978, U.S. Ct. Appeals (1st cir.) 1984. Assoc. Lovett & Linder, Providence, 1978-81; ptnr. Mandell, Goodman, Famiglietti & Schwartz, Providence, 1981—. Mem. R.I. Bar Assn., R.I. Trial Lawyers Assn. Avocation: sports. Office: Mandell Goodman Famiglietti & Schwartz Ltd 1 Park Row Providence RI 02903

SCHWARTZ, MILTON LEWIS, federal judge; b. Oakland, Calif., Jan. 20, 1920; s. Colman and Selma (Lavenson) S.; m. Barbara Ann Moore, May 15, 1942; children: Dirk L., Tracy Ann, Damon M., Brooke. A.B., U. Calif. at Berkeley, 1941, J.D., 1948. Bar: Calif. bar 1949. Research asst. 3d Dist. Ct. Appeal, Sacramento, 1948; dep. dist. atty. 1949-51; practice in Sacramento, 1951-79; partner McDonough, Holland, Schwartz & Allen, 1953-79; U.S. dist. judge Eastern Dist. Calif., 1979—; prof. law McGeorge Coll. Law, Sacramento, 1952-55; Mem. Com. Bar Examiners Calif., 1971-75. Pres. Bd. Edn. Sacramento City Sch. Dist., 1961; v.p. Calif. Bd. Edn., 1967-68; Trustee Sutterville Heights Sch. Dist. Served to maj. 40th Inf. Div. AUS, 1942-46, PTO. Fellow Am. Coll. Trial Lawyers; mem. State Bar Calif., Am. Bar Assn., Am. Bd. Trial Advocates. Jurisprudence. Office: US Courthouse 650 Capitol Mall Sacramento CA 95814

SCHWARTZ, MURRAY M., judge; b. 1931. B.S., Wharton Sch. U. Pa., 1952; LL.B., U. Pa., 1955. Bankruptcy judge Dist. of Del., 1969-74; judge U.S. Dist. Ct. Del., 1974—, now chief judge. Author: The Exercise of Supervisory Power by the Third Circuit Court of Appeals, 1982. Mem. ABA, Del. State Bar Assn., Am. Judicature Soc. Office: Lockbox 44 Federal Bldg 844 King St Wilmington DE 19801 *

SCHWARTZ, PHILIP, lawyer; b. N.Y.C., June 7, 1930; s. Louis and Kate (Brodsky) S.; m. Iris M. Ballin, Nov. 28, 1953 (div. 1979); children—David, Elyse, Donna; m. Monique W. Wagner, July 26, 1982. B.A., George Washington U., 1952, J.D., 1959; LL.M., Georgetown U., 1961. Bar: Va. 1959, D.C. 1966, U.S. Ct. Appeals (D.C. cir.) 1966, U.S. Ct. Mil. Appeals 1966, U.S. Supreme Ct. 1966, U.S. Ct. Appeals (4th cir.) 1982. Sr. intelligence analyst Nat. Security Agy., Washington, 1952-54, 56-63; assoc. Varoutsos, Koutoulakos & Arthur, Arlington, Va., 1963-67; ptnr. Schwartz and Ellis, Ltd., Arlington, 1968—; instr. No. Va. Life Underwriters Tng. Council, Fairfax, Va., 1974, No. Va. Paralegal Inst., Arlington, 1976; moot ct. judge George Washington U., Washington, 1976, Georgetown U., Washington, 1977. Mem. Arlington County Bd. Zoning Appeals, 1972-85, Arlington County Council Human Relations, 1973; bd. dirs. Jewish Community Ctr. Greater Washington, 1975. Served with M.I., U.S. Army, 1954-56. Fellow Am. Acad. Matrimonial Lawyers (sec. 1986—, pres. U.S. chpt.); mem. ABA (chmn. family law sect. com. internat. laws and procedures 1983—, com. fed. legislation 1986—), Internat. Bar Assn. (vice-chmn. family law div. 1984—, liaison officer to IMF), Va. Trial Lawyers Assn. (instr. 1984), Assn. Trial Lawyers Am., Va. State Bar (bd. govs. internat. law sect., liaison to ABA internat. law sect.), D.C. Bar, Arlington County Bar Assn. (cts. com., legis. com.), Brit. Inst. Internat. and Comparative Law, Am. Soc. Internat. Law, Inter-Am. Bar Assn., Internat. Soc. Family Law, Solicitors Family Law Assn. London (assoc.), Arlington Jaycees, Phi Epsilon Pi, Delta Phi Epsilon, Phi Delta Phi. Club: Kiwanis. Family and matrimonial, Private international, General corporate. Office: Schwartz and Ellis Ltd 6950 N Fairfax Dr Arlington VA 22213

SCHWARTZ, RICHARD MORTON, lawyer; b. Bklyn., May 6, 1947; s. Ralph Monroe and Frances (Cohen) S.; m. Lynne J. London, June 7, 1970; children: Allison D., Christopher L. BS, C.W. Post Coll., 1969; JD, Bklyn. Law Sch., 1974. Bar: N.Y. 1975, U.S. Dist Ct. (so. and ea. dists.) N.Y. 1975, Fla. 1976, U.S. Ct. Appeals (2d cir.). Corp. personnel Am. Express Co., N.Y.C., 1971-72; assoc. Schapiro, Wisan, Krassner, N.Y.C., 1975-79, Trager & Trager, Fairfield, Conn., 1979-80; ptnr. Finkelstein, Bruckman, Wohl, Most & Rothamn and predecessor firm Ferziger, Wohl et al, N.Y.C., 1980—. Asst. co-chmn. N.Y.C. Com. to reelect Nelson Rockefeller, 1964; trustee, bd. dirs. Amyotrophic Lateral Sclerosis Assn., N.Y.C., 1981—. Mem. N.Y. State Bar Assn. (corp. bus. and banking sect.), Fla. Bar Assn. (real estate and estate sects.), Am. Arbitration Assn. (arbitrator). Democrat. Jewish. Avocations: tennis, sqaush, baseball. General corporate, Real property, Contracts commercial. Home: 5 Rockridge Rd Rye NY 10580 Office: Finkelstein Bruckman Wohl Most & Rothamn 801 2d Ave New York NY 10017

SCHWARTZ, S. BERNARD, lawyer, educator; b. N.Y.C., May 29, 1949; s. Henry Schwartz and Irene Anis; m. Faina Wajner, Apr. 14, 1956; children: Jordan, Jonathan. BA, NYU, 1970; JD, John Marshall Law Sch., 1974. Bar: N.Y., Ill., U.S. Dist. Ct. (so. and ea. dists.) N.Y., U.S. Ct. Appeals (2d cir.). Atty. immigration and naturalization service U.S. Dept. Justice, Newark, 1974-75; sole practice N.Y.C., 1975—; assoc. adj. prof. law and immigration N.Y. Law Sch., N.Y.C., 1977—. Editor, contbg. author Immigration Practice Manuals, 1976—. Mem. N.Y. County Bar Assn. (lectr.), N.Y. State Bar Assn. (lectr.), Bklyn. Bar Assn., Am. Immigration Lawyers Assn., U.S. Tennis Assn. Avocation: tennis. Immigration, naturalization, and customs, Federal civil litigation.

SCHWARTZ, STEPHEN JAY, lawyer; b. Bklyn., May 28, 1947; s. Morris and Muriel (Scherr) S. BA, Queens Coll., 1969; JD, Bklyn. Law Sch., 1973. Bar: N.Y. 1974, U.S. Dist. Ct. (ea. and so. dists.) N.Y. 1974. Assoc. Aaron J. Broder & F. Lee Bailey, N.Y.C., 1973-74, Harry Grossmun, N.Y.C., 1974-78, Paul A. Gritz, Bklyn., 1978-80; ptnr. Schwartz, Dicker & Gutstein, N.Y.C., 1980—; gen. counsel Hubert Lanz, Inc., Munich, W.Ger., 1980—; bd. dirs. Penstone, Ltd., London; cons. SDVB, Ltd., Graz, Austria; gen. counsel The Am. Theatre Collection, Inc., The Am. Play Co., Authors Research Co. Inc. Mem. ABA, N.Y. Chamber Commerce and Industry, N.Y. State Bar Assn., Queens County Bar Assn. Personal injury, General corporate, Private international. Office: 271 Madison Ave Suite 1800 New York NY 10016

SCHWARTZ, STEVEN GARY, lawyer, insurance executive; b. Newark, Feb. 18, 1954; s. Bert and Maidie (Heimberg) S.; m. Debra Faye Ryals, Apr. 26, 1986. BA in Govt. with honors, Franklin and Marshall Coll., 1975; JD, Washington and Lee U., 1978. Bar: Va. 1978, U.S. Ct. Appeals (4th cir.) 1978, Md. 1986. Assoc. Seawell, Dalton, Norfolk, Va., 1977-83, Scanelli, Shapiro, Norfolk, 1984-85; gen. counsel, mgr. claims Boat Owners Assn. U.S., Alexandria, Va., 1986—. Author: Supreme Court in the Eyes of Presidents, 1975. Chmn. water events Norfolk Harborfest, 1982-84, fireworks 1983-84; chmn. water events Hampton Bay Days, 1985, bd. dirs. Mem. ABA, Va. Bar Assn., Md. Bar Assn., Maritime Law Assn., Young Lawyers Bar Assn. (exec. com. 1979-85, pres. 1985), Phi Beta Kappa, Pi Gamma Mu. Democrat. Jewish. Avocations: carpentry, sailing, softball, racquetball, golf. Admiralty, Insurance, Personal injury. Home: 3504 Fox Ridge Rd Waldorf MD 20601 Office: Boat Owners Assn US 880 S Pickett St Alexandria VA 22304

SCHWARTZ, STUART RANDALL, lawyer; b. Chgo., Feb. 7, 1949; s. Samuel Louis and Marion (Kogon) S.; m. Gayle Ann Jackson, Sept. 15, 1973; children: Sarah, Susan. B.A. in Econ., U. Pa., 1970; J.D. cum laude, Northwestern U., 1973. Bar: Ill. 1973, Fla. 1983, U.S. Dist. Ct. (no. dist.) Ill. 1973. Atty. Merc. Fin. Corp., Chgo., 1973-74, Borg-Warner Corp., Chgo., 1974-77; v.p., asst. gen. counsel Assocs. Comml. Corp., Chgo., 1977-83; assoc. Jacobs, Robbins, Gaynor, Burton, Hampp, Burns, Bronstein & Shasteen P.A., St. Petersburg, Fla., 1983-86; v.p., asst. gen. counsel Sanwa Bus. Credit Corp., Chgo., 1986—. Served to sgt. USAR, 1970-76. Mem. ABA (comml. fin. services com.). Jewish. Contracts commercial, Bankruptcy, Consumer commercial. Home: 4050 Picardy Dr Northbrook IL 60062 Office: Sanwa Bus Credit Corp 1 S Wacker Dr Chicago IL 60606

SCHWARTZ, SUSAN RENEE, lawyer; b. N.Y.C., June 5, 1954; d. Alexander and Martha (Gottesman) Schwartz. B.A. cum laude, Hunter Coll., 1977; J.D., U. Calif. Law Sch., Los Angeles, 1981. Bar: Calif. 1981, U.S. Dist. Ct. (cen. dist.) Calif. 1981, U.S. Ct. Appeals (9th cir.) 1981, U.S. Dist. Ct. (ea. dist.) Calif. 1985, U.S. Supreme Ct. 1985. Atty. Lawler Felix & Hall, Los Angeles, 1981-82, Hayes & Hume, Beverly Hills, Calif., 1983-84, Richards, Watson, Dreyfuss & Geshon, Los Angeles, 1985—; law clk. to judge U.S. Dist. Ct. (ce. dist.) Calif., Los Angeles, 1984-85. Mem. UCLA Law Rev.; editor: Fed Communication Law Jour., Fed. Communications Bar Assn., Washington, 1979-81. Chmn. Univ. Calif. Communications Bd., Los Angeles, 1979-80; bd. dirs. Hollywood-Wilshire Fair Housing Council, Los Angeles, 1982-83. Mem. Women Lawyers Los Angeles (bd. dirs. 1983—), ABA (chmn. com. on intellectual property, tort and ins. practice sect.), Los Angeles County Bar Assn., Barristers (large firm study group). Office: Richards Watson Dreyfuss & Gershon 333 S Hope St 38th Floor Los Angeles CA 90071

SCHWARTZ, SYDNEY JAMES, lawyer; b. N.Y.C., Sept. 27, 1905; s. Morris and Margaret (Harris) S.; m. Rose Knopf, Dec. 20, 1968. LL.B., N.Y. Law Sch., 1928; postgrad. Columbia U. Bar: N.Y. 1929, U.S. Dist Ct. (so. dist.) N.Y. 1930, U.S. Dist Ct. (ea. dist.) N.Y. 1931, U.S. Ct. Appeals (2d cir.) 1938, U.S. Supreme Ct. 1943, U.S. Ct. Appeals (fed. cir.) 1983. Assoc. firm Hollander & Bernheimer, N.Y.C., 1927-43; ptnr. Neustein & Schwartz, N.Y.C., 1943-46; sole practice N.Y.C., 1946-48; assoc. Cronan, Kissel & Roseborough, N.Y.C., 1948-50; sole practice N.Y.C., 1950-69; of counsel Schaeffer, Dale & Vogel, N.Y.C., 1969-76, Greenbaum, Wolff & Ernst, N.Y.C., 1976-81, Pollner, Mezan, Stolzberg & Berger, N.Y.C., 1981—. Pres. N.Y. Fedn. Reform Synagogues, 1976-78, hon pres., 1978—; pres. Parents Without Partners, 1960-61; pres. Met. Synagogue of N.Y., 1974-76. Mem. ABA, Assn. of Bar N.Y.C., N.Y. County Lawyers Assn. Family and matrimonial, General practice, Real property. Home: 140 E 83d St New York NY 10028 Office: Pollner Mezan Stolzberg & Berger 360 Lexington Ave New York NY 10017

SCHWARTZ, THEODORE FRANK, lawyer; b. Clayton, Mo., Aug. 14, 1935; s. Ben and Mary (Roufa) S.; m. Barbara Jean Rader, Aug. 30, 1959; children: Michael D., Kenneth R. JD, Washington U., St. Louis, 1962. Bar: U.S. Dist. Ct. (ea. dist.) Mo. 1962, Mo. 1967, U.S. Dist. Ct. (so. dist.) Ind. 1968, U.S. Dist. Ct. (so. dist.) Tex. 1971, D.C. 1972, Calif. 1974, U.S. Dist. Ct. (no. dist.) Calif. 1976, U.S. Dist. Ct. (cen. dist.) Calif. 1978, N.Y. 1981, U.S. Ct. Appeals (2d, 5th, 7th, D.C., 8th, 9th and 11th cirs.), U.S. Supreme Ct. Assoc. Charles M. Shaw, Clayton, 1962-64; ptnr. Ackerman, Schiller & Schwartz, Clayton, 1964-74; sole practice Clayton, 1975—. Mem. Assn. Trial Lawyer Am., Mo. Assn. Trial Lawyers, Am. Judicature Soc., Nat. Assn. Criminal Def. Lawyers. Antitrust, Federal civil litigation, State civil litigation. Home: 597 Purdue University City MO 63130 Office: 11 S Meramec Suite 1100 Clayton MO 63105

SCHWARTZ, THOMAS D., lawyer; b. Carbondale, Ill., Apr. 1, 1932; s. Walker and Mabel (Smith) S.; m. Kathryn Ann Hooker, Mar. 16, 1957; children: Patricia Ann, Thomas Andrew. B.A., So. Ill. U., 1956; J.D., U. Chgo., 1961. Bar: Ill. 1961, also U.S. Fed. Ct. 1961, U.S. Supreme Ct. 1974, U.S. Tax Ct. 1984. Lectr. bus. law and govt., asst. legal counsel So. Ill. U.,

Carbondale, 1961-62; practice law Carbondale, 1962-63; trust officer, v.p. First Nat. Bank & Trust Co., Mt. Vernon, Ill., 1963-65; asst. to pres. Alton Box Board Co., Ill., 1965-66; corp. sec. Alton Box Board Co., 1966-83; v.p. adminstrn. Smurfit Pension Mgmt. Services, 1978-83, pres., 1980-83; mem. Feirich, Schoen, Mager & Green, Carbondale, Ill., 1983—; bd. dirs. First Nat. Bank & Trust, Carbondale, 1974—. Mem. adv. bd. St. Anthony's Hosp., Alton, Ill., 1973-83, pres., 1980-83; elder First Presbyn. Ch., Alton, 1970—, chmn. bd. trustees, 1972-76; bd. dirs. Pride, Inc.; bd. dirs. Jr. Achievement, pres., 1979-81; founder, bd. dirs. River Bend Civic Progress Assn., Alton, 1980-83 . Served with AUS, 1956-58. Mem. Am., Ill., Jackson County, St. Louis bar assns., Southwestern Ill. Indsl. Assn. (founder, 1st chmn. 1974), Ill. Mfg. Assn. (dir., chmn. So. div. 1977-79). Banking, General corporate, Bankruptcy. Home: Rt 6 Box 126-1 Carbondale IL 62901 Office: Ferich Schoen Mager & Green 2001 W Main St Carbondale IL 62901

SCHWARTZ, WILLIAM, university dean, legal educator; b. Providence, May 6, 1933; s. Morris Victor and Martha (Glassman) S.; m. Bernice Konigsberg, Jan. 13, 1957; children: Alan Gershon, Robin Libby. A.A., Boston U., 1952, J.D. magna cum laude, 1955, M.A., 1960; postgrad., Harvard Law Sch., 1955-56. Bar: D.C. 1956, Mass. 1962. Prof. law Boston U., 1955—, Fletcher prof. law, 1968-70, Roscoe Pound prof. law, 1970-73; dean Sch. of Law, 1980—; of counsel firm Swartz & Swartz, Boston, 1973-80; mem. faculty Frances Glessner Lee Inst., Harvard Med. Sch., Nat. Coll. Probate Judges, 1970, 77, 78, 79; gen. dir. Assn. Trial Lawyers Am., 1968-73; reporter New Eng. Trial Judges Conf., 1965-67; participant Nat. Met. Cts. Conf., 1968; dir. Mass. Probate Study, 1976—; vice chmn. bd. UST Corp.; dir. Sperry and Hutchinson Co., 1979-81, U.S.T. Corp.; mem. legal adv. com. N.Y. Stock Exchange. Author: Future Interests and Estate Planning, 1965, 77, 81, 86, Comparative Negligence, 1970, A Products Liability Primer, 1970, Civil Trial Practice Manual, 1972, New Vistas in Litigation, 1973, Massachusetts Pleading and Practice, 7 vols, 1974-80, others.; Note editor: Boston U. Law Rev, 1954-55; property editor: Annual Survey of Mass. Law, 1960—; Contbr. articles to legal jours. Bd. dirs. Kerry Found.; trustee Hebrew Coll., 1975—; rep. Office Public Info., UN, 1968-73; chmn. legal adv. panel Nat. Commn. Med. Malpractice, 1972-73; examiner of titles Commonwealth of Mass., 1964—; spl. counsel Mass. Bay Transp. Authority, 1979—. Recipient Homer Albers award Boston U., 1955, John Ordronaux prize, 1955; Disting. Service award Religious Zionists Am., 1977; William W. Treat award; William O. Douglas award. Mem. ABA, Am. Law Inst., Mass. Bar Assn. (chmn. task force tortliability), Mass. Trial Lawyers Assn., Nat. Coll. Probate Judges (hon. mem.), Phi Beta Kappa. Estate planning, Federal civil litigation, State civil litigation. Office: 765 Commonwealth Ave Boston MA 02215

SCHWARTZBERG, HUGH JOEL, lawyer, business executive, educator; b. Chgo., Feb. 17, 1933; s. Ralph M. and Celia (Kaplan) S.; m. Joanne Gilbert, July 7, 1956; children: Steven J., Susan Jennifer. BA cum laude, Harvard Coll., 1953; JD, Yale U., 1956. Bar: Ill. 1956, Conn. 1957. Assoc. Ribicoff & Kotkin, Hartford, Conn., 1956-57, Lederer, Livingston, Kahn & Adsit, Chgo., 1957-62; assoc. Marks, Marks & Kaplan, Chgo., 1962-67, ptnr., 1967-70; ptnr. Schwartzberg, Barnett & Schwartzberg, Chgo., 1970-75, Schwartzberg, Barnett & Cohen, Chgo., 1975—; pres. Buffalo Mdse. Distbn. Center, Inc., 1975—; adj. prof. Medill Grad. Sch. Journalism, Northwestern U., 1976, 78; ptnr. Ledgecrest Village, 1970-87, SFS Lambert, Hyde Park Apts.; chmn. Ill. State Adv. Com. to U.S. Civil Rights Commn., 1985—. Bd. dirs. Fund for an Open Soc., Phila., chmn. exec. com.; bd. dirs. Home Health Service of Chgo. North; mem. Cook County (Ill.) Sheriff's Adv. Com., 1972-86; trustee Modern Poetry Assn., pub. Poetry Mag., Chgo., 1980—; chmn. com. in internat. affairs, pub. affairs com. Jewish United Fund, Chgo., 1980-83; bd. govs. Nat. Conf. Soviet Jewry, 1978-83. Recipient testimonial Joint Youth Devel. Com., 1957. Mem. Chgo. Bar Assn. (chmn. com. civil rights 1979-80), ABA (regional atty. sect. on individual rights and responsibilities 1985-86), Ill. State Bar Assn., World Assn. Lawyers, Tau Epsilon Rho. Clubs: Harvard, Yale, Chgo. Lit. (Chgo.); Chgo. Soc. Lodge: B'nai B'rith (pres. dist. 6 1986—). State civil litigation, Real property, Probate. Home: 853 W Fullerton Ave Chicago IL 60614 Office: Schwartzberg Barnett & Cohen 55 W Monroe 2400 Xerox Ctr Chicago IL 60603

SCHWARTZMAN, JACK, lawyer, educator; b. Vinnitsa, Russia, Mar. 22, 1912; came to U.S., 1925; s. Solomon and Anna (Toporoff) S.; m. Vivian Reicher; children—Steven, Marcia, Robert. B.S., CCNY, 1936; LL.B., Bklyn. Law Sch., 1936, J.S.D., 1953; Ph.D., NYU, 1970. Bar: N.Y. 1938. Instr., Henry George Sch., N.Y.C., 1938-40, 46-49, 68-72, Rhodes Sch., N.Y.C., 1956-60; editor, writer Fragments Quar., Floral Park, N.Y., 1963—; prof. Nassau Community Coll., SUNY, Garden City, 1964—; sole practice, N.Y.C., L.I., 1938—; lectr. in field. Author: Rebels of Individualism, 1949; contbr. chpts. to books and over 200 articles to profl. jours. Served to 1st lt. AUS, 1942-46. Decorated Citation for the Army Commendation; recipient Founders Day award NYU, 1971; N.Y. State Chancellor's award for excellence in teaching SUNY, 1974. Mem. N.Y. State Bar Assn. (Disting. Teaching Professorship, rev. com.), MLA, Thoreau Soc., Albert Jay Nock Soc., Council of Georgist Orgns., Univ. Profs. Acad. Order, Acad. of Polit. Sci., Found. for Econ. Edn., Albert Keith Chesterton Soc., Christopher Morley Knothole Assn., Internat. Platform Assn., N.Y. Acad. of Sci., Walt Whitman Birthplace Assn., Henry George Inst. (bd. dirs.), Pi Sigma Alpha, Phi Theta Kappa. General practice, Jurisprudence, Legal education. Office: 146 Jericho Turnpike Floral Park NY 11001

SCHWARTZMAN, JAMES CHARLES, lawyer; b. Kearney, Nebr., Apr. 17, 1945; s. Bernard and Estelle (Lubin) S.; m. Nancy Miriam Hankin, June 26, 1967; children—Kimberly Hankin, Kamian Hankin. B.A., Washington U., St. Louis, 1967; J.D. cum laude, Villanova U., 1972. Bar: Pa. 1972, U.S. Dist. Ct. (ea. dist.) Pa. 1973, U.S. Ct. Appeals (3d cir.) 1973, U.S. Supreme Ct. 1979, U.S. Tax Ct. 1979, U.S. Ct. Claims 1979. Law clk. U.S. Dist. Ct. (ea. dist.) Pa., Phila., 1972-73; asst. U.S. atty. U.S. Dept. Justice, Phila., 1973-77; sr. ptnr. Schwartzman & Hepps, P.C., Phila., 1977—; mem. Disciplinary Bd., Supreme Ct. Pa., 1983—, vice chmn., 1985-86, chmn., 1986—; dir. Bank & Trust Co. of Old York Rd., Willow Grove, Pa., 1983—; mem. Phila. Spl. Trial Ct. Nominating Commn., 1987. Contbr. article to Villanova Law Rev., 1972, mem. editorial staff, 1971-72. Mem. Pa. Bar Assn., Phila. Bar Assn., Pa. Trial Lawyers Assn., Phila. Trial Lawyers Assn., Order of Coif. Federal civil litigation, Criminal, Personal injury. Office: Schwartzman & Hepps 2033 Walnut St Philadelphia PA 19103

SCHWARTZMAN, MARK LEE, lawyer; b. Chgo., Aug. 28, 1928; s. Albert Bernard and Edna Mildred (Kaufman) S. B.S., U. Ill., 1950, J.D., 1952. Bar: Ill. 1952, U.S. Dist. Ct. (no., ea. dist.) Ill. 1952, U.S. Ct. Appeals (7th cir.) 1952. Atty., Wayne & Levine, Chgo., 1954-56; ptnr. Rotenberg & Schwartzman, Chgo., 1956-81, Rosenfeld, Rotenberg, Schwartzman, Hafron & Shapiro, Chgo., 1982—. Served to 1st lt. JAGC, USAF, 1952-54. Mem. ABA, Chgo. Bar Assn. (chmn. social security com., profl. fee com.), Ill. Bar Assn., Nat. Orgn. Social Security Claimants Assn. (Ill. chmn. 1982-84), Assn. Trial Lawyers Am. Jewish. Lodge: Moose. Labor, Workers' compensation, Pension, profit-sharing, and employee benefits. Home: 3130 N Lake Shore Dr Chicago IL 60657 Office: Rosenfeld Rotenberg Schwartzman 221 N LaSalle St Chicago IL 60601

SCHWARTZSTEIN, LINDA ANN, law educator; b. Orange, N.J., June 27, 1952; d. Fred and Jean (Richolson) S.; m. Lee M. Goodwin, June 12, 1977; children: Sarah, Amy. AB magna cum laude, Brandeis U., 1973; JD cum laude, U. Mich., 1976; LLM in Tax, NYU, 1977. Bar: N.J. 1976, N.Y. 1977, D.C. 1977, Md. 1981. Assoc. Groom & Nordberg, Washington, 1977-79; asst. prof. law George Mason U., Arlington, Va., 1979-82, assoc. prof. law, 1982—; exec. dir. Inst. for Law and High Tech., Vienna, Va., 1986—. Contbr. articles to profl. jours. Mem. Phi Beta Kappa. Avocation: computers. Personal income taxation, Computer, Corporate taxation. Office: George Mason U 3401 N Fairfax Dr Arlington VA 22201

SCHWARZ, CARL ALFRED, JR., lawyer; b. N.Y.C., Apr. 27, 1936; s. Carl A. and Genevieve (Byrne) S.; m. Maryellen McGoldrick, Apr. 30, 1966; children—Peter, Elizabeth. B.S., Fordham Coll., 1957, J.D., 1960. Bar: N.Y. 1960, U.S. Dist. Ct. (so. and ea. dists.) N.Y., 1966, U.S. Ct. Appeals (2d cir.) 1975, D.C., 1979, U.S. Ct. Appeals (5th and 9th cirs.) 1980, U.S. Supreme Ct. 1971, U.S. Ct. Appeals (1st cir.) 1984. Assoc. Weil, Gotshal & Manges, N.Y.C., 1965-72, Poletti, Freidin, Prashker, Feldman & Gartner, N.Y.C., 1973-74; ptnr. Fellner & Rovins, N.Y.C., 1974-77, Finley, Kumble, Wagner, Heine, Underberg, Manley & Casey, N.Y.C., 1977—; adj. prof. N.Y. Inst. Tech., 1978-81. Served with USAF, 1961-64. Mem. ABA, Assn. Bar City N.Y., N.Y. State Bar Assn. (chmn. com. on pensions & employee benefits, labor & employment law sect.). Roman Catholic. Clubs: N.Y. Athletic (N.Y.C.); Cherry Valley Country (Garden City, N.Y.); Manhasset Bay Yacht (Port Washington, N.Y.). Lodges: K.C., Knights of Malta. Labor, Pension, profit-sharing, and employee benefits. Office: 425 Park Ave New York NY 10022

SCHWARZ, EARLE JAY, lawyer; b. Memphis, Mar. 7, 1952; s. Maurice Gene and Frances (Lesser) B.; m. Patricia Eldridge Prins, Dec. 17, 1983; children: Linsey, Anna, Susan. BA, Brown U., 1975; postgrad., Memphis State U., 1977-78; JD, Vanderbilt U., 1980. Bar: Tenn. 1980, U.S. Dist. Ct. (we. dist.) Tenn. 1980, U.S. Supreme Ct. 1985, U.S. Ct. Appeals (6th cir.) 1987. Recreational therapist Arlington Devel. Ctr., Memphis, 1972-73; asst. dir. Henry S. Jacobs Camp, Jackson, Miss., 1975-77; assoc. Waring Cox, Memphis, 1980—. mem. pro bono panel for Sr. Citizens, Memphis, 1981—; sec. Memphis Area Legal Services, 1984, pres. 1986—, bd. dirs. 1983-85; bd. dirs. Temple Israel Brotherhood, Memphis, 1980—, v.p. 1983—; bd. dirs. Easter Seals Soc. West Tenn., Memphis, 1984-85. Mem. ABA, Tenn. Bar Assn. Memphis Bar Assn., Shelby County Bar Assn. (bd. dirs. young lawyers div. 1980-81), Assn. Trial Lawyers Am. Federal civil litigation, State civil litigation. Office: Waring Cox 50 N Front St Suite 1300 Memphis TN 38103

SCHWARZ, FREDERICK AUGUST OTTO, JR., lawyer; b. N.Y.C., Apr. 20, 1935; s. Frederick A.O. and Mary Delafield (DuBois) D.; m. Marian Lapsley, June 19, 1959; children: Frederick A.O., Adair L., Eliza Ladd. B.A., Harvard U., 1957, LL.B., 1960. Bar: N.Y. 1961, U.S. Supreme Ct. 1973. Law clk. to chief judge U.S. Ct. of Appeals, 2d Circuit, 1960-61; asst. commr. for law revision Govt. of No. Nigeria, 1961-62; assoc. firm Cravath, Swaine & Moore, N.Y.C., 1963-68; partner firm Cravath, Swaine & Moore, 1969-75, from 1976; now corp. counsel City of N.Y., 1986—; chief counsel Senate Select Com. on Intelligence, 1975-76; dir. F.A.O. Schwarz. Author: The Nation, or the Race, 1966; Contbr. articles to profl. jours. Chmn. Fund for the City of N.Y., 1977-81; pres. Vera Inst. Justice, 1978-81; mem. bd. overseers Harvard U., 1977-83; mem. Com. to Visit Harvard Coll.; trustee Experiment in Internat. Living, 1965—; bd. dirs. Manhattan Bowery Corp., 1970-81, Lawyers for the Public Interest, 1976-81; trustee Legal Action Center, 1973-81, N.Y.C. Criminal Justice Agy., 1977-81, Town Sch., 1972-80, Am. Com. on Africa, 1965-79, Milton Acad., 1960's. Fellow N.Y. Bar Found.; Mem. Am. Law Inst., ABA, Assn. Bar of City of N.Y. (council on criminal justice, chmn. juvenile justice com. 1980-81, chmn. nominating com. 1983). Home: 110 Riverside Dr New York NY 10024 Office: Corp Counsel City of NY 100 Church St New York NY 10007 *

SCHWARZ, JAMES HAROLD, lawyer; b. Hammond, Ind., Dec. 7, 1954; s. Arthur Martin and Agnes (Sternbach) S.; m. Sandra Ellen Gelman, July 30, 1978; children: Jacqueline, Shana. BS, Ind. U., 1977; JD, Ind. U., Indpls., 1980. Bar: Ind. 1980, U.S. Dist. Ct. (so.dist.) Ind. 1980. Assoc. Ice, Miller, Donadio & Ryan, Indpls., 1980-83, Bayh, Tabbert & Capehart, Indpls., 1983; assoc. Dann, Pecar, Newman, Talesnick & Kleiman, Indpls., 1983-86, ptnr., 1986—. Bd. dirs. Bur. Jewish Edn., Indpls., 1985—. Mem. ABA, Ind. Bar Assn., Indpls. Bar Assn. General corporate, Real property, Corporate taxation. Home: 1619 Fern Ct Indianapolis IN 46260 Office: 1 American Sq Suite 2300 PO Box 82008 Indianapolis IN 46282

SCHWARZ, MICHAEL HOWARD, lawyer; b. Brookline, Mass., Oct. 19, 1952; s. Jules Lewis and Estelle (Kosberg) S.; B.A. magna cum laude, U. No. Colo., 1975; postgrad. U. N.Mex., Med. Sch., 1977, U. N.Mex. Law Sch. J.D., 1980; research reader in Negligence Law, Oxford U., summer 1978; diploma in Legal Studies, Cambridge U., 1981. VISTA vol., Albuquerque, 1975-77; research fellow N.Mex. Legal Support Project, Albuquerque, 1978-79; law clk. to field solicitor U.S. Dept. Interior, Santa Fe, summer 1979; admitted to N.Mex. bar, 1980, U.S. Dist. Ct. N.Mex. 1980, U.S. Ct. Appeals (10th cir.) 1982, U.S. Ct. Appeals (D.C. cir.) 1982, U.S. Ct. Internat. Trade, 1982, U.S. Tax Ct. 1982, U.S. Ct. Appeals (fed. cir.) 1982, U.S. Supreme Ct. 1983, N.Y. 1987; supr. in law Cambridge (Eng.) U., 1980-81; law clk. to chief justice Supreme Ct. N.Mex., Santa Fe, 1981-82; sole practice, Santa Fe, 1982—; spl. prosecutor City of Santa Fe, 1985; spl. asst. atty. gen., 1986—. Vice dir. Colo. Pub. Interest Research Group, 1974; scoutmaster Great S.W. Area council Boy Scouts Am., 1977-79; mem. N.Mex. Acupuncture Licensing Bd., 1983. Recipient cert. of appreciation Cambridge U., 1981, Nathan Burkan Meml. award, 1980, 82-83. Mem. ABA (scholar 1983), Fed. Bar Assn. (council on adminstrv. law 1983), N.Y. Trial Lawyers Assn., Assn. Trial Lawyers Am., State Bar N.Mex., First Judicial Dist. Bar Assn. (treas. 1987—) Editorial adv. com. Social Security Reporting Service; co-author N.Mex. Appellate Manual, 1986; contbr. articles to profl. jours. Federal civil litigation, State civil litigation, Civil rights. Home and Office: PO Box 713 Santa Fe NM 87504

SCHWARZBART, ROBERT MORTON, judge; b. N.Y.C., July 20, 1931; s. Hugo and Lilly (Goodfriend) S.; m. Sandra Rae Blockstein, Mar. 26, 1972. B.A., N.Y. U., 1953; J.D., Bklyn. Law Sch., 1958. Bar: N.Y. 1959, U.S. Ct. Appeals (2d and 3d cirs.) 1964. Pvt. pratice, N.Y.C., 1958-61; with NLRB, Chgo., Ill., Newark, and Washington, 1961—, atty., 1961-69, trial specialist, 1969-71, Supervisory atty., 1971-75, adminstrv. law judge, Washington, 1975—; judge Moot Ct., Seton Hall U., 1974; vis. lectr. Fairleigh Dickinson U., 1967. Served with U.S. Army, 1954-56. Recipient cert. commendation Gen. Counsel NLRB, 1973. Mem. ABA (Conf. Adminstrv. Law Judges, sects. on litigation and labor law), Fed. Adminstrv. Law Judges Conf. (exec. bd. 1977-78). Administrative and regulatory, Federal civil litigation, Labor. Office: 1717 Pennsylvania Ave NW Washington DC 20570

SCHWARZER, FRANKLIN JOHN, lawyer; b. Syracuse, Sept. 14, 1922; s. Joseph Karl and Elizabeth A. (Kaufmann) S.; m. Harriet Elizabeth Head, Feb. 1, 1944; children—Anna E. Louise, Joseph Karl, Margaret K., Mary E. B.A., Williams Coll., 1945; J.D., Syracuse Coll. Law, 1952. Bar: N.Y. 1953, U.S. Supreme Ct. 1981. Ptnr., v.p. firm Smith Sovik, Kendrick, Schwarzer & Sugnet, P.C., Syracuse and predecessor firms Smith, Sovik, Kendrick, McAuliffe & Schwarzer, P.C. and Smith, Sovik, Terry, Kendrick, McAuliffe & Schwarzer, 1959—. Chmn. Selective Service, Madison County, 1969. Served with U.S. Army, 1943-46, ETO. Decorated Purple Heart. Mem. ABA, Onondaga County Bar Assn., Madison County Bar Assn. Republican. Episcopalian. Club: Metropolitan (N.Y.C.). Lodge: Masons. Real property assessment reduction, State and local taxation, State civil litigation. Home: 66 Sullivan St Cazenovia NY 13035 Office: Smith Sovik Kendrick Schwarzer & Sugnet PC 300 Empire Bldg Syracuse NY 13202

SCHWARZER, WILLIAM W, federal judge; b. Berlin, Apr. 30, 1925; came to U.S., 1938, naturalized, 1944; s. John F. and Edith M. (Daniel) S.; m. Anne Halbersleben, Feb. 2, 1951; children: Jane Elizabeth, Andrew William. A.B. cum laude, U. So. Calif., 1948; LL.B. cum laude, Harvard U., 1951. Bar: Calif. 1953, U.S. Supreme Ct. 1967. Teaching fellow Harvard U. Law Sch., 1951-52; asso. firm McCutchen, Doyle, Brown & Enersen, San Francisco, 1952-60; partner McCutchen, Doyle, Brown & Enersen, 1960-76; U.S. dist. judge for No. Dist. Calif., San Francisco, 1976—; sr. counsel Pres.'s Commn. on CIA Activities Within the U.S., 1975; mem. faculty Nat. Inst. Trial Advocacy, Fed. Jud. Center, ABA. Author: Managing Antitrust and Other Complex Litigation, 1982; Contbr. articles to legal publs., aviation jours. Trustee World Affairs Council No. Calif., 1961—; chmn. bd. trustees Marin Country Day Sch., 1963-66; chmn. Marin County Aviation Commn., 1969-76; mem. vis. com. Harvard Law Sch., 1981-86. Served with Intelligence U.S. Army, 1943-46. Fellow Am. Coll. Trial Lawyers; mem. ABA (jud. rep. council antitrust sect.) Am. Law Inst., Am., San Francisco bar assns., State Bar Calif. Judicial administration. Office: 450 Golden Gate Ave San Francisco CA 94102

SCHWARZSTEIN, RICHARD JOSEPH, lawyer; b. Yonkers, N.Y., July 6, 1934; s. Jack H. and Beatrice (Florman) S.; m. Ann Sanford Adsley, Aug. 10, 1938; children: Cynthia L., Alisa J., Amy B. AB, Columbia Coll., N.Y.C., 1956; JD, Harvard U., 1959. Bar: N.Y. 1960, U.S. Dist. Ct. (ea. and so. dists.) N.Y. 1974, U.S. Ct. Appeals (2d cir.) Calif. 1974., U.S. Dist. Ct. (cen. dist.) Calif. Clk. White & Case, N.Y.C., 1957-58; assoc. Kramer & Lans, N.Y.C., 1960-62; assoc., then ptnr. Delson & Gordon, N.Y.C., 1961-74; sole practice, Newport Beach, Calif., 1974—; lectr. George Washington U. Law Sch., U. Calif., Irvine, Calif. State U., Fullerton, Long Beach, Orange Coast Coll., U. So. Calif. Contbr. articles to profl. jours. Bd. dirs. Orange County Philharmonic Soc., 1975—, Econ. Devel. Corp. Orange County, 1983-85, Hist. and Cultural Found. Orange County, 1985—. Mem. ABA, Internat. Bar Assn., Calif. Bar Assn. (econ. and law sect. exec. com. 1977-80, exec. com., internat. practice com. 1986—), Orange County Bar Assn. (chmn. internat. law sect. 1984—), World Trade Center Assn. Orange County (bd. dirs. 1976—, chmn. 1986—), Orange County C. of C., Am. Arbitration Assn. (nat. panel), Union Internationale des Avocats. Lodge: Rotary. General corporate, Private international, Computer. Home: 441 El Bosque Laguna Beach CA 92651 Office: 1201 Dove St 6th Fl Newport Beach CA 92660

SCHWED, MICHAEL J., lawyer, administrative law judge; b. Bklyn., July 15, 1945; s. Stanley M. and Lillian (Greenhouse) S.; m. Sandra Elise Rosen, May 29, 1968; children—Laura, Stacy-David. B.A., Queens Coll., 1968; J.D., Bklyn. Law Sch., 1971. Bar: N.Y. State, 1972, U.S. Dist. Ct. (so. and ea. dist.) N.Y. 1974, U.S. Supreme Ct. 1979. Dep. chief Maj. Felony Bur., Queens Dist. Atty., N.Y.C., 1971-77; ptnr. Schwed & Zucker, Kew Gardens, N.Y., 1977—; adminstrv. judge EPA; asst. prof. criminal justice St. Johns U. Vice pres. 13th Dist. Democratic Club, 1978—; mem. Dem. Com. Nassau County, 1978—. Regents N.Y. scholar, 1963; honorarium Mass. Bar Assn., 1978. Mem. ABA, N.Y. Bar Assn., Queens County Bar Assn., Nassau County Bar Assn. Democrat. Jewish. Clubs: Suburban Mens, Rosicrucian Lodge. Criminal, Administrative and regulatory. Office: 125-10 Queens Blvd Kew Gardens NY 11415

SCHWED, PETER GREGORY, lawyer; b. N.Y.C., Feb. 24, 1952; s. Peter and Antonia (Holding) S.; m. Margaret Allen Peters, Feb. 18, 1984; 1 child, Sarah Holding. B.A. summa cum laude, Princeton U., 1973; J.D., Columbia U., 1976. Bar: N.Y. 1977, U.S. Dist. Ct. (so. dist.) N.Y. 1978, U.S. Dist. Ct. (ea. dist.) N.Y. 1978, U.S. Ct. Appeals (2d cir.) 1985. Assoc. Kaye, Scholer, Fierman, Hays & Handler, N.Y.C., 1976-79, Gelberg & Abrams, N.Y.C., 1979-81, Kramer, Levin, Nessen, Kamin & Frankel, N.Y.C., 1981-83; ptnr. Bernstein, Obstfeld & Schwed, P.C., N.Y.C., 1983-86, Austrian, Lance & Stewart P.C., N.Y.C., 1986—. Co-author: Creditors' Rights Handbook, 1982. Harlan Fiske Stone scholar Columbia U. Sch. Law, N.Y.C., 1975-76. Mem. N.Y. State Bar Assn., Assn. Bar City N.Y., Phi Beta Kappa. Bankruptcy, Federal civil litigation, General corporate. Office: Austrian Lance & Stewart PC 30 Rockefeller Plaza New York NY 10112

SCHWEDA, PETER STEVEN, lawyer; b. Spokane, Wash., Jan. 26, 1951; s. Heinz Walter and Margarete Trude (Welz) S.; m. JoAnn Lee Marsh, Sept. 16, 1978; children: Thomas, Samuel. BA, Gonzaga U., 1973, JD, 1976. Bar: Wash. 1977, U.S. Dist. Ct. (ea. dist.) Wash. 1981. Dep. pros. atty. Spokane County, 1976-81; ptnr. Waldo & Schweda P.S., Spokane, 1981—. Bd. dirs. West Valley Sch. Dist., Spokane, 1985—. Mem. Wash. State Bar Assn., Spokane County Bar Assn., Assn. Trial Lawyers Am. Personal injury, Real property, Criminal. Home: 8021 E Maringo Dr Spokane WA 99212 Office: Waldo & Schweda PS 720 N Argonne Rd Spokane WA 99212

SCHWEDOCK, PETER SAUL, lawyer; b. N.Y.C., Jan. 3, 1943; s. Louis Schwedock and Roberta (Schneider) Wiener; m. Roberta Pelzner, Aug. 8, 1965; children: Amy, Alan, Nicole. AB in Communications, U. Miami, Coral Gables, 1965; JD, U. Miami, 1968. Bar: Fla. 1968, U.S. Dist. Ct. (so. dist.) Fla. 1968, U.S. Ct. Appeals (5th cir.) 1969, U.S. Supreme Ct. 1973. Ptnr. Pelzner, Schwedock et al, Miami, Fla., 1968—. Mem. Fla. Bar (exec. com. 1976-82), Dade County Bar Assn. (chmn. workers compensation sect. 1974-77), Assn. Trial Lawyers Am., Acad. Fla. Trial Attys. (pres. 1973-75 workers compensation sect.). Democrat. Jewish. Avocations: snow skiing, tennis, running, aerobics. Workers' compensation, Personal injury, Labor. Home: 28 W Flagler St Suite 800 Miami FL 33130 Office: Pelzner Schwedock et al 28 W Flagler St Suite 800 Miami FL 33130 also: 1922 Tyler St Hollywood FL 33022

SCHWEITZ, MARTHA LEACH, lawyer; b. Mineola, N.Y., May 25, 1954; d. Walter Dalzell and Claire (Ford) Leach; m. Paul William Schweitz, Dec. 27, 1979. BA in History and Spanish, Stanford U., 1976; JD, NYU, 1981. Bar: Ill. 1981. Corr. Baha'i Nat. Ctr., Wilmette, Ill., 1976-79; assoc. Baker & McKenzie, Chgo., 1981-86; asst. prof. U. Oreg. Sch. Law, Eugene, 1986—. Mem. ABA (internat. law sect.), Am. Soc. Internat. Law, Order of Coif. Baha'i. Avocations: ballet, piano. Public international, Private international, General corporate. Office: U Oreg Sch of Law Eugene OR 97403

SCHWEITZER, ERIC CAMPBELL, lawyer; b. Munich, Fed. Republic of Germany, Sept. 12, 1947; s. John Henry and Joan (Campbell) S.; m. Patricia Ritter, May 15, 1971; 1 child, Christopher Campbell. BBA, U. Miss., 1969, JD, 1975. Bar: Miss. 1975, S.C. 1976, U.S. Ct. Appeals (4th cir.) 1978. Assoc. Ogletree, Deakins, Nash, Smoak & Stewart, Greenville, S.C., 1976-79; ptnr. Ogletree, Deakins, Nash, Smoak & Stewart, Greenville, Miss., 1980—. Speaker Leadership Greenville III, 1986—. Served to capt. USAF, 1969-73, PTO. Mem. Carolinas Air Pollution Control Assn. (bd. dirs. 1986—). Avocations: skiing, racquetball, boating. Environment, Labor, Administrative and regulatory. Office: Ogletree Deakins Nash Smoak & Stewart PO Box 2757 Greenville SC 29602

SCHWEITZER, SANDRA LYNN, lawyer; b. San Jose, Calif., Nov. 16, 1952; d. Raymond Oliver and Joanne Rae (Gale) McLean; m. George William Schweitzer, Mar. 26, 1976; children: Brian, Laura, Christopher. BSN, Cornell U., 1974; JD, Georgetown U., 1979. Bar: Md. 1980, U.S. Dist. Ct. Md. 1980, D.C. 1987, U.S. Ct. Appeals (D.C., fed. and 4th cirs.) 1987, U.S. Supreme Ct. 1987. Assoc. Shulman, Rogers, Gandal et al, Silver Spring, Md., 1980-81; sole practice Potomac, Md., 1981-86; assoc. Miller & Chevalier, Washington, 1987—. Served to capt. U.S. Army, 1974-76. Mem. ABA, D.C. Bar Assn., Montgomery County Bar Assn., Women's Bar Assn. D.C., Sigma Theta Tau. Republican. Episcopalian. Health, Insurance. Home: 11304 Tara Rd Potomac MD 20854 Office: Miller & Chevalier 655 15th St NW Washington DC 20005

SCHWENKE, ROGER DEAN, lawyer; b. Washington, Oct. 18, 1944; s. Clarence Raymond and Virginia Ruth (Gould) S.; m. Carol Lynne Flenniken, Nov. 29, 1980; 1 son, Matthew Robert; stepchildren: Tracy L. Wolf, Mary M. Wolf. BA, Ohio State U., 1966; JD with honors, U. Fla., 1969. Bar: Fla. 1970. Instr. Coll. Law, U. Fla., Gainesville, 1969-70; assoc. Carlton, Fields, Ward, Emmanuel, Smith & Cutler, P.A., Tampa, Fla., 1970-74, ptnr., 1975—, adminstr. Real Estate and Land Use Dept., 1978—; adj. prof. Coll. Law, Stetson U., St. Petersburg, Fla. Author chpt. in Environmental Regulation and Litigation in Florida, 1981; contbr. articles to profl. jours. Mem. Diocesan Council, Episcopal Diocese SW Fla., 1978—. Recipient Gertrude Brick Law Rev. prize U. Fla., 1969. Fellow Am. Coll. Real Estate Lawyers (bd. govs. 1985—); mem. ABA (standing com. on environ. law), Fla. Bar Assn., Air Pollution Control Assn., Order of Coif, Greater Tampa C. of C. (chmn. environ. council 1980-81). Democrat. Club: Tampa. Contracts commercial, Environment, Real property. Office: P O Box 3239 1 Harbour Pl Tampa FL 33601

SCHWENN, WILLIAM LEE, lawyer; b. Appleton, Wis., Dec. 23, 1948; s. Lee William and Glenna Edith (Mehne) S.; m. Mary Huey Bledsoe, Aug. 18, 1973. A.B., U. N.C.-Chapel Hill, 1971, J.D., 1973. Bar: Va. 1973, U.S. Dist. Ct. (ea. dist.) Va. 1974, N.C. 1983, U.S. Dist. Ct. (mid. dist.) N.C. 1983. Title examiner, research asst. Phillips, Kendrick, Gearhart & Aylor, Fairfax, Va., 1973-74; assoc. Law Office Frank H. Grace, Jr., Fairfax, 1974-75; atty.-advisor Bankruptcy Div., Adminstrv. Office of U.S. Cts., Washington, 1975-79; clk. of ct. U.S. Bankruptcy Ct. Middle Dist. N.C., Greensboro, 1979—; bd. dirs. Greensboro Fed. Employees Credit Union, 1982-85, chmn. supervisory com., 1981-83. Winner, Holderness Moot Ct. competition U. N.C., Chapel Hill, 1971. Mem. Nat. Conf. Bankruptcy Ct. Clks. (bd. govs. 1980-81), N.C. Bar Assn., Greensboro Bar Assn., Phi Beta Kappa. Independent. Bankruptcy, Family and matrimonial, Environment. Home: 2615 Darden Rd Greensboro NC 27406 Office: US Bankruptcy Ct for Middle Dist NC 202 S Elm St Greensboro NC 27401

SCHWING, ANN TAYLOR, lawyer; b. Berkeley, Calif., Oct. 31, 1946; d. Archer and Hasseltine (Byrd) Taylor; m. Charles Schwing. BA, U. Calif., Berkeley, 1968; JD, Boston U., 1975. Bar: Calif. 1980, U.S. Dist. Ct. (no. and ea. dists.) Calif. 1980, U.S. Ct. Appeals (9th cir.) 1981. Freelance editor Boston, 1975-77; law clk. to chief judge U.S. Dist. Ct. (ea. dist.), Sacramento, Calif., 1977-80; assoc. Weintraub & Genshlea, Sacramento, 1980-82; ptnr. Giattina & Winberry, Sacramento, 1982-84, Burger & Flaherty, Sacramento, 1984-86; of counsel McDonough, Holland and Allen, Sacramento, 1987—; del. 9th Cir. Jud. Conf., 1984-87. Contbr. legal articles to profl jours. Melville M. Bigelow scholar, 1975. Mem. ABA, Calif. Bar Assn. (rules and procedures of court standing com.), Sacramento County Bar Assn. Office: McDonough Holland & Allen PC 555 Capitol Mall Suite 950 Sacramento CA 95814

SCIANNA, RUSSELL WILLIAM, lawyer, legal educator; b. Reading, Pa., Sept. 26, 1956; s. Russell Joseph and Marjorie Louise (Wilson) S.; m. Joanne Frances Melcher, June 24, 1978; children: Russell Jr., Christopher. BS in Fgn. Service, Georgetown U., 1978; JD, Boston U., 1981. Bar: Pa. 1981, U.S. Dist. Ct. (ea. dist.) Pa. 1985. Tax acct. Ernst & Whinney, Reading, 1981-82; sole practice Reading, 1982—; lectr. bus. law and acctg. Penn State U., Reading, 1982-85; pres. Reading Optical Co., Inc., 1982-84; asst. pub. defender, asst. dist. atty. Berks County, Reading, 1985. Mem. Reading Zoning Hearing Bd., 1982—; trustee Reading Area Community Coll., 1985—; bd. dirs. Reading Cen. Br. YMCA, 1982—. Mem. ABA, Pa. Bar Assn., Berks County Bar Assn., Assn. Trial Lawyers Am. Lodge: Sertoma. Avocations: golf, backgammon. General practice, Criminal, Family and matrimonial. Office: 313 N 5th St PO Box 7622 Reading PA 19603

SCIRICA, ANTHONY JOSEPH, federal judge; b. Norristown, Pa., Dec. 16, 1940; s. A. Benjamin and Anna (Sclafani) S.; m. Susan Morgan, May 6, 1966; children—Benjamin, Sara. B.A., Wesleyan U., 1962; J.D., U. Mich., 1965; postgrad., Central U., Caracas, Venezuela, 1966. Bar: Pa. Ptnr. McGrory, Scirica, Wentz & Fernandez, Norristown, Pa., 1966-80; asst. dist. atty. Montgomery County, Pa., 1967-69; mem. Pa. Ho. of Reps, Harrisburg, 1971-79; judge Montgomery County Ct. Common Pleas, Pa., 1980-84, U.S. Dist. Ct. (ea. dist.) Pa., Phila., 1984—; chmn. Pa. Sentencing Commn., 1980-85. Fulbright scholar Central U., Caracas, Venezuela, 1966. Mem. Montgomery Bar Assn., Pa. Bar Assn., ABA. Roman Catholic. Office: US Courthouse Philadelphia PA 19106

SCISM, DANIEL REED, lawyer; b. Evansville, Ind., Aug. 27, 1936; s. Daniel William and Ardath Josephine (Gibbs) S.; m. Paula Anne Sedgwick, June 21, 1958; children: Darby Claire, Joshua Reed. BA, DePauw U., 1958; JD, Ind. U., 1965. Bar: Ind. 1965, U.S. Dist. Ct. (so. dist.) Ind. 1965, U.S. Ct. Appeals (7th cir.) 1967, U.S. Supreme Ct. 1976. Reporter Dayton (Ohio) Jour.-Herald, 1958-59; editor Meade Johnson & Co., Evansville, 1962; first assoc., then ptnr. Roberts, Ryder, Rogers & Scism and predecessor firms, Indpls., 1965-86; ptnr. Barnes & Thornburg, Indpls., 1987—; cons. Ind. Personnel Assn., 1984—. Treas. Marion County chpt. Myasthenia Gravis Found., Indpls., 1970; v.p. Marion County Mental Health Assn., Indpls., 1970-71; pres. The Suemma Coleman Agy., Indpls., 1973-74. Edwards fellow Ind. U., 1964. Mem. ABA, Ind. Bar Assn., Marion County Bar Assn., Ind. State C. of C. (social legis. com. 1970-80). Methodist. Clubs: Indpls. Athletic; Woodland Country (bd. dirs. 1984—) (Carmel, Ind.). Labor. Home: 11070 Winding Brook Ln Indianapolis IN 46280 Office: Barnes & Thornburg 1313 Merchants Bank Bldg 11 S Meridian St Indianapolis IN 46204

SCISM, ROBERT BRUCE, lawyer; b. Evansville, Ind., Feb. 14, 1925; s. Don and Opal (Osman) S.; m. Virginia Cady, Apr. 24, 1971; 1 stepson, Phillip M. Templeton. B.A., DePauw U., 1947; J.D., Drake U., 1964. Bar: Iowa 1964, U.S. Dist. Ct. (so. dist.) Iowa, U.S. dist. ct. (no. dist.) Iowa, U.S. Ct. Appeals (8th cir.), U.S. Supreme Ct. 1971. Asst. atty. gen. State of Iowa, 1965-66; ptnr. Scalise, Scism, Sandre & Uhl, Des Moines, 1967—. Served with USNR, 1943-46. Mem. ABA, Iowa State Bar Assn., Polk County Bar Assn., Assn. Trial Lawyers Am., Assn. Trial Lawyers Iowa, Order of Coif. Democrat. Episcopalian. Clubs: Wakonda, Embassy (Des Moines). Federal civil litigation, State civil litigation, General corporate. Home: 2841 Gilmore Ave Des Moines IA 50312 Office: Scalise Scism Sandre & Uhl 2910 Grand Ave Des Moines IA 50312

SCOCOZZA, MATTHEW VINCENT, government official, lawyer; b. Bklyn., Oct. 13, 1948; s. Frank and Stella (Bartone) S. B.S., Murray State U., Ky., 1970; J.D., U. Tenn.-Knoxville, 1973. Bar: Tenn. 1973, D.C. 1974. Law clk. Tenn. Supreme Ct., 1973-74; minority counsel U.S. Ho. of Reps. com. on Appropriations, subcom. on transp., 1975-76; trial atty. Bur. Investigations and Enforcement, ICC, 1974-75, 76; sr. counsel U.S. Senate Com. on Commerce, Sci. and Transp., 1977-82; dept. asst. sec. U.S. Dept. State, 1977-82; asst. sec. for policy and internat. affairs U.S. Dept. Transp., Washington, 1983—. Contbg. author: Mandate for Leadership, 1980, The First Year, 1982. Recipient Ann. Cooperstown conf. award Cooperstown Rail conf., 1981, Delta Nu Alpha Presdl. award, 1984-85. Mem. ABA, Tenn. Bar Assn., D.C. Bar Assn., Omicron Delta Kappa, Phi Alpha Delta, Delta Nu Alpha, Sigma Phi Epsilon. Roman Catholic. Administrative and regulatory, Public international, Antitrust. Office: US Dept Transp 400 7th St SW Suite 10228 Washington DC 20590

SCOFIELD, MILTON N., lawyer; b. N.Y.C., Aug. 11, 1911; s. Elias and Celia (Neinken) S.; m. Nanette Eisler, Sept. 5, 1945; children—Elizabeth M., Anthony L. A.B., Columbia U., 1932, J.D., 1935. Bar: N.Y. 1935. Asst. N.Y.C. Law Revision Com. 1935; assoc. Stroock & Stroock & Lavan and predecessor Stroock & Stroock N.Y.C., 1942—, 43-45, ptnr., 1945—, sr. ptnr., 1960—; chief counsel food rationing div. Office Price Adminstrn., 1942; adv. on rationing to Sec. War, 1943; police magistrate, Scarsdale, N.Y., 1961-62; dir. Vishay Intertech., Inc. Corp. Mem. ABA, N.Y. County Law Assn., Assn. Bar City N.Y. General corporate, Private international, Securities. Office: 7 Hanover Sq 20th Floor New York NY 10004

SCOGLAND, WILLIAM LEE, lawyer; b. Moline, Ill., Apr. 2, 1949; s. Maurice William and Harriet Rebecca (Lee) S.; m. Vicki Lynn Whitham, Oct. 9, 1976; 1 child, Thomas. BA magna cum laude, Augustana Coll., 1971; JD cum laude, Harvard U., 1975. Bar: Ill. 1975, U.S. Dist. Ct. (no. dist.) Ill. 1975. Assoc. Wildman, Harrold, Allen & Dixon, Chgo., 1975-77, Hughes, Hubbard & Reed, Milw., 1977-81; from assoc. to ptnr. Jenner & Block, Chgo., 1981—. Mem. Phi Beta Kappa. Republican. Mem. Unitarian Ch. Pension, profit-sharing, and employee benefits, Corporate taxation. Office: Jenner & Block One IBM Plaza Chicago IL 60611

SCOLNIK, LOUIS, judge; b. Lewiston, Maine, Feb. 14, 1923; s. Julius and Bessie (Picker) S.; m. Paula Revitz, July 30, 1951; children—Nina, Donna, Julie. B.A., Bates Coll., 1947; LL.B., Georgetown U., 1952. Sole practice Lewiston, 1952-74; justice Maine Superior Ct., 1974-83; assoc. justice Maine Supreme Jud. Ct., Auburn, 1983—. Served to lt. (j.g.) USNR, 1943-46. Mem. ABA, Am. Judicature Soc., Maine Bar Assn. Office: PO Box 768 Auburn ME 04210

SCONYERS, ANTHONY BOOKER, lawyer; b. Chgo., Nov. 25, 1951; s. James Wesley and Helen Hazel (Washington) S.; m. Novella Yvonne Gordon, Sept. 25, 1976; children: Jennifer Elaine, Eric Alan. BA, Loyola U., Chgo., 1971; MA, Roosevelt U., 1976; JD, DePaul U., 1981. Bar: Ill. 1981, U.S. Dist. Ct. (no. dist.) Ill., U.S. Ct. Appeals (7th cir.) 1981. Contract specialist U.S. Army, Ft. Sheridan, Ill., 1974-77; atty., advisor U.S. Army, Rock Island, Ill., 1981—; adminstrv. officer, contracting officer GSA, Chgo., 1977-81; instr. bus. and contract law Blackhawk Coll., Moline, Ill., 1983—; program instr. St. Ambrose Coll., Davenport, 1986. Mem. ABA, Fed. Bar Assn., Ill. Bar Assn., Nat. Contract Mgmt. Assn. Avocations: listening to jazz music, travel. Contracts commercial. Home: 313 Wilshire Dr Colona IL 61241 Office: HQ AMCCOM Attn AMSMC-GCP(R) Rock Island IL 61299

SCORATOW, MARTIN MURRAY, lawyer; b. Pitts., Oct. 20, 1948; s. Sidney Scoratow and Betty (Kapaloff) Freud; m. Renee Rosenfled, Mar. 18, 1972; children: Lee, Ilene, Sarah. BA in Polit. Sci., Am. U., 1970, M in Pub. Adminstrn., 1971; JD, Duquesne U., 1977. Ptnr. Flyer, Eddins & Scoratow, Pitts., 1978-80, Eddins, Scoratow & Dudik, Pitts., 1980-85, Scoratow & Dudik, Pitts., 1985—; legal counsel Colonial Nat. Bank, Phila., 1980—. Cub master Pitts. council Boy Scouts Am., 1984-86; 1st v.p. New Light Congregation, Pitts., 1985-86; bd. dirs. Hebrew Inst. Pitts., 1985-86. Mem. Pa. Bar Assn., Allegheny County Bar Assn., Nat. Trial Lawyers Assn., Trial Atty. Criminal Ct. Allegheny County, Nat. Orgn. for Repeal of Marijuana Laws. Democrat. Jewish. Lodge: B'nai B'rith (sec. Three Rivers lodge 1985-86, treas. 1986, chmn. bequest com. western regional counsel 1985-86). Avocation: over 30 basketball league. Criminal, General corporate, Immigration, naturalization, and customs. Home: 5667 Melvin St Pittsburgh PA 15217 Office: Scoratow & Dedik 510 Lawyers Bldg Pittsburgh PA 15219

SCOTT, BETSY SUE, lawyer; b. Chgo., July 3, 1951; d. Leo and Regina Mackta; m. Thomas Jefferson Scott Jr., Apr. 25, 1981; 1 child, Elspeth Watts. Cert. in French lang., U. Paris, 1971; BA, Hamilton Coll., 1972; JD, Cumberland Coll., 1976. Bar: Pa. 1976, N.Y. 1980, D.C. 1984. Trust adminstr. Mfrs. Hanover Trust, N.Y.C., 1976-78; assoc. Fink, Weinberger et al, N.Y.C., 1978-80; employee benefits officer 1st Va. Bank, Falls Church, 1982-83; mem. Hill, Betts & Nash, Washington, 1983-85; sole practice, litigation cons. Washington, 1985-86; employee benefits atty., Pension and Welfare Benefits Administrn. U.S. Dept. Labor, Washington, 1986—; translator French-English litigation, Washington, 1985—. Mem. Great Falls (Va.) Hist. Soc. Republican. Club: Great Falls Womens. Avocations: sailing, fencing, gardening. Federal civil litigation, State civil litigation, Pension, profit-sharing, and employee benefits. Home: 500 Springvale Rd Great Falls VA 22066

SCOTT, CHARLES LURMAN, lawyer; b. Balt., June 5, 1920; s. Charles Franklin and Clare Agnes (Lurman) S.; m. Doris Petersen, Aug. 30, 1947; children: Charles L. Jr., David Steele. M in Engring., Stevens Tech., 1941; JD, U. Md., 1949. Bar: Md. 1950. Engr. Balt. Gas and Electric Co., 1941-51; contract specialist E.I. Dupont, Wilmington, Del., 1951-82; ptnr. Scott & Scott, Elkton, Md., 1982—; mgr. Thorn Found., Elkton, 1982—. Chmn. County Personnel Bd., Elkton, 1983. Served to lt. USNR, 1942-46, PTO. Mem. Md. Bar Assn. Republican. Episcopalian. Clubs: Balt. Country, Potapskut Sailing Assn., Dupont Country (Wilmington). Avocation: sailing. Personal injury, Family and matrimonial, Probate. Home: 327 Hermitage Dr Elkton MD 21921 Office: Scott & Scott 109 E Main St Elkton MD 21921

SCOTT, DAVID ERNEST, electronics manufacturers' representative, lawyer; b. New Castle, Pa., Aug. 28, 1952; s. David Leroy and Rosemary Anne (Semmes) S.; m. Kristy Lee Logan, Aug. 1, 1976 (div. Dec. 1982); m. Karen Renee Martin, July 27, 1986. B.A. cum laude, U. Santa Clara, 1974, J.D., 1977. Bar: Calif. 1977, U.S. Dist. Ct. (no. dist.) Calif. 1977. Assoc. atty. Royce, Jolly & Hayden, Mountain View, Calif., 1978-80; ptnr. Jolly & Scott, Mountain View, 1980; sr. contracts adminstr. Signetics Corp., Sunnyvale, Calif., 1981, field sales engr., 1981-83; mfr.'s rep. Norcomp, Inc., Santa Clara, Calif., 1983—. Bd. dirs. Valley Inst. Theater Arts, Saratoga, Calif. Calif. State scholar, U. Santa Clara scholar, 1970. Republican. Roman Catholic. Mem. Friends of Winemakers, Mercedes Benz Club Am., Ducks Unltd. Pension, profit-sharing, and employee benefits, Real property. Home: 14269 Quito Rd Saratoga CA 95070 Office: 3350 Scott Blvd #24 Santa Clara CA 95054

SCOTT, DAVID OSCAR, lawyer, educator; b. Bridgeport, Conn., Nov. 16, 1952; s. Oscar A. and Angelina K. (Kordesta) S. BS Mgmt. Engring., Worcester Poly. Inst., 1974; JD cum laude, Western New Eng. Coll., 1982. Bar: Mass. 1982, U.S. Dist. Ct. Mass. 1983, U.S. Ct. Appeals (1st cir.) 1984. Assoc. Fein, Schulman, Resnic, Pearson & Emond, Springfield, Mass., 1982-85, Morisi, O'Connell & Scott, Springfield, 1985—; adj. instr. Fisher Jr. Coll., Easthampton, Mass., 1985—. Mem. Big Brothers Hampden County, Springfield, 1984—; chmn. Greek Orthodox Young Adult League, Springfield, 1986—. Served to capt. U.S. Army, 1974-79, with Res. 1979—. Mem. ABA, Mass. Bar Assn., Hampden County Bar Assn., Assn. Trial Lawyers Am., Mass. Assn. Trial Attys., Am. Hellenic Edn. Progressive Assn., Alpha Epsilon Pi. Club: Ludlow Country (Mass.). Avocations: scuba diving, skiing, golf, reading. General practice, State civil litigation, Administrative and regulatory. Home: 15 Mallowhill Rd Springfield MA 01129 Office: Morisi O'Connell & Scott 101 State St Suite 601 Springfield MA 01103

SCOTT, DORIS PETERSEN, lawyer; b. Balt., June 22, 1925; d. David Steele and Leslie Helena (Suit) Petersen; m. Charles Lurman Scott, Aug. 30, 1947; children—Charles L., David Steele. Student Coll. of Notre Dame of Md., 1945; J.D., U. Md., 1949. Bar: Md. 1949, U.S. Dist. Ct. Md. 1955, U.S. Ct. Appeals (4th cir.) 1956. Assoc. Callahan & Caldwell, Balt., 1949-51; sole practice, Elkton, Md., 1951-82; ptnr. Scott & Scott, Elkton, 1983—, atty. Cecil County Bd. Edn., 1954—; dir. Cecil Fed. Savings & Loan Assn. Trustee Deferred Compensation Bd., State of Md., 1975-79. Mem. ABA, Md. State Bar Assn. (past mem. bd. govs.), Cecil County Bar Assn. (past pres.), Susquehanna Law League. Democrat. Episcopalian. Club: Balt. Country. Probate, Real property, Personal injury. Office Scott & Scott: 103 Burkley Bldg Elkton MD 21921

SCOTT, DOUGLAS WALTER, lawyer; b. Seattle, Apr. 23, 1949; s. James Robert and Helen Ethelen (Clemen) S.; m. Kitty Jo Wladkowski, Dec. 18, 1971: children: Alicia Bernice, Benjamin Walter. BA, Western Wash. State Coll., 1971; JD, Gonzaga U., 1975. Bar: Wash. 1976, U.S. Dist. Ct. (we. dist.) Wash. 1976, U.S. Ct. Appeals (9th cir.) 1977. Sole practice Bellevue, Wash., 1976-77, 84—; ptnr. Creighton, Scott, Schmitt & Cafferty and predecessor firm Creighton & Scott, Bellevue, 1977-80, Scott & Boyle, Bellevue, 1980-84; mem. panel for choosing profl. Wash. State SBA, 1982. Del. County Dem. Conv., Wash. State, 1976; Dem. precinct committeeman, 1976-77; mem. profl. adv. com. Group Health Hosp., Seattle, 1981-83, Indian guide/princesses YMCA, Bellevue, 1983—. Mem. ABA, Wash. State Bar Assn., Seattle-King County Bar Assn., East King County Bar Assn., Sierra Club. Episcopalian. Avocations: skiing, riverrafting, backpacking, tennis, snorkeling. Real property, Personal injury, Construction. Home: 1615 103d Pl NE N-4 Bellevue WA 98004 Office: 320 108th Ave NE Suite 304 Bellevue WA 98004

SCOTT, EARL DANIEL, lawyer; b. Americus, Ga., Aug. 26, 1946; s. Earl Lamar and Clarice (Watson) S.; m. Harriet Coplan, Aug. 27, 1966; children: Riley, Matthew. BS in Banking and Fin., U. S.C., 1968, JD, 1974, M in Criminal Justice, 1977. Bar: S.C. 1974, U.S. Dist. Ct. S.C. 1975. Atty. Wesley Waites, West Columbia, S.C., 1974-75; sole practice West Columbia, 1975-77; ptnr. Setzler, Chewning & Scott, West Columbia, 1977—; atty. Town of Springdale, S.C., 1978—; prosecutor City of West Columbia, S.C., 1983—. Served with U.S. Army, 1969-71, VietNam. Mem. Lexington County Bar Assn., S.C. Bar Assn. Baptist. Avocations: golf, tennis, fishing, hunting. Consumer commercial, Family and matrimonial, Real property. Office: PO Box 4024 1708 Augusta Blvd West Columbia SC 29171

SCOTT, EDDIE ELMER, lawyer; b. Sheridan, Wyo., Oct. 31, 1939; s. Bernard Alfred and Mary Ruth (Aspaas) S.; m. LaQuencis Alene Gibbs, Aug. 24, 1968. BS in Gen. Engring., U. Wyo., 1963, JD, 1966; MS, U. Tex., Dallas, 1972. Bar: Wyo. 1967, Tex. 1970. Examiner U.S. Patent Office, Washington, 1967-68; patent atty. Los Alamos (N.Mex.) Sci. Lab., 1968-69; sr. patent atty. Dresser Industries, Dallas, 1969-79; patent advisor Livermore (Calif.) Nat. Lab., 1979-80; assoc. gen. counsel patents and trademarks Copper Industries Inc., Houston, 1986—. Bd. tech. advisors High Tech. Law Jour. Served with USAF, 1958-63. Mem. Am. Intellectual Property Assn., U.S. Trademark Assn., Assn. Corp. Patent Counsel, Pacific Industrial Property Assn. Avocations: tennis, history. Patent, Trademark and copyright, Computer. Home: 729 Camelot Ln Houston TX 77024 Office: Copper Industries Inc 1001 Fannin Suite 4000 Houston TX 77002

SCOTT, GEORGE MATTHEW, state supreme court judge; b. Clark, N.J., Sept. 14, 1922; s. Francis Patrick and Harriet Ann (O'Donnell) S.; m. Joyce E. Hughes, July 26, 1947; children: Dan, Neil, Brian, George Matthew, Sheila. B.S., U. Minn.; J.D., William Mitchell Coll. Law. Bar: Minn. Practice law 1951-55; dep. atty. gen. State of Minn., 1955; atty. Hennepin County, Mpls., 1955-73; justice Minn. Supreme Ct., St. Paul, 1973—. Contbr. articles to profl. jours. Trustee William Mitchell Coll., 1960; del. Democratic Nat. Conv.; campaign chmn. Hubert H. Humphrey for Senator, 1960. Served with AUS, 1942-45. Mem. ABA, Minn. Bar Assn., Nat. Dist. Atty's. Assn. (pres. 1964-65), Am. Legion. Roman Catholic. Club: Optimists. Office: Minn Supreme Ct 228 Minnesota State Capitol Saint Paul MN 55155 *

SCOTT, HAL S., legal educator; b. 1943. AB, Princeton U., 1965; MA, Stanford U., 1967; JD, U. Chgo., 1972. Law clk. to judge U.S. Ct. Appeals D.C. Cir., Washington, 1972-73, to assoc. justice White, U.S. Supreme Ct., Washington, 1973-74; acting prof. law U. Calif.-Berkeley, 1974-75; asst. prof. law Harvard U. Sch. Law, Cambridge, Mass., 1975-79, prof., 1980—; cons. IBM, N.Y.C., 1977. Contbr. articles to legal jours. Dir. Program on Internat. Fin. Sustems. Mem. Internat. Acad. of Consumer and Comml. Law (pres.). Legal education, Banking. Office: Harvard U Sch Law Cambridge MA 02138

SCOTT, ISAAC ALEXANDER, JR., lawyer; b. Little Rock, Aug. 23, 1934; s. Isaac A. and Sherwin B. (Gilbert) S.; m. Elaine Hoffman, Aug. 24, 1957; children—Melissa E., Caitlin, Bronwen. A.B., Harvard Coll., 1956; LL.B., U. Ark., Fayetteville, 1959. Bar: Ark. 1959. Law clk., U.S. Dist. Ct., 1960-61; assoc. Chowning, Mitchell, Hamilton & Burrow, 1961-65; assoc. Wright, Lindsey & Jennings, Little Rock, 1965-66, ptnr., 1967—, mng. ptnr., 1986—. Bd. dirs. Urban League Greater Little Rock; pres. Chamber Music Soc. Little Rock; mem. discipline council Little Rock Central High Sch., 1976-77. Served with U.S. Army, 1959-62. Mem. Ark. Bar Assn. (ho. of dels. 1972-75), Pulaski County Bar Assn. (incorporator, bd. dirs. legal aid bur. 1967-69). Clubs: Book, Little Rock, Capitol, Harvard of Ark. (v.p.). Bankruptcy, Federal civil litigation, Contracts commercial. Office: Suite 2200 Worthen Bank Bldg Little Rock AR 72201

SCOTT, JANICE GAIL, lawyer; b. St. Petersburg, Fla., Sept. 1, 1949; d. Thomas Arthur and Nell (Van Houten) S.; m. James Corban Massie, June 21, 1975. BA, Fla. State U., 1971, JD cum laude, 1977. Bar: Fla. 1977, U.S. Ct. Appeals (11th and 5th cirs.) 1981, U.S. Supreme Ct. 1984. Asst. pub. defender State of Fla., Tallahassee, 1977-78; trial atty. Fla. Dept. Transp., Tallahassee, 1978-81; asst. gen. counsel Fla. Dept. Bus. Regulation, Tallahassee, 1981-83; ptnr. Massie & Scott, Tallahassee, 1983-84, Taylor Brion Buker & Green, Tallahassee and Miami, 1985—. Mem. ABA, Assn. Trial Lawyers Am., U.S. Dressage Assn., Sierra Club. Democrat. State civil litigation, Administrative and regulatory, General corporate. Office: Taylor Brion Buker & Green 225 S Adams St Suite 250 PO Box 11189 Tallahassee FL 32302

SCOTT, JOHN ANDREW, lawyer; b. N.Y.C., Aug. 17, 1952; s. John Joseph and Virginia (Tiernan) S.; m. Laura Kim Fidanza, Apr. 6, 1954; 1 child, Kathryn Danna. BA summa cum laude, Fordham U., 1974; JD with honors, St. John's U., N.Y.C., 1978. Bar: N.Y. 1979. Assoc. Coudert Brothers, N.Y.C., 1978-81; v.p. Magellan Petroleum Corp., Hartford, Conn., 1981-82, also bd. dirs.; sec., gen. counsel IMS Internat., N.Y.C and London, 1982—; v.p. Can. So. Petroleum Ltd., Calgary, Alta., 1981-82. Contrbg. editor St. John's Law Rev. Club: Hartford. Avocations: tennis, car restoration. Contracts commercial, General corporate, Securities. Home: 90 North Rd, London N6, England Office: IMS Internat Inc, 37 Queen Sq, London WCIN 3BH, England

SCOTT, JOHN JOSEPH, lawyer; b. Chgo., Dec. 30, 1950; s. John Joseph and Alice (Pierzhala) S.; m. Maria Crawford, Aug. 17, 1974. BA, Yale U., 1972; JD, U. Chgo., 1975. Bar: Ill. 1975, U.S. Dist. Ct. (no. dist.) Ill. 1976. Assoc. Kirkland & Ellis, Chgo., 1975-82, ptnr., 1982—. Mem. ABA, Chgo. Bar Assn. (chmn. investment act 1940 subcom. securities law com. 1984—). Roman Catholic. Club: University (Chgo.). Mutual funds, Securities, General corporate. Office: Kirkland & Ellis 200 E Randolph Dr 57th Floor Chicago IL 60601

SCOTT, JOHN ROLAND, oil company executive, lawyer; b. Wichita Falls, Tex., May 13, 1937; s. John Robert and Margaret Willena (Rouse) S.; m. Joan Carol Redding, Sept. 5, 1959; 1 child, John Howard. LL.B., Baylor Sch. Law, Waco, Tex., 1962. Bar: Tex. 1962, Alaska 1970, U.S. Dist. Ct. (we. dist.) Tex. 1965, U.S. Dist. Ct. Alaska 1975. Assoc. litigation sect Lynch & Chappell, Midland, Tex., 1962-65; regional atty. Atlantic Richfield Co., Midland, 1965-79; sr. atty., Anchorage, 1969-77, sr. atty., Dallas, 1977-80; v.p., assoc. gen. counsel Mitchell Energy & Devel. Corp., Houston, 1980-82; asst. gen. counsel Hunt Oil Co., Dallas., 1982-84, v.p., chief counsel, 1984—; bar examiner in Alaska, 1974-77. Mem. State Bar Tex. (lectr.), Dallas Bar Assn., ABA, Phi Alpha Delta. Republican. Baptist. Clubs: Petroleum , Aerobics Ctr., University (Dallas). Oil and gas leasing. Office: Hunt Oil Co 2900 InterFirst One Bldg 1401 Elm St Dallas TX 75202

SCOTT, KENNETH EUGENE, lawyer, educator; b. Western Springs, Ill., Nov. 21, 1928; s. Kenneth L. and Bernice (Albright) S.; m. Viviane H. May, Sept. 22, 1956 (dec. Feb. 12, 1982); children: Clifton, Jeffrey, Linda. B.A., Coll. William and Mary, 1949; M.A., Princeton, 1953; LL.B., Stanford, 1956. Bar: N.Y. bar 1957, Calif. bar 1957, D.C. bar 1967. Practice in N.Y.C., 1956-59, Los Angeles, 1959-61; asso. firm Sullivan & Cromwell, 1956-59, Musick, Peeler & Garrett, Los Angeles, 1959-60; chief dep. savs. and loan commr. State of Calif., 1961-63; gen. counsel Fed. Home Loan Bank Bd., Washington, 1963-67; Parsons prof. law and bus. Stanford Law Sch., 1968—. Co-author: Retail Banking in the Electronic Age, 1977, The Economics of Corporation Law and Securities Regulation, 1980. Mem. Am., Calif. bar assns., Phi Beta Kappa, Order of Coif, Pi Kappa Alpha, Omicron Delta Kappa. Banking, General corporate, Securities. Home: 60 Bear Gulch Dr Portola Valley CA 94025 Office: Stanford Law Sch Stanford CA 94305

SCOTT, L. HAVARD, III, lawyer; b. Shreveport, La., Apr. 20, 1953; s. Leroy Havard and Rebecca (Campbell) S. BA, Centenary Coll. La., 1976; JD, La. State U., 1978. Bar: La. 1979, U.S. Dist. Ct. (ea. and mid. dist.) La. 1980, U.S. Ct. Appeals (5th cir.) 1981, U.S. Dist. Ct. (we. dist.) La. 1982, U.S. Supreme Ct. 1983. Assoc. Chaffe, McCall, Phillips, Toler & Sarpy, New Orleans, 1979-83, jr. ptnr., 1984-85, gen. ptnr., 1986—. Mem. ABA, La. State Bar Assn., New Orleans Bar Assn. Democrat. Episcopalian. Club: World Trade Ctr., Petroleum (New Orleans). Personal injury, Federal civil litigation, State civil litigation. Home: 3805 Carondelet St New Orleans LA 70115 Office: Chaffe McCall Phillips Toler & Sarpy 1500 First NBC Bldg New Orleans LA 70112

SCOTT, LAWRENCE ROWE, lawyer; b. Oklahoma City, May 24, 1956; s. Lawrence Vernon and Elizabeth Buchanan (Rowe) S.; m. Nancy Jo Kreger, Feb. 18, 1984. Student, Am. U., 1976; BA in Polit. Sci., Phillips U., 1978; JD, U. Okla., 1981. Bar: Okla. 1981, U.S. Dist. Ct. (we. dist.) Okla. 1982, U.S. Ct. Appeals (10th cir.) 1982. Asst. dist. atty. Oklahoma County, Oklahoma City, 1981-83; sole practice Oklahoma City, 1983—. Bd. dirs. Campfire, Inc., Oklahoma City, 1985—. Mem. ABA, Nat. Dist. Atty.'s Assn., Assn. Trial Lawyers Am., Okla. Trial Lawyers Assn., Oklahoma County Bar Assn. Democrat. Criminal, General practice. Office: 625 NW 13th Oklahoma City OK 73106

SCOTT, MICHAEL, lawyer; b. N.Y.C., Oct. 11, 1930; s. Irvin Leslie and Dorothy (Chandler) S.; m. Cynthia Ann Meredith, July 17, 1954; children: Elizabeth, Gregory, Andrew. BA, Cornell U., 1952; JD, U. Mich., 1958; diploma, Grad. Inst. of Internat. Studies, Geneva, 1959. Bar: Ohio 1959, D.C. 1971, Calif. 1981. Assoc. Squire, Sanders & Dempsey, Cleve., 1959-67, ptnr., 1967-71; ptnr. Squire, Sanders & Dempsey, Washington, 1971—; pres. Ohio State Legal Services Assn., Columbus, 1969-70, Nat. Capital Area Health Care Coalition, Washington, 1985—. Served to lt. (j.g.) USN, 1952-55. Mem. ABA, Ohio Bar Assn., D.C. Bar Assn., Calif. Bar Assn. Clubs: Met. (Washington), Union (Cleve.). General corporate, Health. Home: 967 Millwood Rd Great Falls VA 22066 Office: Squire Sanders & Dempsey 1201 Pennsylvania Ave NW Washington DC 20004

SCOTT, PAUL EDWARD, lawyer; b. Pitts., July 29, 1947; s. Robert T. and Lillian E. (Bender) S. BA, Colgate U., 1968; MD, U. Pitts., 1972; JD, U. Denver, 1977. Bar: Colo. 1977, U.S. Dist. Ct. Colo. 1977, U.S. Supreme Ct. 1979. Resident in surgery and pathology U. Colo. Med. Ctr., Denver, 1972-74; ptnr. Johnson, Mahoney & Scott P.C., Denver, 1977; asst. clinical prof. U. Colo. Med. Ctr., 1974—; instr. law U. Denver, 1977—. Personal injury, Health. Office: Johnson Mahoney & Scott PC 3773 Cherry Creek Dr N #801 Denver CO 80209

SCOTT, PETER BRYAN, lawyer; b. St. Louis, Nov. 11, 1947; s. Gilbert Franklin and Besse Jean (Fudge) S.; m. Suzanne Rosalee Wallace, Oct. 19, 1974; children: Lindsay W., Sarah W., Peter B. Jr. A.B., Drury Coll., 1969; J.D., Washington U., St. Louis, 1972, LL.M., 1980. Bar: Mo. 1972, Colo. 1980; diplomate Ct. Practice Inst. Sole practice, St. Louis, 1972-80; assoc. firm McKie and Assocs., Denver, 1980-81; ptnr. firm Scott and Chesteen, P.C., Denver, 1981-84, Veto & Scott, Denver, 1984—; tchr. Denver Paralegal Inst. Served to capt. USAR, 1971-79. Mem. ABA, Mo. Bar Assn., Colo. Bar Assn., Denver Bar Assn. Republican. Mem. United Church of Christ. General corporate, Probate, Corporate taxation. Home: 26262 Wolverine Trail Evergreen CO 80439 Office: Veto & Scott 6595 W 14th Ave Suite 200 Lakewood CO 80214

SCOTT, RICHARD WALDO, lawyer; b. N.Y.C., July 8, 1953; s. Walter Vanderbilt Jr. and Ella Louise (Becker) S.; m. Karen Trussell, May 25, 1974 (div. Oct. 1984); children: Richard Jr., Amanda, Margaret; m. Laure Ellen Copland, Mar. 9, 1986. AB, Duke U., 1974, JD, 1977. Bar: N.Y. 1978, Tex. 1980. Assoc. Sullivan & Cromwell, N.Y.C., 1977-79; assoc. Vinson & Elkins, Houston, 1979-84, ptnr., 1984—. Mem. ABA, Tex. Bar Assn., Order of Coif, Phi Beta Kappa. Republican. Presbyterian. Avocations: golf, music, sailing. General corporate, Securities. Home: 122 Paul Revere Dr Houston TX 77024 Office: Vinson & Elkins 3300 1st City Tower 1001 Fannin Houston TX 77002-6760

SCOTT, ROBERT GENE, lawyer; b. Montague, Mass., Aug. 29, 1951; s. Edwin Ray and Barbara Agnes (Painchaud) S.; m. Laura Beth Williams, May 27, 1978; children: Jason Robert, Amanda Marie, Leah Beth. BS, U. Notre Dame, 1973, MS, 1975; postgrad. U. Tex. Med. Br., 1975-76; JD, U. Notre Dame, 1980. Bar: Ind. 1980, Mo. 1981, U.S. Dist. Ct. (no. dist.) Ind. 1980, U.S. Dist. Ct. (we. dist.) Mo. 1981, U.S. Patent Office 1980, U.S. Ct. Appeals (11th cir.) 1986, U.S. Ct. Appeals (8th cir.) 1987. Asst. women's basketball coach U. Notre Dame, Ind., 1977-80; assoc. atty. Oltsch, Knoblock & Hall, South Bend, Ind., 1980-81; atty. Swanson, Midgley, et al, Kansas City, Mo., 1981-82; exec. adminstr. Council of Fleet Specialists, Shawnee Mission, Kans., 1982-83; atty. Levy and Craig, Kansas City, Mo., 1983—. Precinct Committeeman Johnson County Rep. Party, Kans., 1983-84. Mem. ABA, Ind. Bar Assn., Mo. Bar Assn., Kansas City Bar Assn., Kansas City Lawyers Assn. Republican. Roman Catholic. Club: Notre Dame of Kansas City (pres. 1985-86). State civil litigation, Entertainment, Trademark and copyright. Home: 9405 Dice Ln Lenexa KS 66215 Office: Levy and Craig 916 Walnut St Suite 400 Kansas City MO 64106

SCOTT, ROBERT KENT, lawyer; b. New Eagle, Pa., July 25, 1936; s. James Philip Scott and D. Mildred (Jeannot) Scott Crisp; m. Patricia Ann Gamble, Aug. 23, 1958 (div.); children—Elizabeth, Philip, Noelle, David; m. Anne Rodgers, May 29, 1982. B.A., Kenyon Coll., 1958; LL.B., Columbia U., 1961. Bar: Ohio 1962, Ill. 1969, Mich. 1977, Wis. 1979, Fla. 1982. Gen. counsel Cutler-Hammer, Milw., 1978-79; v.p., gen. counsel CF Industries, Long Grove, Ill., 1979-81, A.E. Staley Mfg. Co., Decatur, Ill., 1982-85; v.p., sec., gen. counsel Staley Continental, Inc., Rolling Meadows, Ill., 1985—. Reporter Illinois Criminal Code, 1970. Mem. Ill. Bar Assn., Ohio Bar Assn., Mich. Bar Assn., Wis. Bar Assn., Fla. Bar Assn., Chgo. Crime Commn. Clubs: Biltmore Country (Barrington, Ill.); Country of Decatur; Chicago. General corporate, Antitrust. Office: C/O Staley Continental Inc One Continental Towers 1701 Golf Rd Rolling Meadows IL 60008

SCOTT, ROMAINE SAMPLES, III, lawyer; b. Birmingham, Ala., Jan. 12, 1951; s. Romaine Samples Jr. and Ann Carol (Lindsay) S.; m. Catherine Grace Hartley, Jan. 30, 1982; children: James Grady, Romaine Samples IV, Lindsay Leigh. BA, Washington and Lee U., 1974; JD, Samford U., 1980. Bar: U.S. Dist. Ct. (no. dist.) Ala. 1980, U.S. Ct. Appeals (11th cir.) 1981, U.S. Dist. Ct. (so. dist.) Ala. 1982, U.S. Supreme Ct. 1985. Copy editor Birmingham Post-Herald, 1976-77; assoc. Thomas, Taliaferro, Forman, Burr & Murray, Birmingham, 1980-82; ptnr. Inge, Twitty, Duffy & Prince (later Inge, Twitty, Duffy, Prince & McKean), Mobile, Ala., 1982—. Contbr. article to legal jours.; co-author Foreclosure Law Seminar manual, 1986. Mem. ABA, Ala. Bar Assn. (bankruptcy and comml. law sect. 1984—, bd. editors Ala. Lawyer 1984—), Birmingham Bar Assn., Mobile Bar Assn., Mobile Bankruptcy Com. Presbyterian. Avocations: computer programming, reading, music, tennis, writing. Real property, Bankruptcy, Contracts commercial. Home: 102 N Bayview St Fairhope AL 36532 Office: Inge Twitty Duffy Prince & McKean 56 St Francis St Mobile AL 36602

SCOTT, RONALD CHARLES, lawyer; b. Greenville, S.C., Jan. 8, 1948; s. Robert Claude and Louise Helen (Tinsley) S.; m. Debra Whaley, Aug. 11, 1973; children: Robert Marion, Jordan Whaley. BBA cum laude, The Citadel, 1970; MBA, U. S.C., 1972, M in Acctg., JD, 1976. Bar: S.C. 1976, U.S. Dist. Ct. S.C. 1977, U.S. Tax Ct. 1977. Pres. Scott & Mathews P.A., Columbia, S.C., 1978—; pres. Heritage Title, Columbia, 1980—. Bd. of visitors, pres.'s adv. council Med. U. S.C.; past state pres. Nat. Soc. to Prevent Blindness, past state sec.; state fundraising chmn. Arthritis Found. Served to capt. (adj. gen. corps.) USAR, 1970-76. Named one of Most Outstanding Young Men of Columbia Jaycees, 1982; recipient State Dist. Service award U.S. Jaycees, 1982, Leadership S.C. award Office of the Gov., 1986; recipient Fellowship Regional Finalist award White House, 1984. Mem. ABA (past state rep., significant legis. com., real property com.), S.C. Bar Assn. (sec. subcom. model corp. act panel), Columbia C. of C. (com. of 100, Leadership Columbia award 1981). Democrat. Presbyterian. Clubs: Summit, Palmetto (Columbia), DeBordieu (Georgetown, S.C.), Capital. Administrative and regulatory, Personal income taxation, Real property. Office: Scott & Mathews PA 1331 Laurel St PO Box 2065 Columbia SC 29202

SCOTT, ROSEMARY, lawyer; b. Detroit, July 31, 1921; d. Leonard and Laura B. (Taylor) S. AB in History, U. Mich., 1940, AM in History, 1942, JD, 1946. Bar: Mich. 1946. Sole practice Grand Rapids, Mich., 1948—. Chmn. Mich. Youth Commn. , 1964-71; pres. Mich. Council on Children and Youth, Grand Rapids, 1969-85; pres., exec. sec. Grand Rapids Civic Ballet Co., 1972—. Recipient Meritorious Service award Cath. Social Services, Mich., 1971. Fellow ABA (vice chmn. significant legis., probate and def. com. 1984-85, 86—); mem. Mich. Bar Assn. (chmn. jr. bar 1951-52, chmn. juvenile programs 1966-79), Grand Rapids Bar Assn. (trustee). Republican. Episcopalian. Club: Quota of Grand Rapids. Probate, State civil litigation, Consumer commercial. Office: 714 MetroBanc Bldg Grand Rapids MI 49503

SCOTT, STEPHEN CHARLES, lawyer; b. Sioux City, Iowa, Aug. 8, 1946; s. Charles Marshall and Virginia Eleanor (Dunlap) S.; m. Sandra Ann Davidson, Aug. 26, 1967; children—Stephanie Elaine, Alison Marie, Shelley Lorraine. B.J., U. Mo., 1968, M.A. in Polit. Sci., 1977, J.D. cum laude, 1977. Bar: Mo. 1978, U.S. Dist. Ct. (we. dist.) Mo. 1978; cert. civil trial advocate Nat. Bd. Trial Advocacy. News editor Columbia Tribune, Mo., 1972-73; state editor Globe-Democrat, St. Louis, 1974-75; asst. city editor Columbia Missourian, 1975-77; assoc. Jones & Roper, Columbia, 1978; ptnr. Jones, Scott & Schneider, Columbia, 1979-86; ptnr. Hindman & Scott, Columbia, 1986—. Contbr. articles to legal jours. Counsel, Central Mo. Humane Soc., Columbia, 1978—; mem. session 1st Presbyterian Ch., Columbia, 1981-83, counsel, 1981—; mem. Columbia Sch. Bd., 1985—. Served with USN, 1968-70. Mem. ABA, Mo. Bar (civil procedure com. 1980), Boone County Bar Assn. (treas. 1982-83, sec. 1986-87), Assn. Trial Lawyers Am., Mo. Assn. Trial Attys., Order of Coif. State civil litigation, Insurance, Personal injury. Home: 201 Westwood Ave Columbia MO 65203 Office: Hindman & Scott Law Office 1001 E Walnut St Suite 300 Columbia MO 65201

SCOTT, STEVEN GEORGE, lawyer; b. San Mateo, Calif., Sept. 10, 1948; s. George Osborne and Irene Mae (Tetz) S.; m. Kristin Margaret Houser, June 17, 1977; children: Anna, Nicholas. BA, Stanford U., 1970; JD, U. Pa., 1974. Bar: Oreg. 1974, Wash. 1977, U.S. Dist. Ct. (ea. dist.) Washington 1978, U.S. Dist. Ct. (we. dist.) Washington 1979, U.S. Ct. Appeals (9th cir.) 1980. Law clk. to presiding justice Oreg. Ct. Appeals, Salem, 1974-75; atty., project dir. Instl. Legal Services, Seattle, 1975-76, 78-81; atty. Pub. Def. Assn., Seattle, 1977-78; coordinator litigation Evergreen Legal Services, Seattle, 1981-86; assoc. Kleist & Arnold, Seattle, 1986—; adj. faculty sch. law U. Wash., Seattle, 1978-79; mem. com. corrections Wash. State Bar, Seattle, 1979-82, adv. com. corrections King County, Seattle, 1982-83, council on crime and delinquency State of Wash., Seattle, 1981—; commr. sentencing guidelines com. State of Wash., Olympia, 1981-84; cons. Legal Services Corp., Washington, 1979-81, Nat. Inst. Trial Advocacy, Boulder, Colo., 1986—. Contbr. articles to profl. jours. bd. dirs. Temple Daycare Ctr., Seattle, 1986—. Mem. Wash. State Bar Assn. Democrat. Civil rights, Personal injury, Federal civil litigation. Office: Kleist & Arnold 2209 Eastlake Ave E Seattle WA 98102

SCOTT, TERRENCE VERSON, lawyer; b. Mpls., Jan. 15, 1955; s. Isadore and Lorraine Suzanne (Verson) S. BA, UCLA, 1975, JD, 1978. Bar: Calif. 1978, U.S. Dist. Ct. (no. dist.) Calif. 1982, U.S. Dist. Ct. (cen. dist.) Calif. 1984. Assoc. Law Offices Barry Tarlow, Los Angeles, 1978—. Contbr. articles to profl. jours. Mem. ABA (criminal justice sect. Racketeer Influenced and Corrupt Orgns. com.). Democrat. Jewish. Avocations: baseball, sabrmetrics. Criminal. Office: Law Offices Barry Tarlow 9119 Sunset Blvd Los Angeles CA 90069

SCOTT, THEODORE R., lawyer; b. Mount Vernon, Ill., Dec. 7, 1924; s. Theodore R. and Beulah (Flannigan) S.; m. Virginia Scott, June 1, 1947; children: Anne Sheyka, Sarah Buckland, Daniel, Barbara Gomon. AB, U. Ill., 1947, JD, 1949. Bar: Ill. 1950. Law clk. to judge U.S. Ct. Appeals, 1949-51; sole practice Chgo., 1950—; assoc. Spaulding Glass, 1951-53, Loftus, Lucas & Hammand, 1953-58, Ooms, McDougall, Williams & Hersh, 1958-60; ptnr. McDougall, Hersh & Scott, Chgo., 1960-87; of counsel Jones, Day, Reavis & Pogue, 1987—. Served to 2d lt. USAAF, 1943-45. Decorated Air medal. Fellow Am. Coll. Trial Lawyers.; mem. ABA, Ill. Bar Assn., Chgo. Bar Assn., 7th Circuit Bar Assn. (past pres.), Legal Club Chgo., Law Club Chgo., Patent Law Assn. Chgo. (past pres.), Phi Beta Kappa. Clubs: Union League (Chgo.); Exmoor Country (Highland Park, Ill.). Federal civil litigation, Patent, Trademark and copyright. Home: 1569 Woodvale Ave Deerfield IL 60015 Office: 135 S LaSalle St Chicago IL 60603

SCOTT, THOMAS EMERSON, JR., judge; b. Pitts., Apr. 27, 1948; s. Thomas Emerson Sr. and Marie (Ebel) S.; m. Ginger Claud, Mar. 1978 (div. Aug. 1980); m. Joyce Newman, Aug. 6, 1983. BA in Econs., U. Miami, 1969, JD, 1972. Bar: Fla. 1972, U.S. Dist. Ct. (so. dist.) Fla. 1972, U.S. Ct. Appeals (5th and 11th cirs.) 1972. Assoc. Bradford & Williams, Miami, Fla., 1972-76, Huebner, Shaw & Burrell, Ft. Lauderdale, Fla., 1976-77, Bradford & Williams, Miami, 1977-80; cir. judge State of Fla., Miami, 1980-84; ptnr. Kimbrell, Hamann, Jennings, Womack, Carlson & Kniskern P.A., Miami, 1984-85; judge U.S. Dist. Ct. (so. dist.), Miami, 1985—; instr. U. Miami, Coral Gables, 1984-86. Served to 1st lt. USAR, 1969—. Mem. ABA, Fla. Bar Assn., Dade County Bar Assn. Republican. Roman Catholic. Avocations: running, collectibles. Criminal, State civil litigation, Product liability. Office: US Dist Ct 301 N Miami Ave Fed Courthouse Miami FL 33158

SCOTT, THOMAS STRATTON, JR., lawyer; b. Covington, Va., Mar. 18, 1940; s. Thomas Stratton Sr. and Helen Louise (Jamison) S.; m. Teresa Howell, Nov. 30, 1976; children: Thomas S. III, Patrick H., Carol L. BA, Maryville Coll., 1961; JD, U. Tenn., 1967. Bar: Tenn. 1968, U.S. Dist. Ct. (ea. dist.) Tenn. 1968, U.S. Ct. Appeals (6th cir.) 1984, U.S. Supreme Ct. 1984. From assoc. to ptnr. Arnett, Draper & Hagood, Knoxville, Tenn., 1968—; faculty mem. Tenn. Coll. Trial Adv., Knoxville, 1978—; adj. prof. law trial practice U. Tenn., Knoxville, 1982—. Served to staff sgt. U.S. Army Intelligence, 1961-64. Mem. Am. Bd. Trial Advs., Fedn. Ins. Corp. Counsel, Tenn. Trial Lawyers Assn., Tenn. Def. Lawyers Assn., Def. Research Inst., Am. Judicature Soc. Presbyterian. Lodge: Masons. Avocations: hunting, boating. Federal civil litigation, State civil litigation, Personal injury.

SCOTT, VALERIE WEEKS, lawyer; b. Kansas City, Mo., Nov. 3, 1939; d. William Henry and Elizabeth (Kelley) Weeks; m. Jeffrey J. Scott, June 7, 1962 (div. May 1980); children: Matthew Henry, Emily Louise. BS, Northwestern U., 1960; LLB, Yale U., 1964. Bar: Mont. 1964, U.S. Dist. Ct. Mont. 1965, Nebr. 1972, U.S. Dist. Ct. Nebr. 1974, Calif. 1985, U.S. Dist. Ct. Calif. 1986. Assoc. Sandall, Moses & Cavan, Billings, Mont., 1964-67; ptnr. Scott, Scott & Baugh, Billings, 1967-72; atty. Union Pacific R.R. Co., Omaha, 1973-84, Sci. Applications Internat. Corp., La Jolla, Calif., 1984—. Bd. dirs. San Diego Symphony Assn., 1985—. Mem. ABA, Calif. Bar Assn., San Diego County Bar Assn., Am. Corp. Counsel Assn., Western Pension Conf. Club: Jr. League (San Diego). Avocations: tennis, swimming. General corporate, Pension, profit-sharing, and employee benefits, Securities. Office: Sci Applications Internat Corp 476 Prospect St La Jolla CA 92037

SCOTT, WILLARD PHILIP, lawyer, corporate executive; b. Columbus, Ohio, Jan. 8, 1909; s. Wirt Stanley and Mabel Lynne (Rond) S.; m. Lucille Westrom, June 27, 1936; children: Robert W., David W., Anne L. A.B. with honors, Ohio State U., 1930; LL.B. (dean's scholar), Columbia, 1933. Bar: N.Y. 1934, D.C. 1934. Ptnr. Oliver & Donnally, N.Y.C., 1938-65; Dir. Am. Potash & Chem. Corp., 1951—, v.p., 1955-68, vice chmn. bd., 1968—; v.p., gen. counsel Kerr-McGee Corp., 1968-73, v.p. fin., 1973-75, sr. v.p., 1973-75, cons., 1975—; gen. counsel Nat. Assn. Mut. Savs. Banks and Savs. Banks Assn. N.Y., 1945-60; counsel bondholders coms. r.r. reorgn. C. & N.-W. Ry., Soo Line, Alton, B. & M. R.R., C., M., St. P. & P. Ry., Fla. East Coast, Central N.J., D. & H. R.R.; dir. 1st Nat. Bank & Trust Co. of Oklahoma City, Transocean Drilling Co. Ltd., Bikita Minerals Ltd. Editor: Business Lawyer, 1958-59; Contbr. articles on corporate law to profl. jours. Trustee, Scarsdale, N.Y., 1951-55, police commr., acting mayor, 1953-55, mayor, 1955-57, mem. bd. appeals, 1957-68; Bd. dirs. Oklahoma City Allied Arts Found., Oklahoma City Symphony Soc.; trustee Okla. Sci. and Arts Found.; bd. advisers Mercy Hosp. Fellow Am. Bar Found., Southwestern Legal Found.; Mem. Internat. Bar Assn. (patron), ABA (commn. on corporate laws 1947—, chmn. sect. corporate banking and bus. law 1960-61, ho. of dels. 1961-62, chmn. com. ednl. programs), N.Y. Bar Assn., D.C. Bar Assn., Okla. Bar Assn., Am. Law Inst., Assn. Bar City N.Y., Phi Beta Kappa, Phi Kappa Sigma, Phi Delta Phi, Phi Alpha Theta, Pi Sigma Alpha. Republican. Presbyn. Clubs: Union League (N.Y.C.), Madison Square Garden (N.Y.C.); Metropolitan (Washington); Scarsdale Golf; Oklahoma City Golf and Country (Oklahoma City), Beacon (Oklahoma City), Whitehall (Oklahoma City). Antitrust, General corporate, Private international. Home: 01812 Drury Ln Oklahoma City OK 73116 Office: Kerr-McGee Bldg Oklahoma City OK 73102

SCOULAR, ROBERT FRANK, lawyer; b. Del Norte, Colo., July 9, 1942; s. Duane William and Marie Josephine (Moloney) S.; m. Donna V. Scoular, June 3, 1967; children—Bryan T., Sean D., Bradley R. B.S. in Aero. Engring., St. Louis U., 1964, J.D., 1968. Bar: Mo. 1968, Colo. 1968, N.D. 1968, U.S. Supreme Ct. 1972, Calif. 1979. Law clk. to presiding justice U.S. Ct. Appeals (8th cir.), 1968-69; ptnr. Bryan, Cave, McPheeters & McRoberts, St. Louis, 1969-75; mng. ptnr. Bryan, Cave, McPheeters & McRoberts, Los Angeles, 1979-84, exec. com., 1984-85, sect. leader tech. and computer law sect., 1985—; dir. Mo. Lawyers Credit Union, 1978-79. Contbr. articles to profl. jours. Bd. dirs. St. Louis Bar Found., 1975-76, 79; Eagle Scout leader Boy Scouts Am.; league commr. Am. Youth Soccer Orgn.; mem. alumni council St. Louis U., 1979-82. Mem. ABA (nat. dir. young lawyers div. 1977-78), Am. Judicature Soc., Bar Assn. Met. St. Louis (v.p. 1978-79, sec. 1979, chmn. young lawyers sect. 1975-76), Los Angeles County Bar Assn., Assn. Bus. Trial Lawyers, Calif. Bar. Assn., Mo. Bar (chmn. young lawyers sect. 1976-77, disting. service award), Computer Law Assn., Environ. Bar Assn., Internat. Bar Assn.. Clubs: Mo. Athletic, University Los Angeles. Federal civil litigation, State civil litigation, Computer. Home: 4 Horseshoe Ln Rolling Hills Estates CA 90274 Office: 333 S Grand Ave Suite 3100 Los Angeles CA 90071

SCOWCROFT, JEROME CHILWELL, lawyer; b. Pocatello, Idaho, May 17, 1947; s. Harold and Alberta Mary (Chilwell) S.; m. Corinne Gail Cox, Mar. 12, 1983; 1 child, Jason Trevor. BA, Stanford U., 1969; M in Research Psychology, U. Calif., San Diego, 1973; JD, Duke U., 1978. Bar: N.Y. 1980, Wash. 1986. Assoc. Haight, Gardner, Poor & Havens, N.Y.C., 1978-81, Schwabe, Williamson, Wyatt, Moore & Roberts, Seattle, 1985—; editor, legal advisor Lamorte, Burns & Co., N.Y.C. and Greenwich, Conn., 1981-85. Editor-in-chief Maritime Adv. Services, Arbitration Award Digest, 1981—; contbg. editor U.S. Maritime Arbitration, Internat. Congress Comml. Arbitration, 1983—; case editor Jour. of Maritime Law and Commerce, 1987—; contbr. articles to profl. jours. Vice chmn. com. Seattle-Congquing Sister Cities Assn., 1986. Served with U.S. Army, 1970-72. Fellow HEW, 1975-76. Mem. ABA, Maritime Law Assn. U.S. Republican. Episcopalian. Clubs: Seattle World Trade, Propellor (Seattle). Avocations: math., photography, tennis, hiking. Admiralty, Contracts commercial, Private international. Home: 6305 152d Ave NE Redmond WA 98052 Office: Schwabe Williamson Wyatt & Lenihan 1415 5th Ave Suite 900 Seattle WA 98171

SCREMIN, ANTHONY JAMES, lawyer; b. Miami, Fla., June 20, 1941; s. Anthony Scremin and Rose Marie (Zullo) S.; m. Barbara Jean Thompson, Oct. 22, 1960 (div. July 1977); children: Julie Beth, Sylvia Ann, Ann Marie; m. Iliana Magarita Rodriguez, Mar. 17, 1979. BBA, U. Miami, 1966, JD, 1968. Bar: Fla. 1968, U.S. Dist. Ct. (so. dist.) Fla. 1969, U.S. Ct. Appeals (3d cir.). Assoc. Hawkesworth & Kay, Miami, 1968-69; assoc., trial asst. Steven, Demos, et al, Miami, 1969-70, Welch & Carroll, Miami, 1969-70; head trial atty. Metro Transit Authority, Miami, 1970-71; ptnr., trial atty. Abramson, Scremin et al, Miami, 1971-78; prin., head trial atty. Anthony J. Scremin P.A., Miami, 1978—. Served with USCG, 1959-60. Recipient Cert. of Merit, Bar and Gavel Legal Soc., U. Miami, 1968, Outstanding Service award Labor Law Soc., U. Miami, 1968. Mem. Am. Arbitration Assn., Acad. Trial Lawyers Am., N.Y. State Trial Lawyers Assn., Fla. Bar Assn., Phi Delta Phi. Democrat. Roman Catholic. Avocations: karate, weight-lifting, construction. Criminal, State civil litigation, Personal injury. Home: 12651 SW 20 Ter Miami FL 33175 Office: 37 NE 26 St Miami FL 33137

SCRIBNER, BEVERLY KINNEAR, lawyer; b. Chandler, Okla., Mar. 8, 1941; d. Howard James and Helen Vista (Smith) Kinnear; m. Edward L. Scribner, Aug. 26, 1961 (div. 1970); 1 child, John Edward; m. Don M. Claunch, July 9, 1983; 1 stepchild, Diane Melissa. B.S. with distinction in Math., U. Okla., 1963, J.D., 1977. Bar: Okla. 1977. Office mgr. McAfee & Taft, Attys. at Law, Oklahoma City, 1970-72; adminstrv. asst. GHK Cos., Oklahoma City, 1972; legal asst. Hines & Smith, Oklahoma City, 1972-74; dir. legal assts. program U. Okla. Sch. Law, Norman, 1974-77; assoc. Kerr, Davis, Irvine, Krasnow, Rhodes & Semtner, Oklahoma City, 1977-79; ptnr. Claunch, Bryant & Schribner, Oklahoma City, 1979—. Mem. ABA, Okla. Bar Assn., Okla. County Bar Assn., Okla. City Title Attys. Assn. (pres. 1987), Mineral Lawyers Soc. Okla. City (pres. 1986-87), Okla. City Mgmt. and Profl. Women (pres. 1982), Phi Delta Phi. Republican. Presbyterian. Oil and gas leasing, Real property. Office: Claunch Bryant & Scribner 3030 NW Expressway Suite 710 Oklahoma City OK 73112

SCRIBNER, FRED CLARK, JR., lawyer; b. Bath, Maine, Feb. 14, 1908; s. Fred Clark and Emma Amelia (Cheltra) A.; m. Barbara Curtis Merrill, Aug. 24, 1935; children: Fred Clark, Curtis Merrill, Charles Dewey. A.B., Dartmouth Coll., 1930, LL.D., 1959; LL.B., Harvard U., 1933; LL.D., U. Maine, 1958, Colby Coll., 1959, Bowdoin Coll., 1959, U. Vt., 1960; D.D., Gen. Theol. Sem., 1984. Bar: Maine 1933, Mass. 1933, D.C. 1961. Assoc. Cook, Hutchinson, Pierce, and Connell, Portland, Maine, 1933-35; partner Cook, Hutchinson, Pierce, and Connell, 1935-55, Pierce, Atwood, Scribner, Allen, Smith and Lancaster, Portland, 1961—, Scribner, Hall & Thompson, Washington, 1961—; chmn. bd. Coordinated Apparel, Inc.; dir., gen. counsel, v.p., treas. Bates Mfg. Co., Lewiston, Me., 1946-55; gen. counsel Dept. Treasury, 1955-57, asst. sec. treasury, 1957, under sec., 1957-61; past dir. Sentinel Group Funds, Inc.; mem. commr.'s adv. com. on exempt orgns. Internal Revenue Service; chmn. ad hoc adv. group on presdl. vote for P.R. Mem. nat. council Boy Scouts Am. (Silver Beaver award; mem. exec. com. Region I); pres. Maine Constl. Commn., 1963-64; chmn. Portland Republican City Com., 1936-40, Maine Council Young Rep. Clubs, 1938-40; mem. Maine Rep. State Com., 1940-50 (chmn. exec. com. 1944-50); Rep. nat. committeeman from, Maine, 1948-56; del. Rep. Nat. Conv., 1940, 44, 56, 60, 64, 68; counsel Rep. Nat. Com., 1952-55, 61-73; gen. counsel arrangements com. Nat. Conv., 1956-72; Presdl. elector, 1976; hon. trustee Maine Med. Center, Portland; past bd. dirs. Am. Council Capitol Formation; former pres. bd. trustees Bradford Coll., Haverhill, Mass.; trustee Cardigan Mountain Sch., Canaan, N.H. Recipient Alexander Hamilton award U.S. Treasury; Dartmouth Alumni Council award, 1971. Mem. Am., Fed., Maine, Cumberland County bar assns., Am. Law Inst., Newcomen Soc. in N.Am. (clk.), Phi Beta Kappa, Delta Sigma Rho, Alpha Chi Rho. Episcopalian. (mem. standing com., chancellor Diocese of Maine; del. Gen. Conv. P.E. Ch., 1943, 46, 52, 61, 64, 67, 69, 70, 73, 76, 79, 82). Clubs: Capitol Hill (Washington); Portland, Woodfords. Lodges: Kiwanis, Masons (33 deg.). General corporate, Estate planning, General practice. Home: 335 Foreside Rd Falmouth Foreside ME 04105 Office: 10th Floor One Monument Sq Portland ME 04101 Other: 1875 Eye St NW Washington DC 20006

SCROGGINS, FRANK W., lawyer; b. St. Louis, Feb. 7, 1935; s. John Frank and Ann (Eichmein) S.; m. Gloria Baker, Nov. 11, 1960; children: Deborah L., Frank W. Jr. BS, U. Ala., 1954; JD, Emory U., 1959. Bar: Ga. 1958. Ptnr. Scroggins, Brizendine & Bassler, Atlanta. Mem. Ga. Bar Assn., Atlanta Bar Assn., Lawyers Club Atlanta (bd. dirs.). Bankruptcy. Office: Scroggins Bizendine & Bassler 101 Marietta Tower 3410 Atlanta GA 30303

SCUDDER, CHARLES SEELYE KELLGREN, lawyer; b. London, Feb. 20, 1947; came to U.S., 1964; s. Evarts Seelye and Henrica Antonina (Kellgren) S.; m. Jannette Harris Ericson, June 20, 1970; children: John Whitney, Jocelyn Seelye, Ansley Harris. B.A., Yale U., 1968; B.A. in Law with 2d class honors, Oxford U., 1973; J.D. with honors, U. Conn., 1975; M.A. (hon.), Oxford U., 1980. Bar: N.Y. 1976, U.S. Dist. Ct. N.Y. 1976. Assoc., Winthrop Stimson Putnam & Roberts, N.Y.C., 1975-81; sr. counsel Conoco Inc., Wilmington, Del., 1981-87; assoc. gen. counsel Unisys Corp., Blue Bell, Pa., 1987—. Served with U.S. Army, 1968-71. Editor Conn. Law Review, 1974. Mem. ABA (subcom. on multinat. corps.), N.Y. State Bar Assn., Am. Corp. Counsel Assn. Republican. General corporate, Securities, Private international. Office: Unisys Corp Township Line and Union Meeting Rds Blue Bell PA 19424

SCUDDER, EARL H., JR., lawyer; b. Chgo., Aug. 26, 1942; s. Earl H. and Juliette M. (Bleau) S.; m. Patricia L. Heumann, Aug. 29, 1964; children: Mark, Christine, Barbara. BS, U. Nebr., 1964, JD, 1966. Bar: Nebr. 1966, D.C. 1966, Iowa 1966, U.S. Dist. Ct. (so. and no. dists.) Iowa 1966, U.S. Dist. Ct. Nebr. 1966, U.S. Tax Ct. 1966, U.S. Ct. Appeals (8th cir.) 1970, U.S. Supreme Ct. 1971, U.S. Ct. Appeals (D.C. cir.) 1977. Chmn. Nelson & Harding, Lincoln, Nebr., 1968—; bd. dirs. Heartland Express Inc. Mem. ABA, Nebr. Bar Assn., Lincoln Bar Assn., Iowa Bar Assn., D.C. Bar Assn. Home: 9301 Pioneer Lincoln NE 68520 Office: Nelson & Harding PO Box 82028 Lincoln NE 68501

SCUDDER, THEODORE TOWNSEND, III, lawyer; b. Oak Park, Ill., June 26, 1939; s. Theodore Townsend Jr. and Joan (Kerr) S.; m. Eileen Hesmondhalgh, May 31, 1974; children—Caroline Sarah, Robert Cameron. A.B., Harvard U., 1961; J.D., U. Mich., 1964; postgrad. John Marshall Law Sch., 1965-67, Northwestern Law Sch., 1971. Bar: Ill. 1964, U.S. Dist. Ct. (no. dist.) Ill. 1965. Ct. reporter Ill. Army N.G., Chgo., 1964-70; assoc. willian, Brinks, Olds, Hofer, Chgo., 1963-67, Wilson & McIlvaine, Chgo., 1967-68, Jacobs, Williams & Montgomery, Chgo., 1968-70, asst. U.S. atty. U.S. Dept. Justice, Chgo., 1970-79; ptnr. Ruff Weidenaar & Reidy, Chgo., 1979-87; sole practice, Hoffman Estates, Ill. 1987—; trustee, counsel Pacific Garden Mission, Chgo., 1967—; advisor Ill. Selective Service, Springfield, 1973-79. Editor: Pike-Schaefer Dialog, 1969. Canvasser, Republican Party, Chgo., 1964-67. NEH scholar U. Wis., 1974. Mem. ABA, Christian Legal Soc. (bd. dirs. 1965-67), Am. Judicature Soc., Ill. Bar Assn., Chgo. Bar Assn. Episcopalian. Clubs: Harvard (Chgo.) (asst. treas. 1968-72); Philadelphia Soc. (North Adams, Mich.). Federal civil litigation, Personal injury, Trademark and copyright. Home: 362 Marion St Glen Ellyn IL 60137 Office: 2300 N Barrington Rd Hoffman Estates IL 60195

SCUDI, MORGAN JOHN CLIFT, lawyer; b. N.Y.C., Aug. 1, 1950; s. John Vincent and Mary Elizabeth (Clift) S.; m. Nancy Ann Runion, Mar. 25, 1977 (div. Dec. 1985). BS, U. Tenn., 1975, MS, 1979; JD, Am. U., 1982. Bar: Mich. 1982, U.S. Dist. Ct. (so. dist.) Mich. 1982. Pres. 421 Contractors & Co., Washington, 1972-74, Kingston Constrn. Co., Knoxville, Tenn., 1975-79; assoc. Clark, Klein & Beaumont, Detroit, 1982—; cons., bd. dirs. Runion Assocs., Inc., 1980-82. Editorial advisor Constrn. Litigation Reporter, 1984—. Grantee USDA, 1977. Mem. ABA, Fed. Bar Assn., Mich. Bar Assn., Detroit Bar Assn. Construction, Federal civil litigation, Nuclear power. Home: 843 Beaconsfield Gross Pointe Park MI 48230 Office: Clark Klein & Beaumont 1600 First Fed Bldg Detroit MI 48226

SCULLEN, JAMES ROCHE, lawyer; b. Bklyn., Nov. 14, 1916; s. James and Mary (Ryan) S. B.S., St. Bonaventure U., 1939; postgrad. Montclair State Tchrs. Coll., 1940-41; LL.B., Georgetown U., 1950; postgrad. data processing Prince Georges Community Coll., 1982, post grad computer operations, 1983. Bar: D.C. 1950, Md. 1975, U.S. Ct. Appeals (D.C.) 1955, U.S. Ct. Appeals (4th cir.) 1960, U.S. Supreme Ct. 1958. Sole practice, Washington. Mem. Assn. Plaintiff Trial Attys. (plaintiff's lawyer of yr. Md., Va. D.C. 1970), Assn. Trial Lawyers Am., ABA, Bar Assn. D.C., D.C. Unified Bar Assn., Prince George's County Bar Assn., Md. Bar Assn., Nat. Lawyers Club. Club: N.Y. Athletic (N.Y.C.). Federal civil litigation, General practice, Personal injury. Office: 1701 Pennsylvania Ave NW Suite 450 Washington DC 20006

SCULLIN, FREDERICK JAMES, JR., lawyer; b. Syracuse, N.Y., Nov. 5, 1939; s. Frederick James and Cleora M. (Fellows) S.; m. Veronica Terek Sauro, Aug. 31, 1984; 1 child, Mary Margaret; 1 stepchild, Angel Sauro. B.S. in Econs., Niagara U., 1961; LL.B., Syracuse U., 1964. Bar: N.Y. 1964, Fla. 1976, U.S. Dist. Ct. (no. dist.) N.Y. 1967, U.S. Supreme Ct. 1971. Assoc. Germain & Germain, Syracuse, 1967-68; asst. dist. atty. Onondaga County, Syracuse, 1968-71; asst. atty. gen. N.Y. State Organized Crime Task Force, 1971-78; dir. regional office N.Y. State Organized Crime Task Force, Albany, 1974-78; chief prosecutor, dir. Gov.'s Council on Organized Crime State of Fla., Tallahassee, 1978—; sole practice Syracuse, 1979-82, U.S. atty. for No. Dist. N.Y., 1982—. Served with U.S. Army, 1964-67, Vietnam; col. Res. Decorated Air medal, Bronze Star; Cross of Gallantry (Vietnam). Mem. Am. Judicature Soc., ABA, N.Y. State Bar Assn., Fla. Bar Assn., Nat. Dist. Attys. Assn., N.Y. State Dist. Attys. Assn., Central N.Y. Assn. Chiefs of Police, Fed. Bar Assn., Fed. Bar Council. Home: 4964 Blacksmith Path Liverpool NY 13088 Office: US Attys Office 100 S Clinton St Syracuse NY 13260

SCULLY, JOHN JOSEPH, lawyer; b. Chgo., Mar. 3, 1947; s. Nicholas Henry and Bernice Margaret (Doolan) S.; m. Mary Patrice Crane, Dec. 26, 1969; children—Jeanne, Colleen, AnnMarie, John. B.S., U.S. Naval Acad., 1969; J.D., U. San Diego, 1974. Bar: Calif. 1974, Ill. 1978, U.S. Dist. Ct. (no. dist.) Ill. 1978. Litigation atty. Ill. Bell Telephone, Chgo., 1978-81; asst. states atty. Lake County, Waukegan, Ill., 1981-82; spl. atty. Organized Crime Strike Force, U.S. Dept. Justice, Chgo., 1982—; part-time instr. bus. law Coll. Lake County, Grays Lake, Ill., 1976—. Mem. Police and Fire Commn., Lindenhurst, Ill., 1981; chmn. sch. bd. Prince of Peace Parochial Sch., Lake Village, Ill., 1978-81. Served to lt. comdr., USN, 1965-78. Recipient Brainerd award U.S. Naval Acad., 1969. Roman Catholic. Criminal. Office: US Dept Justice Chgo Strike Force 219 S Dearborn Room 1402 Chicago IL 60604

SCULLY, ROGER TEHAN, lawyer; b. Washington, Jan. 10, 1948; s. James Henry and Marietta (Maguire) S.; m. Martha Anne Seebach, Dec. 29, 1979. BS, U. Md., 1977; JD, Cath. U., 1980. Bar: Md. 1980, D.C. 1981, U.S. Tax Ct. 1982, U.S. Supreme Ct. 1986. V.p. Bogley Related Cos., Rockville, Md., 1971-75; law clk. to presiding justice Superior Ct. of D.C., Washington, 1979-81; assoc. Lerch, Early & Roseman, Bethesda, Md., 1981-82; gen. counsel Westwood Corps., Bethesda, 1982—; of counsel Laszlo N. Tauber, M.D., Bethesda, 1982—; cons. in real estate Order of Friar Minor, N.Y.C. 1977—; lectr. Mortgage Bankers Assn., Washington, 1984—. Mem. Pres.'s Council St. Bonaventure U., Olean, N.Y., 1986—; trustee Edmund Burke Sch., Washington, 1984—; bd. dirs. Nat. Children's Choir, Washington, 1980—, Manor Montessori Sch., Potomac, Md., 1981-84; bd. of govs. Goodwill Industries, Washington, 1987—. Recipient First Order Affiliation Order of Friars Minor, 1985; named one of Outstanding Young Men in Am., 1982. Mem. ABA, Fed. Bar Assn., Md. Bar Assn., D.C. Bar Assn., Assn. Trial Lawyers Am., Am. Judicature Soc., Selden Soc., Phi Delta Phi. Republican. Roman Catholic. Clubs: Nat. Press (Washington); Nat. Aviation (Arlington, Va.). Real property, Contracts commercial, Corporate taxation. Home: 10923 Wickshire Way Rockville MD 20852 Office: Westwood Ctr II 5110 Ridgefield Rd Suite 408 Bethesda MD 20816

SCURO, JOSEPH E., JR., lawyer; b. Jersey City, Mar. 28, 1948; s. Joseph E. and Phyllis (Amato) S.BA, Manhattan Coll., 1970; JD, Ohio State U., 1972. Bar: Tex., Ohio, U.S. Dist. Cts., U.S. Ct. Appeals (5th and 10th cir.), U.S. Tax Ct., U.S. Mil. Appeals, U.S. Supreme Ct. Asst. atty. gen. Ohio, 1973-81; chief legal counsel Ohio State Hwy. Patrol, 1975-81; practice law, 1973—; counsel Nicholas & Barrera, San Antonio, 1982—; atty.-counsel San Antonio Police Officers Assn.; counsel Combined Law Enforcement Assn. Tex., Alamo Heights Police Officers Assn.; Counsel Tex. Mcpl. League; police legal adviser to cities of San Marcos, New Braunfels, Balcones Heights, La Vernia, Poteet, Laredo, Dilley, Kiley, Universal City, Del Rio and others; spl. counsel on tng. San Antonio Police Dept.; counsel to Bexar County Constable's Assn.; condr. seminars. Bd. dirs. Nat. Hispanic Arts Endowment. Served to capt. USAF, 1970-75. Fellow Southwestern Legal Found.; mem. Tex. Bar Assn., Ohio Bar Assn., ABA, San Antonio Bar Assn., Columbus (Ohio) Bar Assn., Am. Trial Lawyers Assn., Police Exec. Research Forum, Internat. Assn. Chiefs of Police (ins. bd. advs., program), Ams. for Effective Law Enforcement (bd. advs.), Southwestern Law Enforcement Inst. (bd. advs.), Internat. Soc. Law Enforcement and Criminal Justice Instrs., Combined Law Enforcement Assn. Tex., Fed. Criminal Investigators Assn., Ohio Assn. Polygraph Examiners. Democrat. Presbyterian. Contbr. articles on police and law enforcement to profl. jours. General corporate, Federal civil litigation, State civil litigation. Office: 424 E Nueva St San Antonio TX 78205

SCZUDLO, RAYMOND STANLEY, lawyer; b. Olean, N.Y., July 5, 1948; s. Raymond Stanley and Ann Marie (Frisina) S.; m. Jane Marie Ehrensberger, May 9, 1970; children: Gregory Martin, Edward James. BChemE, U. Detroit, 1971; JD, Georgetown U., 1974. Bar: D.C., 1975., U.S. Dist. Ct. (fed. dist.) D.C. 1975, U.S. Ct. Appeals (D.C. cir.) 1975, U.S. Ct. Appeals (5th cir.) 1980, U.S. Supreme Ct. 1981. Assoc. Martin, Whitfield, Thaler & Bebchick, Washington, 1974-78, Verner, Liipfert, Bernhard & McPherson, Washington, 1978-80; ptnr. Verner, Liipfert, Bernhard, McPherson & Hand, Washington, 1981—; bd. dirs. Benlink, Inc., Washington, 1984—. Contbr. articles on banking to profl. jours. Mem. corporate bd. Children's Hosp. Nat. Med. Ctr., Washington, 1983—, bd. dirs. 1985—. Mem. ABA, Fed. Bar Assn., D.C. Bar Assn., Washington Internat. Trade Assn., Am. Soc. Internat. Law, Am. Coll. Investment Counsel. Club: University (Washington). Banking, Private international, General corporate. Home: 3913 McKinley St NW Washington DC 20015 Office: Verner Liipfert et al 1660 L St NW Washington DC 20036

SEABOLT, CHARLES FREDERICK, lawyer; b. Danville, Va., Dec. 16, 1946; s. Louie Henry and Sylvia Lucille (Davis) S.; m. Loretta Ann Lysaght, June 26, 1972; children: Erin K., Tara Lea, Charles Jr., Loretta A. BA, U. Va., 1975; JD, La. State U., 1978. Bar: La. 1978, U.S. Dist. Ct. (ea. dist.) La. 1978, U.S. Dist. Ct. (mid. dist.) La. 1980, U.S. Dist. Ct. (we. dist.) La. 1981, U.S. Ct. Appeals (5th cir.) 1981. Assoc. Milling, Benson, Woodward, Hillyer, Pierson & Miller, New Orleans, 1978-84, mem., 1984—; Commr. rd. commn. St. Tammany Parish, La., 1986—. Mem. parish council Our Lady of Lourdes Cath. Ch., Slidell, La., 1982, core group St. Luke The Evangelist Ch., Slidell, 1984—. Served with USN, 1969-73. Mem. ABA, La. Bar Assn., Maritime Lawyer's Assn. Democrat. Roman Catholic. Avocations: outdoor sports, gardening, bird watching. Admiralty, Federal civil litigation, Construction. Home: 718 S Bundicks Lake Ct Slidell LA 70461 Office: Milling Benson Woodward Hillyer Pierson & Miller 1100 Whitney Bldg New Orleans LA 70130

SEABURG, JEAN, lawyer; b. Mpls., May 3, 1935; d. Gunnar Fredrick and Lorraine Elise (Otto) Dahlstrom; m. Paul A. Seaburg, July 27, 1957 (div. Jan. 1973); children—Mark David, Gunnar Paul; m. Richard J. Lee, Feb. 24, 1984 (dec. June 1986). Student U. Minn., 1953-57; B.S.C.E., Marquette U., 1967, J.D., 1974. Bar: Wis. 1974, U.S. Dist. Ct. (ea. and we. dists.) Wis. 1974, Minn. 1986, U.S. Patent Office 1986; registered profl. engr., Wis., Minn. Engr., Howard, Needles, Tammen & Bergendoff, Milw., 1967-71; law clk. Habush, Habush & Davis, Milw., 1973-74, assoc., 1974-77, ptnr., 1977-86; assoc. James E. Olds, Ltd., Mpls., 1986—. Mem. ABA, Assn. Trial Lawyers Am., ASCE, Nat. Soc. Profl. Engrs. Lutheran. Personal injury, Patent, Federal civil litigation. Office: James E Olds Ltd 10800 Lyndale Ave S Minneapolis MN 55420

SEACREST, GARY LEE, lawyer; b. Chambersburg, Pa., July 27, 1946; s. John Alton and Virginia (Robinson) S.; m. Constance Marie Zullinger, Feb. 21, 1970; children—Ryan John, Meredith Marie. B.S., Pa. State U., 1968; J.D. with distinction, Emory U., 1975. Bar: U.S. Dist. Ct. (no. dist.) Ga. 1975, U.S. Ct. Appeals (5th cir) 1978, U.S. Cir. Ct. Appeals (11th cir.) 1982, U.S. Dist. Ct. (mid. dist.) Ga. 1982, U.S. Dist. Ct. (so. dist.) Ga. 1983. Atty. IRS, Atlanta, 1975; assoc. Barwick, Bentley & Binford, Atlanta, 1976-78; ptnr. Barwick, Bentley, Karesh & Seacrest, and Bentley, Karesh, Seacrest, Labovitz & Campbell, Atlanta, 1978—; cons. ins. industry, Atlanta, 1980—; dir. several corps. Mem. German-Am. Relations Com., Berlin, 1971; bd. dirs. Glenridge Civic Assn., Atlanta, 1978; bd. dirs. Branches Civic Assn., Atlanta, 1980-81, pres., 1982. Served with U.S. Army, 1969-72. Mem. ABA, Ga. Bar Assn., Atlanta Bar Assn., Ga. Defense Lawyers Assn., Defense Research Inst., Kappa Delta Rho. Republican. Clubs: Lawyers of Atlanta, Cherokee Town and Country. Insurance, Federal civil litigation, State civil litigation. Home: 1087 Winding Branch Circle Atlanta GA 30338 Office: Bentley Karesh Seacrest et al 3525 Piedmont Rd NE Suite 515 Atlanta GA 30305

SEACRIST, GEOFFREY LYNN, lawyer; b. York, Pa., May 2, 1955; s. George Kenneth and Erla Jean (Weaver) S.; m. Suzanne L. Elling, Apr. 9, 1983; children: Ryan James, Jessica Elizabeth, John Kenneth. BA, Indiana U. Pa., 1977; JD, Dickinson Sch. of Law, 1980. Bar: Pa. 1980. Sole practice Indiana, Pa., 1980—. Treas., bd. dirs. Indiana chpt. Am. Cancer Soc., 1983—, pub. affairs rep. Pa. div., Hershey, 1985—. Mem. Assn. Trial Lawyers Am., Pa. Trial Lawyers Assn., Pa. Bar Assn. (com. on specialization), Indiana U. Pa. Alumni Assn. Republican. Presbyterian. Workers' compensation, Personal injury, Real property. Home: 925 Chestnut St Indiana PA 15701 Office: 942 Philadelphia St Indiana PA 15701

SEADER, PAUL ALAN, lawyer; b. Bklyn., Sept. 6, 1947; s. Philip R. and Beatrice D. (Diamond) S.; m. Marsha Director, Dec. 26, 1970; children: Stephanie, Eric. BA in Polit. Sci., U. Pitts., 1969; JD, N.Y. Law Sch., 1972; LLM in Internat. law, NYU, 1975. Bar: N.Y. 1973, U.S. Dist. Ct. (so. and ea. dists.) N.Y. 1975, U.S. Ct. Appeals (2d cir.) 1975. Atty. Mass Transit Assn., N.Y.C., 1972-74; assoc. Giallorenzi & Stiles, N.Y.C., 1974-76; v.p. Chase Manhattan Bank, N.Y.C., 1976-82; sr. counsel Am. Express Co., N.Y.C., 1982—; bd. dirs. N.Y. Legis. Service, N.Y.C., 1983—. Author: Survey of World Conflicts, 1969; editor N.Y. Legis. Annual, 1971-72. V.p. Chase Polit. Action Com., N.Y.C., 1981-83. Mem. ABA (vice-chmn. fin. services com., adminstrv. law sect. 1985—). Avocations: tennis, running. Banking, Legislative, Private international. Home: 2915 Cheryl Rd Merrick NY 11566 Office: Am Express Co 200 Vesey St New York NY 10285-4900

SEAL, JAMES LEE, lawyer; b. Dayton, Ohio, July 29, 1945; s. M. Thomas and Treva M. (Montgomery) S.; m. Victoria C. Billings, Jan. 10, 1976. B.B.A., U. Cin., 1967; J.D., Harvard U., 1970. Bar: Calif. 1971, U.S. Dist. Ct. (ce. dist.) Calif. 1971, U.S. Dist. Ct. (ea. and so. dists.) Calif. 1976, U.S. Ct. Appeals (9th cir.) 1972, U.S. Supreme Ct. 1974. Assoc., Musick, Peeler & Garrett, Los Angeles, 1970-78; ptnr. Swerdlow, Miller, Seal & Swerdlow, Beverly Hills, Calif., 1978—. Recipient Arthur Young Found. award, 1967. Mem. ABA, Los Angeles County Bar Assn. Federal civil litigation, State civil litigation. Office: 9601 Wilshire Blvd Beverly Hills CA 90210

SEAL, THOMAS DAVID, lawyer, military officer; b. Rantoul, Ill., Mar. 4, 1957; s. Muriel Joseph and Mary J. (Ash) S.; m. Christine Marie Young, June 2, 1982; 1 child, Andrew Robert. AS, St. Leo Coll., 1977; BA, Ind. U., Bloomington, 1979; JD, Ind. U., Indpl., 1982; CSS, Harvard U., 1986. Bar: Ind. 1982. Commd. 2d lt. USAF, 1979, advanced through grades to capt., 1982; govt. contracts atty. Electronics Systems div., judge advocate USAF, Hanscom AFB, Mass., 1982-86; trial atty. USAF, Wright-Patterson AFB, Ohio, 1986—. Mem. ABA (pub. contrat law sect.). Republican. Roman Catholic. Government contracts and claims, Trademark and copyright, Military. Home: 234 S 4th St Richmond IN 47374 Office: USAF Contract Law Ctr Wright-Patterson OH 45433

SEALY, TOM, lawyer; b. Santa Anna, Tex., Feb. 18, 1909; s. Thomas Richard and Elizabeth (Harper) S.; m. Mary Velma McCord, Jan. 16, 1936; 1 child, Nancy. LL.B., U. Tex., 1931. Bar: Tex. 1931. Practice in Midland, 1935—; mem. firm Stubbeman, McRae, Sealy, Laughlin & Browder, 1936—; hon. dir. First City Nat. Bank, Midland; past dir. First Savs. and Loan Assn., Tex. Land & Mortgage Co., Midland, Champlin Petroleum Co., Tex.-N.Mex. Ry. Co. Past mem. city council, Midland.; Past chmn. bd. regents U. Tex., past. chmn. devel. bd.; mem., former chmn. coordinating bd. Tex. Coll. and U. System; past trustee Tex. Presbyn. Found., Presbyn.-Austin Theol. Sem.; hon. trustee Southwestern Legal Found.; past chmn., dir. Tex. Research League; past pres. U. Texas Law Sch. Found., bd. govs. Midland Meml. Found., 1984—. Served to lt. col. USAAF, World War II. Recipient Disting. Alumnus award U. Tex., 1966; Outstanding Alumnus award U. Tex. Law Sch., 1970; 50-yr. award Tex. Bar Fellows, 1985; Tom Sealy research professorship in energy law established in his honor at U. Tex. Law Sch. Atlantic Richfield Co. Fellow Am. Bar Found., Tex. Bar Founds. (50-Yr. award 1985); mem. Midland C. of C. (past pres.), Tex. Assn. Def. Counsel (past pres.), Am. Bar Assn., State Bar of Tex., Internat. Assn. Ins. Counsel, Am. Assn. Petroleum Landmen (hon.), Phi Delta Phi (hon.). Presbyn. Clubs: Midland Petroleum (past pres.), Plaza (vice chmn. bd. govs.) Headliners (Austin); Midland Country, Midland Racquet, Chaparral (Dallas); Century II (Ft. Worth); St. Anthony (San Antonio). Probate, Oil and gas leasing. Home: 915 Harvard St Midland TX 79701 Office: Two First City Center Suite 800 Midland TX 79701

SEAMAN, RICHARD NORMAN, lawyer; b. Trenton, N.J., Mar. 27, 1949; s. Norman Richard and Helen Theresa (Knapp) S.; m. Theresa Mary Immordino, June 24, 1972 (div. Dec. 1978); m. Sabine Staggen, May 22, 1980. BS, U.S. Mil. Acad., 1971; JD, Coll. William & Mary, 1976. Bar: Va. 1976, U.S. Supreme Ct. 1981, U.S. Ct. Appeals (9th cir.) 1984. Commd. 2d lt. U.S. Army, 1971, advanced through grades to maj.; internat. liaison U.S. Army JAGC, Würzburg, Fed. Republic Germany, 1976-77; trial lawyer JAGC U.S. Army, Schweinfurt, Fed. Republic Germany, 1978-80; legis. staff JAGC U.S. Army, Washington, 1981-83; resigned U.S. Army JAGC, 1985; trial atty. U.S. Dept. Justice, Alexandria, Va., 1983-87; sr. assoc. litigation dept. Fried, Frank, Harris, Shriver and Jacobson, Washington, 1987—; lectr. U.S. Army Audit Agy., Alexandria, 1985—. Vol. worker Chesapeake Bay Found., Annapolis, Md. 1985—. Mem. ABA (pub. contract law and litigation sects.), Va. Bar Assn., U.S. Power Squadrons, West Point Soc. of D.C., Fed. Bar Assn., Phi Delta Phi. Republican. Roman Catholic. Club: Spring Cove Yacht (Solomons, Md.). Avocations: sailing, skiing, photography. Criminal, Government contracts and claims. Home: 9021 Blarney Stone Dr Springfield VA 22152 Office: Fried Frank Harris Shriver Jacobsen 1001 Pennsylvania Ave NW Suite 900 Washington DC 20004-2505

SEAMAN, ROBERT E., III, lawyer; b. Chgo., Apr. 2, 1947; s. Robert E. II and Rae June (Blair) S.; m. Edith Agnes McCrackin, June 6, 1970; children: Kimberly Desiree, Charissa Alaine, Robert E. IV, Jason Robert. BA in Polit. Sci., The Citadel, 1969; JD, U. Va., 1972; postdoctoral, N.Y. Inst. Fin., 1975-77, Harvard U., 1979. Bar: N.Y. 1975, S.C. 1978, U.S. Dist. Ct. (so. dist.) N.Y. 1975, U.S. Tax Ct. 1980, U.S. Ct. Appeals (2nd cir.) 1975, U.S. Ct. Appeals (4th cir.) 1979, U.S. Supreme Ct. 1979, U.S. Ct. Mil. Appeals 1980. Assoc. Breed, Abbott & Morgan, N.Y.C., 1972-74; v.p., legal asst., sec. Paine, Webber, Jackson & Curtis, N.Y.C., 1974-77; assoc. gen. counsel Col. Life and Accident Ins. Co., Columbia, S.C., 1977-80; sole practice Columbia, 1980—; gen. counsel, bd. dirs. Jacom Computer Services, Inc., Northvale, N.J., 1977—; pres., chmn. bd. dirs. Leasing Services of Am., Inc., Columbia, 1983—; chmn. bd. dirs., chief exec. officer Piedmont Farms, Inc., Chester, S.C., 1983—; v.p., bd. dirs. Jacom Mgmt. Services, Inc., New City, N.Y., 1983—, D.R.S. Capital Corp., Columbia, 1984; bd. dirs., gen. counsel Internat. Chem. Cons., Ltd., Columbia, 1983—; chmn. bd. dirs., chief fin. officer Titan Trading Co., Inc., Columbia, 1984—; mng. ptnr. Chester Ptnrs., 1984—, Rocky Creek Ptnrs., 1985—; chief exec. officer, pub. Up2Date Market Adv. Service, Columbia, 1985—; pres., chief operating officer Carefree Internat., Ltd., Columbia, 1986—; lectr. various edni. insts. Co-author: How to Use the Relative Strength Index to Increase trading Profits, 1986. Senator S.C. Legis., 1968-69; state dir. presdl. adv. com. Collegiate Counsel of UN, 1968-69; mem. Union Meth. Ch.; trustee Faith United Meth. Ch.; coordinator phon-a-thon campaign Midlands S.C. youth div. YMCA; chpt., campaign, adv. com. chmn., vice chmn. exec. com. Midlands chpt. March of Dimes, 1978-81. Served capt. U.S. Army Mil. Intelligence and Infantry, 1972-77. Robert R. McCormick scholar McCormick Found., and Chgo. Tribune, 1965-69, DuPont scholar U. Va., 1969-72; named Young Man of Yr., S.C. Greater Met. Area Jaycees, 1980; recipient Recognition award Nat. March of Dimes, 1981. Mem. ABA (state regulations of securities com., subcom. on oil and gas, subcom. on regulation of equipment leasing, securities industry assn. complicance div. 1974-77), Nat. Assn. Securities Dealers, Greater Columbia C. of C. (task force on energy conservation for 1980's). Clubs: Com. of 100, Met. Bus., Palmetto Soc. (Columbia); Toastmasters (pres. Lexington chpt., ann. impromptu speech contest champion, Toastmaster of Yr., 1979). Contracts commercial, Securities, General corporate. Home: Rt 2 Box 332C Columbia SC 29210 Office: 121 Executive Ctr Dr Suite 230 Columbia SC 29210

SEAMAN, STEPHEN HENRY, lawyer; b. Houston, Sept. 7, 1949; s. John Gates and Henri Etta (Rester) S.; m. Monica Patricia West, Feb 2, 1980. B.B.A., Tex A&I U., 1973; J.D., Baylor U., 1976. Bar: Tex. 1976, U.S. Dist. Ct. (so. dist.) Tex. 1979, U.S. Supreme Ct. 1980, U.S. Ct. Appeals (5th cir.) 1979, U.S. Ct. Appeals (11th cir.) 1981. Law clk. to presiding judge U.S. Dist. Ct. (so. dist.) Tex., Corpus Christi, 1977-79; assoc. Keys, Russell, Seaman & Mansker, Corpus Christi, 1979-80; assoc., ptnr. Keys, Russell & Seaman, Corpus Christi, 1980-84; ptnr. Seaman & Seaman, Corpus Christi, 1984—. Mem. State Bar Tex., ABA, Am. Judicature Soc., Corpus Christi Assn. Petroleum Landmen. Episcopalian. Oil and gas leasing, Probate, General practice. Home: 4610 Wilma Corpus Christi TX 78412 Office: Seaman & Seaman 1917 First City Bank Tower Corpus Christi TX 78477

SEAR, MOREY LEONARD, judge; b. New Orleans, Feb. 26, 1929; s. William and Yetty (Streiffer) S.; m. Lee Edrehi, May 26, 1951; children: William Sear II, Jane Lee. J.D., Tulane U., 1950. Bar: La. 1950. Asst. dist. atty. Parish Orleans, 1952-55; individual practice law New Orleans, 1955-71; spl. counsel New Orleans Aviation Bd., 1956-60; U.S. magistrate Eastern Dist. La., 1971-76; judge U.S. Dist. Ct. Eastern Dist. La., 1976—, Temporary Emergency Ct. of Appeals; mem. faculty Fed. Jud. Center, Washington, 1971—; adj. prof. Tulane U. Coll. Law; chmn. com. on adminstrn. of the Bankruptcy System, former chmn. adv. com. on bankruptcy rules Jud. Conf. U.S.; former mem. Jud. Conf. Com. on Adminstrn. Fed. Magistrates System. Founding dir. River Oaks Pvt. Psychiat. Hosp., 1968; pres. Congregation Temple Sinai, 1977-79; bd. govs. Tulane Med. Center, 1976—; pres. Tulane Med. Center Hosp. and Clinic, 1976—. Mem. Am., New Orleans, La. bar assns. Jurisprudence. Office: Chambers C-256 US Courthouse 500 Camp St New Orleans LA 70130

SEARCY, CHRISTIAN DEITRICH, SR., lawyer; b. Jacksonville, Fla., Dec. 15, 1947; s. Henry Martin and Christine Marie (Braren) S.; m. Priscilla Gulliford, Oct. 11, 1969; children: Henry Faulk II, Christian Deitrich Jr., Angela Eden, William Eric. BA with distinction, U. Va., 1969; JD, Stetson U., 1973. Bar: Fla. 1973. Assoc. Frates, Floyd, Pearson & Stewart, P.A., Miami, Fla., 1973-74, Howell, Kirby, Montgomery, D'Auito and Dean, P.A., Ft. Lauderdale, Fla., 1974; ptnr. Montgomery, Lytal, Reiter, Denney and Searcy, P.A., West Palm Beach, Fla., 1976-85, Montgomery, Searcy and Denney, P.A., West Palm Beach, 1985—; vis. lectr. med. jurisprudence Stetson U. Law Sch., bd. overseers 1987—. Contbr. articles to profl. jours. Bd. dirs. Palm Beach Ballet Arts Theatre, Seminole Landing Assn., United Cerebral Palsy. Dana Found. scholar. Mem. ABA, Fla. Bar Assn. (vice chmn. rules civil procedure com. 1983-84, chmn. rules civil procedure com. 1984-85, continuing legal edn. com., lectr. statewide seminars, cert. in trial advocacy), Palm Beach County Bar Assn. (continuing legal edn. com.), Assn. Trial Lawyers Am., Acad. Fla. Trial Lawyers (pres. 1986—, bd. dirs. 1979—, chmn. med. jurisprudence com. 1981-82, state chmn. key man program 1980-82, lectr. statewide seminars, key man com. 1981-82), Am. Bd. Trial Advs. (cert. in trial advocacy), Trial Lawyers Pub. Justice, Phi Delta Phi, Delta Si. Democrat. Lutheran. Avocations: tennis, jogging, swimming, basketball. Personal injury, State civil litigation, Federal civil litigation. Office: Montgomery Searcy and Denney PA 2139 Palm Beach Lakes Blvd West Palm Beach FL 33409

SEARCY, WILLIAM NELSON, lawyer; b. Moultrie, Ga., June 26, 1942; s. Floyd Hartsfield and Anna (Pidcock) S.; m. Camille Heery, June 17, 1967; 1 dau., Amelia Ashburn. A.B., U. Ga., 1964, J.D., 1967; LL.M. in Taxation, Washington U., St. Louis, 1968. Bar: Ga. 1967, U.S. Dist. Ct. (so. dist.) Ga. 1970, U.S. Ct. Appeals (5th cir.) 1976, U.S. Ct. Appeals (11th cir.) 1984. Assoc. Bouhan, Williams & Levy, Savannah, Ga., 1970-73; ptnr. Brannen, Wessels & Searcy, Savannah, 1973—; dir. Citizens Bank, Cairo, Ga.; sec. Am. Fed. Savs. and Loan Assn., 1978-81; mem. adv. bd. Liberty Svgs. Bank. Pres. Chatham-Savannah Voluntary Action Ctr., Inc., 1978-80. Served to lt. col. Air N.G., 1967—. Mem. ABA (sec. spl. liaison tax com. S.E. region 1983-84, chmn. 1984-85), State Bar Ga. (chmn. sect. taxation 1983-84, mem.-at-large exec. council Young Lawyers Sect. 1975-78, chmn. conf. with Ga. Soc. C.P.A.s. 1979-81), Savannah Bar Assn. (pres. Younger Lawyers Sect. 1975-76), Am. Judicature Soc., Savannah Estate Planning Council. Clubs: Oglethorpe, Savannah Golf, Plimsoll (Savannah), Georgian (Atlanta). General corporate, Estate planning, Banking. Office: PO Box 8002 Savannah GA 31412

SEARS, DANIEL JOSEPH, lawyer, educator; b. Cedar Rapids, Iowa, Sept. 18, 1942; s. Joseph Eli and Olga Helena (Daniel) S.; m. Cecile Jeane Ray, Nov. 22, 1967. B.S., Colo. State U., 1965; J.D., U. Colo., 1968. Bar: N.Mex. 1968, Colo. 1968, U.S. Dist. Ct. Colo. 1968, U.S. Ct. Appeals (10th cir.) 1972, U.S. Ct. Appeals (2d cir.) 1982, U.S. Supreme Ct. 1975. Dep. dist. atty. Pueblo County, Pueblo, Colo., 1969-72; spl. atty. U.S. Dept. Justice, Denver, 1972-73; asst. U.S. atty. Dist. Colo., Denver, 1973-75; fed. pub. defender Dist. Colo., Denver, 1975-79; sole practice, Denver, 1979—; prof. U. Denver Coll. Law, 1980-83; U. Colo. at Denver, 1979; lectr. Colo. Trial Lawyers Assn., Nat. Assn. Criminal Defense Lawyers, Continuing Legal Edn. Colo. Bar Assn., Fed. Defenders Assn., Colo. Dist. Attys. Council, Bur. Narcotics and Dangerous Drugs, 1975-83. Author: Uninvited Ear in the Defense Camp, 1978. Mem. Gov.'s Council on Crime Control, Denver, 1969-72; mem. Com. on Certification of Lawyers to Fed. Practice, Denver, 1979. Recipient Spl. Commendation, U.S. Dept. Justice, Washington, 1973, Recognition for Outstanding Service U.S. Atty.'s Office, Denver, 1975, Citation for Outstanding Service U.S. Dist. Ct., Denver, 1979. Mem. Pueblo County Bar Assn. (treas. 1971-72), Colo. Bar Assn. (legal fee arbitration com. 1983-84), Nat. Bd. Trial Advocacy (cert. criminal trial advocate 1986), U. Colo. Alumni Assn. Republican. Criminal, State civil litigation. Home: 5904 Meadowbrook Dr Morrison CO 80465 Office: 36 Steele St Suite 210 Denver CO 80206

SEARS, DOUGLAS ALSON, lawyer; b. Oakland, Calif., June 29, 1944; s. Alson Joseph and Zelma Roberta (Lloyd) S.; m. Connie May Delehant, June 21, 1968; children: Aaron Douglas, Ashley Irene. BA in Econs., U. San Francisco, 1966; JD, U. of Pacific, 1970. Bar: Calif. 1971. Atty. dist. atty. office Sacramento County, Calif., 1971-75; assoc. McDonald, Saeltzer, Morris & Caulfield, Sacramento, 1975-79; sr. ptnr. Matheny, Poidmore & Sears, Sacramento, 1979—; tchr., lectr. continuing legal edn. Calif. Bar, Sacramento, 1982—. Bd. dirs. Inst. Design and Exptl. Art, Sacramento, 1985—. Mem. Calif. Bar Assn., Assn. Trial Lawyers Am., Calif. Def. Com., Northern Calif. Def. Assn. Republican. Avocations: golf, snow skiing, art, tennis. State civil litigation, Personal injury, Insurance. Office: Matheny Poidmore & Sears 2100 Northrop Ave Suite 1200 Sacramento CA 95825

SEARS, JOHN WINTHROP, lawyer, administrator; b. Boston, Dec. 18, 1930; s. Richard Dudley and Frederica Fulton (Leser) S.; m. Catherine Coolidge, 1965 (div. 1970). AB magna cum laude, Harvard U., 1952, JD, 1959; MLitt, Oxford U., 1957. Bar: Mass. 1959, U.S. Dist. Ct. Mass. 1982. Rep. Brown Bros. Harriman, N.Y.C., 1959-63, Boston, 1963-66; mem. Mass. Ho. Reps. 1965-68; sheriff Suffolk County, Mass., 1968-69; chmn. Boston Fin. Commn., 1969-70, Met. Dist. Commn., 1970-75; councillor-at-large Boston City Council, 1980-82; trustee Sears Office, Boston, 1975—. Contbr. articles to profl. jours. Trustee Christ's Ch., Longwood, Brookline Mass., 1965—, Haniel, Duisburg, Germany, N.Y.C., 1982—, Sears Trusts, Boston, 1975—; bd. dirs. J.F. Kennedy Library, 1983—, Bostonian Soc., Nichols Mus., Crime and Justice Fedn. Corp., NE Deaconess Hosp., Boys Club Boston, Girls Club Boston, Middlesex Club, NE Hist. Geneal. Soc., 1987—; Rep. candidate Mayor of Boston, 1967, Sec. State, Mass., 1978, Gov. of Mass., 1982; vice chmn. Ward 5 Rep. Com., 1965-69, 75-85; chmn.

Rep. State Com., 1975-76, mem., 80-85; del. Rep. Nat. Conv., 1968, 76, State Conv., 1966—; mem. U.S. Electoral Coll., 1984—; bd. dirs. United South End Settlements, 1966—, chmn., 1977-78. Served as lt. comdr. USN, 1952-54, 61-62. Rhodes scholar, 1955; recipient Outstanding Pub. Servant award Mass. Legis. Assn., 1975. Mem. Mass. Bar Assn., New Eng. Hist. and Geneal. Soc. (bd. dirs., councillor 1977-82), Mass. Hist. Soc., Handel and Hayden Soc. (gov. 1982), Bostonian Soc., Phi Beta Kappa. Republican. Clubs: Spee (pres., trustee) (Cambridge); Tennis and Racquet, Somerset (Boston); The Country (Brookline); Myopia Hunt (Hamilton). Local government, Legislative, Probate. Home: 7 Acorn St Boston MA 02108 Office: 15 Court Sq Room 430 Boston MA 02108 also: New England Hist Geneal Soc 101 Newbury St Boston MA 02116

SEARS, RUTH ANN, lawyer; b. Kansas City, Mo., June 15, 1954; s. Robert Carl and Bessie Bryan (Nicholas) Henderson; m. Irwin Curtis Sears Jr., Aug. 6, 1977. BA, Cen. Meth. Coll., 1976; JD, U. Mo., 1979. Bar: Mo. 1979, Kans. 1980, U.S. Dist. Ct. Kans. Clk. to judge Mo. Supreme Ct., Jefferson City, 1979-80; atty. Southwestern Bell Telephone Co., Topeka, Kans., 1980—. Mem. ABA, Mo. Bar Assn., Kans. Bar Assn., Topeka Bar Assn., Topeka Women's Atty. Assn., Kans. Trial Lawyers Assn. Administrative and regulatory, General corporate, State civil litigation. Office: Southwestern Bell Telephone Co 220 E 6th Rm 515 Topeka KS 66603

SEAVEY, WILLIAM ARTHUR, lawyer, farmer; b. Los Angeles, Aug. 28, 1930; s. Arthur Jones and Dorothy (Keyes) S.; m. Mary Van Beuren, June 25, 1955; children: Dorothy Seavey Jefferson, Arthur B., William G., Frederic A., Charles K. AB, Princeton U., 1952; LLB, Harvard U., 1955; cert., U. Geneva, Switzerland, 1956, D in Polit. Sci., 1970. Bar: Calif. 1957. Assoc. Luce, Forward, Kunzel & Scripps, San Diego, 1956-57; asst. U.S. atty. U.S. Dist. Ct. (so. dist.) Calif., 1957-59; sole practice San Diego, 1959-65, San Francisco, 1978—; lectr., asst. to pres. Mills Coll., Oakland, Calif., 1968-74; ptnr. Richards & Seavey, San Francisco, 1974-76, Davis, Stafford, Kellman & Fenwick, San Francisco, 1976-78. Councilman City of Coronado, Calif., 1960-62, mayor 1962-64; trustee French-Am. Internat. Sch., San Francisco, 1968—; pres. English Speaking Union, San Francisco, 1982-85, v.p. 1985—, Alliance Francaise, San Francisco, 1979-81; mem. Nat. Grad. Fellowship Bd., Washington, 1986—. Mem. ABA, Calif. Bar Assn., San Francisco Bar Assn., Am. Soc. Internat. Law, French-Am. C. of C. (sec. legal com. 1978-86). Republican. Clubs: Pacific Union (San Francisco), World Trade (San Francisco). General corporate, Private international. Home: 303 Pacific Ave Piedmont CA 94611 Office: 425 California St San Francisco CA 94104

SEAY, FRANK H., judge; b. Shawnee, Okla., Sept. 5, 1938; s. Frank and Wilma Lynn S.; m. Janet Gayle Seay, June 2, 1962; children: Trudy Alice, Laura Lynn. Student, So. Meth. U., 1956-57; B.A., U. Okla., 1960, LL.B., 1963. Bar: Okla. bar 1963. Atty. Seminole County, 1963-66; asst. dist. atty. 1967-68, assoc. dist. judge, 1968-74; judge Okla. Dist. Ct. 22, 1974-79; chief judge U.S. Dist. Ct., Eastern Dist. Okla., 1979—. Mem. Am. Bar Assn., Okla. Bar Assn., Seminole County Bar Assn. Democrat. Clubs: Masons, Elks, Lions. Office: U S Courthouse PO Box 828 Muskogee OK 74401 *

SEAY, GEORGE EDWARD, JR., lawyer; b. Dallas, July 22, 1941; s. George Edward and Mary Everman (Saville) S.; m. Nancy Clements, Feb. 13, 1965; children—George Edward III, Pauline Allen. B.B.A., U. Tex., 1964; J.D., So. Methodist U., 1968. Bar: Tex. 1968. Purchasing cost estimator Collins Radio Co., Dallas, 1964; assoc. Trower Still & Keeling, London, 1968-69, Touchstone, Bernays & Johnston, Dallas, 1969-71; gen. mgr. Clemgil Realty Inc., Dallas, 1971-73; sole practice, Dallas, 1973—. Bd. editors Southwestern Law Jour. Chmn. Thomas Jefferson Scholarship Com., Dallas, 1974—; trustee Timberlawn Found., Dallas, 1982—. Served with USAFR, 1964-67. Ward Stephenson scholar Law Sch, So Meth. U., Dallas, 1967; Trower Still & Keeling fellow Southwestern Legal Found., Dallas, 1968. Mem. State Bar Tex., Dallas Bar Assn., ABA, Order of Coif, Phi Delta Phi. Presbyterian. Club: Dallas Country. Real property, Probate, General corporate. Home: 6007 Saint Andrews Dr Dallas TX 75205 Office: 8333 Douglas Suite 1460 Dallas TX 75225

SEAY, GEORGE EDWARD, lawyer; b. Dallas, Jan. 12, 1909; s. Dero Eugene and Pauline Adrienne (Bolanz) S.; m. Mary Everman Saville, Feb. 4, 1937; children—George, John Everman, Edith. B.A., U. Tex.-Austin, 1930, LL.B., with highest honors, 1932. Bar: Tex. 1932, U.S. Ct. Appeals (5th cir.) 1941, U.S. Dist. Ct. (no. dist.) Tex. 1933, U.S. Dist. Ct. (we. dist.) Tex. 1979, U.S. Ct. Appeals (D.C. cir.) 1971. Practiced in Dallas, 1932—, ptnr. Malone Lipscomb & Seay, 1950-60, Malone, Seay & Gwinn, 1960-66, Malone Seay Gwinn & Crawford, 1967-70, Seay Gwinn Crawford & Mebus, 1970-75, Seay Gwinn Crawford Mebus & Blakeney, 1975-82; of counsel Haynes & Boone, Dallas, 1982—; chief pros. staff atty. Nuremberg Trials, 1945-46; speaker Bar Assn. Seminars, Dallas, 1947-49, 78-79. Bd. dirs. Dallas TB Assn., 1948-51, Dallas Day Nursery Assn., 1952-60; mem. bd. elders Highland Park Presbyn. Ch., 1963—. Served to lt. col. AUS, 1942-46. Mem. Southwestern Legal Found. (chmn. labor law sect. 1948-55, mem. planning com. 1970—), State Bar Tex. (chmn. labor law sect. 1952-53), Am. Coll. Trial Lawyers, Tex. Bar Found. (charter mem., fellow), ABA, Dallas Bar Assn., Fed. Bar Assn., Am. Judicature Assn., Chancellors, Order of Coif, Phi Beta Kappa, Phi Delta Phi. Republican. Presbyterian. Clubs: Dallas Country, City. Labor, Probate. Home: 5353 Montrose Dr Dallas TX 75209

SEBASTIAN, WINIFRED MORAN, lawyer; b. Rising Sun, Md., June 9, 1946; d. Thomas Oliver and Bess Mae (Wilson) Moran; m. Randy Lee Sebastian, Dec. 17, 1977; children—Curtis Lee, Melinda Jane. A.B. cum laude, Bryn Mawr Coll., 1974; J.D., Villanova U., 1977. Bar: Pa. 1977, U.S. Dist. Ct. (ea. dist.) Pa. 1979. Sole practice, Oxford, Pa., 1977—; spl. master Chester County Ct. Common Pleas, West Chester, Pa., 1980—. Bd. dirs. YMCA, 1984. Mem. ABA, Pa. Bar Assn., Chester County Bar Assn., Bryn Mawr Alumni of Phila., Oxford Research Club (bd. dirs. 1983-84). Democrat. Methodist. General practice. Home: 453 Locust St Oxford PA 19363 Office: 65 S 3d St PO Box 381 Oxford PA 19363

SEBAT, JOHN EDWARD, lawyer; b. LaSalle, Ill., July 28, 1904; s. John and Agnes Elizabeth (Hudocline) S.; m. Frankie Ladd, Apr. 18, 1953 (dec.); children: Jane Ladd Vredenburgh, Lillie Chriss Firebaugh, Frank; m. Sarah Mires, Nov. 7, 1964. JD, U. Ill., 1929. Bar: Ill. 1929, U.S. Dist. Ct. (ea. dist.) Ill. 1929, U.S. Supreme Ct. 1960. Assoc. Brewer & Grant, Danville, Ill., 1929-52; sr. ptnr. Sebat, Swanson, Banks, Garman & Townsley, Danville, 1952—; bd. dirs. Mervis Industries Inc., Merlan Inc., J & F Industries Inc., Crow's Hybrid Corn Co., Gift Cosmetics Inc., 1st Savings & Loan Co., Danville, Ill. Fireworks Co., World Fireworks Co., H/L Disposal Co. Mem. Danville Housing Authority, 1935-42. Served with USAF, 1942-45. Mem. ABA, Ill. Bar Assn., Vermilion County Bar Assn., Am. Judicature Soc., Probate Council Am. Republican. Roman Catholic. Club: Danville Country. Lodges: Elks, KC. General corporate, Estate planning. Home: 34 Maywood Dr Danville IL 61832 Office: Sebat Swanson Banks Garman & Townsley 306 Adams Bldg Danville IL 61832

SECHEN, GLENN CHARLES, lawyer; b. Chgo., May 16, 1947; s. Charles Arthur and Marion (Zeman) S.; m. Laura Lee Johnson, Feb. 14, 1970; children: William, Michael. BSEE, Purdue U., 1969; JD, John Marshall Law Sch., 1974, LLM in Intellectual Property, 1987. Bar: Ill. 1974, U.S. Dist. Ct. (no. dist.) Ill. 1974, Fla. 1975, U.S. Ct. Appeals (7th cir.) 1975, U.S. Supreme Ct. 1980, U.S. Patent Office 1981. With State's Atty. Cook County, Chgo., 1974-85, chief environ. health tech. litigation div., 1985—; lectr. various seminars, 1985—; co-founder environl. task force Chem Hit, 1986. Author: The Application of Civil RICO to Intellectual Property and Unfair Trade Litigation, 1986. Chmn. founder com. Oak Park (Ill.) Area Jaycees, 1976; chairperson A Day in Our Village, Oak Park, 1977. Recipient Key Man award Oak Park Jaycees, 1976. Mem. ABA, Chgo. Bar Assn. (jud. evaluation com.). Environment, Administrative and regulatory, Federal civil litigation. Home: 424 Selborne Rd Riverside IL 60546 Office: States Atty Cook County 500 Richard J Daley Ctr Chicago IL 60602

SECHEN, ROBERT NICHOLAS, lawyer; b. Roslyn, N.Y., Apr. 26, 1952; s. Bernard L. and Alexsandra Sechen. BA, U. So. Fla., 1975; JD, U. Miami, 1980. Bar: Fla. 1981, U.S. Dist. Ct. (so. dist.) Fla. 1981. Mgr. law firm Dixon, Shear et al, Miami, Fla., 1973-76, Paul & Thomson, Tampa, Fla., 1976-77; mgr. adminstrn. Smith and Mandler, Miami, 1978-80, assoc., 1981-83; assoc. City Atty.'s Office, Miami, 1983-86; ptnr. Blackwell, Walker, Fascell & Hoehl, Miami, 1986—. Mem. ABA (chmn. govt. lawyer com. econ. sect. 1986—), Fla. Bar Assn. (chmn. mid-yr. meeting 1986-87, ann. meeting com., govt. law com., chmn. econ. sect. 1983-85, govt. law com.), Dade County Bar Assn., Acad. Fla. Trial Lawyers, Nimlo (assoc.), Urban Land Inst. Democrat. Roman Catholic. Clubs: Downtown Athletic, The Bankers, Fisher Island. Avocation: sailing. Local government, Development and land use, Administrative and regulatory. Home: 1717 N Bayshore Dr #2940 Miami FL 33132 Office: Blackwell Walker Fascell & Hoehl 2400 Amerifirst Bldg 1 SE 3d Ave Miami FL 33131

SECREST, JAMES SEATON, SR., lawyer; b. Middletown, Ky., Dec. 9, 1930; s. Elmer S. and Linney (Witherbee) S.; m. Mary Sue Corum, Sept. 2, 1950; children—James Seaton, Lynne Suzanne. J.D., U. Louisville, 1954. Bar: Ky. 1954. Ptnr., Goad & Secrest, Scottsville, Ky., 1955-62; sole practice, 1962-77; ptnr. Secrest & Secrest, Scottsville, 1977—. City judge pro tem Scottsville, 1955-58; judge Allen County, 1958-61; city atty. Scottsville, 1962-66; atty. Allen County, 1966—. Mem. Scottsville C. of C. (pres. 1962), Ky. Assn. County Attys. (pres. 1973, bd. dirs. 1985-86), ABA, Am. Judicature Soc., Ky. Bar Assn. Republican. Methodist. Club: Rotary (pres. 1960). General practice. Home: 10055 New Glasgow Rd Scottsville KY 42164 Office: Secrest & Secrest 210 W Main St Scottsville KY 42164

SECREST, RONALD DEAN, lawyer; b. Kansas City, Mo., Nov. 13, 1951; s. William Francis and Corrine Elizabeth (Clarke) S.; m. Stephanie de Jong, Oct. 8, 1983. BS, Stanford U., 1974; JD, U. Va., 1977. Bar: Tex. 1979, U.S. Dist. Ct. (so. dist.) Tex. 1979, U.S. Ct. Appeals (5th cir.) 1980, U.S. Ct. Appeals (11th cir.) 1981, U.S. Dist. Ct. (no. dist.) Tex. 1986. Law clk. to presiding justice U.S. Ct. Appeals (5th cir.), Houston, 1977-78; ptnr. Fulbright & Jaworski, Houston, 1978—. Fellow Tex. Bar Found., Houston Bar Found.; mem. ABA, Tex. Bar Assn., Houston Bar Assn. Federal civil litigation, State civil litigation, Environment. Home: 5588 Doliver Houston TX 77056 Office: Fulbright & Jaworski 1301 McKinney Houston TX 77010

SECREST, STEPHEN FREDERICK, lawyer; b. Boston, Oct. 13, 1947; s. Fred Gilbert and Stephanie (Jenkins) S.; m. Sandra Marie Frank. BA, Alma Coll., 1969; JD, U. Mich., 1972. Bar: Mich. 1972, U.S. Dist. Ct. (ea. dist.) Mich. 1972. Atty. Ford Motor Co., Dearborn, Mich., 1972-77, Ford of Europe, Brentwood, Eng., 1977-80, Ford Motor Credit Co., Dearborn, 1980—. Trustee 1st Presbyn. Ch. of Dearborn, 1975-77; Alumni bd. Alma Coll., 1980-86. Mem. ABA, Mich. Bar Assn. Consumer commercial, Federal civil litigation, State civil litigation. Home: 33085 Biddestone Ln Farmington Hills MI 48018 Office: Ford Motor Credit Co PO Box 6044 Dearborn MI 48121-6044

SEDERBAUM, ARTHUR DAVID, lawyer; b. N.Y.C., Sept. 14, 1944; s. William and Harriet (Warschauer) S.; m. Francine Haba, Dec. 30, 1967 (div. Aug. 1982); children—Rebecca, David; m. Phyllis Padow, Jan. 18, 1986; 1 child, Elizabeth. A.B. cum laude, Columbia U., 1965, J.D., 1968; LL.M., NYU, 1972. Bar: N.Y. 1968, Fla. 1980, U.S. Dist. Ct. (so. and ea. dists.) N.Y. 1972. Assoc. Zissu, Halper & Martin, N.Y.C., 1968-70, Berlack, Israels & Liberman, N.Y.C., 1970-72, Rubin Baum Levin Constant & Friedman, N.Y.C., 1972-76; ptnr. Certilman, Haft, Lebow, Balin, Buckley, & Krener N.Y.C., 1976—. Recipient J. K. Lasser Tax prize, NYU Inst. Fed. Taxation, 1968. Fellow: Am. Coll. Probate Council; mem. ABA, N.Y. State Bar Assn. (vice-chmn. com. on estate planning trusts and estates law sect.), Assn. Bar of City N.Y. (com. surrogates cts.), Practising Law Inst. (chmn. income taxation of estates and trusts program). Probate, Estate planning, Estate taxation. Home: 9 Evergreen Row Armonk NY 10504 Office: 805 3d Ave New York NY 10022

SEDKY, CHERIF, lawyer; b. Alexandria, Egypt, Dec. 10, 1943; came to U.S. 1958; s. Abdalla and Mona Frances (Smith) S.; m. Julie A. Greer, Dec. 18, 1964 (div.); children—Tarik, Mona. B.A., Stanford U., 1966; J.D., Georgetown U., 1969. Bar: D.C. 1969, U.S. Ct. Appeals (D.C. cir.) 1969, U.S. Supreme Ct. 1974. Assoc. Surrey Karasik Greene & Hill, Washington 1969-71, Hill Christopher & Phillips, Washington 1971-72, 73-75; ptnr. Kirkpatrick & Lockhart and predecessor firms, Washington, 1976—; asst. gen. counsel MCI Communications Corp., Washington, 1972-73. Bd. Dirs. Arab-Am. Cultural Found., Am. Near East Refugee Aid. Mem. ABA, D.C. Bar Assn., Phi Delta Phi. Moslem. Clubs: Metropolitan, City Tavern (Washington). Federal civil litigation, General corporate, Private international. Office: 1800 M St NW Washington DC 20036

SEDLAK, JOSEPH ANTHONY, III, lawyer; b. Cleve., Feb. 22, 1952; s. Joseph Anthony Jr. and Winefred Veronica (Nantell) S.; m. Susan Ann Dill, Oct. 1, 1983; children: Joseph Anthony IV and John Warrior Sedlak (twins). BA, Ohio State U., 1974; JD, St. Mary's U., San Antonio, 1977. Bar: Tex. 1977, Colo. 1980, U.S. Dist. Ct. Colo. 1980, U.S. Ct. Appeals (10th cir.) 1980. Assoc. Law Offices of Grady L. Roberts, Piersall, Tex., 1977-80, LoBato, Bliedt & Bliedt, Lakewood, Colo., 1980-81, Vranesic & Visciano, Denver, 1981-85; pres. Sedlak & Vogel P.C., Denver, 1985—. Mem. Colo. Bar Assn., Denver Bar Assn., Am. Trial Lawyers Asn., Denver Jud. Adminstrn. Com., Denver C. of C. Roman Catholic. Clubs: 26, Racquet World (Denver). Avocations: skiing, golf, hunting. State civil litigation, Personal injury, Criminal. Office: 621 17th St Suite 710 Denver CO 80293

SEDOR, GILBERT D., lawyer; b. Wausau, Wis., June 27, 1933; s. Walter and Florence M. (Ways) S.; m. Jean C. Soukup, Aug. 29, 1959 (div. July 1977); children: Daniel P., Rachel J. BS, Marquette U., 1959, JD, 1961. Assoc. Wickem & Consigny, Janesville, Wis., 1961-62; ptnr. Wickem, Consigny & Sedor, Janesville, 1963-69, Wickem, Consigny, Sedor, Andrews & Hemming, Janesville, 1969-75; sole practice Janesville, 1975-79; ptnr. Sedor & McDonald, Janesville, 1979-81, Sedor, McDonald & Hoag, Janesville, 1981-83, Sedor & Hoag S.C., Janesville, 1984—; instr. U. Wis., Madison, 1973-74; v.p. Info. Am., Janesville, 1986—, Maxi-Equipment Distbg. Inc., Janesville, 1986—; bd. dirs. Lenan Corp. Inc., Janesville, Janesville Data Ctr. Inc. Pres. Childrens Services Soc., Janesville, 1871-73; bd. dirs. Rock County United Givers, Janesville, 1970-72, Rock County Hist. Soc., Janesville, 1986—. Served to sgt. USMC, 1952-54, Korea. Named one of Outstanding Young Men Am., U.S. C. of C., 1967, 68, 69. Mem. ABA, Wis. Bar Assn., Wis. Trial Lawyers Assn., Civil Trial Lawyers Wis., Federation Ins. Trial Counsel, Janesville Jaycees (pres. 1966, Distinguished Service award 1966), Phi Delta Phi. Republican. Roman Catholic. Club: Janesville Country. Lodge: Rotary (bd. dirs. 1972-73). Avocations: downhill skiing, waterskiing, sailing, reading, sports. General practice, Personal injury, General corporate. Home: 91 S Huron Janesville WI 53545 Office: Sedor & Hoag SC 111 N Main St Janesville WI 53545

SEDWICK, JOHN WEETER, lawyer; b. Kittanning, Pa., Mar. 13, 1946; s. Jack D. and Marion (Hilton) S.; m. Deborah Brown, Aug. 22, 1966; children: Jack D. II, Whitney Marie. BA summa cum laude, Dartmouth Coll., 1968; JD cum laude, Harvard U., 1972. Bar: Alaska 1972, U.S. Dist. Ct. Alaska 1972, U.S. Ct. Appeals (9th cir.) 1973. Assoc. Burr, Pease and Kurtz, Anchorage, 1972-81, 84—; dir. div. lands State of Alaska, Anchorage, 1981-82; sole practice Anchorage, 1983. Mem. membership com. Commonwealth North, Anchorage, 1985; bd. dirs. South Addition Alaska R.R. Com., Anchorage, 1984. Served to sgt. USNG, 1969-72. Mem. ABA, Alaska Bar Assn. (chmn. environ. law sect. 1980-81, law examiners com. 1985—), Assn. Trial Lawyers Am. Episcopalian. Federal civil litigation, Oil and gas leasing, Personal injury. Home: 1112 S St Anchorage AK 99501 Office: Burr Pease and Kurtz 810 N St Anchorage AK 99501

SEE, ANDREW BRUCE, lawyer; b. St. Louis, Feb. 24, 1949; s. Edward Berry and Mary Lee (Procter) S.; m. Karen Mason, Nov. 24, 1979. BS in Pub. Adminstrn., U. Mo., 1971, JD cum laude, 1978. Bar: Mo. 1978, U.S. Dist. Ct. (we dist.) 1978, U.S. Ct. Appeals (8th cir.) 1982, U.S. Supreme Ct. 1982, U.S. Dist. Ct. (no. dist.) Ohio 1984. Law clk. to presiding judge U.S. Dist. Ct. (we. dist.) Mo., 1978-80; assoc. Shook, Hardy & Bacon, Kansas City, Mo., 1980-84; ptnr. Shook, Hardy & Bacon, Kansas City, 1984—; lectr. law U. Mo., Kansas City, 1982—. Editor in chief Mo. Law Rev., 1977-78. Mem. ABA, Mo. Bar Assn. Methodist. Avocation: sailing. Product liability litigation, Labor, Federal civil litigation. Office: Shook Hardy & Bacon 1101 Walnut 20th Floor Kansas City MO 64106

SEED, THOMAS FINIS, lawyer; b. Springfield, Mo., Aug. 30, 1916; s. William Thomas Haydn and Essye Pearl (Peters) S.; m. Magda Monica Vettos, Dec. 31, 1955. A.B., Kans. State Tchrs. Coll., 1941; J.D., U. Kans., 1948. Bar: Kans. 1948, U.S. Supreme Ct. 1966. Sole practice, Wichita, Kans., 1948-50, 53-59, 81—; county atty. Sedgwick County, Wichita, 1951-53; field atty. VA, Wichita, 1960-77; sec., recorder York Rite, Masons, Wichita, 1978-80. Pres. Wichita Inter-Club Council, 1951. Served to maj. U.S. Army, 1942-46. Mem. Fed. Bar Assn. (pres. Kans. chpt. 1974), Kans. Bar Assn., Wichita Bar Assn., Phi Delta Phi. Republican. Methodist. Club: Nat. Lawyers (Washington). Lodges: Masons. General corporate, General practice, Probate. Home and Office: 1484 Coolidge St Wichita KS 67203

SEELEY, GLENN J., lawyer; b. Wellington, Ohio, Aug. 21, 1926; s. Glen Thompson and Leona Mae (Ensign) S.; m. Ethel A. Sotak, June 7, 1945 (dec. Nov. 1971); 1 child, Gregory Douglas; m. Kristina Rose Ansen, May 29, 1977. BBA, Case Western Res. U., 1950; JD, Cleve. State U., 1955. Sr. ptnr. Jenson & Seeley, Avon Lake, Ohio, 1955-68; mng. ptnr. Marshman, Snyder & Seeley, Cleve., 1968-78; sr. ptnr. Seeley, Savidge & Ausslem, Cleve., 1978—; law dir. City of Avon, Ohio, 1957-63. Served to sgt. U.S. Army Air Corps., 1945-47. Named Man of Yr. Jr. C. of C., 1959. Mem. ABA, Ohio Bar Assn., Cleve. Bar Assn., Lorain County Bar Assn. (chmn. law day 1957-59), Avon Lake Jaycees (pres. 1962-63). Club: Cleve. Athletic. Labor, Insurance, Private international. Office: Seeley Savidge & Aussem 1940 E 6th St Cleveland OH 44114

SEELEY, JAMES J., lawyer; b. Camden, N.J., July 17, 1945; s. James J. and Phyllis (Herman) S.; m. Alexis M. Popoff, June 6, 1968; children: James IV, Thomas, Elizabeth, Alexis. Student, U. Ga., 1963-64; grad., Rutgers U., 1966; LLB, Duke U., 1969. Bar: N.J. 1969, U.S. Dist. Ct. N.J. 1969, Pa. 1971, U.S. Dist. Ct. (ea. dist.) Pa. 1971, Del. 1974, U.S. Dist. Ct. Del. 1974, U.S. Ct. Appeals (3d cir.), U.S. Supreme Ct. Asst. dean, prof. Rutgers U. Law Sch., Camden, N.J., 1969-71; regional counsel U.S. EPA, Phila., 1972-73; assoc. Morris, Nichols, Arsht & Tunnel, Wilmington, Del., 1973-74; ptnr. Stanger & Seeley, Bridgeton, N.J., 1975-83; sole practice Bridgeton, 1983—; prof. law Rutgers Law Sch., Camden, 1969-79; co-adj. prof. Rutgers U., New Brunswick, N.J., 1980—; spl. counsel N.J. Legislature Judiciary Com., Trenton, 1978-79. Mcpl. atty. Greenwich Twp., 1973—, Hopewell Twp., 1980—, Commercial Twp., 1983—, Lawrence Twp., 1981—. Named One of Outstanding Young Men of Am., U.S. Jaycees, 1977. Mem. N.J. State Bar Assn., N.J. Fedn. Planners, Cumberland County Bar Assn. Environment, General practice, Real property. Office: 200 W Commerce St Bridgeton NJ 08302

SEELIE, MICHAEL EDWARD, lawyer; b. Lakewood, Ohio, Nov. 14, 1951; s. Francis Joseph and Helen Bridgette (Walsh) S.; m. Beth Ann Smola, May 28, 1983; children: Christopher Michael, John Brennan Seelie. BA, Fla. State U., 1973; JD, Nova U., 1977. Bar: Fla. 1977, U.S. Dist. Ct. (mid. dist.) Fla. 1978, U.S. Ct. Appeals (5th and 11th cirs.) 1981. From assoc. to ptnr. Penland, McCranie & Shad, P.A., Jacksonville, Fla., 1977-84; sole practice Jacksonville, 1984—. Campaign treas. 1st Coast Legis. Watch com., Jacksonville, 1986; mem. Floridians Against Constl. Tampering, Tallahassee, 1985—, Endowment for Acad. Giving to Law and Edn., Tallahassee, 1985—. Mem. ABA, Fla. Bar Assn., Assn. Trial Lawyers Am., Acad. Fla. Trial Lawyers (amicus curiae com.), Nat. Orgn. Social Security Claimant's Reps., Ctr. Auto Safety. Democrat. Episcopalian. Avocations: hunting, fishing, sailing. State civil litigation, Personal injury. Office: 733 Blackstone Bldg Jacksonville FL 32202

SEELYE, LYNN MCVEIGH, lawyer; b. Bellingham, Wash., Dec. 30, 1939; s. Donald Arthur and Cleone (Haan) S.; m. Vicki Ann Holm, Dec. 30, 1965; children—Kevin McVeigh, Courtney Dawn. B.A. in Bus. Adminstrn., U. Wash., Seattle, 1961; J.D., Gonzaga U., 1965; LL.M. in Taxation, NYU, 1967. Bar: Mont. 1980, Wash. 1965, U.S. Tax Ct. 1967. Assoc., Butler-Lukins, Spokane, Wash., 1967-69; ptnr. Lukins-Seelye-Ran, Spokane, 1969-71, Lukins-Annis, Spokane, 1971-73; assoc. prof. Gonzaga Law Sch., Spokane, 1973-80; assoc. Graybill-Ostrem, Great Falls, Mont., 1980-82; sole practice, Great Falls, 1982—; moderator, lectr. Mont. Annual Tax Inst., Missoula, 1983; chmn., panelist Gonzaga Ann. Tax Inst., Spokane, 1978. Com. mem. City/County Govt. Com., Great Falls, 1984. Mem. Mont. State Bar Assn., Wash. State Bar Assn., Great Falls C. of C. (exec. bd. 1984). Clubs: Meadowlark Country; Spokane. Corporate taxation, Securities, General corporate. Home: 415 Riverview Ct Great Falls MT 59404 Office: 502 Strain Bldg 410 Central Ave Great Falls MT 59401

SEEMAN, ROBERT FOSTER, airline executive, lawyer; b. Mt. Vernon, N.Y., Jan. 17, 1942; s. Clifford Bruno and Eleanor (Foster) S.; m. Isabelle Schuyler Pettit, Nov. 24, 1973. A.B., Stanford U., 1965; M.B.A., Wharton Sch., U. Pa., 1967; J.D., Fordham U., 1973. Bar: N.Y. 1975, Tex. 1981. With Am. Airlines, Inc., 1967—, dir. contract adminstrn., 1975-76, dir. pension and group ins. adminstrn., 1977-86, dir. benefits compliance, 1986—; v.p. Tulsa Bus. Health Group, 1982-86. Pres., 444 Owners Corp., 1978-79; trustee Air Transport Assn. Benefit Plans, 1982—; mem. Forest Hills Homeowners Assn., 1979—. Mem. ABA, Tex. Bar Assn., Assn. Bar City N.Y., Stanford U. Alumni Assn. Republican. Episcopalian. Club: Wharton (Dallas/Ft. Worth). Pension, profit-sharing, and employee benefits, Contracts commercial, Administrative and regulatory. Home: 8442 Garland Rd Dallas TX 75218 Office: Am Airlines Inc MD 3L47 PO Box 619616 DFW Airport TX 75261-9616

SEFCOVIC, HENRY JOHN, lawyer; b. Mt. Clemens, Mich., May 11, 1944; s. Method Wendolyn and Anna (Prchlic) S.; m. Kathleen Ann O'Connor, Jan 27, 1973; children: Natasha, Nadia. BA, Wayne State U., 1969; JD, Detroit Coll. Law, 1975. Bar: Mich. 1975, U.S. Dist. Ct. (ea. dist.) Mich. 1975, U.S. Ct. Appeals (6th cir.) 1975, U.S. Supreme Ct. 1979. Vocat. trainer Detroit Urban League, 1970-75; asst. counsel Genesee County Corp. Counsel, Flint, Mich., 1975-78; county corp. counsel Bay County, Bay City, Mich., 1978-80; city atty. City of Bay City, 1980-85; sole practice Bay City, 1985—. Contbr. articles to profl. jours. Vol. Peace Corps, Washington and Morocco, 1965-67; mem. Bay City Fiscal Task Force, 1983; del. Dem. State Conv., Mich., 1976—; pres. Bay County Community Concert Assn., 1982—; bd. dirs. ARC, Bay City, 1982—, Bay County Econ. Devel. Corp., 1982, Legal Services Eastern Mich., Flint, 1983—, Region 7 Agy. on Aging, Bay City, 1984. Recipient Distinguished Service award Bay County Bd. Commrs., 1980. Mem. ABA, Mich. Bar Assn., Bay County Bar Assn., Am. Arbitration Assn. (arbitrator). Roman Catholic. Lodge: Lions. Avocations: cross country skiing, reading, cooking. General practice, Labor, Personal injury. Home: 617 N Lincoln Bay City MI 48708 Office: 820 N Monroe Bay City MI 48708

SEGAL, BERNARD GERARD, lawyer; b. N.Y.C., June 11, 1907; s. Samuel I. and Rose (Cantor) S.; m. Geraldine Rosenbaum, Oct. 22, 1933; children: Loretta Joan Segal Cohen, Richard Murry. AB, U. Pa., 1928, LLB, 1931, LL.D., 1969; LL.D., Franklin and Marshall Coll., 1953; LLD, Temple U., 1954, Dropsie U., 1966; LL.D., Jewish Theol. Sem. Am., 1977, Vt. Law Sch., 1978, Villanova U., 1980, Georgetown U., 1983; J.S.D., Suffolk U., 1969; D.H.L., Hebrew Union Coll., 1970. Bar: Pa. 1932. Mem. faculty U. Pa., 1928-35, 45-47; legal asst. Am. Law Inst., 1932-33; Am. reporter on contracts Internat. Congress of Law, Hague, Netherlands, 1932; dep. atty. gen. U.S. Atty Gen., 1932-35; mem. firm Schnader, Harrison, Segal & Lewis, Phila., 1936—; chmn. Schnader, Harrison, Segal & Lewis, 1968—; instr. grad. bus., govt. debating Am. Inst. Banking, 1936-39; lectr. law Franklin and Marshall Coll., 1937-38; chmn. Commn. Jud. and Congl. Salaries, U.S. Govt., 1953-55; mem. Bd. Law Examiners, Phila., 1940-46; mem. council World Peace Through Law Ctr., 1973—, also confs. Athens, Geneva, U.S. and Thailand, chmn. demonstration trial, Belgrade, Yugoslavia, 1971, also chmn. com. on internat. communications, world chmn. World Law Day, Madrid, 1979, Berlin, 1985; chmn. World Conf. on Peace and Violence, Jerusalem, 1979; chmn. bd. Council Legal Edn. Opportunities, 1968-71; co-chmn. Lawyers Com. Civil Rights Under Law, 1963-65; adviser Commn. Committment, Detention and Discharge of Prisoners, 1953-55; mem. Atty. Gen.'s Nat. Com. to Study Antitrust Laws, 1953-55; exec. com. Atty. Gen.'s Nat. Conf. on Court Congestion, 1958-61; chmn. jud. nominating commn. Commonwealth of Pa., 1964-64; mem. Appellate Ct. Nominating Commn., 1973-79; standing com. on rules of practice and procedure Jud. Conf. U.S., 1959-76; mem. Nat. Citizens Com. on Community Relations, 1964—; adv. com. U.S. mission UN, 1967-68; adv. panel internat. law U.S. Dept. State,

1967—; mem. Adminstrv. Conf. U.S., 1968-74; chmn. nat. adv. com. on legal services OEO, 1968-74, chmn. exec. com., 1971-74; mem. U.S. Commn. Revision Fed. Ct. Appellate System, 1974-75; mem. Jud. Council Pa., 1968-71; mem. U.S. Commn. on Exec., Legis. and Jud. Salaries, 1976—. Editor-in-chief: Pennsylvania Banking Building and Loan Law, 3 vols., 1941; contbr. articles to law revs., other publs.; editor: The Belgrade Spaceship Trial, 1972; mem. internat. hon. bd. Ency. Judaica. Mem. Commn. on Anti-Poverty Program for Phila., 1967-71; life trustee emeritus, exec. bd. trustees U. Pa., also bd. overseers Law Sch., Faculty Arts and Scis., also fellow joint bd. Annenberg Sch. Communications, bd. overseers, fellow Faculty Arts and Scis.; bd. govs. emeritus, past v.p., past treas. Dropsie U.; chmn. bd. Council Advancement Legal Edn., 1972—; hon. gov. Hebrew U. Jerusalem; trustee Chapel of Four Chaplains; trustee, exec. com. Albert Einstein Med. Ctr.; bd. dirs. NAACP Legal Def. and Ednl. Fund Found. Fed. Bar Assn.; mem. Archdiocese Leadership Com. on Edn. in Cath. Schs., 1979—; bd. dirs. So. Africa Legal Services and Legal Edn. Project, 1979—; trustee Martin Luther King, Jr. Ctr. Nonviolent Social Change, 1984—. Recipient World Lawyer award World Peace through Law Ctr., 1975. Fellow Am. Coll. Trial Lawyers, Inst. Jud. Adminstrn., Am. Bar Found. (pres. 1976-78); mem. Fedn. Jewish Agys., Pa. Bar Assn., Phila. Bar Assn., Pa. Urban Affairs Ptnrship, ABA (pres. 1969-70, Gold medal 1976), Inter-Am. Bar Assn., Internat. Bar Assn. Fed. Bar Assn. (nat. council), Assn. Bar City N.Y., Am. Arbitration Assn. (dir.), Am. Law Inst. (1st v.p. 1976—), Am. Judicature Soc. (dir.), Council Legal Edn. for Profl. Responsibility (dir.), Fed. Jud. Conf. 3d Circuit (life), World Assn. Lawyers (pres. for Ams. 1976—), Nat. Conf. Bar Pres., Taxpayers Forum Pa. (past pres.), Juristic Soc., Brandeis Lawyers Soc., Allied Jewish Appeal (past pres., hon. pres.), Legal Aid Soc. Phila. (dir.), Seldon Soc. Eng., Jewish League Israel (nat. bd.), Jewish Pub. Soc. Am. (trustee, exec. com.), Jewish Family Service (hon. dir.), Order of Coif, Tau Epsilon Rho, Delta Sigma Rho. Republican. Clubs: Socialegal, Locust, Internat. Variety, Pen and Pencil; Union League, Metropolitan (Washington). Home: The Philadelphian 2401 Pennsylvania Ave Philadelphia PA 19130 Office: Suite 3600 1600 Market St Philadelphia PA 19103

SEGAL, FREDERICK LESLIE, lawyer; b. N.Y.C., Oct. 7, 1947; s. Abraham L. and Esther (Kahn) S.; m. Patricia Maclay, July 16, 1972; children—Sabrina Meredith, Elysia Meghan. B.S., U. Pitts., 1970; J.D., Hofstra U., 1973; LL.M., N.Y. U., 1979. Bar: Pa. 1979, N.Y. 1974, U.S. Patent and Trademark Office 1975, U.S. Supreme Ct. 1978, U.S. Ct. Appeals (2d cir.) 1974, U.S. Dist. Ct. (we. dist.) Pa. 1979, U.S. Dist. Ct. (ea. and so. dists.) N.Y. 1974, U.S. Ct. Customs and Patent Appeals 1976, U.S. Ct. Claims 1976, U.S. Ct. Appeals D.C. 1982, U.S. Customs Ct. 1976, U.S. Tax Ct. 1976. Clk., U.S. Dist. Ct. (ea. dist.) N.Y., Bklyn., 1973-74; assoc. Mendes & Mount, N.Y.C., 1974-78; assoc. Hart & Hume, N.Y.C., 1978-79; assoc. Rosenberg & Kirschner, Pitts., 1979-81; assoc. Berger Kapetan, Malakoff & Meyers, Pitts., 1981-83; sole practice, Pitts., 1983—; patent agt., atty. U.S. Patent & Trademark Office, Washington, 1975—; arbitrator Am. Arbitration Assn., 1983—, Ct. Common Pleas Allegheny County, Pitts., 1981—. Served with Army NG, 1970-72. N.Y. State scholar, 1971-73. Mem. ABA, Pa. Bar Assn., Allegheny County Bar Assn., Assn. Trial Lawyers Am., Pa. Trial Lawyers Assn., Men of Achievement, U. Pitts. Golden Panther Alumni Assn. (bd. dirs. 1983—) Democrat. Jewish. State civil litigation, Insurance, Personal injury. Home: 2293 Beechwood Blvd Pittsburgh PA 15217 Office: 564 Forbes Ave Suite 700 Pittsburgh PA 15219

SEGAL, JEROME A., lawyer; b. Haverhill, Mass., June 3, 1931; s. Sydney and Harriet (Goldberg) S.; m. Louise A., June 5, 1955; children: Richard, Steven, Jonathan. AB, Brandeis U., 1953; LLB, Boston U., 1956. Bar: Mass., U.S. Dist. Ct. Mass., U.S. Supreme Ct. Ptnr. Segal, Edelstein & Bussone, Beverly, Mass., 1957—. State rep. Gen. Ct. Mass., Boston, 1965-70. Mem. Mass. Bar Assn., Boston Bar Assn., Salem Bar Assn., Essex Bar Assn. Republican. Jewish. Avocation: bicycle touring. Criminal, Personal injury, Probate. Office: 21 Broadway Beverly MA 01915

SEGAL, MARTIN EDWARD, lawyer; b. Phila., July 2, 1939; s. Samuel Jr. and Rose (Izenberg) S.; divorced; children: Barry David, Ruth Sharon. BBA, U. Fla., 1961; JD, U. Miami, 1964. Bar: Fla. 1964, U.S. Dist. Ct. (so. dist.) Fla. 1964, U.S. Ct. Appeals (5th cir.) 1964. Ptnr. Patton & Kanner, Miami, Fla., 1964—. Author: The Guru is You, 1985, Florida Real Estate Tax Certificates, 1976; editor, author U. Miami Law Rev., 1961-64. Mem. ABA, Fla. Bar Assn., Dade County Bar Assn., Assn. Trial Lawyers Am., Sierra, Author's Guild, Nat. Writers Club, Wig and Robe Soc., Phi Delta Phi, Omicron Delta Kappa. Club: Miami (Fla.), Bankers (Miami), City Club of Miami. Avocations: consciousness growth, writing, reading, wilderness camping, athletics. General corporate, Probate, Real property. Home: PO Box 01-1122 Miami FL 33101 Office: Patton & Kanner 150 SE 2d Ave Suite 300 Miami FL 33131

SEGAL, NORMAN M., lawyer; b. Elizabeth, N.J., Dec. 31, 1926; s. Max and Gladys (Brody) S.; m. Bernice Ginsberg; children—Elizabeth, Daniel. B.A., Columbia U., 1949, LL.B., 1951. With Mudge, Rose, Guthrie, Alexander & Ferdon, N.Y.C., 1951—, ptnr., 1964—; dir. Green Mountain Power Corp., Burlington, Vt.; mem. legal com. Edison Electric Inst., Washington. Served with USN, 1945-46. Mem. Phi Beta Kappa. Home: 26 Cherry St Tenafly NJ 07670 Office: Mudge Rose Guthrie Alexander & Ferdon 180 Maiden Ln New York NY 10038

SEGAL, ROBERT MANDAL, lawyer; b. Worcester, Mass., Mar. 21, 1915; s. Abe Charles and Bella (Perry) S.; m. Sharlee Mysel, June 17, 1941; children—Terry P., Ellen Huvelle. A.B., Amherst Coll., 1936; postgrad., U. Chgo., 1936-38; J.D., Harvard U., 1942. Bar: Mass. 1942, U.S. Dist. Ct. Mass. 1946, U.S. Supreme Ct. 1952. Economist U.S. Steel Corp., 1939; sr. ptnr. Segal & Flamm, Boston, 1955-72; New Eng. counsel AFTRA, 1948-86; sr. ptnr. Segal, Roitman & Coleman, Boston, 1972—; lectr. labor law Harvard Bus. Sch., 1962-82, Boston Coll. Law Sch., 1979-81, Northeastern U. Labor Inst., U.S. State Dept., 1971-73. Contbr. articles to profl. jours. Chmn., Harvard Law Sch. Record Alumni Com., 1973—; pres. Jewish Community Council of Boston, 1975. Served with U.S. Army, 1943-45. Recipient Cushing-Gavin Labor award, 1986; Brookings Instn. fellow, 1938-39. Mem. ABA (ho. of dels. 1957-58, mem. consortium 1975-80, chmn. labor and employment sect. 1957, co-chmn. membership and fin. com. labor sect. 1978—, forum com. 1984-86), Am. Judicature Soc., AFTRA (New England counsel), Screen Actors Guild (New England counsel), Mass. Bar Assn., Boston Bar Assn., Mass. Americans for Dem. Action (chmn. 1960), Harvard Law Sch. Alumni Assn. (mem. council 1970-73), Phi Beta Kappa, Delta Sigma Rho. Jewish. Clubs: World Affairs Council (Boston); Indsl. Relations Assn. Labor, Entertainment. Home: 50 Longwood Ave #1112 Brookline MA 02146 Office: Segal Roitman & Coleman 11 Beacon St Boston MA 02108

SEGAL, TERRY PHILIP, lawyer; b. Boston, July 20, 1942; s. Robert Mandel and Sharlee (Mysel) S.; m. Harriet Lobel, Aug. 3, 1969; children: Jessica, Zachary, Adam. BA, Amherst Coll., 1964; LLB, Yale U., 1967. Bar: Mass. 1967, D.C. 1968. Legal counsel U.S. Senate, Washington, 1967-68; asst. U.S. atty. Dept. Justice, Washington, 1968-70, Boston, 1971-73; of counsel Silverman & Kudisch, Boston, 1975-80; ptnr. Segal, Moran & Feinberg, Boston, 1980—; counsel U.S. Senator Paul Tsongas, Lowell, Mass., 1983-84, Tip O'Neill com., Boston, 1982. Contbr. legal articles to profl. jours. Fellow Am. Coll. Trial Lawyers; mem. ABA (past chmn. criminal law and econ. crime com.), Boston Bar Assn., Yale Law Sch. Assn., (v.p. 1984-86). Democrat. Jewish. Avocations: tennis. Criminal, Federal civil litigation, State civil litigation. Office: Segal Moran & Feinberg 210 Commercial St Boston MA 02109

SEGALL, JAMES ARNOLD, lawyer; b. Columbus, Ohio, Aug. 19, 1956; s. Arthur and Greta Helene (Cohen) S.; m. Janice Faye Wiesen, Mar. 14, 1981; children: Gayle Helene, Aryn Michelle. BA, Coll. of William and Mary, 1978; JD, Washington and Lee U., 1981. Bar: Va. 1981, U.S. Dist. Ct. (ea. dist.) Va. 1981. Assoc. Phelps & King P.C., Newport News, Va., 1981-84, Buxton & Lasris P.C., Yorktown, Va., 1984-85; sole practice Newport News, 1985—. Bd. dirs. ct. appointed spl. adv. program Newport News. Mem. ABA, Newport News Bar Assn., Assn. Trial Lawyers Am., Va. Trial Lawyers Assn. Lodges: Kiwanis, B'nai B'rith, Ruritan (sec. 1985—). Avocations: weightlifting, basketball, boating, history, philosophy. Criminal, Family and matrimonial, General practice. Home: 306 Dogwood Dr Newport News VA 23606 Office: 12284 Warwick Blvd Newport News VA 23606

SEGALL, MARK EDWARD, lawyer; b. N.Y.C., May 30, 1953; s. Harold A. and Edith (Besser) S.; m. Karen Elkin, Aug. 13, 1978; children: Michael, Steven. AB, Harvard U., 1975, JD, 1978. Bar: N.Y. 1979, U.S. Ct. Appeals (9th cir.) 1979. Assoc. Davis, Polk & Wardwell, N.Y.C., 1978-85; from assoc. to ptnr. Finley, Kumble et al, N.Y.C., 1985—. Mem. ABA. Antitrust, Securities, Federal civil litigation. Home: 17 Claremont Rd Scarsdale NY 10583 Office: Finley Kumble Wagner et al 425 Park Ave New York NY 10022

SEGLUND, BRUCE RICHARD, lawyer; b. Lansing, Mich., June 3, 1950; s. Richard Oswald and Josephine Ann (Krause) S.; m. Connie Sue Roberts, June 19, 1970; children: Jennifer Lynne, Nicole Marie. BS, Mich. State U., 1973; JD, Thomas M. Cooley Law Sch., 1979. Bar: Mich. 1981, U.S. DIst. Ct. (ea. dist.) Mich. 1981. Assoc. Michael W. Reeds, P.C., Walled Lake, Mich., 1981-82; sole practice Walled Lake, 1982-85; ptnr. Mick and Seglund, Walled Lake, 1985—. Mem. ABA, Mich. Bar Assn., Oakland County Bar Assn. (lectr. 1984), Mich. Jaycees (pres. Walled Lake 1982-83, excellance award 1982-83, pres. of yr. 1982-83), Walled Lake C. of C. (bd. dirs. scholarship fund 1985—). Roman Catholic. Lodge: KC (adv. 1982—). Family and matrimonial, Real property, General practice. Home: 8618 Buffalo Union Lake MI 48085 Office: Mick and Seglund 2410 S Commerce Rd Walled Lake MI 48088

SEHAM, MARTIN CHARLES, lawyer; b. Jersey City, June 30, 1933; s. Samuel and Libbie (Siegel) S.; m. Phoebe Williams, Apr. 18, 1955; children: Amy, Jenny, Lee, Lucy. BA summa cum laude, Amherst Coll., 1954; JD magna cum laude, Harvard U., 1957. Bar: N.Y. 1957, U.S. Dist. Ct. (ea. and so. dists.) N.Y. 1957, U.S. Supreme Ct. 1963, U.S. Ct. Appeals (D.C. cir.) 1969, U.S. Ct. Appeals (9th cir.) 1973. Assoc. Poletti & Freiden, N.Y.C., 1960-63; ptnr. Kopple & Seham, N.Y.C., 1963-66, Surrey & Morse, N.Y.C., 1966-79, Seham, Klein & Zelman, N.Y.C., 1979—; gen. counsel Am. Maritime Assn., N.Y.C., 1979—, Owners Community Elec. Rates, N.Y.C., 1979—. Author: Federal Wage & Hour Laws, 1962, Chapter Railway Labor Act Kheel Book, 1984; editor: Harvard Law Rev., 1955. Mem. Bergen County (N.J.) Urban League, bd. dirs. 1985—, pres. housing and devel. Corp. 1982—; mem. Bergen County Energy Council, 1982-85. Mem. ABA, N.Y. Bar Assn., Assn. of Bar of City of N.Y., Phi Beta Kappa. Clubs: Harvard (N.Y.C.), Hemisphere (N.Y.C. bd. govs. 1982-86). Labor, Public utilities. Home: 19 Creston Ave Tenafly NJ 07670

SEHEULT, MALCOLM MCDONALD RICHARDSON, solicitor, barrister; b. Port of Spain, Trinidad, July 18, 1949; s. Errol Andre and Laura (Laltoo) S.; m. Robin Lynn Montanye; children: Kristie, Julie, Laura, Aimée. BA in Sociology magna cum laude, U. Toronto, 1971, BEd, 1972, MA, 1973; LLB, U. Toronto, Ottawa, 1976; JD, Kensington U., 1987. Bar: Ontario, Can. 1978; cert. tchr., Toronto, Can. Sole practice Toronto, 1978-85; assoc. Outerbridge, Barristers & Solicitors, Mississquqa, Can., 1985—; lectr. numerous profl. and community groups and orgns. Producer, editor Where Is Tomorrow?, 1969; editor Ottawa Law Rev.; also articles. Mem. Justice for Children, Vanier Inst. of Family, Ont. Sch. Tchrs. Fedn.; bd. dirs. North York Branson Hosp. Mem. ABA, Can. Bar Assn., Assn. Trial Lawyers Am., Law Soc. Upper Can., Medico-Legal Soc., Lawyers Club, Can. Civil Liberties Union, Royal Soc. Arts (fellow 1979), Mensa Internat., Can. Sociology and Anthropology Assn., Nat. Directory Sociology of Edn. and Ednl. Sociology, Am. Philatelic Soc.Soc. Avocations: music, car rally racing, volleyball, swimming, antique furniture restoration. Jurisprudence, Juvenile, Family and matrimonial. Home: 25623 State St Loma Linda CA 92354 Address: 2936 Victoria Park Ave, Willowdale, ON Canada M2J4A6

SEIDEL, ARTHUR HARRIS, lawyer; b. N.Y.C., May 25, 1923; s. Philip and Pearl (Geller) S.; m. Raquel Eliovich, Aug. 21, 1949; children: Stephen A., Paul B., Mary Beth Sharp. B.S., CCNY, 1942; A.M., U. Mich., 1943; J.D. with honors, George Washington U., 1949. Bar: D.C. 1949, Pa. 1956, N.Y. 1955. Atty. patent dept. Gulf Oil Corp., Washington and Pitts., 1947-52; individual practice law 1952-64; sr. ptnr. firm Seidel & Gonda, 1964-68; sr. ptnr. firm Seidel, Gonda & Goldhammer (P.C.), Phila., 1968-72, pres., 1972-84; pres. Seidel, Gonda, Goldhammer & Abbott, P.C., 1984—; lectr. in Intellectual Property Temple U. Law Sch., 1973-86, Am. Law Inst. Editor: George Washington Law Rev, 1949; author: (with others) Trademark Practice, 2 vols, 1963, Monographs on Patent Law and Practice, 4th edit, 1984, Trademarks and Copyrights, 5th edit., 1986, Trade Secrets and Employment Agreements, 2d edit, 1984; also articles. Mem. adv. com. for Restatement of Law of Unfair Competition. Mem. ABA, Pa. Bar Assn., Phila. Bar Assn., Am. Patent Law Assn., Order of Coif. Patent, Trademark and copyright. Home: 904 Centennial Rd Narberth PA 19072 Office: 1800 Two Penn Center Plaza Philadelphia PA 19102

SEIDEL, JOSEPH S., lawyer; b. Elizabeth, N.J., June 30, 1928; A.B., Rutger U., 1950, J.D., 1956. Bar: N.J. 1956, U.S. Supreme Ct. 1963, U.S. Tax Ct. 1972. Assoc., Hannoch, Weisman, Stern and Besser, Newark, 1956-62, ptnr., 1963-71; mcpl. prosecutor Town of Springfield (N.J.), 1962-67, Boro of Hopatcong, 1981—; mem. panel seminar on eminent domain N.Y. Practicing Law Inst., 1967, Rutgers U. Inst. Continuing Legal Edn., 1972-75. Comdg. officer Springfield Police Aux., 1955-67; past chmn. sustaining membership enrollment project Jockey Hollow dist. Boy Scouts Am. Served with USAFR, 1950-61. Mem. ABA, Am. Right-of-Way Assn. (chmn. profl. devel. com. 1974-75), Fed. Bar Assn., N.J. Bar Assn. (chmn. com. revision law of eminent domain 1968-70), Morris County Bar Assn., Sussex County Bar Assn., Assn. Trial Lawyers Am. Contbr. articles to profl. jours. Home and Office: 25 Air Castle Isles PO Box 1003 Hopatcong NJ 07843 Address: care Bellemead Devel Corp 4 Becker Farm Rd Roseland NJ 07068

SEIDEL, SELVYN, lawyer, legal educator; b. Longbranch, N.J., Nov. 6, 1942; s. Abraham and Anita (Stoller) S.; m. Deborah Lew, June 21, 1970; 1 child, Emily. B.A., U. Chgo., 1964; J.D., U. Calif.-Berkeley, 1967; Diploma in Law, Oxford U., 1968. Bar: N.Y. 1970, U.S. Dist. Ct. (so. and ea. dists.) N.Y. 1970, D.C. Ct. Appeals, 1982. Ptnr. Latham & Watkins, N.Y.C., 1984—; adj. prof. Sch. Law, NYU, 1974-85; instr. Practicing Law Inst., 1980-81, 84. Mem. ABA, New York County Bar Assn., N.Y.C. Bar Assn. (mem. fed. cts. com. 1982-85), Boalt Hall Alumni Assn. (bd. dirs. 1980-82), Contbr. articles to profl. jurs. Club: Union League. Federal civil litigation, Private international, Legal education. Home: 110 Riverside Dr New York NY 10024 Office: 885 Third Ave New York NY 10022

SEIDEN, GLENN, lawyer; b. Chgo., Nov. 3, 1947; m. Rochelle Jo Margolis, Mar. 16, 1970; 3 children. BSBA, Roosevelt U., 1970; JD, John Marshall Law Sch., 1974. Bar: Ill. 1974, U.S. Dist. Ct. (no. dist.) Ill. 1974, U.S. Ct. Appeals (7th cir.) 1977, U.S. Supreme Ct. 1979. Sole practice Chgo., 1974-76; ptnr. Del Preto & Seiden, Chgo., 1976-83; prin. Glenn Seiden & Assocs., Chgo., 1983—. Served with USAF, 1970-76. Criminal, Federal civil litigation, State civil litigation. Office: 2050 Clavey Rd Highland Park IL 60085

SEIDENFELD, GLENN KENNETH, JR., real estate developer; b. Oceanport, N.J., Feb. 13, 1944; s. Glenn Kenneth and Mary Louise (Liebenstein) S.; m. Patricia O'Donnell, Sept. 1, 1974; 1 child, Glenn Kenneth, III. B.S., Northwestern U., 1966; J.D., U. Ill., 1969. Atty.-advisor SEC, Washington, 1970-72; atty. McDermott, Will & Emery, Chgo., 1972-76; sec., gen. counsel Bally Mfg. Corp., Chgo., 1977—, v.p., sec., gen. counsel, 1981-85; cons., pres. Catalina West Corp., Tucson, 1985—. Contbr. articles to profl. jours. Mem. Am. Soc. Corp. Secs. (mem. securities law com. 1984—), ABA, Chgo. Bar Assn. General corporate, Contracts commercial, Federal civil litigation. Home: 5010 Valley View Rd Tucson AZ 85702 Office: Catalina West Corp 1200 N El Dorado Pl Tucson AZ 85715

SEIDL, JAMES PETER, lawyer; b. Chippewa Falls, Wis., Dec. 12, 1953; s. Peter James and Majorie Doris (Farmer) S.; m. Holly Catherine Linnehan, Sept. 7, 1985. BA, U. Wis., 1977; JD, Antioch U., 1980. Bar: Wis. 1980, U.S. Mil. Ct. Appeals 1983. Dist. atty. Taylor County, Medford, Wis., 1980-82; judge adv. USAF, Grand Forks AFB, N.D., 1983-86; dep. staff judge adv. USAF, APO N.Y., 1986—; chief of claims USAF, 1984-85, chief of civil, 1985-86. Served to capt. USAF, 1983—. Mem. ABA, Air Force Assn. Roman Catholic. Military. Home: PO Box 2586 APO NY 09224-5368 Office: 7241 ABG/JA APO NY 09224-5000

SEIDLER, B(ERNARD) ALAN, lawyer; b. N.Y.C., Nov. 26, 1946; s. Aaron H. and Ethel T. (Berkowitz) S.; m. Lynne Aubrey, Jan. 21, 1978; children—Jacob A., Morgan H., Lily R. B.A., Colgate U., 1968; J.D., Seton Hall U., 1972. Bar: N.Y. 1973, U.S. Dist. Ct. (ea. and so. dists.) N.Y. 1975, U.S. Ct. Appeals (2d cir.) 1976, U.S. Supreme Ct. 1977, U.S. Ct. Appeals (3rd cir.) 1984. Staff atty. N.Y. Legal Aid Soc., N.Y.C., 1972-75; sole practice, N.Y.C. and Nyack, N.Y., 1975—. Mem. N.Y. County Lawyers Assn. Club: Snedens Landing Tennis Assn. (Palisades, N.Y.). Real property, Federal civil litigation, Probate. Office: 127 S Broadway Nyack NY 10960

SEIDLITS, CURTIS LEE, JR., lawyer; b. Denison, Tex., June 25, 1953; s. Curtis Lee and Betty Ann (Henderson) S.; m. Melody Lynn Ward, Mar., 17, 1979; children: Stephanie Kristin, Sarah Katherine. BA in Polit. Sci., Baylor U., 1975, JD, 1977. Bar: Tex. 1978. Asst. county atty. Grayson County, Sherman, Tex., 1978-80; ptnr. Kennedy, Minshew, Campbell & Seidlits P.C., Sherman, 1980-86. Rep. elect 62 Dem. State Rep., Tex., 1986. Mem. ABA, Grayson County Bar Assn. (pres. 1983-84). Baptist. Lodges: Masons, Hella Shrine Temple. Avocations: golf, water sports, snow skiing. Criminal, Family and matrimonial. Home: 2238 Turtle Creek Sherman TX 75090

SEIDMAN, PAUL JOSEPH, lawyer; b. Phila., Sept. 5, 1948; s. Isadore and Edith (Selditch) S.; m. Jayne I. Levin, May 28, 1972; children—Linda Stacey, David Jeremy. B.B.A., Temple U., 1970; J.D., Georgetown U., 1973. Bar: Pa. 1973, D.C. 1973, Md. 1981, U.S. Ct. Claims 1973, U.S. Tax Ct. 1973, U.S. Dist. Ct. (D.C.) 1981, U.S. Ct. Appeals (fed. cir.) 1982, U.S. Claims Ct., U.S. Ct. Appeals (D.C. cir.) 1983, U.S. Dist. Ct. (Md.) 1984. Law clk. to judge U.S. Ct. Claims, Washington, 1973-74; asst., counsel for claims Naval Sea Systems Command, Washington, 1974-76; staff atty. Machinery and Allied Products Inst., Washington, 1976-78; acting dir. freedom of info. and privacy SBA, Washington, 1978-79, asst. chief counsel for procurement Office Chief Counsel for Advocacy, SBA, 1979-81; prin. Seidman & Assocs., P.C., Washington, 1981—; staff White House Conf. on Small Bus., Washington, 1980. Editorial asst. Tax Lawyer, 1972-73; co-author: Representing Small Business, 1986; writer articles, pamphlet. Mem. ABA, Fed. Bar Assn., Nat. Contract Mgmt. Assn., Nat. Lawyers Club. Government contracts and claims, Administrative and regulatory, Federal civil litigation. Office: 1815 H St NW Washington DC 20006

SEIFERT, STEPHEN WAYNE, lawyer; b. Washington, May 25, 1957; s. Arthur John and Frances E. (Smith) S. BA summa cum laude, Yale U., 1979; JD, Stanford U., 1982. Bar: Colo. 1982, U.S. Dist. Ct. Colo. 1982, U.S. Ct. Appeals (10th cir.) 1982. Ptnr.. Fairfield and Woods P.C., Denver, 1982—. Mem. ABA, Am. Bankruptcy Inst., Colo. Bar Assn., Denver Bar Assn., Yale-Harvard Regatta Com., Phi Beta Kappa. Republican. Episcopalian. Club: University (Denver). Bankruptcy, Contracts commercial, Consumer commercial. Office: Fairfield and Woods 1700 Lincoln St Suite 2400 Denver CO 80203

SEIFFERT, TERRY L., lawyer; b. Billings, Mont., Oct. 3, 1948; s. Joe H. and Berry E. (Bohl) S. B.S., Mont. State U., 1970; J.D., U. Mont., 1973. Bar: Mont. 1973, U.S. dist. ct. Mont. With Mont. Legal Services, 1973-75; sole practice, 1975—. Bd. dirs. Prairie Tower Inc., non-profit housing project for elderly, Concern Inc., non-profit housing project for indigent. Mem. Mont. Bar Assn., ABA. Democrat. Congregationalist. General practice, Landlord-tenant, Administrative and regulatory. Address: 3302 Fourth Ave N Billings MT 59101

SEIGEL, STEPHEN PAUL, lawyer; b. St. Louis, Dec. 5, 1946; s. Paul and Dorothy (Weingart) S.; children: Joseph, Ann. BA in Polit. Sci., U. Mo., 1968, JD, 1971. Bar: Mo., U.S. Dist. Ct. (ea. and we. dists.) Mo., U.S. Ct. Appeals (8th cir.), U.S. Supreme Ct. Assoc. Woolsey & Fisher, Springfield, Mo., 1971-73; prosecuter City of Springfield, 1973-75; sole practice Springfield, 1975—; prosecuter City of Springfield, 1985—. Bd. dirs. Community Alcohol Safety Effort (funding and proposal of safety and ednl. programs), 1985—. Mem. ABA, Mo. Bar Assn., Kansas City Bar Assn., Greene County Bar Assn., Assn. Trial Lawyers Am., Jaycees (legal counsel, bd. dirs. 1975-77). Republican. Jewish. Lodge: Eagles (Springfield) (legal counsel). Avocations: fishing, hunting. General corporate, Personal injury, Real property. Office: 714 Plaza Towers Springfield MO 65804

SEIGER, MARK BRIAN, lawyer; b. N.Y.C., June 18, 1955; s. Harvey Norman and Gloria (Lupatkin) S.; m. Eileen Judy Schor, Oct. 30, 1982. BS summa cum laude, U. Hartford, 1978; JD, Case Western Res. U., 1981; LLM, Georgetown U., 1983. Bar: Conn. 1981, U.S. Dist. Ct. Conn. 1982. Assoc. Halloran, Sage, Phelon & Hagarty, Hartford, Conn., 1981—. Co-inventor zinc electrode for nickel-zinc battery. Leader young fellowship Hartford Jewish Fedn., West Hartford, 1985—. Mem. Conn. Bar Assn. (chmn. subcom. civil justice 1985—), Assn. Trial Lawyers Am., Alpha Chi. Democrat. Club: University (Hartford). Avocations: squash, golf, skiing. Federal civil litigation, State civil litigation, Banking. Home: 39 Penn Dr West Hartford CT 06109 Office: Halloran Sage Phelon & Hagarty One Financial Plaza Hartford CT 06103

SEILLER, BILL VICTOR, lawyer; b. Louisville, Aug. 20, 1931; s. Edward F. and Ruth (Blake) S.; m. Lillian Henseler, Oct. 25, 1958; 1 child, Susan E. BS, U. Ky., 1955; JD, U. Ill., 1958. Bar: Ky. 1958, U.S. Dist. Ct. (ea. and we. dists.) Ky., U.S. Ct. Appeals (5th and 6th cirs.). Ptnr. Jackson & Seiller, Louisville, 1958-62, Seiller & Seiller, Louisville, 1962-64, Ewen, MacKenzic & Peden, Louisville, 1964-84, Rice, Porter & Seiller, Louisville, 1984—; cons. VA, Louisville, 1976-86. Sec. Nature Ctr., Louisville, 1984-87; bd. dirs. Actors Louisville, 1966-86, Citizens for Better Judges, 1985—. Served to 1st lt. U.S. Army, 1955-56. Democrat. Family and matrimonial, State civil litigation, Federal civil litigation. Home: 2316 Crosshill Rd Louisville KY 40206 Office: Rice Porter & Seiller 2200 Meidinger Tower Louisville KY 40202

SEITELMAN, MARK ELIAS, lawyer; b. N.Y.C., Apr. 14, 1955; s. Leo Henry and Pearl (Elias) S. BA, Bklyn. Coll., 1976; JD, Bklyn. Law Sch., 1979. Bar: N.Y. 1980, U.S. Dist. Ct. (ea. and so. dists.) N.Y. 1980, U.S. Dist. Ct. (no. dist.) N.Y. 1985. Law asst. Criminal Ct., Bklyn., 1979; law clk. N.Y. Supreme Ct., Bklyn., 1980; assoc. Gordon & Schectman, N.Y.C., 1981, Lester, Schwab, Katz & Dwyer, N.Y.C., 1981—. Mem. ABA, N.Y. State Bar Assn., N.Y. County Bar Assn., Bklyn. Bar Assn. Insurance, Personal injury, State civil litigation. Home: 920 E 17th St Brooklyn NY 11230 Office: Lester Schwab Katz & Dwyer 120 Broadway New York NY 10271

SEITH, ALEX ROBERT, lawyer; b. Aurora, Ill., July 27, 1934; s. Alex L. and Helen (McKinley) S.; m. Frances Remington, Sept., 1956 (dec. July 1981); children—William, Robert, Kathleen. B.A. magna cum laude, Yale U., 1956; postgrad., U. Munich, Germany, 1956-57; J.D., Harvard U., 1960. Bar: Ill. bar 1961. Assoc. firm Gardner, Carton, Douglas and Carton, Chgo., 1961-63, Lord, Bissell and Brook, Chgo., 1963-69; ptnr. Lord, Bissell and Brook, 1970—; commentator ABC, Chgo.; dir. Paddock Publs. Contbr. numerous articles on fgn. affairs, econs. and politics to various newspapers; syndicated weekly newspaper columnist, 1971—; pub. Inside Ill. Politics newsletter, 1981-84. Mem. Presdl. Adv. Bd. on Ambassadorial Appointments, 1977-81; Democratic candidate for U.S. Senate, Ill., 1978; dep. chmn. Fgn. Affairs Task Force, Dem. Nat. Com., 1974-76; pres. Internat. Visitors Centre of Chgo., 1968-70; chmn. Zoning Bd. of Appeals, Cook County, Ill., 1969—; pres. Chgo. Council Fgn. Relations, 1968-71, chmn. adv. bd., 1971-73; 1st v.p. Young Dem. Clubs Am., 1967-69; county chmn. Young Dems. Cook County, 1965-66. Served to capt. U.S. Army, 1960-61. Decorated Order of Merit, French Legion of Honor, 1974; recipient Superior Public Service award Cook County, Ill., 1975; Woodrow Wilson scholar; Rotary Internat. fellow, 1956-57. Mem. Am. Assn. Comparative Study of Law, Am. Fgn. Law Assn., Chgo. Bar Assn., Am. Bar Assn., Ill. Bar Assn., Harvard Law Assn. (nat. v.p. 1973-74), Harvard Law Soc. Ill. (pres. 1972-73). Private international, General corporate, Insurance. Office: 115 S LaSalle Lord Bissell & Brook Chicago IL 60603

SEITZ, COLLINS JACQUES, judge; b. Wilmington, Del., June 20, 1914; s. George Hilary and Margaret Jane (Collins) S.; m. Virginia Anne Day; children: Virginia Anne, Collins Jacques, Mark, Stephen. A.B., U. Del., 1937, LL.D., 1962; LL.B., U. Va., 1940; LL.D., Widener Coll., 1975, Villanova U. Sch. Law, 1983, Cath. U., 1985. Bar: Del. 1940. Vice chancellor Del., 1946; chancellor 1951-66; judge U.S. Ct. Appeals, 3d Circuit, 1966—, chief judge, 1971-84. Recipient James J. Hoey award, 1954; award NCCJ, 1957; Pro Ecclesia et Pontifice (papal award), 1965. Mem. Am., Del. bar assns. Democrat. Roman Catholic. Club: Wilmington. Office: US Courthouse Federal Bldg 844 King St Wilmington DE 19801 *

SEITZINGER, EDWARD FRANCIS, lawyer; b. Mapleton, Iowa, Apr. 3, 1916; s. John and Catherine Emma (Griffin) S.; m. Marian Bernice Westerberg, June 27, 1943; 1 child, Pam Kathleen. Student Iowa State U., 1935-36, 37-38; B.S., S.D. State U., 1942; J.D. cum laude, U. Iowa, 1947. Bar: Iowa 1947, U.S. Supreme Ct. 1955. Counsel Iowa Farm Bur. Fedn. and Affiliated Cos., 1947-58, asst. gen. counsel, 1958-78, gen. counsel, 1978-82; mem. Iowa Merit Employment Commn., 1982-87, Alcoholic Beverage Comm., 1987—. Bd. dirs. Legal Aid Soc. Polk County, Iowa, 1970-72; trustee Lutheran Home for Aging, 1967-75. Served with U.S. Army, World War II. Mem. ABA, Iowa State Bar Assn. (bd. govs. 1972-73, 73-75), Polk County Bar Assn. (pres. 1969-70), Def. Research Inst. (bd. dirs. 1968-75, v.p. pub. relations 1968-71, v.p. adminstr. 1972-73, pres. 1973-74, chmn. 1974-75), Nat. Conf. Local Def. Groups (chmn. 1973-77), Nat. Assn. Ind. Insurers, Fedn. Ins. Counsel (v.p. 1968-69, bd. dirs. 1970-72, v.p. 1974-75), Internat. Assn. Ins. Counsel, Iowa Def. Counsel Assn. (1st pres. 1964-65, bd. dirs. 1964—), Iowa Conf. Bar Assn. Presidents (bd. dirs. 1969-71, v.p. 1971-73, pres. 1974-79), Iowa Life Ins. Assn. (v.p. 1980-82, bd. dirs. 1979-82), Am. Council Life Ins., Nat. Rifle Assn., Iowa Farm Bur. Fedn., Am. Farm Bur. Fedn. Republican. Lutheran. Clubs: Des Moines Golf & Country, Des Moines. Lodges: Masons, Shriners. General corporate, General corporate, Insurance. Home: 1223 Cummins Pkwy Des Moines IA 50311

SELAK, ROBERT ALLEN, lawyer; b. Wheeling, W.Va., Sept. 5, 1954; s. Frank Robert and Anne Cecilia (Strauss) S.; m. Carla Selak, May 21, 1983. BS, Wheeling Coll., 1976; JD, Harvard U., 1979. Bar: Ohio 1979, U.S. Dist. Ct. (so. dist.) Ohio 1979. Ptnr. Smith & Schnacke, Cin. and Dayton, Ohio, 1979—. Mem. ABA, Ohio Bar Assn., Cin. Bar Assn., Dayton Bar Assn., Nat. Assn. Bond Lawyers. Democrat. Roman Catholic. Avocations: golf, travel. Municipal bonds, Real property, Contracts commercial. Office: Smith & Schnacke 511 Walnut St 2900 Du Bois Tower Cincinnati OH 45202

SELFRIDGE, CALVIN, lawyer; b. Evanston, Ill., Dec. 20, 1933; s. Calvin Frederick and Violet Luella (Bradley) S.; BA, Northwestern U., 1956; JD, U. Chgo., 1960. Admitted to Ill. bar, 1961; trust officer Continental Ill. Nat. Bank & Trust Co. Chgo., 1961-71; individual practice law, Chgo., 1972-76; mem. firm Howington, Elworth, Osswald & Hough, Chgo., 1976-79; individual practice law, 1979—; pres., dir. Des Plaines Pub. Co., Northwest Newspapers Corp. Pres., bd. dirs. Scholarship Fund Found., 1965—; trustee Lawrence Hall Sch. for Boys, 1982—. Served with AUS, 1959. Mem. Chgo., Am., Ill. bar assns., Law Club Chgo., Legal Club Chgo., Chi Psi, Phi Delta Phi. Republican. Congregationalist. Clubs: Attic (gov., sec.), Univ. Racquet (Chgo.); Balboa (Mazatlan); Indian Hill Country. General corporate, Probate, Real property. Home: 1410 N State Pkwy Chicago IL 60610 Office: 135 S LaSalle St Suite 2120 Chicago IL 60603

SELIG, JOEL LOUIS, lawyer, educator; b. Boston, Apr. 12, 1944; s. William Max and Ruth Horton (Berger) S.; m. Ruth Mildred Osterweis, Oct. 6, 1968; children—William Osterweis, Deborah Osterweis. A.B., Harvard U., 1965, J.D., 1968. Bar: Mass. 1968, U.S. Dist. Ct. Mass. 1969, U.S. Supreme Ct. 1973, U.S. Ct. Appeals (9th cir.) 1974, U.S. Ct. Appeals (D.C. cir.) 1974, U.S. Ct. Appeals (5th cir.) 1975, D.C. 1976, U.S. Ct. Appeals (6th cir.) 1976, U.S. Dist. Ct. D.C. 1976, U.S. Ct. Appeals (10th cir.) 1977, U.S. Ct. Appeals (11th cir.) 1981. Atty. Mass. Law Reform Inst., Boston, 1969; atty., employment sect., civil rights div. Dept. Justice, Washington, 1969-73, atty., appellate sect., 1977-78, dep. chief, housing and credit sect., 1978-79, dep. chief, gen. litigation sect., 1979-82, sr. trial atty., fed. enforcement sect., 1982-83; dir. govt. employment discrimination project Lawyers' Com. for Civil Rights Under Law, Washington, 1973-77; vis. prof. law U. Wyo. Coll. Law, Laramie, 1983-84, prof. law, 1984—; temporary recorder Supreme Ct. Wyo. Permanent Rules Adv. Com., 1983-84, mem., reporter, 1984—. Legal education, Federal civil litigation, Civil rights. Office: Univ Wyo Coll Law University Station PO Box 3035 Laramie WY 82071

SELINGER, CARL M., legal educator, dean; b. 1934. B.A., U. Calif.-Berkeley, 1955; J.D., Harvard U., 1958. Bar: Calif. 1958, Hawaii 1976, Mich. 1980, W.Va. 1983. Pvt. practice, Calif., 1958-59; teaching fellow Harvard U., Cambridge, Mass., 1960-61; prof. law Albany (N.Y.) Coll., 1961-63, U. N.Mex., Albuquerque, 1963-68; acad. dean Bard Coll., Annandale-on-Hudson, N.Y., 1968-75; prof. sch. law, assoc. dean U. Hawaii, Honolulu, 1975-79; dean Sch. Law, U. Detroit, 1979-82; dean Coll. Law, W.Va. U., Morgantown, 1982—; cons. Legal education. Office: WVa U Coll Law Morgantown WV 26506

SELINGER, JERRY ROBIN, lawyer; b. Peekskill, N.Y., Nov. 3, 1947; s. Philip R. and Helen D. (Klein) S.; m. Barbara D. Wax, Aug. 2, 1969; children—Elise, Scott. B.S. in Engr. Sci., SUNY-Buffalo, 1969; M.S., Columbia U., 1971; J.D., George Washington U., 1975. Bar: Md. 1975, D.C. 1976, U.S. Ct. Appeals (fed. cir.) 1977, U.S. Supreme Ct. 1978, Tex. 1980, U.S. Ct. Appeals (5th and 11th cirs.) 1981, U.S. Ct. Appeals (3d cir.) 1982. Atty. firm Arent, Fox, Kintner, Plotkin & Kahn, Washington, 1975-79, Richards, Harris & Medlock, Dallas, 1979-82; mem., dir. Baker, Smith & Mills Dallas, 1982—. Contbr. articles to profl. jours. Mem. ABA, Tex. Bar Assn. (treas. intellectual property law sect. 1983), Dallas Bar Assn., Tex. Young Lawyers Assn. (bd. dirs. 1984-86, Pres.'s award 1986), Am. Patent Law Assn., Dallas Assn. Young Lawyers (sec. 1983, treas. 1984), Order of Coif, Phi Delta Phi. Federal civil litigation, State civil litigation, Trademark and copyright. Home: 7318 Yamini Dallas TX 75230 Office: Baker Smith & Mills 500 LTV Ctr 2001 Ross Ave Dallas TX 75201

SELKIRK, ALEXANDER MACDONALD, JR., lawyer; b. Jamaica, N.Y., Oct. 2, 1943; s. Alexander MacDonald and Anne (Roth) S.; m. Joanne Patricia Diskant, July 21, 1974; children: Marianne C., Victoria L. BA in Polit. Sci., St. Johns U., Jamaica, 1965; JD, N.Y. Law Sch., 1970, LLM in Trade Regulation, NYU, 1973. Bar: N.Y. 1971, U.S. Dist. Ct. (so. and ea. dists.) N.Y. 1972, U.S. Ct. Appeals (2d cir.) 1972, U.S. Supreme Ct. 1976. Sr. staff atty. Hartford Ins. Co., N.Y.C., 1971-74; assoc. Richard C. Mooney, Esq., Hempstead, N.Y., 1974-77; sr. trial atty. Home Ins. Co., Huntington Station, N.Y., 1978-80; asst. county atty. Suffolk County, Hauppauge, N.Y., 1980—; arbitrator Suffolk County Dist. Ct. 10th Jud. Dist., 1982—. Contbr. articles to numerous legal publs. Committeeman Suffolk County Rep. Com., Ronkonkoma, N.Y., 1977—; del. 10th Jud. Dist. Conv. Suffolk County, 1981-84; v.p. Holbrook Rep. Club, 1979-81, pres., 1981-83; bd. dirs. Holbrook Youth Devel. Corp., 1985—; pilot legal officer Nassau sr. squadron CAP, 1978-84. Served to capt. JAGC, N.Y. Army Nat. Guard, 1983—. Mem. Am. Arbitration Assn. (comml. arbitrator), Suffolk County Bar Assn., N.Y. State Bar Assn., Internat. Platform Assn., NYU Alumni Assn., Holbrook C. of C. (bd. dirs. 1981—, v.p. 1987—), Aircraft Owners and Pilots Assn., Internat. Platform Assn. Roman Catholic. Club: Great Neck Sportsman's (N.Y.). Lodges: K.C. (adv. 1981-84, trustee 1984—, 3d v.p. 1986—), Lions (bd. dirs. 1985-86, 3d v.p. 1986-87, pres. 1987—). General practice, Personal injury, Trademark and copyright. Home: 12 Glensummer Rd Holbrook NY 11741 Office: Suffolk County Dept Law Vets Meml Hwy Hauppauge NY 11788

SELMAN, ROLAND WOOTEN, III, lawyer; b. Kansas City, Mo., Aug. 16, 1941; s. Roland Wooten Jr. and Dixie R. (Chambliss) S.; m. Deirdre Schumacher, Mar. 10, 1979. Student, U. Kans., 1959-61, Stetson U., 1961-63; BA, U. Mo., Kansas City, 1963; JD, U. Calif., Hastings, 1971. Bar: Calif. 1972, U.S. Ct. Appeals (9th cir.) 1975, U.S. Supreme Ct. 1975, D.C. 1979, U.S. Ct. Appeals (D.C. cir.) 1980, U.S. Ct. Appeals (Fed. cir.) 1983. Assoc. Pillsbury, Madison & Sutro, San Francisco, 1971-79, gen. ptnr., 1979—; judge pro tem Mcpl. Ct., San Francisco, 1984—. Served to lt. USN, 1963-68, Vietnam. Decorated D.F.C., Air medal. Mem. ABA (anti-trust sect., litigation sect.), San Francisco Bar Assn., Bar Assn. of San Francisco, Order of Coif. Republican. Mem. Christian Ch. Avocations: gardening, video, scuba diving. Federal civil litigation, Antitrust, Administrative and regulatory. Home: 130 Currey Ave Sausalito CA 94965 Office: Pillsbury Madison & Sutro 225 Bush St San Francisco CA 94104

SELOVER, R. EDWIN, corporate lawyer; b. 1945. BA, Union Coll., 1967; JD, U. Minn., 1972. With Pub. Service Electric & Gas Co., Newark, 1972-80, gen. counsel, 1980-83, v.p. gen. counsel, 1983—. Served with AUS, 1969-71. Office: Pub Service Electric & Gas Co 80 Park Plaza Newark NJ 07101 *

SELTZER, JEFFREY LLOYD, lawyer, investment banker; b. Bklyn., July 27, 1956; s. Bernard and Sue (Harris) S.; m. Ana Isabel Sifre, Aug. 24, 1985. BS in Econs. cum laude, U. Pa., 1978; JD, Georgetown U., 1981. Bar: N.Y. 1982. Assoc. Austrian, Lance & Stewart, N.Y.C., 1981-85; assoc., gen. counsel, asst. v.p. Shearson Lehman Bros. Inc., N.Y.C., 1986, v.p., dir. swap fin. adminstrn., 1986—. Author: The U.S. Greeting Card Market, 1977, Starting and Organizing a Business, 1984. Mem. nat. adv. council U.S. Small Bus. Adminstrn., Washington, 1982—; mem. small bus. adv. council Rep. Nat. Com., Washington, 1984—; mem. strategy council Fund For Am.'s Future, Washington, 1985—; advisor New Yorkers for Lew Lehrman, N.Y.C., 1981-82; policy analyst Reagan-Bush com., Arlington, Va., 1980. Named one of Outstanding Young Men Am., 1981. Mem. ABA. General corporate, Private international, Securities. Home: 45 W 60th St #21J New York NY 10023 Office: Shearson Lehman Bros Inc Am Express Tower World Financial Ctr New York NY 10285-1200

SELTZER, LEON EUGENE, publisher, copyright lawyer; b. Auburn, Maine, Aug. 14, 1918; s. Samuel and Sadye (Shapiro) S.; m. Lenore Chafetz, Mar. 14, 1948; children—Deborah, Janet, Marcia. A.B., Columbia U., 1940; J.D., Stanford U., 1974. Bar: Calif. 1974, U.S. Dist. Ct. (no. dist.) Calif. 1974. Asst. editor Columbia U. Press, 1939-41, editor, 1946-52, sales promotion mgr., 1952-56; dir. Stanford U. Press, 1956-83, dir. emeritus, 1983—; of counsel Majestic, Gallagher, Parsons, and Siebert, San Francisco, 1983—; asst. editor Columbia Ency., 1946-50; editor Columbia Lippincott Gazetteer of the World, 1946-52; scholar-in-residence Center for Advanced Study in Behavioral Scis., 1975-76. Contbr. short stories, articles and, verse to nat. mags.; author: Exemptions and Fair Use in Copyright, 1977. Vice pres. Santa Clara County Bd. Edn., 1966-71. Served from pvt. to maj. C.E. AUS, 1941-46, PTO. Guggenheim fellow, 1975-76. Mem. Assn. Am. Univ. Presses (pres. 1968-69), Copyright Soc. U.S.A. Trademark and copyright, Entertainment, Computer. Home: 2 Pearce Mitchell Pl Stanford CA 94305 Office: Majestic Gallagher Parsons & Siebert 101 California St San Francisco CA 94111

SELVIN, PAUL PHILLIP, lawyer; b. Hartford, Conn., July 23, 1917; s. Meyer J. and Molly (Podorowsky) S.; m. Marian Glater, Oct. 25, 1946; children—Molly, Peter. A.B. magna cum laude, Harvard, 1939; LL.B. cum laude, U. Conn., 1949. Bar: Calif. 1950. Practice law, specializing in trial and appellate law Los Angeles, 1951—; ptnr. Selvin Weiner, 1962—; teaching fellow, acting asst. prof. law Stanford U. Law Sch., 1949-51; prof., lectr. Loyola U. Law Sch., Los Angeles, 1953-80; lectr. Continuing Edn. of Bar, intermittently, 1961—. Contbr. articles to legal jours., short stories to lit. mags. Served with AUS, 1942-46. Mem. Am. Arbitration Assn. (arbitrator), Am. Civil Liberties Union, State Bar Calif., Los Angeles, Beverly Hills bar assns., Calif. Acad. Appellate Lawyers (pres. 1978-79), Phi Beta Kappa. Club: Harvard of So. Calif. Home: 11556 Coolidge Pl Los Angeles CA 90066 Office: 1900 Ave of the Stars Los Angeles CA 90067

SEMBROSKI, ROBERT EDMUND, lawyer. s. Edmund S. and Catherine A. (Munn) S. BA, Ind. U., 1975, JD, 1978. Bar: Ind. 1979, U.S. Dist. Ct. (no. and so. dists.) Ind. 1979. Sole practice Bloomington, Ind. Bd. dirs. Ind. Guardian ad Litem Ct. Appointed Spl. Adv. Assn., Inc., Monroe County Guardian ad Litem Project, community service council Bloomington and Monroe Counties, Inc. Mem. Ind. Bar Assn., Phi Beta Kappa. Club: Bloomington Bicycle. Juvenile, Family and matrimonial, Consumer commercial. Office: 103 N College 206 Bloomington IN 47401

SEMEL, MARTIN IRA, lawyer; b. N.Y.C., June 26, 1934; s. Joseph and Clara (Rosenblatt) S.; m. Barbara Peltz, June 14, 1956; children—Deborah, Richard, Rhonda. B.A., Cornell U., 1956, LL.B., 1959. Bar: N.Y. 1959, U.S. Dist. Ct. (so. dist.) N.Y. 1963, U.S. Ct. Appeals (2d cir.) 1963, U.S. Supreme Ct. 1964. Assoc., Bierman & Lass, N.Y.C., 1959-62; sole practice, N.Y.C., 1963-64; ptnr. Semel & Patrusky, 1964-69, Semel, Patrusky & Buchsbaum, N.Y.C., 1969—; Chmn. Legal Codes Commn. Inc. Village of Hewlett Bay Park, N.Y., 1974-75. Served as 1st lt. U.S. Army, 1957-63 Res. Mem. N.Y. State Bar Assn., N.Y. State Trial Lawyers Assn., Nat. Bar Assn., Am. Trial Lawyers Assn. Jewish. Admiralty, General corporate, Real property. Home: 159 Meadowview Ave Hewlett NY 11557 Office: Semel Patrusky & Buchsbaum 22 Cortlandt St New York NY 10007

SEMENTO, LAWRENCE JAMES, lawyer; b. West Milford, N.J., Jan. 17, 1952; s. James and Joan A. (Peterson) S.; m. Sharron A. Boone, Nov. 13, 1982; children: Todd, Nicole, Kara. BA, U. S.C., 1974; JD, U. Fla., 1981. Bar: Fla. 1981, U.S. Dist. Ct. (mid. dist.) Fla. 1983. Asst. mgr. Zales Jewelers, Winter Haven, Fla., 1974-77; sales assoc. Associated Realty, Mt. Dora, Fla., 1977-78; ptnr. Huebsch & Semento, Eustis, Fla., 1981—. Mem. ABA, Lake County Bar Assn. Republican. Presbyterian. Lodges: Kiwanis (past pres. Golden Triangle Eustis), Elks. Avocation: tennis. State civil litigation, General practice, Family and matrimonial. Home: 300 W Atwater Ave PO Box 680 Eustis FL 32726-0680 Office: Huebsch & Semento One Park Ave Eustis FL 32726

SEMERJIAN, EVAN YERVANT, lawyer; b. Boston, Feb. 27, 1940; s. Nubar and Alice (Arabian) S.; m. Barbara N. Veach, Dec. 27, 1969; children—Sarah, Jessica, Laura. A.B., Harvard U., 1961, LL.M., 1967; LL.B., U. Pa., 1964. Bar: Mass. 1964, U.S. Tax Ct. 1969, U.S. Supreme Ct. 1974. Law clk. Mass. Supreme Jud. Ct., 1964-65; faculty Harvard U. Law Sch., 1965-67; assoc. Hale & Dorr, Boston, 1967-71, jr. ptnr., 1971-75, sr. ptnr., 1975—, mem. exec. com., 1981-83; faculty, lectr. Mass. Continuing Legal Edn.-New Eng. Law Inst., 1980-85; trustee pvt. trusts, 1978—; Chmn. Citizens Aviation Policy Assn., 1973-76; moderator The Advocates, Nat. Pub. TV, 1973-74; mem. Gov.'s Hanscom Field Task Force, 1974-77; mem. Town of Lincoln (Mass.) Bd. Assessors, 1977-80; mem. Harvard U. 25th Reunion Steering and Gift Coms., 1985-86. Mem. ABA, Mass. Bar Assn. (regional del. 1981-82, chmn. spl. com. appeals tax bd. 1982-85), Boston Bar Assn., Mass. Bar Found., U. Pa. Law Alumni Soc. (bd. mgrs. 1985-87). Clubs: Harvard (Boston); Harvard Faculty (Cambridge, Mass.). Author legal articles and publs. Federal civil litigation, State civil litigation, State and local taxation. Office: Hale & Dorr 60 State St Boston MA 02109

SEMPLE, JAMES WILLIAM, lawyer; b. Phila., Nov. 18, 1943; s. Calvin James and Marie (Robinson) S.; m. Ellen Burns, Nov. 26, 1966; children: Megan Ward, Luke Robinson. AB, St. Josephs U., Phila., 1965; JD, Villanova U., 1974. Bar: Del. 1974, U.S. Dist. Ct. Del. 1974, D.C. 1975, U.S. Ct. Appeals (3d cir.) 1982. Assoc. Flanzer & Isaacs, Wilmington, Del., 1974-83; ptnr. Morris, James, Hitchens & Williams, Wilmington, 1983—; lectr. numerous seminars. Legal advisor Alzheimer's Disease and Related Disorders Greater Phila., Phila. and Wilmington, Del., 1980—. Ashton scholar, 1965-66. Mem. ABA (litigation sect., products liability com., torts and ins. practice sect.), Del. Bar Assn. (mem. exec. com. 1978, 80, 81, asst. sec. 1980, sec. 1981, chmn. torts and ins. practice sect. 1982-84), Def. Research Inst. (products liability sub com.), Fedn. Ins. and Corp. Counsel, Assn. Trial Lawyers Am., Del. Trial Lawyers Assn., Am. Judicature Soc., Am. Soc. Law and Medicine. Democrat. Roman Catholic. Clubs: Wilmington Country (Greenville, Del.). State civil litigation, Insurance, Personal injury. Home: 103 Brook Valley Rd Greenville DE 19807 Office: Morris James Hitchens & Williams PO Box 2306 Wilmington DE 19899

SENESCU, STUART, lawyer; b. Chgo., July 10, 1947; s. Louis and Phyllis (Palace) S.; m. Marlene Rubin. BS, U. Ill., 1969; MBA, No. Ill. U., 1970; JD, Ind. U., 1973. Bar: Ill. 1973, U.S. Dist. Ct. (no. dist.) Ill. 1973. Staff atty. Continental Ill. Nat. Bank, Chgo., 1973-76; from assoc. atty. to atty. to gen. atty. United Air Lines Inc., Chgo., 1976—. Recipient CPR Merit award Lake County chpt. Am. Heart Assn., 1982, 10 yr. Service award Nat. Ski Patrol System, 1986. Mem. ABA. Avocations: skiing, bicycling. Administrative and regulatory, General corporate, Aviation. Office: United Air Lines Law Div PO Box 66100 Chicago IL 60666

SENKER, RICHARD C., lawyer; b. Phila., Dec. 9, 1953; s. A. Leonard and Melva (Carson) S.; m. Patricia A. Abnett, June 7, 1975; 1 child, Erin Hillary. BA, Colgate U., 1975; JD, Villanova U., 1978. Bar: Pa. 1978, U.S. Dist. Ct. (ea. dist.) Pa. 1980, U.S. Supreme Ct. 1981. Assoc. Bacine & Kleitman, Norristown, Pa., 1978-79, Sosnov & Sosnov, Norristown, 1979-80; ptnr. Maida & Senker, Norristown, 1980-84; sole practice Norristown, 1984—. Pres. Eastown Twp. Neighborhood Watch, Devon, Pa., 1984-86. Mem. Pa. Bar Assn., Montgomery Bar Assn., Chester County Bar Assn., Assn. Trial Lawyers Am., Pa. Trial Lawyers Assn., Berwyn Devon Bus. and Profl. Assn. (pres. 1983-85), Wayne Area Jaycees (pres. 1983-84). Avocation: ice hockey. Federal civil litigation, State civil litigation, Personal injury. Office: 526 DeKalb St Norristown PA 19401

SENKEWICZ, MARY E., lawyer; b. N.Y.C., Feb. 22, 1955; d. Peter Michael Senkewicz and Clara Fae (Zoucha) Kennedy. BA, Cabrini Coll., 1976; JD, St. John's U., Jamaica, N.Y., 1980. Bar: N.Y. 1981, Ill. 1981, U.S. Ct. Appeals (7th cir.) 1981, Wyo. 1983, U.S. Dist. Ct. Wyo. 1983, U.S. Ct. Appeals (10th cir.) 1983. Instr. John Marshall Law Sch., Chgo., 1980-82; law clk. to presiding justice U.S. Ct. Appeals (qoth cir.), Cheyenne, Wyo., 1982-83; exec. dir. Wyo. Bar Assn., Cheyenne, 1983—. Mem. tech. staff Cheyenne Civic Ctr., 1983—; campaign worker Mike Sullivan for Gov., Cheyenne, 1986—. Mem. ABA. Democrat. Roman Catholic. Avocations: sports, theatre, reading, movies, hunting. Administrative and regulatory, Jurisprudence. Home: 300 E 26th St Cheyenne WY 82001 Office: Wyo Bar Assn 2111 Central Ave Cheyenne WY 82001

SENN, LAURENCE VAUGHN, JR., lawyer; b. Charlotte, N.C., Jan. 15, 1945; s. Laurence Vaughn and Rose Elaine (McDowell) S.; m. Katharine Ruffner, Sept. 4, 1965; children: Laurence Vaughn, Laura McDowell, Katharine Roberta. AB in Econs., U. N.C., 1965, JD, 1969. Bar: N.Y. 1970, U.S. Dist. Ct. (so., ea. and no. dists.) N.Y. 1971, U.S. Ct. Appeals (2d and 3d dists.) 1972, D.C. 1976, U.S. Supreme Ct. 1978. Assoc. Mudge, Rose, Guthrie, Alexander & Ferdon, N.Y.C., 1969-75, ptnr., 1976—. Editor U. N.C. Law Rev., 1969. Mem. ABA, N.Y. State Bar Assn., Assn. of Bar of City of N.Y., Practising Law Inst. (lectr. 1980—), Order of Coif. Republican. Episcopalian. Clubs: Baltusrol (Springfield, N.J.); Beacon Hill (Summit, N.J.). AVocation: golf. Federal civil litigation, State civil litigation, Construction. Office: Mudge Rose Guthrie Alexander & Ferdon 180 Maiden Ln New York NY 10038

SENSENIG, LANA SMITH, lawyer; b. Estherville, Iowa, July 17, 1952; d. Omer Oakley and Gloria Louise (Hudson) S.; m. Philip Campbell Sensenig, May 6, 1978; 1 child, Laura Campbell. BA, Vanderbilt U., 1974; JD with honors, Emory U., 1981. Bar: Ga. 1981, U.S. Dist. Ct. (no. dist.) Ga. 1981, U.S. Ct. Appeals (11th cir.) 1981. Law clk. U.S. Ct. Appeals (5th and 11th cirs.), Atlanta, 1981-82; assoc. Sutherland, Askill & Brennan, Atlanta, 1982-86, King & Spaulding, Atlanta, 1986—. Participant Atlanta Vol. Lawyers, 1982; bd. dirs. Vis. Nurse Assns. Met. Atlanta (United Way Agy.), 1984-86. Mem. ABA (taxation sect., health law com.), Ga. Bar Assn., Atlanta Bar Assn. (health law com.), Am. Acad. Hosp. Attys., Nat. Health Lawyers Assn., 11th Cir. Hist. Soc., Order of Coif. Republican. Methodist. Club: Vanderbilt, Atlanta Yacht. Health, Corporate taxation. Home: 2060 Black Fox Dr NE Atlanta GA 30345 Office: King & Spalding 2500 Trust Co Tower Atlanta GA 30303

SENTELLE, DAVID BRYAN, judge; b. Canton, N.C., Feb. 12, 1943; s. Horace Richard, Jr., and Maude (Ray) S.; m. Jane LaRue Oldham, July 19, 1965; children—Sharon Rene, Reagan Elaine, Rebecca Grace. A.B., U. N.C., 1965, J.D. with honors, 1968. Bar: N.C. 1968, U.S. Dist. Ct. (we. dist.) N.C. 1969, U.S. Ct. Appeals (4th cir.) 1970. Assoc. firm Uzzell & Dumont, Asheville, N.C., 1968-70; asst. U.S. atty. Charlotte, N.C., 1970-74; dist. judge, Charlotte, N.C., 1974-77; ptnr. firm Tucker, Hicks, Sentelle, Moon & Hodge, P.A., Charlotte, 1977-85; judge U.S. Dist. Ct. (we. dist.) N.C., Charlotte, 1985—; adj. prof. dept. criminal justice U. N.C.-Charlotte. Chmn. Mecklenburg County Republican Com., 1978-80; chmn. N.C. State Rep. Conv., 1979, 80. Demeron fellow, 1967. Mem. ABA, Fed. Bar Assn. (chpt. pres. 1975), Mecklenburg County Bar Assn. Baptist. Lodges: Masons, Scottish Rite, Shrine. Contbr. writings to publs. in field. Criminal, State civil litigation, Federal civil litigation. Office: US Dist Ct PO Box 212 Asheville NC 28802 *

SENTER, LYONEL THOMAS, JR., federal judge; b. Fulton, Miss., July 30, 1933; s. L. T. and Eva Lee (Jetton) S.; (married). B.S., U. So. Miss., 1956; LL.B., U. Miss., 1959. Bar: Miss. 1959. County pros. atty. 1960-64, U.S. commr., 1966-68; judge Miss. Circuit Ct., Circuit 1, 1968-80, U.S. Dist. Ct. for No. Dist. Miss., 1980—. Mem. Miss. State Bar. Democrat. Jurisprudence. Office: PO Box 925 Aberdeen MS 39730

SEQUEIRA, MANUEL ALEXANDRE, JR., lawyer; b. Shanghai, China, Oct. 31, 1931, came to U.S. 1946, naturalized 1954; s. Manuel Alexandre and Cecilia Maria (Xavier) S.; m. Angela Maria Lopes, Feb. 15, 1958; children—Joseph, Michael, Peter, Robert. A.B., U. Notre Dame, 1955, J.D., 1956. Bar: N.Y. 1957, U.S. Dist. Ct. (so. and ea. dists.) N.Y. 1958, U.S. Ct. Appeals (2d cir.) 1967, U.S. Supreme Ct. 1971. Assoc. atty. Hill, Rivkins, Carey, Loesberg, O'Brien & Mulroy, N.Y.C., 1956-67; litigation house counsel Am. Internat. Group (Sequeira, Rienzo & Gillies), N.Y.C., 1967-82; sole practice, Yorktown Heights, N.Y., 1983—. Mem. ABA (tort and ins. practice sect.), N.Y. State Bar Assn. (ins., negligence & compensation law sect.), N.Y. County Lawyers Assn., Maritime Law Assn. U.S. (proctor in admiralty), Assn. Trial Lawyers Am., Def. Research Inst., Def. Assn. N.Y., Christian Legal Soc., Am. Arbitration Assn., (panel of arbitrators), Assn. Average Adjusters of U.S. Roman Catholic. Admiralty, Insurance, Personal injury. Office: 2168 Pondfield Ct Yorktown Heights NY 10598

SERAFINI, LINDA ANN, lawyer; b. Salem, Mass., Nov. 21, 1951; d. John Richard and Ann (Arena) S. BA, U. Pa., 1973; MLS, U. Mich., 1974; JD, Northeastern U., 1981. Bar: Mass. 1981, U.S. Dist. Ct. Mass. 1981. Law clk. to presiding justice Mass. Supreme Jud. Ct., Boston, 1981-82; assoc. Gadsby & Hannah, Boston, 1982-85; atty. The Gillette Co., Boston, 1985—. Mem. ABA, Mass. Bar Assn., Women's Bar Assn. General corporate. Home: 73 Esterbrook Rd Acton MA 01720 Office: The Gillette Co Prudential Tower Bldg Boston MA 02199

SERATA, SAMUEL JACOB, lawyer; b. Bridgeton, N.J., Sept. 6, 1929; s. Lewis and Gertrude C. Serata; m. Meredith Ann McGonigle, Dec. 7, 1951 (dec. Jan. 4, 1978); children: Geoffrey Peter, Christopher Lewis, Tamara Serata Madeiras, Sara Deborah Serata Sharkey. BS, Cornell U., 1951; JD, Dickinson Sch. Law, 1957. Bar: NJ 1957, U.S. Dist. Ct. N.J. 1957, U.S. Supreme Ct. 1966, U.S. Ct. Appeals (3d cir.) 1976. Sole practice, Bridgeton, N.J., from 1958; ptnr. Serata & Stanger, Bridgeton, 1974-78, Serata, Stanger & Seeley, P.C., 1978; sole practice Samuel J. Serata, P.C., Bridgeton, 1978—; mcpl. ct. judge, Vineland, N.J., 1982-85, Sea Isle City, N.J., 1983-87; intermcpl. ct. of Weymouth Twp., Corbin City and Estell Manor; presiding judge mcpl. cts. Vicinage I (Atlantic and Cape May) Counties. Pres. Bridgeton Area United Way, 1971-72, bd. dirs., 1962-82; bd. dirs. Bridgeton YMCA, 1963-82. Served to 1st lt. USAF, 1951-53. Mem. ABA, Am. Judicature Soc., N.J. State Bar Assn., County Bar Assn. Republican. Clubs: Greenwich Yacht, Masons. Jurisprudence, Contracts commercial, Real property. Address: 20 Franklin St Bridgeton NJ 08302

SERBIN, RICHARD MARTIN, lawyer; b. Pitts., Dec. 21, 1947; s. Bernard Serbin and Ella (Stone) Kublanov; m. Francie M. Buncher, June 2, 1974; children: Lawrence B., Haley E., Joshua H. BA, U. Pitts., 1970, JD, Duquesne U., 1974. Bar: Pa. 1974, U.S. Dist. Ct. (mid. dist.) Pa. 1974, U.S. Dist. Ct. (we. dist.) Pa. 1980, U.S. Ct. Appeals (3d cir.) 1981, U.S. Supreme Ct. 1985. Assoc. Barron & Zimmerman, Lewistown, Pa., 1974-77; ptnr. Mullen, Casanave, Carpenter & Serbin, Altoona, Pa., 1977-80, Levine, Reese & Serbin, Altoona, 1981—; asst. dist. atty. Juniata County, Mifflintown, Pa., 1976-77; instr. Pa. State U., Altoona, 1979-83. Bd. dirs. Jewish Fedn., Altoona, 1980-86, Temple Israel, Altoona, 1983-86, Pleasant Valley Community Living, 1982-86; mem. Big Brothers and Friends of Boys, 1978-80.

Mem. ABA, Ass. Trial Lawyers Am., Pa. Trial Lawyers Assn., Blair County Bar Assn., Juniata County Bar Assn., Allegheny County Bar Assn., Am. Bus. Club. Democrat. Jewish. Avocations: tennis, nautilus. Personal injury, State civil litigation. Home: Brushmeade Hollidaysburg PA 16648 Office: Levine Reese & Serbin 85 Logan Blvd Altoona PA 16602

SERCHUK, IVAN, lawyer; b. N.Y.C., Oct. 13, 1935; s. Israel and Freda (Davis) S.; m. Jessica Bonnie Bacal, Oct. 22, 1972; children: Camille, Bruce Mead, Kira Bacal, Vance Foster. BA, Columbia U., 1957, LLB. Bar: N.Y. 1961, U.S. Dist. Ct. (so. dist.) N.Y. 1963, U.S. Ct. Appeals (2d cir.) 1964, U.S. Tax Ct. 1966. Law clk. to judge U.S. Dist. Ct. (so. dist.) N.Y., 1961-63; assoc. Kaye, Scholer, Fierman, Hays & Handler, 1963-68; dep. supt., counsel N.Y. State Banking Dept., N.Y.C. and Albany, 1968-72; mem. Berle & Berle, 1972-73; spl. counsel N.Y. State Senate Banks Com., 1972; mem. Serchuk & Siwek, White Plains, N.Y., 1974; sr. ptnr. Serchuk Wolfe & Zelermyer, White Plains, 1976—; lectr. Practising Law Inst., 1968-71; bd. dirs. United Orient Bank, N.Y.C. Mem. Assn. Bar City of N.Y., N.Y. Bar Assn. Banking, General corporate. Home: Cross River Rd Katonah NY 10536 Office: 81 Main St White Plains NY 10601

SERINI, JOHN PETER, lawyer; b. Boston, July 31, 1948; s. Peter Arthur and Ann Grace (Chiavaro) S. BA, U. Mass., 1972; JD cum laude, New Eng. Sch. Law, 1981. Bar: Mass. 1981, Colo. 1982, U.S. Dist. Ct. Colo. 1982, U.S. Ct. Appeals (10th cir.) 1982, U.S. Ct. Appeals (D.C. cir.). Assoc. Gorsuch, Kirgis, Denver, 1981-83, Schmidt, Elrod & Wills, Denver, 1983-85; sole practice Denver, 1985—. Served with U.S. Army, 1966-69, Vietnam. Decorated Purple Heart, Air medal. Mem. ABA, Colo. Bar Assn., Denver Bar Assn. Republican. Avocations: music, skiing, bicycling, karate, theatre. Construction, Federal civil litigation, State civil litigation. Office: 180 Cook St #215 Denver CO 80206

SERKA, PHILIP ANGELO, lawyer educator; b. Tacoma, Oct. 29, 1950; s. Joseph and Mary Phyllis (Lovrovich) S.; m. Mary Margaret Foote, May 24, 1975; children—Bradley Philip, Lindsay Dumica. A.A., Tacoma Community Coll., 1971; B.A., U. Wash., 1973; J.D., U. Puget Sound, 1976. Bar: Wash. 1976, U.S. Dist. Ct. (we. dist.) Wash. 1979. Dep. prosecutor Whatcom County, Bellingham, Wash., 1976-80; assoc. Flynn, Adelstein, Sharpe, Bellingham, 1980-82, ptnr., 1983-84; ptnr. Adelstein, Sharpe & Serka, 1984-86, Adelstein & Serka, Bellingham, 1987—; lectr. environ. law and zoning Western Wash. U., Bellingham, 1979, 83, 84. Mem. Bellingham Mcpl. Appeals and Code Rev. Bd., 1979-84, chmn., 1979-83; bd. dirs. Whatcom County-Bellingham Vis. and Conv. Bur., 1986—. Mem. Wash. State Bar Assn. (environ. and land use law sect., lectr. at seminar 1986), Wash. State Trial Lawyers Assn., Wash. State Prosecutors Assn. (com. land use legis. 1978-80), Bellingham C. of C. (Devel. Area Recreational Entertainment div. pageant scholarship com. 1983) Democrat. Roman Catholic. Real property, Environment, General practice. Home: 4707 Fir Tree Way Bellingham WA 98226 Office: Adelstein & Serka 400 N Commercial St Bellingham WA 98225

SERNETT, RICHARD PATRICK, publishing company executive, lawyer; b. Mason City, Iowa, Sept. 8, 1938; s. Edward Frank and Loretta M. (Cavanaugh) S.; m. Janet Ellen Ward, Apr. 20, 1963; children: Susan Ellen, Thomas Ward, Stephen Edward, Katherine Anne. BBA, U. Iowa, 1960, JD, 1963. Bar: Ill. 1965. With Scott, Foresman & Co., Glenview, Ill., 1963-80, house counsel, asst. sec., 1967-70, sec., legal officer, 1970-80; with SFN Cos. Inc., Glenview, Ill., 1980—, v.p. law, sec., 1980-83, sr. v.p., sec., gen. counsel, 1983-86, exec. v.p. and gen. counsel, 1986—; mem. adv. panel on internat. copyright U.S. Dept. State, 1972-75; bd. dirs. Iowa State U. Broadcasting Corp. Mem. ABA (chmn. copyright div. sect. patent, trademark and copyright law 1972-73), Ill. Bar Assn. (chmn. copyright law com. 1978-79), Chgo. Bar Assn., Am. Patent Law Assn. (chmn. copyright matters com. 1972-73, bd. mgrs. 1981-84), Patent Law Assn. Chgo. (chmn. copyright com. 1972-73, 77-78, bd. mgrs. 1979-81), Copyright Soc. U.S.A. (trustee 1972-75, 77-80), Am. Judicature Soc., Am. Soc. Corporate Secs., Assn. Am. Pubs. (chmn. copyright com. 1972-73, vice chmn. 1973-75), Phi Delta Phi, Phi Kappa Theta. Clubs: Met. (Chgo.); North Shore Country (Glenview, Ill.). General corporate. Home: 2071 Glendale Ave Northbrook IL 60062 Office: 1900 E Lake Ave Glenview IL 60025

SEROTA, JAMES IAN, lawyer; b. Chgo., Oct. 20, 1946; s. Louis Henry and Phyllis Estelle (Horner) S.; m. Susan Perlstadt, May 7, 1972; children—Daniel Louis, Jonathan Mark. A.B., Washington U., St. Louis, 1968; J.D. cum laude, Northwestern U., 1971. Bar: Ill. 1971, U.S. Dist. Ct. (no. dist.) Ill. 1972, D.C. 1978, U.S. Supreme Ct. 1978, U.S. Ct. Appeals (D.C. cir.) 1978, U.S. Dist. Ct. (D.C. dist.), U.S. Ct. Claims 1980, N.Y. 1981, U.S. Dist. Ct. (so. dist.) N.Y. 1981, (ea. dist.) N.Y. 1981, U.S. Ct. Appeals (2d cir.) 1983. Trial atty. Antitrust div. U.S. Dept. Justice, Washington, 1971-77; assoc. Bell, Boyd & Lloyd, Washington, 1977-81; of counsel Milman, & Shwergold, N.Y.C., 1981-82; ptnr. Werner, Kennedy & French, N.Y.C., 1982-85; ptnr. Levitsky & Serota, 1985-86; sole practice, N.Y.C., 1987—. Recipient Spl. Achievement award U.S. Dept. Justice, 1976. Mem. ABA, N.Y. State Bar Assn., Assn. Bar City N.Y. Contbr. articles to profl. jours. Editor Law Rev. Northwestern U. Antitrust, Federal civil litigation. Office: 711 Third Ave New York NY 10017

SERRAINO, STEPHEN R., lawyer; b. Portland, Oreg., Dec. 14, 1955; s. Joseph T. and Donna R. (Coons) S. BA with distinction, Ohio Northern U., 1978; JD, Ohio State U., 1981. Bar: Ohio 1981, Mo. 1982, U.S. Dist. Ct. (we. dist.) Mo. 1982, U.S. Dist. Ct. (no. dist.) Ohio 1986. Assoc. Miller & Glynn, P.C., Kansas City, Mo., 1981-83, Knipmeyer, McCann, Fish & Smith, Kansas City, 1983-85, Eastman & Smith, Toledo, 1985-87, Robert M. Anspach Assocs., Toledo, 1987—. Vol. arbitrator Better Bus. Bur. Greater Kansas City, 1983-84; recruiter Ohio No. U. Alumni Recruiting Program, 1986—. Mem. ABA, Mo. Bar Assn., Ohio Bar Assn. Federal civil litigation, State civil litigation, Insurance. Office: Robert M Anspach Assocs 1400 National Bank Bldg Madison at Huron Toledo OH 43604

SERRITELLA, JAMES ANTHONY, lawyer; b. Chgo., July 8, 1942; s. Anthony and Angela (Deleonardis) S.; m. Ruby Ann Amoroso, Oct. 3, 1981. B.A., SUNY-S.I., 1965, Pontifical Gregorian U., Rome, 1966; post-grad., DePaul U., 1966-67; M.A., U. Chgo., 1968, J.D., 1971. Bar: Ill. 1971, U.S. Supreme Ct. 1976, U.S. Tax Ct. 1985. Ptnr. Kirkland & Ellis, Chgo., 1978; ptnr. Reuben & Proctor, Chgo., 1978-86, Mayer, Brown & Platt, Chgo., 1986—; lectr. in field. Contbr. articles to profl. jours. Chmn. exec. bd. DePaul U. Coll. Law Ctr. for Ch./State Studies, 1982—, exec. com. Dean's Vis. Com., 1982—; trustee Mundelein Coll., 1982-86, St. Mary of the Lake Sem., 1982-83, WTTW Chgo. Pub. TV, 1978-81; mem. geriatrics/gerontology steering com. McGaw Med. Ctr. of Northwestern U.; exec. com. of govt. relations com. United Way of Chgo., 1979-84; bd. dirs. Child Care Assn. Ill., 1975-79, Lyric Opera Guild, 1979-84; v.p. Comprehensive Community Services of Met. Chgo., 1976-81. Fellow Am. Bar Found.; mem. ABA, Ill. Bar Assn. (bd. govs.), Chgo. Bar Assn. (com. on evaluation of jud. candidates), Fed. Bar Assn., Ill. Trial Lawyers Assn., Cath. Lawyers Guild (bd. govs.), Canon Law Soc. Am., Diocesan Attys. Assn. (exec. com.), Nat. Health Lawyers Assn., NCCJ (adv. com. on ch., state and taxation), Nat. Cath. Cemetery Conf., Justinian Soc. Lawyers, Cath. Health Assn., Am. Hosp. Assn., Ill. Cath. Hosp. Assn., Am. Assn. Homes for Aging, Ill. Assn. Homes for the Aging. Clubs: Attic, Chgo. Literary, Tavern, Chgo. Athletic Assn. General practice. Address: 19 S LaSalle St Chicago IL 60603

SERRITELLA, WILLIAM DAVID, lawyer; b. Chgo., May 16, 1946; s. William V. and Josephine Dolores (Scalise) S. J.D., U. Ill., Champaign, 1971. Bar: Ill. 1971, U.S. Dist. Ct. (no. and cen. dists.) Ill. 1972, U.S. Ct. Appeals (7th cir.) 1974, U.S. Supreme Ct. 1979. Law clk. U.S. Dist. Ct., Danville, Ill., 1971-72; ptnr. Ross & Hardies, Chgo., 1972—; arbitrator Am. Arbitration Assn. Mem. ABA, Ill. Bar Assn., Chgo. Bar Assn., Western Conf. Ry. Counsel, Nat. Assn. R.R. Trial Counsel (Ill.), Soc. Trial Lawyers. Clubs: Legal, Trial Lawyers (Chicago). Federal civil litigation, State civil litigation, Personal injury. Office: Ross & Hardies 150 N Michigan Ave Chicago IL 60601

SERUMGARD, JOHN R., lawyer; b. Rolla, N.D., June 11, 1944; s. John R. and Antoinette R. (Bedard) S.; m. K. Laura Wippich, June 9, 1969; children—Jennie Lynn, John Matthew, Kristen Leigh. A.B., Georgetown U., 1966, J.D., 1969, LL.M., 1974. Bar: Ill. 1969, D.C. 1980, U.S. Sup. Ct. 1975. Staff asst. Office of U.S. Rep. Fred Schwengel, 1967-68; legal editor labor services Bur. Nat. Affairs, Inc., Washington, 1968-70; labor atty. U.S. C. of C., Washington, 1972-75; v.p. labor relations Rubber Mfrs. Assn., Washington, 1975—, treas., 1981—; treas. Natural Rubber Shippers Assn., Inc., 1981—. Bd. dirs. Riverside Manor Civic Assn., 1979-80. Served to capt. U.S. Army, 1970-72. Mem. ABA, Fed. Bar Assn., D.C. Bar Assn., Indsl. Research Assn., Washington Rubber Group. Club: River Bend Golf and Country (Great Falls, Va.). Labor, Corporate taxation. Home: 9504 Arnon Chapel Rd Great Falls VA 22066

SERWER, ALAN MICHAEL, lawyer; b. Detroit, Aug. 31, 1944; s. Bernard Jacob and Marian (Borin) S.; m. Laurel Kathryn Robbert, June 6, 1968; children: David Matthew, Karen Anne. BA in Econs., U. Mich., 1966; JD, Northwestern U., 1969. Bar: Ill. 1969, U.S. Dist. Ct. (no. dist.) Ill. 1970, U.S. Ct. Appeals (7th cir.) 1979, U.S. Supreme Ct. 1979, U.S. Ct. Appeals (D.C. cir.) 1980, U.S. Ct. Appeals (6th cir.) 1982, U.S. Ct. Appeals (5th cir.) 1983, U.S. Ct. Appeals (11th cir.) 1984, U.S. Ct. Appeals (9th cir.) 1986. Trial atty. U.S. Dept. Labor, Chgo., 1969-78, counsel safety and health, 1978-79; assoc. Haley, Bader & Potts, Chgo., 1979-82, ptnr., 1983-87; ptnr. Bell, Boyd & Lloyd, Chgo., 1987—. Mem. Ill. Bar Assn., Chgo. Bar Assn., Assn. Trial Lawyers Am., Fed. Bar Assn. (recipient Milton Gordon award 1977). Labor, Federal civil litigation, Pension, profit-sharing, and employee benefits. Home: 233 Woodland Rd Highland Park IL 60035 Office: Bell Boyd & Lloyd 70 W Madison St Chicago IL 60602

SESSER, GARY DOUGLAS, lawyer; b. Malden, Mass., June 4, 1950; s. Ralph and Esther Anne (Chalfen) S.; m. Rachel Wolkin, June 22, 1979; children: Michael, Benjamin, Anne. BA, Cornell U., 1972; JD, U. Mich., 1975. Bar: Mass. 1975, U.S Dist. Ct. Mass. 1976, N.Y. 1977, U.S. Dist. Ct. (so. and ea. dists.) N.Y. 1977, U.S. Ct. Appeals (2d cer.) 1978, D.C. 1980, U.S. Supreme Ct. 1980, U.S. Ct. Appeals (D.C. cir.) 1987. Assoc. H.M. Kaufman, Boston, 1976; assoc. Haight, Gardner, Poor & Havens, N.Y.C., 1976-84, ptnr., 1984—. Mem. ABA, Assn. of Bar of City of N.Y. (transp. com.), Maritime Law Assn. Antitrust, Admiralty, Federal civil litigation. Home: 520 Upper Mountain Ave Upper Montclair NJ 07043 Office: Haight Gardner Poor & Havens 195 Broadway New York NY 10007

SESSIONS, G. P., lawyer; b. Heber City, Utah, Sept. 2, 1949; s. William Boyd Sessions and Sarah Bonnie (Pyper) Davis; m. Maria J. Piorkowski, Mar. 14, 1969; 1 child, Sean Stefan. BA, U. Puget Sound, 1972, JD, 1977. Bar: Wash. 1978, U.S. Dist. Ct. (we. dist.) Wash. 1978, U.S. Tax Ct. 1982, U.S. Ct. Appeals (9th cir.) 1982. Field rep. Pub. Sch. Employees Wash., Puyallup, 1971-78, gen. counsel, 1978; sole practice Orting, Wash., 1978—; instr. Ft. Steilacoom Community Coll., McChord AFB, Wash., 1982-85. Editor Washington Public Labor Law Reporter, 1981. Served with U.S. Army, 1968-71, Vietnam. Mem. Wash. State Bar Assn., Tacoma Pierce County Bar Assn. Democrat. Lodges: Lions (pres. Orting 1986-87), Eagles. Avocation: leather tooling. General practice, Labor, Real property. Home and Office: 407 E Train Ave Orting WA 98360-0393

SESSIONS, JEFFERSON BEAUREGARD, III, lawyer; b. Selma, Ala., Dec. 24, 1946; s. Jefferson Beauregard and Abbie (Powe) S.; m. Mary Montgomery Blackshear, Aug. 9, 1969; children: Mary Abigail, Ruth Blackshear, Samuel Turner. B.A., Huntingdon Coll., Montgomery, Ala., 1969; J.D., U. Ala., 1973. Bar: Ala. Assoc. Guin, Bouldin & Porch, Russellville, Ala., 1973-75; asst. U.S. atty. U.S. Dept. Justice, Mobile, Ala., 1975-77, U.S. atty., 1981—; ptnr. Stockman & Bedsole Attys., Mobile, Ala., 1977-81. Presdl. elector State of Ala., 1972; chmn. 1st congl. dist. Ala. Republican Party, 1979-81; chmn. adminstrv. bd. Ashland Pl. United Meth. Ch., Mobile, 1982. Served to capt. USAR, 1975-85. Mem. ABA, Ala. Bar Assn., Mobile Bar Assn., Omicron Delta Kappa (hon.). Republican. General practice. Home: 4109 Woodhill Dr Mobile AL 36608 Office: US Atty PO Drawer E Mobile AL 36601 *

SESSIONS, WILLIAM LEWIS, lawyer; b. Waco, Tex., Aug. 19, 1953; s. William Steele and Alice (June) S.; m. Renee Alford, Aug. 21, 1977; children: Dallas Alford, William Harrison. BA in Polit. Sci., Southwestern U., 1975; JD, Baylor U., 1978. Bar: Tex. 1978, U.S. Ct. Appeals (5th cir.) 1978, U.S. Dist. Ct. (we. dist.) Tex. 1981. Asst. atty. gen. State of Tex., Austin, 1978-79; assoc. Foster and Assocs., San Antonio, 1979-80, Wiley, Garwood & Hornbuckle, San Antonio, 1981; sole practice San Antonio, 1981-83; ptnr. Sessions & Sessions, San Antonio, 1983—. Mem. ABA, Tex. Bar Assn., San Antonio Bar Assn. (chmn. law day com. 1982-83, chmn. speakers and program com. 1985—), Fed. Bar Assn. (bd. dirs. San Antonio chpt. 1982-84), Tex. Young Lawyers Assn. (editorial bd. Tex. Practice Guide), San Antonio Young Lawyers Assn., Am. Inns of Ct. (magister San Antonio chpt. 1986—). Republican. Baptist. Bankruptcy, Federal civil litigation, State civil litigation. Home: 11622 Veradero San Antonio TX 78216 Office: 745 E Mulberry Suite 390 San Antonio TX 78212-3179

SESSIONS, WILLIAM STEELE, judge; b. Fort Smith, Ark., May 27, 1930; s. Will Anderson and Edith A. (Steele) S.; m. Alice Lewis, Oct. 5, 1952; children—William Lewis, Mark Gregory, Peter Anderson, Sara Anne. B.A., Baylor U., 1956, J.D., 1958. Bar: Tex. 1959. Ptnr. McGregor & Sessions, Waco, Tex., 1959-61; assoc. Tirey, McLaughlin, Gorin & McDonald, Waco, 1961-63; ptnr. Haley, Fulbright, Winniford, Sessions & Bice, Waco, 1963-69; chief govt. ops. sect. Criminal div. Dept. Justice, Washington, 1969-71; U.S. atty. U.S. Dist. Ct. (we. dist.) Tex., San Antonio, 1971-74, dist. judge, 1974-80, chief judge, 1980—; bd. dirs. Fed. Jud. Ctr., Washington, chmn. bench book com., 1981—. Contbr. articles to profl. jours. Served to capt. USAF, 1951-55. Recipient Rosewood Gavel award St. Mary's U. Sch. of Law, San Antonio, 1982. Mem. Jud. Conf. U.S. (com. on ct. adminstrn., chmn. Jud. Improvements subcom. 1986—), San Antonio Bar Assn. (bd. dirs. 1973-74), Fed. Bar Assn. (pres. San Antonio sect. 1974), Am. Judicature Soc. (exec. com. 1982-84), ABA, Dist. Judges Assn. of 5th Cir. (pres. 1982-83), State Bar of Tex., Waco McLennan County Bar Assn. (pres. 1968). Republican. Methodist. Avocations: hiking; climbing; canoeing. Jurisprudence. Office: US Dist Ct 655 E Durango Blvd San Antonio TX 78206

SESSLER, ALBERT LOUIS, JR., lawyer; b. Davenport, Iowa, May 28, 1925; s. Albert Louis and Eva Ames (Dedrick) S.; m. Irene Helen Seifert, Nov. 20, 1951; children—Curtis N., Scott A., Janice M.; m. Robin Helen Palmer, Mar. 23, 1976. B.S. in Mech. Engring., Iowa State U., 1950; J.D. with honors, George Washington U., 1954. Bar: D.C. 1954, U.S. Patent and Trademark Office 1955, U.S. Supreme Ct. 1972, U.S. Ct. Appeals (Fed. cir.) 1982. Asst. examiner U.S. Patent Office, Washington, 1951-54; patent atty. NCR Corp., Dayton, Ohio, 1955—, div. patent counsel, 1981-84, group intellectual property counsel, 1984-86, assoc. chief, group counsel, 1986—. Mem. bd. zoning appeals, City of Kettering (Ohio), 1970—, Chmn., 1985, mem. zoning task force, 1979—. Served with U.S. Army, 1943-46, to 2d lt., 1951-53. Decorated Bronze Star. Mem. ABA, Am. Intellectual Property Law Assn., D.C. Bar Assn., Dayton Patent Law Assn. (past pres.), Order of Coif. Republican. Lutheran. Patent. Home: 533 Enid Avenue Kettering OH 45429 Office: NCR Corp Law Dept Dayton OH 45479

SESSUMS, STEPHEN WALKER, lawyer; b. Daytona Beach, Fla., Aug. 19, 1934; s. Thomas Little and Dorothy Josephine S.; m. Diana J. Ball, June 21, 1968; children—Laura, Mark, Michael. B.A., U. Fla., 1956, J.D., 1959. Bar: Fla. 1959. Asst. prof. of law, U. Fla., 1959; assoc. firm Hull, Landis Graham & French, De Land, Fla., 1959-60; ptnr. Albritton, Sessums & McCall, Tampa, Fla., 1961-82; pres. Sessums & Mason, P.A., Tampa, 1982—. Past pres., founding dir. Northside Mental Health Community Ctr.; past pres. Greater Tampa chpt. ARC. Fellow Am. Acad. Matrimonial Lawyers (nat. bd. dirs., pres. Fla. chpt.); mem. ABA, Fla. Bar (chmn. subcom. on spl. publs. family law sect., mem. Supreme Ct. Commn. on Matrimonial Law 1982—), Tampa-Hillsborough County Bar Assn. (past pres.), Bay Area Trial Lawyers Assn. (past pres.). Family and matrimonial. Office: 215 Verne St Tampa FL 33602

SESTRIC, ANTHONY JAMES, lawyer; b. St. Louis, June 27, 1940; s. Anton and Marie (Gasparovic) S.; student, Georgetown U., 1958-62; JD, Mo. U., 1965; m. Carol F. Bowman, Nov. 24, 1966; children: Laura Antonette, Holly Nicole, Michael Anthony. Bar: Mo. 1965, U.S. Ct. Appeals (8th cir.) 1965, U.S. Dist. Ct. Mo., 1966, U.S. Tax Ct. 1969, U.S. Supreme Ct. 1970, U.S. Ct. Appeals (7th cir.) 1984, U.S. Dist. Ct. (no. dist.) Tex. 1985, U.S. Claims Ct. 1986. Law clk. U.S. Dist. Ct., St. Louis, 1965-66; ptnr. firm Sestric, McGhee & Miller, St. Louis, 1966-77, Fordyce & Mayne, 1977-78; spl. asst. to Mo. atty. gen., St. Louis, 1968; hearing officer St. Louis Met. Police Dept. Contbr. articles to profl. jours. Mem. St. Louis Air Pollution Bd. Appeals and Varience Rev., 1966-73, chmn., 1968-73; mem. St. Louis Airport Commn., 1975-76; dist. vice chmn. Boy Scouts Am., 1970-76; bd. dirs. Full Achievement, Inc., 1970-77, pres., 1972-77; bd. dirs. Legal Aid Soc. of St. Louis, 1976-77, Law Library Assn. St. Louis, 1976-78; v.p. bd. St. Elizabeth Acad., 1985-86. Mem. ABA (state chmn. judiciary com. 1973-75, circuit chmn. com. condemnation, zoning and property use 1975-77, standing com. bar activities 1982—), Mound City Bar Assn., Chgo. Bar Assn., Fed. Bar Assn., Lawyers Assn., Am. Judicature Soc., Mo. Bar (vice chmn. young lawyers sect. 1973-76, bd. govs. 1974-77), Bar Assn. Met. St. Louis (chmn. young lawyers sect. 1974-75, exec. com. 1974-83, pres 1981-82). Club: Mo. Athletic. Federal civil litigation, State civil litigation, Real property. Home: 3967 Holly Hills Blvd Saint Louis MO 63116 Office: 1015 Locust St Saint Louis MO 63101

SETH, J CABOT, lawyer; b. Ft. Ord, Calif., Apr. 17, 1953; s. Richard George and Rita Barbara (McCooey) S.; m. Tonia Marie Martin, Dec. 20, 1975; children: Hilary, Elissa, Lauren, John. AB, U. Notre Dame, 1975; JD, U. S.C., 1977. Bar: S.C. 1978, U.S. Dist. Ct. S.C. 1983, U.S. Ct. Mil. Appeals 1986. Commd. 2d lt. USAF, 1975, advanced through grades to capt., 1978, resigned, 1983; with USAFR, 1983—; ptnr. Jones & Seth, Sumter, S.C., 1983—; county prosecutor Sumter County, 1983; mcpl. judge City of Sumter, 1984-85. Bd. mem. Sumter Christian Charities, 1983-86; bd. dirs. office of natural family planning Diocese of Charleston, Sumter, 1983—. Named Outstanding Young Man of S.C., S.C. Jaycees, 1984. Mem. ABA (legal econs. sect.), Sumter County Bar Assn., Sumter C. of C. (com. chmn. leadership devel. 1985-86, com. chmn. legis. affairs 1986—), Sumter Jaycees (pres. 1982-86, named outstanding young man of S.C. State div. 1984). Democrat. Roman Catholic. Lodges: Rotary, K.C. (dep. grand knight 1982-83). General practice, Personal injury, State civil litigation. Office: Jones & Seth 5 Law Range Sumter SC 29151

SETO, ROBERT MAHEALANI MING, federal judge; b. Canton, China (parents U.S. citizens), May 12, 1936; s. Yeun Jan and Beatrice Nipoaloha (Lee) S.; m. Elizabeth M. Everhart; children: Michelle Ann Leilani, Craig Kailani, Jeffrey Keakealani, Pamela Beatrice, Scott David. B.S., St. Louis U., 1962, J.D., 1968. Bars: Mo. Sup. Ct., Hawaii Sup. Ct., U.S. Ct. Claims, U.S. Ct. Appeals (D.C.), U.S. Ct. Customs and Patent Appeals, U.S. Dist. Ct. (ea. dist.) Mo., U.S. Dist. Hawaii, U.S. Ct. Apls. (fed. cir.), U.S. Supreme Ct. Asst. circuit atty. felony div. City of St. Louis, 1969; patent counsel Monsanto Chem. Co., 1970; dep. corp. counsel Div. Legal Memorandums and Opinions City and County of Honolulu, 1971; minority counsel U.S. Senate Spl. Com. on Aging, 1971-73; legislative counsel U.S. Senate Judiciary Com., Subcom. on Immigration and Naturalization, 1974; chief patent counsel U.S. Senator Hiram L. Fong for U.S. Senate Judiciary Com., Subcom. on Patents, Trademarks and Copyrights, 1975-76; sr. patent-litigation atty. U.S. Internat. Trade Commn., 1976-81; trial judge U.S. Ct. Claims, Washington, 1981; appointed judge U.S. Claims Ct., Washington, 1982—. Mem. ABA, D.C. Bar Assn., Bar Assn. D.C., Hawaii Bar Assn., Mo. Bar Assn., Am. Patent Law Assn., Govt. Patent Lawyers Assn., Nat. Lawyers Club, Fed. Bar Assn. Patent, Trademark and copyright, Government contracts and claims. Office: Nat Cts Bldg 717 Madison Pl NW Washington DC 20005 *

SETTER, DAVID MARK, lawyer; b. Pueblo, Colo., July 18, 1956; s. Urban Francis and Phyllis Ida (Ward) S.; m. Della Fae McNevin, Sept. 7, 1985. BS with honors, U. So. Colo., 1977; JD with honors, Drake U., 1981. Bar: Colo. 1981, U.S. Dist. Ct. Colo. 1981, U.S. Ct. Appeals (10th cir.) 1981. Law clk. to presiding judge Colo. Ct. Appeals, Denver, 1981-82; assoc. Tilly and Graves, P.C., Denver, 1982—. Assoc. articles editor Drake U. Law Rev., 1980-81. Mem. ABA (antitrust div.), Colo. Bar Assn., Colo. Def. Lawyers Assn., Denver Bar Assn., Order of Coif, Phi Alpha Delta. Democrat. Roman Catholic. Avocations: bicycling, reading, camping. Antitrust, State civil litigation, Insurance. Home: 1973 S Niagara St Denver CO 80224 Office: Tilly and Graves PC 3773 Cherry Creek N Dr Suite 701 Denver CO 80209

SETTERBERG, PATRICIA ANN, lawyer; b. N.Y.C., Nov. 22, 1946; d. J. Lynn and Mary E. (Delaney) Bowen; m. Richard A. Setterberg, Apr. 26, 1969 (div. Sept. 1985); children: Edward Lynn, Alison Brooke; m. John C. Baity, Nov. 9, 1985; children: Michael Paul, Philip James. AB, Vassar Coll., 1968; JD, Cornell U., 1978. Bar: N.Y. 1979, U.S. Dist. Ct. (so. dist.) N.Y. 1979, U.S. Dist. Ct. (no. dist.) N.Y. 1984, U.S. Ct. Claims 1987. Assoc. Donovan, Leisure, Newton & Irvine, N.Y.C., 1978-83, Hunton & Williams, N.Y.C., 1983-84, Baity & Joseph, N.Y.C., 1984-86, Milbank, Tweed, Hadley & McCloy, Los Angeles, 1986—. Mem. ABA, N.Y. State Bar Assn. Avocations: golf, sailing, skiing. Estate planning, Estate taxation, Personal income taxation. Home: 44 Maher Ave Greenwich CT 06830 Office: Milbank Tweed Hadley & McCloy 1 Chase Manhattan Plaza New York NY 10005

SETTLAGE, STEVEN PAUL, lawyer; b. Nashville, Tenn., April 29, 1951; s. Paul Herman and Doris Ruby (Taylor) S.; m. Diane Marie Ribblett, Aug. 11, 1973; children: Christine Marie, Matthew Steven, Jessica Lauren. BS, Vanderbilt U., 1973; JD, Washington and Lee U., 1976. Bar: Va. 1976. Assoc. Hirschler, Fleischer, Weinberg, Cox & Allen, Richmond, Va., 1976-81, ptnr., chmn. real estate sect., 1981-86; exec. v.p. Rowe Devel. Co., 1986—; lectr. Va. Law Found., Charlottesville, 1982. Author: Landlord Tenant Law and Practie, 1978, 84; Real Estate Financing in the '80s, 1982. Trustee Christ the King Lutheran Ch., Richmond, 1982- 83. Mem. Va. State Bar Assn. (real estate com.), ABA, Richmond Bar Assn. (exec. com. real estate sect. 1981-82), Phi Alpha Delta. General corporate, Real property, Landlord-tenant. Home: 3108 Williamswood Rd Richmond VA 23235 Office: Rowe Develepment Co PO Box 32136 Richmond VA 23060

SETTLE, JOHN MARSHALL, lawyer; b. Anadarko, Okla., May 22, 1956; s. H. Marshall and Frances Rose (Reece) S.; m. Paula Gaye Younkin, July 30, 1977; children: Katheryn Suzanne, Lindsey Brooke. BS with honors, Southwestern Okla. State U., 1977; JD, Okla. U., 1980. Bar: Okla. 1980, U.S. Dist. Ct. (we. dist.) Okla. 1980. Asst. dist. atty., 6th prosecution dist. State of Okla., Chickasha, Okla., 1980-81; sole practice Chickasha, 1981—. Bd. dirs. Opportunity Workshop, Chickasha, 1983—, Spl. Young Adults, Chickasha, 1984—. Mem. ABA, Okla. Bar Assn. (bd. dirs. young lawyers div. 1983—), Assn. Trial Lawyers Am. Republican. Christian Scientist. Lodge: Rotary. Avocations: flying, reading, fishing, quail hunting, raquetball. Consumer commercial, Real property, General practice. Office: 212 Chickasha Ave PO Box 1556 Chickasha OK 73203

SETTLE, WILLIAM SYDNOR, lawyer; b. Alberta, Va., Dec. 27, 1933; s. Robert Bruce and Mabel Anne (Jones) S.; m. Stephanie Anne Bauder, Sept. 3, 1955 (div. Aug. 1965); m. Noel Ruth Alverson, Feb. 6, 1968; children: Lisa Anne, William Sydnor. Student, Hampden-Sydney Coll., 1951-55; J.D., U. Va., 1957. Bar: N.Y. 1958. Assoc. Simpson Thacher & Bartlett, N.Y.C., 1957-68, ptnr., 1968—; dir. Canton Drop Forging & Mfg. Co., Ohio, Oloffson Co., Mich., Cordier Group Holdings, Inc. Trustee Hampden-Sydney Coll., Va., 1972—, chmn., 1980—; trustee The Seeing Eye, Inc., Morristown, N.J., 1984—, chmn. 1987—; mem. Morris County Transp. Bd., Morristown, N.J., 1975-79; adv. bd. Morris Mus., Morristown, 1987—. Mem. ABA, Bar Assn. City N.Y., N.Y. State Bar Assn. Republican. Presbyterian. Clubs: Downtown Assn., University (N.Y.C.); Met Golf Assn. (Mamaroneck, N.Y.) (pres. 1982-84). Home: Long Hill Rd New Vernon NJ 07976 Office: Simpson Thacher & Bartlett 1 Battery Park Plaza New York NY 10004

SEVART, DANIEL JOSEPH, lawyer; b. Oswego, Kans., June 25, 1944; s. Vernon Joseph and Alma Bridget (Carland) S.; m. Shoko Kato, Apr. 17, 1968; 1 child, Eric J. AA, Parsons Jr. Coll., 1964; BA, Washburn U., 1973, JD with honors, 1975. Bar: Kans. 1976, U.S. Dist. Ct. Kans. 1976, U.S. Ct. Appeals (10th cir.) 1976. Assoc. Render & Kamas, Wichita, Kans., 1976-78; ptnr. Render & Kamas, Wichita, 1978-82, Schartz & Sevart, Wichita, 1982-83, Sevart & Sevart, Wichita, 1983—. Served to staff sgt. USAF, 1965-72. Mem. Assn. Trial Lawyers Am., Kans. Bar Assn., Wichita Bar Assn., Wichita C. of C. Democrat. Roman Catholic. Avocations: classical music, gardening, fishing, camping, traveling. General practice, Personal injury,

Federal civil litigation. Home: 9508 Harvest Ln Wichita KS 67212 Office: Suite 810 Century Plaza 111 W Douglas Wichita KS 67202

SEVERAID, RONALD HAROLD, lawyer; b. Berkeley, Calif., July 13, 1951; s. J, Harold and Irene Ann (Clark) s.; m. Peggy R. Chappus. B.A., U. Calif.-Davis, 1973; J.D., Georgetown U., 1977. Bar: Calif. 1977, D.C. 1979, U.S. Dist. Ct. (ea. and cen. dists.) Calif. 1977. Assoc. Kindel & Anderson, Los Angeles, 1977-79; exec. v.p., gen. counsel Pacific Mktg. Devel., Sacramento, 1979-80, pres., 1980-81; sec. Aaron-Ross Corp., Glendora, Calif., 1983-84; sole practice, Sacramento, 1979-84; sr. atty. Severaid & Seegmiller, Sacramento, 1984—. Co-editor Internat. Cts. of Justice Opinion Briefs, 1978; sr. topics editor Law and Policy in Internat. Bus., 1975-76; contbr. articles to profl. jours. Asst. sec. Internat. Relations Sect.-Town Hall, Los Angeles, 1978-79; pres. Pacifica Villas Homeowners Assn., 1978-79. Mem. ABA , Calif. State Bar Assn., Sacramento County Bar Assn., Community Assns. Inst., Calif. Trustees Assn. Republican. Roman Catholic. Real property, General corporate, State civil litigation. Office: Severaid & Seegmiller 601 University Ave Suite 125 Sacramento CA 95825

SEVERS, CHARLES A., III, lawyer; b. N.Y.C., Sept. 16, 1942; s. Charles A. and Gertrude (O'Neill) S.; m. Regina Ferrone, Sept. 4, 1965; children: Charles A. IV, Cornelius Forsythe, Rudyard Pierrepont, Olivia Consuelo. BA, Georgetown U., 1964, JD, 1967. Ptnr. Dewey, Ballantine, Bushby, Palmer & Wood, N.Y.C., 1967—. Contbr. articles to profl. jours. Fellow Am. Coll. Probate Counsel; mem. ABA, N.Y. State Bar Assn., Assn. of Bar of City of N.Y. Clubs: Union, Downtown Assn. (N.Y.). Estate taxation, Probate, Personal income taxation. Home: 1095 Park Ave New York NY 10128 Office: Dewey Ballantine Bushby et al 140 Broadway New York NY 10005

SEVERS, ERIC ROBERTSON, lawyer; b. Oberlin, Ohio, Sept. 5, 1948; s. Grover Lawrence and Carol Suzanne (Beachler) S.; m. Diane Marie Reams, Sept. 8, 1984; 1 child, Christopher Jacob. BA in Econs., Denison U., 1970; JD, Cleve-Marshall Law Sch., 1975. Bar: Ohio 1975, Fla. 1975, U.S. Dist. Ct. (no. dist.) Ohio 1975. Ptnr., Severs & Boylan Co., L.P.A., Elyria, Ohio, 1975-86; pres., owner Severs & Severs Co., L.P.A., Elyria, 1986—; city solicitor City of Oberlin, 1980-86. Vice-chmn. Oberlin Civil Service Commn., 1976-79. Mem. ABA, Ohio State Bar Assn., Lorain County Bar Assn., Fla. Bar Ohio Mcpl. Attys. Assn., Nat. Inst. Mcpl. Law Officers. Lodge: Kiwanis (pres. 1977-78). Local government, Probate, General practice. Home: Shipherd Circle Oberlin OH 44074 Office: Severs & Severs Co LPA 28 Lake Ave Elyria OH 44035

SEWALL, WILLIAM DANA, lawyer; b. Boston, Jan. 17, 1948; s. Charles Hull Sewall and Mary (Butler) Spring; m. Lucinda Thames, Oct. 22, 1981; children: Rebecca, Alyssa. BA, Dartmouth Coll., 1970; JD, Boston Coll., 1977. Bar: Mass. 1978, Calif. 1979. Tchr. Concord (N.H.) Sch. Dist., 1970-74; assoc. Csapler & Bok, Boston, 1977-81; gen. counsel LEF & C Corp., San Francisco, 1981-83; sr. v.p. Bankers Leasing, San Mateo, Calif., 1983—; also bd. dirs. Bankers Leasing, San Mateo. Editor Boston Coll. Law Rev., 1975-77. Mem. Am. Assn. Equipment Lessors. Avocations: gardening, whitewater rafting, jogging. General corporate, Leasing. Home: 900 Alsace Lorraine Half Moon Bay CA 94019 Office: Bankers Leasing and Fin Corp 2655 Campus Dr San Mateo CA 94403

SEXTON, DAVID ANDREW, lawyer; b. Louisville, Apr. 24, 1957; s. Russell Gordon and Patricia Ann (Minogue) S.; m. Mary Patricia Gornet, July 20, 1985. BA cum laude, Bellarmine Coll., 1979; JD, U. Ky., 1982. Bar: Ky., U.S. Dist. Ct. (ea. and we. dists.) Ky., U.S. Ct. Appeals (6th cir.). Atty. Ky. Corrections Cabinet, Frankfort, 1982—. Mem. ABA, Ky. Bar Assn., State Govt. Bar Assn. Democrat. Roman Catholic. Civil rights, Federal civil litigation, State civil litigation. Office: Ky Corrections Cabinet High & Holmes Sts 500 State Office Bldg Frankfort KY 40601

SEXTON, DAVID FARRINGTON, lawyer, investment banking executive; b. Montclair, N.J., Aug. 20, 1943; s. Dorrance and Marjorie (McComb) S.; m. Ann Hemmelright, Feb. 27, 1971; children: James, Ashley, Christopher. A.B. cum laude, Princeton U., 1966; J.D. cum laude, U. Pa., 1972. Bar: N.Y. 1972. Assoc. Sullivan & Cromwell, N.Y.C., 1972-77; with First Boston Corp., N.Y.C., 1977—; v.p., gen. counsel First Boston Corp., 1980-83, mng. dir., gen. counsel, 1983-86; mng. dir., pres. First Boston Internat. Ltd., 1986—; adj. prof. law Fordham U., 1985-86. Served to lt. USNR, 1966-69. Mem. ABA, Assn. Bar City N.Y. Republican. Presbyterian. Clubs: Links, Racquet and Tennis (N.Y.C.); Apawamis (Rye, N.Y.); Ivy (Princeton). General corporate, Securities. Office: Park Avenue Plaza New York NY 10055

SEXTON, RICHARD, diversified manufacturing company executive; b. Madison, Wis., May 9, 1929; s. Joseph Cantwell and Eleanor Carr (Kenny) S.; m. Joan Fleming, Feb. 23, 1957; children: Molly, Joseph, Lucy, Michael, Ann, Katherine. Student, Amherst Coll., 1947-49; B.S., U. Wis., 1951; LL.B., Yale U., 1958. Bar: N.Y. 1959, U.S. Supreme Ct. 1968. Assoc. firm Sullivan & Cromwell, N.Y.C., 1958-64; with SCM Corp., N.Y.C., 1964-86; asst. counsel SCM Corp., 1964-67, div. gen. counsel Smith-Corona Marchant div., 1967-72, v.p., gen. counsel parent co., 1972-86, sec., 1977-86. Served to lt. (j.g.) USNR, 1951-55. Mem. Assn. Bar City N.Y., ABA (subcom. on corp. law depts.), U.S. C. of C. (com. on antitrust policy). Club: Yale. General corporate, Antitrust, General practice. Home: 532 3d St Brooklyn NY 11215 Office: SCM Corp 230 Park Ave Suite 1635 New York NY 10169

SEYFARTH, HENRY EDWARD, lawyer; b. Blue Island, Ill., Apr. 16, 1908; s. Ward Richard and Florence Louise (Klein) S.; m. Elizabeth Ellis, Feb. 15, 1965; children: B. Marie, Victoria Fesmire, Richard R. Parkin. B.A., U. Ill., 1928; J.D., U. Chgo., 1930. Asst. State's Atty. Cook County, Ill., 1930-35; partner firm Pope & Ballard, Chgo., 1935-45, Seyfarth, Shaw, Fairweather & Geraldson, Chgo., from 1945; now cons. partner Seyfarth, Shaw, Fairweather & Geraldson; chmn. bd. dirs. Gt. Lakes Fin. Resources, Inc., 1st Nat. Bank of Blue Island, Ill.; bd. dirs. Community Bank of Homewood-Flossmoor (Ill.), Naples (Fla.) Community Hosp. Trustee Northwestern Meml. Hosp., Chgo. Mem. Chgo. Bar Assn., Ill. Bar Assn., Bar Assn. Washington, Assn. for Modern Banking in Ill. (founder, chmn. 1965-75). Republican. Episcopalian. Clubs: Chicago, University; Barrington Hills (Ill.) Country, Naples (Fla.) Yacht, Port Royal, Royal Poinciana Golf. General corporate, Banking, Labor. Office: 55 E Monroe St Chicago IL 60603

SEYKORA, DAVID GERARD, lawyer; b. Owatonna, Minn., June 20, 1955. BA, St. John's U., Collegeville, Minn., 1977; JD, Cornell U., 1980. Bar: Minn. 1980, U.S. Dist. Ct. Minn. 1980, U.S. Ct. Appeals (8th cir.) 1981. Law clk. to presiding judge U.S. Dist. Ct. Minn., Mpls., 1980-82; assoc. Oppenheimer, Wolff & Donnelly, St. Paul, 1982—. Mem. ABA, Minn. Bar Assn., Am. Judicature Soc. Labor, Federal civil litigation, State civil litigation. Office: Oppenheimer Wolff & Donnelly 1700 First Bank Bldg Saint Paul MN 55101

SEYMOUR, MARY FRANCES, lawyer; b. Durand, Wis., Oct. 20, 1948; d. Marshall Willard and Alice Roberta (Smith) Thompson; m. Marshall Warren Seymour, June 6, 1970; 1 foster child, Nghia Pham. BS, U. Wis., LaCrosse, 1970; JD, William Mitchell Coll., 1979. Bar: Minn. 1979, U.S. Dist. Ct. Minn. 1979, U.S. Ct. Appeals (8th cir.) 1979, U.S. Supreme Ct. 1986. With Cochrane and Bresnahan, P.A., St. Paul, 1979—. Mem. Assn. Trial Lawyers Am., Minn. Bar Assn., Ramsey County Bar Assn., Minn. Trial Lawyers Assn. Office: Cochrane and Bresnahan PA 24 E Fourth St Saint Paul MN 55101

SEYMOUR, MCNEIL VERNAM, JR., lawyer; b. St. Paul, Dec. 21, 1934; s. McNeil Vernam and Katherine Grace (Klein) S.; m. Alice Mary Forsythe, June 17, 1961; children—Margaret, McNeil Vernam, James, Benjamin. A.B., Princeton U. 1957; J.D., U. Chgo., 1960. Bar: Minn. 1960, U.S. Dist. Ct. Minn. 1960. Mem. Seymour & Seymour, St. Paul, 1960-71; mem. firm Briggs & Morgan, St. Paul, 1971—, ptnr., 1978—; dir. Webb Co. Pres., treas. White Bear Unitarian Ch., 1964-65; sec. bd. dirs. Ramsey County Law Library, 1972-76. Served with U.S. Army, 1960-62. Mem. Ramsey County Bar Assn., Minn. Bar Assn. Republican. Unitarian. Clubs: University (pres. 1978-80), St. Paul Athletic. Probate, Banking, Real property. Address: W 2200 First Nat Bank Bldg Saint Paul MN 55101

SEYMOUR, STEPHANIE KULP, federal judge; b. Battle Creek, Mich., Oct. 16, 1940; d. Francis Bruce and Frances Cecelia (Bria) Kulp; m. R. Thomas Seymour, June 10, 1972; children: Bart, Bria, Sara, Anna. B.A. magna cum laude, Smith Coll., 1962; J.D., Harvard U., 1965. Bar: Okla. 1965. Practiced in Boston 1965-66, practiced in Tulsa, 1966-67, 71-79, practiced in Houston, 1968-69; assoc. firm Doerner, Stuart, Saunders, Daniel & Anderson, Tulsa, 1971-75; ptnr. firm Doerner, Stuart, Saunders, Daniel & Anderson, 1975-79; judge U.S. Ct. Appeals 10th Circuit, 1979—; asso. bar examiner Okla. Bar Assn., 1973-79; trustee Tulsa County Law Library, 1977-78; mem. legal adv. panel Tulsa Task Force on Battered Women, 1971-77. Mem. various task forces Tulsa Human Rights Commn., 1972-76. Mem. Am. Bar Assn., Okla. Bar Assn., Tulsa County Bar Assn., Phi Beta Kappa. Jurisprudence. Office: US Court Appeals 4562 US Courthouse 333 W 4th St Tulsa OK 74103 *

SEYMOUR, WHITNEY NORTH, JR., lawyer; b. Huntington, W.Va., July 7, 1923; s. Whitney North and Lola Virginia (Vickers) S.; m. Catryna Ten Eyck, Nov. 16, 1951; children—Tryntje Van Ness, Gabriel North. A.B., Princeton U., 1947; LL.B., Yale U., 1950. Bars: N.Y. 1950, U.S. Dist. Ct. (so. dist.) N.Y. 1951, U.S. Supreme Ct. 1960. Assoc. Simpson Thacher & Bartlett, N.Y.C., 1950-53, assoc., 1956-59, ptnr., 1961-70, 1973-83; asst. U.S. atty. So. Dist. N.Y., 1953-56; chief counsel spl. unit N.Y. State Commn. Investigation, 1960-61; U.S. atty. 1970-73; ptnr. Brown & Seymour, N.Y.C., 1983—; mem. N.Y. State Senate, 1966-68; ind. counsel Michael Deaver Investigation, 1986-87. Author: Why Justice Fails, 1973; United States Attorney, 1975; Making a Difference, 1984, others. Served with AUS, 1943-46. Mem. N.Y. State Bar Assn. (pres. 1973-74), Fed. Bar Council (pres. 1981-82), Am. Judicature Soc., Am. Coll. Trial Lawyers, ABA, Assn. Bar City N.Y., N.Y. County Lawyers Assn. Republican. Episcopalian. Clubs: Century, The Players, Overseas Press. General practice. Home: 290 W 4th St New York NY 10014 Office: Brown & Seymour 100 Park Ave New York NY 10017

SEYMOUR, WILLIAM FRANCIS, IV, lawyer; b. Norfolk, Va., Feb. 22, 1957; s. William Francis III and Anne (Holland) S. BA cum laude, Hampden Sydney Coll., 1979; JD, U. Richmond, 1982. Bar: Va. 1982. Assoc. Hugh Thompson Jr., Richmond, Va., 1982-83; mem. Moore, Pollard, Boice & Seymour and predecessor firms, Richmond, 1983-86, Purcell, Cherry, Kerns, Abady & Seymour, Richmond, 1986—. Participating vol. Cen. Va. Legal Aid, Richmond, 1983—. Named one of Outstanding Young Men of Am., U.S. Jaycees, 1984, 85. Mem. ABA, Va. Bar Assn., Richmond Bar Assn., Phi Delta Phi (fraternal). Episcopal. Club: Bull & Bear (Richmond). Consumer commercial, General corporate, Probate. Home: 2711 Salisbury Rd Midlothian VA 23113 Office: Purcell Cherry Kerns Abady & Seymour Mut Bldg Suite 806 909 E Main St Richmond VA 23219

SEYMOUR-HARRIS, BARBARA LAVERNE, lawyer; b. Columbia, S.C., July 9, 1953; d. Leroy Semon and Barbara Lucile (Youngblood) Seymour; m. Canaan L. Harris. BS, S.C. State Coll., 1975; JD, Georgetown U., 1979; MBA, Harvard U., 1985. Bar: S.C. 1979, Tex. 1984, U.S. Dist. Ct. (ea. dist.) Tex. 1983, U.S. Dist. Ct. (so. dist.) Tex. 1985. Tax atty. Texaco Inc., White Plains, N.Y., 1979-80, Houston, 1980—. Troop leader Girl Scouts U.S., White Plains, 1979-80, asst. troop leader, 1981-82; active Leader Houston, 1981-82; treas., bd. dirs. Sickle Cell Disease Research Found. of Tex., Houston, 1986-87. Named One of 50 Outstanding Young Leaders of the Future, Ebony Mag., 1983. Mem. Houston Black Women Lawyers Assn. (sec. 1981-82, treas. 1982-83), Houston Bus. Forum (bd. dirs. 1983, 87), Nat. Bar Assn. (com. chmn. 1982-83), ABA, S.C. Bar Assn., Tex. Bar Assn., Harvard Bus. Sch. Black Alumni Assn. (historian 1985—). Democrat. Roman Catholic. Corporate taxation, Pension, profit-sharing, and employee benefits, State and local taxation. Office: Texaco Inc 1111 Rusk St Houston TX 77052

SFASCIOTTI, MARY L., lawyer; b. Kenosha, Wis., Nov. 5, 1941; d. Joseph Peter and Lilia Mary Louise Sfasciotti. B.A., Ripon Coll., 1962; diplomate Universita Per Stranieri, Perugia, Italy, 1961; J.D., Northwestern U., 1965. Bar: Wis. 1965, U.S. Dist. Ct. (no. dist.) Wis. 1965, U.S. Ct. Appeals (7th cir.) 1966, U.S. Dist. Ct. (no. dist.) Ill. 1967. Atty. Immigrant Service League, Chgo., 1965-68; atty./advisor Bd. Immigration Appeals, Washington, 1968-70; asst. U.S. atty. Dept. Justice, Chgo., 1970-74; assoc. prof. law John Marshall Law Sch., Chgo., 1974-75; assoc. regional counsel EEOC, Chgo., 1975-76; sole practice, Chgo., 1976—. Author chpt. in book Immigration Law and Practice, 1983. Named Outstanding Young Citizen of Chgo., Jr. Chgo. Assn. Commerce and Industry, 1973-74, Outstanding Young Citizen of Ill., Ill. Jr. Assn. Commerce and Industry, 1974-75. Mem. Wis. State Bar Assn., Chgo. Bar Assn., Ill. Bar Assn., Am. Assn. Immigration Lawyers. Federal civil litigation, Family and matrimonial, Immigration, naturalization, and customs. Office: 79 W Monroe St Suite 1215 Chicago IL 60603

SFEKAS, STEPHEN JAMES, lawyer, educator; b. Balt., Feb. 12, 1947; s. James Stephen and Lee (Mesologites) S.; m. Joanne Lorraine Murphy, May 27, 1973; children—James Stephen, Andrew Edward Stephen, Christina Marie. B.S. in Fgn. Service, Georgetown U., 1968; M.A. (Danforth fellow, Woodrow Wilson fellow) Yale U., 1972; J.D., Georgetown U., 1973. Bar: Md. 1973, U.S. Dist. Ct. Md. 1974, U.S. Ct. Appeals (4th cir.) 1974. Law clk. U.S. Dist. Ct., Balt., 1973-74; assoc. firm Frank, Bernstein, Conaway & Goldman, Balt., 1974-75; asst. atty. gen. State of Md., Balt., 1975-81; assoc. firm Tydings & Rosenberg, Balt., 1981-82, ptnr., 1983-86, with firm Miles & Stockbridge, 1986—; instr. legal writing Community Coll. Balt., 1976-79; instr. legal ethics Goucher Coll., Balt., 1979; instr. adminstrv. law U. Md., Balt., 1981—. Editor Georgetown Law Jour., 1972-73; contbr. articles to legal publs. Bd. dirs. Md. region NCCJ, 1981—, co-chmn. Md. region, 1986—; mem. Piraeus Sister City Com., City of Balt., 1983—; mem. parish council Greek Orthodox Cathedral of Annunciation, Balt., 1981-84; mem. internat. com. Balt. region ARC, 1984-85; mem. adv. com. on bread for the world, Dept. Ch. and Soc., Greek Orthodox Archdiocese N. and S.Am., 1984—; pres. Greek Orthodox Counseling and Social Services of Balt. WHO fellow, London, 1979. Fellow Soc. for Values in Higher Edn.; mem. ABA (Grant Morris fellow 1979, forum com. on health law), Md. Bar Assn., Bar Assn. Balt. City, Nat. Health Lawyers Assn., Am. Soc. Hosp. Attys. Democrat. Administrative and regulatory, Health, Federal civil litigation. Office: Miles & Stockbridge 10 Light St Baltimore MD 21202

SHABAZ, JOHN C., federal judge; b. West Allis, Wis., June 25, 1931; s. Cyrus D. and Harriet T.; children: Scott J., Jeffrey J. Student, U. Wis., 1949-53, Marquette U., 1953-54; LL.B., Marquette U., 1957. Sole practice West Allis, Wis., 1957-81; mem. Wis. Ho. of Reps., 1967-81; judge U.S. Dist. Ct. (we. dist.) Wis., 1981—. Judicial administration. Office: US District Court PO Box 2687 Madison WI 53701 *

SHACKLETON, RICHARD JAMES, lawyer; b. Orange, N.J., May 24, 1933; s. S. Paul and Mildred W. (Welsh) S.; m. Katharine L. Richards, June 16, 1956; children: Katharine Margaret, Julia Anne, Forrest Maxwell. Student Kalamazoo Coll., 1957; JD, Rutgers U., 1961. Bar: N.J. 1961, U.S. Dist. Ct. N.J., U.S. Dist. Ct. (ea. dist.) Va., N.Y. 1982, U.S. Dist. Ct. (so. dist.) N.Y., U.S. Ct. Appeals (3d and 4th cirs.), U.S. Supreme Ct. Ltd. atty. Berry Whitson & Berry, 1961; practice, Ship Bottom, N.J., 1961—; sr. ptnr. Shackleton, Hazeltine & Dasti, Ship Bottom, 1965—; dir. Citizens State Bank of N.J., Forked River. Pres., Beach Haven Inlet Taxpayers Assn., 1958-68; pres. Ocean County Vis. Homemakers Assn., 1966-72. Mem. Am. Trial Lawyers Assn., Am. Judicature Soc., ABA, N.J. Bar Assn., N.Y. Bar Assn., Ocean County Bar Assn., Essex County Assn., Ocean County Lawyers Club, Henryville Conservation Club (chmn. bd.), Henryville Flyfishers Club (pres.), Phila. Gun Club. Republican. Clubs: Seaview Country (Absecon, N.J.); Tuscarora. Federal civil litigation, State civil litigation, Local government. Home: 5614 West Ave Beach Haven NJ 08008 Office: 22d St and Long Beach Blvd Ship Bottom NJ 08008

SHADDOCK, ROBERT MONTGOMERY, lawyer; b. Rochester, N.Y., Oct. 27, 1952; s. Warren Montgomery and Gloris (Mulford) S.; m. Mary Agnes Liebel, Sept. 2, 1983; 1 child, John Warren. BA, Hobart Coll., 1975; JD, SUNY, Buffalo, 1978. Bar: N.Y. 1979, U.S. Dist. Ct. (we. dist.) N.Y. 1979. Asst. pub. defender Monroe County, Rochester, 1979-85; trial atty. Law Office of John Alletto, Travelers Ins. Co., Rochester, 1985—. Committeeman Addsford Rep. Com., 1986—. Mem. ABA, N.Y. State Bar Assn., Monroe County Bar Assn. Episcopalian. State civil litigation, Insurance, Personal injury. Office: Law Office of John Alletto 2 State St Suite 810 Rochester NY 14614

SHADDOCK, WILLIAM CHARLES, lawyer; b. Orange, Tex., Aug. 25, 1951; s. Carroll Bitting and Hulda Martha (Gaertner) S.; m. Kim Lei McDonald, Mar. 27, 1982; children: William Charles, Andrew Christopher. B.B.A., Tex. Christian U., 1973; M.B.A., So. Meth. U., 1974; J.D., Baylor U., 1977. Bar: Tex. 1977, U.S. Dist. Ct. (no. dist.) Tex. 1980. Assoc. Turner Hitchins, Webb, McInerney & Strother, Dallas, 1977-83; gen. counsel, v.p. Shaddock & Cook Developers, Inc., Dallas, 1983—; dir. Preston North Nat. Bank, Dallas; bd. dirs. The Colony Municipal Utility Dist., 1974-76. Mem. ABA, Dallas Bar Assn., Tex. Christian U. Alumni Assn. (bd. dirs. 1981-84), Sigma Chi. Contbr. article to profl. jours. Republican. Lutheran. Club: Downtown Dallas Rotary. General corporate, Real property, State civil litigation. Home: 4364 Mockingbird Pkwy Dallas TX 75205 Office: Shaddock & Cook Developers Inc 17330 Preston Rd Suite 200 D Dallas TX 75252

SHADLEY, KAY LEE, lawyer; b. Crawfordsville, Ind., Dec. 30, 1949; d. Kenneth Woodrow Shadley and Wilma Grace (Myer) Wilkinson. BS with highest distinction, Purdue U., 1971; postgrad., Tobe-Coburn Sch. for Fashion Careers, 1972; JD, Bklyn. Law Sch., 1978. Bar: N.Y. 1979. Atty. J.C. Penney Co. Inc., N.Y.C., 1979-83, Allied Stores Corp., N.Y.C., 1983—. Legal counsel Vol. Lawyers for the Arts, N.Y.C., 1979—. Mem. N.Y. State Bar Assn. (antitrust com. corp. cousnel sect. 1984—), N.Y. County Lawyers Assn. (chmn. corp. law depts. com. 1984—), Assn. of Bar of City of N.Y. (profl. responsibility com. 1983—). Methodist. Administrative and regulatory, Contracts commercial, Trademark and copyright. Home: 220 E 63d St Apt 9-P New York NY 10021 Office: Allied Stores Corp 1114 Ave of Americas New York NY 10036

SHADOAN, WILLIAM LEWIS, circuit judge; b. Galesburg, Ill., July 12, 1931; s. William Parker and Hortense (Lewis) S.; m. Katherine E. Thomson, 1961; children—Ann-Wayne Harlan, Kate, Tom. B.S., U. Ky., 1955; J.D., U. Louisville, 1961. Bar: Ky. 1961, U.S. Dist. Ct. (we. dist.) Ky. 1961. City atty., Wickliffe, Ky., 1963-65; county atty. Ballard County, Ky., 1967-79; cir. judge 1st Jud. Dist., Wickliffe, Ky., 1984—. Chmn., Ballard County Democratic Party, 1963; trustee Methodist Ch., Wickliffe, 1961-84; adviser Selective Service, Paducah, Ky., 1968; chmn. Wickliffe C. of C., 1967-71; mem. exec. com. Ky. Hist. Soc., Frankfort. Named assoc. justice Ky. Supreme Ct., 1984. Served to capt. U.S. Army, 1955-59. Mem. Ky. Health Systems Assn. (vice chmn. 1976-82), ABA, Ky. Bar, Assn. Trial Lawyers Am., Ky. County Ofcls. Bd. (chmn. 1976-80), Miss. River Commn. (chmn. 1976-83), Ky. County Attys. Assn. (pres. 1966-77), First Dist. Bar Assn. (pres.). Lodges: Mason (Wickliffe); Shriners (Madisonville, Ky.); Order of Eastern Star, Elks. Jurisprudence. Home: Route 2 Wickliffe KY 42087 Office: Ballard Courthouse 4th St Wickliffe KY 42087

SHADUR, MILTON I., judge; b. St. Paul, June 25, 1924; s. Harris and Mary (Kaplan) S.; m. Eleanor Pilka, Mar. 30, 1946; children: Robert, Karen, Beth. B.S., U. Chgo., 1943, J.D. cum laude, 1949. Bar: Ill. 1949, U.S. Supreme Ct. 1957. Sole practice Chgo., 1949-80; assoc. Goldberg, Devoe & Brussel, 1949-51; ptnr. Shadur, Drupp & Miller and predecessor firms, 1951-80; judge U.S. Dist. Ct. (no. dist.) Ill., Chgo., 1980—; commr. Ill. Supreme Ct. Character and Fitness, 1961-72, chmn., 1971; gen. counsel Ill. Jud. Inquiry Bd., 1975-80. Editor-in-chief: U. Chgo. Law Rev., 1948-49. Chmn. visiting com. U. Chgo. Law Sch., 1971-76, bd. dirs. Legal Assistance Found. Chgo., 1972-78; trustee Village of Glencoe, 1969-74, Ravinia Festival Assn., 1976—, mem. exec. com. Served to lt. (j.g.) USNR, 1943-46. Fellow Am. Bar Found.; mem. ABA (spl. com. on youth edn. for citizenship 1975-79), Ill. State Bar Assn. (joint com. on rules of jud. conduct 1974), Chgo. Bar Assn. (chmn. legis. com. 1963-65, jud. com. 1970-71, profl. ethics com. 1975-76, sec. 1967-69), Chgo. Council Lawyers, Order of Coif. Judicial administration. Office: US Dist Ct 219 Dearborn St Chicago IL 60604 *

SHAEFFER, HENRY WARREN, lawyer; b. Bryn Mawr, Pa., Mar. 1, 1945; s. George and Pauline (Stargle) S.; m. Gail Abrams, June 7, 1970. BS cum laude, U. Pa., 1967; JD magna cum laude, Harvard U., 1971. Bar: Calif. 1973, U.S. Dist. Ct. (no. dist.) Calif. 1973, U.S. Ct. Appeals (9th cir.) 1973, U.S. Dist. Ct. (cen. dist.) Calif. 1981. Legal editor Bancroft-Whitney Co., San Francisco, 1972-75; assoc. O-Melveny & Myers, Los Angeles, 1975-79; dir. investment adminstrn. Coldwell Banker Mgmt. Corp., Los Angeles, 1979; ptnr. Freshman, Marantz, Orlanski, Cooper & Klein, Los Angeles, 1981-86, spl. counsel, 1986—; pres. Downtime, Inc., 1986—. Note editor Harvard Law Rev., Cambridge, 1970-71. Mem. ABA, Am. Mgmt. Assn., Los Angeles County Bar Assn. Avocations: poet, songwriter. Securities. Home: 825 Elyria Dr Los Angeles CA 90065 Office: 9100 Wilshire Blvd 8th Floor E Tower Los Angeles CA 90212

SHAFER, STEPHANIE JANE, lawyer; b. N.Y.C., Apr. 9, 1953; d. Mark and Lillian (Boroff) S. BA, U. Colo., 1974, JD, 1981. Bar: Colo. 1981. Law clk. to presiding justice Colo. Supreme Ct., 1981-82; assoc. Holme, Roberts & Owens, Denver, 1983—. Editor-in-chief U. Colo. Law Rev., 1980-81. Mem. Order of Coif, Phi Beta Kappa. Commercial, General corporate, Real property. Home: 1515 E 9th Ave #209 Denver CO 80718 Office: Holme Roberts & Owens 1700 Broadway Suite 1800 Denver CO 80290

SHAFER, W. O., lawyer; b. Nolan County, Tex., July 6, 1917; m. Margaret Frances Crutsinger, Dec. 22;. Student, Ranger Jr. Coll., 1934-36; JD, Samford U., 1937. Bar: Tex. 1939, U.S. Dist. Ct. (no. dist.) Tex. 1948, U.S. Dist. Ct. (we. dist.) Tex. 1954, U.S. Ct. Appeals (5th cir.) 1955, U.S. Supreme Ct. 1967, U.S. Dist. Ct. (ea. dist.) Tex. 1976, U.S. Ct. Appeals (10th cir.) 1976. Pres. Shafer, Davis, McCollum, Ashley, O'Leary & Stoker, Inc., Odessa, Tex., 1973%; justice of the peace Ector County, Tex., 1941-44, county atty., 1945-50; dist. atty. Ector and Midland Counties, Tex., 1951-52. Mem. ABA (bd. dirs. 1968-72), Tex. Bar Assn. (bd. dirs. 1960-63, chmn. bd. dirs. 1963, pres. 1966-67), Ector Bar Assn. (bd. dirs., pres.), Am. Coll. Trial Lawyers, Internat. Acad. Trial Lawyers (bd. dirs. 1969-73), Tex. Assn. Def. Counsel (bd. dirs., exec. v.p. 1963-67, pres. 1968-69), Fedn. Ins. Counsel, Def. Research Inst., Nat. Conf. Bar Pres.'s (chmn. 1969-70), Odessa C. of C. Federal civil litigation, State civil litigation, Personal injury. Office: Shafer Davis McCollum Ashley O'Leary & Stoker Inc PO Box 1552 Odessa TX 79760

SHAFFER, CHARLES ALAN, lawyer; b. Wilkes-Barre, Pa., July 22, 1938; s. Joseph and Irene G. (Murzin) S.; m. Barbara A. Kurlancheek, July 30, 1961; children—Jonathan D., Susan D. B.S. in Econs., U. Pa., 1960, J.D., 1963. Bar: Pa. 1963, U.S. Dist. Ct. (mid. dist.) Pa. 1968, U.S. Ct. Appeals (3d cir.) 1975, U.S. Supreme Ct. 1976; diplomate Nat. Bd. Trial Advocacy; cert. civil trial adv. Sole practice, 1963-68; asst. pub. defender Luzerne County, Pa., 1965-67; law clk. Ct. Common Pleas of Luzerne County, 1967-69; 1st clk. of Orphans' Ct., dep. register of wills, 1972-83; ptnr. Mahler & Shaffer, Wilkes-Barre, 1968—; mem. faculty Wilkes Coll., 1964-70; nat. panel arbitrators Am. Arbitration Assn. Bd. dirs. Jewish Community Ctr., 1970-76; pres. United Rehab. Services, Inc., 1970-72; incorporator, bd. dirs. Health Services Agy. Northeastern Pa. Mem. Luzerne County Bar Assn. (exec. com. 1976-82), Pa. Bar Assn., ABA, Pa. Trial Lawyers Assn., Assn. Trial Lawyers Am. Clubs: Westmoreland (Wilkes-Barre); Midwest Gentlemen's. Federal civil litigation, State civil litigation, Personal injury. Office: Mahler & Shaffer 46 Public Sq Wilkes-Barre PA 18702

SHAFFER, HERMAN MORRIS, lawyer; b. Kansas City, Mo., June 20, 1951; s. Harry and Muriel B. (Hurst) S. BA, U. Kans., 1973; JD, U. Mo., 1976. Bar: Mo. 1976, U.S. Dist. Ct. (we. dist.) Mo. 1976, U.S. Ct. Appeals (9th cir.) 1978, U.S. Supreme Ct. 1979, U.S. Tax Ct. 1986, U.S. Ct. Appeals (8th cir.) 1986. Assoc. Jolley, Walsh, Hager & Gordon, Kansas City, 1980-83, ptnr., 1983—; mem. AFL-CIO Lawyers Coordinating Com., Washington. Mem. ABA, Mo. Bar Assn., Kansas City Bar Assn., Am. Trial Lawyers Assn., Internat. Found. Employee Benefit Plans. Democrat. Avocations: sports, traveling, politics, history, psychology. Bankruptcy, Labor, Pension, profit-sharing, and employee benefits. Office: Jolley Walsh Hager & Gordon 1125 Grand Kansas City MO 64106

SHAFFER, JAY CHRISTOPHER, lawyer; b. Brookville, Pa., Sept. 18, 1947; s. John Rienard and Laverne (Berding) S.; m. Janice Rita McKenney, May 24, 1972; 1 child, Justin. BA, Ohio State U., 1969; JD, Harvard U., 1974. Bar: Ohio 1974, U.S. Supreme Ct. 1978. Atty. office gen. counsel FTC, Washington, 1974-77; counsel subcom. on oversight, interstate and fgn. com. U.S. Ho. of Reps., Washington, 1977-79, atty. antitrust div., 1979-82; dep. dir. policy planning antitrust div. U.S. Dept. of Justice, Washington, 1982-84, chief legal adv. unit antitrust div., 1984-86; dep. dir. policy bur. competition FTC, Washington, 1986—. Served to sgt. U.S. Army, 1970-72, Korea. Mem. ABA, Fed. Bar Assn. Administrative and regulatory, Antitrust. Home: 7016 Leewood Forest Dr Springfield VA 22151 Office: FTC Room 376 Washington DC 20580

SHAFFER, RICHARD JAMES, lawyer, manufacturing company executive; b. Pe Ell, Wash., Jan. 26, 1931; s. Richard Humphrys and Laura Rose (Faas) S.; m. Donna M. Smith, May 13, 1956; children: Leslie Lauren Shaffer and Stephanie Jane Athenton. B.A., U. Wash.; LL.B., Southwestern U. Bar: Calif. Vice pres., gen. counsel, sec. NI, Inc., Long Beach, Calif., 1974—; gen. counsel Masco Bldg. Products Corp., Long Beach, 1985—. Trustee Ocean View Sch. Dist., 1965-73, pres., 1966, 73; mem. fin. adv. com. Orange Coast Coll., 1966; mem. Long Beach Local Devel. Corp., 1978—. Served in USN, 1954-57. Mem. Am. Bar Assn., Calif. Bar Assn. (exec. com. corporate law dept. com. bus. sect. 1983—), Los Angeles County Bar Assn. Clubs: Huntington Harbour Yacht, Huntington Harbour Ski. General corporate. Office: NI Industries Inc One Golden Shore Long Beach CA 90802

SHAFFER, ROBERTA IVY, law librarian, lawyer. AB, Vassar Coll., 1973; M of Librarianship, Emory U., 1975; JD, Tulane U., 1980; cert. in arts mgmt., Am. U., 1987. Bar: Tex. 1982, U.S. Dist. Ct. (so. dist.) Tex., U.S. Ct. Appeals (5th cir.), U.S. Supreme Ct. Dir. research and writing U. Houston Law Ctr., 1980-84, assoc. dir. law and tech., 1982-84; spl. asst. to law librarian Library of Congress, Washington, 1984—; cons. Coca-Cola Co., Atlanta, 1975-76, Research Info. Service, Houston, 1982-84; edn. rep. Westlaw, St. Paul, 1982-83. Mem. ABA, Inter-Am. Bar Assn., Maritime Law Assn., ALA, Am. Assn. Law Libraries, Internat. Assn. Law Libraries. Avocation: swimming. Computer, Legal history, Comparative law. Office: Library of Congress LM-240 Washington DC 20540

SHAFFER, SANFORD JOEL, lawyer; b. Bronx, N.Y., June 28, 1952; s. Seymour Perry and Gretta Ruth (Young) S. BS, George Washington U., 1974; JD, N.Y. Law Sch., 1977. Bar: Fla. 1978, N.Y. 1978, U.S. Dist. Ct. (so. and ea. dists.) N.Y. 1978, D.C. 1979, U.S. Dist. Ct. (so. dist.) Fla. 1981, U.S. Ct. Appeals (5th and 11th cirs.) 1981, U.S. Supreme Ct. 1981. Assoc. Sidney Sherwin, Queens, N.Y., 1978, Brookman & Brookman, N.Y.C., 1978-81; sole practice Miami, Fla., 1981—. V.p. legal affairs Sunrise (Fla.) Youth Athletic Club, 1983-85; mem. Broward County (Fla.) Young Dems., 1982-84; candidate Sunrise City Council, 1983; corr. sec. Bay Vista Dem. Club, North Bay Village, 1986—. Mem. ABA, Fla. Bar Assn., Phi Delta Phi. General practice, Family and matrimonial, Immigration, naturalization, and customs. Office: Miami Nat Bank Bldg 8101 Biscayne Blvd Suite 500 Miami FL 33138

SHAFFER, WAYNE ALAN, lawyer; b. Reno, Oct. 15, 1954; s. William V. and Shirley Joy (Perry) S.; m. Robin E. Sprung, Jan. 7, 1978. BA, U. Nev., 1977; JD magna cum laude, Calif. Western Sch. Law, 1981. Bar: Nev. 1981, U.S. Dist. Ct. Nev. 1981, Calif. 1982. Dep. dist. atty. Washoe County, Reno, 1981-82; assoc. Lionel, Sawyer & Collins, Reno, 1982-84, Law Office Eugene J. Wait Jr., Reno, 1985—; instr. Old Coll. Sch. Law, Reno, 1982. Mem. ABA, Nev. Bar Assn., Calif. Bar Assn., Assn. Def. Counsel No. Nev., Assn. Def. Counsel No. Calif. Republican. State civil litigation, Insurance, Personal injury. Office: Law Office Eugene J Wait Jr 305 W Moana Ln Suite D Reno NV 89504-0719

SHAFFERMAN, HOWARD HASWELL, lawyer; b. Washington, Aug. 21, 1954; s. Thomas Carlton and Eunice Lucille (Webber) S.; m. Molly Stephens Moore, May 4, 1985. AB, Princeton U., 1975; JD, U. Va., 1978. Bar: D.C. 1978. Assoc. Cadwalader, Wickersham & Taft, Washington, 1978-80, Shaw, Pittman, Potts & Trowbridge, Washington, 1980-86; assoc. solicitor U.S. Dept. Interior, Washington, 1986-87, dep. solicitor, 1987—. Vestryman The Falls Church Episc. Ch., Va., 1986—; mem. source evaluation bd. U.S. Small Bus. Adminstrn., Washington, 1984. Mem. ABA (pub. contracts law com.), D.C. Bar Assn. Republican. Clubs: Princeton Washington (council mem. 1983—, asst. treas. 1986—); Princeton N.Y. Government contracts and claims, Telecommunications, Contracts commercial. Home: 6551 Brooks Pl Falls Church VA 22044 Office: Dept Interior Rm 6351 Washington DC 20240

SHAFFERT, KURT, lawyer, chemical engineer; b. Vienna, July 20, 1929; s. Rudolph and Irma (Altar) S.; m. Judith Pytel, June 12, 1955; children—Elona Ruth, Robin Laurette. B. Ch.E., CCNY, 1951; LL.B. cum laude, NYU, 1963. Bar: N.Y. 1963, D.C. 1965, U.S. Supreme Ct. 1967, U.S. Patent and Trademark Office 1964. Chem. engr. Diamond Alkali Co., Newark, 1951-54; process devel. engr. Am. Cyanamid Co., Stamford, Conn., 1957-59; patent liaison engr. Uniroyal, Inc., 1959-63; assoc. Arthur, Dry & Kalish, N.Y.C., 1963-66, Office of Robert F. Conrad, Washington, 1966-69; sr. ptnr. Shaffert, Miller & Browne, Washington, 1970-74; sr. trial atty. intellectual property sect. Antitrust div. Dept. of Justice, Washington, 1974-85, professions and intellectual property sect., 1985— . Served with U.S. Army, 1955-56. Mem. Profl. Assn. Antitrust Div. Dept of Justice (pres. 1978-79), Bar Assn. D.C. (council del. 1972-74), ABA, D.C. Bar Assn. Federal civil litigation, Patent, Antitrust.

SHAGIN, CRAIG RANDALL, lawyer; b. Paterson, N.J., Jan. 29, 1955; s. Felix Arthur and Elaine Judith (Anderson) S. AB, Haverford Coll., 1977; JD, Villanova U., 1980. Bar: Pa., 1980, U.S. Dist. Ct. (ea. dist.) Pa., 1980. Law clk. to judge Pa. Superior Ct., Phila., 1980-82; assoc. Schnader, Harrison, Segal & Lewis, Phila., 1982-85; gen. counsel Hist. Landmarks for Living, Phila., 1985—. Committeeman Phila. Dems., 1983-85. Presdl. fellow Haverford Coll., 1977. Club: Phila. Sea Horses. Avocations: scuba diving, skiing. Real property, Banking, Construction. Office: Hist Landmarks for Living 30 S Front St Philadelphia PA 19106

SHAINES, ROBERT ARTHUR, lawyer; b. Newburyport, Mass., Nov. 24, 1929; s. Edward I. and Ruth Helena (Diamond) S.; m. Gladys Regger, Dec. 1954 (div. Sept. 1984); children: Stephanie, Pamela, Kate.; m. Denise Kelly, Dec. 30, 1984. Student, U. N.H., 1949; JD cum laude, Boston U., 1951. Assoc. Lobel & Lobel, Boston, 1954; ptnr. Reinhart & Shaines, Portsmouth, N.H., 1954-56, Shaines Brown, Portsmouth, 1956-66, Robert A. Shaines & Assocs., Portsmouth, 1966-70, Shaines, Madrigan & McEachern, Portsmouth, 1970-85, Shaines & McEachern, Portsmouth, 1985—; pres. Strawberry Banke, Inc., Portsmouth, 1977-80. Mayor City of Portsmouth, 1960-61; councilman City of Portsmouth, 1958-67; police commr. City of Portsmouth, 1980-81. Served as capt. USAF, 1950-54, Korea. Mem. N.H. Bar Assn. (sec. 1973-75, gov. at large 1976-79, chmn. prepaid legal services com. 1976-79), Portsmouth Bar Assn. (pres. 1963), Rockingham Bar Assn. (pres. 1972). Federal civil litigation, State civil litigation, General corporate. Home: 81 Garland Rd Rye NH 03870 Office: Shaines & McEachern 25 Maplewood Ave Portsmouth NH 03801

SHAKOOR, ADAM ADIB, judge, educator; b. Detroit, Aug. 6, 1947; s. Harvey Lester and Esther (Hart) S.; m. Nikki Haleema Graves; children—Malik, Sahir, Muhammad, Lateef, Keisha, Khalidah, Koya, Kareena, Jelani. B.S., Wayne State U., 1971, M.Ed., 1974, J.D., 1976. Bar: Mich. 1977, U.S. Dist. Ct. (ea. dist.) Mich. 1977. Prof. Wayne County Community Coll., Detroit, 1971—; mem. Ashford, Cannon, Lumumba, Edison & Shakoor, Detroit, 1978-81, Shakoor & Assocs., 1977-78; judge Common Pleas Ct., State of Mich., Detroit, 1981-82; judge 36th Dist. Ct., Detroit, 1982-85, chief judge, 1985—. Mem. ABA, Assn. Black Judges Mich., Mich. Judges Assn. Islamic. Real property, Civil rights, Entertainment. Home: 2016 W Boston Blvd Detroit MI 48206 Office: 600 Randolph St Courtroom 403 Detroit MI 48226

SHALHOUB, MICHAEL DAVID, lawyer; b. Columbus, Ga., Sept. 10, 1957; s. Michael Elias and Boots Elizabeth (Moon) S. BA, Fordham U., 1979; JD, St. John's U., 1982. Bar: N.Y. 1983, U.S. Dist. Ct. (ea. and so. dists.) N.Y. 1985. Assoc. Smith & Laquercia P.C., N.Y.C., 1982-85, Heidell, Pittoni, Murphy & Bach, N.Y.C., 1985—. Mem. ABA, N.Y. Bar Assn., Am. Assn. Trial Lawyers, N.Y. State Trial Lawyers Assn. Roman Catholic. Avocations: sports, reading, travel. Insurance, State civil litigation, Personal injury. Home: 7 Wesleyan Ct Smithtown NY 11787 Office: Heidell Pittoni Murphy & Bach 100 Park Ave New York NY 10017

SHAMBAUGH, STEPHEN WARD, lawyer; b. South Bend, Ind., Aug. 4, 1920; s. Marion Clyde and Anna Violet (Stephens) S.; m. Marilyn Louise Pyle; children—Susan Wynne Shambaugh Hinkle, Kathleen Louise Shambaugh Thompson. Student San Jose State Tchrs. Coll., 1938-40, U. Ark., 1951; LL.B., U. Tulsa, 1954. Bar: Okla. 1954, Colo. 1964. Mem. staff Reading & Bates, Inc., Tulsa, 1951-54; v.p., gen. mgr., legal counsel Reading & Bates Drilling Co. Ltd., Calgary, Alta., Can., 1954-61; sr. ptnr. Bowman, Shambaugh, Geissinger & Wright, Denver, 1964-81; sole practice, Denver, 1981—; dir., fin. counsel various corps. Served to col. USAF ret. Mem. ABA, Fed. Bar Assn., Colo. Bar Assn., Okla. Bar Assn., Denver Bar Assn., P-51 Mustang Pilots Assn., Phi Alpha Delta. Clubs: Spokane; Petroleum of Bakersfield (Calif.); Masons, Shriners, Elks. Banking, General corporate, Oil and gas leasing.

SHANABERGER, CAROL JEAN, lawyer, paramedic; b. Burlington, Iowa, Dec. 5, 1952; d. Mark E. and Paula (Concino) S. BS, Western State Coll. Colo., 1975; JD, U. Denver, 1977. Bar: Colo. 1978, U.S. Dist. Ct. Colo. 1978, U.S. Ct. Appeals (10th cir.) 1978; cert. paramedic. Sole practice Crested Butte, Colo., 1978-80, Golden and Longmont, Colo., 1982—; assoc. Sessions and Silver, Denver, 1980-82; paramedic A-1 Ambulance, Golden and Longmont, 1982—; med. investigator State of Colo., Denver, 1985—; instr. med.-legal, advanced cardiac life support St. Anthony Hosp., Denver, Luth. Hosp., Wheatridge, Colo., 1983—, Community Coll., Greeley, Colo., 1984—; cons. pre-hosp. law Rockwell Industries, Arapahoe Community Coll. Contbr. articles to profl. jours. Mem. Assn. Trial Lawyers Am. (assoc.), Nat. Assn. EMS Physicians. Personal injury, Health, Pre-hospital care and emergency medical services liabilty. Home: 25 B Centaur Ct Lafayette CO 80026 Office: State of Colo 1525 Sherman St #110 Denver CO 80203

SHANAHAN, JAMES PATRICK, lawyer; b. Syracuse, N.Y., Jan. 28, 1934; s. Patrick F. and Mary M. (Donnelly) S. B.S., LeMoyne Coll., 1955; LL.B., Georgetown U., 1959, LL.M., 1961. Bar: N.Y. 1961, U.S. Dist. Ct. (no. dist.) N.Y. 1964, U.S. Ct. Appeals (2d cir.) 1968, U.S. Supreme Ct. 1970, U.S. Dist. Ct. (we. dist.) N.Y. 1974. Assoc. Covington & Burling, Washington, asst. U.S. atty. No. Dist. N.Y., 1964-70; 1st asst. corp. counsel City of Syracuse (N.Y.), 1970-72; sole practice, Syracuse, 1972—. Chmn. bd. trustees St. John the Evangelist Ch.; nat. bd. govs. LeMoyne Coll. Alumni Assn.; regional vice chmn. Syracuse Diocese Hope Appeal; mem. Georgetown U. Nat. Law Alumni Bd., 1986—. Mem. Onondaga County Bar Assn., N.Y. State Bar Assn., ABA. Democrat. Roman Catholic. Clubs: University (Syracuse); Cavalry (Manlius, N.Y.); Indian Spring Country (Boynton Beach, Fla.). Federal civil litigation, State civil litigation, Criminal. Address: 8321 Decoy Run Manliuse NY 13104

SHANAHAN, THOMAS M., state supreme court justice; b. Omaha, May 5, 1934; m. Jane Estelle Lodge, Aug. 5, 1956; children—Catherine Anne Shanahan Trofholz, Thomas M., Jr., Mary Elizabeth, Timothy F. A.B. magna cum laude, U. Notre Dame, 1956; J.D., Georgetown U., 1959. Bar: Nebr. Mem. McGinley, Lane, Mueller, Shanahan, O'Donnell & Merritt, Ogallala, Nebr.; assoc. justice Nebr. Supreme Ct., Lincoln, 1983—. Mem. Nebr. State Bar Assn. (Legal Services Lawyers Referral Service, ho. of dels. 13th jud. dist. 1983, rep. exec. council 1979-83), ABA, Western Nebr. Bar Assn. (pres. 1975-76, sec.-treas. 1969-70), Nebr. Assn. Trial Attys., Assn. Trial Lawyers Am. Judicial administration. Office: Nebr Supreme Ct State Capitol Bldg 1445 K St Lincoln NE 68509 *

SHANDELL, RICHARD ELLIOT, lawyer; b. N.Y.C., Dec. 23, 1932; s. Edward and Dorothy (Glass) S.; m. Helene Hicken, Aug. 28, 1954; children: Andrea, Thomas, Deborah. BS in Econs., U. Pa., 1953; JD, Columbia U., 1956. Bar: N.Y. 1957. Ptnr. Katz, Shandell, Katz & Erasmous, N.Y.C, Glaser, Shandell & Blitz, N.Y.C, 1981—. Author: The Preparation and Trial of Medical Malpractice Cases, 1981; contbg. author: Medical Malpractice: Strategic and Practical Principles 1986. Mem. Assn. Trial Lawyers Am. (gov.), N.Y. State Trial Lawyers Assn. (past pres.). Home: 214 W 17th St New York NY 10011 Office: Glaser Shandell & Blitz 150 Broadway New York NY 10038

SHANDOR, BOHDAN DONALD, lawyer; b. Paterson, N.J., May 21, 1952; s. Vincent and Oksana (Sichynsky) S.; m. Maria Christina Koczerzuk, June 15, 1975; children—Christina Romana, Alexander Vincent. B.S. cum laude in Econs., U. Pa., 1973; M.B.A. in Fin., N.Y.U., 1977, J.D., 1977, LL.M. in Corp. Law, 1982. Bar: N.J. 1977, U.S. Dist. Ct. N.J. 1977, N.Y. 1986. Assoc. Crummy, Del Deo, Dolan & Vecchione, Newark, 1977-80; div. atty. CPC N.Am., Englewood Cliffs, N.J., 1980-82; mgr. bus. planning and devel. CPC Internat., Englewood Cliffs, 1982-83, counsel, 1983-86; div. counsel Best Foods Div., 1986—; dir. Acme Resin Corp., Forest Park, Ill., Food Opinions, Inc., Union, N.J., Amerchol Corp., Edison, N.J., 1984-86. Marcus Nadler fellow NYU, 1975. Mem. ABA, N.J. State Bar Assn., Am. Corp. Counsel Assn., Ukrainian Am. Bar Assn. (pres. 1983-84). Clubs: U. Pa. Alumni of N.J., Wharton Bus. Sch. General corporate, Private international, Mergers and acquisitions. Home: 21 Pleasant Pl Brunswick NJ 08902 Office: CPC Internat Inc International Plaza Englewood Cliffs NJ 07632

SHANE, B(ENJAMIN) JEROME, lawyer; b. Phila., Aug. 2, 1928; s. Hyman and Evelyn (Oistatcher) S.; m. Rhona Sally Chenetz, Dec. 25, 1966; children: Corey, Meredith. AB, U. Pa., 1950, JD, 1953. Bar: Pa. 1954, U.S. Dist. Ct. (ea. dist.) Pa., U.S. Ct. Appeals (3d cir.), U.S. Supreme Ct. 1961. Assoc. Hyman Shane, Phila., 1953-56; sole practice Phila., 1956-75, 79-86; ptnr. Shane & Rubin, Phila., 1975-79. Lodge: Masons. Family and matrimonial, Personal injury, State civil litigation. Home: 1601 Riverview Rd Gladwyne PA 19035 Office: Suite 712 GSB Bldg Bala Cynwyd PA 19004

SHANE, PETER MILO, law educator, lawyer; b. Oceanside, N.Y., July 12, 1952; s. Albert and Ann (Semanoff) S.; m. Martha Elisabeth Chamallas, June 27, 1981; 1 child, Elisabeth Ann. AB, Harvard U., 1974; JD, Yale U., 1977. Bar: N.Y. 1978, U.S. Ct. Appeals (5th cir.) 1978, D.C. 1979, U.S. Ct. Appeals (8th cir.) 1983, U.S. Supreme Ct. 1984. Law clk. to presiding justice U.S. Ct. Appeals (5th cir.), New Orleans, 1977-78; atty., advisor office of legal counsel, U.S. Dept. Justice, Washington, 1978-81; asst. gen. counsel Office of Mgmt. and Budget, Washington, D.C., 1981; assoc. prof. law U. Iowa, Iowa City, 1981-85, prof. law, 1985—; adj. lectr. Am. U., Washington, D.C., 1979-80; vis. prof. law Duke U., Durham, N.C., 1986; cons. U.S. Dept. Edn., Washington, D.C., 1980; cooperating atty. Iowa Civil Liberties Union, Des Moines, 1982—, bd. dirs., 1987—. Mem. Dem. cen. com. Johnson County, Iowa, 1982—. Old Gold Summer fellow U. Iowa, 1981-84, Mellon Found fellow, 1982. Mem. ABA (vice chmn. com. on govt. orgn. and separation of powers adminstrv. law sect. 1983-87, exec. com. adminstrv. law sect.1987, chmn. com. on edn. 1987—). Jewish. Legal education, Administrative and regulatory, Constitutional. Office: U Iowa Coll Law Iowa City IA 52242

SHANEY, KEVIN ROBERT, lawyer; b. Cleve., Apr. 12, 1950; s. Robert and Ramona (Reynolds) S.; m. Monica Ruth Martinez, Nov. 23, 1979. BA in Polit. Sci., Mich. State U., 1972; M Pub. Health, U. Hawaii, 1974; JD, U. Colo., 1977; LLM in Taxation, U. Denver, 1981. Bar: Colo. 1977, U.S. Dist. Ct. Colo. 1977, U.S. Tax Ct. 1983, Tex. 1985. Assoc. Lattimer, Bollinger, Young & Drummond P.C., Pueblo, Colo., 1977-79; asst. atty. Pueblo County, 1980; atty. tax Shell Oil Co., Houston, 1981-85; mgr. tax research and planning Castle & Cooke, San Francisco, 1985, dir. tax research and planning, 1986—. Author: (with others) Taxation of Real Estate Dispositions, 1982; Selected Legal Aspects of China's Conduct of Foreign Trade, 1977, The Basic Requirements for Having and Operating a Foreign Sales Corporation, 1985, Mobil Oil: Have Captive Insurance Companies Run Out Of Gas, 1986. Profl. Fellow NEH, U. Chgo., 1979. Mem. ABA, Colo. Bar Assn., Tex. Bar Assn. Avocations: rare books, tennis. Corporate taxation, Private international. Home: 483 S Hamel Rd Los Angeles CA 90048 Office: Castle & Cooke 10900 Wilshire Blvd Suite 1500 Los Angeles CA 90024

SHANK, SUZANNE, lawyer; b. Kansas City, Mo., Nov. 13, 1946; d. Howard Howe and Bettie Ann (Winkler) Hettick; m. Neil Alan Shank, Nov. 3, 1973; children—Andrew David, Michael Darrin, Pamela Suzanne. B.J., U. Mo., 1972; M.Pub.Adminstrn. in Health Adminstrn., U. Mo.-Kansas City, 1982, J.D., 1982. Bar: Mo. 1982, U.S. Dist. Ct. (we. dist.) Mo. 1982. Journalist, U. Kans. Med. Ctr., Kansas City, 1972-73; asst. editor Am. Family Physician, Kansas City, Mo., 1973-75; exec. dir. Shank Med. Clinic, Kansas City, Mo., 1975-80; assoc. firm Shughart, Thomson & Kilroy, Kansas City, 1982—. Mem. Friends of Zoo, Kansas City., Mo., 1981—, Menorah Med. Ctr. Aux., Kansas City., Mo., 1982—. Named one of Outstanding Young Women Am., 1983. Mem. Am. Soc. Hosp. Attys., Mo. Soc. Hosp. Attys., ABA, Mo. Bar Assn., Kansas City Bar Assn., Kappa Tau Alpha. Health, Insurance, Personal injury. Home: 701 S Prairie Ln PO Box 686 Raymore MO 64083 Office: Shughart Thomson & Kilroy PO Box 13007 Kansas City MO 64199

SHANK, WILLIAM O., lawyer; b. Hamilton, Ohio, Jan. 11, 1924; s. Horace Cooper and Bonnie (Winn) S.; m. Shirleen Allison, June 25, 1949; children—Allison Kay, Kristin Elizabeth. B.A., Miami U., Oxford, O., 1947; J.D., Yale, 1950. Bar: Ohio, Ill. bars, also U.S. Supreme Ct. bar. Practice in Hamilton, Ohio, 1950-55, Chgo., 1955—; mem. firm Shank, Briede & Spoerl, 1950-55; asso. Lord, Bissell & Brook, 1955-58; atty. Chemetron Corp., 1958-60, sr. atty., 1960-61, gen. atty., asst. sec., 1961-71, sec., gen. counsel, 1971-78; v.p., gen. counsel, sec. Walgreen Co., Deerfield, Ill., 1978—; Mem. bus. adv. council Miami U., Oxford, 1975—; dir. Midwest Securities Trust Co. Bd. dirs. Council for Community Services Met. Chgo., 1973-77; trustee Library Internat. Relations, 1971-78; bd. dirs. Chgo. Civic Fedn., 1984—; mem. Chgo. Crime Commn., 1985—. Served to 1st lt. USAAF, World War II, ETO. Fellow Am. Bar Found.; mem. ABA, Ill. Bar Assn., Chgo. Bar Assn., Am. Soc. Corp. Secs. (sec., pres. Chgo. regional group 1983-84, nat. dir. 1984—), Yale Law Sch. Assn. (past pres. Ill., exec. com. New Haven), Legal Club (pres. 1979-80), Law Club, Northwestern U. Corp. Counsel Inst. (chmn. planning com. 1973), Sigma Chi, Omicron Delta Kappa, Phi Delta Phi. Clubs: Yale (N.Y.C.); University (Chgo.), Economic (Chgo.). General corporate, Securities. Home: 755 S Shore Dr Crystal Lake IL 60014 Office: 200 Wilmot Rd Deerfield IL 60015

SHANKS, HERSHEL, lawyer, publisher, editor; b. Sharon, Pa., Mar. 8, 1930; s. Martin and Mildred (Freedman) S.; m. Judith Alexander Weil, Feb. 20, 1966; children: Elizabeth Jean, Julia Emily. B.A., Haverford (Pa.) Coll., 1952; M.A., Columbia, 1953; LL.B., Harvard, 1956. Bar: D.C. 1956. Trial atty. Dept. Justice, 1956-59; pvt. practice Washington, 1959—; partner firm Glassie Pewett, Beebe & Shanks, 1964—; editor Bibl. Archaeology Rev., Washington, 1975—; Pres. Bibl. Archaeology Soc., 1974—. Author: The Art and Craft of Judging, 1968, The City of David, 1973, Judaism in Stone, 1979; also articles.; co-editor: Recent Archeology in the Land of Israel, 1984; editor Bible Rev., 1985—; editor, publisher Moment mag., 1987—. Mem. Am., Fed., D.C. bar assns., Am. Schs. Oriental Research, Phi Beta Kappa. Clubs: Nat. Lawyers (Washington); Nat. Press. Administrative and regulatory, Federal civil litigation, Real property. Home: 5208 38th St NW Washington DC 20015 Office: Biblical Archaeology Review 3000 Connecticut Ave NW Suite 300 Washington DC 20008

SHANKS, WILLIAM ENNIS, JR., lawyer; b. Jackson, Miss., Sept. 5, 1950; s. William Ennis and Alice Josephine (Crisler) S.; m. Jean F. Steinschneider, Sept. 7, 1974; 1 child, William E. III. B.A., Harvard U., 1972; J.D. cum laude, Emory U., 1976; LL.M. with highest honors in Taxation, Ala. U., 1979. Bar: Ga. 1976, Ala. 1976, Ptnr. Balch & Bingham, Birmingham, Ala., 1976—. Bd. dirs. Birmingham Festival Theatre, 1980—, treas., 1980-84. Mem. Birmingham Estate Planning Council, Birmingham Employee Benefit Forum, Birmingham Profit Sharing Group, ABA (tax sect.), Order of Coif. Presbyterian. Clubs: Downtown, Exchange (bd. dirs. 1984-85, sec. 1985-86, v.p. 1985-86). Corporate taxation, Pension, profit-sharing, and employee benefits, Estate planning. Home: 1050 32d St S Birmingham AL 35205 Office: Balch & Bingham 600 N 18th St Birmingham AL 35203

SHANMAN, JAMES ALAN, lawyer; b. Cin., Aug. 1, 1942; s. Jerome D. and Mildred Louise (Bloch) S.; m. Marilyn Louise Glassman, June 11, 1972; 1 dau., Ellen Joan. B.S., U. Pa., 1963; J.D., Yale U., 1966. Bar: N.Y. 1967, U.S. Supreme Ct. 1971, U.S. Ct. Mil. Appeals 1971, U.S. Ct. Appeals (2d cir.) 1972, U.S. Dist. Ct. (so. and ea. dists.) N.Y. 1972, U.S. Ct. Internat. Trade, 1976. Assoc. Cahill Gordon & Reindel, N.Y.C., 1971-74, Freeman, Meade, Wasserman, Sharfman & Schneider, N.Y.C., 1974-76; mem. Sharfman, Shanman, Poret & Siviglia, P.C., N.Y.C., 1976—. Served to capt. USAF, 1966-71. Decorated Air Force Commendation medal. Mem. ABA, N.Y. State Bar Assn., Assn. Bar City N.Y. (com. on ins. law, 1985—), Am. Arbitration Assn. (comml. panel arbitrators), Air Force Assn. Club: Lotos. Federal civil litigation, State civil litigation, Insurance. Office: 1370 Ave of Americas New York NY 10019

SHANNON, JAMES MICHAEL, lawyer; b. Methuen, Mass., Apr. 4, 1952; s. Martin J. and Mary J. (Sullivan) S.; m. Silvia de Araujo Castro; 1 child, Sarah. BA, Johns Hopkins U., 1973; JD, George Washington U., 1975. Sole practice Lawrence, Mass., 1976-78; U.S. Rep. 5th Dist. U.S. Ho. of Reps., Mass., 1979-84; ptnr. Hale & Dorr, Boston, 1984-86; atty. gen. Commonwealth of Mass., Boston, 1987—. Mem. Mass. Bar Assn., D.C. Bar Assn. Democrat. Roman Catholic. Home: 401 Prospect St Lawrence MA 01842 Office: Atty Gens Office 1 Ashburton Pl Room 2010 Boston MA 02108

SHANNON, JOE, JR., lawyer; b. Fort Worth, Nov. 9, 1940; s. Joe and Juanita Elizabeth (Milliorn) S.; m. Carol Jean Tinsley, Aug. 10, 1968 (div. 1978); children—Kelley Jane, Joseph Patrick, Shelley Carol. B.A., U. Tex., 1962, LL.B., 1963. Bar: Tex. 1963, U.S. Supreme Ct. 1977, U.S. Dist. Ct. (no. dist.) Tex. 1970, U.S. Ct. Appeals (5th cir.) 1977; cert. family and criminal law Tex. Bd. Legal Specialization. Ptnr. Shannon & Shannon, Fort Worth, 1963-72; adminstrv. asst. to speaker, Tex. Ho. of Reps., Austin, 1970; chief criminal div. Tarrant County Dist. Atty., Fort Worth, 1972-78; sole practice, Fort Worth, 1978-86; ptnr. Snakard & Gambill, Ft. Worth, 1986— . Mem. Tex. Ho. of Reps., 1964-70. Mem. State Bar of Tex. (chmn. dist. grievance com. 1973-76, chmn. 1975-76), Tex. Criminal Def. Attys. Assn., Tex. Dist. and County Attys. Assn., North Tex. Family Law Specialists Assn., Fort Worth Jr. Bar Assn., Phi Alpha Delta. Lodges: Masons, Shriners. Criminal, Family and matrimonial, Insurance. Office: 3200 Tex Am Bank Bldg Fort Worth TX 76102

SHANNON, MALCOLM LLOYD, JR., lawyer; b. Phila., Jan. 27, 1946; s. Malcolm L. and Rosalia U. (Yanura) S.; m. Jeanne Marie Halle, Dec. 28, 1974; children—Travis Alan, Kate Meredith. B.B.A., U. N.Mex., 1968, J.D., 1971. Bar: N.Mex. 1971, Tex. 1981, U.S. Supreme Ct. 1976, Colo. 1984, Calif. 1986. Landman, clk. Ranchers Exploration & Devel. Co., Albuquerque, 1969-71; assoc. Ahern, Montgomery & Albert, Albuquerque, 1971-72; atty. Ranchers Exploration, 1972-73; assoc. Kool, Bloomfield & Eaves, Albuquerque, 1973-75; ptnr. Matthews, Shannon & Hooker, Albuquerque, 1975-78; gen. counsel, corp. sec. Koppen Mining Constrn. Co., Albuquerque, 1978-79; atty. Phillips Petroleum Co., Albuquerque, 1979-81; atty., land rep. Chevron Resources Co., San Antonio, 1981-82, dist. supr., 1982-85, div. mgr. land and legal dept., Englewood, Colo., 1985—, San Francisco, 1986—; lectr. mining and pub. land law U. N.Mex. Adv. com. solar energy application Tech. Vocat. Inst. of Albuquerque Pub. Schs., 1976; judge N.Mex. State Sci. Fair 1978-80; mem. ednl. accountability com. Cherry Creek Sch. Dist., 1984-86. Mem. ABA, Rocky Mountain Mineral Landmen Assn., AIME. Republican. Roman Catholic. Author publs. in field. Oil and gas leasing, General corporate, Real property. Office: 595 Market St Suite 2406 San Francisco CA 94105

SHANNON, MICHAEL GEORGE, lawyer; b. N.Y.C., Sept. 7, 1949; s. Michael George Shannon and Alice Miriam (O'Connor) Lover; m. Karen S. Craddock, Mar. 21, 1970; children: Heather, Jennifer, Kimberly. BA cum laude, St. Francis Coll., Bklyn., 1971; JD, St. John's U., Jamaica, N.Y., 1974; LLM in Trade Regulation, NYU, 1979. Bar: N.Y. 1975, U.S. Dist. Ct. (ea. and so. dists.) N.Y. 1975, U.S. Ct. Appeals (2d cir.) 1975, U.S. Dist. Ct. (no. dist.) N.Y. 1978, U.S. Dist. Ct. (we. dist.) 1980, U.S. Supreme Ct. 1978, U.S. Supreme Ct. 1980. Assoc. Amen, Weisman & Butler, N.Y.C., 1974-77; assoc. Summit, Rovins & Feldesman, N.Y.C., 1977-81, ptnr.,

1982—. Assoc. editor St. John's U. Law Rev., 1973-74, symposium editor, 1974; assoc. editor periodical The Catholic Lawyer, 1973-74. Mem. ABA (antitrust and litigation sects.), N.Y. State Bar Assn., Assn. of Bar of City of N.Y. Republican. Roman Catholic. Lodge: KC (adv. 1978-79). Federal civil litigation, State civil litigation, Antitrust. Office: Summit Rovins & Feldesman 445 Park Ave New York NY 10022

SHANNON, PETER MICHAEL, JR., lawyer; b. Chgo., Oct. 13, 1928; s. Peter Michael Sr. and Marian (Burke) S.; m. Anne M. Mueller, April 3, 1969; children: Peter III, Stephen, Heather, Eamon. BA, St. Mary of the Lake, Mundelein, Ill., 1949, MA, 1952, STL, 1953; JCL, Gregorian U., Rome, 1958; JD, U. Calif., Berkeley, 1971. Bar: Calif. 1972, D.C. 1972, U.S. Dist. Ct. Md. 1972, U.S. Dist. Ct. D.C. 1972, U.S. Ct. Appeals (1st, 2d, 3d, 4th, 5th, 6th, 7th, 8th, 9th and 10th cirs.) 1972-75, U.S. Supreme Ct. 1975. Supervisory atty. litigation U.S. Dept. of Justice, Washington, 1971-75; ptnr. Shannon, Moseman et al, Washington, 1980-82, Keck, Mahin & Cate, Chgo., 1982—; sr. appellate atty. ICC, Washington, 1975-78, dir. enforcement, 1976-80. Author: Energy and Transportation Implications of Ratemaking Policy Concerning Sources of Energy, 1980, Disposition of Real Estate by Religious Institutions, 1987. Mem. ABA (chmn. transp. com., adminstrv. law sect. 1984—), Am. Acad. Hosp. Attys., Assn. Transp. Practitioners, Canon Law Soc. (pres. 1965-66). Administrative and regulatory, Ecclesiastical law, Health. Home: 4546 S Wolf Rd Western Springs IL 60558 Office: Keck Mahin & Cate 8300 Sears Tower Chicago IL 60606

SHANNON, WILLIAM JAMES, lawyer; b. Cambridge, Mass., Feb. 27, 1939; s. William Holesworth and Virginia Nora (Keenan) S.; m. Naomi Sakamoto, July 9, 1980; 1 dau., Julia Mariko; children from previous marriage: Katherine Anne, Tracey Kristina. B.S. cum laude, U.S. Mcht. Marine Acad., 1961; J.D. in Internat. Affairs, Cornell U., 1971. Bar: Hawaii 1971, U.S. Ct. Appeals (9th cir.) 1971, N.Y. 1987. Sr. spl. agt. Office Naval Intelligence. Keflavik, Iceland, 1964-66, resident agt., Greenock, Scotland, 1966-68; assoc. Damon Key, Char & Bocken, Law Corp., Honolulu, 1971-74, ptnr., 1974-79; pres., dir. Shannon & Sakamoto, Law Corp., Honolulu, 1979—; fgn. legal cons. Braun, Moriya, Hoashi & Kubota, Tokyo, 1985—. Served as lt. USN, 1961-63. Mem. ABA, Hawaii Bar Assn. Assoc. note editor Cornell Internat. Law Jour., 1970-71. General corporate, Private international, Admiralty. Office: 911 Iino Bldg, 1-1 2-Chome Uchisaiwai-cho, Chiyoda-ku Tokyo 100, Japan

SHANNONHOUSE, JOSEPH GRANBERRY, IV, lawyer; b. Alexandria, La., May 27, 1945; s. Joseph Granberry, III, and Edna Christine (Parmelee) S.; m. Linda K. Bettis, Aug. 4, 1967; children—Joseph, Stephanie, Justin. B.S., Central State Coll., 1967; J.D., U. Okla., 1970; LL.M. in Taxation, NYU, 1972. Bar: Okla. 1970. Mem. Andrews Davis Legg Bixler Milsten & Murrah, Inc. and predecessors, Oklahoma City, 1972—. Mem. ABA, Okla. Bar Assn., Oklahoma County Bar Assn. Republican. Mem. Dutch Reform Ch. Author: Basic Tax for the Landman, Landman Handbook on Basic Land Management, 1978. Corporate taxation, Personal income taxation. Office: 500 W Main Suite 500 Oklahoma City OK 73102

SHANNONHOUSE, ROYAL GRAHAM, III, lawyer, educator; b. New Bern, N.C., May 18, 1929; s. Royal Graham and Mary Sue (Poe) S.; m. Myra Welsh, July 5, 1952; children: Royal Graham IV, William Welsh, Elliot McCarten. BA, U. N.C., 1950, JD with honors, 1955. Bar: N.C. 1955, U.S. Dist. Ct. (ea. dist.) N.C. 1967, U.S. Ct. Appeals (4th cir.) 1969, U.S. Dist. Ct. Md. 1974. Asst. dir. Inst. of Govt., Chapel Hill, N.C., 1955-60; asst. prof. law U. Ga., Athens, 1960-65; sole practice Rocky Mount, N.C., 1965-69; prof. law U. Balt., 1969-83; counsel Blumenthal, Wayson, Downs & Offutt P.A., Annapolis, Md., 1983—; instr. Police Acad., Balt., 1970-74, Md. Bar Rev., Balt. 1973-74; speaker Harford Co. Vestry Assn., 1973, Waxter Sr. Citizens Ctr., 1974-75, Montgomery Coll. Forum, 1975; reporter Md. Jud. Conf., 1973-74, U.S. Dist. Ct. Md., Balt., 1976-80, Speedy Trial Act; adj. prof. U. Balt., 1983—. Contbr. articles to profl. jours. Cons. Mayor's Council Criminal Justice, 1976. Served with USNR, 1950-52, Korea. Democrat. Episcopalian. Avocation: studying law. State civil litigation, Real property, Legal education. Office: Blumenthal Wayson Downs & Offutt PA 80 West St Box 868 Annapolis MD 21404

SHAPIRO, ALVIN DALE, lawyer; b. N.Y.C., Apr. 30, 1930; s. Samuel and Fannie (Korman) S.; m. Patricia Nan Swaden, Nov. 8, 1959; children: Peter, Julia, Molly, Anthony. BS, U. Mo., 1951; LLB, Yale U., 1958. Bar: Fla. 1958, Mo. 1959, U.S. Supreme Ct. 1966. Assoc. Sams, Anderson & Assocs., Miami, Fla., 1958-59; ptnr. Stinson, Mag & Fizzell, Kansas City, Mo., 1959-80; sole practice Kansas City, 1980—; mem. Yale Law Sch. Exec. Com., 1982—. Exec. bd. dirs., v.p. Hyman Brand Hebrew Acad., Kansas City, 1966—; bd. dirs. Beth Shalom Congregation, Kansas City, 1970—. Served with USN 1951-55. Mem. ABA, Mo. Bar Assn., Fla. Bar Assn. Democrat. Jewish. Club: Yale. Federal civil litigation, State civil litigation, General practice. Home: 816 W 52nd Terr Kansas City MO 64112 Office: 911 Main Kansas City MO 64105

SHAPIRO, ANITA RAE, commissioner superior court; b. Omaha, May 16, 1941; d. Harry and Jesse (Shiloff) Lavine; m. Mark Howard Shapiro, June 8, 1961; children: David Gregory, Diane Elaine, Lisa Michelle. BA, Mills Coll., Oakland, Calif., 1961; LLB, U. Pa., 1965; student UCLA, summer 1959, U. Calif.-Berkeley, summer 1960, NYU Grad. Sch. Law Div., 1965-66. Bar: Calif. 1966, U.S. Dist. Ct. (cen. dist.) Calif. 1967, N.Y. 1969. Sole practice, Pasadena, Calif., 1967; dep. city prosecutor City Prosecutor's Office, Pasadena, Calif., 1968; assoc. legal editor Lawyers Co-op Pub. Co., Rochester, N.Y., 1969-70; sr. jud. atty. Calif. Cts. Appeal, Los Angeles, 1971-76, San Bernardino, Calif., 1977-82; commr. Superior Ct., Los Angeles County, Calif., 1982—, asst. liaison commr., 1985-86; adj. prof. Western State U. Coll. Law, Fullerton, Calif., 1979-83. Vice-pres. Friends Outside, 1979-80, pres., 1980-81, nat. bd. dirs., 1978-81, 83-86; referee Calif. State Bar Ct., 1980-84; Judge Incamp lectr. Constl. Rights Found., 1983—; lectr. workshops and symposia. NYU Law Sch. scholar, 1965-66. Mem. State Bar of Calif. (commn. on corrs., chmn. 1983-84, vice-chmn. 1982-83, legis. com. family law sect. 1985—, editor jour. 1977-81), Orange County Bar Assn., Los Angeles County Bar Assn., Los Angeles Women Lawyers Assn., Calif. Women Lawyers (past treas., bd. govs.) Women Lawyers Orange County, Inland Counties Women at Law (founder, pres. 1979-80), Calif. Ct. Commrs. Assn. (bd. dirs. 1986—), Calif. Judges Assn., Am. Judicature Soc. Family and matrimonial, Juvenile, Criminal. Office: Los Angeles Superior Ct 12720 Norwalk Blvd Norwalk CA 90650

SHAPIRO, BARRY ROBERT, lawyer; b. Bklyn., Apr. 10, 1947; s. Sam and Jean (Moak) S.; m. Marjorie Spiegelman, Dec. 24, 1968; children: Andrew, Daniel. BA, Hofstra U., 1968; JD, Columbia U., 1973. Bar: N.Y., U.S. Dist. Ct. (so. dist.) N.Y., U.S. Ct. Appeals (2d cir.). Assoc. Shereff, Friedman et al, N.Y.C., 1973-74; v.p., gen. counsel Avis, Inc., Garden City, N.Y., 1974-83; ptnr. Farrell, Fritz, Caemmerer, Cleary, Barnosky & Armentano P.C., Uniondale, N.Y., 1983—. Contbr. article to profl. jours. Pres. Camerata Youth Orch., Mineola, 1985-86; bd. dirs. L.I. Philharm., Melville, N.Y., 1986—, Friends of Arts, Locust Valley, N.Y., 1986—; bd. govs. Am. Jewish Com., Great Neck, N.Y., 1986—. Mem. ABA, N.Y. State Bar Assn., Nassau County Bar Assn. (lectr. 1985-86). Club: Hofstra (Hempstead, N.Y.). Avocations: sports, music. Contracts commercial, General corporate, Securities. Office: Farrell Fritz Caemmerer Cleary Barnosky & Armentano PC EAB Plaza Uniondale NY 11556

SHAPIRO, BENJAMIN LOUIS, lawyer; b. N.Y.C., June 5, 1943; s. Leonard and Henrietta (Cohen) S.; m. Madeleine Fortin, May 28, 1968 (div. Oct. 1982); m. Carol Ann McLaughlin, May 18, 1986. B.A., L.I. U., 1966; J.D., New Eng. Law Sch., 1972; LL.M., NYU, 1973. Bar: Mass. 1975, U.S. Dist. Ct. Mass. 1975, U.S. Ct. Appeals (1st cir.) 1975. Ct. planner Gov.'s Commn. on Adminstrn. of Justice, Montpelier, Vt., 1973-74; staff atty. Nat. Ctr. for State Cts., Boston, 1974-76; regional counsel U.S. Dept. Justice Law Enforcement Assistance Adminstrn., Boston, 1976-77; ct. specialist, 1977-80, exec. asst. to adminstr., 1980-81; atty. advisor U.S. Dept. Justice, Office Justice Assistance, Washington, 1981-82, program mgr., dep. asst. adminstr. Office Juvenile Justice and Delinquency Prevention, 1982—. Asst. editor-in-chief New Eng. Law Rev. Chmn. host com. Nat. Salute to Vietnam Vets., v.p. D.C. Chpt. Vietnam Vets. Am., 1982. Served with U.S. Army, 1966-69. Mem. ABA (mem. victims com. criminal justice sect.). Democrat. Jewish. Criminal, Administrative and regulatory, Legislative. Home: 801 S Pitt St Apt 326 Alexandria VA 22314 Office: US Dept Justice Juvenile Justice and Delinquency Prevent 633 Indiana Ave NW Washington DC 20351

SHAPIRO, DANIEL MURRY, lawyer; b. N.Y.C., Feb. 28, 1926; s. Rubin and Laura (Balton) S.; m. Olga Werchola, Apr. 14, 1981; children—Robert, Suzanne, Stephen. B.A., George Washington U., 1948, M.A., 1949; M.D., U. Lausanne, Switzerland, 1957; J.D., Bklyn. Law Sch., 1977. Bar: N.Y. 1978, Pa. 1984, U.S. Dist. Ct. (ea. and so. dists.) N.Y. 1978. Assoc. Gair, Gair & Conason, N.Y.C., 1977-81, Fuchsberg & Fuchsberg, N.Y.C., 1981-82; ptnr. Katz, Katz, Shapiro & Brand, N.Y.C., 1982-83, Shapiro, Baines & Saesto, N.Y.C., 1983—; clin. asst. prof. community health NYU, N.Y.C., 1978—. Editor Trial Lawyers Quar., 1981-84, Med. Malpractice Reporter, 1981—, Med. Malpractice, 1983. Mem. ABA, Am. Trial Lawyers Assn., Pa. Bar Assn., N.Y. State Trial Lawyers, Met. Womans Bar Assn. (bd. trustees), Pike County Bar Assn., Assn. Bar N.Y., AMA, Acad. Opthalmology, N.Y. State Med. Soc., Bronx County Med. Soc. Patentee in field. State civil litigation, Personal injury, Insurance. Home: PO Box 312 Foster Hill Rd Milford PA 18332 Office: Shapiro Baines & Saasto 55 Mineola Blvd Mineola NY 11501

SHAPIRO, DAVID LOUIS, lawyer, educator; b. N.Y.C., Oct. 12, 1932; s. Louis and Sara (Grabelsky) S.; m. Jane Wilkins Bennett, June 19, 1954; 1 child, Lynn Mayson. Grad., Horace Mann Sch., 1950; A.B. magna cum laude, Harvard U., 1954, LL.B. summa cum laude, 1957. Bar: D.C. 1957, Mass. 1964. Assoc. atty. firm Covington & Burling, Washington, 1957-62; law clk. Supreme Ct. Justice John M. Harlan, 1962-63; faculty Harvard Law Sch., 1963—, prof. law, 1966—, William Nelson Cromwell prof. law, 1984—, asso. dean, 1971-76; Mem. labor arbitration and commercial arbitration panels Am. Arbitration Assn., 1966—; reporter, adv. com. on fair trial and free press Am. Bar Assn., 1965-68. Author: (with others) The Federal Courts and the Federal System, 1973; Editor: The Evolution of a Judicial Philosophy: Selected Opinions of Justice John M. Harlan, 1969; directing editor: Univ. Casebook Series, Foundation Press, 1980—; Contbr. articles to profl. jours. Mem. Soc. Profls. in Dispute Resolution, Am. Law Inst. (asst. reporter study of div. of jurisdiction 1963-65, reporter Restatement of Judgments 2d 1970-74). Administrative and regulatory, Federal civil litigation, Legal education. Home: 17 Wendell St Cambridge MA 02138

SHAPIRO, DONALD ALLAN, lawyer; b. Chgo., Apr. 29, 1950; s. Arthur Louis and Shirley (Steinberg) S.; m. Robbin Marlee Alpert, June 25, 1972; children: Lauren Deena, Brittany Lynn. BA in Econs. with highest distinction, U. Ill., Urbana, 1971; JD, U. Chgo., 1974. Bar: Ill. 1974, U.S. Dist. Ct. (no. dist.) Ill. 1974, U.S. Ct. Appeals (7th cir.) 1974, U.S. Supreme Ct. 1974. Assoc. Aaron, Aaron, Schimberg & Hess, Chgo., 1974-78; pres. Donald A. Shapiro, Ltd., Chgo., 1978—; of counsel Levine, Wittenberg, Eisner, Newman and Silverman, Ltd., 1978—; instr. IIT, Chgo., 1978-80. Mem. Ill. Bar Assn., Chgo. Bar Assn., Assn. Trial Lawyers Am., Ill. Trial Lawyers Assn. Jewish. Club: Highland Park (Ill.) Country. Avocations: jogging, tennis. Personal injury. Home: 3801 Brett Ln Glenview IL 60020 Office: 180 N LaSalle Chicago IL 60601

SHAPIRO, FRED DAVID, lawyer; b. Cleve., Nov. 10, 1926; s. Isadore R. and Lottie (Turetsky) S.; m. Helen Solomon, Sept. 5, 1948; children—Gary N., Ira R., Diane S. B.A. cum laude, Ohio State U., 1949; LL.B., Harvard U., 1954. Bar: Ohio 1954. Since practiced in Cleve.; sr. partner firm Shapiro, Turoff, Gisser & Belkin, 1976—. Served with USNR, 1945-46. Mem. Ohio Bar Assn., Greater Cleve. Bar Assn., Cuyahoga County Bar Assn., Phi Beta Kappa. Jewish. Estate planning, Probate, Estate taxation. Home: 29226 S Woodland Rd Pepper Pike OH 44124 Office: Shapiro Turoff Gisser & Belkin 1200 Standard Bldg Cleveland OH 44113

SHAPIRO, GARY JOEL, lawyer; b. Bethpage, N.Y., Aug. 28, 1956; s. Jerome and Mildred (Gorby) S.; m. Janice Joan Wolf, Sept. 5, 1982; children: Steven Scott, Douglas Jay. BA, SUNY, Binghamton, 1977; JD, Georgetown U., 1980. Bar: D.C. 1980, Va. 1981, U.S. Dist. Ct. D.C. 1981, U.S. Ct. Appeals (D.C. cir.) 1981, U.S. Supreme Ct. 1987. Legis. asst. Congressman Edwards, Washington, 1977; assoc. Squire Sanders & Dempsey, Washington, 1980-82; gen. counsel Consumer Electronics Show, Washington, 1982—; v.p. govt. and legal affairs Electronic Industries Assn./Consumer Electronics Group, Washington, 1982—; dir. COPIAT, Washington. V.P., treas. Audio/Home Recording Rights Coalition, Washington, 1983—. Mem. ABA, Phi Beta Kappa. General corporate, Legislative, Trademark and copyright. Home: 8502 Bromley Ct Annandale VA 22003 Office: Electronic Industries Assn 2001 Eye St NW Washington DC 20006

SHAPIRO, GEORGE M., lawyer; b. N.Y.C., Dec. 7, 1919; s. Samuel N. and Sarah (Milstein) S.; m. Rita V. Lubin, Mar. 29, 1942; children: Karen Shapiro Spector, Sanford. B.S., LIU, 1939; LL.B. (Kent scholar), Columbia U., 1942; LL.D. (hon.), L.I. U., 1986. Bar: N.Y. 1942. Mem. staff gov. N.Y. 1945-51, counsel to gov., 1951-54; partner firm Proskauer, Rose, Goetz & Mendelsohn, N.Y.C., 1955—, mem. exec. com., mng. ptnr., 1974-84; pres. Edmond de Rothschild Found., 1964—; dir. Bank of Calif., 1973-84; counsel, majority leader N.Y. Senate, 1955-59; counsel N.Y. Constl. Revision Commn., 1960-61. Chmn. council State U. Coll. Medicine, N.Y., 1955-71; mem. Gov.'s Com. Reapportionment, 1964, Mayor's Com. Jud. Selection, 1966-69; chmn. Park Ave. Synagogue, 1973-81. Served with USAAF, 1943-45. Mem. Council on Fgn. Relations. Club: Harmonie. Banking, General corporate, Private international. Home: 1160 Park Ave New York NY 10128 Office: 300 Park Ave New York NY 10022

SHAPIRO, HADASSAH R(UTH), lawyer; b. N.Y.C., June 20, 1924; d. Bernard and Ida Pauline (Turitz) S. AB, Wellesley Coll., 1945; LLB, Columbia U., 1948. Bar: N.Y. 1948. Assoc. Mulligan & Jacobson, N.Y.C., 1968-73, ptnr., 1973—. Mem. adv. bd. Wellesley Coll. Hillel, Wellesley, Mass., 1984—. Mem. ABA, Assn. of Bar of City of N.Y., Assn. Trial Lawyers Am., Selden Soc., N.Y. County Lawyers Assn. Clubs: Wellesley (N.Y.C.), Columbia U. (N.Y.C.). Family and matrimonial, State civil litigation. Office: Mulligan Jacobson & Langenus 25 W 45th St Suite 1405 New York NY 10036

SHAPIRO, IRVING, law educator, author; b. N.Y.C., Aug. 23, 1917; s. Isidor and Bessie (Hecht) S.; m. Rosalind Leonora Roth, Sept. 14, 1941; children—Deanne, Susan, Joyce. B.A., NYU, 1946, J.D., 1942. Bar: N.Y. 1943. Spl. asst. to adminstrv. judge N.Y. Supreme Ct., Bklyn., 1949-74; prof. St. John's U., Jamaica, N.Y., 1974—; dir. programs Ct. Careers, N.Y.C., 1960—; arbitrator Small Claims Ct., N.Y.C., 1977—. Author: Dictionary of Legal Terms, 1969; New Dictionary of Legal Terms, 1984. Editor N.Y. Statutes, 1963-73. Contbr. articles to law jours. Served with U.S. Army, 1943-46. Decorated Army Commendation medal. Fellow Inst. for Ct. Mgmt.; mem. Criminal Justice Educators Assn. Democrat. Jewish. Criminal, Legal education. Office: St Johns U Bent Hall 425 Jamaica NY 11439

SHAPIRO, IVAN, lawyer; b. N.Y.C., Nov. 11, 1928; s. Archie M. and Auguste (Reiff) S.; m. Florence Goodstein, June 24, 1951 (div. Oct. 1958); 1 child, Lisa J. Kubiske; m. Maria Schaffner, Sept. 16, 1960; 1 child, Alexandra. B.S.S., CCNY, 1948; J.D., Harvard U., 1951. Bar: N.Y. 1952. Assoc. Wien, Lane, Klein & Purcell, N.Y.C., 1954-59; ptnr. Wien, Lane & Klein, 1959-74, Greenbaum, Wolff & Ernst, N.Y.C., 1974-81, Willkie Farr & Gallagher, N.Y.C., 1981—; lectr. Real Estate Inst., NYU Sch. Continuing Edn., N.Y.C., 1978-81. Author: Case Studies in Real Estate Finance, 1980; author pamphlets on ethical issues, 1973-80, articles on civil liberties issues, 1966-80. Trustee Ethical Culture Soc., N.Y.C., 1970—, pres., 1972-78; chmn. Ethical Culture Schs., N.Y.C., 1980-82; bd. visitors Grad. Sch., Univ. Ctr. CUNY, 1986—; bd. dirs. N.Y. Civil Liberties Union, N.Y.C., 1966-80, 86—. Served to 1st lt. U.S. Army, 1952-54. Mem. Assn. Bar City N.Y., Phi Beta Kappa. Democrat. Real property. Office: Willkie Farr & Gallagher 153 E 53d St New York NY 10022

SHAPIRO, JEROME GERSON, lawyer; b. N.Y.C., May 12, 1924; s. Joseph Louis and Beatrice Rebecca S.; m. Marjorie Kemble Mackay, Dec. 31, 1959; children—Jeffrey Kemble, Jill Dara, Eric Paul. A.B. summa cum laude, N.Y. U., 1946; LL.B. magna cum laude, Harvard U., 1948. Bar: N.Y. State bar 1949, U.S. Supreme Ct. bar 1955. Asso. mem. firm Hughes Hubbard & Reed, N.Y.C., 1949-51, 52-57; spl. asst. atty. gen., sr. asst. counsel N.Y. State Crime Commn., 1951-52; ptnr. firm Hughes Hubbard & Reed, N.Y.C., 1957-75; chmn. Hughes Hubbard & Reed, 1975—; prof. law N.Y. Law Sch., 1951-53. Vice chmn. trustees James W. Johnson Community Centers, Inc., N.Y.C., 1975-78; trustee Lawyers Com. for Civil Rights Under Law, 1976—. Served with AUS, 1943-45. Decorated Purple Heart. Mem. Assn. Bar City N.Y. (exec. com. 1967-73), N.Y. State Bar Assn., N.Y. County Lawyers Assn., Am. Bar Found. (research com.), PhiBeta Kappa.; Fellow Am. Coll. Trial Lawyers. Jewish. Clubs: Harvard, City Midday. Federal civil litigation, Antitrust, State civil litigation. Office: Hughes Hubbard & Reed 1 Wall St New York NY 10005

SHAPIRO, MARGE DIANA, lawyer; b. Sapporo, Japan, Jan. 12, 1949; d. Daniel William and Ruth (Hines) Rachal; m. Richard Stephen Shapiro, May 27, 1972. Student Agnes Scott Coll., 1966-68; B.A., Duke U., 1970; postgrad. U. S.C., 1970-72; J.D., Emory U., 1976. Bar: Ga. 1976. Teaching asst. U. S.C., Columbia, 1970-72; sole practice law, Decatur, Ga., 1977-80, Dunwoody, Ga., 1980-81; mng. atty. Hyatt Legal Services, Stone Mountain, Ga., 1981-85, UAW Legal Services Plan, 1985; sole practice law, Norcross, Ga., 1986—. Mem. adv. com. Ga. Vietnam Vets. Leadership Program, Atlanta, 1983, 84; legal adviser Atlanta Day Vets. Day's Parade, Atlanta, 1983. Mem. ABA, Ga. Bar Assn., Atlanta Bar Assn., Nat. Council Jewish Women (life), Jewish War Vets Aux., Gwinnett County Bar Assn. (women and law sect.), Delta Theta Phi (historian). Jewish. Family and matrimonial, General practice.

SHAPIRO, MARTIN, legal educator; b. 1933. B.A., UCLA, 1955; Ph.D., Harvard U., 1961. Instr. polit. sci. Harvard U., Cambridge, Mass., 1960-62; prof. Harvard U., 1971-74; asst. prof. Stanford U., Calif., 1962-65; assoc. prof. U. Calif.-Irvine, 1965-70, prof., 1970; prof. polit. sci. U. Calif.-Berkeley, 1971, prof. law, 1977—; prof. U. Calif.-San Diego, 1974-77. Author: Law and Politics in the Supreme Court, 1964, Freedom of Speech, The Supreme Court and Judicial Review, 1966, Supreme Court and Administrative Agencies, 1968, Courts, 1981. Mem. Law and Soc. Assn. (trustee 1970-77), Western Polit. Sci. Assn. (pres. 1978), Am. Acad. Arts and Scis. Legal education. Office: U Calif Law Sch 225 Boalt Hall Berkeley CA 94720

SHAPIRO, MICHAEL BRUCE, lawyer; b. Great Neck, N.Y., Jan. 3, 1957; s. Edward and Vera (Messing) S. BA in Polit. Sci., Emory U., 1978, JD, 1981. Bar: Ga. 1982, U.S. Dist. Ct. (no. and mid. dists.) Ga. 1981, U.S. Ct. Appeals (11th cir.) 1981, U.S. Supreme Ct. 1985. Assoc. Ronnie K. Batchelor, P.C., Decatur, Ga., 1981-82; sole practice Atlanta, 1982-84; mng. ptnr. Fambrough & Shapiro, P.C., Chamblee, Ga., 1984—; counsel Phoenix Properties Inc., 1985—. Mem. ABA, Assn. Trial Lawyers Am., Ga. Assn. Criminal Defense Lawyers, Audubon Soc., Cousteau Soc., Phi Gamma Delta, Pi Sigma Alpha. Jewish. Avocations: scuba diving, sailing, backpacking, white water canoeing, photography. Criminal, Family and matrimonial, General practice. Home: 5733 Musket Ln Stone Mountain GA 30087 Office: Fambrough & Shapiro PC 3604 Chamblee Tucker Rd Chamblee GA 30341

SHAPIRO, NELSON HIRSH, lawyer; b. Washington, Feb. 3, 1928; s. Arthur and Anna (Zenitz) S.; m. Helen Lenora Sykes, June 27, 1948; children—Ronald Evan, Mitchell Wayne, Jeffrey Mark, Julie Beth. B.E.E., John Hopkins U., 1948; J.D., George Washington U., 1952. Bar: D.C. 1952, Va. 1981. Patent examiner U.S. Patent Office, 1948-50; patent advisor U.S. Signal Corps, 1950-52; mem. Shapiro & Shapiro, Arlington, Va., 1952—. Mem. ABA, Am. Patent Law Assn., Bar Assn. D.C., Order of Coif, Tau Beta Pi. Patentee; contbr. articles to legal publs. and Ency. of Patent Practice and Invention Management, 1964. Patent, Trademark and copyright. Home: 7001 Old Cabin Ln Rockville MD 20852 Office: Shapiro and Shapiro 1100 Wilson Blvd Suite 1701 Arlington VA 22209

SHAPIRO, NORMA SONDRA LEVY, judge; b. Phila., July 27, 1928; d. Bert and Jane (Kotkin) Levy; m. Bernard Shapiro, Aug. 21, 1949; children: Finley, Neil, Aaron. B.A. in Polit. Theory with honors, U. Mich., 1948; J.D. magna cum laude, U. Pa., 1951. Bar: Pa. 1952, U.S. Supreme Ct. 1978. Law clk. to justice Pa. Supreme Ct., 1951-52; instr. U. Pa. Law Sch., 1951-52, 55-56; asso. Dechert Price & Rhoads, Phila., 1956-58, 67-73; partner Dechert Price & Rhoads, 1973-78; judge U.S. Dist. Ct. Eastern Dist. Pa., 1978—; assoc. trustee U. Pa. Law Sch., 1978—; trustee Women's Law Project, 1978—, Albert Einstein Med. Center, 1979—, Fedn. Jewish Agys., 1980—, Jewish Publ. Soc., 1980—; mem. lawyer's adv. panel Pa. Gov.'s Comm. on Status of Women, 1974; legal adv. Regional Council Child Psychiatry. Guest editor: Shingle, 1972. Mem. Lower Merion County (Pa.) Bd. Sch. Dirs., 1968-77, pres., 1977, v.p., 1976; v.p. Jewish Community Relations Council of Greater Phila., 1975-77; chmn. legal affairs com., 1978; pres. Belmont Hills Home and Sch. Assn., Lower Merion Twp.; legis. chmn. Lower Merion Sch. Dist. Intersch. Council; mem. Task Force on Mental Health of Children and Youth of Pa.; treas., chmn. edn. com. Human Relations Council, Lower Merion; v.p., parliamentarian Nes Ami Penn Valley Congregation, Lower Merion Twp. Named Woman of Yr., Oxford Circle Jewish Community Center, 1979, Woman of Distinction, Golden Slipper Club, 1979; Gowen fellow, 1954-55. Mem. Am. Law Inst., Am. Bar Found., ABA (vice chmn. com. law and mental health sect. family law), Pa. Bar Assn. (ho. of dels. 1979—), Phila. Bar Assn. (chmn. com. women's rights 1972, 74-75, chmn. bd. govs. 1977—, chmn. public relations com. 1978), Fed. Bar Assn., Nat. Assn. Women Lawyers, Phila. Trial Lawyers Assn., Am. Judicature Soc., Phila. Fellowship Commn., Order of Coif (chpt. pres. 1973-75), Tau Epsilon Rho. Jurisprudence. Office: US District Courthouse 10614 US Courthouse Independence Mall West Philadelphia PA 19106 *

SHAPIRO, PAUL STUART, lawyer; b. Chgo., May 5, 1947; s. Benjamin and Ethel (Bornstein) S.; m. Patricia Olsen, Oct. 5, 1985. BA, So. Ill. U., 1970; JD, DePaul U., 1973. Bar: Ill. 1973. Sole practice Chgo., 1974—. General practice, Probate, Real property. Home: 2800 N Lake Shore Dr Chicago IL 60657 Office: 188 W Randolph St Ste 927 Chicago IL 60601

SHAPIRO, ROBYN SUE, lawyer, educator; b. Mpls., July 19, 1952; d. Walter David and Judith Rae (Sweet) S.; m. Charles Howard Barr, June 27, 1976; children: Tania Shapiro-Barr, Jeremy Shapiro-Barr, Michael Shapiro-Barr. BA summa cum laude, U. Mich., 1974; JD, Harvard U., 1977. Bar: D.C. 1977, Wis. 1979. Assoc. Foley, Lardner, Hollabaugh & Jacobs, Washington, 1977-79; ptnr. Barr & Shapiro, Menomonee Falls, Wis., 1980—; adj. asst. prof. law Marquette U., Milw., 1979-83; assoc. dir. bioethics ctr. Med. Coll. Wis., Milw., 1982-85, dir., 1985—; asst. clin. prof. health law Med. Coll. Wis., 1984—. Contbr. articles to profl. jours. Mem. ethics com. St. Luke's Hosp., Milw., 1983—, Elmbrook Meml. Hosp., Milw., 1983-86, Community Meml. Hosp., Menomonee Falls, 1984—, Good Samaritan Hosp., Milw., 1986—, Milw. County Med. Complex, 1985—; mem. subcom. organ transplantation Wis. Health Policy Council, Madison, Wis., 1984, bioethics com., 1986—; mem. com. study of bioethics Wis. Legis. Council, Madison, 1984-85. James B. Angell scholar, 1971-72. Mem. ABA (forum com. health law), Am. Soc. Law and Medicine, Wis. Bar Assn. (mem. council health law sect.), Assn. Women Lawyers, Phi Beta Kappa. Health, Legal education, Jurisprudence. Home: 7360 N Seneca Rd Milwaukee WI 53217 Office: Barr & Shapiro N88 W17015 Main St Menomonee Falls WI 53051 also: Med Coll Wis Bioethics Ctr 8701 Watertown Plank Rd Milwaukee WI 53226

SHAPIRO, STEPHEN M., lawyer; b. Chgo., May 3, 1946; s. Samuel H. and Dorothy A. (D'Andrea) S.; m. Joan H. Gately, Oct. 30, 1982. BA, Yale U., 1968, JD, 1971. Bar: Ill. 1971, Calif. 1972, U.S. Supreme Ct. 1975. Ptnr. Mayer, Brown & Platt, Chgo., 1977-78, 83—; asst. to soliciter gen. U.S. Dept. Justice, Washington, 1978-80, dep. soliciter gen., 1981-82. Author: Supreme Court Practice, 1986; cintbr, articles to profl. jours. Mem. ABA, Am. Law Inst., Supreme Ct. Hist. Soc. Republican. Jewish. Federal civil litigation, Antitrust, Banking. Office: Mayer Brown & Platt 190 S LaSalle St Chicago IL 60604

SHAPO, HELENE S., law educator; b. N.Y.C., June 5, 1938; d. Benjamin Martin and Gertrude (Kahaner) Seidner; m. Marhsall S. Shapo, June 21, 1959; children: Benjamin Mitchell, Nathaniel Saul. BA, Smith Coll., 1959; MA in Teaching, Harvard U., 1960; JD, U. Va., 1976. Bar: Va. 1976, U.S. Dist. Ct. (we. dist.) Va. 1977. Tchr. Dade County, Miami, Fla., 1960-64; assoc. Robert Musselman & Assocs., Charlottesville, Va., 1976-77; law clk. to presiding justice U.S. Dist. Ct. Va., Charlottesville, 1977-78; asst. prof. law Northwestern U., Chgo., 1978-81, assoc. prof. law, 1981-83, prof. law,

1983—; instr. Sweet Briar Coll., Va., 1976-77, U. Va., Charlottesville, 1976-78; mem. com. law sch. admissions council/testing and devel., 1983—; cons. in field. Mem. ABA, Va. Bar Assn., Assn. of Am. Law Schs. (sect. chairperson 1985—), Women's Bar Assn. Chgo. Legal education. Office: Northwestern U Sch Law 357 East Chicago Ave Chicago IL 60611

SHAPO, MARSHALL SCHAMBELAN, lawyer, educator; b. Phila., Oct. 1, 1936; s. Mitchell and Norma (Schambelan) S.; m. Helene Shirley Seidner, June 21, 1959; children: Benjamin, Nathaniel. A.B. summa cum laude, U. Miami, 1958, J.D. magna cum laude, 1964; A.M., Harvard U., 1961; S.J.D., 1974. Bar: Fla. 1964, Va. 1977. Copy editor, writer Miami (Fla.) News, 1958-59; instr. history U. Miami, 1960-61; asst. prof. law U. Tex., 1965-67, asso. prof., 1967-69, prof., 1969-70; prof. law U. Va., 1970-78, Joseph M. Hartfield prof., 1976-78; Frederic P. Vose prof. Northwestern U. Sch. Law, Chgo., 1978—; vis. prof. Juristisches Seminar U. Gottingen (W. Ger.), 1976; cons. on med. malpractice and tort law reform U.S. Dept. Justice, 1978-79; mem. panel on food safety Inst. Medicine, Nat. Acad. Scis., 1978-79; vis. fellow Centre for Socio-legal Studies, Wolfson Coll., Oxford, vis. fellow of Coll., 1975; mem. Center for Advanced Studies, U. Va., 1976-77; cons. Pres.'s Commn. for Study of Ethical Problems in Medicine and Biomed. and Behavioral Research, 1980-81; reporter Spl. Com. on Tort Liability System Am. Bar Assn., 1980-84; delegation leader People to People Citizen Ambassador program, 1986; delegation to East Asia Tort and Ins. Law, 1986. Author: Towards a Jurisprudence of Injury, 1984; Tort and Compensation Law, 1976, The Duty to Act: Tort Law, Power and Public Policy, 1978, A Nation of Guinea Pigs, 1979, Products Liability, 1980, Public Regulation of Dangerous Products, 1980, The Law of Products Liability, 1987; (with Page Keeton) Products and the Consumer: Deceptive Practices, 1972, Products and the Consumer: Defective and Dangerous Products, 1970; editorial bd.: Jour. Consumer Policy, 1980—; author: A Representational Theory of Consumer Protection: Doctrine, Function and Legal Liability for Product Disappointment, 1974; contbr. articles to legal and med. jours. NEH sr. fellow, 1974-75. Mem. Am. Law Inst., Am. Assn. Law Schs. (chmn. torts compensation systems sect. 1983-84, torts round table council 1970). Personal injury, Health, Legal education. Home: 1910 Orrington Ave Evanston IL 60201 Office: Northwestern U Sch Law 357 E Chicago Ave Chicago IL 60611

SHAR, MARCUS Z., lawyer; b. Columbus, Ohio, May 14, 1951; s. Farrell K. and Adeline (Thall) S.; m. Gwen Ellen Abrams, Aug. 13, 1972; children—Jonathan Carrie, Debra Erin, David Eric, Helaine Beth. B.A., Ohio State U., 1973; J.D., U. Md., 1976. Bar: Md. 1976, U.S. Dist. Ct. Md. 1976, U.S. Bankruptcy Ct. Md. 1984. Assoc. Peter G. Angelos, Balt., 1976-79; sr. ptnr. Bierer & Shar P.A., Balt., 1979—; mem. faculty Nat. Coll. Trial Advocacy, Washington, 1983—; med. malpractice corr. Md. Daily Record, Balt., 1984—; lectr. profl. assns. Author: Medical Malpractice Law of Maryland. Contbr. articles to legal jours., model pleadings to legal treatises. Mem. youth commn. Union of Orthodox Congregations of Am., Atlantic Seaboard Region, 1978; mem. adv. com. Nat. Conf. Synagogue Youth, Atlantic Seaboard Region, 1979; mem. adv. com. Project Yedid, Balt., 1983-84; bd. govs. Union of Orthodox Congregations, 1985. Recipient cert. merit Moot Ct., U. Md. Sch. Law, 1974. Mem. Balt. City Bar Assn., Md. State Bar Assn. (com. 1984), Md. Trial Lawyers Assn. (bd. govs. 1985—), Assn. Trial Lawyers Am. (com. 1981, 84). U. Md. Law Sch. Alumni Assn. Democrat. Jewish. Personal injury, State civil litigation, Federal civil litigation. Home: 2506 Shelleydale Dr Baltimore MD 21209 Office: Bierer & Shar PA 926 Saint Paul St Baltimore MD 21202

SHARE, RICHARD HUDSON, lawyer; b. Mpls., Sept. 6, 1938; s. Jerome and Millicent S.; m. Carolee Martin, 1970; children—Mark Lowell, Gregory Martin, Jennifer Hillary, Ashley. B.S., UCLA, 1960; J.D., U. So. Calif., 1963. Bar: Calif. Sup. Ct. 1964, U.S. Dist. Ct. (cen. and so. dists.) Calif., U.S. Supreme Ct. 1974. Field agt. IRS, 1960-63; mem. law div., asst. sec. Avco Fin. Services, 1963-72; ptnr. Frandzel and Share and predecessor firm Foonberg and Frandzel, Beverly Hills, Calif., 1972—; lectr. in field. Mem. Calif. Bankers Assn., Fin. Lawyers Assn. Clubs: Rivera Tennis, Pacific Palisades. Consumer commercial, Bankruptcy. Office: 8383 Wilshire Blvd Suite 400 Beverly Hills CA 90211 also: Fed Res Bank Bldg 101 Market St San Francisco CA 94105 also: 18300 Von Karman Ave Irvine CA 92715

SHAREEF, MICHAEL T., lawyer; b. Chgo., Sept. 28, 1953; s. George and Julia (Walker) Taylor; m. Evelyn F. Waltrous, Sept. 28, 1981; children: Rastafian A.; Zoe S. BA, Tougaloo Coll., 1976; JD, Howard U., 1979. Bar: Miss. 1979, U.S. Dist. Ct. (no. dist.) Miss. 1979, U.S. Ct. Appeals (5th and 11th cirs.) 1981, N.Y. 1986, U.S. Ct. Appeals (2d cir. 1986). Sr. atty. No. Miss. Rural Legal Services, Oxford, 1979-85; staff atty. Harlem Legal Services, N.Y.C., 1985. Served with USMC, 1973-75. Mem. ABA, Nat. Conf. Black Lawyers, Miss. State Bar Assn., Magnolia Bar Assn. (committeeman 1985—). Republican. Islam. Lodge: Masons. Avocations: swimming, dancing, photography, reading, travel. Government contracts and claims, Landlord-tenant, Civil rights.

SHARETT, ALAN RICHARD, lawyer; b. Hammond, Ind., Apr. 15, 1943; s. Henry S. and Frances (Givel) Smulevitz; divorced, children—Lauren Ruth, Charles Daniel. Student Ind. U., 1962-65; J.D., DePaul U., 1968. Bar: N.Y. 1975, Ind. 1969, U.S. Ct. Appeals (2d cir.) 1975, U.S. Ct. Appeals (7th cir.) 1974, U.S. Supreme Ct. 1973. Assoc. Call, Call, Borns & Theodoros, Gary, Ind., 1969-71; judge protem Gary City Ct., 1970-71; environ. dep. prosecutor 31st Jud. Circuit, Lake County, Ind., 1971-75; mem. Cohan, Cohan & Smulevitz, 1971-75; judge pro tem Superior Ct., Lake County, Ind., 1971-75; professorial dir. NYU Pub. Liability Inst., N.Y.C., 1975-76; asst. atty. gen. N.Y. State, N.Y.C., 1976-78; sole practice, Flushing, N.Y., 1980-82, Miami Beach, Fla., 1982—; chmn. lawyers panel for No. Ind., ACLU, 1969-71; mem. Nat. Dist. Attys. Assn., 1972-75, mem. environ. protection com. Recipient Honors award in medicolegal litigation Law-Sci. Acad. Am., 1967. Mem. ABA, Assn. Bar City N.Y., N.Y. County Lawyers Assn. (com. on fed. cts. 1977-82), Am. Judicature Soc., Assn. Trial Lawyers Am., N.Y. State Trial Lawyers Assn., N.Y. State Bar Assn., Ind. State Bar Assn., Queens County Bar Assn., Am. Acad. Poets. Democrat. Contbr. articles to profl. jours. Federal civil litigation, Labor, Family and matrimonial. Address: B1418 2371 Collins Ave Miami Beach FL 33139

SHARFMAN, HERBERT, judge; b. Northampton, Pa., July 29, 1909; s. Meyer and Minnie (Caplan) S.; m. Dorothy Muriel Cohen, Feb. 8, 1932; children—Richard M., Jo-Ellen Crews. A.B., U. Pa., 1930; LL.B., Columbia U., 1933. Bar: Pa. 1933, U.S. Dist. Ct. (ea. dist.) Pa. 1935, U.S. Supreme Ct., 1945. Sole practice, Lehigh and Northampton Counties, Pa., 1933-44; atty.-adv. pub. utilities br. OPA, Washington, 1944-46, FCC, Washington, 1946-52; adminstrv. law judge FCC, Washington, 1952-74, Postal Rate Commn. Washington, 1974-76, part-time adminstrv. law judge, 1976—. Mem. ABA, Pa. State Bar Assn., Lehigh County Bar Assn. Jewish. Administrative and regulatory. Home: 162 W Center Ave Sebring FL 33870

SHARP, ALLEN, judge; b. Washington, Feb. 11, 1932; s. Robert Lee and Frances Louise (Williams) S.; m. Sara J. Roberts, Dec. 7, 1982; children: Crystal Catholyn, Scarlet Frances. Student, Ind. State U., 1950-53; A.B., George Washington U., 1954; J.D., Ind. U., 1957; postgrad., Butler U., 1970-73. Bar: Ind. 1957. Practiced in Williamsport, 1957-68; judge Ct. of Appeals Ind., 1969-73; U.S. dist. judge No. Dist. Ind., Hammond, 1973—. Bd. advisers Milligan (Tenn.) Coll. Served to JAG USAFR. Mem. Ind. Judges Assn., Blue Key, Phi Delta Kappa, Pi Gamma Mu, Tau Kappa Alpha. Republican. Mem. Christian Ch. Club: Mason. Office: U S Dist Ct 325 Fed Bldg 204 S Main St South Bend IN 46601 *

SHARP, CHRISTOPHER GLENN, lawyer; b. Dallas, Nov. 11, 1952; s. Luther W. and Genevieve Sadie (Graffeo) S.; m. Kydie Elizabeth Franklin, June 25, 1977; 1 child, Elizabeth. BBA, U. Tex., 1975; JD, So. Meth. U., 1978. Bar: Tex. 1978, U.S. Dist. Ct. (no. dist.) Tex. 1978, U.S. Ct. Appeals (5th cir.) 1978, U.S. Supreme Ct. 1978. Ptnr. Coffee, Coffee & Sharp, Dallas, 1978—. Mem. planning and zoning commn. City of Univ. Park, 1984—, Greater Dallas Crime Commn., 1983—, participant protection rev. bd. Inst. of Aerobics Research, Dallas, 1984—. Mem. ABA, Dallas Bar Assn. Republican. Clubs: Aerobics Activity Ctr., Park City, Premier (Dallas). Avocations: jogging, swimming, cycling, golf, hunting. Banking, Real property, General corporate. Office: Coffee Coffee & Sharp 6201 Hillcrest Dallas TX 75205

SHARP, GEORGE KENDALL, U.S. district judge; b. Chgo., Dec. 30, 1934; s. Edward S. and Florence S.; m. Mary Bray; children—Florence Kendall, Julia Manger. B.A., Yale U., 1957; J.D., U. Va., 1963. Bar: Fla. 1963. Atty. Sharp, Johnston & Brown, Vero Beach, Fla., 1963-78; pub. defender 19th Circuit, 1964-68; sch. bd. atty. Indian River County, Fla., 1968-79; judge 19th Circuit Ct., Vero Beach, 1978-83; judge U.S. Dist. Ct. (mid. dist.) Fla., Orlando, 1983—. Judicial administration. Office: US Dist Ct 611 US Courthouse 80 N Hughey Ave Orlando FL 32801 *

SHARP, JOHN, lawyer; b. Detroit, Aug. 25, 1952; s. John Pershing and Florence Marie (Morris) S.; m. Diana Lyn Reynolds, Aug. 25, 1973; children: Erica, Jessica, Jamie. AB, U. Mich., 1974; JD, Wayne State U., 1978. Bar: Mich. 1978, U.S. Dist. Ct. (ea. dist.) Mich. 1978, U.S. Ct. Appeals (6th cir.) 1984, U.S. Dist. Ct. (we. dist.) Mich. 1985. Assoc. Plunkett, Cooney et al, Detroit, 1979—. Sec., trustee First Ch. of God, Farmington Hills, Mich., 1983-84. Mem. ABA, Fed. Bar Assn., Mich. Bar Assn., Oakland County Bar Assn., Detroit Bar Assn. Democrat. General corporate, Securities, Banking. Office: Plunkett & Cooney 900 Marquett Bldg Detroit MI 48226

SHARP, ROBERT WEIMER, lawyer; b. Cleve., Feb. 12, 1917; s. Isaac Walter and Ruth (Weimer) S.; m. Norine Wines, Nov. 13, 1948; children—Kathleen L. (Mrs. Larry J. Samuel), Pamela J. (Mrs. David N. Adamson), Janet E. (Mrs. Marcus V. Schoon), Andrea L. (Mrs. David A. Bobak), Gail N. A.B., Oberlin Coll., 1939; LL.B., Harvard U., 1942. Bar: Ohio 1944. Practiced in Cleve; ptnr. Gallagher, Sharp, Fulton & Norman and predecessors, 1958—; dir. Bulkley Bldg. Co., 1964-70, pres., 1966-70; dir. Nat. Terminals Corp. Trustee St. Luke's Hosp. Assn.; trustee Ohio East Area United Meth. Found., 1974—, sec., 1967-74, 83-86, pres., 1974-80; adv. trustee Ohio div. Am. Cancer Soc. Served with USNR, 1942-46. Mem. ABA, Ohio Bar Assn., Cleve. Bar Assn. Republican. Methodist. Probate, State and local taxation, General corporate. Home: 3090 Fairmount Blvd Cleveland OH 44118 Office: Gallagher Sharp Fulton & Norman 600 Bulkley Bldg Cleveland OH 44115

SHARP, STARKEY, V, lawyer; b. Ahoskie, N.C., Feb. 23, 1956; s. Starkey Jr. and Jean Lois (McGehee) S.; m. Lisa Gaye Beale, Aug. 8, 1981; 1 child, Sarah Wildes. BS in Sci., Davidson Coll., 1978; JD, Wake Forest U., 1982. Bar: N.C. 1982. Ptnr. Hartsell, Hartsell & Mills, P.A., Concord, N.C., 1982—. Sec. Cabarrus Civic Found., N.C., 1985—; bd. dirs. Cabarrus Arts Council, 1985—. Mem. N.C. Bar Assn. (young lawyers div. 1986—), Cabarrus County Bar Assn. (sec. 1983-86), Charlotte Estate Planning Council. Democrat. Presbyterian. Avocations: golf, tennis. Probate, General corporate, Contracts commercial. Home: 137 Glendale Ave SE Concord NC 28025 Office: Hartsell Hartsell & Mills PA 77 McCachern Blvd SE Concord NC 28025

SHARP, STEPHEN ALAN, lawyer; b. Columbus, Ohio, June 10, 1947; s. William George and Barbara Martin (Baughan) S.; m. Lynn Cawley, Dec. 30, 1971; children: Sarah Cawley, A.J. Tucker. AB, Washington and Lee U., 1969; JD, U. Va., 1973. Bar: Va. 1973, D.C. 1973, U.S. Supreme Ct. 1976. Legal clk., staff atty. Office Gen. Counsel FCC, Washington, 1972-74, staff atty. litigation div., 1974-76, legal asst. to commr., 1976-78, gen. counsel, 1981-82, commr., 1982-83, chmn. adv. com. on tech. standards for direct broadcast satellite service, 1983-84; atty. Schnader, Harrison, Segal & Lewis, Washington, 1978-81; ptnr. Skadden, Arps, Slate, Meagher & Flom, Washington, 1983—; counsel, impeachment inquiry U.S. Ho. of Reps. Com. on Judiciary, 1974; adj. prof. law George Mason U., Arlington, Va., 1977-82; lectr. U. Va. Sch. Law, Charlottesville, 1979-80; mem. Adminstrv. Conf. U.S., Washington, 1981-82. Pres. Charlottesville Lacrosse League, 1971-72; chmn. City of Alexandria Consumer Affairs Commn., 1979-81; bd. dirs. Alexandria Soccer Assn., 1983—; pres., 1986—; capt. U.S. Ry. Assn. Transition Team; mem. FCC Transition Team Office of Pres. Elect, Washington, 1980-81. Mem. ABA (sect. adminstrv. law chmn. election law com. 1980-81, council mem. 1981-85, mem. standing com. on law and electoral process 1981—, chmn. 1983-86), Fed Bar Assn. (chmn. polit. campaign and election law com. 1978-81, Disting. Service award). Republican. Episcopalian. Administrative and regulatory, Legislative, Communications. Home: 204 W Walnut St Alexandria VA 22301 Office: Skadden Arps Slate Meagher & Flom 1440 New York Ave Washington DC 20005

SHARPE, CHRISTOPHER GRANT, lawyer; b. Seattle, Feb. 18, 1949; s. Grant W. and Wenonah (Finch) S. BA, U. Wash., 1973; JD, U. Puget Sound, 1977. Bar: Wash. 1978, U.S. Dist. Ct. (we. dist.) Wash. 1978, U.S. Ct. Appeals (9th cir.) 1978, U.S. Supreme Ct. 1982. Sole practice Seattle, 1978—. Served with U.S. Army, 1969-71, Vietnam. Decorated Purple Heart, Bronze Star with four oak leaf clusters. Mem. ABA, Wash. State Trial Lawyers Assn. Personal injury, Workers' compensation. Office: 1333 N Northlake Way Seattle WA 98103

SHARPE, LEON EDWARD, lawyer; b. Kendall, Fla., Oct. 2, 1952; s. Joe Edward and Dorothy Mae (Saunders) S.; m. Esther Wyllie, Aug. 16, 1975; children—Rashad D., Aaron I., Adam P., Richard A. B.A., Harvard U., 1974; J.D. cum laude, Columbia U., 1977. Bar: Fla. 1978, U.S. Dist. Ct. (so. dist.) Fla. 1978, U.S. Ct. Appeals (5th cir.) 1978, U.S. Ct. Appeals (11th cir.), U.S. Supreme Ct. Assoc. firm Frates, Floyd Pearson, Stewart, Richman & Greer, P.A., Miami, Fla., 1977-80, Hall & Hauser, P.A., Miami, 1980-81; ptnr. firm McGhee & Sharpe, Miami, 1981-84, Leon E. Sharpe, P.A., 1985—; pres. Dade Employment and Econ. Devel. Corp., 1986—; legal cons. NAACP Urban Affairs Office, Miami, 1982; regional dir. Police Violence Project, Miami, 1981-82; mem. rules of evidence com. Fla. Bar. Author booklet: Miami Model City Expo, 1974; contbg. author: NAACP Police Violence, 1982. Dir. Dade Employment and Econ. Devel. Corp., 1982—; bd. dirs. Legal Service of Greater Miami, Inc., 1981-83; dir. Operation PUSH, Miami, 1982. Alexander H. White scholar, Harvard U., 1970-74; recipient Super Achiever's award Boy Scouts Am., 1982. Mem. ABA, Nat. Bar Assn., Dade County Bar Assn., Assn. Trial Lawyers Am., Dade County Black Lawyers Assn. Democrat. Roman Catholic. General corporate, General practice. Home: 10671 SW 137th St Miami FL 33176 Office: 4770 Biscayne Blvd Suite 970 Miami FL 33137

SHARPE, NORAH G., lawyer; b. Lloydminster, Saskatchewa, Can., Aug. 6, 1938; came to U.S., 1960; d. Wilfred Daniel and Irene Elizabeth (Adams) S.; m. Norman Clement Stone, June 1, 1986. RN, U. Alberta, 1960; JD, San Francisco Law Sch., 1975. Atty. Pacific Telephone and Telegraph Co., San Francisco, 1975-83; sr. atty., asst. sec. Pacific Telesis Group, San Francisco, 1983—. Commr. San Rafael Parks and Recreation Commn., Calif., 1980-82; bd. dirs. Internat. Visitors Ctr., San Francisco, 1984—. Mem. ABA, San Francisco Bar Assn., As. Soc. Corp. Secs. (v.p. 1986—). Republican. Anglican. Club: San Francisco Bay. General corporate, Public utilities. Office: Pacific Telesis Group 140 New Montgomery Suite 1618 San Francisco CA 94105

SHARPE, ROBERT FRANCIS, JR., lawyer; b. Long Branch, N.J., Mar. 9, 1952; s. Robert Francis and Audrey Carolyn (Rembe) S.; m. Joan Huntington Yerges, July 21, 1975; 1 child, Robert Francis III. BA, DePauw U., 1975; BSE, Purdue U., 1975; JD, Wake Forest U., 1978. Bar: N.C. 1978. Atty. Capital Synergistics Corp., Winston-Salem, N.C., 1977-80; asst. counsel R.J. Reynolds Industries, Winston-Salem, 1980-82, assoc. counsel, 1983-85, counsel, 1985-86; corp. and comml. counsel R.J. Reynolds Tobacco Co., Winston-Salem, 1986-87; sr. counsel, asst. sec. R.J. Reynolds Nabisco, Inc., Atlanta, 1987—. Bd. dirs. Lewisville (N.C.) Fire Dept. Mem. ABA, N.C. Bar Assn., Forsyth County Bar Assn. Republican. Episcopalian. Avocation: retriever training. Securities, Contracts commercial, General corporate. Office: RJ Reynolds Nabisco Inc 300 Galleria Pkwy NW Atlanta GA 30339

SHARPNACK, JOHN TRENT, lawyer; b. Columbus, Ind., May 7, 1933; s. Lew G. Sharpnack and Mary Harvey (Lingle) Moody; m. Helen E. Carroll, Dec. 26, 1960; children: Rosanne, Christopher. BA, U. Cin., 1955, LLB, 1960. Bar: Ohio 1960, Ind. 1963, U.S. Dist. Ct. (so. dist.) Ind. 1963. Atty. antitrust div. U.S. Dept. Justice, Washington, 1960-63; ptnr. Sharpnack, Bigley, David & Rumple, Columbus, 1963—; mem. com. rules of practice and procedure Ind. Supreme Ct., 1986—. Fellow Am. Coll. Trial Lawyers; mem. Ind. Bar Assn. (chmn. trial sect. 1983-84, chmn. ho. of dels. 1986-87, ethics com.). State civil litigation, Personal injury, Libel. Home: 9682 W Harrison Ct Columbus IN 47201 Office: Sharpnack Bigley David & Rumple 321 Washington Columbus IN 47201

SHATZ, PHILLIP, lawyer, banker, insurance executive; b. White Plains, N.Y., Sept. 1, 1926; s. Hyman and Ruth (Futoran) S.; m. Bettie Dorsey, Oct. 18, 1957 (dec.); children—Phillip Dorsey, Sallie Dean. B.S., Syracuse U., 1948; LL.B., Columbia U., 1954. Bar: N.Y. 1954, U.S. Dist. Ct. (so. dist.) N.Y. 1955, U.S. Supreme Ct. 1960. Pres., chmn. bd. Rich, Shatz and Duncan, Inc., Mahopac, N.Y., 1948-75; v.p. Putnam County Fed. Savs. and Loan Assn., 1953-63, pres., chmn. bd., 1963-78; sole practice, Mahopac, 1954-70; ptnr. Shatz & Braatz, Mahopac, 1970-74, Shatz & Thomsen, Mahopac, 1974-77, Shatz, Thomsen & Mace, Mahopac, 1977-80, McCabe & Mack, Poughkeepsie, 1980—; spl. prosecutor Putnam County; dir. Mid-Hudson Legal Services. Chmn. Putnam County Young Republicans. Served with USNR, 1943-46. Mem. ABA, N.Y. State Bar Assn., Dutchess County Bar Assn., Assn. Bar City N.Y. Clubs: Amrita (Poughkeepsie); University (N.Y.C.). General corporate, State civil litigation, Family and matrimonial. Other: PO Box 2467 Poughkeepsie NY 12603 Office: McCabe & Mack Esqs 63 Washington St Poughkeepsie NY 12601

SHAUGHNESSY, JAMES MICHAEL, lawyer; b. Rockville Centre, N.Y., Feb. 1, 1945; s. James Gregory and Frieda Louise (Brosche) S.; m. Linda Ann Bonfiglio, Aug. 17, 1968; m. 2d, Kari Marie Thoring, Nov. 19, 1977; children—Brendan Michael, Megan Ann. B.A., Adelphi U., 1967; J.D., NYU, 1969. Bar: N.Y. 1970, U.S. Dist. Ct. (so. and ea. dists.) N.Y. 1971, U.S. Ct. Appeals (2d cir.) 1974, Calif. 1977, U.S. Dist. Ct. (so. dist.) Calif. 1977, U.S. Ct. Appeals (9th cir.) 1977, U.S. Ct. Appeals (5th cir.) 1983, U.S. Supreme Ct. 1979, U.S. Dist. Ct. (no. dist.) N.Y. 1982, N.J. 1983, U.S. Dist. Ct. N.J. 1983, U.S. Tax Ct. 1983. Assoc. Casey, Lane & Mittendorf, N.Y.C., 1969-76, ptnr., 1976-82; ptnr. Haythe & Curley, N.Y.C., 1982—. Served with N.Y. N.G., 1969-70. Recipient Benjamin F. Butler award Sch. Law NYU, 1969. Mem. ABA, Assn. Bar City of N.Y., N.Y. State Bar Assn., Fed. Bar Council, N.J. State Bar Assn. Republican. Roman Catholic. State civil litigation, Family and matrimonial, Real property. Office: The Yorktown Commons 1830 Commerce St Yorktown Heights NY 10598

SHAULIS, NORMAN ALBERT, county judge; b. Somerset, Pa., July 13, 1927. B.S., Temple U., 1949, J.D., 1952; grad. Nat. Coll. State Judiciary, U. Nev., 1972. Bar: Pa. 1952. Ptnr. Coder & Shaulis, Somerset, Pa., 1952-56; sole practice, Somerset, 1956-64; ptnr. Shaulis & Rascona, Somerset, 1964-67, Shaulis, Kimmel & Rascona, Somerset, 1967-72; judge Somerset County Ct. Common Pleas, Pa., 1972—; U.S. commr. for we. dist. Pa., 1957-61; legal officer Pa. Wing CAP, 1965—. Editor Somerset Legal Jour., 1960. Recipient Commendation, Pa. Senate, Harrisburg, 1984. Mem. ABA, Am. Judicature Soc., Lawyer-Pilot Bar Assn., Pa. Bar Assn., Somerset County Bar Assn., Phi Delta Phi. Club: Somerset Country (bd. dirs. 1984—, pres. 1985). Lodges: Masons, Shriners. Judicial administration. Home: 707 Cannel Dr Somerset PA 15501 Office: PO Box 527 Courthouse Somerset PA 15501

SHAVELL, STEVEN, law educator; b. 1946. AB, U. Mich., 1968; PhD, MIT, 1973. Asst. prof. Harvard U., Cambridge, Mass., 1974-79, 80-82, assoc. prof., 1979-80, prof., 1982—. Office: Harvard U Law Sch Cambridge MA 02138 *

SHAW, A. REID, lawyer; b. Chgo., Sept. 9, 1956; s. Allan Robert and Patricia (Ringley) S.; m. Karen Elizabeth Davis, June 21, 1980; children: Caitlin Elizabeth, Alec Riordan. BA, Carleton Coll., 1978; JD, Stanford U., 1981. Bar: Minn. 1981, U.S. Dist. Ct. Minn. 1981, U.S. Supreme Ct. 1987. Assoc. Oppenheimer Wolff & Donnelly, Mpls., 1981—. Article editor Stanford U. Law Rev., 1980-81. Mem. ABA, Minn. Bar Assn., Hennepin County Bar Assn., Phi Beta Kappa. Federal civil litigation, State civil litigation. Home: 2619 Robbins Minneapolis MN 55410 Office: Oppenheimer Wolff & Donnelly 4800 IDS Ctr Minneapolis MN 55402

SHAW, ARNOLD H(AROLD), lawyer, arbitrator; b. Pittston, Pa., Mar. 15, 1914; s. Jonas W. and Sadie (Tunick) S.; m. Belle G., May 20, 1945; children—Jonas W., Lawrence S. B.S., L.I. U., 1939; J.D., Bklyn. Law Sch., 1941. Bar: N.Y. 1942, U.S. Ct. Appeals (2d cir.) 1947, U.S. Dist. Ct. (so. dist.) N.Y. 1946, U.S. Dist. Ct. (ea. dist.) N.Y. 1946, U.S. Supreme Ct. 1947. Sole practice law, N.Y.C., 1942—; spl. master Supreme Ct. N.Y., 1978-86; arbitrator Civil Ct. N.Y.C., 1978—, Dist. Ct. Nassau County, N.Y., 1979—, Small Claims Div. N.Y. Civil Ct., 1972-86; dir., gen. counsel Safe Flight Instrument Corp., White Plains, N.Y., 1967—; gen counsel Inland Pension Fund, Corageous Syndicate, Inc.; ret. gen. counsel Warehousemen's Assn. N.Y. and N.J., Inland Dry Storage Labor Com., Assn. Am. Weighmasters, Young Adult Inst. and Workshop, Inc., also past chmn. Trustee, counsel Inst. for Socioecon. Studies; ret. trustee South Shore Assn. for Ind. Living. Administrative and regulatory, General corporate, Probate. Office: One Madison Ave New York NY 10010

SHAW, DAVID ANTHONY, lawyer; b. Gary, Ind., July 31, 1948; s. James Anthony and Martha Fay (McCulloch) S.; m. Kathy Louise McCullough, June 11, 1971; children—Amanda Louise, Jason Anthony. B.S., Ind. U., 1970, J.D., 1973. Bar: Ind. 1973, D.C. 1974, U.S. Dist. Ct. (so. dist.) Ind. 1973, U.S. Dist. Ct. D.C. 1974, U.S. Ct. Claims 1977, U.S. Ct. Mil. Appeals 1973, U.S. Tax Ct. 1974, U.S. Ct. Appeals (D.C. cir.) 1974, U.S. Ct. Appeals (4th cir.) 1976, U.S. Ct. Appeals (5th cir.) 1976, U.S. Ct. Appeals (10th cir.) 1976, U.S. Supreme Ct. 1976. Atty. appellate div. U.S. Army, Washington, 1973-75, litigation div., 1975-76; spl. asst. U.S. atty. Dept. Justice, Washington, 1976-77; counsel Senate Select Com. on Intelligence, Washington, 1977-81; exec. v.p. Software div. Gould, Inc., Urbana, Ill., 1981-84; ptnr. Eastham & Shaw, Washington, 1985—; mng. dir. New Venture Devel. Corp., 1985—, Venture Lease Inc., 1985—; v.p. Triad Leasing Corp., 1985—; advisor, dir. various cos. Contbr. articles to profl. publs. Chmn. bd. Devel. Services Ctr., Champaign, Ill., 1983—. Served to capt. U.S. Army, 1973-77. Mem. ABA, Fed. Bar Assn., D.C. Bar Assn., Ind. Bar Assn. General corporate, Entrepreneural. Home: 10117 New London Dr Potomac MD 20854 Office: Eastham & Shaw 1024 Thomas Jefferson St NW Suite 400 Washington DC 20007

SHAW, DONALD RAY, lawyer; b. Hugo, Okla., Nov. 29, 1945; s. Jesse Vernon and Velma Lee (Atkinson) S.; m. Nelda Jan Finley, May 31, 1969; children: Britton, Taylor. BBA, U. Okla., 1968, JD, 1975. Bar: Okla. 1975, U.S. Dist. Ct. Okla. 1978, U.S. Ct. Appeals (10th cir.) 1980. Sole practice Idabel, Okla., 1975-77, 87—; dist. atty. Dist. 17, Idabel, 1978-87. Served to capt. USAFR, 1969-72. Mem. ABA, Okla. Bar Assn., Okla. CPA's, Gideons (treas. 1980-86), Am. Legion (comdr. 1976—). Democrat. Presbyterian. Lodges: Lions (bd. dirs. 1985-86), Elks. Criminal, State civil litigation, Civil rights. Home: 1312 E Madison Idabel OK 74745 Office: 8 NW 1st St PO Box 957 Idabel OK 74745

SHAW, ELWIN SCOTT, lawyer; b. Columbus, Ohio, Aug. 18, 1949; s. William R. and Helen (Dunipace) S.; m. Marjorie E. Farrier, Feb. 1, 1980 (div. Aug. 1984). BA, Ohio State U., 1971; JD, Capital U., 1976. Bar: Ohio 1976, U.S. Dist. Ct. (so. dist.) Ohio 1976. Sole practice Columbus, 1976—; sec. BFI Inc., Columbus, 1983—. Served with USAFR, 1968-74. Mem. ABA, Ohio Bar Assn., Columbus Bar Assn., Frank County Trial Lawyers, Ohio Assn. Trial Lawyers, Assn. Trial Lawyers Am. Republican. Presbyterian. Avocations: gliders, travel. Criminal, Personal injury, Consumer commercial. Office: 39 E Whittier St Columbus OH 43206

SHAW, JOHN FREDERIC, JR., lawyer; b. Elyria, Ohio, July 7, 1944; s. John Frederic and Georgianna Mayre (Hessler) S.; m. Carolyn Dickinson, Nov. 26, 1966; children: Jennifer Sara, Samuel Archer. BA, Oberlin Coll., 1966; JD, U. Conn., 1972. Bar: Conn. 1972, U.S. Dist. Ct. Conn. 1973. Assoc. Fortuna & Cartelli, Middletown, Conn., 1972-73, Dzialo, Pickett & Allen, Middletown, 1973-75; ptnr. Shaw, Howard & McMillan, Middletown, 1975-85; sole practice Middletown, 1985—; instr. real property law Middlesex Community Coll., Middletown, 1985—. Dir. exec. com. Conn. Conf. United Ch. Christ, 1982—, chmn. bd. dirs., 1986—. Mem. ABA (real property and probate sect.), Conn. Bar Assn. (exec. com. real property sect. 1984—), Middlesex County Bar Assn. Office: 234 Court St Middletown CT 06457

SHAW, JOHN LEROY, JR., lawyer; b. Charleston, S.C., May 27, 1944; s. John LeRoy and Mary (Buley) S.; m. Joanna M. Pampena, Nov. 18, 1967;

children—Amy Jo, Maryann Elizabeth, Alison Patricia, Katie Marietta. B.S., Calif. State U.-Los Angeles, 1966; J.D., Southwestern U., Los Angeles, 1973. Bar: Calif. 1973, U.S. Dist. Ct. (cen. dist.) Calif. 1973. Ptnr. Shaw, Shaw & Shaw, Temple City, Calif., 1973—; dir. N.Am. Real Estate Co., Arcadia, Calif. Chmn. Parks and Recreation Commn., Temple City, 1983-84. Served to sgt. U.S. Army, 1966-69; Vietnam. Recipient commendation Los Angeles County, 1983. Mem. San Gabriel Valley Bar Assn. (pres. 1984-85), Los Angeles County Bar Assn., Calif. Bar Assn., ABA, Temple City C. of C., Am. Legion. Republican. Mormon. Club: Temple City High Twelve (pres. 1976-77). Lodges: Masons, Rotary (pres. local club 1976-77, gov.'s citation 1977). General practice, Probate, Real property. Home: 6453 N Livia Ave Temple City CA 91780 Office: Shaw Shaw & Shaw 5816 Temple City Blvd PO Box 1 Temple City CA 91780

SHAW, JOHN MALACH, fed. judge; b. Beaumont, Tex., Nov. 14, 1931; s. John Virgil Shaw and Ethel (Malach) Newstadt; m. Glenda Ledoux, Nov. 11, 1970; children: John Lewis, Stacy Anne. Student, Tulane U., 1949-50; B.S. with spl. attainments in Commerce, Washington and Lee U., 1953; LL.B., J.D., La. State U., 1956. Bar: La. bar 1956. Partner firm Lewis and Lewis, Opelousas, La., 1958-79; U.S. dist. judge Western Dist. La., Opelousas, 1979—; Govt. appeal agt. Local Bd. 60, La., 1965-72. Mem.: La. Law Rev, 1954-56; asso. editor, 1955-56; author articles, 1954-56. Served with U.S. Army, 1956-58. Recipient Presdl. cert. of appreciation for services as appeal agt. Mem. Fifth Circuit Dist. Judges Assn., Am. Judicature Soc., La. State Bar Assn., Opelousas C. of C. (pres. 1966). Democrat. Methodist. Club: Kiwanis. Jurisprudence. *

SHAW, LEANDER JERRY, JR., Florida supreme court justice; b. Salem, Va., Sept. 6, 1930; s. Leander J. and Margaret S.; m. Vidya B. Lye. BA, W.Va. State Coll., 1952, LLD (hon.), 1986; JD, Howard U., 1957. Asst. prof. law Fla. A&M U., 1957-60; sole practice Jacksonville, Fla., 1960-69, 72-74; asst. pub. defender Fla., 1965-69; asst. state's atty. Fla., 1969-72; judge Fla. Indsl. Relations Commn., 1974-79, Fla. Ct. Appeals (1st dist.), 1979-83; justice Fla. Supreme Ct., Tallahassee, 1983—. Judicial administration. Office: Supreme Ct Bldg Tallahassee FL 32301

SHAW, LEE CHARLES, lawyer; b. Red Wing, Minn., Feb. 17, 1913; s. Marvil Thomas and Bernice (Quinland) S.; m. Lorraine Schroeder, July 1, 1939; children—Lynda Lee, Robert, Candace Jean, Lee Charles. B.A., U. Chgo., 1936, J.D., 1938. Bar: Ill. Assoc. Pope & Ballard, Chgo., 1938-44, ptnr., 1944-45; founding ptnr. Seyfarth, Shaw, Fairweather & Geraldson, Chgo., 1945—; mem. arbitration services adv. com. Fed. Mediation and Conciliation Service; dir. Walker Forge, Inc., Racine, Wis. Contbr. articles on labor law to profl. jours. Mem. ABA, Chgo. Bar Assn. (bd. mgrs. 1956-57), U. Chgo. Alumni Assn. Republican. Episcopalian. Clubs: Tavern, Union League (Chgo.); Lomas Santa Fe Country (Solano Beach, Calif.). Labor, Pension, profit-sharing, and employee benefits. Home: 434 Loma Larga Solana Beach CA 92075 Office: Suite 4200 55 E Monroe St Chicago IL 60603

SHAW, NANCY ANN, lawyer; b. Pitts., May 15, 1955; d. Harry Edward and Patricia Ann (Hussey) S.; m. James A. Goldsmith, Sept. 10, 1983. B.A., U. Iowa, 1977; J.D., 1980. Bar: Ohio 1980. Assoc. Squire, Sanders & Dempsey, Cleve., 1980-85, Spieth, Bell, McCurdy & Newell, Cleve., 1985-87, ptnr., 1987—. Articles editor Jour. Corp. Law, 1979-80. Mem. jr. womens com. Cleve. Playhouse; mem. Children's Oncology Soc. Northeast Ohio. Mem. ABA, Ohio Bar Assn., Cuyahoga County Bar Assn., Def. Research Inst., Mortar Bd. Club: Women's City. Labor, State civil litigation, Federal civil litigation. Home: 19220 Lomond Blvd Shaker Heights OH 44122 Office: Spieth Bell McCurdy & Newell 2000 Huntington Bldg Cleveland OH 44115

SHAW, STANFORD EUGENE, lawyer; b. Poteau, Okla., Dec. 27, 1934; s. Leland Stanford and Corrine (Francis) S.; m. Regina Nell Bagube, July 3, 1965; children—Stanford F., Stephanie R. A.A., Santa Ana Coll., 1963; J.D., Southwestern U., 1968. Bar: Calif. 1970, U.S. Ct. Mil. Appeals 1971, U.S. Tax Ct. 1970, U.S. Dist. Ct. (cen. dist.) Calif. 1970. Chief clk. criminal dept. Grand Jury, Orange County, Calif., 1963-66; law librarian Orange County, 1966-72; assoc. prof. law Western State U. Coll. Law, 1969-72; sole practice, Santa Ana, Calif., 1972—. Served with USCG, 1953-64. Mem. Orange County Bar Assn., Calif. Trial Lawyers Assn., ABA. Democrat. Roman Catholic. Columnist, Orange County Bar Jour., 1966-72. State civil litigation, Family and matrimonial, General practice. Address: 2021 E 4th St Suite 217A Santa Ana CA 92705

SHAW, SUSAN BOYCE, lawyer; b. Memphis, May 10, 1955; d. Richard William Sr. and Willie Mae (Prestage) Boyce; m. Larry Russell Shaw, Mar. 19, 1983; 1 child, Richard Russell, Aug. 23, 1986. BA, Miss. State U., 1976; JD, U. Miss., 1978. Bar: Miss. 1979, U.S. Dist. Ct. (no. dist.) Miss. 1979. Staff atty. N. Miss. Rural Legal Services, Clarksdale, 1979-82; staff atty. N. Miss. Rural Legal Services, Tupelo, 1983-85, mng. atty., 1985—. Adv. bd. Retired Sr. Vols., Tupelo, 1985—, vice chmn., 1986. Named one of Outstanding Young Women of Am., 1981. Mem. Lee County Bar Assn., Miss. Bar Assn., Bus. and Profl. Womens. Democrat. Baptist. Avocations: horseback riding, tennis, travel. Bankruptcy, Family and matrimonial, Pension, profit-sharing, and employee benefits. Home: 1403 W Bristow Tupelo MS 38801 Office: N Miss Rural Legal Services PO Box 139 104 E Franklin Tupelo MS 38802

SHAW, TEX RONNIE, lawyer; b. Lubbock, Tex., Sept. 13, 1946; s. Clyde Bailey and Lucille Tennie (Luna) S.; m. Patricia Jean Lumsden, July 16, 1966; children: Jennifer Diane, Jonathan Porter. BS, East Tex. State U., 1973; JD, Tex. Tech U., 1981. Bar: U.S. Dist. Ct. (no. dist.) Tex. 1982, U.S. Dist. Ct. (ea. dist.) Tex. 1983; cert. in personal injury and in civil trial by Tex. Bd. Legal Specialization. Sole practice Sulpher Springs, Tex., 1981-82; assoc. Windle Turley, P.C., Dallas, 1982-84; ptnr. Stark & Shaw, Gainesville, Tex., 1984-85, Sullivant, Woodlock, Underwood, Meurer, Shaw & Zielinski, Gainesville, 1985—. V.p. Camp Fire Girls, Gainesville, 1985, bd. dirs., 1986—; leader Boy Scouts Am., Gainesville, 1986—. Mem. Tex. Bar Assn., Assn. Trial Lawyers Am., Tex. Trial Lawyers Assn., Dallas Trial Lawyers Assn., Cooke County Bar Assn. Democrat. Baptist. Lodge: Masons. Avocations: reading, fishing, boating. Personal injury, Workers' compensation, State civil litigation. Home: 616 Lindsay Gainesville TX 76240 Office: Sullivant Woodlock Underwood et al 209 S Dixon PO Box 1517 Gainesville TX 76240

SHAW, WILLIAM ALBERT, lawyer; b. Fort Dodge, Iowa, Dec. 28, 1943; s. William Francis and Irene Catherine (Rafferty) S. BS in Pharmacy, Drake U., 1966; JD, U. Iowa, 1969. Lic. real estate broker, Calif.; bar: Iowa 1969, U.S. Dist. Ct. (no. dist.) Iowa 1969, Calif. 1971, U.S. Dist. Ct. (cen. dist.) Calif. 1971, U.S. Supreme Ct. 1972, U.S. Dist. Ct. (so. dist.) Calif. 1974, U.S. Ct. Appeals (9th cir.) 1974, U.S. Ct. (D.C. cir.) 1981, U.S. Dist. Ct. (no. dist.) Calif. 1981, N.Y. 1987. Assoc. Shaw & Shaw, Pocahontas, Iowa, 1969-70; dept. dist. atty. Los Angeles County, 1971-74; asst. U.S. atty. U.S. Dist. Ct. (so. dist.) Calif., Los Angeles, 1974-76; assoc. Kirkland & Packard, Los Angeles, 1976; ptnr. Reed & Shaw, Beverly Hills, Calif., 1977—; asst., staff mem. office pub. liaison White House, Washington, 1975; pres. Controlled Investment, Beverly Hills, 1979—. Mem. ABA (nat. v.p. law student div. 1968), Calif. Bar Assn., Iowa Bar Assn., D.C. Bar Assn., Los Angeles County Bar Assn., South Cen. Los Angeles Bar Assn. (bd. dirs. 1973-74), Am. Pharm. Assn., Calif. Pharm. Assn., Assn. Trial Lawyers Am., Calif. Trial Lawyers Assn., Los Angeles Trial Lawyers Assn., Colina Los Angeles area and Beverly Hills C. of C. Republican. Roman Catholic. Avocations: skiing, running. Personal injury, Real property, Entertainment. Home: 9131 Callejuela Dr Beverly Hills CA 90210 Office: Reed & Shaw 425 S Beverly Dr Beverly Hills CA 90212

SHAY, MICHAEL PATRICK, lawyer; b. Plainfield, N.J., July 20, 1950; s. Elwood Kenneth and Gertrude Frances (Yeager) S.; m. Ulvia Stammherr, Aug. 11, 1973; children: Bryan, Colin, Erin. BA, Lehigh U., 1972; JD, U. Pa., 1975. Bar: Pa. 1975, U.S. Dist. Ct. (ea. dist.) Pa. 1976, U.S. Ct. Appeals 1977, U.S. Supreme Ct. 1986. Ptnr. Sigmon & Ross, Bethlehem, Pa., 1975-85, Shay & Santee, Bethlehem, 1985—; solicitor Bath (Pa.) Zoning Hearing Bd., 1979—, Forks Twp. (Pa.) Zoning Hearing Bd., 1986—. Bd. dirs. Lehigh U. Home Club, Bethlehem, 1983—. Named one of Outstanding Young Alumnus award Lehigh U., 1982. Mem. ABA, Pa. Bar Assn., Northampton County Bar Assn. Democrat. Avocations: golf, running. Insurance, Workers' compensation, General practice. Office: Shay & Santee 44 E Broad St PO Box 1005 Bethlehem PA 18016

SHAYNE, DAVID, lawyer; b. Chgo., Nov. 6, 1934; s. Philip Shapiro and Doris (Smoler) S.; m. Mette Hannover, July 10, 1960; children: Philip, Adam, Ralph. B.A., Yale U., 1956; LL.B., Harvard U., 1959. Bar: Ill. Ptnr. Sidley & Austin, Chgo., 1971—. Mem. ABA, Chgo. Bar Assn., Ill. Bar Assn., Chgo. Estate Planning Council. Probate, Estate taxation, Personal income taxation. Home: 507 W Roscoe St Chicago IL 60657 Office: Sidley & Austin One First Nat Plaza Chicago IL 60603

SHAYNE, NEIL T., lawyer; b. N.Y.C., May 2, 1932. Graduate, NYU; LLB, Bklyn. Sch. Law, 1954. Bar: N.Y. 1954. Sole practice Mineloa, N.Y. Columnist N.Y. Law Journal, 1973—; also articles. Mem. ABA (lectr.), Nassau County Bar Assn. (bd. dirs. 1983—, chmn. profl. ethics com. 1982-84, dean acad. law), Assn. Trial Lawyers Am. (lectr.), W.Va. Trial Lawyers Assn. (speaker), N.Y. State Trial Lawyers Assn. (lectr.), Medicine for Attys. (speaker), Practising Law Inst. (lectr.). Office: 1501 Franklin Ave Mineloa NY 11501

SHEA, DAVID MICHAEL, justice; b. Hartford, July 1, 1922; s. Michael Peter and Margaret (Agnes) S.; m. Rosemary Anne Sasseen, Apr. 28, 1956; children—Susan, Kathleen, Margaret, Rosemary, Christina, Michael, Maura, Julie. B.A., Wesleyan U., 1944; LL.B., Yale U., 1948. Bar: Conn. 1948. Assoc. Tunick & Ferris, Greenwich, Conn., 1948-49; assoc. Bailey & Wechsler, Hartford, 1949-57; ptnr. Bailey, Wechsler & Shea, Hartford, 1957-65; judge Conn. Superior Ct., Hartford, 1966-81; justice Conn. Supreme Ct., Hartford, 1981—. Served with U.S. Army, 1943-46. Democrat. Roman Catholic. Office: Conn Supreme Ct 231 Capitol Ave Hartford CT 06106

SHEA, DONALD FRANCIS, justice Supreme Court Rhode Island; b. Pawtucket, R.I., Sept. 14, 1925; s. Edward Leo and Lucy Rose (Read) S.; m. Ursula V. Rafferty, June 17, 1950; children: Donald Edward, Michaela Theresa, Christopher John, Sara Elizabeth, Ellen Marie. A.B., Providence Coll., 1950; J.D., Georgetown U., 1954. Bar: R.I. Trial atty. firm Boss, Conlan, Keenan, Bulman and Rice, Providence, 1955-72; assoc. justice Superior Ct. R.I., 1972-81, Supreme Ct. R.I., 1981—; part-time instr. law Roger Williams Coll., Providence.; Mem. R.I. Ho. of Reps., 1960-68; exec. asst. to gov. R.I., 1968-72. Served with USNR, 1943-46. Mem. ABA, R.I. Bar Assn. *

SHEA, EDWARD EMMETT, lawyer, educator; b. Detroit, May 29, 1932; s. Edward Francis and Margaret Kathleen (Downey) S.; m. Ann Marie Conley, Aug. 28, 1957; children: Michael, Maura, Ellen. AB, U. Detroit, 1954; JD, U. Mich., 1957. Assoc. Simpson Thacher & Bartlett, N.Y.C., 1960-63, Dykema, Wheat & Spencer, Detroit, 1963-69, Cadhalader Wickersam & Taft, N.Y.C., 1969-71; v.p., gen. counsel, chmn. Reichold Chems., White Plains, N.Y., 1971-81; adj. prof. Grad. Sch. Bus. Pace U., N.Y.C., 1982—; adj. prof. Law Sch. U. Detroit, 1965-69; bd. dirs. GAF Corp., Wayne, N.J. Contbr. articles to profl. jours. Served to 1st lt. JAGC, USAF, 1957-60. Clubs: N.Y. Athletic, Chemist's (N.Y.C.). General corporate, Environment, Private international. Office: GAF Corp 1361 Alps Rd Wayne NJ 07470

SHEA, FRANCIS MICHAEL, lawyer; b. Manchester, N.H., June 16, 1905; s. Michael Francis and Margaret (Muldoon) S.; m. Hilda Droshnicop, July 22, 1936; 1 child, Richard. A.B., Dartmouth Coll., 1925; LL.B., Harvard U., 1928. Bar: N.Y. 1930, D.C. 1946. On research project for Bernard Flexner, N.Y., 1928-29; asso. Slee, O'Brian, Hellings and Ulsh, Buffalo, 1929-33; chief of opinion sect., legal div. A.A.A., 1933-35; specialist, legal div. SEC, Feb.-July 1935; gen. counsel P.R. Reconstrn. Adminstrn., 1935-36; dean and prof. law U. Buffalo Law Sch., 1936-41; on leave of absence July 1939-Feb. 1941, asst. atty. gen. of U.S., 1939-Oct. 1945, asso. counsel for the prosecution of major Axis war criminals, 1945; sr. ptnr. Shea & Gardner., Washington, 1947—; Chmn. Atty. Gen.'s Com. on Bankruptcy Adminstrn., 1941-45, Jud. Conf. Com. Laws Pertaining Mental Disorders; dir. Joint Conf. Legal Edn., N.Y. State; exec. com., 1936-40. Contbr. to law jours. Mem. ABA, New York State Bar Assn., D.C. Bar Assn., Assn. Bar City N.Y., Maritime Law Assn., Am. Law Inst. (life). Democrat. Roman Catholic. Clubs: Metropolitan, Cosmos (Washington). Federal civil litigation, Antitrust, Environment. Home: 505 S Lee St Alexandria VA 22314 Office: 1800 Massachusetts Ave NW Washington DC 20036

SHEA, GERALD MACDONALD, lawyer, petroleum company executive; b. N.Y.C., Nov. 10, 1942; s. John Anthony and Grace (Deery) S.; m. Claire Marie Antoinette Elisabeth de Gramont, Dec. 5, 1981; children—Penelope Mahot de la Querantonnais, Sebastian John Andrew, Alexander George Edward. B.A., Yale U., 1964; J.D., Columbia U., 1967. Bar: N.Y. 1968. Assoc. Debevoise & Plimpton, N.Y.C., 1967-72, 75-76, Paris, France, 1972-75; sr. counsel Mobil Oil Corp., N.Y.C., 1976-83; v.p., gen. counsel Mobil Saudi Arabia Inc., Jeddah, 1983—. Jerome Michael scholar, 1966. Mem. Assn. Bar City N.Y. Club: Racquet and Tennis (N.Y.C.). General corporate, Private international. Home: care of E Zervos Mobil Oil Corp New York NY 10017 Office: Mobil Saudi Arabia Inc, Jeddah Saudi Arabia

SHEA, J. MICHAEL, lawyer; b. Tampa, Fla., May 24, 1942; s. John Henry and Mary (Bryon) S.; m. Virginia Tarr; 1 child, Sean Michael; stepson: Will Burnett. BA in Polit. Sci., U. S. Fla., 1965; JD, Fla. State U., 1969; postdoctoral, Fla. State U. Dept. Urban & Regional Planning, 1969-70. Bar: Fla. 1969, U.S. Dist. Ct. (mid. dist.) Fla. 1969, U.S. Ct. Appeals (5th cir.) 1978, U.S. Ct. Appeals (11th cir.) 1982. Ptnr. Shea & Assocs., P.A., 1971—; cons. city planner Milo, Smith & Assocs., Tampa, 1970-72; chmn. bd. dirs., chief exec. officer Mid South Home Health Agys., Birmingham, Ala., 1979—. Contbr. articles to profl. jours. Pres. Suncoast chpt. Leukemia Soc. Am., 1978-80; Fla. rep. Dem. Nat. Com., 1980-84. Recipient Commencation City of Tampa, 1971. Mem. ABA, Fla. Bar Assn., Hillsborough County Bar Assn., Assn. Trial Lawyers Am., Health Planning Lawyers Assn., Maritime Law Assn. (proctor in admiralty, com. on navigation and USCG matters). Episcopalian. Clubs: Tampa Rowing, Propellor (Tampa). Lodges: Masons (32 degree), Palma Ceia. Avocation: scullying. Admiralty, Real property, Personal injury. Home: 3312 Perry Tampa FL 33603 Office: Shea & Assocs PA 419 W Platt St Tampa FL 33606

SHEA, JAMES WILLIAM, lawyer; b. N.Y.C., July 10, 1936; s. William Peter and Mildred E. (McCaffrey) S.; m. Ann Marie Byrne, June 6, 1964; children: James T., Kathleen A., Tracy A. BS, St. Peters Coll.; LLD, Fordham U.; LLM in Taxation, NYU. Bar: N.Y. 1963, U.S. Dist. Ct. (so. and ea. dists.) N.Y. 1966, U.S. Supreme Ct. 1967. Revenue agent U.S. Treasury Dept., N.Y.C., 1961-63; tax atty. Kennecott Copper Corp., N.Y.C., 1963-67; tax counsel CBS Inc., N.Y.C., 1968-71; ptnr. Hunton & Williams and predecessor firm Conboy, Hewitt, O'Brien & Boardman, N.Y.C., 1971—; bd. dirs. Victory Van Lines Inc., N.Y.C. Rep. committeeman, Staten Island, N.Y., 1980. Served to capt. JAGC, 1957-61. Mem. N.Y. State Bar Assn. Republican. Roman Catholic. Club: Richmond County Country (Staten Island). Probate, State and local taxation, Personal income taxation. Home: 399 Tysens Ln Staten Island NY 10306 Office: Hunton & Williams 100 Park Ave New York NY 10017

SHEA, JOSEPH WILLIAM, III, lawyer; b. Cin., Jan. 3, 1947; s. Joseph W. Jr. and Gertrude Mary (Reardon) S.; m. Elaine N. Miller, May 29, 1971; children: J. Blaine, Doyle Reardon, C. Lauer. BA, U. Cin., 1969; JD, No. Ky. U., 1974. Bar: Ohio 1974 (bd. examiners 1984—), U.S. Dist. Ct. Ohio 1974, U.S. Ct. Appeals (6th cir.) 1983, U.S. Supreme Ct. 1983. Ptnr. Shea & MacKay, Cin. Author: Shea's Forms for Ohio Trial Practice, 1983, Wrongful Death Manual, 1984; editor Verdict Reporter, vols. 1-127, 1976—; contbr. articles to profl. jours. Mem. Gov.'s Ins. Task Force, Columbus, 1985—. Fellow Ohio Acad. Trial Lawyers (pres. ednl. found. 1981, pres. 1982-83, editor mag. 1981); mem. Assn. Trial Lawyers Am. (del. nat. conv. 1983-85, bd. govs. 1985—), Ky. Acad. Trial Lawyers, ABA, Ohio State Bar Assn. (negligence law com.), Cin. Bar Assn. (negligence law com.), Nat. Conf. Bar Examiners. Roman Catholic. Personal injury, Federal civil litigation, State civil litigation. Home: 8575 Kugler Mill Rd Cincinnati OH 45243 Office: Shea & MacKay 1500 Columbia Plaza 250 E 5th St Cincinnati OH 45202

SHEA, MICHAEL ALAN, lawyer; b. Iowa City, Oct. 9, 1946; s. Robert Wallace and Florence (Foley) S.; m. La Donna Reiner, Mar. 3, 1979. BA, U. Iowa, 1968, JD, 1974; LittB, Oxford U., Eng., 1973. Bar: Hawaii 1974, U.S Tax Ct. 1974, U.S. Dist. Ct. Hawaii 1974, U.S. Ct. Appeals (9th cir.) 1974, U.S. Supreme Ct. 1983. From assoc. to ptnr. Cades, Schutte, Fleming & Wright, Honolulu, 1974-83; ptnr. Goodsill, Anderson, Quinn & Stifel, Honolulu, 1983—. Mem. Gov.'s adv. com. on adoption of Tax Reform Act, 1986; bd. dirs. Arts Council Hawaii, Honolulu, 1975—, Honolulu Community Theatre, 1976-82. Mem. ABA (exempt orgns. com. tax sect.), Hawaii Bar Assn. (chmn. tax sect. com. 1986, chmn. elect tax sect. 1987—), Honolulu C. of C. (chmn. tax com. 1985—, pub. health com.). Clubs: Honolulu, Hawaii Yacht (Honolulu); Plaza. Corporate taxation, Personal income taxation, State and local taxation. Home: 3430B Keahi Pl Honolulu HI 96822 Office: Goodsill Anderson Quinn & Stifel PO Box 3196 Honolulu HI 96801

SHEA, MICHAEL MURT, lawyer; b. Billings, Mont., June 26, 1937; s. Murt Edward and Vera Virginia (Seifert) S.; m. Phyllis Ann Lopes, Jan. 2, 1961; children: Michael, Lisa, Patrick, Brigid, Annie. BS, U. Santa Clara (Calif.), 1959, JD, 1965. Bar: Calif. 1966, Wash. 1966, U.S. Dist. Ct. (no. dist.) Calif. 1966, U.S. Ct. Appeals (9th cir.) 1966. Assoc. DeKoltz & Hayes, San Jose, Calif., 1966-67; ptnr. Wool, Richardson, Colbert & Shea, San Jose, 1967-70; sole practice, San Jose, 1970—. Author exclusionary clauses in automobile liability policies, 1983. Served to capt. U.S. Army, 1959-60. Mem. Santa Clara Trial Lawyers Assn. (pres. 1980-81), Calif. Trial Lawyers Assn. (bd. govs. 1981—), Assn. Trial Lawyers Am. Democrat. Roman Catholic. Personal injury, Insurance, State civil litigation. Office: James Square Bldg Suite 190 255 N Market St San Jose CA 95110

SHEA, PATRICK A., lawyer; b. Salt Lake City, Feb. 28, 1948; s. Edward J. and Ramona (Kilpack) S.; m. Deborah Fae Kern, Sept. 1, 1980. B.A., Stanford U., 1970; M.A., Oxford U. (Eng.), 1972; J.D., Harvard U., 1975. Bar: Utah 1976, D.C. 1979. Mem. profl. staff, majority leader's office U.S. Senate, 1971, asst. staff dir. intelligence com., 1975-76; assoc. VanCott, Bagley, Salt Lake City, 1976-79, ptnr., 1980—; counsel fgn. relations com. U.S. Senate, 1979-80; gen. counsel KUTV, Communications Investment Corp., and Standard Communications; cons. judiciary com. U.S. Ho. of Reps., 1972-73; adj. prof. polit. sci. U. Utah, Salt Lake City, 1981—. Chmn. Utah Democratic Party, Salt Lake City, 1983-85; v.p. Tomorrow-Today Found., Salt Lake City, 1982-84. Mem. Am. Rhodes Scholar Assn., Utah Bar Assn., D.C. Bar Assn., Stanford Alumni Assn. (pres.-elect 1983-84). Roman Catholic. Club: Alta. Libel, Entertainment, Federal civil litigation. Office: Communications Investment Corp 2185 S 3600 W Salt Lake City UT 84119

SHEA, WILLIAM ALFRED, lawyer; b. N.Y.C., June 21, 1907. J.D., Georgetown U., 1931, L.H.D. (hon.), 1971; L.H.D. (hon.), St. Johns U., 1973, St. Francis Coll., 1974; LL.D. (hon.), L.I. U., 1986. Bar: D.C. 1932, N.Y. 1932. Now partner firm Shea & Gould, N.Y.C.; counsel liquidation bur. N.Y. State Banking Dept., 1934-36; asst. gen. counsel to supt. ins. N.Y. State, 1936-41; mem. N.Y. State Ins. Bd., 1956; trustee emeritus, sec., gen. counsel Cross Land Savs., FSB; dir., gen. counsel Interboro Mut. Indemnity Ins. Co., N.Y.C.; bd. dirs. Nat. Benefit Life Ins. Co., N.Y.C., Companion Life Ins. Co. Vice chmn. bd. Benjamin N. Cardozo Sch. Law, N.Y.C., North Shore Univ. Hosp., Manhasset, N.Y., Taft Inst. Two-Party Govt. Banking, Federal civil litigation, General corporate. Office: 330 Madison Ave New York NY 10017

SHEAFFER, WILLIAM JAY, lawyer; b. Carlisle, Pa., Jan. 18, 1948; s. Raymond Jay and Barbara Jean (Bell) S.; m. Carol Ann Madison, Jan. 5, 1974. BA, U. Cen. Fla., 1975; JD, Nova U., 1978. Bar: Fla. 1978, U.S. Dist. Ct. (mid. dist.) Fla. 1979, U.S. Dist. Ct. (so. and no. dists.) Fla. 1981, U.S. Ct. Appeals (5th and 11th cirs.) 1981, U.S. Supreme Ct. 1983. Atty. State of Fla., Orlando, 1978-79; sole practice Orlando, 1979—. Served to ensign class 4 USN, 1967-71. Mem. ABA, Fla. Bar Assn., Orange County Bar Assn., Nat. Assn. Criminal Def. Attys., Cen. Fla. Criminal Def. Attys. Assn. Republican. Avocation: sailing. Juvenile, Personal injury, Criminal. Office: 609 E Central Blvd Orlando FL 32801

SHEAHAN, JOSEPH D., lawyer; b. Rock Island, Ill., Oct. 25, 1946; s. Joseph L. and Muriel (Bogart) S.; m. Judith Richards, Nov. 26, 1965; children: Michelle Lynn, Jessica Michelle. B.A., Augustana Coll., Rock Island, Ill.; J.D., Washburn U., 1978; postgrad. Georgetown U., 1978-80; honor grad. U.S. Dept. Justice, Washington, 1980. Bar admittee: Kans., 1978, Ill., 1979. Law clk. U.S. Ct. Appeals for 10th Circuit, Denver, 1978; asso. McGehee, Boling & Whitmire, Ltd., Silvis, Ill., 1980-82; sole practice, East Moline, Ill., 1982—; owner Ill.-Iowa Claim Service, Davenport; city atty. City of Green Rock (Ill.), 1980—; village atty. Village of Carbon Cliff, 1984—. Served with U.S. Army, 1967-70; Vietnam. Mem. ABA, Ill. Bar Assn., Rock Island County Bar Assn., Upper Rock Island C. of C. (dir. 1980-82). Democrat. Contbr. articles to legal jours. State civil litigation, Local government, Personal injury.

SHEAHAN, ROBERT EMMETT, lawyer, management labor and employment consultant; b. Chgo., May 20, 1942; s. Robert Emmett and Lola Jean (Moore) S. B.A., Ill. Wesleyan U., 1964; J.D., Duke U., 1967; M.B.A., U. Chgo., 1970. Bar: Ill. 1967, La. 1975, N.C. 1978. VISTA vol., N.Y.C., 1967-68; trial atty. NLRB, Milw. and New Orleans, 1970-75; mem. Jones, Walker, Waechter, Poitevent, Carrere & Denegre, New Orleans, 1975-78; pvt. practice, High Point, N.C., 1978—; cons., tchr. Robert Pearlman & Assocs. Author: Employees and Drug Abuse—An Employer's Handbook; contbg. author: The Developing Labor Law, 1975—; editor: The World of Personnel; contbg. editor: Employee Testing and the Law. Bd. dirs. High Point United Way, 1979—; congressional action com. High Point C. of C., 1979—. Mem. ABA, N.C. Bar Assn., High Point Bar Assn., Ill. Bar Assn., La. Bar Assn. Republican. Roman Catholic. Clubs: Sedgefield (N.C.) Country, String and Splinter (High Point). Labor. Home: 101 Bellwood Ct Jamestown NC 27282 Office: Eastchester Office Ctr 603-B Eastchester Dr High Point NC 27260

SHEAN, OWEN JOSEPH, lawyer; b. Arlington, Va., Aug. 30, 1956; s. Thomas L. and Ursula M. (Hunt) S. BA, U. Va., 1978, JD, 1982. Bar: Va. 1982, U.S. Dist. Ct. (ea. dist.) Va. 1982, U.S. Ct. Appeals (4th cir.) 1985. Assoc. Seawell, Dalton, Hughes & Timms, Norfolk, Va., 1982-86, Wickwire, Gavin & Gibbs, Washington, 1986—. Mem. ship invitation com. Harborfest, Norfolk, 1984, Va. Symphony Ball Com., Norfolk, 1986. Named one of Outstanding Young Men of Am., U.S. Jaycees, 1985. Mem. ABA, Va. State Bar, Norfolk-Portsmouth Bar Assn. (bd. dirs. young lawyers sect.), YMCA Mens Club. Roman Catholic. Federal civil litigation, State civil litigation, Insurance. Home: 1700 N Quebec St Arlington VA 22207 Office: Wickwire Gavin & Gibbs 1133 21st St NW 2 Lafayette Ctr Suite 500 Washington DC 20036

SHEAR, KENNETH, association executive; b. Phila., July 2, 1945; s. Edward Burr and Lillian (Granoff) S.; m. Susanne Coren, Nov. 27, 1969; children: Adena Leah, Jonathan Aaron. B.A., Temple U., 1967, M.A., 1969. Adminstrv. analyst City of Phila., 1969-72; asst. dir. Citizens Crime Commn., Phila., 1972-76; exec. dir. Phila. Bar Assn., 1976—; adj. prof. Temple U., Phila., 1974-76; cons. ABA. Contbr. articles to profl. jours. Chmn. urban affairs com. Jewish Community Relations Council, Phila., 1981-82. Mem. Am. Soc. Assn. Execs. (merit award 1980), Nat. Assn. Bar Execs., Am. Soc. for Pub. Adminstrn., ABA. Avocations: sports; photography; reading; jazz/classical recordings. Office: Phila Bar Assn One Reading Ctr 10th Floor Philadelphia PA 19107 *

SHEAR, STEPHEN BARRETT, lawyer; b. Washington, Dec. 8, 1943; s. Cornelius Barrett and Hetty Louise (Harkness) S.; m. Beatrix Weinberg, Feb. 9, 1969; children: Judith, Michael, Matthew. BS, Tulane U., 1966; MS, N.Mex. State U., 1969; JD, George Washington U., 1974. Bar: Va. 1974, N.Y. 1977. Law clk. to presiding justice U.S. Dist. Ct. Del., Wilmington, 1974-76; assoc. Kenyon & Kenyon, N.Y.C., 1976-83; assoc. Felte & Lynch, N.Y.C., 1983-85, ptnr., 1986—. Contbr. articles to profl. jours. Served with U.S. Army, 1969-71. Mem. ABA, Va. Bar Assn. (assoc.), N.Y. County Lawyers Assn., N.Y. Patent Law Assn., Am. Chem. Soc. Patent, Trademark and copyright, Federal civil litigation. Home: 101 Oakview Terr Short Hills NJ 07078 Office: Felte & Lynch 805 3d Ave New York NY 10022

SHEARIN, KATHRYN KAY, lawyer, publisher; b. Norfolk, Va., Dec. 24, 1946; d. John Willis and Kathryn (Riecken) S.; m. James Charles Bray, June 1, 1969 (div. May 1973). BA, U. N.C., Greensboro, 1968; MA, Boston U., 1971; MS, N.C. State U., 1978; JD, Rutgers U., 1980; LLM in Taxation, Georgetown U., 1983. Bar: N.J. 1980, U.S. Dist. Ct. N.J. 1980, D.C. 1981, Md. 1982, U.S. Tax Ct. 1982, U.S. Supreme Ct. 1984, U.S. Dist. Ct. Del. 1986. Law clk. to presiding justice U.S. Dist. Ct. N.J., Newark, 1978-79; prin. stat. State of N.J., Trenton, 1979-80; atty., adviser U.S. Dept. of Justice, Washington, 1982-83; editor tax law BNA Tax Mgmt., Washington, 1983-84; editor common law revue, pub. CapriComp, Wilmington, Del., 1984—; cons., lectr. on computers in law and estate planning, 1983—; trust counsel, v.p., corp. sec., E.F. Hutton Trust Co., Wilmington, 1984-86. Mem. ABA, D.C. Bar Assn., Del. Bar Assn., Md. Bar Assn., N.J. Bar Assn., Fed. Bar Assn., Am. Chem. Soc., Geol. Soc. of Am., Am. Math. Soc., Marine Tech. Soc., AAAS, Wilmington Tax Group Estate Planning Counsel of Del., Mensa Intertel. Estate planning, Estate taxation, Legal humor. Home and Office: 1301 Maple Ave Wilmington DE 19805

SHEBLE, WALTER FRANKLIN, lawyer; b. Chestnut Hill, Pa., Sept. 14, 1926; s. Franklin and Harriett Elizabeth (Smith) S.; m. Nancy Altemus, July 7, 1956; 3 children. A.B., Princeton U., 1948; J.D., George Washington U., 1952, LL.M., 1953. Bar: U.S. Dist. Ct. D.C. 1952, U.S. Ct. Appeals D.C. 1952, U.S. Supreme Ct. 1953, U.S. Ct. Appeals Md. 1960. Assoc. Hudson & Creyke, Washington, 1953-56, H. William Tanaka, Washington, 1956-61, 63-66; cons. Office of Pres., Washington, 1961-63; spl. asst. to postmaster gen., U.S. rep. to Univ. Postal Union, Bern, Switzerland, 1966-70; spl. asst. to gen. counsel Interam. Devel. Bank, Washington, 1970—. Trustee, New Eng. Coll.; sec. bd. mgrs. Chevy Chase Village, 1985—; pres. Parents Assn. Nat. Cathedral Sch., 1969-70, mem. governing bd. 1970. Mem. ABA (exec. council gen. practice sect. 1982—), Bar Assn. D.C. Clubs: Colonial, Barristers, Metropolitan, Chevy Chase. General practice, Public international, Legislative. Office: 7401 Wisconsin Ave Bethesda MD 20814

SHEEDY, PATRICK THOMAS, judge; b. Green Bay, Wis., Oct. 31, 1921; s. Earl P. and Elsie L. (Brauel) S.; m. Margaret P. Mulvaney, Sept. 6, 1952; children: Michael, Mary Kathleen, Pat Jr., Ann, Maureen. BS in Bus. Adminstrn., Marquette U., 1943, JD, 1948; LLM in Taxation, John Marshall Law Sch., 1972. Bar: Wis. 1948. Sole practice Milw., 1948-80; judge Wis. Cir. Ct., Milw., 1980—. Vice chmn. Archdiocesean Sch. Bd., Milw. Served to col. USAR, 1942-73. Decorated Legion of Merit. Mem. ABA (state del. 1983-85, bd. govs. 1985—), Wis. Bar Assn. (pres. 1974-75, bd. govs., exec. com.). Roman Catholic. Club: Exchange (pres.).

SHEEHAN, CHARLES WINSTON, JR., lawyer; b. Montgomery, Ala., Aug. 27, 1947; s. Charles Winston and Marion (Moody) S.; m. Katherine Flannagan Sheehan, July 16, 1977; children: Charles Winston, William Allen. BA, U. of South, 1969; JD, U. Ala., 1972. Bar: Ala. 1972, U.S. Ct. Mil. Appeals 1973, U.S. Dist. Ct. (mid. and no. dists.) Ala. 1977, U.S. Supreme Ct. 1976. Asst. atty. gen. State of Ala., Montgomery, 1977; assoc. Ball, Ball, Duke, et al, Montgomery, 1977-82, ptnr., 1982—. Chmn. No. Cen. Dist. Tukabatchee Area council Boy Scouts Am., 1983-86. Mem. Ala. State Bar Assn., Montgomery County Bar Assn. Episcopalian. Lodges: Masons, Shriners. Insurance, State civil litigation, Federal civil litigation. Home: 2618 Essex Pl Montgomery AL 36111

SHEEHAN, KENNETH EDWARD, lawyer, business executive; b. N.Y.C., Aug. 12, 1946; s. William Arvis and Anne (Murphy) S.; m. Julie Babka, Aug. 16, 1969 (div. 1980); children—Megan, Kristen, Elaine; m. Cynthia Leigh Davis, Sept. 10, 1982; 1 child, Abigail Elizabeth. B.S. in Bus. Adminstrn., Georgetown U. 1968; postgrad. U. Akron Law Sch., 1968-69; J.D., Fordham U., 1972. Bar: N.Y. 1973, N.J. 1973, U.S. Dist. Ct. (so. and ea. dists.) N.Y. 1973, U.S. Ct. Appeals (2d cir.) 1973, U.S. Ct. Appeals (3rd cir.) 1973, U.S. Supreme Ct. 1976. Assoc., Kirlin, Campbell & Keating, N.Y.C., 1973-76, ptnr., 1976; counsel Am. Bur. Shipping N.Y.C., 1976-77, v.p., gen. counsel, 1977—; dir., office-in-charge Marine and Indsl. Ins., Hamilton, Bermuda, 1982—, ABS Boiler and Marine Ins., Burlington, Vt., 1982—; dir., v.p., gen. counsel ABS Group Cos., N.Y.C., 1978—, ABS Worldwide Tech. Services, Inc., 1978, ABS Properties, Inc., 1978, Armory Properties, Ltd., 1981; frequent expert witness before congress, mcht. marine safety and liability. Contbr. articles to profl. publs. Served with N.Y. Army N.G., 1970-76. Mem. Maritime Law Assn., Soc. Naval Architects, ABA, N.Y. State Bar Assn., N.J. State Bar Assn. Clubs: Essex Fells Country (N.J.); Whitehall Lunch (N.Y.C.). Corporate taxation, Insurance, Admiralty. Home: 14 Cypress Ave North Caldwell NJ 07006 Office: Am Bur Shipping 65 Broadway New York NY 10006 also: 45 Eisenhower Dr Paramus NJ 07653-0910

SHEEHAN, LAWRENCE JAMES, lawyer; b. San Francisco, July 23, 1932. A.B., Stanford U., 1957, LL.B., 1959. Bar: Calif. 1960. Law clk. chief judge U.S. Ct. Appeals 2d Cir., N.Y.C., 1959-60; assoc. O'Melveny & Myers, Los Angeles, 1960-68, ptnr., 1969—. Pres.: Stanford Law Rev., 1958-59. Mem. Los Angeles County Bar Assn., Calif. Bar Assn., Fed. Bar Assn., ABA, Order of Coif. Banking, General corporate, Securities. Office: O'Melveny & Myers 1800 Century Park E Los Angeles CA 90067-1589

SHEEHAN, RICHARD JERE, lawyer; b. St. Louis, Jan. 8, 1934; s. George Henry and Pearl (Murphy) S.; m. Barbara Lee Rogers, Nov. 27, 1957 (div. Jan. 1970); children: Beth, Molly; m. Kathryn Kirk, July 21, 1984. BBA, Washington U., St. Louis, 1958, JD, 1962. Bar: Mo. 1962, U.S. Dist. Ct. (ea. dist.) Mo. 1962, U.S. Ct. Appeals (8th cir.) 1962, U.S. Tax Ct. 1979, Ky. 1985, D.C. 1986, U.S. Dist. Ct. D.C. 1986. Assoc. Armstrong, Teasdale, Kramer & Vaughan, St. Louis, 1962-69, ptnr., 1970-73; ptnr. Popkin, Stern, Heifetz, Lurie, Sheehan, Reby & Chervitz, St. Louis, 1973-86; asst. chief trial atty. SEC, Washington, 1986—; lectr. bus. and pharmaceutical law St. Louis Coll. Pharmacy, 1966-71. Contbg. editor Washington U. Law Quarterly, 1961-62. Mem. adv. bd. Psychoanalytic Found. St. Louis, 1962-68; bd. dirs. St. Louis Bi-State chpt. ARC, 1970-73; precinct capt. Jefferson Twp., 1962-65; active United Fund Greater St. Louis, 1962-64, Boy Scouts Am., 1966; big brother, Big Bros. Orgn. of Am., 1961-64. Served with U.S. Army, 1954-56. Van Blarcom scholar Washington U., 1960-62. Mem. ABA, Mo. Bar Assn., D.C. Bar Assn., Bar Assn. Met. St. Louis, William Greenleaf Eliot Soc., Phi Delta Phi. Club: University (St. Louis), John Marshall (membership com.). Securities, Federal civil litigation, State civil litigation. Home: 2555 Pennsylvania Ave NW #816 Washington DC 20037 Office: SEC 450 5th St #4027 4-2 NW Washington DC 20549

SHEEHY, EDMUND FRANCIS, JR., lawyer; b. Butte, Mont., Oct. 12, 1952; s. Edmund Francis and Catherine Elizabeth (Nielsen) S.; m. Donna Mae McConnaha, Sept. 8, 1978. BA in Polit. Sci., Carroll Coll., 1974; JD, Gonzaga U., 1978. Bar: Mont. 1978, U.S. Dist. Ct. Mont. 1980, U.S. Supreme Ct. 1983, U.S. Tax Ct. 1984, U.S. Ct. Claims 1985, U.S. Ct. Appeals (Fed. cir.) 1986. Law clk. to presiding justice Mont. Supreme Ct., Helena, 1978; assoc. Cannon & Gillespie, Helena, 1979-82; ptnr. Cannon & Sheehy, Helena, 1982—. Criminal, General practice, State civil litigation. Home: 301 N California Helena MT 59601 Office: Cannon & Sheehy 2031 11th Ave Helena MT 59601

SHEEHY, JOHN C., state supreme court justice; b. Butte, Mont., Jan. 27, 1918. Ed., Mont. Sch. Mines; LL.B., Mont. State U., 1943. Bar: Mont. 1943, U.S. Tax Ct. 1969. Chief dep. ins. commr. State of Mont., 1944-47; sole practice Billings, Mont., 1947-78; assoc. justice Mont. Supreme Ct., 1978—; mem. Mont. Ho. of Reps., 1959, 65, Mont. Senate, 1969. Mem. ABA, Yellowstone County Bar Assn. (pres. 1968-69), Mont. Bar Assn. (sec.-treas. 1953-58). Judicial administration. Office: Supreme Court Justice Bldg 215 N Sanders St Helena MT 59620 *

SHEETS, THOMAS WADE, lawyer; b. Decatur, Ind., July 23, 1956; s. Lewis Lindberg and Mary Alice (Lee) Hoffman S. Student Purdue U., 1974-75; B.S. in Edn., Ind. U.-Fort Wayne, 1978; J.D., Valparaiso U., 1981. Bar: Ind. 1981, U.S. Dist. Ct. (so. dist.) Ind. 1981, U.S. Dist. Ct. (no. dist.) Ind. 1982. Sole practice, Decatur, Ind., 1981—; baliff Rentner Senate, 1980-81; pub. defender, Decatur, 1981-82; dep. pros. atty. 26th Jud. Cir., Decatur, 1982-86. Chmn. bd. Adams County Red Cross, 1984; v.p. bd. dirs. Adams/Wells chpt. Big Bros./Big Sisters, 1984. Recipient Am. Jurisprudence award Lawyers Coop. Pub. Co., 1979. Mem. Assn. Trial Lawyers Am., Ind. State Bar Assn., Adams County Bar Assn. (pres. 1985-86). Delta Theta Phi. Democrat. Lutheran. Family and matrimonial, General practice, Consumer commercial. Home: Rt 8 PO Box 187 Decatur IN 46733 Office: 221 W Jefferson St PO Box 333 Decatur IN 46733

SHEETZ, RALPH ALBERT, lawyer; b. Dauphin County, Pa., June 13, 1908; s. Harry Wesley and MaNora (Enders) S.; m. Ruth Lorraine Bender, May 19, 1938; 1 son, Ralph Bert. Ph.B., Dickinson Coll., 1930; J.D., U. Ala., 1933. Bar: Pa. 1934, U.S. Dist. Ct. (mid. dist.) Pa. 1944. Solicitor, East Pennsboro Twp., Pa., 1937-53, Peoples Bank of Enola (Pa.), 1935-75; atty. Lawyers Title Ins. Corp., Richmond, Va., 1956—, Commonwealth Land Title Ins. Co., Phila., 1957—; atty. Employees Loan Soc., 1966-76. Ofcl. Appeal Area no. 4, SSS, Pa., assoc. legal adviser to Draft Bd. No. 2, adviser to registrants to Local Bd. No. 55, Harrisburg, Pa., 1974—; counselor Camp Kanestake, Huntingdon County, Pa., Methodist Ch.; treas., atty. Enola Boys Club, from 1950; pres. East Pennsboro Twp. PTA, 1951-52; atty. hon. mem. Citizens Fire Co. No. 1, Enola, 1951; sec., treas. West Shore Regional Coordinating Com., Cumberland County, 1956-66; mem. bd. adjustments East Pennsboro Twp., 1959, chmn., 1959, mem. planning commn, 1956-59, vice-chmn., mem. zoning commn., 1958, chmn., 1959; mem. East Pennsboro Twp. Republican Club, from 1936. Recipient numerous awards and honors from Pres. of U.S. for service to SSS; Order of the Silver Trowel, Council of Anointed Kings Commonwealth of Pa., Altoona, 1948. Mem. Dauphin Bar Assn. (social com. 1934—), Cumberland County Bar Assn., Pa. Bar Assn., ABA. Clubs: Tall Cedars of Lebanon (historian Harrisburg Forest No. 43 1980—, exec. com.), Shriners, Masons (York cross of honor), K.T. (comdr. 1946). Family and matrimonial, General practice, Probate.

SHEETZ, WILLIAM DEAN, lawyer; b. Wichita, Kans., May 1, 1951; s. Jack A. and Parthene Florence (Duval) S.; m. Susan Marian deVries, June 8, 1982; 1 child, William Aaron. BA, U. Tex., Arlington, 1971, Baylor U., 1973; JD, S. Tex. Coll. of Law, Houston, 1977. Bar: Tex. 1978, U.S. Dist. Ct. (no. dist.) Tex. 1983, U.S. Ct. Appeals (5th cir.) 1984, U.S. Supreme Ct. 1985, U.S. Dist. Ct. (we. dist.) Tex. 1986. Assoc. Law Offices of Gus J. Zgourides, Houston, 1978-80; asst. dist. atty. Dallas County, 1980-86; asst. U.S. atty. for no. dist. U.S. Dept. Justice, Lubbock, Tex., 1986—. Named Outstanding Young Man, Jaycees, 1982. Mem. ABA, State Bar Assn. Tex., Tex. Young Lawyers Assn., Dallas Assn. Young Lawyers, S. Tex. Coll. of Law Alumni Assn., Phi Alpha Delta Legal Frat. (justice, treas. Samuel Houston chpt. 1974), Lubbock Bar Assn., Lubbock Assn. Young Lawyers. Democrat. Roman Catholic. Club: St. Elizabeth's Men's. Criminal, Federal civil litigation, Bankruptcy. Office: US Attys Office 1205 Texas Lubbock TX 79401

SHEFFIELD, FRANK ELWYN, lawyer; b. Tallahassee, Jan. 4, 1946; s. Byron Elmer and Essie Faustine (West) S.; m. Judith Elizabeth Powell, July 26, 1968 (div. July 1971); m. Janice Alicia Gentry, Feb. 22, 1975; stepchildren: Lorimer H. Blitch, Richard S. Noles; children: Brett Elwyn, Jennifer Alicia. BS in Mktg., Fla. State U., 1968, JD, 1972. Bar: Fla. 1972, U.S. Dist. Ct. (no. dist.) Fla. 1972, U.S. Ct. Appeals (5th cir.) 1975. Sole practice Tallahassee, 1972, 73-78, 80—; assoc. Dye & Conner, Tallahassee, 1973; ptnr. Michaels, Sheffield, Perkins & Collins, Tallahassee, 1978-80. Mem. ABA, Fla. Bar Assn., Tallahassee Bar Assn., Assn. Trial Lawyers Am., Acad. Fla. Trial Lawyers, Delta Sigma Pi. Democrat. Mem. Assembly of God. Ch. Avocations: woodworking, scuba diving, automobile restoration. State civil litigation, Criminal, Family and matrimonial. Home: 4028 Old Bainbridge Rd Tallahassee FL 32303 Office: 906 Thomasville Rd PO Box 10645 Tallahassee FL 23202

SHEFFIELD, WALTER JERVIS, lawyer; b. Petersburg, Va., Mar. 20, 1946; s. John Courtney and Betty Lou (Loftis) S.; m. Susan Jarrett Moore, May 4, 1968 (div. June 1980); children: John Courtney II, Walter Alexander; m. Christina Meredith Shipp, Jan. 23, 1982; 1 child, Margaret Ashbrooke. BA magna cum laude, Old Dominion U., 1971; LLD, Emory U., 1973; LLM in taxation, NYU, 1974. Bar: Va. 1975, U.S. Dist. Ct. (ea. dist.) Va. 1975, U.S. Ct. Appeals (4th cir.) 1975, U.S. Ct. Claims 1975, U.S. Tax Ct. 1975, U.S. Supreme Ct. 1979. Asst. to Sec. of Commonwealth Office of Gov. of Commonwealth of Va., Richmond, 1974-75; assoc. Cox, Woodbridge, Smith, Scott & VanLear, Fredericksburg, Va., 1975-76; city atty. City of Fredericksburg, 1976-86; pres. Sheffield & Bricken, Fredericksburg, 1976—; bd. dirs. Spotsylvania (Va.) Cable TV Network, Inc., Detention Devel. Corp., Nashville. Mem. 7th Dist. Dem. Com., 1985, state Dem. Cen. com., 1985; com. on Instnl. Relatinships Va. Ann. Conf. United Meth. Ch., 1975; cons. atty. Fredericksburg Area Mus. and Cultural Ctr., Inc., 1986. Recipient Disting. Service award Fredericksburg Jaycees, 1978. Mem. Va. Trial Lawyers Assn., Va. Bar Assn., Va. Local Govt. Attys. Assn., Phi Alpha Theta, Phi Delta Phi (magister 1972-73). Club: Fredericksburg Country. Lodge: Kiwanis. Local government, Contracts commercial, Probate. Home: 1314 Sophia St Fredericksburg VA 22401 Office: Sheffield & Bricken PC PO Box 7818 Fredericksburg VA 22404-7818

SHEFTE, DALBERT UHRIG, lawyer; b. Evanston, Ill., Sept. 17, 1927; s. Frederick William and Edna Helena (Uhrig) S.; m. Adelaide Morrison, May 9, 1953; children: William Scarr, Scarlett Ann, Robert Uhrig, John Dalbert. BS in Mech. Engring., Northwestern U., 1949, JD, 1952. Bar: Ill. 1952, N.C. 1960, U.S. Supreme Ct. 1960, U.S. Dist. Ct. N.C., U.S. Ct. Appeals (4th, 7th and fed. cirs.). Assoc. Hofgren, Schroeder et al, Chgo., 1954-56, Ooms & Dominik, Chgo., 1956-58, Parrott & Richards, Charlotte, N.C., 1958-61; ptnr. Shefte, Pickney & Sawyer and predicessor firm Richards & Shefte, Charlotte, 1961—. Mem. com., bd. dirs. United Way, Charlotte, 1971—; v.p., chmn., com. mem. Boy Scouts Am., Charlotte, 1963—. Served to sgt. U.S. Army, 1952-54. Mem. ABA (various coms.), N.C. Bar Assn. (various coms.), Mecklenburg County Bar Assn. (com. mem., bd. dirs.), N.C. Patent, Trademark and Copyright Law Assn. (pres. 1982-83). Republican. Presbyterian. Clubs: Charlotte Eng. (pres. 1966-67), Myers Park Country (pres. 1985-86). Lodge: Rotary (pres. 1984-85). Patent, Trademark and copyright, Unfair competition. Home: 1430 Coventry Rd Charlotte NC 28211 Office: Shefte Pinkney & Sawyer 2150 Charlotte Plaza Charlotte NC 28244

SHEFTMAN, HOWARD STEPHEN, lawyer; b. Columbia, S.C., May 20, 1949; s. Nathan and Rena Mae (Kantor) S.; m. Sylvia Elaine Williams, Nov. 30, 1974; children: Amanda Elaine, Emily Catherine. BS in Bus. Adminstrn., U. S.C., 1971, JD, 1974. Bar: S.C. 1974, U.S. Dist. Ct. 1975, U.S. Ct. Appeals (4th cir.) 1982. Assoc. Kirkland, Taylor & Wilson, West Columbia, S.C., 1974-75; ptnr. Sheftman, Oswald & Holland, West Columbia, 1975-77, Finkel, Georgaklis, Goldberg, Sheftman and Korn, P.A., Columbia, 1977—. Mem. Assn. Trial Lawyers Am., S.C. Bar Assn. (jud. modernization com. 1978—), S.C. Trial Lawyers Assn. (chmn. domestic relations sect. 1982-83), Richland and Lexington Bar Assn. Jewish. Club: Met. Sertoma (Columbia) (S.C. pres. 1986-87). Family and matrimonial, State civil litigation, Federal civil litigation. Office: Finkel Georgaklis Goldberg Sheftman & Korn PO Box 1799 Columbia SC 29202

SHEILS, JAMES BERNARD, lawyer; b. New Rochelle, N.Y., May 18, 1950; s. Richard Anthony and Jeanne Bernadette (Berrigan) S.; m. Cheryl Ann Girouard, Aug. 19, 1973; children—Siobhan, Caitrin, Daniel. A.B. with honors, Holy Cross Coll., 1972; J.D., Boston Coll., 1975. Bar: Mass. 1975, U.S. Dist. Ct. Mass 1977, U.S. Supreme Ct. 1983. Assoc. Kamberg, Berman, Gold & West, P.C., Springfield, 1975-80, ptnr., 1980-85; ptnr. Shatz, Schwartz & Fentin, 1985—; dir. Springfield Leadership Inst., 1979—. Author: What the General Practitioner Needs to Know About Consumer Protection, 1982; (with others) Don't Get Left Picking Up the Check; Negotiable Instruments Under UCC, 1984. Contbr. editor: Massachusetts Collection Law, 1984. Mem. Zoning Bd. Appeals, East Longmeadow, Mass., 1983—, chmn. 1985—; bd. dirs. Goodwill Industries of Springfield/Hartford, 1980—; mem. Democratic Town Com., East Longmeadow, 1981—. Mem. ABA, Mass. Bar Assn., Hampden County Bar Assn., Assn. Comml. Fin. Attys., Smaller Bus. Assn. New Eng. (bd. dirs. 1983—). Contracts commercial, Banking. Home: 170 Tanglewood Dr East Longmeadow MA 01028 Office: 1441 Main St Springfield MA 01103

SHEIMAN, RONALD LEE, tax lawyer; b. Bridgeport, Conn., Apr. 26, 1948; s. Samuel Charles and Rita Doris (Feinberg) S.; m. Deborah Joy Lovitky, Oct. 16, 1971; children—Jill, Laura. B.A., U. Mich., 1970; J.D., U. Conn., 1973; LL.M. in Taxation, NYU, 1974. Bar: Conn. 1973, U.S. Ct. Appeals (2d cir.) 1975, U.S. Dist. Ct. Conn. 1975, U.S. Tax Ct. 1975, U.S. Supreme Ct. 1977, D.C. 1978, N.Y. 1981. Sr. tax atty. Office of Regional Counsel, IRS, Phila., 1974-78; sole practice, Westport, Conn., 1978—. Adv. bd. Early Childhood Resource and Info. Ctr., N.Y. Pub. Library, N.Y.C., 1984. Mem. ABA, Conn. Bar Assn., Westport Bar Assn. Estate taxation, Corporate taxation, Personal income taxation. Home: 128 Random Rd Fairfield CT 06432 Office: 1804 Post Rd E Westport CT 06880

SHEIMAN, STUART MELVYN, lawyer; b. Bridgeport, Conn., Apr. 29, 1942; s. Sidney A. and Edith Raichelson S.; m. Deborah K. Kaufman, Mar. 31, 1979. BBA, U. Mich., 1964; JD, Ind. U., 1969. Bar: Conn. 1969. Sole practice, Bridgeport, 1969—. Mem. ABA, Conn. Bar Assn., Bridgeport Bar Assn., Conn. Trial Lawyers Assn., Am. Trial Lawyers Assn. Democrat. Jewish. Personal injury, Family and matrimonial, Workers' compensation. Office: 4270 Main St Suite 208 Bridgeport CT 06606

SHEINFELD, MYRON M., lawyer, educator; b. Mass., Mar. 18, 1930; s. Robert and Sadye (Rosenberg) S.; mChristina Trzcinski, Mar. 30, 1985; children—Scott, Astrid, Tom. B.A., Tulane U., 1951; J.D., U. Mich., 1954. Bar: Mich. 1954, Tex. 1956. Researcher Legis. Research Inst. U. Mich., 1954; asst. U.S. atty. So. Dist. Tex., 1958-60; law clk. U.S. Dist. Judge, 1960-61; ptnr. Strickland, Gordon & Sheinfeld, Houston, 1961-68, Sheinfeld, Maley & Kay, Houston, 1968—; lectr. law U. Tex. Served with JAG U.S. Army, 1955-58. Mem. State Bar Tex., Phi Beta Kappa, Phi Sigma Alpha. Club: Ramada, Houstonian. Contbg. editor: Collier on Bankruptcy; contbr. articles to profl. jours. Bankruptcy, Banking. Office: Sheinfeld Maley & Kay 3700 1st City Tower Houston TX 77002

SHELDON, HARVEY M., lawyer; b. Chgo., Dec. 7, 1942; s. Richard A. and Beatrice (Gutensky) S.; children—Paul (dec.), Timothy. A.B., Amherst Coll., 1965; J.D., Harvard U., 1968. Bar: Ill. 1968, U.S. Ct. Appeals (7th and D.C. cirs.) 1978, U.S. Supreme Ct. 1980. Assoc. Schiff, Hardin & Waite, Chgo., 1968-70; asst. atty. gen. spl. prosecutions State of Ill., 1970-71, chief environ. control div., 1972-73; regional counsel U.S. EPA, 1973-74; ptnr. Nisen, Elliott & Meier, Chgo., 1974-85; ptnr. Coffield, Ungaretti, Harris & Slavin, Chgo., 1985—; instr. environ. law and equity law John Marshall Law Sch., 1974-76; adj. prof. environ. law Loyola U., Chgo., 1983—. Active Chgo. Crime Commn.; mem. Mayor's Task Force on Air Quality, 1978-82; spl. counsel Ill. Dept. Mines & Minerals, 1977-86. Mem. ABA, Ill. Bar Assn., Fed. Bar Assn., Chgo. Bar Assn., Air Pollution Control Assn., Environ. Law Inst. (assoc.), Chgo. Assn. Commerce and Industry (dir., chmn. environ. control com., dir.). Republican. Club: University (Chgo.). Contbr. to environ. law handbooks. Environment, State civil litigation, Federal civil litigation. Office: COF/UNG/HAR/SLAV Three First Nat Plaza Suite 3500 Chicago IL 60602-4208

SHELDON, JEFFREY LEE, lawyer; b. Johnstown, Pa., Apr. 18, 1956; s. George P. and Alma R. (Helman) S.; m. Sharon L. O'Brien, June 7, 1980. BA magna cum laude, Drew U., 1978; JD, Georgetown U., 1981. Bar: D.C. 1981, U.S. Dist. Ct. D.C. 1982, U.S. Ct. Appeals (D.C. cir.) 1982. Assoc. Pellegrin & Levine, Chartered, Washington, 1981—. Mem. ABA, D.C. Bar Assn., Fed. Communications Bar Assn., Pi Sigma Alpha. Republican. Methodist. Avocations: photography, personal computing. Administrative and regulatory, Trademark and copyright. Office: Pellegrin & Levine Chartered 1140 Connecticut Ave NW Washington DC 20036

SHELDON, MICHAEL RICHARD, law educator, lawyer; b. Schenectady, Apr. 6, 1949; s. Richard Charles and Evelyn Marie (Delisle) S.; m. Diane Mary Micklos, May 29, 1971; children—Graham Andrew, Conor Michael, Rowan Richard. A.B., Princeton U., 1971; J.D., Yale U., 1974; postgrad. Georgetown U., 1974-76. Bar: D.C. 1975, U.S. Dist. Ct. D.C. 1975, U.S. Ct. Appeals (D.C. cir.) 1975, U.S. Dist. Ct. (no. dist.) N.Y. 1976, Conn. 1976, U.S. Dist. Ct. Conn. 1976. Legal intern Georgetown U. Law Ctr., Washington, 1974-76; prof. law U. Conn. Sch. Law, West Hartford, 1976—; vis. prof. U. Aix-Marseille, 1986; bd. dirs. Conn. Civil Liberties Union, Hartford, 1979-83. Contbg. author: Handbook on the Connecticut Law of Evidence, 1982. Bd. dirs. Legal Aid Soc. of Hartford County, 1978—. Recipient Outstanding Faculty Mem. award Student Bar Assn. U. Conn. Sch. Law, 1979, 82. Mem. Conn. Trial Lawyers Assn., Assn. Trial Lawyers Am., Conn. Bar Assn. (exec. com. sect. on human rights and responsibilities, exec. com. sect. on criminal justice 1978—). Criminal, Civil rights. Home: 20 Pond View Dr Canton CT 06019 Office: U Conn Sch Law 65 Elizabeth St Hartford CT 06105

SHELDON, SCOTT JEFFREY, lawyer; b. Newark, Nov. 20, 1957; s. Jack Benjamin and Gloria Lois (Bratter) S.; m. Kathleen Laurel McCue, Sept. 15, 1978; children: Rebekah, Marshall. BA, Rutgers U., 1978, JD with high honors, 1982. Bar: N.J. 1982. Law sec. to presiding judge Appellate Div., N.J. Superior Ct., 1982-83; assoc. Carpenter, Bennett & Morrissey, Newark, 1983—. Vol. lawyer Essex-Newark Legal Services Corp., Newark, 1983—. Named Vol. Lawyer of Month Essex-Newark Legal Services Corp., 1985. Mem. ABA (antitrust law com., local govt. law award 1982), N.J. Bar Assn., Essex County Bar Assn., Am. Judicature Soc. Democrat. Jewish. Avocations: songwriting for guitar and piano, short story writing, home renovation. Antitrust, Federal civil litigation, Contracts commercial. Home: 304 Lupine Way Short Hills NJ 07078 Office: Carpenter Bennett & Morrissey Gateway Three Newark NJ 07102

SHELL, LOUIS CALVIN, lawyer; b. Dinwiddie County, Va., Dec. 8, 1925; s. Roger LaFayette and Susie Ann (Hill) S.; m. Barbara Marie Pamplin, Aug. 5, 1950; children—Pamela Shell Baskervill, Patricia Shell Caulkins. B.A., U. Va., 1946, LL.B., 1947. Bar: Va. 1947. Assoc. White, Hamilton, Wyche & Shell and predecessor White, Hamilton & Wyche, Petersburg, Va., 1948-50, ptnr., 1950—, now chief trial counsel. Chmn. Petersburg Electoral Bd., 1952, vice mayor city council, 1957-60; trustee Petersburg Dist. United Methodist Ch. Named Outstanding Young Man, Petersburg Jr. C. of C., 1956. Fellow Am. Coll. Trial Lawyers; mem. ABA, Va. State Bar Assn., Petersburg Bar Assn., Am. Judicature Soc., Va. State Bar (council 1972-75). Democrat. Club: Kiwanis (Petersburg). Personal injury, State civil litigation. Home: 1612 E Tuckahoe St Petersburg VA 23805 Office: 20 E Tabb St Petersburg VA 23803

SHELLEY, HEYWOOD, lawyer; b. N.Y.C., May 2, 1927; s. Robert and Jessie (Sinick) S.; m. Maritza Farkas, Dec. 31, 1959; 1 child, Alexandra. AB, Columbia U., 1947, LLB, 1950. Bar: N.Y. 1950, U.S. Supreme Ct. 1970. Assoc. Columbia Law Sch., 1950-51; assoc. Carter, Ledyard & Milburn, N.Y.C., 1951—, now ptnr., chmn. real estate dept. Served with U.S. Army, 1946-47. Mem. ABA, N.Y. State Bar Assn., Assn. Bar City N.Y. Democrat. Jewish. Clubs: City Midday (N.Y.C.); Heights Casino (Bklyn.). General corporate, Real property, General practice. Office: 2 Wall St New York NY 10005

SHELLEY, JOHN FLETCHER, lawyer; b. Des Moines, Oct. 7, 1943; s. John DeWane and Catherine Hilma (Fletcher) S.; m. Karan Antonette Early, Aug. 27, 1966; children—Jack, Joseph. A.B., Harvard Coll., 1965; LL.B., Harvard U., 1968. Bar: Ohio 1968. Assoc., Squire, Sanders & Dempsey, Cleve., 1968, 72-78, ptnr., 1978—; coordinator Employee Benefits Practice Area, 1984—. Vice-pres., trustee Child Guidance Ctr. of Cleve., 1980—. Served with USNR, 1968-71. Mem. Bar Assn. Greater Cleve. (mem. council estate planning and probate sect.), Ohio State Bar Assn., Bar Assn., ABA. Democrat. Club: Clevelander. Pension, profit-sharing, and employee benefits, Probate, Estate taxation. Home: 3283 Norwood Rd Shaker Heights OH 44122 Office: Suite 1800 Union Commerce Bldg Cleveland OH 44115

SHELLEY, SUSANNE MARY, lawyer, mathematics educator; b. Vienna, Austria, Feb. 2, 1928; came to U.S., 1946; d. Joseph and Paula (Grunbaum) Langer; m. Robert E. Shelley, July 21, 1946; children: Frances S. MacCallum, Mark Robert. BA, Calif. State U., Sacramento, 1961, MA, 1963; JD, U. Pacific, 1980. Bar: Calif. 1980, U.S. Dist. Ct. (ea. dist.) Calif. 1980. Tchr. math. Johnson High Sch., Sacramento, 1961-65; prof. math. Sacramento City Coll., 1965-84; gen. counsel Los Rios Community Coll. Dist., Sacramento, 1984—. Author 13 math. textbooks. Named Outstanding Educator, Sacramento City Coll., 1967. Mem. ABA, Calif. State Bar Assn., Sacramento County Bar Assn., Sacramento Women Lawyers, Order of Coif. Republican. Roman Catholic. Labor, Legal education, Government con-

tracts and claims. Home: 28 Shoreline Circle Sacramento CA 95831 Office: Los Rios Community Coll Dist 1919 Spanos Ct Sacramento CA 95831

SHELTON, DAVID COCHRAN, lawyer; b. Memphis, Dec. 9, 1952; s. William Donnie and Mary Agnes (Gwinn) S.; m. Judith Ann Hodgson, Aug. 24, 1974; children: Heather Ann, Jessica Faith. BA, Memphis State U., 1974, JD, 1979. Bar: Tenn. 1979, U.S. dist. Ct. (we. dist.) Tenn. 1979, U.S. Ct. Appeals (6th cir.) 1985. Assoc. Winchester, Huggins, Charlton, Leake, Brown & Slater, Memphis, 1979-83, Borod & Huggins, Memphis, 1982-85; ptnr. The Winchester Law Firm, Memphis, 1985—. Contbrg. author: Marketing Life Insurance in a Bank or Thrift, 1986, Self-directed IRA's: Investment, Marketing and Trust Administration, 1986. Bd. dirs. Sr. Citizens Services, Inc., Memphis. Recipient Am. Jurisprudence award. Mem. ABA, Memphis and Shelby County Bar Assn., Tenn. Bar Assn. Banking, Insurance, General corporate. Home: 2077 Newfields Germantown TN 38138 Office: The Winchester Law Firm 8 Third St S Memphis TN 38103

SHELTON, DONALD E., lawyer; b. Jackson, Miss., June 28, 1944; m. Marjorie K. Whitman; children: Tracy, Gregory. BA, Western Mich. U., 1966; JD, U. Mich., 1969. Atty. litigation div. U.S. Army Pentagon, Washington, 1973-74; ptnr. Forsythe, Campbell, Vandenberg, Clevenger & Bishop, Ann Arbor, Mich., 1974-78, Bishop & Shelton P.C., Ann Arbor, 1978—; mayor pro tem City of Saline, 1977-78, mayor, 1978-86; lectr. bus. law U. Md., 1971-73, legal asst. program Washtenaw Community Coll., 1976-79, legal asst. program Oakland U., 1977-79, Inst. Continuing Legal Edn. Sr. editor U. Mich. J.LawRef., 1968-69; contbr. articles to numerous jours. Mem. City of Saline (Mich.) Planning Commn., 1976—, Gov.'s Small city Adv. Council, 1983-86, City Council of Saline, 1976-78; chmn. Saline Tax Increment Fin. Authority, 1982-86, Southeast Mich. Council of Govts., 1983-85, vice-chmn., 1980-83; bd. dirs. Washtenaw Devel. Council, 1983—; regent Ea. Mich. U., 1987—. Served to capt. (JAGC) U.S. Army, 1969-74. Recipient Dist. Service award City of Saline, 1985. Mem. ABA (litigation sect., econs. sect.), Mich. Bar Assn. (exec. com. econs. sect.), Washtenaw County Bar Assn. (judiciary com.), Assn. Trial Lawyers Am., Mich. Trial Lawyers Assn. (exec. bd. 1984—, legis. com.), Washtenaw Trial Lawyers Assn. (sec. 1982, pres. 1983-84), Saline Jaycees (legal counsel, past bd. dirs., named Man of Yr. 1976). Office: Bishop & Shelton PC 709 W Huron Ann Arbor MI 48103

SHELTON, FINCOURT BRAXTON, lawyer; b. Cin., July 24, 1951; s. S. McDowell Shelton and Melvina James; m. Vivian Gibson, July 24, 1981; children: Sarai Keturah, Indirah Julia, Melech Adam. Baccalaureal, U. Dakar, Senegal, 1969; BA in Polit. Sci. and French, Dickinson Coll., 1975; JD, Widener U., 1979. Bar: Pa. 1980, U.S. Dist. Ct. (ea. dist.) Pa. 1980, U.S. Ct. Appeals (3d cir.) 1984. Pres. W.T. Pub. and Broadcasting, Phila., 1975-79; sole practice Phila., 1980-85; sr. ptnr. Shelton & DeLeon, Phila., 1985—; asst. counsel Phila. Housing Authority, 1980-84. Candidate Phila. Mcpl. Ct., 1985; bd. dirs. Sch. Ln. Villa, Phila., 1983—, African studies Temple U., Phila., 1984—; trustee Ch. Lord Jesus Christ, Phila., 1973—. Mem. ABA, Assn. Trial Lawyers Am., Phila. Bar Assn. Clubs: 21st Century Polas, 74 (Phila.). Avocation: youth counseling. Personal injury, State civil litigation, Criminal. Home: 5963 Woodbine Ave Philadelphia PA 19131 Office: 1 E Penn Sq Suite 309 Philadelphia PA 19107

SHEMWELL, ARTHUR LUTHER, JR., lawyer; b. Paris, Tenn., Jan. 12, 1927; s. Arthur Luther and Valerie Fay (Bell) S.; m. Joan Erthal, June 7, 1950; children: Andrea S. Jones, Gale A., Arthur L. III, Eric J. BS, U.S. Mil. Acad., 1950; MA, Columbia U., 1961; JD, U. S.C., 1979. Bar: S.C. 1979, U.S. Dist. Ct. S.C. 1979, U.S. Ct. Appeals (4th cir.) 1979. Commd. 2d lt. U.S. Army, 1950, advanced through grades to lt. col., 1966, ret., 1973; sole practice Gaffney, S.C., 1979—; bd. dirs. Piedmont Legal Services, 1983—. Mem. ABA, S.C. Bar Assn., S.C. Trial Lawyers Assn., Cherokee County Bar Assn. (sec., treas. 1980). General practice, Family and matrimonial, Real property. Home: 121 Fernwood Dr Gaffney SC 29340 Office: 225 E Baker Blvd Gaffney SC 29342

SHENEFIELD, JOHN HALE, lawyer; b. Toledo, Jan. 23, 1939; s. Hale Thurel and Norma (Bird) S.; m. Judy Simmons, June 16, 1984; children: Stephen Hale, Christopher Newcomb. A.B., Harvard U., 1960, LL.B., 1965. Bar: Va. 1966, D.C. 1966. Mem. firm Hunton & Williams, Richmond, Va., 1965-77; dep. asst. atty. gen. antitrust div. Dept. Justice, Washington, 1977; asst. atty. gen. Dept. Justice, 1977-79, assoc. atty. gen., 1979-81; mem. firm Milbank, Tweed, Hadley & McCloy (Washington office), 1981-86, Morgan, Lewis & Bockius, Washington, 1986—; assoc. prof. law U. Richmond, 1975; prof. law Georgetown Law Center, 1981-83; chmn. Nat. Commn. for Rev. Antitrust Law and Procedures, 1978-79. Contbr. articles on law to profl. jours. Sec. Va. Democratic Com., 1970-72, treas., 1976-77; chmn. Richmond Dem. Party, 1975-77; bd. govs. St. Albans Sch., 1983—. Served as 2d lt. U.S. Army, 1961-62; to capt. Res. 1965. Fellow Am. Bar Found.; mem. ABA (mem. standing com. on law and nat. security), Va. Bar Assn. Antitrust, Federal civil litigation. Home: 4615 4th Rd N Arlington VA 22203 Office: Morgan Lewis & Bockius 1800 M St NW Suite 800 Washington DC 20036

SHENG, JACK TSE-LIANG, law librarian; b. Hsiang Ying, Hunan, China, Nov. 15, 1929; m. Helen S. Sheng, Sept. 20, 1939; children: Paul, Henry. LLB, Soochow U., Taiwan, 1963; LLM, Yale U., 1966; MS, La. State U., 1967; JD, Wayne State U., 1969. Teaching asst. Soochow U. Law Sch., Taipei, Taiwan, 1963-64; librarian I and II, cataloger Detroit Pub. Library, 1967-70; head librarian, assoc. prof. Soochow U., 1970-72; asst. law librarian Ohio No. U., Ada, 1972-75; law librarian Duval County Law Library, Jacksonville, Fla., 1975—; editorial asst. Gale Research Co., Detroit, 1969; law library cons. Del. Law Sch., Wilmington, 1973, CSX Corp., Jacksonville, Fla., 1983-85; instr. Fla. Jr. Coll., Jacksonville, 1976-83. Author: Index to Chinese Legal Periodicals, 1963-70, 1972. Mem. Am. Assn. Law Libraries. Democrat. Librarianship. Home: 4080 Old Mill Cove Trail W Jacksonville FL 32211 Office: Duval County Law Library 330 E Bay St Jacksonville FL 32202

SHEPARD, ADAM HOFFMAN, lawyer; b. Boston, Jan. 2, 1953; s. Jerome Howard and Carolyn Ora (Radnofsky) H. BA, John Hopkins U., 1974; JD, Boston U., 1978. Bar: Mass. 1978, Md. 1978, Pa. 1986, U.S. Dist. Ct. Md., U.S. Tax Ct., U.S. Ct. Appeals (4th cir.). Assoc. Venable, Baetjer & Howard, Balt., 1978-80, Offices of Peter G. Angelos, Balt., 1981-87; ptnr. Offices of Shepard A. Hoffman, Balt., 1987—; com. mem. Johns Manville Bankruptcy Asbestos Health Claimants Creditors Com., N.Y.C., 1982—. Trustee Johns Hopkins U., 1974-78. Henry Luce scholar, N.Y.C., 1975. Mem. Am. Trial Lawyers Assn. Federal civil litigation, State civil litigation, Personal injury. Home: 2628 N Calvert St Baltimore MD 21218 Office: B&O Bldg Suite 800 Charles & Baltimore Sts Baltimore MD 21201

SHEPARD, ALLAN GUY, state chief justice; b. Gardner, Mass., Dec. 18, 1922; s. Guy H. and May (Kendall) S.; m. Donna K. Soderlund, 1972; children: Lynn Kendall, Paul Vernon, Ann Kendall. Student, Boston U., 1942-43; B.S., U. Washington, 1948, J.D., 1951; LL.M., U. Va., 1984. Bar: Idaho 1951. Asst. atty. gen. Idaho, 1951-57; chief counsel Idaho Dept. Hwys., 1952-57; pvt. practice Boise, 1957-63; mem. Idaho Ho. of Reps. from Ada County, 1958-63; atty. gen. Idaho, 1963-69; justice Idaho Supreme Ct., 1969—, chief justice, 1974—; Mem. Western States Hwy. Policy Com., 1959-63. Mem. youth and govt. com. YMCA Idaho, 1953—, chmn., 1969; Adv. bd. Booth Meml. Hosp., Boise. Mem. Am., Idaho, 3d Dist. bar assns., Western Assn. Attys. Gen. (chmn. 1965-66), Nat. Assn. Attys. Gen. (pres. 1968), Delta Theta Phi. Republican. Episcopalian. Judicial administration. Home: 4023 Del Monte St Boise ID 83704

SHEPARD, DARRELL ROYCE, lawyer; b. Lincoln, Nebr., Aug. 14, 1941; s. John Creath and Inez Lucille (Wiedeman) S. BA, U. Nebr., 1962, PhD, 1967; BD, Lexington Theol. Sem., 1965; JD, Ind. U., 1981. Bar: Ohio 1981, U.S. Dist. Ct. (so. dist.) Ohio 1981, U.S. Ct. Appeals (6th cir.) 1986. Prof. philosophy Washburn U., Topeka, Kans., 1967-78; assoc. Porter, Wright, Morris & Arthur, Columbus, Ohio, 1981—; cons. Agcy. for Instructional TV, Bloomington, Ind., 1977-79. Contbr. articles to profl. jours. Republican. Methodist. Avocations: bridge, racquetball. Workers' compensation, Personal injury, Insurance. Home: 6380 Birkewood Columbus OH 43229 Office: Porter Wright Morris & Arthur 41 S High Columbus OH 43215

SHEPARD, PAUL COOPER, lawyer; b. N.Y.C., Apr. 28, 1948; s. Edward Morse and Elizabeth (Yates) S.; m. Claudia Cadman Prichard, June 6, 1970; children: Colin Williams, Jean Adams. Student, Williams Coll., 1966-69; BA, Vassar Coll., 1970; JD, Wake Forest U., 1976. Bar: N.C. 1976. Ptnr. Hayes & Shepard, Winston-Salem, N.C., 1976-85; sole practice Winston-Salem, 1985—. Pres. West End Assn., Winston-Salem, 1980; mem. New Horizons Fair Housing Com., Winston-Salem, 1979-80, 85—, city-county planning bd., Winston-Salem and Forsyth County, 1981-85, Winston-Salem Human Relations Commn., 1985—. Mem. ABA, N.C. Bar Assn., N.C. Trial Lawyers Assn., Forsyth County Bar Assn. Democrat. Episcopalian. General practice, Personal injury, Probate. Home: 1406 Jarvis St Winston-Salem NC 27101 Office: 245 BB&T Bldg 8 W 3d St Winston-Salem NC 27101

SHEPARD, ROBERT PAYNE, lawyer; b. Port Arthur, Tex., Mar. 15, 1953; s. Louis Victor and Irene Louise (Payne) S.; m. Nancy Elizabeth Eubanks, May 15, 1981; 1 child, Zachary Robert. BA, U. So. Ala., 1975; JD, U. Miss., 1977. Bar: Miss., U.S. Dist. Ct. (no. and so. dists.) Miss., U.S. Dist. Ct. (so. dist.) Ala., U.S. Ct. Appeals (5th and 11th cirs.), U.S. Supreme Ct. Ptnr. Law Offices of Murphy & Shepard, Lucedale, Miss., 1978—; atty. City of Lucedale, Miss., 1980—; spkr. U. Miss. Continuing Legal Edn., 1985. Mem. ABA, Miss. Bar Assn. (resolutions com. 1986—), George-Greene County Bar Assn. (pres. 1985—), Assn. Trial Lawyers Am., Miss. Trial Lawyers Assn., Am. Judicature Soc. Avocations: remodeling old hotel, collecting antiques. Insurance, Local government, Probate. Office: Law Offices of Murphy & Shepard 309 Ratliff St Lucedale MS 39452

SHEPARD, TAZEWELL TAYLOR, III, lawyer; b. Washington, Jan. 8, 1954; s. Tazewell Taylor Jr. and Julia Ann (Sparkman) S.; m. Cynthia MAdeline Chastain, June 3, 1978. AA, Eton Coll., 1972; BA, Dartmouth Coll., 1976; JD, U. Ala., 1979. Bar: Ala. 1979, U.S. Dist. Ct. (no. dist.) Ala. 1979, U.S. Ct. Appeals (5th & 11th cirs.) 1981, U.S. Supreme Ct. 1982. Assoc. Sparkman & Shepard, Huntsville, Ala., 1979-83; ptnr. Bell, Richardson, Herrington, Sparkman & Shepard P.A., Huntsville, 1983—; trustee in Bankruptcy, Huntsville, 1980—. Pres. Madsion County Young Dems., Huntsville, 1980; chmn. Hunsville crusade Am. Cancer Soc., 1983. Mem. ABA (bus. bankruptcy com.), Ala. Bar Assn. (sec. bankruptcy and comml. law sect. 1983-84), Comml. Law League. Club: Acme (Huntsville) (pres. 1984). Avocations: golf, tennis, writing, music. Bankruptcy, Consumer commercial, Contracts commercial. Office: Bell Richardson Herrington et al PO Box 2008 Huntsville AL 35804

SHEPHERD, CAROL NELSON, lawyer; b. West Point, N.Y., July 2, 1952; d. Arthur D. and Sarah (Burton) Nelson; m. William J. Henwood, June 5, 1982; children: Teagan Sarah, Alexander William. Student, Wells Coll., 1970-72; BA in Sociology and English, Ariz. State U., 1975; JD, Syracuse U., 1978. Bar: Pa. 1978, U.S. Dist. Ct. (ea. dist.) Pa. 1978, U.S. Ct. Appeals (3d cir.) 1980. Assoc. Shrager, McDaid & Loftus, Phila., 1978-87; ptnr. Shrager, McDaid, Loftus, Shepherd & Flum, Phila., 1987—. Contbr. articles to profl. jours. Mem. Pa. Bar Assn., Phila. Bar Assn. (bd. govs. 1985—), Assn. Trial Lawyers Am., Pa. Trial Lawyers Assn. (bd. govs. 1982—, spl. merit award 1981), Phila. Trial Lawyers Assn. (pres. 1987—). Democrat. Personal injury, Federal civil litigation, State civil litigation. Office: Shrager McDaid Loftus et al 8 Penn Ctr Philadelphia PA 19103

SHEPHERD, JAMES EDWARD, lawyer; b. Roswell, N.Mex., Apr. 24, 1953; s. Max Gordon and Edith (French) S.; m. Donna Gwen Moerbe, Jan. 3, 1981; children: Ellen Janine, Lisa Diane. BBA, Baylor U., 1976, JD, 1977. Bar: Tex. 1978, U.S. Dist. Ct. (no. dist.) Tex. 1980, U.S. Ct. Appeals (5th cir.) 1981, U.S. Ct. Mil. Appeals 1981. Tax atty. Arthur Young & Co., Dallas, 1977-78; assoc. Noah & Assocs., Richardson, Tex., 1978-81; sole practice Richardson, 1981—; judge Town of Buckingham, Tex., 1985—. Bd. dirs. Neighborhood Youth Services, Richardson, 1985—, YMCA, Richardson, 1985-87. Mem. ABA, Tex. Bar Assn., Dallas Bar Assn., Richardson Bar Assn., Richardson C. of C. (vice-chmn. 1986—). Republican. Methodist. Lodge: Lions (pres. Richardson Noon club 1985-86). Avocations: boating, hunting, skiing. General practice, Family and matrimonial, Personal injury. Office: 1204 First City Bank Ctr Richardson TX 75080

SHEPHERD, JOHN MICHAEL, lawyer; b. St. Louis, Aug. 1, 1955; s. John Calvin and Bernice Florence (Hines) S.; m. Deborah Tremaine Fenton, Oct. 10, 1981; 1 child, Elizabeth White. BA, Stanford U., 1977; JD, U. Mich., 1980. Bar: Calif. 1981, U.S. Dist Ct. (no. dist.) Calif. 1981. Assoc. McCutchen, Doyle, Brown & Enersen, San Francisco, 1980-82; spl. asst. to asst. atty. gen. U.S. Dept. Justice, Washington, 1982-84, dep. asst. atty gen., 1984-86; assoc. counsel to The President The White House, Washington, 1986-87; sr. dep. comptroller of the currency Dept. Treasury, Washington, 1987—. Asst. dir. policy Reagan-Bush Presdl. Transition Team, Washington, 1980-81; bd. dirs. Regan Dep. Asst. Secs., Washington, 1985—. Named one of Outstanding Young Men Am., U.S. Jaycees, 1984; Wardack Research fellow Washington U., 1976. Mem. ABA (internat. law and practice sect., banking law com. 1983—), D.C. Bar Assn. (internat. law com.). Club: University (N.Y.). Banking, Administrative and regulatory, Private international. Home: 5318 Blackstone Rd Bethesda MD 20816 Office: Office Comptroller of Currency 490 L'enfant Plaza SW Washington DC 20219

SHEPHERD, RICHARD EARNSHAW, lawyer; b. Youngstown, Ohio, Sept. 24, 1934; s. Richard Carlton and Mary Emma (Earnshaw) S.; m. Charlotte Diane Eckel, June 1, 1957; children: Sara, Martha. AB magna cum laude, W.Va. U., 1957, JD, 1978. Bar: W.Va. 1978, U.S. Dist. Ct. (no. and so. dists.) W.Va. 1978, U.S. Ct. Appeals (4th cir.) 1978. Purchasing agt. Elkins (W.Va.) Limestone Co., 1957-65, pres., 1965-75; sole practice Elkins, 1978—; ptnr. Health Services Cons., Phila., 1970-76; cons. W.Va. Regional Med. Program, Margantown, 1969-76; chmn. adminstrv. div. Nat. Crushed Stone Assn., Washington, 1969-72; pres. Elkins Asphalt Co., 1968-74. Dir. gen. Mountain State Forest Festival, Elkins, 1962; bd. dirs. Appalachian Highlands Assn., Elkins, 1965-67, Elkins Indsl. Devel. Corp., 1965-68. Mem. ABA, W.Va. Bar Assn., Randolph County Bar Assn., Cmml. Law League Am., Elkins C. of C. (bd. dirs. 1963-66), Phi Beta Kappa, Phi Alpha Theta, Delta Sigma Rho. Episcopalian. Antitrust, Pension, profit-sharing, and employee benefits, General corporate. Home and Office: Fern Hill Norton Rd Elkins WV 26241

SHEPHERD, ROBERT EDWARD, JR., law educator; b. Richmond, Va., 1937; m. Julia Ann Jett, 1960; 3 children. BA in History, Washington and Lee U., 1959, LLB, 1961; postgrad., Georgetown U. Bar: Va. 1961, U.S. Ct. Mil. Appeals 1962, U.S. Dist. Ct. Va. 1964, U.S. Supreme Ct. 1971, U.S. Ct. Appeals (4th cir.) 1972, U.S. Ct. Appeals (5th cir.) 1975, Md. 1976, U.S. Dist. Ct. Md. 1976. Sole practice Richmond, 1964-71; asst. atty. gen. State of Va., 1971-75; lectr. law Marshall-Wythe Sch. Law, Coll. William & Mary, Williamsburg, Va., 1975; assoc. prof. law U. Balt. Law Sch., 1975-78; prof. law T.C. Williams Sch. Law, U. Richmond, 1978—; instr. legal medicine Med. Coll. Va., Richmond, 1966-69; adj. assoc. prof. law T.C. Williams Sch. Law U. Richmond, 1973-74; instr. law and social work Sch. Social Work Va. Commonwealth U., Richmond, 1974; mem. criminal law and family law sects. Va. State Bar. Editor: Children and the Law in Maryland, 1978; author: Legal Manual for Abuse and Neglect, Foster Care Review, Termination of Parental Rights and Adoption Cases in Virginia, 1978; also articles. Chmn. Chesterfield County Dem. Com., Va. Criminal Justice Services Bd., Va. Juvenile Justice and Delinquency Prevention Adv. Council; mem. Va. Dem. State Cen. Com., 3d Dist. Dem. Com., adv. bd. New Community Sch., Richmond, Va. Com. on Continuing Legal Edn., adv. com. Va. Conf. Early Adolescence, James Madison Meml. Com., Va. Bapt. Extension Bd.; Sunday sch. tchr., co-chmn. missions com. River Road Bapt. Ch.; bd. dirs. Learning Disabilities Council, Va. chpt. Nat. Com. for Prevention of Child Abuse. Recipient Outstanding Child Adv. award Va. Div. for Children, 1980, Pub. Service award Va. chpt. Am. Acad. Pediatrics, 1982, Juvenile Justice Community Service award Va. Juvenile Officers Assn., 1983. Mem. ABA (chmn. com. on juvenile justice criminal justice sect., family law sect., forum com. on entertainment and sports industries), Va. Bar Assn. (chmn. commn. on needs of children), Nat. Council of Juvenile and Family Ct. Judges (learning disabilities com., legal edn. com.), Va. Juvenile Officers Assn., Nat. Counsel for Children, Assn. Am. Law Schs. (clinical law sect., criminal law sect., family and juvenile law sect., sports law sect.), Assn. Trial Lawyers Am., Richmond Bar Assn., Washington and Lee Law Sch. Assn. Juvenile, Legal education, Family and matrimonial. Home: 8600 Gem St Richmond VA 23235 Office: U Richmond TC Williams Coll Law Richmond VA 23173

SHEPPARD, BERTON SCOTT, lawyer; b. Zanesville, Ohio, Aug. 6, 1936; s. Isaac and Ruth (Scott) S.; m. Regina Polka, Oct. 6, 1962; children—Kristina M., Cynthia A. B.S. in Agr. Engring., Mich. State U., 1958; J.D., Northwestern U., 1961. Bar: Ill. 1962, U.S. Dist. Ct. (no. dist.) Ill. 1962, U.S. Dist. Ct. Md. 1965, U.S. Ct. Appeals (4th cir.) 1970, U.S. Ct. Appeals (7th cir.) 1974, U.S. Ct. Customs and Patent Appeals 1976, U.S. Supreme Ct. 1976. With Leydig, Voit & Mayer, Ltd. and predecessor firms, Chgo., 1959—, assoc., 1970-71, ptnr., 1971—. Served with USAR, 1961. Mich. State U. scholar, 1954-58; Hardy scholar Northwestern U., 1958-61. Mem. ABA, Am. Patent Law Assn., Fed. Bar Assn. 7th Cir., Patent Law Assn. Chgo., Law Club Chgo. Republican. Mem. Northwestern Law Rev., 1960-61. Patent, Trademark and copyright. Office: Leydig Voit & Mayer One IBM Bldg Suite 4600 Chicago IL 60611

SHEPPARD, NICHOLAS JOSEPH, lawyer; b. N.Y.C., Dec. 6, 1926; s. William Anthony and Agnes Frances (Adrian) S.; m. Mary Elizabeth Albert, Nov. 19, 1955; children: Sandra Marie, Stuart John, Robert James, Susan Elizabeth. AB, Dartmouth Coll., 1949; JD, St. John's U., 1955; LLM, NYU, 1962. Bar: N.Y. 1956, U.S. Dist. Ct. (so. dist.) 1957, U.S. Ct. Appeals (2d cir.) 1957, U.S. Supreme Ct. 1971. Assoc. Wilkie, Farr & Gallagher, N.Y.C., 1955-61; assoc. gen. counsel Continental Can Co., Inc., Norwalk, Conn., 1961—; bd. dirs. Continental Can Hong Kong, Ltd., Doosan Continental Can Mfg. Co., Ltd., Seoul, Republic of Korea, Envases Generales Continental, Mexico City, Dominguey Continental, Caracas, Venezuela; v.p., gen. counsel Continental Can Internat. Corp. Rep. dist. leader, Chappaqua, N.Y., 1970-74. Served to col. with USMCR, 1944-78, PTO, Korea. Mem. ABA, Westchester Fairfield Corp. Counsel Assn. Republican. Roman Catholic. Avocations: tennis, CCD teaching. Home: 9 Chatham Rd Chappaqua NY 10514 Office: Continental Can Co Inc 800 Connecticut Ave Norwalk CT 06854

SHEPPARD, THOMAS RICHARD, lawyer; b. Pasadena, Calif., Aug. 8, 1934; s. James Carroll and Ruth Mary (Pashgian) S.; m. Arlene Clubb, June 23, 1956; children—Eileen Diana, Pamela Lynn, Thomas Richard. A.B., Stanford U., 1956; LL.B., Harvard U., 1961. Bar: Calif. bar 1962. Asso. firm Sheppard, Mullin, Richter & Hampton, Los Angeles, 1961-66; partner Sheppard, Mullin, Richter & Hampton, 1966—; dir. numerous small corps.; pres. Legal Aid Found. Los Angeles, 1973. Trustee Harold Lloyd Found., Los Angeles, 1971—, Della Martin Found., 1979—. Served to lt. (j.g.) USN, 1956-58. Mem. Am. Bar Assn., State Bar Assn. Calif., Los Angeles County Bar Assn., Am. Law Inst., Am. Coll. Real Estate Lawyers, Beta Theta Pi. Club: Calif. (Los Angeles) (bd. dirs. 1985-86, sec. 1987). Real property, Corporate taxation, Personal income taxation. Home: 1680 Oak Grove Ave San Marino CA 91108 Office: 333 S Hope St Suite 4800 Los Angeles CA 90071

SHEPPEARD, SARAH Y., lawyer; b. Lawrence, Kans., Jan. 30, 1955; d. Lee Channing and Nancy Lee (Lawrence) S.; m. Benjamin F. Alford III, June 7, 1974; children: Jennifer Sheppeard Alford, Lee Sheppeard Alford. BA, U. Tenn., 1976, JD, 1979. Bar: Tenn. 1980, U.S. Dist. Ct. (ea. dist.) Tenn. 1980, U.S. Tax Ct. 1984, U.S. Supreme Ct. 1986. Assoc. Lockridge & Becker P.C., Knoxville, Tenn., 1980-83, ptnr., 1983-85; ptnr. Allen & Taylor, Knoxville, 1986—. Mem. ABA, Am. Judicare Soc., East Tenn. Legal Assn. for Women, Tenn. Bar Assn., Knoxville Bar Assn., Assn. Trial Lawyers Am., Phi Delta Phi. Episcopalian. State civil litigation, Probate, Family and matrimonial. Office: Allen & Taylor 1016 E Weisgarber Rd Knoxville TN 37909

SHER, BYRON D., legal educator; b. 1928. B.S., B.A., Washington U., St. Louis, 1949; J.D., Harvard U., 1952. Bar: Mass. 1952. Sole practice, Boston, 1952-54; teaching fellow Harvard U., Cambridge, Mass., 1954-55; asst. prof. law So. Methodist U., Dallas, 1955-57; asst. prof. Stanford (Calif.) U. Law Sch., 1957-59, assoc. prof., 1959-62, prof., 1962—; cons. Fulbright research scholar Victoria U., Wellington, N.Z., 1964. Mem. Nat. Conf. Commrs. Uniform State Laws. Co.-author: Law and Society, 1960. Legal education. Office: Stanford U Law Sch Stanford CA 94305 *

SHER, LEOPOLD ZANGWILL, lawyer; b. New Orleans, May 1, 1953; s. Joseph and Rachel (Israelowiec) S.; m. Karen Baumgarten, June 7, 1975; children: Rose Sarah, Samantha Jill. BA, Tulane U., 1974, JD, 1976. Bar: La., U.S. Dist. Ct. (ea. dist.) La., U.S. Ct. Appeals (5th cir.), U.S. Supreme Ct. Ptnr. McGlinchey, Stafford, Mintz, Cellini & Lang, P.C., New Orleans, 1979—. Mem. Leman-Stern Young Leadership Tng., New Orleans, 1980, Met. Area Com. Young Leadership Tng./Leadership Forum, New Orleans, 1982; chmn. Preservation Action Tax Task Force, La., 1985-86. Mem. ABA (vice chmn. real estate fin. subcom. of comml. fin. services com. of corps. banking and bus. sec., real property sect., probate and trust sect., corp. banking and bus. sect.), La. Bar Assn., New Orleans Bar Assn. Democrat. Jewish. Real property, Contracts commercial, Landlord-tenant. Home: 471 Topaz St New Orleans LA 70124 Office: McGlinchey Stafford Mintz Cellini & Lang 643 Magazine St New Orleans LA 70130

SHER, RICHARD PHILIP, lawyer; b. Kansas City, Mo., Oct. 30, 1950; s. Abbott J. and Martha (Abend) S.; m. Linda Zellinger, May 7, 1972; children: Jennifer, Amanda. BA, Northwestern U., 1972; JD with distinction, U. Mo., Kansas City, 1974. Bar: Mo. 1975. Ptnr. Peper, Martin, Jensen, Maichel & Hetlage, St. Louis, 1975—. Mem. Am. Judicature Soc. Club: Media (St. Louis). Federal civil litigation, State civil litigation, Securities. Office: Peper Martin Jensen Maichel & Hetlage 720 Olive St 24th Floor Saint Louis MO 63101

SHERER, FRANK AUDEMARS, JR., lawyer; b. N.Y.C., Dec. 3, 1947; s. Frank Audemars and Sally (Harding) S.; m. Marie Saydah, May 5, 1973; children: Frank, Edward, Marie. BA, Yale U., 1969; JD, Boston U., 1972. Bar: N.Y. 1973. Assoc. Chadbourne & Parke, N.Y.C., 1972-77; counsel Timex Corp., Middlebury, Conn., 1977-78, acting asst. gen. counsel, 1978; asst. gen. counsel, asst. sec. Timex Group Ltd., Middlebury, Conn., 1979-86, gen. counsel, sec., 1986—. Mem. ABA, Westchester Fairfield Corp. Counsel Assn. General corporate, Antitrust, Private international. Office: Timex Group Ltd Park Rd Extension Middlebury CT 06762

SHERER, RONALD BRIAN, lawyer; b. Buffalo, June 25, 1935; s. Andrew Joseph and Amelia (Moreau) S.; m. Betty Ann Charles, May 12, 1962; children: Maria A., Michael B., Charles A. BS, Canisius Coll., Buffalo, 1957; JD Georgetown U., 1961. Bar: Pa. 1962, U.S. Supreme Ct. 1969, U.S. Ct. Appeals (fed. cir.) 1984. Examiner, U.S. Patent Office, Washington, 1957-61; patent adviser U.S. Naval Ordnance Lab., White Oak, Md., 1961-62; assoc. Busser, Smith & Harding, Phila., 1962-63; div. patent counsel Air Products & Chem. Inc., Allentown, Pa., 1963-80; asst. gen. counsel Internat. Coal Refining Co., Allentown, Pa., 1980-82; corp. dir. patents, trademarks and licenses Black & Decker Mfg. Co., Towson, Md., 1982—. Bd. dirs. Ancient Oak Homeowners Civic Assn., Allentown, 1966-70; vice chmn. Salisbury Planning Commn. (Pa.), 1972; Mem. parish council, counsel St. Thomas More Ch., Allentown, 1972-73. Mem. ABA, Fed. Bar Assn., Lehigh County Bar Assn., Am. Patent Law Assn., N.Y. Patnet Law Assn., Md. Patent Law Assn., Phila. Patent Law Assn., Assn. Corp. Patent Counsels, Am. Corp. Counsels Assn., Am. Intellectual Property Law Assn., Licensing Execs. Soc., Washington Patent Lawyers Club. Patent, Trademark and copyright, Federal civil litigation. Home: 1437 Forest Park Ave Baltimore MD 21207 Office: 701 E Joppa Rd Towson MD 21204

SHERESKY, NORMAN M., lawyer; b. Detroit, June 22, 1928; s. Harry and Rose (Lieberman) S.; m. Elaine B. Lewis, Oct. 30, 1977; 1 child, from previous marriage, Brooke Hillary. A.B., Syracuse U., 1950; LL.B., Harvard U., 1953. Bar: N.Y. 1953. Assoc. Gold & Pollack, N.Y.C., 1954-60; sole practice, N.Y.C., 1960-72; ptnr. Sheresky & Kalman, N.Y.C., 1972-77, Colton, Hartnick, Yamin & Sheresky, N.Y.C., 1977—; adj. prof. matrimonial litigation N.Y. Law Sch., 1979—. Mem. Am. Acad. Matrimonial Lawyers (gov., past pres. N.Y. chpt.), N.Y. State Bar Assn., Assn. Trial Lawyers Am., Met. Trial Lawyers Assn., Internat. Acad. Matrimonial Lawyers (bd. govs. 1986—). Author: (with Marya Mannes) Uncoupling,

1972; On Trial, 1977; contbr. editor: Fairshare mag. Family and matrimonial. Office: 79 Madison Ave New York NY 10016

SHERIDAN, JOHN KRESS, II, lawyer; b. Logansport, Ind., Jan. 17, 1948; s. John Kress and Alice (Davis) S.; m. Lou Ann, Apr. 28, 1982 (div. Nov. 1983); 1 child, Mary Alice. BS, BA, U. N.C., 1969; JD, Ind. U., 1974. Bar: Ind. 1975, U.S. Dist. Ct. (so. dist.) Ind. 1975. Mgr. pensions Am. United Life Ins. Co., Indpls., 1970-75; v.p., gen. counsel The Howard E. Nyhart Co., Inc., Indpls., 1975-79; ptnr. Fogle, Sheridan & Assocs., Indpls., 1979-84; pres. Sheridan & Assocs., Inc., Indpls., 1984—. Mem. lawyer's panel Ind. Civil Liberties Union, Indpls., 1978-79. Mem. ABA, Ind. Bar Assn., Indpls. Bar Assn., Midwest Pension Conf. Republican. Roman Catholic. Club: Broadmoor Country (Indpls.). N. Am. Men's Pairs Contract Bridge winner, 1978. Represented US in World Bridge Championship, 1978. Pension, profit-sharing, and employee benefits. Home: 5243 N Meridian St Indianapolis IN 46208 Office: Sheridan & Assocs Inc 10333 N Meridian St Suite 110 Indianapolis IN 46290

SHERIDAN, JOHN ROBERT, lawyer; b. Upland, Pa., Oct. 8, 1944; s. John Paul and Theresa Valerie (Dawson) S.; m. Barbara Ann Bigelow, Aug. 18, 1973; children—Daniel, Timothy. B.A., U. Del., 1966; J.D., U. Balt., 1972. Bar: Pa. 1973, Del. 1975, U.S. Dist. Ct. Del. 1976. Law clk. Herlihy & Herlihy, Wilmington, Del., 1971-72; asst. city solicitor Wilmington, 1973—. Pres., Forty Acres Restoration, Inc., Wilmington, 1975-81; staff mem. Maloney for U.S. Senate, Wilmington, 1976; mem. City Democratic Com., Wilmington, 1977—; alt. del. State Dem. Conv., Del., 1984, regular del., 1986; mem. exec. com. Frawley for Wilmington, 1984, Citizens for Biden, 1987. Served with USAR, 1966-72. Mem. ABA, Pa. Bar Assn., Del. Bar Assn., Am. Mgmt. Assn., Del. Assn. Pub. Adminstrs., Sierra Club. Democrat. Roman Catholic. Local government, Legislative, Antitrust. Home: 1611 Mt Salem Ln Wilmington DE 19806 Office: Office of City Solicitor 800 French St Wilmington DE 19801

SHERIDAN, PETER N., lawyer; b. N.Y.C., Feb. 27, 1944; s. Stephen S. and Beatrice (Zimmer) S.; 1 child, Elizabeth. B.A., U. Vt., 1965; J.D., Bklyn. Law Sch., 1968. Bar: N.Y. 1969, U.S. Ct. Mil. Appeals 1970, U.S. Dist. Ct. (ea. and so. dist.) N.Y. 1972, U.S. Ct. Appeals 1972, U.S. Supreme Ct. 1974. Assoc., Mendes & Mount, N.Y.C., 1971-74; asst. gen. counsel CIBA-GEIGY Corp., Ardsley, N.Y., 1974—. Bd. editors: Leader's Product Liability Newsletter, 1982—; lectr. Contbr. articles to profl. jours. Bd. dirs. Concerned Com. for Indo-Chinese Relations, N.Y.C., 1980-81; regional bd. dirs. Cystic Fibrosis Found., Greater N.Y. region, 1982—. Served to capt. U.S. Army, 1969-71, Vietnam. Mem. ABA (vice chair products gen. liability and consumer law com., sect. of torts and ins. practice 1981—), Am. Corp. Counsel Assn. (chair indsl. def. library 1983—). General corporate, product liability. Home: 232 W Norwalk Rd Norwalk CT 06850 Office: CIBA-GEIGY Corp 444 Saw Mill River Rd Ardsley NY 10502

SHERK, GEORGE WILLIAM, lawyer; b. Washington, Mo., June 23, 1949; s. George William Sr. and Lorraine Martha (Meyer) S. AA, St. Louis Community Coll., 1970; BA, Colo. State U., 1972, MA, 1974; JD, U. Denver, 1978. Bar: Am. Samoa 1978, Colo. 1979, U.S. Dist. Ct. Colo. 1979, U.S. Ct. Claims 1984, U.S. Supreme Ct. 1985. Cons. office of legis. counsel Govt. of Am. Samoa, Pago Pago, 1978-79; atty. advisor Western Area Power Adminstrn., U.S. Dept. Energy, Colo., 1979-80; sole practice Denver, 1980-82; staff assoc. Nat. Conf. State Legis., Denver, 1980-82; spl. asst. office of water policy U.S. Dept. Interior, Washington, 1982-83; atty. lands and natural resources div. U.S. Dept. Justice, Washington, 1984—; lectr. various colls. and univs. Co-author: State and Local Management Actions to Reduce Colorado River Salinity, 1977; contbr. articles on water law and alternative energy law to profl. jours. Mem. ABA, Fed. Bar Assn., Colo. Bar Assn., Washington Ind. Writers. Democratic. Presbyterian. Avocations: automobile racing and rallying, sports, reading, outdoor activites. Water Law, Environment, Federal civil litigation. Home: 546 N Saint Asaph St Alexandria VA 22314 Office: US Dept of Justice PO Box 7415 Benjamin Franklin Sta Washington DC 20044-7415

SHERMAN, CARL LEON, lawyer; b. Pitts., Sept. 3, 1945; s. Julius Louis Sherman and Ida (Schooler) Sherman Cohodas; m. Selma Bonderow, Oct. 14, 1973; children: Alyssa B., Dana B. BA, U. Pitts., 1967, JD, 1970. Bar: Pa. 1970, U.S. Supreme Ct. 1974. Law clk. to presiding justice Allegheny-Ct. Common Pleas, Pitts., 1970-71; sole practice Pitts., 1971-73; ptnr. Miller & Sherman, Pitts., 1974-77; assoc. Tucker Arensberg et al, Pitts., 1977-79, ptnr., 1979-85; ptnr. Sherman & Picadio and predecessor firm Karlowitz, Sherman & Picadio, Pitts., 1985—. Bd. dirs. Am. Wind Symphony, Pitts., 1974-82; mem. Ross Twp. Planning Commn., Pitts., 1976-78, chmn., 1978-80. Mem. Pa. Bar Assn., Allegheny County Bar Assn., Def. Research Inst. Clubs: Rivers (Pitts.), Downtown (Pitts.). Avocations: sports, exercising. Federal civil litigation, State civil litigation. Office: Sherman & Picadio 3180 600 Grant St Pittsburgh PA 15219

SHERMAN, CHARLES ISRAEL, lawyer; b. Hartford, Conn., June 9, 1939; s. Joseph and Ruth Sherman; children from previous marriage: Pamela, Jeffrey; m. Pamela J. Sherman, Mar. 24, 1984; 1 child, Katherine Daniel-le. B in Metall. Engring., Rensselaer Poly. Inst., 1961; postgrad., Georgetown U., 1961-64; JD, NYU, 1965. Bar: Conn. 1965, U.S. Patent Office 1965, U.S. Dist. Ct. Conn. 1967, U.S. Dist. Ct. (so. and ea. dists.) N.Y. 1969, U.S. Ct. Appeals (2d cir.) 1969, U.S. Supreme Ct. 1971, N.Y. 1980. Ptnr. St. Onge, Cahill and Mayers, Stamford, Conn., 1965-71; asst. chief patent and trademark counsel Gulf and Western, Inc., N.Y.C., 1971-85; gen. patent and trademark counsel Wickes Cos., Inc., N.Y.C., 1985—. Patentee in field. Pres., bd. dirs. Nor-West Condominium Assn., Norwalk, Conn., 1980-82. NSF grantee 1960-61. Mem. ABA, Conn. Bar Assn., Conn. Patent Law Assn., Licensing Execs. Soc., U.S. Trademark Assn., Tau Beta Pi. Patent, Trademark and copyright, Licensing. Home: 218 Sport Hill Rd Easton CT 06612 Office: Wickes Cos Inc 1285 Ave of the Americas New York NY 10019

SHERMAN, DANA, lawyer; b. Los Angeles, Apr. 1, 1953; s. Harry P. and Lillie (Epstein) S. BA in Math., UCLA, 1975; JD, Loyola U., Los Angeles, 1978; MBA, Claremont Coll., 1980; M in Bus. Tax, U. So. Calif., 1984. Bar: Calif. 1978, U.S. Dist. Ct. (cen. dist.) Calif. 1979, U.S. Ct. Appeals (9th cir.) 1981, U.S. Tax Ct. 1982, U.S. Supreme Ct. 1983; registered real estate broker, Calif., investment advisor, SEC. Assoc. Pachter, Gold & Schaefer, Los Angeles, 1978-82; sole practice Los Angeles, 1982—; lectr. sch. engring. U. So. Calif., Los Angeles, 1979—; adj. prof. Claremont (Calif.) Coll. Grad. Sch., 1985—; judge pro tem Los Angeles Mcpl. Ct., 1985. V.p. Mental Health Assn. Calif., 1985—; pres. Mental Health Assn. Los Angeles County, 1986—. Mem. St. Thomas More Soc. Avocations: sports, travel. State civil litigation, General corporate, Contracts commercial. Home and Office: 611 W 6th St #3200 Los Angeles CA 90017-3109

SHERMAN, ELLIOT MARK, lawyer; b. Brookline, Mass., Aug. 6, 1952; s. Daniel and Elizabeth (Bromfield) S. BA, U. Mass., 1974; JD, Western New England Coll., 1977. Bar: Mass. 1977, U.S. Dist. Ct. Mass. 1977, U.S. Tax Ct. 1981. Sole practice Braintree, Mass., 1977—. Mem. town meeting Town of Amherst, Mass., 1977. Mem. Mass. Bar Assn. (mem. council law practice section 1985—), Boston Bar Assn., Norfolk County Bar Assn., Mass. Acad. Trial Attys., Am. Trial Lawyers Assn. Democrat. Avocations: sailing, skiing, carpentry, scuba diving. State civil litigation, Family and matrimonial, General practice. Office: 1 Rockdale St Braintree MA 02184

SHERMAN, FREDERICK HOOD, lawyer; b. Deming, N.Mex., Aug. 9, 1947; s. Benjamin and Helen (Hood) S.; m. Janie Carol Jontz, Oct. 23, 1973; children: Jerah, Jakub. BBA, Southern Meth. U., 1970, JD, 1972. Bar: Tex. 1972, N.Mex. 1973, U.S. Dist. Ct. N.Mex. 1973, U.S. Dist. Ct. (we. dist.) Tex. 1974, U.S. Supreme Ct. 1979. Assoc. Sherman & Sherman, Deming, 1973-74, ptnr., 1974-78; prin. Sherman & Sherman P.C., Deming, 1978—; assoc. prof. Western N.Mex. U., Silver City, 1975-77, mem. specialization com. US. Supreme Ct. Chmn. Lupa County Planning Commn., Deming, 1976-78. Mem. N.Mex. Bar Assn. (supreme ct. specialization bd., 1986—, commr. 1978-86, com. on alt. dispute resolutions practice 1980, jud. selection com. 1985, co-chmn. legal retreat 1987—), Tex. Bar Assn., 6th Jud. Bar Assn., Assn. Trial Lawyers Am. (notably large award 1983, 84, 85), N.Mex. Trial Lawyers Assn. (bd. dirs. 1986—). Democrat. Roman Catholic. Lodge: Toastmasters. Avocations: skiing, investments, camping. Personal injury, Workers' compensation, Social security. Office: Sherman & Sherman PC 210 S Silver Deming NM 88031-0850

SHERMAN, GLENN TERRY, lawyer; b. Los Angeles, Sept. 11, 1954; s. Sidney L. and Marilyn S. (Bloom) S.; m. Cindy L. Pallock, July 30, 1977; children: Melanie Nicole, Brent Daniel. BA, UCLA, 1976; JD cum laude, Southwestern U., 1979. Bar: Calif. 1979, U.S. Dist. Ct.(cen. dist.) Calif. 1980, U.S. Ct. Appeals (9th cir.) 1980. Gen. counsel Conroy's Florists, Culver City, Calif., 1979-84; assoc. Freeman, Freeman & Smiley, Los Angeles, 1984-86, ptnr., 1986—; lectr. Pepperdine U., Los Angeles, 1984-85. Mem. ABA, Calif. Bar Assn., Los Angeles Bar Assn., Beverly Hills Bar Assn., Assn. Corp. Real Estate Execs., Internat. Council Shopping Ctrs., Los Angeles Breakfast Club. Club: The Guardians (Los Angeles). Avocations: running, golf, backpacking, fishing. Real property, Construction, Franchising. Office: Freeman Freeman & Smiley 3415 Sepulveda Blvd Penthouse Los Angeles CA 90034

SHERMAN, JEFFREY SCOTT, lawyer; b. Bklyn., Oct. 26, 1955; s. Martin and Beatrice (Matrick) S.; m. Susan Ellen Ganz, Aug. 13, 1981; 1 child, Elisabeth Faye. BA cum laude, SUNY, Albany, 1976; JD magna cum laude, Bklyn. Law Sch., 1980. Bar: N.Y. 1980. Assoc. Proskauer, Rose et al, N.Y.C., 1980-83, Shereff, Friedman, Hoffman and Goodman, N.Y.C., 1983—. Mem. ABA, Assn. of the Bar of the City of N.Y. (young lawyers com. 1983-86). General corporate, Securities, Contracts commercial. Office: Shereff Friedman Hoffman and Goodman 919 3d Ave New York NY 10022

SHERMAN, JOSEPH ALLEN, lawyer; b. St. Joseph, Mo., Sept. 18, 1929; s. Joseph Allen and Faye Louise (Anthony) S.; m. Mary Jane Phipps, July 2, 1949; children—Joseph Allen, David Phipps, Mark Eden, John William. LL.B., U. Mo.-Kansas City, 1955. Bar: Mo. 1956, U.S. Dist. Ct. (we. dist.) Mo. 1961, U.S. Ct. Apls. (8th and 5th cirs.) 1975, U.S. Sup. Ct. 1977, U.S. Ct. Apls. (10th cir.) 1978. Claims atty. Western Casualty & Surety Co., Kansas City, Mo., 1955-56; spl. agt. FBI, San Francisco, 1956-57; home office rep. Prudential Ins. Co., Kansas City, Mo., 1957-59; assoc. Deacy & Deacy, Kansas City, after 1959, ptnr., to 1967; ptnr. Jackson, Barker & Sherman, Kansas City, 1967-69, Jackson & Sherman, Kansas City, 1969-83; pres. Sherman Wickens Lysaught & Speck, P.C., Kansas City, 1983—; lectr. continuing legal edn. Mem. Bd. Edn. Elem. Sch. Dist. 49, Shawnee Mission, Kans., 1963-69, pres., 1967-68; mem. Bd. Edn. Shawnee Mission Unified Sch. Dist. 512, 1969-70; mem. City Plan Commn., Weatherby Lake, Mo., 1973—. Recipient Gavel award Def. Research Inst., 1984. Fellow Internat. Acad. Trial Lawyers, Internat. Soc. Barristers; mem. Am. Bd. Trial Advocates (nat. exec. com.), Internat. Assn. Def. Counsel, Def. Research Inst. (pres. 1982, chmn. bd. 1983, hon. chmn. bd. 1984), Westmo Def. Lawyers (pres. 1973-74), Kansas City Bar Assn. (pres. 1976-77). Republican. Presbyterian. Club: Kansas City. State civil litigation, Federal civil litigation, Personal injury. Home: 10009 NW 75th St Kansas City MO 64152 Office: Sherman Wickens et al 1100 Main St Top of City Ctr Sq PO Box 26530 Kansas City MO 64105

SHERMAN, LAWRENCE M., lawyer; b. N.Y.C., May 23, 1940; s. Philip and Goldie (Brown) S.; m. Barbara Zuckerman, June 10, 1962; children: Roger, Jacqueline. B.A., NYU, 1962, LL.B., 1965. Bar: N.Y. 1965, Calif. 1977. Asso. firm Proskauer Rose Goetz & Mendelsohn, N.Y.C., 1965-71, Nickerson Kramer Lowenstein Nessen Kamin & Soll, N.Y.C., 1971-74, Fried Frank Harris Shriver & Jacobson, N.Y.C., 1974-76; exec. v.p. legal and adminstrn. The Fed Mart Corp., San Diego, 1976-82, pres., 1982-83; mng. ptnr. Finley, Kumble, Wagner, Heine, Underberg, Manley & Casey, San Diego, 1983—. General corporate, Real property, Securities. Office: 101 W Broadway Suite 1500 San Diego CA 92101

SHERMAN, LENORE SHUSTAK, lawyer; b. Bronx, N.Y., Aug. 7, 1956; d. Charles Jack and Florence (Garfinkel) Shustak; m. Neil Hamilton Sherman, Aug. 23, 1981; 1 child, Alexander Michael. BA in Sociology, SUNY, Albany, 1977; JD, Emory U., 1980. Bar: Ga. 1980, U.S. Dist. Ct. (no. dist.) Ga. 1980, N.Y. 1984. Staff atty. Oxford Industries Inc., Atlanta, 1981-83; assoc. Cadwalader, Wickersham & Taft, N.Y.C., 1983-84; asst. gen. counsel On-Line Software Internat., Inc., Ft. Lee, N.J., 1984—. Mem. ABA, Ga. Bar Assn., Bar Assn. State of N.Y. Computer, General corporate, Securities. Office: On-Line Software Internat Inc 2 Executive Dr Fort Lee NJ 07024

SHERMAN, LESTER IVAN, lawyer; b. Flagler, Colo., June 1, 1936; s. Lester B. and Helen E. S.; m. Lois E. Hafling, July 19, 1958 (div. Mar. 1986); children—Kathi, Scott, Brett. Student Colo. State U., 1954-55; B.S.B.A., U. Denver, 1958, J.D., 1961. Bar: Colo. 1961, U.S. Dist. Ct. Colo. 1961. Sole practice, Denver, 1961-62; assoc. Harold C. Greager, Ft. Collins, Colo., 1962-65; sole practice, Durango, Colo., 1965-67; ptnr. Hamilton, Sherman, Hamilton & Shand, P.C., Durango, 1967-78; sole practice, Durango, 1979-81; ptnr. Sherman Rhodes & Wright, P.C., Durango, 1981-86; sole practice, Durango, 1986—; judge La Plata County (Colo.) Ct., 1966-76; cons. in field; mem. Colo. Commn. on Jud. Qualifications, 1974-76. Mem. La Plata County Bd. for Mentally Retarded and Seriously Handicapped, Inc., 1968-75, pres., 1970-73; bd. dirs. Colo. County Judges Assn., 1973-74. Mem. S.W. Colo. Bar (pres. 1969-70), Colo. Bar Assn. (gov. 1970-72, 74-76), ABA, Phi Delta Phi, Sigma Chi. Republican. Club: Petroleum (Durango). Lodge: Elks. General corporate, Estate planning, Real property. Home: 495 County Rd 203 Durango CO 81301 Office: 1022 1/2 Main Suite 4 PO Box 2199 Durango CO 81302

SHERMAN, MARTIN PETER, lawyer; b. N.Y.C., May 2, 1940; m. Susan Randall, Feb. 16, 1969; children—David, Timothy, Peter. B.A., UCLA, 1961; J.D., U. Chgo., 1964; LL.M., U. So. Calif., 1969. Bar: Calif. 1965, Pa. 1972. Law clk. Los Angeles Superior Ct., 1964-65; dep. county counsel Los Angeles County, 1965-66; atty. Antipoverty Program, Ventura, San Francisco and Los Angeles, 1966-69; counsel Atlantic Richfield Co., Los Angeles and Phila., 1969-73; asst. gen. counsel Ampex Corp., Redwood City, Calif., 1973-87, corp. counsel Amgen, Inc., Thousand Oaks, Calif., 1987—. Mem. ABA, Palo Alto Bar Assn., Am. Corp. Counsel Assn. (nat. pro bono com.), Am. Soc. Corp. Secs. Contbr. articles to law jour. Antitrust, Private international, Contracts commercial. Office: Amgen Inc 1900 Oak Terrace Ln Thousand Oaks CA 91320

SHERMAN, MICHAEL PAUL, lawyer; b. N.Y.C., June 7, 1952; s. Louis J. and Muriel F. (Kroman) S.; m. Ruth Schlesinger, Sept. 16, 1973; children: Joshua, Laura, Jonathan. Student, Hebrew U., Jerusalem, 1971-72; BA cum laude, Syracuse U., 1973; JD, Rutgers U., 1977. Bar: N.Y. 1978, N.J. 1978, U.S. Dist. Ct. N.J. 1978, U.S. Dist. Ct. (so. dist.) N.Y. 1983. Assoc. Nixon, Hargrave, Devans & Doyle, N.Y.C., 1977-80; asst. corp. counsel Joseph E. Seagram and Sons, Inc., N.Y.C., 1980-83; sr. v.p., gen. counsel and sec. The Horn & Hardart Co., N.Y.C., 1983—. Mem. ABA, Assn. Bar of City of N.Y., N.J. Bar Assn. General corporate, General practice, Securities. Home: 15 Tamarack Rd Edison NJ 08820 Office: The Horn & Hardart Co 730 5th Ave New York NY 10019

SHERMAN, WILLIAM DELANO, lawyer; b. White Plains, N.Y., Nov. 11, 1942; s. Edgar Jay S.; children from previous marriage: Jennifer W., Andrea B.; m. Vickie R. McGraw, July 31, 1982; children: Peter M., Sarah D. BA, Princeton U., 1964; MBA, JD, U. Calif., Berkeley, 1972. Bar: Calif., U.S. Dist. Ct., U.S. Ct. Appeals. Teaching, research asst. various orgns., 1961-72; assoc. Pillsbury, Madison & Sutro, San Francisco, 1972-79, ptnr., 1979-87; ptnr. Morrison & Foerster, San Francisco, 1987—; lectr. grad. sch. bus. U. Calif., Berkeley, 1976—; judge pro tem Mcpl. Ct., San Francisco, 1978—; panelist, moderator various orgns. Bd. dirs. Youth for Service, 1975-76, Town Sch. for Boys, pres. alumni assn., trustee 1976-77, The Head-Royce Sch., Oakland, Calif., 1977-86, chmn. 1985-86, treas. 1979-82, chmn. devel. com., 1978-79, chmn. fin. com., 1979-82, Phillips Acad., Andover, Mass., 1984—, alumni council, 1984—. Mem. ABA (fed. regulation of securities com., 1981—, state regulation securities com., 1981—, banking and bus. law sect., charter mem. fed. securities law com. young lawyers div. 1977-80), Calif. Bar Assn. (corps. com. bus. law sect. 1986—), San Francisco Bar Assn. (bd. dirs. 1977-78, chmn. corps. com. Barristers club 1974-76, sec., bd. dirs. 1977-78). Episcopalian. Securities, General corporate. Office: Morrison & Foerster 345 California St San Francisco CA 94104

SHERR, MORRIS MAX, lawyer; b. Marysville, Calif., Oct. 3, 1930; s. Alfred and Alice Carrie (Peters) S.; m. Bobbie Gray, June 27, 1954; children—David, Rodney. B.A., Calif. State U., 1952; J.D., U. Calif.-San Francisco, 1956. Bar: Calif. 1956. Prin. elem. sch., Stanislaus County, Calif., 1952-54; instr. Golden Gate Coll., 1954-55; instr. Calif. State U.-San Francisco, 1955-56; asst. prof. Calif. State U.-Fresno, 1956-59; assoc. Thompson & Rose, C.P.A.s, Fresno, Calif., 1959-61; ptnr. Blumberg, Sherr & Kerkorian, Fresno, Calif., 1961-84, Morris M. Sherr & Assocs., Fresno, 1984—. Mem. adv. council St. Agnes Hosp. Found., 1978-83. Mem. Am. Inst. C.P.A.s, Fresno Estate Planning Council (dir. 1977-79), Fresno County Bar, Christian Legal Soc., Calif. State Bar (cert. tax specialist). Baptist (chmn. trustees 1967-69, deacon 1969-73). Mem. Am. Baptist Chs. of West (moderator). Clubs: Fresno Kiwanis, Elks, Masons, Shriners. Estate taxation, Personal income taxation, Probate. Office: 1540 E Shaw St Suite 109 Fresno CA 93710

SHERRARD, ALEXANDER CONN, lawyer; b. Brownsville, Pa., July 5, 1923; s. Jacob Henderson Sherrard and Mary Milholland (McConnell); m. Dorothy A. Lind, Nov. 28, 1953; children: Amy Sherrard Weaver, Alexander C. III. Student, Washington & Jefferson U., 1943; BA, Amherst Coll., 1947; LLB, Yale U., 1950. Bar: Pa. 1951, U.S. Dist. Ct. (we. dist.) Pa. 1951, U.S. Ct. Appeals (3d cir.) 1951. Prin. Campbell, Sherrard & Burke P.C., Pitts., 1951—; lectr. various seminars. 1st v.p. Mendelssohn Choir, Pitts., 1986—. Served with U.S. Army, 1943-45. Fellow Am. Bar Found.; mem. ABA, Pa. Bar Assn., Allegheny County Bar Assn., Maritime Law Assn. U.S. Presbyterian. Clubs: Univ., Duquesne (Pitts.). Consumer commercial, Banking, General practice.

SHERRELL, JOHN BRADFORD, lawyer; b. Indpls., Jan. 27, 1951; s. Carl and Mary Jean (Bell) S.; m. Sherry Naomi Calhoun, Apr. 28, 1974; children: David Alan, Corinne Elizabeth. BA, Yale U., 1973; JD, U. Mich., 1977. Bar: Calif. 1977. Ptnr. Latham & Watkins, Los Angeles, 1977—. Mem. ABA, Calif. Bar Assn., Los Angeles County Bar Assn. (barrister's exec. com. 1978-80). Real property, Secured financing, Landlord-tenant. Office: Latham & Watkins 555 S Flower St Los Angeles CA 90071

SHERRER, CHARLES WILLIAM, lawyer, writer; b. Denton, Kans., July 24, 1922; s. Charles Eric and Pearl Bearl (McClellan) S.; m. Marion Sylva Webb, Aug. 27, 1948; children—Gary L., Carol J. Sherrer McGehee. B.S., U. Kans., 1948; J.D., U. Mo.-Kansas City, 1951. Bar: Mo. 1950, Kans. 1958, U.S. Supreme Ct. 1959. Atty., U.S. Army C.E., 1955—; div. counsel South Pacific div., Lafayette, Calif., 1983—. Served with AUS, 1942-45; to 1st lt., 1950-52. Mem. ABA, Fed. Bar Assn., Mensa, Soc. Am. Mil. Engrs. Author: (with Sherrer) Ethical and Professional Standards for Academic Psychologists and Counsellors, 1980: contbr. articles to legal jours. Government contracts and claims, Antitrust, Labor. Home: 3933 Woodside Ct Lafayette CA 94549

SHERRY, JOHN SEBASTIAN, lawyer; b. Homestead, Pa., Apr. 18, 1946; s. Sebastian John and Margaret Josephine (Coyne) S.; m. Joan Carol Paulsen, Aug. 9, 1969; children: Brendan P., Michael S., Conor J. BA, U. Dayton, 1968; JD, Duquesne U., 1971. Bar: Pa. 1971, U.S. Dist. Ct. (we. dist.) Pa. 1971, U.S. Supreme Ct. 1975, U.S. Ct. Appeals (3d cir.) 1976, U.S. Tax Ct. 1977, U.S. Claims Ct. 1977, U.S. Ct. Mi. Appeals 1977, U.S. Ct. Internat. Trade 1977. Sole practice Pitts., 1971—; mng. atty. The Travlers Ins. Co., Pitts., 1972-78; mng. trial atty. The CNA Ins. Cos., Pitts., 1978—; lectr. Trial Advocacy Found., Pitts., 1984. Assoc. opinion editor Pitts. Legal Jour., 1977-78, editor YLS newsletter, 1980. Chmn. Bd. Auditors, South Park, Pa., 1977-85. Named One of Outstanding Young Men of Am., 1979. Fellow Acad. Trial Lawyers Allegheny County; mem. Allegheny County Bar Assn. (continuing legal edn. com. 1978—, council civil litigation sect. 1985—), ABA, Pa. Def. Inst., Pa. Bar Assn., South Park C. of C. (pres.). Democrat. Roman Catholic. Clubs: Rivers, South Hills Country (Pitts.). Lodge: Lions (treas. South Park club 1980-81). Avocations: fishing, hunting, lit. Federal civil litigation, State civil litigation, Insurance. Home: 181 Vernon Dr Pittsburgh PA 15228 Office: 608 Grant Bldg Pittsburgh PA 15219

SHERTZ, PERRY JACK, lawyer; b. Wilkes-Barre, Pa., May 26, 1928; s. William Charles and Fannie (Jackier) S.; m. Shirlee Jean Rosenzweig, Aug. 31, 1952; children—Dori Hope Shertz Sobin, Judy Ellen Shertz Sofer, Marcy Lynn Shertz Stein, Lawrence Mitchell. B.A., Dickinson Coll., 1952; J.D., Temple U., 1956. Bar: Pa. 1957, U.S. Dist. Ct. (ea. dist.) Pa. 1957, U.S. Dist. Ct. (mid. dist.) Pa. 1960, U.S. Ct. Appeals (3d cir.) 1980. In-house trial counsel Empire Mut. Ins. Co., Phila., 1957-59; assoc. Rosenn, Jenkins & Greenwald, Wilkes-Barre, Pa., 1959-61, ptnr., 1961-80, 82—; judge Superior Ct. of Pa., 1980-82; commr. Gov.'s Pa. Heritage Affairs Adv. Commn.; mem. hearing com. Disciplinary Bd. of U.S. Supreme Ct. Pa.; lectr. Continuing Legal Edn. seminars and profl. orgns.; permanent mem. Jud. Conf. 3d Jud. Cir. U.S. Pres. Dist. Grand Lodge No. 3 B'nai B'rith, 1971-72, chmn. dist. flood disaster allocations com., 1972-74, mem. Adult Jewish Edn. Commn., B'nai B'rith Internat., 1973-75, planning and research com., 1971-75, commn. on community vol. services, 1975-78, 80—, chmn. Nat. Disaster Relief Com., 1974-76, Nat. Young Leadership Devel. Com., 1967-69, mem. Pa. Regional Bd. Anti-Defamation League, 1972—; chmn. Gen. Mcpl. Authority City of Wilkes-Barre, 1966-71; bd. dirs. Health Care Mgmt. Corp., 1975-80; bd. dirs. Health Systems Agy. N.E. Pa., Inc., 1975-78, parliamentarian, 1976-78; bd. dirs. Jewish Community Ctr., 1964-70, 82—, chmn. Jewish Ctr. Youth Com., 1965-67, chmn. Youth Dept. 1966-67; bd. dirs. Jewish Home Ea. Pa., 1966-82; mem. nat. services com. Jewish Welfare Bd., 1966-70; bd. dirs. Northeastern Pa. Heart Assn., 1966-74, exec. com., 1967-74; bd. dirs. Ohav Zedek Synagogue, 1965—, chmn., 1973-74, v.p., 1974-80; hon. bd. mem. Pennsylvanians for Human Life, 1975-80; chmn. lawyers sect. United Fund, 1973; mem. sch. bd. United Hebrew Inst., 1963—, pres., 1965-67; founder Upper Darby (Pa.) Citizens Com., 1958, chmn., 1958-59; pres. Westbrook Park Civic Assn., 1957-58; mem. Wilkes-Barre Planning Comm., 1965-66; del. Wyo. Valley Jewish Com., 1962-64, 65-67, 73-80, exec. com., bd. dirs. 1982— chmn. Wyo. Valley Jewish Community Relations Com., 1978-80, 82—. Served with USN, 1946-48, with USNR, 1948-49, with USMCR, 1949-52, 54-76; served with USMC, 1952-54; to lt. col. USMCR. Recipient Temple Law Alumni Legal Aid award. Fellow Am. Coll. Trial Laywers (state com.); mem. ABA, Pa. Bar Assn. (council mem. Ins., Negligence and Compensation Sect. 1970-77, chmn. 1975-77, mem. pres.'s select com. on med. malpractice 1975-76, council mem. jud. adminstrn. sect. 1976—, chmn. superior ct. sub com. 1982-84, mem. judiciary com. 1982-85, spl. com. on product liability), Phila. Bar Assn., Luzerne County Bar Assn. (pres. 1974-76), Pa. Trial Lawyers Assn. (bd. govs. 1969-71), Assn. Trial Lawyers Am., Am. Legion, AMVETS, Jewish War Vets., Marine Corps League, Marine Corps Res. Officers Assn., Res. Officers Assn., VFW. Republican. Club: Kiwanis. State civil litigation, Federal civil litigation, Personal injury. Office: 15 S Franklin St Wilkes-Barre PA 18711

SHERWOOD, ALLEN JOSEPH, lawyer; b. Salt Lake City, Sept. 26, 1909; s. Charles Samuel and Sarah (Abramson) Shapiro; m. Edith Ziff, Jan. 19, 1941; children—Mary (Mrs. John Marshall), Arthur Lawrence. Student, UCLA, 1927-30; A.B., U. So. Calif., 1933, LL.B., 1933. Bar: Calif. 1933, U.S. Supreme Ct. 1944. Practice Los Angeles, 1933-54; practice Beverly Hills, 1954—; legal counsel Internat. Family Planning Research Assn., Inc., 1970-76; bd. dirs. Family Planning Ctrs. Greater Los Angeles, Inc., 1968-84, pres., 1973-76. Mem. editorial bd. So. Calif. Law Rev., 1932-33. Contbr. articles to profl. jours. Mem. Calif. Atty. Gen.'s Vol. Adv. Council and its legis. subcom., 1972-78. Recipient alumni award U. So. Calif. Law Sch., 1933. Fellow Med.-Legal Soc. So. Calif. (bd. dirs. 1966-74); mem. ABA, Los Angeles County Bar Assn., Beverly Hills Bar Assn., State Bar of Calif., Am. Arbitration Assn. (nat. panel arbitrators 1965—), Order of Coif, Tau Delta Phi. Club: Brentwood Country (Los Angeles). Lodge: Masons. General practice, State civil litigation, Probate. Home: 575 Moreno Ave Los Angeles CA 90049 Office: 9033 Wilshire Blvd Penthouse Beverly Hills CA 90211

SHERWOOD, ARTHUR LAWRENCE, lawyer; b. Los Angeles, Jan. 25, 1943; s. Allen Joseph and Edith (Ziff) S.; m. Frances Merele, May 1, 1970; children—David, Chester. B.A. magna cum laude, U. Calif.-Berkeley, 1964; M.S., U. Chgo., 1965; J.D. cum laude, Harvard U., 1968. Bar: Calif. 1969, US. dist. cts. (cent. dist.) Calif. 1968 (no. dist.) Calif. 1971 (so. dist.) Calif. 1973 (ea. dist.) Calif. 1973, U.S. Ct. Appeals (9th cir.) 1973, U.S. Supreme Ct. 1980. Instr., UCLA Law Sch., 1968-69; assoc. Gibson, Dunn &

Crutcher, Los Angeles, 1968-75, ptnr., 1975—; judge pro tem Los Angeles Mcpl. Ct., 1980—; arbitrator N.Y. Stock Exchange. NASA fellow U. Chgo., 1964-65. Mem. ABA, Los Angeles County Bar Assn., Phi Beta Kappa. Republican. Jewish. Contbr. articles to profl. jours. Antitrust, Federal civil litigation, State civil litigation. Home: 18800 Wells Dr Tarzana CA 91356 Office: Gibson Dunn & Crutcher 333 S Grand Ave Los Angeles CA 90071

SHERWOOD, JAMES CRUZE, lawyer; b. Rockville Centre, N.Y., Aug. 12, 1950; s. Charles Gilbert and Agnes (Cruze) S. BA, Yale U., 1972; JD, Columbia U., 1977. Bar: N.Y. 1978, U.S. Dist. Ct. (so. and ea. dists.) N.Y. 1978, U.S. Ct. Appeals (2d cir.) 1980, U.S. Tax Ct. 1982. Assoc. Donovan Leisure Newton & Irvine, N.Y.C., 1977-82, Kostelanetz & Ritholz, N.Y.C., 1982-86; ptnr. Kostelanetz, Ritholz, Tigue & Fink, N.Y.C., 1986—. Mem. ABA (vice chmn. young lawyers' div., criminal justice com.), N.Y. State Bar Assn. (tax sect., com. criminal and civil penalties), Assn. of Bar of City of N.Y., N.Y. County Lawyers Assn. Roman Catholic. Avocation: theatre. Criminal, Personal income taxation, Federal civil litigation. Office: Kostelanetz Ritholz Tigue & Fink 80 Pine St New York NY 10005

SHERWOOD, LINDA KATHLEEN, lawyer; b. Houston, May 11, 1947; d. Mack Hayes and Dorothy Clare (Sullender) D.; m. Don Curtis Sherwood, Nov. 28, 1981; children: Matthew Curtis, Patrick Hayes, Timothy Michael. BS in Home Econs., U. Tex., 1969, JD, 1972. Bar: Calif. 1972, Tex. 1972, U.S. Dist. Ct. (cen. dist.) Calif. 1973, U.S. Ct. Appeals (9th cir.) 1973. From assoc. to ptnr. Latham & Watkins, Los Angeles, 1972—. Mem. ABA, Los Angeles Bar Assn., Women Lawyers Los Angeles. Episcopalian. General corporate, Contracts commercial, Securities. Office: Latham & Watkins 555 S Flower St Los Angeles CA 90071

SHERWOOD, RICHARD EDWIN, lawyer; b. Los Angeles, July 24, 1928; s. Benjamin Berkley and Jennie (Goldeen) S.; m. Dorothy Lipsey Romonek, July 25, 1953; children: Elizabeth Deirdre, Benjamin Berkley II. B.A., Yale U., 1949; LL.B., Harvard U., 1952, Sheldon traveling fellow, 1953-54. Bar: Calif. 1953. Law clk. to Justice Felix Frankfurter, U.S. Supreme Ct., 1954-55; with firm O'Melveny & Myers, Los Angeles, 1955—; ptnr. O'Melveny & Myers, 1964—; vis. lectr. Yale Law Sch., 1981; vis. prof. Sophia U., Tokyo, 1982; research scholar U. Tokyo, 1982; Mem. Calif. Little Hoover Commn., 1961-67, White House Task Force Antitrust Policy, 1967-68. Trustee Los Angeles County Mus. Art, 1966—, pres., 1974-78; chmn., overseers Rand/UCLA Ctr. for Study Soviet Internat. Behavior, 1986—; mem. vis. com. Harvard Law Sch., 1969-75, 86—, Harvard Art Museums, 1975—; trustee Asia Soc., 1978—; bd. dirs. Center Theatre Group, Los Angeles Music Center, pres., 1982-85, chmn., 1985—; bd. dirs. Japanese Am. Cultural and Community Ctr.; mem. Council on Fgn. Relations, Internat. Council, Mus. Modern Art., N.Y.C., Internat. Inst. for Strategic Studies, London . Served to 2d lt. USAF, 1952-53. Mem. Am. Bar Assn., Calif. Bar Assn., Los Angeles County Bar Assn. (chmn. human rights sect. 1970-71). Antitrust, Federal civil litigation, State civil litigation. Home: 803 N Elm Dr Beverly Hills CA 90210 Office: O'Melveny & Myers 400 S Hope St Los Angeles CA 90071-2899

SHESTACK, JEROME JOSEPH, lawyer; b. Atlantic City, N.J., Feb. 11, 1925; s. Isidore and Olga (Shankman) S.; m. Marciarose Schleifer, Jan. 28, 1951; children—Jonathan Michael, Jennifer. A.B., U. Pa., 1944; LL.B., Harvard U., 1949. Bar: Ill. 1950, Pa. 1952. Teaching fellow Northwestern U. Law Sch., Chgo., 1949-50; asst. prof. law, faculty editor La. State Law Sch., Baton Rouge, 1950-52; dep. city solicitor City of Phila., 1952, 1st dep. solicitor, 1952-55; ptnr. Schnader, Harrison, Segal & Lewis, Phila. and Washington, 1956—; adj. prof. law U. Pa. Law Sch., 1956; U.S. rep. to UN Human Rights Commn., 1979-80; U.S. del. to Econ. and Soc. Council UN, 1980; pres. Internat. League Human Rights, 1972—; bd. dirs., sec. Internat. Com. Jurists Am.; co-chmn. Lawyers Com. Internat. Human Rights, 1979-80; mem. nat. adv. com. legal services OEO, 1965-72; bd. dirs., mem. exec. com. Lawyers Com. Civil Rights Under Law, Washington, 1963—. Editor: (with others) Rights of Americans, 1971, Human Rights, 1979. Mem. fin. com. Democrat. Nat. Com., 1975—; bd. dirs. Fedn. Jewish Agys., 1962—; bd. overseers Jewish Theol. Soc. Am., 1968—; bd. govs. Hebrew U., 1969—; pres. Am. Poetry Ctr., 1986—, chmn. bd. dirs.; trustee Free Liberty of Phila., 1986—. Served with USNR, 1943-46. Fellow Am. Bar Found.; mem. ABA (nomination com., mem. ho. dels. 1971-73, 77—, chmn. numerous coms.), Am. Law Inst., Am. Coll. Trial Lawyers, Jewish Pub. Soc. (pres. 1973-76, trustee 1955—), Nat. Legal Aid and Defender Assn. (dir., mem. exec. com. 1970-80), Order of Coif. Clubs: Harvard, Varsity (Phila.). Antitrust, Federal civil litigation, Communications. Home: Parkway Houst 2201 Pennsylvania Ave Philadelphia PA 19130 Office: Schnader Harrison Segal & Lewis 1600 Market St Suite 3600 Philadelphia PA 19103

SHEVLIN, BRIAN CHARLES, lawyer; b. N.Y.C., May 12, 1940; s. Charles Joseph and Kathleen Gertrude (Walsh) S.; m. Rose Marie Schneider, Mar. 19, 1965; children: Michael, Meaghan, Maureen, Matthew. BA, U. Notre Dame, 1962, BS, 1963; JD, Am. U., 1969. Bar: Va. 1969, D.C. 1973. Pros. atty. Commonwealth Attys. Office, Arlington, Va., 1970-73; assoc. Doherty, Sheridan, Fairfax, Va., 1973-76, ptnr., 1976-80; ptnr. Shevlin, Artz & Curtis, Arlington, 1980—; malpractice panelist Supreme Ct. Va., 1983—. Tchr. Saint Leos, Fairfax, 1982-83. Served to 1st lt. U.S. Army, 1963-66. Mem. ABA, Am. Trial Lawyers Assn., Va. Trial Lawyers Assn., Commonwealth Attys. Assn., Va. Bar Assn., D.C. Bar Assn. Republican. Roman Catholic. Avocations: golf, tennis, running. Personal injury, Insurance, Federal civil litigation. Office: Shevlin Artz & Curtis 1700 N Moore St #1010 Arlington VA 22209

SHEWARD, RICHARD S., lawyer; b. Jackson, Ohio, May 21, 1944; s. D.J. and M.A. (Rapp) S.; m. Kathryn L. Wagner, Sept. 26, 1975; children—Carrin E., Alison M. B.B.A., Ohio U., 1967; J.D., Capital U., 1974. Bar: Ohio 1974, U.S. Dist. Ct. (so. dist.) Ohio 1975, U.S. Supreme Ct. 1978. Asst. pros. atty. Franklin County (Ohio), 1974-76; ptnr. Sheward & Weiner, Columbus, Ohio, 1976—; instr. real estate law Columbus Tech. Inst., 1977-80. Mem. Upper Arlington (Ohio) Civic Assn.; mem. Franklin County Republican Central Com., 1978—. Served with U.S. Army, 1968-71. Decorated Bronze Star, Air medal. Mem. ABA, Ohio Bar Assn., Columbus Bar Assn. (common please ct., chmn. criminal law com. 1985-86, 86-87), Franklin County Trial Lawyers Assn. (pres. 1984-85), Am. Arbirtation Assn. (labor panel), Franklin County Pros. Atty. Alumni Assn. (chmn. 1979—) Republican. Methodist. Clubs: Buckeye Rep. (pres. 1981), Touchdown, Agonis, Charity Newsies. Lodge: Masons (32 deg.). Criminal, Real property, Contracts commercial. Home: 3086 Leeds Rd Upper Arlington OH 43221 Office: 743 S Front St Columbus OH 43206

SHIBLEY, RAYMOND NADEEM, lawyer; b. State College, Pa., Oct. 7, 1925; s. Jabir and Adma (Hammam) S.; m. Jean Alene Phillips, Mar. 10, 1951 (dec. Oct. 1979). B.S. in Chemistry, Pa. State U., 1947; LL.B., Yale U., 1950. Bar: D.C. 1951, U.S. Supreme Ct. 1960. Ptnr. Steptoe & Johnson, Washington, 1950-60; ptnr. Patterson, Belknap, Farmer & Shibley, Washington, 1960-70, Farmer, Shibley, McGuinn & Flood, Washington, 1970-80, LeBoeuf, Lamb & MacRae, Washington, 1980—; gen. counsel Panhandle Eastern Corp., Houston, 1968-74. Mem. exec. com. Nat. Campaign for Pa. State U., 1985—, chmn. mid. Atlantic region. Served as lt. j.g. U. S. Maritime Service, 1944-46. Mem. ABA (council pub. utilities sect.), Fed. Energy Bar Assn. (pres. 1973-74), Order of Coif, Phi Lambda Upsilon, Phi Delta Phi, Alpha Chi Sigma. Republican. Presbyterian. Clubs: City Tavern, Yale of Washington (Washington). Federal civil litigation, FERC practice, Public utilities. Home: 2240 Decatur Pl NW Washington DC 20008 Office: LeBoeuf Lamb Leiby & & MacRae 1333 New Hampshire Ave NW Washington DC 20036

SHIELDS, FRANCIS EDWARD, lawyer; b. Phila., Apr. 1, 1919; s. Daniel J. and Sara (McNamee) S.; m. Margaret P. O'Shaughnessy, Sept. 19, 1944; children—Maureen F. Manion, Donna Marie Kausek, Agnes Finigan, Meg, Frank Jr. B.A., Temple U., 1947, LL.B., 1951. Bar: Pa. 1952, U.S. Dist. Ct. Pa. 1952, U.S. Supreme Ct. 1962. Law clk Supreme Ct. Pa., Phila., 1951-52; ptnr. Pepper, Hamilton & Scheetz, Phila., 1953—. Contbr. articles to profl. jours. Pres. Lower Merion Fedn. Civic Assns., 1970-71; pres., bd. dirs. Neighborhood Club Bala Cynwyd, Pa., 1960-70. Served to 1st lt. USAF, 1942, 46, PTO. Decorated Air medal with five oak leaf clusters, five battle stars. Fellow Am. Coll. Trial Lawyers; mem. Internat. Assn. Ins. Counsel, Phila. Def. Assn., Pa. Def. Inst., ABA, Pa. Bar. Assn., Phila. Bar Assn., Brehon Soc. Republican. Roman Catholic. Club: Union League (Phila.). Avocation: golf. Federal civil litigation, State civil litigation, Personal injury. Home: 815 Larkspur Ln Penn Valley PA 19072 Office: Pepper Hamilton Scheetz 2001 The Fidelity Bldg Philadelphia PA 19109

SHIELDS, JEFFREY WESTON, lawyer; b. Salt Lake City, Mar. 14, 1955; s. Jed W. and Shirlee (Hurst) S.; m. Carla Ann Collram, Dec. 4, 1980; 1 child, Lauren Marie. BS, U. Utah, 1977; JD, Pepperdine U., 1980. Bar: Utah 1980, U.S. Dist. Ct. Utah 1980, U.S. Supreme Ct. 1986. Ptnr. Shields, Shields & Holmgren, Salt Lake City, 1980-86; assoc. gen. counsel Comml. Security Bank, Salt Lake City, 1986—. Author: Commercial Laws of Utah, 1985. Mem. Comml. Law League Am. (sustaining), Assn. Trial Lawyers Am. (supporting), Utah Trial Lawyers Assn., Am. Inst. Banking, Alpha Kappa Psi (bd. dirs. dist. 1983—), Pepperdine U. Alumni Assn. (pres. Salt Lake City chpt. 1983—). Republican. Mormon. Club: Salt Lake City Track. Avocations: long distance running, tennis. General corporate, Federal civil litigation, State civil litigation. Office: Comml Security Bank 50 S Main Suite 2011 Salt Lake City UT 84144

SHIELDS, KAREN BETHEA, lawyer; b. Raleigh, N.C., Apr. 29, 1949; d. Bryant William and Grace Louise (Parrish) Bethea; m. Kenneth R. Galloway, 1971 (div. 1976); m. Linwood B. Shields, Dec. 1984. A.B. in Psychology, East Carolina U., 1971; J.D., Duke U., 1974. Bar: N.C. 1974. Ptnr., Paul, Keenan, Rowan & Galloway, Durham, N.C., 1974-77, Loflin, Loflin, Galloway, Leary & Acker, Durham, 1977-80; ct. judge 14th Judicial Dist., Durham, N.C., 1980-85; sole practice, Durham, 1986—; mem. faculty Nat. Inst. Trial Advocacy. Recipient Cert. of Recognition, City of Detroit, 1975; recipient Cert. of Appreciation N.C. State Assn. Black Social Workers, 1979; Disting. Achievement award NAACP, 1981. Mem. ABA, Am. Judicature Soc., Nat. Conf. Black Lawyers (Lawyer of Yr. 1977), Nat. Assn. Black Women Attys., N.C. Bar Assn., N.C. Acad. Trial Lawyers, Nat. Assn. Women Judges. Democrat. Baptist. Criminal, Juvenile, Family and matrimonial. Home and Office: 3525 Mayfair Rd Durham NC 27707

SHIELDS, LLOYD NOBLE, lawyer; b. Longview, Tex., Dec. 11, 1951; s. Lloyd Leon and Carolyn Lynch (Noble) S.; m. Lynn Ellen Hufft, June 15, 1974; children—Carolyn Elise, Ellen Lynch, Audrie Menville. B. Arch., Tulane U., 1974, J.D., 1977. Bar: La. 1977, U.S. Dist. Ct. (ea., we. and mid. dists.) La., U.S. Ct. Appeals (5th cir.) 1978, U.S. Patent Office 1981. Law clk. Civil Dist. Ct., New Orleans, 1977-78; assoc. Deutsch, Kerrigan & Stiles, New Orleans, 1978-79; ptnr. Simon, Peragine, Smith & Redfearn, New Orleans, 1979—; instr. New Orleans Bar Review, Inc., 1980—, Loyola U. Law Sch., 1987—. Bd. dirs. Preservation Resource Ctr., New Orleans, 1983—, pres. 1986—. Mem. ABA (chmn. automobile law com. torts and ins. practice sect. 1984-85), Am. Arbitration Assn. (constrn. industry panel). Presbyterian. Construction, Federal civil litigation, State civil litigation. Office: Simon Peragine Smith & Redfearn 3000 Energy Ctr New Orleans LA 70163

SHIELDS, PERRY, judge; b. Townsend, Tenn., Jan. 12, 1925; s. Fred David and Alice Elizabeth (Dorsey) S.; m. Bonnie Manning Davis, Nov. 1, 1951; children: Bailey Davis, Leslie, Beth. LL.B., Duke U., 1950. Bar: Tenn. 1950, U.S. Ct. Appeals (6th cir.) 1973, U.S. Supreme Ct. 1981. Revenue agt. IRS, Knoxville, Tenn., 1950-52, tax atty. office chief counsel, Washington, Atlanta and Greensboro, N.C., 1952-56; sole practice, Knoxville, 1956-58, Chattanooga, 1958-60; ptnr. Stone & Bozeman, Knoxville, 1960-63, Ford & Shields, Knoxville, 1963-70, Shields, Rainwater & Humble, Knoxville, 1970-82; judge U.S. Tax Ct., Washington, 1982—; trustee Tenn. Fed. Tax Inst., 1963-64. Served with U.S. Army, 1943-45. Mem. Nat. Lawyers Club, Tenn. Bar Assn. (past chmn. tax sect.). Republican. Baptist. Club: LeConte (Knoxville). Corporate taxation, Estate taxation, Personal income taxation. Home: 5506 Holston Dr Knoxville TN 37914 Office: US Tax Ct 400 Second St NW Washington DC 20217 *

SHIELDS, ROBERT LLOYD, III, lawyer; b. Birmingham, Ala., Oct. 19, 1945; s. Robert L. and Patricia M. (Lavette) S.; m. Bonnie L. Murray, June 30, 1968; children: Erin, Robyn, Rebecca. BS, U. Ala., 1967; JD cum laude, Samford U., 1975. Bar: Ala. 1975, U.S. Dist. Ct. (no. and so. dist.) Ala. 1975, U.S. Ct. Appeals (5th and 11th cirs.) 1975. Sole practice Birmingham, 1975-82; assoc. Balch & Bingham, Birmingham, 1982-87, Berkowitz, Lefkovits, Isom & Kushner, Birmingham, 1987—. Served to lt. USN, 1967-71. Mem. ABA, Ala. Bar Assn., Birmingham Bar Assn., Assn. Trial Lawyers Am., Am. Bankruptcy Inst. Baptist. Bankruptcy, Federal civil litigation, State civil litigation. Home: 3468 Birchwood Ln Birmingham AL 35243 Office: Berkowitz Lefkovits Isom & Kushner 1100 Financial Ctr Birmingham AL 35201

SHIELDS, WILLIAM GILBERT, lawyer; b. Charleston, W.Va., June 11, 1945; s. Alston Burkley and Marguerite Louise (Gilbert) S.; m. Linda Jeanne May, Oct. 4, 1968; children—William Gilbert, Jr. and Robert Alston. B.A., U. N.C., 1967; J.D., U. Va., 1974. Bar: Va. 1974, U.S. Dist. Ct. (ea. and we. dists.) Va. 1975, U.S. Ct. Appeals (4th cir.) 1975, U.S. Supreme Ct. 1980. Law clk. Supreme Ct. of Va., Richmond, 1974-75; assoc. atty. May, Miller & Parsons, Richmond, 1975-78; ptnr. Beale, Eichner, Wright, Denton & Shields, Richmond, 1978-83, Anderson, Parkerson & Shields, Richmond, 1983—; guest lectr. Va. Commonwealth U., Richmond, 1978-81, Va. Welfare Dept., Richmond, 1984—, tort seminar Va. Trial Lawyers Assn., 1987—. Chmn., Central Richmond Jaycee's Venereal Disease Project, 1975; mem. Richmond Democratic Com., 1978-79; vol. for Juvenile and Domestic Relations Ct. After Care Program, 1978-81; mem. parish council St. Peters Ch., Richmond, 1979-81. Served to 1st lt. U.S. Army, 1968-72. Named An Outstanding Young Man of Am., Jaycees, 1976, 80. Roman Catholic. Personal injury, Federal civil litigation, State civil litigation. Home: 13531 Kingsmill Rd Midlothian VA 23113 Office: Anderson Parkerson Shields PO Box 7439 3437 W Cary St Richmond VA 23221

SHIELDS, WILLIAM HENRY, lawyer; b. Walland, Tenn., Apr. 11, 1929; s. John Elmer and Matilda Belle (Williams) S.; m. Jeane Ione Pelton, Oct. 12, 1952; children: David William, Kathy Jean. BA, Maryville Coll., 1950; JD, U. Tenn., 1953. Bar: U.S. Dist. Ct. (ea. dist.) Tenn. 1963, Fla. 1964, U.S. Tax Ct. 1956, U.S. Dist. Ct. (mid. and so. dists.) Fla. 1964, U.S. Supreme Ct. 1966, U.S. Ct. Appeals (5th cir.) 1967. Sole practice Maryville, Tenn., 1953-63; ptnr. Pavese, Shields et al, Ft. Myers, Fla., 1963—; chmn. 2d Jud. Nominating Com., 1976-82. Contbr. articles to profl. jours. Mem. Lee County Indsl. Devel. Authority, Ft. Myers, 1976—; chmn. Lee County Port Adv. Com., 1970-81; chmn. bd. trustees First Presbyn. Ch., Ft. Myers. Mem. Fla. Bar Assn. (pres. Lee County chpt. 1981-82), Tenn. Bar Assn. (pres. Blount County chpt. 1961-62). Republican. Presbyterian. Club: U.S. Power Squadron (Ft. Myers). Lodge: Masons. Avocations: sailing, baseball, piano. Bankruptcy, Federal civil litigation, Personal injury. Home: 1399 Whiskey Creek Dr Fort Myers FL 33907 Office: Pavese Shields et al 1833 Hendry St Fort Myers FL 33902

SHIELY, JOHN STEPHEN, lawyer; b. St. Paul, June 19, 1952; s. Vincent Robert and Mary Elizabeth (Hope) S.; m. Helen Jane Pauly, Aug. 29, 1981; 1 child, Michael. B.B.A. in Acctg., U. Notre Dame, 1974; J.D., Marquette U., 1977. Bar: Wis. 1977, U.S. Dist. Ct. (ea. and we. dists.) Wis. 1977. Sr. assoc. Arthur Andersen & Co., Milw., 1977-79, Hughes Hubbard & Reed, N.Y.C. and Milw., 1979-83; asst. sec. Allen-Bradley Co., Milw., 1983-86; asst. gen. counsel Rockwell Internat. Corp., Milw. and Pitts., 1985-86; gen. counsel Briggs & Stratton Corp., Milw., 1986—; adj. lectr. in law Marquette Univ., Milw., 1986—. Vice chmn. St. Charles Boys' Home, Milw., 1978—; mem. planned giving com. Arthritis Found., Milw., 1980-86; chmn. Wauwatosa (Wis.) Bd. Tax Rev., 1984-87. Mem. Wis. Bar Assn., ABA, Milw. Bar Assn., Am. Corp. Counsel Assn. (pres., bd. dirs. Wis. chpt. 1984—). General corporate, Pension, profit-sharing, and employee benefits, Corporate taxation. Home: 15270 Briaridge Ct Elm Grove WI 53122 Office: Briggs & Stratton Corp PO Box 702 Milwaukee WI 53201

SHIFF, ALAN HOWARD WILLIAM, judge; b. New Haven, June 2, 1934; s. Philip Robert and Harriet (Panikoff) S.; divorce; children—Daniel Stuart, Andrew Reuben; m. Carol Sweeterman Brumbaugh. B.A., Yale U., 1957; LL.B., U. Va., 1960. Bar: Conn. 1960, U.S. Dist. Ct. Conn. 1960, U.S. Ct. Appeals (2d cir.) 1969. Ptnr. Shiff, Shiff and Schancupp, New Haven, 1960-81; judge U.S. Bankruptcy Ct., Dist. Conn., Bridgeport, 1981—; spl. counsel Conn. Gen. Assembly Pub. Energy and Pub. Utilities Com., 1979-80; lectr. to various bar assns., other groups Recipient cert. appreciation Pres. Lyndon B. Johnson, 1967, ofcl. citation Conn. Gen. Assembly, 1980. Mem. New Haven County Bar Assn., Conn. Bar Assn. Clubs: Mory's Assn., Quinnipiak (New Haven). Bankruptcy. Office: 319 US Courthouse 915 Lafayette Blvd Bridgeport CT 06604

SHIFFRIN, STEVEN H., law educator; b. 1941. BA, Loyola U., Chgo., 1963, JD, 1975; MA, Calif. State U., Northridge, 1964. Assoc. Irell & Manella, Los Angeles, 1976-77; acting prof. UCLA, 1977-81, prof., 1981—. Office: U Calif Sch Law 405 Hilgard Ave Los Angeles CA 90024 *

SHIFRIN, DEBRA SUE, lawyer; b. Cleve., Sept. 10, 1956; d. Alan Robert and Lois Ruth (Cohen) S.; m. Steven Howard Newman, Mar. 24, 1985. BA in Polit. Sci., Am. U., 1977; JD, Case Western Res. U., 1981. Bar: Ohio 1981, U.S. Dist. Ct. (no. dist.) Ohio 1982. Assoc. Kaufmann & Devany, Akron, Ohio, 1981-82, Moss & Friedman, Barberton, Ohio, 1982-85; sole practice Akron, 1985-86; ptnr. Whited, Pritchard and Shifrin, Akron, 1986—. Precinct person Summit County Dems., Fairlawn, Ohio, 1982-84, Akron, 1985-86; bd. dirs. Blick Clinic for Devel. Disabilities, Inc., 1982—. Recipient Young Leadership award Akron Jewish Community Fedn., 1985. Mem. ABA, Ohio Bar Assn., Akron Bar Assn., Assn. Trial Lawyers Am., Ohio Acad. Trail Lawyers. Democrat. Jewish. Avocations: singing, reading. General practice. Office: 999 N Main St Akron OH 44310

SHIHATA, IBRAHIM FAHMY IBRAHIM, lawyer, banker; b. Damietta, Egypt, Aug. 19, 1937; s. Ibrahim and Neamat (El Ashmawy) S.; m. Samia S. Farid, June 18, 1967; children—Sharif, Yasmine, Nadia. LL.B., U. Cairo, 1957, diploma in pub. law, 1958, diploma in pvt. law, 1959; S.J.D., Harvard U., 1964. Mem. Conseil d'Etat, UAR, 1957-60; mem. Tech. Bur. of Pres., UAR, 1959-60; assoc. prof. internat. law Ain-Shams U., Cairo, 1964-66, 70-72; gen. counsel Kuwait Fund for Arab Econ. Devel., 1966-70, 72-76; dir. gen. OPEC Fund for Internat. Devel., Vienna, 1976-83; exec. dir. Internat. Fund for Agrl. Devel., Rome, 1977-83; v.p., gen. counsel World Bank, Washington, 1983—; sec. gen. Internat. Centre for Settlement of Investment Disputes, Washington, 1983—; chmn. bd. Internat. Devel. Law Inst., Rome, 1983—; mem. bd. Internat. Law Inst., Washington, 1975—; bd. dirs. Internat. Fertilizer Devel. Ctr., Muscle Shoals, Ala., 1979-84; mem. internat. law adv. council Am. U., Washington, 1984—; adv. com. Research Ctr. Internat. Law, Cambridge, Eng., 1985—; founding adv. dir. Inst. Transnat. Arbitration, Houston, 1986—. Author books including: The Power of the International Court to Determine Its Own Jurisdiction, 1965; International Air and Space Law, 1966; International Joint Economic Ventures, 1969; Treatment of Foreign Investment in Egypt, 1972; The Arab Oil Embargo, 1978; The Other Face of OPEC, 1982; The OPEC Fund for International Development, The Formative Years, 1983. Decorated Grosse Silverne Ehrenzeichen am Bande fuer Verdienste (Austria); recipient Kuwait prize for sci. progress in social scis., 1983. Mem. Am. Soc. Internat. Law (exec. council 1984—), Institut de Droit Internat. (assoc.). Private international, Public international, Development finance. Office: World Bank 1818 H St NW Washington DC 20433

SHILLMAN, JEFFREY NATHANIEL, lawyer; b. Detroit, Nov. 9, 1945; s. Morris H. and Esther F. (Cantor) S.; m. Marlene R. Weinberger, May 29, 1969 (div. Oct. 1983); children: Randall, Tracey; m. Barbara Susan Feldman, Apr. 27, 1984. BA, Wayne State U., 1967, JD cum laude, 1969. Bar: Mich. 1969, U.S. Dist. Ct. (ea. dist.) Mich. 1976. Ptnr. Sommers, Schwartz, Silver & Schwartz, Southfield, Mich., 1981—; mediator Mediation Tribunal Assn., Detroit, Oakland County Circuit Court, Pntiac. Mem. ABA, Met. Detroit Trial Lawyers Assn. (pres.), Oakland County Trial Lawyers Assn. (pres.), Mich. Trial Lawyers Assn. (pres. 1980-81), Southfield Bar Assn. (v.p.), Assn. Trial Lawyers Am., Oakland County Bar Assn. Jewish. Personal injury, State civil litigation. Home: 7137 Pebble Park Dr West Bloomfield MI 48033 Office: Sommers Schwartz Silver & Schwartz 26555 Evergreen Rd Suite 1800 Southfield MI 48076

SHIMER, CHARLES PURINTON, lawyer; b. Exeter, N.H., Dec. 7, 1956; s. Stanley Reiss and Helen (Purinton) S.; m. Leslie Ann Sciarra, Aug. 11, 1979. AB with high honors, Coll. William and Mary, 1978; MBA, JD magna cum laude, Boston Coll., 1982. Bar: Va. 1982. Assoc. Hunton & Williams, Richmond, Va., 1982-86, Hayes & Smith P.C., Richmond, 1986—. Del. Norfolk (Va.) State Rep. Conv., 1985. Mem. ABA, Richmond Bar Assn., Chesterfield County Bar Assn., Nat. Assn. Bond Lawyers, Order of Coif, Richmond Jaycees. Presbyterian. Club: Richmond First. Avocations: boating, golf, hiking. Corporate taxation, Estate taxation, Municipal bonds. Home: 8349 Charlise Rd Richmond VA 23235 Office: Hayes & Smith PC 1001 Chinaberry Blvd Suite 340 Richmond VA 23225

SHIMM, MELVIN G., legal educator; b. 1926. A.B., Columbia U., 1947; J.D., Yale U., 1950. Bar: N.Y. 1950. Assoc., Cahill, Gordon, Zachry & Reindel, N.Y.C., 1950-51; atty. Wage Stblzn. Bd., Washington, 1951-52; Bigelow fellow U. Chgo., 1952-53; asst. prof. Duke U. Law Sch., Durham, N.C., 1953-56, assoc. prof., 1956-59, prof., 1959—, assoc. dean, 1978-83; vis. prof. U. Mich., Ann Arbor, 1973, U. Tex.-Austin, 1976; chmn. Durham (N.C.) Bd. Adjustment, 1966-70; dir. Orientation Program in Am. Law, 1968-70; cons. The Brookings Instn., 1965-67. Served to lt. U.S. Army. 1943-46. Mem. Order of Coif, Phi Beta Kappa. Editor-in-chief Law & Contemporary Problems, Jour. Legal Edn., Yale Law Jour., Am. Edn. Jour. Bus. Law. Legal education. Office: Duke U Sch Law Durham NC 27706

SHIMOFF, PAUL MARTIN, lawyer; b. San Francisco, Nov. 1, 1947; s. Marcus and Louise Barbara (Jacobs) S.; m. Susan Louise Richmond, Aug. 27, 1972; children: Aaron, Jared. AB, UCLA, 1969; JD, U. Calif., San Francisco, 1972. Bar: Calif. 1972, U.S. Dist. Ct. (so. and cen. dists.) 1972, U.S. Ct. Appeals (9th cir.) 1972, U.S. Tax Ct. 1973, U.S. Ct. Claims 1973; cert. specialist in taxation law Calif. Bd. Legal Specialization. Ptnr. McPeters, McAlearney & Shimoff, San Bernardino, Calif., 1985—. Bd. dirs. San Bernardino Legal Aid Soc., 1985-86; advisor San Bernardino Community Law-Related Edn., 1985; bd. dirs. Inland Empire Symphony, San Bernardino, 1981. Mem. San Bernardino County Bar Assn. (pres. 1985-86), Estate Planning Council for San Bernardino County (pres. 1985-86), Calif. Bd. Legal Specialization (cert.). Personal income taxation, Estate taxation, Corporate taxation. Home: 12912 Hilary Way Redlands CA 92373 Office: 290 N D St Suite 303 San Bernardino CA 92401

SHINALL, ROBERT PHILLIP, III, lawyer; b. Atlanta, Jan. 20, 1947; s. Robert P. Jr. and Alice Weekes (Clements) S.; m. Ellen Greer Thomas, Dec. 5, 1970; children: Wimberly Greer, Robert Phillip IV, Alice Weekes. BA, Vanderbilt U., 1969; MBA, Ga. State U., 1973; LLB, Emory U., 1975. Bar: Ga. 1976, U.S. Dist. Ct. (no. dist.) Ga. 1976, Fla. 1976, U.S. Ct. Appeals (5th and 11th cirs.) 1976. From assoc. to ptnr. Weekes & Canler, Decatur, Ga., 1976—; bd. dirs. Fidelity Nat. Bank, Atlanta. Bd. dirs. DeKalb Community Coll. Found., North Atlanta Club Area Civic Assn., 1984-86; adminstrv. bd. dirs. Northside United Meth. Ch., Atlanta, 1984—. Served to capt. U.S. Army, 1969-73. Clubs: Capital City, Lawyers, German (Atlanta). Lodge: Rotary (bd. dirs. 1984—). Avocations: golf, tennis, fishing. State civil litigation, Workers' compensation, Personal injury. Home: 2655 Rivers Rd NW Atlanta GA 30305 Office: Weekes & Candler 150 E Ponce de Leon Ave Suite 300 Decatur GA 30030

SHINKLE, JOHN THOMAS, lawyer; b. Albany, N.Y., May 9, 1946; s. Robert Thomas and Margery Joan (Kneip) S.; m. Csilla Elizabeth Bekasy, Sept. 2, 1967; children—Reka, Ildiko. B.A., Yale U., 1967; J.D., Harvard U., 1970. Bar: D.C. 1971, U.S. Supreme Ct. 1974, N.Y. 1983. Law clk. U.S. Ct. Appeals for D.C. Circuit, Washington, 1970-71; assoc. Caplin & Drysdale, Washington, 1971-77, ptnr., 1977-80; assoc. dir. div. corp. fin. SEC, Washington, 1980-81, dep. gen. counsel, 1981-82; v.p., gen. counsel Salomon Bros. Inc., N.Y.C., 1982—. Contbr. articles to profl. jours. Mem. ABA, Assn. Bar City N.Y., Securities Industry Assn. (fed. regulation com.), Futures Industry Assn. (law and compliance div.). Club: Downtown Athetic (N.Y.C.). General corporate, Administrative and regulatory. Home: 16 Cove Rd Old Greenwich CT 06870 Office: Salomon Bros Inc One New York Plaza New York NY 10004

SHINN, CLINTON WESLEY, lawyer; b. Haworth, Okla., Mar. 7, 1947; s. Clinton Elmo and Mary Lucille (Dowdy) S.; m. Beverly Ann Laborde, Jan.

20, 1968; children: Laura Kathryn, Clinton Wesley Jr. BS, McNeese State U., 1969; JD, Tulane U., 1972; LLM, Harvard U., 1973. Bar: La. 1972, U.S. Dist. Ct. (ea. dist.) La. 1975, U.S. Dist. Ct. (we. dist.) La. 1980, U.S. Ct. Appeals (5th cir.) 1981, U.S. Ct. Appeals (11th cir.) 1982, U.S. Tax Ct. (1982). Asst. prof. law Tulane U., New Orleans, 1973-75; assoc. Stone, Pigman et al, New Orleans, 1975-78, ptnr., 1979—; Editor Tulane Law Rev., 1971-72. Mem. Nat. Rep. Com., Washington, 1980—; fund raiser Mandeville (La.) Leukemia Found.; mem. Christ Episcopal Sch. PTA, Covington, La., 1985—. Served to capt. USAR, 1969-77. Mem. ABA, La. Bar Assn., New Orleans Bar Assn., Order of Coif, Assn. Employee Benefit Planners for New Orleans, Assn. Henri Capitant, Nat. Wildlife Fedn. (life). Avocations: backpacking, gardening. Probate, General corporate, Environment. Home: 195 Beau Rivage Dr Mandeville LA 70448 Office: Stone Pigman Walther Wittman & Hutchinson 546 Carondelet St New Orleans LA 70130

SHIPMAN, MARK SAMUEL, lawyer; b. Hartford, Conn., Apr. 16, 1937; s. Paul David and Reeva (Joseph) S.; m. Sonia S. Sosensky, Aug. 28, 1960; children—Paul, Lawrence, William. B.A., U. Conn. Hartford, 1959, LL.B., 1962. Bar: Conn. 1962, U.S. Dist. Ct. Conn. 1963, U.S. Ct. Appeals (2d cir.) 1967, U.S. Supreme Ct. 1973. Assoc. Schatz & Schatz, Hartford, 1962-64; asst. state's atty. State of Conn., 1964-66; ptnr. Schatz & Schatz, Ribicoff & Kotkin, Hartford, 1967—. Mem. Greater Hartford Transp. Dist., 1973-86, chmn., 1978-86; mem. council Town of Newington (Conn.), 1966-68, 73-75; mem. Bd. of Edn., Newington, 1979-81; town atty., Newington, 1975-77, 81-86; sec., vice-chmn. state commn. Med. Legal Investing, 1986—; chmn. Charter Rev. Commn., Newington, 1969, 71. Mem. ABA, Conn. Bar Assn., Hartford County Bar Assn., Assn. Trial Lawyers Am., Conn. Trial Lawyers Assn., Am. Acad. Forensic Sci. (chmn. juris sect. 1977, exec. com. 1980-83, v.p. 1983-84), Nat. Def. Lawyers Assn. Democrat. Jewish. Clubs: Lions, Tumblebrook Country, Masons. State civil litigation, Federal civil litigation, Administrative and regulatory. Home: 83 Kenmore Rd Bloomfield CT 06002 Office: 1 Financial Plaza Hartford CT 06103

SHIPP, H(AMILTON) THOMAS, lawyer, banker; b. Bullard, Tex., Feb. 19, 1941; s. James Joseph and Julia Jewell (Goldman) S.; m. Shirley Ann Moore, Jan. 2, 1965; children—Laura, Rhonda. B.S., S.F. Austin State U., 1964; J.D., U. Houston, 1970. Bar: Tex. 1971, U.S. Dist. Ct. (so. dist.) Tex. 1975, U.S. Supreme Ct. 1975, U.S. Ct. Appeals (5th cir.) 1978. Bank examiner FDIC, Tyler, Tex., 1965-66; claims rep. HEW, Pasadena, Tex., 1966-71; v.p., gen. counsel Houston Bank for Coops., Houston, 1971-79; prin., atty. H. Tom Shipp & Assocs., Houston, 1979—; dir. First City Bank, North Belt, Houston; nat. chmn. 37 Farm Credit Banks Com.; expert witness, corp. fin. Bd. dirs. Family Time Found., Kingwood, Tex., 1984—. Mem. ABA, Houston Bar Assn. State Bar Tex., Tex. Trial Lawyers Assn., Greenspoint Exchange Club, Houston Northwest C. of C. (dir. 1982—, Pres.'s Club award 1984). Republican. Methodist. Clubs: Kingwood Country; Greenspoint (Houston). Bankruptcy, General corporate, Real property. Home: 3002 Forest Laurel Dr Kingwood TX 77339 Office: H Tom Shipp & Assocs PC 333 North Belt Suite 240 Houston TX 77060

SHIPP, JOHN E., lawyer; b. Oklahoma City, Aug. 6, 1942; s. Edward Monroe and Margaret (Craig) S.; m. Barbara Jo Gaines, Sept. 28, 1961; children: Brian, Susan, Beth Ann. LLB, Okla. U., 1966. Bar: Okla. 1966, U.S. Dist. Ct. (ea. and we. dists.) Okla., U.S. Dist. Ct. (we. dist.) Tex., U.S. Dist. Ct. (ea. dist.) Ark., U.S. Ct. Appeals (10th cir.). Ptnr. Shipp & deWitt, Idabel, Okla., 1966—. Mem. ABA, Okla. Bar Assn. (bd. govs. 1981-83, pres. 1985—), McCurtain County Bar Assn. (pres. 1970-76), Idabel C. of C. Democrat. Presbyterian. Office: Shipp & DeWitt 100 North Central Idabel OK 74745

SHIRAISHI, SHERMAN T., lawyer; b. Waimea, Hawaii, Sept. 8, 1954; s. Clinton Ikuzo and Fumiko (Okada) S.; m. Molly E. Kuboyama, Aug. 12, 1978; children: Mari, Mia. BA, U. Hawaii, 1976; JD, John Marshall Law Sch., 1979. Bar: Hawaii 1979, U.S. Dist. Ct. Hawaii 1979. Ptnr. Shiraishi & Yamada, Lihue, Hawaii, 1979—. State dir., v.p. Easter Seal Soc. Hawaii, Honolulu, 1985. Named One of Outstanding Young Men of Am., U.S. Jaycees, 1984. Mem. ABA, Hawaii Bar Assn, Jaycees (bd. dirs. Lihue chpt.). Lodge: Kiwanis. General corporate, Probate, Real property. Home: 2909 Ohiohi St Lihue HI 96766 Office: PO Box 1246 Lihue HI 96766

SHIRE, HAROLD RAYMOND, legal educator, author; b. Denver, Nov. 23, 1910; s. Samuel Newport and Rose Betty (Herrmann) S.; m. Cecilia Goldhaar; children: Margaret, David, Donna, Darcy, Esti. M.B.A., Pepperdine U., 1972; LL.D. (hon.), 1975; J.D., Southwestern U., Los Angeles, 1974; M.Liberal Arts, U. So. Calif., 1977; Ph.D. in Human Behavior, U.S. Internat. U., San Diego, 1980. Bar: Calif. 1937, U.S. Dist. Ct. (so. dist.) Calif. 1939, U.S. Supreme Ct. 1978. Dep. dist. atty. Los Angeles County, Calif., 1937-38; asst. U.S. atty. So. Dist. Calif., Los Angeles and San Diego, Justice Dept., 1939-42; sole practice, Los Angeles, 1946-56; pres., chmn. bd. Gen. Connectors Corp., U.S. and Eng., 1956-73; prof. mgmt. and law Pepperdine U., Malibu, Calif., 1974-75, U.S. Internat. U., San Diego, 1980-83; dir. Bestobell Aviation, Eng., 1970-74. Bd. dirs. Pepperdine U., 1974-80; nat. bd. govs. Union Orthodox Jewish Congregations Am., 1973—. Served with U.S. Army, 1942-46. Author: Cha No Yu and Symbolic Interactionism: Method of Predicting Japanese Behavior, 1980; The Tea Ceremony, 1984. Patentee aerospace pneumatics; invented flexible connectors. Decorated chevalier du vieux moulin (France); companion Royal Aero. Soc. (U.K.). Mem. Am. Legion (service officer). Republican. Jurisprudence, Legal education, Japanese. Office: PO Box 1352 Beverly Hills CA 90213

SHIRLEY, JAMES THEO, JR., lawyer; b. Charleston, S.C., Feb. 14, 1943; s. James Theo Sr. and Martha (McCrary) S.; m. Patricia Devlin, May 7, 1966; children: Elizabeth Jane, Jennifer Ann, Heather Marie. BS, U.S. Merchant Marine Acad., 1965; JD, Rutgers U., 1981. Bar: N.J. 1981, U.S. Dist. Ct. N.J. 1981, U.S. Dist. Ct. N.Y. 1982, N.Y. 1982. Assoc. Haight, Gardner, Poor & Havens, N.Y.C., 1981—. Served to lt. USNR, 1965-75. Mem. ABA, Fed. Bar Council, Council Am. Master Mariners. Republican. Mormon. Club: Downton Athletic (N.Y.C.). Avocations: sailing, motor boating, water skiing, travel, family camping. Admiralty. Home: 28 Brophy Dr Trenton NJ 08638 Office: Haight Gardner Poor & Havens 195 Broadway New York NY 10007

SHIRLEY, RAYMOND ANDREW, JR., lawyer; b. Sheffield, Ala., Oct. 5, 1947; s. Raymond Andrew and Patricia Anne (Myers) S.; m. Jane Francis Perla, July 25, 1970 (div. 1979); children—Stephen Andrew, Michael Andrew; m. Anita Katherine Ray, Dec. 29, 1979 (div. 1986); children—John Christopher, Mark Aaron. B.S., U. Tenn., 1969, J.D., 1977. Bar: Tenn. 1977, U.S. Dist. Ct. (ea. dist.) Tenn. 1981, U.S. Ct. Appeals (6th cir.) 1981. Asst. dist. atty. gen. 2d Jud. Cir. Ct., Sevierville, Tenn., 1977-80, Knox County Atty. Gens. Office, Knoxville, 1980-81; mem. firm Lockett, Slovis & Weaver, 1981—. Knox County Jud. Commr., 1982. Served to lt. (j.g.) USN, 1969-74. Mem. ABA, Am. Assn. Trial Lawyers, Tenn. Trial Lawyers Assn. Methodist. Personal injury, Workers' compensation, Criminal. Home: 1704 Loflin Circle Knoxville TN 37919 Office: Lockett Slovis & Weaver 626 Market St Knoxville TN 37922

SHIRLEY, ROBERT PRESTON, lawyer; b. Ft. Worth, Nov. 14, 1912; s. James Preston and Nevra (Boykin) S.; student Tex. Christian U., 1928-30; LL.B., U. Tex., 1933; m. Elizabeth Hodgson, Nov. 13, 1936; children—Susan E. Shirley Eckel, Carolyn D. Shirley Wimberly, Sarah J. Shirley-White. Bar: Tex. 1933. Partner firm Boykin, Ray & Shirley, Ft. Worth, 1933-36; assoc. prof. law U. Tex., Austin, 1936-40; partner firm Kelley & Looney, Edinburg, Tex., 1940-41, Holloway, Hudson & Shirley, Ft. Worth, 1945-47, Mills, Shirley, McMicken & Eckel, Galveston, Tex., 1947—; sr. chmn. bd. InterFirst Bank Galveston, N.A.; dir. Am. Indemnity Co., Am. Fire & Indemnity Co., Tex. Gen. Indemnity Co.. Mem. U. Tex. Devel. Bd., Austin, chmn., 1965-66, 66-67; mem. devel. bd. U. Tex. Med. Br., Galveston, 1967—; pres. First Bapt. Found., Galveston. Chmn. Galveston Charter Rev. Commn., 1968, 72, mem., 74, 1970; mem. Planning Commn. City of Galveston, 1961-69; mem. Tex. Constl. Revision Commn., 1973—; mem. Gov.'s Task Force on Higher Edn., 1981; bd. dirs., exec. v.p. Sealy & Smith Found. for John-Sealy Hosp., Galveston; bd. dirs. U. Tex. Found., Pres., 1970-72; life trustee, pres. U. Tex. Law Sch. Found.; trustee Mary Hardin Baylor Coll., Belton, Tex., 1974-78. Served from 2d lt. to lt. col., AUS, 1942-45; CBI. Named Disting. Alumnus, U. Tex., 1982; Outstanding Alumnus award U. Tex. Law Sch., 1984. Fellow Am. Coll. Trial Lawyers, Am. Coll. Probate Counsel, Am. Bar Found., Tex. Bar Found. (Outstanding 50-yr. Lawyer 1983); mem. Tex. Assn. Def. Counsel (pres. 1963-64), Galveston County (pres. 1954-55), ABA, State Bar Tex. (com. adminstrn. justice 1952-72), Internat. Assn. Ins. Counsel, Assn. Ins. Attys., Order of Coif, Phi Delta Phi, Phi Kappa Psi. Club: Galveston Arty. State civil litigation, Oil and gas leasing, Personal injury. Home: 39 Colony Park Circle Galveston TX 77551 Office: 2228 Mechanic Galveston TX 77550

SHIYOU, ORVIS A., JR., lawyer, bank executive; b. Bay Saint Louis, Miss., June 7, 1955; s. Orvis A. and Lola A. (Sorey) S. AA, Copiah-Lincoln Jr. Coll., 1975; BS, U. So. Miss., 1977; JD, Miss. Coll., 1982. Bar: Miss. 1982, U.S. Dist. Ct. (so. dist.) Miss. 1982. Agt. State of Miss., Jackson, 1977-81, Nationwide Ins. Co., Jackson, 1981-82; staff counsel, trust officer, v.p. Trustmark Nat. Bank, Hattiesburg, Miss., 1982—. Named one of Outstanding Young Men in Am., 1985, 86. Mem. Miss. Bar Assn. (young lawyers sect.), Miss. Young Lawyers Assn. (south cen. bd. dirs. 1983—, local rep. 1983—, chmn. bar admissions 1986—). Baptist. Lodges: Lions (bd. dirs. 1984-86), Rotary, Masons (degree team 1985—). Probate, Contracts commercial, Banking. Home: 1705 Adeline Hattiesburg MS 39401 Office: Trustmark Nat Bank #1 Trustmark Plaza Hattiesburg MS 39401

SHKLOV, MARK THOMAS, lawyer; b. Vernon, B.C., Can., June 14, 1950; came to U.S., 1953; s. Nathan and Agnes (White) S.; m. Cheryl M. Kiyosaki, Sept. 7, 1985. Student, Sophia U., Tokyo, 1970-71; BA in English and History, Whitman Coll., 1972; JD, U. Puget Sound, 1976. Bar: Hawaii 1976, U.S. Dist. Ct. Hawaii 1976, U.S. Ct. Claims 1977, U.S. Ct. Appeals (9th cir.) 1977, U.S. Ct. Internat. Trade 1978, U.S. Ct. Appeals (fed. cir.) 1982, N.Y. 1987. From assoc. to ptnr. Shirley & Jordan, Honolulu, 1976-82; ptnr. Smith, Himmelmann & Shklov, Honolulu, 1982-86; assoc. Ezra, O'Connor, Moon & Tam, Honolulu, 1986—; broker Mark Shklov Real Estate, Honolulu, 1977—; chmn. bd. dirs. Asia-Pacific Network. Mem. ABA, Internat. Bar Assn., Hawaii Bar Assn. (chmn. internat. sect. 1985—, ad hoc com. 1985—), Asia-Pacific Lawyers Assn., Japan-Hawaii Lawyers Assn. (pres. 1981—, chmn. conv. 1985, 86). Avocations: writing, reading, sports. Consumer commercial, General corporate, Private international. Office: Ezra O'Connor Moon & Tam 220 S King St Honolulu HI 96813

SHKOLNICK, RODNEY, educator, lawyer; b. Davenport, Iowa, Dec. 3, 1931; s. Jake Sam and Jeanette Rose (Rohrbach) S.; B.A., U. Iowa, 1953, J.D., 1955; m. Lois Ann Greenblatt, Aug. 22, 1954; children—Jeffrey Mark, Stuart Craig. Admitted to Iowa bar, 1955, Nebr. bar, 1961; mem. faculty Sch. Law, Creighton U., Omaha, 1961—, asso. dean, 1972-77, dean, 1977—; partner firm McGrath, North, Nelson, Shkolnick & Dwyer, 1965-71. Served with U.S. Army, 1955-57. Mem. Am. Bar Assn., Iowa Bar Assn., Nebr. Bar Assn. Jewish. Club: Rotary. Legal education. Office: Creighton Univ Sch of Law Omaha NE 68178

SHMUKLER, STANFORD, lawyer; b. Phila., June 16, 1930; s. Samuel and Tessye (Dounne) S.; m. Anita Golove, Mar. 21, 1951; children—Jodie Lynne Shmukler Girsh, Joel Mark, Steven David. B.S. in Econs., U. Pa., 1951, J.D., 1954. Bar: D.C. 1954, Pa. 1955; U.S. Ct. Appeals (2d cir.), 1959, U.S. Supreme Ct. 1959, U.S. Ct. Appeals (3d cir.), 1960, U.S. Ct. Claims, 1966, U.S. Tax Ct., 1966, U.S. Ct. Mil. Appeals 1966. Atty., U.S. Bur. Pub. Roads, 1954-55, cons., 1955-57; sole practice, Phila., 1955—; lectr. Temple U. Law Sch., 1975-78; mem., past sec., exec. dir. crminal procedural rules com. Pa. Supreme Ct., 1971—; mem. lawyers adv. com. Ct. Appeals for 3d cir., 1977-80; selection com. Criminal Justice Act Panel, 1979-84. Bd. dirs. Ecumenical Halfway House, 1967-71. Served to col. JAGC, USAR, from 1955 (ret.). Recipient Phila. Bar Assn. Criminal Justice Sect. award, 1972; Legion of Honor, Chapel of the Four Chaplains, 1983. Mem. ABA, Pa. Bar Assn., Phila. Bar Assn. (bd. govs. 1971-73, past chmn. criminal justice com. and mil. justice com.), Fed. Bar Assn., Pa. Trial Lawyers Assn. Democrat. Jewish. Lodges: Justice Lodge, B'nai B'rith. Contbr. articles to profl. jours. Criminal. Home: 1400 Melrose Ave Melrose Park PA 19126 Office: 24th Floor Packard Bldg 15th and Chestnut Sts Philadelphia PA 19102

SHNIDERMAN, HARRY LOUIS, lawyer; b. Erie, Pa., Sept. 26, 1916; s. Frank and Sophie (Barber) S.; m. Lenore Hyman, Nov. 29, 1942; children—Craig Mitchell, Neal Barber. A.B., U. Mich., 1938; LL.B., Harvard U., 1941. Bar: D.C. bar 1941, Pa. bar 1945, U.S. Supreme Ct. bar 1945. With litigation div. OPA, 1941-44; law clk. to Justice Rutledge, U.S. Supreme Ct., 1944-45; partner firm Covington & Burling, Washington, 1945—; lectr. Continuing Legal Edn. Programs, 1955—. Author: Price Discrimination in Perspective, 1977; Contbr. articles to profl. jours. Mem. Am. Bar Assn., D.C. Bar Assn., Am. JudicatJudicature Soc., Harvard Law Sch. Assn., Phi Beta Kappa, Phi Kappa Phi, Delta Sigma Rho. Clubs: Harvard, City Tavern. Office: Covington & Burling 1201 Pennsylvania Ave NW PO Box 7566 Washington DC 20044

SHOAF, CHARLES JEFFERSON, lawyer; b. Roanoke, Va., July 22, 1930; s. Cash Jefferson and Elizabeth Wilder (Cure) S.; m. Mary LaSalle, May 30, 1958; children: Susan Elizabeth, Sarah Ann. BS in Chemistry, Va. Mil. Inst., 1952; MS, Purdue U., 1954, PhD, 1957; JD, Del. Law Sch., 1980. Bar: Pa. 1980. Research chemist E.I. du Pont, Kinston, N.C., 1957-63; patent chemist E.I. du Pont, Wilmington, Del., 1963-74, patent agt., 1974-80, patent atty., 1980-85, patent counsel, 1985—. Patentee in field, inventor epoxy adhesive. Served to capt. USAFR, 1952-65. Mem. ABA, Pa. Bar Assn., Am. Chem. Soc., Am. Intellectual Property Law Assn. Republican. Episcopalian. Avocations: photography, golf. Patent. Home: 1113 Independence Dr West Chester PA 19382 Office: EI du Pont Legal Dept Wilmington DE 19898

SHOCKEY, GARY LEE, lawyer; b. Casper, Wyo., Sept. 25, 1950; s. Bernis L. and Shirley E. (Diehl) S.; m. Dona K. Galles, June 1, 1979; children: Amber, Jeremy, Kimberly. AB in Polit. Sci. and Sociology, Yale U., 1973; JD, U. Wyo., 1976. Bar: Wyo. 1976, U.S. Dist. Ct. Wyo. 1976, U.S. Ct. Appeals (10th cir.) 1984. Pub. defender State of Wyo. and City of Casper, 1976-78; sole practice, Casper, 1976-79; assoc. Spence, Moriarty & Schuster, Casper and Jackson, Wyo., 1978-82, ptnr., Jackson, 1982—. Mem. ABA, Wyo. State Bar (continuing legal edn. com. 1984-85), Assn. Trial Lawyers Am., Wyo. Trial Lawyer's Assn. (bd. dirs. 1984-87). Personal injury, State civil litigation, Federal civil litigation. Home: 480 Wister Jackson WY 83001 Office: Spence Moriarty & Schuster PO Box 548 Jackson WY 83001

SHOCKLEY, GARY CLARK, lawyer; b. Chattanooga, May 28, 1957; s. Russell Porter and Deane (Hamby) S.; m. Penny J. White, Sept. 24, 1983. BA in History with highest honors, U. Tenn., 1979, JD with high honors, 1982. Bar: Tenn. 1982, U.S. Dist. Ct. (ea. dist.) Tenn. 1986. Law clk. to presiding justice Tenn. Ct. Appeals, Knoxville, 1982-83; trial atty. Dept. Agr., Washington, 1983-85; assoc. Baker, Worthington, Stansberry & Woolf, Johnson City, Tenn., 1985—. Contbr. articles to law jours. Adult reading tutor Johnson City Area Literacy Council, 1983; instr. mock trial competition Sequoyah Area council Boy Scouts Am., 1986. Stevens-Hoffman scholar U. Tenn., 1978-79. Mem. ABA (litigation sect.), Tenn. Bar Assn., Washington County Bar Assn. (sec. 1986). Democrat. Methodist. Avocations: guitar, writing fiction, sports. Federal civil litigation, State civil litigation, Personal injury. Office: Baker Worthington Crossley et al 207 Mockingbird Ln Johnson City TN 37601

SHOEMAKE, BRANSFORD HUNT, lawyer; b. Tulsa, Sept. 28, 1956; s. Shockley Taliaferro and Hazel Ann (Hunt) S.; m. Vickie Lynn Wright, Apr. 28, 1984; children: Jill Ann, Mandy Lynn, Jacquelyn Lauren. Student, Oxford U., Eng., 1977; BA in History, Okla. U., 1978, JD, 1981. Bar: Okla 1982, U.S. Dist. Ct. (no. dist.) Okla. 1983, U.S. Ct. Appeals (10th cir.) 1985, U.S. Supreme Ct. 1986. Legal intern Shoemake & Briggs, Pawhuska, Okla., 1980; ptnr. Shoemake & Shoemake, Pawhuska, 1981—; legal intern Cleve. County Dist. Atty.'s Office, Norman, Okla., 1980-81. V.p., bd. dirs. Osage County Youth Services, Pawhuska; pres. Tallgrass Prairie Preserve Assn., Pawhuska, 1985—; mem. Downtown Revitalization Com., Pawhuska, 1984—. Mem. ABA, Okla. Bar Assn., Osage County Bar Assn. (pres. 1984—), Assn. Trial Lawyers Am., Okla. Trial Lawyers Assn. Democrat. Baptist. Lodges: Rotary (local pres. 1984-85), Elks. Avocations: flying, golf, tennis, weightlifting. Family and matrimonial, Personal injury, Probate. Home: Box 23 6 Mile N of City Pawhuska OK 74056 Office: 106 W Main Box 177 Pawhuska OK 74056

SHOEMAKER, JAMES MARSHALL, JR., lawyer; b. La Jolla, Calif., Aug., 1932; s. James M. and Frances (Little) S.; m. Mary Hunter Sloan, Jan. 3, 1959; children—James M. III, Edward Sloan, Jonathan Evans. B.A., U. Va., 1955, J.D., 1965. Bar: S.C. 1965. Fgn. service officer U.S. Dept. State, 1958-62; with Bur. Cultural Affairs, Washington, 1958-60; vice consul Am. Embassy, Tokyo, 1960-62; mem. Wyche, Burgess, Freeman & Parham, Greenville, S.C., 1965—; dir. Palmetto Bank, Ryan's Family Steak Houses, Inc., Engineered Custom Plastics Corp., Palmetto Spinning Corp., Woven Electronics Corp. Served with USMC, 1955-58, to maj., USMCR. Bd. dirs. Greater Greenville YMCA, 1980-82; bd. dirs. Greenville Urban League, 1980-84, pres., 1983-84; chmn. City of Greenville Civil Service Commn., 1977-78; mem. Greenville City Council, 1971-73; pres. Family and Children Service, Greenville County, 1969; mem. Little Theatre Council, 1967-71; United Fund. Div. chmn. Mem. ABA, Am. Judicature Soc., S.C. Bar Assn., Greenville County Bar Assn., Greater Greenville C. of C. (bd. dirs. 1977-82, pres. 1979), S.C. C. of C. (bd. dirs. 1983-85). Republican. Episcopalian. Clubs: Greenville Country, Poinsett, Commerce, Cotillion, St. Andrews Soc. General corporate, Federal civil litigation, State civil litigation. Home: 109 Pine Forest Dr Greenville SC 29601 Office: PO Box 10207 Greenville SC 29603

SHOGAN, ALEXANDER JOE, JR., Lawyer; b. Spokane, Wash., Sept. 27, 1948; s. Alexander Joe Sr. and Eloise Marie (Slavens); m. Maureen Eileen Gordon, May 27, 1978. BS in Polit. Sci., Gonzaga U., 1970, JD, 1978. Ptnr. Gordon, Hipperson, Shogan & Devlin, Profl. Assocs., Spokane, 1978—. Chmn. Human Services Adv. Bd., Spokane, 1986, Homelessness Task Force, Spokane, 1986. Served to capt. U.S. Army, 1970-74, Vietnam, served to maj. USAR. Decorated Bronze Star with Oak Leaf Cluster, 1972. Mem. ABA, Wash. State Bar Assn., Spokane County Bar Assn. Democrat. Roman Catholic. Lodge: N.E. Kiwanis. Avocations: jogging, swimming, snow skiing, water skiing. Personal injury, Probate, Bankruptcy. Office: Gordon Hipperson et al W 24 Indiana Spokane WA 99205

SHOLEM, DAVID BENNETT, lawyer; b. Champaign, Ill., Oct. 5, 1953; s. Myron J. and Sonya M. (Ades) S.; m. Janis Mecklenburger, Oct. 27, 1979; children: James Alan, Kathryn Faye. BA, Brown U., 1975; postgrad., U. Ill., 1976-77; JD, Case Western Res. U., 1978. Bar: Ill. 1978, U.S. Dist. Ct. (cen. dist.) Ill. 1980. Assoc. Meyer, Capel, Hirschfeld, Muncy, Jahn & Aldeen P.C., Champaign, 1978-80, ptnr., 1980—. Mem. Champaign County Bar Assn. (pres. 1984-85). General corporate, Real property, Communications. Office: Meyer Capel Hirschfeld et al 306 W Church St Champaign IL 61820

SHOLK, STEVEN HOWARD, lawyer; b. Newark, July 6, 1956. BA with highest honors, Rutgers U., 1978; JD with honors, U. N.C., 1981. Bar: N.J. 1982, U.S. Ct. Claims 1984, U.S. Tax Ct. 1984, U.S. Ct. Appeals (3d cir.) 1985. Law clk. to presiding judge Appellate Div. Superior Ct. N.J., Flemington, 1981-82; assoc. Sills, Beck et al, Newark, 1982-1986, Gern, Dunetz, Davison, Borteck & Weinstein, Roseland, N.J., 1986—. Research editor N.C. Jour. Internat. Law and Comml. Regulation, 1980-81. Mem. ABA (taxation sect.), N.J. State Bar Assn., Phi Beta Kappa. Jewish. General corporate, Probate, Corporate taxation. Home: 135 Berkshire Ct Piscataway NJ 08854 Office: Gern Dunetz et al 103 Eisenhower Pkwy Roseland NJ 07068

SHOLLENBERGER, ELIZABETH ANN, legal educator; b. Alliance, Ohio, Mar. 26, 1956; d. Herbert Russell and Nancy Marie (Craven) S. AB, Princeton U., 1978; JD, Yale U., 1981. Bar: N.Y. 1982, U.S. Dist. Ct. (so. and ea. dists.) N.Y. 1983. Assoc. Rosenman, Colin, Freund, Lewis & Cohn, N.Y.C., 1981-83, Milberg, Weiss, Bershad, Specthrie & Lerach, N.Y.C., 1983-85; corp. atty. Hess, Segall, Guterman, Pelz, Steiner & Barovick, N.Y.C., 1985-86; faculty NYU Sch. Law, 1986—. Pres. Village Reform Dem. Club, N.Y.C., 1983-86; Dem. dist. leader, Greenwich Village, 1986—; mem. Community Bd. 2, N.Y.C., 1986—. Federal civil litigation, State civil litigation, Landlord-tenant. Home: 60 E 9th St Apt 533 New York NY 10003

SHOLLENBERGER, LEWIS WINNBERT, JR., lawyer; b. Washington, Jan. 3, 1940; s. Lewis Winnbert and Florence Elizabeth (Long) S.; m. Sydney Ann Crawford, Aug. 18, 1962. B.A., Allegheny Coll., 1961; J.D., Rutgers U., 1964. Bar: D.C. 1965, Tex. 1970, U.S. Supreme Ct. 1974, U.S. Ct. Mil. Appeals 1982. Atty. NASA, Houston, 1968-72, Washington, 1972-77; dep. asst. gen. counsel U.S. Dept. Energy, Washington, 1977-83; regional counsel NRC, San Francisco, 1983—. Mem. Falls Ch. Law Enforcement Adv. Commn., Va., 1976-77; chmn. Falls Ch. Bd. Zoning Appeals, 1978-82; pres. Falls Ch. Village Preservation and Improvement Soc., 1982-83. Served to Capt. JAGC, USAF, 1965-68, lt. col. Res. Named Outstanding Res. Judge Adv. of Yr., U.S. Air Force, 1982; Recipient Skylab Achievement award NASA, 1974, Superior Achievement award Dept. Energy, 1980, Meritorious Service medal Dept. Air Force, 1982, Joint Services Commendation medal Dept. Def., 1984. Mem. ABA, Fed. Bar Assn., Am. Judicature Soc., D.C. Bar Assn., State Bar Tex., Res. Officers Assn. (pres. Air Force chpt. 1 1977-78), Phi Delta Phi. Clubs: Army-Navy Country (Arlington, Va.); Commonwealth of Calif. (San Francisco). Administrative and regulatory, Nuclear power, Military. Office: US NRC 1450 Maria Ln Suite 210 Walnut Creek CA 94596

SHOOB, MARVIN H., federal judge; b. Walterboro, S.C., Feb. 23, 1923; s. Michael Louis and Lena (Steinberg) S.; m. Janice Paradies, Nov. 14, 1979; children: Michael, Wendy. J.D., U. Ga., 1948. Bar: Ga. 1948. Ptnr. Brown & Shoob, Atlanta, 1949-55; ptnr. Phillips, Johnson & Shoob, Atlanta, 1955-56, Shoob, McLain & Merritt, Atlanta, 1956-79; judge U.S. Dist. Ct., Atlanta, 1979—; chmn. Juvenile Ct. Com., 1964-70; mem. Ga. State Bar Grievance Tribunal, 1975-79; chmn. Ga. State Bar Fed. Legislation Com., 1977-79; guest lectr. Continuing Legal Edn., Athens, Ga., 1975-77. Chmn. 5th Dist. Democratic Exec. Com., 1974-76. Mem. Phi Eta Sigma, Phi Kappa Phi. Jewish. Judicial administration. Office: US Dist Ct 1921 US Courthouse 75 Spring St SW Atlanta GA 30303 *

SHOOP, DEBORAH, lawyer; b. Detroit, May 15, 1948; d. F. W. and E. M. Shoop; m. Charles John Bopp III, Jan. 31, 1982; 1 child, Charles John IV. BA, U. Mich., 1970, MLS, 1972; JD, Wayne State U., 1977. Bar: Mich. 1977, U.S. Dist. Ct. (ea. dist.) Mich. 1977, U.S. Ct. Appeals (6th cir.) 1980. Asst. v.p., sr. counsel Alexander Hamilton Life Ins. Co. Am., Farmington Hills, Mich., 1979—; arbitrator Better Bus. Bur., Detroit, 1983—. Mem. ABA, Mich. Bar Assn. General corporate, Insurance, Banking. Home: 22420 Clear Lake Farmington Hills MI 48024 Office: Alexander Hamilton Life Ins Co Am 33045 Hamilton Blvd Farmington Hills MI 48018

SHOOP, ROGER THOMAS, lawyer; b. Wilmington, Del., Feb. 1, 1949; s. Kimber Lee and Katherine (Hack) S.; m. Melinda Suzanne DiCarlo, May 11, 1985. BA, Lehigh U., 1971; JD, Dickinson Sch. Law, 1974. Bar: Pa. 1974, U.S. Dist. Ct. (mid. dist.) Pa. 1976, U.S. Ct. Appeals (3d cir.) 1982. Asst. atty. gen. Pa. Dept. Transp., Harrisburg, 1974-77; ptnr. Thomas & Thomas, Harrisburg, 1977—. Mem. ABA, Pa. Bar Assn., Dauphin County Bar Assn., Pa. Def. Inst., Phi Beta Kappa, Phi Sigma Kappa Alumni Assn. (Watts scholar 1971, legal advisor 1977—). Republican. Presbyterian. Avocations: golf, racquetball. State civil litigation, Federal civil litigation, Personal injury. Home: 4 Timberline Pl Hummelstown PA 17036 Office: Thomas & Thomas 212 Locust St Harrisburg PA 17108

SHOPSIN, (MARC) MOSHE, lawyer; b. Bklyn., Feb. 17, 1952; s. Robert and Selma (Kreisberg) S.; m. Donna Marie Taylor, Dec. 28, 1983; 1 child, Joseph Michael. Student, Fla. Bible Coll., 1970-71; A in Jewish Studies, U. Miami, 1974; BA in History, Fla. Internat. U., 1976; JD, Potomac Sch. Law, 1979. Bar: Ga. 1979, U.S. Dist. Ct. (no. dist.) Ga. 1979, U.S. Tax Ct. 1979, U.S. Ct. Customs and Patent Appeals 1979, U.S. Ct. Mil. Appeals 1979, U.S. Ct. Appeals (5th cir.) 1979, U.S. Dist. Ct. (mid. dist.) Ga. 1980, U.S. Ct. Appeals (11th cir.) 1981. Sole practice Miami, Fla., 1979-80; ptnr. Friedman, Shopsin & Woodard, Atlanta, 1980-83; mfr. Pera Fashions, Inc., Miami, 1983-84; legal coordinator Hayt, Hayt & Landau, Miami, 1984-86, assoc., supervising atty., 1986—; v.p., gen. counsel Ficor Ltd., Atlanta, 1980-83. Author various poems; artist comic strip, 1969. Spl. aide to Pres. James E. Carter, Washington, 1977. Mem. ABA, Ga. Bar Assn., Atlanta Lawyers Assn., Assn. Trial Lawyers Am., Immigration and Nationality Lawyers Assn., Phi Alpha Delta. Republican. Lodge: Masons. Avocations: music,

art, acting, writing, community service. Health, Consumer commercial, Immigration, naturalization, and customs.

SHORE, ELBERT RUSSELL, lawyer; b. St. Louis, Nov. 28, 1945; s. Elbert Russell Sr. and Helen (Brissenden) S.; m. Dale Carol Eno, Oct. 14, 1977; 1 child, Noble Alexander. BA, Western Md. Coll., 1967; JD, U. Md., 1970. Bar: Md. 1971, U.S. Ct. Mil. Appeals 1975, U.S. Ct. Appeals (D.C. and 4th cirs.) 1977, U.S. Tax Ct. 1977, U.S. Dist. Ct. D.C. 1979., U.S. Dist. Ct. Md. 1977. Ptnr. Bell, Cornelius & Shore, Rockville, Md., 1974—. Served to capt. JAGC U.S. Army, 1971-74. Mem. ABA, Md. Bar Assn., Bar Assn. Montgomery County, Assn. Trial Lawyers Am., Nat. Hist. Railway Soc. Democrat. Presbyterian. Federal civil litigation, State civil litigation, Family and matrimonial. Home: 7404 Miller Fall Rd Rockville MD 20855 Office: Bell Cornelius & Shore 101 W Jefferson St Rockville MD 20850

SHORE, MICHAEL ALLAN, lawyer, accountant; b. Cleve., Dec. 6, 1931; s. Herman and Genevieve Elizabeth (Cohen) S.; m. M. Kay Shore; children: Debbie E., Steven J. BS in Econs., U. Pa., 1953, JD, Cleve. State U., 1959, postdoctoral studies Sch. Law, Case Western Res. U. Bar: Ohio, U.S. Supreme Ct. CPA, Ohio. Prin. Michael A. Shore Co., L.P.A., Cleve.; pres., ptnr. Shore, Shirley & Co., CPA's, Cleve.; dir. various corps.; lectr. taxation Case Western Res. U., Cleve.; acting judge Shaker Heights Municipal Ct., 1983-84; arbitrator Am. Arbitration Assn. Served with U.S. Army, 1953-55. Mem. Ohio Bar Assn., Cleve. Bar Assn., Am. Assn. Atty.-CPA's, Am. Inst. CPA's. Republican. Jewish. Lodge: Masons. General corporate, Probate. Office: 23200 Chagrin Blvd Cleveland OH 44122

SHORES, JANIE LEDLOW, state justice; b. Georgiana., Ala., Apr. 30, 1932; d. John Wesley and Willie (Scott) Ledlow; m. James L. Shores, Jr., May 12, 1962; 1 dau., Laura Scott. J.D., U. Ala., Tuscaloosa, 1959. Bar: Ala. 1959. Pvt. practice Selma, 1959; mem. legal dept. Liberty Nat. Life Ins. Co., Birmingham, Ala., 1962-66; asso. prof. law Cumberland Sch. Law, Samford U., Birmingham, 1)66-74; asso. justice Supreme Ct. Ala., 1974—; legal adviser Ala. Constn. Revision Commn., 1973; mem. Nat. Adv. Council State Ct. Planning, 1976—. Contbr. articles to legal jours. Mem. Am. Bar Assn., Am. Judicature Soc., Farrah Order Jurisprudence. Democrat. Episcopalian. Judicial administration. Office: Supreme Court 445 Dexter Ave PO Box 218 Montgomery AL 36130 *

SHORR, MATTHEW SAM, lawyer; b. Los Angeles, July 16, 1953. BA, Calif. State U., Northridge, 1976; JD, Southwestern U., 1980; LLM with honors, U. Cambridge, Eng., 1985. Bar: Calif. 1982, U.S. Dist. Ct. (cen. dist.) Calif. 1982. Resident counsel bus. affairs D.I.C. Enterprises Inc., Studio City, Calif., 1982-83; assoc. Barry K. Rothman, Los Angeles, 1983-84, Iwasaki, Thomas & Sheffield, Los Angeles, 1986—. Mem. ABA (internat. law and practice sect.), Los Angeles County Bar Assn. (internat. law and intellectual property sects.), Los Angeles Ctr. Internat. Comml. Arbitration (legis. com.). Private international, General corporate, State civil litigation. Office: Iwasaki Thomas & Sheffield 420 Boyd St 4th Floor Los Angeles CA 90013

SHORT, DERONDA MINIARD, lawyer; b. Hazard, Ky., Jan. 18, 1943; d. Arthur Shepherd and Margaret (Roddle) Miniard; m. Lester L. Hudgins Jr., Sept. 24, 1961 (div. Nov. 1980); 1 child, Stephanie Elaine; m. W. Dean Short, June 18, 1983. AA, Christopher Newport Coll., Newport News, Va., 1968, BA, 1975; JD, Coll. William and Mary, 1978. Bar: Va. 1978, U.S. Ct. Appeals (4th cir.) 1978, U.S. Dist. Ct. Va. 1983. Ptnr. Short, Short, Telstad & Kerr, PC, Newport News, 1978—. Mem. Va. Symphony Guild, Newport News, 1975-84, Va. State Ballet, Newport News, 1977-81, Peninsula Estate Planning Council, 1983—; commr. Penisula Ports Authority Va., Newport News, 1977-86; bd. visitors Christopher Newport Coll., 1979-83. Mem. ABA, Va. State Bar Assn., Newport News Bar Assn., Am. Trial Lawyers Assn., Va. Trial Lawyers Assn, Peninsula Women's Network. Republican. Baptist. Club: Towne Point (Norfolk, Va.). Family and matrimonial, Personal injury, Consumer commercial. Home: 52 Settlers Rd Newport News VA 23606 Office: Short Short Telstad & Kerr PC 710 Denbigh Blvd Bldg 1A Newport News VA 23602

SHORT, MARIANNE DOLORES, lawyer; b. Mpls., Mar. 12, 1951; d. Robert Earl and Marion (McCann) S.; m. Raymond Louis Skowyra Jr., Nov. 1, 1980; 1 child, R. Louis III. BA in Philosophy and Polit. Sci., Newton Coll. of Sacred Heart, 1972; JD, Boston Coll., 1976. Bar: Minn. 1976, U.S. Dist. Ct. Minn. 1976, Mass. 1977, U.S. Ct. Appeals (8th cir.) 1980. Spl. asst. atty. gen. St. Paul, 1976-77; assoc. Dorsey & Whitney, Mpls., 1977-82, ptnr., 1983—, mem. policy com., 1987—; chmn. recruiting com. Dorsey & Whitney, Mpls., 1985—. Trustee Boston Coll., 1985—, Visitation Convent, St. Paul, 1985—. Mem. ABA, Mass. Bar Assn., Minn. Bar Assn., Hennepin County Bar Assn. (ethics com.), Ramsey County Bar Assn., Am. Arbitration Assn. (arbitrator). Mem. Democratic Farm Labor Party. Club: Town and Country (St. Paul), Mpls. Athletic. Avocations: skiing, running. Federal civil litigation, State civil litigation, Civil rights. Home: 2215 Summit Ave Saint Paul MN 55105 Office: Dorsey & Whitney 2000 1st Bank Pl E Minneapolis MN 55402

SHORT, SKIP, lawyer; b. N.Y.C., July 13, 1951; s. Albert Joseph and Gertrude B. (Johnson) S. B.A., Fordham Coll., 1972; J.D., Georgetown U., 1975. Bar: N.Y. 1976, U.S. Dist. Ct. (ea. dist.) N.Y. 1976, U.S. Dist. Ct. (so. dist.) N.Y. 1978, D.C. 1979, U.S. Ct. Appeals (1st cir.) and D.C. Cir. 1983, U.S. Supreme Ct. 1984. Assoc. Russakoff & Weiss, Bklyn., 1975-76; sole practice, N.Y.C., 1976-79; ptnr. Short & Billy, N.Y.C., 1979—; cons. ins. seminars, 1978—; arbitrator N.Y. Civil Ct., 1981—; adminstrv. law judge N.Y. Environ. Control Bd., 1980-82; arbitrator Am. Arbitration Assn., N.Y.C., 1981—, U.S. Dist. Ct. (ea. dist.) N.Y., 1986—. Spl. envoy Internat. Human Rights Found., 1986—. Author: First Party Claims, 1979; co-author: First Party Claims Under the New York Comprehensive Automobile Reparations Act, 3d edit., 1984. Mem. N.Y. State Bar Assn., N.Y. County Lawyers Assn. Federal civil litigation, Insurance, Private international. Office: Short & Billy 217 Broadway New York NY 10007

SHORT, TIMOTHY ALLEN, lawyer; b. Russell, Kans., July 17, 1952; s. H. Francis and Ruth (Teeter) Short; m. Barbara Diane Phillips, June 30, 1979; children: Justin Corey, Kisha Erin. BA in Speech Communication, Kans. U., 1974, JD, 1977. Bar: Kans. 1977. Atty. Fred Spigarelli, P.A., Pitts., 1976-82; ptnr. Spigarelli, McLane & Short, Pitts., 1982—. Mem. ABA, Kans. Bar Assn., Southeast Kans. Bar Assn., Crawford County Bar Assn. (sec. 1979), Kans. Trial Lawyers Assn., Assn. Trial Lawyers Am. Democrat. Presbyterian. Avocations: canoeing, softball, computers, basketball. Personal injury, Workers' compensation, State civil litigation. Home: 601 W Kansas Pittsburg KS 66762 Office: Spigarelli McLane & Short PO Box 1447 100 S Broadway Suite 200 Pittsburg KS 66762

SHORTER, JAMES RUSSELL, JR., lawyer; b. N.Y.C., June 10, 1946; s. James Russell and Helen (Ibert) S. AB, Columbia Coll., 1968; JD, Harvard U., 1975; LLM in Taxation, NYU, 1979. Bar: N.Y. 1976, U.S. Dist. Ct. (so. and ea. dists.) N.Y. 1976, U.S. Tax Ct. 1987. Assoc. Thacher Proffitt & Wood, N.Y.C., 1975-84, ptnr., 1984—. Serves as commdr. USNR, 1968—. Mem. ABA (tax, corps., banking and bus. law sect.). Republican. Club: Harvard (N.Y.C.). Corporate taxation, Personal income taxation. Home: 345 E 80th St #9A New York NY 10021 Office: Thacher Proffitt & Wood 2 World Trade Ctr 39th Fl New York NY 10048

SHORTRIDGE, MICHAEL L., lawyer; b. Grundy, Va., May 26, 1957; s. Leon and Mavis S.; m. Judy Beth Copenhaver, July 27, 1984. BA with distinction, U. Va., 1979, JD, 1982. Bar: Va. 1982, U.S. Dist. Ct. (we. dist.) Va. 1982, U.S. Ct. Appeals (4th cir.) 1984, U.S. Tax Ct. 1985. Assoc. Mullins, Winston, Keuling-Stout, Thomason & Harris, Norton, Va., 1982-84; sole practice Norton, 1984—; bd. dirs. Client Centered Legal Services, Castlewood, Va., Big Stone Gap (Va.) Bank and Trust. Mem. ABA, Va. Bar Assn., Wise County Bar Assn., , Assn. Trial Lawyers Am., Va. Assn. Def. Attys., Va. Trial Lawyer's Assn., Def. Research Inst. Club: Lonesome Pine Country (Big Stone Gap, Va.). Lodge: Kiwanis. Federal civil litigation, State civil litigation, Personal injury. Office: 1122 Park Ave NW Norton VA 24273

SHORTZ, RICHARD ALAN, lawyer; b. Chgo., Mar. 11, 1945; s. Lyle A. and Wilma Warner (Wildes) S.; m. Jennifer A. Harrell; children: Eric, Heidi. BS, Ind. U., 1967; JD, Harvard U., 1970. Bar: Calif. 1971, U.S. Supreme Ct. 1980. Assoc. Gibson, Dunn & Crutcher, Los Angeles, 1970-73; sr. v.p., gen. counsel, sec. Tosco Corp., Los Angeles, 1973-83; ptnr. Jones, Day, Reavis & Pogue, Los Angeles, 1983—. Mem. Los Angeles World Affairs Inst., 1983—, Town Hall Los Angeles, 1983—. Served to 2d lt. U.S. Army, 1970-71. Mem. ABA, Los Angeles Bar Assn. Republican. Episcopalian. Clubs: Calif. (Los Angeles), Beach (Santa Monica). Oil and gas leasing, Securities, Banking. Home: 1343 Pavia Pl Pacific Palisades CA 90272 Office: Jones Day Reavis & Pogue 355 S Grand Ave Suite 3000 Los Angeles CA 90071

SHOSS, CYNTHIA RENEE, lawyer; b. Cape Girardeau, Mo., Nov. 29, 1950; s. Milton and Carroll Jane (Duncan) S.; m. David Goodwin Watson, Apr. 13, 1986. BA, Newcomb Coll., 1971; JD, Tulane U., 1974; LLM in Taxation, NYU, 1980. Bar: La. 1974, Mo. 1977, Ill. 1978. Law clk. to presiding justice La. Supreme Ct., New Orleans, 1974-76; assoc. Stone, Pigman et al, New Orleans, 1976-77, Lewis & Rice, St. Louis, 1977-79, Curtis, Mallet-Prevost, N.Y.C., 1980-82; ptnr. LeBoeuf, Lamb, Leiby & MacRae, N.Y.C., 1982—. Contbr. articles to profl. jours. Mem. ABA. Corporate taxation, Personal income taxation, Private international. Office: LeBoeuf Lamb Leiby & MacRay 520 Madison Ave New York NY 10022

SHOSTAK, STANLEY RICHARD, lawyer; b. Omaha, July 16, 1931; s. Max R. and Reva R. (Gross) S.; m. Carole Ruth Blumenthal, July 4, 1953; children—Stuart Robert, Dennis Alan, Cynthia Robin. Student Northwestern U., 1949-51; A.A., U. Calif.-Berkeley, 1951, A.B. in History with honors, 1953, J.D., Boalt Hall, 1956. Bar: Calif. 1956, U.S. Dist. Ct. (no. dist.) Calif. 1956, U.S. Ct. Appeals (9th cir.) 1956, U.S. Dist. Ct. (so. dist.) Calif. 1960, U.S. Customs Ct. 1957, Ct. Internat. Trade 1981, U.S. Ct. Customs and Patent Appeals 1960, U.S. Ct. Appeals (Fed. cir.) 1982, U.S. Supreme Ct. 1960, D.C. 1980. Assoc. Geary, Spridgen & Moskowitz, Santa Rosa, Calif., 1956-57; dep. dist. atty. Sonoma County, Calif., 1957-59; ptnr. Stein & Shostak, 1959-76; v.p. Stein Shostak Shostak & O'Hara, Los Angeles and Washington, 1976—; hearing examiner Los Angeles Police Commn. and Civil Service Commn., 1964-79; lectr. UCLA Extension, 1975—. Pres. Fgn. Trade Assn. So. Calif., 1973, bd. dirs., 1962-84. Mem. ABA, D.C. Bar Assn., Wilshire Bar Assn., Assn. of Customs Bar, Fed. Cir. Bar Assn. (bd. dirs. 1987—), Los Angeles C. of C. (chmn. World Trade Week 1976). Democrat. Jewish. Clubs: Braemar Country, Masons, Scottish Rite, Shrine. Contbr. article to legal publ. Immigration, naturalization, and customs, Public international. Office: 3580 Wilshire Blvd Suite 1240 Los Angeles CA 90010 Office: 1101 17th St NW Washington DC 20036

SHOSTROM, EARL RUSSELL, lawyer; b. Dayton, Iowa, May 2, 1921; s. Russell Elmer and Elvina Christina (Chinburg) S.; m. Sarah Louise Homeier, Nov. 19, 1944; children: Karen, Keith. BA, U. Iowa, 1943, JD, 1947. Bar: Iowa 1947. Asst. atty. gen. State of Iowa, Des Moines, 1947-48, 49-53; sole practice Winterset, Iowa, 1948-49; counsel, law dept. Prin. Mut. Life Ins. Co. and predecessor firm Bankers Life Co., Des Moines, 1953—. Big Eight football referee. 1960-78; supr. officials Iowa Girls' High Sch. Athletic Union, 1968—. Served to capt. inf., U.S. Army, 1943-46, ETO. Mem. ABA, Am. Land Title Assn. (life ins. counsel), Am. Life Ins. Assn. (legal Sect.), Iowa Bar Assn., Polk County Bar Assn., Des Moines Civil War Round Table (comdr. 1984—), Phi Beta Kappa. Republican. United Methodist. Lodges: Sertoma (pres. Des Moines club 1960), Lions. Real property, Contracts commercial. Office: Prin Mut Life Ins Co 711 High St Des Moines IA 50309

SHOULDERS, BOBBY HARRIS, lawyer; b. Westmoreland, Tenn., Feb. 15, 1936; s. Roey Dewey and Minnie Aline (Harris) S.; m. Patricia Ann Watkins, June 9, 1956; children: Bobby H. Jr., Beverly Hope S. Andrews. BA magna cum laude, David Lipscomb Coll., 1958; JD, Vanderbilt U., 1961. Bar: Tenn. 1961, U.S. Dist. Ct. (mid. dist.) Tenn. 1961, U.S. Ct. Appeals (5th and 11th cirs.) 1981. Assoc. Clement, Sanford & Fisher, Nashville, 1961-64; atty. So. Bell Tel.&Tel. Co., Nashville, 1964-68; atty. South Cen. Bell Telephone Co., Birmingham, Ala., 1968-84, solicitor, 1984-86; gen. atty. South Cen. Bell Telephone Co., Birmingham, 1986—; mem. bd. pardons and paroles State of Tenn., Nashville, 1963-64. Bd. dirs. Children's Home Riverwood Ch. of Christ, Nashville, 1962-68. Mem. ABA, Tenn Bar Assn., Birmingham Bar Assn., Am. Judicature Soc., Alpha Kappa Psi. Democrat. Antitrust, Federal civil litigation, State civil litigation. Home: 3140 Warrington Rd Mountain Brook AL 35223 Office: S Cen Bell Legal Dept 600 N 19th St Birmingham AL 35203

SHOULDERS, PATRICK ALAN, lawyer; b. Evansville, Ind., Mar. 26, 1953; s. Harold Ray and Jeanne Marie (Nicholson) S.; m. Lisa Lou Iaccarino, July 12, 1975; children—Samantha Alain, Andrew Patrick. B.A., Ind. U., 1975, J.D. magna cum laude, 1978. Bar: Ind. 1978, U.S. Dist. Ct. (so. dist.) Ind. 1978, U.S. Ct. Appeals (7th cir.) 1979, U.S. Supreme Ct. 1985, Ky. 1986, U.S. Dist. Ct. (we. dist.) Ky. 1987. Assoc. Kahn, Dees, Donovan & Kahn, Evansville, Ind., 1978-81, ptnr., 1981-87; ptnr. Early, Arnold & Ziemer, Evansville, 1987—; adj. prof. law of evidence U. Evansville, 1980-82; mem. instl. rev. bd. St. Mary's Med. Ctr., Evansville, 1980—. Pres. Evansville Parks Found., 1982-83, Vanderburgh Law Library Found., Evansville, 1983-84; bd. dirs. Evansville Mus. Arts and Sci., 1982—; mem. Bd. Park Commrs., Evansville, 1984—; bd. dirs. Democrats for Better Govt., 1981-83. Recipient Cert. of Achievement, City of Evansville, 1982, Civic Service award Ind. Assn. Cities and Towns, 1983. Mem. ABA (litigation sect.), Ind. Bar Assn., Ind. Trial Lawyers Assn., Seventh Cir. Bar Assn., Evansville Bar Assn. (pres. 1984-85). Methodist. Federal civil litigation, State civil litigation, Personal injury. Home: 417 S Alvord Blvd Evansville IN 47714 Office: Early Arnold & Ziemer 1507 Old National Bank Bldg PO Box 916 Evansville IN 47706

SHOUSE, AUGUST EDWARD, lawyer; b. Houston, Aug. 12, 1949; s. Earl Edward Shouse and Mary Ann (Myers) Carrico; m. Ann Tucker Thompson, June 27, 1975; children: William Bundy, Edward Booth. BS, Stanford U., 1971; JD, U. Tex., 1974. Bar: Tex. 1974. From assoc. to ptnr. Vinson & Elkins, Houston, 1974—; bd. dirs. 1st Nat. Bank Mo., Missouri City, Tex. Bd. dirs. Greater Houston Area Chpt. ARC, 1982-86. Mem. Order of Coif, Phi Beta Kappa, Tau Beta Pi. Episcopalian. Real property, Landlord-tenant, General corporate. Home: 3645 Ella Lee Ln Houston TX 22027 Office: Vinson & Elkins 1001 Fannin #2628 Houston TX 77002-6760

SHOWERS, H. ROBERT, JR., lawyer; b. Canton, Ohio, May 16, 1955; s. H. Robert and Marguerite Y. (Froehlich) S.; m. Evelyn Jean Pruitt, Sept. 8, 1984. BA in History cum laude, Wake Forest U., 1977, JD, 1980. Assoc. Westmoreland, Sawyer & Miller, Winston-Salem, N.C., 1980-81; asst. U.S. Atty.'s Office, Raleigh, N.C., 1982-83, chief civil sect., 1983—; spl. prosecutor U.S. Atty. and N.C. Atty. Gen., Raleigh, 1985-86; asst. to atty. gen. U.S. Atty. Gen. Office, Raleigh, 1986—; chmn. N.C. LECC on Pornography, Organized Crime and Child Abuse, 1984—; chief N.C. Pornography Task Force, 1986—; cons. in field. Contbr. articles to profl. jours. Commr. N.C. Gov.'s Commn. Child Victimization, 1985—; bd. dirs. North Carolinians Against Alcohol and Drug Abuse, 1983-85, Christian Conciliation Service, 1983—, N.C. Baptist Men, 1985—, chmn. statewide com., 1985—. Recipient Spl. Achievement awards Dept. Justice, 1982, 84; Hankins scholar, Kirkpatrick-Howell scholar; named Outstanding Atty. 1985. Mem. ABA, N.C. State Bar Assn., Wake County Bar Assn., Ams. for Pub. Justice Assn., N.C. Sexual Violence Task Force, Christian Legal Soc. (pres. N.C. chpt. 1985—), Mortar Bd., Phi Alpha Theta, Omicron Delta. Republican. Avocations: golf, tennis, hiking, basketball, racquetball. Federal civil litigation, Criminal, Personal injury.

SHOWERS, JACK PAUL, lawyer; b. Montgomery, Ala., Nov. 18, 1945; s. Jack Roy and Julia Lucille (Baria) S.; m. Pamela Kathlyn Hammond, June 12, 1981; 1 child, Elizabeth Hammond Gray. J.D., La. State U., 1976. Bar: La. 1976, U.S. Dist. Ct. (mid. and we. dists.) La. 1977, U.S. Ct. Appeals (5th cir.) 1979, U.S. Ct. Appeals (11th cir.) 1981, U.S. Supreme Ct. 1981. Sr. ptnr. Showers & Guidry, Lafayette, La., 1977-81, Litigation Firm of Jack Paul Showers, Lafayette, New Orleans and Baton Rouge, 1981—; sec., dir. TBC Corp., Lafayette, 1981—; v.p., dir. La. Brass, Inc., Lafayette, 1981—, Lafayette Acquisitions, Inc., 1981—. Mem. Acadiana Arts Council, Lafayette, 1978—, Fine Arts Found., Lafayette, 1978—; bd. dirs. Lafayette Community Theatre, 1984. Named judge ad hoc Lafayette City Ct., 1984. Mem. Assn. Trial Lawyers Am., La. Trial Lawyers Assn., ABA, La. State Bar Assn., Greater Lafayette C. of C. (vol. 1977—). Democrat. Methodist. Clubs: Cypremort Yacht, City, Lafayette Townhouse. Lodge: Krewe of Troubadour. State civil litigation, Personal injury. Office: 311 Rue Louis XIV Suite IV Lafayette LA 70508

SHOWLEY, LON DUANE, lawyer; b. Rochester, Ind., May 3, 1944; s. Harold D. and Doveda G. (Rouch) S.; 1 child, Matthew. B.A., Butler U., 1966; J.D., Ind. U., 1969. Bar: Ind. 1970, Calif. 1972. Dep. atty. gen. State of Ind., Indpls., 1969-71; sole practice, San Diego, 1972—; instr. Cabrillo Pacific Coll. of Law, San Diego, 1972-75. Mem. Calif. Bar Assn., San Diego Bar Assn., San Diego County Bar (chmn. estate planning, trust and probate sect. 1985). Estate planning, Probate. Home: 1450 Hidden Mesa Trail El Cajon CA 92019 Office: Suite 1750 530 B St San Diego CA 92101

SHREVE, GENE RUSSELL, law educator, consultant; b. San Diego, Aug. 6, 1943; s. Ronald D. and Hazel (Shepherd) S.; m. Marguerite Russell, May 26, 1973. A.B. with honors, U. Okla., 1965; LL.B. Harvard U., 1968, LL.M., 1975. Bar: Mass. 1969, Vt. 1981, U.S. Dist. Ct. (no. dist.) Tex. 1969, U.S. Dist. Ct. Mass. 1970, U.S. Ct. Appeals (1st cir.) 1971, U.S. Dist. Ct. Vt. 1976. law clk. U.S. Dist. Ct., Dallas, 1969-70; assoc. prof. Vt. Law Sch., Royalton, 1975-81; vis. assoc. prof. George Washington U., Washington, 1981-83; assoc. prof. law N.Y. Law Sch., N.Y.C., 1983-84, prof., 1984—; vis. prof. law Ind. U., Bloomington, 1986, prof., 1987—; appellate atty. and state extradition hearing examiner Office of Mass. Atty. Gen., 1968-69; ; staff and supervising atty. Boston Legal Assistance Project, 1970-73; cons. Conn. Bar Examiners, Hartford, 1978—, Vt. Bar Examiners, Montpelier, 1980; reporter Speedy Trial Planning Group, U.S. Dist. Ct., Montpelier, 1976-77. Contbr. numerous articles to legal jours. Mem. Am. Arbitration Assn. Democrat. Episcopalian. Club: Harvard Faculty. Federal civil litigation, Legal education, State civil litigation. Office: Ind U Sch of Law Bloomington IN 47405

SHROYER, THOMAS JEROME, lawyer; b. Morris, Minn., Mar. 18, 1952; s. Virgil Earnest and Muriel June (Hanson) S.; m. Nan Kenwood Sorensen, June 30, 1979; 1 child, Eric Sorensen. BA in Polit. Sci., U. Minn., 1974, JD, 1977. Bar: Iowa 1977, Minn. 1978, U.S. Dist. Ct. (no. and so. dists.) Iowa, U.S. Dist. Ct. Minn. Assoc. Thoma, Schoenthal, Davis, Hockunberg & Wine, Des Moines, 1977-78, Chadwick, Johnson & Condon, Bloomington, Minn., 1978-80, Moss & Barnett, Mpls., 1980—. Mem. ABA, Minn. Bar Assn., Def. Research Inst., Minn. Def. Lawyers Assn. Democrat. Federal civil litigation, State civil litigation. Home: 121 S Washington Ave Minneapolis MN 55401 Office: Moss & Barnett 200 S 6th St Minneapolis MN 55402

SHUFFETT, JAMES AVERY, lawyer; b. Greensburg, Ky., Jan. 7, 1943; m. Laura Sue Morrison, Aug. 8, 1981; 1 child, Leah. BA, U. Ky., 1964, JD, 1965. Bar: Ky. 1966, U.S. Dist. Ct. (ea. dist.) Ky. 1966, U.S. Ct. Appeals (6th cir.) 1973, U.S. Supreme Ct. 1973, U.S. Dist. Ct. (we. dist.) Ky. 1977. Sr. ptnr. Shuffett & Shuffett, Lexington, Ky., 1966—. Criminal, Federal civil litigation, State civil litigation. Home: 541 W Short St #1 Lexington KY 40508 Office: Shuffett & Shuffett 403 Security Trust Bldg Lexington KY 40507

SHUGART, JAMES ELMER, lawyer; b. Winona, Minn., Dec. 26, 1929; s. George and Bertha Anna (Schaale) S.; m. Ernestine Levere Boylan, Nov. 26, 1955. Student, Winona State Coll., 1950-52; B in Gen. Edn., U. Omaha, 1965; MA, St. Mary's U., San Antonio, 1978, JD, 1980. Bar: Tex. 1980. Commd. 2d lt. USAF, 1952, advanced through grades to lt. col., 1970, served in U.S., Eng., Vietnam, ret., 1975; sole practice San Antonio, 1980—. Adminstrv. asst. 21st Congl. Dist., San Antonio, 1977; mem. Vision 2000 Com., Bexar County, Tex., 1985. Decorated Silver Star, 1966, DFC, 1966, Cross of Gallantry (Republic of Vietnam), 1966. Mem. ABA, Tex. State Bar Assn., San Antonio Bar Assn., Assn. Trial Lawyers Am. Lutheran. Avocations: flying, golf. Criminal, General practice. Home: 34 Campden Circle San Antonio TX 78218 Office: 110 E Nueva St San Antonio TX 78204

SHUGHART, DONALD LOUIS, lawyer; b. Kansas City, Mo., Aug. 12, 1926; s. Henry M. and Dora M. (O'Leary) S.; m. Mary I. Shughart, July 25, 1953; children—Susan C. Shughart Hosgett, Nancy J. Goede. A.B., U. Mo., Columbia, 1949, J.D., 1951. Bar: Mo. 1951, U.S. Dist. Ct. (we. dist.) Mo. 1951, U.S. Tax Ct. 1979. Sr. ptnr. Shughart, Thomson & Kilroy, P.C., Kansas City, Mo., 1962—, exec. v.p., 1980—; dir. K.C. Mack Sales & Service Inc., Kaw Transport Co., R.D. Mann Carpet Co., TOP Co. Investments, Inc.; mem. Mo. Carriers Assn. Pub. Service Com. Bd. dirs. Rockhurst Coll. Served with AC, U.S. Army, 1944-46. Mem. ABA, Kansas City Bar Assn., Lawyers Assn. Kansas City, Westmo Def. Lawyers (pres. 1971-72, sec. 1975-78), Mo. Bar Assn. (chmn. corp. com. 1980-81, 82-83), Internat. Assn. Ins. Counsel, Am. Judicature Soc., Westmo Def. Lawyers (pres. 1971-72), Phi Delta Phi. Republican. Roman Catholic. Clubs: Univ., Homestead Country; Brookfield (Mo.) Country. General corporate, Estate planning, Corporate taxation.

SHULAW, RICHARD ALLEN, lawyer; b. Bowling Green, Ohio, Oct. 14, 1934; s. Francis Marion and Mary Frances (Morehead) S.; m. Jeanette H. Hagan, Feb. 21, 1970; children: Richard B., Katherine Elizabeth. AA, Ferris State Coll., 1958; JD, Detroit Coll. of Law, 1963. Bar: Mich., U.S. Dist. Ct. (ea. and we. dists.) Mich., U.S. Ct. Appeals (6th cir.), U.S. Supreme Ct. Sole practice Owosso, Mich., 1963—; chief asst. pros. atty. Shiwassee County, Mich., 1971, cir. ct. commr., 1965-67. Served to specialist 4th class U.S. Army, 1954-55. Mem. ABA, Mich. Bar Assn. (ins. sect., negligence sect., law sect., grievance com., arbitration of disputes between lawyers), Shiawassee County Bar Assn. (v.p.), Assn. Trial Lawyers Am., Mich. Trial Lawyers Assn., Mich. Def. Trial Counsel, Inc., Fed. Bar Assn. Republican. Roman Catholic. Clubs: University (Flint, Mich.), Owosso Country. Lodges: K.C., Elks. Avocations: golf, boating. Insurance, Personal injury, Family and matrimonial. Home: 969 Marguerite Dr Owosso MI 48867

SHULL, WILLIAM EDGAR, JR., lawyer; b. Quincy, Ill., Aug. 8, 1947; s. William Edgar and Elizabeth Estelle (Stuhr) S.; m. Sharon Elaine Watt, May 27, 1969; children: Shari, Jennifer, William III, Robert, Rebecca, Katherine, Brian, Matthew. BA, Wichita State U., 1968; postgrad., U. Utah, 1968-69; JD, U. Mo., Kansas City, 1972. Bar: Mo. 1972, U.S. Dist. Ct. (we. dist.) Mo. 1972, U.S. Ct. Appeals (8th cir.) 1973, U.S. Ct. Appeals (5th and 10th cirs.) 1976, U.S. Supreme Ct. 1976, Kans. 1985. Assoc. Duncan & Russell, Kansas City, 1972-76; ptnr. Gettig, Coulson & Shull, Kansas City, 1976-82; gen. counsel Billings Corp., Independence, Mo., 1982-85; atty. litigation Koch Industries, Wichita, Kans., 1985—. Mem. sch. bd., Kearney, Mo., 1981-84, v.p., 1983-84; bd. dirs. Soccer Club, Kearney, 1982-84. Mem. ABA, Mo. Bar Assn., Kans. Bar Assn., Wichita Bar Assn., Kansas City Bar Assn., Assn. Trial Lawyers Am. Mormon. Federal civil litigation, State civil litigation, General corporate. Home: 1107 Partridge Derby KS 67037 Office: Koch Industries 4111 E 37th St Wichita KS 67220

SHULMAN, STEPHEN NEAL, lawyer; b. New Haven, Apr. 6, 1933; s. Harry and Rea (Karrel) S.; m. Sandra Paula Still, Aug. 14, 1954; children—Harry, Dean, John. B.A., Harvard, 1954; LL.B. cum laude (editor-in-chief Law Jour. 1957-58), Yale, 1958. Bar: Conn. bar 1958, also U.S. cts 1958. Indsl. relations Bendix Aviation Corp., 1954-55; law clk. to Justice Harlan, U.S. Supreme Ct., 1958-59; vis. asst. pro. U. Mich. Law Sch., 1959; asso. firm Covington & Burling, Washington, 1959-60; asst. U.S. atty. Washington, 1960-61; exec. asst. to sec. labor 1961-62, dept asst. sec. of def., 1962-65; gen. counsel U.S. Air Force, 1965-66; chmn. Equal Employment Opportunity Commn., 1966-67; mem. firm Kane, Shulman & Schiei, Washington, 1967-70, Cadwalader, Wickersham & Taft, N.Y.C., also Washington, 1971—; vis. prof. mgmt. U. Okla., 1965-66. Mem. Order of Coif, Cum Laude Soc., Phi Alpha Delta, Book and Gavel. Home: 1332 Skipwith Rd McLean VA 22101 Office: 1333 New Hampshire Ave NW Washington DC 20036

SHULMAN, WARREN SCOTT, lawyer, photofinishing company executive; b. St. Petersburg, Fla., Oct. 8, 1942; s. Arnold and Mary Frances (Johnson) S.; m. Stella Esther Thompson, Sept. 6, 1980; 1 child, Zachary Scott; children by previous marriage: Dedee, Robert, Allison. BBA, U. Ga., 1964, JD, 1966. Bar: Ga. 1965. Assoc. Shulman & Alembik, Atlanta, 1966-67; staff

officer CIA, Washington, 1967-72; ptnr. Shulman & Bauer, Atlanta, 1972-77, Shulman, Bauer, Deitch, Raines & Hester, Atlanta, 1977-79, Stolz & Shulman, Atlanta, 1979—; pres., chmn. bd. Colonial Hospitality Mgmt. Corp., Colonial Equities, Inc.; bd. dirs. Ray Net Communications Systems, Inc.; instr. Atlanta Law Sch., 1973-74. Author: Georgia Practice and Procedure, 1975; contbr. articles to legal jours. Mem. bus. and industry com. Clean City Commn., Atlanta, 1980-81, So. Ctr. for Internat. Studies, 1979-81; trustee Congregation Beth Jacob, Atlanta, 1976-79; bd. dirs. Atlanta Jewish Welfare Fedn., 1980-82; Fulton County Rep. dist. chmn., 1982; candidate for mayor of Atlanta, 1981. Mem. ABA, Ga. Bar Assn., Atlanta Bar Assn., Assn. Trial Lawyers Am., Ga. Assn. Trial Lawyers, Lawyers Club Atlanta, Am. Judicature Soc., Am. Soc. Writers on Legal Subjects, Assn. Profl. Color Labs., Pres.'s Assn., Atlanta C. of C. (internat. relations task force 1977-80). Clubs: Atlanta City, Men's ORT of Atlanta. Lodge: B'nai B'rith. Avocations: skiing, golf, tennis, karate. State civil litigation, General corporate, Family and matrimonial. Home: 6400 Green Island Dr Columbus GA 31904 Office: Colonial Equities Inc 1017 Virginia St Columbus GA 31902

SHULTZ, JOHN DAVID, lawyer; b. Los Angeles, Oct. 9, 1939; s. Edward Patterson and Jane Elizabeth (Taylor) S.; m. Joanne Person, June 22, 1968; children—David Taylor, Steven Matthew. Student Harvard Coll., 1960-61; B.A., U. Ariz., 1964; J.D., Boalt Hall, U. Calif.-Berkeley, 1967. Bar: N.Y. 1968, Calif. 1978. Assoc. Cadwalader, Wickersham & Taft, N.Y.C., 1968-77; ptnr. Lawler, Felix & Hall, Los Angeles, 1977-83 , mem. exec. com., chmn. planning com., co-chmn. recruiting and hiring com.; ptnr. Morgan, Lewis & Bockius, Los Angeles, 1983—, mem. ptnr. lateral entry com., mgmt. com., profl. evaluation com., chmn. recruiting com.; sec., counsel Copy Tech., Inc., 1971-73; trustee St. Thomas Ch., N.Y.C., 1969-72, Shore Acres Point Corp., Mamaroneck, N.Y., 1975-77; mem. adv. bd. Internat. and Comparative Law Center, Southwestern Legal Found., 1981—. Mem. Republican Nat. Com. Mem. Assn. Bar City N.Y., State Bar Calif., N.Y. State Bar Assn., ABA, Phi Delta Phi, Sigma Chi. Episcopalian. Club: University (Los Angeles). General corporate, Contracts commercial. Office: 801 S Grand Ave 22d Fl Los Angeles CA 90017-3189

SHUMAKER, ROGER LEE, lawyer; b. Auburn, Ind., Sept. 6, 1950; s. Donald E. and Helen Jeannette (Gary) S.; m. Cheralyn Jean Fee, Aug. 28, 1971; children—Donald Lawrence, William Lee, Cristin Leigh. B.A., Manchester Coll., 1972; J.D., Case Western Res. U., 1976. Bar: Ind. 1976, Ohio 1976. Assoc. Kiefer, Knecht, Rees, Meyer & Miller, Cleve., 1976-79; ptnr. Knecht, Rees, Meyer, Mekedis & Shumaker, Cleve. 1979-86; prin. McDonald, Hopkins & Hardy Co., L.P.A., Cleve., 1986—. council, mem. faculty Notre Dame Estate Planning Inst., 1986. Trustee Manchester Coll., Ind., 1983—; mem. Breckenridge Village Council, Ohio Presbyn. Homes, Willoughby, Ohio, 1981—; mem. devel. com. Salvation Army Adv. Bd., Cleve., 1986—; faculty mem. Notre Dame Estate Planning Inst., 1986. Mem. ABA (chmn. software evaluation com. 1983-85, chmn. com. on tech. and econs. in probate and planning 1985—), Ohio State Bar Assn., Bar Assn. Greater Cleve. (chmn. estate planning inst. 1983), Estate Planning Council (chmn. Program Com., 1987). Democrat. Methodist. Probate, Estate taxation, General corporate. Office: McDonald Hopkins & Hardy Co LPA 1100 E Ohio Bldg Cleveland OH 44114

SHUMAN, MARK PATRICK, lawyer; b. Lawton, Okla., Jan. 22, 1952; s. Billy Joe and Jeane (Keating) Shuman. BA in Econs., U. Colo., 1975, MA in Econs., 1977, JD, 1980. Bar: Colo. 1980. Assoc. Brenman, Raskin, Friedlob & Tenenbaum, Denver, 1980-85, ptnr., 1986-87; gen. counsel, sec. Matrix Med., Inc., Wheat Ridge, Colo., 1987—. Mem. ABA, Colo. Bar Assn. (chmn. uniform state law com. 1986—), Denver Bar Assn. Securities, General corporate. Home: 242 S Nome Denver CO 80012 Office: Matrix Med Inc 4050 Youngfield St Wheat Ridge CO 80033

SHUPE, LARRY LEWIS, lawyer; b. Hampton, Iowa, June 19, 1933; s. Eldred Charles and Zella Irene (Shirk) S.; m. Frances Ellen Furber, July 14, 1956; children: Douglas, Polly, Andrea. BSEE, Iowa State U., 1955; JD, Marquette U., 1979. Bar: Wis. 1979, U.S. Dist. Ct. (ea. and we. dists.) Wis. 1979, U.S. Ct. Appeals (7th cir.) 1979. Field engr. Square D Co., Pitts., 1958-64; account rep. Applied Power Inc., Milw., 1964-70, mgr. field sales, 1970-73, mgr. nat. sales, 1973-76; assoc. Whyte & Hirschboeck, Milw., 1979-82; atty. Johnson Controls, Inc., Milw., 1982—. Pres. Our Saviors, Hartland, 1984—. Served to 1st lt. USMC, 1955-57. Mem. Wis. Intellectual Property Law Assn. (treas. 1984-85, pres. 1985-86). Republican. Lutheran. Avocations: hunting, fishing, photography. Patent, Trademark and copyright, Computer. Office: Johnson Controls Inc x75 PO Box 591 Milwaukee WI 53201

SHUPING, C(LARENCE) LEROY, JR., lawyer; b. Greensboro, N.C., Jan. 11, 1920; s. Clarence Leroy and Ruth (Hampton) S.; m. Bobbie Anne Clay, Sept. 22, 1949; children—Clay L., Nancy Anne. B.S. in Commerce, U. N.C.-Chapel Hill, 1941, J.D., 1947. Bar: N.C. 1947, U.S. Ct. Apls. (4th cir.) 1959. Spl. agent FBI, 1942-43; mem. Shuping and Shuping, Greensboro, 1947—. Mem. State N.C. Veterans Commn., 1952-53; chmn. bd. trustees Christ Methodist Ch., Greensboro, 1956-59, bd. stewards, 1956-59; mem. Guilford County (N.C.) Democratic Exec. Com., 1956-58. Served with AUS, 1944-46. Recipient cert. appreciation Sec. War Henry L. Stimson, 1945, cert. appreciation N.C. State Democratic Exec. com., 1966, citations of appreciation Am. Legion Dept. N.C., 1967, 70, 76, 77, 78, 79; citation of appreciation N.C. Vets. Council, 1979. Mem. N.C. State Bar, N.C. Bar Assn., Greensboro Bar Assn., Phi Alpha Delta. Democrat. Methodist. Club: Am. Legion (N.C. comdr. 1952-53, judge adv., 1951-52, 75—, vice chmn. Nat. Americanism council 1978-84, nat. legis. council 1976-80, 82—). practice, Corporate. State civil litigation, General practice, General corporate. Home: 610 Whittier Dr Greensboro NC 27403 Office: 430 Southeastern Bldg PO Drawer 239 Greensboro NC 27402

SHURN, PETER JOSEPH, III, lawyer; b. Queens, N.Y., Aug. 30, 1946; s. Peter J. Jr. and Vivienne M. (Tagliarino) S.; m. Ingrid Kelbert; children—Steven Douglas, Vanessa Leigh, David Michael. B.S.E.E. magna cum laude, Poly. Inst. Bklyn., 1974; J.D. magna cum laude, New Eng. Sch. Law, 1977; LL.M. in Patent and Trade Regulation Law, George Washington U., 1981. Bar: N.C., 1977, Va., 1979, Tex., 1982. Research scientist GTE Labs., 1965-77; sole practice, Raleigh, N.C., 1977-78; asso. Burns, Doane, Swecker & Mathis, Alexandria, Va., 1978-80; tech. advisor to judge U.S. Ct. Appeals (fed. cir.), 1980-81; ptnr. Arnold, White & Durkee, Houston, 1981—; adj. prof. South Tex. Coll. Law, 1984—. Served with U.S. Army, 1966-68; Korea. Mem. ABA, Houston Bar Assn., Am. Patent Law Assn. (Robert C. Watson award 1981), Houston Patent Law Assn., Assn. Trial Lawyers Am., IEEE, Sigma Xi. Contbr. articles to legal jours. State civil litigation, Patent, Federal civil litigation. Office: PO Box 4433 Houston TX 77210

SHUST, DIANE MARIE, lawyer, educator; b. Binghamton, N.Y., Aug. 17, 1954; d. Joseph E. and Rose Lillian (Ondrusek) S. BA, MS, U. Pa., 1976; JD, Georgetown U., 1979. Bar: D.C. 1980. Law clk. to presiding justice D.C. Superior Ct., Washington, 1979-80; atty. alts. for jailed children project Nat. Ctr. on Insts. and Alts., Washington, 1980-82; atty. human services com. D.C. Council, Washington, 1982; sr. supervising atty. juvenile services program Pub. Defender Service of D.C., Washington, 1982—. Bd. dirs. Oak Hill Scholarship Club, Washington, 1983—, sec., 1985—; bd. dirs. Visitors Services Ctr., Washington, 1982—, pres., 1984-85, sec., 1986—. Mem. ABA (juvenile justice com.), D.C. Bar Assn. (contbr., panelist Criminal Practice Inst. and Manual 1983— young lawyers sect.). Democrat. Roman Catholic. Avocations: cooking, tennis, running. Juvenile, Criminal. Office: Pub Defender Service DC 451 Indiana Ave NW Washington DC 20001

SHUSTER, MORRIS MYER, lawyer; b. Phila., Apr. 14, 1930; s. Philip and Miriam (Mokrin) S.; m. Lorna T. Greenspun, Dec. 25, 1960; children—Stephen B., Pamela L. B.S. in Econs., U. Pa., 1951, J.D., 1954; postgrad. Temple U., 1956-57. Bar: Pa. 1954, U.S. Dist. Ct. (ea. dist.) Pa. 1957, U.S. Ct. Appeals (3d cir.) 1959, U.S. Supreme Ct. 1967. Assoc. Freedman, Landy and Lorry, Phila., 1957-60, ptnr., 1960-66; sole practice, Phila., 1966-73; ptnr. Shuster and Beckman, Phila., 1973-84; spl. litigation counsel Cohen, Shapiro, Polisher, Shiekman & Cohen, Phila., 1984—; mem. panel arbitrators Am. Arbitration Assn.; lectr., clin. supr. clin. edn. U. Pa. Law Sch. 1981; guest lectr. on various legal subjects U. Pa. Law Sch., Med. Sch. and Dental Sch., Drexel U. Bd. govs. Reconstructionist Rabbinical Coll.; mem. steering com. Friends of Reconstructionist Rabbinical Coll. Served with U.S. Army, 1954-56. Mem. Phila. Bar Assn. (chmn. com. on civil jud. procedure state cts. 1974, bd. dirs. 59th St. Legal Clinic 1976-77, gov. 1976-78, assn. counsel in litigation 1977-79 and as amicus in case before Pa. Supreme Ct. 1981, mem. jud. commn. 1979-85, vice chmn. commn. 1981, chmn. commn. 1982-84, chmn. on civil legis./legis. liaison 1979, mem. vol. panel to provide legal services for indigent 1982-87), Phila. Trial Lawyers' Assn. (pres. 1975-76, dir.), Pa. Bar Assn., ABA, Pa. Trial Lawyers' Assn., Assn. Trial Lawyers Am., Am. Judicature Soc., U. Pa. Law Alumni Soc. (bd. mgrs. 1978-83, chmn. law alumni giving Phila. region 1979-80, treas. 1981-83, class agt. 1954—). State civil litigation, Personal injury. Home: 254 Lloyd Ln Wynnewood PA 19151 Office: PSFS Bldg 22nd Floor 12 S 12th St Philadelphia PA 19107

SHYER, HERBERT PAUL, lawyer, insurance company executive; b. Los Angeles, Apr. 29, 1930; s. Nathaniel and Cele (Caine) S. A.B., UCLA, 1950, M.A., 1952; postgrad., Grad. Sch. Arts and Scis., Harvard U., 1951-53; LL.B., Harvard U., 1956; postgrad. (Fulbright scholar), Oxford U., 1956-57. Bar: N.Y. 1957. Teaching fellow dept. govt. Harvard U., 1952-56; assoc. firm Cleary, Gottlieb, Steen & Hamilton, N.Y.C., 1957-67; with Equitable Life Assurance Soc. of U.S., N.Y.C., 1967—; gen. counsel Equitable Life Assurance Soc. of U.S., 1975—, exec. v.p., 1980—. Fellow Am. Bar Found.; mem. Am., N.Y. State bar assns., Assn. Bar City N.Y., Assn. Life Ins. Counsel, Phi Beta Kappa Assocs. (pres., dir. 1979-82, hon. dir. 1982—). General corporate. Home: 24 W 55th St New York NY 10019 Office: Equitable Life Assurance Soc US 787 7th Ave Suite 4701 New York NY 10019

SIBLEY, JAMES MALCOLM, lawyer; b. Atlanta, Aug. 5, 1919; s. John Adams and Nettie Whitaker (Cone) S.; m. Karen Norris, Apr. 6, 1942; children: Karen Mariea, James Malcolm Jr., Jack Norris, Elsa Alexandria Victoria, Quintus Whitaker. A.B., Princeton U., 1941; student, Woodrow Wilson Sch. Law, 1942, Harvard Law Sch., 1946. Bar: Ga. 1942. Asso. King & Spalding, Atlanta, 1942-47; partner King & Spalding, 1947—; dir. Trust Co. of Ga., also chmn. exec. com.; dir. Trust Co. Bank, SunTrust Banks, Inc., The Coca Cola Co., Ga. U.S. Corp., John H. Harland Co., Life Ins. Co. of Ga., Rock-Tenn Co. Trustee Joseph B. Whitehead Found., Lettie Pate Evans Found., Emory U., A. G. Rhodes Home, Inc., Robert W. Woodruff Found., Inc. (formerly Trebor Found.); trustee David, Helen and Marian Woodward Fund, also vice-chmn.; chmn. bd. trustees Jesse Parker Williams Hosp., Berry Coll., Inc.; bd. dirs. Callaway Gardens Found. Served with USAAF, 1942-45. Mem. ABA, Ga. Bar Assn., Atlanta Bar Assn., Atlanta Lawyers Club, Am. Coll. Probate Counsel, Am. Bar Found., Am. Law Inst. Episcopalian. Clubs: Piedmont Driving, Commerce, Capital City. Banking, General corporate, Probate. Home: 63 Peachtree St NE Atlanta GA 30309 Office: 2500 Trust Co Tower Atlanta GA 30303

SICILIANO, GERARD MICHAEL, lawyer; b. St. Louis, July 10, 1952; s. Gavin William and Marie E. (Madden) S.; m. Paula Jane McCray, Aug. 5, 1979; 1 child, Christina Louise. BA summa cum laude, Marshall U., 1978; JD, U. Tenn., 1981. Bar: Tenn. 1981, U.S. Dist. Ct. (ea. dist.) Tenn. 1982. Asst. dist. atty. Hamilton County, Tenn., 1982-84; assoc. Luther, Anderson, Cleary & Ruth, Chattanooga, 1984—. Mem. ABA, Tenn. Bar Assn., Chattanooga Bar Assn., Chattanooga Trial Lawyers Assn. Avocations: golf, racquetball, woodworking. Federal civil litigation, State civil litigation, Banking. Home: 6608 White Sands Ln Hixson TN 37343 Office: Luther Anderson Cleary & Ruth 99 Walnut St Chattanooga TN 37403

SICKLER, SANDRA DAVIS, lawyer; b. Waterloo, Iowa, Apr. 15, 1943; d. Benjamin and Lucile (Bard) Davis; m. Sheldon O. Sickler, June 9, 1962; children: Sherene, Shawn. BA magna cum laude, Eastern Nazarene Coll., 1975; JD, U. San Diego, 1980. Bar: Calif. 1980, U.S. Dist. Ct. (so. dist.) Calif. 1980. Assoc. Toone, Knowlton & Kimball, San Diego, 1981-82; ptnr. Knowlton & Sickler, San Diego, 1982—. Lectr. various seminars and ch. groups, 1982—. Mem. Calif. Bar Assn., San Diego County Bar Assn. (co-chmn. community services com. 1986—, co-chmn. sr. services subcom. 1986, client relations com. 1987). Mem. Nazarene Ch. Avocation: skiing. Probate, General corporate, Estate planning. Home: 4582 Adair St San Diego CA 92107 Office: Knowlton & Sickler 555 W Beech Suite 400 San Diego CA 92101

SIDAK, JOSEPH GREGORY, lawyer; b. Des Moines, Aug. 17, 1955. AB, Stanford U., 1977, MA, JD, 1981. Bar: Calif. 1982. Law clk. to judge U.S. Ct. Appeals (7th cir.), Chgo., 1981-82; assoc. O'Melveny & Myers, Los Angeles, 1982-84; cons. Boston Cons. Group, Los Angeles, 1984-86; sr. counsel Council of Econ. Advisors, Washington, 1986—. Contbr. articles to profl. jours. Republican. Office: Council of Econ Advisers The White House Washington DC 20500

SIDEBOTTOM, WILLIAM JEFFREY, lawyer; b. Washington, Nov. 5, 1947; s. John H. and Dorothy (Winlock) S.; m. Nancy Whitley, Oct. 14, 1972; 1 child, Katherine. BA, Bucknell U., 1969; JD, Villanova U., 1972. Bar: Pa. 1972. Assoc. Barley, Snyder, Cooper & Barber, Lancaster, Pa., 1972-75, ptnr., 1976—; Spkr. on worker's compensation issues, various orgns. Pres. March of Dimes, Lancaster, 1980-82; treas. Planned Parenthood of Lancaster, 1982-83; pres. bd. trustees Fulton Opera House Found., Lancaster, 1985-86. Mem. Am. Judicial Soc., Am. Soc. Law and Medicine, Pa. Bar. Assn. (workers compensation sect.). Republican. Episcopalian. Lodge: Rotary. Avocations: skiing, tennis, sailing. Workers' compensation. Home: 1412 Ridge Rd Lancaster PA 17601 Office: Barley Snyder Cooper & Barber 126 E King St Lancaster PA 17602

SIDES, JACK DAVIS JR., lawyer; b. Dallas, Sept. 18, 1939; s. Jack Davis Sr. and Edith Eugenia (Lowrie) S.; m. Nancy Pauline Cantwell, July 22, 1967 (div. Sept. 1976); children: Mary Katharine, Jack Davis III; m. Laura Gail Miller, Aug. 2, 1979; children: Susan Ashley, Stacy Anne. BBA, U. Tex., 1962, JD with honors, 1963. Bar: Tex. 1963. Assoc. Jackson, Walker, et al, Dallas, 1963-67, White, McElroy, White, Sides & Rector, Dallas, 1968-78; sole practice Dallas, 1978—. Editor: U. Tex. Law Review, 1963. Served with USAF, 1963-69. Mem. ABA, Tex. Bar Assn., (grievance com. 1979—), Dallas Bar Assn. (ethics com. 1973-77), Tex. Assn. Def. Counsel, Dallas Assn. Def. Counsel (sec. 1973-74). Republican. Methodist. Club: Brook Hollow Golf (Dallas). Avocations: tennis, jogging. Federal civil litigation, State civil litigation. Office: 2001 Bryan Tower Suite 1550 Dallas TX 75201

SIDO, KEVIN RICHARD, lawyer; b. Alton, Ill., Nov. 22, 1951; s. Robert Frederick and Mary (Colligan) S.; m. Mary O'Neil, July 28, 1984. BA, U. Ill., 1972, JD, 1975. Bar: Ill. 1975, U.S. Dist. Ct. (no. dist.) Ill. 1975, U.S. Tax Ct. 1976, U.S. Ct. Appeals (7th cir.) 1977, U.S. Supreme Ct. 1979. Assoc. Hinshaw, Culbertson, Moelmann, Hoban & Fuller, Chgo., 1975-82, ptnr., 1982—; lectr. Ill. Inst. Continuing Legal Edn., 1977—. Bd. dirs. Lake Barrington Shores (Ill.) Homeowners Assn., 1979. Mem. ABA, Ill. Bar Assn., Chgo. Bar Assn., Def. Research Inst. (lectr. 1983—), Ill. Def. Counsel Assn. (bd. dirs. 1982-83, editor 1984—), Union League, Phi Beta Kappa. Avocations: photography, antiques. State civil litigation, Insurance, Federal civil litigation. Office: Hinshaw Culbertson Moelmann Hoban & Fuller 69 W Washington #2700 Chicago IL 60602

SIEDZIKOWSKI, HENRY FRANCIS, lawyer; b. Chester, Pa., Dec. 27, 1953; s. Henry W. and Virginia (Szymanski) S. BA cum laude, Juniata Coll., 1975; JD magna cum laude, Villa Nova U., 1979. Bar: Pa. 1979, U.S. Dist. Ct. (ea. dist.) Pa. 1979, U.S. Ct. Appeals (3d cir.) 1979, U.S. Ct. Appeals (8th cir.) 1981, U.S. Dist. Ct. (we. dist.) Pa. 1986. Assoc. Dilworth, Paxson, Kalish & Kauffman, Phila., 1979-86; ptnr. Baskin, Flaherty, Elliot & Mannino P.C., Phila., 1986—; mem. hearing com. Disciplinary bd., Supreme Ct. Pa., 1985—. Mem. ABA (chmn. Lanham act subcom. of bus. torts com. of litigation sect. 1986—, rotating editor Newsletter of Anti-trust, sect. franchise com.), Pa. Bar Assn., Phila. Bar Assn. (chmn. subcom. disiplinary rules for profl. responsibility com. 1984—). Democrat. Roman Catholic. Federal civil litigation, Bankruptcy, Franchising and distribution. Office: Baskin Flaherty Elliot & Mannino PC 3 Mellon Bank Ctr 18th Fl Philadelphia PA 19102

SIEGAN, BERNARD HERBERT, lawyer, educator; b. Chgo., July 28, 1924; s. David and Jeannette (Seitz) S.; m. Sharon Goldberg, June 15, 1952 (dec. Feb. 5, 1985). Student, Herzl. Jr. Coll., Chgo., 1943, 46, Roosevelt Coll., Chgo., 1946-47; J.D., U. Chgo., 1949. Bar: Ill. 1950. Practiced in Chgo.; partner firm Siegan & Karlin, 1952-73; pres., sec. various small corps. and gen. partner in partnerships engaged in real estate ownership and devel. 1955-70; weekly columnist Freedom newspaper chain, other papers, 1974-79; cons. law and econs. program U. Chgo. Law Sch., 1970-73; adj. prof. law U. San Diego Law Sch., 1973-74, prof., 1974-75, disting. prof., 1975—; cons. windfalls and wipeouts project HUD, 1973-74; cons. FTC, 1985-86. Author: Land Use Without Zoning, 1972, Other People's Property, 1976, Economic Liberties and the Constitution, 1980; Editor: Planning without Prices, 1977, The Interaction of Economics and the Law, 1977, Regulation, Economics and the Law, 1979, Government, Regulation and the Economy, 1980. Mem. Pres.-Elect's Task Force on Housing, 1980-81; mem. Pres.'s Commn. on Housing, 1981-82; mem. Nat. Commn. on Bicentennial of U.S. Constn., 1985—; chmn. adv. com. Affordable Housing Conf., San Diego, 1985, Rights of Regulated Conf., Coronado, Calif., 1976; mem. devel. bd. Mingei Internat. Mus. of World Folk Art, 1981—. Served with AUS, 1943-46. Research fellow law and econs. U. Chgo. Law Sch., 1968-69; Urban Land Inst. research fellow, 1976—; recipient Leander J. Monks Meml. Fund award Inst. Humane Studies, 1972; George Washington medal Freedom Founds. at Valley Forge, 1981. Mem. ABA, Chgo. Bar Assn., Am. Judicature Soc. 1985—. Constitutional, Real property. Home: 6005 Camino de la Costa La Jolla CA 92037

SIEGAN, JEROLD NATHAN, lawyer; b. Chgo., Feb. 27, 1947; s. Harold A. and Bernice (Rubinoff) S.; m. Barbara G. (Gerber), July 29, 1969; children: Bradley J., Matthew B., Elizabeth A. BA, U. Ill., 1968; JD, De Paul U., 1972. Bar: Ill. 1972, D.C. 1973. Atty. SEC, Chgo., 1972-73, Washington, 1973-75; assoc. Arvey, Hodes, Costello & Burman, Chgo., 1975-77, Friedman & Koven, Chgo., 1977-78; sole practice Chgo., 1978-79; ptnr. Siegan, Barbakoff & Gomberg, Chgo., 1979—. Mem. Ill. Sec. State Securities Law Com., 1975-76; bd. dirs. Young Men's Jewish Council, Chgo., 1976-82, Ctr. for Enriched Living, Highland Park, Ill., 1986—. Recipient Future Interest award Am. Jurisprudence, 1976, Ill. Pub. Service award Ill. Sec. State Securities Law Com., 1976. Mem. Chgo. Bar Assn. (chmn. subcom. securities law com. 1978-79, 81-82). Securities, General corporate. Office: Siegan Barbakoff et al 20 N Clark St Suite 1000 Chicago IL 60602

SIEGEL, ALLEN GEORGE, lawyer; b. Chgo., May 19, 1934; s. David Harry and Jeanette (Morris) S.; m. Rochelle Robin, Mar. 12, 1961; children: Dina Robin, Jonathan Joseph. B.B.A., CCNY, 1957; LL.B. with distinction, Duke U., 1960. Bar: Fla. 1960, D.C. 1965. Sole practice Jacksonville, Fla., 1960-62; field atty. NLRB, 1962-64; assoc. Arent, Fox, Kintner, Plotkin & Kahn, Washington, 1964-70, ptnr., 1970-80, sr. ptnr., 1980—; sr. lectr. in law Duke U., Durham, N.C., 1979—. Author: Confidential Supervisors Guide to Labor Relations, 1980, Confidential Supervisors Guide to Equal Employment, 1981; contbr. articles. Past pres. United Cerebral Palsy D.C.; founder David H. Siegel Meml. Scholarship Duke U. Sch. Law, bd. dirs. pvt. ajudication ctr., 1986—. Served with U.S. Army, 1955-56, 61-62. Mordecai Soc. scholar. Mem. ABA, Am. Judicature Soc., Fla. Bar Assn., D.C. Bar Assn., Order of Coif. Republican. Jewish. Clubs: International of Washington. Labor, Workers' compensation, Administrative and regulatory. Home: 7505 Connecticut Ave Chevy Chase MD 20815 Office: Washington Square 1050 Connecticut Ave NW Washington DC 20036

SIEGEL, ARTHUR BERNARD, lawyer; b. Bklyn., Mar. 22, 1932; s. Abraham and Sarah (Hecht) S.; m. Miriam Ann Barck, Dec. 22, 1963; children: Hugh David, Susan Barck. BA, Syracuse U., 1954; M in Indsl. and Labor Relations, Cornell U., 1958; JD, Columbia U., 1971. Bar: Pa. 1972, U.S. Dist. (mid. dist.) Pa. 1979. Ptnr. Finan, Beecher, Wagner & Rose, P.A., Milford, Pa., 1972-79, Beecher, Wagner, Rose, Siegel & Klemeyer, Milford, 1979; sole practice Milford, 1979—; pub. defender Pike County (Pa.), Milford, 1980-82; solicitor Pa. twps. Porter, Blooming Grove, Greene and municipal authority Borough Milford. Contbr. articles Pike County Dispatch. Treas. Pike County Rep. com., Milford, 1982-84. Served to 1st lt. USAF, 1955-57, served to capt. USAFR, 1967. Mem. ABA, Pa. Bar Assn., Pike County Bar Assn., Columbia U. Law Sch. Alumni Assn., Pike County Legal Aid Soc. (founder 1979), Phi Beta Kappa, Phi Kappa Phi, Sigma Delta Chi. Jewish. Club: Cornell Club (N.Y.C.). Lodges: Rotary, Lions, Elks, Masons. Avocations: photography, music, collecting memorabilia, travel. Real property, Family and matrimonial, Local government. Home: Pine Acres Milford PA 18337 Office: 511 Broad St Milford PA 18337

SIEGEL, EDWARD, lawyer; b. Asbury Park, N.J., Jan. 15, 1931; s. Nathan Albert and Fannie (Kahn) S.; m. Helen Dorothy Haber, Aug. 29, 1954; children—Sharon, Frances. B.A., U. Fla., 1952, J.D., 1955. Bar: Fla. 1955. Spl. asst. atty. gen. Office Atty. Gen. Fla., Tallahassee, 1955; ptnr. Adams, Rothstein & Siegel, Jacksonville, Fla., 1957—. Author: How to Avoid Lawyers, 1969; Defend Yourself! The Moneysworth Legal Adviser, 1972. Mem. editorial bd. Fla. Bar Jour., 1979-86. Trustee Jacksonville Library Bd., 1978-82; bd. dirs. Jacksonville Jewish Ctr., 1968-70; bd. dirs., v.p. Jewish Family and Childrens Services, 1970-75. Served as 1st lt. USAF, 1955-57. Mem. ABA, Fla. Bar Assn., Jacksonville Bar Assn. (chmn. fee arbitration com. 1976-77), Assn. Trial Lawyers Am., Blue Key, Order of Coif, Phi Beta Kappa. Democrat. Real property, Consumer commercial, Family and matrimonial. Home: 6855 San Sebastian Ave Jacksonville FL 32217 Office: Adams Rothstein & Siegel 1530 First Union Bldg Jacksonville FL 32202

SIEGEL, EDWARD M., lawyer, management and administrative services professional; b. N.Y.C., Apr. 14, 1934; s. Charles and Rose (Fritzhand) S.; m. Elyse R. Roth, Mar. 9, 1969; children—Eric, Eve-Lynn. B.A., Columbia Coll., 1955, M.A. in Polit. Sci., 1957; J.D., 1960. Bar: N.Y. 1961. Legal asst. to dean Columbia U. Law Sch., 1960-65; gen. counsel Transp. Displays, Inc., N.Y.C., 1965-75, corp. sec., 1968-75, v.p., 1972-73, sr. v.p., dir. adminstrn., 1973-75; mgr. pub. affairs Fin. Services div. J.C. Penney Co., N.Y.C., 1975-77; gen. counsel Electro Audio Dynamics, Inc., Great Neck, N.Y., 1977-85, corp. sec., 1977-85, v.p., 1981-85; first v.p. legal affairs East View Co., N.Y.C., 1985—. Mem. staff Columbia Law Rev., 1958-59, editor, 1959-60. Harlan Fiske Stone scholar, 1957-58; recipient Kenneth M. Spence prize, 1958. Mem. Columbia Law Sch. Alumni Assn. (dir. 1966-70), N.Y. State Bar Assn., Am. Corp. Counsel Assn. General corporate. Home: 1036 Park Ave Apt 6D New York NY 10028 Office: East View Co 150 E 58th St Suite 2710 New York NY 10155

SIEGEL, GERALD WILLIAM, lawyer; b. Waterloo, Iowa, Sept. 21, 1917; s. Samuel and Rebecca (Wartey) S.; m. Helene Louise Jacober, Aug. 22, 1948; children: Robin Elizabeth, Robert Arthur. AB, Iowa U., 1941; LLB, Yale U., 1947. Bar: U.S. Dist. Ct. D.C. 1948, U.S. Ct. Appeals (D.C. cir.) 1948, U.S. Supreme Ct. 1952. Atty., exec. asst. to chmn. SEC, Washington, 1947-53; chief counsel dem. policy com. U.S. Senate, Washington, 1953-58; faculty Harvard U., Boston, 1958-61; v.p., counsel The Washington Post, Washington, 1961-75; of counsel Clifford, Warnkle, McIlwain & Finney, Washington, 1975-79; Dem. chief counsel U.S. Senate Com. on Rules and Adminstrn., Washington, 1979—; cons. United Research Inc., Boston, 1958-61. Served to maj. USAFR, 1942, 46-70. Mem. Fed. Bar Assn. Jewish. Club: Cosmos (Washington). Legislative, Administrative and regulatory, Securities. Home: 4921 30th Pl NW Washington DC 20008 Office: US Senate Com Rules & Adminstrn Russell Senate Office Bldg Washington DC 20510

SIEGEL, HAROLD ARYAI, lawyer; b. N.Y.C., Jan. 1, 1931; s. Jacob and Ruth (Eisen) S.; m. Valerie L. Rose, June 18, 1978; children: Brandy R. McNeil, Sandra M. Stimson, Marc A., P.J., Kevin, Trevor, Shelly, Sean Arthurs. BS, MIT, 1951; JD, Georgetown U., 1962. Bar: Md. 1963, U.S. Supreme Ct. 1966. Ptnr. Siegel & Siegel, Greenbelt, Md., 1962—; gen. counsel Radiation Systems Inc., Sterling, Va., 1966—. Republican. Jewish. Contracts commercial, Government contracts and claims, Personal injury. Home: 16 Maplewood Ct Greenbelt MD 20770 Office: Siegel & Siegel PO Box 25 Greenbelt MD 20770

SIEGEL, HOWARD JEROME, lawyer; b. Chgo., July 29, 1942; s. Leonard and Idele (Lehrner) S.; m. Diane L. Gerber; children—Sari D. and Allison J. B.S., U. Ill., 1963; J.D., Northwestern U., 1966. Bar: Ill. 1966, U.S. Dist. Ct. (no. dist.) Ill. 1967. Assoc., Ancel, Stonesifer & Glink, Chgo., 1966-70; ptnr. Goldstine & Siegel, Summit, Ill., 1970-75; sole practice, Chgo., 1975-77; pres.

Wexler, Siegel & Shaw, Ltd., Chgo., 1978-82; ptnr. Keck, Mahin & Cate, Chgo., 1982—; village atty., Willow Springs, Ill., 1973-75, Westhaven, Ill., 1973-75, Harwood Heights, Ill., 1967-70; dir. various corps. Mem. Deerfield Sch. Bd., Ill., 1978-80. Mem. ABA, Chgo. Bar Assn., Ill. Bar Assn., Internat. Council Shopping Ctrs., Urban Land Inst., Chgo. Real.Estate Bd. Clubs: Standard (Chgo.); Ravisloe Country (Homewood, Ill.). Real property, General corporate. Office: Keck Mahin & Cate 8300 Sears Tower Chicago IL 60606

SIEGEL, JULIAN LEE, patent attorney; b. Washington, July 22, 1928; s. Harry Alec and Etta (Schofer) S. BS, George Washington U., 1955, JD, 1959. Bar: Mass. 1969, U.S. Ct. Appeals (D.C. cir.) 1960, U.S. Supreme Ct. 1980, U.S. Ct. Appeals (fed. cir.) 1982; registered patent atty. U.S. Patent and Trademark Office. Mathematician, U.S. Naval Obs., Washington, 1954-62; patent atty. U.S. Air Force, Waltham, Mass., 1962-76, Hanscom AFB, Mass., 1976—, chief patent and data br. electronics systems div. Served with USN, 1946-48. Mem. Fed. Bar Assn., Boston Patent Law Assn., Nat. Contract Mgmt. Assn. Republican. Club: North Medford (Boston) (pres. 1976-78). Patent, Government contracts and claims. Home: 56 Fifer Ln Lexington MA 02173 Office: ESD/JAT Hanscom Air Force Base MA 01731

SIEGEL, LEWIS WOLFE, lawyer; b. N.Y.C., Oct. 24, 1949; s. Marcus S. and Edith (Davis) S. BA, Hobart Coll., 1970; JD, Georgetown U., 1974. Bar: N.Y. 1975, U.S. Dist. Ct. (so. and ea. dists.) 1975, U.S. Ct. Appeals, 1982, U.S. Ct. Appeals (2d cir.) 1982. House counsel C. Iton and Co. Inc., N.Y.C., 1974-79; assoc. Glass & Howard P.C., N.Y.C., 1979-83; sole practice N.Y.C., 1983—; exec. bd. U.S. Olympic Com., Colorado Springs, Colo., 1984—. Mem. ABA, Assn. Bar of City of N.Y., U.S. Fencing Assn. (pres. 1984—). Avocation: fencing. Bankruptcy, Contracts commercial, General corporate. Home: 201 W 85th St New York NY 10024 Office: 10 E 40th St New York NY 10016

SIEGEL, MARK JORDAN, lawyer; b. Dallas, Feb. 22, 1949; s. Jack H. and Zelda (Sikora) S. BS in Psychology, North Tex. State U., 1972; JD, Southwest Tex. Coll. Law, 1977. Bar: Tex. 1977, U.S. Dist. Ct. (no. dist.) Tex., U.S. Ct. Appeals (11th and 5th cirs.) 1982, U.S. Supreme Ct. 1982. Sole practice, Dallas, 1977—; bd. dirs. Intercontinental Bank, San Antonio, Scotch Corp., Dallas. Mem. N. Dallas 40. Named one of Outstanding Young Men Am., 1985, 86. Mem. Tex. Trial Lawyers Assn., Dallas Trial Lawyers Assn., Assn. Trial Lawyers Am. Personal injury, Workers' compensation, State civil litigation. Office: 3607 Fairmount St Dallas TX 75219

SIEGEL, MARLENA, lawyer; b. Phila., Apr. 7, 1953; d. Isadore Siegel and Libby (Oppenheim) Siegel Forman. B.A., Rutgers U., 1974; J.D., Temple U., 1979. Bar: Pa. 1979, U.S. Dist. Ct. (ea. dist.) Pa. 1979, U.S. Ct. Appeals (3d cir.) 1985, U.S. Supreme Ct. 1986. Law clk. firm Barsky, Golden & Remick, Phila., 1978-79, assoc., 1979-80; arbitrator Phila. Mcpl. Ct., 1982—; ptnr. Starr & Siegel, P.C., Phila., 1980-82, Zion & Siegel Assocs., 1986—; sole practice, Phila., 1982-85; instr. seminar, 1983. Bd. dirs. Phila. Ctr. Human Devel., Inc., 1982-86, counsel to bd., 1982-86. Mem. ABA, Pa. Bar Assn. (jud. adminstrn. com. 1985—), Phila. Bar Assn. (chmn. mcpl. ct. com. 1982—), Comml. Law League Am. (laws and legis. com. 1985—, pamphlet com. 1985—), Phila. Trial Lawyers Assn., Tau Epsilon Rho (exec. com. 1980—, asst. corr. sec. 1982-85, corr. sec. 1985—). Republican. Club: Phila. Lawyers'. Contracts commercial, Bankruptcy. Home: 7314 Germantown Ave Philadelphia PA 19119 Office: Zion & Siegel 1422 Chestnut St Philadelphia PA 19102 also: Rosemont Bus Campus 919 Conestoga Rd Bryn Mawr PA 19010

SIEGEL, NEIL YAHR, lawyer; b. Pitts., July 9, 1954; s. Edmond Harold and Edith Adele (Yahr) S.; m. Debra Helen Soybel, Aug. 20, 1978; children: Ann, Sarah. AB, Boston Coll., 1976, JD, 1979. Bar: Pa., 1979, U.S. Dist. Ct. (we. dist.) Pa. 1979, U.S. Supreme Ct. 1984. Assoc. Conte & Courtney, Conway, Pa., 1979-80; assoc. Hyatt Legal Services, Bridgeville, Pa., 1980-83, mng. atty., 1983-85; assoc. Bernstein & Bernstein, P.C., Pitts., 1985—. Part-time mem. Pitts. Opera Chorus; past mem. Mendelssohn Choir of Pitts. Mem. ABA, Pa. Bar Assn., Comml. Law League, Allegheny County Bar Assn., Phi Beta Kappa. Democrat. Jewish. Club: Beth El Men's (Pitts.) (past pres.). Bankruptcy, General practice, Consumer commercial. Home: 107 Mitchell Dr Pittsburgh PA 15241 Office: Bernstein & Bernstein PC 1133 Pennsylvania Ave Pittsburgh PA 15222

SIEGEL, PAUL, lawyer; b. Troy, N.Y., May 7, 1938; s. Benjamin and Mary (Silverman) S.; m. Elaine Beverly Kramer, May 19, 1973 (div. 1979); 1 child, Mark Aron. B.S. in Physics, U. Miami, 1958, LL.B., 1962. Bar: Fla. 1963, D.C. 1964, U.S. Supreme Ct. 1967, U.S. Ct. Appeals (5th cir.) 1967, U.S. Ct. Appeals (11th cir.) 1982. Cert. civil trial lawyer Fla. Bar. Mem. gen. counsel's office AEC, Washington, 1962-65; ptnr. Sinclair, Louis, Siegel, Heath, Nussbaum & Zavertnik, P.A., Miami, Fla., 1972—. Editor-in-chief U. Miami Law Rev. Chmn. bd. dirs. Alliance Francaise of Dade County, 1983—. Democrat. Jewish. Personal injury, Family and matrimonial, State civil litigation. Home: 235 E San Marino Dr Miami Beach FL 33139 Office: Sinclair Louis Siegel Heath Nussbaum & Zavertnik PA 11 25 Alfred I duPont Bldg Miami FL 33131

SIEGEL, ROBERT IRWIN, lawyer; b. N.Y.C., Nov. 7, 1954; s. Arthur Bernard and Edith (Kleinman) S.; m. Maria Kulmatycki, June 23, 1984. Undergrad., U. Ill., 1972-73; BA, SUNY, Binghamton, 1976; JD, Loyola U., New Orleans, 1979. Bar: La. 1979, U.S. Dist. Ct. (ea., mid. and we. dists.) La. 1979, U.S. Ct. Appeals (5th and 11th cirs.) 1979. Assoc. Camp, Carmouche, Gray & Hoffman, New Orleans, 1979-82; ptnr. Carmouche, Gray & Hoffman, New Orleans, 1982—, also bd. dirs., treas. Mem. ABA, La. Assn. Def. Counsel, New Orleans Assn. Def. Counsel, Def. Research Inst., Maritime Law Assn. Democrat. Jewish. Clubs: City Club, Lakewood Country (New Orleans). Avocations: golf, softball. Admiralty, Federal civil litigation, Insurance. Home: 95 S Wren St New Orleans LA 70124 Office: Carmouche Gray & Hoffman 2100 Poydras Ctr New Orleans LA 70130

SIEGEL, STANLEY, legal educator, lawyer; b. N.Y.C., Mar. 2, 1941; s. David Aaron and Rose (Minsky) S.; m. Karina Haum, July 20, 1986; children: Mark Leonard, Janet Valerie, Toby Caron. B.S. summa cum laude, NYU, 1960; J.D. magna cum laude, Harvard U., 1963. Bar: N.Y. 1963, D.C. 1964, Calif. 1976, Mich. 1970. Atty. Office Sec. of Air Force, 1963-66; asst. prof. law U. Mich., Ann Arbor, 1966-69, assoc. prof., 1969-71, prof., 1971-74; ptnr. Honigman, Miller, Schwartz & Cohn, Detroit, 1974-76; prof. law UCLA, 1976-86, NYU, 1986—; vis. prof. Stanford Law Sch., 1973; cons. reorgn. U.S. Postal Service, 1969-71; exec. sec. Mich. Law Revision Commn., 1973; bd. examiners Am. Inst. C.P.A.s, 1980-83. Author: (with Schulman and Moscow) Michigan Business Corporations, 1979, (with Conard and Knauss) Enterprise Organization, 4th edit., 1987, (with D. Siegel) Accounting and Financial Disclosure: A Guide to Basic Concepts, 1983. Served to capt. USAF, 1963-66. Mem. ABA, D.C. Bar Assn., Calif. Bar Assn., Assn. Bar City N.Y., Am. Inst. C.P.A.s. Legal education, General corporate, Corporate taxation. Office: NYU Law Sch 40 Washington Sq South New York NY 10012

SIEGEL-BAUM, JUDITH ELLEN, lawyer; b. Washington, Pa., Dec. 9, 1946; d. Sherman Harold and Miriam (Danzinger) S. BA, U. Wis., 1968; MA, Emerson Coll., 1969; JD, New Eng. Sch. of Law, 1978. Bar: N.Y. 1979, U.S. Dist. Ct. (so. and ea. dists.) N.Y. 1981. Asst. staff atty. N.Y. State Commn. Jud. Conduct, N.Y.C., 1979; asst. atty. gen. State of N.Y., N.Y.C., 1979-82; ptnr. Weidman & Siegel-Baum, N.Y.C., 1982-86; sole practice N.Y.C., 1986—; guest lectr. continuing legal edn. Yeshiva U., N.Y.C., 1984—. Mem. Murray Hill Com., N.Y.C., 1981—. Mem. ABA, N.Y. State Bar Assn. (trust and estates com.), Assn. of Bar of City of N.Y., N.Y. County Lawyers Assn. Jewish. Probate, State civil litigation, Family and matrimonial. Home: 40 Park Ave Box 128 New York NY 10016 Office: 120 E 37th St New York NY 10016

SIEGELMAN, DON EUGENE, state official; b. 1946. B.A., U. Ala.; J.D., Georgetown U., 1972; postgrad., Oxford U., Eng., 1972-73. Bar: Ala. 1972. Sec. of state State of Ala., Montgomery, 1979—. Office: Office of Sec of State State Capitol Montgomery AL 36130

SIEGFRIED, DAVID CHARLES, lawyer; b. N.Y.C., Feb. 15, 1942; s. Charles Albert and Marjorie Claire (Young) S.; m. Meri Stephanie Smith; children: Karin Elisabeth, Christine Elise. AB summa cum laude, Princeton U., 1964; JD, Harvard U., 1967. Bar: N.Y. 1970. Assoc. Milbank, Tweed, Hadley & McCloy, N.Y.C., 1968-76, ptnr., 1977-79, 83-85; resident ptnr. Milbank, Tweed, Hadley & McCloy, Hong Kong and Singapore, 1979-83, 85—; speaker at confs. and seminars. Served to 1st lt. USAR, 1967-74. Mem. ABA, N.Y. State Bar Assn., Internat. Bar Assn., Internat. Law Inst., Am. Soc. Internat. Law. Congregationalist. Clubs: Princeton (New York/Hong Kong) (v.p., schs. chmn.), Short Hills (N.J.), Am. (Hong Kong/Singapore), Tanglin (Singapore), Cricket. Avocations: running, tennis, historic reading. Banking, Private international, Contracts commercial. Home: 25 Claymore Rd #1802 A, Singapore Singapore 0922

SIEGLER, LORA CELIA, lawyer; b. Paterson, N.J., May 13, 1957; d. Harry and Helen (Fox) Siegler. B.A. in English, U. Pa., 1977; J.D., Rutgers U., 1980. Bar: N.Y. 1981, Utah 1983. Research asst. Rutgers U., Camden, N.J., 1978-80; securities analyst Utah Securities Div., Salt Lake City, 1980-83; sole practice law, Salt Lake City, 1983—; legal cons. Dept. Fin. Inst., Salt Lake City, 1983-85. Mem. ACLU. U. Pa. scholar, 1974. Mem. ABA, Utah Bar Assn., N.Y. State Bar Assn. (corp. sec. 1983—), Salt Lake County Bar Assn. Securities, General corporate, Contracts commercial. Office: 1399 S 700 E #12 Salt Lake City UT 84105

SIEMER, DEANNE C., lawyer; b. Buffalo, Dec. 25, 1940; d. Edward D. and Dorothy J. (Helsdon) S.; m. Howard P. Willens; 1 child, Jason L. BA, George Washington U., 1962; LLB, Harvard U., 1968. Bar: N.Y. 1968, D.C. 1969, Md. 1972, Trust Ter. 1976. Economist Office of Mgmt. and Budget, Washington, 1964-67; from assoc. to ptnr. Wilmer, Cutler & Pickering, Washington, 1968—; gen. counsel U.S. Dept. of Def., Washington, 1977-79; spl. asst. to sec. U.S. Dept. of Energy, Washington, 1979-80. Author: Tangible Evidence, 1984, Understanding Modern Ethical Standards, 1985, Manual on Litigation Support Databases, 1986. Mem. exec. com. Lawyers for Civil Rights, Washington, 1973—; mediator multidoor program D.C. Superior Ct., Washington, 1986. Recipient Citation Air Force Assn., 1977, Dist. Pub. Service medal Sec. of Def., 1979, Commendation Pres. of U.S. 1981. Mem. ABA, D.C. Bar Assn., No. Marianas Bar Assn., Womens Bar Assn., Assn. Trial Lawyers Am. Episcopalian. Federal civil litigation, State civil litigation, Administrative and regulatory. Office: Wilmer Cutler & Pickering 2445 M St NW Washington DC 20037

SIEMON, JOYCE MARILYN, lawyer, writer; b. Bridgeport, Conn., Dec. 4, 1944; d. George Lewis and Rita (Siegel) Nissenson; 1 child, Alyssa Karen. BA in English, Carnegie Inst. Tech., 1966; JD with high honors, Fla. State U., 1980. Bar: Fla. Tech. writer Computer Sci. Research Ctr. Carnegie Inst. Tech., Pitts., 1966-67; tchr. Leesville (La.) Jr. High Sch., 1967-68, Leesville State Sch., 1968; mag. editor VanTrump, Zeigler and Shane, Pitts., 1969; news editor Pitts. Press, 1970; staff writer Dade County Pub. Safety Dept., Miami, 1971-75; reporter North Dade Jour., Miami, 1977; freelance writer, 1977—; instr. legal writing and research Coll. Law Fla. State U., Tallahassee, 1979-80; intern. Fla. Supreme Ct., 1980; law clk. Office Gen. Counsel, Fla. Dept. Gen. Services, Tallahassee, 1980; assoc. Young, Stern & Tannenbaum, P.A., North Miami Beach, Fla., 1981, Greenberg, Traurig, Askew, Hoffman, Lipoff, Quentel & Wolff, P.A., Miami, Fla., 1981-82, Hornsby & Whisenand, Miami, 1982-85; sole practice, North Miami Beach, 1985—. Editor: Lawrenceville: A Short History, 1969; author weekly humor column Siemon Says, North Date Jour., 1977; author employee manual, advt. brochures, newspaper articles and ads, book revs.; author, editor, contbr. articles to legal and non-legal publs. Dade County coordinator Network, 1983; corr. sec. Democratic Club of North Dade; bd. dirs. The Forum of North Dade, Inc. Mem. ABA, Fla. Bar (various coms.), Am. Judicature Soc., Dade County Bar Assn., Order of Coif, Phi Alpha Delta. Jewish. General practice, State civil litigation, Real property. Office: Senator Bldg 13899 Biscayne Blvd North Miami Beach FL 33181

SIERATZKI, STEVEN SOLOMON, lawyer; b. N.Y.C., Aug. 28, 1954. BA, CUNY Queens Coll., Flushing, 1976; JD, Hofstra U., 1979. Bar: N.Y. 1980, U.S. Dist. Ct. (so. and ea. dists.) N.Y. 1980. Staff atty. Community Action for Legal Services, N.Y.C., 1979-81; assoc. Rosenberg & Estis, N.Y.C., 1981-84; ptnr. Jacobs, Sieratzki & Zinns, N.Y.C., 1984—. Real property, Landlord-tenant, State civil litigation. Home: 85-19 Chelsea St Jamaica Estates NY 11432

SIFFERT, JOHN SAND, lawyer, educator, author; b. N.Y.C., Mar. 26, 1947; s. Robert Spencer and Miriam (Sand) S.; m. Goldie Alfasi-Siffert, June 1, 1975; children: David Alfasi, Matthew Alfasi. BA, Amherst Coll., 1969; JD, Columbia U., 1972. Bar: N.Y. 1973, U.S. Dist. Ct. (so. dist.) N.Y. 1974, (ea. dist.) N.Y. 1974, U.S. Ct. Appeals (2d cir.) 1974, U.S. Supreme Ct. 1979. Law clk. to Hon. Murray I. Gurfein, U.S. Dist. Ct. (so. dist.) N.Y., 1972-74; asst. U.S. atty., 1974-79; ptnr. firm Fulop & Hardee and predecessor firm Barovick, Konecky, et al, N.Y.C., 1979-83, Lankler & Siffert, N.Y.C., 1983-84, Lankler, Siffert & Wohl, N.Y.C., 1984—; adj. assoc. prof., NYU, 1979—. Co-author: Business Crime, 1981, Modern Federal Jury Instructions-Criminal, 1984, Modern Federal Jury Instructions-Civil, 1985. Mem. ABA, N.Y. State Bar Assn., Bar Assn. City of N.Y. Democrat. Jewish. Federal civil litigation, State civil litigation, Criminal. Office: Lankler Siffert & Wohl 1120 Ave of Americas New York NY 10036

SIFTON, CHARLES PROCTOR, judge; b. N.Y.C., Mar. 18, 1935; s. Paul F. and Claire G. S.; m. Susan Scott Rowland, May 20, 1986; children: Samuel, Tobias, John. A.B., Harvard U., 1957; LL.B., Columbia U., 1961. Bar: N.Y. 1961. Assoc. Cadwalader, Wickersham & Taft, 1961-62, 64-66; staff atty. U.S. Senate Fgn. Relations Com., 1962-63; asst. U.S. atty. N.Y.C., 1966-69; partner LeBoeuf, Lamb, Leiby and MacRae, N.Y.C., 1969-77; judge U.S. Dist. Ct. Eastern Dist. N.Y., Bklyn., 1977—. Mem. Bar Assn. City of N.Y. Jurisprudence. Office: 225 Cadman Plaza E Brooklyn NY 11201

SIGAL, MICHAEL STEPHEN, lawyer; b. Chgo., July 9, 1942; s. Carl I. and Evelyn (Wallack) S.; m. Kass M. Flaherty, May 16, 1971; 1 child, Sarah Caroline. B.S., U. Wis.-Madison, 1964; J.D., U. Chgo., 1967. Bar: Ill. 1967, U.S. Dist. Ct. (no. dist.) Ill. 1967. Assoc. firm Sidley & Austin and predecessor firm, Chgo., 1967-73, ptnr., 1973—. Mem. U. Chgo. Law Rev., 1965. Bd. dirs. EMRE Diagnostic Services, Inc., affiliate Michael Reese Hosp., Chgo., 1982—, The Mary Meyer Sch., Chgo., 1986—. Mem. Chgo. Bar Assn., Ill. State Bar Assn., ABA, Phi Beta Kappa, Phi Kappa Phi, Phi Eta Sigma. Jewish. Clubs: Law, Monroe (Chgo.); Mill Creek Hunt (Wadsworth, Ill.). General corporate, Securities. Home: 2821 N Pine Grove Ave Chicago IL 60657 Office: Sidley & Austin 1 First National Plaza Chicago IL 60603

SIGALL, MICHAEL WILLIAM, lawyer, legal educator; b. N.Y.C., July 10, 1944; s. Leon and Hertha (Dubiner) S.; m. Roberta Diane Kramer, Mar. 9, 1975; children: Jessica Sarah, Jeremy Karl. BA, The City Coll., 1966; PhD, CUNY, 1970; JD, Fordham U., 1977. Bar: N.Y. 1978, U.S. Dist. Ct. (so. and ea. dists.) N.Y. 1978. Assoc. Shea, Gould, Climenko & Casey, N.Y.C., 1977-79; ptnr. Green, Sigall & Zich, P.C., N.Y.C., 1979-85; sole practice N.Y.C., 1985—; asst. prof. Finch Coll., N.Y.C., 1970-73, Wagner Coll., Staten Island, N.Y., 1973-77; adj. assoc. prof. N.Y. Law Sch., N.Y.C., 1981—. Co-author: Political Bargaining, 1976; co-editor The American Political Reality, 1972, New Patterns in American Politics, 1975. Emergency med. technician Hatzoloh Vol. Ambulance Corps., N.Y.C., 1985—. Mem. ABA, Assn. of Bar of City of N.Y. Jewish. Avocation: breeding pet fish. Probate, Immigration and naturalization, Real property. Office: 505 Fifth Ave New York NY 10017

SIGUENZA, PETER C., JR., territory judge. Judge U.S. Superior Ct., Agara, Guam. Office: Superior Ct of Guam Judiciary Bldg Agara GU 96910 *

SIKORA, FREDERICK JOSEPH, lawyer; b. Elizabeth, N.J., June 25, 1945; s. Joseph and Stephanie S.; m. Vera Jeanne Nolan, Dec. 26, 1976; children: Douglas Frederick, Matthew Frederick, Christopher Frederick. BA, Seton Hall U., 1967, JD, 1970. Bar: N.J. 1971, U.S. dist. ct. N.J. 1971. Assoc. Sachar, Bernstein & Rothberg, Plainfield, N.J., 1971-76; ptnr. Sachar, Bernstein, Rothberg, Sikora & Mongello, Esqs., Plainfield, 1976-81, Sachar & Sikora, P.A., Plainfield, 1981-86; pres. Frederick J. Sikora, P.A., Warren, N.J., 1986—; mem. exec. com. family law sect. State Bar N.J., 1982-86. Pub. N.J. Family Lawyer, 1986. Mem. ABA, N.J. Bar Assn., State Bar N.J. (mem. exec. com. family law sect. 1982), Union County Bar Assn. (speaker matrimonial law), PLainfield Bar Assn., Somerset County Bar Assn., Am. Acad. Matrimonial Lawyers, Phi Alpha Delta. Roman Catholic. Club: Plainfield Country (Edison, N.J.). Family and matrimonial. Office: 51 Mount Bethel Rd PO Box 4912 Warren NJ 07060-4912

SIKORA, TED ROBERT, II, lawyer; b. Gary, Ind., May 21, 1946; 1 child, Zachary. BA in History, The Citadel, Mil. Coll. S.C., 1968; JD, Northwestern U., 1973. Bar: Wis. 1973. Atty. Northwestern Mut. Life Ins. Co., Milw., 1973-76; sr. atty. Joseph Schlitz Brewing Co., Milw., 1976-81; gen. counsel Koss Corp., Milw., 1981-84; v.p., assoc. gen. counsel The Marine Corp., Milw., 1985—. Served with U.S. Army, 1968-70. Mem. ABA, Wis. Bar Assn., Milw. Bar Assn. General corporate, Banking, Securities. Office: The Marine Corp 111 E Wisconsin Ave Milwaukee WI 53202

SIKORA, WARREN, lawyer; b. Chgo., May 6, 1921; s. Paul Arthur and Mae Theresa (Hampl) S.; m. Jean Pessell, Nov. 20, 1943; children: Paul Elliott, Catherine Ann, Michael Warren. BA, U. Chgo., 1942, MBA, 1946; JD, UCLA, 1952. Bar: Calif. 1953, U.S. Dist. Ct. (cen. dist.) Calif. 1953, U.S. Ct. Appeals (9th cir.) 1960, U.S. Supreme Ct. 1962. Acct. Arthur Andersen, Los Angeles, 1946-47, Roberts & Coombs, Los Angeles, 1947-49; assoc. Paul Hastings & Janofsky, Los Angeles, 1952-54; ptnr. Rutan & Tucker, Santa Ana, Calif., 1954-66, Sikora & Price Inc., Santa Ana, 1966—. Served to capt. USMCR, 1942-46. Mem. ABA (vice chmn. sales and fin. trans. com. tax sect. 1985). Republican. Episcopalian. Clubs: Santa Ana Country, LaQuinta Country. Lodges: Masons, Shriners, Elks. Avocations: golf, travel. Probate, Real property, Personal income taxation. Home: 22801 Corralejo Mission Viejo CA 92692 Office: Sikora & Price Inc 2913 Pullman PO Box 15707 Santa Ana CA 92705

SILBAUGH, PRESTON NORWOOD, savings and loan consultant, lawyer; b. Stockton, Cal., Jan. 15, 1918; s. Herbert A. and Della Mae (Masten) S.; m. Maria Sarah Arriola; children—Judith Ann Silbaugh Freed, Gloria Silbaugh Stypinski, Ximena Carey Silbaugh Braun, Carol Lee Silbaugh Morgan. A.B. in Philosophy, U. Wash., 1940; J.D., Stanford U., 1953. Bar: Calif. With Lockheed Aircraft Corp., 1941-44, Pan Am. World Airways, 1944, Office Civilian Personnel, War Dept., 1944-45; engaged in ins. and real estate in Calif., 1945-54; mem. faculty Stanford Law Sch., 1954-59, asso. prof. law, 1956-59, asso. dean, 1956-59; chief dep. savs. and loan commnr. for Calif., 1959-61, bus. and commerce adminstr., dir. investment, savs. and loan commr., mem. gov.'s cabinet, 1961-63; dir. Chile-Calif. Aid Program, Sacramento and Santiago, 1963-65; chmn. bd. Beverly Hills Savs. & Loan Assn., Calif., 1965-84; dir. Wickes Cos., Inc.; chmn. bd., pres. Simon Bolivar Fund, Del Mar, Calif.; of counsel firm Miller, Boyko & Bell, San Diego. Author: The Economics of Personal Insurance, 1958; also articles. Mem. pres.'s real estate adv. com. U. Calif., 1966—; mem. Beverly Hills Pub. Bldg. Adv. Com., 1970—. Served with USMCR, 1942-43. Mem. ABA, San Diego County Bar Assn., Soc. Internat. Devel., U.S., Nat., Calif. Savs. and Loan Leagues, Inter-Am. Savs. and Loan Union, Internat. Union Building Socs., U. Wash., Stanford Alumni Assns., Calif. Aggie Alumni Assn., Order of Coif, Phi Alpha Delta. Clubs: Commonwealth (San Francisco), Town Hall (Los Angeles). Banking. Home: 13059 Caminito del Rocio Del Mar CA 92014 also: Costenera del Sur, Zapallar Chile

SILBER, NORMAN JULES, lawyer; b. Tampa, Fla., Apr. 18, 1945; s. Abe and Mildred (Hirsch) S.; m. Linda Geraldine Hirsch, June 10, 1979; 1 child, Michael Hirsch. BA, Tulane U., 1967, JD, 1969; postgrad. in bus. adminstrn. NYU, 1970-72. Bar: Fla. 1970, U.S. Dist. Ct. (so. dist. Fla.) 1975, U.S. Tax Ct. 1975, U.S. Ct. Appeals (5th cir.) 1975, U.S. Ct. Appeals (11th cir.) 1981. With legal dept. Fiduciary Trust Co. N.Y., N.Y.C., 1969-72, asst. trust officer, 1971-72; exec. v.p. I.R.E. Fin. Corp., Miami, Fla., 1972-76; mng. atty. Norman J. Silber, P.A., Miami, 1973-85; ptnr. McDermott, Will & Emery, 1985—. Mem. ABA, Fla. Bar (chmn. 11th jud. cir. grievance com. I 1982-84), Dade County Bar Assn., Am. Judicature Soc., Assn. Trial Lawyers Am., Acad. Fla. Trial Lawyers. Republican. Jewish. Club: Standard (Miami). Real property, General corporate, General practice. Home: 1232 Palermo Ave Coral Gables FL 33134 Office: 700 Brickell Ave Miami FL 33131

SILBERBERG, HENRY J., lawyer; b. Paris, Tenn., Jan. 30, 1944; s. Joseph and Lila (Boch) S.; m. Jeanne Fenmore, Aug. 16, 1969; children: Lori, Douglas. BS, CCNY, 1965; JD, NYU, 1968. Bar: N.Y 1968, U.S Ct. Appeals (2d cir.) 1968, U.S. Supreme Ct. 1973, Calif. 1976, U.S. Ct. Appeals (9th cir.) 1979, U.S. Dist. Ct. (so. and ea. dists.) N.Y., U.S. Dist. Ct. (no. and so. dists.) Calif. Law clk. to presiding justice U.S. Ct. Appeals (2d cir.), N.Y.C., 1968-69; instr. law UCLA, Los Angeles, 1969-70; from assoc. to ptnr. Stroock & Stroock & Lavan, Los Angeles, 1970—. Pomeroy scholar NYU, 1966-68. Mem. Calif. Bar Assn., Los Angeles County Bar Assn., Assn. Bus. Trial Lawyers, NYU Sch. Law Alumni Assn. (class rep. 1985—), Am. Arbitration Assn. (arbitrator 1972—), Practising Law Inst. (lectr.), Order of Coif. Federal civil litigation, State civil litigation. Home: 3104 Hutton Dr Beverly Hills CA 90210 Office: Stroock & Stroock & Lavan 2029 Century Park E Los Angeles CA 90067

SILBERBLATT, JAY NED, lawyer; b. Clearfield, Pa., Nov. 23, 1955; s. Paul and Gloria (Kolb) S.; m. Lori A. Sisson, Sept. 26, 1985. BA cum laude, Allegheny Coll., 1977; JD, U. Pitts., 1980. Bar: Pa. 1980, U.S. Dist. Ct. (we. dist.) Pa. 1980, U.S. Ct. Appeals (3d cir.) 1986, U.S. Supreme Ct. 1986. From assoc. to ptnr. Sikov & Love P.A., Pitts., 1980—. Mem. exec. com. Allegheny Coll. Alumni Congress, Meadville, Pa., 1985—; pres. Temple Sinai Brotherhood, Pitts., 1984-86, asst. fin. sec.; bd. dirs. Nat. Fedn. Temple Brotherhoods. Mem. ABA, Pa. Bar Assn., Allegheny County Bar Assn. (civil litigation sect. council), Assn. Trial Lawyers Am., Pa. Trial Lawyers Assn., Allegheny Coll. Alumni Assn. (treas. 1984-86, pres. 1986—), Pi Gamma Mu. Democrat. Avocations: golf, racquetball, swimming, travel. State civil litigation, Federal civil litigation, General practice. Home: 225 E Swissvale Ave Pittsburgh PA 15218 Office: Sikov & Love PA 1400 Lawyers Bldg Pittsburgh PA 15219

SILBERGELD, ARTHUR F., lawyer; b. St. Louis, June 1, 1942; s. David and Sabina (Silbergeld) S.; m. Carol Ann Schwartz, May 1, 1970; children—Diana Lauren, Julia Kay. B.A., U. Mich., 1968; M.City Planning, U. Pa., 1971; J.D., Temple U., 1975. Bar: N.Y. 1976, Calif. 1978, D.C. 1983, U.S. Dist. Ct. (so. and ea. dists.) N.Y. 1976, U.S. Dist. Ct. (cen., no., ea. and so. dists.) Calif. 1978, U.S. Ct. Appeals (2d, 9th and D.C. cirs.). Assoc. Vladeck, Elias, Vladeck & Lewis, N.Y.C., 1975-77; field atty. NLRB, Los Angeles, 1977-78; ptnr., head employment law practice group McKenna, Conner & Cuneo, Los Angeles, 1978—; instr. extension div. UCLA, 1981—. Contbr. articles to profl. jours. Founding mem. Los Angeles Mus. Contemporary Art; bd. dirs. Bay Cities unit Am. Cancer Soc., Calif., 1981-85, Jewish Family Service Los Angeles, 1981-85 . Mem. ABA, Def. Research Inst., Los Angeles County Bar Assn. (exec. bd. labor law sect. 1984—). Labor. Office: McKenna Conner & Cuneo 3435 Wilshire Blvd Los Angeles CA 90010

SILBERING, ROBERT HOWARD, lawyer; b. N.Y.C., June 6, 1947; s. Morris and Tessie (Kushner) S.; m. Rochelle Melamed, Nov. 12, 1972; children: Jill, David. BA, Fairleigh Dickinson U., 1969; JD, Bklyn. Law Sch., 1974. Bar: N.Y. 1975, U.S. Dist. Ct. (so. and ea. dists.) N.Y. 1975, U.S. Ct. Appeals (2d. cir.) 1975. Asst. dist. atty., bur. chief N.Y. County, N.Y.C., 1974—; chief asst. dist. atty. Office of Prosecution, Spl. Narcotics Cts., 1984—; lectr. bur. prosecution and def. services N.Y. State Div. Criminal Justice Services. Mem. ABA, N.Y. State Bar Assn. (lectr.), N.Y. County Bar Assn. (lectr.), Nat. Coll. Dist. Attys. (lectr.). Criminal. Office: NY County Dist Atty's Office New York NY 10013

SILBERMAN, CURT C., lawyer; b. Wuerzburg, Germany; came to U.S., 1938, naturalized, 1944; s. Adolf and Ida (Rosenbusch) S.; m. Else Kleemann, 1935. Student U. Berlin, U. Munich; J.D. summa cum laude, Wuerzburg U., 1931; J.D., Rutgers U., 1947. Bar: N.J. 1948, U.S. Supreme Ct., 1957. Sole practice internat. pvt. law, Florham Park, N.J., 1948—; counsel to Arnold R. Kent, Florham Park; lectr. internat. pvt. law, 1954, 81,

82; prin. guest lectr. at Univ.'s 400th anniversary U. Wuerzburg, 1982. Pres., Am. Fedn. Jews from Central Europe, N.Y., 1962-86, chmn. bd., 1986—; pres. Jewish Philanthropic Fund of 1933, Inc., N.Y., 1971—; trustee Leo Baeck Inst., N.Y., 1962—, N.Y. Found. Nursing Homes, Inc.; hon. trustee Jewish Family Service of Metro-West, N.J.; co-chmn. Council of Jews from Germany, 1974—; chmn. Research Found. for Jewish Immigration Inc. N.Y.; dir. Conf. on Jewish Material Claims Against Germany. Recipient Golden Doctoral Diploma U. Wuerzburg Law faculty, 1982, Festschrift dedicated to him by Am. Fedn. Jews from Cen. Europe in N.Y., 1969, recipient Pub. Service medal. Mem. N.J. Bar Assn. (chmn. com. comparative jurisprudence 1966-73, chmn. com. internat. trade 1974-78), Essex County Bar Assn., German-Am. Lawyers Assn., German-Am. C. of C. Contbr. articles to legal jours.; also lectr. on polit. edn. and contemporary Jewish history. Private international.

SILBERMAN, JOHN ALAN, lawyer; b. Balt., Sept. 20, 1951; s. Ronnie A. and Dovera (Gogel) S. BA, Northwestern U., 1973; JD, Harvard U., 1976. Bar: N.Y. 1977, U.S. Dist. Ct. (so. and ea. dists.) N.Y. 1977. Assoc. Paul, Weiss, Rifkind, Wharton & Garrison, N.Y.C., 1976-84, ptnr., 1985—; bd. dirs. N.Y. Stage and Film Co., N.Y.C. Bd. dirs. Council on Econ. Priorities, N.Y.C., 1986—. Entertainment, Advertising. Office: Paul Weiss Rifkind Wharton & Garrison 1285 Ave of Americas New York NY 10019

SILBERSTEIN, N. RONALD, lawyer; b. Boston, Feb. 23, 1927; s. Moses and Rose (Silverman) S.; m. Ruth Gerst, Dec. 26, 1954; children: Peter, Margery, Amy. A.B., Yale U., 1949; LL.B., Harvard U., 1952. Bar: Mass. 1952, N.Y. 1955. Clk. Judge John C. Knox, Chief Judge U.S. Dist. Ct., N.Y.C., 1955; v.p., gen. counsel Sheraton Corp. Am., Boston, 1956-73; sec. Sheraton Corp. Am., 1969-73, sr. v.p., gen. counsel, 1973—, also dir. Served with AUS, 1944-46. Office: Sheraton Corp 60 State St Boston MA 02109

SILER, EUGENE EDWARD, JR., judge; b. Williamsburg, Ky., Oct. 19, 1936; s. Eugene Edward and Lowell (Jones) S.; m. Christy Dyanne Minnich, Oct. 18, 1969; children—Eugene Edward, Adam Troy. B.A. cum laude, Vanderbilt U., 1958; LL.B., U. Va., 1963; LL.M., Georgetown U., 1964. Bar: Ky. 1963. Individual practice law Williamsburg, 1964-65; atty. Whitley County, Ky., 1965-70; U.S. atty. Eastern Dist. Ky., Lexington, 1970-75; judge U.S. Dist. Ct., Eastern and Western Dists., Ky., 1975—. Campaign co-chmn. Congressman Tim L. Carter, 1966, 5th Congl. Dist.; campaign co-chmn. U.S. Senator J.S. Cooper, 1966; trustee Cumberland Coll., Williamsburg, 1965-73. Served with USNR, 1958-60. E. Barrett Prettyman fellow, 1963-64; recipient medal Freedom's Found., 1968. Mem. Fed. Bar Assn., Ky. Bar Assn., D.C. Bar Assn., Va. State Bar. Republican. Baptist. Lodge: Optimists (pres. Williamsburg 1969). Jurisprudence. Home: PO Box 129 Williamsburg KY 40769 Office: US Courthouse Room 207 London KY 40741

SILETS, HARVEY MARVIN, lawyer; b. Chgo., Aug. 25, 1931; s. Joseph Lazarus and Sylvia (Dubner) S.; m. Elaine Lucy Gordon, June 25, 1961; children: Hayden Leigh, Jonathan Lazarus (dec.), Alexandra Rose. B.S. cum laude, DePaul U., 1952; J.D. (Frederick Leckie scholar), U. Mich., 1955. Bar: Ill. 1955, N.Y. 1956, U.S. Supreme Ct. 1959, U.S. Ct. Appeals (2d, 5th, 6th, 7th and 11th cirs.), U.S. Tax Ct., U.S. Ct. Mil. Appeals, U.S. Dist. Ct. (no. dist.) Ill. Assoc. Paul, Weiss, Rifkind, Wharton & Garrison, N.Y.C., 1955-56; asst. atty. U.S. Dist. Ct. (no. dist.) Ill., 1958-60; chief tax atty. U.S. atty. No. Dist. Ill., Chgo., 1960-62; ptnr. Harris, Burman & Silets, Chgo., 1962-79; firm Silets & Martin, Ltd., Chgo., 1979—; asst. advance tng. program IRS, U. Mich., 1952-53; law lectr. advance fed. taxation John Marshall Law Sch., 1962-66; adj. prof. taxation Chgo.-Kent Coll. Law, 1985—; gen. counsel Nat. Treasury Employees Union, 1968—; mem. Chgo. Crime Commn., 1975—; mem. adv. com. tax litigation U.S. Dept. Justice, 1979-82; mem. Tax Reform Com., State of Ill., 1982-83; mem. Speedy Trial Act Planning Group U.S. Dist Ct (no. dist.) Ill., 1976—; lectr. in field. Contbr. articles to profl. jours. Trustee Latin Sch., Chgo., Rodfei Zedek; mem. Gov.'s Commn. Reform Tax Laws, Ill. 1982-83. Served with AUS, 1956-58. Fellow Am. Coll. Trial Lawyers (chmn. com. on fed. rules of criminal procedure 1982—), Am. Coll. Tax Counsel, Internat. Acad. Trial Lawyers; mem. Bar Assn. 7th Fed. Cir. (chmn. com. criminal law and procedure 1972-82, bd. govs. 1983-86, sec. 1986—), Internat. Acad. Trial Lawyers, ABA (active various coms.), Fed. Bar Assn. (bd. dirs. 1971—, pres. 1977-78, v.p. 1976-77, sec. 1975-76, treas. 1974-75, active various coms.), Fed. Cir. Bar Assn. (jud. selection com. 1985—, tax appeals com. 1985—), Chgo. Bar Assn. (tax com. 1958-66, com. devel. law 1966-72, 78—, com. fed. taxation 1968—, com. evaluation candidates 1978-80), Am. Bd. Criminal Def. Lawyers, Chgo. Soc. Trial Lawyers, Decalogue Soc. Lawyers, BAr Assn. City of N.Y., Nat. Assn. Criminal Def. Lawyers, Ill. Soc. Trial Lawyers, Phi Alpha Delta, Pi Gamma Mu. Clubs: Standards Chgo., Cliff Dwellers (Chgo.), Biltmore Country, Law of City of Chgo. Office: Silets & Martin Ltd 15th Floor 140 S Dearborn St Chicago IL 60603

SILK, ROBERT HOWARD, lawyer; b. Detroit, Dec. 23, 1925; s. Israel Herbert and Gertrude (Nurko) S.; m. Susan Thumin, July 16, 1955; children: Nina, Caroline. LLB, U. Mich., 1951. Bar: Mich. 1951, N.Y. 1952, U.S. Dist. Ct. (so. dist.) N.Y. 1955, U.S. Ct. Appeals (2d cir.) 1977, U.S. Supreme Ct. 1978. Ptnr. Silk & Burks P.C., N.Y.C. Assoc. editor: Trial Lawyers Quarterly. Alt. del. Dem. Conv., Chgo., 1968. Mem. ABA, Assn. Trial Lawyers Am., N.Y. County Lawyers Assn., N.Y. State Trial Lawyers Assn. (bd. dirs.). State civil litigation, Personal injury, Family and matrimonial. Office: Silk & Burks PC 401 Broadway New York NY 10013

SILK, THOMAS, lawyer; b. Beaver, Pa., Dec. 12, 1937; s. Thomas and Alice Genevieve (Beck) S.; m. Susan Clark, Aug. 5, 1979; 1 dau., Nicole Amory. AB, U. Calif.-Berkeley, 1959, LLB, 1963. Bar: Calif. 1964, U.S. Dist. Ct. (no. dist.) Calif. 1964, U.S. Ct. Appeals (D.C., 2-10th cirs.) 1966-68, U.S. Supreme Ct. 1967. Appellate atty. tax div. U.S. Dept. Justice, Washington, 1964-66; spl. asst. to asst. atty. gen. tax div., 1966-68; assoc. Brobeck, Phleger & Harrison, San Francisco, 1968-71; sole practice, San Francisco, 1972-82; pres., owner Silk & Marois and Silk & Adler, San Francisco, 1982—; adj. prof. U. San Francisco, lectr. in field. Gen. counsel, trustee Oceanic Soc. Mem. ABA, State Bar Calif., San Francisco Bar Assn. (award of merit and outstanding pro bono lawyer award, 1986). Democrat. Contbr. articles to profl. jours. Corporate taxation, General corporate. Office: Silk & Adler Russ Bldg Suite 1010 235 Montgomery St San Francisco CA 94104

SILKENAT, JAMES ROBERT, lawyer; b. Salina, Kans., Aug. 2, 1947; s. Ernest E. and Mildred R. (Iman) S.; m. Pamela J. Thomas; children: David Andrew, Katherine Anne. BA, Drury Coll., 1969; JD, U. Chgo., 1972; LLM, NYU, 1978. Bar: N.Y. 1973, D.C. 1980. Assoc. Cravath, Swaine & Moore, N.Y.C., 1972-80; counsel Internat. Fin. Corp., Washington, 1980-86; ptnr. Morgan, Lewis & Bockius, N.Y.C., 1986—; chmn. Council N.Y. Law Assocs., 1978-79, Lawyers Com. Internat. Human Rights, 1978-80. Contbr. over 60 articles on law and public policy to profl. jours. Served to capt. U.S. Army, 1972-73. Fellow NEH, 1977, U.S. Dept. State, 1981. Mem. ABA (vice chmn. internat. law sect. 1985—). Private international, Public international, General corporate. Office: Morgan Lewis & Bockius 101 Park Ave New York NY 10178

SILL, LAUREN ANN, lawyer; b. Smithtown, N.Y., Jan. 28, 1958; d. Laurence Randolph and Alice Eileen (Krause) S. BA, U. So. Fla., 1978; JD, Stetson U., 1980. Bar: Fla. 1981, U.S. Dist. Ct. (mid. dist.) Fla. 1981. Assoc. Law Offices of Helen Hansel, St. Petersburg, 1982-83; sole practice St. Petersburg, Fla., 1983. Bd. dirs. Hospice Care, Inc., Pinellas Park, Fla. Mem. ABA. Republican. Episcopalian. Club: Presidents (St. Petersburg). Probate, Real property, General practice. Home: 1885 County Rd 193 Clearwater FL 33519 Office: 572 2d Ave S Saint Petersburg FL 33701

SILL, PETER LEWIS, real estate company executive, lawyer; b. New Rochelle, N.Y., May 15, 1940; s. Jerome and Ethel (Streusand) S.; m. Marcia H. Joslyn, Aug. 22, 1965; children—Jennifer Joslyn, Randolph Joslyn. B.A. cum laude, Amherst Coll., 1962; LL.B. cum laude, Harvard U., 1965; LL.M., NYU, 1967. Bar: N.Y. 1966, Wash. 1972, U.S. Dist. Ct. (we. dist.) N.Y. 1968, U.S. Dist. Ct. (so. dist.) N.Y. 1966, U.S. Dist. Ct. (we. dist.) Wash. 1973, U.S. Tax Ct. 1968, U.S. Ct. Appeals (2d cir.) 1966, U.S. Supreme Ct. 1969. Assoc., Cadwalader, Wickersham & Taft, N.Y.C., 1965-72; tax counsel Weyerhaeuser Co., Tacoma, 1972-84; mgr. spl. projects Weyerhaeuser Real Estate Co., Tacoma, 1984-86, v.p., 1986—. Trustee East Shore Unitarian Ch., Bellevue, Wash., 1980-82, treas., 1980-82; mem. Bellevue Sch. Dist. Fiscal Com., 1977-79; youth sport officer, coach, 1976-86. Mem. ABA, Wash. State Bar Assn. Contbr. articles to profl. jours. Home: 14845 SE 50th St Bellevue WA 98006 Office: Weyerhaeuser Co Tacoma WA 98477

SILLECK, HARRY GARRISON, lawyer; b. Putnam Valley, N.Y., Mar. 19, 1921; s. Harry Garrison and Bertha May (Barrett) S.; m. June Baird, Mar. 4, 1977. B.A., Union Coll., 1940; LL.B., Columbia U., 1943. Bar: N.Y. 1944, U.S. Supreme Ct. 1966, U.S. Ct. Appeals (2d cir.) 1966 (6th cir.) 1976. Assoc. Dorr Hand Whittaker & Watson, N.Y.C., 1945-55, ptnr., 1955-63; ptnr. Mudge Rose Gurthrie Alexander & Ferdon, N.Y.C., 1963-86; of counsel Mudge Rose Gurthrie Alexander & Ferdon, 1986—, chmn., 1978-85. Served to 1st lt. AC, U.S. Army, 1943-45, ETO. Mem. Phi Beta Kappa. Home: 131 E 69th St New York NY 10021 Office: Mudge Rose Guthrie Alexander & Ferdon 180 Maiden Ln New York NY 10038

SILLER, STEPHEN I., lawyer; b. Bklyn., May 8, 1949; m. Helen Seewald, June 6, 1971. B.A., Bklyn. Coll., 1970, J.D., 1973; LL.M., NYU, 1978. Bar: N.Y. 1974, U.S. Dist. Ct. (so. and ea. dists.) N.Y. 1974, U.S. Ct. Appeals (2d cir.) 1974. Assoc. Fried, Frank, Harris, Shriver & Jacobson, N.Y.C., 1973-78; assoc. Feit & Ahrens, N.Y.C., 1978-80, ptnr., 1981—. Mem. ABA (partnership law com.), Assn. Bar City N.Y. (transp. com.). General corporate, Securities, Private international. Office: Feit & Ahrens 488 Madison Ave New York NY 10022

SILLIMAN, RICHARD GEORGE, lawyer, farm machinery company executive; b. Elgin, Ill., Aug. 11, 1922; s. Charles B. and Mabel Ellen (Winegar) S.; m. Mary L. Yost, June 12, 1945; children—Martha Jane, Charles R. B.A. in History, Cornell Coll., Mt. Vernon, Iowa, 1946; J.D., Northwestern U., 1949. Bar: Ill. 1949. Atty. various U.S. agys., Chgo., 1949-52; atty., asst. sec. Elgin Nat. Watch Co., Ill., 1952-59, sec., gen. atty., 1959-62; asst. gen. counsel Deere & Co., Moline, Ill., 1962-75, assoc. gen. counsel, 1975-82, sec., assoc. gen. counsel, 1982—. Mem. editorial bd. Ill. Law Rev., 1948-49. Contbr. articles to profl. jours. Bd. dirs., past pres. Quad-City Symphony Orch., Moline and Davenport, Iowa, 1968—; bd. dirs., trustee Upper Rock Island County YMCA, Moline, 1965—; bd. dirs. Police-Fire Commn., Elgin, 1957-61; bd. dirs., sec. Elgin YMCA, 1955. Served with USN, 1943-46. Mem. Ill. State Bar Assn. (chmn. com. on corp. law dept.), ABA. Clubs: Short Hills Country (Moline); Union League (Chgo.). Avocations: golf; music; sailing; gardening. General corporate, Securities. Home: 3104 26th St Moline IL 61265 Office: Deere & Co John Deere Rd Moline IL 61265

SILLS, JOHN DENNIS, lawyer; b. Detroit, Nov. 20, 1934; s. John J. and Namoi (Schaar) S.; m. Marlene K. Jaeger, June 29, 1957; children: Lisa Sills Zimmerman, Leslie, Lori. BA, U. Mich., 1956; JD, Detroit Coll. Law, 1959. Bar: Mich. 1960, U.S. Dist. Ct. (ea. dist.) Mich. 1960. House counsel Sentry Ins. Co., Grand Rapids, Mich., 1960-63; ptnr. Moore, Sills et al, Birmingham, Mich., 1963-84, Vandeveer, Garzia, Tonkin, Kerr, Heaphy, Moore, Sills & Poling P.C., Detroit, 1984—. Mem. 20001 com. City of Southfield, Mich., 1982. Mem. ABA, Am. Judicature Soc., Fed. Bar Assn. (mediator), Oakland County Bar Assn. (mediator), Wayne County Bar Assn. (mediator), Am. Arbitration Assn. (arbitrator), Def. Research Inst., Assn. Trial Lawyers Am. Clubs: Plum Hollow Golf (Southfield) (pres. 1982); Piper's Landing (Fla.). State civil litigation, Federal civil litigation, General corporate. Home: PO Box 156 Bloomfield Hills MI 48013 Office: Vandeveer Garzia Tonkin et al 333 W Fort St Suite 1600 Detroit MI 48011

SILLS, NANCY MINTZ, lawyer; b. N.Y.C., Nov. 3, 1941; d. Samuel and Selma (Kahn) Mintz; m. Stephen J. Sills, Apr. 17, 1966; children: Eric Howard, Ronnie Lynne. BA, U. Wis., 1962; JD cum laude, Albany Law Sch., 1976. Bar: N.Y. 1977, U.S. Dist. Ct. (no. dist.) N.Y. 1977, U.S. Tax Ct. 1984. Asst. editor fin. news Newsweek mag., N.Y.C., 1962-65; staff writer, reporter Forbes mag., N.Y.C., 1965; research assoc. pub. relations Eastern Airlines, N.Y.C., 1965-67; asst. editor Harper & Row, N.Y.C., 1968-69; freelance writer, editor N.Y.C. and Albany, N.Y., 1967-70; confidential law sec. N.Y. State Supreme Ct., Albany, 1976-79; assoc. Whiteman, Osterman & Hanna, Albany, 1979-81, Martin, Noonan, Hislop, Troue & Shudt, Albany, 1981-83; ptnr. Martin, Shudt, Wallace & Sills, Albany, 1984; of counsel Krolick & DeGraff, Albany, 1984—; asst. counsel N.Y. State Senate, 1983—; cons. The Ayco Corp., 1975; bd. dirs. Albany Law Sch. Estate Planning Inst. Editor: Reforming American Education, 1969, Up From Poverty, 1968; researcher The Negro Revolution in America, 1963; contbr. articles to mags. Bd. govs. Jewish Philanthropies Endowment, 1983-86; bd. dirs. Albany Jewish Community Ctr., 1984—. Mem. ABA, N.Y. State Bar Assn., Bar Assn. Albany County, Estate Planning Council Eastern N.Y., Women's Aux. Albany County Med Soc., Albany Med. Coll. Faculty Wives, Women's Am. O.R.T., Phi Beta Kappa, Sigma Epsilon Sigma. Democrat. Clubs: Colonie Country, Hudson River (Albany). Lodge: B'nai B'rith Women. Probate, Estate taxation, Personal income taxation. Home: 16 Hiawatha Dr Guilderland NY 12084 Office: Krolick & DeGraff 3 City Sq Albany NY 12207

SILVA, EUGENE JOSEPH, lawyer; b. Gloucester, Mass., May 23, 1942; s. Edward Joseph and Rose (Lebre) S.; m. Nancy Blue-Pearson, Jan. 8, 1972; children: Eugene Joseph II, Michael Joseph. BS with honors, Maine Maritime Acad., 1964; JD, U. Notre Dame, 1972. Bar: Calif. 1972, U.S. Dist. Ct. (so. and cen. dists.) Calif. 1972, Tex. 1977, U.S. Dist. Ct. (so. and ea. dists.) Tex. 1978, U.S. Ct. Appeals (5th, 2d and 11th cirs.) 1978, U.S. Supreme Ct. 1981. Assoc. Luce, Forward, Hamilton & Scripps, San Diego, 1972-77; assoc. Vinson & Elkins, Houston, 1977-79, ptnr., 1980—. Bd. dirs. Cabrillo Festival Inc., San Diego, 1974-77. Served to lt. USN, 1967-69. Recipient Master Mariner award U.S. Coast Guard, 1967. Mem. ABA, Houston Bar Assn., Internat. Bar Assn., Grays Inn U. Notre Dame Sch. Law (pres. 1970-72), Southeastern Admiralty Law Inst., Maritime Law Assn. U.S. (proctor in admiralty 1974—), Portugese Union Calif. (bd. dirs. 1973-74), Portugese Am. League San Diego (pres. 1974-75), Asia-Pacific Lawyers Assn. Roman Catholic. Club: Notre Dame (San Diego) (pres. 1976-77). Admiralty, Private international, Federal civil litigation. Home: 811 Monte Cello Houston TX 77024 Office: Vinson & Elkins 2620 1st City Tower 1001 Fannin Houston TX 77002-6760

SILVER, COLE BRIAN, lawyer; b. Phila., Dec. 19, 1956; s. Stan I. and Geri A. (Levy) S. BA, George Washington U., 1978; JD, Antoich Sch. Law, 1981. Bar: Pa. 1981, U.S. Dist. Ct. (ea., mid and we. dists.) Pa. 1981, N.J. 1983, U.S. Dist. Ct. N.J. 1983. Assoc. Samuel Katz, Phila., 1981-84, Mark Koral, Phila., 1984-85, Goodman, Schneidert & Cohen, Marlton, N.J., 1985—; tchr. A.I.P.S., Cherry Hill, N.J., 1981-84. Mem. ABA, Assn. Trial Lawyers Am. General corporate, Federal civil litigation, State civil litigation. Home: 1 N Syracuse Dr Cherry Hill NJ 08034 Office: Goodman Schneidert & Cohen 3 Greentree Ctr Suite 305 Rt 73 Marlton NJ 08053

SILVER, DANIEL BEN, lawyer; b. Phila., Aug. 14, 1941; s. Samuel and Marjorie (Euster) S.; m. Sybil F. Michelson, Jan. 20, 1963; children—Abigail Ruth, Rachel Ann, Alexander Joseph. A.B., U. Calif.-Berkeley, 1961; M.A., Harvard U., 1965, Ph.D., 1967, LL.B., 1968. Bar: D.C. 1968, U.S. Ct. Appeals (D.C. cir.) 1975, U.S. Supreme Ct. 1975. Assoc. Cleary, Gottlieb, Steen & Hamilton, Washington, 1968-70, 73-76, Brussels, Belgium, 1973-76, ptnr., Washington, 1976-78, 81—; gen. counsel NSA, Washington, 1978-79, CIA, Washington, 1979-81; adj. prof. Georgetown U. Law Ctr., 1981-83. Recipient Exceptional Civilian Service award NSA, 1979; Disting. Intelligence medal CIA, 1981. Mem. ABA (standing com. law and nat. security, sects. antitrust law, pub. contract law, internat. law). Democrat. Jewish. Author: (with P. Fabrega) Illness and Shamanistic Curing in Zinacantan, 1975. Administrative and regulatory, General corporate, Private international. Office: 1752 N St NW Washington DC 20036

SILVER, ELAINE TERRY, lawyer; b. Balt., May 11, 1953. Student, Hebrew U., 1972-73; BA with honors, Bucknell U., 1974; JD, NYU, 1977. Bar: Conn. 1977, U.S. Dist. Ct. Conn. 1977, U.S. Ct. Appeals (2d cir.) 1980. Assoc. Glazer, Seelig & Glazer, Stamford, Conn., 1977-81, 82-83; vis. prof. law Beijing U., 1981-82; ptnr. Fleisher, Trow & Silver, Stamford, 1983—; counsel Domestic Violence Service, Stamford, 1983-85. Pres., bd. dirs. Rape and Sexual Abuse Crisis Ctr., Inc., Stamford, 1985-87. Mem. ABA (family law sect.), Conn. Bar Assn. (exec. com. family law sect.), Stamford Bar Assn. Clubs: Midday, Newfield (sec. 1984-85) (Stamford). Family and matrimonial, State civil litigation, Probate. Office: Fleisher Trow & Silver PC 30 Oak St Stamford CT 06905

SILVER, GRAY, III, lawyer; b. Martinsburg, W.Va., June 4, 1953; s. Gray Jr. and Kathleen Lucille (Usak) Silver. BA, U. Va., 1975; JD, W.Va. U., 1979. Bar: W.Va. 1979, U.S. Dist. Ct. (so. and no. dists.) W.Va. 1979, U.S. Ct. Appeals (4th cir.) 1980, U.S. Supreme Ct. 1982. Asst. atty. gen. State of W.Va., Charleston, 1979-82; assoc. Martin & Seibert, Martinsburg, 1982-84; ptnr. Avey & Steptoe, Martinsburg, 1984—. Mem. exec. com. Berkeley County Dems., Martinsburg, 1984-86; bd. deacons, treas. First Presbyn. Ch., Martinsburg, 1984-87. Mem. ABA, W.Va. Bar Assn., Berkeley County Bar Assn., Def. Research Inst., Def. Trial Counsel W.Va., Martinsburg Jaycees. Avocations: tennis, jogging, biking, hunting, gardening. Insurance, State civil litigation, Federal civil litigation. Home: 501 S Queen St Martinsburg WV 25401 Office: Avey & Steptoe 126 E Burke St Martinsburg WV 25401

SILVER, HARRY R., lawyer; b. Phila., Aug. 8, 1846; s. Jerome Benjamin Silver and Josephine Sandler (Steinberg) Furr; m. Jessica Dunsay, Nov. 23, 1972; children: Gregory, Alexander. BA, Temple U., 1968; JD, Columbia U., 1971. Bar: N.Y. 1972, D.C. 1973, U.S. Dist. Ct. D.C., U.S. Ct. Claims, U.S. Ct. Appeals (1st, 4th, 5th, 7th, 8th, 9th, 10th fed. and D.C. cirs.), U.S. Supreme Ct. Law clk. to judge U.S. Ct. Appeals (2d cir.), N.Y.C., 1971-72; assoc. Arent, Fox, Kintner, Plotkin & Kahn, Washington, 1972-74; atty. U.S. Dept. Justice, Washington, 1974-77, U.S. Dept. Energy, Washington, 1977-78; assoc. Akin, Gump, Strauss, Hauer & Feld, Washington, 1978-81, ptnr., 1981—. Mem. ABA, Fed. Bar Assn. Avocations: running, music, travel. Administrative and regulatory, Federal civil litigation, Government contracts and claims. Home: 6829 Wilson Ln Bethesda MD 20817 Office: Akin Gump Strauss Hauer & Feld 1333 New Hampshire Ave NW Suite 400 Washington DC 20036

SILVER, IRVING, lawyer; b. Holyoke, Mass., May 7, 1940; s. Herman and Esther Lena (Orlen) S.; m. Frances Grodsky, June 18, 1961; children: Hedy Marlene, Evan Bernard. BS in Commerce, U. Ala., 1964, LLB, 1965. Bar: Ala. 1965, U.S. Dist. Ct. (so. dist.) Ala. 1966, U.S. Ct. Appeals (5th cir.) 1966, U.S. Supreme Ct. 1970, U.S. Ct. Appeals (11th cir.) 1979. Gen. counsel Merit Fin. Corp., Mobile, Ala., 1965-68; sole practice Mobile, 1968-70; ptnr. Feibleman & Silver, Mobile, 1970-74, Feibleman, Silver & Grodsky, Mobile, 1974-75; pres. Silver, Voit & Inge P.C., Mobile, 1976—. Co-author: Alabama Enforcing Secured Transactions, 1985, Alabama Mortgage Foreclosure, 1985. Pres. Mobile Community Action Com., 1974; active Fedn. Jewish Charities, 1975-86. Served with USAF, 1959-62. Mem. Comml. Law League Am. Lodge: B'nai B'rith (local dist. v.p. 1978-83, local dist. pres. 1983-84, commr. nat. adult Jewish edn. 1984—). Bankruptcy, General corporate, Probate. Home: 5951 N Shenandoah Rd Mobile AL 36608 Office: Silver Voit & Inge PC 4317-A Midmost Dr Mobile AL 36609

SILVER, LOUIS EDGAR, lawyer; b. Montreal, Que., Can., Mar. 15, 1953; came to U.S., 1975; s. Sidney and Edith (Edgar) S.; m. Laurie Morgan, Aug. 16, 1975; 1 child, Rachel. AB magna cum laude, Princeton U., 1974; JD with honors, U. Tex., 1978. Bar: Tex. 1978, Fla. 1979. Assoc. Schlanger, Cook, Cohn, Mills & Grossberg, Houston, 1978-83, ptnr., 1984—. Bd. dirs. S.W. Regional Anti-Defamation League, Houston, 1984—, mem. nat. civil rights com., 1985—. Mem. ABA, Houston Bar Assn. Real property, Bankruptcy. Office: Schlanger Cook Cohn Mills & Grossberg 5847 San Felipe Suite 1700 Houston TX 77057

SILVER, MARK STEVEN, lawyer; b. N.Y.C., Dec. 7, 1952. AA, Nassau Community Coll., 1972; BS, Western State U., 1979, JD, 1980. Bar: Calif. 1981, U.S. Dist. Ct. (cen. dist.) Calif. 1981, U.S. Dist. Ct. (so. dist.) 1982, U.S. Ct. Appeals (9th cir.). Assoc. Marlin & Assocs., Tustin, Calif., 1981; atty. O.C. Lawyers Group, Santa Ana, Calif., 1981; assoc. Mackey & Sullivan, Orange, Calif., 1982; prin. Silver & Assocs., Santa Ana, 1982—; cons. in field. Mem. ABA, Calif. Bar Assn., Orange County Bar Assn. (speaker bridging the gap com. 1983), Orange County Barristers, Counsel Better Bus. Burs. (arbitrator, nat. panel consumer arbitrators 1982—). Avocations: travel, baseball, tennis, golf. Contracts commercial, General corporate, State civil litigation. Office: Silver & Assocs 1182 SE Bristol Suite 200 Santa Ana CA 92707 Office: PO Box 3504 Huntington Beach CA 92605-3504

SILVER, MARVIN S., lawyer; b. Portland, Maine, Nov. 21, 1951; s. Jacob L. and Jean (Mitchell) S.; m. Laura M. Black, June 26, 1977. B.S., Syracuse U., 1974; J.D., Boston U., 1977, LL.M., 1981. Bar: Mass. 1977, U.S. Dist. Ct. Mass. 1978, U.S. Tax Ct. 1981. Atty. Seder & Seder, Worcester, Mass., 1977-82; atty., ptnr. Seder & Chandler, Worcester, 1983—. Bd. dirs. Jewish Community Ctr. of Worcester, Inc., Mass., 1982-84. Mem. Comml. Law League Am., Mass. Bar Assn. (chmn. estate planning com. tax sect. 1982-84, mem. tax sect. council 1983-86, mem. bus. law sect.), Worcester County Bar Assn. (co-chmn. tax law sect. 1981-84, 86—. Club: Exchange of Tri-Towns, Inc. (pres. 1984-85) (Shrewsbury, Mass.). General corporate, Estate planning, Estate taxation. Office: Seder & Chandler 339 Main St Worcester MA 01608

SILVER, MELVIN JACOB, lawyer; b. St. Paul, Nov. 12, 1903; s. Alexander and Edith (Silberstein) S.; m. Eleanor Kaufman, Jan. 12, 1930; 1 child, Sandra Joy Silver Alch. BA, U. Minn., 1923; JD, St. Paul Coll. Law, 1927. Bar: Minn. 1927, U.S. Dist. Ct. (no. dist.) Ill. 1934. Spl. counsel atty. gen. office State of Minn., St. Paul, 1944-45; sr. ptnr. Silver, Ryan & Smith (and predecessor firm Silver, Goff, Murphy Ryan and Dillon), St. Paul, 1945—; atty. Montgomery Wards, 1938-55; gen. counsel Ralph R. Kriesel Co., St. Paul, 1943-76, ATR Electronics, St. Paul, 1950-80, Minn. Capital Corp., St. Paul, 1960-63; gen. counsel, chmn. bd. dirs. Sacred Design Assn., Mpls., 1965-70. Mem. St. Paul Bd. Edn., 1950-53; chmn. Univ. Scholarship Com., Mpls., 1951-75, bond com. State of Israel, Minn., 1952-56. Mem. ABA, Minn. Bar Assn., Ramsey County Bar Assn. Clubs: St. Paul Athletic, Hillcrest Country. Lodge: B'nai B'rith (pres. St. Paul club 1932-34). General corporate, Personal injury, Probate. Home: 2029 Upper St Dennis Rd Saint Paul MN 55116 Office: Silver Ryan & Smith 1300 Minnesota Bldg 4th and Cedar Saint Paul MN 55101

SILVER, ROGER ALLEN, lawyer, court administrator, general master; b. Melbourne, Fla., Oct. 19, 1945; s. Morton Henry and Rose May (Reed) S.; m. Esther Leach, May 17, 1986. BA, U. Miami, 1968; JD, U. Fla., 1973. Bar: Fla. 1974, U.S. Ct. Appeals (5th cir.) 1978, U.S. Supreme Ct. 1979. Tchr. Dade County (Fla.) Sch. Dist., Miami, 1968-70; dir. and staff atty. Dade County Child Support IVD Program, Miami, 1974-76; exec. officer 11th Judicial Cir. Fla., Miami, 1978—, gen. master, 1981—; adj. mem. faculty clinical program U. Miami Sch. Law, Coral Gables, Fla., 1980—, guest lectr. Sch. Law and Fla. Internat. U., Miami. Contbr. articles to profl. jours. Mem. adv. bd. Guardiam Ad Litem Program, Miami, 1984—; participant Metro-Miami Crime Symposium, 1986. Fellow Inst. for Ct. Mgmt.; mem. ABA, Fla. Bar Assn. (research asst. tort litigation rev. comm.), Dade County Bar Assn., Nat. Ctr. for State Cts. (assoc.). Club: Rotary (bd. dirs. 1987—). Family and matrimonial, Judicial administration, General practice. Office: 11 Judicial Cir of Fla 73 W Flagler St 900 Courthouse Miami FL 33130

SILVER, STUART ROBERT, lawyer; b. Bridgeport, Conn., June 28, 1949; s. Bennett N. and Deborah B. Silver. Bar: Fla. 1974, U.S. Dist. Ct. (so. dist.) Fla. 1974, U.S. Ct. Appeals (5th cir.) 1974, U.S. Supreme Ct. 1980, U.S. Ct. Appeals (11th cir.) 1981, U.S. Dist. Ct. (mid. dist.) Fla. 1982, N.Y. 1985, Pa. 1985. Assoc. J. Dermer, Miami Beach, Fla., 1974-78; assoc. to ptnr. Britton Cohen et al, Miami, 1978-85; of counsel Edward Kaufman, P.A., Miami, 1985—; assoc. Bernstein, Bernstein & Harrison, P.C., Phila., 1986—. Mem. Phila. Bar Assn., Fla. Bar Assn., N.Y. State Bar Assn., Assn. Trial Lawyers Am., Pa. Trial Lawyers Assn., Acad. Fla. Trial Lawyers. Personal injury, State civil litigation, Federal civil litigation. Office: Bernstein Bernstein & Harrison PC 1600 Market St Suite 2500 Philadelphia PA 19103

SILVERBERG, SHELDON, lawyer; b. Bklyn., Apr. 19, 1929; s. Harry N. and Shirley (Novick) S.; m. Elissa Nenner, May 30, 1960; children: Jay, Roy. Student, NYU, 1946-48; LLB, Bklyn. Law Sch., 1951. Bar: N.Y. 1951, U.S. Dist. Ct. (so. dist.) N.Y. 1954, U.S. Dist. Ct. (so. dist.) N.Y.

1954, U.S. Dist. Ct. (ea. dist.) N.Y. 1955, U.S. Ct. Appeals (2d cir.) 1959. Assoc. Schwartz & Stoll, N.Y.C., 1951-54, Ruben & Schwartz, N.Y.C., 1954-66; ptnr. Ruben, Schwartz & Silverberg, N.Y.C., 1966-77; sr. ptnr. Silverberg, Stonehill & Goldsmith, P.C., N.Y.C., 1978—. Pres. Jewish Community Council Oceanside, 1977-81, Manhattan Credit Group, 1979-80, Decorum Credit Club, 1980-81. Served with N.Y. N.G., 1948-56. Mem. Assn. Lawyers Textile and Apparel Industries, N.Y. County Lawyers Assn. Consumer commercial, General corporate, Bankruptcy. Home: 1064 Channel Rd Hewlett Harbor NY 11557 Office: Silverberg Stonehill & Goldsmith PC 111 W 40th St New York NY 10018

SILVERBERG, STANLEY J., lawyer; b. N.Y.C., June 19, 1940; s. Max and Dorothy (Baron) S.; m. Hazel L. Janover; children: Russell, Amanda. BSEE, Poly. U. N.Y., 1961; JD, NYU, 1965. Bar: N.Y. 1965, U.S. Dist. Ct. (so. and ea. dists.) N.Y. 1967, U.S. Ct. Claims 1968, U.S. Ct. Appeals (2d and fed. cirs.) 1982, U.S. Supreme Ct. 1982. Trademark counsel The Singer Co., N.Y.C., 1970-79; trademarks and copyrights atty. Warner Communications, Inc., N.Y.C., 1979-81, Am. Cyanamid Co., Wayne, N.J., 1981—; lectr. U.S. Trademark Assn., 1985. Mem. N.Y. State Bar Assn., U.S. Trademark Assn. (chmn. com. on product substitution 1984-85, chmn. anti-counterfeiting subcom., bd. dirs. 1987—), N.Y. Patent Trademark and Copyright Law Assn. (chmn. com. on pub. info. and edn. 1985—, chmn. subcom. on U.S. trademark practice), Am. Arbitration Assn. (nat. panel arbitrators 1980—). Home: 320 Orenda Circle Westfield NJ 07090 Office: Am Cyanamid Co 1 Cyanamid Plaza Wayne NJ 07470

SILVERBERG, STEVEN MARK, lawyer; b. Bklyn., June 7, 1947; m. Arlene Leopold, July 4, 1971; 2 children. BA, Bklyn. Coll., 1969; JD, NYU, 1972. Bar: N.Y. 1973, U.S. Dist Ct. (so. and ea. dist.) N.Y. 1974, U.S. Supreme Ct. 1976, U.S. Ct. Appeals (2d cir.) 1978. Asst. dist. atty. Kings County Dist. Atty., Bklyn., 1972-75; dep. town. atty. Town of Greenburgh, N.Y., 1975-79; ptnr. Stowell, Kelly & Silverberg, White Plains, N.Y., 1979-83, Hoffman, Silverberg & Wachtell, Elmsford, N.Y., 1983-86, Hoffman, Silverberg, Wachtell & Koster, Elmsford, 1986—. Counsel Greenburgh Housing Authority, 1979-84, Town of Mamaroneck, N.Y., 1984—; bd. dirs. Temple Beth Torah, Upper Nyack, N.Y., pres. 1984-86. Real property, Environment, Government contracts and claims. Office: Hoffman Silverberg Wachtell & Koster 45 Knollwood Rd Elmsford NY 10523

SILVERGLADE, BRUCE A., lawyer; b. Milw., July 19, 1953. BA in Polit. Sci., U. Ill., Champaign, 1975; JD, Boston Coll., 1978. Bar: D.C. 1978, U.S. Ct. Appeals (5th and D.C. cirs.) 1978. Atty., advisor Fed. Trade Commn., Washington, 1978-81; atty. Ctr. for Sci. in Pub. Interest, Washington, 1981—. Mem. ABA, Fed. Bar Assn. (chmn. rulemaking com. 1986—), Phi Beta Kappa. Administrative and regulatory, Environment, Food and drug. Office: Ctr for Sci in Pub Interest 1501 16th St NW Washington DC 20036

SILVERIA, LINDA LORRAINE, lawyer; b. San Jose, Calif., Oct. 1, 1950; d. Lester and Lorraine (Morgante) S. LLB, Lincoln Law Sch., 1982. Bar: Calif. 1982. Sole practice San Jose, 1982—. Mem. ABA, Santa Clara County Bar Assn., Calif. Trial Lawyers Assn., Assn. of Owners and Pilots. Probate, Personal injury, Family and matrimonial. Office: 2021 The Alameda #310 San Jose CA 95126

SILVERMAN, ARNOLD BARRY, lawyer; b. Sept. 1, 1937; s. Frank and Lillian Lena (Linder) S.; m. Susan L. Levin, Aug. 7, 1960; children: Michael Eric, Lee Oren. B. Engring. Sci., Johns Hopkins U., 1959; LL.B. cum laude, U. Pitts., 1962. Bar: U.S. Dist. Ct. (we. dist.) Pa. 1963, Pa. 1964, U.S. Patent and Trademark Office 1965, U.S. Supreme Ct. 1967, Can. Patent Office 1968, U.S. Ct. Claims 1975, U.S. Ct. Appeals (3d cir.) 1982, U.S. Ct. Appeals (fed. cir.) 1985. Patent atty. Alcoa, New Kensington, Pa., 1962-67, 68-72, sr. patent atty., 1972-76; ptnr. Price and Silverman, Pitts., 1967-68; v.p., gen. patent counsel Joy Mfg. Co., Pitts., 1976-80; ptnr. Murray Silverman & Keck, Pitts., 1980-81, Buell, Blenko, Ziesenheim & Beck, Pitts., 1981-84, Eckert, Seamans, Cherin & Mellott, Pitts., 1984—; spl. counsel patents U. Pitts., 1975—; speaker on patents, trademarks, copyright, computer law. Contbr. articles to profl. jours. on property law and computer law. Mem. Churchill CSC (Pa.), 1967—, chmn., 1975—; mem. Pitts. law com. Anti-Defamation League, 1981, regional adv. to bd., 1982—, co-chmn. Pitts. region ann. dinner, 1983, mem., chmn. by-laws com., 1983; bd. govs. Slippery Rock U. Found., 1985—; Pitts. steering com. MIT Enterprise Forum. Served with U.S. Army, 1963-64. Recipient Cert. of Recognition Project on Pub. Policy and Tech. Transfer of Council of Ams. and Internat. C. of C. Joint Com. on Tech. Transfer, 1978; Univ scholar U. Pitts., 1960-62. Mem. ABA, Allegheny County Bar Assn. (chmn. pub. relations com. 1978-80, vice-chmn. intellectual property sect. 1981-83 chmn.), Pitts. Patent Law Assn. (chmn. pub. relations com., 1968-69, chmn. patent laws com., 1970-72, chmn. nominating com., 1973, chmn. legis. action com., 1972-75, bd. mgrs. 1974—newsletter editor 1974-77, sec.-treas. 1976-84, v.p. 1984-85, pres. 1985-86), Am. Intellectual Property Law Assn., U.S. Trademark Assn. (chmn. task force on advt. agys. 1981), Assn. Corp. Patent Counsel, D.C. Bar Assn., Pa. Bar Assn., Nat. Assn. Coll. and Univ. Attys., Am. Chem. Soc., ASME, Licensing Execs. Soc., Brit. Inst. Chartered Patent Agts. (fgn. mem.), Johns Hopkins U. Alumni Assn. (chmn. publicity com. 1963-66, exec. com. 1966—, v.p. 1969-70, pres. 1971-72), U. Pitts. Gen. Alumni Assn., U. Pitts. Law Alumni Assn., Robert Bruce Soc., Golden Panthers, Stratford Community Assn. (v.p. 1966-67, gov. 1966-70, pres. 1967-68), Amen Corner, Mensa (charter fellow lawyers in Mensa 1978—, nat. assoc. counsel patents and trademarks copyrights 1980-82, inventors' spl. interest group 1980—), Intertel (treas. Pitts. Forum 1983—), Order of Coif, Tau Epsilon Rho, Psi Chi. Republican. Jewish. Clubs: Churchill Valley Country, Duquesne, Downtown of Pitts. (sec. and bd. dirs. 1985-87). Patent, Trademark and copyright, Computer. Home: 221 Thornberry Dr Pittsburgh PA 15235 Office: 600 Grant St 42d Floor Pittsburgh PA 15219

SILVERMAN, BRUCE STANLY, lawyer; b. San Francisco, Mar. 26, 1943; m. Robin Kaplan, Sept. 3, 1967; children—Stefani, Laney. A.B., U. Calif., Berkeley, 1964, J.D., U. Calif., San Francisco, 1967; cert. specialist in family law, Calif., 1980. Bar: Calif., 1967. Ptnr., Silverman, Ballard & Landey, San Francisco, 1970-85; instr. family law Calif. State U., San Francisco, 1976, 77; adminstrv. asst. to State Sen. Milton Marks, 1967-70. Fellow Am. Acad. Matrimonial Lawyers Assn.; mem. Assn. Joint Bay Area Family Law Sects. (chmn. 1980), Bar Assn. San Francisco (chmn. family law sect. 1977-80, dir., award of merit), Jud. Council, Assn. Family Conciliation Cts., Family Mediation Assn. Club: Concordia-Argonaut (San Francisco). Author: Family Law Manual and Form Guide, 1979. Family and matrimonial, State civil litigation. Office: 2 Embarcadero Ctr 26th Floor San Francisco CA 94111

SILVERMAN, ELLIOT, lawyer; b. Bklyn., Mar. 15, 1954. BA, CUNY, 1975; JD, Harvard U., 1978. Bar: N.Y. 1979, U.S. Dist. Ct. (so. and ea. dists.) N.Y. 1979, U.S. Tax Ct. 1979, U.S. Ct. Appeals (5th cir.) 1979, U.S. Ct. Appeals (2d cir.) 1980. Assoc. Kostelanetz & Ritholz, N.Y.C., 1978-86; ptnr. Gold & Wachtel, N.Y.C., 1986—. Co-author: Tax Fraud: Audits, Investigations, Prosecutions, 1980; contbr. articles to profl. jours. Mem. ABA, N.Y. County Lawyers Assn., Assn. Bar City N.Y. (sec. criminal law com. 1982-83). Personal income taxation, Criminal, Federal civil litigation. Office: Gold & Wachtel 10 E 53 St New York NY 10022

SILVERMAN, KAREN FAY, lawyer; b. Syracuse, N.Y., Nov. 15, 1956; d. Herbert Allen and Joan Ruth (Rakov) S.; m. Richard E. Haftel. BA, U. Wis., 1978; JD, Am. U., 1981. Bar: N.Y. 1982, U.S. Dist. Ct. (so. and ea. dists.) N.Y. 1982, U.S. Ct. Appeals (2d cir.) 1984, U.S. Dist. Ct. (no. dist.) N.Y. 1985. Assoc. LaRossa Mitchell and Ross, N.Y.C., 1981—. Mem. ABA, Bar Assn. of City of N.Y., Nat. Assn. Women Lawyers, Criminal Bar Assn. Democrat. Jewish. Criminal, Federal civil litigation, State civil litigation. Office: LaRossa Mitchell and Ross 41 Madison Ave New York NY 10010

SILVERMAN, LEON, lawyer; b. N.Y.C., June 9, 1921. B.A., Bklyn. Coll., 1942; LL.B., Yale U., 1948; postgrad., London Sch. Econs., 1948-49. Bar: N.Y. 1949. Assoc. firm Riegelman, Strasser, Schwartz & Spiegelberg, N.Y.C., 1949-53; asst. U.S. atty. So. Dist. N.Y., 1953-55; asst. dep. atty. gen. Dept. Justice, Washington, 1958-59; partner firm Fried, Frank, Harris, Shriver & Jacobson, N.Y.C., 1960—; counsel N.Y. Gov.'s Com. to Rev. N.Y. Laws and Procedure in the Area of Human Rights, 1967-68, Com. to Rev. Legis. and Jud. Salaries, 1972-73; mem. adv. com. on criminal rules to com. on rules of practice and procedure Jud. Conf. U.S.; mem. joint com. to monitor N.Y. drug laws; pres. N.Y. Legal Aid Soc., 1970-72, dir., 1966—. Trustee William Nelson Cromwell Found., 1983—. Recipient Judge Learned Hand Human Relations award, 1981, Emory Buckner Pub. Service medal, Judge Joseph M. Proskauer award, 1982. Mem. ABA, N.Y. State Bar Assn., Fed. Bar Assn., Am. Coll. Trial Lawyers (regent 1979—, pres. 1982-83), Am. Law Inst., Am. Judicature Soc., Practising Law Inst. (trustee), Assn. Bar City N.Y., Fed. Bar Council. Federal civil litigation, State civil litigation. Home: 16 Oak Dr Great Neck NY 11021 Office: Fried Frank Harris Shriver & Jacobson 1 New York Plaza New York NY 10004

SILVERMAN, MILTON JOSEPH, SR., lawyer; b. Denver, Dec. 19, 1917; s. Samuel Rosebluth and Amelia Josephine (Zeibel) S.; m. Audrey Mae Parrette, June 1, 1943 (dec. Nov. 1954); 1 child, Milton Joseph Jr.; m. Frances Genevieve McKenna (div. 0ct. 1979), 1 child, Mary Frances; m. Carol Ann Tracy, Oct. 2, 1980. BS, U.S. Naval Acad., 1941; MBA, Long Beach State U., 1968; JD, Western State U., San Diego, 1978. Bar: Calif. 1979. Commd. ensign USN, 1941, advanced through grades to comdr., 1952, ret., 1961; sole practice San Diego, 1979—. Mem. Calif. Bar Assn., Assn. Trial Lawyers Am., Calif. Trial Lawyers Assn., San Diego Trial Lawyers Assn. Personal injury. Home: 10441 Sierra Vista Ave La Mesa CA 92041 Office: Quartermass-Wilde House 2404 Broadway San Diego CA 92102

SILVERMAN, MOSES, lawyer; b. Bklyn., Mar. 3, 1948; s. Bernard and Anne (Barlia) S.; m. Betty B. Robbins, Jan. 19, 1980; 1 child, Benjamin. AB, Colby Coll., 1969; JD, NYU, 1973. Bar: N.Y. 1974, U.S. Dist. Ct. (so. and ea. dists.) N.Y. 1974, U.S. Ct. Appeals (2d cir.) 1974, U.S. Ct. Appeals (D.C. cir.) 1977, U.S. Supreme Ct. 1977, D.C. 1982, U.S. Ct. Appeals (fed. cir.) 1985, U.S. Ct. Appeals (11th cir.), 1986 . Assoc. Paul, Weiss, Rifkind, Wharton & Garrison, N.Y.C., 1973-81, ptnr., 1981—. Vol. U.S. Peace Corps., Istanbul, Turkey, 1969-70. Mem. ABA, Assn. of Bar of City of N.Y. Federal civil litigation, State civil litigation, Antitrust. Home: 350 E 78th St New York NY 10021 Office: Paul Weiss Rifkind Wharton & Garrison 1285 Ave of the Americas New York NY 10019

SILVERMAN, PETER RAY, lawyer; b. Toledo, Dec. 26, 1955; s. Irwin J. and Inez (Okun) S. Student, Hebrew U., Jerusalem, 1975-76; BA, George Washington U., 1977; JD, U. Mich., 1982. Assoc. Debevoise & Plimpton, N.Y.C., 1981-84, Shumaker, Loop & Kendrick, Toledo, 1984—. Vice chmn. young men's div. United Jewish Appeal, Toledo, 1985, allocations com. United Way, Toledo, 1985; trustee Dem. Roundtable, Toledo, 1986—; bd. of trustees Darlington Ho., Toledo, 1985. Mem. ABA, Ohio Bar Assn., Toledo Bar Assn. Federal civil litigation, State civil litigation, General corporate. Office: Shumaker Loop & Kendrick 1000 Jackson St Toledo OH 43624

SILVERMAN, ROBERT ALAN, educational administrator, historian; b. Phila., Dec. 22, 1947; s. Milton Edward and Rhoda (Pasternack) S.; m. Fran Stukelman, Mar. 30, 1969; 1 son, David. B.S., Drexel U., 1969; M.A., Harvard U., 1973, Ph.D., 1977. Fin. analyst Harvard U., Cambridge, Mass., 1977-78, v.p. Harvard Real Estate, 1978-84; dir. planning Harvard U., 1984—. cons. Served with U.S. Army, 1969-72. Jewish. Author: Law and Urban Growth, 1981; editor: The Corporate Real Estate Handbook, 1986. Legal history. Office: Holyoke Ctr Room 912 Cambridge MA 02138

SILVERMAN, ROBERT J(OSEPH), lawyer; b. Mpls., Apr. 4, 1942; s. Maurice and Toby (Goldstein) S.; 1 son, Adam. B.A., U. Minn., 1964, J.D., 1967. Bar: Minn. 1967, U.S. Dist. Ct. Minn. 1967. Assoc. Dorsey & Whitney, Mpls., 1967-72, ptnr., 1972—; lectr. William Mitchell Coll. Law, 1978, Minn. Continuing Legal Edn., Advanced Legal Edn. Bd. dirs. Courage Ctr., 1978-84, 85—, v.p., 1983-86. Served with USAR, 1967-73. Mem. ABA, Minn. Bar Assn., Hennepin County Bar Assn. Club: Mpls. Athletic. Real property, Contracts commercial. Office: Suite 2200 First Bank Pl E Minneapolis MN 55402

SILVERMAN, SCOTT JAY, lawyer; b. Silver Springs, Md., June 25, 1957; s. Murray Silverman and Reeva Ina (Hurwitz) Fainberg. BBA magna cum laude, U. Miami, 1978; JD, U. Tulsa, 1981. Bar: Okla. 1981, U.S. Dist. Ct. (no., ea. and we. dists.) Okla. 1981, U.S. Ct. Appeals (10th cir.) 1981, Fla. 1983, U.S. Dist. Ct. (so. dist.) Fla. 1984. Asst. atty. gen. State of Okla., Oklahoma City, 1981-82; law clk. to presiding judge Fla. Cir. Ct., Miami, 1982-83; assoc. Marlow, Shofi et al, Miami, 1983-86; sole practice Miami, 1986—. Mem. ABA, Fla. Bar Assn., Okla. Bar Assn., Dade County Bar Assn., Assn. Trial Lawyers Am., Acad. Fla. Trial Lawyers, Am. Arbitration Assn. (arbitrator 1984—), Beta Gamma Sigma, Phi Kappa Phi, Phi Delta Phi, Omicron Delta Epsilon, Alpha Lambda Delta. Democrat. Personal injury, State civil litigation, Civil rights. Home: 1270 Kane Concourse Bay Harbor Islands FL 33154

SILVERMAN, WILLIAM MICHAEL, lawyer; b. N.Y.C., Feb. 7, 1942; s. Marvin David and Beverly (Roth) S.; m. Lynn M. Gozan, Aug. 30, 1964; children—Kim, John, Scott. B.A., Brown U., 1963; LL.B., N.Y.U., 1966. Bar: N.Y. 1966, U.S. Ct. Appeals (2d cir.) 1974, U.S. Supreme Ct. 1975. Assoc. Otterbourg, Steindler, Houston & Rosen, P.C., N.Y.C., 1966-69, 70-71, ptnr., 1972—; gen. counsel First Republic Corp. Am., 1970; dir. First Republic Corp. Am. Mem. Assn. Bar City N.Y., ABA, Fed. Bar Council, Assn. Comml. Fin. Attys., Lawyers Assn. Textile Industry. Banking, Bankruptcy, Consumer commercial. Office: 230 Park Ave New York NY 10169

SILVERNAIL, JESSE PRESTON, lawyer; b. Walker County, Ala., Aug. 24, 1947; s. Jesse William and Betty Jean (Humpries) S.; m. Sarah Elizabeth O'Kelley, Sept. 4, 1971. BA, U. Fla., 1972, MBA, 1974; JD, St. Mary's U., San Antonio, 1977. Bar: Fla. 1977, U.S. Dist. Ct. (mid. dist.) Fla. 1977. Mgr. contracts Harris Corp., Melbourne, Fla., 1978-79; ptnr. Rossetler, Maxwell & Silvernail, Melbourne, 1979-81; sole practice Melbourne, 1981-83; ptnr. Vaughn, Vaughn, Vaughn, Silvernail & Cary, Melbourne, 1983—; adj. prof. Brevard Community Coll., Melbourne, 1985—. Vice chmn. parks and recreation bd. Brevard County; mem. Fla. Blue Key. Served to sgt. U.S. Army, 1967-69. Mem. ABA, Omicron Delta Kappa. Lodge: Kiwanis (bd. dirs. Melbourne 1986—). State civil litigation, Family and matrimonial. Home: 551 Inverness Ave Melbourne FL 32940 Office: Vaughn Vaughn Vaughn Silvernail & Cary 2007 S Melbourne Ct Melbourne FL 32901

SILVERNALE, LAWRENCE DUGGAN, lawyer; b. Walla Walla, Wash., June 9, 1930; s. Grant J. and Leanor (Hall) S.; m. Joanne Ellis Klasell, Sept. 17, 1955; children: Ann, Marya, Lisa, Meighan. BA in History, U. Wash., 1952, JD, 1957. Bar: Wash. 1957, U.S. Dist. Ct. (ea. and we. dists.) Wash. 1960, U.S. Ct. Appeals (9th cir.) 1961, U.S. Supreme Ct. 1963. Asst. atty. gen. State of Wash., Olympia, 1957-60; atty. Great Northern R.R., Seattle, 1960-70, Burlington Northern R.R., Seattle, 1970-86; assoc. Rosenow, Hale & Johnson, Seattle, 1986—. Served to 1st lt. U.S. Army, 1953-55. Mem. ABA, Wash. Bar Assn., Seattle-King County Bar Assn. Personal injury, Railroad law, Labor. Office: Rosenow Hale & Johnson 999 3d Ave Seattle WA 98104

SILVERS, EILEEN S., lawyer; b. N.Y.C., Sept. 21, 1948; d. Sidney and Ethel Lynne (Starobin) Swertloff; m. Kenneth Roth Silvers, Aug. 31, 1969; children—Steven Jay, Sharron Roth. B.A. magna cum laude, SUNY-Buffalo, 1970; J.D., Columbia U., 1975. Bar: N.Y. 1977, U.S. Tax Ct. 1981, U.S. Ct. Claims 1983, D.C., 1984. Assoc., Paul, Weiss, Rifkind, Wharton & Garrison, N.Y.C., 1975-83, ptnr., 1983—. Mem. ABA (tax sect. mem. of com. on U.S. Activities of Foreigners and Tax Treaties 1986—), N.Y. State Bar Assn. (chmn. personal income com. tax sect. 1983-85 , exec. com. 1982-85), Inst. Ice Age Studies (bd. dirs.), D.C. Bar Assn. Corporate taxation, Personal income taxation. Home: 9 Sleepy Hollow Rd Chappaqua NY 10514 Office: Paul Weiss Rifkind et al 1285 Ave of Americas New York NY 10019

SILVERSTEIN, CAROL KAUFFMAN, lawyer; b. Phila., May 18, 1948; d. Abraham L. and Sarah (Levin) Kauffman; m. Elliot M. Silverstein, June 10, 1973; children: Scott Andrew, Alan Joseph. BA, U. Pa., 1969; JD, Temple U., 1972. Bar: Pa. 1972, N.C. 1975. Ptnr. Hollowell and Silverstein P.A., Raleigh, N.C., 1974—. Bd. dirs. Learning Together Inc., Raleigh, 1975-79. Mem. N.C. Soc. Health Care Attys. (pres. 1979, bd. dirs. 1977-79, 84), ABA, N.C. Bar Assn., Wake County Bar Assn., Am. Acad. Hosp. Attys. Democrat. Jewish. Health, Estate planning, Pension, profit-sharing, and employee benefits. Office: Hollowell and Silverstein PA 1100 Dresser Ct Raleigh NC 27609

SILVERSTEIN, ELIZABETH BLUME, lawyer; b. Newark, Nov. 2, 1892; d. Selig and Goldie (Arahowitz) Blume; m. Max Silverstein, Aug. 23, 1934 (dec. 1955); 1 son, Nathan Royce. LL.B., N.J. Law Sch. (now Rutgers U. Sch. Law), 1911. Bar: N.J. 1913, U.S. Supreme Ct. 1921, U.S. Tax Ct. 1960. First woman lawyer in N.J. in practice law, 1913, 1st woman in N.J. to represent defendant, unassisted in homicide case, 1916, 1st woman on legal adv. bd. of Draft Bd. during World War I, Essex County, N.J. Del. First Am. Jewish Congress, 1916, 23, exec. bd. dirs., mem. immigration com., 1923, del. 1st World Jewish Congress, 1936; leader Balfour parade, Newark. Mem. Woman's Lawyers Assn. (v.p. 1920s), ABA, Essex County Bar Assn., Am. Judicature Soc., N.J. State Bar Assn., Nat. Assn. Women Lawyers (N.J. state del.). Republican. (del. Republican conv. 1932). Club: Heinberg Rep. (pres. 1920's). Lodges: Ind. Order Brith Abraham (1st woman to serve nat. order exec. positions, asst. to Grand Master, chmn. Jewish rights, chmn. com. on disability), Louis D. Brandies Lodge (pres. 1920s). Home: 62 Osborne Terr Newark NJ 07108

SILVERSTEIN, LEONARD LEWIS, lawyer; b. Scranton, Pa., Jan. 21, 1922; s. Robert Philip and Blanche (Raker) S.; m. Elaine Wise, June 24, 1951; children: Thomas, Susan. A.B., Yale U., 1943; LL.B., Harvard U., 1948. Bar: Pa. 1949, D.C. 1953. Practiced in Scranton, 1949-51, Washington, 1954—; atty. Office Chief Counsel, IRS, Washington, 1951-52; mem. legal adv. staff Dept. Treasury, Washington, 1952-54; mem. firm Silverstein and Mullens, Washington, 1959—; adj. prof. Law Sch., Georgetown U., Washington, 1960-61; spl. tax counsel SBA, Washington, 1958-59; lectr. law N.Y. U., N.Y.C., 1954-60. Chief editor: Tax Mgmt. Inc, 1959—. Chmn. exec. com. Nat. Symphony Orch., Washington, 1978-79; exec. dir. Commn. on Pvt. Philanthropy and Pub. Needs, 1973-77; mem. task force Council on Environ. Quality, 1970-71; Mem. adv. group House Ways and Means Com., 85th Congress; mem. task force on taxes Pres.-elect Nixon, 1968-69; trustee Corcoran Gallery of Art, Washington, 1974—; pres. Nat. Symphony Orch. Assn., 1980-83, bd. dirs., 1971—; mem. U.S. Adv. Commn. on Public Diplomacy, 1980-83, chmn., 1981-82; mem. Presdl. Task Force on Arts and Humanities, 1981—; mem., chmn. tax working group President's Com. on Arts and Humanities, 1982—; bd. dirs. French-Am. Found., 1983—, Bur. Nat. Affairs,1985—; mem., vice chmn. bd. trustees John F. Kennedy Ctr. for Performing Arts, 1985—Served to lt. (j.g.) USNR, 1943-46. Mem. ABA, Pa. Bar Assn., D.C. Bar, Am. Law Inst. Corporate taxation, Estate taxation, Personal income taxation. Home: 5402 Goldsboro Rd Bethesda MD 20817 Office: Silverstein and Mullens 1776 K St NW #800 Washington DC 20006

SILVEY, CHARLES DELBERT, II, lawyer; b. Yankton, S.D., Aug. 10, 1947; s. Charles Delbert and Doris Jean (Long) S.; m. Mary Ann Wiese, Jan. 14, 1974; children: Charles Delbert III, William Scott. BA, St. Olaf Coll., 1969; JD, Vanderbilt U., 1971. Bar: Colo. 1972, U.S. Ct. Mil. Appeals 1972, U.S. Supreme Ct. 1976, Alaska 1977, U.S. Dist. Ct. Alaska 1977, U.S. Ct. Appeals (9th cir.) 1985. From assoc. to ptnr. Schaible, Staley, DeLisio & Cook Inc., Fairbanks, Alaska, 1976—, pres., 1985-87; pres. Staley, DeLisio, Cook & Sherry Inc., Fairbanks, 1987—. Pres. Fairbanks Luth. Ch., Fairbanks, 1984; coach Women's softball, Fairbanks, 1985—. Served to capt. JAGC, USAF, 1972-76. Mem. ABA, Alaska Bar Assn., Tanana Valley Bar Assn. Avocations: reading, softball, travel, fishing, hunting. State civil litigation, Consumer commercial, Personal injury. Home: PO Box 1350 Fairbanks AK 99707 Office: Staley DeLisio Cook & Sherry Inc 330 Barnette St Fairbanks AK 99701

SIMBURG, MELVYN JAY, lawyer; b. San Francisco, June 15, 1946; s. Earl J. and Pearl Estelle (Garmaise) S.; m. Barbara Sherri Frost, Jan. 1, 1981; 2 children. A.B., U. Calif.-Berkeley, 1968; J.D., Columbia U., 1972, M.Internat. Affairs, 1972. Bar: Wash. 1972, U.S. Ct. Appeals (9th cir.) 1972. Assoc. Perkins, Cole, Stone, Olsen & Williams, Seattle, 1972-76; sole practice, Seattle, 1976-81; pres. Melvyn Jay Simburg, P.S., A Profl. Service Corp., Seattle, 1981-83, Simburg, Ketter, Haley, Sheppard & Purdy, P.S., Seattle, 1983—; adj. prof. Law Sch., U. Puget Sound, Tacoma, 1972-74; chmn. ann. seminar on U.S. Can. bus. trans. of Bar Assn. B.C. and Wash. State. Former pres. Leschi Improvement Council, Seattle; active Seattle Film Soc., Seattle Art Mus. Mem. ABA (com. on fgn. investment in U.S. sect. internat. law and practice, com. on internat. bus. law sect. corp., bus. and banking law), Wash. State Bar Assn. (chmn. sect. internat. law and practice 1986-87), Seattle-King County Bar Assn. (former chmn. sect. internat. and comparative law), World Trade Club Seattle (bd. dirs. 1983-86), World Affairs Council Seattle, Seattle C. of C. (vice chmn. internat. trade and devel. com. 1984-86). Contbr. to Columbia U. Jour. Law and Soc. Private international, Real property, Bankruptcy. Home: 235 Lake Dell Ave Seattle WA 98122 Office: 2525 First Interstate Ctr 3d & Marion Sts Seattle WA 98104

SIMCHAK, MATTHEW STEPHEN, lawyer; b. Washington, Sept. 29, 1947; s. Matt Szymczak and Morag (MacLeod) Simchak; m. Jane Flues, Aug. 28, 1971; children: Thomas, Philip, Stephen. BA in History, Trinity Coll., 1969; JD, U. Va., 1972. Bar: D.C. 1973, Mass. 1985. Assoc. McKenna, Conner & Cuneo and predecessor firm Sellers, Conner & Cuneo, Washington, 1972-74; from assoc. to ptnr. Pettit & Martin, San Francisco and Washington, 1974-84; ptnr. Ropes & Gray, Boston and Washington, 1984—; instr. govt. contract law continuing legal edn. program D.C. Bar, 1984; advisor Fed. Contracts Report Bur. Nat. Affairs, 1984—. Trustee St. Albans Sch., Washington, 1978-83. Mem. ABA (pub. contract sect., editor-in-chief Pub. Contract Law Jour., 1982—), D.C. Bar Assn. (steering com. 1983—). Democrat. Episcopalian. Club: Metropolitan (Washington). Government contracts and claims. Home: 3719 Morrison St NW Washington DC 20015 Office: Ropes & Gray 1001 22d St NW Washington DC 20037 also: Ropes & Gray 225 Franklin St Boston MA 02110

SIMKANICH, JOHN JOSEPH, lawyer, engineer; b. Clairton, Pa., Aug. 7, 1941; s. John and Emily G. (Frenock) S. BSEE, Drexel Inst. Tech., 1964; MSEE, Purdue U., 1966; JD, George Washington U., 1972. Bar: U.S. Patent Office 1970, Pa. 1973, U.S. Ct. Customs and Patent Appeals 1974, U.S. Dist. Ct. (ea. dist.) Pa. 1977, U.S. Supreme Ct. 1977, U.S. Ct. Appeals (Fed. cir.) 1982. Elec. engr. U.S. Steel Co., Fairless Hills, Pa., 1963-65; engr. Westinghouse Aerospace, Balt., 1966-69; systems developer TRW Systems, Washington, 1969-70; patent atty. Burroughs Corp., Paoli, Pa., 1970-74, Johnson & Johnson, New Brunswick, N.J., 1974-77, Paul, Paul, Ferrill & Logan, Phila., 1977-85; ptnr. Simkanich & Green, Newtown, Pa., 1985—; adv. Soup, Inc., Washington, 1970-72. Patentee in field. Mem. ABA, Pa. Bar Assn., Bucks County Bar Assn., Phila. Patent Law Assn., Am. Intellectual Property Law Assn., Delta Theta Phi, Eta Kappa Nu. Patent, Computer, Trademark and copyright. Office: Simkanich & Green 1701 Newtown-Langhonre Rd Box 671 Newtown PA 18940

SIMMENTAL, DAVID ANTHONY, lawyer; b. El Paso, Tex., Sept. 12, 1953; m. Dorothy Ann Simmental, July 21, 1977. BA in History, U. Tex., 1976; JD, U. Houston, 1981. Bar: Tex. 1981, U.S. Ct. Appeals (5th cir.) 1982, U.S. Dist. Ct. (so. dist.) Tex. 1982, U.S. Dist. Ct. (we. dist.) Tex. 1983. Atty., mgr. real estate Cooper Industries Inc., Houston, 1981-82; asst. city atty. City of El Paso, 1982-83; sole practice El Paso, 1983—. V.p. El Paso chpt. Tex. Ex.'s, 1985. Mem. ABA, Assn. Trial Lawyers Am., El Paso Bar Assn., El Paso Young Lawyers Assn., Jaycees (sec. East El Paso chpt. 1984), Sierra Club. Roman Catholic. Avocations: skiing, golf, sailing. Personal injury, Federal civil litigation, General corporate. Home: 2344 Robert Wynn Dr El Paso TX 79936 Office: 6040 Surety Dr El Paso TX 79905

SIMMONDS, JAMES HENRY, lawyer; b. Lynchburg, Va., Apr. 19, 1905; s. Sidney J. Simmonds and Elsie Amelia Febrey; m. Elizabeth Welch, Nov. 23, 1934 (div. 1953); children: James G., John S.; m. Jeane Deeley, Feb. 6, 1954; children: Sidney, Susan. BS, U. Va., 1927, JD, 1930; LLM, Columbia U., 1931. Bar: Va. 1930, N.Y. 1933, U.S. Dist. Ct. (ea. dist.) 1933, U.S. Ct. Appeals (4th cir.) 1935, U.S. Supreme Ct. 1940. Asst. commonwealth atty. Arlington County, Va., 1933-39; ptnr. Simmonds, Coleburn & Towner, Arlington, 1939—; bd. dirs. 1st Am. Bank Va., Arlington. Columbia U. fellow, 1930-31. Fellow Am. Coll. Trial LAwyers, Am. Bar Found.; mem. Va. Bar Assn. (pres. 1958-59), Arlington Bar Assn. (pres. 1948-49, distinguished service award 1983), Order of Coif, Raven Soc., Phi Beta Kappa. Club: Washington Golf and Country (Arlington) (bd. dirs.). Estate plan-

ning, Contracts, Probate. Office: Simmonds Coleburn & Towner 2041 N 15th St Arlington VA 22201

SIMMONS, ALAN RUSSELL, lawyer; b. Huntington, W.Va., Aug. 21, 1949; s. Howard Russell and Louise Barbara (Stefanelli) S.; m. Jean Anne Ramsey, Sept. 29, 1984. BA cum laude, Marshall U., 1971; JD, Emory U., 1974. Bar: W.Va. 1974, U.S. Dist. Ct. (so. dist.) W.Va. 1974. Tax analyst W.Va. State Tax Dept., Charleston, W.Va., 1974-77; dep. W.Va. Sec. of State, Charleston, 1975-77; staff atty. W.Va. Senate Judiciary Com., Charleston, 1977; assoc. Ducker & McCreight, Huntington, W.Va., 1977-80; v.p., trust officer Huntington Trust and Savings Bank, 1980-85; sr. trust officer 1st Huntington Nat. Bank, 1985—; realtor, assoc. Simmons Realty Co, Huntington, 1969—. Pres., bd. dirs. Goodwill Industries Kyowva Area, Huntington, 1982-83; alt. del. Rep. Nat. Conv., Dallas, 1984; mem. W.Va. State Election Commn., Charleston, 1985. Mem. ABA, W.Va. Bar Assn., Cabell County Bar Assn., Am. Bankers Assn. (cert. fin. services counselor 1983), Estate Planning Council Huntington, Marshall U. Alumni Assn. (v.p., bd. dirs.), Phi Alpha Theta. Methodist. Pension, profit-sharing, and employee benefits, Probate, Banking. Home: 2201 Cherry Ave Huntington WV 25701 Office: 1st Huntington Nat Bank 1000 5th Ave Huntington WV 25701

SIMMONS, BRENT ELLIOTT, lawyer; b. Albion, Mich., Mar. 17, 1949; s. Rufus and Marjorie Mae (Broughton) S.; m. Kathryn Ann King, Aug. 19, 1972; children—Michael David, Rachel Anne. B.A. with honors, Albion Coll., 1971; J.D., U. Mich., 1977; M.A., George Washington U., 1981. Bar: Mich. 1977, U.S. Ct. Appeals (4th cir.) 1979, U.S. Supreme Ct. 1980, U.S. Ct. Appeals (D.C. cir.) 1981, U.S. Ct. Appeals (5th cir.) 1981, U.S. Ct. Appeals (11th cir.) 1981, U.S. Ct. Appeals (6th cir.) 1983, U.S. Dist. Ct. (ea. and we. dists.) Mich. 1984. Asst. counsel NAACP Legal Defense and Ednl. Fund, Inc., Washington 1977-84; asst. atty. gen. State Mich., Lansing, 1984—; mem. lawyers com. Lansing Br., ACLU, 1984-86. Mem. editorial staff U. Mich. Jour. Law Reform, 1977. Commr., chmn. East Lansing (Mich.) Bd. Zoning Appeals, 1984-87. Served to lt. commdr. USN, 1971-75, with Res., 1984—. Mem. ABA (co-chmn. com. minority rights and equal opportunity 1983-84), Nat. Bar Assn., State Bar Mich., Lansing Black Lawyers Assn. (pres. 1986—, chmn. scholarship com. 1985-86), Omicron Delta Kappa. Environment, Government contracts and claims, Civil rights. Home: 1308 Woodingham Dr East Lansing MI 48823 Office: Atty Gen Dept 720 Law Bldg Lansing MI 48913

SIMMONS, BRYAN J., corporate lawyer; b. Springfield, Pa., Sept. 12, 1955; s. Alfred John and Priscilla Theresa (O'Donnell) S.; m. Carol Lynn Hoffman, Aug. 11, 1979; children: Brett, Kristen. BS in Meteorology, Pa. State U., 1977; JD, Dickinson Law Sch., 1981. Bar: Pa. 1981, U.S. Dist. Ct. (mid. dist.) 1982, U.S. Ct. Appeals (3d cir.) 1982. Law clk. Lancaster County (Pa.) Ct. of Common Pleas, 1981-82; counsel Hershey (Pa.) Foods Corp., 1982—. Trustee Elizabethtown (Pa.) Public Library, 1985—. mem. ABA, Pa. Bar Assn., Lancaster County Bar Assn., Dauphin County Bar Assn., Nat. Weather Assn. Avocations: fishing, softball. Environment, Patent, Private international. Home: 2331 Elizabethtown Rd Elizabethtown PA 17022 Office: Hershey Foods Corp 14 E Chocolate Ave Hershey PA 17033

SIMMONS, CHARLES BEDFORD, JR., lawyer; b. Greenville, S.C., Dec. 4, 1956; s. Charles Bedford and Mary Margaret (Mason) S.; m. Claudia Elizabeth Spencer, Apr. 26, 1986. AA magna cum laude, Spartanburg Meth. Coll., 1977; BS magna cum laude, E. Tenn. State U., 1979; JD, U. S.C., 1982. Bar: S.C. 1982, U.S. Dist. Ct. S.C. 1983, U.S. Ct. Appeals (4th cir.) 1986. Law clk. to presiding justice S.C. Cir. Ct., Greenville, 1982-83; with Carter Law Firm, Greenville, 1983-86; assoc. Wilkins, Wilkins, Nelson & Kittredge, Greenville, 1986—. Leadership Greenville Class XIII, bd. dirs. Big Bros./Big Sisters, Greenville, 1985—; bd. dirs., sec. Crimestoppers Inc., Greenville, 1985—. Mem. S.C. Bar Assn. (young lawyer liason 1985—), Greenville Bar Assn. (sec. young lawyers 1985—, v.p. 1986—), Assn. Trial Lawyers Am., S.C. Trial Lawyers Assn., Gamma Beta Phi, Pi Gamma Mu, Phi Delta Phi. Republican. Presbyterian. Clubs: Greenville City, Textile (v.p. 1985—), Revelers (Greenville). Personal injury, Family and matrimonial. Home: 11 W Hillcrest Dr Greenville SC 29609 Office: Wilkins Wilkins Nelson & Kittredge 408 E North St Greenville SC 29601

SIMMONS, DONALD CHARLES, lawyer, anthropologist, educator; b. Evanston, Ill., Apr. 10, 1926; s. Donald F. and Madeline R. (Carnahan) S.; m. Nancy Taylor, Mar. 27, 1951; children—Charles T., Donald C. B.Sc., Northwestern U., 1948; M.A., Yale U., 1950, Ph.D., 1954; J.D., U. Conn., 1967; M.Sc. in Taxation, U. Hartford, 1976. Bar: Conn. 1967, U.S. Dist. Ct. Conn. 1967, U.S. Supreme Ct. 1971. Sole practice, Waterbury, Conn., 1969—. Author: Efik Tone Riddles, 1981. Served with USNR, 1944-46, PTO. Fellow Am. Anthropology Assn.; mem. ABA, Conn. Bar Assn., Waterbury Bar Assn. Lodge: Elks. Administrative and regulatory, Civil rights, Criminal. Office: 440 Meadow St Waterbury CT 06107

SIMMONS, HOWARD KOORKEN, lawyer; b. Providence, May 29, 1902; m. Ann Mary Carroll, Aug. 20, 1929 children—Howard Carroll, Robert Lewis. LL.B., Boston U., 1924. Bar: R.I. 1925, U.S. Dist. Ct. R.I. 1926. Assoc. Walling & Walling, Providence, 1925-79; sole practice, Providence, 1979; partner Simmons & Simmons, Providence, 1979—. Mem. Assn. Trial Lawyers Am., R.I. Trial Def. Attys. Club: Club: Fraternal Order Police Assocs. Roman Catholic. Criminal, Family and matrimonial, Personal injury. Office: 10 Nate Whipple Hwy Cumberland RI 02864 Office: 31 Tanglewood Dr East Providence RI 02915

SIMMONS, KERMIT MIXON, lawyer; b. Winnfield, La., Oct. 7, 1935; s. Kermit Carson and Mamie Rose (Mixon) S.; m. Nina Underwood, Jan. 30, 1960; children—Kermit Mixon, Susan Elizabeth, Alfred Lee. B.A., La. Tech. U., 1956; J.D., La. State U., 1959. Bar: La. 1959, U.S. Dist. Ct. (we. dist.) La. 1965, U.S. Ct. Appeals (5th cir.) 1965. Law clk. La. 2d Cir. Ct. Appeals, Shreveport, 1961-62; assoc. Lowe & Benton, Minden, La., 1962-63; ptnr. Peters & Simmons, Winnfield, La., 1963-69; sole practice, Winnfield, 1969-74; ptnr. Simmons & Derr, Winnfield, 1974—; 1st asst. 8th Jud. Dist. Atty., Winnfield, 1965—; chmn. spl. com. malpractice ins. La. Bar, 1984-85. Trustee Winn Parish Bd. Library Trustees, 1966—. Mem. La. Trial Lawyers Assn., Winn Parish Bar Assn. (pres. 1981—). Lodges: Rotary (pres. Winnfield 1967), Masons. Banking, State civil litigation, Probate. Home: Simmons & Derr 200 Church Winnfield LA 71483

SIMMONS, PAUL ALLEN, judge; b. Monongahela, Pa., Aug. 31, 1921; s. Perry C. and Lilly D. (Allen) S.; m. Gwendolyn O. Gladden, Sept. 2, 1950; children—Paul A., Gwendolyn Dale, Anne Marie. B.A., U. Pitts., 1946; J.D., Harvard U., 1949. Mem. faculty dept. law S.C. State Coll. Law, 1949-52; prof. law N.C. Central U., 1952-56; pvt. practice law Monongahela, 1956-73; judge Ct. of Common Pleas, Washington County, Pa., 1973-78, U.S. Dist. Ct., Western Dist. Pa., Pitts., 1978—. Mem. Pa. Human Relations Commn., 1963-68; mem. Pa. Minor Jud. Edn. Bd., 1970—, Washington County Redevel. Authority, 1970-73. Mem. Pa. Bar Assn., N.C. Bar Assn., Am. Bar Assn., Washington County Bar Assn., Pa. Bar Assn., Am. Judicature Soc., NAACP. Democrat. Mem. African Meth. Episcopal Ch. Clubs: Masons, Elks. Jurisprudence.

SIMMONS, PETER, law educator, university dean; b. N.Y.C., July 19, 1931; s. Michael L. and Mary A. S.; m. Ruth J. Tanfield, Jan. 28, 1951; children: Sam, Lizzard. A.B., U. Calif., Berkeley, 1953, LL.B., 1956; postgrad. (Alvord fellow), U. Wis., 1956-58. Prof. SUNY, Buffalo, 1963-67; mem. faculty Ohio State U., 1967-75, U. Ill., 1972, Case Western Res. U., 1974-75; prof. law and urban planning Rutgers U. Coll. Law, Newark, 1975—, dean, 1975—. Contbr. articles to profl. jours. Mem. Ohio Housing Commn., 1972-74; commr. Ohio Reclamation Rev. Bd., 1974-75; chmn. N.J. Criminal Disposition Commn., 1983-84; mem. N.J. Law Revision Commn., 1987—. Mem. Am. Planning Assn., Urban Land Inst., Am. Law Inst., AAUP (nat. council 1973-75). Legal education. Office: 15 Washington St Newark NJ 07102

SIMMONS, RAYMOND HEDELIUS, JR., lawyer; b. Salinas, Calif., May 27, 1958; s. Raymond Hedelius and Antoinette (Lynch) S. BA magna cum laude, U. Calif., San Diego, 1979; JD magna cum laude, U. Calif., San Francisco, 1982. Bar: Calif. 1982, U.S. Dist. Ct. (no. dist.) Calif. 1982. Assoc. Farella, Braun & Martel, San Francisco, 1982-85; atty., v.p. Barnett-Range Corp., Atlanta, 1985-86; counsel Nationwide Capital Corp. sibs. Home Fed. Savings and Loan Assn. San Diego, Atlanta, 1986—. Mem. ABA, Calif. Bar Assn., Calif. Scholarship Fedn. (life), Order of Coif, Thurston Soc. Real property, Contracts commercial, General corporate. Home: 2054 Cottage Ln NW Atlanta GA 30318 Office: Nationwide Capital Corp 3500 Piedmont Rd NE Suite 610 Atlanta GA 30305

SIMMONS, ROBERT MICHAEL, lawyer; b. Milw., Jan. 27, 1948; s. Keith Rexford and June Antoinette (Schimmels) S.; m. Judy Ann Whelan, July 6, 1978; children: Paul Michael, Michael David. BA in Econs., U. Wis., 1970, JD, 1973; ML, George Washington U., 1979. Bar: D.C. 1973, U.S. Supreme Ct. 1976, U.S. Claims Ct. 1978. Atty. advisor USDA, Washington, 1973-78; atty. advisor USDA, Portland, Oreg., 1978-85, asst. regional atty., 1985-87; regional atty. USDA, San Francisco, 1987—. Recipient Superior Service award USDA, 1985. Mem. ABA (forest resources subcom., vice chmn. 1986—), Fed. Bar Assn. (v.p. 1986-87). Environment, Government contracts and claims, Federal civil litigation. Office: USDA Office of Gen Counsel 211 Main St Suite 1060 San Francisco CA 94105-1924

SIMMONS, SAMUEL LEE, lawyer; b. St. Louis, Dec. 27, 1929; s. David Mayo and Mayme Pearle (Looney) S.; m. Joan Miller, Oct. 8, 1959; children—Lesley, Samuel Lee. B.A. with honors, Principia Coll., 1951; J.D. cum laude, Harvard U., 1957. Bar: N.Y. 1958. Atty. Standard Oil Co. N.J., N.Y.C., 1957-59; firm Arthur, Dry & Dole, N.Y.C., 1959-63; with ITT, 1963-75; staff counsel, gen. counsel ITT Credit Corp., 1963-67; v.p. parent co., gen. counsel European hdqrs. Europe Inc., Brussels, Belgium, 1967-75; v.p., gen. counsel Revlon Inc., N.Y.C., 1975-76; sr. v.p., gen. counsel Revlon Inc., 1976-86, dir., 1976-85, corp. sec., 1979-86; sr. v.p. dir. corp. devel. ITT Credit Corp., 1987—. Served with U.S. Army, 1952-54. Mem. Bar Assn. City N.Y., Am. Bar Assn. Home: 800 Park Ave New York NY 10021

SIMMONS, STEPHEN JUDSON, lawyer; b. Columbus, Ohio, Feb. 19, 1946; s. Samuel A. and Jane A. (McGrath) S.; m. Claire Maxine Schriber, Aug. 15, 1970; children—Darren, Judson. B.A., Ohio State U., 1968; J.D., U. Cin., 1972. Bar: Tex. 1982, Ohio 1973. Sr. law clk. U.S. Dist. Ct. (ea. dist.) Tenn., Knoxville, 1972-74; asst. atty. gen. Office of Atty. of Ohio, Columbus, 1974-75; assoc. McGrath & Shirey, Columbus, 1975; corp. counsel Wendys Internat., Inc., Columbus, 1975-79; sr. v.p., gen. counsel Precision Tune, Inc., Beaumont, Tex., 1979—, also dir. Bd. editors U. Cin. Law Rev., 1971-72. Mem. ABA, Tex. Bar Assn. Roman Catholic. Franchising, General corporate, Trademark and copyright. Home: 895 Shakespeare St Beaumont TX 77706 Office: Precision Tune Inc 755 S 11th St Beaumont TX 77705

SIMMS, ROBERT D., justice Supreme Court Oklahoma; b. Tulsa, Feb. 6, 1926; s. Matthew Scott and Bessie L. (Moore) S.; m. Patricia C., Feb. 16, 1950; 1 son, Robert D. Student, Milligan Coll., Phillips U.; LL.B., U. Tulsa. Bar: Okla. 1950. Practiced law Sand Springs, Okla., from 1950; asst. county atty. Tulsa County, 1953-54; chief prosecutor County Atty.'s Office, 1955-58, county atty., 1958-62; judge Okla. Dist. Ct., Dist. 14, 1962-71, Okla. Ct. Criminal Appeals, 1971-72; justice Okla. Supreme Ct., 1972—; mem. Okla. Crime Commn. Mem. Gov.'s Spl. Com. on Drug Abuse, 1970; sponsor and coach Pee-Wee Baseball. Served with USN, 1943-46. Mem. Tulsa County Bar Assn., Okla. Bar Assn. (chmn. dist. atty. sect. 1959). Office: Supreme Ct Okla 202 State Capitol Bldg Oklahoma City OK 73105 •

SIMMS, SANDRA ARLENE, lawyer; b. Chgo., July 26, 1948; d. Gerald Raymond Sr. and Vera Mae (Clemons) Nuckolls; m. Henry Simms, June 15, 1974; children: Sharon Anita, Richard Henry, Vera Iwalani. BA, U. Ill., 1970; JD, DePaul U., 1978. Bar: Hawaii 1980, U.S. Dist. Ct. Hawaii 1980. Flight attendant United Airlines, Chgo., 1972-77; law clk. to presiding justice Ill. Appelate Ct., Chgo., 1978, Intermediate Ct. Appeals, Honolulu, 1980-82; dep. corp. counsel City and County of Hawaii, Honolulu, 1982—. Mem. Mililani Uka Sch. Parent Tchrs. Guild, 1981—, Mililani-Waipio-Melemonu Neighborhood Bd., 1983—. Named one of Outstanding Young Women of Am., 1984. Mem. ABA, Hawaii Women Lawyers (bd. dirs. 1981), Hawaii Afro-Am. Lawyers Union, Hawaii State Bd. Bar Examiners, NAACP (legal redress com.), Abundant Life Ctr. Family and matrimonial, Local government. Home: 94-444 Keehuhiwa Pl Mililani HI 96789 Office: City and County Honolulu Dept Corp Counsel 530 S King St Honolulu HI 96813

SIMON, ALEXANDER NATHAN, lawyer; b. East Orange, N.J., May 22, 1951; s. Seymour and Dina (Gross) S. BA, U. Va., 1973, JD, 1978. Bar: Va. 1978, U.S. Dist. Ct. (ea. dist.) Va. 1979, U.S. Ct. Appeals (4th cir.) 1979, U.S. Supreme Ct. 1982. Law clk. to presiding judge U.S. Dist. Ct., Richmond, Va., 1978-79; assoc. Wallerstein, Goode & Dobbins, Richmond, 1979-86; ptnr. Woodley & Simon, Richmond, 1986—; prin., dir. The Innovative Capital Group, Richmond, Washington, Boston. Served to capt. U.S. Army, USAR, 1973-80. Mem. ABA, Richmond Bar Assn., Va. Small Bus. Advanced Tech. Assn. Jewish. Club: Downtown (Richmond). Lodge: Masons. General corporate, Contracts commercial, Real property. Home: 2 S Boulevard Richmond VA 23220 Office: Woodley & Simon 1 N 5th St Suite 301 Richmond VA 23219

SIMON, BRUCE LEE, lawyer; b. San Francisco, Nov. 19, 1953; s. Sidney Lee and Nancy Helen (Simon) S.; m. Carolyn Jane Flint, June 25, 1983. AB, U. Calif., Berkeley, 1977; JD, U. Calif., Hastings Coll. Law, 1980. Bar: Calif. 1980, U.S. Dist. Ct. (no. dist.) Calif. 1980, U.S. Supreme Ct. 1985. Assoc. Liccardo, Hartsell & Caselli, San Jose, Calif., 1980-82, Gordon & Rees, San Francisco, 1982-84, Cotchett & Illston, Burlingame, Calif., 1984—; pro tem commr. San Mateo County Mcpl. Ct., 1985—. Mem. ABA, Calif. Bar Assn., San Mateo County Bar Assn. (bench, bar, media and community affairs coms.), Assn. Trial Lawyers Am., Calif. Trial Lawyers Assn. Avocations: skiing, racquetball, jogging, reading. Federal civil litigation, State civil litigation, Construction. Office: San Francisco Office Ctr 840 Malcolm Rd Suite 200 Burlingame CA 94010

SIMON, DAVID FREDERICK, lawyer; b. El Paso, Tex., Apr. 14, 1953; s. Maurice and Susan (Bendekovits) S.; m. Deborah Hart, Mar. 1, 1980; children: Alison Mallory, Joshua Alan. BS magna cum laude, U. Buffalo, 1974; JD cum laude, U. Pa., 1977. Bar: Pa. 1979, N.J. 1980. Law clk. to presiding judge Phila. Ct. Common Pleas, 1977-79; assoc. Wolf, Block, Schorr & Solis-Cohen, Phila., 1979-85, ptnr., 1985—. Mem. Phila. Bar Assn. (exec. com. young lawyers sect. 1983-85, chmn. computer law com. 1984-85). Avocations: photography, electronics. Computer, State civil litigation, Construction. Home: 218 Jefferson Ave Haddonfield NJ 08033 Office: Wolf Block Schorr & Solis-Cohen Packard Bldg 12th Floor Philadelphia PA 19102

SIMON, DAVID ROBERT, lawyer; b. Newton, Mass., June 21, 1934; m. Myrna B. Kiner, June 28, 1959; children—Marianne, Geoffrey. A.B., Harvard U., 1956, LL.B., 1960. Bar: Mass. 1960, N.J. 1963, N.Y. 1980. Law sec. to judge U.S. Dist. Ct., Newark, 1961-63; assoc. Newark Law Firm, 1964-68; ptnr. Simon & Allen, Newark, 1968-86; ptnr. Kirsten, Simon, Friedman, Allen, Cherin & Linken, Newark, 1987—. Served with USAR, 1956-64. Mem. ABA, N.J. State Bar Assn., Essex County Bar Assn., Assn. Trial Lawyers Am. Antitrust, Federal civil litigation, State civil litigation. Home: 22 Saratoga Way Short Hills NJ 07078 Office: One Gateway Ctr Newark NJ 07102

SIMON, DENNIS LEE, lawyer; b. South Bend, Ind., May 15, 1946; s. Ralph H. and Marjorie A. (Bassett) S.; m. Veronica M. Vodicka, Aug. 24, 1968; children: Daria L., Jeremy D. BBA, U. Notre Dame, 1968; JD, U. Colo., 1973. Bar: Wis. 1973. Atty. Alvin H. Eisenberg Law Office, Milwaukee, 1974-76, Di Renzo & Bomier Law Office, Neenah, Wis., 1976—. Mem., trustee St. Patrick's Cath. Parish Fin. Com., Menasha, Wis., 1985—. Served with U.S. Army, 1968-70. Mem. ABA, Wis. Bar Assn., Winnebago County Bar Assn. (pres. 1985-86). Democrat. Roman Catholic. Club: Oshkosh Power Boat. Avocations: gardening, camping. Real property, Contracts commercial, Family and matrimonial. Home: 415 Park Dr Neenah WI 54956 Office: Di Renzo & Bomier 231 E Wisconsin Ave Neenah WI 54956

SIMON, GARY RICHARD, lawyer; b. N.Y.C., May 25, 1949; s. Seymour and Florence (Lowenthal) S.; m. Stephanie Jane Heyman, Jan. 8, 1981. BBA summa cum laude, Syracuse U., 1971; JD, Fordham U., 1974. Bar: N.Y., U.S. Dist. Ct. (so. dist.) N.Y., U.S. Ct. Appeals (2d cir.). Assoc. Donovan, Leisure, Newton & Irvine, N.Y.C., 1974-76; atty. Lever Bros. Co., N.Y.C., 1976-80; v.p., gen. counsel OPM Leasing Services, Inc., N.Y.C., 1980-82, Pony, Inc., Rutherford, N.J., 1982—. Mem. ABA, N.Y. State Bar Assn., Assn. of Bar of City of N.Y., Phi Kappa Psi, Beta Gamma Sigma. Republican. Jewish. Avocation: sports. General corporate. Home: 3 Old Scots Rd Marlboro NJ 07746 Office: Pony Inc 201 Rt 17 N Rutherford NJ 07070

SIMON, GILBERT STANLEY, lawyer; b. Chgo., May 24, 1941; s. Louis L. and Kate A. Simon; m. Dale Suzanne Simon, Jan. 23, 1965; children: Michael Scott, Laurence Stewart. BA, U. Chgo., 1963, JD, 1966; MBA, Dayton U., 1985. Bar: Ill. 1966, U.S. Dist. Ct. (no. dist.) Ill. 1967, U.S. Supreme Ct. 1974. Assoc. counsel Aldens Inc., Chgo., 1966-68; assoc. gen. counsel Playboy Enterprises Inc., Chgo., 1968-75, dir. new bus., 1975-76; gen. corp. counsel S. Rosenfeld & Assocs., Northbrook, Ill., 1977-78; asst. gen. counsel Wendy's Internat. Inc., Dublin, Ohio, 1978—; bd. dirs. Food Service & Lodging Inst., Washington. Trustee, referee Westerville (Ohio) Amateur Soccer Program, 1979—. Mem. Ill. Bar Assn. Jewish. General corporate. Home: 84 Spring Creek Dr Westerville OH 43081 Office: Wendy's Internat Inc PO Box 256 Dublin OH 43017

SIMON, HINDA BOOKSTABER, lawyer; b. Newark, Jan. 13, 1942; d. Irving Bookstafer and Olga Marguerite (Serlui) Small; m. Barry P. Simon, Feb. 9, 1964; children: Alan, John, Eric. BA, Conn. Coll., 1964; JD, Rutgers U., 1981. Bar: N.J. 1981, Calif. 1983, Tex. 1984. Assoc. McCarter and English, Newark, 1981-82, Rintala, Smoot and Jaenicke, Los Angeles, 1982-83; exec. dir. Tex. Accts. and Lawyers for the Arts, Houston, 1984—. Mem. ABA, State Bar Tex. (com. legal aspects of the arts), N.J. Bar Assn., Nat. Soc. Fund Raising Execs., Jr. League of Houston. Republican. Jewish. Clubs: Houston Raquet, Montclair Golf. Entertainment, Art, Exempt organizations. Office: Tex Accts and Lawyers for Arts 1540 Sul Ross Houston TX 77006

SIMON, H(UEY) PAUL, lawyer; b. Lafayette, La., Oct. 19, 1923; s. Jules and Ida (Rogere) S.; m. Carolyn Perkins, Aug. 6, 1949; 1 child, John Clark. B.S., U. Southwestern La., 1943; J.D., Tulane U., 1947. Bar: La. 1947; CPA, La. Practiced in New Orleans, 1947—; asst. prof. advanced acctg. U. Southwestern La., 1944-45; prin. Haskins & Sells, CPA's, New Orleans, 1945-57; gen. ptnr. law firm Deutsch, Kerrigan & Stiles, 1957-79; founding sr. partner law firm Simon, Peragine, Smith & Redfearn, 1979—. Author: Louisiana Income Tax Law, 1956, Changes Effected by the Louisiana Trust Code, 1965, Gifts to Minors and the Parent's Obligation of Support, 1968, Deductions-Business or Hobby, 1975, Role of Attorney in IRS Tax Return Examination, 1978; assoc. editor: The Louisiana CPA, 1956-60; bd. editors Tulane Law Rev., 1945-46; estates, gifts and trusts editor The Tax Times, 1986—. Mem. ABA (mem. tax sect. com. ct. procedure 1958—), La. Bar Assn. (com. on legislation and adminstrv. practice 1966-70), New Orleans Bar Assn., Inter-Am. Bar Assn., Internat. Bar Assn. (com. on securities issues and trading 1970—), Am. Judicature Soc., Am. Inst. CPA's, Am. Assn. Atty.-CPA's, Soc. La. CPA's, New Orleans Assn. Notaries, Tulane Alumni Assn., New Orleans C. of C. (council 1952-66), New Orleans Met. Area Com., Council for Better La., NYU Tax Conf.-New Orleans (co-chmn. 1976), Tulane Tax Inst. (program com. 1960—), La. Tax Conf. (program com. 1968-72), Bur. Govtl. Research, New Orleans Bd. Trade, Pub. Affairs Research Council, Internat. Platform Assn., Met. Crime Commn., Phi Delta Phi (past pres. New Orleans chpt.), Sigma Pi Alpha. Roman Catholic. Clubs: Young Men's Bus., (legislation com.), Petroleum, City, Press, Toastmasters Internat., New Orleans Country, International House (dir. 1976-79, 82-85), Pendennis, World Trade Ctr. (dir. fin. com. 1985-86) (New Orleans). Estate planning, General corporate, Corporate taxation. Office: Energy Centre 30th Floor New Orleans LA 70163

SIMON, JACK HUNT, lawyer; b. Mesa, Ariz., June 6, 1947; s. Sam Eli and Ruby (Hunt) S. AA, Phoenix Coll., 1967; BS, No. Ariz. U., 1970; JD, Ariz. State U., 1973. Bar: Ariz. 1973, U.S. Dist. Ct. Ariz. 1973. Sole practice Mesa, Ariz., 1973—. Pres. Ariz. Wildlife Fedn., Scottsdale. Mem. ABA, Ariz. Bar Assn. Republican. Mormon. Personal injury, Real property, Consumer commercial. Office: 20 E Main Suite 785 Mesa AZ 85201

SIMON, JAMES LOWELL, lawyer; b. Princeton, Ill., Nov. 8, 1944; s. K. Lowell and Elizabeth Ann (Unholz) S.; m. Deborah Ann Wolf, Dec. 27, 1966; children: Heather Lyn, Brandon James. Student, U. Ill., 1962-63; BSEE magna cum laude, Bradley U., 1967; JD with honors, 1975. Bar: Fla. 1975, U.S. Dist. Ct. (mid. dist.) Fla. 1976, U.S. Ct. Appeals (11th cir.) 1981, U.S. Patent Office 1983. Engineer Pan Am. World Airways, Cape Kennedy, Fla., 1967-68; assoc. Akerman, Senterfitt & Eidson, Orlando, Fla., 1975-80; ptnr. Bogin, Munns, Munns & Simon, Orlando, 1980-87, Holland & Knight, 1987—. Active Seminole County Sch. Adv. Council, Fla., 1981—, Forest City Local Sch. Adv. Com., Altamonte Springs, Fla., 1981-84, Code Enforcement Bd., Altamonte Springs, 1983-84, Central Bus. Dist. Study com., Altamonte Springs, 1983-85, Rep. Council of '76, Seminole County, 1982-87. Served to capt. USAF, 1968-72. Named one of Outstanding Young Men in Am., 1981. Mem. ABA, Orange County Bar Assn. (jud. relations com. 1982-83, fee arbitration com. 1983—), Phi Kappa Phi, Tau Beta Pi, Sigma Tau, Eta Kappa Nu. Republican. Mormon. Contracts commercial, Construction, Trademark and copyright. Home: 620 Longmeadow Circle Longwood FL 32779 Office: 255 S Orange Ave Suite 750 PO Box 1526 Orlando FL 32802

SIMON, MICHAEL SCOTT, lawyer; b. Bronx, Feb. 9, 1954; s. Philip and Miriam C. (Feller) S.; m. Elayne Robin Baer, May 26, 1974; children: Joshua Seth, Sarah Emily. BA, SUNY, Stony Brook, 1976; JD, Boston U., 1979. Bar: N.Y. 1980, U.S. Dist. Ct. (ea. and so. dists.) N.Y. 1980, U.S. Ct. Appeals (2d cir.) 1981, U.S. Tax Ct. 1983, U.S. Supreme Ct. 1983. Asst. corp. counsel N.Y.C. Law Dept., 1979-82; assoc. Tenzer, Greenblatt, Fallon & Kaplan, N.Y.C., 1982—. Mem. ABA, N.Y. State Bar Assn., Assn. of Bar of City of N.Y., Pi Sigma Alpha. Avocations: travel, music. State civil litigation, Real property, Landlord-tenant. Home: 8 Kantor Ave Dix Hills NY 11746 Office: Tenzer Greenblatt Fallon & Kaplan 405 Lexington Ave New York NY 10174

SIMON, MORTON SONNY, lawyer; b. N.Y.C., Dec. 15, 1935; s. Irving and Lily (Miller) S.; m. Marcia J. Langsner, Aug. 12, 1961; children: Ellen S., Matthew D. BS, Columbia U., 1957; MS, Coll. Pharm. Scis., 1959; JD, NYU, 1968. Bar: N.Y. 1968, U.S. Patent Office 1969, U.S. Ct. Appeals (2d cir.) 1969, U.S. Dist. Ct. (so. and ea. dists.) N.Y. 1970, U.S. Supreme Ct. 1979, U.S. Ct. Appeals (fed. cir.) 1982. Mgr. pharmacy dept. Library Drug Corp., N.Y.C., 1958-63; research chemist Colfax Labs. div. Shulton, Inc., Clifton, N.J., 1963-68; sr. assoc. Bierman & Bierman, N.Y.C., 1968-73; sr. internat. patent atty. Bristol-Myers Co., N.Y.C., 1973-76, asst. patent counsel licensing div., 1976-77, sr. asst. patent counsel licensing div., 1978-79, patent counsel dermatological products, 1980-83, patent counsel consumer products group, 1984—. Bristol Myers Research fellow, 1958-59. Mem. N.Y. State Bar Assn., Am. Intellectual Property Law Assn., N.Y. Patent Trademark and Copyright Law Assn., Licensing Execs. Soc., Soc. Cosmetic Chemists (legis. chmn. 1974). Patent, Trademark and copyright. Home: 3 Roseland Ct New City NY 10956 Office: Bristol Myers Co 345 Park Ave Suite 6-54 New York NY 10154

SIMON, RICHARD HEGE, lawyer; b. Englewood, Colo., Jan. 15, 1911, A.B., U. Denver, 1934, J.D., 1936. Bar: Colo. 1938, U.S. Supreme Ct. 1970. Practice, Englewood, 1941—; mem. Simon, Lee & Shivers and predecessors, 1942-49; ptnr. Simon, Kelley, Hoyt & Malone, 1967-69; ptnr. Simon, Eason, Hoyt & Malone, 1969-76; sole practice, 1977—; dist. atty. First Jud. Dist. Colo., 1941-49; dir. First Nat. Bank Englewood, Key Savs. and Loan Assn. Founder, pres., dir. Arapahoe County (Colo.) Fair Assn., 1946—; bd. dirs., pres. Sch. Dist 1, Arapahoe County; sec., pres., chmn. bd., gen. counsel Centennial Turf Club, Inc., 1949-83; bd. dirs., pres. Arapahoe Park, Inc., 1983—; trustee Denver Met. United Way; state and county chmn. Republican Central Com.; pres., trustee Iliff Sch. Theology, 1960—; pres., dir. Arapahoe Mental Health Ctr., 1960-75, Arapahoe County Mile High United Way, 1958-74. Fellow Am. Bar Found.; mem. Arapahoe County Bar Assn. (rep. to bd. govs. Colo. Bar Assn. 1958-67) ABA, Colo. Bar Assn. (pres.

1969-70), Am. Judicature Soc. Clubs: Denver Athletic, Columbine Country. Banking, Probate, Legal education.

SIMON, ROY D., JR., law educator; b. Highland Park, Ill., June 27, 1949; s. Roy D. and Fannie (Bowman) S.; m. Karen Schwarzschild, Aug. 29, 1977; children: Daniel, Nicole, Joshua. BA, Williams Coll., 1973; JD, NYU, 1977. Bar: U.S. Ct. Appeals (4th cir.) 1978, U.S. Ct. Appeals (7th cir.) 1982, Mo. 1983, U.S. Dist. Ct. (ea. dist.) Mo. 1983, U.S. Ct. Appeals (1st cir.) 1986. Law clk. U.S. Dist. Ct. (ea. dist.) Va., Richmond, 1977-78; assoc. Jenner & Block, Chgo., 1978-82, Hannafan & Handler, Chgo., 1982-83; assoc. prof. law Washington U., St. Louis, 1983—. Contbr. articles to law revs. Bd. dirs. Eastern Mo. chpt. ACLU, 1986—. Mem. ABA (litigation sect., sect. on legal edn.), Am. Assn. Law Schs. (civil procedure, alternative dispute resolution, evidence, clin. legal edn. sects.). Federal civil litigation, Legal education, Civil rights. Office: Washington U Law Sch Campus Box 1120 Saint Louis MO 63130

SIMON, SAMUEL ALAN, consumer advocate, lawyer, educator; b. El Paso, Tex., July 18, 1945; s. Marcus and Frieda (Alfman) S.; m. Susan Meryl Kalmans, Aug. 25, 1966; children: Marcus Bertram, Rachael Lara. BA, U. Tex.-El Paso, 1967; JD, U. Tex., 1970. Bar: U.S. Dist. Ct. D.C. 1971, U.S. Ct. Appeals D.C. 1971, U.S. Ct. Mil. Appeals 1971, U.S. Supreme Ct. 1973. Atty. Pub. Interest Research Group, Washington, 1970-71; assoc. Fried, Frank, Harris, Shriver & Kampelman, Washington, 1975-76; legis. dir. U.S. Senator John Durkin, Washington, 1976-77; dir. energy program Bur. Consumer Protection FTC, Washington, 1977-78; exec. dir. Telecommunications Research Action Ctr., Washington, 1978-82, pres., 1982-85; pres. Issue Dynamics Inc., Washington, 1985—; treas., dir. Nat. Coalition on TV Violence, Washington, 1979-84; sec.-treas. Citizens TV System, Washington, 1981—; dir. Nat. Consumers League, Washington, 1982—; adj. prof. N.Y.C. Law Sch., 1982—. Author: Reverse the Charges: How to Save Money on Your Phone Bill, 1983, Teleconsumers and the Future, 1983, After Divestiture: What the AT&T Settlement Means for Business and Residential Phone Service, 1985, Phonewriting: A Consumers Guide to the New World of Electronic Information Services, 1986; editor: Access, 1978-85; contbr. articles to profl. jours. Vice chmn. Fairfax Schs. Com. on Human Relations, Va., 1982-83; sec., bd. dirs. McLean Community Ctr., Va., 1983-85; pres. Temple Rodef Shalom, Falls Church, Va., 1980-82. Served to capt. U.S. Army, 1971-75. Decorated Disting. Service medal. Mem. ABA, Fed. Communication Bar Assn., Order of Coif. Democrat. Jewish. Communications, Legal education, Legislative. Office: Issue Dynamics Inc 1660 L St NW Washington DC 20036

SIMON, SEYMOUR, Illinois supreme court justice; b. Chgo., Aug. 10, 1915; s. Ben and Gertrude (Rusky) S.; m. Roslyn Schultz Biel, May 26, 1954; children: John B., Nancy Harris, Anthony Biel. B.S., Northwestern U., 1935, J.D., 1938; LL.D. (hon.), John Marshall Law Sch., 1982, North Park Coll., 1986. Bar: Ill. 1938. Spl. atty. Dept. Justice, 1938-42; practice law Chgo., 1946-74; judge Ill. Appellate Ct., Chgo., 1974-80; presiding justice Ill. Appellate Ct. (1st Dist., 3d Div.), 1977, 79; justice Ill. Supreme Ct., 1980—; former dir. Nat. Gen. Corp., Bantam Books, Grosset & Dunlap, Inc., Gt. Am. Ins. Corp. Mem. Cook County Bd. Commrs., 1961-66, pres., 1962-66; pres. Cook County Forest Preserve Dist., 1962-66; mem. Pub. Bldg. Commn., City Chgo., 1962-67; Alderman 40th ward, Chgo., 1955-61, 67-74, Democratic ward committeeman, 1960-74; bd. dirs. Schwab Rehab. Hosp., 1961-71, Swedish Covenant Hosp., 1969-75. Served with USNR, 1942-45. Decorated Legion of Merit; recipient citation for disting. service North Park Coll., Chgo., 1967, 9th Ann. Pub. Service award Tau Epsilon Rho, 1963, alumni award of merit Northwestern U., 1982, Hubert L. Will award Am. Vets. Com., 1983, Decalogue Soc. of Lawyers award of Merit, 1986, Freedom award John Marshall Law Sch., 1987. Mem. ABA, Ill. Bar Assn., Chgo. Bar Assn., Chgo. Hist. Soc., Decalogue Soc. Lawyers, Izaak Walton League, Chgo. Hort. Soc., Phi Beta Kappa Assocs., Phi Beta Kappa, Order of Coif. Clubs: Standard, Variety (Chgo.). Jurisprudence. Home: 1555 N Astor St Chicago IL 60610 Office: Supreme Ct Bldg Springfield IL 62706 also: 3088 Richard J Daley Center Chicago IL 60602

SIMONDS, MARSHALL, lawyer; b. Boston, Sept. 17, 1930; s. Sidney Lawrence and Evelyn (Peterson) S.; m. Katharine Blewett, May 9, 1969; children: Robert Bradley, Joshua Lawrence. B.A., Princeton U., 1952; LL.B., Harvard U., 1955. Bar: Mass. 1955. Since practiced in Bosto; partner Goodwin, Procter & Hoar, Boston, 1965—; counsel Mass. Crime Commn., 1963-65; spl. asst. atty. gen. Commonwealth of Mass., 1964-66; dir. Dynatech Corp., 1960-85, Data Packaging Corp., 1972-79; trustee Middlesex Instn. Savs., 1974-79. Moderator of Carlisle, Mass., 1967—; trustee Trustees for Reservations, 1972-78; bd. dirs. South Boston Neighborhood House, 1972-78. Served with USMCR, 1955. Fellow Am. Coll. Trial Lawyers, Am. Bar Found.; mem. Am. Bar Assn., Mass. Bar Assn., Boston Bar Assn. (council 1980-82), New Eng. Legal Found. (dir.). Clubs: Harvard (Boston); Princeton (N.Y.C.). Federal civil litigation, State civil litigation. Office: Exchange Pl Boston MA 02109

SIMONE, MARTIN MASSIMO, lawyer; b. New Haven, Sept. 26, 1946; s. Nicholas and Grace Loretta S.; m. Christine Irene, June 25, 1977; children—Lisa Marie, Bridgett Lynn. B.A. in History, Loyola U., Los Angeles, 1968, J.D., 1971. Bar: Calif. bar, 1972, U.S. Supreme Ct. 1983. Law clk. Judge Campbell M. Lucas, 1972-74, supervising research atty. Los Angeles Superior Ct., 1973-74; assoc. Schwartz, Steinsapir, Dorhmann & Krepack, Los Angeles, 1974-79, ptnr., 1980; assoc. Frank & Greenberg Inc., 1980; ptnr. Frank, Greenberg, Simone & Winston, P.C., Beverly Hills Calif., 1982-84, Frank, Greenberg & Simone, 1984—. Mem. local sch. adv. bd., 1973-75. Mem. Los Angeles County Bar Assn., Calif. Bar Assn., ABA, Lawyers Club Los Angeles, Am. Judicature Soc. Contbr. articles to profl. jours. State civil litigation, Public international, Immigration, naturalization, and customs. Office: 8484 Wilshire Blvd #730 Beverly Hills CA 90211

SIMONELLI, JAMES JOHN, lawyer; b. Bklyn., Feb. 15, 1937; s. John and Margaret (Esposito) S.; m. Joan Edna Papke, Mar. 9, 1962 (div. Oct. 1981); children: John, Daniel, Peter; m. Jennifer Ann Roberts, Oct. 31, 1981; step-children: Zoe, Kim, Kelly. AB, U. Notre Dame, 1958; LLB, U. Calif., Berkeley, 1961. Bar: Calif. 1962, U.S. Dist. Ct. (ea. and no. dists.) Calif., U.S. Ct. Claims, U.S. Ct. Appeals (9th cir.). Asst. U.S. atty. U.S. Dist. Ct. (ea. and no. dists.) Calif., San Francisco and Sacramento, 1965-70; ptnr. Simonelli & Carash, Stockton, Calif., 1971—; bd. dirs. Golden Bear Ins. Co., Stockton. bd. dirs. Easter Seal Soc., Stockton, 1972-73. Served to capt. USMC, 1962-65. Mem. Calif. State Bar Assn. (com. fed. cts. 1976-77), San Joaquin County Bar Assn. (bd. dirs. 1977-78), Calif. Trial Lawyers Assn. (pres. San Joaquin chpt. 1975-76). Democrat. Roman Catholic. Club: West Lane Tennis (Stockton) (pres. 1975). Lodge: Kiwanis (bd. dirs. 1986—). Avocations: tennis, rare books, travel. State civil litigation, Criminal, Family and matrimonial. Office: 333 E Channel St 3d Floor Stockton CA 95202

SIMONELLI, JERRY, lawyer; b. N.Y.C., Jan. 27, 1952; s. James A. and Rose Simonelli. BA, John Carroll U., 1972; JD, U. Toledo, 1976; LLM in Taxation, George Washington U., 1982. Bar: Ohio 1977, D.C. 1977, U.S. Dist. Ct. D.C. 1978, U.S. Tax Ct. 1978. Legis. asst. Congressman Charles Vanik, Washington, 1976-78; sole practice Washington, 1978—; pres., counsel Tax Mgmt. Systems, Inc., Stamford, Conn., 1977—; legislator State of Conn., Hartford, 1979-81. Mem. ABA (taxation com.). Democrat. Avocations: jogging, boating. Personal income taxation, Corporate taxation, General corporate. Home: 219 G St SW Washington DC 20024 Office: Tax Mgmt Systems Inc 1 Landmark Sq Suite 424 Stamford CT 06901

SIMONETT, JOHN E., state supreme court justice; b. Mankato, Minn., July 12, 1924; m. Doris Bogut; 6 children. B.A., St. John's U., 1948; LL.B., U. Minn., 1951. Practice law Little Falls, Minn., 1951-80; asso. justice Supreme Ct. of Minn., 1980—. Office: Supreme Ct State Capitol Saint Paul MN 55155 *

SIMONINI, DAVID MICHAEL, lawyer; b. San Rafael, Calif., Jan. 15, 1948; s. Aldo Joseph and Lola Anita S.; children—Clinton, Jeanne; m. Maria Cara Melletta, Nov. 3, 1984. B.A., U. San Francisco, 1970, J.D., 1974. Bar: Calif. 1975, U.S. Dist. Ct. (no. dist.) Calif. 1975, Hawaii 1983. Pres., Pacific Porterwall Inc., 1970-75; assoc. Pisor, Vadney, George & Bennett; sole practice, David M. Simonini, P.C.; ptnr. Vadney, George & Simonini, San Rafael. Mem. Marin County, L.R.S., Bd. Appeals. Mem. Calif. Trial Lawyers Assn., ABA, Assn. Trial Lawyers Am., Marin County Bar Assn. Republican. Roman Catholic. Clubs: Marin Yacht, Canon Tennis (Marin County); Harbor Point Beach and Tennis; Elks. State civil litigation, Insurance, Personal injury. Office: 36 Professional Center Pkwy San Rafael CA 94903

SIMONS, BERNARD PHILIP, lawyer; b. N.Y.C., Nov. 14, 1942; s. Harold J. and Lila (Orchant) S.; m. Eve C. Simons, Nov. 28, 1971; B.A., Rutgers U., 1964; J.D., Hastings Coll. Law, 1967. Bar: Calif. 1967, U.S. Dist. Cts. (cen., no. and so. dists.) Calif. 1967, U.S. Supreme Ct. 1974. Ptnr. Gendel, Raskoff, Shapiro & Quittner, Los Angeles, 1974—; lectr. continuing edn. of bar, 1977-85; instr. Hastings Coll. Law Ctr. for Trial and Appellate Advocacy, San Francisco, 1986-87; arbitrator Los Angeles County Superior Ct., 1980-83; judge pro tem Beverly Hills Mcpl. Ct., 1978-80. Served to capt. U.S. Army, 1977-79. Decorated Bronze Star. Mem. ABA (chmn. discovery com. litigation sect. Dist. 9), Calif. Bar Assn., Los Angeles County Bar Assn., Thurston Soc., Assn. Trial Lawyers Am., Calif. Trial Lawyers Assn., Order of Coif. Club: Friars (Los Angeles) Federal civil litigation, State civil litigation. Office: 1801 Century Park E Los Angeles CA 90067

SIMONS, CHARLES EARL, JR., U.S. judge; b. Johnston, S.C., Aug. 17, 1916; s. Charles Earl and Frances (Rhoden) S.; m. Jean Knapp, Oct. 18, 1941; children—Charles Earl III, Paul Knapp, Richard Brewster, Jean Brewster. A.B., U. S.C., 1937, LL.B. cum laude, 1939. Bar: S.C. bar 1939. Mem. firm Lybrand, Simons and Rich, Aiken, S.C., 1939-64; U.S. dist. judge Dist. S.C., 1964—; Mem. S.C. Constl. Revision Com., 1948; mem. Bd. Discipline and Grievance S.C. Bar, 1958-61; Fourth Circuit dist. judge rep. Jud. Conf. of U.S., 1973-79; mem. ethics adv. panel, chmn. subcom. on fed. jurisdiction of com. on ct. adminstrn., mem. com. on ct. adminstrn.; mem. S.C. House Reps., 1942, 1947-48, 1961-64, S.C. House Reps. (mem. ways and means com.), 1947-48, 61-64; chmn. Met. Dist. Chief Judges Assn. 1986-89. bd. dirs. S.C. Athletic Hall of Fame. Served with USN, World War II. Recipient Algernon Sidney Sullivan award, 1937, 64. Mem. S.C. Bar Assn. (mem. exec. com.), ABA, Am. Law Inst., Am. Judicature Soc., Am. Legion, VFW, U. S.C. Alumni Assn. (past pres.). Baptist (past mem. bd. deacons, past chmn. finance com.). Clubs: Rotarian (hon.), Aiken Business Men's. Office: US Courthouse Aiken SC 29801

SIMONS, DAVID WARREN, lawyer; b. Pitts., Apr. 16, 1943; s. Dalton Henry and Beryl Elaine (Lacey) S.; m. Pamela Ruth Stalter, Feb. 1, 1969; children: Catherine Anne, Mary Elisabeth, Gregory Joseph. AB, Waynesburg Coll., 1965; M Div., Gen. Theol. Sem., 1968; JD, U. Balt., 1978. Bar: Md. 1978, U.S. Dist. Ct. Md. 1979; ordained priest Episcopal Ch., 1968. Pastor various chs., Pa., Mich. and Md., 1968-82; sole practice Balt., 1978—. Contbr. articles to profl. jours. Panel chmn. Health Claims Arbitration Office, Balt., 1980—; bd. dirs. Md. right to Life, Inc., 1984—. Served to capt. Md. CAP, 1977—. Mem. ABA, Md. Bar Assn., Bar Assn. Balt. Republican. Roman Catholic. General practice, Family and matrimonial, Personal injury. Home: 6509 Loch Hill Ct Baltimore MD 21239 Office: 5718 Harford Rd Baltimore MD 21214

SIMONS, MORTON LEONARD, lawyer; b. Windsor, Ont., Can., Aug. 8, 1928; came to U.S., 1943, naturalized, 1949; s. Benjamin and Sarah (Nadell) S.; m. Barbara Malitz, Sept. 2, 1951; 1 dau., Claudia. B.A., U. Mich., 1950, J.D., 1952. Bar: N.Y. 1953, U.S. Supreme Ct. 1959, U.S. Ct. Appeals (D.C. cir.) 1962, U.S. Ct. Appeals (5th cir.) 1964, U.S. Ct. Appeals (10th cir.) 1966, U.S. Ct. Appeals (3d cir.) 1976. Asst. counsel Pub. Service Commn. N.Y., Albany also N.Y.C., 1952-57; counsel Gas Distbrs. Info. Service, Washington, 1957-61; ptnr. Simons & Simons, Washington, 1962—; advisor Georgetown U. Law Center Inst. Pub. Interest Representation, 1971—; lectr. Nat. Jud. Coll., Nat. Acad. Sci., Mich. State U., Northwestern U., ABA, Am. Law Inst. Mem. ABA, Fed. Energy Bar Assn., Phi Beta Kappa, Phi Kappa Phi, Phi Eta Sigma, Order of Coif. Bd. editors Mich. Law Rev. 1951-52. FERC practice, Public utilities, Administrative and regulatory. Home: 5025 Linnean Ave NW Washington DC 20008 Office: 1629 K St NW Washington DC 20006

SIMONS, RICHARD DUNCAN, state judge; b. Niagara Falls, N.Y., Mar. 23, 1927; s. William Taylor and Sybil Irene (Swick) S.; m. Muriel E. Genung, June 9, 1951; children: Ross T., Scott R., Kathryn E., Linda A. A.B., Colgate U., 1949; LL.B., U. Mich., 1952; LLD (hon.), Albany Law Sch., 1983. Bar: N.Y. 1952. Pvt. practice law Rome, N.Y., 1952-63; asst. corp. counsel City of Rome, 1955-58, corp. counsel, 1960-63; justice 5th jud. dist. N.Y. Supreme Ct., 1964—, asso. justice appellate div. 3d dept., 1971-72, asso. justice appellate div. 4th dept., 1973-82; assoc. judge N.Y. Ct. Appeals, 1983—. Editorial staff: N.Y. Pattern Jury Instructions, 1979-83. Chmn. Republican City Com., 1958-62; vice chmn. Oneida County Rep. Com., 1958-62; bd. mgrs. Rome Hosp. and Murphy Meml. Hosp., 1953. Served with USN, World War II. NEH fellow U. Va. Law Sch., 1979. Fellow Am. Bar Found.; mem. ABA, Am. Law Inst., Inst. Jud. Adminstrn., N.Y. State Bar Assn., Oneida County Bar Assn., Rome Bar Assn. Home: 1410 N George St Rome NY 13440 Office: Ct Appeals Hall Eagle Street Albany NY 12207

SIMONS, STEVEN J(AY), lawyer; b. Akron, Ohio, Oct. 30, 1946; s. Alex and Bella Simons; m. Harriet Fishman, Aug. 29, 1971; children: Sara, Rebecca, David. BA, Harvard U., 1969, JD, 1972. Bar: Ohio 1972, Mass. 1975. Assoc. Squire, Sanders & Dempsey, Cleve., 1972-74; assoc. Ropes & Gray, Boston, 1974-81, ptnr., 1981—. Mem. Wellesley (Mass.) Town Meeting, 1983—. Rotary Internat. fellow, 1969. Mem. ABA, Nat. Assn. Bond Lawyers. Municipal bonds, Contracts commercial, Banking. Office: Ropes & Gray 225 Franklin St Boston MA 02181

SIMONSEN, DAVID RAYMOND, JR., lawyer; b. Rochester, N.Y., June 7, 1952; s. David Raymond and Lillie May (Fuller) S.; m. Vickey Ann Verwey, Aug. 25, 1973; children: Kathleen Ann, Kristen Elizabeth. BA, Duke U., 1974; MA in Tech., Vanderbilt U., 1976, JD, 1980. Bar: Va. 1980, U.S. Dist. Ct. (ea. and we. dists.) Va. 1980, U.S. Ct. Appeals (4th cir.) 1980, Maine 1986. Assoc. McGuire, Woods, Battle & Boothe, Richmond, Va., 1980—. Mem. ABA., Va. Bar Assn., Va. State Bar Assn., Richmond Bar Assn., Am. Arbitration Assn. Office: McGuire Woods Battle & Boothe One James Ctr Richmond VA 23219

SIMONSON, MICHAEL, lawyer, judge; b. Franklin, N.J., Feb. 5, 1950; s. Robert and Eleanor (Weiss) S. BA, U. Ariz., 1973; JD, Southwestern U., Los Angeles, 1976; LLM in Taxation, Washington U., St. Louis, 1978. Bar: Ariz. 1977, U.S. Dist. Ct. Ariz. 1979, U.S. Tax Ct. 1978. Bailiff, law clk. Superior Ct. Maricopa County Div. 2, Phoenix, 1976-77; sole practice, Scottsdale, Ariz., 1978-79; ptnr. Simonson, Groh, & Lindteigen, Scottsdale, 1979-81, Simonson & Preston, Phoenix, 1984-86, Simonson, Preston & Arbetman, 1986-87, Simonson & Arbetman, 1987—; judge pro tempore Mcpl. Ct., City of Phoenix, 1984—; adj. prof. Ariz. State U Coll. Bus., Tempe, 1984—, Coll. for Fin. Planning, Denver, 1984—, Maricopa County Community Colls., 1984—, Western Internat. U., Phoenix, 1984—; prof. law Univ. Phoenix, 1985—, area chmn. legal studies, 1986—. Mem. Maricopa County Foster Child Care Rev. Bd. No. 17, 1978-81; pres. Camelback Mountainview Estates Homeowners Assn., 1980-81, Congregation Tiphereth Israel, 1979-81. Mem. ABA (taxation sect., various coms.), State Bar Ariz. (cert. specialist in tax law), Maricopa County Bar Assn., Cen. Ariz. Estate Planning Council, Internat. Assn. Fin. Planners, Ariz. Inst. CPA's, Internat. Platform Assn., Phoenix C. of C. (taxation and fin. council 1984—). Democrat. Jewish. Club: Nucleus. Lodge: Masons. Corporate taxation, Estate taxation, Personal income taxation. Office: Simonson & Arbetman 4645 N 32d St Suite 200 Phoenix AZ 85018

SIMONTON, ROBERT BENNET, lawyer; b. N.Y.C., Feb. 23, 1933; s. Theodore E. and Beulah H. (Hulsebus) S.; m. Tanya Wood, Aug. 24, 1957; children: Sheri, Robert B. Jr., Scott S. Student Amherst Coll., 1950-52; B.S. in Engring., Columbia U., 1954; LL.B., Syracuse U., 1959. Bar: 1959. Patent agt., atty. Theodore E. Simonton, Cazenovia, N.Y., 1956-60; assoc. Hancock, Dorr, Ryan and Shove, Syracuse, N.Y., 1960-64; staff atty. Bristol-Myers Co., Syracuse, 1967, counsel, 1967-71, v.p., counsel Bristol Labs., 1971-74; v.p., sec., gen. counsel Crouse Hinds Co., Syracuse, 1974-75; staff atty. Sterling Drug Inc., N.Y.C., 1975-78, sec., asst. gen. counsel, 1978—; trustee Syracuse Savs. Bank, 1973-76. Bd. govs. Citizens' Found., Syracuse, 1969-70; bd. dirs. Urban League of Syracuse, 1967-72, pres., 1967-71, chmn., 1971-72; bd. visitors Syracuse U. Coll. Law, 1968—; bd. dirs. Graham Windham. Served with U.S. Army, 1954-56. Recipient Justinian Honor Soc. award Syracuse U. Coll. Law, 1959. Mem. ABA, N.Y. State Bar Assn., Am. Soc. Corp. Secs., Mfg. Assn. Syracuse (chmn. state legis com. 1973-74), Greater Syracuse C. of C. (chmn. state legis com. 1968-70). General corporate, Antitrust, Pension, profit-sharing, and employee benefits. Office: Sterling Drug Inc 90 Park Ave New York NY 10016

SIMOSON, WILLIAM EUGENE, lawyer; b. N.Y.C., Mar. 20, 1949; s. William Eugene and Agnes Veronica (Fisher) S.; m. Laurinda Roxanne Bennett, Mar. 16, 1950; children: Keri Elizabeth, Kristen Rebecca. BA, SUNY, Plattsburgh, 1971; studied for bar under, The N.Y. State Law Clerkship Program, 1971-76. Bar: N.Y. 1977, U.S. Dist. Ct. (so. dist.) N.Y. 1978, U.S. Dist. Ct. (ea. dist.) N.Y. 1979, U.S. Ct. Appeals (2d cir.) 1979, U.S. Supreme Ct. 1981. Assoc. Herzfeld & Rubin, P.C., N.Y.C., 1977-1982; atty. Pepsico, Inc., Purchase, N.Y., 1982-83, sr. litigation atty., 1983-85, counsel litigation div., 1985—. Mem. ABA, N.Y. State Bar Assn., Def. Research Inst. Democrat. Roman Catholic. Lodge: Elks (sec. Westport 1983-85). Personal injury, State civil litigation, Trademark and copyright. Office: Pepsico Inc 700 Anderson Hill Rd Purchase NY 10577

SIMPKINS, MARY NELL, lawyer; b. Panama City, Fla., Sept. 18, 1956; d. Carl N. Jr. and Dorothy (McKee) S. BS, Vanderbilt U., 1977; JD, U. Va., 1980; LLM in Taxation, NYU, 1984. Bar: N.Y. 1981, Fla. 1984, U.S. Dist. Ct. (so. and ea. dists) N.Y. 1982, U.S. Tax Ct. 1983. Assoc. Liddle & Henze, N.Y.C., 1982-83, Johnson, Blakely, Pope, Bokor & Ruppel, Clearwater, Fla., 1984-86, Finley, Kumble, Wagner, Heine, Underberg, Manley, Myerson & Casey, Washington, 1986—. Mem. Nat. Assn. Bond Lawyers, Phi Beta Kappa. Municipal bonds, Corporate taxation, Personal income taxation. Office: Finley Kumble et al 1120 Connecticut Ave NW Washington DC 20036

SIMPSON, A. W. B., law educator; b. 1931. Fellow Oxford U., Eng., 1955-72; prof. U. Kent, Canterbury, Eng., 1972-84, U. Chgo., 1984—. Office: U Chgo Law Sch 1111 East 60th St Chicago IL 60637 *

SIMPSON, CHARLES REAGAN, U.S. judge; b. Danville, Ill., June 16, 1921; s. Frank and Mamie (Moreland) S.; m. Ruth V. Thomason, June 5, 1948. B.A. with highest honors, U. Ill., 1944, J.D. with high honors, 1945; LL.M., Harvard U., 1950. Bar: Ill. 1945. Practiced in Champaign, Ill., 1946-49; atty. OPS, 1951-52; with legislation and regulations div. Office Chief Counsel, IRS, 1952-65, dir. office, 1964-65; judge U.S. Tax Ct., 1965—; Teaching fellow Harvard Law Sch., 1950-51. Chmn. Champaign County chpt. Nat. Found. Infantile Paralysis, 1947-49; Mem. Ill. Gen. Assembly from 24th Dist., 1947-50. Recipient Justice Tom C. Clark award Fed. Bar Assn., 1964. Mem. ABA, Am. Law Inst., Am. Judicature Soc., Phi Beta Kappa, Order of Coif, Phi Kappa Phi. Corporate taxation, Estate taxation, Personal income taxation. Office: US Tax Court 400 2d St NW Washington DC 20217

SIMPSON, DANIEL REID, lawyer; b. Glen Alpine, N.C., Feb. 20, 1927; s. James R. and Margaret Ethel (Newton) S.; m. Mary Alice Leonard, Feb. 25, 1930; children—Mary Simpson Beyer, Ethel B. Simpson Todd, James R. II. B.S., Wake Forest U., 1949, LL.B., 1951. Bar: N.C. 1951, U.S. Dist. Ct. (we. dist.) N.C. 1951, U.S. Ct. Appeals (4th cir.) 1980, U.S. Ct. Appeals (5th cir.) 1976. Pres., Simpson, Aycock, Beyer & Simpson, P.A., 1976—; dir. Western Steer-Mom n' Pop's, Inc. Mem. N.C. Ho. of Reps., 1959-65; now mem. N.C. Senate; del. Republican Nat. Conv., 1968, 76. Served with USN, 1943-45, PTO. Mem. ABA, N.C. Bar Assn., Burke County Bar Assn. Baptist. Club: Masons. General corporate. Office: Simpson Aycock Beyer & Simpson 204 E McDowell St Marganton NC 28655

SIMPSON, DAVID EUGENE, lawyer, youth educator; b. Greencastle, Ind., Aug. 15, 1951; s. David Ernest and Ruth Elmyra (Ridge) S.; m. Wanda Carolyn Binnicker, Aug., 1971; children: David Erik, Keri Alysia. BA, Lee Coll., 1973; postgrad., Ind. U., 1973-74; JD, U. S.C., 1977. Bar: S.C. 1977, U.S. Dist. Ct. S.C. 1977, U.S. Ct. Appeals (4th cir.) 1982. Assoc. Ackerman, Woodard & Campbell, Walterboro, S.C., 1978-79; from staff atty. to mng. atty. Piedmont Legal Services, Inc., Rock Hill, S.C., 1979-86; ptnr. Pearce & Simpson, Rock Hill, 1987—; active Council of Advisors on Consumer Credit, Columbia, S.C., 1985—; instr. S.C. Dept. Youth Services Streetlaw Program; instr. real estate law courses York Tech. Bible tchr. Mt. Gallant Ch. of God; del. York (S.C.) County Dems., 1986—; chmn. sports com. S.C. Area II Spl. Olympics, Rock Hill, 1986-87. Mem. S.C. Bar Assn. (consumer law sect. chmn. 1987-88), York County Bar Assn., Christian Legal Soc. Democrat. Lodge: Civitan (S.C. chpt. lt. gov. 1983-84, pres. 1982-83, chaplain 1984-86, dist. pres. 1983, bd. dirs. 1986-87). Avocations: softball, family outings. Landlord-tenant, Real property, Consumer commercial. Home: 1340 Decatur Dr Rock Hill SC 29731 Office: Pearce & Simpson 234 Johnston St PO Box 10893 Rock Hill SC 29731

SIMPSON, JAMES MARLON, JR., lawyer; b. Little Rock, June 9, 1952; s. James Marlon Sr. and Wanda Louise (Garrison) S. m. Karen Brooks, Dec. 30, 1977. B.S., U. Ark., 1974, J.D., 1976. Bar: U.S. Dist. Ct. (ea. and we. dists.) Ark. 1977, U.S. Ct. Appeals (8th cir.) 1977. Ptnr. Friday, Eldridge & Clark, Little Rock, 1976—. Contbr. articles to legal publs. Mem. ABA, Ark. Bar Assn. (ho. of dels. 1983—), Pulaski County Bar Assn. Republican. Baptist. Lodge: Rotary. Federal civil litigation, State civil litigation, Antitrust. Home: 30 River Ridge Ct Little Rock AR 72205 Office: Friday Eldridge & Clark 2000 First Commercial Bldg Little Rock AR 72201

SIMPSON, JAMES REID, II, lawyer; b. Morganton, N.C., Sept. 7, 1954; s. Daniel Reid and Mary Alice (Leonard) S.; m. Helen Lanning Gaskill, May 31, 1986. BA, Stanford U., 1976; JD, Duke U., 1979. Bar: N.C. 1979, U.S. Dist. Ct. (we. dist.) N.C. 1979, U.S. Ct. Appeals (4th cir.) 1980. Ptnr. Simpson, Aycock, Beyer & Simpson P.A., Morganton, 1979—; trustee Southmountain Inc., Marganton. Trustee Western Piedmont Community Coll., Morganton, 1985—. Mem. ABA, N.C. Bar Assn., Burke County Bar Assn. Republican. Baptist. Lodge: Rotary. General corporate, Probate. Home: Church St Box 595 Glen Alpine NC 28628 Office: Simpson Aycock Beyer & Simpson PA 204 E McDowell St Morganton NC 28655

SIMPSON, LYLE LEE, lawyer; b. Des Moines, Oct. 15, 1937; s. R. Clair and Martha B. (Accola) S.; m. Sharon Kay Insko, June 13, 1970; children—Sondra Sue, Donald Scott; m. 2d Marcene Eliane Tesdell, Sept. 9, 1978. B.A., Drake U., 1960, J.D., 1963. Bar: Iowa 1963, U.S. Dist. Ct. (so. and no. dists.) Iowa 1963, U.S. Ct. Appeals, 1963; U.S. Supreme Ct. 1970, U.S. Tax Ct. 1963, U.S. Ct. Mil. Appeals 1972. Sole practice law, Des Moines, 1963; mem. firm Beving and Swanson, Des Moines, 1964-68; sr. ptnr. Peddicord, Simpson & Sutphin, Des Moines, 1964-83; mng. ptnr. Dreher, Wilson, Simpson, Jensen and Adams, 1984—; gen. counsel campaign com. Gov. Iowa, 1978—. Chmn. bd. trustees Broadlawns Med. Ctr., 1974-80; mem. Iowa Inaugural Com., 1983, 87; bd. dirs. YMCA Boys Camp, 1967—; pres. First Unitarian Ch., 1958-70; bd. dirs. Home, Inc., 1981-85, Project H.E.L.P.E.R., 1983-87, Batten Found.; pres., bd. dirs. Polk County Health Services, 1972—. Served to capt. U.S. Army N.G., 1955-68, comdr., USNR, 1968-86. Recipient Oren E. Scott award, Class of 1915 award in liberal arts Drake U., 1960. Mem. ABA, Polk County Bar Assn., Iowa Bar Assn., Am. Arbitration Assn. (pres.), Am. Humanist Assn. (bd. dirs.). Republican. Congregationalist. Clubs: Prairie, Morning, Le Chevaliers de vin, Masons (Shriner). Contbr. articles to profl. jours. General corporate, Estate planning, Probate. Address: 1200 Hub Tower Des Moines IA 50309

SIMPSON, ROBERT EDWARD, economist; b. Chgo., July 7, 1917; s. James Albert and Mabel Grace (Farrell) S.; m. Anna Margareta Nelson, May 22, 1954; children—Karen Anne, Heather Margot, John Frederick. A.B., Amherst Coll., 1938; student, Nat. Inst. Pub. Affairs, 1939; M.A., George Washington U., 1964. Student U.S. Central Statis. Bd., 1938-39; economist U.S. Nat. Resources Com., 1939-40; personnel work Office Sec. of War, 1941; economist civilian supply div. WPB, 1941-42; econ., adminstrv. work Nat. Housing Adminstrn., 1946-47; asst. dir. European div., later dept. asst. dir. for econ. affairs Office Internat. Trade U.S. Dept. Commerce, 1947-53; dir. Office Econ. Affairs, Bur. Fgn. Commerce, 1953-61, Office Regional Econs., Bur. Internat. Commerce, 1961-70, Office Internat. Comml. Relations, 1970-73; counsellor for econ. and comml. affairs Am. embassy,

Canberra, Australia, 1973-77; dir. Office Country Affairs, U.S. Dept. Commerce, Washington, 1978-79; cons. economist 1980—; mem. pub. adv. com. Met. Washington Council of Govts., 1987—; assigned Nat. War Coll., Washington, 1961-62. Mem. U.S. dels. to various internat. confs., 1948-79; bd. examiners for U.S. Fgn. Service; mem. gov. bd. Common Cause, Md., 1985—, v.p., 1987—; v.p. Montgomery County Civic Fedn., 1985—. Served with USNR, 1942-46, PTO; and in U.S.S. Europa comdr. Res.; mem. pub. adv. com. Met. Washington Council Govts., 1987—. Decorated Bronze Star. Mem. Nat. Economists Club, Am. Econ. Assn., Phi Beta Kappa, Delta Tau Delta, Kappa Theta. Home: 10317 Riverwood Dr Potomac MD 20854 Address: Simpson Assocs PO Box 386 Glen Echo MD 20812

SIMPSON, ROBERT EDWARD, JR., lawyer; b. Harrisburg, Pa., Oct. 17, 1951; s. Robert Edward and Jacqueline (Rupp) S.; m. Christine Patricia Durkee, Aug. 25, 1973; children: Jennifer Leigh, Robert Edward III. BS magna cum laude, Dickinson Coll., 1973, JD, 1976. Bar: Pa. 1976, U.S. Dist. Ct. (mid. dist.) Pa. 1976, U.S. Dist. Ct. (ea. dist.) Pa. 1978, U.S. Ct. Appeals (3d cir.) 1980. Law clk. to presiding justice Commonwelath Ct. Pa., Harrisburg, 1976-78; assoc. Teel, Stettz, Shimer & DiGiacomo, Ltd., Easton, Pa., 1978-83, ptnr., 1983—; instr. Am. Inst. Banking, Harrisburg, 1977. Bd. dirs. Nazareth (Pa.) YMCA, 1984. Mem. ABA, Pa. Def. Inst., Pa. Trial Lawyers Assn., Def. Research Inst., Nat. Bd. Trial Advocacy (diplomate 1984). Democrat. Mem. United Ch. Christ. Lodges: Rotary, Lions (v.p. Nazareth club 1982-83). State civil litigation, Federal civil litigation, Insurance. Home: 40 S Green St Nazareth PA 18064 Office: Teel Stettz Shimer & DiGiacomo 616 Alpha Bldg Easton PA 18042

SIMPSON, RONALD VINCENT, lawyer; b. Boston, Aug. 11, 1930; s. Alfred Vincent and Eleanor J. (Raynor) S.; m. Virginia Louise Knight, June 7, 1952 (dec. July 1965); children: Carole, Diane; m. Nancy Lee Corbett, Apr. 5, 1980. AB, Duke U., 1952; LLB, U. Louisville, 1954. Bar: Ky. 1957, U.S. Dist. Ct. (we. dist.) Ky. 1961, U.S. Ct. Appeals (6th cir.). Atty. claims dept. Travelors Ins. Co., Louisville, 1957-60; sole practice Louisville, 1961-78; ptnr. Goldberg & Simpson, Louisville, 1978—. Republican. Presbyterian. Insurance, Personal injury, Workers' compensation. Office: Goldberg & Simpson 2800 1st nat Tower Louisville KY 40202

SIMPSON, RUSSELL AVINGTON, law firm administrator; b. Greybull, Wyo., June 19, 1935; s. William Avington and Margaret E. (Draper) S.; m. Margarita A. del Valle, Dec. 19, 1960; children—Margaret E., Robert A., Alexandra P., Christina M. B.S. with honors, U. Wyo., 1957; LL.B., Harvard U., 1965. Bar: Tex. 1965, Mass. 1966. Assoc. firm Bonilla, de Pena, Read & Bonilla, Corpus Christi, Tex., 1965-66; asst. dean, dir. admissions Harvard Law Sch., Cambridge, Mass., 1966-75, asst. dean, dir. fin. aid, 1972-78, asst. dean for fin. and gen. adminstrn., 1978-84; dir. adminstrn. firm Hill & Barlow, Boston, 1984—; chmn. devel. com. Law Sch. Data Assembly Service, 1969; pres. bd. dirs. Law Sch. Admissions Services, Newtown, Pa., 1979-80. Mem. town meeting Town of Belmont (Mass.), 1975—; mem. Belmont Sch. Com., 1977-83. Served to capt. USAF, 1957-62. Mem. Tex. Bar Assn., Law Sch. Admission Council (trustee 1968-70, 72-78, 81-82, chmn. services com. 1972-74, chmn. test devel. and research com. 1976-78), Grad. and Profl. Sch. Fin. Aid Council (founding), Phi Kappa Phi. Democrat. Club: Belmont Rotary (bd. dirs. 1978-80). Law firm management. Home: 49 Elizabeth Rd Belmont MA 02178 Office: Hill & Barlow One International Pl Boston MA 02110

SIMPSON, RUSSELL GORDON, lawyer; b. Springfield, Mass., May 22, 1927; s. Archer Roberts and Maude Ethel (Gordon) S.; married, Sept. 11, 1954; children: Barbara G., Elisabeth Pires-Fernandes, Helen Blair. B.A., Yale U., 1951; J.D., Boston U., 1956; postgrad., Parker Sch. Internat. Law. Advt. mgr. Burden Bryant Co., Springfield, 1951-53; assoc. Goodwin, Procter & Hoar, Boston, 1956-64, ptnr., 1965—; hon. consul New Eng. of Bolivia, 1958-82; mem. spl. com. to revise Mass. Corrupt Practices Act, 1961-62; dir. Fishery Products, Inc., Bolsa Corp., Haskell Investment Corp. Author: The Lawyer's Basic Corporate Practice Manual, 1971, rev. edit., 1978, 84. Bd. overseers Boston U. Sch. Mgmt., 1969-74; mem. exec. com. Sch. Law Boston U., 1978—; mem. Mass. Rep. Com., 1959-67, exec. com., 1959-67, chmn., 1962-67; del. Rep. Nat. Conv., 1964, state convs., 1960, 62, 64, 66, 67, 70; exec. dir. Mass. Del. Rep. Nat. Conv., 1968; vice chmn. Milton Rep. Town Com., 1970-71; mem. Milton Town Meeting, 1978-87; adv. com. ambulatory care service Beth Israel Hosp., 1969-71; bd. dirs. Greater Boston Arts Fund, Inc., Milton Hosp., Mass., 1983-86; mem. housing and regional orgn. coms. Met. Boston Area Planning Council, 1969-75; mem. Milton Town Warrant Com., 1976-80, chmn., 1978-80; mem. adv. com. Mass. Mediation Service, 1986—; mem. various coms. Served with USN, 1945-46. Named Outstanding Young Man of Greater Boston, 1963. Fellow Am. Bar Found., Mass. Bar Found.; mem. Mass. Bar Assn. (chmn. banking and bus. law sect. 1980-83, bd. dels., exec. com. 1983—, v.p. 1985—), ABA (corp. banking and bus. law sect., com. on law firms, cochmn. com. on law firm governance, panel on corp. law ednl. programs), Boston Bar Assn., World Affairs Council, Ambassadors Club. Clubs: The Country (Brookline, Mass.), Edgartown Yacht (Mass.), Edgartown Reading Room, Golf (Edgartown), Edgartown, Squibnocket Assocs. (Martha's Vineyard, Mass.), Jupiter Island (Hobe Sound, Fla.), Bay (Boston), Yale (N.Y.C.). General practice, General corporate, Contracts commercial. Home: Down Harbor Estates Edgartown MA 02539 Office: Goodwin Procter & Hoar Exchange Pl Boston MA 02109

SIMPSON, SEARCY LEE, JR., lawyer; b. Ft. Benning, Ga., Feb. 20, 1947; s. Searcy Lee Sr. and Jean (James) S.; m. Carol Ann Bitter, Jan. 25, 1969 (div. Apr. 1980); m. Jana Jo, Sept. 21, 1985; 1 child, Kyle. BA, Tex. A&I U., 1969; JD, St. Marys Law Sch., San Antonio, 1974. Bar: Tex. 1975, U.S. Ct. Mil. Appeals 1975, U.S. Dist. Ct. (no. dist.) Tex. 1982, U.S. Ct. Appeals (5th cir.) 1982. Commd. USAF, 1969; atty. USAF, Washington, 1969-81; advanced through grades to maj. USAF; asst. dist. atty. Dallas Dist. Atty. Office, 1981-82; asst. U.S. atty. U.S. Atty.'s Office, Dallas, 1982-85; atty. Southwestern Bell Telephone, Dallas, 1985—; judge USAF, Washington, 1980-81; asst. gen. counsel Air Force Exchange Service, Dallas, 1982—. Sunday sch. tchr. Prestonwood Bapt. Ch., Dallas, 1985. Served to maj. USAF, 1969-81. Recipient Cert. of Merit Dallas Police Dept., 1985, Ross Perot award; named Top Narcotics Prosecutor in Tex., 1984. Mem. ABA, Fed. Bar Assn., Tex. Bar Assn., Dallas Bar Assn., Semper Fidelis Soc. (pres.), Sigma Chi. Republican. Avocation: running. General corporate, Military, Criminal. Home: 6039 Wind Break Trail Dallas TX 75252 Office: Southwestern Bell Telephone Co One Bell Plaza Suite 2900 Dallas TX 75265

SIMPSON, STEVEN DREXELL, lawyer; b. Sturgis, Mich., Sept. 20, 1953; s. Drexell and Loraine Simpson; m. Peggy Deibert, April 28, 1979; children: Andrew Drexell, Christine Elizabeth. BA, Hillsdale (Mich.) Coll., 1975; JD, Wake Forest U., 1978; LLM in Taxation, Georgetown U., 1981. Bar: Fla. 1978, D.C. 1980, N.C. 1984. Assoc. Bradford, Williams et al, Miami, Fla., 1978-80, Webster & Chamberlain, Washington, 1980-82, Fisher, Wayland et al, Washington, 1982-84, Maupin, Taylor, Ellis & Adams, Raleigh, N.C., 1984—. Author: Taxation of Broadcasters, 1984, Charitable Organizations: Operations and Reporting Requirements, 1987; contbr. articles to profl. jours. Precinct chmn. Funderburk for Senate, Raleigh, 1986—. Mem. ABA (exemp orgns. com., mem. exec. com. young lawyers tax com.). Republican. Methodist. Lodge: Rotary (bd. dirs. Raleigh chpt. 1986—). Avocations: golf, running. Corporate taxation, Estate taxation, Exempt organizations. Home: 820 Purdue St Raleigh NC 27609 Office: Maupin Taylor Ellis & Adams PC PO Drawer 19764 Raleigh NC 27619

SIMS, E. JANE, lawyer; b. Hutchinson, Kans., Feb. 25, 1938; d. Laurence C. and Nina H. (Hill) Forker; m. Jack K. Sims, July 31, 1959 (div.); children: Gregory K., Stephen E. L. AS, Eastern Mont. U., 1958; BS, Mont. State U., 1965; JD, Lewis U., 1978. Bar: Ill. 1979, U.S. Dist. Ct. (no. dist.) Ill. 1979, U.S. Ct. Appeals (7th cir.) 1979. Trust adminstr. Bank of Wheaton, Ill., 1978-80; sole practice Wheaton, Ill., 1980-83; assoc. Mountcastle & DaRosa, Wheaton, 1983—. Bd. dirs. DuPage Council Girl Scouts U.S., 1980-85; vol. legal advisor West Suburban YWCA, Lombard, Ill., 1980—. Mem. Ill. State Bar Assn., DuPage County Bar Assn. Probate, Real property, Family and matrimonial. Home: 1102 Sunset Rd Wheaton IL 60187 Office: Mountcastle & DaRosa 208 N West PO Box 48 Wheaton IL 60189

SIMS, GARLAND DWIGHT, lawyer; b. Washington, Mar. 11, 1949; s. George Creel and Mary Virginia (Biedler) S. BA, Lehigh U., 1971; MA, U. Chgo., 1972; JD, U. Va., 1978. Bar: N.Y. 1979, U.S. Dist. Ct. (so. and ea. dists.) N.Y. 1979. Assoc. Wickes, Riddel, Bloomer, Jacobi & McGuire, N.Y.C., 1978-79, Morgan, Lewis & Bockius, N.Y.C., 1979-81; jr. assoc. counsel Chase Manhattan Bank, NA, N.Y.C., 1981-85, v.p., sr. assoc. counsel, 1985—. Mem. ABA. Banking, Contracts commercial. Home: 181 7th Ave Apt 14A New York NY 10011 Office: Chase Manhattan Bank NA 1 Chase Manhattan Plaza New York NY 10081

SIMS, JAMES CHRISTIAN, lawyer; b. Seattle, Sept. 26, 1944; s. Donald Andrew and Alida Gertrude (Hamel) S.; m. Jacquelyn Clare Sims, Aug. 2, 1979. Degree in Polit. Sci., UCLA, 1967; J.D., Loyola U., Los Angeles, 1970. Bar: Calif. 1973, Oreg. 1974. Sole practice, Ashland, Oreg., 1973-84; ptnr. Kelly and Cogan, P.C., Santa Monica, Calif., 1984—; editor, pub. Lithia Times newspaper, 1976-78; dir. Ashland Community Fed. Credit Union, 1975-78; dir. Oreg. League Environ. Voters, 1978. Dir. Ashland C. of C., 1975; coach UCLA varsity crew, 1986; mem. Ashland City Planning Commn., 1975, Ashland City Council, 1979-82; chmn. Ashland City Hist. Commn., 1977-78; mem. Ret. Sr. Vol. Program, 1973-76, Jackson County Air Quality Adv. Com., 1981-82, Bear Creek Greenway Com., 1981, Jackson County Democratic Central com., 1979-81. Served to 1st lt. U.S. Army, 1970-72, Vietnam. Decorated Bronze Star, Army Commendation medal. Mem. Los Angeles Trial Lawyers Assn., Calif. Trial Lawyers Assn. Home: 14020 Old Harbor Ln Apt #203 Marina Del Rey CA 90291 Office: Kelly and Cogan PC 2632 Lincoln Blvd Santa Monica CA 90405

SIMS, JOE, lawyer; b. Phoenix, Sept. 29, 1944; s. Joe and Pauline Jane (Saunders) S.; m. Robin Ann Reed, Jan. 30, 1965; 1 child, Shannon Dane. B.S., Ariz. State U., 1967, J.D., 1970. Bar: Ariz. 1970, U.S. Supreme Ct. 1975, D.C 1978. Trial atty. antitrust div. Dept. Justice, Washington, 1970-73; spl. asst. to asst. atty. gen., 1973-74; dep. asst. atty. gen. for policy planning and legislation, 1975-77, dep. asst. atty. gen. for regulatory matters and fgn. commerce, 1977-78; mem. firm Jones, Day, Reavis & Pogue, Washington, 1978-79; partner firm Jones, Day, Reavis & Pogue, 1979—; resident fellow Am. Enterprise Inst. for Public Policy Research, Washington, 1978-79; vis. fellow Am. Enterprise Inst. for Public Policy Research, 1979-82, adj. scholar, 1982—. Mem. Am. Bar Assn., D.C. Bar Assn., Ariz. State Bar Assn.. Antitrust, Administrative and regulatory. Home: 2020 Upper Lake Dr Reston VA 22091 Office: 655 15th St NW Washington DC 20005

SIMS, MURRAY WILLIAM, JR., lawyer; b. Chgo., Nov. 15, 1932; s. Murray William and Gertrude (Rammer) S.; m. Anne Marie Gartner, May 4, 1963; children—Mary Therese, Colleen Marie. A.B. in History, St. Joseph's Coll., Collegeville, Ind., 1954; LL.B., John Marshall Law Sch., 1958; student Lawyers Inst., Chgo., 1959-60. Bar: Ill. 1959, U.S. Dist. Ct. (no. dist.) Ill. 1961. Ptnr. Zimbehl, Sims & Zuckerman, Chgo., 1960-62, Parillo, Sims & Bressler, Chgo., 1966-74, Piacenti, Cifelli & Sims, Chgo. Heights, 1974-80, Watson & Sims, Chgo., 1983—; assoc. Brody & Gore, Chgo., 1962-66; sole practice, Chicago Heights, 1980-83; lectr. law day com. Chgo. Bar Assn., 1964-65. Republican candidate cir. ct. judge Cook County, Ill., 1980; pres. Hickory Hills Park Dist., 1971-72, Mem. Assn. Trial Lawyers Am., Ill. Trial Lawyers Assn., Ill. State Bar Assn., Am. Arbitration Assn. Roman Catholic. State civil litigation, Insurance, Personal injury. Home: 2849 Kathleen Ln Flossmoor IL 60422 Office: Watson & Sims 100 W Monroe St Chicago IL 60602

SIMS, RICKY REECE, lawyer; b. Lubbock, Tex., Sept. 20, 1954; s. Dwight Reece and Dorla Vene (Pruitt) S.; m. Jo Ann Holloway, Dec. 22, 1975; 1 child, Sean Reece. Student McLennan Community Coll., 1973-74; B.A., Baylor U., 1976, J.D., 1977. Bar: Tex. 1977, U.S. Dist. Ct. (ea. dist.) Tex. 1979, U.S. Dist. Ct. (we. dist.) Tex. 1980; cert. residential/farm and ranch real estate law Tex. Bd. Legal Specialization. Sole practice, Teague, Tex., 1977—; city atty. Cities of Teague, Buffalo, Jewett and Coolidge, Tex. Mem. Freestone County Bar Assn. (treas. 1984), Teague C. of C. (pres. 1978-79), State Bar Coll. Baptist. Lodge: Rotary (pres. 1979). Real property, General practice, Criminal. Home: 28 Mimosa Ln Teague TX 75860 Office: PO Drawer 299 Teague TX 75860

SIMS, RONALD LOUIS, lawyer; b. Ocala, Fla., Aug. 18, 1950; s. Joseph L. Sims and Sophie (Mickwee) Samya: m. Joyce Willcox, Dec. 28, 1971; children: Mark G., Karen M., Madeline A. BS, Spring Hill Coll., 1972; JD, U. Ala., 1975. Bar: Ala. 1975, U.S. Dist. Ct. (so. dist.) Ala. 1975, U.S. Dist. Ct. (no. dist.) Ala. 1980. Assoc. Gallalee, Denniston & Edington, Mobile, Ala., 1975-79; counsel Amsouth Bank N.A., Birmingham, Ala., 1979—. Mem. ABA, Ala. Bar Assn., Bench and Bar Honor Soc., Mobile Jaycees (com. chmn. 1977-79). Roman Catholic. Avocations: coaching youth soccer and basketball. Banking, Contracts commercial, General corporate. Office: Amsouth Bank NA PO Box 11007 Birmingham AL 35288

SIMS, TERRANCE LEE, lawyer; b. Garden City, Kans., May 12, 1953; s. Francis Joe and Ruth Edna (Reschke) S. BA summa cum laude, Mo. So. State Coll., 1975; JD, U. Mo., 1978. Bar: Mo. 1978, Ariz. 1984. Law clk. to presiding judge Mo. Ct. Appeals, Springfield, 1978-79, U.S. Dist. Ct. Kans., Wichita, 1979-83; mem. Tower, Byrne & Beaugureau, P.C., Phoenix, 1983—. Mem. ABA, Mo. Bar Assn., Ariz. Bar Assn., Maricopa County Bar Assn. Democrat. Avocations: classical music, snow skiing, racquetball. Federal civil litigation, State civil litigation, Jurisprudence. Office: Tower Byrne & Beaugureau PC 2111 E Highland Suite 255 Phoenix AZ 85016

SIMS, WILSON, lawyer; b. Nashville, Dec. 24, 1924; s. Cecil and Grace (Wilson) S.; m. Linda Bell, Aug. 12, 1948; children: Linda Rickman, Suzanne, Wilson. B.A., U. N.C., 1946; J.D., Vanderbilt U., 1948. Bar: Tenn. bar 1948. Since practiced in Nashville; partner firm Bass, Berry & Sims, 1948—; gen. counsel, dir. Baird Ward Printing Co., Tenn., 1950-76, Martha White Foods, Synercon Corp., 1968-76, Charter Co., 1983-84. Chmn. Tenn. Commn. for Human Devel., 1970, Tenn. Commn. on Continuing Legal Edn., 1987—; Mem. Tenn. Gen. Assembly, 1959; bd. dirs. Nashville YMCA, 1955-65, United Cerebral Palsy, Kidney Found.; trustee Meharry Med. Coll., Webb Sch., Bell Buckle, Tenn.; adv. bd. Jr. League. Served to 1st lt. USMCR, 1942-45, 50-52. Fellow Am. Bar Found.; mem. ABA, Tenn. Bar Assn. (ho. dels. chmn. 1973-75, pres. 1985-86), Nashville Bar Assn. (past pres., dir.), Tenn. Bar Found. (chmn.), Am. Judicature Soc., Am. Acad. Polit. Sci., Vanderbilt Law Alumni (pres. 1974-75), Nashville C. of C. (bd. govs. 1965-70, 83-85). Mem. Christian Ch. Clubs: Belle Meade Country (Nashville) (dir. 1969-72), Cumberland (Nashville); Bay Point Yacht and Country (Panama City, Fla.). Federal civil litigation, State civil litigation, General corporate. Home: 405 Westview Ave Nashville TN 37205 Office: Bass Berry & Sims 2700 First Am Ctr Nashville TN 37238

SIMSON, GARY JOSEPH, legal educator; b. Newark, Mar. 18, 1950; s. Marvin and Mildred (Silberg) S.; m. Rosalind Slivka, Aug. 15, 1971; 1 child, Nathaniel. B.A., Yale Coll., 1971; J.D., Yale U., 1974. Bar: Conn. 1974, N.Y. 1980. Law clk. to judge U.S. Ct. Appeals 2d Cir., 1974-75; asst. prof. law, U. Tex., 1975-77, prof. law, 1977-80; vis. prof. law Cornell U., Ithaca, N.Y., 1979-80, prof. law, 1980—; vis. prof. law U. Calif., Berkeley, 1986; chair adv. bd. law casebook series Carolina Acad. Press. Author: Issues and Perspectives in Conflict of Laws, 1985. Mem. ABA, ACLU, Phi Beta Kappa. Contbr. articles to legal publs. Legal education. Office: Cornell U Law Sch Ithaca NY 14853

SINAK, DAVID LOUIS, lawyer; b. Detroit, Oct. 3, 1953; s. Joseph and Edwina Mae (Collarini) S.; m. Barbara Louise Hoving, Aug. 27, 1976; 1 child, Jeffrey David. BA, U. Notre Dame, 1975; student, London Sch. Econs., 1975-76; JD, Boston Coll., 1979. Bar: Tex. 1979, U.S. Ct. Claims 1981, U.S. Tax Ct. 1981, U.S. Dist. Ct. (no. dist.) Tex. 1984, U.S. Ct. Appeals (fed. cir.) 1982, U.S. Ct. Appeals (5th cir.) 1984. Assoc. Hughes and Luce (formerly Hughes and Hill), Dallas, 1979-84, ptnr., 1984—; speaker Miss. Tax Inst., 1981, Ark. Natural Resources Law Inst., 1981, Nat. Assn. Home Builders Tax Conf., 1983, Southwest Legal Found. Symposium on Tax Reform Act, 1984, State Bar Tex. Advanced Real Estate Law course, 1985, A Bus. Guide to REMICs, 1987. Co-founder, bd. dirs. Incest Recovery Assn., Dallas, 1983—; participant Leadership Dallas, 1983-84. Mem. ABA, Tex. Bar Assn., Dallas Bar Assn. Corporate taxation, Personal income taxation, State and local taxation. Office: Hughes and Luce 1000 Dallas Bldg Dallas TX 75201

SINAS, GEORGE THOMAS, lawyer; b. Detroit, June 1, 1950; s. Thomas George and Martha (Gikas) S.; m. Sheryl Ann Hogan, June 24, 1972; children—Thomas, Stephen. B.A. in Polit. Sci., U. Mich., 1972; J.D., Wayne State U., 1975. Bar: Mich. 1975, U.S. Dist. Ct. (ea. dist.) Mich. 1976, U.S. Ct. Appeals (6th cir.) 1976, U.S. Dist. Ct. (we. dist.) Mich. 1980. Ptnr. Sinas, Dramis, Brake, Boughton, McIntyre & Reisig, P.C., Lansing, Mich., 1975—; faculty Mich. Jud. Inst., 1979—; mediator Ingham and Wayne County Cir. Cts., 1980—; mem. Supreme Ct. Com. on Standard Jury Instructions, Detroit, 1984—. Author: Michigan No Fault Auto Insurance Decisions, 1978 (Mich. Trial Lawyers Assn. Spl. award 1979). Mem. Mich. Trial Lawyers Assn. (pres. 1982-83), Assn. Trial Lawyers Am. (nat. gov. 1984—). Personal injury, Insurance. Office: 520 Seymour Lansing MI 48933

SINCERBEAUX, ROBERT ABBOTT, lawyer, foundation executive; b. N.Y.C., July 22, 1913; s. Frank Huestis and Jessie Marian (Batterson) S.; m. Elizabeth Morley, Apr. 19, 1940; children—Richard M., Suzanne Sincerbeaux Brian, Charles M. B.A. cum laude, Princeton U., 1936; LL.B., Yale U., 1939. Bar: N.Y. 1940. Assoc. White & Case, N.Y.C., 1939-42, Simpson, Thacher & Bartlett, N.Y.C., 1942-43; assoc. Sincerbeaux & Shrewsbury, N.Y.C., 1946-52, ptnr., 1952-72, of counsel, 1972—. Pres., Eva Gebhard-Gourgaud Found., N.Y.C., 1959—, trustee, 1947—; mng. trustee Cecil Howard Charitable Trust, N.Y.C., 1968—; trustee Woodstock Hist. Soc., Vt., 1972—; trustee Woodstock Found., 1976—, Preservation Trust Vt., 1980—; chmn. design rev. bd. Village of Woodstock, 1983—. Served to lt. comdr. USNR, 1943-46. Recipient Preservation award Preservation Trust Vt., 1983 84; Honor award Nat. Trust for Historic Preservation, 1984. Fellow Met. Mus. Art (life). Episcopalian. Clubs: Woodstock Country, Lakota, Round Table; Nassau (Princeton), Belleair Country (Fla). Probate, Estate taxation. Home: Uphill Farm RR 1 Box 391 N Bridgewater Rd Woodstock VT 05091 Office: One The Green Woodstock VT 05091

SINCLAIR, RICHARD CARROLL, lawyer; b. Modesto, Calif., July 15, 1948; s. Carroll Burns and Katherine Louise (Miller) S.; m. Deborah Ann Romine, June 14, 1974; children: Brandon, Justin, Megan. BA in Sociology, U. Calif., Santa Barbara, 1970; JD, U. Pacific, 1975; LLM in Taxation, U. Miami, Fla., 1976. Computer analyst, fin. aids office U. Calif., Santa Barbara, 1967-69; pvt. practice real estate Modesto, 1970-71; referee and adminstrv. hearing officer, office of chief referee State Dept. Benefit Payments, Sacramento, Calif., 1973-74; cert. officer State Dept. Benefit Payments, Sacramento, 1974-75; sole practice Modesto and Oakdale, 1976—. Mem. ABA, Stanislaus County Bar Assn., Calif. Bar Assn., Sigma Pi. Mormon. Club: Sportsman of Stanislaus (Modesto). Office: 8212 Oakview Dr Oakdale CA 95361

SINCLAIR, VIRGIL LEE, JR., lawyer, writer; b. Canton, Ohio, Nov. 10, 1951; s. Virgil Lee and Thelma Irene (Dunlap) S.; m. Judy Ann Montgomery, May 26, 1969 (div. Mar. 1980); children: Kelly, Shannon. BA, Kent State U., 1973; JD, U. Akron, 1976; postgrad. Case Western Res. U., 1979. Adminstr. Stark County Prosecutor's Office, Canton, 1974-76; mem. faculty Walsh Coll., Canton, 1976-78; asst. pros. atty. Stark County, Canton, 1976-77; ptnr. Amerman Burt Jones Co. LPA, Canton, 1976—; legal adviser Mayor's Office, City of North Canton, Ohio, 1978-79; referee Stark County Family Ct., Canton, 1981; spl. referee Canton Mcpl. Ct., 1985-86. Author: Law Enforcement Officers' Guide to Juvenile Law, 1975, Lay Manual of Juvenile Law, 1976; editor U. Akron Law Rev.; contbr. to Ohio Family Law, 1983, also articles to profl. jours. Mem. North Canton Planning Comm., 1979-82; bd. mgrs. North Canton YMCA, 1976—, Camp Tippecanoe, Ohio, 1981—; profl. adviser Parents Without Partners, 1980—; spl. dep. Stark County Sheriff Dept., 1983—; trustee Palace Theatre Assn., Canton, 1982—. Recipient Disting. Service award U.S. Jaycees, 1984. Mem. ABA, Ohio Bar Assn., Stark County Bar Assn. (lectr. 1984), Ohio Trial Lawyers Assn., Assn. Trial Lawyers Am., Nat. Dist. Attys. Assn., Delta Theta Phi (bailiff 1976; nat. key winner 1975-76), Jaycees. Republican. Methodist. Lodge: Elks. Personal injury, State civil litigation, Family and matrimonial. Home: 6069 Paris Ave NE Louisville OH 44641

SINDELL, DAVID IRWIN, lawyer; b. Cleve., Jan. 30, 1912; s. Isadore and Jennie (Miller) S.; m. Grace Tabakin, June 26, 1938; children—Roger, Gerald, Laura. B.A. cum laude, Case Western Res. U., 1932, LL.D., 1936; postgrad. U. Mich. Law, U. Wis. Law Sch., Case Western Res. U. Bar: Ohio 1936, U.S. Supreme Ct. 1969. Tchr., Cleve. Sch. System, 1932-34; ptnr. Sindell Sindell & Rubenstein, Cleve., 1936—. Co-author: Settlement (personal injury cases), 1963. Pres., Civil Service Commn. of Cleve., 1969-74. Recipient Outstanding Law Alumnus award of merit Case Western Res. Law Sch., 1973; Pres.'s award Assn. Trial Lawyers Am., 1967. Fellow Internat. Acad. Trial Lawyers (co-founder); mem. Black Shield Police Assn. Cleve. (Community Service award), Case Western Res. U. Law Sch. Law Soc. (hon.; pres. Bencher's Soc. 1982-85), Cuyahoga County Bar Assn. (award of merit 1973-74, pres. 1973-74). Democrat. Jewish. Personal injury. Home: 14818 Shaker Blvd Shaker Heights OH 44120 Office: Sindell Sindell & Rubenstein Nat City E Bldg Cleveland OH 44114

SINDON, GEOFFREY STUART, lawyer; b. Bklyn., Dec. 3, 1952; s. Arlen Earle and Rita Nathalie (Dillon) S.; m. Deborah Jean Mull, Oct. 22, 1977; children: Jennifer Lorraine, Darryl Aaron. BS cum laude, U. Utah, 1973; JD, Pepperdine U., 1976. Bar: Calif. 1976, U.S. Dist. Ct. (cen. dist.) Calif. 1977, U.S. Dist. Ct. (no. dist.) Calif. 1980, U.S. Dist. Ct. Appeals (9th cir.) 1980. Mem. Litt and Wells, Los Angeles, 1977-78, Cohen and Steinhart, Los Angeles, 1978-82, Trope and Trope, Los Angeles, 1982-83, Sindon and Vogt, Los Angeles, 1983—; mediator Los Angeles Superior Ct., 1983—. Mem. ABA, Los Angeles County Bar Assn., State Bar Calif. (family law sect.), Calif. Copyright Conf. Family and matrimonial, Probate, State civil litigation. Office: Sindon and Vogt 1900 Ave of the Stars Los Angeles CA 90067

SING, WILLIAM BENDER, lawyer; b. Houston, Oct. 16, 1947; s. William B. Sr. and Alice Irene (Detmers) S.; m. Doris Anne Spradley, Sept. 1, 1967; children: Erin Elaine, Emily Elizabeth. BS cum laude, U. Houston, 1968, JD magna cum laude, 1971. Bar: Tex. 1971. Ptnr. Fulbright & Jaworski, Houston, 1973—. Served to 1st lt. USAR, 1971-77. Mem. ABA, Tex. Bar Assn., Houston Bar Assn. Presbyterian. Club: Houston Center. Office: Fulbright & Jaworski 1301 McKinney St Houston TX 77010

SINGER, DANIEL MORRIS, lawyer; b. Bklyn., Oct. 10, 1930; s. Samuel W. and Fannie G. (Sabloff) S.; m. Maxine Frank, June 15, 1952; children—Amy E., Ellen R., David B., Stephanie F. B.A. with honors, Swarthmore Coll., 1951; LL.B., Yale U., 1954. Bar: N.Y. 1956, U.S. Dist. Ct. D.C. 1957, U.S. Ct. Appeals (D.C. cir.) 1957, U.S. Supreme Ct., 1959. Motions clk. U.S. Ct. Appeals D.C. Cir., 1956-57, law clk. to Judge George T. Washington, 1957-58; assoc. Fried, Frank, Harris, Shriver & Kampelman, Washington, 1958-64, ptnr., 1965—; vol. atty. Lawyers Com. for Civil Rights Under Law, 1965, 66; mem. exec. com. Washington Lawyers Com. for Civil Rights Under Law, 1973—. Bd. dirs., sec.-treas. Nat. Com. Tithing in Investment, 1964-65; dir. sec.-treas. Council for a Livable World, 1962-64; mem. gov. council, exec. com. Am. Jewish Congress, 1986—; pres. Am. Soc. for the Protection of Nature in Israel, 1986—. Served with Signal Corps, U.S. Army, 1954-56. Recipient 2d prize Nathan Burkan Meml. Competition, 1954. Mem. ABA, D.C. Bar, Bar Assn. D.C. Real property, Contracts commercial. Home: 5410 39th St NW Washington DC 20015 Office: Fried Frank Harris Shriver et al 1001 Pennsylvania Ave NW Suite 800 Washington DC 20004

SINGER, DAVID HARRIS, lawyer; b. Wilkes-Barre, Pa., Apr. 3, 1947; s. Julian B. and Bernice (Albert) S.; m. Carol S. Seeherman, July 5, 1970; children—Julie Elayne, Shellie Hope. A.B., George Washington U., 1969; J.D., U. Miami, 1972. Bar: Fla. 1972, Pa. 1972, U.S. Dist. Ct. (mid. and so. dists.) Fla., U.S. Ct. Appeals (5th cir.), U.S. Ct. Appeals (11th cir.). Sole practice Law Offices D.H. Singer, Miami, Fla., 1973—. Mem. Fla. Bar, Dade County Trial Lawyers Assn., Acad. Fla. Trial Lawyers, Assn. Trial Lawyers Am. Contracts commercial, Consumer commercial, General corporate. Office: 7000 SW 62d Ave Miami FL 33143

SINGER, NORMAN BRUCE, lawyer, management company executive; b. St. Paul, Sept. 16, 1947; s. Abraham and Ruth (Ehrlich) S.; m. Linda Ellen Birkeland, May 26, 1972. BA, U. Minn., 1969, JD, 1972. Bar: Minn. 1972, U.S. Dist. Ct. Minn. 1972. Assoc. Nilva & Frisch, P.A., St. Paul, 1972-77; founder, exec. dir. Nat. Practice Inst., Inc., Mpls., 1976-84; chief exec. officer

Law Office Mgmt. Corp., Mpls., 1984—; co-founder, bd. dirs. Minn. Bar Rev., Inc., Mpls., 1972—. Editor (newsletter) Law Office Mgmt., 1986—. Mem. ABA, Minn. Bar Assn. Continuing legal education, Law office administration. Office: Law Office Mgmt Corp 701 4th Ave S Suite 500 Minneapolis MN 55415

SINGER, PAUL MEYER, lawyer; b. Pitts., May 20, 1943; s. Sidney Morris and Doris (Lyttle) S.; m. Sue Friedberg, 1976 (div.). BS in Bus., U. Minn., 1965; JD, U. Pitts., 1968; LLM, Harvard U., 1970. Law clk. to presiding justice Pa. Supreme Ct., Pitts., 1970-71; atty. Am. Express Credit Corp., N.Y.C., 1971-73; ptnr. Reed, Smith, Shaw & McClay, Pitts., 1973—. Jewish. Clubs: Harvard Yale Princeton, Duquesne (Pitts.). Banking, Bankruptcy, General corporate. Office: Reed Smith Shaw & McClay 435 6th Ave Pittsburgh PA 15219-1886

SINGER, STUART H., lawyer; b. Miami, Fla., July 20, 1956; s. Marvin and Rose (Gordon) S. BS, MA, Northwestern U., 1978; JD, Harvard U., 1981. Law clk. to assoc. justice Byron White U.S. Supreme Ct., Washington, 1981-83; assoc. Greenberg, Traurig, Askew, Hoffman, Lipoff, Rosen & Quentel P.A., Miami, 1983—. Pres. Harvard U. Law Rev., 1980-81. Counsel Mondale-Ferraro for Pres., Fla., 1984. Mem. ABA, Fla. Bar Assn., Dade County Bar Assn., Assn. Trial Lawyers Am. Trademark and copyright, Securities, Federal civil litigation. Office: Greenberg Traurig Askew et al 1401 Brickell Ave Miami FL 33131

SINGLETARY, ALVIN D., lawyer; b. New Orleans, Sept. 27, 1942; s. Alvin E. and Alice (Pastoret) S.; m. Judy Louise Singletary, Dec. 3, 1983; children: Kimberly Dawn, Shane David, Kelly Diane. B.A., La. State U., 1964; J.D., Loyola U., New Orleans, 1969. Bar: La. 1969, U.S. Dist. Ct. (ea. dist.) La. 1972, U.S. Ct. Appeals (5th cir.) 1972, U.S. Supreme Ct. 1978, U.S. Ct. Appeals (11th cir.) 1981, U.S. Ct. Internat. Trade 1981, U.S. Ct. Customs and Patent Appeals 1982. Instr. Delgado Coll., New Orleans, 1976-77; sole practice, Slidell, La., 1970—; sec.-treas. St. Tammany Pub. Trust Fin. Authority, Slidell, 1978—; interim mayor City of Slidell, Spring 1985. Councilman-at-large City of Slidell, 1978—, interim mayor, 1985; mem. Democratic State Central Com., 1978-82; del. La. Constl. Conv., 1972-73; chmn. sustaining membership enrollment Cypress dist. Boy Scouts Am. Mem. Delta Theta Phi. Baptist. Lodge: Lions. General practice, State civil litigation, Probate. Office: PO Box 1158 Slidell LA 70459

SINGLETON, JOHN VIRGIL, JR., judge; b. Kaufman, Tex., Mar. 20, 1918; s. John Virgil and Jennie (Shelton) S.; m. Jane Guilford Tully, Apr. 18, 1953. J.D., U. Tex., 1942. Bar: Tex. 1942. Mem. firm Fulbright & Jaworski, 1946-54; partner Bates, Riggs & Singleton, 1954-56, Bell & Singleton, 1957-61, Barrow, Bland, Rehmet & Singleton, 1962-66; judge U.S. Dist. Ct. So. Dist. Tex., 1966—, chief judge, 1979—; pres. Houston Jr. Bar Assn., 1952-53; co-chmn. 5th circuit dist. judges div. Jud. Conf., 1969, chmn., 1970, rep. from 5th cir., 1980-83, also chmn. legis. com.; mem. Fifth Circuit Jud. Council, 1984—; dir. Central Nat. Bank, Houston, 1964-66. Mem. Tex. Depository Bd., 1963-66; co-chmn. Harris County Lyndon B. Johnson for Pres. Com., 1960-61; del.-at-large Democratic Nat. Conv., 1956, 60, 64; regional coordinator 7-state area Dem. Nat. Com., Lyndon B. Johnson-Hubert Humphrey Campaign for Pres., 1964; mem. exec. com., chmn. fin. com. Tex. Dem. Com., 1962-66; former bd. dirs. Houston Speech and Hearing Center; trustee Houston Legal Found.; mem. chancellor's council U. Tex.; mem. exec. com. Lombardi Awards Trophy; mem. Tex. Longhorn Edn. Found.; sponsor Found. for Tex. Excellence. Served to lt. comdr. USNR, 1942-46. Mem. ABA (mem. litigation sect. ad hoc com. on tng. for spl. masters), Fed. Judges Assn. (bd. dirs. 1974—), Houston Bar Assn. (v.p. 1956-57, editor Houston Lawyer 1954-55, chmn. unauthorized practice law com.), Tex. Bar Found. (charter mem. fellows), Tex. Bar Assn. (dist. dir.), State Bar Tex. (chmn. grievance com. for Harris County 1963-66, dir. 1965-66, mem. standing com. liaison with fed. judiciary 1981—, ex-officio mem. bd. dirs. 1984-85), U. Tex. Ex-Students Assn. (life mem., pres. Houston 1961-62, mem. exec. com., chmn. scholarship com., at large mem. 1969-80), Cowboys (foreman, straw boss), Am. Judicature Soc., Delta Tau Delta (pres. 1940-41), Phi Alpha Delta. Episcopalian. Club: Lakeside Country (Houston) (past sec., dir.). Lodge: Rotary. Jurisprudence. Office: Room 11144 US Courthouse 515 Rusk St Houston TX 77002

SINGLETON, SARAH MICHAEL, lawyer; b. Ann Arbor, Mich., Apr. 2, 1949; d. Palmer Christie and Susan (Ballard) S. B.A., Sarah Lawrence Coll., 1971; J.D., Ind. U., 1974. Bar: N. Mex. 1974, U.S. Dist. Ct. N.Mex. 1974, U.S. Ct. Appeals (10th cir.) 1976, U.S. Supreme Ct. 1978. Asst. appellate defender Pub. Defender Office, Santa Fe, N.Mex., 1974-76; ptnr. Pickard & Singleton, Santa Fe, 1976-81; sole practice, Santa Fe, 1981-85; assoc. Montgomery & Andrews, P.A., Santa Fe, 1985—; bd. visitors U. N.Mex. Sch. Law, 1983—. Contbr. to Women & The Law: The Situation in New Mexico, 1975, also articles; editor (with Pamela B. Minzner) Women's Legal Rights Newsletter, 1983. Pres. bd. trustees No. N.Mex. Legal Services, 1982; chmn. N.Mex. Bd. Bar Examiners, 1983—. Mem. ABA, State Bar N.Mex. (Outstanding Contbn. award 1983), 1st Jud. Dist. Bar Assn. (pres. 1978). Democrat. Club: Blue Sox Softball (coach 1984). State civil litigation, Federal civil litigation. Office: Montgomery & Andrews PA PO Box 2307 Santa Fe NM 87504

SINNOTT, JOHN PATRICK, lawyer, law educator; b. Bklyn., Aug. 17, 1931; s. John Patrick and Elizabeth Muriel (Zinkand) S.; m. Rose Marie Yuppa, May 30, 1959; children—James Alexander, Jessica Michelle. B.S., U.S. Naval Acad., 1953; M.S., U.S. Air Force Inst. Tech., 1956; J.D., Chase Coll. Law, 1960. Bar: Ohio 1961, N.Y. 1963, U.S. Patent Office 1963, N.J. 1970, U.S. Supreme Ct. 1977. Assoc. firm Brumbaugh, Graves, Donohue & Raymond, N.Y.C., 1961-63; patent atty. Bell Telephone Labs., Murray Hill, N.J., 1963-64; patent atty. Schlumberger Ltd., N.Y.C., 1964-71; asst. chief patent counsel Babcock & Wilcox, N.Y.C., 1971-79; asst. chief patent and trademark counsel Am. Standard Inc., N.Y.C., 1979—; adj. lectr. N.J. Inst. Tech., Newark, 1974—. Author: World Patent Law and Practice, Vols. 2-2M, 1974; A Practical Guide to Document Authentication, 1984; also numerous articles. Bd. dirs. New Providence Community Swimming Pool (N.J.), 1970; mem. local Selective Service Bd., Plainfield, N.J., 1971. Served to capt. USAF, 1953-61, Col. JAGC Res. Decorated Nat. Def. Service medal. Mem. N.Y. Patent Law Assn. (bd. dirs. 1974-82), N.J. Patent Law Assn. (com. chmn. 1981-82). Republican. Roman Catholic. Clubs: Squadron A (N.Y.C.); Army and Navy (Washington). Patent, Trademark and copyright, Legal education. Home: Two Blackburn Pl Summit NJ 07901 Office: Am Standard Inc 40 W 40th St New York NY 10018

SINNOTT, RANDOLPH PAUL, lawyer; b. Mineola, N.Y., Apr. 21, 1954; s. John and Joan Martha (Guggisberg) S.; m. Denise Shawn Kociemba, July 21, 1979; children: Randolph Paul Jr., Erica Shawn. AB, U. Mich., 1976; JD, U. So. Calif., 1982. Bar: Calif. 1982, U.S. Dist. Ct. (cen. dist.) Calif. 1982, U.S. Ct. Appeals (9th cir.) 1982, U.S. Dist. Ct. (no. ea. and so. dists.) Calif. 1983. Assoc. Gibson, Dunn & Crutcher, Los Angeles, 1982—. Served to 1st lt. USMC, 1976-79. Mem. ABA, Los Angeles Bar Assn., State Bar Assn. of Calif. Lutheran. Antitrust, Federal civil litigation, State civil litigation. Office: Gibson Dunn & Crutcher 333 S Grand Ave Los Angeles CA 90071

SINOWSKI, THOMAS CHARLES, lawyer; b. Youngstown, Ohio, Jan. 2, 1953; s. Joseph Thomas and Anna (Dedeck) S.; m. Cathy T. Tibbits, May 21, 1977; children: Kyleen Elizabeth, Thomas Charles. BS cum laude, Youngstown State U., 1977; JD, Western State U., 1980. Bar: Ga. 1982. Assoc. Thrasher & Whitley, Atlanta, 1982-84; ptnr. Sinowski & Jones, Marietta, Ga., 1984—. Mem. ABA (young lawyers div., bus. law sect.), Atlanta Bar Assn., Sandy Springs Bar Assn. Securities, Real property, Corporate taxation. Office: Sinowski & Jones PC 274 Washington Ave Marietta GA 30060

SINRICH, DIANE WINGARD, lawyer; b. Cambridge, Mass., May 31, 1950; s. Sumner Lawrence and Peggy Helene (Hahn) S. BA, Hofstra U., 1972; EdM, Suffolk U., 1974; JD, New Eng. Sch. of Law, 1980. Bar: Mass. 1980, U.S. Dist. Ct. Mass. 1981, U.S. Ct. Appeals (1st cir.) 1981. Law clk. to chief justice Mass. Land Ct., Boston, 1981-83; gen. counsel Mass. Exec. Office of Labor, Boston, 1983—. Mem. ABA, Mass. Bar Assn., Boston Bar Assn., Mass. Assn. Women Lawyers. Legislative, Labor. Office: Exec Office of Labor 1 Ashburton Place Suite 2112 Boston MA 02108

SINSHEIMER, ALAN J., lawyer; b. New Rochelle, N.Y., Jan. 11, 1956; s. Warren J. and Florence (Dubin) S.; m. Lisa A. Meshier, Sept. 12, 1981. AB, Princeton U., 1978; JD, NYU, 1981. Bar: N.Y. 1982. Assoc. Sullivan & Cromwell, N.Y.C., 1981—. Mem. ABA, Order of Coif. Democrat. Jewish. Mergers and acquisitions, General practice, Securities. Office: Sullivan & Cromwell 125 Broad St New York NY 10004

SIPHRON, JOSEPH RIDER, lawyer; b. Cin., Apr. 15, 1933; s. Joseph William and Florence (Rider) S.; m. Mary John Wilson, June 22, 1957; 1 son, John Rider. B.A., Yale U., 1955; postgrad., Oxford U., Eng., 1955-56; LL.B., Yale U., 1959. Bar: N.Y. 1960. Assoc. Milbank, Tweed, Hadley & McCloy, N.Y.C., 1959-67, ptnr., 1968—. Trustee The Buckley Sch., N.Y.C., 1975-80; trustee The Hotchkiss Sch., Lakeville, Conn., 1978-80, Southampton Hosp., N.Y., 1981-84; bd. dirs. Lab. of Ornithology, Cornell U., 1983—. Mem. Internat. Bar. Assn., ABA, N.Y. State Bar Assn., N.Y. Country Bar Assn., Assn. Bar City N.Y., Nat. Audubon Soc. (dir. 1982—). Clubs: Union, Down Town Assn; Yale (N.Y.C.); Quogue Beach (Quogue, N.Y.). Contracts commercial, Private international, Securities. Home: 50 E 72d St New York NY 10021 Office: Milbank Tweed Hadley & McCloy 1 Chase Manhattan Plaza New York NY 10005

SIPLIN, GARY ANTHONY, lawyer; b. Orlando, Fla., Oct. 21, 1954. BA, Johnson C. Smith U., 1975; M in Pub. and Internat. Affairs, U. Pitts., 1976; JD, Duquesne U., 1981. Law clk. to presiding justice U.S. Dist. Ct., Miami, Fla., 1981-82; asst. county atty. County Atty.'s Office, Miami, 1982—; judge Dade County Bar Moot Ct., Miami, 1983-84. Author: Prosecutorial Misuse of Peremptory Challenges on Black Veniremen: The Reasons, Impacts and Remedies, 1981. Asst. co-dir. Ctr. for Internat. Policy, Washington, 1976; staff writer Dade County Bar Bull., 1985; bd. dirs. Informed Families, 1985; chairperson Inner City Task Force, 1985. Named one of Outstanding Young Men in Am., 1984. Mem. ABA, Dade County Bar Assn. (bd. dirs. young lawyers sect. 1987—), Nat. Bar Assn., Dade County Nat. Bar Assn. (chairperson jud. reception com. 1984, bd. dirs. 1985—, bd. govs. 1985). Federal civil litigation, State civil litigation, Insurance. Home: 20580 SW 126th Ave Miami FL 33177

SIPPEL, WILLIAM LEROY, lawyer; b. Fon du Lac, Wis., Aug. 14, 1948; s. Alfonse Aloysious and Virginia Laura (Weber) S.; m. Barbara Jean Brost, Aug. 23, 1970; children: Katharine Jean, David William. BA, U. Wis., JD. Bar: Wis. 1974, U.S. Dist. Ct. (we. dist.) Wis. 1974, Minn. 1981, U.S. Dist. Ct. Minn. 1981, U.S. Ct. Appeals (10th cir.) 1984, U.S. Ct. Appeals (8th cir.) 1985. Research assoc. dept. agrl. econs. U. Wis., Madison, 1974-75; counsel monopolies and comml. law subcom. Ho. Judiciary Com., Washington, 1975-80; spl. asst. to asst. gen. antitrust div. U.S. Dept. of Justice, Washington, 1980-81; from assoc. to ptnr. Doherty, Rumble & Butler, Mpls. and St. Paul, Minn., 1981—. Mem. program com. Minn. World Trade Assn., Mpls., St. Paul, 1985-86, bd. dirs., 1986—, Minn. Served with USAR, 1971-77. Mem. Minn. Bar Assn. (co-chmn. antitrust sect. 1986—, internat. law sect. 1985-86, sect. council 1986—), Nat. Council of Farmer Coops. (legal tax and acctg. com. 1984—), Phi Beta Kappa. Democrat. Roman Catholic. Avocations: computers, reading. Antitrust, Private international, Federal civil litigation. Home: 1448 Pinewood Dr Woodbury MN 55125 Office: Doherty Rumble & Butler PA E-1500 First National Bank Bldg Saint Paul MN 55101

SIRES, BRUCE DAVID, lawyer; b. Milwaukee, Mar. 29, 1948; s. Melvin K. and Harriet June (Kahn) S.; children: Sean F., Marisa A. AB in Econs., UCLA, 1969; JD, Hastings Coll., 1972; LLM, NYU, 1976. Bar: Calif. 1972, U.S. Dist. Ct. (cen. dist.) Calif. 1972, U.S. Tax Ct. 1980, U.S. Ct. Appeals (9th cir.) 1972. Assoc., ptnr. Brawerman & Kopple, Beverly Hills, Calif., 1976-81, Halperin & Halperin, Los Angeles, 1981-84; ptnr. Hoffman, Sabban, Brucker & Sires, Los Angeles, 1984; sole practice Los Angeles, 1984—; lectr. continuing edn. of the bar, Los Angeles, 1981—; adj. prof. law U. San Diego, 1984-85. Bd. dirs. Jewish Free Loan Assn., 1985—, Met. Region Jewish Fedn. Council of Greater Los Angeles, 1986—. Mem. ABA (taxation and real property, probate and trust sects.), Beverly Hills Bar Assn. (gov., taxation, probate, trust and estate planning sects.). Democrat. Avocations: sailing, swimming, photography, reading. Probate, Corporate taxation, Personal income taxation. Office: 9595 Wilshire Blvd Suite 1010 Beverly Hills CA 90212-2510

SIRIS, MICHAEL JOHN, lawyer; b. N.Y.C., Sept. 11, 1945; s. Joseph Herbert and Muriel (Lazerus) S.; m. Teresa Pickman, Dec. 14, 1969 (div. Dec. 1982); children: Elizabeth Anne, John P. BA cum laude, Yale U., 1967; JD, NYU, 1970. Bar: N.Y. 1971, U.S. Dist. Ct. (so. and ea. dists.) N.Y. 1974, U.S. Ct. Appeals (2d cir.) 1975. Assoc. Kissam & Halpin, N.Y.C., 1970-71; producer films Witty Siris Prodns., N.Y.C., 1971-73; atty. Erie Lackawanna R.R. Co., N.Y.C., 1973-76; assoc. Gilmartin, Poster & Shafto, N.Y.C., 1976-79; sole practice N.Y.C., 1979—. Sec., bd. dirs. 139 E. 33d St. Corp., N.Y.C., 1985. Mem. N.Y. County Bar Assn., Assn. of Bar of City of N.Y. Clubs: Yale (N.Y.C.); Knickerbocker Yacht (Port Washington, N.Y.). Avocations: guitar, skiing, tennis, squash, jogging. State civil litigation, Transportation.

SISCO, THOMAS EDWARD, II, lawyer; b. Plainfield, N.J., June 29, 1943; s. Irwin Lloyd Sisco and Ethel (Baker) Vachon; m. Joy LaRae Wilbur, Mar. 17, 1963 (div. 1965). MA, Harvard U., 1961; BS, Fla. State U., 1965; JD, Southwestern U., 1978. Bar: Fla. 1981, U.S. Dist. Ct. (so. dist.) Fla. 1981, U.S. Ct. Appeals (5th and 11th cirs.) 1981, U.S. Supreme Ct. 1986. Admissions officer Wentworth Coll., Boston, 1967-68; asst. dean for admission Rensselaer Poly. Inst., Troy, N.Y., 1968-70; exec. dir. World Federalists, Boston, 1970-71; cons. various orgns. worldwide, 1971-76; law clk. to presiding justice Calif. Superior Ct., Los Angeles, 1978-80; sole practice West Palm Beach, Fla., 1981-86; sr. ptnr. Sisco & West, P.A., 1986—. Author: Collected Thoughts, 1964, Personality Theory, 1965. Non-govt. rep. Peace Talks, Paris, 1970-71; pres. Council on Child Abuse and Neglect, Palm Beach County, Fla., 1982-86, Juvenile Service Program, 1986—, Fla. Fedn. Young Reps. Clubs, 1963-66. Named Leading Man of Palm Beach, 1986. Mem. Fla. Bar Assn., Palm Beach County Bar Assn., Assn. Trial Lawyers Am., SAR (pres. Boston and Palm Beach 1968-83, pres.'s medal 1970, 83). Episcopalian. Clubs: Palm Beach Yacht, Forum (Palm Beach); Flotilla. Lodge: Kiwanis (bd. dirs. 1983-86). Contracts commercial, Entertainment, Real property. Home: 206 36th St West Palm Beach FL 33407 Office: 805 Belvedere Rd West Palm Beach FL 33405

SISK, PAUL DOUGLAS, lawyer; b. Colorado Springs, Colo., Mar. 30, 1950; s. Charles Ray Sisk and Patricia Joann (Linville) Botzler; m. Patricia Rizzo, Aug. 8, 1981. AB, Brown U., 1972; JD, Temple U., 1979; postgrad., U. Pa., 1987—. Bar: Pa. 1979, U.S. Ct. Appeals (3d cir.) 1980, U.S. Supreme Ct. 1983, U.S. Dist. Ct. (ea. dist.) Pa. 1985. Atty. U.S. Ct. Appeals (3d cir.), Phila., 1979-80, supervising atty., 1980—, sr. staff atty., 1981—. Jr. Warden Episc. Ch., Springfield, Pa., 1979-81; bd. dirs. Springfield Pastoral Care Found., 1979-82. Mem. ABA, Am. Judicature Soc., Com. Appellate Staff Attys. (exec. bd. 1986—). Democrat. Judicial administration, Federal civil litigation, Civil rights. Home: 8 Windsor Circle Springfield PA 19064 Office: US Ct Appeals 3d Cir 601 Market St Philadelphia PA 19106

SISKIND, DONALD H., lawyer; b. Providence, Dec. 25, 1937; s. Samuel and Sadie (Wasserman) S.; m. Beth Mohel, July 15, 1962; children—Steven M., Edward M. B.S., U. Pa., 1959; LL.B., Columbia U., 1962. Bar: Mass. 1962, N.Y. 1963. Assoc. Marshall Bratter Greene Allison & Tucker, N.Y.C., 1962-69, ptnr., 1969-82; ptnr. Rosenman & Colin, N.Y.C., 1982—; dir. Cadillac Fairview Corp. Ltd., Toronto, Ont. Can., Chgo. Title Ins. Co.; chmn. various seminars Practicing Law Inst., 1974—. Contbr. articles to profl. jours. Pres. Greenville Community Council, 1974-76; pres. bd. edn. Union Free Sch. Dist., Scarsdale, N.Y., 1978-81. Mem. Am. Coll. Real Estate Lawyers, ABA, N.Y. State Bar Assn., Assn. Bar City of N.Y., Phi Alpha Psi. Real property. Home: 876 Park Ave New York NY 10021 Office: Rosenman & Colin 575 Madison Ave New York NY 10022

SISSON, JERRY ALLAN, lawyer; b. Memphis, Oct. 13, 1956; s. Thomas E. and Jewel O. (Hipps) S.; m. Debra Elaine Martin, Aug. 13, 1977; children: Jennifer Elaine, Elizabeth Diane, Meredith Lydia. BBA, Memphis State U., 1977, JD, 1979. Bar: Tenn. 1980, U.S. Dist. Ct. (we. dist.) Tenn. 1980. Ptnr. Sisson & Sisson, Memphis, 1980—. Named one of Outstanding Young Men Am., 1981. Mem. ABA, Tenn. Bar Assn., Memphis-Shelby County Bar Assn., Memphis Jaycees (legal counsel 1985, v.p. community action 1986—, v.p. individual devel. 1987). Republican. Mem. Ch. Christ. Real property, General corporate, Probate. Home: 2966 Savannah Way S Germantown TN 38138 Office: Sisson & Sisson 5350 Poplar Ave Suite 415 Memphis TN 38119

SISTARE, SUSAN POWELL, lawyer; b. Ft. Lauderdale, Fla., July 23, 1949; d. Robert Preston and Margaret Susan (Pierce) Powell; m. Charles Warren Sistare, Nov. 27, 1982. BS, Auburn U., 1971; JD, U. Fla., 1982. Bar: Fla. 1982, U.S. Dist. Ct. (so. and mid. dists.) Fla. 1983, U.S. Ct. Appeals (11th cir.) 1983, U.S. Supreme Ct. 1986. Assoc. Saunders, Curtis, Ginestra & Gore, Ft. Lauderdale, 1982-83, FitzGerald & Taylor, Ft. Lauderdale, 1983-85; ptnr. Monast & Sistare P.A., Ft. Lauderdale, 1985; sole practice Ft. Lauderdale, 1985—. Mem. ABA, Broward County Bar Assn., Assn. Trial Lawyers Am. State civil litigation, General practice, Contracts commercial. Home: 720 SE 5th Ct Fort Lauderdale FL 33301

SITES, RICHARD LOREN, lawyer; b. Tiffin, Ohio, Feb. 16, 1948; s. Loren Richard and Frances Mary (Tellaro) S.; m. Karen Ann Heazlit, Oct. 6, 1979; children—Brian, David. B.A., Coll. Wooster, 1970; J.D., Coll. Law, U. Denver, 1973, M.S., 1975; cert. in health care fin. mgmt. Ohio State U., 1984. Bar: Colo. 1973, Ohio 1975, U.S. Dist. Ct. 1973, U.S. Supreme Ct. 1977. Sole practice, Columbus, 1973—; atty. HHS, Columbus, Ohio, 1975-85, Ohio Hosp. Assn., Columbus, 1985—. Author: Closed Medical Malpractice Claims in Ohio Hospitals, 1970 to 1984, 1986, 1st rev. edit., 1987. Alumni admissions rep. Coll. Wooster, Ohio, 1979-85, fund raiser, 1984; v.p. Sycamore Hills Residents Assn., Columbus, 1983, pres., 1984. Recipient awards, including merit award, 1979, 81, spl. achievement award, 1982 (all HHS). Mem. Am. Soc. for Health Care Risk Mgrs., Risk and Ins. Mgmt. Soc., Am. Soc. Hosp. Engring. Democrat. Health, Pension, profit-sharing, and employee benefits, Legal education. Office: Ohio Hosp Assn 21 W Broad St Columbus OH 43215

SITKIN, PETER EDWARD, lawyer; b. N.Y.C., July 14, 1940; s. Louis and Beatrice (Maly) S.; m. Wanda Marie Wilkerson, Oct. 15, 1982; children: Lisa, Jennifer, Brian. BA, Cornell U., 1961; JD cum laude, Columbia U., 1964. Bar: N.Y. 1964, Calif. 1966. Assoc. Baker & McKenzie, N.Y.C., 1964-66; atty. San Francisco Legal Services, 1966-71; ptnr. Pub. Advs., San Francisco, 1971-73; sole practice Berkeley, Calif., 1973—; assoc. prof. U. Calif. Hastings Coll. Law, San Francisco, 1970—; lectr. U. Calif. Berkeley, 1970-85. Active VISTA, San Jose, Calif., 1966; chmn. San Pablo Ave. Revitalization Com., Oakland, Calif., 1980-84; gen. counsel SYDA Found., South Fallsburg, N.Y., 1976-83, sec., trustee, bd. dirs. 1976-84; counsel Berkeley Womens Crew, 1986—. Mem. Calif. Bar Assn., Berkeley Bar Assn., Alamedy County Bar Assn. Avocations: jogging, tennis, meditation, yoga. Federal civil litigation, State civil litigation, Real property. Home: 216 Moraga Way Orinda CA 94563 Office: 1950 Addison St Suite 109 Berkeley CA 94704

SITLINGER, LEROY EDWARD, JR., lawyer; b. Harrisburg, Pa., Apr. 12, 1946; s. Leroy Edward Sr. and Mary (Mickalo) S.; m. Marjorie Sue Whiteley, Jan. 28, 1967 (div. Aug. 1978); children: Curtis Lee, Shannon Renee; m. Deborah Dee Carson, Aug. 19, 1983; 1 child, Justin Lee. BA, U. Louisville, 1968, JD, 1973. Bar: U.S. Ct. Appeals (6th cir.) 1974, Ky., U.S. Dist. Ct. (we. and ea. dists.) Ky. Assoc. Bennett, Bowman, Triplett & Vittitow, Louisville, 1974-85; ptnr. Sitlinger, McGlincy & Steiner, Louisville, 1985—. Pres. Navy League Louisville council, 1980-85; mem. exec. com. Jefferson County 4-H Council, Louisville, 1980—, Citizens for Better Judges, Louisville, 1983—, also v.p. Served to lt. USN, 1968-70. Mem. ABA, Ky. Bar Assn. (ho. dels. 1984—), Louisville Bar Assn. (chmn. litigation sect. 1985—), Louisville Bar Found. (bd. dirs. 1983—), U. Louisville Law Sch. Alumni Assn. (bd. dirs. 1980—). Democrat. Lodge: Masons (32d degree). Personal injury, Insurance, State civil litigation. Home: 2611 Evergreen Ct Louisville KY 40223 Office: Sitlinger McGlincy & Steiner 1506 Kentucky Home Life Bldg Louisville KY 40202

SIVERD, ROBERT JOSEPH, lawyer; b. Newark, N.J., July 27, 1948; s. Clifford David and Elizabeth Ann (Klink) S.; m. Bonita Marie Shulock, Jan. 8, 1972; 1 child, Robert J. Siverd, Jr. A.B. in French, Georgetown U., 1970; J.D., 1973; student LaSorbonne, Paris, summer 1969. Bar: N.Y. 1974, U.S. Dist. Ct. (so. and ea. dists.) N.Y. 1974, U.S. Dist. Ct. (ea. dist.) Pa. 1984, U.S. Ct. Appeals (2nd cir.) 1974, (3rd cir.) 1984, (6th cir.) 1985, U.S. Supreme Ct. 1980. Assoc. Donovan Leisure Newton & Irvine, N.Y.C., 1973-83; staff v.p., litigation counsel The Penn Central Corp., Greenwich, Conn., 1983-86, v.p. litigation counsel, 1986—. Mem. ABA, Westchester Fairfield County Corp. Counsel Assn., Am. Corp. Counsel Assn., Assn. Bar of City of NY. Republican. Roman Catholic. Antitrust, Federal civil litigation, General corporate. Office: The Penn Central Corp 500 W Putnam Ave Greenwich CT 06836

SKAAR, HARVEY ENGAARD, lawyer; b. Mpls., Dec. 30, 1922; s. Iver Joseph and Gurina Josephine (Hendrickson) S.; m. Audrey Edith Oestreich, July 23, 1949; children—Cynthia, Heather Skaar Catania, Randall, Daniel. B.B.A., U. Minn., 1946; B.S. in Law, Mpls. Coll. Law, 1955; J.D. cum laude, William Mitchell Coll. Law, 1957. Bar: Minn. 1957, U.S. Ct. Appeals (8th cir.) 1957, U.S. Dist Ct. Minn. 1958. Practice law, Mpls., 1957—, ptnr. Skaar & McCullough, Mpls., 1978—. Chmn. bd. trustees Emmanuel Lutheran Ch., Mpls., 1948-52; trustee Calvary Luth. Ch., Golden Valley, Minn., 1966-68; bd. dirs. Mpls. Boys Work, Am. Luth. Ch., Mpls., 1966-68. Served to capt. USN, 1942-46, 50-52; PTO. Decorated D.F.C. (7) Air medal (7). Mem. ABA, Hennepin County Bar Assn., Minn. Bar Assn., Assn. Trial Lawyers Am., Am. Pilots Assn. Republican. Club: Mpls. Athletic. Lodge: Masons. Federal civil litigation, State civil litigation, Family and matrimonial. Home: 1285 Black Oaks Ct Plymouth MN 55447 Office: Skaar & McCullough 1900 First Bank Pl W Minneapolis MN 55402

SKADOW, RONALD ROBERT, lawyer; b. Chgo., Mar. 17, 1942; s. Robert H. and Lois R. (Daumke) S.; m. Patricia A. Coon, May 24, 1968; 1 son, Peter Coon. B.S., Northwestern U., 1963, J.D., 1966. Bar: Ill. 1966. Assoc. Chapman, Pennington, Montgomery, Holmes & Sloan, Chgo., 1967-69; asst. gen. counsel Allied Products Corp., Chgo., 1969-75; assoc. gen. counsel Canteen Corp., Chgo., 1975-86, gen. counsel, 1986—, v.p., 1987—. Vestryman St. Michael's Episcopal Ch., Barrington, Ill., 1983-85, jr. warden, 1986— . Served in USMCR, 1966-72. Mem. ABA, Chgo. Bar Assn. Republican. Club: Meadow (Rolling Meadows, Ill.). General corporate. Home: 254 Donlea Rd Barrington Hills IL 60010 Office: Canteen Corp 1430 Merchandise Mart Chicago IL 60654

SKAFF, ANDREW JOSEPH, lawyer, public utilities, energy and transportation; b. Sioux Falls, S.D., Aug. 30, 1945; s. Andrew Joseph and Alice Maxine (Skaff) S.; m. Lois Carol Phillips, Oct. 4, 1971; children—Amy Phillips, Julie Phillips. B.S. in Bus. Adminstrn, Miami U., Oxford, Ohio, 1967; J.D., U. Toledo, 1970. Bar: Calif. 1971, U.S. Supreme Ct. 1974. Prin., sr. counsel Calif. Public Utilities Commn., 1977; gen. counsel Delta Calif. Industries, Oakland, 1977-82; sec. Delta Calif. Industries, 1978-82; mem. Silver Rosen, Fischer & Stecher, San Francisco, 1982-84; sr. ptnr. Skaff and Anderson, San Francisco, 1984—; officer Delta Calif. Industries and subs. Contbr. articles to legal jours.; contbg. mem. law rev. U. Toledo, 1970. Mem. Calif. Bar Assn., Assn. Transp. Practitioners, Conf. Calif. Pub. Utilities Counsel (Calif. Cogeneration Council and Conf.), San Francisco Bar Assn.,. Administrative and regulatory, Public utilities, General corporate. Office: Skaff & Anderson 353 Sacramento St 19th Floor San Francisco CA 94611

SKAGGS, SANFORD MERLE, lawyer; b. Berkeley, Calif., Oct. 24, 1939; s. Sherman G. and Barbara Jewel (Stinson) S.; m. Sharon Ann Barnes, Sept. 3, 1976; children—Stephen, Paula, Barbara, Darren Peterson. B.A., U. Calif.-Berkeley, 1961, J.D., 1964. Bar: Calif. 1965. Atty. Pacific Gas and Electric Co., San Francisco, 1964-73; gen. counsel Pacific Gas Transmission Co., San Francisco, 1973-75; ptnr. firm Van Voorhis & Skaggs, Walnut Creek, Calif., 1975-85, McCutchen, Doyle, Brown & Enersen, San Francisco and Walnut Creek, 1985—; dir. Civic Bank Commerce, Oakland, Calif. Councilman City of Walnut Creek, 1972-78, mayor, 1974-75, 76-77; bd. dirs. East Bay Mcpl. Utility Dist., 1978—, pres., 1982—; trustee Regional Arts Ctr., Inc., 1980—, Contra Costa County Law Library, 1978—. Mem. Calif. State Bar Assn., Contra Costa County Bar Assn., Calif. Trial Lawyers Assn., Alpha Delta Phi, Phi Delta Phi. Republican. Club: World Trade. State civil litigation,

Local government, Real property. Office: McCutchen Doyle Brown & Enersen Suite 111 1855 Olympic Blvd Walnut Creek CA 94596

SKALLERUP, WALTER THORWALD, JR., lawyer; b. Chgo., Feb. 17, 1921; s. Walter Thorwald and Ruth (White) S.; m. Nancy McGhee Baxter, Dec. 16, 1950 (dec.); children: Paula Skallerup Osborn, Walter Thorwald III, Andrew (dec.), Nancy.; m. Margaret Perkins Bouhafa, Dec. 24, 1983. B.A., Swarthmore Coll., 1942; LL.B., Yale U., 1947. Bar: D.C. 1948. Atty. AEC, 1947-52; partner Volpe, Boskey & Skallerup, Washington, 1953-61; dep. asst. sec. for security policy U.S. Dept. Def. 1962-67; partner Cox, Langford & Brown, Washington, 1968-71; pvt. practice law 1973-81; gen. counsel Dept. Navy, Washington., 1981—; spl. cons. to undersec. state, 1968-69; legal cons. Joint Congressional Com. on Atomic Energy, 1973-74; mem. panel U.S. AEC Atomic Safety and Licensing Bd., 1970-71. Treas. Citizens for Senator Henry M. Jackson campaign, 1971-72; treas., counsel Senator Henry M. Jackson for Pres. Com., 1974-76; bd. mgrs. Swarthmore (Pa.) Coll., 1977—. Served with USNR, 1943-45. Home: 1155 Crest Ln McLean VA 22101 Office: Gen Counsel of Navy Washington DC 20350 *

SKARDA, LYNELL GRIFFITH, lawyer, banker; b. Clovis, N.Mex., Aug. 28, 1915; s. Albert S. and Bertha V. (Taylor) S.; m. Kathryn Burns Skarda, Dec. 25, 1939; children—Jeffrey J., Patricia Lyn, Katrina A., Gregory A.F. B.S., U. Calif., Berkeley, 1937; J.D., Washington & Lee U., 1941. Bar: N.Mex. 1941. Sole practice, Clovis, 1941—; chmn. bd. Citizens Bank of Clovis 1968—; mem. Uniform Jury Instrn. Com., 1963-83. Served to capt. JAG Corps, U.S. Army, World War II. Mem. ABA, N.Mex. Bar Assn., Am. Judicature Soc. General practice, Banking, Contracts commercial. Home: 1512 Fairmont Ct Clovis NM 88101 Office: Citizens Bank Bldg PO Box 400 Clovis NM 88101

SKARE, ROBERT MARTIN, lawyer; b. Fargo, N.D., Jan. 13, 1930; s. Martin Samuel and Verna Adelle (Forseth) S.; m. Marilyn Hutchinson, Aug. 28, 1954; children—Randolph, Robertson, Rodger, Richard. Student St. Olaf Coll., 1947-48; B.S., U. Minn., 1951, J.D., 1954. Bar: Minn. 1956. Assoc., Best and Flanagan, Mpls., 1956-60, ptnr., 1960—, sr. ptnr., 1970—; gen. counsel, v.p. Luth. Brotherhood Mut. Funds, Mpls., 1970—; corporate mcpl. counsel City of Golden Valley (Minn.), 1963—; adv. dir. Norwest Bank Mpls., N.A. Nat. trustee Am. Luth. Ch.; bd. dirs. Search Inst., Mpls, Vesper Soc. Group, San Francisco, 1985—. Served to 1st. lt. CIC, U.S. Army, 1954-56. Recipient Disting. Alumni Service award Sigma Alpha Epsilon Minn., 1978, Pres. award Luth. Human Relations Assn. Am., 1979. Mem. Am. Bar Assn., Minn. State Bar Assn., Hennepin County Bar Assn., Sigma Alpha Epsilon. Lutheran. Clubs: Minneapolis, Golden Valley Country, Torske Klubben. General corporate, Local government, Real property. Home: 109 Paisley Ln Golden Valley MN 55422 Office: 3500 IDS Center Minneapolis MN 55402

SKEEL, PETER BROOKS, lawyer; b. Cleve., Sept. 10, 1954; s. Thomas Ellis and Jane (Henss) S.; m. Susan Joyce Blair, Aug. 22, 1981; 1 child, Robert Ellis. Bar: Pa. 1979, U.S. Dist. Ct. (we. dist.) Pa. 1979, U.S. Ct. Appeals (3d cir.) 1982, U.S. Supreme Ct. 1984. Assoc. Damian and DeLuca, Pitts., 1979-81; law clk. to presiding judge Ct. Common Pleas Allegheny County, Pitts., 1980; trial atty. Allegheny County Pub. Defender's Office, Pitts., 1980-81; assoc. Swensen and Perer, Pitts., 1981-85, ptnr., 1985—; lectr. retail theft diversionary program Allegheny Service Inst., Pitts., 1985—. Bd. dirs. West Pa. Leadership Seminar Hugh O'Brian Youth Found., 1986—; bd. deacons Sunset Hills United Presby. Ch., Pitts., 1985—. Mem. Pa. Bar Assn., Allegheny County Bar Assn., Soc. Vectors (Pitts. bd. dirs. 1982-85, Outstanding Adminstrv. award 1983, Outstanding Youth Program award 1984). Democrat. Avocations: running, squash, golf. Insurance, State civil litigation, Criminal. Home: 335 Jonquil Pl Pittsburgh PA 15228 Office: Swensen & Perer 2201 Lawyers Bldg Pittsburgh PA 15219

SKEFOS, HARRY J(ERRY), lawyer; b. Memphis, Mar. 12, 1951; s. Jerry H. and Katherine (Fillon) S.; m. Catherine Chrysanthe Hetos, June 21, 1975; 1 child, Chrystan Maria. B.S. in Econs., U. Pa., 1972, M.S. in Acctg., 1973; J.D., George Washington U., 1976. Bar: Tenn. 1976, U.S. Dist. Ct. (we. dist.) Tenn. 1980, U.S. Tax Ct. 1981. Assoc. firm Martin, Tate, Morrow & Marston, Memphis, 1979—. Bd. dirs. Annunciation Greek Orthodox Ch., Memphis, 1980—. Mem. ABA, Shelby County Bar Assn., Tenn. Bar Assn. Eastern Orthodox. Corporate taxation, Probate, Real property. Home: 3981 Walnut Grove Memphis TN 38111

SKELLY, JOSEPH GORDON, lawyer; b. Oil City, Pa., June 2, 1935; s. Daniel Joseph and Ruth Mary (Mansfield) S.; m. Barbara Ossoff, Apr. 30, 1966; children—Mame, Meghan, Stephen. B.S., U. Notre Dame, 1957; J.D., Villanova U., 1962. Bar: Pa. 1963, U.S. Supreme Ct. 1967, U.S. Ct. Appeals (3d cir.) 1967, U.S. dist. ct. (ea. dist.) Pa. 1969, U.S. dist. ct. (mid. dist.) Pa. 1970. Assoc., Breene, Frame & Magee, Oil City, Pa., 1963-67; asst. counsel Pa. Catholic Conf., Harrisburg, 1967-68; ptnr. Ball, Skelly, Murren & Connell and predecessor firm Ball & Skelly, Harrisburg, 1968—. Bd. dirs. Keystone council Boy Scouts Am., New Cumberland Youth Baseball Assn.; pres., bd. dirs. Alcoholism Services, Inc., Harrisburg, 1980-82. Served with USNR, 1957-59. Mem. Pa. Bar Assn., Dauphin County Bar Assn., Pa. Trial Lawyers Assn. Republican. Club: Allenberry (Boiling Springs, Pa.). State civil litigation, Federal civil litigation, Administrative and regulatory. Home: 232 Poplar Ave New Cumberland PA 17070 Office: 511 N 2d St PO Box 1108 Harrisburg PA 17108

SKELTON, DARRELL JEAN, lawyer; b. Pratt, Kans., May 4, 1924; s. Roy Daniel and Cora Bell (Pennington) S.; m. Lucille Evelyn McMerney, Mar. 17, 1948; children—Michael D., Darrilyn J. Skelton Girard, Mark Roy, Kathleen Louise Skelton Kuenning, Mary Skelton Perrella, Martha Skelton Langin. Student U. Florence (Italy), 1945; B.S.B.A., U. Denver, 1950, J.D., 1952. Bar: Colo. 1952, U.S. Dist. Ct. Colo. 1953, U.S. Ct. Appeals (10th cir.) 1954, U.S. Supreme Ct. 1957. Ptnr., Tilly and Skelton, Oviatt and O'Dell, Wheat Ridge, Colo., 1966—; mem. Colo. Ho. of Reps., 1964-65. Pres. Colo. Horsemen's Council; instr. Westernaires youth horse mounted drill team, Jefferson County, Colo., 1958—; chmn. Colo. Recreational Trails Com., 1971-75, Jefferson County Open Space Advisement Com., 1973-77; past capt. Jefferson County Sheriff's Mounted Posse. Mem. ABA, Colo. Bar Assn., 1st Jud. Dist. Bar Assn., Denver Bar Assn. Republican. Roman Catholic. Club: Kiwanis (past pres. East Denver, past lt. gov. div. 3). Federal civil litigation, State civil litigation, General corporate. Office: 4350 Wadsworth Suite 320 Wheat Ridge CO 80033

SKENYON, JOHN MICHAEL, lawyer; b. Providence, May 10, 1947; s. John Thomas and Eleanor Mary (Gaudet) S.; m. Margaret Mary McNamara, Oct. 7, 1978; children: Stephanie, Matthew, Heather. BSEE, Cath. U., 1969, JD, 1973. Bar: R.I. 1973, U.S. Dist. Ct. R.I. 1973, Conn. 1974, U.S. Dist. Ct. Conn. 1974, Mass. 1978, U.S. Dist. Ct. Mass. 1978, U.S. Ct. Appeals (1st cir.) 1978, U.S. Ct. Appeals (Fed. cir.) 1982, U.S. Supreme Ct. 1982. Elec. engr. Singer/Link Co., Silver Spring, Mo., 1969-70; assoc. Wooster, Davis & Cifelli, Bridgeport, Conn., 1973-77; assoc. Fish & Richardson, Boston, 1977-84, ptnr., 1985—. Mem. ABA, Conn. Patent Law Assn., Am. Intellectual Property Assn., Boston Patent Law Assn. (treas. 1985, v.p. 1986—, pres.-elect 1987). Patent, Trademark and copyright. Office: Fish & Richardson 1210 Fleet Ctr Providence RI 02903

SKILTON, ROBERT HENRY, law educator, lawyer; b. Phila., Jan. 17, 1909; s. Robert Henry and Margaret Thompson (Beaton) S.; m. Margaret Rittenhouse Neisser, Aug. 22, 1936; children—Robert Henry, III, John Singleton, Margaret S. Prince, David Hamilton. A.B., U. of Pa., 1930, M.A., 1931, LL.B., 1934, Ph.D., 1943. Bar: Pa. 1934, Wis. 1962, U.S. Supreme Ct. 1945. Inst. in English Swarthmore Coll., Pa., 1930-31; assoc. Edmonds Obermayer Rebmann, Phila. Pa., 1934-37; instr. asst. to assoc. prof., Wharton Sch. U. of Pa., 1937-53; assoc. prof. to prof. Law Sch. U. of Wis., Madison, 1953-76; vis. prof. Southern Ill. Law Sch., 1976, 78-79, 80-81, 81-83, McGeorge Sch. of Law, Sacramento, Calif., 1977-78, Williamette Coll. of Law, Salem, Oreg., 1979, Wayne State Law Sch., Detroit, 1981-82, U. of Wis. Law Sch., 1983-84. Author: Government and the Mortgage Debtor, 1929-39, 1943, Industrial Discipline and the Arbitration process, 1952. Editor: Annals on Our Servicemen and Economic Security, 1942. Contbr. articles to prof. jours. Served to lt., USN, 1943-46. Mem. ABA, Wis. Bar Assn. Contracts commercial, Insurance. Home: 4106 Cherokee Dr Madison WI 53711

SKINKER, DONALD RAY, lawyer; b. Richmond, Va., Apr. 4, 1949; s. Benjamin Montague and Mary Gravett (Shackelford) S. BA, U. Richmond, 1971, JD, 1974. Bar: Va. 1974, U.S. Dist. Ct. (ea. dist.) Va. 1974. Spl. asst. Atty. Gen. of Va., Richmond, 1974; sole practice Fredericksburg, Va., 1974—. Mem. Econ. Devel. Commn., Fredericksburg, 1983-86. Mem. Assn. Trial Lawyers Am., Va. State Bar, Va. Trial Lawyers Assn., Fredericksburg Trial Lawyers Assn. General practice, Personal injury, State civil litigation. Home: 1308 William St Fredericksburg VA 22401 Office: 1818 Charles St Fredericksburg VA 22401

SKINNER, JACK MERLE, lawyer; b. Sallisaw, Okla., Aug. 28, 1954; s. Jerald P. and Evelyn Hazel (Siple) S.; m. Vallorie Janice Dipboye, Mar. 24, 1981; children: Jason, Justin. BA in Physics, U. Ark., 1976, BA in Polit. Sci., 1976, JD, 1979. Bar: Ark. 1979, U.S. Dist. Ct. (we. dist.) Ark. 1980. Researcher U. Ark., Fayetteville, 1976-78; sole practice Greenwood, Ark., 1979—. Committeman Sebastian County Rep. Com. Ft. Smith, Ark., 1982—; chmn. Scott-Sebastian Regional Library Bd., Greenwood, 1983—; del. Ark. Rep. Conv., Little Rock, 1984. Named Spl. Judge, Greenwood Mcpl. Ct., Ark., 1980-82. Mem. ABA (committeeman), Ark. Bar Assn.(committeeman), Am. Trial Lawyers Assn., Ark. Trial Lawyers Assn., Alpha Iota Alumni (chartered), Alpha Gamma Rho. State civil litigation, Federal civil litigation, Personal injury. Office: Two Town Sq Greenwood AR 72936

SKINNER, ROBERT STANLEY, lawyer; b. St. Louis, July 12, 1920; s. Stanley David and Hilda (Grothe) S.; m. Mary Jean Elliott, Dec. 3, 1945; children: Jeffrey, Scott, Leslie Anne. AB, Washington U., St. Louis, 1942; LLB, Colo. U., 1946. Bar: Mo. 1942, Colo. 1946, N.Mex. 1947. Assoc. Crampton & Robertson, Raton, N.Mex., 1946-51; ptnr. Crampton, Robertson & Skinner, Raton, 1951-63; sole practice Raton, 1963—; bd. dirs. Blue Cross and Blue Shield, N.Mex. Served as sgt. U.S. Air Corps, 1942-45, ETO. Fellow Am. Bar Found., N.Mex. Bar Found.; mem. ABA, N.Mex. State Bar (bd. bar commrs. 1958-70, pres. 1964-65, Outstanding Mem. 1985). Democrat. Episcopalian. Lodge: Kiwanis (pres. Raton chpt. 1951-52). Real property, General practice. Home: 317 S 7th Raton NM 87740 Office: 210 Cook Ave PO Box 220 Raton NM 87740

SKINNER, SAMUEL KNOX, lawyer; b. Chgo., June 10, 1938; s. Vernon Orlo and Imelda Jane (Curran) S.; m. Susan Ann Thomas; children—Thomas, Steven, Jane. B.S., U. Ill., 1960; J.D., DePaul U., 1966. Bar: Ill. 1966. Asst. U.S. atty. No. Dist. Ill., Chgo., 1968-74, 1st asst. U.S. atty., 1974-75, U.S. atty., 1975-77; ptnr. Sidley & Austin, Chgo., 1977-84; chmn. Regional Transp. Authority, Chgo., 1984. Chmn. Ill. Capitol Devel. Bd, 1977-84. Served as 1st lt. U.S. Army, 1960-61. Mem. ABA, Ill. Bar Assn., Chgo. Bar Assn. Republican. Presbyterian. Clubs: Chgo. Ontwentsia, Shoreacres. Criminal, Federal civil litigation, Antitrust. Office: Sidley & Austin 1 First Nat Plaza Chicago IL 60603

SKINNER, WALTER JAY, judge; b. Washington, Sept. 12, 1927; s. Frederick Snowden and Mary Waterman (Comstock) S.; m. Sylvia Henderson, Aug. 12, 1950; 4 children. A.B., Harvard, 1948; J.D., 1952. Bar: Mass. bar 1952, U.S. Dist. Ct. bar 1954. Assoc. firm Gaston, Snow, Rice & Boyd, Boston, 1952-57; pvt. practice law Scituate, Mass., 1957-63; asst. dist. atty. Plymouth County, 1957-63; town counsel Scituate, 1957-63; asst. atty. gen., chief Criminal Div., Commonwealth of Mass., 1963-65; mem. firm Wardwell, Allen, McLaughlin & Skinner, Boston, 1965-74; U.S. dist. judge Mass., 1974—. Bd. dirs. Douglas A. Thom Clinic, 1966-70. Mem. Am. Bar Assn. Clubs: Longwood Cricket, City; Eight O'Clock (Newton, Mass.). Jurisprudence, Judicial administration. Office: 1503 Post Office and Courthouse Boston MA 02109

SKINNER, WILLIAM POLK, lawyer; b. St. Louis, Apr. 4, 1951; s. Edwin Lemoine Jr. and Grizelda Gilchrist (Polk) S.; m. Karen Kenny, Aug. 2, 1975; children: Suzanne, William. BA, Harvard U., 1972, JD, 1975. Bar: Mo. 1976, D.C. 1976. Assoc. Covington & Burling, Washington, 1976-83, ptnr., 1983—. Federal civil litigation, Insurance, Labor. Home: 5903 Skyline Heights Ct Alexandria VA 22311 Office: Covington & Burling 1201 Pennsylvania Ave NW PO Box 7566 Washington DC 20044

SKIPPER, NATHAN RICHARD, JR., lawyer; b. Wilmington, N.C., May 29, 1934; s. Nathan Richard and Mary Dell (Sidbury) S.; m. Barbara Lynn Renton, Sept. 5, 1959 (div. June 1978); children: Nathan Richard III, Valerie Lynne. AB, Duke U., 1956, JD, 1962; AAS, Oakland Community Coll., 1980. Bar: N.Y. 1963, U.S. Dist. Ct. (so. dist.) N.Y. 1964, Mich. 1971, U.S. Dist. Ct. (ea. dist.) Mich. 1979. Assoc. Cravath, Swaine & Moore, N.Y.C., 1962-70; counsel financings Ford Motor Co., Dearborn, Mich., 1970-78; gen. counsel, sec. Volkswagen Am., Inc., Troy, Mich., 1978—. Served to capt. USAF, 1956-59, USAFR, 1962-75. Mem. ABA, Mich. Bar Assn., N.Y. State Bar Assn., Phi Delta Phi. Club: Grosse Pointe (Mich.) Yacht. Avocations: photography, boating. General corporate, Administrative and regulatory, Other. Office: Volkswagen Am Inc 888 W Big Beaver Troy MI 48007-3951

SKLAMBA, STEPHEN GERARD, lawyer; b. New Orleans, Apr. 9, 1948; s. Carl John and Marjorie Claire (Wimberly) S.; m. Mary Kathleen Caldwell, Aug. 2, 1969; children—Jennifer Elizabeth, Stephanie Marie. Student La. State U., New Orleans, 1966-68; J.D., Tulane U., 1971. Bar: La. 1971. Assoc. Walter F. Marcus, New Orleans, 1971-80; assoc. David L. Campbell, New Orleans, 1980-82; sole practice, New Orleans, 1982-83, Metairie, La., from 1983; now ptnr. firm Sklamba & Thomas, P.C. Mem. ABA. Democrat. Roman Catholic. Banking, Consumer commercial, Insurance. Office: 3017 Kingman St Suite 103 Metairie LA 70002

SKLAR, STANLEY LAWRENCE, judge; b. N.Y.C., Jan. 25, 1932; s. Julius and Rebecca (Skerker) S.; m. Margot Algase, Dec. 10, 1972; 1 child, Deborah. BA, Columbia U., 1953, LLB, 1956. Bar: N.Y. 1957, U.S. Supreme Ct. 1967. Assoc. Zipser & Levitt, N.Y.C., 1957-60, Wolf, Popper, Ross, Wolf & Jones, N.Y.C., 1960-64; assoc. Rubin, Baum, Levin, Constant & Friedman, N.Y.C., 1964-67, ptnr., 1967-76; judge N.Y.C. Civil Ct., 1977-78; acting justice N.Y. State Supreme Ct., N.Y.C., 1978-85, justice, 1986—. Author: Shoplifting: What You Need to Know About the Law, 1982; contbr. articles to profl. jours. Mem. ABA, N.Y. State Bar Assn., Assn. of Bar of City of N.Y., N.Y. County Lawyers Assn., Am. Judicature Soc., Inst. Jud. Adminstrn., Scribes. Office: NY Supreme Ct 60 Centre St New York NY 10007

SKLAR, STANLEY PAUL, lawyer; b. Bklyn., Apr. 25, 1938; s. Hyman and Rae (Winston) S.; m. Sandra Rae Leboe; children—Steven H., Daniel A. B.S., U. Ill., 1960; J.D., Northwestern U., 1964. Bar: Ill. 1964, U.S. Dist. Ct. (no. dist.) Ill. 1964, U.S. Ct. Appeals (7th cir.) 1965, U.S. Supreme Ct. 1968. Assoc. Fein & Pesmen, Chgo., 1964-70; ptnr. Mann, Cogan, Sklar and Lerman, Chgo., 1970-82; mem. Pretzel & Stouffer, Chartered, Chgo., 1982—; instr. real estate Oakton Community Coll.; atty. Northbrook (Ill.) Park Dist., 1973-79. Mem. Northbrook Zoning Bd. Appeals, 1973—; bd. dirs. Constrn. Law Inst., Chgo. Kent Sch. Law; trustee B'nai Joshua Beth Elohim Congregation. Served with USAR, 1960-66. Mem. Recipient Service award Lawyers Title Ins. Corp., 1980; Recognition award Property Mgmt. Counsel Chgo., 1982. Mem. Chgo. Bar Assn. (cert. appreciation 1981), ABA (constrn. industry forum com.), Am. Arbitration Assn. (arbitrator constrn. adv. panel), Chgo. Real Estate Bd., Real Estate Educators Assn., Assn. Ill. Real Estate Educators, Am. Subcontractors Assn. (dir., Appreciation award 1980). Co-author: Illinois Mechanics Liens, Illinois Construction Law, Illinois Mortgage Foreclosures and Workouts, Illinois Construction Lending. Contbr. articles to profl. jours. Construction, Real property. Office: One S Wacker Dr Suite 2500 Chicago IL 60606

SKLAR, STEVEN J., lawyer, legal educator, accountant; b. N.Y.C., Dec. 26, 1956; s. Jerry and Martha (Kolin) S. BS in Econs., U. Pa., 1978, MS in Acctg., 1978; JD, Columbia U., 1981; LLM in Taxation, NYU, 1985. Bar: N.Y. 1982, U.S. Dist. Ct. (so. and ea. dists.) N.Y. 1982, U.S. Tax Ct. 1982. Ptnr. Botein, Hays & Sklar, N.Y.C., 1981-85; prof. NYU Sch. of Law, N.Y.C., 1985—. Editor-in chief Tax Law Rev., 1985—. Mem. ABA (taxation sect. com. real estate tax problems 1982—), N.Y. State Bar Assn. (taxation sect. com. tax acctg. problems 1983—) Bar Assn. City N.Y. Corporate taxation, Personal income taxation, Pension, profit-sharing, and employee benefits.

SKOL, ARMAND GEORGE, lawyer; b. N.Y.C., Aug. 26, 1943; s. Joseph and Doris (Karp) S.; m. Sara Elizabeth Jenkins, Aug. 26, 1967; children—Edward Van Huysen, Caroline Golda. A.B. with honors, Clark U., 1964; J.D., Georgetown U., 1967. Bar: D.C. 1968, Calif. 1974, U.S. Supreme Ct. 1971, U.S. Ct. Appeals (D.C. cir.) 1968, U.S. Dist. Ct. D.C. 1968, U.S. Dist. Ct. (no. dist.) Calif. 1977. Atty. fgn. commerce sect., antitrust div. U.S. Dept. Justice, Washington, 1967-72; counsel boiling water reactor ops. Gen. Electric Co., San Jose, Calif., 1973-78; sr. atty. Crown Zellerbach Corp., San Francisco, 1978-85, assoc. gen. counsel, 1985, assoc. gen. counsel E&J Gallo Winery, 1985—; alt. del. Calif. State Bar Conv., 1982. Served with USAR, 1969. Recipient awards Lawyers' Coop. Pub. Assn., 1966, 67. Mem. ABA, State Bar Calif. (sec. 1981-84, mem. exec. com. 1981—, chmn. antitrust and trade regulation law sect. 1984-85). Jewish. Antitrust, Labor. Home: 1206 St Francis Ave Modesto CA 95356

SKOLAN-LOGUE, AMANDA NICOLE, lawyer, consultant; b. Los Angeles, Feb. 19, 1954; d. Carl Charles and Estelle (Lubin) Skolan; m. James Edward Logue, Dec. 10, 1983. BS, U. Calif., Los Angeles, 1973; MBA, U. So. Calif., 1976; JD, Southwestern U., Los Angeles, 1982. Bar: Calif. 1982, U.S. Dist. Ct. (cen., no. and ea. dists.) Calif. 1982, N.Y. 1986. Sr. internal cons. Getty Oil Co., Los Angeles, 1976-80; atty. litigation ACLU of So. Calif., Los Angeles, 1982-83; corp. atty. Am. Can Co., Greenwich, Conn., 1983-86; assoc. Shereff, Friedman, Hoffman & Goodman, N.Y.C., 1986—. Mem. ABA, Westchester-Fairfield County Corp. Counsel Assn., Soc. Creative Anachronism. Republican. General corporate, Securities. Home: 33 Musket Ridge Rd New Fairfield CT 06812 Office: Shereff Friedman Hoffman & Goodman 919 3d Ave New York NY 10022

SKOLER, DANIEL LAWRENCE, lawyer, adminstrv. law judge, educator; b. Newark, Jan. 15, 1929; s. Arthur Emil and Marian June (Bardack) S.; m. Shirley Weiss, Sept. 20, 1953; children—Glen David, Michael James, Deborah. Student Rutgers U., 1945-47, U. Chgo., 1947-49; J.D. cum laude, Harvard U., 1952. Bar: N.Y. 1953, Ill. 1963, D.C. 1968. Assoc. Willkie Farr Gallagher Walton & Fitzgibbon, N.Y.C., 1955-59; staff atty. U.S. Industries, Inc., N.Y.C., 1959-61; asst. dir. Am. Judicature Soc., Chgo., 1961-62; exec. dir. Nat. Council Juvenile Ct. Judges, Chgo., 1962-65; dir. Commn. on Correctional Facilities and Services ABA, 1971-75, Commn. on Mentally Disabled, Washington, 1976-77; dir. public service activities ABA, 1977-80; dir. office law enforcement assistance Law Enforcement Assistance Adminstrn., Dept. Justice, Washington, 1965-71; vis. fellow Nat. Inst. Law Enforcement and Criminal Justice, 1975-76; chmn. Trademark and Appeal Bd., Dept. Commerce, Washington, 1982-84, dep. asst. commr. for Trademarks, 1984-86 ; dep. assoc. commr. Hearings and Appeals, Social Security Adminstrn., Washington, 1980-82; adj. prof. Georgetown U., George Washington U., American U.; mem. Commn. on Accreditation for Corrections, 1974-78, chmn., 1976-77. Dir. Edn. and training Fed. Jud. Ctr., 1986—, Am. Justice Inst., 1978-80. Recipient Certificate of Commendation Atty. Gen. U.S., 1968; Meritorious Service award Nat. Council Juvenile Ct. Judges, 1965; Silver medal Dept. Commerce, 1983. Fellow Nat. Acad. Public Adminstrn.; mem. ABA Commn. on Legal Problems of the Elderly. Author: Organizing the Non System: Government Structuring of Criminal Justice Services, 1977. Administrative and regulatory, Jurisprudence, Trademark and copyright. Home: 7036 Buxton Terr West Bethesda MD 20817

SKOLNICK, JEROME H., legal educator; b. 1931. B.B.A., CCNY, 1952, M.A., 1953; Ph.D., Yale U., 1957. Research assoc. Yale U., New Haven, 1956-60, asst. prof., 1960-62; asst. prof. U. Calif.-Berkeley Law Sch., 1962-67, prof., 1970—; vis. assoc. prof. NYU, 1966; vis. prof. U. Denver, 1967; assoc. prof. U. Chgo., 1967-69; prof. U. Calif.-San Diego, 1969-70; dir. Ctr. Study of Law and Soc., 1972—; cons. Bd. dirs. Pres.'s Commn. on Causes and Prevention of Violence, 1968-69. Carnegie fellow, 1956-66; Guggenheim fellow, 1980. Mem. Am. Criminol. Assn., ACLU, Law and Soc. Assn. (trustee). Author: (with D. Bayley) The New Blue Line, 1986, Justice Without Trial, 1966; House of Cards, 1978; (with R.D. Schwartz) Society and the Legal Order, 1970. Legal education. Office: U Calif Berkeley Law Sch 225 Boalt Hall Berkeley CA 94720

SKOLNICK, S. HAROLD, lawyer; b. Woonsocket, R.I., June 17, 1915; s. David and Elsie (Silberman) S.; m. Shirley Marshall. A.B. cum laude, Amherst Coll., 1936; J.D., Boston U., 1940. Bar: R.I. 1940, D.C. 1947, U.S. Supreme Ct. 1946, Fla. 1952, U.S. Dist. Ct. (so. dist.) Fla. 1953, U.S. Ct. Appeals (5th cir.) 1960, U.S. Ct. Appeals (11th cir.) 1981. Atty., Dept. War, Washington, 1940-42; asst. gen. counsel, asst. chief legal dept. Office Chief Ordnance, Dept. Army, Washington, 1947-50; assoc. Francis I. McCanna, Providence, 1951-52; ptnr. French & Skolnick, Miami, 1953-60; sole practice, Miami, 1961—. Trustee Beth David Congregation. Served to lt. col. U.S. Army, 1942-47. Mem. ABA, R.I. Bar Assn., D.C. Bar Assn., Dade County Bar Assn., Am. Judicature Soc., Am. Def. Preparedness Assn., Estate Planning Council of Greater Miami. Clubs: Mason, Shriners. Insurance, Probate. Home: 6521 SW 122 St Miami FL 33156 Office: Suite 1531 AI duPont Bldg 169 E Flagler St Miami FL 33131

SKOLNIK, BRADLEY WILLIAM, lawyer; b. Benton Harbor, Mich., Nov. 27, 1955; s. Louis S. and Faye (Kritt) S.; m. Gayle Lynn Smith, Oct. 9, 1982. BA in Polit. Sci., Mich. State U., 1978; JD, Ind. U., 1981. Bar: Ind. 1981, U.S. Dist. Ct. (so. dist.) Ind. 1981, U.S Ct. Appeals (7th cir.) 1983. Law clk. to presiding justice Ind. Ct. Appeals, Indpls., 1981-82; assoc. Bayh, Tabbert and Capehart, Indpls., 1982-86, Dann, Pecar, Newman, Talesnick & Kleiman, Indpls., 1986—. State vol. coordinator com. Bowen for Sec. of State, 1986; v.p. 4th Dist. Rep. Cen. Com., Mich., 1976-77. Mem. ABA, Ind. Bar Assn. (ho. of dels. 1985—), Indpls. Bar. Assn., Hon. Order Ky. Cols. Jewish. State civil litigation, Federal civil litigation, General practice. Home: 3401 Bando Ct W Indianapolis IN 46220 Office: Dann Pecar Newman Talesnick One American Sq Suite 2300 PO Box 82008 Indianapolis IN 46282

SKOLROOD, ROBERT KENNETH, lawyer; b. Stockton, Ill., May 17, 1928; s. Myron Clifford and Lola Mae (Lincicum) S.; m. Marilyn Jean Riegel, June 18, 1955; children: Cynthia, Mark, Kent, Richard. BA, Ohio Wesleyan U., 1952; JD, U. Chgo., 1957. Bar: Ill. 1957, U.S. Dist. Ct. (no. dist.) Ill. 1959, Okla. 1981, U.S. Ct. Appeals (7th cir.) 1970, U.S. Dist. Ct. (no. dist. Okla.) 1982, U.S. Supreme Ct. 1982, U.S. Ct. Appeals (10th cir.) 1983, U.S. Ct. Dist. (so. dist.) Ala. 1985, U.S. Ct. Dist. (so. dist.) N.Y. 1985, U.S. Dist. Ct. (ea. and we. dists.) Va. 1985, U.S. Ct. Appeals (8th cir.) 1985, U.S. Dist. Ct. D.C. 1987, U.S. Ct. Appeals (11th cir.) 1987. Ptnr. Reno, Zahm, Folgate, Skolrood, Lindberg & Powell, Rockford, Ill., 1957-80; prof. Ohio Wesleyan U. Coburn Sch. Law; prof. Oral Roberts U., Tulsa, 1980-81, exec. dir., gen. counsel Nat. Legal Found., Virginia Beach, Va., 1984—. Contbr. articles to legal jours. Pres., John Ericsson Rep. Club, 1964; trustee No. Ill. conf. United Meth. Ch., 1957-74, chmn., 1972-74; pres. Ill. Home and Aid Soc. Served with U.S. Army, 1952-54, Korea. Fellow Am. Coll. Trial Lawyers; mem. ABA, Ill. Bar Assn., Okla. Bar Assn., Winnebago County Bar Assn., Assn. Trial Lawyers Am., Va. Trial Lawyers Assn., Tex. Trial Lawyers Assn., Ill. Trial Lawyers Assn., Okla. Trial Lawyers Assn., Nat. Assn. Coll. and Univ. Attys., Christian Legal Soc., Kappa Delta Pi, Pi Sigma Kappa. Mem. Evangelical Free Ch. Civil rights, Federal civil litigation, Jurisprudence. Home: 4800 Orchard Ln Virginia Beach VA 23464 Office: Nat Legal Found 6477 College Park Sq Suite 306 Virginia Beach VA 23464

SKOPIL, OTTO RICHARD, JR., judge; b. Portland, Oreg., June 3, 1919; s. Otto Richard and Freda Martha (Boetticher) S.; m. Janet Rae Lundy, July 27, 1956; children: Otto Richard III, Casey Robert, Shannon Ida, Molly Jo. BA in Econs., Willamette U., 1941, LLB, JD (hon.), 1946, LLD (hon.), 1983. Bar: Oreg. 1946, IRS, U.S. Treasury Dept., U.S. Dist. Ct. Oreg., U.S. Ct. Appeals (9th cir.), U.S. Supreme Ct. 1946. Assoc. Skopil & Skopil, 1946-51; ptnr. Williams, Skopil, Miller & Beck (and predecessors), Salem, Oreg., 1951-72; judge U.S. Dist. Ct., Portland, 1972-79; chief judge U.S. Dist. Ct., 1976-79; judge U.S. Ct. Appeals (9th cir.), Portland, 1979—; chmn. com. adminstrn. of fed. magistrate system U.S. Jud. Conf.; co-founder Oreg. chpt. Am. Leadership Forum. Hi-Y adviser Salem YMCA, 1951-52; appeal agt. SSS, Marion County (Oreg.) Draft Bd., 1953-66; master of ceremonies 1st Gov.'s Prayer Breakfast for State Oreg., 1959; mem. citizens adv. com., City

of Salem, 1970-71; chmn. Gov.'s Com. on Staffing Mental Instns., 1969-70; pres., bd. dirs. Marion County Tb and Health Assn., 1958-61; bd. dirs. Willamette Valley Camp Fire Girls, 1946-56, Internat. Christian Leadership, 1959, Fed. Jud. Ctr., 1979; trustee Willamette U., 1969-71; elder Mt. Park Ch., 1979-81. Served to lt. USNR, 1942-46. Recipient Oreg. Legal Citizen of Yr. award, 1986. Mem. ABA, Oreg. Bar Assn. (bd. govs.), Marion County Bar Assn., Am. Judicature Soc., Oreg. Assn. Def. Counsel (dir.), Def. Research Inst., Assn. Ins. Attys. U.S. and Can. (Oreg. rep. 1970), Internat. Soc. Barristers, Prayer Breakfast Movement (fellowship council). Clubs: Salem, Exchange (pres. 1947), Illahe Hills Country (pres., dir. 1964-67). Jurisprudence. Office: Pioneer Courthouse Portland OR 97204

SKORA, SUSAN SUNDMAN, lawyer; b. Chgo., Jan. 5, 1947; d. Gordon Manley and Julia Walker (Firebaugh) Sundman; m. Alan Patrick Skora, May 1, 1977. AB, U. Ill., Chgo., 1970; JD, Ill. Inst. Tech., 1980. Bar: Ill. 1980, Mich. 1983, U.S. Dist. Ct. (we. dist.) Mich. 1983. Dir. Chgo. programs U. Ill. Found., 1973-79; asst. dir. bus. affairs U. of Ill., Chgo., 1980-81, exec. asst., exec. v.p., 1981-83; 2d v.p. Nat. Bank of Detroit, Grand Rapids, 1983—; v.p., dept. head bus. devel. Union Bank, Grand Rapids, 1986—. Author: Cuneen Linguist, 1975. Bd. dirs. Kent County Aux. to Osteopathic Physicians and Surgeons, Grand Rapids, 1984-86; v.p. West Mich. U. Ill. Alumni Club, Grand Rapids, 1983-86; mem. Womens Symphony Com., Grand Rapids, 1986—. Mem. ABA, Mich. Bar Assn., Grand Rapids Bar Assn., Women Lawyers of Mich. Club: University (Grand Rapids). Avocations: gardening, fishing. Banking, Estate planning, Probate. Home: 2424 Village Dr Grand Rapids MI 49506 Office: Nat Bank of Detroit 200 Ottawa Ave NW Grand Rapids MI 49503

SKORD, JENNIFER LYNNE, patent lawyer; b. Chgo., Oct. 3, 1948; d. Joseph and Jean (Bobeyka) S. BA in Chemistry, Bradley U., 1970; cert. of summer law study, U. Exeter, Eng., 1978; JD, DePaul U., 1980. Bar: Ill. 1980, U.S. Dist. Ct. (no. dist.) Ill. 1980, U.S. Patent Office 1982, U.S. Ct. Appeals (D.C. cir.) 1983, U.S. Supreme Ct. 1984, Ind. 1985, U.S. Dist. Ct. (no. dist.) Ind. 1985. Assoc. patent counsel Ladas & Parry, Chgo., 1980-83; patent counsel Eltech Systems, Chardon, Ohio, 1983-84; patent atty. Miles Labs., Elkhart, Ind., 1984-86, W.R. Grace & Co., Duncan, S.C., 1986—. Mem. ABA, Ill. Bar Assn., Am. Intellectual Property Law Assn., Phi Alpha Delta. Avocations: aerobics, lifting weights. Patent. Home: 201 Powell Mill Rd Apt L-208 Spartanburg SC 29301 Office: WR Grace & Co Cryovac Div PO Box 464 (Legal Div/Patent Dept) Duncan SC 29334

SKORDAS, GREGORY G., lawyer; b. Salt Lake City, July 15, 1957; s. William Gene and Beverly (Butler) S.; m. Michelle Carter, Jan. 29, 1983 (div.); 1 child, Nicolas James; m. Charlotte Miller, Dec. 6, 1986. BS in Metall. Engring., U. Utah, 1979, JD, 1982. Bar: Utah 1982, U.S. Ct. Appeals (10th cir.) 1982, U.S. Tax Ct. 1985. Assoc. Barber, Verhock & Yocom, Salt Lake City, 1982-85, Salt Lake Legal Defenders, 1985—; adj. prof. law U. Utah, Salt Lake City, 1985—; judge Small Claims Cir. Ct., Salt Lake City, 1983—; judge, coach Statewide Mock Trial Competition, Salt Lake City, 1983—. Mem. ABA, Utah State Bar (chairperson criminal law sect. 1985-86, sec., treas. young lawyer's sect.), Salt Lake County Bar Assn., U.S. Ski Patrol. Democrat. Criminal. Office: Salt Lake Legal Defenders 333 S 200 E Salt Lake City UT 84111

SKOTYNSKY, WALTER JOHN, lawyer; b. Youngstown, Ohio, June 28, 1946; s. Walter and Kathleen Marie (Adams) S.; m. Sandra Lee Wiebeck, July 17, 1971; 1 child, Nicholas James. BSME, U. Mich., 1971; JD, U. Toledo, 1976. Bar: Ohio 1976, Mich. 1979. Engr. Andersons, Toledo, 1965-68, Libbey-Owens-Ford, Toledo, 1971-73; sole practice Toledo, 1976—; instr. real estate law U. Toledo, U. Mich., Ann Arbor, Bowling Green (Ohio) State U., Davis Bus. Coll., Toledo, 1976-80. Mem. Mich. Bar Assn., Ohio Bar Assn., Toledo Bar Assn., Lucas County Bar Assn.. U. Mich. ALumni Toledo (pres. 1986—). Republican. Roman Catholic. Clubs: U. Mich. Alumni Toledo (pres. 1986—); Ukranian/Am. Citizens (Toledo). Family and matrimonial, General practice, Real property. Home: 4830 Oakridge Dr Toledo OH 43623 Office: 1018 Adams St Toledo OH 43624

SKULINA, THOMAS RAYMOND, lawyer; b. Cleve., Sept. 14, 1933; s. John J. and Mary B. (Vesely) S. A.B., John Carroll U., 1955; J.D., Case Western Res. U., 1959, LL.M., 1962. Bar: Ohio 1959, U.S. Supreme Ct. 1964, ICC 1965. Ptnr. Skulina & Stringer, Cleve., 1967-72, Riemer Oberdank & Skulina, Cleve., 1978-81, Skulina, Fillo, Walters & Negrelli, 1981-86, Skulina & McKeon, Cleve., 1986—; atty. Penn Cen. Transp. Co., Cleve., 1960-65, asst. gen. atty., 1965-78, trial counsel, 1965-76; with Consol. Rail Corp., 1976-78; dir. High Temperature Systems, Inc., Active Chem. Systems, Inc.; tchr. comml. law Practicing Law Inst., N.Y.C., 1970. Contbr. articles to legal jours. Income tax and fed. fund coordinator Warrensville Heights, Ohio, 1970-77; spl. counsel City of N. Olmstead, Ohio, 1971-75; pres. Civil Service Commn., Cleve., 1977-86, referee, 1986—, fact-finder SERB, Ohio, 1986—; spl. counsel Ohio Atty. Gen., 1983—. Served with U.S. Army, 1959. Mem. Nat. Assn. R.R. Trial Counsel, Internat. Assn. Law and Sci., ABA, Cleve. Bar Assn., Ohio Bar Assn. (bd. govs. litigation sect. 1986—), Fed. Bar Assn., Pub. Law Practitioners Assn., Ohio Trial Lawyers Assn., Pub. Sector Labor Relations Assn. Democrat. Roman Catholic. Clubs: River Run Racquet, Lakewood Country. Federal civil litigation, State civil litigation, Railroad. Home: 3162 W 165th St Cleveland OH 44111 Office: Skulina & McKeon 709 Ohio Savings Plaza 1801 E 9th St Cleveland OH 44113

SKURET, DANIEL D., lawyer; b. Derby, Conn., Oct. 15, 1942; s. Daniel D. and Helen (Kolakowski) S.; m. Marcia E. Hine, Oct. 16, 1965; children—Lisa H., Daniel D. III, Patrick D. B.A., Fairfield U., Conn., 1964; J.D., U. Conn., 1967. Bar: Conn. 1967, U.S. Dist. Ct. Conn. 1982. Assoc. Edward J. Donohue, Atty., Derby, 1967-71; pres. Law Offices of Daniel D. Skuret, P.C., Ansonia, Conn., 1971—. Mem. Assn. Trial Lawyers Am., Conn. Trial Lawyers Assn., Nat. Criminal Def. Lawyers Assn., Conn. Bar Assn., Valley Bar Assn. Democrat. Roman Catholic. Personal injury, Criminal, Real property. Home: 2 Elmwood Dr Seymour CT 06483 Office: 215 Division St PO Box 158 Ansonia CT 06401

SLABACH, STEPHEN HALL, lawyer; b. Oklahoma City, Nov. 15, 1934; s. Carl Edward and Alvine A. (Woellner) S.; m. Elizabeth Havard Cartwright, Feb. 15, 1958; children—Elizabeth Havard, Stephen Edward, William Cartwright. B.S.M.E., Northwestern U., 1957; postgrad. George Washington U. Sch. Law, 1957-59; LL.B., Stanford U., 1961. Bar: Calif. 1962, U.S. Dist. Ct. (no. dist.) Calif. 1962, U.S. Ct. Appeals (9th cir.) 1973, U.S. Supreme Ct. 1976. Law clk. to judge Calif. First Dist. Ct. Appeal, San Francisco, 1961-62; assoc. Cooley, Crowley, Gather, Godward, Castro & Huddleson, San Francisco, 1962-65; assoc. Cushing, Cullinan, Hancock & Rothert, San Francisco, 1965-73, ptnr., 1973-75; sole practice, Burlingame, Calif., 1975—; legal aid vol. San Mateo County; mem. San Mateo County Law Library Com.; bd. dirs. Pacific Locomotive Assn., 1980-82, gen. counsel, 1980—. Bd. dirs. Notre Dame High Sch., Belmont, Calif., 1976-84, pres., bd., 1981-82. Mem. State Bar Calif., ABA, Am. Judicature Soc. Republican. Episcopalian. Club: Kiwanis (Burlingame). Estate planning, General business. Office: 20 Park Rd Suite H Burlingame CA 94010

SLADE, GEORGE KEMBLE, JR., business educator, lawyer; b. Bridgeton, N.J., July 16, 1949; s. George Kemble Sr. and Leona (Fleetwood) S. Student, City of London Coll., 1970; BA, Lehigh U., 1971; JD, Temple U., 1977. Bar: N.J. 1977, U.S. Dist. Ct. N.J. 1977. Assoc. Law Offices of Arnold Bauer, Bridgeton, N.J., 1977; sole practice Vineland, N.J., 1978-85; capt., bus. instr. Valley Forge Mil. Acad., Wayne, Pa., 1985-86; of counsel Law Offices of Seymour Wasserstrum, Vineland, 1986—; adj. prof. bus. law Glassboro (N.J.) State Coll., 1983-84; arbitrator U.S. Dist. Ct. N.J., 1985—. Mem. ABA, N.J. Bar Assn., Cumberland County Bar Assn. Republican. Presbyterian. Avocations: music, arts. General practice. Home: 312 Mulberry St Millville NJ 08332

SLADE, JEFFREY CHRISTOPHER, lawyer; b. Los Angeles, June 4, 1946; s. Sherman Richard and Afton Audre (Johnson) S.; m. Ruth Anne Diem, Mar. 5, 1983; 1 child, Katharine Anne. BA, Pomona Coll., 1967; MDiv., Union Theol. Sem., 1970; JD cum laude, NYU, 1976. Bar: N.Y. 1977, U.S. Dist. Ct. (so. and ea. dists.) N.Y. 1978, U.S. Dist. Ct. (no. dist.) Tex. 1978, Tex. 1979, U.S. Ct. Appeals (5th cir.) 1979, U.S. Dist. Ct. (ea. dist.) Ky. 1985, U.S. Ct. Appeals (2d and 3rd cirs.) 1985, U.S. Supreme Ct. 1985, U.S. Ct. Appeals (6th cir.) 1986. Law clk. to presiding justice U.S. Dist. Ct. (so. dist.), N.Y.C., 1976-78; assoc. Akin, Gump, Strauss, Hauer & Feld, Dallas, 1978-80, Paul, Weiss, Rifkind et al, N.Y.C., 1980-84; ptnr. Meister Leventhal & Slade, N.Y.C., 1984—. Mem. ABA, N.Y. State Bar Assn. Federal civil litigation, State civil litigation, Criminal. Office: Meister Leventhal & Slade 777 Third Ave New York NY 10017

SLADKUS, HARVEY IRA, lawyer; b. Bklyn., Mar. 5, 1929; s. Samuel Harold and Charlotte Dorothy Sladkus; m. Harriet Marcia Barske, Dec. 31, 1940 (div.); children—Steven David, Jeffrey Brandon; m. Roberta Frances Pope, Oct. 24, 1986. A.B., Syracuse U., 1950; J.D., N.Y.U., 1961. Bar: N.Y. 1962, Conn. 1981, U.S. Supreme Ct. 1967. Assoc. Morris Ploscowe, N.Y.C., 1961-66; sole practice, N.Y.C., 1966-67; ptnr. Dweck & Sladkus and Feiden, Dweck & Sladkus, N.Y.C., 1968—; lectr. family and matrimonial law; small claims ct. arbitrator N.Y.C. civil ct. 1977—. Served to 1st lt. U.S. Army 1952-53; Korea. Decorated Bronze Star medal; recipient George Washington Honor medal Freedoms Found. Valley Forge, 1953. Mem. ABA, N.Y. State Bar Assn., Assn. Bar City N.Y., Conn. Bar Assn., Am. Acad. Matrimonial Lawyers, Am. Judges Assn., Am. Arbitration Assn. (nat. panel arbitrators). Jewish. Contbg. author: Practice under New York's Matrimonial Law, 1971-79; editor-in-chief Family Law Practice, 1982; contbr. articles on family and matrimonial law to legal publs. Family and matrimonial, State civil litigation, Federal civil litigation. Office: 295 Madison Ave New York NY 10017

SLAGLE, JAMES WILLIAM, lawyer; b. Marion, Ohio, Nov. 8, 1955; s. Gene and Emily Frances (Weber) S.; m. Heidi Ann Schweinfurth, Feb. 12, 1983. BA in Polit. Sci., Ohio State U., 1977, JD, 1980. Bar: Ohio 1980, U.S. Dist. Ct. (no. dist.) Ohio 1982. Sole practice Marion, 1980—; spl. counsel Ohio Atty. Gen., Cols, 1984—; pros. atty. Marion County, 1985—. Dist. chmn. Evergreen Dist. Boy Scouts Am., Marion and Morrow County, 1986—. Mem. ABA, Ohio Bar Assn., Marion County Bar Assn., Ohio Pros. Attys. Assn. Democrat. Methodist. Local government, Criminal, General practice. Home: 380 Bradford St Marion OH 43302 Office: Marion County Pros Atty Courthouse Marion OH 43302

SLANINGER, FRANK PAUL, lawyer; b. Lake City, Iowa, Sept. 19, 1944; s. Paul Vincent and Loveda Laura (Peterson) S. B.A., Loras Coll., Dubuque, Iowa, 1966; J.D., Harvard U., 1969. Bar: Colo. 1970, U.S. dist. ct. Colo. 1970, U.S. Ct. Appeals (10th cir.) 1970, U.S. Supreme Ct. 1973. Assoc. Schwartz & Snyder, Denver, 1970-73; staff atty. SEC, Denver, 1973-75; estate planner Mfrs. Life Ins. Co., Denver, 1976; sole practice, Denver, 1977—; co-pres. Champagne, 1983-84; bd. dirs. AMC Cancer Research Ctr. fund raiser, 1983—. Active Am. Cancer Soc. Mem. ABA, Colo. Bar Assn., Denver Bar Assn., Colo. Assn. Trial Lawyers. Democrat. Roman Catholic. Clubs: Schussbaumer Ski, Fiddlesteppers Square Dance (Denver). General practice, Personal injury, Real property. Office: 1776 S Jackson Suite 800 Denver CO 80210

SLATER, BRENT R., lawyer; b. Dexter, Maine, Mar. 10, 1947; s. George R. and Janice M. (Dorr) S.; 1 child, Daniel R. BS, U. Maine, Orono, 1970; JD, U. Maine, Portland, 1973. Bar: Maine, U.S. Dist. Ct. Maine. Ptnr. Slater & Austin, Dexter, 1974-83, Linscott & Slater, Bangor, Maine, 1983—. Mem. ABA, Maine Bar Assn., Assn. Trial Lawyers Am., Maine Trial Lawyers Assn. General practice, Real property, General corporate. Office: Linscott & Slater 82 Columbia Bangor ME 04401

SLATER, JILL SHERRY, lawyer; b. N.Y.C., Apr. 8, 1943. BA with distinction and honors, Cornell U., 1964; JD cum laude, Harvard U., 1968. Bar: Mass. 1968, Calif. 1970, U.S. Dist. Ct. (cen. dist.) Calif. 1970, U.S. Ct. Appeals (9th cir.) 1974, U.S. Dist. Ct. (so. dist.) Calif. 1977, U.S. Dist. Ct. (ea. dist.) Calif. 1984, U.S. Dist. Ct. (no. dist) Calif. 1985, U.S. Ct. Appeals (Fed. cir.) 1982, U.S. Supreme Ct. 1986. Atty. Boston Redevel. Authority, 1968-70; assoc. Latham & Watkins, Los Angeles, 1970-78, ptnr., 1978—. Woodrow Wilson fellow, 1964. Mem. ABA, Los Angeles County Bar Assn. (trial lawyers exec. com.), Am. Intellectual Property Law Assn., Assn. Bus. Trial Lawyers, Phi Beta Kappa. Federal civil litigation, State civil litigation, Trademark and copyright. Office: Latham & Watkins 555 S Flower St Los Angeles CA 90071-2466

SLATTERY, DAVID EDMUND, lawyer, consultant; b. Omaha, Feb. 9, 1956; s. Timothy Lee and Thelma Elizabeth (Haggarty) S.; m. Elizabeth Martin Danberg, Dec. 26, 1981; children: David, Erin. BBA, Creighton U., 1978, JD, 1981. Assoc. Knoles & Assocs., Omaha, 1981-82; pres. ComFed Capital Corp., Omaha, 1982—, also bd. dirs.; bd. dirs. C.F. Realty Investors, Omaha, 1982—, pres. 1983—. Co-author How to Operate a Broker/Dealer Firm, 1982. Mem. Ak-Sar-Ben Floor Com., Omaha, 1985—; bd. dirs. sch. bus. Creighton U., Omaha, 1983—. Mem. ABA, Nebr. Bar Assn., Omaha Bar Assn., Real Estate Securities and Syndication Inst. (pres. Nebr. chpt. 1986—). Republican. Roman Catholic. Club: Omaha Country. Lodge: Rotary. Real property, Securities, Personal income taxation. Home: 9912 Harney Pkwy N Omaha NE 68114 Office: ComFed Capital Corp 2428 S 130th Circle Omaha NE 68144

SLATUS, ROBERT EARL, lawyer; b. Bklyn., Dec. 7, 1943; s. Arthur S. and Anne (Mallenbaum) S.; m. Karen Janet Rubin, Aug. 17, 1975; children: Jeffrey Charles, David Jonathan, Judith Deborah. BA, Hunter Coll., 1965; JD, Bklyn. Law Sch., 1973. Bar: NY. 1973, U.S. Dist. Ct. (ea. and so. dist.) 1974, U.S. Ct. Appeals (2d cir.) 1974, U.S. Ct. Appeals (6th cir.) 1975. Assoc. Blecher and Mendel, N.Y.C., 1973-77; sole practice N.Y.C., 1977-86; ptnr. Slatus & Schwartz, N.Y.C., 1986—; legal counsel to Senator Albert Lewis, N.Y., 1973. Trustee Community Assn. West Hempstead, N.Y., 1986, pres. 1987—. Democrat. Jewish. Immigration, naturalization, and customs. Home: 719 Wildwood Rd West Hempstead NY 11552 Office: Slatus & Schwartz 50 E 42d St New York NY 10017

SLAUGHTER, DAVID ALAN, lawyer; b. Kingsport, Tenn., July 24, 1955; s. George Harold and Carrie Sue (Robinette) S.; m. Renae Millstid, May 25, 1985. BA magna cum laude, U. Houston, 1977, JD with honors, 1980. Bar: Tex. 1980, U.S. Dist. Ct. (so. dist.) Tex. 1981, U.S. Ct. Appeals (5th and 11th cirs.) 1981, U.S. Dist. Ct. (ea. dist.) Tex. 1984. Ptnr. McConnico, Houchins, Slaughter & Purcell, Houston, 1981-84; sole practice Texas City, 1984-85; assoc. Krist, Gunn, Weller, Neumann & Morrison, Houston, 1985—. Mem. ABA, Am. Trial Lawyers Assn., State Bar Tex., Tex. Trial Lawyers Assn., Bay Area Bar Assn., Phi Kappa Phi, Phi Delta Phi. Democrat. Personal injury, State civil litigation, Workers' compensation. Home: 18519 Egret Bay Blvd 1405 Houston TX 77058 Office: Krist Gunn et al 17050 El Camino Houston TX 77058

SLAUGHTER, DAVID WAYNE, lawyer; b. Rexburg, Idaho, Nov. 4, 1951; s. Richard Del and Ruth Julienne (Hill) S.; m. Connie Jo Brower, July 2, 1975; children: Shad, R. Colby, Nathan. BA magna cum laude, Brigham Young U., 1975, JD magna cum laude, 1981. Bar: Utah 1981, U.S. Dist. Ct. Utah 1881, U.S. Ct. Appeals (10th cir.) 1981, U.S. Ct. Appeals (D.C. cir.) 1982. Law clk. to presiding judge U.S. Ct. Appeals (D.C. cir.), 1981-82; assoc. Snow, Christensen & Martineau, Salt Lake City, 1982-86, ptnr., 1986—. Served to 1st lt. U.S. Army, 1975-78. Mem. ABA, Utah Bar Assn., Salt Lake County Bar Assn. Republican. Mormon. Avocations: hiking, photography, raquetball. Insurance, Federal civil litigation, State civil litigation. Office: Snow Christensen & Martineau 10 Exchange Pl 11th Floor Salt Lake City UT 84110

SLAUGHTER, MARSHALL GLENN, lawyer; b. Wauchula, Fla., Jan. 15, 1940; s. Glenn S. and Carrie Melissa (Shelfer) S.; m. Marsha Ann Miller, May 30, 1981 (div. June 1982); children: Glenn Scott II, Todd Harvey. BBA, U. Fla., 1961; JD, Stetson U., 1979. Bar: Fla. 1979, U.S. Dist. Ct. (mid. dist.) Fla. 1980. Pres. Slaughter Motor Sales, Wauchula, 1965-77; assoc. McDaniel & Smith, Lakeland, Fla., 1979-80, Edmund & McDaniel, Bartow, Fla., 1980-84; sole practice Bartow, 1984—. Served to lt. USNR, 1961-65. Mem. Fla. Bar Assn. (evidence com. 1982—, computer law com. 1984—), Criminal Def. Lawyers Assn., Polk County Trial Lawyers Assn. Republican. Baptist. Lodge: Elks. Avocations: scuba diving, travel. Family and matrimonial, Criminal, Juvenile. Home: 316 Carlisle Rd Lakeland FL 33803 Office: 245 S Central Ave Bartow FL 33830

SLAVIN, FRANCIS JOHN, JR., lawyer; b. Olean, N.Y., Oct. 1, 1942; s. Francis John and Justina Grace (Baldoni) S.; m. Carol Jane Shelly, June 25, 1966; children: Patrick Francis, Jacquelyn Anne, Daniel Joseph. B.A., U. Cin., 1965, J.D., 1968. Bar: Ohio 1968, U.S. Tax Ct. 1970, Ariz. 1972, U.S. Dist. Ct. Ariz. 1973. Assoc. Krugliak, Wilkins, Griffiths & Dougherty, Canton, Ohio, 1968-71; v.p., corp. counsel Continental Homes, Inc., Phoenix, 1971-73; dir. Fennemore, Craig, von Ammon, Udall & Powers, Phoenix, 1973-83; ptnr. Slavin, Kane & Paterson, Phoenix, 1983—. Mem. Zoning Ordinance Revision Commn. Phoenix, 1981—; judge pro tem Maricopa County Superior Ct., 1981—; trustee Washington Elementary Sch. Dist. Employee BenefitsTrust and Worker's Compensation Bd., 1986—; mem. fin. com. Cath. Diocese of Phoenix, 1984— . Mem. ABA, State Bar Ariz. (disciplinary bd. 1976-84, chmn. 1981-84; jud. evaluation com. 1974—, chmn. 1974-80; chmn. conv. 1974-80), Maricopa County Bar Assn. Republican. Roman Catholic. Contracts commercial, Landlord-tenant, Real property. Office: Slavin Kane & Paterson 2198 E Camelback Rd Suite 285 Phoenix AZ 85016

SLAVIN, HOWARD LESLIE, lawyer, real estate broker, law educator; b. Bklyn., Aug. 13, 1951; s. Benjamin David and Pauline (Rothenberg) S.; m. Rhea Englander, Feb. 16, 1986. BA, SUNY, Stony Brook, 1972; MS, U. Utah, 1975; JD, U. Denver, 1978. Bar: Colo. 1979, U.S. Dist. Ct. Colo. 1979, U.S. Ct. Appeals (10th cir.) 1985. Assoc. Law Offices of Arthur M. Frazin, Denver, 1979-82; sole practice Denver, 1982-86; ptnr. Slavin & Donnelly, Denver, 1986—; investigator, subcontractor USDA, Denver, 1983-85; instr. Denver Para legal Inst., 1982—; mediator Ctr. for Dispute Resolution, Denver, 1980. Lectr. Community Assn. Inst., Denver, 1986; mentor U. Denver Alumni Mentor Program, 1986. N.Y. Bd. Regents scholar, 1968-72; N.Y. State Dept. Labor grantee, 1974-75. Mem. ABA, Colo. Bar Assn., Denver Bar Assn. Jewish. Club: Law (Denver). Avocations: classical guitar, running, sailing, ski touring. Contracts commercial, Bankruptcy, Real property. Office: Slavin & Donnelly 1133 Pennsylvania Denver CO 80203

SLAVIN, JOHN JEREMIAH, lawyer, corporation director; b. Yonkers, N.Y., Apr. 5, 1921; s. John Lawrence and Carolyn (Lyons) S.; m. Jean Celeste Murphy, Aug. 23, 1943; children: Jean, Susan, Paul, Thomas, Margaret. BA, Manhattan Coll., 1943; JD, Harvard U., 1949. Bar: Mich. 1949. Atty. Detroit Edison Co., Detroit, 1949-51; ptnr. Freud, Markus, Slavin & Galgan and predecessor firms, Troy, Mich., 1951—; bd. dirs. Fed. Screw Works, Detroit, Mac Valves, Inc., Wixom, Mich., various other corps. Served to 1st lt. USAAC, 1942-46, ETO. Mem. ABA, Mich. Bar Assn., Detroit Bar Assn., Oakland County Bar Assn., Am. Judicature Soc. Clubs: Birmingham (Mich.) Athletic (pres. 1967-68), Hillsboro (Fla.). Avocations: tennis, squash, flying. General corporate, General practice, Contracts commercial. Home: 4688 Haddington Ln Bloomfield Hills MI 48013 Office: Freud Markus Slavin & Galgan PC 100 E Big Beaver Rd Suite 900 Ameritech Bldg Troy MI 48083

SLAVITT, BEN J., lawyer; b. Newark, Dec. 31, 1934; s. Arthur and Berdie (Goodman) S.; children—Lauri, Julie, Donna, John. B.A., Bucknell U., 1956; LL.B., U. Va., 1959. Bar: N.J. 1959, U.S. dist. ct. N.J. 1959, U.S. Supreme Ct. 1973. Ptnr., Slavitt, Fish & Cowen, and predecessors, Newark, 1959—. Served with U.S. Army, 1959-60. Mem. N.J. Bar Assn. Democrat. Jewish. State civil litigation, Family and matrimonial, Real property. Office: 17 Academy St Suite 415 Newark NJ 07102

SLAWSKY, NORMAN JOEL, lawyer; b. N.Y.C., June 22, 1949; s. Samuel Slawsky and Lillian (Freizer) Alexander; m. Sigrid Wagner, Dec. 22, 1974; children: Stephen, Lynn. BA, SUNY, Binghamton, 1970; MA, CUNY, 1976; JD, U. Ga., 1980. Bar: Ga. 1980, U.S. Dist. Ct. (no. and mid. dists.) Ga. 1980, U.S. Ct. Appeals (11th cir.) 1980. Tchr. math. N.Y.C. Bd. Edn., Bklyn., 1976; instr. math. dept. U. Ga., Athens, 1977, legal research assoc., 1980-81; assoc. Nelson & Sweat, P.A., Athens, 1981-83, Jacobs & Langford, P.A., Atlanta, 1983—; atty. Oglethorpe County, Lexington, Ga., 1981—. Contbr. articles to profl. jours. Mem. Atlanta Jewish Community Ctr. Mem. ABA, Ga. Bar Assn., Atlanta Bar Assn., Fed. Bar Assn., Am. Arbitration Assn. Democrat. Labor, Federal civil litigation, Pension, profit-sharing, and employee benefits. Home: 190 Tuxedo Rd Athens GA 30606 Office: Jacobs & Langford PA 134 Peachtree St NW Suite 1000 Atlanta GA 30303

SLAYDON, KATHLEEN AMELIA, lawyer; b. Ft. Worth, June 1, 1951; d. A. Glynn and E. Jeanne (Miller) S.; m. John Mayer. B.A., Rice U., 1973; J.D., U. Tex., 1976. Bar: Tex. 1977, U.S. Dist. Ct. (so. dist.) Tex. 1978, U.S. Ct. Appeals (5th cir.) 1978, U.S. Ct. Appeals (11th cir.) 1981, U.S. Dist. Ct. (we. dist.) Tex. 1984. Assoc. Reynolds, Allen Cook, Houston, 1977-78; assoc. Ross, Banks, May Cron & Cavin, Houston, 1978-83, ptnr., 1983—; speaker continuing legal edn. State Bar Tex., 1983-86. Chairperson Rice Alumni 1973 Fund Dr., Houston, 1978. Mem. Tex. Assn. Bank Counsel, State Bar Tex., Houston Bar Assn., Rice Alumni Assn. Banking, Contracts commercial, Bankruptcy. Home: 725 E Creekside Dr Houston TX 77024 Office: Ross Banks May Cron & Cavin 9 Greenway Plaza 20th Floor Houston TX 77046

SLAYDON, ROGER JAMES, lawyer; b. Winston-Salem, N.C., June 18, 1949; s. Ralph James and Doris (Greer) S.; Nancy Watkins, Aug. 6, 1972 (div. Oct. 1977); 1 child, Layla Melissa; m. Sandra Ruth Taylor, Mar. 9, 1986;. BA in Polit. Sci., U. Fla., 1975, JD, 1978. Bar: U.S. Ct. Appeals (5th cir.) 1978, Fla. 1979, U.S. Dist. Ct. (so. dist.) Fla. 1979. Asst. pub. defender 15th Jud. Cir., West Palm Beach, Fla., 1978-79; assoc. Dell & Casey, West Palm Beach, 1979-82; assoc. Walton, Lantaff, Schroder & Carson, West Palm Beach, 1982-86, ptnr., 1986—. Served with USN, 1968-72. Mem. ABA, Palm Beach County Bar Assn., Assn. Trial Lawyers Am., John Marshall Bar Assn. Democrat. Avocations: tennis, sailing, snow skiing, fishing, camping. Personal injury, Insurance, State civil litigation. Home: 14-F Lexington Ln East Palm Beach Gardens FL 33418 Office: Walton Lantaff Schroeder & Carson 1615 Forum Place West Palm Beach FL 33401

SLAYTON, JOHN HOWARD, business lawyer, financial consultant; b. Sparta, Wis., July 6, 1955; s. Rex Gordon and Elizabeth (Ward) S. BA in Polit. Sci. with honors, Marquette U., 1977; JD with honors, George Washington U., 1980, MBA in Fin., 1982; LLM in Taxation, Georgetown U., 1986. Bar: D.C. 1981, U.S. Ct. Appeals (D.C. cir.) 1981, U.S. Dist. Ct. (D.C. dist.).1981. Assoc. Metzger, Shadyac & Schwarz, Washington, 1980-83, Pillsbury, Madison & Sutro, Washington, 1983-87, Vallejo Co., Washington, 1987—; instr. real estate syndication, Arlington (Va.) County Continuing Edn./Realty Bd., 1982. Contbr. articles to profl. jours. Mem. ABA (mem. com. fed. regulation of securities), D.C. Bar Assn. Roman Catholic. Avocations: sailing, golf, racquetball. General corporate, Securities, Corporate taxation. Home: 6802 McLean Province Circle Falls Church VA 22043 Office: Vallejo Co 600 New Hampshire Ave NW Suite 953 Washington DC 20037

SLEDGE, JAMES SCOTT, lawyer; b. Gadsden, Ala., July 20, 1947; s. L. Lee and Kathryn (Privott) S.; m. Joan Nichols, Dec. 27, 1969; children—Joanna Scott, Dorothy Privott. B.A., Auburn U., 1969; J.D., U. Ala., 1974. Bar: Ala. 1974, U.S. Ct. Appeals (5th cir.) 1975, U.S. Ct. Appeals (11th cir.) 1981. Ptnr. Inzer, Suttle, Swann & Stivender, P.A., Gadsden, 1974—; mcpl. judge, Gadsden, 1975—; instr. U. Ala., Gadsden, 1975-77. Lay minister, vestryman Holy Comforter Episc. Ch., Gadsden, 1976—; incorporator Episc. Day Sch., Gadsden, 1976, Kyle Home for Devel. Disadvantaged, Gadsden, 1979; bd. dirs. Salvation Army, 1984—, Etowah County Health Dept., 1975—; mem. Etowah County Dem. Exec. Com., 1984—; county coordinator U.S. Senator Howell Heflin, Etowah County, Ala., 1978, 84; founder Gadsden Cultural Arts Found., 1983. Served to capt. U.S. Army, 1969-71, Vietnam. Decorated Bronze Star; Legion of Honor (Vietnam); Mem. Ala. State Bar (charter mem. bankruptcy sect., vice chmn. 1984, regional liaison bankruptcy bench and bar 1984), Gadsden-Etowah C. of C. (bd. dirs. 1986—), Phi Kappa Phi, Phi Eta Sigma. Lodge: Kiwanis (bd. dirs. 1981-84). Federal civil litigation, Bankruptcy, General practice. Home: 435 Turrentine Ave Gadsden AL 35901 Office: Inzer Suttle Swann & Stivender PA 601 Broad St Gadsden AL 35901

SLEHOFER, RICHARD DONALD, lawyer; b. Billings, Mont., Oct. 24, 1945; s. Albert John and Elsie Elaine (Kuyala) Schlehofer; m. Terry Lynn

Marcus, May 7, 1983; children: Christopher, Joseph. BS in Chemistry, U. Puget Sound, 1967; JD, Lewis and Clark Coll., 1975. Bar: Washington 1975, Calif. 1976, U.S. Dist. Ct. (cen. dist.) Calif. 1981. Assoc. Jessup & Beecher, Sherman Oaks, Calif., 1979-84; ptnr. Jessup, Beecher & Slehofer, Westlake Village, Calif., 1984—. Mem. Conejo Bar Assn., Los Angeles Patent Law Assn. (bd. dirs. 1984—). Patent, Trademark and copyright. Home: 3520 Ridgeford Dr Westlake Village CA 91361 Office: Jessup Beecher & Slehofer 875 Westlake Blvd 205 Westlake Village CA 91361

SLENKER, NORMAN FREDERICK, lawyer; b. Washington, Pa., Oct. 12, 1929; s. Fred William and Esther Lenore (Lamp) S.; m. Berta King Ray, Sept. 20, 1952; children: Susan Slenker Brewer, Donald P., Martha Ball Slenker Haggerty. AB, Wesleyan U., Delaware, Ohio, 1951; JD, George Washington U., 1955. Bar: Va. 1956, U.S. Ct. Appeals (4th cir.) 1962, U.S. Supreme Ct. 1967. Assoc. Russell & Hulvey, Arlington, Va., 1956-59, Jesse, Phillips, Klinge & Kendrick, Arlington, 1959-62; ptnr. Slenker, Brandt, Jennings & Johnston, Fairfax, Va., 1962—; instr. Adult Edn. Program, Arlington County, 1956-59, U. Va., 1974-75, 80; lectr. No. Va. Community Coll., 1970-74; speaker various orgns. and schs. Fellow Am. Coll. Trial Lawyers, Internat. Soc. Barristers; mem. ABA, Va. Bar Assn., Fairfax County Bar Assn., Am. Judicature Soc., Internat. Assn. Ins. Counsel, Va. Trial Lawyers Assn., Def. Research Inst. Republican. Methodist. Club: Washington Golf (Arlington). Avocations: tennis, scuba diving. Personal injury, State civil litigation, Insurance. Home: 3861 N Ridgeview Rd Arlington VA 22207 Office: Slenker Brandt Jennings & Johnston 3026 Javier Rd Fairfax VA 22031

SLEZ, ANTHONY FRANCIS, JR., lawyer; b. Westport, Conn., May 23, 1946; s. Anthony Francis and Vanetta (Benos) S.; m. Margaret Joan Gorczynski, Jan. 27, 1973; 1 child, Adam Francis. B in Elective Studies, U. Bridgeport, 1975; JD, Western New Eng. Coll., 1979. Bar: Conn. 1979, U.S. Dist. Ct. Conn., 1980. Ptnr. Slez & O'Grady, Westport, 1979—; bd. dirs. Vaamp Devel. Corp. Mem. Rep. Town Commn., Westport, 1984—. Mem. ABA, Conn. Bar Assn., Bridgeport Bar Assn., Assn. Trial Lawyers Am., Conn. Trial Lawyers Assn., Phi Delta Phi. Roman Catholic. Lodge: Kiwanis (bd. dirs. Westport club 1985—). Avocations: computers, skiing, flying. Civil rights, Federal civil litigation, State civil litigation. Home: 13 Parsell Ln Westport CT 06880 Office: 793 Post Rd E Westport CT 06880

SLIFKIN, IRVING, lawyer; b. Tarrytown, N.Y., Jan. 5, 1922; s. Samuel and Rebecca (Velitzkin) S.; m. Judith Nover, Apr. 4, 1952; children: Amy Jean, Laurie Bea, Lawrence Scott. AB with distinction, U. Mich., 1943, JD with distinction, 1948. Bar: N.Y. 1948, Colo. 1954, Conn. 1971. Sr. atty., asst. sec. Shell Oil Co., N.Y.C. and Denver, 1948-77; gen. counsel, asst. sec. Condec Corp., Greenwich, Conn., 1977-81; v.p., gen. counsel HMW Industries, Stamford, Conn., 1981-83; v.p., sec., gen. counsel Consol. Westway Group Inc., Englewood Cliffs, N.J., 1983—; bd. dirs. HMW Industries, Stamford. Contbr. articles to profl. jours. Vice chmn. Stamford Sewer Commn., 1979-80, mem., 1975-80; alt. mem. City of Stamford Zoning Bd., 1981—. Served as lt. (j.g.) USN, 1942-46. Mem. ABA, N.Y. State Bar Assn., Conn. Bar Assn., Assn. of Bar of City of N.Y., Am. Petroleum Inst., Southwestern Conn. Area Commerce and Industry Assn., N.Y. State Petroleum Council, Westchester Fairfield Corp. Counsel Assn. Republican. Jewish. Avocations: boating, golf, travel. General corporate, Antitrust, Federal civil litigation. Home: 332 Mill Rd Stamford CT 06903 Office: Consol Westway Group Inc 464 Hudson Terr Englewood Cliffs NJ 07632

SLOAN, F(RANK) BLAINE, law educator; b. Geneva, Nebr., Jan. 3, 1920; s. Charles Porter and Lillian Josephine (Stiefer) S.; m. Patricia Sand, Sept. 2, 1944; children—DeAnne Sloan Riddle, Michael Blaine, Charles Porter. A.B. with high distinction, U. Nebr., 1942, LL.B. cum laude, 1946; LL.M. in Internat. Law, Columbia U., 1947. Bar: Nebr. 1946, N.Y. 1947. Asst. to spl. counsel Intergovtl. Com. for Refugees, 1947; mem. Office Legal Affairs UN Secretariat, N.Y.C., 1948-78, gen. counsel Relief and Works Agy. Palestine Refugees, Beirut, 1958-60, dir. gen. legal div., 1966-78, rep. of Sec. Gen. to Commn. Internat. Trade Law, 1969-78, rep. to Legal Sub-com. on Outer Space, 1966-78; rep. UN delegation Vietnam conf., Paris, 1973; rep UN Conf. on Carriage of Goods by sea, Hamburg, 1978; prof. internat. law and orgn. Pace U., 1978—. Cons. UN Office of Legal Affairs, 1983-84, UN Water Resources Br., 1983. Served with AC, U.S. Army, 1943-46. Decorated Air medal. Mem. Am. Soc. Internat. Law, Am. Acad. Polit. and Social Sci., Am. Arbitration Assn. (panel of arbitrators), Order of Coif, Phi Beta Kappa, Phi Alpha Delta (hon.). Republican. Roman Catholic. Contbr. articles to legal jours. Public international, Water Law. Home: 23 Hall Rd Briarcliff Manor NY 10510 also: Fox Hill-Forbes Park Fort Garland CO 81133 Office: 78 N Broadway White Plains NY 10603

SLOAN, SHELDON HAROLD, lawyer; b. Mpls., Dec. 25, 1935; s. Leonard Norman and Mary (Wasserman) S.; m. Loraine Bayer, Nov. 28, 1964; children: Stephen Howard, Jennifer Blair. BSBA, UCLA, 1958; JD, U. So. Calif., 1961. Bar: Calif. 1962, U.S. Dist. Ct. (so. and cen. dists.) Calif. 1962, U.S. Claims Ct. 1962, U.S. Supreme Ct. 1962. Atty. U.S. Dept. Justice, Washington, 1962-63; assoc. Brown & Brown, Los Angeles, 1963-73, ptnr., 1976-79; judge Los Angeles Mcpl. Ct., 1973-76; sole practice Los Angeles, 1980—; bd. dirs. ACA JOE, San Francisco, Pioneer Magnetics Inc., Santa Monica, Calif. Trustee, treas. Westlake Sch. for Girls, Los Angeles, 1980—; pres., chmn. Coro Found., Los Angeles, 1980-81, Frater Friends Music Ctr., Los Angeles, 1981-85; chmn. Senator Pete Wilson's Jud. Selection Com., 1982-84, 85—; pres. Guardians Jewish Homes for the Aged, Los Angeles, 1986. Mem. Los Angeles County Bar Assn. (chmn. jud. appointments com. 1984—). Republican. Avocations: tennis, golf, skiing. General corporate, Real property, Landlord-tenant. Office: 1801 Ave of the Stars Los Angeles CA 90067

SLOAN, STEVEN KENT, general counsel; b. McPherson, Kans., Jan. 25, 1944; s. Edward K. and Dorothy (Nordling) S.; m. Suzan Chan, Feb. 19, 1972; children: Michelle, Angela. BA, U. Okla., 1966, JD, 1969. Bar: Okla. 1969. Asst. dist. atty. Office of Dist. Atty., Tulsa, Okla., 1972-77; atty., then sr. atty. Williams Bros. Engring. Co., Tulsa, Okla., 1977-81; atty. M.W. Kellogg Co., Houston, 1981-82; assoc. gen. counsel Williams Bros. Engring. Co., Tulsa, Okla., 1982-84; gen. counsel Williams Bros. Engring. Co., Tulsa, 1984—; atty. M.W. Kellogg Co., Houston, 1982-84; bd. dirs. Williams Bros. Engring. Co., Tulsa, Okla., Williams Bros., Engring. Ltd., London, Resource Scis. Corp., Tulsa, Okla. Served as capt. U.S. Army, 1970-72, Vietnam. Republican. Methodist. Avocations: classical music, reading. General corporate, Private international. Office: Williams Bros Engring Co 6600 S Yale Tulsa OK 74136

SLOANE, OWEN JAY, lawyer, educator; b. N.Y.C.; m. Beverly Hope Gorlin; children—Meredith Jean, Lindsay Ann, Brooke Leslie. B.A. with distinction, Cornell U., 1962; J.D. cum laude, Yale U., 1965. Bar: Calif. 1966, U.S. Dist. Ct. (cen. dist.) Calif. 1966. Assoc. O'Melveny & Myers, Los Angeles, 1965-68, Greenberg & Glusker, Los Angeles, 1968-71; prin. Owen J. Sloane, P.C., 1971-78; sr. ptnr. Mason, Sloane & Gilbert, Los Angeles and Santa Monica, Calif., 1978—; lectr. UCLA Grad. Sch. Mgmt. Mem. ABA, Calif. Bar Assn., Los Angeles Bar Assn., Beverly Hills Bar Assn., Copyright Soc. Entertainment. Office: 1299 Ocean Ave Penthouse Santa Monica CA 90401

SLOANE, WILLIAM MARTIN, lawyer, legal educator; b. Harrisburg, Pa., Nov. 28, 1951; s. William and Margaret Mater (Martin) S.; m. Susan Marie Ankney, June 16, 1984. BA, York Coll. of Pa., 1972; cert. in English Law, London Poly., Eng., 1973; JD, Widener U., 1975; LLM, Temple U., 1979; D in Juridical Sci., Heed U., 1982. Bar: Pa. 1976, U.S. Dist. Ct. (mid. dist.) Pa. 1980, Md. 1985. Lectr. St. Francis Coll., Harrisburg, 1979-83; asst. prof. Millersville (Pa.) U., 1985—; instr. Elizabethtown (Pa.) Coll., 1987—; pres. Profl. Edn. Research Group, Carlisle, Pa., 1975—; legal counsel Ho. of Reps., Harrisburg, 1976—; v.p. Tan Tan, Inc., Mechanicsburg, Pa., 1981—, Maker & Sloane, Inc., Mechanicsburg, 1982—; adj. asst. prof. Heed U., Christiansted, V.I., 1982—; sec. Halmark Constrn., Camp Hill, Pa., 1983—; lectr. Wilson Coll., Chambersburg, Pa., 1981—; adj. faculty Newport U., Newport Beach, Calif., 1983—; mem. faculty Fairfax U., New Orleans, 1987—. Contbg. author: Fate of the Oceans, 1972; editor Young Electorate mag., 1974-77. Exec. com. mem. Cumberland County Dems., Carlisle, Pa., 1976-84, Pa. Dem. State Com., Harrisburg, 1976-84; gen. counsel Young Dems. of Pa., Harrisburg, 1976-86; chmn. Am.-European Community Youth Assn., London, 1980—. Recipient Citizen in Action award Sta. WSBA Radio, 1972. Mem. ABA (3d cir. Brass Key award student div. 1973), Md. Bar Assn., Pa. Bar Assn., Assn. Trial Lawyers Am., Pa. Trial Lawyers Assn., Am. Soc. Internat. Law, Mansfield Law Club, Mensa, Scottish Lawyers, Phi Alpha Delta. Democrat. Presbyterian. Club: Stair Soc. Avocations: church and community work, cons., chiropractic research. General practice, Banking, Legal education. Home and Office: Rt 174 RD 1 Box 84 Newville PA 17241-9510

SLOAT, GERALD CHARLES, lawyer; b. Bklyn., Jan. 12, 1945; s. Bernard H. and Pauline (Schartz) S.; m. Gail Harris, Sept. 13, 1981; children: Adam D., Daniel E., Emily I. AB, U. Rochester, 1966; JD, Syracuse U., 1969. Bar: N.Y. 1970, Colo. 1971. Assoc. Bressler, Meislin, Taubert & Bressler, N.Y.C., 1969-70, Frederick & Hackett, Farmingdale, N.Y., 1970-73; ptnr. Kayne & Sloat, Boulder, Colo., 1971-74, Sloat & Warren, Boulder, 1975-76; sole practice Boulder, 1976—; spl. dep. atty. gen. Election Funds Bur., N.Y., 1970; atty. Town of Superior, Colo. 1972; tchr. Community Free Sch., Boulder, 1982-83. Cubmaster Boy Scouts Am., Boulder, 1982; trustee Boulder Jewish Congregation, 1973-74. Recipient Cert. Appreciation, Boulder County Legal Services, 1976, Cert. Appreciation, Arapahoe Community Coll., 1978; named one of Outstanding Young Men of Am., 1982. Mem. ABA, Colo. Bar Assn., Boulder County Bar Assn., Assn. Trial Lawyers Am., Colo. Trial Lawyers Assn., Jaycees (bd. dirs. Boulder 1972-74). Avocations: photography, skiing. Personal injury, General corporate, Real property. Home: 3785 Orange Ln Boulder CO 80302 Office: 1823 Folsom St Boulder CO 80302

SLOCUM, SHAUN MICHAEL, lawyer; b. Plattsburg, N.Y., Jan. 22, 1951. BA, Fairfield U., 1973; JD, U. Bridgeport, 1981. Bar: Conn. 1981, U.S. Dist. Ct. Conn. 1981. Asst. clk. Conn. Superior Ct., New Haven, 1979-81; assoc. Vincent T. McManus Jr., Wallingford, Conn., 1982-83; ptnr. Shay, Thompson & Slocum, New Haven, 1983—; counsel Cheshire Land Trust, 1986—, also bd. dirs. Bd. dirs. Wallingford (Conn.) Boys and Girls Club, 1982-84; counsel Cheshire Land Trust, 1986—. Mem. ABA, Conn. Bar Assn., New Haven County Bar Assn., Assn. Trial Lawyers Am., Conn. Trial Lawyers Assn. State civil litigation, Insurance, Personal injury. Office: Shay Thompson & Slocum 250 Church St New Haven CT 06510

SLOMAN, MARVIN SHERK, lawyer; b. Fort Worth, Apr. 17, 1925; s. Richard Jack and Lucy Janette (Sherk) S.; m. Margaret Jane Dinwiddie, Apr. 11, 1953; children: Lucy Carter, Richard Dinwiddie. AB, U. Tex., 1948, LLB with honors, 1950. Bar: Tex. 1950, N.Y. 1951. Assoc., Sullivan & Cromwell, N.Y.C., 1950-56, Carrington, Coleman, Sloman & Blumenthal, Dallas, 1956-60, ptnr., 1960—. Fellow ABA, Tex. Bar Found.; mem. Tex. Bar Assn., Bar Assn. 5th Fed. Cir. (pres. 1984-85, bd. govs. 1984—), Dallas Bar Assn. (chmn. com. on judiciary 1979), Assn. Bar City of N.Y. Clubs: City (bd. dirs. 1970—), Crescent (Dallas). General practice. Office: Carrington Coleman Sloman & Blumenthal 200 Crescent Ct Suite 1500 Dallas TX 75201

SLONAKER, JERRY PAUL, lawyer; b. Harrisonburg, Va., Nov. 25, 1945; s. Paul Jeremiah and Ethel Mae (Houtz) S.; m. Sandra Kay Brooks, July 3, 1966; children—Jeri Suzanne, Heather Anne. B.A., Lebanon Valley Coll., 1968; J.D., U. Richmond, 1971. Bar: Va. 1971, U.S. Ct. Mil. Appeals, 1971, U.S. Supreme Ct. 1974, U.S. Ct. Appeals (4th cir.) 1975, U.S. Dist. Ct. (ea. and we. dists.) Va. 1975, U.S. Ct. Appeals (3d cir.) 1983. Asst. atty. gen. State of Va., Richmond, 1975—; adj. prof. Park Coll., Kansas City, Kans., 1975; instr. Va. Forensic Sci. Acad., Richmond, 1975—. Pres. Chestnut Oaks Recreation Assn., Richmond, 1981. Served as capt. JAGC, U.S. Army, 1971-75. Decorated Army Commendation medal; recipient Disting. Service award Va. Atty. Gen., 1983. Mem. ABA, Va. Trial Lawyers Assn., Va. State Bar Assn., Phi Alpha Delta (treas. Patrick Henry chpt. 1970-71), Pi Gamma Mu. Methodist. Federal civil litigation, State civil litigation, Criminal. Home: 9311 Fordson Rd Richmond VA 23229 Office: Office of Atty Gen of Va 101 N 8th St Richmond VA 23219

SLOTE, EDWIN MICHAEL, lawyer; b. N.Y.C., Mar. 28, 1905; s. Abraham and Ida (Levine) S.; m. Tisha Kunst, July 2, 1940; children: Michael Anthony, Wendy Slote Kleinbaum. LLB, NYU, 1925; postgrad. Columbia U. Bar: N.Y. 1927. Sec., counsel World Habeas Corpus, Washington, 1952-65; panel Am. Arbitration Assn., N.Y.C., 1950—; gen. counsel No. R.R. of N.J., 1939-43, Bondholders Com. Central R.R. of N.J., 1940-45; mem. law com. Real Estate Bd. N.Y., 1940-45; spl. master N.Y. Supreme Ct., 1982—; organizer blind lawyers Supreme Ct. recs. with Library of Congress. Contbr. articles to profl. jours. Counsel, dir. North Westchester Sr. Assembly, 1960-75. Mem. Am. Judges Assn., ABA, Internat. Assn. Jewish Lawyers-Jurists (v.p.), N.Y. State Bar Assn., New York County Bar Assn., U.S. Navy League. Club: Yale. State civil litigation, Private international, Probate. Home: 32 E 64 St New York NY 10021 Office: 790 Madison Ave New York NY 10021

SLOUGH, JOHN EDWARD, corporation executive, lawyer; b. Phila., May 29, 1942; s. Herbert Edward and Barbara Bane (Holahan) S.; m. Karin Lesley Bendel, June 1, 1974; children—Lara, John Edward. B.A., San Francisco State U., 1965; J.D., U. Calif., 1972; LL.M., U. London, 1973. Bar: Calif. 1973, Md., 1974, Fla., 1975, D.C. 1976, U.S. Supreme Ct. 1976, Mass. 1978, N.Y. 1980; C.P.A., Md. Atty. Bank of Am., San Francisco, 1973-74; asst. counsel Easco Corp., Balt., 1974-76; sr. v.p., gen. counsel Snelling and Snelling, Inc., Sarasota, Fla., 1976-82, also dir.; v.p., sec., gen. counsel Williamhouse-Regency, Inc., N.Y.C., 1982—; dir. Plant Maintenance Inc. of Calif. Served to 1st lt. U.S. Army. Decorated Bronze Star (2), Purple Heart. Mem. ABA, Calif. Bar Assn., D.C. Bar Assn., Fla. Bar Assn., Nat. Assn. Corp. Dirs. General corporate, Trademark and copyright, Labor. Home: 35 School House Ln Morristown NJ 07960 Office: 28 W 23d St New York NY 10010

SLOUGH, J(OSEPHINE) HELEN, lawyer; b. Elyria, Ohio, Feb. 10, 1908; d. Frank Merrill and Josephine Caroline (Herbert) S.; m. Harold H. Jurgens, May 17, 1930; 1 child, Robert Slough. JD, Cleve. State Law Sch., 1929. Bar: Ohio 1929, U.S. Dist. Ct. (no. dist.) Ohio 1930, U.S. Dist. Ct. (ea. dist.) Mich. 1930, U.S. Ct. Appeals (2d, 4th, 5th, 6th, 7th, 8th, 9th and 10th cirs.). Ptnr. Slough & Canfield, 1929-37, Slough & Slough, 1937-73; of counsel Squire, Sanders & Dempsey, Cleve., 1973-79; sole practice, Cleve., 1979—; bd. dirs. Rolec, Inc. Bd. dirs. Women's City Club of Cleve., 1983—. Recipient Internat. Women's Year Disting. Service award Cleve. State U., 1975, YWCA Career Woman of Year award, 1979. Mem. ABA, Cleve. Bar Assn., Nat. Assn. Women Lawyers (pres. 1950-51), Licensing Execs. Soc., Internat. Lawyers Group of Cleve., Cleve. Pat. Bar, Cuyahoga Women's Polit. Caucus, Women's City Club Fedn. Republican. Roman Catholic. Clubs: Women's City, University, Westwood Country. Federal civil litigation, Patent, Trademark and copyright. Office: Room 200 21010 Center Ridge Rd Cleveland OH 44116

SLOVITER, DOLORES KORMAN, federal judge; b. Phila., Sept. 5, 1932; d. David and Tillie Korman; m. Henry A. Sloviter, Apr. 3, 1969; 1 dau., Vikki Amanda. A.B. in Econs. with distinction, Temple U., Phila., 1953, L.H.D. (hon.), 1986; LL.B. magna cum laude, U. Pa., 1956; LL.D. (hon.), The Dickinson Sch. Law, 1984. Bar: Pa. 1957. Assoc., then partner Dilworth, Paxson, Kalish, Kohn & Levy, Phila., 1956-69; mem. firm Harold E. Kohn (P.A.), Phila., 1969-72; assoc. prof, then prof. law Temple U. Law Sch., 1972-79; judge U.S. Ct. Appeals 3d Circuit, Phila., 1979—; mem. Disciplinary Bd. Supreme Ct. Pa., 1978-79. Mem. S.E. region Gov. Pa. Council Aging, 1976-79; mem. Com. of 70, 1976-79; trustee Jewish Publ. Soc. Am., 1983—. Mem. ABA, Am. Law Inst., Fed. Bar Assn., Fed. Judges Assn., Phila. Bar Assn. (gov. 1976-78), Phi Beta Kappa, Order of Coif (pres. U. Pa. chpt. 1975-77). Jurisprudence. Office: US Court of Appeals 18614 US Courthouse Independence Mall W-601 Market St Philadelphia PA 19106

SLOWIACZEK, JOHN STEVEN, lawyer; b. Sioux City, Iowa, Apr. 15, 1950; s. Walter Anthony and Lena (Surmack) S.; m. Shannon Henry, Aug. 21, 1971; children—Kara Nicole, Anlee Colleen, Mary Katherine. B.A. cum laude, Briar Cliff Coll., 1971; J.D., Creighton U., 1973. Bar: Nebr. 1974, Iowa 1974, U.S. Dist. Ct. Nebr. 1974, U.S. Dist. Ct. Iowa 1974. Atty. Douglas County, Omaha, 1974-75; ptnr. Starr, Slowiaczek & Washburn, Omaha, 1975-79, Erickson & Sederstrom, Omaha, 1979—. Mem. Omaha Bar Assn., Nebr. State Bar Assn., ABA, Iowa State Bar Assn., Nebr. Trial Lawyers Assn., Assn. Trial Lawyers of Am. Democrat. Roman Catholic. Club: Regency Lake & Tennis. Family and matrimonial, Computer.

SLUGG, RAMSAY HILL, lawyer; b. Hamilton, Ohio, May 7, 1953; s. Roger Hill and Ellen (Ramsay) S.; m. Rebecca Pope, Oct. 12, 1985; 1 child, Elliott. BA in History, Wittenberg U., 1975; JD, Ohio State U., 1978. Bar: Ohio 1978, U.S. Tax Ct. 1979, Tex. 1983, U.S. Dist. Ct. (no. dist.) Tex. 1983, U.S. Ct. Appeals (5th cir.) 1983, U.S. Supreme Ct. 1983. Assoc. Mayer, Terakedis & Blue, Columbus, Ohio, 1978-81; ptnr. Gandy, Michener, Swindle, Whitaker & Pratt, Ft. Worth, 1981—. Contbr. articles to Ressi Region Quarterly, 1985—. Mem. Am. Agrl. Law Assn., Real Estate Securities and Syndication Inst. Republican. Episcopalian. Club: Ohio State U. Pres. (Columbus). Securities, General corporate, Personal income taxation. Home: 208 Lindenwood Dr Fort Worth TX 76107 Office: Gandy Michener Swindle et al 2501 Parkview #600 Fort Worth TX 76102

SLUTSKY, KENNETH JOEL, lawyer; b. N.Y.C., Sept. 18, 1953; s. Clement and June (Gross) S.; m. Nancy Ellen Goldfarb, Jan. 15, 1978; children: Rachel, Jason. BA, Columbia U., 1975; JD, Harvard U., 1978. Bar: N.J. 1978, U.S. Dist. Ct. N.J. 1978. Assoc. Lowenstein, Sandler, Brochin, Kohl, Fisher & Boylan, Roseland, N.J., 1978-83, ptnr., 1984—. V.p. met. N.J. chpt. Am. Jewish Com., Millburn; bd. dirs. Jewish Family Service Metrowest N.J., Millburn. Mem. ABA, N.J. Bar Assn. Estate planning, Estate taxation, Corporate taxation. Home: 4 Page Pl Livingston NJ 07039 Office: Lowenstein Sandler et al 65 Livingston Ave Roseland NJ 07068

SMAIL, LAURENCE MITCHELL, lawyer, educator; b. Pitts., May 2, 1937; s. Samuel Percy and Kathryn Jeanette (Mitchell) S.; m. Katherine Sylvia Carr, Nov. 30, 1964; 1 child, Leslie Anne. B.A., Washington and Lee Univ., 1959, J.D., 1962; M.B.A., Coll. William and Mary, 1973. Bar: Va. 1964, U.S. Ct. Claims 1967, U.S. Supreme Ct. 1968, U.S. Ct. Appeals (Fed. cir.) 1982; cert. profl. contracts mgr. Assoc. Hoyle & Short, Newport News, Va., 1965-66; atty., advisor USAAV Labs., Fort Eustis, Va., 1966-74; counsel SUPSHIP, Newport News, Va., 1974; counsel U.S. Army Aviation Applied Tech. Div., Fort Eustis, 1974—; dir. Fort Eustis Fed. Credit Union, 1973—; instr. U. Va., 1974—; sec. Med. Security Card, Inc., Newport News, 1980—. Contbr. articles to profl. jours. Pres., Brentwood Civic League, 1969; chmn. Newport News Taxpayers Assn., 1973. Served to capt. U.S. Army, 1962-65. Fellow Nat. Contract Mgmt. Assn. (nat. v.p. 1979-80), Am. Helicopter Soc., Fed. Bar Assn., Va. Bar Assn., Phi Delta Phi. Republican. Presbyterian. Clubs: Warwick Yacht, Pegasus (past pres.). Government contracts and claims, Legal education. Home: 507 Beech Dr Newport News VA 23601 Office: US Army Aviation Applied Tech Div Bldg 401 Fort Eustis VA 23604

SMALL, DANIEL I., lawyer; b. Boston, Jan. 2, 1954; s. Martin I. and Joanne (Goldfine) S. BA, Harvard U., 1975, JD, 1979. Bar: Mass. 1979, U.S. Ct. Appeals (1st, 5th, 11th and D.C. cirs.). Trial atty. U.S. Dept. Justice, Washington, 1979-82; asst. U.S. atty. State of Mass., Boston, 1982—; lectr. Harvard U. Law Sch. Recipient Dir.'s award Tex. Dept. Pub. Safety, 1983. Avocations: sailing, football referee. Criminal. Office: US Attys Office 1107 McCormack Courthouse Boston MA 02109

SMALL, HAROLD S., lawyer; b. Chgo., Jan. 22, 1945; s. James Milman and Miriam Bernice (Elenbogen) S.; m. Susan I. Small, June 22, 1969; children: Matthew Howard, Hillary Shayne, Allison Blythe. BS, San Diego State U., 1967; JD, U. Calif.-Hastings Coll. Law, 1970. Bar: Calif. Pres. Profl. Corp., Attys., San Diego, 1982—; instr. U. Calif., San Diego, 1972—. Bd. dirs. The Children's Mus. of San Diego, 1982—, pres. 1983-85. Mem. Am. Inst. CPA's, Soc. CPA's, Estate Planning Council of San Diego (pres. 1986-87). Avocations: photography, travel, enology, skiing. Probate, General corporate, Real property. Office: 110 W C St #2112 San Diego CA 92101

SMALL, JONATHAN ANDREW, lawyer; b. N.Y.C., Dec. 26, 1942; s. Milton and Teresa Markell (Joseph) S.; m. Cornelia Mendenhall, June 8, 1969; children: Anne, Katherine. B.A., Brown U., 1964; student, U. Paris, 1962-63; LL.B., Harvard U., 1967; M.A., Tufts U., 1968; LL.M., NYU, 1974. Bar: N.Y. 1967. VISTA vol. Washington and Cambridge, Mass., 1968; law clk. to judge U.S. Ct. Appeals (2d cir.), 1968-69; assoc. Debevoise & Plimpton, N.Y.C., 1969-75, ptnr., 1976—; cons. Spl. Task Force on N.Y. State Taxation, 1976. Trustee Brearley Sch., 1985—; bd. dirs. Nonprofit Coordinating Com. of N.Y., 1985—, Muscular Dystrophy Assn., 1986—. Mem. ABA, N.Y. State Bar Assn. (chmn. tax sect. com. exempt orgns. 1980-82), Assn. Bar City N.Y., Phi Beta Kappa. Corporate taxation, Personal income taxation, State and local taxation. Address: 60 East End Ave New York NY 10028

SMALL, JOSEPH CHAUNCEY, lawyer; b. N.Y.C., Mar. 23, 1943; s. Fred and Frances (Katsh) S.; m. Alice Kay Schwedock, Sept. 27, 1970; children: Adlai Jonathan Jacob, Emily Frances. BA, Williams Coll., 1965; JD, Columbia U., 1975. Bar: N.J. 1975, U.S. Dist. Ct. N.J. 1975, N.Y. 1976, U.S. Tax Ct. 1981. Asst. dir. Mathematica, Princeton, N.J., 1971-74; assoc. Shearman & Sterling, N.Y.C., 1975-77; dept. atty. gen., exec. asst. to atty. gen. Trenton, N.J., 1977-81; assoc. Liebman & Flaster, Cherry Hill, N.J., 1981-83; coordinator tax evasion task force, counsel N.J. Div. Taxation, Trenton, 1983—. Orgn. for Econ. Cooperation and Devel. fellow, 1965-66. Mem. ABA, N.J. Bar Assn. (exec. com. tax sect., lawyers in pub. employment com.), Mercer County Bar Assn., Nat. Assn. Tax Adminstrs. (chmn. criminal enforcement sect., chmn. collection enforcement sect.), Assn. Govt. Accts. State and local taxation. Home: 277 Hawthorne Ave Princeton NJ 08540 Office: NJ Div Taxation 50 Barrack St Trenton NJ 08646

SMALL, MARC JAMES, lawyer; b. Los Angeles, Jan. 13, 1950; s. James Garfield and Betty Ellen (Martin) S.; m. Tempy Glenn Larew, Nov. 1, 1975 (div. Dec. 1985); 1 child, Ian Marc. BA, Washington and Lee U., 1972; MA, Yale U., 1974; JD, William and Mary U., 1981. Bar: Va. 1981, U.S. Dist. Ct. (we. dist.) Va. 1981, U.S. Ct. Appeals (4th cir.) 1981. Assoc. J.H. Krasnow Law Office, Roanoke, Va., 1981-85; ptnr. Melton & Small, Roanoke, 1985-87; sole practice Roanoke, 1987—. Mem. Roanoke City Rep. Com., 1981—, King Canute Soc., Roanoke City, 1965—, Roanoke Valley Astron. Assn., 1985—; candidate Ho. of Dels., Roanoke City, 1985. Served to capt. U.S. Army, 1974-78. Mem. ABA, Assn. Trial Lawyers Am., Va. Trial Lawyers Assn. Episcopalian. Avocations: car restoration, classical music, langs. and lit., sci. fiction, herpetology, camping. General practice, Family and matrimonial, State civil litigation. Home and Office: 713 First St SW Roanoke VA 24016

SMALL, MARSHALL LEE, lawyer; b. Kansas City, Mo., Sept. 8, 1927; s. Phillip and Lillian (Mendelsohn) S.; m. Mary Rogell, June 27, 1954; children: Daniel, Elizabeth. B.A., Stanford U., 1949, J.D., 1951. Bar: Mo. 1951, Calif. 1955. Law clk. to Justice William O. Douglas U.S. Supreme Ct., Washington, 1951-52; assoc. Morrison & Foerster, San Francisco, 1954-60, ptnr., 1961—; reporter corp. governance project Am. Law Inst., 1982-86. Served as 1st lt. U.S. Army, 1952-54. Mem. ABA (com. corp. laws 1975-82), Phi Beta Kappa, Order of Coif. General corporate. Office: Morrison & Foerster 345 California St San Francisco CA 94104

SMALLEY, DAVID VINCENT, lawyer; b. N.Y.C., Mar. 27, 1935; s. Vincent R. and Ethel A. (Sullivan) S.; m. Patricia Doyle Tolles, Nov. 28, 1964; children—Brian W., Gregory T. B.A., Hamilton Coll.; LL.B., Harvard U. Bar: N.Y. 1960. Assoc. Debevoise & Plimpton, N.Y.C., 1959-67, ptnr., 1968—. Mem. ABA, Assn. Bar City N.Y. General corporate. Home: 14 E 90th St New York NY 10128 Office: Debevoise & Plimpton 875 3d Ave New York NY 10022

SMART, IRENE BALOGH, judge; b. Cleve., Mar. 24, 1921; d. John and Elizabeth (Szaszak) Balogh; m. Charles Eugene Smart, May 17, 1945 (dec. Apr. 1986); children: Charles Eugene II, Jennifer Lynn Smart Sargus. BS, Wittenberg U., 1942; cert. in physical therapy, Harvard U., 1981; LLB, William McKinley Sch. Law, 1955. Bar: Ohio 1956. Ptnr. Smart & Smart, Canton, Ohio, 1956-78; judge Canton Mcpl. Ct., 1978-85, Ct. Common Pleas, Canton, 1985—. Councilwoman Canton City Council, 1959-72; rep. Ohio Ho. of Reps., Columbus, 1973-78; mem. Dem. Women's Club, Canton Art Inst. Recipient Outstanding Service award Ohio Firefighters, 1976,

Fraternal Order Police, 1976, Excellent Jud. Service award Ohio Supreme Ct., 1984. Mem. ABA, Ohio Bar Assn., Stark County Bar Assn., Am. Judges Assn., U.S. Women Judges Assn. (del. to Peoples Republic China), Canton C. of C., Manzer Camera Club. Presbyterian. Avocations: violinist, oil and water color painting, photography, econs. State civil litigation, Criminal, Personal injury. Home: 3807 3d St NW Canton OH 44708 Office: Ct Common Pleas Stark County Courthouse Market Ave Canton OH 44702

SMART, JAMES HUDSON, lawyer; b. Dallas, Dec. 6, 1906; s. James Hudson and Ann Virginia (Oldham) S.; m. Martha Van Brunt, Mar. 27, 1942; children: Martha Smart Bennett, James Hudson Jr., Robert Oldham. BBA, U. Ariz., 1929; LLB, U. Tex., 1937. Bar: Tex. 1937, U.S. Dist. Ct. (no. dist.) Tex. 1937, U.S. Ct. Appeals (5th cir.) 1950, U.S. Dist. Ct. (we. dist.) Tex. 1971. Pilot Ford Motor Co., 1930-32, United Airlines, 1932-34; ptnr. T.J. McMahon, Abilene, Tex., 1940—; sr. ptnr. McMahon, Smart, Surovik, Suttle, Buhrmann & Cobb, Abilene. Mayor City of Abilene, 1949-51; pres. Abilene Community Theater, Abilene Fine Arts Mus.; bd. dirs. YMCA, Abilene. Served to col. AC, 1942-46. Decorated D.F.C. Mem. ABA, Tex. Bar Assn., Abilene Bar Assn. (dir.), Am. Judicature Soc., Abilene C. of C. Episcopalian. Clubs: Abilene Country, Petroleum (Abilene). Probate, Real property, Oil and gas leasing. Home: 3758 Woodridge Abilene TX 79605 Office: McMahon Smart et al PO Box 1440 Abilene TX 79604

SMARTT, MICHAEL STEWART, lawyer; b. Missoula, Mont., Mar. 5, 1951; s. George Madison and Alice Marion (Haggarty) S.; m. Sheila Boetcher, Aug. 15, 1975; children: Seanna Dawn, Heather Lynn, Michael Stewart. BA, U. Mont., 1974; JD, Gonzaga U., 1977. Bar: Montana 1977. Law clk. to presiding judge Mont Dist. Ct. (8th dist.), Great Falls, 1977; assoc. Hartelius & Assocs., Great Falls, 1977; assoc. atty. pub. defenders Great Falls, 1980-84; pres. The Law Ctr., Great Falls, 1982-84; assoc. Big Sky Law Ctr., Great Falls, 1985—. Active participant Cursillo and Cum Cristo, Great Falls, 1978-85. Mem. ABA, Mont. Bar Assn., Cascade County Bar Assn. (bd. dirs. 1986—). Avocations: music, gardening, carpentry. Criminal, Family and matrimonial, Bankruptcy. Home: 212 3rd Ave N Great Falls MT 59401 Office: Big Sky Law Ctr PC PO Box 2323 503 1st Ave N Great Falls MT 59403

SMAY, STEPHEN LEROY, association executive; b. Sioux City, Iowa, May 16, 1944; s. John LeRoy and Mary Louise (Sargent) S. B.A., Drake U., 1966; J.D., U. Mich., 1968. Asst. prof. bus. law Mich. State U., East Lansing, 1968-70; assoc. atty. Cleary, Gottlieb, et al, N.Y.C., 1970-72; asst. to pres. Council on Fgn. Relations, N.Y.C., 1972-73; grant dir. ABA, Chgo., 1974-77; exec. dir. State Bar Wis., Madison, 1978—. Office: State Bar Wisconsin 402 W Wilson St Madison WI 53703 *

SMEDINGHOFF, THOMAS J., lawyer; b. Chgo., July 15, 1951; s. John A. and Dorothy M.; m. Mary Beth Smedinghoff. B.A. in Math., Knox Coll., 1973; J.D., U. Mich., 1978. Bar: Ill. 1978, U.S. Dist. Ct. (no. dist.) Ill. 1978. Assoc. McBride, Baker & Coles and predecessor McBride & Baker, Chgo., 1978-84, ptnr., 1985—. Author: Legal Guide to Developing, Protecting and Marketing Software, 1986. Mem. Chgo. Bar Assn. (chmn. computer law com. 1984-85), Ill. State Bar Assn., ABA, Computer Law Assn., Assn. Computing Machinery. Computer, Trademark and copyright, General corporate. Office: McBride Baker & Coles 3 First Nat Plaza Suite 3800 Chicago IL 60602

SMEGAL, THOMAS FRANK, JR., lawyer; b. Eveleth, Minn., June 15, 1935; s. Thomas Frank and Genevieve (Andreachi) S.; m. Susan Jane Stanton, May 28, 1966; children: Thomas Frank, Elizabeth Jane. BS in Chem. Engring., Mich. Technol. U., 1957; JD, George Washington U., 1961. Bar: Va. 1961, D.C. 1961, Calif. 1964, U.S. Supreme Ct. 1976. Patent examiner U.S. Patent Office, Washington, 1957-61; staff patent atty. Shell Devel. Co., San Francisco, 1962-65; patent atty. Townsend and Townsend, San Francisco, 1965—, now mng. ptnr.; mem. U.S. del. to Paris Conv. for Protection of Indsl. Property. Pres. bd. dirs. Legal Aid Soc. San Francisco, 1982-84, Youth Law Ctr., 1973-84; bd. dirs. Nat. Ctr. for Youth Law, 1978-84, San Francisco Lawyers Com. for Urban Affairs, 1972—, Legal Services for Children, 1980—, Legal Services Corp., 1984—. Served to capt. Chem. Corps, U.S. Army, 1961-62. Recipient St. Thomas More award, 1982. Mem. ABA, Calif. Bar Assn. (v.p. bd. govs. 1986-87), Nat. Council Patent Law Assn. (dir.), Am. Patent Law Assn. (bd. dirs., pres. 1986), Internat. Assn. Intellectual Property Lawyers (dir.), Bar Assn. San Francisco, Patent Law Assn. San Francisco. Republican. Roman Catholic. Clubs: World Trade, Commonwealth, Olympic, Golden Gate Breakfast (San Francisco); Claremont (Berkeley); University (Washington). Contbr. articles to publs. in field. Patent, Trademark and copyright. Office: Townsend and Townsend 1 Market Plaza San Francisco CA 94105

SMETHILLS, HAROLD REGINALD, business executive, lawyer; b. Denver, Jan. 16, 1948; s. Harold Reginald and Nona Myrtle (Pickett) S.; m. Diane Smethills. B.S.B.A., U. Denver, 1970, M.B.A., 1971, J.D., 1975. Bar: Colo. 1975. Mem. staff United Bank of Denver, 1967-71, exec. banking officer, 1971-73, asst. v.p. nat. accounts, 1972-75, v.p. compliance, 1975-79, v.p. corp. services, 1979-81; v.p. legal and sec. United Banks of Colo., Denver, 1981-85; exec. v.p. corp. fin. and adminstrn. Adolph Coors Co., Golden, Colo., 1986—, also bd. dirs. Served to lt. col. Air N.G., 1970—. Named Outstanding Airman of Colo. Air N.G., 1971. Mem. Bank Adminstrn. Inst. (mem. ednl. council), Colo. Assn. Corp. Counsel (chmn. com.), Aircraft Owners and Pilots Assn. Republican. Episcopalian. Lodge: Rotary. Banking, General corporate, Legislative. Office: Adolph Coors Co Golden CO 80401

SMIDDY, JAMES DALLAS, lawyer; b. Flint, Mich., Nov. 26, 1925; s. Barney Cecil and Carrie Mae (Boling) S.; m. Linda Claiborne O'Riordan, Sept. 9, 1972. BA, Mich. State U., 1950; JD, Vt. Law Sch., 1979. Bar: Pa. 1981, Conn. 1982, U.S. Dist. Ct. (so. and ea. dists.) N.Y. 1983, U.S. Dist. Ct. Conn. 1983. Acct. Gen. Motors Co., Flint, 1950-56; systems engr., mktg. rep., instr. IBM, Flint, Chgo., Yorktown, N.Y., 1956-75; litigation analyst IBM, White Plains, N.Y., 1979-82; market developer Satellite Bus. Systems, Stamford, Conn., 1975-77; assoc. Cummings & Lockwood, Stamford, 1983-86; ptnr. Smiddy & Smiddy, Greenwich, Conn., 1986—; mem. Com. on Computer Crime, Hartford, Conn., 1983-84, SBA Computer Security and Edn. Council, Washington, 1985—. Contbr. numerous articles to profl. jours. Served with USN, 1944-46, PTO. Mem. ABA (corp. and bus. law sect. 1983—), Conn. Bar Assn. (co-chmn. legis. com. 1983-86, computer law sect.). Club: Exchange. Avocations: skiing, jogging, golf, tennis. Computer, General corporate, Contracts commercial. Office: Smiddy & Smiddy 2 Greenwich Plaza Suite 100 Greenwich CT 06830 also: 61 Central St Woodstock VT 05091

SMIDDY, LINDA O'RIORDAN, lawyer; b. Houston, Sept. 17, 1942; d. John Eldridge and Beatrice Elma (Trudeau) O'Riordan; m. James Dallas Smiddy, Sept. 9, 1972. BA, Northwestern U., 1964; MAT, Harvard U., 1965; JD, Vt. Law Sch., 1979; LLM, Yale U., 1983. Instr., systems engr. IBM, Chgo., 1968-74, mgr., Kingston, N.Y., 1974-75; editor Hudson Valley Mag., Pleasant Valley, N.Y., 1975-76; law clk. Hon. J.S. Holden, Fed. Dist. Ct., Vt., 1980-81; assoc. Cravath, Swaine & Moore, N.Y.C., 1981-83, Cummings & Lockwood, Stamford, Conn., 1983-86; ptnr. Smiddy & Smiddy, Greenwich, Conn., 1986—; co-chmn. Com. on Computer Crime, Hartford, Conn., 1983-84. Recipient Am. Pen Women's award Northwestern U., 1964; Learned Hand award for acad. excellence Vt. Law Sch., South Royalton, Vt., 1976. Mem. Conn. Bar Assn. (co-chmn. legis. com. computer law sect.), Phi Lambda Theta. Computer, General corporate, Legal education. Office: Smiddy & Smiddy 2 Greenwich Plaza Suite 100 Greenwich CT 06830 also: 61 Central St Woodstock VT 05091

SMIETANKA, JOHN ALLEN, lawyer; b. Chgo., June 28, 1941; s. Allen J. and Virginia C. (Conerty) S.; m. Robin Zollar, Dec. 30, 1978; 1 child, Cara. B.A. in Philosophy, Oblate Fathers Scholasticate, Pass Christian, Miss., 1964; J.D., John Marshall Law Sch., Chgo., 1968. Bar: Mich. Ill., U.S. Dist. Ct. (no. dist.) Ill., U.S. Dist. Ct. (we. dist.) Mich., U.S. Ct. Appeals (6th cir.), U.S. Supreme Ct. Atty. Smietanka & Garrigan, Chgo., 1969-70; asst. pros. atty. Berrien County, St. Joseph, Mich., 1970-74; pros. atty. Berrien County, 1974-81; U.S. atty. Dept. Justice, Grand Rapids, Mich., 1981—; mem. Mich. Environ. Rev. Bd., Lansing, 1977-81. Mem. Mich. Republican State Com., Lansing, 1978-81. Mem. State Bar Mich., Grand Rapids Bar Assn., Fed. Bar Assn. (chpt. v.p. 1982-83), ABA, Am. Soc. Internat. Law, Pros. Attys. Assn. of Mich. (pres., dir. 1975—). Republican. Roman Catholic. Lodges: Rotary (St. Joseph, Grand Rapids). Criminal, Federal civil litigation, State civil litigation. Office: US Atty's Office 399 Federal Bldg Grand Rapids MI 49503

SMILEY, GUY IAN, lawyer; b. N.Y.C., July 30, 1938; s. Edward and Minerva June (Silverman) S.; m. Constance Ann Rodbell, July 30, 1967; children: Erica, Andrew. BA, Cornell U., 1960; JD, Columbia U., 1963. Bar: N.Y 1964, U.S. Dist. Ct. (so. dist.) N.Y. 1965, U.S. Dist. Ct. (ea. dist.) N.Y. 1965, U.S. Ct. Appeals (2d cir.) 1967, U.S. Supreme Ct. 1970. Assoc. Law Offices of Harry H. Lipsig, N.Y.C., 1964-68; ptnr. Smiley, Schwartz & Captain, N.Y.C., 1968—; arbitrator Am. Arbitration Assn., N.Y. 1974—, Civil Ct. City of N.Y., 1974-80; co-chmn. Combined Jud. Screening Panel City of N.Y., 1983—. Contbr.: (book) The Lawyers Secretary, 1972. V.p., gen. counsel Westchester Emergency Communications Assn., White Plains, N.Y., 1979—; vol. counsel Am. Radio Relay League, 1983—. Served to lt. (JAGC) USN 1966-70. Mem. Assn. Trial Lawyers Am. (sustaining), N.Y. State Trial Lawyers Assn. (mem. legis. com., 1979-85, bd. dirs. 1982—, editor-in-chief newsletter, 1984—, dep. treas. 1986), Jewish Lawyers Guild (sec. 1984—). Avocations: amateur radio, tennis, skiing. Personal injury, State civil litigation, Federal civil litigation. Home: 294 Trenor Dr New Rochelle NY 10804 Office: Smiley Schwartz & Captain 60 E 42d St New York NY 10165

SMILEY, ROBERT RENNSLAER, III, lawyer; b. Chgo., Nov. 20, 1933; s. Robert Rennslaer II and Vera Eloise (McCord) S.; m. Antonia Browning, Dec. 29, 1956; children—Sim E., Robert Rennslaer IV, Nicholas. B.S. with distinction, U.S. Naval Acad., 1956; postgrad. in law U. Florence (Italy); J.D. with honors, George Washington U., 1970. Bar: D.C. 1970; U.S. Ct. Appeals (D.C. cir.) 1973, U.S. Appeals (4th cir.) 1974, U.S. Ct. Claims 1973, U.S. Supreme Ct. 1975, U.S. Ct. Appeals (9th cir.) 1982; lic. comml. pilot. Trial atty. air crash unit Civil div. U.S. Dept. Justice, 1970-72; sole practice, Washington, 1972-73; sr. ptnr. Smiley & Lear, Washington, 1973-78, Smiley Olson Gilman & Pangia, Washington and Charleston, S.C., 1980—. Served to capt. USNR 1956-68. Decorated Navy Commendation medal with combat V, Air medal with 11 oak leaf clusters; George Olmsted Found. fellow, 1961. Mem. ABA, D.C. Bar, Bar Assn. D.C., Fed. Bar Assn., Assn. Trial Lawyers Am., Lawyer-Pilot Bar Assn., Soc. Air Safety Investigators, Order of Coif. Asst. editor George Washington Law Rev.; contbr. articles to profl. jours. Aviation, Personal injury, Federal civil litigation. Home: 71 E Bay St Charleston SC 29401 Office: Smiley Olson Gilman & Pangia 39 Broad St Charleston SC 29402

SMILEY, STANLEY ROBERT, lawyer; b. N.Y.C., Feb. 19, 1947; s. Arthur and Rose Smiley; m. Anita Kape, June 28, 1970; children—Wayne Alan, Lori Patricia. B.A., SUNY-Buffalo, 1968; J.D., St. John's U., 1971. Bar: N.Y. 1971, Calif. 1977, U.S. Tax Ct. 1972, U.S. Ct. Mil. Appeals 1972, U.S. Ct. Appeals (9th cir.) 1979, U.S. Dist. Ct. (cen. dist.) Calif. 1978, U.S. Dist. Ct. (no. dist.) Calif. 1979, U.S. Dist. Ct. (so. dist.) Calif. 1979, U.S. Dist. Ct. (ea. dist.) Calif. 1979. Atty., Office of Chief Counsel, IRS, Newark, 1971-72, Los Angeles, 1976-78; ptnr. McLaughlin and Irvin, Los Angeles, San Francisco and Newport Beach, Calif., 1978—; guest instr. U. Md., Madrid, 1974-76. Served with JAGC, USAF, 1972-76. Decorated Air Force Commendation medal. Mem. ABA (com. tax ct. procedure 1981—), State Bar N.Y., State Bar Calif., Los Angeles County Bar Assn., Bar Assn. San Francisco, Phi Delta Phi. Club: Stock Exchange (Los Angeles). Assoc. editor St. John's Law Rev., 1969-71. Pension, profit-sharing, and employee benefits, Probate, Corporate taxation. Home: 2525 Camino Del Sol Fullerton CA 92633 Office: 801 S Grand Ave 3d Floor Los Angeles CA 90017

SMIT, HANS, law educator, academic administrator, lawyer; b. Amsterdam, Netherlands, Aug. 13, 1927; came to U.S. 1952; s. Eylard Albertus and Trijntje (de Jong) S.; m. Beverly M. Gershgol, Aug. 1, 1954; children: Robert Hugh, Marion Tina. LLB with highest honors, U. Amsterdam, 1946, JD with highest honors, 1949; AM, Columbia U., 1953, LLB with highest honors, 1958. Bar: Supreme Ct. Netherlands 1946, N.Y. 1974. Mem. Bodenhausen, Blackstone, Rueb, Bloemsma & Smit, The Hague, 1952-58; assoc. Sullivan & Cromwell, N.Y.C., 1958-60; mem. faculty law Columbia U., 1960—, assoc. prof., 1960-62, prof., 1962—, Stanley H. Fuld prof. law, 1978—, dir. Parker Sch. Fgn. and Comparative Law, 1980—; vis. prof. U. Paris, Sorbonne-Pantheon, 1975-76; dir. Project on Internat. Proc., Columbia U., 1960—; reporter U.S. Com. on Internat. Rules Jud. Procedure, 1960-67; dir. Project on European Legal Inst., 1968—; dir. Leyden-Amsterdam-Columbia Summer Program in Am. Law, 1963—; cons. intenat. comml. transactions, internat. litigation; arbitrator ICC and AAA. Author: International Cooperations in Litigation, 1963, (with others) Elements of Civil Procedure, International Law, 1980, 4th edit., 1986, World Arbitration Reporter, 1986, (with Herzog) The Law of the European Economic Community, 1978. Mem. All-Dutch Waterpolo team 1946-48, All-Am. Waterpolo team, AAU, 1954. Mem. ABA, Internat. Bar Assn., Internat. Law Assn., Am. Fgn. Law Assn., Assn. Bar City N.Y., Am. Soc. Internat. Law, German-Am. Lawyers' Assn., Internat. Assn. Jurists of U.S.A.-Italy, Internat. Acad. Comparative Law, Royal Dutch Soc. Arts and Scis. (assoc.). Office: Columbia U Sch Law 435 W 116th St New York NY 10027

SMITH, ANDREW LOVGREN, lawyer; b. Mobile, Ala., Dec. 2, 1951; s. Curtis Andrew and Sonja Louise (Goller) S.; m. Kaye Geiger, Aug. 2, 1975; children: Kami, Justin, Nathan. BS, U. South Ala., 1973; JD, U. Ala., 1976; LLM in Taxation, NYU, 1977. Bar: Ala. 1976, U.S. Dist. Ct. (so. dist.) Ala. 1980, U.S. Ct. Appeals (5th and 11th cirs.) 1980. Assoc. Johnstone, Adams, May, Howard & Hill, Mobile, 1977-81; ptnr. Smith & Hill, Mobile, 1981-82, Brown, Hudgens & Richardson, Mobile, 1982—. Republican. Methodist. General corporate, Real property, Probate. Office: Brown Hudgens Richardson 1495 University Blvd Mobile AL 36609

SMITH, ARTHUR ALLAN, lawyer; b. Detroit, May 22, 1931; s. Arthur M.; m. Lois C. Crutchfield, June 14, 1955; children: Mark, Scott, Amy. Student Mich. State U., 1949-52; LLB, U. Va., 1955, JD, 1970. Bar: Mich. 1956. Asst. U.S. Atty. ea. dist. of Mich., 1957-59; ptnr. Watson, Lott & Wunsch, Detroit, 1959-63; ptnr. Fildew, Degree, Gilbride & Smith, Detroit, 1963-71; ptnr. Smith, Poplar & Kalis, Dearborn, Mich., 1971-83, Smith & Smith, Dearborn, 1983—; instr. Henry Ford Community Coll.; chmn. com. on specialization State Bar of Mich., mem. com. on profl. and jud. ethics, com. on client security fund. Chmn. bd. mgmt. Fairlane YMCA, 1966-69; commr. Indian Affairs for Mich., 1961-71. Served to 1st lt. U.S. Army, 1955-57. Mem. ABA, Fed. Bar Assn. (pres. Detroit chpt.), Detroit Bar Assn., Dearborn Bar Assn. Republican. Methodist. Lodge: Rotary (pres. Dearborn 1978-79, pres. found. 1982—). General practice, State civil litigation, Federal civil litigation. Office: 5th Floor Village Plaza Tower Dearborn MI 48124

SMITH, ARTHUR B(EVERLY), JR., lawyer; b. Abilene, Tex., Sept. 11, 1944; s. Arthur B. and Florence B. (Baker) S.; m. Marya Argetsinger, Dec. 30, 1968; children—Arthur C., Sarah R. B.S., Cornell U., 1966; J.D., U. Chgo., 1969. Bar: Ill. 1969, N.Y. 1976. Assoc. Vedder, Price, Kaufman & Kammholz, Chgo., 1969-74; asst. prof. law N.Y. State Sch. Indsl. and Labor Relations, Cornell U., 1975-77; ptnr. Vedder, Price, Kaufman & Kammholz, Chgo., 1977-86, Murphy, Smith & Polk, Chgo., 1986—; guest. lectr. Northwestern U. Grad. Sch. Mgmt., 1979, Sch. Law, spring 1980; mem. hearing bd. Ill. Atty. Registration and Disciplinary Commn. Recipient award for highest degree of dedication and excellence in teaching N.Y. State Sch. Indsl. and Labor Relations, Cornell U., 1977. Mem. Chgo. Bar Assn., N.Y. State Bar Assn., ABA (co-chmn. com. on devel. law under Nat. Labor Relations Act, Sect. Labor Relations Law 1976-77). Presbyterian. Clubs: Chgo. Athletic Assn., Monroe (Chgo.). Author: Employment Discrimination Law Cases and Materials, 1978, supplement, 1980, 2d edit., 1982,supplement, 1986; Construction Labor Relations, 1984; co-editor: Cumulative Supplement to Morris, The Developing Labor Law, 1976; co-editor-in-chief 1976 Annual Supplement to Morris, The Developing Labor Law, 1977; assoc. editor: The Developing Labor Law (Morris), 2d edit., 1983; contbr. articles to profl. jours. Labor, Civil rights, Federal civil litigation. Office: Murphy Smith & Polk Two First National Plaza 24th Floor Chicago IL 60603

SMITH, ARTHUR LEE, lawyer; b. Davenport, Iowa, Dec. 19, 1941; s. Harry Arthur Smith (dec.) and Ethel (Hoffman) Duerre; m. Georgia Mills, June 12, 1965 (dec. Jan. 1984); m. Jean Bowler, Aug. 4, 1984; children—Juliana, Christopher, Andrew. B.A., Augustana Coll., Rock Island, Ill., 1964; M.A., Am. U., 1968; J.D., Washington U., St. Louis, 1971. Bar: Mo. 1971, D.C. 1983. Telegraph editor Davenport Morning Democrat, 1962-64; ptnr. Peper Martin Jensen Maichel & Hetlage, St. Louis, 1971-82, Washington, 1983—; arbitrator Nat. Assn. Security Dealers, 1980—, Am. Arbitration Assn., 1980—. Served to lt. USN, 1964-68. Mem. ABA, D.C. Bar Assn., Mo. Bar Assn. (vice-chair ins. programs com. 1981-83, vice-chair antitrust com. 1983-86), Am. Judicature Soc., Order of Coif. Federal civil litigation, Pension, profit-sharing, and employee benefits, Securities. Home: 1321 Darnall Dr McLean VA 22101 Office: Peper Martin Jensen Maichel & Hetlage 1730 Pennsylvania Ave NW Suite 400 Washington DC 20006

SMITH, BAKER ARMSTRONG, construction company executive, lawyer; b. Brunswick, Ga., Oct. 3, 1947; s. William Armstrong and Priscilla (Baker) S.; m. Deborah Elizabeth Ellis, Nov. 13, 1982; children: Ellis Armstrong, Elizabeth Anne. BS, U.S. Naval Acad., 1969; MBA, Northeastern U., 1975; JD cum laude, Suffolk U., 1977; LLM in Labor, Georgetown U., 1981. Bar: Ga. 1977, D.C. 1978, U.S. Supreme Ct. 1980. Commd. ensign U.S. Navy, 1969, advanced through grades to lt., 1974; exec. dir., founder The Center on Nat. Labor Policy, Inc., North Springfield, Va., 1977-81; asst. to sec., dir. labor relations U.S. Dept. HUD, Washington, 1981-83; exec. v.p. U.S. Bus. and Indsl. Council, Nashville, 1983-84; pres. Am. Quality Builders, Inc., Nashville, 1984-86; v.p. Hopeman Bros., Inc., Waynesboro, Va., 1986—; sec., founder U.S. Constitutional Rights Legal Def. Fund, Inc., Atlanta, 1983—; trustee Leadership Inst., Springfield, Va., 1978—; mem. Council for Nat. Policy, Washington, 1981-86, Civil Rights Reviewing Authority U.S. Dept. Edn., Washington, 1984—; transition team leader Office of the Pres.-Elect of the U.S., NLRB, Occupational Safety and Health Review Commn., Fed. Mediation and Conciliation Service, Nat. Mediation Bd., Fed. Labor Relations Authority, Washington, 1980-81; instr. law, faculty sec. No. Va. Law Sch., Alexandria, Va., 1980-83; instr. law D.C. Law Sch., Washington, 1978-80. Contbg. author: Mandate for Leadership, 1981; contbr. articles to profl. jours. Served to lt. USN, 1969-74. Mem. St. George's House, Windsor Castle (assoc.), ABA (Nat. Law Day chmn. 1976-77, Silver Key award 1977), Phila. Soc., U.S. Supreme Ct. Hist. Soc., Federalist Soc., Beta Gamma Sigma, Phi Delta Phi (council mem. 1981—, sr. council mem. 1985—). Republican. Presbyterian. Club: Capitol Hill (Washington). Civil rights, Labor. Home: 5 Hickory Hill Ln Waynesboro VA 22939

SMITH, BARNEY OVEYETTE, JR., lawyer; b. Mobile, Ala., July 29, 1952; s. Barney O. Sr. and Delores (Long) S.; m. Rita Ward, May 31, 1975; children: Barney O. III, Berkley Lauren. BA, Furman U., 1973; JD, U. S.C., 1976. Bar: S.C. 1976, U.S. Dist. Ct. S.C. 1976, U.S. Ct. Appeals (4th cir.) 1981, U.S. Supreme Ct. 1981. Ptnr. Smith & McKinney, P.A., Greenville, S.C., 1976—. Fellow Nat. Bd. Trial Adv.; mem. ABA, Assn. Trial Lawyers Am. (sustaining) , S.C. Trial Lawyers Assn. (bd. dirs. 1984—, pres. elect 1986—). Democrat. Personal injury, Insurance. Home: 502 Sugar Valley Ct Greer SC 29651 Office: 1024 E North St Greenville SC 29601

SMITH, BRIAN DAVID, lawyer, educator; b. Fayetteville, Ark., Oct. 29, 1953; s. Samuel Charles and Janelle (McCaskill) S.; m. Sharon Kay Wilson, June 16, 1979; children: Garrett Walker, Brian Austin. JD, La. State U., 1977. Bar: La. 1978, U.S. Dist. Ct. (we. dist.) La. 1979, U.S. Tax Ct. 1980, U.S. Ct. Appeals (5th cir.) 1980. Law clk. to presiding justice 1st Jud. Cir. Ct. La., Shreveport, La., 1978-79; assoc. Nelson, Hammons & Johnson, Shreveport, 1979-84, Lunn, Irion, Johnson, Salley & Carlisle, Shreveport, 1984—; instr. legal asst. cirriculum La. State U., Shreveport, 1984—. Mem. Shreveport Young Reps., 1985—. Mem. ABA, La. Bar Assn., La. Trial Lawyers Assn., Assn. Trial Lawyers Am. Methodist. Club: Shreveport Country. Avocations: golf, snow skiing, tennis. Personal injury, Insurance, Federal civil litigation. Home: 9912 Beaver Creek Shreveport LA 71106 Office: Lunn Irion Johnson Salley & Carlisle PO Box 1534 Shreveport LA 71165-1534

SMITH, BRIAN JOSEPH, lawyer; b. Albany, N.Y., Jan. 3, 1952; s. Joseph Peter Smith and mary Ellen (Milot) Dolan; m. Lori Alisa Barraco, Aug. 7, 1977. BS, SUNY, Brockport, 1974; JD, N.Y. Catholic U., 1977. Bar: N.Y. 1979, U.S. Dist. Ct. (no. dist.) N.Y. 1979. Sr. atty. N.Y. State Dept. Law, Albany, 1978—; lectr. SUNY, Albany, 1982. Dem. committeeman Albany County, 1978-84; mem. exec. bd. N.Y. Pub. Employees Fedn., AFL-CIO, Albany, 1984—; pres. Poestenkill County for Arts, Inc., Sand Lake, N.Y., 1985—. Mem. ABA (subcom. chmn. 1980), N.Y. State Bar Assn., Albany County Bar Assn. Avocation: baseball. Consumer commercial, State civil litigation, Administrative and regulatory. Home: 119-A Taborton Rd Sand Lake NY 12153 Office: NY State Dept Law The Capitol Albany NY 12224

SMITH, BRIAN WILLIAM, lawyer, former govt. ofcl.; b. N.Y.C., Feb. 3, 1947; s. William Francis and Dorothy Edwina (Vogel) S.; m. Donna Jean Holverson, Apr. 24, 1976; children—Mark Holverson, Lauren Elizabeth. B.A., St. John's U., 1968, J.D., 1971; M.S., Columbia U., 1981. Bar: N.Y. 1972, D.C. 1975, U.S. Supreme Ct. 1976, U.S. Dist. Ct. N.Y. 1975, U.S. Dist. Ct. D.C. 1986. Atty., Am. Express Co., N.Y.C., 1970-73, CIT Fin. Corp., N.Y.C., 1973-74; assoc. counsel, mng. atty. Interbank Card Assn., N.Y.C., 1974-75, sr. v.p., corp. sec., gen. counsel, 1975-82; chief counsel to comptroller of currency, Washington, 1982-84; mng. ptnr. Stroock & Stroock & Lavan, Washington, 1984-86; mng. ptnr., 1986—. Served to capt., USAR, 1970-78. Mem. N.Y. State Bar Assn., ABA, D.C. Bar Assn., Assn. Bar City N.Y., Fed. Bar Assn., Computer Law Assn. Clubs: N.Y. Athletic, City Washington. Banking, Antitrust, General corporate. Home: 3646 Upton St NW Washington DC 20008 Office: 1150 17th St NW Washington DC 20036

SMITH, BRISCOE R., lawyer; b. Orange, N.J., Mar. 29, 1938; s. Theodore H. and Mary Virginia (Ranson) S.; m. Lee Sanders, Sept. 8, 1962; children: Radford, Ranson, Brewster. BA, Williams Coll., 1960; LLB, U. Va., 1963. Bar: N.Y. 1964, U.S. Dist. Ct. (so. and ea. dists.) N.Y., U.S. Ct. Appeals (2d, 4th, 5th and 6th cirs.). Law clk. to presiding justice U.S. Ct. Appeals, N.Y.C., 1963-64; assoc. Millbank, Tweed, Hadley & McCloy, N.Y.C., 1964-72, ptnr., 1972—. Elder Reformed Ch. Bronxville, N.Y., 1986—. Mem. ABA, Assn. of Bar of City of N.Y., Fed. Bar Council. Club: Siwanoy Country (gov. 1986—) (Bronxville). Federal civil litigation, State civil litigation. Office: Milbank Tweed Hadley & McCloy 1 Chase Manhattan Plaza New York NY 10005

SMITH, BROOK MCCRAY, lawyer; b. Ft. Wayne, Ind., Nov. 19, 1947; s. Frederick Charles and Marjorie (Kuhn) S.; m. Melinda Jean Watson, Aug. 22, 1974 (div. Dec. 1984); 1 child, Morgan McCray; m. Martha Eddlemon, Feb. 6, 1987. BS in Indsl. Engring., U. Mich., 1970, JD, 1974. Bar: Mich. 1974, U.S. Dist. Ct. (ea. dist.) Mich. 1975, U.S. Ct. Appeals (6th cir.) 1980. Sole practice Ann Arbor, Mich., 1974—. Mem. Mich. Bar Assn., Washtenaw County Bar Assn. Presbyterian. Clubs: Huron Portage Yacht (chmn. race com.), Interlake Fleet 22 (Pickney, Mich.) (capt. 1985). Avocations: sailboat racing, computer programming. General corporate, Real property, General practice. Office: 101 W Liberty St Ann Arbor MI 48104

SMITH, BRUCE ARTHUR, lawyer; b. Terre Haute, Ind., Jan. 4, 1952; s. Wayne Coakley and Stella Inez S.; m. Jacalyn Marie Harker, Sept. 4, 1983; children: Ashley Nicole, Haley Marie. BS, Ind. State U., 1973; JD cum laude, Ind. U., 1976. Bar: Ind. 1976, U.S. Dist. Ct. (so. dist.) Ind. 1976, U.S. Tax Ct. 1977, Ill. 1984, U.S. Supreme Ct. 1983. Ptnr. Sturm, Smith & Webster, Vincennes, Ind., 1976—; instr. para legal edn. Vincennes U., 1977-81, mem. adv. bd. dept. small bus. edn., 1984-86; dep. pros. atty. Knox County Prosecutor's Office, Vincennes, 1976-82. Mem. ABA, Ind. Bar Assn., Ill. Bar Assn., Knox County Bar Assn. (pres. 1982-83), Assn. Trial Lawyers Am., Ind. Trial Lawyers Assn., Knox County C. of C. (bd. dirs., pres. 1985-86), Vincennes Area C. of C. (bd. dirs., pres. 1985-86), Phi Delta Phi. Lodges: Kiwanis (pres. 1981-82), Elks (exalted ruler 1983-84). Banking, Contracts commercial, General practice. Home: 1918 McDowell Vincennes IN 47591 Office: Sturm Smith & Webster 302 Main St PO Box 393 Vincennes IN 47591

SMITH, CAROL ANN, lawyer; b. Birmingham, Ala., Apr. 23, 1949; d. James William and Mildred Viola (Ferguson) S. BA, Birmingham So. Coll., 1971; J.D., U. Ala.-Tuscaloosa, 1975; LL.M., NYU, 1977. Bar: Ala. 1975,

U.S. Dist. Ct. (no. dist.) Ala. 1977, U.S. Dist. Ct. (mid. dist.) Ala. 1976, U.S. Ct. Appeals (11th cir.) 1981, U.S. Ct. Appeals (5th cir.) 1979. Law clk. Ala. Supreme Ct., Montgomery, 1975-76; assoc. Lange, Simpson, Robinson & Somerville, Birmingham, 1977-81; assoc. Starnes & Atchison, Birmingham, 1981-83, ptnr., 1983—. Editorial bd. Ala. Law Rev., 1973-75. Mem. bd. mgmt. Downtown YMCA, Birmingham, 1984-85, mem. exec. com., 1985—. Mem. Birmingham Bar Assn. (pres. young lawyers sect. 1984), Ala. Bar Inst. for Continuing Legal Edn. (exec. com. 1979—), Ala. Bar Assn. (editorial bd. The Ala. Lawyer 1979—, assoc. editor 1984—, exec. com. young lawyers sect. 1983-84, chmn. continuing legal edn. com. of young lawyers sect. 1984, mem. pres.'s adv. task foce 1984-85), Eleventh Cir. Jud. Conf. (alt. del. 1985—), Phi Beta Kappa. Methodist. Club: Birmingham Jr. Music Bd. Federal civil litigation, Insurance, State civil litigation. Home: 1511 Ridge Rd Homewood AL 35209 Office: Starnes & Atchison One Daniel Plaza Daniel Bldg Birmingham AL 35233

SMITH, CAROL JEAN, lawyer; b. Anniston, Ala., Oct. 12, 1947; d. Claudous Sellers and Hester (Ledbetter) S. BS, Jacksonville State U., 1970; JD, U. Ala., 1973. Bar: Ala. 1973, U.S. Dist. Ct. (mid. dist.) Ala. 1974, U.S. Ct. Appeals (5th cir.) 1974, U.S. Supreme Ct. 1977, U.S. Dist. Ct. (no. dist.) Ala. 1981, U.S. Ct. Appeals (11th cir.) 1981, U.S. Dist. Ct. (so. dist.) Ala. 1985. Law clk. to presiding justice Supreme Ct. Ala., Montgomery, 1973-74; asst. atty. gen. State of Ala., Montgomery, 1974—. Named one of Outstanding Young Women Am., 1974, 84, Outstanding Alumna, Jacksonville State U., 1985. Mem. ABA, Ala. Bar Assn., Montgomery County Bar Assn., Farrah Law Soc., Bench and Bar Soc., Am. Assn. Univ. Women, League Women Voters (bd. dirs. Montgomery chpt. 1985—), Phi Alpha Delta (treas. 1972-73), Alpha Xi Delta (pres. 1974-76, nat. fin. v.p. 1978-82, nat. alumnae v.p. 1982-84), Kappa Delta Epsilon, Sigma Tau Delta, Pi Gamma Mu. Democrat. Baptist. Lodge: Zonta (recording sec. 1986—). Avocations: vol. work, Ala. football. Local government, Administrative and regulatory. Home: 2014 Rexford Rd Montgomery AL 36116 Office: Office of Atty Gen 11 S Union Montgomery AL 36130

SMITH, CHARLES F., JR., lawyer; b. Rhinelander, Wis., July 16, 1918; s. Charles F. Sr. and Jeanette (Burnsen) S.; m. Joan Sampson, Feb. 7, 1948; children: Nancy, Kathryn, Charles, Richard. BA, U. Wis., 1941, JD, 1948. Bar: Wis. 1948, U.S. Dist. Ct. (ea. and we. dists.) Wis. Ptnr. Tinkham, Smith, Bliss, Patterson, Richards & Hessert, Wausau, Wis., 1948—. Mem. city council, Wausau, 1950-60; state senator, Madison, Wis., 1963-67; supr. Marathon County Bd., Wausau, 1950-60, chmn. 1957-58; past pres. Cancer Soc., Wausau; past bd. dirs. ARC, YMCA, Wausau Club, Little League, United Fund, Ch. Vestry. Served to 1st lt. U.S. Army, 1942-46, PTO. Mem. ABA, Wis. Bar Assn., Marathon County Bar Assn. (past pres.), Internat. Assn. Ins. Council, Am. Legion. Republican. Episcopalian. Lodges: Elks, Rotary (pres. Wausau 1957-58, past bd. dirs.). Avocations: sports. Personal injury, State civil litigation, Workers' compensation. Office: Tinkham Smith Bliss et al PO Box 1144 630 4th St Wausau WI 54401

SMITH, CHARLES LYNWOOD, JR., judge; b. Talladega, Ala., Feb. 25, 1943; s. Charles Lynwood and Ann Lou (Riley) S.; children—Ashley Lauren, Carlton Riley. Student Ga. Inst. Tech., 1961-63; B.A., U. Ala., 1966; M.A., Rutgers U., 1967; J.D., U. Ala., 1971. Bar: Ala. 1971; U.S. Dist. Ct. (no. dist.) Ala. 1971, U.S. Dist. Ct. (no. dist.) Tex., 1974, U.S. Ct. Appeals (5th cir.) 1973. Instr. polit. sci. Rutgers U., 1968-69; cons. Fla., Miss. and Ala. State Legislatures, 1968-70; law clk. to chief judge U.S. Dist. Ct. (no. dist.) Ala., Birmingham, 1971-72; mem. Bell, Richardson, Cleary, McLain & Tucker, Huntsville, Ala., 1972-75, Hornsby, Blankenship, Smith & Robinson, 1975-81; dist. judge 23d Jud. Cir. Ala. (Madison County), Huntsville, 1981, cir. judge, 1981—; instr., lectr. polit. sci. Rutgers U., 1968-69, U. Ala., Huntsville, 1967, 1972-75. Mem. Madison County Democratic Exec. Com., 1974-81; mem. Huntsville Electric Utility Bd., 1978-81, chmn., 1980-81; chmn. Hist. Huntsville Found. 1974-76; pres. Madison County Young Dems., 1977-78; dist. chmn. Chickasaw Dist., Tenn. Valley Council, Boy Scouts Am., 1981-82. Recipient Henderson M. Somerville Law prize U. Ala. Law Sch., 1971; named Outstanding Grad. Phi Delta Phi, U. Ala., 1971. Mem. Ala. State Bar (pres. Young Lawyers sect. 1978-79), ABA, Ala. Assn. Cir. Judges, Fed. Bar Assn., Ala. Trial Lawyers Assn., Omicron Delta Kappa, Pi Sigma Alpha. Methodist. Club: Rotary (Huntsville). Author: Strengthening the Florida Legislature, 1970. Contbr. articles to profl. jours. State civil litigation, Criminal, Jurisprudence. Office: Madison County Courthouse Huntsville AL 35801

SMITH, CHARLES STERLING, lawyer; b. Monroe, La., Aug. 3, 1948; s. William Ernest and Byrnie (Handy) S., Jr. BS, La. State U., 1970, JD, 1973. Bar: La. 1973, U.S. Dist. Ct. (we. dist.) La. 1973, U.S. Ct. Appeals (5th cir.) 1974. Ptnr. Hayes, Harkey, Smith, Cascio & Mullens, Monroe, La., 1973—. Mem. La. Young Lawyers Assn. (council mem. 1976-83), La. State Bar Assn. (Ho. of Dels. 1981—). Republican. Methodist. Insurance, Federal civil litigation, State civil litigation. Office: Hayes Harkey Smith Cascio & Mullens 2811 Kilpatrick Blvd PO Box 8032 Monroe LA 71211

SMITH, CHRISTOPHER MICHAEL, lawyer; b. New Orleans, La., Dec. 8, 1951; s. Jack Haynes and Helen Hilda (Lotz) S.; m. Lilly Rose Mary Fournier, Aug. 3, 1973; children: Christine, Chad. BA in Polit. Sci., La. State U., 1973, JD, 1976. Bar: La. 1976, U.S. Dist. Ct. (ea. and we. dists.) La. 1976. Assoc. Law Office of M. Serpas, Galliano, La., 1976-77; sole practice Golden Meadow, La., 1977-79; ptnr. Smith & Main, Slidell, La., 1979-80, Cheramie & Smith, Cutoff, La., 1984—; sole practice Cutoff, 1980-83. Mem. St. Tammany Planning and Zoning Commn., Covington, Va., 1980-83. Mem. ABA, La. Bar Assn., La. Trial Lawyers Assn., Lafourche Parish Bar Assn. Presbyterian. Club: City (New Orleans). Avocations: fishing, boating. Personal injury, Family and matrimonial, General practice. Office: Cheramie & Smith 2024 W Main PO Box 640 Cutoff LA 70345

SMITH, CODY WALKER, JR., lawyer; b. Rock Hill, S.C., Oct. 15, 1945; s. Cody Walker and Jean R. (Mills) S.; m. Betty Oliver Anglin, May 27, 1971; children—Cody Walker III, Jennifer Lynn, Shannon Elizabeth. B.A., Clemson U., 1967; J.D., U. S.C., 1971. Bar: S.C. 1971, U.S. Dist. Ct. S.C. 1971, U.S. Ct. Appeals (4th cir.) 1974, U.S. Supreme Ct. 1974. Law clerk U.S. Dist. Ct., Columbia, S.C., 1971-72; ptnr. Solomon, Kahn, Smith & Baumil, Charleston, S.C., 1972—. Contbr. chpt. to book, articles to profl. jours. Served with USAR, 1968-72. Mem. ABA, S.C. Bar Assn., S.C. Trial Lawyers Assn. (pres. 1982-83), Assn. Trial Lawyers Am. (state committeeman 1974-78, bd. govs. 1986—), Order of Wig and Robe, Phi Delta Phi. Democrat. Presbyterian. Federal civil litigation, State civil litigation, General practice. Home: 1003 Casseque Province Mount Pleasant SC 29464 Office: Solomon Kahn Smith & Baumil 39 Broad St PO Drawer P Charleston SC 29402

SMITH, CORNELIUS C., JR., lawyer, chemical company executive; b. N.Y.C., Oct. 30, 1941; s. Cornelius C. Sr. and Mary (Foley) S.; m. Katherine Moroney; children: Douglas, Michael, Bradley. BS in History, Holy Cross Coll., 1963; JD, NYU, 1966. Bar: N.Y. 1966. Assoc. Haight, Gardner, Poor & Havens, N.Y.C., 1969-72; chief environ. counsel Texaco, Inc., N.Y.C., 1972-76; assoc. Le Boeuf, Lamb, Leiby & MacRae, N.Y.C., 1976-78; chief environ. counsel Union Carbide Corp., Danbury, Conn., 1978-85; asst. gen. counsel Union Carbide Corp., Danbury, 1985, v.p. community and employee health, safety environ. protection, 1985—. Contbr. articles to profl. jours. Served to maj. (JAGC) USMC, 1966-69. Mem. ABA (natural resources sect.), Westcheser-Fairfield Corp. Counsel Assn., Ctr. for Pub. Resources (hazardous waste com.), Soc. of Chem. Industry, Environ. Law Inst. (assoc.). Republican. Roman Catholic. Avocations: boating, tennis, fishing. Environment, Health, Administrative and regulatory. Home: 23 Joann Circle Westport CT 06880 Office: Union Carbide Corp J-3 Old Ridgebury Rd Danbury CT 06817-0001

SMITH, DAVID BURNELL, lawyer; b. Charleston, W.Va., Apr. 8, 1941; s. Ernest Dayton and Nellie Dale (Tyler) S.; m. Rita J. Hughes. Sept. 25, 1967. B.A., U. Charleston, 1967; J.D., U. Balt., 1972. Bar: Colo. 1972, Md. 1972, U.S. Supreme Ct. 1980, Ariz. 1983, U.S. Dist. Ct. Md. 1972, U.S. Dist. Ct. Colo. 1972, U.S. Ct. Appeals (4th cir.) 1972, U.S. Ct. Appeals (9th cir.) 1972, U.S. Ct. Appeals (10th cir.) 1983. Sales rep. Gulf Oil, Washington, 1967-72; sole practice, Littleton, Colo., 1972-83, Glendale, Ariz., 1983-86, Phoenix, 1986—. Vice pres. South Jefferson County Republicans, Lakewood, Colo., 1979, pres., 1980. Served with USCG, 1959-66. Mem. Nat. Assn. Criminal Lawyers, Am. Judicature Soc., ABA (vice-chmn. family law), Colo. Bar Assn., Ariz. Bar Assn., Md. Bar Assn., Assn. Trial Lawyers Am., Colo. Trial Lawyers Assn., Ariz. Trial Lawyers Assn. Maricopa County Bar Assn. Lodges: Masons, Shriners, Elks. State civil litigation, Personal injury, Criminal. Home: 36418 N Wildflower PO Box 5145 Carefree AZ 85377-5145 Office: 16042 N 32d St Suite C-1 Phoenix AZ 85032

SMITH, DAVID OLIVER, lawyer; b. Ft. Worth, Dec. 30, 1942; s. Oliver Wolcott and Jo Ellen (Haywood) S.; m. Barbara Anne Britt, Mar. 9, 1968; children: Kirby Wolcott, Cambria Anne. BA, U. Colo., 1965; JD, Duke U., 1972. Bar: Tex. 1972. From assoc. to ptnr. McGown, Godfrey et al, Ft. Worth, 1972-81; sr. tax specialist, chief tax counsel Diamond Shamrock Corp., Dallas, 1981—. Pres. Ft. Worth Boys Club, 1982, bd. dirs. 1980-82. Served to lt. USN, 1965-69. Mem. ABA, Tax Execs. Inst. Club: Colonial Country (Ft. Worth). Avocations: theatre, performing arts. Corporate taxation, State and local taxation. Home: 4208 Tanbark Trail Fort Worth TX 76109 Office: Diamond Shamrock Corp 717 N Harwood Dallas TX 75201

SMITH, DAVID ROBINSON, lawyer; b. Loveland, Ohio, Sept. 27, 1946; s. William E. and Mamie (Robinson) S.; m. Wessylyne French, Apr. 12, 1969; 1 child, Kimberly. BA, Central State U., 1969; JD, DePaul U., 1974. Bar: Ill. 1975. Asst. chief counsel U.S. Dept. Energy, Argonne, Ill., 1972-83; ptnr. Cole & Smith, Chgo., 1983-85; corp. v.p., gen. counsel, sec. Maxima Corp., Rockville, Md. Mem. ABA (state chmn. pub. contract law 1984), Nat. Bar Assn., Ill. Bar Assn., Nat. Contract Mgmt. Assn. (seminar chmn. 1984), Alpha Phi Alpha. Baptist. General corporate, Government contracts and claims. Home: 13924 Wagon Way Silver Spring MD 20906 Office: The Maxima Corp 2101 E Jefferson St Rockville MD 20852

SMITH, DIANE RAPP, lawyer; b. New Orleans, Oct. 10, 1946; d. William Lennox and Lillian Rose (Varnado) Rapp; m. Thaddeus Mitchell Nastich, Nov. 2, 1968 (div. 1978); 1 child, Summer Lea; m. Sherman Uhler Smith, Aug. 6, 1983. AB, U. Calif., Berkeley, 1972, JD, 1975. Atty. Dept. Energy, Oakland, Calif., 1975-82; sr. counsel Fluor Tech., Inc., Irvine, Calif., 1982-84; asst. gen. counsel Fluor Corp., Irvine, Calif., 1986—; gen. counsel Fluor Tech., Inc., Irvine, Calif., 1984-86, asst. gen. counsel, 1986—; vis. lectr. environ. law U. Calif., Irvine, 1984-86. Contbr. articles to Pub. Law Section Newsletter. John Woodman Ayer fellow U. Calif. Berkeley, 1975. Mem. ABA, Calif. Bar Assn., Phi Beta Kappa. Construction, Environment, Government contracts and claims. Home: 3 Springwood Irvine CA 92714 Office: Fluor Tech Inc 3333 Michelson Dr Irvine CA 92730

SMITH, DONALD PERRY, lawyer, electrical engineer; b. Bklyn., Feb. 23, 1912; s. Harry N. and Lucy (Perry) S.; m. Frances Carrington, Aug. 1946 (div. 1963); m. Doris Marie Ten Brock, Jan. 12, 1971; 1 child, George A. B.E.E., NYU, 1938; J.D., Am. U., 1951. Bar: D.C. 1951, U.S. Supreme Ct. 1954, N.Mex. 1975. Elec. engr. U.S. Maritime Adminstrn., Washington, 1946; patent examiner U.S. Patent Office, Washington, 1951; div. patent counsel ACF Industries, Riverdale, Mo., 1954; patent counsel Dept. Def., Washington, 1960; ptnr., dir. patent operation Singer, Smith & Powell, P.A., Albuquerque, 1981—. Author: Understanding Patents, 1968. Patentee in field. Recipient Meritorious Civilian Service award U.S. Air Force, Kirtland AFB, 1975, cert. of appreciation St. John's Cathedral, Albuquerque, 1981. Mem. Am. Patent Law Assn., Albuquerque Bar Assn., Sigma Nu Phi. Republican. Episcopalian. Lodges: Masons. Patent, Trademark and copyright. Home: 6432 Louise Pl NE Albuquerque NM 87109 Office: Singer Smith & Powell PA 300 Central St SW Box 25565 Albuquerque NM 87125

SMITH, DRAYTON BEECHER, II, lawyer; b. Memphis, Apr. 15, 1949; s. Drayton Beecher and Margaret (Williams) S.; m. Ann Wallace Dewey, Aug. 25, 1973; children—Ann Margaret Wallace, Stephanie Dewey. B.A., Millsaps Coll., 1971; J.D., U. Tenn., 1974. Bar: Tenn. 1974, U.S. Tax Ct. 1975, U.S. Dist. Ct. (we. dist.) Tenn. 1979. Assoc. Montedonico, Heiskell & Davis, Memphis, 1974-77; sr. assoc. tax dept. Glankler, Brown, Gilliland & Chase, Memphis, 1977-82; sr. ptnr. tax dept. Beaty & Smith, Memphis, 1982—; gen. counsel Elvis Presley Enterprises, Inc., Memphis, 1980—; pres. D. Beecher Smith II, P.C., Memphis, 1982—; gen. counsel K-Sun Co., Memphis, 1984—. Pres. Episcopal Young Churchmen, Calvary Ch., Memphis, 1966-67, Youth Guidance Commn., Memphis, 1967; mem. estate planning council, Millsaps Coll., Jackson, Miss., 1986. Recipient cert. of appreciation, City of Memphis, 1982. Mem. ABA (taxation sect. 1974—), Tenn. Bar Assn. (com. on profl. responsibility), Memphis-Shelby County Bar Assn. (chmn. cts. com.), Kappa Sigma (alumnus adviser Rhodes Coll.; Man of Yr. award Alumni Assn. 1982, Outstanding 1st Yr. Vol. award 1983, cert. of appreciation 1983). Republican. Episcopalian. Club: University (Memphis). Probate, Entertainment, Federal civil litigation. Home: 237 Windover Rd Memphis TN 38111 Office: Beaty & Smith 44 N 2d St Memphis TN 38103

SMITH, DUNCAN MCLAURIN, JR., lawyer, engineer, educator; b. Mobile, Ala., July 24, 1926; s. Duncan McLaurin and Louise J. (Davies) S.; m. Sallie Coco June 25, 1955; children—Duncan McLaurin III, Sherrill L., Allison L., Ashley C., Stuart M. Student N.E. Jr. Coll. of La. State U., 1943-44, U.S. Mil. Acad., 1945-46; B.S. in Petroleum Engring., La. State U., 1949, J.D., 1953. Bar: La. 1953, Tex. 1957, U.S. Dist. Ct. (we. dist.) La. 1953, U.S. Dist. Ct. (ea. dist.) La., U.S. Ct. Appeals (5th cir.) 1963, U.S. Dist. Ct. (mid. dist.) La. 1964, U.S. Supreme Ct. 1970, U.S. Ct. Appeals (11th cir.) 1981; registered profl. engr., La., Tex. Drilling and prodn. engr. California Co., various locations, 1949-52; assoc. Hargrove, Guyton, VanHook & Hargrove, Shreveport, La., 1953-56; Louisiana div. atty. Tidewater Oil Co., Houston, 1956-58; sole practice, Lafayette, La., 1958—; adj. prof. petroleum engring. U. Southwestern La., 1973—. Mem. adv. bd. Salvation Army, Lafayette; pres. Lafayette Natural History Mus. and Planetarium; trustee La. Moral and Civic Found., 1976-79. Served with USNR, 1944-45, U.S. Army, 1945-46. Mem. La. State Bar Assn., State Bar Tex., ABA, Am. Assn. Petroleum Geologists, Soc. Petroleum Engrs., Lafayette Bar Assn., 15th Jud. Dist Bar Assn., Lafayette Geol. Soc., Greater Lafayette C. of C., Am. Legion, Kappa Sigma, Phi Delta Phi. Democrat. Methodist. Clubs: Petroleum of Lafayette, Masons, Shriners. Oil and gas leasing, Probate, General practice. Home: 205 Whitcomb Rd Lafayette LA 70503 Office: PO Box 51643 203 Oil Center Dr Lafayette LA 70505

SMITH, EDWARD JEROME, lawyer; b. Kittanning, Pa., Sept. 18, 1944; s. Edward Chester and Sophie Elizabeth (Solack) S.; m. Roxie Kae Ruhlman, Dec. 23, 1965; 1 child, Morgan Diana. BA in Math. and Chemistry, Clarion State Coll., 1965; MA in Legal Anthropology, U. N.C., 1970-72; JD, Duke U., 1975; LLM, DePaul U., 1985. Bar: N.C. 1975. Sole practice Chapel Hill, N.C., 1975-78; mng. editor Callaghan & Co., Wilmette, Ill., 1978—. Served to capt. USMC, 1965-70, Vietnam. Nat. Merit Found. scholar, 1971. Mem. ABA. Avocation: sports. General corporate, Corporate taxation, Personal income taxation. Home: 533 Madison Glencoe IL 60022 Office: Callaghan & Co 3201 Old Glenview Rd Wilmette IL 60091

SMITH, EDWARD MICHAEL, lawyer; b. Grand Rapids, Mich., Mar. 29, 1939; s. Andrew Patrick and Margaret Mary (McGavin) S.; m. Patricia A. Geer; children: Edward M. Jr., Timothy R., Katherine M., Matthew T. BA, Aquinas Coll., 1961; JD, Wayne State U., 1965. Bar: Mich. 1965, U.S. Dist. Ct. (we. dist.) Mich. 1965, U.S. Ct. Appeals (6th cir.) 1965. Assoc. Morse & Kleiner, Grand Rapids, 1965-70; ptnr. Morse, Kleiner & Smith, Grand Rapids, 1970-75; sole practice Grand Rapids, 1975-80; ptnr. Pinsky, Smith & Soet, Grand Rapids, 1980—; pub. adminstr. Kent County, Mich., 1979-84; mem. appointed by Gov. to Workers Compensation Qualification Adv. Com. Mem. appeals com. Mich. Dems., 1978—, exec. bd. Cath. Cen. Boosters, 1982—; chmn. Kent County Dems., Grand Rapids, 1972-74; bd. trustees Aquinas Coll., Grand Rapids, 1973-86; bd. dirs. St. John's Home, Grand Rapids, 1970. Recipient Boss of Yr. award Grand Rapids Legal Sec. Assn., 1975. Mem. Fed. Bar Assn., Mich. Bar Assn., Grand Rapids Bar Assn., Mich. Trial Lawyers Assn., Aquinas Coll. Alumni Assn. (pres. 1970-72), Cath. Cen.-West Cath. Alumni Assn. (pres. 1979-83). Workers' compensation, Personal injury, Labor. Home: 2300 Shawnee SE Grand Rapids MI 49506 Office: Pinsky Smith & Soet 1400 McKay Tower Grand Rapids MI 49503

SMITH, EDWARD PHILIP, legal association administrator; b. Providence, Dec. 24, 1923; s. Joseph E. and Madge F. (Lynch) S.; m. Barbara Masterson, July 18, 1954; children: Anne Marie, Susan, Edward. BBA, U. R.I., 1948. Sales rep. Burroughs Bus. Machines, Providence and Detroit, 1948-51; alumni sec. U. R.I., Kingston, 1951-54; personnel mgr. Acushnet Process, New Bedford, Mass., 1954-58; exec. dir. R.I. Bar Assn., Providence, 1958-87, exec. dir. emeritus, 1987—. Mem. Nat. Assn. Bar Execs. (pres. 1973-74, treas., Bolton award 1981), New Eng. Bar Assn. (treas./sec. 1980-81), Am. Soc. Assn. Execs. (New Eng. bd. dirs. 1975), U. R.I. Alumni Assn. (pres. 1964). Administrative and regulatory. Office: RI Bar Assn 91 Friendship St Providence RI 02903

SMITH, EDWARD SAMUEL, judge; b. Birmingham, Ala., Mar. 27, 1919; s. Joseph Daniel and Sarah Jane (Tatum) S.; m. Innes Adams Comer, May 5, 1942; children: Edward Samuel, Innes Smith Cameron Richards. Student, Ala. Poly. Inst., 1936-38; B.A., U. Va., 1941, J.D., 1947. Bar: Va. 1947, D.C. 1948, Md. 1953. Asso., then partner firm Blair, Korner, Doyle & Appel, Washington, 1947-54; partner firm Blair, Korner, Doyle & Worth, 1954-61; chief trial sect., tax. div. Dept. Justice, 1961, asst. for civil trials, 1961-63; partner firm, head tax dept. Piper & Marbury, Balt., 1963-78; mng. partner Piper & Marbury, 1971-74; asso. judge U.S. Ct. Claims, Washington, 1978-82; judge U.S. Ct. Appeal (Fed. Cir.), Washington, 1982—. Bd. dirs. Roland Park Civic League, Inc., Balt., 1977-78; past pres., trustee St. Andrew's Soc. Washington. Served to lt. USNR, 1941-46; to comdr. USNR, Ret. 1968. Mem. Am. Bar Assn. (chmn. com. on tax litigation 1977-78), Fed. Bar Assn., Md. State Bar Assn. (chmn. sect. on taxation 1971-72), Balt. City Bar Assn., D.C. Bar Assn., Va. State Bar, Lambda Chi Alpha. Democrat. Episcopalian. Clubs: Met. (Washington), Nat. Lawyers (Washington); Chevy Chase (Md.); Mountain Brook (Birmingham). Home: 3708 Taylor St Chevy Chase MD 20815 Office: 717 Madison Pl NW Washington DC 20439

SMITH, EDWARD (TED) LEWIS, JR., lawyer; b. Covington, Ky., Nov. 17, 1937; s. Edward Lewis and Mary Eva (Thomas) S.; m. Renate Hildegard Markefka, June 11, 1960; children: Steven Mark, Inge Karen. BA, Ohio Wesleyan U., 1961; JD, No. Ky. U., 1979. Bar: Ky. 1979, Ohio 1980, U.S. Dist. Ct. (so. dist.) Ohio 1980, U.S. Dist. Ct. (ea. dist.) Ky. 1980. Atty. state and local govt. relations Procter & Gamble, Cin., 1963—. Chmn. Kenton County Reps., Ky., 1984—; mem. Ky. Rep. Cen. Com., 1984—, 4th Congl. Dist. Com., Ky., 1984—; bd. dirs. No. Ky. Mental Health/Mental Retardation Regional Bd. Inc., 1985—, chmn. fin. com., 1986—. Mem. ABA, Ky. Bar Assn., No. Ky. Bar Assn. Methodist. Legislative, General practice. Home: 831 Aberdeen Rd Park Hills KY 41011 Office: Procter & Gamble 1 Procter & Gamble Plaza Cincinnati OH 45201

SMITH, EDWARD VANCE, III, lawyer; b. Dallas, May 24, 1937; s. Edward Vance Jr. and Helen Louetta (Pitts) S.; m. Nikki Deshazo Smith, Feb. 7, 1987. B.A., N.Tex. State U., 1960; J.D., So. Meth. U., 1963. Bar: Tex. 1963, U.S. Dist. Ct. (no. dist.) Tex. 1965, U.S. Ct. Appeals (5th cir.) 1974, U.S. Dist. Ct. (ea. dist.) Tex. 1981. Ptnr. Taylor & Mizell, Dallas, 1970—, dir., officer; spl. judge Probate Ct. 2, Dallas County, 1985-86. Bd. regents N.Tex. State U., 1978-79; trustee Coll. Ozarks, 1985—, The Grace Found., Presbyn. Retirement Home North, Dallas, Profl. Devel. Inst., N. Tex. State U. Found. Recipient Outstanding Alumni Service award N.Tex. State U., 1974; named N.Tex. State U. Alumnus of Yr., Kappa Sigma, 1979. Fellow Am. Coll. Probate Counsel; mem. Dallas Bar Assn. (chmn. probate sect. 1982-83), Tex. State Bar (speaker, author advanced family law course 1981, advanced estate planning and probate course 1977-79, 85—). Presbyterian. Author, lectr., 1979, 80. Estate planning, Probate, Estate taxation. Office: Lincoln Plaza Suite 3000 Dallas TX 75201

SMITH, FRANK FORSYTHE, JR., lawyer; b. Crystal City, Tex., June 5, 1942; s. Frank F. and Allyne (Allen) S.; m. Martha Strack, Aug. 7, 1965; children: Martha Lee, Amanda Louise. BA, U. Tex., 1964; MA, U. Mich., 1965; LLB, U. Tex., 1968. Bar: Tex. 1968. Ptnr. Vinson & Elkins, Houston, 1968—; bd. dirs. Tex. Commerce Bank-Stafford. Mem. Am. Coll. Real Estate Lawyers. Republican. Methodist. Club: Houston Ctr. Construction, Landlord-tenant, Real property. Home: 5733 Shady River Houston TX 77057 Office: Vinson & Elkins 1001 Fannin 2638 1st City Tower Houston TX 77002-6760

SMITH, FRANK TUPPER, lawyer; b. Englewood, N.J., May 21, 1929; s. Frank T. and Mary Elizabeth S.; m. Anita K. Jacobsen, Mar. 9, 1957; children—Delia, Lisa Noel, Kathryn. B.A., Columbia Coll., 1951, J.D., Columbia U., 1954, M.B.A., NYU, 1963; cert. estate planning and probate law specialist, Tex. Bar: N.Y. 1956, Calif. 1966, Tex. 1974, U.S. Supreme Ct. 1963. Assoc., Vaughn & Lyons, N.Y.C., 1956-60; assoc. Edward R. Peckerman, N.Y.C., 1960-63; v.p. Bank of Calif., San Francisco, 1963-69; assoc. Paul Hastings Janofsky & Walker, Los Angeles, 1969-72; v.p., trust officer Republic Nat. Bank, Dallas, 1972-74; ptnr. Smith, Miller & Carlton, Dallas, 1975—; lectr. estate and tax shelter planning U. Tex., Dallas, Dallas Community Coll. Dist. Bd. dirs. Am. Heart Assn., 1979-82, Tex. chmn. planned giving com. 1980-82, nat. chmn. planned giving com., 1983-86. Served with AUS, 1954-56. Mem. Calif. State Bar Assn., Tex. State Bar Assn., Dallas Bar Assn., ABA. Clubs: Columbia University Notre Dame (pres. 1980-86), University, Rush Creek Yacht (Dallas). Corporate taxation, Estate taxation, Pension, profit-sharing, and employee benefits. Home: 5949 Sherry Ln Dallas TX 75225 Office: Sterling Plaza Bldg 5949 Sherry Ln Dallas TX 75225

SMITH, GEORGE CURTIS, lawyer, judge; b. Columbus, Ohio, Aug. 8, 1935; s. George B. and Dorothy R. S.; m. Barbara Jean Wood, July 10, 1963; children—Curt, Geof, Beth Ann. B.A., Ohio State U., 1957, J.D., 1959. Bar: Ohio 1959. Asst. city atty. City of Columbus, 1959-62; exec. asst. to Mayor of Columbus, 1962-63; asst. atty. gen. State of Ohio, 1964; chief counsel to pros. atty. Franklin County, Ohio, 1965-70, pros. atty., 1971-80; judge Franklin County Mcpl. Ct., Columbus, 1980-85; judge Franklin County Common Pleas Ct., 1985—. faculty Ohio Jud. Coll.; Bd. elders Covenant Ch., trustee Central Ohio sect. Am. Lung Assn.; trustee Leukemia Soc. Central Ohio; men's bd. Project Hope; trustee Crime Solvers Anonymous, Teen Challenge, Inc.; pres. Young Republican Club, 1963, Buckeye Rep. Club, 1968; exec. com. Franklin County Rep. Party, 1971-80. Recipient Superior Jud. Service award Supreme Ct. Ohio, 1980, 81, 82, 83, 84; Resolution of Honor, Columbus Bldg. and Constrn. Trades Council, 1980; award Eagles, 1980; Mem. Ohio Common Pleas Judges Assn., Ohio Pros. Attys. Assn. (life, pres., Ohio Prosecutor of Yr, Award of Honor, Leadership award), Columbus Bar Assn., Ohio Bar Assn., Assn. Trial Lawyers Am., Ohio Common Pleas Judges Assn., Ohio Mcpl.-County Judges Assn. 2d v.p., trustee). Presbyterian. Clubs: Columbus Athletic (pres., dir.), Columbus Maennerchor, Germania, Lawyers Club of Columbus (pres. 1975), Shamrock. Lodges: Fraternal Order Police Assocs., Eagles, Masons, Shriners. Office: Franklin County Common Pleas Ct 369 S High St Columbus OH 43215

SMITH, GEORGE DUFFIELD, JR., lawyer; b. Dallas, Dec. 23, 1930; s. G. Duffield and Gladys (Cassle) S.; m. Ann L. Suggs, Aug. 29, 1956; children—Jeanie, Christina, Duffield. B.S. in Bus. Adminstrn., U. N.C.-Chapel Hill, 1952; LL.B., So. Meth. U., 1957. Bar: Tex. 1957, U.S. Dist. Ct. (no., ea. and western dists.) Tex. 1960, U.S. Ct. Appeals (5th and 10th cirs.) 1983. Assoc. Lyne, Blanchett & Smith, Dallas, 1957-60, Touchstone, Bernays & Johnson, Dallas, 1960-65; ptnr. Gardere, Porter & DeHay, Dallas, 1965-79, Gardere & Wynne, Dallas, 1979—; instr. Internat. Assn. Ins. Counsel Trial Acad., 1982. Elder, Highland Park Presbyn. Ch., Dallas; pres. Shakespeare Festival, Dallas, 1976; bd. dirs. Hope Cottage, Dallas, Ctr. Pastoral Care & Counseling, 1979-81. Served to capt. USAF, 56. Fellow Tex. Bar Found.; mem. ABA, Tex. Bar Assn. (dir. 1985—), Dallas Bar Assn., Tex. Assn. Def. Counsel (pres.), Def. Research Inst. (regional v.p. 1980-83, dir. 1983-86, v.p. pub. relations 1986—), Internat. Assn. Ins. Counsel, Am. Bd. Trial Advs., Trial Attys. Assn. Am. Republican. Club: Brook Hollow Golf (Dallas). Federal civil litigation, State civil litigation, Insurance. Office: Diamond Shamrock Tower Suite 1500 Dallas TX 75201

SMITH, GEORGE EMMETT, lawyer, business executive; b. Glens Falls, N.Y., Aug. 2, 1928; s. George Lester and Julia Mae (O'Connell) S.; m. Therese Marie Deschambault, Dec. 28, 1950; children—Mark Christopher, Laura Ann, Claire Louise, Lydia Margaret. B.S. in Econs., Fordham U., 1953, J.D., 1956; M.A. in Econs., N.Y. U., 1959. Bar: N.Y. 1956, Tex. 1976. atty. Union Carbide Corp., N.Y.C., 1956-67; asst. sec., asst. gen. counsel

Xerox Corp., Stamford, Conn., 1967-75; sr. v.p., gen. counsel, sec. LTV Corp., Dallas, 1975—. Trustee, Cath. Found. Served with Signal Corps, AUS, 1947-48. Mem. ABA (corporate bus. and banking sect. com. corporate law depts. 1977), N.Y. State, Dallas bar assns., State Bar Tex. (chmn. corporate Counsel Sect. 1984-85). Clubs: Bent Tree Country, Dallas. General corporate, Antitrust. Home: 900 Park Ave New York NY 10028 Office: LTV Corp 299 Park Ave New York NY 10171

SMITH, GEORGE MAYNARD, lawyer; b. Cairo, Ga., Oct. 5, 1907; s. John Quincy and Nona (Hathorn) S.; m. Helen Miller, Oct. 5, 1936; 1 child, Helen Maynard Hull. AB in Law, Mercer U., 1929. Bar: D.C. 1933. Pros. atty City of Cairo, 1935-42; spl. asst. U.S. Atty. Gen., Washington, 1942-44; spl. asst. to chief of naval ops. USN, Washington, 1944-47; ptnr. Smith, Currie & Hancock, Atlanta, 1947—; bd. dirs. Genuine Parts Co., Atlanta, Douglas & Lomason Co., Detroit. Club: Breakfast (Atlanta) (pres. 1951). Lodge: Kiwanis (Atlanta dist. gov. 1942, pres. 1951, 76). Avocation: golf. Labor. Home: 3085 Slaton Dr #6 Atlanta GA 30305 Office: Smith Currie & Hancock 233 Peachtree St NE Atlanta GA 30043

SMITH, GEORGE PATRICK, II, educator, lawyer; b. Wabash, Ind., Sept. 1, 1939; s. George Patrick and Marie Louise (Barrett) S. B.S., Ind. U., 1961, J.D., 1964; certificate, Hague Acad. Internat. Law, 1965; LL.M., Columbia U., 1975. Bar: Ind. 1964, U.S. Supreme Ct. 1968. Kannert teaching fellow Ind. U. Sch. Law, 1964-65; instr. law U. Mich. Sch. Law, 1965-66; practiced in Ind. and Washington, 1965—; legal adviser Fgn. Claims Settlement Commn., Dept. State, Washington, 1966; asst. prof., asst. dean State U. N.Y. at Buffalo Law Sch., 1967-69; vis. asst. prof. law George Washington U., Nat. Law Center, summer 1968; assoc. prof. law U. Ark., 1969-71; spl. counsel EPA, Washington, 1971-74; adj. prof. law Catholic U. Law Sch., Washington, 1973-74; prof. Catholic U. Law Sch., 1977—; adj. prof. law Georgetown U. Law Center, 1971-75; asso. prof. law U. Pitts. Sch. Law, 1975-78; Commonwealth fellow in law, sci. and medicine Yale, 1976-77; vis. prof. law U. Conn., 1977; distinguished vis. scholar Kennedy Bioethics Inst., Georgetown U., 1977-81; vis. scholar Inst. Soc., Ethics and Life Scis., Hastings Center, N.Y., 1981; vis. Lilly scholar Lilly Rare Books Library, Ind. U., July 1981; Rockefeller Found. resdl. scholar, Bellagio, Italy, 1980; lectr. Sch. Medicine, Uniformed Services U. Health Scis., Bethesda, Md., 1979—; cons. environ. legislation Govt. of Greece, 1977; spl. counsel to Gov. Ark. for environ. affairs, 1969-71; cons. Ark. Planning Commn., 1970-71; mem. Ark. Waterway Commn., 1970-71; chmn. Ark. Com. on Environ. Control, 1970-71; mem. com. on hwy. research NRC, Nat. Acad. Sci., 1971-81; Life mem. Ind. U. Found.; Univ. fellow Columbia Law Sch., 1974-75; vis. scholar Cambridge (Eng.) U., summer 1975, spring 1978, 79, Hoover Instn. on War, Revolution and Peace, Stanford U., summer 1982; fellow Max Planck Inst., Heidelberg, summer 1983; mem. Pres. Reagan's Pvt. Sector Survey on Cost Control, 1982; vis. fellow Clare Hall Cambridge U., 1983-84, summer 87; Fulbright vis. prof. U. New South Wales, Syndey, Australia, 1984; vis. fellow Inst. Advanced Study, Ind. U., 1985; vis. prof. law U. Notre Dame, 1986; vis. scholar Am. Bar Found., Chgo., 1986, 87. Author: Genetics, Ethics and the Law, 1981, Restricting the Concept of Free Seas, 1980, Legal, Ethical and Social Issues of the Brave New World, 1980, Medical-Legal Aspects of Cryonics, 1983; contbr. articles to profl. jours. U. Ark. del. Pacem In Maribus Conf., Malta, 1970. Recipient Disting. Alumni award Ind. U. Bd. Trustees, 1985, citation for Path-Breaking Work; establishment of George P. Smith II Disting. Research Professorship, Ind. U., Bloomington, 1986. Mem. Nat. Cathedral Assn. Washington, Am. Bar Assn. (rep. UN Conf. on Human Environment, Stockholm 1972, rep. Law of Sea Conf., UN, N.Y.C. 1976, Switzerland 1979), Ind. Bar Assn., Am. Friends of Cambridge U., Am. Law Inst., Alpha Kappa Psi, Phi Alpha Delta, Sigma Alpha Epsilon, Order of Omega. Republican. Club: Cosmos (Washington). Environment, Legal education, Real property. Office: 2500 Que St NW Suite 521 Washington DC 20007

SMITH, GLEE SIDNEY, JR., lawyer; b. Rozel, Kans., Apr. 29, 1921; s. Glee S. and Bernice M. (Augustine) S.; m. Geraldine B. Buhler, Dec. 14, 1943; children—Glee S., Stephen B., Susan K. A.B., U. Kans., 1943, J.D., 1947. Bar: Kans. 1947, U.S. Dist. Ct. 1951, U.S. Supreme Ct. 1973. Ptnr. Smith, Burnett & Larson, Larned, Kans., 1947—. Kans. state senator, 1957-73, pres. Senate, 1965-73; mem. Kans. Bd. Regents, 1975-83, pres., 1976; bd. govs. Kans. U. Law Soc., 1967—; mem. Kans. Jud. Council, 1963-65; county atty. Pawnee County, 1949-53; Kans. commr. Nat. Conf. Commn. on Uniform State Laws, 1963—. Bd. dirs. Nat. Legal Services Corp., 1975-79. Served to 1st lt. U.S. Army, 1943-45. Recipient Leadership award Kans. Bar Assn., 1973; Disting. Service award, U. Kans. Law Sch., 1976; Disting. Service citation U. Kans., 1984. Fellow Am. Coll. Probate Counsel, Am. Bar Found.; mem. ABA (bd. of govs. 1987—), Kan. Bar Assn. (del. to ABA ho. of dels. 1982—), Southwest Kans. Bar Assn., Am. Judicature Soc. Republican. Presbyterian. Clubs: Kiwanis, Masons. General practice, Probate, Estate taxation. Home: 616 W 4th St Larned KS 67550 Office: 111 E 8th St Larned KS 67550

SMITH, GREGORY HAYES, lawyer; b. Concord, N.H., Apr. 5, 1946; s. Erville Hayes and Natalie (Painting) S.; m. Marcia Ruth Blodgett, June 6, 1968; children: Geoffrey Hayes, Stuart Blodgett. BA in Chemistry, U. N.H., 1969; JD, U. Maine, 1973. Bar: N.H. 1973, U.S. Supreme Ct. 1979. With N.H. Atty. Gen., Concord, 1973-78; dep. atty. gen. N.H. Atty. Gen., 1978-80, acting atty. gen., 1980, atty. gen., 1981-84; mem. McLane, Graf, Raulerson & Middleton, P.A., Manchester, N.H., 1984—; chmn. N.H. Jud. Council, Concord, 1984—, mem. 1980—. Mem. N.H. Crime Commn., 1980-84, Gov.'s Task Force on Drunk Driving, 1982; chmn. Gov.'s Commn. on Gambling, 1982, Leadership Manchester, 1986—. Mem. ABA, N.H. Bar Assn., Merrimack County Bar Assn., Manchester Bar Assn., U. Maine Law Sch. Alumni Assn. (bd. dirs. 1987—). Administrative and regulatory, Environment, General practice. Office: McLane Graf et al 40 Stark St PO Box 326 Manchester NH 03105

SMITH, HARDY BOLTON, lawyer; b. Mobile, Ala., Apr. 22, 1930; s. Gregory Hardy and Carolyn Theresa (Bolton) S.; m. Donna Jenkins, July 18, 1953; children—Diane Smith Conklin, Cynthia Anne Smith Kirk. Student, Spring Hill Coll., 1947-48; B.A. in Econs., U. Ala., 1950; J.D., U. Wis., 1957. Bar: Wis. 1957, Ala. 1958, U.S. Supreme Ct. 1961. Ptnr., Gaillard & Smith, Mobile, 1958-63, Gaillard, Wilkins & Smith, Mobile, 1963-76, Gaillard, Smith & Little, Mobile, 1976-79; sole practice, Mobile, 1979—. Deacon, Spring Hill Presbyn. Ch., 1968-75; mem. Ala. Republican Exec. Com., 1968-72. Served with USAF, 1951-55; lt. col. Res. ret. Decorated Air Force Commendation medal. Mem. ABA, State Bar Wis., Ala. Bar Assn., Air Force Assn., Alpha Tau Omega, Phi Delta Phi. Lodge: Kiwanis. Probate, Real property, Personal income taxation. Office: 2504 Dauphin St Mobile AL 36606

SMITH, HAROLD DELANE, lawyer; b. Artemus, Pa., Nov. 7, 1932; s. Dewey Lester and Helen Viola (Norris) S.; m. Betty Jo McWhorter, Sept. 14, 1963. BBA in Indsl. Relations, Kent State U., 1961; JD, Cleve. State U., 1972. Bar: Ohio 1972, Fla. 1974, U.S. Dist. Ct. (so. dist.) Fla. 1974, U.S. Dist. Ct. (mid. and no. dists.) Fla. 1979, U.S. Ct. Appeals (5th cir.) 1979, U.S. Supreme Ct. 1979, U.S. Ct. Appeals (11th cir.) 1981, U.S. Ct. Appeals (fed. cir.) 1984. Rep. labor relations B.F. Goodrich Co., Akron, Ohio, 1961-66; mgr. employee relations Harshaw Chem. Co., Cleve., 1966-68; staff asst. employee relations Texaco Inc., N.Y.C., 1968-69; supr. labor and employee relations Gen. Electric Co., Warren, Ohio, 1969-73; labor atty. Eastern Airlines, Miami, Fla., 1973-76; sole practice Hollywood, Fla., 1976-86; ptnr. Carpenter, Brown & Smith, Ft. Lauderdale, Fla., 1986—. Served with USNR, 1950-56. Mem. ABA, Broward County Bar Assn., Am. Arbitration Assn., Christian Legal Soc. Republican. Presbyterian. Avocation: golf. Labor, Federal civil litigation, State civil litigation. Home: 5841 SW 37th Ave Fort Lauderdale FL 33312 Office: Carpenter Brown & Smith Saar Bldg Suite 100 701 E Commercial Blvd Fort Lauderdale FL 33334

SMITH, HAYDEN, JR., lawyer; b. Long Branch, N.J., Jan. 2, 1947; s. Hayden and Rosalie (Neilson) S.; m. Elizabeth Gerrard, May 9, 1970; children: Samuel Hayden, Daphne Madelaine. BA, Princeton U., 1969; JD, Rutgers U., 1974. Bar: N.J. 1974, U.S. Dist. Ct. N.J. 1974., U.S. Dist. Ct. (ea. and so. dists.) 1985. Ptnr. McCarter & English, Newark, 1975—. Served with USMC, 1969-71. Mem. ABA, N.J. Bar Assn., Essex County Bar Assn. Republican. Episcopalian. Avocation: tennis. Bankruptcy, Federal civil litigation, State civil litigation. Home: 32 Wheat Sheaf Ln Princeton NJ 08540

SMITH, HERMAN EUGENE, lawyer; b. Ceredo, W.Va., Sept. 12, 1926; s. Leonard P. and Evelyn J. (Melson) S.; m. Charlotte Virginia Toney, July 13, 1945; children—Mary, Herman, Michael W. Student Marshall U., 1944-47; B.S. in Mech. Engring., Va. Poly. Inst. and State U., 1949; J.D., John Marshall Law Sch., 1961. Bar: Ill. 1961, U.S. Dist. Ct. (no. dist.) Ill. 1981, U.S. Supreme Ct. 1976. Engr. Bituminous Coal Research, Inc., Huntington, W.Va., 1949-51; engr. Goodman Mfg. Co., Chgo., 1951-61, house counsel, 1961-64; patent atty. Borg Warner Corp., Chgo., 1964-78; fgn. patent dir., 1978-87; ret., 1987. Mem. health council Village of Park Forest, Ill., 1977-82, mem. profl. adv. com., 1976-82. Served wtih U.S. Army, 1945-46, PTO. Mem. ABA, Am. Intellectual Property Law Assn., Ill. State Bar Assn., Patent Law Assn. Chgo. (chmn. fgn. patent com.). Lodge: Kiwanis. Patent. Office: Borg Warner Corp 200 S Michigan Ave Chicago IL 60604

SMITH, HORACE, JR., lawyer; b. Orangesburg, S.C., Nov. 22, 1942; s. Horace Sr. and Margaret (Dankin) S.; m. Teresa Crisp, Jan. 19, 1985. BA, Fla. State U., 1964; JD, Samford U., 1967. Bar: Fla. 1967, U.S. Dist. Ct. Fla. 1977, U.S. Ct. Appeals (11th cir.) 1971, U.S. Supreme Ct. 1971. Sole practice Daytona Beach, Fla., 1967-78; ptnr. Dunn, Smith, Withers & Hart, Daytona Beach, 1978—; adj. prof. Daytona Beach Community Coll., 1976—; atty. City of Burnell, Fla., 1974-82. Mem. Fla. Bar Assn. (bd. of govs. 1986—), Volusia County Bar Assn. (pres. 1977-78), Criminal Def. Lawyers of Volusia County (pres. 1984-85, exec. council criminal law sect.). Club: QuarterBack (Daytona Beach). Lodge: Kiwanis. Criminal, Family and matrimonial. Office: Dunn Smith Withers & Hart 347 S Ridgewood Ave Daytona Beach FL 32015

SMITH, J. ARTHUR, III, lawyer; b. Monroe, La., Feb. 5, 1946; s. J. Arthur Jr. and Sydnie (Calongne) S.; m. Jane Wood, 1971; children: J. Arthur IV, Grace Wood. BS, La. State U., 1968, JD, 1971. Bar: La. 1973, U.S. Dist. Ct. (mid. and ea. dists.) La. 1973, U.S. Ct. Appeals (5th cir.) 1974, U.S. Supreme Ct. 1977, U.S. Dist. Ct. (we. dist.) La. 1978. Legal assoc. adv. commn. on coastal and marine resources State of La., Baton Rouge, 1971-72; sole practice Baton Rouge, 1972—; town atty. Wilson, La., 1981—. Contbr. articles to profl. jours. Mem. session Clinton (La.) Presbyn. Ch., 1985—. Mem. ABA, La. Bar Assn., Baton Rouge Bar Assn., La. Trial Lawyers Assn., Phi Kappa Phi, Omicron Delta Kappa, Lambda Chi Alpha (pres. LSU alumni 1985). Democrat. Avocation: fishing. Federal civil litigation, State civil litigation, Criminal. Office: 524 France St Baton Rouge LA 70802

SMITH, JACK DAVID, lawyer; b. Honolulu, Jan. 4, 1946; s. Jack David and Gloria June (Slater) S.; m. Mary Elizabeth Zasadny, Sept. 17, 1977; children: Amy Elizabeth, Amanda Marie. BA in Polit. Sci., George Washington U., 1968, JD, 1971. Bar: Va. 1971, U.S. Ct. Mil. Appeals 1971, U.S. Ct. Appeals (1st and D.C. cirs.) 1975, U.S. Ct. Appeals (2d and 7th cirs.) 1976, U.S. Supreme Ct. 1976, D.C. 1986. Atty. litig. div. FCC, Washington, 1974-81, dept. chief common carrier bur., 1981-83, chief common carrier bur., 1983-84, gen. counsel, 1984-86; dep. gen. counsel Fed. Home Loan Bank Bd., Washington, 1986—. Served to capt. USMC, 1971-74. Mem. Va. Bar Assn. Avocations: tennis, swimming. Administrative and regulatory, Banking, Federal civil litigation. Home: 7824 Telegraph Rd Alexandria VA 22310 Office: Fed Home Loan Bank Bd 1700 G St NW Washington DC 20552

SMITH, JAMES ALEXANDER, JR., lawyer; b. Highland Park, Ill., Nov. 14, 1948; s. James Alexander and Dorothy (Banker) S.; m. Susan Wilcox Thomas, Dec. 27, 1982; children: Deirdre, Kara. BA cum laude, U. Notre Dame, 1970; JD, Cornell U., 1973. Bar: Wash. 1973, U.S. Dist. Ct. (ea. and we. dists.) Wash. 1973, U.S. Ct. Appeals (9th cir.) 1984, U.S. Supreme Ct. 1984. Assoc. Bogle & Gates, Seattle, 1973-78, ptnr., 1978-82; ptnr. Perey & Smith, Seattle, 1982-86, Smith & Leary, Seattle, 1986—; bd. dirs. Children's Montessori Sch., Bainbridge Island, Wash., 1981—. Research editor Cornell U. Law Rev., 1972-73. Mem. ABA (litigation sect.), Wash. State Bar Assn. (trustee trial practice sect. 1983-86), Assn. Trial Lawyers Am., Wash. State Trial Lawyers Assn. Roman Catholic. Clubs: Wing Point Country, Notre Dame (bd. dirs. 1977-78). Avocations: soccer, outdoor sports, sailing, creative writing. Federal civil litigation, State civil litigation, Securities. Home: 108 Lake Dell Ave Seattle WA 98122 Office: Smith & Leary 316 Occidental Ave S Suite 500 Seattle WA 98104

SMITH, JAMES BONNER, lawyer; b. Dallas, Jan. 11, 1950; s. B. J. and Mary Louise (Landrum) S.; m. Shelly Smith, May 1, 1977; 1 child, Bonny Leigh. B.S., Midwestern U., 1972; J.D., Tex. Tech U., 1977. Bar: Tex. 1977. Law clk. Wichita County Dist. Atty.'s Office, Wichita Falls, Tex., 1975, law firm Vickers, Moreau & Huckaby, Wichita Falls, 1976, Hance, Thompson & Thomas, Lubbock, Tex., 1976; asst. city atty. City of Lubbock, 1977-78; asst. criminal dist. atty. Lubbock County, 1978; assoc. firm Wicks & Lee, 1979-80; sole practice law, Lubbock, 1980; ptnr. Freeman, McNeely & Smith, Lubbock, 1982-84; ptnr. McNeely & Smith, Lubbock, 1984—; instr. law Continuing Edn. div. Tex. Tech Univ., Lubbock; instr. health law Wayland Bapt. U., Lubbock. Mem. Leadership Lubbock, 1986-87. Served to maj. USAFR, 1973—. Mem. Tex. Bar Assn., ABA, Lubbock County Bar Assn., West Tex. Bankruptcy Bar Assn., Tex. Criminal Def. Lawyers Assn., Tex. Assn. Bank Counsel, Tex. City Attys. Assn., Air Force Assn., Am. Bus. Club (v.p. 1985-86), Lubbock C. of C. (health and med., oil and gas coms.), Tau Kappa Epsilon (chmn. bd. trustees Tex. Tech chpt. 1976—, nat. real estate adv. group, sec., treas. housing corp. 1986—), Res. Officers Assn. U.S. (chpt. pres.). Lodges: Order Daedalians, Lions, Rotary. State civil litigation, Oil and gas leasing, Health. Home: 4309 92d St Lubbock TX 79423 Office: 6400 Quaker Suite B Lubbock TX 79413

SMITH, JAMES EDWIN, JR., lawyer; b. Jackson, Ms., Mar. 28, 1952; s. James Edwin Sr. and Marcelene (Cobb) S.; m. Karen Davis, Aug. 12, 1973; children: James Edwin III, Jennifer Jill. BBA, U. Ms., 1974, JD, 1976. Bar: Miss. 1976. Assoc. Smith & McLemore, Carthage, Ms., 1976-79; ptnr. Smith, McLemore & Smith, Carthage, 1980-82, Smith & Smith, Carthage, 1983—; asst. chmn. East Ms. Legal Services, Forest, 1979-86; state legal counsel Ms. Jaycees, Meridian, 1978. Pres. Leake County Cancer Soc., Carthage, 1978-79; bd. dirs. Andrew Jackson council Boy Scouts Am., Jackson, 1984—. Recipient Leadership Ms. award Miss. Econ. Council, 1981. Mem. ABA, Ms. Bar Assn., Leake County Bar Assn., Assn. Trial Lawyers Am., Ms. Trial Lawyers Assn., Leake County C. of C. (pres. 1986-87), Leadership Ms. Alumni Assn., Sq. County Jaycees (v.p. 1979), Ms. Bankruptcy Conf. Baptist. Lodge: Rotary (pres. Carthage 1984-85). Avocations: sports, bicycling, playing music. General practice, Federal civil litigation, State civil litigation. Home: 1100 Pinehill Dr Carthage MS 39051 Office: Smith & Smith PO Box 387 Carthage MS 39051

SMITH, JAMES HIBBERT, lawyer; b. Orange, N.J., Sept. 11, 1946; s. Cecil Reginald and Helen (Little) S.; m. Sheila Patricia Tournet, Aug. 28, 1971. JD, U. Fla., 1970. Bar: Fla. 1970. Atty. legis. revision sect. Fla. Legislature, 1971; atty. Spl. Disability Trust Fund, Fla. Dept. Commerce, Tallahassee, 1971-72, chief atty. and conservator Spl. Disability Trust Fund, 1972-74; assoc. Marlow, Shofi, Smith, Hennen, Smith & Jenkins, P.A., and predecessors, Tampa, 1974-75, ptnr., 1976—. Served to capt. USAR, 1970-78. Mem. Fla. Bar Assn., Hillsborough County Bar Assn. Democrat. Workers' compensation, Insurance, Personal injury. Home: 2915 Walcraft Tampa FL 33629 Office: 2907 Bay to Bay Suite 201 Tampa FL 33626

SMITH, JAMES IGNATIUS, III, association executive; b. Grosse Pointe, Mich., May 23, 1931; s. James I. and Jacqueline Mary (Moran) S.; m. Deborah L. Eyler, Mar. 17, 1983. BS, U. Notre Dame, 1953. Sales mgr., gen. mgr. Esmeralda Canning Co., Circleville, Ohio, 1955-57; gen. reporter The Herald, Circleville, 1957-60; asst. exec. sec., dir. pub. relations Ohio State Bar Assn., Columbus, 1960-62; exec. dir. Allegheny County Bar Assn., Pitts., 1963—; pres. Profl. Seminars and Designs, Pitts., 1972—. Chmn. Reapportionment com., Bethel Park, Pa., 1969-71. Served with U.S. Army, 1953-55. Recipient Journalism award Ohio State Bar Assn., Columbus, 1959; named Man of Yr., Notre Dame Club Pitts., 1972. Mem. Nat. Assn. Bar Execs. (pres. 1977-78), Legal Services Assn. (bd. dirs., 1st sec. 1966—), Pitts. Soc. Assn. Execs. (pres. 1973-74), Assn. Continuing Legal Edn. Adminstrs., Pitts. C. of C. Democrat. Roman Catholic. Clubs: Notre Dame (pres. 1970-71), Serra (dir. 1971-72). Lodge: Elks. Home: 350 Jonquil Pl Pittsburgh PA 15228 Office: Allegheny County Bar Assn 420 Grant Bldg Pittsburgh PA 15219

SMITH, JAMES PAYTON, lawyer, state legislator; b. Texarkana, Ark., Oct. 17, 1950; s. T.P. and Frances Ann (Dallashyde) S.; m. Cheryl Hart, July 28, 1984. BA in Polit. Sci., U. Ala., Huntsville, 1973; JD, U. Ala., Tuscaloosa, 1976. Assoc. Ford & Payne, Huntsville, 1976-78; ptnr. Harrison & Smith, Huntsville, 1978-83, Smith & Stevens, Huntsville, 1983-84, Smith & Waldrop, Huntsville, 1984—. State rep. Ala. Ho. of Reps., Montgomery, 1978-82; state sen. Ala. State Senate, Montgomery, 1982-86, re-elected, 1987—. Recipient Nat. Commdrs. award DAV, Legis. Crime Fighting award, Ala. Dist. Atty.s Office, 1982, Election Law Reform award, Ala. Sec. of State, 1982; named Outstanding Alabamian, Ala. Jaycees, 1981. Mem. ABA, Ala. Bar Assn., Madison County Bar Assn., Order of Coif, Pi Sigma Alpha, Omicron Delta Epsilon, Delta Tau Kappa. Democrat. Methodist. Avocations: tennis, jogging, hunting. Office: Smith & Waldrop 108-A South Side Sq Huntsville AL 35801

SMITH, JAMES RANDOLPH, JR., lawyer; b. Martinsville, Va., Mar. 7, 1945; s. James Randolph and Ruth (Boykin) S. B.A., Randolph-Macon Coll., 1967; LL.B., U. Va., 1970. Bar: Va. 1970, U.S. Dist. Ct. (we. dist.) Va. 1972, U.S. Supreme Ct. 1973, U.S. Ct. Appeals (4th cir.) 1976. Law clk. to judge U.S. Dist. Ct., Wilmington, Del., 1970-71; asst. commonwealth atty. City of Martinsville, 1971-81, commonwealth atty. 1981—; ptnr. Smith & Penn, P.C., Martinsville, 1981-86; instr. New River Criminal Justice Acad., 1980—. Vice chmn. Martinville Rep. Com., 1986—. Mem. ABA, Martinsville-Henry County Bar Assn. (v.p. 1983-84, pres. 1984-85), Am. Judicature Soc., Phi Delta Phi. Mem. Disciples of Christ Ch. Home: 817 Mulberry Rd Martinsville VA 24112 Office: 26 W Church St PO Box 1311 Martinsville VA 24114-1311

SMITH, JANET DIANE, lawyer; b. N.Y.C., Dec. 16, 1948; d. Saul and Lillian (Reasenberg) S.; m. Scott Jay Zevon, Nov. 23, 1986. BS, Cornell U., 1969; MS, SUNY, Stony Brook, 1973; JD, Boston U., 1976. Bar: N.Y. 1977, Mass. 1977. Atty. EPA, Boston, 1976-79, chief legal rev. sect., 1979-81; assoc. Sive, Paget & Riesel, P.C. and predecessor firm Winer, Newburger & Sive, N.Y.C., 1981-84; staff counsel NL Industries, Inc., N.Y.C., 1984—. Contbr. articles to profl. jours. V.p., bd. dirs. Maple Arms Townhouse Condominium, Westbury, N.Y., 1985—. Mem. ABA (natural resources sect.). Environment, Federal civil litigation. Home: 175 Maple Ave Westbury NY 11590 Office: NL Industries 1230 Ave of Americas New York NY 10020

SMITH, JEFFERSON VERNE, JR., lawyer; b. Greenville, S.C., Oct. 10, 1948; s. J. Verne and Jean (Myers) S.; m. Susie Brannon, June 24, 1972. BA, Furman U., 1970; JD, U. S.C., 1973. Bar: S.C. 1973, U.S. Dist. Ct. S.C. 1973, U.S. Ct. Appeals (4th cir.) 1974. Assoc. Carter, Philpot & Johnson, Greenville, 1974-75; ptnr. Carter, Philpot, Johnson & Smith, Greer, S.C., 1975-80, Carter, Smith, Merriam, Rogers & Traxler and predecessor firms Carter, Smith, Merriam & Rogers and Carter, Smith, Johnson & Merriam, Greer, 1980—; mcpl. judge City of Greer, 1974-77; mem. S.C. Bd. Grievances and Discipline, 1979-82; bd. dirs. Bank of Greer, United Carolina Bank. Chmn. Greenville County Dems., 1978-80, Atty. Gen.'s Citizen's Com. on High Tech. Crime, 1983; mem. adv. bd. C&S Nat. Bank, Greer, 1981-83; Dem. nominee for U.S. Congress, 1984; trustee Greenville County Library, 1979-85; bd. dirs. Greer Community Ministries, 1981—, chmn., 1983, 86. Served to capt. Q.M.C., USAR, 1973-78. Mem. S.C. Bar Assn., Greenville County Bar Assn., S.C. Trial Lawyers Assn. Presbyterian. Personal injury, State civil litigation, Family and matrimonial. Home: Rt 2 Hwy 14 Greer SC 29651 Office: Carter Smith Merriam Rogers & Traxler 200 N Main St Greer SC 29651

SMITH, JEFFREY ALLEN, lawyer; b. Cleve., Feb. 2, 1944; s. William R. and Esther Mae Smith; m. Ruth Ann Sweeton, June 10, 1967; children—Amy Esther, Adam Minor. A.B., Clark U., 1966; J.D., Boston U., 1969. Bar: Maine 1971, U.S. Dist. Ct. Maine 1971, U.S. Supreme Ct. 1980. Clk. to judge Maine Probate Ct., 1970; assoc. Law Offices of Harold J. Shapiro, Gardiner, Maine, 1971-73; ptnr. Smith Stein Bernotavicz & Orbeton, Hallowell, Richmond & Bath and predecessor firms Smith & Stein, and Smith Stein & Bernotavicz, Hallowell, Richmond, Hallowell, Maine, 1973-85, mng. ptnr., 1980-84, Smith & Assoc. P.A., Hallowell, 1985—; instr. trusts and estates and legal writing Beal Bus. Coll., Brunswick, Maine, 1981-82. Mem., Monmouth (Maine) Planning Bd., 1978-85; cubmaster Pine Tree council Boy Scouts Am., 1982—; Vista vol. Alaska Legal Services, 1969-70. Mem. ABA, Maine Bar Assn., Kennebec County Bar Assn., Assn. Trial Lawyers Am., Maine Trial Lawyers Assn. (bd. govs. 1986—), Nat. Council Sch. Attys., Maine Council Sch. Attys., Maine Organic Farmers and Gardeners Assn. Democrat. Methodist (lay leader 1978—). Author: Santa's Will, 1978; Santa's Codicil, 1979; Letter to Smith Stein & Bernotavicz From Santa, 1982; also articles. Federal civil litigation, General practice, Personal injury. Home: Blue Heron Farm Town Farm Rd Monmouth ME 04259 Office: PO Box 351 144 Water St Hallowell ME 04347

SMITH, JEFFREY G., lawyer; b. Mineola, N.Y., Feb. 21, 1948; s. Robert R. and Helen E. (Graham) S.; m. Lynn J. Fielden, June 16, 1974; children: Allyson M., Graham H., Brendan C. AB, Vassar Coll., 1974; M in Pub. Adminstrn., Princeton U., 1977; JD, Yale U., 1978. Bar: N.Y. 1979, U.S. Dist. Ct. (so. and ea. dists.) N.Y. 1979, U.S. Tax Ct. 1979, U.S. Supreme Ct. 1984, U.S. Ct. Appeals (6th, 8th and 9th cirs.) 1985. Assoc. Fried, Frank, Harris, Shriver & Jacobson, N.Y.C., 1978-81; assoc. Wolf Haldenstein Adler Freeman & Herz, N.Y.C., 1981-86, ptnr., 1987—; bd. dirs. The South Forty Corp., N.Y.C. Mem. ABA, N.Y. State Bar Assn., Assn. of Bar of City of N.Y. Republican. Avocations: science fiction, sailing. Federal civil litigation, State civil litigation, Securities. Office: Wolf Haldenstein et al 270 Madison Ave New York NY 10016

SMITH, JEFFREY MICHAEL, lawyer; b. Mpls., July 9, 1946; s. Philip and Gertrude E. (Miller) S.; 1 son, Brandon Michael. BA summa cum laude, U. Minn., 1970; student U. Malaya, 1967-68; JD magna cum laude, U. Minn., 1973. Bar: Ga. 1973. Assoc. Powell, Goldstein, Frazier & Murphy, 1973-76; ptnr. Rogers & Hardin, 1976-79; ptnr. Bondurant, Stephenson & Smith, Atlanta, 1979-85, Arnall, Golden & Gregory, Atlanta, 1985—; vis. lectr. Duke U., 1976-77, 79-80; adj. prof. Emory U.; lectr. Vanderbilt U., 1977-82. Bd. visitors U. Minn. Law Sch., 1976-82. Mem. ABA (vice chmn. com. profl. officers and dirs. liability law 1979-83, chmn. 1983-84, vice chmn. com. profl. liability 1980-82, mem. standing com. lawyer's profl. liability 1981-85, chmn. 1985-87), State Bar of Ga. (chmn. profl. liability and ins. com. 1978—, trustee Inst. of Continuing Legal Edn. in Ga. 1979-80), Order of Coif, Phi Beta Kappa. Legal malpractice litigation, Accounting malpractice litigation, Directors and officers malpractice litigation. Home: 145 15th St Unit 811 Atlanta GA 30361 Office: Arnall Golden & Gregory 55 Park Pl Atlanta GA 30335

SMITH, JOHN ANTHONY, lawyer; b. Poughkeepsie, N.Y., Sept. 10, 1942; s. John Charles and Eunice C. (Hatfield) S.; m. Carol A. Bechtel; children: Jessica R., Michael Anthony. B.S., Cornell U., 1964, J.D., 1971. Bar: U.S. Dist. Ct. Alaska 1971, Alaska 1971, U.S. Supreme Ct. 1978, U.S. Ct. Appeals (9th cir.) 1971. Assoc. firm Kay, Miller, Libbey, Kelly, Christie & Fuld, 1971, ptnr., 1972-73; ptnr. Gruenberg, Willard & Smith, 1973-74; sole practice, Anchorage, Alaska, 1974-77; ptnr. Smith & Taylor, 1978; ptnr. Smith, Taylor & Gruening, Anchorage, 1979, sr. partner, 1979-84; sr. ptnr. Smith, Robinson & Gruening, 1984-85; sr. ptnr. Smith, Robinson, Gruening & Brecht, 1985-86, Smith, Gruening, Brecht, Evans & Spietzfodeu, 1986—; commr. of communication and econ. devel. State of Alaska, 1987—; adj. prof. U. Alaska Sch. Criminal Justice; mem. exec. com. House-Senate Dem. Council; pres. Alaska Inst. Research and Pub. Service; coordinator U. Alaska Paralegal Program; chmn. Bush Justice Com.; chmn. Gov.'s Bodily Injury Reparation Commn., 1979-80. Bd. dirs. Alaska Bus. Monthly; mem. Internat. Relations com. Nat. Olympic Com., 1986—; mem. exec. com. Anchorage Organizing Com. for the Winter Olympics. Columnist Anchorage Times; contbg. editor Alaska Jour. Commerce. Bd. dirs., counsel Anchorage Olympic Devel. Com.; dir. Glacier Creek Acad. Served to lt. (j.g.), USN, 1964-67. Mem. Alaska Bar Assn. (chmn. specialization com.), ABA, Am. Judicature Soc., Am. Trial Lawyers Assn., Anchorage C. of C. Democrat. Quaker. Administrative and regulatory, Admiralty, Federal civil litigation. Address: 6861 Covitt Circle Anchorage AK 99576 Address: PO Box

D Juneau AK 99811 Office: Smith Robinson & Gruening 801 B St Suite 300 Anchorage AK 99501

SMITH, JOHN CHURCHMAN, lawyer; b. Phila., May 16, 1931. BA, Dickinson U., 1953, JD, 1956. Bar: Pa. 1962, U.S. Ct. Appeals (3d cir.) 1962, U.S. Dist. Ct. (ea. dist.) Pa. 1969, U.S. Supreme Ct. 1969; cert. civil trial advocacy. Ptnr. Gibbons, Buckley, Smith, Palmer & Proud, Media, 1970—. Mem. ABA, Pa. Bar Assn. (ins. trustee), Delco Bar Assn. (bd. dirs., sec., v.p., pres. 1985), Internat. Assn. Ins. Counsel, Pa. Trial Lawyers Assn. Club: Rolling Green Golf (Springfield, Pa.). State civil litigation, Personal injury, Civil rights. Office: Gibbons Buckley Smith Palmer Proud 14 W 2d St Media PA 19063

SMITH, JOHN FRANCIS, III, lawyer; b. White Plains, N.Y., Sept. 24, 1941; s. John Francis and Mary Dake (Mairs) S.; m. Susan Brown; children—John, Stephen, Peter. A.B., Princeton U., 1963; LL.B., Yale U., 1970. Bar: Pa. 1970, U.S. Supreme Ct. 1985. Assoc. Dilworth, Paxson, Kalish & Kauffman, Phila., 1970-75, ptnr., 1975-86, sr. ptnr., 1986—. Mem. exec. com. Employment Discrimination Referral Project, 1971-74; pres. Society Hill Civic Assn., 1975-76, Phila. Chamber Ensemble, 1977-80; mem. exec. com. Radnor Dem. Com., 1982—; bd. govs. Pa. Economy League, 1983—; bd. dirs. World Affairs Council Phila., 1983—, chmn. program com., 1986—; moderator Main Line Unitarian Ch. Served to lt. (j.g.) USNR, 1963-67; Vietnam. Mem. ABA, Pa. Bar Assn., Phila. Bar Assn., Yale Law Sch. Alumni Assn. (exec. com. 1982—, treas. 1986—, sec. 1987—). Club: Princeton (Phila.). Federal civil litigation, Labor, Business negotiations. Office: 2600 Fidelity Bldg Philadelphia PA 19109

SMITH, JOHN GELSTON, lawyer; b. Chgo., Aug. 10, 1923; s. Fred G. and Ferne (Keiser) S.; m. JoAnn Stanton, Aug. 17, 1944; children: Carey S., JoAnne G. B.S., U. Notre Dame, 1949, LL.B., 1950. Bar: Ill. 1950. Assoc. Lord, Bissell & Brook, Chgo., 1950-54, 57, ptnr., 1958—; asst. atty. gen. State of Ill., Springfield, 1954-56; lectr. ins. law Northwestern U., Evanston, 1952, 56-57. Chmn. Gov.'s Transition Task Force, Ill. Dept. Ins., Springfield, 1969; chmn. Gov.'s Adv. Bd. Ill. Dept. Ins., 1969-73; atty.-in-fact Underwriters at Lloyd's, London, 1974—; adv. com. William J. Campbell Library of U.S. Cts., Chgo., 1963—; trustee Lake Bluff (Ill.) Village Bd., 1965-69. Served to 1st lt. USAAF, 1942-45. Mem. Chgo. Bar Assn., Ill. Bar Assn., ABA, Law Club Chgo. Clubs: Union League, Knollwood Country. Insurance. Home: 382 E Ravine Park Dr Lake Forest IL 60045 Office: 115 S LaSalle St Chicago IL 60603

SMITH, JOHN JOSEPH, JR., lawyer; b. Birmingham, Ala., Sept. 28, 1945; s. John Joseph and Ruth Lee (Snavely) S.; m. Sandra Ann Prater, May 25, 1975; 1 dau., Leigh Galbraith, B.A. in English, Vanderbilt U., 1967; J.D., U. Ala.-Tuscaloosa, 1970, LL.M. in Taxation cum laude, 1979. Bar: Ala. 1970, U.S. Dist. Ct. (no. dist.) Ala. 1970, U.S. Ct. Appeals (5th cir.) 1976, U.S. Ct. Appeals (11th cir.) 1982, U.S. Tax Ct. 1973, U.S. Supreme Ct. 1977. Ptnr. Smith & Smith, Birmingham, 1970—. Served to sgt. USNG, 1968-74. Mem. ABA, Assn. Trial Lawyers Am., Ala. Bar Assn., Ala. Trial Lawyers Assn., Ala. Criminal Def. Attys. Assn., Birmingham Bar Assn. (chmn. grievance com. 1982-83, mem. speakers bur. 1981-83, exec. com. 1985-87), Nat. Legal Aid and Defender Assn., Bench and Bar, Birmingham Estate Planning Council, Birmingham Tax Club, Birmingham C. of C. Democrat. Methodist. Clubs: Santa Rosa (Fla.) Golf and Beach, Downtown Democratic, Kiwanis (dir. club), Birmingham Tip-Off, Altadena Valley Country, Relay House, Birmingham Venture (Birmingham). Lodge: Masons. General corporate, Probate, Estate taxation. Home: 132 Lake Dr Birmingham AL 35213 Office: Smith & Smith 1111 John A Hand Bldg Birmingham AL 35203

SMITH, JOHN JOSEPH, lawyer; b. Pitts., Nov. 14, 1911; s. John J. and Alta Ethel (McGrady) S.; m. Ruth Lee Snavely, July 11, 1942; children: John Joseph Jr., Robert William. AB, Birmingham So. Coll., 1931; AM, U. Va., 1932, postgrad. in Econs., 1932-34; JD, U. Ala., 1937. Bar: Ala. 1937, U.S. Dist. Ct. (no. dist.) Ala. 1940, U.S. Supreme Ct. 1945, U.S. Ct. Appeals (5th cir.) 1950. Assoc. Murphy, Hanna & Woodall, Birmingham, Ala., 1937; asst. prof. U. Va., Charlottesville, 1937-39; office solicitor U.S. Dept. Labor, Washington, 1939-42; enforcement atty. Office of Price Adminstrn., Atlanta, 1942-43; legal counsel Bechtel-McCone Corp., Birmingham, 1943-46; sole practice Birmingham, 1946—. Author: Selected Principles of the Law of Contracts, Sales and Negotiable Instruments, 1938. Founder, commr. Homewood (Ala.) Joy Open Baseball League, 1958-72, dir., 1972—; gov's staff Ala., 1963-71; chmn. Homewood Citizens Action Com. Against Annexation. Recipient Youth Service award Pop Warner Conf., Phila., 1961, Clifford Crow Meml. Community Service award, Shades Valley Civitan Club, Homewood, 1981, Key to City, Homewood, 1982. Mem. ABA, Ala. Bar Assn., Birmingham Bar Assn., Order of Coif (founder Farrah order of jurisprudence, pres. 1969-73). Democrat. Methodist. Clubs: The Club (Homewood); City Salesmen's (Birmingham) (Man of Yr. award 1986). Lodges: Masons (life mem., master 1956-57, legal adv. com. for grand lodge), Shriners. Probate, Real property, General corporate. Home: 1506 Primrose Pl Birmingham AL 35209 Office: Smith & Smith 1111 John Hand Bldg Birmingham AL 35203

SMITH, JOHN STUART, lawyer; b. Rochester, N.Y., Sept. 4, 1943; s. Cecil Y. and Helen M. (Van Patten) S.; m. Nancy Schauman, Aug. 28, 1965; children—Kristan, Debra. A.B. magna cum laude, Harvard U., 1965, LL.B. cum laude, 1968. Bar: N.Y. 1968, D.C. 1968, U.S. dist. ct. (we. dist.) N.Y. 1969, U.S. dist. ct. (so. dist.) N.Y. 1973, U.S. dist. ct. (no. dist.) N.Y. 1977, U.S. dist. ct. (no. dist.) Tex. 1980, U.S. Ct. Apls. (5th cir.) 1971, (2d cir.) 1972, (9th cir.) 1980, U.S. Sup. Ct. 1978. Assoc. Nixon, Hargrave, Devans & Doyle, Rochester, N.Y., 1968-74, mem., 1975—. Bd. dirs. Rochester Chamber Orch., 1970-75. Mem. ABA, N.Y. State Bar Assn. (past chmn. criminal procedure subcom. antitrust sect.), Monroe County Bar Assn. Antitrust, Federal civil litigation, Trademark and copyright. Office: Lincoln First Tower Rochester NY 14603 also: 1 Thomas Circle Washington DC 20005

SMITH, JONATHAN SCOTT, lawyer; b. Elmira, N.Y., May 4, 1956; s. Alfred John Smith Jr. and Eloise Mary (Reitz) Rand. AA, Howard Community Coll., 1975; BA in Jurisprudence magna cum laude, U. Balt., 1977, JD magna cum laude, 1979. Bar: Md. 1979, U.S. Dist. Ct. Md. 1979, U.S. Ct. Appeals (4th cir.) 1986. Asst. state's atty. Balt. County, Towson, Md., 1980-84; sole practice Ellicott City, Md., 1984—. Mem. ethics panel Howard County Pub. Sch. System, Ellicott City, 1984-87. Republican. Criminal, State civil litigation, Personal injury. Home: 5590-8 Vantage Point Rd Columbia MD 21044 Office: 3525 N Ellicott Mills Dr Ellicott City MD 21043

SMITH, JUDY GOLDSTEIN, lawyer; b. Chgo., June 15, 1950; s. Sidney Julius and Rose Ellen (Crane) Goldstein; m. Willard S. Smith Jr., Aug. 14, 1982; children: Adam David, Charles Jacob. BA, U. Wis., 1972; JD, Northwestern U., 1975. Bar: Ill. 1975, D.C. 1980. Staff atty. antitrust div. U.S. Dept. Justice, Washington, 1975-80; asst. atty. U.S. Atty.'s Office, Phila., 1980-1986, chief, pres. drug task force and narcotics sect., 1986—. Mem. ABA (chairwoman newsletter subcom. 1983-85, Racketeer Influenced and Corrupt Organizations com. criminal law sect. 1984—, govt. atty. litigation com. litigation sect.). Criminal, Antitrust. Office: US Attys Office 601 Market St Suite 3310 Philadelphia PA 19106

SMITH, KENNETH MCKAY, lawyer; b. Provo, Utah, Mar. 1, 1947; s. Oliver R. and Barbara F. (McKay) S.; m. JoAnne King, Mar. 27, 1970; children: Shannon, Brent K., Ryan K., Kevin K. BS in Acctg., Brigham Young U., 1971, JD, 1977; MBA, U. Utah, 1973. Bar: Ariz. 1978, Utah 1978; CPA, Tex. Ptnr. Carson Messinger, Phoenix, 1978-86, Andersen & Smith, Mesa, Ariz., 1986—. Coordinator Boy Scouts Am., Mesa, 1980—. Served to 1st lt. USAF, 1971-75, Korea. Mem. ABA, Am. Inst. CPA's. Republican. Mormon. General corporate, Estate planning, Real property. Home: 1256 E Harvest Mesa AZ 85203 Office: Andersen & Smith 6053 E University Dr Mesa AZ 85205

SMITH, KIM LEROY, lawyer; b. Boone, Iowa, June 17, 1955; s. George LeRoy Smith and Karen Jean (Price) Nystrom; m. Carol Ann Chapman, Mar. 25, 1978; children: Stephanie Nicole, Austin Jameson. BS in Acctg., Iowa State U., 1977; JD, U. Iowa, 1980. Bar: Iowa 1980; CPA, Iowa. Law clerk Stanley Lande Coulter & Pearce, Muscatine, Iowa, 1978, Claypool & Claypool, Williamsburg, Iowa, 1980; tax mgr. Peat, Marwick, Mitchell & Co., Des Moines, 1980-85; pres. K.L. Smith, P.C., West Des Moines, 1985—. Mem. Des Moines Estate Planning Council, 1984—; pres. Employee Retirement Income Security Act Forum, 1984—. Mem. ABA, Iowa Bar Assn., Internat. Assn. for Fin. Planning (mem. local program com. 1985—), Am. Soc. CPAs, Iowa Soc. CPAs. Presbyterian. Avocations: popular music, tennis, science fiction. Personal income taxation, Estate taxation, Pension, profit-sharing, and employee benefits. Office: 3737 Woodland Ave Suite 130 West Des Moines IA 50265

SMITH, KIM RIDGELY, lawyer, university administrator; b. Preston, Idaho, July 25, 1954; d. Dell Walker and Carmen Ann (Roper) S. BS, BA, U. Idaho, 1976; JD, George Washington U., 1979. Bar: D.C. 1979, U.S. Ct. Appeals (D.C. cir.) 1979. Patent assoc. Battelle Meml. Inst., Richland, Wash., 1979-83; patent adminstr. Oreg. State U., Covallis, 1983—. Pres. Benton County Chpt. ACLU, 1982-83. Mem. Oreg. Patent Law Assn., Soc. Univ. Patent Adminstrs., Licensing Execs. Soc. Patent, Trademark and copyright, Administrative and regulatory. Office: Oreg State U Corvallis OR 97339

SMITH, KIRK BERTON, judge; b. Cogswell, N.D., Feb. 5, 1930; s. Harry William and Adeline Marie (McCauley) S.; m. Mary Joan Bushaw July 2, 1960; children: Ellen, Thomas, James. PhB, U. N.D., 1956, JD, 1957. Bar: N.D. 1957. Law clk. to presiding justice U.S. Ct. Appeals (8th cir.), Fargo, N.D. and St. Louis, 1957-58; ptnr. Bangert & Smith, Enderlin, N.D., 1958-59, Arnason & Smith, Grand Forks, N.D., 1959-63; judge Grand Forks County Ct., 1963-77, N.D. Dist. Ct., Grand Forks, 1977—; mem. N.D. Spl. Procedures Commn., Bismarck, N.D., 1967—; chmn. N.D. Sentencing Commn., Bismarck, 1975-77, N.D. Jud. Immunity Commn., Bismarck, 1985—. Served with USN, 1951-54, Korea. Mem. ABA, Am. Judicature Soc. (bd. dirs. N.D. chpt. 1982-86). Roman Catholic. Lodges: Kiwanis (pres. Grand Forks 1975), Elks. Avocation: automobiles. Office: Dist Ct Courthouse 125 S 4th St PO Box 1476 Grand Forks ND 58206-1476

SMITH, LEN YOUNG, editor, lawyer; b. Nicholasville, Ky., Oct. 20, 1901; s. Walden Rogers and Margaret (Young) S.; m. Helen Tuttle, Aug. 7, 1930; children—Margaret Helen Smith Smith, William R. T. B.A., Northwestern U., 1923, M.A., 1924, J.D., 1927. Bar: Ill. 1927. Assoc. Church, Traxler and Kennedy, Chgo., 1927-33; law sec. to justices Ill. Supreme Ct., Chgo., 1933-58; chmn. dept. bus. law Northwestern U., 1948-70; mem. staff Nat. Conf. Bar Examiners, Chgo., 1966-84, chmn., 1955-56, editor The Bar Examiner, 1966-84; mem. Ill. Bd. Law Examiners, 1947—, pres., 1951—. Recipient Signal Contbn. and Disting. Service award Ill. Supreme Ct., 1978; cert. appreciation Nat. Conf. Bar Examiners, 1956. Fellow Am. Bar Found. (life); mem. Chgo. Bar Assn. (sec. 1954-58, 50-yrs. Service plaque 1978), Ill. Bar Assn., ABA, Order of Coif, Beta Gamma Sigma. Republican. Congregationalist. Clubs: University (Chgo.); Skokie Country (Glencoe, Ill.). Coauthor numerous books on bus. law, including: (with G. Gale Roberson) Essentials of Business Law, 1983, 2d rev. edit., 1986; (with Richard Mann and Barry Roberts) Business Law and the Regulation of Business, 1984, 1986. Legal education, General practice. Home: 109 Fuller Ln Winnetka IL 60093 Office: 203 N Wabash Ave Chicago IL 60601

SMITH, LEO EMMET, b. Chgo., Jan 6, 1927; J.D., DePaul U., 1950. Admitted to Ill. bar, 1950; asso. with law firm also engaged in pvt. industry, 1950-54; asst. states atty. Cook County, Ill., 1954-57; asst. counsel Traffic Inst., Northwestern U., Evanston, Ill., 1957-60; asst. exec. sec. Comml. Law League Am., Chgo., 1960-61, exec. dir., 1961-83, editor Comml. Law Jour., 1961—. Fellow Chgo. Bar Found.; mem. ABA, Ill. Bar Assn., Chgo. Bar Assn. (chmn. library com. 1983), Am. Acad. Matrimonial Lawyers (exec. dir. 1982-84), Friends of Northwestern Sta. (spokesperson 1984). Contbr. articles to legal jours. Home: 1104 S Knight St Park Ridge IL 60068 Office: 222 W Adams St Chicago IL 60606

SMITH, LESLIE CLARK, lawyer; b. Balt., July 15, 1941; s. Leslie McClure and Evelyn (Clark) S.; m. Linda J. Whitley, Oct. 5, 1974; children—Gerre Ann, Randy Lee. B.A., Vanderbilt U., 1962; J.D., U. Ky., 1971; LL.M., U. Western Australia, 1978. Bar: N.Mex. 1971, U.S. Dist. Ct. N.Mex. 1971, U.S. Tax Ct. 1972, U.S. Supreme Ct. 1975, U.S. Ct. Appeals (10th cir.) 1982. Ptnr. firm Buhler, Smith, Fitch & Stout, Truth or Consequences, N.Mex., 1971-76, Smith & Filosa, Truth or Consequences, 1976—; dir. 1st Sierra Nat. Bank; instr. U. Western Australia, Perth, 1975. Contbr. articles to profl. jours. Articles editor U. Ky. Law Rev., 1970-71. Pres. Fiesta Bd., Truth or Consequences, 1982, 87, mem. Bd. Bar Commrs., 1986—. Served to capt. USAF, 1962-68, Vietnam, Congo, Dominican Republic. Mem. N.Mex. Trial Lawyers (bd. dirs. 1982—), Assn. Trial Lawyers Am., N.Mex. Bar Assn. (mem. bd. bar commrs., bd. dirs. criminal sect. 1982—, judiciary com. 1982—). Episcopalian. Club: Rotary (pres. Truth or Consequences 1983). Banking, General practice, State civil litigation. Home: 707 Sierra Vista St Truth or Consequences NM 87901 Office: Smith & Filosa 501 Main St PO Box 391 Truth or Consequences NM 87901

SMITH, LISA MARGARET, lawyer; b. Hamilton, N.Y., Apr. 25, 1955; d. Robert Virgil and Rosalind E. (Walls) S.; m. Joseph L. Hedrick, May 19, 1979. BA, Earlham Coll., 1977; JD, Duke U., 1980. Bar: N.Y. 1981, U.S. Dist. Ct. (ea. and so. dists.) N.Y. 1984, U.S. Ct. Appeals (2d cir.) 1984, U.S. Dist. Ct. (no. dist.) N.Y. 1985, U.S. Supreme Ct. 1985. Asst. dist. atty. Kings County Dist. Atty.'s Office, Bklyn., 1980-85; asst. atty. gen. N.Y. Dept. of Law, Albany, N.Y., 1985-86; supervising sr. asst. dist. atty. Kings County Dist. Atty.'s Office, Bklyn., 1986—. Mem. ABA, N.Y. State Bar Assn., Capital Dist. Women's Bar Assn., N.Y. Dist. Atty.'s Assn. Democrat. Methodist. Criminal, Federal civil litigation. Office: Office of Dist Atty Kings County Mcpl Bldg Brooklyn NY 11201

SMITH, MALCOLM PERCY, lawyer; b. Selma, Ala., Jan. 30, 1943; s. Percy Chesnut and Ella (Spurlin) S.; m. Dovrannah Connor, Aug. 6, 1974; 1 child, Malcolm Percy Jr. BA, U. Ala., 1965; JD, U. Va., 1968. Bar: Ala. 1968, Ga. 1970, U.S. Dist. Ct. (no. dist.) Ga. 1972, U.S. Ct. Appeals (11th cir.) 1981, U.S. Supreme Ct. 1982. Law clk. to presiding justice Ala. Supreme Ct., Montgomery, 1968-69; assoc. Ross & Finch, Atlanta, 1970-73, N. Forrest Montet, P.C., Atlanta, 1973-84. Mem. Ga. Conservancy, Atlanta, 1986, Appalachian Trail Conf., Harper's Ferry, W.Va., 1986. Mem. ABA (contbr., mem. study com. tort liability report 1986), Am. Trial Lawyers Assn., Ga. Bar Assn., Ala. Bar Assn., Def. Research Inst., Nat. Parks Conservation Assn., Regenerative Agr. Assn., Trout Unltd. Republican. Avocations: conservation, fishing, hiking, gardening, reading. Insurance, Federal civil litigation, State civil litigation. Office: Talmadge Mallis & Smith 10 Park Pl S Suite 200 Atlanta GA 30342

SMITH, MARK P., association executive; b. Charleston, W.Va., July 27, 1949; s. Bernard Henry and Josephine (Polan) S.; m. Jane Stephens, May 6, 1978; children: Stephen Noble, Allison Baxter. B.A., Princeton U., 1971; J.D., Yale U., 1978. Asst. to exec. dir. ABA, Chgo., 1976-79; exec. dir. W.Va. State Bar, Charleston, 1979—; treas. W.Va. Legal Services Plan, Inc., Charleston, 1982—, Found. for Youth and Govt., Charleston, 1983—. Bd. dirs. Coalition for Homeless, Charleston, 1984—. Mem. Nat. Assn. Bar Execs. (chmn. continuing edn. com. 1981-83, mem. exec. com. 1984—). Office: W Va State Bar E-400 State Capitol Charleston WV 25305 *

SMITH, MARK RICHARD, lawyer; b. Hastings, Mich., Nov. 6, 1955; s. Bruce Leroy and Betty Jean (Washburn) J.; m. Denise Kay Blair, Oct. 10, 1981. AA, Kellogg Community Coll., 1976; BBA, Western Mich. U., 1978; JD, Coll. William and Mary, 1981. Bar: Mich. 1981, U.S. Dist. Ct. (we. dist.) Mich. 1981. Assoc. Clary, Nantz, Wood, Hoffius, Rankin & Cooper, Grand Rapids, Mich., 1981—. Mem. ABA, Mich. Bar Assn., Grand Rapids Bar Assn. (chairperson young lawyers sect. 1985-86), Assn. Trial Lawyer Am., Mich. Trial Lawyers Assn. Workers' compensation, Liquor liability, Personal injury. Office: Clary Nantz et al 500 Calder Plaza Grand Rapids MI 49503

SMITH, MARVIN HUGH, judge; b. Federalsburg, Md., Aug. 10, 1916; s. Charles Henry and Jeannette (Brown) S.; m. Rebecca Groves, Feb. 21, 1942; children—Melissa (Mrs. Charles O. Waggoner, Jr.), Marvin Hugh, Sarah Jeannette (Mrs. John L. Pettegrew). A.B., Washington Coll., Chestertown, Md., 1937, LL.D., 1980; LL.B., U. Md., 1941. Bar: Md. bar 1941. Practice in Denton, 1946-68; asso. judge Ct. Appeals Md., 1968-86; asst. atty. gen. Md., 1953-55. Chmn. trustees Client's Security Trust Fund of Bar of Md., 1966-68; Mem. Caroline County Bd. Edn., 1951-53, pres., 1952-53; mem. Commn. to Revise Criminal Law of Md., 1952; del. from Caroline County to Md. Constl. Conv., 1967; mem. exec. bd. Del-Mar-Va Area council Boy Scouts Am., 1967—, v.p., 1969-71, pres., 1971-73. Served with CIC AUS, 1941-45. Recipient Silver Beaver award Boy Scouts Am., 1968, Distinguished Eagle Scout award, 1975. Mem. ABA, Md. Bar Assn. (past gov.), Caroline County Bar Assn., Am. Legion, Omicron Delta Kappa. Methodist. Lodges: Rotary (past pres.), Masons, Shriners. Home: 318 Maple Ave Federalsburg MD 21632

SMITH, MAXINE STEWARD, lawyer; b. Delaware County, Okla., Jan. 25, 1921; d. Clay Dillard and Frankie Gladys (Wolford) Steward; m. Gordon Daniel Smith, May 22, 1947 (div. Apr. 1970). LL.B., LaSalle Extension U., 1961; postgrad. U. Calif., 1962-65. Bar: Calif. 1962, U.S. Dist. Ct. (so. dist.) Calif. 1962. Sole practice, San Diego, 1962-65; staff atty. Legal Aid Soc. of San Diego, Inc., 1965-72; dep. dist. atty. child support div. San Bernardino County, Calif., 1973; sole practice, San Diego, 1974-81, Ramona, Calif., 1981—; instr. adult edn. San Diego City Schs., 1962-64. Trustee, Crossroads Found., 1971-77. Served with Women's Air Force Service Pilots, 1943-44. Mem. San Diego County Bar Assn. (various sects.), Am. Judicature Soc., Calif. Women Lawyers, Ninety-Nines, Inc., Am. Assn. Retired Persons (semi retired), Silver Wings. Republican. Probate, Administrative and regulatory, General practice. Office: 520 D St Ramona CA 92065

SMITH, MAXWELL PAUL, lawyer; b. Elyria, Ohio, Jan. 8, 1924; s. Maxwell P. and Hilma Lillian (Holmgren) S.; m. Vaunceil Hulda Tiarks, Nov. 10, 1928; children—Mark Paul, Terri Smith Lindvall, Amy, Laura. J.D., Valparaiso U.,. 1950. Bar: Ind. 1950, U.S. Dist. Ct. (no. dist.) Ind. 1950, U.S. Dist. Ct. (so. dist.) Ind. 1950, U.S. Ct. Appeals (6th cir.) 1982. Pres. Krueckeberg and Smith, P.C., Ft. Wayne, Ind., 1982—; Pres. bd. trustees, elder First Presbyterian Ch., Ft. Wayne; pres. Neighbors, Inc., Ft. Wayne; bd. dirs. Samaritan Counseling, Inc. Served to 1st lt. JAGC, U.S. Army, 1952-53. Decorated Army Commendation medal. Mem. Allen County Bar Assn., Ind. State Bar Assn. (citation for article 1982). Club: Wildwood Racquet (Ft. Wayne). Contbg. author: Professional Corporations, 1978, Indiana Continuing Legal Edn. Forum, 1983. General corporate, Probate. Office: 622 S Calhoun St Fort Wayne IN 46802

SMITH, MICHAEL ALAN, lawyer, educator; b. Craig, Colo., Apr. 20, 1954; s. William James and Olive Jean (Kline) S. BSBA, U. Denver, 1976, BA, 1977; JD, Harvard U., 1980. Bar: Colo. 1980, U.S. Dist. Ct. Colo. 1980, U.S. Ct. Appeals (10th cir.) 1980. Mem. Ireland, Stapleton, Pryor & Pascoe P.C., Denver, 1980—; barrister's cup judge U. Denver Coll. Law, 1981—; lectr. in field, 1984—. Dir. student jud. affairs, U. Denver, 1986—. Mem. Denver Bar Assn. (sec. young lawyers conv. com. 1984-85, mem. meeting com. 1985—), Colo. Bar Assn. (mem. meeting com. 1985—, chmn. conv. com. 1985—), U. Denver Mile High Alumni Club (bd. dirs. 1981—, pres. 1985—), U. Denver Alumni Admissions Council (chmn. 1984—), Centennial Colo. Conf. (staff mem. 1976-81, bd. dirs. 1981—), Harvard Law Sch. Assn. Colo. (sec. 1985—). Republican. Baptist. Avocations: skiing, running. Real property, Contracts commercial, Landlord-tenant. Home: 1123 Sherman #D Denver CO 80203 Office: Ireland Stapleton et al 1675 Broadway Suite 2600 Denver CO 80202

SMITH, MICHAEL GLEN, lawyer; b. Batesville, Ark., Aug. 14, 1955; s. Bobby Glen and Bonnie (Wiley) S. BA, U. Md., 1977; JD with honors, U. Ark., 1981. Bar: Ark. 1981, U.S. Dist. Ct. (ea. and we. dists.) Ark. 1981, U.S. Ct. Appeals (8th cir.) 1981, U.S. Supreme Ct. 1985. From assoc. to ptnr. Friday, Eldredge & Clark, Little Rock, 1981—. Articles editor U. Ark. Law Rev., 1980-81. Mem. ABA, Ark. Bar Assn. (lectr. bar exam preperation course 1982), Pulaski County Bar Assn., Assn. Trial Lawyers Am., Ark. Trial Lawyers Assn. (lectr. constrn. litigation seminar 1986). Avocations: classical and jazz guitar, eng. lit. Federal civil litigation, State civil litigation. Home: 5208 F St Little Rock AR 72205 Office: Friday Eldredge & Clark 200 First Comml Bldg Little Rock AR 72201

SMITH, MICHAEL LOUIS, lawyer; b. Detroit, Dec. 23, 1947; s. Jesse H. and Mary M. (Zemke) S.; m. Patricia Eileen Hagerty, Sept. 11, 1970; children: David Brian, Jessica Colleen. BA magna cum laude, U. Detroit, 1970, postgrad., 1970-71; JD, Wayne State U., Detroit, Mich., 1974. Bar: Mich. 1974, U.S. Dist. Ct. (ea. dist.) Mich. 1974, U.S. Dist. Ct. (we. dist.) Mich. 1975, Colo. 1978, U.S. Dist. Ct. Colo. 1978. Intern dir. City of Detroit, 1969-73; research asst. Mich. Civil Rights, Detroit, 1973; assoc. Keller & Thoma, Detroit, 1973-78, Mulligan & Damas, Denver, 1978-79; ptnr. Damas and Smith, P.C., Denver, 1979—; bd. dirs. Family Tree, Inc., Denver. Mem. Colo. Nursing Bd., Denver, 1985—. Mem. ABA (labor law com.), Colo. Bar Assn. (labor law com.), Nat. Assn. Sch. Attys., Colo. Assn. Sch. Bds. Avocations: racquetball, running, travel. Civil rights, Labor, Local government. Office: Damas and Smith PC 1900 Grant Suite 730 Denver CO 80203

SMITH, MILAN DALE, JR., lawyer; b. Pendleton, Oreg., May 19, 1942. BA cum laude, Brigham Young U., 1966; JD, U. Chgo., 1969. Bar: Calif. 1970, D.C. 1972, U.S. Supreme Ct. 1977, U.S. Tax Ct. 1978. Assoc. O'Melveny & Myers, Los Angeles, 1969-72; ptnr. Smith & Hilbig, Torrance, Calif., 1972—. Pres. Los Angeles State Office Bldg. Authority, 1984—, Informed Voters League, Torance, 1975-77; vice chmn. bd. Ettie Lee Homes for Youth, 1973-82. Nat. Honor scholar, 1966-69. Mem. ABA (coordinator real estate syndicate subcom. 1973-75), Calif. Bar Assn. (chmn. real estate fin. subsect. 1982-84, real property sect.), Los Angeles County Bar Assn., Brigham Young U. Alumni Assn. (bd. dirs. 1982-86). Banking, Contracts commercial, Real property. Office: Smith & Hilbig 21515 Hawthorne Blvd Torrance CA 90503

SMITH, MILTON LOVETT, lawyer; b. Camden, N.J., Feb. 6, 1951; s. Milton L. Smith and Dorothy S. (Shaner) Hare. BS, USAF Acad., 1973; JD, George Washington U., 1976; LLM in Air and Space Law, McGill U. Inst., 1985. Bar: N.J. 1976, D.C. 1978. Commd. 2d lt. USAF, advanced through grades to maj., 1983; def. counsel trial judiciary USAF, Peterson AFB, Colo., 1976-81, atty. aviation law sect., 1981-83, dir. space law hdqrs. air force command, 1984—. Bd. dirs. Big Bros. Orgn., Colorado Springs, Colo., 1985—. Mem. ABA, AIAA, Am. Soc. Internat. Law, U.S. Space Found. Avocations: scuba diving, skiing, sailing. Public international, Space law. Home: 3785 Windmill Ct Colorado Springs CO 80907 Office: USAF Space Command Hdqrs Peterson AFB CO 80914-5001

SMITH, NORMAN BARRETT, lawyer, legal educator; b. Iron Mountain, Mich., Oct. 28, 1938; s. Donald Barrett and Kathryn Muriel (Sturtz) S.; m. Gabriella Palmer Wilson, July 21, 1962; children: Catherine Muriel, Julian Barrett, Gabrielle Palmer, Alexa McColl. AB, U. N.C., 1960; LLB, Harvard U., 1965. Bar: N.C. 1965, U.S. Dist. Ct. (mid. dist.) N.C. 1965, U.S. Ct. Appeals (4th cir.) 1969, U.S. Supreme Ct. 1969, U.S. Dist. Ct. (ea. and we. dists.) N.C. 1970, U.S. Ct. Appeals (7th cir.) 1973, U.S. Ct. Appeals (D.C. cir.) 1976, U.S. Dist. Ct. (we. dist.) Tex. 1982, U.S. Ct. Appeals (5th cir.) 1982. Assoc. Smith, Moore, Smith, Schell & Hunter, Greensboro, N.C., 1965-69; ptnr. Smith, Patterson, Follin, Curtis, James & Harkavy, Greensboro, 1969—; adj. prof. environ. law U. N.C., Chapel Hill, 1978; adj. prof. law enforcement Guilford Coll., Greensboro, 1970-74; gen. counsel N.C. Civil Liberties Union, 1969—. Author: (with Michael Curtis, Martha Johnston, John Kernodle, Jr.) Domestic Relations in North Carolina Law Practice Systems, 1983; (with Marion Follin, III and John Dusenbury, Jr.) Collections: A North Carolina Law Practice System, 1983; contbr. numerous articles to profl. jours. Served to comdr. USNR, 1956-82. Recipient Frank Porter Graham Civil Liberties award N.C. Civil Liberties Union, 1978; named Hon. Admiral in New River Navy by Gov. James B. Holshouser, 1975. Mem. ABA, N.C. Bar Assn., Greensboro Bar Assn., 18th Dist. Bar Assn., N.C. Acad. Trial Lawyers. Democrat. Mem. Unitarian Ch. State civil litigation, Civil rights, Federal civil litigation. Home: 3502 Madison Ave Greensboro NC 27403 Office: Smith Patterson Follin Curtis James & Harkavy 700 Southeastern Bldg Greensboro NC 27401

SMITH, NORMAN CHARLES, lawyer; b. St. Johnsbury, Vt., July 13, 1955; s. Stewart Clinton and Cecile M. (Prevost) S.; m. Nadia Schreiber, July

28, 1984. BS, Mass. Inst. Tech., 1977; JD, Boston U., 1980. Bar: Vt. 1981, U.S. Dist. Ct. Vt. 1981. Law clk. to presiding justice Vt. Supreme Ct., Montpelier, 1980-81; assoc. Whitcomb, Clark & Moeser, Springfield, Vt., 1981-82, Bloomberg & Greenberg, Burlington, Vt., 1981-85, Bloomberg & Assocs., Burlington, 1985-86, John J. Bergeron, Burlington, 1986—. Bd. dirs. Green Mountain Habitat for Humanity, Burlington, 1984—, pres. 1985—, Mt. Calvary Cemetery Assn., Burlington, 1986—. Mem. ABA, Vt. Bar Assn., Chittenden County Bar Assn. Roman Catholic. Avocations: christian ministry, basketball. Real property, General corporate, State civil litigation. Home: 70 Drew St Burlington VT 05401 Office: Law Offices John J Bergeron 96 S Union St PO Box 925 Burlington VT 05402

SMITH, ORA EVERETT, corporate executive, lawyer; b. Kennett, Mo., Dec. 24, 1947; s. Everett and Thelma May (Johnson) S.; m. Sue Ellen Caldwell, Sept. 3, 1972; children: Everett Eugene, Nathan Thomas. BME and MME, MIT, 1970; JD, Harvard U., 1976. Bar: Mass. 1977, D.C. 1977, U.S. Dist. Ct. Mass. 1977, Calif. 1983, U.S. Dist. Ct. (cen. dist.) Calif. 1983, U.S. Ct. Appeals (9th cir.) 1983. Mgr. engring. U.S. EPA, Cin., 1970-73; atty. New Eng. Telephone, Boston, 1976-77; mng. dir. Gordian Assocs. Inc., Washington, 1977-79; dir. structural materials integrity Rockwell Internat., Thousand Oaks, Calif., 1979-81, dir. physics and chem., 1981-85, dir. external tech. devel., 1985—; cons. Exec. Office of Pres. of U.S., Washington, 1985—; bd. dirs. N.Mex. TechnetInc., Albuquerque. Patentee impact sensor and coding apparatus; contbr. articles to profl. jours. Trustee Conejo Future Found., Thousand Oaks. Served with USPHS, 1970-72. Mem. ABA, Indsl. Research Inst. (White House fellow 1984-85, program com.), Consortium for Advanced Tech. Edn. (bd. dirs.). Republican. Lodge: Rotary. General corporate, Private international. Home: 447 Arcturus St Thousand Oaks CA 91360 Office: Rockwell Internat PO Box 1085 Thousand Oaks CA 91360

SMITH, PAUL RAY, lawyer; b. Santa Fe, Nov. 23, 1955; s. Paul W. and Nola P. (Sims) S. BA in Polit. Sci., Ariz. State U., 1976; JD, N.Mex. Law Sch., 1979. Bar: N.Mex. 1979, U.S. Dist. Ct. N.Mex. 1979, U.S. Ct. Appeals (10th cir.) 1979, Ariz. 1980. Assoc. Danoff & Assocs., P.C., Albuquerque, 1979-80; pres. Visual Prodns., Albuquerque, 1981-84; ptnr. Smith & Sandager, P.A., Albuquerque, 1983-84; sole practice Albuquerque, 1984—; sec. various restaurants and bus. computer systems, Albuquerque, 1984—. Mem. N.Mex. Trial Lawyers Assn. Avocations: ballooning, boardsailing, skiing. Real property, Personal injury. Office: 237-B Eubank Blvd NE Albuquerque NM 87123

SMITH, PETER JOHN, lawyer; b. Orange, N.J., Jan. 5, 1956; s. John Philip and Marie Ann (Miller) S.; m. Karen Marie Pretzer, July 21, 1984. BA, U. Notre Dame, 1978; JD, Rutgers U., 1981. Bar: N.J. 1981, U.S. Dist. Ct. N.J. 1981, U.S. Ct. Claims 1985, U.S. Supreme Ct. 1985. Jud. clk. law div. N.J. State Ct., Elizabeth, 1981-82; assoc. Connell, Foley & Geiser, Roseland, N.J., 1982—. Contbg. author: New Jersey Construction Law, 1984, Construction Litigation: Representing the Contractor, 1985. Mem. ABA (pub. contract law com. 1983—), N.J. Bar Assn. (pub. contract law com. 1982—). Democrat. Roman Catholic. Avocations: running, music. Construction, Federal civil litigation, State civil litigation. Office: Connell Foley & Geiser 85 Livingston Ave Roseland NJ 07068

SMITH, PHILLIP NOLAN, JR., lawyer; b. Pittsburg, Tex., Nov. 16, 1942; s. Phillip Nolan and Emma Lee (George) S. B.B.A., U. Tex., 1966; LL.B., Baylor U., 1969; LL.M., Harvard U., 1970. Bar: Tex. bar 1970. Partner firm Baker & Botts, Dallas, 1987—. Antitrust, Federal civil litigation, State civil litigation. Home: 11706 Forest Ct Dallas TX 75230 Office: 800 LTV Ctr 2001 Ross Ave Dallas TX 75201

SMITH, RICHARD B., lawyer; b. Lancaster, Pa., July 9, 1928; s. Richard H. and May F. (Blottenberger) S.; children: Landis, Leslie, Thompson, Eliza. B.A., Yale U., 1949; LL.B., U. Pa., 1953. Bar: N.Y. 1955, U.S. Supreme Ct. 1972. Assoc. Reavis & McGrath, N.Y.C., 1953-55, 57-63, ptnr., 1963-67; atty. W.R. Grace Co., N.Y.C., 1955-57; ptnr. Reavis & McGrath, N.Y.C., 1963-67; commr. SEC, Washington, 1967-71; ptnr. firm Davis, Polk & Wardwell, N.Y.C., 1971—; mem. council Adminstrv. Conf. U.S., 1971-74. Trustee N.Y.C. Citizens Budget Commn., 1976—, vice chmn. 1976-84. Mem. ABA (vice chmn. commn. on law and economy 1975-79, mem. council sect. on corp., banking and bus. law 1979-84, nat. conf. lawyers and C.P.A.s, 1982—), N.Y. State Bar Assn., Assn. of Bar of City of N.Y., Internat. Bar Assn., Am. Judicature Soc., Am. Law Inst. (adviser Fed. Securities Code 1970-80, corp. governance project 1981—). Office: Davis Polk & Wardwell 1 Chase Manhattan Plaza New York NY 10005 Office: Davis Polk & Wardwell 1575 I St NW Washington DC 20005

SMITH, RICHARD WENDELL, lawyer; b. Lincoln, Nebr., May 29, 1912; s. Walter Charles and Mary Frances (Goodale) S.; m. Patricia Adelle Lahr, Apr. 8, 1947; children—Laurie Patricia, Barton Richard. A.B., Nebr. Wesleyan U., 1933; J.D., Harvard U., 1938. Bar: Nebr. 1938, U.S. Dist. Ct. Nebr. 1938, U.S. Ct. Claims 1949, U.S. Ct. Appeals (7th and 8th cirs.), U.S. Supreme Ct. 1955. Spl. agt. FBI, Dept. Justice, Washington, 1942-44; Ptnr. Woods, Aitken, Smith, Greer, Overcash & Spangler, Lincoln; apptd. by U.S. Dist Ct. as trustee in reorgn. of Am. Buslines, Inc., 1954-58; lectr. constrn. law Fed. Publs., Washington, 1974—. Contbr. articles to profl. jours. Bd. dirs., sec. Nebr. Wesleyan U., Lincoln, 1958-74; sec. Harvard Schs. and Scholarship Com., Lincoln, 1948—; treas. Nebr. Art Assn., Lincoln, 1984—; bd. dirs. Lincoln Symphony Orch. Assn., Lincoln Community Theater, 1982—. Served to lt. USNR, 1944-46. Mem. ABA (governing com. forum on constrn. industry 1983—), Nebr. Bar Assn. Republican. Lodge: Rotary (pres. 1981-82). Construction, Government contracts and claims, Probate. Home: 916 Fall Creek Rd Lincoln NE 68510 Office: Woods Aitken Smith Greer et al 1500 American Charter Ctr Lincoln NE 68508

SMITH, ROBERT ANTHONY, lawyer; b. Edison, N.J., May 11, 1954; s. Robert J. and Helen (Dugansky) S.; m. Therese Fleurie, Aug. 13, 1977; 1 child, Kristen Fleurie. BA, Cath. U., 1976, JD, 1979. Bar: D.C. 1979, U.S. Dist. Ct. D.C. 1980, U.S. Ct. Appeals (D.C. cir.) 1980, U.S. Ct. Appeals (11th cir.) 1982. Assoc. Brownstein, Zeidman and Schomer, Washington, 1979-74; atty. Marriott Corp., Bethesda, Md., 1984-87; asst. sec. Marriott Family Restaurants, Inc., Bethesda, 1985-87; sec. Big Boy Nat. Advt. Coop., Inc., Bethesda, 1985-87; assoc. Reed, Smith, Shaw & McClay, Washington, 1987—; speaker in field. Mem. ABA, D.C. Bar Assn., Internat. Franchise Assn. (legal legis. com. 1984—), Phi Beta Kappa. Democrat. Roman Catholic. Franchising, Contracts commercial, Real property. Home: 2436 Henslowe Dr Potomac MD 20854 Office: Reed Smith Shaw & McClay 1150 Connecticut Ave NW Suite 900 Washington DC 20036

SMITH, ROBERT BLAKEMAN, lawyer; b. Mt. Vernon, N.Y., June 18, 1949; s. William Blakeman and Helen Theresa (Curley) S. BS, Rensselaer Polytech. Inst., 1971, ME, 1973; JD, Boston U. Sch. Law, 1976. Bar: N.Y. 1977, U.S. Dist. Ct. (so. and ea. dist.) N.Y. 1977, U.S. Dist. Ct. (no. dist.) N.Y. 1981, U.S. Patent and Trademark Office 1977, U.S. Ct. Appeals (7th cir.) 1979, U.S. Ct. Appeals (fed. cir.) 1983, U.S. Supreme Ct. 1981. Assoc. Brumbaugh, Graves, Donohue & Raymond, N.Y.C., 1976-84, ptnr. 1984—; lectr. IEEE, N.Y.C., 1983—. Trustee Delta Phi Found., Ithaca, N.Y., 1978-86, St. Elmo Found., Ithaca, 1986—. Mem. ABA, N.Y. Patent, Trademark and Copyright Law Assn., Am. Intellectual Property Law Assn. Republican. Club: St. Anthony (N.Y.C.). Patent, Trademark and copyright. Home: 245 W 104 St New York NY 10025 Office: Brumbaugh Graves Donohue & Raymond 30 Rockefeller Plaza New York NY 10112

SMITH, ROBERT CATLETT, lawyer; b. Brookings, S.D., July 29, 1926; s. Homer William and Marguerite Hill Catlett S.; m. Josephine Trygstad, July 31, 1949; children: Carl, Susan (Smith) Burchiel, Philip, Amy Jo. BSEE, S.D. State U., 1949, JD, 1952. Bar: S.D. 1952, U.S. Patent and Trademark Office 1953. Patent atty. Bendix Aviation Corp., South Bend, Ind., 1952-61; atty. patent div. The Bendix Corp., Towson, Md., 1961-63, North Hollywood, Calif., 1963-66; counsel regional patent The Bendix Corp., North Hollywood, 1966-71, Sylmar, Calif., 1971-82; counsel patent Allied Corp., Sylmar, 1982—. Served as cpl. U.S. Army, 1945. Mem. Los Angeles Patent Law Assn. (bd. govs. 1976-78). Republican. Lutheran. Patent, Government contracts and claims, Trademark and copyright. Home: 5854 Le Sage Ave Woodland Hills CA 91367 Office: Allied Corp Law Dept 15825 Roxford St Sylmar CA 91342

SMITH, ROBERT EVERETT, lawyer; b. N.Y.C., Mar. 15, 1936; s. Arthur L. and Augusta (Cohen) S.; m. Emily Lucille Lehman, July 17, 1960; children: Amy, Karen, Victoria. BA, Dartmouth Coll., 1957; LLB, Harvard U., 1960. Bar: N.Y. 1960, U.S. Dist. Ct. (so. dist.) N.Y. 1962, U.S. Ct. Appeals (2d cir.) 1963, U.S. Supreme Ct. 1967, U.S. Dist. Ct. (ea. dist.) N.Y. 1969, U.S. Ct. Appeals (3d cir.) 1982. Assoc. Paul, Weiss, Rifkind, Wharton & Garrison, N.Y.C., 1960-65; from assoc. to ptnr. Baar, Bennett & Fullen, N.Y.C., 1965-74; ptnr. Guggenheimer & Untermyer, N.Y.C., 1974-85, Rosenman & Colin, N.Y.C., 1985—; bd. dirs. U.S. Realty and Investment Co., Newark, The Zweig Fund, Inc., N.Y.C. Mem. ABA, N.Y. State Bar Assn., Assn. of Bar of City of N.Y., Fed. Bar Counsel, N.Y. County Lawyers Assn., Am. Arbitration Assn. (nat. panel arbitrators). Federal civil litigation, State civil litigation, General corporate. Office: Rosenman & Colin 575 Madison Ave New York NY 10022

SMITH, ROBERT JOHN, lawyer; b. Waupaca, Wis., Jan. 20, 1944; s. Lawrence J. and Doris (Danielson) S.; m. Marjorie Costello, June 3, 1967; children: Alicia, Scott, Robyn, Carly, Colin. BCE, U. Wis., 1967, JD cum laude, 1974. Bar: Wis. 1974, U.S. Dist. Ct. (we. dists.) Wis. 1975, U.S. Supreme Ct. 1978, U.S. Dist. Ct. (ea. dist.) 1985, D.C. 1987. Assoc. prof. engring. U. Wis., Madison, 1974-79; chmn. Wis. Transp. Commn., Madison, 1979-81; mem. Wickwire, Gavin & Gibbs, Madison, 1982—. Author: Wisconsin Construction Law, 1985. Served to lt. USN, 1967-71. Mem. ASCE, ABA, Wis. Bar Assn. Construction, Environment, Government contracts and claims. Office: Wickwire Gavin & Gibbs 152 W Johnson Madison WI 53701

SMITH, ROBERT MCDAVID, lawyer; b. Birmingham, Ala., Oct. 5, 1920; s. Maclin F. and Virginia (McDavid) S.; m. Eugenia Wimberly, Aug. 27, 1946; children—Eugenia Wimberly, Robert Patton, Felton Wimberly. B.A., U. N.C., 1942; LL.B., U. Ala., 1948; LL.M., Harvard U., 1949. Bar: Ala. 1949, U.S. Dist. Ct. (no. dist.) Ala. 1950, U.S. Ct. Appeals (5th cir.) 1952, U.S. Ct. Appeals (11th cir.) 1981, U.S. Supreme Ct. 1957. Assoc. Lange, Simpson, Robinson & Somerville, 1949-52, ptnr. 1952—; mem. Nat. Defendant Project, 1963-69. Mem. exec. com. Jefferson County (Ala.) Republican Party, 1965-68. Served to capt. AUS, 1942-46. Decorated Bronze Star. Fellow Am. Coll. Trial Lawyers; mem. ABA (chmn. sect. legal edn. and admission to bar), Am. Judicature Soc., Ala. Bar Assn. (chmn. com. legal edn.), Fed. Bar Assn. Republican. Methodist. Clubs: Kiwanis, Country, The Club, Downtown (Birmingham). Federal civil litigation, State civil litigation, Estate planning. Office: Lange Simpson Robinson & Somerville 1700 First Alabama Bank Bldg Birmingham AL 35203

SMITH, ROBERT SHERLOCK, lawyer; b. N.Y.C., Aug. 31, 1944; s. Robert and Janet W. (Welt) S.; m. Dian Goldston Smith, Aug. 31, 1969; children—Benjamin Eli, Emlen Matthew, Rosemary Friedman. B.A., Stanford U., 1965; LL.B., Columbia U., 1968. Bar: N.Y. 1968, U.S. Dist. Ct. (so. dist.) N.Y. 1969, U.S. Ct. Appeals (2d cir.) 1970, U.S. Tax Ct. 1974, U.S. Dist. Ct. (ea. dist.) N.Y. 1977, U.S. Supreme Ct. 1979. Assoc., Paul, Weiss, Rifkind, Wharton & Garrison, N.Y.C., 1968-76, ptnr., 1976—; vis. prof. Columbia Law Sch., N.Y.C., 1980-81, lectr. law, 1981—. Mem. ABA (sect. litigation 1977—), Assn. Bar City N.Y. (com. fed. legis. 1981-84, com. on judiciary 1984—). Democrat. Mem. Reformed Ch. Federal civil litigation, State civil litigation. Office: Paul Weiss Rifkind Et Al 1285 Ave of Americas New York NY 10019

SMITH, ROGER THEODORE, lawyer; b. Copaigue, N.Y., Apr. 27, 1954; s. Sidney Malcolm and Jeanne Clara (Widyn) S.; m. Mary Anne Rhymer, May 27, 1984; 1 child, Adam. BA, U. N.C., 1976; JD, Pepperdine U., 1979. Bar: N.C. 1979, U.S. Dist. Ct. (we. dist.) N.C. 1979, U.S. Ct. Appeals (4th cir.) 1985. Assoc. Lentz & Ball, P.A., Asheville, N.C., 1979-80; sole practice Asheville, 1981—. Chmn. Irene Wortham Ctr. Inc., Asheville, 1985—; pres. Santa Pal Inc., Asheville, 1986; mem. Asheville Tree Commn., 1984—. Mem. ABA, N.C. Bar Assn. (ethics and environ. law com.), 28th Jud. Dist. Bar Assn., N.C. Acad. Trial Lawyers, Sierra Club (chmn. We. N.C. group 1983-85, atty. 1985). Democrat. Roman Catholic. Lodge: DeMolay (Chevalier award, 1975), Optimists (v.p. Asheville 1983-85). Avocations: photography, music, basketball, volleyball, outdoors. Family and matrimonial, Criminal, Personal injury. Home: 40 Wanoca Ave Asheville NC 28803 Office: Asheville Legal Clinic 108 College St Suite 201 Asheville NC 28801

SMITH, RUFUS RANDOLPH, JR., lawyer; b. Birmingham, Sept. 14, 1949; s. Rufus Randolph and Jo (Bogus) S.; m. Miriam Jane Whatley, Sept. 12, 1980; children—Jason Randolph, Caroline Jane. B.S., Troy State U., 1971; J.D., Cumberland Sch. Law Samford U., 1974. Bar: Ala. 1974, U.S. Dist. Ct. (mid. dist.) Ala. 1974, U.S. Ct. Appeals (5th cir.) 1979, U.S. Ct. Appeals (11th cir.) 1981, U.S. Supreme Ct. 1980. Ptnr. Carter & Smith, Dothan, Ala., 1974-77, Byrd, Carter & Smith, Dothan, 1977-82, Farmer, Price & Smith, Dothan, 1982-85; spl. asst. atty. gen. State of Ala., 1977-79, 79-83. Author: Decedent Estates & Trusts, 1973; Uniform Commercial Code, 1974. Bd. dirs. Selective Service Bd., Dothan, 1982—. Mem. Ala. Trial Lawyers Assn. (bd. govs. 1980-81, exec. com. 1982—), Assn. Trial Lawyers Am., ABA, Ala. Jud. Coll. Faculty Assn., Phi Alpha Delta. Baptist. Club: Dothan Exchange (pres. 1980-81). Lodge: Elks. Personal injury, Federal civil litigation, State civil litigation. Home: Number 1 Brannon Ridge Dothan AL 36303 Office: Farmer Price & Smith PO Box 2228 Dothan AL 36303

SMITH, RUSSELL BRYAN, lawyer; b. Fort Worth, Nov. 1, 1936; s. Russell B. and Marie Antoinette (Hornick) S.; children—Robert B., Donna Sue. B.B.A., So. Meth. U., 1959, J.D., 1962. Bar: Tex. 1962, U.S. dist. ct. (no., ea., we., so. dists.) Tex., U.S. Ct. Appeals (5th cir.) 1962, (8th cir.) 1981 (11th cir.) 1982, U.S. Supreme Ct. 1967, U.S. Ct. Claims 1987. Assoc. Woodruff, Hill & Bader, Dallas, 1962-65; ptnr. Woodruff, Hill Kendall & Smith, Dallas, 1965-75; sole practice, Dallas, 1975—. Concession chmn. Byron Nelson Golf Class, 1975, 77, 80, 83, 85, 87; mem. Dallas Assembly, 1973-87; Dallas Big Bros., 1967—; bd. trustees Dallas Hist. Soc., 1978-87, Dallas 40, 1967—; bd. dirs. Dallas Police Athletic Assn., 1979-86, Dallas Urban League, 1978-86, Dallas Zool. Soc., 1980—; bd. dirs. Greater Dallas Planning Council, 1978-87; bd. dirs. State Fair Tex., 1972—, v.p., 1973—; adv. council St. Paul Hosp., 1974—; mem. Dallas City Council, 1971-75, dep. mayor pro tem, 1973-75; bd. dirs. Greater Dallas Sesquicentennial Commn., 1982-87. Served with USNR, 1955-62. Recipient Disting. Service award Dallas Jaycees 1976, award Tex. Jaycees 1972; named Outstanding Man in Dallas 1975; Ky. col. Mem. ABA, Tex. Bar Assn., Am. Bd. Trial Advs., Dallas Trial Lawyers Assn., Tex. Trial Lawyers Assn., Am. Trial Lawyers Assn., Dallas Bar Assn., Dallas Estate Council, Am. Judicature Soc., Dallas Bar Found., Phi Alpha Delta. Methodist. Clubs: Salesmanship, All Sports Assn. (pres. 1977), Dallas Athletic, 2001 (Dallas), Woodvale Fishing, Rock Creek Barbecue. Federal civil litigation, State civil litigation, General corporate. Home: 11342 Dalron Dr Dallas TX 75218 Office: Two Turtle Creek Village Dallas TX 75219

SMITH, RUTH HUNTER, lawyer; b. Columbus, Ohio, Dec. 23, 1949; d. Richard F. and Bernice E. (Strawser) Hunter; m. J. T. Smith, Jan. 23, 1970 (div. May 1972); 1 son, Jason C. B.S. in Edn., Ohio State U., 1973, J.D., 1977. Bar: Ohio 1977. Tchr. English, Columbus Pub. Schs., 1973-74; cons. Franklin County Mcpl. Ct., Columbus, 1975-76; research asst. Coll. Law, Ohio State U., Columbus, 1976; law clk. Vorys, Sater, Seymour & Pease, Columbus, 1976-77; legal counsel John W. Galbreath & Co., Columbus and Denver, 1977—; lectr. N.W. Ctr. for Profl. Edn., Portland, Oreg., 1984. Vol. Am. Cancer Soc., Columbus, 1984, March of Dimes, Columbus, 1984. Coll. Law scholar Ohio State U., 1974-76; Milton R. Bierly scholar Ohio State U., 1972. Mem. ABA, Ohio State Bar Assn., Columbus Bar Assn., Franklin County Women Lawyers Assn. Republican. Roman Catholic. Real property, General corporate. Office: John W Galbreath & Co 188 E Broad St Columbus OH 43215

SMITH, SCOTT ORMOND, lawyer; b. Altadena, Calif., Mar. 30, 1948; s. Donald Ormond and Jerry Ann (Shaw) S.; m. Antoinette Tribolet, Aug. 23, 1968 (div. 1983); children—Victoria, Jeffrey Ormond, Meagan Ashley; m. Barbara Lockert, May 8, 1985. B.S., U. So. Calif., 1971; J.D., Loyola U., Los Angeles, 1974. Bar: Calif. 1974, U.S. Dist. Ct. (so., no., cen. and ea. dists.) Calif. 1975, U.S. Ct. Appeals (9th cir.) 1975, U.S. Supreme Ct. 1984. Assoc. Foonberg & Frandzel, Beverly Hills, Calif., 1974-77; ptnr. Nelsen & Smith, Los Angeles, 1977-80; ptnr. Morganstern, Mann & Smith, Beverly Hills, 1980-83; sr. ptnr. Smith & Smith, Los Angeles, Calif., 1983—; lectr. Rutter Group, Calif., 1982—, Continuing Edn. of Bar, Calif., 1983—. Mem. ABA, Calif. State Bar, Los Angeles County Bar (treas. prejudgement remedies sect. 1984-85), Fin. Lawyers Conf. (bd. govs. 1982-86), Bankruptcy Study Group, Phi Alpha Delta, Beta Gamma Sigma. Republican. Presbyterian. Consumer commercial, Bankruptcy, Banking. Office: Smith & Smith 888 S Figueroa St 9th Floor Los Angeles CA 90017

SMITH, SEYMOUR ALAN, lawyer; b. N.Y.C., Nov. 15, 1913; s. Sol and Esther (Och) S.; m. Marjorie H. Heft, June 1, 1939; children—Lawrence D., Robert T., Peter J. LL.B. cum laude, John Marshall Coll., 1935. Bar: N.J. 1936, N.J. 1940, U.S. Supreme Ct. 1956, U.S. Dist. Ct. (so. dist.) N.Y. 1957. Assoc., Abram A. Lebson, Englewood, N.J., 1935-44; ptnr. Hein, Smith & Berezin and predecessor, Hackensack, N.J., 1944—; mem. adv. com. profl. ethics N.J. Supreme Ct., 1973—. Mem. ABA, N.J. State Bar Assn., Bergen County Bar Assn. Club: Preakness Hills Country (pres. 1975-77). Probate, Family and matrimonial, Real property. Home: 50 Walnut Ct Englewood NJ 07631 Office: 2 University Plaza Hackensack NJ 07601

SMITH, SHARON LOUISE, lawyer, consultant; b. Williamsport, Pa., Apr. 21, 1949; d. Stuart Mallory and Phyllis Virginia (Hartzell) S. Student, Schiller Coll., Heidelberg, Fed. Republic Germany, 1969-70; AB, Grove City Coll., 1971; MA, Kent State U., 1973; JD, Temple U., 1978. Bar: Pa. 1978, U.S. Dist. Ct. (we. dist.) Pa. 1980. Assoc. Laurel Legal Services, Brookville, Pa., 1980-82; sole practice Brookville, 1982—; cons. Prothonotary, Brookville, 1984—. Mem. multidisciplinary team for child abuse Jefferson County Child Welfare Dept., Brookville, 1985; bd. dirs. Clarion-Jefferson Community Action, Brookville, 1982, Clearfield-Jefferson Drug and Alcohol Commn., DuBois, Pa., 1983-84. Mem. ABA, Pa. Bar Assn., Jefferson County Bar Assn. Presbyterian. Avocations: swimming, reading. Family and matrimonial, Juvenile, General practice. Home: 124 Franklin Ave Brookville PA 15825 Office: 173 Main St Brookville PA 15825

SMITH, SHELDON HAROLD, lawyer, law educator; b. Denver, Apr. 27, 1948; s. Marvin and Goldie Ruth (Cohen) S.; m. Lucy Bea Silverberg, July 16, 1970; children: Adam Paul, Amanda Jill. BA, Washington U., St. Louis, 1970; JD, U. Denver, 1973, LLM in Taxation, 1980. Bar: Colo. 1974, U.S. Dist. Ct. Colo. 1974, U.S. Tax Ct. 1974, U.S. Ct. Appeals (10th cir.) 1975. Assoc. Deisch & Marion P.C., Denver, 1974-79; tax ptnr. Pryor, Carney & Johnson P.C., Denver, 1979—; adj. prof. U. Denver, 1980—. Author: Methods of Compensating Employees, 1984. Bd. dirs. Univ. Ctr. at Greenwood Plaza, Englewood, Colo., 1985-86. Named One of Fifty to Watch Denver Mag., 1986. Mem. ABA, Colo. Bar Assn., Denver Bar Assn., Denver Tax Group (pres. 1982-83), Southeast Denver Law Assn., Colo. Soc. CPAs (lectr. 1982—, teaching award 1985). Republican. Corporate taxation, Pension, profit-sharing, and employee benefits, Estate planning. Home: 6785 E Orchard Rd Englewood CO 80111 Office: Pryor Carney & Johnson PC 6200 S Syracuse Way #400 Englewood CO 80111

SMITH, SHERMAN N., III, lawyer; b. Vero Beach, Fla., Feb. 22, 1946; s. Sherman N. Jr. and Olive S. (Heath) S.; m. Melodee Ann Moore, Dec. 30, 1978. BA, Fla. Presbyn. Coll., 1968; JD, U. Fla., 1970. Ptnr. Smith, Heath, Smith, & O'Haire, Vero Beach, Fla., 1971-79; sole practice Vero Beach, 1980-82; ptnr. Reed Smith Shaw & McClay, Vero Beach, 1982-85; sole practice Sherman N. Smith III, Vero Beach, 1985—. Mem. ABA, Acad. Fla. Trial Lawyers Assn., Fla. Bar Assn. (chmn. 19th jud. cir. grievance com. 1982-83), Indian River County Bar Assn. (pres. 1983). Democrat. Clubs: Vero Beach Country, John's Island Club (Vero Beach). State civil litigation, General practice, Probate. Office: Mus-Archives of the Sumter County Historical Society Inc PO Box 1456 Sumter SC 29150

SMITH, SPENCER THOMAS, lawyer; b. N.Y.C., May 3, 1943; s. Spencer H. and Marie K. (Walter) S.; m. Jenny Matilda Anderson, Aug. 15, 1965; children—S. Anders, J. Kirsten. B.M.E., Cooper Union Sch. Engring., 1965; J.D., American U., 1968. Bar: N.Y. 1969, U.S. Dist. Ct. (ea. and so. dists.) N.Y. 1971, U.S. Ct. Appeals (fed. cir.) 1983. Assoc. atty. Nolte & Nolte, N.Y.C., 1968-70, Nims, Halliday, Whitman, Howes, Collison & Isner, 1970-72; group patent and licensing counsel Litton Industries, Inc., Hartford, Conn., 1972-84; sole practice, Hartford, 1984-85; sr. group patent atty. Emhart Corp., Farmington, Conn., 1985—. Author: Primarily Merely, 1973. Coach Farmington Valley YMCA basketball program, Simsbury, Conn., 1976-80, Simsbury Youth Soccer Assn., 1976—. Mem. Licensing Execs. Soc., Greater Hartford C. of C. (mem. high tech. continuing edn. task force 1981—). Republican. Methodist. Patent, Federal civil litigation, Trademark and copyright. Home: 22 Wheeler Rd Simsbury CT 06070 Office: 426 Colt Hwy Farmington CT 06032

SMITH, STANLEY DAVID, lawyer; b. Los Angeles, Apr. 12, 1935; s. Samuel Joseph and Edna (Bridge) S.; m. Natalie Cailin, July 11, 1964; children: Samantha Dionn, Joshua David. Student, UCLA, 1956; JD, Southwestern U., 1964. Bar: Calif. 1965, U.S. Dist. Ct. (so. dist.) Calif. 1965. Claims mgr. Safeco Ins. Co., Los Angeles, 1960-65; assoc. Kinkle, Rodiger & Spriggs, Santa Ana, Calif., 1965-80; sr. mng. ptnr. Kinkle, Rodiger & Spriggs, San Diego, 1980—; prof. law Southwestern U., Los Angeles, 1965-70, 73. Recipient of Commendation Orange County Bd. of Suprs., 1977, Pub. Service award Orange County Bar Assn., 1980. Mem. ABA, Def. Research Inst., Assn. So. Calif. Def. Counsel. Democrat. Avocations: tennis, surfing. State civil litigation, Insurance, Personal injury. Home: 512 Santa Carina Solana Beach CA 92075 Office: Kinkle Rodiger & Spriggs 1620 5th Ave Suite 900 San Diego CA 92101

SMITH, STANLEY QUINTEN, lawyer; b. Lake Village, Ark., July 27, 1954; s. Jake Quinten and Carolyn (Hicks) S.; m. Angelia Gay Mullins, June 23, 1984. BBA in Acctg., U. Miss., 1976, JD, 1979. Bar: Miss. 1980, U.S. Dist. Ct. (no. and so. dists.) Miss. 1980, U.S. Ct. Appeals (5th cir.) 1981. Assoc. Stennett, Wilkinson & Ward, Jackson, Miss., 1980-85; ptnr. Stennett, Wilkinson & Ward, Jackson, 1985—. Fund raiser Boy Scouts Am., Jackson, 1984. Named one of Outstanding Young Men Am., 1982, 85, 86; Clifford H. Williams scholar, 1975-76. Mem. ABA (vice chmn. pub. utility law com. 1983-84), Miss. Bar Assn. (chmn. elections for young lawyers 1983-84), Hinds County Bar Assn., Jackson Young Lawyers Assn., Fed. Bar Assn., Miss. Bankruptcy Conf., Alpha Gamma of Chi Psi Assn. (bd. dirs. 1977-85), Alph Gamma of Chi Psi Found. Baptist. Lodge: Kiwanis (edn. chmn. Jackson 1982-84, bd. dirs. Jackson 1983-84). Avocations: jogging, tennis, water skiing, music, reading. Public utilities, Bankruptcy, Administrative and regulatory. Home: 124 Bent Creek Dr Brandon MS 39042 Office: Stennett Wilkinson & Ward 100 Congress St S Jackson MS 39201

SMITH, STANTON KINNIE, JR., utility executive; b. 1931; m. B.A., Yale U., 1953; J.D., U. Wis., 1956. Ptnr. firm Sidley & Austin, 1956-84; with Am. Natural Resources Co., Detroit, 1973-83; corp. gen. counsel Am. Natural Gas Service Co., 1975-83, vice chmn., gen. counsel, 1984—, also dir.; also dir. J.L. Clark Mfg. Co., Mich. Nat. Corp., Mich. Nat. Bank, Gt. Lakes Gas Transmission Co., Coastal Corp. General corporate. Office: Am Natural Resources Co 1 Woodward Ave Detroit MI 48226

SMITH, STEPHANIE MARIE, lawyer; b. Manhattan, Kans., May 15, 1955; d. William C. and Joyce A. (Davis) S. BS in Fgn. Studies, Georgetown U., 1977; JD, U. Mich., 1980. Bar: Colo. 1980, U.S. Dist. Ct. Colo. 1980, U.S. Ct. Appeals (10th cir.) 1980, Ariz. 1985, Nev. 1985, U.S. Dist. Ct. Nev. 1985. Assoc. Fishman & Geman, Denver, 1980-81, Hart & Trinen, Denver, 1982-85, Jolley, Urga, Wirth & Woodbury, Las Vegas, Nev., 1985—. Mem. ABA, Nev. Bar Assn., Colo. Bar Assn., Assn. Trial Lawyers Am., Cath. Lawyers Guild (treas. Denver 1984-85). Federal civil litigation, Bankruptcy, State civil litigation. Office: Jolley Urga Wirth & Woodbury 300 S 4th #800 Las Vegas NV 89101

SMITH, STEPHEN JEROME, lawyer; b. Princeton, W.Va., Mar. 7, 1956; s. Glen C. and Gladys (White) S. AB magna cum laude, Davidson Coll., 1978; JD, Harvard U., 1981. Bar: W.Va. 1981, N.C. 1982. Assoc. Bell, Davis & Pitt, Winston-Salem, N.C., 1981-83; trust officer United Carolina Bank, Monroe, N.C., 1983-84, Charlotte, 1984-85; asst. v.p., trust officer United Carolina Bank, Raleigh, 1985-87; asst. v.p., Moore County trust exec. United Carolina Bank, Souther Pines, N.C., 1987—. Bd. dirs. N.C. Human Rights Fund, Raleigh, 1983-86. Nat. Merit scholar, 1974-78. Mem. ABA,

N.C. Bar Assn., Pi Kappa Alpha, Phi Beta Kappa, Omicron Delta Epsilon. Republican. Episcopalian. Club: Hasty Pudding (Cambridge, Mass.); Harvard (N.Y.C.); Capitol City (Raleigh); Pinehurst (N.C.) Country. Avocations: tennis, genealogy, racquetball. Probate, Estate taxation, General corporate. Home: PO Box 30213 Raleigh NC 27622 Office: PO Box 17389 Raleigh NC 27619

SMITH, STEVEN IRA, lawyer; b. Los Angeles, May 27, 1954; s. Byron Arnold and Bernice Lillian (Glickman) S. BA, UCLA, 1976; JD, Southwestern U. Sch. Law, 1979. Bar: Calif. 1980, U.S. Dist. Ct. (cen. dist.) Calif. 1980, U.S. Ct. Appeals (9th cir.) 1980. Assoc. Smaltz & Neelley, Los Angeles, 1980-81, Law Offices Schell & Delamer, Los Angeles, 1982-86, Law Offices of Frydrych & Webster Inc., Beverly Hills, Calif., 1986—; vol. judge pro tem Los Angeles Mcpl. Ct., 1985—. Assoc. editor Computer Law Jour., 1978-79. Assoc. mem., bd. dirs. Beckman Research Inst. City of Hope, 1985—, Com. to Recruit Young Adults of City of Hope, Los Angeles and Duarte, Calif., 1985—. Mem. ABA, Calif. Bar Assn. (vol. atty. trial counsel office 1986—), Los Angeles County Bar Assn., Assn. Southern Calif. Def. Counsel. Democrat. Jewish. State civil litigation, Contracts commercial, Federal civil litigation. Office: Law Offices Frydrych & Webster Inc 9777 Wilshire Blvd Suite 1018 Beverly Hills CA 90212

SMITH, STEVEN LEE, lawyer; b. San Antonio, Apr. 19, 1952; s. Bill Lee and Maxine Rose (Williams) S.; m. Rebecca Ann Brimmer, Aug. 5, 1978; 1 child, William Christopher. B in Music Edn. magna cum laude, Abilene Christian U., 1974; JD, U. Tex., 1977. Bar: Tex. 1977. U.S. Dist. Ct. (so. dist.) Tex. 1979, U.S. Dist. Ct. (we. dist.) Tex. 1980. Assoc. Dillon & Giesenschlag, Bryan, Tex., 1977-80, ptnr., 1980-84; ptnr. Dillon, Lewis, Elmore & Smith, Bryan, 1985—. Mem. devel. bd. Abilene Christian U., 1982—, vis. com. Dept. Music, 1983-86; chmn. March of Dimes Brazos Valley Chpt., 1983-84; Leadership Brazos Valley Devel. Program, Bryan/Coll. Sta. C. of C., 1984-85; pres. Meml. Student Ctr. Opera and Performing Arts Soc., Coll. Sta., 1985—. Recipient Charles Plum Distinguished Service award Tex. A&M U., 1986. Mem. ABA, Assn. Trial Lawyers Am., Tex. Trial Lawyers Assn., Abilene Christian U. Alumni Bd. Mem. Ch. of Christ. Lodge: Optimists (pres. 1982-83). Avocations: golf, flying. Banking, State civil litigation, General practice. Home: 19 Cedar Ridge Dr College Station TX 77840 Office: Dillon Lewis Elmore & Smith PO Box 4067 Bryan TX 77805

SMITH, S(YDNEY) STROTHER, III, lawyer, priest; b. Ft. Knox, Ky., Aug. 1, 1941; s. Sydney Strother and Elizabeth (Oglesby) S.; m. Barbara Beville, July 9, 1966; children—Jacqulyn Ambler, Sydney Ann, Nancy Elizabeth. Student Va. Mil. Inst., 1959-60; A.B., U. Richmond, 1963; B.C.L., Coll. William and Mary, 1966, J.D., 1968; postgrad. U. Va., 1966-67. Bar: Va. 1967, U.S. Supreme Ct. 1973, U.S. Dist. Ct. (ea. and we. dists.) Va., U.S. Ct. Appeals (4th cir.) 1967. Ptnr. Moore and Smith, Abingdon, Va., 1967-69; dir., gen. counselor dept. compensation Dist. 28 of United Mine Workers Am., Norton, Va., 1970-74; sr. mem. Smith, Robinson & Vinyard, Abingdon, 1975-80; sole practice, Abingdon, 1980—; ordained to deacon Anglican Catholic Ch., 1981, priesthood, 1986; chancellor Diocese of Mid-Atlantic State, 1978-80, pres. standing com., 1983-85; dir. Anglican Hour Radio Series, 1978-80; rector Anglican Ch. of the Good Shepherd, Abingdon, 1981—, St. Columba Anglican Ch., Lebanon, Va., 1984—; mem. bus. law faculty Va. Highlands Community Coll.; officer, dir. various corps.; trustee in bankruptcy U.S. Dist. Ct. (we. dist.) Va., 1969-71; v.p. Bicentennial Investment Corp., 1975-80; pres. L.S. Richards Co., Inc., 1980—; atty. Russell County, 1977, Washington County, 1979-80. Chmn. Washington County (Va.) Republican Party, 1976-80; mem. Va. Rep. Central Com., 1980—; mem. exec. council Sequoia council Boy Scouts Am., 1982—. Named Outstanding Grad., Coll. William and Mary Law Sch., 1966. Mem. Va. Trial Lawyers Assn. (life), Assn. Trial Lawyers Am., ABA, Dist. 28 United Mine Workers Am., (hon. life), Omicron Delta Kappa, Phi Delta Phi, Tau Kappa Alpha, Pi Sigma Alpha. Author Va. Black Lung Act, 1972, 73; contbr. poems, sketches and articles to mags., articles to legal revs.; author radio broadcast sermons Anglican Hour, 1980-82, The Via Media: Devotions for Anglicans, 1983. Criminal, Personal injury, Labor. Home: Winter Spring Farm Abingdon VA 24210 Office: I 81 at Exit 9 Abingdon VA 24210

SMITH, TAD RANDOLPH, lawyer; b. El Paso, July 20, 1928; s. Eugene Rufus and Dorothy (Derrick) S.; B.B.A., U. Tex., 1952, LL.B., 1951; m. JoAnn Wilson, Aug. 24, 1949; children—Laura, Derrick, Cameron Ann. Admitted to Tex. bar, 1951; assoc. firm Kemp, Smith, Duncan & Hammond, El Paso, 1951, partner, 1952—, mng. ptnr., 1971—; dir. El Paso Electric Co., M-Bank El Paso N.A., Property Trust Am.. Greater El Paso Devel. Corp., El Paso Indsl. Devel. Corp. Active United Way of El Paso; chmn. El Paso County Reps., 1958-61, Tex. Rep. State Exec. Com., 1961-62; alt. del. Rep. Nat. Conv., 1952, 62, del., 1964; trustee Robert E. and Evelyn McKee Found. 1970—; mem. devel. bd. U. Tex. El Paso, 1973-81, v.p., 1975, chmn. 1976; dinner treas. Nat. Jewish Hosp. and Research Ctr., 1977, chmn. 1978, presenter of honoree, 1985; bd. dirs. Southwestern Children's Home, El Paso, 1959-78, Nat. Conf. Christians and Jews, 1965-76, chmn. 1968-69, adv. dir. 1976—, Renaissance 400, El Paso, 1982—. Named Outstanding Young Man El Paso, El Paso Jaycees, 1961; recipient Humanitarian award El Paso chpt. NCCJ, 1983. Fellow Tex. Bar Found.; mem. ABA, Tex. Bar Assn., El Paso Bar Assn. (pres. 1971-72), El Paso C. of C. (dir. 1979-82), Sigma Chi. Republican. Methodist. General corporate, Securities. Home: 1202 Thunderbird El Paso TX 79912 Office: Kemp Smith Duncan & Hammond 221 N Kansas 2000 MBank Plaza El Paso TX 79901

SMITH, TEMPLETON, JR., lawyer; b. Pitts., May 20, 1952; s. Templeton Sr. and Nellie Margaret (Fergus) S.; m. Lea Elizabeth Anderson, Aug. 2, 1980; 1 child, Templeton III. BA, Washington & Lee U., 1974; JD, U. Pitts., 1977. Bar: Pa. 1977, U.S. Dist. Ct. (we. dist.) Pa. 1977, U.S. Tax Ct. 1982, U.S. Supreme Ct. 1982, U.S. Ct. Appeals (3d cir.) 1983. Assoc. Rose, Schmidt & Dixon, Pitts., 1977-83; ptnr. Rose, Schmidt, Chapman, Duff & Hasley, Pitts., 1983—. Mem. com. Mt. Lebanon (Pa.) Reps., 1984—; elder, trustee Southminster Presbyn. Ch., Mt. Lebanon, Pa., 1984—. Mem. ABA (litigation sect., natural resource law sect.), Pa. Bar Assn. (profl. responsibility sect.). Republican. Clubs: Duquesne, Univ. (Pitts.). Federal civil litigation, State civil litigation, Local government. Office: rose Schmidt Chapman Duff & Hasley 900 Oliver Bldg Pittsburgh PA 15222

SMITH, TERRY J., lawyer; b. Detroit, Mar. 7, 1938; s. Russell A. and Anna M. (Chape) S.; m. Lorene M. Yocum, May 17, 1980. B.A. with high honors, Mich. State U., 1960; J.D., U. Chgo., 1965. Bar: 1965, U.S. Supreme Ct. 1972. Mem. Deming & Smith, Grand Ledge, Mich., 1965-72; research assoc. to Chief Judge Protem, Mich. Ct. Appeals, 1965-67; mem. Smith & Smith, Grand Ledge, 1973-76; pres. Smith Bros. Law Office, P.C., Grand Ledge, 1976—; dir. Debt Relief Legal Clinic of Mich., P.C., 1981—; mem. Mich. State Boundries Commn., 1970—; dir. First of Am. Bank of Grand Ledge, 1975—, Pro-Bono Legal Services; city atty., Grand Ledge, 1977—. Mem. Eaton County Social Services Bd., 1970-77; bd. dirs. Grand Ledge Area Community Chest, 1964-73, v.p., 1970-73. Recipient Book award W. Pub. Co., 1964. Mem. ABA, Eaton County Bar Assn. (pres. 1968-69), Grand Ledge Area C. of C. (dir. 1968-73, 80—). Club: Rotary. Family and matrimonial, Real property, Local government. Home: 221 E Scott St Grand Ledge MI 48837 Office: 207 E Jefferson St PO Box 56 Grand Ledge MI 48837

SMITH, THEODORE FREDERICK, JR., lawyer; b. Anderson, Ind., Oct. 19, 1951; s. Theodore Frederick Sr. and Nancy Ann (Morrison) S.; m. Jill Camille Denny, Nov. 9, 1979; children: Jessica Louise, Theodore Frederick III. BA, Notre Dame U., 1973, JD, 1976. Bar: Ind. 1976, U.S. Dist. Ct. (so. dist.) Inc. 1976, D.C. 1978, U.S. Ct. Appeals (7th cir.) 1983. Assoc. Campbell & Campbell, Anderson, 1976-78; sole practice Anderson, 1979-85; ptnr. Smith & Farrell P.C., Anderson, 1985—; dep. prosecutor Madison County, Anderson, 1977; master commr. Madison County Superior Ct., Anderson, 1979-83; panel chmn. social security disability seminar, 1987. Mem. ABA, D.C. Bar Assn., Ind. Bar Assn. (spl. com. to form gen. practice, panelist merger and acquisitions seminar 1986). Democrat. Roman Catholic. Lodge: Rotary (pres. 1983). State civil litigation, Personal injury, Administrative and regulatory. Home: 340 Winding Way Anderson IN 46011 Office: Smith & Farrell PC 215 W 8th St Anderson IN 46016

SMITH, THOMAS FENTON, lawyer; b. New Rochelle, N.Y., Sept. 27, 1948; s. Robert L. and Ruth (Hawkins) S.; m. Laura Carmichael, May 1, 1982; children: Lilia Marie, Nathaniel Jacob. BA in English, U. Notre Dame, 1970; JD, U. Colo., 1974. Bar: Colo. 1975, U.S. Dist. Ct. Colo. 1975, Del. 1976, U.S. Dist. Ct. Del. 1976. Asst. atty. gen. State of Del., Dover, 1975-79, State of Colo., Denver, 1979-83; county atty. Pitkin County, Aspen, Colo., 1983—; commr. Colo. Water Quality Control Commn., Denver, 1984—; cons. law and stress project, Jackson Place Counseling & Research Ctr., Denver, 1986—. Fellow Gates Found., 1986. Mem. ABA, Colo. Bar Assn., Pitkin County Bar Assn., Colo. County Attys. Assn. Democrat. Roman Catholic. Avocations: literature, music, skiing, fishing, golf. Administrative and regulatory, Environment, Local government. Office: Pitkin County Atty 530 E Main St Suite I Aspen CO 81611

SMITH, THOMAS SHORE, lawyer; b. Rock Springs, Wyo., Dec. 7, 1924; s. Thomas and Anne E. (McTee) S.; m. Jacqueline Emily Krueger, May 25, 1952; children: Carolyn Jane, Karl Thomas, David Shore. BS in Bus. Adminstrn., U. Wyo., 1950, JD, 1959. Bar: U.S. Dist. Ct. Wyo. 1960, U.S. Ct. Appeals (10th cir.) 1960, U.S. Tax Ct. 1969, U.S. Supreme Ct. 1971. Ptnr. Smith, Stanfield & Scott, Laramie; city atty. City of Laramie, Wyo., 1963-86; instr. mcpl. law U. Wyo., 1987. Dir. budget and fin. Govt. Am. Samoa, 1952-56; bd. dirs. Bur. Land Mgmt., Rawlins, Wyo., 1984—, Ivinson Hosp. Found., 1986—. Served 2d lt. USAF, 1944-46, ETO. Francis Warren scholar, 1958. Mem ABA, Wyo. Bar Assn. (pres. 1984-85), Albany County Bar Assn., Western States Bar Conf. (pres. 1985-86). Republican. Episcopalian. Lodges: Elks, Rotary. Avocations: golf, tennis. Local government, Probate, Real property. Office: Smith Stanfield & Scott 515 Ivinson PO Box 971 Laramie WY 82070

SMITH, THORN MCCLELLAN, lawyer; b. Peoria, Ill., Feb. 19, 1958; s. Lester Berry and June Edda (Kopal) S. BS in Fgn. Service, Georgetown U., 1979; JD, Northwestern U., 1982. Bar: Ill. 1982, U.S. Dist. Ct. (so. dist.) Ill. 1983, S.C. 1984, U.S. Dist. Ct. S.C. 1985. Assoc. Law Offices of Lester Berry Smith, Peoria, 1982-83, Law Offices of C.R. Dunbar, Spartanburg, S.C., 1983-85; sole practice Spartanburg, 1985—. Mem. ABA, Comm. Law League Am., Spartanburg C. of C. Lodge: Lions. Bankruptcy, Consumer commercial, Contracts commercial. Office: Suite 545 Montgomery Bldg Spartanburg SC 29301

SMITH, TIMOTHY DALY, legal educator, lawyer; b. Cleve., Nov. 9, 1943; s. Ralph W. and Bettie (Daly) S.; m. Jane Louise Andrews, June 18, 1966; children: Randall Knowles, Rachel West, Bryan Daly. BA, Ohio State U., 1965, MA, 1971; JD, U. Akron, 1977. Bar: Ohio 1977. Reporter UPI, Columbus, Ohio, 1966-67; reporter, asst. editor Akron (Ohio) Beacon Jour., 1976-80, asst. mng. editor, 1980-84, mng. editor, 1984-86; prof. Kent (Ohio) State U., 1986—; chmn. FOI com. AP, Ohio, 1985-86. Mem. ABA, Am. Press Inst. (lectr. 1972—). Democrat. Methodist. Legal education, Libel, Probate. Home: 3901 Silverwood Dr Stow OH 44224

SMITH, VINCENT MILTON, lawyer; b. Barbourville, Ky., Nov. 21, 1940; s. Virgil Milton and Louis (McGalliard) S.; m. Mary Eleanor Lindgren, Aug. 21, 1965; 1 child, Jessica Todd. BA, Harvard U., 1962; LLB, Yale U., 1965. Bar: N.Y. 1966. Assoc. Breed, Abbott & Morgan, N.Y.C., 1965-70; assoc. Debevoise & Plimpton, N.Y.C., 1970-75, ptnr., 1975—; mem. adv. bd. Chgo. Title Ins. Co., N.Y.C., 1979—. Trustee Chatham Players, N.J., 1967-77, 87—, Summit Friends Meeting, Chatham, 1973—, N.J. Shakespeare Festival, Madison, 1975-80. Mem. ABA, N.Y. State Bar Assn., Assn. of Bar of City of N.Y., Am. Land Title Assn., Urban Land Inst. Mem. Soc. of Friends. Clubs: Harvard, N.Y. Athletic. Real property, Landlord-tenant. Office: Debevoise & Plimpton 875 3d Ave New York NY 10022

SMITH, WALTER HENRY, lawyer; b. Tallahassee, Fla., Dec. 13, 1955; s. Walter Douglas and Rhondda (Miller) S.; m. Mary Ann Edwards. BA, U. Ala., 1978; JD, U. S.C., 1981. Bar: S.C. 1981, U.S. Dist. Ct. S.C. 1981, U.S. Ct. Appeals (4th cir.) 1981, U.S. Supreme Ct. 1986. Ptnr. Bolt & Smith, Columbia, S.C., 1981—. Mem. S.C. Bar Assn., Richland County Bar Assn., S.C. Trial Lawyers Assn. (legis. coordinator). Avocations: sailing competitively. State civil litigation, Personal injury, Criminal. Office: Bolt & Smith 1720 Main St Suite 105 Columbia SC 29201

SMITH, WALTER JOSEPH, JR., lawyer, educator; b. N.Y.C., Feb. 23, 1936; s. Walter J. and Florence W. (Watson) S.; m. Felicitas U. Von Zeschau, Oct. 5, 1968; children—Caroline, Alexandria, Christopher. A.B., Hamilton Coll., 1958; LL.B., Columbia U., 1961. Bar: U.S. Ct. Mil. Appeals 1967, U.S. Dist. Ct. (D.C. dist.) 1967, U.S. Ct. Appeals (D.C. cir.) 1967, U.S. Supreme Ct. 1974, U.S. Ct. Claims 1975. Mem. Judge Advocate Gen.'s Office, U.S. Navy, Washington, 1966-68; trial atty., Washington, 1968-75; ptnr. Wilson, Elser, Moskowitz, Edelman & Dicker, Washington, 1975—; mng. ptnr., 1979—; adj. prof. law Antioch Sch. Law, 1981—. Pres. Dogwood Assn., 1982-83. Served to lt. USN, 1962-67. Recipient Pres.'s award Am. Soc. Pharmacy Law, 1984. Mem. ABA, Def. Research Inst., Counsellors, D.C. Bar Assn. Democrat. Roman Catholic. Clubs: Tuckahoe. Author: Insurance Protection in Product Liability. Federal civil litigation, Insurance, Private international. Office: Suite 880 600 Maryland Ave SW Washington DC 20024

SMITH, WALTER S., federal judge; b. Marlin, Tex., Oct. 26, 1940; s. Walter S. and Mary Elizabeth Smith; children—Debra Elizabeth, Susan Kay. B.A., Baylor U., 1964, J.D., 1966. Bar: Tex. Assoc. Dunnam & Dunnam, Waco, Tex., 1966-69; ptnr. Wallace & Smith, Waco, 1969-78, Haley & Fulbright, Waco, 1978-80; judge Tex. Dist. Ct., 1980-83; U.S. magistrate Western Dist. Tex., 1983-84; judge U.S. Dist. Ct. for Western Dist. Tex., Waco, 1984—. Office: PO Box 1906 Waco TX 76703

SMITH, WAYNE RICHARD, lawyer; b. Petoskey, Mich., Apr. 30, 1934; s. Wayne Anson and Frances Lynetta (Cooper) S.; m. Carrie J. Swanson, June 18, 1959; children: Stephen, Douglas, Rebecca. AB, U. Mich., 1956, JD, 1959. Bar: Mich. 1959. Asst. atty. gen. State of Mich., 1960-62; pros. atty. Emmet County (Mich.), 1963-68; dist. judge 90th Jud. Dist. Mich., 1969-72; sr. ptnr. Marco, Litzenburger, Smith, Brown & Wynn, P.C., Petoskey; city atty. City of Petoskey, 1976—; lectr. real estate law U. Mich. Trustee North Central Mich. Coll., 1981—; mem. No. Mich. Community Mental Health Bd., 1972—, chmn. 1979-81. Mem. ABA, Am. Judicature Soc., Emmet-Charlevoix Bar Assn. (pres. 1967). Presbyterian. Lodges: Kiwanis (pres. 1967), Elks. Real property, Probate, Local government. Address: 201 Sunset Ave Petoskey MI 49770

SMITH, WILBUR COWAN, lawyer; b. Aledo, Ill., July 16, 1914; s. Fred Harold and Anna Elizabeth (Cowan) S.; m. Teressa Phyllis Stout, Sept. 10, 1938; children—Roger Allen, Judith Ellen Smith Adams; m. Florence Ann Mackie, June 21, 1964; 1 dau., Donna Lee Pinkes; step-children—Diane Marie Linhart, Wayne Douglas Griffith, Nancy Ann LaFraugh. Student Colo. U., 1932-33, N.Mex. U., 1933; B.A., U. Iowa, 1937; J.D., Creighton U., 1954. Bar: Nebr. 1954, U.S. Dist. Ct. Nebr. 1954, U.S. Ct. Appeals (8th cir.) 1974. Salesman Gen. Foods Corp., 1939; civilian chemist U.S. Naval Ordnance, 1942-45; mgr. Omar Flour Mills, 1945-47; account exec. C.A. Swanson & Sons, 1948-49; dist. mgr. Brown-Forman Distillery, 1950-51; adminstrv. asst. to judge Douglas County, 1954-55; asst. city prosecutor Omaha, 1956; sole practice, Omaha, 1956-73; ptnr. Smith & Hansen, Omaha, 1973—. Pres., North High Sch. PTA, 1959-61, Belvedere Sch., 1954-56, Oak Valley, 1965-67; mem. bldg. com. YMCA, 1954-56; membership com. Boy Scouts Am., 1956-61; county del. Republican Party, 1962-82. Mem. ABA, Nebr. Bar Assn., Omaha Bar Assn., Am. Judicature Soc., Phi Alpha Delta. Methodist. Clubs: Odd Fellows, Masons, Shriners, United Comml. Travelers Protective Assn., Order Eastern Star. General practice, Family and matrimonial, Criminal. Office: Smith & Hansen 1st Nat Bank Bldg Suite 1022 Omaha NE 68102

SMITH, WILLARD MARK, lawyer; b. Kansas City, Mo., May 7, 1955; s. Willard G. and Phyllis E. (Potter) S.; m. Joan E. Spaith, May 29, 1976; children: W. Ryan, Brent E., Erin E. BA, Kans. U., 1977; JD, Cornell U., 1980. Bar: D.C. 1981. Law clk. to presiding judge U.S. Ct. Appeals (4th cir.), Greenville, S.C., 1980-81; assoc. Sutherland, Asbill & Brennan, Washington, 1981—. Editor-in-chief Cornell U. Law Rev., Ithaca, N.Y., 1979-80. Mem. ABA. Methodist. Pension, profit-sharing, and employee benefits, Securities. Office: Sutherland Asbill & Brennan 1666 K St NW Washington DC 20006

SMITH, WILLIAM FRENCH, lawyer, former U.S. attorney general; b. Wilton, N.H., Aug. 26, 1917; s. William French and Margaret (Dawson) S.; m. Jean Webb, Nov. 6, 1964. A.B. summa cum laude, U. Calif., 1939; LL.B., Harvard U., 1942; hon. degrees, Pepperdine U., DePaul U., U. San Diego. Bar: Calif. 1942. Atty., sr. ptnr. Gibson, Dunn & Crutcher, Los Angeles, 1946-81, 85—; atty. gen. U.S., Washington, 1981-85; mem. Pres. Fgn. Intelligence Adv. Bd., Washington, 1985—; bd. dirs. Pacific Lighting Corp., Los Angeles, NBC Corp., N.Y.C., Am. Internat Group, N.Y.C., Pacific Telesis Group, Pacific Bell, San Francisco, Gen. Electric Co., N.Y.C., H.F. Ahmanson & Co., Los Angeles, Earle M. Jorgensen Co., Los Angeles, Fisher Sci. Group Inc., Weintraub Entertainment Croup Inc. Mem. U.S. Adv. Commn. on Internat. Ednl. and Cultural Affairs, 1971-78, Stanton Panel on Internat. Info., Edn. and Cultural Relations, 1974-75; U.S. del. The East-West Ctr. for Cultural and Tech. Interchange, Hawaii, 1975-77; mem. adv. council Sch. Govt., Harvard U., 1977—, mem. visiting com. Ctr. Internat. Affairs, 1986—; mem. adv. bd. Ctr. for Strategic and Internat. Studies, Georgetown U., Washington, 1978-82, 85—; mem. nat. bd. advisors Fedn. for Am. Immigration Reform (FAIR), 1985—; mem. nat. adv. com. Internat. Tennis Found. and Hall of Fame, Inc., 1985—, Nat. Legal Ctr. for the Pub. Interest, 1985—; mem. exec. com. The Calif. Roundtable, 1976-81, 85—, Calif. Community Found., 1980-81, 85—; bd. regents U. Calif., 1968—, chmn., 1970-72, 74-75, 76; bd. dirs. Legal Aid Found. Los Angeles, 1963-72; bd. dirs. Los Angeles World Affairs Council, 1970—, pres., 1975-78; bd. fellows Inst. Jud. Adminstn., Inc., 1981—; trustee Claremont McKenna Coll., 1967—, Ind. Colls. of So. Calif., 1969-74, Ctr. Theatre Group, Los Angeles Music Ctr., 1970-81, Henry E. Huntington Library and Art Gallery, 1971—, The Cate Sch., 1971-78, Northrop Inst. Tech., 1973-75, The Ronald Reagan Presdl. Library Found., 1985—; nat. trustee Nat. Symphony Orch., Washington, 1974—; mem. bd. fellows The Inst. Jud. Adminstrn., Inc., 1981—; chmn. Calif. Delegation to Rep. Nat. Conv., 1968, vice chmn., 1971, 76, 80. Served to lt. USNR, 1942-46. Fellow Am. Bar Found.; mem. ABA (fellow sect. of litigation 1985—, standing com. law and nat. security 1985—), Los Angeles County Bar Assn., Am. Judicature Soc., Am. Law Inst., Calif. C. of C. (bd. dirs. 1963-80, pres. 1974-75), Order of Coif, Phi Beta Kappa, Pi Gamma Mu, Pi Sigma Alpha, Phi Delta Phi. Club: Chancery. Office: Gibson Dunn & Crutcher 333 S Grand Ave Los Angeles CA 90071

SMITH, WILLIAM HERBERT, JR, lawyer; b. Boston, Apr. 29, 1944; s. William Herbert and Jean Cathryn (Hagen) S.; m. Jean Wilson Douglas, Sept. 13, 1969; children: Douglas Tyson, Elizabeth McBrien, Ellen Marcy, Timothy Charles Derrick. BA, Yale U., 1965; JD, Cornell U., 1968. Bar: D.C. 1972, N.Y. 1973. Atty. Fed. Maritime Commn., Washington, 1972-76, Gen. Services Adminstn., Washington, 1976-80; legal adv. to commr. Fed. Energy Regulatory Commn., Washington, 1980-84; atty. Broadhurst, Brook, Mangham & Hardy, Washington, 1985; chief bur. rate and safety Iowa State Utilities Bd., Des Moines, 1986—. Treasr. Adv. Neighborhood Commn., Washington, 1978-79. Served to 1st lt. USAR, 1968-72. Mem. ABA, Fed. Energy Bar Assn., Fed. Communications Bar Assn., Phi Gamma Delta, Phi Alpha Delta. Republican. Episcopalian. Club: Genesee Valley (Rochester, N.Y.). Avocation: hockey. Public utilities, FERC practice, Administrative and regulatory. Home: 4816 Pleasant St Des Moines IA 50312 Office: Iowa State Utilities Bd Lucas Bldg Des Moines IA 50319

SMITH, WILLIAM HOLT, lawyer; b. Auburn, Ala., Nov. 2, 1949; s. Clyde Earl and Helen Marie (Holt) S.; m. Deborah Morrison, June 2, 1971 (div. May 1980); children: William Holt Jr., Bryan Edward; m. Barbara Jo Cagle, June 26, 1980. BS, E. Tenn. State U., 1971; JD, U. Tenn., 1976. Bar: Tenn. 1976, U.S. Dist. Ct. (ea dist.) Tenn. 1976, U.S. Ct. Appeals (6th cir.) 1979. Assoc. Michael & Michael, Sweetwater, Tenn., 1976-78; ptnr. Lee & Smith, Sweetwater, 1978-80; sole practice Madisonville, Tenn., 1980—. Mem. ABA, Am. Trial Lawyers Assn., Tenn. Bar Assn. Democrat. Presbyterian. Lodges: Rotary, Kiwanis. Personal injury, Workers' compensation, Federal civil litigation. Home: Rt 5 Box 256 D Madisonville TN 37354 Office: 209 Tellico St Madisonville TN 37354

SMITH, WILLIAM RANDOLPH, lawyer; b. Houston, July 30, 1928; s. Angie Frank and Bess Patience (Crutchfield) S.; m. Margaret Ann Pickett, Nov. 25, 1950; children: Sherren Bess, William Randolph Jr., Margaret Moody, David Christian. B.A., So. Meth. U., 1948; LL.B., U. Tex., 1951. Assoc. Vinson & Elkins, Houston, 1951-64, ptnr., 1965—; dir. Weatherford Internat., Houston, 1979—, several pvt. corps. Dir. Methodist Hosp., Houston, 1968—; trustee M.D. Anderson Hosp., 1975—, So. Meth. U., Dallas, 1975—, Briarwood Sch., Houston, 1970—. Served to 1st lt. USAF, 1952-53. Clubs: Houston Country, Ramada (sec. 1978). Oil and gas leasing. Home: 58 E Broad Oaks Houston TX 77056 Office: Vinson & Elkins 3501 First City Tower 1001 Fannin St Houston TX 77002

SMITH, WILLIAM REECE, JR., lawyer; b. Athens, Tenn., Sept. 19, 1925; s. William Reece and Gladys (Moody) S.; m. Marlene Medina, Aug. 8, 1963; 1 son, William Reece III. B.S., U. S.C., 1946; J.D., U. Fla., 1949; Rhodes scholar, Oxford U., 1949-52; LL.D., U. So. Fla., 1973, Rollins Coll., 1980, U. Fla., 1980, U. S.C., 1981, Stetson U., 1985; D.C.L., Central Meth. Coll., 1980, New Eng. Coll., 1980; D.H.L., Calif. West Sch. Law, 1981. Bar: Fla. 1949. Mem. firm Carlton, Fields, Ward, Emmanuel, Smith & Cutler (and predecessor firm), Tampa, 1955—; now chmn.; interim pres. U. So. Fla., 1976-77; city atty. Tampa, 1963-72; asst. prof. law U. Fla., 1952-53; adj. prof. law Stetson U., 1954-59; past pres. Am. Bar Endowment, Fla. Legal Services, Inc. Past pres. Tampa Philharmonic Assn., Fla. Gulf Coast Symphony, Inc.; sec. Fla. Rhodes Scholar Selection Com., 1969—. Served to ensign USNR, 1943-46. Named Outstanding Young Man of Tampa, 1961; recipient Good Govt. award Fla. Jr. C. of C., 1965, Disting. Am. award Tampa Chpt. Nat. Football Found., 1977, Humanitarian award B'nai B'rith Found., 1977, Pres.'s award Fla. Assn. Retarded Citizens, 1978, Von Briesen award Nat. Legal Aid and Defender Assn., 198, Brotherhood award NCCJ, 1980, Herbert Harley award Am. Judicature Soc., 1983, Citizen of Yr. award Civitan Club, 1986, Algernon Sydney Sullivan award, U. S.C., 1987. Fellow Am. Coll. Trial Lawyers, Internat. Acad. Trial Lawyers, Am. Bar Found., Fla. Bar Found. (past pres.); mem. Internat. Soc. Barristers, Am. Law Inst. (mem. council), Internat. Bar Assn. (v.p.), ABA (chmn. jr. bar conf. 1960-61, life, ho. of dels., sec. 1967-71, pres. 1980-81), Inter-Am. Bar Assn. (mem. exec. council), Fla. Bar (pres. 1972-73), Hillsborough County Bar Assn. (pres. 1963), Nat. Conf. Bar Pres. (pres.), Greter Tampa C. of C. (pres. 1986-87). Methodist. Antitrust, Federal civil litigation, State civil litigation. Home: PO Box 3239 Tampa FL 33601 Office: Box 3239 Tampa FL 33601

SMITH, WILLIAM SIDNEY, lawyer; b. Clearwater, Fla., Feb. 25, 1944; s. Sidney Bankhead and Daphne (Guptile) S.; m. Caroline L. Holley, June 12, 1967 (div. Jan. 1982); children: Cynthia Ann, Charles W., Craig W.; m. Bobbi Ann Trachta, Sept. 18, 1983. BBA, U. Iowa, 1966, JD, 1968. Bar: Iowa 1968, U.S. Tax Ct. 1972, U.S. Dist. Ct. (so. dist.) Iowa 1976, U.S. Dist. Ct. (no. dist.) Iowa 1977, U.S. Ct. Claims 1978, U.S. Ct. Appeals (8th cir.) 1978, U.S. Supreme Ct. 1979, U.S. Ct. Appeals (fed. cir.) 1982; CPA, Ill., Iowa. Tax acct. Price Waterhouse & Co., Chgo., 1968-70; tax ptnr. Sidney B. Smith & Co., Des Moines, 1970-75; prin. Smith, Schneider & Stiles, P.C., Des Moines, 1975—. Mem. ABA (litigation sect.), Iowa State Bar Assn. (tax com.), Polk County Bar Assn., Am. Inst. CPA's (Elijah Watt Sell award 1969), Jaycees (pres. 1971-72), Order of Coif. Episcopalian. Federal civil litigation, Corporate taxation, Criminal. Home: 4301 Walnut West Des Moines IA 50265 Office: Smith Schneider & Stiles PC 4717 Grand Ave Des Moines IA 50312

SMITH, WILLIAM WAYNE, lawyer; b. Birmingham, Ala., Aug. 28, 1941; s. Wayne C. and Mary R. (Patton) S.; m. E. Jan Gray, Aug. 13, 1983; 1 child, William Wayne Jr. BBA, Auburn U., 1963; JD, Samford U., 1966. Bar: Ala. 1966, U.S. Dist. Ct. (no. dist.) Ala. 1966, U.S. Ct. Mil. Appeals 1968, U.S. Ct. Appeals (5th and 11th cirs.) 1971. Ptnr. Hogan, Smith, Alspaugh, Samples & Pratt, P.C., Birmingham, 1967—; lectr. various orgns. Served to capt. JAGC, USAR, 1966-73. Mem. ABA, Ala. Bar Assn., Birmingham Bar Assn. (past chmn. entertainment com., econs. of law practice com.), Am. Bd. Trial Advs., Am. Acad. Forensic Scis. Inc., Assn. Trial Lawyers Am. (bd. govs. 1979-80), Ala. Trial Lawyers Assn. (sec., treas., v.p. no. dist., pres. 1977-78, exec. com. 1973—), Omicron Delta Kappa, Phi

Alpha Delta, Pi Kappa Alpha. Personal injury, State civil litigation, Workers' compensation. Home: 4501 Old Brook Way Birmingham AL 35243 Office: Hogan Smith Alspaugh Samples & Pratt PC 1000 City Fed Bldg Birmingham AL 35203

SMITH, WREDE HOWARD, JR., lawyer; b. Sioux City, Iowa, May 11, 1949; s. Wrede Howard Sr. and Barbara (Katherman) S.; m. Melissa Uelk, Aug. 10, 1974; 1 child, Wrede Howard III. BA in Econs., DePauw U., 1971; JD, Northwestern U., 1974. Bar: Wis. 1974, U.S. Dist. Ct. (we. dist.) Wis. 1974. From assoc. to ptnr. Ross & Stevens S.C., Madison, Wis., 1974—; lectr. U. Wis. Law Sch. Bd. dirs. Community Support Services, Madison, 1979—, pres. 1983-86. Mem. ABA, Wis. Bar Assn., Dane County Bar Assn. (exec. com. 1981-84), Phi Beta Kappa. Republican. Presbyterian. Lodge: Kiwanis. Avocations: golf, softball, singing barbershop quartet. Consumer commercial, General corporate, Pension, profit-sharing, and employee benefits. Home: 4022 Mandan Crescent Madison WI 53711 Office: Ross & Stevens SC 402 Gammon Pl Madison WI 53719

SMITHER, J. MICHAEL, lawyer, educator; b. Rantoul, Ill., July 31, 1956; s. Robert L. and Betty W. (Allen) S.; m. Vicki Lynn Bechtel, Sept. 18, 1978; children: Justin Michael, Ryan Clark, Allison Attaway. BA, Western Ky. U., 1978; JD, U. Louisville, 1982. Instr. Jefferson Community Coll., Louisville, 1982—; assoc. Amshoff & Amshoff, Louisville, 1982-85; sole practice Louisville, 1985—. Assoc. editor Louisville Lawyer Mag., 1982-86. Mem. ABA, Louisville Bar Assn., Ky. Bar Assn. (Continuing Edn. award 1983), Assn. Trial Lawyers Am., Ky. Acad. Trial Atty.'s. Democrat. Episcopalian. Avocations: golf, boating. State civil litigation, Personal injury, Family and matrimonial. Home: 4031 St Ives Ct Louisville KY 40207 Office: 304 W Liberty St Suite 308 Louisville KY 40202

SMITHYMAN, LEE MILLER, lawyer; b. Pitts., Jan. 23, 1947; s. William Earl and Geraldine Fern (Miller) S.; m. Nancy Louise Blackburn, Mar. 24, 1973; children: William E., Michael L., Amy L. BS, Carnegie-Mellon U., 1969, MS in Indsl. Adminstrn., 1970; JD, Washburn U., 1976. Bar: Kans. 1977, U.S. Dist. Ct. Kans. 1977, U.S. Ct. Appeals (10th cir.) 1980. Ptnr. Weeks, Thomas & Lysaught, Kansas City, Kans., 1977-86, Smithyman & Zakoura, Kansas City, 1986—. Served to capt. U.S. Army, 1970-74. Mem. ABA, Kans. Bar Assn., Kansas City Bar Assn., Wyandotte County Bar Assn. Presbyterian. Federal civil litigation, State civil litigation, Personal injury. Home: 8415 W 98th Circle Overland Park KS 66212 Office: Smithyman & Zakoura PO Box 1233 Kansas City KS 66101

SMITTER, RONALD WARREN, lawyer; b. Pasadena, Calif., Nov. 14, 1951; s. Robert Claude and Kathryn Margaret (Brown) S.; m. Shannon Elaine Neilson, June 9, 1973; children: Sarah Kay, Robert William. B.A., U. Redlands, 1973; J.D., So. Meth. U., 1976. Bar: Tex. 1976, Calif., 1978, U.S. Dist. Ct. (so. dist.) Calif. 1978, U.S. Ct. Appeals (9th cir.) 1978. Assoc. Bonne, Jones & Bridges, Los Angeles, 1978-80, Morres, Polich & Purdy, Tustin, Calif., 1980-83; sole practice, Walnut, Calif., 1984—; judge pro tem Orange County Superior Ct., 1985—, mem. panel arbitrators, 1985—. Mem. ABA. Republican. Personal injury, Insurance, Construction. Address: 2362-A Altisma Way Carlsbad CA 92009

SMOAK, LEWIS TYSON, lawyer; b. Orangeburg, S.C., Feb. 11, 1944; s. William B. and Louise (Dempsey) S.; m. Elizabeth Adams Babb, July 16, 1969; children—Katherine, Blair, Tyson. B.A., Furman U., 1966; J.D., U. S.C., 1969. Bar: S.C. 1969, D.C. 1982. Ptnr., Ogletree, Deakins, Nash, Smoak and Stewart, Greenville, S.C., 1969—. Mem. ABA, Greenville County Bar Assn., S.C. Bar Assn., D.C. Bar Assn., Environ. Law Inst. (assoc.). Clubs: Poinsett, Greenville Country, Rotary (Greenville); Kiawah Island. Labor, Environment. Home: 76 Stonehaven Greenville SC 29607 Office: 1000 E North St Greenville SC 29601

SMOLEN, JASON DAVID, lawyer; b. Bklyn., Nov. 8, 1952; s. Benjamin and Judith Selma (Berman) S.; m. Marilyn Berzin, Apr. 23, 1983; 1 child, Gregory Matthew. BA, CUNY, 1974; JD, George Mason U., 1977. Bar: Va. 1977, U.S. Dist. Ct. (ea. dist.) Va. 1977, U.S. Ct. Appeals (D.C. cir.) 1977, D.C. 1978, U.S. Dist. Ct. D. C. 1978, U.S. Tax Ct. 1978, U.S. Ct. Appeals (4th cir.) 1978, U.S. Supreme Ct. 1981. Ptnr. Smolen & Plevy P.C., Fairfax, Va., 1977—; judge moot ct. Cath. U., Washington, 1981—; adj. prof. George Mason U., Fairfax, 1982-83. Mem. Fairfax Bar Assn. (cir. ct. com., chmn. membership com. 1984-85). Democrat. Jewish. General corporate, Contracts commercial, Family and matrimonial. Home: 7124 Armat Dr Bethesda MD 20817 Office: Smolen & Plevy PC 3905-S Railroad Ave 2d Floor Fairfax VA 22030

SMOLIAR, BURTON BRUCE, lawyer; b. Bklyn., Oct. 6, 1943; s. Milton J. and Esther (Edwin) S.; m. Barbara A. Gollance, June 12, 1963; children: Laura, David. BA, Columbia U., 1964, LLB, 1967, MBA, 1967; LLM, NYU, 1968. Bar: N.Y. 1967, Mich. 1977. Assoc. Kaye, Scholer, Fierman, Hayes & Handler, N.Y.C., 1968-77; sr. supervisory atty. Ford Motor Co., Dearborn, Mich., 1977-80, mgr., 1980-86, assoc. gen. counsel, 1986—. Corporate taxation. Office: Ford Motor Co The American Rd Dearborn MI 48013

SMOLINSKY, SIDNEY JOSEPH, lawyer; b. Phila., July 17, 1932; s. Max and Bertha (Goldberg) S.; m. Phyllis Landis, Feb. 14, 1960 (div. Aug. 1983); children: Susan, Joel; m. Phyllis Albert, Aug. 3, 1986. BS, Temple U., 1954, LLB, 1956. Bar: Pa. 1956, U.S. Dist. Ct. (ea. dist.) Pa., U.S. Ct. Appeals (3d cir.), U.S. Tax Ct., U.S. Supreme Ct. Ptnr. Pechner, Dorfman, Wolffe, Rounick & Cabot, Phila., 1958-74, sr. ptnr., 1974—. Police practices com. mem. Phila. br. ACLU, 1960-65. Served with U.S. Army, 1956-58. Mem. ABA, Assn. Trial Lawyers Am., Pa. Bar Assn., Phila. Bar Assn., Pa. Trial Lawyers Assn., Phila. Trial Lawyers Assn., Phi Alpha Delta. Democrat. Jewish. Avocations: skiing, cooking, travel, theatre, music. Federal civil litigation, State civil litigation, Personal injury. Office: Pechner Dorfman Wolffe Rounick & Cabot 3 Parkway 17th Floor Philadelphia PA 19102

SMOLKER, GARY STEVEN, lawyer; b. Los Angeles, Nov. 5, 1945; s. Paul and Shayndy Charolette (Sirott) S.; children: Terra, Judy. BS, U. Calif.-Berkeley, 1967; MS, Cornell U., 1968; JD cum laude, Loyola U., Los Angeles, 1973. Bar: Calif. 1973, U.S. Dist. Ct. (cen. dist.) Calif. 1973, U.S. Tax Ct. 1973, U.S. Ct. Appeals (9th cir.) 1973, U.S. Supreme Ct. 1978, U.S. Dist. Ct. (so., ea. and no. dists.) Calif. 1981. Guest researcher Lawrence Radiation Lab., U. Calif., 1967; teaching fellow Sch. Chem. Engring., Cornell U.; mem. tech. staff Hughes Aircraft Co., Culver City, Calif., 1968-70; in advanced mktg. and tech. TRW, Redondo Beach, Calif., 1970-72; sole practice, Beverly Hills, Calif., 1973—; guest lectr. UCLA Extension, 1973-74, Loyola U. Law Sch., 1979; speaker, panelist in field; adv. Loyola U. Law Sch., 1973—. Contbr. articles to profl. jours.; inventor self-destruct aluminum tungstic oxide films, electrolytic anticompromise process. Bd. dirs. Women's Clinic. Mem. ABA, Calif. State Bar Assn., Los Angeles County Bar Assn., Beverly Hills Bar Assn. (sr. editor jour. 1978-79, contbg. editor jour. 1980-82, 86—, editor-in-chief 1984-86), Assn. Real Estate Attys. (contbg. editor real estate rev. 1987—), Nat. Assn. Homebuilders, Bldg. Industry Assn. So. Calif. (bd. dirs. Los Angeles chpt., editor-in-chief Los Angeles Builder 1983-85), Nat. Audubon Soc., N.Y. Met. Mus. Art. Republican. Jewish. Club: Beverly Hills Lincoln (bd. dirs.). Lodge: B'nai B'rith (anti-defamation league). Real property, Construction. Office: 9401 Wilshire Blvd Suite 830 Beverly Hills CA 90212

SMOOT, THURLOW TED, lawyer; b. Glendive, Mont., Dec. 30, 1910; s. Marvin A. and Ivah (Cook) S. JD, U. Colo., 1933. Bar: Mont. 1933, Ohio 1934, U.S. Supreme Ct. 1964. Sole practice Cleve., 1933-37, 45—; trial atty., examiner, appellate atty. NLRB, Washington, 1937-47; instr. labor law Cuyahoga Community Coll., Cleve., 1982—; adj. faculty labor studies, Cuyahoga Community Coll., Cleve., 1982—. contbg. editor Baldwin Legal Forms Inc., 1978-79. Served with U.S. Army, 1942-45. Mem. ABA (chmn. labor relations law sect. 1966-67, del. ho. of dels. 1970-71) , Ohio Bar Assn., Greater Cleve. Bar Assn., Cuyahoga County Bar Assn., Panel Legal Arbitrators, Fed. Mediation and Conciliation Service, Assn. Trial Lawyers Am., Ohio Acad. Trial Lawyers, Am. Arbitration Assn. (panel), Fed. Mediation Conciliation Service. Labor. Home: 12700 Lake Ave Lakewood OH 44107 Office: 118 St Clair Ave Suite 806 Mall Bldg Cleveland OH 44114-1261

SMOOTS, CAROL ANNE, lawyer; b. Wenatchee, Wash., Jan. 25, 1953; d. Jesse C. and Sadie E. (Yeager) S.; m. P. Jay Hines, July 12, 1980; 1 child, Patrick Charles Hines. Student, Seattle Pacific U., 1971-72; BA, Cen. Wash. U., 1975; student, U. Wash. Sch. Law, 1976; JD, Willamette U., 1978. Bar: Oreg. 1978, D.C. 1981, U.S. Supreme Ct. 1985, U.S. Ct. Appeals (5th and D.C. cirs.) 1986. Legis. asst. U.S. Congressman Mike McCormack, Washington, 1974-75; law clk. U.S. Atty. Oreg., Portland, 1977; assoc. atty. and mcpl. judge City of Lafayette, Oreg., 1978-79; pub. utility specialist and atty. Bonneville Power Adminstrn., Washington, 1979-83; counsel Am. Gas Assn., Arlington, Va., 1983—. Co-author (chpt.) The Legal Aspects of Doing Business in North America, 1984; editor-in-chief The Natural Gas Lawyers Jour., 1985—. Vol. legal advisor Oregonians to Save the Boat People, 1982; tutor Alexandria (Va.) Vol. Bur., 1986. Recipient acad. scholarship Cen. Wash. U., 1974, Pres. award, 1975; recipient acad. scholarships and grants Seattle Pacific U. Mem. ABA, Fed. Energy Bar Assn. (judicial review com. 1985—), Corp. Counsel Assn., Wash. Met. Area Corp. Counsel Assn., Women's Bar Assn. Democrat. Avocations: sailing, fishing, reading, skiing. FERC practice, General corporate, Administrative and regulatory. Office: Am Gas Assn 1515 Wilson Blvd Arlington VA 22209

SMOUSE, H(ERVEY) RUSSELL, lawyer; b. Oakland, Md., Aug. 13, 1932; s. Hervey Reed and Vernie (Rush) S.; m. Creta M. Staley, June 15, 1955; children—Kristin Anne, Randall Forsyth, Gregory Russell. A.B., Princeton U., 1955; LL.B., U. Md., 1958. Bar: Md. 1958, U.S. Tax Ct. 1979, U.S. Ct. Appeals (4th cir.) 1960, U.S. Supreme Ct. 1974. Atty., Atty. Gen.'s Honors Program, Dept. Justice, Washington, 1958-60, asst. atty. Dist. Md., 1960-62; assoc. Pierson and Pierson, Balt., 1962-64; atty. B.&O. R.R., Balt., 1964-66; mem. Pierson and Pierson, 1966-69; mem. Clapp, Somerville, Black & Honemann, Balt., 1969-74; sole practice, Balt., 1974-81; mem. Melnicove, Kaufman, Weiner & Smouse, P.A., Balt., 1981—; v.p. Legal Aid Bur. Balt. City, 1972-73; bd. dirs. Md. Legal Services Corp., 1987—. Fellow Am. Coll. Trial Lawyers; mem. ABA, Md. State Bar Assn. (gov. 1981-83), Bar Assn. Balt. City (chmn. grievance com. 1969-70, chmn. judiciary com. and nominating com. 1980, mem. exec. com. 1969-70, 80), Nat. Assn. Criminal Def. Lawyers, Nat. Assn. R.R. Trial Counsel (exec. com., v.p. eastern region 1986—). Republican. Presbyterian. Federal civil litigation, State civil litigation. Office: 36 S Charles St Suite 600 Baltimore MD 21201

SMYK, STEPHEN DOUGLASS, lawyer; b. White Plains, N.Y., Mar. 8, 1944; s. Stephen and Lillian Mae (Faruolo) S.; m. Diane Elaine Dittman, Aug. 25, 1965; children: Stephen P., Rebecca A. BA, Syracuse U., 1967, JD, 1970. Bar: N.Y. 1971, U.S. Dist. Ct. (no. dist.) N.Y. 1971, U.S. Dist. Ct. (mid. dist.) Pa. 1977. Assoc. White, Berry & Reiter, Binghamton, N.Y., 1971, Stearns & Stearns, Binghamton, 1971-75; ptnr. Stearns & Smyk, Binghamton, 1975-77, Kramer, Wales & McAvoy, Binghamton, 1977-78, Smyk & Smyk, Binghamton, 1978—. Clk., vestry Trinity Episc. Ch., Binghamton, 1978-84; trustee Binghamton Gen. Hosp., 1976-80; bd. dirs. Vols. Am., Binghamton, 1977-79. Federal civil litigation, State civil litigation, Insurance. Office: Smyk & Smyk 111-115 Court St Binghamton NY 13901

SMYSER, (CHARLES ARVIL) SKIP, senator, lawyer; b. Caldwell, Idaho, Nov. 14, 1949; s. Samuel H. and Mildred (Skelton) S.; m. Melinda Sloviaczek, Sept. 22, 1981; 1 child, Lincoln. BA, Eastern Wash. U., 1972; JD, Gonzaga U., 1977. Dep. pros. atty. Ada County, Boise, Idaho, 1977-79; dep. atty. gen. State of Idaho, Boise, 1979-80; ptnr. Connolly & Smyser, Boise and Parma, Idaho, 1980—; senator State of Idaho, 1982—; bd. dirs. Idaho State Sch. and Hosp., Nampa, 1983—. Rep. Idaho Ho. of Reps., Canyon County, 1980-82. Served to capt. Q.M.C., U.S. Amry, 1972-74. Named Legis. of Yr., Idaho Prosecuting Atty.'s Assn., one of Outstanding Young Men of Am., U.S. Jaycees, 1977-86. Mem. Idaho State Bar Assn. Republican. Presbyterian. Lodges: Lions (zone chmn. 1985-86), Masons. Avocations: sports, stamp collecting. General practice, Family and matrimonial, Personal injury. Home: Rt 1 Box 1357 Parma ID 83660 Office: Connolly & Smyser 134 S 5th Boise ID 83702

SNAID, LEON JEFFREY, lawyer; b. Johannesburg, Transvaal, Republic of South Africa, Dec. 24, 1946; came to U.S., 1981; s. Mannie and Hene (Blume) S.; m. Alva Ann Robson, Aug. 12, 1979; children: Jedd, Nicole. Diploma in Law, U. Witwatersrand, Johannesburg, 1969. Bar: Supreme Ct. Republic South Africa 1971, High Ct. of the Kingdom of Lethoso 1976, Calif. 1982, U.S. Dist. Ct. (so. and cen. dists.) Calif. 1982. Assoc. Reeders, Teeger & Rosettenstein, Johannesburg, 1972; sole practice Johannesburg, 1973-76; ptnr. Snaid & Snaid, Johannesburg, 1976-81; sole practice San Diego, 1982—; lectr. legal edn. seminars, San Diego, 1984—. Author, pub. quar. newsletter Immigration and Internat. Law. Mem. ABA, Am. Immigration Lawyers Assn. (past chmn. continuing legal edn. San Diego chpt.), San Diego County Bar Assn. (past chmn. immigration com.). Lodge: Rotary. Immigration, naturalization, and customs, Private international. Home: 5060 Via Papel San Diego CA 92122 Office: 5030 Camino De La Siesta Suite 305 San Diego CA 92108

SNAIDER, BENSON ABRAM, lawyer; b. New Haven, Oct. 2, 1937; s. Morris B. and Lena (Bisnov) S.; children: Brian, Meredith, Elizabeth; m. Nadya J. Cardenas, Dec. 22, 1985. BA, U. Vt., 1959; LLB, U. Va., 1962. Bar: Conn. 1962, Fla. 1966, U.S. Ct. Appeals (2d cir.) 1966, U.S. Supreme Ct. 1966, U.S. Ct. Appeals (8th cir.) 1985. Asst. atty. gen. Conn. Atty. Gen. Office, Hartford, 1966-70; assoc. Slavitt & Connery, Norwalk, Conn., 1970-72; ptnr. Snaider & Sullivan, New Haven, 1972-74; sole practice New Haven, 1974—. Sec. Shubert Theater, New Haven, 1984—. Served to capt. U.S. Army, 1962-66. Mem. Conn. Bar Assn. (exec. com. real property sect.), New Haven Bar Assn. (bd. dirs. 1976—, sec. 1984—), Assn. Trial Lawyers Am., Conn. Trial Lawyers Assn. Democrat. Jewish. Club: Graduates (New Haven). Avocations: skiing, fishing, theater. Condemnation, Personal injury, Real property. Office: 181 Edwards St New Haven CT 06511

SNECKENBERG, WILLIAM JOHN, lawyer; b. Mpls., Dec. 16, 1946; s. William Albert and Shirley (Elvig) S.; m. Kathleen Gilman, Jan. 2, 1981. BBA, U. Nebr., 1969; JD, Creighton U., 1972. Bar: Ill. 1972, Nebr. 1972, U.S. Dist. Ct. (no. dist.) Ill. 1972, U.S. Ct. Appeals (7th cir.) 1975, U.S. Ct. Appeals (8th cir.) 1982. Assoc. Clausen, Miller et al, Chgo., 1972-77; ptnr. Lev & Sneckenberg, Chgo., 1977-81, William J. Sneckenberg & Assocs., Ltd., Chgo., 1981—; cons. Provisio Assoc., Chgo., 1986—. Editor, author: Creighton U. Law Rev., 1972, Property Ins. Law Newsletter, 1977-82. Chmn. bd. Am. with Distinction, Chgo., 1982—. Law Rev. scholar Creighton U., 1971-72. Mem. ABA, Fed. Bar Assn., Ill. Bar Assn., Chgo. Bar Assn., Ill. Appellate Lawyers Assn. (bd. dirs. 1982-84). Roman Catholic. Clubs: Evanston Country (Ill.), Rider (Chgo.). Avocations: sports, horses. Civil rights, Federal civil litigation, State civil litigation. Home: 327 W Belden #2 Chicago IL 60614

SNEED, JAMES H., lawyer; b. Bartlesville, Okla., Nov. 27, 1947; s. James H. and Genevieve (Harris) S.; m. Maree Sneed, Dec. 27, 1969. BA, U. Okla., 1969, JD, 1972. Bar: D.C. 1974, Ill. 1982, U.S. Dist. Ct. (no. dist.) Ill., U.S. Dist. Ct. D.C., U.S. Ct. Appeals (9th, 10th, 11th and D.C. cirs.). Trial atty. FTC, Washington, 1972-74, gen. counsel, dir. bur. consumer protection, asst. dir. bur. competition, 1977-82; assoc. Hogan & Hartson, Washington, 1974-77; ptnr. McDermott, Will & Emery, Chgo., 1982-86, Washington, 1986—. Mem. ABA (chmn. competition sub., FTC com., antitrust sect.), Order of Coif. Antitrust, Federal civil litigation. Office: McDermott Will & Emery 1850 K St NW Suite 500 Washington DC 20006

SNEED, JOSEPH TYREE, judge; b. Calvert, Tex., July 21, 1920; s. Harold Marvin and Cara (Weber) S.; m. Madelon Juergens, Mar. 15, 1944; children—Clara Hall, Cara Carleton, Joseph Tyree IV. B.B.A., Southwestern U., 1941; LL.B., U. Tex., Austin, 1947; S.J.D., Harvard, 1958. Bar: Tex. bar 1948. Instr. bus. law U. Tex., Austin, 1947; asst. prof. law U. Tex., 1947-51, asso. prof., 1951-54, prof., 1954-57, asst. dean, 1949-50; counsel Graves, Dougherty & Greenhill, Austin, 1954-56; prof. law Cornell U., 1957-62, Stanford Law Sch., 1962-71; dean Duke Law Sch., 1971-73; dep. atty. gen. U.S. justice dept., 1973; judge U.S. Ct. Appeals, 9th Circuit, San Francisco, 1973—; Cons. estate and gift tax project Am. Law Inst., 1960-69. Author: The Configurations of Gross Income, 1967; Contbr. articles to profl. jours. Served with USAAF, 1942-46. Mem. ABA (chairperson appellate judges conf. jud. adminstrn. div.), State Bar Tex., Am. Law Inst., Order of Coif. Address: PO Box 547 San Francisco CA 94101

SNEED, SPENCER CRAIG, lawyer; b. Juneau, Alaska, Dec. 30, 1951; s. Gene Eric and Sarah Anne (McNeil) S.; m. Magna Cyd Coster, Sept. 19, 1981; children: Kenneth Craig, Joseph Bernard. BA in Philosophy magna cum laude, Ariz. State U., 1975; JD, Willamette U., 1978. Bar: Alaska 1978. Assoc. Hartig, Rhodes, Norman, Mahoney & Edwards, Anchorage, Alaska, 1978-82, ptnr., 1982—. Mem. ABA, Alaska Bar Assn., Phi Kappa Phi. Banking, Bankruptcy, Consumer commercial. Home: 6731 Spectrum Circle Anchorage AK 99516 Office: Hartig Rhodes Norman et al 717 K St Anchorage AK 99501

SNEEDEN, EMORY MARLIN, lawyer, former judge, retired army officer; b. Wilmington, N.C., May 30, 1927; s. Silas and Helen (Boynton) S.; m. Margie Jeanette Carden, Dec. 29, 1945; children—Sharon Sneeden Clapper, David Michael. B.S., Wake Forest U., 1949, J.D., 1953. Bar: S.C. 1953, U.S. Supreme Ct. 1959. Enlisted man U.S. Army, 1944-46, commd. 2d lt., 1951, advanced through grades to brig. gen., 1974; staff judge adv. 1st Air Cavalry Div., U.S. Army, Vietnam, 1966-67; exec. to JAG U.S. Army, 1971-72; staff judge adv. XVIII Airborne Corps, U.S. Army, 1972-74; chief judge U.S. Army, 1974-75; chief U.S. Army Legal Services Agy., 1974-75; ret. U.S. Army, 1975; counsel and minority chief counsel, subcom. on antitrust and monopoloy, minority chief counsel, chief counsel, com. on judiciary U.S. Senate, Washington, 1975-81; assoc. dean, lectr. Sch. Law, U. S.C., 1978-82; counsel, ptnr. McNair, Glenn, Konduros, Corley, Singletary, Porter & Dibble, 1981-84, ptnr., 1986—; judge U.S. Ct. Appeals (4th cir.), Columbia, S.C., 1984-86; mem. U.S. Ct. Appeals (4th cir.) Jud. Conf., 1986—; cons. jud. br. com. Jud. Conf. U.S. Contbr. articles to profl. jours. Trustee Fork Union Mil. Acad., 1976-79, 80-84; bd. visitors Wake Forest U. Sch. Law, 1986—; mem. Founders Strom Thurmond Ctr., Clemson U., 1981-84, 86—. Decorated Legion of Merit with two oak leaf clusters, Meritorious Service medal, Air medal, Army Commendation medal with 3 oak leaf clusters, Cross of Gallantry (Vietnam); recipient Disting. Alumni award Wake Forest U. Sch. Law, 1985. Mem. ABA Fed. Bar Assn., Am. Judicature Soc., Ret. Officers Assn., 11th Airborne Div. Assn., Phi Delta Phi, Lambda Chi Alpha. Republican. Baptist. Clubs: Army and Navy; Nat. Lawyers (Washington). Home: 9 Trotwood Dr Columbia SC 29209 Office: NCNB Tower 18th Floor Columbia SC 29201 also: Madison Office Bldg 1155 15th St NW Suite 400 Washington DC 20005

SNEERINGER, STEPHEN GEDDES, lawyer; b. Lancaster, Ohio, Mar. 27, 1949; s. Stanley Carlylle and Mary Eleanor (Fry) S.; m. Kristine Karen Serfling, Oct. 6, 1974; children: Mary Rhonda, Robyn Kathleen. BA magna cum laude, Denison U., 1971; JD, Washington U., 1974. Bar: Mo. 1974. V.p. A.G. Edwards & Sons Inc., St. Louis, 1974—; arbitrator N.Y. Stock Exchange. Editor: Urban Law Ann., 1973-74. Am. Jurisprudence scholar, 1974. Mem. ABA, Securities Industries Assn., Futures Industries Assn., Nat. Assn. of Securities Dealers (arbitrator), Nat. Futures Assn. (arbitrator). Securities, State civil litigation, Federal civil litigation. Office: AG Edwards & Sons Inc 1 N Jefferson Saint Louis MO 63103

SNELL, THADDEUS STEVENS, III, retired building materials manufacturing company executive, lawyer; b. Ida Grove, Iowa, Feb. 23, 1919; s. Thaddeus Stevens and Catharine (Noble) S.; m. Mary Ward, Nov., 1951 (div. 1965); children: William, Kathleen, Pamela, Debra, Robert; m. Gloria Cramer Brent, July, 1966 (dec. 1981); m. Eleanor Larson Hawes, Nov. 24, 1982. BS, Northwestern U., 1941, postgrad. Law Sch., 1941-42; postgrad. U.S. Naval Acad. Postgrad. Sch., 1944-45; LLB, Yale U., 1947. Bar: Ill. 1948, Iowa 1948. Assoc. Keck, Mahin & Cate and predecessors, Chgo., 1947-58, ptnr., 1959-71; v.p., corp. counsel U.S. Gypsum Co., Chgo., 1971-82, v.p., gen. counsel, 1982-84; v.p., gen. counsel USG Corp., 1984-85; sole practice, Chgo., 1986—. Deacon Glenview (Ill.) Community Ch., 1958-61; pres. Kenilworth (Ill.) Citizens Adv. Com., 1973-74; mem. Chgo. Crime Commn. Served to lt. USNR, 1942-46. Mem. ABA, Ill. Bar Assn., Iowa Bar Assn., Chgo. Bar Assn., Legal Club Chgo., Am. Judicature Soc. Clubs: University, Metropolitan (Chgo.); Sunset Ridge Country (Northbrook, Ill.); Quail Ridge (Boynton Beach, Fla.). Lodge: Masons. General corporate, Antitrust. Home: 1901 Somerset Ln Northbrook IL 60062 Office: 101 S Wacker Dr Chicago IL 60606

SNIDER, DONALD STEPHEN, lawyer; b. Bklyn., Oct. 16, 1943; s. Leon Snider and Winifred (Scharfman) Novello; m. Elaine Daniels, June 18, 1966; children: Jacqueline Leigh, Jordan Lee. BA cum laude, NYU, 1965; JD magna cum laude, Harvard U., 1968. Bar: N.Y. 1969, U.S. Dist. Ct. (so. dist.) N.Y. 1972, U.S. Supreme Ct. 1974, Fla. 1975, U.S. Ct. Appeals (2d cir.) 1976, U.S. Dist. Ct. (ea. dist.) N.Y. 1980. Assoc. Finley, Kumble, Wagner, Underberg, Manley, Myerson & Casey, N.Y.C., 1968-74, ptnr., 1974—; advisor restatement, second, landlord and tenant property Am. Law Inst. 1972-77; lectr. law Fordham U., 1986—. Co-author: Cases and Text on Property, 2d edit., 1969, 3d edit., 1984; contbr. several articles on litigation, real estate devel. and environment to profl. jours. Mem. ABA, Fla. Bar Assn., N.Y. State Bar Assn. (lectr. environ. law sect. 1984), Assn. of Bar of City of N.Y. (com. on profl. responsibility 1984—, chmn. subcom. on atty. competence 1985—), Practising Law Inst. (lectr. comml. leasing 1975-81), Am. Arbitration Assn. (arbitrator 1978—), N.Y. State Planning Fedn. (lectr. 1985), Phi Beta Kappa. Jewish. Club: Fenway Golf (Scarsdale, N.Y.) (bd. govs. 1985—, co-chmn. law com. 1985—, admissions com. 1985-86). Real property, State civil litigation, Environment. Home: 48 Noh Ct New Rochelle NY 10804 Office: Finley Kumble Wagner et al 425 Park Ave New York NY 10022

SNIDER, JEROME GUY, lawyer; b. Lakewood, N.J., Mar. 14, 1950; s. Theodore Charles and Minnie Snider; m. Naomi S. Herman, Sept. 20, 1981; 1 child, Benjamin Herman. AB, Rutgers U., 1972; JD, U. Pa., 1975. Bar: N.Y. 1976, U.S. Dist. Ct. (so. and ea. dists.) N.Y. 1976, U.S. Dist. Ct. (no. dist.) Calif. 1979, U.S. Supreme Ct. 1980, U.S. Dist. Ct. D.C. 1983, U.S. Ct. Appeals (6th cir.) 1984, U.S. Ct. Appeals (D.C. cir.) 1986. Law clk. to chief judge U.S. Dist. Ct. (so. dist.) N.Y., N.Y.C., 1975-77; assoc. Davis Polk & Wardwell, N.Y.C., 1977-82, ptnr., Washington, 1983—. Mem. ABA, Fed. Bar Assn. Jewish. Federal civil litigation, State civil litigation. Home: 4821 43d St NW Washington DC 20016 Office: Davis Polk & Wardwell 1575 I St NW Washington DC 20005

SNIDER, RONALD ALBERT, lawyer; b. Selma, Ala., Aug. 13, 1948; s. Carl Edwards Snider and Lou Ella (Edwards) West; m. Virginia Creary Smith, Aug. 30, 1980; children: Virginia, George Chaffin. Bar: Ala. 1973. Staff atty. Fed. Home Loan Bank Bd., Washington, 1973-75, asst. sec., 1975-79; ptnr. Miller, Hamilton, Snider and Odom, Mobile, Ala., 1979—. Mem. ABA (banking sect.), Ala. Bar Assn., Mobile Bar Assn., Fed. Bar Assn. Democrat. Banking.

SNIERSON, RICHARD S., lawyer; b. Cambridge, Mass., Sept. 4, 1944; s. Bernard I. and Muriel S. (Goldberg) S.; m. Joyce B. Freedman, June 9, 1968; children: Daniel, Jennifer. BA, Yale U., 1966; JD, Boston U., 1969. Bar: N.H. 1969, U.S. Dist. Ct. N.H. 1969, U.S. Ct. Appeals (1st. cir.) 1977. Law clk. to presiding judge N.H. Supreme Ct., Concord, 1969-70; from assoc. to ptnr. McLane, Graf, Raulerson & Middleton P.A., Manchester, N.H., 1973—. Served to capt. JAG, USMC, 1970-73. General practice, General corporate, Federal civil litigation. Home: 3 Vassar St Manchester NH 03104 Office: McLane Graf Raulerson & Middleton PA 40 Stark St Manchester NH 03105

SNIPES, G(EORGE) WILLIAM, lawyer; b. N.Y.C., Dec. 20, 1956; s. George W. and Doreen (Gollop) S.; m. Nancy Carr, June 11, 1978; 1 child, Amanda Beth. BA magna cum laude, St. Lawrence U., Canton, N.Y., 1977; JD, Stanford U., 1980. Bar: Calif. 1981, U.S. Dist. Ct. (no. dist.) Calif. 1981, U.S. Dist. Ct. (ea. dist.) Calif. 1985. Atty. Landels, Ripley & Diamond, San Francisco, 1980-83, McCutchen, Doyle, Brown & Enersen, Walnut Creek, Calif., 1983-85; counsel Bechtel Civil, Inc., San Francisco, 1986—. Pres., bd. dirs. View Park Homeowners Assn., Rodeo, Calif., 1984-86. Mem. ABA, Calif. Bar Assn., Am. Arbitration Assn. (arbitration panel community disputes service program), Phi Beta Kappa. Avocations: softball, football, basketball. Contracts commercial, Construction. Office: Bechtel Civil Inc 50 Beale St San Francisco CA 94105

SNITE, ALBERT JOHN, JR., lawyer; b. Phila., Mar. 3, 1948; s. Albert John and Florence H. (Davison) S.; m. Julia Ann Conover, Sept. 12, 1981. B.S., U. Pa., 1969; J.D., Dickinson Sch. Law, 1973. Bar: Pa. 1973, U.S. Dist.

Ct. (ea. dist.) Pa. 1977, U.S. Ct. Appeals (3d cir.) 1978, U.S. Supreme Ct., 1980. Staff atty. Defender Assn. Phila., 1973-77, fed. ct. div., 1977-81; assoc. Rutter, Turner, Stein & Solomon, Phila., 1981-83; sole practice, Phila., 1984-85; ptnr. Fiechter, Hartmann & Snite, 1985—; cons. criminal practice Phila. Community Legal Services, Inc., 1975. Bd. dirs. Oak Lane Community Action Assn., Phila., 1983—; chmn. race relations com. St. James United Methodist Ch., Phila., 1983—; bd. dirs. Wesley Shared Housing Corp., 1985—. Mem. ABA, Assn. Trial Lawyers Am., Pa. Trial Lawyers Assn., Phila. Bar Assn. (legis. liason, fed. cts., criminal law coms.). Club: Germantown Cricket (Phila.). Lodge: Artisans Order Mut. Protection. Criminal, Federal civil litigation, State civil litigation. Office: Fiechter Hartmann & Snite 2040 PSFS Bldg 12 S 12th St Philadelphia PA 19107

SNODERLY, JOHN ALLEN SHELBY, lawyer; b. Akron, Ohio, June 6, 1929; s. William E. Snoderly and Alma (Shelby) Snoderly Sebaugh Ostroff; m. Donna Gover (div.); children—Lynn Marie, John II, Catherine C., Elizabeth; m. Joyce Evelyn Poth (div.); 1 child, Rebecca N.; m. B. Catherine Barnett, May 22, 1975. A.A., Tenn. Wesleyan Coll., 1948; B.A., U. Akron, 1952, J.D., 1959. Bar: Ohio 1959. Sole practice, Akron, 1959—. Trustee Akron Law Library, 1962-82, Lakemore Meth. Ch., Akron, 1973-85. Served with USAF, 1949-50. Mem. Akron Bar Assn., Ohio State Bar Assn. Avocations: farming; flying; golfing; fishing; camping. General practice. Office: 77 E Mill St Akron OH 44308

SNOOK, JOHN LLOYD, III, lawyer; b. Plainfield, N.J., Apr. 11, 1953; s. John Lloyd Jr. and Helen Alexandria (Buchanan) S.; m. Sheila Cowles Haughey, May 13, 1979; children: Christopher Haughey, Michael Haughey. AB, Stanford U., 1974; JD, U. Mich., 1979. Bar: Va. 1979, U.S. Dist. Ct. (ea. and we. dists.) Va. 1979, U.S. Ct. Appeals (4th cir.) 1983, U.S. Supreme Ct. 1983. Assoc. Lowe, Gordon, Jacobs & Snook Ltd., Charlottesville, Va., 1979-84, Paxson, Smith, Gilliam & Scott, Charlottesville, 1984-85; sole practice Charlottesville, 1985—; pres. Va. Coalition on Jails and Prisons Inc., Richmond, 1984—. Adminstrv. editor Mich. Yearbook of Internat. Legal Studies, 1979. Mem. Charlottesville Planning Commn., 1981—; pres. Community Energy Conservation Program, Charlottesville, 1981—. Mem. ABA, Va. Bar Assn., Nat. Assn. Criminal Def. Lawyers, Assn. Trial Lawyers Am., Va. Trial Lawyers Assn. Democrat. Presbyterian. Avocations: tennis, politics. Criminal, Personal injury, State civil litigation. Home: 2408 Hillwood Pl Charlottesville VA 22901 Office: 230 Court Sq Charlottesville VA 22901

SNOUFFER, WILLIAM CAMPBELL, judge; b. Fort Monmouth, N.J., Oct. 14, 1939; s. William Noel and Florence Corinne (Campbell) S. A.B., Antioch Coll., Yellow Springs, Ohio, 1962; student U. Edinburgh (Scotland), 1959-60; J.D., U. Chgo., 1965. Bar: Oreg. 1965. Law clk. to justice Oreg. Supreme Ct., 1965-66; dep. dist. atty. Multnomah County, 1966-68; assoc. Lindsay, Nahstoll, Hart, Duncan, Dafoe & Krause, Portland, 1968-72; prof. law Lewis & Clark Law Sch., 1972-76; judge Multnomah County Dist. Ct., 1976-78, 80-84; judge pro tem Cir. Ct., 1979-80; judge Circuit Ct. 4th Jud. Dist., 1984—; mem. Oreg. Jud. Conf.; exec. sec. Jud. Fitness Commn., 1975-76; dir. Oreg. Jud. Coll., 1979. Trustee, Met. Pub. Defender, Portland, 1972-76; mem. exec. bd. Oreg. chpt. ACLU, 1974-76; chmn. Sandy River Gorge com. Nature Conservancy, 1981-83. Mem. ABA, Oreg. State Bar (criminal law sect.), Multnomah County Bar Assn., Circuit Judges Assn. (treas. 1986—). Clubs: City, Mazamas (Portland). Contbr. articles to profl. jours.; author: Criminal Justice Standards in Oregon, 1975, Oregon Criminal Law, 1986. Criminal, State civil litigation, Legal history. Office: Multnomah County Courthouse Portland OR 97204

SNOW, CHARLES, lawyer; b. Bklyn., May 3, 1932; s. Irving S. and Bessie (Siegel) S.; m. Deanna Friedman, Jan. 15, 1961; children: Lisa C., Amy M. BA, U. Vt., 1954; LLB, Bklyn. Law Sch., 1959. Bar: N.Y. 1959, U.S. Dist. Ct. (ea. dist.) N.Y. 1961, U.S. Dist. Ct. (so. dist.) N.Y. 1961, U.S. Ct. Appeals (2d cir.) 1961, U.S. Supreme Ct. 1965. Dep. asst. atty. gen. N.Y. Dept. Law, N.Y.C., 1959-60; asst. U.S. atty. U.S. Dist. Ct. (ea. dist.) N.Y., Bklyn., 1960-61; asst. regional adminstr. SEC, N.Y.C., 1961-68; ptnr. Wofsey Certilman Haft Snow & Becker, P.C., N.Y.C., 1968-77, Snow Becker Krauss, P.C., N.Y.C., 1977—; bd. dirs. Walker Color, Inc., Yonkers, N.Y., Stone Med. Supply, Hempstead, N.Y., Celcom Corp., N.Y.C., Congregate Care Ctrs. Am., Inc., San Diego. Chmn. Harrison Planning Bd., N.Y., 1977—; bd. dirs. Am. Mus. Hist. Documents, Chartered, Las Vegas, Nev. Mem. ABA, N.Y. Bar Assn., Assn. Bar City N.Y. Republican. Jewish. Securities, Federal civil litigation, General corporate. Office: 605 3d Ave New York NY 10158

SNOW, DAVID FORREST, lawyer; b. Boston, Mar. 15, 1932; s. Albert Grindle and Hope (Farrington) S.; m. Rosemary Allsman, Oct. 7, 1957 (div. Jan. 1982); children: Nicholas David, Sarah Alison, Catherine Ann; m. Joyce Neiditz, Mar. 15, 1985. BA, Dartmouth Coll., 1954; JD, Harvard U., 1960. Ptnr. Jones, Day, Reavis & Pogue, Cleve., 1960-67, 68—; asst. prof. law U. Iowa, Iowa City, 1967-68. Mem. ABA, Ohio Bar Assn., Cleve. Bar Assn. Bankruptcy, Contracts commercial. Home: 2330 Ardleigh Dr Cleveland Heights OH 44106 Office: Jones Day Reavis & Pogue 1700 Huntington Bldg Cleveland OH 44115

SNOW, ROBERT BRIAN, lawyer; b. Rochester, N.Y., Apr. 9, 1953; s. Warren Buffington and Betty (Thrash) S.; m. Laura Rudman, May 11, 1976 (div. Sept. 1981); m. Patricia M. Lindsay, April 29, 1984; 1 child, Robert Kyle. BA in Polit. Sci., Communications, U. N.H., 1975; postgrad., Suffolk U., 1975-76; JD, Boston Coll., 1978. Bar: N.H. 1979, U.S. Dist. Ct. N.H. 1979, U.S. Supreme Ct. 1982, Mass. 1985, U.S. Dist. Ct. Mass. 1985, U.S. Ct. Appeals (1st, and D.C. cirs.) 1985, D.C. 1985, U.S. Ct. Claims 1985. Asst. supr. Dept. Atty. Gen., Boston, 1977-78; dir. crime prevention and pub. info. State Dept. of Safety, Concord, N.H., 1978-79; atty., adminstr. subcontracts Kollsman Indsl. Co. div. Sun Chem. Corp., Merrimack, N.H., 1979-81; sole practice Nashua, N.H., 1982—; atty. contracts div. youth and adult services State Dept. Human Services, Concord, 1983—, state div. Children & Youth Services; instr. faculty Hesser Coll., Manchester, N.H., 1983—, U. N.H., 1986—; bd. dirs., legal counsel Mt. Hope Bd. of Edn., Nashua, N.H., 1983—; chmn. appellate div. State Dept. Employment, Concord, 1983-85; prosecutor p.t. Hudson (N.H.) Police Dept., 1985-86. Candidate N.H. Reps., Concord, 1982; cand. State Senate, Merrimack, 1983; del. State Constl. Convention, Concord, 1983. Named one of Outstanding Young Men in Am., 1985, 86. Mem. ABA, N.H. Bar Assn. (profl. code rev. com., criminal practice rev. com.), N.H. Trial Lawyers Assn., Assn. Trial Lawyers Am., N.H. Trial Lawyers Assn., So. N.H. Bus. and Indsl. Club, Merrimack C. of C. Club: Merrimack Exchange (chartered). Avocations: sports. Criminal, General corporate, Personal injury. Home: 6 Valleyview Dr Merrimack NH 03054 Office: 2 Wellman Ave Nashua NH 03060

SNOW, TOWER CHARLES, JR., lawyer; b. Boston, Oct. 28, 1947; s. Tower Charles and Margaret (Harper) S. AB cum laude, Dartmouth Coll., 1969; JD, U. Calif., Berkeley, 1973. Bar: Calif. 1973, U.S. Dist. Ct. (no. dist.) Calif. 1973, U.S. Dist. Ct. (ea. dist.) Calif. 1979, U.S. Ct. Appeals (fed. cir.) 1980, U.S. Ct. Claims 1980, U.S. Supreme Ct. 1976. Ptnr., chmn. litigation dept. Orrick, Herrington & Sutcliffe, San Francisco, 1973—; arbitrator Nat. Assn. Securities Dealers, N.Y. Stock Exchange, Pacific Coast Stock Exchange, Superior Ct. City and County San Francisco; lectr. Author: numerous law handbooks and articles to prof. jours. Mem. San Francisco Museum Soc., San Francisco Symphony. Mem. ABA (assoc., chmn. subcom. pub. offering litigation), Continuing Edn. Bar (bus. law inst. planning com.), San Francisco Bar Assn., Securities Industry Assn., Nat. Inst. Trial Advocacy. Democrat. Club: Commonwealth (San Francisco). Avocations: internat. travel, skiing, running, scuba diving, photography. Securities, Federal civil litigation, State civil litigation. Home: 9 Wyngaard Ave Piedmont CA 94611 Office: Orrick Herrington & Sutcliffe 600 Montgomery St San Francisco CA 94111

SNOWBARGER, VINCENT KEITH, lawyer, state representative; b. Kankakee, Ill., Sept. 16, 1949; s. Willis Edward and Wahnona Ruth (Horger) S.; m. Carolyn Ruth McMahon, Mar. 25, 1972; children: Jeffrey Edward, Matthew David. BA in History, Bethany Nazarene Coll., 1971; MA in Polit. Sci., U. Ill., 1974; JD, U. Kans., 1977. Bar: Kans. 1977, U.S. Dist. Ct. Kans. 1977. Instr. Mid-Am. Nazarene Coll., Olathe, Kans., 1973-76; ptnr. Haskin, Hinkle, Slater & Snowbarger, Olathe, 1977-84, Dietrich, Davis, Dicus et al, Olathe, 1984—. Rep. Kans. Legislature, Topeka, 1984—; mem. Olathe Planning Commn., 1982-84; bd. dirs. Olathe Area C. of C., 1984; div. chmn. United Way, Olathe, 1985-86; participant Leadership Olathe. Mem. ABA, Am. Soc. Hosp. Attys., Kans. Bar Assn., Kans. Assn. Hosp. Attys., Johnson County Bar Assn. Republican. Nazarene. Avocations: politics, flying. Contracts commercial, Health, Legislative. Home: 1451 Orleans Olathe KS 66062 Office: Dietrich Davis et al PO Box 484 Olathe KS 66061

SNOWDEN, ELTON GREGORY, lawyer; b. Meridian, Miss., May 30, 1954; s. Elton Monroe and Almeta (Covington) S.; m. Renee Campbell, Dec. 20, 1975; children: Emily Gay, Katharine Covington. BA magna cum laude, U. Ala., 1976; JD, Vanderbilt U., 1979. Bar: Fla. 1979, U.S. Ct. Appeals (5th cir.) 1979, Miss. 1981, U.S. Ct. Appeals (11th cir.) 1981. Assoc. Holland & Knight, Bartow, Fla., 1979-80, Lakeland, Fla., 1980-81; assoc. Bourdeaux & Jones, Meridian, 1981-84, ptnr., 1984—. Assoc. editor Vanderbilt U. Law Rev., 1978-79. Treas. Polk County Reps., Lakeland, 1980-81; mem. Lauderdale County Reps., Meridian, 1981—. Mem. ABA, Lauderdale County Bar Assn., Meridian Jaycees (pres. 1985, Outstanding Local Pres. award 1985). Republican. Baptist. Avocations: hist. research and writing, amateur theater acting. Real property, Banking, General corporate. Home: 6136 14th Ave Meridian MS 39305 Office: Bourdeaux & Jones 505 21st Ave Meridian MS 39302-2009

SNOWDEN, JAMES ARTHUR, lawyer; b. Lincoln, Nebr., Oct. 8, 1948; s. John Kenneth and Mary Ann (Beard) S.; m. Nancy Jean Bess, Aug. 9, 1969; children: Kristine, Kathryn, Kerrie. BA, U. Nebr., 1970, JD, 1972. Bar: Nebr. 1972, U.S. Dist. Ct. Nebr. 1972, U.S. Ct. Appeals (8th cir.) 1972. Assoc. Knudsen & Berkheimer, Lincoln, 1972-76; ptnr. Knudsen, Berkheimer, Richardson & Endacott, Lincoln, 1976—; dist. rep. Nebr. Bar Ho. Dels., Lincoln, 1984—. Mem. 3d Dist. Judicial Nominating Com., Lincoln. Served to capt. U.S. Army, 1972-73. Personal injury, Federal civil litigation, Medical malpractice defense. Home: 940 Piedmont Rd Lincoln NE 68510 Office: Knudsen Berkheimer Richardson & Endacott 1000 NBC Center Lincoln NE 68508

SNYDER, ALLEN ROGER, lawyer; b. Washington, Jan. 26, 1946; s. Henry and Sylvia (Oxenburg) S.; m. Susan Port, Aug. 10, 1969; children: Joanna, Carolyn. BA with distinction, George Washington U., 1967; JD magna cum laude, Harvard U., 1971. Bar: D.C. 1973, U.S. Dist. Ct. D.C., Md., U.S. Ct. Appeals (D.C., 4th, 5th, 6th, 8th, 11th cirs.), U.S. Supreme Ct. Temp. assoc. Williams, Connolly & Califano, Washington, 1971; law clk. to assoc. justice W. Harlan U.S. Supreme Ct., 1971, law clk. to assoc. justice J. Rehnquist, 1972; assoc. Hogan & Hartson, Washington, 1972-78, ptnr., 1979—; mem. D.C. Jud. Conf., D.C. Cir. Comm. on Admissions and Grievances, D.C. Cir. Adv. Com. on Procedures; chmn. D.C. Ct. Appeals Bd. Profl. Responsibility, 1978-84. Bd. dirs. Jewish Found. Group Homes, Rockville, Md., 1982-86. Served with USAR, 1968-74. Mem. D.C. Bar Assn. (chmn. steering com. div. cts., lawyers and adminstrn. justice 1974-77, long range planning com. 1976, bd. govs. 1977-78), Washington Council Lawyers (bd. dirs. 1976—), Am. Psychiat. Assn. (exec. sec. com. jud. action 1974-77). Federal civil litigation, State civil litigation, Civil rights. Home: 7616 Arrowood Rd Bethesda MD 20817 Office: Hogan & Hartson 555 13th St Washington DC 20004

SNYDER, ARTHUR KRESS, lawyer, government official; b. Los Angeles, Nov. 10, 1932; s. Arthur and Ella Ruth (Keck) S.; m. Mary Frances Neely, Mar. 5, 1953; children—Neely Arthur, Miles John; m. 2d, Michaele Maggie Noval, May 14, 1973; 1 dau., Erin-Marisol Michele; m. 3d, Delia Wu, Apr. 18, 1981. B.A., Pepperdine U., 1953; J.D., U. So. Calif., 1958; LL.D., Union U., 1980. Bar: Calif. 1960, U.S. Supreme Ct. 1982. Sole practice, Los Angeles, 1960-67; founder, pres. Arthur K. Snyder Law Corp., Los Angeles, 1981—; mem. City Council Los Angeles, 1967-85; pres. Marisol Corp., real estate and fgn. trade, 1978—; past instr. Los Angeles City Schs. Served to capt. USMC. Decorated La Tizona de El Cid Compeador (Spain), medal Legion of Honor (Mex.), Hwa Chao Zee You medal (Republic of China); numerous other commendations, medals, awards. Mem. Los Angeles County Bar Assn., Calif. Bar Assn., ABA, Internat. Bar Assn., Am. Trial Lawyers Assn., Am. Immigration Lawyers Assn., Am. Judicature Soc. Baptist. Club: Masons. Local government, Administrative and regulatory, Real property. Office: 355 S Grand Ave Suite 3288 Los Angeles CA 90071

SNYDER, BROCK ROBERT, lawyer; b. Topeka, Sept. 18, 1935; s. Ralph and Helen (Fritze) S.; m. Carol Lee Cunningham, June 5, 1957 (div. Nov. 1976); children: Lori, Holli, Staci; m. Sheryl Anita Clarke, Apr. 1, 1985; children: Brock Robert II, Samantha. BS, U. Kans., 1957; JD, Washburn U., 1964. Bar: Kans. 1964. Ptnr. Eidson, Lewis, Porter & Haynes, Topeka, 1964-82; sole practice Topeka, 1982—; lectr. on sch. discipline and due process, 1975-80; pres. Kans. Legal Services, Topeka, 1977-80. Served to capt. USMC, 1957-61. Fellow Kans. Bar Assn. (chmn. legal assts. com. 1983-84); mem. ABA, Trial Lawyers Assn., Topeka Bar Assn., Topeka Legal Aid Soc. (pres. 1976-78). Republican. Lutheran. Avocation: scuba. Personal injury, General practice, General corporate. Office: 1403 SW Topeka Blvd Topeka KS 66612

SNYDER, CHARLES AUBREY, lawyer; b. Bastrop, La., June 19, 1941; s. David and Shirley Blossom (Haas) S.; m. Sharon Rae Veta, Aug. 29, 1963; children: David Veta, Shelby Haas, Claire Frances. B.B.A., Tulane U., 1963; J.D., La. State U., 1966. Bar: La. 1966. Assoc. firm. Milling, Benson, Woodward, Hillyer, Pierson & Miller, and predecessors, New Orleans, 1966-69, ptnr., 1969—; dir. Delta Petroleum Co., Petroleum Helicopters, Inc., Inc. Corp., La. Motel and Investment Corp. Trustee Kathlyn O'Brien Found., 1970, Touro Infirmary, bd. mgrs.; bd. dirs. New Orleans Speech and Hearing Ctr., pres., 1978-80; fellow La. Coll. Securities Counsel. Mem. ABA, La. Bar Assn. (chmn. sect. on corp. and bus. law 1982-83), New Orleans Bar Assn., La. Law Inst. (coms. on mineral code and revision of partnership law and community property law), Beta Gamma Sigma. Clubs: Metairie Country, Petroleum, Internat. House, Plimsoll. General corporate, State and local taxation, Estate planning. Home: 1659 Burbank Dr New Orleans LA 70122 Office: Milling Benson Woodward Hillyer Pierson & Miller 1100 Whitney Bldg New Orleans LA 70130

SNYDER, DEAN EDWARD, lawyer, pharmacist; b. Kittery, Maine, Sept. 4, 1946; s. David William and Leota Ruth (Peters) S.; m. Sally Jane Groves, June 10, 1967 (div. 1982); children—Sarah Elizabeth, Thomas Craig. B.S. in Pharmacy, Purdue U., 1969; J.D., U. Mich., 1972. Bar: Ill., 1972. Atty., First Nat. Bank of Chgo., 1972-74, Am. Hosp. Supply Corp., Evanston, Ill., 1974-76; regulatory affairs mgr. Arnar-Stone Labs., Mt. Prospect, Ill., 1976-77; sr. atty. Travenol Labs. Inc., Deerfield, Ill., 1977-84; ptnr. Otto & Snyder, Park Ridge, Ill., 1984—; contbg. editor AMA publ., Chgo., 1973—. Author: Keyword Guide to Drug Labeling Regulation, 1986; contbr. articles to profl. jours. Mem. ABA, Chgo. Bar Assn., Am. Pharm. Assn., Am. Soc. for Pharmacy Law. Presbyterian. Personal injury, Food and drug. Home: 189 Happ Rd Northfield IL 60093 Office: Otto & Snyder 3 S Prospect Park Ridge IL 60068

SNYDER, EUGENE I., lawyer, chemist; b. Phila., Oct. 18, 1933; s. William and Bessie (Press) S.; children: Gwendolyn, Jordan, Lynne. BS, Temple U., 1955; PhD, U. Chgo., 1959; JD, Loyola U., Chgo., 1978. Bar: Ill. 1978, U.S. Patent Office 1980. Research chemist Exxon Corp., Linden, N.J., 1961-63; asst. prof. U. Conn., Storrs, 1963-69; vis. prof. East Tenn. State U., Johnson City, 1969-70; chemist Kraft, Inc., Glenview, Ill., 1970-79; patent atty. Signal-Allied Corp., Des Plaines, Ill., 1979—. Patent. Home: 1748 Carib Ln Mount Prospect IL 60056 Office: Signal UOP Group Algonquin & Mt Prospect Des Plaines IL 60016

SNYDER, FREDERICK EDWARD, legal educator; b. Kingston, N.Y., Apr. 3, 1944; s. John I. and Agatha (Flick) S. A.B., Georgetown U., 1966, J.D., 1974; M.Phil., Yale U., 1969, Ph.D., 1970; LL.M., Harvard U., 1977. Bar: Conn. 1974, N.Y. 1976, Mass. 1981. Law clk. to chief justice Conn. Supreme Ct., 1974; assoc. Baker & McKenzie, N.Y.C., 1975; assoc. Bingham Dana & Gould, Boston, 1976; fellow in law and humanities Harvard U. Law Sch., 1977, asst. dean, lectr. on law, dir. clin. programs, assoc. dir. East Asian legal studies, 1978-83, asst. dean for internat. and comparative legal studies, lectr. Latin Am. law, adminstr. grad. program, assoc. dir. East Asian legal Studies, 1983—; bd. dirs. Cambridge and Somerville Legal Services. Named Fulbright Disting. Vis. Lectr., Universidad de Los Andes, Columbia, 1987. Mem. Ateneo Mexicano de Jurisprudencia (hon.), Inst. Politics and Constl. Law of U. La Plata (hon.), ABA, Critical Legal Studies Conf., Assn. Am. Law Schs. (pres. Sect. Grad. Studies). Democrat. Club: Harvard Faculty (bd. mgrs. 1980-83). Author: Law Politics and Revolution in Latin America: A Research Guide and Selected Bibliography, 1982; Latin American Society and Legal Culture, 1985; (with S. Sathirathai) Third World Attitudes Toward International Law, 1987. Private international, Public international, Comparative. Office: Harvard U Law Sch Cambridge MA 02138

SNYDER, GEORGE EDWARD, lawyer; b. Battle Creek, Mich., Feb. 7, 1934; s. Leon R. and Edith (Dullabahn) S.; m. Mary Jane Belt, July 27, 1957 (div. Sept. 23, 1982); children: Sara Lynn, Elizabeth Jane; m. Claudia Gage Brooks, Feb. 25, 1984. B.S., Mich. State U., 1957; J.D., U. Mich., 1960. Bar: Mich. 1961, U.S. Dist. Ct. (we. and ea. dists.) Mich. 1961. With Gen. Electric Co., 1957-58; asso. firm Miller, Johnson, Snell & Commisky, Grand Rapids, 1960-62, Goodenough & Buesser, Detroit, 1962-66; partner firm Buesser, Buesser, Snyder & Blank, Detroit and Bloomfield Hills, 1966-85, Meyer, Kirk, Snyder & Safford, Bloomfield Hills, 1985—; dir. Bill Knapps Mich., Inc. Chmn. E. Mich. Environ. Action Council, 1974-78; pub. mem. inland lakes and streams rev. com. Mich. Dept. Natural Resources, 1975-76. Served as 2d lt. AUS, 1957. Fellow Am. Acad. Matrimonial Lawyers, Am. Bar Found.; mem. State Bar Mich. (chmn. family law com. 1968-72, mem. rep. assembly 1972-78, chmn. rules and calendar com. 1977-78, mem. family law sect. council 1973-76, environ. law sect. council 1980-85, prepaid legal services com. 1973-82, com. on judicial selection 1974, com. on specialization 1976-82), ABA, Detroit Bar Assn. (chmn. family law com. 1966-68), Oakland County Bar Assn., Am. Judicature Soc., Am. Arbitration Assn. (panel arbitrators), Delta Upsilon (chmn. trustees, alumni chpt. dep. 1965-70), Tau Beta Pi, Pi Tau Sigma, Phi Eta Sigma. Conglist. Clubs: Detroit Athletic, Thomas M. Cooley, Birmingham (Mich.) Athletic. Federal civil litigation, State civil litigation, Family and matrimonial. Home: 32965 Outland Trail Birmingham MI 48010 Office: Meyer Kirk Snyder & Safford 100 W Long Lake Rd Suite 100 Bloomfield Hills MI 48013

SNYDER, JOHN BENNETT, lawyer, trust company executive; b. Evanston, Ill., July 8, 1929; s. Erwin Paul and Fern Kathryn (Bennett) S.; m. Ann Walker Bross, June 16, 1956; children—John B., Elizabeth, Daniel. A.B., Williams Coll., 1951; LL.B., Harvard U., 1957. Bar: Ill. 1957. Ptnr. Chadwell & Kayser, Chgo., 1957-73; asst. gen. counsel No. Trust Co., Chgo., 1973-78, gen. counsel, 1978, sec., exec. v.p., 1983—; exec. v.p., gen. counsel, sec. No. Trust Corp., Chgo. Pres. Chgo. Commons Assn., 1965-66, Winnetka Community House, Ill., 1979. Served to lt. (j.g.) USNR, 1951-54; Korea. Mem. ABA, Ill. Bar Assn., Chgo. Bar Assn., Fellows of ABA, Legal Club Chgo. (pres. 1985-86), Law Club Chgo., Phi Beta Kappa. Republican. Episcopalian. Avocations: fishing; golf. Home: 592 Cherry St Winnetka IL 60093 Office: No Trust Co 50 S LaSalle St Chicago IL 60675

SNYDER, JOHN FREEMAN, lawyer; b. Washington, July 4, 1922; s. Peter Frederick and Ruth (Freeman) S.; m. Betsy McCoy, Dec. 5, 1943; 1 dau., Susan Snyder Toth. A.B., U. Md., 1948; J.D., Georgetown U., 1950. Bar: D.C. 1950, Md. 1969, U.S. Ct. Claims 1965, U.S. Supreme Ct. 1975, U.S. Ct. Internat. Trade 1986. Asst. legal officer Applied Physics Lab., Johns Hopkins U., Silver Spring, Md., 1950-52; staff counsel Thieblot Aircraft Co., Bethesda, Md. and Martinsburg, W.Va., 1952-57; patent coordinator Vitro Corp., Silver Spring, Md., Ft. Walton Beach, Fla. and West Orange, N.J., 1957-59; asst. mgr. legal dept., assoc. counsel Atlantic Research Corp. subs. Susquehanna Corp., Alexandria, Va., 1959-68; pvt. practice, 1968-70, 72—; atty. Melpar subs. Am. Standard, Inc., McLean, Va., 1970-72; law lectr. CloseUp Fedn., 1984—; panel chmn. Md. Health Claims Arbitration Act, 1983—. Clk., permanent jud. com. Nat. Capitol Presbytery, 1980-85; bd. dirs. ARC, 1983—, Montgomery County Ch.; mem. bd. arbitrators NASD, 1986—; counsel Nat. Assn. of the Deaf, 1976—. Served to capt. AUS, 1942-46. Decorated Bronze Star. Mem. Nat. Assn. Security Dealers (bd. arbitrators 1986—), St. Andrew's Soc. Washington, Am. Legion. Club: Chatterbox (Washington). General corporate, Family and matrimonial, Probate. Office: 800 Securities Bldg 729 15th St NW Washington DC 20005-2120

SNYDER, KENT VICTOR, lawyer; b. Kansas City, Mo., Dec. 18, 1952; s. Marvin Kinyon and Emelie Annette (Kirk) S.; m. Janice Lynn Simons, Aug. 11, 1974 (div. Apr. 1978). BS cum laude, Kansas State U., 1975; JD, Lewis and Clark Coll., 1978. Bar: Oreg. 1978, U.S. Dist. Ct. Oreg., U.S. Ct. Appeals (9th cir.). Legal intern gen. counsel U.S. EPA, Washington, 1977; law clk. to presiding justice Oreg. Ct. Appeals, Salem, 1978-79; sole practice Portland, Oreg., 1979-82; prin. Snyder Bankruptcy Legal Services, Portland, 1982—. Author: Chapter 13, 1987; editor Lewis and Clark Law Rev., 1977-78. Founding dir., treas. Community Action Agy. Portland, 1983. Mem. ABA, Oreg. Bar Assn. (debtor-creditor sect.), Multnomah Bar Assn., Comml. Law League Am., Am. Banking Inst. Avocations: rowing, sailing. Bankruptcy. Office: Snyder Bankruptcy Legal Services 424 NW 19th Ave Portland OR 97209

SNYDER, MARIE ELIZABETH, nurse lawyer; b. Kingston, Pa., Oct. 21, 1945; d. Robert and Madge June (Dymond) S. BS, U. Pa., 1967; MS, Boston U., 1969; JD, Suffolk U., 1977. Bar: Mass. 1977, U.S. Dist. Ct. Mass. 1982, U.S. Supreme Ct. 1982. Staff nurse psychiatry Inst. Pa. Hosp., Phila., 1967-68; clin. specialist adult psychiat. nursing Boston City Hosp., 1969-70; instr. community and mental health nursing Boston City Hosp. Sch. Nursing, 1970-73; project coordinator mental health integration grant Newton (Mass.) Jr. Coll., 1973-74; project dir. mental health and social services, adolescent services North End Community Health Ctr., Boston, 1975-79; sole practice Boston, 1977-81; assoc. clinic mgr. pvt. group practice South Shore Counseling Assocs. Inc., Quincy, Mass., 1979-81; clin. assoc. Ronal G. Rosso and Assocs., South Weymouth, Mass., 1981—; ptnr. Snyder and Sweeney, Boston, 1981—; cons. Glover Meml. Hosp., Needham, Mass., 1975—, Quincy City Hosp., 1981—, Edith Nourse Rodgers VA Hosp., Bedford, Mass., 1983—, D.C. Nurses' Assn. 1985; adj. assoc. prof. Boston U. Sch. Nursing, 1981-83; mem. clin. faculty Harvard Sch. Pub. Health, Mass. Gen. Hosp., Erich Lindemann Mental Health Ctr. 1975-77. Contbr. articles to profl. jours. Bd. dirs. Planned Parenthood League of Mass., 1976—; mem. mental health task force Mass. League of Neighborhood Health Ctrs., 1974-77. Mem. ABA, Mass. Nurses Assn. (bd. dirs. 1981—, mem. various coms., Outstanding Leadership award 1983), Am. Assn. Nurse Attys. (pres. New Eng. chpt. 1985-87), Mass. Bar Assn., Women's Bar Assn., Am. Soc. Law and Medicine. Health, Family and matrimonial, Probate. Home: 185 Norton St Weymouth MA 02191 Office: Snyder and Sweeney 102 Union Wharf Boston MA 02109

SNYDER, PAUL, JR., lawyer; b. Hollywood, Calif., Jan. 18, 1943; s. Paul and Helen Jean (Trayan) S.; m. Kathy Jane Pope, Oct. 7, 1945 (div.); m. 2d, Martha Kate Frick, May 15, 1948; children—Jeffrey Randall, Suzanne Leigh. B.A., U. Colo., 1965, J.D., 1967. Bar: Colo. 1967. Assoc. Williams, Taussig & Trine, 1967-70; ptnr. Taussig, McCarthy & Snyder, 1970-73; of counsel Taussig & Cobb, 1974-75; pres. Snyder, Neuman & Enwall, P.C., 1978-81, Paul Snyder, Jr., P.C., Boulder, Colo., 1981-83; ptnr. Martin and Snyder, 1983-85, Brauchli, Snyder, Jevons and Johnson, 1986—; faculty Nat. Inst. Trial Advocacy, 1982—. Chmn. Boulder Growth Mgmt. Task Force, 1980-81. Mem. Colo. Bar Assn., Boulder Bar Assn., Assn. Trial Lawyers Am., Colo. Trial Lawyers Assn. State civil litigation, Personal injury. Home: 2444 10th St Boulder CO 80302 Office: 2010 14th St Boulder CO 80302

SNYDER, PAUL STEWART, lawyer; b. Ashland, Ky., Mar. 11, 1949; s. James Thomas and Martha Mayo (Stewart) S. BA, U. Ky., 1971, JD, 1974. Bar: Ky. 1974, U.S. Dist Ct. (ea. dist.) Ky. 1977. Sole practice Ashland, 1975—; pres. Info. Systems Inc., 1978—. Mem. ABA (contbr. articles to jour.), Ky. Bar Assn. Presbyterian. Avocations: tennis, computers. Computer, Bankruptcy, General practice. Home: 810 20th St Ashland KY 41101 Office: 306 Kitchen Bldg PO Box 1067 Ashland KY 41105-1067

SNYDER, RICHARD JOSEPH, lawyer; b. Boston, June 18, 1939; s. Harris H. and Ruth (Galner) S.; m. Joyce Marshall Snyder Serwitz, Aug. 19, 1962; children—Robert M., Lauren E., John K.; m. 2d Susana Gohiman, Apr. 11, 1982. B.S. in Bus. Adminstrn. with honors, Babson Coll., 1960; LL.B. with honors, Boston U., 1963; LL.M., Georgetown U., 1966. Bar: Mass. 1963, U.S. Dist. Ct. Mass. 1968, U.S. Tx Ct. 1966, U.S. Ct. Appeals (1st Cir.)

1968, U.S. Supreme Ct. 1968. Trial atty. Dept. Justice, 1963-66; sole practice Boston, 1966-75; adminstrv. mng. sr. ptnr. Goldstein & Manello, Boston, 1976—; lectr. in law Babson Coll., 1966—. Contbr. articles to profl. jours. Bd. dirs. The Sunday Sch., Inc., 1974-85, pres., 1976-85: trustee Babson Coll., 1977—, mem. exec. com., 1979—, chmn., 1984—; mem. bus. and profl. leadership com. Boston Symphony Orch.; bd. dirs. Babson Recreation Ctr., chmn., 1987—; trustee Mass. Corp. for Ednl. Telecommunications, 1985—, vich chmn., 1986—. Fellow Mass. Bar Found.; mem. ABA, Mass. Bar Assn., Boston Bar Assn., Am. Bus. Law Assn. (chmn. real property com. 1976-77, pres. North Atlantic region 1976-77), Nat. Assn. Coll. and Univ. Attys., Mass. Conveyancers Assn., New Eng. Land Title Assn., Babson Coll. Alumni Assn. (pres. 1977-79). Clubs: Minuteman Yacht, Downtown. Real property, Landlord-tenant, General corporate. Home: 12 Harborwatch Rd Burlington VT 05401 Office: Goldstein & Manello 265 Franklin St Boston MA 02110

SNYDER, ROBERT JOHN, lawyer; b. Phila., June 2, 1952; s. Robert John and Lilja (Anderson) S. B.A., St. John's U., 1974; J.D., U. N.D., 1977. Bar: N.D. 1977, Minn. 1977, U.S. Dist. Ct. N.D. 1977, U.S. Ct. Appeals (8th cir.) 1982, U.S. Supreme Ct. 1982. Ptnr. Bickle, Coles & Snyder, Chartered, Bismarck, N.D., 1977—; alt. bd. dirs. Legal Aid N.D., Bismarck, 1982-84. Vol. Bismarck United Way, 1979; active talking book S.D. State Program for Handicapped, Pierre, 1983-84. Named one of Outstanding Young Men of Am., 1979. Mem. ABA, Assn. Trial Lawyers Am., N.D. Bar Assn. (com. revision of pattern jury instrns. 1981, revision code of profl. responsibility 1983-87), Internat. Platform Assn., Mensa, Intertel. Bismarck Jaycees (outstanding officer 1979, Outstanding Young Bismarcker 1985). Lodge: Elks. Criminal, Personal injury, State and federal civil litigation. Office: Bickle Coles & Snyder Chartered PO Box 2071 311 N Mandan St Bismarck ND 58502

SNYDER, SAM A., oil company executive, lawyer; b. Helen, W.Va., Sept. 11, 1930; s. Russell Brown and Bess Kate (Swim) S.; m. Dorothy Martha Berry, Oct. 26, 1973. Student, Concord Coll., Athens, W.Va., 1947-50; LL.B., So. Meth. U., 1953. Bar: Tex. 1953, Calif. 1962. Landman Union Oil Co., Midland, Tex., 1955-60; atty. Union Oil Co., 1961-69, asst. counsel, 1969-73, asst. gen. counsel, 1973-85, v.p., gen. counsel, 1985—. Served with U.S. Army, 1953-55. Mem. ABA, Angeles County Bar Assn., Am. Soc. Internat. Law, Fgn. Law Assn., Soc. Mining Law Antiquarians. Republican. Clubs: Petroleum, Jonathan (Los Angeles). Avocations: collecting books, home computers; reading. Home: 3740 Greenhill Rd Pasadena CA 91107 Office: Unocal Corp 1201 W 5th St Los Angeles CA 90051 *

SNYDER, STUART JAY, lawyer, real estate broker; b. Balt., May 15, 1945; s. Bernard Ben-Zion and Louise (Guliere) S. Bar: Md. 1968, U.S. Dist. Ct. Md. 1968, U.S. Tax Ct. 1970, U.S. Ct. Appeals (4th cir.) 1969. Sole practice Balt., 1968—. Federal civil litigation, Personal injury, Criminal. Office: 231 St Paul Pl Baltimore MD 21202

SNYDER, VERNON GILBERT, III, lawyer; b. Greensboro, N.C., Mar. 23, 1952; s. Vernon Gilbert Jr. and Evelyn Rose (Fields) S.; m. Jessica Gay Fleming, Dec. 23, 1978; 1 child, Vernon Gilbert, IV. AB, U. N.C., 1977; JD cum laude, Campbell U., Buies Creek, N.C., 1980. Bar: N.C. 1980, U.S. Dist. Ct. (ea. dist.) N.C. 1981, U.S. Supreme Ct. 1984. Assoc. Gaylord, Singleton & McNally, P.A., Greenville, N.C., 1980-83; ptnr. Gaylord, Singleton, McNally, Strickland & Snyder, Greenville, 1984—. Bd. editors Campbell U. Law Rev., 1979-80. Bd. dirs. Pitt County Mental Health Assn., Greenville, 1985—. Recipient Am. Jurisprudence awards Lawyers Cooop. Pub. Co., 1979, 80; Campbell U. Law scholar, 1978-80; research scholar Campbell U. Sch. Law, 1979. Mem. ABA, N.C. Bar Assn., Pitt County Bar Assn. Democrat. Methodist. General practice, Personal injury, Real property. Home: 101 Woodhaven Rd Greenville NC 27834 Office: Gaylord Singleton et al 206 S Washington St PO Box 545 Greenville NC 27835

SNYDER, WILLIAM ARTHUR, JR., lawyer; b. Balt., July 11, 1940; s. William Arthur and Nelda Merle (Bailey) S.; m. Robin E. Siver, June 29, 1968. B.A., Johns Hopkins U., 1960; J.D., U. Md., 1964. Bar: Md. 1964, D.C. 1976. Law clk. Ct. Appeals Md., 1964-65; assoc. Ober, Kaler, Grimes & Shriver, Balt., 1965-70, ptnr., 1971—. Fellow Am. Coll. Probate Counsel. Mem. ABA, Md. Bar Assn., Balt. City Bar Assn. Lutheran. Probate, State civil litigation, Estate taxation. Office: 1600 Maryland Nat Bank Bldg Baltimore MD 21202

SNYDERMAN, PERRY JAMES, lawyer; b. Chgo., Oct. 9, 1932; s. Max and Frances (Kaplan) S.; m. Elaine Pomper, Aug. 14, 1955; children: Michelle, Sol, Robin. BS, Bradley U., 1954; JD, DePaul U., 1959. Sr. ptnr. Rudnick & Wolfe, Chgo., 1960—; pvt. practice gen. real estate; resort property time-sharing project adminstr.; lectr. in field; instr. Real Estate Securities and Syndication Inst. Contbr. articles to profl. publs. Bd. dirs. Jewish Community Ctrs. Chgo., 1980; bd. overseers Chgo. Kent Coll. Law; mem. Urban Land Inst., 1980, Ill. Devel. Fin. Authority, Capital Devel. Bd. Served with U.S. Army 1956-58. Mem. ABA, Ill. State Bar Assn., Chgo. Bar Assn., Chgo. Council Lawyers. Real property. Home: 254 Hazel Ave Highland Park IL 60035 Office: Rudnick & Wolfe 30 N LaSalle St Chicago IL 60602

SOBECKI, THOMAS ALVA, lawyer; b. Toledo, Aug. 11, 1956; s. Raymond A. and Louise (Kretz) S. BA, U. Toledo, 1978; JD, Northwestern U., 1981. Bar: Ohio 1981, Ill. 1985, U.S. Dist. Ct. (no. dist.) Ill. 1986. Assoc. Rudnick & Wolfe, Chgo., 1985-86; sole practice Toledo, 1986—. Served to capt. JAGC, U.S. Army, 1981-85. Mem. Assn. Trial Lawyers Am., Fed. Bar Assn., ABA, Ill. State Bar Assn., Chgo. Bar Assn., Ohio Bar Assn., Toledo Bar Assn. Democrat. Roman Catholic. Avocations: tennis, jogging. State civil litigation, Federal civil litigation, Administrative and regulatory. Home: 3404 River Rd Toledo OH 43614 Office: 811 Spitzer Bldg Toledo OH 43604

SOBEL, ERWIN, lawyer; b. Kosice, Czechoslovakia, Apr. 24, 1938; came to U.S., 1952; s. Alexander and Ella (Eisner) S.; m. Rebecca Blooming, Aug. 21, 1960 (div. 1968); children: Michael, Jessica: m. Valerie Vayda, Aug. 29, 1971; children Andre, Simone. JD, Southwestern U. Sch. Law, Los Angeles, 1964. Bar: Calif. 1965, U.S. Dist. Ct. (cen. dist.) Calif. 1965, U.S. Ct. Appeals (9th cir.) 1969. Sole practice Los Angeles, 1965-66, 68—; sr. ptnr. Grayson, Green, Sobel, Vodnoy, Los Angeles, 1965-68; bd. dirs. Microvision Inc., Orange, Calif., 1977-78; lectr. med. law U. So. Calif. Dental Sch., Los Angeles, 1977. Served to sgt. U.S. Army, 1957-63. Mem. ABA, Nat. Trial Lawyer Assn., Calif. Trial Lawyers Assn., Los Angeles County Bar Assn. Republican. Avocation: chess. Personal injury, Insurance, State civil litigation. Home: 8930 St Ives Dr Los Angeles CA 90069 Office: Law Offices of Erwin Sobel 5820 Wilshire Blvd #200 Los Angeles CA 90036

SOBEL, LARRY D., lawyer; b. Phila., Apr. 22, 1951; s. Herman and Sylvia (Nagel) S.; m. Suzanne Sobel, Dec. 20, 1950; children: Kimberly, Evan. BS, Drexel U.; JD, U. Pa. Bar: Pa. 1976, N.Y. 1984, Calif. 1984, D.C. 1985. Assoc. Ballard, Spahr, Andrews & Ingersoll, Phila., 1976-84; ptnr. Mudge, Rose, Guthrie, Alexander & Ferdon, Los Angeles, 1984-86, Orrick, Herrington & Sutcliffe, Los Angeles, 1986—; faculty mem., lectr. U. Pa., Phila., 1982, Northwest Ctr. for Profl. Edn., Denver, 1982-83. Mem. ABA (com. tax exempt financing), N.Y. Bar Assn., Calif. Bar Assn., D.C. Bar Assn., Pa. Bar Assn., Phila. Bar Assn., Pa. Bar Inst., Nat. Assn. Bond Lawyers (com. on arbitrage 1983—), Practising Law Inst. (lectr., faculty mem. 1985—), Bond Atty.'s Workshop (lectr., faculty mem. 1979—). Republican. Jewish. Avocations: tennis, jogging. Municipal bonds, Corporate taxation. Home: 29031 Warnick Rd Rancho Palo Verde CA 90274 Office: Orrick Herrington & Sutcliffe 444 S Flower St Los Angeles CA 90017

SOBIESKI, WANDA GRAHAM, lawyer; b. Kansas City, Mo., Nov. 7, 1947; d. Frank Jr. and V. Juanita (Parker) G.; m. Robert W. Glenn, Aug. 23, 1969 (div. May 1981); children: Daran, Alana, Elise. BA, Wichita State U.; MA, U. Tenn., JD. Bar: Tenn., U.S. Dist. Ct. (ea. dist.) Tenn., U.S. Ct. Appeals (6th cir.), U.S. Claims Ct. Tchr. Hanover (N.H.) High Sch., 1969-70, Lebanon (N.H.) High Sch., 1970-71; instr. U. Tenn., Knoxville, 1971-79; assoc. Baker, Worthington, Crossley, Stansberry & Woolf, Knoxville, 1982—. Regional dir. Women Against Violence Against Women, 1976-79; bd. dirs. Knoxville Women's Ctr., 1975-80; mem. Council on Adoptive Children, Knoxville, 1982—. Named Regional Best Oralist, Am. Coll Trial Lawyers, 1982; recipient Nat. Moot Ct. championship Am. Coll. Trial Lawyers and N.Y. City Bar., N.Y.C., 1982. Mem. ABA, Tenn. Bar Assn., Knoxville Bar Assn., Assn. Trial Lawyers Am., East Tenn. Lawyers Assn. for Women, NOW (pres. Knoxville chpt. 1978-79). Federal civil litigation, Construction, Civil rights. Home: 5105 Wyndcroft Dr Knoxville TN 37914 Office: Baker Worthington Crossley Stansberry & Woolf 530 Gay SE Knoxville TN 37902

SOBLE, JAMES BARRY, lawyer; b. Chgo., Apr. 14, 1942; s. Julius R. and Bernyce (Morris) Rossuck; children—Debra, Jeffrey, Tony, Leslie; m. Ann S. Valenstein, June 29, 1980. B.A., Grinnell Coll., 1963; J.D., Northwestern U., 1966. Bar: Ill. 1966, Fla. 1974. Assoc. Deutsch & Peskin, Chgo., 1966-68; ptnr. Siegel & Soble, 1969-71 Peskin & Soble, 1972-73; exec. v.p., corp. counsel Millstream Corp., Sunrise, Fla., 1973-79; pvt. developer, Ft. Lauderdale, Fla., 1979-81; ptnr., shareholder Jacobs, Robbins, Gaynor, Hampp, Burns, Cole & Shasteen, P.A., St. Petersburg, Fla., 1981-83; ptnr. Taub & Williams, Tampa, Fla., 1984—; lectr. Law Forum, Inc., 1982—, St. Petersburg Bar Assn., 1982—. Pres., bd. dirs. Gulf Coast Jewish Family Services of Pinellas County, 1984—. Mem. ABA, Fla. Bar Assn., Ill. Bar Assn., St. Petersburg Bar Assn., Hillsborough County Bar Assn. Jewish. Real property, Banking. Home: 3029 Gull Pl Clearwater FL 33520 Office: 100 S Ashley Dr Suite 2100 Tampa FL 33602

SOBLE, STEPHEN M., lawyer; b. Rochester, N.Y., Aug. 15, 1951; s. Jack and Zella (Allen) S.; m. Judith Ann Schoenberg; children: Alexandra, Maya. BA with honors, Syracuse U., 1972; postgrad., London Sch. Econs. and Polit. Sci., 1971-75, The Sch. of Oriental and African Studies, London, 1973-74, U. B.C., Vancouver, Can., 1974, Stanford U., 1974-75, Nat. Taiwan U., Taipei, 1974-75; JD, Harvard U., 1978. Bar: D.C. 1978, U.S. Dist. Ct. D.C. 1978, U.S. Ct. Appeals (D.C. cir.) 1978, U.S. Ct. Internat. Trade 1985, U.S. Supreme Ct. 1985. Assoc. Surrey & Morse, Washington, 1978-84; of counsel Morgan, Lewis & Bockius, Washington, 1984-86; ptnr. Goodwin & Soble, Washington, 1986—; lectr. internat. tax program Harvard U. Law Sch., Cambridge, Mass., 1977-78; gen. counsel Assn. for South-East Asian Nations-U.S. Bus. Council, Washington, 1984—. Sr. editor East Asian Exec. Reports, 1979—; editor Mid. East Exec. Reports, 1980—. Mem. ABA (internat. law sect.), Am. Soc. Internat. Law, Nat. Com. on U.S.-China Relations, N.Y. Acad. of Scis., U.S. Assn. for South-East Asian Nations Ctr. for Tech. Exchange. Private international, Contracts commercial, General corporate. Home: 504 E St NE Washington DC 20002 Office: Goodwin & Soble 1300 19th St NW Washington DC 20036

SOBOL, ALAN J., lawyer; b. Newark, Dec. 18, 1948; s. Max and Marjorie (Namorovsky) S.; m. Kathreen Miriam Campbell, June 2, 1984; 1 child, Laura Emily. B.A. with honors, U. Md., 1971; J.D., U. Akron, 1974. Bar: Ohio 1974, U.S. Ct. Appeals (2d cir.) 1975, U.S. Ct. Appeals (1st and 6th cirs.) 1976, U.S. Supreme Ct. 1978, D.C. 1978, Md. 1978, U.S. Ct. Appeals (4th cir.) 1979, U.S. Ct. Appeals (5th, 9th and 11th cirs.) 1982, U.S. Dist. Ct. D.C. 1983, Conn. 1986, U.S. DIst. Ct. Conn. 1986. Trial atty. criminal div. U.S. Dept. Justice, Washington, 1974-79, spl. asst. U.S. atty., Alexandria, Va., 1979-80, Key West, Fla., 1980, San Francisco, 1980-81, trial atty. gen. litigation criminal div., Washington, 1980-82; assoc. gen. counsel Nat. RR Passenger Corp., Washington, 1982-86; assoc. Tyler, Cooper & Alcorn, New Haven, 1986—. Case & Comments editor Akron Law Rev., 1972-74. Recipient U.S. Atty. Gen.'s Honor Law Grad. award U.S. Dept. Justice, 1974. Mem. ABA (litigation sect. 1982—), D.C. Bar Assn. (litigation sect. 1982—), Phi Alpha Delta, Phi Sigma Alpha, Phi Sigma Delta (house master 1969-70). Federal civil litigation, Contracts commercial, Labor. Home: 39 Filbert St Hamden CT 06517 Office: Tyler Cooper & Alcorn 205 Church St New Haven CT 06509

SOBOL, LAWRENCE RAYMOND, lawyer; b. Kansas City, Mo., May 8, 1950; s. Haskell and Mary (Press) S.; m. Maureen Patricia O'Connell, May 29, 1976; children: David, Kevin. BBA, U. Tex., 1972; JD, U. Mo., 1975. Bar: Mo. 1975, U.S. Dist. Ct. (ea. dist.) Mo. 1975. Gen. counsel, gen. ptnr. Edward D. Jones & Co., Maryland Heights, Mo., 1975—; allied mem. N.Y.C. Stock Exchange, 1977—; sec. Lake Communications Corp., Conroe, Tex., 1984-86; sec., bd. dirs. Cornerstone Mortgage Inc., St. Louis, 1986; v.p., bd. dirs. Tempus Corp., St. Louis, 1984—. Omar Robinson Meml. scholar U. Mo., 1974-75. Mem. ABA (securities law com. 1982—), Met. St. Louis Bar Assn. (securities law sect.), Nat. Assn. Securities Dealers (dist. bus. com., registered prin. officer), Phi Eta Sigma. Republican. Jewish. Club: Woodsmill Racquet (St. Louis). Avocations: tennis, golf. Securities, Real property. Office: Edward D Jones & Co 201 Progress Pkwy Maryland Heights MO 63043

SOBOTA, JOHN RAYMOND, lawyer; b. Wilkes-Barre, Pa., May 21, 1956; s. Raymond John and Anne Jane (Dugan) S. Student, Rider Coll., 1974-77; BA, Wilkes Coll., 1978; JD, Drake U., 1981. Bar: Iowa 1982, Pa. 1983, U.S. Dist. Ct. (mid. dist.) Pa., 1984. Assoc. F.G. Wieslander P.C., Altoona, Iowa, 1982-83; sole practice Wilkes-Barre, 1983—; asst. pub. defender Luzerne County, Wilkes-Barre, 1986—. Mem. ABA, Pa. Bar Assn., Assn. Trial Lawyers Am., Pa. Trial Lawyers Assn., West Side Jaycees (bd. dirs. 1985, sec. 1986—), Phi Alpha Delta. Republican. Roman Catholic. Club: Wyo. Valley Striders (Wilkes-Barre). Lodge: Fraternal Order of Police. Avocations: running, flying. Criminal, Family and matrimonial, Real property. Office: 1120 United Penn Bank Bldg Wilkes-Barre PA 18701

SOCOL, MELINDA, lawyer; b. N.Y.C., Jan. 22, 1952; d. Edward Socol and Ann (Lesser) Rosenstein. BA summa cum laude, CCNY, 1972; JD, Fordham U., 1977. Bar: N.Y. 1978, U.S. Dist. Ct. (so. dist.) N.Y. 1978, U.S. Dist. Ct. (ea. dist.) N.Y. 1979, U.S. Ct. Appeals (2d cir.) 1986. Assoc. Davis, Polk & Wardwell, N.Y.C., 1977-83, Stuart, Zavin, Sinnreich & Wasserman, N.Y.C., 1983-84; ptnr. Gaynin & Socol, N.Y.C., 1985—; mem. faculty Nat. Inst. Trial Advocacy N.E. Regional Seminar, Hempstead, N.Y., 1981—; instr. trial technique Hofstra Law Sch., Hempstead, 1981—; moot ct. judge Fordham Law Sch., N.Y.C., 1982—; instr. trial advocacy Benjamin Cardozo Law Sch., N.Y.C., 1983—. Recipient N.Y. State Regents scholarship. Mem. ABA (litagation and copyright sects.), Fed. Bar Council, N.Y. State Bar Assn., N.Y.C. Bar Assn. (entertainment com.), Phi Beta Kappa. Avocations: writing, acting, singing. Federal civil litigation, State civil litigation, Trademark and copyright. Office: Gaynin & Socol 600 Madison Ave New York NY 10022

SODEN, PAUL A., lawyer; b. N.Y.C., Feb. 3, 1944; s. Leo J. and Mildred E. (Callahan) S.; m. Irene M. Davis, Aug. 3, 1968; children—Christina M., Paul A. A.B., Fordham U., 1965, J.D., 1968. Bar: N.Y. State bar 1968. Assoc. Cahill, Gordon & Reindel, N.Y.C., 1968-74; corp. counsel Technicon Corp., Tarrytown, N.Y., 1974-76, asst. gen. counsel, asst. sec., 1976-78, sr. v.p., gen. counsel, sec., 1978-87; v.p., dir. internat. law Sterling Drug Inc., 1987—. Mem. Am. Bar Assn., N.Y. State Bar Assn. Club: Scarsdale (N.Y.) Golf. General corporate, Antitrust, Contracts commercial. Office: Technicon Instruments Corp 511 Benedict Ave Tarrytown NY 10591

SODERMAN, KENNETH JOHN, lawyer; b. Putnam, Conn., Jan. 19, 1951; s. John W. and Virginia J. (Ruisniemi) S.; m. Vivian P. Hale, July 19, 1980 (div. May 1986); 1 child, Erik K.H.; m. Jill G. Jones, July 26, 1986. BA, Clark U., 1971; MBA, U. Conn., 1974, JD, 1975. Bar: Conn. 1975. Tax acct. Arthur Young & Co., Stamford, Conn., 1975-78; fed. tax adminstr. RCA Corp., N.Y.C., 1978; tax editor Research Inst. Am., N.Y.C., 1979-85; tax mgr. Forbes Inc., N.Y.C., 1985-87; editor Prentice-Hall Info. Services, Paramus, N.J., 1987—; lectr. 41st annual inst. on fed. taxation, NYU, 1982. Mem. ABA (tax sect.), Conn. Bar Assn. (tax and corps. sects.). Corporate taxation, Estate taxation, Personal income taxation. Office: Prentice Hall Info Services Inc 240 Frisch Ct Paramus NJ 07652

SODERQUIST, LARRY DEAN, lawyer, educator, cons.; b. Ypsilanti, Mich., July 20, 1944; s. Hugh E. and Emma A. (Johnson) S.; m. Ann Mangelsdorf, June 15, 1968; children—Hans, Lars. B.S., Eastern Mich. U., 1966; J.D., Harvard U., 1969. Bar: N.Y. 1971, Tenn. 1981. Assoc. Milbank, Tweed, Hadley & McCoy, N.Y.C., 1971-76; assoc. prof. law U. Notre Dame, South Bend, Ind., 1976-80, prof. 1980-81; vis. prof. law Vanderbilt U. Law Sch., Nashville, 1980-81, prof. 1981—. Cons. to various law firms; spl. master U.S. Dist. Ct. (no. dist.) Ohio, 1977. Served from 1st lt. to capt. U.S. Army 1969-71. Decorated Army Commendation medal. Mem. ABA, Am. Law Inst. Presbyterian. Author: Corporations: A Problem Approach, 1979, 2d edit., 1986, Understanding the Securities Laws, 1987; Securities Regulation: A Problem Approach, 1982; Law of Federal Estate and Gift Taxation: Code Commentary, 1978, Analysis, 1980; contbr. numerous articles to legal jours. Legal education, General corporate, Securities. Home: 421 Sunnyside Dr Nashville TN 37205 Office: Vanderbilt U Law School Nashville TN 37240

SOET, HENRY DAVID, lawyer; b. Grand Rapids, Mich., Oct. 20, 1935; s. John Charles and Marian Josephine (Vandermeulen) S.; m. Christine Clara Hubacker, June 4, 1964 (div. July 1975); children: Peter Hendrik, Johanna Eastman; m. Ann Sullivan, Jan. 21, 1978. AB, U. Mich., 1957, JD, 1960. Bar: Mich. 1961, U.S. Dist. Ct. (we. dist.) Mich. 1962, U.S. Ct. Appeals (6th cir.) 1965, U.S. Dist. Ct. (ea. dist.) 1974. Asst. U.S. atty. U.S. Dept. Justice, Grand Rapids, 1961-64, dep. atty., 1964-65; ptnr. Bergstrom, Slykhouse & Shaw, Grand Rapids, 1965-73, Pinsky & Soet and Pinsky, Smith & Soet, Grand Rapids, 1973—; chmn. Mich. Probate Judges Retirement Bd., 1982. Mem. Grand Rapids Human Relations Com., 1970; chmn. Kent County Dems., Grand Rapids, 1974, sec., 1972. Mem. Mich. Bar Assn., Assn. Trial Lawyers Am., Mich. Trial Lawyers Assn. Mem. Unitarian Ch. Club: Peninsular (Grand Rapids). Personal injury, State civil litigation, Federal civil litigation. Office: Pinsky Smith & Soet 1400 McKay Tower Grand Rapids MI 49503

SOFAER, ABRAHAM DAVID, legal advisor, judge, legal educator; b. Bombay, India, May 6, 1938; came to U.S., 1948, naturalized, 1959; m. Marian Bea Scheuer, Oct. 23, 1977; children: Daniel E., Michael J., Helen R., Joseph S., Aaron R. B.A. magna cum laude in History, Yeshiva Coll., 1962, LL.D., 1980; LL.B. cum laude (Root-Tilden scholar), NYU, 1965. Bar: N.Y. 1965. Law clk. U.S. Ct. Appeals, Washington, 1965-66, to; Hon. William J. Brennan, Jr., U.S. Supreme Ct., Washington, 1966-67; asst. U.S. atty. So. Dist. N.Y., N.Y.C., 1967-69; prof. law Columbia U., N.Y.C., 1969-79, Meyer prof. law and social research, 1974-75; adj. prof. law 1979-80; judge U.S. Dist. Ct. for So. Dist. N.Y., 1979-85; legal advisor Dept. State, Washington, 1985—; Brainerd Currie lectr. Duke U., Durham, N.C., 1975; hearing officer N.Y. Dept. Environ. Conservation, 1975-76. Author: War, Foreign Affairs and Constitutional Power: The Origins, 1976; contbr. articles to legal jours.; editor-in-chief: NYU Law Rev, 1964-65. Bd. dirs. Citizens Union and Moblzn. for Youth Legal Services, 1976-78. Served with USAF, 1956-59. Mem. Fed. Bar Assn., Am. Bar Assn., N.Y. Bar Assn., Am. Law Inst. Jewish. Jurisprudence. Office: Dept State Office Legal Advisor Washington DC 20520

SOFORENKO, JOEL FREDRICK, lawyer; b. Providence, Sept. 29, 1954; s. Irwin S. and Norma (Gladstone) S.; m. Rhonda Blazer, Dec. 2, 1978; 1 child, Julie Beth. AB, Franklin & Marshall Coll., 1976; JD, Suffolk U., 1979. Bar: Mass. 1979, U.S. Dist. Ct. Mass. 1980, U.S. Supreme Ct. 1984. Assoc. Burstein & DuPont, Springfield, Mass., 1980-81; sole practice Springfield, 1981-84; sr. ptnr. Soforenko & Assocs., P.C., Springfield, 1984—. State rep., aide Mass. Ho. of Reps., Boston, 1977-78; pres. Outer Belt Civic Assn., Springfield, 1986; bd. dirs. ACLU, Springfield, 1982-84. Named one of Outstanding Young Men of Am., 1981. Mem. ABA, Mass. Bar Assn., Hampden County Bar Assn., Assn. Trial Lawyers Am., Mass. Assn. Trial Attys., Springfield Jaycees (pres. 1982). Avocation: real estate. Personal injury, Real property, General corporate. Home: 170 Forest Hills Rd Springfield MA 01128 Office: Soforenko & Assocs PC 122 School St Springfield MA 01105

SOGG, WILTON SHERMAN, lawyer; b. Cleve., May 28, 1935; s. Paul P. and Julia (Cahn) S.; m. Saralee Frances Krow, Aug. 12, 1962 (div. July 1975); 1 child, Stephanie.; m. Linda Rocker Lehman, Dec. 22, 1979. A.B., Dartmouth Coll., 1956; J.D., Harvard U., 1959; Fulbright fellow, U. London, 1959-60. Bar: Ohio 1960, D.C. 1970, Fla. 1970, U.S. Supreme Ct., N.Y. 1985, U.S. Tax Ct. Assoc. Gottfried, Ginsberg, Guren & Merritt, 1960-63, ptnr., 1963-70; ptnr. Guren, Merritt, Feibel, Sogg & Cohen, Cleve., 1970-84; of counsel Hahn, Loeser, Freedheim, Dean and Wellman, Cleve., 1984-85; ptnr. Hahn Loeser & Parks, 1986—; trustee, pres. Cleve. Jewish News; adj. prof. Cleve. State Law Sch., 1960—; lectr. Harvard U. Law Sch., 1978-80. Author (with Howard M. Rossen); new and rev. vols. of Smith's Review Legal Gems series, 1969—; editor: Harvard Law Rev; Contbr. articles to profl. jours. Trustee Jewish Community Fedn. of Cleve., 1966—; bd. overseers Cleve. Marshall Coll. Law, Cleve. State U., 1969—; mem. State of Ohio Holocaust commn. Recipient Kane Meml. award Jewish Community Fedn., Cleve., 1970; named one of 10 outstanding young men Cleve. Jaycees, 1967, 68. Mem. German Philatelic Soc., ABA, Ohio Bar Assn., Cleve. Bar Assn., Cuyahoga County Bar Assn., Fla. Bar Assn., D.C. Bar Assn., N.Y. State Bar Assn., Am. Law Inst., Am. Soc. Corp. Secs., Phi Beta Kappa. Clubs: Oakwood (trustee), Chagrin Valley Hunt. General corporate, Legal education, Real property. Home: 5150 Three Village Dr Unit 2E Lyndhurst OH 44124 Office: 800 National City East 6th Bldg Cleveland OH 44114

SOKOL, MICHAEL BRUCE, lawyer; b. St. Paul, Feb. 19, 1954; s. Theodore Harvey Margulis and Harriet Sokol; m. Stacy Perl, July 4, 1976; children: Joshua Adam, Amy Beth. BS, U. Wis., 1976; JD, Hamline U., 1979. Bar: U.S. Dist. Ct. Minn. 1979, U.S. Ct. Appeals (8th cir.) 1979. Assoc. Deparcq Law Firm, Mpls., 1979-85; sole practice Mpls., 1985-86; ptnr. Resnick, Bartsh & Sokol, P.A., Mpls., 1985-86, Michael B. Sokol and Assocs., Mpls., 1986—; commr. No. Dakota County Cable Commn. Mem. ABA, Minn. Bar Assn., Assn. Trial Lawyers Am., Minn. Assn. Trial Lawyers, Hennepin County Bar Assn. State civil litigation, Personal injury, Workers' compensation. Office: 1800 Foshay Tower 821 Maquette Ave Minneapolis MN 55402

SOKOLOW, ASA D., lawyer; b. N.Y.C., Apr. 22, 1919; s. Harry J. and Dorothy (Turkeltaub) S.; m. Phyllis E. Cahen, Jan. 31, 1943 (dec. Apr. 1982); children—Jeffrey, Judith, Jonathan; m. Renee J. Ginsberg, June 11, 1984. Grad., Phillips Acad., Andover, Mass., 1936; B.A., Yale U., 1940, LL.B., 1947. Assoc. Cahill, Gordon and Reindel, N.Y.C., 1947-59; ptnr. Rosenman & Colin (and predecessor firm Rosenman Colin Freund Lewis & Cohen), N.Y.C., 1960—. Author: The Political Theory of Arthur J. Penty, 1940; co-author: Discovery Proceedings Under the Federal Rules, 1955. Past v.p., past trustee Park Ave. Synagogue, N.Y.C.; trustee Soc. for Advancement Judaism, N.Y.C., 1972—; bd. dirs. Lawyers Com. for Civil Rights Under Law, 1965—. Served to capt. U.S. Army, 1941-45; NATOUSA, ETO. Recipient Leadership award State of Israel Bonds, 1980. Mem. Assn. Bar City N.Y., N.Y. State Bar Assn., ABA. Democrat. Clubs: Morys (New Haven); Harmonie (N.Y.C.); Sunningdale Country (Scarsdale, N.Y.). Antitrust. Home: 141 E 88th St New York NY 10128 Office: Rosenman & Colin 575 Madison Ave New York NY 10022

SOKOLOW, LLOYD BRUCE, lawyer, psychotherapist; b. N.Y.C., Nov. 3, 1949; s. Edwin Jay and Harriet (Corman) S.; m. Christina Carol Smolinski, Jan. 27, 1979; 1 child, Joshua. BA, U. Buffalo, 1971, MS, 1974, JD, 1978, PhD, 1979. Bar: N.Y. 1979, U.S. Dist. Ct. (we. dist.) N.Y. 1979, U.S. Dist. Ct. (no. dist.) N.Y. 1982, Conn. 1985, U.S. Supreme Ct. 1985, U.S. Dist. Ct. Conn. 1986. Research scientist Research Inst. on Alcoholism, Buffalo, 1976-80; legal cons. N.Y. Gov.'s Task Force on Drinking and Driving, Albany, 1979-82; pvt. practice health law Albany, N.Y., 1980—; counsel, dir. Conifer Park, Scotia, N.Y., 1982-84; consult. dir. alcohol treatment Inst. of Living, Hartford, Conn., 1984-86; pres. Lifestart Health Services, Schenectady, N.Y., 1986—; bd. dirs. Lifestart Health Services; cons. Constn. Health Network, Hartford, 1984-86; atty. Town of Knox, N.Y., 1980—. Bd. dirs. Schenectady (N.Y.) Community Service Bd., 1982—. Regent scholar NY State, 1967; Baldy fellow U. Buffalo, 1974, 78. Mem. ABA (task force on youth alcohol and drug abuse 1986), N.Y. State Bar Assn., Conn. Bar Assn. (chmn. lawyers impairment com. 1985-86), Am. Psychol. Assn. Health, Family and matrimonial, Real property. Office: 89 Columbia St Albany NY 12210

SOLA, ANTHONY MARCE, lawyer; b. Glen Cove, N.Y., Oct. 19, 1951; s. Marce S. and Mary Elizabeth (Boulon) S.; m. Maria Rosario Perez, Jan. 17, 1975; children—Robert Anthony, Kevin Marce, Thomas Anthony. B.S., Cornell U., 1973; J.D., St. John's U., Jamaica, N.Y., 1977. Bar: N.Y. 1978, U.S. Dist. Ct. (ea. and so. dists.) N.Y. 1978, D.C. 1979. Assoc. Martin,

Clearwater & Bell, N.Y.C., 1977-83, ptnr., 1983—. Mem. Assn. Bar City of N.Y., N.Y. State Bar Assn., N.Y. County Trial Lawyers Assn. Republican. Roman Catholic. Personal injury, Insurance, State civil litigation. Home: 53 Lake Dr Manhasset Hills NY 11040 Office: Martin Clearwater & Bell 220 E 42d St New York NY 10017

SOLANO, CARL ANTHONY, lawyer; b. Pittston, Pa., Mar. 26, 1951; s. Nick D. and Catherine A. (Occhiato) S. BS magna cum laude, U. Scranton, 1973; JD cum laude, Vilanova U., 1976. Bar: Pa. 1976, U.S. Dist. Ct. (ea. dist.) Pa. 1978, U.S. Ct. Appeals (3rd cir.) 1980, U.S. Ct. Appeals (5th cir.) 1981, U.S. Supreme Ct. 1982, U.S. Ct. Appeals (9th cir.) 1986. Law clerk Hon. Alfred L. Luongo U.S. Dist. Ct., Ea. Dist. Pa., Phila., 1976-78; assoc. Schnader, Harrison, Segal & Lewis, Phila., 1978-84, ptnr., 1985—. Mem. ABA, Pa. Bar Assn. (statutory law com. 1980—), Phila. Bar Assn., St. Thomas More Soc., Justinian Soc., Order of Coif, Pi Gamma Mu. Roman Catholic. Federal civil litigation, State civil litigation, Libel. Home: 619 Heritage Manor Ardmore PA 19003 Office: Schnader Harrison Segal & Lewis 1600 Market St Suite 3600 Philadelphia PA 19103

SOLBACH, JOHN MARTIN, III, lawyer, state legislator; b. Clay Center, Kans., July 30, 1947; s. Roy and W. Jeanne (Swenson) Meek; m. Mary Patricia Kennedy, May 22, 1974. B.S., Kans. State U., 1973; postgrad. U. Kans., 1973-74; J.D., Washburn Law Sch., 1977. Bar: Kans. 1977, U.S. Dist. Ct. Kans. 1977. Sole practice, Lawrence, Kans., 1977—; mem. Kans. Ho. of Reps., 1979—, ranking minority mem. judiciary; Served with USMC, 1966-69, Vietnam. Decorated Purple Heart. Mem. Douglas County Bar Assn., Kans. Bar Assn. (Certs. Appreciation 1979-86), ABA. Democrat. Lodge: Sertoma. General practice, Legislative. Home: Route 1 Lawrence KS 66044 Office: Solbach Law Office 901 Kentucky St Suite 201 Lawrence KS 66044

SOLBERG, THOMAS ALLAN, lawyer, author; b. Parkers Prairie, Minn., Mar. 23, 1933; s. Francis A. and Gladys K. S.; m. Alla K. Swanton, June 27, 1981. B.B.A. in Fin., U. Miami, 1956; J.D., U. Mich., 1959, Bar: N.Y. 1959, U.S. Dist. Ct. (we. dist.) N.Y. 1959, Mich. 1959, Fla. 1975. Assoc. Harter, Secrest & Emery, Rochester, N.Y., 1959-68, ptnr., 1968—; lectr. Am. Coll. Bd. dirs. Rochester Rehab. Ctr. Served with USAFR, 1959-65. Mem. ABA (com. on closely held corps., tax sect.), N.Y. State Bar Assn., Monroe County Bar Assn., Estate Planning Council of Rochester. Club: Monroe Golf. Contbr. articles to legal and profl. publs. General corporate, Estate planning, Estate taxation. Office: Harter Secrest & Emery 700 Midtown Tower Rochester NY 14604

SOLBERG, WAYNE O., lawyer; b. Aneta, N.D., Apr. 4, 1932; s. George and Olga M. (Hovde) S.; m. Patricia A. Lind, Aug. 26, 1950; children: Ronald W., Mary P., Daniel G., Rebecca A., Roberta J., Jennifer L. BS in Archtl. Engring., N.D. State U., 1957, MS in Civil Engring., 1961; JD, U. N.D., 1966. Bar: N.D. 1966, U.S. Dist. Ct. N.D. 1966, U.S. Ct. Appeals (8th cir.) 1976, U.S. Supreme Ct. 1983. Ptnr. Solberg, Stewart, Boulger & Miller, Fargo, N.D., 1966—. Served to col. USAF and Air Nat. Guard, 1953-86. Lutheran. Lodges: Masons, Shriners, Lions (v.p. 1986—). State civil litigation, Construction, General practice. Office: Solberg Stewart Boulger & Miller 1129 5th Ave S PO Box 1897 Fargo ND 58107

SOLECKI, TRINA ANNE, lawyer; b. New Haven, Conn., June 6, 1955; d. Henry Joseph and Stephanie Anne (Paszynski) S. Student, Mt. Holyoke Coll., 1973-74; BA, So. Conn. State U., 1977; JD, U. Bridgeport, 1980. Bar: Conn. 1982, U.S. Dist. Ct. Conn. 1982. Law. clk. to presiding judge Conn. Superior Ct., Middletown, 1980-81, asst. clk., 1981-85; asst. city atty. City of Middletown, 1985—. Named one of Outstanding Young Women Am., 1983. Mem. ABA, Conn. Bar Assn., Middlesex County Bar Assn. (sec. 1986—), U. Bridgeport Sch. Law Alumni Assn. (sec. 1980-85, v.p. 1985—), Altrusa Profl. Women. Roman Catholic. Avocation: softball. Civil rights, Government contracts and claims, Local government. Home: 805 Chamberlain Hill Rd Middletown CT 06457 Office: City of Middletown 245 DeKoven Dr PO Box 1300 Middletown CT 06457

SOLIS, CARLOS, lawyer; b. Managua, Nicaragua, May 15, 1945; came to U.S., 1952; s. Carlos and Luisa (Serrano) S.; m. Debra-Lynne Stean, Aug. 15, 1981. BA, U. San Francisco, 1967, JD, 1969. Bar: Calif. 1970, U.S. Dist. Ct. (cen. and no. dists.) Calif. 1970, U.S. Ct. Appeals (9th cir.) 1970, U.S. Dist. Ct. (ea. dist.) Calif. 1972, U.S. Dist. Ct. (so. dist.) Calif. 1973, U.S. Supreme Ct. 1973. Assoc. Kindel & Anderson, Los Angeles, 1976-76, ptnr., 1976—; bd. advisors Los Angeles Internat. Trade Devel. Corp., 1981—. Assoc. editor U. San Francisco Law Rev., 1968-69; contbr. articles to profl. jours. Bd. dirs. Los Angeles ARC, 1978—, Los Angeles March of Dimes, 1982—, Am. Diabetes Assn., 1986—, Los Angeles Pub. Theater Found., 1978-81, Young Musicians Found., 1979-80; vice chmn. bd. Los Angeles United Way, 1982—, bd. dirs., 1980—, corp. bd. dirs. 1982—. Mem. Los Angeles Jr. Chamber (Most Improved com. award 1975, Dir. of Yr. award 1977, Outstanding Bus. Leader award 1980), Assocs. Los Angeles C. of C., U. San Francisco Alumni Assn. (pres. San Gabriel Valley chpt. 1976-80), Latin Am. Ctr. Assocs. (pres. 1980-82, bd. advisors 1980—), Alpha Sigmu Nu, Phi Delta Phi. Club: Jonathan (Los Angeles). Federal civil litigation, State civil litigation, Consumer commercial. Home: 590 Bradford St Pasadena CA 91105 Office: Kindel & Anderson 555 S Flower St Los Angeles CA 90071

SOLISH, JONATHAN CRAIG, lawyer; b. Monticello, N.Y., May 27, 1949; s. David Julius and Gertrude (Hellman) S.; m. Dhana Krushkhov, Dec. 30, 1981; 1 child, Nickolas Brewster. BA, U. Calif., Santa Cruz, 1971; JD, UCLA, 1975. Bar: Calif. 1975, U.S. Dist. Ct. (cen. dist.) Calif. 1977, U.S. Ct. Appeals (9th cir.) 1979. Ptnr. Solish, Jordan & Wiener, Los Angeles, Calif., 1977—. Mem. Los Angeles Olympics Citizens Adv. Com., 1981-84, Los Angeles Olympics Cultural and Fine Arts Adv. Com., 1981-84. Mem. ABA (forum com. on franchising, litigation com.), Calif. Bar Assn., Los Angeles Bar Assn. (client relations com. 1984—), Century City Bar (tort litigation com.), Los Angeles Trial Lawyers Assn. Franchise law, State civil litigation, Personal injury. Home: 4107 Holly Knoll Dr Los Angeles CA 90027 Office: Solish Jordan & Wiener 12100 Wilshire Blvd #1550 Los Angeles CA 90025

SOLIZ, JOSEPH GUY, lawyer; b. Corpus Christi, Tex., June 25, 1954; s. Oscar and Ola Mae (Trammell) S.; B.A. with highest honors, S.W. Tex. State U., 1976; J.D., Harvard U., 1979; m. Juanita Solis, June 3, 1978; 1 child, Lauren Michelle. Bar: Tex. 1979, U.S. Dist. Ct. (no. dist.) Tex. 1980, U.S. Ct. Appeals (5th and 11th cirs.) 1980, U.S. Dist. Ct. (so. dist.) 1987. atty. Gulf Oil Corp., Houston, 1979-81; ptnr. firm Chamberlain, Hrdlicka, White, Johnson & Williams, Houston, 1981—. Mem. Am. Bar Assn., Tex. Bar Assn., Mexican-Am. Bar Assn. Houston, Houston Bar Assn., Houston Young Lawyers Assn., Tex. Bd. Legal Specialization (cert.), Coll. of State Bar, Internat. Bar Assn., Tex. Ind. Producers and Royalty Owners Assn., Delta Tau Kappa, Alpha Chi, Pi Gamma Mu. Democrat. Roman Catholic. Oil and gas leasing, FERC practice, Nuclear power. Home: 9406 Beverly Hill Houston TX 77063 Office: Chamberlain Hrdlicka White et al 1400 Citicorp Ctr 1200 Smith St Houston TX 77002

SOLK, GERALD, law educator; b. Chgo., July 20, 1942; s. Louis and Serene (Lazar) S. B.A., Pepperdine U., 1964; J.D., U. Calif.-Berkeley, 1967; LL.M., NYU, 1972; Ph.D., Sussex Coll., 1981; postgrad. Harvard U., 1983-85. Bar: Hawaii 1968, N.Y. 1970, Calif., 1973, D.C. 1980, Ohio 1980, Mass. 1981. Assoc., Carlsmith, Wichman & Case, Honolulu, 1967-69, Olwine, Connelly, Chase, O'Donnell & Weyher, N.Y.C., 1969-70, Bellen, Belli & Bailey, Frankfort, W.Ger., 1970-71; vis. asst. prof. U. Santa Clara Law Sch., 1973-74; asst. prof. Gonzaga Law Sch., Spokane, 1974-76; assoc. prof., assoc. dean U. La Verne (Calif.), 1976-80; prof. law Suffolk U. Law Sch., Boston, 1981—; chief economist Shulamith Mgmt. Ltd., Nashua, N.H., 1982—; judge pro tem Los Angeles Mcpl. Ct., 1979-81; arbitrator Los Angeles County Superior Ct., 1979-81, law program Mass. Dept. Consumer Affairs. Recipient Disting. Service award San Fernando Valley Bar Assn., 1980; Nat. Council State Cts. grantee, 1973-74. Mem. ABA (mem. com. on legal edn. 1981), Soc. Legal Writers, Mass. Bar Assn., Boston Bar Assn.,ACLU (outstanding service award 1970), Am. Arbitration Assn., Inst. Advanced Law Study (bd. of trustees 1986—), Bar Assn. U.S. Supreme Ct. (sec.-treas. 1982—). Contracts commercial, General corporate, Legal education. Office: Beacon Hill 41 Temple St Boston MA 02114

SOLKOFF, JEROME IRA, lawyer, consultant, lecturer; b. Rochester, N.Y., Feb. 15, 1939; s. Samuel and Dorothy (Krovetz) S.; m. Doreen Hurwitz, Aug. 11, 1963; children: Scott Michael, Anne Lynn. BS, Sch. Indsl. and Labor Relations, Cornell U., 1961; JD, U. Buffalo, 1964. Bar: N.Y. 1965, Fla. 1974, U.S. Dist. Ct. (we. dist.) N.Y. 1965. Assoc. Nusbaum, Tarricone, Weltman, Bilgore & Silver, Rochester, N.Y., 1964-66, Mousaw, Vigdor, Reeves, Heilbronner & Kroll, Rochester, 1966-70; sr. mcpl. atty. Urban Renewal Agy., Rochester, 1970-73; sole practice, Rochester, 1970-73; chief legal counsel Arlen Realty Mgmt., Inc., Miami, Fla., 1973-75; assoc. Britton, Cohen, Kaufman, Benson & Schantz, Miami, 1975-76; chief legal counsel First Mortgage Investors, Miami Beach, Fla., 1976-79; ptnr. Cassel & Cassel, P.A., Miami, 1979-82; sole practice, Deerfield Beach, Fla., 1982—; lectr. on fgn. investment practices in U.S., Eng., 1981-84, Montreal, Que., Can., 1981. Author: Fundamentals of Foreign Investing in American Real Estate and Businesses, 1981, Checklist of N.Y. Mortgage Foreclosure Procedures, 1970, History of Municipal Employee Unions, 1964. Bd. dirs. Jewish Community Ctrs. of South Broward, Fla., 1979—. Mem. ABA (sects. real property, trust and probate law), Fla. Bar Assn. (sects. real property, trust and probate law). Real property, General corporate, Estate planning.

SOLL, ARTHUR MARTIN, lawyer; b. Phila., July 3, 1901; s. Simon and Bertha Soll; widowed; children—Kenneth H., Melvin E. B.A., U. Pa., 1923, LL.B., 1925; student Gratz Coll., 1917-21. Bar: Pa. 1926, U.S. Dist. Ct. (ea. dist.) Pa. 1940. Atty. inheritance tax div. Orphans' Ct., Commonwealth of Pa., Phila., 1939-55; sole practice, Phila., 1926—. Mem. ward com. Republican Party, Phila., 1926-66; bd. dirs. Congregation B'rith Israel, 1944—. Recipient commendation for vol. legal service Pres. Johnson. Mem. Phila. Bar Assn. Club: Pussmaraniens (Phila.) (chmn. bd. dirs.). Lodge: Masons (master, trustee 1964—). Probate. Home: 1919 Chestnut St #1817 Philadelphia PA 19103

SOLMONSON, STEVEN JAY, lawyer, investment banking executive; b. Providence, Mar. 22, 1954; s. Louis I. and Irene (Zitwer) S.; m. Leslie Ann Morgan, June 24, 1978; Children: Samantha M., Isabel A. BA, Columbia U., N.Y.C., 1975; postgrad., London Sch. Econ., 1976; JD, Bklyn. Law Sch., 1979. Bar: N.Y. 1980. 1st v.p. Drexel Burnham Lambert Inc., N.Y.C., 1979—; alt. dir. Winchester Diversified Ltd., Bermuda, 1985—; bd. dirs. DBL Trade Fin. Inc., N.Y.C. Editor: Millenium Jour. of Internat. Relations, 1976, Bklyn. Law Sch. Jour. of Internat. Law, 1978. Mem. ABA, N.Y. State Bar Assn., Futures Industry Assn. Clubs: University, Town. Commodities, Private international. Home: 965 Fifth Ave New York NY 10021 Office: Drexel Burnham Lambert Inc 60 Broad St New York NY 10004

SOLO, GAIL DIANNE, lawyer; b. Sacramento, Calif., Aug. 29, 1950; d. Myron B. and Betty (Codron) S.; 1 child, Rebecca Joy. AB, UCLA, 1972, JD, 1975. Bar: Calif. 1975, U.S. Dist. Ct. (cen. dist.) Calif. 1976, U.S. Dist. Ct. (no. dist.) Calif. 1976. Aide to Senator Robbins, Calif. State Senate, Sacramento, 1975; assoc. McKay & Byrne, Los Angeles, 1976-78, Joseph Shalant Law Corp., Los Angeles, 1978-79; prin. Solo & Baron, Los Angeles, 1979-87; of counsel McKay, Byrne, Graham & Van Dam, Los Angeles, 1987—; co-founder Women's Legal Clinic, Los Angeles, 1979—, Attys. Against Discrimination, Los Angeles, 1981—. Mem. United Jewish Welfare Fund, 1976—, Los Angeles World Affairs Council, 1980—, mem. Am. Jewish Congress Commn. on Law and Social Action. Recipient Outstanding Service award Women's Legal Clinic, 1979. Mem. Am. Judicature Soc., Affiliated Network Exec. Women, Women Lawyers Assn. Los Angeles, Los Angeles County Bar Assn., Los Angeles Trial Lawyers Assn., Beverly Hills Bar Assn. (women and law com.), NOW. Democrat. Jewish. Labor, Personal injury. Office: McKay Byrne Graham & Van Dam 3250 Wilshire Blvd Suite 603 Los Angeles CA 90010

SOLOMON, DOUGLAS PAUL, lawyer, real estate broker; b. Far Rockaway, N.Y., Nov. 13, 1944; s. Charles Milton and Evelyn Loretta (Mandel) S. BA, U. Rochester, 1966; JD, NYU, 1969. Bar: N.Y. 1970, Fla. 1976, U.S. dist. ct. (so. dist.) N.Y., U.S. dist. ct. (so. dist.) Fla. Assoc. Demov, Morris, Levin & Shein, N.Y.C., 1969-72, Dreyer & Traub, N.Y.C., 1972-73; ptnr. Mandel & Solomon, P.C., N.Y.C., 1973-77; prin. Douglas Paul Solomon, P.A., Miami, Fla., 1977—; real estate broker. Mem. ABA. Real property, Federal civil litigation, Franchising. Office: 520 Brickell Key Dr Suite 305 Miami FL 33131

SOLOMON, MARK RAYMOND, law educator, lawyer; b. Pitts., Aug. 23, 1945; s. Louis Isadore and Fern Rhea (Josselson) S. BA, Ohio State U., 1967; MEd, Cleve. State U., 1971; JD with honors, George Washington U., 1973; LLM in Taxation, Georgetown U., 1976. Bar: Ohio, Mich. Tax law specialist corp. tax br. Nat. Office of IRS, 1973-75; assoc. Butzel, Long, Gust, Klein & Van Zile, Detroit, 1976-78; dir., v.p. Shatzman & Solomon, P.C., Southfield, Mich., 1978-81; prof., chmn. tax and bus. law dept., dir. MS in Taxation Program, Walsh Coll., Troy, Mich., 1981—; of counsel in tax matters Meyer, Kirk, Snyder and Safford, Bloomfield Hills, Mich., 1981—; adj. prof. law U. Detroit, 1977-81. Editor: Cases and Materials on Consolidated Tax Returns, 1978. Mem. ABA, Mich. Bar Assn., Phi Eta Sigma. Lodge: Kiwanis (bd. dirs). Avocation: bridge (life master). Legal education, Corporate taxation, Estate planning. Home: 2109 Golfview Dr Apt 102 Troy MI 48084 Office: Meyer Kirk Snider and Safford 100 W Long Lake Rd Suite 100 Bloomfield Hills MI 48013

SOLOMON, RAYMAN LOUIS, research foundation executive; b. Helena, Ark., June 5, 1947; s. David and Miriam (Rayman) S.; m. Carol Avins, Aug. 10, 1975. BA, Wesleyan U., 1968; MA in History, U. Chgo., 1972, JD, 1976, PhD in History, 1986. Bar: Ill. 1976, U.S. Ct. Appeals (7th cir.) 1978, U.S. Ct. Appeals (6th cir.) 1979. Dir. court history project U.S. Ct. Appeals (7th cir.), Chgo., 1976-78; law clk. to presiding judge U.S. Ct. Appeals (6th cir.), Cin., 1978-79; Bigelow fellow instr. U. Chgo. Law Sch., 1979-80; research fellow Am. Bar Found., Chgo., 1980-86, asst. exec. dir., 1986—; instr. Kent-Ill. Inst. Tech. Coll. Law, Chgo. 1982, Northwestern U., Evanston, Ill. 1986. Author: History of the Seventh Circuit, 1981; editor Am. Bar Found. Research Jour. 1985—. Bd. dirs. Family Counseling Service of Evanston, 1985—. Served with USN, 1969-70. Mem. ABA, Law and Soc. Assn., Selden Soc., Am. Soc. Legal Hist. (bd. dirs. 1985—). Democrat. Jewish. Club: Univ. (Chgo.). Legal history. Office: Am Bar Found 750 N Lake Shore Dr Chicago IL 60611

SOLOMON, STEPHEN L., lawyer; b. N.Y.C., Aug. 15, 1942; s. Sam and Ruth (Goldblum) S.; m. Regina Fisher, Aug. 14, 1969; children—Todd, Lisa. A.B., Columbia Coll., 1964; LL.B., N.Y.U., 1967. Bar: N.Y. 1967, U.S. Dist. Ct. (so. and ea. dist.) 1969, U.S. Ct. Customs 1970, U.S. Supreme Ct. 1975. Assoc. Burns, Jackson, Summit, N.Y.C., 1969-74; ptnr. Miller, Singer, Michaelson & Raives, N.Y.C., 1974-79; ptnr., pres. Jarblum, Solomon & Fornari, PC, N.Y.C., 1979—. Contbr. articles to profl. jours. Active Com. on Philanthropic Orgns., N.Y.C., 1980-83; bd. dirs. Emanu-El Midtown YM/YWHA, N.Y.C., 1979—. Mem. Assn. Bar City of N.Y. Democrat. General corporate, Real property. Home: 40 Fifth Ave New York NY 10011 Office: Jarblum Solomon & Fornari PC 650 Fifth Ave New York NY 10019

SOLON, JAMES DAVIS, lawyer; b. Oak Park, Ill., Aug. 24, 1940; s. John James and Mary (Davis) S.; m. Nancy Van Schelven, June 15, 1963; children: Elizabeth, Jennifer. BS, Ill. Inst. Tech., 1963; JD, U. Kans., 1974. Bar: Kans. 1974, Ill. 1975. Commd. ensign USN, 1963, advanced through grades to lt. comdr., 1971, with nuclear submarine program, 1963-72, resigned, 1972; atty. Lord, Bissell & Brook, Chgo., 1974-78; ptnr. Martin, Pringle, Oliver, Wallace & Swartz, Wichita, Kans., 1978—. Mem. ABA, Kans. Bar Assn., Wichita Bar Assn. Federal civil litigation, State civil litigation, Insurance. Home: 7 English Ave Wichita KS 67202 Office: Martin Pringle Oliver Wallace & Swartz 300 Page Ct Wichita KS 67202

SOLOWAY, LOUIS, lawyer; b. Bklyn., Apr. 23, 1932; s. George and Anna (Wachtel) S.; m. Ruth Soloway, 1956; children—Ann, Marc; m. 2d, Linda Soloway, 1966; 1 dau., Susan; m. 3d, Joan Soloway, Aug. 21, 1981. B.A., Columbia U., 1953, LL.B., 1956. Bar: N.Y. 1956, U.S. Dist. Ct. (ea. and so. dists.) N.Y. 1957, U.S. Supreme Ct. 1961. Assoc., Bernstein, Margolin & Balin, 1956-61; ptnr. Wydler, Balin, Pares & Soloway, 1961-81, Wofsey, Certilman, Haft, Lebow, Balin, Buckley & Kremer, Valley Stream, N.Y., 1981—; lectr. Hofstra U., 1979-80, L.I. Builders Inst., Builders Tng. Course C.W. Post Coll. Mem. Oyster Bay Bd. Ethics, 1964-67; bd. dirs. L.I. Builders Inst., 1981—. Mem. Nassau County Bar Assn. (grievance com. 1977-78), N.Y. State Bar Assn., Nassau Lawyers Assn. (chmn. real property com. 1963-64). Real property. Home: 444 E 82d St Apt 5-X Great Neck NY 11021

SOLTIS, ROBERT ALAN, lawyer; b. Gary, Ind., Jan. 30, 1955; s. George William and Frances Marie (Jakob) S. AB (scholar), Ind. U., 1977; JD, DePaul U., 1982. Bar: Ill. 1982, Ind. 1982, U.S. Dist. Ct. (no. dist.) Ill. 1982, U.S. Dist. Ct. (no. and so. dists.) Ind. 1982, U.S. Ct. Apls. (7th cir.) 1983, U.S. Dist. Ct. Trial (no. dist.) Ill. 1984, Ind. Indsl. Bd. 1982; lic. instrument-rated pilot. Photographer Herald Newspapers, Merrillville, Ind., 1971-72; dep. coroner Lake County, Ind., 1972-78, spl. dep. sheriff, 1972-78; dep. coroner, Monroe County, Ind., 1975-76; area dir. Mayors Office of Urban Conservation, Gary, 1977-80; title examiner Law Bull. Title Services, Chgo., 1980; field clm. rep. Employers Ins. of Wausau, River Forest, Ill., 1980-82; assoc. Perz & McGuire, P.C., Chgo., 1982-84, McKenna, Storer, Rowe, White & Farrug, Chgo., 1984—. Co-host twice weekly TV show: Cancer and You, Bloomington, Ind., 1975-76; contbr. articles in field of cancer. Dir. pub. info. Am. Cancer Soc., Gary, 1977-79, Monroe County unit, 1975-76; pres. Gary Young Dems., 1977-78; precinct committeeman Dem. Party, Gary, 1978-82; bd. dirs. N.W. Ind. Urban League; chmn. Com. to Retain State Rep. William Drozda, 1978-82. Recipient Outstanding Reporter award Lake County Mar. of Dimes, 1973, Disting. Service award Am. Cancer Soc. Ind. Div., 1975-76. Mem. Ill. Bar Assn., Chgo. Bar Assn., Ind. Bar Assn., Lawyer-Pilots Bar Assn., Aircraft Owners and Pilots Assn., Glen Park Jaycees (founder, charter pres. 1977), Nat. Press Photographers Assn., Am. Soc. Mag. Photographers, Ind. U. Alumni Assn. (life). Roman Catholic. Club: Slovak (Gary). Workers' compensation, Personal injury. Home: 1711 W 105th Pl Chicago IL 60643 Office: McKenna Storer Rowe White & Farrug 135 S LaSalle St #4200 Chicago IL 60603

SOLTOW, WILLIAM DONALD, JR., lawyer; b. Cleve., Sept. 19, 1924; s. William Donald and Sophie (Novotny) S.; m. Shirley Elaine Martin, Aug. 25, 1951; 1 dau., Willow Ann. B.S.M.E., Rensselaer Poly. Inst., 1948; J.D., George Washington U., 1953. Bar: D.C. 1953. Patent examiner U.S. Patent Office, Washington, 1948-54; patent lawyer Firm of Harold B. Hood, Indpls., 1954-55, Metals & Controls Corp., Attleboro, Mass., 1955-58; patent lawyer Pitney Bowes Inc., Stamford, Conn., 1958-61, corp. patent counsel, 1961—. Served to lt. (j.g.) USN, 1943-46. Mem. ABA (patent, trademark and copyright sect.), Assn. Corp. Patent Counsel, Am. Intellectual Property Law Assn., Conn. Patent Law Assn., U.S. Trademark Assn., NAM (patents com.). Patentee electronic lock. Patent, Trademark and copyright. Home: 80 Riverside Ave Riverside CT 06878 Office: Pitney Bowes Inc World Headquarters Stamford CT 06926

SOLUM, GREGORY RANDAL, lawyer; b. Mpls., Jan. 9, 1948; s. Darryl R. and Elouise M. (Marlow) S. BA, U. Minn., 1969; JD, William Mitchell Coll. Law, 1980. Bar: Minn. 1980. Sole practice Mpls., 1980—. Bd. dirs. West Bank Sch. Music, Mpls., 1980—, Lawyers Concerned for Lawyers, St. Paul, 1985—. Mem. ABA, Minn. Trial Lawyers Assn., Order of Barristers. General practice. Home: 3520 12th Ave S Minneapolis MN 55407 Office: 7250 France Ave S Suite 410 Edina MN 55435

SOMER, STANLEY JEROME, lawyer; b. N.Y.C., Oct. 29, 1943; s. David Meyer and Rose (Bleifeld) S.; m. Janice Somer, June 20, 1965 (div. May 1980); children: Penny Lynn, Andrew Michael. BBA in Acctg., Hofstra U., 1966; JD, New York Law Sch., 1969. Bar: N.Y. 1970, U.S. Dist. Ct. (ea. and so. dists.) N.Y. 1972, U.S. Tax Ct. 1983. Assoc. Halpin, Keough & St. John, N.Y.C., 1970-71, Bodenstein & Gumson, N.Y.C., 1971-73; counsel Heatherwood Comm., Hauppauge, N.Y., 1973-74; ptnr. Somer & Wand, P.C., Commack and Smithtown, N.Y., 1974—; lectr. N.Y. Law Sch., N.Y.C., 1970-73, Income Property Cons., Huntington, N.Y., 1976-85. Commiteeman Suffolk Reps., East Northport, N.Y., 1978. Mem. N.Y. State Bar Assn., Suffolk Bar Assn., Comm. Assoc. Inst., L.I. Builders Inst. Lodge: Lions (pres. East Northport chpt. 1977-78). Landlord-tenant, Real property, General practice. Office: Somer & Wand PC 1030 W Jericho Turnpike Smithtown NY 11787

SOMERS, CLIFFORD LOUIS, lawyer; b. Portland, Maine, Dec. 27, 1940; s. Norman Louis and Adeline Wilhemina (Witzke) S.; m. Barbara Suzanne Berry, Aug. 1, 1961; children: Alan Mark, Penelope Lee. BA, U. Fla., Gainsville, 1965, JD, 1967. Bar: Fla. 1967, U.S. Ct. Mil. Appeals 1968, U.S. Dist. Ct. (mid. dist.) Fla. 1972. Assoc. Miller & McKendree, Tampa, Fla., 1972-75; ptnr. Burton, Somers & Reynolds, Tampa, 1975-77, Miller, McKendree & Somers, Tampa, 1977-85, McKendree & Somers, Tampa, 1985—; instr. law U. Fla., Gainesville, 1967. Contbr. article to profl. jours. Served as sgt. U.S. Army, 1961-64, Vietnam; served as capt. JAG U.S. Army, 1968-72. Mem. Assn. Trial Lawyers Am., Fla. Bar Assn., Def. Research Inst. (coordinator Fla. west coast 1985-86), Am. Legion (comdr. Post 278, 1975), Brandon Vet.'s Post and Park (pres. 1985). Avocations: writing, running, weight lifting. State civil litigation, Insurance, Personal injury. Home: 512 E Davis Blvd Tampa FL 33606 Office: McKendree & Somers 3315 Henderson Blvd Tampa FL 33609

SOMERS, CONSTANCE REYNOLDS, lawyer; b. Dallas, Feb. 9, 1951; d. William S. and Jean V. (Ferebee) Reynolds; m. Richard D. Somers, Sept. 11, 1976; children: Emily Susanne, Alan William. BA, Vanderbilt U., 1972; postgrad., Ariz. State U., 1977-78, U. Wash., 1978-79; JD, St. Mary's U., San Antonio, 1980. Bar: Tex. 1981, U.S. Dist. Ct. (we. dist.) Tex. 1983. Assoc. Tinsman & Houser Inc., San Antonio, 1981-85; sole practice San Antonio, 1985—; alt. mcpl. judge City of Shavano Park, San Antonio, 1985—. Mem. Tex. State Bar, San Antonio Trial Lawyers Assn., Bexar County Women's Bar Assn., Tex. Trial Lawyers Assn., San Antonio Young Lawyers Assn. Personal injury, Workers' compensation, Family and matrimonial. Home: 114 Fawn Dr San Antonio TX 78231 Office: 711 Navarro Suite 777 San Antonio TX 78205

SOMERS, FRED LEONARD, JR., lawyer; b. Orange, N.J., July 5, 1936; A.B., U. Va., 1958, LL.B., 1961. Bar: Va. 1961, Mo. 1963, Ga. 1967, U.S. Tax Ct. 1971, U.S. Supreme Ct. 1978. Assoc. Lewis, Rice, Tucker, Allen & Chubb, St. Louis, 1962-65; asst. regional counsel AT&T, Atlanta, 1965-67; assoc. Kaler, Karish & Reuben, Atlanta, 1968; ptnr. Stack & O'Brien, Atlanta, 1968-70, Somers & Altenbach and predecessors, Atlanta, 1970—. Mem. Citizens Adv. Park Com., DeKalb County, Ga., 1969, Citizens Bond Commn. DeKalb County, 1970; chmn. DeKalb County Charter Commn., 1970; vice chmn. DeKalb County Planning Commn., 1971-77; chmn., trustee Callanwolde Found., 1971-83; chmn. Oglethorpe Housing Devel. Authority, De Kalb County, 1974; bd. dirs., pres.Nat. Club Assn., 1982—; bd. govs. Ravinia Club, 1986—. Mem. ABA, Altanta Bar Assn., Computer Law Assn. Securities, Real property, General corporate. Home: 105 Cliffside Crossing Atlanta GA 30338 Office: 2 Ravinia Dr Atlanta GA 30346

SOMERS, HANS PETER, lawyer; b. Berlin, Germany, Nov. 11, 1922; came to U.S., 1938; s. Fritz A. and Karoline E. (Neuert) S.; m. Claudia C. Schuette, May 3, 1947; children: Daniel E., Stephen A., Deborah J., Conrad S. B.A., Cornell Coll., 1946; M.A., U. Iowa, 1948; LL.B. magna cum laude, Harvard U., 1951. Bar: Mass. 1951, Pa. 1957. Assoc. Hill & Barlow, Boston, 1951-56; assoc. Morgan, Lewis & Bockius, Phila., 1956-60, ptnr., 1960—; lectr. law Northeastern U. Law Sch., Boston, 1951-53, Boston U. Law Sch., 1953-55; lectr. Villanova U. Law Sch., Phila., 1959-63; research assoc. Am. Law Inst., Cambridge, Mass., 1955-56. Editor: Harvard Law Rev., 1949-51; contbr. articles to legal jours. Served to 2d lt. AUS, 1943-46, ETO. Mem. ABA (chmn. com. tax sect. 1967-69, real property, probate and trust law 1974-77), Nat. Conf. Lawyers and Corp. Fiduciaries (chmn. 1978-81), Am. Coll. Probate Counsel (mem. editorial bd. dirs. 1976-77), Internat. Acad. of Estate and Trust Law (exec. council 1974-78, 81—). Clubs: Radnor Hunt (Malvern, Pa.) (bd. govs.); Union League (Phila.). Home: 8024 Goshen Rd Newtown Square PA 19073 Office: Morgan Lewis & Bockius 2000 One Logan Sq Philadelphia PA 19103

SOMERVILLE, FRANK WALKER, lawyer; b. Charlottesville, Va., Feb. 21, 1952; s. Atwell Wilson and Anne Carter (Walker) S.; m. Laura Adair Farmer, June 4, 1977; children: Laura Adair, John Walker. AB in History with honors, Davidson Coll., 1974; JD, U. Va., 1979. Bar: Va. 1979. Assoc. Somerville, Moore & Joyner, Ltd., Orange, Va., 1979-82; ptnr. Somerville, Moore & Somerville, Ltd., Orange, 1982—. Pres. Orange County

Unit of Am. Cancer Soc., 1981; bd. dirs., treas. Friends and Alumni of Orange County High Sch., Inc., 1985. Mem. ABA (litigation sect., family law sect.), Va. Bar Assn., Va. Trial Lawyers Assn. Baptist. Club: Charlottesville (Va.) Track. Lodge: Lions (pres. 1985-86). Avocation: running. State civil litigation, Insurance, Personal injury. Office: Somerville Moore & Somerville Ltd PO Box 629 Orange VA 22960

SOMERVILLE, WILLIAM GLASSELL, JR., lawyer; b. Memphis, July 27, 1933; s. William Glassell and Hilda (Deeth) S.; m. Mary Hateley Quincey, June 13, 1959 (div. Oct., 1985); children—William Glassell, John Quincey, Mary Campbell, Sarah Guerrant. A.B., Princeton U., 1955; LL.B., U. Va., 1961. Bar: Ala. 1961, U.S. Ct. Appeals (5th cir.) 1963, U.S. Supreme Ct. 1964, U.S. Ct. Appeals (8th cir.) 1968, U.S. Ct. Appeals (11th cir.) 1981. Law clk. to chief judge U.S. Dist. Ct. (no. dist.) Ala., 1961-63; assoc. Lange, Simpson, Robinson & Somerville, Birmingham, Ala., 1963-66, ptnr., 1966—; mem. supreme ct. adv. com. on rules of Ala. appellate procedure, 1972-77; mem. standing com. on Ala. rules of appellate procedure, 1979-86. Served with CIC, U.S. Army, 1955-58. Mem. ABA, Ala. Bar Assn., Am. Judicature Soc. Clubs: Ivy (Princeton), Birmingham Country, Rotary. Insurance, Federal civil litigation, Antitrust. Office: Suite 1700 F A B Bldg Birmingham AL 35203

SOMMER, ALPHONSE ADAM, JR., lawyer; b. Portsmouth, Ohio, Apr. 7, 1924; s. A.A. and Adelaide (Orlett) S.; m. Storrow Cassin, June 13, 1951; children: Susan, Edward, Nancy. A.B., U. Notre Dame, 1948; LL.B., Harvard U., 1950; LL.D., Cleve. State U., 1976. Bar: Ohio 1951, D.C. 1976. Assoc. Calfee, Halter, Calfee, Griswold & Sommer, Cleve., 1950-60; ptnr. Calfee, Halter, Calfee, Griswold & Sommer, 1960-73; commr. SEC, 1973-76; ptnr. Morgan, Lewis & Bockius, Washington, 1979—. Contbr. articles to profl. jours. Served with AUS, 1943-46. Mem. Am. Inst. C.P.A.s (chmn. pub. oversight bd.). Administrative and regulatory, General corporate. Home: 7105 Heathwood Ct Bethesda MD 20817 Office: 1800 M St NW Washington DC 20036

SOMMER, EVELYN MORRISON, lawyer; b. N.Y.C.; s. H. and Sarah (Drucker) Morrison; m. Rudolph Sommer, Apr. 18, 1948; children—Peter, Cathy, Timothy. B.A., Hunter Coll., 1945; postgrad. N.Y.U. Grad. Sch. Arts and Scis., 1946-48; J.D., Bklyn. Law Sch., 1955. Bar: N.Y. 1956, U.S. Patent Office 1957, U.S. Dist. Ct. (so. and ea. dists.) N.Y., U.S. Ct. Appeals (fed. cir.), U.S. Supreme Ct. Research chemist Mt. Sinai Hosp., N.Y.C., 1945-46, N.Y.U. Med. Sch., 1946-55; sr. asso. Burgess, Dinklage & Sprung, N.Y.C., 1955-69, Nolte & Nolte, N.Y.C., 1969-71, GAF, N.Y.C., 1971-73; sr. counsel Champion Internat., Stamford, Conn., 1973—; instr. Practicing Law Inst., Bur. Nat. Affairs, Am. Mgmt. Assn., U. Bridgeport (Conn.) Law Sch.; judge moot ct. Regional (NE), U. Bridgeport Law Sch. Mem. ABA, Am. Patent Law Assn., N.Y. Patent Law Assn. Contbr. articles on law to profl. jours. Patent, Intellectual property law. Home: 16 Emery Dr E Stamford CT 06902 Office: Champion Internat Corp 1 Champion Plaza Stamford CT 06921

SOMMERFELD, DONALD DROVDAL, lawyer; b. Billings, Mont., Apr. 7, 1951; s. Edward T. and Ruth (Drovdal) S.; m. Susan Kennedy, Aug. 15, 1981. BS, Mont. State U., 1974; JD, U. Mont., 1979. Bar: Mont. 1979, U.S. Dist. Ct. Mont. 1979, U.S. Ct. Appeals (9th cir.) 1980. Tchr. Missoula (Mont.) Hellgate High Sch., 1974-76; assoc. Towe, Ball, Enright & Mackey, Billings, 1979-83, ptnr., 1983—. Mem. Billings Symphony Chorale, 1980—; advisor Am. Field Service, Billings, 1980—; bd. dirs. Billings Symphony Soc., 1980—. Mem. ABA, Yellowstone County Bar Assn., Assn. Trial Lawyers Am., Mont. Trial Lawyers Assn., Yellowstone Valley Claimants Attys. (bd. dirs. 1981-84)., Phi Kappa Phi, Phi Sigma Kappa, Phi Delta Phi. Lutheran. Avocations: fly fishing, snow skiing, travel. Insurance, Personal injury, Workers' compensation. Office: Towe Ball Enright & Mackey 2525 6th Ave N Billings MT 59101

SOMMERS, ELIZABETH BOONE, lawyer; b. Corinth, Miss., June 24, 1945; d. Nelms Burnett Boone and Fay (Mauldin) Dickinson; m. Richard Henry Sommers, June 17, 1967 (div. June 1983); children: Richard Benjamin, Kelly Elizabeth. BS, U. S.C., 1969; JD, SUNY, Buffalo, 1982. Bar: N.Y. 1982, U.S. Ct. Appeals (7th cir.) 1983. Ptnr. Van Horn & Sommers, Geneva, N.Y., 1982-83; staff atty. U.S. Ct. Appeals (7th cir.), Chgo., 1983-85; law asst. N.Y. Ct. Appeals, Albany, 1985-86; dep. counsel N.Y. Commn. Correction, Albany, 1986-87; law clk. to presiding judge N.Y. Ct. Calims, Albany, 1987—. Appellate and trial court research, drafting and case management. Home: 27 Melrose Ave Albany NY 12203

SOMMERS, LOUISE, lawyer; b. Jersey City, May 19, 1948; d. Moe R. and Estelle Sylvia (Sachs) S.; m. Mark Glen Sokoloff, Feb. 6, 1983. BA with honors, Douglas Coll., 1969; JD magna cum laude, Bklyn. Law Sch., 1976. Bar: N.Y. 1977, U.S. Dist. Ct. (ea. and so. dists.) N.Y. 1977, U.S. Ct. Appeals (2d cir.). Law clk. to presiding justice U.S. Dist. Ct. (so. dist.) N.Y., N.Y.C., 1976-78; ptnr. Rogers & Wells, N.Y.C., 1978—; adj. prof. Bklyn. Law Sch., 1986—. Mem. ABA, N.Y. State Bar Assn., Assn. of Bar of City of N.Y. Federal civil litigation, Libel, State civil litigation.

SOMRAK, DAVID JOSEPH, lawyer; b. Cleve., Jan. 25, 1958; s. Donald Joseph and Mary Somrak; m. Noreen Hartnett, May 29, 1982. BA, John Carroll U., 1978; JD, Case Western Res. U., 1982. Bar: Ohio 1982, U.S. Dist. Ct. (no. dist.) Ohio 1983, U.S. Ct. Appeals (6th cir.) 1984. Assoc. Squire, Sanders & Dempsey, Cleve., 1982—. Mem. ABA, Ohio State Bar Assn., Cleve. Bar Assn., Order of Coif, Am. Numismatic Assn. Democrat. Byzantine Catholic. Labor, Workers' compensation, Federal civil litigation. Home: 1700 E 13th St Apt 23S-E Cleveland OH 44114 Office: Squire Sanders & Dempsey 1800 Huntington Bldg Cleveland OH 44115

SOMSEN, HENRY NORTHROP, lawyer; b. New Ulm, Minn., Aug. 12, 1909; s. Henry N. and Meta (Koch) S.; m. Anne Elizabeth Duncan, Sept. 12, 1936; children: Pennell Anne, Stephen Duncan. BA, U. Minn., 1932, JD, 1934. Bar: Minn. 1934. Practice law, New Ulm, Minn., 1934-85, ptnr. Somsen, Dempsey Johnson & Somsen, 1934-40, Somsen Dempsey & Somsen, 1940-46, Somsen & Somsen, 1946-55; sole practice, 1955-64; ptnr. Somsen & Dempsey, 1964-71; sr. ptnr. Somsen Dempsey & Schade, 1971-85, of counsel, 1985—. Bd. editors U. Minn. Law Rev., 1932-33. Trustee Minn. State Parks Found., 1967-77; bd. dirs. Minn. Council State Parks, 1956—, pres., 1974-75; bd. dirs., pres. New Ulm Community Concert Assn., 1947-85; bd. dirs. Union Hosp., New Ulm, 1959-77, Highland Homes, Inc., 1970-79, New Ulm Meml. Found., 1958-79; bd. dirs. New Ulm Industries Inc., 1952-85, pres., 1968-77; bd. dirs. New Ulm Industries Found., Inc., 1953-85, pres., 1968-77; mem. City Charter Commns., 1940, 51, 66, pres., 1966. Served to capt. JAGC, AUS, 1943-46. Mem. ABA, Minn. Bar Assn., Am. Judicature Soc., Am. Arbitration Assn. (panel of arbitrators 1967-85). Episcopalian. Clubs: Mpls., Mpls. Athletic. Lodges: Masons, Rotary, Shriners. Home: 211 2d St NW Apt 1907 Rochester MN 55901 Office: Somsen Dempsey & Schade 106 1/2 N Minnesota St New Ulm MN 56073

SONBERG, MICHAEL ROBERT, lawyer; b. Bklyn., Oct. 17, 1947; s. Harold R. and Betty (March) S. AB, CUNY, 1968; JD, Harvard U., 1971. Bar: N.Y. 1972. Assoc. Weiss, Rosenthal, Heller & Schwartzman, N.Y.C., 1971-79, Moore, Berson, Lifflander, Eisenberg & Mewhinney, N.Y.C., 1979-82; ptnr. Moore, Berson, Lifflander & Mewhinney, N.Y.C., 1983—. Mem. Overseers' Com. to Visit Harvard Law Sch., 1978-83; bd. Dirs., chmn. com. on legis. Citizens Union of City of N.Y., 1978—. Mem. ABA, N.Y. State Bar Assn., Assn. of Bar of City of N.Y. (chmn. com. on state cts. of Superior jurisdiction), Fed. Bar Council, Queens Coll. Alumni Assn. (trustee 1983—). Federal civil litigation, State civil litigation. Home: 380 W 12th St Apt 3F New York NY 10014 Office: Moore Berson Lifflander Eisenberg & Mewhinney 595 Madison AVe New York NY 10022

SONDE, THEODORE IRWIN, lawyer; b. N.Y.C., Jan. 7, 1940; s. Martin and Anne (Greenbaum) S.; m. Grace Suzanne Kolisch, Sept. 10, 1964; children—Andrea Martine, David Ian. B.A., CCNY, 1961; LL.B., NYU, 1964; LL.M., Georgetown U., 1967. Bar: N.Y. 1964, D.C. 1978, U.S. Supreme Ct. With SEC, Washington, 1964-80, asst. gen. counsel, office of Gen. Counsel, 1970-74, assoc. dir. div. of enforcement, 1974-80; dir. Office of Enforcement, Fed. Energy Regulatory Commn., 1980-81; mem. Cole & Corette, Washington, 1982—; adj. prof. Georgetown U. Law Sch. 1977—, George Washington U. Nat. Law Ctr., 1976-82. Contbr. articles to legal jours. Administrative and regulatory, Federal civil litigation. Office: Cole & Corette 1110 Vermont Ave NW Washington DC 20005

SONDOCK, RUBY KLESS, judge; b. Houston, Apr. 26, 1926; d. Herman Lewis and Celia (Juran) Kless; m. Melvin Adolph Sondock, Apr. 22, 1944; children—Marcia Cohen, Sandra Marcus. A.A., Cottey Coll., Nevada, Mo., 1944; B.S., U. Houston, 1959, LL.B., 1961. Sole practice, Houston, 1961-73; judge Harris County Ct. Domestic Relations, 1973-77, 234th Jud. Dist. Ct., Houston, 1977-82, 83—; justice Tex. Supreme Ct., Austin, 1982. Mem. ABA, Tex. Bar Assn., Houston Bar Assn., Nat. Assn. Women Lawyers, Houston Assn. Women Lawyers, Order of Barons, Phi Theta Phi, Kappa Beta Pi, Phi Kappa Phi, Alpha Epsilon Pi. Democrat. Jewish. Judicial administration. Office: 234th Dist Ct 301 Fannin St Houston TX 77002

SONGSTAD, STEVEN BOOTH, lawyer; b. Moscow, Idaho, Oct. 1, 1946; s. Merle Pitman and Marjorie Elisabeth (Booth) S. BA, U. Wash., 1970; JD, U. Puget Sound, 1975. Bar: Hawaii 1975, U.S. Dist. Ct. Hawaii 1975. Sole practice Law Office of Steven Booth Songstad and Assocs., Wailuku, Maui, Hawaii, 1976—; bd. dirs. Legal Aid Soc. Hawaii, Honolulu. Bd. dirs. Maui Assn. for Children with Learning Disabilities, Wailuku, 1976-84, Neighborhood Justice Ctr., Wailuku, 1980-84, Maui Mediation Services, Wailuku, 1985—. Mem. ABA, Hawaii Bar Assn., Maui County Bar Assn., Assn. Trial Lawyers Assn., Hawaii Criminal Def. Lawyers Assn., ACLU, Kahului Jaycees (legal officer 1981-82), Sierra Club. Avocations: civil liberties, diving, skiing, baseball, climbing. Personal injury, Criminal, State civil litigation. Office: Law Office Steven Booth Songstad 2180 Main St #700 Wailuku, Maui HI 96793

SONNENFELD, MARC JAY, lawyer; b. Bryn Mawr, Pa., Sept. 16, 1946; s. Burton David and Rochelle (Galant) S. BA, Swarthmore Coll., 1968; JD, Harvard U., 1971. Bar: Pa. 1971, Mass. 1971, U.S. Supreme Ct. 1976, D.C. 1977. Lectr. Wellesley (Mass.) Coll., 1971-72; law clk. to presiding judge U.S. Dist. Ct. (ea. dist.) Pa., Phila., 1972-73; assoc. Ewing & Cohen, Phila., 1973-74; assoc. Morgan, Lewis & Bockius, Phila., 1974-78, ptnr., 1978—. Dem. committeeman, Phila., 1980-84. Mem. ABA, Pa. Bar Assn., Phila. Bar Assn. (exec. com. young lawyers sect. 1976-79, appellate cts. com., fed. cts. com., state civil jud. procedures com., nominating com., city policy com., chmn. profl. responsibility com. 1985, bus. banking and corp. law sect., vice chmn. bd. govs. 1986, chmn. 1987), Harvard Law Sch. Assn. of Phila. (pres.), Swarthmore Coll. Annual Fund (gen. chmn.). Jewish. Club: Locust (Phila.). Avocations: reading, sailing. Federal civil litigation, State civil litigation. Home: 322 S Juniper St Philadelphia PA 19107 Office: Morgan Lewis & Bockius 2000 One Logan Sq Philadelphia PA 19103

SONNTAG, RICHARD ARTHUR, lawyer; b. Ft. Ord, Calif., Apr. 12, 1955; s. Richard Norman Sonntag and Joyce Hagen; m. Janice Kay Borgerson, Sept. 5, 1982; 1 child, William Frederick Cody. BA, U. Calif., Santa Barbara, 1975; JD, Harvard U., 1979. Bar: Colo. 1979, U.S. Dist. Ct. Colo. 1979, Tex. 1986. Assoc. Davis, Graham & Stubbs, Denver, 1979-82; counsel Colo. region Mobil Land Devel. Corp., Denver, 1982-85, counsel Colo. and Tex. region, 1985—. Treas. Denver County Young Reps., 1983-85, bd. dirs. 1983—, Denver Forum, 1985—, The Marguarita Soc., 1985—. Mem. Tex. Bar Assn., Colo. Bar Assn., Denver Bar Assn., El Paso County Bar Assn., Douglas/Elbert County Bar Assn. Presbyterian. Real property, Local government, Municipal bonds. Home: 1380 Bellaire St Denver CO 80220 Office: Mobil Land Devel Corp 7315 E Orchard Rd Suite 400 Englewood CO 80111

SOPER, E. PHILLIP, legal educator; b. 1942. B.A., 1964; M.A., Washington U., St. Louis, 1965, Ph.D., 1972; J.D., Harvard U., 1969. Bar: D.C. 1970. Law clk. to Justice Byron R. White, U.S. Supreme Ct., 1969-70; recognized student Oxford (Eng.) U., 1970-71; with Office Gen. Counsel, Council on Environ. Quality, Washington, 1971-73; asst. prof. U. Mich. Law Sch., 1973-76, assoc. prof., 1976-78, prof., 1978—. Former supreme ct. and note editor Harvard Law Rev. Legal education. Office: U Mich Law Sch Ann Arbor MI 48109 *

SORENSEN, MURRAY JIM, lawyer; b. Blackfoot, Idaho, Feb. 10, 1948; s. Murray L. and Lona Mae (Clegg) S.; m. Gay Grimshaw, May 25, 1974; children—Benjamin Jim, Joshua John, Matthew Murray, Daniel Henry, Adam Michael. Student in Political Sci., Brigham Young U., 1965-72; J.D., U. Idaho, 1975. Bar: Idaho 1975, U.S. Dist. Ct. Idaho 1975. Asst. prosecutor Bingham County, Idaho, 1975-77, pub. defender, 1979-82; city atty. City of Blackfoot, 1978-79; ptnr. Blasen & Sorensen Chartered, Blackfoot, 1981—; city atty. City of Basalt, Idaho, 1984—. Chmn. Eastern Idaho Fair Parade, Blackfoot, 1978-79, United Fund, Blackfoot, 1979, Ducks Unltd., Blackfoot, 1983-84. Named to Outstanding Young Men Am., U.S. Jaycees, 1982. Mem. ABA, Assn. Trial Lawyers Am., Idaho Trial Lawyers Assn., Blackfoot C. of C. (bd. dirs. 1979-80). Mormon. Lodge: Kiwanis (bd. dirs. local lodge 1983-84). Personal injury, Bankruptcy, General practice. Office: Blaser & Sorensen Chartered 265 NW Main St PO Box 1047 Blackfoot ID 83221

SORENSEN, THEODORE CHAIKIN, lawyer, former special counsel to U.S. president; b. Lincoln, Nebr., May 8, 1928; s. Christian Abraham and Annis (Chaikin) S.; m. Gillian Martin, June 28, 1969; 1 child, Juliet Suzanne; children from previous marriage: Eric Kristen, Stephen Edgar, Philip Jon. B.S. in Law, U. Nebr., 1949, LL.B., 1951, LL.D. (hon.), 1969; LL.D. (hon.), U. Canterbury, 1966, Alfred U., 1969, Temple U., 1969, Fairfield U., 1969. Bar: Nebr. 1951, N.Y. 1966, U.S. Supreme Ct. 1966, D.C. 1971. Atty. Fed. Security Agy., 1951-52; mem. staff joint com. r.r. retirement U.S. Senate, 1952; asst. to Sen. John F. Kennedy, 1953-61; sec. New Eng. Senators' Conf., 1953-59; spl. counsel to pres. U.S., 1961-64; mem. firm Paul, Weiss, Rifkind, Wharton & Garrison, N.Y.C., 1966—; mem. Pres.'s Adv. Com. Trade Negotiations, 1978; commentator nat. affairs Metromedia Channel 5, 1971-73. Editor: Nebr. Law Rev, 1950-51; author: Decision Making in the White House, 1963, Kennedy, 1965, The Kennedy Legacy, 1969, Watchmen in the Night: Presidential Accountability After Watergate, 1975, A Different Kind of Presidency, 1984, (with Ralf Dahrendorf) A Widening Atlantic? Domestic Change and Foreign Policy, 1986. Democratic candidate for N.Y. Senate, 1970; chmn. Dem. Nat. Com. task force on polit. action, 1981-82, mem. task force on fgn. policy, 1986; chmn. N.Y. Dem. Com. on Ethical Conduct, 1986—; mem. Internat. Trade Roundtable, 1986. Named by Jr. C. of C. as one of ten Outstanding Young Men of Year, 1961. Mem. Phi Beta Kappa, Order of Coif. Private international, Public international, Administrative and regulatory. Office: Paul Weiss Rifkind Wharton & Garrison 1285 Ave of Americas New York NY 10019

SORGE, JAY WOOTTEN, lawyer; b. Detroit, July 27, 1917; s. Ervin H. and Harriet Louise (Wootten) S.; m. Mary Jane Peterson, June 19, 1943. Student Washington and Lee U., 1935-36; A.B., U. Mich., 1939, J.D., 1942. Bar: Mich. 1942. Assoc. Hill Lewis Adams Goodrich & Tait, Detroit, 1945-52, ptnr., 1952-85; of counsel, 1986—; lectr. corp. law Detroit Coll. Law and Wayne State U. Law Sch., 1945-55. Trustee Fund for Henry Ford Hosp.; pres. Friends of Grosse Pointe Pub. Library, 1955-56, others. Served with USCG, 1942-45. Mem. Detroit Bar Assn., Mich. Bar Assn., ABA, Order of the Coif. Republican. Episcopalian. Clubs: Detroit, Country of Detroit. General corporate, Non-profit organizations, Securities. Home: 88 Tourine Rd Grosse Pointe Farms MI 48236 Office: Suite 3200 100 Tower Renaissance Center Detroit MI 48243

SORKIN, LAURENCE TRUMAN, lawyer; b. Bklyn., Oct. 20, 1942; s. Sidney and Lilly (Kowensky) S.; m. Joan Carol Ross, June 25, 1972; children—Andrew Ross, Suzanne Ross. A.B. summa cum laude, Brown U., 1964; LL.B., Yale U., 1967; LL.M., London Sch. Econs. and Polit. Sci., 1968. Bar: N.Y. 1968, U.S. Ct. Appeals (2d cir.) 1969, U.S. Dist. Ct. (so. and ea. dists.) N.Y. 1971, D.C. 1972, U.S. Ct. Appeals (D.C. cir.) 1972, U.S. Supreme Ct. 1973. Law clk. to presiding judge U.S. Ct. Appeals (2d cir.), Hartford, Conn., 1968-69; assoc. Cahill Gordon & Reindel, N.Y.C., 1969-75, ptnr., 1975—; vis. lectr. Yale U., 1972, 73; lectr. Practicing Law Inst., 1977—; research asst. to Lester and Bindman for book Race and Law in Great Britain, 1972. Contbr. to State Antitrust Law (Lifland), 1984; co-author: (with Lifland, Sorkin and Van Cise) Understanding the Antitrust Laws, 1986. Fulbright scholar, 1967-68. Mem. N.Y. State Bar Assn. (mem. antitrust sect. 1978—, sec. 1979-80, chmn. com. on legis. 1978-79, vice chmn. com. on mergers 1982—), Assn. Bar City N.Y. (mem. com. trade regulation 1974-77, com. on electronic funds transfer 1979-80), ABA (mem. antitrust law sect. 1978—), Phi Beta Kappa. Antitrust, Federal civil litigation. Office: Cahill Gordon & Reindel 80 Pine St New York NY 10005

SOROKIN, ETHEL SILVER, lawyer; b. Hartford, Conn.; d. Jacob M. and Jennie (Klein) Silver; m. Milton Sorokin, June 25, 1950; children—Rachel B., Sharon L., Leo T. B.A., Vassar Coll., 1950; LL.B. with honors, U. Conn., 1953. Bar: Conn. 1953, U.S. Dist. Ct. Conn. 1955, U.S. Ct. Appeals (2d cir.), U.S. Supreme Ct. 1960. Assoc. Levine & Katz, Hartford, Conn., 1953-56; ptnr. Sorokin & Sorokin, Hartford, 1956—; lectr. law., advisor law rev. U. Conn., 1955-58, 61-66; mem., sec. Conn. Jud. Rev. Council, 1978—; trustee U. Conn. Law Found., Hartford, 1976—; lectr. Two Career Marriage, Vasser Coll. and others, 1979—, Conn. Women Artists, U. Hartford, 1984, Understanding the Law series, Hartford Coll. for Women, 1985. Editor-in-chief U. Conn. Law Rev., 1953; mem. bd. editors Conn. Bar Jour., 1951-56. Contbr. to legal jours. Mem. ABA (family law, litigation, probate, antitrust, trademark sects., 1st amendment com.), Conn. Bar Assn. (family law sect., chmn. legis. com. 1984-87, chmn. UMPA study com. 1986); Assn. Trial Lawyers Am. Personal injury, Legislative, Family and matrimonial. Office: Sorokin & Sorokin PC 1 Corporate Ctr Hartford CT 06103 also: 760 Hopmeadow St Simsbury CT 06070

SORTLAND, PAUL ALLAN, lawyer; b. Powers Lake, N.D., July 30, 1953; s. Allan Berdette and Eunice Elizabeth (Nystuen) S.; m. Carolyn Faye Anderson, June 23, 1979; children: Joseph Paul, Martha Marie. BA, St. Olaf Coll., 1975; JD, U. Minn., 1978. Bar: Minn. 1978, U.S. Dist. Ct. Minn. 1979, U.S. Dist. Ct. N.D. 1980, N.D. 1981. Assoc. Alderson & Ondov, Austin, Minn., 1978-80, Qualley, Larson & Jones, Fargo, N.D., 1980-83; ptnr. Holand, Lochow & Sortland, Fargo, 1983-85; pres. Sortland Law Office, Fargo, 1985—. Mem. N.D. State Bar Assn., Minn. State Bar Assn., Assn. Trial Lawyers Am., N.D. Trial Lawyers, U. Minn. Alumni Assn. (v.p. 1986). Lutheran. Lodge: Kiwanis (bd. dirs. Fargo 1985—). State civil litigation, Federal civil litigation, Contracts commercial. Home: 1725 S 10th St Fargo ND 58103 Office: 710 Black Bldg PO Box 1882 Fargo ND 58107

SOSA, DAN, JR., justice Supreme Court New Mexico; b. Las Cruces, N.Mex., Nov. 12, 1923; s. Dan and Margaret (Soto) S.; m. Rita Ortiz, Aug. 31, 1950; 7 children. BSBA, N.Mex. State U., 1947; JD, U. N.Mex., 1951. Bar: N.Mex. 1951. Tchr., coach, public schs. Mesilla, N.Mex., 1947-48; practiced law Las Cruces, 1952-75; judge Las Cruces City Ct., 1952-55; spl. agt. Office of Price Stblzn., 1951-52; asst. dist. atty., then dist. atty. N.Mex. 3d Jud. Dist., 1956-64; spl. asst. atty. gen. for prosecution capital criminal cases Dept. Justice, 1965-66; justice N.Mex. Supreme Ct., 1975—, former chief justice. Served to 1st lt. AC U.S. Army, 1942-45. Democrat. Roman Catholic. Jurisprudence. Office: Supreme Ct N Mex 327 Don Gaspar Ave Santa Fe NM 87504

SOSHNIK, ROBERT MARK, lawyer; b. Omaha, Dec. 6, 1951; s. Joseph and Miriam (Saks) S.; m. Marguerite Jean Pappenheimer, Nov. 29, 1982; children: Michael Andrew, Leah Gail. AB with high distinction, U. Mich., 1970-73; JD with distinction, U. Nebr., 1977. Bar: Nebr. 1977, U.S. Dist. Ct. Nebr. 1977, Mo. 1983. Atty. Zweiback, Kasher, Flaherty & DeWitt, Omaha, 1977-82; asst. counsel Gen. Am. Life Ins., St. Louis, 1982-84; counsel May Dept. Stores Co., St. Louis, 1985—; lectr. Omaha Metropolitan Tech. Community Coll., 1980-82. Mem. ABA, Nebr. Bar Assn., Mo. Bar Assn., St. Louis Bar Assn., Order of Coif, Order of Barristers. Jewish. Real property. Home: 420 Country Oak Dr Saint Louis MO 63017 Office: May Dept Stores Co 611 Olive St Saint Louis MO 63101

SOSLAND, KARL Z., lawyer; b. Springfield, Mass., Apr. 3, 1933; s. Saul and Bessie (Shub) S.; m. June L. Sosland, Mar. 31, 1975; children—Daniel, Cynthia, Jayne, Rachel, Elizabeth. B.A., U. Conn., 1955; LL.B., Columbia U., 1959. Bar: N.J. 1960. Assoc. firm Robert Gruen, Hackensack, N.J., 1960-64, Gruen & Sosland, Hackensack, 1964-65, Scangarella and Sosland, Pompton Plains, N.J., 1965-70; sole practice, Pompton Plains and Paramus, N.J., 1970—; atty. Bd. Adjustment Norwood (N.J.), 1965-74; mcpl. atty. Pequannock Twp., N.J., 1971-80; judge Mcpl. Ct. Pompton Lakes, 1976-78. Mem. Fairlawn (N.J.) Bd. Edn., 1964-66; pres. Kinnelon (N.J.) Bd. Edn., 1971. Mem. ABA, N.J. Bar Assn., Morris County Bar Assn. Real property, Contracts commercial, State civil litigation. Home: 11 Tecumseh Trail Oakland NJ 07436 Office: 95 Route 17 Paramus NJ 07652

SOSNOV, STEVEN ROBERT, lawyer; b. Phila., June 10, 1942; s. Michael and Edna Sosnov; m. Amy L. Wiener, Aug. 9, 1943; children: Jonathan, Elizabeth. BS, Temple U., 1963; JD, NYU, 1966. Bar: N.Y. 1966, U.S. Ct. Internat. Trade 1966, D.C. 1967, U.S. Ct. Appeals (Fed., 2d, 3d, and D.C. cirs.) 1967, U.S. Dist. Ct. N.Y. 1967, U.S. Dist. Ct. D.C. 1967, Pa. 1970, U.S. Dist. Ct. Pa. 1970. Trial atty. customs sect. U.S. Dept. of Justice, N.Y.C., 1966-69; asst. corp. counsel Aamco Industries, Bridgeport, Pa., 1969-70; asst. atty. gen. Pa. Dept. of Justice, Phila., 1971-72; ptnr. Sosnov and Assocs., Phila., N.Y.C., Washington, 1972—. Mem. N.Y. State Bar Assn., Pa. Bar Assn., D.C. Bar Assn., Inter-Am. Bar Assn., Customs and Internat. Trade Bar Assn. Private international, Administrative and regulatory. Home: 113 Yellowstone Rd Plymouth Meeting PA 19462 Office: Sosnov and Assocs 410 Lafayette Bldg Philadelphia PA 19106

SOSTARICH, MARK EDWARD, lawyer; b. Milw., Apr. 10, 1953; s. Edward Michael and Sophia (Hibler) S.; m. Karen Sue Baranek, June 12, 1976; children: Samantha Nicole, Alex Edward. BA with distinction, U. Wis., 1975, JD cum laude, 1978. Bar: Wis. 1978, U.S. Dist. Ct. (ea. and we. dists.) Wis. 1978. Assoc. Godfrey & Kahn, Milw., 1978-84, ptnr., 1984—; mem. bd. visitors U. Wis., Madison, 1983—. Editor-in-chief U. Wis. Law Rev., 1978. Commr. South Milw. Housing Authority, Wis., 1985-86, South Milw. Police and Fire Commn., 1986—; chmn. State of Wis. Dem. Platform and Resolutions Com.; chairperson Milw. County Dem. Party. Mem. ABA, Wis. Bar Assn., Milw. Bar Assn. Avocations: state and local politics, softball, tennis. Federal civil litigation, State civil litigation, Criminal. Home: 1785 Tamarack St South Milwaukee WI 53172 Office: Godfrey & Kahn 780 N Water St Milwaukee WI 53202

SOTIR, RICHARD LOUIS, JR., lawyer; b. Jamestown, N.Y., May 18, 1948; s. Richard Louis Sr. and Naoma Joyce (Lawson) S.; m. Barbara Jane Zinck, Dec. 21, 1970; children: Richard L. III, Laura Ann. BA cum laude, SUNY, Fredonia, 1970; JD, Syracuse U., 1973. Bar: N.Y. 1974, U.S. Dist. Ct. (we. dist.) N.Y. 1985. Sole practice Jamestown, 1974-82; ptnr. Sotir & Goldman, Jamestown, 1983—; assoc. corp. counsel City of Jamestown, 1974-75, corp. counsel, 1976—. Pres. Jamestown (N.Y.) High Sch. Alumni Assn., 1986—; bd. dirs. Jamestown (N.Y.) Babe Ruth Baseball, Inc., 1986—; bd. dirs. Jamestown Boy and Girls Club, Inc. Recipient Service to Youth award Jamestown Boys Club, Inc., 1985, Disting. Service award Jamestown Boys and Girls Club Inc., 1986. Mem. ABA, N.Y. State Bar Assn., Jamestown Bar Assn. (pres. 1982-83), Am. Aribtration Assn. Democrat. Club: Maplehurst Country (v.p. 1986, pres. 1987). Lodge: Masons. Avocations: golf, Babe Ruth Baseball. General practice, Local government, Real property. Office: Sotir & Goldman 8 E 4th St Thurston Terr Jamestown NY 14701

SOUDER, SUSAN, lawyer; b. Washington, Sept. 20, 1956; m. Carl Koziol, June 4, 1978. BA, U. Md., 1978; JD, Georgetown U., 1981. Bar: Md. 1981. Trial atty. U.S. Dept. Justice, Washington, 1981-85; spl. asst. U.S. atty. Los Angeles, 1983; assoc. Gordon, Feinblatt, Rothman, Balt., 1985—. Mem. ABA, Md. State Bar Assn., Balt. City Bar Assn., Women's Bar Assn. (program chair Balt. County chpt. 1985-86, v.p. Balt. City chpt. 1986-87). Tax litigation, Federal civil litigation, State civil litigation. Office: Gordon Feinblatt & Rothman 233 E Redwood St Baltimore MD 21202

SOUERS, LOREN EATON, JR., municipal court judge; b. Canton, Ohio, Apr. 3, 1947; s. Loren Eaton and Mildred Mae (McCollum) S.; m. Beth Ellen Porter, Aug. 2, 1969; children—Jennifer Ellen, Danner Eaton, Theodore Edmunds. B.A., Denison U., 1969; J.D., Case Western Res. U., 1974. Bar: Ohio 1974; U.S. Dist. Ct. (no. dist.) Ohio, 1975; U.S. Supreme Ct. 1978. Asst. prosecutor civil div. Stark County (Ohio), 1977-81; judge Canton Mcpl. Ct., 1982—. Trustee Canton Montessori Sch., 1979, 82; bd. deacons Christ United Presbyn. Ch., 1979-81, v.p., 1980; active United Arts Campaign, Downtown YMCA, Boy Scouts Am.; trustee United Way,

1986—. Served with USAR, 1970-76. Mem. ABA (nat. conf. spl. ct. judges), Ohio State Bar Assn., Ohio Mcpl. Judges Assn., Ohio Legal Ctr. Inst., Canton Jaycees (dir. 1975-76), Phi Delta Theta. Mem. staff Jour. Internat. Law, 1972, mem. editoral bd., 1972-73, editor, 1972-74. Jurisprudence, State civil litigation, Contracts commercial. Home: 1174 Sprucewood SE North Canton OH 44720

SOURS, JOHN DELMAR, lawyer; b. Harrisburg, Pa., Dec. 23, 1944; s. M. Delmar and F. Kathryn (Fowler) S.; m. Lelia Ruth Eye, Aug. 20, 1966; children—Cynthia L., Matthew J., David A. A.B., Coll. William and Mary, 1966, J.D., 1969; LL.M., Georgetown U., 1973. Bar: Va. 1969, Ga. 1973. Assoc., Smith, Currie & Hancock, Atlanta, 1973-77, ptnr., 1978-79; ptnr., prin. Wasson, Sours & Harris, P.C., Atlanta, 1979—; adj. prof. Ga. Inst. Tech., 1979—; seminar lectr. Fed. Publs., Inc., 1976—. Served to capt. U.S. Army, 1969-73. Decorated Bronze Star medal. Mem. Nat. Constrn. Industry Panel, Am. Arbitration Assn., Fed. Bar Assn., ABA, Calif. State Constrn. Arbitration Panel, Atlanta Bar Assn., Lawyers Club Atlanta. Republican. Episcopalian. Government contracts and claims, Labor, Construction. Home: 6490 River Chase Circle NW Atlanta GA 30328 Office: 235 Peachtree St Suite 1000 Atlanta GA 30303

SOURWINE, JULIEN GILLEN, lawyer; b. Washington, Aug. 2, 1939; s. Julien Goode and Mary Elizabeth (Gillen) S.; m. Bonnie P. Seeley, Apr. 14, 1962 (div. Aug. 1986); children: Amanda L. Durante, Jay Andrew. AB, U. Md., 1961; JD, Georgetown U., 1964. Bar: D.C. 1964, U.S. Dist. Ct. D.C. 1965, U.S. Ct. Appeals (D.C. cir.) 1965, U.S. Dist. Ct. Nev. 1966, U.S. Ct. Appeals (9th cir.) 1966, U.S. Supreme Ct. 1976. Law clk. to presiding justice U.S. Ct. Appeals (D.C. cir.), Washington, 1964-65, U.S. Dist. Ct. Nev., Reno, 1965-66; asst. U.S. atty. U.S. Dept. Justice, Reno, 1966-70; ptnr. Mortimer, Sourwine, Mousel, Sloane & Knobel and predecessor firms, Reno, 1971—; council, adj. faculty Nev. Sch. Law, Reno, 1982—. Trustee Old Coll., Reno, 1985—. Fellow Am. Coll. Trial Lawyers; mem. Nev. Bar Assn. (bd. govs.), Assn. Trial Lawyers Am., Nev. Trial Lawyers Assn., Assn. Def. Counsel Nev. (pres. 1981-82). Republican. Methodist. Federal civil litigation, State civil litigation, General practice. Office: Fahrenkopf Mortimer Sourwin et al 333 Marsh Ave Reno NV 89509

SOUTER, DAVID HACKETT, state supreme court justice; b. Melrose, Mass., Sept. 17, 1939; s. Joseph Alexander and Helen Adams (Hackett) S. B.A., Harvard U., 1961, LL.B., 1966; Rhodes scholar, Oxford U., 1961-63. Bar: N.H. Assoc. firm Orr & Reno, Concord, 1966-68; asst. atty. gen. N.H. 1968-71, dep. atty. gen., 1971-76, atty. gen., 1976-78; assoc. justice Superior Ct. N.H., 1978-83, N.H. Supreme Ct., 1983—. Trustee Concord Hosp., 1973-85, pres. bd. trustees, 1978-84; bd. overseers Dartmouth Med. Sch., 1981—. Mem. Am. Bar Assn., N.H. Bar Assn., N.H. Hist. Soc. (v.p. 1980-85, trustee 1976-85), Phi Beta Kappa. Republican. Episcopalian. Judicial administration. Home: Weare NH 03281

SOUTER, DON VERN, lawyer; b. Detroit, July 7, 1923; s. Alfred Lavern and Elizabeth Agnes (Muhlitner) S.; m. Dona-Jean Ann Palmatier, July 12, 1958; children: Sarah, Thomas. Student, Grand Rapids (Mich.) Jr. Coll., 1941-43; B in Mech. Engring., Marquette U., 1944; JD, U. Mich., 1949. Bar: Mich. 1949, U.S. Dist. Ct. (we. dist.) Mich. 1954. Assoc. Cholette, Perkins & Buchanan, Grand Rapids, 1949-59, ptnr., 1959—. Mem. Grand Rapids Bd. of Zoning Appeals, 1957-60, Grand Rapids Bd. of Library Commrs., 1968-79, Kent County Library Commn., 1973-78, Grand Rapids Bd. of Edn., 1985—. Served to lt. comdr. USNR, 1942-65. Fellow Am. Coll. Trial Lawyers; mem. ABA, Mich. Bar Assn., Grand Rapids Bar Assn., Am. Judicature Soc., Internat. Assn. Def. Counsel, Grand Rapids Jaycees (pres. 1954-55), Delta Theta Phi. Republican. Lodge: Masons. Avocations: skiing, sailing. Federal civil litigation, State civil litigation, Insurance. Home: 2637 Littlefield NE Grand Rapids MI 49506 Office: Cholette Perkins & Buchanan 900 Campau Sq Bldg Grand Rapids MI 49503

SOUTH, MARK OMEGA, lawyer; b. Ft. Knox, Ky., Aug. 15, 1957; s. Robert Lee and Johanna Teresa (Palisek) S. BS summa cum laude, So. Benedictine Coll., 1978; JD, U. Ala., 1981. Bar: Ala. 1981, U.S. Dist. Ct. (no. dist.) Ala. 1983. Assoc. Law Office of S. Wayne Fuller, Cullman, Ala., 1981-83; ptnr. Davis and South, Cullman, 1983-86; sole practice Cullman, 1986—. Named one of Outstanding Young Men of Am., 1983. Mem. Assn. Trial Lawyers Am., Ala. Trial Lawyers Assn. Democrat. Avocations: softball, white-water rafting, water skiing. General practice, Personal injury, Real property. Home: Rt 3 Box 88 Vinemont AL 35179 Office: PO Box 1221 Cullman AL 35056

SOUTHERN, ROBERT ALLEN, lawyer; b. Independence, Mo., July 17, 1930; s. James Allen and Josephine (Ragland) S.; m. Cynthia Agnes Drews, May 17, 1952; children: David D., William A., James M., Kathryn A. B.S. in Polit. Sci., Northwestern U., 1952, LL.B., 1954. Bar: Ill. 1955. Assoc. Mayer, Brown & Platt, Chgo., 1954-64, ptnr., 1965—, mng. ptnr., 1978—. Editor-in-chief: Northwestern U. Law Rev., 1953-54. Trustee, v.p., gen. counsel LaRabida Children's Hosp. and Research Ctr., Chgo., 1974—; trustee, gen. counsel Kenilworth Union Ch., Ill., 1980—; hon. trustee Joseph Sears Sch. Found., Kenilworth, 1981—; pres. Joseph Sears Sch. Bd., 1977-79; trustee Rush-Presbyn.-St. Luke's Med. Ctr., 1983—; bd. dirs. Boys and Girls Clubs of Chgo., 1986— . Served with U.S. Army, 1955-57. Mem. ABA, Chgo. Bar Assn., Law Club of Chgo., Legal Club of Chgo., Order of Coif, Econ. Club of Chgo. Clubs: Indian Hill (Winnetka), Sky (N.Y.C.), Chicago, Metropolitan, Monroe. Banking, General corporate, Securities. Office: Mayer Brown & Platt 190 S LaSalle St Chicago IL 60603

SOUTHGATE, (CHRISTINA) ADRIENNE GRAVES, lawyer; b. Biloxi, Miss., Feb. 26, 1951; d. James Henry Jr. and Helen Alvera (Mataya) Graves; m. Theodore John Southgate, June 26, 1972; children: Edward James Leyland, Colin Scott Christian. BA, Wellesley (Mass.) Coll., 1973; postgrad., Gordon-Conwell Theol. Sem., South Hamilton, Mass., 1973-75; JD, Wayne State U., 1978, postgrad. Bar: Mich. 1979, U.S. Ct. Appeals (6th cir.) 1980, U.S. Ct. Appeals (5th, 7th and 11th cirs.) 1982, U.S. Supreme Ct. 1982, U.S. Ct. Appeals (3d, 4th, 8th, 9th, 10th and D.C. cirs.) 1983, U.S. Ct. Appeals (1st, 2d and fed. cirs.) 1984, R.I. 1985. Law clk. to presiding justice Mich. Supreme Ct., Detroit, 1979-81; chief appellate counsel Charfoos, Christensen & Archer, P.C., Detroit, 1981-85; assoc. Carroll, Kelly & Murphy, Providence, R.I., 1985—; adj. instr. legal writing Detroit Coll. Law, 1979-81; counsel exec. com. Emma Willard Sch., Troy, N.Y., 1985—; cons. Jr. League of Providence, R.I., 1986—. Contbr. articles to profl. jours. Vol. atty. R.I. Protection and Advocacy Services, Inc.; mem. fin. stewardship com. Episcopal Diocese R.I.; bd. dirs. alumnae fund and exec., council Emma Willard Sch.; bd. dirs. Big Sisters Assn. R.I. Mem. ABA (editorial bd. gen. practice sect. 1982—, various coms.), R.I. Bar Assn. (specialization com. 1985—), Fed. Bar Assn., Nat. Assn. Women Lawyers, Am. Judicature Soc., Christian Legal Soc., R.I. Wellesley Club. Republican. Federal civil litigation, State civil litigation, Health. Home: 16 Edwin St Barrington RI 02806 Office: Carroll Kelly & Murphy 155 S Main St Providence RI 02903

SOUTHWICK, LESLIE HARBURD, lawyer, educator; b. Edinburg, Tex., Feb. 10, 1950; s. Lloyd M. and Ruth (Tarpley) S.; m. Sharon E. Polasek, Aug. 18, 1973; children: Philip, Catherine. BA cum laude, Rice U., 1972; JD, U. Tex., 1975. Bar: Tex. 1975, Miss. 1977. Law clk. to presiding judge Tex. Ct. Criminal Appeals, Austin, 1975-76, U.S. Ct. Appeals (5th cir.), Jackson, Miss., 1976-77; assoc. Brunini, Grantham, Grower & Hewes, Jackson, 1977-83, ptnr., 1983—; adj. prof. Miss. Coll. Sch. Law, Jackson, 1985—; mem. Miss. Constn. Study Commn., 1985-86. Author: Presidential Also-Rans and Running Mates, 1984 (ALA best reference book award 1985). Pres. Hinds County Mental Health Assn., Jackson, 1981-82; Miss. campaign mgr. George Bush for Pres., 1980; alternate del. Rep. Nat. Conv., 1984. Named Vol. of Yr., Hinds County Mental Health Assn., 1981, 85. Mem. ABA, Miss. Bar Assn. Republican. Roman Catholic. Lodge: Kiwanis. Oil and gas leasing, Legal education, Public education. Home: 6 Pond Side Dr Jackson MS 39211 Office: Brunini Grantham Grower & Hewes PO Box 119 1400 Trustmark Nat Bank Jackson MS 39205

SOVEREIGN, KENNETH LESTER, lawyer, consultant, educator, writer; b. Sartell, Minn., Feb. 20, 1919; s. Lester Clark and Myrtle (Frank) S.; m. Janet Lucille Olson, July 19, 1947; children—David Paul, Jeffrey Clark. B.S., U. Minn., 1941, postgrad. Sch. Bus., 1946-47, J.D., Wm. Mitchell Coll. Law, 1955; Advanced Mgmt. Program, Harvard U., 1964. Bar: Minn. 1955, U.S. Dist. Ct. Minn. 1973, U.S. Ct. Appeals (8th cir.) 1973. Asst. state labor conciliator State of Minn., 1949-53; personnel and safety dir. Waldorf Paper Products Co., 1953-60, corp. indsl. and pub. relations dir., 1960-66; corp. indsl. relations dir. Hoerner Waldorf Corp., St. Paul, 1966-68, v.p. indsl. relations, 1968-71, v.p., sr. atty., 1971-77; assoc. counsel, asst. sec. Champion Internat. Corp., St. Paul, 1977-81; sole practice, St. Paul, 1981—; cons., seminar leader; lectr. indsl. relations U. Minn.; mem. Faculty Mgmt. Ctr., St. Thomas Coll., 1965-82; lectr. on workers and unemployment compensation, personnel law Minn. Assn. Commerce and Industry, 1980—. Mem. indsl. relations adv. council U. Minn., 1955-70; pres. Don El Guia Owners Assn., Mex., 1974-77, chmn. bd., 1978-79; mem. Minn. Occupational Safety and Health Rev. Bd., 1975—, chmn., 1980—; bd. dirs. Tri-Lakes Assn., 1955—. Served with AUS, 1942-46, PTO. Fellow Soc. for Advancement Mgmt.; mem. ABA (labor law sect., OSHA and EEO coms. 1971—), Minn. Bar Assn. (labor law sect.), Am. Soc. Personnel Adminstrn. (lectr. 1980-85, seminar leader personnel mgmt. and law 1980—, contbg. author Handbook on Personnel and Indsl. Relations 1980). Author: Personnel Law, 1984. Republican. Lutheran. Club: Masons. Author: Personnel Law, 1984. Labor, Workers' compensation, Pension, profit-sharing, and employee benefits. Home: 4415 Olson Lake Trail N Lake Elmo MN 55042 Office: 2218 University Ave Saint Paul MN 55114

SOVERN, JEFF, law educator; b. Mpls., Dec. 26, 1956; s. Michael Ira Sovern and Lenore Judith (Goodman) Sanders; m. Gail Beckenstein, June 30, 1985. AB, Columbia U., 1977, JD, 1980. Bar: N.Y. 1982, U.S. Dist. Ct. (ea. and so. dists.) N.Y. 1982, U.S. Dist. Ct. Md. 1982, U.S. Ct. Appeals (4th cir.) 1982. Law clk. to chief judge U.S. Dist. Ct. Md., Balt., 1980-81; assoc. Paul, Weiss, Rifkind, Wharton & Garrison, N.Y.C., 1981-83; asst. prof. sch. law St. John's U., Jamaica, N.Y., 1983-85, assoc. prof. sch. law, 1985—; reporter discovery oversight com. U.S. Dist. Ct. (ea. dist.) N.Y., Bklyn., 1985—. Mem. ABA, N.Y. State Bar Assn., Assn. of Bar of City of N.Y. Jewish. Contracts commercial, Federal civil litigation. Home: 123-40 83d Ave Kew Gardens NY 11415 Office: St John's U Sch Law Fromkes Hall Jamaica NY 11439

SOVERN, MICHAEL IRA, university president; b. N.Y.C., Dec. 1, 1931; s. Julius and Lillian (Arnstein) S.; m. Lenore Goodman, Feb. 21, 1952 (div. Apr. 1963); children: Jeffrey Austin, Elizabeth Ann, Douglas Todd; m. Eleanor Leen, Aug. 25, 1963 (div. Feb. 1974); 1 dau., Julie Danielle; m. Joan Wit, Mar. 9, 1974. A.B. summa cum laude, Columbia U., 1953, LL.B. (James Ordronaux prize), 1955, LL.D. (hon.), 1980; Ph.D. (hon.), Tel Aviv U., 1982. Bar: N.Y. 1956, U.S. Supreme Ct. 1976. Asst. prof., then assoc. prof. law U. Minn. Law Sch., 1955-58; mem. faculty Columbia Law Sch., 1957—, prof. law, 1960—, Chancellor Kent prof., 1977—, dean Law Sch., 1970-79; chmn. exec. com. faculty Columbia U., 1968-69, provost, exec. v.p., 1979-80, univ. pres., 1980—; research dir. Legal Restraints on Racial Discrimination in Employment, Twentieth Century Fund, 1962-66; spl. counsel N.Y. State Joint Legis. Com. Indsl. and Labor Conditions, 1962-63; spl. counsel to gov. N.J., 1974-77; cons. Time mag., 1965-80; dir. Chem. Bank, AT&T, GNY Ins. Group.; mem. N.J. Bd. Mediation Panel of Arbitrators; mem. panel arbitrators Fed. Mediation and Conciliation Service; bd. dirs. Asian Cultural Council, Shubert Orgn., Shubert Found., NAACP Legal Def. Fund; chmn. N.Y.C. Charter Revision Commn., 1982-83; co-chmn. 2d Circuit Commn. on Reduction of Burdens and Costs in Civil Litigation, 1977-80; chmn. Commn. on Integrity in Govt., 1986. Author: Legal Restraints on Racial Discrimination in Employment, 1966, Law and Poverty, 1969. Fellow Am. Acad. Arts and Scis.; mem. Council Fgn. Relations, Assn. Bar City N.Y., ABA, Am. Arbitration Assn. (panel arbitrators), Am. Law Inst., Nat. Acad. Arbitrators. Office: Columbia Law Sch 435 W 116th St New York NY 10027

SOWALD, HEATHER GAY, lawyer, hearing examiner; b. Columbus, Ohio, Dec. 26, 1954; d. Martin M. and Beatrice (Kronick) S.; m. Robert Marc Kaplan, June 12, 1977; children: Andrew Scott, Alexis Beth. BA, Case Western Res. U., 1976; JD, Capital U., 1979. Bar: Ohio 1979, U.S. Dist. Ct. (so. dist.) Ohio 1980, U.S. Ct. Appeals (6th cir.) 1981. Ptnr. Sowald & Sowald, Columbus, 1979-85, Sowald & Daneman, Columbus, 1985—; hearing officer Cert. Need Rev. Bd. State of Ohio, 1982—, Dept. Adminstrv., 1982—, Dept. Mental Health, 1986—, Dept. Mental Retardation, 1986—, Dept. Health, 1986—. Bd. dirs. Wilderness Bond, Inc., Franklin County, Ohio, 1982—, Youth Services Adv. Bd., Franklin County, 1984—; legal advisor United Way League Against Child Abuse, Franklin County, 1986—. Mem. Ohio State Bar Assn. (council of dels. 1986—), Columbus Bar Assn. (chmn. juvenile law com. 1982-84, chmn. admissions to bar 1984—), Franklin County Trial Lawyers Assn. (trustee 1985—), Women Lawyers of Franklin County (pres. 1984-85), Capital U. Alumni Assn. (pres. 1984-86). Democrat. Jewish. Family and matrimonial, Juvenile, Probate. Office: Sowald & Daneman 575 S 3d St Columbus OH 43215

SOWELL, JACK ROBSON, lawyer; b. San Antonio, Jan. 29, 1932; c. Charles L. and Alleen (Reese) S.; m. Patricia M. Stone, Aug. 6, 1954; children: Michael, Laura K., Sowell Brown. B.B.A., U. Tex., 1953, LL.B., 1956. Bar: Tex. 1956. Atty. Humble Oil and Refining Co. (Exxon), Houston, 1956-57; from assoc. to ptnr. Vinson & Elkins, Houston, 1957—; mem. ursury com. Tex. State Bar; bd. dirs. First Continental Real Estate Investment Trust, Houston, Nat. Tile Ins. Co. Mem. ABA, Houston Bar Assn., Houston Real Estate Lawyers Council, Am. Coll. Investment Counsel, Am. Coll. Real Estate Lawyers, Houston C. of C. Methodist. Clubs: River Oaks Country, Houston Center. Office: Vinson & Elkins 3300 First City Tower 1001 Fannin Houston TX 77002-6760

SOWERS, DAVID ERIC, lawyer; b. Marceline, Mo., Nov. 15, 1946; s. Alvin P. and Carol (Wheeler) S.; m. Vickie Diane Sanders, Dec. 28, 1968; 1 child, Courtney Evan. BS in Physics, Russian Lang., U. Mo., 1968, JD, 1974. Bar: Mo. 1975, U.S. Dist. Ct. (we. dist.) Mo. 1975, U.S. Supreme Ct. 1979, U.S. Ct. Claims 1980, U.S. Tax Ct. 1980, U.S. Dist. Ct. (ea. dist.) Mo. 1983, U.S. Ct. Appeals (8th cir.) 1983. Mem. Clandestine Service CIA, Washington, 1976-79; asst. prosecutor Boone County, Columbia, Mo., 1975-76; sole practice Brunswick, Mo., 1979-83; ptnr. Kennedy & Sowers, St. Charles, Mo., 1983-85; chief litigator Friedman, Weitzman & Friedman P.C., St. Louis, 1985—; pres. 9th Jud. Cir., 1981-82; pros. atty. Chariton County, Mo., 1980-83. Del. Dem. State Conv., Columbia, 1980; candidate for State Rep. Mo. Legislature, 18th Legis. Dist., 1984. Served to capt. USMC, 1968-72. Mem. Mo. Bar Assn., Bar Assn. of Met. of St. Louis, Assn. Trial Lawyers Am., Mo. Assn. Trial Attys. (gov. 1983—), Am. Legion. Methodist. Lodge: Masons. Avocation: tennis, sailing. Federal civil litigation, State civil litigation, Labor. Office: Friedman Weitzman & Friedman PC 1133 Pine St Saint Louis MO 63101

SOWLES, MARCIA KAY, lawyer; b. Elkhart, Ind., Oct. 29, 1950; d. Charles H. and Maxine (Sprinkle) S. BA, Manchester Coll., 1972; JD, Valparaiso U., 1975; LLM, Yale U., 1980. Bar: Ind. 1975, D.C. 1983. Atty. Legal Services Program No. Ind., South Bend, 1975-79; trial atty. Dept. Energy Econ. Regulatory Adminstrn., Washington, 1980-84, dep. asst. gen. counsel, 1984-85, asst. chief counsel, 1985-86, assoc. solicitor, 1986—. Fellow Yale U., 1979-80. Mem. ABA, Ind. Bar Assn., D.C. Bar Assn. Mem. Brethren Ch. Clubs: Washington Figure Skating; North Va. Skating (Fairfax). Administrative and regulatory, Federal civil litigation. Home: 2525 N 10th St Apt 519 Arlington VA 22201 Office: Econ Regulatory Adminstrn Dept Energy Dept Energy 1000 Independence Ave SW Washington DC 20585

SOYSTER, MARGARET BLAIR, lawyer; b. Washington, Aug. 5, 1951; s. Peter and Eliza (Shumaker) S. AB magna cum laude, Smith Coll., 1973; JD, U. Va., 1976. Bar: N.Y. 1977, U.S. Dist. Ct. (so. and ea. dists.) N.Y. 1977, U.S. Ct. Appeals (2d cir.) 1979, U.S. Supreme Ct. 1981, U.S. Ct. Appeals (4th cir.) 1982. Assoc. Rogers & Wells, N.Y.C., 1976-84, ptnr., 1984—. Mem. ABA, Assn. of Bar of City of N.Y., Nat. Assn. Coll. and Univ. Attys., Phi Beta Kappa. Episcopalian. Labor, Libel, Federal civil litigation. Office: Rogers & Wells 200 Park Ave New York NY 10128

SPADONI, PETER ANTHONY, lawyer; b. Tacoma, Oct. 12, 1955; s. Rudolph Michael and Jacquelline Belle (Mellican) S.; m. Elizabeth Anne Scott, Dec. 17, 1982; children: Anne Jacquelline, Evan McLaren. BA, Wash. State U., Pullman; JD cum laude, U. Puget Sound; LLM in Taxation, U. Fla. Bar: Wash. 1980, Fla. 1981, U.S. Dist. Ct. (so. dist.) Fla. 1981, U.S. Dist. Ct. (we. dist.) Wash. 1981, U.S. Tax Ct. 1981, U.S. Dist. Ct. (ea. dist.) Wash. 1985. Assoc. Smathers & Thompson, Miami, Fla., 1981-83, Jeffers, Danielson, Sonn & Aylward P.S., Wenatchee, Wash., 1983—; adj. prof. econs. Heritage Coll., Wenatchee, Wash., 1984, bus. law Wenatchee Valley Coll., 1985; keynote speaker Greater Miami Tax Inst., 1983. Mem. fin. com. St. Joseph's Ch., Wenatchee, 1985—, legal com. United Way, Wenatchee, 1986—. Mem. ABA (tax sect., continuing legal edn. com.), Wash. State Bar Assn. (tax sect.), Fla. Bar Assn. (1st Place award 1983), Aircraft Owners and Pilots Assn. Avocations: writing, flying, hunting. Corporate taxation, Securities, Contracts commercial. Home: 1215 Castlerock Wenatchee WA 98801 Office: Jeffers Danielson Sonn & Aylward PS 317 N Mission Wenatchee WA 98801

SPAEDER, ROGER CAMPBELL, lawyer; b. Cleve., Dec. 20, 1943; S. Ferd N. and Luceil (Campbell) S.; m. Frances DeSales Sutherland, Sept. 7, 1968; children—Michael, Matthew. B.S., Bowling Green U., 1965; J.D. with honors, George Washington U., 1970. Bar: D.C. 1971, U.S. Dist. Ct. D.C. 1971, U.S. Ct. Appeals (D.C. cir.) 1971, U.S. Supreme Ct. 1976, U.S. Ct. Claims 1979, U.S. Dist. Ct. Md. 1984, U.S. Ct. Appeals (2d and 4th cirs.) 1985. Asst. U.S. atty. D.C., Washington, 1971-76; ptnr. Zuckerman, Spaeder, Goldstein, Taylor & Kolker, Washington, 1976—; faculty Atty. Gen. Advocacy Inst., 1974-76, Nat. Inst. Trial Advocacy, 1978-79; adj. faculty Georgetown U. Law Ctr., 1979-80, Am. U. Ctr. Adminstrn. Justice, 1976-79; lectr. D.C. Bar Continuing Legal Edn. Programs, 1980—; mem. Recipient Spl. Achievement award Dept. Justice, 1971. Mem. Bar Assn. D.C. (lectr. Criminal Practice Inst. 1977-80), D.C. Bar (com. criminal jury instrns. 1972, div. courts, lawyers, adminstrn. of justice, 1976-78; adv. com. continuing legal edn. 1986), ABA (litigation, antitrust law sects.; co-chair Washington complex crimes subcom.), Def. Research Inst., Assn. Trial Lawyers Am., Assn. Plaintiffs' Trial Attys., Nat. Assn. Criminal Def. Lawyers, Omicron Delta Kappa. Federal civil litigation, Criminal. Home: 7624 Georgetown Pike McLean VA 22102 Office: Zuckerman Spaeder Goldstein et al 1201 Connecticut Ave NW 12th Floor Washington DC 20036

SPAETH, GARY LEWIS, lawyer; b. Billings, Mont., Jan. 13, 1945; s. Alfred George and Lucy Jane Spaeth. BA, Mont. State U., 1968; JD, U. Mont., 1974. Bar: Mont. 1974, U.S. Dist. Ct. Mont. 1974, U.S. Ct. Claims 1976. Legal counsel Mont. Dept. Natural Resources, Helena, 1974-78, asst. chief counsel, 1978-82; sole practice Joliet and Red Lodge, Mont., 1982—; rep. Mont. State Legislature, Helena, 1982—; chmn. Interim Legis. Code Com., 1985—. City atty. Town of Fromberg, Mont., 1983—, Town of Joliet, 1986—; bd. dirs. Mont. Regional Rehab. Corp., Billings, 1985. Served with U.S. Army, 1968-72. Recipient Civic Achievement award Mont. High Sch. Assn., 1986. Mem. ABA (fellow young lawyers div., chmn. explorer law com. 1982-84, council 1980-82, energy coordination com. 1984—); mem. Mont. Bar Assn. (trustee 1978-80, sec., treas. 1982—), Am. Judicature Soc., Am. Legion, Mont. Stock Growers. Democrat. Mem. Disciples of Christ Ch. Lodges: Elks, Masons. State civil litigation, Legislative, General practice. Office: Box 193 Joliet MT 59041 Office: Box 1661 Red Lodge MT 59068

SPAETH, NICHOLAS JOHN, state attorney general; b. Mahnomen, Minn., Jan. 27, 1950. A.B., Stanford U., 1972, J.D., 1977; B.A., Oxford U., Eng., 1974. Bar: Minn. 1979, U.S. Dist. Ct. (Minn.) 1979, U.S. Ct. Appeals (8th cir.) 1979, N.D. 1980, U.S. Dist. Ct. (N.D.) 1980, U.S. Supreme Ct. 1984. Law clk. U.S. Ct. Appeals (8th cir.), Fargo, N.D., 1977-78; law clk. to Justice Byron White U.S. Supreme Ct., Washington, 1978-79; pvt. practice 1979-84; atty. gen. State of N.D., Bismarck, 1984—; adj. prof. law U. Minn., 1980-83. Rhodes scholar, 1972-74. Democrat. Roman Catholic. Criminal. Office: Office of Atty Gen State Capitol Bismarck ND 58505 •

SPAIN, LARRY ROBERT, law educator; b. Newton, Iowa, Apr. 20, 1951; s. Robert M. and Colleen M. (Edwards) S.; m. Amelia L. Churchill, July 17, 1974; children: Kristina, Jodi, Robin. BA, U. Iowa, 1973; JD, Creighton U., 1976. Bar: Nebr. 1976, U.S. Dist. Ct. Nebr. 1976, N.D. 1983, U.S. Dist. Ct. N.D. 1983. Atty. Western Nebr. Legal Services, Scottsbluff, 1976-78, Legal Aid Soc., Omaha, 1978-83; asst. clin. prof. law, dir. legal clinic U. N.D., Grand Forks, 1983—; mem. spl. com. civil legal services N.D. Supreme Ct., 1985—. Mem. ABA, Nebr. Bar Assn., N.D. Bar Assn. (lawyer referral service com.). Democrat. Lutheran. Avocations: gardening, home remodeling. Legal education, Family and matrimonial, General practice. Home: 714 Cottonwood St Grand Forks ND 58201 Office: U ND Sch Law Grand Forks ND 58202

SPAIN, PATRICK JAMES, lawyer; b. Karachi, Pakistan, Apr. 22, 1952; came to U.S., 1953; s. James William and Edith (James) S. BA, U. Chgo., 1974; JD, Boston U., 1979. Bar: Ill. 1979. Staff counsel Extel Corp., Northbrook, Ill., 1979-83, gen. counsel, 1983—, v.p., 1986—; gen. ptnr. Lakeshore Properties, Chgo., 1983—. Mem. ABA, Ill. Bar Assn., No. Ill. Exporters Council. General corporate, Computer, Real property. Office: Extel Corp 4065 Commercial Ave Northbrook IL 60062

SPAINHOUR, TREMAINE HOWARD, lawyer; b. Rural Hall, N.C., Jan. 15, 1924; s. T. Hobart and Martha (Vaughn) S.; m. Nancy Williamson, Dec. 2, 1944; 1 child, Robert H. B.A., Coll. William and Mary, 1954, J.D., 1956. Ptnr. Kaufman, Obernorfer & Spainhour, Norfolk, Va., 1962-77; ptnr. Spainhour & Hall, Norfolk, 1977-80, McGuire, Woods, Battle & Boothe, Norfolk, 1980—. Served to capt. USAF, 1948-53. Mem. ABA, Va. State Bar, Va. Bar Assn. Methodist. Clubs: Harbor, Town Point (Norfolk); Cedar Point (Suffolk, Va.). Avocations: golf; fishing. Probate, Corporate taxation, Estate taxation. Home: 1406 Buckingham Ave Norfolk VA 23508 Office: McGuire Woods Battle & Boothe 9000 World Trade Ctr Norfolk VA 23510

SPAK, WALTER JOSEPH, lawyer; b. New Kensington, Pa., July 23, 1951; s. Walter and Virginia B. (Fontana) S. Student, Sophia U., Tokyo, 1970-71; BA, U. Notre Dame, 1973; JD, Georgetown U., 1977; postgrad., Ctr. for Internat. Studies, Salzburg, Austria, 1977-78. Bar: D.C. 1978, Pa. 1978, U.S. Ct. Internat. Trade. Assoc. Loesheider, Heuking, Kühn & Partner, Dusseldorf, Fed. Republic of Germany, 1978, Arter, Hadden & Hemmendinger, Washington, 1978-83, Wald, Harkrader & Ross, Washington, 1983-85; ptnr. Wald, Warkraper & Ross, Washington, 1985, Willkie, Farr & Gallagher, Washington, 1985—. Mem. D.C. Bar Assn. Democrat. Roman Catholic. Private international, Public international, Administrative and regulatory. Home: 4417 Volta Pl Washington DC 20007 Office: Willkie Farr & Gallagher 818 Connecticut Ave Washington DC 20006

SPALDING, MICHAEL FREDRICK, lawyer; b. Louisville, Apr. 14, 1945; s. Robert William and Lillian (Waters) S.; m. Shirley Taylor, Mar. 19, 1967; 1 child, Taylor. B Mech. Engring., U. Louisville, 1968, JD, 1972, M in Engring., 1973. Bar: Ky. 1972, U.S. Dist. Ct. (we. dist.) Ky. 1982, U.S. Ct. Appeals (6th cir.) 1982. Engr. Ford Motor Co., Louisville, 1966-78, sr. engr., 1978-82; sole practice Louisville, 1972-82; asst. atty. U.S. Dept. Justice, Louisville, 1982-85, chief civil sect., 1984—; ptnr. Specialties by Spalding, Louisville, 1972—; sec. Printing Plus Inc., Louisville, 1980—. Deacon Walnut St. Bapt. Ch., Louisville, 1972—, dir. sunday sch., 1974—. Named Christian Sportsperson of Yr. Walnut St. Bapt. Ch, 1981. Mem. ABA, Ky. Bar Assn., Louisville Bar Assn., Fed. Bar Assn. Republican. Club: Classic Thunderbird (Louisville) (treas. 1974-84). Avocations: old cars, running. Federal civil litigation, State civil litigation, Bankruptcy. Home: 3014 Falmouth Dr Louisville KY 40205 Office: US Atty Office 510 W Broadway 10th Floor Louisville KY 40202

SPALDING, WALLACE HUGH, JR., lawyer; b. Lebanon, Ky., Nov. 21, 1921; s. Wallace H. and Nell (Hill) S.; m. Martha R. Ratterree, July 20, 1946; children: Janet, Carol, Wallace H. III, Thomas. AB, St. Joseph's Coll., 1943; JD, U. Louisville, 1951. Bar: Ky. 1951, U.S. dist. Ct. (we. dist.) Ky. 1958, U.S. Ct. Appeals (6th cir.) 1959, U.S. Supreme Ct. 1960, U.S. Dist. Ct. (so. dist.) Ind. 1972. Pros. atty. City of Louisville, 1960-62; sole practice Louisville, 1954—; part-time prof. U. Louisville Law Sch., 1969-71; trustee in Bankruptcy Ct., 1962-84. Active Louisville Dem. politics, 1956-74, St. Agnes Parish Council, Louisville, 1980-83. Served to sgt. U.S. Army, 1943-46, ETO. Mem. ABA, Ky. Bar Assn., Louisville Bar Assn. Democrat. Roman Catholic. Lodge: KC. Avocations: hunting, fishing. Bankruptcy, Estate planning, Probate. Home: 1438 Rosewood Ave Louisville KY 40204 Office: Old Portland Bldg 539 W Market Suite 300 Louisville KY 40202

SPALTY, EDWARD, lawyer; b. New Haven, Conn., Oct. 1, 1946; s. Kermit and Elinor (Phelan) Turgeon. AB, Emory U., 1968; JD, Columbia U., 1973. Bar: Mo. 1975, U.S. Dist. Ct. (we. dist.) Mo. 1975, U.S. Ct. Claims 1977, U.S. Ct. Appeals (8th cir.) 1984. Assoc. Webster & Sheffield, N.Y.C., 1973-74; from assoc. to ptnr. Dietrich, Davis, Dicus, Rowlands, Schmitt & Gorman, Kansas City, Mo., 1974—; adv. bd. dirs. Operation Discovery Sch., Kansas City. Regional adv. bd., VIP panel chmn., state bd. dirs. Mo. Easter Seals Soc., Kansas City, 1984—; bd. dirs. Kansas City Track Club. Served to specialist U.S. Army, 1968-70. Mem. ABA (litigation sect., franchising forum com.), Mo. Bar Assn. (civil rules and procedures com.), Kansas City Met. Bar Assn. (franchise law com., co-chmn. 9th ann. Franchise Law Inst.), Lawyers Assn. Kansas City, Mo. Orgn. Def. Attys., Def. Research and Trial Lawyers Assn., Am. Judicature Soc., Sigma Nu. Clubs: Kansas City (Mo.); Columbia, Princeton (N.Y.C.). Federal civil litigation, State civil litigation, Franchising. Home: 618 W 39th Terr 2E Kansas City MO 64111 Office: Dietrich Davis Dicus Rowlands et al 1700 City Ctr Sq Kansas City MO 64105

SPANGLER, EDWIN LEROY, lawyer; b. Denver, Dec. 2, 1924; s. Edwin Lewis and Vera (Vern) S.; m. Rebecca Muldrow, Aug. 19, 1943; children: Gregory Scott, Ronald Stephen, Kent Stanley. BS in Chem. Engring., U. Colo., 1948, JD, 1951. Bar: Colo. 1951, Mo. 1952, U.S. Patent Office 1955. House counsel Malinckrodt Chem. Works, St. Louis, 1951-53; ptnr. Anderson & Spangler, Denver, 1953-56; sr. ptnr. Anderson, Spangler & Wymore, Denver, 1956-73; ptnr. Edwards, Spangler, Wymore & Klaas, Denver, 1972-75; sole practice Denver, 1975—. Served to lt. USN, 1943-46. Mem. ABA, Fed. Bar Assn., Colo. Bar Assn., Denver Bar Assn., Am. Patent Law Assn., Denver Law Club, Phi Gamma Delta, Phi Delta Phi. Republican. Presbyterian. Clubs: Denver Country, Executive, Gyro (Denver); Deans U. Colo. Lodge: Rotary. Patent, Trademark and copyright, Federal civil litigation. Office: 200 Trinity Pl 1801 Broadway Denver CO 80202

SPANN, RONALD THOMAS, lawyer; b. Chgo., Aug. 27, 1949; s. Daniel Anthony and Lorraine Marie (Gervasio) S. Student Sophia U., Tokyo, 1969, St. Mary's Coll., Rome, 1970; AB, U. Notre Dame, 1971; postgrad. Fordham Law Sch. Inst. State and Law, Warsaw, Poland, 1976, Trinity Coll., Cambridge U., 1976; JD, John Marshall Law Sch., Chgo., 1977; diploma internat. trade law. Bar: Ill. 1977, D.C. 1980, U.S. Dist. Ct. (no. dist.) Ill., U.S. Ct. Appeals (7th cir.), N.Y. 1984, Fla. 1984, U.S. Dist. Ct. (so. dist.) Fla., U.S. Supreme Ct., U.S. Ct. Appeals (11th cir.) Fla., 1985; lic. real estate and mortgage broker. Assoc. solicitor U.S. Dept. Labor; trial atty. EEOC; law clk. to chief judge U.S. Dist. Ct. (no. dist.) Ill.; lobbyist Trade Assn. Execs. Food Industry, Ill., D.C., Va., Baker & McKenzie, Chgo., 1972-74; ptnr. firm Newman & Spann, Chgo.; sr. ptnr. Spann & Assocs., P.A., Miami and Fort Lauderdale, Fla.; pres. panel U.S. Arbitration and Mediation Service of S.E., Am. Arbitration Assn.; pres. AMERI-TRUST, Inc. Bd. dirs. Edgewater Community Council, Advs. for Human Dignity, Advs. for Human Rights; corr. Amnesty Internat., U.S.A.; co-founder AID-Ctr. One, Gay Rights Nat. Lobby, Lamda Legal Def. and Edn. Fund, Inc. Recipient Real Estate Rehabilitator award Chgo. City Council, 1981. Mem. ABA (chmn. internat. human rights com., drafter Monec "Whistleblower" and mcpl. civil rights codes), Chgo. Bar Assn., Fed. Bar Assn. (bd. dirs. Chgo. chpt., chmn. internat. human rights com.), Assn. Trial Lawyers Am., Christian Legal Soc., Lawyers in Mensa, Fla. Bar Assn., Broward County Bar Assn., Soc. Profls. Dispute Resolution, Nat. Assn. Realtors, Assn. Mortgage Bankers (chair alt. dispute resolution com.). Arbitration and mediation, Real property, Civil rights. Office: 1001 S Andrews Ave #102 Fort Lauderdale FL 33316

SPARKES, JAMES EDWARD, lawyer; b. Syracuse, N.Y., Oct. 29, 1948; s. Edward William and Kathryn Claire (MacDonald) S.; m. Karen M. Kelley, June 28, 1975; children: Matthew Kelley, Bryan Kelley. BA, Coll. Holy Cross, 1971; MA, Nelson A. Rockefeller Coll. Pub. Affairs and Policy, SUNY-Albany, 1974; JD cum laude, Syracuse U., 1976. Bar: N.Y. 1977, U.S. Dist. Ct. (no. dist.) N.Y. 1977, U.S. Tax Ct. 1977, U.S. Supreme Ct. 1986. Dep. dir. ct. adminstrn. N.Y. State Office Ct. Adminstrn., Rochester, 1972-73; asst. dist. atty. Onondaga County, Syracuse, 1977-79; assoc. Hancock & Estabrook, Syracuse, 1979-83, ptnr., 1983—; instr. polit. sci. Adirondack Community Coll., Glens Falls, N.Y., 1973-74. Youth racing coach, instr. Toggenburg Ski Sch., U.S. Eastern Amateur Ski Assn., 1972—, Profl. Ski Instrs. Am., 1985—; advisor Explorers div. Boy Scouts Am., Syracuse, 1977-80. Mem. ABA, N.Y. State Bar Assn., Assn. Trial Lawyers Am., Onondaga County Bar Assn., Am. Arbitration Assn. (comml. arbitration panel 1983—), N.Y. State Trial Lawyers Assn. Democrat. Roman Catholic. Clubs: Cavalry (Manlius, N.Y.); Bellevue Country (Syracuse). Avocation: skiing. Federal civil litigation, State civil litigation, Real property. Home: 237 Whitestone Circle Syracuse NY 13215 Office: Hancock & Estabrook 1400 One Mony Plaza Syracuse NY 13202

SPARKIA, ALISA A., lawyer; b. Grand Rapids, Mich., Oct. 1, 1955; d. Roy B. and Renee Anne (Nemerov) Sparkia; m. John T. Moore, 1985. B.A., Mich. State U., 1977; J.D., U. Mich., 1981; cert. Nat. Inst. Trial Advocacy, 1983. Bar: N.Mex. 1981, U.S. Dist. Ct. N.Mex. 1982, U.S. Ct. Appeals (10th cir.) 1981. Assoc., Civerolo, Hansen & Wolf, Albuquerque, 1981-82, Faurot & Titus, P.A., Farmington, N.Mex., 1982-83, Ferguson & Lind, P.C., Albuquerque, 1983-84; sole practice, Albuquerque, 1984—. Active polit. campaigns and orgns. Mem. ABA, Assn. Trial Lawyers Am., N.Mex. Trial Lawyers Assn., Albuquerque Bar Assn., N.Mex. Bar Assn., Solo Practitioners Assn., Greater Albuquerque C. of C. Club: Civitan. State civil litigation, Personal injury, Workers' compensation. Office: 500 Marquette NW Suite 301 Albuquerque NM 87102

SPARKMAN, ROY T., lawyer; b. Huntsville, Tex., Feb. 14, 1951; s. Byford Henry and Melva Nalene (Dickerson) S.; m. Donna Ann Hill, June 12, 1970; children—Mindy Marie, Amy Allison, Roy Curtis. B.B.A., Midwestern State U., 1973; J.D., Baylor U., 1976. Bar: Tex. 1976, Wichita County 1976, U.S. Dist. Ct. (no. dist.) Tex. 1977, U.S. Ct. Appeals (5th cir.) 1983. Cert. in civil trial law, Tex. Sole practice, Wichita Falls, Tex., 1976-80; ptnr. Sparkman & Cantrell, Wichita Falls, 1980-83; assoc. Sherrill & Pace, Wichita Falls, 1983-84, share holder, 1984—; mem. Dist. 14-A Grievance Com., Wichita Falls, 1982-85. Trustee Wichita Falls Sch. Dist., 1984—; active pub. responsibility com. Wichita Falls State Hosp., 1977-80; deacon, tchr. First Baptist Ch., Wichita Falls, 1976—. Rotary Club scholar 1969. Mem. Wichita County Bar Assn. (treas. 1981, dir. 1979-80). Lodge: Kiwanis. Federal civil litigation, State civil litigation. Home: 2503 Amherst Falls TX 76308 Office: Sherrill & Pace 1100 Hamilton Bldg Wichita Falls TX 76307

SPARKS, BERTEL MILAS, legal educator, lawyer; b. 1918. B.S., Eastern Ky. U., 1938; LL.B., U. Ky., 1948; LL.M., U. Mich., 1949, S.J.D., 1955. Bar: Ky. 1948. Instr. NYU, 1949-50, asst. prof., 1950-52, assoc. prof., 1952-54, prof., 1954-67; prof. law Duke U., Durham, N.C., 1967—; cons. subcom. on constrn. rights Com. Judiciary of U.S. Senate, 1966; mem. drafting com. for rev. laws relating to adminstrn. estates N.C. Gen. Statutes Commn., 1967—; mem. drafting com. multi-state bar exam Nat. Conf. Bar Examiners, 1970—. Author: Contracts to Make Wills, 1956, Cases on Trusts and Estates, 1965; former editor-in-chief: Ky. Law Jour. Served as spl. agt. CIC U.S. Army, 1941-45. Mem. Order of Coif. Legal education. Office: Duke University Law School Durham NC 27706

SPARKS, BILLY SCHLEY, lawyer; b. Marshall, Mo., Oct. 1, 1923; s. John and Clarinda (Schley) S.; A.B., Harvard, 1945, LL.B., 1949; student Mass. Inst. Tech., 1943-44; m. Dorothy O. Stone, May 14, 1946; children—Stephen Stone, Susan Lee Sparks Raben, John David. Admitted to Mo. bar, 1949; partner Langworthy, Matz & Linde, Kansas City, Mo., 1949-62, firm Linde, Thomson, Fairchild Langworthy, Kohn & Van Dyke, 1962—. Mem. Mission (Kans.) Planning Council, 1954-63; mem. Kans. Civil Service Commn., 1975—. Mem. dist. 110 Sch. Bd., 1964-69, pres., 1967-69; mem. dist. 512 Sch. Bd., 1969-73, pres., 1971-72; del. Dem. Nat. Conv., 1964; candidate for representative 10th Dist., Kans., 1956, 3d district, 1962; treas. Johnson County (Kans.) Dem. Central com., 1958-64. Served to lt. USAAF, 1944-46. Mem. Kansas City C. of C. (legis. com. 1956-82), Am., Kansas City bar assns., Mo. Bar, Law Assn. Kansas City, Harvard Law Sch. Assn. Mo. (past dir.), Nat. Assn. Sch. Bds. (mem. legislative com. 1968-73), St. Andrews Soc. Mem. Christian Ch. (trustee). Clubs: Harvard (v.p. 1953-54), The Kansas City (Kansas City, Mo.); Milburn Golf and Country. General practice, State civil litigation, Federal civil litigation. Home: 8517 W 90th Terr Shawnee Mission KS 66212 Office: City Center Sq 12th & Baltimore Sts Kansas City MO 64105

SPARKS, JOHN EDWARD, lawyer; b. Rochester, Ind., July 3, 1930; s. Russell Leo and Pauline Ann (Whittenberger) S.; m. Margaret Joan Snyder, Sept. 4, 1954; children: Thomas Edward, William Russell, Kathryn Chapman. A.B., Ind. U., 1952; LL.B., U. Calif., Berkeley, 1957; postgrad., London Sch. Econs., 1957-58. Bar: Calif. 1958. Assoc. Brobeck, Phleger & Harrison, San Francisco, 1958-66, ptnr., 1967—; adj. prof. law U. San Francisco, 1967-69; pres. Legal Aid Soc. San Francisco, 1978-79, dir., 1971-81; trustee Pacific Legal Found., Sacramento, 1975-80. Editor U. Calif. Law Rev., 1956-57. Served to 1st lt. Q.M.C. U.S. Army, 1952-54, Korea. Recipient Wheeler Oak Meritorious award U. Calif., Berkeley, 1986. Fellow Am. Coll. Trial Lawyers; mem. State Bar Calif., Bar Assn. San Francisco (dir. 1974-75), ABA, Am. Judicature Soc. Democrat. Club: Bankers, Pacific Union (San Francisco). Antitrust, Federal civil litigation, State civil litigation. Office: One Market Plaza San Francisco CA 94105

SPARKS, JOHN O., lawyer; b. Woodward, Okla., Apr. 7, 1939; s. Reuben K. and Mary Sue (Simpson) S.; m. Marcia Cleary, Nov. 25, 1963; children; Lisa, Grant. BA, U. Okla., 1961, JD, 1966. Bar: Okla. 1966, U.S. Dist. Ct. (we. dist.) Okla. 1968, U.S. Ct. Appeals (10th cir.) 1968. Asst. dist. atty. City of Woodward, 1967-68, Oklahoma City, 1968-69; asst. U.S. atty. U.S. Dist. Ct. (we. dist.) Okla., Oklahoma City, 1969-70; sole practice Woodward, 1970—; city atty. Woodward, 1974-78; bd. dirs. the Bank of Woodward. Commnr. Okla. Transp. Commn., 1987—. Served to capt. U.S. Army, 1961-63. Fellow Am. Bar Found., Okla. Bar Found.; mem. Okla. Bar Assn. (bd. govs. 1982-85, probate ct. com.), U. Okla. Alumni Assn. (adv. bd. 1982—), Woodward C. of C. Republican. Lodge: Kiwanis, Elks. Banking, Probate, Oil and gas. Home: 3611 Cedar Ridge Ln Woodward OK 73801 Office: Sparks & Stake PO Box 968 Woodward OK 73802

SPARKS, ROBERT W., lawyer; b. Passaic, N.J., Feb. 18, 1938; s. Perry Sparks and Cecilia Howley; m. Myrna M. Raker, Nov. 28, 1961; children: Jonathan, Elizabeth. BA, Ithaca Coll., 1960; LLB, NYU, 1963. Bar: N.Y. 1964, U.S. Dist. Ct. (so. dist.) N.Y. 1966, U.S. Ct. Appeals (3d cir.) 1979, U.S. Dist. Ct. (ea. dist.) Mich. 1983. Assoc. J. Robert Morris, N.Y.C., 1964-70, William H. Morris, N.Y.C., 1970-74, Johnson and Johnson, New Brunswick, N.J., 1974-82; of counsel Bower and Gardner, N.Y.C., 1982—; lectr. Seton Hall Sch. Law, Newark, 1976—, Rutgers U. Sch. Medicine, New Brunswick, 1979—. Federal civil litigation, State civil litigation, Personal injury. Home: 35 Knight Rd Wayne NJ 07470 Office: Bower and Gardner 110 E 59th St New York NY 10022

SPARKS, STEPHEN STONE, lawyer; b. Kansas City, Mo., June 21, 1954; s. Billy Schley and Dorothy (Stone) S.; m. Martha Nelson, Oct. 19, 1979; 1 child, Matthew Nelson. BA, New Coll. of U. of South Fla., 1976; JD with distinction, U. Mo., Kansas City, 1979. Bar: Mo. 1979, U.S. Dist. Ct. (we. dist.) Mo. 1979. Assoc. Linde, Thomson, Fairchild, Langworthy, Kohn & Van Dyke P.C., Kansas City, 1979-82, ptnr., 1982—. Mem. ABA, Kansas City Bar Assn., Lawyers Assn. K.C. Mo., Nat. Assn. Bond Lawyers. Democrat. Club: Milburn Country (Overland Park, Kans.). Avocations: golf, soccer. Municipal bonds, Real property, General corporate. Home: 10818 W 102d St Overland Park KS 66214 Office: Linde Thomson Fairchild et al 2700 City Ctr Sq Kansas City MO 64196

SPARKS, THOMAS E., JR., lawyer; b. Little Rock, Jan. 11, 1942; s. Thomas E. and Marie Christine Lundgren, Sept. 11, 1976; children: Thomas Gunnar, Erik Richard, Andrew Pal. BS, Washington and Lee U., 1963; JD, U. Ark., 1968; LLM, Harvard U., 1970. Bar: Ark. 1968, Calif. 1970. Assoc. Pillsbury, Madison & Sutro, San Francisco, 1970-76, ptnr., 1977-84; ptnr. Baker & McKenzie, San Francisco, 1984—; bd. dirs. InSite Vision Inc., San Francisco. Bd. dirs. Netherlands-Am. Amity Trust, Amsterdam, Holland, 1985—. Served to 1st lt. U.S. Army, 1965. Mem. ABA, Calif. Bar Assn. Club: Olympic (San Francisco). Securities. Office: Baker & McKenzie 580 California St San Francisco CA 94104

SPARKS, WILLIAM JAMES ASHLEY, lawyer, educator; b. Victoria, B.C., Can., Jan. 27, 1949; came to U.S., 1970; s. John Ashley and Elizabeth (Enoch) S. BA, U. Victoria, 1970; JD, Duke U., 1973. Bar: N.Y. 1974, U.S. Dist. Ct. (so. and ea. dists.) N.Y. 1974, U.S. CT. Appeals (2d cir.) 1974. Assoc. Dewey, Ballantine, Bushby, Palmer & Wood, N.Y.C., 1973-78; counsel Olin Corp., Stamford, Conn., 1979—; adj. prof. Pace U. Sch of Law, White Plains, N.Y., 1984—. Mem. ABA, Assn. of Bar of City of N.Y., Westchester and Fairfield Counties Corp. Counsel Assn. Democrat. Club: N.Y. Athletic. Product Liability, Federal civil litigation, General corporate. Home: 155 W 68th St New York NY 10023 Office: Olin Corp. 120 Long Ridge Rd Stamford CT 06904

SPATH, GREGG ANTHONY, lawyer; b. New Rochelle, N.Y., Nov. 13, 1952; s. Richard Dennis and Renee (Turtletaub) S.; m. Lois Lang, Mar. 18, 1979. Student Coll. William and Mary, 1970-72; B.A. in English, U. Rochester, 1974; J.D., New Eng. Sch. Law, 1977; LL.M. in Trade Regulation, NYU, 1979. Bar: N.Y. 1978; U.S. Supreme Ct., 1984. Spl. legal cons. Western Electric Co., N.Y.C., 1978-81; atty. St. Regis Paper Co., N.Y.C., 1981-82; asst. gen. counsel, sec. patent com. United Mchts. and Mfrs., Inc., N.Y.C., 1982—, legal counsel mgmt. bd. Decora Div., Ft. Edward, N.Y., 1984—. Contbr. New Eng. Law Rev., 1976, tech. editor, 1976-77. Mem. ABA (sects. of antitrust and patent, trademark and copyright law). Avocations: sports; music; theatre; cinema. Trademark and copyright, Computer, Patent. Office: United Mchts and Mfrs Inc 1407 Broadway New York NY 10018

SPATT, ROBERT EDWARD, lawyer; b. Bklyn., Mar. 26, 1956; s. Milton E. and Blanche S. (Bakstansky) S.; m. Lisa B. Malkin, Aug. 11, 1979; 1 child, Mark Eric. AB, Brown U., 1977; JD magna cum laude, U. Mich., 1980. Bar: N.Y. 1981. Assoc. Simpson Thacher & Bartlett, N.Y.C., 1980—. Mem. ACLU, ABA, N.Y. State Bar Assn., Order of Coif. Avocations: photography, boating, reading. General corporate, Securities, Mergers and acquisitions. Home: 526 Fairmount Ave Chatham NJ 07928 Office: Simpson Thacher & Bartlett 1 Battery Park Plaza New York NY 10004

SPATZ, ALAN BRENT, lawyer; b. Charleston, W.Va., May 19, 1954; s. Dale and Pauline (Lewis) S.; m. Michele Joy Kohan, June 29, 1985. BA, U. Mich., 1976; JD, U. Calif., Berkeley, 1979. Bar: Calif. 1979. Ptnr. Hill Wynne Troop & Meisinger, Los Angeles, 1979—. Mem. ABA, Calif. Bar Assn., Los Angeles County Bar Assn. General corporate, Securities, Banking. Home: 1870 Kelton Ave #201 Los Angeles CA 90025 Office: 10920 Wilshire Blvd 9th Floor Los Angeles CA 90024

SPEARS, FRANKLIN SCOTT, state supreme court justice; b. San Antonio, Aug. 20, 1931; s. Jacob Franklin and Lois Louise (Harkey) S.; m. Rebecca Nell Errington, Dec. 4, 1977; children: Franklin Scott, Carleton Blaise, John Adrian. Student, So. Methodist U., 1948-50; B.B.A., U. Tex., 1954, J.D., 1954. Bar: Tex. bar 1954, U.S. Dist. Ct. bar for Western Dist. Tex 1956, 5th Circuit Ct. bar 1961, U.S. Supreme Ct. bar 1966. Practiced law San Antonio, 1956-68; mem. Tex. Ho. of Reps., 1958-61, Tex. Senate, 1961-67; dist. judge 57th Jud. Dist. Tex., 1968-78; justice Tex. Supreme Ct., 1979—. Exec. com. Frontier dist. Boy Scouts Am., 1964-68. Served with U.S. Army, 1955-56. Mem. San Antonio Bar Assn., Tex. Bar Assn., State Bar Tex., YMCA, Soc. Preservation and Encouragement Barbershop Quartet Singing in Am, SAR. Democrat. Presbyterian. Clubs: Masons, Shriners. Office: Office Supreme Ct Box 12248 Capitol Station Austin TX 78711

SPEARS, LARRY JONELL, lawyer; b. Webb, Miss., Jan. 10, 1953; s. John Spears and Lillian Belle Embrey; m. Nancy Ellen King, Aug. 1, 1976 (div. Dec. 1984). BS, U. Ill., 1976, JD, 1979; postdoctoral, So. Ill. U., 1984—. Bar: Ill. 1980. Asst. atty gen. Ill. Atty. Gen.'s Office, Murphysboro, 1980-84; asst. pub. defender Jackson County Pub. Defender's Office, Murphysboro, 1985; lectr. Crime Study Ctr., Carbondale, Ill., 1985; sole practice Carbondale, 1985-86; asst. state's atty. Peoria (Ill.) State's Atty. Office, 1986; cons. Minority Contractors Assn., Carbondale, 1985; mem. Inmate Advocacy Group, Murphysboro, 1985—. Elijah P. Lovejoy scholar, 1972. Mem. ABA, Ill. State Bar Assn., Peoria County Bar Assn., Jackson County Bar Assn., Adminstrn. of Justice Assn. (treas. 1984-85), Am. Soc. Criminology (discussant 1984—), Midwest Criminal Justice Assn., Am. Judicature Soc., LWV, Phi Alpha Delta (treas. 1979), Alpha Phi Sigma. Republican. Methodist. Clubs: Sphinx (Carbondale); River City Athletic (Pearia). Avocations: songwriting, tennis, volleyball. Criminal, Family and matrimonial. Home: 6516 N University #815 Peoria IL 61614 Office: Peoria County State's Atty Peoria County Courthouse Peoria IL 61602

SPEARS, MICHAEL EUGENE, lawyer; b. Columbia, S.C., June 21, 1949; s. Vernon Alexander and Edna Elizabeth (Stephenson) S.; m. Sylvia Ann Bankhead, Aug. 5, 1979; children: Lauren Virginia, Michael Thomas. BS, U. S.C., 1971, JD, 1977. Bar: S.C. 1977, U.S. Dist. Ct. S.C. 1978, U.S. Ct. Appeals (4th cir.) 1978, U.S. Supreme Ct. 1981. Ptnr. Swofford, Turnipseed, Allen, Smith & Spears, Spartanburg, S.C., 1978-79, Swofford & Spears, Spartanburg, 1979-80, Swofford, Poliakoff & Spears, Spartanburg, 1980—; Mem. bd. commrs. Spartanburg County Pub. Defenders, 1979-82; bd. commrs. States Reorgn. Commn. on Prison Overcrowding, 1983—, subcom. intensive supervision, 1984—; instr. legal internship program Converse Coll., 1978-80. Mem. com. to honor S.C. chief justice, Spartanburg, 1984; chmn. security and violence com. Hillbrook Neighborhood Assn., Spartanburg, 1981-82; pres. U. of S.C. New Carolinians, Spartanburg, 1981-82. Mem. ABA, S.C. Bar Assn., Spartanburg County Bar Assn. (grievance com. 1984-85, chmn. entertainment and placques & memls. coms. 1987—), Assn. Trial Lawyers Am., S.C. Trial Lawyers Assn., Nat. Assn. Coll. Univ. Attys., Spartanburg Young Lawyers Assn. (chmn. 1978-79, vice chmn. 1981-83), 7th Jud. Cir. (vice chmn. gen. sessions com. 1984-86). Personal injury, Criminal, State civil litigation. Home: 101 Kearse Ct Spartanburg SC 29302 Office: Swofford Poliakoff & Spears 251 Magnolia St Spartanburg SC 29301

SPEARS, RONALD DEAN, lawyer; b. Michigan City, Ind., July 30, 1951; s. Lonnie and Frances Ellen (Benad) S.; m. Annette Jean Greffe, Dec. 22, 1973; 1 child, Donald Dean. BA, U. Ill., 1974; JD, So. Ill. U. 1977. Bar: Ill. 1977, U.S. Dist. Ct. (cen. and so. dists.) Ill. 1977, U.S. Ct. Appeals (7th cir.) 1977, U.S. Supreme Ct. 1983. Law clk. U.S. Dist. Ct., Springfield, Ill., 1977-79; ptnr. Miley, Meyer, Austin Spears & Romano, P.C., Taylorville, Ill., 1979—; city atty. for Taylorville, 1985—. Pres., drive chmn. United Fund Taylorville, 1981, YMCA, 1986— (pres. 1987). Served to capt. (JAGC) Ill. NG. Mem. ABA, Ill. State Bar Assn., Ill. Trial Lawyers Assn., Christian County Bar Assn. (pres. 1987), So. Ill. U. Law Sch. Alumni Assn. (pres. 1984). Lodge: Optimists (sec. 1986—, pres. 1986, lt. gov. 1986-87). State civil litigation, Personal injury, Federal civil litigation. Home: 1204 Brown Ct Taylorville IL 62568 Office: Miley Meyer Austin Spears & Romano PC 210 S Washington Taylorville IL 62568

SPECCHIO, MICHAEL RONALD, lawyer, judge; b. Huntington, N.Y., Aug. 27, 1942; s. R. Fred Specchio; m. Patricia Rose, Jan. 16, 1976; 1 child, Lisa A. AA, U. San Francisco, 1962; JD, U. Pacific, 1970. Bar: Nev. 1971, U.S. Ct. Claims, U.S. Ct. Appeals (9th and 10th cirs.) 1974, U.S. Tax Ct. 1977, U.S. Supreme Ct. 1977. Chief trial dep. pub. defender office Washoe County, Reno, 1971-76; sole practice Reno, 1976—; spl. dep. pub. defender office Washoe County, 1978-84; juvenile ct. master 2d Jud. Dist. Ct., Washoe County, 1980—; judge pro tem Reno Mcpl. Ct., 1985—. Mem. ABA, Assn. Trial Lawyers Am., Nat. Assn. Criminal Def. Lawyers, Nev. Trial Lawyers Assn., Nat. Dist. Attys. Assn., Am. Judges Assn. Republican. Roman Catholic. Lodges: Elks, Italian Benevolent Soc. Criminal, General practice, Juvenile. Home: 335 Hillcrest Dr Reno NV 89509 Office: 556 California Ave Reno NV 89509

SPECHT, RANDOLPH STEPHEN, lawyer; b. Lawton, Okla., Dec. 19, 1951; s. Homer Leo and Madelyn (O'Keefe) S.; m. Renee Lobodinski, Aug. 12, 1979. BS, Okla. State U., 1978; JD, U. Okla., 1981. Bar: Okla. 1981. Trial examiner Okla. Corp. Commn., Oklahoma City, 1981-82, asst. chief trial examiner, 1982, referee oil and gas, 1982—; lectr. U. Okla. Sch. of Law, Norman, 1985. Mem. steering com. Linwood Neighborhood Assn., Oklahoma City, 1986—. Mem. ABA, Okla. Bar Assn. (mineral lawyer sect., young lawyers div.), Okla. County Bar Assn.,. Democrat. Roman Catholic. Oil and gas leasing, Administrative and regulatory, Real property. Home: 3129 NW 22d Oklahoma City OK 73107 Office: Oklahoma Corp Commn Jim Thorpe Bldg Oklahoma City OK 73105

SPECTER, HOWARD ALAN, lawyer; b. Pitts., Dec. 1, 1939; s. Ben and Ethel (Gorn) S.; m. Elaine Spatz, Jan. 1, 1986. B.A., U. Pitts., 1961, J.D., 1964. Bar: Pa. 1964, U.S. Ct. Appeals (3d cir.) 1973, U.S. Supreme Ct. 1974, U.S. Ct. Appeals (5th and 9th cirs.) 1976, U.S. Ct. Appeals (11th cir.) 1981, U.S. Ct. Appeals (10th cir.) 1983. Assoc. Litman Litman & Harris, Pitts., 1964-67; ptnr. Litman Litman Harris & Specter, P.A., Pitts., 1967-82; sr. ptnr. Specter & Buchwach, P.C., Pitts., 1982—; mem. faculty, chmn. Nat. Coll. Advocacy, 1977-79. Contbr. articles to legal publs. Fellow Roscoe Pound-Am. Trial Lawyers Assn. (trustee); mem. ABA (bus. torts com. litigation sect. 1975, subcom. on multidist. litigation antitrust law sect. 1975), Pa. Trial Lawyers Assn., Pa. Bar Assn., Acad. Trial Lawyers Allegheny County, Tex. Trial Lawyers Assn., Acad. Fla. Trial Lawyers, Assn. Trial Lawyers Am. (chmn. comml. litigation sect. 1976-77, sec. 1979-80, v.p., pres. elect. 1980-81, pres. 1982-83), Belli Soc. (trustee 1979, pres. 1983-84). Democrat. Jewish. Antitrust, Personal injury, Securities. Office: Specter & Buchwach PC 2230 Grant Bldg Pittsburgh PA 15219

SPECTER, MELVIN H., lawyer; b. East Chicago, Ind., July 12, 1903; s. Moses and Sadie (Rossuck) S.; A.B., U. Mich., 1925; J.D., U. Chgo., 1928; m. Nellie Rubenstein, Feb. 1, 1927; children—Lois, Michael Joseph. Admitted to Ind. bar, 1928; individual practice law, East Chicago, Ind. 1928—. Bd. dirs. ARC (chpt. chmn. 1940-46), Community Chest Assn., Salvation Army Adv. Bd., pres., 1930-35; bd. dirs. Vis. Nurse Assn., pres., 1943-44; bd. dirs. East Chgo. Boys Club, 1958-65; trustee East Chicago Pub. Library, 1956-80, pres., 1957-67; pres. Anselm Forum, 1957-58; chmn. Brotherhood Week NCCJ, East Chicago, 1958-61; exec. bd. Twin City council Boy Scouts Am.; city chmn. U. Chgo. Alumni Found. Fund, 1951-55. Awarded James Couzen Medal for Inter-collegiate debate, U. Mich., 1924; citation for distinguished pub. service, U. Chgo. Alumni Assn., 1958. Citizenship award Community Chest Assn., 1965. Mem. Am. Ind. (del.), East Chicago (pres. 1942-44) bar assns., Am. Judicature Soc., Comml. Law League Am., Community Concert Assn. (dir. 1950-55), Wig and Robe Frat., Phi Beta Kappa, Delta Sigma Rho. Elk (exalted ruler 1945), K.P., Kiwanian (dir. 1946, 49-51, 52-55, pres. 1961); mem. B'nai B'rith. General practice. Home: 4213 Baring Ave East Chicago IN 46312 Office: 804 W 145th St East Chicago IN 46312

SPECTER, RICHARD BRUCE, lawyer; b. Phila., Sept. 6, 1952; s. Jacob E. and Marilyn B. (Kron) S.; m. Jill Ossenfort, May 30, 1981; children: Lauren Elizabeth, Lindsey Anne. BA cum laude, Washington U., St. Louis, 1974; JD, George Washington U., 1977. Bar: Mo. 1977, U.S. Dist. Ct. (ea. and we. dists.) Mo. 1977, U.S. Ct. Appeals (8th cir.) 1977, Ill. 1978, Pa. 1978, U.S. Dist. Ct. (ea. dist.) Ill. 1979, U.S. Ct. Appeals (7th cir.) 1979, Calif. 1984, U.S. Dist. Ct. (cen. dist.) Calif. 1985, U.S. Ct. Appeals (9th cir.) 1986. Assoc. Coburn, Croft, Shepherd, Herzog & Putzell, St. Louis, 1977-79; ptnr. Herzog, Kral, Burroughs & Specter, St. Louis, 1979-82; exec. v.p. Uniqey Internat., Santa Ana, Calif., 1982-84; sole practice Los Angeles and Irvine, Calif., 1984-87; of counsel Corbett & Steelman, Irvine, 1987—; instr. Nat. Law Ctr. George Washington U. 1975. Mem. ABA, Ill. Bar Assn., Mo. Bar Assn., Pa. Bar Assn., Calif. Bar Assn. Jewish. Federal civil litigation, State civil litigation, General corporate. Home: 37 Bull Run Irvine CA 92720 Office: 18200 Von Karman Ave Suite 200 Irvine CA 92715

SPECTOR, BRIAN F., lawyer; b. Bklyn., Aug. 24, 1952; s. Harry and Mildred S.; m. Meryl Joy Linder, June 22, 1975; children—Randi Jill, Andrew Jay. B.A. in Polit. Sci. cum laude, Syracuse U., 1974; J.D. magna cum laude, U. Miami (Fla.), 1978. Bar: Fla. 1978, U.S. dist. ct. (so. and mid. dists.) Fla. 1978, U.S. Ct. Appeals (5th cir.) 1978, U.S. Ct. Appeals (11th cir.) 1981, U.S. Supreme Ct. 1985. Jud. clk. to sr. judge U.S. Ct. Appeals (5th cir.), Jacksonville, Fla., 1978-79; instr. in law U. Miami, 1980-81, adj. faculty, 1985. Mem. ABA, Fla. Bar, Am. Judicature Soc., Fed. Bar Assn., Dade County Bar Assn., Wig and Robe, Bar and Gavel, Omicron Delta Kappa. Former articles and comments editor U. Miami Law Rev.; bd. editors So. Dist. Digest, 1982-87, chmn., 1984-85. Federal civil litigation, Securities, Trademark and copyright. Home: 13551 SW 57 Ct Miami FL 33156 Office: 400 Edward Ball Bldg Miami Ctr 100 Chopin Plaza Miami FL 33131

SPEER, WILSON EDWARD, lawyer; b. Kansas City, Mo., Nov. 14, 1929; s. Paul and Hazel Imogene (Craft) S.; m. Ailie Deem, Oct. 7, 1956; children: Paul Wilson, Edward Deem. BA, U. Kans., 1952, LLB, 1954. Bar: Kans. 1954. Gen. counsel Water Dist. #1, Johnson County, Kans., 1978—; with firm Speer, Autsin, Holliday, Ruddick & Taylor, Olathe, Kans. Mem. Friends of the Johnson County Library (pres. 1983-84), Johnson County Charter Com., 1975-76; Rep. precinct committeman, Overland Park, Kans. Served with U.S. Army, 1954-56. Mem. ABA, Johnson County Bar Assn. (pres. 1975-76), Kans. Bar Assn. Republican. Presbyterian. Administrative and regulatory, Contracts commercial, Real property. Home: 8813 W 106th Circle Overland Park KS 66212 Office: Speer Austin Holliday et al PO Box 1000 Olathe KS 66061

SPEERS, THOMAS JAMES, lawyer; b. Phila., June 29, 1954; s. James Wilson and Katherine (Roberts) S.; m. Donna Burke, Feb. 12, 1984; children: Charles John, William Gordon, James Dennis. BA, Villanova U., 1976; JD, Dickinson Sch. Law, 1979. Bar: Pa. 1979, U.S. Dist. Ct. (ea. dist.) Pa. 1980, U.S. Ct. Appeals (3d cir.) 1981, U.S. Supreme Ct. 1983. Atty. Montgomery County Pub. Defenders Office, Norristown, Pa., 1979; law clk. to judge Montgomery Ct. Common Pleas, Norristown, 1980-81; assoc. McTighe, Weiss & Stewart P.C., Norristown, 1981-86; ptnr. McTighe, Weiss, Stewart, Bacine & O'Rourke P.C., Norristown, 1986—, also bd. dirs. Leader Boy Scouts Am., Montgomery County, 1972-76, 85—; mem. Montgomery County Rep. Com., 1986—. Mem. ABA, Pa. Bar Assn., Montgomery County Bar Assn. Roman Catholic. Lodge: Lions (bd. dirs. Montgomery County 1979—). Avocations: camping, hiking, travel. Banking, Real property, Civil rights. Home: 3004 Jolly Rd Norristown PA 19401 Office: McTighe Weiss Stewart et al 11 E Airy St PO Box 510 Norristown PA 19404

SPEICHER, JOHN ALLAN, lawyer; b. Indpls., Apr. 18, 1954; s. Kenneth Earl and Helen Ross (Smith) S. BA, DePauw U., 1976; JD, U. Toledo, 1979. Bar: Ind. 1979. Atty. Highland Realty, Indpls. Recipient God and Country award Boy Scouts Am. Mem. ABA, Ind. Bar Assn. Jurisprudence, Construction, Landlord-tenant. Home: 7777 W Washington St Indianapolis IN 46231

SPEIDEL, RICHARD ELI, lawyer, educator; b. Cin., May 27, 1933; s. Russell Frazier and Grace (Jarbo) S.; m. Elizabeth West; children: Rae Ann, Richard Scott. B.A., Denison U., 1954; J.D., U. Cin., 1957; LL.M., Northwestern U., 1958. Bar: Ohio 1958, Va. 1968. Teaching assoc. Northwestern U. Law Sch., 1957-58; asst. prof. law U. Va., 1961-63, assoc. prof. law, 63-66, prof. law, 1966-70, Doherty prof., 1970-77; dean, prof. Boston U. Sch. Law, 1977-80; prof. law Northwestern U. Law Sch., 1980—; Comml. arbitrator; vis. prof. U. Calif., Berkeley, 1965-66; sr. Fulbright lectr. in law and and guest prof. U. Vienna, Austria, 1974-75; vis. scholar Harvard Law Sch., 1980; cons. in field. Author: (with E.J. Murphy) Studies in Contract Law, 1970, 4th revised edit., 1987, (with R.S. Summers and J.J. White) Commercial and Consumer Transactions, 4th rev. edit, 1987; contbr. numerous articles to law jours. Trustee Denison U., 1971—. Served as capt. JAGC USAR, 1958-61. Decorated D.S.M.; Recipient Emil Brown Preventive Law award Emil Brown Found., 1964. Mem. Am. Bar Assn., Am. Law Inst., Order of Coif. Democrat. Methodist. Contracts commercial, Legal education, Government contracts and claims. Home: 3717 N Pine Grove Apt 3 Chicago IL 60613 Office: 357 E Chicago Ave Chicago IL 60611

SPEIGHT, JOHN B., lawyer; b. Cheyenne, May 29, 1949; s. Jack B. and Kathryn Elizabeth (Schmidt) S.; m. Sally Karolee Sullivan, Aug. 20, 1960; children—Sheryl, Tricia, Jackie; m. Carol Ann McBee, Sept. 16, 1979. B.A., U. Wyo., 1962, J.D., 1965. Bar: Wyo. 1966, U.S. Dist. Ct. Wyo. 1967, U.S. Dist. Ct. Colo. 1967, U.S. Ct. Appeals (10th cir.) 1967, U.S. Supreme Ct. 1970. Atty., Standard Oil Co. of Calif., 1965-67; asst. atty. gen. State of Wyo., 1967-69; adminstrv., legal asst. to Gov. Wyo., 1969-71; atty. for Reorgn. Commn., State of Wyo., 1969-71; asst. U.S. atty. Litigation div., 1971-72; cons. sec. interior, 1975; ptnr. firm Hathaway, Speight & Kunz, Cheyenne, 1972—; dir., First Wyo. Bank, East Cheyenne; dir. Laramie County Legal Service Inc. Bd. dirs. Laramie County United Fund. Mem. Wyo. Bar Assn., ABA, Wyo. Trial Lawyers Assn., Am. Trial Lawyers Assn., Laramie County United Fund. Mem. Wyo. Bar Assn., ABA, Wyo. Trial Lawyers Assn. (bd. dirs. 1982—), Am. Trial Lawyers Assn., Laramie County Bar Assn. (pres. 1982-83), Commrs. for Uniform State Laws from the State of Wyo., Jud. Supervisory Commn. Republican. Roman Catholic. Clubs: Cheyenne Kiwanis (dir.), Cheyenne Vocation. Federal civil litigation, Personal injury, State civil litigation. Office: 1 Pioneer Center 2424 Pioneer Ave Cheyenne WY 82001

SPEISER, STUART MARSHALL, lawyer; b. N.Y.C., June 4, 1923; s. Joseph and Anne (Jonath) S.; m. Mary J. McCormick, Feb. 12, 1950 (dec.); 1 son, James Joseph; m. Maxine Sprouse, June 24, 1985. Student, U. Pa., 1939-42; LL.B., Columbia U., 1948. Bar: N.Y. 1948. Practiced in N.Y.C., 1948—; mem. Speiser, Shumate, Geoghan & Krause, 1957-68; mem. firm Speiser, Shumate, Geoghan, Krause & Rheingold, 1968-70, Speiser & Krause (P.C.), 1971—; Chmn. bd. Aerial Application Corp., 1968-71, Hydrophilics Internat., 1971-77; Hon. atty. gen., La., 1958—. Author: Preparation Manual for Aviation Negligence Cases, 1958, Death in the Air, 1957, Liability Problems in Airline Crash Cases, 1957, Private Airplane Accidents, 1958, Speiser's Negligence Jury Charges, 1960, Speiser's Aviation Law Guide, 1962, Lawyers Aviation Handbook, 1964, Recovery for Wrongful Death, 2d edit., 1975, Lawyers Economic Handbook, 1970, 2d edit., 1979, Attorney's Fees, 1972, Res Ipsa Loquitur, 1973, A Piece of the Action, 1977, Aviation Tort Law, 1978, Lawsuit, 1980, Superstock, 1982, The American Law of Torts, 1983, How to End the Nuclear Nightmare, 1984, The USOP Handbook, 1986; bd. editors: Jour. Post Keynesian Econs, 1977—. Pilot USAAF, 1943-46. Fellow Internat. Soc. Barristers; mem. Am. Bar Assn., N.Y. County Lawyers Assn. (chmn. subcom. law outer space 1958—), Am. Trial Lawyers Assn. (chmn. aviation law 1955-64), AIAA (asso.). Federal civil litigation, State civil litigation, Personal injury. Home: 511 W Lyon Farm Dr Greenwich CT 06831 Office: Pan Am Bldg 200 Park Ave New York NY 10166

SPELFOGEL, EVAN J., lawyer; b. Boston, Jan. 28, 1936; s. Morris R. and Helen S. (Steinberg) S.; m. Beverly Kolenberg; children—Scott, Douglas, Karen. A.B., Harvard U., 1956; J.D., Columbia U., 1959. Bar: Mass. 1959, N.Y. 1964, U.S. Supreme Ct. 1969. Atty., Office of Solicitor, U.S. Dept. Labor, Washington and Boston, 1959-60; atty. NLRB, Boston and N.Y.C., 1960-64; assoc. Simpson, Thacher & Bartlett, N.Y.C., 1964-69, Dewey, Ballantine, Bushby, Palmer & Wood, N.Y.C., 1969-77; ptnr. Fellner, Rovins & Gallay, N.Y.C., 1977-80, Summit, Rovins & Feldesman, N.Y.C., 1981—; adj. prof. law Baruch Coll., CCNY. Mem. ABA (sect. on labor and employment law, exec. council 1978-86, co-editor sect. newsletter 1976—), Fed. Bar Assn. (council on labor law), N.Y. State Bar Assn. (chmn. labor and employment law sect. 1977-78, exec. council 1975—, ho. of dels. 1978-79), Assn. Bar City N.Y. (labor com. 1968-71), Am. Arbitration Assn. (nat. panel labor arbitrators), Phi Alpha Delta. Club: Harvard Varsity. Bd. editors Developing Labor Law: The Board, The Courts and the National Labor Relations Act, also co-editor-in-chief Supplements. Contbr. articles to profl. jours. Labor. Home: 17 Parkside Dr Great Neck NY 11021 Office: 445 Park Ave New York NY 10022

SPELLACY, JOHN FREDERICK, lawyer; b. Steubenville, Ohio, Mar. 24, 1930; s. Joseph Roland and Thelma Fay (Stone) S.; m. Martha Jane Manning June 18, 1955; children—Joseph, James, John, Lawrence. Ph.B., Loyola Coll. Balt., 1952; LL.D., U. Miami (Fla.) 1958. Bar: Fla. 1960, U.S. Dist. Ct. (so. dist.) Fla. 1961. Ptnr., Kirsch & Spellacym Fort Lauderdale, Fla., 1958-69, DiGiulian, Spellacy, Ft. Lauderdale, 1969-83, Spellacy & McFann, Ft. Lauderdale, 1983—; municipal judge City of Plantation, Fla., 1971-75. Mem. City Council, Plantation, 1962-71. Served to capt. USMC, 1952-54. Fellow Fla. Trial Lawyers Assn.; mem. Am. Arbitration Assn., ABA, Fed. Bar Assn., Fla. Bar, Assn. Trial Lawyers Am., Am. Judicature Soc., Broward County Mcpl. Judges Assn. (pres. 1974-75), Broward County. Trial Lawyers Assn. (pres. 1978-79). Democrat. Roman Catholic. Club: Civitan (v.p. Plantation 1965-70). Lodge: Elks. Personal injury, Insurance. Home: 1313 Ponce de Leon Dr Fort Lauderdale FL 33316 Office: Spellacy & McFann 888 S E 3d Ave Fort Lauderdale FL 33316

SPELLMAN, EUGENE PAUL, judge; b. N.Y.C., Sept. 16, 1930; s. Michael Francis and Mary Elizabeth (Loftus) S.; m. Roberta J. Recht, July 16, 1959; children: James Kevin, Michael Patrick. A.A., U. Fla., 1951, B.A., 1953, J.D., 1955; J.D., U. Fla., 1967; D.H.L., Biscayne Coll., 1977. Bar: Fla. 1956. Research aide to chief judge 3d Dist. Ct. Appeals, Miami, Fla., 1957-58; asst. atty. gen. (Criminal Appeals Div.), Tallahassee, 1958-59, 60-61; asst. state atty. Dade County (Fla.), also head (Rackets and Frauds div.), 1959-61; apptd. spl. prosecutor Judge Curtis E. Chillingsworth murder case by Govs. Leroy Collins and Farris Bryant, 1969-70; apptd. spl. asst. atty. gen. 1969-70; gen. counsel Biscayne Coll., 1970-80; judge so. dist. Fla. U.S. Dist. Ct., Miami, 1979—. Chmn. Fla. Council for Blind, 1963-65; pres. Southeastern Inst. Human Devel., 1977; bd. dirs. Marian Center Inc.; mem. South Miami Hosp. Found. Hon. mem. Order St. Augustine Rome; recipient Outstanding Achievement award Fla. Assn. Rehab. Facilities. Mem. Am., Fla., Dade County bar assns., Am., Fla. trial lawyers assns., Supreme Ct. Hist. Soc., Am. Judicature Soc., Dade County Assn. Retarded Citizens, Fla. Assn. Rehab. Facilities. Democrat. Roman Catholic. Jurisprudence. Office: US Courthouse PO Box 13170 Miami FL 33101 *

SPELMAN, JOHN HENRY, lawyer; b. South Haven, Mich., Feb. 28, 1921; s. Ohel Bostwick and Gertrude Marie (Englesby) S.; m. Jean Collingwood, June 21, 1947; children—Michael, John, Katherine. A.B., Mich. State U., 1943; J.D., U. Mich., 1949. Bar: Mich., 1949. Chief asst. pros. atty. Berrien County, Mich., 1950-54, pros. atty., 1955-58; pres. mem. Spelman, Taglia, Meek, Burdick & Sauer, P.C., St. Joseph, Mich., 1973—; cts. adv. council 2d Jud. Cir., Mich., 1974—; chmn. 4th Congl. Dist. Grievance Com., 1965-70; mem. hearing panel Berrien Cir., 1980—; chmn. hearing panel 4, 4th Congl. Dist., 1971-79; criminal law com. State Bar Mich., 1957-60. Chmn. Mich. State U. Alumni Adv. Council, 1962; vice chmn. Berrien County Bldg. Authority, 1967—. Served to 1st lt. armored div. AUS, 1943-46. Decorated Bronze Star; named Young Man of Yr., St. Joseph-Benton Harbor Jaycees, 1953. Mem. Berrien County Bar Assn. (pres. 1970-71), ABA, Mich. Prosecutors Assn., Am. Judicature Soc., Ft. Miami Hist. Soc. Republican. Congregationalist. Clubs: Benton Harbor-St. Joseph Rotary, Elks, Berrien Hills Country. General practice, Local government. Home: 390 Ridgeway Saint Joseph MI 49085 Office: 414 Main St Saint Joseph MI 49085

SPELTS, RICHARD JOHN, lawyer; b. Yuma, Colo., July 29, 1939; s. Richard Clark and Barbara Eve (Pletcher) S.; children—Melinda, Meghan, Richard John. B.S. cum laude, U. Colo., 1961, J.D., 1964. Bar: Colo. bar 1964, U.S. Supreme Ct. bar 1968. With Ford Motor Internat., Cologne, W. Ger., 1964-65; legis. counsel to U.S. Senator, 89th and 90th Congresses, 1967-68; minority counsel U.S. Senate Subcom., 90th and 91st Congresses, 1968-70; asst. U.S. atty., 1st asst. U.S. atty Dist. of Colo., 1970-77; owner, pres. Richard J. Spelts P.C. (P.C.), Denver, 1977—. Recipient cert. for outstanding contbns. in drug law enforcement U.S. Drug Enforcement Adminstrn., 1977; spl. commendation for criminal prosecution U.S. Dept. Justice, 1973; spl. commendation for civil prosecution, 1976. Mem. Colo. Bar Assn. (gov. 1976-78), Fed. Bar Assn. (chmn. govt. torts seminar 1980), Denver Bar Assn., Leadership Denver, Colo. Trial Lawyers Assn., Order of Coif. Republican. Presbyterian. Club: Denver Law. Federal civil litigation, State civil litigation, Criminal. Office: 200 Blake St Bldg 1441 18th St Denver CO 80202

SPENCE, GERALD LEONARD, lawyer, writer; b. Laramie, Wyo., Jan. 8, 1929; s. Gerald W. and Esther Sophie (Pfleeger) S.; m. Anna Wilson, June 20, 1947; children: Kip, Kerry, Kent, Katy; m. LaNelle Hampton Peterson, Nov. 18, 1969. B.S.L., U. Wyo., 1949, LL.B., 1952. Bar: Wyo. 1952, U.S. Ct. Claims 1952. Sole practice Riverton, Wyo., 1952-54; county and pros. atty. Fremont County, Wyo., 1954-62; ptnr. various law firms, Riverton and Casper, Wyo., 1962-78; sr. ptnr. Spence, Moriarity & Schuster, Jackson, Wyo., 1978—; lectr. legal orgns. and law schs. Author: (with others) Gunning for Justice, 1982, Of Murder and Madness, 1983; Trial By Fire, 1986. Mem. Wyo. Bar Assn., ABA, Wyo. Trial Lawyers Assn., Assn. Trial Lawyers Am., Nat. Assn. Criminal Def. Lawyers. Criminal, Personal injury, Product liability. Office: Spence Moriarity & Schuster Box 548 Jackson WY 83001

SPENCE, HOWARD TEE DEVON, insurance executive; b. Corinth, Ms., Sept. 29, 1949; s. T. P. and Dorothy M. (Bowers) S.; m. Diane Earl Williams, Feb. 26, 1977 (div. June 1986); children: Derek, Tina, Steven. BA, Mich. State U., 1970, M in Criminal Justice Adminstrn., 1975, M in Labor-Indsl. Relations, 1981, MBA, 1983; JD, U. Mich., 1976, M in Pub. Adminstrn., 1977. Bar: Mich. 1976, U.S. Dist. Ct. (ea. dist.) Mich. 1976, U.S. Ct. Appeals (6th cir.) 1976, U.S. Supreme Ct. 1980, U.S. Dist. Ct. (we. dist.) Mich. 1986. Counselor State Prison of So. Mich., Jackson, 1971-76; personnel adminstr. Mich. Dept. Commerce, Lansing, 1976-77; asst. dir. Mich. Pub. Service Commn., Lansing, 1977-78; asst. commr. Mich. Ins. Bur., Lansing, 1978—; ptnr., cons. Spence & Assocs., Lansing, 1983—; arbitrator U.S. Dist. Ct. (we. dist.) Mich., Grand Rapids, 1986; adj. law prof. Thomas M. Cooley Law Sch., Lansing, 1977-80. Author short stories. Sec., v.p. Ingham County Housing Commn., Okemos, Mich., 1985—; mem. Ingham County Dems., Lansing, 1985—; bd. dirs. Econ. Devel. Corp. City of Lansing, 1981—. Mem. ABA, Mich. Bar Assn., Nat. Bar Assn., NAACP (life), Blue Key, Alpha Phi Alpha. Mem. Ch. of Christ. Club: Renaissance, Economic (Detroit). Avocations: tennis, racquetball, camping, dancing. Administrative and regulatory, Criminal, Labor. Home: 4462 Seneca Okemos MI 48864 Office: Spence & Assocs PO Box 20133 Lansing MI 48901

SPENCE, KRISTI COTTON, lawyer; b. San Mateo, Calif., Jan. 23, 1942; s. Aylett Borel and Martha Jane (Knecht) Cotton; m. Robert L. Spence, Apr. 1, 1963; children: Brooksley, Kimberley, Alexander, Jonathan. AB, Stanford U., 1963, JD, 1981. Bar: Calif. 1981, U.S. Dist. Ct. (no. dist.) Calif. 1981. Tchr. Crystal Spring-Uplands Sch., Hillsborough, 1964; assoc. Carr, McClellan, Ingersoll, Thompson & Horn, Burlingame, Calif., 1981—. Pres. North Calif. Assn. Adoption Agys., 1976-78; mem. Stanford U. Law Sch. Bd. Visitors; bd. dirs. Childrens Home Soc. Calif., 1970-78, Pacific Sch. Religion, Berkeley, 1985—; v.p., bd. dirs. San Mateo County Legal Aid Soc., 1982—. Mem. San Mateo Bar Assn. (chmn. family law sect., 1986—, Am. Women for Internat. Understanding, Crystal Springs Alumni Assn. (pres. 1970—). Republican. Family and matrimonial. Office: Carr McClellan Ingersoll et al 216 Park Rd Burlingame CA 94010

SPENCER, FREDERICK S., lawyer; b. El Dorado, Ark., May 28, 1947; s. James Victor and Mary Margaret (Strawn) S.; m. Coralee Faith Eck, Aug. 6, 1971; 1 child, Sarah Faith. BBA, U. Ark., 1970, JD, 1975. Bar: Ark. 1975, U.S. Dist. Ct. (ea. and we. dists.) Ark. 1975, U.S. Ct. Appeals (8th cir.) 1975, U.S. Supreme Ct. 1981. Sole practice, Mountain Home, Ark., 1975—; dir., atty. Ark. Inst. Theology, Fayetteville, 1984—; lectr. in law. Contbr. articles to profl. jours. Dir., atty. Johnson Brothers Youth Ranch, Bruno, Ark., 1981—; pres., founder Ark. Injured Worker's Assn., 1982-84, mem. exec. com. 1985—; dir., atty. Christian Broadcasting Group, Mountain Home, Ark., 1983—; witness U.S. Congress, 1984. Winner Environ. Law Essay Contest Assn. Trial Lawyers Am. 1974; mem. ABA, Ark. Bar Assn. (Reaching Out to Serve award 1983), Baxter County Bar Assn. (sec. 1977-78), Christian Legal Soc., Ark. Injured Worker's Assn., Nat. Orgn. Social Security Claimant's Reps. Baptist. Clubs: Racquet, Athletic (Mountain Home). Federal civil litigation, Personal injury, Workers' compensation. Home: Rt 6 PO Box 431 Mountain Home AR 72653-9147 Office: 409 E 6th St Mountain Home AR 72653

SPENCER, GEORGE HENRY, lawyer; b. Vienna; s. Frank Henry and Lillian (Godin) S.; m. Joan Betty Spencer, Sept. 16, 1956 (dec.); children—Lucy, Margaret, Robert, Nancy. B.E., Yale U., 1948; J.D., Cornell U., 1952. Bar: D.C., N.Y. Examiner, U.S. Patent Office, 1952-54; sole practice, N.Y.C. and Washington, 1954-62; ptnr. Spencer & Frank, Washington, 1962—; lectr. World Trade Inst. Served to capt. JAGC, U.S. Army, 1956-62. Mem. ABA, Am. Patent Law Assn., Lawyer-Pilots Bar Assn., Am. Arbitration Assn. (panel of arbitrators). Club: Cosmos (Washington). Patent, Trademark and copyright. Office: 1111 19th St NW Washington DC 20036

SPENCER, GREGORY SCOTT, lawyer; b. San Mateo, Calif., Dec. 17, 1953; s. Robert Daffron and Lina Margaret (Spencer) S. BA in Econs., U. Calif., Davis, 1976; JD, Hastings Coll. Law, San Francisco, 1980. Bar: Calif. 1980, U.S. Dist. Ct. (no. dist.) Calif. 1980, U.S. Dist. Ct. (cen. dist.) Calif. 1981, U.S. Dist. Ct. (so. dist.) Calif. 1983, U.S. Dist. Ct. (ea. dist.) Calif. 1984, U.S. Ct. Appeals (9th cir.) 1981, U.S. Ct. Appeals (5th cir.) 1984, U.S. Supreme Ct. 1984. Law clk. Cotchett, Dyer & Illston, San Mateo, 1978-80; assoc. Cotchett & Illston, San Mateo, 1980-85; counsel Bank of Am., San Francisco, 1986—; co-chmn. State Bar Fed. Cts. Trial Subcom. and Pretrial Practice Com., San Francisco, 1984-85; mem. moot ct. bd. U. Calif. Hastings Coll. Law, San Francisco, 1979-80. Mem. ABA, Phi Alpha Delta, Kappa Sigma, Omicron Delta Epsilon. Republican. Federal civil litigation, State civil litigation, Antitrust. Office: Bank of Am Legal Dept #3017 PO Box 37000 San Francisco CA 94137

SPENCER, JAMES VICTOR, III, lawyer; b. Morgantown, W.Va., June 29, 1944; s. James Victor Jr. and Mary (Strawn) S.; m. Diane Chowning, Apr. 25, 1970; children: Mary Carol, Christopher, Elizabeth Anne. BA, U. Ark., 1966, JD, 1968. Bar: Ark. 1968, U.S. Supreme Ct. 1972. Ptnr. Spencer, Spencer, Depper & Guthrie and predecessor firm, El Dorado, Ark., 1968—; atty. City of El Dorado, 1971-78; spl. assoc. justice Ark. Supreme Ct., Little Rock, 1979. Dist. chmn. Union Dist. Boy Scouts Am., 1973; exec. bd. mem. DeSoto Area Council Boy Scouts Am.; cubmaster El Dorado Boy Scouts Am. Pack 17; chmn. United Way Campaign, 1978; adv. bd. mem. Salvation Army; vice chmn. Union County chpt. Am. Heart Assn.; bd. dirs. S. Ark. Arts Ctr.; active 1st United Meth. Ch. El Dorado. Mem. ABA, Ark. Bar Assn. (judicial nominations com.), Assn. Trial Lawyers Assn., U. Ark. Alumni Assn., El Dorado Jaycees (pres. 1969), Ark. Jaycees (named to ten outstanding young men in state). Club: Civitan Club (El Dorado) (pres. 1977). Lodge: Rotary (pres. El Dorado 1984-85) (named outstanding young man 1977). Avocations: hunting, fishing, bridge. Probate, Oil and gas leasing, General practice. Home: 1414 N Jefferson El Dorado AR 71730 Office: Spencer Spencer Depper & Guthrie 215 N Washington El Dorado AR 71730

SPENCER, JESSE NEAL, lawyer; b. Portland, Oreg., Jan. 7, 1953; s. Forrest Glenn and Martha May (Yost) S.; m. Elizabeth Cash, June 23, 1983. BA, Portland State U., 1975, MBA, 1978; JD, U. Puget Sound, 1981. Bar: Oreg. 1981, U.S. Dist. Ct. Oreg. 1982. Mng. ptnr. Bernardi & Spencer, Portland, 1982—. Mem. Oreg. Bar Assn., Multnomah Bar Assn. Lodge: Elks. Avocation: writing and speaking Spanish. State civil litigation, Family and matrimonial, Bankruptcy. Home: 1344 SE Miller St Portland OR 97202 Office: Bernardi & Spencer 3717 SE 39th Ave Portland OR 97202

SPENCER, MARY ELIZABETH, lawyer; b. Park Forest, Ill., Aug. 15, 1955; d. Frank Lawrence and Helen Terese (Zezulak) S. BA, Miss. U. for Women, 1977; JD, U. S.C., 1980. Bar: S.C. 1980, U.S. Dist. Ct. S.C. 1985, U.S. Ct. Appeals (4th cir.) 1986. Atty. S.C. Commn. on Aging, Columbia, 1981-85; atty., auditor S.C. Legis. Audit Council, Columbia, 1985—. Mem. ABA, S.C. Bar Assn. (chmn. com. of young lawyers div. 1984-85). Roman Catholic. Administrative and regulatory, Legislative. Home: 619 King St #503 Columbia SC 29205 Office: SC Legis Audit Council 620 NCNB Tower Columbia SC 29201

SPENCER, PATTI S., lawyer, educator; b. Waynesboro, Pa., Aug. 12, 1954; d. Robert Grevell and Peggy Spencer; m. Donald S. Feldman, June 17, 1984. BA, Dickinson Coll., 1975; JD, Boston U., 1978, LLM, 1984. Bar: Mass. 1978, Pa. 1979, U.S. Dist. Ct. Mass. 1979, U.S. Tax Ct. 1979. Assoc. H.M. Kaufman, Boston, 1974-77, Hoffman & Hoffman, Boston, 1977-81, Wyman & Gulick, Boston, 1981-85, Vacovec, Miller & Rothenberg, Brookline, Mass., 1985-87, Deutsh, Williams, Brooks, DeRensis, Holland & Drachman P.C., Waltham, Mass., 1987—; prof. estate and gift tax Boston U. Grad. Tax Program, 1985—. Mem. ABA, Mass. Bar Assn., Boston Bar Assn., Brookline C. of C., Phi Beta Kappa. Estate planning, Legal education, Estate taxation. Home: 38 Fuller St Brookline MA 02146 Office: Vacovec Miller & Rothernberg 1330 Beacon St Brookline MA 02146

SPENCER, PHILIP POLMER, lawyer; b. New Orleans, June 13, 1929; s. Harry and Estelle Polmer (Rabin) Slipakoff; m. Rochelle Terebelo, Apr. 27, 1957; m. 2d, Marilyn Lemoine, Dec. 24, 1978; children—Michelle, Harry, Sharon, Bonnie, Susan. B.B.A., Tulane U., 1949, J.D., 1952. Bar: La., U.S. Supreme Ct. Sole practice, New Orleans; atty. for pub. adminstrn. Parish of Orleans (La.); real estate investor. chmn. adv. bd. Salvation Army of New Orleans. Served to 1st lt. USAF. Mem. ABA, La. State Bar Assn., New Orleans Bar Assn., Apt. Assn. New Orleans (pres.), Apt. Assn. La. (pres.). Democrat. Jewish. Clubs: Masons, Shriners. Real property, Probate, Family and matrimonial. Home: 600 Lakeshore Pkwy New Orleans LA 70124 Office: 100 Robert E Lee Blvd New Orleans LA 70124

SPENCER, SAMUEL, lawyer; b. Washington, Dec. 8, 1910; s. Henry Benning and Katharine (Price) S.; children from previous marriage: Henry B., Janet Spencer Dougherty, Richard A.; m. June Byrne, May 29, 1982. Student, Milton (Mass.) Acad., 1924-29; A.B. magna cum laude, Harvard U., 1932, LL.B., 1935. Bar: N.Y. 1937, D.C 1938, U.S. Supreme Ct 1950. Assoc. Shearman & Sterling, N.Y.C., 1935-37, Covington, Burling, Rublee, Acheson & Shorb, Washington, 1937- 40, 45-47; partner firm Spencer, Whalen & Graham, 1947—; pres. bd. commrs., D.C., 1953-56; pres., chmn. bd. Tennessee R.R. Co., 1956-73; dir. C.N.O. & T.P. Ry. Co. Bd. dirs. Nat. Symphony Orch., 1949-51, Garfield Hosp., 1947-53, 56-62; bd. dirs. Children's Hosp., 1948-53, sec., 1951-53; trustee Potomac Sch., 1947-53; pres. Washington Hosp. Center, 1958-60, dir., 1958-65; mem. Washington Nat. Monument Soc., 1958—. Served to comdr. USNR, 1940-45. Decorated Bronze Star with combat V. Mem. ABA, Bar Assn. D.C., Am. Cancer Soc. (trustee D.C. chpt. 1951-53), AIA (hon.), Washington Inst. Fgn. Affairs (bd. dirs. 1961—, sec. 1961-81), Jud. Council D.C. Circuit (com. on adminstrn. of justice 1966-70), Soc. of Cincinnati, Phi Beta Kappa. Episcopalian (sr. warden). Clubs: Metropolitan of Washington (bd. govs. 1949-53, 56-61, pres. 1959-60); Chevy Chase (Md.). General practice, Probate, Personal income taxation. Home: 5904 Cedar Pkwy Chevy Chase MD 20815 Office: 2000 Massachusetts Ave Washington DC 20006

SPENCER, THOMAS LEE, lawyer; b. Escondido, Calif., Apr. 15, 1956; s. Earl and Lynn Elizabeth (Torstrup) S.; m. Marsha Lou Stinson, Aug. 11, 1979; children: Daniel, Laura. BS in Bus., Oklahoma City U., 1978; JD, U. Okla., 1981. Bar: Okla. 1981, U.S. Dist. Ct. (no., ea. and we. dists.) Okla. 1981. Assoc. John Lampton Belt & Assocs., Oklahoma City, 1980-83; asst. atty. gen. State of Okla., Oklahoma City, 1983—. Mem. ABA, Okla. Bar Assn., Phi Delta Phi. Democrat. Methodist. Administrative and regulatory, State civil litigation, Municipal bonds. Home: 3219 NW 42d St Oklahoma City OK 73112 Office: Okla Atty Gen 112 State Capitol Bldg Oklahoma OK 73105

SPENCER, W(ALTER) THOMAS, lawyer; b. Crawfordsville, Ind., Aug. 6, 1928; s. Walter White and Jean Anna (Springer) S.; m. Patricia Audrey Raia, Mar. 30, 1974; children—Thomas Alfred, Jamie Raia. Student Wabash Coll., Crawfordsville, 1946-47; A.B., U. Miami-Coral Gables, 1950, J.D., 1956. Bar: Fla. 1956, U.S. Dist. Ct. (so. dist.) Fla. 1957, U.S. Dist. Ct. (no. dist.) Fla. 1963, U.S. Ct. Appeals (11th cir.) 1981, U.S. Supreme Ct. 1984. Assoc., Dean, Adams & Fischer, Miami, 1957-63; ptnr. Spencer, Taylor & George, Miami, 1963-81, Spencer, Taylor & Arthur, Miami, 1981—; mem. Fla. Ho. Reps., 1963-66; mem. Fla. Senate, 1966-68. Served to lt. USNR, 1952-55. Mem. ABA, Dade County Bar Assn., Am. Judicature Soc., Def. Research Inst., Fla. Def. Lawyers Assn. Democrat. Methodist. Clubs: Riviera Country, Coral Gables Country (Coral Gables); Bath (Miami Beach, Fla.). Insurance, Personal injury, General practice. Home: 4520 Santa Maria St Coral Gables FL 33146 Office: 1107 Biscayne Bldg 19 W Flagler St Miami FL 33130

SPENGLER, DANIEL GEORGE, lawyer; b. Bethlehem, Pa., Nov. 22, 1950; s. Elias Walter and Miriam Cecelia (Hess) S.; m. Mary Patricia Connolly, June 5, 1981; children: Adam Elias, Ariel Jean. BA, Muhlenberg Coll., 1968-72; MA, Boston Coll., 1973-74; JD, Villanova U., 1974-77. Bar: Pa. 1977, U.S. Dist. Ct. (ea. dist.) Pa. 1979. Assoc. Elias W. Spengler, Bath, Pa., 1977-82; ptnr. Spengler & Spengler, Bath, 1982—; asst. pub. defender Northampton County, Easton, Pa., 1978-80, asst. dist. atty., 1980—. Served with N.G., 1968-74. Mem. ABA, Pa. Bar Assn., Northampton County Bar Assn. Democrat. Mem. United Ch. Christ. Lodge: Lions (pres. local club 1985-86). Criminal, General practice. Office: Spengler & Spengler 110 E Main St Bath PA 18014

SPERBER, MARK DAVID, lawyer; b. Albany, Ga., Oct. 25, 1950; s. Michael and Beatrice (Koch) S.; m. Toby Claire Schack, Dec. 30. 1982; 1 child, Brian Isaac. AB, Franklin & Marshall Coll., 1972; JD, Widener U., 1975. Bar: N.J. 1975, U.S. Dist. Ct. N.J. 1975, U.S. Ct. Appeals (3d cir.) 1978, U.S. Supreme Ct. 1980. Asst. dep. pub. defender appellate sect. State of N.J., East Orange, 1976—, in charge designated counsel sect., 1980—. Coordinator athletic statistics Jersey City State Coll., 1986. Mem. ABA, N.J. Bar Assn. (sports com. young lawyers div., appellate practice seminar young lawyers div. 1984-86). Avocations: football, hockey, writing, tennis, gardening. Criminal, Antitrust, Appellate practice. Office: NJ Pub Defender Office Appellate Sect 20 Evergreen Pl East Orange NJ 07018

SPERO, KEITH ERWIN, lawyer; b. Cleve., Aug. 21, 1933; s. Milton D. and Yetta (Silverstein) S.; m. Carol Kohn, July 4, 1957 (div. 1974); children—Alana, Scott, Susan; m. 2d, Karen Weaver, Dec. 28, 1975. B.A., Western Res. U. 1954, LL.B., 1956. Bar: Ohio 1956. Assoc. Sindell, Sindell & Bourne, Cleve., 1956-57, Sindell, Sindell, Bourne, Markus, Cleve., 1960-64; ptnr. Sindell, Sindell, Bourne, Markus, Stern & Spero, Cleve., 1964-74, Spero & Rosenfield, Cleve., 1974-76, Spero, Rosenfeld & Bourne, L.P.A., Cleve., 1977-79, Spero & Rosenfield Co. L.P.A., 1979—; tchr. bus. law U. Md. overseas div., Eng., 1958-59; lectr. Case-Western Res. U., 1965-69; instr. Cleve. Marshall Law Sch. of Cleve. State U., 1968—; nat. panel arbitrators Am. Arbitration Assn. Trustee Western Res. Hist. Soc., 1984—. Served as 1st lt. JAGC, USAF, 1957-60; capt. Res., 1960-70. Mem. ABA, Ohio Bar Assn., Cleve. Bar Assn., Cuyahoga County Bar Assn., Ohio Acad. Trial Lawyers (pres. 1970-71), Assn. Trial Lawyers Am. (state committeeman 1971-75, bd. govs. 1975-76, sec. family law litigation sect. 1975-76, vice-chmn. 1976-77, chmn. 1977-79), Order of Coif, Phi Beta Kappa, Zeta Beta Tau, Tau Epsilon Rho. Jewish (trustee, v.p. congregation 1972-78). Clubs: Cleve. Racquet, Dugway Creek Yacht (commodore 1984—). Lodge: Masons. Author: The Spero Divorce Folio, 1966; Hospital Liability for Acts of Professional Negligence, 1979. State civil litigation, Personal injury, Family and matrimonial. Home: 2 Bratenahl Pl Bratenahl OH 44108 Office: Suite 500 113 St Clair Cleveland OH 44114

SPERO, MORTON BERTRAM, lawyer; b. N.Y.C., Dec. 6, 1920; s. Adolph and Julia (Strasburger) S.; m. Louise Thacker, May 1, 1943; children—Donald S., Carol S. Roen. B.A., U. Va., 1942, LL.B., 1946. Bar: Va. 1946, U.S. Supreme Ct. 1961. Mem. legal staff NLRB, Washington, 1946-48; sole practice, Petersburg, Va., 1948-70; sr. ptnr. Spero & Levinson, Petersburg, 1970-75; sr. ptnr. Spero & Diehl, Petersburg, 1975-85; sole practice, Petersburg, 1985—; chmn. The Community Bank, Petersburg, 1976-79, dir., 1976—. Chmn. United Fund Drive, 1960; pres. Dist. IV Petersburg Council Social Welfare, Southside Sheltered Workshop, 1965, Congregation B'rith Achim, 1973. Served to lt. USNR, 1943-45. Recipient Outstanding Mem. award Petersburg chapt. B'nai B'rith, 1966; Service to Law Enforcement award Petersburg Police Dept., 1965. Mem. Va. Bar Assn., Petersburg Bar Assn. (pres. 1981-82), Va. State Bar (council 1981-84, chmn. criminal law sect. 1972, chmn. family law sect. 1979, bd. dirs. litigation sect. 1983-86), Assn. Trial Lawyers Am., Va. Trial Lawyers Assn. (v.p. 1972). Democratic. Jewish. Clubs: Civitan (hon.), Rotary. Lodge: Elks (exalted ruler 1968). State civil litigation, Family and matrimonial, Criminal. Home: 9706 Bunker Ct Petersburg VA 23805 Office: 135 S Adams St PO Box 870 Petersburg VA 23804

SPEROS, JAMES MANDAMADIOTIS, lawyer; b. Pitts., Sept. 22, 1952; s. Dimitrios M. and Marinel Boyd (Calhoun) S.; m. Janet Elaine Woodworth, June 17, 1976; children: Benjamin, Carolyn. BS in Journalism, Boston U., 1975; JD, Cleveland-Marshall Coll. Law, 1980. Bar: Ohio 1980, U.S. Dist. Ct. (no. dist.) Ohio 1980, U.S. Ct. Appeals (6th cir.) 1981. Law clk. to judge U.S. Dist. Ct. Ohio, Cleve., 1980-83; assoc. Gallagher, Sharp, Fulton & Norman, Cleve., 1983—; trustee Lake Hosp. System, Inc., Painesville, Ohio, 1985—; gen. counsel Western Res. Health Plan, Cleve., 1983—, bd. dirs. Mem. Painesville City Planning Commn., 1980-85. Mem. Nat. Health Lawyers Assn., Ohio Civil Trial Lawyers Assn. Democrat. Congregationalist. Health, Administrative and regulatory, Federal civil litigation. Home: 7356 Williams Rd Concord OH 44077 Office: Gallagher Sharp Fulton & Norman 1501 Euclid Ave 6th Floor Cleveland OH 44115

SPEROS, MICHAEL CARL, lawyer; b. Memphis, Jan. 15, 1949; s. Nick Speros and Katherine (Hines) Speros Somers; m. Carolyn I. Ijams, Mar. 24, 1973; children—Kristina, Alexis. B.A., Vanderbilt U., 1971; J.D., Emory U., 1974. Bar: Tenn. 1974, U.S. Dist. Ct. (we. dist.) Tenn. 1976, U.S. Ct. Appeals (6th cir.) 1979, U.S. Supreme Ct. 1979. Law clk. Tenn. Supreme Ct., Memphis, 1974-75; asst. city atty. City of Memphis, 1975-80; asst. U.S. atty. Dept. Justice, Memphis, 1980-83; assoc. Young & Perl P.C., Memphis, 1983—. Mem. ABA (employment and labor relations law com. litigation sect.), Tenn. Bar Assn., Memphis and Shelby County Bar Assn., Am. Hellenic Edn. Progressive Assn. (treas. 1983-87), Phi Beta Kappa. Greek Orthodox. Labor, Federal civil litigation, State civil litigation. Home: 2031 Heather Circle Memphis TN 38119 Office: Young & Perl PC 1 Commerce Sq Suite 2380 Memphis TN 38103

SPERRY, FLOYD BENJAMIN, lawyer; b. Denhoff, N. Dakota, Aug. 3, 1905; s. James S. and Mary P. (Johnson) S.; m. Ruth E. Hovda (dec.). JD, U. N.D., 1927, LLB (hon.), 1927. Bar: N.D. 1927, U.S. Dist. Ct. N.D., U.S. Ct. Appeals (8th cir.). Asst. atty. gen. states atty.; ptnr. Sperry and Erickson, Bismark, N.D. Served to lt. U.S. Army, 1927. Fellow ABA, (life, state bar del., code of ethics com.), N.D. Bar Assn. (pres., continuing edn. com.), Assn. Trial Layers Am., Res. Officers Assn., Order of Coif. Lodges: Elks, Masons (32 degree), Shriners. Condemnation, Estate planning, Personal injury. Home: 319 Nova Dr Bismarck ND 58501 Office: 1022 E Divide Ave Bismarck ND 58501

SPERRY, MARTIN J., lawyer; b. Troy, N.Y., May 15, 1947; s. Raymond Leon and Selma (Jenkins) S.; m. Faith Arden Saal, Dec. 24, 1969; children: Jana, Douglas, Jill. BSBA, U. Fla., 1969, JD, 1971. Bar: Fla. 1972, U.S. Dist. Ct. (mid. dist.) Fla. 1972, U.S. Dist. Ct. (so. dist.) Fla. 1974, U.S. Supreme Ct. 1976, N.Y. 1983. Sr. law clk. to presiding justice U.S. Dist. Ct. (mid. dist.) Fla., Orlando, 1972-74; ptnr. Carey, Dwyer, Cole, Selwood & Bernard, Ft. Lauderdale, Fla., 1974-78, Krathen & Sperry, Ft. Lauderdale, Fla., 1978-84, Selwood & Sperry, Ft. Lauderdale, Fla., 1984-85; sole practice Ft. Lauderdale, Fla., 1985—. Contbg. author: Casebook of Florida Constitutional Law, 1971. Served as capt. U.S. Army, 1969-77. Mem. Acad. Fla. Trial Lawyers (diplomate), Assn. Trial Lawyers Am. (sustaining), N.Y. State Bar Assn., Fla. Bar Assn., Fed. Bar Assn., Nat. Bd. Trial Adv. (cert. civil trial lawyer). Democrat. Jewish. Lodge: B'nai B'rith. Avocations: sports, traveling. Personal injury, State civil litigation, Insurance. Office: 305 E Broward Blvd Suite 200 Fort Lauderdale FL 33301

SPETRINO, RUSSELL JOHN, utility company executive, lawyer; b. Cleve., Apr. 22, 1926; s. John Anthony and Madeline S.; July 17, 1954 (dec.); children—Michael J., Ellen A. B.S., Ohio State U., 1950; LL.B., Western Res. U., 1954. Bar: Ohio 1954. Asst. atty. gen. Ohio, 1954-57; atty.-examiner Public Utilities Commn. of Ohio, Columbus, 1957-59; atty. Ohio Edison Co., Akron, 1959-69; sr. atty. Ohio Edison Co., 1970-73, gen. counsel, 1973-78, v.p., gen. counsel, 1978—. Served with inf. U.S. Army, 1944-46. Mem. Edison Electric Inst., Ohio Electric Utility Inst., Akron Bar Assn., Ohio State Bar Assn., Am. Bar Assn., Summit County Law Library Assn., Fed. Energy Bar Assn. Republican. Episcopalian. Clubs: Portage Country, Akron City. General corporate, Public utilities. Home: 867 Lafayette Dr Akron OH 44303 Office: Ohio Edison Co 76 S Main St Akron OH 44308

SPICER, S(AMUEL) GARY, lawyer; b. Dickson, Tenn., Jan. 8, 1942; s. Clark and E. Maybelle (Hogin) S.; m. Katherine M. Stettner, May 12, 1972; children—Victoria, Gary Jr., Matt, Katie, Mark, David. B.A., Adrian Coll., 1964; M.B.A., Wayne State U., 1965; J.D., Detroit Coll. Law, 1969. Bar: Mich. 1969, Tenn. 1969. With personnel dept. Gen. Motors, Pontiac, Mich., 1964-66, trust dept. Nat. Bank Detroit, 1966-69; acct. Price Waterhouse & Co., Detroit, 1969-71; sr. ptnr. Spicer & Assocs., P.C., Detroit, 1973—; dir. Peninsular Steel Co., Clarklift of Detroit, Inc., Detroit Country Inc.; numerous others. Trustee, Adrian Coll., Grosse Pointe Acad., Don and Dolly Smith Found., Wayne State U. Med. Sch. Funding, Elvis Presley Meml. Found.; pres. Ronnie Milsap Found.; treas. Richard Sterban Entertainers and Athletes Found.; mem. adv. bd. Kresge Eye Inst.; mem. citizens adv. bd. Wayne County Juvenile Ct. Com.; trustee, pres. Renaissance Concerts; elder Presbyterian Ch. Served with USAR, 1966-72. Mem. Mich. Bar Assn., Tenn. Bar Assn., Detroit Bar Assn. Clubs: Detroit Country, Detroit Athletic. General corporate, Entertainment, Corporate taxation. Home: 320 Provencal Grosse Pointe Farms MI 48236

SPIEGEL, GEORGE, lawyer; b. Salem, Mass., Sept. 16, 1919; s. Charles and Lena A. Spiegel; m. Ruth H. Weinstein, Mar. 17, 1949; children: John, Ladd, Charles. BA magna cum laude, Amherst Coll., 1941; LLB, Harvard U., 1949. Bar: Mass. 1949, D.C. 1952, U.S. Ct. Appeals (D.C. cir.) 1954, D.C. Ct. Appeals 1972, U.S. Ct. Appeals (5th cir.) 1979, U.S. Ct. Appeals (11th cir.) 1981, U.C. Ct. Appeals (4th cir.) 1983. Atty., advisor USN, Washington, 1950-60; legal mem. Navy Contract Adjustment Bd., Washington, 1958-60; ptnr. Goldberg & Spiegel, Washington, 1960-67, Spiegel & McDiarmid, Washington, 1968—. Served to lt. USN, 1942-45. Mem. ABA, Fed. Bar Assn., Fed. Energy Bar Assn. Administrative and regulatory, Antitrust, FERC practice. Office: Spiegel & McDiarmid 1350 New York Ave NW Washington DC 20024

SPIEGEL, HART HUNTER, lawyer; b. Safford, Ariz, Aug. 30, 1918; s. Jacob B. and Margaret (Hunter) S.; m. Genevieve Willson, Feb. 12, 1946; children: John Willson, Claire Spiegel Brian, Jennifer Emily Wilkinson. BA, Yale U., 1940, LLB, 1946. Bar: Calif. 1946, D.C. 1960. Assoc. Brobeck, Phleger & Harrison, San Francisco, 1947-55, ptnr., 1955—; chief counsel IRS, Washington, 1959-61, mem. adv. group to commr., 1975. Served to lt. USMC, 1942-46, PTO. Fellow Am. Coll. Tax Counsel, Am. Bar Found.; mem. Am. Law Inst., ABA (council mem. tax sect. 1966-68), Bar Assn. San Francisco (pres. 1983). Clubs: Pacific Union (San Francisco); Berkeley Tennis (pres. 1964-65). Corporate taxation, State and local taxation. Home: 3647 Washington St San Francisco CA 94118 Office: Spear St Tower 1 Market Plaza San Francisco CA 94105

SPIEGEL, JERROLD BRUCE, lawyer; b. N.Y.C., Apr. 11, 1949; s. Seymour S. and Estelle (Minsky) S.; m. Helene Susan Cohen, Mar. 3, 1972; children: Dana Sean, Amy Barrett, Evan Tyler. BS, Queens Coll., 1970; JD cum laude, NYU, 1973. Bar: N.Y. 1974. Assoc. Austrian, Lance & Stewart, N.Y.C., 1973-75, Gordon Hurwitz Butowsky Baker Weitzen & Shalov, N.Y.C., 1975-79; ptnr. Shapiro Spiegel Garfunkel & Driggin, N.Y.C., 1979-86, Frankfurt, Garbus, Klein & Selz P.C., N.Y.C., 1986—; adj. faculty Hofstra U., Hempstead, L.I., N.Y., 1986—; bd. dirs. Atlantic Computer Systems Inc., N.Y.C. Editor Ann. Survey Am. Law, 1972-73,. Mem. ABA (corp. law sect.), Order of the Coif, Omicron Delta Epsilon. General corporate, Securities, Contracts commercial. Office: Frankfurt Garbus et al 485 Madison Ave New York NY 10022

SPIEGEL, LAURENCE HAROLD, lawyer; b. Portland, Oreg., Oct. 13, 1947; s. Sidney Irwin and Eloise (Durkheimer) S.; m. Corinne Bacharach, Nov. 14, 1976; children: Samuel, Nathan, Joel. BA, U.S. Internat. U., 1969; MLS, Syracuse U., 1973; JD, Lewis and Clark Coll., 1981. Bar: Oreg. 1981. Sole practice Lake Oswego, Oreg., 1981—. Mem. Library Task Force, Tualatin, Oreg., 1977-78, Conservancy Commn., Lake Oswego, 1982-83; v.p. Northwest Adoptive Family Assn., Portland, 1984-85; pres. Amigos Adoptive Parent Assn., Portland, 1985—. Mem. ABA (adoption com. sect. on family law 1984—). Democrat. Jewish. Lodge: B'nai B'rith. Avocations: hiking, camping, travel. Family and matrimonial, Adoption, Librarianship. Home: 4321 Bernard Lake Oswego OR 97034 Office: 4040 Douglas Way Lake Oswego OR 97034

SPIEGEL, ROBERT ALAN, lawyer; b. N.Y.C., Apr. 1, 1952; s. Benjamin and Pauline (Neus) S. BA, CUNY, 1974; JD, NYU, 1977; MPA, Syracuse U., 1984. Bar: Pa. 1978, D.C. 1985. Exec. rep. Found. Press., Mineola, N.Y., 1978-81; asst. prof. urban studies CUNY, Flus, N.Y., 1982; budget analyst Metro Studies Syracuse (N.Y.), 1982-83; policy analyst Nat. Conf. State Legislatures, Washington, 1983; fin. mgmt. analyst, atty.-advisor U.S. Dept. Housing and Urban Devel., Washington, 1984—. Contbg. author: Middle-class Blacks in a White Society, 1975, The President's National Urban Policy Report, A State Legislator's Guide to Public Pensions, 2d edit., 1983. editor: An Analytical Legislative History of the Medical Device Amendments of 1976, 1976. Mem. ABA, Pa. Bar Assn., D.C. Bar Assn., Am. Soc. for Pub. Adminstrn. Jewish. Administrative and regulatory, Legislative, Real property. Home: 6040 Richmond Hwy 315 Alexandria VA 22303 Office: US Dept Housing and Urban Devel 451 7th St SW Washington DC 20410

SPIEGEL, ROBERT IRA, lawyer; b. Chgo., Apr. 13, 1940; B.A., U. Mich., 1961; J.D., Northwestern U., 1965. Bar: Ill. 1965, U.S. Dist. Ct. (no. dist.) Ill. 1965, U.S. Ct. Appeals (7th cir.) 1969, U.S. Supreme Ct. 1971. Practice, Chgo., 1969—; labor arbitrator Am. Arbitration Assn., 1968—; contbr. to seminars on immigration law. Mem. ABA, Ill. Bar Assn., Am. Immigration Lawyers Assn. (past pres. Chgo. chpt.), Chgo. Bar Assn. (past chmn. immigration law com.), Decalogue Soc. Lawyers. Immigration, naturalization, and customs. Office: 53 W Jackson Blvd Chicago IL 60604

SPIEGEL, ROBERT JOSEPH, lawyer; b. Phila., Apr. 15, 1920; s. Carl and Beatrice Louise (Shoeneman) S.; m. Dean Ida Silverman, Jan. 9, 1955; children—Karen, Roger. A.B., U. Pa., 1941, LL.B., 1948. Bar: Pa. 1949, U.S. Dist. Ct. (ea. dist.) Pa. 1954, U.S. Ct. Appeals (3d cir.) 1954, U.S. Supreme Ct. 1955. Assoc. Earl Jay Gratz, Phila., 1948-53; asst. U.S. Atty. ea. dist. Pa., chief criminal div., 1953-57; ptnr. firm Gratz, Sperling & Spiegel, Phila., 1957-72, firm Gratz, Tate, Spiegel, Ervin & Ruthrauff, Phila., 1972—; instr. trial practice seminars Ct. Practice Inst., Chgo., Willamette Law Sch., Salem, Oreg., Trial Advocacy, Phila. Co-founder Young Republican Orgn., Montgomery County, Pa., 1950; bd. dirs., treas. Defender Assn. Phila., 1960—; bd. dirs. Eagleville Hosp. and Rehab. Ctr., 1974-78; pres. Lower Abington Civic Assn., 1970. Served to maj. M.I., U.S. Army, 1941-45. Decorated Bronze Star. Mem. ABA, Pa. Bar Assn., Phila. Bar Assn. (mem. coms.), Pi Gamma Mu. Jewish. Clubs: Lawyers of Phila. (bd. dirs. 1978-80); Philmont Country (past pres., bd. dirs.). Contbr. articles to legal publs. Federal civil litigation, State civil litigation, Antitrust. Office: 25th Floor Two Girard Plaza Philadelphia PA 19102

SPIEGEL, S. ARTHUR, judge; b. Cin., Oct. 24, 1920; s. Arthur Major and Hazel (Wise) S.; m. Louise Wachman, Oct. 31, 1945; children—Thomas, Arthur Major, Andrew, Roger Daniel. B.A., U. Cin., 1942, postgrad., 1949; LL.B., Harvard U., 1948. Assoc. Kasfir & Chalfie, Cin., 1948-52; assoc. Benedict, Bartlett & Shepard, Cin., 1952-53, Gould & Gould, Cin., 1953-54; ptnr. Gould & Spiegel, Cin., 1954-59; assoc. Cohen, Baron, Druffel & Hogan, Cin., 1960; ptnr. Cohen, Todd, Kite & Spiegel, Cin., 1961-80; judge U.S. Dist Ct. Ohio, Cin., 1980—. Served to capt. USMC, 1942-46. Mem. ABA, Ohio Bar Assn., Cin. Bar Assn., Fed. Bar Assn. Democrat. Jewish. Club: Cin. Lawyers. Home: 4031 Egbert Ave Cincinnati OH 45220 Office: US Dist Ct 838 US Courthouse Cincinnati OH 45202

SPIEGELBERG, FRANK DAVID, lawyer; b. Washington, Aug. 21, 1948; s. Joseph H. and Ruth (May) S.; m. Linda Rae Gordesky, June 28, 1970; children: Adam Jay, Kimberly Joy. BA, Kent State U., 1970; JD, Duke U., 1973. Bar: Md. 1973, Tex. 1977, Okla. 1978, U.S. Ct. Mil. Appeals 1974, U.S. Dist. Ct. (ea. dist.) Okla. 1978, U.S. Ct. Appeals (10th cir.) 1978, U.S. Dist. Ct. (we. dist.) Okla. 1985, U.S. Supreme Ct. 1985. Assoc. Dukes, Troese, Mann & Wilson, Landover, Md., 1973; litigation atty. Cities Service Co., Tulsa, 1978-82, sr. litigation atty., 1982; atty. Apache Corp., Tulsa, 1982-86; of counsel Boesche, McDermott & Eskridge, Tulsa, 1982—. Pres., bd. dirs. Burning Tree Homeowners Assn., Tulsa, 1981-85; mem. redistricting com. Union Sch. Bd., Tulsa, 1984. Served as capt. USAF, 1974-77. Recipient Air Force Commendation medal, 1977, cert. of Appreciation for seminar, Okla. Assn. Def. Counsel, 1982. Mem. Okla. Bar Assn., Tex. Bar Assn., Tulsa County Bar (grievance com.), Tulsa County Bar Assn., Assn. Trial Lawyers Am., Kent State U. Alumni Assn., Duke U. Alumni Assn., Sigma Phi Epsilon Alumni Assn. State civil litigation, Oil and gas leasing, General corporate. Home: 9032 E 67th St Tulsa OK 74133 Office: Boesche McDermott & Eskridge 800 Oneok Plaza 100 W 5th St Tulsa OK 74103

SPIER, RICHARD GARY, lawyer; b. N.Y.C., Feb. 7, 1948; s. Alvin and Doris Jean (Saul) S.; m. Jennifer Celeste Jasaitis, Sept. 21, 1971; children: Zachary Daniel, Ethan E., Ezra Jasaitis. BA, Stanford U., 1969; postgrad., Yale U., 1969-70; JD, Cornell U., 1976. Bar: Oreg. 1976, U.S. Dist. Ct. Oreg. 1977, U.S. Ct. Appeals (9th cir.) 1978, U.S. Supreme Ct. 1979. Law clk. to judge U.S. Dist. Ct. Oreg., Portland, 1976-78; assoc. Bullivant, Houser et al, Portland, 1978-80; from assoc. to ptnr. Sussman, Shank, Wapnick, Caplan & Stiles, Portland, 1980—; judge pro tem Multnomah County Cir. Ct., Portland, 1986—. Chmn. regional appeal program Stanford U., Oreg., 1985-86. Served with USNR, 1970-73. Mem. Oreg. Bar Assn. (chmn. com. fed. practice and procedures 1981-82, bd. examiners), Am. Arbitration Assn. (arbitrator). Federal civil litigation, State civil litigation, Insurance. Office: Sussman Shank Wapnick Caplan & Stiles 1001 SW 5th Ave Suite 1111 Portland OR 97204

SPIES, HOWARD A., real estate company executive, lawyer; b. Hays, Kans., Mar. 31, 1936; s. Adolph A. and Margaret R. (Coltrane) S.; m. Carolyn C. Hain, Aug. 13, 1960; children—Christine, Howard, Cathleen, Karen. B.S., Fort Hays State Coll., 1958; J.D., Washburn U. of Topeka, 1961. Bar: Kans. 1961, U.S. Dist. Ct. Kans. 1961, U.S. Ct. Appeals (10th cir.) 1964, U.S. Supreme Ct. 1971, U.S. Tax Ct. 1971. With Alcoholic Beverage Control, Atty. Gen.'s Office, State of Kans., 1961-63; ptnr. Schroeder, Heeney, Groff, Spies & Hiebert, Topeka, 1963-77; sole practice, Kansas and Ohio, 1977-80 (bd. dirs.); v.p., gen. counsel Cardinal Industries, Columbus, Ohio, 1980—. Served with U.S. Army, 1955-57. Mem. ABA, Phi Alpha Delta. Republican. Roman Catholic. Club: Worthington Hills (Ohio) Country. General corporate, Real property, Securities. Office: Cardinal Industries Inc 2040 S Hamilton Rd Columbus OH 43227

SPIES, LEON FRED, lawyer; b. Blue Grass, Iowa, Oct. 8, 1950; s. Fred William and Alma Lois (Lineburg) S.; m. Janet Rae Peterson, July 15, 1979; children: Caitlin, Allison. BBA with distinction, U. Iowa, 1972, JD with distinction, 1975. Bar: Iowa 1975, U.S. Dist. Ct. (no. and so. dists.) Iowa 1975, U.S. Ct. Appeals 1975, U.S. Supreme Ct. 1987. Assoc. Heintz & Mellon, Iowa City, 1975-76; ptnr. Mellon & Spies, Iowa City, 1976—; magistrate jud. dept. State of Iowa, 1978-83. Bd. chmn. Johnson County Red Cross, Iowa City, 1982-84; bd. dirs. Big Bros./ Big Sisters, Johnson County, Iowa, 1985—. Mem. ABA, Iowa Bar Assn., Assn. Trial Lawyers Am., Assn. Trial Lawyers of Iowa, Am. Judicature Soc. Democrat. Presbyterian. State civil litigation, Criminal, Personal injury. Home: 709 Caroline Ave Iowa City IA 52240 Office: Mellon & Spies 102 S Clinton St Iowa City IA 52240

SPIKE, MICHELE KAHN, lawyer; b. Paterson, N.J., Oct. 1, 1951; d. Nathan and Clara (Spinella) Kahn; m. John Thomas Spike, May 26, 1973; 1 child, Nicholas Nathan. BA summa cum laude, Conn. Coll., 1973; JD cum laude, Boston U., 1976. Bar: N.Y. 1977, U.S. Dist. Ct. (so. and ea. dists.) N.Y. 1977. Assoc. Hale, Russell & Gray, N.Y.C., 1976-82; sole practice, N.Y.C., 1982-86; ptnr. Dolgenos, Bergen & Newman, N.Y.C., 1986—. Editor: (exhbn. catalogue) Italian Still Life Paintings, 1983, Baroque Portraiture in Italy, 1984. Mem. ABA, Bar Assn. City N.Y., Phi Beta Kappa. Art, Real property, General corporate. Home: 85 East End Ave New York NY 10028 Office: Dolgenos Bergen & Newman 101 Wooster St New York NY 10012

SPILLANE, DENNIS KEVIN, lawyer; b. N.Y.C., Sept. 15, 1953; s. Denis Joseph and Mary Kate (Sullivan) S. BA magna cum laude, Manhattan Coll., 1974; JD, NYU, 1978; MS in Taxation, Pace U., 1986. Bar: N.Y. 1979, U.S. Dist. Ct. (ea. and so. dists.) N.Y. 1979, U.S. Tax Ct. 1986. Asst. dist. atty. Borough of Bronx, N.Y.C., 1978-85; prin. atty. N.Y. State Tax Dept., N.Y.C., 1985—; prof. law Pace U., 1987—. Contbr. articles to profl. jours. Mem. ABA, N.Y. State Bar Assn., N.Y. County Lawyers Assn. Democrat. Roman Catholic. State and local taxation, State civil litigation, Criminal. Office: NY State Tax Dept 2 World Trade Ctr Rm 4776 New York NY 10047

SPILLER, WILLIAM, JR., lawyer; b. Los Angeles, Feb. 19, 1947; s. William and Goldie (Norman) S.; m. Donna M. DuPuy, Sept. 11, 1976; 1 child, Sydney N. AA, Los Angeles Harbor Coll., 1970; BA, U. Calif., Carson, 1971; postgrad., U. So. Calif., 1971-73; JD, Northrop U., 1981. Bar: Calif. 1983, U.S. Dist. Ct. (cen. dist.) Calif. 1983, U.S. Ct. Appeals (9th cir.) 1983. Sole practice Los Angeles, 1983-84; assoc. Norby & Brodeur, Torrance, Calif., 1984-85, McKay, Byrne et al, Los Angeles, 1985—; cons. Watts Labor Community Action Com., Los Angeles, 1972-75, Los Angeles County Probation, 1975-79. Editor Northrop U. Law Rev., 1981. Served with U.S. Army, 1967-69. Recipient Proclamation U.S. senator John V. Tunney, Washington, 1978, mayor Thomas Bradley, Los Angeles, 1978-81, City Council, Los Angeles, 1979-81. Mem. ABA, Assn. So. Calif. Def. Council, Assn. Trial Lawyers Am. Republican. Club: Fun Boys Inc. (Los Angeles). Avocations: tennis, photography, travel, counseling. Federal civil litigation, State civil litigation, Insurance.

SPINA, ANTHONY FERDINAND, lawyer; b. Chgo., Aug. 15, 1937; s. John Dominic and Nancy Maria (Ponzio) S.; m. Anita Phyllis, Jan. 28, 1961; children—Nancy M., John D., Catherine M., Maria J., Felicia M. B.S. in Social Sci., Loyola U., Chgo., 1959; J.D., DePaul U., 1962. Bar: Ill. 1962. Assoc. Epton, Scott, McCarthy, & Bohling, Chgo., 1962-64; sole practice, Elmwood Park, Ill., 1964-71; pres. Anthony & Spina, P.C., 1971-84, Spina, McGuire & Okal, P.C., 1985—; atty. Leyden Twp., Ill., 1969—, Village of Rosemont, Ill., 1971; counsel for Pres. and dir. Cook County Twp. Ofcls. of Ill., 1975—; counsel for exec. dir. Ill. State Assn. Twp. Ofcls.; counsel Elmwood Park Village Bd. and various Cook County Twps. (DuPage, 1980-82, Maine, 1981—, Norwood Park, 1982—, Wayne, 1982-84); mem. Elmwood Park Bldg. Code Planning Commn. Bd. Appeals. Recipient Lacodaire medal Dean's Key Loyola U.; Loyola U. Housing awards, 1965, 71, 76; award of appreciation Cook County Twp. Ofcls. Mem. Ill. Bar Assn., ABA, Chgo. Bar Assn., Am. Judicature Soc., Justinian Soc. Lawyers, Ill. State Twp. Attys. Assn. (past v.p., pres. 1982-86, dir. 1986—, sec., Ill. del. Nat. Assn. Towns and Twps.), Nat. Assn. Twp Attys. (sec. 1986—), Edgebrook C. of C. (bd. dirs.), Nat. Assn. Italian Am. Lawyers, Blue Key, Delta Theta Phi, Tau Kappa Epsilon, Pi Gamma Mu. Roman Catholic. St. Rocco Soc. of Simbario (auditor-trustee Chgo.), KC (scribe, past grand knight). Author Rosemont Village Ordinances, 1971; Elmwood Park Bldg Code, 1975, Leyden Twp. Codified Ordinances, 1987. State civil litigation, General practice, Local government. Office: 7608-7610 W North Ave Elmwood Park IL 60635

SPINA, GEORGE CHARLES, lawyer; b. Newark, Nov. 1, 1947; s. George John and Lillian Evelyn (Greb) S. B.A., Seton Hall U., 1969; J.D., Georgetown U., 1976; LL.M., Columbia U., 1977; M.A., U. So. Calif., 1977. Bar: N.J. 1977, U.S. Customs Ct. 1978, D.C. 1979. Exec. dir. Internat. Law Inst., Washington, 1977-81; pres. George C. Spina Assocs., Washington, 1981—; sec., dir. Biog. Archives Corp., Maplewood, N.J., 1984—. Editor: Career Opportunities in International Law, 1977; OECD Guidelines for Multinational Enterprises: A Business Appraisal, 1977; Interface I: Proc. on the Application of U.S. Antidumping and Countervailing Duty Laws to Imports from State-Controlled Economies and State-Owned Enterprises, 1980; co-editor numerous books on law. Contbr. articles to profl. jours. Pres. bd. trustees Meml.-West Presbyterian Ch., Newark, 1984—. Served with USAF, 1970-74. Mem. ABA (exec. sec. com. on jud. edn. and internat. law 1980-82), Am. Soc. Internat. Law, Internat. Law Assn. (sec. com. on law and the internat. econ. order 1980-82), N.J. Bar Assn., D.C. Bar Assn. U.S. C. of C. (founding mem. internat. service industry com. 1977-80). Republican. Presbyterian. Club: Princeton (N.Y.C.). Lodge: Masons. Private international, Antitrust. Home: 10 Vermont St Maplewood NJ 07040 Office: 4301 Massachusetts Ave NW Washington DC 20016

SPINGLER, FRANK JOSEPH, lawyer; b. Poughkeepsie, N.Y., Dec. 29, 1945; s. Frank J. and Catherine W. Spingler; m. Susan Hueth, Apr. 25, 1986; 1 child, Erin. BA in English, St. Bonaventure U., 1967; JD, Georgetown U., 1970. Bar: D.C. 1972. Dir. real estate So. Ry. Co., Washington, 1976-80; gen. atty. Norfolk So. Ry., Washington, 1980-84; v.p. B.F. Saul Co., Chevy Chase, Md., 1984-87, Potomac Capital Investment Corp., Washington, 1987—. Serves as capt. USAR, 1971—. Mem. ABA, D.C. Bar Assn. Office: Potomac Capital Investment Corp 1020 19th St NW Washington DC 20036

SPINKS, HUGH FRANKLIN, JR., lawyer; b. Little Rock, Nov. 30, 1949; s. Hugh Franklin Sr. and Gertrude (Carmack) S.; m. Debra Ann Kendrick,

June 30, 1972; children: Scott, Stacey. BA, Hendrix Coll., 1970; JD with honors, U. Ark., 1975. Bar: Ark. 1975, U.S. Dist. Ct. (ea. dist.) Ark. 1975. Assoc. Eubanks, Files & Hurley, Little Rock, 1975-77; ptnr. Eubanks & Spinks, Little Rock, 1977-79; assoc. Gary Eubanks and Assocs., Little Rock, 1979—. Editor-in-chief U. Ark. Law Rev., 1974. Served with U.S. Army, 1970-72. Mem. Ark. Bar Assn., Pulaski County Bar Assn., Assn. Trial Lawyers Am., Ark. Trial Lawyers Assn. Baptist. Personal injury. Home: 214 Alanbrook Sherwood AR 72116 Office: Gary Eubanks and Assocs 708 W 2d Little Rock AR 72201

SPINRAD, MAX, lawyer; b. Newark, June 10, 1939; s. Joseph and Dora (Zimmerman) S.; m. Myrna Zigman, June 25, 1961; 1 son, Larry. B.A., Rutgers U., 1960; LL.B., U. Pa., 1963. Bar: N.J. 1963, U.S. Dist. Ct. N.J. 1963, U.S. Supreme Ct. 1969, N.Y. 1982, U.S. Ct. Appeals (3d cir.) 1982. Clk. to judge Superior Ct., 1963-64; dep. atty. gen., 1964-65; asst. counsel to gov. N.J., 1965-67; practice, East Orange and Livingston, N.J., 1967-78; ptnr. Miele, Cooper, Spinrad & Kronberg, Milburn, N.J., 1979—; counsel N.J. Optometric Assn., 1968-79, chmn. legal advs. com., 1972. Pres., East Orange Democratic Club, 1968; bd. dirs. Hebrew Youth Acad. Essex County, 1970-76; v.p. West Orange Jewish Ctr. Recipient Meritorious Service award N.J. Optometric Assn., 1978. Mem. ABA, N.J. Bar Assn. (mem. environ. law, equity jurisprudence, pub. utilities law coms.), Essex County Bar Assn. (chmn. legis. com. 1973). Jewish. Environment, Personal injury, Administrative and regulatory. Home: 35 Edgemont Rd West Orange NJ 07041 Office: 90 Millburn Ave Millburn NJ 07041

SPIRE, ROBERT M., attorney general of Nebraska; b. Omaha, Sept. 20, 1925. B.S., Harvard U., 1949, J.D., 1952; student, Juilliard Sch. Music, 1952; D.H.L. (hon.), U. Nebr.-Omaha, 1971. C.P.A., Nebr. Ptnr. Ellick, Spire & Jones, Omaha; atty. gen. State of Nebr., Lincoln, 1985; adj. assoc. prof. med. jurisprudence U. Nebr. Coll. Medicine, 1968-84; mem. Nebr. Fourth Jud. Dist. Com. on Inquiry, 1959-81, vice chmn., 1974-81. Contbr. articles to profl. jours. Mem. Gov.'s Citizens Comm. for Study Higher Edn. in Nebr., 1984. Served with U.S. Army, 1943-46. Recipient numerous awards for profl. and civic contbns., including Spl. Contbn. to Black Heritage award Omaha Black Heritage Series, 1983, Whitney M. Young Meml. award Urban League Nebr., 1983. Fellow Am. Bar Found.; mem. Am. Judicature Soc. (bd. dirs. 1983-84), ABA (spl. com. on lawyers' pub. service responsibility 1983-84), Am. Guild Organists, Nebr. State Bar Assn. (pres. 1981-82), Nebr. Continuing Legal Edn. (pres. 1978-80), Urban League Nebr. (bd. dirs. 1977-80), Omaha Bar Assn. (pres. 1978-79), Legal Aid Soc. Omaha (bd. dirs. 1971-79, pres. 1972-75). Criminal. Office: Nebr Dept Justice Office Atty Gen Lincoln NE 68509 *

SPIRN, STUART DOUGLAS, lawyer; b. Manchester, N.H., Sept. 27, 1945; s. Sidney and Eve (Avedon) S.; children by previous marriage—Daniel Todd, Eve Avedon; m. Nancy Deborah Brenegan, Aug. 4, 1984; 1 child, Alexander Jonathan. AB in History, Coll. William and Mary, 1967, JD, 1970. Bar: Va. 1970. Assoc. D.R. Taylor, Williamsburg, Va., 1970; mem. staff div. justice Office of Gov., Commonwealth of Va., 1973-75; sole practice, Williamsburg, 1975—; guest lectr. Marshall Wythe Sch. Law, Coll. William and Mary; cons. Nat Manpower Survey, Am. Inst. Research, Am. Acad. Jud. Edn. Nat. Ctr. for State Cts.; exec. sec. Va. Supreme Ct. Trustee Norge (Va.) Civic Assn., 1974-75; bd. dirs. James City-County Soc. Services, 1974-76; commr. Housing & Redevelopment Authority, City of Williamsburg, 1985—, vice chmn., 1986-87, chmn. 1987—; coach Williamsburg Volleyball Club, 1981-82; pres. Williamsburg Soccer Club, 1978—; coach men's volleyball team Coll. William and Mary 1982—. Served to capt. JAGC, U.S. Army, 1970-73. Mem. ABA, Am. Soc. Internat. Law, Va. Trial Lawyers Assn., Am. Judicature Soc., Va. Bar Assn, Nat. Volleyball Coaches Assn., U.S. Volleyball Assn. (bd. dirs. 1982-87), Collegiate Volleyball Coaches Assn. Jewish. Club: Kiwanis (Williamsburg, Va.). Author: Practical Instructions for Jury Management, 1975. State civil litigation, General corporate, General practice. Office: Francis and Blair Sts PO Box 584 Williamsburg VA 23187

SPITAL, SAMUEL E., lawyer; b. Detroit, Mar. 4, 1944; children: Barry, Joel, Robyn, Cheryl. BA, Calif. State U., Los Angeles, 1962; JD, Loyola U., Los Angles, 1966. Bar: Calif. 1971, U.S. Dist. Ct. (cen. and so. dists.) Calif. 1971, U.S. Ct. Appeals (9th cir.) 1971. Dep. atty. gen. Office of Atty. Gen., Los Angeles and San Diego, Calif., 1970-78; sole practice San Diego, 1978—. Contbr. articles to profl. jours. Mem. ABA, San Diego County Bar Assn., San Diego County Trial Lawyers Assn. Office: 1200 3d Ave Suite 1524 San Diego CA 92101-4109

SPITZ, HUGO MAX, lawyer; b. Richmond, Va., Aug. 17, 1927, s. Jacob Gustav and Clara (Herzfeld) S.; m. Barbara Steinberg, June 22, 1952; children—Jack Gray, Jill Ann Levy, Sally. A.A., U. Fla., 1948, B.Laws, 1951, J.D., 1967. Bar: Fla. 1951, S.C., 1955, U.S. Dist. Ct. (so. dist.) Fla. 1951, U.S. Dist. Ct. (ea. dist.) S.C. 1956, U.S. Ct. Appeals (4th cir.) 1957. Asst. atty. gen. State of Fla., Tallahassee, 1951; assoc. Williams, Salomon & Katz, Miami, Fla., 1951-54, Steinberg & Levkoff, Charleston, S.C., 1954-57; sr. ptnr. Steinberg, Levkoff, Spitz & Goldberg, Charleston, 1957—; lectr. S.C. Trial Lawyers Assn., Columbia, 1958—, S.C. U. Sch. Law, Columbia, 1975, S.C. Bar Assn., 1955—. Assoc. mcpl. judge Charleston, 1972-74, mcpl. judge, 1974-76; commr. Charleston County Substance Abuse Commn., 1976-79; bd. govs. S.C. Patient's Compensation Fund, Columbia, 1978-89; adv. mem., atty. S.C. Legis. Council for Workers' Compensation; chmn. bd. dirs. Franklin C. Fetter Health Ctr., Charleston, 1977-78; mem. S.C. Appellate Def. Commn., 1985-86; founding sponsor Civil Justice Found., 1986—; bd. dirs. Charleston Jewish Fedn., 1986—. Served with USN, 1945-46. Fellow S.C. Bar Assn., U. S.C. Ednl. Found; mem. ABA, Civil Justice Found., S.C. Law Inst., S.C. Trial Lawyers Assn. (pres. 1985-86), S.C. Claimants' Attys. for Worker's Compensation, S.C. Worker's Compensation Ednl. Assn. (bd. dirs. 1978—), S.C. Law Inst., Am. Judicature Soc., N.Y. State Trial Lawyers Assn., Pa. Trial Lawyers Assn., Assn. Trial Lawyers Am. (mem. pres. council 1986—), Nat. Rehab. Assn., Nat. Orgn. Social Security Claimants' Reps. S.C. Bar (chmn. trial and appellate sect. 1982-83; ho. of dels. 1984-85), So. Assn. Workmen's Compensation Adminstrs., Nat. Inst. for Trial Advocacy (com. chmn. 1985). Democrat. Jewish. Clubs: Hebrew Benevolent Soc. (pres. 1974-75), Jewish Community Ctr. (v.p. 1972-74) (Charleston). Workers' compensation, Personal injury, State civil litigation. Home: 337 Confederate Circle Charleston SC 29407 Office: Steinberg Levkoff Spitz & Goldberg PO Box 9 Charleston SC 29402

SPITZ, ROBERT JOHN, lawyer; b. N.Y.C., May 26, 1947; s. Charles H. and Ola G. (Monroe) S.; m. Suzie Choi, Dec. 8, 1979; 1 child, Danory Michael Carleton. BS in Aero. Engring., Purdue U., 1969; JD, U. So. Calif., 1975. Bar: Calif. 1975, D.C. 1978, N.Y. 1979. Gen. counsel News World Communications, Inc., N.Y.C., 1978-87; exec. dir. Am. Constn. Com., Calif., 1987—. Editor: Legal Audits for Corporations, 1984. Mem. ABA (gen. practice sect., chmn. corp. counsel com. 1986—, chmn. ann. meeting com. 1986—). Republican. Avocations: tennis, golf, swimming. General corporate. Home: 39408 Stratton Common Fremont CA 94538 Office: Am Constn Com 955 L'Enfant Plaza SW Suite 500 Washington DC 20024

SPITZBERG, IRVING JOSEPH, JR., association executive, lawyer; b. Little Rock, Feb. 9, 1942; s. Irving Joseph and Marie Bettye (Seeman) S.; m. Roberta Frances Alprin, Aug. 21, 1966; children—Edward Storm, David Adam. B.A., Columbia U., 1964; B.Phil., Oxford U., 1966; J.D., Yale U., 1969. Bar: Calif. 1969, D.C. 1985. Asst. prof. Pitzer Coll., Claremont, Calif., 1969-71; fellow Inst. Current World Affairs, N.Y.C., 1971-74; vis. lectr. Brown U., Providence, 1973; prof. SUNY, Buffalo, 1980; dean of coll. SUNY, 1974-78; gen. sec. AAUP, Washington, 1980-84; exec. dir. Council for Liberal Learning of Assn. Am. Colls., Washington, 1985—; pres. The Knowledge Co., Bethesda, Md., 1985—; coordinator Alvan Ikoku coll., Nigeria, 1979-80; cons. Bd. Adult Edn., Kenya, 1973-74, Philander Smith Coll., Little Rock, 1978-80. Author and editor: Exchange of Expertise, 1978, Universities and the New International Order, 1979, Universities and the International Exchange of Knowledge, 1980; author: Campus Programs on Leadership, 1986, Racial Politics in Little Rock, 1987. Founder Coalition for Ednl. Excellence, Western N.Y., 1978-80; founding mem. Alliance for Leadership devel., Washington, 1985; counsel GASP, Pomona, (Calif.), 1969-71; Democratic Committeeman, Erie County, (N.Y.), 1978-80; founding pres. Internat. Found for St. Catherine's Coll., Oxford, 1986—. Recipient 1st place award Westinghouse sci. Talent Search, 1960; Kellett scholar Trustees of Columbia U., 1964-66. Mem. AAAS, Internat. Soc. Ednl., Cultural, and Sci. Exchanges. Jewish. Clubs; Federal, Columbia, Yale (Washington). Avocations: kids; microcomputing. Education and Schools, Labor, Legislative. Office: 7612 Winterberry Pl Bethesda MD 20817

SPITZER, MARC LEE, lawyer; b. Pitts., Sept. 12, 1957; s. Richard A. and Edith (Brodie) S. BA in History and Polit. Sci. summa cum laude, Dickinson Coll., 1979; JD cum laude, U. Mich., 1982. Bar: Ariz. 1982, U.S. Dist. Ct. Ariz. 1982, U.S. Tax Ct. 1982, U.S. Ct. Appeals (9th cir.) 1985. Assoc. Fennemore, Craig et al, Phoenix, 1982—. Mem. Ariz. Rep. Caucus, Phoenix, 1982—; chmn. Ariz. Reps. for Choice, 1984-86, Atty.'s Council Planned Parenthood, 1985-86; mem. devel. com. Dickinson Coll., Carlisle, Pa., 1985-86; elected rep. committeeman Ariz. 18th Dist., Phoenix, 1986. Mem. ABA (tax sect.), State Bar Ariz. (tax sect.), Ariz. Tax Research Found. (bd. dirs. 1984—), Ariz. Tax Research Assn., Maricopa County Bar Assn. Jewish. Club: Arizona, Phoenix City, Captain's (bd. dirs.). Avocations: fishing, prospecting, classical music, racquetball. Personal income taxation, Corporate taxation, Tax litigation. Home: 36 E Harmont Dr Phoenix AZ 85020

SPITZLI, DONALD HAWKES, JR., lawyer; b. Newark, Mar. 19, 1934; s. Donald Hawkes and Beatrice (Banister) S.; m. Jacqueline Anne Spitzli, Mar. 3, 1979; m. Rita Angell, June 17, 1956; children—Donald Hawkes III, Peter Gilbert, Lori Anne, Seth Armstrong. A.B., Dartmouth Coll., 1956; LL.B., U. Va. 1963. Bar: Va. 1963. Assoc. Willcox, Savage, Lawrence, Dickson & Spindle, Norfolk, Va., 1964-67; atty. Eastman Kodak Co., Rochester, 1967-68; assoc. Willcox, Savage, Lawrence, Dickson & Spindle, Norfolk, Va., 1968-70, ptnr., 1971-77; pres. Marine Hydraulics Internat., Inc., Chesapeake, Va., 1978-80; sole practice, Virginia Beach, Va., 1980—; gen. counsel Chieftain Motor Inn, Inc., Jadon Farms, Ltd., Ocean Breeze Condominium, Ltd. Served to comdr. USNR, 1956-70. Mem. ABA, Va. Bar Assn. Episcopalian. Club: Yale (N.Y.C.). General corporate, General practice, Trademark and copyright. Office: PO Box 6059 Virginia Beach VA 23456

SPIVACK, EDITH IRENE, lawyer; b. N.Y.C., Apr. 19, 1910; d. Harry A. and Ethel Y. (Mantell) Spivack; m. Bernard H. Goldstein, Dec. 22, 1933; children: Rita Goldstein Christopher, Amy Goldstein Bass. BA, Barnard Coll., 1929; LLB, Columbia U., 1932; hon. doctorate St. John's U. Bar: N.Y. 1933, U.S. Dist. Ct. (so. dist.) N.Y. 1949, U.S. Cts. Appeals 1950, 75, U.S. Supreme Ct. 1969, U.S. Dist. Ct. (ea. dist.) Pa. 1973. Assoc. asst. Corp. Counsel's Office, City of N.Y., 1934-76, exec. asst., 1976—; mem. panel to rev. qualifications for ea. dist. ct. bankruptcy judges. Active Planned Parenthood, Legal Aid Soc.; Columbia Law Sch. rep. to Alumni Council, also past bd. dirs. Recipient William Nelson Cromwell award N.Y. County Law Assn., 1976, Fund for City of N.Y. Pub. Service award, 1975, Disting. Service award Mayor Koch, 1981, Columbia award for Conspicuous Service, 1975, NIMLO award for Outstanding Pub. Service, 1976, Disting. Alumnae award Barnard Coll., 1984, Disting. and Dedicated Corp. Counsel Service award, 1986. Fellow N.Y. Bar Found. (Community Service award); mem. Am. Bar Found., Assn. Bar City N.Y. (cts. and membership coms., judiciary com.), N.Y. State Bar Assn. (judiciary com., del., status of women in cts. com., Service plaque, Fifty-yr. Lawyer award 1984), N.Y. County Lawyers Assn. (bd. dirs., fin. com., women's rights com., judiciary com.), N.Y. County Lawyers Found., Am. Judicature Soc., Columbia U. Law Sch. Alumni Assn. (medal for excellence com.). Democrat. Jewish. Clubs: Sands Point Bath and Tennis (L.I.); Princeton (N.Y.C.). Bankruptcy, Condemnation, Real property. Office: City New York Law Dept 100 Church St New York NY 10007

SPIVACK, GORDON BERNARD, lawyer, lecturer; b. New Haven, June 15, 1929; s. Jacob and Sophie (Ocheretianski) S.; m. Dolores Olivia Traversano, Jan. 16, 1956; children—Michael David, Paul Stephen. B.S. with philosophic orations and honors and exceptional distinction, Yale U., 1950, LL.B. magna cum laude, 1955. Bar: Conn. 1955, U.S. Supreme Ct. 1962, N.Y. 1970. Trial atty. antitrust div. Dept. Justice, Washington, 1955-60; asst. chief field ops. antitrust div. Dept. Justice, 1961-64, chief field ops. antitrust div., 1964-65, dir. ops. antitrust div., 1965-67; assoc. prof. law Yale U., New Haven, 1967-70; vis. lectr. Yale U., 1970-78; ptnr. Lord, Day & Lord, N.Y.C., 1970-86, Coudert Bros., N.Y.C., 1986—; speaker on antitrust law; mem. Pres.'s Nat. Commn. for Rev. Antitrust Law and Procedures, Washington, 1978-79. Contbr. numerous articles on antitrust law to profl. jours. Served with U.S. Army, 1950-52. Recipient Sustained Superior Performance award Dept. Justice, 1955-60. Fellow Am. Coll. Trial Lawyers; mem. ABA, N.Y. State Bar Assn., Bar Assn. City N.Y. Jewish. Clubs: The Sky, Yale (N.Y.C.); Woodbridge Country (Conn.). Avocation: detective stories. Antitrust. Home: 118 Townsend Terr New Haven CT 06512 Office: Coudert Bros 200 Park Ave New York NY 10166

SPIVAK, PETER BEECHING, lawyer, football club executive; b. Phila., Jan. 9, 1934; s. Alexander Avery and Marguerite Elizabeth (Beeching) S.; m. Anne Markley, Jan. 3, 1974; children—Frank, Jeffery, Michelle, Peter Beeching. B.A., Ohio Wesleyan U., 1955; J.D., Northwestern U., 1957. Bar: Mich. 1958, U.S. Supreme Ct. 1962. Asst. U.S. atty. Eastern Dist. Mich., 1958-60; law clk. to judge U.S. Dist. Ct. Eastern Dist. Mich., 1960-62; mem. firm Dyer, Meek, Ruegsegger & Bullard, Detroit, 1960-62, Spivak & James, Detroit, 1962-63, Fenton, Nederlander, Tracy & Dodge, Detroit, 1963-64; chmn. Mich. Pub. Service Commn., 1964-68; judge Wayne County (Mich.) Common Pleas Ct., 1968-72, presiding judge, 1971; judge Wayne County 3d Jud. Circuit Ct., 1972-81, exec. com., 1978-81; pub. adminstr. Wayne County, 1963-64; of counsel Jaffe, Snider, Raitt & Huer, Detroit, 1982-84, Fitzgerald Young Peters Dakmak & Bruno, Detroit, 1984—. pres. Mich. Panthers Profl. Football Club, 1981-83. Trustee, exec. com. New Detroit, Inc., 1971—; exec. com., dir. Music Hall Ctr. Performing Arts, Detroit, 1972—, chmn. bd., 1972-74; trustee Detroit City Theatre, U. Wash. Inst. Study Contemporary Social Problems, Internat. Assn. Met. Research and Devel. of Toronto, Detroit Symphony, 1981—; dir. Detroit Pub. Library Film Council, 1973—; chmn. Assocs. of Detroit Inst. Arts, 1981—; chmn. owners, acting commr. U.S. Football League, 1980-82. Mem. Detroit Bar Assn., Mich. Bar Assn., ABA, NAACP. Contbr. articles to legal publs., book revs. to Detroit Free Press. General corporate, Family and matrimonial, Entertainment. Address: 2580 Penobscot Bldg Detroit MI 48226

SPLITT, CODY, lawyer; b. Wausau, Wis., Aug. 13, 1919; d. Anne Monahan Wendt; m. Harley B. Splitt, Apr. 17, 1948; 1 child, Leigh Rogers. B.A., U. Wis.-Madison, 1947, LL.B., 1949. Bar: Wis. 1949, U.S. Dist. Ct. (we. dist.) Wis. 1949. Sole practice, Appleton, Wis., 1949—; asst. dir. U.S. Agr. Census, 1955; dist. dir. U.S. Census, 1960; lectr., moderator Law for Laymen, Appleton, 1975-80; dir. Legal Service Northeastern Wis., Inc., 1984-85. Mem. Equal Rights Council, Wis., 1966-73, Equal Opportunities, Appleton, 1973-81; vice chmn. Outagamie County Republican Club, 1965; pres. Outagamie County Rep. Women's Club, 1951; co-pres. Appleton PTA, 1971; v.p. Appleton Big Sisters, 1974. Served with WAVES, 1942-45. Named Woman of Yr. Outagamie County, NOW, 1974. Mem. State Bar Wis. (sect. sec. 1974), Outagamie County Bar Assn. (exec. com. 1978-85, sec. 1985-86, pres. 1986-87), Fed. Bus. and Profl. Women (v.p. 1978), Fedn. Rep. Women. Family and matrimonial, Probate, Real property. Home: 1611 W Glendale Ave Appleton WI 54914 Office: 1213 N Superior St Appleton WI 54911

SPLITT, DAVID ALAN, lawyer, writer; b. Ripon, Wis., Nov. 28, 1945; s. Orville Sylvester and Joyce Eileen (Anson) S.; m. Martha Ann Corson, Mar. 19, 1966; children—Amy Emmeline, Sarah Daisy. B.A. in English, Va. Poly. Inst. & State U., 1966; J.D., Am. U., 1971. Bar: D.C. 1971, U.S. Supreme Ct. 1981. Tchr., Bowie (Md.) High Sch., 1966-68; freelance journalist and photographer, Washington, 1968-70; ptnr. Christensen, Splitt & King, Washington, 1971-74; gen. csl. D.C. Bd. Edn., 1974-79; dir. documents, D.C., 1979-82; of counsel Stein, Miller, Brodsky & Beerman, Washington, 1983-84; spl. asst. city adminstr. for fin. mgmt. systems, dir. city computer center, Washington, 1980-81. Dir., vice chmn. Choral Arts Soc. of Washington, 1974-84, chmn., 1984-85; dir., v.p. Traditional Music Documentation Project, Washington. Recipient Outstanding Service awards and merit promotion D.C. Govt., 1976, 78, 79, Mayor's Disting. Pub. Service award, 1983. Mem. ABA, Inter-Am. Bar Assn., Aircraft Owners and Pilots Assn., Lawyer-Pilots Bar Assn. Democrat. Club: Indian Spring Country (Montgomery County, Md.). Author: Post-Conviction Relief for Federal Prisoners, 1973; The Resolution of Detainers for Federal and State Prisoners, 1971; columnist The Executive Educator, 1978—; editor: Inquiry & Analysis, 1977-79; Becoming a Better Board Member, 1982; D.C. Rulemaking Handbook & Publications Style Manual. General corporate, Contracts commercial. Home: 6111 Utah Ave NW Washington DC 20015

SPOLLEN, JOHN W., lawyer; b. Bklyn., Aug. 26, 1944; s. Laurence and Annie F. (Johnston) S.; m. Mary Twomey; children: Moira, Laurence, Claire. AB, Fordham U., 1966, JD, 1973. Ptnr. Simpson, Thacher & Bartlett, N.Y.C., 1973—. Bd. dirs. Larchmont Jr. Soccer League, N.Y., 1986. Served to 1st lt, U.S. Army, 1967-69. Mem. ABA, N.Y. State Bar Assn., N.Y. County Lawyers Assn., Cath. Lawyers Guild. Club: Larchmont Shore. Banking, General corporate. Office: Simpson Thacher & Bartlett 1 Battery Park Plaza New York NY 10004

SPONG, WILLIAM BELSER, JR., lawyer, educator; b. Portsmouth, Va., Sept. 29, 1920; s. William Belser and Emily (Nichols) S.; m. Virginia Wise Galliford, June 3, 1950; children: Martha Kingman, Thomas Nichols. Student, Hampden-Sydney Coll., 1937-40, LL.D. (hon.); LL.B., U. Va., 1947; postgrad., U. Edinburgh, Scotland, 1947-48; LL.D. (hon.), Roanoke Coll., Washington and Lee U. and Coll. William and Mary. Bar: Va. 1947. Lectr. law Coll. William and Mary, 1948-49, 75-76; practice law Portsmouth, 1949-76; mem. Va. Ho. Dels., 1954-55, Va. Senate, 1956-66, U.S. Senate, 1966-73; gen. counsel Comm. for Conduct Fgn. Policy, 1973-75; dean Marshall-Wythe Sch. Law Coll. William and Mary, 1976-85, Woodbridge prof. emeritus, 1985—; spl. master Va. Electric & Power Co., et al vs. Westinghouse Corp., 1977-80, re Dalkon Shield litigation, 1983-85; guest scholar Woodrow Wilson Center Smithsonian Instn.; vis. scholar U. Va. Sch. Law, 1973; adj. prof. law U. Richmond, 1974-75, Salzburg Seminar, 1979; sr. visitor Inst. Advanced Legal Studies, U. London, 1985; vis. prof. Washington and Lee U., 1986; Ewald disting. vis. prof. U. Va. Sch. Law, 1987. Chmn. Va. Commn. Pub. Edn., 1958-62, Gov.'s Comm. on Va.'s Future, 1982-84; mem. Va. Council Higher Edn., 1985—; trustee Hampden-Sydney Coll.; bd. visitors Air Force Acad., 1970, Naval Acad., 1971. Mem. Va. Bar Assn. (pres. 1976), Portsmouth Bar Assn. (past pres.), Order of Coif, Phi Beta Kappa, Phi Alpha Delta, Omicron Delta Kappa, Pi Kappa Alpha. Legal education. Home and office: 111 Montague Circle Williamsburg VA 23185

SPONZILLI, EDWARD GEORGE, lawyer, history educator; b. Newark, Mar. 30, 1948; s. Edward James and Dorothy Maria (Murillo) S. B.A. in History with high honors, Rutgers U., 1971, J.D., 1975; summer diploma Cath. Inst. of Paris, 1971; M.A., Columbia U., 1972. Bar: N.J. 1975, U.S. Dist. Ct. N.J. 1975, U.S. Ct. Appeals (3d cir.) 1976, U.S. Supreme Ct. 1979, U.S. Ct. Appeals (D.C. cir.) 1979, N.Y. 1981. Law clk. Essex County Pros.'s Office, Newark, summer 1974, Sr. Judge James A. Coolahan, Sr. U.S. Dist. Ct. N.J., Newark, 1975-77; assoc. Pitney, Hardin & Kipp, Morristown, N.J., 1975-81, Cummins, Dunn, Horowitz & Pashman, Hackensack, N.J., 1981-83; ptnr., 1984—; co-adj. prof. Rutgers U., New Brunswick, N.J., 1980-81; mcpl. pros. Rutgers U., 1981—; counsel Judo of N.J. Inc., Cranford, 1983—; mem. 1975 Rutgers Jessup Internat. Law Moot Ct. Team; judge Seton Hall Law Sch. Moot Ct. Competitions, 1977-79, 81. Lectr. Biennial Grand Conclave, New Orleans, 1981. Recipient Nancy Higgenson Dorr award Rutgers U., 1971; Disting. Service award Animals Need You-Kindness Corp., N.J., 1981; Henry Rutgers scholar. Mem. N.J. State Bar Assn., Fed. Bar Assn. (N.J. chpt.), Assn. Fed. Bar N.J., ABA (trial practice com. of litigation sect.), Assn. Trial Lawyers Am., N.J. Trial Lawyers Assn., Trial Lawyers of N.J. (trustee), Bergen County Bar Assn., Essex County Bar Assn., Middlesex County Bar Assn., Am. Hist. Assn., So. Hist. Assn., Orgn. Am. Historians, Civil War History Assn., Rutgers Law Sch. Alumni Assn. (exec. counsel, nominating com. 1982, program dir. 1982, alumni fedn. rep.), "Scarlet R" Round Table Alumni Assoc., Columbia Grad. Faculties Alumni Assn., Phi Beta Kappa, Kappa Sigma (dist. grand master, 1986—, alumnus advisor 1978—, trustee Gamma Upsilon chpt., sec. 1978-79, v.p. 1979-82, pres. 1982-86), Phi Alpha Delta. Federal civil litigation, State civil litigation, Labor. Home: 37 Brookside Ave Caldwell NJ 07006 Office: Cummins Dunn & Pashman Continental Plaza II 411 Hackensack Ave Hackensack NJ 07601

SPOONER, ARTHUR ELMON, JR., lawyer; b. Mobile, Ala., Oct. 22, 1946; s. Arthur Elmon and Mamie (Pierce) S.; children: Bradford D., William D. BA, U. Ark., 1969, JD, 1974; LLM, So. Meth. U., 1976. Bar: Ark. 1974, Tex. 1975, U.S. Tax Ct. 1978, U.S. Dist. Ct. (so. dist.) Tex. 1980, U.S. Ct. Appeals (5th cir.) 1980, U.S. Ct. Claims 1985, U.S. Ct. Internat. Trade 1985, U.S. Supreme Ct. 1986. Contract atty. Gen. Dynamic Corp., Ft. Worth, 1975-76; tax atty. Aramco Services Co., Houston, 1976—. Mem. ABA (taxation sect.). Corporate taxation, Personal income taxation, Pension, profit-sharing, and employee benefits. Home: 1201 McDuffie #184 Houston TX 77019 Office: Aramco Services Co PO Box 4535 Houston TX 77210

SPOONER, RALPH CHARLES, lawyer; b. Milw., June 12, 1946; s. Ralph C. and Sylvia M. (Troyk) S.; m. Denice Lynn Prevendar, Dec. 14, 1968; children: Melissa, Robin, Robert, Thomas. BA, U. Ill., 1968; JD cum laude, Ill. Inst. Tech., 1973. Bar: Oreg. 1973, Ill. 1973, U.S. Dist. Ct. Oreg. 1973. Assoc. Bruce W. Williams P.C., Salem, Oreg., 1973-75; ptnr. Williams, Spooner and Graves, Salem, 1976-80, Williams and Spooner, Salem, 1981-83, Williams Spooner and Much, Salem, 1983-84, Spooner and Much, Salem, 1984—. Contbr. articles to profl. assn. jours. Mem. civil service commn. Marion County Fire Dist. 1, Salem, 1975-76; mem. fin. commn., Sun. sch. tchr. St. Marys Ch., Shaw, Oreg., 1981-86. Mem. Oreg. Assn. Def. Counsels (bd. dirs. 1980-86, pres. 1986), Marion County Bar Assn. (bd. dirs. 1980-86, pres. 1986), Assn. Ins. Attys., Def. Research Inst. Democrat. Roman Catholic. Club: Illahe Country (Salem). Avocations: pvt. pilot, skiing, river rafting, fishing, golf. Insurance, Personal injury, Federal civil litigation. Home: 7231 Bethel Rd Salem OR 97301 Office: Spooner and Much 530 Center St Suite 722 Salem OR 97301

SPOTSWOOD, ROBERT KEELING, lawyer; b. Balt., July 11, 1952; s. William Syson and Helen Marie (Fairchild) S.; m. Ashley Hayward Wiltshire, Aug. 19, 1978; children: Robert Keeling, Mary Hayward. BS with highest distinction in Applied Math., U. Va., 1974, JD, 1977. Bar: Ala. 1977, U.S. Dist. Ct. (no. dist.) Ala. 1979, U.S. Dist. Ct. (so. dist.) Ala. 1980, U.S. Ct. Appeals (5th cir.) 1979, U.S. Ct. Appeals (11th cir.) 1981, U.S. Dist. Ct. (mid. dist.) Ala. 1986. Ptnr. Bradley, Arant, Rose & White, Birmingham, Ala., 1977—. Mem. Birmingham Bar Assn., ABA. Roman Catholic. Club: Mountain Brook. Labor. Home: 428 Dexter Ave Birmingham AL 35213 Office: Bradley Arant Rose & White 1400 Park Pl Tower Birmingham AL 35203

SPRADLIN, THOMAS RICHARD, lawyer, throughbred horse farm owner; b. Pauls Valley, Okla., June 9, 1937; s. Julius Everett and Mary Jane (Thompson) S.; m. Carol Birk, July 12, 1980; children—Trevor, Joseph, Shane; A.A. with distinction, George Washington U., 1958, B.A. with distinction, 1959, J.D. with honors, 1963. Bar: Va. 1963, D.C. 1968, U.S. Ct. Mil. Appeals 1963, U.S. Ct. Appeals (3d, 4th, 5th, 9th and D.C. cirs.), U.S. Supreme Ct. 1967. Clk., FBI, 1955-56; asst. to U.S. Senator A.S. Mike Monroney, Washington, 1956-63; assoc. Clifford & Warnke, Washington, 1967-72, ptnr., 1972-83; ptnr. Stovall, Spradlin, Armstrong & Israel, 1983-86, Stovall & Spradlin, 1986—; dir. Am. Trade & Fin. Co., Arlington, Va., University Assocs., Inc., Washington, Calcusearch, Inc., Atlanta, Tanner Resources, Inc., Oklahoma City Re-Top USA, Inc., Arlington Sci. and Aviation Systems Ltd., Nassau, Dimel Ltd., Nassau/Onshoco, Inc., Houston. pres., dir. Gandhara Farm, Ltd., Poolesville, Md., Served to capt. Judge Adv. Gen. U.S. Army, 1963-67. Eugene and Agnes E. Meyer scholar, 1958. Mem. ABA, Fed. Bar Assn., D.C. Bar, Va. Bar, Md. Horse Breeders Assn., Order of Coif, Phi Beta Kappa, Phi Delta Phi. Unitarian. Clubs: Potomac Hunt (Md.); Pisces (Washington). Contbr. articles on law to profl. jours. Administrative and regulatory, Private international, General corporate. Home: 6118 Tilden Ln Rockville MD 20852 Office: 2600 Virginia Ave NW The Watergate Suite 820 Washington DC 20037

SPRANG, KENNETH ALLYN, lawyer; b. Kenton, Ohio, July 25, 1947; s. Ralph Allyn Sprang and Mary Alice (Conley) McCord; m. Viera Leng, Sept. 16, 1967; children: Todd Christopher, Heidi Noel. BS in Edn., Ohio State U., 1969; postgrad., Princeton U. Theol. Sem., 1971-72; MA, U. Mich., 1973; JD, Case Western Res. U., 1978. Bar: Pa. 1978, U.S. Dist. Ct. (ea. dist.) Pa. 1978, Ohio 1985, U.S. Dist. Ct. (so. dist.) Ohio 1986. Assoc. Morgan, Lewis and Bockius, Phila., 1978-80; atty., asst. sec. Calgon Corp., Pitts., 1980-81; assoc. Cyclops Corp., Pitts., 1981-83; asst. prof. law U. Dayton, Ohio, 1983-

85; adj. prof. U. Dayton, 1985—; assoc. Sebaly, Shillito and Dyer, Dayton, 1986-87; ptnr. Bogin & Patterson, Dayton, 1987—. Contbr. articles to profl. jours. Mem. ABA, Ohio State Bar Assn. (bd. govs. labor sect. 1984—), Dayton Bar Assn., Order of the Coif. Democrat. Presbyterian. Lodge: Optimists. Avocations: travel, reading, theater, golf. General corporate, Legal education, Labor. Home: 1801 Shafor Blvd Dayton OH 45419 Office: Bogin & Patterson 1200 Talbott Tower Dayton OH 45402

SPRANSY, JOSEPH WILLIAM, corporate lawyer; b. Durham, N.C., July 17, 1946; s. George Brower and Marion Elizabeth (Dibble) S.; m. Lillian Drew Darden, Aug. 8, 1970; children: Katherine Leigh, Joseph William II. AB in Math., King Coll., Bristol, Tenn., 1968; JD, U. N.C., 1973. Bar: Ala. 1973, U.S. Dist. Ct. (no. dist.) Ala. 1973, U.S. Ct. Appeals (5th cir.) 1976, U.S. Supreme Ct. 1980, U.S. Ct. Appeals (11th cir.) 1981. Math. tchr. Castlewood (Va.) High Sch., 1968-70; program dir. Camp Monroe, Laurel Hill, N.C., 1968-70; assoc. Bradley, Arant, Rose & White, Birmingham, Ala., 1973-79; counsel U.S. Pipe and Foundry Co., Birmingham, 1979—. Moderator Birmingham Presbytery, Presbyn. Ch. USA, 1987—, vice moderator, 1986—; elder Mountain Brook Presbyn. Ch., 1982-84, 1986—. Mem. ABA, Ala. State Bar Assn., Birmingham Bar Assn., Assn. Corp. Counsel in Am. (bd. dirs. Ala. chpt. 1985—), U. N.C. Alumni Assn. (pres. Ala. chpt. 1983-84), Phi Alpha Delta. Club: Birmingham Sailing. Avocations: woodworking, sailing, running. General corporate, Antitrust, Labor. Home: 4000 Hunters Ln Birmingham AL 35243 Office: US Pipe and Foundry Co 3300 First Ave N Birmingham AL 35222

SPREITZER, JOHN RICHARD, lawyer; b. Chgo., June 30, 1953; s. John Peter and Eleanor May (Salow) S.; m. Judith Ann Belcher, Dec. 14, 1974; children: Karl, Luke, Erik. BS in Edn., Cen. Mich. U., 1976; JD, Brigham Young U., 1979. Bar: Mich. 1979, U.S. Dist. Ct. (ea. dist.) Mich. 1979, U.S. Ct. Appeals (6th cir.) 1982. Assoc. Clark, Klein & Beaumont, Detroit, 1979-81; sr. counsel Mich. Nat. Corp., Farmington Hills, Mich., 1981—. Mem. ABA, Oakland County Bar Assn. Mormon. Avocations: soccer coaching, indoor soccer. Banking, Federal civil litigation, State civil litigation. Home: 1723 Crestline Troy MI 48083 Office: Mich Nat Corp Legal Dept 30445 Northwestern Hwy Suite 204 Farmington Hills MI 48018

SPRIGGS, EVERETT LEE, lawyer; b. Safford, Ariz., July 30, 1930; s. Claude E. and Evelyn (Lee) S.; m. Betty Medley, Aug. 22, 1953; children: Claudia Lynn, Lee M., Scott B. B.S., Ariz. State U., 1955; J.D., U. Ariz., 1958. Bar: Calif. 1960, U.S. Supreme Ct. 1983. City atty. criminal dept. Los Angeles, 1960-61; mem. firm Kinkle & Rodiger, Riverside, Calif., 1961-64; pres. firm Kinkle, Rodiger & Spriggs (P.C.), Riverside, 1965—; dir. Mission Bank, Sea Pointe Estate, Analysts, Inc.; mem. Am. Bd. Trial Advocates. Bd. dirs., mem. adv. bd. Riverside Symphony Orch.; mem. com. performing arts, Riverside. Served with AUS, 1951-52. Mem. Calif. State Bar; ABA; Mem. Riverside County Bar Assn., Los Angeles County Bar Assn., Def. Research Inst., So. Calif. Def. Counsel (editorial staff 1970—), Assn. Trial Lawyers Am. Personal injury. Home: 1456 Muirfield Riverside CA 92506 Office: Kinkle Rodiger & Spriggs 3393 14th St Riverside CA 92501

SPRIGGS, KENT, lawyer; b. Syracuse, N.Y., Jan. 1, 1939; s. James Orville and Virginia (Story) S.; m. Tanya Castiglione, Mar. 1, 1963 (div. Aug. 1965); 1 child, Jennifer Lynn; m. Christina Jo Talbot, May 30, 1987. AB, Bowdoin Coll., 1961; postgrad. in design, Harvard U., 1962-63; LLB, NYU, 1965. Bar: N.Y. 1965, Fla. 1967, D.C. 1969, Calif. 1970, U.S. Dist. Ct. (no. dist.) Fla. 1971, U.S. Ct. Appeals (5th cir.) 1968, U.S. Supreme Ct. Assoc. Rabinowitz & Boudin, N.Y.C., 1965-66; dep. dir. So. Fla. Rural Legal Service, Miami, 1967-68, No. Miss. Legal Services, 1968-70; exec. dir. Los Angeles Legal Services, 1970-71; ptnr. Spriggs & Warren, Tallahassee, 1971—; cons. Legal Services Corp., Boston Legal Services, Mexican Am. Legal Services. Contbr. articles to profl. jours. Commr. City of Tallahassee, 1981-85, mayor, 1984-85. Recipient James Hudson award NAACP, 1981, CK Steele award NAACP, 1985, Good Neighbor award Red Cross, 1986; named Hon. Chmn., March of Dimes, 1985. Mem. ABA, Tallahassee Bar Assn. Democrat. Baptist. Civil rights, Administrative and regulatory, Environment. Home: 1006 Washington St Tallahassee FL 32303 Office: Spriggs & Warren 117 S Martin Luther King Tallahassee FL 32301

SPRIGGS, WILLIAM JAMES, lawyer; b. Bloomington, Ind., Oct. 1, 1939; s. Joseph William and Susan (Steinmetz) S.; m. Mary Adrin Burrus, Aug. 26, 1961; children: Russell Burrus, Benjamin Steinmetz, Jennifer Lynn. BA, Abilene Christian U., 1961; JD, Washburn U., 1964. Bar: Kans. 1964, Colo. 1970, D.C. 1982, U.S. Claims Ct. 1964. Atty. Boeing Co., Wichita, Kans., 1968-69; assoc. Martin Marietta Corp., Denver, 1969-72; ptnr. McKenna, Conner & Cuneo, Washington, 1972-82, Spriggs, Bode & Hollingsworth, Washington, 1982—; lectr. various profl. groups. Contbr. articles to profl. jours. Served to capt., USMC, 1964-67. Fellow Nat. Contract Mgmt. Assn.; mem. ABA. Democrat. Mem. Ch. of Christ. Administrative and regulatory, Federal civil litigation, Government contracts and claims. Home: 9020 Old Mt Vernon Rd Alexandria VA 22309 Office: Spriggs Bode & Hollingsworth 1015 15th St NW Washington DC 20005

SPRING, MAX EDWARD, lawyer; b. Seattle, Dec. 26, 1947; s. Myron J. and Ruth (Moskowitz) S.; m. Frances Kremen, Aug. 15, 1971; children: Joel B., Aaron M. BA, U. Wash., 1970; JD, U. Calif., Berkeley, 1973. Bar: Wash. 1974, Calif. 1974. Law clk. U.S. Dist. Ct. (we. dist.), Washington, 1973-74; ptnr. Oseran, Hahn, Kelley, Spring & Maimon P.S., Bellevue, Wash., 1974—. Bd. dirs. Youth Eastside Services, Bellevue, 1978—, Northwest Sch. for Hearing Impaired Children, Seattle, 1983—, Stroum Jewish Community Ctr., Mercer Island, Wash., 1981—. Mem. ABA, Wash. State Bar Assn., Seattle/King County Bar Assn., Order of Coif, Phi Beta Kappa. General corporate, Real property, Probate. Office: Oseran Hahn Kelley Spring & Maimon PS 10900 NE 4th St 850 Skyline Tower Bellevue WA 98004

SPRINGER, BYRON EUGENE, lawyer; b. Lawrence, Kans., June 25, 1932; s. Charles A. and Vivian E. (Kagi) S.; m. Marion J. Peltier, June 13, 1959; children—Byron Eugene, Allison A., Carolyn J. B.A., U. Kans., 1955, J.D., 1960. Bar: Kans. 1960, U.S. Dist. Ct. Kans. 1960, U.S. Ct. Appeals (10th cir.) 1981. Ptnr. Springer & Springer, Lawrence, Kans., 1960-71; ptnr. Barber, Emerson, Six, Springer & Zinn, Lawrence, 1971—; instr. bus. law U. Kans., 1960. Mem. Kans. Ho. of Reps., 1961-62. Served with U.S. Army, 1955-57. Mem. ABA, Kans. Bar Assn., Lawrence C. of C. (v.p. 1976-77). Probate, Real property, Estate taxation. Home: PO Box 666 Lawrence KS 66044

SPRINGER, CHARLES EDWARD, state justice; b. Reno, Feb. 20, 1928; s. Edwin and Rose Mary Cecelia (Kelly) S.; m. Jacqueline Sirkegian, Mar. 17, 1951; 1 dau., Kelli Ann. B.A., U. Nev., Reno, 1950; LL.B., Georgetown U., 1953; LL.M., U. Va. Bar: Nev. 1953, D.C. 1953. Practiced in Reno, 1953-80; atty. gen. State of Nev., 1962, legis. legal adv. to gov., 1958-62; legis. bill drafter Nev. Legislature, 1955-57; mem. faculty Nat. Coll. Juvenile Justice, 1978—, U. Nev., Reno, McGeorge Sch. Law, 1982—; juvenile master 2d Jud. Dist. Nev., 1973-80; justice Supreme Ct. Nev., 1981—; chmn. Jud. Selection Commn., 1981—; trustee Nat. Council Juvenile and Family Ct. Judges, 1983-85. Served with AUS, 1945-47. Recipient Outstanding Contbn. to Juvenile Justice award Nat. Council Juvenile and Family Ct. Judges, 1980. Mem. Am. Judicature Soc., Am. Trial Lawyers Assn., ABA. Jurisprudence. Office: Supreme Ct Bldg Carson City NV 89710

SPRINGER, ERIC WINSTON, lawyer; b. N.Y.C., May 17, 1929; s. Owen Winston and Maida Christina (Stewart) S.; m. Cecile Marie Kennedy, Oct. 25, 1958; children: Brian, Christina. AB, Rutgers U., 1950; LLB, NYU, 1953. Bar: N.Y. 1953, Pa. 1975, U.S. Dist. Ct. (we. dist.) Pa. 1978. Law clk. to presiding justice N.Y. State Supreme Ct., 1955-56; research assoc. U. Pitts., 1956-58, asst. prof. law, 1958-64, assoc. prof. law, 1965-68; dir. compliance EEOC, 1967; v.p., dir. Publs. Aspen Systems Corp., Pitts., 1968-71; ptnr. Horty, Springer & Mattern, Pitts., 1971-82; mem. Horty, Springer & Mattern, P.C., Pitts., 1982—; dir. Duquesne Light Co., Pitts. Author: Group Practice and the Law, 1969. Editor Nursing and the Law, 1970; Automated Medical Records and the Law, 1971; contbg. editor monthly newsletter Action-Kit for Hosp. Law, 1973—. Bd. dirs. Presbyn. Univ. Hosp., Pitts., 1966—, Hosp. Utilization Project., Pitts., 1975-86; mem. Pitts. Commn. on Human Relations, 1963-68, chmn., 1964-68. Fellow Am. Coll. Healthcare Execs. (hon.), Am. Pub. Health Assn.; mem. ABA, Nat. Bar Assn., Allegany County Bar Assn., Am. Acad. Hosp. Attys. (charter), Order of Coif. Democrat. Health. Home: 5665 Bartlett St Pittsburgh PA 15217 Office: Horty Springer & Mattern PC 4614 Fifth Ave Pittsburgh PA 15213

SPRINGER, JEFFREY ALAN, lawyer; b. Denver, Feb. 26, 1950; s. Stanley and Sylvia (Miner) S.; m. Nicki Hirsh, Sept. 24, 1978; 1 child, Cydney Erin. AB, Princeton U., 1972; JD, U. Colo., 1975. Bar: Colo. 1975, U.S. Dist. Ct. Colo. 1975, U.S. Ct. Appeals (10th cir.) 1975, U.S. Supreme Ct. 1978, U.S. Ct. Appeals (8th cir.) 1986. Assoc. Gerash & Springer, Denver, 1975-79; sole practice Denver, 1979—; active com on Mcpl. Ct. rules U.S. Supreme Ct., Colo. 1985-86. Mem. ABA, Assn. Trial Lawyers Am. (sustaining), Colo. Criminal Def. Bar (bd. dirs. 1985-86). Criminal, Personal injury. Office: 1600 Broadway Suite 1500 Denver CO 80202

SPRINGER, JOHN WHATLEY, lawyer; b. Montgomery, Ala., Oct. 20, 1953; s. Curtis Howe and Mary Haden (Whatley) S.; m. Glenn King, Aug. 20, 1977; children: Lillian Glenn, Mary Haden Whatley. BA in Econs. with honors, U. Va., 1975; JD, U. Ala., 1978; LLM in Taxation, NYU, 1981. Bar: Ga. 1978. Assoc. Hatcher, Stubbs, Land, Hollis & Rothschild, Columbus, Ga., 1978-80; gen. counsel, v.p. fin., sec. Callaway Chem. Co., Columbus, 1981-85; ptnr. Sprouse, Tucker & Ford, Columbus, 1985—. Sec. LIKE Found., Columbus, 1985; bd. dirs., treas. Springer Opera House Arts Assn., Columbus, 1984; bd. dirs. Met. Boys Club, Columbus, 1982. Mem. ABA, Ga. Bar Assn., Columbus Lawyers Club. Club: Country Club (Columbus); Bid Eddy (N.Y.C.). Avocations: golf, tennis, sailing, hunting, fishing. Office: Sprouse Tucker & Ford 1025 1st Ave Columbus GA 31902

SPRINGER, PAUL DAVID, lawyer, motion picture company executive; b. N.Y.C., Apr. 27, 1942; s. William W. and Alma (Markowitz) S.; m. Mariann Frankfurt, Aug. 16, 1964; children: Robert, William. BA, U. Bridgeport, 1963; JD, Bklyn. Law Sch., 1967. Bar: U.S. Dist. Ct. (so. and ea. dists.) N.Y. 1968, U.S. Ct. Appeals (2d cir.) 1970, U.S. Supreme Ct. 1973. Assoc. Johnson & Tannenbaum, N.Y.C., 1968-70; assoc. counsel Columbia Pictures, N.Y.C., 1970; assoc. counsel Paramount Pictures, N.Y.C., 1970-79, v.p., theatrical distbn. counsel, 1979-85, sr. v.p., chief resident counsel East Coast, 1985—. Trustee West Cunningham Park Civic Assn., Fresh Meadows, N.Y., 1978—. Mem. ABA, Assn. of Bar of City of N.Y. Antitrust, General corporate, Federal civil litigation. Home: 73-59 189th St Fresh Meadows NY 11366 Office: Paramount Pictures Corp 1 Gulf and Western Plaza New York NY 10023-7799

SPRINGER, STEVE EDWARD, lawyer; b. Indpls., June 25, 1948; m. Judy Springer; children: Cindy, Clay. BS in Aero Engring., Purdue U., 1971; JD, Ind. U., 1979. Bar: Ind. 1979. Engr. Bay Equipment Co., San Francisco, 1975-77; gen. ptnr. Kightlinger & Gray, Indpls., 1979—. Served to lt. cmdr. USNR, 1971—. Mem. ABA, Ind. Bar Assn., Indpls. Bar Assn., Lawyer/Pilot Bar Assn. Lodge: Kiwanis. State civil litigation, Insurance, Personal injury. Office: Kightlinger & Gray 151 N Delaware 660 Market Sq Ctr Indianapolis IN 46260

SPRINGMEYER, DON, lawyer; b. Miami, Fla., Apr. 11, 1954; s. Archie Eugene Evans and Sally (Springmeyer) Zanjani; m. Pati Parnell Acres, May 31, 1982; 1 child, Parnell Alexander. BA cum laude, Yale U., 1976; JD cum laude, U. Wis., 1979. Bar: Nev. 1980, U.S. Dist. Ct. Nev. 1980, U.S. Dist. Ct. (no. dist.) Calif. 1983, U.S. Ct. Appeals (9th cir.) 1983, U.S. Dist. Ct. (cen. dist.) Calif. 1984. Law clk. to presiding justice U.S. Dist. Ct. Nev., Reno, 1980-81; assoc. Lionel, Sawyer & Collins, Reno, 1981, Law Offices Eugene J. Wait Jr., P.C., Reno, 1983—; bd. dirs. Carson (Nev.) Brewing Co., Council on Econ. Priorities, N.Y.C., 1981-82. Candidate Springmeyer for Congress Com., Reno, 1981-82; mem. cen. com. Douglas County, Nev., 1981-82, Washoe County, Nev., 1983-85; co-chmn. Sferraza for Congress Com., Washoe, 1985-86; bd. dirs. Citizen Alert, Reno, 1983-86. Mem. ABA, Washoe County Bar Assn., Assn. Def. Counsel No. Nev., Assn. Def. Counsel Calif. Democrat. Avocations: skiing, gardening. Personal injury, Insurance. Office: Law Offices Eugene J Wait Jr PC 305 W Moana Ln Reno NV 89509

SPRITZER, RALPH SIMON, lawyer, educator; b. N.Y.C., Apr. 27, 1917; s. Harry and Stella (Theuman) S.; m. Lorraine Nelson, Dec. 23, 1950; children: Ronald, Pamela. B.S., Columbia U., 1937, LL.B., 1940. Bar: N.Y. bar 1941, U.S. Supreme Ct. bar 1950. Atty. Office Alien Property, Dept. Justice, 1946-51; anti-trust div. Dept. Justice, 1951-54, Office Solicitor Gen., 1954-61; gen. counsel FPC, 1961-62; 1st asst. to solicitor gen. U.S. 1962-68; prof. law U. Pa., Phila., 1968-86, Ariz. State U., Tempe, 1986—; gen. counsel AAUP, 1983-84; Adj. prof. law George Wasington U., 1967; cons. Adminstrv. Conf. U.S., Ford Found., Pa. Gov.'s Justice Commn. Served with AUS, 1941-46. Recipient Superior Service award Dept. Justice, 1960; Tom C. Clark award Fed. Bar. Assn., 1968. Mem. Am. Law Inst. Administrative and regulatory, Antitrust, Criminal. Home: 1024 E Gemini Dr Tempe AZ 85283

SPRIZZO, JOHN EMILIO, federal judge; b. Bklyn., Dec. 23, 1934; s. Vincent James and Esther Nancy (Filosa) S.; children—Ann Esther, Johna Emily Sprizzo Bolka, Matthew John. B.A., St. John's U., Jamaica, N.Y., 1956; LL.B., St. John's U., 1959. Bar: N.Y. 1960. Asst. U.S. atty. so. dist. N.Y. Dept. Justice, N.Y.C., 1963-68, chief appellate atty., 1965-66, asst. chief criminal div., 1966-68; assoc. prof. Fordham U. Law Sch., N.Y.C., 1968-72; ptnr. Curtis, Mallet-Prevost, N.Y.C., 1972-81; dist. judge U.S. Dist. Ct. (so. dist.) N.Y., N.Y.C., 1981—; cons. Nat. Com. for Reform of Criminal Laws, N.Y.C., 1971-72; mem. Knapp Commn., 1971-72; assoc. atty. Com. of Ct. on Judiciary, N.Y.C., 1971-72. Co-contbr. articles to profl. law revs. Mem. ABA, Assn. of Bar City N.Y., N.Y. State Bar Assn., New York County Lawyers Assn. Judge. Office: US Dist Court US Courthouse Foley Square New York NY 10007

SPROLES, DONALD RAY, lawyer; b. Kingsport, Tenn., Nov. 8, 1950; s. Ralph N. and Laura L. (Miller) S.; m. Karen Ann Brown, July 3, 1982; 1 child, Matthew Anderson. BA, U. Tenn., 1976, JD, 1978. Bar: Tenn. 1979, U.S. Dist. Ct. (ea. dist.) Tenn., 1979, U.S. Ct. Appeals (6th cir.) 1981. Assoc. Gilreath, Pryor et al, Knoxville, Tenn., 1978-81; prin. Coffey, Sproles & Brasfield, Knoxville, 1981—. Vestry mem. Ch. of Good Samaritan, Knoxville, 1985-87, jr. warden, 1986—. Served with USN, 1970-73. Mem. ABA, Tenn. Bar Assn. (chmn. com. on st. law young lawyers div. 1979-81), Assn. Trial Lawyers Am., Tenn. Trial Lawyers Assn., Knoxville Barristers Club (pres. 1982). Episcopal. Family and matrimonial, Personal injury, Workers' compensation. Office: Coffey Sproles & Brasfield 709 Concord St Knoxville TN 37919

SPROULL, FREDERICK ANTHONY RAYMOND, lawyer, educator; b. Pitts., May 20, 1949; s. Frederick T. and Ann C. (Raymond) S. BA in Biology, Clarion U., 1971; PhD in Biology, U. Pitts., 1977; JD, Duquesne U., 1982. Assoc. prof. biomed. sci. La Roche Coll., Pitts., 1979—; sole practice Pitts., 1982—; mem. instl. rev. bd. Biodecision Lab., Pitts., 1984—. Contbr. articles to profl. jours. Mem. AAAS, ABA, Allegheny County Bar Assn., Pa. Bar Assn. Democrat. Roman Catholic. General practice, Estate planning, Personal injury. Home: 302 Brilliant Ave Pittsburgh PA 15215 Office: 445 Fort Pitt Blvd Pittsburgh PA 15219

SPROULS, JOSEPH WALTER, lawyer; b. Summit, N.J., Oct. 21, 1950; s. Walter A. and Alice C. (Van Pevenage) S.; m. Barbara Anne Russo, Jan. 9, 1982; 1 child, Cara Elise. BA, Georgetown U., 1972; JD, Seton Hall U., 1976. Bar: N.J. 1976, U.S. Dist. Ct. N.J. 1976, D.C. 1978. Assoc. Lamb, Hutchinson, Chappell, Ryan & Hartung, Jersey City, 1976-77; assoc. regional counsel Prudential Ins. Co., Washington, 1977-82; regional gen. counsel Boston Properties, Washington, 1982-83; regional counsel Travelers Ins. Co., Washington, 1983-87; ptnr. Finley, Kumble, Wagner, Heine, Underberg, Manley, Myerson & Casey, Palm Beach, Fla., 1987—. Mem. ABA. Real property. Home: 13264 Whispering Lakes Ln Palm Beach Gardens FL 33410 Office: Finley Kumble Wagner Heine et al 125 Worth Ave Palm Beach FL 33480

SPROUSE, JAMES MARSHALL, fed. judge; b. Williamson, W.Va., Dec. 3, 1923; s. James and Garnet (Lawson) S.; m. June Dolores Burt, Sept. 25, 1952; children: Tracy Sprouse Ferguson, Jeffrey Marshall, Andrew Michael, Sherry Lee, Shelly Lynn. A.B., St. Bonaventure (N.Y.) U., 1947; LL.B., Columbia U., 1949; postgrad. in internat. law, U. Bordeaux, France, 1950. Bar: W.Va. bar. Agt. CIA, 1952-57; pvt. practice W.Va., 1957-72, 75-79; asst. atty. gen. State of W.Va., 1949; justice W.Va. Supreme Ct. Appeals, 1972-75; judge U.S. Circuit Ct. Appeals 4th Circuit, Charleston, 1979—. Served with AUS, 1942-45. Fulbright scholar. Mem. Am. Bar Assn., W.Va. State Bar, W.Va. Bar Assn., W.Va. Trial Lawyers Assn., Kanawha County Bar Assn., VFW, Am. Legion. Democrat. Presbyterian. Clubs: Shriners, Aheppa. Jurisprudence. Office: US Court Appeals 122 N Court St Lewisburg WV 24901 *

SPROWL, CHARLES RIGGS, lawyer; b. Lansing, Mich., Aug. 22, 1910; s. Charles Orr and Hazel (Allen) S.; m. Virginia Lee Graham, Jan. 15, 1938; children: Charles R., Robert A., Susan G., Sandra D. A.B., U. Mich., 1932, J.D., 1934. Bar: Ill. 1935. Pvt. practice 1934—; of counsel Taylor, Miller, Sprowl, Hoffnagle & Merletti, 1986—; Dir. Simmons Engring Corp., Busch & Schmitt, Inc., Petersen Aluminum Corp. Mem. Bd. Edn., New Trier Twp. High Sch., 1959-65, pres., 1962-65; mem. Glencoe Zoning Bd. of Appeals, 1965-76, chmn., 1966-76; mem. Glencoe Plan Commn., 1962-65; Bd. dirs. Glencoe Pub. Library, 1953-65, pres., 1955-56; trustee Highland Park Hosp., 1959-69; bd. dirs. Cradle Soc. Fellow Am. Coll. Trial Lawyers; mem. Chgo. Bar Assn. (bd. mgrs. 1949-51), Ill. Bar Assn., ABA, Juvenile Protective Assn. (dir. 1943-53), Northwestern U. Settlement (pres. 1963-70, dir.), Soc. Trial Lawyers, Delta Theta Phi, Alpha Chi Rho. Presbyn. Clubs: Law (pres. 1969-70), Legal (pres. 1953-54), Univ, Monroe, Skokie Country. General corporate, Probate, Estate taxation. Home: 558 Washington Ave Glencoe IL 60022 Office: 33 N LaSalle St Chicago IL 60602

SPROWLS, PAUL ALAN, lawyer; b. Louisville, Dec. 27, 1951; s. Paul Harris and Nelle (Oldacre) S.; m. Ellen Virginia Culpepper, Apr. 11, 1981. BA, Tulane U., 1973, JD, 1976. Bar: Fla. 1977, La. 1981, U.S. Dist. Ct. (we. dist.) La. 1981, U.S. Ct. Appeals (5th and 11th cirs.) 1981, U.S. Supreme Ct. 1984. Spl. agt. FBI, Washington, 1977-81; assoc. Coleman, Dutrey & Thomson, New Orleans, 1981; asst. U.S. atty. Dept. Justice, Lafayette, La., 1981-83, Tallahassee, 1983—; evaluation staff Dept. Justice, Washington, 1983—, instr. 1985. V.p. Foxcroft Civic Assn., Tallahassee, 1985—. Served with USNR, 1985—. Mem. ABA, Am. Judicature Soc. Republican. Avocations: tennis, golf, sailing. Criminal, Federal civil litigation. Office: U S Atty 227 N Bronough Tallahassee FL 32301

SPRY, DONALD FRANCIS, II, lawyer; b. Bethlehem, Pa., Nov. 17, 1947; s. Donald Francis and Carol Annette (Bolger) S.; m. Mary Frances, June 20, 1981; stepchildren—Michael Matlaga, Michelle Matlaga. B.A., Moravian Coll., 1969; J.D., U. Pitts., 1972. Bar: Pa. 1972, U.S. Dist. Ct. (ea. dist.) Pa. 1975. Assoc. Law Offices of Edmund P. Turtzo, Bangor, Pa., 1973-76; ptnr. Turtzo, Spry, Powlette & Sbrocchi, P.C., Bangor, 1976-83, Turtzo Spry Powlette Sbrocchi & Faul, P.C., Bangor and Stroudsburg, Pa., 1983—. Served to capt. USAR 1979-80. Mem. ABA (family law sect.), Pa. Bar Assn. (family law sect.), Northampton County Bar Assn. (chmn. family law com.), Pa. Sch. Bds. Assn., Nat Sch. Bds. Assn., ACLU, Nat. Orgn. Legal Problems of Edn. Republican. Methodist. Club: Pomfret. Family and matrimonial, Education and schools. Office: 109 Broadway Bangor PA 18013 also: 930 N 9th St Stroudsberg PA 18360

SPUEHLER, DONALD ROY, lawyer; b. Elmhurst, Ill., Sept. 28, 1934; s. Ernst Albert and Ruth Esther (Hinesley) S.; m. Jane Romm, Oct. 1, 1966; children: Sean Jason, Tracy Ariana. AB in Econs. magna cum laude, Harvard U., 1956, AM in Econs., 1958, LLB magna cum laude, 1964; postgrad., Cambridge U., Eng., 1956-57. Bar: Calif. 1965, U.S. Dist. Ct. Calif. 1965. Assoc. O'Melveny & Myers, Los Angeles, 1964-72, tax ptnr., 1972—; bd. dirs. Mercury Gen. Corp., Los Angeles. Contbr. articles on tax law to profl. jours. Cons. Filer Commn. on Charitable Orgns., Washington, 1973-74; bd. dirs. Amateur Chamber Music Players Inc., End Hunger Network; mem. mens com. Los Angeles Philharmonic, Los Angeles County Mus. Art. Served with U.S. Army, 1958-61. Knox fellow, 1956-57, Rockefeller Found. fellow, 1957-58; recipient John Harvard award Harvard U., 1953-56. Mem. ABA (exempt orgn. com., employee benefit com.), Calif. Bar Assn. (exempt orgn. som., employee benefit com.), Los Angeles County Bar Assn. Democrat. Buddhist. Avocations: spiritual study, tennis, community work. Pension, profit-sharing, and employee benefits, General practice, Exempt organizations. Office: O'Melveny & Myers 400 S Hope St Los Angeles CA 90071-2899

SPURGEON, ROBERTA KAYE, lawyer; b. Genoa, Ohio, Sept. 2, 1938; d. Donald Howard and Audrey June (Schimmel). BS, U. Cin., 1963; MS, Yale U., 1965; JD, U. Calif., Berkeley, 1976. Bar: Ohio 1977, U.S. Dist. Ct. (no. dist.) Ohio 1977. Staff nurse Vis. Nurse Service, Toledo, 1960-61, VA Hosp., Cin., 1963; instr. Boston U. Coll. Nursing, 1965-67; asst. prof. Coll. Nursing, Boston Coll., Chestnut Hills, Mass., 1967-71; chmn., asst. prof. Yale U. Coll. Nursing, New Haven, Conn., 1971-73; assoc. Squire, Sanders & Dempsey, Cleve., 1976—. Contbr. articles to profl. jours. Adv. council Mus. Arts Assn., Cleve., 1982-83; mem. Holden Arboretum, Cleve., 1981—, Cleve. Mus. Art, 1980—. Mem. ABA, Fed. Bar Assn., Def. Research Inst., Ohio State Bar Assn., Greater Cleve. Bar Assn. Unitarian. Avocations: flute, poetry, aviation. State civil litigation, Federal civil litigation, Personal injury. Home: 2660 Edgehill Rd Cleveland Heights OH 44106 Office: Squire Sanders & Dempsey 1800 Huntington Bldg Cleveland OH 44115

SPURLOCK, JOE CLARENCE M., judge U.S. Ct. Appeals, 2d Supreme Jud. Dist.; b. Throckmorton, Tex., Aug. 31, 1910; s. Joseph G. and Annie (Dooley) S.; m. Clarice Stiles, June 3, 1933 (dec. Apr. 1977); m. 2d, Monica Basil; children—Kay Heigert, Joe C.M., Dean. Bar: Tex. 1933, U.S. Dist. Ct. (no. dist.) Tex. 1935, U.S. Supreme Ct. 1964, U.S. Ct. Appeals (5th cir.) 1936. Sole practice, Ft. Worth, 1933-71; judge. U.S. Dist. Ct. Tex., 1971; judge Appellate Ct., 1975-83; now judge U.S. Ct. Appeals, 2d Supreme Jud. Dist. Mem. Secret Service. Mem. Tex. State Bar Assn., Fed. Bar Assn., Tarrant County Bar Assn. Methodist. Club: Fort Worth, Petroleum. Home: 709 Green River Trail Fort Worth TX 76103 Office: 5201 W Freeway Suite 102 Fort Worth TX 76107

SQUARCY, CHARLOTTE VAN HORNE, lawyer; b. Chgo., June 8, 1947; d. Charles Marion and Ruth (Van Horne) S. BA, Smith Coll., 1969; JD, Ind. U., 1977. Bar: Ind. 1977, U.S. Tax Ct. 1977, Mich. 1978, U.S. Supreme Ct. 1980, D.C. 1981, Conn. 1983, Calif. 1986. Law clk. to presiding judge Ind. State Ct., Hammond, 1976-77; dep. atty. gen. State of Ind., 1977-78; mem. legal staff Gen. Motors Corp., Detroit, 1978-81; assoc. counsel Olin Corp., Norwalk, Conn., 1981-85; sr. assoc. Bishop, Barry, Howe & Reid, San Francisco, 1985—. Mem. ABA (vice chmn. products liability com., tort and ins. practice, del. jud. adminstrn. div. competitions com.), Westchester-Fairfield County Corp. Counsel Assn. Republican. Methodist. Avocation: sports. Insurance, Environment, Personal injury. Home: 51 Sulgrave Ln Peacock Gap San Rafael CA 94901 Office: Bishop Barry Howe & Reid 465 California St 11th Floor San Francisco CA 94104

SQUIRE, SIDNEY, lawyer; b. N.Y.C., Dec. 27, 1906; s. Julius and Eva (Medwedick) S.; m. Helen Friedman, Sept. 24, 1942; children—Walter Charles, Jason Edward. LL.B., Bklyn. Law Sch., 1928. Bar: N.Y. 1928, U.S. Dist. Ct. (ea. dist.) N.Y. 1928, U.S. Dist. Ct. (so. dist.) N.Y. 1929, U.S. Ct. Appeals (2d cir.) 1930, U.S. Supreme Ct. 1970. Exec. dep. sec. State of N.Y., 1955-56; judge N.Y. Ct. Claims, State of N.Y., 1956-77; sole practice, N.Y.C., 1977—. Pres. Bklyn. Talmud Torah Council; dir., chmn. resolutions com. Bklyn. Jewish Community Council; hon. pres. Bklyn. Lawyers Club Fedn. Jewish Philanthropies; chmn. Flatbush Fund Raising Com. Boy Scouts Am.; Bklyn. chmn. United Jewish Appeal; Bklyn. Lawyers Com. United Hosp. Appeal, Red Cross and Greater N.Y. Fund; Bklyn. dinner chmn. NCCJ; trustee East 55th St. Conservative Synagogue; dir. Bd. Jewish Edn. N.Y.; bd. overseers Jewish Theol. Sem. Served with U.S. Army, 1944-45. Mem. Bklyn. Bar Assn. (trustee, chmn. centennial dinner 1972), N.Y. State Bar Assn. (jud. sect. continuing edn.), ABA (litigation sect., com. trial practice), N.Y. County Lawyers Assn. (com. arbitration). State civil litigation, Probate, Condemnation. Home and Office: 300 E 57th St New York NY 10022

SQUIRES, JOHN HENRY, lawyer; b. Urbana, Ill., Oct. 21, 1946; s. Henry Warrick and Nell Catherine (McDonough) S.; m. Mary Kathleen Damhorst, June 7, 1969; children—Jacqueline Marie, Mary Elizabeth, Katherine Judith, Emily Jean. A.B. cum laude, U. Ill., 1968, J.D., 1971. Bar: Ill. 1971, U.S.

Dist. Ct. (cen. dist.) Ill. 1972, U.S. Tax Ct. 1978. Assoc. Brown, Hay & Stephens, Springfield, Ill., 1971-76, ptnr., 1977—; trustee in bankruptcy, 1984—; lectr. Ill. Inst. Continuing Legal Edn. Bd. dirs., mem. lay adv. bd. St. Joseph's Home, Springfield, 1980-84, sec., 1982-84, v.p., 1983-84. Served with USAF, 1969. Mem. ABA, Ill. State Bar Assn., Sangamon County Bar Assn. Roman Catholic. Clubs: Sangamo, Am. Bus. (Springfield); K.C., Elks. Bankruptcy, Contracts commercial, State civil litigation. Office: First Nat Bank Bldg Suite 700 Springfield IL 62701

SQUIRES, MARK ELLIOTT, lawyer; b. Phila., Oct. 3, 1953; s. Anthony Louis and Davora (Udelson) S. BA in Communications summa cum laude, Temple U., 1975, JD cum laude, 1978. Bar: Pa. 1978, U.S. Dist. Ct. (ea. dist.) Pa. 1978, U.S. Ct. Appeals (3d cir.) 1978, U.S. Supreme Ct. 1984. Assoc. Morgan, Lewis & Bockius, Phila., 1978-82; assoc. Taylor & Taylor, Phila., 1982-83, ptnr., 1983—. Mem. ABA, Pa. Bar Assn., Phila. Bar Assn. Lodge: B'nai B'rith (nat. law com. anti-defamation league 1982). Civil rights, Federal civil litigation, State civil litigation. Office: Taylor & Taylor 10 Penn Ctr Suite 811 Philadelphia PA 19103

SQUIRES, WILLIAM RANDOLPH, III, lawyer; b. Providence, Sept. 6, 1947; s. William Randolph and Mary Louise (Gress) S.; children: Shannon, William R. IV; m. Elisabeth McAnulty, June 23, 1984. BA in Econs., Stanford U., 1969; JD, U. Tex., 1972. Bar: Wash. 1973, U.S. Dist. Ct. (we. dist.) Wash. 1973, U.S. Dist. Ct. (ea. dist.) Wash. 1976, U.S. Ct. Appeals (9th cir.) 1976, U.S. Supreme Ct. 1976, U.S. Ct. Claims 1982. Assoc. Oles, Morrison, Rinker, Stanislaw, & Ashbaugh, Seattle, 1973-78; ptnr. Davis, Wright & Jones (formerly Davis, Wright, Todd, Riese & Jones), Seattle, 1978—. Mem. ABA, Wash. State Bar Assn., Seattle-King County Bar Assn. Episcopalian. Clubs: Wash. Athletic, Rainier (Seattle). Construction, Federal civil litigation, Labor. Home: 2312 30th W Seattle WA 98199 Office: Davis Wright & Jones 2600 Century Sq 1501 Fourth Ave Seattle WA 98101-1688

SSEKANDI, FRANCIS MUZINGU, lawyer; b. Mbarara, Uganda, Sept. 29, 1940; came to U.S. 1979; m. Joanne Binder, July 5, 1969; 1 child, Christina Nabunya. LLB with honors, U. London, 1965; LLM, Columbia U., 1966. Bar: Uganda 1966, N.Y. 1981. State atty. Ministry of Justice, Uganda, 1965-71; dir. Law Devel. Ctr., Uganda, 1971-74; puisne judge High Court, Uganda, 1974-78; justice Ct. Appeals, Uganda, 1978-79; prof. Wayne State U., Detroit, 1980-81; sr. legal officer UN, N.Y.C., 1981—; judge Jessup Moot Ct. Competition, 1983-86. Editor: Uganda Law Reports, 1971-74; mem. bd. editors N.Y. Law Sch. Jour. Internat. and Comparative Law, 1983—. Mem. ABA, Am. Soc. Internat. Law. Public international, Contracts commercial, Jurisprudence. Home: 10 O'Donnell St Westwood NJ 07675 Office: UN Office Legal Affairs New York NY 10017

STABBE, MITCHELL HOWARD, lawyer; b. Bklyn., Oct. 12, 1955; s. Alfred and Evelyn (Mann) S. BA, U. Rochester, 1977; JD, U. Chgo., 1980. Bar: D.C. 1980, U.S. Dist. Ct. D.C. 1981, U.S. Ct. Claims 1981, U.S. Ct. Appeals (D.C. cir.) 1981, Md. 1982, U.S. Dist. Ct. Md. 1983, U.S. Supreme Ct. 1984. Assoc. Pope, Ballard & Loos, Washington, 1980-81, Holland & Knight, Holland & Knight, 1982—. Mem. ABA, Fed. Bar Assn., Def. Research Inst., Bar Assn. of D.C., Md. Bar Assn. Avocations: film, cuisine, literature. Federal civil litigation, State civil litigation, Insurance. Office: Holland & Knight 888 17th St NW Suite 400 Washington DC 20006

STABLER, LEWIS VASTINE, JR., lawyer; b. Greenville, Ala., Nov. 5, 1936; s. Lewis Vastine and Dorothy Daisy S.; m. Monteray Scott, Sept. 5, 1958; children: Dorothy Monteray, Andrew Vastine, Monteray Scott, Margaret Langston. B.A., Vanderbilt U., 1958; J.D. with distinction, U. Mich., 1961. Bar: Ala. 1961. Assoc. firm Cabaniss & Johnston, Birmingham, Ala., 1961-67; assoc. prof. law U. Ala., 1967-70; partner firm Cabaniss, Johnston, Gardner, Dumas & O'Neal (and predecessor firms), Birmingham, 1970—; Mem. com. of 100 Candler Sch. Theology, Emory U. Bd. editors: Mich. Law Rev, 1960-61. Mem. Am. Law Inst., Ala. Law Inst. (mem. council, dir. 1968-70), ABA, Ala. Bar Assn., Birmingham Bar Assn., Am. Judicature Soc., Am. Assn. Railroad Trial Counsel, Order of Coif. Methodist (cert. lay speaker). Clubs: Country of Birmingham, Rotary. Federal civil litigation, State civil litigation, Antitrust. Home: 3538 Victoria Rd Birmingham AL 35223 Office: 1900 First National Southern Natural Bldg Birmingham AL 35203

STACEY, JAMES ALLEN, judge; b. Norwalk, Ohio, Dec. 26, 1925; s. James Calvin and Glenna (Cleveland) S.; m. Marlyn Frederick, Aug. 21, 1948; children—James A., Libbie M. Romigh, Lorrie Stacey Singler, David F., CamAllison Shenigo, Tricia Stacey Berger. Student Bucknell U., 1943-44, Ohio Wesleyan U., 1944, 46, 47, U. N.C., 1944-45; J.D., Cleveland-Marshall Law Sch., 1951. Bar: Ohio 1952, U.S. Dist. Ct. (n.w. dist.) Ohio 1955. Ptnr., McGory & Stacey, Sandusky, Ohio, 1954-56; assoc. Steinemann & Zeiher, Sandusky, 1956-60; ptnr. Work, Stacey & Moyer, 1960-67; judge Sandusky Mcpl. Ct., 1967—; mem. Ohio State Traffic Law Com., 1969—, chmn., 1978-82. Mem., Erie-Ottawa Mental Health Bd., 1968—; mem. Ex-Offenders for Help Bd., 1975-81; bd. dirs. Camp Fire Girls, 1956-60, L.E.A.D.S., 1984-86, Sandusky C. of C., 1984-86. Served with USNR, 1943-46. Mem. Ohio State Bar Assn., Ohio Mcpl. Judges Assn. (exec. bd. 1970-80), Am. Judicature Soc., Am. Judges Assn., Erie County Bar Assn., Amvets. Republican. Presbyterian. Clubs: Sandusky Exchange, Elks, Eagles. Judicial administration, Jurisprudence. Home: 3407 Columbus Ave Sandusky OH 44870 Office: City Bldg 222 Meigs St Sandusky OH 44870

STACHOWSKI, MICHAEL JOSEPH, lawyer, consultant; b. Buffalo, Feb. 27, 1947; s. Stanley Joseph and Pearl (Wojcik) S.; children—Lisa Ann, Evan Michael; m. Deborah Ann Jakubczak, Oct. 19, 1979. B.A., Canisius Coll., 1970; J.D., SUNY-Buffalo, 1973; cert. Hague Acad. Internat. Law, Netherlands, 1976. Bar: N.Y. 1974, U.S. Dist. Ct. (we. dist.) N.Y. 1974, U.S. Ct. Appeals (2d cir.) 1974. Atty. Sportservice, Inc., Buffalo, 1973-74; assoc. Siegel & McGee, Buffalo, 1974-75; confidential clk. 8th dist. N.Y. Supreme Ct., Buffalo, 1975-77; research counsel N.Y. State Assembly, Albany, 1977-80; sole practice, Buffalo, 1976-86, dep. atty. Town of Cheektowaga, N.Y., 1986—; cons. in field. Campaign mgr. various jud. candidates, Buffalo, 1977—; fund raiser Erie County Democrats, Buffalo, 1979—. Fellow Am. Acad. Matrimonial Lawyers; mem. Erie County Bar Assn., East Clinton Profl. Businessmen's Assn. (v.p. 1976—, pres. 1985). Roman Catholic. Family and matrimonial, State civil litigation, Construction. Home: 12 Beaverbrook Ct Depew NY 14043 Office: 2130 Clinton St Buffalo NY 14206

STACK, CHARLES RICKMAN, lawyer; b. Boston, Sept. 26, 1935; s. John Joseph and Caroline Benradet (Rickman) S.; m. Barbara Alice Levine, Oct. 12, 1963; children—Caroline K., Kevin C., Constance K. B.S. in Bus. Adminstrn., U. Fla. 1957, J.D., 1960; diplomate Nat. Bd. Trial Advocacy; cert. Fla. Bd. Trial Certification. Bar: Fla. 1960, U.S. dist. ct. (so. dist.) Fla. 1960. Assoc. Macfarlane, Ferguson, Allison & Kelly, Tampa, Fla., 1960-62; ptnr. High, Stack, Lazenby, Bender, Palahach & Lacasa, Miami, Fla., 1962—, sr. ptnr. 1968—; mem., sec. U.S. Dist. Ct. Peer Rev. commn., 1983—; instr. bus. law U. South Fla. 1960-62; instr. comml. law Am. Inst. Banking, Tampa, 1960-62. Chmn. Fla. Jud. Nominations Commn. for 11th Cir., 1970-76; Dade County campaign chmn. Ruebin Askew for Gov., 1970, Steve Clark for Mayor, 1972; mem. Fla. Constn. Revision Com., 1968; chmn. Fla. Corp. Income Tax Com., 1972; mem. Fla. Democratic Conv. Com., 1972; mem. City of Miami Downtown Devel. Authority, 1979-82. Mem. ABA, Fla. Bar, Am. Trial Lawyers Assn., Lawyers for Pub. Justice, Acad. Fla. Trial Lawyers, Tex. Trial Lawyers, Dade County Trial Lawyers, Com. of 100, Dade County Bar Assn. Democrat. Episcopalian. Clubs: Univ. (Miami); Riviera Country (Coral Gables, Fla.). Contbr. numerous articles to profl. jours. State civil litigation, Federal civil litigation, Personal injury. Home: 11900 SW 67th Ct Miami FL 33156 Office: 3929 Ponce de Leon Blvd Coral Gables FL 33134

STACK, DANIEL, lawyer, financial consultant; b. Bklyn., July 29, 1928; s. Charles and Gertrude (Heller) S.; m. Jane Marcia Gordon, Apr. 18, 1953; children: Joan, Gordon. B.A. cum laude, Bklyn. Coll., 1949; LL.B., Columbia U., 1952; LL.M., Georgetown U., 1955. Bar: N.Y. 1956. Asst. counsel ABC-TV, N.Y.C., 1959-60; gen. counsel IFC Securities Corp., N.Y.C., 1961-63; sec. pension com. Consol. Foods Corp., Chgo., 1967-69; v.p. legal Seaway Multi Corp. Ltd., Toronto, Ont., Can., 1969-72; v.p. mergers and acquisitions Acklands Ltd., Toronto, 1972-74; sr. v.p., sec., counsel Greenwich Savs. Bank, N.Y.C., 1978-81; sole practice, N.Y.C., 1982-85; ptnr. Brenne and Stack, N.Y.C., 1986—; cons. venture capital, corp. fin., mining, and oil, N.Y.C., 1982—; pres. Bus. and Fin. Resources, Inc., 1982-84; officer and dir. various public cos.; lectr., guest speaker on mergers and acquisitions; gen. counsel Greater N.Y. Safety Council, 1980— Mem. Congl. mil. service acads. nominations com. and Civil Service intern selection com., 1978—; info. officer U.S. Naval Acad., 1972—. Served to lt. j.g. USNR, 1952-55, capt. Res. ret. 1981. Decorated Joint Service Commendation medal, 1981. N.Y. State Regents scholar, 1945-49. Mem. N.Y. State Bar Assn., N.Y. County Lawyer's Assn., ABA. Republican. General corporate, Banking, Oil and gas leasing. Home: 8 Linda Dr Suffern NY 10901 Office: Brenne and Stack 11 Broadway New York NY 10004

STACK, JOANNE TUNNEY, lawyer, editor; b. N.Y.C., Aug. 8, 1952; d. Patrick Francis and Mary (Rowland) Tunney; m. William Michael Stack, Feb. 1, 1975; 1 child, Liam Patrick. BA in Psychology, Manhanttanville Coll., 1974; JD, Fordham U., 1977. Bar: N.Y. 1978. Legal editor West Pub. Co., Mineola, N.Y., 1977-85; sr. editor Research Inst. Am., N.Y.C., 1985-86; mgr. Price Waterhouse, N.Y.C., 1986—; editor U.S. Taxes, Views and Reviews, N.Y.C., 1986—; cons., legal advisor Readers Digest, N.Y.C., 1983—. Editor: Family Legal Guide, 1981 (Best Reference Work 1982), Guide To American Law, 1984 (Best Reference Work 1985), How To Do Just About Anything, 1985. Mem. ABA. Avocations: travel, art. Probate, Personal income taxation, Explaining law in plain english to general public. Home: 119 Cocks Ln Locust Valley NY 11560 Office: Price Waterhouse 1251 Ave of Americas New York NY 10020

STACK, MICHAEL J., lawyer; b. Phila., June 14, 1927; s. Michael J. and Mary Catherine (Dolan) S.; m. Felice, Nov. 15, 1958; children: Mary Theresa, Michael Patrick, Eileen, Carol. BS, St. Joseph's U., Phila., 1951; LLD, U. Pa., 1954. Dep. atty. gen. Justice Dept., Pa., 1958-60; gen. counsel Phila. Parking Authority, 1967-72, Hosp. Authority Phila., 1974-79; ptnr. Stack & Gallagher, Phila., 1972—; adj. prof. law Georgetown U., Washington, 1964-67. Dist. dir. Poverty Program, Pa., 1965-66; ward leader Dem. Exec. Com., Phila., 1970. Served with U.S. Army, 1945-47, ETO. Mem. Pa. Bar Assn., Phila. Bar Assn., Brehon Law Soc. (mem. exec. bd., past pres.), St. Joseph's Law Alumni Assn. (past pres.). Democrat. Roman Catholic. Club: Racquet (Phila.). General corporate, Criminal, State civil litigation. Home: 1247 Southampton Rd Philadelphia PA 19116 Office: Stack & Gallagher 1600 Locust St Philadelphia PA 19103

STACK, PAUL FRANCIS, lawyer; b. Chgo., July 21, 1946; s. Frank Louis and Dorothy Louise Stack; m. Nea Waterman, July 8, 1972; children—Nea Elizabeth, Sera Waterman. B.S., U. Ariz., 1968; J.D., Georgetown U., 1971. Bar: Ill. 1971, U.S. Ct. Claims 1975, U.S. Tax Ct. 1974, U.S. Ct. Customs and Patent Appeals 1977, U.S. Supreme Ct. 1975. Law clk., U.S. Dist. Ct., Chgo., 1971-72; asst. U.S. atty. No. Dist. Ill., Chgo., 1972-75; ptnr. Stack & Filpi, Chgo., 1976—. Bd. dirs. Riverside Pub. Library, 1977-83, Suburban Library System, Burr Ridge, Ill., 1979-82, Suburban Health Systems Agy., Inc., Oak Park, Ill., 1983. Mem. ABA, Chgo. Bar Assn. Presbyterian. Club: Union League. Immigration, naturalization, and customs, Administrative and regulatory, Federal civil litigation. Home: 238 N Delaplaine Rd Riverside IL 60546 Office: 140 S Dearborn St Suite 411 Chicago IL 60603

STACY, RICHARD A., lawyer; b. Eldorado, Ark., Mar. 7, 1942; s. Jack Leonard S. and Estelle (Mabry) Carrier; m. Karen Kay King, Aug. 20, 1961; children: Mark Leonard, Andrea May. B.A., U. Wyo., 1965, J.D., 1967. Bar: Wyo. 1967, Colo. 1967, U.S. Supreme Ct. 1972. Revisor Wyo. Statute Revision Com., Cheyenne, 1967-69; asst. atty. gen. State of Wyo., 1969-72; asst. U.S. atty. Dept. Justice, Cheyenne, 1972-75, U.S. atty., 1981—; sole practice law Wheatland, Wyo., 1975-81; mem. atty. gen's adv. com. of U.S. attys. Dept. Justice, 1981-84. Mem. ABA, Wyo. Bar Assn., Laramie County Bar Assn., Wyo. Trial Lawyers Assn. Republican. Episcopalian. Club: Kiwanis (charter pres. Wheatland 1977). Office: US Atty Dist Wyo 2120 Capitol Ave Cheyenne WY 82003

STADTMUELLER, JOSEPH PETER, lawyer; b. Oshkosh, Wis., Jan. 28, 1942; s. Joseph Francis and Irene Mary (Kilp) S.; m. Mary Ellen Brady, Sept. 5, 1970; children: Jeremy, Sarah. B.S. in Bus. Adminstrn., Marquette U., 1964, J.D., 1967. Bar: Wis. 1967, U.S. Supreme Ct. 1980. Asst. U.S. atty. Dept. Justice, Milw., 1969-74; 1st. asst. U.S. atty. Dept. Justice, 1974-75, asst. U.S. atty., 1977-78, dep. U.S. atty., 1978-81, U.S. atty., 1981—; ptnr. Stepke, Kossow, Trebon & Stadtmueller, Milw., 1976; instr. Atty. Gen.'s Advocacy Inst., Washington, 1975—. Recipient Spl. Commendation award Atty. Gen. U.S., 1974, 80. Mem. Milw. Young Lawyers (exec. bd. 1974-78, sec. 1977-78), State Bar Wis. (bd. govs. 1979-83, exec. com. 1982-83), ABA, Am. Law Inst. Republican. Roman Catholic. Club: University (Milw.). Federal civil litigation, Criminal. Office: US Attorneys Office 330 Fed Bldg 517 E Wisconsin Ave Milwaukee WI 53202 *

STAEHLE, SANDRA JOHNSON, lawyer; b. Bridgeport, Conn., Feb. 11, 1952; d. Otto John and Pearl Julia (Toth) S.; m. Keith Godfrey Johnson, Sept. 10, 1983. BA, Temple U., 1973, JD, 1976, LLM in Taxation, 1978. Bar: Pa., 1976, N.J. 1976, U.S. Dist. Ct. N.J. 1976, U.S. Dist. Ct. (ea. dist.) Pa. 1977, U.S. Tax Ct. 1978. Sr. trust tax adminstr. Phila. Nat. Bank, 1976-77; house counsel Birchminster Industries, Inc., Telford, Pa., 1977-78; atty. broadcast systems div. RCA Corp., Camden, N.J., 1978-81; broadcast systems div. and Princeton Labs RCA Corp., Gibbsboro and Princeton, N.J., 1983-84; counsel solid state div. and Princeton Labs RCA Corp., Somerville, N.J. and Princeton, 1984-85; counsel service dept. RCA Corp., Cherry Hill, N.J., 1985-86; atty. to counsel RCA Internat. Ltd., Sunbury-on-Thames, Eng., 1981-83; counsel comml. and telephone dept. Gen. Electric Co., Cherry Hill, 1986—. Mem. Society Hill Civic Assn., Phila., 1985—. Mem. ABA, Am. Corp. Counsel Assn. (Internat. Law Com.), Am. Soc. Internat. Law, Pa. Bar Assn., Am. C. of C. (liason Internat. Trade Com. London 1981-83), Phi Alpha Delta, Sigma Delta Pi. General corporate, Contracts commercial, Private international. Office: Gen Electric Co Comml and Telephone dept Route 38 Bldg 204-2 Cherry Hill NJ 08358

STAFFORD, WILLIAM HENRY, JR., U.S. district judge; b. Masury, Ohio, May 11, 1931; s. William Henry and Frieda Gertrude (Nau) S.; m. Nancy Marie Helman, July 11, 1959; children: William Henry, Donald Helman, David Harrold. B.S., Temple U., 1953, LL.B., 1956; J.D., 1968. Bar: Fla. 1961, U.S. Supreme Ct. 1970, U.S. 5th Circuit Ct. Appeals bar 1969. Asso. firm Robinson & Roark, Pensacola, 1961-64; individual practice law Pensacola, 1964-67, state atty., 1967-69, U.S. atty., 1969-75; U.S. dist. judge No. Dist. Fla., Tallahassee, 1975—; now chief judge No. Dist. Fla.; instr. Pensacola Jr. Coll., 1964, 68. Served to lt. (j.g.) USN, 1957-60. Mem. Am., Tallahassee bar assns., Fla. Bar (chmn. fed. funding com., mem. exec. council trial lawyers sect. 1972-75), Soc. Bar First Jud. Circuit Fla., Sigma Phi Epsilon, Phi Delta Phi. Republican. Episcopalian. Clubs: Masons, Shriners, Rotary, Pensacola Yacht. Office: US Courthouse 110 E Park Ave Tallahassee FL 32301 *

STAGEMAN, RICHARD FREDERICK, judge; b. Omaha, Sept. 25, 1926; s. Frederick William and Claire Emilia (Huth) S.; m. Mary Ellen Desenberg, July 16, 1982; m. Grace Adele Yeiser, Jan. 20, 1950; children—Susan Stageman Fejes, Richard Wayne, William Maurice, Emily Grace Rollison. B.S., Creighton U., 1949, J.D., 1951. Bar: Iowa, 1951, Nebr. 1951, U.S. Tax Ct. 1958. Mem. firm Smith, Pogge & Stageman, Council Bluffs, Iowa, 1951-62; U.S. bankruptcy judge U.S. Ct. So. Dist. Iowa, Des Moines, 1962-86; assoc., Davis, Hockenberg, Wine, Brown & Koehn, 1986—. Mem. 59th Gen. Assembly Iowa from Pottawattamie County, 1961-62; treas. Tabitha Home Lutheran Ch. Am., Lincoln; bd. dirs. Augustana Coll., Rock Island, Ill., Central Theol. Sem., Fremont, Nebr. Served with USN, 1944-46: PTO. Mem. ABA (former chmn. contitution and by laws com. of spl. ct. judges), Iowa Bar Assn., Polk County Bar Ass., Pottawattamie County Bar Assn., Southwest Iowa Bar Assn., Comml. Law League, Nat. Conf. Bankruptcy Judges. Republican. Lutheran. Contracts commercial. Home: 827 Main St Norwalk IA 50211 Office: 2300 Financial Ctr Des Moines IA 50309

STAGG, TOM, judge; b. Shreveport, La., Jan. 19, 1923; s. Thomas Eaton and Beulah (Meyer) S.; m. Margaret Mary O'Brien, Aug. 21, 1946; children: Julie, Margaret Mary. B.A., La. State U., 1943, J.D., 1949. Bar: La. 1949. With firm Hargrove, Guyton, Van Hook & Hargrove, Shreveport, 1949-53; pvt. practice Shreveport, 1953-58; sr. partner firm Stagg, Cady & Beard, Shreveport, 1958-74; U.S. dist. judge Western Dist. of La., 1974—, chief judge, 1984—; Pres. Abe Meyer Corp., 1960-74, Stagg Investments, Inc., 1964-74; mng. partner Pierremont Mall Shopping Center, 1963-74; v.p. King Hardware Co., 1955-74; Mem. Shreveport Airport Authority, 1967-73, chmn., 1970-73; chmn. Gov.'s Tidelands Adv. Council, 1969-70; del. La. Constl. Conv., 1973-74; chmn. rules com., com. on exec. dept.; mem. Gov.'s Adv. Com on Offshore Revenues, 1972-74. Active Republican party, 1950-74, del. convs., 1956, 60, 64, 68, 72; mem. Nat. Com. for La., 1964-72, mem. exec. com., 1964-68; Pres. Shreveport Jr. C. of C., 1955-56; v.p. La. Jr. C. of C., 1956-57. Served to capt., inf. AUS, 1943-46, ETO. Decorated Bronze Star, Purple Heart with oak leaf cluster. Mem. Am., La., Shreveport bar assns., Photog. Soc. Am. Jurisprudence. Office: US Court House Room 2B15 500 Fannin St Shreveport LA 71101

STAGNER, ROBERT DEAN, lawyer; b. Simi, Calif., May 23, 1950; s. Cecil William and Mary Jane (Davis) S.; m. Barbara Ann Crosby, Dec. 27, 1974; children: Rebecca Lyn, Brenda Deann. BA in History and Polit. Sci., Pasadena Coll., 1972; JD, Western State U., Fullerton, Calif., 1977. Bar: Calif. 1977, U.S. Dist. Ct. (cen. dist.) Calif. 1979. Ptnr. Stagner & Gregg, Orange, Calif., 1978—; officer, cons. Richard Walker Inc., Anaheim, Calif., 1976—, sec. 1978-81, bd. dirs.; gen. counsel Greater Am. Produce, Anaheim, 1978-84, acting pres. 1984; pres. Orion Constrn., Tustin, Calif., 1980-82; counsel Whittier Police Officers Assn., 1982—; cons. ballistics Kraemer Industries, Anaheim, 1985—, Exodus One Mktg., Placentia, Calif., 1985—, A.W. Schnitger, Encinada, Mexico, 1985—. Trainer USN Sea Cadet Corps, El Toro, Calif., 1984—; adult edn. Nazarene Ch., Chino, Calif., 1982-85. Named one of Outstanding Young Men Am., 1981. Avocations: hunting, fishing, woodworking. General practice, Private international, Labor. Office: Stagner & Gregg 2745 E Chapman #202 Orange CA 92669

STAHL, STANLEY PAUL, lawyer; b. Pitts., June 10, 1946; s. Sam and Evelyn (Sheck) S.; m. Laurie Nan Hallet, June 14, 1969; children—Chad Harmon, Joanna Michelle. A.B., U. Miami, 1967; J.D., N.Y. Law Sch., 1970. Bar: D.C., 1970, U.S. Ct. Mil. Appeals 1972, U.S. Supreme Ct. 1974, Pa. 1975, U.S. Dist. Ct. (ea. dist.) Pa. 1975, U.S. Ct. Appeals (3d cir.) 1975, N.J. 1976, U.S. Dist. Ct. N.J. 1976. Assoc. Sellers, Connor and Cuneo, Washington, 1970-71; assoc. LaBrum and Doak, Phila., 1974-79; ptnr. Post & Schell, P.C., Phila., 1979—; sole practice, Camden County, N.J., 1981—. Served to lt. comdr. USNR, 1971-74. Mem. ABA, N.J. State Bar Assn., Pa. Bar Assn., Phila. Bar Assn., Camden County Bar Assn., Pa. Def. Inst., Pa. Trial Lawyers Assn. Club: Masons. Personal injury, Insurance. Office: 1800 JFK Blvd Philadelphia PA 19103 also: Ashland Office Ctr Evesham & Alpha Aves Voorhees NJ 08043

STAHR, THOMAS JAMES, lawyer; b. Horseheads, N.Y., May 5, 1951; s. Donald W. and Mildred (Havard) S.; m. Deborah M. Pharr, May 22, 1976; 1 child, Jessica M. AS, Corning Community Coll., 1973; BA, SUNY, Buffalo, 1975, JD, 1978. Bar: N.Y. 1979, U.S. Dist. Ct. (we. dist.) N.Y. 1979. Assoc. Bradstreet & Bradstreet, Bath, N.Y., 1979-80; ptnr. Bradstreet & Stahr, Bath, 1980-81, Bradstreet, Stahr & Curran, Bath, 1981-85, Stahr & Curran, Bath, 1985—; asst. dist. atty. Steuben County, Bath, 1980-81; instr. local justice cert. program Steuben County. NIMH fellow, 1976; recipient criminal justice cert. NIMH, 1978. Mem. ABA, N.Y. State Bar Assn., Steuben County Bar Assn., Bath Village Bar Assn., Steuben County Magistrates Assn., Steuben County Assn. Chiefs of Police. Democrat. Methodist. Lodge: Elks. Personal injury, Criminal, Family and matrimonial. Home: 221 W Washington St Bath NY 14810 Office: Stahr & Curran 7 W Morris St Bath NY 14810

STAINE, ROSS, lawyer; b. El Paso, Tex., July 13, 1924; s. Adelbert Claire and Dennie Joe (Stowe) S.; m. Mary Louise Sibert, Aug. 15, 1947; children: Martha Louise, Julie Ann, Ross. B.A., Tex. A&M U., 1947; LL.B., U. Tex., 1950. Bar: Tex. Assoc. Baker & Botts, Houston, 1947, ptnr., 1962—. Served with AUS, 1943-46; served to 1st lt. U.S. Army, 1950-52, PTO. Mem. State Bar Tex., Houston Bar Assn., ABA, Tex. Law Rev. Assn., Order of Coif, Phi Delta Phi. Baptist. Clubs: Forest (Houston), Coronado (Houston), Univ. (Houston). Home: 5555 Del Monte Houston TX 77056 Office: Baker & Botts 3000 One Shell Plaza Houston TX 77002

STAKER, ROBERT JACKSON, U.S. district judge; b. Kermit, W.Va., Feb. 14, 1925; s. Frederick George and Nada (Frazier) S.; m. Sue Blankenship Poore, July 16, 1955; 1 child, Donald Seth; 1 stepson, John Timothy Poore. Student, Marshall U., Huntington, W.Va., W.Va. U., Morgantown, U. Ky., Lexington; LL.B, W.Va. U., 1952. Bar: W.Va. 1952. Practiced in Williamson, 1952-68; judge Mingo County Circuit Ct., Williamson, 1969-79; U.S. dist. judge So. Dist. W.Va., Huntington, 1979—. Served with USN, 1943-46. Mem. ABA, Am. Judicature Soc., W.Va. Bar Assn., W.Va. State Bar. Democrat. Presbyterian. Jurisprudence.

STALEY, JOHN FREDRIC, lawyer; b. Sidney, Ohio, Sept. 26, 1943; s. Harry Virgil and Fredericka May (McMillin) S.; m. Sue Ann Bolin, June 11, 1966; children—Ian McMillin, Erik Bolin. A.B. in History, Fresno State Coll., 1965; postgrad. in pub. adminstrn. Calif. State U.-Hayward, 1967-68; J.D., U. Calif. 1972. Bar: Calif. 1972. Ptnr. Staley, Jobson & Bernal, Livermore, Calif., 1972—; assoc. Paul Eisler, San Francisco, 1974-75; lectr. Hastings Coll. Law, 1973-74; founding mem., shareholder Bank of Livermore; bd. dirs. Erickson Land Devel. Co. Mem. Livermore City Council, 1975-82, vice mayor, 1978-82; bd. dirs. Alameda County Tng. and Employment Bd., Alameda-Contra Costa Emergency Med. Services Agy., Valley Vol. Ctr. Served with M.I., U.S. Army, 1966-67. Mem. ABA, Calif. State Bar, Alameda Bar Assn., Contra Costa Bar Assn., Amador Valley Bar Assn., Calif. Assn. Cert. Family Law Specialists (sec.), Lawyer Friends of Wine. Family and matrimonial, Real property, Contracts commercial. Office: Staley Jobson & Bernal 5776 Stoneridge Mall Rd #310 Pleasanton CA 94566

STALFORT, JOHN ARTHUR, lawyer; b. Balt., June 9, 1951; s. John Irving and Libby Jean (Adams) S.; m. Anne Cheesman, July 19, 1985. BA, U. Va., 1973, MBA, JD, 1977. Bar: Md. 1977. Assoc. Miles & Stockbridge, Balt., 1977-84, ptnr., 1984—. Author: Commercial Financing Forms-Maryland, 1986. Mem. ABA, Md. State Bar Assn., Balt. City Bar Assn., Nat. Assn. Bond Lawyers, Phi Beta Kappa. Republican. Presbyterian. Clubs: Balt. Country, Center, Merchants. Avocations: skiing, tennis, golf, running. Contracts commercial, Municipal bonds, Banking. Office: Miles & Stockbridge 10 Light St Baltimore MD 21202

STALKER, TIMOTHY WAYNE, lawyer; b. Kansas City, Mo., July 24, 1950; s. Earl Judson Stalker and Florence Elva (Herter) Arpajian; m. Lee Margaret Blakeslee, Sept. 4, 1971; children: Scott Andrew and Keith William. AB, Rutgers U., 1972; JD, N.Y. Law Sch., 1977. Bar: Pa. 1977, U.S. Dist. Ct. (ea. dist.) Pa. 1981, U.S. Supreme Ct. 1982. Atty. claims Am. Ins. Group, N.Y.C, 1979-80; mgr. claims and re-ins. counsel PMA Re-ins., Phila., 1980-83.; corp. sec., counsel GRE-Re Am., Princeton, N.J., 1983—; v.p., corp. sec. Albany-Atlas Group, Princeton, 1985—. Mem. ABA, Pa. Bar Assn. Democrat. Methodist. Insurance, Admiralty, General corporate. Home: 1493 Scarlet Oak Rd Yardley PA 19067 Office: Albany-Atlas Group 1020 US Rt 1 Princeton NJ 08540

STALLARD, WAYNE MINOR, lawyer; b. Onaga, Kans., Aug. 23, 1927; s. Minor Regan and Lydia Faye (Randall) S.; B.S., Kans. State Tchrs. Coll., Emporia, 1949; J.D., Washburn U., 1952; m. Wanda Sue Bacon, Aug. 22, 1948; children—Deborah Sue, Carol Jean, Bruce Wayne (dec.). Admitted to Kans. bar, 1952 pvt. practice, Onaga, 1952—; atty. Community Hosp. Dist. No. 1, Pottawatomie, Jackson and Nemaha Counties, Kans., 1955—; Pottawatomie County atty., 1955-59; city atty. Onaga, 1953-79; atty Unified School Dist. 322, Pottawatomie County, Kans., 1966-83. Bd. dirs. North Central Kans. Guidance Ctr., Manhattan, 1974-78; lawyer 2d dist. jud. nominating commn., 1980—; atty. Rural Water Dist. No. 3, Pottawatomie County, Kans., 1974—; chmn. Pottawatomie County Econ. Devel. Com., 1986—. Fund dr. chmn. Pottawatomie County chpt. Nat. Found. for Infantile Paralysis, 1953-54. Served from pvt. to sgt., 8th Army, AUS, 1946 to 47. Mem. ABA, Pottawatomie County, Kans. bar assns., Onaga Businessmen's Assn., Am. Judicature Soc., City Attys. Assn. Kan. (dir. 1963-66), Phi Gamma Mu, Kappa Delta Pi, Delta Theta Phi, Sigma Tau Gamma. Mem. United Ch. of Christ. Mason (Shriner); mem. Order Eastern Star. Estate

planning, Estate taxation, Real property. Home: 720 High St Onaga KS 66521 Office: Stallard & Flattery 307 Leonard Onaga KS 66521

STALLINGS, ROBERT GEORGE, lawyer, educator; b. Louisville, Dec. 4, 1942; s. Samuel James Sr. and Edna (Bauer) S.; children: Stephen David, Linda Price. AB, Bellarmine U., 1965; JD, Samford U., 1968. Bar: Ala. 1968, Ky. 1969, U.S. Dist. Ct. (we dist.) Ky. 1969. Ptnr. Stallings & Stallings, Louisville, 1968—; prof. bus. law U. Louisville, 1981—. Mem. Ky. Bar Assn., Ala. Bar Assn., Louisville Bar Assn. Democrat. Roman Catholic. Clubs: Louisville Quarterback (pres. 1975-86), Big Spring Country (Louisville). State civil litigation. Home: 279 Stonehenge Dr Apt 102 Louisville KY 40207 Office: Stallings & Stallings 412 Ky Home Life Bldg Louisville KY 40202

STALMACK, JOSEPH, lawyer; b. Chgo., Sept. 1, 1949; s. Joseph Sr. and Mary Theresa (Petriska) S.; m. Deborah Kathleen Soczyk, Aug. 22, 1970; children: Todd Joseph, Allison Lee, Jessica Claire. BA, Coe Coll., 1971; JD, Loyola U., Chgo., 1974. Bar: Ill. 1974, Ind. 1975. Assoc. Galvin & Galvin, Hammond, Ind., 1974-82; ptnr. Galvin, Stalmack & Kirschner, Hammond, 1982-85, Galvin, Stalmack, Kirschner & Clark, Hammond, 1985—. Mem. ABA, Ind. Bar Assn., Def. Research Inst., Ind. Def. Lawyers Assn. State civil litigation, Federal civil litigation, Construction. Office: Galvin Stalmack et al 5253 Hohman Hammond IN 46320

STAMATO, PHILOMENA, lawyer; b. Red Bank, N.J., May 17, 1958; d. Nicholas Patrick and Mary Ann (Leombrone) S. BA, SUNY, Buffalo, 1980; JD, Syracuse U., 1982. Bar: N.Y. 1983, N.J. 1984, U.S. Dist. Ct. (no. dist.) N.Y. 1983, U.S. Dist. Ct. N.J. Assoc. Law Firm of Jerome Nealon, Binghamton, N.Y., 1983-85; asst. corp. counsel City of Binghamton, N.Y., 1985-87; asst. atty. County of Broome, Binghamton, 1987—. Mem. Bd. Broome Legal Assistance Corp., Broome County Pro Bono Project. Mem. N.Y. State Bar Assn., N.J. Bar Assn., Broome County Bar Assn. (continuing legal edn. com., lawyers reference service com.), Assn. Trial Lawyers Am., N.Y. State Trial Lawyers Assn., So. Tier Affiliates Trial Lawyers Assn. (sec.). Democrat. Roman Catholic. Avocations: swimming, photography, travel. Local government. Office: County of Broome Law Dept Govtl Plaza Binghamton NY 13901

STAMBERG, LOUIS MANN, lawyer; b. Ukraine, June 14, 1902; came to U.S., 1904, naturalized, 1906; m. Marjorie Salinger Bing, June 25, 1952; children—Louis Collins, Catherine Bing Lipkin. B.S. in Civil Engring., U. Pa., 1924; LL.B., Temple U., 1929. Bar admittee Pa. 1929, U.S. dist. ct. (ea. dist.) Pa. 1929. Jr. ptnr. Sundheim, Folz & Sundheim, Phila., 1929-31; sr. ptnr. Stamberg, Caplan & Calnan, 1965-81; sr. mem. Stamberg & Caplan, Allentown, Pa., 1982—; legal counsel, v.p., dir. mem. exec. com. Coplay Cement Co., Bath, Pa., 1950-82, chief exec. officer, chmn. bd., 1971-80, hon. chmn. bd. and mem. exec. com., 1980—; legal counsel, dir. Rodale Press, Inc., Emmaus, Pa., 1945-82; bd. dirs., legal counsel Soil and Health Soc., 1947-82; legal counsel, bd. dirs., exec. com. United Way of Lehigh County, 1947-82; chmn. Allentown Zoning Bd., 1951-56. Mem. ABA, Pa. Bar Assn., Lehigh County Bar Assn., Phila. Bar Assn., Engrs.' Club Lehigh Valley. Republican. Club: Lehigh Valley. General corporate, Probate. Office: 534 Turner St Allentown PA 18102

STAMPER, JOE ALLEN, lawyer; b. Okemah, Okla., Jan. 30, 1914; s. Horace Allen and Ann (Stephens) S.; m. Johnnie Lee Bell, June 4, 1936; 1 child, Jane Allen (Mrs. Ernest F. Godlove). B.A., U. Okla., 1933, LL.B., 1935, J.D., 1970. Bar: Okla. bar 1935. Practice in Antlers, 1935-36, 46—; mem. firm Stamper, Otis & Burrage, 1974—; atty. Pushmataha County, 1936-39; spl. justice Okla. Supreme Ct., 1948. Mem. Okla. Indsl. Commn., 1939-40; pres. Antlers Sch. Bd., 1956-67, Pushmataha Found., 1957—; mem. Okla. Bicentennial Com., 1971—; vice chmn. bd. U. Okla. Law Center, 1975-78; mgr. Okla. Democratic party, 1946, dist. chmn., 1946-50; alt. del. Dem. Nat. Conv., 1952. Served to col. AUS, 1935-46, E O. Decorated Bronze Star. Fellow Am. Bar Found., Am. Coll. Trial Lawyers; mem. ABA (del. 1974, state del. 1975-86, mem. com. on law book pub. practices 1974-76, bd. govs. 1986—), Okla. Bar Assn. (bd. govs. 1969-73, Pres.'s award 1977, 80), Okla. Bar Found. (pres. 1977), S.A.R., Mil. Order World Wars, Pi Kappa Alpha. Baptist (deacon). Clubs: Whitehall (Oklahoma City). Lodges: Masons, Shriners, Lions. Federal civil litigation, State civil litigation, General practice. Home: 1000 NE 2d St Antlers OK 74523 Office: PO Box 100 Antlers OK 74523

STAMPER, RANDALL LEE, lawyer; b. Spokane, Wash., July 9, 1949; s. Lyman D. and Ida Rebecca (Olmsted) S.; m. Mary Costello, Nov. 10, 1966 (div. June 1973); m. Conni L. Stradley, June 28, 1975. BA, U. Idaho, 1969; JD, U. Notre Dame, 1972. Bar: Idaho 1972, U.S. Dist. Ct. Idaho 1972, Wash. 1973, U.S. Dist. Ct. (ea. dist.) Wash. 1973. Law clk. to presiding justice Idaho Supreme Ct., Boise, 1972-73; ptnr. MacGillivary & Jones, Spokane, 1973-85; sr. ptnr. Stamper & Taylor P.S., Spokane, 1986—. Mem. ABA, Wash. Bar Assn., Idaho Bar Assn., Spokane Bar Assn., Wash. Soc. Hosp. Attys., Am. Acad. Hosp. Attys., Wash. State Trial Lawyers Assn. Lodges: Rotary, Shriners. General corporate, Health, Personal injury. Home: 7507 N Cedar Spokane WA 99208 Office: Stamper & Taylor PS W 720 Boone Suite 200 Spokane WA 99201

STAMPS, THOMAS PATY, lawyer; b. Mineola, N.Y., May 10, 1952; s. George Moreland and Helen Leone (Paty) S.; m. Regina Ruth Thomas, May 23, 1981; 2 children: Katherine Camilla, George Belk. BA, U. Ill., 1973; postgrad. Emory U., 1975-76, JD, Wake Forest U., 1979. Bar: Ga. 1979, N.C. 1979. Personnel dir. Norman Jaspan, N.Y.C., 1973-74; assoc. Macey & Zusmann, Atlanta, 1979-81; owner Zusmann, Small, Stamps & White PC, Atlanta, 1981-85; cons. GMS Cons., Oxford, Ga., 1975—; ptnr. Destin Enterprises, Atlanta, 1983-85. Author: Study of a Student, 1973, History of Coca-Cola, 1976. Chmn. Summer Law Inst., Atlanta, 1981-85; mem. Dem. Party of Ga., Atlanta, 1983—; atty. Vol. Lawyers for Arts, Atlanta, 1981-85. Recipient Service award Inst. Continuing Legal Edn., Athens, Ga., 1981, 86. Mem. ABA, Atlanta Bar Assn. (com. chmn. 1981-85), N.C. Bar Assn., Internat. Bar Assn., Hon. Order Ky. Cols., Phi Alpha Delta (justice, Atlanta 1982-83, emeritus 1983). Clubs: Lawyers, Sporting (Atlanta). Bankruptcy, Contracts commercial, General practice. Home: 1210 Sheridan Rd Atlanta GA 30324 Office: 460 E Paces Ferry Rd Atlanta GA 30305

STANBACK, CLARENCE FREEMAN, JR., lawyer; b. Washington, May 28, 1949; s. Clarence Freeman and Cassie Elzena (Hawkins) S.; m. Denise Carol Rutherford, May 20, 1978; 1 child, Clarence F. III. BA in Econs., Tufts U., 1972, BSEE, 1972; JD, George Washington U., 1976. Bar: Va. 1977, D.C. 1979, Md. 1981. Mem. tech. mktg. staff Gen. Electric Co., Phila., 1972; proposition engr. Gen. Electric Co., Lynn, Mass., 1972-73; patent engr. Gen. Electric Co., Arlington, Va., 1973-77, patent atty., 1977; sole practice Arlington, 1977—. Bd. dirs. Legal Services of No. Va., Arlington, Family Stress Services, Washington; mem. Guest House/Friends of Women Prisoners, Alexandria, Va., 1982-84. Recipient Class Prize of 1898, Tufts U., 1970. Mem. ABA, Am. Trial Lawyers Assn., Va. Trial Lawyers Assn. Avocations: tennis, cards, dancing. State civil litigation, Personal injury, Patent. Home: 104 Alexandria Dr Oxon Hill MD 20745 Office: 2009 N 14th St Suite 307 Arlington VA 22201

STANCATI, JOSEPH ANTHONY, lawyer; b. Endicott, N.Y., Sept. 9, 1947; s. Joseph Frank and Ann (Conti) S.; m. Diane E. Engel, Dec. 9, 1972; children: Joseph Michael, Michael Benjamin, Jennifer Ann. BA, LeMoyne Coll., 1969; JD, U. Toledo, 1972. Bar: Ohio 1972, U.S. Dist. Ct. (no. dist.) Ohio 1972. Atty. Toledo Legal Aid Soc., 1972-74; asst. prosecutor Lucas County, Toledo, 1974-77; chief prosecutor atty. gen. office State of Ohio, Columbus, 1977-79; counsel Owens Corning Fiberglas Co., Toledo, 1979-86; ptnr. Cooper, Straub, Walinski & Cramer, Toledo, 1986—. Editor in chief U. Toledo Law Rev., 1972. Mem. ABA, Ohio Bar Assn., Toledo Bar Assn. Avocations: sailing, tennis, golf. Antitrust, Federal civil litigation, State civil litigation. Home: 2637 Barrington Toledo OH 43606 Office: Cooper Straub et al 900 Adams Toledo OH 43624

STANDEL, RICHARD REYNOLD, JR., communications company executive, lawyer; b. N.Y.C., Nov. 20, 1936; s. Richard Reynold and Antoinette (Pfinder) S.; m. Elizabeth Hughes, Dec. 5, 1963. AB, Columbia U., 1956, JD, 1959; LLM, NYU, 1972. Bar: N.Y. 1960, Colo. 1974, Tenn. 1978. Assoc. Wickes, Riddell, Bloomer, Jacobs & McGuire, N.Y.C., 1959-64; assoc. gen. counsel Manville Corp., Denver, 1964-71; dir. acquisitions and divestments Johns-Manville Corp., Denver, 1972-76; v.p., gen. counsel, sec. No Telecom Inc., Nashville, 1976—. Bd. dirs. Nashville Urban League, 1984-86, Tenn. Bus. Roundtable, Nashville, 1985-87. Ford Found. scholar, 1952-56; Columbia U. Law Sch. scholar, 1956-59. Mem. Am. Soc. Corp. Secs., ABA, Tenn. Bar Assn. Presbyterian. Club: Richland Country (Nashville). Antitrust, General corporate. Office: No Telecom Inc 200 Athens Way Nashville TN 37228

STANDISH, WILLIAM LLOYD, judge; b. Pitts., Feb. 16, 1930; s. William Lloyd and Eleanor (McCargo) S.; m. Marguerite Oliver, June 12, 1963; children: Baird M., N. Graham, James H., Constance S. Bar: Pa. 1957, U.S. Supreme Ct. 1967. Assoc. Reed, Smith, Shaw & McClay, Pitts., 1957-63, ptnr., 1963-80; judge Ct. Common Pleas of Allegheny County (Pa.), 1980—; solicitor Edgeworth Borough Sch. Dist., 1963-66. Bd. dirs. Sewickley (Pa.) Community Ctr., 1981-83, Staunton Farm Found.; corporator Sewickley Cemetary; trustee Mary and Alexander Laughlin Children's Ctr.; trustee Leukemia Soc. Am., 1978-80, trustee western Pa. chpt., 1972-80, Western Pa. Sch. for the Deaf. Recipient Pres. award Leukemia Soc. Am., 1980. Mem. ABA, Pa. Bar Assn., Allegheny County Bar Assn., Am. Judicature Soc., Acad. Trial Lawyers Allegheny County (treas. 1977-78, bd. dirs. 1979-80). State civil litigation, Family and matrimonial. Office: City-County Bldg Suite 626 Pittsburgh PA 15219

STANDRIDGE, RICHARD E., lawyer; b. Camp Chaffee, Ark., Jan. 28, 1953; s. Eldon E. and Nema (Freeman) S.; m. Linda D. Tarpley, Feb. 2, 1985. BS cum laude, Southwest Mo. State U., 1976; JD, U. Mo., Kansas City, 1980. Bar: Mo. 1980, U.S. Dist. Ct. (we. dist.) Mo. 1980. Assoc. Buck, Bohm & Stein P.C., Kansas City, 1980-85, Copilevitz, Bryant, Gray & Jennings P.C., Kansas City, 1985—. Research editor U. Mo., Kansas City Law Rev., 1979. Mem. Friends of the Kansas City Zoo, 1984—, Kansas City NEAR, 1985—, Dem. Victory Coalition, Kansas City, 1985—, bd. dirs., 1986—. Mem. Mo. Bar Assn. (bd. of govs. 1986—, vice chmn. young lawyers council 1986—, rep. to young lawyers council 1984-86), Kansas City Met. Bar Assn. (chmn. assoc. cts. com. 1985—), Comml. Law League Am., Am. Arbitration Assn. (comml. arbitrator 1983—), Phi Delta Phi. Avocations: photography, astronomy. Bankruptcy, State civil litigation, Contracts commercial. Office: Copilevitz Bryant Gray & Jennings PC 1812 Commerce Tower 911 Main Kansas City MO 64105

STANFIELD, JAMES CALEB, lawyer; b. Paris, Ill., Oct. 16, 1923; s. Foster and Smyrna Grace (Guthridge) S.; m. Melissa Lee Shaffner, Oct. 5, 1979; m. Florence Cole Hodge, Dec. 18, 1943; children—Judith Ann Young, James Foster. B.A., Washington and Lee U., 1947, LL.B., J.D., 1948. Bar: Ill. 1949. Asst. atty. gen. Ill., 1952-54; hearing officer Ill. Commerce Commn., 1954-60; sole practice law, Paris, Ill., 1949—; v.p. Nelson Title Co. Bd. dirs. Paris Pub. Library, 1958-68, pres., 1968-69; mem. Edgar County Republican Central Com., 1954—, county chmn., 1954-64. Served with USN, 1943-46. Mem. Ill. Bar Assn., Edgar County Bar Assn. (pres. 1967-68), Am. Legion. Presbyterian. Clubs: Mo. Athletic (St. Louis); Elks. General practice, Family and matrimonial, Probate. Home: Rural Route 2 Box 313 Paris IL 61944 Office: 227 W Court St Paris IL 61944

STANFIELD, JOHN EDMISTON, lawyer; b. Laramie, Wyo., June 22, 1934; s. Kenneth Edison and Marie Lois (Lovercheck) S.; m. Randi Helvard, Jan. 15, 1959 (div.); m. 2d Leila Rita Bruno, Dec. 18, 1970; children—Kenneth, Kristina Maj; stepchildren—Jeffrey, Jennifer. B.S. in Law, U. Wyo., 1956, J.D., 1960. Bar: Wyo. sup. ct. 1960, U.S. Dist. Ct. Wyo. 1960, U.S. Ct. Apls. (10th cir.) 1963, U.S. Sup. Ct. 1969. Assoc., Pence & Millett, Laramie, 1960-63; ptnr. Smith, Stanfield & Scott and predecessors, Laramie, 1963—; lectr. evidence and trial practice U. Wyo., 1965—; lectr. in field; asst. atty. City Laramie, 1963—. Served to capt. U.S. Army, 1957-59. Mem. Wyo. Trial Lawyers Assn. (pres. 1977, dir. 1970—), Wyo. State Bar., Assn. Trial Lawyers Am. (wyo. state del. 1976—), Albany County Bar, Assn (pres. 1967). Republican. Clubs: Laramie Country, Fox Acres Country, Red Feather Lakes, Colo., Mason, Elks. Contbr. articles in field to profl. jours. Federal civil litigation, State civil litigation, Personal injury. Office: 416 S 25th St Laramie WY 82070

STANFIELD, SALLY FITE, lawyer; b. Balt., Feb. 1, 1956; d. Edward Fite Jr. and Virginia Brantly (Tolzman) S. BA, Western Md. Coll., 1978; JD, Washington and Lee U., 1981. Bar: Md. 1981, Wash. 1983, U.S. Dist. Ct. (we. dist.) Wash. 1983. Dep. pros. atty. Office of King County Pros. Atty., Seattle, 1984—. Mem. Wash. Council on Crime and Delinquency. Mem. Md. Bar Assn., Wash. State Bar Assn. Avocations: lacrosse, coaching recreational youth programs. Criminal. Office: Office of King County Pros Atty W554 King County Courthouse Seattle WA 98104

STANFORD, KENNETH CHARLES, lawyer; b. San Diego, Nov. 7, 1955; s. Charles Hiljmar and Louise Jane (Yankovic) S. BA, U. Ariz., 1976, JD, 1979. Sole practice Tucson, 1980-85; ptnr. Duncan & Stanford, Tucson, 1985—. Active Big Brothers/Big Sisters Orgn., Tucson, 1984, Hands Across Am., Ariz., 1986. Mem. ABA, Pima County Bar Assn. (pres. young lawyers sect. 1985-86, Disting. Service award 1986), Assn. Trial Lawyers Am., Ariz. Young Lawyers Assn. (exec. council). Democrat. Personal injury, Family and matrimonial. Office: Duncan & Stanford 548 E Speedway Tucson AZ 85703

STANGER, DOUGLAS SCOTT, lawyer; b. Bklyn., Sept. 12, 1956; s. Philip and Faye (Laster) S.; m. Gail Herring, Dec. 15, 1978; chilren: Alan Doniel, Ari Hillel. B in Psychology, Tel Aviv U., 1977; B in Religion, Emory U., 1978; BA in Pschology and Religion; JD, Benjamin N. Cordoza Sch. Law, 1981. Bar: N.Y. 1982, N.J. 1982, U.S. Dist. Ct. N.J. 1982, U.S. Ct. Appeals 1982, U.S. Supreme Ct. 1986. Law clk. to judge N.J. Tax Ct., Atlantic City, 1981-82; ptnr. Blatt, Mairone, Biel, Zlotnick, Feinberg & Griffith, Atlantic City, 1982—. Bd. dirs. Jewish Family Services, Ventnor, N.J., 1982, N.J. Regional Adv. Bd. of Anti-Defamation League, Livingston, 1985-86; mem. South Jersey Adv. Council Anti-Defamation League, Sewel, 1984—; mem. N.J. panel trustees, 1986. Strumph scholar Temple E'Manuel of Lynbrook, N.Y., 1977. Mem. ABA, N.J. Bar Assn., Atlantic County Bar Assn. Bankruptcy, Real property, State and local taxation. Office: Blatt Mairone Biel Zlotnick Feinberg & Griffith 3201 Atlantic Ave Atlantic City NJ 08401

STANHAUS, JAMES STEVEN, lawyer; b. Evergreen Park, Ill., Oct. 22, 1945; s. Wilfrid Xavier and Mary (Komanecky) S.; m. Naomi Evelyn Miller, June 27, 1971; 1 child, Heather. AB magna cum laude, Georgetown U., 1966; JD magna cum laude, Harvard U., 1970. Bar: Ill. 1970, U.S. Dist. Ct. (no. dist.) Ill. 1970. Assoc. Mayer, Brown & Platt, Chgo., 1971-76, ptnr., 1977—. Mem. ABA, Ill. Bar Assn., Chgo. Bar Assn., Chgo. Council Lawyers, Chgo. Estate Planning Council, Phi Beta Kappa. Club: River (Chgo.). Avocations: computers, tennis, racquetball. Estate planning, Probate, Personal income taxation. Office: Mayer Brown & Platt 190 S LaSalle St Chicago IL 60603

STANISCI, THOMAS WILLIAM, lawyer; b. Bkln., Nov. 16, 1928; s. Vito and Angela Marie (Martino) S.; m. Catherine Ellen Cullen, June 4, 1955; children—Thomas, Marianne, Ellen, William, Peter. B.A., St. John's Coll. Men, 1949, J.D., 1953, postgrad., 1954. Bar: N.Y. 1953, U.S. Dist. Ct. (so. and ea. dists.) N.Y. 1956; diplomate Am. Bd. Profl. Liability Attys. Assoc. Diblas Marasco & Simone, White Plains, N.Y., 1954-60; mem. Simone Brant & Stanisci, White Plains, 1960-66; mem. Shayne Dachs Stanisci & Harwood, Mineola, N.Y., 1966-83; sr. mem. Shayne Dachs Stanisci & Corker, Mineola, 1983—; lectr. Practising Law Inst., 1975-79; instr., lectr. Am. Mgmt. Assn., 1976-77; guest instr. Adelphi U., Hofstra U., 1975-79. Served with U.S. Army, 1950-52. Mem. Am. Arbitration Assn., Nassau Suffolk Trial Lawyers Assn. (dir., 1978—), Nassau County Bar Assn., Assn. Trial Lawyers Am., Contbr. articles in field. State civil litigation, Insurance, Personal injury. Office: 1501 Franklin Ave Mineola NY 11501

STANKEE, GLEN ALLEN, lawyer; b. Clinton, Iowa, Sept. 27, 1953; s. Glen Earl and Marilyn Jean (Clark) S.; m. Carol Ann Prowe, Feb. 19, 1984. BSBA, Drake U., 1975; MBA, Mich. State U., 1977; JD, U. Detroit, 1979; LLM in Taxation, U. Miami, 1983. Bar: Mich. 1980, U.S. Dist. Ct. (ea. dist.) Mich. 1980, U.S. Ct. Appeals (6th cir.) 1980, U.S. Tax Ct. 1980, Fla. 1981, U.S. Ct. Appeals (11th cir.) 1981, U.S. Dist. Ct. (so. dist.) Fla. 1982, U.S. Dist. Ct. (mid. dist.) 1984; CPA, Fla. Assoc. Raymond & Dillon P.C., Detroit, 1980-81; assoc. Raymond & Dillon P.C., West Palm Beach, Fla., 1981-85, prin., 1985-86; prin. Raymond & Dillon P.C., Ft. Lauderdale, Fla., 1987—; instr. Person/Wolinsky CPA Rev., West Palm Beach, 1985—. Contbr. articles to profl. jours. Mem. ABA, Fed. Bar Assn., Fla. Bar Assn., Mich. Bar Assn., Am. Assn. Attys./CPA's, Am. Inst. CPA's, Fla. Inst. CPA's, Palm Beach County Bar Assn., South Fla. JD/MBA Assn. (treas. 1985—). Republican. Avocation: golf. Federal and state tax litigation (civil & criminal), Federal civil litigation, Corporate taxation. Office: Raymond & Dillon PC 1 E Broward Blvd Suite 1705 Fort Lauderdale FL 33301

STANLEY, BRIAN KEITH, lawyer; b. South Bend, Ind., Dec. 19, 1950; s. Milton L. Jr and Phyllis L. (Lillie) S. BA with distinction, Ariz. State U., 1972; JD cum laude, Cornell U., 1976. Bar: Ariz. 1976, U.S. Dist. Ct. Ariz. 1976, U.S. Ct. Appeals (9th cir.) 1979. Law clk. to presiding justice Ariz. Superior Ct., Phoenix, 1976-77; assoc. Jones, Hunter & Lerch, Phoenix, 1977-79; sole practice Phoenix, 1980—. Sec./treas. Ariz. Christian Lawyers' Fellowship, Phoenix; bd. dirs. Christian Conciliation Service Cen. Ariz., Phoenix. Mem. ABA, Maricopa County Bar Assn. Republican. Episcopalian. Real property, Bankruptcy. Office: 122 W Osborn Rd Phoenix AZ 85013

STANLEY, BRUCE MCLAREN, lawyer; b. Cleve., May 13, 1948; s. Willard Cyrus and Isabel (Anderson) S.; m. Pamela Soderholm, June 23, 1984; children: Bruce Jr., Willard Charles. BA with high honors, Coll. William and Mary, 1970; JD, U. Va., 1974. Bar: Fla. 1974, U.S. Supreme Ct. 1978, U.S. Dist. Ct. (so. dist.) Fla. 1974, U.S. Dist. Ct. (mid. dist.) U.S. Ct. Appeals (5th cir.) 1975, U.S. Ct. Appeals (11th cir.) 1982. Assoc. Bradford, Williams, McKay, Kimbrell, Hamann & Jennings, Miami, Fla., 1974-79; ptnr. Blackwell, Walker, Gray, Powers, Flick, & Hoehl, Miami, 1979-85; assoc. Henderson, Franklin, Starnes & Holt, 1985—. Mem. Fla. Bar Assn. (cert. in trial civil law 1984), Dade County Bar Assn. (bd. dirs. 1982-85), Dade County Def. Bar (bd. dirs. 1980-85), ABA, Lee County Bar Assn. Presbyterian. Federal civil litigation, State civil litigation, Personal injury. Home: 2506 McGregor Blvd Fort Myers FL 33901-5828 Office: Franklin Starnes & Holt 2100 2d St PO Box 280 Fort Myers FL 33902-0280

STANLEY, JUSTIN ARMSTRONG, lawyer; b. Leesburg, Ind., Jan. 2, 1911; s. Walter H. and Janet (Armstrong) S.; m. Helen Leigh Fletcher, Jan. 3, 1938; children: Janet Van Wie Hoffmann, Melinda Fletcher Douglas, Justin Armstrong, Harlan Fletcher. A.B., Dartmouth Coll., 1933, A.M. (hon.), 1952, LL.D. (hon.), 1983; LL.B., Columbia U., 1937; LL.D. (hon.), John Marshall Law Sch., 1976, Suffolk U., 1976, Vt. Law Sch., 1977, Norwich U., 1977, Ind. U., 1981, Oklahoma City U., 1981. Bar: Ill. 1937. Since practiced in Chgo.; assoc. Isham, Lincoln & Beale, 1937-48, partner, 1948-66; partner Mayer, Brown & Platt, 1967—; v.p. Dartmouth Coll., 1952-54; asst. prof. law Chgo.-Kent Coll. Law, 1938-43, prof., 1943-46; Dir. Charles H. Shaw Co., Ellsworth Fin. Corp.; Pub. mem. disputes sect. Nat. War Labor Bd., 1943-44. Trustee Presbyn.-St. Luke's Hosp., Wells Coll., 1960-69, Rockford Coll., 1962-70; trustee Ill. Childrens Home and Aid Soc., pres., 1963-64. Served as lt. USNR, 1944-46. Recipient medal for excellence Columbia U. Law Sch., 1984. Fellow Am. Bar Found., Am. Coll. Trial Lawyers; mem. ABA (chmn. pub. utility sect. 1970-71, ho. of dels. 1973—, pres. 1976-77, commn. on professionalism. 1985-86, ABA medal 1986), Fed. Energy Bar Assn., Chgo. Bar Assn. (pres. 1967-68), Ill. Bar Assn. (Disting. Service award 1986), Alumni Council Dartmouth (pres. 1952), Am. Law Inst., Am. Judicature Soc., Alpha Delta Phi. Episcopalian. Clubs: Chicago (Chgo.), University (Chgo.), Legal (Chgo.), Commercial (Chgo.), Commonwealth (Chgo.), Law (Chgo.); Wausaukee (Wis.); Cosmos (Washington); Univ. (N.Y.C.), Century Assn. (N.Y.C.); R & A (St. Andrews, Scotland). State civil litigation, Real property, General practice. Home: 1630 Sheridan Rd Wilmette IL 60091 Office: 231 S LaSalle St Chicago IL 60604

STANLEY, KEITH EUGENE, lawyer; b. Syracuse, N.Y., Mar. 15, 1951; s. Eugene Ridgway and Margeret Alice (Lake) S. BS, Mich. State U., 1973; JD, U. Mich., 1981. Bar: D.C. 1981. Atty. Office of Chief Counsel, IRS, Washington, 1981—. Mem. ABA, Fed. Bar Assn. Avocation: athletics. Corporate taxation. Office: IRS Office of Chief Counsel CC:LR:2 1111 Constitution Ave NW Washington DC 20226

STANLEY, SABRINA ANN, lawyer; b. Jefferson City, Mo., Aug. 4, 1956; d. Arthur F. and Jean T. (Powers) S.; m. Steven P. Howarth, Oct. 12, 1985. BA, Ind. U., 1978; JD, Georgetown U., 1981. Bar: D.C. 1981, Calif. 1983. Assoc. McKenna, Conner & Cuneo, Washington and Los Angeles, 1981-83; counsel FMC Corp., San Jose, Calif., 1983—. Named Twin Honoree YWCA, San Jose, 1986. Mem. D.C. Bar Assn. Calif. Bar Assn., Am. Corp. Counsel Assn. (chmn. young lawyers com. 1986—). Labor, Government contracts and claims, State civil litigation. Home: 2444 Villanueva Way Mountain View CA 94040

STANLEY, WILLIAM, JR., lawyer; b. Laurel, Md., Sept. 30, 1919; s. William and Mary Jane (Gilbert) S.; m. Margaret Fleming Bell, Jan. 15, 1943; m. Janina Hanin, Jan. 14, 1969; children—Amy (Anthony), William III, Robert H., Margaret S. B.A., Princeton U., 1941, J.D., Harvard U., 1944. Bar: D.C. 1948, Md. 1948. Law clk. U.S. Ct. Appeals D.C. 1948; assoc. Covington & Burling, Washington, 1948-58, ptnr., 1958—. Served with USNR, 1942-45. Mem. ABA, D.C. Bar Assn. Democrat. Episcopalian. Clubs: Met., City Tavern, Pisces, Md. Probate, Real property, General corporate. Office: 1201 Pennsylvania Ave NW PO Box 7566 Washington DC 20044

STANTON, ELIZABETH MCCOOL, lawyer; b. Lansdale, Pa., Apr. 12, 1947; d. Leo J. and Helen M. (Gillooly) McCool; m. Robert J. Stanton, June 13, 1970; children: Jonathan R., James Alfred. BBA, Drexel U., 1969; JD magna cum laude, U. Houston, 1979. Bar: Tex. 1979, U.S. Dist. Ct. (so. dist.) Tex. 1980, Ohio 1982, U.S. Dist. Ct. (so. dist.) Ohio 1983. Assoc. Friedman & Chaffin, Houston, 1979-80, Law Offices of Elaine Brady, Houston, 1980-81, Moots, Cope & Kizer Co., L.P.A., Columbus, Ohio, 1982—. Campaign worker Susan Walker for Judge Campaign, Columbus, 1983; mem. legal com. Met. Womens Ctr., Columbus, 1983-84. Drexel Bd. Trustees scholar, 1965-67, Internat. Ladies Garment Workers Union scholar, 1965-69. Mem. ABA, Ohio Bar Assn., Columbus Bar Assn., Nat. Assn. Women Lawyers, Plantiff Employment Lawyers Assn., Women's Lawyers Franklin County, Phi Kappa Phi, Beta Gamma Sigma. Democrat. Roman Catholic. Labor, State civil litigation, Administrative and regulatory. Office: Moots Cope & Kizer Co LPA 3600 Olentangy River Rd Columbus OH 43214

STANTON, GEORGE PATRICK, JR., lawyer; b. Fairmont, W.Va., Nov. 21, 1933; s. George Patrick and Wilma Roberta (Everson) S.; m. Shirley Jean Champ, Sept. 3, 1956; children—George Patrick, Edward Scott. B.S. in Bus. Adminstrn., Fairmont Coll., 1956; M.B.A. in Fin., U. Dayton, 1969; J.D., U. Balt., 1977. Bar: Md. 1978, U.S. Dist. Ct. Md. 1978, W.Va. 1979, U.S. Dist. Ct. (so. dist.) W.Va. 1979, U.S. Dist. Ct. (no. dist.) W.Va. 1980, U.S. Ct. Appeals (4th cir.) 1985.Auditor 1st Nat. Bank Fairmont, 1955-61; asst. cashier S.C. Nat. Bank, Columbia, 1961-64; sr. systems analyst Chase Manhattan Bank, N.Y.C., 1964-65; asst. v.p. Winters Nat. Bank, Dayton, Ohio, 1965-69, Md. Nat. Bank, Balt., 1969-74; v.p. Equitable Trust Co., Balt., 1974-79; gen. ptnr. Stanton & Stanton Attys. at Law, Fairmont, 1979—; staff sect. leader, mem. faculty Sch. for Bank Adminstrn. U. Wis.-Madison, 1978—. Treas. Mountaineer Area council Boy Scouts Am., Fairmont, 1982—; pres. Three Rivers Coal Festival, Inc., Fairmont, 1984-85, pres., 1985—; mem. adv. bd. Inst. for Living, Fairmont, 1983—. Mem. ABA, Assn. Trial Lawyers Am., Comml. Law League Am., W.Va. State Bar Assn., Marion County Bar Assn., Md. State Bar Assn., W.Va. Trial Lawyers Assn., Marion County C. of C. (bd. dirs. 1983—), Fairmont State Coll. Alumni Assn. (bd. dirs. 1982—). Club: Fairmont Field. Lodges: Rotary, Masons. Home: 2 West Hills Dr Fairmont WV 26554 Office: Stanton & Stanton Suite 707 First National Bank Bldg Fairmont WV 26554

STANTON, LOUIS LEE, judge; b. N.Y.C., Oct. 1, 1927; s. Louis Lee and Helen Parsons (La Fétra) S.; m. Berit Elconora Rask; children: I Lee, Susan Helen Benedict, Gordon R., Fredrik S. BA, Yale U., 1950; JD, U. Va., 1955. Assoc. Davis Polk Wardwell Sunderland & Kiendl, N.Y.C., 1955-66; assoc. Carter, Ledyard & Milburn, N.Y.C., 1966-67, ptnr., 1967-85; judge

U.S. Dist. Ct. (so. dist.) N.Y., N.Y.C., 1985—. Served to 1st lt. USMCR, 1950-52. Fellow Am. Coll. Trial Lawyers, N.Y. Bar Found. *

STANTON, ROGER D., lawyer; b. Waterville, Kans., Oct. 4, 1938; s. George W. and Helen V. (Peterson) S.; m. Judith L. Duncan, Jan. 27, 1962; children: Jeffrey B., Brady D., Todd A. AB, U. Kans., 1960, JD, 1963. Bar: Kans. 1963, U.S. Dist. Ct. Kans. 1963, U.S. Ct. Appeals (10th cir.) 1972, U.S. Supreme Ct. 1973. Assoc. Stanley, Schroeder, Weeks, Thomas & Lysaught, Kansas City, Kans., 1963-68; ptnr. Weeks, Thomas, Lysaught, Bingham & Johnston, Kansas City, 1968-72; bd. dirs. Weeks, Thomas & Lysaught, 1969-80; bd. dirs., chmn. exec. com., 1981-82; ptnr. Stinson, Mag & Fizzell, 1983—. Active Boy Scouts Am., 1973-79; pres. YMCA Youth Football Club, 1980-82. Fellow Am. Coll. Trial Lawyers (state chmn. 1984-86); mem. Internat. Assn. Def. Counsel, Def. Research Inst. (state co-chmn., Exceptional Performance award 1979), Kans. Bar Assn. (Pres.'s award 1982), Kans. Assn. Def. Counsel (pres. 1977-78), U. Kans. Sch. Law Alumni Assn. (bd. dirs. 1972-75). Chmn. bd. editors Jour. Kans. Bar Assn., 1975-83; contbr. articles to legal jours. Federal civil litigation, State civil litigation. Office: The Mast Bldg 7500 W 110th St Overland Park KS 66210

STANWYCK, STEVEN JAY, lawyer; b. N.Y.C., Sept. 21, 1944; m. Joan Mary Ciapciak, Jan. 18, 1969; children: Kirsten Jane, Michael Peter, Devin Marie, Mark Peter, Joseph Robert. BA, U. Denver, 1967; MBA, U. Calif.-Berkeley, 1971, JD, 1970. Bar: N.Y. 1972, Calif., 1971, U.S. Dist. Ct. (cen. dist.) Calif. 1981, U.S. Ct. Appeals (9th cir.) 1971, U.S. Tax Ct. 1982, U.S. Supreme Ct. 1980. Assoc. Dewey, Ballantine, Bushby, Palmer & Wood, N.Y.C., 1971-73; assoc. Kadison, Pfaelzer, Woodard, Quinn & Rossi, Los Angeles, 1973-74; ptnr. Steven J. Stanwyck, P.C., Los Angeles, 1974—. Corp. adv. bd. Nat. Ctr. for Hyperactive Children. Served with AUS, 1962-64. Recipient Calif. Real Estate Scholarship Found. award 1971; Phi Alpha Delta Nat. scholar, 1970. Mem. Assn. Bar City N.Y., Los Angeles County Bar Assn., N.Y. State Bar Assn., Am. Mgmt. Assn., Calif. Bar Assn., Am. Judicature Soc., ABA, Am. Mgmt. Assn., Phi Alpha Delta. Episcopalian. Club: Regency (Los Angeles). Corporate finance, Commercial, Criminal and civil litigation. Office: 880 W 1st St Suite 300 Los Angeles CA 90012

STANZIOLA, JAMES ALAN, lawyer; b. Burlington, Vt., June 29, 1955; s. Thomas Neil and Patricia (Blaise) S.; m. Lori Anderson, May 25, 1985. BA, U. Vt., 1977; JD, Drake U., 1981. Bar: Iowa 1981, Mo. 1986. Examiner Iowa Dept. Banking, Des Moines, 1981-82; advanced underwriter Cen. Life, Des Moines, 1982-85; corp. gen. counsel B.C. Christopher Securities Co., Kansas City, Mo., 1985—. Counselor Polk County Juvenile Ct., Des Moines, 1982; arbitrator Better Bus. Bur., Des Moines, 1984; mediator Polk County Mediation Ctr., Des Moines, 1982. Mem. ABA, Mo. Bar Assn., Kansas City Bar Assn. Republican. Roman Catholic. Avocations: running, musician. Securities, General corporate. Home: 115 E 58th St Kansas City MO 64113

STAPLES, LYLE NEWTON, lawyer; b. Radford, Va., Feb. 16, 1945; s. Lester Lyle and Velma Jean (King) S.; m. Christie Mercedes Carr, Feb. 1, 1971; children—Scott Andrew, John Randolph, Brian Matthew, Melissa Ann. B.A., U. Md., 1967, J.D., 1972; LL.M. in Taxation, Georgetown U., 1977. Bar: Md. 1973, U.S. Supreme Ct. 1978, U.S. Tax Ct. 1981, U.S. Dist. Ct. Md. 1981, U.S. Ct. Appeals (4th cir.) 1981. Tax law specialist IRS, Washington, 1972-77; assoc. Hessey & Hessey, Balt., 1978-82, Rosenstock, Burgee & Welty, Frederick, Md., 1982-84; sole practice, Hampstead, Md., 1984—; vis. asst. prof. Towson State U., Md., 1981-82; Active, Carroll County ARC, Md., Hampstead Bus. Assn., Hampstead Elem. Sch. PTA, North Carroll Middle Sch. PTO, Greenmount, Md., Balt. Council Fgn. Affairs, Inc. Served with U.S. Army, 1968-69, Vietnam. Mem. ABA, Md. Bar Assn. Democrat. Methodist. General practice, Estate planning, General corporate. Home: 4304 Royal Ave Hampstead MD 21074 Office: 926 S Main St Hampstead MD 21074

STAPLETON, JOHN OWEN, lawyer; b. Montgomery, Ala., July 24, 1951; s. Max O. Stapleton and Margaret (Lois) Gardner; m. Andrea Carole White, Apr. 1973 (div. June 1975); 1 child, Stefani Michele; m. Nancy Jean Corbett, Sept. 20, 1980; 1 child, Kellie Nichole. BS, U. of Montevallo, 1976; JD, Samford U., 1980. Bar: Fla. 1981, U.S. Dist. Ct. (no. dist.) Fla. 1981, U.S. Ct. Appeals (11th cir.) 1982, U.S. Ct. Appeals (Fed. cir.) 1985. Assoc. Shimek & Sutherland P.A., Pensacola, Fla., 1981-83, Dye Law Firm P.A., Pensacola, 1984; sole practice Pensacola, 1984—; contract atty. Local 1960, Pensacola, 1984, guardian ad litem program 1st Jud. Cir., 1984—. Mem. ABA, Fla. Bar Assn., Escambia-Santa Rosa Bar Assn., Assn. Trial Lawyers Am. Democrat. Avocations: fishing, woodworking, boardgaming, reading, World War II ETO info. Labor, Civil rights, Juvenile. Office: 16 W La Rua St Pensacola FL 32501

STAPLETON, WALTER KING, judge; b. Cuthbert, Ga., June 2, 1934; s. Theodore Newton and Elizabeth Grantland (King) S.; m. Patricia Chappelle Ames, Oct. 27, 1956; children—Russell K., Theodore N., Teryl J. B.A., Princeton, 1956; LL.B., Harvard, 1959; LL.M., U. Va., 1984. Bar: Del. Asso. mem. firm Morris, Nichols, Arsht & Tunnell, Wilmington, Del., 1959-65; partner Morris, Nichols, Arsht & Tunnell, 1966-70; judge U.S. Dist. Ct. Del., Wilmington, 1970-85; chief judge U.S. Dist. Ct. Del., 1983-85; judge U.S. Ct. Appeals (3d cir.), 1985—; Dep. atty. gen., Del., 1964; mem. Jud. Conf. U.S., 1984-85. Bd. dirs. Am. Bapt. Chs., U.S.A., 1978. Baptist. Jurisprudence. Office: Federal Bldg Wilmington DE 19801

STAR, RONALD H., lawyer; b. N.Y.C., Feb. 29, 1956; s. Irving and Lita (Friedman) S.; m. Faye Tiano, Aug. 15, 1982. Bar: Calif. 1980. Ptnr. Howard, Rice et al, San Francisco, 1980—. Mem. ABA, Calif. Bar Assn., Phi Beta Kappa. Democrat. Computer, Securities, General corporate. Office: Howard Rice et al 3 Emarcadero Ctr #700 San Francisco CA 94111

STARCEVIC, JOSEPH FRANCIS, lawyer; b. Ottumwa, Iowa, Apr. 19, 1956; s. Francis Joseph and Virgene Elizabeth (Flahive) S.; m. Dixie Lee Reierson, June 21, 1986. AA, Ottumwa Heights Coll., 1975; BA, U. Iowa, 1977, JD, 1981. Bar: Iowa 1981. Trust officer Peoples Bank & Trust Co., Cedar Rapids, 1981-86; staff atty. Teleconnect, Cedar Rapids, 1986—. Mem. ABA, Linn County Bar Assn., Phi Beta Kappa. Republican. Roman Catholic. Lodge: KC. General corporate. Home: 120 2d St SW #2 Cedar Rapids IA 52404 Office: Teleconnect 500 2d Ave SE Cedar Rapids IA 52401

STARING, GRAYDON SHAW, lawyer; b. Deansboro, N.Y., Apr. 9, 1923; s. William Luther and Eleanor Mary (Shaw) S.; m. Joyce Lydia Allum-Poon, Sept. 1, 1949; children: Diana Hilary Agnes, Christopher Paul Norman. Student, Colgate U., 1943-44; A.B., Hamilton Coll., 1947; J.D., U. Calif.-Berkeley, 1951. Bar: Calif. 1952, U.S. Supreme Ct. 1958. Atty. Office Gen. Counsel, Navy Dept., San Francisco, 1952-53; atty. admiralty and shipping sect. U.S. Dept. Justice, San Francisco, 1953-60; assoc. Lillick McHose & Charles, San Francisco, 1960-64, ptnr., 1965—; titulary mem. Internat. Maritime Com.; bd. dirs. Marine Exchange at San Francisco, 1984—, pres. 1986—; instr. pub. speaking Hamilton Coll., 1947-48. Assoc. editor: Am. Maritime Cases, 1966—; contbr. articles to legal jours. Mem. San Francisco Lawyers Com. for Urban Affairs, 1972—; bd. dirs. Legal Aid Soc., San Francisco, 1974—, v.p., 1975-80, pres., 1980-82. Served with USN, 1943-46, comdr. Res. ret. Fellow Am. Bar Found., Am. Coll. Trial Lawyers; mem. ABA (chmn. maritime ins. com. 1975-76, mem. standing com. on admiralty law 1976-82, 86—), Fed. Bar Assn. (pres. San Francisco chpt. 1968), Bar Assn. San Francisco (sec. 1972, treas. 1973), Calif. Acad. Appellate Lawyers, Maritime Law Assn. U.S. (exec. com. 1977—, v.p. 1980-84, pres. 1984-86), World Trade Club San Francisco, Mayor's San Francisco Shanghai Friendship Com. Club: Propeller of U.S. Republican. Episcopalian. Admiralty, Insurance, General Appellate. Home: 195 San Anselmo Ave San Francisco CA 94127 Office: Two Embarcadero Ctr Suite 2600 San Francisco CA 94111

STARK, FRANKLIN CULVER, lawyer; b. Unityville, S.D., Apr. 16, 1915; s. Fred H. and Catherine (Culver) S.; m. Alice C. Churchill, Sept. 16, 1941 (dec. May 1975); children: Margaret C., Wallace C., Judith C., Franklin Culver; m. Carlyn Kaiser Stark, July 18, 1976. J.D., Northwestern U., 1940; A.B., Dakota Wesleyan U., 1937, LL.D., 1959. Bar: Ill. 1940, U.S. Supreme Ct. 1945, U.S. Tax Ct. 1945, U.S. Ct. Appeals (10th cir.) 1945, Calif. 1946; cert. taxation law specialist, Calif. Assoc. firm Sidley, McPherson, Austin & Burgess, Chgo., 1940-41, Fitzgerald, Abbott & Beardsley, Oakland, Calif., 1946-47; sr. mem. firm Stark, Wells, Rahl, Field & Schwartz, Oakland, 1947—; lectr. comml. law U. Calif. Sch. Bus., 1946-66. Editor: Ill. Law Rev, 1939-40; Contbr. articles to legal publs. Staff Office Gen. Counsel, OPA, Washington, 1941-42; Bd. dirs. Merritt Peralta Found., Claremont Sch. Theology, Dakota Wesleyan U., Fred Finch Youth Center, 1970-82, Calif.-Nev. United Meth. Found., 1974-80, Oakland Meth. Found., 1952-82; chmn. bd. trustees Calif.-Nev. Meth. Homes, 1966-73; pres. Oakland Council of Chs., 1954-56; charter mem. World Peace Through Law Center; nat. pres. Campaign for UN Reform. Served with USNR, 1942-45. Named Alumnus of Year for notable achievement Dakota Wesleyan U., 1966. Mem. Am., Calif., Alameda County bar assns., Oakland C. of C., Am. Trial Lawyers Assn., Phi Kappa Phi, Pi Kappa Delta, Phi Alpha Delta, Order Coif. Methodist. Clubs: Lakeview (Oakland); Commonwealth (San Francisco). Lodges: Masons; Shriners. Estate planning, Probate, Estate taxation. Home: 333 Wayne Ave Apt E Oakland CA 94606 Office: Stark Wells Rahl Field & Schwartz 1999 Harrison St Suite 1300 Oakland CA 94612 also: Peri Exec Centre Suite 900 2033 N Main St Walnut Creek CA 94596

STARK, KELLY SHIRA, lawyer; b. Ft. Warren, Wyo., Nov. 23, 1942; d. Malcolm D. and June (Buxton) Gish. BA, Tex. Tech U., 1965, MA, 1966; JD, Memphis State U., 1982. Bar: Tenn. 1982, U.S. Dist. Ct. Tenn. 1982. Prof. U. Oreg., Memphis State U. and others, Eugene, Oreg. and St. Louis, 1966-76; mem. Towery Press, Inc., Memphis, 1976-79; sole practice Memphis, 1982-83; ptnr. Dice, Burson & Stark, Memphis, 1983-86, Bernstein, Bernstein, McLean, Stark & Robinson, Memphis, 1986—; prof. law Memphis State U., 1982-85, mgmt. skills evaluator, 1986—. Mem. Vollintine-Evergreen Community Assn., Memphis, 1985—. Mem. ABA, Memphis-Shelby County Bar Assn., Tenn. Trial Lawyers Assn., Assn. Women Attys. (treas. 1984-86), LWV, ACLU, NOW. Avocations: flower growing, reading, camping, water skiing. Family and matrimonial, Probate, State civil litigation. Office: Bernstein Bernstein McLean et al 5521 Murray Ave Memphis TN 38119

STARK, MAURICE EDMUND, lawyer; b. Ft. Dodge, Iowa, Sept. 22, 1921; s. Max Martin and Lillian Veronica (O'Rourke) S.; m. Mary Murray, Dec. 27, 1952; children—Michelle, Diane, Stephen, Thomas, Julie, David. B.C.S., U. Iowa, 1942, J.D., 1949. Bar: Iowa. Law clk. to judge U.S. Dist. Ct., 1949-50; spl. atty. criminal div. Dept. Justice, Washington, 1951; trial atty. Office Chief Counsel, IRS, N.Y.C., 1951, 53-55; mem. Stark, Crumley & Jacobs, Ft. Dodge, 1955—; mem. Fed. Tax Liaison Com. in Iowa, 1968-82; mem. adv. group Commr. Internal Revenue, 1969-70; Iowa. mem. Midwest Region Liaison Com. with IRS, 1962-71, vice chmn., 1974-76, ABA rep., 1976-80. Sec. Trinity Regional Hosp. of Ft. Dodge, 1973-76. Served as lt., inf. U.S. Army, 1943-46, to capt., 1951-52. Decorated Bronze Star with Oak leaf cluster, Combat Infantry Badge with star; recipient Meritorious Pub. Service award Commr. Internal Revenue, 1971. Mem. Am. Judicature Soc., Webster County Bar Assn. (treas. 1955-62, pres. 1976-77), Iowa State Bar Assn. (chmn. com. taxation 1967-69), ABA, Order Artus, Delta Theta Phi, Beta Gamma Sigma, Omicron Delta Kappa. Roman Catholic. Club: Rotary (pres. club 1966-67). Notes editor Iowa Law Rev., 1948-49. Corporate taxation, Estate taxation, Personal income taxation. Office: Stark Crumley & Jacobs Warden Plaza Fort Dodge IA 50501

STARK, MICHAEL LEE, lawyer, educator; b. Watseka, Ill., Apr. 29, 1936; s. Lee J. and Enid Lucille (Pickett) S.; m. Mary Elizabeth Campbell, Aug. 29, 1958; children—Robert C., Charles H., David M. B.B.A., Miami U., Oxford, Ohio, 1958; J.D., U. Ind., 1961. Bar: Ind. 1961, Ohio 1967. Trust officer A.M. Fletcher Nat. Bank, and Trust, Indpls., 1961-66; v.p. First Nat. Bank, Akron, Ohio, 1966-69; assoc. Roetzel & Andress, Akron, 1969-70, ptnr., from 1970, mng. ptnr., from 1980; now ptnr. Stark & Knoll, Akron; adj. prof. taxation U. Akron, 1981—; lectr. Ohio Continuing Legal Edn. V.p. United Way, Akron, 1970-75. Fellow Am. Coll. Probate Lawyers; mem. Akron Estate Planning Assn., (past pres.), Ohio Bar Assn. (council dels. 1980—), ABA, Akron Pension Council, Akron Probate Ct. Commn. (pres. 1975), Phi Beta Kappa, Beta Alpha Psi, Omicron Delta Kappa. Republican. Mem. Disciples of Christ Ch. Clubs: Cascade (bd. govs. 1983—), Portage (Akron). Probate, Pension, profit-sharing, and employee benefits, Corporate taxation. Office: Stark & Knoll 1512 Ohio Edison Bldg 76 S Main St Akron OH 44308

STARK, RICHARD ALVIN, lawyer; b. Ann Arbor, Mich., Apr. 6, 1921; s. Judson Luther and Evelyn (Briley) S.; m. Barbara Jones, Feb. 5, 1944; children: Susan S. Woglom, Sarah S. Oldham, Margaret S. Worthington, Barbara Stark Baxter. AB, DePauw U., 1943; MBA, Harvard U., 1947; JD, Ind. u., 1948. Bar: N.Y. 1949, Ind. 1948. Assoc. Milbank, Tweed, Hadley & McCloy, N.Y.C., 1948-56, ptnr., 1957—; bd. dirs. Raymark Corp., Trumbull, Conn., Buttonwood Petroleum Corp., Tulsa; chmn. bd. dirs. Savance Corp., San Francisco. Justice Village of Centre Island, Oyster Bay, N.Y., 1981—; vice chmn. L.I. U., N.Y., 1981—; trustee St. Frances Hosp., Roslyn, N.Y., 1986—. Served to lt. (j.g.) USNR, 1943-46. Mem. ABA, N.Y. State Bar Assn., Assn. of Bar of City of N.Y., Am. Law Inst. Clubs: Creek (Locust Valley, N.Y.); Wall St., Downtown Athletic (N.Y.C.); John's Island (Vero Beach, Fla.). Home: 219 Centre Island Rd Oyster Bay NY 11771 Office: Milbank Tweed Hadley & McCloy 1 Chase Manhattan Plaza New York NY 10005

STARK, THOMAS MICHAEL, justice N.Y. Supreme Court; b. Riverhead, N.Y., Feb. 13, 1925; s. John Charles and Mary Ellen (Gaynor) S.; B.S. cum laude, Holy Cross Coll., 1945; LL.B., Harvard U., 1949; m. Jane Claire Crabtree, Dec. 30, 1954; children—Elizabeth Mary, Ellen Gaynor. Admitted to N.Y. bar, 1950; asso. firm Zaleski & Jablonka, Riverhead, 1949-51; individual practice, Riverhead, 1951-63; town atty., Riverhead, 1953; justice of peace, mem. town bd., Riverhead, 1956-57; mem. Riverhead Bd. Edn., 1960-63; judge county ct., County of Suffolk, 1963-68; justice 10th Jud. Dist. Supreme Ct. N.Y., Riverhead, 1969—, assoc. justice appellate term, 1985—; supervising judge Suffolk County Superior Criminal Cts., 1978—; panel discussion leader Ann. Conf. N.Y. State Trial Judges, 1970-81; chmn. criminal law subcom. N.Y. State Trial Judges Benchbook, 1970-75; vice chmn. com. on criminal jury instrns. N.Y. State Office Ct. Adminstrn., 1975—; lectr. N.Y. State Office Ct. Adminstrn., 1977-87; mem. N.Y. State Ct. Facilities Task Force, 1980-84. Mem. exec. bd., v.p. Suffolk County council Boy Scouts Am., 1955-58. Mem. exec. com., co-leader Riverhead, Suffolk County Republican Com., 1961-62. Served as ensign USNR, World War II. Recipient Silver Beaver award Boy Scouts Am., 1957, Disting. Eagle Scout, 1974; named Judge of Yr., Suffolk County Criminal Bar Assn., 1984. Mem. N.Y. State Bar Assn. (chmn. com. evidence 1978-84), Suffolk County Bar Assn. (sec. 1959-62, 3d v.p. 1962-63). Judicial administration. Home: Bay Woods Aquebogue NY 11931 Office: Suffolk County Courthouse Riverhead NY 11901

STARKES, DALE JOSEPH, lawyer; b. New Milford, Conn., Jan. 18, 1953; s. Paul John Cicileo and ElVera (Haunfelder) Starkes; m. Elizabeth Ann Henry, June 18, 1978. BA in History and Eng., Valparaiso U., 1973, JD, 1976. Bar: Ind. 1976, U.S. Dist. Ct. (no. and so. dists.) Ind. 1976. Sole practice Winamac, Ind., 1976—; dep. pros. atty. 59th Jud. Cir., Winamac, Ind., 1982-86; atty. First Nat. Bank of Monetery, Ind., 1984—; pros. atty. 59th Jud. Cir., Winamac, 1976-82, dep. pros. atty. 1982—; staff atty. 1st Nat. Bank Monterey, Ind., 1984—. Mem. ABA, Ind. Bar Assn. (ho. of dels. 1985—), Assn. Trial Lawyers Am. Republican. Lutheran. Avocations: reading, skiing, sailing. Personal injury, Consumer commercial, Banking. Home: Winamac IN 46996 Office: 111 N Monticello St PO Box 134 Winamac IN 46996

STARKMAN, GARY LEE, lawyer; b. Chgo., Sept. 2, 1946; s. Oscar and Sara (Ordman) S. A.B., U. Ill., 1968; J.D. cum laude, Northwestern U., 1971. Bar: Ill. 1971, U.S. Dist. Ct. (no. dist.) Ill. 1972, U.S. Ct. Appeals (7th cir.) 1972, U.S. Supreme Ct. 1974, Trial Bar U.S. Dist. Ct. (no. dist.) Ill. 1982, U.S. Ct. Appeals (3d cir.) 1984, U.S. Ct. Appeals (D.C. cir.) 1984. Asst. U.S. Atty. No. Dist. Ill., 1971-75; gen. counsel, dir. research Citizens for Thompson Campaign Com., 1975-77; counsel to Gov. of Ill., 1977-81; ptnr. Arvey, Hodes, Costello & Burman, Chgo., 1981—, chmn. litigation dept., 1985—; mem. admissions com. U.S. Dist. Ct. (no. dist.) Ill.; mem. Chgo. Crime Commn. State agys. chmn. Jewish United Fund Met. Chgo., 1974-81; mem. community adv. bd. Jr. League of Chgo. Recipient John Marshall award for appellate litigation, Atty. Gen. U.S., 1974, nat. service award Tau Epsilon Phi, 1968; named to Ten Outstanding Young Citizens, Chgo. Jr. C. of C., 1978. Mem. ABA (litigation sect.), Chgo. Bar Assn. (constl. law com.), Decalogue Soc., Chgo. Council of Lawyers, Northwestern U. Law Alumni Assn. (dir.). Co-author textbook: Cases and Comments on Criminal Procedure, 1974, 2d edit., 1980, 3d edit., 1987; contbr. writings to profl. publs., book revs. to periodicals including Chgo. Sun-Times. Federal civil litigation, Criminal, State civil litigation. Office: Suite 3800 180 N La Salle St Chicago IL 60601

STARNES, JAMES WRIGHT, lawyer; b. East St. Louis, Ill., Apr. 3, 1933; s. James Adron and Nell (Short) S.; m. Helen Woods Mitchell, Mar. 29, 1958 (div. 1978); children: James Wright, Mitchell A., William B. II; m. Kathleen Israel, Jan. 26, 1985. Student St. Louis U., 1951-53; LLB, Washington U., St. Louis, 1957. Bar: Mo. 1957, Ill. 1957. Assoc. Stinson, Mag & Fizzell, Kansas City, Mo., 1957-60, ptnr., 1960—; ptnr. Mid-Continent Properties Co., 1959—, Fairview Investment Co., Kansas City, 1971-76, Monticello Land Co., 1973—; sec. Packaging Products Corp., Mission, Kans., 1972—. Bd. dirs. Mo. Assn. Mental Health, 1968-69, Kansas City Assn. Mental Health, 1966-78, pres., 1969-70; bd. dirs. Heed, 1965-73, 78-82, pres., 1966-67, fin. chmn. 1967-68; bd. dirs. Kansas City Halfway House Found., exec. com., 1966-69, pres., 1966; bd. dirs. Joan Davis Sch. for Spl. Edn., 1972—, v.p., 1972-73, 79-80, pres., 1979-82; bd. dirs. Sherwood Ctr. for Exceptional Child, 1977-79, v.p., 1978-79. Served with AUS, 1957. Mem. ABA, Mo. Bar Assn., Kansas City Bar Assn., Kansas City Lawyers Assn. Presbyterian (deacon). Mem. adv. bd. Washington U. Law Quar., 1957—. General corporate, Banking, Contracts commercial. Home: 1246 Huntington Rd Kansas City MO 64113 Office: Stinson Mag & Fizzell 2100 Boatmen's Ctr Kansas City MO 64105

STARNES, OSCAR EDWIN, JR., lawyer; b. Raleigh, N.C., May 3, 1924; s. Oscar and Marion (Fletcher) S.; m. Lida Martin Starnes, July 8, 1978; children by previous marriage—Oscar Edwin, Amy Elizabeth, Jane Marion. B.S., Davidson Coll., 1947; LL.B., U. N.C., 1950. Bar: N.C., 1950. Mem. Van Winkle, Walton & successor firm Van Winkle, Buck, Wall, Starnes & Davis, Asheville, N.C., 1950—, pres., 1973—; corp. counsel City of Asheville, 1958-67; town atty. Town of Biltmore Forest, 1981—. Served with U.S. Army, 1943-46. Decorated Purple Heart. Fellow Am. Coll. Trial Lawyers (state chmn. 1979-80); mem. N.C. Bar Assn., ABA. Democrat. Presbyterian. State civil litigation, Federal civil litigation, Insurance. Office: Van Winkle Buck Wall Starnes & Davis PA 18 Church St Asheville NC 28807

STARR, ISIDORE, lawyer, educator; b. Bklyn., Nov. 24, 1911. B.A., CCNY, 1932; M.A., Columbia U., 1939; LL.B., St. John's U., Jamaica, N.Y., 1936; J.S.D., Bklyn. Law Sch., 1942; Ph.D., New Sch. Social Research, 1957. Bar: N.Y. 1937. Tchr. N.Y.C. high schs., 1934-61; assoc. prof., prof. edn. Queens Coll., 1961-75, emeritus, 1975—; dir. Inst. on Law-Related Edn., Lincoln-Filene Center, Tufts U., 1963; dir. Law Studies Inst., N.Y.C., 1974; mem. adv. bd. LEAP, Constl. Rights Found., Ariz. Ctr. for Law-Related Edn.; cons. in field. Bd. dirs. Phi Alpha Delta Juvenile Justice Program, 1981—. John Hay fellow, 1952-53. Mem. ABA (Isidore Starr award for Spl. Achievement in Law Studies), AAUP, Am. Judicature Soc., Am. Soc. for Legal History, Am. Legal Studies Assn., Nat. Council Social Studies (past pres.), Phi Beta Kappa. (cert. of appreciation 1981). Author: The Lost Generation of Prince Edward County, 1968; The Gideon Case, 1968; The Feiner Case, 1968; The Supreme Court and Contemporary Issues, 1968; The Mapp Case, 1968; The Supreme Court and Contemporary Issues, 1968; Human Rights in the United States, 1969; Living American Documents, 1971; The American Judicial System, 1972; The Idea of Libery, 1978; Justice: Due Process of Law, 1981. Legal education, Juvenile, Legal history. Address: 6043 E Harvard St Scottsdale AZ 85257

STARR, IVAR MILES, lawyer; b. N.Y.C., Sept. 19, 1950; s. Charles S. Scholnicoff and Rosalie (Paletz) Starr. AA, Nassau Community Coll., 1970; BA, Queens Coll., 1972; JD, U. Miami, 1980. Bar: Fla. 1981, U.S. Dist. Ct. (so. dist.) Fla. 1981. Rep. securities sales Aetna Variable Life Ins. Co., Garden City, N.Y., 1973-75; freelance real estate broker New Fairfield, Conn., 1973-79; assoc. Law Offices of Peter Lopez, Miami, Fla., 1981-82, Mills & London P.A., Miami, 1982; sole practice Miami, 1982—; lectr. Dade County (Fla.) Consumer Advs. Office, 1984—. Recipient Outstanding Service award Miami Beach Bd. Realtors, 1986. Mem. ABA, Dade County Bar Assn., Miami Beach Bar Assn. (bd. dirs. 1984—), Econ. Soc. South Fla., Omicron Delta Epsilon, Miami Beach C. of C. (lectr. 1985—), Better Bus. Bur. South Fla. (arbitrator 1984—, cert. of appreciation 1985), Queens Coll. Alumni in South Fla. (chmn. 1986—). Avocations: boating, swimming, music. State civil litigation, General practice, Real property. Home: 5055 Collins Ave #5J Miami Beach FL 33140 Office: 1000 Lincoln Rd Suite 206 Miami Beach FL 33139-2502

STARR, KENNETH WINSTON, judge; b. Vernon, Tex., July 21, 1946; s. William Douglas and Vannie Maude (Trimble) S.; m. Alice Jean Mendell, Aug. 23, 1970; children: Randall Postley, Carolyn Marie. B.A., George Washington U., 1968; M.A., Brown U., 1969; J.D., Duke U., 1973. Bar: Calif. 1973, D.C. 1979, Va. 1979. Law clk. presiding justice U.S. Ct. Appeals (5th cir.), Miami, Fla., 1973-74; assoc. Gibson, Dunn & Crutcher, Los Angeles, 1974-75; law clk. to Chief Justice Warren E. Burger, U.S. Supreme Ct., Washington, 1975-77; assoc., ptnr. Gibson, Dunn & Crutcher, Washington, 1977-81; counselor to atty gen. of U.S. Dept. Justice, Washington, 1981-83; judge U.S. Ct. Appeals (D.C. circuit), Washington, 1983—. Contbr. articles to legal jours. Mem. com. on edn. McLean Citizens Assn., McLean, Va., 1980—; mem. Fairfax County Va. Republican Com., 1979-81; ops. chmn. Fairfax County Rep. Party Dranesville Dist., Va., 1979-80; legal advisor CAB transition team office of pres.-elect, 1980-81, legal advisor SEC transition team, 1980-81. Mem. Am. Judicature Soc., Inst. Jud. Adminstrn., Supreme Ct. Hist. Soc., Calif. Bar Assn., D.C. Bar Assn., Va. Bar Assn., Order of Coif, Phi Delta Phi (Hughes chpt. Man of Yr. 1973). Office: US Courthouse Washington DC 20001 *

STARR, MARK TOBY, lawyer; b. N.Y.C., Apr. 11, 1946; s. Reubin J. and Sylvia (Anfang) S.; m. Renee Reiss, Aug. 16, 1972; children: Steven, David. BSEE, Fairleigh Dickinson U., 1967; MSEE, PolyTech. U., 1971; JD, John Marshall Law Sch., 1975. Bar: Ill. 1975, N.Y. 1976, Pa. 1977, N.J. 1979, Fla. 1979, D.C. 1980. Engr. IBM Corp., Poughkeepsie, N.Y., 1967-71; litigation analyst IBM Corp., White Plains, N.Y., 1975-76; group patent counsel Burroughs Corp., Paoli, Pa., 1976-86; sr. patent counsel Unisys Corp., Blue Bell, Pa., 1986—. Mem. ABA, Pa. Bar Assn., Am. Intellectual Property Law Assn., Phila. Patent Law Assn. Patent, Computer, Trademark and copyright. Home: 8 Kent Ln Paoli PA 19301 Office: Unisys Corp Law Dept PO Box 500 Blue Bell PA 19424

STARR, RICHARD MARC, lawyer; b. Jersey City, Oct. 13, 1951; s. Harry Alan and Carol Bernice (Schustrin) S. AB, Harvard U., 1973; JD, Cath. U., 1979; LLM, Georgetown U., 1981. Bar: D.C. 1979, N.J. 1981, N.Y. 1983. Atty. Securities & Exchange Commn., Washington, 1979-83; assoc. Paul, Weiss, Rifkind, Wharton & Garrison, N.Y.C., 1983—. Recipient Am. Jurisprudence award Lawyer Coop. Pub. Co., 1977, 79. Mem. ABA, N.Y. State Bar Assn., N.Y. City Bar Assn. General corporate, Securities. Home: 300 E 54th St New York NY 10022

STARRETT, LOYD MILFORD, lawyer; b. St. Louis, Aug. 13, 1933; s. Loyd George and Edna (Switzer) S.; m. Michelle Miller, June 21, 1953 (div. Oct. 1965); children: Lucinda, Sarah Jean, Loyd Benjamin, Patricia Mary; m. Elaine Virginia MacGray, Apr. 8, 1967; children: A. Thomas Bower, Jo Ellen Bower, Amy S. Bower, Charles D. AB magna cum laude, Harvard U., 1953, LLB magna cum laude, 1958. Bar: Mass. 1959, U.S. Ct. Appeals (1st cir.) 1959, U.S. Dist. Ct. Mass. 1960, U.S. Supreme Ct. 1965, U.S. Ct. Appeals (5th cir.) 1973, U.S. Ct. Appeals (11th cir.) 1984. Law clk. to chief judge U.S. Ct. Appeals (1st cir.), Boston, 1958-59; assoc. Foley, Hoag & Eliot, Boston, 1959-62; ptnr. Faley, Hoag & Eliot, Boston, 1963-85, Fordham & Starrett, Boston, 1985—; v.p., sec. Modern Health Care Services, North Miami Beach, Fla., 1971—; bd. dirs. A.W. Hastings & Co., Manchester, N.H., clk., 1973—. moderator City of Rockport, Mass., 1975—, chmn. bd. appeals, 1976—; treas., bd. dirs. North Bay council Boy Scouts Am., Danver, Mass., 1986—; moderator, bd. dirs. Adoniram Judson Bapt. Assn., Malden, Mass., 1974—; bd. dirs. Am. Bapt. Chs. Mass., Boston, 1978—, Bapt. Home Mass., Kingston, 1984—, Am. Bapt. Chs.,

USA, Valley Forge, Pa., 1987—. Served to 1st lt. USAF, 1953-55. Mem. ABA, Mass. Bar Assn., Boston Bar Assn., Am. Acad. Hosp. Attys., Mass. Moderators Assn. (bd. dirs. 1981-85, 86—). State civil litigation, Local government, Federal civil litigation. Home: 23 Granite St Rockport MA 01966 Office: Fordham & Starrett 260 Franklin St Boston MA 02110

STARRS, ELIZABETH ANNE, lawyer; b. Detroit, Jan. 1, 1954; d. John Richard and Mabel Angeline (Gilchrist) S. BA, U. Mich., 1975; JD, Suffolk U., 1980. Bar: Mass. 1980, U.S. Dist. Ct. Mass. 1980, U.S. Ct. Appeals (1st. cir.) 1980, Colo. 1983, U.S. Dist. Ct. Colo. 1983, U.S. Ct. Appeals (10th cir.) 1983. Assoc. Denner & Benjoya P.C., Boston, 1980-83; assoc. Cooper & Kelley P.C., Denver, 1983-86, ptnr., 1986—; instr. bus. law Bay State Community Coll., Boston, 1981-82. Leader Girl Scouts U.S., Denver, 1984-85; mem. Denver Young Dems., 1983; sec., adv. council Colo. Taxpayers for Choice, Denver, 1985—. Mem. Mass. Bar Assn., Colo. Bar Assn., Denver Bar Assn., Mass. Assn. Women Lawyers, Colo. Women's Bar Assn., Colo. Def. Lawyers Assn. Roman Catholic. Malpractice defense, Federal civil litigation, State civil litigation. Home: 115 S Clarkson Denver CO 80209 Office: Cooper & Kelley PC 1660 Wynkoop #900 Denver CO 80202-1197

STASACK, STEPHEN ANDREW, lawyer; b. Troy, N.Y., Sept. 28, 1950; s. Samuel Paul and Helen Mildred (Kupic) S.; m. Yvonne A. Vannier, Dec. 26, 1981; 1 child, James Henry. B.S., Siena Coll., 1972; J.D., Albany Law Sch., 1975. Bar: N.Y. 1976, U.S. Dist. Ct. (no. dist.) N.Y. 1976. Assoc. atty. George B. Caresia, Jr., Troy, 1976-79; town atty. town of North Greenbush, N.Y., 1978-79, 84-86, spl. dist. atty., 1979-84; law clk. to judge Family Ct., Rensselaer County, N.Y., 1984-86; sole practice, Troy, 1976-86; prin. law clk. to justice F. Warren Travers, U.S. Supreme Ct., 1986—; examiner guardian's accounts Rensselaer County Surrogate Ct., Troy, 1975-86; lectr. in field. Treas. softball league, North Greenbush, N.Y., 1973-78; treas., mgr. various polit. campaigns, Rensselaer County, 1974-84. Mem. N.Y. State Bar Assn., ABA, Rensselaer Bar Assn., Capitol Dist. Trial Lawyers Assn., Comml. Law League. Democrat. Roman Catholic. Clubs: Albany Yacht (commodore 1981), Golf League (pres. 1978). General practice, Probate. Home: 19C Menemsha Ln Troy NY 12180 Office: 106 3d St Troy NY 12180

STASSEN, JOHN HENRY, lawyer; b. Joliet, Ill., Mar. 22, 1943; s. John H. and Florence C. (McCarthy) S.; m. Sara A. Gaw, July 6, 1968; children: John C., David A. BS, Northwestern U., 1965, JD, Harvard U., 1968. Bar: Ill. 1968. Assoc. Kirkland & Ellis, Chgo., 1968, 73-76, ptnr. 1977—. Contbr. articles to legal jours. Served to lt. comdr. JAGC, USN, 1969-72. Mem. ABA (chmn. com. on futures regulation), Ill. Bar Assn., Chgo. Bar Assn., Phila. Soc. Club: Mid-America (Chgo.). Administrative and regulatory, Federal civil litigation, General corporate. Home: 1310 N Astor St Chicago IL 60610 Office: Kirkland & Ellis 200 E Randolph Dr Suite 5700 Chicago IL 60601

STASSON, SHELLEY ANDREA, lawyer; b. Detroit, Apr. 23, 1953; d. Jerome and Betty (Kowalksy) S. BA in Psychology, U. Mich., 1975; JD, Thomas M. Cooley, 1978. Bar: Mich. 1979, D.C. 1983, U.S. Supreme Ct. 1983, U.S. Dist. Ct. (mid. dist.) Pa. 1984, U.S. Ct. Appeals (3d cir.) 1984. Sole practice Harrisburg, Pa., 1981—; atty. Legis. Reference Bur., Harrisburg, 1981-87, Valentine & Assocs., West Bloomfield, Mich., 1987—; guest speaker various interest groups, Pa., 1983—. Contbr. articles to numerous jours. Del. Nat. Conf. State Legislators, Denver, 1983, 84. Republican. Jewish. Avocations: dance, jogging, languages, business, politics. Administrative and regulatory, Legislative, Contracts commercial. Office: Valentine & Assocs 5767 W Maple Rd West Bloomfield MI 48033

STATKUS, JEROME FRANCIS, lawyer; b. Hammond, Ind., June 13, 1942; s. Albert William and Helen Ann (Vaicunas) S.; m. Carol Ann Wipperman, July 25, 1970; children—Wesley Albert, Nicholas Jerome. B.A., So. Ill. U., 1964; J.D., U. Louisville, 1968; M.A., U. Wyo., 1974. Bar: Wyo. 1971, U.S. Dist. Ct. Wyo. 1971, U.S. Ct. Claims 1973, U.S. Supreme Ct. 1974, U.S. Ct. Appeals (10th and D.C. cirs.) 1975. Law clk. U.S. Dist. Ct., So. Dist. Ill., Peoria, 1968-69; asst. atty. gen. State of Wyo., Cheyenne, 1971-75; legis. asst. to U.S. Senator Clifford Hansen, Washington, 1975-76; asst. U.S. atty. U.S. Dept. Justice, Cheyenne, 1976-77; ptnr. Carmichael & Statkus, Cheyenne, 1977-78; sole practice, Cheyenne, 1978-79; assoc. Horisky, Bagley & Hickey, Cheyenne, 1979-81; ptnr. Rooney, Bagley, Hickey Evans & Statkus, Cheyenne, 1981—. Pres. Ret. Sr. Vol. Program, Cheyenne, 1982-83; treas. Pathfinder (drug rehab.), Cheyenne, 1982-85; bar commr. 1st Jud. Dist., 1985—, Bd. Legal Services, 1986—. Served with USNR, 1969-70. Mem. Wyo. Bar Assn., D.C. Bar Assn., Wyo. Trial Lawyers Assn. (bd. dirs.), Am. Arbitration Assn. (panel). Democrat. Roman Catholic. General practice, Criminal, Personal injury. Home: 300 E 3d Ave Cheyenne WY 82001 Office: Rooney Bagley et al 1712 Carey Ave Cheyenne WY 82003

STATLAND, EDWARD MORRIS, lawyer; b. Washington, Aug. 20, 1932; s. Harry and Rebecca (Berman) S.; m. Pearl Axelrod, June 1, 1958; children: Stuart J., Carole B. AB, George Washington U., 1954, JD with honors, 1959. Bar: D.C. 1959, Md. 1959. Asst. corp. counsel D.C. Washington, 1960-62; assoc. Miller, Brown & Gildenhorn, Washington, 1962-70; ptnr. Brown, Gildenhorn & Statland, Washington, 1970-75; sr. ptnr. Statland & Zaslav, Washington, 1975-83; ptnr. Statland, Nerenberg, Nassau, Buckley & Squires, Washington, 1984—. Pres., bd. dirs. Hebrew Home of Greater Washington, D.C. Served with U.S. Army, 1954-56. Mem. ABA, Md. State Bar Assn., Montgomery County Bar Assn., D.C. Bar Assn. (panel mem.), Am. Arbitration Assn., Nat. Assn. Securities Dealers, Assn. Plaintiffs Trial Attys., Am. Judicature Soc. Family and matrimonial, Personal injury, Federal civil litigation. Home: 3003 Van Ness St NW Washington DC 20008 Office: 1101 17th St NW Suite 406 Washington DC 20036

STATMORE, KENNETH T., lawyer; b. Passaic, N.J., Feb. 17, 1935; s. Benjamin A. and Helen (Wruble) S.; m. June Mesirow, Dec. 27, 1959; children: Elizabeth K., Michael A. BA, Ohio State U., 1956; LLB, Georgetown U., 1959. Bar: N.J. 1960, D.C. 1960, U.S. Dist. Ct. N.J. 1960, U.S. Dist. Ct. D.C. 1960, U.S. Supreme Ct. 1964, U.S. Ct. Appeals (3d cir.) 1969. Atty. FAA, Washington, 1963-64; sole practice Passaic, 1964-68; staff v.p., sr. counsel RCA Corp., Cherry Hill, N.J., 1968—. Served to capt. USAF, 1960-63. Mem. ABA, N.J. Bar Assn., Am. Corp. Counsel Assn. Avocations: running, tennis, photography, pvt. pilot. Contracts commercial, General corporate, Government contracts and claims. Office: RCA Corp Rt 38 Cherry Hill NJ 08358

STAUBER, RONALD JOSEPH, lawyer; b. Toledo, Nov., 8, 1940; s. Frederick I. and Anna R. (Kline) S.; m. Doreen Lynn Toll, Aug., 19, 1967 (div.); children—Brandon, Deborah. B.B.A., U. Toledo, 1962; J.D., Ohio State U., 1965. Bar: Calif. 1967; U.S. Dist. Ct. (cen. and ea. dists.) Calif. 1967, U.S. Supreme Ct. 1972. Corp. counsel, Div. Corps., Dept. Investments, State of Calif., Los Angeles, 1965-67; ptnr. Blacker & Stauber, Beverly Hills, Calif., 1967-77; ptnr. Ronald J. Stauber, Inc., Beverly Hills and Los Angeles, 1978-86; ptnr. Stauber & Gersh, Beverly Hills and Washington, 1986—. Bd. dirs. Jewish Free Loan; bd. dirs. Pico Robertson Redevel. Assn. Served in USNG. Mem. Beverly Hills Bar Assn. (corps. com., real estate com.), Los Angeles Bar Assn. (bus. and corp. sect., judge pro tem Mcpl. Ct.), ABA (corps., banking and bus. law sect.) Democrat. Jewish. Real property, General corporate. Home: 508 N Sierra Dr Beverly Hills CA 90210 Office: 2029 Century Park E Suite 3335 Los Angeles CA 90067

STAUBITZ, ARTHUR FREDERICK, lawyer, pharmaceutical company executive; b. Omaha, Nebr., Mar. 14, 1939; s. Herbert Frederick Staubitz and Barbara Eileen (Dallas) Alderson; m. Linda Medora Miller, Aug. 18, 1962; children: Michael, Melissa, Peter. AB cum laude, Wesleyan U., Middletown, Conn., 1961; JD cum laude, U. Pa., 1964. Bar: Ill. 1964, U.S. Dist. Ct. Ill. (no. dist.) Ill. 1964, U.S. Ct. Appeals (7th cir.) 1964, Pa. 1972. Assoc. Sidley & Austin, Chgo., 1964-71; sr. internat. atty., asst. gen. counsel, dir. Japanese ops. Sperry Univac, Blue Bell, Pa., 1971-78; from asst. to assoc. gen. counsel Baxter Travenol Labs., Deerfield, Ill., 1978-85, v.p., dep. gen. counsel, 1985—. Mem. Planning Commn., Springfield Twp., Montgomery County, Pa., 1973-74, Zoning Hearing Bd., 1974-78; bd. dirs. Twp. High Sch. Dist. #113, Deerfield and Highland Park, Ill., 1983—. Mem. ABA, Chgo. Bar Assn. Episcopalian. General corporate, Antitrust, Private international. Home: 1144 Walden Ln Deerfield IL 60015 Office: Baxter Travenol Labs Inc One Baxter Pkwy Deerfield IL 60015

STAUFFER, SCOTT WILLIAM, lawyer, CPA; b. Oshkosh, Wis., Aug. 17, 1954; s. Robert Edward and Shirley Lydia (Wrasse) S.; m. Janet Margaret Spalding, June 19, 1976 (div. Sept. 1985). BBA in Acctg., U. Wis., 1975; JD, U. Denver, 1979. Bar: Colo. 1979. Tax acct. Arthur Andersen & Co., Denver, 1979-82; tax mgr. Gary-Williams Oil, Englewood, Colo., 1982-85; sole practice law, acct. Denver, 1986—; Treas. Colo. Mining and Exploration, Denver, 1984—. Pres. Colo. Chorale, Denver, 1984-85; asst. treas. Patten Inst. for Arts, Denver, 1985. Mem. ABA, Am. Inst. CPA's, Colo. Bar Assn., Denver Bar Assn., Colo. Soc. CPA's, Ind. Petroleum Assn. Mountain States, Petroleum Accts. Soc. Colo. Lutheran. Club: Petroleum (Denver). Avocations: golf, travel, reading, skiing, tennis. Personal income taxation, Corporate taxation, Probate. Home: 8147 W Frost Pl Littleton CO 80123 Office: 15200 E Grand Suite 4800 Aurora CO 80014

STAVELY, RICHARD WILLIAM, lawyer; b. Lyndon, Kans., May 14, 1927; s. A.K. and Bertha May (Patton) S.; m. Gladys Edith Voetmann, June 8, 1958; children: Jill Elizabeth, Jocelyn Carita. AB, U. Kans., 1950, LLB, 1954. Bar: Kans., U.S. Dist. Ct. Kans. 1954, U.S. Ct. Appeals (10th cir.) 1956. Assoc. Lilleston, Spradling, Gott & Stallwitz, Wichita, Kans., 1954-63; gen. counsel MISCO Industries, Inc., Wichita, 1964—, sec., 1966—, v.p., 1968—; co-trustee MISCO charitable trust. Editor: U. Kans. Law Rev., 1952-53. Mem. exec. com. Wichita area Devel. Inc. 1st v.p. 1982-83, pres. 1984-86, chmn. bd. dirs. 1986—. Served with USNR, 1945-46. Mem. ABA (chmn. div. jud. adminstrn. Kans. sect. 1958-68, Kans. rep. Lawyers Conf., 1979—), Kans. Bar Assn., Wichita Bar Assn. (chmn. pro-bono com. 1984—), Am. Judicature Soc., Wichita Corp. Counsel Soc. (pres. 1978-79), Am. Assn. Equipment Lessors (lawyers com. 1977-80, co-chmn. 1980), Wichita Area C. of C., Phi Alpha Delta. Republican. Presbyterian. Clubs: Wichita, University. Insurance, Contracts commercial, Pension, profit-sharing, and employee benefits. Home: 120 S Pinecrest Wichita KS 67218 Office: MISCO Industries Inc 257 N Broadway Room 200 Wichita KS 67202

STAVES, MARION COLE, lawyer; b. Bellingham, Wash., Apr. 17, 1927; s. Marion Cole and Edith (Krayer) S.; m. Monique Kennell, July 29, 1954; children: George VR., Elizabeth J. BS, Am. U., 1952; MS, Georgetown U., 1954; LLB, Goerge Washington U., 1959. Bar: D.C. 1962, U.S. Supreme Ct. 1976, Pa. 1978, U.S. Ct. Appeals (fed. cir.) 1982. Patent counsel Hercules Inc., Wilmington, Del., 1959—. Chmn. bd. trustees West Chester (Pa.) State U., 1980-83. Served with USN, 1944-46. Mem. Phila. Patent Law Assn. Democrat. Patent, Antitrust, Trademark and copyright. Home: 1603 East Street Rd Kennett Square PA 19348 Office: Hercules Inc Hercules Plaza Wilmington DE 19894

STAVIG, ALF RUSTEN, lawyer; b. Rosholt, S.D., Oct. 26, 1917; s. Edwin Lars and Lydia Agnethe (Rusten) S.; m. Dorothy Emily Glorvick, July 5, 1944; children—Susan J. Searle, Barbara Stavig Doane. B.A., Concordia Coll., 1939; LL.B., Harvard U., 1946. Bar: S.D. 1947, Calif. 1949. Spl. agt. FBI, 1941-45; spl. agt. in charge Compliance Enforcement div. War Assets Adminstrn. and GSA, Denver, Salt Lake City, Honolulu and San Francisco, 1946-49; sole practice, Sacramento, 1950—. Govt. appeal agt. SSS, 1950-55; mem. state bldg. standards com. State of Calif., 1969-81. Recipient award of merit Republican Assocs. of Sacramento, 1962. Mem. Calif. Bar Assn., S.D. Bar Assn., ABA. Republican. Lutheran. Clubs: Book of Calif., Rotary; Harvard of Sacramento (founding pres.). Author: The Employers Right of Free Speech, 1946. State civil litigation, General practice, Probate. Home: 1600 Del Dayo Dr Carmichael CA 95608 Office: 901 H St Suite 604 Sacramento CA 95814

STEADMAN, JAMES ROBERT, lawyer; b. Girard, Pa., Aug. 28, 1950; s. Robert Emmet and Ruth Harriet (Blair) S.; m. Alison Terry, June 16, 1973; children—Elizabeth, Kathryn, Anne. B.A. in Polit. Sci., Grove City Coll., 1972; J.D., Dickinson Sch. Law, 1975. Bar: Pa. 1975, U.S. Dist. Ct. (we. dist.) Pa. 1976, U.S. Supreme Ct. 1981. Atty., advisor Small Bus. Adminstrn., Harrisburg, Pa. 1975-76; sole practice, Girard, 1976—; dir. Penn. Attys. Title Ins. Co., Erie. Councilman, Girard Borough, 1978-82; treas. Willcox Library, Girard, 1982-86; bd. dirs. Battles Village Sr. Citizen Housing, Girard, 1981—. Mem. Pa. Bar Assn., Erie County Bar Assn. (bd. dirs. 1983-86). Republican. Episcopalian. Club: Girard-Lake City Exchange (bd. dirs. 1977-79). Lodge: Masons. Probate, Real property, Family and matrimonial. Home: 205 Penn Ave Girard PA 16417 Office: PO Box 87 24 Main St E Girard PA 16417

STEADMAN, JOHN MONTAGUE, judge; b. Honolulu, Aug. 8, 1930; s. Alva Edgar and Martha (Cooke) S.; m. Alison Storer Lunt, Apr. 8, 1961; children—Catharine N., Juliette M., Eric C. Grad., Phillips Acad., Andover, Mass., 1948; B.A. summa cum laude, Yale, 1952; LL.B. magna cum laude, Harvard, 1955. Bar: D.C. 1955, Calif. 1956, U.S. Supreme Ct. 1964, Hawaii 1977. Assoc. Pillsbury, Madison & Sutro, San Francisco, 1956-63; atty. Dept. Justice, 1963-64; dep. under sec. army for internat. affairs 1964-65; spl. asst. to sec. and dep. sec. def. Dept. Def., 1965-68; gen. counsel Dept. Air Force, 1968-70; vis. prof. law U. Pa. Law Sch., 1970-72; prof. law Georgetown U. Law Ctr., Washington, 1972-85, assoc. dean, 1979-84; assoc. judge D.C. Ct. Appeals, 1985—; instr. Lincoln Law Sch., San Francisco, 1961-62, San Francisco Law Sch., 1962-63; vis. prof. U. Mich. Sch. Law, 1976, U. Hawaii Sch. Law, 1977; of counsel firm Pillsbury, Madison & Sutro, Washington, 1979-85. Editor: Harvard Law Rev, 1953-55. Sinclair-Kennedy Traveling fellow, 1955-56. Mem. Am. Law Inst., Phi Beta Kappa, Delta Sigma Rho, Zeta Psi. Episcopalian. Judicial administration. Home: 2960 Newark St NW Washington DC 20008 Office: DC Ct Appeals 500 Indiana Ave NW Washington DC 20001

STEADMAN, RICHARD ANDERSON, JR., lawyer; b. Charleston, S.C., Sept. 17, 1954; s. Richard A. and Elizabeth (Barber) S.; m. Sarah Stokes, Aug. 5, 1978. B.A., Wofford Coll., 1976; J.D., U. S.C., 1981. Bar: S.C. 1981, U.S. Dist. Ct. S.C. 1982. Assoc. Willis Fuller, P.A., Charleston, 1981-82; sole practice, Charleston, 1982—; assoc. Lewis, Lewis, Bruce & Truslow, Charleston, 1982-86, Joye Law Firm, North Charleston, 1986—. Dir. East Cooper Lifestyles, Inc., Mt. Pleasant, S.C., 1983-85. Mem. S.C. Bar Assn. (publs. editor Real Estate Lawyer 1982-83), Charleston County Bar Assn., S.C. Trial Lawyers Assn., Assn. Trial Lawyers Am., ABA, Lawyer's Club, Charleston Young Lawyers Club. Lodge: Optimists (bd. dirs. 1984-85, Yearling award 1983). General practice, State civil litigation, Consumer commercial. Home: 1476 Short St Mount Pleasant SC 29464 Office: Joye Law Firm 5861 Rivers Ave North Charleston SC 29418

STEADMAN, SUSAN KIRKPATRICK, lawyer; b. Salina, Kans., Aug. 6, 1954; d. James Frank and Pellerree Aletha (Jackson) Kirkpatrick; m. R. Garland Steadman Jr., Sept. 8, 1979; 1 child, Pellerree Amelia. AA, Miss. Gulf Coast Jr. Coll., 1974; BSE, Delta State U., 1976; JD, U. Miss., 1979. Bar: Mo., 1979. Assoc. Morris & Fair P.A., Hattiesburg, Miss., 1979-83, Law Offices of Eugene L. Fair, Hattiesburg, 1983—. Named one of Outstanding Young Women in Am., 1985, 86. Mem. ABA, Miss. Bar Assn., South Cen. Miss. Bar Assn., South Cen. Miss. Women Lawyers Assn., Phi Alpha Delta. Republican. Presbyterian. Consumer commercial, Bankruptcy, Contracts commercial. Office: Law Offices of Eugene L Fair 522 Main St PO Box 455 Hattiesburg MS 39401

STEAGALL, HENRY B., II, state judge. Judge Ala. Supreme Ct., Montgomery. Office: Jud Bldg PO Box 218 Montgomery AL 36104 *

STECKLER, WILLIAM ELWOOD, judge; b. Mt. Vernon, Ind., Oct. 18, 1913; s. William Herman and Lena (Menikheim) S.; m. Vitallas Alting, Oct. 15, 1938; children: William Rudolph, David Alan. LL.B., Ind. U., 1936, J.D., 1937; LL.D., Wittenberg U., Springfield, Ohio, 1958; H.H.D., Ind. Central U., 1969. Bar: Ind. 1936. Practiced in Indpls., 1937-50; mem. firm Key & Steckler; pub. counselor Ind. Pub. Service Commn., 1949-50; judge U.S. Dist. Ct. So. Dist., Ind., 1950—; chief judge U.S. Dist. Ct. So. Dist., 1954-82; faculty mem. for judges confs. Fed. Jud. Ctr., 1973-74. Mem. Ind. Election Bd., 1946-48; chmn. speakers bur. Democratic State Central Com., 1948; bd. dirs. Community Hosp., Indpls.; bd. visitors Ind. U. Sch. Law, Indpls. Served with USNR, 1943. Recipient Man of Yr. award Ind. U. Sch. Law, Indpls., 1970, Disting. Alumni Service award, 1985; Disting. Alumni Service award Ind. U., 1985. Mem. Am., Fed., Ind., Indpls. bar assns., Am. Judicature Soc. Nat. Lawyers Club, Jud. Conf. U.S. (dist. judge rep. from 7th fed. circuit 1961-64, mem. study group pretrial com. 1956-60, pretrial procedure com. 1960-65, trial practice and procedure com. 1965-69, coordinating com. for multiple litigation 1966-69, operation of jury system com. 1969-75, jud. ethics com. 1985—), Am. Legion, St. Thomas More Soc., Order of Coif, Sigma Delta Kappa. Lutheran. Club: Indianapolis Athletic. Lodges: Masons (33 deg.), Shriners, Order DeMoley, Royal Order Jesters. Home: 30 Jurist Ln Lamb Lake Trafalgar IN 46181 Office: 204 US Courthouse 46 E Ohio Indianapolis IN 46204

STEDHAM, BRENDA SMITH, lawyer; b. Birmingham, Ala., Feb. 22, 1954; d. James William and Mildred (Ferguson) Smith; m. Michael Eugene Stedham, June 4, 1983; 1 child, Jennifer Elizabeth. BA, Birmingham-So. Coll., 1976; JD, U. Ala., 1980. Bar: Ala. 1980, U.S. Dist. Ct. (mid. and no. dists.) Ala. 1981. Law clk. to presiding justice Ala. Ct. of Civil Appeals, Montgomery, 1980-81; assoc. Merrill, Porch, Doster & Dillon, Anniston, Ala., 1981-83, ptnr., 1983—; adj. faculty mem. Jacksonville (Ala.) State U., 1981-85. Mem. Jr. Service League of Anniston-Calhoun County, 1985-86. Mem. ABA. Calhoun County Bar Assn. (treas. 1983-84), Phi Delta Phi. General practice, General corporate, State civil litigation. Home: 1428 Kilby Terr Anniston AL 36201 Office: Merrill Porch Doster & Dillon PO Box 580 Anniston AL 36202

STEEDLE, ROGER CRAIG, lawyer; b. Phila., Sept. 17, 1942; s. Robert H. and Marjorie K. Steedle; m. Jean Marie Ruhl, June 19, 1965 (div. Dec. 1976); m. Maryanne Ryan, Sept. 1, 1978; children: Melissa, Ryan, Andrew. AB, Dickinson Coll., 1964, JD, 1967. Bar: N.J. 1967, U.S. Dist. Ct. N.J. 1967, U.S. Supreme Ct. 1977, U.S. Ct. Appeals (3d cir.) 1981. Ptnr. Lloyd, Megargee & Steedle, Pleasantville, N.J., 1969-75; sr. ptnr. Lloyd, Megargee, Steedle & Connor and successor firms, Pleasantville, N.J., 1975-85; sr. mem. Law Offices of Roger C. Steedle, Atlantic City, 1985—; solicitor Hamilton Twp. Planning Bd., 1972-75; mem. fee arbitration com. N.J. Supreme Ct., 1979-82. Mem. council City of Linwood, N.J., 1973-74; elected Rep. County Committeeman, 1975-79, 81-83; bd. dirs. Atlantic City Friend's Sch., 1971-73, Atlantic County YMCA, 1974-75; bd. trustees Margate Community Ch., 1986—. Served with JAGC USAR,N.J. Air N.G., 1968-74. Mem. ABA, N.J. Bar Assn. (joint county jud. selection com. 1972-74, 76, civil case mgmt. com. 1984-85, vice chmn. civil case implementation com. 1985-86), N.J. Bar Found. (so. dist. co-chmn. bar ctr. campaign 1985-86), Atlantic County Bar Assn. (pres. 1983-84), Def. Research Inst. (chmn. N.J. State), Assn. Ins. Attys. (prime mem.), Fedn. Ins. and Corp. Counsel, Trial Attys. N.J. (trustee 1987—), Am. Arbitration Assn. (panel of arbitrators), Am. Judicature Soc., N.J. Def. Assn. (pres. 1982-83), Dickinson Sch. of Law Gen. Alumni Assn. (v.p. 1981-83), Greater Altantic City C. of C., Mainland C. of C., N.J. Jaycees and Greater Atlantic Jaycees (v.p. 1972), N.J. State C. of C., Am. Legion. Lodges: Kiwanis, Masons. Insurance, Federal civil litigation, State civil litigation. Home: 1050 Bartlett Dr Linwood NJ 08221 Office: 1125 Atlantic Ave PO Box 900 Atlantic City NJ 08404-0900

STEELE, ANITA (MARGARET ANNE MARTIN), law librarian, legal educator; b. Haines City, Fla., Dec. 30, 1927; d. Emmett Edward and Esther Majulia (Phifer) Martin; m. Thomas Dinsmore Steele, June 10, 1947 (div. 1969); children—Linda Frances, Roger Dinsmore, Thomas Garrick, Carolyn Anne; m. James E. Beaver, Mar. 1980. B.A., Radcliffe Coll., 1948; J.D., U. Va., 1971; M.Law Librarianship, U. Wash., 1972. Asst. prof. law U. Puget Sound, Tacoma, 1972-74, assoc. prof. law, 1974-79, prof. law, 1979—, dir. law library, 1972—. Contbr. articles to profl. jours.; mem. editorial adv. bds. various law book pubs., 1980—. Treas., Congl. Campaign Orgn., Tacoma, 1978, 80; mem. adv. bd. Clover Park Vocat.-Tech. Sch., Tacoma, 1980-82. Mem. Am. Assn. Law Libraries, Internat. Assn. Law Libraries, Am. Soc. Info. Sci. Republican. Legal education, Librarianship. Home: 1502 Fernside Dr S Tacoma WA 98465 Office: U Puget Sound Sch of Law 950 Broadway Tacoma WA 98402

STEELE, GLENN HORACE, JR., lawyer; b. Jasper, Tex., Sept. 14, 1955; s. Glenn H. and Jo Kathry (Smyly) S.; m. Sherry Gale Roberts, June 18, 1983; 1 child, Laura Lee. BA, U. Tex., 1977; JD, S. Tex. Coll. Law, 1980. Assoc. Patterson, Boyd, Lowery et al, Houston, 1980-82; assoc. Provost, Umphrey, Swearingen & Eddins, Pt. Arthur, Tex., 1982—, ptnr., 1982—. Mem. Jefferson County Young Bar Assn., Pt. Arthur Bar Assn. Methodist. Banking, Consumer commercial, Real property. Office: Provost Umphrey et al PO Box 3837 Port Arthur TX 77640

STEELE, JOHN ROBERT, lawyer; b. Chattanooga, July 16, 1951; s. James Russell and Hazel Virginia (Meyers) S.; m. Susan Faye Nielsen, Aug. 22, 1970; children—Amanda, Corey James. B.A., U. Central Fla., 1974; J.D., U. S.D., 1978. Bar: S.D. 1978, U.S. Dist. Ct. S.D. 1979. Pres., Steele Law Office, Plankinton, S.D., 1978—; state's atty. Aurora County, Plankinton, 1978—; city atty., Plankinton, 1980-84; adminstrv. hearing officer S.D. Dept. Edn., Pierre, 1978—; adj. instr. Dakota Wesleyan U., Mitchell, S.D., 1979—. Chmn. bd. trustees Plankinton United Methodist Ch., S.D., 1981-82; state committeeman Aurora County Democratic Com., Plankinton, 1982-85. Mem. ABA, Nat. Dist. Attys. Assn., S.D. Bar Assn., S.D. State's Atty. Assn. Democrat. Methodist. Home: 107 Vine St Plankinton SD 57368 Office: Steele Law Office PC 405 S Main St Plankinton SD 57368-0577

STEELE, JOSEPH ROBERT, lawyer; b. Jasper, Tex., Aug. 21, 1952; s. Glenn Horace Sr. and Jo Katherine (Smyly) S.; m. Debra Kay McAlister Apr. 12, 1980 (div. July 1985); 1 child, Julie Anne; m. Tammy Lyn Daniel, Feb. 14, 1986; children: Joel Scott, Emily Jolyn. BA, U. Tex., 1975, MA, 1977, JD, 1979. Bar: Tex. 1980, U.S. Dist. Ct. (ea. dist.) Tex. 1980, U.S. Ct. Appeals (5th cir.) 1980, U.S. Dist. Ct. (so. dist.) Tex. 1984, U.S. Supreme Ct. 1984. Law clk. to presiding justice U.S. Dist. Ct. (ea. dist.) Tex., Beaumont, 1980-81; assoc., ptnr. Provost, Umphrey, Swearingen & Eddins, Port Arthur, Tex., 1981-86; ptnr. Smith, Cable & Steele, Houston, 1986—. Named one of Outstanding Young Men of Am., 1981. Mem. ABA, Tex. Bar Assn., 5th Cir. Bar Assn., Assn. Trial Lawyers Am., Tex. Trial Lawyers Assn. Democrat. Methodist. Avocations: golf, collecting antique automobiles. Personal injury, Federal civil litigation, State civil litigation. Home: 13826 Trailville Houston TX 77077 Office: Smith Cable & Steele 2 Houston Center 8th Floor Houston TX 77010

STEELE, KATHIE FAY, lawyer; b. Oregon City, Oreg., Jan. 17, 1953; d. Donald R. and Lorna F. (Carley) S.; m. Stephen George Altishin, Aug. 15, 1981. BA, Stanford U., 1977; JD, Northwestern Sch. of Law, 1980. Bar: Oreg. 1981, U.S. Dist. Ct. Oreg. 1981, U.S. Ct. Appeals (9th cir.) 1981. Assoc. Redman, Carkadon et al, Milwaukie, Oreg., 1981-83, Crist, Stewart et al, Oregon City, 1983-84; ptnr. Stewart & Steele, Oregon City, 1984—. Bd. dirs. Clackamas Assn. for Retarded Citizens, Marylhurst, Oreg., 1983—, pres. 1985-86, ACLU, Multnomah County, 1980-83. Mem. Oreg. Bar Assn., Clackamas County Bar Assn., Assn. Trial Lawyers Am., Oreg. Criminal Def. Lawyers Assn., ACLU (bd. dirs. 1980-83). Democrat. Criminal, Personal injury, Real property. Office: Stewart & Steele 294 Warner Milne Rd Oregon City OR 97045

STEELE, RICHARD PARKS, lawyer; b. Amarillo, Tex., May 12, 1940; s. Rufus Byron and Lillian (Parks) S.; m. Mary J. McKerall, Mar. 29, 1980; children—Martha Jane, Byron Danforth. B.S. in Geology, West Tex. State U., 1965; J.D., St. Mary's U., San Antonio, 1972. Bar: Tex. 1972, U.S. Dist. Ct. (so. dist.) Tex. 1977, U.S. Ct. Appeals (5th cir.) 1977, U.S. Supreme Ct. 1977. Engr., Core Labs. Inc., Dallas, 1966-72; contract atty. Offshore Co., Houston, 1972-74; internat. atty. Union Tex. Petroleum, Houston, 1974-76; gen. counsel Western Oceanic Inc., Houston, 1976-77; v.p. Citco Internat. Petroleum Co., Houston, 1977-83; sole practice, Houston, 1983—. dir., chief exec. officer ERG Co., Houston. Recipient Leslie C. Meriam award Delta Theta Phi, 1972. Mem. ABA, Maritime Law Assn., U.S. C. of C., Delta Theta Phi, Delta Sigma Phi. Democrat. Oil and gas leasing, Private international, Admiralty. Home: 3132 University Blvd Houston TX 77005 Office: PO Box 25234 Houston TX 77265

STEELE, ROBERT MICHAEL, lawyer; b. Arlington, Va., Aug. 23, 1956; m. Betty Koppelman. BA in History summa cum laude, Furman U., 1978; JD, Vanderbilt U., 1981. Bar: Fla. 1981, U.S. Dist. Ct. (mid. and so. dists.) Fla. 1981. Assoc. Carlton, Fields, Ward, Emmanuel, Smith, Cutler & Kent, Tampa, Fla., 1981—. Articles editor Vanderbilt U. Law Rev.; contbr. articles to profl. jours. Trustee Elliott Cheatham Scholarship Fund, Vanderbilt Law Sch., Nashville, 1981—. Recipient Endel History medal Furman U., 1978. Mem. ABA (real property sect.), Fla. Bar Assn. (land use

and environmental law sect., reporter com. 1984-85, manual editorial com. 1984—), Order of Coif, Phi Beta Kappa. Real property, Environment, Administrative and regulatory. Office: Carlton Fields Ward et al PO Box 3239 Tampa FL 33601

STEELMAN, DAVID CARL, lawyer, educator; b. Worcester, Mass., Aug. 24, 1944; s. George Russell and Ruth Ann (Gregson) S.; stepson Lillian Rita (McNamara) Steelman; m. Virginia Theodosopoulos, Apr. 18, 1969. B.A., U. N.H., 1967, M.A., 1970; J.D., Boston U., 1974. Bar: Mass. 1975, N.H. 1975, U.S. Dist. Ct. Mass. 1976, U.S. Dist. Ct. N.H. 1976, U.S. Supreme Ct. 1980. Asst. to dean of students U. N.H., Durham, 1968-69; human resources intern Maine Mcpl. Assn., Augusta, 1971-72; law intern N.H. Legal Assistance, Nashua, 1972-73; staff atty. Nat. Ctr. for State Cts., Boston, 1974-77, sr. staff atty., North Andover, Mass., 1977—; adj. prof. Boston Coll. Evening Coll., Chestnut Hill, Mass., 1977-83; v.p. Va. Theo-Steelman Cons. Services, Inc., Manchester, N.H., 1983-86; mem. core faculty Inst. Ct. Mgmt., 1986—. Author: (with others) Maine Traffic Court Study, 1975; Maine Superior Court Benchbook, 1976; Lessons of Philadelphia Justice Information System, 1978; Options for Reducing Civil Volume and Delay, 1980; Traffic Court Procedure and Administration, 2d edit., 1983; Rhode Island Family Court Benchbook, 1984, Settlement Conferences: An Experiment in Appellate Justice, 1986; assoc. editor Justice System Jour., 1984-86. Served to 1st. lt. U.S. Army, 1969-71, Vietnam. Decorated Bronze Star; Ford Found. teaching fellow, 1967-68; recipient Excellence award Nat. Ctr. State Cts., 1985. Mem. ABA (traffic ct. com.), Am. Judicature Soc., Nat. Com. Uniform Traffic Laws and Ordinances, Manchester Hist. Soc., Friends of N.H. Symphony, Phi Beta Kappa. Democrat. Judicial administration, Legal education, Legal history. Home: 792 Maple St Manchester NH 03104 Office: Nat Ctr for State Cts 1545 Osgood St North Andover MA 01845

STEELMAN, JACOB DEHART, lawyer; b. Camden, N.J., Dec. 13, 1946; s. J.D. and Elaine (Bonner) S.; m. Deborah Leasure, Jan. 17, 1970 (dec. Sept. 1971); m. Anne Hudson, June 14, 1980; children: Stephanie, John. BA in Polit. Sci., Econs., Grove City Coll., 1969; JD, Baylor U., 1974; acctg. degree, Mercer U., 1976; mgmt. degree, Duke U., 1986. Bar: Tex. 1974, Ga. 1975, Okla. 1977, U.S. Dist. Ct. (no. dist.) Ga. 1975, U.S. Supreme Ct. 1978, U.S. Dist. Ct. (ea. dist.) Okla. 1982, U.S. Ct. Appeals (5th cir.) 1984. Sales rep. PBSW Inc., Phoenix, 1971-72; atty. Cities Service Co., Atlanta, Tulsa, Houston, 1974-80; counsel Occidental Petroleum Corp., Grand Junction, Colo. and Tulsa, 1980-83; asst. gen. counsel The Williams Cos., Tulsa, 1983—; ptnr., gen. counsel Mill Creek Assn., Phila., 1984—; bd. dirs. Gafco Inc., Tulsa, Denmar Products Inc., Tulsa, EMRx Corp., Palisade, Colo. Mem. Tulsa Philharmonic, 1984—; arbitrator Better Bus. Bur., Tulsa, 1984—. Found. for Econ. Edn. fellow, 1969, 70. Mem. ABA, Tex. Bar Assn., Ga. Bar Assn., Okla. Bar Assn., Am. Corp. Counsel Assn., Fed. Energy Bar Assn., Phi Delta Phi. Episcopalian. Avocations: golf, tennis, swimming, gardening, reading. General corporate, Private international, Administrative and regulatory. Home: Box 1915 Tulsa OK 74101 Office: The Williams Cos 3600 Bank of Okla Tower 2d and Cincinnati Tulsa OK 74102

STEEN, JOHN THOMAS, JR., lawyer, savings and loan executive; b. San Antonio, Dec. 27, 1949; s. John Thomas and Nell (Donnell) S.; m. Ida Louise Clement, May 12, 1979; children—John Thomas, Ida Louise Larkin. A.B., Princeton U., 1971; J.D., U. Tex., 1974. Bar: Tex. 1974, U.S. Dist. Ct. (we. dist.) Tex. 1976. Assoc. firm Matthews & Branscomb, San Antonio, 1977-82; ptnr. firm Soules, Cliffe & Reed, San Antonio, 1982-83; sr. v.p., gen. counsel Commerce Savs. Assn., San Antonio, 1983—, also dir.; bd. dirs. North Frost Bank, San Antonio, 1982-84. Trustee San Antonio Acad., 1976-81; v.p. Bexar County Easter Seal Soc., San Antonio, 1976-77; trustee, vice chmn. San Antonio Community Coll. Dist., 1977-82; bd. dirs. Tex. Easter Seal Soc., Dallas, 1977-80, San Antonio Research and Planning Council, 1978-81, Community Guidance Ctr., 1983-84, Nix Med. Found., 1987—; vice-chmn. Leadership San Antonio, 1978-79; mem. Fiesta San Antonio Commn., 1982-83; Bexar County commr., San Antonio, 1982,Tex. Commn. on Economy and Efficiency in State Govt., 1985—; Coliseum Adv. Bd., 1985—; pres. San Antonio Performing Arts Assn., 1984-85; chmn. World Affairs Council San Antonio, 1984-86; bd. dirs. United Way San Antonio, 1985—, Nix Med. Found., 1987—. Served to 1st lt. USAR, 1973-81. Mem. Tex. Bar Assn., San Antonio Bar Assn., Santa Gertrudis Breeders Internat., Tex. and Southwestern Cattle Raisers Assn., San Antonio Acad. Alumni Assn. (pres. 1976-77). Clubs: Ivy (Princeton, N.J.); San Antonio German (pres. 1982-83), Order of Alamo, Tex. Cavaliers, San Antonio Country, Argyle, Conopus, Princeton (San Antonio and South Tex.) (pres. 1980-81). General corporate, Banking, Administrative and regulatory. Home: 207 Ridgemont Ave San Antonio TX 78209 Office: Commerce Savs Assn 111 Soledad St Suite 1300 San Antonio TX 78205

STEEN, WESLEY WILSON, bankruptcy judge; b. Abbeville, La., Feb. 15, 1946; s. John Wesley and Margaret (Chauvin) S.; m. Evelyn Finch, Aug. 29, 1970; children—Anna Frances, John Wesley, Lee Wilson. B.A. in English, U. Va., 1968; J.D., La. State U., 1974. Bar: La. 1974. Assoc. atty. Sanders, Downing, et al, Baton Rouge, 1974-77, ptnr., 1977-80; sole practice law, Baton Rouge, 1980-83; pres., atty. Steen, Rubin, et al, Baton Rouge, 1983-84; bankruptcy judge U.S. Bankruptcy Ct., Middle Dist. La., part time, 1983-84, full time, Baton Rouge, 1984—; mem. La. State Law Inst. Continuous Revision Com., La. Trust Code, 1980—; mem. Baton Rouge Estate and Bus. Planning Council, 1980—, State Bar Com. on Bar Admissions, Baton Rouge, 1981-85; adj. asst. prof. law La. State U., 1979—, So. U. Law Sch., 1981; congl. page U.S. Ho. of Reps., 1963-64. Contbr. articles to profl. jours. Vestryman, St. James Episcopal Ch., 1980-83; bd. dirs. Baton Rouge Symphony Assn., 1976-87, St. James Place, 1985—, Cerebral Palsy Ctr., 1981, Baton Rouge Gallery, 1982. Mem. Baton Rouge Bar Assns., La. Bar Assn., Order of Coif, Omicron Delta Kappa. Republican. Episcopalian. Lodge: Rotary. Avocations: jogging, computers. Bankruptcy, Judicial administration. Office: US Bankruptcy Ct Mid Dist La 412 N 4th St Suite 302 Baton Rouge LA 70802

STEENO, DAVID LAWRENCE, legal educator; b. Green Bay, Wis., June 20, 1944; s. Paul Wilbur and Grace Nina (Martell) S.; m. Mary Joanne Shea, Aug. 7, 1971; children—Karen Marie, John Paul. B.S., U. Wis., 1966; M.S., Mich. State U., 1973; J.D., Cooley Law Sch., 1976. Bar: Mich. 1976, U.S. Dist. Ct. (ea. dist.) Mich. 1977, U.S. Ct. Appeals (6th cir.) 1977, U.S. Ct. Appeals (7th cir.) 1979, U.S. Ct. Appeals (8th cir.) 1982. Instr. U. Ill. Police Tng. Inst., Champaign, 1973; dist. security mgr. Venture Stores, St. Louis, 1971-73; assoc. Schneider, Handlon & Steeno, Midland, Mich., 1976-78; assoc. prof. dept. law enforcement adminstrn. Western Ill. U., Macomb, 1978-85; Ferris State Coll., Big Rapids, Mich., 1985—; cons. in field. Contbr. articles to profl. jours., chpt. to book. Bd. dirs. Western Ill. U. Found., 1983-85. Served to capt. USAF, 1966-70, Vietnam. Mem. Nat. Dist. Attys. Assn., Midwestern Assn. Criminal Justice Educators, Security Law Inst., Am. Soc. Indsl. Security, Alpha Phi Sigma, Phi Alpha Delta. Lodge: Elks. Legal education, Criminal, Legal aspects of private security industry, police civil liability. Home: 520 Mecosta Ave Big Rapids MI 49307 Office: Ferris State Coll 501 Bishop Hall Big Rapids MI 49307

STEER, REGINALD DAVID, lawyer; b. N.Y.C., July 16, 1945; s. Joseph D. and Rozica (Yusim) S.; Marianne Spizzy, July 22, 1984; 1 child, Derek Brandon. BA, U. Minn., 1966, JD, 1969. Bar: Minn. 1969, Calif. 1973, U.S. Dist. Ct. (no., ea. and cen. dists.) Calif., U.S. Ct. Mil. Appeals, U.S. Ct. Appeals (9th cir.), U.S. Supreme Ct. Assoc. Pillsbury, Madison & Sutro, San Francisco, 1973-79, ptnr., 1979—; lectr. Calif. Continuing Edn. of Bar, San Francisco, 1981. Served to capt. U.S. Army, 1969-73. Mem. ABA (antitrust and litigation sects.). Club: Olympic (San Francisco). Avocations: piano, tennis, photography. Federal civil litigation, State civil litigation, Antitrust. Office: Pillsbury Madison & Sutro 225 Bush St PO Box 7880 San Francisco CA 94104

STEER, RICHARD LANE, lawyer; b. Bklyn., July 20, 1949; s. Irving and Sheila Peggy (Rothman) S.; m. Carole Marcia Liebman, Aug. 20, 1972; children—Stephanie Jill, Adam Benjamin. B.A., Alfred U., 1971; J.D. cum laude, New Eng. Sch. Law, 1974; cert. in EEO, Cornell U., 1978. Bar: N.Y. 1975, U.S. Dist. Ct. (so. dist.) N.Y. 1975, U.S. Dist. Ct. (ea. dist.) N.Y. 1975, U.S. Ct. Appeals (2d cir.) 1977, U.S. Supreme Ct. 1980. Asst. corp. counsel City of Yonkers, N.Y., 1975-78; assoc. Stein, Davidoff & Malito, N.Y.C., 1978-80; sr. labor assoc. Epstein, Becker, Borsody & Green, P.C., N.Y.C., 1980-84; counsel Stein, Davidoff & Malito, N.Y.C., 1984—; lead trial counsel Yonkers Police Dept., U.S. Dist. Ct. (so. dist.) N.Y., 1984—. adj. prof. law Pace U., 1984—. Researcher: AT Will Termination in Texas, 1983; author: Labor Trends (Mcpl. Lawyer mag.). Served to capt. JAGC, USAR, 1979-80. Recipient Am. Jurisprudence award Lawyers Coop., 1972-73. Mem. Am. Arbitration Assn. (lectr.), ABA, N.Y. State Bar Assn. (lectr. annual meeting 1986), Fed. Bar Council, Adminstrv. Mgmt. Soc. (lectr.), Indsl. Relations Research Assn. (lectr. 1984), N.Y. State Pub. Employer Labor Relations Assn., Def. Research Inst., Westchester County Bar Assn., Yonkers Lawyers Assn., Blue Key, Delta Theta Phi. Democrat. Jewish. Labor, Federal civil litigation, State civil litigation. Office: Stein Davidoff & Malito 100 E 42d St New York NY 10017

STEFANI, RANDALL H., lawyer; b. Des Moines, July 19, 1956; s. Raymond R. and Phyllis J. Stefani. BBA, U. Iowa, 1978, JD, 1981. Bar: Iowa 1981, U.S. Dist. Ct. (so. and no. dists.) Iowa 1981, U.S. Ct. Appeals (8th cir.) 1981. From assoc. to ptnr. Ahlers Law Firm, Des Moines, 1981—. Mem. ABA, Iowa State Bar Assn., Iowa Soc. CPA's. Avocation: sports. Personal injury, Insurance, Federal civil litigation. Office: Ahlers Law Firm Liberty Bldg Suite 300 Des Moines IA 50309

STEFFEL, VERN JOHN, JR., lawyer; b. Chgo., July 10, 1950; s. Vern John and Adeline T. (Safranski) S.; m. Cynthia Lousie Corkum, Aug. 4, 1973. BS, Western Mich. U., 1972; postgrad., U. Notre Dame, London, summer 1974; JD, Ohio No. U., 1975. Bar: Mich. 1975, U.S. Dist. Ct. (ea. and we. dists.) Mich. 1980. Assoc. Allen, Worth & Hatch, Battle Creek, Mich., 1975-78; sole practice Battle Creek, 1978-85; sr. ptnr. Steffel & Steffel, Battle Creek, 1985—; bd. dirs. Steffel Design Studio, Battle Creek. Editor Ohio No. U. Law Review, 1974. Bd. dirs. Y-Ctr. Battle Creek, 1984—. Mem. ABA, Assn. Trial Lawyers Am., Comml. Law League Am., Mich. Bar Assn., Mich. Trial Lawyers Assn., Calhoun County Bar Assn. (sec. 1981-84). Roman Catholic. Avocations: marathons, racquetball, skiing. Contracts commercial, Real property, Banking. Home: 564 Breezy Bluff Battle Creek MI 49015 Office: Steffel & Steffel 332 E Columbia Suite A Battle Creek MI 49015

STEFFEN, JOSEPH JOHN, JR., lawyer; b. Chgo., Nov. 20, 1957; s. Joseph John Steffen Sr. and Carol Jane (Kuczon) Waddell. BA in History cum laude, Wake Forest U., 1979; JD, Coll. of William and Mary, 1982. Bar: Va. 1982, U.S. Dist. Ct. (we. dist.) Va. 1983. Assoc. Vaught & Steffen, Galax, Va., 1982-85, ptnr., 1985—; instr. Radford U., 1983-84, city councilman, Galax, 1984—. Chmn. Dem. Party, Galax, 1984—; mem. State Cen. Com., Richmond, Va., 1985. Mem. Assn. of Trial Lawyers of Am., ABA, Galax Jaycees. Education law, Workers' compensation, Family and matrimonial. Home: Box 227 Galax VA 24333 Office: Vaught & Steffen 111 W Grayson St Box 227 Galax VA 24333

STEFFEN, THOMAS LEE, state supreme court justice; b. Tremonton, Utah, July 9, 1930; s. Conrad Richard and Jewel (McGuire) S.; m. Lavona Ericksen, Mar. 20, 1953; children—Elizabeth, Catherine, Conrad, John, Jennifer. Student, U. So. Calif., 1955-56; B.S., U. Utah, 1957; J.D. with honors, George Washington U., 1964. Bar: Nev., U.S. Dist. Ct. Nev. 1965, U.S. Tax Ct. 1966, U.S. Ct. Appeals 1967, U.S. Supreme Ct. 1977. Contracts negotiator U.S. Bur. Naval Weapons, Washington, 1961-64; private practice Las Vegas, 1965-82; justice Supreme Ct. Nev., Carson City, 1982—; chmn. Nev. State-Fed. Jud. Council, 1986—. Mem. editorial staff George Washington U. Law Rev., 1963-64; contbr. articles to legal jours. Bd. dirs. So. Nev. chpt. NCCJ, 1974-75; mem. exec. bd. Boulder Dam Area council Boy Scouts Am., 1979-83; chmn. Nev. State-Fed. Jud. Council, 1986—; bd. visitors Brigham Young U., 1985—. Recipient merit citation Utah State U., 1983. Mem. Nev. Bar Assn. (former chmn. So. Nev. med.-legal screening panel), Nev. Trial Lawyers Assn. (former dir.). Republican. Mem. Ch. of Jesus Christ of Latter-day Saints. Avocations: reading, spectator sports. Judicial administration. Office: Supreme Ct of Nev Capitol Complex Carson City NV 89710

STEGALL, DANIEL RICHARD, lawyer, educator; b. Portsmouth, Va., Oct. 4, 1946; s. Earl and Theresia Loyce (Barlow) S.; m. Linda Elaine Gehman, Aug. 17, 1968; children—Justin Daniel, Joshua Gehman. Student, Ga. Inst. Tech., 1964; B.S., Va. Poly. Inst., 1969; M.B.A., U. Va., 1973, J.D., 1973. Bar: Va. 1973, D.C. 1974, Calif. 1981. Assoc., Hogan & Hartson, Washington, 1974-76; ptnr. Melrod, Redman & Gartlan, 1976-80, Rose & Stegall, Los Angeles, 1982-84, Dreisen, Kassoy & Freiberg, Los Angeles, 1984—; of counsel Lawler, Felix & Hall, 1980-81; adj. prof. U. So. Calif., Los Angeles, 1983-84, Loyola Law Sch., 1982—; lectr. in field. Contbr. tax articles to law rev. jours. Mem. ABA (chmn. subcom.), Calif. State Bar, Va. State Bar, D.C. Bar, Order of Coif, Phi Kappa Phi, Tau Beta Pi. Republican. Presbyterian. Club: Riverbend Country (Great Falls, Va.). Personal income taxation, Corporate taxation, Real property. Office: Dreisen Kassoy & Freiberg 1801 Century Park E Suite 740 Los Angeles CA 90067

STEGEMAN, THOMAS ALBERT, lawyer; b. Quincy, Ill., Mar. 9, 1948; m. Cynthia J. Taylor, Aug. 11, 1973; 1 son, Corey A.T. A.B., U. Ill., 1970; J.D., Washington U., 1973. Bars: Mo. 1973, Ill. 1974, D.C. 1985. Assoc., James C. Moloney, Inc., Clayton, Mo., 1973-75, Thompson & Mitchell, St. Louis, 1975-79; v.p., gen. counsel Roosevelt Fed. Savs. & Loan Assn., St. Louis, 1979-84; atty. Akin, Gump, Strauss, Hauer & Feld, 1984-86, Thomas & Fiske P.C., Fairfax, Va., 1986—. Capt., Friends of Scouting, 1974. Mem. Ill. State Bar Assn., Mo. Bar Assn., ABA, Chgo. Bar Assn., St. Louis Bar Assn. (exec. com. 1979-80). Editor, Washington U. Law Quar., 1972-73. Banking, Real property, General corporate. Home: 21 River Falls Ct Potomac MD 20854 Office: Thomas & Fiske 3110 Fairview Park Dr Suite 1400 Fairfax VA 22042

STEGER, EVAN EVANS, lawyer; b. Indpls., Oct. 24, 1937; s. Charles Franklin and Alice (Hill) S.; m. Suzy Gillespie, July 18, 1964; children—Cynthia Anne, Emily McKee. A.B., Wabash Coll., 1959; J.D., Ind. U., 1962. Bar: Ind. 1962, U.S. Dist. Ct. (so. dist.) Ind. 1962, U.S. Ct. Appeals (7th cir.) 1972, U.S. Tax Ct. 1982, U.S. Supreme Ct. 1982. Assoc. Ice, Miller, Donadio and Ryan, and predecessor firm Ross, McCord, Ice and Miller, Indpls., 1962-69, ptnr., 1970—. Fellow Am. Coll. Trial Lawyers; mem. ABA, Ind. Bar Assn., Indpls. Bar Assn., Internat. Assn. Def. Counsel. Democrat. Congregationalist. Federal civil litigation, State civil litigation. Office: One American Sq Box 82001 Indianapolis IN 46282

STEGER, SUSAN ST. JOHN, lawyer; b. Nashville, Oct. 18, 1945; d. William Augustus and Beverly Head (Pickup) St. John; m. Frank McAlister Steger, Sept. 7, 1969. B.A., Furman U., 1967; J.D., Walter F. George Sch. Law, Mercer U., 1970. Bar: Ga. 1970. Assoc. Martin, Snow, Grant & Napier, 1971-76; sole practice, Macon, Ga., 1976—. Bd. dirs. Middle Ga. council Girl Scouts U.S.A.; mem. adv. council Central Ga. Comprehensive Mental Health Ctr.; mem. adv. council Macon Probation and Parole Bd.; tech. adviser, bd. dirs. Crisis Line of Macon-Bibb County, Inc. Mem. Macon Bar Assn., State Bar Ga., Ga. Trial Lawyers Assn. Democrat. Episcopalian. Family and matrimonial, General practice, Juvenile. Home: 1074 Ave of Pines Macon GA 31204 Office: 740 Mulberry St Macon GA 31201

STEGER, WILLIAM MERRITT, judge; b. Dallas, Aug. 22, 1920; s. Merritt and Lottie (Reese) S.; m. Ann Hollandsworth, Feb. 14, 1948; 1 son, Merritt Reed (dec.). Student, Baylor U., 1938-41; LL.B., So. Meth. U., 1950. Bar: Tex. bar 1951. Pvt. practice Longview, 1951-53; apptd. U.S. dist. atty. Eastern Dist. Tex., 1953-59; mem. firm Wilson, Miller, Spivey & Steger, Tyler, Tex., 1959-70; U.S. dist. judge Eastern Dist. Tex. Tyler, 1970—. Republican candidate for gov. of Tex., 1960; for U.S. Ho. of Reps., 1962; mem. Tex. State Republican Exec. Com., 1966-69; chmn. Tex. State Republican Party, 1969-70. Served as pilot with ranks 2d lt. to capt. USAAF, 1942-47. Mem. Am. Bar Assn., State Bar Tex. Club: Mason (32 deg., Shriner). Home: 801 Meadow Creek Tyler TX 75703 Office: PO Box 1109 Tyler TX 75710 *

STEHLIK, FREDERICK D., lawyer; b. Lincoln, Nebr., Jan. 9, 1952; s. Norman F. and Dorothy E. (Rogers) S.; m. Charlene G. Lutz, May 17, 1974; children: Jason, Jennifer, Jessie, Jill, James. BS, Peru State Coll., 1974; JD, U. Nebr., 1977. Bar: Nebr. 1977, U.S. Dist. Ct. Nebr. 1977. Assoc. Law Offices of Russell S. Daub PC, Omaha, 1977-80; ptnr. Daub, Stehlik & Smith, Omaha, 1980-82, Stehlik, Smith, Trustin & Schweer, Omaha, 1982-86, Fitzgerald & Stehlik, Omaha, 1986—; bd. dirs. Norman IGA, Nebraska City, 1977—. Mem. Nebr. Bar Assn., Omaha Bar Assn. Republican. Methodist. Lodge: Rotary. Avocations: skiing, golf, reading. Contracts commercial, Government contracts and claims, Real property.

STEIL, GEORGE KENNETH, SR., lawyer; b. Darlington, Wis., Dec. 16, 1924; s. George John and Laura (Donahue) S.; m. Mavis Elaine Andrews, May 24, 1947; children: George Kenneth, John R., Michelle Steil Bryski, Marcelaine K. Student, Platteville State Tchrs. Coll., 1942-43; J.D., U. Wis., Madison, 1950. Bar: Wis. 1950, U.S. Tax Ct. 1971. Asso. firm J. G. McWilliams, Janesville, 1950-53; partner firm McWilliams and Steil, Janesville, 1954-60, Brennan, Steil, Ryan, Basting & MacDougall (S.C., and predecessor), Janesville, 1960-72; pres. Brennan, Steil, Ryan, Basting & MacDougall (S.C., and predecessor), 1972—; lectr. in law U. Wis., 1974; chmn. bd. Marine First Nat. Bank, Janesville, 1979—; dir. Marine Trust Co., N.A., Milw., Heritage Mut. Ins. Co., Sheboygan, Wis.; chmn. Wis. Supreme Ct. Bd. Atty. Profl. Responsibility, 1982-83, chmn. 1983—; chmn. Gov.'s adv. council jud. selection State of Wis., 1987—, chmn. Gov.'s jud. selection com. 1987—. Bd. dirs. St. Coletta Sch. for Exceptional Children, Jefferson, Wis., 1972-76, 78-84, chmn. bd., 1982-83. Served with U.S. Army, 1943-45. Fellow Am. Bar Found., Am. Coll. Probate Counsel; mem. Janesville Area C. of C. (pres. 1970-71), State Bar Wis. (pres. 1977-78), Am. Bar Assn., Wis. Bar Found. (dir. 1976—). Roman Catholic. General corporate, Probate. Home: 431 Apache Dr Janesville WI 53545 Office: Brennan Steil Ryan Basting & MacDougall SC 1 E Milwaukee St Janesville WI 53547

STEIMEL, NORMAN CLEMENS, III, lawyer; b. Spokane, Wash., Dec. 30, 1953; s. Norman Clemens Jr. and Margaret Mary (Rufkahr) S.; m. Libby Christine Toney, June 17, 1978; children: Nathan Andrew, Daniel Joseph, Amanda Jane, Jason Paul, Susanna Christine. AB, Washington U., St. Louis, 1975, JD, 1978. Bar: Mo. 1979, U.S. Dist. Ct. (we. dist.) Mo. 1979, Ill. 1980, U.S. Dist. Ct. (ea. dist.) Mo. 1980, U.S. Ct. Appeals (8th cir.) 1980, U.S. Supreme Ct. 1986. Law clk. to presiding justice Mo. Ct. Appeals (so. dist.), Springfield, 1979-80; assoc. Niedner, Niedner, Ahlheim & Bodeux L.A., St. Charles, Mo., 1980—. Mem. Mo. Citizens for Life, Families for Home Edn. Mem. Ill. Bar Assn., Mo. Bar Assn., Mo. Assn. Trial Attys., Lawyers for Life, Christian Legal Soc., Phi Alpha Delta. Republican. Mem. Evangelical Free ch. General practice, State civil litigation, Family and matrimonial. Office: Niedner Niedner Ahlheim & Bodeux 131 Jefferson St Saint Charles MO 63301

STEIMEL, WALTER EARL, JR., lawyer; b. Austin, Tex., Oct. 13, 1956; s. Walter Earl Sr. and Margaret Lucile (Brady) S. BBA in Acctg., Tex. Christian U., 1978; JD, U. Tex., 1981. Bar: Tex. 1981, U.S. Dist. Ct. (no. dist.) Tex. 1982; CPA, Tex. Legal assoc. Bechtel, Inc., San Francisco, 1980; assoc. Bracewell & Patterson, Houston, 1981-82; legis. counsel to Tex. Senator Parmer, Austin, 1982-83; counsel to chmn. Pub. Utility Commn. Tex., Austin, 1983—; speaker in field. mem. Space Bus. Roundtable, Austin, 1985—; bd. dirs. Austin Lawyers and Accts. for Arts, 1985—. Named Most Valuable Legis. Aide, Ft. Worth News Tribune, 1983. Mem. Assn. Trial Lawyers Am., Tex. Trial Lawyers Assn., Tex. Bar Assn. (various sects.), Phi Delta Phi, Beta Gamma Sigma, Omicron Delta Epsilon, Beta Alpha Psi. Democrat. Episcopalian. Club: Austin Rowing (v.p., regatta chmn.). Avocations: rowing, tennis, bicycling, investments, backpacking. Administrative and regulatory, Public utilities, Legislative. Home: 1333 Bonham Terr Austin TX 78704 Office: Pub Utility Commn Tex 7800 Shoal Creek Blvd #450N Austin TX 78757

STEIN, ALLAN MARK, lawyer; b. Montreal, Quebec, Can., Oct. 18, 1951; came to U.S., 1977; s. Boris and Beatrice (Fishman) S. B in Commerce, Sir George Williams, 1972; BA, Loyola, Montreal, 1973; B in Civil Law, McGill U., 1976, LLB, 1977; JD, Nova U., 1979. Bar: Fla. 1979, U.S. Dist. Ct. (so. dist.) Fla. 1979, U.S. Ct. Appeals (5th cir.) 1980, U.S. Ct. Appeals (11th cir.) 1983. Assoc. Law Offices of Paul Landy Beiley, Miami, Fla., 1980, Heitner & Rosenfeld, Miami, 1980-85; ptnr. Rosenfeld & Stein, Miami, 1985—. Mem. North Dade Bar Assn. (bd. dirs. 1985—). Republican. Jewish. Avocation: photography. Consumer commercial, Contracts commercial, Bankruptcy. Office: Rosenfeld & Stein 18260 NE 19 Ave #202 North Miami Beach FL 33162

STEIN, CAREY M., lawyer; b. Chgo., July 15, 1947; s. Daniel and Shirley (Weinstein) S.; m. Seena R. Silverman, July 8, 1972; children: Allison, Amy. BS, So. Ill. U., 1970; JD, DePaul U., 1974. Bar: Ill. 1974. Tax examiner IRS, Chgo., 1973-75; atty. Ill. Dept. Revenue, Chgo., 1975-77; asst. corp. counsel Hart, Schaffner & Marx, Chgo., 1977-83; Assoc. gen. counsel, asst. sec. Hartmarx Corp., Chgo., 1983-84, v.p., sec., gen. counsel, 1984—. V.p., bd. dirs. Ctr. for Enriched Living, Highland Park, 1984—; adv. bd. Northwestern U. Corp. Counsel Ctr., Chgo., 1984—; bd. dirs. Jewish Edn. Met. Chgo., 1987—. Mem. ABA, Ill. Bar Assn., Chgo. Bar Assn., Am. Soc. Corp. Secs., Am. Apparel Mfrs. Assn. (legal com. 1985—). Jewish. General corporate. Office: Hartmarx Corp 101 N Wacker Dr Chicago IL 60606

STEIN, CRAIG EDWARD, lawyer; b. Erie, Pa., Feb. 24, 1955; s. David and Phyllis Patricia (Lancet) S. BA with high honors, Swarthmore Coll., 1978; LLD, Emory U., 1981. Bar: Pa. 1981, U.S. Dist. Ct. (we. dist.) Pa. 1981, Fla. 1984, U.S. Dist. Ct. (so. dist.) Fla. 1986. Law clk. to presiding justice Pa. Supreme Ct., 1981-83; assoc. Stearns, Weaver, Miller, Weissler, Alhadeff & Sitterson P.A., Miami, Fla., 1984—. Mem. ABA, Pa. Bar Assn., Fla. Bar Assn., Am. Arbitration Assn., Swarthmore Coll. Alumni Council. Jewish. Federal civil litigation, State civil litigation. Home: 4245 Lennox Dr Miami FL 33133 Office: Stearns Weaver Miller et al 150 W Flagler St 2200 Museum Tower Miami FL 33130

STEIN, ELEANOR BANKOFF, judge; b. N.Y.C., Jan. 24, 1923; d. Jacob and Sarah (Rashkin) Bankoff; m. Frank S. Stein, May 27, 1947; children—Robert B., Joan Jenkins, William M. Student, Barnard Coll., 1940-42; B.S. in Econs., Columbia U., 1944; LL.B., NYU, 1949. Bar: N.Y. 1950, Ind. 1976, U.S. Supreme Ct. 1980. Atty. Hillis & Button, Kokomo, Ind., 1975-76, Paul Hillis, Kokomo, 1976-78, Bayliff, Harrigan, Kokomo, 1978-80; judge Howard County Ct., Kokomo, 1980—; co-juvenile referee Howard County Juvenile Ct., 1976-78. Mem. Republicans Women's Assn. Kokomo, 1980—; bd. dirs. Howard County Legal Aid Soc., 1976-80; dir. Howard County Ct. Alcohol and Drug Services Program, 1982—; bd. advisors St. Joseph Hosp., Kokomo, 1979—; commn. mem. Kokomo Bd. Human Relations, 1967-70. Mem. law rev. bd. NYU Law Rev., 1947-48. Mem. Am. Judicature Soc., Ind. Jud. Assn., Nat. Assn. Women Judges, ABA, Ind. Bar Assn., Howard County Bar Assn. Jewish. Clubs: Kokomo Country, Altrusa. Criminal, State civil litigation, Landlord-tenant. Home: 3204 Tally Ho Dr Kokomo IN 49602 Office: Howard County Ct Howard County Courthouse Kokomo IN 46901

STEIN, ERNEST D., corporate lawyer. BA, Bklyn. Coll.; LLB, NYU. With Mfrs. Hanover Co., N.Y.C., 1966-68, asst. sec., 1968-70, asst. v.p., 1970-72, v.p., 1972-77, sr. v.p., 1977-82, sr. v.p. gen. counsel, 1982-85, exec. v.p. gen. counsel, 1985—. Office: Mfrs Hanover Co 270 Park Ave New York NY 10017 *

STEIN, GARY, justice; b. Newark, June 13, 1933; s. Morris J. and Mollie (Goldfarb) S.; married, July 1, 1956; children—Jill, Carrie, Michael, Terri, Jo; m. Et Tilchin, July 1, 1956. A.B., Duke U., 1954, LL.B. with distinction, 1956; D.H.L. (hon.), N.J. Inst. Tech., 1985. Bar: D.C. 1956, Ohio 1957, N.Y. 1958, N.J. 1963. Research asst. U.S. Senate AntiTrust and Monopoly Subcom., Washington, 1955; assoc. Kramer, Marx, Greenlee & Backus, N.Y.C., 1956-65; sole practice Paramus, N.J., 1966-72; ptnr. Stein & Kurland, Esquires, Paramus, N.J., 1972-82; dir. Gov.'s Office of Policy and Planning, Trenton, N.J., 1982-85; assoc. justice Supreme Ct. N.J., Hackensack, 1985—; mcpl. atty., Paramus, 1967-71; counsel N.J. Election Law Revision Commn., 1970; atty. Bd. Adjustment, Teaneck, N.J., 1973-82. Mem. editorial bd. Duke Law Jour., 1954-56, assoc. editor, 1955-56. mem. Dist. Ethics Com. for Bergen County, N.J., 1977-80, chmn. 1981. Served with U.S. Army, 1957-58, 61-62. Mem. ABA (antitrust sect.), N.J. State Bar Assn. (com. on state legislation 1973-79, chmn. 1973-76, jud. selection com. 1976-81, Constl. amendment com. 1977-79, court modernization com. 1976-79), N.J. State Bar Assn., Bergen County Bar Assn., Order of Coif. Repub-

lican. Jewish. Avocation: tennis. Judicial administration. Office: Supreme Ct of NJ 25 Main St Hackensack NJ 07601

STEIN, LESLIE E., lawyer; b. N.Y.C., Dec. 25, 1956; d. Samuel and Barbara E. (Ellen) S. Student, Union Coll., 1974-76; BA, Macalester Coll., 1978; postgrad., U. Minn., 1978-79; JD, Albany Law Sch., 1981. Assoc. McNamee, Lochner, Titus & Williams P.C., Albany, N.Y., 1983—. Mem. adv. bd. Schenectady (N.Y.) Community Dispute Resolution, 1982-83; bd. dirs. Schenectady YWCA, 1983-84, Mens Coalition Against Battering, Inc., Albany, 1985—. Mem. N.Y. State Bar Assn., Womens Bar Assn. N.Y. (bd. dirs. 1986—), Albany County Bar Assn., Schenectady County Bar Assn. Family and matrimonial. Office: McNamee Lochner Titus & Williams 75 State St PO Box 459 Albany NY 12201-0459

STEIN, LESLIE REICIN, lawyer; b. Chgo., June 30, 1946; d. Frank Edward and Abranita (Rome) Reicin; m. Richard Nathan Stein, Nov. 25, 1967; 1 child, Michael Bennett. AB, U. Mich., 1967; MA in History, U. So. Fla., 1973; JD, Stetson U., 1976. Bar: Fla. 1976, U.S. Supreme Ct. 1981. Assoc. gen. counsel U. So. Fla., Tampa, 1968-80, lectr., instr., 1976-80; sr. atty. Gen. Telephone Co. of Fla., Tampa, 1983—; adj. prof. law Stetson U., St. Petersburg, Fla., 1983—; adv. bd. dirs. dispute resolution Ctr. For Labor Mgmt., St. Petersburg, 1983—; bd. dirs. Instl. Rev. Bd. for Human Subjects., Tampa. Editor in chief Stetson U. Law Rev., 1975; contbr. articles to profl. jours. Chmn. Civil Service Bd., Tampa, 1984-86; bd. dirs., chmn. personnel com. The Children's Home, Inc., Tampa, 1978—; bd. dirs. Sch. Enrichment Resource Vols. in Edn., Tampa, 1983-85, Retinitis Pigmentosis Found., Tampa, 1983-85. Mem. ABA (mgmt. com., labor com.), Fla. Bar Assn. (chmn. corp. counsel com. 1986—), Hillsborough County Bar Assn. (chmn. corp. counsel sect. 1982—), Am. Arbitration Assn. (corp. com.), Fla. Assn. for Women Lawyers (bd. dirs., sec., pub. affairs officer 1983—), Hillsborough Assn. for Women Lawyers (bd. dirs., pres. 1981—), Athena Soc., Inc. (chmn. com. 1981-83), Fla. Women's Network, U. So. Fla. Alumni Assn. (treas., bd. dirs. 1982—), Indsl. Relations Resource Assn. (pres. 1986—). Club: Tower. Labor, General corporate, Administrative and regulatory. Home: 99 Ladoga Ave Tampa FL 33606 Office: Gen Telephone Co of Fla One Tampa Center PO Box 110 MC 7 Tampa FL 33601

STEIN, MARK S., lawyer; b. Natchez, Miss., June 2, 1950; s. William and Lillian (Shiff) S.; m. Nancy Davies, May 16, 1977; children: Andrew Mark, Gregory Scott, Melissa Anne. BA, Duke U., 1972; JD, Tulane U., 1975; LLM in Taxation, NYU, 1976. Bar: La. 1975. Ptnr. Lemle, Kelleher, Kohlmeyer, Dennery, Hunley, Moss & Frilot, New Orleans, 1975-86, Lowe, Stein, Hoffman & Allweiss, New Orleans, 1986—; lectr. law Tulane U. Mem. profl. adv. com. Jewish Endowment Found., New Orleans, exec. com. Congregation Temple Sinai, New Orleans, 1980—, New Orleans Estate Planning Council. Mem. ABA (specialization bd. taxation sect. 1986—), La. Bar Assn. (chmn. taxation sect. 1984-85). Office: Lowe Stein et al 650 Poydras St Suite 2450 New Orleans LA 70130

STEIN, ROBERT ALLEN, law educator; b. Mpls., Sept. 16, 1938. B.S. in Law, U. Minn., 1960, J.D. summa cum laude, 1961. Bar: Wis. 1961, Minn. 1967. Asso. Foley, Sammond & Lardner, Milw., 1961-64; prof. Law Sch. U. Minn., Mpls., 1964—; assoc. dean U. Minn., 1976-77, v.p. adminstrn. and planning, 1978-80, dean Law Sch., 1979—, faculty rep. men's intercollegiate athletics, 1981—; of counsel Mullin, Weinberg & Daly, P.A., Mpls., 1970-80, Gray, Plant, Mooty, Mooty & Bennett, Mpls., 1980—; vis. prof. UCLA, 1969-70, U. Chgo., 1975-76; mem. Uniform State Laws Commn. Minn., 1973—; acad. fellow Am. Coll. Probate Counsel, 1975—; vis. scholar Am. Bar Found., Chgo., 1975-76; mem. trust com. Northwestern Nat. Bank St. Paul, 1977-81; trustee Gt. No. Iron Ore Properties, 1982—; advisor Restatement of Law Second, Property, 1977—. Author: Stein on Probate, 1976, Estate Planning Under the Tax Reform Act of 1976, 2d edit, 1978, In Pursuit of Excellence: A History of the University of Minnesota Law School, 1980, others; contbr. articles to legal jours. Founding bd. dirs. Park Ridge Ctr., 1985—; co-chair Gov.'s Task Force on Ctr. for Treatment of Torture Victims, 1985. Fellow Am. Bar Found., Am. Coll. Tax Counsel; mem. ABA, Minn. Bar Assn. (bd. govs. 1979—, mem. exec. council, probate and trust law sect. 1972-77), Hennepin County Bar Assn., Am. Judicature Soc. (bd. dirs. 1984—), Am. Law Inst., Internat. Acad. Estate and Trust Law. Estate planning, Probate, Real property. Home: 6005 Manchester Dr Minneapolis MN 55422 Office: Law Sch U Minn Minneapolis MN 55455

STEIN, SHELDON IRVIN, lawyer, investment banker; b. Bklyn., Aug. 11, 1953; s. Sidney and Esther (Gold) S.; m. Barbara Brickman, Aug. 18, 1974; children: Shane Randall, Kyle Noah, Reid Jordan. BA, Brandeis U., 1974; JD, Harvard U., 1977. Bar: Calif. 1977, Tex. 1978. Assoc. Fulop, Rolston, Burns & McKittrick, Beverly Hills, Calif., 1977-78; assoc. Hughes & Luce, Dallas, 1978-83, ptnr., 1983-86; assoc. dir. Bear, Stearns & Co., Inc., Dallas, 1986—; bd. dirs. BSN Corp., Dallas. Mem. leadership cabinet United Jewish Appeal, N.Y., 1984—; bd. dirs. Jewish Fedn. Dallas, 1985—, Jewish Community Ctr. Dallas, 1985—, Akiba Acad. Dallas, 1985—. Mem. ABA, Tex. Bar Assn., Calif. Bar Assn., Dallas Assn. Young Lawyers, Phi Beta Kappa. Clubs: Tower, Lincoln City (Dallas). Lodge: B'nai B'rith (bd. dirs. anti-defamation league Dallas 1983—). Avocations: sports, wine collecting, photography. Securities, General corporate. Office: Bear Stearns & Co Inc 1601 Elm St Dallas TX 75201

STEIN, STEPHEN, lawyer; b. Bklyn., Oct. 22, 1943; s. Alex and Rachel (Osbrach) S.; m. Susan Helane Cooper, Dec. 23, 1965; children: Sharyn Beth, David Marc. BA, NYU, 1964; JD, Bklyn. Law Sch., 1967. Bar: N.Y. 1967, U.S. Ct. Appeals (3d cir.) 1973, Nev. 1974, U.S. Dist. Ct. Nev. 1974, U.S. Ct. Appeals (9th cir.) 1974, U.S. Supreme Ct. 1974, U.S. Ct. Appeals (5th cir.) 1975, U.S. Ct. Appeals (4th cir.) 1976, U.S. Ct. Appeals (10th cir.) 1979, U.S. Ct. Appeals (8th and 11th cirs.) 1982. Spl. atty. U.S. Dept. Justice, Washington, 1971-74; ptnr. Goodman, Stein & Quintana, Las Vegas, Nev., 1974—. Pres. Temple Beth Am, Las Vegas, 1985—. Served to lt. commdr. USN, 1967-71. Mem. Nev. Trial Lawyers Assn. (bd. dirs. 1985—). Republican. Jewish. Criminal. Office: Goodman Stein & Quintana 520 S 4th St Las Vegas NV 89101

STEIN, STUART LEONARD, lawyer; b. Bklyn., Aug. 31, 1946; s. Sidney Sam and Ada (Schlaifer) S.; m. Joanne Eskind Lanza, July 3, 1968 (div. Aug. 1979); children: Andrew H., Jordan L.; m. Barbara McCann White, Apr. 25, 1982; 1 child, Jessica S. White. BS, Adelphi U., 1974; JD, Nova U., 1977. Bar: Fla. 1977, U.S. Supreme Ct. 1982, U.S. Dist. Ct. (so. and midl dists.) Fla. 1977, U.S. Ct. Appeals (5th and 11th cirs.) 1981. Ptnr. Gedrich & Stein, Ft. Lauderdale, Fla., 1977-78; sole practice Ft. Lauderdale, 1979—. Cand. Fla. Ho. of Reps., 1978, 80, 82; bd. dirs. Broward County Right to Life, 1980-83. Mem. ABA, Broward Bar Assn., Supreme Ct. Hist. Soc., Broward County Criminal Defense Lawyers, Nova U. Law Alumni Assn. (pres. 1980). Republican. Jewish. Lodge: B'nai B'rith (founding mem. justice unit). Criminal, Personal injury, General practice. Office: 150 N Federal Hwy Suite 220 Fort Lauderdale FL 33301

STEIN, WILLIAM ROBERT, lawyer; b. N.Y.C., Mar. 23, 1952; s. Norman William and Alyce Josephine (Amorosino) S.; m. Victoria Jane Griffiths May 30, 1981; 1 child, Katherine Jane. BA magna cum laude, Columbia U., 1974, JD, 1977. Bar: N.Y. 1978, U.S. Ct. Appeals (3d cir.) 1978, U.S. Dist. Ct. (so. dist.) N.Y. 1979, D.C. 1980, U.S. Dist. Ct. D.C. 1980, U.S. Ct. Appeals (D.C. cir.) 1980, U.S. Supreme Ct. 1981. Law clk. to presiding justice U.S. Ct. Appeals (3d cir.), Newark, 1977-78; assoc. Hughes, Hubbard & Reed, Washington, 1978-85, ptnr., 1985—. Harlan Fiske Stone scholar Columbia U. Law Sch., 1975, 76, James Kent scholar Columbia U. Law Sch., 1977. Mem. ABA, D.C. Bar Assn., Phi Beta Kappa. Federal civil litigation. Home: 8812 Altimont Ln Chevy Chase MD 20815 Office: Hughes Hubbard & Reed 1201 Pennsylvania Ave NW Washington DC 20004

STEINBACH, HAROLD I., lawyer; b. The Bronx, N.Y., Aug. 31, 1956; s. Aaron and Phyllis (Feldfeber) S.; m. Beryl Joy Schwartz, Mar. 14, 1982; 1 child, Sarah Brandl. BA, SUNY, Binghamton, 1978; JD, NYU, 1981. Bar: N.Y. 1982, N.J. 1983, U.S. Dist. Ct. (so. dist.) N.Y. 1982. Assoc. Flemming, Zulack & Williamson, N.Y.C., 1981-83, Kleinberg, Kaplan, Wolff & Cohen, P.C., N.Y.C., 1983—. Mem. ABA (corp. law sect., small bus. com.), N.Y. State Bar Assn., Assn. Bar City N.Y., Phi Beta Kappa. Jewish. General corporate, Real property. Home: 665 Ogden Ave Teaneck NJ 07666 Office: Kleinberg Kaplan Wolff & Cohen 522 5th Ave New York NY 10036

STEINBERG, ELLIOT GERSHOM, lawyer; b. San Francisco, Oct. 15, 1937; William and Pauline (Finkelstein) S.; m. Sarah Jane Staats, Apr. 3, 1965 (div. 1973); children: John Michael, Aaron William, Scott Anthony; m. Janet Beth Goldberg, June 12, 1982. BA, U. Calif., Berkeley, 1960, JD, 1964. Bar: Calif., U.S. Dist. Ct. (no. dist.) Calif., U.S. Ct. Appeals (9th cir.); cert. specialist in taxation. Assoc. Thorne & Stanton, San Jose, Calif., 1965-66, ptnr., 1966-70; ptnr. Levenfeld & Kanter, San Francisco, 1970-79, Flynn & Steinberg, San Francisco, 1979-83; gen. ptnr. European Am. Securities Ventures L.P., San Francisco, 1984-85; v.p., gen. counsel Itel Corp., San Francisco, 1985—; cons. Itel Corp., 1985; bd. dirs. Kimco Mgmt. Co., San Francisco. Co-author: Closely Held Corporations, 1977, (book) Tax Reform Act of 1976, 1976, Income Taxation of Foreign Related Transactions, 1971; editor Jour. Taxation of Investments, 1984—. Chmn. bd. dirs. San Francisco Art Inst., 1982—; trustee Urban High Sch. of San Francisco, 1983—, Wright Inst., Berkeley, 1980-83. Served with USN, 1955-57. Mem. ABA, Calif. Bar Assn., Bar Assn. of San Francisco, Internat. Fiscal Assn. Democrat. Jewish. Clubs: Tiburon (Calif.) Peninsula, Bay (San Francisco), San Francisco Lawyers. Avocations: skiing, tennis. Corporate taxation, Estate taxation, Personal income taxation. Office: Itel Corp 220 Jackson St San Francisco CA 94111

STEINBERG, HARVEY LAURANCE, lawyer; b. N.Y.C., May 14, 1942; s. Jack and Pearl (Abberbock) S.; m. Karen Lynn Nelson, June 28, 1970; children: Tanya Janelle, Justin Drew. BA, Drew U., 1963; JD, U. Pa., 1966. Bar: N.Y. 1967, Ind. 1971, Mich. 1978. Atty. FTC, N.Y.C., 1966-70; asst. counsel Miles Labs., Elkhart, Ind., 1970-77; food and drug counsel Dow Corning Corp., Midland, Mich., 1977—. Pres. Friends of the Library, Midland, 1986-87. Mem. ABA, Mich. Bar Assn., Health Industry Mfrs. Assn. (legal sect. steering com. 1979—). Administrative and regulatory, General corporate, Health. Home: 1403 W St Andrews Rd Midland MI 48640 Office: Dow Corning Corp PO Box 994 2200 Salzburg Rd Midland MI 48686

STEINBERG, HOWARD E., lawyer, holding company executive; b. N.Y.C., Nov. 19, 1944; s. Herman and Anne Rudel (Sinnreich) S.; m. Judith Ann Schucart, Jan. 28, 1968; children: Henry Robert, Kathryn Jill. A.B., U. Pa., 1965; J.D., Georgetown U., 1969. Bar: N.Y. 1970, U.S. Dist. Ct. (so. and ea. dists.) N.Y. 1973, U.S. Ct. Appeals (2d cir.) 1976. Assoc. Dewey, Ballantine, Bushby, Palmer & Wood, N.Y.C., 1969-76, ptnr., 1977-83; sr. v.p., gen. counsel, corp. sec. Reliance Group Holdings Inc., N.Y.C., 1983—; corp. sec. Data Resources, Inc., Lexington, Mass., 1978-79; bd. dirs. Days Inn Corp., Telemundo Group, Inc. Editor case notes: Georgetown Law Jour., 1968-69. Served to capt. JAGC AUS, 1972-74. Mem. ABA, N.Y. Bar Assn., Assn. Bar of City N.Y. Jewish. Club: University. General corporate, Securities. Office: Reliance Group Holdings Inc 55 E 52d St New York NY 10055

STEINBERG, MARVIN BERNARD, judge; b. Balt., Sept. 10, 1929; s. Israel and Dorothy (Pinkner) S.; m. Ilene Abel, Aug. 3, 1952 (div. 1975); children: John, Jill, Scott; m. Kathryn Burch, Aug. 29, 1975. AA, U. Balt., 1949, LLB cum laude, 1952. Bar: Md. 1952, U.S. Supreme Ct. 1960. Ptnr. Hyman Rubenstein, Balt., 1954-56, Steinberg & Steinberg, Balt., 1961-70, Gomborov, Steinberg, Schlachman & Harris, Balt., 1971-77, Steinberg, Schlachman, Potler & Belsky, Balt., 1978-79, Steinberg, Schlachman, Potler, Belsky & Weiner, Balt., 1980-85; judge Cir. Ct. of Balt., 1985—; mem. Jud. Nominating Commn., 1974-78. Bd. dirs. Alzheimer's Assn., Zionists Am., 1984-86. Served with USAF, 1953-54. Mem. Md. State Bar Assn. (bd. govs. 1971-72, chmn. section legal edn. and adminstrn. 1971), Balt. City Bar Assn (chmn. workmen's compensation com. 1964,). Democrat. Jewish. Avocations: travelling, mountain climbing, camping. Judicial administration. Home: 3007 Cresmont Ave Baltimore MD 21211 Office: Cir Ct of Balt City 111 N Calvert St Baltimore MD 21202

STEINBERG, MORTON M., lawyer; b. Chgo., Feb. 13, 1945; s. Paul S. and Sylvia (Neikrug) S.; m. Miriam C. Bernstein, Aug. 25, 1974; children—Adam Michael, Shira Judith. A.B. with honors U. Ill., 1967; J.D., Northwestern U., 1971. Bar: Ill. 1971, U.S. Dist. Ct. (no. dist.) Ill. 1971, U.S. Ct. Appeals (7th cir.) 1971, U.S. Supreme Ct. 1974. Assoc. Caffarelli & Wiczer, Chgo., 1971-73; assoc. Arnstein, Gluck, Lehr, Barron & Milligan, Chgo., 1974-76, ptnr., 1977-86, Rudnick & Wolfe, 1986—; speaker in field. Sr. editor Jour. Criminal Law and Criminology, Northwestern U., 1969-71. Bd. dirs., v.p. Camp Ramah in Wis., Inc., Chgo., 1974—; dir. North Suburban Synagogue Beth-El, Highland Park, Ill., 1978—, corp. sec., 1983-87; mem. Nat. Ranch Commn., 1987—; dir. Found. Conservative Judaism in Israel. Served with USAR, 1969-75. Recipient Youth Leadership award Nat. Fedn. Jewish Men's Clubs, N.Y.C., 1963; cert. of merit U.S. Dist. Ct. Fed. Defender Program, Chgo., 1969. Mem. ABA, Ill. Bar Assn., Chgo. Bar Assn., Am. Land Devel. Assn. Jewish. Club: Metropolitan (Chgo.). Real property, Contracts commercial, General corporate. Home: 1320 Lincoln Ave S Highland Park IL 60035 Office: Rudnick & Wolfe 30 N LaSalle St Chicago IL 60602

STEINBERGER, JEFFREY WAYNE, lawyer, consultant; b. Bronx, N.Y., Nov. 27, 1947; s. Martin and Shirley (Blumen) S.; m. Marlene Zimmelman, Apr. 28, 1976 (div. June 1983); 1 child, Darren William. BS, Queens Coll., 1968; JD, U. Western Los Angeles, 1976. Sole practice 1979—; owner Jeridean Industries, Los Angeles, 1968-75; mgr., artist Clout Agy., Beverly Hills, Calif., 1972-76; real estate broker Nat. Real Estate, Beverly Hills, 1974—; dist. atty. City of Los Angeles, 1976-77; cons. City of Hope, San Fernadino, Calif., 1979; judge pro tem Los Angeles Mcpl. Ct., 1984—. Producer, developer, host TV show Jeffs Law, 1979—. Developer, founder Coalition for Child Care, Beverly Hills, 1985. Served with USAR, 1969-70. Mem. Los Angeles Bar Assn., Beverly Hills Bar Assn., Assn. Trial Lawyers Am., Calif. Trial Lawyers Assn., Beverly Hills Trial Lawyers Assn., Los Angeles Bd. of Realtors, Beverly Hills Bd. of Realtors, Mensa. Avocations: karate-do, scuba exploration, hatha yoga, triathalons. Personal injury, Criminal, Entertainment. Office: 9665 Wilshire Blvd #801 Beverly Hills CA 92012

STEINBRECHER, WILLIAM JOHN, lawyer; b. Jamaica, N.Y., June 14, 1928; s. William J. and Mary (Ryan) S.; m. Mary E. Gilmartin, Dec. 26, 1959; children—Mary Ellen, Karen William, David, Nancy. B.S., Fordham U., 1950; J.D., N.Y. U., 1953. Bar: N.Y. 1954, U.S. dist. ct. (so. and ea. dists.) 1956, U.S. Supreme Ct. 1970. Mem. firm Maurice, McNamee & Dart, N.Y.C.; with Aetna Life & Casualty, N.Y.C.; mem. firm Walter F. Doyle, Esq., Mineola, N.Y.; sole practice, Garden City, N.Y.; lectr. Hofstra Law Sch., Nassau County Bar Assn., Judiciary Com. Nassau County. Mem. ABA, Am. Trial Lawyers Assn., N.Y. Trial Lawyers Assn., N.Y. State Bar Assn., Nassau County Bar Assn., Suffolk County Bar Assn., Queens County Bar Assn., New York County Lawyers Assn. Democrat. Clubs: Cherry Valley Country, Elks (past pres. N.Y. State). Personal injury, Federal civil litigation, State civil litigation. Home: 59 First St Garden City NY 11530 Office: 161 Willis Ave Mineola NY 11501

STEINER, BRUCE DARRELL, lawyer; b. N.Y.C., Apr. 17, 1950; s. Julius and Terry (Pruslin) S.; m. Sandra Renée Shaiman, Jan. 21, 1979; children: Michèle Robin, David Benjamin. AB, Cornell U., 1972; JD, SUNY, Buffalo, 1975; LLM in Taxation, NYU, 1976. Bar: N.Y. 1976, U.S. Ct. Claims 1976, U.S. Tax Ct. 1976, N.J. 1978, Fla. 1978, U.S. Dist. Ct. N.J. 1978. Assoc. Young, Kaplan & Edelstein, N.Y.C., 1976-77, Gannet & Apfel, Newark, 1978-80, Orloff, Lowenbach, Stifelman & Siegel, Roseland, N.J., 1980-86; of counsel Meltzer, Lippe & Goldstein, Mineola, N.Y., 1986—; lectr. Fairleigh Dickinson U. Tax Inst., Madison, N.J., 1986-87. Mem. Nassau County Dem. Com., N.Y., 1973-74. Mem. ABA, N.Y. State Bar Assn., N.J. Bar Assn., Assn. of Bar of City of N.Y., Essex County Bar Assn. (lectr. 1982, 84), Fla. Bar Assn., Nassau County Bar Assn. Jewish. Corporate taxation, Personal income taxation, Probate. Home: 821 Jersey Ave Elizabeth NJ 07202 Office: Meltzer Lippe & Goldstein 190 Willis Ave Mineola NY 11501

STEINER, HENRY J., legal educator; b. 1930. B.A., 1951; M.A., 1955; LL.B., Harvard U., 1955. Bar: N.Y. 1956, Mass. 1963. Law clk. to Justice John M. Harlan, U.S. Supreme Ct., 1957-58; assoc. Sullivan and Cromwell, N.Y.C., 1958-62; asst. prof. Harvard U. Sch. Law, 1962-65, prof., 1965—, dir. Human Rights Program, 1984—; vis. prof. CEPED, Rio de Janeiro, Brazil, 1968-69; vis. prof. Yale U., 1972-73, Stanford U., 1965; with San Diego-Paris Inst. on Internat. and Comparative Law, 1978, 81; cons. AID, 1962-64, Ford Found., 1966-69. Author: (with others) Transnational Legal Problems, 3d edit., 1986, Tort and Accident Law, 1983, Moral Argument and Social Vision in the Courts, 1987; former devels. editor Harvard Law Rev. Legal education. Office: Harvard U Law Sch Cambridge MA 02138

STEINER, JULIUS MICHAEL, lawyer; b. Phila., Aug. 18, 1946; s. Raymond J. and Selma E. (Lipschutz) S.; m. Sherry Handsman, Jan., 1970; m. 2d, Darlene Landwehr, Oct. 18, 1978; 1 dau., Joan Michelle. B.S., Temple U., 1968; J.D., U. Louisville, 1972. Bar: Pa. 1973, Wis. 1974, U.S. Sup. Ct. 1980. Field atty. NLNB, Pitts., 1973-74; ptnr. Pechner, Dorfman, Wolffe, Rounick & Cabot, Phila., 1975—; gen. counsel, dir. Annenberg Research Inst., Phila. Contbr. articles on labor law to profl. jours. Mem. ABA, Pa. Bar Assn., Phila. Bar Assn., Am. Soc. Hosp. Attys., Union Internat. Des Avocats, Phi Kappa Phi, Omicron Delta Kappa. Labor. Home: 811 Nagys Ford Rd Narberth PA 19072 Office: Pechner Dorfman Wolffe Rounick & Cabot 3 Parkway Philadelphia PA 19102

STEINER, PETER OTTO, educator; b. N.Y.C., July 9, 1922; s. Otto Davidson and Ruth (Wurzburger) S.; m. Ruth E. Riggs, Dec. 20, 1947 (div. 1967); children: Alison Ruth, David Denison; m. Patricia F. Owen, June 2, 1968. A.B., Oberlin Coll., 1943; M.A., Harvard, 1949, Ph.D., 1950. Instr. U. Calif. at Berkeley, 1949-50, asst. prof. econs., 1950-57; asso. prof. econs. U. Wis., Madison, 1957-59; prof. U. Wis., 1959-68; prof. econs. and law U. Mich., Ann Arbor, 1968—; chmn. dept. econs. U. Mich., 1971-74, dean Coll. Lit., Sci. and Arts, 1981—; vis. prof. U. Nairobi, Kenya, 1974-75; Cons. U.S. Bur. Budget, 1961-62, Treasury Dept., 1962-63, various pvt. firms, 1952—. Author: An Introduction to the Analysis of Time Series, 1956, (with R. Dorfman) The Economic Status of the Aged, 1957, (with R.G. Lipsey) Economics, 8th edit., 1987, On the Process of Planning, 1968, Public Expenditure Budgeting, 1969, Mergers: Motives, Effects, Policies, 1975, also articles. Served to lt. USNR, 1944-46. Social Sci. Research Council Faculty Research fellow, 1956; Guggenheim fellow, 1960; Ford Faculty Research fellow, 1965. Mem. Am. Econ. Assn., Econometric Soc., AAUP (chmn. com. Z 1970-73, pres. 1976-78). Legal education, Antitrust, Economics and law. Home: 2611 Hawthorne Rd Ann Arbor MI 48104 *

STEINER, PHILIP, lawyer; b. Yonkers, N.Y., Aug. 5, 1914; s. Henry Joseph and Gertrude (Davis) S.; m. Dorothy Ruvkun, Jan. 18, 1941; children—Paul, Lawrence, Stephen; m. 2d, Lorraine Simon, Nov. 19, 1978. B.S. in Bus. Adminstrn., U. Calif.-Berkeley, 1937; J.D., U. San Francisco, 1948. Bar: Calif. 1948, U.S. Dist. Ct. (no. dist.) Calif. 1948, U.S. Ct. Appeals (9th cir.) 1948, U.S. Supreme Ct. 1966, U.S. Ct. Mil. Appeals 1968, N.Y. 1986. Casualty underwriter Hartford Accident & Indemnity Co., San Francisco, 1937-38, Pacific Nat. Fire Ins. Co., San Francisco, 1938-40; investigator Calif. Dept. Ins., San Francisco, 1940-42; chief underwriter Gen. Am. Insurance Group, San Francisco, 1946-48; assoc. Long & Levit, San Francisco, 1948-50; ptnr. Steiner & Steiner, San Francisco, 1950—. Served with U.S. Army 1942-46. Mem. ABA, State Bar Calif., Bar Assn. San Francisco, Phi Alpha Delta. Republican. Clubs: Presidio Golf and Country, Presidio Officers, Concordia-Argonaut (San Francisco). Lodges: Shriners; Masons. Administrative and regulatory, Insurance, General practice. Office: 400 Montgomery St 4th Floor San Francisco CA 94104-1297

STEINER, SANFORD LEE, lawyer; b. Detroit, Oct. 6, 1941; s. Paul and Evelyn (Stolman) S.; m. Kathleen Wolf; children: Mark, Wendi. BA, Wayne State U., 1963, JD, 1966. Bar: Mich. 1966, U.S. Dist. Ct. (ea. and we. dists.) Mich. 1966, U.S. Ct. Appeals (6th cir.) 1974, U.S. Supreme Ct. 1976. Assoc. Ripple, Chambers & DeWitt, Detroit, 1966-68, Ripple & Chambers, Detroit, 1968-72; ptnr. Chambers, Steiner, Mazur et al, Kalamazoo, 1972—; instr. law Wayne State U., Detroit, 1966-69. Exec. bd. dirs. Kalamazoo County Dems., 1982-84. Mem. Assn. Trial Lawyers Am., Mich. Trial Lawyers Assn., State Bar Mich. (treas. workers compensation council 1984-85, sec. workers compensation council 1985-86). Federal civil litigation, State civil litigation, Personal injury. Office: Chambers Steiner Mazur et al 965 W Milham Kalamazoo MI 49002

STEINGER, CHARLES STANFORD, lawyer; b. St. Louis, Jan. 3, 1944; s. George Charles and Paula May (Yawitz) S.; m. Elaine May Ladin, July 24, 1965; children: Shayna Rebecca, Jessica Claire. BA, U. Colo., 1965; MA, Ohio State U., 1967, PhD, 1971; postgrad., U. London, 1968-69; JD, Drake U., 1981. Bar: Iowa 1982, U.S. Ct. Appeals (8th cir.) 1982, U.S. Dist. Ct. (so. dist.) Iowa 1983, U.S. Ct. Internat. Trade 1985, U.S. Tax Ct. 1985, U.S. Supreme Ct. 1985. Editor D.C. Heath Ltd., London, 1971-73, Macmillan Ltd., London, 1973-76; mgr. consumer products Ladin Industries Inc., Des Moines, 1976-81; assoc. Davis, Hockenberg, Wine, Brown, Koehn & Shors, Des Moines, 1982-86, ptnr., 1986—; Mem. Gov.'s adv. com. on Internat. Trade, State of Iowa, 1985—. Mem. ABA, Internat. Bar Assn., The Law Soc. Eng., Iowa State Bar Assn., Polk County Bar Assn. Office: Davis Hockenberg Wine Brown & Shors 2300 Financial Ctr Des Moines IA 50309

STEINGOLD, FRED SAUL, lawyer; b. Highland Park, Mich., Apr. 16, 1936; s. Nathaniel and Rosaline S.; m. Sarah Ruth Rubenstein, Jan. 25, 1959; children—Mark Ross, David Michael. A.B., U. Mich., 1957, J.D., 1960. Bar: Mich. 1961. Chief asst. city atty. City of Ann Arbor, 1965-69; ptnr. Fahrner & Steingold, Ann Arbor, 1969—; pres. Bus. Enterprise Inst., Inc., Ann Arbor, 1981—. Author: The Practical Guide to Michigan Law, 1983, Legal Master Guide for Small Business, 1983; editor: Basic Michigan Practice Handbook, 1981. Mem. ABA, State Bar Mich., Washtenaw County Bar Assn., Am. Trial Lawyers Assn. Jewish. General corporate, Real property, Federal civil litigation. Home: 3410 Andover Rd Ann Arbor MI 48105 Office: 320 N Main St Suite 102 Ann Arbor MI 48104

STEINGOLD, STUART GEOFFREY, lawyer; b. N.Y.C., Apr. 6, 1945; m. Celia Anne Newberg; children: Marissa Leigh, Alison Clare. BA, Princeton U., 1966; Cd'EP, Institut d'Etudes Politiques, Paris, 1967; JD, Harvard U., 1970. Bar: N.Y. 1971, U.S. Dist. Ct. (so. dist.) N.Y. 1974, D.C. 1984. Assoc. White & Case, N.Y.C. and Paris, 1970-80; ptnr. White & Case, N.Y.C., 1981-83, Perkins Coie, Washington, 1983—. Mem. ABA. Clubs: Princeton, Aero (Washington). Contracts commercial, Private international, Banking. Office: Perkins Coie 1110 Vermont Ave NW Washington DC 20005

STEINHAUS, RICHARD ZEKE, lawyer, lobbyist; b. N.Y.C., Dec. 27, 1927; s. Jacob and Rose Ornstein; m. Joan G., June 24, 1951 (div.); children—Peter Michael, Richard Zeke; m. 2d, Mary K. Kopley, Sept. 25, 1982. B.S., N.Y. U., 1951; J.D., Bklyn. Law Sch., 1955; L.H.D. (hon.), N.Y. Coll. Podiatric Medicine, 1975. Bar: N.Y. 1956, D.C. 1960. Sole practice, 1956-60; ptnr. Reeves, Robinson, Washington, 1960-63, Blinder & Steinhaus, 1965-73, Steinhaus & Hochhauser, 1973-76; sole practice Tarrytown, N.Y., and Albany, N.Y., 1976-82; ptnr. Richard Z. Steinhaus Assocs., Albany, 1981—; asst. prof. N.Y. Coll. Podiatric Medicine; vis. lectr. Ithaca Coll., 1973-85; acting village judge Village of Dobbs Ferry (N.Y.), 1965. Served with USN, 1945-47. Mem. ABA, N.Y. State Bar Assn., N.Y. State Magistrates Assn., Albany Bar Assn., Westchester Bar Assn., Assn. Bar City N.Y. Democrat. Jewish. Clubs: Ft. Orange (Albany); Swiss Alpine (Zermatt). Legislative, General practice. Address: 90 S Swan St Albany NY 12210

STEINHILBER, AUGUST WILLIAM, association executive, consultant; b. Cleve., Jan. 19, 1932; s. William August and Clara Augusta (Steinbrucker) S.; m. Dolores Ables, Nov. 3, 1956; children—August William, Lisa, Paula. B.A., Case Western Res. U., 1954; J.D., Georgetown U., 1961. Bar: Ohio 1962, D.C. 1963, U.S. Supreme Ct. 1966. Dep. asst. U.S. Commr. of Edn., HEW, 1960-68; asst. exec. dir. Nat. Sch. Bd. Assn., Washington, 1968-78, assoc. exec. dir., 1978—, legal counsel, 1978-85, gen. counsel, 1985—; cons. sch. fin., lectr. numerous colls. Pres. Prince Georges County Boys and Girls Club; v.p. Prince Georges County Fedn. Recreation Councils. Served to 1st lt., USMC, 1955-58. Recipient Superior Service award HEW, 1968. Mem. ABA, Nat. Orgn. Legal Problems in Edn. (pres., chmn. ad hoc com. on copyright), Am. Judicature Soc., Fed. Bar Assn. (v.p. Va. chpt.). Lutheran. Author: Education Consolidation and Improvement Act, a Manual, 1982; State Laws on Compulsory Attendance; The Copyright Law and Education, 1983; asst. editor Jour. Law and Edn., 1972—. Local government, Legislative, Trademark and copyright. Home: 12437 Surrey Circle Dr Tantallon MD 20744 Office: 1680 Duke St Alexandria VA 22314

STEINHORN, IRWIN HARRY, lawyer, educator, corporate executive; b. Dallas, Aug. 13, 1940; s. Raymond and Libby L. (Miller) S.; m. Linda Kay Shoshone, Nov. 30, 1968; 1 child, Leslie Robin. BBA, U. Tex., 1961, LLB, 1964. Bar: Tex. 1964, U.S. Dist. Ct. (no. dist.) Tex. 1965, Okla. 1970, U.S. Dist. Ct. (we. dist.) Okla. 1972. Assoc. Oster & Kaufman, Dallas, 1964-67; ptnr. Parness, McQuire & Lewis, Dallas, 1967-70; sr. v.p., gen. counsel LSB Industries, Inc., Oklahoma City, 1970—; adj. prof. law Oklahoma City U. Sch. Law, 1979-84; lectr. in field. Mem. adv. com. Okla. Securities Commn., 1986—. Served to capt. USAR, 1964-70. Mem. ABA, Tex. Bar Assn., Okla. Bar Assn., Com. to Revise Okla. Bus. Corp. Act, Phi Alpha Delta. Republican. Jewish. Lodge: Kiwanis. General corporate, Securities, Contracts commercial. Home: 6205 Avalon Oklahoma City OK 73118 Office: LSB Industries Inc 16 S Pennsylvania Oklahoma City OK 73107

STEINHOUSE, CARL LEWIS, lawyer; b. N.Y.C., July 18, 1931; s. Samual A. and Sophia (Schwartz) S.; m. Diana Joan Wasserman, Aug. 16, 1953; children: Samuel A., Jane W., Laura A. BS in Acctg., NYU, 1952; LLB, Bklyn. Law Sch., 1959. Bar: N.Y. 1959, U.S. Dist. Ct. (so. dist.) N.Y. 1960, U.S. Dist. Ct. Hawaii 1962, Ohio 1971, U.S. Dist. Ct. (no. dist.) Ohio, U.S. Dist. Ct. (no. dist.) N.Y., U.S. Ct. Appeals (fed. and 6th cirs.) 1983, U.S. Supreme Ct. 1983. Acct. D. Grossman & Co., N.Y.C., 1954-59; trial atty. anti-trust div. U.S. Dept. Justice, N.Y.C., 1959-61, Hawaii, 1961-65; chief great lakes div. U.S. Dept. Justice, Cleve., 1965-73; assoc. Jones, Day, Reavis & Pogue, Cleve., 1973-75, ptnr., 1975—. Editor: Jury Instructions in Criminal Law Antitrust Cases, 1982, Sample Antitrust Jury Instruction Criminal, 1984; contbr. articles to profl. jours. Mem. com. Soviet Jewry Jewish Community Fedn., Cleve., 1985—, older persons services, 1983-85; trustee Pepper Pike Civic League, Ohio, 1979-80. Served to sgt. U.S. Army, 1952-54. Mem. ABA (antitrust council 1984—, antitrust com. Sherman Act Com. 1982-84, criminal com. 1979-82, litigation sect.). Avocations: tennis, computer science. Antitrust, Federal civil litigation, Criminal. Home: 28599 S Woodland Pepper Pike OH 44124 Office: Jones Day Reavis & Pogue 1700 Huntington Bldg Cleveland OH 44115

STEINMAN, JOAN ELLEN, lawyer, educator; b. Bklyn., June 19, 1947; d. Jack and Edith Ruth (Shapiro) S.; m. Douglass Watts Cassel, Jr., June 1, 1974 (div. July 1986); children—Jennifer Lynn, Amanda Hilary. Student U. Birmingham, Eng., 1968; A.B. with high distinction, U. Rochester, 1969; J.D. cum laude, Harvard U., 1973. Bar: Ill. 1973. Assoc., Schiff, Hardin & Waite, Chgo., 1973-77; asst. prof. Ill. Inst. Tech. Chgo.-Kent. Coll. Law, 1977-82, assoc. prof., 1982-86, prof., 1986—; cons. in atty. promotions Met. San. Dist. Greater Chgo., 1981, 85. Coop. atty. ACLU Ill., Chgo., 1974, Leadership Council for Met. Open Communities, Chgo., 1975, Better Govt. Assn., 1975; arbitrator Better Bus. Bur. Met. Chgo., 1984; appointed to Ill. Gov.'s Grievance Panel, 1987. Mem. Chgo. Council Lawyers, Phi Beta Kappa. Democrat. Jewish. Legal education, Federal civil litigation, Civil rights. Office: IIT Chgo Kent Coll Law 77 S Wacker Dr Chicago IL 60606

STEINMANIS, KARL SVEN, lawyer; b. Köping, Sweden, Mar. 19, 1948; s. Fricis J. and Alma (Berzins) S.; m. Anda L. Straume, Oct. 5, 1974; 1 child, Laura. AB, Dartmouth Coll., 1970; JD, Ind. U., 1973. Bar: Ohio 1973, U.S. Dist. Ct. (so. dist.) Ohio 1973. Atty. Procter & Gamble, Cin., 1973-75, counsel, 1975-79, sr. counsel, 1979-87, div. counsel, 1987—; arbitrator Hamilton County, Cin., 1974—. Chmn. campaign sect. United Appeal, Cin., 1975—. Mem. Ohio Bar Assn., Cin. Bar Assn., Equal Employment Adv. Council (case selection com.). Republican. Lutheran. Club: Turpin Hills Swim & Racquet (Cin.) (bd. dirs., counsel 1980—). General corporate, Labor. Office: Procter & Gamble One Procter & Gamble Plaza Cincinnati OH 45202

STEINMETZ, DONALD WALTER, justice Wis. Supreme Ct.; b. Milw., Sept. 19, 1924. B.A., U. Wis., 1949, J.D., 1951. Bar: Wis. bar 1951. Individual practice law Milw., 1951-58; asst. city atty. City of Milw., 1958-60; 1st asst. dist. atty. County of Milw., 1960-65; spl. asst. atty. gen. State of Wis., 1965-66; judge Milwaukee County (Wis.) Ct., 1966-80; justice Wis. Supreme Ct., 1980—; chmn. Wis. Bd. County Judges; sec.-treas. Wis. Bd. Criminal Ct. Judges; mem. State Adminstrv. Commn. Cts., Chief Judge Study Com., Study Com. for TV and Radio Coverage in Courtroom, Wis. Council on Criminal Justice. Mem. ABA, Wis. bar assns., Am. Judicature Soc. Office: Wis Supreme Ct 231 E State Capitol Madison WI 53702 *

STEINTHAL, KENNETH L., lawyer; b. N.Y.C., Aug. 28, 1952; s. Arthur Donald Steinthal and Roslynn (Sturman) Wachtel; m. Wendy E. Frankel, May 21, 1978; children: Andrew, Jason. BA, Williams coll., 1974; JD, Fordham U., 1978. Bar: N.Y. 1979, U.S. Dist. Ct. (so. and ea. dists.) N.Y. 1979, U.S. Tax Ct. 1986. Assoc. then ptnr. Weil, Gotshal and Manges, N.Y.C., 1978—; adj. prof. law Fordham U., N.Y.C., 1982-84. Contbr. articles Fordham U. Law Rev., 1975. Mem. ABA, N.Y. State Bar Assn. Democrat. Jewish. Federal civil litigation, State civil litigation, Private international. Office: Weil Gotshal and Manges 767 5th Ave New York NY 10153

STELL, JOHN ELWIN, JR., lawyer; b. Atlanta, June 19, 1954; s. John E. and Juanita (Bush) S.; m. Juliet Genene Saunders, Dec. 29, 1979; children: Carrie Juanita, John E. III, Charles Stapler. BA summa cum laude, Mercer U., 1975; JD cum laude, U. Ga., 1978. Bar: Ga. 1978, U.S. Dist. Ct. (no. dist.) Ga. 1978, U.S. Ct. Appeals (5th cir.) 1978, U.S. Dist. Ct. (mid. dist.) Ga. 1981, U.S. Ct. Appeals (11th cir.) 1981. Ptnr. Russell, Adamson & Stell P.C., Winder, Ga., 1978—. Trustee Project Adam, Winder, 1982—; city atty., Winder, 1986—. Mem. ABA, Ga. Bar Assn., Piedmont Bar Assn. (pres. 1983), Barrow County C. of C. (bd. dirs. 1985—). Baptist. Insurance, Real property, State civil litigation. Home: PO Box 1045 Winder GA 30680 Office: Russell Adamson & Stell PC 109 N Broad St Winder GA 30680

STELLA, DANIEL FRANCIS, lawyer; b. Sedalia, Mo., Aug. 1, 1943; s. Frank D. and Martha T. Stella; m. Kaethe Reiff, Aug. 31, 1968; children: Dante, Davidde, Ciara. AB, Holy Cross Coll., 1965; JD, Harvard U., 1968; LLM, London Sch. Econs. and Polit. Sci. (Eng.), 1974. Bar: Mich. 1968, U.S. Dist. Ct. (ea. dist.) Mich. 1968, U.S. Ct. Appeals (6th cir.) 1968, Calif. 1975, U.S. Dist. Ct. (no. dist.) Calif. 1975, U.S. Ct. Appeals (9th cir.) 1975, U.S. Dist. Ct. (we. dist.) Mich. 1977, U.S. Ct. Mil. Appeals 1980. Assoc. Dykema, Gossett, Spencer, Goodnow & Trigg, Detroit, 1968-69, 77-78, ptnr., 1979—; assoc. Pillsbury, Madison & Sutro, San Francisco, 1974-76. Mem. Founder Soc., Detroit Art Inst.; pres. Friends Internat. Inst. of Detroit. Served to capt. USNR, 1969—. Mem. ABA, Calif. Bar Assn., Mich. Bar Assn., Detroit Bar Assn., Holy Cross Coll. Alumni Assn., London Sch. Econs. and Polit. Sci. Soc. Clubs: Fairlane (Dearborn, Mich.); Harvard of Eastern Mich. Federal civil litigation, State civil litigation, Private international. Office: Dykema Gossett Spencer 400 Renaissance Center Detroit MI 48243

STELLMAN, L. MANDY, lawyer; b. Toronto, Ont., Women, ABA, Milw. Bar Assn., Aug. 22, 1922; came to U.S., 1946, naturalized, 1948; d. Abraham and Rose (Rubinoff) Mandlsohn; m. Samuel David Stellman, July 11, 1943; children—Steven D., Leslie Robert. B.Sc. summa cum laude, Ohio State U., Columbus, 1966; J.D., Marquette U., 1970. Bar: Wis. 1971. Tchr., Toronto Pub. Schs., 1943-46; recreation specialist, Toronto, 1942-46; educator, social worker Columbus (Ohio) Jewish Ctr., 1951-64; instr. U. Wis. Extension, Milw., 1970-76; sole practice, Milw., 1971—. Bd. dirs. Women's Crisis Line, Women's Coalition, Milw. Jewish Home for Aged. Recipient Disting. Alumni award Ohio State U., 1976; Hannah G. Solomon award Nat. Council Jewish Women, 1984. Mem. Assn. Trial Lawyers Am., Lawyers Assn. for Women, ABA, Milw. Bar Assn., Wis. Assn. Trial Lawyers, Nat. Council Jewish Women (life), Women's Polit. Caucus, Common Cause, NOW (Milw. Woman of Yr. 1977). Jewish. Family and matrimonial, Criminal, Juvenile. Home: 1545 W Fairfield Ct Glendale WI 53209 Office: 606 W Wisconsin Ave Suite 308 Milwaukee WI 53203

STELTZLEN, JANELLE HICKS, lawyer; b. Atlanta, Sept. 18, 1937; d. William Duard and Mary Evelyn (Embrey) Hicks; m. Gerald William Steltzlen, Jr., 1958; children: Gerald William III, Christa Diane. BS, Okla. State U., 1958; MS, Kans. State U., 1961; JD, U. Tulsa, 1981. Bar: Okla. 1981 U.S. Dist. Ct. (no., ea. and we. dists.) Okla. 1981, U.S. Tax Ct. 1981, U.S. Ct. Claims 1981, U.S. Ct. Appeals (10th and Fed. cirs.) 1981, U.S. Supreme Ct. 1981. Sole practice Tulsa, 1981—; lectr. Coll. of DuPage, Ill., 1976, Tulsa Jr. Coll., 1981—. Christian counselor 1st United Meth. Ch., Tulsa, 1986—. Mem. Okla. Bar Assn., Tulsa County Bar Assn., Delta Zeta. Republican. Methodist. Avocations: swimming, sewing, biking, reading, painting. General corporate, Probate, Real property. Home: 6636 S Jamestown Place Tulsa OK 74136 Office: 1150 E 61st St Tulsa OK 74136

STENFELDT, LILLIAN GERDA, lawyer; b. Providence, Sept. 28, 1955; s. Nils and Gerda Stenfeldt; m. Nicolas Mansour, Aug. 21, 1976; 1 child, Marie. Student, Syracuse U., 1973-74; BA in Econs., Stanford U., 1976, MA in Orgn. Behavior, 1977; postgrad., U. San Francisco, 1977-78, U. Mich., 1978; JD magna cum laude, U. Detroit, 1980. Bar: Calif. 1982, Mich. 1982, U.S. Dist. Ct. (no. dist.) Calif. 1982, U.S. Dist. Ct. (ea. dist.) Mich. 1982, U.S. Ct. Appeals (9th cir.) 1984, D.C. 1986. Staff atty. Gen. Motors, Ann Arbor, Mich., 1980-82; assoc. Bronson, Bronson & McKinnon, San Francisco, 1982—; adj. prof. law U. Detroit, 1981-82. Mem. Calif. Bar Assn. Pro Bono award, 1983), Mich. Bar Assn., D.C. Bar Assn., Barrister Club (comml. law sect. 1984—), Stanford Alumni Assn., Queens Bench, Alpha Sigma Nu, Phi Alpha Delta (dist. justice 1981-86), Stanford Bay Area Profl. Women's Club. Clubs: Commonwealth, Metropolitan. Contracts commercial, Bankruptcy, Real property. Office: Bronson Bronson & McKinnon 555 California St Suite 3400 San Francisco CA 94080

STENGEL, JAMES LAMONT, lawyer; b. Decatur, Ill., Jan. 1, 1956; s. Richard Lamont and Jean (Kizer) Blake; m. Beverly Jean Bartow, June 4, 1978. BA, U. Ill., 1977; JD, U. Mich., 1980. Bar: N.Y. 1981, U.S. Dist. Ct. (so. dist.) N.Y. 1981, U.S. Ct. Appeals (2d cir.) 1982. Assoc. Donovan Leisure Newton & Irvine, N.Y.C., 1980—. Mem. ABA. Democrat. Avocation: automobile racing. Federal civil litigation, Securities, Antitrust. Home: 61 W 73d St Apt 2A New York NY 10023 Office: Donovan Leisure Newton & Irvine 30 Rockefeller Plaza New York NY 10112

STENGEL, MARK ALLEN, lawyer; b. Bklyn., Oct. 16, 1952; s. Leonard and Gloria (Sandler) S.; m. Agneta Neuman, Dec. 23, 1978; children: Jennifer Lee, Kimberly Brooke. Student, Adelphi U., 1970-73; AB, U. Miami, 1974, postgrad., 1974-75; JD, N.Y. Law Sch., 1977. Bar: N.Y. 1978, Fla. 1979, U.S. Dist. Ct. (ea. and so. dists.) N.Y. 1978, U.S. Ct. Appeals (2d cir.) 1982. Assoc. Montfort, Healy, Macguire & Salley, Mineola, N.Y., 1977-78, Law Office Harry H. Lipsig, N.Y.C., 1978-79; sole practice Mineola, 1979—; lectr. Lawyer in Classroom Series, Nassau County, N.Y., 1981. Mem. ABA (forum com. on entertainment and sports industries), Assn. Trial Lawyers Am., N.Y. State Bar Assn., N.Y. State Trial Lawyers Assn. (forum com. on entertainment and sports industries), Fla. Bar Assn. Republican. Jewish. Avocations: musician, songwriter, musical producer. Personal injury, Contracts commercial, Entertainment. Office: 114 Old Country Rd Mineola NY 11501

STEPAN, M(ARGARET) JEAN, judge; b. Lincoln, Nebr., Aug. 23, 1947; d. Alfred Henry and Mary Jane (Thomsen) S.; m. John Michael Tancabel, Aug. 16, 1974; children: Leah Marie, John Andrew, David Anthony. BA in Math. and English, Coll. of St. Catherine, St. Paul, 1969; JD, William Mitchell Coll. of Law, 1978. Bar: Minn. 1978, U.S. Dist. Ct. Minn. 1979. Spl. asst. atty. gen. Minn. Atty. Gen.'s Office, St. Paul, 1978-84; judge Minn. Tax Ct., St. Paul, 1985—. Bd. dirs. YMCA, St. Paul, 1986. Mem. Nat. Assn. Women Judges, Minn. Women Lawyers Assn., Minn. Women's Consortium (steering com. 1984). Roman Catholic. State and local taxation. Office: Minn Tax Ct 520 Lafayette Rd 2d Floor Saint Paul MN 55155

STEPANIAN, STEVEN ARVID, II, lawyer, financial consultant; b. Charleroi Penn., Apr. 15, 1935; s. Steven A. and Edithmarion M. (McElligott) S.; m. Pamela A. Abbey, Feb. 15, 1979. A.B. magna cum laude, U. Pitts., 1957; LL.B., Harvard U., 1963. Bar: Pa. 1964, U.S. Supreme Ct. 1967. Assoc. Reed Smith Smith Shaw and McClay, 1963-69, ptnr., 1970-78; sole practice, 1978—; dir., gen. counsel Civic Arena Corp., Midec, Inc., Mid State Foods, Inc., The Igloo. Nat. Football League Alumni Assn., Reserve Petroleum Co. Served to maj. USAF, 1957-60, 68-69. Mem. ABA, Pa. Bar Assn., Nat. Football League Alumni Assn. Democrat. Catholic. Clubs: Duquesne, University (past pres.), Nemacolin Encampment (Pitts.). General corporate, Real property, Corporate finance. : Office: 436 7th Ave 1550 Koppers Bldg Pittsburgh PA 15219

STEPHAN, EDMUND ANTON, lawyer; b. Chgo., Oct. 7, 1911; s. Anton Charles and Mary Veronica (Egan) S.; m. Evelyn Way, July 3, 1937; children: Miriam, Edmund Anton, Martha (Mrs. Robert McNeill), Donald, Christopher, Evelyn, Gregory, Joan. A.B., U. Notre Dame, 1933; LL.B., Harvard, 1939. Bar: N.Y. 1940, Ill. 1945. Assoc. firm Carter, Ledyard & Milburn, N.Y.C., 1939-42; atty. charge N.Y. office U.S. Alien Property Custodian, 1943-45; assoc. firm Mayer, Brown & Platt (and predecessors), Chgo., 1945-47; partner Mayer, Brown & Platt (and predecessors), 1947—; dir. (hon.) Brunswick Corp., Marsh & McLennan Cos. Emeritus chmn. bd. trustees U. Notre Dame. Mem. Am., Ill., Chgo. bar assns. Roman Catholic. Clubs: Legal (Chgo.), Mid-Day (Chgo.), Chicago (Chgo.), Law (Chgo.); Michigan Shores (Wilmette, Ill.), Westmoreland Country (Wilmette, Ill.); Harvard (N.Y.C.); Bob-O-Link Golf (Highland Park, Ill.). General corporate. Home: 1410 Sheridan Rd Wilmette IL 60091 Office: Mayer Brown & Platt 190 S LaSalle St Chicago IL 60603

STEPHAN, H. PESKIN, lawyer; b. N.Y.C., Oct. 31, 1943; s. Michael Peskin and Ruth Berger; m. Victoria Bond, Jan. 27, 1974. BA, NYU, 1965; JD, Bklyn. Law Sch., 1968. Bar: N.y. 1968, U.S. Supreme Ct. 1972, D.C. 1974, Pa. 1979. Assoc. Rothblatt & Rothblatt, 1968-70; ptnr. Rothblatt, Rothblatt, Seijas & Peskin, 1970-79, Tolmage, Peskin, Harris & Falick, N.Y.C., 1979—; sr. mem. faculty Nat. Coll. Trial Adv. Commanding officer N.Y.C. Police Dept., Cen. Park Precinct. Mem. ABA, N.Y. State Bar Assn. (exec. com.), Assn. Trial Lawyers Am. (chmn. criminal justice sect. 1978-80, chmn. tort sect. 1986—, bd. govs. 1985—), N.Y. State Trial Lawyers Assn. (v.p. 1986—, treas. 1981-85, chmn. criminal justice sect. 1980—), N.Y. County Lawyers Assn. Criminal, Federal civil litigation, Personal injury. Home: 256 W 10th St New York NY 10014 Office: Tolmadge Peskin Harris & Falick 20 Vesey St New York NY 10007

STEPHAN, ROBERT JOSEPH, JR., lawyer; b. Montgomery, Ala., Aug. 17, 1947; s. Robert J. Sr. and Doris Stephan; m. Patricia Jolley, Mar. 18, 1978; children: Angela, Robert J. III, Michael Porter, Alan Ronald. BA, Ariz. State U., 1969, JD, 1972. Bar: Ariz. 1972, U.S. Dist. Ct. Ariz. 1972, U.S. Ct. Appeals (9th cir.) 1977, U.S. Supreme Ct. 1978. Sole practice Phoenix, 1972—. Author: Arizona Law of Medical Malpractice, 1983. Mem. Assn. Trial Lawyers Am., Ariz. Trial Lawyers Assn. bd. dirs. 1981—), Ct. Practice Inst. (diplomate 1979), Nat. Bd. Trial Advocacy (cert.). Democrat. Latter Day Saints. Avocations: fishing, camping, travel. Personal injury. Office: 3300 N Central #1400 Phoenix AZ 85012

STEPHAN, ROBERT TAFT, attorney general of Kansas; b. Wichita, Kans., Jan. 16, 1933; s. Taft and Julia S.; children: Dana, Lisa. BA, Washburn U., 1954, JD, 1957; grad., Nat. Coll. State Trial Judges, U. Pa., 1967. Bar: Kans. 1957. Sole practice 1957-63; judge Wichita (Kans.) Mcpl. Ct., 1963-65, Kans. Dist. Ct., 18th Jud. Dist., 1965-78; atty. gen. State of Kans., 1979—; chmn. Kans. Jud. Conf., 1977; mem. adv. bd. Shawnee County Ct.-Appointed Spl. Adv. Program. Hon. crusade chmn. Kans. div. Am. Cancer Soc., 1979-81; mem. adv. bd. Kans. Big Bros.-Big Sisters, Kans. Spl. Olympics, Shawnee County Ct.-Appointed Spl. Advocate Program; bd. dirs. Accent on Kids, Am. Cancer Soc., state chpt. and Sedgwick County unit, Parents Against Leukemia and Malignancies Soc., Kans. chpt. Leukemia Soc. Am. Named Kans. Trial Judge of Yr. Kans. Trial Lawyers Assn., 1977. Mem. Am. Judges Assn., Am. Judicature Soc., ABA (mem. adv. commn. youth alcohol and drug problems), Nat. Assn. Attys. Gen. (past pres.). Republican. Club: Wagonmasters. Lodges: Elks; Moose; Masons; Shriners. Office: Office Atty Gen Kans Judicial Center Topeka KS 66612

STEPHENS, FERRIS W., lawyer; b. Birmingham, Ala., Aug. 22, 1955; s. William John and Mildred Ann (Ritchey) S. BA, U. Ala., Tuscalousa, 1978; JD, Samford U., 1981; postgrad., Northwestern U., 1985. Bar: Ala. 1981, U.S. Dist. Ct. (no., mid. and so. dists.) Ala. 1982, U.S. Ct. Internat. Trade 1982, U.S. Ct. Customs and Patent Appeals 1982, U.S. Ct. Mil. Appeals 1982, U.S. Ct. Appeals (11th cir.) 1982. Law clk. to presiding justice Ala. Ct. Criminal Appeals, Montgomery, 1981-82; asst. atty. gen. State of Ala., Montgomery, 1982—; instr. Huntington Coll., Montgomery, 1983-84; bd. dirs. welfare fraud State of Ala.; mem. State Jud. System Study Commn., 1986. Narrator (cable TV) Legal Education Program, 1982-84; news dir. Sta. WVSU, Birmingham, 1980-81. V.p. Ala. Young Dems., 1979-82; mem. Election Reform Commn., 1979-82. Recipient Nathan Burkan award ASCAP, 1981. Mem. Am. Trial Lawyers Assn., Ala. Bar Assn. (lawyer pub. relations and media relations commn.), Dist. Attys. Assn., Young Lawyers Assn. Montgomery Jaycees (v.p. 1984, legal counsel 1983). Democrat. Roman Catholic. Avocations: basketball, tennis. Criminal, Federal civil litigation, Legislative. Home: 406 Gardendale Dr Montgomery AL 36110 Office: Atty Gen's Office State House Montgomery AL 36130

STEPHENS, GEORGE EDWARD, JR., lawyer; b. Lawrence, Kans., Mar. 26, 1936; s. George Edward and Mary Helen (Houghton) S.; m. Gretel Geiser, Dec. 31, 1965; children: Thaddeus Geiser, Edward Houghton, Mary Schoentgen. Student. U. Colo., Boulder, 1954-57, U. Colo. Sch. Medicine, Denver, 1957-59; LLB, Stanford U., 1962. Bar: Calif. 1963, U.S. Dist. Ct. (cen. dist.) Calif. 1963, U.S. Ct. Appeals (9th cir.) 1971. Law clk. to judge U.S. Dist. Ct., Los Angeles, 1962-64; ptnr. Pollock & Palmer, Los Angeles, 1964-69, Gates, Morris, Merrill & Stephens, Los Angeles, 1969-72, Paul, Hastings, Janofsky & Walker, Los Angeles, 1972—; Mem. coordinating council on Lawyer Competence, Conf. Chief Justices, 1983—; chmn. porbate sect. Los Angeles County Bar Assn., 1979-80. Nat. chmn. Stanford (Calif.) U. Law Fund Quad Program, 1980-87; mem. bd. visitors Stanford Law Sch., 1982-85; founder Mus. Contemporary Art, Los Angeles, 1982. Recipient Stanford Assocs. award, 1982. Fellow Am. Bar Found., Am. Coll. Probate Counsel, Internat. Acad. Probate and Trust; mem. ABA (chmn. standing com. specialization 1979-82, rep. to coordinating council on lawyer competence, 1982-87); mem. Stanford Law Soc. (pres. 1972-73). Episcopalian. Clubs: Chancery (Los Angeles), Amandale Golf (Pasadena, Calif.), Balley Hunt (Pasadena). Probate, Estate planning, Estate taxation. Office: Paul Hastings Janofsky & Walker 555 S Flower Floor 22 Los Angeles CA 90071

STEPHENS, (HOLMAN) HAROLD, lawyer; b. Enterprise, Ala., Nov. 29, 1954; s. Holman Harrison and Louise (Bass) S. BA, U. Ala., 1976, JD, 1980. Bar: Ala. 1980, U.S. Dist. Ct. (no. dist.) Ala. 1980, U.S. Ct. Appeals (5th and 11th cirs.) 1981. Asst. dist. atty. U.S. Dist. Ct. (no. dist.) Ala., Birmingham, 1980-82; assoc. Lanier, Shaver & Herring, Huntville, Ala., 1982-84; ptnr. Lanier, Shaver & Herring, Huntville, 1985—; lectr. U. Ala., Huntsville, 1982—, So. Jr. Coll., Huntsville, 1984-86. Bd. dirs. Huntsville-Madison County Mental Health Ctr., 1983—, Big Bros./Big Sisters of N. Ala., Huntsville, 1983—, Friends of Pub. Radio, Huntsville, 1984-86. Mem. ABA, Ala. Bar Assn., Huntsville-Madison County Bar Assn. (v.p. young lawyers div. 1986-87). Mem. Huntsville-Madison (Ala.) County Bar Assn. (v.p. young lawyers div. 1986-87, pres. 1987—). Baptist. Avocations: tennis, golf, hiking. Federal civil litigation, State civil litigation, Insurance. Home: 8421 Hogan Dr SE Huntsville AL 35802 Office: Lanier Shaver & Herring PC 404 Madison St Huntsville AL 35801

STEPHENS, HENRY L., JR., law educator; b. Nashville, Tenn., Aug. 31, 1949; s. Henry L. and Barbara (Sugg) S.; m. Mary Kathryn Kaiser, July 26, 1980; 1 son, Andrew Gregory. B.A., Western Ky. U., 1972; J.D., U. Ky., 1975. Bar: Ky. 1975, U.S. Dist. Ct. (we. dists.) Ky. 1975, U.S. Ct. Appeals (6th cir.) 1977. Trial atty. Middleton, Reutlinger & Baird, Louisville, 1975-78; asst. counsel Louisville-Jefferson County Bd. Health, 1976-78; spl. asst. atty. gen. Ky. Dept. Natural Resources, Frankfort, 1978-79; environ. counsel Newport Steel Corp., Ky., 1980—; assoc. dean, prof. No. Ky. U., Highland Heights, 1979—, interim dean, 1985-86, dean, 1986—. Co-author: Coal Law and Regulation, 1982; contbr. articles to profl. jours. Mem. exec. com. Campbell County Democratic Party, Newport, Ky., 1984; mem. Ky. Bar Found. (v.p.), Campbell County Pub. Def. Bd., 1981—, No. Ky. U. Found. Bd., 1985—, No. Ky. U. Found. Devel. Com. Mem. Eastern Mineral Law Found. (trustee and teaching com. chmn. 1982—), Am. Arbitration Assn. (arbitrator 1980—), Kenton County CETA Bd. (hearing officer 1980-81), Ky. Bar Found. (v.p. 1986—), Ky Bar Assn. (bd. govs. 1983-84, chmn. young lawyers sect., co-founder natural resources sect.), Jaycees (Outstanding Young Man of Yr. 1983). Episcopalian. Club: Fort Mitchell Country. Environment, Mining and minerals.

STEPHENS, JOHN F., JR., lawyer; b. Dallas, Aug. 27, 1948; s. John F. and Ruth T. Stephens. BA, Vanderbilt U., 1970; JD, U. Tex., 1974. Bar: Tex. 1984. Trial atty. antitrust FTC, Washington, 1974-83; atty. internat. law ENSERCH Corp., Dallas, 1983—. Bd. dirs. Dallas Zoological Soc., YMCA. Mem. ABA, Tex. Bar Assn., Dallas Bar Assn., Delta Kappa Epsilon. Avocations: scuba diving, hunting, fishing, squash. Antitrust, General corporate, Private international. Home: 6338 Woodland Dallas TX 75225 Office: Enserch Corp 300 S St Paul Dallas TX 75201

STEPHENS, MARLIN GERARD, lawyer; b. Pitts., July 28, 1946; s. Marlin Bingham and Mary Alice (Kunzelman) S.; divorced. BA in Polit. Sci., Calif. (Pa.) U., 1970; JD, Duquesne U., 1974; postdoctoral, LaRoche Coll. Bar: Pa. 1974, U.S. Dist. Ct. (we. dist.) Pa. 1974, U.S. Supreme Ct. 1987. Assoc. Law Office Donald P. Monti, Pitts., 1975-77, Hanna & Assocs., Pitts., 1979—; atty. Legal Service Northwestern Pa., St. Marys, 1977-78; sole practice Allison Park, Pa., 1978-79. Chmn. bd. dirs. Hampton Twp. Zoning Commn., Allison Park. Mem. Allegheny County Bar Assn., Assn. Trial Lawyers Am., Am. Arbitration Assn. (bd. arbitrators). Democrat. Roman Catholic. Lodge: Elks. Avocations: restoring antique cars and furniture, hunting, fishing, golf. Construction, Contracts commercial, General corporate. Home: 2847 McCully Rd Allison Park PA 15101 Office: Hanna & Assocs III Rivers Bank Bldg Pittsburgh PA 15236

STEPHENS, MARY ELIZABETH GIULIANI, lawyer; b. Danville, Pa., Apr. 23, 1955; d. Emilio Romolo and Georgene May (Peterman) G.; m. R. Gregory Stephens, June 9, 1984; children: Jane Monroe Stephens. BA with distinction, U. Mich., 1977; postgrad., Cambridge U., summer 1979; JD cum laude, William Mitchell Coll. of Law, 1981. Bar: Minn. 1981, U.S. Dist. Ct. Minn. 1981. Assoc. Moore, Costello & Hart, St. Paul, 1981—; hearing examiner human rights cases, St. Paul, 1985—. Mem. staff William Mitchell Law Rev., Vol. VI, 1980. Recipient cert. of merit William Mitchell Coll. of Law Alumni Assn., St. Paul, 1981. Mem. ABA, Minn. Bar Assn. (tort sect., ins. practice litigation sect.). Avocations: photography, swimming, skiing, knitting. Construction, Government contracts and claims, Personal injury. Home: 1233 Shannon Ct Woodbury MN 55125 Office: Moore Costello & Hart 55 E Fifth St Suite 1400 Saint Paul MN 55101

STEPHENS, ROBERT F., chief justice Kentucky Supreme Court; b. Covington, Ky., Aug. 16, 1927. Student, Ind. U.; LL.B., U. Ky., 1951. Bar: Ky. 1951. Asst. atty. Fayette County, Ky., 1964-69; judge Fayette County, 1969-75; atty. gen. Ky. Frankfort, 1976-79; justice Supreme Ct. Ky., Frankfort, 1979—; chief justice Supreme Ct. Ky., 1982—. Staff: Ky. Law Jour. Bd. dirs. Nat. Assn. Counties, 1973-75; 1st pres. Ky. Assn. Counties; 1st chmn. Bluegrass Area Devel. Dist.; chmn. Ky. Heart Assn. Fund Drive, 1976-78. Served with USN, World War II. Named Outstanding County Judge of Ky. Ky. Bar Assn., 1972, 86; recipient Herbert Harley award Am. Judicature Soc. Mem. Order of Coif. Democrat. Office: Ky Supreme Ct State Capitol Bldg Frankfort KY 40601

STEPHENS, R(OBERT) GARY, lawyer; b. Lindsay, Okla., Sept. 21, 1942; s. William Denno and Leta Mildred (Jones) S.; m. Lurinda Lou Osborne; children: Trent Delno, Skyler Wynne. Student U. Okla., 1960-62, U. Houston, 1968-72; JD, South Tex. Coll., 1975. Bar: Tex. 1975, U.S. Dist. Ct. (so. dist.) Tex. 1976, (ea. dist.) Tex. 1976, (no. dist.) Tex. 1984, U.S. Ct. Appeals (5th cir.) 1979, U.S. Supreme Ct. 1984. Assoc. Kronzer, Abraham & Watkins, Houston, 1975-81; ptnr. R. Gary Stephens, P.C., Houston, 1981-84, Stephens & Garner, P.C., Houston, 1985—; dir. Longhorn Express Co., Inc.; adj. prof. South Tex. Coll. of Law, Houston, 1980—. Trustee Terrace Meth. Ch., Houston, 1981-85. Served with USAF, 1963-67. Mem. Am. Trial Lawyers Assn., Tex. Trial Lawyers Assn. (bd. dirs. 1986—), Houston Trial Lawyers Assn., ABA (vice chmn. products liability com. 1979-84). Club: Texas (Houston). Federal civil litigation, State civil litigation, Personal injury. Home: 8332 Merlin Houston TX 77055 Office: 5 Post Oak Park Suite 1630 Houston TX 77027 also: 1301 Capital of Texas Hwy S Austin TX 78746

STEPHENS, WALTER DAVID, lawyer; b. Lufkin, Tex., Dec. 1, 1955; s. Ralph A. Stephens and Winnie Dell (Shotwell) Melancon. BA with honors, U. Tex., 1977; JD with honors, U. Houston, 1979. Bar: Tex. 1980, U.S. Dist. Ct. (ea. and so. dists.) Tex. 1982, U.S. Ct. Appeals (5th cir.) 1982. Assoc. Law Office George Chandler, Lufkin, 1980, Flournoy & Deaton, Lufkin, 1980-82; ptnr. Flournoy, Deaton & Stephens, Lufkin, 1982—; instr. bus. and real estate law Angelina Jr. Coll., Lufkin, 1983—. Mem. Tex. Bar Assn., Angelina County Bar Assn., Angelina County Jr. Bar Assn. Avocations: private pilot, guitar, sports. Personal injury, Federal civil litigation, State civil litigation. Office: Flournoy Deaton & Stephens 118 S 2d St Lufkin TX 75901

STEPHENS, WILLIAM TAFT, lawyer; b. Huntsville, Ala., Dec. 3, 1943; s. Roy Carl and Mary Francis (Taft) S. B.S. in Aero. Engring., Auburn (Ala.) U., 1966; J.D., Harvard U., 1969. Bar: Ala. 1969, N.Y. 1970, U.S. Dist. Ct. (so. and ea. dists.) N.Y. 1970, U.S. Ct. Appeals (2d cir.) 1970, U.S. Supreme Ct. 1972, U.S. Dist. Ct. (mid. dist.) Ala. 1973, U.S. Ct. Appeals (5th cir.) 1973, U.S. Dist. Ct. (so. dist.) Ala. 1978, U.S. Dist. Ct. (no. dist.) Ala. 1983, U.S. Ct. Appeals (11th cir.) 1983, U.S. Ct. Appeals (Fed. cir.) 1984. Engr. trainee NASA, 1963-65, 67; propulsion engr. Boeing Co., 1966; assoc. Kenyon & Kenyon, N.Y.C., 1969-70; assoc. Sullivan & Cromwell, N.Y.C., 1970-73; chief civil div. State of Ala. Atty. Gen.'s Office, Montgomery, 1973-80; gen. counsel Retirement Systems of Ala., Montgomery, 1980—; spl. counsel Ala. Legis., 1976-77, 1983; mem. permanent Study Commn. of State Jud. System, 1977-80; adj. prof. Auburn U., Montgomery, 1979-81. Contbr. articles to profl. jours. Candidate for State Atty. Gen., 1978; mem. exec. com. Auburn U. Alumni Engring. Council, 1981—; coach Little League Baseball, Football, Basketball, Montgomery, 1979—; bd. dirs. Boys Clubs of Montgomery, 1985—. Mem. Ala. Bar Assn., Montgomery County Bar Assn., Harvard Law Sch. Assn., Auburn U. Alumni Assn. Methodist. Pension, profit-sharing, and employee benefits, State civil litigation, Administrative and regulatory. Home: 2662 The Meadows Montgomery AL 36116 Office: Retirement Systems Ala 135 S Union St Montgomery AL 36130

STEPHENS, WILLIAM THEODORE, lawyer, business executive; b. Balt., Mar. 31, 1922; s. William A. and Mildred (Griffin) S.; m. Arlene Alice Lesti, June 2, 1958; children: William Theodore, Renee Adena. Student, Balt. City Coll., 1939-41, U. Md., 1946-47; A.B., J.D., George Washington U., 1950, postgrad., 1951. Bar: D.C. 1951. Mem. firm J.L. Green, Washington, 1950-51, J.M. Cooper, Washington, 1952-54; ptnr. firm Stephens & Carlson, Washington, 1955—; sec. gen. counsel, bd. dirs. Exotech, Inc., Gaithersburg, Md.; bd. dirs., prin. owner BARBCO, Inc., Nev., Fairfax Racquet Club; gen. counsel various nat. corps.; mem. exec. com. Nat. Com. on Uniform Traffic Laws and Ordinances, 1967—. Trustee Am. Bikeways Found., Washington. Served to 1st lt. AUS, 1941-45. Mem. Bar Assn. D.C. (sec. taxation 1959-68), ABA (sec. taxation 1959—, sec. corps, banking and bus. law 1960—), Md. Bar Assn., Va. Bar Assn., XVI Corps Assn. (pres. 1967), Kappa Alpha Order, Delta Theta Phi. Clubs: Commonwealth (Calif.); University, Capitol Hill (Washington); Army-Navy Country (Arlington, Va.); Regency Racquet (McLean, Va.); Jockey, Racquet Club Internat. (Miami, Fla.). General corporate, Legislative, Administrative and regulatory. Home: 881 Ocean Dr Key Biscayne FL 33149 Office: Regency at McLean Suite 119 1800 Old Meadow Rd PO Box 1096 McLean VA 22101 also: Stephens & Carlson 1200 18th St Suite 710 Washington DC 20036

STEPHENSON, ALAN CLEMENTS, lawyer; b. Wilmington, N.C., Nov. 7, 1944; s. Abram Clements and Ruth (Smith) S.; m. Sherri Jean Miller, Dec. 19, 1970; children: Edward Taylor, Anne Baldwin. AB in Hist., U. N.C., 1967; JD, U. Va., 1970. Bar: N.Y. 1971. Assoc. Cravath, Swaine & Moore, N.Y.C., 1970-78, ptnr., 1978—; bd. dirs. Met. Assistance Corp., N.Y.C. Bd. dirs. Travelers Aid Soc. N.Y., N.Y.C., 1979-82. Morehead scholar John M. Moorehead Found., 1963. Mem. ABA, N.Y. State Bar Assn., Assn. of Bar of City of N.Y., Phi Beta Kappa. Republican. Episcopalian. Clubs: Union (N.Y.C.); Tuxedo (Tuxedo Park, N.Y.). General corporate, Securities. Office: Cravath Swaine & Moore One Chase Manhattan Plaza New York NY 10005

STEPHENSON, JAMES BENNETT, state justice; b. Greenup, Ky., Jan. 26, 1916; s. Elmer D. and Emabel (Bennett) S.; m. Elizabeth Campbell Paddison, June 28, 1941; children—Martha Bennett, Jane Marsh. A.B., U. Ky., Lexington, 1938, LL.B., 1951. Bar: Ky. bar 1939. Practice in Pikeville, Ky., 1940-57; circuit judge Div. I 35th Jud. Dist., Pike County, 1957-73; justice Ky. Ct. Appeals, 1973-75, Supreme Ct. Ky., 1975—; Mem. Jud. Council Ky., 1959-61. Bd. dirs. Meth. Hosp., Pikeville. Served to capt. USAAF, 1942-45. Mem. Sigma Chi, Phi Delta Phi. Democrat. Methodist (chmn. finance com. 1955-70; chmn. ofcl. bd. 1971-72; Ky. Conf. Com. on World Service and Finance 1969-72). Home: 37 Timberlawn Circle Frankfort KY 40601 Office: 239 State Capitol Frankfort KY 40601

STEPHENSON, MICHAEL MURRAY, lawyer; b. San Pedro, Calif., July 31, 1943; s. George Murray and Josephine Ann (Wathen) S. Student, U. Okla., 1961, 62, 65, 66; student Harbor Coll., 1962-63, Universidad Ibero-Americana, Mexico City, summer 1964; A.B., U. So. Calif., 1965; J.D., Southwestern U., 1970. Bar: Calif. 1971. Dep. dist. atty. Los Angeles County, 1971-74; ptnr. Stephenson, Stephenson & Holmes, San Pedro, Calif., 1974—; legal advisor Los Angeles County Underwater Instrs. Assn.; dir. Los Angeles County Underwater Instrs. Assn.; staff instr. Los Angeles Underwater Instrs. Certification Progrm and Advanced Diving progrm. Bd. dirs. ARC, San Pedro, 1975-76; alt. mem. Los Angeles County Dem. Central Com. Recipient Outstanding Teaching award, 28th Underwater Instrs. Cert. Course, Los Angeles, 1980. Mem. State Bar Calif., Los Angeles Trial Lawyers Assn., Am. Trial Lawyers Assn., ABA, Calif. Trial Lawyers Assn. (lectr. underwater instr. liability), Harbor Bar Assn. (pres.), S. Bay Bar Assn., Nat. Assn. Underwater Instrs., Profl. Assn. Diving Instrs. Democrat. Roman Catholic. Lodge: Elks. Contbr. articles to profl. jours. State civil litigation, Personal injury, Family and matrimonial. Office: 255 W 5th St Suite 104 San Pedro CA 90731

STEPHENSON, ROSCOE BOLAR, JR., state supreme court justice; b. Covington, Va., Feb. 22, 1922. A.B., Washington and Lee U., 1943, J.D., 1947, LL.D. (hon.), 1983. Bar: Va. 1947. Ptnr. Stephenson & Stephenson, Covington, 1947-52; commonwealth's atty. Alleghany County, Va., 1952-64; ptnr. Stephenson, Kostel, Watson, Carson and Snyder, Covington, 1964-73; judge 25th Jud. Cir. Ct. Commonwealth Va., Covington, 1973-81; justice Va. Supreme Ct., Richmond, 1981—. Recipient Covington Citizen of Yr. award, 1973; recipient Outstanding Alumni award Covington High Sch., 1973. Fellow Am. Coll. Trial Lawyers; mem. Va. State Bar (council 1969-73), Va. Bar Assn., Va. Trial Lawyers Assn., Order of Coif. Jurisprudence. Home: Clearwater Park Covington VA 24426 Office: Va Supreme Ct Supreme Ct Bldg Richmond VA 23219 Office: 214 W Main St Covington VA 24426

STEPP, KENNETH STEPHENSON, lawyer; b. Greenville, S.C., Sept. 8, 1947; s. James Marvin and Vivian Olivia (Pittman) S.; m. Ann Watts, July 20, 1969 (dec. Aug. 1984); children: Brian Stephen, Mark Gregory (dec.). BS in Indsl. Mgt., Clemson U., 1968; MS in Mgt., U.S. Naval Postgrad. Sch., 1970; JD, U. Ga., 1976. Bar: Ga. 1976, U.S. Dist. Ct. (mid. dist.) Ga. 1976, Fla. 1977, U.S. Dist. Ct. (mid. dist.) Fla. 1979, U.S. Ct. Appeals (5th cir.) 1978. Assoc. Law Offices of H. Norwood Pearce, Columbus, Ga., 1976-77; ptnr. Hawkins, Fitt, Messner & Stepp, Columbus, 1977-78; sole practice Inverness, Fla., 1979-85; ptnr. Stepp & Travis, Inverness, 1985—; atty. City of Inverness, 1980; bd. dirs. Withlacoochie Area Legal Services, Inc., Ocala, Inverness, Brooksville and Bushnell, Fla., 1982-85. Mem. precinct committee Citrus County Dem. Exec. Com., Inverness, 1984-87, sec. 1984-86; candidate Dem. Primary U.S. Congress, 1986. Served to lt. (j.g.) USN, 1968-73. Mem. Assn. Trial Lawyers Am., Ga. Bar Assn., Fla. Bar Assn., Tri-County Bar Assn., Citrus County Bar Assn. Methodist. Probate, Personal injury, General practice. Home: 100 N Edinburgh Dr Inverness FL 32650 Office: Stepp & Travis PA 220 S Pine Ave Inverness FL 32652

STERLING, A(MERICA) MARY FACKLER, lawyer; b. Pioneer, Ohio, Sept. 4, 1955; d. Harland L. and Nina M. (Essex) Fackler; m. Edward E. Sterling. AB cum laude, Harvard U., 1976; MA, Ohio State U., 1977; JD, NYU, 1980. Bar: Mo. 1980, U.S. Dist. Ct. (we. dist.) Mo. 1980, U.S. Ct. Appeals (8th cir.) 1983, U.S. Dist. Ct. (we. and no. dists.) Okla. 1985, U.S. Dist. Ct. Kans. 1985, U.S. Ct. Appeals (10th cir.) 1985. Assoc. Watson, Ess, Marshall & Enggas, Kansas City, Mo., 1980-82; asst. U.S. atty. we. dist. Mo. U.S. Dept. Justice, Kansas City, 1982-85, fed. prosecutor organized crime and racketeering strike force, 1985—; instr. U.S. Atty. Gen.'s Advocacy Inst., Washington, 1986; guest lectr. NYU Sch. Law, 1986. Sec. 8th cir. Root-Tilden Scholarship program, NYU, 1982—; mem. Urban Crime Prevention Authority, Kansas City, 1980-81, Friends of Art, Kansas City, Friends of Symphony, Kansas City. Root-Tilden scholar NYU, 1977-80; recipient Whittaker award Lawyers Assn. Kansas City, 1985, 86.; named one of ten Outstanding Young Working Women in Am., 1986-87. Mem. ABA (assmebly del. 1986—, ho. of dels. 1986—, assembly resolutions com. 1986—, com. on govt. litigation counsel litigation sect.), Mo. Bar Assn. (bd. govs. 1986—, chmn. pro bono task force, young lawyers council, Outstanding Service award 1984, Pro Bono Publico award 1986), Kansas City Met. Bar Assn. (fed. cts. and bench bar coms.), Nat. Assn. Women Lawyers (chmn. torts and litigation sect. 1982-83, 85—, state del. 1981-83, 85, recording sec. 1986—, exec. com. 1986—), Greater Kansas City Assn. Women Lawyers, Am. Soc. Pub. Adminstrn. Club: Harvard (Kansas City). Avocations: pilot, ventriloquist. Federal civil litigation.

STERLING, EDWARD EMANUEL, lawyer; b. New York, Oct. 5, 1953; s. Eduard and Martha (Krein) S.; m. A. Mary Fackler, Oct. 27, 1978. AB, Princeton U., 1975; JD, NYU, 1978. Bar: Mo. 1978, U.S. Dist. Ct (we. dist.) Mo. 1978. Assoc. Stinson, Mag & Fizzell, Kansas City, Mo., 1978-83; ptnr. Stinson, Mag & Fizzell, Kansas City, 1983—. Pres. Armour Blvd. Community Devel. Corp., Kansas City, 1983-85; atty. mem. Landmarks Commn. of City of Kansas City, 1981-85; bd. dirs. Kansas City Neighborhood Alliance, 1984-87; counsel Jackson County Young Reps., Kansas City; chmn. Jackson County Rep. Party, Kansas City, 1986—. Mem. ABA (vice chmn. title ins. com. real property, probate and trust sect.), Mo. Bar Assn., Kansas City Met. Bar Assn. (chmn. real estate law com. 1986-87), Lenders Counsel Group of Am. Land Title Assn., Am. Underground Space Assn. (affiliate). Republican. Baptist. Real property. Office: Stinson Mag & Fizzell 2100 Boatmens Ctr 920 Main St Kansas City MO 64105

STERLING, HAROLD G., lawyer, real estate developer, bank executive; b. Bklyn., Jan. 23, 1925; s. Philip and Rosalind (Mendel) S.; m. Elaine Ruth Druckman, June 28, 1953; children: Robin Patricia, Brian Richard. BA, NYU, 1950; JD, Yale U., 1954. Bar: N.Y. 1956, N.J. 1955, U.S. Dist. Ct. (so. dist.) N.Y. 1956. Assoc. Lum, Fairlie & Foster, Newark, 1954-56, 57-58, Gordon, Brady, Caffrey & Keller, N.Y.C., 1957; asst. gen. counsel Tishman Realty & Constrn., N.Y.C., 1958-62; v.p., gen. counsel Met. Structures, N.Y.C. and Balt., 1962-63; chmn. bd., gen. counsel Sutton Constrn. Co., Clifton, N.J., 1964—; bd. dirs., exec. com. Berkeley Fed. Savs., Millburn, N.J., 1975-85; chmn. bd. dirs. Berkeley Fin. Corp., Milburn, 1983-86; pres, chief exec. officer Berkeley Realty Group Millburn, 1983—; lectr. real estate and devel. Soc. Indsl. Realtors, N.J. Mortgage Bankers Assn., N.J. Home Builders Assn., Inst. Continuing Legal Edn., Exec. Enterprises. Trustee Temple B'nai Abraham, Livingston, 1965—, Newark Beth Israel Med. Ctr., 1974—; cons. West Orange Bd. Edn., N.J. Served with Signal Corps, U.S. Army, 1943-48, ETO. Mem. ABA, Phi Alpha Delta. Club: Green Brook Country (West Caldwell, N.J.). Real property, Construction. Home: 14 Devonshire Terr West Orange NJ 07052 Office: Berkeley Realty Group 21 Bleeker St Millburn NJ 07041

STERLING, ROSS N., federal judge; b. 1931. B.A., U. Tex., 1956, LL.B., 1957. With Vinson & Elkins, 1958-76; judge U.S. Dist. Ct. (so. dist.) Tex., 1976—. Judicial administration. Office: US Courthouse PO Box 61527 Houston TX 77208 *

STERN, ARNOLD JAY, lawyer; b. Omaha, Nov. 10, 1931; s. Samuel H. and Bess (Haykin) S.; m. Carolyn R. Cohn, Nov. 23, 1958; children: John, Richard, Jeffrey. BS in Law, U. Nebr., 1954; JD, Creighton U., 1957. Bar: Nebr. 1957, U.S. Dist. Ct. Nebr. 1957., U.S. Ct. Appeals (8th cir.) 1960. Assoc. Stern, Harris & Feldman, Omaha, 1961-65; ptnr. Fellman & Stern, Omaha, 1965-74, Eisenstatt, Higgins et al, Omaha, 1974-79; ptnr., pres. Arnold J. Stern & Assocs., Omaha, 1979-86, Stern, Swanson & Stickman, Omaha, 1986—. Pres. Variety Club Nebr., Omaha, 1970-74, Beth El Synagogue, Omaha, 1975-76, Meyer Inst. Bd., Omaha, 1978-80. Served to 1st lt. U.S. Army, 1954-56. Recipient award Meyer Children's Rehab. Inst. Mem. ABA, Nebr. Bar Assn., Omaha Bar Assn., Omaha Estate Planning Council, Omaha Tennis Assn. (pres. 1977-79). Democrat. Jewish. Estate planning, General corporate, General practice. Home: 1312 S 78th St Omaha NE 68124 Office: Stern Swanson & Stickman 7901 Wakeley Plaza Omaha NE 68114

STERN, DUKE NORDLINGER, lawyer, consultant; b. Chgo., Apr. 14, 1942. B.S. in Econs., U. Pa., 1963; postgrad. U. Va. Law Sch., 1964; J.D., Temple U., 1968; M.B.A., U. Mo., 1969; Ph.D., 1972. Admitted to Mo. bar, 1969, U.S. Supreme Ct., 1978; dir. Center for Adminstrn. Legal Systems, Duquesne U., Pitts., 1974-75; exec. dir., gen. counsel W.Va. State Bar, Charleston, 1975-79; pres. Risk & Ins. Services Cons., Inc., St. Petersburg, Fla., 1979-80, Duke Nordlinger Stern & Assos., Inc., St. Petersburg, 1980-85, Duke Nordlinger Stern and Assocs., Ltd., London, 1985—, Duke Nordlinger Stern and Assocs., Ltd., Bermuda, 1986—. Pres., W.Va. Legal Services Plan, Inc., 1978-79. Mem. Am. Soc. Assn. Execs. (cert.), Am. Arbitration Assn., Nat. Assn. Corp. Dirs., Am. Judicature Soc., ABA. Author: An Attorney's Guide to Malpractice Liability, 1977, Case in Labor Law, 1977, An Accountant's Guide to Malpractice Liability, 1979, Avoiding Accountant's Malpractice Claims, 1982, Avoiding Legal Malpractice Claims, 1982; A Practical Guide to Preventing Legal Malpractice, 1983. Insurance, Personal injury, Legal education. Address: Duke Nordlinger Stern & Assocs Inc 1336 54th Ave NE Saint Petersburg FL 33703

STERN, EDWARD MAYER, lawyer; b. Albany, N.Y., Feb. 18, 1946; s. William Barnet and Louise (Mayer) S.; m. Ann Swanson, Jan. 22, 1972; children: Jared William, Jordan Carl. BCE, Tufts U., 1968; JD, Boston U., 1972. Bar: Mass. 1972, U.S. Dist. Ct. Mass. 1973, U.S. Supreme Ct. 1980, N.Y. 1983. Staff atty. Boston Legal Assistance Project, 1972-74; counsel Treatment Alternative to Street Crime-Juvenile, Boston, 1974-75; atty., project dir. Action Plan for Legal Services, Boston, 1976; lawyer in residence U. Mass., Boston, 1976-77; sole practice Newton Centre, Mass., 1976—; prelaw advisor Boston U., 1977—; vis. lectr. U. Mass., 1977—; bd. dirs. PreLaw Advisors Nat. Council, 1986. Author: (with others) NAPLA PreLaw Advising Guide, 1984, 85, 86; contbr. articles to profl. jours. Mem. ABA, Mass. Bar Assn., Northeast Assn. Pre-Law Advisors (pres.-elect 1986). Jewish. General practice, General corporate, Real property. Home: 38 Morseland Ave Newton Centre MA 02159-1150 Office: 93 Union St Suite 312 Newton Centre MA 02159-2291

STERN, GERALD DANIEL, lawyer; b. N.Y.C., May 16, 1933; s. Solomon Stern and Stella Schoen; m. Doris Stern, Mar. 21, 1960; children: Nelson M., Andrew L., Teri H. BA, NYU, 1954, LLB, 1957. Bar: N.Y. 1957, U.S. Ct. Appeals (2d cir.) 1959, U.S. Dist. Ct. (no. dist.) N.Y. 1965, U.S. Dist. Ct. D.C. 1969, U.S. Ct. Appeals (D.C. cir.) 1969, U.S. Dist. Ct. Md. 1970, U.S. Supreme Ct. 1970, U.S. Tax Ct. 1971. Assoc. Paul, Weiss, Rifkind, Wharton & Garrison, N.Y.C., 1957-67, ptnr., 1967—; adj. prof. law NYU, 1983—. Chmn. legal com., trustee Westchester Reform Temple, Scarsdale, N.Y., 1983—. Mem. ABA, N.Y. State Bar Assn., Assn. of Bar of City of N.Y., N.Y. County Bar Assn., Fed. Bar Council. Jewish. Clubs: Beach Point (Mamaroneck, N.Y.); Boca West (Boca Raton, Fla.). Federal civil litigation, State civil litigation. Home: 20 Morris Ln Scarsdale NY 10583 Office: Paul Weiss Rifkind Wharton & Garrison 1285 Ave of the Americas New York NY 10019

STERN, GERALD M., lawyer, oil company executive; b. Chgo., Apr. 5, 1937; s. Lloyd and Fannye (Wener) S.; m. Linda Stone, Dec. 20, 1969; children: Eric, Jesse, Maia. B.S. in Econs., U. Pa., 1958; LL.B. cum laude, Harvard, 1961. Bar: D.C. 1961, U.S. Supreme Ct. 1971. Trial atty. civil rights div. U.S. Dept. Justice, 1961-64; assoc. firm Arnold & Porter, Washington, 1964-68; partner Arnold & Porter, 1969-76; founding partner firm Rogovin, Stern & Huge, Washington, 1976-81; exec. v.p., sr. gen. counsel Occidental Petroleum Corp., Washington, 1981-82, Los Angeles, 1982—. Author: The Buffalo Creek Disaster, 1976; co-author: Southern Justice, 1965. Bd. dirs. Facing History and Ourselves Nat. Found., Inc., Bet Tzedek. Mem. ABA. Office: Occidental Petroleum Corp 10889 Wilshire Blvd Los Angeles CA 90024

STERN, HERBERT JAY, lawyer; b. N.Y.C., Nov. 8, 1936; s. Samuel and Sophie (Berkowitz) S.; children: Jason Andrew and Jordan Ezekiel (twins), Samuel Abraham, Sarah Kathrine. B.A., Hobart Coll., 1958; J.D. (Ford Found. scholar), U. Chgo., 1961; LL.D. (hon.), Seton Hall Law Sch., 1973, Hobart Coll., 1974; L.H.D. (hon.), Newark State Coll., 1973; D.C.L. (hon.), Bloomfield Coll., 1973; Litt.D. (hon.), Montclair State Coll., 1973. Bar: N.Y. 1961, N.J. 1971. Asst. dist. atty. New York County, 1962-65; trial atty. organized crime and racketeering sect. Dept. of Justice, 1965-69; chief asst. U.S. atty. dist. of N.J., Newark, 1969-70; U.S. atty. Dist. of N.J., 1971-74, U.S. dist. judge, 1974-87; ptnr. Hellring, Lindeman, Goldstein, Siegal & Stern, Newark, 1987—; mem. adv. com. U. Chgo. Law Sch. Author: Judgment in Berlin, 1984 (Valley Forge award Freedom Found. 1984). Named One of America's 10 Outstanding Young Men U.S. Jr. C. of C., 1971. Fellow ABA, Am. Law Inst. (Clarence Darrow award), Internat. Platform Assn.; mem. ABA, N.J. Bar Assn., Fed. Bar Assn. (past pres. Newark chpt.), Essex County Bar Assn., Am. Judicature Soc., Phi Alpha Delta. Subject of book Tiger in the Court, 1973. Office: Hellring Lindeman et al 1180 Raymond Blvd Newark NJ 07102

STERN, JOHN JULES, lawyer; b. Paterson, N.J., Apr. 15, 1955; s. Howard and Muriel (Lubowitt) S.; m. Holly Anne Cohn, Aug. 12, 1979; 1 child, Julianne Lauren. Student, Northwestern U., 1972-73; BA, Brandeis U., 1976; M in Pub. Adminstrn., U. So. Calif., 1979, JD, 1979. Bar: Calif. 1979, U.S. Dist. Ct. (cen. dist.) Calif. 1979, U.S. Ct. Appeals (9th cir.) 1979, N.J. 1980, U.S. Dist. Ct. N.J. 1980, U.S. Ct. Appeals (3d cir.) 1982, U.S. Supreme Ct. 1982. Law sec. to chancery judge N.J. Superior Ct., Paterson, 1979-80; assoc. Stern, Steiger, Croland, Tanenbaum & Schielke, Paramus, N.J., 1980-83, ptnr., 1983—. Mem. ABA (jud. adminstrn. div., antitrust div. 1979—), N.J. Bar Assn., Calif. Bar Assn., Trial Attys. N.J. (trustee 1987—), Passaic County Bar Assn. (chmn. equity jurisprudence com. 1984—, chmn. com. civil and constl. rights 1984—), Bergen County Bar Assn., Morris County Bar Assn., Am. Judicature Soc. Democrat. Jewish. Avocations: sailing. State civil litigation, Federal civil litigation, Antitrust. Office: Stern Steiger Croland Tanenbaum & Schielke 1 Mack Centre Dr Paramus NJ 07652

STERN, LEWIS ARTHUR, lawyer; b. Pitts., Apr. 28, 1934; s. John C. and Belle (Maretsky) S.; children: Isobel, Gillian, Emily, Thomas. B.A., Yale U., 1955, LL.B., 1958. Bar: N.Y. 1959. Law clk. to chief judge U.S. Ct. Appeals (2d cir.), N.Y.C., 1958-59; assoc. Fried, Frank, Harris, Shriver & Jacobson, N.Y.C., 1959-67, ptnr., 1967—. General corporate, Securities. Office: Fried Frank Harris Shriver & Jacobson 1 New York Plaza New York NY 10004

STERN, PETER R., lawyer; b. East Orange, N.J., Nov. 2, 1947; s. Ralph and Jacqueline Rene (Piot) S.; B.A., Columbia U., 1969, J.D., 1972. Bar: N.Y. 1973, U.S. Dist. Ct. (so. and ea. dists.) 1973, U.S. Ct. Appeals (2nd cir.) 1975, U.S. Supreme Ct. 1979. Law clk. to judge U.S. Dist. Ct., N.Y.C., 1972-74; assoc. Winthrop, Stimson, Putnam & Roberts, N.Y.C., 1974-80; founder, ptnr. Berger, Steingut, Weiner, Fox & Stern, N.Y.C., 1980-85, ptnr. Berger & Steingut, 1986— ; dir. Kitchen Ctr., N.Y.C., 1978—. Mem. ABA, N.Y.C. Bar Assn., Fed. Bar Council, N.Y. State Bar. Federal civil litigation, State civil litigation, General practice. Office: Berter & Steingut 600 Madison Ave New York NY 10022

STERN, RICHARD HARVEY, lawyer; b. N.Y.C., Sept. 9, 1931; s. Harold and Syd Stern; m. Janice Chaleen Teisberg, Apr. 23, 1983; children: Noah, Robert. AB cum laude, Columbia U., 1953, BSEE, 1954; LLB cum laude, Yale U., 1959. Bar: Conn. 1959, U.S. Dist. Ct. Md. 1960, U.S. Ct. Appeals (2d cir.) 1960, U.S. Dist. Ct. Conn. 1961, U.S. Patent Office 1961, U.S. Ct. Appeals (D.C. cir.) 1962, U.S. Ct. Appeals (7th cir.) 1965, U.S. Ct. Appeals (4th cir.) 1967, U.S. Supreme Ct. 1971, D.C. 1980, U.S. Ct. Appeals (fed. cir.) 1986. Trial atty. U.S. Dept. Justice, Washington, 1959-62, 66-68, chief intellectual property sect., 1970-78; law clk. to Justice Byron R. White U.S. Supreme Ct., Washington, 1962-63; trial atty. FTC, Washington, 1963-66; atty. U.S. Dept. Commerce, Washington, 1968-69, Iron & Sears, P.C., 1978; ptnr. Baker & Hostetler, 1979-82, Stern & Roberts, 1982-83; sole practice Washington, 1983—; disting. vis. prof. law U. Minn., 1974; cons. U.S. Semiconductor Assn., San Jose, Calif., 1983—, MITI Govt. Japan, Tokyo, 1984—, World Intellectual Property Orgn. United Nations, Geneva, Switzerland, 1984—, World Bank, Washington, 1987—; lectr. on computer related law. Author: Semiconductor Chip Protection, 1986; mem. editorial bd. various legal jours.; contbr. articles to profl. jours. Served with U.S. Army, 1955-56. Mem. ABA (chmn. subcom. on new forms intellectual property protection for high tech. patent and copyright sect. 1983-86), IEEE (assoc. editor computer soc. jour. Micro 1984—, writer bimonthly column), Am. Intellectual Property Law Assn., Order of Coif, Eta Kappa Nu. Computer, Patent, Trademark and copyright. Home: 3936 Rickover Rd Silver Spring MD 20902 Office: 2101 L St #800 NW Washington DC 20037

STERN, SAMUEL ALAN, lawyer; b. Phila., Jan. 21, 1929. A.B., U. Pa., 1949; LL.B., Harvard U., 1952. Bar: Mass. 1952, D.C. 1958. Assoc. Cox, Langford, Stoddard & Cutler, Washington, 1956-62; ptnr. Wilmer, Cutler & Pickering, Washington, 1962—, mem. mgmt. com., 1986; vis. prof. law Harvard U., Cambridge, Mass., 1976; dir. Internat. Law Inst., Georgetown U., 1971—, adj. prof. law, 1979—; asst. counsel Warren Commn., 1964; cons. UN, 1974—, WHO, 1978—; bd. dirs. ADEC Inc., David Adamson Ltd., Interjura Consultancy Services (China) Ltd., Ninth Moon Inc. Contbr. articles to legal jours. Mem. ABA, Am. Law Inst., Am. Soc. Internat. Law, D.C. Bar Assn. Legal education. Home: 2336 California St NW Washington DC 20008 Office: 2445 M St NW Washington DC 20037

STERN, WARREN ROGER, lawyer; b. Amsterdam, N.Y., Aug. 20, 1952; s. Edward Donald and Irene (Northman) S.; m. Susan Schickler, Aug. 11, 1974; 1 child, Jordan Michael. BA, Columbia U., 1974; JD, Harvard U., 1978. Bar: N.Y. 1980, U.S. Dist. Ct. (so. and ea. dists.) N.Y. 1980. Law clk. to presiding sr. judge U.S. Ct. Appeals (2d cir.), N.Y.C., 1978-79; assoc. Wachtell, Lipton, Rosen & Katz, N.Y.C., 1979-84, ptnr., 1985—; adj. faculty N.Y. Law Sch., N.Y.C., 1985—. Contbr. articles to profl. jours. Mem. ABA, N.Y. State Bar Assn., Fed. Bar Council, Assn. of Bar of City of N.Y. (com. on legal edn. and admission to bar 1984-86), Harvard Club. Securities, Federal civil litigation, State civil litigation. Home: 4 Cross Rd Darien CT 06820 Office: Wachtell Lipton Rosen & Katz 299 Park Ave New York NY 10171

STERNBERG, DAVID J., lawyer; b. Cleve., Nov. 27, 1948; s. Harry and Katherine (Kantor) S.; m. Marlene S. Harris, Nov. 14, 1982. BS, Miami U., Oxford, Ohio, 1970; JD cum laude, Ohio State U., 1973. Bar: Ohio 1973, U.S. Dist. Ct. (no. dist.) Ohio 1975, U.S. Supreme Ct. 1977, U.S. Dist. Ct. (ea. dist.) Mich. 1982. Atty. Ohio EPA, Columbus, 1974, Lake County Pros. Atty. Offices, Painesville, Ohio, 1974-77; trial atty. NLRB, Cleve., 1977; assoc. Kenen & Snider Co., LPA, Mentor, Ohio, 1978-81; sole practice Mentor, 1982; ptnr. Sternberg & Zeid Co., LPA, Mentor, 1983—. Mem. community relation com. Jewish Community Fedn., 1986—; trustee Big Bros. Big Sisters of Lake County, Painesville, 1978—, v.p. 1981, pres. 1982; pres. Western Res. City Club, Mentor, 1983; trustee United Way of Lake County, Painesville, 1984—. Mem. ABA, Am. Trial Lawyers Assn., Am. Arbitrators Assn., Ohio State Bar Assn., Ohio Trial Lawyers Assn., Lake County Bar Assn. Avocations: racquetball, bowling. Labor, Personal injury, Family and matrimonial. Office: Sternberg & Zeid Co LPA 7547 Mentor Ave Mentor OH 44060

STERNBERG, MELVIN, lawyer, accountant; b. Bklyn., Dec. 13, 1939; s. Sidney and Gussie (Bach-Le Boyer) S.; m. Janet M. Hoffman, Jan. 11, 1964 (div. 1974); 1 child, Daryl S.; m. Katheryne Ann Allison, Oct. 7, 1975; children—Colette M., Allison K. B.S., Ariz. State U., 1958; LL.B., U. Ariz. 1961. Bar: Ariz. 1961, U.S. Dist. Ct. Ariz. 1961. Ptnr. Sternberg, Sternberg & Rubin, Phoenix, 1961—; judge pro-tem Maricopa County Superior Ct., 1981—; Contbr. articles to profl. jours. Bd. dirs. Phoenix Jewish Community Ctr., 1965. Mem. ABA, State Bar Ariz. (chmn. continuing legal edn. family law div. 1983, 84), Maricopa County Bar Assn. (chmn. continuing legal edn., family law com.), Assn. Trial Lawyers Am. Republican. Jewish (dir. 1979—). Family and matrimonial. Office: Sternberg Sternberg & Rubin 80 E Columbus St Phoenix AZ 85012

STERNBERG, RICHARD, lawyer; b. Akron, Ohio, Mar. 30, 1928; s. Howard Coleman and Sarah (Krupsky) S.; m. Fredi Burnes Narkin, July 12, 1954; children: Liam, Ethan, Leslie. BA, U. Chgo., 1948; BS, U. Akron, 1949; LLB, Case Western Res. U., 1952. Bar: Ohio 1952, U.S. Dist. Ct. (no. dist.) Ohio 1959, U.S. Ct. Appeals (6th cir.) 1961. Of counsel Castle Homes, Inc., Akron, 1954-59; sole practice Akron, 1959-72; ptnr. Oesterícher, Sternberg & Manes, Akron, 1972-85, Sternberg, Newman & Assocs., Akron, 1985—. Mem. Summit County Facilities Rev. Bd., Akron, 1985—. Cert. of Trial Adv., Nat. Bd. Trial Adv., Washington, 1983. Mem. ABA, Assn. Trial Lawyers Am., Ohio Bar Assn., Akron Bar Assn. Clubs: University, Cascade (Akron). Personal injury, Civil rights, General practice. Office: 146 S High St Suite 905 Akron OH 44308

STERNS, JOEL H., lawyer; b. N.Y.C., Apr. 13, 1934; s. Barney and Yetta S.; m. Joanne Glickman, Nov. 19, 1961; children—Rachael, Leslie, David. B.S. in Journalism, 1956; M.P.A., Princeton U., 1958; J.D., N.Y. U., 1967. Bar: N.J. bar, D.C. bar. Exec. asst. to commr. N.J. Dept. Conservation and Econ. Devel., 1958-61; exec. asst. to adminstr. Bur. Security and Consular Affairs, Dept. State, 1961-62; regional programs coordinator Alliance for Progress, 1962-64; exec. asst. to pres. Export-Import Bank U.S., 1964; dep. commr. N.J. Dept. Community Affairs, 1967-68; counsel to gov. N.J., 1968-70; pres. firm Sterns, Herbert & Weinroth (P.A.), Trenton, N.J., 1970—. Mem. Am. Bar Assn., Am. Law Inst., Am. Judicature Soc., N.J. Bar Assn. (trustee), Mercer County Bar Assn., Assn. Princeton U. Grad. Alumni (trustee 1975-77), NYU Alumni Assn. N.J. (Disting. Alumni award 1987). Administrative and regulatory, State civil litigation, Legislative. Home: River Rd PO Box 307 Washington Crossing NJ 08560 Office: 186 W State St PO Box 1298 Trenton NJ 08607

STERNSTEIN, ALAN BARRY, lawyer; b. Tucson, Dec. 27, 1950; m. Joyce Lee Kramer, Oct. 22, 1977; children: Aliya, Rachel. BA, U. Ariz., 1972, JD, 1975. Bar: D.C. 1976, Md. 1987. Law clk. to presiding justice Supreme Ct., Washington, 1975-76; assoc. Wilmer, Cutler & Pickering, Washington, 1976-82; gen. atty. STC/COMSAT, Washington, 1982-84; ptnr. Dilworth, Paxson, Kalish & Kauffman, Washington, 1984-87, Baskin, Flaherty, Eliott, Mannino & Gordon, P.C., Washington, 1987—. Mem. Fed. Communications Bar Assn., Order of Coif, Phi Beta Kappa. Jewish. Avocations: meteorology, tennis. Administrative and regulatory, Antitrust, Public utilities. Home: 908 Twin Oaks Dr Potomac MD 20854 Office: Baskin Flaherty Eliott et al 818 Connecticut Ave Washington DC 20006

STERRETT, JAMES KELLEY, II, lawyer; b. St. Louis, Nov. 26, 1946; s. James Kelley and Anastasia Mary (Holzer) S. AB, San Diego State U., 1968; JD, U. Calif., Berkeley, 1971; LLM, U. Pa., 1973. Bar: Calif. 1972, U.S. Dist. Ct. (so. dist.) Calif. 1972. From assoc. to ptnr. Gray, Cary, Ames & Frye, San Diego, 1972-83; ptnr. Lillick, McHose & Charles, San Diego, 1983—. Contbr. articles to profl. jours. Bd. dirs. Holiday Bowl, San Diego, 1980—, Mus. Photog. Arts, San Diego, 1985—; bd. dirs., sec. Greater San Diego Sports Assn, 1980—. Served to capt. USAFR, 1972. Fellow U. Pa. Ctr. Study Fin. Instns., 1971-72. Mem. ABA, Calif. Bar Assn., San Diego County Bar Assn., San Diego Fin. Lawyers Group. Republican. Episcopalian. Clubs: Fairbanks Ranch Country (Rancho Santa Fe) (bd. dirs. 1985—); Cuyamaca (San Diego). Avocation: golf. Banking, General corporate, Securities. Office: Lillick McHose & Charles 101 W Broadway Suite 1800 San Diego CA 92101

STERRETT, MALCOLM MCCURDY BURDETT, federal executive; b. Norwalk, Conn., Sept. 21, 1942; s. Raymond Arthur and Grace Mildred (Burdett) S.; m. Joan Place DeChant, June 11, 1966; 1 dau., Anne. B.A., Princeton U., 1964; postgrad. The Hague Acad. Internat. Law, 1966; J.D., Vanderbilt U., 1967. Bar: D.C. 1968. Atty. advisor ICC, Washington, 1967-72, commr., 1982, vice chmn., 1983, commr., 1984—; minority staff counsel U.S. Senate Com. on Commerce, 1972-76, minority staff dir., counsel com. on commerce, sci. and transp., 1976-80; v.p., gen. counsel U.S. Ry. Assn., 1980-82. Mem. D.C. Bar Assn. Republican. Episcopalian. Administrative and regulatory, Legislative. Office: Interstate Commerce Commn 12th St and Constitution Ave NW Washington DC 20423

STERRETT, SAMUEL BLACK, judge; b. Washington, Dec. 17, 1922; s. Henry Hatch Dent and Helen (Black) S.; m. Jeane McBride, Aug. 27, 1949; children: Samuel Black, Robin Dent, Douglas McBride. Student, St. Albans Sch., 1933-41; grad., U.S. Mcht. Marine Acad., 1945; B.A., Amherst Coll., 1947; LL.B., U. Va., 1950; LL.M. in Taxation, N.Y.U., 1959. Bar: D.C. 1951, Va. 1950. Atty. Alvord & Alvord, Washington, 1950-56; trial atty. Office Regional Counsel, Internal Revenue Service, N.Y.C., 1956-60; ptnr. Sullivan, Shea & Kenney, Washington, 1960-68; municipal cons. to office vice pres. U.S. 1965-68; judge U.S. Tax Ct., 1968—, chief judge, 1985—. Bd. mgrs. Chevy Chase Village, 1970-74, chmn., 1972-74; 1st v.p. bd. trustees, mem. exec. com. Washington Hosp. Center, 1969-79, chmn. bd. trustees, 1979-84; chmn. bd. trustees Washington Healthcare Corp., 1982-87; chmn. bd. trustees Medlantic Healthcare Group, 1987—; mem. Washington Cathedral chpt., 1973-81; mem. governing bd. St. Albans Sch., 1977-81; trustee Louise Home, 1979—. Served with AUS, 1943; Served with U.S. Mcht. Marine, 1943-46. Mem. Am., Fed., Va., D.C. bar assns., Soc. of the Cincinnati, Beta Theta Pi. Episcopalian. Clubs: Chevy Chase (bd. govs. 1979-84, pres. 1984), Metropolitan, Lawyers, Alibi, Lake Placid, Church of N.Y. Jurisprudence. Office: US Tax Ct 400 2d St Washington DC 20217

STETLER, NEVIN, lawyer; b. Newberrytown, Pa., Sept. 29, 1918; s. Daniel Edward and Ruth (Hays) S.; m. Frances Jeannette Lose, Aug. 29, 1942; children—Smith Georgianna Stetler Snowden, Stephen Hays. B.A., Duke U., 1940; LL.B., Yale U., 1947. Bar: Pa. 1948, U.S. Dist. Ct. (mid. dist.) Pa. 1952, U.S. Tax Ct. 1965. Sole practice York, Pa., 1948-62; sr. ptnr. Stetler & Gribbin, York, 1962—. Mem. Pa. App. Ct. Nominating Commn. 1973-79. Chmn. Housing Authority City of York 1969-74; bd. dirs., sec.-treas. York Benevolent Assn. 1956—; sec.-treas. Hahn Home of York 1958-82, pres. 1982—; pres. York County Tb Soc. 1959-63. Served to lt. comdr. USN 1942-46, 51-52. Recipient citation of merit for outstanding contbns. to judiciary Gov. of Pa., 1978. Mem. ABA, Pa. Bar Assn., York County Bar Assn., Am. Judicature Soc. (sustaining). Democrat. Clubs: Country of York, Lafayette (York). Insurance, Probate, Corporate taxation.

STETTER, ROGER ALAN, lawyer; b. N.Y.C., Mar. 12, 1947; s. William Adolphe, Jr. and Dorothy Shirley (Adler) S.; m. Barbara Jean Hensley, Dec. 25, 1974; children: David O'Neill, John Roger. B.S. in Indsl. and Labor Relations, Cornell U., 1968; J.D., U. Va., 1971. Bar: Va. 1971, N.Y. 1978, La. 1982. Atty. Legal Aid Soc., Roanoke, Va., 1971-72; asst. prof. law La. State U., Baton Rouge, 1972-76; litigation assoc. Mudge Rose Guthrie Alexander & Ferdon, N.Y.C., 1977-82; ptnr. Lemle, Kelleher, Kohlmeyer, Dennery, Hunley, Moss & Frilot, New Orleans, 1983—; dir., vis. asst. prof. criminal def. unit U. Tenn. Legal Clinic, Knoxville, 1975-76; adj. assoc. prof. Benjamin N. Cardozo Sch. Law, N.Y.C., 1978-81. Editor in chief La. Appellate Practice Handbook (Lawyers Co-op 1986), Manual of Recent Devels. in the Law (La. Bar Assn. 1985); contbr. articles to legal jours. Bd. dirs. Community Service Ctr., Inc., New Orleans, 1983—; Legal Aid Bur. of New Orleans, 1985. Mem. Am. Law Inst., La. Bar Assn., Va. Bar Assn., New Orleans Bar Assn., Assn. Bar City N.Y., U. Va. Alumni Assn. La. Democrat. Federal civil litigation, Environment, Antitrust. Home: 4429 Baronne St New Orleans LA 70115 Office: Lemle Kelleher Kohlmeyer et al 601 Pydras St New Orleans LA 70130-6097

STEUER, RICHARD MARC, lawyer; b. Bklyn., June 19, 1948; s. Harold and Gertrude (Venga) S.; m. Audrey F. Forchheimer, Sept. 9, 1973; children: Hilary, Jeremy. BA, Hofstra U., 1970; JD, Columbia U., 1973. Ptnr. Kaye, Scholer, Fierman, Hays & Handler, N.Y.C., 1973—; adj. assoc. prof. law NYU, 1985; lectr. various orgns. Contbr. articles to profl. jours. Mem. ABA (chmn. monograph com. refusals to deal and exclusive distributorships 1983, various others, editorial bd. antitrust devel. volume 1984—, antitrust law sect., lectr. 1978, 85), Assn. of Bar of City of N.Y. (antitrust and trade regulation, lectures and continuing edn. coms., lectr. 1983-85). Antitrust, Trademark and copyright, Federal civil litigation. Office: Kaye Scholer Fierman Hays & Handler 425 Park Ave New York NY 10022

STEUER, ROBERT KARL, lawyer; b. Fredericksburg, Va., Dec. 17, 1940; s. Ulrick B. and Edith (Rosenthal) S.; m. Elizabeth Mufson, June 20, 1964; children—Jonathan, David, Ellen. A.B., Ind. U., 1962; J.D., Northwestern U., 1965. Bar: Wis. 1965, U.S. Dist. Ct. (ea. dist.) Wis. 1965, U.S. Ct. Appeals (7th cir.) 1973. Assoc. Lorinczi & Weiss, Milw., 1965-70, ptnr., 1970-74; ptnr. Weiss, Steuer, Berzowski & Kriger, Milw., 1974-81; ptnr. Weiss, Steuer, Berzowski, Brady & Donahue, Milw., 1981-85; ptnr. Polacheck & Harris, Milw., 1985—. Democrat. Jewish. Federal civil litigation, State civil litigation, Contracts commercial. Address: care of Polacheck & Harris 710 N Plankinton Milwaukee WI 53203

STEVENS, BEN DEE, lawyer; b. San Angelo, Tex., Jan. 13, 1942; s. Rex W. and Nettie Marie (Evans) S.; m. Joyce Irene Dymke, June 22, 1964 (div. 1966); children—Mark Richard, Samantha Ann, Andrew Duncan; m. Paula Sue Smith, June 4, 1983; 1 stepchild, Shan Michelle Spear. B.B.A., U. Houston-Clear Lake, 1978; J.D., S. Tex. Coll., 1981. Bar: Tex. 1981, U.S. Tax Ct. 1982, U.S. Dist. Ct. (so. dist.) Tex. 1982, U.S. Ct. Appeals (5th cir.) 1982. Sole practice, Houston, 1981-84; gen. counsel Cantrell & Co., Houston, 1984—. Mem. ABA, Tex. Bar Assn., Houston Bar Assn., Am. Trial Lawyers Assn., Phi Alpha Delta. Republican. Episcopalian. Office: 4204 Bellaire Blvd Suite 204 Houston TX 77025

STEVENS, BRADFORD LEE, lawyer; b. Clayton, Mo., Oct. 14, 1951; s. Laddie Lee and Velma Louise (Thompson) S.; m. Rachel Sue Harshaw, Mar. 24, 1973; children: Rachel Louise, Hannah Leigh, Adam William. BA magna cum laude, U. Mo., St. Louis, 1973; JD, Washington U., St. Louis, 1976. Bar: Mo. 1976, U.S. Dist. Ct. (ea. dist.) Mo. 1977, U.S. Ct. Appeals (8th cir.) 1979, U.S. Supreme Ct. 1981. Assoc. Law Offices of Conway B. Briscoe Jr., St. Louis, 1976-77, Barksdale, Adams, Chorlins & Young, St. Louis, 1977-78, Chused, Strauss, Chorlins, Golfarb, Bini & Kohn, St. Louis, 1978-83; prin. Newman, Goldfarb, Freyman & Stevens, P.C., Clayton, Mo., 1983—. Alderman City of Rock Hill, Mo., 1977—; deacon McKnight Rd. Ch. of Christ, Ladue, Mo., 1980—. Mem. Mo. Bar Assn., Met. Bar of St. Louis. Estate planning, Real property, General corporate. Home: 9783 Sherrell Ct Rock Hill MO 63105 Office: Newman Golfarb et al 7777 Bonhomme Clayton MO 63105

STEVENS, CHARLES PAUL, lawyer; b. Hinsdale, Ill., Sept. 20, 1955; s. William Edward and Nancy Margarite (Hoover) S.; m. Barbara Ann Retzlaff, June 27, 1981; children: William Wayne, Nancy Louise. BBA, U. Wis., 1977; JD, Marquette U., 1981. Bar: Wis. 1981, U.S. Dist. Ct. (ea. and we. dists.) Wis. 1981. Assoc. Godfrey, Trump & Hayes, Milw., 1981-85, Linder & Marsack S.C., Milw., 1985—. Mem. ABA, Wis. Bar Assn., Wis. Retirement Plan Profls. Ltd. Pension, profit-sharing, and employee benefits, Labor, Federal civil litigation. Home: 8021 W Hillcrest Dr Wauwatosa WI 53213 Office: Linder & Marsack SC 700 N Water St Milwaukee WI 53202

STEVENS, DOUGLAS ROBERT, lawyer; b. Dallas, Sept. 22, 1955; s. Robert Lewis and Doris (Petersen) S.; m. Deborah Else, July 7, 1979. BA, Ind. U., 1977; JD, U. Tex., 1982. Bar: Ill. 1982, U.S. Dist. Ct. (no. dist.) Ill. 1982, U.S. Ct. Appeals (7th cir.) 1984. Assoc. Foran, Wiss & Schultz, Chgo., 1982—. Mem. ABA, Ill. Bar Assn., Chgo. Bar Assn. Federal civil litigation, State civil litigation, Condemnation. Office: Foran Wiss & Schultz 30 N LaSalle St Suite 3000 Chicago IL 60602

STEVENS, EDWIN DAN, lawyer; b. Raleigh, N.C., May 2, 1943; s. Ross Oliver and Rose Elizabeth (Askew) S.; m. Karen Diane Colby, Jan 22, 1966; children: Joseph O., Kirsten R. BS, U. Mich., 1965, MA, 1970; JD, Thomas M. Cooley Sch. Law, 1977. Bar: Mich. 1977, Fla. 1983, U.S. Dist. Ct. (ea. dist.) Mich. 1978, U.S. Ct. Appeals (6th cir.) 1981, U.S. Supreme Ct. 1982, U.S. Dist. Ct. (so. dist.) Fla. 1986. Tchr. White Lake (Mich.) High Sch., 1965-67; exec. dir. Summer Sci. Inc., Ann Arbor, Mich., 1967-72; pres. Stevens Real Estate Inc., Atlanta, Mich., 1972-77; ptnr. Stevens, Tibbetts & Kundinger, Atlanta, 1977-85; sole practice Ft. Myers, Fla., 1985-86; sr. atty. Fla. Dept. Labor, Miami, 1986—. Mem. Atlanta Bd. Edn., 1972, Mich. Ho. of Reps., 1975-78. Recipient Edison Sci. Teaching award Edison Found., 1967. Republican. Probate, Real property, Contracts commercial. Home: Rt 2 Box 929 D Alva FL 33920 Office: Fla Dept Labor 108 NE 1st St Fort Lauderdale FL 33301

STEVENS, GERALD M., lawyer; b. Detroit; married; 3 children. B.S. in Forestry, Mich. State U., 1951; LL.B., U. Detroit, 1957. Mem. legal div. Bd. Wayne County Rd. Commrs., 1955-61; assoc. Langs, Molyneaux & Armstrong, Detroit, 1961-65; sole practice, Owosso, Mich., 1965—; pros. atty. County of Shiawassee (Mich.), 1968-72. Trustee, atty. Nardin Park Meth. Ch.; mem. Taylor Twp. Sch. Bd.; bd. dirs. YMCA; bd. dirs. Community Concert, Inc.; bd. dirs. Shiawassee County unit Am. Cancer Soc.; pres. Owosso Day Care Center; v.p. bd. trustees First United Meth. Ch., Owosso; pres. Lung Assn. Genesee Valley. Served to 1st. lt. U.S. Army, 1951-53. Mem. ABA, State Bar Mich., Detroit Bar Assn., Shiawassee County Bar Assn., Assn. Trial Lawyers Am., Mich. Trial Lawyers Assn., Aircraft Owners and Pilots Assn. (approved atty. prepaid legal plan), Owosso-Corunna C. of C. Clubs: Masons, Kiwanis. General practice, State civil litigation, Personal injury. Office: 319 E Main St PO Box 757 Owosso MI 48867 Office: White House G-3247 Beecher Rd Suite 300 Flint MI 48504

STEVENS, HAROLD BURR, lawyer; b. Uniontown, Pa., June 14, 1948; s. Harold Burr Sr. and Nancy (Behre) S.; m. Carol Deckelman, Sept. 7, 1950; children: Christopher Burr, Katherine Neff. BA, Bowdoin Coll., 1971; JD, Cleve.-Marshall Sch. Law, 1975; LLM in Corps., NYU, 1976. Bar: Conn., Vt., U.S. Dist. Ct. Conn., U.S. Dist. Ct. Vt., U.S. Ct. Appeals (2d cir.). Assoc. Thompson, Weir & Barclay, New Haven, Conn., 1976-77, Law Offices Richard M. Hubbard, Stowe, Vt., 1978-79; ptnr. Stevens & Vogl, Stowe, 1980—. Mem. Stowe Rescue Squad, 1979-80, Environ. Def. Fund, N.Y.C., 1986—. Mem. Conn. Bar Assn. (chmn. adminstrn. justice com. young lawyers div. 1976-77), Vt. Bar Assn. Episcopalian. Club: Squash (Stowe) (sec. 1981-84). Lodge: Rotary. Avocations: skiing, ice hockey, running, carpentry, golf. General practice, State civil litigation, Consumer commercial. Home: Mountain Rd Stowe VT 05672 Office: Stevens & Vogl Main St PO Box 1200 Stowe VT 05672

STEVENS, HAROLD SANFORD, lawyer; b. Phila., Mar. 30, 1950; s. Irvin R. and Betty (Schimel) S.; m. Patricia Madeline Douglass, Aug. 10, 1974; children: Caryn Alicia, Brian Jonathan. BA in Econs., Temple U., 1971; JD, U. Miami, 1975. Bar: Fla. 1975, Pa. 1976, U.S. Dist. Ct. (so. dist.) Fla. 1976, U.S. Ct. Appeals (5th cir.) 1976, D.C. 1977, U.S. Ct. Appeals (11th cir.) 1981. Asst. corp. counsel Sage Corp., Hallandale, Fla., 1975-76; trial atty. Vernis & Bowling, Miami, Fla., 1976-78, Allstate Ins. Co., Miami, 1978-82, Ins. Co. of N.Am., Miami, 1982-83, Dixon, Dixon, Hurst & Nicklaus, Miami, 1983-84; mng. trial counsel Colonial Penn Ins. Co., Phila., 1984—. Mem. ABA, Dade County Bar Assn., Fla. Def. Lawyers Assn. Avocations: golf, home remodeling and repairs. State civil litigation, Insurance, Personal injury. Office: Colonial Penn Ins Co 2699 Stirling Rd Suite C304 Fort Lauderdale FL 33312

STEVENS, HENRY LEONIDAS, III, judge; b. Warsaw, N.C., May 12, 1923; s. Henry Leonidas and Mildred (Beasley) S.; m. Vernell Abernethy, June 6, 1957; children—Mildred Beasley, Henry Leonidas IV. B.A., U. N.C., 1947; J.D., Wake Forest U., 1951. Bar: N.C. 1951, U.S. Dist. Ct. (ea. dist.) N.C. 1951. Ptnr. Beasley and Stevens, Kenansville, N.C., 1951-77; sr. resident judge Superior Ct., 4th Jud. Dist. of N.C., Kenansville, 1977—. Served to capt. USMC, 1943-48, 51-52. Democrat. Presbyterian. Judicial administration. Office: PO Box 26 Kenansville NC 28349

STEVENS, HENRY PATRICK, patent attorney; b. Detroit, Mar. 31, 1918; m. Marjorie Clare Peiffer, 1943; m. Dolores Dawn Debayona, 1982; children—Patrick Henry, Michael John, Suzanne Marie. B.S. in Applied Sci., Mich. State U., 1939; M.S. in Chemistry, U. Mich., 1941; J.D., U. Akron, 1951. Bar: U.S. Patent Office 1955. Patent atty. Dow Chem. Co., Midland, Mich., 1954-58; sr. patent counsel Abbott Labs., North Chicago, Ill., 1958-65; patent dir. Schick Safety Razor Co., Culver City, Calif., 1965-69; sr. patent atty. Miles Labs., Elkhart, Ind., 1969-71; sr. patent counsel Owens-Illinois, Toledo, 1971-78; patent atty. Calif. Inst. Tech., Pasadena, 1978—. Patentee rubber antiozone agts., rubber stabilizers, rubber vulcanizers. Served to lt. USNR, 1941-45. Patent, Trademark and copyright. Home: 2624 Summer Lilac Dr Palmdale CA 93550 Office: Calif Inst Tech 4800 Oak Grove Dr Pasadena CA 91109

STEVENS, JERON LYNN, lawyer; b. Abilene, Tex., Nov. 24, 1942; s. J.L. and Thelma (Owen) S.; m. Rena Jo Cottrell, June 2, 1965; children: David, Lara. BS, N. Tex. State U., 1965; JD, U. Houston, 1968. Bar: Tex. 1968, U.S. Ct. Appeals (5th and D.C. cirs.) 1972, U.S. Supreme Ct. 1972, U.S. Ct. Appeals (9th cir.) 1975, U.S. Ct. Appeals (3d cir.) 1978, U.S. Ct. Appeals (11th cir.) 1981, U.S. Ct. Appeals (10th cir.) 1984. Ptnr. Baker & Botts, Houston, 1968—. Pres. Inverness Forest Owners Com., Inverness Forest Residents Civic Club, Inc. Mem. Tex. Bar Assn., Houston Bar Assn., Fed. Energy Bar Assn., U. Houston Law Alumni Assn. (pres. 1981-82). Clubs: Inns of Cts., Houston. FERC practice, Administrative and regulatory. Home: 1107 Old Mill Ln Houston TX 77073 Office: Baker & Botts One Shell Plaza Houston TX 77002

STEVENS, JOHN PAUL, assoc. justice U.S. Supreme Ct.; b. Chgo., Apr. 20, 1920; s. Ernest James and Elizabeth (Street) S.; m. Elizabeth Jane Sheeren, June 7, 1942; children: John Joseph, Kathryn Stevens Jedlicka, Elizabeth Jane Stevens Sesemann, Susan Roberta; m. Maryan Mulholland Simon, Dec. 1979. A.B., U. Chgo., 1941; J.D. magna cum laude, Northwestern U., 1947. Bar: Ill. 1949. Practiced in Chgo.; law clk. to U.S. Supreme Ct. Justice Wiley Rutledge, 1947-48; assoc. firm Poppenhusen, Johnston, Thompson & Raymond, 1948-52; assoc. counsel sub-com. on study monopoly power, com. on judiciary U.S. Ho. of Reps., 1951; partner firm Rothschild, Stevens, Barry & Myers, 1952-70; U.S. circuit judge 1970-75; asso. justice U.S. Supreme Ct., 1975—; Lectr. anti-trust law Northwestern U. Sch. Law, 1953, U. Chgo. Law Sch., 1954-55; Mem. Atty. Gen.'s Nat. Com. to Study Anti-Trust Laws, 1953-55. Served with USNR, 1942-45. Decorated Bronze Star. Mem. Chgo. Bar Assn. (2d v.p. 1970), Am., Ill., Fed. bar assns., Am. Law Inst., Order of Coif, Phi Beta Kappa, Psi Upsilon, Phi Delta Phi. Jurisprudence. Office: US Supreme Ct 1 First St NE Washington DC 20543

STEVENS, JOHN SHORTER, lawyer; b. Asheville, N.C., May 30, 1933; s. John H. and Viola (Shorter) S.; m. Imogene R. Radeker, Aug. 21, 1965; children: John B., Wyatt S., Scott R. AB in Econs., U. N.C., 1956, LLD, 1961. Bar: N.C. 1961, U.S. Dist. Ct. (we. dist.) N.C. 1975, U.S. Ct. Appeals (4th cir.) 1973. Assoc. Law Offices of Anthony Redmond, Asheville, 1961-64; ptnr. Redmond & Stevens, Asheville, 1964-73, Redmond, Stevens, Loftin & Currie, Asheville, 1973-86, Roberts, Stevens, Cogburn, P.A., Asheville, 1986—; bd. dirs. Lawyers Mutual Liability Ins. Co., Raleigh, N.C. Chmn. Meml. Mission Hosp. Bd. Dirs. Found., 1984-86, pres., 1976-78; mem. N.C. Ho. Reps., 1969-76. Served to cpl. U.S. Army, 1957-58. Mem. ABA, N.C. Bar Assn., Phi Beta Kappa. Democrat. Episcopalian. Club: Balt. Forest Country (sec. 1978-82). General corporate, Contracts commercial. Home: 83 Forest Rd Asheville NC 28803 Office: Roberts Stevens & Cogburn PO Box 7146 Asheville NC 28807

STEVENS, JOSEPH EDWARD, JR., judge; b. Kansas City, Mo., June 23, 1928; s. Joseph Edward and Mildred Christian (Smith) S.; m. Norma Jeanne Umlauf, Nov. 25, 1956; children—Jennifer Jeanne, Rebecca Jeanne. B.A., Yale U., 1949; J.D., U. Mich., 1952. Bar: Mo., U.S. Supreme Ct. Assoc. Lombardi, McLean, Slagle & Bernard, Kansas City, Mo., 1955-56; assoc. then ptnr. Lathrop, Koontz, Righter, Clagett & Norquist, Kansas City, Mo., 1956-81; judge U.S. Dist. Ct. Mo., Kansas City, 1981—. Bd. govs. Citizens Assn. Kansas City, 1959-70; bd. dirs., exec. com. Truman Med. Ctr., Kansas City; trustee Central United Methodist Ch., Kansas City, 1978—, Barstow Sch., Kansas City, 1978—; bd. dirs. Truman Med. Ctr., 1978—. Served with USNR, 1952-55. Recipient Lon O. Hocker Meml. Trial Lawyer award, 1963. Mem. ABA (ho. of dels.), Am. Judicature Soc., Kansas City Bar Assn., Lawyers Assn. Kansas City, Mo. Bar (pres. 1980-81, bd. govs. 1976-82). Clubs: University, Carriage, Mercury, Vanguard. U.S. district judge. Home: 425 W 55th St Kansas City MO 64113 Office: US Dist Ct 811 Grand Ave 404 US Courthouse Kansas City MO 64106

STEVENS, LEE, talent agency executive; b. Bklyn., Mar. 10, 1930; s. Joseph and Helen (Zlotnik) Silverman; m. Lizabeth Silverman, Apr. 11, 1954; children—Todd Lowell, Claudia Michelle, Jennifer Susan. B.S., NYU, 1951, J.D., 1957. Bar: N.Y. 1957. Sec. William Morris Agy., N.Y.C., 1953-57, with bus. affairs dept., 1957-62, exec. asst. to pres., 1962-80, exec. v.p., chief operating officer N.Y. office, 1980-84, pres., dir., chief exec. officer, 1984—; vice chmn. adv. bd. Tisch Sch. of Arts, NYU, N.Y.C., 1983—. Pres. Grace Harbor Assn., Kings Point, N.Y., 1967-69; chmn. Show Biz Bash East, Big Bros.-Big Sisters, N.Y.C., 1979—; mem. exec. com. United Jewish Appeal/Fedn.-Entertainment Div., N.Y.C., 1982—; mem. arts and entertainment adv. com. N.Y.C. Partnership, 1984; bd. dirs. USO of Met. N.Y., N.Y.C., 1985—. Served to cpl. U.S. Army, 1951-53. Mem. Internat. Radio and TV Soc., Nat. Acad. TV Arts and Scis., Country Music Assn., Acad. Motion Picture Arts and Scis., Psi Chi Omega, Phi Lambda Delta. Clubs: City Athletic (N.Y.C.); Hillcrest Country (Los Angeles). Avocations: tennis; golf; music. Entertainment. Office: 1350 Ave of Americas New York NY 10019 also: William Morris Agy Inc 151 El Camino Dr Beverly Hills CA 90212

STEVENS, MICHAEL DEAN, lawyer; b. Brownwood, Tex., Apr. 13, 1950; s. Garland Wayne and Virginia Ruth (Sutton) S.; m. Barbara Denise Vaden, June 3, 1972; children: Michael Blake, Brittany Michelle. BA, U. Houston, 1972, M in Pub. Adminstrn., 1974, JD, 1977. Bar: Tex. 1978. Assoc. Urban & Coolidge, Houston, 1978-80; ptnr. Fitzgerald, Majors & Stevens, Wimberley and San Marcos, Tex., 1980—. Pres. bd. Wimberley Ind. Sch. Dist., 1986—; bd. sec. Hays Consol. Ind. Sch. Dist., Wimberley and Kyle, Tex., 1983-85. Mem. ABA, Tex. Bar Assn., Hays County Bar Assn. (sec., v.p., pres. 1985), Wimberley C. of C. (pres. 1984). Democrat. Baptist. Avocation: tennis. Real property. Home: 25 Shady Grove Wimberley TX 78676 Office: Fitzgerald Majors & Stevens PO Box 727 Wimberley TX 78676

STEVENS, PAUL LAWRENCE, lawyer; b. Glen Ridge, N.J., Aug. 18, 1947; s. Mead Ferrin and Mary Nealtha (Cherry) S.; m. Cathy Lee Danskin, Sept. 13, 1969; children: Todd Benjamin, Laura Catherine. BA, U. N.H., 1969; JD cum laude, Dickinson U., 1975. Bar: Pa. 1975, U.S. Dist. Ct. (ea. and mid. dists.) Pa. 1975, U.S. Ct. Appeals (3d cir.) 1979, U.S. Supreme Ct. 1980. Law clk. to presiding justice Pa. Superior Ct., Carlisle, 1975-76; assoc. Curtin and Heefner, Morrisville, Pa., 1976-82, ptnr., 1982—. Editor Dickinson Law Rev., 1975. Asst. cubmaster Boy Scouts Am., Makefield, Pa., 1983-85, Doylestown, Pa., 1985-86; mem. Lenape Dist. Com. Boy Scouts Am., Doylestown, 1986—. Served to 1st lt. U.S. Army, 1969-82. Mem. ABA (Spl. Achievement award 1983), Pa. Bar Assn. (bd. govs. 1981-84, chmn. coms., Spl. Achievement award 1986), Bucks County Bar Assn. (bd. dirs. 1978-80), Pa. Sch. Bd. Solicitors' Assn. (v.p. 1985-87, pres. 1987—). Republican. Avocations: photography, skiing. Local government, Labor, Education law. Home: 56 Sandywood Dr Doylestown PA 18901 Office: Curtin and Heefner 140 E State St Doylestown PA 18901

STEVENS, PETER NICHOLAS, lawyer; b. Bklyn., Feb. 21, 1949; s. Alexander Michael and Sophie (Zahalkowitz) S.; m. Mary Elizabeth Donohue, June 12, 1971; children: Michael, Alexandra. BA, Columbia U., 1970, JD, 1973. Bar: N.Y. 1974, U.S. Dist. Ct. (so. dist.) N.Y. Asst. dist. atty. N.Y. County, N.Y.C., 1973-80; counsel litigation Bristol-Myers Co., N.Y.C., 1980—. Mem. Assn. of Bar of City of N.Y. State civil litigation, Personal injury, Civil rights. Office: Bristol Myers Co 345 Park Ave New York NY 10154

STEVENS, ROGER EDWARD BOUCHER, lawyer; b. Chgo., Nov. 7, 1929; s. Edward Boucher and Sophie (Solow) S.; m. Annlouise Rupert (div.); children: Naomi Caroline Goff, Paul Eric, Joshua Boucher, Wendy Welsh, Sydney Diane; m. Jane Ormsby, Feb. 4, 1977. BA in English, UCLA, 1953; JD, Colo. U., 1957. Mcpl. judge Boulder, Colo., 1957-59; ptnr. Wims, Stevens, Tausig & Trine, Boulder, 1959-65, Stevens & Miller, Boulder, 1967-69, Stevens & Littman, Boulder, 1982—. Office: Stevens & Littman PO Box 2140 Boulder CO 80306

STEVENSON, DONALD W., lawyer; b. Louisville, Mar. 12, 1948; s. Edward Van and Addie Ann (Quick) S.; m. June 7, 1970; 1 child, Imari. BS, Murray (Ky.) State U., 1970; MBA, U. Ky., 1976; JD, Cin. U., 1979. Bar: Ohio. Tax atty. IRS, Washington, 1979-84, Standard Oil Co., Cleve., 1984—. Author: Tax Shelters Are For Everyone, 1984. Served to capt. U.S. Army, 1970-74. Mem. ABA, Assn. Trial Lawyers Am. Democrat. Baptist. General corporate, Corporate taxation, Personal income taxation. Home:

33053 Leafy Mill Ln North Ridgeville OH 44039 Office: Standard Oil Co 200 Public Sq Cleveland OH 44014

STEVENSON, JOCKE SHELBY, lawyer; b. N.Y.C., June 12, 1934; s. Lincoln L. and Shirley (Grodnick) S.; m. Barbara Winokar, Oct. 7, 1970; 1 son, Marshall Lincoln. B.A., Yale U., 1956, J.D., 1959. Bar: N.Y. 1960, U.S. Dist. Ct. (ea. and so. dists.) N.Y. 1976, U.S. Ct. Internat. Trade 1978, U.S. Supreme Ct. 1981. Assoc. Marshall, Bratter, Greene, Allison & Tucker, N.Y.C., 1960-66; house counsel Burnham & Co., N.Y.C., 1966-70; sole practice, N.Y.C., 1971-77; ptnr. Hershcopf, Sloame & Stevenson, N.Y.C., 1978-80, Hershcopf, Stevenson, Tannenbaum & Glassman, N.Y.C., 1980—; adj. asst. prof. bus. law and polit. sci. Marymount Manhattan Coll., 1978—; arbitrator N.Y.C. Small Claims Ct., 1977—, N.Y.C. Civil Ct., 1981—. Trustee Park Ave. Synagogue, N.Y.C. Mem. Assn. Bar City N.Y., N.Y. State Bar Assn. (com. on trusts and estates), ABA (com. sole practitioners and small firms). Clubs: Yale, University Glee (treas. 1987—) (N.Y.C.). General practice, Probate, Real property. Home: 400 E 85th St New York NY 10028 Office: 230 Park Ave Suite 3330 New York NY 10169

STEVENSON, JOHN REESE, lawyer; b. Chgo., Oct. 24, 1921; s. John A. and Josephine R. S.; m. Patience Fullerton, Apr. 10, 1943 (dec. 1982); children: Elizabeth F., Sally H. Stevenson Fischer, John Reese, Patience Stevenson Scott; m. Ruth Carter Johnson, May 21, 1983. A.B., Princeton U., 1942; LL.B., Columbia U., 1949, D.J.S., 1952. Bar: N.Y. 1949, U.S. Supreme Ct. 1964. With firm Sullivan & Cromwell, N.Y.C., 1950—; mem. Sullivan & Cromwell, 1956-69, 75-87, of counsel, 1973-75, chmn., sr. partner, 1979-87, counsel, 1987—; legal adv. with rank of asst. sec. U.S. Dept. State, 1969-72; adviser U.S. del. Gen. Assembly UN, 1969-74; chmn. U.S. del. Internat. Conf. on Air Law, The Hague, 1970; mem. U.S. del. Internat. Conf. on Law of Treaties, Vienna, 1969; ambassador, spl. rep. of Pres. Law of the Sea Conf., 1973-75; U.S. mem. Permanent Ct. of Arbitration, The Hague, 1969-79, 84—; U.S. rep. Internat. Ct. Justice, Namibia (S.W. Africa) case, 1970; spl. counsel U.S. del. Delimitation of Maritime Boundary in Gulf of Maine (Can. vs. U.S.A.), 1984; dir. Bank of N.Y., Bank of N.Y. Co., Inc. Author: The Chilean Popular Front, 1952; Contbr. articles to legal jours. Trustee Andrew W. Mellon Found.; trustee U.S. council ICC; vice chmn. ICC Ct. of Arbitration; pres., trustee Nat. Gallery Art. Fellow Am. Bar Assn. (hon.); mem. Am. Soc. Internat. Law (pres. 1966-68), N.Y. State Bar Assn. (chmn. com. on internat. law 1963-65), Internat. Law Assn., Institut de Droit Internat., Assn. Bar City N.Y. (chmn. com. on internat. law 1958-61), Am. Arbitration Assn. (dir., chmn. exec. com.; chmn. internat. sect. law com.), Council on Fgn. Relations, Am. Law Inst. Clubs: Links (N.Y.C.); Met. (Washington); Chevy Chase. International arbitration, Private international, Public international. Home: 1819 Kalorama Sq NW Washington DC 20008 Office: 1775 Pennsylvania Ave NW Washington DC 20006

STEVENSON, JUSTIN JASON, III, lawyer; b. Cin., Nov. 4, 1941; s. Justin Jason and Anne (Hollister) S.; m. Ann Robinson, Oct. 23, 1971; children—Justin Jason, Christopher R., Catherine F. A.B., Princeton U., 1963; LL.B., Harvard U., 1966. Bar: N.Y. 1966. Assoc. Shearman & Sterling, N.Y.C., 1966-76, ptnr., 1976—. Served to 1st lt. AUS, 1966-69. Mem. Phi Beta Kappa. Banking, Contracts commercial, Private international. Office: Shearman & Sterling 53 Wall St New York NY 10005

STEVENSON, NOEL C., lawyer, author; b. Sacramento, Dec. 24, 1907; s. Ernest E. and Emma (Walker) S.; m. Mary Elizabeth Galton, Oct. 15, 1965. J.D., Pacific Coast U., 1943. Bar: Calif. 1944, U.S. Supreme Ct. 1951. Dist. atty. Sutter County, Calif., 1951-55; sole practice, Laguna Hills, Calif., 1956—. Author: Search and Research, 1951, rev., 1977; How To Build a More Lucrative Law Practice, 1967; Successful Cross Examination Strategy, 1971; Genealogical Evidence, 1979. Contbr. articles to legal and hist. jours. Fellow Am. Soc. Genealogists; mem. State Bar Calif., Am. Name Soc., Supreme Ct. Hist. Soc. General practice, Legal writing, Real property. Office: 5338-A Bahia Blanca Laguna Hills CA 92653

STEVES, EDWARD MICKEL, lawyer; b. N.Y.C., Sept. 29, 1953; s. Paul J. and Clemen (Garced) S.; m. Gladys E. Sanchez, Feb. 4, 1979; 1 child, Cristina. BA, Columbia U., 1975, JD, 1978. Bar: N.Y. 1979, U.S. Dist. Ct. (so. and ea. dists.) N.Y 1980. Asst. corp. counsel N.Y.C. Law Dept., 1978-81; ptnr. Aranda & Steves P.C., N.Y.C., 1981-83; sole practice N.Y.C., 1983—; bd. dirs., officer Taino Internat. Airways Inc.; hearing officer Family Ct., State of N.Y., 1985. Mem. ABA, N.Y. Bar Assn., Puerto Rican Bar Assn. General practice, Personal injury, Consumer commercial. Office: 15 Park Row Suite 1100 New York NY 10038

STEWART, ALLEN WARREN, lawyer; b. Manchester, N.H., Dec. 12, 1938; s. Ellwyn F. and Aelene W. (Harriman) S.; m. Mary Ann Schubert, Apr. 14, 1973; children—William, Paul, Geoffrey. B.S., U.S. Naval Acad., 1961; M.S., George Washington U., 1967; J.D., U. Pa., 1970. Bar: Pa. 1970, U.S. Ct. Appeals (3d cir.) 1971, U.S. Supreme Ct. 1980. Assoc. Morgan, Lewis & Bockius, Phila., 1970-77, ptnr., 1977—; dir. Affiliated Holdings, Ltd., Equi-Realty Mgmt. Corp., Equitable Beneficial Life Ins. Co. Served as naval aviator, lt. comdr. USN, 1961-66. Mem. ABA, Pa. Bar Assn., Phila. Bar Assn. Pa. Club: Phila. Racquet. Contbr. articles to legal jours. Administrative and regulatory, Insurance, Public utilities. Office: One Logan Sq Philadelphia PA 19103

STEWART, ANNETTE, judge; b. Paris, Tex., Jan. 1, 1928; d. Ray Bryan and Mary Christene (Plumer) Stewart. B.A., U. Tex.-Austin, 1949, M.Ed., 1952; LL.B. summa cum laude, So. Meth. U., 1966. Bar: Tex. 1966. Assoc. Parnass, McGuire & Handy, 1966-67; ct. reporter Ct. Domestic Relations, Dallas, 1957-66, 67-74; judge, 1975-77; judge 301st Dist. Ct., Dallas, 1977-83, Ct. of Appeals, Dallas, 1983-84, 305th Dist. Ct., 1985-86, Ct. Appeals, Dallas, 1986—. Fellow Tex. Bar Found.; mem. State Bar Tex., Dallas Bar Assn., ABA, Nat. Conf. State Trial Judges, Nat. Assn. Women Lawyers, Am. Judicature Soc., P.E.O., Phi Beta Kappa. Democrat. Presbyterian. Club: Town and Gown (Dallas). Family and matrimonial, State civil litigation, Criminal. Home: 1822 Marydale Dr Dallas TX 75208

STEWART, CAROL HARDWICK, lawyer; b. Mooresville, N.C., Jan. 18, 1953; d. Lawrence Glenn and Eloise (Estes) Hardwick; m. Lewis M. Stewart Jr., May 2, 1986. BS, U. N.C., 1975; JD, Samford U., 1982; MS, U. Ala., 1983. Bar: Ga. 1982, Ala. 1982, Fla. 1982. Scientist forensics Charlotte (N.C.) Crime Lab, 1977-78, Ala. Dept. Forensic Sci., Mobile, 1978-79; law clk. to chief judge U.S. Dist. Ct. (no. dist.) Ala., Birmingham, 1982-83; assoc. Burr & Forman, Birmingham, 1983—; instr. U. Ala., Birmingham, 1983—; prof. Cumberland Sch. Law Samford U., 1987—. Mem. Ala. Bar Assn., Ga. Bar Assn., Fla. Bar Assn. Office: Burr & Forman 3000 South Trust Tower Birmingham AL 35203

STEWART, CHARLES EVAN, lawyer; b. N.Y.C., Mar. 4, 1952; s. Charles Thorp and Jenifer Jennings (Barbour) S.; m. Cathleen Bacich, June 26, 1982. B.A. cum laude, Cornell U., 1974, J.D., 1977. Bar: N.Y. 1978, U.S. dist. ct. (so. and ea. dists.) N.Y. 1978, U.S. Ct. Appeals (2d cir.) 1978, U.S. Ct. Appeals (D.C. and 7th cirs.) 1980, U.S. Ct. Appeals (3d, 9th and 5th cirs.) 1981, U.S. Supreme Ct. 1981, U.S. Ct. Appeals (10th cir.) 1982, U.S. Claims Ct. 1983, U.S. Ct. Appeals (6th cir.) 1986. Assoc., Donovan Leisure Newton & Irvine, N.Y.C., 1977-87, 1st v.p., assoc. gen. counsel E.F. Hutton and Co., Inc., 1987—; spl. asst. dist. atty. N.Y. County, 1979-80. Contbr. articles to legal jours. Mem. Cornell U. Council; adv. council Cornell U. Coll. Arts and Scis.; exec. com. Westminster Sch. Alumni Assn.; v.p., dir. Cornell Alumni Assn. Mem. Fed. Bar Council (com. on 2d circuit cts. 1978—), N.Y.C. Bar Assn. (young lawyers com. 1979-83, uniform laws com. 1984—). ABA, Am. Soc. Internat. Law. Democrat. Episcopalian. Clubs: Downtown Athletic, Univ. (N.Y.C.); Kennebunk River, Arundel Beach (Kennebunkport, Maine). Federal civil litigation, Antitrust. Home: 153 E 57th St New York NY 10022 Office: EF Hutton and Assoc Inc 1 Battery Park Plaza New York NY 10004

STEWART, DAVID PENTLAND, lawyer, educator; b. Milw., Dec. 24, 1943; s. James Pentland and Frederica (Stockwell) S.; m. Jennifer Kilmer, June 21, 1986; 1 child, Daniel; children from a previous marriage: Jason, Jonathan. AB, Princeton U., 1966; JD, MA, Yale U., 1971; LLM, N.Y.U., 1975. Bar: N.Y. 1972, U.S. Dist. Ct. (ea. and so. dists.) N.Y. 1973, U.S. Ct. Appeals (2d cir.) 1973, D.C. 1976. Assoc. Donovan, Leisure, Newton & Irvine, N.Y.C., 1971-76; atty. adviser, office of legal adviser U.S. Dept. State, Washington, 1976-82, asst. legal adviser, 1982—; adj. prof. law Georgetown U., Washington, 1984—, Am. U., Washington, 1985—. Contbr. articles to profl. jours.; also editorial adv. bd. Mem. dean's adv. council internat. law Am. U., 1984—. Served to major USAR, 1970—. Mem. ABA, Fed. Bar Assn., Am. Soc. Internat. Law., Internat. Law Assn. (adv. council procedural aspects internat. law inst.). Public international, Private international, Antitrust. Office: US Dept State Office of the Legal Adviser Washington DC 20520

STEWART, DUNCAN JAMES, lawyer; b. Amsterdam, N.Y., Apr. 24, 1939; s. William James and Maybelle Veronica (Matthews) S.; m. Susan Cobb Stewart, June 18, 1966; children: Benjamin Ross, Matthew Schuyler. AB, Cornell U., 1961, LLB, 1964. Bar: N.Y. 1964, U.S. Dist. C.t (no. dist.) N.Y. 1964. Assoc. Willkie Farr & Gallagher, N.Y.C., 1964-66, ptnr., 1967—. Served to capt. U.S. Army, 1965-67. Democrat. Presbyterian. General corporate, Securities. Home: 264 Berkeley Pl Brooklyn NY 11217 Office: Willkie Farr & Gallagher 153 E 53d St New York NY 10022

STEWART, EUGENE LAWRENCE, lawyer, trade association executive; b. Kansas City, Mo., Feb. 9, 1920; s. Edmund Dale and Mary Elizabeth (Raef) S.; m. Jeanne Ellen Powers, Oct. 19, 1945; children—Timothy, Terence, Brian. B.S., S.S., Georgetown U., 1947, J.D., 1951. Bar: D.C., U.S. Tax Ct., U.S. Ct. of Customs and Patent Appeals, U.S. Ct. Appeals Fed. Circuit, U.S. Ct. Appeals (3d cir.), U.S. Ct. Appeals (D.C. cir.), U.S. Ct. Internat. Trade, U.S. Supreme Ct. Assoc. Steptoe & Johnson, Washington, 1951-56, ptnr., 1956-58; ptnr. Hume & Stewart, Washington, 1958-64; sole practice Law Offices of Eugene L. Stewart, Washington, 1964-69, 1978-83; ptnr. Lincoln & Stewart, Washington, 1969-73, Stewart & Ikenson, Washington, 1974-78, Stewart and Stewart, Washington, 1983—; adj. prof. law Georgetown U. Law Ctr., Washington, 1955-58; exec. sec. Trade Relations Council of U.S., Washington, 1962—. Contbr. articles to profl. publs. Pres., Sursum Corda, Inc. (low-income housing project), Washington, 1964-78. Served to lt. col. USAF, 1941-52; PTO. Recipient John Carroll award Georgetown U., 1966. Mem. ABA, D.C. Bar, Georgetown U. Alumni Assn. Inc. (pres. 1964-66). Republican. Roman Catholic. General practice, Immigration, naturalization, and customs, Federal civil litigation. Office: Stewart and Stewart 1001 Connecticut Ave NW Washington DC 20036

STEWART, HELEN MARGERY, lawyer; b. Racine, Wis., Dec. 18, 1925; d. George Adrian and Christine Julia (Smith) Gregory; m. Stanley George Stewart, July 4, 1943 (div. May 1961); children: Stanley George III, Dean Lynn. AA, Fresno Community Coll., 1970; JD, Humphreys Coll. Law, 1974. Bar: CAlif. 1974, U.S. Dist. Ct. (ea. dist.) Calif. 1974. Sole practice Fresno, Calif., 1975-77; chief of claims U.S. Army, Ft. Ord, Calif., 1977-79; atty., advisor U.S. Army, Ft. Meade, Md., 1979-85; gen. counsel IBAR Settlement Co., Pasadena, Calif., 1985—. Mem. Fresno County Commn. on Status Women, 1975-77, Parks and Recreation Commn., Laurel, Md., 1983-85; bd. dirs. Family Service Ctr., Fresno, 1974-77. Mem. Calif. Women Lawyers. Democrat. Avocations: golf, sewing, knitting, reading. Insurance, Personal injury, Personal income taxation. Office: IBAR Settlement Co Inc 35 N Lake Ave 7th Floor Pasadena CA 91101

STEWART, ISAAC DANIEL, JR., associate chief justice Utah Supreme Court; b. Salt Lake City, Nov. 21, 1932; s. Isaac Daniel and Orabelle (Iverson) S.; m. Elizabeth Bryan, Sept. 10, 1959; children: Elizabeth Ann, Shannon. B.A., U. Utah, 1959, J.D., 1962. Bar: Utah 1962. Atty. Dept. Justice, 1962-65; asst. prof., then asso. prof. U. Utah Coll. Law, 1965-70; partner firm Jones, Waldo, Holbrook & McDonough, Salt Lake City, 1970-79; justice Utah Supreme Ct., 1979-86, now assoc. chief justice, 1986—; lectr. in field; dir. Med. Devel. Corp.; Mem. Utah Bd. Oil, Gas and Mining, 1976-78, chmn., 1977-78; Utah rep. Interstate Oil Compact Commn., 1977-78, exec. com. 1978-79; mem. adv. com. rules of procedure Utah Supreme Ct., 1983—. Contbr. articles to legal jours. Chmn. subcom. on legal rights and responsibilities of youth Utah Gov's Com. on Youth, 1972; pres. Salt Lake Chpt. Council Fgn. Relations, 1982; bd. dirs. U. Utah Alumni. Named Apellate Judge of Year, 1986. Mem. ABA, Am. Judicature Soc., Utah Bar Assn. (Appellate Judge of Yr. 1986), Salt Lake County Bar Assn., U. Utah Alumni Assn. (bd. dirs. 1985—), Phi Beta Kappa, Order of Coif, Phi Kappa Phi, Sigma Chi (Significant Sig award 1987). Mormon. Jurisprudence. Address: 332 State Capitol Bldg Salt Lake City UT 84114

STEWART, JAMES, lawyer; b. Paterson, N.J., Dec. 26, 1954; s. Joseph F. and Margaret (Gallagher) Stewart. BA, Seton Hall U., 1976; JD, NYU, 1981. Bar: N.J. 1981, U.S. Dist. Ct. N.J. 1981, N.Y. 1982, U.S. Dist. Ct. N.H. 1986, U.S. Dist. Ct. (so. and ea. dists.) N.Y. 1987. Law clk. to assoc. justice N.J. Supreme Ct., Morristown, 1981—; assoc. Lowenstein, Sandler, Kohl, Fisher & Boylan, Roseland, N.J., 1982—. Note and comment editor N.Y.U. Law Rev., 1980-81. Mem. Dem. Nat. Com. Mem. ABA, N.J. Bar Assn., Order of Coif. Roman Catholic. Federal civil litigation, Environment, Personal injury. Office: Lowenstein Sandler et al 65 Livingston Ave Roseland NJ 07068

STEWART, JAMES KEVIN, government official; b. Berkeley, Calif., Nov. 28, 1942; s. Berthold and Myrle (Minson) S.; m. Marise Rene Duff, Oct. 26, 1985; children: Daphne Brooks, Andrew MacLaren. B.S., U. Oreg., 1964; M.P.A., Calif. State U.-Hayward, 1977; grad. cert., U. Va., 1978; grad., FBI Nat. Acad., 1978. Chief of detectives Oakland Police Dept., 1976-81; instr. San Jose (Calif.) State U., 1978-81; spl. asst. atty. gen. Dept. Justice, Washington, 1981-82; dir. Nat. Inst. Justice, Washington, 1982—; guest lectr. U. Calif., Berkeley, Harvard U.; U.S. del. Council of Europe, Strasborg, France, 1984, U.N. Conf. on Crime Offenders, Milan, Italy, 1984. Bd. dirs. Alameda County Bd. Mental Health, 1979. White House fellow, 1981-82; named Police Officer of Yr. Kiwanis Club of Oakland, 1976. Mem. Internat. Assn. Chiefs of Police (dir. 1981-82), Police Mgmt. Assn. (founder, pres. 1979-81), White House Fellows Alumni, Nat. Acad. Assoc., Calif. Homicide Investigation Assn., Nat. Inst. Corrections (bd. dirs.), Crime Stoppers Internat. (bd. dirs.), Am. Judicature Soc., Calif. Peace Officers Assn. Delta Upsilon. Republican. Episcopalian. Club: University (Washington). Criminal, Judicial administration, Juvenile. Home: 6427 Lakeview St Falls Church VA 22041 Office: Nat Inst Justice 633 Indiana Ave NW Washington DC 20531 *

STEWART, JOSEPH WARD, lawyer; b. Lufkin, Tex., Jan. 12, 1933; s. Thomas Mahlon and Catherine Elizabeth (Kerr) Noyce S.; m. Bobby Nell Wilson, Sept. 4, 1954 (div. 1969); children—Timothy Kerr, Paul Lindsay, Terrence Mahlon; m. Elaine Moss, Aug. 20, 1976; children—Amy Elaine Moss, J. Patrick Moss. Student Rice Inst., 1951-52, U. Houston, 1952-53; B.A., Baylor U., 1956; B.Div., Southwestern Theol. Sem., Ft. Worth, 1960; J.D., So. Meth. U., 1965. Bar: Tex. 1965, U.S. Dist. Ct. (no. dist.) Tex. 1967. Assoc. atty. Harris, Ball & Stewart, Arlington, Tex., 1965-69; sole practice, Arlington, 1969-80; pres. Joseph W. Stewart, P.C., attys. at law, P.C., Arlington, 1980—; instr. bus. law Tarrant County Jr. Coll., Fort Worth, 1973-78. Charter mem. Republican Presidential Task Force, Washington, 1983. Diplomate Civil trial law Tex. Bd. Legal Specialization. Mem. Defense Research Inst., State Bar Tex., Tex. Assn. Defense Counsel. Baptist. Club: Ambucs (Arlington, Tex.) (pres. 1977-78). Insurance, State civil litigation, Federal civil litigation. Office: 2415 Ave J Suite 100 Arlington TX 76006

STEWART, JULIA SMEDS, lawyer; b. Ft. Benning, Ga., June 26, 1951; d. Erling Thorvald Smeds and Dorothy (Killcrease) Burtenshaw; m. Merrill Harpe Stewart Jr., June 30, 1984; 1 child, Merrill Harpe III. BA with honors, U. Ala., Tuscaloosa, 1973, JD, 1977. Bar: Ala. 1977, U.S. Dist. Ct. (no. dist.) Ala. 1977, U.S. Dist. Ct. (mid. dist.) Ala. 1979, U.S. Ct. Appeals (5th cir.) 1979, D.C. 1980, U.S. Dist. Ct. (so. dist.) Ala. 1980, U.S. Ct. Appeals (11th cir.) 1982. Law clk. to presiding judge U.S. Dist. Ct. (no. dist.) Ala., Birmingham, 1977-78; assoc. Smith, Bowman, Montgomery, Ala., 1978-80, Burr & Forman, Birmingham, 1980-86; sole practice Birmingham, 1987—. Democrat. Presbyterian. Avocation: horseback riding. State civil litigation, Federal civil litigation. Office: 2160 Highland Ave Birmingham AL 35205

STEWART, LARRY S., lawyer; b. Ft. Myers, Fla., Nov. 19, 1939; s. F.B. and Eleanor (Riebling) S.; m. Pat Korodin, June 13, 1960; children: Scott, Todd, Drew. BA, U. Fla., 1960, JD with honors, 1963. Bar: Fla. 1963, U.S. Dist. Ct. (so. and mid. dists.) Fla. 1963, U.S. Ct. Appeals (5th cir.) 1965, U.S. Supreme Ct. 1967, U.S. Ct. Appeals (11th cir.) 1981. Ptnr. Floyd, Pearson, Stewart, Richman et al, Miami, Fla., 1963-84, Stewart, Tilghman, Fox & Bianchi P.A., Miami, 1984—; lectr. numerous orgns. Exec. editor U. Fla. Law Rev. Bd. dirs. Univ. Club, 1970-76, pres., 1975-76; bd. trustees Palmer Prep. Sch., 1978—, chmn., 1982-84; mem. com. Dade County Art in Pub. Pls., 1979-81; chmn. art auctions WPBT TV, 1984, 85, bd. dirs., 1986—. Fellow Internat. Acad. Trial Lawyers, Am. Coll. Trial Lawyers; mem. ABA (litigation sect.), Fla. Bar Assn. (chmn. trial lawyers sect. 1975-76, mem. exec. council trial lawyers sect. 1972-82, chmn. civil trial cert. com. 1984-86, vice chmn. continuing legal edn. com. 1972-74, vice chmn. rules com. 1971-73, bd. of govs. young lawyers sect. 1967-73, treas. young lawyers sect. 1970-71), Dade County Bar Assn., Acad. Fla. Trial Lawyers (pres. 1978-79, sec. 1976, bd. dirs. 1972—), John Marshall Bar Assn. (pres.), Fla. Blue Key, Order of Coif, Order of Ky. Cols., Assn. Trial Lawyers Am. (bd. of govs. 1983—), Phi Delta Phi. Club: Grove Isle Club (bd. of govs. 1980—). Personal injury, Federal civil litigation, State civil litigation. Home: 10500 Snapper Creek Rd Miami FL 33156 Office: Stewart Tilghman Fox & Bianchi PA 44 W Flagler St Suite 1900 Miami FL 33130

STEWART, LAWRENCE EDWARD, lawyer; b. Cleve., Mar. 15, 1925; s. Samuel E. and Sarah (Gamble) S.; m. Barbara Joan Metcalfe, Aug. 19, 1950; children—Scott E., Brian P., Kerry T., Jennifer M., Bruce J. B.S.C. with honors, Ohio U., 1949; J.D., Western Res. U., 1950. Bar: Ohio 1950, U.S. Dist. Ct. (no. dist.) Ohio 1952, U.S. Ct. Appeals (6th cir.) 1957, U.S. Supreme Ct. 1966, U.S. Ct. Appeals (D.C. cir.) 1980, U.S. Ct. Appeals (3d and 11th cirs.). Assoc. Edward E. Lurie, 1950-56; sole practitioner, from 1956; now pres. Stewart & DeChant Co., L.P.A., Cleve.; mem. nat. panel arbitrators Am. Arbitration Assn., 1961—; mem. med.-legal com. Cleve. Acad. Medicine, 1963-75. Served with U.S. Army, 1943-46; ETO. Fellow Am. Coll. Trial Lawyers (Ohio state chmn. 1986—), Internat. Acad. Trial Lawyers; mem. Am. Coll. Legal Medicine (assoc.-in-law), Am. Soc. Law and Medicine, Am. Judicature Soc. (bd. dirs. 1986—), Greater Cleve. Bar Assn. (trustee 1969-72, chmn. ct. mgmt. project 1973-75, pres. 1976-77), Cuyahoga County Bar Assn. (chmn. med.-legal com. 1962-63, co-chmn. com. 1963), Ohio Bar Assn., ABA (ho. of dels. 1978-80), Assn. Trial Lawyers Am., Cleve. Acad. Trial Attys. (trustee 1972-74, pres. 1977-78), Ohio Acad. Trial Lawyers (trustee 1973-75, v.p. 1976-77), Soc. of Benchers. Clubs: Cleve. Athletic, Cleve. Yacht, River Oaks Tennis, East Chop Beach, E.C. Tennis. State civil litigation, Federal civil litigation, Personal injury. Office: Atrium Office Plaza 668 Euclid Ave Suite 850 Cleveland OH 44114

STEWART, MARK STEVEN, lawyer; b. Palestine, Tex., Jan. 1, 1950; s. Bruce F. and Diana Wilba (Franks) S.; m. Dianne Marie Cochran, May 26, 1973; 1 son, Steven Andrew. B.A., U. Tex., 1971, J.D., 1975. Bar: Tex. 1975, U.S. Dist. Ct. (no. dist.) Tex. 1976. Assoc. McDonald, Sanders et al., Ft. Worth, 1975-78; ptnr. Kugle, Stewart, Dent & Frederick, Ft. Worth, 1978—; dir. Tarrant County Trial Lawyers, Ft. Worth, 1984—. Mem. Assn. Trial Lawyers Am., Tex. Trial Lawyers Assn., Tarrant County Bar Assn. Personal injury, Workers' compensation. Home: 8103 N New Braunfels #18 San Antonio TX 78209 Office: Kugle Stewart Dent & Frederick 111 Soledad Suite 700 San Antonio TX 78205

STEWART, MELINDA JANE, lawyer; b. Picayune, Miss., Mar. 11, 1951; d. Argie Thomas and Myrtis (Smith) S.; 1 child, Melanie Jane Kilpatrick. BA, U. So. Miss., 1974; JD, U. Miss., 1976. Bar: Miss. 1976, U.S. Dist. Ct. (no. dist.) Miss. 1976, La. 1982. Atty. Shell Oil Co., New Orleans, 1976—. Mem. fin. com. Rayne Meml. United Meth. Ch., New Orleans, 1984—, adminstrv. bd. dirs., 1985—. Mem. ABA, La. Bar Assn., Miss. Bar Assn., Miss. Oil and Gas Lawyers Assn., Phi Delta Phi, Phi Gamma Mu. Republican. Oil and gas leasing, General corporate, Administrative and regulatory. Home: 5870 Vicksburg St New Orleans LA 70124 Office: Shell Oil Co 701 Poydras Dr New Orleans LA 70139

STEWART, MERYLE RICHARD, oil company executive, lawyer; b. Seminole, Okla., Aug. 20, 1943; s. Horace Medford and Francis May (Watson) S.; 1 dau., Michele. B.A., U. Tex., 1965, J.D., 1967. Bar: Tex. 1967, Okla. 1967. Staff atty. Phillips Petroleum Co., Oklahoma City, 1967-71, Bartlesville, Okla., 1972-74; staff atty. Tesoro Petroleum Co., San Antonio, 1974-75; sr. atty. Tesoro Petroleum Co., 1975-79, v.p., gen. counsel, sec., 1979-80, sr. v.p., gen. counsel, sec., 1981—; Mem. adv. bd. Internat. Oil and Gas Edn. Center, Southwestern Legal Found.; mem. adv. bd. Internat. and Comparative Law Center, Southwestern Legal Found. Mem. Tex. Bar Assn., Okla. Bar Assn., Am. Bar Assn., San Antonio Bar Assn. Office: Tesoro Petroleum Corp 8700 Tesoro Dr San Antonio TX 78286 *

STEWART, MURRAY BAKER, lawyer; b. Muskogee, Okla., May 16, 1931; s. Francis and Fannie Penelope (Murray) S.; m. Roseanna Furgason; children—Melinda, Jeffrey, Cheryl. B.A., U. Okla., 1953, LL.B., 1955; postgrad. Georgetown U., 1958-59; C.L.U., Am. Coll., 1980, chartered fin. cons., 1984; fellow Life Mgmt. Inst., 1983. Bar: Okla. 1955, U.S. Tax Ct. 1957, U.S. Supreme Ct. 1958, U.S. Ct. Mil. Appeals 1958. Partner, Stewart & Stewart, Tulsa and Muskogee, Okla., 1955, 62-72; asst. v.p. First Nat. Bank and Trust Co. of Tulsa, 1959-62, 77-78; mem. Hutchins, Stewart, Stewart & Elmore, Tulsa, 1972-77; atty., pvt. cons. advanced underwriting Met. Life Ins. Co., N.Y.C., 1978—; lectr. univ. campuses. Served to capt. U.S. Army, 1955-59. Mem. Okla. Bar Assn., Am. Soc. Chartered Life Underwriters, Life Office Mgmt. Assn., Assn. Investment Advs., Nat. Assn. Security Dealers (registered), Tulsa Estate Planning Forum, Tulsa Employee Benefits Group, Phi Delta Phi. s. Estate planning, Corporate taxation, Pension, profit-sharing, and employee benefits. Office: PO Box 500 Tulsa OK 74102

STEWART, RICHARD BURLESON, lawyer, educator; b. Cleve., Feb. 12, 1940; s. Richard Siegfreid and Ruth Dysert (Staten) S.; m. Alice Peck Fales, May 13, 1967; children—William, Paul. A.B., Yale U., 1961; M.A. (Rhodes scholar), Oxford (Eng.) U., 1963; LL.B., Harvard U., 1966. Bar: D.C. 1968, U.S. Supreme Ct 1971. Law clk. to Justice Potter Stewart, U.S. Supreme Ct., 1966-67; assoc. Covington & Burling, Washington, 1967-71; asst. prof. law Harvard U., 1971-75, prof., 1975—, Byrne prof. adminstrv. law, assoc. dean, 1984—; spl. counsel U.S. Senate Watergate Com., 1974; vis. prof. law U. Chgo. Law Sch., 1986-87. Author: (with J. Krier) Environmental Law and Policy, 1978, (with S. Breyer) Administrative Law and Regulation, 1979, 2d edit., 1985, (with others) Integration Through Law: Environmental Protection Policy. Trustee Environ. Def. Fund, Found. for Research on Econs. and Environ. Mem. ABA (standing com. on environ. law), Am. Law Inst. (chief reporter project or enterprize personal injuries). Legal education. Office: Harvard U Law Sch Cambridge MA 02138

STEWART, ROBERT DESBROW, JR., lawyer; b. Manchester, N.H., Mar. 26, 1942; s. Robert D. and Ruth E. (Burgess) S.; m. Patricia Ann Byrne, Dec. 3, 1966; children—Kimberly, Robert, Deborah. B.A., U. Okla., 1966, J.D., 1971. Bar: Okla. 1972, U.S. Supreme Ct. 1982. Assoc. Horsley Epton & Culp, Wewoka, Okla., 1972-73, ptnr., 1973-79; sr. staff counsel Okla. Corp. Commn., Oklahoma City, 1979, gen. counsel, 1979-82; staff atty. Okla. Gas & Electric Co., Oklahoma City, 1983—; instr. U. Okla. Law Center, 1982. Served with U.S. Army, 1966-70, Okla. Army N.G., 1973-85. Decorated Bronze Star, Army Commendation medal. Mem. Okla. Bar Assn., ABA. Democrat. Roman Catholic. Club: Rotary (pres. 1978). Lodge: KC. Author: Overview of Utility Regulation, 1982; A Bankrupt Electric Utility-What If?, 1983, The Law of Cogeneration in Oklahoma, 1986. Public utilities, General corporate, Oil and gas leasing. Office: Oklahoma Gas & Electric Co 321 N Harvey St Oklahoma City OK 73101

STEWART, TERENCE PATRICK, lawyer; b. Washington, June 30, 1948; s. Eugene Lawrence and Jeanne Ellen (Powers) S.; m. Ellen Guraa Blendheim, June 14, 1970; children—Natalie, Melissa, Hanna. B.A. magna cum laude, Coll. of Holy Cross, 1970; M.B.A., Harvard U., 1972; J.D. magna cum laude, Georgetown U., 1979. Bar: U.S. Ct. Appeals (D.C. cir.) 1979, D.C. 1979, U.S. Dist. Ct. D.C. 1980, U.S. Customs Ct. 1980, U.S. Ct. Internat. Trade 1980, U.S. Ct. Customs and Patent Appeals 1980-82, U.S. Ct. Appeals (fed. cir.) 1982, U.S. Supreme Ct. 1983, U.S. Ct. Appeals (3d cir.) 1985. Asst. buyer J.C. Penny Co., N.Y.C., 1972-73; merchandise mgr. Kroehler Mfg. Co., Naperville, Ill., 1973-75, mgr. mktg. info. systems, 1975-76; assoc. Eugene L. Stewart, Washington, 1979-83; mng. ptnr. Stewart and Stewart, Washington, 1983—. Mem. ABA, D.C. Bar Assn., Customs and Internat. Trade Bar Assn., Assn. Trial Lawyers Am., Internat. Trade Commn. Trial Lawyers Assn. Roman Catholic. Private international, Immigration, naturalization, and customs, Administrative and regu-

latory. Home: 7004 Delaware St Chevy Chase MD 20815 Office: Stewart & Stewart 1001 Connecticut Ave NW Washington DC 20036

STEWART, THOMAS WILSON, lawyer; b. Miami, Fla., Oct. 23, 1926; s. Thelmar Wilson and Katherine (Smith) S.; m. Priscilla Ann Mabie, Aug. 28, 1949. B.S., Miami U., Oxford, Ohio, 1948; J.D. with distinction, State U. Iowa, 1951. Bar: Iowa 1951, Fla. 1952, U.S. Supreme Ct. 1969. Assoc. Daniel & Woodward, Bradenton, Fla., 1952-57; ptnr. Daniel, Woodward & Stewart, 1957-68, sole practice, Bradenton, 1968-73, 86—; asst. prof. bus. law Fla. State U., Tallahassee, 1951-52. Chmn. Manatee County Republican Com., 1970-71; Fla. state Rep. committeeman, 1970-71. Served with USN, 1944-46. Mem. Manatee County Bar Assn. (pres. 1968-69), Fla. Bar Assn., Mensa, Intertel, Manatee County Hist. Soc. Republican. Episcopalian. Club: Masons. Author: Labor Laws of Iowa, 1951. Real property, Probate, Estate planning. Home: 2705 Riverview Blvd W Bradenton FL 33505 Office: 406 13th St W Bradenton FL 33505

STEYER, HUME RICHMOND, lawyer; b. N.Y.C., Dec. 25, 1953; s. Roy Henry and Margaret (Fahr) S. BA, U. Pa., 1975; JD, Harvard U., 1978. Assoc. Hughes Hubbard & Reed, N.Y.C., 1978-86, Morris & McVeigh, N.Y.C., 1987—. Bd. nat. advisors Mus. Am. Folk Art, N.Y.C., 1983—. Mem. ABA (com. on drafting), Assn. of Bar of City of N.Y. (com. on trusts, estates and surrogate's cts.). Democrat. Clubs: University (N.Y.C.), Shinnecock Hills Country (Southampton, N.Y.). Estate planning, Private international, Probate. Home: 118 E 93rd St # 9C New York NY 10128 Office: Morris & McVeigh 767 Third Ave New York NY 10017

STEYER, ROY HENRY, lawyer; b. Bklyn., July 1, 1918; s. Herman and Augusta (Simon) S.; m. Margaret Fahr, Feb. 21, 1953; children: Hume R., James P., Thomas F. A.B. with honors in Govt. and Gen. Studies, Cornell U., 1938; LL.B. cum laude, Yale U., 1941. Bar: N.Y. 1941, various fed. cts. from 1947, U.S. Supreme Ct. 1955. Assoc. firm Sullivan & Cromwell, N.Y.C., 1941-42, 46-52, ptnr., 1953—. Trustee N.Y.C. Sch. Vol. Program, 1974-78. Served to lt. USNR, 1943-46. Mem. Am. Coll. Trial Lawyers, ABA (chmn. com. on antitrust problems in internat. trade antitrust sect. 1959-62), N.Y. State Bar Assn., Assn. Bar City N.Y. (chmn. com. on trade regulation 1962-64), N.Y. County Lawyers Assn. (bd. dirs. 1972-78), Am. Judicature Soc., Am. Soc. Internat. Law, N.Y. Law Inst., Order of Coif, Phi Beta Kappa, Phi Kappa Phi. Clubs: Century Assn. (N.Y.C.), Broad Street (N.Y.C.), Yale (N.Y.C.). Federal civil litigation, State civil litigation, General corporate. Home: 112 E 74th St New York NY 10021 Office: Sullivan & Cromwell 125 Broad St New York NY 10004

STICH, LAWRENCE PAUL, lawyer; b. Dayton, Ohio, June 22, 1930; s. Lawrence Andrew and Pauline Louise (Sieverding) S.; m. Patricia Metzger; children: Joseph, Matthew, Elizabeth, Patricia, Lawrence Bernard, Laura, Christopher, Martin. Student, U. Dayton, 1947-51; BS, Ohio State U., 1953, JD, 1955. Bar: Ohio 1955, N.Y. 1957, D.C. 1978. Counsel to div. mil. applications AEC, Albuquerque, 1957-60; counsel aerospace/def. IBM Corp., Bethesda, Md., 1961—. Bd. govs. Antioch U. Coll. Law, Washington, 1970—. Mem. ABA, Nat. Security Indsl. Assn. (chmn. legal and spl. task com. 1984), U.S. Govt. Procurement Commn., Electronic Industries Assn. (chmn. law com. 1971-76, Service and Leadership award 1973.). Home: 8401 Sparger St McLean VA 22102 Office: IBM Corp 6600 Rockledge Dr Bethesda MD 20854

STICKEL, FREDERICK GEORGE, III, lawyer; b. Newark, Oct. 7, 1915; s. Frederick G. and Helen Muriel (Walker) S.; m. Elizabeth Tobin, Sept. 23, 1940; children—Fred G., Virginia H., Jane, Elizabeth Louise, Kathryn; m. 2d, Doris B. Asdal, May 19, 1979; stepchildren—William C. Asdal, Robert K. Asdal. A.B., Princeton U., 1937; J.D., Columbia U., 1940. Bar: N.J. 1941, U.S. Dist. Ct. N.J. 1941, U.S. Supreme Ct. 1952. Assoc., Stickel & Stickel, Newark, 1941-46; ptnr. Stickel Kain & Stickel, Newark, 1946-78; sr. ptnr. Stickel & Koenig, Cedar Grove, 1978—, mcpl. atty. Roseland, N.J., 1948-68, Verona, N.J., 1961-63, Cedar Grove, 1945-55; v.p. N.J. State, County and Mcpl. Study Commn., 1966—; counsel City of Orange Redevel. Agy. 1977—; gen. counsel N.J. State League of Municipalities, 1984—; judge Mcpl. Ct. of Roseland, 1985—. Recipient Disting. Service award Nat. Inst. Mcpl. Attys., 1955; N.J. League of Municipalities, 1980. Mem. ABA, N.J. State Bar Assn., Essex County Bar Assn., West Essex Bar Assn., N.J. Inst. Mcpl. Attys., N.J. Assn. Sch. Bd. Attys., Nat. Assn. Sch. Bd. Attys., Am. Judicature Soc., Columbia Law Assn., Class of 1937 Princeton U. (v.p. 1982-87). Republican. Clubs: Nassau of Princeton (N.J.); Rotary of Cedar Grove (past pres. 1941); Masons (West Essex). Contbr. articles on law to profl. jours. Local government, Probate, General practice. Home: 15 Birch Dr Roseland NJ 07068 Office: 571 Pompton Ave Cedar Grove NJ 07009

STICKNEY, PAUL DOUGLAS, lawyer; b. Evanston, Ill., Jan. 10, 1953; s. John James and Marion A. (Lewis) S.; m. Mary C. Lochridge, Aug. 19, 1978; children: Andrea Megan, Jenny Lynn, John James. BS, U. S.D., 1978, JD, 1981. Bar: S.D. 1981, U.S. Dist. Ct. S.D. 1981, U.S. Ct. Appeals (8th cir.) 1981. Intern Office of U.S. Attorney, Sioux Falls, S.D., 1981; ptnr. Breit & Stickney, Sioux Falls, 1981—; instr. Kilian Community Coll., Sioux Falls, 1981; mem. Joint Task Force on Prompt Disposition of Criminal Cases, Sioux Falls, 1986—. Served to sgt. USAF, 1972-75. Mem. ABA, Comml. Law League. Democrat. Lutheran. Avocations: racquetball, golf, children. Criminal, Family and matrimonial, General practice. Home and Office: 3610 S Western Ave Sioux Falls SD 57105

STIEFEL, CHARLES WERNER, lawyer; b. Catskill, N.Y., Oct. 30, 1950; s. Werner K. and Catherine M. (Pierson) S.; m. Daneen C. Waldstein, Aug. 20, 1972; children: Todd, Brent. BS, Yale U., 1972; JD, Albany Law Sch., 1975. Bar: N.Y. 1976, U.S. Dist. Ct. (no. and so. dists.) N.Y. 1976. Law research asst. appellate div. N.Y. State Supreme Ct., Albany, 1975-76; assoc. Pulver & Stiefel, Catskill, 1976-79, ptnr., 1979-82; gen. counsel Stiefel Labs. Inc., Coral Gables, Fla., 1982—; also bd. dirs. Stiefel Labs. Inc., Coral Gables; bd. dirs. Durham Pharmacal Corp., Oak Hill, N.Y., Bank N.Y., Catskill. Bd. dirs. Mid-Hudson Heart Assn., Kingston, N.Y., 1980-82, Catskill Boys Club, 1980-82. Mem. ABA, N.Y. State Bar Assn., Greene County Bar Assn. (treas. 1980-82). Republican. Roman Catholic. Lodge: Rotary (pres., bd. dirs. Catskill 1981-82). General corporate. Home: 8500 SW 108th St Miami FL 33156 Office: Stiefel Labs Inc 2801 Ponce de Leon Blvd Coral Gables FL 33134

STIEGLITZ, ALBERT BLACKWELL, lawyer; b. Warrenton, Va., May 21, 1936; s. Valentine Henry and Mary (Blackwell) S.; m. Rosemary Jeanne Dommerich, Nov. 11, 1971; children—Albert Blackwell Jr., John Dommerich. Student U. Fla., 1954-1955; B.A., U. Miami, 1958, LL.B., 1964. Bar: Fla. 1964, U.S. Dist. Ct. (so. dist.) Fla. 1964, U.S. Ct. Appeals (5th and 11th cirs.) 1964. Ptnr. Fowler, White, Burnett, Hurley, Banick and Strickroot, Miami, Fla., 1969—. Served to 1st lt. USAF, 1958-61. Mem. ABA, Fla. Bar Assn., Internat. Assn. Ins. Counsel (exec. com. 1981-84), Dade County Def. Bar Assn. (pres. 1978-79), Delta Theta Phi. Republican. Episcopalian. Clubs: Riviera Country (Coral Gables); Com. of 100, Bath (Miami Beach, Fla.); University, Bankers (Miami). Lodge: Rotary. Federal civil litigation, State civil litigation, Personal injury. Office: Fowler White Burnett Hurley et al City Nat Bank Bldg 5th Floor Miami FL 33130

STIEL, DAVID HAROLD, III, lawyer; b. New Orleans, Dec. 5, 1951; s. David Harold Jr. and Patricia (Palfrey) S.; m. Tonya Marxsen, May 25, 1974; children: Allison Todd, Sally Palfrey, Stacey Gates. Student, Trinity U., 1969; BS, La. State U., 1973, JD, 1976. Bar: La. 1976, U.S. Dist. Ct. (we. dist.) La. 1976. Assoc. Aycock, Horne, Caldwell, Coleman & Duncan, Franklin, La., 1976-79; ptnr. Aycock, Horne & Coleman, Franklin, 1979—; atty. City of Franklin, 1981—. Bd. drs. Franklin Little Theatre Inc., 1979. Mem. ABA, La. Bar Assn. (ho. of dels. 1986—), St. Mary Parish Bar Assn. (pres. 1981-82), La. Bankers Assn. (bank counsel sect.), La. Assn. Def. Counsel, La. City Attys. Assn., Def. Research Inst. Republican. Episcopalian. Lodges: Optomists (Franklin v.p. 1979-80), Rotary (bd. dirs. 1983-85). Insurance, Banking, Real property. Home: 1008 Perret St PO Box 293 Franklin LA 70538 Office: Aycock Horne & Coleman 519 Main St Franklin LA 70538

STIERBERGER, EDWARD ALBERT, lawyer; b. St. Louis, Nov. 2, 1933; s. Edward Albert and Amelia Louise (Wiesendanger) S.; m. Sandra Lee Bentz, Sept. 3, 1966. BA, Westminster Coll., 1955; JD, U. Wis., 1958. Bar: Wis. 1958, Mo. 1958, U.S. Dist. Ct. (ea. dist.) Wis. 1962, U.S. Dist. Ct. (ea. dist.) Mo. 1973, U.S. Supreme Ct. 1965. Sole practice, Sheboygan, Wis., 1959-65, Union, Mo., 1965—; v.p. Linmark Machine Products, Union, 1970—; chmn. bd. United Bank of Union, 1967—. Chmn. Cen. Com. Rep. Party, Sheboygan, 1963-65; bd. dirs. Union R-11 Sch. Dist., 1969-72; atty. City of Gerald (Mo.) 1966-86, City of Pacific (Mo.), 1977—. Served with U.S. Army, 1958. Mem. Mo. Bar Assn., Wis. Bar Assn., ABA, Am. Trial Lawyers Assn. Republican. Mem. United Ch. Christ. Lodges: Masons, Elks. Personal injury, Banking, Probate. Home: 1 Stierberger Ct Union MO 63084 Office: Hansen Stierberger Downard & Melenbrink 311 Main St Union MO 63084

STILES, WILLIAM NEIL, lawyer; b. Portland, Oreg., Mar. 28, 1938; s. Charles W. and Luella J. (Dahl) S.; m. C. Arlene Kelsay, Feb. 7, 1976; children: Eric, Craig. BA, Yale U., 1960, LLB, 1963. Bar: Calif. 1964, U.S. Dist. Ct. (cen. dist.) Calif. 1964, U.S. Ct. Appeals (9th cir.) 1964, Oreg. 1965, U.S. Dist. Ct. Oreg. 1965. Law clk. U.S. Ct. Appeals (9th cir.), Los Angeles, 1963-64; assoc. Miller, Nash, Wiener, Hager & Carlsen and predecessor firms, Portland, 1964-71, Sussman, Shank & Wapnick, Portland, 1972-74; ptnr. Sussman, Shank, Wapnick, Caplan & Stiles, Portland, 1975—. Contbr. articles to profl. jours. Elder Valley Community Presbyn. Ch., Portland, 1986—; bd. dirs. Oreg. Law Inst., Portland, 1986—. Mem. Oreg. Bar Assn. (chmn. debtor creditor sect. 1979-80), Yale Alumni Assn. Oreg. (pres. 1984-86). Club: Multnomah Athletic (Portland). Avocation: golf. State civil litigation, Contracts commercial, Real property. Home: 1870 SW Parkwood Dr Portland OR 97225 Office: Sussman Shank Wapnick Caplan & Stiles 1001 SW 5th Ave 1111 Orbanco Bldg Portland OR 97204

STILL, EDWARD, lawyer, historian; b. Augusta, Ga., Feb. 22, 1946; s. Wilson Edward and Ollie (Williams) S.; m. Elizabeth Ann Rich, Oct. 2, 1976; 1 son, Griffith Williams Frazer. B.A. with honors, U. Ala., 1968, J.D., 1971. Bar: Ala. 1971, U.S. Dist. Ct. (no. dist.) Ala. 1971, U.S. Dist. Ct. (mid. dist.) Ala. 1972, U.S. Dist. Ct. (so. dist.) Ala. 1972, U.S. Ct. Appeals (11th cir.) 1981, U.S. Supreme Ct. 1974. Ptnr., Drake, Knowles & Still, Tuscaloosa, Ala., 1971-75; sole practice, Birmingham, Ala., 1975—; ptnr. Reeves & Still, Birmingham, 1979—; instr. continuing legal edn. programs. Gen. counsel State Democratic Exec. Com., 1980-85; alt. del. Nat. Dem. Policy Conf., 1982, Nat. Dem. Conv., 1984; pres. Ala. Citizens for Equal Rights Amendment, 1977. Mem. Birmingham Bar Assn., Ala. State Bar, ABA, Assn. Trial Lawyers Am., Am. Polit. Sci. Assn., Ala. Hist. Assn., So. Hist. Assn. Episcopalian. Contbg. author: Minority Vote Dilution, 1984. Civil rights, Elections and voting, Federal civil litigation. Office: 714 S 29th St Birmingham AL 35233

STILLER, JENNIFER ANNE, lawyer; b. Washington, May 4, 1948; d. Ralph Sophian and Joy (Dancis) S.; m. Ray Redd, Jan. 24, 1987. AB in Econs. and History, U. Mich., 1970; JD, NYU, 1973. Bar: Pa. 1973, Ill. 1979; U.S. Dist. Ct. (mid. dist.) Pa. 1977, U.S. Dist. Ct. (no. dist.) Ill. 1979, U.S. Dist. Ct. (ea. dist.) Pa. 1983; U.S. Ct. Appeals (3d cir.) 1983; U.S. Supreme Ct. 1978. Dep. atty. gen. Pa. Dept. Justice, Harrisburg, 1973-75, Pa. Dept. Health, Harrisburg, 1975-78; sr. staff atty. Am. Hosp. Assn., Chgo., 1978-80, mgr., Dept. Fed. Law, 1980-81; gen. counsel Ill. Health Fin. Authority, 1981-82; sr. assoc. Berriman & Schwartz, King of Prussia, Pa., 1983-85, Wolf, Block, Schorr & Solis-Cohen, Phila., 1985—. Contbr. health law articles to profl. pubs. Mem. Nat. Health Lawyers Assn., Am. Acad. Hosp. Attys., ABA, Phila. Bar Assn., Bicycle Coalition of Del. Valley, Pa. Democrat. Avocations: bicycling, hiking, music. Health, Administrative and regulatory, Federal civil litigation. Office: Wolf Block Schorr & Solis-Cohen 15th and Chestnut Sts Philadelphia PA 19102

STILLMAN, BERNARD M., lawyer; b. Niagara Falls, N.Y., Oct. 13, 1929; s. Jack and Pearl (LaBell) S.; m. Marcia E. Borins, Nov. 5, 1960; children: Alan, Michelle. Bsc in Bus. Adminstrn., U. Buffalo, 1952, LLB, 1953, JD, 1957. Bar: N.Y. 1956. Sole practice Buffalo, N.Y., 1957—. Served with U.S. Army, 1954-56. Mem. N.Y. State Bar Assn., Erie County Bar Assn. Jewish. Lodge: B'Nai Brith (pres. 1980). Contracts commercial, General practice, Real property. Home: 44 Heritage Rd W Williamsville NY 14221 Office: 411 Brisbane Bldg Buffalo NY 14203

STILLPASS, JOHN EDWARD, lawyer; b. Cin., May 13, 1956; s. Stanford J. and Josephine (Goodman) S.; m. Merrie Lynn Stewart, June 5, 1983. BS in Econs., U. Pa., 1978; JD, Case Western Res. U., 1981. Bar: Ohio 1981, U.S. Dist. Ct. (so. dist.) Ohio 1981, U.S. Ct. Appeals (6th cir.) 1981, Fla. 1982. Asst. zone mgr. A.B. Volvo, Gothenburg, Sweden, 1974-78; assoc. Goodman & Goodman, Cin., 1981—. Mem. ABA, Ohio Bar Assn., Fla. Bar Assn., Cin. Bar Assn. (fed. cts. com., common pleas ct. com.). Contracts commercial, General corporate, Federal civil litigation. Home: 1815 William H Taft Rd Apt 910 Cincinnati OH 45206 Office: Goodman & Goodman 123 E 4th St 5th Floor Cincinnati OH 45202

STIMMEL, TODD RICHARD, lawyer; b. Freeport, N.Y., Jan. 20, 1954; s. Leonard E. and Lorraine Joyce (Greenfield) S.; m. Andrea Jane Katz, Aug. 20, 1978. BA, Columbia U., 1976; JD, Harvard U., 1979. Bar: N.Y. 1980. Assoc. Cravath, Swaine & Moore, N.Y.C., 1979-83, O'Sullivan Graev & Karabell, N.Y.C., 1983-85; ptnr. O'Sullivan, Graev, Karabell & Grosi, N.Y.C., 1985—. Phi Beta Kappa. Club: Harvard. Avocation: Sports. General corporate, Securities. Home: 1199 Park Ave Apt 2H New York NY 10128 Office: O'Sullivan Graev et al 30 Rockefeller Plaza New York NY 10112

STIMSON, JUDITH NEMETH, lawyer; b. Hammond, Ind., Oct. 30, 1942; d. John G. and Pearl (Lemish) Nemeth; m. Clare M. Stimson, June 5, 1965 (div. Oct. 1981); children: Justin D., Seth C., Sarah L.; m. John R. Conolly, Dec. 30, 1982. BS, St. Mary of the Woods Coll., Terre Haute, Ind., 1964; MS in Clothing and Textiles, Ind. U., 1968; JD, Ind. U., Indpls., 1981. Bar: Ind. 1982. Tchr. pub. schs. Ind., 1964-79; assoc. Buck, Berry, Landau & Breunig, Indpls., 1982—; instr. Ind. Continuing Legal Edn. Forum, Indpls., 1983—. Named one of Outstanding Young Women in Am., 1974. Mem. ABA, Ind. Bar Assn., Indpls. Bar Assn. (chmn. family law sect. 1985, exec. mem. continuing legal edn. com. 1986-87), Assn. Trial Lawyers Am. Avocation: travel. Family and matrimonial, Civil rights, Personal injury. Office: Buck Berry Landau & Breunig 302 N Alabama Indianapolis IN 46204

STINCHFIELD, JOHN EDWARD, lawyer; b. Alameda, Calif., July 31, 1947; s. John Eastwood and Pauline Finch (Acker) S.; m. Niall O'Melia, May 15, 1976; children: John Ryan, Noel O'Neil. BA, Wesleyan U., Middletown, Conn., 1969; JD, U. Calif., 1973. Bar: Calif. 1974, D.C. 1980. Atty. advisor div. corp. fin. U.S. SEC, 1974-76; atty. advisor investment mgmt. div. SEC, 1976-77; atty., advisor Bur. of Competition, FTC, 1977-79; corp. counsel The Donohoe Cos., Inc., Washington, 1979—, also bd. dirs.; bd. dirs. Fed. Ctr. Plaza Corp., also sec. Mem. ABA, Bar Assn. of D.C. Episcopalian. Clubs: Columbia Country (Chevy Chase, Md.), Chevy Chase Athletic. Construction, General corporate, Real property. Office: The Donohoe Cos Inc 2101 Wisconsin Ave NW Washington DC 20016

STINE, JOHN, corporate lawyer; b. Yonkers, N.Y., May 4, 1955; s. John and Hildegard (Penitz) S.; m. Michele Porto, Aug. 8, 1981. BA, Columbia U., 1977; JD, Fordham U., 1980. Bar: N.Y. 1981, U.S. Dist. Ct. (so. and ea. dists.) N.Y. 1981. Staff atty. N.Y. Life Ins Co., N.Y.C., 1980-83, asst. counsel, 1983-85, assoc. counsel, 1985—. Mem. N.Y. State Bar Assn. Democrat. Roman Catholic. Avocations: automobiles, travel. Securities, Insurance, State civil litigation. Home: 142 Chittenden Ave Crestwood NY 10707 Office: New York Life Ins Co 51 Madison Ave New York NY 10010

STINEHART, WILLIAM, JR., lawyer; b. Los Angeles, Dec. 15, 1943; s. William and Martha T. Stinehart; m. Patricia Kidney, June 22, 1968; children: Jacqueline Elaine, William III. BA, Stanford U.; JD, U. Calif., Los Angeles. Bar: Calif. 1970, U.S. Dist. Ct. (cen. dist.). Assoc. Gibson, Dunn & Crutcher, Los Angeles, 1969-76, ptnr., 1977—. Trustee Harvard Sch., North Hollywood, Calif., 1983—, Southwest Mus., 1986—. Mem. Los Angeles County Bar Assn., Order of Coif. Republican. Episcopalian. Clubs: Los Angeles Country; Beach (Santa Monica, Calif.). Estate planning, Probate, Estate taxation. Office: Gibson Dunn & Crutcher 2029 Century Park East Suite 4100 Los Angeles CA 90067

STINNETT, MARK ALLAN, lawyer; b. Jackson, Miss., Sept. 15, 1955; s. Allan J. and Joan (Mouser) S. BA in Polit. Sci., Tex. Tech U., 1977; JD, U. Tex., 1980. Bar: Tex. 1980, U.S. Dist. Ct. (no. and ea. dists.) Tex. 1981. Atty. Cowles & Thompson, Dallas, 1980—. Mem. ABA, State Bar of Tex., Dallas Bar Assn., Tex. Assn. Def. Counsel, Dallas Assn. Def. Counsel. Avocations: backpacking, softball. State civil litigation, Personal injury, Federal civil litigation. Home: 7340 Skillman 1224 Dallas TX 75231 Office: Cowles & Thompson 4000 Interfirst Plaza 901 Main St Dallas TX 75202

STINNETT, TERRANCE LLOYD, lawyer; b. Oakland, Calif., July 22, 1940; s. Lloyd Monroe and Gertrude (Hyman) S. B.S., Stanford U., 1962; J.D. magna cum laude, U. Santa Clara, 1969. Bar: Calif. 1970, U.S. Dist. Ct. (no. dist.) Calif. 1970, U.S. Dist. Ct. (ea. and so. dists.) Calif. 1975, U.S. Ct. Appeals (9th cir.) 1970, U.S. Supreme Ct. 1975. Law clk. to judge Calif. Ct. Appeals, San Francisco, 1969-70; assoc. Hyman, Rhodes & Aylward, Fremont, Calif., 1970-71, Glicksberg, Kushner & Goldberg, San Francisco, 1972-77; mem. Goldberg, Stinnett & Macdonald, San Francisco, 1977—. Mem. ABA, Bar Assn. San Francisco. Republican. Roman Catholic. Bankruptcy. Home: 131 Alamo Hills Ct Alamo CA 94507-2245 Office: Goldberg Stinnett & McDonald 44 Montgomery St Suite 1700 San Francisco CA 94104

STINSON, STEVEN ARTHUR, lawyer; b. Rochester, Ind., Dec. 14, 1946; s. Dean King and Lavonna Jeannette (Bailey) S.; m. Sherry Elizabeth Overton, Mar. 23, 1968; children: Nathaniel Overton, Stephanie Noelle. B.A., Vanderbilt U., 1969, J.D., 1972; M.A.L.S., U. Mich., 1977; LL.M. in Air and Space Law, McGill U., 1982. Bar: Ind. 1972, Fla. 1972, U.S. Supreme Ct. 1976, D.C. 1980, U.S. Ct. Appeals (5th and 11th cirs.) 1981. Sole practice, Rochester, 1973-76; prosecutor 41st Jud. Circuit, Rochester, 1975-76; assoc. Walton, Lantaff, Schroeder & Carson, West Palm Beach, Fla., 1978-82, ptnr., 1983-85; sole practice, West Palm Beach, 1985-86; mem. Jordan & Stinson, P.A., West Palm Beach, 1986—. Contbr. articles to profl. publs. Legal counsel Palm Beach County Republican Exec. Com., 1980—; alt. del. Rep. Nat. Conv., Dallas, 1984. Named Jaycee of Yr., Rochester Jaycees, 1973. Mem. ABA, Am. Soc. Internat. Law, Fla. Bar, Ind. Bar Assn., D.C. Bar Assn., Palm Beach County Bar Assn. (pres. young lawyers sect. 1983-84, bd. dirs. 1984-86, treas. 1986-87, sec. 1987—). Club: Governor's (West Palm Beach). Lodges: Masons, Shriners, Kiwanis, (bd. dirs. West Palm Beach 1981-83). State civil litigation, Insurance, Personal injury. Home: 3117 Medinah Circle Lake Worth FL 33467 Office: 324 Datura St #324 West Palm Beach FL 33401

STIPANOV, KENNETH JEROME, lawyer; b. Ontario, Calif., Sept. 27, 1957; s. Jerome A. and Mary (Harvey) S.; m. Julie S. Mebane, Jan. 21, 1984. AB in History, Stanford U., 1978; JD, UCLA, 1981. Bar: Calif. 1981. Assoc. Adams, Duque & Hazeltine, Los Angeles, 1981-82; assoc. Aylward, Kintz, Stiska, Wassenaar & Shannahan, San Diego, 1983-85, ptnr., 1985-87; assoc. Brobeck, Phleger & Harrison, San Diego, 1987—. Mem. ABA, San Diego Bar Assn., La Jolla Bar Assn. Real property. Office: Brobeck Phleger & Harrison 225 Broadway Suite 2100 San Diego CA 92101

STIPANOWICH, THOMAS JOSEPH, law educator; b. Evanston, Ill., Oct. 5, 1952; s. Joseph Jean and Mary (Forsythe) S.; m. Celia Marks, May 22, 1976; children: Laura J., Thomas M. BS in Architecture with highest honors, U. Ill., 1974, MArch, 1976, JD magna cum laude, 1980. Bar: Ga. 1980, U.S. Dist. Ct. (no. dist.) Ga. 1980, Ill. 1981. Assoc. Smith, Currie & Hancock, Atlanta, 1980-84; asst. prof. U. Ky., Lexington, 1984—. Contbr. articles to profl. jours. Bd. dirs. Samaritan Ctr. Bluegrass, Lexington, 1986—. Ryerson Traveling fellow, 1976-77. Mem. ABA (forum com. on constrn. 1984—, architect/engr. and profl. services com. pub. contracts sect. 1984—). Contracts commercial, Construction, Government contracts and claims. Office: U Ky Coll Law Law Bldg Lexington KY 40506-0048

STIRBA, ANNE MELINDA MORR, lawyer; b. Orrville, Ohio, July 12, 1951; d. Robert Shuey and Grace Roberta (McClaran) Morr; m. Peter Stirba, June 19, 1973; children: Emily, Melissa. BA, Coll. of Wooster, 1973; JD, U. Utah, 1978. Bar: Utah 1978, U.S. Dist. Ct. Utah 1978, U.S. Ct. Appeals (10th cir.) 1980. Law clk. Utah Atty. Gen.'s Office, Salt Lake City, 1976-78; teaching fellow U. of Utah, Salt Lake City, 1977; research atty. Utah Supreme Ct., Salt Lake City, 1978-80; asst. atty. gen. Utah Atty Gen.'s Office, Salt Lake City, 1980-86; adminstrv. law judge Utah Pub. Service Commn., Salt Lake City, 1986—; instr. Utah State Bar Legal Edn. Program, 1978-79. Trustee Columbus Community Found. for Mentally Retarded and Physically Disabled, Salt Lake City, 1984—; officer Utah div. Am. Cancer Soc., 1985—. Mem. ABA (exec. council young lawyers div. 1983-84), Utah Bar Assn. (commr. 1984—, pres. young lawyers sect. 1980-81), Salt Lake County Bar Assn., Women Lawyers of Utah Inc., Nat. Assn. Women Judges. Oil and gas leasing, Public utilities, Administrative and regulatory. Office: Utah Pub Service Commn 160 E 300 South 4th Fl Salt Lake City UT 84111

STIRTON, CHARLES PAUL, lawyer; b. Cedar City, Utah, Mar. 24, 1950; s. John K. and Idonna G. (Gower) S. BS in Math., U. Ariz., 1972, BS in Chemistry, 1972, JD, 1975. Bar: Ariz. 1975, U.S. Dist. Ct. Ariz. 1975, U.S. Ct. Appeals (9th cir.) 1975. Assoc. Laber, Lovallo & Colarich, Tucson, 1975-77; ptnr. Lovallo & Stirton, Tucson, 1977-85; sole practice Tucson, 1985—. Contbr. articles to newspapers. Mem. Big Brothers Tucson, 1973-80, adv. bd. Tucson Fitness Marathon, 1984-85, adv. bd. Wellness Council Tucson, 1986—. Mem. Ariz. Bar Assn., Pima County Bar Assn. (ethics com. 1982—), Assn. Trial Lawyers Am., Phi Beta Kappa, Order of Coif. Democrat. Roman Catholic. Avocations: running, hiking, skiing, swimming, biking. General corporate, Probate, Real property. Office: 1325 N Wilmot Suite 310 Tucson AZ 85712

STITH, JOHN STEPHEN, lawyer; b. Cin., Apr. 15, 1939; s. David Clyde and Dorothy Mae S.; m. Carolyn Liles, June 24, 1961; children—Stephen Liles, Laura Elizabeth, Sarah Anne. A.B. cum laude, Princeton U., 1961; J.D. summa cum laude, U. Cin., 1964. Bar: Ohio 1964. Assoc., Frost & Jacobs, Cin., 1964-70, ptnr., 1970—; instr. U. Cin. Coll. Law, Chase Coll. Law, Cin. Mem. ABA, Ohio State Bar Assn., Cin. Bar Assn., Am. Judicature Soc. Presbyterian. Clubs: Cin. Country, Queen City (Cin.); Queen City Anglers. General corporate, Securities, Private international. Office: 2500 Central Trust Ctr 201 East Fifth St Cincinnati OH 45202

STITT, LEMOINE DONALDSON, lawyer; b. Chgo., Sept. 24, 1925. Ph.B., U. Chgo., 1945, J.D., 1949. Bar: Ill. 1949. Mem. Johnson, Zahler, Campbell & Stitt, Chgo., 1960-65; mem. Stitt, Kearns & Szala, Palatine, Ill., 1965-71; mem. Stitt, Moore, Kearns & Szala, Arlington Heights, Ill., 1971-76; mem. Stitt, Moore & Lennon and predecessors, Rolling Meadows, Ill., 1976-85, Stitt & Klein, Inverness, Ill., 1985—. Mem. ABA, Ill. Bar Assn., Chgo. Bar Assn. (matrimonial com. 1971—), Am. Judicature Soc., Am. Matrimonial Acad. Club: Inverness Golf. Family and matrimonial, State civil litigation, Local government. Office: 1620 Colonial Pkwy Inverness IL 60067

STIVISON, DAVID VAUGHN, lawyer; b. Logan, Ohio, Oct. 11, 1946; s. Robert Woodrow and Freda Mae (Smith) S.; m. Sandra Kay Geiger, July 12, 1985. B.A. in Philosophy, Ohio U., 1969, B.S. in Chemistry, 1969; J.D., Harvard U., 1979. Bar: Ohio 1979, U.S. Dist. Ct. (so. dist.) Ohio 1980, Pa. 1983. Dir. commn. on poverty Ohio Council Churches, Columbus, 1975-76; assoc. firm Bricker and Eckler, Columbus, 1979-83, Morgan, Lewis and Bockius, Phila., 1983-85. Co-author: Housing Needs in Appalachian Ohio, 1972. Contbg. author: Homosexuals and the Constitution, 1982, 1986 Public Utility Research Handbook, 1986, Anatomy of an Administrative Proceeding, 1986. Contbr. articles to legal publs. Pres. Ohio Housing Coalition, Columbus, 1973-75; chmn. bd. dirs. Hunger Task Force Ohio, Columbus, 1980-82; bd. dirs. Ohio State Legal Services Assn., Columbus, 1980-83. Mem. ABA, Internat. Bar Assn., Ohio Bar Assn. (chmn. com. 1983), Columbus Bar Assn.(com. chmn. 1980-82, community service award 1981), Pa. Bar Assn., Phila. Bar Assn. (com. chmn. 1986), Selden Soc. (sec. Ohio Chpt. 1982-83), Mensa, Harvard Club Phila. Democrat. Mem. Met. Community Ch. Public utilities, Nuclear power, Legal history. Home: 870 N 30th St Philadelphia PA 19130-1104 Office: PO Box 15877 Philadelphia PA 19103

STOCKBURGER, JEAN DAWSON, lawyer; b. Scottsboro, Ala., Feb. 4, 1936; d. Joseph Mathis Scott and Mary Frances (Alley) Dawson; m. John Calvin Stockburger, Mar. 23, 1963; children: John Scott, Mary Staci, Christopher Sean. Student, Gulf Park Coll., 1954-55; BA, Auburn U., 1958; M in Social Work, Tulane U., 1962; JD, U. Ark., Little Rock, 1979. Bar: Ark. 1979, U.S. Dist. Ct. (ea. dist.) Ark. 1980. Assoc. Mitchell, Williams, Selig & Tucker, Little Rock, 1979-85, ptnr., 1985—; bd. dirs., sec. Cen. Ark. Estate Planning Council, Little Rock, 1984-85, 2d v.p., 1985-86; pres. Cen. Ark. Estate Council, 1987-88. Assoc. editor U. Ark. Law Rev., 1978-79. Bd. dirs. Sr. Citizens Activities Today, Little Rock, 1983-86, treas., 1986—; bd. dirs. Vol. Orgn. for Cen. Ark. Legal Services, 1986—, sec., 1987-88. Mem. ABA (real property, probate and trust sect.), Ark. Bar Assn. (chmn. probate and trust law sect. 1986—), Pulaski County Bar Assn. Democrat. Methodist. Estate planning, Probate. Office: Mitchell Williams Selig & Tucker 1000 Savers Fed Bldg Little Rock AR 72201

STOCKER, THOMAS EDWIN, lawyer; b. Canton, Ohio, Oct. 12, 1953; s. Homer Eugene and Doris Verna (Schweitzer) S.; m. Patricia Ann Popko, Mar. 7, 1981; 1 child, Joshua Adam. BA, Grove City Coll., 1976; JD, U. Akron, 1979. Bar: Ohio 1979, U.S. Dist. Ct. (no. dist.) Ohio 1980. Law clk. to presiding justice U.S. Bankruptcy Ct., Canton, 1979-81; sole practice Canton, 1981—; tchr. Career Studies Inst., Canton, 1984—. Mem. ABA, Ohio Bar Assn., Stark County Bar Assn. (chmn. young lawyers com. 1982-84, bankruptcy com. 1984-86), Plain Twp. Jaycees (pres. 1981-82). Family and matrimonial, Probate, Real property. Home: 921 24th St NE Canton OH 44714 Office: 132 15th St NW Canton OH 44703

STOCKHOLM, KENDALL RAY, criminal justice educator; b. Beaumont, Tex., July 18, 1939; s. Charles Allen and Ruth Ellen (Moye) S.; m. Helen Kathryn Derzapf, Apr. 19, 1965; children: Kurt R., Kathy R. BA, Lamar U., 1971; MA, Sam Houston State U., 1973, PhD, 1984. Cert. police instr. Patrolman, Tex. Dept. Pub. Safety, Wichita Falls, 1960-62; owner, mgr. L&L Detective Agy., Beaumont, 1962-70, Spl. Investigations, Beaumont, 1970-73; prof. Blinn Coll., Brennem, Tex., 1973-74; dir. criminal justice U. Alaska, Fairbanks, 1974—, chmn. polit. sci./justice dept.; dir. Criminal Justice Ctr., Anchorage; founder Interior Police Acad., Fairbanks, 1981. Author: Research Methods in Criminal Justice, 1983; (booklet) The Impact of Presumptive Sentencing, 1984. Del. Rep. Party, Fox, Alaska, 1970; asst. scoutmaster Boy Scouts Am., Fairbanks, 1980. CETA grantee, 1981, 82. Mem. Am. Soc. Criminology, Acad. Criminal Justice Scis., Internat. Assn. Chief of Police, Pacific N.W. Assn. Criminal Justice Educators, Alaska Peace Officers Assn. Baptist. Club: Marine Corps League (sgt. at arms 1973) (Beaumont). Lodge: Lions. Legal education, Criminal. Home: 4437 Stanford Dr Fairbanks AK 99701 Office: U Alaska Fairbanks AK 99701

STOCKMAN, HARRY MICHAEL, lawyer; b. Iowa City, Mar. 29, 1954; s. Leo Cornelius and Mary Dorothy (Florang) S. AB, St. Louis U., 1976, JD, 1979. Bar: Mo. 1979, U.S. Dist. Ct. (ea. and we. dists.) Mo. 1979, Ill. 1980. Assoc. Riethmann & Soebbing, St. Louis, 1979—. Mem. ABA, Met. St. Louis Bar Assn., Lawyers Assn. St. Louis. Roman Catholic. Insurance, Personal injury, Workers' compensation. Home: 2608 Park Ave Saint Louis MO 63104 Office: Riethmann & Soebbing 10805 Sunset Office Dr Saint Louis MO 63127

STOCKTON, RALPH MADISON, JR., lawyer; b. Winston-Salem, June 22, 1927; s. Ralph Madison and Margaret (Thompson) S.; m. Frances Bowles, July 15, 1950; children: Mary Ellen Sartin, Ralph Madison III, David Anderson, James Alexander. B.S., U. N.C., 1948, LL.B. cum laude, 1950; LL.D. (hon.), Winston-Salem U., 1983. Bar: N.C. 1950. Assoc. firm Dwight, Royal, Harris Koeger & Caskey, Washington, 1950-51; with firm Petree Stockton & Robinson (and predecessors), Winston-Salem, 1951—; partner Petree, Stockton & Robinson (and predecessors), 1956—; Mem. jud. conf. 4th Circuit U.S. Ct. Appeals, 1958—. Trustee Winston-Salem State U., 1958-84, vice chmn., 1973-84; trustee Forsyth County Legal Aid Soc., 1966-70, pres., 1969; trustee Meth. Children's Home, 1966-84, chmn. exec. com., 1969-75, past pres. bd. trustees, 1975-84; bd. mgrs. Meth. Home, Charlotte, N.C., 1967-70; bd. dirs. Winston-Salem Found., 1979-86, chmn. bd., 1985-86; mem. Leadership Winston-Salem, 1984-85, alumni council, 1987—; co-chmn. N.C. Legis. Com. on Evidence and Comparative Negligence, 1980-82; mem. Gov.'s Jud. Nominating Com., 1982-85; chmn. adminstrv. bd. local United Meth. Ch., 1984-86. Mem. ABA, (Ho. of Dels. 1986—), N.C. Bar Assn. (bd. govs. 1957-60, chmn. comml. banking and bus. law com. 1958-60, chmn. appellate rules study com. 1973-75, pres. 1976-77), Forsyth County Bar Assn. (pres. 1965-66), Internat. Assn. Ins. Counsel, Am. Judicature Soc. (dir. 1976-82), Am. Coll. Trial Lawyers (state chmn. 1984-86), Nat. Conf. Bar Presidents, Fellows of Am. Bar Found., Law Alumni Assn. U. N.C. (pres. 1964, dir. gen. 1970-73), Order of Coif, Phi Delta Phi. Democrat. Methodist. Lodge: Rotary (pres. Winston-Salem 1965-66). Federal civil litigation, State civil litigation, Personal injury. Home: 2696 Reynolds Dr Winston-Salem NC 27104 Office: 1001 W 4th St Winston-Salem NC 27101

STOCKWELL, DAVID MICHAEL, lawyer, consultant; b. Dhahran, Saudi Arabia, Aug. 10, 1951; came to U.S., 1969; s. Gilbert Wesley and Jane Emma (Miller) S.; m. Melanie Patricia Blanco, May 23, 1981. BA, U. Pa., 1973; JD, Villanova U., 1976. Bar: Tex. 1976. Sole practice Houston, 1976-77; comml. attache U.S. Embassy, Kuwait, 1977-79; country officer U.S. Dept. of State, Washington, 1979-80; U.S. consul gen. U.S. Consulate, Dubai, United Arab Emirates, 1982-85; assoc., legal counsel Sidley & Austin, Dubai, 1985-87; of counsel Bryan, Cave, McPheeters & McRoberts, Dubai, 1987—; fgn. service officer U.S. Dept. State, Washington, 1977-85. Sustaining mem. Rep. Nat. Com., 1983. Mem. ABA, Houston Bar Assn., Tex. Bar Assn., Am. Bus. Council Dubai, Nat. Rifle Assn. (life). Clubs: Passport (Dubai) (bd. dirs. 1985—), Hilton Beach (Dubai). Avocations: scuba diving, tennis. General corporate, Private international, Local government. Home: PO Box 6750 Deira, Dubai United Arab Emirates Office: Bryan Cave McPheeters & McRoberts, PO Box 6750 Deira, Dubai United Arab Emirates

STOCKWELL, OLIVER PERKINS, lawyer; b. East Baton Rouge, La., Aug. 11, 1907; s. William Richard and Lillie Belle (Dawson) S.; m. Roseina Katherine Holcombe, June 24, 1936; 1 dau., Angell Roseina (Mrs. William C. Wright). LL.B., La. State U., 1932, J.D., 1968. Bar: La. 1932. Since practiced in Lake Charles; partner firm Stockwell, Sievert, Viccellio, Clements & Shaddock (and predecessor firm), 1933—; Dir. Lakeside Nat. Bank of Lake Charles; past dir. Gulf States Utilities Co.; past mem. jud. council La. Supreme Ct.; past mem. La. Commn. on Law Enforcement and Adminstrn. Criminal Justice; referee bankruptcy U.S. Dist. Ct. (we. dist.) La., 1938-46. Contbr. to La. Law Rev. Pres. Lake Charles Centennial; bd. dirs., mem. exec. com. Council for a Better La., pres., 1972; past bd. dirs. Pub. Affairs Research Council La.; past bd. dirs. La. State U. Found.; past bd. suprs. La. State U., chmn., 1977-78; past chmn. legal services adv. com. La. Joint Legis. Commn. on Intergovtl. Relations.; chmn. Paul H. Hebert Law Ctr. Council La. State U.; mem. Task Force on Excessive Govtl. Regulations. Served to lt. USNR, 1943-45. Research fellow Southwestern Legal Found. Fellow Am. Bar Found., Am. Coll. Trial Lawyers, Am. Coll. Probate Counsel; mem. Inter-Am. Bar Assn., Am. Judicature Soc., Internat. Bar Assn., ABA (past state chmn. jr. bar sect., mem. spl. com. adoption jud. conduct code;, chmn. La. membership com., sr. lawyers div.), La. Bar Assn. (past pres.), S.W. La. Bar Assn. (pres. 1942), Mid-Continent Oil and Gas Assn. (exec. com.), Comml. Law League, Internat. Assn. Ins. Counsel, Fedn. Ins. Counsel, Am. Law Inst. (life mem.), La. Law Inst. (past pres., chmn. mineral code com. 1986, chmn. of counsel 1987), Lake Charles C. of C. (past pres., Civic award 1978), State Assn. Young Men's Bus. Clubs (past pres. Lake Charles), La. State U. Law Sch. Alumni Assn. (past pres.), Order of Coif, Henri Capitant, Lambda Alpha, Omicron Delta Kappa. Clubs: Kiwanis, Pioneer, City, Lake Charles Country, Boston of New Orleans, L of La. State U. (past pres.). Oil and gas leasing, Federal civil litigation, State civil litigation. Home: 205 Shell Beach Dr Lake Charles LA 70601 Office: One Lakeside Plaza Lake Charles LA 70601

STODDARD, CHARLES WARNER, III, lawyer; b. Tucson, Mar. 13, 1943; s. Charles Warner and Hortense Elizabeth (Shahan) S.; m. Linda Margaret Murphy, July 5, 1965; m. 2d, Verna Marie Howard, Jan. 29, 1972; children—Sarah Ashley, Kristine Elizabeth. A.A., N.Mex. Mil. Inst., 1963; B.S. in Bus. Adminstrn., U. Ariz., 1965, J.D., 1968. Bar: Ariz. 1968, U.S. Dist. Ct. Ariz. 1968, U.S. Ct. Appeals (9th cir.) 1977. Law clk. Ariz. Ct. Appeals, 1968-69; staff atty. Maricopa County Legal Aid, 1969-70; asst. atty. gen. State of Ariz., 1970-71; sole practice, Page, Ariz., 1971—; city atty. City of Page; dep. county atty. Coconino County, Ariz.; instr. Yavapai Community Coll. Vestry St. David's Episcopal Ch.; bd. dirs. John Wesley Powell Mus. Mem. Ariz. Bar Assn., Coconino County Bar Assn., ABA, Lawyer-Pilots Bar Assn., Nat. Dist. Attys. Assn., Nat. Inst. Mcpl. Law Officers. Republican. Clubs: Elks, Page-Lake Powell Boating (founder, dir.), Masons, Shriners, Page Rotary (past pres.). General practice, Local government, Real property. Office: PO Box M Page AZ 86040

STODOLA, MARK ALLEN, lawyer; b. Mpls., May 18, 1949; s. Robert Allen and Elizabeth (Abeler) S.; 1 child, Allison. BA in Journalism and Polit. Sci., U. Iowa, 1971; JD, U. Ark., 1974. Bar: Ark. 1974, U.S. Dist Ct. (we. and ea. dists.) Ark. 1975, U.S. Ct. Appeals (8th cir.). Assoc. Givens & Buzbee, Little Rock, 1974-75; dep. pub. defender Pulaski County, Little Rock, 1975-76; pub. defender North Little Rock City, Ark., 1976-85; ptnr. Stodola & Smith, North Little Rock, 1976-85; city atty. City of Little Rock, 1985—; instr. criminal justice U. Ark, Little Rock, 1976-85. Mem. exec. com. Dem State Com., Little rock, 1976—; mem. exec. com. Dem. Nat. Com., Washington, 1981-83; nat. pres. Young Dems. Am., Washington, 1981-83. Served to 1st lt. USAFR, 1969-74. Mem. ABA, Ark. Bar Assn., Pulaski Bar Assn. (Lawyer's award, 1981), Nat. Inst. Mcpl. Law Officers, Am. Trial Lawyers Assn. Lodge: Rotary. Avocations: rugby, hist. preservation. Real property, Labor, Legislative. Home: 1418 Louisiana St Little Rock AR 72202 Office: City Attys Office Markham and Broadway Sts Little Rock AR 72201

STOETZER, GERALD LOUIS, lawyer; b. Detroit, Apr. 6, 1914; s. Albin August and Ida Henrietta (Kuhlman) S.; m. Muriel Simons, Aug. 16, 1941; children: Gerald Louis Jr., James Brian, Susan Hart Stoetzer Bockelman. AB cum laude, Valparaiso U., 1935; JD cum laude, U. Mich., 1938. Bar: Mich. 1938, U.S. Dist. Ct. (ea. dist.) Mich. 1938, U.S. Supreme Ct. 1955. Ptnr. Clark, Klein & Beaumont and predecessor Clark, Klein, Winter, Parsons & Prewitt and Clark Klein, Brucker & Waples, Detroit, 1938—; lectr. U. Mich. Law Sch. Inst. Continuing Legal Edn., 1964—. Sec. 14th Congressional Dist. Mich. Rep. Com., 1950-54; mem. Grosse Pointe (Mich.) Symphony Orch., 1955—, pres. support orgn., 1979-81. Served to capt. JAG Dept., U.S. Army, 1942-46. Decorated Bronze Star. Mem. ABA, Mich. State Bar (chmn. corp. and securities com. 1961-65, chmn. corp., fin. and bus. law sect. 1965-68), Detroit Bar Assn., Judge Advs. Assn., Am. Judicature Soc., Mich. Assn. of Professions, Fine Arts Soc. Detroit, Order of Coif, Phi Delta Theta, Delta Theta Phi. Lutheran. Clubs: Univ., Players (Detroit); Lochmoor (Grosse Pointe Woods, Mich.); Hidden Valley (Gaylord, Mich.). Bd. editors U. Mich. Law Rev., 1937-38. General corporate, Administrative and regulatory, Securities. Home: 1949 Littlestone Rd Grosse Pointe Woods MI 48236 Office: 1600 First Fed Bldg Detroit MI 48226

STOFFER, JAMES MYRON, JR., lawyer; b. Cape Girardeau, Mo., Mar. 17, 1952; s. James Myron Sr. and Barbara June (Campbell) S.; m. Diane Elizabeth House, June 24, 1978; children: James Myron III, Megan Campbell. BBA, Murray State U., 1974; JD, S. Tex. Coll. of Law, 1977. Bar: Tex. 1978, U.S. Dist. Ct. (so. dist.) Tex. 1978, U.S. Supreme Ct. 1980. Assoc. Hirch & Westheimer, Houston, 1977-80, Sawtell & Goode, San Antonio, 1981-83; assoc. Davis & Smith, San Antonio, 1983-84, ptnr., 1985-86; ptnr. Smith, Barshop, Stoffer & Millsap, Inc., San Antonio, 1986—; bd. dirs. 1st Tex. Corp., San Antonio. Chmn. Spicewood (Tex.) Vol. Fire Dept. Fund Raiser, 1985, Terrell Hills Property Owners Assn., San Antonio, 1986; vol. Am. Cancer Soc., San Antonio, 1981—. Mem. ABA (land surveys sect.), San Antonio Bar Assn., Houston Bar Assn., Tex. Land Title Assn., Tex. Bd. Legal Specialization (cert. in residential, farm and ranch real estate law). Methodist. Club: Horseshoe Bay Country (Marble Falls, Tex.). Avocations: snow skiing, golf, reading. Banking, Real property. Home: 117 Ivy Ln San Antonio TX 78209 Office: Smith Barshop Stoffer & Millsap Inc 700 N St Mary's St Suite 1000 San Antonio TX 78205

STOGSDILL, DANIEL RAY, lawyer; b. Bloomington, Ind., Aug. 18, 1957; s. Paul E. and Jacquelin J. (Sims) S.; m. Melinda J. Wilson, Aug. 25, 1979. Student, U.S. Mil. Acad., 1975-76; BBA in Internat. Fin. with highest distinction, U. Hawaii, 1977; JD cum laude, Ind. U., 1979. Bar: Nebr. 1980, U.S. Dist. Ct. Nebr. 1980, U.S. Ct. Appeals (D.C. cir.) 1984, U.S. Tax Ct. 1986, US. Supreme Ct. 1986. Assoc. Cline, Williams, Wright, Johnson & Oldfather, Lincoln, Nebr., 1979-84, ptnr., 1985—. Lawyer ACLU, 1979—. Mem. ABA. Democrat. Mem. Ch. of Christ. Probate. Home: 8000 Pioneer Blvd Lincoln NE 68506 Office: Cline Williams Wright et al 1900 FirsTier Bldg Lincoln NE 68508

STOKER, ARLON L., JR., lawyer; b. Espanola, N.Mex., Apr. 11, 1955; s. Arlon L. and Elizabeth B. (Butler) S.; m. Nancy A. Gallenberger, Dec. 7, 1984. BA in Polit. Sci., U. N.Mex., 1978; JD, Tex. Tech. U., 1982. Bar: N.Mex. 1982, U.S. Ct. Appeals (10th cir.) 1982, U.S. Dist. Ct. N.Mex., Mar. 23, 1983. Assoc. Beall, Stoker & Clifford (formerly Larry D. Beall, P.A.), Albuquerque, 1982-84; sole practice Albuquerque, 1984—. Mem. ABA, Assn. Trial Lawyers Am., N.Mex. Bar Assn., N.Mex. Trial Lawyers Assn., N.Mex. Def. Lawyers Assn., Albuquerque Bar Assn., N.Mex. Workmen's Compensation Assn. Democrat. Avocations: camping, fishing, hunting, animal enthusiast. Workers' compensation, Personal injury, Insurance. Office: 8200 Mountain Rd NE #203 Albuquerque NM 87110

STOKER, ROBIN JEFFREY, lawyer; b. Idaho Falls, Idaho, Nov. 23, 1946; s. Sheldon and Martha (Bradshaw) S.; m. Rosemary Kay Morrill, Aug. 2, 1974; children: Melissa, Amanda, Jeffrey, Christopher. BA in Polit. Sci., Brigham Young U., 1971; JD, U. Idaho, 1974. Bar: Idaho 1974, U.S. Dist. Ct. Idaho 1974. Pros. atty. Twin Falls County, Idaho, 1978-80; sole practice Twin Falls, Idaho, 1980—; mem. Idaho Ho. of Reps., Boise, 1985-87. Mem. Assn. Trial Lawyers Am. Republican. Mormon. Insurance, Personal injury, Legislative. Home: 79 Rim View Ln W Twin Falls ID 83301 Office: PO Box 1597 Twin Falls ID 83303

STOKES, CARL NICHOLAS, lawyer; b. Memphis, Jan. 26, 1907; s. John William and Edith Isabell (Burgess) S. 1 dau., Vicki Stokes Koehn. LL.B., U. Memphis, 1934. Bar: Tenn. 1934. Assoc., Norvell & Monteverde, 1934-38; clk. City Ct., Memphis, 1938-42; clk. Criminal Cts., Shelby County, Tenn., 1946-50; judge City Ct. and 1st Traffic Ct., Memphis, 1950-52; assoc. Shea and Pierotti, Memphis, 1952-62; v.p., gen. counsel Allen & O'Hara, Inc., Memphis, 1962-72; of counsel McDonald, Kuhn, Smith, Gandy, Miller & Tait, Memphis, 1972-76, Stokes, Kimbrough, Grusin & Kizer, P.C., Memphis 1976-82, Stokes, May, Grusin, Surprise & Kizer, P.C., Memphis, 1982-84. Hon. dir. Mid South Fair Assn.; life mem. Salvation Army Adv. Bd., Memphis, chmn., 1973-75; trustee Shrine Sch. for Handicapped Children; life elder Lindenwood Christian Ch. Served to capt. AUS, 1942-46. Recipient T.E. Kirkpatrick Ann. award Kiwanis Club Memphis, 1978; James W. Bodley Americanism award Am. Legion, 1980. Mem. Tenn. Bar Assn. (Merit award for pub. service 1958), ABA, Memphis Bar Assn., Shelby County Bar Assn. Clubs: Economic, English Speaking Union, Masons, Shriners (Memphis). Estate planning, Probate, General corporate. Home: 2237 Massey Rd Memphis TN 38119 Office: Johnson Grusin Kee & May 780 Ridge Lake Blvd Memphis TN 91934

STOKES, DOUGLAS LEON, lawyer; b. Pawnee City, Nebr., Nov. 23, 1951; s. Douglas Leon and Mary Jane (Robertson) S.; m. Dora Ann Klassen, Sept. 8, 1973; children: Jocelyn Denise, Juliet Danille. BA, U. Manitoba, Winnipeg, Can., 1973; JD, La. State U., 1977. Bar: La., 1977, U.S. Dist. Ct. (we. dist.) La. Assoc. Emmons, Henry & Reeves, Jonesborg, La., 1977-80; ptnr. Emmons, Reeves & Stokes, Jonesborg, La., 1980, Emmons & Stokes, Jonesborg, La., 1981—. Mem. ABA, La. Bar Assn., Jackson Parish Bar Assn. (pres. 1984—). Republican. Baptist. Lodge: Kiwanis (dir. 1982-83). Criminal, Probate, Real property. Office: Emmons & Stokes PO Drawer 726 Jonesboro LA 71251

STOKES, JAMES CHRISTOPHER, JR., lawyer; b. Orange, N.J., Mar. 19, 1944; s. James Christopher and Margaret Mary (Groome) S.; m. Eileen Marie Brosnan, Sept. 7, 1968; children—Erin Margaret, Michael Colin, Courtney Dorothy. A.B., Holy Cross Coll., 1966; J.D., Boston Coll., 1975. Bar: Hawaii 1975, U.S. Ct. Appeals (1st and 9th cirs.) 1976, Mass. 1977 Assoc., Carlsmith, Carlsmith, Wichman and Case, Honolulu, 1975-76; assoc., then ptnr. firm Bingham, Dana & Gould, Boston., 1976-79, 84—, ptnr, London, 1980-84. mem. steering com. New Eng. British Bus. Council, 1986—, gov.'s council on Internat. Trade and Investment, 1985—. Contbr. articles to Jour. Maritime Law and Commerce. Mem. personnel bd. Town of Wellesley (Mass.), 1984—, vice chmn., 1986—. Served to capt. USMC, 1966-72, Vietnam. Mem. Hawaii Bar Assn., Boston Bar Assn., Mass. Bar Assn., Internat. Bar Assn. Roman Catholic. Club: Travellers' (London). Private international, General corporate, Contracts commercial. Office: Bingham Dana & Gould 100 Federal St Boston MA 02110

STOKES, JOHN REYNOLDS, lawyer; b. Loma Linda, Calif., Aug. 13, 1917; s. John Reynolds and Maynie Lee (Coleman) S.; m. Edith Bishop, July 16, 1946; children: Katherine, John Reynolds, Mary, Lucy, Emily. AB, U. Calif., Berkeley, 1946, LLB, 1948. Bar: Calif., 1948. Atty. City of Blue Lake, Calif., 1948-57, City of Arcata, Calif., 1950-73; gen. counsel Humboldt Bay (Calif.) Wastewater Authority, 1975-83; ptnr. Stokes, Steeves & Schaub, Arcata, 1987—; mem. Calif. com. Bar Examiners, 1983-87, chmn. 1985-86. Chmn. Dem. Cen. Com., Humboldt County, 1952-62, mem. state exec. com., Calif., 1962. Served to capt. U.S. Army, 1942-45, ETO. Decorated D.F.C., Air medal with 10 oak leaf clusters. Mem. State Bar Calif. Assn. (bd. govs. 1979-82, v.p. 1981-82), Humboldt County Bar Assn. (pres. 1950). General practice. Home: 916 13th St Arcata CA 95521 Office: PO Box 1109 381 Bayside Rd Arcata CA 95521

STOKES, RICHARD FRANCIS, lawyer; b. Teaneck, N.J., Jan. 7, 1946; s. Edwin Matthew and Norma S. (Bonn) S.; m. Sally Scott, Mar. 28, 1970; children—Sarah S., Richard Hunter. B.A., Colgate U., 1967; J.D., Duke U., 1970. Bar: Del. 1970, U.S. Dist. Ct. Del. 1970. Law clk. Superior Ct., Wilmington, Del., 1970; ptnr. Tunnell & Raysor, Georgetown, Del., 1978—; counsel Beebe Hosp., Lewes, Del., 1983—; dir. Seaside Med. Assoc., Lewes. Bd. dirs. Community Legal Aid, Georgetown, Del., 1978-82; elder Rehoboth Beach Presbyterian Ch., Del., 1983—; chmn. Sussex County Dem. Exec. Com. 1986-88. Served to capt. USAF, 1971-75. Mem. Bd. Profl. Responsibility. Democrat. Lodge: Rotary (sec. 1983). General practice, State civil litigation, Personal injury. Home: 36 Sycamore Dr Lewes DE 19958 Office: Tunnell & Raysor PO Box 151 Georgetown DE 19947

STOKES, ROBERT JEROME, lawyer; b. Benton Harbor, Mich., Jan. 2, 1942; s. John R. and Marjorie M. (Van Voorst) S.; m. Kathleen D. Stokes, Aug. 20, 1966; children: Robert J., Christine M., James M. BS magna cum laude, Boston Coll., 1964; LLB, Yale U., 1967; LLM in Taxation, NYU, 1971. Bar: N.Y. 1968, U.S. Tax Ct. 1978. Tax atty. Met. Life Ins. Co., N.Y.C., 1967-72; atty. Weil, Gotshal & Manges, N.Y.C., 1972-75; v.p. Pension Planning Co. Inc., N.Y.C., 1975-76; assoc. Cravath, Swaine & Moore, N.Y.C., 1976-86, sr. atty., 1986—. Pres. town council Twp. of River Vale (N.J.), 1983-84, councilman, 1979-84. Mem. ABA (tax sect. employee benefits com.), N.Y. State Bar Assn. (tax sect., employee benefits com.). Democrat. Pension, profit-sharing, and employee benefits. Office: Cravath Swaine & Moore 1 Chase Manhattan Plaza New York NY 10005

STOLL, NEAL RICHARD, lawyer; b. Phila., Nov. 7, 1948; s. Mervin Stoll and Goldie Louise (Serody) Stoll Wilf; m. Linda G. Seligman, May 25, 1972; children—Meredith Anne, Alexis Blythe. B.A. in History with distinction, Pa. State U., 1970; J.D., Fordham U., 1973. Bar: N.Y. 1974, U.S. Dist. Ct. (ea. dist.) N.Y. 1974, U.S. Ct. Appeals (2d cir.) 1974, U.S. Ct. Appeals (11th cir.) 1982, U.S. Dist. Ct. (ea. dist.) Mich. 1983, U.S. Dist. Ct. (so. dist.) N.Y. 1984, Assoc. Skadden, Arps, Slate, Meagher & Flom, N.Y.C., 1973-81, mem., 1981—; lectr. Practicing Law-Inst., N.Y.C. Contbr. articles to profl. publs. Author: (with others) Aquisitions Under the Hart Scott Rodino Antitrust Improvements Act, 1980. Mem. Assn. Bar City of New York (mem. trade regulation com. 1983—), ABA, N.Y. State Bar Assn. Democrat. Antitrust, Federal civil litigation. Office: Skadden Arps Slate Meagher & Flom 919 3d Ave New York NY 10022

STOLLER, LARRY ALAN, lawyer, consultant; b. Spirit Lake, Iowa, Apr. 6, 1956; s. Leonard H. and Elayne M. (Cohn) S.; m. Marlene Marie Zahradnik, Apr. 28, 1985. BA in Communications cum laude, Ariz. State U., 1977; JD, Creighton U., 1980. Bar: Iowa 1980, U.S. Dist. Ct. (no. dist.) Iowa 1980, U.S. Ct. Claims 1980, U.S. Tax Ct. 1980, U.S. Ct. Customs and Patent Appeals 1980, U.S. Ct. Appeals (8th cir.) 1980. Sole practice Spirit Lake, 1980-81; ptnr. Stoller & Larson, Spirit Lake, 1981-84; pres., gen. counsel Progressive Cos. Inc., Spirit Lake, 1983—; pres. Dickinson County Bar, Spirit Lake, 1982. Liason Iowa Heart Assn., Spirit Lake, 1983—; bd. dirs. Maritime Mus., Arnolds Park, Iowa, 1984—. Mem. ABA, Iowa Bar Assn., Nat. Assn. Criminal Def. Lawyers, Lakes Area C. of C. (bd. dirs. 1982—, pres. elect 1986—). Democrat. Jewish. Lodge: Masons. Avocations: golf, boating, car racing, dogs. Contracts commercial, Real property, Consumer commercial. Office: PO Box 441 Spirit Lake IA 51360

STOLPMAN, THOMAS GERARD, lawyer; b. Cleve., June 2, 1949; s. Joseph Eugene and Katherine Ann (Berry) S.; m. Marilyn Heise, Aug. 17, 1974; children: Jennifer, Peter. BA, UCLA, 1972; JD, Los Angeles, 1976. Bar: Calif. 1976, U.S. Dist. Ct. (cen. dist.) Calif. 1976, U.S. Dist. Ct. (ea. dist.) Calif. 1985. Ptnr. Silver, McWilliams, Stolpman, Mandel and Katzman, Wilmington and Los Angeles, Calif., 1976—. Editor-in-chief The Advocate legal jour., 1984—; contbr. articles to profl. jours. Bd. dirs. Miraleste Recreation and Park Dist., Rancho Palos Verdes, Calif., 1982—, Citizens Against Forced Annexation, Rancho Palos Verdes, 1978-83; del. Rancho Palos Verdes Council of Homeowners Assns., 1979-86, v.p. 1986; v.p., gov. Miraleste Assn., Rancho Palos Verdes, 1976-82. Named Trial Lawyer of Yr. So. Calif., Verdictum Juris, 1984. Mem. Los Angeles Trial Lawyers Assn. (treas. 1984, sec. 1985, v.p. 1986-87, bd. govs., 1979-83), Calif. Trial Lawyers Assn. (bd. govs. 1987—), Assn. Trial Lawyers of Am., Am. Bd. Trial Advocates, Nat. Bd. Trial Advocacy (cert.), Los Angeles County Bar Assn., South Bay Bar Assn., Long Beach Bar Assn. Democrat. Roman Catholic. Personal injury, Admiralty, Federal civil litigation. Office: Silver McWilliams Stolpman Mandel & Katzman 1121 N Avalon Blvd Wilmington CA 90744-3598

STOLTZ, JOHN ROBERT, lawyer; b. Milw., Aug. 4, 1944; s. Robert John and Kathleen (Kullmann) S.; m. Mary Ellen Ross; children: Melissa, Megan, Maren. AB, U. Notre Dame, 1966; JD, Marquette U., 1969. Bar: Wis. 1969, U.S. Dist. Ct. (ea. dist.) Wis. 1969, U.S. Dist. Ct. (we. dist.) Wis. 1971, U.S. Supreme Ct. 1976. Atty. Milw. Ins. Co., 1969-71; assoc. Callahan & Arnold, Columbus, Wis., 1971-78; sole practice Columbus, 1978—. Bd. dirs., pres. Cane Palm Beach Condominium Assn., Ft. Meyers Beach, Fla., 1979-83, Columbus Community Hosp., 1980-86, pres., 1985-86; bd. dirs. Ryan-Powell-Carroll Scholarship, U. Notre Dame, 1969—. Mem. Wis. Bar Assn., Columbia County Bar Assn., Assn. Trial Lawyers Am., Wis. Trial Lawyers Assn., Nat. Notre Dame Monogram Club (bd. dirs. 1986—). Roman Catholic. General practice, State civil litigation, Family and matrimonial. Home: 308 Fairway Dr Columbus WI 53925 Office: 132 Ludington St PO Box D Columbus WI 53925

STOLTZ, MICHAEL RAE, lawyer; b. Hobbs, N.Mex., Nov. 23, 1951; s. Jacque Rae and Marguerite Evelyn (Johnson) S.; m. Barbara Ann Douglas, July 15, 1978; children: Christopher, Stephen, Michael. BA in Polit. Sci., Tex. Tech U., 1973, JD, 1976. Bar: Tex. 1976. Assoc. Stubbeman, McRae, Sealy, Laughlin and Browder, Midland, Tex., 1976-81, ptnr., 1981—. Pres. St. Ann's Cath. Ch. parish council, Midland, 1979-80. Mem. ABA, State Bar Assn. of Tex., Phi Delta Phi. Club: Ranchland Hills Country (treas., bd. dirs.). Avocation: golf. Oil and gas leasing, Probate. Home: 2303 Keswick Midland TX 79705 Office: Stubbeman McRae Sealy Laughlin Browder PO Box 1540 Midland TX 79702

STOLZ, PREBLE, legal educator, lawyer; b. 1931. J.D., U. Chgo., 1956. Bar: Calif., 1957. Law clk. to judge U.S. Ct. Appeals (9th cir.), 1956-57; law clk. to Hon. Harold H. Burton, 1957-58; dep. atty. gen. State of Calif., 1958-61; prof. U. Calif. Law Sch.-Berkeley, 1961—; scholar-in-residence Am. Bar Found., Chgo., spring 1967; vis. prof. Yale U., 1970-71; asst. to Calif. Gov. for Programs and Policies, 1975-76; reporter U.S. Admiralty Rules Com., 1968-72. Mem. Order of Coif. Former editor-in-chief U. Chgo. Law Rev. Legal education. Office: U Calif Law Sch 225 Boalt Hall Berkeley CA 94720 *

STOMMEL, R. ROBERT, lawyer; b. Columbus, Ga., Feb. 5, 1957; m. Jayne Wainscott, Nov. 28, 1981; 1 child, Jon Michael. BBA, U. Wis., 1979;

JD cum laude, Ind. U., 1982. Bar: Ind. 1982, U.S. Dist. Ct. (no. and so. dists.) Ind. 1982, U.S. Ct. Appeals (7th cir.) 1983, U.S. Ct. Appeals (11th cir.) 1985. Assoc. Lewis, Bowman, St. Clair & Wagner, Indpls., 1982—; Contbr. articles to law jour.; devel. editor: Ind. Law Rev., 1981-82. Mem. ABA, Ind. Bar Assn. (civil litigation and labor law sects.), Indpls. Bar Assn. Federal civil litigation, State civil litigation, Labor. Office: Lewis Bowman St Clair & Wagner 5101 Madison Ave Indianapolis IN 46227

STONE, ALAN G., lawyer; b. Bronx, June 2, 1950; s. Robert R. and Shirley (Weliky) S.; m. Jane Ellen Ruthberg, July 16, 1972; children: Benjamin, Amy. BA, Boston U., 1972; JD, Washington U., 1975. Bar: Maine 1975, U.S. Dist. Ct. Maine 1975. Atty., examiner Pub. Utilities Commn., Augusta, Maine, 1975-79; ptnr. Samp & Stone, Auburn, Maine, 1979-82, Clifford, Clifford & Stone, Lewiston, Maine, 1982—; instr. law Res. Police Acad., Lewiston, 1985. Mem. Sch. Bd., Raymond, Maine, 1984—, Govt. Study Com., Raymond, 1983; alt. del. Augusta Dems., 1984. Mem. ABA, Maine Bar Assn. (gov. 1986—), Androscoggin County Bar Assn. (v.p. 1986, pres. 1986-87), Assn. Trial Lawyers Am., Maine Trial Lawyers Assn. Avocations: horseback riding, sports, art, music. State civil litigation, Criminal, Public utilities. Office: Clifford Clifford & Stone 640 Main St Lewiston ME 04240

STONE, BERTRAM ALLEN, lawyer; b. Chgo., Nov. 14, 1915; s. David and Fannie (Abrams) S.; m. Idelle Shirley Kotz, Nov. 25, 1951; children—Robert A., Ronald W., Judith Stone Weiss. Student U. Ill.; LL.B., J.D., Chgo. Kent Coll. Law, 1938. Bar: Ill. 1938, U.S. Dist. Ct. (no. dist.) Ill. 1939. Ptnr. Cherkas, Rosenberg & Stone, 1950-58, Cherkas, Stone & Pogrund, 1958-61, Stone, Pogrund & Korey, 1961—; gen. counsel Chgo. Metal Finishers Inst., 1982—, Twin Cities Assn. Metal Finishers, 1961—, Fabric Salesmen's Club Chgo., 1961-86, Stone, Pogrund, Korey and Spagat, 1986—. Bd. overseers. IIT-Chgo.-Kent Coll. Law; sec. Ill. Water, Waste and Sewage Group. Served to maj. USAF, 1941-45. Recipient award of merit, award of spl. recognition Nat. Assn. Metal Finishers. Mem. Ill. State Bar Assn., Chgo. Bar Assn. IIT Chgo.-Kent Coll. Law Alumni Assn. (past pres.), Alpha Epsilon Pi. Lodge: B'nai B'rith. Environment, General corporate, Probate. Address: 221 N LaSalle St Chicago IL 60601

STONE, BRIAN, lawyers' foundation adminstrator; b. N.Y.C., July 26, 1937; s. Julian Bernard and Frances W. (Stone) Rosenthal; m. Betsey Beach, Dec. 28, 1960; children—Jennifer Frances, Meredith Leslie, Brian. A.B., Marietta Coll., 1960; LL.B., Duke U., 1963. Bar: Ga. 1965. Assoc., Edenfield, Heyman & Sizemore, Atlanta, 1964-66; dir. Duke U. Atlanta Devel. Office, 1966-70; ptnr. Stone and Pennington, Atlanta, 1970-79; exec. dir. Atlanta Vol. Lawyers Found., 1979—. Mem. adv. bd. Atlanta Legal Aid Soc.; nat. bd. dirs. Close Up Found., 1971—; trustee Leadership Atlanta, 1977-78, 79-82. Mem. ABA, State Bar Ga., Atlanta Bar Assn., Assn. Bar City N.Y., Nat. Conf. Bar Pres.'s, Lawyers Club Atlanta (pres. 1985-86). Presbyterian. Family and matrimonial, Legal services and aid. Home: 900 W Wesley Rd NW Atlanta GA 30327 Office: 606 The Equitable Bldg Atlanta GA 30303

STONE, DENNIS J., law librarian, professor; b. Sacramento, May 25, 1948; s. Edward F. and Irene V. (Johnson) S.; m. Judith Stone; children: Monica, Marjorie, Jonathan, Emily. BA, U. Calif., Berkeley, 1970, MLS, 1971; JD, U. of Pacific, 1977. Bar: Calif. 1977. Asst. law librarian McGeorge Sch. of Law, Sacramento, 1974-77, lectr., asst. law librarian, 1977-79; law librarian, asst. prof. Gonzaga Sch. of Law, Spokane, 1979-83; law librarian, assoc. prof. law U. Conn. Sch. of Law Library, Hartford, 1983—. Founder Can.-Am. Law Jour., 1983; contbr. articles to profl. jours. Mem. Am. Assn. Law Libraries (exec. bd. 1983—), New Eng. Law Library Consortium (bd. dirs. 1983—, pres. 1986—), Law Librarians of New Eng., So. New Eng. Law Libraries, Am. Assn. Law Libraries (spl. interest sect.). Admiralty, Librarianship, Computer. Office: U Conn Sch Law Library 120 Sherman Hartford CT 06105-2289

STONE, EDWARD HERMAN, lawyer; b. July 20, 1939; s. Sidney and Ruth S.; m. Pamela G. Gray; children: Andrew, Matthew. BS in Acctg., U. Ill., 1961; JD, John Marshall Law Sch., 1967. Bar: Ill. 1967, Calif. 1970. With IRS, 1963-71; assoc. Eilers, Baranger, Myers & Smith, 1971-72; sole practice, Newport Beach, Calif., 1972-84; mem. Davis, Samuelson, Goldberg & Blakely (formerly Cohen Stokke & Davis), Santa Ana, Calif., 1984-87; instr. IRS, 1968-69; del. State Bar Conf., 1978-86, chmn. probate legis., 1979, 83-86; instr. income and estate taxes Western States U. Sch. Law, 1971-72. Bd. dirs. Eastbluff Homeowners Community Assn., Newport Beach, 1980-82, pres., 1981-82; pres. Jewish Family Services Orange County, 1975; v.p., bd. dirs. Orange County Jewish Community found., 1985—; founder, officer community Found. United Jewish Fedn. of Orange County. Recipient Outstanding award IRS, 1970. Mem. Orange County Bar Assn. (vice chmn. estate planning probate and trust law sect. 1976-77, chmn. sect. 1977-78, instr. Probate Clinic 1980, speaker in substantive law; dir. 1977-82; chmn. Profl. Ednl. Council 1980-82), ABA, Los Angeles Bar Assn., Phi Alpha Delta (pres. alumni chpt. 1975-76). Successful Estate Planning Ideas and Methods Service; contbr. articles to jour. ABA Young Atty.'s Sect. on Estate Taxes. Probate, General corporate, Estate planning.

STONE, FREDDIE RAY JOSH, lawyer; b. Staunton, Va., Jan. 1, 1955; s. Freddie Ray and Gladys Elizabeth (Wampler) S.; m. Wanda Lee Higgins, Aug. 12, 1972 (div. Feb. 1979); 1 child, Stephanie. BS in Commerce, U. Va., 1977, JD, 1980. Bar: Va., Ga., U.S. Dist. Ct. (no. and so. dists.) Ga., U.S. Ct. Appeals (5th, 10th and 11th cirs.). Assoc. Stokes & Shapiro, Atlanta, 1980-82, King & Spalding, Atlanta, 1982—. Arbitrator Fulton County Civil Arbitration Program, Atlanta, 1986—. Mem. ABA, Ga. Bar Assn., Va. Bar Assn., Va. Soc. CPA's, Am. Arbitration Assn. (arbitrator 1986—). Club: Atlanta Renegades Rugby Football (treas. 1983-85, capt. 1983-84). Federal civil litigation, Construction, Real property. Home: 3558Y Ashford-Dunwoody Rd Atlanta GA 31219 Office: King & Spalding 2500 Trust Co Tower Atlanta GA 30303

STONE, GEOFFREY R., legal educator, lawyer; b. 1946. B.A., U. Pa., 1968; J.D., U. Chgo., 1971. Bar: N.Y. 1972. Law clk. to judge U.S. Ct. Appeals (D.C. cir.), 1971-72; law clk. to Hon. William J. Brennan, Jr., U.S. Supreme Ct., 1972-73; asst. prof. U. Chgo., 1973-77, assoc. prof., 1977-79, prof., 1979-84, Harry Kalven Jr. prof., 1984—; dean Law Sch., 1987—. Bd. dirs. Ill. div. ACLU, 1978-84. Mem. Chgo. Council Lawyers (bd. govs. 1976-77), Order of Coif. Former editor-in-chief U. Chgo. Law Rev. Legal education. Office: U Chgo Law Sch 1111 E 60th St Chicago IL 60637

STONE, HENRY, lawyer; b. N.Y.C., Feb. 8, 1908; s. Joshua and Mathilda (Michaelson) S.; m. Babette Rosmond, Apr. 2, 1944; children: James Martin, Eugene Robert. BA, U. Pa., 1929; LLB, Columbia U., 1932. Served as cpl. U.S. Army, 1940-42. Mem. Bar Assn. of City of N.Y. Club: Williams. Family and matrimonial, Probate. Home: 245 E 40th 6E New York NY 10016 Office: 22 E 40th St New York NY 10016

STONE, HOWARD LAWRENCE, lawyer; b. Chgo., Sept. 16, 1941; s. Jerome Richard Stone and Ceale (Perlik) Stone Tandet; m. Susan L. Saltzman, June 2, 1963; children—Lauren, David. Student U. Ill.-Chgo., 1960-61, U. Ill., Champaign, 1961; B.S.B.A., Roosevelt U., 1963; J.D., DePaul U., 1972. Bar: Ill. 1972, U.S. Dist. Ct. (no. dist.) Ill. 1972, U.S. Tax Ct. 1972, U.S. Supreme Ct. 1982; C.P.A., Ill. Agt. IRS, Chgo., 1964-72; spl. asst. U.S. atty. and chief fin. auditor and investigator No. Dist. Ill., Dept. Justice, Chgo., 1972-76; sr. ptnr. Stone, McGuire & Benjamin, Chgo., 1976—; lectr. in taxation. Author: Defending the Federal Tax Case: What To Do When the IRS Steps In, 1978; Client Tax Fraud—A Practical Guide to Protecting Your Rights, 1984. Co-editor, co-author: Handling Criminal Tax Cases: A Lawyers Guide, 1982; co-author: Federal Civil Tax Law, 1982; co-author: Negotiating to Win, 1985. Campaigner lawyers div. Jewish United Fund, Chgo., 1982—; com. mem., bd. dirs. Israel Bonds, Chgo., 1982—, U. Chgo.; chmn. U. Ill. Found. Geriatric Research Fund, 1984; bd. dirs. Gastro Intestinal Research Found., Chgo., 1978—. Mem. Chgo. Bar Assn., Ill. State Bar Assn., Fed. Bar Assn., ABA, Decalogue Soc. Lawyers, Am. Inst. C.P.A.s, Ill. C.P.A. Found., Am. Assn. Atty.-C.P.A.s, Ill. C.P.A. Soc. (resident lectr. in tax fraud 1976-84, chmn. Investment Advisers Act task force 1983-84). Jewish. Lodges: B'nai B'rith, Shriners. Criminal, Personal income taxation, Health. Office: Stone McGuire & Benjamin 55 E Monroe Suite 3740 Chicago IL 60603

STONE, HUGH WILLIAM, lawyer; b. Atlanta, Sept. 27, 1934; s. Noah John and Alma Louise (Leathers) S.; m. Rebecca Evans, Oct. 1, 1966; children: Hugh William Jr., Elizabeth Louise. AB, North Ga. Coll., 1955; LLB, Emory U., 1960. Bar: Ga. 1960, U.S. dist. Ct. (no. dist.) Ga. 1960, U.S. Ct. Appeals (5th and 11th cirs.) 1960. Ptnr. Stone & Stone, Atlanta, 1961-73; assoc. Liston, Van Norte, Welch & Stone, Atlanta, 1973-75; ptnr. Woodside & Stone, Blairsville, Ga., 1975-77; sole practice Blairsville, 1977-81; ptnr. Stone & Williams, Blairsville, 1981—. Editor-in-chief Emory U. Law Rev., 1960. Mem., vice mayor Blairsville City Council, 1976-79; bd. dirs. Union County Hist. Soc., Blairsville, 1978. Served with USAR, 1955-77. Mem. ABA, Ga. State Bar Assn., Mountain Jud. Cir. Bar Assn., Blairsville/Union County C. of C. (sec., bd. dirs. 1981-82), Res. Officer's Assn. (jr. v.p. dept. Ga. 1975). Democrat. Lodge: Kiwanis (v.p. Blairsville 1980). Local government, Probate, Real property. Home: Bucksnort Rd PO Box 421 Blairsville GA 30512 Office: Stone & Williams PO Box 639 Blairsville GA 30512

STONE, JAMES DORSEY, lawyer; b. Balt., June 15, 1940; s. Luke Dorsey and Florence (Gibson) S.; m. Anne Luetkemeyer, July 16, 1970; children: John L., James D. BS, U. Pa., 1962; JD, U. Md., 1966. Bar: Md.; 1966, U.S. Dist. Ct. Md., 1966. Law clk. Supreme Bench Baltimore City, 1964-65; atty. 1st Nat. Bank Md., 1969-72; assoc. White, Mindel, Clarke & Hill, Towson, 1972-75, ptnr., 1975—; dir., sec. Evapco, Inc., 1976—; dir. Internat. Tech. Equipment, Inc. Trustee St. Marys Coll. Md. Found., 1979—, v.p., 1985—; bd. dirs. Family and Children's Soc., 1982—, Valleys Planning Council, 1986—. Served with U.S. Army, 1966-69. Mem. Md. Bar Assn., ABA, Balt. Estate Planning Council, Md. Hist. Soc. Clubs: University, Elkridge, Bachelors Cotillion. Probate, Estate taxation. Home: 825 Hillside Rd Brooklandville MD 21022 Office: 29 W Susquehanna Ave Suite 600 Towson MD 21204

STONE, JEAN, lawyer; b. Los Angeles, Nov. 10, 1934; d. Robert Guy and Mary (Temple) Sherman; m. James Bernard Stone, Aug. 5, 1959 (dec. May 1987); children: Aeleen, Todd, Craig, Patti. Student, U. So. Calif., 1952-54; JD cum laude, U. San Fernando, 1977. Bar: Calif. 1977, U.S. Dist. Ct. (cen. dist.) Calif. 1977. Assoc. Gage & Cooper, Beverly Hills, Calif., 1977-80; sr. litigation assoc. Hillsinger & Costanzo, Los Angeles, 1980-87, ptnr., 1987—. Bd. editors U. San Fernando Law Rev., 1976-77. Mem. Am. Acad. Hosp. Attys., Am. Soc. Law and Medicine, Assn. So. Calif. Def. Counsel, Los Angeles County Bar Assn. Republican. Episcopalian. State civil litigation, Health, Personal injury. Home: 15049 Florentine Sylmar CA 91342 Office: Hillsinger & Costanzo 3055 Wilshire Blvd Los Angeles CA 90010

STONE, JED, lawyer; b. Chgo., Sept. 30, 1949; s. William P. and Bernice (Birenhotz) S.; m. Terri Deimler, Dec. 19, 1978; children—Meghan Elizabeth, Allison Leigh, Benjamin William. B.A. with honors, Lake Forest Coll., 1971; J.D. Chgo.-Kent U. 1975. Bar: Ill. 1976, Wis. 1984, U.S. Dist. Ct. (no. dist.) Ill. 1976, U.S. Ct. Appeals (7th cir.) 1983, U.S. Ct. Appeals (5th cir.) 1985, U.S. Ct. Appeals (11th cir.) 1986, U.S. Supreme Ct. 1984. Cert. Criminal Trial Adv.; diplomate Nat. Bd. Trial Advocacy, 1984. Staff atty. Lawyer's Com. Civil Rights Under Law and Land of Lincoln Legal Aid, Cairo, Ill., 1975; sr. staff atty. Prairie State Legal Services, Waukegan, Ill., 1975-77; pres. The Law Offices of Jed Stone, Ltd., Waukegan. Life mem. NAACP, Urban League; mem. Ill. Coalition Against the Death Penalty; pres., bd. dirs. Prairie State Legal Services, Inc., 1982-84; bd. dirs., Lake County Urban League, Waukegan, 1981—; bd. mem. alumni bd. gov.'s Lake Forest College, Ill., 1981—, treas., bd. dirs. Ill. Attys. for Criminal Justice. Mem. Assn. Trial Lawyers Am., Nat. Assn. Criminal Def. Lawyers (various coms.), Ill. Attys. Criminal Justice (bd. dirs., treas. 1986—), Lake County Bar Assn. (chmn. criminal law sect. 1983-86). Democrat. Jewish. Criminal. Office: 415 Washington St Suite 206 Waukegan IL 60085

STONE, KATHLEEN GALE, criminal justice educator, researcher, consultant; b. Birmingham, Eng., May 9, 1943; came to U.S., 1970; d. Eric Harold and Gertrude Alice (Taylor) Johnson; m. Christopher Stephen Lange, July 11, 1964 (div. Nov. 1971); 1 child, Tamara Alice Merry; m. Sheldon Leslie Stone, Nov. 24, 1971. children—Rosalinda Dawn, Adam Douglas. B.A. in Econs. 1st class with honors, U. Manchester (Eng.), 1965, M.A. in Econs. with distinction, 1967, Ph.D., 1976. Research asst. U. Manchester, 1969-70; instr. anthropology SUNY,-Geneseo, 1970-72; vis. lectr. George Peabody Coll., 1974-76; program coordinator women's studies Vanderbilt U., 1976-77; asst. prof. sociology Tenn. State U., 1979; asst. prof. Wells Coll., Aurora, N.Y., 1980-82; lectr. sociology Elmira Coll., N.Y., 1982—, asst. prof. criminal justice, 1982—. Vol., Tompkins County Info. and Referral, N.Y., 1982-83. Mem. Am. Anthrop. Assn., S.E. Women's Studies Assns. (conf. organizer), Acad. Criminal Justice Scis. Quaker. Legal education, Family and matrimonial, General practice. Home: 1345 Slaterville Rd Ithaca NY 14850 Office: Elmira Coll Dept Criminal Justice Elmira NY 14901

STONE, LAURA WILLIAMS, lawyer; b. Springville, N.Y., July 15, 1957; d. Lee C. and Lois (Botsford) W.; m. Harlan S. Stone, May 27, 1984. BA with distinction, George Washington U., 1979, JD with honors, 1982. Bar: Pa. 1982, U.S. Dist. Ct. (we. dist.) Pa. 1982. Assoc. Eckert, Seamans, Cherin & Mellott, Pitts., 1982-84, Rose, Schmidt, Chapman, Duff & Hasley, Pitts., 1984—; counsel Equibank/Equimark Corp., Pitts., 1986—. Mem. ABA, Pa. Bar Assn., Allegheny Bar Assn., Phi Beta Kappa. Securities, General corporate, Banking. Office: Rose Schmidt Chapman Duff & Hasley 900 Oliver Bldg Pittsburgh PA 15222

STONE, MICHAEL K., lawyer; b. Houston, Apr. 26, 1954; s. Donald J. and Norma (Karchmer) S.; m. Elizabeth S. Scarf; children: Deborah L., Sarah S. BA, Yale U., 1976, JD, 1979. Bar: Tex. 1979, U.S. Dist. Ct. (no. dist.) Tex. 1980, U.S. Tax Ct. 1982. Law clk. to presiding judge U.S. Dist. Ct. (so. dist.) N.Y., N.Y.C., 1979-80; assoc. Jenkens & Gilchrist, Dallas, 1980-84, ptnr., 1984—. Advisor Dallas Theater Ctr., 1985—; vol. Goals for Dallas, 1984-85; bd. dirs. Tex. Accts. and Lawyers for Arts, Houston, 1984—, Anti-Defamation League, Dallas, 1984—. Mem. ABA (subcom. chmn. tax sect. 1985—), Tex. Bar Assn. (contbg. author newsletter tax sect. 1985—), Dallas Bar Assn. (council tax sect. 1985—). Corporate taxation, Personal income taxation, Municipal bonds. Office: Jenkens & Gilchrist 1445 Ross Ave 3200 Allied Bank Tower Dallas TX 75202

STONE, PAULA LENORE, lawyer; b. N.Y.C., Nov. 1, 1942; s. Milton H. and Pauline (Smith) Stone; m. Richard J. Chodoff, July 29, 1969 (dec. 1983). AB in Biology, Muhlenberg Coll., 1961; student Lehigh U., 1960, Jefferson Med. Sch., 1961-63; JD, Temple U., 1981. Bar: Pa. 1982. Med. cons. to trial lawyers, Bala Cynwyd, Pa., 1963-85, N.Y., 1985—; sole practice, Bala Cynwyd, 1982-85, N.Y., 1985—; of counsel firm Turrey Kepler, Norristown, Pa., 1985—. Editor Psychopharmacology Abstracts, Cancer Chemotherapy Abstracts, 1961-64; author: (with R. J. Chodoff) Doctor for the Prosecution, 1983. Mem. Assn. Trial Lawyers Am., Coll. Physicians, Phila., ABA, N.Y. Acad. Scis. (adv. com.), Pa. Bar Assn., ACLU. Democrat. Jewish. Personal injury, Federal civil litigation, State civil litigation. Address: Suite 8B 870 United Nations Plaza New York NY 10017

STONE, RALPH KENNY, lawyer; b. Bainbridge, Ga., Aug. 7, 1952; s. Ralph Patrick and Joyce (Mitchell) S.; m. Julie Ann Waldren, Aug. 24, 1974; children—Laura Lee, Rebecca. B.B.A. magna cum laude, U. Ga., 1974, J.D. cum laude, 1977. Bar: Ga. 1977, U.S. Dist. Ct. (so. dist.) Ga. 1977, U.S. Supreme Ct. 1980, U.S. Ct. Appeals (11th cir.) 1981. Staff acct. Price Waterhouse & Co., Columbia, S.C., 1974; assoc. Calhoun & Donaldson, Savannah, Ga., 1977; ptnr. Franklin & Stone, Statesboro, Ga., 1977—; instr. taxation Ga. So. Coll., Statesboro, 1979-80. Sect. chmn. United Way Bulloch County, 1982, div. chmn., 1983, vice chmn. campaign, 1984, v.p., 1985-86; charter pres. Leadership Bulloch, Inc., 1984; chmn. Bulloch County Democratic Com., 1984—, Bulloch 2000 Com. 1986—; sec. Ga. Assn. Dem. County Chairs, 1985; dist. chmn. Boy Scouts Am., 1985; pres. Forward Bulloch Inc., 1986; participant Leadership Ga., 1986—. Mem. ABA, State Bar Ga., Bulloch County Bar Assn. (pres. 1982-83), Statesboro-Bulloch County C. of C. (participant Tomorrow's Leaders program 1978, bd. dirs. 1982-83, chmn. govtl. affairs com. 1982-83, v.p. 1984-85, pres. 1986, chmn. bd. dirs. 1987), Phi Kappa Phi, Beta Alpha Psi. Baptist. Club: Optimist (bd. dirs. Statesboro 1978-79, 83-84, pres. 1980-81, dist. lt. gov. 1981-82, dist. youth activities and community service chmn. 1983-84). Bankruptcy, State civil litigation, General practice. Home: PO Box 2072 Statesboro GA 30458 Office: Franklin & Stone PO Box 964 Statesboro GA 30458

STONE, RICHARD B., legal educator; b. 1943. A.B., Harvard U., 1963, LL.B., 1967. Bar: La. 1967. Assoc. Covington & Burling, Washington, 1967-69; asst. to solicitor gen. Office Solicitor Gen., Dept. Justice, Washington, 1969-73; now prof. law Columbia U., N.Y.C. Legal education. Office: Columbia U Sch Law 435 W 116th St New York NY 10027 * *

STONE, RICHARD JAMES, lawyer; b. Chgo., Apr. 30, 1945; s. Milton M. and Ruth Jean (Manaster) S.; m. Lee Lawrence, Sept. 1, 1979; children—Robert Allyn, Katherine Jenney, Grant Lawrence. B.A. in Econs., U. Chgo., 1967; J.D., UCLA, 1970. Bar: Calif. 1971. Assoc., O'Melveny & Myers, Los Angeles, 1971-77; dep. asst. gen. counsel U.S. Dept. Def., Washington, 1978-79; asst. to sec. U.S. Dept. Energy, Washington, 1979-80; counsel Sidley & Austin, Los Angeles, 1981, ptnr., 1982—; del. Calif. State Bar Conf. of Dels., 1982—. Mem. Pub. Sector Task Force, Calif. State Senate Select Com. on Long Range Policy Planning, 1985-86, U.S. del. Micronesian Polit. Status Negotiations, 1978-79; mem. adv. panel Council Energy Resource Tribes, 1981—; elder Presbyterian Ch. Recipient Amos Alonzo Stagg medal and Howell Murray Alumni medal U. Chgo., 1967; honoree Nat. Conf. Black Mayors, 1980; recipient spl. citation for outstanding performance Sec. Dept. Energy, 1981. Mem. ABA, Calif. Bar Assn., Los Angeles County Bar Assn. (trustee 1986—), Assn. Bus. Trial Lawyers, Phi Gamma Delta. Editor-in-chief UCLA Law Rev., 1970. Federal civil litigation, State civil litigation, Antitrust. Office: 2049 Century Park E 35th Floor Los Angeles CA 90067

STONE, SAMUEL SPENCER, lawyer, accountant; b. Parkersburg, W.Va., Oct. 10, 1947; s. James Marvin and Juanita (Tracewell) S.; m. Jerilyn Van Beneden, May 24, 1975; children: Morgan Rebecca, Joshua Samuel, Lara MacKenzie. BS, W.Va. U., 1969, JD, 1976. Bar: W.Va. 1976, U.S. Dist. Ct. (no. dist.) W.Va. 1976, U.S. Tax Ct. 1981; CLU. Staff acct. Arthur Andersen & Co., Houston, 1969-71; sole practice Morgantown, W.Va., 1976—; speaker various orgns. Contbr. articles to profl. jours. Advisor Council Internat. Programs, Morgantown, 1984, Monongalia County Youth Services Ctr., Morgantown, 1984. Served with U.S. Army, 1969-71. Mem. ABA, W.Va. State Bar Assn. (speaker), W.Va. Trial Lawyers Assn., Monongalia County Bar Assn., Am. Inst. CPA's, W.Va. Soc. CPA's, North Cen. Chpt. W.Va. Soc. CPA's (speaker), Am. Soc. Cert. Life Underwriter, Internat. Assn. for Fin. Planning. Democrat. Presbyterian. Lodge: Rotary. General corporate, Estate planning, Arbitration. Office: 221 Willey St Morgantown WV 26505

STONE, SAUL, lawyer; b. New Orleans, Dec. 15, 1906; s. Lazard David and Laura (Singer) S.; m. Sara Berenson, Apr. 7, 1938; children—David L., Richard B., Harvey M., Carol R. Stone Wright. LL.B., Tulane U., 1929. Bar: La. 1929, U.S. Ct. Appeals (5th cir.) 1930, U.S. Supreme Ct. 1950. Asst. U.S. atty., Eastern Dist. La., 1933-37; founder, ptnr. Wisdom and Stone and successor firm, Stone, Pigman, Walther, Wittmann and Hutchinson, New Orleans, 1967—. Mem. New Orleans Bar Assn., La. Bar Assn., ABA, Am. Law Inst. Real property, Corporate taxation, Probate. Home: 2503 Jefferson Ave New Orleans LA 70115

STONE, SHELDON, lawyer; b. Jersey City, June 16, 1947; s. Leonard and Claire (Orlean) S.; m. Esther Curland, Dec. 19, 1970; children: Lesley-Anne, Jaime. BA, Rutgers U., 1969; JD, Seton Hall U., 1972. Bar: N.J. 1972, U.S. Dist. Ct. N.J. 1972, N.Y. 1980. Ptnr. Stone & Stone, Teaneck, N.J., 1972—; tchr. New Milford (N.J.) Bd. Edn., 1974-76; investigator Atty. Ethics Com., Bergen County, N.J., 1984; settlement referee Superior Ct., Bergen County, 1984—; lectr. Eastern Bergen Multiple Listing System, Bergen County, periodically. Mem. ABA, N.J. Bar Assn., Bergen County Bar Assn., Major League Baseball Players Assn. (approved player rep.), Nat. Collegiate Athletic Assn. (approved player rep.). Lodge: Lions (v.p.). Real property, General corporate, Contracts commercial. Home: 135 Birchwood Rd Old Tappan NJ 07675 Office: Stone & Stone 517 Cedar Lane Teaneck NJ 07666

STONE, STEVEN DAVID, lawyer, consultant; b. N.Y.C., July 6, 1952; s. Harris Bobby and Ray (Masin) S.; m. Lynn Jason, May 4, 1986. AB, Princeton U., 1974; JD, U. Richmond, 1977. Bar: Va. 1977, U.S. Dist. Ct. (ea. dist.) Va. 1977, U.S. Ct. Appeals (4th cir.) 1977. Legis. asst. Va. Senate, Richmond, 1975-76; assoc. McClandish, Lillard, Church & Best, Fairfax, Va., 1977-79; assoc. Fried, Fried & Klewans, Springfield, Va., 1980-83, ptnr., 1983-86; sole practice Springfield and Alexandria, Va., 1986—; legal counsel Va. Assn. Ind. Spa Owners, Springfield, 1984—. Chmn. Lee Dist. Dem. Com., Fairfax County, 1981-85; sec., treas. Lee Dist. Assn. Civic Orgns., 1981—, Northern Va. Assn. Retarded Citizens; sec. Va. Bd. Rights of Disabled, Richmond, 1985—; mem. com. of 100, Fairfax County, 1979—, found. bd. Northern Va. Community Coll., adv. bd. Sch. Contemporary Edn., Parent-Ednl. Advocacy Tng. Ctr., pub. affairs com. Am.-Israel Orgn., gov.'s overall adv. com. on Needs of Handicapped Persons, 1981-85, Nat. Orgn. of Legal Problems in Edn. William DuBose Sheldon Meml. scholar. Mem. ABA, Assn. Trial Lawyers Am., Va. Bar Assn., Va. Trial Lawyers Assn., Fairfax Bar Assn. (lobbyist), Alexandria Bar Assn., Fairfax County C. of C. (chmn. legis. affairs com. 1980-81), Lee-Mt. Vernon C. of C. Democrat. Jewish. Club: Princeton (Washington). State civil litigation, Condemnation, Legislative. Office: 114 N Columbus St PO Box 1417-A45 Alexandria VA 22313

STONE, VICTOR J., b. Chgo., Mar. 11, 1921; s. Maurice Albert and Ida (Baskin) S.; m. Susan Abby Cane, July 14, 1951; children—Mary Jessica, Jennifer Abby, Andrew Hugh William. A.B., Oberlin Coll., 1942; J.D., Columbia U., 1948; LL.D. hon., Oberlin Coll., 1983. Bar: N.Y. 1949, Ill. 1950. Assoc. Columbia U., N.Y.C., 1948-49; assoc. Sonnenschein, Chgo., 1949-53; research assoc. U. Chgo., 1953-55; asst. prof. law U. Ill., Champaign, 1955-57, assoc. prof. law, 1957-59, prof. law, 1959—, assoc. v.p. acad. affairs, 1975-78; mem. jud. adv. council State Ill., 1959-61; mem. com. jury instructions Ill. Supreme Ct., 1963-79, reporter, 1973-79; mem. Ill. State Appellate Defender Commn., 1973-83, vice chmn., 1973-77, 79-83. Trustee Oberlin Coll., 1982—; trustee AAUP Found., 1983—. Served as lt. USNR, 1942-46. Ford Found. fellow, 1962-63. Mem. ABA, Ill. Bar Assn. (chmn. individual rights and responsibilities 1971-72, mem. council civil practice and procedure 1978-82), Chgo. Bar Assn., Am. Judicature Soc., AAUP (gen. counsel 1978-80, pres. 1982-84, pres. Ill. conf. 1968-70, pres. Ill. chpt. 1964-65, mem. council 1982—), ACLU (bd. dirs. Ill. div. 1986—). Co-editor: Ill. Pattern Jury Instructions, 1965, 71, 77; Civil Liberties and Civil Rights, 1977. Federal civil litigation, State civil litigation, Legal education. Office: Coll Law U Ill 504 E Pennsylvania St Champaign IL 61820

STONEKING, GARY EDWIN, lawyer; b. Chgo., Mar. 21, 1949; s. Harold Edwin and Gwendolyn (Peterson) S.; m. Diane Marie Smith, June 27, 1970; children: Henry, Harold, Patrick, Margaret. BA, U. Minn., 1977, JD, 1977. Bar: Minn. 1977, U.S. Dist. Ct. Minn. 1977, U.S. Ct. Appeals (8th cir.) 1977, U.S. Supreme Ct. 1981. Ptnr. Hvass, Weisman & King, Mpls., 1977—, also bd. dirs. Author: Minnesota Pleading and Practice Forms: Personal Injury, 1981. Served to sgt. USMC, 1966-70, Vietnam. Mem. ABA, Minn. Bar Assn., Assn. Trial Lawyers Am., Minn. Trial Lawyers Assn., Hennepin County Bar Assn. Roman Catholic. Club: Mpls. Athletic. Avocation: flying. Personal injury. Home: 18 Barton Ave SE Minneapolis MN 55414 Office: Hvass Weisman & King 100 S 5th St Suite 2100 Minneapolis MN 55402

STOPFORD, JEFFREY MORGAN, lawyer; b. Great Barrington, Mass., July 26, 1944; s. Robert M. and Ann (Woodhall) S.; m. Jane M. Lloyd, Mar. 16, 1968; 1 child, Justin M. BA, Harvard Coll., 1966; LLB, U. Pa., 1969. Bar: Pa. 1970, U.S. Dist. Ct. Pa. 1970, U.S. Ct. Appeals (3d cir.) 1970. Law clk. to judge U.S. Ct. Appeals (3d cir.), Phila., 1969-70; assoc. Beasley, Hewson, Casey & Stopford, Phila., 1970-78; ptnr. Litvin, Blumberg, Matusow & Young, Phila., 1979-82; sole practice Media, Pa., 1983—. Agt. class 1969 U. Pa. Law Sch., Phila., 1984—; tutor Del. County Literacy Council, Chester, Pa., 1986—. Fellow Nat. Bd. Trial Advocacy; mem. Assn. Trial Lawyers Am., Pa. Bar Assn., Crime Prevention Assn. (chmn. exec. com. 1975-77, 86—), Order of Coif. Avocations: gardening, golf, white water paddling. Personal injury. Office: 341 W Baltimore Ave Media PA 19063

STOPHER, ROBERT ESTES, lawyer; b. Louisville, Oct. 16, 1952; s. Joseph Earley and Marie (Estes) S.; m. Nancy Judson Stanger, Sept. 3, 1977; children: James Alexander, David Wesley. BA, Davidson Coll., 1974; JD, U. Va., 1977. Bar: Ky. 1977, U.S. Dist. Ct. (we. dist.) Ky. 1978, U.S. Ct. Appeals (6th cir.) 1982, U.S. Dist. Ct. (ea. dist.) Ky. 1984. Assoc. Boehl, Stopher, Graves & Deindoerfer, Louisville, 1977-79, ptnr., 1979—. Mem. Louisville Bar Assn. (bench and bar coms. 1986), Louisville Bar Found. (bd. dirs. 1985—). State civil litigation, Insurance, Federal civil litigation. Home: 2100 Twin Hill Rd Louisville KY 40207 Office: Boehl Stopher Graves et al One Riverfront Plaza Suite 2300 Louisville KY 40202

STORCK, ROBERT EMIL, lawyer; b. Slinger, Wis., June 27, 1925; s. Raymond Charles and Viona Elizabeth (Arndt) S.; m. Caroline Elizabeth Feutz, Aug. 26, 1950; children: Ellen, John, Carol. BS, U. Wis., 1949, LLB, 1952. Bar: Wis. 1952. Ptnr. Thiel, Allan & Storck, Mayville, Wis., 1952-68, Allan & Storck, Mayville, 1968-75; sole practice Mayville, 1975—; chmn. bd. Mayville Savs. & Loan, Mayville, 1970—. Served with U.S. Army, 1945-46. Republican. Methodist. Lodge: Rotary (local pres.). Avocations: sailing, snorkeling, swimming, golf. State civil litigation, Personal injury, Probate. Office: 116 S Main St Mayville WI 53050

STORETTE, RONALD FRANK, lawyer; b. N.Y.C., June 20, 1943; m. Monique Storette; 1 child, Ronald. BA summa cum laude, U. Va., 1966; JD, Harvard U., 1969; Diploma of Internat. Law, Stockholm Faculty of Law, 1970. Bar: D.C. 1973, U.S. Ct. Appeals (D.C. cir.) 1976, U.S. Supreme Ct. 1976, U.S. Dist. Ct. (so. and ea. dists.) N.Y. 1977, U.S. Dist. Ct. D.C. 1977, U.S. Ct. Appeals (2d cir.) 1978, U.S. Ct. Internat. Trade. 1978. Lectr. law Stockholm Faculty of Law, 1970-71; assoc. Jean-Pierre De Bandt, Brussels, 1971-73; chief legal counsel Textron Atlantic S.A., Brussels, 1973-75; assoc. Donovan, Leisure, Newton & Irvine, N.Y.C., 1975-79; ptnr. Fragomen, Del Rey & Bernsen, P.C., N.Y.C., 1979—. Author: The Politics of Integrated Social Investment; An American Study of the Swedish LAMCO Project in Liberia, 1971, The Administration of Equality; An American Study of Sweden's Bilateral Development Aid, 1972; also articles. Cassal Found. fellow U. Stockholm, Sweden, 1969. Mem. ABA, N.Y. State Bar Assn., Assn. of Bar of City of N.Y., Am. Immigration Lawyers Assn., Phi Beta Kappa. Immigration and naturalization, Consular law. Office: Fragomen Del Rey & Bernsen PC 515 Madison Ave New York NY 10022

STOREY, SCOTT ALFRED, lawyer; b. Ann Arbor, Mich., Jan. 14, 1954; s. Alfred W. and Margaret M. (Kearns) S.; m. Sandra M. Wonnacott, July 31, 1976; children: Ryan, Matthew. B in Gen. Studies, U. Mich., 1976; JD, Washington and Lee U., 1979. Bar: Mich. 1979, U.S. Dist. Ct. (ea. and we. dists.) Mich. 1980, U.S. Supreme Ct. 1986. Assoc. Foster, Swift, Collins & Coey, Lansing, Mich., 1979—. Chmn. Capital Area Substance Abuse Council, Ingham County, Mich., 1980—; mem. Lansing Civic Ctr. Bd., 1984—. Methodist. Avocations: woodworking, photography, sports. Oil and gas leasing, Insurance, Personal injury. Home: 2500 Provincial House Dr Lansing MI 48910 Office: Foster Swift Collins & Coey 313 S Washington Sq Lansing MI 48933

STORMS, CLIFFORD BEEKMAN, lawyer; b. Mount Vernon, N.Y., July 18, 1932; s. Harold Beekman and Gene (Pertak) S.; m. Barbara H. Grave, 1955 (div. 1975); m. Valeria N. Parker, July 12, 1975; children: Catherine Storms Fischer, Clifford Beekman. B.A. magna cum laude, Amherst Coll., 1954; LL.B., Yale U., 1957. Bar: N.Y. 1957. Assoc. atty. firm Breed, Abbott & Morgan, N.Y.C., 1957-64; with CPC Internat., Inc., Englewood Cliffs, N.J., 1964—; v.p. legal affairs CPC Internat., Inc., 1973-75, v.p., gen. counsel, 1975—. Trustee Food and Drug Law Inst., 1976—; mem. adv. com. Parker Sch. Fgn. and Comparative Law, Columbia U. Mem. ABA (com. on corp. law depts.), N.Y. State Bar Assn., Assn. Bar City N.Y. (sec., com. on corp. law depts. 1979-81), Assn. Gen. Counsel, Phi Beta Kappa. Clubs: Indian Harbor Yacht, Yale (N.Y.C.); Milbrook, Board Room. General corporate, Antitrust, Private international. Home: 11 Serenity Ln Cos Cob CT 06807 Office: CPC Internat Inc Internat Plaza Englewood Cliffs NJ 07632

STORROW, CHARLES FISKE, lawyer; b. Houston, Mar. 14, 1957; S. Charles Henry Fiske and Margaret (Hubbard) S.; m. Melissa Cary, Aug. 22, 1981. BA, U. Maine, 1979; JD, Vt. Law Sch., 1982. Bar: Vt. 1982, U.S. Dist. Ct. Vt. 1983. Law clk. to sr. judge U.S. Ct. Appeals (2d cir.), N.Y.C., 1982-83; assoc. Paul, Frank & Collins, Inc., Burlington, Vt., 1983—. Mem. ABA, Vt. Bar Assn., Chittenden County Bar Assn., Am. Jurisprudence Soc. Mem. Unitarian Ch. Avocation: fly fishing. Public utilities, Environment, State civil litigation. Office: Paul Frank & Collins 1 Church St Burlington VT 05401

STORY, CLEMENT, III, lawyer; b. New Orleans, May 31, 1939; s. Clement Jr. Story and Lois (Jacomet) deLatour; m. Merrilyn Checkan, Aug. 25, 1968; children: Laura Marie, Heather Jean. BS, Southeastern La. U., 1961; JD, Loyola U., New Orleans, 1970. Bar: La., U.S. Dist. Ct. (ea., we. and mid. dists.) La., U.S. Ct. Appeals (5th and 11th cirs.), U.S. Supreme Ct., Fla. 1986. Atty. litigation div. U.S. Govt., 1966-70; asst. dist. atty. New Orleans Dist. Atty.'s Office, 1970-72; sole practice Lafayette, La., 1972—; chief disaster counsel State of La., 1969-70, rackets and fraud div. Dist. Atty.'s Office, New Orleans, 1970-72; instr. La. State Police Inst., Lafayette, 1974-77; lectr. Acadiana Tng. Police Inst., Lafayette, 1975-80. Mem. Assn. Trial Lawyers Am., La. Trial Lawyers Assn., SAR. Republican. Roman Catholic. Avocations: snow skiing, yachting. Admiralty, Oil and gas leasing, Insurance. Home: 1508 Sturbridge Ct Dunedin FL 33528-1508 Office: 115 W Main St Lafayette LA 70502-0115

STORY, JOHN HAROLD, lawyer, accountant; b. Utica, N.Y., June 1, 1950; s. John Harold and Aniela (Szafranski) S. AB, Hamilton Coll., 1972; JD, Cornell U., 1975, postgrad., 1973-75. Bar: N.Y. 1976, U.S. Tax Ct. 1978. Tax acct. Arthur Andersen & Co., Rochester, N.Y., 1975-77; ptnr. Evans, Severn, Bankert & Peet, Utica, 1977—; adj. prof. tax law, acctg. Utica Coll., 1978—; adj. faculty Utica Sch. of Commerce, 1986—; adminstr. Assigned Legal Counsel, Oneida County, N.Y., 1979—, bd. dirs. Author: Pension Facts, 1986. Fundraiser United Way, Utica, 1984—; bd. dirs. Logos World U., Phoenix, 1985—. Mem. N.Y. State Bar Assn., Oneida County Bar Assn. (treas. 1978-85), N.Y. State Soc. CPA's. (pres. Utica chpt. 1986—), Nat. Assn. Accts. (treas. upstate regional council 1979-82, pres. Mohawk Valley chpt. 1981-82). Republican. National Catholic. Lodge: Rotary. Avocations: golf, reading, computers. General corporate, Pension, profit-sharing, and employee benefits, Corporate taxation. Home: RD 2 Box 55 Barneveld NY 13304 Office: Evans Severn Bankert & Peet 231 Genesse St Utica NY 13501

STOTLER, ALICEMARIE H., federal judge; b. Alhambra, Calif., May 29, 1942; d. James R. and Loretta M. Huber; m. James A. Stotler, Sept. 11, 1971. B.A., U. So. Calif., 1964, J.D., 1967. Dep., Orange County Dist. Atty.'s Office, 1967-73; mem. Stotler & Stotler, Santa Ana, Calif., 1973-76, 83-84; judge Orange County Mcpl. Ct., 1976-78, Orange County Superior Ct., 1978-83, U.S. Dist. Ct. (cen. dist.) Calif., Los Angeles, 1984—. Mem. ABA, Orange County Bar Assn., Calif. Judges Assn. Judicial administration. Office: US District Court 312 N Spring St Los Angeles CA 90012 *

STOTTER, LAWRENCE HENRY, lawyer; b. Cleve., Sept. 24, 1929; s. Oscar and Bertha (Lieb) S.; m. Ruth Rapoport, June 30, 1957; children—Daniel, Jennifer, Steven. B.B.A., Ohio State U., 1956, LL.B., 1958, J.D., 1967. Bar: Calif. 1960, U.S. Supreme Ct. 1973, U.S. Tax Ct. 1976. Individual practice law San Francisco, 1963-65, 78—; ptnr. firm Stotter, Samuels & Chamberlain, San Francisco, 1981-83; mem. faculty Nat. Judicial Coll.; mem. Calif. Family Law Adv. Commn., 1979-80. Editor in chief: Am. Bar Family Advocate mag, 1977-82; TV appearances on Phil Donahue Show, Good Morning America. Pres. Tamalpais Conservation Club, Marin County, Calif.; U.S. State Dept. del. Hague Conf. Pvt. Internat. Law, 1979-80; legal adv. White House Conf. on Families, 1980—. Served with AUS, 1950-53. Mem. Am. Bar Assn. (past chmn. family law sect.), Am. Acad. Matrimonial Lawyers (past nat. v.p.), Calif. State Bar (past chmn family law sect.). Family and matrimonial. Home: 2244 Vistazo St E Tiburon CA 94920 Office: 1735 Franklin St San Francisco CA 94109

STOUDENMIRE, WILLIAM WARD, lawyer; b. Charlotte, N.C., Apr. 8, 1944; s. Sterling and Betty Zane (Scott) S. B.A. in Polit. Sci., Furman U., 1966; J.D., U. S.C., 1970. Bar: Ala. 1970, U.S. Dist. Ct. (so. dist.) Ala. 1970, U.S. Ct. Appeals (5th cir.) 1971, U.S. Supreme Ct. 1973, U.S. Tax Ct. 1982, U.S. Ct. Appeals (11th cir.) 1982, U.S. Ct. Appeals (D.C. cir.) 1982, D.C. bar 1982. Sole practice, Mobile, Ala., 1982—; legal research asst. Select Com. on Crime, U.S. Ho. of Reps., 1969; mem. law day com. Ala. State Bar, 1975-78, chmn., 1978. Mem. Leadership Mobile Adv. Council on Govt., 1982; mem. transition adv. com. Ala. Gov.-Elect Guy Hunt, 1986, Mobile County Rep. Exec. Com., 1976—, vice chmn., 1976-81, chmn., 1979—; mem. Ala. Rep. Exec. Com., 1979-86, vice chmn., 1982— , platform com., 1976, 78; co-chmn., 1978, vice-chmn., 1985—; sec., bd. trustees Wilmer Hall Episcopal Diocese Children's Home. Served with USCGR, 1966-72. Mem. Mobile Bar Assn. (law day com. 1974-78, chmn. 1977, del. young lawyers sect. ABA conv. 1976, 77), ABA (internat. sect. human rights subcom. 1975—, chmn. 1976-79), Internat. Bar Assn., Phi Delta Phi. Contracts commercial, General corporate, Probate. Home: 212 C Nack Ln Mobile AL 36608

STOUGH, CHARLES DANIEL, lawyer; b. Mound Valley, Kans., Dec. 6, 1914; s. Charles Daniel and Narka Pauline (Ice) S.; m. Mary Juliet Shipman, Feb. 13, 1936; children—Vera Rubin, Sally Randall Stough Bartlett. A.A., Kemper Mil. Sch., 1934; A.B., U. Kans., 1936, LL.B., 1938, J.D., 1968. Bar: Kans. 1938, Ill. 1938. City atty. City of Lawrence, Kans., 1947-67, City of Eudora (Kans.), 1949-85; spl. counsel, Douglas County Kans., 1951-85; sole practice, Lawrence, 1939-82; with firm Stough & Heck, 1982—; prof. local govt. law U. Kans., 1969-70. Mem. U. Kans. Spencer Mus., 1986; mem. Kans. Ho. of Reps., 1947-55, majority leader, 1951-53, speaker of house, 1953-55. Trustee, U. Kans. Endowment Assn., Nat. Parks and Conservation Assn., Washington. Served to lt. j.g. USNR, 1943-46. Recipient Ellsworth award U. Kans., 1980; named one of Outstanding Kansans U. Kans., 1986; named to Gallary of Outstanding Kansans, 1986. Trustee Hertzler Research Found., Halstead, Kans., 1983—. Mem. ABA (chmn. Local Govt. Law Sect. 1964-67), Kans. Bar Assn. (chmn. world Peace Through Law Sect. 1970—), Nat. Inst. Mcpl. Law Officers (trustee 1964-65), City Attys. Assn. (exec. com.). Republican. Congregationalist. Clubs: Kiwanis, Masons (Lawrence); Republican Vets. of Kans. (state pres. 1959-60). Local government, Probate, Real property.

STOUP, ARTHUR HARRY, lawyer; b. Kansas City, Mo., Aug. 30, 1925; s. Isadore and Dorothy (Rankle) S.; m. Kathryn Jolliff, July 30, 1948; children—David C., Daniel P., Rebecca Ann, Deborah E. Student, Kansas City Jr. Coll., Mo. 1942-43; B.A., U. Mo., 1950; J.D., 1950. Bar: Mo. 1950, D.C. 1979. Practice law Kansas City, Mo., 1950—; mem. firm Stoup & Thompson; mem. Lawyer to Lawyer Consultation Panel-Litigation, 1976—; chmn. U.S. Merit Selection Com. for Western Dist. Mo., 1981. Chmn. com. to rev. continuing edn. U. Mo., 1978-79; trustee, pres. U. Mo.-Kansas City Law Found., 1979-82; trustee U. Kansas City, 1979—. Served with USNR, 1942-45. Recipient Alumni Achievement award U. Mo.-Kansas City Alumni Assn., 1975. Fellow Internat. Soc. Barristers, Am. Bar Found. (life mem.); mem. Kansas City Bar Assn. (pres. 1966-67), Mo. Bar Assn. (bd. govs. 1967-76, v.p. 1972-73, pres. 1974-75), ABA (ho. dels. 1976-80), Lawyers Assn. Kansas City, Mo. Assn. Trial Attys., Assn. Trial Lawyers Am. (sustaining), So. Conf. Bar Pres.'s (life), Mobar Research Inc. (pres. 1978-86), Phi Alpha Delta Alumni (justice Kansas City area 1955-56). Lodges: Optimists (pres. Ward Pkwy. 1961-62, lt. gov. Mo. dist. internat. 1963-64), Sertoma, B'nai B'rith. Federal civil litigation, Construction, Personal injury. Home: 9002 Western Hills Dr Kansas City MO 64114 Office: Home Savs Bldg Kansas City MO 64106

STOUT, A(RTHUR) WENDEL, III, lawyer; b. New Orleans, Nov. 16, 1949; s. Arthur Wendel Jr. and Rowena (Lee) S.; m. Elizabeth Jane Marsal, Dec. 17, 1978; children: Arthur W. IV, Andrew Winston. BA, Tulane U., 1971, JD, 1978. Bar: La. 1978, U.S. Dist. Ct. (ea. dist.) La. 1978, U.S. Dist. Ct. (we. dist.) La. 1979, U.S. Dist. Ct. (mid. dist.) La. 1980, U.S. Ct. Appeals (5th cir.) 1981. Assoc. Deutch, Kerrigan & Stiles, New Orleans, 1978-84, ptnr., 1985—. Served to lt. USNR, 1971-74. Mem. ABA, Fed. Bar Assn., Maritime Law Assn., Southeastern Admiralty Law Inst., La. Bar Assn. Admiralty, Federal civil litigation, Personal injury. Home: 619 Nashville Ave New Orleans LA 70115 Office: Deutsch Kerrigan & Stiles 755 Magazine St New Orleans LA 70130

STOUT, GEORGE MCBRIDE, lawyer; b. Great Neck, N.Y., Jan. 16, 1947; s. Charles Holt and Katherine (Black) S. B.S., U. of Ariz., 1969, J.S., 1973. Bar: Nev. 1973, U.S. Dist. Ct. Nev. 1975, U.S. Ct. Appeals (9th cir.) 1977. Dep. atty. gen. Atty. Gen. Office, Nev., Carson City, 1973-77; staff atty. Sierra Pacific Power, Reno, 1977-79; ptnr. Dyer & Stout, Reno, 1979-82; sole practice, Reno, 1982-85; pres., bd. dirs. Earlee West Printing, Anaheim, Calif., 1985—; chmn., dir. Reno Printing, Inc.; v.p., sec., dir. Diamond S. Corp., Reno. Served with U.S. Army, 1969-75. Mem. Washoe County Bar Assn., ABA. Republican. Clubs: Prospectors (Reno), Balboa Bay (Newport Beach). General corporate, Bankruptcy, General practice.

STOUT, GREGORY STANSBURY, lawyer; b. Berkeley, Calif., July 27, 1915; s. Verne A. and Ella (Moore) S.; m. Virginia Cordes, Apr. 23, 1948; 1 son, Frederick Gregory. A.B., U. Calif., 1937, LL.B., 1940. Bar: Calif. 1940. Practice law San Francisco, 1946, 52—; asst. dist. atty., 1947-52; mem. Penal Code Revision Commn. Calif.; chmn. com. State Bar Calif. Contbr. articles to profl. jours. Served to master sgt. AUS, 1942-45. Fellow Am. Coll. Trial Lawyers, Am. Bar Found.; mem. ABA, Fed. Bar Assn., Am. Bd. Trial Advocates, Nat. Assn. Def. Lawyers in Criminal Cases (sec. 1958-59, pres. 1962-63). Democrat. Episcopalian. Club: Bohemian. Federal civil litigation, State civil litigation, Criminal. Home: 2389 Washington St San Francisco CA 94115 Office: 220 Montgomery St Suite 1010 San Francisco CA 94104

STOUT, JAMES DUDLEY, lawyer; b. Lawrence County, Ill., June 22, 1947; s. Donald K. and Myrtle Irene (Pullen) S.; m. Susan A. West, Jan. 3, 1976 (div. Feb. 1985); children: Lindsey Diane, Kristi Lynn. BA, So. Ill. U., 1969; JD, U. Ill., 1974. Bar: Tex. 1974, U.S. Dist. Ct. (so. dist.) Tex. 1974, Ill. 1978, U.S. Dist. Ct. (cen. dist.) Ill. 1979, U.S. Dist. Ct. (so. dist.) Ill. 1986. Sole practice Humble, Tex., 1974-78; assoc. Law office Robert W. Dodd, Champaign, Ill., 1978-79; ptnr. Dodd, Stout, Martinkus, et al, Champaign, 1979-81, Zimmerly, Gadau, Stout, Selin & Otto, Champaign, 1981-85, Correll and Stout, Bridgeport, Ill., 1985-86; sole practice Bridgeport, 1986—. Served with U.S. Army, 1969-71. Mem. Assn. Trial Lawyers Am., Ill. Bar Assn., Tex. Bar Assn. Lodges: Elks, Shriners. Avocations: golf, tennis, reading. General practice, Federal civil litigation, Oil and gas leasing. Office: 324 N Main Bridgeport IL 62417

STOVALL, CARLA JO, lawyer; b. Hardner, Kans., Mar. 18, 1957; d. Carl E. and Juanita Jo (Ford) S. BA, Pittsburg State U., Kans., 1979; JD, U. Kans., 1982. Bar: Kans. 1982, U.S. Dist. Ct. Kans. 1982. Sole practice Pittsburg, 1982-85; atty. Crawford County, Pittsburg, 1984—; lectr. law Pittsburg State U. 1982-84. Bd. dirs., sec. Pittsburg Family YMCA, 1983—. Mem. ABA, Kans. Bar Assn., Crawford County Bar Assn. (sec. 1984-85, v.p. 1985-86, pres. 1986—), Kans. County and Dist. Attys. Assn., Nat. Coll. Dist. Attys., Pittsburg State U. Alumni Assn. (bd. dirs. 1983—), Pittsburg Area C. of C. (bd. dirs. 1983-85, Leadership Pitts. 1984), Bus. and Profl. Women Assn. (Young Careerist 1984), Kans. Assn. Commerce and Industry (Leadership Kans. 1983), AAUW (bd. dirs. 1983—). Republican. Methodist. Avocations: travel, photography, tennis. Criminal, Local government. Home: RR#1 Pittsburg KS 66762 Office: Crawford County Atty 4th and Pine Pittsburg KS 66762

STOVALL, JAMES TRUMAN, III, lawyer; b. Montgomery, Ala., Nov. 6, 1937; s. James Truman and Mary Virginia (Dawsey) S.; m. Lou Ann Barno, Aug. 18, 1962; children—Marlan Elizabeth, Pamala Dorsey. B.A., U. Ala., 1959, J.D., 1960; postgrad. Hague Acad. Internat. Law, Netherlands, 1965. Bar: D.C. 1968, U.S. Ct. Appeals (D.C. cir.) 1968. Assoc. Clifford & Warnke, Washington, 1967-72, ptnr., 1973-83; ptnr. Stovall & Spradlin1983—. Served to maj. JAGC, U.S. Army, 1960-67. Mem. Farrah Law Soc., ABA, Fed. Bar Assn., Phi Delta Phi. Presbyterian. Clubs: Univ., Kenwood (Bethesda, Md.). Private international, Public international, Administrative and regulatory. Office: 2600 Virginia Ave NW Suite 820 Washington DC 20037

STOVALL, THOMAS J., JR., judge; b. Houston, Oct. 31, 1920; s. Thomas Jackson and Mary Ella (Hutchison) S.; m. Martha Lou Barnett, Nov. 15, 1945; children: Thomas J. III, David Barnett, Timothy Hutchison. BA, Rice U., 1943; JD, U. Tex., 1948. Bar: Tex. 1948, U.S. Dist. Ct. (so. dist.) Tex. 1954, U.S. Ct. Appeals 1980. Ptnr. Stovall, O'Bryant & Stovall, Houston, 1948-58; judge 129 Jud. Dist. Ct. of Tex., Houston, 1958-83, 2d Adminstrv. Jud. Region of Tex., La Porte, 1983—; bd. dirs. Search Group, Inc., Sacramento. Contbr. articles to law jours. Served to Lt. (j.g.) USNR, 1941-45, PTO. Recipient Service award Tex. Ctr. for Judiciary, 1973-82. Mem. ABA (jud. adminstrn. div.), Houston Bar. Assn., Tex. Bar Assn. (chmn. Jud. sect. 1966-67, Service award 1967), Inst. Ct. Mgmt. (bd. dirs. 1980—), Nat. Conf. Met. Cts. (bd. dirs. 1984—, Tom C. Clark award 1975), Nat. Ctr. State Cts. (bd. dirs. 1985—). Democrat. Methodist. Club: Houston Yacht (Shoreacres, Tex.) (bd. dirs. 1958-62). Judicial administration, Legal education, State civil litigation. Home: 4718 Hamblen Ct Seabrook TX 77586 Office: 2d Adminstrv Jud Region of Tex PO Box 40 Seabrook TX 77586

STOVER, DAVID FRANK, lawyer; b. Phila., May 15, 1941; s. Emory Frank and Beatrice Norah (Spinelli) S. A.B., Princeton U., 1962; J.D., U. Pa., 1965. Bar: D.C. 1966, U.S. Ct. Appeals (D.C. cir.) 1968, U.S. Ct. Appeals (9th cir.) 1969, U.S. Ct. Appeals (4th cir.) 1972. Atty. FPC, Washington, 1965-71, Tally & Tally, Washington, 1972-75; asst. gen. counsel Postal Rate Commn., Washington, 1975-79, gen. counsel, 1979—. Author: (with Bierman, Lamont, Nelson) Geothermal Energy in the Western United States, 1978. Mem. Fed. Bar Assn. Episcopalian. Administrative and regulatory. Office: Postal Rate Commn 1333 H St NW Washington DC 20268

STOVER, KATHY ANN, lawyer, financial consultant; b. Kansas City, Kans., Mar. 14, 1956; s. Martin D. and Jo Ann (Lumley) S. BA cum laude, Washburn U., 1978, JD, 1981. Bar: Kans., Mo., U.S. Dist. Ct. Kans., U.S. Dist. Ct. (we. dist.) Mo. Asst. gen. counsel Kans. Corp. Commn., Topeka, 1981-82; fin. cons. Stover Fin. Services, Topeka, 1983—; jud. law clk. to chief judge U.S. Bankruptcy Ct., Kansas City, 1985-86; v.p. Electronic Processing, Inc., 1986—. Congl. intern U.S. Ho. Reps., Washington, 1978; legis. intern Kans. Ho. Reps., Topeka, 1978. Named one of Outstanding Young Women in Am., 1982. Mem. ABA, Kans. Bar Assn., Mo. Bar Assn., Kansas City Met. Bar Assn., Assn. Trial Lawyers Am., Comml. Law League, Am. Bankruptcy Inst., Phi Kappa Phi, Omicron Delta Epsilon. Methodist. Bankruptcy, Personal income taxation, General corporate. Home: 3017 Sowers Ct Topeka KS 66604

STOVITZ, CHUCK, lawyer; b. Alhambra, Calif., Nov. 11, 1950; s. Benjamin and Helene Stovitz. Cert., Pasadena Playhouse, 1968; JD, Loyola U., Los Angeles, 1974. Bar: Calif. 1974, U.S. Ct. Appeals (9th cir.) 1974. Counsel Southwest Leasing Inc., Los Angeles, 1975-79, Videography Inc., Los Angeles, 1980-81; sole practice Bervely Hills, Calif., 1981-84, Bervely Hills, 1986—; atty. U.S. Antarctic Service, South Pole, 1984-85; cons. NSF, Washingion, 1986—; assoc. NASA, 1986—; assoc. prof. West Los Angeles Law Sch., 1978-79. Contbr. articles on space law to profl. jours. Researcher project NASA Hastings Law Sch., San Francisco, 1985, 86. Recipient Antarctic Service medal U.S. Congress. Mem. ABA (space and tech. div., forum com. on air space law), Internat. Inst. Space Law. Real property, Contracts commercial, Space law. Office: 2505 Ocean Front Walk Marina Del Rey CA 90291

STOW, ELIZABETH GLENN, law assistant; b. Atlanta, Feb. 5, 1925; d. Alsa Candler and Harriet May (Finney) Glenn; m. James Robertson Stow, Nov. 26, 1947; children: Thomas William, Sarah Elizabeth Stow Wallingford. BA magna cum laude, Agnes Scott Coll., 1945; MRE, Emory U., 1948, PhD, 1970, JD, 1981. Bar: Ga. 1981, U.S. Dist. Ct. (no. dist.) Ga. 1981. Tchr. pub. schs. various locations, 1948-53; asst. prof. English Ga. State U., Atlanta, 1962-65, 66-68, 70-77; freelance editorial cons. Atlanta, 1975-81; law clk. to presiding justice U.S. Dist. Ct. (no. dist.) Ga., Atlanta, 1981-82; law asst. Ga. Ct. Appeals, Atlanta, 1982—; part-time editorial cons., USDA, Atlanta, 1977-81. Author: Venus in Spenser's "Faerie Queene", 1970; author various poems; also articles. Chmn. pub. relations Alamance County council Girl Scouts U.S., Burlington, N.C., 1956-58; v.p. Atlanta Flower Show Assn., 1965-66; chmn. judges com. Camellia Soc. Ga., Atlanta, 1968-77. Mem. ABA, Ga. Bar Assn., Atlanta Bar Assn., Ga. Assn. for Women Lawyers (corr. sec. 1985—), League of Women Voters, World Peace Through Law Assn., Innovative Investors, Atlanta Agnes Scott Alumnae (exec. bd. 1947-48, 84-85), Gardeners Club (pres. 1980-81), Phi Beta Kappa. Presbyterian. Club: Gardeners (Atlanta) (pres. 1980-81). Avocations: art, theater, music, traveling, hiking. Judicial administration. Home: 3050 Margaret Mitchell Dr NW Apt 48 Atlanta GA 30327 Office: Ga Ct Appeals 416 Judicial Bldg Atlanta GA 30334

STOWE, CHARLES ROBINSON BEECHER, management consultant, educator; b. Seattle, July 18, 1949; s. David Beecher and Edith Beecher (Andrade) S.; m. Laura Everett, Mar. 9, 1985. B.A., Vanderbilt U., 1971; M.B.A., U. Dallas, 1975; J.D., U. Houston, 1982. Bar: Tex. 1982, U.S. Dist. Ct. (so. dist.) Tex., 1984, U.S. Tax Ct., 1984. Account exec. Engleman Co., pub. relations and advt., Dallas, 1974-75; instr. Richland Coll., Dallas, spring 1976; acct. Arthur Andersen & Co., Dallas, 1976-78; part-time pub. relations cons.; dir. Productive Capital Corp.; gen. ptnr. Productive Capital Assocs.; pres. Stowe & Co., mgmt. cons., Dallas, 1978—; asst. prof. dept. gen. bus. and fin. Coll. Bus. Adminstrn., Sam Houston State U., 1982—, dir. Office Free Enterprise and Entrepreneurship, 1982—; adminstrv. intern, asst. to pres., spring 1985. Trustee, Stowe-Day Found., 1979-82; mem. nat. adv. bd. Young Am.'s Found., 1979—. Served as officer USNR, 1971-74; comdr. Res. Recipient Freedoms Found. award, 1969; Navy Achievement medal, 1973, Gold Star, 1985; Disting. Service award U. Houston Coll. Law, 1982. Mem. Am. Bar Assn., State Bar Tex., Walker County Bar Assn. (pres. 1987—), Pub. Relations Soc. Am., Tex. Assn. Realtors, U.S. Navy League, Naval Res. Assn., Res. Officers Assn., Sigma Iota Epsilon. Club: Dallas Vanderbilt (pres. 1977-78). Co-author CPA Review, contbr. articles; editor Houston Jour. Internat. Law, 1981-82. General corporate, Legal education, Securities. Office: PO Box 2676 Huntsville TX 77341

STOWERS, HARRY E., JR., state supreme court justice; b. 1926. B.A., U. N.Mex.; J.D., Georgetown U. Former judge N.Mex. 2d Jud. Dist., Albuquerque; assoc. justice N.Mex. Supreme Ct., Santa Fe, 1983—. Judicial administration. Office: Supreme Court New Mexico Supreme Ct Bldg 327 Don Gasper Ave Santa Fe NM 87501 *

STOYANOFF, DAVID JOSEPH, taxes executive, lawyer; b. Sioux City, Iowa, Oct. 2, 1953; s. John J. and Hazel M. (Giles) S.; m. Susan L. Park, Aug. 17, 1974. Student, Kearney (Nebr.) State Coll., 1971; BS, Wayne (Nebr.) State Coll., 1974; JD, U. Nebr., 1979. CPA, Nebr.; bar: Nebr. 1979, U.S. Dist. Ct. Nebr. Tax acct. Arthur Andersen & Co., Omaha, 1979-82; tax mgr. Pacesetter Corp., Omaha, 1982-85; mgr. taxes and fin. controls The Pinkerton Tobacco Co., Richmond, Va., 1985—; tax cons. Omaha, 1979-85. Mem. ABA, Nebr. Bar Assn., Nebr. Soc. CPAs. Roman Catholic. Avocations: running, woodworking, cooking. Corporate taxation, Personal income taxation, State and local taxation.

STRACENER, CAROL ELIZABETH, lawyer; b. Baton Rouge, Mar. 28, 1951; d. Nealon and Mary Helen (Langlois) S.; m. John Joseph Nicholson, June 2, 1973; 1 dau., Courtney Elizabeth. B.S., La. State U., 1973; J.D., So. U., 1977. Bar: La., U.S. Dist. Ct. (mid. dist.) La. 1985. Ptnr. Stracener, Stracener and Stracener, Baton Rouge, 1978—. Mem. ABA, La. Bar Assn., East Baton Rouge Bar Assn., La. Assn. for Women Attys., Baton Rouge Assn. for Women Attys., Am. Judicature Soc., Alpha Xi Delta. Republican. Methodist. Family and matrimonial, Probate, General practice. Home: 3695 Ridgemont Dr Baton Rouge LA 70814 Office: Stracener Stracener & Stracener 3155 Weller Ave Baton Rouge LA 70805

STRADER, JAMES DAVID, lawyer; b. Pitts., June 30, 1940; s. James Lowell and Tyra Fredrika (Bjorn) S.; m. Ann Wallace, Feb. 8, 1964; children: James Jacob, Robert Benjamin. BA, Mich. State U., 1962; JD, U. Pitts., 1965. Bar: Pa. 1966, U.S. Dist. Ct. (we. dist.) Pa. 1966, U.S. Dist. Ct. (ea. dist.) Pa. 1973, U.S. Ct. Appeals (4th and 5th cirs.), U.S. Ct. Appeals (3d and 11th cirs.) 1981, U.S. Supreme Ct. 1982, U.S. Dist. Ct. (mid. dist.) Pa. 1985. Assoc. Peacock, Keller & Yohe, Washington, 1967-68; atty. U.S. Steel Corp., Pitts., 1968-77, gen. atty. workman's compensation, 1977-84; assoc. Caroselli, Spagnolli & Beachler, Pitts., 1984-87, ptnr., 1987; ptnr.

Dickie, McCame & Strader, Pitts., 1987—. Del. Dem. Mid-Yr. Conv., 1974; mem. Dem. Nat. Platform Com., 1976; commr. Mt. Lebanon Twp., Pa., 1974-78. Served to capt. U.S. Army, 1965-67. Mem. ABA (sr. vice chmn. worker's compensation com. 1978—), Pa. Bar Assn., Allegheny County Bar Assn., Assn. Trial Lawyers Am., Pa. Trial Lawyers Assn. Democrat. Presbyterian. Club: Rivers (Pitts.). Workers' compensation, Personal injury. Office: Dickie McCame & Chilcote 2 PTG Pl Pittsburgh PA 15222

STRADLEY, WILLIAM JACKSON, lawyer; b. Houston, Oct. 27, 1939; s. Samuel H. and Mary Stradley; m. Emmalee H. Stradley, Apr. 16, 1960; children—Lisa D., William M. B.S., U. Houston, 1964; J.D., 1967. Bar: Tex. 1967, U.S. Dist. Ct. (so. dist.) Tex., U.S. Ct. Appeals (5th cir.), U.S. Supreme Ct. Pres., Stradley, Barnett & Stein, P.C., Houston; mem. faculty trial advocacy course Law Sch. U. Houston, 1982. Pres., Police Adv. Com. 1981-84, sec., 1980-81; bd. dirs. Houston Council Human Relations, 1982-84; mem. adminstrv. bd. St. Luke's United Meth. Ch. Recipient Pub. Service award Houston Police Dept., 1984. Mem. Houston Bar Found. (charter), Am. Bd. Trial Advocates (treas., pres. 1980-82, v.p. 1983-84 Houston), State Bar of Tex. (chmn. grievance com., mem. profl. ethics com.), Houston Trial Lawyers Assn. (bd. dirs. 1980-82, v.p. 1983-84, pres. 1985-86), Houston Bar Assn. (chmn. tort and compensation sect. 1980-81), Tex. Trial Lawyers Assn., Assn. Trial Lawyers Am., Am. Judicature Soc., Am. Acad. Polit. and Social Scis. Clubs: Briar, Met. Racquet, Inns of Court (bd. dirs. 1984). Personal injury, State civil litigation, Federal civil litigation. Home: 2521 Reba Dr Houston TX 77019 Office: 440 Louisiana St Suite 2000 Houston TX 77002

STRANAHAN, ROBERT PAUL, JR., lawyer; b. Louisville, Oct. 29, 1929; s. Robert Paul and Anna May (Payne) S.; m. Louise Perry, May 12, 1956; children: Susan Dial, Robert Paul, Carol Payne. A.B., Princeton U., 1951; J.D., Harvard U., 1954. Bar: D.C. 1954, Md. 1964. Assoc. Wilmer & Broun, Washington, 1957-62; ptnr. Wilmer, Cutler & Pickering, Washington, 1963—; professional lectr. in law Nat. Law Center, George Washington U., 1969-72. Served to 1st lt. USMCR, 1954-57. Mem. ABA, Fed. Bar Assn., D.C. Bar Assn., Md. Bar Assn. Clubs: Metropolitan (Washington), Gridiron (Washington); Chevy Chase (Md.). General corporate. Home: 5316 Cardinal Ct Bethesda MD 20816 Home: 286 Beach Rd N Figure Eight Island Wilmington NC 28405 Office: 2445 M St NW Washington DC 20037

STRAND, ALFRED BENJAMIN, JR., lawyer; b. Knoxville, Tenn., Feb. 13, 1940; s. Alfred Benjamin Sr. and Margaret Irene (Boynton) S.; m. Louisa Mae Woodard, Mar. 4, 1967; children: Margaret Loudora, Alfred Benjamin III, Nathaniel Craig. BA, Carson-Newman Coll., 1962; BS, U. Tenn., 1964; JD, Samford U., 1967. Bar: Tenn. 1967, U.S. Dist. Ct. (ea. dist.) Tenn. 1969, U.S. Tax Ct. 1971, U.S. Ct. Appeals (6th cir.) 1974, U.S. Supreme Ct. 1978. Sole practice Dandridge, Tenn., 1967-75; judge Tenn. 2d Cir. Ct., 1975-76; ptnr. Strand & Goddard, Dandridge, 1976—; prof. bus. adminstrn. Carson-Newman Coll., Jefferson City, Tenn., 1967-71; bd. dirs. Top Flite Oil Co., Morristown, Tenn. State and local officer, Tenn. Jaycees, 1967-75, internat. senator, 1975. Served with Tenn. Air Force N.G., 1957-63. Mem. ABA, Tenn. Bar Assn., Jefferson County Bar Assn. (pres. 1976-79), Tenn. Trial Law Assn., Dandridge Jaycees (pres., v.p., state dir., state protocol officer, Outstanding Young Man award 1973), Phi Alpha Delta, Alpha Kappa Psi. Democrat. Baptist. State civil litigation, General practice. Office: Strand & Goddard PO Drawer H Dandridge TN 37725

STRAND, ROGER GORDON, federal judge; b. Peekskill, N.Y., Apr. 28, 1934; s. Ernest Gordon Strand and Lisabeth Laurine (Phin) Steinmetz; m. Joan Williams, Nov. 25, 1961. AB, Hamilton Coll., 1955; LLB, Cornell U., 1961; grad., Nat. Coll. State Trial Judges, 1968. Bar: Ariz. 1961, U.S. Dist. Ct. Ariz. 1961, U.S. Supreme Ct. 1980. Assoc. Fennemore, Craig, Allen & McClennen, Phoenix, 1961-67; judge Ariz. Superior Ct., Phoenix, 1967-85, U.S. Dist. Ct. Ariz., Phoenix, 1985—; assoc. presiding judge Ariz. Superior Ct., 1971-85; lectr. Nat. Jud. Coll., Reno, 1978-87. Past pres. cen. Ariz. chpt. Arthritis Found. Served to lt. USN, 1955-61. Mem. ABA, Ariz. Bar Assn., Maricopa County Bar Assn., Nat. Conf. Fed. Trial Judges, Phi Delta Phi, Aircraft Owners and Pilots Assn. Lodge: Rotary. Avocations: golf, fishing. Judicial administration. Home: 5825 N 3d Ave Phoenix AZ 85013 Office: US Courthouse 230 N 1st Ave Room 6077 Phoenix AZ 85025

STRANDBERG, REBECCA NEWMAN, lawyer; b. Ft. Smith, Ark., Apr. 22, 1951; d. Russell Lynn and Doris Jean (Lindsey) Newman; m. Jeffrey Eugene Strandberg, Nov. 23, 1979; children—Lindsey Katherine, Russell Jeffrey. B.A., Tex. Christian U., 1973; J.D., So. Meth. U., 1976. Bar: Tex. 1976, Md. 1981, D.C. 1983. Field atty. NLRB, New Orleans, 1976-79; legis. asst. Senator Dale Bumpers, Washington, 1979-81; sole practice, Montgomery County, 1981—. Vice-pres. bd. dirs. Share-A-Ride Corp., Montgomery County, Md., 1984; dir. children's choir Glenmont Meth. Ch., Silver Spring, Md., 1984. Mem. Silver Spring C. of C., Montgomery County Women's Bar Assn. (chmn. membership 1982-83), Md. Women's Bar Assn., Silver Spring Bus. and Profl. Women (pres. 1984-85). Federal civil litigation, State civil litigation, Labor. Home: 1504 Ballard St Silver Spring MD 20910 Office: 8630 Fenton St Suite 430 Silver Spring MD 20910

STRASBURGER, JOSEPH JULIUS, lawyer; b. Albia, Iowa, Aug. 29, 1913; s. Joseph and Elsa (Gottlieb) S.; m. Lucile C. Lapidus, Oct. 11, 1957; 1 dau., Susan A. (dec. Jan. 1970). A.B., Knox Coll., 1934; J.D., Harvard, 1937. Bar: Ill. 1937. Assoc. firm Moses, Kennedy, Stein & Bachrach, Chgo., 1938-39; asso. gen. counsel's office Middle West Service Co., Chgo., 1939-44; partner firm Altheimer & Gray (and predecessor firms), Chgo., 1944—; Sec., dir. Vitamins, Inc., 1956—; Chmn. lawyer's handbook editorial com. Jewish Fedn. Chgo., 1968-73; mem. adv. council Ill. Inst. Continuing Legal Edn., 1970-76, exec. com., 1971-76, chmn., 1974-75; lectr. probate and tax subjects. Contbr. articles to legal jours. Mem. devel. com. Knox Coll., 1964-70, trustee, 1982—; trustee Latin Sch. Chgo., 1978-84. Fellow Am. Coll. Probate Counsel, Am. Bar Found.; mem. ABA, Ill. Bar Assn., Chgo. Bar Assn. (chmn. probate practice com. 1960-61, chmn. continuing legal edn. com. 1968-69, chmn. legal edn. com. 1972-73), Chgo. Estate Planning Council (pres. 1975-76), Phi Beta Kappa, Delta Sigma Rho, Beta Theta Pi. Jewish. Clubs: Tavern (Chgo.), Mchts. and Mfrs. (Chgo.), Harvard (Chgo.). Probate, Estate taxation. Home: 1335 N Astor St Chicago IL 60610 Office: 333 W Wacker Dr Chicago IL 60606

STRASER, RICHARD ALAN, lawyer; b. Washington, Feb. 11, 1945; s. Woodward John and Nina Louise (Weaver) S.; m. Beverly Jean Brickhouse, May 9, 1981. B.A., George Washington U., 1971; J.D., Wake Forest U., 1974. Bar: Pa. 1975, Va. 1977, U.S. Ct. Appeals (5th cir.) 1979, U.S. Supreme Ct. 1980. Mgmt. asst. NASA Hdqrs., Washington, 1972, 1973; primary trademark atty. U.S. Patent and Trademark Office, Crystal City, Arlington, Va., 1974—. Dep. dir. Herndon Community Chorus, Va., 1981-82. Served with U.S. Army 1963-64. Mem. Delta Phi Alpha, Phi Alpha Delta. Democrat. Roman Catholic. Federal civil litigation, Trademark and copyright. Office: US Patent and Trademark Office Dept of Commerce Washington DC 20231

STRASHUN, JEFFREY MARC, lawyer; b. Elizabeth, N.J., Mar. 2, 1954; s. Harold and Ruth (Sheinwald) S.; m. Brenda Pilchick, Mar. 25, 1984. BA, Yeshiva U., 1976, JD, 1979. Bar: N.Y. 1980, N.J. 1980, U.S. Dist. Ct. N.J. 1980, U.S. Ct. Appeals (5th cir.) 1981, U.S. Dist. Ct. (so. and ea. dists.) N.Y. 1986, U.S. Supreme Ct. 1986. Appellate atty. U.S. Dept. Labor, Washington, 1979-81; sole practice Union, N.J., 1981—; counsel govt. relations Bd. Jewish Edn. Greater N.Y., 1985—. Mem. ABA, Union County Bar Assn., Middlesex County Bar Assn., Assn. Trial Lawyers N.J., Yeshiva U. Alumni Assn. (treas. to v.p. 1986—). Jewish. Avocations: collecting autographs, travel. State civil litigation, Personal injury, General practice. Home: 194 Surrey Rd Hillside NJ 07205 Office: 2424 Morris Ave Union NJ 07083

STRASSER, WILLIAM IGNATIUS, lawyer; b. N.Y.C., Sept. 12, 1949; s. Richard J. and Lillian M. (Murray) S.; m. Marianne Elizabeth Malespina, July 21, 1973; children: Michael, Gregory, Christopher, Daniel. BA, Seton Hall U., 1971, JD, 1974. Bar: N.J. 1974, U.S. Supreme Ct. 1980, N.Y. 1983, U.S. Ct. Appeals (3d cir.) 1986. Assoc. Donohue, Donohue, Costenbader & Beck, Nutley, N.J., 1974-78; ptnr. Donohue, Donohue, Costenbader & Strasser, Nutley, 1978—; lectr. Citizen's Com. on Bio-med. Ethics, Inc., Summit, N.J., 1983—. Contbr.: By No Extraordinary Means, Lynn, 1986. Mem. legal and ethical problems in delivery of health care commn. State of N.J., Trenton, 1986—. Mem. ABA, Assn. Trial Lawyers Am., N.J. Trial Lawyers Assn., N.J. Bar Assn., Essex County Bar Assn., Bergen County Bar Assn., Bloomfield Lawyers Club. Roman Catholic. Health, State civil litigation, Real property. Home: 24 Fox Hill Upper Saddle River NJ 07458 Office: Donohue Donohue Costenbader & Strasser 391 Franklin Ave Nutley NJ 07110

STRASSNER, KENNETH ALLEN, lawyer; b. St. Louis, Jan. 18, 1946; s. Ernest Alexander and Audrey Marie (Ausmussen) S.; m. Margaret Lee McCarteney, Mar. 17, 1973; children: Allen Cleveland, Jennifer Lee. Student, Harvard U., 1967; BA, Yale U., 1968, JD, 1974. Bar: D.C. 1975, U.S. Dist. Ct. D.C. 1975. Assoc. Kirkland & Ellis, Washington, 1974-75; exec. asst. U.S. Dept. of Labor, Washington, 1975-76; regulatory atty. Kimberly-Clark, Washington, 1976-83; asst. gen. counsel Kimberly-Clark, Atlanta, 1983—; participant, speaker various profl. confs. in environ. and energy fuel. Mem. Yale Alumni Schs. Com., Atlanta, 1985—; treas. parents council Holy Innocent Episc. Sch., Atlanta, 1985—; bd. dirs. Leukemia Soc. of Ga., Atlanta, 1984—, Riverside Club, Atlanta, 1985—. Mem. ABA, Fed. Bar Assn., Am. Corp. Counsel Assn., Phi Beta Kappa. Clubs: Met. (Washington), Chevy Chase (Md.), Cherokee Country Club (Atlanta). Environment, FERC practice, Public utilities. Home: 6140 Weatherly Dr NW Atlanta GA 30328 Office: Kimberly-Clark Corp 1400 Hotcomb Br Rd Roswell GA 30328

STRATAKIS, CHRIST, lawyer; b. Chios, Greece, June 6, 1928; s. John and Sophie (Kazdaglis) S.; m. Mary C. Skinitis, Oct. 25, 1959; children—Sophia, John, Irene. B.S. in Econs., Drexel U., 1951; J.D., NYU, 1955. Bar: N.Y. 1956, U.S. Dist. Ct. (so. and ea. dists.) 1957, U.S. Ct. Appeals (2d cir.) 1958, U.S. Ct. Customs 1965, U.S. Supreme Ct. 1970. Gen. counsel Nat. Shipping & Trading Corp., N.Y.C., 1955-59; with firm Poles, Tublin, Patestides & Stratakis, N.Y.C., 1960—, jr. ptnr., 1961—, sr. ptnr., 1962—. Chmn. sch. bd. Sch. of the Transfiguration, Corona, N.Y., 1967-78; mem. Adv. Council N.Y. dist. SBA, 1971-73. Recipient St. Paul's award Greek Orthodox Archdiocese of N.Am. and S.Am., 1976; medal of honor Govt. of Greece, 1974; Knight Holy Sepulchre of Jerusalem. Mem. ABA, Maritime Law Assn. U.S., United Chios Socs. Am. (supreme legal advisor 1960-82), Sigma Rho, Phi Alpha Delta. Greek Orthodox. Clubs: Whitehall (N.Y.C.); Douglaston (N.Y.); Greek-Am. Dem. of Queens (chmn. law com. 1960-74). Contbr. articles to profl. jours. Admiralty, Contracts commercial, General corporate. Office: 5th Floor 46 Trinity Pl New York NY 10006

STRATTON, EVELYN JOYCE, lawyer; b. Bangkok, Thailand, Feb. 25, 1953; came to U.S., 1971; d. Elmer John and Corrine Sylvia (Henricksen) Sahlberg; m. R. Stephen Stratton, June 16, 1973; children: Luke Andrew, Tyler John. A.A., U. Fla., 1973; B.A., Akron U., 1975; J.D., Ohio State U., 1978. Bar: Ohio 1979, U.S. Dist. Ct. (so. dist.) Ohio 1979, U.S. Ct. Appeals (6th cir.) 1983. Teaching asst. history LeTourneau Coll., Longview, Tex., 1973-74; law clk. Knepper, White, Columbus, 1978-79, Crabbe & Brown, Columbus, 1977-79; assoc. Hamilton, Kramer, Myers & Cheek, Columbus, 1980-85; ptnr. Wesp, Osterkamp & Stratton, 1985—; trustee Linc Resources, Columbus, 1980-86, chmn. bd. dirs., 1984-86 ; speaker legal seminars. Worker Republic Party Campaign, Columbus, 1983-84; vice chmn. fund drive United Way Columbus, 1984; fundraisor Easter Seal Telethon, 1986, Columbus Mus. Art, 1986. Recipient Gold Key award LeTourneau Coll., Gainesville, Fla., 1974; service commendation Ohio Ho. of Reps., 1984. Mem. Columbus Bar Assn. (com. chmn. 1982-84, bd. govs. 1984—), Ohio Bar Assn., ABA, Ohio Assn. Civil Trial Attys., Columbus Def. Assn., Columbus Bar Found. (trustee 1985—, officer, sec. 1986—), Am. Arbitration Assn., Phi Delta Phi (pres. 1982-83). Clubs: Civitan (trustee 1982-83), Exec. Club of Columbus (bd. dirs. 1986—). State civil litigation, General corporate, Personal injury. Office: Wesp Osterkamp & Stratton 42 E Gay St Suite 812 Columbus OH 43215

STRATTON, HAL, state attorney general; b. Muskogee, Okla., Dec. 6, 1950; s. Mr. and Mrs. H. Duane S. BS in Geology, U. Okla., 1973, JD, 1976. Bar: N.Mex., Okla., U.S. Dist. Ct. N.Mex., U.S. Dist. Ct. (we. dist.) Okla., U.S. Ct. Appeals (10th cir.), U.S. Supreme Ct. Spl. asst. dist. atty. Bernalillo County Dist. Atty.'s Office, Albuquerque, 1978; mem. N.Mex. Ho. Reps., 1979-86, mem. house jud. com., 1979-86, chmn. house jud. com., 1985-86, mem. house energy and natural resources com., 1979-82, 85-86, vice-chmn. house energy and natural resources com., 1981-82, mem. house transp. com., 1983-84, mem. house rules and order of bus. com., 1981-82, mem. radioactive wast consultation com., 1979-81, mem. N.Mex. mortgage fin. authority oversight com., 1983-84; mem. N.Mex. workmens compensation com. Coors, Singer and Broullire, 1986; assoc. Coors, Singer and Broullire, Albuquerque, 1977-81; ptnr. Stratton and Barnett, Albuquerque, 1981-86; atty. gen. State of N.Mex., 1987—; mem. N.Mex. Supreme Ct. com. on rules governing magistrate cts., mcpl. cts. and met. ct., 1984-86; mem. N.Mex. Jud. Council, 1981-82. Sec./treas., bd. dirs. N.Mex. Rep. legis. campaign com., 1981-85; state counsel Rep. Nat. Com., 1984—; mem. juvenile justice project adv. bd. Rose Inst., Claremont-McKenna Coll., 1984—, Bur. of Land Mgmt. Citizens Adv. Com., Albuquerque, 1983-86; state dir. The Conservative Caucus; state chmn. Nat. Tax Limitation Com., Citizens for Am.; founding chmn. N.Mexicans for Tax Limitation. Phillips petroleum scholar, 1969, Union Oil of Calif. scholar, 1969-73, George Wyatt Brown scholar, 1972-73; recipient George Wyatt Brown award, 1971-72. Mem. Council of State Govts. (western conf. 1981-84), Nat. Conf. of Commrs. on Uniform State Laws. Office: Office of Atty Gen PO Drawer 1508 Santa Fe NM 87504-1508

STRATTON, RICHARD JAMES, lawyer; b. Sandwich, Ill., May 17, 1946; s. James L. and Dorothy (Olson) S.; m. Michele Disario, June 13, 1970; children: Matthew A., Laura D. AB, Harvard U., 1968, JD, 1972; MS, London Sch. of Econs., 1969. Bar: Calif. 1972, U.S. Dist. Ct. (no. dist.) Calif. 1972, U.S. Ct. Appeals (9th cir.) 1972, U.S. Dist. Ct. (cen. dist.) Calif. 1978, U.S. Dist. Ct. (so. and ea. dists.) Calif. 1979, U.S. Supreme Ct. 1979. Assoc. Bronson, Bronson & McKinnon, San Francisco, 1972-79, ptnr., 1980—. Mem. ABA, Bar Assn. of San Francisco, Calif. Bar Assn., Def. Research Inst. (chmn. subcom. on real estate brokers and agts. 1986—), No. Calif. Assn. Def. Counsel., San Francisco Barristers Club. Clubs: Stock Exchange, Harvard (San Francisco). Federal civil litigation, State civil litigation, Real property. Office: Bronson Bronson & McKinnon 555 California St San Francisco CA 94104

STRATTON, WALTER LOVE, lawyer; b. Greenwich, Conn., Sept. 21, 1926; s. John McKee and June (Love) S.; children—John, Michael, Peter (dec.), Lucinda. Student, Williams Coll., 1943; A.B., Yale U., 1948; LL.B., Harvard U., 1951. Bar: N.Y. 1952. Assoc. Casey, Lane & Mittendorf, N.Y.C., 1951-53; assoc. Donovan, Leisure, Newton & Irvine, N.Y.C., 1956-63; partner Donovan, Leisure, Newton & Irvine, 1963-84, Gibson, Dunn & Crutcher, 1984—; asst. U.S. atty. So. Dist. N.Y., N.Y.C., 1953-56; lectr. Practising Law Inst. Served with USNR, 1945-46. Fellow Am. Coll. Trial Lawyers; mem. ABA, N.Y. Bar Assn. Clubs: Round Hill, Indian Harbor Yacht (Greenwich, Conn.); Colo. Arlberg (Winter Park). Antitrust, Federal civil litigation, State civil litigation. Home: 434 Round Hill Rd Greenwich CT 06830 Office: 9 W 57th St New York NY 10019

STRAUB, CHESTER JOHN, lawyer; b. Bklyn., May 12, 1937; s. Chester and Ann (Majewski) S.; m. Patricia Morrissey, Aug. 22, 1959; children: Chester, Michael, Christopher, Robert. AB, St. Peter's Coll., 1958; JD, U. Va., 1961. Bar: N.Y. State 1962, U.S. Dist. Ct. (so. and ea. dists.) N.Y. 1963, U.S. Ct. Appeals (2d cir.) 1967, U.S. Supreme Ct. 1978. Assoc. firm Willkie Farr & Gallagher, N.Y.C., 1963-71; partner Willkie Farr & Gallagher, 1971—; Mem. N.Y. State Assembly, 1967-72, N.Y. State Senate, 1973-75; mem. Democratic Nat. Com., 1976-80; chmn. law com. N.Y. State Dem. Com., 1975-76; chmn. Gov. Cuomo's First Dept. Jud. Screening Com.; mem. N.Y. Jud. Screening Com., Senator Moynihan's Jud. Selection Com. Mem. Cardinal's Com. of Laity for Cath. Charities N.Y.; trustee Lenox Hill Hosp., N.Y. League for Histadrut, Collins Found. Served with U.S. Army, 1961-63. Mem. Am. Bar Assn., N.Y. State Bar Assn., Assn. Bar City N.Y., Kosciuszko Found., Assn. Sons of Poland. Administrative and regulatory, Federal civil litigation, State civil litigation. Office: Willkie Farr and Gallagher 1 Citicorp Center 153 E 53d St New York NY 10022

STRAUB, J(AMES) KURT, lawyer; b. Norristown, Pa., May 6, 1953; s. James S. and Carol E. (Strode) S.; m. Jane M. Goodfellow, June 26, 1979; children: James David, Sandra Jeanine, Stephen Paul. AB in Govt. with highest honors, Coll. of William & Mary, 1975; JD cum laude, Villanova U., 1978. Bar: Pa. 1978, U.S. Dist. Ct. (ea. dist.) Pa. 1979, U.S. Ct. Appeals (3d cir.) 1979, U.S. Ct. Appeals (5th cir.) 1984. Law clk. to presiding justice Pa. Superior Ct., Phila., 1978-79; assoc. Pepper, Hamilton & Scheetz, Phila., 1979—. Mem. ABA, Pa. Bar Assn., Phila. Bar Assn., Phi Beta Kappa, Order of Coif. Republican. Presbyterian. Federal civil litigation, State civil litigation, Products liability defense. Home: 1863 Cleveland Ave Abington PA 19001 Office: Pepper Hamilton & Scheetz 123 S Broad St Philadelphia PA 19109

STRAUCH, JOHN L., lawyer; b. Pitts., Apr. 16, 1939; s. Paul L. and Delilah M. (Madison) S.; m. Patricia Ann Gulas, June 16, 1962 (div. Oct. 1985); children: Paul L., John M., Lisa E. BA, U. Pitts., 1960; JD, N.Y. Sch. Law, 1963. Law clk. to presiding justice U.S. Ct. Appeals (2d cir.), St. Johnsbury, Vt., 1963-64; assoc. Jones, Day, Reavis & Pogue, Cleve., 1964-70, ptnr., 1970—. Mem. Statutory Com. on Selecting Bankruptcy Judges, Cleve., 1985—; pres. trustee Cleve. Task Force on Violent Crimes, Cleve., 1985-86; trustee Legal Aid Soc., Cleve., 1978, Cleve. Greater Growth Assn., 1985-86. Fellow Am. Coll. Trial Lawyers (life); mem. ABA, Ohio Bar Assn., Cleve. Bar Assn. (trustee 1980-83, pres. 1985-86), Fed. Bar Assn. (trustee Cleve. chpt. 1978-79, v.p. Cleve. chpt. 1979-80), Sixth Jud. Conf. (life), Eighth Jud. Conf. (life), Order of Coif, Phi Beta Kappa. Clubs: Oakmont (Pitts); Cleve. Racquet. Federal civil litigation, State civil litigation. Office: Jones Day Reavis & Pogue North Point 901 Lakeside Ave Cleveland OH 44114

STRAUGHN, ROBERT OSCAR, III, lawyer; b. Vallejo, Calif., Nov. 1, 1942; s. Robert Oscar Jr. and Phyllis Ruth (Main) S.; m. Mavis Marie Ann Turpeinen, May 25, 1975; 1 child, Megan Marie. BS, U. Minn., 1965, MSCE, 1971; JD, William Mitchell Coll. Law, 1976. Bar: Minn. 1976, U.S. Dist. Ct. Minn. 1979. Staff engr. Arctic Health Research Ctr., Fairbanks, Alaska, 1967-70; sr. design engr. Ellison-Pihlstrom, Inc., St. Paul, 1971-77; asst. atty. City of St. Paul, 1977-79; counsel, v.p. legal Oxford Properties, Inc., Mpls., 1979-84; ptnr. O'Connor & Hannan, Mpls., 1984—. Mem. program com. Ramsey County Hist. Soc., St. Paul, 1985-86, bd. dirs., 1986—; del. community council St. Paul Dist. 12, 1986—. Mem. ABA, Minn. Bar Assn., Hennepin County Bar Assn., Christian Legal Soc., Nat. Assn. Indsl. and Office Parks, Chi Epsilon. Republican. Presbyterian. Club: Mpls. Athletic, Toastmasters (Mpls.) (adminstrv. v.p. 1985). Real property, Construction, Environment. Home: 2200 W Hoyt Ave Saint Paul MN 55108 Office: O'Connor & Hannan 3800 IDS Tower Minneapolis MN 55402

STRAUS, JOSEPH PENNINGTON, lawyer; b. Phila., May 30, 1911; s. M. Franklin and Ella (Pennington) S.; m. Ruth Wolstenholme, June 24, 1933 (dec. Dec. 17, 1977); children: Anne S. (Mrs. John M. Rusk), Susan S. (Mrs. William H. Rorer III), Helen H. (Mrs. Alexander Stephens Clay IV); m. Rosemary Teresa Ioele, Dec. 30, 1978. A.B., U. Pa., 1932, LL.B., 1935. Bar: Pa. 1935. Counsel RFC, 1938-42; partner firm Schnader, Harrison, Segal & Lewis, Phila., 1948—; dir. Precision Tube Inc. Alt. Contbr. articles to profl. publs. U.S. rep. Internat. Conf. Wills, U.S. State Dept., 1973; Pres. Chestnut Hill Community Assn., 1957-58, mem. bd., 1960-66; exec. com. Com. of Seventy, 1960—, chmn., 1962-66; exec. com. Citizens Council on City Planning, 1961-64; vice chmn. Citizens Charter Com., 1956-64; bd. govs. Settlement Music Sch., Phila, vice chmn., 1962-67, mem. central bd. trustees, counsel, 1967—; chmn. bd. mgrs. All Saints Hosp., Phila., 1980—; Phila. co-chmn. White House Conf. on Children and Youth, 1970; mem., past chmn. bd. govs. Heart Assn. S.E. Pa.; bd. dirs., treas. Theodore F. Jenkins Meml. Law Library, 1974—; past vestryman St. Martin-in-the Fields; trustee Police Athletic League Phila.; bd. govs. Epis. Community Services, Diocese of Pa., 1979—; bd. dirs. Amici Center for Italian Studies, U. Pa., 1979—. Served to lt. USNR, 1944-46. Recipient William Treat award Nat. Coll. Probate Judges, 1979. Fellow Am. Bar Found., Internat. Acad. Estate and Trust Law; mem. Am. Bar Assn. (ho. of dels. 1974-78, past chmn., council sect. real property, probate and trust law, chmn. com. nat. conf. groups), Pa. Bar Assn. (past chmn. sect. real property, probate trust law), Phila Bar Soc. (bd. govs. 1968-71), Am. Judicature Soc., Juristic Soc., Pa., Germantown hist. socs., Chestnut Hill Hist. Soc. (pres. 1986—), Pa. Acad. Fine Arts, Am. Coll. Probate Counsel (past pres.), Am. Law Inst. (co-chmn. joint editorial bd. uniform probate code, adv. com. Pa. joint state govt. commn. 1971—), World Assn. Lawyers, Newcomen Soc., Phila. Musical Fund Soc., Independence Hall Soc. (bd. dirs.), Welcome Soc. Pa. (trustee 1977—), Colonial Soc. Pa. (councillor 1985—), Pa. Soc. Colonial Wars, Phi Beta Kappa. Clubs: Racquet, Phila. Cricket, Corinthian Yacht, Peale, Urban. Estate planning, Probate, Estate taxation. Home: 719 Glengarry Rd Philadelphia PA 19118 Office: 1600 Market St Philadelphia PA 19103

STRAUS, WILLIAM MARC, lawyer; b. Orange, N.J., June 26, 1956; s. Howard and Helaine (Nelkin) S.; m. Kerry Ann Shortle, June 15, 1985. BA, Middlebury Coll., 1977; JD, Georgetown U., 1982. Bar: Va. 1982, Mass. 1982, U.S. Ct. Appeals (4th cir.) 1982, U.S. Dist. Ct. Mass. 1983. Editorial asst. The New Republic, Washington, 1976; aide U.S. Senate, Washington, 1978-80; ptnr. Lang, Straus, Xifaras & Bullard P.A., New Bedford, Mass., 1983—. Mem. ABA, Mass. Bar Assn., Assn. Trial Lawyers Am., Sierra Club. Avocation: skiing. Labor, Pension, profit-sharing, and employee benefits, Federal civil litigation. Office: Lang Straus Xifaras & Bullard PA 81 Hawthorn St New Bedford MA 02740

STRAUSS, EDWARD KENNETH, lawyer; b. Santa Monica, Calif., Jan. 14, 1944; s. Harold Heumann and Henrietta (Gottesman) S.; m. Henria Sue Hyman, Aug. 8, 1971; children: Aaron, Rebecca. SB, MIT, 1965, SM, 1969; JD, U. Pitts., 1974. Bar: Pa. 1974, U.S. Dist. Ct. (mid. dist.) Pa. 1974, U.S. Dist. Ct. (we. dist.) Pa. 1975, Republic of Palau 1986. Sole practice Selinsgrove, Pa., 1974-75; assoc. Berkman, Ruslander, Pohl, Lieber & Engel, Pitts., 1975-79, ptnr., 1979—. Editor U. Pitts. Law Rev., 1973-74. Mem. ABA, Assn. Trial Lawyers Am., Nat. Assn. Bond Lawyers, Order of Coif. Clubs: Westmoreland Country (Export, Pa.), Rivers (Pitts.). Avocations: golf, tennis, squash, flying, skiing. Municipal bonds, Securities, International finance. Home: 3822 Burnaby Dr Pittsburgh PA 15235 Office: Berkman Ruslander Pohl Lieber & Engel 4000 One Oxford Ctr Pittsburgh PA 15219

STRAUSS, GARY JOSEPH, lawyer; b. N.Y.C., July 6, 1953; s. Stanley Vinson and Frieda (Fischoff) S. BA magna cum laude, City Coll. of N.Y., 1974; JD, NYU, 1977. Bar: N.Y. 1978, Fla. 1980. Assoc. Finley, Kumble, Wagner, Heine & Underberg, N.Y.C., 1977-79; ptnr. Phillips, Nizer, Benjamin, Krim & Ballon, N.Y.C., 1979-87, Gaston Snow Beekman & Bogue, N.Y.C., 1987—. Mem. ABA (chmn. N.Y. com. current literature and real property law 1977), Fla. Bar Assn., N.Y. State Bar Assn. Real property. Home: 20 E 35th St Apt 8H New York NY 10016 Office: Gaston Snow Beekman & Bogue 14 Wall St New York NY 10005

STRAUSS, PETER L(ESTER), legal educator, consultant; b. N.Y.C., Feb. 26, 1940; s. Simon D. and Elaine Ruth (Mandle) S.; m. Joanna Burnstine, Oct. 1, 1964; children—Benjamin, Bethany. A.B. magna cum laude, Harvard U., 1961; LL.B. magna cum laude, Yale U., 1964. Bar: D.C. 1965, U.S. Supreme Ct., 1968. Law clk. U.S. Ct. Appeals D.C. Cir., 1964-65, U.S. Supreme Ct., 1965-66; lectr. Haile Selassie U. Sch. Law, Addis Ababa, Ethiopia, 1966-68; asst. to solicitor gen. Dept. Justice, Washington, 1968-71; assoc. prof. law Columbia U., 1971-74, prof., 1974—, Betts Prof., 1985—; gen. counsel NRC, 1975-77; pub. mem. Adminstrv. Conf. U.S., nominating com. Am. Assn. Law Schs. Recipient John Marshall prize Dept. Justice, 1970, Disting. Service award NRC, 1977. Mem. ABA (chmn. separation of powers com. sect. adminstrv. law), Am. Law Inst. Author: (with Abba Paulos, translator) Fetha Negast: The Law of the Kings, 1968; (with others) Administrative Law Cases and Comments, 1986; (with Paul Verkuil) Administrative Law Problems, 1983; contbr. articles to law revs. Administrative and regulatory, Legal education, Constitutional. Office: Columbia U Sch Law 435 W 116 St New York NY 10027

STRAUSS, ROBERT SCHWARZ, lawyer; b. Lockhart, Tex., Oct. 19, 1918; s. Charles H. and Edith V. (Schwarz) S.; m. Helen Jacobs, 1941; children: Robert A., Richard C., Susan. LL.B., U. Tex., 1941. Bar: Tex.

1941, D.C. 1971. Spl. agt. FBI, 1941-45; ptnr. Akin, Gump, Strauss, Hauer & Feld, Dallas, 1945-77, 81—; pres. Strauss Broadcasting Co., 1964; Dem. nat. committeeman from Tex. 1968-72; mem. exec. com. Dem. Nat. Com., 1969-77, treas., 1970-72, chmn., 1972-77; spl. rep. for trade negotiations with rank of ambassador Office of Pres., 1977-79; chmn. Pres. Carter's reelection campaign, 1979-81; Pres.'s personal rep. for Mid. East negotiations 1979-81; dir. Lone Star Industries Inc., Greenwich, Conn., Archer-Daniels-Midland Co., Decatur, Ill., Music Corp. Am., Los Angeles, Pepsico, Purchase, N.Y., Xerox, Rochester, N.Y. Recipient Presdl. medal of freedom, 1980. Mem. ABA, Dallas Bar Assn., D.C. Bar Assn. Jewish. Banking, General corporate, Public international. Office: Akin Gump Strauss Hauer & Feld 4100 First City Center Dallas TX 75201 also: 1333 New Hampshire Ave NW Suite 400 Washington DC 20036 also: 900 MBank Tower Austin TX 78701 also: 700 N St Mary's San Antonio TX 78205 also: 445 Park Ave New York NY 10022 also: 31 Curzon St, London England W1 also: 2604 Tex Am Bank Bldg Fort Worth TX 76102

STRAWN, DAVID UPDEGRAFF, lawyer, consultant, lecturer, researcher; b. DeLand, Fla., May 21, 1936; s. Robert Richey and Marian (Warner) S.; m. Frances Freeland, Aug. 30, 1974; children—Glynn Laurel, Kirk Cabell, Trisha Weyand. B.A., U. Fla., 1958, J.D., 1961. Bar: Fla. 1961. With Akerman, Turnbull, Senterfitt & Edison, Orlando, Fla., 1961-62, Gleason & Strawn, Melbourne, Fla., 1962-67, Strawn and Rumberger, Melbourne, 1967-70; judge 18th Jud. Cir. Ct. Fla., Titusville, 1972-78; sheriff Brevard County (Fla.), 1978-79, vis. professorial lectr. Holland Law Ctr., U. Fla., Gainesville, 1979; ptnr. Akerman, Senterfitt and Edison, Orlando, 1979-83; faculty Nat. Jud. Coll., 1976—; chmn. Fla. Legis. Study Commn. Alternative Dispute Resolution for Cts., 1984-85. Bd. dirs. Fla. Endowment for Humanities, 1976-79; v.p. U. Central Fla. Found., 1977-79; chmn. bd. dirs. Inst. Study of Trial, U. Central Fla., Orlando, 1978—. Recipient Disting. Service award Fla. Council Crime and Delinquency, 1977, Sunshine award Soc. Profl. Journalists Central Fla., 1978. Mem. ABA, Fla. Bar Assn., Fla. Bar, Fla. Bar Found., Am. Judicature Soc. (bd. dirs. 1984—). Author: Communication and Courtroom Advocacy; contbr. articles to legal jours. and gen. interest periodicals. Federal civil litigation, State civil litigation, Family and matrimonial. Office: 100 W Lucerne Circle Suite 602 Orlando FL 32801

STRAWN, JAMES ROY, lawyer; b. Bloomington, Ill., June 15, 1956; s. Roy William and Carol Ann (Wilson) S. BA, Okla. State U., 1978; JD, U. Tulsa, 1981. Bar: Okla. 1981, U.S. Dist. Ct. (we. dist.) Okla. 1982, Tex. 1985. Trial examiner Okla. Corp. Commn., Oklahoma City, 1981-83; assoc. Conoco Inc., Houston, 1983—. Mem. Okla.-Kans. Mid-Continent Oil and Gas Assn., Phi Delta Phi. Computer, Oil and gas leasing, Administrative and regulatory. Office: Conoco Inc 600 N Dairy Ashford Houston TX 77079

STRAYHORN, RALPH NICHOLS, JR., lawyer; b. Durham, N.C., Feb. 16, 1923; 27101 Ralph Nichols and Annie Jane (Cooper) S.; m. Donleen Carol MacDonald, Sept. 10, 1949; children—Carol Strayhorn Rose, Ralph Nichols III. B.S. in Bus. Adminstrn., U. N.C., 1947, LL.B., 1950. Bar: N.C. 1950, U.S. Dist. Ct. (mid. and ea. dists.) N.C. 1950, U.S. Ct. Appeals (4th cir.) 1950. Assoc. Victor S. Bryant, Sr., Durham, 1950-55; ptnr. Bryant, Lipton, Strayhorn & Bryant, Durham, 1956-62; sr. ptnr. Newson, Graham, Strayhorn & Hedrick, Durham, 1962-78; gen. counsel Wachovia Corp., Wachovia Bank and Trust Co., N.A., Winston-Salem, N.C., 1978-86, 1st Wachovia Corp., 1986—; mem. legal adv. com. to N.Y. Stock Exchange; adv. dir. Wachovia Bank and Trust Co., Durham, 1973-78; chmn. bd. 1st Fed. Savs. & Loan Assn., Durham, 1976-78; mem. N.C. Gen. Assembly, 1959-61; bd. of visitors U. N.C., Wake Forest U Law Sch. Served to lt. comdr. USN, 1943-46. Fellow Am. Coll. Trial Lawyers, Am. Bar Found.; mem. N.C. Bar Assn. (pres. 1971-72), Newcomen Soc. of U.S., 4th Jud. Conf., Forsyth Bar Assn., ABA. Democrat. Episcopalian. Clubs: Twin City, Old Town, Rotary (Winston-Salem); Hope Valley Country (Durham). Federal civil litigation, State civil litigation, Banking. Office: First Wachovia Corp 301 N Main St Winston-Salem NC 27101

STRAZZELLA, JAMES ANTHONY, legal educator, lawyer; b. Hanover, Pa., May 18, 1939; s. Anthony F. and Teresa Ann (D'Alonzo) S.; m. Judith A. Coppola, Oct. 9, 1965; children—Jill M., Steven A., Tracy Ann, Michael P. Student U. Del., 1957-58; A.B. Villanova U., 1961; J.D., U. Pa., 1964. Bar: Pa. 1964, U.S. Ct. Appeals (3d cir.) 1964, D.C. 1965, U.S. Dist. Ct. D.C. 1965, U.S. Ct. Appeals (D.C. cir.) 1965, U.S Dist Ct. (ea. dist.) Pa. 1969, U.S. Supreme Ct. 1969, U.S. Ct. Appeals (4th cir.) 1983. Law clk. to justice Pa. Supreme Ct., 1964-65; asst. dept. chief appeals, spl. asst. to U.S. Atty., Washington, D.C., 1965-69; vice dean, asst. prof. law U. Pa., Phila., 1969-73; faculty Temple U. Sch. Law, Phila., 1973—, prof., 1974—, acting dean, 1987—; chief counsel Kent State investigation Pres.'s Commn. Campus Unrest, 1970; chmn. Atty. Gen.'s Task Force on Family Violence, Pa., 1985—; mem., chmn. justice ops. Mayor's Criminal Justice Coordinating Commn., Phila., 1983-85; Pa. Joint Council Criminal Justice, 1979-82; Com. to Study Pa.'s Unified Jud. System, 1980-82; Jud. Council Pa., 1972-82; chmn. criminal procedural rules com. Pa. Supreme Ct., 1972-85; mem. task force on prison overcrowding Pa. Commn. on Crime and Delinquency, 1983-85; designate D.C. Com. on Adminstrv. Justice Under Emergency Conditions, 1968; Cons. Am. Acad. Jud. Edn. Dir., past pres. A Better Chance in Lower Merion; dir. Hist. Fire Mus., Phila.; dir. Neighborhood Civic Assn. Bala, 1984—; active Boy Scouts Am. Recipient Lindback Found. award for disting. teaching, 1983. Mem. Am. Law Inst., ABA (faculty appellate judges' seminars 1977—, chair various coms.), Pa. Bar Assn. (commn. profl. standards 1981-84, chmn. criminal law sect., 1986—), D.C. Bar (Chair various coms.), Phila. Bar Assn. (criminal justice sect., appellate cts. com., del. D.C. Jud. Conf. 1985), Order of the Coif (exec. bd. Phila.), St. Thomas More Soc. (pres., 1985-86, dir. Phila. area). Roman Catholic. Contbr. articles to legal jours. Legal education, Criminal, Federal civil litigation. Office: Temple U Law Center 1719 N Broad St Philadelphia PA 19122

STREETER, BENJAMIN ARRINGTON, III, lawyer; b. Portsmouth, Va., June 18, 1954; s. Benjamin Arrington Jr. and Kee Soon (Lee) S.; m. Andrea Baldassarre, Nov. 28, 1975; children: Benjamin Arrington IV, Courtney Meagan. BA, Mich. State U., 1976; JD, U. Chgo., 1979. Bar: D.C. 1979, U.S. Ct. Appeals (D.C. cir.) 1980, U.S. Dist. Ct. (no. dist.) Ill. 1983. Assoc. Covington & Burling, Washington, 1979-81, Jenner & Block, Chgo., 1981-83; ptnr. Benjamin A. Streeter III, Chgo., 1985—. Nat. bd. dirs. Ams. for Dem. Action, Washington. Mem. ABA, D.C. Bar Assn. Federal civil litigation, Civil rights. Office: Benjamin A Streeter III Ltd 332 S Michigan Ave Suite 1000 Chicago IL 60604

STREETER, TOM, lawyer; b. Worcester, Mass., July 30, 1948; s. Thomas W. and Barbara (Brown) S.; m. Patricia Wimmer, July 31, 1971; children: Karen, Kathryn. Student, Rice U., 1966-69; BS in Polit. Sci., U. Houston, 1972; JD, U. Tex., 1975; BS in Physics summa cum laude, U. Tex., Dallas, 1986. Bar: Tex. 1975, U.S. Dist. Ct. (ea. dist.) Tex. 1977, U.S. Ct. Appeals (5th cir.) 1977, U.S. Supreme Ct. 1978, U.S. Dist. Ct. (no. dist.) Tex. 1979, U.S. Patent Office 1985. Asst. county atty. Grayson County, Sherman, Tex., 1975-77; sole practice Sherman, 1977-79, Richardson, Tex., 1986; asst. dist. atty. Dallas County, 1979-85; assoc. Law Offices Allan R. Fowler, Irvine, Calif., 1986—. Served with U.S. Army, 1969-71, Vietnam. Decorated Bronze Star, Air medal. Mem. ABA (patent sect.), Tex. Bar Assn. (patent sect.). Democrat. Episcopalian. Patent, Criminal. Home: 62 Greenbough Irvine CA 92714 Office: 18662 MacArthur Blvd #460 Irvine CA 92714

STREICHER, JAMES FRANKLIN, lawyer; b. Ashtabula, Ohio, Dec. 6, 1940; s. Carl Jacob and Helen Marie (Dugan) S.; m. Sandra JoAnn Jennings, May 22, 1940; children—Cheryl Ann, Gregory Scott, Kerry Marie. B.A., Ohio State U., 1962; J.D., Case Western Res. U., 1966. Bar: Ohio 1966, U.S. Dist. Ct. (no. dist.) Ohio 1966. Assoc., Calfee, Halter & Griswold, Cleve., 1966-71, ptnr., 1972—; mem. Div. Securities Adv. Bd., State of Ohio; lectr. Case Western Res. U., Cleve. State U., Ctr. for Venture Devel. Trustee Cottillion Soc., Hiram House Camp, Soc. Crippled Children. Mem. ABA, Ohio State Bar Assn., Greater Cleve. Bar Assn. (chmn. corp., banking and bus. law sect. 1980-84), Ohio State U. Alumni Assn., Case Western Res. U. Alumni Assn., Newcomen Soc., Beta Theta Pi, Phi Delta Phi. Republican. Roman Catholic. Clubs: Hermit, Mayfield Country (bd. dirs. 1985—), Tavern, Union. General corporate, Real property, Partnership. Home: 50 Windrush Moreland Hills OH 44022

STREICKER, RICHARD DANIEL, lawyer; b. Chgo., Aug. 1, 1952; s. Ned Charles and Dolores May (Tronsky) S. BA, U. Mich., 1974; JD, Harvard U., 1978. Bar: Ill. 1978, U.S. Dist. Ct. (no. dist.) Ill. 1979, Calif. 1980, U.S. Dist. Ct. (cen. dist.) Calif. 1981. Assoc. Mayer, Brown & Platt, Chgo., 1978-79, Mitchell, Silberberg & Knupp, Los Angeles, 1980-81; sr. dir. bus. affairs Warner Bros. Records Inc., Burbank, Calif., 1982—. Mem. Ill. Bar Assn., Calif. Bar Assn. Avocations: literature, music. Entertainment. Home: 409 N Norton Ave Los Angeles CA 90004 Office: Warner Bros Records Inc 3300 Warner Blvd Burbank CA 91510

STRENSKI, ROBERT FRANCIS, lawyer; b. Chgo., Oct. 10, 1947; s. Bernard F. and Harriet L. (Prokopiak) S. B.S., U. Ill., 1969; J.D., Washington U., St. Louis, 1973; postgrad. U. Colo., 1975. Bar: Mo. 1973, Colo. 1974. Acct. Motorola, Inc., Chgo., 1970; acct. City and County of Denver, 1973-74, asst. city atty., 1974—. Precinct committeeman Denver Democratic Com., 1976-78, dist. fin. chmn., 1977-78; arbitrator Better Bus. Bur., Denver, 1977—; mediator Ctr. for Dispute Resolution, Denver, 1980. Mem. Colo. Bar Assn., Denver Bar Assn., Nat. Inst. Mcpl. Law Officers (ethics com. 1985-87), Am. Arbitration Assn. (arbitrator). Democrat. Roman Catholic. Administrative and regulatory, State and local taxation, Local government. Home: 410 Pearl St Denver CO 80203 Office: Law Dept City and County of Denver 353 City and County Bldg Denver CO 80202

STRIBLING, GRAY CARROLL, JR., lawyer; b. St. Louis, Apr. 23, 1941; s. Gray Carroll Sr. and Jane Polk (Forder) S.; m. Madeline Traugott, June 3, 1967 (div. Aug. 1983); 1 child, William C.M.; m. Maryella Kelly, Apr. 6, 1986. BA, Trinity Coll., Hartford, Conn., 1963; JD, Washington U., St. Louis, 19 67. Bar: Mo. 1967, U.S. Dist. Ct. (ea. dist.) Mo. 1967, U.S. Ct. Appeals (8th cir.) 1968, U.S. Tax Ct. 1972, U.S. Supreme Ct. 1979, U.S. Ct. Appeals (6th cir.) 1986. Assoc. Fordyce & Mayne P.C., St. Louis, 1967-72, ptnr., 1972—. V.p., bd. dirs. Consol. Neighborhood Services, Inc., St. Louis, 1985—; pres., bd. dirs. Bach. Soc. St. Louis, 1985—. Mem. ABA, Mo. Bar Assn., Am. Arbitration Assn. (comml. panel 1983—). Federal civil litigation, State civil litigation. Office: Fordyce & Mayne PC 120 S Central Suite 1100 Saint Louis MO 63105

STRICKLAND, DELPHENE COVERSTON, lawyer, administrative law judge; b. Ponca City, Okla.; d. Harry Ethelbert and Mary Louise (Reed) Coverston; m. Thomas Whitney Strickland, Aug. 31, 1946; children—Mary Evalyn, Thomas Whitney. B.A., John B. Stetson U., 1944; J.D., U. Fla.-Gainesville, 1945; postgrad. student Fla. State U., 1965, 70. Bar: Fla. 1945, U.S. Dist. Ct. (so. dist.) Fla. 1946, U.S. Dist. Ct. (no. dist.) Fla. 1966, U.S. Dist. Ct. (no. dist.) Tex. 1979, U.S. Dist. Ct. Hawaii, 1980, U.S. Supreme Ct. 1980, U.S. Ct. Appeals (11th dist.) 1983. Assoc., Rogers & Morris, Ft. Lauderdale, Fla., 1945-46, Clayton, Arnow, Johnson & Duncan, Gainesville, Fla., 1946-51; sole practice Delphene Strickland Law Offices, Gainesville, 1951-59; legal research asst. Fla. Supreme Ct., 1960-68, exec. asst., 1968-70; adj. prof. U. Fla., Gainesville, Fla. State U., Tallahassee; Fla. del. to 1983 11th Cir. Jud. Conf.; mem. Fla. Bd. Bar Examiners, 1970-80; mem. Fla. Traffic Ct. Rev. Com., 1970—, Fla. Supreme Ct. Efficiency Com., 1984—. . Mem. ABA (chmn. nat. conf. adminstrv. law judges 1983-84 exec. council 1985—), Fla. Assn. Women Lawyers (past pres.), Fla. Govt. Bar Assn. (past pres.), Tallahassee Women Lawyers Assn. (past pres.), Nat. Assn. Women Lawyers (Fla. del.), Nat. Assn. Women Judges, Am. Arbitration Assn., AAUW (past pres. Gainesville), Supreme Ct. Hist. Soc., Fla. Supreme Ct. Hist. Soc. (organizer, charter, trustee), Phi Alpha Delta. Clubs: Capital City Country, Zonta. Contbr. articles to legal jours. Administrative and regulatory, Legislative, General practice. Office: 2802 Sterling Dr Tallahassee FL 32312

STRICKON, HARVEY ALAN, lawyer; b. Bklyn., Nov. 9, 1947; s. Milton and Norma (Goodhartz) S.; m. Linda Carol Meltzer, July 2, 1972; children: Joshua Andrew, Meredith Cindy, Erica Stacey. BBA, CCNY, 1968; JD, NYU, 1971. Bar: N.Y. 1972, U.S. Dist. Ct. (so. and ea. dists.) N.Y. 1973, U.S. Ct. Appeals (2d cir.) 1973, U.S. Supreme Ct. 1975, U.S. Dist. Ct. (no. dist.) N.Y. 1980, U.S. Dist. Ct. (we. dist.) N.Y. 1981. Law clk. U.S. Dist. Ct. (ea. dist.) N.Y., Bklyn., 1971-73; assoc. Moses & Singer, N.Y.C., 1973-80; from assoc. to ptnr. Kaye, Scholer, Fierman, Hays & Handler, N.Y.C., 1980—. Mem. Nassau County Rep. Com., Great Neck, N.Y., 1982—; chmn. bd. dirs. Flushing Community Vol. Ambulance Corps. Inc., N.Y., 1981-86. Mem. ABA, N.Y. State Bar Assn., Assn. of Bar of City of N.Y., Am. Judicature Soc., Assn. Comml. Fin. Attys., N.Y. Law Inst., Bankruptcy Lawyers Bar Assn. Republican. Jewish. Bankruptcy, Contracts commercial. Home: 27 Carriage Rd Great Neck NY 11024-1445 Office: Kaye Scholer Fierman Hays & Handler 425 Park Ave New York NY 10022

STRIMBU, VICTOR, JR., lawyer; b. New Philadelphia, Ohio, Nov. 25, 1932; s. Victor and Veda (Stancu) S.; m. Kathryn May Schrote, Apr. 9, 1955; children—Victor Paul, Michael, Julie, Sue. B.A., Heidelberg Coll., 1954; postgrad. Western Res. U., 1956-57; LL.B., Columbia U., 1960. Bar: Ohio 1960, U.S. Supreme Ct. 1972. With Baker & Hostetler, Cleve., 1960—, ptnr., 1970—. Mem. Bay Village (Ohio) Bd. Edn., 1976-84, pres., 1977-81; mem. Cleve. State U. Indsl. Relations Adv. Com., 1979—, chmn., 1982; mem. Bay Village Planning Commn., 1967-69; life mem. Ohio PTA; mem. Greater Cleve. Growth Assn.; bd. of trustees New Cleve. Campaign, 1987—. Served as pfc AUS, 1955-56. Recipient Service award Cleve. State U., 1980. Mem. Ohio Bar Assn., ABA, Greater Cleve. Bar Assn., Ohio Newspaper Assn. (minority affairs com. 1987—). Republican. Presbyterian. Clubs: Order of Nisi Prius, Cleve. Athletic. Labor. Office: Baker & Hostetler 3200 National City Center Cleveland OH 44114

STRINGER, EDWARD CHARLES, lawyer, food company executive; b. St. Paul, Feb. 13, 1935; s. Philip and Anne (Driscoll) S.; m. Mary Lucille Lange, June 19, 1957; children: Philip, Lucille, Charles, Carolyn. BA, Amherst Coll., 1957; LLD, U. Minn., 1960. Bar: Minn. Ptnr. Stringer, Donnelly & Sharood, St. Paul, 1960-69, Briggs & Morgan, St. Paul, 1969-79; sr. v.p., gen. counsel Pillsbury Co., Mpls., 1980-82, exec. v.p., gen. counsel, 1982-83, exec. v.p., gen. counsel, chief adminstrv. officer, 1983—. Trustee William Mitchell Coll. Law, Minn. Pvt. Coll. Fund; bd. dirs. Minn. Planned Parenthood, 1983, Mpls. United Way, 1983, Northland Coll. Mem. ABA, Minn. State Bar Assn., Ramsey County Bar Assn. (sec. 1977-80), Order of Coif. Unitarian. Clubs: Mpls.; Somerset Country; Madeline Island Yacht (La Pointe, Wis.). Home: 795 Hilltop Ct Saint Paul MN 55118 Office: Pillsbury Co 200 S 6th St Minneapolis MN 55402

STRINGHAM, JACK FRED, II, bank holding company executive, lawyer; b. Cookeville, Tenn., Sept. 4, 1946; m. Anne Ramsey, Dec. 19, 1969; children: Sara Ramsey, John Ross. B.A., Vanderbilt U., 1968, J.D., 1974. Atty. Barksdale, Whalley, Gilbert & Frank, Nashville, 1973-77; asst. gen. counsel First Am. Corp., Nashville, 1977-79, sec., 1979-81, sr. v.p., gen. counsel, 1981—. Served to 1st lt. U.S. Army, 1969-71. Recipient Man of Yr. award. Nashville Area Jaycees, 1980. Mem. ABA, Tenn. Bar Assn., Nashville Bar Assn. Presbyterian. General corporate, Banking. Home: 4437 Sheppard Pl Nashville TN 37205 Office: First Am Corp First Am Ctr Nashville TN 37237

STRITMATTER, PAUL LESTER, lawyer; b. Aberdeen, Wash., Apr. 23, 1943; s. Lester Otho and Dolcia Ruth (Rice) S.; m. JoAnn Harriet Rhebeck, Mar. 23, 1963; children: Daniel, Lynn. BA in Econs., U. Wash., 1966; JD magna cum laude, Willamette Law Sch., Salem, Oreg., 1969. Bar: Wash. 1969, U.S. Dist. Ct. (we. dist.) Wash. 1973. Law clk. to presiding justice Wash. State Supreme Ct., Olympia, 1969-70; ptnr. Stritmatter & Stritmatter, Hoquiam, Wash., 1970-82, Stritmatter, Kessler & McCauley, Hoquiam, 1982—; judge City of Ocean Shores, Wash., 1970—. Chmn. Sch. Levy Drives, Hoquiam, 1975-76; pres. Hoquiam YMCA, 1979. Fellow Am. Acad. Trial Lawyers, Am. Coll. Trial Lawyers, Internat. Soc. Barristers; mem. ABA, Wash. State Bar Assn., Assn. Trial Lawyers Am. (del. 1986), Wash. Trial Lawyers Assn. (pres. 1985, Brandeis award 1982), Damage Atty.'s Roundtable, Am. Bd. Trial Advs., Internat. Acad. Trial Lawyers, Hoaquim C. of C. (bd. dirs. 1978). Lodge: Lions. State civil litigation, Insurance, Personal injury. Home: 306 Semler Ct Hoquiam WA 98550 Office: Stritmatter Kessler & McCauley 407 8th St Hoquiam WA 98550

STRIZEVER, WILLIAM J(AY), lawyer; b. N.Y.C., July 14, 1950; s. Milton B. and Sylvia S. B.A., Johns Hopkins U., 1972; J.D., Georgetown U., 1975; LL.M. in Taxation, NYU, 1979. Bar: N.Y. 1976, U.S. Dist. Ct. (so. and ea. dists.) N.Y. 1976. Assoc. Phillips, Nizer, Benjamin, Krim & Ballon, N.Y.C., 1975-77, Paul, Weiss, Rifkind, Wharton & Garrison, N.Y.C., 1977-79; ptnr. Bressler, Lipsitz & Rothenberg, N.Y.C., 1979-84; sole practice, N.Y.C., 1984—. Editor: Georgetown Law Jour., 1974. Mem. Assn. Bar City N.Y., N.Y. State Bar Assn., ABA, Phi Beta Kappa. Corporate taxation, Personal income taxation. Office: 650 Fifth Ave New York NY 10019

STROBEL, MARTIN JACK, motor vehicle and industrial component manufacturing and distribution company executive; b. N.Y.C., July 4, 1940; s. Nathan and Clara (Sorgen) S.; m. Hadassah Orenstein, Aug. 15, 1965; children: Gil Michael, Karen Rachel. BA, Columbia U., 1962; JD, Cleve. Marshall Law Sch., 1966; completed advanced bus. mgmt. program, Harvard U., 1977. Bar: Ohio bar 1966. Counsel def. contract adminstrn. services region Def. Supply Agy., Cleve., 1966-68; with Dana Corp., Toledo, 1968—; gen. counsel Dana Corp., 1970—, dir. govt. relations, 1970-71, asst. sec., 1971—, v.p., 1976—, sec., 1982—; adv. com. C.A. Dana Inst. Internat. and Comparative Legal Studies. Mem. Am. Bar Assn., Fed. Bar Assn., Machinery and Allied Products Inst., Ohio Bar Assn., Toledo Bar Assn. General corporate. Office: 4500 Dorr St Toledo OH 43615

STRODE, JOSEPH ARLIN, lawyer; b. DeWitt, Ark., Mar. 5, 1946; s. Thomas Joseph and Nora (Richardson) S.; m. Carolyn Taylor, Feb. 9, 1969; children—Tanya Briana, William Joseph. B.S.E.E. with honors, U. Ark., 1969; J.D., So. Meth. U., 1972. Bar: Ark. 1972. Design engr. Tex. Instruments Inc., Dallas, 1969-70, patent agt., 1970-72; assoc. Bridges, Young, Matthews, Holmes & Drake, Pine Bluff, Ark., 1972-74, ptnr., 1975—. Bd. dirs. United Way Jefferson County, Pine Bluff, 1975-77, campaign chmn., 1983, pres., 1986, exec. com., 1983-87; bd. dirs. Leadership Pine Bluff, 1983-85. Mem. ABA, Ark. Bar Assn., Jefferson County Bar Assn., Pine Bluff C. of C. (dir. 1981-84), Ark. Wildlife Fed. (dir. 1979-81), Jefferson County Wildlife Assn. (dir. 1973-80, pres. 1974-76), Order of Coif, Tau Beta Pi, Eta Kappa Nu. Club: Kiwanis (lt. gov. Mo.-Ark. div. 1983-84, chm. lt. govs. 1983-84). Contracts commercial, General practice. Home: Route 9 Box 908 Pine Bluff AR 71603 Office: 315 E 8th St PO Box 7808 Pine Bluff AR 71611

STRODEL, ROBERT CARL, lawyer; b. Evanston, Ill., Aug. 12, 1930; s. Carl Frederick and Imogene (Board) S.; m. Mary Alice Shonkwiler, June 17, 1956; children: Julie Ann, Linda Lee, Sally Payson. B.S., Northwestern U., 1952; J.D., U. Mich., 1955. Bar: Ill. 1955, U.S. Supreme Ct. 1970. Mem. firm Davis, Morgan & Witherell, Peoria, Ill., 1957-59; sole practice Peoria, 1959-69; prin. Strodel, Kingery & Durree Assoc., Peoria, Ill., 1969—; asst. state's atty. Peoria, 1960-61; instr. bus. law Bradley U., Peoria, 1961-62; lectr. Belli seminars, 1969-83; lectr. in trial practice; mem. U.S. Presdl. Commn. German-Am. Tricentennial, 1983. Author books and articles in med.-legal field. Gov. appointee Ill. Dangerous Drugs Advisory Council, 1970-73; gen. chmn. Peoria-Tazewell Easter Seals, 1963, Cancer Crusade, 1970; pres. Peoria Civic Ballet, 1969-70; mem. Mayor's Commn. on Human Relations, 1962-64; chmn. City of Peoria Campaign Ethics Bd., 1975; Peoria County Rep. Sec., 1970-74; campaign chmn. Gov. Richard Ogilvie, Peoria County, 1972, Sen. Ralph Smith, 1970; treas. Michel for Congress, 1977—, campaign coordinator, 1982—; bd. dirs. Crippled Children's Center, 1964-65, Peoria Symphony Orchestra, 1964-68. Served with AUS, 1956-57. Decorated Officer's Cross of Order of Merit (Fed. Republic Germany), 1984; named Outstanding Young Man Peoria Peoria Jr. C. of C., 1963. Mem. Assn. Trial Lawyers Am., Ill. Trial Lawyers Assn., ABA, Ill. Bar Assn. (Lincoln awards for legal writing 1961, 63, 65), Am. Coll. Legal Medicine, Am. Soc. Law and Medicine. Club: Mason (Shriner). Federal civil litigation, State civil litigation, Personal injury. Home: 3908 N Pinehurst Ct Peoria IL 61614 Office: 915 First Nat Bank Bldg Peoria IL 61602

STROHL, PAUL E., lawyer; b. Honolulu, Oct. 13, 1953; s. Paul E. and Mary A. (Ernster) S.; m. Sigrid C. Schroder, Oct. 18, 1980. BA in Govt., Dartmouth Coll., 1974; JD, Harvard U., 1977. Bar: Tex. 1977. Assoc. Butler & Binion and predecessor firm Butler, Binion, Rice, Cook & Knapp, Houston, 1977-83; assoc. Johnson & Swanson, Dallas, 1983-85, ptnr., 1985—. Contbg. editor Natural Gas mag. Mem. ABA (vice chmn. nat. gas marketing and transp. com., nat. resources sect.), Dallas Bar Assn. (council oil gas and mineral law sect., editor newsletter), Internat. Bar Assn., Rocky Mountain Mineral Law Inst. (oil and gas subcom.), Dallas Energy Forum, Harvard Law Sch. Alumni Assn. Republican. Avocations: golf, reading, music. FERC practice, Oil and gas leasing, General corporate. Home: 4626 Hallmark Dr Dallas TX 75229 Office: Johnson & Swanson 300 Founders Sq 900 Jackson St Dallas TX 75202-4499

STROM, LYLE ELMER, federal judge; b. Omaha, Jan. 6, 1925; s. Elmer T. and Eda (Hanisch) S.; m. Regina Ann Kelly, July 31, 1950; children: Mary Bess, Susan Frances, Amy Claire, Cassie A., David Kelly, Margaret Mary, Bryan Thomas. Student, U. Nebr., 1946-47; AB, Creighton U., 1950, JD cum laude, 1953. Bar: Nebr. 1953. Assoc. Fitzgerald, Brown, Leahy, Strom, Schorr & Barmettler and predecessor firm, Omaha, 1953-60, ptnr., 1960-63, gen. trial ptnr., 1963-85; judge U.S. Dist. Ct. Nebr., Omaha, 1985—; bd. dirs. World of Sleep Inc., Unpainted Furniture Ctr. Inc.; adj. prof. law Creighton U., 1959—; mem. com. pattern jury instrns. and practice and proc. Nebr. Supreme Ct., 1965—; spl. legal counsel Omaha Charter Rev. Commn., 1973. Mem. exec. com. Covered Wagon council Boy Scouts Am., 1953-57; chmn. bd. trustees Marian High Sch., 1969-71. Served as ensign USNR and with U.S. Maritime Service, 1943-46. Fellow Am. Coll. Trial Lawyers, Internat. Acad. Trial Lawyers; mem. Citizens for Ednl. Freedom, ABA, Nebr. Bar Assn. (ho. of dels. 1978-81, exec. council 1981—), Omaha Bar Assn. (pres. 1980-81), Am. Judicature Soc., Midwestern Assn. Amateur Athletic Union (pres. 1976-78), Alpha Sigma Nu (pres. alumni chpt. 1970-71). Republican. Roman Catholic. Lodge: Rotary. Office: U S Dist Ct PO Box 607 Omaha NE 68101 *

STROM, MICHAEL A., lawyer; b. Chgo., Dec. 14, 1952; s. David H. and Sylvia (Abelson) S.; m. Sherry Sinett, May 29, 1977; children—Eric M., Shayna D. B.A., U. Ill., 1974; J.D., Boston U., 1977. Bar: Ill. 1977, U.S. Dist. Ct. (no. dist.) Ill. 1977, U.S. Dist. Ct. (no. dist.) Ill., 1982. Assoc. Schaffenegger, Watson & Peterson, Chgo., 1978-85; ptnr., 1985—. Mem. Ill. State Bar Assn., Chgo. Bar Assn., Trial Lawyers Club Chgo., Ill. Trial Lawyers Assn., Chgo. Coalition for Law Related Edn. (instr. 1984—). Jewish. Personal injury, State civil litigation, Federal civil litigation. Office: Schaffenegger Watson & Peterson 69 W Washington Chicago IL 60602

STROM, MILTON GARY, lawyer; b. Rochester, N.Y., Dec. 5, 1942; s. Harold and Dolly (Isaacson) S.; m. Barbara A. Simon, Jan. 18, 1975; children: Carolyn, Michael, Jonathan. BS in Econs., U. Pa., 1964; JD, Cornell U., 1967. Bar: N.Y. 1968, U.S. Dist. Ct. (we. dist.) N.Y. 1968, U.S. Ct. Claims 1969, U.S. Ct. Mil. Appeals 1969, U.S. Ct. Appeals ((D.C. cir.) 1970, U.S. Supreme Ct. 1972, U.S. Dist. Ct. (so. dist.) N.Y. 1975. Atty. SEC, Washington, 1968-71; assoc. Skadden, Arps, Slate, Meagher & Flom, N.Y.C., 1971-77, ptnr., 1977—. Served with USCGR, 1967-68. Mem. ABA, N.Y. State Bar Assn. (corp. law sect.), Assn. of Bar of City of N.Y. Republican. Jewish. Club: Beach Point, Marco Polo. Avocations: tennis, skiing. General corporate, Securities. Office: Skadden Arps et al 919 3d Ave New York NY 10022

STROMBERG, CLIFFORD DOUGLAS, lawyer; b. N.Y.C., June 1, 1949; s. George M. and Greta (Netzow) S.; m. Ava S. Feiner, June 25, 1972; 1 child, Kimberly. BA summa cum laude, Yale U., 1971; JD, Harvard U., 1974. Bar: N.Y. 1975, D.C. 1975, U.S. Dist. Ct. (so. and ea. dists.) N.Y. 1975, U.S. Ct. Appeals (D.C. cir.) 1975, U.S. Ct. Appeals (2nd cir.) 1975, U.S. Supreme Ct. 1980. Law clk. to presiding justice U.S. Dist. Ct. (ea. dist.) N.Y., 1974-75; assoc. Arnold & Porter, Washington, 1975-78, 80-83; dep. exec. sec. HHS, Washington, 1978-79; cons. FTC, Washington, 1979-80; ptnr. Dorsey & Whitney, Washington, 1983-84, Hogan & Hartson, Washington, 1984—. Author: (with Alan Stone, M.D.) Mental Health and Law: A System in Transition, 1975; co-author and editor: Alternatives to the Hospital: Ambulatory Surgery Centers and Emergicenters, 1984, Entrepreneurial Health Care: How to Structure Successful New Ventures, 1985; editorial bd. Harvard Law Rev., 1972, Psychiat. Times; editor in chief Healthspan: The Report of Health Business and Law, 1984—; contbr. articles to profl. jours. Bd. dirs. Nat. Children's Eye Care Found., Washington, 1985—. Teaching fellow in govt. Harvard U., 1973-74. Fellow Am. Bar Found.; mem. ABA (state membership chmn., 1984, forum com. health law, individual rights and responsibilities sect., exec. council, 1980, sec.

1984—, legal aid and indigent defendants com.), Am. Acad. Hosp. Attys., Nat. Health Lawyers Assn., Phi Beta Kappa. Health, Antitrust, Federal civil litigation. Office: Hogan & Hartson 815 Connecticut Ave Washington DC 20006

STROMME, GARY L., lawyer, law librarian, author, lecturer; b. Willmar, Minn., July 8, 1939; s. William A. and Edla A. (Soderberg) S. B.A., Pacific Lutheran U., 1965; B.L.S., U. B.C. (Can.), Vancouver, 1967; J.D., Hastings Coll. of Law; 1973. Bar: Calif. 1973, U.S. Sup. Ct. 1977. Serials librarian U. Minn. St. Paul Campus Library, 1967-69; asst. librarian McCutchen, Doyle, Brown and Enersen, San Francisco, 1970-71, Graham & James, San Francisco, 1971-73; ind. contracting atty., 1973-74; law librarian Pacific Gas and Electric Co., San Francisco, 1974—; lectr. in field. Served with USAF, 1959-63. Mem. Am. Assn. Law Libraries (chmn. com. on indexing of legal periodicals, 1986—), Western Pacific Assn. Law Libraries, No. Calif. Assn. Law Libraries, Pvt. Law Libraries, Corp. Law Libraries, ABA (chmn. library com. of sect. econs. of law practice 1978-82). Author: An Introduction to the use of the Law Library, 1974, 76; Basic Legal Research Techniques, 1979. Librarianship, Public utilities, General corporate. Home: 2589 LeConte Ave Berkeley CA 94709 Office: PO Box 7442 San Francisco CA 94120

STRONE, MICHAEL JONATHAN, lawyer; b. N.Y.C., Feb. 26, 1953; s. Bernard William and Judith Semel (Sogg) S.; m. Andrea Nan Acker, Jan. 27, 1979; 1 child, Noah Gregory. B.A. cum laude, Colby Coll., 1974; J.D., Fordham Law Sch., 1978. Bar: N.J. 1978, N.Y. 1979, U.S. Ct. Appeals (2d and 3d cirs.) 1979, U.S. Dist. Ct. (so. and ea. dists.) N.Y. 1979, U.S. Dist. Ct. N.J. 1979. Assoc. Ratheim Hoffman et al, N.Y.C., 1978-80, Botein Hays et al, N.Y.C., 1980-84; v.p., assoc. gen. counsel Gen. Electric Investment Corp., 1984—. Vice chmn., bd. dirs. N.Y. chpt. Juvenile Diabetes Found., N.Y.C., 1981—, mem. fin. com. Juvenile Diabetes Found. Internat.; pres., chmn. bd. dirs., asst. prin. bassist Westchester Symphony Orch., Scarsdale, N.Y., 1982; vice-chmn. ann. dinner NCCJ, 1987. Mem. ABA (erisa and significant legis. coms. 1985—). Republican. Jewish. Real property, Pension, profit-sharing, and employee benefits, General corporate. Home: Genesee Trail Harrison NY 10528 Office: Gen Electric Investment Corp 292 Long Ridge Rd Stamford CT 06904

STRONG, GEORGE GORDON, JR., litigation and management consultant; b. Toledo, Apr. 19, 1947; s. George Gordon and Jean Boyd (McDougall) S.; m. Annsley Palmer Chapman, Nov. 30, 1974; children: George III, Courtney, Meredith, Alexis. BA, Yale U., 1969; MBA, Harvard U., 1971; JD, U. San Diego, 1974. Bar: Calif. 1974, U.S. Dist. Ct. (cen. dist.) Calif. 1974; CPA, Calif., Hawaii, cert. mgmt. cons., U.S. customs house broker. Controller Vitredent Corp., Beverly Hills, Calif., 1974-76; sr. mgr. Price Waterhouse, Los Angeles, 1976-82, ptnr., 1987—; exec. v.p., chief operating officer Internat. Customs Service, Long Beach, Calif., 1982-84; chief fin. officer Uniform Software Systems, Santa Monica, Calif., 1984-85; exec. v.p. and chief operating officer Cyberlink Corp., 1986; pres. Woodleigh Lane, Inc., Flintridge, Calif., 1985-87; ptnr. Price Waterhouse, 1987—. Active Verdugo Hills Hosp. Adv. Council, Glendale, Calif., 1985. Mem. ABA, Calif. State Bar Assn., Los Angeles County Bar Assn., Am. Inst. CPA's, Calif. Soc. CPA's, Inst. of Mgmt. Cons., Harvard Bus. Sch. Assn. So. Calif. (v.p. 1986—). Republican. Presbyterian. Clubs: Jonathan (Los Angeles), Flint Canyon Tennis (Flintridge); Olympic (San Francisco), La Canada Flintridge Country (San Francisco); Coral Beach and Tennis (Bermuda). Avocations: golf, tennis, bridge. Computer, Federal civil litigation, State civil litigation. Home: 4251 Woodleigh Ln Flintridge CA 91011 Office: 1880 Century Park E West Los Angeles CA 90067

STRONG, JOHN VAN RENSSELAER, lawyer; b. New Brunswick, N.J., Apr. 30, 1912; s. Theodore and Cornelia Livingston (Van Rensselaer) S.; m. Katharine Bayard Bonsall, Apr. 18, 1942 (divorced); children: Katharine Strong Berge, John V. R., Jr., Robert L., Sarah H. JD, Harvard U., 1934, postgrad. Bar: N.J. 1936, U.S. Dist. Ct. N.J. 1939, U.S. Ct. Appeals (3d cir.) 1963, U.S. Supreme Ct. 1965. Sr. ptnr. Strong, Strong, Gavarny & Longhi, New Brunswick, N.J., 1968-75, Strong, Gavarny & Lane, New Brunswick, 1975-79, Strong & Strong, New Brunswick, 1979-85, Strong & Metallo, New Brunswick, 1985—; bd. dirs. Fastcrete Corp., N.Y.C., Am. Internat. Petroleum Corp.; bd. dirs., sec. Chemtree Corp., Cen. Valley, N.Y. Atty. Borough of East Millstone, N.J.; councilman Borough Council, Highland Park, N.J., 1962; treas. Am. Cancer Soc. Middlesex (N.J.) chpt., 1965-75. Served to 1st lt. U.S. Army, 1943-45. Mem. N.J. Bar Assn., Middlesex County Bar Assn., New Brunswick Bar Assn., Nat. Assn. R.R. Trial Counsel, Lords of Manor, Soc. Col. Wars, Descendants of Signers of Declaration of Independence. Republican. Clubs: Somerset Hill Country Club (Bernardsville, N.J.), Nassau (Princeton, N.J.), Harvard (N.J.) (bd. trustees 1965-75). Personal injury, Probate, General practice. Home: Rural Delivery 2 382 Suydam Rd Somerset NJ 08873 Office: Strong & Metallo 303 George St Plaza Bldg PO Box 11 New Brunswick NJ 08903

STRONG, THOMAS GORMAN, lawyer; b. Boston, Dec. 6, 1931; s. Frank Noble and Blanche (Gorman) S.; m. Wilma R. Owens, Nov. 5, 1955; children: John Thomas, Stephanie Sue, David Kevin. BS, Southwest Mo. State U., 1952; JD, U. Mo., 1955. Bar: Mo. 1955, U.S. Dist. Ct. (we. dist.) Mo. 1958, U.S. Ct. Appeals (8th cir.) 1959, U.S. Supreme Ct. 1981. Instr. bus. law U. Mo., Columbia, 1954-55; ptnr. Farrington, Curtis & Strong, Springfield, Mo., 1957-75, Strong & Wooddell P.C., Springfield, 1975—; instr. various orgns. Contbr. articles to profl. jours. Bd. dirs. YMCA, 1971-77. Named one of Outstanding Young Men of Am., 1967. Mem. Mo. Bar Assn. (chmn. tort com. 1980-81, legis. com., chmn. medico legal relations com. 1974, code of evidence com. 1982-83), Greene County Bar Assn. (pres. 1978), Assn. Trial Lawyers Am., Mo. Assn. Trial Attys. (v.p. 1986—), Nat. Bd. Trial Adv., Inner Circle Advs., Fed. Cts. Com., Mo. Appellate Jud. Commn., Mo. Bd. Law Examiners (pres. 1979-80), Southwest Mo. State U. Alumni Assn. (pres. 1965-66), Order of Barristers, Order of Coif. Republican. Methodist. Club: Southwest Mo. State U. Basketball Booster (pres. 1974). Lodge: Kiwanis (pres. South Springfield 1968). Avocations: mountain climbing, snow skiing, racquetball, bicycle riding, horseback riding. Federal civil litigation, State civil litigation, Personal injury. Home: 1366 E Loren Springfield MO 65804 Office: Strong & Wooddell PC 901 E Battlefield Rd Springfield MO 65807

STROTHER, JAMES FRENCH, lawyer; b. Detroit, Jan. 3, 1938; s. John Cover Strother and Dorothy (Baskett) Turner; m. Mary Logan de Butts, Aug. 21, 1965. Student, Woodberry Forest U., 1956; BS in Mech. Engring., U. Va., 1960, LLB, 1966. Bar: Va. 1966, U.S. Ct. Appeals (4th cir.) 1967, D.C. 1968, U.S. Ct. Appeals (2d cir.) 1968. Assoc. Covington & Burling, Washington, 1967-75; gen. counsel Grant Thornton and predecessor firms, Chgo., 1975-86; ptnr. Mayer, Brown & Platt, Washington, 1986—. Served to lt. USN, 1960-63. Mem. ABA, D.C. Bar Assn., Va. Bar Assn. Accountants liability, General corporate, Securities. Office: Mayer Brown & Platt 2000 Pennsylvania Ave NW Washington DC 20006

STROTHER, LANE H., lawyer; b. Altus, Okla., Mar. 26, 1945; s. Lynn H. and Elwanda (Melton) S.; m. Judith L. Cook, Dec. 17, 1966; children: Jodi L., Megan K., Mica J. BA, Ouachita Bapt. U., 1968; MEd, U. Ark., 1970, JD, 1979. Bar: Ark., U.S. Dist. Ct. (we. and ea. dists.) Ark. Gen. agt. Res. Life Ins. Co., Dallas, 1968-70; assoc. dir. devel. Ouachita Bapt. U., Arkadelphia, Ark., 1971-76; agt. Northwestern Nat. Life Ins. Co., Little Rock, 1976-79; ptnr. Osmon, Wilber & Strother, Mountain Home, Ark., 1979-81, Strother Firm, Mountain Home, 1981—; cons. Our Way, Little Rock, 1976-77; bd. dirs. Ark. Bapt. Newsmagazine. Sec. Ouachita Bapt. U. Devel. Council, Arkadelphia, 1979-83. Served to 1st lt. U.S. Army, 1970-71. Named one of Outstanding Young Men of Am., 1971. Mem. ABA, Ark. Bar Assn., Baxter County Bar Assn. Democrat. Baptist. Lodge: Rotary. Avocation: tennis. General practice, Estate planning, Consumer commercial. Home: 940 E 4th St Mountain Home AR 72653 Office: 210 E 7th St PO Box 1166 #1 Cedar Sq Mountain Home AR 72653

STROUD, ALAN NEIL, lawyer; b. Kinston, N.C., Apr. 2, 1953; s. Walter Lee and Winnie Lee (Manning) S.; m. Helen Gayle Jackson, Nov. 17, 1973. Student, E. Carolina U., 1975-77; BA with highest honors, U. N.C., 1979, JD, 1982. Bar: N.C. 1982, U.S. Dist. Ct. (mid. dist.) N.C. 1982, U.S. Ct. Mil. Appeals 1984. Assoc. Pulley, Watson, King & Hofler, Durham, N.C., 1982-84; judge adv. U.S. Army, Baumholder, Fed. Republic Germany, 1984-86, atty. trial def. service, 1986—. Mem. ABA, Assn. Trial Lawyers Am. Avocations: running, sailing, golf, skiing. General practice, Government contracts and claims, Military. Home: Hemelrijkstraat II, Valkenburg-Sibbe The Netherlands Office: US Army Trial Def Service USMC-The Netherlands APO NY 09011

STROUD, JOHN FRED, JR., state supreme court justice; b. Hope, Ark., Oct. 3, 1931; s. John Fred and Clarine (Steel) S.; m. Marietta Kimball, June 1, 1958; children: John Fred III, Ann Kimball, Tracy Steel. Student, Hendrix Coll., 1949-51; B.A., U. Ark., 1959, LL.B., 1960. Bar: Ark. bar 1959. Since practiced in Texarkana; partner Stroud & McClerkin, 1959-62; legislative asst. to U.S. senator John L. McClellan, 1962-63; partner Smith, Stroud, McClerkin, Dunn & Nutter, 1962—; city atty. Texarkana, 1961-62; asso. justice Ark. Supreme Ct., 1980-81. Chmn. Texarkana Airport Authority, 1966-67; chmn. TexarKana United Way Campaign; pres. Caddo Area council Boy Scouts Am., 1971-73. Served to Lt. Col. USAF, 1951-56. Recipient award of exceptional accomplishment Ark. State C. of C., 1972, 1986, Silver Beaver and Disting. Eagle awards Boy Scouts Am.; named Outstanding Young Man of Texarkana, 1966, One of Five Outstanding Young Men of Ark., 1967. Fellow Am. Bar Found.; Mem. ABA, Ark. Bar Assn. (chmn. exec. council 1979-80, pres. 1987-88), Miller County Bar Assn. (pres.), Texarkana Bar Assn. (pres. 1982-83), Ark. Bar Found. (pres.), Am. Coll. Probate Counsel (chmn. Ark. chpt. 1986-87), Texarkana C. of C. (pres. 1969). Methodist (chmn. ofcl. bd., chmn. council ministries). Lodge: Rotary (pres. Texarkana club 1965-66). Probate, Estate planning, Real property. Office: State First Nat Bank Bldg Texarkana AR 75502

STROUD, JOSEPH E., JR., lawyer; b. Raleigh, N.C., Jan. 4, 1951; s. Joseph E. Sr. and Mary (Hall) S.; m. Rhonda Hall, Aug. 23, 1980; 1 child, Daniel Joseph. BA, East Carolina U., 1973, postgrad., 1973-74; JD, Wake Forest U., 1977. Bar: N.C., 1977, U.S. Dist. Ct. (ea. dist.) N.C. Asst. dist. atty., 4th pros. dist. State of N.C., Jacksonville, 1977-84; sole practice Jacksonville, 1984-86; ptnr. Merritt & Stroud, Jacksonville, 1986—. Mem. ABA, N.C. Bar Assn., Onslow County Bar Assn., N.C. Acad. of Trial Lawyers. Democrat. Baptist. State civil litigation, Criminal, General practice. Home: 201 Elm St Swansboro NC 28584 Office: Merritt & Stroud PO Box 728 410 New Bridge St Office Park NC 28540

STROUGO, ROBERT, lawyer; b. N.Y.C., May 23, 1943; s. Victor and Mary Strougo; m. Barbara Lieb, June 27, 1976; children—Debra, David. B.A., CCNY, 1965; J.D., N.Y. Law Sch., 1970. Bar: N.Y. 1971, U.S. Dist. Ct. (so. and ea. dists.) N.Y. 1975. Sole practice, N.Y.C., 1971—; also investment and fin. adviser; arbitrator Civil Ct. of N.Y. First v.p. Democracy for Stockholders, N.Y.C., 1971—; active Republican Nat. Com.; bd. dirs. 505 E 79th St. Coop., N.Y.C., 1975—. Recipient certs. of recognition Nat. Rep. Congl. Com., 1982-84. Mem. ABA, Kings County Bar Assn., N.Y. State Legis. Com., Nat. Defenders Assn., Legal Def. Panel for Indigent, Assn. Bar City of N.Y., N.Y. Trial Lawyers Assn., N.Y. State Com. on Trial Cts., Bklyn. Bar Assn., Am. Judges Assn., Assn. Legal Aid Attys., Am. Arbitration Assn. (arbitrator civil ct., C.J.A. panel ea. dist.). General practice, Real property, Securities. Home: 505 E 79th St New York NY 10021 Office: 60 E 42d St New York NY 10165

STROUP, STANLEY STEPHENSON, lawyer; b. Los Angeles, Mar. 7, 1944; s. Francis Edwin and Marjory (Weimer) S.; m. Sylvia Douglass, June 15, 1968; children—Stacie, Stephen, Sarah. A.B., U. Ill., 1966; J.D., U. Mich., 1969. Bar: Calif., Ill., Minn. Atty. First Nat. Bank Chgo., 1969-80; chief legal officer Bank of Calif., San Francisco, 1980-84; gen. counsel sec. Norwest Corp., Mpls., 1984—; mem. adj. faculty Coll. Law, William Mitchell Coll., St. Paul, 1985. Mem. ABA, Ill. Bar Assn., State Bar Calif., Minn. Bar Assn. Banking, Contracts commercial. Office: Norwest Corp 1200 Peavey Bldg Minneapolis MN 55479

STROYD, ARTHUR HEISTER, lawyer; b. Pitts., Sept. 5, 1945; s. Arthur Heister and Anne (Griffiths) S.; m. Susan Fleming, July 21, 1973; 1 child, Elizabeth. AB, Kenyon Coll., 1967; JD, U. Pitts., 1972. Bar: Pa. 1972, U.S. Dist. Ct. (we. dist.) Pa. 1972, U.S. Ct. Appeals (3d cir.) 1972. Law clk. to judge U.S. Ct. Appeals (3d cir.), Phila., 1972-75; ptnr. Reed, Smith, Shaw & McClay, Pitts., 1975—; mem. Nat. Adv. Council on Child Nutrition, U.S. Dept. Agriculture, 1984-85. Treas. Mt. Lebanon Civil League, Pitts., 1977-80; sec. Mt. Lebanon Zoning Hearing Bd., 1978-81; pres. Mt. Lebanon Sch. Dist. Bd. Dirs., 1981—; bd. dirs. Ctr. for Theater Arts, Pitts., 1984-87. Served to lt. USNR, 1969-71. Mem. Pa. Bar Assn., Allegheny County Bar Assn., Acad. Trial Lawyers. Republican. Episcopalian. Clubs: Chartiers Country, Pitts. Press. Avocations: skiing, running. Federal civil litigation, State civil litigation, Construction. Home: 17 Saint Clair Dr Pittsburgh PA 15228 Office: Reed Smith Shaw & McClay 435 6th Ave Pittsburgh PA 15219

STROZDAS, JEROME MARK, lawyer; b. Paducah, Ky., July 26, 1953; s. Alfred Peter and Mary Eunice (Brennan) S.; m. Dee Ann Williamson, Dec. 28, 1982. BS, U. Cin., 1975; cert. in teaching, Wittenberg U., 1975; JD, U. Dayton, 1980. Bar: Ohio 1980, U.S. Dist. Ct. (so. dist.) Ohio 1980. Law clk. Common Pleas Ct., Dayton, Ohio, 1978-80; assoc. Schwer, Taggart, Wehler, Emerich & Winks, Springfield, Ohio, 1980-81, ptnr., 1982—; spl. counsel City of Logan, Ohio, 1982—, City of Greenville, Ohio, 1983—, City of London, Ohio, 1985—, City of Springfield, Ohio, 1983—. Football coach Cath. Cen. High Sch., Springfield, 1977—; sec. Clark County Dems., Springfield, 1977-78. Mem. ABA, Ohio Bar Assn. (modern cts. com.), Clark County Bar Assn., Clark County Law Library Assn. Club: Northwood Hills Country (Springfield) (v.p. 1986—). Avocation: golf. Bankruptcy, Labor, Agriculture. Home: 7757 Garlough Rd Springfield OH 45502 Office: 22 S Limestone St PO Box 1406 Springfield OH 45501

STRULL, JAMES RICHARD, lawyer; b. N.Y.C., Oct. 31, 1946; s. Abraham Arthur and Beverly Ann (Lamot) S.; m. Catherine Koziel, Sept. 25, 1983. B.B.A., Coll. Ins. N.Y.C., 1971; J.D., N.Y. Law Sch., 1974. Bar: N.J. 1974, U.S. Dist. Ct. N.J. 1974, N.Y. 1980, U.S. Supreme Ct. 1983. Ins. broker Strull Garber Corp., N.Y.C., 1967-74; assoc. Ludmer & Slaff, Wood Ridge, N.J., 1974; ptnr. Ludmer, Slaff & Strull, Wood Ridge, 1975-78; with Ludmer & Strull, Wood Ridge, 1978-81; ptnr. La Fianza and Strull, Hackensack, N.J., 1981—; staff atty., bd. advisers Fin. Road Maps, Inc., Clifton, N.J., 1983—. Bd. dirs. Bergen County Catholic Youth Orgn., Paramus, 1978-80; mem. Greater N.J. Estate Planning Council, 1984—. Lodge: Lions (pres. 1979). Probate, General corporate, Real property. Office: LaFianza and Strull Continental Plaza III 433 Hackensack Ave Hackensack NJ 07601

STRUTT, DAVID STANLEY, lawyer; b. Dodgeville, Wis., Oct. 17, 1953; s. Donald Frost and JoAnne Lucille (Reese) S.; m. Marci Lynn Henkes, June 19, 1976; children: Jennifer Lynn, Katherine JoAnne, Jonathan Rhys, Rebecca Marie, Robert Arthur. BSBA, Drake U., 1976; JD, U. Iowa, 1979. Bar: Iowa 1979, U.S. Dist. Ct. (no. and so. dists.) Iowa 1979, U.S. Tax Ct. 1979, U.S. Ct. Appeals (8th cir.) 1979, U.S. Claims Ct. 1982, U.S. Supreme Ct. 1983; CPA, Iowa. Assoc. Davis, Hockenberg, Wine, Brown & Koehn, Des Moines, 1979-83, jr. ptnr., 1983-85, sr. ptnr., 1985-86; gen. counsel The Weitz Corp., Des Moines, 1986—. Contbg. author: Closely Held Corpations in Business and Estate Planning, 1982; contbr. articles to jours. Mem. ABA (tax sect., constrn. law sect.), Polk County Bar Assn. (alternatives to resolving disputes com.), Thursday Tax Club (Des Moines), Order of Coif. Republican. Methodist. Club: Embassy, Bohemian (Des Moines). Avocations: bibliophile, water activities, family. Construction, General corporate, Corporate taxation. Office: The Weitz Corp 800 2nd Ave Des Moines IA 50309

STRUVE, GUY MILLER, lawyer; b. Wilmington, Del., Jan. 5, 1943; s. William Scott and Elizabeth Bliss (Miller) S.; m. Marcia Mayo Hill, Sept. 20, 1986; children—Andrew Hardenbrook, Catherine Tolstoy, Frank Leroy Hill. A.B. summa cum laude, Yale U., 1963; LL.B. magna cum laude, Harvard U., 1966. Bar: N.Y. State 1967, U.S. Supreme Ct. 1971, U.S. Ct. Appeals 1969, 73, 76, 79, U.S. Dist. Ct. 1970, 73, 79, 87, D.C. 1985. Law clk. Hon. J. Edward Lumbard, Chief Judge United States Ct. Appeals for 2d Circuit, 1966-67; asso. firm Davis Polk & Wardwell, 1967-72, partner, 1973—; partner Ind. Counsel's Office, 1987—. Mem. Am. Bar Assn., N.Y. State Bar Assn., Assn. Bar City N.Y. (chmn. com. antitrust and trade regulation, 1983-86), Am. Law Inst. Antitrust, Federal civil litigation, State civil litigation. Home: 116 E 63d St New York NY 10021 Office: 1 Chase Manhattan Plaza New York NY 10005

STUART, ALICE MELISSA, lawyer; b. N.Y.C., Apr. 7, 1957; d. John Marberger and Marjorie Louise (Browne) S. BA, Ohio State U., 1977; JD, U. Chgo., 1980; LLM, NYU, 1982. Bar: N.Y. 1981, Ohio 1982, N.Y. 1982, U.S. Dist. Ct. (so. dist.) Ohio 1983, U.S. Dist. Ct. (so. and ea. dists.) N.Y. 1985. Assoc. Schwartz, Shapiro, Kelm & Warren, Columbus, Ohio, 1982-84, Paul, Weiss, Rifkind, Wharton & Garrison, N.Y.C., 1984-85, Kassel, Neuwirth & Geiger, N.Y.C., 1985-86, Phillips, Nizer, Benjamin, Krim & Ballon, N.Y.C., 1987—. Surrogate Speakers' Bur. Reagan-Bush Campaign, N.Y.C., 1984. Mem. ABA, N.Y. State Bar Assn., Winston Churchill Meml. Library Soc., Phi Beta Kappa, Phi Kappa Phi, Alpha Lambda Delta. Republican. Presbyterian. Club: Women's Nat. Rep. (N.Y.C.). Banking, Contracts commercial, General corporate. Office: Philips Nizer Benjamin Krim & Ballon 40 W 57th St New York NY 10019

STUART, JOHN BRUCE, lawyer; b. Tulsa, Sept. 9, 1948; s. Horace Isaac and Helen Louise (Spavor) S.; m. Letitia Ann Peitz, Apr. 17, 1982; 1 child, Jonathan Isaac. BS in Econs. and Bus. Mgmt., Tulsa U., 1971, JD, 1974. Bar: Okla. 1974, U.S. Dist. Ct. (no. dist.) Okla. 1975, U.S. Dist. Ct. (ea. and we. dists.) Okla. 1977, U.S. Ct. Appeals (10th cir.) 1980, U.S. Supreme Ct. 1980. Sole practice Tulsa, 1974; trial atty. Knight, Wagner, Stuart & Wilkerson & Lieber, Tulsa, 1974—; lectr. Tulsa U., 1979. Atty. rep. 1986 United Way Lawyers Drive; lector Madalene Cath. Ch., Tulsa, 1980-84; mem. com. Big Bros./Big Sisters Green County, Tulsa, 1986. Served with U.S. Air N.G., 1970-76. Mem. ABA, Okla. Bar Assn., Tulsa County Bar Assn., Okla. Trial Lawyers Assn., Okla. Assn. Def. Counsel. Roman Catholic. Civil rights, Insurance, Personal injury. Office: Knight Wagner Stuart Wilkerson & Lieber 233 W 11th St Tulsa OK 74119

STUART, JOHN M., lawyer, author; b. N.Y.C., Apr. 3, 1927; s. Winchester and Maude Ruth (Marberger) S.; m. Marjorie Louise Browne, Dec. 11, 1954; children—Jane, Alice, Richard. B.A., Columbia U., 1948, J.D., 1951. Bar: N.Y. 1951, U.S. Supreme Ct. 1955. Assoc., Reid & Priest, N.Y.C., 1951-64, ptnr., 1965—; asst. sec. Minn. Power & Light Co., 1951-64. Recipient Internat. Brotherhood Magicians award, 1958-60, 1st prize in sci. fiction Phila. Writers Conf., 1958. Mem. ABA, N.Y. County Bar Assn., Sr. Republican. Methodist. Author: A Re-examination of the Replacement Fund, 1968; Avoiding Costly Bond Problems, 1980; (with Louis H. Willenken) Utility Mortgages Should be Reexamined, 1984; (with Majorie L. Stuart) (play) Make Me Disappear, 1969; (novel) You Don't Have to Slay a Dragon, 1976. Contbr. articles to mags. Magician, W. German TV magic spl., 1965; appeared in Spy at the Magic Show benefit for Project Hope, Manhasset, N.Y., 1967. Public utilities. Home: 31 Westgate Blvd Plandome NY 11030 Office: 40 W 57th St New York NY 10019

STUART, MICHAEL GEORGE, lawyer; b. N.Y.C., May 24, 1951; s. George Bernard and Diana (Porikos) S.; 1 child, Jennifer. BBA, Pace U., 1973, JD, 1980. Bar: Oreg. 1981, U.S. Dist. Ct. Oreg. 1981, U.S. Tax Ct. 1981, U.S. Ct. Appeals (9th cir.) 1982; CPA, Oreg. Acct. Cambridge Instrument Inc., Ossining, N.Y., 1973-76; fin. cons. Bronxville, N.Y., 1976-78; legal asst. Frank B. Hall & Co., Briarcliff Manor, N.Y., 1978-79; supr. tax specialist Coopers & Lybrand, Portland, Oreg., 1979-81; sole practice Beaverton, Oreg., 1981—; com. mem. Atty. Realtors, Beaverton, 1986. Pres. Young Adult League, Portland, 1983-85; sec. Portland Parish Council, 1983, treas. 1984; mem. Greek Civic Club Oreg., Portland, 1982—. Mem. Washington County Bar Assn., Oreg. State Bar Assn. (tax bus. sect.), ABA (econs. of law practice sect.), Beaverton C. of C., Am. Hellenic Ednl. Progressive Assn. Democrat. Greek Orthodox. Lodge: Masons. Avocations: guitar, backpacking, woodworking, racquetball. Corporate taxation, Estate taxation, Pension, profit-sharing, and employee benefits. Home: 3950 SW 102d St #72 Beaverton OR 97005 Office: 4540 SW 110th Ave Beaverton OR 97005

STUART, PAMELA BRUCE, lawyer; b. N.Y.C., Feb. 13, 1949; d. J. Raymond and Marion Grace (Cotins) S. AB with distinction, Mt. Holyoke Coll., 1970; JD cum laude, U. Mich., 1973. Bar: N.Y. 1974, D.C. 1975, U.S. Dist. Ct. D.C. 1979, U.S. Ct. Appeals (D.C. cir.) 1980, U.S. Supreme Ct. 1980. Trial atty., deputy asst. dir. Bur. of Consumer Protection, FTC, Washington, 1973-79; asst. U.S. atty. U.S. Atty's Office, Washington, 1979-85; trial atty. Office of Internat. Affairs, U.S. Dept. Justice, Washington, 1985—. Mem. Bar Assn. of D.C., Women's Bar Assn. of D.C., Alumnae Assn. of Mt. Holyoke Coll. (bd. dirs.). Avocations: flying, home restoration. Public international, Federal civil litigation, Criminal. Home: 4601 Davenport St NW Washington DC 20016 Office: US Dept of Justice 1400 New York Ave NW Washington DC 20530

STUART, PETER FRED, lawyer; b. Savona, N.Y., June 23, 1939; s. Chester M. and Gertrude (Manning) S.; m. Karin Sandal, May 30, 1964; children: Peter Christopher, Sandal Clay, Grant Alan. AB, Dartmouth Coll., 1961; JD, Dickinson Sch. Law, 1969. Bar: Conn. 1970, U.S. Ct. Appeals (2d cir.) 1974, U.S. Ct. Mil. Appeals 1974, U.S. Supreme Ct. 1974. Commd. ensign USN, 1961, advanced through ranks to commdr., 1979, resigned, 1981; staff atty. Conn. Gen. Life Ins. Co., Hartford, 1969-72; ptnr. O'Brien, Shafner, Bartinik, Stuart & Kelly P.C., Groton, Conn., 1972—; corporator New Eng. Savings Bank, New London, Conn., 1979-86. City councilor Town of Groton, 1974-78. Mem. Ct. Corps. Com. (exec. com. mem.). Lodge: Rotary (local pres. 1982-83). Avocation: gardening. Consumer commercial, General practice, General corporate. Office: 500 Bridge St Ext Box 929 Groton CT 06340

STUART, WALTER BYNUM, IV, lawyer; b. Grosse Tete, La., Nov. 23, 1946; s. Walter Bynum III and Rita (Kleinpeter) S.; m. Lettice Lee Binnings May 18, 1968; children: Courtney Lyon, Walter Burke. Student Fordham U., 1964-65; BA, Tulane U., 1968, JD, 1973. Bar: La. 1973, U.S. Dist. Ct. (ea. and we. dists.) La. 1974, U.S. Tax Ct. 1974, U.S. Supreme Ct. 1981, U.S. Dist Ct. (so. dist.) N.Y. 1983. Ptnr. Stone, Pigman, Walter, Wittman and Hutchinson, New Orleans, 1973-78, Singer, Hutner Levine, Seeman and Stuart, New Orleans, 1978-81, Gordon, Arata, McCollam and Stuart, New Orleans, 1981—; instr. Tulane U. Law Sch., 1978-82; mem. faculty Baulurg Sch. of the South; bd. dirs. Inst. Politics; mem. adv. bd. City Atty.'s Office, New Orleans, 1978-79. Mem. ABA, N.Y. State Bar Assn., La. Bar Assn., New Orleans Bar Assn., La. Bankers Assn. (chmn. bank counsel com.). Democrat. Roman Catholic. Banking, Contracts commercial, Federal civil litigation. Office: 201 St Charles Suite 4000 New Orleans LA 70170

STUBBLEFIELD, JOSEPH STEPHEN, lawyer; b. Jackson, Miss., Mar. 28, 1947; s. Joseph Murat and Mary Alice (Ragland) S.; m. Mary Margaret McRae, Mar. 7, 1970; children: Mary Lindsay, David Stephen. BS, Miss. State U., 1969; JD, U. Miss., 1974. Bar: Miss. 1974, U.S. Dist. Ct. (no. and so. dists.) Miss. 1974, U.S. Ct. Appeals (5th cir.) 1974. Atty. IRS, Jackson, 1974-78; ptnr. Peterson, Harper & Bellan, Jackson, 1978-82, Wells, Crecink, Wells & Stubblefield, Jackson, 1982-83, Wells, Moore, Simmons & Stubblefield, Jackson, 1983—; sec., treas. Profl. Planning Council, Jackson, 1986—. Mem. Fellowship Christian Fin. Advisors, Jackson, 1985. Served to 1st lt. U.S. Army, 1970-71. Mem. ABA, Miss. Bar Assn., Hinds County Bar Assn., Internat. Assn. Fin. Planners, Miss. Estate Planning Council, Miss. Assn. Petroleum Landmen, Mid-Continent Oil and Gas Assn., Miss. Oil and Gas Lawyers Assn., Phi Delta Phi. Republican. Baptist. Club: University (Jackson). Avocations: fishing, hunting, gardening. Estate planning, Probate, General corporate. Home: 1921 Bellewood Rd Jackson MS 39211 Office: Wells Moore Simmons & Stubblefield 2120 Deposit Guaranty Plaza Jackson MS 39205

STUBBS, SIDNEY ALTON, lawyer; b. Gainesville, Fla., Nov. 29, 1938; s. Sidney Alton and Esther Ann (Witt) S.; m. Annette McIntosh, Feb. 7, 1938; children: Melanie K., Natalie K., Scott M. BS in History, Fla. State U., 1960; JD with honors, U. Fla., 1965. Bar: Fla. 1966, U.S. Dist. Ct. (so. dist.) Fla. 1967, U.S. Ct. Appeals (5th &11th cirs.) 1981, U.S. Ct. Supreme Ct. 1985. Mem. Jones & Foster, P.A., West Palm Beach, Fla., 1972—; spl. counsel to Fla. Gov. Bob Graham, 1983-84; mem. adv. bd. Southwestern Legal Found., 1983. Trustee U. Fla. Law Ctr. Found. Served with USAF, 1960-63. Fellow Am. Coll. Trial Attys., Am. Bar Found., Internat. Soc. Barristers; mem. Fla. Bar Assn. (bd. govs. 1980-84), Palm Beach County Bar Assn. (pres. 1978-79), U. Fla. Law Alumnae Council (pres. 1985). Lodge: Kiwanis (pres. West Palm Beach chpt. 1978-79). Condemnation, Federal civil litigation, State civil litigation. Office: PO Drawer E West Palm Beach FL 33402

STUBBS, WILLIAM PERRY, JR., tax attorney; b. Wisner, La., Mar. 6, 1947; s. William Perry Sr. and Barnie Lee (Cloy) S.; m. Carol Lee Maeser, Aug. 22, 1970; children: John William, Nathan Robert, Andrew Michael. BS in Acctg., La. State U., 1969, JD, 1973. Bar: La. 1973; CPA, La., Tex. Staff acct. Ernst & Whinney, Houston, 1973-75; tax atty. Wright, Dawkins, et al, Ruston, La., 1975-76, Ledbetter, Percy & Stubbs, Alexandria, La., 1976-80; tax dept. head Broadhurst, Brook et al, Lafayette, La., 1980-82; sole practice Lafayette, 1983-86; chmn. bd. Cajun Capital, Lafayette; chmn. bd. C-Cap Properties, Inc., Lafayette. Del. state conv. La. Rep. Party, 1980, alt. del. nat. conv., 1984; session elder Grace Presbyterian Ch., 1984-86, chmn. nominations, 1986. Mem. ABA, La. Bar Assn., La. Soc. CPA's, Tex. Soc. CPA's, Am. Inst. CPA's. Clubs: Riverside Swim (bd. dirs. 1985-86), Krewe of Bonaparte (Lafayette). Estate taxation, Probate, General corporate.

STUCKEY, CHARLES EDWARD, lawyer; b. Fairbury, Ill., Apr. 29, 1955; s. James D. and Helenjean (Lauterbach) S.; m. Marilyn Snook, July 2, 1983; 1 child, Charlotte. BA, Wesleyan U., Bloomington, Ill., 1977; JD, U. Ill., 1980. Bar: Ill. 1980, N.Mex. 1980, U.S. Dist. Ct. N.Mex. 1980, U.S. Ct. Appeals (10th cir.) 1980. Assoc. Modrall, Sperling, Roehl, Harris & Sisk P.A., Albuquerque, 1980-85, Rodey, Dickason, Sloan, Akin & Robb P.A., Albuquerque, 1985—; instr. bus. law Cert. Profl. Secs., Albuquerque, 1984—, trial practice N.Mex. Legal Secs., Albuquerque, 1985. Mem. ABA, Ill. Bar Assn., N.Mex. Bar Assn. (bd. dirs., pres. young lawyers div. 1985—), N.Mex. Def. Lawyers Assn., N.Mex. Trial Lawyers Assn. Episcopalian. Federal civil litigation, State civil litigation, Insurance. Office: Rodey Dickason Sloan Akin & Robb PA PO Box 1888 Albuquerque NM 87103

STUHLDREHER, GEORGE WILLIAM, lawyer; b. Mansfield, Ohio, Nov. 20, 1923; s. George Henry and Clara Sophia (Gabel) S.; m. Fay McClurg, Jan. 7, 1956 (div.); children—Karen Louise, Diane Marie; m. Norah Constance Burran, July 1, 1978. Student, Kans. State Coll., 1943-44, U. Detroit, 1946-47; B.A., Ohio State U., 1948, J.D. summa cum laude, 1951. Bar: Ohio 1951, U.S. Dist. Ct. (no. dist.) Ohio 1953, U.S. Ct. Appeals (6th cir.) 1955, U.S. Supreme Ct. 1979. Atty., ptnr. Gallagher, Sharp, Fulton & Norman and predecessor firms, Cleve., 1951—; dir. Bulkley Bldg. Co., Cleve. Mem. Citizen's League Cleve. Served to cpl. U.S. Army, 1943-46. Mem. ABA, Am. Judicature Soc., Internat. Assn. Ins. Counsel, Def. Research Inst., Ohio State Bar Assn., Ohio Assn. Civil Trial Attys., Cleve. Bar Assn., Cleve. Assn. Civil Trial Attys. (pres. 1973), Phi Sigma Kappa, Phi Delta Phi, Order of Coif. Editor-in-chief Ohio State Law Jour., 1951. Federal civil litigation, State civil litigation, Professional liability defense. Home: 6 Edgewater Sq Lakewood OH 44107 Office: Gallagher Sharp Fulton & Norman 630 Bulkley Bldg Cleveland OH 44115

STUKENBERG, MICHAEL WESLEY, lawyer; b. Freeport, Ill., Feb. 22, 1951; s. Wesley W. and Nancy Jack (Baker) S.; m. Amanda Reed Eggert, July 21, 1973; children—Sarah Reed, William Robinson. B.A., Princeton U., 1973; J.D., Vanderbilt U., 1976. Bar: Tex. 1977, U.S. Tax Ct. 1977, U.S. Dist. Ct. (so. dist.) Tex. 1982. Assoc. firm Matthews & Branscomb, Corpus Christi, Tex., 1976-81, ptnr., 1981—. Trustee Art Mus. South Tex., Corpus Christi, 1978—, Corpus Christi YMCA, 1979—; vice chmn. planning council United Way-Coastal Bend, Corpus Christi, 1979; chmn. Young People for Lloyd Bentsen, Nueces County, Tex., 1982. Mem. ABA (chmn. subcom. on gross estate and gift taxes 1982), Tex. Bar Assn. (tax sect.) Republican. Episcopalian. Clubs: Corpus Christi Country, Corpus Christi Yacht; Causeway (Southwest Harbor, Maine). Estate taxation, Corporate taxation, Personal income taxation. Home: 155 Rossiter St Corpus Christi TX 78411 Office: Matthews & Branscomb 1800 First City Bank Tower Corpus Christi TX 78477

STULL, GORDON BRUCE, lawyer; b. Dighton, Kans., Aug. 3, 1945; s. Eldon W. and Mildren M. (Zink); m. Carol Joyce Hampton, Aug. 1, 1973; children—Megen, Colby, Braden. B.A., Ft. Hays U., 1967; J.D., U. Kans., 1975. Bar: Kans. 1975. Assoc., Morris, Laing et al., Wichita, Kans., 1975-76; ptnr. Hampton, Hampton, Stull et al., Pratt, Kans., 1976-81; exec. v.p., gen. counsel Tex. Energies, Inc., 1981-83. also dir.; pres., dir. Wheatstate Oilfield Services, Inc., 1983-84; pres. Gordon B. Stull, Atty., P.A., Pratt, 1984—. Bd. editors Kans. Bar Assn., Oil and Gas Handbook. County coordinator Nancy Landon Kassebaum Senate campaign, Pratt County, 1980; elder Pratt Presbyterian Ch., 1978-81. Served to sgt. U.S. Army, 1968-71. Mem. ABA, Kans. Bar Assn. (Merit award for coordinating agr. law seminar 1980), Pratt County Bar Assn. (pres. 1980, 86); Pratt Jaycees (Disting. Service award 1980). Lodges: Lions, Elks (jud. advisor 1976—). Oil and gas leasing, General corporate, Real property. Home: RR 1 Pratt KS 67124 Office: 1320 E 1st St Pratt KS 67124

STUMPF, FELIX FRANKLIN, legal educator; b. Boston, Feb. 10, 1918; s. Karl Heinrich and Annette (Schreyer) S.; m. Martha Wickland, May 29, 1948; m. Betty-Jo Danielson, Aug. 5, 1959; children: Eric, Kenneth, Kirk, Mark, Paul. AB magna cum laude, Harvard U., 1938, LLB, 1941. Bar: Mass. 1941, Calif. 1946, Nev. 1975, U.S. Dist. Ct. (no. dist.) Calif. 1946, U.S. Dist. Ct. Nev. 1981, U.S. Ct. Appeals (9th cir.) 1948, U.S. Supreme Ct. 1967. Assoc. Hale & Dorr, Boston, 1941-42, McCutchen, Thomas, Matthews, Griffiths & Greene, San Francisco, 1946-50, Livingston, Leeker & Feldman, San Francisco, 1950-53; adminstr. Calif. Continuing Edn. of Bar, U. Calif. Extension, Berkeley, 1953-70; staff atty. U.S. Dist. Ct. No. Dist. Calif., San Francisco, 1971-73; acad. dir. Nat. Jud. Coll.-U. Nev., Reno, 1973-84; prof. Old Coll. Nev. Sch. Law, Reno, 1984-85, dean, 1985—. Contbr. articles to profl. jours. Served to 1st lt. AC, U.S. Army, 1942-46. Recipient First Harrison Tweed award Assn. Continuing Legal Edn. Adminstrs., 1969. Mem. ABA, Nev. Bar Assn., Washoe County Bar Assn., Am. Judicature Soc., Nev. Bar Found. (past trustee). Democrat. Legal education, Civil rights. Office: Old Coll Nev Sch Law Reno NV 89503

STUNTZ, LINDA GILLESPIE, lawyer; b. Bellefontaine, Ohio, Sept. 11, 1954; d. J. Bradshaw Gillespie and Freda Taylor; m. Reid P.F. Stuntz, May 23, 1981; 1 child, Joseph Gillespie. AB, Wittenberg U., 1976; JD, Harvard U., 1979. Bar: D.C. 1979, U.S. Dist. Ct. D.C. 1980, U.S. Temp. Emergency Ct. Appeals 1980, U.S. Ct. Appeals (D.C. cir.) 1980, U.S. Supreme Ct. 1983. Assoc. Jones, Day, Reavis & Pogue, Washington, 1979-81, 87—; assoc. minority counsel Energy and Commerce Com., U.S. Ho. of Reps., Washington, 1981-86, minority counsel, staff dir., 1986—. Mem. Fed. Energy Bar Assn. Republican. FERC practice, Legislative. Office: Jones Day Reavis & Pogue 655 15th St NW Washington DC 20005-5701

STUNTZ, REID PENDLETON FITZHUGH, lawyer; b. Arlington, Va., July 2, 1952; s. Mayo Sturdevant and Constance (Pendleton) S.; m. Linda Gillespie, May 23, 1981; 1 child, Joseph Gillespie. AB, Princeton U., 1974; JD, Harvard U., 1977. Bar: Pa. 1977, U.S. Dist. Ct. (ea. dist.) Pa. 1978, D.C. 1982. Assoc. Dechert, Price & Rhoads, Phila., 1977-79; trial atty. antitrust div. U.S. Dept. Justice, Washington, 1979-82; assoc. Popham, Haik, Schnobrich, Kaufman & Doty Ltd., Washington, 1982-84, sr. atty., 1984—. Democrat. Presbyterian. Avocations: fishing, tennis. Antitrust, Administrative and regulatory, Criminal. Office: Popham Haik Schnobrich Kaufman & Doty Ltd 1800 M St Suite 300S Washington DC 20036

STURDEVANT, PATRICIA TENOSO, lawyer; b. Portland, Oreg.; m. James C. Sturdevant. BA, UCLA, 1965, JD, 1972. Bar: U.S. Ct. Appeals (9th cir.) 1972, U.S. Dist. Ct. (cen. dist.) Calif. 1972, U.S. Supreme Ct. 1978, U.S. Ct. Appeals (D.C. cir.) 1978, U.S. Dist. Ct. (ea. dist.) Calif. 1979, U.S. Dist. Ct. (no. dist.) Calif. 1981. Atty. San Fernando Valley Neighborhood Legal Services, Los Angeles, 1972-75; sr. counsel Western Ctr. Law and Poverty, Los Angeles, 1975-81; assoc. Alioto & Alioto, San Francisco, 1981-86; ptnr. Sturdevant & Elion, San Francisco, 1986—. Mem. Retail Credit Adv. Com., Sacramento, Calif., 1981-82. Mem. Assn. Trial Lawyers Am., Calif. Trial Lawyers Assn., San Francisco Trial Lawyers Assn., Calif. Women Lawyers Assn., San Francisco Women Lawyers Alliance (bd. dirs.), Order of Coif. Consumer commercial, Federal civil litigation, State civil litigation. Office: Sturdevant & Elion 120 Montgomery St Suite 1800 San Francisco CA 94104

STURM, WILLIAM CHARLES, lawyer; b. Milw., Aug. 4, 1941; s. Charles William and Helen Ann (Niesen) S.; m. Kay F. Sturm, June 10, 1967; children—Patricia, Elizabeth, Katherine, William, Susan. B.S. in Bus. Adminstrn., Marquette U., 1963, J.D., 1966. Bar: Wis. 1966, U.S. Dist. Ct. (ea. dist.) Wis. 1966, U.S. Supreme Ct. 1980. Sole practice, Milw., 1966-78; ptnr. Rausch, Hamell, Ehrle & Sturm, S.C., Milw., 1978-81, Rausch, Hamell, Ehrle, Sturm & Blom, Milw., 1981-83, Rausch, Hamell, Ehrle & Sturm, 1983—; asst. prof. Marquette U., 1982—; lectr. in field. Mem. adv. bd. Pallotine Order, 1985—. Recipient Editors award Wis. Med. Credit Assn., 1980. Mem. ABA, Wis. Bar Assn., Comml. Law League Am. (exec. council midwestern dist. 1981-83, 86—, chmn. state membership com. 1981—, nat. nominating council 1984-86), Nat. Speakers Assn., Am. Bus. Law Assn., Internat. Platform Assn., Midwest Bus. Law Assn., Wis. Profl. Speakers Assn., Healthcare Fin. Mgmt. Assn., Beta Alpha Psi (faculty v.p. Psi chpt. 1985—). Clubs: Westmoor Country (Milw.); Kiwanis (pres. 1979, lt. gov. div. 5, 1980) (Wauwatosa, Wis.). Contbr. articles to profl. jours. Consumer commercial, Bankruptcy. Office: 7500 W State St Milwaukee WI 53213

STURTEVANT, BRERETON, government official, lawyer; b. Washington, Nov. 24, 1921; d. Charles Lyon and Grace (Brereton) S. B.A., Wellesley Coll., 1942; J.D., Temple U., 1949; postgrad., U. Del., 1969-71. Bar: D.C. 1949, Del. 1950. Research chemist E.I. duPont DeNemours & Co., 1942-50; law clk. Del. Supreme Ct., 1950; gen. practice law Wilmington, Del., 1950-57; partner Connolly, Bove & Lodge, Wilmington, 1957-71; examiner-in-chief U.S. Patent and Trademark Office Bd. Appeals, Washington, 1971—; Adj. prof. law Georgetown U., 1974-79. Trustee Holton-Arms Sch., Bethesda, Md., 1977—, mem. edn. and fin. coms., bldg. and grounds com. Mem. Am., Del. bar assns., Patent Office Soc., Govt. Patent Lawyers Assn., Exec. Women in Govt. (charter mem., chmn. 1978-79). Episcopalian. Clubs: Wellesley College, Washington-Wellesley (pres. 1982-84). Federal civil litigation, Patent. Home: 1227 Morningside Ln Alexandria VA 22308 Office: US Patent and Trademark Office Washington DC 20231

STUTMAN, MICHAEL DAVID, lawyer; b. N.Y.C., June 21, 1954; s. Herbert Irving and Ilse Marion (Buehler) S.; m. Nancy Helen Butts, June 7, 1975 (div. Jan. 1982); m. Linda Kay Congram, June 1, 1984. Ba, Knox Coll., 1975; JD, U. Tulsa, 1978. Bar: Okla. 1978, U.S. Dist. Ct. (no. dist.) Okla. 1978, N.Y. 1985, U.S. Dist. Ct. (so. and ea. dists.) N.Y. 1985. Sole practice Tulsa, 1978-82; ptnr. Bagley & Stutman, Tulsa, 1983-84; of counsel Bagley, Stutman & Carpenter, Tulsa, 1985—. Bd. dirs. Local Devel. Corp. Del Barrio, N.Y.C., 1985—. Mem. Okla. Bar Assn., N.Y. State Bar Assn., N.Y. County Bar Assn., Assn. Trial Lawyers Am. Republican. Jewish. Clubs: Tsa-La-Gi Yacht (Wagoner, Okla.); North Minneford Yacht (City Island, N.Y.); Sheldrake Yacht (Mamaroneck, N.Y.). Avocations: sailing, yacht racing, cross country skiing. Construction, Environment, Personal injury. Home: 205 3d Ave Apt 2V New York NY 10003 Office: Stutman & Stutman PC 244 E 13th St New York NY 10003

STUTT, JOHN BARRY, lawyer; b. Phila., Feb. 1, 1948; m. Dena Lieberman; children: Timothy, Margaret. BBA, U. Wis., 1971, MBA, 1973, JD, 1974. Bar: Wis. 1974, Mo. 1974. Asst. counsel Mo. Dept. Revenue, Jefferson City, 1974-75; asst. gen. counsel Mo. Hwy. Dept., Jefferson City, 1975-77; assoc. Stewart, Peyton, Crawford & Crawford, Racine, Wis., 1978-83; ptnr. Stewart, Peyton, Crawford, Crawford & Stutt, Racine, 1983—. Mem. Wis. Bar Assn. (sec., bd. dirs. young lawyers div. 1983, environ. law com. 1985—), Acad. Trial Lawyers, Jaycees (pres. Racine). Personal injury, Real property, Banking. Home: 4830 Alcyn Dr Racine WI 53402 Office: Stewart Peyton Crawford et al 840 Lake Ave Racine WI 53403

SUBAK, JOHN THOMAS, chemical company executive; b. Trebic, Czechoslovakia, Apr. 19, 1929; came to U.S., 1941, naturalized, 1946; s. William John and Gerda Maria (Subakova) S.; m. Mary Corcoran, June 4, 1955; children—Jane, Kate, Thomas, Michael. A.B., Yale U., 1950, LL.B., 1956. Bar: Pa. bar 1957. Asso., then partner firm Dechert, Price & Rhoads, Phila., 1956-76; v.p., gen. counsel Rohm & Haas Co., Phila., 1976-77; group v.p., gen. counsel Rohm & Haas Co., 1977—, also dir.; dir., mem. exec. Milton Roy Co. Editor: Bus. Lawyer, 1978—. Served as lt. (j.g.) USN, 1950-53. Mem. ABA (officer sect.). Democrat. Roman Catholic. Clubs: Merion Cricket, Philadelphia, Down Town. General corporate. Home: 214 Ivy Ln Haverford PA 19041 Office: Rohm and Haas Co Independence Mall W Philadelphia PA 19105

SUDBURY, DAVID M., corporate lawyer; b. 1945. BA, So. Meth. U., 1967, JD, 1970. Asst. sec., atty. Wilson & Co. Inc., Oklahoma City, 1970-74; sole practice Houston, 1974-76; gen. counsel, asst. sec. Comml. Metals Co., Dallas, 1976-77, v.p., sec. gen. counsel, 1977—. Office: Comml Metals Co 7800 Stemmons Freeway Dallas TX 75247 *

SUDDARD, OLIVER VINCENT, lawyer; b. Newark, Apr. 29, 1926. AB, Duke U., 1947, JD, 1950. Bar: Del. 1950, U.S. Dist. Ct. Del. 1950, U.S. Ct. Appeals (3d cir.) 1950, U.S. Supreme Ct. 1950. Assoc. Smith & Keith, Wilmington, Del., 1951, Southerland, Berl & Potter, Wilmington, 1951-52; ptnr. Wise & Suddard, Wilmington, 1952-67; sole practice Wilmington, 1967—. Mem. ABA, Del. Bar Assn., Lawyer-Pilots Bar Assn., Assn. Trial Lawyers Am. (state committeeman), Del. Trial Lawyers Assn. (pres. 1968-76). Republican. Personal injury, Workers' compensation. Home: 503 Country Club Dr Wilmington DE 19803 Office: 8 E 13th St Wilmington DE 19801-3273

SUDOL, WALTER EDWARD, lawyer, corporate professional; b. Passaic, N.J., Jan. 13, 1942; s. Walter and Ann (Kopec) S.; m. June Ann Jancio, Oct. 14, 1967; children: Karen Ann, Alyson Anne. BA, Tulane U., 1963; JD, Seton Hall U., 1975. Bar: N.J. 1975, U.S. Dist. Ct. N.J. 1975, N.Y. 1985. Indsl. engr. Westinghouse Electric Co., Jersey City, 1969-72, indsl. relations mgr., 1972-75; atty., mgr. contracts Westinghouse Electric Co., Millburn, N.J., 1975-80; gen. counsel, sec. Internat. Computers Ltd., East Brunswick, N.J., 1980-81, Belco Pollution Control Corp., Parsippany, N.J., 1981-85; v.p., gen. counsel, sec. H-R Internat., Inc., Edison, N.J., 1985—; cons. constrn. claims Westinghouse Electric Co., Washington, 1977-79, Foster Wheeler Energy Corp., Livingston, N.J., 1983-84. Pres. St. Andrew's Parish Council, Clifton, N.J., 1980. Served to capt. USNR, 1963—, Vietnam. Mem. ABA, N.J. Bar Assn., Passaic County Bar Assn., Nat. Constructors Assn. (chmn. gen. counsels com. 1985—), Am. Legion, VFW. Republican. Roman Catholic. Lodge: Masons. Avocations: sailing, tennis. General corporate, General practice, Private international. Home: 67 Village Rd Clifton NJ 07013 Office: H-R Internat Inc 2045 Lincoln Hwy Edison NJ 08817

SUEDHOFF, CARL JOHN, JR., lawyer; b. Ft. Wayne, Ind., Apr. 22, 1925; s. Carl John and Helen (Lau) S.; m. Carol Mulqueeney, Apr. 10, 1954; children—Thomas Lau, Robert Marshall, Mark Mulqueeney. B.S., U. Pa., 1948; J.D., U. Mich., 1951. Bar: Ind. 1951. Assoc. mem. firm Hunt & Mountz, Ft. Wayne, 1951-54; ptnr. Hunt, Suedhoff, Borrorr & Eilbacher and predecessors, Ft. Wayne, 1955—; officer, dir. Inland Chem. Corp., Ft. Wayne, 1952-81; pres., dir. Lau Bldg. Co., Ft. Wayne, 1951-78, S.H.S. Realty Corp., Toledo, 1960-78; officer, dir. Inland Chem. P.R., Inc., San Juan, 1972-81, Northeast Cogen, Inc., others. Mem. Allen County Council, 1972-76, pres., 1974-76; mem. Allen County Tax Adjustment Bd., 1973-74, N.E. Ind. Regional Coordinating Council, 1975-76; bd. dirs. Ft. Wayne YMCA, 1961-63. Served with AUS, 1943-45. Mem. VFW (comdr. 1958-59), ABA, Ind. Bar Assn., Allen County Bar Assn., Beta Gamma Sigma, Phi Delta Phi, Psi Upsilon. Republican. Lutheran. Clubs: Univ. Mich. (pres. 1965-66), Friars, Ft. Wayne Country, Mad Anthony's. Federal civil litigation, Probate, General corporate. Office: 900 Paine Webber Bldg Fort Wayne IN 46802

SUFLAS, STEVEN WILLIAM, lawyer; b. Camden, N.J., Oct. 7, 1951; s. William V. and Dorothy (Stafre) S.; m. Rochelle B. Volin, Apr. 15, 1978; children: Allison, Rebecca. BA, Davidson Coll., 1973; JD with honors, U. N.C., 1976. Bar: N.J. 1976, Pa. 1978, U.S. Dist. Ct. N.J., U.S. Ct. Appeals (3d cir.). Field atty. NLRB, Phila., 1976-80; assoc. Archer & Greiner P.C., Haddonfield, N.J., 1980-86, ptnr., 1986—. Mem. ABA, Pa. Bar Assn., Phila. Bar Assn., N.J. Bar Assn. (exec. com. labor law sect. 1985—, co-chmn. employment at will subcom. 1985—), Order of Coif, Omicron Delta Kappa. Labor. Office: Archer & Greiner PC 1 Centennial Sq Haddonfield NJ 08033

SUGARMAN, PAUL WILLIAM, lawyer; b. Cambridge, Mass., July 31, 1947; s. Louis Edward and Natalie (Waldman) S.; m. Susan Lee Richard, July 16, 1978; children: Sarah, Emily, Hannah. BA, Harvard U., 1969; JD, Yale U., 1975. Bar: Calif. 1976, U.S. Dist. Ct. (no. dist.) Calif. 1976, U.S. Ct. Appeals (9th cir.) 1976. Law clk. to judge U.S. Dist. Ct. (no. dist.) Calif., San Francisco, 1975-76; assoc. Heller, Ehrman, White & McAuliffe, San Francisco, 1976-81, ptnr., 1982—. Vol. U.S. Peace Corps, Ethiopia, 1969-72. Mem. ABA, Calif. Bar Assn., San Francisco Bar Assn., Phi Beta Kappa. Federal civil litigation, State civil litigation. Home: 907 Longridge Rd Oakland CA 94610 Office: Heller Ehrman White & McAuliffe 333 Bush St San Francisco CA 94104

SUGARMAN, ROBERT GARY, lawyer; b. Bronx, Sept. 3, 1939; s. Eugene L. and Frances (Solomon) S.; m. Surie Rudoff, June 16, 1985 children: Dana, Alison. B.A., Yale U., 1960, LL.B., 1963. Bar: N.Y. 1963, Fla. 1963, U.S. Supreme Ct. 1971, U.S. Dist. Ct. (so. dist.) N.Y. 1966, U.S. Dist. Ct. (ea. dist.) N.Y. 1982, U.S. Ct. Appeals (2d cir.) 1970, U.S. Ct. Appeals (10th cir.) 1971. Assoc. Sugarman, Kuttner & Fuss, N.Y.C., 1965-66; assoc. firm Sullivan & Cromwell, N.Y.C., 1966-72; assoc. Weil, Gotshal & Manges, N.Y.C., 1972-75, ptnr., 1975—. Co-author: Deposition Strategy Law and Forms, 1980. Pres. B'nai B'rith Hillel-Jewish Assn. Coll. Youth, 1984-86. Served as capt. U.S. Army, 1963-65. Mem. Am. Coll. Trial Lawyers, ABA, N.Y. State Bar Assn. Lodge: B'nai B'rith (bd. govs. internat. 1975-85, nat. commn. Anti-Defamation League 1981—). Federal civil litigation, Trademark and copyright, Libel. Office: Weil Gotshal & Manges 767 Fifth Ave New York NY 10022

SUGARMAN, STEPHEN D., law educator; b. 1942. JD, Northwestern U., 1967. Assoc. O'Melveny & Myers, Los Angeles, 1967-72; prof. U. Calif., Berkeley, 1972—. Office: U Calif Sch Law Berkeley CA 94720 *

SUGG, REED WALLER, lawyer; b. Morganfield, Ky., Dec. 1, 1952; s. Matt Waller and Iris (Omer) S. BA, Furman U., 1975; JD, Vanderbilt U., 1978. Bar: Mo. 1978, Ill. 1979, U.S. Ct. Appeals (8th, 9th and 7th cirs.), U.S. Dist. Ct. (ea. dist.) Mo., U.S. Dist. Ct. (so. dist.) Ill. Atty. Coburn, Croft, Shepherd & Herzog, St. Louis, 1978-79, Shepherd, Sandberg & Phoenix, St. Louis, 1979—. Mem. ABA, Bar Assn. Met. St. Louis, Christian Legal Soc., Assn. Trial Lawyers Am., Aviation Ins. Assn., Lawyer-Pilots Bar Assn., Phi Beta Kappa. Republican. Presbyterian. Clubs: Mo. Athletic, Westborough Country(St. Louis). Avocations: basketball, golf, tennis, reading. Federal civil litigation, State civil litigation, Personal injury. Home: 6 Cricket Ln Saint Louis MO 63144 Office: Shepherd Sandberg & Phoenix One City Centre Suite 1500 Saint Louis MO 63101

SUGGS, FRED WILSON, JR., lawyer; b. Montgomery, Ala., Nov. 18, 1946; s. Fred W. Suggs Sr. and Frances (Woodruff) Gray; m. Judith Irene Hysom, May 9, 1970; children: Fred W. III, David Hysom. BS, Kans. State U., 1970; JD, U. Ala., 1975. Bar: Ala. 1975, Fla. 1975, S.C. 1976. Assoc. Ogletree, Deakins, Nash, Smoak & Stewart, Greenville, S.C., 1975-80, ptnr., 1980—. Mem. bd. regents Leadership Greenville, 1985—; commr. Donaldson Devel. Commn., Greenville, 1986—. Served to capt. USAR, 1970-72. Mem. ABA, Ala. Bar Assn., Fla. Bar Assn., S.C. Bar Assn. (chmn. program com. labor and employment sect., editor newsletter 1985—), S.C. Def. Trial Attys. Assn. Republican. Methodist. Clubs: Greenville Country, Poinsett (Greenville). Lodge: Rotary (bd. dirs. North Greenville club 1985—). Labor. Home: 104 Augusta Dr Greenville SC 29605 Office: Ogletree Deakins Nash Smoak & Stewart 1000 E North St Greenville SC 29602

SUGRUE, THOMAS JOSEPH, lawyer; b. Bklyn., Feb. 9, 1947; s. Francis J. and Elizabeth W. (Connolly) S.; m. Patricia A. Mannion, Aug. 5, 1972; children: Erin, Kerry. BS magna cum laude, Boston Coll., 1968; M in Pub. Policy and JD magna cum laude, Harvard U., 1975. Bar: Mass. 1975, D.C. 1982, U.S. Dist. Ct. D.C. 1982, U.S. Ct. Appeals (D.C. cir.) 1982, U.S. Supreme Ct. 1982. Law clk. to presiding justice Mass. Supreme Ct., Boston, 1975-76; atty., advisor FTC, Washington, 1976-78; assoc. Wilmer, Cutler & Pickering, Washington, 1978-83; spl. counsel for competition policies FCC, Washington, 1983-84, chief policy div. common carrier bur., 1985—. Mem. ABA, D.C. Bar Assn. Avocations: running, music, N.Y. Giants fan. Administrative and regulatory, Public utilities. Home: 1048 Palmer Pl Alexandria VA 22304 Office: FCC 1919 M St NW Washington DC 20554

SUHRE, CAROL ANN, law librarian; b. Youngstown, Ohio, Feb. 22, 1958; d. Russell Arnold and Mary Agnes (Rodzen) O'Connor; m. James Albert Suhre, Aug. 31, 1985. BA, Kent State U., 1980; postgrad., U. Ky., 1984—. Asst. to curator Kent (Ohio) State U. Libraries, 1976-80; microfilm clk. Blue Cross Northeast Ohio, Youngstown, 1981-82; law librarian Clermont County Law Library, Batavia, Ohio, 1983—; specialist west law West Pub., St. Paul, 1986; book reviewer Law Library Alert, Chgo., 1985—. Bd. dirs. Am. Cancer Soc., Cin., 1986. Mem. Am. Assn. Law Libraries (scholarship com.), Ohio Regional Assn. Law Libraries (newsletter com.). Roman Catholic. Avocations: writing, boating, traveling. Librarianship. Home: 600 Brandy Way Cincinnati OH 45244 Office: Clermont County Law Library Main St Courthouse Batavia OH 45103

SUHRE, KAREN KAY, lawyer; b. Libertyville, Ill., June 17, 1958; d. Wilbert F. and Phyllis Ann (Martin) S.; m. Jeffrey Mark Cotter, Mar. 20, 1982. B in Music with highest honors, So. Ill. U., 1979; JD magna cum laude, U. Ill., 1982. Bar: Tex. 1982, U.S. Dist. Ct. (no. dist.) Tex. 1983, U.S. Tax Ct. 1985. Assoc. Hughes & Luce, Dallas, 1982—. Topics editor U. Ill. Law Review, Champaign, 1981-82. Vol. income tax asst., Dallas, 1984-85. Mem. ABA, State Bar Tex., Dallas Bar Assn., Dallas Assn. Young Lawyers (co-chmn. benefits survey com. 1987), Order of Coif. Avocations: music, wilderness adventures. Pension, profit-sharing, and employee benefits, Corporate taxation, Personal income taxation. Home: 3033 San Jacinto Apt 311 Dallas TX 75204 Office: Hughes & Luce 1000 Dallas Building Dallas TX 75201

SUHRE, WALTER ANTHONY, JR., brewery executive; b. Cin., Jan. 17, 1933; s. Walter A. and Elizabeth V. (Heimbuch) S.; m. Judy Lee Carrington, June 7, 1975. B.S. in Bus. Adminstrn., Northwestern U., 1956; LL.B. with honors, U. Cin., 1962. Bar: Ohio 1962, Mo. 1982. Assoc. Taft, Stettinius & Hollister, Cin., 1962-65; with Eagle-Picher Industries, Inc., Cin., 1965-82, sr. v.p., gen. counsel, 1980-82; v.p., gen. counsel Anheuser-Busch Cos., Inc., St. Louis, 1982—. Served with USMC, 1956-59. Mem. ABA, Mo. Bar Assn. Republican. Presbyterian. Clubs: Queen City (Cin.), Old Warson Country (St. Louis). General corporate. Home: 7 Cricklewood Pl Saint Louis MO 63131 Office: Anheuser-Busch Cos Inc One Busch Pl Saint Louis MO 63118

SUHRHEINRICH, RICHARD F., federal judge; b. 1936. B.S., Wayne State U., 1960; J.D. cum laude, Detroit Coll. Law, 1963. Bar: Mich. Assoc. Moll, Desenberg, Purdy, Glover & Bayer, 1963-67; asst. prosecutor Macomb County, 1967; ptnr. Rogensues, Richard & Suhrheinrich, 1967; assoc. Moll, Desenberg, Purdy, Glover & Bayer, 1967-68; ptnr. Kitch, Suhrheinrich, Saurbier & Drutchas, 1968-84; judge U.S. Dist. Ct. (ea. dist.) Mich., Detroit, 1984—. Office: US Dist Ct US Courthouse 231 W Lafayette Blvd Room 235 Detroit MI 48226 *

SUJACK, EDWIN THOMAS, lawyer; b. Chgo., Jan. 9, 1927; s. Frank Thomas and Florence Mary (Meyer) S.; m. Vivijeanne Therese Foley, Aug. 8, 1953; children: Stephen, Donald, Gregory, Julie. Ph.B., Loyola U., Chgo., 1948; LL.B., Harvard U., 1951. Bar: Ill. 1951, U.S. Ct. Appeals (7th cir.) 1963, U.S. Supreme Ct. 1964. Assoc. kirkland & Ellis, Chgo., 1952-60; ptnr. Kirkland & Ellis, Chgo., 1961—. Served with USN, 1945-46. Mem. ABA, Ill. State Bar Assn., Chgo. Bar Assn., Catholic Lawyers Guild. Clubs: Chgo. Athletic Assn, Mid-Am, Olympia Fields (Ill.) Country. General corporate, Contracts commercial. Home: 34 Danube Way Olympia Fields IL 60461 Office: Kirkland & Ellis 200 E Randolph Dr Chicago IL 60601

SULKES, CAROL FAY, lawyer; b. Detroit, Feb. 25, 1953; d. Emanuel M. and Jean (Kaplan) S.; m. Michael C. Krauss, Mar. 1, 1981; children: Matthew Stephen, Jonathan Andrew. BA, U. Mich., 1975, JD, 1977. Bar: Ill. 1978, U.S. Dist. Ct. (no. dist.) Ill. 1978. Assoc. Fox & Grove, Chgo., 1978-79; atty. Centel Corp., Chgo., 1979-80, staff atty., 1980-86, gen. staff atty., asst. sec., 1986—. Angell scholar, 1974. Mem. ABA (labor law sect.), Chgo. Bar Assn. (corp. law dept. com.), Phi Beta Kappa. Avocations:

bridge, bicycling. General corporate, Labor. Home: 844 Marion Ave Highland Park IL 60035 Office: Centel Corp 8725 Higgins Rd Chicago IL 60631

SULLENBARGER, DANIEL JAMES, lawyer; b. Greenville, Ohio, Apr. 25, 1951; s. James Lee and Lois Evelyn (Roark) S.; m. Lauren Jean Drehs, Aug. 10, 1974; children: Jennifer Ann, Erin Michelle. BA, Bowling Green State U., 1973; JD, Ohio No. U., 1976. Bar: Ohio 1976, U.S. Dist. Ct. (no. dist.) Ohio 1977, U.S. Ct. Appeals (7th cir.) 1978, U.S. Ct. Appeals (5th cir.) 1985, Tex. 1985. Atty. pipeline div. Marathon Oil, Findlay, Ohio, 1976-78, atty. mktg. div., 1978-80; legal adviser prodn. div. Marathon Oil, London, 1980-84; atty. prodn. pipeline div. Marathon Oil, Houston, 1984-86, sr. counsel refining, mktg., supply, transp. and adminstrn., 1986—. Bd. dirs. Hancock County Mental Health Assn., Findlay, 1976-80; chmn. Cityof Findlay Bd. of Zoning Appeals, 1978-80. Recipient awards for Excellence Lawyer's Coop. Pub. Co., 1975,76. Mem. ABA, Ohio Bar Assn., Tex. State Bar Assn., Houston Bar Assn. Avocation: recreational and competitive running. Oil and gas leasing, Private international, General corporate. Home: 12722 Cloverwood Dr Cypress TX 77429 Office: Marathon Oil Co 5555 San Felipe PO Box 3128 Houston TX 77253

SULLIVAN, ALFRED A., judge; b. Yonkers, N.Y., Feb. 27, 1926; s. Alfred A. and Clara B. (Kennepohl) S.; m. Virginia R. Secrest, Aug. 27, 1949; children—Alfred A., Brian E., Kathleen P., Theresa A., A.B., U. Mich., 1949, J.D., 1951. Bar: Ohio 1951, Mich. 1952, U.S. Dist. Ct. (ea. dist.) Mich. 1952, U.S. Supreme Ct. 1958. Legal analyst, legal tax analyst Kaiser Motors Corp., Willow Run, Mich., 1951-54; title examiner, escrow officer and v.p. Lawyers Title Ins. Corp., Ann Arbor, Mich., 1954-67; head legal dept. Am. Title Ins. Co., Detroit, 1967-69; hearing examiner Mich. Pub. Service Commn., Lansing, 1969-71, chief hearings examiner, 1971-75, chief adminstrv. law judge, 1975-84, sr. adminstrv. law judge, 1984—; part-time sole practice, 1951-67; atty. Washtenaw County Drain Commn., 1955-65; mem. faculty Cleary Coll., Ypsilanti, Mich., 1956-59, Lansing Community Coll., 1983-85; faculty advisor Nat. Jud. Coll., Reno, 1978-79; justice of peace, Ypsilanti Twp., 1963-65. Served with U.S. Army, 1942-45. Mem. State Bar of Mich. (former chmn. adminstrv. law sect.), ABA. Republican. Roman Catholic. Club: K.C. (3d and 4th degree). Administrative and regulatory, Public utilities. Address: 6545 Mercantile Way Lansing MI 48910

SULLIVAN, BARRY, lawyer; b. Newburyport, Mass., Jan. 11, 1949; s. George Arnold and Dorothy Bennett (Furbush) S.; m. Winnifred Mary Fallers, June 14, 1975; children: George Arnold, Lloyd Ashton. AB cum laude, Middlebury Coll., 1970; JD, U. Chgo., 1974. Bar: Mass. 1975, Ill. 1975, U.S. Dist. Ct. (no. dist.) Ill. 1976, U.S. Ct. Appeals (7th cir.) 1976, U.S. Ct. Appeals (10th cir.) 1977, U.S. Supreme Ct. 1978, U.S. Ct. Appeals (11th cir.) 1986. Law clk. to presiding justice U.S. Ct. Appeals (5th cir.), New Orleans, 1974-75; assoc. Jenner & Block, Chgo., 1975-80; asst. to solicitor gen. of U.S. U.S. Dept. of Justice, Washington, 1980-81; ptnr. Jenner & Block, Chgo., 1981—; lectr. in law Loyola U., Chgo., 1978-79. Assoc. editor U. Chgo. Law Rev., 1973-74; contbr. articles to profl. jours. Mem. vis. com. U. Chgo. Divinity Sch., 1987—. Yeats Soc. scholar, 1968; Woodrow Wilson fellow, Woodrow Wilson Found., 1970. Mem. ABA, Ill. Bar Assn., Bar Assn. 7th Fed. Cir. (vice chmn. adminstrv. justice com. 1985-86), Am. Law Inst., Phi Beta Kappa. Democrat. Roman Catholic. Federal civil litigation, State civil litigation. Home: 5733 S Kimbark Ave Chicago IL 60637 Office: Jenner & Block One IBM Plaza Chicago IL 60611

SULLIVAN, CARROLL HART, lawyer; b. Mobile, Ala., Jan. 4, 1950; s. John Dominique and Doris Frances (Hart) S.; m. Carol Jan Heacock, Aug. 5, 1972; children: Frances Rebecca, John Warren. BS in Econs., Auburn U., 1972; JD cum laude, Samford U., 1975. Bar: Ala. 1975, U.S. Dist. Ct. (no. and so. dists.) Ala. 1975, U.S. Ct. Appeals (5th cir) 1976, U.S. Ct. Appeals (11th cir.) 1981. Law clk. to presiding judge U.S. Dist. Ct., Birmingham, Ala., 1975-76; from assoc. to ptnr. Inge, Twitty, Duffy & Prince, Mobile, Ala., 1976-82; ptnr. Hume & Sullivan, Mobile, 1982-86, Clark, Scott & Sullivan, Mobile, 1986—. Mem. editorial bd. Samford U. Cumberland Sch. Law Rev., 1974-75, Ala. Lawyer, 1985—; contbr. articles to profl. jours. Bd. dirs. Cerebral Palsy Mobile Inc., 1983—. Mem. ABA, Ala. Bar Assn., Moblie Bar Assn. (fed. ct. com.), Def. Research Inst., Ala. Def. Lawyers Assn. (amicus curiae com.), Omicron Delta Epsilon. Clubs: Country Mobile, Athelstan (Mobile). Avocations: golf, tennis, boating. State civil litigation, Insurance, Personal injury. Home: 3814 Mordecai Ln Mobile AL 36608 Office: Clark Scott & Sullivan PO Box 1034 Mobile AL 36633

SULLIVAN, CHARLES WILLIAM, lawyer; b. Natick, Mass., Mar. 13, 1924; s. Charles F. Sullivan and Mary E. Costello; m. Anne Lyons, May 19, 1951; children: Anne P., Charles W. Jr., MaryElise. BBA, Babson Coll., 1949; MBA in Mgmt., Boston U., 1950; JD, Boston Coll., 1957; LLM in Taxation, Boston U., 1965. Bar: Mass. 1957. Agent IRS, Boston, 1951-57; ptnr. Sullivan, Sorgi & Dimmock, Boston, 1957—; bd. dirs. The Trans. Lease Group, Westwood, Mass., UTT Distbg. Co. Inc., Cambridge, Mass. Mem. Estate Planning Council, Boston Coll., Newton, 1960—, Suffolk U., Boston, 1983—. Served with USN, 1942-46, ETO and PTO. Democrat. Roman Catholic. Corporate taxation, Estate taxation, Personal income taxation. Home: 14 Slocum Rd Jamaica Plain MA 02130 Office: Sullivan Sorgi & Dimmock 50 Staniford St Boston MA 02114

SULLIVAN, EDWARD JOSEPH, lawyer, educator; b. Bklyn., Apr. 24, 1945; s. Edward Joseph and Bridget (Duffy) S.; m. Patte Hancock, Aug. 7, 1982; children: Amy Belieu, Molly Belieu, Mary Christine. BA in Polit. Sci., St. John's U., 1966; JD, Willamette U., 1969; MA, Portland State U., 1974; LLM, University Coll., Oxford, London, 1978, Diploma Law, 1984. Bar: Oreg. 1969, D.C. 1978, U.S. Dist. Ct. Oreg. 1970, U.S. Ct. Appeals (9th cir.) 1970, U.S. Supreme Ct. 1972. Counsel Washington County, Hillsboro, Oreg., 1969-75; legal counsel Gov. of Oreg., Salem, 1975-77; ptnr. O'Donnell, Sullivan & Ramis, Portland, Oreg., 1978-84, Sullivan, Josselson, Roberts, Johnson & Kloos, Portland, Salem and Eugene, Oreg., 1984-86, Mitchell, Lang & Smith, Portland, 1986—; bd. dirs., pres. Oreg. Law Inst. Contbr. numerous articles to profl. jours. Chmn. Capitol Planning Commn., Salem, 1975-77, 78-81. Mem. ABA (local govt. sect., com. on planning and zoning, adminstrv. law sect.) Oreg. State Bar Assn., D.C. Bar Assn., Am. Judicature Soc., Am. Polit. Sci. Assn. Democrat. Roman Catholic. Administrative and regulatory, Jurisprudence, Planning and zoning. Office: Mitchell Lang & Smith 101 SW Main 2000 One Main Pl Portland OR 97204

SULLIVAN, EDWARD PAUL, lawyer; b. Chgo., Aug. 30, 1955; s. Edward Joseph and Ann (Jeno) S. BS in Law Enforcement, Western Ill. U., 1977; JD, Oklahoma City U., 1981. Bar: Okla. 1982, U.S. Dist. Ct. Okla. 1982. Sole practice Oklahoma City, 1982-84; assoc. Levine and Assocs., Oklahoma City, 1984-85; atty., restaurateur Red Byrd Restaurant and Motel, Keedysville, Md., 1985-86; assoc. Tulsa Law Clinic, 1986-87, John J. Tanner, Atty., Tulsa, 1987—. Ill. State scholar, 1973-76, Otis P. Graves scholar, 1973-77. Mem. ABA, Okla. Bar Assn., Okla. Wildlife Assn. Roman Catholic. Avocations: fishing, softball, basketball, shooting, travel. Criminal, Family and matrimonial, General practice. Home: 1143 S Wheeling Tulsa OK 74104 Office: John J Tanner Atty 3315 E 39th St Tulsa OK 74135

SULLIVAN, EUGENE JOHN, lawyer; b. Chestertown, Md., May 13, 1946; s. Eugene John and Dorothy Ann (Douglas) S. BA with high honors, U. Md., 1969; JD, Columbia U., 1972. Bar: N.Y. 1973, Pa. 1980, U.S. Dist. Ct. (so. and ea. dists.) N.Y. 1973, U.S. Ct. Appeals (2d cir.) 1975, N.J. 1976, U.S. Supreme Ct. 1976, U.S. Ct. Appeals (3d cir.) 1976, U.S. Dist. Ct. N.J. 1976, U.S. Ct. Appeals (D.C. cir.) 1977, U.S. Ct. Claims 1978, U.S. Ct. Customs and Patent Appeals 1978. Assoc. Kirlin, Campbell & Keating, N.Y.C., 1972-75; dep. atty. gen. div. law N.J. Dept. Law and Pub. Safety, Trenton, 1976-81, asst. atty. gen., 1981—; mem. com. on civil model jury charges N.J. Supreme Ct., 1983—, com. on civil case mgmt. and procedure, 1983—. Author, editor: Division of Law Litigation Manual, 1983. Served with USN, 1964-67. Mem. ABA (sec. litigation, sect. anti-trust law, sect. pub. contract law), N.J. Bar Assn., Pa. Bar Assn., Columbia Law Sch. Alumni Assn., Phi Beta Kappa, Phi Kappa Phi, Phi Eta Sigma, Phi Alpha Theta. Roman Catholic. Federal civil litigation, State civil litigation. Home: 480 Valley Rd Upper Montclair NJ 07043 Office: Richard J Hughes Justice Complex NJ Dept Law and Public Safety Div of Law CN112 Trenton NJ 08625

SULLIVAN, EUGENE RAYMOND, federal judge; b. St. Louis, Aug. 2, 1941; s. Raymond Vincent and Rosemary (Kiely) S.; m. Lis Urup Johansen, June 18, 1966; children—Kim, Eugene II. B.S., U.S. Mil. Acad., 1964; J.D., Georgetown U., 1971. Bar: Mo. 1972, D.C. 1972. Law clk. to judge U.S. Ct. Appeals (8th cir.), St. Louis, 1971-72; assoc. Patton Boggs & Blow, Washington, 1972-74; asst. spl. counsel The White House, Washington, 1974; trial counsel U.S. Dept. of Justice, Washington, 1974-82; dep. gen. counsel U.S. Air Force, Washington, 1982-84; gen. counsel U.S. Air Force, 1984-86; judge U.S. Ct. Mil. Appeals, Washington, 1986—. Served to capt. U.S. Army, 1964-69, Vietnam. Decorated Bronze Star, Air medal, others. Republican. Roman Catholic. Criminal, Government contracts and claims, Federal civil litigation. Home: 6307 Massachusetts Ave Bethesda MD 20816 Office: US Ct Mil Appeals 450 E St NW Washington DC 20442-0001

SULLIVAN, FRANCIS CHARLES, legal educator, college dean; b. Chgo., Jan. 14, 1927; s. Frank Colby and Mary Cecilia (Burke) S.; m. Dolores Gray, June 11, 1955; children: Brian, Eugene, Laurence. B.S., Loyola U., Chgo., 1947, J.D., 1949; LL.M., NYU, 1961. Bar: Ill. 1950, Tenn. 1986. Ptnr. McKinley, Price & Appleman, Chgo., 1949-56; prof. law Loyola U., Chgo., 1956-66; prof. La. State U., 1966-85, assoc. dean, 1970-77, dean, 1977-78; prof. law emeritus C.C. Humphreys Sch. Law, Memphis State U., 1986—, dean, 1985—; disting. vis. prof. law U. Okla., 1979, U. San Diego, 1981-82, UCLA, 1985; dir. La. Jud. Coll., 1975-81, Ctr. Criminal Justice, Policy and Mgmt., 1981-82; cons. in field. Author: The Adminstration of Criminal Justice, 1965, 2d edit., 1968, Evidence, 1969, Louisiana Evidence, 1983, 2d edit., 1984, Louisiana Criminal Justice, 1983, 2d edit., 1985; contbr. articles to profl. jours. Served with U.S. Army, 1945-46, 50-52. Named Papal Knight of Holy Sepulchre; Ford Found. Travel fellow, 1958-59; Ford Found. fellow, 1959-61. Mem. Baton Rouge Bar Assn., Chgo. Bar Assn., Ill. Bar Assn., La. Bar Assn., Am. Bar Assn. (recipient award 1978), Tenn. Bar Assn., Shelby County Bar Assn., Council La State Law Inst., Am. Law Inst., Order of Coif, Blue Key. Roman Catholic. Clubs: City of Baton Rouge, Nat. Lawyers, Summit, Chickasaw Country, Camelot; University (San Diego). Home: 275 Central Park W Apt 4 Memphis TN 38111 Office: Memphis State University CC Humphreys Sch Law Memphis TN 38152

SULLIVAN, JAMES ANDERSON, lawyer; b. Wabash, Ind., July 1, 1925; s. Lawrence James and Mildred (Anderson) S.; m. Marily June Allen, Oct. 4, 1947; children—Timothy J., Patrick F., Katherine M. Sullivan Luce, Thomas S., James Anderson. A.B. magna cum laude, Ind. U., 1952, J.D. magna cum laude, 1954. Bar: Calif. 1955, U.S. Dist. Ct. (so. dist.) Calif. 1955, U.S. Ct. Appeals (9th cir.) 1955, U.S. Supreme Ct. 1963. Assoc. Gibson, Dunn & Crutcher, Los Angeles, 1954-56; mem. corp. legal staff Hughes Aircraft Co., Culver City, Calif., 1956-58, div. counsel, El Segundo, Calif., 1958-63, aerospace group counsel, Culver City, 1963-65; of counsel Sweeney Cozy & Diederich, Torrance, Calif., 1965-72; ptnr. Buck, Sullivan, Govendo & Bavetta, Redondo Beach, Calif., 1973-75; sole practice, Redondo Beach, 1975-84, Torrance, 1984—; mem. panel arbitrators Am. Arbitration Assn., Fed. Mediation and Conciliation Service; bd. dirs. LES Enterprises, Inc., Anaheim, Calif., Pro-File Sports Inc., Oxnard, Calif., Coast Wire & Cable Corp., Gardena, Calif., EDP Environments, Inc., Torrance, Calif., Palos Verdes Breakfast Club, Palos Verdes Estates, Calif. Bd. dirs. South Bay Children's Health Ctr. Assn., Torrance, Calif. Served with USNR, 1943-46, 50-51; PTO. John H. Edwards fellow, 1953-54. Mem. South Bay Estate Planning Council (pres. 1967-68), Order of Coif, Phi Beta Kappa, Phi Eta Sigma, Phi Delta Phi. Republican. Clubs: South Bay Athletic (Redondo Beach); Kiwanis (pres. Redondo Beach club 1981-82, Riviera Village club. 1985-86), Palos Verdes Breakfast (bulletin editor 1982-86, bd. dirs. 1986—). Probate, Contracts commercial, Estate planning. Address: Madrona Bldg Suite 201 3246 W Sepulveda Blvd Torrance CA 90505

SULLIVAN, JAMES WASHBURN, lawyer; b. N.Y.C., June 4, 1948; s. James Frederick Sullivan and Ariel (Williams) Schaffer; m. Catherine Elizabeth Brennan, Apr. 24, 1977; children: Jonathan, Michael. BA, Harvard U.; JD, Stanford U. Bar: Calif. 1975, U.S. Dist. Ct. (no. dist.) Calif. 1975. Atty. Community Legal Services, San Jose, Calif., 1975-79, Calif. Agrl. Labor Relations Bd., Salinas, Calif., 1979-84; v.p., gen. counsel Castle & Cooke Fresh Vegetables, Salinas, 1984-86; sole practice Salinas, 1986—; bd. dirs Legal Aid Soc. Monterey County, Calif., chmn. 1982-84. Mem. Santa Clara Housing and Community Devel. Citizens Adv. Com., San Jose, 1979; mediator Salinas Housing Mediation Bd., 1981-83. Mem. ABA, Calif. Bar Assn. (bus. sect., labor and employment sect.), Monterey County Bar Assn. Democrat. Avocations: swimming, soccer, tennis, skiing, windsurfing. Labor, Contracts commercial, General practice.

SULLIVAN, JOSEPH CHARLES, lawyer; b. N.Y.C., Dec. 6, 1927. B.E.E., Manhattan Coll., 1950; LL.B., St. John's U., 1954; LL.M., N.Y.U., 1958. Bar: N.Y. 1955, U.S. Dist. Ct. (so. and ea. dists.) N.Y. 1956, U.S. Dist. Ct. (no. dist.) N.Y. 1960, U.S. Ct. Appeals (2d cir.) 1960, U.S. Ct. Customs and Patent Appeals 1963, U.S. Supreme Ct. 1976, U.S. Ct. Claims 1981. Design engr. Sperry Corp., Long Island City, N.Y., 1950-54; atty. Control Instrument Co. subs. Burroughs Corp., Bklyn, 1954-55; assoc. Kane, Dalsimer, Kane, Sullivan & Kurucz, N.Y.C., 1955-60, ptnr., 1960—. Lectr. Practicing Law Inst., 1960—. Mem. IEEE, Am. Patent Law Assn., N.Y. Patent Law Assn., N.Y. Bar Assn., Assn. Bar City N.Y. Contbr. articles to profl. jours. Patent, Trademark and copyright. Home: 82 Eton Rd Garden City NY 11530 Office: Kane Dalsimer Kane Sullivan 420 Lexington Ave New York NY 10017

SULLIVAN, KEVIN PATRICK, lawyer; b. Waterbury, Conn., June 9, 1953; s. John Holian Sullivan and Frances (McGrath) Coon; m. Peggy Hardy, June 13, 1975 (div. Jan. 1985); m. Jarnine Welker, Feb. 15, 1985; children: S. Craig Lemmon, Michael Scott Lemmon, Lindsay Michelle Lemmon. BS in Polit. Sci., BS in Police Sci. cum laude, Weber State Coll., 1979; JD, Pepperdine U., 1982. Bar: Utah 1982, U.S. Dist. Ct. Utah 1982, U.S. Ct. Appeals (10th cir.) 1986, U.S. Supreme Ct. 1986. Assoc. Farr, Kaufman & Hamilton, Ogden, Utah, 1982—; judge pro tem Utah 3d Cir. Ct. Mem. Eccles Community Art Ctr. Mem. Weber County Bar (criminal law sect.), Utah State Bar (criminal law sect., young lawyer sect.), Assn. Trial Lawyers Am., Weber County Pub. Defenders Assn. (assoc. dir.), Phi Kappa Phi. Roman Catholic. Lodge: Elks. Avocations: skiing, golf, tennis, fishing. Criminal, Personal injury, State civil litigation. Home: 945 Fillmore Ave Ogden UT 84404 Office: Farr Kaufman & Hamilton 205 26th St #34 Ogden UT 84401

SULLIVAN, LAWRENCE A., legal educator, lawyer; b. 1923. J.D., Harvard U., 1951. Bar: Mass. 1952. Law clk. to chief judge U.S. Ct. Appeals (1st cir.), 1951-52; assoc. Foley, Hoag & Eliot, Boston, 1952-54, 56-59, ptnr., 1959-65; vis. assoc. prof. U. Calif. Law Sch.-Berkeley, 1954-56, prof., 1966—; mem. Nat. Com. for Revision Antitrust Laws and Procs., 1978-79. Served to sgt. USAAF, 1942-46. Guggenheim fellow, 1978. Author: Handbook on the Law of Antitrust, 1977; former mem. editorial bd. Harvard Law Rev. Legal education. Office: U Calif Law Sch 225 Boalt Hall Berkeley CA 94720

SULLIVAN, LOVELL WAYNE, lawyer; b. Heidelberg, Fed. Republic Germany, May 21, 1957; s. Gerald Wayne Sullivan and Rita Joyce (Click) Weimer; m. Susan Jo Eastin, May 31, 1980; 1 child, Megan Ann. BS in Bus., Kans. State U., 1979, BS Agr. Econs., 1979; JD, U. Kans., 1982. Bar: Okla. 1975, U.S. Dist. Ct. (no. dist.) Okla. 1975. Tax specialist Peat, Marwich, Mitchell & Co., Tulsa, 1982-83; sole Practice Jenks, Okla., 1983—; v.p. Sullo, Inc., Sabetha, 1982—; pres. Vanberg, Jenks, Okla., 1985—. Bd. dirs. Coll. Reps. Region 7, 1979. Named Real Trojan of Month Jenks Jour., 1985. Mem. ABA (taxation sect.), Okla. Bar Assn., Tulsa County Bar Assn., Tulsa Estate Planning Forum, Jenks C. of C. (pres. 1986, named citizen of yr. 1985). Lodge: Kiwanis (bd. dirs. Jenks club 1985). Avocations: snow skiing, golf. Probate, Real property, Securities. Home: 8212 S Florence Pl Tulsa OK 74137 Office: 123 E Main Jenks OK 74037

SULLIVAN, MARK EDWARD, lawyer; b. Rockeville Ctr., N.Y., Jan. 1, 1950; s. William Daniel and Catherine Mary (Lynch) S. BA in Philosophy, U. Va., 1973; JD, Marshall Coll. Law, 1981. Bar: Ohio 1982. Asst. pros. atty. Cuyahoga County, Cleve., 1982-86; sole practice Cleve., 1982—; adminstrv. gen. ptnr. Bradley Assocs. Ltd., Cleve., 1983—. Mem. ABA, Ohio Bar Assn. Criminal, Personal injury, Real property. Home: 1220 W Sixth Apt 800 Cleveland OH 44113 Office: 1220 W 6th Bradley Bldg Cleveland OH 44113

SULLIVAN, MAUREEN, lawyer; b. Bklyn., June 2, 1954; d. John Joseph and Mary Virginia (McCabe) Sullivan; m. John Quincy Landers, Jr., Sept. 8, 1979. B.A. summa cum laude (Durant scholar) Wellesley Coll., 1976; J.D., U. Pa., 1979. Bar: N.Y. 1979, Calif. 1980. Assoc. firm Milbank, Tweed, Hadley & McCloy, N.Y.C., 1979-80, Brobeck, Phleger & Harrison, San Francisco, 1980—. Mem. ABA, Calif. State Bar Assn., Phi Beta Kappa. Club: Meadow. Real property. Home: 2811 Adeline Dr Burlingame CA 94010 Office: Brobeck Phleger & Harrison Two Embarcadero Pl 2200 Geng Rd Palo Alto CA 94303

SULLIVAN, MICHAEL D., Mississippi supreme court justice; b. Hattiesburg, Miss., Dec. 2, 1938; s. Curran W. and Mittie (Chambers) S.; m. Nancy Ezell, Dec. 20, 1959; children—Kathleen, David Paul, Rachel Michel. B.S., U. So. Miss., 1960; J.D., Tulane U., 1966. Atty. Hattiesburg, Miss., 1967-75; chancellor Miss. Chancery Ct. Dist. 10, 1975-84; justice Miss. Supreme Ct., Jackson, 1984—. Judicial administration. Office: PO Box 117 Jackson MS 39205 *

SULLIVAN, MICHAEL MAURICE, lawyer; b. Hartford, Conn., Mar. 14, 1942; s. Charles John and Katherine (Moriarity) S.; m. Tina Noel Petro, Oct. 8, 1966; children: Tara Noel, Megan Alexandra. BA in Govt., Fairfield U., 1965; JD, Cath. U., 1972. Bar: N.Y. 1972, U.S. Dist. Ct. (so. and ea. dists.) N.Y. 1972, U.S. Ct. Appeals (2d cir.) 1972. Assoc. Sullivan & Cromwell, N.Y., 1972-75; dir. legal and govt. affairs Allied Stores Corp., N.Y., 1975-78; counsel U.S. div. Singer Co., N.Y., 1978-80; counsel internat. group Singer Co., Stamford, Conn., 1980-84; v.p., gen. counsel ITEC Inc., Huntsville, Ala., 1984—. Contbr. articles to profl. jours. V.P. Internat. Juvenile Diabetes Found., Fairfield, Conn., 1982-84. Served to lt. USN., 1965-69. Mem. ABA, N.Y. Bar Assn., Assn. Bar City of N.Y., Westchester-Fairfield County Corp. Counsel Assn. Avocations: running, tennis, golf. General corporate, Private international, Trademark and copyright. Home: 1321 Chandler Rd Huntsville AL 35801 Office: ITEC Inc 520 Green Cove Rd Huntsville AL 35803

SULLIVAN, MICHAEL PATRICK, lawyer; b. Mpls., Dec. 5, 1934; s. Michael Francis and Susan Ellen (Doran) S.; m. Marilyn Emmer, June 27, 1964; children—Katherine, Michael, Maureen, Bridget, Daniel, Thomas. Bar: Minn. 1962, U.S. Dist. Ct. Minn. 1962, U.S. Supreme Ct. 1975, U.S. Ct. Appeals (8th cir.) 1978. Assoc., Gray, Plant, Mooty, Mooty & Bennett, Mpls., 1962-67, ptnr., 1968—, mng. ptnr., 1976—; instr. U. Minn. Law Sch., 1962-67; lectr. continuing legal edn.; spl. counsel to atty. gen. Minn., 1971-79, 82-84. Bd. dirs. Legal Aid Soc. Mpls.; bd. trustees Coll. St. Catherine; chmn. exec. com. Uniform Law Commn. Served with USN, 1956-59. Mem. ABA (ho. of dels.), Minn. Bar Assn. (gov.), Hennepin County Bar Assn. (pres. 1978-79), Am. Bar Found., Order of Coif. Democratic Farmer Labor Party. Roman Catholic. Clubs: Serra, Mpls., KC. Contbr. articles to profl. jours. General corporate, Antitrust, Contracts commercial. Office: 3400 City Center Minneapolis MN 55402

SULLIVAN, MORTIMER ALLEN, JR., lawyer; b. Buffalo, N.Y., Sept. 19, 1930; s. Mortimer Allen Sr. and Gertrude (Hinkley) S.; m. Maryanne Calella, Nov. 20, 1965; children: Mark Allen, Michael John. BA, U. Buffalo, 1954. Bar: N.Y. 1964, U.S. Dist. Ct. (we. dist.) N.Y. 1966, U.S. Dist. Ct. (no. dist.) N.Y. 1967, U.S. Supreme Ct. 1970. Counsel liability claims Interstate Motor Freight System, Grand Rapids, Mich., 1964-82; v.p. J.P.M. Sullivan, Inc., Elmira, N.Y., 1959-67; govt. appeal agt. U.S. Selective Service System, 1967-71; dep. sci. div. Erie County (N.Y.) Sheriff's Dept., 1971—, lt., 1986—. Inventor (with others) in field; creator, dir. video depiction JudiVision, 1969; composer High Flight, 1983. Chmn. com. on Constn. and Canons Episcopal Diocese of Western N.Y., 1975—. Served with USAF, 1954-57; col. res. ret. Decorated Legion of Merit. Mem. N.Y. State Bar Assn., Erie County Bar Assn. (chmn. laws and tech. com. 1970-81), Transp. Lawyers Assn., Kappa Alpha Soc. Republican. Clubs: Saturn (Buffalo); Wanakah (N.Y.) Country. Avocation: aviation. General practice, Insurance. Home: 19 Knob Hill Rd Orchard Park NY 14127 Office: 530 Convention Tower Buffalo NY 14202

SULLIVAN, PATRICK ARTHUR, lawyer; b. Bellingham, Wash., July 21, 1935; s. James Edward and Maribel (Bailey) S.; m. Diane S. Zack, Feb. 27, 1960; children—Kevin Patrick, Kathleen Diane, Colleen Michelle, Meaghan Mari, Elizabeth. J.D., Gonzaga U., 1959; M.B.A. in Govt. Contracts, U. Va., 1960; Bar: Wash. 1959. Tchr. music pvt. schs., Spokane, Wash., 1949-62; performed with own jazz band, Spokane, 1959-62; mem. legal staff Boeing Corp., Seattle, 1962-63, chief contracts counsel Saturn br., New Orleans, 1963-64; assoc. Winston & Cashatt, Spokane, Wash., 1964-66, ptnr., 1966—, pres., chmn. bd., 1981—; pres., dir. Squire Motor Inns, Grand Canyon Airlines, N.Am. Helicopter Corp., 1968-76; internat. arbitrator Geneva; lectr. on constrn. law and claims throughout U.S. Bd. dirs. Am. Heart Assn., YMCA, Spokane; adv. bd. Spokane Interplayers Ensemble. Served with JAGC, U.S. Army, 1959-62. Mem. ABA (state chmn. constrn. litigation 1976-80, state chmn. pub. contracts sect. 1981-83), Wash. State Bar Assn., Assoc. Gen. Contractors, Internat. Arbitration Assn. Methodist. Clubs: Spokane, Spokane Racquet. Co-author seminar book on constrn. law and claims, 1982. Construction. Home: 920 Melinda Ln Spokane WA 99203 Office: 20th Floor Seat-First Tower Spokane WA 99201

SULLIVAN, PATRICK JAMES, lawyer; b. Orange, Calif., Sept. 17, 1943; s. Leo Charles Sullivan and Virginia (Wohosky) Souza; m. Pamela Pressler, Aug. 17, 1974; children—Shannon, Erin. B.A., U. So. Calif., 1965; J.D., Loyola U., Los Angeles, 1974. Bar: Calif. 1974, U.S. Ct. Appeals (9th cir.) 1978, U.S. Supreme Ct. 1979, U.S. Ct. Appeals (3rd cir.) 1983, U.S. Tax Ct. 1986. Trial atty. U.S. Dept. Justice, Washington, 1974-75; ptnr. Sullivan, Jones & Archer, San Diego and San Francisco, 1975-82, Sullivan & Jones, San Diego, 1982-83, Hewitt, Sullivan & Marshall, San Diego, 1983-85, Sullivan, DuVall & Noya, San Diego, 1986—; arbitrator San Diego Superior Ct., 1979-83; lectr. U. Calif. Securities Regulations Inst. Served to 1st lt. U.S. Army, 1966-69; Vietnam. Decorated Bronze Star. Mem. ABA (litigation and antitrust sects.), Nat. Inst. Trial Adv. (faculty 1986—). Republican. Roman Catholic. Lodge: Rotary (Newhall, Calif.). Antitrust, Federal civil litigation, Securities. Home: 335 Whitewood Pl Encinitas CA 92024 Office: Sullivan DuVall & Noya Wells Fargo Bank Bldg 101 W Broadway Suite 1400 San Diego CA 92101

SULLIVAN, RICHARD FRANCIS, lawyer; b. Fairhaven, Vt., Mar. 3, 1928. BS, Fordham U., 1952; JD, Union U., 1957. Bar: Vt. 1957, U.S. Dist. Ct. Va. 1959, U.S. Ct. Appeals (7th cir.) 1959, U.S. Supreme Ct. 1962. Atty. City of Rutland, Vt., 1959-62; judge Rutland Dist. Ct., 1962-67; mem. dist. environ. commn. Environ. Conservation Agy. State of Vt., 1972-77; U.S. magistrate 1977-78; ptnr. Sullivan & McClallen, Rutland, 1980-86, Richard Francis & Assocs., Rutland, 1986—. Mem. Vt. Bar Assn., Rutland County Bar Assn., Assn. Trial Lawyers Am., Vt. Trial Lawyers Assn. General practice, General corporate. Office: 82 Merchants Row Rutland VT 05701-5993

SULLIVAN, RICHARD MORRISSEY, lawyer; b. Louisville, Feb. 22, 1942; s. Richard John and Margaret Crossland (Brown) S.; m. Kathleen Harvey Sanders, May 9, 1964 (div. 1976); chidren: Amy Crossland, Nathan Brown; m. Cinda Dixon, May 8, 1979. BS in Commerce, Eastern Ky. U., 1964; JD, U. Louisville, 1970. Bar: U.S. Dist. Ct. (we. dist.) 1970, U.S. Dist. Ct. (ea. dist.) Ky., U.S. Claims Ct., U.S. Ct. Appeals (6th cir.) 1975, U.S. Supreme Ct. 1983. Assoc. Conliffe, Sandmann, Gorman & Sullivan, Louisville, 1970-74, ptnr., 1974-82, mng. ptnr., 1982—; asst. atty. Jefferson County, Louisville, 1975—; bd. dirs. Tower Mut. Funds, Louisville. Bd. dirs. Mose Green Dem. Party, Louisville, 1977. Fellow Am. Bar Found. (life); mem. ABA (ho. of dels. 1985—), Ky. Bar Assn., Louisville Bar Assn., Am. Judicature Soc. (bd. dirs. 1983—), Assn. Trial Lawyers Am., Ky. Trial Lawyers Assn. Avocations: hunting, fishing, backgammon. State civil litigation, Federal civil litigation, Personal injury. Home: 4 Overbrook Rd Louisville KY 40207 Office: Conliffe Sandmann Gorman & Sullivan 621 W Main St Louisville KY 40202

SULLIVAN, ROBERT JOSEPH, lawyer; b. N.Y.C., July 4, 1949; s. Robert J. and Rosemary T. (Considine) S.; m. Maria Felicia Panarese, Aug. 25, 1974; 1 child, R. Jason. BA in Polit. Sci., Fordham U., 1971; JD, N.Y. Law Sch., 1974. Bar: N.Y. 1985, U.S. Dist. Ct. (so. and ea. dists.) N.Y. 1985, U.S. Tax Ct. 1985, U.S. Ct. Appeals (2d cir.) 1985. Asst. counsel Am. Ins. Assn., N.Y.C., 1974-76; assoc. counsel Swiss Re Holding, N.Y.C., 1976-

77; v.p. govt. affairs Crum and Foster, Morristown, N.J., 1977—. Mem. ABA. Roman Catholic. Insurance, Legislative, Workers' compensation. Home: 7 Buckley Hill rd Morristown NJ 07960 Office: Crum and Foster 305 Madison Ave Morristown NJ 07960

SULLIVAN, STEPHEN JOSEPH, lawyer, geologist; b. Oklahoma City, Jan. 27, 1955; s. John J. and Tosca (Pieretti) S.; m. Joan Marie Roberge, Jan. 12, 1985. BA, Princeton U., 1977; MS, U. Calif., Berkeley, 1979; JD, U. Denver, 1982. Bar: Colo. 1982, U.S. Dist. Ct. Colo. 1983. Assoc. Welborn, Dufford, Brown & Tooley, Denver, 1982—. Mem. Vols. for Outdoor Colo., Denver, 1984—. Mem. Colo. Bar Assn., Denver Bar Assn., Rocky Mountain Assn. of Geologists, Order of St. Ives, Sigma Xi. Avocations: mountaineering, music. Oil and gas exploration geology, Oil and gas leasing. Home: 6973 E Jewell Ave Denver CO 80224-2235 Office: Welborn Dufford Brown & Tooley 1700 Broadway Suite 1100 Denver CO 80290

SULLIVAN, THOMAS EUGENE, lawyer; b. Kansas City, Mo., Sept. 30, 1948; s. Maurice David and Virginia Adams (Pope) S.; m. Nancy Jane Petty, Apr. 26, 1969 (div.); 1 child, Bryan Jeffrey. AA, Kans. Jr. Coll., Kansas City, 1969; BS in Edn., U. Kans., 1971; JD, U. Mo., Kansas City, 1974. Bar: Kans. 1975, U.S. Dist. Ct. Kans. 1975. Assoc. Bronston Law Offices, Overland Park, Kans., 1975-77; ptnr. firm Cleaver & Sullivan, Chartered, Overland Park, 1977-83; pres. Law Offices of Thomas E. Sullivan, P.A., Overland Park, 1983—. Contbr.: Modern Trials (by Melvin Belli), 2d edit. 1982. Bd. dirs. Mid-Am. Cerebral Palsy Games, Inc., Shawnee Mission, Kans., 1983—, Bishop Meige High Sch. Scholarship com., Shawnee Mission, 1984—. Named Boss of Yr., Johnson County Legal Secs., 1983; recipient cert. appreciation YMCA of Greater Kansas City, 1982-83, Bishop Miege High Sch., 1984. Mem. Kans. Trial Lawyers Assn. (gov. 1976—, exec. com., parliamentarian 1982-83, v.p. 1985-86, pres.-elect 1986), Assn. Trial Lawyers Am. (Kans. state del. 1983-85), Kans. Bar Assn., Johnson County Bar Assn., Wyandotte County Bar Assn., Am. Soc. Legal Medicine, Trial Lawyers for Pub. Justice (life), U. Kans. Alumni Assn. Roman Catholic. Club: Jayhawk (Kansas City, Mo.). Personal injury, Federal civil litigation, State civil litigation. Home: 12005 Cherokee St Leawood KS 66209 Office: 7300 W 110th St Suite 900 Overland Park KS 66210

SULLIVAN, TIMOTHY JOSEPH, lawyer; b. Detroit, Oct. 31, 1942; s. Joseph A. and Teresa M. (Stackpole) S.; m. Anna Marie DeMarco, July 16, 1968; children: Joseph, Molly. BS, U. Detroit, 1964, JD, 1967. Bar: Mich. 1968, U.S. Dist. Ct. (ea. dist.) Mich. 1968. Staff atty. Auto Club Mich., Detroit, 1968-70; ptnr. Coticchio, Zotter & Sullivan, Detroit, 1970—. Vol. atty. Boniface Community Action Corp., Detroit, 1968-76, Family Life Council of Grosse Pointe, Mich., 1983-85. Mem. Assn. Trial Lawyers Am., Def. Research Inst., Def. Trial Counsel Mich., Comml. Law League, U. Detroit Alumni Assn. Roman Catholic. Clubs: Gowanie Golf (Mt. Clemens, Mich.). Insurance, Personal injury, Contracts commercial. Office: Coticchio Zotter & Sullivan 500 Marquette Bldg Detroit MI 48226

SULLIVAN, WILLIAM FRANCIS, lawyer; b. Boston, June 15, 1957; s. William Henry and Susan (White) S.; m. Mary Lou Hutchinson, June 13, 1982; 1 child, William H. BA, U. Notre Dame, 1979; JD, Boston Coll., 1982. Bar: Mass. 1982, U.S. Dist. Ct. Mass. 1984. Assoc. Murphy, Lamere & Murphy, Braintree, Mass., 1982; asst. dist. atty. Norfolk County, Dedham, Mass., 1983-84; assoc. Barry, Masterson, Sullivan & Largey, Quincy, Mass., 1985—. Coach, referee Canton (Mass.) Youth Soccer, 1981—; mem. council Parish Youth Commn., 1984-85. Mem. ABA, Mass. Bar Assn., Norfolk County Bar Assn., Quincy Bar Assn., Assn. Trial Lawyers Am., Mass. Acad. Trial Attys. Democrat. Roman Catholic. Club: Monogram (South Bend, Ind.). Criminal, Personal injury, General practice. Home: 135 Vassall St Quincy MA 02170 Office: Barry Masterson Sullivan & Largey 339 Hancock St Quincy MA 02171

SULLIVAN, WILLIAM FRANCIS, lawyer; b. San Francisco, May 6, 1952; s. Francis Michael and Jane Frances (Walsh) S.; m. Joanne Mary Nebeling; children: Matthew, Meghan, Kathleen. AB, U. Calif., Berkeley, 1974; JD, UCLA, 1977. Bar: Calif. 1977, U.S. Dist. Ct. (no. dist.) Calif. 1977, U.S. Ct. Appeals (9th cir.) 1977, U.S. Dist. Ct. (ea. dist.) Calif. 1978, U.S. Ct. Appeals (D.C. cir.) 1979, U.S. Ct. Appeals (fed. cir.) 1985, U.S. Dist. Ct. (so. dist.) Calif. 1986, U.S. Supreme Ct. 1986. Assoc. Chickering & Gregory, San Francisco and Washington, 1977-81; assoc. Brobeck, Phleger & Harrison, San Francisco, 1981-84, ptnr., 1984—; panelist Calif. Continuing Edn. Bar; instr. fed. practice program U.S. Dist. Ct. (no. dist.) Calif., 1980. Mem. ABA, Calif. Bar Assn., San Francisco Bar Assn., Barristers Club San Francisco (bd. dirs. 1984—, pres. 1985), Calif. Young Lawyers Assn. (bd. dirs. 1986—). Democrat. Roman Catholic. Club: Commonwealth of Calif. Federal civil litigation, State civil litigation, Banking. Office: Brobeck Phleger & Harrison One Market Plaza Spear Tower San Francisco CA 94105

SULLY, IRA BENNETT, lawyer; b. Columbus, Ohio, June 3, 1947; s. Bernie and Helen Mildred (Koen) S.; m. Nancy Lee Pryor, Oct. 2, 1983. B.A. cum laude, Ohio State U., 1969, J.D. summa cum laude, 1974. Bar: Ohio 1974, U.S. Dist. Ct. (so. dist.) Ohio 1974. Assoc. Schottenstein, Garel, Swedlow & Zox, Columbus, 1974-78; atty. Borden Inc., Columbus, 1978-80; sole practice, Columbus, 1980—; instr. Real Estate Law Columbus Tech. Inst., 1983—; title ins. agt. Sycamore Title Agy., Columbus, 1983—. Commentator Sta. WOSU, Columbus, 1980. Treas. Leland for State Rep., Columbus, 1982, 84, Leland for City Atty., Columbus, 1985; asst. treas. Pamela Conrad for City Council, Columbus, 1979; bd. dirs. Research Franklin County Celeste for Gov., Columbus, 1978. Mem. Columbus Bar Assn., Ohio Bar Assn., ABA. Democrat. Jewish. Club: Agonis (Columbus). Avocations: running, coin collecting. Real property, Consumer commercial, Contracts commercial. Home: 305 E Sycamore Columbus OH 43206 Office: 844 S Front St Columbus OH 43206

SULLY, WILLIAM LESLIE, JR., lawyer; b. N.Y., Sept. 14, 1949; s. William Leslie and Emily Hone (Winslow) S.; m. Cheryl Lynn Schurke, Oct. 11, 1980; children—David Adam, Emily Rose, Rachel Leslie. B.S., U. Montevallo, 1971; J.D., Samford U., 1974; LL.M., NYU, 1976. Bar: Ala 1974, Nev. 1975, U.D. Dist. Ct. Nev. 1976, U.S. Tax Ct. 1976. Law clk. 8th Jud. Dist. Ct., Las Vegas, Nev., 1974-75; assoc. Jones, Jones, Close & Brown, Las Vegas, 1976-79; mem. Sully, Lenhard & Raizin, Las Vegas, 1979—. Atty., cons. Nathan Adelson Hospice, Las Vegas; atty., trustee Candlelighters Clark County, Las Vegas; atty. U. Nev.-Las Vegas Found., Las Vegas, VanHowd Wildlife Fedn. Mem. ABA, Clark County Bar Assn., Democrat. Roman Catholic. Corporate taxation, Estate taxation, Personal income taxation. Office: Sully Lenhard & Raizin 300 S 4th St Suite 1515 Las Vegas NV 89101

SULZBERGER, EUGENE WILLIAM, lawyer; b. Bklyn., July 12, 1926; s. Charles Vincent and Elizabeth Gertrude (Stehlin) S.; m. Beverley Roberta Leonard, Jan. 24, 1963; children: Eugene Charles, Eric William. JD, U. Miami, 1951. Bar: Fla. 1951. Sole practice Bay Harbor Islands, Fla., 1951—. Advisor Florida Will and Trust Manuel, 1984. Mcpl. judge Town of Surfside, Fla., 1953-73; trustee, chmn. bd. St. Thomas U., Miami, Fla., 1983-87; trustee Miami Country Day Sch., 1980-85; bd. dirs. Am. Cancer Soc., Miami, 1980-85, Miami Heart Inst., Miami Beach, 1985—. Served with USN, 1944-46. Named one of ten Outstanding Young Men in Fla., U.S. Jr. C. of C.; recipient Disting. Service award Rec. for the Blind. Mem. Dade County Bar Assn., Estate Planning Council of Greater Miami, Phi Delta Phi. Roman Catholic. Lodges: Kiwanis (pres. Miami Beach club 1956), KC (sec. 1951-56). Avocations: golf, tennis. Probate. Office: 1090 Kane Concourse Bay Harbor Islands FL 33154

SULZER, JOSEPH PAUL, lawyer; b. Chillicothe, Ohio, Sept. 21, 1947; s. John Robert Sr. and Rita Colleen (Haggerty) S.; m. Linda Lou Post, Apr. 28, 1973; children: Joseph P. Jr., James Patrick. BGS, Ohio U., 1972; JD, Capitol U., 1982. Bar: Ohio 1982, U.S. Dist. Ct. (so. dist.) Ohio 1982, U.S. Supreme Ct. 1986. Bailiff, referee Juvenile Ct., Chillicothe, 1973-78; sole practice Chillicothe, 1982; environ. adv. bd. Goodyear Atomic Corp., Piketon, Ohio, 1985—, Martin-Marietta Energy Systems, Inc., Piketon, 1985—. Councilman City of Chillicothe, 1982—; trustee David Meade Massie Trust, Chillicothe, 1981—, Juvenile Detention Ctr., Chillicothe, 1984—. Served with U.S. Army, 1966-68, Vietnam. Democrat. Roman Catholic. Lodges: Kiwanis (local v.p. 1977-78), KC (local treas. 1974-78). State civil litigation, Personal injury, Probate. Home: 146 Plum St Chillicothe OH 45601 Office: 2 W 4th St Chillicothe OH 45601

SUMIDA, GERALD AQUINAS, lawyer; b. Hilo, Hawaii, June 19, 1944; s. Sadamu and Kimiyo (Miyahara) S.; m. Sylvia Whitehead, June 23, 1970. AB summa cum laude, Princeton U., 1966, cert. in pub. and internat. affairs, 1966; JD, Yale U., 1969. Bar: Hawaii 1970, U.S. Dist. Ct. Hawaii 1970, U.S. Ct. Appeals (9th cir.) 1970, U.S. Supreme Ct. 1981. Research assoc. Ctr. Internat. Studies, Princeton U., 1969; assoc. Carlsmith, Wichman, Case, Mukai & Ichiki, Honolulu, 1970-76, ptnr., 1976—; mem. cameras in courtroom evaluation com. Hawaii Supreme Ct., 1984—. Mem. sci. and statis. com. Western Pacific Fishery Mgmt. Council, 1979—; mem. study group on law of armed conflict and the law of the sea Comdr. in Chief Pacific, U.S. Navy, 1979—; pres. Pacific and Asian Affairs Council Hawaii, 1982—, bd. govs., 1976—, Paul S. Bachman award, 1978; chmn. internat. com. Hawaii chpt. ARC, 1983—; vice chmn. Honolulu Com. on Fgn. Relations, 1983—; pres., dir., founding mem. Hawaii Ocean Law Assn., 1978—; mem. Hawaii Adv. Group for Law of Sea Inst., 1977—; pres. Hawaii Inst. Continuing Legal Edn., 1979-83, dir., 1976—; pres., founding mem. Hawaii Council Legal Edn. for Youth, 1980-83, dir., 1983—; chmn. Hawaii Commn. on Yr. 2000, 1976-79; exec. com. Honolulu Community Media Council, 1976—, legal counsel, 1979-83; bd. dirs. Hawaii Imin Centennial Corp., 1983—, Hawaii Pub. Radio, 1983—. Legal Aid Soc. Hawaii, 1984; mem. Pacific Alliance Trade and Devel., 1984—. Recipient cert. of appreciation Gov. of Hawaii, 1979, resolutions of appreciation Hawaii Senate and Ho. of Reps., 1979; grantee Japan Found., 1979. Mem. ABA, Hawaii Bar Assn. (pres. young lawyers sect. 1974, v.p. 1984—), Japan-Hawaii Lawyers Assn., Am. Soc. Internat. Law, Japan-Hawaii Lawyers Assn., Hawaii C. of C. (energy com. 1981—, chmn. 1985—), Am. Judicature Soc., AAAS, Asia Pacific Lawyers Assn., Real Estate Securities and Syndication Inst., Phi Beta Kappa. Democrat. Clubs: Yale (N.Y.C.); Plaza (Honolulu); Colonial (Princeton). Author: (with others) Legal, Institutional and Financial Aspects of An Inter-Island Electrical Transmission Cable, 1984, Alternative Approaches to the Legal, Institutional and Financial Aspects of Developing an Inter-Island Electrical Transmission Cable System, 1986, Alternative Approaches to he Legal, Institutional and Financial Aspects of Developing an Inter-Island Electrical Transmission Cable System, 1986; editor Hawaii Bar News, 1972-73; contbr. chpts. to books. Antitrust, General corporate, Private international. Home: 1130 Wilder Ave #1401 Honolulu HI 96822 Office: Pacific Trade Center 190 S King St Suite 2200 Honolulu HI 96813 also: Carlsmith Wichman Case Mukai Ichiki 1001 Bishop St Pacific Tower Suite 2200 Honolulu HI 96813

SUMMERS, CLYDE WILSON, legal educator; b. Grass Range, Mont., Nov. 21, 1918; s. Carl Douglas and Anna Lois (Yontz) S.; m. Evelyn Marie Wahlgren, Aug. 30, 1947; children: Mark, Erica, Craig, Lisa. B.S., U. Ill., 1939, J.D., 1942; LL.M., Columbia, 1946, J.S.D., 1952; LL.D., U. Leuven, Belgium, 1967, U. Stockholm, 1978. Bar: N.Y. 1951. Mem. law faculty U. Toledo, 1942-49, U. Buffalo, 1949-56; prof. law Yale, 1956-66, Garver prof. law, 1966-75; Jefferson B. Fordham prof. law U. Pa., 1975—; Hearing examiner Conn. Commn. on Civil Rights, 1963-71. Co-author: Labor Cases and Material, 1968, 82; co-author: Rights of Union Members, 1979; Co-editor: Labor Relations and the Law, 1953, Employment Relations and the Law, 1959. Chmn. Gov.'s Com. on Improper Union Mgmt. Practices N.Y. State, 1957-58; chmn. Conn. Adv. Council on Unemployment Ins. and Employment Service, 1960-72; mem. Conn. Labor Relations Bd., 1966-70, Conn. Bd. Mediation and Arbitration, 1964-72. Guggenheim fellow, 1955-56; Ford fellow, 1963-64; German-Marshall fellow, 1977-78; NEH fellow, 1977-78, Fullbright fellow, 1984-85. Mem. Am. Arbitration Assn., Internat. Soc. Labor Law and Social Legislation. Congregationalist. Legal education, Labor, State and local taxation. Home: 753 N 26th St Philadelphia PA 19130 Office: U Pa Law Sch 3400 Chestnut St Philadelphia PA 19104

SUMMERS, GERALD (JERRY) HOWARD, lawyer; b. Chattanooga, May 28, 1941; s. Homer Howard and Millie (Dean) S. B.A. in Bus. Adminstrn. with honors, U. of South, 1963; LL.B., U. Tenn., 1966. Bar: Tenn. 1966, U.S. Ct. Appeals (6th cir.) 1970, U.S. Supreme Ct. 1972. Asst. dist. atty. City of Chattanooga, 1966-69; sole practice, Chattanooga, 1969—; mem. Tenn. Law Revision Commn. 1976; city judge City of Soddy-Daisy (Tenn.), 1976-83; mem. Tenn. Supreme Ct. Com. on Jud. Planning, 1976, Commn. on Advt., 1978; guest instr. in criminal law Cleveland (Tenn.) State Coll., 1973-76; mem. bd. advisers paralegal program Cleveland State Community Coll., 1975-76; mem. faculty polit. sci. U. Tenn., 1982; mem. Law Enforcment Commn. Hamilton County; bd. dirs. Project First Offender; mem. br. adv. bd. United Bank Chattanooga; mem. Speedy Trial Planning Commn. for Eastern Dist. Tenn. 1977-78; mem. Commn. on Criminal Rules, Tenn. Supreme Ct., 1982-83; lectr. in field. Named Young Man of Yr., Chattanooga Jaycees, 1973, 76-77, Outstanding Young Man Am., U.S. Jaycees, 1974; U. Tenn. univ. scholar, 1963-64. Fellow Tenn. Bar Found., Am. Bd. Trial Advs. (pres. Tenn. chpt. 1986-87), Internat. Soc. Barristers; mem. ABA, Tenn. Bar Assn. (chmn. criminal justice sect. 1976), Assn. Trial Lawyers Am. (chmn. young lawyers sect. 1975, bd. govs. 1985-87), Tenn. Trial Lawyers Assn. (v.p. 1972-73, pres. 1977-78), Nat. Assn. Criminal Def. Lawyers (gov. 1975-76), Tenn. Assn. Criminal Def. Lawyers (pres. 1975-76), Chattanooga Bar Assn. (chmn. continuing legal edn. 1976, gov. 1978, pres. 1983), Chattanooga Trial Lawyers Assn. (pres. 1972-73), Central High Alumni Assn. (pres. 1971-73), Phi Gamma Delta (v.p. chpt. 1962-63). Club: Civitan (Chattanooga). Author: Law Office Management Manual, 1974. Criminal, Labor, Personal injury. Home: 199 S Crest Rd Chattanooga TN 37402 Office: 500 Lindsay St Chattanooga TN 37402

SUMMERS, HUGH SCOTT, lawyer; b. Hannibal, Mo., Mar. 31, 1956; s. Hugh L. and Marjorie A. (Smith) S.; m. Jan Denise Rood, Feb. 5, 1983. BBA, U. Mo., 1978, JD, 1981. Bar: Mo. 1981, U.S. Dist. Ct. (we. dist.) Mo. 1981, U.S. Dist. Ct. (ea. dist.) Mo. 1984. Assoc. J. Patrick Wheeler, Canton, Mo., 1981-84; sole practice Kahoka, Mo., 1984—; bd. dirs. Legal Services of N.E. Mo., Hannibal. Bd. dirs. Northeast Mo. Library Service, Kahoka, Indsl. Opportunities Inc., Kahoka; trustee Clark County Hist. Soc. Mus. Mem. ABA, Mo. Bar Assn., Mo. Assn. Trial Attys., Assn. Trial Lawyers Am., Kahoka C. of C. Democrat. Mem. Christian Ch. Club: Keokuk (Iowa) Country. Personal injury, Contracts commercial, Criminal. Home: 714 W Clark St Kahoka MO 63445 Office: 540 N Johnson PO Box 247 Kahoka MO 63445-0247

SUMMERS, ROBERT SAMUEL, lawyer, author, educator; b. Halfway, Oreg., Sept. 19, 1933; s. Orson William and Estella Belle (Robertson) S.; m. Dorothy Millicent Kopp, June 14, 1955; children: Brent, William, Thomas, Elizabeth, Robert. B.S. in Polit. Sci., U. Oreg., 1955; postgrad. (Fulbright scholar), U. Southampton, Eng., 1955-56; LL.B., Harvard U., 1959; postgrad. research, Oxford (Eng.) U., 1964-65, 74-75. Bar: Oreg. 1959, N.Y. 1974. Asso. King, Miller, Anderson, Nash and Yerke, Portland, Oreg., 1959-60; asst. prof. law U. Oreg., 1960-63, asso. prof., 1964-68; vis. asso. prof. law Stanford U., 1963-64; prof. U. Oreg., 1968-69; prof. Cornell U., 1969-76, McRoberts prof. law, 1976—; summer vis. prof. Ind. U., 1969, U. Mich., 1974, U. Warwick (Eng.), 1975, U. Miami (Fla.), 1976-78, Australia Nat. U., U. Sydney (Australia), 1977; research fellow Merton Coll., Oxford U., 1981-82; cons. Cornell Law Project in public schs., N.Y., 1969-74, Law in Am. Soc. project Chgo. Bd. Edn., 1968-69; instr. Nat. Acad. Jud. Edn., 1976—. Author: (with Howard) Law, Its Nature, Functions and Limits, 1972, (with Hubbard and Campbell) Justice and Order Through Law, 1973, (with Bozzone and Campbell) The American Legal System, 1973, (with Speidel and White) Teaching Materials on Commercial Transactions, 1974, Collective Bargaining and Public Benefit Conferral—A Jurisprudential Critique, 1976, (with White) The Uniform Commercial Code, 1980, (with Speidel and White) Teaching Materials on Commercial and Consumer Law, 1981, Het Pramatisch Instrumentalisme, 1981, Instrumentalism and American Legal Theory, 1982, Lon L. Fuller—Life and Work, 1984; contbr. book revs. and articles to profl. jours.; editor: Essays in Legal Philosophy, vol. 1, 1968, vol. 2, 1971. Social Sci. Research Council fellow, 1964-65. Mem. Am. Law Inst., Assn. Am. Law Schs. (chmn. sect. jurisprudence 1972-73), Am. Soc. Polit. and Legal Philosophy (v.p. 1976-78), Internat. Assn. Philosophers of Law, Phi Beta Kappa. Republican. Congregationalist. Office: Cornell Law Sch Ithaca NY 14853 *

SUMMIT, PAUL ELIOT, lawyer; b. N.Y.C., Oct. 24, 1949; s. Leon Gershon and Annette (Sanders) S. BA, Harvard U., 1972; JD, Columbia U., 1977. Bar: N.Y. 1978, Mass. 1979, U.S. Dist. Ct. (so. and ea. dists.) N.Y. 1979, U.S. Ct. Appeals 1983. Law clk. to judge U.S. Dist. Ct. Mass., Boston, 1977-78; assoc. Orans, Elsen & Lupert, N.Y.C., 1978-82; asst. atty. U.S. Dist. Ct. (so. dist.) N.Y., N.Y.C., 1982-87; mem. Graham & James, N.Y.C., 1987—. Mem. Assn. Bar of City of N.Y. (fed. cts. com. 1983-86, career law com. 1987—). Federal civil litigation, Criminal. Home: 280 Riverside Dr #5K New York NY 10025 Office: Graham & James 885 3d Ave New York NY 10022

SUMMIT, STUART A., lawyer; b. Canton, Ohio, Apr. 18, 1936; s. William A. and Dorothy Jean (Cohen) S.; children from previous marriage: Joshua, Ian. BS, Ohio State U., 1957, JD summa cum laude, 1959. Bar: Ohio 1960, N.Y. 1965, U.S. Dist. Ct. (so. dist.) N.Y., 1965, U.S. Dist. Ct. (ea. dist.) N.Y. 1965, U.S. Ct. Appeals (2d cir.) 1966, U.S. Supreme Ct. 1973, U.S. Ct. Appeals (5th cir.) 1975, D.C. 1978. Law clk. to judge Appellate Div., Supreme Ct. N.Y., 1962-63; assoc. Mudge, Stern, Baldwin & Todd, and successors, N.Y.C., 1960-62, 63-66; ptnr. Miller & Summit, N.Y.C., 1967-76; ptnr. Summit Rouins & Feldesman and predecessor firm, N.Y.C., 1976—; counsel N.Y. Commn. Jud. Nomination, 1978—; exec. sec. Mayor's Com. on Judiciary, N.Y.C., 1966-77. Chmn. alumni adv. council Ohio State U.; mem. nat. council Ohio State U. Law Coll. Mem. Ohio State U. Law Alumni Assn. (pres. 1978-79), trustee Boys Club Am., 1980—, N.Y.C. Bar Assn., N.Y. State Bar Assn., ABA, Fed. Bar Assn., Am. Judicature Soc. Federal civil litigation, State civil litigation. Home: 1000 Park Ave Apt 12B New York NY 10028 also: 492 N Main St Southampton NY 11968 Office: 445 Park Ave 5th Floor New York NY 10022

SUMNER, JAMES DUPRE, JR., lawyer, educator; b. Spartanburg, S.C., Nov. 30, 1919; s. James DuPre and Frances Grace (Harris) S.; m. Evvie Lucille Beach, Apr. 1, 1945 (dec.); children: Chery Erline (Mrs. Horacek), James DuPre III; m. Doris Kaiser Malloy, Oct. 20, 1972; children: John L. Malloy III, Mary Margaret Purdy, Kenneth S. Malloy, James M. Malloy. A.B., Wofford Coll., 1941; LL.B., U. Va., 1949; LL.M., Yale, 1952, J.S.D., 1955. Bar: Va. 1948, Calif. 1957. Practice law Los Angeles, 1957—; instr. law U. S.C., 1949-52; asso. prof. U. Calif. at Los Angeles, 1952-55, prof., 1955—; distinguished vis. prof. Instituto Luigi Sturzo, Rome, 1959; vis. prof. U. Tex., 1962, U. So. Calif., 1971; lectr. Calif. Bar Rev. Co-author: An Anatomy of Legal Education; Contbr. articles to profl. jours. Served from 2d lt. to lt. col. inf. AUS, 1941-46, ETO. Decorated Silver Star, Purple Heart with oak leaf cluster. Mem. Calif. Bar Assn., Va. Bar Assn., Westwood Village Bar Assn. (pres.). Republican. Methodist. Clubs: Westwood Village Rotary, Los Angeles Country, Braemar Country, Bel Air Assn. (bd. dirs.). Home: 10513 Rocca Pl Los Angeles CA 90077

SUMNERS, LESTER FURR, lawyer; b. Blytheville, Ark., June 2, 1926; s. Chester L. and Bessie (Furr) S.; m. Mary Joyce Bonner, Feb. 12, 1956; children: Thomas Bonner, Melinda Watson, Leslie Elizabeth. BA, U. Miss., 1949, LLB, 1950. Bar: Miss. 1950. Staff atty. USDA, Washington, 1951-52; ptnr. Darden & Sumners, New Albany, Miss., 1952-76, Darden, Sumners, Carter & Trout, New Albany, 1976-83, Sumners, Carter, Trout & McMillin, New Albany, 1983—. Assoc. editor U. Miss. Law Rev., 1950. Scoutmaster Boy Scouts Am., New Albany, 1953-75; trustee NE Miss. Jr. Coll., Booneville, 1961-66. Recipient Silver Beaver award Boy Scouts Am., 1966. Fellow Internat. Acad. Trial Lawyers, Am. Coll. Trial Lawyers; mem. Miss. State Bar Assn. (commr. 1950-63, 65-67, complaint commr. 1963, 65, pres. 1971-72), Miss. Bar Found. (pres. 1979-80), U. Miss. Law Alumni Chpt. (pres. 1976-77). Federal civil litigation, State civil litigation, General practice. Office: Sumners Carter Trout et al PO Box 730 New Albany MS 38652

SUMNERS, WILLIAM GLENN, JR., lawyer; b. Pueblo, Colo., Feb. 23, 1928; s. William Glen Sr. and Ruth Priscilla (Carmody) S.; 1 child from previous marriage, William Glenn III; m. Virginia Christine Thomson, June 16, 1985. BA, MA, U. Colo., 1951; postgrad., Colo. Sch. of Mines, 1954; LLB, U. Denver, 1954. Bar: Colo. 1954, U.S. Dist. Ct. Colo. 1954, U.S. Supreme Ct. 1962, U.S. Ct. Appeals (10th cir.) 1963, U.S. Ct. Claims 1982. Sole practice Denver, 1954-75; ptnr. Sumners & Fowler, Denver, 1975-80, Sumners & Miller, Denver, 1980-85, Sumners & Eppich, Denver, 1985—. Contbr. articles to profl. jours. Judge Denver Mcpl. Ct., 1962. Served with U.S. Army, 1945-47, PTO. Mem. ABA (chmn. internat. ins. law com. 1980-81, ins., negligence and compensation sect., internat. energy law sect.), Rocky Mountain Mineral Law Found. (trustee 1960-63, 80-85), Mountain States Legal Found. (bd. of litigation 1977—), Colo. Mining Assn. (bd. dirs. 1962—, pres. 1977), Internat. Bar Assn., Internat. Assn. Ins. Counsel, Ind. Petroleum Assn. Mountain States (bd. dirs. 1975). Oil and gas leasing, Private international, Reinsurance risk management. Office: Sumners & Eppich 600-17th St #2600 S Denver CO 80202

SUMPTER, JERRY LEE, lawyer; b. Detroit, Aug. 13, 1942; s. Joseph Edward Sumpter and Telcie (Crager) Church; m. Santina Marie Cervi, Feb. 14, 1970; children—J.L., Shaundra. B.S. in Edn., Ball State U., 1966; J.D., Detroit Coll. Law, 1970. Bar: Mich. 1970. Cert. Nat. Bd. Trial Advocacy. Sole practice, Cheboygan, Mich., 1970—; prosecuting atty. County of Cheboygan, 1972-74; instr. criminal justice Alpena Community Coll., Mich., 1970—; speaker in field. Author: Civil Trial Strategy and Technique Notebook (2 vols.), 1983, Personal Injury: Discovery and Trial, 1986. Contbr. articles to profl. jours. Mem. Assn. Trial Lawyers Am., Mich. Bar Assn., Mich. Trial Lawyers Assn., Belli Soc., Delta Theta Phi. Federal civil litigation, State civil litigation, Personal injury. Home: 10805 Moonlight Bay Rd Cheboygan MI 49721 Office: PO Box 286 Cheboygan MI 49721

SUMPTER, RODNEY EVERT, lawyer; b. Wichita, Kans., July 17, 1954; s. Dearl E. and Merlyn Joyce (Johnson) S. BA, U. Nev.; JD, U. Pa. Bar: Nev. 1980, U.S. Dist. Ct. Nev. 1980. Assoc. Grubic, Lyon & Barnette, Reno, 1980-82; ptnr. Bunce, Sumpter & McDonald, Reno, 1982-84; sole practice Reno, 1984—. Mem. Nat. Gay Task Force, Washington, 1985—; chmn. bd. dirs. River Mountain Services, Reno, 1982-86. Mem. ABA, Am. Judicature Soc., Nev. Bar Assn., Washoe County Bar Assn. (pro bono atty. 1984—), Assn. Trial Lawyers Am., Nev. Trial Lawyers Assn. Republican. Avocations: snow skiing, biking, pianist, photography. Bankruptcy, Family and matrimonial, Personal injury. Office: Liberty Ctr Suite 350 350 S Center St Reno NV 89501

SUN, COSSETTE TSUNG-HUNG WU, law librarian; b. Taipei, Taiwan, July 14, 1937; d. Lin Tsung and Chiu Ching (Wu) Hsieh; m. Stanley Siann-Shyang Sun, Nov. 23, 1961; children—Louise Caroline, Marina Sheree, Olivia Cossette. LL.B., Nat. Taiwan U., Taipei, 1960; M.A., U. Houston, 1963; M.S., Simmons Coll., Boston, 1965. Asst. prof. law, assoc. librarian St. Louis U., 1965-73; assoc. librarian U. Calif.-Berkeley, 1974-75; br. librarian Alameda County Law Library, Hayward, Calif., 1975-77, law library dir., Oakland, 1978—. W.H. Anderson scholar, 1966; Matthew Bender scholar, 1971. Mem. Am. Assn. Law Libraries (cert. 1969), ALA, Spl. Libraries Assn., Asian-Pacific Librarians Assn. Legislative, Legal education, Librarianship. Office: Alameda County Law Library Rm 200 Court House Oakland CA 94612

SUNDERLAND, THOMAS ELBERT, lawyer, business executive; b. Ann Arbor, Mich., Apr. 28, 1907; s. Edson R. and Hannah Dell (Read) S.; m. Mary Louise Allyn, Dec. 21, 1946; children: Louise Allyn, Anne Read, Thomas Edson (dec.), Mary Compton, Alice Elizabeth (dec.). Student, in England and Sorbonne, Paris, France, 1924-25; A.B. summa cum laude, U. Mich., 1928, student Law Sch., 1927-29; J.D., U. Calif.-Berkeley, 1930; postgrad. advanced mgmt. program, Harvard U. Grad. Sch. Bus. Adminstrn., 1948. Bar: Mich. 1930, N.Y. 1933, D.C. 1948, Ill. 1948, U.S. Supreme Ct., 1948, Mass. 1962, Ariz. 1969. Practiced law Detroit, 1930-31, N.Y.C., 1931-48, Chgo., 1948-60; with firm Cadwalader, Wickersham and Taft, N.Y.C., 1931-33, Milbank, Tweed, Hope and Webb, N.Y.C., 1931-36, Townley, Updike and Carter, N.Y.C., 1936-40, Snell & Wilmer, Phoenix, 1969-79; gen. counsel Pan Am. Petroleum and Transport Co., Am. Oil Co., N.Y.C., 1940-48; dir., mem. exec. com. Pan Am. Petroleum and Transport Co., Am. Oil, 1947-54; v.p., gen. counsel, dir. Standard Oil Co. (Ind.), Chgo., 1948-60, also bd. dirs.; pres., chief exec. officer, chmn. bd., dir. United Fruit Co., Boston, 1959-68; dir. First Nat. Bank of Boston, Nat. Cash Register Co., Liberty Mut. Ins. Co., Johns-Manville Corp.; mem. com. on pub. affairs Am. Petroleum Inst., 1948-59. Nat. trustee Lake Forest Coll.; trustee Lawrence Hall of Sci., U. Calif. at Berkeley, Boston Hosp. for Women, Winsor Sch., Boston; mem. vis. com. Harvard Grad. Sch. Bus. Adminstrn.,

Harvard Law Sch., Harvard Sch. Pub. Health, U. Chgo. Law Sch., Stanford U. Sch. Law; chmn. nat. com. Mich. Sch. Law, also vis. com.; trustee Phoenix Symphony, pres., 1979-81; mem. corp. Northeastern U., Boston; vis. com. Stanford Law Sch., Palo Alto, Harvard Bus. Sch., Harvard Law Sch. and Harvard Sch. Public Health, Law Sch. U. Mich., U. Chgo. Law Sch.; bd. dirs. Nat. Merit Scholarship Corp.; trustee Phoenix Country Day Sch. Served from 1st lt. to lt. col. USAAF, 1942-46, ETO. Decorated Bronze Star; recipient Bus. Leadership award U. Mich., 1966, also Outstanding Achievement award, 1970. Mem. Am. Law Inst., Council on Fgn. Relations, ABA (com. on jurisprudence and law reform 1940-41, chmn. sect. antitrust law 1953-58), Ill., Chgo., Ariz. bar assns., Assn. Bar City N.Y., Nat. Indsl. Conf. Bd. (sr. mem.), Squadron A Assn. (N.Y.C.), Inter-Am. Bar Assn., Assn. Gen. Counsel (co-founder), Phi Beta Kappa, Phi Delta Phi, Phi Gamma Delta, Phi Kappa Phi. Clubs: Wianno (Cape Cod, Mass.); The Beach (Centerville, Mass.); Bohemian (San Francisco); Phoenix Country; The Country (Brookline, Mass.); Chicago; Glenview (Golf, Ill.); Metropolitan (Washington); Union League (N.Y.C.); Paradise Valley Country (Scottsdale, Ariz.). Home: 5840 E Starlight Way Paradise Valley Scottsdale AZ 85253 Summer Address: 66 Fernwood Rd (Brookline) Chestnut Hill MA 02167 Office: Suite A-201 6991 E Camelback Rd Scottsdale AZ 85251

SUOJANEN, WAYNE WILLIAM, lawyer; b. Salem, Oreg., July 5, 1950; s. Waino Wiljam and Doris Grace (Stinson) S.; m. Deborah Kindler, Mar. 22, 1970; children: Rachel, Noah, Sarah. BA, Northwestern U., Evanston, Ill., 1972; SM, MIT, 1974, PhD, 1977; JD, U. Pa., 1980. Bar: Pa. 1980, U.S. Dist. Ct. (ea. dist.) Pa. 1981, U.S. Ct. Appeals (3d cir.) 1981. Assoc. Pepper, Hamilton & Scheetz, Phila., 1980-84, Hoyle, Morris & Kerr, Phila., 1985—. Coach Rosemont-Villanova Civic Assn., 1985-86. Joseph Scanlon fellow, MIT, 1974-75. Mem. ABA, Pa. Bar Assn., Phila. Bar Assn., Indsl. Relations Research Assn. Democrat. Federal civil litigation, State civil litigation, Personal injury. Home: 970 Lafayette Rd Bryn Mawr PA 19010 Office: Hoyle Morris & Kerr 1424 Chestnut St Philadelphia PA 19102

SUPINA, GERALD JOSEPH, judge, lawyer; b. Ionia, Mich., July 1, 1941; s. Joseph Edward and Adeline Ruth (Feuerstein) S.; m. Janet A.; children—Joseph G., Elizabeth M., Suzanne K. B.Arch., U. Detroit, 1965; J.D., Detroit Coll. Law, 1970. Bar: Mich. 1970, U.S. Dist. Ct. (we. dist.) Mich. 1979. Archtl. coop. student Gen. Motors, Detroit, 1963-65; architect-in-tng. Greimel-Malcomson-James, Detroit, 1965-71; sole practice, Portland, Mich., 1971-81; judge Ionia County Probate Ct., 1981—; city atty. City of Portland, 1974-81; instr. Mich. Jud. Inst., Lansing, 1984—; mem. caseflow mgmt. com. Mich. Supreme Ct., 1986-87. Author ct. forms, 1981—. Bd. dirs. Econ. Devel. Corp., Portland, 1978-84; active Ionia County Child Abuse and Neglect Council; chmn. ad hoc com. Prevention of Adolescent Depression/Suicide. Recipient Jud. scholarship Mich. Jud. Inst., 1984, Person of Yr. award, 1986. Mem. State Bar Mich., Mich. Probate and Juvenile Judges Assn. (chmn. resolutions com. 1986—, chmn. chief justices com. to rev. proposed juvenile ct. rules), Nat. Coll. Probate Judges, Ionia Montcalm Bar Assn. (sec./treas., v.p., pres.), Southwestern Probate and Juvenile Judges Assn. (pres. 1984). Roman Catholic. Clubs: Kiwanis Internat. (trustee 1973-79), Rotary, K.C. Juvenile, Probate, Judicial administration. Office: Probate Ct Courthouse Ionia MI 48846

SURACI, JOSEPH ANTHONY, lawyer; b. N.Y.C., Mar. 21, 1951; s. Anthony and Caroline Ann (Ferri) S.; m. Carol Ann Gaddis, June 29, 1985. BA with honors, Manhattan Coll., 1972; JD, St. John's U., Jamaica, N.Y., 1975. Bar: N.Y. 1976, U.S. Dist. Ct. (so. dist.) N.Y. 1978, U.S. Dist. Ct. (ea. dist.) N.Y. 1979, U.S. Ct. Appeals (2d cir.) 1980, U.S. Supreme Ct. 1982. Assoc. criminal def. div. Legal Aid Soc., N.Y.C., 1976—. Candidate N.Y. State Assembly, Queens, 1982, 84; mem. community council 108th precinct, Queens, 1982—, community bd. #2 com. Queens City Services, 1985—; pres. United Reps. Western Queens, 1985—; v.p. Woodside Sr. Assistance Ctr., Queens, 1986—; bd. dirs. Sunnyside Drum Corps., Inc., Queens, 1984—, Gateway Community Restoration, Inc., Queens, 1985—. Mem. ABA, N.Y. State Bar Assn., Queens County Bar Assn., St. Thomas More Law Soc. (pres. 1971-72), Phi Beta Kappa, Epsilon Sigma Pi. Republican. Roman Catholic. Avocations: reading, guitar, collecting stamps, astronomy, baseball. Criminal, Legislative, Local government. Office: Legal Aid Soc Criminal Def Div 80 Lafayette St New York NY 10013

SURAN, ROBERT HERMAN, lawyer; b. Milw., Oct. 14, 1934; s. Arthur N. and May (Levy) S.; m. Karen J. Kohne, June 3, 1962; children: Laurie L., Alaina K. BS, U. Wis., 1956, JD, 1959. Bar: Wis. 1959, U.S. Dist. Ct. (ea. dist.) Wis. 1959. Sole practice Milw., 1959-71; ptnr. Suran & Suran, Milw., 1971—. Past mem. Glendale (Wis.) Bd. of Appeals, Glendale Planning Commn., Glendale Aux. Police; mcpl. judge City of Glendale, 1979—. Served with USAR, 1955-63. Real property, State civil litigation, Contracts commercial. Home: 1151 W Acacia Rd Glendale WI 53217

SURPRENANT, MARK CHRISTOPHER, lawyer; b. Providence, Oct. 12, 1951; s. William and Margaret Surprenant; m. Monica Tufano; children: Christopher, Jennifer. BA, Fordham U., 1973; JD, Loyola U., New Orleans, 1977. Ptnr. Adams & Reese, New Orleans, 1977—. Pres. Southwest Edn. Devel. Lab, Austin, Tex., 1986—. Mem. ABA, La. Bar Assn., New Orleans Def. Counsel (bd. dirs. 1983—), Loyola Law Alumni Assn. (pres. 1983-84), Loyola U. Alumni Assn. (pres. 1986-87), Greater New Orleans Athletic League, New Orleans C. of C. (met. edn. com.). Civil rights, Environment, Products liability law. Office: Adams & Reese One Shell Sq Suite 4500 New Orleans LA 70139

SURRATT, JOHN RICHARD, lawyer; b. Winston-Salem, N.C., Aug. 7, 1928; s. Wade Talmage and Julia (Efird) S.; m. Estella Eason, Dec. 2, 1961; children: Margaret Virginia, Estella Elizabeth, Susan Efird. BS In Commerce, U.N.C., 1948; JD, Duke U., 1951. Bar: N.C. 1951. Sole practice Winston-Salem, 1951—; judge mcpl. ct. Winston-Salem; lectr. law Wake Forest U., Winston-Salem, 1976-80. Mayor City of Winston-Salem 1961-63, chmn. city planning bd., 1972-78; sec., mem. Forsyth County Dem. Exec. Com., N.C.; mem. bar candidate com. N.C. Bd. Law Examiners. Served to capt. U.S. Army Reserve, 1951-53, Korea. Mem. ABA, N.C. Bar Assn., Estate Planning Council, Forsyth County Bar Assn. (pres. 1984, exec. com. 1986). Club: Old Town, Twin City. Lodge: Rotary (pres. local chpt. 1983). General corporate, Probate, Estate taxation.

SUSI, MART SVEN, lawyer; b. Fremont, Ohio, Sept. 2, 1955; s. Kalev and Ada (Post) S.; m. Harriet Faith Pinck, Aug. 17, 1980; 1 child, Kara Amanda. BA in Polit. Sci., SUNY, Buffalo, 1977; JD, Golden Gate U., 1980. Bar: Calif. 1981, U.S. Dist. Ct. (no. dist.) Calif. 1981. Assoc. Toomajian & Manoogian, Oakland, Calif., 1981-82, Law Office J.E. Manoogian, Walunt Creek, Calif., 1982-84; sole practice Fremont, Calif., 1984-85; mng. atty. Jacoby & Meyers, Fremont, 1985-87, regional dist. mgr., 1987—. Mem. ABA (arts and law com. 1981-82), Alameda Bar Assn., Assn. Trial Lawyers Am., Alameda/Contra Costa Trial Lawyers Assn. Democrat. Lutheran. Avocations: performing in musical comedies, singing opera. Family and matrimonial. Office: Jacoby & Meyers Law Offices 38950 Blacow Rd Suite F Fremont CA 94536

SUSMAN, KAREN LEE, lawyer; b. Austin, Tex., Oct. 26, 1942; d. Paul and Dorothy (Goudchaux) Hyman; m. Stephen D. Susman, Dec. 26, 1965; children: Stacy M., Harry P. BA, U. Tex., 1964; JD, U. Houston, 1981. Bar: Tex. 1981. Tchr. high schs. Houston and Washington, 1964-68; realty broker Susman Realty, Houston, 1968-78; assoc. Saccomanno, Clegg, Martin & Kipple, Houston, 1981-83, Marian S. Rosen & Assocs., Houston, 1983-86; of counsel Webb & Zimmerman, Houston, 1986—. Editor Internat. Law Jour., 1980-81. Bd. dirs. Downtown YWCA, Houston, 1969-74, pres. 1974; bd dirs. Tex. Arts Alliance, Houston, 1975-78, Antidefamation League B'nai Brith, Houston, 1983-86, Lawyers and Accts. for Arts, Houston, 1985—; chmn. PBS TV Art Auction, Houston, 1975; mem. Tex. State Dem. Fin. Council, 1983—, Harris County Dem. Chmn.'s Council, 1984—, Candidate Selection Com., 1986—; bd. dirs. Houston Symphony, 1985—. Fellow Houston Bar Found.; mem. ABA, Tex. Bar Assn., Houston Bar Assn., A.A. White Soc., U. Houston Alumni (bd. dirs., v.p., sec. 1983—), Phi Delta Phi. Club: Houstonian. Avocations: marathon running, snow skiing, collecting modern art. Home: 10 Shadder Way Houston TX 77019 Office: 1990 S Post Oak Blvd Post Oak Cen Suite 1400 Houston TX 77056

SUSMAN, MORTON LEE, lawyer; b. Detroit, Aug. 6, 1934; s. Harry and Alma (Koslow) S.; m. Nina Meyers, May 1, 1958; 1 son, Mark Lee. B.B.A., So. Meth. U., 1956, J.D., 1958. Bar: Tex. 1958, U.S. Dist. Ct. (so. dist.) Tex. 1961, U.S. Ct. Appeals (5th cir.) 1961, U.S. Supreme Ct. 1961, U.S. Ct. Appeals (11th cir.) 1981. Asst. U.S. atty., Houston, 1961-64, 1st asst. U.S. atty., 1965-66, U.S. atty., 1966-69; ptnr. Weil, Gotshal & Manges and predecessor firm Susman & Kessler, Houston, 1969—. Served to lt. USNR, 1958-61. Recipient Younger Fed. Lawyer award Fed. Bar Assn., 1968. Fellow Am. Coll. Trial Lawyers; mem. ABA, Tex. Bar Assn., Houston Bar Assn. Democrat. Jewish. Club: Houston. Federal civil litigation. Home: 338 Hunters Trail Houston TX 77024 Office: Weil Gotshal & Manges 1600 Republic Bank Ctr Houston TX 77002

SUSMAN, ROBERT M., lawyer; b. St. Louis, Jan. 15, 1951; s. Bernard and Lorraine (Abramson) S.; m. Shelby Zarick, Aug. 14, 1977; children—Jane, Stephanie. B.A., Ind. U., 1973. J.D., St. Louis U., 1976. Bar: Mo. 1976, U.S. Dist. Ct. (ea. dist.) Mo. 1976. Ptnr. firm Susman & Susman, St. Louis, 1976—. Mem. Lawyers Assn. St. Louis (exec. com. 1980-83, sec. 1983-85, v.p. 1985-86), Met. Bar Assn. St. Louis, Assn. Trial Lawyers Am. (basic course trial advocacy Nat. Coll. Advocacy 1983), Mo. Assn. Trial Attys. Personal injury, Workers' compensation, State civil litigation. Home: 1711 Shallowbrook Saint Louis Mo 63146 Office: Susman & Susman 1015 Locust St Suite 808 Saint Louis MO 63101

SUSMARSKI, RONALD JAMES, lawyer; b. Erie, Pa., Mar. 10, 1954; s. Edward Edmund and Eileen Caroline (Riso) S.; m. Stephanie Domitrovich, Sept. 1, 1979; children: Adam James, Aaron Edward. BA, Mercyhurst Coll., 1975; JD, Duquesne U., 1978. Bar: Pa., U.S. Dist. Ct., U.S. Supreme Ct. Sole practice Erie, 1978—. Co-dir. legal explorer program Boy Scouts Am., 1980-84; solicitor Community Drop-In Ctr., Erie, 1983—. Mem. ABA, Pa. Bar Assn., Erie County Bar Assn. Republican. Roman Catholic. Lodge: Lions. Probate, Family and matrimonial, Real property. Home and Office: 4036 W Lake Rd Erie PA 16505

SUSSER, STUART J., lawyer; b. Bklyn., Nov. 25, 1945; s. George and Iris (Engler) S.; m. Robin H. Lipkovitz, Aug. 14, 1981; 1 child, Heather. BA, Bklyn. Coll.; JD, Ariz. State U. Bar: Ariz. 1970, Fla. 1973, N.Y. 1981. Assoc. gen. counsel ITT, Miami, Fla., 1972-74; sole practice Miami, 1974-81; asst. atty. gen. N.Y. State, N.Y.C., 1981-83; sole practice N.Y.C., 1983-85; sr. litigation counsel Barst & Mukamal, N.Y.C., 1985-87; sole practice Mousey, N.Y., 1987—. Mem. ABA, Assn. Trial Lawyers Am., N.Y. State Trial Lawyers Assn. Environment, Federal civil litigation, General corporate. Office: PO Box 292 Mousey NY 10952

SUSSMAN, ALEXANDER R., lawyer; b. Bronx, N.Y., Sept. 24, 1946; s. Herman R. and Claire (Blumenson) S.; m. Edna Rubin, Mar. 24, 1973; Children; Jason, Carl. AB, Princeton U., 1968; JD, Yale U., 1972. Bar: N.Y., U.S. Dist. Ct. (so. and ea. dists.) N.Y., U.S. Ct. Appeals (2d and 5th cirs.), U.S. Supreme Ct. Law clk. to presiding justice U.S. Dist. Ct., N.Y.C., 1972-73; assoc. Cravath, Swaine & Moore, N.Y.C., 1974-76; assoc. Fried, Frank, Harris, Shriver & Jacobson, N.Y.C., 1977-79, ptnr., 1979—. Contbr. articles to profl. jours. Bd. dirs. N.Y. Lawyers for the Pub. Interests., 1983—. Mem. ABA, N.Y. State Bar Assn., Assn. of Bar of City of N.Y. (fed. cts. com.) 1984—. Federal civil litigation, State civil litigation, Securities. Home: 685 West End Ave New York NY 10025 Office: Fried Frank Harris Shriver et al 1 NY Plaza New York NY 10004

SUSSMAN, DANIEL LEONARD, lawyer; consultant; b. Bklyn., Apr. 21, 1947; s. Hyman and Sonia Sussman; m. Roberta Silverstein, June 23, 1968; children—Bradley Ward, Emily Janine. B.S., Harpur Coll., SUNY-Binghamton, 1967; J.D., SUNY-Buffalo, 1970. Bar: N.Y. 1971, Pa. 1973, U.S. Tax Ct. 1972, U.S. Supreme Ct. 1974. Assoc. Weingold, Schneider, Eisenstat, Berman & Wohl, N.Y.C., 1970-71; assoc. Allan Bakst, N.Y.C., 1971-72; asst. regional dir. pensions, Aetna Life & Casualty, Hartford, Conn., 1972-75; ptnr. Sussman & Forster, N.Y.C., Washington, 1975-80; sr. ptnr. Simon Sussman Uncyk Forster & Borenkind, N.Y.C. and Washington, 1980-83; sr. ptnr. Sussman Forseter & Krongold, 1983—; v.p., counsel DCP Adminstrs. Inc., N.Y.C. and Washington; cons. pensions; adj. prof. Northampton Community Coll.; instr. Hofstra U.; mem. faculty N.Y.U. Tax Inst.; lectr. Fed. Publs. Served to sgt. JAGC, USAR, 1968-73. Mem. N.Y. State Bar Assn., ABA. Co-author: Administering Pension Plans, 1979. Pension, profit-sharing, and employee benefits, Corporate taxation. Home: 4 Cove Meadow Ln Oyster Bay Cove NY 11771

SUSSMAN, EDNA RUBIN, lawyer, lecturer; b. Tel-Aviv, Nov. 10, 1948; d. Jacob Abraham and Aliza (Sass) Rubin; m. Alexander Ralph Sussman, Mar. 24, 1973; children: Jason Rubin, Carl Philip. BA, Barnard Coll., 1970; JD, Columbia U., 1973. Bar: N.Y. 1974, U.S. Dist. Ct. (so. and ea. dists.) N.Y. 1974, U.S. Ct. Appeals (2d cir.) 1975, U.S. Supreme Ct. 1977. Assoc. White & Case, N.Y.C., 1974-81, ptnr., 1981—. Co-author Litigation Lookout monthly column Legal Times, 1983—. Mem. ABA (lectr.), N.Y. State Bar Assn., Assn. of Bar of City of N.Y., Banking Law Inst. (co-editor semi-monthly newsletter Letters of Credit Report 1986—, lectr.), Practicing Law Inst. (lectr.), Law and Bus. Inc. (lectr.). Democrat. Jewish. Federal civil litigation, Banking, Bankruptcy. Office: White & Case 1155 Ave of Americas New York NY 10036

SUSSMAN, HOWARD S(IVIN), lawyer; b. N.Y.C., Feb. 12, 1938; s. Joseph and Dora (Sivin) S.; m. Michele Keesee, Oct. 24, 1981. AB cum laude, Princeton U., 1958; LLB, Columbia U., 1962. Bar: N.Y. 1964, U.S. Dist. Ct. (so. and ea. dists.) N.Y. 1967, U.S. Ct. Appeals (2d cir.) 1967, U.S. Tax Ct. 1969, U.S. Dist. Ct. (no. dist.) N.Y. 1970, U.S. Supreme Ct. 1970, Tex. 1979, U.S. Dist. Ct. (so. dist.) Tex. 1982, U.S. Ct. Appeals (5th cir.) 1982. Assoc. Chadbourne, Parke, Whiteside & Wolff, N.Y.C., 1963-71; asst. U.S. atty. So. Dist. N.Y., 1971-77; assoc. prof. law U. Houston, 1977-82; of counsel Wood, Lucksinger & Epstein, Houston, 1982-83; sole practice N.Y.C.; instr. continuing legal edn. U. Houston. Editor Columbia U. Law Rev., 1960-62; contbr. articles to profl. jours. Harlan Fiske Stone scholar, 1959-61, Edvard Cassels Stiftelse vis. scholar, Stockholm, 1962-63; travelling fellow Parker Sch. Fgn. and Comparative Law Columbia U., 1962-63. Mem. ABA, Tex. Bar Assn., Houston Bar Assn., N.Y. State Bar Assn., Assn. of Bar of City of N.Y. (com. adminstrv. law 1974-76, profl. conf. 1979, com. fed. legis. 1984—), Fed. Bar Council. Club: Princeton N.Y. Federal civil litigation, Criminal, General practice. Office: 140 Broadway New York NY 10005

SUSSMAN, MARK RICHARD, lawyer; b. Bklyn., Feb. 4, 1952; s. Vincent E. and Rhoda (Urowsky) S.; m. Lisa Rosner, Aug. 19. 1952; children: Corey, Randi. BS in Civil Engring., Tufts U., 1974; JD, U. Pa., 1977. Bar: Pa. 1977, D.C. 1980, Conn. 1981. Trial atty. land and natural resources div. U.S. Dept. Justice, Washington, 1977-81; ptnr. Murtha, Cullina, Richter & Pinney, Hartford, Conn., 1981—. Chmn. conservation commn. Windsor, Conn., 1984—. Mem. Conn. Bar Assn. (chmn. conservation and environ. quality sect., faculty continuing legal edn.), Tau Beta Pi. Environment, Federal civil litigation, State civil litigation. Home: 62 Timothy Terr Windsor CT 06095 Office: Murtha Cullina Richter & Pinney City Place PO Box 3197 Hartford CT 06103

SUSSMAN, MITCHELL REED, lawyer, real estate executive; b. Bklyn., Feb. 9, 1951; s. Sy and Pauline (Frank) S. B.B.A., George Washington U., 1973; J.D., Pepperdine U., 1976. Bar: Calif. 1977, D.C. 1980. Founder, pres. Legal Research Assn., Newport Beach, Calif., 1974-80; prin. Sussman & Assocs., Newport Beach, 1977—; owner, mgr. New Horizon Realty, Beverly Hills, Calif., 1977—. Mem. Calif. Bar Assn., D.C. Bar Assn., Real property, Bankruptcy, Personal injury. Office: Sussman & Assocs 3345 Newport Blvd #213 Newport Beach CA 92663 Office: 9465 Wilshire Blvd Beverly Hills CA 90012 also: 673 N Palm Canton Dr Palm Springs CA 92262

SUSSWEIN, RONALD, lawyer; b. Trenton, N.J., Aug. 10, 1956; s. Irving David and Joyce Elaine (Gars) S. BS in Polit. Sci. summa cum laude, Am. U., 1978; JD cum laude, Georgetown U., 1981. Bar: N.J. 1981, U.S. Dist. Ct. N.J. 1981. Dep. atty. gen., chief of policy and legis. N.J. Div. Criminal Justice, Trenton, 1981—; adj. prof. Mercer County Community Coll.; cert. spl. instr. N.J. Police Tng. Commn; del. N.J. Supreme Ct. Model Jury Charge Com. Mem. ABA, Assn. Trial Lawyers Am., N.J. Bar Assn., Georgetown Law Alumni Assn. (charter mem. N.J. chpt.). Avocations: violin, astronomy. Criminal, Legislative. Office: NJ Div Criminal Justice Hughes Complex CN 085 Trenton NJ 08625

SUTCLIFFE, ROLAND ALTON, JR., lawyer; b. Dublin, Ga., Feb. 21, 1946; s. Roland A. Sr. and Ernestine (Shearouse) S.; m. Madge Fitzpatrick, Aug. 10, 1968; children: Madge Mershon, Jennifer, Lauren. BA, Emory U., 1968; JD, U. Fla., 1971. Bar: Fla. 1971, U.S. Supreme Ct. 1975. Assoc. Howell, Kirby et al, Orlando, Fla., 1971-73; ptnr. Akerman, Senterfitt & Eidson, Orlando, 1973-84, Zimmerman, Shuffield, Kiser & Sutcliffe, Orlando, 1984—. Mem. ABA, Def. Research Inst., Internat. Assn. Ins. Attys., Fla. Def. Lawyers Assn. (sec.-treas. 1984, pres. 1985—). Republican. Presbyterian. Lodge: Rotary. Avocations: tennis, fishing, golf. State civil litigation, Insurance, Construction. Office: Zimmerman Shuffield Kiser & Sutcliffe PO Box 3000 Orlando FL 32802

SUTER, BERNARD REYNOLD, lawyer; b. Sacramento, Dec. 14, 1954; s. Alexander Frederick and Anne Ida (De Bergen) S.; m. Lizanne Bouchard, Dec. 23, 1979; children: Tycho Benjamin, Hadley Theadora. BA in Philosophy, U. Calif., Santa Barbara, 1978; JD, U. Calif., San Francisco, 1982. Bar: Calif. 1982, U.S. Dist. Ct. (cen., ea., no. and so. dists.) Calif. 1982, U.S. Ct. Appeals (9th cir.) 1982, Ariz. 1983, Hawaii 1984. Assoc. Keesal, Young & Logan, San Francisco and Long Beach, Calif., 1982-87, ptnr., 1987—. Securities, Admiralty, Real property. Office: Keesal Young & Logan 455 The Embarcadero San Francisco CA 94111

SUTER, CAROL JOAN, lawyer; b. Highland Park, Mich., Mar. 5, 1949; d. Francis and Doris I. (Weis) Salucci; m. Eugene W. Suter, Mar. 21, 1970; children: Leanne M., Tracy L. Student, Taylor U., 1967-69; BS in Edn., Bowling Green State U., 1971; JD, Ohio No. U., 1981. Bar: Ohio 1981, U.S. Dist. Ct. (no. dist.) Ohio 1982. Of counsel Schroeder, Schroeder & O'Malley, Ottawa, Ohio, 1981—; dir. devel. Gen. Conf. Mennonite Ch., Newton, Kans., 1984—; mem. jud. qualification and endorsement com. Ohio Supreme Ct., Columbus, 1983-84. Bd. dirs. Putnam County Mental Health Clinic, Inc., Ottawa, 1982—, Appleseed Ridge Girl Scout Council, Inc., Lima, Ohio, 1984—, pres. 1984—. Mem. ABA (Gold Key award 1981), Ohio State Bar Assn., Northwest Ohio Bar Assn., Putnam County Bar Assn. (v.p. 1984, pres. 1985). Democrat. Mennonite. Estate planning, General corporate, General practice. Home: Rt 1 PO Box 380 Pandora OH 45877 Office: Gen Conf Mennonite Ch Bluffton Coll PO Box 1328 Bluffton OH 45817

SUTHERLAND, LOWELL FRANCIS, lawyer; b. Lincoln, Nebr., Dec. 17, 1939; s. Lowell Williams and Doris Genevieve (Peterson) S.; A.B., San Diego State Coll., 1962; LL.B., Hastings Coll. Law, 1965; m. Sandra Gaylynne Stengel, June 12, 1965; children—Scott Thorpe, Mark James, Sandra Doris. With Cooper, White & Cooper, attys., San Francisco, 1963-66; admitted to Calif. bar, 1966; with Wien & Thorpe, attys., El Centro, 1966-67; ptnr. Wien, Thorpe & Sutherland, El Centro, 1967-74, Wien, Thorpe, Sutherland & Stamper, 1973-74, Sutherland, Stamper & Feingold, 1974-77, Sutherland & Gerber, 1977—; ptnr. Sutherland & Sutherland, Ivy Shoppe; instr. bus. law Imperial Valley Coll., 1967. Pres. El Centro Active 20-30 Club, 1968-69; finance chmn. Salvation Army, 1972. Pres. bd. dirs. Boys Club of El Centro, 1969-71; bd. dirs. Imperial Gen. Hosp., 1971. Mem. Am., Calif., Imperial County bar assns., Am., Calif. (Recognition of Experience awards), San Diego (named outstanding trial lawyer April 1981, Oct. 1983 trial lawyer of yr. 1982), trial lawyers assns., Thurston Soc., Am. Bd. Trial Advocates (diplomate), Theta Chi. Mem. editorial staff Hastings Law Jour., 1964-65. Condemnation, Insurance, Personal injury. Home: 1853 Sunset Dr El Centro CA 92243 Office: 300 S Imperial Ave 7 El Centro CA 92243

SUTHERLAND, RICHARD THOMAS, lawyer; b. Houston, May 8, 1946; s. Daniel James and Helen Eva (Hayes) S.; m. Elizabeth Anne Fergeson, Dec. 26, 1970 (div. Aug. 1973); m. Alexis Jones, June 5, 1982. BS, U. Tex., 1969; JD, Okla. City U., 1976. Bar: Tex. 1976, U.S. Dist. Ct. (no. dist.) Tex. 1977. Sole practice Dallas, 1977; assoc. Gibson, Darden & Hotchkiss, Wichita Falls, Tex., 1977-1980; ptnr. Gibson & Hotchkiss, Wichita Falls, 1980-83, Towery & Sutherland, Wichita Falls, 1984—. Bd. dirs. Big Brothers and Sisters, Wichita Falls, Tex., 1985—. Mem. ABA (conv. speaker 1983), Tex. Bar Assn., Tri-County Bar Assn. (pres. 1985-86), Wichita County Bar Assn. (bd. dirs. 1982-83), Assn. Trial Lawyers Am., Tex. Trial Lawyers Assn. Democrat. Methodist. Avocations: trout fishing, model railroading. Family and matrimonial, Consumer protection and deceptive trade practices, State civil litigation. Home: 3000 10th St Wichita Falls TX 76309 Office: Towery & Sutherland 1400 Hamilton Bldg Wichita Falls TX 76301

SUTHERLUND, DAVID ARVID, lawyer; b. Stevens Point, Wis., July 20, 1929; s. Arvid E. and Georgia M. (Stickney) S. BA, U. Portland, 1952; JD, U. N.Mex., 1957; postgrad., U. Wis., 1957. Bar: D.C. 1957, U.S. Supreme Ct. 1961. Atty. ICC, Washington, 1957-58; counsel Am. Trucking Assn., Washington, 1958-62; assoc. and ptnr. Morgan, Lewis & Bockius, Washington and Phila., 1962-72; ptnr. Fulbright & Jaworski, Washington and Houston, 1975-83; spl. counsel LaRoe, Winn & Moerman, Washington, 1983—; bd. dirs., gen. counsel Nat. Film Service, 1962-75; mem. family div. panel Public Defender Service for D.C., 1972-76. Founder, chmn. bd. govs. Transp. Law Jour, 1969-74. Vice chmn. Nat. Capitol Area council Boy Scouts Am., 1975-78; bd. regents U. Portland, 1985—. Served as spl. agt. CIC U.S. Army, 1952-54. Mem. ABA, Fed. Bar Assn., D.C. Bar Assn., Transp. Lawyers Assn., Am. Arbitration Assn. (nat. panel arbitrators 1970—), Am. Judicature Soc., Smithson Soc. (Smithsonian Instn.). Clubs: Nat. Lawyers; International, Lakewood (Washington). Civil rights, State civil litigation. Home: 2130 Bancroft Pl NW Washington DC 20008 Office: 1120 G St NW Washington DC 20005

SUTHERS, JOHN WILLIAM, lawyer; b. Denver, Oct. 18, 1951; s. William Dupont and Marguerite A. (Ryan) S.; m. Janet Gill, May 21, 1976; children: Alison, Catherine. BA in Govt. magna cum laude, U. Notre Dame, 1974; JD, U. Colo., 1977. Bar: Colo. 1977, U.S. Dist. Ct. Colo. 1977, U.S. Ct. Appeals (10th cir.) 1979. Dep. dist. atty. 4th jud. dist. State of Colo., Colorado Springs, 1977-79, chief dep. dist. atty. 4th jud. dist., 1979-81; assoc. Sparks, Dix, Enoch, Colorado Springs, 1981-82; ptnr. Sparks, Dix, Enoch, Suthers & Winslow, Colorado Springs, 1982—; mem. adv. bd. Sec. of state, Denver, 1983—. Author: Fraud and Deceit, 1982, How to Liquidate a Lemon, 1983. Pres., chmn. bd. dirs. Community Corrections of Pikes Peak Region Inc., 1984—; precinct committeeman El Paso County Reps., Colorado Springs, 1985—; county campaign chmn. Natalie Meyer for Sec. State, Colorado Springs, 1982, 86; bd. dirs. Crimestoppers Inc., Colorado Springs, 1985—. Zimmerman Found. scholar, 1970-74. Mem. ABA, Colo. Bar Assn. (com. chmn.), El Paso County Bar Assn. (com. chmn.), Assn. Trial Lawyers Am., Colo. Assn. Trial Lawyers. Roman Catholic. Club: Notre Dame Colorado Springs (pres. 1983-84). Avocation: tennis. State civil litigation, Federal civil litigation, Administrative and regulatory. Home: 2561 Scorpio Dr Colorado Springs CO 80906 Office: Sparks Dix Enoch Suthers & Winslow 128 S Tejan Suite 304 Colorado Springs CO 80906

SUTPHEN, ROBERT LOUIS, lawyer; b. Odessa, Tex., Oct. 15, 1954; s. Bob L. and Joyce Ann (Shipman) S.; m. Ellen Ruth Woodall, June 15, 1979. BS, Abilene Christian U., 1977; JD, U. Tex., 1980. Bar: Tex. 1980. Asst. dist. atty. Midland County, Tex., 1980-81; assoc. Turpin, Smith, Dyer, Saxe & MacDonald, Midland, Tex., 1981-86; atty. El Paso Products Co., Odessa, Tex., 1986—. Pres., bd. dirs. Friends Midland Pub. Library, 1981-86; tenor Midland-Odessa Symphony Chorale, 1983—. Mem. ABA, Tex. Bar Assn., Midland County Bar Assn., Tex. Assn. Bank Counsel, Midland County Young Lawyers Assn. Mem. Ch. of Christ. Lodge: Lions (Midland). Avocations: reading, classical music. Environment, Labor, General corporate. Home: 2403 Arbor Circle Midland TX 79707 Office: El Paso Products Co PO Box 3986 Odessa TX 79760

SUTRO, JOHN ALFRED, lawyer; b. San Francisco, July 3, 1905; s. Alfred and Rose (Newmark) S.; m. Elizabeth Hiss, Oct. 16, 1931; children: Caroline Sutro Mohun, Elizabeth Sutro Mackey, John A., Stephen (dec.). A.B., Stanford U., 1926; LL.B., Harvard U., 1929. Bar: Calif. 1929. Since practiced in San Francisco; with firm Pillsbury, Madison & Sutro, 1929—, ptnr., 1935—, adv. ptnr., 1971—; adv. dir. Bank of Calif. (N.A.), 1976-81; Adv. dir. BanCal Tri-State Corp., 1976-81; chmn. sr. adv. bd. U.S. Ct. Appeals

9th Circuit. Mem. Calif. Commn. on Uniform State Laws, 1968; mem. legal adv. com. Criminal Justice Legal Found.; mem. Calif. Commn. on Interstate Cooperation, 1968; chmn. exec. com. Friends of Stanford Law Library; vice chmn. San Francisco Airports Commn., 1970-74; bd. councilors U. So. Calif. Law Center; trustee Hastings Law Center Found.; bd. visitors U. Santa Clara Sch. Law, Stanford U. Law Sch., 1967-86; pres., trustee San Francisco Law Library (hon. mem.); bd. dirs. St. Luke's Hosp., 1975-85; pres. U.S. Dist. Ct. No. Dist. Calif. Hist. Soc.; v.p. 9th Judicial Cir. Hist. Soc.; mem. USCA 9th Cir. Atty. Admission Fund Com. Served as comdr. USNR, 1940-45. Recipient Navy Disting. Pub. Service award, 1958, ann. award St. Thomas More Soc., 1971, Brotherhood award NCCJ, 1975, Torch of Liberty award Anti-Defamation League of B'nai Brith, 1980. Fellow Am. Bar Found. (chmn. 1973); mem. Am. Judicature Soc. (dir. 1964-70, exec. com. 1967-70, Herbert Harley award 1974), Navy League (nat. v.p. and dir. 1954-67, mem. nat. adv. council), Calif. Acad. Scis. (trustee 1966-80, hon. trustee 1980—), Am. Law Inst., Am. Bar Assn. (standing com. fed. judiciary 1968-74, chmn. 1973-74, chmn. com. jud. selection and tenure 1975-78, vice chmn., dir. Nat. Jud. Coll. 1975-80, mem. exec. com. lawyers conf. jud. adminstrn. div., div. council), State Bar Calif. (bd. govs. 1962-66, pres. 1965-66), Bar Assn. San Francisco (pres. 1962, John A. Sutro award for legal excellence 1975), San Francisco C. of C. (pres. 1973, life dir.), Nat. Center for State Cts. (bus. and profl. friends com., independence support fund com., Disting. Service award), Rodeo Cowboys Assn. (life), Phi Alpha Delta. Clubs: Family (San Francisco), Stock Exchange (San Francisco), Commonwealth (San Francisco) (bd. govs. 1957-59). Federal civil litigation, General corporate, Estate planning. Office: 225 Bush St San Francisco CA 94104

SUTTER, WILLIAM FRANKLIN, lawyer, food products executive; b. Rock Port, Mo., Oct. 5, 1938; s. Otto Lee and Hattie May (Moody) S.; m. Carolyn Ann Oliver, Dec. 27, 1960; children: William Scott, Bryan Lee, Stephen Brent. BS in Bus. Adminstrn., Northwest Mo. State U., 1960; JD, U. Mo., 1965. Bar: Mo. 1965. Asst. bank examiner FDIC, Washington, 1960-62; assoc. Shughart, Thomsen & Kilroy, Kansas City, 1965-68; v.p., gen. counsel, sec. Pet Inc., St. Louis, 1968—. Contbg. editor U. Mo. Law Rev., 1964. Recipient Chmn.'s awd. IC Industries, 1986. Mem. ABA (corp. banking and bus. law sect., antitrust and real property sect.), Mo. Bar Assn., Met. St. Louis Bar Assn., Am. Soc. Corp. Secs. Inc., Am. Corp. Counsel Assn., Practicing Law Inst. Republican. Lodge: Rotary. Avocations: tennis, golf. General corporate, Real property, Contracts commercial. Home: 1509 Greening Kirkwood MO 63122 Office: Pet Inc 400 S Fourth St Saint Louis MO 63102

SUTTLE, STEPHEN HUNGATE, lawyer; b. Uvalde, Tex., Mar. 17, 1940; s. Dorwin Wallace and Ann Elizabeth (Barrett) S.; m. Rosemary Williams Davison, Aug. 3, 1963; children—Michael Barrett, David Paull, John Stewart. B.A., Washington and Lee U., 1962; LL.B., U. Tex., 1965. Bar: Tex. 1965, U.S. Dist. Ct. (no. and we. dists.) Tex. 1965, U.S. Ct. Appeals (5th cir.) 1967, U.S. Supreme Ct. 1970. Law clk. to presiding justice U.S. Dist. Ct., No. Dist. Tex., Ft. Worth, 1965-67; ptnr. McMahon, Smart, Surovik, Suttle, Buhrmann & Cobb, Abilene, Tex., 1970—. Pres. Abilene Boys Clubs, Inc., 1975-76; bd. dirs. Abilene Community Theater, 1979-80, Abilene Fine Arts Mus., 1977-78. Fellow Am. Coll. Trial Lawyers, Tex. Bar Found.; mem. Abilene Young Lawyers Assn. (outstanding young lawyer 1976), Tex. Young Lawyers Assn. (chmn. bd. dirs. 1973-76), Am. Judicature Soc. (bd. dirs. 1981-84), Abilene Bar Assn. (pres.), Tex. Bar Assn. (mem. coms. various sects.), ABA (chmn. young lawyers sect., award of merit 1976). Democrat. Episcopalian. Club: Abilene Country. Federal civil litigation, State civil litigation, Personal injury. Home: 1405 Woodland Trail Abilene TX 79605 Office: McMahon Smart Surovik Suttle Buhrmann & Cobb PO Box 3679 Abilene TX 79604

SUTTON, JOHN F., JR., law educator, university dean, lawyer, rancher; b. Alpine, Tex., Jan. 26, 1918; s. John F. and Pauline Irene (Elam) S.; m. Nancy Ewing, June 1, 1940; children: Joan Sutton Parr, John Ewing. J.D., U. Tex., 1941. Bar: Tex. 1941, U.S. Dist. Ct. (we. dist.) Tex. 1947, U.S. Ct. Appeals (5th cir.) 1951, U.S. Supreme Ct. 1960. Assoc. Brooks, Napier, Brown & Matthews, San Antonio, 1941-42; spl. agt. FBI, Washington, 1942-45; assoc. Matthews, Nowlin, Macfarlane & Barrett, San Antonio, 1945-48; ptnr. Kerr, Gayer & Sutton, San Angelo, Tex., 1948-50, Sutton, Steib & Barr, San Angelo, 1951-57; prof. U. Tex.-Austin, 1957-65, William Stamps Farish prof., 1965-84, A.W. Walker centennial chair, 1984—, dean Sch. Law, 1979-84; mem. com. on rules of profl. conduct State Bar Tex., 1983-87. Editor: (with McCormick and Wellborn) Materials on Evidence, 6th edit., 1987; contbr. articles to profl. jours. Served to 1st lt. JAGC USAR, 1948-54. Fellow Am Bar Found., Tex. Bar Found. (life); mem. ABA (commn. on ethics 1970-76), Order of Coif, Phi Delta Phi. Presbyterian. Clubs: Metropolitan, North Austin Rotary (pres. 1969). Federal civil litigation, State civil litigation, Legal education. Home: 8705 Parkfield Dr Austin TX 78758 Office: U Tex Law Sch 727 E 26th St Austin TX 78705

SUTTON, MICHAEL FERRIS, lawyer; b. Orlando, Fla., Apr. 3, 1952; s. Rousselle Alton and Dorothy Ann (Railsback) S.; m. Adrienne Mary Brunelle, Jan. 8, 1972; 1 child, Jennifer Michelle. AA, Valencia Comm. Coll., 1973; BA, Fla. Tech. U., 1975; JD, U. Fla., 1977. Bar: Fla. 1978, U.S. Dist. Ct. (no. dist.) Fla. 1978, U.S. Dist. Ct. (mid. dist.) Fla. 1980. Assoc. Sherrill, Moore & Hill, Pensacola, Fla., 1978-80; assoc. atty. Gurney, Gurney & Handley, Orlando, 1980-83; ptnr. Gurney & Handley, Orlando, 1983—. Mem. ABA, Def. Research Inst., Fla. Def. Lawyers Assn., Orange County Bar Assn. Republican. Roman Catholic. Personal injury, State civil litigation, Insurance. Home: 5121 Contour Dr Orlando FL 32810 Office: Landmark Ctr Two 225 E Robinson St Suite 450 Orlando FL 32801

SUTTON, PAUL J., lawyer; b. N.Y.C., June 16, 1939; s. Jack and Frances (Drexler) Schwartzberg; m. Edith Diane Bers Sutton, Sept. 18, 1976; children: Daniel Richard, Lily Anna Bers. Student Indsl.Mgmt., Columbia U., 1960; student Welding Metallurgy, UCLA, 1963; BME, NYU, 1962; JD, Bklyn. U., 1967. Cer. Welder, Calif. Patent atty. Nolte & Nolte, N.Y.C., 1965-67, Darby & Darby, N.Y.C., 1967-69; patent counsel Gulf & Western Industries, Inc., N.Y.C., 1969-71; ptnr. Miskin & Sutton, N.Y.C., 1971-74, Sutton & Magidoff, N.Y.C., 1974-82; sr. ptnr. Sutton, Magidoff & Amaral, N.Y.C., 1982—. Author: Commercial Law, 1971; patentee telephone multidialing systems. Arbitrator civil court, City Of N.Y., 1979-86; co-founder Hallen Ctr. Edn., Mamaroneck, N.Y., 1975; chief judge Am. Patent Law Assn., N.Y.C., 1981. Mem. ABA (ethics and profl. responsibilities com., patent, trademark and copyright sect.), N.Y. Bar Assn. (antitrust law, patent and trademarks sects.), D.C. Bar Assn., Am. Intellectual Property Law Assn., N.Y. Patent, Trademark and Copyright Assn., Am. Judges Assn., Assn. Trial Lawyers Assn., Licensing Execs. Soc. Club: East Hampton, Yacht. Avocations: sailing, photography, computers. Patent, Trademark and copyright, Federal civil litigation. Home: 300 Central Park West New York NY 10024 Office: Sutton Magidoff & Amaral 420 Lexington Ave New York NY 10170

SUZUKI, NORMAN HITOSHI, lawyer; b. Honolulu, Dec. 5, 1935; s. Hajime and Mildred (Fujimoto) S.; m. Lois A. Tatsuguchi, Aug. 19, 1962; children: Grant T., Brandon A. BA, U. Mich., 1957; LLB, Harvard U., 1960. Bar: Hawaii 1960, U.S. Dist. Ct. Hawaii 1960, U.S. Ct. Appeals (9th cir.) 1962. Sole practice Honolulu, 1960—. Served to capt. USAR, 1960-66. Mem. ABA, Hawaii Bar Assn., Assn. Trial Lawyers Am. General corporate, Legislative, Probate. Home: 3517 Kahawalu Dr Honolulu HI 96819 Office: 1188 Bishop St Century Sq Suite 1805 Honolulu HI 96813

SVEEN, JEFFREY T., lawyer; b. Omaha, Nov. 18, 1953; s. John A. and Doris (Bieberdorf) S.; m. Marcia Eilers, Aug. 16, 1975; children: Andrew John, Peter Joseph. BA, U. S.D., 1976, JD, 1979. Bar: S.D. 1979, U.S. Dist. Ct. S.D. 1979. Assoc. Siegal, Barnett & Schutz, Aberdeen, S.D., 1979-81, ptnr., 1981—. Pres. Parks and Recreation Bd., Aberdeen, 1981—; bd. dirs. ARC, Aberdeen, 1985—, St. Mark's Episc. Ch., Aberdeen, 1984—. Mem. S.D. Bar Assn. (commr. 1984—), S.D. Trial Lawyers Assn., Aberdeen Jaycees (bd. dirs. 1983). Republican. Avocations: skiing, golf, flying, backpacking, hunting. State civil litigation, Federal civil litigation, Bankruptcy. Homw: 410 E Melgaard Aberdeen SD 57401 Office: Siegel Barnett & Schutz 500 Capitol Bldg Aberdeen SD 57402-0490

SVENGALIS, KENDALL FRAYNE, law librarian; b. Gary, Ind., May 16, 1947; s. Frank Anthony and Alvida Linnea (Matheus) S.; m. Deborah Kay Andrews, May 23, 1970; children: Hillary Linnea, Andrew Kendall. BA, Purdue U., 1970, MA, 1973; MLS, U. R.I., 1975. Reference librarian Roger Williams Coll., Bristol, R.I., 1975, Providence (R.I.) Coll., 1975-77; asst. law librarian R.I. State Law Library, Providence, 1976-82, state law librarian, 1982—. Contbr. articles to profl. jours. Chmn. jud. branch United Way Com. R.I., 1980. Mem. Am. Assn. Law Libraries, Law LibrariansNew England (treas. 1983-85, v.p. 1985-86, pres. 1986—0, State, Court, and County Law Libraries (spl. interest sect., bd. dirs. 1986—), R.I. Coordinating Council State Library, Archival and Info. Services. Republican. Lutheran. Librarianship, Judicial administration. Home: 37 Brentwood Ave Providence RI 02908 Office: Providence County Courthouse RI State Law Library 250 Benefit St Providence RI 02903

SVENSON, CHARLES OSCAR, investment banker; b. Worcester, Mass., June 28, 1939; s. Sven Oscar and Edahjane (Castner) S.; m. Sara Ellen Simpson, Nov. 15, 1968; children: Alicia Lindall, Tait Oscar. A.B., Hamilton Coll., 1961; LL.B., Harvard U., 1964; LL.M., Bklyn. Law Sch., 1965. Bar: N.Y. 1965, U.S. Dist. Ct. (so. dist.) N.Y. 1965, U.S. Ct. Appeals (2d. cir.) 1965. Atty. Dewey, Ballantine, Bushby, Palmer & Wood, N.Y.C., 1964-68; v.p. Goldman Sachs & Co., N.Y.C., 1968-75; sr. v.p. Donaldson, Lufkin & Jenrette, N.Y.C, 1975—. Trustee Kirkland Coll., Clinton, N.Y., 1976-78; trustee Hamilton Coll., Clinton, 1979-83. Mem. ABA, N.Y. State Bar Assn., Asn. Bar City N.Y. Clubs: Tuxedo (Tuxedo Park, N.Y.); Harvard (N.Y.C.). Oil and gas leasing. Home: 1185 Park Ave New York NY 10128 Office: Donaldson Lufkin & Jenrette 140 Broadway New York NY 10005

SWAGART, HARRY AUGUSTUS, III, lawyer; b. Evanston, Ill., Apr. 27, 1945; s. Harry Augustus, Jr. and Lorraine Genevieve (Gibney) S.; m. Aline Conard Williamson, Aug. 14, 1976; children—Heather Williamson, Russell Gibney. A.B. in Econs., Duke U., 1971; J.D. cum laude, U. S.C., 1976. Bar: S.C. 1976, U.S. Dist. Ct. S.C. 1978, D.C. 1977, U.S. Ct. Appeals (4th cir.) 1978, U.S. Ct. Appeals (11th cir.) 1982. Assoc., Howrey & Simon, Washington, 1976-78, Quinn & Smith, Columbia, S.C., 1979-82; asst. dean, lectr. U. S.C. Sch. of Law, 1978-79; ptnr. McKay & Swagart, P.A., 1982; of counsel Kennedy & Price, Columbia, 1982—; instr. legal writing, research U. S.C., 1975-76; cons. Atty. Gen. of S.C. sect. on antitrust and consumer fraud, 1978-82. Editor: Jour. S.C. Law Rev. 1975-76. Contbr. articles to profl. jours. Vol. United Way. Columbia, 1984. Served with U.S. Army, 1967-70. Recipient Am. Jurisprudence award for torts Lawyers Coop. Pub. Co., 1974. Mem. ABA (com. mem.). S.C. Bar Assn. (chmn. seminar on antitrust law 1981, speaker seminars on def. modern crimes and torts 1982-83). Republican. Roman Catholic. Clubs: Forest Lake Country, Gamecock. Antitrust, Federal civil litigation, Securities. Home: 6125 Rutledge Hill Rd Columbia SC 29209 Office: Kennedy & Price 1722 Main St Bouchier Bldg Suite 220 Columbia SC 29202 Address: PO Box 7787 Columbia SC 29202

SWAIM, JOHN JOSEPH, lawyer; b. Phila., Mar. 19, 1949; s. John J. and Dorothy A. (Brown) S.; m. Janet Linda Lutz, June 3, 1972; children—John, Jessica, Justin. B.A., Pa. State U., 1971; J.D., Widener U., 1977. Bar: Pa. 1977, U.S. Dist. Ct. (ea. dist.) Pa. 1979, U.S. Ct. Appeals (3d cir.) 1979, U.S. Supreme Ct. 1980. Ptnr. Swaim & Duffy, Phila., 1978-80; mem. Pa. Ho. of Reps., Harrisburg, 1980-82; sole practice, Phila., 1982—. Counsel, Democratic Campaign Com., 1977—; treas. 57th Ward Dem. Com., 1980—. Mem. Phila. Bar Assn., Brehon Law Soc., Phi Alpha Delta, Alpha Xi Omega. Democrat. Roman Catholic. Lodge: K.C. Personal injury, Criminal, Legislative. Home: 9322 Academy Rd Philadelphia PA 19114 Office: 42 S 15th St Robinson Bldg Suite 1120 Philadelphia PA 19102

SWAIM, R(OBERT) KURT, lawyer; b. Bloomfield, Iowa, Oct. 29, 1950; s. F. Basil and Betty J. (Adams) S.; m. Julie R. Morlan, June 19, 1971; children: Justin, Mandy, Joshua. BS, Iowa Wesleyan Coll., 1972; JD, U. Iowa, 1975. Bar: Iowa 1975, U.S. Dist. Ct. (no. and so. dists.) Iowa 1975, U.S. Ct. Appeals (8th cir.) 1979. Assoc. Lunty, Butler, Wilson & Hall, Eltora, Iowa, 1975-78; sr. staff atty. Legal Services Corp. Iowa, Dubuque, 1978-81; ptnr. Harris & Swaim, Bloomfield, 1981-83; sole practice Bloomfield, 1983—; atty. Davis County, Bloomfield, 1982—; instr. Indian Hills Community Coll., Ottumwa, Iowa, 1985; bd. dirs. Citizens Mut. Telephone Co., Bloomfield. Mem. Iowa Bar Assn., Davis County Bar Assn. (sec. 1981-83), Order of Coif. Democrat. Methodist. Lodge: Masons. General practice. Home: 307 N Washington Bloomfield IA 52537 Office: 105 E Locust Bloomfield IA 52537

SWAIN, DENNIS MICHAEL, lawyer; b. Jackson, Mich., June 15, 1948; s. Donald Elliot and Rose Therese (Flynn) S.; m. Jacque Lee Wallace, Mar. 20, 1971; 1 child, Jason Patrick. BA, Mich. State U., 1974; JD, Thomas M. Cooley Law Sch., 1978. Bar: Mich. 1979, U.S. Dist. Ct. (we. dist.) Mich. 1983. Assoc. Law Office of Zerafa P.C., Elk Rapids, Mich., 1978-81; ptnr. Gockerman & Swain, Manistee, Mich., 1981-85; pros. atty. Manistee County, 1985—; instr. West Shore Community Coll., Scottville, Mich., 1985—, bd. dirs. law enforcement adv. bd.; bd. chmn. Region 10 Detectives, Manistee, 1985—. Fellow Mich. Bar Found.; mem. ABA, Mich. Bar Assn. (rep. state assembly 1983—), Manistee County Bar Assn. (pres. 1985-86), Assn. Trial Lawyers Am., Pros. Attys. Assn. of Mich., Nat. Dist. Attys. Assn. Republican. Episcopalian. Lodge: Elks. Avocations: hunting, fishing, skiing, shooting. Criminal, Local government, General practice. Home: 410 Pine St Manistee MI 49660 Office: Manistee County Prosecutor 402 Maple St Manistee MI 49660

SWAIN, JOHN BARRY, lawyer; b. Oak Park, Ill., Jan. 1, 1947; s. John Henry Swain and Jean Adele (Boyle) Janssen; m. Kathleen Jo Kengott, Feb. 21, 1969; children: Shawn Marie, John Charles. AA, Coll. DuPage, 1974; BA, No. Ill. U., 1976, JD, 1980. Bar: Ill. 1980, U.S. Dist. Ct. (no. dist.) Ill. 1980, U.S. Ct. Appeals (7th cir.) 1981. Dep. sheriff patrolman DuPage County Sheriff's Office, Wheaton, Ill., 1970-74; assoc. William E. Hourigan, Wheaton, 1980-81, Garretson & Santora, Chgo., 1982-83; sole practice Wheaton, 1983—. Served as cpl. USMC, 1966-70, Vietnam. Mem. Ill. Bar Assn., DuPage County Bar Assn. Republican. Baptist. Criminal, Family and matrimonial, Personal injury. Office: 112 W Liberty Dr Wheaton IL 60187

SWAN, GEORGE STEVEN, law educator; b. St. Louis, Feb. 9, 1948; s. Raymond A. and Lorene (Kennedy) S. B.A., Ohio State U., 1970; J.D., U. Notre Dame, 1974; LL.M., U. Toronto, 1976, S.J.D., 1983. Bar: Ohio 1974. Asst. atty. gen. state of Ohio, Columbus, 1974-75; jud. clk. Supreme Ct. Ohio, Columbus, 1976-78; asst. prof. Del. Law Sch., Wilmington, 1980-83, assoc. prof., 1983-84; prof. law St. Thomas U. Law Sch., Miami, Fla., 1984—. Contbr. articles to law jours. Mem. ABA, Ohio State Bar Assn., Am. Polit. Sci. Assn. Republican. Roman Catholic. Legal education, Civil rights, Public international. Office: St Thomas U Law Sch 16400 NW 32d Ave Miami FL 33054

SWAN, MICHAEL ROBERT, lawyer; b. Passaic, N.J., Oct. 8, 1957; s. Harry A. and Marilyn P. (Wells) S.; m. Katherine L. Goldman, May 24, 1982. BA in English cum laude, Montclair State Coll., 1979; JD with honors, U. Tex., 1982. Bar: N.Mex. 1982, U.S. Dist. Ct. N.Mex. 1982, Tex. 1984, U.S. Dist. Ct. (no. dist.) Tex. 1984, U.S. Ct. Appeals (5th cir.) 1985. Assoc. Poole, Tinnin & Martin, Albuquerque, 1982-84, Lippe & Lay, Dallas, 1984-85, Brice & Mankoff, Dallas, 1985—. cert. arbitrator Better Bus. Bur., Dallas, 1985—. Mem. Phi Delta Phi, Phi Kappa Phi. Avocations: basketball, swimming. Federal civil litigation, State civil litigation, Labor. Home: 13009 Fall Manor Dr Dallas TX 75243 Office: Brice & Mankoff 300 Crescent Ct Suite 700 Dallas TX 75201

SWANEY, THOMAS EDWARD, lawyer; b. Detroit, Apr. 25, 1942; s. Robert Ernest and Mary Alice (Slinger) S.; m. Patricia Louise Nash, Sept. 9, 1967; children: Julia Bay, Mary Elizabeth, David Paul. AB, U. Mich., 1963, JD, 1967; postdoctoral, London Sch. Econs., 1967-68. Bar: Ill. 1968. From assoc. to ptnr. Sidley & Austin, Chgo., 1968—. Officer, pres. bd. trustees 1st Presbyn. Ch., Evanston, Ill., 1984-87. Mem. ABA, Ill. Bar Assn., Chgo. Bar Assn. Clubs: Monroe (Chgo.), Mich. Shores (Wilmette). Estate planning, Probate, Estate taxation. Office: Sidley & Austin One First National Plaza Chicago IL 60603

SWANN, ELIZABETH WALKER, lawyer; b. Magnolia, Ark., Oct. 16, 1956; d. Benjamin Thomas Jr. and Helen Jolene (Corlew) Walker; m. William Dickinson Swann, May 29, 1982. BS in Elementary Edn., Southeast Mo. State U., 1978; JD, U. Mo., 1982. Bar: Mo. 1982, U.S. Dist. Ct. (ea. and we. dists.) Mo. 1982. Ptnr. James & Swann, Wentzville, Mo., 1982-86, Swann & Boeckman, O'Fallon, Mo., 1986—. Mem. St. Charles County Bar Assn. Family and matrimonial, General practice, Workers' compensation. Home: 4 Horizon Dr Saint Peters MO 63376 Office: Swann & Boeckman 120C O'Fallon MO 63366

SWANN, RICHARD HILL MCRAE, lawyer; b. Cairo, Ga., Aug. 16, 1923; s. Joseph Paul and Mae (Shriver) S.; m. Norma Marie Pinder, Aug. 12, 1947; children—Cheryl Swann Babcock, Lynette Norma. J.D., U. Miami, 1950; LL.D. (hon.), La Academia de Derecho Internacional, Mexico, 1982. Judge City of Miami, Fla., 1956-58; judge 3d Dist. Ct. of Appeals Fla., Miami, 1965-72; ptnr. Hall & Swann, Coral Gables, Fla., 1980—; spl. atty. City of Miami, 1954-56. hon. counsul gen. of Japan, Miami, 1974—bd. dirs. U. Miami-Jackson Meml. Burn Ctr., 1983—, Leukemia Soc. South Fla., Miami, 1983—; mem. Citizens Bd. Miami, 1978—. Mem. Iron Arrow, Pi Kappa Alpha, Pi Alpha Delta. Democrat. Baptist. Clubs: Miami, Riviera Country, Beach Colony, Consular Corps, Cotillion, Vizcayans, Biltmore. Home: 5890 SW 117th St Miami FL 33156 Office: Hall & Swann 2801 Ponce de Leon Blvd Coral Gables FL 33134

SWANSON, ARTHUR DEAN, lawyer; b. Onida, S.D., Apr. 19, 1934; s. Obert W. and Mary I. (Barnum) S.; m. Paula Swanson, Aug. 22, 1965 (div. Feb. 1984); children: Shelby, Dean, Sherry. BA, Wash. State U., 1956; JD, U. Wash., 1963. Bar: Wash. 1963. Dep. prosecutor King County, Seattle, 1964-65; ct. commr. Renton and Issaquah Dist. Cts., Wash., 1966-68; sole practice Renton, Wash., 1969—; lectr. various orgns.; former counsel Wash. State Law Enforcement Assn., Wash. State Dep. Sheriff's Assn. Served with Fin. Corps, U.S. Army, 1956-58. Fellow Am. Coll. Trial Lawyers; mem. Wash. State Bar Assn. (past sec. trial sect.), Seattle-King County Bar Assn. (bd. trustees 1977-80), Assn. Trial Lawyers Am., Wash. State Trial Lawyers Assn. (past pres.), Am. Bd. Trial Advs., Damages Attys. Roundtable. Democrat. Avocation: tennis. Personal injury, Insurance, State civil litigation. Office: 4512 Talbot Rd S Renton WA 98055

SWANSON, CHARLES WALTER, lawyer; b. Bluefield, W.Va., Mar. 6, 1954; s. Don B. and Ann (Hughes) S.; m. Linda Susan Doak, Aug. 12, 1978. BA, Pfeiffer Coll., 1976; JD, U. Tenn., 1979. Bar: Tenn. 1979, U.S. Dist. Ct. (ea. dist.) Tenn. 1979, U.S. Ct. Appeals (6th cir.) 1983. Spl. judge juvenile ct. Knoxville (Tenn.) County, 1979-81; asst. city atty. City of Knoxville, 1981-84; assoc. Pryor, Flynn, Priest & Harber, Knoxville, 1984—; atty. city council Knoxville, 1985—. Mem. ABA, Tenn. Bar Assn., Knoxville Bar Assn., Tenn. Trial Lawyers Assn., Knoxville Barristers (exec. com.). Democrat. Methodist. Avocations: softball, tennis, golf, hiking. Personal injury, Local government, General practice. Home: 304 Oran Rd Knoxville TN 37922 Office: Pryor Flynn Priest & Harber 706 Walnut St Suite 600 Knoxville TN 37902

SWANSON, DAVID WARREN, lawyer; b. Fairmont, Minn., Mar. 30, 1932; s. Raymond Clifford and Lucille May (Warren) S.; m. Elizabeth Joan Berkaw, July 14, 1962; children: Karen, Lynn, Paul. A.A., Flint Jr. Coll., 1951; A.B., Augustana Coll., 1953; J.D., U. Mich., 1956. Bar: Mich. 1956, N.Y. 1958. Assoc. White & Case, N.Y.C., 1956-66, ptnr., 1967—. Trustee Henry M. Blackmmer Found., Inc., 1967—. Served with U.S. Army, 1957-59. Mem. ABA, N.Y. Bar Assn., Assn. Bar City N.Y. Republican. Lutheran. Clubs: Wall Street; Montclair Golf (N.J.). General corporate, Contracts commercial, Private international. Office: White and Case 1155 Ave of the Americas New York NY 10036

SWANSON, LENARD CHARLES, lawyer; b. Oak Park, Ill., Apr. 5, 1937; s. Carl Gustave and Luella Katherine (Pingel) S.; m. Grace Cecelia Rickman, Dec. 28, 1963; children—Stephen, Jennifer, Elizabeth. B.S., U. Ill., 1963, J.D., 1967. Bar: Ill. 1967, U.S. Dist. Ct. (no. dist.) Ill. 1967. Assoc. Chadwell, Keck, Kayser, Ruggles & McLaren, Chgo., 1967-69; ptnr. Wildman, Harrold, Allen & Dixon, Chgo., 1969—. Mem. Glen Ellyn (Ill.) Zoning Bd. Appeals, 1975-80; bd. dirs. B.R. Ryall YMCA, 1982-86, Marianjoy Rehab. Hosp., 1985—. Served as sgt. USMC, 1957-60. Mem. ABA, Ill. State Bar Assn., DuPage County Bar Assn., Ill. Trial Lawyers Club, Soc. Trial Lawyers. Club: Glen Oak Country. General practice, Personal injury, Insurance. Office: Wildman Harrold Allen & Dixon Suite 3000 1 IBM Plaza Chicago IL 60611

SWANSON, MARK DOUGLAS, lawyer; b. Red Oak, Iowa, Dec. 14, 1951; s. R. John and Margaret (Seibert) S.; m. Kristine Marie Ranallo, May 31, 1986. BA, Yale U., 1974; JD, Boston U., 1977. Bar: Iowa 1978, U.S. Dist. Ct. (so. dist.) Iowa 1979. Ptnr. Swanson, Boeye & Bloom, Red Oak, 1978—; asst. atty. Montgomery County, Red Oak, 1978-82, atty., 1982—. Republican. Roman Catholic. General practice, Real property, Personal injury. Home: Rt 4 Box 14 Red Oak IA 51566 Office: Swanson Boeye & Bloom Box 78 Red Oak IA 51566

SWANSON, RICHARD PAUL, lawyer; b. New Haven, June 22, 1955; s. Edward Stanley and Irene (Crowe) S.; m. Caryn Ruth Steinfeld, Aug. 3, 1980; 1 child, Douglas. BA summa cum laude, Wesleyan U., Middletown, Conn., 1977; JD cum laude, Harvard U., 1980. Bar: N.Y. 1981, U.S. Dist. Ct. (so. and ea. dists.) N.Y. 1981, U.S. Ct. Appeals. (2d cir.) 1984. Assoc. Milbank, Tweed, Hadley & McCloy, N.Y.C., 1980-83, Spengler Carlson Gubar Brodsky & Frischling, N.Y.C., 1983—. Co-author: The Expanded Liability of Accountants for Negligence, 1984. Mem. ABA, N.Y. State Bar Assn. (sec. fed. legis. com. 1984—), Assn. of Bar of City of N.Y., N.Y. County Lawyers Assn., Council N.Y. Law Assocs. Federal civil litigation, Securities, Antitrust. Office: Spengler Carlson Guber Brodsky & Frischling 280 Park Ave New York NY 10017

SWANSON, STEVEN RICHARD, law edcator; b. Brookings, S.D., Oct. 30, 1956; s. Charles Richard and Edith May (Nystul) S.; m. Carol Jean Beaumont, May 19, 1978. AB summa cum laude, Bowdoin Coll., 1978; JD, Vanderbilt U., 1981; LLM, Yale U., 1984. Bar: N.Y. 1982, U.S. Dist. Ct. (so. and ea. dists.) N.Y. 1982. Assoc. Milbank, Tweed, Hadley & McCloy, N.Y.C., 1981-83; asst. prof. law Hamline U., St. Paul, 1984-86, assoc. prof. law, 1986—. Mem. ABA, Order of Coif. Public international, Private international, Probate. Home: 5 Woodcrest Dr Circle Pines MN 55014 Office: Hamline U Sch Law 1536 Hewitt Ave Saint Paul MN 55104

SWANSON, WARREN LLOYD, lawyer; b. Chgo., Sept. 2, 1933; s. Martin W. and Esther Swanson; m. Rosalie Elaine Simpson, June 23, 1963; 1 son, Christopher; m. 2d, Kathryn Ann Jasperson, Oct. 16, 1979 (dec. Sept. 1986). B.A., U. Chgo., 1953; J.D., Northwestern U., 1957. Bar: Ill. 1957, U.S. Dist. Ct. (no. dist.) Ill, 1958, U.S. Ct. Appeals (7th cir.) 1959. Lectr., Northwestern U. Law Sch., 1958-59; ptnr. Stoffrls & Swanson, Chgo., 1959-63; spl. asst. states atty. Cook County, Ill., 1960-62; sole practice, Chgo., 1963-80; ptnr. Swanson, Ross & Block, Chgo., 1980-84, Swanson & Brown, Palos Heights, Ill., 1984—; city atty. Palos Heights, Ill., 1959—, co-counsel City of Park Ridge, 1957-63. Pres., Easter Seal Soc. Met. Chgo., 1970-74; mem. Chgo. Crime Commn., 1963—. Recipient John Howard Assn. Disting. Service award, 1961, 63. Mem. Chgo. Bar Assn., Ill. Bar Assn., ABA, Writers Guild Am. Clubs: Cliff Dwellers, Rotary. Head writer daytime serials As the World Turns, 1970-72, Somerset, 1973-75; co-writer daytime serials Another World, 1963-66, Love is a Many Splendored Thing, 1966-68, Edge of Night, 1968-70; author: Museums of Chicago, 1976, Recreation Guide to Chicago and Suburbs, 1980. Banking, Real property, Local government. Office: 12602 S Harlem Ave Palos Heights IL 60464 also: 20 W Wacker Dr Chicago IL 60602

SWARTWOUT, WILLIS BREWSTER, III, lawyer. s. Willis B. II and Evelyn B. (Keepman) S.; m. Sharon L. Steinke, Aug. 15, 1953; children: Cheryl, Craig, Scott, Brian. BS in Social Studies, U. Wis., 1954, LLB, 1958. Bar: U.S. Patent Office 1958, U.S. Dist. Ct. (ea. dist.) Wis. 1958, U.S. Supreme Ct. 1958, U.S. Ct. Appeals (7th cir.) 1979, U.S. Dist. Ct. (we. dist.) Wis. 1985. Assoc. Allis Chalmers, Milw., 1957-59, Wheeler, Wheeler & Wheeler, Milw., 1959-60, Hovey, Schmidt, Johnson & Hovey, Kansas City, Mo., 1960; gen. counsel Mortgage Assocs., Milw., 1961-65; gen. counsel,

pres. Cen. Mortgage, Milw., 1966-67; sole practice Milw., 1967-72; claims mgr., fraud investigator Mortgage Guarantee Ins., Milw., 1972-75; ptnr. Swartwout & Ryan, Brookfield, Wis., 1975—. Pasr patron Order of Eastern Star, Pewaukee chpt. Served to 1st lt. U.S. Army Mil. Police, 1956-64. Mem. Wis. Bar Assn., Waukesha County Bar Assn. Lodge: Masons (past grand master). Avocations: lapidary, golf, boating. Patent, Trademark and copyright, Family and matrimonial. Home: 617 Oxford Dr Hartland WI 53029 Office: Swartwout & Ryan SC 15850 W Bluemound Rd #220 PO Box 1068 Brookfield WI 53008-1068

SWARTZ, CHRISTIAN LEFEVRE, lawyer; b. Mechanicsburg, Pa., Aug. 14, 1915; s. Christian Ira and Anna Frances (LeFevre) S.; m. Jean Althan Vanderbilt, Nov. 30, 1946 (div. 1964); children—Christian Arthur, James Vanderbilt, B.S., U. Pa., 1937; LL.B., Temple U., 1946; LL.M., George Washington U., 1950. Bar: Pa. 1947, D.C. 1947, U.S. Dist. Ct. D.C. 1947, U.S. Supreme Ct. 1955, U.S. Ct. Claims 1959, U.S. Ct. Appeals (D.C. cir.) 1959, U.S. Ct. Customs and Patent Appeals 1963. Assoc. James W. Batchelor Law Office, Washington, 1947-50, Julia B. Hopkins Law Office, 1950-51; asst. counsel facilities br. Naval Air Systems Command, Office of Gen. Counsel, Dept. Navy, Washington, 1951-72; sole practice, Washington, 1972—. Exhibited woodcarving in numerous shows. Served to lt. USNR, 1941-46. Mem. Fed. Bar Assn., D.C. Bar Assn., Nat. Woodcarvers Assn., No. Va. Carvers Assn. Republican. Presbyterian. Clubs: Capitol Hill, Capital Yacht (Washington); Corinthian Yacht (Ridge, Md.). Government contracts and claims, General practice, Patent. Home: 1900 S Eads St Apt 908 Arlington VA 22202 Office: 2000 L St NW Suite 504 Washington DC 20036

SWARTZ, DEAN ELLIOT, lawyer; b. Hollywood, Calif., Sept. 20, 1949. AB, Stanford U., 1971; JD, U. Toledo, 1974. Bar: Ohio 1974, D.C. 1976, U.S. Tax Ct. 1978, U.S. Ct. Mil. Appeals 1978. Litigation atty. torts div. office judge adv. gen. USN, 1974-78; spl. asst. gen. counsel Occupational Safety and Health Rev. Commn., Washington, 1978-81; of counsel The Boccardo Law Firm, 1982-84; ptnr. Swartz & Reed, Washington, 1984—. Mem. ABA (torts and ins. practice sect.), Va. Bar Assn., D.C. Bar Assn., Assn. Trial Lawyers Am., Trial Lawyers Assn. Met. Washington, Order of Barristers. Federal civil litigation, State civil litigation, Personal injury. Office: Swartz & Reed 1232 17th St NW Washington DC 20036

SWARTZ, LEE CARTER, lawyer; b. Harrisburg, Pa., July 20, 1936. BS in Econs., Albright Coll., 1958; JD, Dickinson Sch. of Law, 1961. Bar: Pa. 1962, U.S. Dist. Ct. (mid. dist.) Pa. 1962, U.S. Ct. Appeals (2d cir.) 1965, U.S. Supreme Ct. 1966, U.S. Dist. Ct. (ea. dist.) Pa. 1969, U.S. Ct. Appeals (3d cir.) 1976. Assoc. H. Joseph Hepford Law Offices, Harrisburg, 1962-69; ptnr. Hepford, Zimmerman & Swartz, Harrisburg, 1970-80, Hepford, Swartz, Menaker & Wilt, Harrisburg, 1981-83, Hepford, Swartz, Menaker & Morgan, Harrisburg, 1983—; lectr. Dickinson Sch. of Law, Nat. Coll. Adv. Contbr. articles of profl. jours. Mem. Council for Human Services of Cumberland, Dauphi and Perry Counties; bd. dirs. Tri-County Mental Health Assn. and Child Guidance Ctr. Mem. ABA, Pa. Bar Assn. (ho. of dels. 1981—, chmn. civil litigation sect., various coms.), Dauphin Bar Assn. (pres. 1981, bd. dirs. 1970-82), Dauphin County Assn. Young Lawyers (pres. 1968), Assn. Trial Lawyers Am. (bd. govs. 1977-80, 85—, various coms.), Pa. Trial Lawyers Assn. (pres. 1977-78, various coms.), Pa. Bar Inst. (pres. 1976-77), Am. Judicature Soc., Pitts. Inst. Legal Medicine. Republican. Federal civil litigation, State civil litigation, Personal injury. Office: Hepford Swartz Menaker & Morgan 111 N Front St PO Box 889 Harrisburg PA 17108

SWARTZ, MELVIN JAY, lawyer, author; b. Boston, July 21, 1930; s. Jack M. and Rose (Rosenberg) S.; m. Beth Ames, Dec. 27, 1959 (div.); children: Julianne, Jonathan Samuel. B.A., Syracuse U., 1953; LL.D., Boston U., 1957. Bar: N.Y. 1959, Ariz. 1961. Assoc., Alfred S. Julian, N.Y.C., 1957-59; ptnr. Finks & Swartz, Youngtown, Sun City, Phoenix, Ariz., 1961-70, Swartz & Jeckel, P.C., Sun City, Youngtown, Scottsdale, Ariz., 1971-82; pres. Melvin Jay Swartz Retirement Seminar, The Strategic Learning Ctr., Scottsdale, Ariz. Bd. dirs. Valley of the Sun Sch. for Retarded Children, 1975-79. Mem. ABA, Ariz. Bar Assn., N.Y. Bar Assn., Maricopa County Bar Assn., Scottsdale Bar Assn., Central Ariz. Estate Planning Council. Jewish. Club: Masons (Phoenix). Author: Don't Die Broke, A Guide to Secure Retirement, 1974, 3d revised edit., 1985, Money in Your Pocket (How to Keep What You Own), 1987; columnist News-Sun, Sun City, 1979-83; author column Swartz on Aging. Probate, Estate taxation, Legal Problems of Aging. Office: 6623 N Scottsdale Rd Scottsdale AZ 85253

SWARTZBAUGH, MARC L., lawyer; b. Urbana, Ohio, Jan. 3, 1937; s. Merrill L. and Lillian K. (Hill) S.; m. Marjory Anne Emhardt, Aug. 16, 1958; children: Marc Charles, Kathleen Marie, Laura Kay. BA magna cum laude, Wittenberg Coll., 1958; LLB magna cum laude, U. Pa., 1961. Bar: Ohio 1961, U.S. Dist. Ct. (no. dist.) Ohio 1962, U.S. Ct. Appeals (6th cir.) 1970, U.S. Supreme Ct. 1973, U.S. Ct. Appeals (3d. cir.) 1985. Law clk. to judge U.S. Ct. Appeals (3d cir.), Phila., 1961-62; assoc. Jones, Day, Reavis & Pogue, Cleve., 1962-69, ptnr., 1970—. Note editor U. Pa. Law Rev., 1960-61. Co-chmn. Suburban Citizens for Open Housing, Shaker Heights, Ohio, 1966; v.p. Lomond Assn., Shaker Heights, Ohio, 1965-68; trustee The Dance Ctr., Cleve., 1980-83; ambassador People to People Internat., 1986. Mem. ABA (litigation sect.), Cleve. Bar Assn., Order of Coif, Beta Theta Pi. Democrat. Club: 13th St Racquet (Cleve.). Avocations: poetry, painting, music, skiing, squash. Federal civil litigation, State civil litigation. Office: Jones Day Reavis & Pogue North Point 901 Lakeside Ave Cleveland OH 44114

SWEEBE, RICHARD DALE, lawyer; b. Akron, Ohio, Aug. 13, 1951; s. Delbert Henry and Yvonne Rose (Gray) S. BA in Polit. Sci. cum laude, Kent State U., 1975; JD, U. Akron, 1979. Bar: Ohio 1979, U.S. Dist. Ct. (no. dist.) Ohio 1980, U.S. Ct. Appeals (6th cir.) 1980. Asst. prosecuter Summit County, Akron, 1979-82; assoc. Ulmer, Berne, Laronge, Glickman & Curtis, Cleve., 1982—; speaker ins. and law enforcement seminars, 1980—. Mem. planning com. Ohio Arson Sch., Columbus, 1985—. Served with U.S. Army, 1970-72. Recipient commendation Akron Fire Dept., 1981, Akron Police Dept., 1982, FBI, 1981, Ohio Arson Sch. and Internat. Assn. Arson Investigators, 1984-85. Mem. ABA, Ohio Bar Assn., Greater Cleve. Bar Assn., Akron Bar Assn., Soc. Profl. Ins. Investigators (com. 1985—, seminar chmn. 1984—). Democrat. Avocations: boating, snow skiing. Insurance, Federal civil litigation, State civil litigation. Office: Ulmer Berne Laronge Glickman & Curtis 900 Bond Ct Bldg Cleveland OH 44114

SWEENEY, ASHER WILLIAM, justice Supreme Court Ohio; b. Canfield, Ohio, Dec. 11, 1920; s. Walter William and Jessie Joan (Kidd) S.; m. Bertha M. Englert, May 21, 1945; children: Randall W., Ronald R., Garland A., Karen M. Student, Youngstown U., 1939-42; LL.B., Duke U., 1948. Bar: Ohio 1949. Practiced law Youngstown, Ohio, 1949-51; judge adv. gen. Dept. Def., Washington, 1951-65; chief Fed. Contracting Agy., Cin., 1965-68; corp. law 1968-77; justice Ohio Supreme Ct., Columbus, 1977—. Democratic candidate for Sec. of State Ohio, 1958. Served with U.S. Army, 1942-46; col. Res. 1951-68. Decorated Legion of Merit, Bronze Star; named to Army Hall of Fame Ft. Benning, Ga., 1981. Mem. Ohio Bar Assn., Phi Delta Phi. Democrat. Jurisprudence. Home: 6690 Drake Rd Cincinnati OH 45243 Office: 30 E Broad Columbus OH 43215

SWEENEY, DEIDRE ANN, lawyer; b. Hackensack, N.J., Mar. 17, 1953; d. Thomas Joseph and Robin (Thwaites) S. AB cum laude, Mt. Holyoke Coll., 1975; JD, Fordham U., 1978. Assoc. Curtis, Mallet-Prevost, Colt & Mosle, N.Y.C., 1978-84, Eaton & Van Winkle, N.Y.C., 1984-86; ptnr. Jacobs, Persinger & Parker, N.Y.C., 1986—; adj. instr. Adelphi U., N.Y.C., 1982—. Class agt. Mt. Holyoke Coll. Alumni Fund, South Hadley, Mass., 1975-80. Mem. Assn. of Bar of City of N.Y. (uniform state laws com. 1982-85). Democrat. Roman Catholic. Club: Mt. Holyoke N.Y. (asst. treas. 1982-85). Probate, Estate planning, Estate taxation. Office: Jacobs Persinger & Parker 70 Pine St New York NY 10270

SWEENEY, EILEEN CECILIA, lawyer; b. Balt., May 16, 1952; d. John J. Jr. and Mary Rosewin (Tewey) S.; m. Kirby C. Smith, Apr. 21, 1979. BA, Georgetown U., 1974; JD, U. Balt., 1977. Bar: Md. 1977, U.S. Dist. Ct. Md. 1978.,. Law clk. to presiding justice Md. Ct. Appeals, 1977-78; assoc. Whiteford, Taylor, Preston, Trimble & Johnston, Balt., 1978-84; mem. O'Conor & Sweeney, Balt., 1984-86. Recent legis. and articles editor U. Balt. Law Rev., 1976-77. Vol. Long Green Nursing Home, Balt., 1980; speaker Pre-Cana Program St. Marys of Assumption, Balt., 1983—; mem. Lawyers' Alliance for Nuclear Arms Control, Balt., 1984—, Balt. City Commn. on Women, 1986, co-chmn. child task force, 1986, sec., 1987—. Mem. Md. Bar Assn., Balt. Bar Assn., Women's Bar Assn. (bd. dirs. 1986—), St. Thomas More Soc. (bd. dirs. 1986—). Democrat. Roman Catholic. State civil litigation, Federal civil litigation, General practice. Office: O'Conor & Sweeney 1513 Fidelity Bldg Baltimore MD 21212

SWEENEY, GERALD BINGHAM, lawyer; b. Waterbury, Conn., July 4, 1946; s. James W. and Aletha E. (Bingham) S.; m. Carolyn S. Chin, Sept. 18, 1976; 1 child, Patricia M. Chin-Sweeney. BS in Engring., Rensselaer Poly. Inst., 1968; JD, Columbia U., 1971. Bar: N.Y. 1972, N.J. 1976, Calif. 1986, U.S. Dist. Ct. (so. dist.) N.Y. 1973, U.S. Dist. Ct. N.J. 1976, U.S. Dist. Ct. (no. dist.) Calif. 1986. Assoc. Owen and Turchin, N.Y.C., 1971-74; atty. Avon Products, Inc., N.Y.C., 1974-76; sr. counsel Revlon, Inc., N.Y.C., 1976-81, regulatory counsel, 1981-83, v.p., div. counsel, 1983—. Exec. v.p. N.J. Common Cause, Trenton, N.J., 1983; trustee Hosp. Ctr. at Orange, N.J., 1986—. Named one of Outstanding Young Men Am., 1976. Mem. ABA, N.Y. Bar Assn., N.J. Bar Assn., Calif. Bar Assn. Administrative and regulatory, Contracts commercial, General practice. Home: Oak Bend Llewellyn Pk West Orange NJ 07052 Office: Revlon Inc 2147 Route 27 Edison NJ 08818

SWEENEY, GREGORY LOUIS, lawyer; b. Fairborn, Ohio, Aug. 20, 1945; s. Henry Morrow and Marie Anna (Boisfontaine) S.; m. Sarah Ann Jarrell, Mar. 29, 1969; children: Jason N., Jeffrey M., Colin J. BA, U. Tex., 1967; JD, U. Houston, 1970. Bar: Tex. 1970, U.S. Supreme Ct. 1973, Okla. 1975. Staff atty. Cities Service Co., Tulsa and Houston, 1974-77; internat. counsel The Coastal Corp., Houston, 1977-79; sr. counsel, asst. sec. Damson Oil Corp., Houston, 1979-80; gen. acquisitions atty. Tenneco Oil Co., Houston, 1980-81; div. counsel GHR Energy Corp., Houston, 1981-82; of counsel Barnhart, Mallia, Cochran & Luther, Houston, 1982-84; ptnr. Solomon, Foley, Sweeney & Moran, Houston, Detroit and Washington, 1984-86, Pinedo, Cezeaux & Sweeney, Houston, 1986—; comml. arbitrator Am. Arbitration Assn. Pres. Houston Assn. for Big Bros. and Big Sisters, Inc., 1981. Served to maj. USAF, 1970-74. Recipient Dean's Award U. Houston Law Ctr., 1981. Mem. Okla. Bar Assn., ABA, Houston Bar Assn. (chmn. corp. counsel 1981), U. Houston Law Alumni Assn. (v.p. 1979), Kappa Alpha, Phi Delta Phi. Republican. Roman Catholic. Club: Junipero Serra. Lodges: Rotary, Ancient Order of Hibernians. Federal civil litigation, Securities, State civil litigation. Office: Pinedo Cezeaux & Sweeney 1200 Smith St #1600 Houston TX 77002

SWEENEY, JOHN FRANCIS, lawyer; b. Washington, Nov. 26, 1946; s. Albert Eugene and Mildred (Mattimore) S.; m. Noreen Marie Castelli, Aug. 9, 1969; children—Matthew John, Laura Marie. B.S. in Math,. Carnegie-Mellon U., 1968; J.D., Georgetown U., 1973. Bar: N.Y. 1974, U.S. Supreme Ct. 1980, U.C. Ct. Appeals (Fed. cir.) 1982, U.S. Ct. Appeals (2d cir.) 1975, U.S. Ct. Appeals (3d cir.) 1981, U.S. Dist. Ct. (so. dist.) N.Y. 1975, U.S. Dist. Ct. (ea. dist.) N.Y. 1984. Mathematician, U.S. Army Strategy and Tactics Analysis Group, Bethesda, Md., 1968-70; computer analyst U.S. Army Computer Systems Support and Evaln Command, Arlington, Va., 1970-73; assoc. Morgan & Finnegan and predecessor firm Morgan Finnegan Pine Foley & Lee, N.Y.C., 1973-81, ptnr., 1981—, mem. exec. com. 1983—. Author: (poems) Rhymes, 1984. Mem. Assn. Bar City N.Y. (mem. patent com. 1983—), N.Y. Patent, Trademark and Copyright Law Assn., ABA. Democrat. Roman Catholic. Club: Head of the Bay (Huntington Bay, N.Y.). Patent, Trademark and copyright, Federal civil litigation. Home: Tulipwood Lloyd Ln Lloyd Neck NY 11743 Office: Morgan & Finnegan 345 Park Ave New York NY 10154

SWEENEY, KEVIN MICHAEL, lawyer; b. Washington, Nov. 20, 1956; s. Timothy Dennis and Naomi (Rosen) S.; m. Joanne Cranney, June 28, 1986. BA, Coll. of William and Mary, 1978; JD, George Washington U., 1981. Bar: D.C. 1982, U.S. Ct. Appeals (D.C., 3d and 5th cirs.) 1982, U.S. Ct. Appeals (7th cir.) 1984, U.S. Ct. Appeals (4th, 10th and 11th cirs.) 1986. Assoc. Grove, Jaskiewicz, Gilliam & Cobert, Washington, 1981—. Polit. action dir. Arlington (Va.) Young Dems., 1984-86, treas. 1986—; task force mem. Commn. on Arlingtons Future, 1986. Mem. ABA, Fed. Energy Bar Assn. FERC practice, Administrative and regulatory. Home: 800 N Garfield St Arlington VA 22201 Office: Grove Jaskiewicz et al 1730 M St NW Washington DC 20036

SWEENEY, NEAL JAMES, lawyer; b. Patterson, N.J., Nov. 1, 1957; s. Bernard Thomas and Mary Agnes (Kenneally) S.; m. Mary Elizabeth Finocchiaro, Oct. 27, 1984; 1 child, Daniel Fulton. BA in History and Polit Sci., Rutgers U., 1979; JD, George Wash. U., 1982. Bar: Ga. 1982, U.S. Dist. Ct. (no. dist.) Ga. 1982, U.S. Dist. Ct. (no. dist.) Tex. 1982, U.S. Claims Ct. 1984, U.S. Ct. Appeals (5th cir.) 1987. Assoc. Smith, Currie & Hancock, Atlanta, 1982—. Co-author: Construction Business Handbook, 1985, Holding Subcontractors to Their Bids, 1986, Subcontractor Default, 1987. Mem. ABA (pub. contract law sect., forum com. on constrn. industry), Atlanta Bar Assn., Am. Arbitration Assn. (panel of arbitrators). Construction, Government contracts and claims, Federal civil litigation. Home: 223 Clarion Ave Decatur GA 30030 Office: Smith Currie & Hancock 2600 Harris Tower 233 Peachtree St Ne Atlanta GA 30043

SWEENEY, ROBERT JOHN, lawyer; b. Glendale, N.Y., Mar. 5, 1918; s. John P. and Claire M. (Evers) S.; m. Martha A. Sweeney, Oct. 31, 1942; children—Robert, Martha Sweeney Green. B.B.A., Pace Coll., 1950; LL.B., St. John's U., 1956. Bar: N.Y. 1957, U.S. Dist. Ct. (so. dist.) N.Y. 1959, U.S. Supreme Ct. 1960, U.S. Dist. Ct. (ea. dist.) N.Y. 1973. Mayor, Village of Freeport (N.Y.), 1961-73, spl. counsel 1973—; sole practice, Freeport, 1956—; dep. atty. County of Nassau, 1973-76, sr. dep. atty., 1976-77, chief dep. exec., 1977-78. Mem. Gov.'s Electric Power Com., 1966-67. Served to capt. U.S. Army, 1940-46; 51-52. Mem. Nassau County Bar Assn., Mcpl. Electric Utilities Assn. (pres. 1966-67), Nassau County Village Ofcls. Assn. (pres. 1967-68). Republican. Roman Catholic. State civil litigation, Personal injury, General practice.

SWEENEY, WILLIAM JONES, JR., lawyer; b. New Britain, Conn., Nov. 5, 1947; s. William J. and Katharine Agnes (Kenney) S.; m. Christine Breslin, June 12, 1981; 1 child, Liam Breslin. AB, Fairfield U., 1969; JD, Suffolk U., 1974. Bar: Conn. 1975, U.S. Dist. Ct. Conn. 1975, U.S. Ct. Appeals (2d cir.) 1975, U.S. Supreme Ct. 1983. Ptnr. Webb, Sweeney, Clebowicz & Griffen, New Britain, 1975—; trial referee State of Conn., 1985—. Corporator New Britain Gen. Hosp., 1980—, New Britain YMCA, 1984—, New Britain Boys Club, 1986—; bd. dirs. United Community Services, New Britain, 1981—. Mem. ABA, Conn. Bar Assn. (ho. of dels. 1984—), Hartford County Bar Assn., New Britain Bar Assn. (pres. civil justice sect. 1983-84), Assn. Trial Lawyers Am., Conn. Trial Lawyers Assn., Nat. Assn. Criminal Def. Lawyers. State civil litigation, Criminal, Personal injury. Home: 7 Foxcroft Rd West Hartford CT 06119 Office: Webb Sweeney Clebowicz & Griffin 233 Main St New Britain CT 06051

SWEENY, PETER MICHAEL, lawyer; b. Boston, Aug. 17, 1947; s. John Sweeny and Marguerite Veronica (Caulfield) Shine; m. Sousan Fakhry Omana, Dec. 18, 1981; children—Kaitlin Anne, Lauren Elizabeth. B.A., Georgetown U., 1971; J.D., Seton Hall U., 1974. Bar: Va. 1976, U.S. Dist. Ct. (ea. dist.) Va. 1977, U.S. Ct. Appeals (4th cir.) 1977, D.C. 1978, U.S. Dist. Ct. D.C. 1978, U.S. Ct. Appeals (D.C. cir.) 1978, U.S. Supreme Ct. 1979. Staff atty. Occupational Safety and Health Rev. Commn., Washington, 1974-76; assoc. Ashcraft & Gerel, Alexandria Va. and Washington, D.C., 1977-84, ptnr., 1985-86; ptnr. Thacher, Swiger, Sweeny & Day, Fairfax, Va., 1986—. Mem. ABA, Va. State Bar, Alexandria Bar Assn., Assn. Trial Lawyers Am., Ct. Practice Inst. (diplomate). Democrat. Mem. Ch. of Jesus Christ of Latter-day Saints. Personal injury, Workers' compensation, State civil litigation. Home: 8531 Monticello Ave Alexandria VA 22308 Office: Thacher Swiger Sweeny & Day 3975 University Dr Suite 450 Fairfax VA 22030

SWEET, JOSEPH CHURCH, JR., lawyer, historian; b. Winsted, Conn., Aug. 27, 1918; s. Joseph Church and Grace Garland (Grey) S.; m. Jane Helen Goodman, Sept. 27, 1958; children—Grace Elizabeth, Pamela Jane. B.E., Yale U., 1940, LL.B., 1943. Bar: Conn. 1943, N.Y. 1947, U.S. Dist. Ct. (so. dist. N.Y.) 1948, U.S. Ct. Appeals (2d cir.) 1948, U.S. Dist. Ct. (ea. dist.) N.Y. 1949, U.S. Supreme Ct. 1961, U.S. Ct. Appeals (fed. cir.) 1978. Instr. Yale U., New Haven, 1940; elec. cost engr. United Illuminating Co., New Haven, 1941-43; assoc. Kenyon & Kenyon, N.Y.C., 1946-51; lawyer IBM, N.Y.C. and Armonk, N.Y., 1951—; spl. dep. atty. gen. N.Y. Dept. Law, N.Y.C., 1956-65. Contbr. columns to newspaper and music mag. Vice pres., bd. govs. New Canaan Hist. Soc., 1967—; mem. New Canaan Town Bd., 1970—. Served to lt. USN, 1943-46. Mem. Conn. Bar Assn., N.Y. State Bar Assn., N.Y. Patent Law Assn., Litchfield County Bar Assn., Yale Engring. Assn., Tau Beta Pi. Republican. Episcopalian. Clubs: New Canaan Field, Gridiron, Poinsetta (New Canaan). Antitrust, Patent, Contracts commercial. Home: 45 Wee Burn Dr New Canaan CT 06840 Office: IBM Old Orchard Rd Armonk NY 10504

SWEET, JUSTIN, legal educator, lawyer; b. 1929. B.A., 1951; LL.B., U. Wis., 1953. Bar: Wis. 1953, Calif. 1960. Atty. State Atty. Gen., Madison, Wis., 1953-54; atty., Milw., 1957-58; assoc. prof., 1958-63; prof. U. Calif. Law Sch.-Berkeley, 1963—; Fulbright lectr. U. Rome, 1965-66; vis. prof. Hebrew U., Jerusalem, 1970; vis. prof. U. Leuven (Belgium), 1973-74; vis. prof. Osgoode Hall, 1977; with U. Calif. Hastings Sch. Law, summers 1974-78; on leave at Hebrew U. and U. Tel Aviv, 1980-81. Served to 1st lt. JAGC, U.S. Army, 1954-57. Mem. Order of Coif, Phi Beta Kappa. Author: Role of the State Social Welfare Board in the Administration of ANC Program in California, 1961; Legal Aspects of Architecture, Engineering and the Construction Process, 1970, 77; former note editor Wis. Law Rev. Legal education. Office: U Calif Sch Law 225 Boalt Hall Berkeley CA 94720 *

SWEET, LOWELL ELWIN, lawyer; b. Flint, Mich., Aug. 10, 1931; s. Leslie E. and Donna Mabel (Latta) S.; m. Mary Ellen Ebben, Aug. 29, 1953; children—Lawrence Edward, Diane Marie, Sara Anne. B.A. in Psychology, Wayne State U., 1953, LL.B., U. Wis., 1955. Bar: Wis. 1955, U.S. dist. ct. (ea. dist) Wis. 1955, U.S. dist. ct. (no. dist.) Ill. 1958. Ptnr., Morrissy, Morrissy, Sweet & Race and predecessors, Elkhorn, Wis., 1957-70; sr. ptnr. Sweet & Leece, and predecessor, Elkhorn, 1970—. Instr. gen. practice sect. U. Wis. Law Sch. 1978, 79, 86; lectr. real estate law Wis. Bar, Gateway Tech. Inst., 1974—; dir. Citizens State Bank, Genoa City, Wis. Mem. Walworth County Republican Com.; sect. Wis. Joint Survey Commn. on Debt Mgmt. Served with CIC, U.S. Army, 1955-57. Named Outstanding Young Man, Elkhorn Jaycees, 1966; recipient citation for service in drafting Wis. Condominium Law, Wis. Legislature, 1978. Mem. ABA, Wis. Bar Assn. (gov. 1972-75), Walworth County Bar Assn., Am. Judicature Soc., Assn. Trial Lawyers Am., Am. Coll. Real Estate Lawyers. Roman Catholic. Clubs: Kiwanis, Lions, Moose, KC. Co-author, co-editor: Condominium Law Handbook, 1981. Real property, Probate, General corporate. Home: 411 W Marshall St Elkhorn WI 53121 Office: Sweet & Leece 114 N Church Elkhorn WI 53121

SWEET, ROBERT WORKMAN, dist. judge; b. Yonkers, N.Y., Oct. 15, 1922; s. James Allen and Delia (Workman) S.; m. Adele Hall, May 12, 1973; children by previous marriage—Robert, Deborah, Ames, Eliza. B.A., Yale U., 1944, LL.B., 1948. Bar: N.Y. State bar 1949. Asso. firm Simpson, Thacher & Bartlett, 1948-53; asst. U.S. atty. So. Dist. N.Y., 1953-55; asso. firm Casey, Lane & Mittendorf, 1955-65, partner, 1957-65; counsel Interdepartmental Task Force on Youth and Juvenile Delinquency, 1958-78; dep. mayor City of N.Y., 1966-69; partner firm Skadden, Arps, Slate, Meagher & Flom, N.Y.C., 1970-77; mem. hearing office N.Y.C. Transit Authority, 1975-77; U.S. dist. judge So. Dist. N.Y., N.Y.C., 1978—. Pres. Community Service Soc., 1961-78; trustee Sch. Mgmt. Urban Policy, 1970—, Taft Sch.; vestryman St. Georges Epis. Ch., 1958-63. Served to lt. (j.g.) USNR, 1943-46. Recipient various awards, citations for service as dept mayor N.Y.C. Mem. Assn. Bar of City of N.Y., N.Y. Law Inst., N.Y. County Lawyers Assn., Am. Bar Assn., N.Y. State Bar Assn., Am. Legion (comdr. Willard Straight Post). Clubs: Quaker Hill Country, Century Assn, Merchants. Jurisprudence. Office: US Dist Ct US Courthouse 2601 Foley Sq New York NY 10007

SWEITZER, HARRY AVERIL, lawyer; b. Madison, Wis., Aug. 30, 1943; s. Harry Averil and Eleanore Grace (Halvorson) S. B.A., St. Olaf Coll., Northfield, Minn., 1965; J.D., So. Methodist U., 1968. Bar: Tex. 1968, U.S. Dist. Ct. (no. dist.) Tex. 1970, U.S. Supreme Ct. 1971, U.S. Dist. Ct. (we. dist.) Wis. 1979, U.S. Ct. Appeals (5th cir.) 1979, U.S. Ct. Appeals (11th cir.) 1982. Sole practice, 1968-77; gen. counsel, v.p. Cert. Optical Labs. Inc. Brucks Pharm., Inc., 1977-78; sr. ptnr. Sweitzer, Attys., Dallas, 1979—; pres. Tex. Advt. Lawyers League, 1982—; lectr. Tex. Family Law Seminar, Belize, 1983. Mem. Citizen for Rep. Govt., 1971—, pres., 1971-73; gen. counsel Tex. Young Republicans Fedn., 1977-78. Mem. Tex. Bar Assn., Dallas Bar Assn. Lutheran. Club: Mason. Polit. columnist East Dallas Banner Newspaper, 1976-78. Family and matrimonial. Office: Sweitzer Attys 4308 N Central Expressway Suite 105 Dallas TX 75206

SWENDIMAN, ALAN ROBERT, lawyer; b. Arlington, Va., Apr. 5, 1947; s. Robert Charles and Jessie (Birse) S.; m. Kathleen Shea, Oct. 8, 1977; children: Shelley Christine, Robert Alan. A.B. in Polit. Sci., U. N.C., 1969; J.D., Georgetown U., 1973. Bar: Md. 1973, D.C. 1974, U.S. Dist. Ct. D.C. 1974, U.S. Dist. Ct. Md. 1974, U.S. Ct. Appeals (D.C. cir.) 1974, U.S. Ct. Appeals (4th cir.) 1974, U.S. Supreme Ct. 1980. Law clk. to chief judge U.S. Dist. Ct. Md., 1973-74; ptnr. Jackson & Campbell, Washington, 1974—; mem. Edn. Appeal Bd., Dept. Edn., 1982—; gen. counsel Legal Services Corp., Washington, 1983-84. Election judge Montgomery County Bd. Elections, 1978-82; precinct chmn. Montgomery County Rep. party, 1981-83; active Md. Reagan-Bush campaign, 1984, dep. site coordinator inaugural, 1985; elder United Presbyn. Ch., Kensington, Md., 1982-84; counselor Boy Scouts Am., Kensington; bd. of govs. Goodwill Industries; bd. of advisors Columbia Lighthouse for the Blind. Mem. ABA, Am. Judicature Soc., D.C. Bar Assn., Md. Bar Assn., Montgomery County Bar Assn., Jud. Conf. D.C. Circuit, Greater Washington Soc. Assn. Execs., U. N.C. Alumni Assn., Phi Beta Kappa, Phi Eta Sigma. Clubs: Barristers, St. Andrews Soc. (Washington). Lodge: Rotary (Washington). General corporate, Administrative and regulatory, Probate. Office: Jackson & Campbell PC 1120 20th St NW Suite 300S Washington DC 20036

SWENSEN, JAN CLOVIS, lawyer; b. Pitts., July 16, 1937; s. Clifford Henry and Edith Cora (Clovis) S.; m. Sonja Ramona Gohn; children: Erik David, Andrew Jon. BS, U. Pitts., 1959; postgrad., Dickinson Sch. Law, 1959-60; JD, U. Pitts., 1962. Bar: Pa. 1963, U.S. Dist. Ct. (we. dist.) Pa. 1963, U.S. Ct. Appeals (D.C. cir.) 1965, U.S. Supreme Ct. 1974, U.S. Ct. Appeals (3d cir.) 1982. Assoc. Brandt, Riester, Brandt & Malone, Pitts., 1965-67; ptnr. Scott, Swensen and Scott, Pitts., 1967-80, Swensen & Perer, Pitts., 1980—. Bd. dirs. Edgewood (Pa.) Sch. Dist., 1978-84; pres. Edgewood Sch. Dist. Bd. Sch. Dirs., 1983-84; bd. dirs. Edgewood Found., 1984—; v.p. Woodland Hills Sch. Dist. Bd. Sch. Dirs., Pitts., 1984. Mem. ABA, Pa. Bar Assn., Allegheny County Bar Assn., Pa. Def. Inst., Pitts. Athletic Assn. Republican. Clubs: Edgewood (pres. 1985—); Edgewood Country (Churchill, Pa.). Avocations: tennis, golf, skiing, community service. State civil litigation, Federal civil litigation, Personal injury. Home: 421 Locust St Pittsburgh PA 15218 Office: 428 Forbes Ave Pittsburgh PA 15219

SWERDLOFF, DAVID ALAN, lawyer; b. Buffalo, Sept. 19, 1948; s. John and Joan (Harris) S.; m. Shelley Ann Taylor, Oct. 6, 1974; children: Joan Taylor, Laura Taylor, Carolyn Taylor. AB, Brown U., 1970; MS, Northwestern U., 1974; JD, U. Conn., 1979. Bar: Conn. 1979, U.S. Dist. Ct. Conn. 1981. Assoc. Day, Berry & Howard, Hartford, Conn., 1979-83; assoc. Day, Berry & Howard, Stamford, Conn., 1983-86, ptnr., 1986—; sec., bd. dirs. Teen Life Ctr. Inc., Stamford, 1984—. Mem. ABA, Conn. Bar Assn., Stamford-Darien Bar Assn. General corporate, Contracts commercial. Home: 87 Alexandra Dr Stamford CT 06903 Office: Day Berry & Howard 3 Landmark Sq Stamford CT 06901

SWHIER, ROBERT DEWAIN, JR., lawyer; b. Portland, Ind., Sept. 17, 1949; s. Robert Dewain and Sammie (Boyd) S.; m. Claudia Versfelt, June 5, 1974; children: James Robert, Jeffrey William. BS in Econs. with honors and highest distinction, Purdue U., 1971; MS, London Sch. Econs., 1972; JD magna cum laude, Harvard U., 1975. Bar: Ind. 1975, U.S. Dist. Ct. (so. dist.) Ind. 1975, U.S. Ct. Appeals (7th cir.) 1979. Assoc. Baker & Daniels, Indpls., 1975-82, ptnr., 1982—. Mem. Ind. com. Harvard U. Law Sch.

Fund; asst. chmn. ward Marion County Reps., Ind.; del. Rep. State Conv., 1984, 86. Mem. ABA, 7th cir. Bar Assn., Ind. Bar Assn., Indpls. Bar Assn., Nat. Assn. Bond Lawyers, Pike Twp. Rep. Club (pres. 1986—). Phi Beta Kappa, Beta Gamma Sigma. Methodist. Lodge: Rotary (fellow). Avocation: tennis. Securities, Municipal bonds, General corporate. Home: 7216 Chablis Ct Indianapolis IN 46278 Office: Baker & Daniels 810 Fletcher Trust Bldg Indianapolis IN 46204

SWIFT, AUBREY EARL, lawyer, petroleum engineer; b. Tulsa, Sept. 21, 1933; s. Virgil and Edith (Jackson) S.; m. Modell Paulding, Oct. 5, 1951 (div.); children—Terry Earl, Vannessa Suzanne; m. Glenda Kay Arnce, Apr. 8, 1978 (div.); 1 son, Nickolas Gorman. B.S. in Petroleum Engring., U. Okla., 1955; J.D., S. Tex. Coll. Law, 1968. Bar: Tex. 1968, U.S. Supreme Ct. 1977. Petroleum engr. Humble Oil Co. div. Exxon, Houston, 1955-62; v.p. Mich.-Wis. Pipe Line, Houston, 1962-79, Am. Natural Gas Prodn., Houston, 1962-79; pres., chmn., chief exec. officer Swift Energy Co., Houston, 1979—; dir. Inter First Bank Greenspoint, Houston; cons. Northwest Ala. Gas Dist., Hamilton, 1979—. Served to 1st lt. U.S. Army, 1956-57. Mem. Tex. Soc. Profl. Engrs., Soc. Petroleum Engrs. AIME, Order of Lytae, Tau Beta Pi. Presbyterian. General corporate, Oil and gas leasing.

SWIFT, EVANGELINE WILSON, lawyer; b. San Antonio, May 2, 1939; d. Raymond E. and Josephine (Woods) Wilson; 1 son, Justin Lee. Student So. Meth. U., 1956-59; LL.B., St. Mary's U., San Antonio, 1963. Bar: Tex. 1963, U.S. Ct. Appeals (5th cir.) 1972, D.C. 1976, U.S. Dist. Ct. D.C. 1976, U.S. Supreme Ct. 1980, U.S. Ct. Appeals (11th cir.) 1981, U.S. Ct. Appeals (10th cir.) 1982, U.S. Ct. Appeals (D.C. cir.) 1982, U.S. Ct. Appeals (fed. cir.) 1983. Atty.-adv. ICC, Washington, 1964-65; staff atty. Headstart Program, OEO, Washington, 1965; exec. legal asst. to chmn., spl. asst. to vice chmn. EEOC, Washington, 1965-71, chief decisions div., 1971-75, asst. gen. counsel, 1975-76; cons. to sec. Employment Standards Adminstrn., Dept. Labor, Washington, 1977-79; ptnr. Swift & Swift, P.C., Washington, 1977-79; gen. counsel Merit Systems Protection Bd., Washington, 1979-86, mng. dir., 1986—; chmn. jud. conf. Merit Systems Protection Bd. U.S. Ct. Appeals (fed. cir.) 1983—, bd. govs., 1984—. guest lectr. Drake U., U. Pa., MIT; mem. U.S. del. 3d Sessions UN Econ. and Social council Commn. on Status of Women, Geneva, 1970. Recipient Meritorious Service award Fed. Govt., 1967, Fed. Women's award, 1975; Performance award Merit Systems Protection Bd., 1981-86, Gold award 1986; Presdl. CFC award, 1984, EEO award Merit Systems Protection Bd., 1985. Methodist. Administrative and regulatory. Office: Merit System Protection Bd Office of the Chmn 1120 Vermont Ave NW Washington DC 20419

SWIFT, JOHN GOULDING, lawyer; b. Lake Charles, La., Nov. 12, 1955; s. Goulding William Jr. and Betty Jane (Richardson) S. BS, La. State U., 1977, JD, 1980. Bar: La. 1980, U.S. Dist. Ct. (we. dist.) La. 1982, U.S. Ct. Appeals (5th cir.) 1983, U.S. Dist. Ct. (mid. dist.) La. 1985, U.S. Dist. Ct. (ea. dist.) Tex. 1986, U.S. Dist. Ct. (ea. dist.) La. 1986. Law clk. to presiding justice U.S. Dist. Ct. (we. dist.) La., Lake Charles, 1980-81; assoc. Davidson, Meaux, Sonnier & McElligott, Lafayette, La., 1981-85, ptnr., 1985—. Mem. Gulf Coast Conservation Assn., Houston, 1985-86. Mem. ABA, La. Trial Lawyers Assn., La. Def. Counsel, Am. Judicature Soc. Democrat. Methodist. Avocations: tennis, skiing, scuba, fishing, hunting. Personal injury, Insurance, Admiralty. Home: Hidden Hills Community Rt 3 Lot 104 Arnaudville LA 70512 Office: Davidson Meaux Sonnier & McElligott 810 S Buchanan PO Box 2908 Lafayette LA 70502

SWIFT, STEPHEN JENSEN, judge; b. Salt Lake City, Sept. 7, 1943; s. Edward A. and Maurine (Jensen) S.; m. Lorraine Burnell Facer, Aug. 4, 1972; children: Carter, Stephanie, Spencer, Meredith, Hunter. BA, Brigham Young U., 1967; JD, George Washington U., 1970. Trial atty. U.S. Dept. Justice, Washington, D.C., 1970-74; asst. U.S. atty. U.S. Atty.'s Office, San Francisco, 1974-77; v.p., sr. tax counsel Bank Am. Corp., San Francisco, 1977-83; judge U.S. Tax Ct., Washington, 1983—; adj. prof. Golden Gate U., San Francisco, 1978-83. Mem. ABA, Calif. Bar Assn., D.C. Bar Assn. Corporate taxation, Federal civil litigation. Office: US Tax Court 400 2d St NW Washington DC 20217

SWIFT, THEODORE WELLS, lawyer; b. Battle Creek, Mich., June 8, 1928; s. Leland Miller and Frances (Brewer) S.; m. Anne Gilbert, Aug. 22, 1953; children—Timothy W., Sarah F., Thomas W. B.A., DePauw U., 1950; J.D., U. Mich., 1955. Assoc., Foster, Swift, Collins & Coey, P.C., Lansing, Mich., 1955; ptnr., 1957—; vis. prof. Thomas M. Cooley Law Sch., Lansing, 1980-81. Chmn., Mich. State Bd. Ethics, 1974-80. Served to capt. USMCR, 1952-55. Named Outstanding Young Man of Year, Lansing Jr. C. of C., 1962, Boss of Year, Lansing Legal Secs. Assn., 1979. Fellow Am. Bar Found.; mem. ABA, State Bar of Mich. (chmn. ethics com. 1972-74), Ingham County Bar Assn. (pres. 1980-81), Am. Arbitration Assn. Republican. Episcopalian. Clubs: Automobile, Rotary (pres. 1974-75); University (East Lansing). Administrative and regulatory, Labor, Health. Address: 313 S Washington Ave Lansing MI 48933

SWIGER, MICHAEL ANDRE, lawyer; b. Hawthorne, Nev., June 24, 1955; s. L.A. and Mary Belle (Kinney) S.; m. Suzzanne Haywood, June 13, 1981; 1 child, Adam. AB in Polit Sci., Kenyon Coll., 1977; MA in Polit. Sci., MPhil. in Polit. Sci., Yale U., 1982, JD, 1982. Bar: D.C. 1982. Assoc. Shaw, Pittman, Potts and Trowbridge, Washington, 1982-85, Van Ness, Feldman, Sutcliffe and Curtis, Washington, 1986—. Pres. Valleigh Homeowners Assn. Inc., Alexandria, Va., 1985—. Mem. ABA. Administrative and regulatory, FERC practice, Nuclear power. Home: 6206 Little Valley Way Alexandria VA 22310 Office: Van Ness et al 1050 Thomas Jefferson St NW Washington DC 20007

SWIGERT, JAMES MACK, lawyer; b. Carthage, Ill., Sept. 25, 1907; s. James Ross and Pearl (Mack) S.; m. Alice Francis Titcomb Harrower, July 7, 1931; children: Oliver, David Ladd, Sally Harper (Mrs. Hamilton). Student, Grinnell Coll., 1925-27; S.B., Harvard U., 1930, LL.B., 1935. Bar: Ill. 1935, Ohio 1937. With Campbell, Clithero & Fischer, Chgo., 1935-36, Taft, Stettinius & Hollister, Cin., 1936—; ptnr. Taft, Stettinius & Hollister, 1948-79, sr. ptnr. and chmn. exec. com., 1979-85, of counsel, 1985—; dir., mem. exec. com. Union Cen. Life Ins. Co., 1963-79; dir., chmn. audit com. Philips Industries, 1975-82. Author articles labor relations labor law. Past bd. dirs. Cin. Symphony Orch., 1976-78. Republican. Presbyterian. Clubs: Queen City (past dir.), Cincinnati Country (past v.p., dir.), Queen City Optimists, Tennis (past pres.), Recess (past pres.), Harvard Law (past pres.) (Cin.). Labor. Home: 196 Green Hills Rd Cincinnati OH 45208 Office: 1800 1st Nat Bank Cent Cincinnati OH 45202

SWIHART, FRED JACOB, lawyer; b. Park Rapids, Minn., Aug. 19, 1919; s. Fred and Elizabeth Pauline (Judnitsch) S.; m. Edna Lillian Jensen, Sept. 30, 1950; 1 child; Frederick Jay. BA, U. Nebr., 1949, JD, 1954; M in Russian Lang., Middlebury Coll., 1950; grad., U.S. Army Command and Staff Coll., 1965. Bar: Nebr. 1954, U.S. Dist. Ct. Nebr. 1954, U.S. Ct. Appeals (8th cir.) 1977, U.S. Supreme Ct. 1972. Claims atty. Chgo. & Eastern Ill. R.R., 1954-56; atty. Assn. Amer. R.R.s, Chgo., 1956-60; assoc. Wagener & Marx, Lincoln, Nebr., 1960-61; prosecutor City of Lincoln, 1961-68; sole practice Lincoln, 1968—. Editor Law for the Aviator, 1969-71. Served to lt. col. U.S. Army, 1943-46, ETO, Korea, ret. col., USAR, 1979. Mem. ABA, Nebr. Bar Assn. Fed. Bar Assn., Assn. Trial Lawyers Am., Am. Judicature Soc., Aircraft Owners and Pilots Assn (legis. rep.), Nebr. Criminal Def. Attys. Assn. Republican. Presbyterian. Lodges: Masons (knight comdr. of ct. of honor 1983), Shriners (potentate 1983), Elks. Avocations: collecting art, music, pistol competition. Personal injury, State civil litigation, Criminal. Home: 1610 Susan Circle Lincoln NE 68506 Office: 4435 O St Suite 130 Lincoln NE 68510

SWIMLEY, GARY WALLACE, lawyer; b. Mooreland, Okla., Mar. 8, 1946; s. Charles L. and Vivian Mary (Biggs) S.; m. Barbara Jean Newshutz, Dec. 28, 1985. BS in Physics, U. Okla., 1967, JD, 1975. Bar: Okla. 1975, Calif. 1975, U.S. Dist. Ct. (cen. dist.) Calif. 1976, U.S. Dist. Ct. (we. dist.) Okla. 1980. Geophysicist Standard Oil Ind., Houston, 1967-69, Tulsa, 1969-71; sole practice Newport Beach, Calif., 1976-80; staff atty. Legal Aid Western Okla., Stillwater, 1980-83, mng. atty., 1983—. Del. for Hart to Dem. precinct, county, dist. and state Convs., Okla., 1984. Mem. Payne County Bar Assn., Logan County Bar Assn., Sierra Club (exec. com. Okla. chpt. 1983-85). Avocations: photography, construction. Pension, profit-sharing, and employee benefits, Administrative and regulatory, Unemployment benefits. Home: Rt 1 PO Box 19A Ripley OK 74062 Office: Legal Aid Western Okla 920 S Main Stillwater OK 74074

SWINDLE, MACK ED, lawyer; b. Abilene, Tex., Nov. 25, 1948; s. Edgar Lloyd and Maxine (Brown) S.; m. Sharon Humphreys, Dec. 20, 1970; children—Cameron, Sommer. B.S., Abilene Christian U., 1971; J.D., Baylor U., 1974. Bar: Tex. 1974, U.S. Dist. Ct. (no. dist.) Tex. 1975, U.S. Ct. Appeals (5th cir.) 1983, U.S. Supreme Ct. 1983. Atty., Nelson, McCleskey, Harriger & Brazill, Lubbock, Tex., 1974-77, Owen & Swindle, Ft. Worth, 1977-78, Owen, Michener, Swindle, Whitaker & Pratt, Ft. Worth, 1978-83, Gandy, Michener, Swindle, Whitaker & Pratt, 1983—. Assoc. editor: Baylor U. Law Sch. Rev., 1973. Recipient Harvey M. Ritchey award Baylor U., 1973. Mem. ABA, Fort Worth/Tarrant County Bar Assn. Republican. Mem. Ch. of Christ. Federal civil litigation, State civil litigation, Trademark and copyright. Home: 6700 Riverbend Fort Worth TX 76132 Office: Gandy Michener Swindle Whitaker & Pratt Suite 600 2501 Parkview Dr Fort Worth TX 76102

SWINFORD, JOHN WALKER, lawyer, cons.; b. Stillwater, Okla., May 2, 1909; s. William B. and Velma (Walker) S.; m. Lois Eaton Steele, Dec. 25, 1938; children—William S., John W. A.B., U. Okla., 1931, LL.B., 1933. Bar: Okla. 1933. Ptnr. Chandler Shelton Fowler & Swinford, Oklahoma City, 1934-42; ptnr. Crowe Dunlevy Thweatt Swinford & Burdick (now Crowe & Dunlevy), Oklahoma City, 1947-78, of counsel, 1978—; Pres. Legal Aid Soc., 1963-64. Mem. C. of C., Order of Coif. Republican. Episcopalian. Club: Petroleum (Oklahoma City). Banking, Bankruptcy, Contracts commercial. Home: 837 NW 41st St Oklahoma City OK 73118 Office: 20 N Broadway Suite 1800 Oklahoma City OK 73102

SWIRE, JAMES BENNETT, lawyer; b. Bklyn., July 10, 1942. A.B., Princeton U., 1963; LL.B., Harvard U., 1966. Bar: N.Y. 1967, D.C. 1976. Assoc., Rogers Hoge & Hills, N.Y.C., 1966-73, ptnr., 1974-82; ptnr. Townley & Updike, N.Y.C., 1982—; guest lectr. food and drug law Seton Hall Law Sch., 1977. Trustee Nat. Cancer Care Found. and Cancer Care, Inc., 1978—, v.p., 1982—, chmn. exec. com., 1986—. Mem. Assn. Bar City N.Y. (chmn. com. medicine and law 1977-80, sec. com. on trademarks and unfair competition 1982-85, chmn. trademarks and unfair copetition, 1985—), ABA, N.Y. State Bar Assn., U.S. Trademark Assn. (assoc.). Trademark and copyright, Food and drug. Office: Chrysler Bldg 405 Lexington Ave New York NY 10174

SWIRSKY, STEVEN MITCHELL, lawyer; b. N.Y.C., Oct. 29, 1953; s. I. Robert and Dorothy Irene (Rosen) S. BS in Indsl. and Labor Relations, Cornell U., 1975; JD, Fordham U., 1978. Bar: N.Y. 1979, U.S. Dist. Ct. (ea. and so. dists.) N.Y. 1980, U.S. Ct. Appeals (2d cir.) 1983. Field atty. NLRB, Bklyn., 1978-83; assoc. Wender, Murase & White, N.Y.C., 1983-86; ptnr. Marks, Murase & White, N.Y.C., 1986—. Mem. ABA (labor law sect.), N.Y. State Bar Assn. (labor law sect, com. on practice and procedure before the NLRB and N.Y. State Labor Relations Bd.). Labor. Office: Marks Murase & White 400 Park Ave New York NY 10022

SWITZER, DONALD HUGH, lawyer; b. Atlanta, May 31, 1950; s. Hugh Ernest and Ruth Isabelle (Otto) S. BA, Tex. A&M U., 1972; JD, U. Va., 1978. Bar: Ohio 1978. Ptnr. Weston, Hurd, Fallon, Paisley & Howley, Cleve., 1978—. Served to capt. U.S. Army, 1972-75. Mem. ABA, Ohio Bar Assn., Cleve. Bar Assn., Ohio Assn. Civil Trial Attys. (quarterly editor 1983-84, case editor 1985—), Def. Research Inst. Personal injury, Insurance, Construction. Home: 13891 Edgewater Dr Lakewood OH 44107 Office: Weston Hurd Fallon Paisley & Howley 2500 Terminal Tower Cleveland OH 44113

SWITZER, ROBERT EARL, lawyer, educator, military law and criminal justice consultant; b. Buffalo, Nov. 24, 1929; s. Earl Alexander and Verne (Nowak) S.; m. Suzanne Marion Van Slyke, May 11, 1957; children—Tracey Ann, Beth Ann. BA with distinction in History, Bethany (W.Va.) Coll., 1951; JD, U. Buffalo, 1956; postgrad. Nat. Jud. Coll., Reno, 1978. Bar: N.Y. 1958, U.S. Ct. Mil. Appeals, 1966, U.S. Supreme Ct. 1976. Estate planner M & T Trust Co., Buffalo, 1956-58; sole practice, Buffalo, 1959-65; asst. county atty. Erie County, Buffalo, 1962-65; commd. 2d lt. U.S. Marine Corps, 1951, advanced through grades to col., 1973; inf. officer, 1951-53; trial csl., def. csl., 1965-66, dep. staff judge adv., 1967-69; staff judge adv., 1969-70, 75-77; dir. Law Ctr., 1971-72; cir. mil. judge, 1973-74, 1978-81; ret., 1981; instr. law criminal justice dept. Coastal Carolina Community Coll., Jacksonville, N.C., 1981—; mil. law cons., 1981—; lectr. on criminal law and trial advocacy, 1970—, v.p. faculty assembly, 1986—. Bd. dirs. Onslow County chpt. Am. Cancer Soc.; dist. committeeman Erie County Republican Com., 1960-65; del. 8th Jud. Dist. Nominating Conv., 1962-64; scoutmaster Boy Scouts Am., Quantico, Va., 1952-53, advisor Explorer scout post, Jacksonville, 1981-82. Decorated Navy Commendation medal; named Eagle Scout with gold palm Boy Scouts Am., 1947. Mem. ABA, Fed. Bar Assn. (pres. Hawaii chpt. 1977-78), Assn. Trial Lawyers Am., Acad. Criminal Justice Scis., N.C. Assn. Criminal Justice Edn. (chmn. long-range planning com. 1986—), Inst. for Criminal Justice Ethics, So. Assn. Criminal Justice Educators. Episcopalian. Club: Masons. Legal education, Criminal, Military. Home: 1112 Keating Ct Jacksonville NC 28540 Office: Coastal Carolina Community Coll 444 Western Blvd Jacksonville NC 28540

SWITZER, ROBERT JOSEPH, lawyer; b. N.Y.C., Aug. 18, 1950; s. Sidney and Claire Devera (Bier) S. A.B., UCLA, 1972; postgrad. Notre Dame U., London, 1973; J.D., Southwestern U., 1975. Bar: Calif., 1976, U.S. Dist. Ct. (cen. dist.) Calif. 1976, U.S. Sup. Ct. 1983. Legis. counsel Office of Chief Legislative Counsel Los Angeles City Council, 1977-79; assoc. editor Casenotes Publishing Co., Inc., Los Angeles, 1979—; congressional page U.S. Ho. of Reps., 1965. Commr. City of West Hollywood Commn. on Rent Stabilization, 1987—. Recipient Calif. State Senate Rules Com. Resolution in Honor of work as chmn. of UCLA Govt. Internship Program, 1971. Mem. Calif. Bar Assn. (standing com. on human rights 1985-87, conf. dels. 1985-86, conf. bar leaders 1984-85), Los Angeles County Bar Assn. (conf. bar leaders 1984-86, del. to State Bar Conf. Dels. 1987), Lawyers for Human Rights (gov. 1981—, pres. 1984-85), Mcpl. Elections Com. Los Angeles (chmn. com. legislation). Legal writing, Legislative, Trademark and copyright. Home: 851 N Kings Rd #309 West Hollywood CA 90069

SWOPE, DEREK CRAIG, lawyer; b. Balt., Apr. 26, 1953; s. Norman Emmet and Norma Lena Maud (Evans) S.; m. Anna Louise Johnson, Mar. 30, 1984; 1 child, Stuart Norman George; stepson: Mark D. Mills. BA, Coll. William & Mary, 1975; JD, Washington & Lee U., 1978. Bar: W.Va. 1978, U.S. Dist. Ct. (so. dist.) W.Va. 1978. Assoc. Sanders, Austin & Swope, Princeton, W.Va., 1978—; asst. pros. atty. Mercer County, Princeton, 1983—. Mem. W.Va. Bar Assn., Mercer County Bar Assn., Assn. Trial Lawyers Am., W.Va. Trial Lawyers Assn. Democrat. Methodist. Lodge: Kiwanis. Avocation: toy soldier collecting. Personal injury, State civil litigation, Criminal. Home: 1905 E River Ave Bluefield WV 24701 Office: Sanders Austin & Swope 320 Courthouse Rd Princeton WV 24740

SWORD, CARL H(ARRY), lawyer; b. N.Y.C., May 14, 1947; s. Carl Harry and Alfreda Dorothy (Larson) S.; m. Barbara Ellen Donoghue, July 12, 1981. BS, Wittenberg U., 1968; JD cum laude, Bklyn. Law Sch., 1976. Bar: N.Y. 1977, U.S. Dist. Ct. (so. and ea. dists.) N.Y. 1977, U.S. Ct. Appeals (2d cir.) 1983, U.S. Supreme Ct. 1984. Research chemist Mearl Corp., Ossining, N.Y., 1968-73; assoc. Costello and Shea, N.Y.C., 1976-81, ptnr., 1982—. Mem. ABA, N.Y. State Bar Assn., N.Y. County Lawyers Assn. Democrat. Lutheran. Avocation: golf. Federal civil litigation, State civil litigation, Personal injury. Office: Costello and Shea 50 Broadway New York NY 10004

SWYGERT, MICHAEL IRVEN, legal educator; b. Hammond, Ind., Nov. 20, 1939; s. Luther Merritt and Mildren (Kercher) S.; m. Dianne Margaret Jeffrey, Sept. 2, 1961; children—Jeffrey Michael, Gregory Robert. A.B. cum laude, Valparaiso U., 1965, J.D. summa cum laude, 1967; LL.M., Yale U., 1968. Bar: Ill. 1967, U.S. Dist. Ct. (no. dist.) Ill. 1969, U.S. Ct. Appeals (7th cir.) 1971, U.S. Ct. Appeals (D.C. cir.) 1971. Assoc. Hopkins, Sutter, Owen, Mulroy, Wentz & Davis, Chgo., 1968-70; asst. prof., asst. dean Sch. Law Valparaiso (Ind.) U., 1969-72; prof. law DePaul U., Chgo., 1972-80, Stetson U., St. Petersburg, Fla., 1980—; mediator, conciliator Ind. Employment Relations Bd., Indpls., 1974—, hearing officer, 1974-79; lectr. Sch. Pub. Affairs, Ind. U., Gary, 1974-78; vis. prof. law Cambridge U., Eng., 1986-87. Co-author, editor Maximizing the Law School Experience, 1983; co-author The Legal Handbook of Business Transactions, 1987. Contbg. author Creditor Rights, 1974. Vol. atty. Ch. Fedn. Chgo., 1968-70. Mem. Soc. Profls. in Dispute Resolution, Chgo. Bar Assn., Ill. Bar Assn., Am. Arbitration Assn. (arbitrator), Phi Alpha Delta. Presbyterian. Legal education, Jurisprudence, Consumer commercial. Home: 2600 70th Ave S Saint Petersburg FL 33712 Office: Stetson U Coll Law 1301 61st St S Saint Petersburg FL 33707

SYDLOW, HOLLY TAFT, lawyer; b. Charleston, S.C., Jan. 4, 1951; d. Eugene John and JoAnn (Galberach) S.; m. Frederick Hill McDonald, May 15, 1976; children: William Thomas, Charles Robert. BA, Coll. Wooster, 1971; JD, U. Toledo, 1975. Bar: Ohio 1975, U.S. Dist. Ct. (no. dist.) Ohio, 1983. Research atty. 6th Dist. Ct. Appeals Ohio, Toledo, 1975-78; asst. city prosecutor City of Toledo Law Dept., 1978-82, civil atty., 1982—. Editor: U. Toledo Law Rev., 1974-75. Mem. Toledo Bar Assn., Toledo Woman's Bar Assn. (pres.), Women's Equity Action League, Phi Kappa Phi. Republican. Presbyterian. Club: Zonta (com. chmn. 1980-82). Local government, Federal civil litigation, State civil litigation. Office: City Law Dept One Govt Ctr Suite 2250 Toledo OH 43604

SYDOW, MICHAEL DAVID, lawyer; b. Cuero, Tex., Dec. 12, 1950; s. Vernon Emil Sydow and Carolyn Marie (Peters) Sydow Rogas; m. Cheryl Lynn Lawson, Aug. 4, 1973; children—Kristen, David. B.A., Southwestern U., 1973; J.D., U. Tex., 1976. Bar: Tex. 1976, U.S. Ct. Claims 1977, U.S. Ct. Appeals (5th cir.) 1977, U.S. Dist. Ct. (so. dist.) Tex. 1977, U.S. Dist. Ct. (ea. dist.) Tex. 1979, U.S. Supreme Ct. 1980; cert. in civil trial law Tex. Bd. Legal Specialization. Trial atty. Office Gen. Counsel U.S. Navy, Arlington, Va., 1976-77; mem. firm Eastham, Watson, Dale & Forney, Houston, 1977-84, O'Quinn & Hagans, Houston, 1984-85, Hagans & Sydow, Houston, 1986—. Mem. Tex. Trial Lawyers Assn., Assn. Trial Lawyers Am., Houston Bar Assn., Maritime Law Assn. U.S. (mem. com. on gen. average 1977—), State Bar Tex., Phi Delta Phi. Episcopalian. Clubs: Texas, Houston Ctr. Federal civil litigation, Admiralty, Personal injury. Home: 13118 Highwood St Houston TX 77079 Office: Hagans & Sydow 1415 Louisiana Houston TX 77002

SYKES, PETER M'CREADY, lawyer; b. Boise, Idaho, Oct. 10, 1914; s. M'Cready and Beatrice (Evans) S.; m. Barbara Craig, Dec. 27, 1941 (dec. Oct. 1969); children: Michael, Barbara, Sarah; m. Elizabeth Hastings, July 7, 1970 (dec. May, 1983); m. Jean Margot Sweet, June 1, 1985. BA, Princeton U., 1937; LLB, Harvard U., 1941. Bar: N.Y. 1941, Mass. 1947. Assoc. Stewart & Shearer, N.Y.C., 1941-47; ptnr. Wilson & Sykes, Hyannis, Mass., 1947-60, Sykes & Cole, Hyannis, 1970—; sole practice Hyannis, 1960-70; clk. Cape Cod Coop. Bank, Yarmouth Port, Mass., 1985—, bd. dirs. Past moderator Town of Yarmouth, mem. various coms. Served with USCG, 1943. Mem. Mass. Bar Assn., Barnstable County Bar Assn. Republican. Episcopalian. Avocation: fishing. Probate, Real property. Home: 120 Storrow Rd Brewster MA 02631 Office: Sykes & Cole 420 South St Hyannis MA 02601

SYKES, THOMAS DALE, lawyer; b. Rice Lake, Wis., July 26, 1954; s. Dale Leroy and Glenna Marie (Amundson) S.; m. Deborah Ann Custer, Aug. 25, 1985. BA, U. Wis., Eau Claire, 1976; JD, Ohio State U., 1979. Bar: Wis. 1979, U.S. Dist. Ct. (we. dist.) Wis. 1979, Minn. 1981, U.S. Ct. Appeals (7th cir.) 1983. Asst. dist. atty. Barron County, Barron, Wis., 1979-80, dist. atty., 1980-82; asst. U.S. atty. U.S. Dept. Justice, Madison, Wis., 1982-84; trial atty. U.S. Dept. Justice, Washington, 1984—. Mem. Wis. Bar Assn. Republican. Lutheran. Avocations: golf, skiing. Federal civil litigation, Criminal, Personal income taxation. Office: US Dept Justice Tax div Washington DC 20530

SYLVESTER, JON HOWARD, law educator, consultant; b. Berkeley, Calif., June 7, 1952; s. Odell Howard Sylvester and Joyce K. (Palmer) Wood; m. Felicia Jeter, June 7, 1984. AB, Stanford U., 1973; MA in Journalism, U. Calif., Berkeley, 1975; JD, Harvard U., 1981. Bar: Calif. 1981, D.C. 1982, U.S. Dist. Ct. D.C. 1982, U.S. Dist. Ct. (no. dist.) Calif. 1982, U.S. Ct. Appeals (D.C. cir.) 1983. News producer ABC, San Francisco, 1975; news reporter Cox Broadcasting, San Francisco, 1975-76, CBS, Los Angeles, 1976-78; assoc. Rogers & Wells, Washington, 1981-83, Anderson & Baker, Washington, 1983-84; asst. prof. law Tex. Southern U., Houston, 1984—; cons. HUD, San Francisco, 1977-80, Sta. KTSU-FM, Houston, 1984—; bd. dirs. Houston Cable Corp. Mem. ABA, Nat. Bar Assn., Houston Bar Assn. Private international, Contracts commercial, Legal education. Office: Tex Southern U Law Sch 3100 Cleburne Houston TX 77004

SYMMERS, WILLIAM GARTH, international maritime lawyer; b. Bronxville, N.Y., Nov. 30, 1910; s. James Keith and Agnes Louise (Shuey) S.; m. Marina Baruch, Apr. 25, 1936; children: Benjamin Keith, Ann (Mrs. Edward L. Reed); m. Anne H. Ellis, Mar. 20, 1946; children: Barbara (Mrs. Thomas M. Bancroft, Jr.), Susan Friedman, Deborah. Grad., Lawrenceville (N.J.) Sch., 1929; AB, U. Va., 1933, JD, 1935. Bar: N.Y. 1937, U.S. Supreme Ct. 1940, D.C. 1953. Assoc. Bigham, Englar, Jones & Houston, N.Y.C., 1935-37; mem. Dow and Symmers, N.Y.C., 1940-56; ptnr. Symmers, Fish & Warner, N.Y.C., 1956—; admiralty counsel U.S. Maritime Commn., 1937-40; spl. counsel to naval affairs com. U.S. Ho. of Reps.; active investigation loss of SS Normandie, 1942; U.S. del., v.p. Antwerp Conf., Comité Maritime Internat.; also del. Maritime Law Assn. U.S. to succeeding confs., Amsterdam, 1949, Brighton, 1952, Madrid, 1955, N.Y.C., 1966, Tokyo, 1968, Rio de Janeiro, 1977, Montreal, 1981; titular mem. Comité Maritime Internat., 1955—; mem. adv. com. on admiralty rules U.S. Supreme Ct., 1962-71. Contbr. articles to maritime publs. Mem. ABA, N.Y. State Bar Assn., Bar Assn. City N.Y. (chmn. admiralty com. 1953-56), Am. Soc. Internat. Law, Maritime Law Assn. (chmn. com. revision U.S. Supreme Ct. admiralty rules 1952-56, mem. exec. com. 1958-61, 1st v.p. 1964-66), Internat. Maritime Arbitration Orgn. (U.S. rep. 1978-81), Phi Delta Theta, Phi Delta Phi. Clubs: Down Town Assn., N.Y. Yacht (N.Y.C.); Indian Harbor Yacht; Field (Greenwich); Hillsboro (Pompano Beach, Fla.). Admiralty, Federal civil litigation, State civil litigation. Home: 444 E 52d St New York NY 10022 Office: 111 E 50th St New York NY 10022

SYMONS, ROBIN SUZANNE TAYLOR, lawyer; b. Atlanta, Apr. 1, 1960; d. Robert Thomas and Ella Sherrill (Smith) T. BS, Fla. So. Coll.; JD, U. Miami. Bar: Fla. 1982, U.S. Dist. Ct. (so. dist.) Fla. 1983, U.S. Dist. Ct. (mid. dist.) Fla. 1984. Assoc. Preddy, Kutner, Hardy, Rubinoff, Brown & Thompson P.A., Miami, Fla., 1982—. Judge Dade County Schs. Mock Trial Competition, 1984-85, U. Miami Mock Trial Competition, 1985-86. Mem. ABA, Dade County Bar Assn. (exec. com. young lawyers sect. 1985, referral service com. 1986), Assn. Trial Lawyers Am., Acad. Fla. Trial Lawyers, Fla. Assn. Women Lawyers. State civil litigation, Insurance, Personal injury. Office: Preddy Kutner Hardy et al 501 NE 1 Ave Miami FL 33132

SZALKOWSKI, CHARLES CONRAD, lawyer; b. Amarillo, Tex., Apr. 14, 1948; s. Chester Casimer and Virginia Lee (Hess) S.; m. Jane Howe, Dec. 28, 1971; children: Jennifer Lee, Stephen Claude. BA, BS in Acctg., Rice U., 1971; MBA, JD, Harvard U., 1975. Bar: Tex. 1975; CPA, Tex. Assoc. Baker & Botts, Houston, 1975-82, ptnr., 1983—; speaker in field. Vice chmn., chmn. Rice U. Annual Fund Class Campaign, Houston, 1982—; mem. adminstrn. bd. St. Luke's United Meth. Ch., Houston, 1983-85, 87—; co-chmn. profl. div. United Fund, Houston, 1985-86. Mem. ABA (fed. regulation of securities com.), Tex. Bar Assn. (council corp. banking and bus. law sect.), Houston Bar Assn. (sec. corp. counsel sect. 1985—), Harvard Law Sch Assn. Tex. (pres. 1983-84), Assn. Rice U. Alumni (chmn. various coms. 1981—), Lincoln's Inn Soc. Club: Briar (Houston). General corporate, Securities. Office: Baker & Botts 3000 One Shell Plaza Houston TX 77002

SZCZEPANIAK, JOSEPH DENNIS, lawyer; b. Phila., Nov. 25, 1953; s. John Paul and Jane Mary (Feltowicz) S.; m. Peggy Simmons, Sept. 17, 1982; children: Joseph Simmons, John Alexander. BA, St. Joseph's Coll., Phila., 1975; JD summa cum laude, The Del. Law Sch., 1982. Bar: Pa. 1982, N.J. 1983, U.S. Dist. Ct. (ea. dist.) Pa. 1983, U.S. Dist. Ct. N.J. 1983, U.S. Ct. Appeals (3d cir.) 1983. Law clk. to presiding justice Pa. Commonwealth Ct., West Chester, 1982-83; assoc. Curran, Mylotte, David & Fitzpatrick, Phila.,

1983-85, White & William, Phila., 1985-87; dep. corp. counsel SMS, Inc., Malvern, Pa., 1987—. Served as lt. USNR, 1975-84. Mem. ABA, Pa. Bar Assn., Phila. Bar Assn. Computer, General corporate, State civil litigation. Home: 291 Bickley Rd Glenside PA 19038 Office: SMS Inc 51 Valley Stream Parkway Malvern PA 19355

SZCZEPANSKI, SLAWOMIR ZBIGNIEW STEVEN, lawyer; b. Lodz, Poland, Mar. 9, 1948; s. Wladyslaw and Janina Szczepanski; m. Cynthia Ellen Weagley, Sept. 30, 1972; children: Christine, Diana. BS in Chem. Engring., Rensselaer Poly. Inst., 1971; MS in Chem. Engring., Rensselaer Poly. Inst., 1972; JD, Union U., Albany, N.Y., 1975. Bar: N.Y. 1976, D.C. 1976, Ill. 1977, U.S. Dist. Ct. (no. dist.) Ill. 1977. Atty. Philips Petroleum Co., Washington, 1975-77; from assoc. to ptnr. Willian, Brinks, Olds, Hofer, Gilson & Lione Ltd., Chgo., 1977—; bd. dirs. Richards Tire Co., Montgomery, Ill. Editor: Licensing in Foreign and Domestic Operations, 1985—; editor (legal periodical) Licensing Law and Business Report, 1986—; contbr. articles to profl. jours. Mem. ABA, Am. Intellectual Property Law Assn., Am. Inst. Chem. Engrs., Internat. Assn. Protection Indsl. Property. Club: University (Chgo.). Avocations: tennis, fencing, squash, racquetball. Patent, Federal civil litigation, Licensing of intellectual property. Home: 641 N Willow St Apt 107 Chicago IL 60614 Office: Willian Brinks Olds Hofer et al One IBM Plaza Suite 4100 Chicago IL 60611

SZEWCZYK, STEPHEN MICHAEL, lawyer; b. East St. Louis, Ill., Mar. 8, 1949; s. Thaddeus Stanislaus and Loretta Helen Szewcyk; m. Kathleen Annette Gula, July 10, 1982; children: Stephen Thaddeus, Christopher Joseph. AB, St. Louis U., 1972; JD, 1981; MBA, So. Ill. U., 1976; LLM, Washington U., St. Louis, 1984. Assoc. Charles Kolker Law Office, Belleville, Ill., 1981-83; sole practice Belleville, 1983—; tchr. Belleville Area Coll., 1980-82. Mem. ABA, Ill. State Bar Assn., St. Clair County Bar Assn. Republican. Roman Catholic. Estate taxation, Personal income taxation, Family and matrimonial. Home: #2 Lake Lorraine Dr Belleville IL 62223 Office: 7616 W Main St Belleville IL 62223

SZWALBENEST, BENEDYKT JAN, lawyer; b. Poland, June 13, 1955; s. Sidney and Janina (Bleishtif) S.; m. Shelley Joy Leibel, Nov. 8, 1981. BBA, Temple U., 1978, JD, 1981. Law clk. Fed. Deposit Ins. Corp., Washington, 1980; law clk. to presiding justice U.S. Dist. Ct. (ea. dist.) Pa., Phila., 1980-81; staff atty., regulatory specialist Fidelcor, Inc. and Fidelity Bank, Phila., 1981-86; spl. asst. to head of compliance and examinations dept. Fed. Res. Bank of N.Y., N.Y.C., 1986—. Author: Federal Bank Regulation, 1980. Mem. Commonwealth of Pa. Post-secondary Edn. Planning Commn., Harrisburg, 1977-79; trustee Pop Warners Little Scholars, Phila., 1981—. Mem. ABA (nat. sec., treas. law student div. 1980-81, Silver Key award 1980, Gold Key award 1981), Am. Judicature Soc., Am. Bankers Assn. (cert. compliance specialist, lectr. 1984—), Temple U. Sch. Bus. Alumni Assn. (sec. 1982-84, v.p. 1984-86, pres. 1986—, bd. dirs. gen. alumni assn. 1986—), Tau Epsilon Rho, Omicron Delta Epsilon. Avocations: baseball, tennis, skiing. Banking, Administrative and regulatory, Securities. Home: 1107 Bryn Mawr Ave Bala Cynwyd PA 19004 Office: Fed Res Bank of NY 33 Liberty St New York NY 10045

SZYBALA, RENEE LESLIE, lawyer; b. Bklyn., Mar. 6, 1952; s. Adolph and Bernice (Schwartz) Cohen; m. Dennis Edward Szybala, Jan. 11, 1981; children: Valerie, Julia. BA, SUNY, Binghamton, 1973; JD summa cum laude, Syracuse U., 1976. Bar: N.Y. 1977, U.S. Dist. Ct. (so. and ea. dists.) N.Y. 1978, U.S. Supreme Ct. 1980, U.S. Ct. Appeals (D.C. and fed. cirs.) 1985, U.S. Dist. Ct. D.C. 1986. Assoc. Patterson, Belknap, Webb & Tyler, N.Y.C., 1976-81, 84—; spl. asst. to assoc. atty. gen. U.S. Dept. Justice, Washington, 1981-82, dep. assoc. atty. gen., 1982-83. Mem. ABA, D.C. Bar Assn., Order of Coif, Phi Beta Kappa. Federal civil litigation, State civil litigation, Libel. Office: Patterson Belknap Webb & Tyler 1730 Pennsylvania Ave NW Washington DC 20006

SZYMANSKI, BARRY WALTER, lawyer; b. Chgo., Apr. 6, 1943; s. Walter F. and Rose (Mazurek) S.; m. Susan E., Jan. 27, 1968; 1 dau., Sarah Ann. B.A., St. Edward's U., 1965; J.D., Marquette U., 1973. Bar: Wis. 1973, U.S. Dist. Cts. (ea. and we. dists.) Wis. 1973, U.S. Ct. Appeals (7th cir.) 1977; lic. real estate broker. Ct. Commr. for County of Milw., 1980-82; ptnr., prin. Barry W. Szymanski, S.C., Milw., 1978—; tchr. U. Wis. Law Sch.; lectr. Waukesha County Tech. Inst.; instr. Milw. Area Tech. Coll. ; arbitrator Am. Arbitration Assn. Contbr. articles to profl. jours. Mem. State Bar of Wis. (sec. law office mgmt. sect.), ABA, Milw. Bar Assn., (speaker's bur. and fee arbitrations comss., co-chmn. litigation sect.), Wauwatosa C. of C. (bd. dirs.). Club: Rotary of Wauwatosa . General corporate, Real property, State civil litigation. Home: 2151 Ludington Ave Wauwatosa WI 53226 Office: 2300 N Mayfair Rd Milwaukee WI 53226

SZYMANSKI, FRANK S(TANISLAUS), JR., lawyer; b. Detroit, Oct. 16, 1952; s. Frank S. Sr. and Lillian (Mikula) S. BA in History, U. Notre Dame, 1974; JD, U. Detroit, 1980. Bar: Mich. 1980, U.S. Dist. Ct. (ea. and we. dists.) Mich. 1980. Assoc. Warner, Norcross & Judd, Grand Rapids, Mich., 1980-82; sole practice Detroit, 1982—. Mem. ABA, Mich. Bar Assn., Detroit Bar Assn. Probate, State civil litigation, General practice. Home: 20274 Woodmont Harper Woods MI 48225 Office: 3080 Penobscot Bldg Detroit MI 48226

TAALMAN, JURI E., lawyer; b. Tartu, Estonia, Nov. 1, 1940; s. Aarne and Linda (Kutt) T.; m. Tania J. Taalman, June 1, 1944; children—Laura, Linda, Alina. S.B. in Math., U. Chgo.; J.D., U. Conn. Bar: Conn. 1969, U.S. dist. ct. Conn. 1971, U.S. Supreme Ct. 1975. Assoc., Brown, Jacobson, Jewett & Laudone, P.C., Norwich, Conn., dir., 1972-82; ptnr. Taalman & Phillips, Norwichtown, Conn. Vice chmn. Windham Regional Planning Agy., Norwichtown, 1977-81. Served with USAR, 1964-70. Mem. ABA, Conn. Bar Assn., New London County Bar Assn., Assn. Trial Lawyers Am., Am. Arbitration Assn. (panel arbitrators). State civil litigation, Personal injury, General practice. Home: Cemetery Rd RFD 1 Baltic CT 06330 Office: Suite 215 12 Case St Norwichtown CT 06360

TABACHNIK, DOUGLAS T., lawyer; b. Bronx, N.Y., Dec. 22, 1955. BA, George Washington U., 1977; JD, MBA, Syracuse U., 1980. Bar: N.Y. 1981, U.S. Dist. Ct. (so. and ea. dists.) N.Y. 1982. Assoc. Hayt, Hayt & Landau, Great Neck, N.Y., 1981-83, Lipsig, Sullivan & Liapakis, N.Y.C., 1983-85; v.p., gen. counsel, sec. John B. Stetson Co. Inc., N.Y.C., 1985-86; assoc. Mazur, Carp & Barnett P.C., N.Y.C., 1986—. Mem. ABA, N.Y. State Bar Assn. (securities, fin. and corp. law com., governance com. corp. counsel sect., SEC com., fin. and corp. law and governance, spl. com. on patents and trademarks), Assn. of Bar of City of N.Y., Nassau County Bar Assn., N.Y. County Lawyers Assn. (com. on corp. law), U.S. Trademark Assn. (dictionary listings com.). Republican. Avocations: windsurfing, tennis. General corporate, Contracts commercial, Real property. Office: Mazur Carp & Barnett PC 2 Park Ave Suite 2200 New York NY 10016

TABAK, MICHAEL L., lawyer; b. N.Y.C., July 3, 1946; s. Abraham S. and Frieda C. Tabak; m. Roxanne Kelber, Dec. 12, 1982; 1 child, Alan Joseph. BA, Harvard U., 1968; JD, Yale U., 1975. Law clk. to chief presiding judge U.S. Ct. Appeals (2d cir.), 1975-76; assoc. Davis Polk & Wardwell, N.Y.C., 1976-78; dep. chief counsel Spl. Commn., Boston, 1978-80; asst. U.S. atty. U.S. Atty.'s Office (so. dist.) N.Y., N.Y.C., 1980-87, U.S. atty. in charge White Plains br., 1987—. Editor: Yale Law Jour., 1974-75. Mem. ABA, Assn. Bar of City of N.Y. Avocation: flutist. Criminal, Litigation. Office: US Attys Office 101 E Post Rd White Plains NY 10601

TABAK, MORRIS, lawyer; b. Warsaw, Poland, July 23, 1944; came to U.S. 1953, naturalized, 1957; s. Joseph Irving and Zina T. (Basista) T.; m. Karen Elaine Tomber, Aug. 31, 1969; children—Adam Jason, Jessica Lee, Joshua Paul. B.S., Ind. U., 1970, J.D. magna cum laude, 1972. Bar: Ind. 1972, Tex. 1984. Assoc. Talesnick & Kleiman, Indpls., 1972-73; ptnr. Kilroy & Tabak, Indpls., 1973-74, Stivers & Tabak, Indpls., 1974-77; labor relations rep. Coastal Corp., Houston, 1978-82; atty., Alameda Corp., Houston, 1982-84; mem. Brochstein & Slobin, Houston, 1984—. Bd. dirs. Beth El, Stafford, Tex., 1981—. Served with U.S. Spl. Forces, 1965-67, Vietnam. Named Ky. Col., 1982. Mem. Ind. Bar Assn., Harris Bar Assn., Tex. Bar Assn., Ft. Bend Bar Assn., Beta Gamma Sigma. Jewish. Clubs: Houston City, Sweetwater Country. Federal civil litigation, State civil litigation, Labor. Home: 2746 Raintree Sugarland TX 77478 Office: Brochstein & Slobin 9301 Southwest Freeway Suite 510 Houston TX 77074

TABAS, ALLAN M., lawyer, engineer; b. Phila., Jan. 30, 1926; s. Abraham and Anna (Cohen) T.; m. Evelyn Psaki, Sept. 7, 1952; children—Maxine, Joel, Jeffrey. B.S. in M.E., Drexel U., 1948; J.D., Temple U., 1952. Bar: Pa. 1953. Various partnerships, Phila., 1953-80; sr. ptnr. Tabas & Rosen, Phila., 1980—; nat. counsel Am. Guild Patient Account Mgrs. Mem. com. on studies involving humans Albert Einstein Med. Ctr., Phila., 1972—; mem. Recombinant DNA research com. Temple U. Sch. Medicine, Phila., 1979—. Served with USN, 1944-46; PTO. Recipient Presdl. citations Pres. Ford, Pres. Nixon; Masada award State of Israel, 1974. Mem. ABA, Pa. Bar Assn., Phila. Bar Assn., Am. Trial Lawyers Assn., Pa. Trial Lawyers Assn., Phila. Trial Lawyers Assn., Nat. Health Lawyers Assn., Am. Hosp. Assn., Hosp. Assn. Pa. Clubs: B'nai B'rith; Lawyers of Phila. Contbr. articles to profl. jours. Health, General practice, State civil litigation. Home: 1 Steeplechase Ln Blue Bell PA 19422 Office: 260 S Broad St 10th Floor Philadelphia PA 19102

TABAS, LAWRENCE JEFFREY, lawyer; b. Phila., Mar. 30, 1953; m. Libby A. White, Aug. 7, 1983. BA, MA, U. Pa., 1975; JD, Georgetown U., 1978. Bar: Pa. 1978, U.S. Dist. Ct. (ea. dist.) Pa. 1978, U.S. Ct. Appeals (3d cir.) 1984. Assoc. Stradley, Ronan, Stevens & Young, Phila., 1978-84; ptnr. Goldberg, Dickman, Shalita & Tabas, Phila., 1984-86, Charen & Goldberg, Phila., 1986—; instr. pub. election law, course planner Pa. Bar Inst., 1986; bd. dirs. Paint Mfg. Firm, Norristown, Pa. Co-author: Planning for Your Family's Future. Rep. nominee Phila. City Controller, 1985, Pa. Ho. of Reps., 1980; chmn. ballot integrity com., Phila. County, 1984—; mem. Nat. Rep. Lawyer's Com., 1986—. Named Knight Comdr., Italian-Am. Press, 1985. Mem. ABA (corp. sect., bankruptcy com.), Pa. Bar Assn. (instr. and moderator in election law 1986), Phila. Bar Assn. (bankruptcy com.), Am. Bankruptcy Inst., Nat. Assn. Bankruptcy Trustees. Avocations: politics, reading. Bankruptcy, General corporate, Public election law. Office: Charen & Goldberg 260 S Broad St 16th Floor Atlantic Bldg Philadelphia PA 19102

TABB, CHARLES JORDAN, law educator; b. Dallas, Nov. 1, 1955; s. William Herschel and Jeanne Mitchell (Jordan) T.; m. Linda Lee Smith, Mar. 8, 1980; children: Rebecca Marie, Natalie Ann. BA, Vanderbilt U., 1977; JD, U. Va., 1980. Bar: Tex. 1980. Assoc. Carrington, Coleman, Sloman & Blumenthal, Dallas, 1980-84; asst. prof. U. Ill., Champaign, 1984—. Recipient Best Instr. award U. Ill. Coll. Law, Champaign, 1986. Mem. ABA, State Bar Tex., Assn. Am. Law Schs., Order of Coif, Phi Beta Kappa. Republican. Episcopalian. Club: Urbana Country. Avocations: sports, travel. Bankruptcy, Contracts commercial, Probate. Home: 505 W Delaware Urbana IL 61801 Office: U Ill Coll Law 504 E Pennsylvania Ave Champaign IL 61820

TABIS, BRUNO WALTER, JR., lawyer; b. Chgo., May 23, 1946; s. Bruno Walter and Anne Helen (Dziak) T.; m. Martha Ann Sorgatz, Jan. 25, 1969; 1 child, Elizabeth Katherine. B.S., U. Ill.-Urbana, 1973; J.D. with distinction, Ill. Inst. Tech.-Kent Coll. Law, 1973. Bar: Ill. 1973, U.S. Dist. Ct. (no. dist.) Ill. 1973. Atty. EPA, Chgo., 1973-75; sole practice, Chgo., 1975-77; ptnr. Anderson, McDonnell, Miller & Tabis, Chgo., 1977—; instr. Ill. Inst. Tech.-Kent Coll. Law, Chgo., 1980-81. Editor-in-chief: CBA-Communicator, 1983-86; editor CBA Record, 1986—; contbr. articles to profl. jours. Mem. ch. counsel St. Paul Luth. Ch., Wheaton, Ill., 1982—, v.p., 1984-86; commr. Lawyers Trust Fund Implementation Commn., Chgo., 1983-85; bd. dirs. Legal Clinic for Disabled, 1985—. Mem. Chgo. Bar Assn. (chmn. young lawyers sect. 1982-83, bd. mgrs. 1984-86), Ill. State Bar Assn., ABA (chmn. directory com. young lawyers div. 1982-83), Legal Assistance Found. Chgo. (chmn. pvt. atty. involvement com. 1984—), Lawyers for Creative Arts (dir. 1979—, sec. 1980-81). Real property, Banking, Contracts commercial. Home: 1223 Howard Circle Wheaton IL 60187 Office: Anderson McDonnell Miller & Tabis 200 S Wacker Dr Suite 420 Chicago IL 60606

TACHNA, RUTH C., lawyer, educator; b. N.Y.C.; d. Max and Rose (Rosenblatt) T.; m. Paul Bauman (dec.); children—Leslie Bauman Levy, Lionel, B.A., Cornell U., 1935; LL.B. cum laude, Bklyn. Law Sch., 1937. Bar: N.Y. 1938, U.S. Supreme Ct. 1956, U.S. Dist. Ct. (so. dist.) N.Y. 1966, U.S. Ct. Appeals (2d cir.), Calif. 1978. Founding atty. Legal Aid, Westchester, N.Y., 1960-64; sr. ptnr., of counsel Tachna & Krassner, White Plains, N.Y., 1964—; group mng. editor Matthew Bendor, N.Y.C., 1968-77; staff. atty., founder Legal Aid for Srs., Santa Monica, Calif., 1980-83; prof. law Northrop U. Sch. Law, Los Angeles, 1977-85. Mem. Calif. Bar Assn., Los Angeles County Bar Assn. Legal education, General practice. Office: 13900 Marquesas Way Marina del Rey CA 90292

TACHNER, LEONARD, lawyer; b. Bklyn., Jan. 18, 1944. B.E.E., CCNY, 1965; M.S. in E.E., Calif. State U.-Long Beach, 1969; J.D., Western State U., Fullerton, Calif., 1973. Bar: Calif. 1973, U.S. Patent Office 1972. Supr. electronic counter measures sect. Ford Aerospace Corp., Newport Beach, Calif., 1969-73; patent atty. Reed C. Lawlor, Los Angeles, 1973-76, Rockwell Internat. Corp., Anaheim, Calif., 1976-78; ptnr. Fischer, Tachner & Strauss, Newport Beach, Calif., 1978-84, law offices of Leonard Tachner, Newport Beach, 1984—; instr. intellectual property Calif. State U.-Long Beach, 1979—; mem. com. maintenance profl. competence Calif. State Bar, 1978—. Mem. Calif. Bar Assn., Orange County Bar Assn., Los Angeles Patent Law Assn., Orange County Patent Law Assn., Greater Irvine Indsl. League, Phi Kappa Phi. Recipient Am. Jurisprudence award, 1970, 71. Assoc. editor Western State U. Law Rev., 1972-73; author column: Jurisprudent Computerist, Interface Age mag., 1979—, Bus.-to-Bus. mag., 1983—. Patent, Trademark and copyright. Office: 3990 Westerly Pl Suite 295 Newport Beach CA 92660

TAFFET, RICHARD S., lawyer; b. N.Y.C., Mar. 5, 1955; s. Sam and Laura (Atlas) T.; m. Jane Gottlieb, Feb. 19, 1984. BA, Sarah Lawrence Coll., 1977; JD, Bklyn. Law Sch., 1980. Bar: N.Y. 1981, U.S. Dist. Ct. (so. and ea. dists.) N.Y. 1981. Assoc. Weil, Gotshal & Manges, N.Y.C., 1980—. Antitrust, Trademark and copyright. Office: Weil Gotshal & Manges 767 Fifth Ave New York NY 10153

TAFT, FREDERICK IRVING, lawyer; b. New Haven, June 26, 1945; s. Seth Chase and Frances (Prindle) T.; m. Susan Hoefflinger, July 28, 1973; children: Amanda, Joshua. BA, Yale U., 1967, JD, 1971. Bar: Ohio 1972. Probation officer Ohio Dept. Corrections, Norwalk, 1971-72; asst. atty. gen. State of Ohio, Columbus, 1972-73; sole practice Cleve., 1973-77; ptnr. Spieth, Bell, McCurdy & Newell Co. L.P.A., Cleve., 1977—; bd. dirs. Sturges Pub. Co., Princeton, N.J., Griswold Inc., Cleve. Author: Stan Mahoney, 1978. Pres. Your Schs., Cleveland Heights and University Heights, Ohio, 1986—; trustee Children's Aid Soc., Cleve., 1982—, Ohio Venture Assn., 1984—, Family Health Assn., Cleve., 1985—. Grantee AHS Found., 1976. Mem. ABA, Cleve. Bar Assn. (vice chmn. corp., banking and bus. law sect. 1985—). Democrat. Mem. Unitarian Ch. Avocations: squash, tennis, snorkeling. General corporate, Contracts commercial, Real property. Home: 2989 Washington Blvd Cleveland Heights OH 44118 Office: Spieth Bell McCurdy & Newell Co LPA 2000 Huntington Bldg Cleveland OH 44115

TAFT, LEE MCCREARY, lawyer; b. Monroe, Mich., May 31, 1950; s. William Lee and Patricia Anne (Pheeney) T. BS with Honors, Mich. State U., 1972; JD, St. Mary's U., San Antonio, 1975. Bar: Tex. 1975. Ptnr. Carter, Jones, Magee, Rudberg & Mayes, Dallas, 1980—. Bd. dirs. Maple Ave. Econ. Devel. Corp., Dallas, 1984-86. Mem. Tex. Trial Lawyers Assn., Dallas Trial Lawyers Assn. (bd. dirs.), Dallas Assn. Young Lawyers (chmn. com. 1978-82, bd. dirs. 1983, 84), Tex. Bd. Legal Specialization (bd. cert. in trial law, personal injury trial law). Avocation: swimming. Federal civil litigation, State civil litigation, Personal injury. Office: Carter Jones Magee Rudberg & Mayes One Main Place Suite 2400 Dallas TX 75250

TAFT, PERRY HAZARD, lawyer; b. Los Angeles, Jan. 23, 1915; s. Milton and Sarah T.; m. Callie S. Taft, Aug. 15, 1968; children by previous marriage—Stephen D., Sally L., Sheila R. Student U. Calif.-Berkeley, 1932-35; A.B., UCLA, 1936; LL.B., George Washington U., 1940. Bar: Calif. 1940. Spl. atty. Antitrust div. U.S. Dept. Justice, Los Angeles, 1941-42; dep. atty. gen. State of Calif., San Francisco, 1943-44; regional rep. Council State Govts., San Francisco, 1944-45; regional dir. govt. affairs Trans World Airlines, Los Angeles, 1945-47; Pacific coast mgr. Am. Ins. Assn., San Francisco, 1948-66; gen. counsel Assn. Calif. Ins. Cos., Sacramento, 1967-73; asst. city atty. City of Stockton, Calif., 1973-79; pres. Perry H. Taft, P.C., Stockton, 1979-85; dir. Compair, Inc., Burlingame, Calif. ; arbitrator Surplus Line Assn. Calif., 1965—. Contbr. articles to profl. jours. Bd. dirs. Stockton East Water Dist., 1979-83, pres., 1981-83; mem. San Joaquin County Water Adv. Com., 1982-85. Mem. State Bar of Calif., Psi Upsilon. Democrat. Clubs: Elkhorn Country, Yosemite. General corporate, Legislative, Local government. Home: 8615 Stonewood Dr Stockton CA 95209 Office: PO Box 7453 Stockton CA 95207

TAFT, SETH CHASE, lawyer; b. Cin., Dec. 31, 1922; s. Charles Phelps and Eleanor K. (Chase) T.; m. Frances Prindle, June 19, 1943; children: Frederick, Thomas, Cynthia, Tucker. B.A., Yale U., 1943, LL.B., 1948. Bar: Ohio 1948. Assoc. firm Jones, Day, Reavis & Pogue, Cleve., 1948-59, ptnr., 1959—. Mem. bd. commrs. Cuyahoga County, Ohio, 1971-78, pres., 1977-78; mem. Cuyahoga County Charter Commn., 1958-59, Republican candidate for gov. of Ohio, 1982; pres. Fedr. for Community Planning, Cleve., 1986—. Served with USNR, 1943-46. General corporate. Home: 6 Pepper Ridge Rd Cleveland OH 44124 Office: Jones Day Reavis & Pogue 901 Lakeside Ave Cleveland OH 44114

TAINTOR, FREDERICK GILES, lawyer; b. Cambridge, Mass., Mar. 14, 1923; s. Charles Wilson and Elizabeth Wood (Taber) T.; m. Jane Florence Skelton, July 2, 1951; children—Frederick Skelton, Anne Taintor Lemieux, Elizabeth Agnes, Christopher Skelton, Ellen Skelton. B.A., Yale U., 1945, J.D., 1951. Bar: Maine 1951, U.S. Dist. Ct. Maine 1952, U.S. Tax Ct. 1964, U.S. Ct. Appeals (1st cir.) 1964, U.S. Supreme Ct. 1964. Assoc. Skelton & Mahon, Lewiston, Maine, 1951-55, ptnr., 1956; ptnr. Skelton & Taintor, 1956-65; ptnr. Skelton, Taintor & Abbott, Lewiston, 1965-69, v.p., 1970-75, pres., 1975-82; pres. Skelton, Taintor, Abbott & Orestis, P.A., Lewiston, 1983-86, pres. Skelton, Taintor & Abbott, 1987—; city atty., Lewiston, 1981-86. Fire commr. City of Lewiston, 1968-71. Served to 1st lt. U.S. Army, 1942-46. Mem. ABA, Am. Bar Found., Maine Bar Assn., Androscoggin County Bar Assn. Republican. Labor, General corporate, Banking. Office: Skelton Taintor Abbott & Orestis 95 Main St PO Box 3200 Auburn ME 04210

TAIT, JOHN REID, lawyer; b. Toledo, Ohio, Apr. 7, 1946; s. Paul Reid and Lucy Richardson (Rudderow) T.; m. Christina Ruth Bjornstad, Mar. 12, 1972; children—Gretchen, Mary. B.A., Columbia Coll., 1968; J.D., Vanderbilt U., 1974. Bar: Idaho 1974, U.S. Dist. Ct. Idaho 1974. Assoc. Keeton & Tait, Lewiston, Idaho, 1974-76, ptnr. Keeton & Tait, 1976-86, Keeton, Tait & Petrie, 1986—. Chmn. bd. No. Rockies Action Group, Helena, Mont., 1985-86; bd. dirs. Lewiston Hist. Preservation Commn., Idaho, 1975—, Idaho Legal Aid Services, Boise, 1975—, Idaho Housing Agy., Boise, 1984—. Served with U.S. Army, 1968-71. Mem. ABA, Assn. Trial Lawyers Am., Idaho Trial Lawyers Assn., Clearwater Bar Assn. (sec. 1974-76, pres. 1984-86). Democrat. General practice, Workers' compensation, State civil litigation. Office: Keeton Tait & Petrie 312 Miller St PO Box E Lewiston ID 83501

TAIT, ROBERT ED, lawyer; b. Lima, Ohio, Sept. 3, 1946; s. Robert and Helen (Smith) T.; m. Donna G. Dome, June 22, 1968; children: Heather, Jennifer, Robert. BA, Kenyon Coll., 1968; JD, U. Mich., 1973. Bar: Ohio 1973, U.S. Dist. Ct. (so. dist.) Ohio. 1976, U.S. Dist. Ct. (no. dist.) Ohio 1976, U.S. Dist. Ct. Md. 1980, U.S. Ct. Appeals (6th cir.) 1981, U.S. Supreme Ct. 1982. Ptnr. Vorys, Sater, Seymour & Pease, Columbus, Ohio, 1973—. Staff counsel Govs. Select Com. on Prevention Indsl. Accidents, Columbus, 1977-78. Seved with U.S. Army, 1969-70. Mem. ABA, Ohio Bar Assn., Columbus Bar Assn., Def. Research Inst., Columbus Def. Assn., Assn. Ins. Attys. Clubs: Capital, Columbus Country. Workers' compensation, Personal injury, State civil litigation. Home: 2045 Wickerford Rd Columbus OH 43221 Office: Yorys Sater Seymour & Pease Box 1008 Columbus OH 43216

TAITZ, STEVEN CARTER, lawyer; b. Bronx, N.Y., Feb. 19, 1956; s. Arthur and Phyllis (Manta) T. BS, Johns Hopkins U., 1978; JD, U. Miami, 1982. Bar: Fla. 1982, U.S. Dist. Ct. (so. dist.) Fla. 1986. Asst. state atty. Dade County, Miami, 1982-86; atty. Samuel I. Burstyn P.A., Miami, Fla., 1986—. Mem. ABA, Dade County Bar Assn., Assn. Trial Lawyers Am., Nat. Inst. Trial Advocacy, Nat. Coll. Dist. Attys., Southwest Fla. Inst. Criminal Justice (instr. 1982—), Greater Miami Jaycees. Avocations: sailing, boating. Federal civil litigation, State civil litigation, Criminal. Office: Samuel I Burstyn PA 3050 Biscayne Blvd Suite 701 Miami FL 33137

TAKAS, MARIANNE HEATH, lawyer, writer; b. New Rochelle, N.Y., Sept. 16, 1955; d. Andrew and Jane (Heath) T.; m. Edward Warner, May 3, 1986. BS in Polit. Sci. and Philosophy with high honors, Mich. State U., 1976; JD, Emory U., 1980. Bar: Ga. 1980, Mass. 1987. Law clk. to presiding justice Superior Ct. of Fulton County, Atlanta, 1980-82; sole practice Cambridge, Mass., 1982—. Author: Child Support: A Complete, Up-to-Date, Authoritative Guide, 1987, Child Custody: A Complete Guide for Concerned Mothers, 1985; contbr. articles to popular mags. Mem. council on Battered Women, Atlanta, legal adv. com., 1980-82, chmn., organizer, atty. edn. seminars, 1981; active in numerous child support groups and events. Mem. ABA (mem. child support project), Ga. Bar Assn. (continuing legal edn. award 1982). Democrat. Avocations: swimming, bicycling, camping, photography. Family and matrimonial, Writing, legal, Juvenile. Office: 32 Soden St Cambridge MA 02139

TAKASHIMA, HIDEO, lawyer, accountant; b. Kobe, Hyogo-Ken, Japan, Mar. 2, 1919; came to U.S., 1956; s. Yoshimitsu and Yoshie (Akagi) T.; m. Adrianna Elizabeth Selch Coe, Oct. 31, 1961 (div. Apr. 1984); children—James, George K., Oliver Sachio; m. Chizu Kojima, Mar. 14, 1986. Chartered Acct., Kanagawa U., Yokohama, Japan, 1941; LL.M., Taihoku Imperial U., Japan, 1943; LL.M. in Bus. Law Yale U., 1957; S.J.D. in Antitrust Laws, N.Y. Law Sch., 1959; postgrad. Yale Sch. Law, 1961-62. Bar: D.C. 1973, U.S. Tax Ct. 1973, U.S. Ct. Appeals (D.C. cir.) 1973, N.J. 1974, U.S. Dist. Ct. N.J. 1974, U.S. Ct. Claims 1974, U.S. Ct. Appeals (3d cir.) 1977, U.S. Supreme Ct. 1977. Lectr. criminology Yen Ping Coll., Taipei, Taiwan, 1946-47; mgr. Taiwan br. Warner Bros. F.N. Pix, Inc., Taipei, 1947-52; with labor union activities dept. FOA MSM/C, Am. embassy, Taipei, 1953-54; tax editor Prentice-Hall, Inc., Englewood Cliffs, N.J., 1961-66; editor-in-chief Washington Publs., Inc., N.Y.C., 1966-69; tax atty., editor Am. Inst. C.P.A.s, N.Y.C., 1971-72; pres., Charles Hideo Coe, P.A., Jersey City, 1973—; dir. Coe & Coe, Inc., Park Ridge, N.J., 1973—; pvt. practice acctg., N.J. 1980—. Author: My Unsuspecting Formosa, 1944. Editor-in-chief The Tax Barometer, 1966-69. Capt. Chinese Kuo-Min-Tang, Taipei, 1945; Judo-Kendo instr. New Milford Recreation Commn., N.J., 1963-69, Park Ridge Recreation Com., 1969-72, Pascack Valley Kendo Club, Park Ridge, 1969-71. Yale Law Sch. fellow, 1956-57; N.Y. Law Sch. scholar, 1958, Prentice-Hall, Inc. scholar grad. div. NYU Sch. Law, 1961-63. Mem. Am. Immigration Lawyers Assn. (sec. N.J. chpt. 1978-83), Assn. Trial Lawyers Am., N.J. Assn. Pub. Accts., Yale Law Sch. Alumni Assn., NYU Law Alumni Assn. Republican. Am. Assn. N.Y. Clubs: Yale (N.Y.C.); Japanese Community Pioneer Ctr. (Los Angeles), Japanese Am. Assn. of N.Y. General practice, Immigration, naturalization, and customs, Antitrust. Home: 15377 Shefford St Hacienda Heights Los Angeles CA 91745 Address: Charles Hideo Coe Journal Sq Station PO Box 16702 Jersey City NJ 07306 Office: 303 Fifth Ave New York NY 10016

TAKASUGI, ROBERT MITSUHIRO, federal judge; b. Tacoma, Sept. 12, 1930; s. Hidesaburo and Kayo (Otsuki) T.; m. Dorothy O. Takasugi; children: Jon Robert, Lesli Mari. BS, UCLA, Los Angeles, 1953; LLB, JD, U. So. Calif., 1959. Bar: Calif. bar 1960. Practiced law Los Angeles, 1960-73; judge East Los Angeles Municipal Ct., 1973-75, adminstrv. judge, 1974, presiding judge, 1975; judge Superior Ct., County of Los Angeles, 1975-76; U.S. dist. judge U.S. Dist. Ct. for Central Dist. Calif., 1976—; nat. legal counsel Japanese Am. Citizens League; guest lectr. law seminars Harvard U. Law Sch. Careers Symposium; commencement speaker; mem. Atty. Liaison/Lawyers Rep. Circuit Conf. Com.; chmn. affirmative action com., calendar relief com., new judges' calendar com.; mem. pub. defender and indigent def. panel com.; mem. Legion Lex U. So. Calif. Law Center. Mem. editorial bd. U. So. Calif. Law Rev., 1959; contbr. articles to profl. jours. Mem. Calif.

adv. com. Western Regional Office, U.S. Commn. on Civil Rights. Served with U.S. Army, 1953-55. Recipient U.S. Mil. Man of Yr. award for Far East Theater U.S. Army, 1954; certificate of merit Japanese-Am. Bar Assn.; other awards; Harry J. Bauer scholar, 1959. Mem. U. So. Calif. Law Alumni (dir.). Club: Optimists (Los Angeles) (hon. dir. local club). Jurisprudence. Office: US Dist Ct US Courthouse 312 N Spring St Los Angeles CA 90012

TAKAYAMA, KEN HIDESHI, lawyer; b. Honolulu, Nov. 13, 1951; s. Mitsuo and Amy (Yamauchi) T.; m. Diane Sachi Kishimoto, July 1, 1979. AB, Occidental Coll., 1973; JD, U. Calif., Berkeley, 1976. Bar: Hawaii 1976, U.S. Dist. Ct. Hawaii 1976. Atty. Legal Aid Soc. of Hawaii, Honolulu, 1976-77, also bd. dirs., 1984—; atty. Office of Council Services, City and County of Honolulu, 1977-79, Legis. Reference Bur., Honolulu, 1979—. Mem. Hawaii State Bd. Cosmetology, Honolulu, 1986—; mediator Neighborhood Justice Ctr. of Honolulu, 1979—. Served with JAGC, Hawaii Army N.G., 1982—. Mem. ABA (state and local govt. sect.), Hawaii State Bar Assn. Democrat. Avocations: jogging, stamp and coin collecting, ballroom dancing. Legislative, Local government, Administrative and regulatory. Office: Legis Reference Bur State Capitol Room 004 Honolulu HI 96813-2407

TALAFOUS, JOSEPH JOHN, lawyer; b. N.Y.C., Sept. 6, 1929; s. Karol J. and Anna (Sulik) T.; m. Louise Lukac, June 18, 1955; children—Mary Lou, Joseph J., Caroline, Theresa. A.B., Rutgers U., 1954; J.D., Seton Hall U., 1958. Bar: N.J. 1959, U.S. Dist. Ct. N.J. 1959, U.S. Dist. Ct. (so. dist.) N.Y. 1959, U.S. Dist. Ct. (ea. dist.) N.Y. 1965, U.S. Supreme Ct. 1965. Sole practice, Jersey City, 1959—; asst. prosecutor Hudson County, N.J., 1962-63; asst. corp. csl. City of Jersey City, 1965-72; judge Mcpl. Ct., Jersey City, 1974-77. Pres., Slovak Am. Heritage Found., Inc., 1976—. Served with U.S. Army, 1951-53, Korea. Mem. ABA, N.J. Bar Assn., Hudson County Bar Assn., Hague Acad. Internat. Law. Democrat. Roman Catholic. General practice, Private international, Probate. Office: 924 Bergen Ave Jersey City NJ 07306

TALAREK, WALTER GLENN, lawyer; b. N.Y.C., Aug. 3, 1946; s. Walter M. and Phyllis M. (Werst) T.; m. Paula L. Heins; 1 child, Walter G. Jr. BS in Indsl. Engring., Fairleigh Dickinson U., 1969; JD, U. Md., 1974. Bar: Md. 1975, D.C. 1976, U.S. Dist. Ct. D.C. 1979, Va. 1982, U.S. Ct. Appeals (D.C. cir.) 1982. Chief state and local programs sect., imports sect. U.S. EPA, Washington, 1974-79, chief field coordination and program devel. br., 1980-81; regulatory analyst U.S. Dept. Energy, Washington, 1979-80; gen. counsel Am. Wood Preservers Inst., Vienna, Va., 1981-86; sole practice Tysons Corner, Va., 1986—; pres. Talarek and Assocs., Tysons Corner, 1986—. Mem. ABA, Fed. Bar Assn., Am. Wood Preservers Assn., Phi Zeta Kappa, Phi Omega Epsilon. Avocations: jogging, international travel. Administrative and regulatory, Environment, Legislative. Office: 7779 Leesburg Pike Suite 900 Tysons Corner VA 22043

TALBOTT, FRANK, III, lawyer; b. Danville, Va., Mar. 26, 1929; s. Frank and Margaret (Jordan) T.; m. Mary Beverley Chewning, July 11, 1952; children: Beverley, Frank IV. B.A., U. Va., 1951, LL.B., 1953. Bar: Va. 1952. Gen. practice law Danville, 1956-66; with Dan River Inc., 1966-76, v.p., gen. counsel, 1968-76; partner firm Clement, Wheatley, Winston, Talbott & Majors, Danville, 1977-78; individual practice law Danville, 1979—; chmn. adv. bd. Sovran Bank, Danville. Vice chmn. Danville Sch. Bd., 1964-70; Sec. Danville Democratic Com., 1962-63; Trustee Va. Student Aid Found., 1963-68; bd. dirs. United Fund Danville, 1959-63, Meml. Hosp., Danville, 1977—. Served with AUS, 1953-56. Decorated Commendation medal. Fellow Am. Bar Found.; mem. ABA, Va. Bar Assn. (v.p. 1965-66, exec. com. 1967-70), Danville Bar Assn. (pres. 1965-66), Am. Judicature Soc., Newcomen Soc., U. Va. Alumni Assn. (bd. mgrs.), Delta Psi, Phi Alpha Delta. Methodist. Clubs: Golf (Danville), German (Danville); Farmington Country (Charlottesville, Va.); Commonwealth (Richmond, Va.). General corporate, Legislative. Home: 420 Maple Ln Danville VA 24541 Office: 326 Masonic Bldg Danville VA 24541

TALCOTT, KENT PATTERSON, lawyer; b. Dearborn, Mich., Feb. 26, 1938; s. Horace Patterson and Marian (Procknow) T.; m. M. Jane Shurtleff, June 22, 1957; children: Vance Patterson, Rita Lynn. Student, U. Mich., 1956-59, BBA, 1962; postgrad., Wayne State U., 1962-63; JD with distinction, U. Mich., 1965. Bar: Mich. 1965, U.S. Dist. ct. (ea. dist.) Mich. 1966, U.S. Ct. Appeals (6th cir.) 1966, U.S. Tax Ct. 1966. Assoc. Wunsch, Aikens & Lungershausen, Detroit, 1965-67; asst. pros. atty. Washtenaw County, Ann Arbor, Mich., 1967-69; mng. ptnr. Ellis, Talcott, Ohlgren & Ferguson, Ann Arbor, 1969—; bd. dirs. VSP Labs., Ann Arbor, C & H Stamping, Inc., Jackson, Mich. Mem., past pres. Manchester (Mich.) Bd. of Edn., 1981-86, Ann Arbor Bd. of Canvassers, 1971-73, Washtenaw County Plat Bd., Ann Arbor, 1971-73, Washtenaw County Bd. of Auditors, Ann Arbor, 1971-73; 3d ward dir. Ann Arbor Reps., 1st ward dir.,; pres. bd. dirs. Washtenaw Red Cross, 1973-81; bd. dirs. Chelsea (Mich.) Community Hosp., 1986—. Mem. ABA, Washtenaw County Bar Assn., Order of Coif. Republican. Lodge: Optimists (past pres. Ann Arbor chpt., bd. dirs. Manchester chpt.). General corporate, Private international, Corporate taxation. Home: 6886 Ernst Rd Manchester MI 48158 Office: Ellis Talcott Ohlgren & Ferguson 320 N Main St Suite 300 Ann Arbor MI 48104

TALDONE, NICHOLAS JOHN, lawyer; b. N.Y.C., Feb. 2, 1954; s. John S. and Lena S. (Capelli) T.; m. Suzanne Green, May 8, 1986. Student, SUNY, Stony Brook, 1972-74; BS, SUNY, Albany, 1976, JD, 1979. Bar: N.Y. 1980, U.S. Dist. Ct. (so. dist.) N.Y. 1980, N.J 1983, U.S. Dist. Ct. N.J. 1983, U.S. Supreme Ct. 1985, Calif. 1986. Assoc. Jackson, Lewis, Schnitzler & Krupman, N.Y.C., 1979-84; labor counsel Grandmet USA, Montvale, N.J., 1984—. Contbr. articles to profl. jours. Bd. dirs. Hudson Riverfront Mus., 1986—. Mem. ABA (chmn. corp. counsel com. young lawyers div., 1986—), N.J. State Bar Assn. (del. to ABA 1987—, trustee 1986—, editor-in-chief labor and employment law newsletter 1987—), N.Y. State Bar Assn., Calif. Bar Assn. Labor, Environment, Pension, profit-sharing, and employee benefits. Office: Grandmet USA 100 Paragon Dr Montvale NJ 07645

TALESNICK, ALAN LEE, lawyer; b. Indpls., Aug. 12, 1945; s. Irvin and Ruth (Newman) T. AB, Harvard U., 1967, MBA, JD, 1972. Bar: Colo. 1972. Assoc. Holme, Roberts & Owen, Denver, 1972-76, ptnr., 1977-78; ptnr. Parcel, Talesnick, Meyer & Schwartz, Denver, 1978-83, Bearman, Talesnick & McNulty PC, Denver, 1983—. Trustee Colo. Women's Coll., Denver, 1979-82; mem. adv. com. Denver Ctr. Theater, 1986—. Mem. ABA, Colo. Bar Assn., Denver Bar Assn. (exec. com. young lawyers council 1977-79, chmn. securities com. 1984-85). Jewish. Avocations: tennis, reading, skiing, theater. General corporate, Securities. Home: 5030 Bow Mar Dr Littleton CO 80123 Office: Bearman Talesnick & McNulty PC 1675 Larimer St Denver CO 80202

TALIAFERRO, BRUCE OWEN, lawyer; b. Kansas City, Mo., Feb. 13, 1947; s. Paul Everett and Irene Winifred (Warden) T.; m. Gail Ann Niesen, Aug. 16, 1969; children—Tracy Ann, Patrick Andrew. B.A., U. Ark., 1969; J.D., U. Tulsa, 1971. Bar: Okla. 1972, U.S. Dist. Ct. (no. dist.) Okla. 1972, U.S. Ct. Appeals (10th cir.) 1975, U.S. Sup. Ct. 19. Assoc. Dennis J. Downing & Assocs., Tulsa, 1972-78; ptnr. Taliaferro, Malloy & Elder, Tulsa, 1979-84; sole practice, Tulsa, 1984—. Served to maj. USAFR, 1976—. Mem. ABA, Okla. Bar Assn., Tulsa County Bar Assn. (chmn. law day com. 1973), Am. Judicature Soc., Am. Soc. Law and Medicine, Okla. Assn. Def. Csl., Tulsa Claim Men Assn., Delta Theta Phi. Republican. Mem. Ch. of Christ. Club: Candlewood (Tulsa). Workers' compensation, Estate planning, Personal income taxation. Home: 5678 S Utica Ave Tulsa OK 74105 Office: Suite 310 Elmcrest Park Office Ctr 2700 E 51st St Tulsa OK 74105

TALLANT, DAVID, JR., lawyer; b. Oak Park, Ill., Mar. 16, 1931. A.B., Claremont Men's Coll., 1953; J.D., Duke U., 1956. Bar: Ill. 1956. Assoc. Chapman & Cutler, Chgo., 1956-65, ptnr., 1965—. Mem. ABA, Ill. Bar Assn., Chgo. Bar Assn. Banking, Contracts commercial. Office: Chapman & Cutler 111 W Monroe St Chicago IL 60603

TALLENT, STEPHEN EDISON, lawyer; b. Columbus, Nebr., Aug. 10, 1937; s. William E. and Helen T.; m. Martha Sutcliffe, Apr. 6, 1971; 1 child, Jennifer Diane. B.A., Stanford U.; J.D., U. Chgo. Bar: Calif. 1963, U.S. Dist. Ct. (so. and cen. dists.) Calif. 1965, U.S. Ct. Appeals (9th cir.) 1968, U.S. Ct. Mil. Appeals 1965, U.S. Supreme Ct. 1973, U.S. Ct. Appeals (3d cir.) 1980, U.S. Ct. Appeals (4th cir.) 1982, D.C. Ct. Appeals 1981. Ptnr. Gibson, Dunn & Crutcher, Los Angeles, 1962—; former adj. prof. Loyola Law Sch., Los Angeles; mem. vis. com. U. Chgo. Law Sch. Mem. Calif. Atty. Gen.'s adv. com. for Evaluation of Anti-Organized Crime Programs; mem. Los Angeles Town Hall, Los Angeles World Affairs Council. Served with AUS. Mem. ABA, Calif. Bar Assn., D.C. Bar Assn., N.Y. Bar, Los Angeles County Bar Assn., Indsl. Relations Research Assn. Club: University of Los Angeles. Labor, Administrative and regulatory, Legislative. Home: 7020 Glenbrook Rd Bethesda MD 20814 Office: Gibson Dunn & Crutcher 333 S Grand Ave Los Angeles CA 90071 also: 1050 Connecticut Ave NW Washington DC 20036

TALLERICO, THOMAS JOSEPH, lawyer; b. Detroit, Oct. 24, 1946; s. Joseph Louis and Irene Marie (Srock) T.; m. Ellen Marie Donnelly, May 12, 1973; children—Brian Thomas, Anne Elizabeth. B.A. cum laude, Sacred Heart Sem., 1968; J.D. cum laude, U. Mich., 1973. Bar: Mich. 1974, D.C. 1976. Atty.-adviser Dept. State, Washington, 1973-76; assoc. Jaffe, Snider, Raitt & Heuer, Detroit, 1976-81, ptnr., 1981—; spl. asst. atty. gen. Mich., 1983—. Trustee Met. Detroit Youth Found., 1983—. Mem. ABA, Detroit Bar Assn., Oakland County Bar Assn. Club: Detroit Athletic. Federal civil litigation, State civil litigation, Antitrust. Office: Jaffe Snider Raitt & Heuer PC 1800 1st Nat Bldg Detroit MI 48226

TALLEY-MORRIS, NEVA BENNETT, lawyer; b. Judsonia, Ark., Aug. 12, 1909; d. John W. and Erma (Rhew) Bennett; m. Cecil C. Talley, Jan. 1, 1946 (dec. Oct. 1948); m. Joseph H. Morris, Mar. 22, 1952 (dec. Dec. 1974). BA magna cum laude, Ouachita Coll., 1930; MEd, U. Tex., 1938, postgrad., 1939-41, PhD in Law, 1984; PhD in Law, World U., 1984. Bar: Ark. bar 1947, U.S. Supreme Ct. bar 1950. Tchr. high sch., prin. White County, Ark., 1930-42; student asst. U. Tex., summers 1937-41; ordnance insp. war service appointment U.S. Army Service Forces, 1942-45; law office apprentice, pvt. tutor North Little Rock, Ark., 1945-47; practiced in Little Rock, 1947—; del., mem. program coordinating com. World Peace through Law Conf., Manila, 1977, mem. pre-biennial goals and planning com., Madrid, 1978; program participant World Peace through Law Conf., Jerusalem conf., 1979, Brazil, 1981, Cairo, 1983; mem. com. on Client Security Fund, Ark. Supreme Ct., 1978-82, chmn. client security com., 1980-82; mem. Ark. Lawyers Com. for Appellate Cts., 1978; chmn. com. for Ark. lawyer writing awards Ark. Bar Assn. Found., 1981-86; program speaker 12th Biennial Conf. World Peace through Law, Berlin, 1985. Author: Family Law Practice and Procedure Handbook, 1973, Appellate Civil Practice and Procedure, 1975; contbr. articles to profl. publs. Chmn. Ark. Council on Children and Youth, 1952-54; participant People to People Program, citizen ambassador to Peoples Republic China, Beijing, 1985. Named hon. mayor-pres. City of Baton Rouge, 1985. Fellow Ark. Bar Found. (bd. fellows), Internat. Biog. Assn., Am. Acad. Matrimonial Lawyers (gov. 1974-79), Phi Alpha Delta (hon.); mem. Nat. Assn. Women Lawyers (life, council del., pres. 1956-57, pres. NAWL Found. 1958, Achievement award 1962, hon. chmn. family law com. 1970-71), Ark. Assn. Women Lawyers (Outstanding Achievement award 1971, program chmn. 1977), Little Rock Assn. Women Lawyers, pres. 1950-51), North Little Rock Bus. and Profl. Women's Club (pres. 1951-52), AAUW (life), Am. Bar Assn. (mem. family law council 1958—, chmn. family law sect. 1969-70, ho. of dels., com. on late reports 1972-73, com. on hearings 1973-74, standing com. on memberships 1974-80, cert. of merit ann. conv. 1979, 80, judge Schwab legal essay contest 1980, sr. div. com. on alternates for dispute resolution 1986—), Ark. Bar Assn. (Distinguished Service to Legal Profession award 1970, chmn. family law reform com. 1960-61, ho. of dels. 1957-58, 74-78, Outstanding Lawyer-Citizen award 1978), Pulaski County Bar Assn. (chmn. com. on continuing legal edn. and programs 1978), World Assn. Lawyers (founding), Am. Judicature Soc. (cert. of appreciation 1979), Nat. Conf. Lawyers and Social Workers (exec. bd. 1962-66, 70-74), Smithsonian Assocs., U.S. Supreme Ct. Hist. Soc., Scribes-Legal Writers Assn., Phi Alpha Delta (1st woman hon.). Family and matrimonial, Probate, Federal civil litigation. Office: 1013 W Markham St Little Rock AR 72201

TALLIS, ALAN LOUIS, hotel executive; b. Suffern, N.Y., Apr. 16, 1946; s. Sam Tallis and Emily Helen (Sabel) Raze; m. Shirley Ann Abraham, Dec. 30, 1977; children: Bryan, Scott. BA, U. Miami, 1968, JD, 1972; MBA, U. Tex., 1983. Sole practice Orlando, Fla., 1972-77; v.p., gen. counsel LR Property Mgmt., Inc., S. Daytona, Fla., 1977-78, Internat. Community Corp., Orlando, 1978-80; sr. corp. atty. La Quinta Motor Inns, Inc., San Antonio, 1980-82, dir. devel., adminstrn., 1982-83, v.p., gen. counsel, 1983-86, sr. v.p. devel. programs, gen. counsel, 1986—. Fund raiser Elf Louise, San Antonio. Served with USAR, 1968-74. Named one of Outstanding Young Men of Am., U.S. Jaycees, 1982. Mem. ABA, Tex. Bar Assn., Fla. Bar Assn., Am. Hotel Motel Assn. (gen. counsels com.), Nat. Assn. Corp. Real Estate Execs., Urban Land Inst., Phi Beta Kappa. Republican. Jewish. Avocations: swimming, sailing, cooking. General corporate, Real property. Office: La Quinta Motor Inns Inc 10100 San Pedro San Antonio TX 78216

TALMADGE, JEFFREY DAVID, lawyer; b. Uvalde, Tex., Feb. 18, 1953; s. John Mills and Marjorie (Beach) T. BA, Duke U., 1975; JD, U. Tex., 1980. Bar: Tex. 1980, U.S. Dist. Ct. (so. dist.) Tex. 1980, U.S. Ct. Appeals (5th and 11th cirs.) 1981, U.S. Dist. Ct. (we. dist.) Tex. 1984. Assoc. Fulbright & Jaworski, Houston and Austin, Tex., 1980-85, Mullen, Berliner, MacInnes & Redding, Austin, 1985—. Bd. dirs. Austin Lawyers and Accts. for the Arts, Austin, 1983-85; mem. Leadership Austin, 1983-84. Mem. ABA, Tex. Young Lawyers Assn., Austin Young Lawyers Assn. (bd. dirs. 1983-86). Democrat. State civil litigation. Office: Mullen Berliner MacInnes & Redding 812 San Antonio Penthouse Austin TX 78701

TALMO, RONALD VICTOR, lawyer, educator; b. Wilmington, Del., May 16, 1951; s. Victor Rinaldo and Jessie (Rash) T.; m. Gale Loraine Taplin, Sept. 16, 1984; 1 child, Ellery. B.A. in Sociology, U. Del., 1974; J.D., Pepperdine U., 1977. Bar: Calif. 1977, U.S. Dist. Ct. (cen. dist.) Calif. 1977. Sole practice, Santa Ana, Calif., 1977-82; ptnr. firm Wallin, Roseman & Talmo, Tustin, Calif., 1982-85; prof. law, Western State U., Fullerton, Calif., 1979—. Contbr. articles to law revs. Legal dir. Orange County chp. ACLU, Costa Mesa, Calif., 1978-82. Recipient Civil Rights award ACLU, 1984. Mem. Orange County Bar Assn. (mem. faculty coll. trial advocacy 1984-86). Democrat. Civil rights, Criminal. Office: Western State U Coll of Law 1111 N State College Blvd Fullerton CA 92631

TALPOS, JOHN C., lawyer; b. Detroit, Oct. 31, 1944; s. John C. and Mildred G. (Rogan) T.; m. Beatrice MaryAnn Malensky, Sept. 11, 1970; children: Sara K., John C. III. BA, U. Detroit, 1966, JD cum laude, 1969; LLM in Criminal Justice, NYU, 1971. Bar: Mich. 1969, U.S. Dist. Ct. (ea. dist.) Mich. 1969, U.S. Supreme Ct. 1980, U.S. Ct. Appeals (6th cir.) 1981. Research atty. Mich. Ct. Appeals, Detroit, 1969-70, law clk. to presiding justice, 1970-71; asst. pros. atty. Oakland County, Mich., 1971-72; ptnr. Talpos & Arnold P.C., Troy, Mich., 1973—. Commr. Pleasant Ridge (Mich.) Planning Commn., 1981-85, City of Pleasant Ridge Commn., 1985—. Fellow Ford Found. Mem. ABA (sect. criminal justice, drunk driving com. 1983-85, grand jury com. 1982-83, publs. com. 1981-82, continuing legal edn. com. 1974-76), Mich. Bar Assn. (rep. assembly 1975-81, prisons and corrections com. 1978—, criminal jurisprudence com. 1978-81, criminal procedure revision com. 1978-80), Union Internat. De Advocats, Criminal Def. Attys. Mich., Assn. Trial Lawyers Am., Mich. Trial Lawyers Assn. (jud. endorsement com. 1982-84), Am. Judicature Soc., Am. Arbitration Assn. Avocations: fishing, reading, skiing. Personal injury, Family and matrimonial, Criminal. Office: Talpos & Arnold PC 2855 Coolidge Suite 109 Troy MI 48084

TAM, JAMES KELLETT, lawyer; b. Paia, Hawaii, Feb. 3, 1949; s. Edward Kum and Amy (Chang) T.; m. Linda Frances Woolley, Aug. 24, 1975; children: Emily, Mary, Jason. BA, Williams Coll., 1971; JD, Georgetown U., 1974. Ptnr. Hoddick, Reinwald, O'Connor & Marrack, Honolulu, 1974-83; v.p., dir. Ezra, O'Connor, Moon & Tam, Honolulu, 1984—. Pres., dir. emergency youth shelter Hale Kipa, Honolulu, 1984—; deacon Cen. Union Ch., Honolulu, 1984—. Mem. ABA, Small Bus. Council of Am., Internat. Found. Employee Benefit Plans, Hawaii State Bar (bd. dirs. 1986—, sec. real property, fin. Services sect., 1985-86). Club: Pacific. Avocations: athletics, outdoor activities. Contracts commercial, Pension, profit-sharing, and employee benefits, Real property. Office: Ezra O'Connor Moon & Tam 220 S King St 20th Floor Honolulu HI 96813

TAMKIN, ALVIN CHASIN, lawyer; b. Boston, June 19, 1924. B.S. in Bus. Adminstrn., Boston U., 1946, LL.B., 1948. Bar: Mass. 1948, U.S. Dist. Ct. Mass. 1949. Sole practice, Boston, 1948-63; presiding justice Mass. Dist. Ct., Hingham, 1963—; mem. civil adv. com. Supreme Jud. Ct., 1970-84; chmn. civil rules com. and edn. com. Dist. Cts. Mass., 1970-76, assoc. justice appelate div., 1975-79; gov.'s councillor, Mass. 1960-62; mem. Mass. Ho. of Reps., 1955-62. Hon. pres. New England region Am. Jewish Congress; hon. trustee Combined Jewish Philanthropies. Mem. ABA, Mass. Bar Assn., Plymouth County Bar Assn., Boston U. Law Sch. Alumni Assn (past pres.). Home: 79 Woodcliff Rd Brookline MA 02167 Office: 28 George Washington Blvd Hingham MA 02043

TAMMANY, DONALD TIMOTHY, lawyer; b. Wilmington, Del., Apr. 11, 1951; s. Donald Tammany and Patsy Randolph (Mayerberg) Guthrie; m. Ann Ramona Steiner, June 23, 1973 (div. Sept. 1983); m. Elissa Mabel Lewis, Dec. 31, 1983; 1 child, Hope Madeleine. BA, Haverford Coll., 1974; MBA, U. Pa., 1978, JD, 1978; LLM in Taxation, NYU, 1981. Bar: Pa. 1978, U.S. Dist. Ct. (ea. dist.) Pa. 1978, U.S. Tax Ct. 1979, U.S. Ct. Claims 1979. Assoc. Obermayer, Rebmann, Maxwell & Hippel, Phila., 1978-83; counsel CIGNA Corp., Phila., 1983—; lectr. in law Temple U., Phila., 1980—; adj. asst. prof. Drexel U., Phila., 1985—. Author, lectr. Pa. Bar Inst., 1982-84, Temple U., 1984-86. V.p. Wynnewood (Pa.) Civic Assn., 1987—; Vestryman Ch. of Good Shepherd, Rosemont, Pa., 1984—; pres. Phila. chpt. Evang. and Cath. Mission, 1986—. Mem. ABA, Phila. Bar Assn., Tax Study Group, Federalist Soc. Republican. Episcopalian. Corporate taxation, Personal income taxation. Home: 1345 Morris Rd Wynnewood PA 19096 Office: CIGNA Corp One Logan Sq Philadelphia PA 19103

TAMULONIS, FRANK LOUIS, JR., lawyer; b. Pottsville, Pa., Sept. 26, 1946; s. Frank Louis Sr. and Cecelia Florence (Hoffman) T.; m. Jane Alice Troutman, June 26, 1976; children: Kathryn Lydia, Frank Louis III. AB, Cornell U., 1968; JD, Villanova Law Sch., 1971. Bar: Pa. 1971, U.S. Supreme Ct. 1975, U.S. Ct. Appeals (3d cir.) 1981. Law clk. to presiding justice U.S. Dist. Ct. (ea. dist.), Phila., 1971-74; assoc. Kassab, Cherry & Archbold, Media, Pa., 1974-76, Zimmerman, Lieberman & Derenzo, Pottsville, 1976—. Contbr. articles to profl. jours. Mem. Am. Trial Lawyers Assn., Def. Research Inst., Pa. Def. Inst., Inst. Pa. Trial Lawyers Assn., Pa. Bar Assn., Schuylkill County Bar Assn. Republican. Roman Catholic. Personal injury, Workers' compensation, State civil litigation. Office: Zimmerman Lieberman & Derenzo 111 E Market St PO Box 238 Pottsville PA 17901

TAN, WILLIAM LEW, lawyer; b. West Hollywood, Calif., July 25, 1949; s. James Tan Lew and Choon Guey Louie. BA, U. Pa., 1971; JD, U. Calif. Hastings Coll. Law, San Francisco, 1974. Bar: Calif. 1975, U.S. Dist. Ct. (cen. dist.) Calif. 1975, U.S. Ct. Appeals (9th cir.) 1975, U.S. Supreme Ct. 1979. Assoc. Hiram W. Kwan, Los Angeles, 1974-79; ptnr. Mock & Tan, Los Angeles, 1979-80; sole practice Los Angeles, 1980-81; ptnr. Tan & Sakiyama, P.C., Los Angeles, 1981—; bd. dirs. Pacific Career Opportunities, Los Angeles, Am. Bus. Network, Los Angeles; pres., bd. dirs. Asian Research Cons., Los Angeles. Founder Asian Pacific Am. Roundtable, Los Angeles, 1981; chmn. bd. dirs. Leaderhip Edn. for Asian-Pacifics, Los Angeles, 1984; alt. del. Dem. Nat. Conv., San Francisco, 1984; mem. Calif. State Bd. Pharmacy, Sacramento, 1984, Los Angeles City and County Crime Crisis Task Force, Los Angeles, 1981, Los Angeles Asian Pacific Heritage Week Com., 1980—, Asian Pacific Women's Network, Los Angeles, 1981, Los Angeles City Atty.'s Blue Ribbon Con. of Advisors, 1981, community adv. bd. to Mayor of Los Angeles, 1984, allocations vol. liaison team health and therapy div. United Way, Los Angeles, 1986; bd. dirs. Chinatown Service Ctr., Los Angeles, 1983; conf. advisor U.S.-Asia, Los Angeles, 1981-83; atty. Los Angeles City Housing Adv. Com. Named one of Outstanding Young Men of Am., 1979. Mem. ABA (mem. numerous coms.), Calif. State Bar Assn. (vice chmn. com. ethnic minority relations 1983-85, chmn. pub. affairs com. 1981-82, mem. others), Los Angeles County Bar Assn. (vice chmn. 1980-82, mem. numerous coms.), So. Calif. Chinese Lawyers Assn. (pres. 1980-81, mem. various coms.), Minority Bar Assn. (chmn. 1981-82, sec. 1980-81, chmn. adv. bd. 1982-83), Asian Pacific Bar of Calif., Nat. Asian Pacific Am. Bar, Japanese Am. Bar Assn., Assn. Trial Lawyers Am., Bench and Bar Council, Calif. Trial Lawyers Assn., Soc. Intercultural Edn. (conf. coordinator, advisor panelist tng. and research com. 1983),. Club: Marina City (Marina del Rey, Calif.). Avocations: gourmet cooking, bicycling, swimming, tennis, water color painting. Administrative and regulatory, Immigration, naturalization, and customs, Real property. Office: Tan & Sakiyama 711 W College St Suite 610 Los Angeles CA 90012

TANAKA, AKIHIKO, lawyer; b. Tokyo, Apr. 25, 1953; s. Tsutomu and Kyoko (Kuranari) T. Ed., U. Tokyo, 1972-75; M.A.L.D., Fletcher Sch. Law and Diplomacy, 1978. Econ. officer Am. Affairs Bur. Japanese Fgn. Ministry, Tokyo, 1975-76; press sec., then aide to ambassador Embassy of Japan, Washington, 1978-80; legal adviser Treaties Bur., Japanese Fgn. Ministry, Tokyo, 1980-82, dep. bd. dirs. Multilateral Corp., 1985-86; counsel legal dept. World Bank, Washington, 1982—; lectr. on diplomacy and internat. law at univs. Mem. Am. Soc. Internat. Law, Japanese Assn. Internat. Law. Anglican. Banking, Private international, Public international. Office: World Bank 1818 H St NW Washington DC 20433

TANAKA, LEILA CHIYAKO, lawyer; b. Honolulu, Mar. 11, 1954; d. Masami and Bernice Kiyoka (Nakamura) T. BA in Japanese Lang., Am. Studies with distinction, U. Hawaii, Manua, 1977; JD, U. Santa Clara, 1980. Bar: Hawaii 1980, U.S. Dist. Ct. Hawaii 1980. Sole practice 1980-81; law clk. to presiding justice State Cir. Ct. (2d cir.), Waikaku, Maui, Hawaii, 1981-82; spl. dep. atty. gen. Dept. of Atty. Gen., Honolulu, 1982-83; dep. atty. gen. Dept. of Atty. Gen., Hawaii, 1983—; br. chief Hawaii Housing Authority, 1987—; trial examiners eviction hearings Hawaii Housing Authority, 1986—. Mem. ABA, Assn. Trial Lawyers Am., Phi Kappa Phi. Democrat. Buddhist. Avocations: reading, needlework, crafts, cooking, music. Condemnation, State civil litigation. Office: State of Hawaii Dept Atty Gen 465 S King St Room 203 Honolulu HI 96813

TANCREDI, LAURENCE RICHARD, law and psychiatry educator, administrator, consultant; b. Hershey, Pa., Oct. 15, 1940; s. Samuel N. and Alvesta (Pera) T. A.B. in English, Franklin and Marshall Coll., 1962; M.D., U. Pa., 1966; J.D., Yale U., 1972. Diplomate Am. Bd. Neurology and Psychiatry. Bar: N.Y. 1982. Sr. profl. assoc. Inst. of Medicine, Nat. Acad. Scis., Washington, 1972-74; fellow dept. psychiatry Columbia U. Coll. Physicians and Surgeons, N.Y.C., 1974-75; postdoctoral fellow in psychiatry Yale Med. Sch., New Haven, 1975-77; assoc. prof. psychiatry and law NYU Med. Sch., 1977-84, adj. prof. law Sch. of Law, 1977-84; Kraft Eidman prof. medicine and law U. Tex. Health Sci. Ctr., Houston, 1984—, dir. Health Law Program, U. Tex. Health Sci. Ctr., Houston, 1984—; mem. bd. tech. dirs. Milbank Meml. Fund, N.Y.C., 1981-84; mem. adv. com. on heart transplantations Health Care Fin. Adminstrn., Dept. HHS, 1981-84, other coms.; cons. Commn. on Med. Profl. Liability, co-prin. investigator study ABA, 1978-80. Co- author 5 books. Editor and contbg. author 4 books. Contbr. articles to profl. jours. Mem. editorial bd. Ann. Bibliography on Bioethics, Kennedy Inst. Bioethics, 1979—. Mem. Am. Psychiat. Assn. (chmn. council on govt. policy and the law 1979-81), Am. Soc. Law and Medicine, Soc. Med. Jurisprudence (trustee 1983-85). Health, Legal education.

TANENBAUM, BRIAN IRA, lawyer; b. Chgo., Mar. 16, 1957; s. Fred Samuel and Dressel Cheryl (Alpert). BA in Am. History with high distinction, U. Mich., 1978; JD, Hofstra U., 1981. Bar: Ill. 1981, N.Y. 1982, U.S. Dist. Ct. (no. dist.) Ill. 1984. Assoc. Reisman, Peirez & Reisman, Garden City, N.Y., 1981-84, Mathewson, Hamblet & Casey, Chgo., 1984—. Mem. ABA, Ill. Bar Assn. Democrat. Jewish. Club: Am. Bridge League. Avocations: bridge, hockey, football. Bankruptcy, State civil litigation, Contracts commercial. Home: 2341 1/2 N Geneva Terr Chicago IL 60614

TANENBAUM, JAY HARVEY, lawyer; b. N.Y.C., Nov. 17, 1933; s. Leo Aaron and Regina (Stein) T.; m. Linda Goldman, May 28, 1960; children: Susan Hillary, Steven Eric. BA, Hobart and William Smith Colls., 1954;

LLB, Union U., 1957, JD, 1961. Bar: N.Y. 1957, U.S. Dist. Ct. (so. dist.) N.Y. 1961, U.S. Supreme Ct. 1967. Internat. trader Associated Metals and Minerals Corp., N.Y.C., 1960-64; sole practice N.Y.C., 1964—; corp. counsel Internat. Gate Corp., Gen. Gate Corp. Mem. N.Y. State Bar Assn., N.Y. Trial Lawyers Assn., Bronx County Bar Assn. Jewish. Club: St. James (London), Le Club (N.Y.). Personal injury, Commercial litigation, General corporate.

TANENBAUM, RICHARD HUGH, lawyer; b. Washington, July 10, 1947; s. Joseph M. and Shirley (Levin) T.; m. Linda Jorgensen, Nov. 14, 1969; children—Brian J., Drew S. B.S., Bradley U., 1969; J.D., Cath. U. of Am. Sch. Law, 1974. Bar: Md. 1974, D.C. 1975, U.S. Ct. Claims 1975, U.S. Dist. Ct. D.C. 1975, Md. 1979, U.S. Ct. Appeals (D.C. cir.) 1975, U.S. Ct. Appeals (4th cir.) 1982, U.S. Tax Ct. 1982, U.S. Supreme Ct. 1982. Consumer edn. developer, tchr. Peoria (Ill.) Pub. Sch. System, 1969-71; legal asst. Pay Bd., Exec. Office of Pres., Washington, 1971-72; acct. Alexander Grant & Co., Washington, 1972; assoc. Jones, Day, Reavis & Pogue, Washington, 1973-78; ptnr. Lerch, Early, Roseman & Frankel, Chartered, Bethesda, Md., 1978-85; sole practice, Bethesda, Md., 1985—. Mng. editor Cath. U. Law Rev., Washington, 1974. Recipient Superior Performance award Exec. Office of Pres., Washington, 1972. Mem. ABA, Montgomery County Bar Assn., D.C. Bar Assn., Bethesda-Chevy Chase C. of C. (bd. dirs. 1980-83. Club: Bethesda Country. Lodge: Rotary (charter mem., bd. dirs. 1980—). Real property, Contracts commercial, General corporate. Office: 7315 Wisconsin Ave Bethesda MD 20814

TANENBAUM, TED JAY, lawyer; b. Bklyn., Oct. 21, 1948. BA, Temple U., 1970; JD, Bklyn. Law Sch., 1974. Bar: U.S. Dist. Ct. (ea. and so. dists.) N.Y. 1975, U.S. Ct. Appeals (2d cir.) 1975, U.S. Ct. Appeals (D.C. cir.) 1978. Sr. assoc. Rivkin, Leff, Sherman & Radler, Garden City, N.Y., 1983-84; sr. ptnr. Russo & Tanenbaum, Westbury, N.Y., 1984—; arbitrator Am. Arbitration Assn., Garden City, 1983—, Dist. Ct. Nassau County, Mineola, N.Y., 1984—. Mem. Nassau-Suffolk Trial Lawyers Sect., Nassau Bar Assn., N.Y. State Trial Lawyers Assn., ABA, D.C. Bar Assn. Insurance, Personal injury, State civil litigation. Home: 2600 Glenn Dr Bellmore NY 11710 Office: Russo & Tanenbaum 466 Maple Ave Westbury NY 11590

TANENBAUM, WILLIAM ALAN, lawyer; b. Rochester, N.Y., Feb. 16, 1954; s. Burton David and Millicent (Kroll) T.; m. Judy Ellen Hertz, June 15, 1986. BA magna cum laude, Brown U., 1976; JD, Cornell U., 1979. Assoc. Proskauer, Rose, Goetz & Mendelsohn, N.Y.C., 1979-82, Phillips, Nizer, Benjamin, Krim & Ballon, N.Y.C. and Los Angeles, 1982—; lectr. computer law Practicing Law Inst., N.Y.C., 1984—. Editor-in-chief The Computer Law Bull., 1986—; contbr. articles to profl. jours. Recipient 1st Place Cup Adirondack Sailing Assn., 1972-83. Mem. ABA, N.Y. State Bar Assn., Computer Law Assn., Am. Arbitration Assn. (panel arbitrators), Phi Beta Kappa. Avocation: sailing. Computer, Federal civil litigation, Contracts commercial. Office: Phillips Nizer Benjamin Krim & Ballon 40 W 57th St New York NY 10019

TANG, THOMAS, judge; b. Phoenix, Jan. 11, 1922. B.S., U. Santa Clara, 1947, law student, 1948-50; LL.B. with distinction, U. Ariz., 1950. Bar: Ariz. 1950, Calif. 1951. Dep. county atty. Maricopa County, Ariz., 1953-57; asst. atty. gen. State of Ariz., 1957-58; judge Ariz. Superior Ct., 1963-70; mem. firm Sullivan, Mahoney & Tang, Phoenix, 1971-77; councilman City of Phoenix, 1960-62, vice mayor, 1962; judge U.S. Ct. of Appeals 9th Circuit, Phoenix, 1977—. Mem. State Bar Ariz. (bd. govs. 1971-77, pres. 1977), State Bar Calif. Jurisprudence. Office: US Ct of Appeals Federal Bldg 230 N 1st Ave Phoenix AZ 85025

TANGEN, JON PAUL, laywer; b. Quincy, Mass., Apr. 7, 1944; s. George Henry and Bertha Marie (Backius) T.; m. Valerie Ann Clayton, June 27, 1964; children: Nathaniel Clayton, Kristoffer Willis, Thomasine Deyo. BA, Washington and Jefferson Coll., Pa., 1966; LLB, U. Va., 1969; LLM, George Washington U., 1976. Bar: Va. 1969, Alaska 1975, U.S. Dist. Ct. Alaska 1975, U.S. Ct. Appeals (9th cir.) 1977. Atty., advisor Office Gen. Counsel, U.S. Dept. Commerce, Washington, 1973-75; mem. Robertson, Monagle, Eastaugh & Bradley, Juneau, Alaska, 1975-86; sole practice, Juneau, 1986—. Served to capt. U.S. Army, 1969-73. Mem. ABA, Va. Bar Assn., Alaska Bar Assn., Alaska State C. of C. (chmn. bd. dirs. 1983-84), Alaska Miners Assn. (pres. 1978-80), N.W. Mining Assn. (trustee 1979-80). Democrat. Episcopalian. Lodges: Rotary, Masons. Environment, Mining and minerals, Insurance. Office: 105 Municipal Way Suite 303 Juneau AK 99801

TANICK, MARSHALL HOWARD, lawyer, educator; b. Mpls., May 9, 1947; s. Jack and Esther (Kohn) T.; m. Cathy E. Gorlin, Feb. 20, 1982; 1 child, Lauren. BA, U. Minn., 1969; JD, Stanford U., 1973. Bar: Calif. 1973, Minn. 1974. Law clk. to presiding justice U.S. Dist. Ct., Mpls., 1973-74; assoc. Robins, Davis & Lyons, Mpls., 1974-76; ptnr. Tanick & Heins, P.A., Mpls., 1976—; prof. constrn., real estate and media law U. Minn., Mpls., 1983—. Editor: Hennepin Lawyer and Litigation mag.; contbr. articles to mags. Avocation: writing. Federal civil litigation, State civil litigation, Libel. Home: 1230 Angelo Dr Golden Valley MN 55422 Office: Tanick & Heins PA 701 S 4th Ave Minneapolis MN 55415

TANKERSLEY, GLENN RAYBURN, lawyer, educator; b. Appalachia, Va., Apr. 4, 1948; s. Roy and Stella Pearl (Swecker) T.; m. Debra Lee Dalton, May 25, 1973; 1 child, David Glenn. BA, Berea Coll., 1970; JD, U. Richmond, 1976. Bar: Va. 1976. Assoc. H. Ronnie Mongtgomery, Jonesville, Va., 1976-77; sole practice Big Stone Gap, Va., 1977—; instr. Mountain Empire Community Coll., Big Stone Gap, 1979—. Candidate for Va. Ho. of Dels. 2d Legis. dist., 1985. Mem. ABA, Va. Bar Assn., Wise County Bar Assn. (pres. 1985). Republican. Methodist. Avocations: softball, bicycling. Contracts commercial, State civil litigation, Real property. Home: Rt 1 Box 484 Big Stone Gap VA 24219 Office: 502 E Wood Ave Big Stone Gap VA 24219

TANKERSLEY, MICHAEL WAYNE, lawyer; b. Dallas, Apr. 5, 1956; s. Ewell L. and Sylvia (Sikes) T.; m. Lisa Dunlevy, May 20, 1978; children: Jennifer Lauren, Amy Elizabeth. BA, Rice U., 1977, M in Acctg., 1978; JD with high honors, U. Tex., 1980. Bar: Tex. 1981; CPA, Tex. Assoc. Hughes & Luce, Dallas, 1980-86, ptnr., 1986—; adj. prof. law U. Tex., 1987. Contbg. author: Texas Corporation Law and Practice, 1984; editor, contbr. articles Bull. of Corp. Banking and Bus. Law, 1985—. Mem. Tex. Bar Assn. (chmn. communications and newsletter com., corp. banking and bus. law sect. 1985—), Dallas Bar Assn., Dallas Assn. Young Lawyers (bd. dirs. 1986-87), Order of Coif. Securities, General corporate. Office: Hughes & Luce 1000 Dallas Bldg Dallas TX 75201

TANKERSLEY, THOMAS CHANNING, lawyer; b. Newport News, Va., June 25, 1949; s. Channing Ford and Dorothy M. (Dakin) T.; m. Janet Ficken, Aug. 26, 1972; children: James, Daniel. BA in Polit. Sci., Econs. with highest honors, U. Calif., Santa Barbara, 1971; JD, UCLA, 1975. Bar: Oreg. 1975, U.S. Dist. Ct. Oreg. 1979, U.S. Tax Ct. 1982. Law clk. to chief justice Oreg. Supreme Ct., Salem, 1975-76; assoc. Rutherford & Drabkin, McMinnville, Oreg., 1976-79; ptnr. Drabkin & Tankersley, McMinnville, 1980-83, Drabkin, Tankersley & Richardson, McMinnville, 1984—; mcpl. judge City of Dayton, Oreg., 1977-80. Sr. warden St. Barnabas Episcopal Ch., McMinnville, 1978-79, 85-86. Mem. Oreg. Bar Assn. (uniform state laws com.), Yamhill County Bar Assn. (pres. 1981-82), Order of Coif, Phi Beta Kappa. Democrat. Lodge: Rotary. Avocations: hunting, fishing, camping, canoeing. Real property, General corporate, State civil litigation. Home: 1841 Thomsen Ln McMinnville OR 97128 Office: Drabkin Tankersley & Richardson 625 N Evans St McMinnville OR 97128

TANKSLEY, RAYMOND RICHARD, JR., judge; b. Spokane, June 9, 1931; s. Raymond Richard and Frances Josephine (Demigne) T.; m. Kathleen Sorensen, Aug. 6, 1960; children: Claire, Michael, Edward, Ann Marie. JD, Gonzaga U., 1955. Bar: Wash. 1955, U.S. Dist. Ct. (ea. and we. dist.) Wash. 1956. Sole practice Spokane, 1957-85; judge Spokane County Dist. Ct., 1985—. state committeeman Wash. Rep. Party, 1968-72. Mem. Assn. Trial Lawyers Am., Wash. State Bar Assn., Spokane County Bar Assn., Wash. State Dist. and Mcpl. Ct. Judges Assn. Judicial administration, Criminal, State civil litigation. Home: S 2418 Manito Blvd Spokane WA 99203 Office: Spokane County Dist Ct W 1100 Mallon Spokane WA 99260

TANNEN, EDWARD COOPER, lawyer, railroad executive; b. Hampton, Va., May 31, 1948; s. Joseph Sherman and Rhea (Cooper) T.; m. Millie Kolb, June 4, 1977; children—Samuel Louis, Jonathan Scott. B.A., U. Va., 1970, J.D., 1973. Bar: Va. 1973, U.S. Dist. Ct. (ea. dist.) Va. 1980, U.S. Ct. Appeals (4th cir.) 1973, Fla. 1982, U.S. Dist. Ct. (mid. dist.) Fla. 1982, U.S. Ct. Appeals (11th cir.) 1982. Atty., Seaboard Coast Line R.R., Richmond, Va., 1973-78, asst. gen. atty., 1978-81; asst. gen. solicitor Seaboard System R.R., Jacksonville, Fla., 1981-86; gen. atty. CSX Transp., Inc., 1986—. Bd. dirs. Jacksonville Jewish Ctr., 1984—. Mem. ABA, Va. State Bar, Fla. Bar, Jacksonville Bar Assn., Conf. R.R. and Airline Labor Lawyers, Am. Com. on the History of the Second World War, Phi Beta Kappa. Jewish. General corporate, Labor. Home: 8643 Osprey Ln Jacksonville FL 32217 Office: Seaboard System RR Inc 500 Water St Jacksonville FL 32202

TANNENBAUM, BERNARD, lawyer; b. N.Y.C., July 14, 1928; s. Jacob and Lillian (Jupiter) T.; m. Elinor Fried June 3, 1950; children—Jody, Ilene, Carol, Jeffrey. B.A. in Edn., NYU, 1950, J.D., 1953; M.A. (hon.), Internat. U. Communications, 1974. Bar: N.Y. 1954, D.C. 1980, U.S. Dist. Ct. (so. and east. dists.) N.Y. 1961, U.S. Ct. Claims 1964, U.S. Supreme Ct. 1964. Assoc. Halperin, Natanson, Shivitz & Scholar, N.Y.C., 1952-54; sole practice, Mineola, N.Y., 1954-60, N.Y.C., 1969—; ptnr. Fried, Beck, Tannenbaum & Field, N.Y.C., 1960-69, counsel to Meltzer, Lippe & Goldstein, Mineola, N.Y., 1987—; spl. counsel U.S. Senate Subcom. on Juvenile Delinquency, Washington, 1965-70, subcom. on Panama Canal U.S. Ho. of Reps., Washington, 1970-71, com. on mcht. marine and fisheries U.S. Ho. of Reps., 1977-80; arbitrator Am. Arbitration Assn., N.Y.C., 1965—, Small Claims Div. Civil Ct., N.Y.C., 1975—. Editor NYU Law Rev. Editor, pub., The Democratic Forum, 1967-73. Contbr. articles to profl. jours. Vice chmn. N.Y. City Democratic Com., 1960-73; bd. dirs., trustee Daytop Village Inc., N.Y.C., 1983—; bd. advisors Assn. Children with Retarded Mental Devel., N.Y.C., 1984-86. Mem. N.Y. State Bar Assn., Internat. Narcotics Law Enforcement Officers Assn. Real property, Contracts commercial, Legislative. Office: 190 Willis Ave Mineola NY 11501

TANNENBAUM, CALVIN MICHAEL, lawyer; b. Bklyn., Feb. 15, 1949; s. Lawrence Tannenbaum and Roslyn Rumain; m. Adele Fuchsberg, July 19, 1970 (div. Jan. 1982); children: Leonard Mark, David Gary; m. Lana Iny, Nov. 25, 1984; 1 child, Jessica Kara. BA, Syracuse U., 1971, JD, 1973. Bar: N.Y. 1974, U.S. Dist. Ct. (ea. and so. dists.) N.Y. 1975. Assoc. Fuchsberg & Fuchsberg, N.Y.C., 1974-82; ptnr. Johnson, Tannen, Brecher, Fishman, Feit & Heller, N.Y.C., 1982—. Editor Syracuse U. Law Rev., 1972-73. Mem. Assn. Trial Lawyers Am., N.Y. State Trial Lawyers Assn. (cert. commendation 1981, cert. appreciation 1976, assoc. editor quarterly 1978-80, assoc. editor notes 1986). Democrat. Jewish. Avocations: sports, investment. Workers' compensation, Personal injury, State civil litigation. Home: 135 W 70 New York NY 10023 Office: Johnson Tannen Brecher et al 225 Broadway New York NY 10007

TANNENBAUM, HERBERT WALTER, lawyer; b. N.Y.C., May 13, 1935; s. Hyman Jack and Regina (Izan) T.; m. Muriel Golde, June 25, 1961; children—Ross, Eric, Brett. A.B., Amherst Coll., 1957; J.D., Georgetown U., 1967. Bar: Va. 1961, Fla. 1961. Sr. ptnr. Young, Stern & Tannenbaum, P.A., North Miami Beach, Fla., 1962—; chmn. bd. Turnberry Savs. and Loan Assn., North Miami Beach. Served with USAR, 1960, to lt., USCGR, 1961-68. Mem. North Dade Bar Assn. (pres. 1966-68), ABA. Democrat. Jewish. Real property. Address: 4800 Cleveland St Hollywood FL 33021

TANNER, DOUGLAS ALAN, lawyer; b. Palo Alto, Calif., Aug. 30, 1953; s. Bernard R. and Caroline (Orris) T.; m. Carol Scilacci, May 27, 1977; children: Lauren Elizabeth, Wynn Ann. AB in History, Stanford U., 1974, JD, MBA, 1978. Bar: Calif. 1978, U.S. Dist. Ct. (no. dist.) Calif. 1978, U.S. Ct. Appeals (9th cir.) 1979. Law clk. to judge U.S. Ct. Appeals (9th cir.), San Francisco, 1978-79; assoc. Orrick, Herrington & Sutcliffe, San Francisco, 1979-83; ptnr. Orrick, Herrington & Sutcliffe, San Jose, Calif., 1983-86, N.Y.C., 1986—. Mem. San Francisco Barristers (chmn. corps. com. 1981-82), Order of Coif, Phi Beta Kappa. Republican. Episcopalian. Securities, General corporate. Office: Orrick Herrington & Sutcliffe 1211 Ave of Americas New York NY 10036

TANNER, MICHAEL GRANT, lawyer; b. Ann Arbor, Mich., Nov. 24, 1953; s. Richard G. and Marjorie (Hehn) T.; m. Sharon Howard. AB, Davidson Coll., 1975; JD, U. Fla., 1978. Bar: Fla. 1978, U.S. Dist. Ct. (mid. dist.) Fla. 1979, U.S. Ct. Appeals (3d cir.) 1980, U.S. Ct. Appeals (11th cir.) 1981, U.S. Dist. Ct. (so. dist.) Fla. 1982, U.S. Dist. Ct. (no. dist.) Fla. 1984. Assoc. Mahoney Hadlow, et al, Jacksonville, Fla., 1980-82; ptnr. Gallagher, Baumer, Mikals, Bradford, Cannon & Walters, P.A., Jacksonville, 1982—. Coordinator Duval County campaign Pajcic for Gov., Jacksonville, 1985—. Mem. Fla. Bar Assn., Jacksonville Bar Assn., Assn. Trial Lawyers Am. Clubs: Fla. Yacht, River (Jacksonville). Home: 4651 Arapahoe Ave Jacksonville FL 32210 Office: Gallagher Baumer Mikals et al 2000 Independent Sq Jacksonville FL 32202

TANNER, SHERYL MALICK, lawyer; b. Houston, Nov. 6, 1956; d. James and Leah (Reservitz) Malick; m. Allen Mark Tanner, Oct. 21, 1984. BBA, U. Tex., 1977, JD, 1981. Bar: Tex. 1981, U.S. Dist. Ct. (so. dist.) Tex. 1982, U.S. Ct. Appeals (5th cir.) 1982. Atty. Shell Oil Co., Houston, 1981—. Mem. Houston Bar Assn., Tex. Bar Assn., U. Houston Law Sch. Alumni Assn., Phi Kappa Phi. Lodge: Order of the Barons. Antitrust, Trademark and copyright, Environment. Office: Shell Oil Co Legal Dept PO Box 2463 Houston TX 77001

TANNIAN, JOY, lawyer, utility executive; b. N.Y.C., Sept. 30, 1932; d. Constantine and Aphrodite (Menex) Xenis; 1 child, Sean P. B.A., U. Mich., 1953, J.D., 1956. Bar: N.Y. 1957. Atty. Consol. Edison Co. N.Y. Inc., N.Y.C., 1957-73, asst. v.p., asst. gen. counsel, 1973-76, v.p., 1976-80, v.p., assoc. gen. counsel, 1980-84, sr. v.p., gen. counsel, 1984—. Mem. N.Y. State Bar Assn. (exec. com. corp. counsel sect. 1982—), Edison Electric Inst. (econ. exec. adv. com. 1981—, legal com. 1984—), Order of Coif, Phi Beta Kappa. Home: Sycamore Dr Sands Point NY 11050 Office: Consol Edison Co NY Inc 4 Irving Pl New York NY 10003

TANNON, JAY MIDDLETON, lawyer; b. Augusta, Ga., Feb. 24, 1956; m. Elizabeth M. Gabhart; 1 child, Katherine. BA, U. N.C., 1978; JD, U. Va., 1982; MBA, U. Louisville, 1983. Bar: Ky. 1982. Assoc. Brown, Todd & Heyburn, Louisville, 1982—; chmn., founder Comml. Dispute Resolution Inc., Louisville, 1986—. Contbr. articles to profl. jours. Bd. dirs. U. Louisville Sch. Bus., 1985—; mem. 3d Century, Louisville. Hearst Found. scholarship, 1974, Johnston scholar U. N.C., 1976, Phillips scholar U. N.C., 1977, du Pont scholar U. Va., 1979. Mem. ABA, Ky. Bar Assn., Louisville Bar Assn. General corporate, Mergers and acquisitions, Alternative dispute resolution. Office: Brown Todd & Heyburn 1600 Citizens Plaza Louisville KY 40202

TANOUS, JAMES JOSEPH, lawyer; b. Olean, N.Y., Sept. 11, 1947; s. Michael F. and Philomena M. (Eade) T.; m. Constance M. Griffin, Nov. 27, 1982; children: James M., Michele P. BA, St. Bonaventure U., 1969; JD, U. Va., 1972. Bar: N.Y. 1973, U.S. Dist. Ct. (we. dist.) 1973, U.S. Ct. Appeals (2d cir.) 1973. Ptnr. Jaeckle, Fleischmann, & Mugel, Buffalo, 1973—. Served to capt. USAR, 1971-79. Mem. ABA, N.Y. State Bar Assn., Erie County Bar Assn. Securities, General corporate. Home: 29 Tillinghast Pl Buffalo NY 14216 Office: Jaeckle Fleischmann & Mugel Norstar Bldg Buffalo NY 14202

TANSILL, FREDERICK JOSEPH, lawyer; b. Washington, Feb. 27, 1948; s. Frederick Riker and Mary Eileen (Loftus) T.; m. Joan Louise Trefsgar, July 10, 1971; children: Brendan Frederick, Brooke Charlotte, Charlotte Trefsgar. BA with honors, Brown U., 1970; JD, Georgetown U., 1974, LLM in Taxation, 1982. Bar: D.C. 1974, U.S. Tax Ct. 1976., Va. 1982. Assoc. Cross, Murphy & Smith, Washington, 1974-77; ptnr. Bird & Tansill, Washington, 1977-79; assoc. Ober, Grimes & Shriver, Washington, 1979-81; ptnr. Lewis, Mitchell & Moore, Vienna, Va., 1981-86; counsel Boothe, Prichard & Dudley, McLean, Va., 1986-87, McGuire, Woods, Battle & Boothe, McLean, 1987—. V.p., bd. dirs. Evanboro Homeowners Assn., Great Falls, Va., 1984—. Mem. ABA, Va. Bar Assn., Fairfax County Bar Assn. (chmn. will sect. 1986, vice chmn. 1985, chmn. tax. sect. 1987—), Northern Va. Estate Planning Council (bd. dirs. 1987—, exec. com.). Corporate taxation, Probate, General corporate. Office: McGuire Woods Battle & Boothe 8280 Greensboro Dr McLean VA 22102

TANSILL, FREDERICK RIKER, retired judge; b. Washington, July 12, 1914; s. Frederick Guida and Elizabeth Estele (Riker) T.; m. Mary Eileen Loftus, Dec. 31, 1940; children: Claire Tansill Hermann, Constance Tansill Gelfuso, Fred, Celine Tansill Kramer, Eileen. BSS, Georgetown U., 1936, JD, 1941; postgrad., Benjamin Franklin U., 1951-53. Bar: D.C. bar 1940. Credit reporter Dun & Bradstreet, Washington, 1938; instr. R.O.T.C., Georgetown U., 1940-42; spl. atty. IRS, N.Y.C., 1945-48; ptnr. Goodwin, Rosenbaum & Meacham, Washington, 1948-68, Cox, Langford & Brown, Washington, 1968-69, McInnis, Wilson, Munson & Woods, Washington, 1969-72, Bird & Tansill, Washington, 1972-79, Ober, Grimes & Shriver, Balt. and Washington, 1979-80; spl. trial judge U.S. Tax Ct., 1980-86; sole practice Washington, 1986—; instr. tax Ben Franklin U., 1956-57, instr. econs., 1967. Acting gen. counsel Children to Children, Inc., Washington, 1975-79; bd. dirs. Woodley Park Community Assn., Washington, 1968-76, v.p., 1975-76; pres. parish council Roman Cath. ch., 1973-76, 78-79. Served with AUS, 1940-45. Mem. ABA, Fed. Bar Assn., D.C. Bar Assn., Delta Theta Phi. Republican. Clubs: Army and Navy, Nat. Lawyers. Federal civil litigation. Home: 2740 Cortland Pl NW Washington DC 20008

TANSKI, JAMES MICHAEL, lawyer; b. Bristol, Conn., Feb. 11, 1946; s. John William and Stephanie J. (Kasek) T.; m. Janet E. Burlingame, Sept. 5, 1975; children: John Matthew, Susan Burlingame. BS, U.S. Mil. Acad., 1968; JD, U. Conn., 1976. Bar: Conn. 1976, U.S. Dist. Ct. Conn. 1977, U.S. Ct. Appeals (2d cir.) 1977. Commd. 2d lt. U.S. Army, 1968, advanced through ranks to capt., 1970, resigned, 1973; assoc. Law Offices of F. Timothy McNamara, Hartford, Conn., 1976-77, Adinolfi, O'Brien & Hayes, P.C., Hartford, 1977-80; ptnr. O'Brien & Tanski, Hartford, 1980—. Decorated Purple Heart with oak leaf cluster, Bronze Star, Air medal with 4 oak leaf clusters and 3 silver leaf clusters, Army Commendation medal with oak leaf cluster. Mem. ABA, Conn. Bar Assn. (profl. ethics com. 1982-83), Conn. Defense Lawyers Assn., Hartford County Bar Assn., Defense Research Inst. Roman Catholic. Federal civil litigation, State civil litigation. Office: O'Brien & Tanski 185 Asylum St Cityplace Hartford CT 06103-3402

TAPLEY, JAMES LEROY, lawyer, railway corporation executive; b. Greenville, Miss., July 10, 1923; s. Lester Leroy and Lillian (Clark) T.; m. Priscilla Moore, Sept. 9, 1950; children: Lane, Taylor, Cameron, James Clark, Meredith. AB, U. N.C., 1947, JD, 1950. Bar: N.C. 1951, D.C. 1962. With So. Ry. Co., Washington, 1953-83; gen. solicitor So. Ry. Co., 1967-74, asst. v.p. law, 1974-75, v.p. law, 1975-83; v.p. Washington counsel Norfolk So. Corp., Washington, 1983—. Mem. Phi Beta Kappa, Kappa Sigma. Clubs: Chevy Chase, Univ. Administrative and regulatory, Antitrust, General corporate. Office: Norfolk So Corp 1050 Connecticut Ave NW Suite 740 Washington DC 20036

TAPP, RICHARD N., lawyer; b. Memphis, Dec. 28, 1943; s. Charles Hall and Sarah Agnes (Brown) T.; m. Delia Sutherland Gaffney; 1 child, Richard Elliott. BA, Furman U., 1966; JD, U. S.C., 1972. Bar: S.C. 1972, U.S. Dist. Ct. S.C. 1973, U.S. Ct. Appeals (4th cir.) 1973. Ptnr. Abrams, Bowen & Tapp, Greenville, S.C., 1974-80; sole practice Greenville, 1980-83; ptnr. Brown & Hagins, Greenville, 1983—. Served to 1st lt. U.S. Army, 1966-68, Vietnam. Decorated Bronze Star. Mem. S.C. Bar Assn. (ethics adv. com.), Assn. Trial Lawyers Am., S.C. Trial Lawyers Assn. Presbyterian. Clubs: Poinsett, Greenville. Avocations: jogging, golf, tennis. Family and matrimonial, Federal civil litigation, State civil litigation. Home: 214 Rockwood Dr Greenville SC 29605 Office: Brown & Hagins 106 Williams St Greenville SC 29601

TARANGELO, RICHARD MICHAEL, lawyer, educator; b. Bklyn., June 30, 1927; s. Angelo and Mary Catherine (Sisti) T.; m. Nancy Colro, Sept. 19, 1957; children—Carol, Richard. B.A., Bklyn. Coll., 1950; J.D., St. John's U., 1954. Bar: N.Y. 1957, U.S. Supreme Ct. 1973, U.S. Dist. Ct. (ea. dist.) N.Y. 1979. Spl. dep. supt. N.Y. Ins. Dept., 1975-79; asst. v.p., house counsel GEICO, Woodbury, N.Y., 1979—. Mem. ABA, N.Y. State Bar Assn. Roman Catholic. Contbr. articles to mags. Federal civil litigation, Personal injury, Insurance. Address: 760 Woodbury Rd Woodbury NY 11797

TARCZA, ROBERT EMMET, lawyer; b. Alton, Ill., Jan. 26, 1956; s. Fred J. and Roberta (Howard) T.; m. Laura Puneky, May 23, 1981; children: Erin, Walter. BA, Loyola U., New Orleans, 1978, JD, 1981. Bar: La. 1981, U.S. Dist. Ct. (ea. dist.) La. 1981, U.S. Dist. Ct. (no. dist.) Miss. 1982, U.S. Ct. Appeals (5th cir.) 1982, U.S. Dist. Ct. (so. dist.) Ill. 1983, U.S. Supreme Ct. 1984. Dir. Feingerts & Kelly P.L.C., New Orleans, 1985—. Contbr. articles to profl. jours. Mem. ABA, La. Bar Assn. (bd. cert. tax atty. specialization program), New Orleans Bar Assn., New Orleans Estate Planning Council. Estate planning, Estate taxation, Probate. Office: Feingerts & Kelly PLC 650 Pondras St Suite 2750 New Orleans LA 70130

TARGOFF, CHERI KAMEN, lawyer; b. N.Y.C., Feb. 28, 1946; s. Alfred and Phyllis (Rozofsky) Kamen; m. Michael B. Targoff, June 11, 1966; children: Ramie, Josh, Jason, Hannah. Student, Barnard Coll., 1966-67; BA magna cum laude, Conn. Coll., 1967; MA, Columbia U., 1969; JD, NYU, 1980. Bar: N.Y. 1981, U.S. Dist. Ct. (so. dist.) N.Y. 1982. Assoc. Law Offices of Sondra M. Miller, White Plains, N.Y., 1981-83; sole practice White Plains, 1983—; adj. instr. history County Coll. Morris, Dover, N.J., 1973-75. Bd. dirs. Am. Diabetes Assn., 1982-85, Juvenile Diabetes Assn., 1986—. Mem. ABA, N.Y. State Bar Assn., Women's Bar Assn. State N.Y., Westchester Bar Assn., Westchester Women's Bar Assn., Phi Beta Kappa. Avocations: running, skiing. Family and matrimonial, Probate, Real property. Office: 50 Main St White Plains NY 10601

TARGOFF, MICHAEL BART, defense corporation executive, lawyer; b. N.Y.C., July 20, 1944; s. Jerome H. and Tillie R. T.; m. Cheri Kamen, June 11, 1966; children: Ramie, Joshua, Jason, Hannah. AB, Brown U., 1966; JD cum laude, Columbia U., 1969. Bar: N.Y. 1969. Law clk. to presiding justice U.S. Dist. Ct. Mass., 1969-70; assoc. Willkie, Fair & Gallagher, N.Y.C., 1970-76, ptnr., 1976-80; gen. counsel, v.p. Savin Corp., Valhalla, N.Y., 1980-81; gen. counsel, v.p., sec. Loral Corp., N.Y.C., 1981—. Harlan Fiske Stone scholar, 1968-69. Mem. ABA, N.Y. State Bar Assn., Assn. of Bar of City of N.Y. Antitrust, General corporate. Office: Loral Corp 600 Third Ave New York NY 10016

TARKENTON, JEFFREY L., lawyer; b. Portsmouth, Va., June 28, 1956; s. Henry L. and Ruby (Parisher) T. BA high honors, Coll. of William and Mary, 1978, JD, 1981. Bar: Va. 1981, D.C. 1984. Law clk. to presiding justice U.S. Bankruptcy Ct., Richmond, Va., 1981-83; assoc. Hunton & Williams, Washington, 1983—. V.p. Stephen's Housing, Inc., Washington, 1986—. Mem. ABA, Va. Bar Assn., D.C. Bar Assn. Episcopalian. Bankruptcy. Office: Hunton & Williams 2000 Pennsylvania Ave NW Washington DC 20006

TARKOFF, MICHAEL HARRIS, lawyer; b. Phila., Oct. 3, 1946. B.A., U. Miami, 1968, J.D., 1971. Bar: Fla. 1973, U.S. Supreme Ct. 1976, N.Y. 1983, U.S. Tax Ct. 1984. Asst. pub. defender Miami Pub. Defender's Office, Fla., 1973-77; guest lectr. U. Miami Sch. Law, 1977; ptnr. Flynn, Rubio & Tarkoff, Miami, 1977-83; ptnr. Flynn and Tarkoff, Miami, 1983—; mem. substancial asst. in trafficing cases com. criminal law sect. Fla. Bar. Mem. Dade County Democratic Exec. Com., 1970-72; pres. Young Dems. of Dade County, Fla., 1971, trustee, 1973-75; legal counsel Dade County Dem. Com., 1978. Sponsor, South Fla. council Boy Scouts Am. Mem. ABA, Fla. Bar Assn., Nat. Assn. Criminal Def. Lawyers (membership com., NORML legal com.), Fla. Criminal Def. Lawyers Assn. Criminal. Office: 1414 Coral Way Miami FL 33145

TARLOW, MARC GARY, lawyer; b. Phila., Aug. 18, 1951; s. Stanley and Ellen (Meinberg) T.; m. Elyana Eisenstadt, June 2, 1974; 1 child, Joshua. BA in History magna cum laude, U. Pa., 1973; JD cum laude,

Temple U., 1976. Bar: Pa. 1976, U.S. Dist. Ct. (mid. dist.) Pa. 1979, U.S. Ct. Appeals (3d cir.) 1980, U.S. Supreme Ct. 1983., Md. 1985. Assoc. Shawn Rosenthal, Balt., 1976; counsel to speaker of house Pa. Legis., Harrisburg, 1977, atty. joint state gov. commn., 1977-80; ptnr. Seidensticker, Keiter, Tarlow & Baughman, P.C. and predecessor firm Markowitz & Seidensticker, P.C., York, Pa., 1980—. Contbr. articles to profl. jours. Mem. ABA, Pa. Bar Assn. (statutory law com. 1982—), Assn. Trial Lawyers Am., Pa. Trial Lawyers Assn. (subcom. comml. litigation 1982—, labor com. 1983—). Democrat. Jewish. Lodge: B'nai B'rith. Avocation: tennis. Federal civil litigation, Labor, Securities. Home: 209 Maywood Rd York PA 17402 Office: Seidensticker Keiter Tarlow & Baughman 55 S Queen St York PA 17403

TARNACKI, DUANE L., lawyer; b. Detroit, Dec. 21, 1953; s. Leo A. and Dorothy O. (Roginski) T.; m. Anne Marie Prokop, Sept. 10, 1982. BA in Psychology with high distinction and high honors, U. Mich., 1976; MBA with honors, JD cum laude, U. Notre Dame, 1980. Bar: Mich. 1980, U.S. Dist. Ct. (so. dist.) Mich., 1980. Ptnr. Clark, Klein & Beaumont, Detroit, 1980—. Author: Establishing a Charitable Foundation in Michigan, 1986; assoc. editor Notre Dame Lawyer, 1977-80. Mem. Increasing Philanthropy Com., Council Mich. Founds. Mem. ABA (corp. law, real property, probate and trust law and tax sects.), Mich Bar Assn. (nonprofit corp. subcom. corp., fin. and bus. law sect., probate and trust law and tax sects.), Detroit Bar Assn. Republican. Roman Catholic. Club: Economic (Detroit). General corporate, Tax exempt organizations, Estate planning. Home: 22166 Doxtator Dearborn MI 48128 Office: 1001 Woodward Ave 1600 1st Fed Bldg Detroit MI 48226-1962

TARNOFF, JEROME, lawyer; b. Bklyn., June 22, 1931; s. Meyer and Anne (Sosnick) T.; children: Marcy Jane, Margery Lynne. AB, Syracuse U., 1952; JD, Columbia U., 1957. Bar: N.Y. 1957, Pa. 1983, U.S. Dist. Ct. (so. and ea. dists.) N.Y. 1960, U.S. Ct. Appeals (2d cir.) 1961. Ptnr., Sheldon and Tarnoff, N.Y.C., 1957-78, Feldesman, D'Atri, Tarnoff & Lubitz, N.Y.C., 1978, Baskin and Sears, P.C., N.Y.C., 1979-84, Baskin & Steingut P.C., 1984-85, Berger & Steingut, 1986—. Contbr. article to legal jour. Chmn. policy com. N.Y. Democratic Party, 1975-78, vice chmn. N.Y. County, 1978—, mem. nat. com., 1980—; mem. Community Planning Bd. #8, 1966-75; trustee Grand St. Settlement, Assoc. Y's of N.Y. Served with U.S. Army, 1952-54. Recipient Disting. Service award NAACP, 1975, cert. Achievement El Diario-La Prensa, 1977. Mem. ABA, Pa. State Bar, N.Y. State Bar Assn., Assn. Bar City N.Y., N.Y. County Lawyers, Am. Arbitration Assn. (nat. panel arbitrators), Phi Alpha Delta. Jewish. Clubs: Hollywood Golf (Deal, N.J.), Audubon. Lodge: Masons. Federal civil litigation, State civil litigation, Family and matrimonial. Home: 444 E 86th St New York NY 10028 Office: 600 Madison Ave New York NY 10022

TARPY, THOMAS LYNN, lawyer; b. Knoxville, Tenn., Feb. 10, 1951; s. Marvin Lawrence and Betty Lynn (Ghormley) T.; m. Elizabeth Ann McNew, Mar. 15, 1980. BA, U. Tenn., 1973, JD, 1977. Bar: Tenn. 1978, U.S. Dist. Ct. (ea. dist.) Tenn. 1978, U.S. Ct. Appeals (6th cir.) 1978. Legal counsel, dir. personnel pay cash div. Scrivner, Knoxville, 1977-82; sole practice Knoxville, 1982-85; assoc. Robertson, Williams, Ingram & Overbey, Knoxville, 1985—. State civil litigation, Bankruptcy. Home: 4925 Asheville Hwy Knoxville TN 37914 Office: Robertson Williams Ingram & Overbey Andrew Johnson Plaza 10th Floor Knoxville TN 37902

TARR, RALPH W., federal government official; b. Bakersfield, Calif., Sept. 29, 1948. BA, Dartmouth Coll., 1970; M of Pub. Adminstrn., Calif. State U., 1973; JD, U. Calif., Berkeley, 1976. Sole practice 1977-81; dir., mem. exec. com. Baker, Manock & Jensen, Fresno, Calif., 1981-82; mem. adminstrv. com. Fed. Registar, Washington, 1982-85; dep. asst. atty. gen. U.S. Dept. Justice, Washington, 1982-84, acting asst. atty. gen., 1984-85; solicitor U.S. Dept. Labor, Washington, 1985-86, U.S. Dept. Interior, Washington, 1986—. Office: Dept Labor Solicitor 200 Constitution Ave NW Washington DC 20210 *

TARTT, BLAKE, lawyer; b. Houston, Mar. 16, 1929; s. Herbert Blake and Bernice (Schwalm) T.; m. Barbara Jean Moore, Jan. 30, 1960; children: Blake III, Courtnay M. B.B.A., So. Methodist U., 1949, J.D. cum laude, 1959. Bar: Tex. 1959. Sole practice Houston, 1959-70; ptnr. Fulbright & Jaworski, 1970—; dir. Hycel, Inc., 1972-78. Served to 1st. lt. USAF, 1951-55, Korea. Decorated Air medal. Fellow Am. Bar Found. (chmn. Tex. 1981-85, vice chmn. fellows 1986-87), Tex. Bar Found. (chmn. bd. 1974-75, chmn. fellows 1978-79), Am. Coll. Trial Lawyers, Am. Bd. Trial Advocates (advocate); mem. ABA (ho. dels. 1976-82), Fed. Bar Assn., Internat. Assn. Ins. Counsel, Am. Judicature Soc. (bd. dirs. 1984—), So. Conf. Bar (pres. 1984), State Bar Tex. (dir. 1972-75, exec. com. 1975-76, pres. 1983-84), Houston Bar Assn., Delta Theta Phi, Alpha Tau Omega. Episcopalian. Clubs: Coronado, Forest, Houston, Houstonian. Nuclear power, Federal civil litigation, State civil litigation. Home: 3690 Inwood Dr Houston TX 77019 Office: MBank Bldg Houston TX 77002

TARTT, TYRONE CHRIS, lawyer; b. Detroit, Apr. 1, 1955; s. Albert James and Louise (Savare) T.; m. Dianne Marie Hersey, Nov. 24, 1979. AB, U. Mich., 1976, JD, 1978. Bar: Mich. 1979, U.S. Dist. Ct. (ea. dist.) Mich. 1980, U.S. Ct. Appeals (6th cir.) 1980, U.S. Dist. Ct. (no. dist.) Ohio 1987, U.S. Supreme Ct. 1987. Sr. assoc. Plunkett, Cooney & Rutt, Detroit, 1978-84; counsel Ameritech Pub. Inc., Troy, Mich., 1985—; cons. Mich. Student Assembly, Ann Arbor, 1976-78; bd. dirs. Univ. Cellars Inc., Ann Arbor., Fletcher Hall, Ann Arbor. Mem. Civic Searchlight Inc., Detroit, 1981—; bd. dirs. Oakland Citizens League, Detroit, 1987—. Mem. ABA, Mich. Bar Assn., Detroit Bar Assn., Am. Corp. Counsel Assn., Assn. Def. Trial Counsel, Econ. Club Detroit, Licensing Execs. Soc. of U.S./Can., U. Mich. Alumni Assn. Republican. Roman Catholic. Club: Detroit Athletic. Avocations: Caribbean travel, real estate investment. Trademark and copyright, Federal civil litigation, General corporate. Office: Ameritech Pub Inc 100 E Big Beaver Rd Suite 1300 Troy MI 48018

TARUN, ROBERT WALTER, lawyer; b. Lake Forest, Ill., Sept. 1, 1949; s. Donald Walter and Bonnie Jean (Cruickshank) T. AB, Stanford U., 1971; JD, DePaul U., 1974; MBA, U. Chgo., 1982. Bar: Ill. 1974, U.S. Dist. Ct. (no. dist.) Ill. 1974, Calif. 1975, U.S. Ct. Appeals (7th cir.) 1975, U.S. Supreme Ct. 1978, U.S. Dist. Ct. (we. dist.) Ark. 1986. Asst. atty. gen. State of Ill., Chgo., 1974-76; asst. U.S. atty. U.S. Dept. Justice, Chgo., 1976-79, dep. chief criminal div., 1979-82, exec. asst. U.S. atty. no. dist. Ill., 1982-85; ptnr. Reuben & Proctor, Chgo., 1985-86, Isham, Lincoln & Beale, Chgo., 1986—; lectr. criminal law practice Northwestern U. Sch. Law, 1986—. Mem. ABA, Chgo. Bar Assn., U. Chgo. Grad. Sch. Bus. Alumni Assn. (bd. dirs. 1986—). Presbyterian. Club: Racquet of Chgo. Avocations: hockey, architecture. Federal civil litigation, State civil litigation, Criminal. Home: 554 W Fullerton Pkwy Chicago IL 60614 Office: Isham Lincoln & Beale 3 First National Plaza Suite 5000 Chicago IL 60602

TARVER, TIMOTHY STEPHEN, lawyer; b. Gillette, Wyo., Sept. 12, 1951; s. Stephen C. and Ruth L. (Shrieves) T.; m. Carole A., May 18, 1973; children: Charles E., Hilary J. BS, U. Wyo., 1973, postgrad., 1974; JD, U. Va., 1976. Bar: Wyo. 1976, U.S. Dist. Ct. Wyo. 1976. Assoc. Burgess & Davis, Sheridan, Wyo., 1976-80; ptnr. Koester & Tarver, Sheridan, 1980-84; sole practice Sheridan, 1984—; bd. dirs. Prill Mfg. Co., Sheridan. Bd. dirs. Sheridan Community Council, 1982—, chmn., 1984, 85; trustee No. Wyo. Community Coll. Found., Sheridan, 1984, 85. Mem. ABA, Wyo. Bar Assn., Wyo. Trial Lawyers Assn.. Sheridan County Bar Assn. General practice, State civil litigation, Probate. Home: 374 Kilbourne Sheridan WY 82801 Office: PO Box 6284 Sheridan WY 82801

TASHIMA, ATSUSHI WALLACE, judge; b. Santa Maria, Calif., June 24, 1934; s. Yasutaro and Aya (Sasaki) T.; m. Nora Kiyo Inadomi, Jan. 27, 1957; children: Catherine Y., Christopher I., Jonathan I. A.B. in Polit. Sci., UCLA, 1958; LL.B., Harvard U., 1961. Bar: Calif. 1962. Dep. atty. gen. State of Calif., 1962-67; atty. Spreckels Sugar div. Amstar Corp., 1968-72, v.p., gen. atty., 1972-77; partner Morrison & Foerster, Los Angeles, 1977-80; judge U.S. Dist. Ct. Central Dist. Calif., Los Angeles, 1980—; mem. Calif. Com. Bar Examiners, 1978-80. Served with USMC, 1953-55. Mem. ABA, State Bar Calif., Los Angeles County Bar Assn. Democrat. Office: US Courthouse 312 N Spring St Los Angeles CA 90012 *

TASKER, JOSEPH, lawyer, educator; b. Tulsa, May 6, 1950; s. Joseph and Kathryn Lucille (Ahlstrom) T.; m. Constance Lee Sontheimer, May 28, 1971; 1 child, Joseph III. BA, U. Okla., 1972; JD, George Washington U., 1975. Bar: D.C. 1975, U.S. Dist. Ct. D.C. 1981, U.S. Ct. Appeals (D.C. cir.) 1981, U.S. Ct. Internat. Trade 1981, U.S. Ct. Appeals (fed. cir.) 1984. Staff atty. Bur. of Competition FTC, Washington, 1975-79, asst. to dir., 1979-81; assoc. Bishop, Liberman, Cook, Purcell & Reynolds, Washington, 1981-85, ptnr., 1986—; lectr. in sociology George Washington U., 1974, 77, lectr. George Washington U. Law Sch., 1982. Mem. ABA, D.C. Bar Assn., Order of Coif, Phi Beta Kappa. Democrat. Antitrust, Private international, Federal civil litigation. Office: Bishop Liberman Cook Purcell Reynolds 1200 17th St NW Washington DC 20036

TASKER, MICHAEL KENNETH, lawyer; b. Auburn, Wash., Sept. 14, 1948; s. Kenneth Glenn and Genevieve Anne (Kitna) T.; m. Lynn Adaire Chamberlain, June 19, 1971; children: Gavin Joseph B.H., Campbell Elizabeth C.T. BA, Western Wash. U., 1971; JD with distinction, George Mason U., 1980. Bar: U.S. Dist. Ct. (we. dist.) Wash. 1982. Spl. agt. FBI, Washington, 1972-81; ptnr. Hindman & Tasker, Bellingham, Wash., 1982—; pro bono panel Western Dist. Wash., 1982—. Mem. ABA, Wash. State Bar Assn. (lectr. annual conv. 1985), Fed. Bar Assn., Assn. Trial Lawyers Am., Wash. Trial Lawyers Assn., Soc. Former Spl. Agts. of FBI. Personal injury, Insurance, Civil rights. Office: Hindman & Tasker 306 Flora Bellingham WA 98225

TATE, DAVID KIRK, lawyer; b. Detroit, Apr. 20, 1939; s. Andrew Golden and Izona (Kirk) T.; m. Lucy Arlayne Carter, Nov. 19, 1961; children—De Marcus David, Lisa Arlayne. B.S. in Math., Mich. State U., 1963; J.D., U. Detroit, 1973. Bar: Mich. 1973, U.S. Dist. Ct. (ea. dist.) Mich. 1973, U.S. Tax Ct. 1973, N.C. 1983. Assoc., Patmon, Young & Kirk, P.C., Detroit, 1973-76; staff atty. Detroit Edison Co., 1976-77; asst. counsel R.J. Reynolds Industries, Inc., Winston-Salem, N.C., 1977-79; assoc. counsel R.J. Reynolds Tobacco Co., Winston-Salem, 1979-82, counsel corp. and comml., 1982-86, sr. counsel, 1986—, asst. sec., 1984; dir. Legal Services of N.C., Raleigh; negotiator, author numerous multi-million dollar contracts. Bd. dirs. Dearborn Med. Ctr., Mich., 1975-77; mem. U.S. Selective Service Appeals Bd., Middle dist. N.C., 1982; mem. coll./industry cluster St. Augustine's Coll., Raleigh, 1983; bd. dirs. N.C. Vietnam Vets Leadership Program, Inc., 1985—. Served to capt. inf. U.S. Army, 1963-68; Vietnam. Decorated Bronze Star, Air medal. Mem. ABA (contracts com. 1984-86), State Bar Mich., N.C. Bar Assn., Forsyth County Bar Assn., Alpha Phi Alpha (chpt. pres. 1961-63). Democrat. Mem. United Ch. of Christ. Contracts commercial, Construction, Landlord-tenant. Home: 340 Lynhaven Dr Winston-Salem NC 27104 Office: RJ Reynolds Tobacco Co 401 N Main St Winston-Salem NC 27102

TATE, JAMES SOLOMON, JR., lawyer; b. Louisville, July 4, 1954; s. James S. Sr. and Margaret Keyes (Clark) T.; m. Anne Marsden, May 19, 1979; 1 child, James Solomon III. BA, Vanderbilt U., 1976, JD, 1980. Bar: Tenn. 1980, U.S. Dist. Ct. (mid. dist.) Tenn. 1980. Assoc. Bass, Berry & Sims, Nashville, 1980-86, ptnr., 1986—. Mem. ABA, Tenn. Bar Assn., Nashville Bar Assn., Order of Coif. Avocations: aviation, hunting, fishing. Banking, Contracts commercial, Real property. Office: Bass Berry & Sims 2700 First American Ctr Nashville TN 37238-0070

TATE, MILTON YORK, JR., lawyer; b. Giddings, Tex., May 14, 1939; s. Milton Y. and Miriam (Phillips) T.; m. Twila Tate, June 4, 1960; children—Rebecca Lynn, Rachel Kelley. B.B.A., U. Tex., Austin, 1960, J.D., 1963. Bar: Tex. 1963. Ptnr., Moorman, Tate, Moorman & Urquhart, Brenham, Tex., 1965—; pres. Washington County Abstract Co., 1965—; dir. Tex. Nat. Bank Brenham; city atty. Brenham, 1982—. Bd. dirs. Bohne Meml. Hosp., Brenham Indsl. Found., Inc. General practice. Address: PO Box 1808 Brenham TX 77833

TATE, S. SHEPHERD, lawyer; b. Memphis, Dec. 19, 1917; m. Janet Graf; children: Adele Shepherd, Shepherd Davis, Janet Reid Walker. B.A., Southwestern at Memphis, 1939; J.D., U. Va., 1942; LL.D. (hon.), Samford U., 1979, Suffolk U., 1982. Bar: Va. 1941, Tenn. 1942. Mem. firm Martin, Tate, Morrow & Marston, P.C. (and predecessor firms), Memphis, 1947—. Sec. bd. trustees Southwestern at Memphis, 1968-77, from 1979; pres. Episcopal Churchmen of Tenn., 1961-62; sec. standing com. Episcopal Diocese of Tenn., 1969-71; pres. Chickasaw Council Boy Scouts Am., 1967-78. Served with USNR, 1942-46; comdr. USNR; ret. Decorated Order of Cloud Banner (China).; recipient Silver Beaver award Boy Scouts Am., 1963, Disting. Eagle Scout award, 1980, Disting. Service medal Southwestern at Memphis, 1978; Memphis Rotary Club Civic Recognition award, 1983; Paul Harris fellow, 1985. Fellow Am. Bar Found., Tenn. Bar Found., Memphis and Shelby County Bar Found., Am. Coll. Probate Counsel, Internat. Acad. Estate and Trust Law; mem. Am. Judicature Soc. (past bd. dirs.), ABA (past chmn. task force on lawyer advt. 1977, past chmn. standing com. on scope and correlation of work 1976-77, past. chmn. standing com. profl. discipline 1973-77, chmn. standing com. on lawyer competence 1986, pres. 1978-79), Tenn. Bar Assn. (pres. 1963-64), Memphis and Shelby County Bar Assn. (pres. 1959-60), Nat. Conf. Bar Pres. (pres. 1972-73), Am. Law Inst., U. Va. Law Sch. Alumni Assn. (mem. exec. council 1974-77), Order of Coif, Raven Soc., Phi Beta Kappa, Omicron Delta Kappa, Phi Delta Phi, Sigma Alpha Epsilon (highest effort award N.Y.C. Alumni Assn. 1979). Lodge: Rotary (pres. 1982-83, bd. dirs. 1974, 80-84). General corporate, Estate planning, Probate. Office: Martin Tate Morrow & Marston PC The Falls Bldg 11th Floor 22 N Front St Memphis TN 38103

TATE, THOMAS HARRISON, lawyer; b. Washington, Mar. 7, 1948; s. Samuel George Tate and Jean Anita (Harrison) Slovensky; m. Tracey Sandlyn Brown Elliot, Nov. 29, 1986. BS, Towson State U., Balt., 1967-71; JD, Hamline U., 1975-77. Bar: D.C. 1980, U.S. Dist. Ct. (D.C. dist.) 1980, U.S. Ct. Appeals (D.C. cir.) 1981, U.S. Ct. Claims 1981. Ptnr. Eaton & Tate, Washington, 1980-82, Paulson, Nace & Norwind, Washington, 1982—. Named one of Outstanding Young Men Am., U.S. Jaycees, 1981. Mem. ABA, Assn. Trial Lawyers Am., Assn. Plaintiffs' Trial Attys. Met. Washington, Sigma Nu Phi (nat. pres. 1980-82, 1987—). Democrat. Lutheran. Avocations: racquetball, football, hiking, motorcycling. Personal injury, Drug product liability, Birth defect product liability litigation. Office: Paulson Nace & Norwind 1814 N St NW Washington DC 20036

TATLOW, GARY ARTHUR, lawyer; b. Huntington Park, Calif., Mar. 11, 1939; s. Chester A. and Rosa May (Hallmark) T.; m. Marilyn Rose Silvey, June 2, 1962; children—Jennifer Gay, Phillip Arthur, Rebecca Jane. A.B., U. Mo., 1961; J.D., U. Mo., 1964. Bar: Mo. 1964, U.S. Ct. Appeals Mo. 1964, U.S. Dist. Ct. Mo. 1964. Asst. atty. gen. State of Mo., 1964-65; city atty. City of Moberly, 1965-80; spl. asst. Mo. atty. gen., 1967-69, spl. pros. atty., 1970-71; ptnr. Hulen, Hulen, Tatlow & Gump, Moberly, Mo., 1968—. Bd. dirs., chpt. chmn. ARC, Randolph County, 1968-69; mem. Randolph County Health Council, 1970-73; chmn. Randolph County Com. for Mo. Sch. of Religion, 1966-69; bd. dirs. Randolph County Day Care Ctr., 1968-70; deacon Central Christian Ch. of Moberly, 1976-80, elder, 1980—; mem. Moberly Police Dept. promotion rev. com., 1975-80, Randolph County Bd. Visitors, 1968-70; trustee Woodhaven Learning Ctr.; bd. dirs. Mo. Symphony Soc., Great River City council Boy Scouts Am. Recipient Atty. Gen.'s Outstanding Citizenship award, 1968. Mem. Assn. Trial Lawyers Am., Randolph County Bar Assn. (pres. 1972-73, Mo. Bar Assn., ABA, Mo. Mcpl. Attys. Assn., Mo. Assn. Trial Attys., U. Mo. Alumni Assn. (chmn. Randolph County chpt.), Phi Delta Phi. Clubs: Masons, Rotary (past pres.). General corporate, State civil litigation, Federal civil litigation. Office: Hulen Hulen Tatlow & Gump 110 N 5th St Moberly MO 65270

TATTERSALL, WILLIAM JAMES, industrial association executive, lawyer; b. Wilkes-Barre, Pa., May 11, 1932; s. James and Harriett (Moreau) T.; m. Joan M. Burns, Aug. 12, 1957; children—William J., James T., Christine M. B.A. in English, Moravian Coll., 1960; J.D., DePaul U., 1967. Bar: Ill. 1967. With Bethlehem Steel Corp., 1956-85, labor atty. indsl. relations dept., Bethlehem, Pa., 1967-73, mgr. state govt. affairs, 1973-79; asst. to mgr. Bethlehem Mines Corp., 1970-73; rep., negotiator 1974 Nat. Bituminous Coal Wage Agreement; dep. sec. gen. Internat. Iron and Steel Inst., Brussels, 1979—; Pres. Am. Club of Brussels, 1984-85, 85-86; counselor Boy Scouts Am., Brussels, 1984-85; lectr. Internat. Sch. Brussels, 1979-86; Mem. ABA, Ill. Bar Assn. Am. Iron and Steel Inst., The Metals Soc., Mid-Atlantic Legal Found., Pa. Soc., Institut Royal Des Relations Internats., Antique Automobile Club of Am. Club: Saucon Valley Country (Bethlehem). Lodge: Rotary. Labor, Legislative, Private international. Office: Rue Colonel Bourg 120, B-1140 Brussels Belgium

TATUM, FRANKLIN M., III, lawyer; b. Hattiesburg, Miss., July 4, 1946; s. Franklin M. Jr. and Doris Elaine (Trimmer) T.; m. Kathryn Hardcastle, Dec. 23, 1966; children: Susan, Ann. BA, Tex. Christian U., 1969; JD, Vanderbilt U., 1972. Bar: Va. 1973. Assoc. McGuire, Woods & Battle, Richmond, Va., 1972-78, ptnr., 1978-86; ptnr. Wright, Robinson, McCammon & Tatum, Richmond, 1986—. Mem. ABA, Def. Research Inst., Mng. Counsel Group, Va. Bar Assn., Richmond Bar Assn., Va. Assn. Def. Attys. Methodist. Federal civil litigation, State civil litigation, Securities. Home: 814 Westover Rd Richmond VA 23220 Office: Wright Robinson McCammon & Tatum 629 E Main St Suite 400 Richmond VA 23219

TATUM, FRED MENEFEE, JR., lawyer; b. Dothan, Ala., Dec. 5, 1927; s. Fred Menefee and Eunice Jewell (Butts) Baker; m. Agnes Grantham, Feb. 14, 1953 (div. 1961); m. Mary Irwin, Oct. 15, 1961 (div. 1972); 1 child, John Francis; m. Minnye Carson Roberts, Sept. 5, 1972 (dec. 1977). B.S. in Law, U. Ala., 1957, LL.B., 1958, J.D., 1969. Bar: Ala. 1958, U.S. Ct. Appeals (5th cir.) 1975, U.S. Ct. Appeals (11th cir.) 1981, Tex. 1975, U.S. Supreme Ct. 1979, U.S. Ct. Mil. Appeals 1980, U.S. Tax Ct. 1981, U.S. Ct. Appeals (Fed. cir.) 1984. Sole practice, Dothan, Ala., 1958—, Daleville, Ala., 1965-69; ptnr. Robert P. Jungman & Assocs., Houston, 1974-79; sole practice, Dothan, 1980—; cons. in law. Served with USMC, 1943-45, 1949-53. Mem. ABA, Nat. Assn. Criminal Def. Lawyers, Ala. Bar Assn., Tex. Bar Assn., Tex. Criminal Def. Lawyers Assn., Ala. Criminal Def. Lawyers Assn. (organizer), Houston County Bar Assn., Houston Bar Assn., VFW (post judge advocate 1984, 85), Phi Alpha Delta (vice justice 1957). Methodist. Lodge: Elks (past exalted ruler). Criminal, Family and matrimonial, State civil litigation. Home: 2004 W Main St Dothan AL 36301 Office: 119-121 N Oates St Dothan AL 36303

TAUB, ELI IRWIN, lawyer; b. N.Y.C., July 6, 1938; s. Max and Belle (Slutsky) T.; m. Nancy Denise Bell, May 15, 1983. 1 child, Jennifer. B.A., Bklyn. Coll., 1960; LL.B., NYU, 1963. Bar: N.Y. 1964, U.S. Dist. Ct. (no. dist.) N.Y. 1979. Assoc. Silver & Silverman, Schenectady, 1964-71; ptnr. Silverman, Silverman & Taub, Schenectady, 1971-77; pres. Eli I. Taub, P.C., Schenectady, 1978—; chmn. Bd. Assessment Review, Schenectady, 1972-81; arbitrator Am. Arbitration Assn., N.Y.C., 1966—. Pub. Employee Relations Bd., Albany, N.Y., 1984—. Chmn. trustees Joseph Egan Supreme Ct. Library, Schenectady, 1980, 81, 84; pres. Schenectady County Republican Club, 1985-86; v.p. Jewish Fedn. Schenectady, 1983-86; asst. treas., bd. dirs. Northeast Parent and Child Soc., Schenectady; 1st v.p. Jewish Community Ctr.; bd. dirs. Alcoholism Council Schenectady County, Jewish Fedn. of NE N.Y. Mem. Assn. Trial Lawyers Am., Am. Arbitration Assn., Indsl. Relation Research Assn., N.Y. State Bar Assn., N.Y. State Trial Lawyers Assn., Schenectady County Bar Assn. Republican. Jewish. Lodge: B'nai B'rith (pres. 1976-77, spl. award 1982, youth services award 1985). Family and matrimonial, Personal injury, General practice. Home: 105 N Ferry St Schenectady NY 12305 Office: 115 Clinton St Schenectady NY 12305

TAUB, SHEILA KURZROCK, law educator; b. N.Y.C., May 6, 1939; d. Jonas and Esther(Wollman) Kurzrock; m. Arthur Taub, June 16, 1963; 1 child, Ethan. BA cum laude, Brandeis U., 1961; JD, Harvard U., 1968. Bar: Conn. 1969. Assoc. Sachs, Sachs & Sachs, New Haven, Conn., 1969-72; researcher sch. medicine Yale U., New Haven, 1972-73; sole practice New Haven, 1974-78; prof. law U. Bridgeport, Conn., 1978—. Assoc. editor: Law, Medicine, and Health Care, Boston, 1981-87; contbr. numerous articles on law and medicine to profl. jours. Mem. New Haven Bd. Police Commrs., 1976-79. Brandeis Nat. fellow, Brandeis U., 1957-61, NSF fellow, 1958, Mellon Research grantee, 1984. Mem. Conn. Bar Assn. (mental healt law com., legal medicine com.), Am. Soc. Law and Medicine, Pitts. Inst. of Legal Medicine, Conn. Health Lawyers Assn. (founding). Avocations: photography, flute. Legal education, Health. Home: 30 Conrad Dr New Haven CT 06515 Office: U Bridgeport Sch of Law 303 University Ave Bridgeport CT 06601

TAUBENFELD, HARRY SAMUEL, lawyer; b. Bklyn., June 27, 1929; s. Marcus Isaac and Anna (Engelhard) T.; m. Florence Spatz, June 17, 1956; children—Anne Gail, Stephen Marshall. B.A., Bklyn. Coll., 1951; J.D., Columbia U., 1954. Bar: N.Y. 1955, U.S. Supreme Ct. 1965, U.S. Dist. Ct. (so. and ea. dists.) N.Y. 1976. Assoc., Benjamin H. Schor, Bklyn., 1955-58; ptnr. Zuckerbrod & Taubenfeld, Cedarhurst, N.Y. and N.Y.C., 1958—; village atty. Village of Cedarhurst, 1977—; legis. chmn. counsel to Nassau County Village Ofcls., 1979-86; mem. legis. com. N.Y. State Conf. Mayors, 1979—; arbitrator small claims ct. Civil Ct. City N.Y., 1970—; arbitrator Small Claims Assessment Rev. Bd., Dist. Ct. Nassau County, 1980—, Supreme Ct. Nassau County, 1981—. Assoc. chmn. Am. Zionist Fedn., 1985-87; pres. Herut Zionists Am., 1977-79; v.p. Hartman YMHA; del. World Zionist Congress, 1977, 82, mem. gen. Zionist council, 1977-83; bd. govs. Jewish Agy., World Zionist Orgn.; exec. Am. sect. bd. dirs. United Israel Appeal; trustee United Jewish Appeal; bd. dirs. Jewish Nat. Fund. Served with USAR, 1948-56. Recipient Centennial award Jabotinsky Found., 1981; Betar Youth award World Betar 1982; award Internat. League for Repatriation of Russian Jews; Youth Towns of Israel Leadership award Israel Bonds Leadership; cert. of appreciation City N.Y. Mem. ABA, Nassau County Bar Assn., Internat. Assn. Jewish Lawyers and Jurists. Club: B'nai B'rith. Real property, Local government, Contracts commercial. Home: 288 Leroy Ave Cedarhurst NY 11516 Office: PO Box 501 575 Chestnut St Cedarhurst NY 11516

TAUBER, FREDERIC J., lawyer; b. N.Y.C., Aug. 22, 1949; s. Maurice F. and Rose A. (Begner) T.; m. Carolyn A. Lippel, Dec. 30, 1973. BA, Columbia U., 1971, JD, 1974. Bar: N.J. 1974, U.S. Dist. Ct. N.J., U.S. Ct. Appeals (2d cir.). Assoc. Pitney, Hardin & Kipp, Morristown, N.J., 1974-80; sr. atty. Warner-Lambert Co., Morris Plains, N.J., 1980-83; counsel div. Sony Corp. Am., Park Ridge, N.J., 1983—. Mem. ABA. Antitrust, General corporate, General practice. Home: 2100 Linwood Ave Fort Lee NJ 07024 Office: Sony Corp Am Sony Dr Park Ridge NJ 07656

TAUBMAN, GLENN MATTHEW, lawyer; b. Manhasset, N.Y., Feb. 15, 1956; s. Isaac and Elaine (Lewis) T.; m. Marie Jennifer Rose, Apr. 15, 1984; 1 child, Helen Rose. BA in Polit. Sci., SUNY, Stony Brook, 1977; JD with distinction, Emory U., 1980; grad., Nat. Inst. Trial Advocacy, 1983; LLM in Labor Law, Georgetown U., 1985. Bar: Ga. 1980, N.Y. 1981, D.C. 1985, U.S. Ct. Appeals (11th cir.) 1981, U.S. Supreme Ct. 1983, U.S. Ct. Appeals (6th cir.) 1985. Staff atty. U.S. Dist. Ct. (mid. dist.), Jacksonville, Fla., 1980-81; law clk. to judge U.S. Ct. Appeals (11th cir.), Jacksonville, 1981-82; staff atty. Nat. Right to Work Legal Def. Found., Springfield, Va., 1982—. Mem. ABA, Order of Coif. Republican. Jewish. Labor, Constitutional Law, Civil rights. Office: Nat Right to Work Legal Def Found 8001 Braddock Rd Springfield VA 22160

TAULANE, JOHN BAPTIST, JR., lawyer; b. Phila., Nov. 14, 1933; s. John Baptiste and Frances (Devine) T.; m. Margaret Mary Bradley, Aug. 1, 1941; children: Joan, Margaret Mary, John, Elizabeth, Anne, Mary Kathleen. BS, St. Joseph U., 1955; LLB, Villanova U., 1962. Bar: Pa. 1963, U.S. Dist. Ct. (ea. dist.) Pa. 1963. Law clk. to presiding justice Phila. County Common Pleas Ct. 2, 1962-71; ptnr. Gilfillan Gilpin & Brehman, Phila., 1965—; bd. dirs. E. Girard Savs. and Loan, Phila. Commr., coach Huntingdon Valley (Pa.) Athletic Assn., 1978-86; Sunday sch. tchr.St. Albert's Ch., Huntingdon Valley, 1981-83; lector Our Lady of Good Counsel Ch., South Hampton, Pa., 1980-81. Served to lt. USNR, 1955-59. Mem. Phila. Bar Assn., Phila. C. of C. (100 Club award 1951), Order of Coif. Democrat. Roman Catholic. Avocations: golf, skiing. Landlord-tenant, Estate planning, Probate. Home: 281 Coachlight Terr Huntingdon Valley PA 19006 Office: Gilfillan Gilpin & Brehman 1201 Chestnut St 11th Floor Philadelphia PA 19107

TAUNT, CHARLES JOSEPH, lawyer; b. Pontiac, Mich., Jan. 17, 1949; s. Joseph L. and Elsie Bernadine (Omans) T.; m. Cheri L. Hazard; children: Charles Joseph, Sarah Elizabeth, Matthew Paul. BA, Mich. State U., 1971; JD, Detroit Coll. Law, 1974. Bar: Mich. 1974, U.S. Dist. Ct. (we. and ea.

dists.) Mich. 1975, U.S. Ct. Appeals (6th cir.) 1983. Sole practice Birmingham, Mich., 1975—; instr. bus. law Detroit Coll. Bus., Dearborn, 1975-78; trustee U.S. Bankruptcy Ct. (ea. dist.) Mich., 1986—. Chmn. bd. dirs. Rubicon Odyssey House, Inc., Detroit. Mem. Oakland County Bar Assn. (chmn. fed. ct. com. 1984-85). Republican. Roman Catholic. Club: Economic (Detroit). Pension, profit-sharing, and employee benefits, Federal civil litigation, Bankruptcy. Office: 401 S Woodward Ave Suite 365 Birmingham MI 48011-1621

TAURO, JOSEPH LOUIS, federal judge; b. Winchester, Mass., Sept. 26, 1931; s. G. Joseph and Helen Maria (Petrossi) T.; m. Elizabeth Mary Quinlan, Feb. 7, 1959 (dec. 1978); children—Joseph L., Elizabeth H., Christopher M. m. Ann Lefavour Jones, July 12, 1980. A.B., Brown U., 1953; LL.B., Cornell U., 1956; J.D. (hon.), U. Mass., 1985; D.Laws (hon.), Suffolk U., 1986. Bar: Mass. 1956, D.C. 1960. Assoc. Tauro & Tauro, Lynn, Mass., 1958-59; asst. U.S. atty. Dept. Justice, Boston, 1959-60; ptnr. Jaffee & Tauro, Boston and Lynn, Mass., 1960-71; chief legal counsel Gov. of Mass., Boston, 1965-68; U.S. atty. Dept. Justice, Boston, 1972; judge U.S. Dist. Ct., Boston, 1972—; exec. com. Cornell Law Assn., Ithaca, N.Y., 1968-71; adv. council Cornell Law Sch., Ithaca, 1975-80; dir. Security Nat. Bank, Lynn, 1961-72; lectr. Boston U. Law Sch., Boston, 1977; trustee Brown U., 1978—. trustee Mass. Gen. Hosp., Boston, 1968-72, Children's Hosp. Med. Ctr., Boston, 1979—, Brown U., 1978—. Served to 1st lt. U.S. Army, 1956-58. Recipient Ten Outstanding Young Men award Greater Boston Jaycees, 1966. Fellow Am. Bar Found.; mem. ABA, Mass. Bar Assn., Boston Bar Assn. (council 1968-71), D.C. Bar Assn. Republican. Roman Catholic. Club: Corinthian Yacht (Marblehead, Mass.). Avocations: sports; reading; music; films; theater. Jurisprudence. Office: U S Dist Ct Suite 1615 Post Office Sq Boston MA 02109

TAUS, ARMIN KENNETH, lawyer; b. N.Y.C., June 14, 1950; s. Julius B. and Lois (Baum) T.; m. Nina Gendelman, July 3, 1975; children: David, Sarah. BA, U. Wis., 1972; JD, Harvard U., 1975. Bar: Wis. 1975, U.S. Dist. Ct. (ea. and we. dists.) Wis. 1976, U.S. Ct. Appeals (7th cir.) 1976. Law clk. to chief judge U.S. Dist. Ct. (ea. dist.) Wis., 1975-76; assoc. Herz, Levin, Teper, Sumner & Croysdale, Milw., 1976-81, ptnr., 1981-85; ptnr. Michael, Best & Friedrich, Milw., 1985—. Mem. ABA, Wis. Bar Assn., Milw. Bar Assn., Nat. Assn. Bond Lawyers. Club: Brynwood Country Club (Milw.). Real property, Municipal bonds, Contracts commercial. Office: Michael Best & Friedrich 250 E Wisconsin Ave Milwaukee WI 53202

TAUSSIG, ERIC ALFRED, lawyer; b. London, May 13, 1944; came to U.S., 1946; s. Walter and Gerda (Nass) T.; m. Marlene Carole Pollack, Apr. 25, 1976; children: Melanie Gayle, Richard Walter. BA, Adelphi U., 1966; MA, NYU, 1968, JD, 1971. Bar: N.Y. 1972, D.C. 1975, U.S. Dist. Ct. (so. and ea. dists.) N.Y. 1974, U.S. Ct. Appeals (2d cir.) 1974, U.S. Ct. Appeals (4th cir.) 1985. Asst. corp. counsel City of N.Y., 1971-74; sr. atty. CBS, Inc., N.Y.C., 1974-77; asst. gen. counsel Philip Morris Cos., Inc., N.Y.C., 1978—. Contbr. articles to profl. jours. Mem. ABA, N.Y. State Bar assn., Assn. of the Bar of the City of N.Y. Labor, Federal civil litigation, Pension, profit-sharing, and employee benefits. Home: 29 Crest Dr White Plains NY 10607 Office: Philip Morris Cos Inc 120 Park Ave New York NY 10017

TAVERNI, LINDA TROY, lawyer; b. Little Falls, N.Y., Mar. 3, 1950; d. John and Marguerite Jean (Reardon) Troy; m. Anthony F. Taverni, April 14, 1973; children: Matthew, Elisa. BA, U. Rochester, 1972; postgrad., Cornell U., 1976-77; JD, Union U., Albany, N.Y., 1980. Bar: N.Y. 1981, U.S. Dist. Ct. (no. dist.) N.Y. 1981. Assoc. McNamee, Lochner, Titus & Williams, P.C. and predecessor firm Lifset & Lifset, Albany, 1980—. Mem. ABA, N.Y. State Bar Assn., N.Y. State Women's Bar Assn. Democrat. Roman Catholic. Bankruptcy, Consumer commercial, Banking. Office: McNamee Lochner Titus & Williams PC 75 State St Albany NY 12207

TAVROW, RICHARD LAWRENCE, lawyer, transportation executive; b. Syracuse, N.Y., Feb. 3, 1935; s. Harry and Ida Mary (Hodess) T.; m. Barbara J. Silver, Mar. 22, 1972; children—Joshua Michael, Sara Hallie. A.B. magna cum laude, Harvard U., 1957, LL.B., 1960, LL.M., 1961; postgrad., U. Copenhagen, 1961-62, U. Luxembourg, 1962. Bar: N.Y. bar 1961, U.S. Supreme Ct. bar 1969, Calif. bar 1978. Atty. W.R. Grace & Co., N.Y.C., 1962-66; asst. chief counsel Gen. Dynamics Corp., N.Y.C., 1966-68; chief counsel office of fgn. direct investments U.S. Dept. Commerce, Washington, 1969-71; ptnr. Schaeffer, Dale, Vogel & Tavrow, N.Y.C., 1971-75; v.p., sec., gen. counsel Prudential Lines, Inc., N.Y.C., 1975-78; v.p., sec., gen. counsel Am. Pres. Lines Ltd., Oakland, Calif., 1978-80, sr. v.p., sec., gen. counsel, 1980-82, sr. v.p. legal and govt. affairs, 1982—, also bd. dirs.; sr. v.p., sec., gen. counsel, bd. dirs. Am. Pres. Cos., Ltd., Oakland, 1983—; instr. Harvard Coll., 1959-61; lectr. Am. Mgmt. Assn., Practising Law Inst. Contbg. author: Private Investors Abroad - Problems and Solutions in International Business, 1970. Recipient Silver Medal award Dept. Commerce, 1970; Fulbright scholar, 1961-62. Mem. ABA, State Bar Calif., Internat. Bar Assn., Am. Soc. Internat. Law, Maritime Law Assn., San Francisco Bar Assn., Asia-Pacific Lawyers Assn., Transp. Lawyers Assn., Am. Steamship Owners Mut. Protection and Indemnity Assn. (dir.), Pacific Mcht. Shipping Assn. (dir., chmn. bd. dirs.), Am. Corp. Counsel Assn., Am. Soc. Corp. Secs. Inc., Calif. C. of C. (state transp. com.), Harvard Law Sch. Assn., Navy League. Democrat. Jewish. Clubs: World Trade, Alpine Hills Swimming and Tennis, Lakeview (Oakland), Harvard (N.Y.C. and San Francisco). General corporate, Administrative and regulatory. Office: Am President Cos Ltd 1800 Harrison St Oakland CA 94612

TAYLOR, ANNA DIGGS, U.S. district judge; b. Washington, Dec. 9, 1932; d. Virginius Douglass and Hazel (Bramlette) Johnston; m. S. Martin Taylor, May 22, 1976; children: Douglass Johnston Diggs, Carla Cecile Diggs. B.A., Barnard Coll., 1954; LL.B., Yale U., 1957. Bar: Mich. 1961. Atty. Office Solicitor, Dept. Labor, W, 1957-60; asst. prosecutor Wayne County, Mich., 1961-62; asst. U.S. atty. Eastern Dist. of Mich., 1966; partner firm Zwerdling, Maurer, Diggs & Papp, Detroit, 1970-75; asst. corp. counsel City of Detroit, 1975-79; U.S. dist. judge Eastern Dist. Mich. Detroit, 1979—; adj. prof. labor law Wayne State U. Law Sch., Detroit, 1976. Trustee Receiving Hosp. Detroit, Episcopal Diocese Mich., Detroit Symphony, Sinai Hosp., United Found., Community Found. Southeastern Mich. Mem. Fed. Bar Assn., Nat. Lawyer's Guild, State Bar Mich., Wolverine Bar Assn., Women Lawyers Assn. Mich. Democrat. Episcopalian. Jurisprudence. Office: US District Court 231 W Lafayette Blvd Detroit MI 48226

TAYLOR, BRENT DOUGLAS, lawyer; b. New Castle, Ind., Jan. 14, 1957; s. Delmar Lee and Judith Ann (Cronk) T.; m. Rhonda Sue Jenkins, May 26, 1979; children: Jennifer Kay, Tamara Renée. BA in Econs. summa cum laude, Butler U., 1979; JD, Harvard U., 1982. Bar: Ind. 1982, U.S. Dist. Ct. (so. and no. dists.) Ind. 1982. Assoc. Baker & Daniels, Indpls., 1982—. Mem. ABA, Ind. Bar Assn., Indpls. Bar Assn. (litigation sect.), Phi Kappa Phi. Democrat. Mem. Soc. of Friends. Federal civil litigation, State civil litigation. Home: 9631 Lincoln Blvd Indianapolis IN 46280 Office: Baker & Daniels 810 Fletcher Trust Bldg Indianapolis IN 46204

TAYLOR, BRIAN LAWRENCE, lawyer; b. Plattsburgh, N.Y., Mar. 7, 1947; s. Walter Lawrence and Helen Elizabeth (Bourdon) T. BA in English, Fordham U., 1969; MFA, Tulane U., 1973; postdoctoral, Brandeis U., 1974-78; JD cum laude, Boston Coll., 1981. Bar: N.Y. 1982, U.S. Dist. Ct. (so. and ea. dists.) N.Y. 1982. Assoc. Proskauer, Rose, Goetz & Mendelsohn, N.Y.C., 1981-84, Sage & Gray, N.Y.C., 1984-85, Reid & Priest, N.Y.C., 1985—. Mydans fellow, Remis fellow. Mem. ABA, N.Y. State Bar Assn. Real property. Office: Reid & Priest 40 W 57th St New York NY 10019

TAYLOR, CARL LARSEN, lawyer; b. Honolulu, Apr. 9, 1937; s. William Henry and Dorothy (Gray) T.; m. Linda Ann Farrell, Aug. 3, 1963. AB, Harvard U., 1958, LLB, 1961. Bar: U.S. Ct. Appeals (D.C. cir.) 1965, U.S. Supreme Ct. 1969, U.S. Ct. Appeals (9th cir.) 1975, U.S. Ct. Appeals (2d cir.) 1977, U.S. Ct. Appeals (3d cir.) 1981, U.S. Ct. Appeals (7th cir.) 1982, U.S. Ct. Appeals (5th cir.) 1986. Assoc. Hogan & Hartson, Washington, 1966-69, ptnr., 1978-80; gen. counsel Retail Clerks Internat. Assn., Washington, 1969-76; assoc. gen. counsel NLRB, Washington, 1976-78; ptnr. Kirkland & Ellis, Washington, 1980—. Served to lt. (j.g.) USN, 1961-65. Mem. Barristers. Club: Belle Haven (Alexandria, Va.). Federal civil litigation, Labor, Pension, profit-sharing, and employee benefits. Office: Kirkland & Ellis 655 15th St NW Washington DC 20005

TAYLOR, CARROLL STRIBLING, lawyer; b. Port Chester, N.Y., Jan. 14, 1944; s. William H. Jr. and Anna P. (Stribling) T.; m. Nancy S. Tyson, Apr. 7, 1968; children: Heather, Kimberly, Tori, Tiffany, Tacy. AB, Yale U., 1965; JD, U. Calif., Berkeley, 1968. Bar: Hawaii 1969, Calif. 1969, U.S. Dist. Ct. Hawaii 1969, U.S. Dist. Ct. (cen. dist.) Calif. 1975, U.S. Ct. Appeals (9th cir.) 1975. Researcher Legis. Reference Bur., Honolulu, 1968-70; reporter Jud. Council Probate Code Revision Project, Honolulu, 1970-71; assoc. Chun, Kerr & Dodd, Honolulu, 1971-75; ptnr. Hamilton & Taylor, Honolulu, 1975-80; officer, dir. Char, Hamilton, Taylor & Thom, Honolulu, 1980-82, Carroll S. Taylor Atty. at Law, A Law Corp., Honolulu, 1982-86; ptnr. Taylor & Leong, Honolulu, 1986—; adj. prof. U. Hawaii Richardson Sch. Law, Honolulu, 1981—. Fellow Am. Coll. Probate Counsel; mem. ABA, Calif. Bar Assn., Hawaii Bar Assn., Hawaii Inst. Continuing Legal Edn. (v.p. 1984-86, pres. 1986—). Episcopalian. Club: Plaza (Honolulu). Probate, Real property, State civil litigation. Home: 46-429 Hololio St Kaneohe HI 96744 Office: 737 Bishop St Suite 2060 Honolulu HI 96813

TAYLOR, DANE EDWARD, lawyer; b. Cumberland, Md., Mar. 27, 1957; s. Casper Rohman and Mary Lenore (Young) T.; m. Linda Marie Perrin, Sept. 25, 1982; children: Mallory Aileen, Colin Andrew, Devin Patrick. BA, U. Notre Dame, 1979; JD, U. Md., 1982. Bar: Md. 1982. Assoc. Walsh, Walsh & Reinhart, Cumberland, 1982—; bd. dirs. Archway Sta., Inc., Cumberland, 1983—. Bd. dirs. YMCA, Cumberland, 1984. Mem. ABA, Md. Bar Assn., Allegheny County Bar Assn., Assn. Trial Lawyers Am. Democrat. Roman Catholic. Club: Dapper Dan (Cumberland) (bd. dirs. 1983—). Avocation: weightlifting. State civil litigation, Banking, Consumer commercial. Home: 501 Patterson Ave Cumberland MD 21502 Office: Walsh Walsh & Reinhart 504 Liberty Trust Bldg Cumberland MD 21502

TAYLOR, DANIEL EDWIN, lawyer, army officer; b. Hartford, Conn., Mar. 13, 1943; s. Leonard W. and Margaretta (O.) T.; m. Gayna L. Burrie; children—Daniel, Aubryn. B.A., U. Fla., 1965, J.D., 1967; LL.M., NYU, 1975. Bar: Fla. 1968, U.S. Ct. Mil. Appeals, U.S. Supreme Ct. Commd. U.S. Army, 1968, advanced through grades to col.; asst. prof. law U.S. Mil. Acad., West Point, N.Y., 1973-75; chief legal sect. USDAO, Am. embassy, Paris, 1975-78; dep. staff judge adv., Fort Huachuca, Ariz., 1979-82; chief internat. law div. Judge Adv. Gen.'s Sch., Charlottesville, Va., 1983-86; staff judge advocate, U.S. Command, Berlin, 1986—. Sec., Charlottesville Com. on Fgn. Relations, 1984-86.. Mem. Assn. Trial Lawyers Am., Internat. Soc. Mil. Laws and Laws of War (Am. corr. 1983—). Public international, Military.

TAYLOR, DAVID AFTON, lawyer; b. Independence, Mo., Jan. 31, 1949; s. Herbert and Roberta Claire (Staihr) T.; m. Tina Mari Van Oosbree, Dec. 21, 1975; children: Derek Afton, Laura Mari. AB in History, U. Mo., 1971, JD, 1975. Ptnr. Taylor and Murphy, Kansas City, Mo., 1975-84; asst. atty. gen. Mo. Atty. Gen., Jefferson City, 1984—. Dir. Friends of Truman Campus, U. Mo.-Kansas City, 1982-84. Mem. ABA, Mo. Bar Assn. (chmn. com. on energy and nat. resources 1981-84). Methodist. Avocations: sports, travel, amateur radio. Environment. Home: 111 Forest Hill Ave Jefferson City MO 65101 Office: Mo Atty Gens Office PO Box 899 Jefferson City MO 65102

TAYLOR, EDWARD MCKINLEY, JR., lawyer; b. Dayton, Ohio, Apr. 19, 1928; s. Edward McKinley and Margaret Helen (Gaessler) T.; m. Mary Joan McMahon; 1 dau., Mary Margaret Taylor Neises. J.D. with distinction, 1951. Bar: Ohio 1951, U.S. Supreme Ct. 1971, U.S. Ct. Mill. Appeals 1973, U.S. Dist. Ct. (so. dist.) Ohio 1959. Ptnr. Taylor & Taylor, Dayton, 1957—; asst. city atty. City of Dayton, 1957-77; solicitor Village of Union (Ohio), 1978-82, law dir., 1982, law dir. emeritus, 1982—. Served to col. JAGC, USAF. Mem. ABA, Ohio State Bar Assn., Dayton Bar Assn., Judge Advocate Assn. Clubs: Shriners, Racquet (Dayton). Probate, Real property, Local government. Address: 7417 N Main St Dayton OH 45415

TAYLOR, GEORGE MALCOLM, III, lawyer; b. Montgomery, Ala., Sept. 12, 1953; s. George Malcolm Jr. and Marion (Hall) T.; m. Judy Grace Howall, May 24, 1986. BA summa cum laude, U. of the South, 1975; JD, Vanderbilt U., 1978. Bar: Ala. 1978, U.S. Dist. Ct. (no. dist.) Ala. 1978, U.S. Ct. Appeals (5th cir.) 1979, U.S. Tax Ct. 1980, U.S. Ct. Appeals (11th cir.) 1982. Law clk. to chief judge U.S. Dist. Ct. (no. dist.) Ala., Birmingham, 1978-79; assoc. Burr & Forman, Birmingham, 1979-84, ptnr., 1984—; mem. bd. examiners Ala. State Bar, 1987—. Treas. Ind. Presbyn. Ch., Birmingham, 1986—. Mem. ABA, Ala. Bar Assn. (bd. editors jour. 1984-86), Internat. Bar Assn., Phi Beta Kappa, Order of Coif, Omicron Delta Kappa. Club: Birmingham Sailing. Avocation: sailing. General corporate, Banking, Securities. Home: 2864 Canterbury Rd Birmingham AL 35223 Office: Burr & Forman 3000 S Trust Tower Birmingham AL 35203

TAYLOR, GREGORY FREDERICK, lawyer; b. Washington, Apr. 9, 1946; s. Francis Mortimer and Victoria Jean (DeVoe) T.; m. Roberta Elmina Cashwell, Oct. 12, 1985. BA, U. Va., 1968; JD, Boston U., 1971. Bar: N.Y. 1973. Atty. Am. Stock Exchange, N.Y.C., 1972-74; spl. counsel N.Y. Stock Exchange, N.Y.C., 1974-79, dir. fin., 1975-76; assoc. Law Dept. of Morgan Stanley, N.Y.C., 1979-81; asst. v.p., gen. sr. counsel Merrill Lynch, N.Y.C., 1981-84, v.p., gen. counsel money markets, 1984—. Mem. steering com. Lawyers Pro-Choice, N.Y.C., 1979-81; bd. dirs. Bklyn. Heights (N.Y.) Assn., 1975-87, treas., 1981-83. Served to capt. U.S. Army, 1971. Mem. ABA, Assn. of Bar of City of N.Y., Securities Industry Assn. Episcopalian. Club: Princeton (N.Y.C.). Avocations: collecting Am. antiques, landscaping, cinema. Securities, General corporate, Banking. Home: 93 Vanderveer Ave Holland PA 18966 Office: Merrill Lynch Money Markets 165 Broadway New York NY 10080

TAYLOR, HENDRIX ARTHUR, JR., judge, farmer; b. Pine Bluff, Ark., Jan. 18, 1941; s. Hendrix Arthur and Mary Marie (Mariscallo) T.; m. Marcella Joanne Harvey, Feb. 8, 1969; children—Kirk Ann, Anastasia Belle. B.A. in Bus. Adminstrn., U. Ark., 1962, J.D., 1965. Bar: Ark. 1965, U.S. Dist. Ct. (ea. dist.) Ark. 1969, U.S. Ct. Appeals (8th cir.) 1974, U.S. Supreme Ct. 1974. Assoc. Reinberger, Eilbott, Smith & Staten, Pine Bluff, 1969-72; city atty. City of Pine Bluff, 1972-74; judge 11th. Jud. Cir. Ct. Ark., 1975—; mem. S.E. Ark. Criminal Justice Planning Council, 1974-76; mem. Ark. Criminal Detention Facilities Bd., 1976-80, Ark. Jud. Compensation Com., 1986—; mem. Ark. Jud. Council, 1975—, co-chmn. com. on continuing jud. edn., 1984—; bd. dirs. Ark. Inst. Continuing Legal Edn., 1975—; co-chmn. S.E. Ark. Trial Practice Com., 1986—. Mem. adv. bd. Pine Bluff Opportunity Industrialization Ctr. 1972-74; bd. dirs. Jefferson County (Ark.) Farm Bur., 1972-74; mem. Ark. Dem. Cen. Com., 1972-74; state exec. committeeman Ark. Young Dems., 1971-72; mem. Jefferson County Young Dems., 1971-73. Served to capt. JAGC, U.S. Army, 1965-69; Vietnam. Decorated Army Commendation medal, Bronze Star medal. Mem. ABA, Ark. Bar Assn., Jefferson County Bar Assn., Pine Bluff C. of C. Democrat. Roman Catholic. Clubs: Kiwanis (Pine Bluff); Order Police (assoc.). Jurisprudence, State civil litigation, Criminal. Office: PO Box 8705 Pine Bluff AR 71601

TAYLOR, HILARY SHELDON, lawyer; b. Cleve., Nov. 6, 1944; s. Hilary Oliver and Sally (Wilkins) T.; Catherine Fears, Oct. 16, 1971; children: Hilary Sterling, Jeremy Fears. BS, Cen. State U., 1967; JD, Cleve. State U., 1977. Bar: Ohio 1977, U.S. Dist. Ct. (no. dist.) Ohio 1977, U.S. Ct. Appeals (6th cir.) 1983, U.S. Supreme Ct. 1984. Ptnr. Weston, Hurd, Fallon, Paisley & Howley, Cleve., 1985—; trustee Legal Aid Soc., Cleve., 1983—. Served to capt. U.S. Army, 1968-70, Vietnam. Decorated Bronze Star. Mem. Scabbard and Blade , Alpha Phi Alpha, Phi Alpha Theta, Pershing Rifle Soc. Republican. Mem. United Ch. of Christ. Personal injury, Civil rights, State civil litigation. Office: Weston Hurd Fallon Paisley & Howley 2500 Terminal Tower Cleveland OH 44113

TAYLOR, HOWARD HARPER, lawyer; b. Detroit, June 5, 1926; s. Howard Francis and Helen (Hawken) T.; m. Mary L. Maddox, Mar. 28, 1953 (div. Oct. 1967); 1 child, Steven. BA, Stanford U., 1949, JD, 1951. Bar: Calif. 1952., U.S. Dist. Ct. (so. dist.) Calif. 1952. Sole practice San Diego, 1952—; instr. bus. law and real estate law Mesa Coll., San Diego, 1962—. Editor Stanford U. Law Rev., 1950-51. Served to petty officer 3d class USN, 1944-46, PTO. Mem. ABA, Calif. Bar Assn., San Diego County Bar Assn. Republican. Lodge: Masons, Shriners. Family and matrimonial, Probate. Home: 980 Scott St San Diego CA 92106 Office: 1200 3d Ave Suite 1200 San Diego CA 92101

TAYLOR, JAMES DANFORTH, lawyer; b. Sioux Falls, S.D., Apr. 27, 1954; s. William George and Marit Gertrude (Danforth) T.; m. Margo Joyce Oakland, Dec. 29, 1979; 1 child, Adrienne. BA, St. Olaf Coll., 1976; JD, U. S.D., 1982. Bar: S.D. 1982, U.S. Dist. Ct. S.D. 1982. From assoc. to ptnr. Tinan, Smith & Saukerson, Mitchell, S.D., 1982—; bd. dirs. Mitchell Area Adjustment Tng. Ctr. Mem. ABA, S.D. Bar Assn., Davison County Bar Assn. (pres. 1985—), S.D. Trial Lawyers Assn. Republican. Congregationalist. Club: Davison County Sportsmans (Mitchell). Lodge: Kiwanis (bd. dirs. 1984-85). Avocations: upland game bird and waterfowl hunting, gardening. General practice, Banking, Contracts commercial. Office: Tinan Smith & Taylor 305 N Kimball PO Box 488 Mitchell SD 57301

TAYLOR, JERRY FRANCIS, lawyer; b. Memphis, Oct. 2, 1934; s. Rex Brewster and Naomi (Robertson) T.; m. Jo(dy) Evelyn Katz, Mar. 5, 1971; 1 child, Deborah Pagan. B.S., Memphis State U., 1956; J.D., U. Tenn., 1963. Bar: U.S. Dist. Ct. (we., mid. and ea. dists.) Tenn. 1965, U.S. Dist. Ct. (mid. dist.) Miss. 1963, U.S. Ct. Appeals (6th cir.) 1970. Assoc. Krivcher & Cox, Memphis, 1963-65; sr. ptnr. Holt, Batchelor, Taylor & Spicer, 1965-80, Wilkes, McCullough & Taylor, Memphis, 1980—. Fund raiser United Way Memphis, 1982; bd. dirs. Jeff Steinberg Ministries, 1983—, Outreach to Youth, Inc., 1983—. Served to capt. USAF, 1957-60. Law Sch. scholar Memphis-Shelby County Bar Assn., 1961. Mem. Memphis-Shelby County Bar Assn., ABA, Assn. Trial Lawyers Am. (state committeeman 1968), Tenn. Trial Lawyers Assn. (bd. govs. 1984). Lodges: Masons, Shriners. Personal injury, Insurance. Home: 1830 Kimbrough St Germantown TN 38138 Office: Wilkes McCullough & Taylor 1140 Sterick Bldg Memphis TN 38103

TAYLOR, JOB, III, lawyer; b. N.Y.C., Feb. 18, 1942; s. Job II and Anne Harrison (Flinchbaugh) T.; m. Mary C. August, Oct. 24, 1964 (div. Oct. 1978); children: Whitney August, Job IV; m. Sally Lawson, May 31, 1980. BA, Washington & Jefferson Coll., 1964; JD, Coll. William and Mary, 1971. Bar: N.Y. 1972, U.S. Dist. Ct. (ea. and no. dists.) N.Y. 1973, U.S. Ct. Appeals (2d cir.) 1973, U.S. Ct. Claims 1974, U.S. Tax Ct. 1974, U.S. Supreme Ct. 1975, U.S. Ct. Appeals (9th cir.) 1976, U.S. Ct. Mil. Appeals 1977, U.S. Ct. Appeals (D.C. and 10th cirs.) 1977, D.C. 1981, U.S. Ct. Internat. Trade 1981, U.S. Ct. Appeals (fed. cir.) 1982, U.S. Dist. Ct. (no. dist.) Calif. 1983, U.S. Ct. Appeals (6th cir.) 1987. Ptnr. Olwine, Connelly, Chase, O'Donnell & Weyher, N.Y.C., 1971-85, Latham & Watkins, N.Y.C., 1985—. Served to lt. USN, 1964-68. Mem. ABA, Assn. of Bar of City of N.Y. Republican. Episcopalian. Clubs: Racquet and Tennis (N.Y.C.); The Wee Burn Country (Darien, Conn.). Avocations: squash, tennis, golf, reading. Antitrust, Computer, Federal civil litigation. Office: Latham & Watkins 885 3d Ave New York NY 10022-4802

TAYLOR, JOE CLINTON, judge; b. Durant, Okla., Mar. 28, 1942; s. Luther Clinton and Virena (Parker) T.; m. Margaret Pearl Byers, June 8, 1963; children: Marna Joanne, Leah Alison, Jocelyn Camille. Student, Southeastern State Coll., 1960-62; B.A., Okla. State U., 1965; J.D., U. Okla., 1968. Bar: Okla. 1968. Practice law Norman, Okla., 1968-69; apptd. spl. dist. judge Durant, 1969-72; asso. dist. judge Bryan County, Okla., 1972-76; dist. judge, chief judge 19th Dist. Ct., 1976—; presiding judge Southeastern Okla. Jud. Adminstrv. Dist.; judge trial div. Okla. Ct. on the Judiciary; presiding judge Choctaw Tribal Ct., 1979-83; chmn. bd. dirs Durant Youth Services, 1976—; bd. dirs. Bryan County Youth Services, Inc., 1971—. Served to maj. USAR. Mem. Phi Sigma Epsilon, Delta Theta Phi. Mem. Ch. of Christ. Club: Lion. State civil litigation, Criminal, Juvenile. Home: 424 W Olive St Durant OK 74701 Office: Bryan County Courthouse Durant OK 74701

TAYLOR, JOHN ANTHONY, lawyer, legal educator; b. Boston, Mar. 17, 1954; s. Amos Leavitt Jr. and Jean Barker (McMann) T. BA with honors, Brown U., 1977; JD cum laude, New Eng. Sch. of Law, 1980; postdoctoral, Temple U., 1983-85. Bar: Mass. 1980, U.S. Dist. Ct. Mass. 1981, U.S. Ct. Appeals (1st cir.) 1981, Pa. 1983. Assoc. Adams & Blinn, Boston, 1980-83, mng. ptnr., 1985—; supr. atty. Temple U. Legal Aid Office, Phila., 1983-85; instr. law New Eng. Sch. of Law, Boston, 1980-83, Newbury Coll. Paralegal Inst., Boston, 1985—; grad. teaching fellow Temple U. Sch. of Law, 1983-85. Speaker Sch. Vols. for Boston, Inc., 1982-83; atty. Crittenton Hastings House, Inc., Alston, Mass., 1981—, High Sch. Mock Trial Competition, Phila., 1984-85; bd. dirs. Mass. Vols. of Am., Boston, 1982-84. Abraham L. Friedman fellow Temple U., 1983; named one of Outstanding Young Men in Am. American Jaycees, 1983; recipient Cert. of Achievement Sch. Vols. for Boston, Inc., 1983. Mem. ABA, Mass. Bar Assn. Republican. Mem. Unitarian Ch. Avocations: sailing, racquet sports, bridge. Probate, Real property, Legal education. Home: 214 Hemenway St Boston MA 02115 Office: Adams & Blinn 43 Thorndike St Cambridge MA 02141

TAYLOR, JOHN MCKOWEN, lawyer; b. Baton Rouge, Jan. 20, 1924; s. Benjamin Brown and May (McKowen) T.; 1 son, John McKowen. B.A., La. State U., 1948, J.D., 1950. Bar: La. 1950, U.S. Supreme Ct. 1960. Asso., Taylor, Porter, Brooks, Fuller & Phillips, Baton Rouge, 1951-55, Huckaby, Seale, Kelton & Hayes, Baton Rouge, 1955-58; ptnr. Kelton & Taylor, Baton Rouge, 1958-61; sole practice, Baton Rouge, 1961—. Served with AUS, 1943-46; to maj. USAR, 1946—; ATO, ETO, PTO. Mem. ABA, La. State Bar Assn., Baton Rouge Bar Assn., AAAS, Mil. Order of World Wars, Am. Radio Relay League, Sigma Chi. Republican. Presbyterian. Clubs: Baton Rouge Country, City of Baton Rouge, Baton Rouge Amateur Radio, Camelot. Oil and gas leasing, Real property, Family and matrimonial. Home and Office: 2150 Kleinert Ave Baton Rouge LA 70806

TAYLOR, JOSEPH WILLIAM, lawyer; b. Uvalde, Tex., May 3, 1952; s. Robert Augustus and Epsie Belle (Thompson) T. B.A. in Econs., Southwestern Tex., U. 1974, B.B.A. in Fin., 1974; J.D. U. Houston, 1977. Bar: Tex. 1977. Ptnr. firm Taylor & Taylor, Crystal City, Tex., 1977-80, firm Dodson, Nunley & Taylor, Crystal City and 5 other locations, 1980—; cons. Zavala Water Dist., Zavala and Dimmit counties, Tex., 1977—; dir., owner Zavala County Bank, Crystal City; dir., v.p. Nueces River Authority; county judge Zavala County, 1980; mem. com. on admissions Tex. Bar. Mem. Tex. Bar Assn., ABA, Zavala County Bar Assn. (pres. 1983-85), Uvalde County Bar Assn. (sec.-treas. 1983-84, v.p. 1984-85), Border Dist. Bar Assn., Medina County Bar. Democrat. Methodist. Real property, Oil and gas, Banking. Office: Dodson Nunley & Taylor PC 123 E Uvalde St Crystal City TX 78839

TAYLOR, KENNETH DAVID, lawyer; b. Perry, Okla., Nov. 19, 1950; s. Kenneth Vincent and Mary Vincent (Higdon) T.; m. Deborah Kathleen McGraw, June 7, 1970 (div. Oct. 1978); 1 child, Brian David; m. Margaret Ruth Dawkins, May 23, 1981. BS, Okla. State U., 1972; JD, Okla. City U., 1979. Bar: Okla. 1980, U.S. Dist. Ct. (we. dist.) Okla. 1980. Assoc. Brogden & Behrens, Oklahoma City, 1980-83; ptnr. Murray, Behrens & Taylor, Oklahoma City, 1983—. Mem. Okla. Bar Assn., Okla. County Bar Assn., Assn. Trial Lawyers Am., Okla. Trial Lawyers Assn., Okla. City Assn. Petroleum Landmen. Democrat. Roman Catholic. Avocations: tennis, golf, music. Oil and gas leasing, Workers' compensation. Home: 909 NW 33rd Oklahoma City OK 73118 Office: Murray Behrens & Taylor 6 NE 63d St Suite 400 Oklahoma City OK 73105

TAYLOR, KERNS BOWMAN, administrative law judge, lawyer; b. Austin, Tex., June 27, 1920; s. Q.C. and Marian (Kerns) T.; m. Rosemary Parrish, Nov. 29, 1963. J.D. U. Tex., 1948. Bar: Tex. 1948. Assoc. Taylor & Chandler, Austin, 1948-52; spl. asst. U.S. atty. Dept. Justice, Austin, 1953; ptnr. Cain & Taylor, Liberty, Tex., 1953-59; asst. atty. gen. State Atty. Gen., Austin, 1965-72; U.S. adminstrv. law judge HHS, Social Security Adminstrn., Houston, 1973—. Served to capt. Q.M.C., AUS, 1940-45, to col. JAGC, USAR, 1965-70. Mem. Houston Fed. Bar Assn. (pres. 1978-79), Houston Ret. Officers Assn. (pres. 1979), Am. Legion (comdr. 1963). Lodge: Capital City Kiwanis (pres. 1968-69) (Austin). Administrative and regulatory. Home: 10324 Briar Forest Houston TX 77042 Office: Office Hearings and Appeals Social Security Adminstrn 3100 Wesleyan Suite 440 Houston TX 77027

TAYLOR, KNEELAND LAMOUREUX, lawyer; b. N.Y.C., Nov. 17, 1947; s. John Read and Patricia Lamoureux (Green) T.; m. Beth Lee Pennington, June 1, 1984; children: Heidi Dahl, Jodi Dahl. BA, U. Pa., 1970; JD, U. Denver, 1975. Bar: Alaska 1975, U.S. Dist. Ct. Alaska 1975. Assoc. Groh, Benkert, and Walter, Anchorage, 1975-77; ptnr. Smith, Taylor, and

Gruening, Anchorage, 1977-79, Vollintine, Taylor and Carey, Anchorage, 1979—. Bd. dirs. Common Sense for Alaska, Anchorage, 1981—; candidate for Alaska State Legis., Anchorage, 1980. Recipient President's award Common Sense Alaska, 1982. Mem. Anchorage Bar Assn., Am. Trial Lawyers Assn. Republican. Club: Mountaineering (Anchorage). Avocations: mountain climbing, running, swimming. Personal injury, State civil litigation, General practice. Home: 2108 Dawson St Anchorage AK 99503 Office: 801 B St Suite 200 Anchorage AK 99501

TAYLOR, LAWRENCE ERIC, lawyer; b. Los Angeles, Apr. 1, 1942; s. Forrest Everett and Lyla (Sherwood) T.; m. Linda Sue Colello, June 5, 1978 (div. Apr. 1983); 1 child, Christopher. B.A., U. Calif.-Berkeley, 1966; J.D., UCLA, 1969. Bar: Calif. 1969. Dep. county counsel, Los Angeles, 1969-70; dep. pub. defender, Los Angeles, 1970-71; dep. dist. atty., Los Angeles, 1971-72; sole practice, Los Angeles, 1972-81; vis. assoc. prof. Sch. of Law, Pepperdine U., Malibu, Calif., 1981-82; assoc. prof. Sch. of Law, Gonzaga U., Spokane, Wash., 1982-84; ptnr. Giometti, Powell and Taylor, Glendale, Calif., 1984-86; prof. Western State U. Sch. Law, Fullerton, Calif., 1986—; Fulbright prof. U. Kobe, U. Osaka, Japan, 1985; lectr. profl. confs. and seminars. Author: Trail of the Fox, 1980; Handling Criminal Appeals, 1980; A Trial of Generals, 1981; Drunk Driving Defense, 1981; Witness Immunity, 1983; Eyewitness Identification, 1983; Born to Crime, 1984; Scientific Interrogation: Polygraphy, Hypnosis, Truth Serum, Voice Stress and Pupillometrics, 1984; contbr. legal articles to various mags. Served with USMC, 1960-63. Mem. Nat. Assn. Criminal Def. Lawyers, Am. Bd. Criminal Lawyers, Calif. Bar Assn. Criminal. Office: Western State U Sch Law 1111 N State College Blvd Fullerton CA 92631 Home: 7126 Marina Pacifica S Long Beach CA 90803

TAYLOR, MARK EDWARD, lawyer; b. Waukegan, Ill., Jan. 27, 1956; s. John Hayes and Eleanor Adelaide (Folkerts) T. BA, Monmouth Coll., 1978; JD, U. Mich., 1981. Bar: Tex. 1981, U.S. Ct. Appeals (5th cir.) 1982. Assoc. Liddell, Sapp and Zivley, Houston, 1981—. Mem. ABA, Houston Bar Assn., Tex. Assn. Bank Counsel, Am. Judicature Soc., ACLU. Democrat. Methodist. Club: Houston. Avocations: skiing, camping. Banking, Contracts commercial. Home: 1511 Kipling Houston TX 77006 Office: Liddell Sapp and Zivley 3400 Texas Commerce Tower Houston TX 77002

TAYLOR, MICHAEL CONRAD, lawyer; b. Tulsa, Feb. 17, 1955; s. Conrad Wayne Taylor and Sue Marie (Young) Ellingsworth; m. Cindy Lynn Polson, Aug. 20, 1978; 1 child, Trevin Conrad. BS, Drury Coll., 1977; JD, U. Tulsa, 1981. Bar: Okla. 1982, U.S. Dist. Ct. (no. dist.) Okla. 1982, U.S. Ct. Appeals (10th cir.) 1982, U.S. Dist. Ct. (ea. and we. dists.) Okla. 1984. Intern Best, Sharp, et.al., Tulsa, 1981; land atty., landman Ozark Mahoning, Tulsa, 1981-83; assoc. atty. Gibbon, Gladd & Assocs., Tulsa, 1983-84, E. Terrill Corley & Assocs., Tulsa, 1984-85; mng. atty. Daniel W. Lowe & Assocs., Tulsa, 1985-86; sole practice Tulsa, 1986-87; ptnr. Michael C. Taylor & Assocs., Tulsa, 1987—. Mem. ABA, Okla. Bar Assn., Assn. Trial Lawyers Am., Okla. Trial Lawyers Assn., Tulsa County Bar Assn. Republican. Avocation: golf. Personal injury, Insurance, State civil litigation. Home: 1625 S Boston Ave Tulsa OK 74119

TAYLOR, MICHAEL WILLIAM, lawyer; b. Little Rock, May 29, 1947; s. Orville Walters and Evelyn Adella (Bonham) T.; m. Susan Gaye Chandler, Aug. 14, 1977; children: William Chandler Bonham, Samuel Michael Gathright. AB with honors, U. N.C., 1969, JD, 1978; MA in Classical Archaeology, Harvard U., 1972, PhD in Classical Archaeology, 1975. Bar: N.C. 1978, U.S. Dist. Ct. (ea. dist.) N.C. 1978, U.S. Dist. Ct. (mid. dist.) N.C. 1983. Law clk. to presiding justice N.C. Ct. Appeals, Raleigh, 1978-79; assoc. atty. gen. State of N.C., Raleigh, 1979-80; asst. counsel med. ctr. Duke U., Durham, N.C., 1980-81; sole practice Albemarle, N.C., 1981—. Author: The Tyrant Slayers, 1981. Mem. Stanly County Hist. Preservation Commn., Albemarle, 1981—, chmn. 1986—; mem. gen. bd. N.C. State Bapt. Conv., Raleigh, 1984—. Served to lt. USN, 1969-71, Vietnam. Charles Eliot Norton fellow, 1973-74. Mem. ABA, N.C. Bar Assn., Stanly County Bar Assn., Phi Beta Kappa. Democrat. Lodge: Rotary. Avocations: archaeology, sailing. General practice, State civil litigation, Personal injury. Office: 112 E North St Albemarle NC 28002-0065

TAYLOR, REESE HALE, JR., lawyer, former government administrator; b. Los Angeles, May 6, 1928; s. Reese Hale and Kathryn (Emery) T.; m. Lucille Langdon, Dec. 29, 1948 (div. 1959); children: Reese Hale (dec.), Stuart Langdon, Anne Kathryn, Lucille Emery; m. Jolene Yerby, June 30, 1972. B.A. with distinction, Stanford U., 1949; LL.B., Cornell U., 1952. Bar: Calif. 1954, Nev. 1966. Assoc. Gibson, Dunn & Crutcher, Los Angeles, 1952-58; sole practice Los Angeles, 1958-65; assoc. Wiener, Goldwater & Galatz, Las Vegas, Nev., 1966-67; chmn. Nev. Pub. Service Commn., Carson City, 1967-71; ptnr. Laxalt, Berry & Allison, Carson City, 1971-78, Allison, Brunetti, MacKenzie & Taylor, Carson City, 1978-81; chmn. ICC, Washington, 1981-85; ptnr. Heron, Burchette, Ruckert & Rothwell, Washington, 1986—; vice chmn. Nev. Tax Commn., Carson City, 1967-69; mem. Nev. Gov.'s Cabinet, Carson City, 1967-70, Carson City Bd. Equalization, 1979-81, chmn., 1979-80; bd. dirs. U.S. Rail Assn., Washington, 1981-85. Del. Republican Nat. Conv., Kansas City, Mo., 1976, mem. platform com., 1976, alt. del., Detroit, 1980; mem. Rep. Nat. Com., 1980-81. Mem. ABA, Am. Judicature Soc., Order of Coif, Phi Gamma Delta, Phi Delta Phi. Episcopalian. Clubs: Prospectors (Reno, Nev.); Washington Golf and Country (Arlington, Va.). Administrative and regulatory. *

TAYLOR, RICHARD LEE, lawyer; b. Des Moines, Mar. 23, 1954; s. Glen Charles and Erma Arlene Taylor. B.S., Iowa State U., 1976; J.D., Drake U., 1979. Bar: Iowa 1979, Ill. 1980, U.S. Dist. Ct. (so. dist.) Iowa 1979. Staff atty. Am. Farm Bur. Fedn., Park Ridge, Ill., 1979-82; corp. atty. United Fed. Savs. Bank, Des Moines, 1982—. Mem. ABA, Iowa State Bar Assn., Polk County Bar Assn., Des Moines Civic Ctr. Republican. Presbyterian. Banking, Consumer commercial, Real property. Office: United Fed Savs Bank 400 Locust Des Moines IA 50308

TAYLOR, RICHARD POWELL, lawyer; b. Phila., Sept. 13, 1928; s. Earl Howard and Helen Moore (Martin) T.; m. Barbara Jo Anne Harris, Dec. 19, 1959; 1 child, Douglas Howard. BA, U. Va., 1950, JD, 1952. Bar: Va. 1952, D.C. 1956. Law clk. U.S. Ct. Appeals for 4th Circuit, 1951-52; assoc. Steptoe & Johnson, Washington, 1956-61, ptnr., 1962—, chmn. transp. dept., 1978—; sec., corp. counsel Slick Corp., 1963-69, asst. sec., 1969-72, also bd. dirs., 1965-68; sec., corp. counsel Slick Indsl. Co., 1963-72; sec., bd. dirs. Slick Indsl. Co. Can. Ltd, 1966-72; bd. dirs. Intercontinental Forwarders, Inc., 1969-72. Mem. Save the Children 50th Anniversary Com., 1982; gen. counsel Am. Opera Scholarship Soc., 1974—; mem. lawyer's com. Washington Performing Arts Soc., 1982—; mem. adv. com. Rock Creek Found. Mental Health, 1982—; mem. nat. adv. bd. DAR, 1980-83, chmn., 1983—; mem. men's com. Project Hope Ball, 1980—; nat. vice chmn. for fin. Reagan for Pres., 1979-80; mem. exec. fin. com. 1981 Presdl. Inauguration; mem. President's Adv. Com. for Arts, 1982—, Rep. Nat. Com., 1983—; fin. chmn. Reagan-Bush '84. Served to lt (j.g.), Air Intelligence USNR, 1952-56. Mem. ABA (co-chmn. aviation com. 1964-76, chmn. 1976-77), Fed. Bar Assn., D.C. Bar Assn., Va. Bar Assn., Fed. Energy Bar Assn., Am. Judicature Soc., Assn. Transp. Practitioners, Internat. Platform Assn., Raven Soc., Order of Coif. Episcopalian. Clubs: International, Capitol Hill, Nat. Aviation, Aero, Congl. Country (Washington); Potomac (Md.) Polo. Administrative and regulatory, General corporate. Home: 14309 Brickhowe Ct Germantown MD 20874 Office: Steptoe and Johnson 1330 Connecticut Ave NW Washington DC 20036

TAYLOR, RICHARD TRELORE, lawyer; b. Kewanee, Ill., Aug. 5, 1917; s. Earl G. and Lucile (Cully) T.; m. Maureen Hoey, Feb. 9, 1946. B.S., U. Ill., 1939, J.D., 1946; LL.M., Columbia U., 1947. Bar: Ill. 1946, N.Y. 1947. Assoc. Cadwalader, Wickersham & Taft, N.Y.C., 1947-57, ptnr., 1957—, presiding ptnr., 1977—; dir. RHM Holdings (USA) Inc. Trustee Marlboro Coll., Vt. Served with U.S. Army, 1941-45. Decorated Bronze Star. Mem. ABA, N.Y. State Bar Assn., Assn. Bar City N.Y. Clubs: Downtown Assn. (N.Y.C.), University (N.Y.C.), The Pilgrims (N.Y.C.). General corporate, Banking. Home: 870 United Nations Plaza New York NY 10017 Office: 100 Maiden Ln New York NY 10038

TAYLOR, ROBERT LOVE, arbitrator, retired judge, consultant; b. Trenton, Tenn., Mar. 30, 1914; s. Hillsman and Katherine (Taylor) T.; m. Jerry C., Sept. 30, 1943 (dec. July 1972); children—Robert Love, Martha Taylor Smith; m. Virginia W., Feb. 14, 1974. LL.B., So. Law Coll.; J.D. (hon.), Memphis State U., 1967. Bar: Tenn. 1944, U.S. Supreme Ct. 1958, U.S. Ct. Appeals (6th cir.) 1952, U.S. Ct. Appeals (5th cir.) 1957, U.S. Tax Ct. 1977, Tex. 1979. Commr. ins. and banking State of Tenn., Nashville, 1951-52; chancellor Tenn. Chancery Ct., Memphis, 1960-68; judge Tenn. Ct. Appeals, Jackson, 1968-76; spl. atty. State of Tenn., Memphis, 1948-50, State of Miss., Memphis, 1950-51; cons. in field; bd. dirs. Bank of Leon Springs, San Antonio, Tex. Author report Black Market Sales of Infants in Tennesee, 1950. Mem. United Congl. Adv. Bd.; del. Democratic Nat. Conv., Chgo., 1957; chmn. Shelby County Dem. Exec. Com., Memphis, 1949-53; state comdr. Air Res. Assn., Nashville, 1946-47, judge adv., Washington, 1947-48. Recipient Cert. of Merit, Am. Legion, 1949; hon. life mem. DAV, Tenn. Hist. Commn., 1966. Mem. Tenn. Jud. Council, Tenn. Bar Assn. (chmn. labor sect. 1965). Methodist. Club: Fair Oaks Country (Boerne, Tex.). Lodges: Rotary, Masons, K.T., Shriners. Real property, Labor, Probate. Home: 102 S Frey Boerne TX 78006 Office: Affiliated Profl Services Inc 216 E Blanco Boerne TX 78006

TAYLOR, ROBERT LYNN, lawyer; b. Denver, Apr. 4, 1947; s. Melvin Sebrine and F. Shirley (Roberts) T.; m. Elizabeth Susan Smith, Sept. 6, 1969 (div. Nov. 1975); children: Sarah Ellen, Alison Elizabeth. BS, U. Colo., 1969; JD, Denver U., 1972. Bar: Colo. 1972, U.S. Dist. Ct. Colo. 1972. Sole practice Denver, 1972—. Author (pamphlet) Drinking, Driving and You, 1984, 85. Mem. ABA, Colo. Bar Assn., Denver Bar Assn., Assn. Trial Lawyers Am., Colo. Trial Lawyers Assn. Republican. Avocations: golf, cooking, bicycling, scuba diving, photography. Personal injury, Family and matrimonial, State civil litigation. Office address: 200 Filmore St Suite 101 Denver CO 80206

TAYLOR, ROBERT STANLEY, lawyer; b. Boston, May 11, 1950; s. Harold Ralph and Henrietta Irene (Medalia) T.; m. Vicki Carla Jackson, Sept. 17, 1978; children: Jacob Louis, Michael Julius. AB, Harvard U., 1972, JD, 1975. Bar: D.C. 1975, U.S. Supreme Ct. 1983. Law clk. to judge U.S. Ct. Appeals (3d cir.), Phila., 1975-76; assoc. Leva, Hawes, Symington, Martin & Oppenheimer, Washington, 1976-82, Swidler, Berlin & Strelow, Washington, 1982-83; ptnr. Swidler & Berlin, Washington, 1983—. Coauthor Product Risk Reduction in the Chemical Industry, 1985; also articles. Mem. ABA. Democrat. Jewish. Environment, Administrative and regulatory. Office: Swidler & Berlin 1000 Thomas Jefferson St NW Washington DC 20007

TAYLOR, RONALD LOUIS, lawyer; b. Memphis, July 18, 1942; s. George Festus and Ina Dell (Sanderson) T.; m. Elsa Juanita Parker, Dec. 28, 1969; children: Anna-Kathryn, Benjamin Louis. BA magna cum laude, Miss. State U., 1964; JD, U. Miss., 1970. Bar: Miss. 1970, U.S. Ct. Appeals (5th cir.) 1976, U.S. Supreme Ct. 1976. Assoc. B.G. Perry, Southaven, Miss., 1970-71; ptnr. Perry & Taylor, Southaven, 1971-73, Perry, Taylor & Whitwell, Southaven, 1973-75, Taylor & Whitwell, Southaven, 1976-85, Taylor, Jones, Alexander, Greenlee, Seale & Ryan, Ltd., Southaven, 1985—; mcpl. judge City of Horn Lake, Miss., 1975-77; city atty. City of Southaven, 1983—. Vice chmn. Southaven Libary Bd., 1973-76. Served to lt. col. USAR, 1964—. Fellow Miss. Bar Found.; mem. Assn. Trial Lawyers Am., Miss. Trial Lawyers (bd. govs. 1980), DeSoto County Bar Assn. (pres. 1978, 86). Republican. Baptist. Club: Exchange (Southaven) (pres. 1973). Lodge: Shriners. Personal injury, Local government, Family and matrimonial. Home: 5872 Rolling Hills Dr Olive Branch MS 38654 Office: Taylor Jones Alexander Greenlee Seale & Ryan 961 State Line Rd W PO Box 188 Southaven MS 38671

TAYLOR, SAMUEL WAYNE, judge; b. Mobile, Ala., Aug. 8, 1935; s. George Samuel and Oclis (Waldrip) T.; m. Emily Allen Thrasher, June 3, 1960; children—Samuel Wayne, George Samuel II, Emily Allen Thrasher. B.S. in Bus. Adminstrn., U. Ala., 1956, J.D., 1958; LL.M., NYU, 1959. Bar: Ala. 1958. Sole practice, Montgomery, Ala., 1965-75; judge Montgomery County Ct., Montgomery, 1975-77, Dist. Ct., Montgomery, 1977, Cir. Ct., Montgomery, 1977-83, Ct. of Criminal Appeals, State of Ala., Montgomery, 1983—; prof. Jones Law Inst., Montgomery, 1965-73. Mem. Ala. Ho. of Reps., 1971-75. Served to capt. U.S. Army, 1962-64. Mem. ABA (jud. administr. div. and criminal law sect.), Ala. State Bar, Montgomery Bar Assn., Dist. Judges Assn. (pres. Ala. 1977), Pi Kappa Alpha, Phi Alpha Delta. Democrat. Methodist. Club: Lions (mem. 1983-86) (Montgomery). Lodge: Toastmasters. Judicial administration. Home: 2429 Woodley Rd Montgomery AL 36111 Office: Court of Criminal Appeals State of Ala PO Box 351 Montgomery AL 36101

TAYLOR, TED, lawyer; b. Fayette, Ala., June 3, 1940; B.S., U. Ala., 1962, J.D., 1966. Bar: Ala. 1966. Law clk. de Graffenried, deGraffenried & deGraffenried, Tuscaloosa, Ala., 1964-66; assoc. Hamilton, Denniston, Butler & Riddick, Mobile, Ala., 1966-67; ptnr. McDowell & Taylor, Prattville, Ala., 1967-74; sole practice, Prattville, 1974—; mem. Ala. Bd. Bar Commrs., 1981. Fellow Roscoe Pound Found.; mem. 19th Jud. Cir. Bar Assn. (pres. 1973), Ala. Bar Assn., Ala. Trial Lawyers Assn. (pres. 1978), Assn. Trial Lawyers Am. (gov. 1979-80), Farrah Law Soc., U. Ala. Nat. Alumni Assn. (v.p. 1972), Autauga County Bar Assn. (pres. 1976), Am. Bd. Trial Advocacy (advocate). Personal injury. Office: 114 E Main St Prattville AL 36067

TAYLOR, THOMAS ALAN, lawyer; b. Houston, Aug. 15, 1950; s. Thomas Alfonso and Marion Elizabeth (Tidmore) T.; children—Elizabeth Louise, Lindsay Anne. B.B.A., U. Tex.-Austin, 1972; J.D., S. Tex. Coll. Law, 1977; LL.M., So. Meth. U., 1978. Bar: Tex. 1977, U.S. Dist. Ct. (no. dist.) Tex. 1978, U.S. Ct. Appeals (5th cir.) 1984, U.S. Tax Ct. 1985. Landman, Exxon Co., U.S.A., Midland, Tex., 1972-74; sole practice, Dallas, 1978—. Mem. Republican Nat. Com., 1978-85. Mem. Dallas Bar Assn. Republican. Methodist. Clubs: Argyle (sec. 1983-84), Energy. Oil and gas leasing, Real property, Banking. Home: 8406 Chadbourne Dallas TX 75209 Office: Robertson Miller & Taylor 5956 Sherry Ln Dallas TX 75225

TAYLOR, VAUGHAN EDWARD, lawyer, law educator; b. Portland, Maine, Oct. 3, 1947; s. Henry Landes and Elinor (Paine) T.; m. Kathy Anne Webb, May 19, 1984. B.A. cum laude, Dartmouth Coll., 1969; J.D., U. Va., 1972. Bar: Maine 1972, Va. 1972, N.C. 1982, U.S. Ct. Mil. Appeals 1976, U.S. Supreme Ct. 1976. Commd. def. counsel U.S. Army, 1972, advanced through grades to maj., 1974; assoc. prof. U.S. Army JAG Sch., Charlottesville, Va., 1977-80; sr. ptnr. Taylor & Kripner Attys Mil. Law, Jacksonville, N.C., 1981—; sr. instr., maj. U.S. Army Res. JAG Sch., Charlottesville, 1980—. Contbr. to jour. Army Lawyer. Recipient Army Commendation medal (W. Ger.), Meritorious Service medal. Mem. ABA, Am. Assn. Trial Lawyers Republican. Military, Administrative and regulatory, Criminal. Office: Taylor & Kripner 824 Gem Branch Rd Jacksonville NC 28540

TAYLOR, WALLACE L., lawyer; b. Maquoketa, Iowa, Jan. 12, 1947; s. Wallace O. and Nona M. (Dague) T.; m. Pamela Jo Mackey, Nov. 1, 1975; children: Jeffrey, Michele. BS, Iowa State U., 1969; JD, Drake U., 1972. Bar: Iowa 1972, U.S. Dist. Ct. (so. dist.) Iowa 1972, U.S. Ct. Appeals (8th cir.) 1977, U.S. Dist. Ct. (no. dist.) Iowa 1978. Jud. magistrate Boone County, Iowa, 1973-74; atty. Boone County, 1975-77; sole practice Boone, 1972-78, Cedar Rapids, Iowa, 1978-80; ptnr. Keyes, Bennett & Kucera, Cedar Rapids, 1980-84, Bennett, Kucera & Taylor, Cedar Rapids, 1984—. Mem. Iowa Bar Assn., Assn. Trial Lawyers Am., Assn. Trial Lawyers Iowa, Sierra Club (vice chmn. Cedar Rapids 1980—, conservation chmn. Des Moines 1982—, vice chmn. Midwest region 1984—, Distinguished Service award, 1985). Democrat. Methodist. Avocations: hiking, camping, cross country skiing, bicycling, raquetball. Federal civil litigation, State civil litigation, Personal injury. Office: Bennett Kucera & Taylor 425 2d St SE Suite 330 Cedar Rapids IA 52401

TAYLOR, WARREN ANTHONY, lawyer; b. Muncie, Ind., Oct. 10, 1950; s. William Jacob and Mabel Helen (Henderson) T. BA, U. Ky., 1976, JD, 1979. Bar: Ky. 1979, Nev. 1985. Sole practice Frakes, Ky., 1979-80; asst. pub. adv. Ky. Dept. Pub. Advocacy, Hazard, 1985—. Served to capt. U.S. Army, 1970-72, Vietnam, as def. counsel JAGC, 1980-83. Criminal. Office: Dept Pub Advocacy 233 Birch St Suite 3 Hazard KY 41701

TAYLOR, WILLIAM JAMES, lawyer; b. Milw., Jan. 26, 1948; s. William Elmer and Elizabeth Emily (Lupinski) T.; m. Marlou Belyea, Sept. 20, 1975; children: Danielle Belyea, James Zachary Belyea. BA in Econs., Yale U., 1970; JD, Harvard U., 1976. Bar: Calif. 1976, U.S. Dist. Ct. (cen., ea. and no. dists.) Calif., U.S. Ct. Appeals (9th cir.), U.S. Supreme Ct. 1980. Law clk. to presiding judge U.S. Ct. Appeals (9th cir.), Los Angeles, 1976-77; assoc. Broebeck, Phleger and Harrison, San Francisco, 1977-83, ptnr., 1983—. Bd. editors No. Dist. of Calif. Digest, 1978-83. Bd. dirs. Legal Services for Children, San Francisco, 1984—, pres., 1986; co-chair Attorneys Task Force for Children, 1984—. Served with U.S. Army, 1970-73. Mem. Bar Assn. San Francisco (bd. dirs. 1986-87, chair antitrust sect. 1987), ABA. Democrat. Club: Barristers of San Francisco (bd. dirs. 1980-82, v.p. 1982-83). Antitrust, Federal civil litigation, State civil litigation. Office: Brobeck Phleger & Harrison Spear Tower Market Plaza San Francisco CA 94105

TAYLOR, ZACHARY, III, lawyer; b. Jackson, Miss., Sept. 23, 1951; s. Zachary Jr. and Dorothy Irene (Jones) T.; m. Jan Foster, Feb. 10, 1979; children: Zachary IV, Jenny Katheryn. BA with honors, Harvard U., 1973; JD with high honors, U. Miss., 1977. Bar: Miss. 1977, U.S. Dist. Ct. (no. dist.) Miss. 1977. Assoc. Watkins, Ludlam & Stennis, Jackson, 1977-82, ptnr., 1982—. Pres. Goodwill Industries Miss., Jackson, 1986; elder Fondren Presbyn. Ch., Jackson, 1986; bd. dirs. New Stage Theatre, Jackson, 1986. Mem. ABA, Miss. Bar Assn., Hinds County Bar Assn. Club: Harvard (Jackson) (pres. 1986). Lodge: Kiwanis. Municipal bonds, Local government, Finance. Home: 5411 River Thames Rd Jackson MS 39211 Office: Watkins Ludlam & Stennis 633 N State St Jackson MS 39205-0427

TAYLOR-HANINGTON, PAULA KAY, lawyer; b. Colquitt, Ga., May 20, 1956; d. Buford LaVon and India R. (Lofton) Taylor; m. John F. Hanington, May 3, 1986. BA in Polit. Sci., Valdosta State U., 1978; JD, U. Ga., 1981. Bar: Ga. 1981, U.S. Dist. Ct. (mid. dist.) Ga. 1983, U.S. Ct. Appeals (11th cir.) 1983. Assoc. Law Office of John H. Hayes, Albany, Ga., 1981-83, Gilberg & Kraselsky, Albany, 1983-85; sole practice Albany, 1985—; pub. defender City of Albany, 1983—; spl. asst. atty. gen. State of Ga., 1986—. Named one of Outstanding Young Women of Am., 1983-84. Mem. ABA, Women in Network. Democrat. Baptist. Criminal, State civil litigation, Family and matrimonial. Home: 2112 Lullwater Albany GA 31707 Office: PO Box 1805 Albany GA 31702

TEAGUE, DEWEY WAYNE, lawyer; b. Franklin, Ga., June 12, 1955; s. Wayne and Eleanor Josephine (Jones) T.; m. Kathryn Lee Timberlake, Sept. 4, 1976; children: Dylan Wayne, Jacie Lee. BS, Auburn U., 1977; JD, U. Ala., 1980. Bar: Ala. 1980, U.S. Dist. Ct. (mid. dist.) Ala. 1980, U.S. Ct. Appeals (11th cir.) 1985. Assoc. Whittelsey, Ray & Tipton, Opelika, Ala., 1980-83; ptnr. Whittelsey, Ray, Tipton & Teague, Opelika, 1983-85, Spear & Teague, Auburn, Ala., 1985—. Fund-raiser Am. Heart Assn., Lee County, Ala., 1986—; pres. Lee County Unit of Am. Cancer Soc., 1987—; campaign dir. Jim Folsom, Jr. for Lt. Gov., Lee County, 1986—. Hugo L. Black scholar, 1979. Mem. ABA, Lee County Bar Assn., Assn. Trial Lawyers Am., Ala. Trial Lawyers Assn., Ala. Criminal Def. Lawyers Assn. (v.p. 1984-85). Methodist. Clubs: Saugahatchee Country Club, Auburn U. Touchdown (Auburn, Ala.). Avocations: golf, collecting records and baseball cards, family. Bankruptcy, Consumer commercial, General practice. Home: 648 Shawnee Auburn AL 36830 Office: Spear & Teague PO Box 710 Auburn AL 36831-0710

TEAGUE, RANDAL CORNELL, SR., lawyer; b. Durham, N.C., May 19, 1944; s. Roy M. Sr. and Lottie (Rhew) T.; m. Jessica Townsend, Oct. 29, 1977; children: R. Cornell, R. Townsend, Mary Robb Durham. BA, Am. U., 1967; JD, George Washington U., 1971, LLM with highest honors, 1972; LLD (hon.), Allen U., 1973. Bar: D.C. 1972, Fla. 1972, U.S. Dist. Ct. D.C. 1972, U.S. Tax Ct. 1972, U.S. Ct. Mil. Appeals 1972, U.S. Ct. Appeals (D.C. and fed. cirs.) 1972, U.S. Ct. Appeals (5th cir.) 1973, U.S. Supreme Ct. 1975, Mass. 1979, U.S. Ct. Appeals (1st cir.) 1979. Coordinator policy devel. OEO, Washington, 1971-73; adminstrv. asst., legis. counsel to Rep. Jack F. Kemp Ho. of Reps., Washington, 1973-79; div. counsel Cabot Corp., 1979-81; counsel Vorys, Sater, Seymour & Pease, Washington, 1981-83, ptnr., 1984—. Pres. Internat. Exchange Council, 1984—, Am. Council Young Polit. Leaders, Washington, 1982-83, sec. 1986—; trustee Fund Am. Studies, Washington, 1976—, Air Force Acad. Found., Colorado Springs, Colo., 1983—. Named one of Outstanding Young Men Am., 1973; recipient George Washington medal Freedoms Found., 1978. Mem. ABA, Fed. Bar Assn., Fla. Bar Assn., Internat. Exchange Council (pres. 1984—). Republican. Episcopalian. Clubs: Union (Boston); University (Washington). Legislative, General corporate, Corporate taxation. Office: Vorys Sater Seymour & Pease 1828 L St NW Suite 1111 Washington DC 20036-5401

TEASE, RALPH JOSEPH, JR., lawyer; b. Green Bay, Wis., Sept. 19, 1956; s. Ralph Joseph Sr. and Katherine Elizabeth (Wanish) T.; m. Susan Beth Lambert, Sept. 15, 1984; 1 child, Rebecca Elizabeth. BBA in Acctg., St. Norbert Coll., 1978; JD, Marquette U., 1981. Bar: Wis. 1981, U.S. Dist. Ct. (ea. and we. dists.) Wis. 1981. Assoc. Arthur Andersen & Co., Milw., 1981, Liebmann, Conway, Olejniczak & Jerry, S.C., Green Bay, 1981—. Mem. bd. mgrs. YMCA, Green Bay, 1986—. Mem. ABA, Wis. Bar Assn., Wis. Acad. Trial Lawyers, Assn. Trial Lawyers Am. Lutheran. Lodge: Optimists. State civil litigation, General corporate, Real property. Office: Liebmann Conway et al 231 S Adams St PO Box 1241 Green Bay WI 54305

TEBELIUS, MARK ALAN, lawyer; b. Harvey, N.D., Jan. 25, 1953; s. Ervin E. and Edna P. (Smestad) T.; m. Linda Margaret Irons, June 27, 1976; children: Brock Alan, Lindsay Ann. BBA in Acctg., U. N.D., 1975, JD, 1979. Bar: N.D. 1979, U.S. Dist. Ct. N.D. 1979. Assoc. John J. Tebelius, Harvey, 1979-82; ptnr. Tebelius Law Firm, Harvey, 1982—. Recipient Am. Jurisprudence award Bancroft-Whitney Co., 1978. Mem. ABA, N.D. State Bar Assn., Harvey C. of C. (bd. dirs. 1981-82, pres. 1983). Republican. Adventist. Lodge: Kiwanis (bd. dirs. 1982-84), Eagles. Avocations: golf, racquetball, gardening. Probate, General practice. Home: 521 Pleasant St Harvey ND 58341 Office: Tebelius Law Firm 1012 Lincoln Ave Harvey ND 58341

TEBLUM, GARY IRA, lawyer; b. Phila., Apr. 25, 1955; s. Milton and Marlene Ann (Rosenberg) T.; m. Lisa Ida Goldsmith, May 13, 1979; children: Corey Harris, Jeremy Brett. BS, U. Del., 1976; JD cum laude, U. Pa., 1979. Assoc. Trenam, Simmons, Kemker, Scharf, Barkin, Frye & O'Neill, Tampa, Fla., 1979-84, ptnr., 1984—. Editor U. Pa. Law Rev., 1978-79. Mem. ABA, Fla. Bar Assn., Hillsborough County Bar Assn. Jewish. Banking, Contracts commercial, Corporate taxation. Home: 14039 Shady Shores Dr Tampa FL 33613 Office: Trenam Simmons Kemker et al 2700 Barnett Plaza Tampa FL 33601

TECLAFF, LUDWIK ANDRZEJ, law educator, consultant, author, lawyer; b. Czestochowa, Poland, Nov. 14, 1918; came to U.S., 1952, naturalized, 1958; s. Emil and Helena (Tarnowska) T.; m. Eileen Johnson, May 30, 1952. Mag Iuris, Oxford (Eng.) U., 1944; M.S., Columbia U., 1955; LL.M., N.Y. U., 1961, J.S.D., 1965. Attaché Polish Fgn. Ministry, London, 1943-46; consul in Ireland, Polish Govt. in London, 1946-52; student librarian Columbia U. Sch. Library Sci., 1953-54; librarian Bklyn. Pub. Library, 1954-59; research librarian Fordham U. Sch. Law, 1959-62, asst. prof. law, 1962-65, assoc. prof. law, 1965-68, prof. 1968—, dir. law library, 1962-86; cons. in field. Bd. dirs. Polish Inst. Arts and Scis. Am.; trustee Pilsudski Inst., N.Y.C. Served with Polish Army, 1940-43; France, Eng. Recipient Clyde Eagleton award in internat. law N.Y. U., 1965. Mem. Am. Soc. Internat. Law, Internat. Law Assn., Am. Law Libraries Assn., Internat. Council Environ. Law, Internat. Water Law Assn. Roman Catholic. Author: The River Basin in History and Law, 1967; Abstraction and Use of Water, 1972; Legal and Institutional Responses to Growing Water Demand, 1978; Economic Roots of Oppression, 1984, Water Law in Historical Perspective, 1985; editor: (with Albert E Utton) International Environmental Law, 1974, Water in a Developing World, 1978, International Groundwater Law, 1981; contbr. articles on water law, law of the sea and environ. law to law jours. Legal education, Jurisprudence, Public international. Office: Fordham USch Law Lincoln Sq 140 W 62 St Room 226 New York NY 10023

TEDDER, CECIL A., circuit judge; b. Ft. Smith, Ark., Mar. 24, 1929; s. Cecil A. Sr. and Nettie E. (Hart) T.; m. Virginia Ruth Bartlett, Apr. 24, 1949; children: Martha Carol, Andrew G. BS in Pub. Adminstrn. with

honors, U. Ark., 1955, JD, 1957. Bar: Ark. 1957. Sole practice Searcy, Ark., 1957-78; cir. judge Ark. 17th Jud. Dist., Searcy, 1979—. Chmn. White County Election Commn., Searcy, 1970, White County Dem. Com., 1970. Served to staff sgt. USAF, 1948-52. Mem. Ark. Jud. Council, Ark. Adult Probation Commn. (vice chmn. 1986—), Searcy C. of C. (pres. 1967, Exceptional Accomplishment award Ark. 1967). Democrat. Baptist. Lodge: Lions (Searcy) (pres. 1964-65). Avocations: golf, fishing, hunting. Judicial administration. Office: Wilbur D Mills Cts Bldg Searcy AR 72143

TEDESCO, MICHAEL J., lawyer; b. N.Y.C., Dec. 14, 1952; s. Vincent James and Angela Agnes (Letterell) T.; children: Elizabeth, David. BA in History, Coll. William & Mary, 1975; JD, Southwestern U., 1978. Bar: Oreg. 1978. Asst. atty. gen. Oreg. Dept. Justice, Portland, 1978-80; atty. Richardson & Murphy, Portland, 1980-83, Doblie & Francesconi, Portland, 1983-84, Tedesco & Wilson, Portland, 1984—. Author: Monograph Subcontracting in Public Sector, 1985. Democrat. Labor. Home: 9572 Wagner Creek Rd Talent OR 97540

TEEPLE, RICHARD DUANE, lawyer; b. Portland, Ind., Oct. 31, 1942; s. Joseph Carlise and Sylvia Ann (Bailey) T.; m. Julie Favorite, June 5, 1965; children: Laura, Darin. BA, Purdue U., 1964; JD, U. Cin., 1967. Bar: Ohio 1967. Assoc. Wilke & Goering, Cin., 1967-72; atty. Gen. Motors Corp., Dayton, Ohio, 1972-77; gen. counsel Cooper Tire & Rubber Co., Findlay, Ohio, 1977—. Mem. advisory bd. Salvation Army, Findlay, 1982—. Mem. ABA, Ohio Bar Assn. (bd. govs. corp. counsel sect. 1984—), Findlay/Hancock Bar Assn. General corporate. Home: 3249 Gleneagle Dr Findlay OH 45840 Office: Cooper Tire & Rubber Co Lima & Western Aves Findlay OH 45840

TEER, JANET, lawyer, risk manager; b. Taiwan, Oct. 21, 1954; d. James Ellis and Ernestine (Tilley) T. BA, Judson Coll., 1975; JD, U. Ala., 1978. Bar: Ala. 1978. Claims rep. State Farm Ins., Huntsville, Ala., 1978-80; risk mgr. DCH Regional Med. Ctr., Tuscaloosa, Ala., 1980—. Dir. Kentuck Bd., Northport, Ala., 1981-86. Named Most Outstanding Non-Member, Ala. State Nurses Assn., Montgomery, 1984. Mem. ABA, Am. Soc. Hosp. Risk Management. Baptist. Avocations: shooting, music, basketball. Office: DCH Regional Med Ctr 809 University Blvd E Tuscaloosa AL 35403

TEGENKAMP, GARY ELTON, lawyer; b. Dayton, Ohio, Nov. 27, 1946; s. Elmer Robert and Dorothy Ann (Hummerich) T.; m. June Evelyn Barber, Aug. 2, 1969; children: Emily Stratton, Andrew Elton. BA in Polit. Sci., U. South Fla., 1969; JD, Coll. William and Mary, 1972. Bar: Va. 1972, U.S. Dist. Ct. (we. and ea. dists.) Va. 1972, U.S. Ct. Appeals (4th cir.) 1973. Law clk. to presiding judge U.S. Dist. Ct. (we. dist.) Va., U.S. Ct. Appeals (4th cir.), Abingdon, Va., 1972-73; assoc. Hunter, Fox & Trabue, Roanoke, Va., 1973-77; ptnr. Fox, Wooten and Hart P.C., Roanoke, 1977—. Active United Way, Roanoke Valley, 1976; legal advisor Roanoke Jaycees, 1976-77. Mem. ABA (tort and ins. sects), Va. Bar Assn., Va. Trial Lawyers Assn., Va. Assn. Def. Attys., Roanoke Bar Assn. (chmn. com. continuing legal edn. 1983-86). United Methodist. Club: Jefferson. Lodge: Elks. Avocations: coin collecting, youth sports programs. Federal civil litigation, State civil litigation, Insurance. Home: 2524 Stanley Ave SW Roanoke VA 24014 Office: Fox Wooten & Hart PC 707 S Jefferson St Suite 310 Roanoke VA 24011

TEGTMEIER, RICHARD LEWIS, lawyer; b. Lincoln, Nebr., July 11, 1946; s. Oscar Lewis and Ila Mae (Bradford) T.; children: Holly Anne, Margaret Mae. BS, U. Nebr., 1968, JD, 1971. Bar: Nebr. 1971, Colo. 1971, U.S. Dist. Ct. Nebr. 1971, U.S. Dist. Ct. Colo. 1971, U.S. Supreme Ct. 1978. Staff lawyer Colorado Pub. Defender, Colo. Springs, 1971-73; dir. office Colo. Pub. Defender, Colorado Springs, 1973-74; ptnr. Tegtmeier & Sears P.C. and predecessor firm, Colorado Springs, 1974—. Mem. ABA (chmn. def. function com. 1985-87), Colo. Bar Assn. (chmn. criminal justice sect. 1985-86), Colo. Trial Lawyers Assn., Colo./ Criminal Def. Bar (bd. dirs. 1979-83). Democrat. Club: Broadmoor Golf (Colorado Springs). Criminal, Personal injury. Office: Tegtmeier & Sears PC 518 N Nevada Ave Colorado Springs CO 80903

TEHAN, JOHN BASHIR, lawyer; b. Utica, N.Y., May 13, 1948; s. Louis Bashir and Frances Mary (Argenzia) T.; m. Regina Anne Callahan, Aug. 1, 1970; children—Aaron J., Lauren R., Eileen L. B.A., LeMoyne Coll., 1970; J.D., Catholic U., Washington, 1973. Bar: N.Y. 1974, U.S. Dist. Ct. (so. and ea. dists.) N.Y. 1975, U.S. Ct. Appeals (2d cir.) 1975. Assoc. Sullivan & Cromwell, N.Y.C., 1973-81; ptnr. Simpson Thacher & Bartlett, N.Y.C., 1981—. Roman Catholic. General corporate, Securities, Banking. Home: 10 Warwick Rd Rockville Centre NY 11570 Office: Simpson Thacher & Bartlett One Battery Park Plaza New York NY 10004

TEICHER, MARK L., lawyer; b. Boston, Aug. 14, 1956; s. Harry and Charlotte (Leavy) T.; m. Julie Beth Klein; 1 child, Perry Isaac. BA, Mich. State U., 1979; JD, U. Detroit, 1982. Bar: Mich. 1982, U.S. Dist. Ct. (ea. dist.) Mich. 1982, U.S. Ct. Appeals (6th cir.) 1982. Assoc. Bain & Shapero, P.C., Southfield, Mich., 1982-84, Matz & Rubin P.C., Birmingham, Mich., 1984-87; ptnr. Schaden, Heldman, Lampert, Katzman & Teicher, Birmingham, 1987—; adj. magistrate Garden City (Mich.) Dist. Ct., 1984—. Bd. dirs. Big Bros./Big Sisters of Met. Detroit, Southfield, Mich., 1987—; pres., bd. dirs. Doherty Estates, West Bloomfield, Mich., 1984-85; bd. dirs. Internat. Inst. of Met. Detroit, Inc., 1985—. Mem. ABA, Mich. Bar Assn., Oakland Bar Assn., Southfield Bar Assn., Am. Trial Lawyers Assn., Mich. Trial Lawyers Assn. Personal injury, Insurance. Office: Schaden Heldman Lampert et al 800 N Woodward Ave Suite 102 Birmingham MI 48011

TEICHER, MARTIN, lawyer; b. N.Y.C., Nov. 16, 1945; s. Aaron and Gertrude (Mark) T.; m. Barbara Langner, Sept. 13, 1970; children: Nina Rebecca, Ira Kenneth. BA, CUNY, Flushing, 1967; JD, NYU, 1970. Bar: N.Y. 1971, U.S. Dist. Ct. (so. and ea. dists.) N.Y. 1972, U.S. Ct. Appeals (2d cir.) 1975, U.S. Supreme Ct. 1976. Assoc. Kronish, Lieb, Shainswit, Weiner & Hellman, N.Y.C., 1970-79; atty. spl. litigation dept. Am. Cyanamid Co., Wayne, N.J., 1980—; speaker drug liability seminars Def. Research Inst., 1985, 86, 87. Bd. of trustees Ahavath Torah Congregation, Englewood, N.J., 1983—. Mem. N.Y. State Bar Assn., Assn. of Bar of City of N.Y. (product liability com., 1981-86, tort litigation com. 1986—), Assn. Corp. Counsel N.J. Jewish. Federal civil litigation, State civil litigation, Personal injury. Home: 453 Cape May St Englewood NJ 07631 Office: Am Cyanamid Co 1 Cyanamid Plaza Wayne NJ 07470

TEITELBAUM, STEVEN ALAN, lawyer; b. N.Y.C., July 30, 1956; s. Arnold and Hilda (Strenger) T.; m. Susan Kitt, Aug. 26, 1984. AB, Columbia U., 1977, JD, 1980. Bar: D.C., 1980, N.Y., 1983. Assoc. Melrod, Redman & Gartlan, Washington, 1980-82, Rosenman, Colin, Freund, Lewis & Cohen, N.Y.C., 1982-84, Hale & Dorr, Washington, 1984-85, Jones, Day, Reavis & Pogue, Washington, 1985—. Mem. D.C. com. Am. Planning Assn., Washington, 1984—. Mem. ABA. Real property. Office: Jones Day Reavis & Pogue 655 15th St NW Washington DC 20005

TEITELBAUM, STEVEN USHER, lawyer; b. Chgo., Nov. 29, 1945; s. Jerome H. and Marion Judith (Berlin) T.; m. Cathy Ann Rosenblatt, Mar. 11, 1984. A.B., Boston U., 1967; J.D., Union U., 1975. Bar: N.Y. 1976, U.S. Dist. Ct. (no. dist.) N.Y. 1976, U.S. Supreme Ct. 1980. Sr. atty. N.Y. State Dept. Health, Albany, 1976-79; counsel N.Y. State Office Bus. Permits, Albany, 1979-83; sole practice, Albany, 1983—; staff judge advocate U.S. Army Res. Wateruliet Arsenal, N.Y., 1978-84. Author: Streamlining the Regulatory Procedures of the Department of Agriculture, 1982. Served with U.S. Army, 1968-69. Mem. Am. Arbitration Assn. (arbitrator 1979—), N.Y. State Bar Assn. (com. on pub. health 1976-80, faculty on adminstrv. law 1980, com. on adminstrv. law 1980-84, labor and employment sect. 1985—). Clubs: Fort Orange (Albany); Colonie Country (Voorheesville, N.Y.). Administrative and regulatory, State civil litigation, Civil rights. Home: 17 Carstead Dr Slingerlands NY 12159 Office: 1 Columbia Pl Albany NY 12207

TEITLER, HAROLD HERMAN, lawyer, family psychotherapist, mediator; b. San Francisco, Feb. 14, 1936; s. Max Herman and Elsie (Kaplan) T.; m. Joan Barbara Teitler; children—Deborah, Leah, Rebekah. A.B., U. Calif.-Berkeley; M.A., Chapman Coll.; J.D., Lincoln U., 1977. Bar: Calif., 1977. Sole practice, 1977—; mem. faculty Lincoln U. Law Sch., 1982—. Bd. dirs. United Jewish Community Ctrs.-Brotherhoodway Ctr., 1979-82; mem. youth com. Central YMCA, San Francisco. USPHS grantee, 1962. Mem. Calif. Bar Assn., San Francisco Bar Assn., Calif. Assn. Marriage and Family Therapists, Am. Arbitration Assn. (panelist), Psi Chi, Alpha Phi Sigma. Mem. Lincoln U. Law Rev. Family and matrimonial, Jurisprudence, Contracts commercial. Home: 1343 43d Ave San Francisco CA 94122

TEITLER, PAUL HUGH, judge; b. N.Y.C., Apr. 30, 1935; s. Jules R. and Sarah (Cheson) T.; m. Lenore S. Kirshner, Sept. 29, 1972; children: Avery Scott, Brooke Dara. BA, NYU, 1956; JD, Bklyn. Law Sch., 1959. Bar: N.Y. 1960, U.S. Dist Ct. (ea. and so. dists.) N.Y. 1971, U.S. Dist. Ct. (no. dist.) Tex. 1979, U.S. Supreme Ct. 1979. Ptnr. Teitler & Teitler, Bklyn., 1960-1974; chief judge HHS, Camden, N.J., 1974-85; dist. chief judge Dept. Labor, Camden, 1985—; adminstrv. law judge, N.Y.C., 1970-74; mem. jud. adminstrn. div. Nat. Conf. Adminstrv. Law Judges. Mem. prof. ethics com. Bklyn. Bar Assn., 1970-74. Mem. ABA (exec. com. 1982—), Assn. Adminstrv. Law Judges (jud. adminstrn. div., bd. dirs region II 1980-85). Lodges: Masons (did. dep. grand master 1971-72, grand standard bearer 1973-74), Assn. Kings (2d dist. pres., charities fund pres.), Tuscan #704 (master 1969). Administrative and regulatory. Office: US Dept Labor Office of Adminstrv Law 2600 Mount Ephriam Ave Camden NJ 08104

TEKLITS, JOSEPH ANTHONY, lawyer; b. Bellville, Ill., July 18, 1952; s. Frank Anthony and Mary (Bodish) T.; m. Deborah Ann Keevill, June 1, 1974; children—Jessica, Joseph, Michael. B.A., Allentown Coll. St. Francis de Sales, 1974; J.D., U. Notre Dame, 1977. Bar: Ind. 1977, U.S. Dist. Ct. (no. dist.) Ind. 1977, U.S. Dist. Ct. (so. dist.) Ind. 1977. Legal counsel CTS Corp., Elkhart, Ind., 1977-80; mng. labor counsel Sperry Corp. (name now Unisys Corp.), Blue Bell, Pa., 1980-87, asst. gen. counsel Unisys Corp., 1987—. Mem. mgmt. com. Equal Employment Opportunity Law, bd. advisors Employer's Guide to Equal Employment Opportunity Law, Bus. Laws, Inc. Mem. ABA (labor and employment law sec., EEO com.), Assn. Trial Lawyers Am. (assoc.), Delta Epsilon Sigma (pres. chpt. 1974). Republican. Roman Catholic. Labor, Federal civil litigation, Administrative and regulatory. Office: Unisys Corp Hdqrs PO Box 500 Blue Bell PA 19424

TELEPAS, GEORGE PETER, lawyer; b. Kingston, N.Y., Nov. 20, 1935; s. Peter G. and Grace T.; m. Regina Tisiker, Sept. 6, 1969 (div.). B.S., U. Fla., 1960; J.D., U. Miami, 1965. Bar: Fla., 1965. Assoc., Preddy, Haddad, Kutner, & Hardy, 1966-67; assoc. Williams & Jabara, 1967-68; sole practice, Miami, Fla., 1968—; dir. First City Bank. Mem. citizens bd. U. Miami. Served with USMC, 1954-56. Mem. ABA, Fla. Bar Assn., Dade County Bar Assn., Assn. Trial Lawyers Am., Fla. Trial Lawyers Assn., Dade County Trial Lawyers Assn., Delta Theta Phi, Sigma Nu. Personal injury. Home: 1 Grove Isle Dr Apt 910 Coconut Grove FL 33133 Office: 1933 SW 27 Ave Miami FL 33145

TELESCA, MICHAEL ANTHONY, federal judge; b. Rochester, N.Y., Nov. 25, 1929; s. Michael Angelo and Agatha (Locurcio) T.; m. Ethel E. Hibbard, June 3, 1935; children: Michele, Stephen. A.B., U. Rochester, 1952; J.D., U. Buffalo, 1955. Bar: N.Y. 1957, U.S. Dist. Ct. (we. dist.) N.Y. 1958, U.S. Ct. Appeals (2d cir.) 1960, U.S. Supreme Ct. 1967. Ptnr. Lamb, Webster, Walz, Telesca, Rochester, N.Y., 1957-73; surrogate ct. judge Monroe County, N.Y., 1973-82; judge U.S. Dist. Ct. (we. dist.) N.Y., Rochester, 1982—. Bd. govs. Genesee Hosp., Rochester; mem. adv. bd. Assn. for Retarded Citizens, Al Sigl Ctr., Rochester. Served to 1st lt. USMC, 1955-57. Recipient Civic medal Rochester C. of C., 1983. Mem. ABA, Am. Judicature Soc., Justinian Soc. Jurists, N.Y. State Bar Assn., Monroe County Bar Assn. Republican. Roman Catholic. Jurisprudence. Office: 272 US Courthouse 100 State St Rochester NY 14614 *

TELKER, ELLEN MELINDA, lawyer; b. Milford, Conn., Oct. 10, 1951; d. Eugene and Ella (Roller) T. BA, Mount Holyoke Coll., 1973; JD, Union U., Albany, N.Y., 1976. Bar: Conn. 1976. Law clk. to presiding justice Conn. Superior Ct., New Haven, 1978-81; asst. counsel Senate Rep. Caucus, Hartford, Conn., 1982; sole practice Milford, Conn., 1983—. Vol. legal counsel Milford Ind. Disabled Com., 1983—; bd. dirs. Cen. for Ind. Living, Bridgeport, Conn., 1985—. Recipient Community Service award Mil. Ind. Persons Com., 1985. Mem. ABA, Conn. Bar Assn., Am. Blind Lawyers Assn., Milford Bus. and Profl. Women's Club (women of yr. award 1985, 86), Jaycee Women (young woman of yr. 1985). Republican. Mem. United Ch. Christ. Lodge: Indian River and Conn. State Grange. Avocation: ch. choir. Family and matrimonial, Probate, Juvenile. Home: 42 Roller Terr Milford CT 06460 Office: 564 Boston Post Rd Milford CT 06460

TELL, A. CHARLES, lawyer; b. Chgo., May 9, 1937; s. William K and Virginia S (Snook) T.; m. Wendy Thomsen, June 16, 1962; children—Tracey, Melissa, A. Charles, Jr. A.B., Dartmouth Coll., 1961; J.D., Ohio State U., 1963. Ptnr. George, Greek, King & McMahon, Columbus, Ohio, 1964-78, Baker & Hostetler, Columbus, 1978—; dir. Kaplan Trucking Co., Cleve. Editor Your Letter of the Law, 1984. Contbr. articles to profl. jours. Served with U.S. Army, 1958-60. Mem. ABA, Am. Judicature Soc., Ohio State Bar Assn., Columbus Bar Assn., Transp. Lawyers Assn. (pres. 1986-87). Republican. Presbyterian. Clubs: City (pres. 1985), Columbus Country (trustee 1985—), Athletic. Administrative and regulatory, Labor, Public utilities. Office: Baker & Hostetler 65 E State St Suite 2200 Columbus OH 43215

TELL, RONALD J., lawyer, savings and loan association executive; b. Newark, June 16, 1934; s. Frank and Agnes (Amberg) T.; m. Jean P. Stirrup; children—Stephen Gregory, Kristin Elizabeth. A.B., Woodrow Wilson Sch. Pub. and Internat. Affairs, Princeton U., 1956; postgrad., Bklyn. Law Sch., 1956-57; LL.B., Seton Law U., 1963; grad., Sch. Savs. and Loans, Grad. Sch. Bus., Ind. U., 1975; grad. program for lawyers, Harvard U., 1980. Bar: N.J. 1963, U.S. Dist. Ct. N.J. 1963. With Prudential Ins. Co. Am., 1956-61; with City Fed. Savs. Bank, Bedminster, N.J., 1961—; corp. sec. City Fed. Fin. Corp., 1972-73; sr. v.p.-br. adminstrn. City Fed. Savs. Bank, 1973-74, exec. v.p.-div. mgmt., 1974-77, exec. v.p.-customer services, 1977-79, exec. v.p., gen. counsel, 1979—; AID rep., cons. Jordan Housing Bank, 1974. Mem. ABA, N.J. Bar Assn., Summit Bar Assn. Office: City Fed Savs Bank Bedminster One Route 202-206 Bedminster NJ 07921

TELLERIA, ANTHONY F., lawyer; b. Nicaragua, June 6, 1938; s. Carlos E. and Melida (Amador) T.; m. Dolores A. Rockey, Nov. 3, 1962; children—Matthew J., Andrea F. LL.B., Southwestern U., 1964. Bar: Calif 1964. Sr. partner Telleria, Townley & Doran, Los Angeles, 1971-75; sole practice, Los Angeles, 1964-71, 75—. Mem. Calif. Trial Lawyers Assn., Los Angeles County Bar Assn., Am. Arbitration Assn. (Los Angeles adv. council, accident claims com.), Internat. Platform Assn. Personal injury, State civil litigation, Criminal. Home: 1615 Rose Ave San Marino CA 91108 Office: Civic Center Law Bldg 205 S Broadway Suite 402 Los Angeles CA 90012

TELLINGHUISEN, ROGER A., state official. Atty. gen. State of S.D., Pierre, 1987—. Office: Attorney General's Office State Capitol Pierre SD 57501 *

TELSEY, NORMAN, judge; b. Bklyn., Dec. 23, 1925; s. Albert and Anna Telsey; m. Claire Leah Colton, Mar. 9, 1952; children—Yona, Albert, Benjamin, Adam. B.S., Albright Coll., Reading, Pa., 1949; J.D., Bklyn. Law Sch., 1951. Bar: N.Y. 1952, N.J. 1956, U.S. Ct. Appeals (3d cir.) 1956. Sole practice, Cumberland and Salem, N.J., 1956-76; judge Salem County Ct., 1976-78; judge N.J. Superior Ct., 1978-83, presiding judge criminal div. Superior Ct. Salem, Gloucester, Cumberland, 1983—. Mem. Deerfield Twp. (N.J.) Com., 1959-61. Served with USN, 1943-45; PTO. Mem. Am. Judicature Soc., ABA, N.J. Bar Assn., Salem County Bar Assn. Criminal, State civil litigation. Office: Courthouse Market St Salem NJ 08079

TEMPLE, L. PETER, lawyer; b. Chgo., Mar. 24, 1948; s. John Albert and Helene (Psiharis) T.; m. Susan Schneider, Sept. 4, 1971; children—Peter J., Benjamin L. B.A., Haverford Coll., 1970; J.D., Boston U., 1973. Bar: Pa. 1973. Gen. counsel State Dept. Mental Health, Concord, N.H., 1972-73; assoc. Larmore & Scarlett, Kennett Square, Pa., 1973-75; mng. ptnr. Larmore, Scarlett, Myers & Temple, Kennett Square, 1975—; dir. Elmwood Savs. Bank, Kennett Square, Abstracting Co. Chester County, West Chester, Pa. Mem. Chester County Bar Assn. (bd. dirs. 1981-83, chmn. jud. qualifications com. 1980-81), ABA, Pa. Bar Assn. Probate, Estate taxation, Real property. Home: 139 E Doe Run Rd PO Box 476 Unionville PA 19375 Office: Larmore Scarlett Myers & Temple 123 E Linden St PO Box 384 Kennett Square PA 19348

TEMPLE, LARRY EUGENE, lawyer; b. Plainview, Tex., Dec. 26, 1935; s. Herman Edward and Grace Eileen (Ivey) T.; m. Laura Louann Atkins, Feb. 23, 1963; children: Laura Allison, John Lawrence. BBA, U. Tex., 1957, LLB, 1959. Bar: Tex., U.S. Dist. Ct. (we. dist.) Tex., U.S. Ct. Appeals (5th cir.), U.S. Supreme Ct. Law clk. to justice Tom Clark U.S. Supreme Ct., Washington, 1959-60; assoc. Powell, Rauhut, McGinnis, Reavley & Lochridge, Austin, Tex., 1960-63; legal adminstrn. asst., exec. asst. Tex. Gov. John B. Connally, Austin, 1963-67; spl. counsel to pres. Lyndon Baines Johnson, Washington, 1967-69; sole practice Austin, 1969—; bd. dirs. Tex. Lawyers Ins. Exchange, Austin. Mem. U. Tex. Cancer Found., Houston, 1978-85, U. Tex. Devel. Bd., Austin, 1980-85; chmn. Select Com. for Higher Edn., Austin, 1985—, coordinating bd. Tex. Coll. and U. System, Austin, 1983—. Fellow Tex. Bar Found.; mem. ABA, Tex. Bar Assn. (chmn. legis. com. 1980, 83-86), Tex. Jr. Bar Assn. (chmn. bd. dirs. 1967), Austin Jr. Bar Assn. (pres. 1962-63). Democrat. Episcopalian. Administrative and regulatory, Banking, Legislative. Home: 2606 Escondido Cove Austin TX 78703 Office: 400 W 15th St 1510 United Bank Tower Austin TX 78701

TEMPLEMAN, JAMES EDWIN, lawyer; b. Wewoka, Okla., Oct. 30, 1942; s. Edwin Arthur and Ruth LaVelle (Hightower) T.; m. Sandra Kay Bradshaw, Aug. 12, 1966; children: Lisa Christine, Robin Leigh, James David. BA, Eastern N.Mex. U., 1964; JD, U. Tex., 1972. Bar: N.Mex. 1972, Tex. 1972, U.S. Dist. Ct. N.Mex. 1972, U.S. Ct. Appeals (10th cir.) 1974, U.S. Claims Ct. 1981. Assoc. Sanders & Snipes, Lovington, N.Mex., 1972-75; ptnr. Sanders & Templeman, Lovington, 1975-77, Templeman & Crutchfield, Lovington, 1977—. Mem. Lovington Bd. Edn., 1981—; bd. dirs. Door of Opportunity, Inc., Artesia, N.Mex., 1982—; trustee Coll. of the Southwest, Hobbs, N.Mex, 1985—. Served to 1st lt. U.S. Army, 1966-69. Named Boss of Yr., Lea County Legal Secs. Assn., 1980. Mem. Assn. Trial Lawyers Am. Democrat. Methodist. Lodge: Rotary (pres. Lovington 1975-76). Banking, Insurance, General practice. Office: Templeman and Crutchfield Reed McCrory Bldg 2d Floor Lovington NM 88260

TENDLER, PAUL MARC, lawyer; b. N.Y.C., Oct. 22, 1943; s. Leonard and Gladys (Steisel) T.; m. Elaine Lynn Isaacson, Mar. 28, 1971; children—Jamie Meredith, Seth Evan. B.A., Queens Coll., N.Y.C., 1965; M.S., So. Ill. U., Carbondale, 1966; J.D., Howard U., 1969; postgrad. U. Pitts., 1969-70. Bar: D.C. 1980. Press asst to Congressman Begich, Washington, 1971; legis. asst. to Congressman Halpern, Washington, 1972, Congressman Rinaldo, 1973; dir. legis. research Cost of Living Council, Washington, 1973-74; asst. dir. govt. affairs Am. Nurses Assn., Washington, 1974-75; pres. Paul Tendler Assocs., Washington, 1975—; mng. ptnr. Tendler & Biggins, 1982—; adj. prof. Georgetown U., 1980-83, asst. prof., 1975-80; dir. bus. program Trinity Coll., Washington, 1983—. Author: The Federal Government at Work, 1976; An LPNs Guide to the Federal Government, 1978, 84. Ford Found. scholar, 1967-69. Mem. D.C. Bar Assn., Am. Arbitration Assn., ABA, Assn. Trial Lawyers Am., Delta Sigma Rho, Tau Kappa Alpha. Democrat. Jewish. Administrative and regulatory, Legislative, Private international. Home: 1090 Vermont Ave Washington DC 20005 Office: 1090 Vermont Ave NW Washington DC 20005

TENDY, WILLIAM MICHAEL, JR., lawyer; b. N.Y.C., Apr. 19, 1954; s. William Michael Sr. and Anna Rose (Appignani) T.; m. Christine Marie Giannini, Apr. 26, 1980; children: Lauren, William III. BA in Polit. Sci. cum laude, St. John's U., Jamaica, N.Y., 1976, JD, 1979. Bar: N.Y. 1980, U.S. Dist. Ct. (ea. and so. dists.) N.Y. 1982. Asst. dist. atty. N.Y. County, 1979-83; assoc. Meiselman, Farber, Stella & Eberz P.C., Poughkeepsie, N.Y., 1983-85; ptnr. Tendy, Ellis & Cantor, Poughkeepsie, 1985—. Mem. ABA, N.Y. State Bar Assn., Duchess County Bar Assn., N.Y. State Trial Lawyers Assn. Republican. Roman Catholic. Lodge: Lions. Avocations: fishing, reading. Criminal, Personal injury. Home: Mountain Dr Pleasant Valley NY 12569 Office: Tendy Ellis & Cantor PO Box 8220 Poughkeepsie NY 12601

TENGI, FRANK R., lawyer, ins. co. exec.; b. Garfield, N.J., Aug. 11, 1920; s. John and Mary (Fedush) T.; m. Shirley H. Mitchell, May 17, 1952; children—Christopher, Nancy. B.S., Georgetown U., 1946; LL.D., Fordham U., 1951. Bar: N.Y. 1955, U.S. Supreme Ct. 1967, U.S. Ct. Claims 1967, U.S. Dist. Ct. (so. dist.) N.Y. 1967, U.S. Dist. Ct. (ea. dist.) N.Y., 1967, U.S. Tax Ct. 1968. Asst. sec. Am. Internat. Aviation Agy., Inc., N.Y.C., 1961-69; assoc. Lee Mulderig & Celentano, N.Y.C., 1965-70; asst. sec. Am. Internat. Underwriting Corp., N.Y.C., 1965—, Am. Internat. Underwriters Assn., 1965—, Starr Tech. Risks Agy., Inc., 1967-78; asst. comptroller taxation A.I.G., Inc., N.Y.C., 1971-75; asst. sec. C.V. Starr & Co., Inc., N.Y.C., 1965—; pres. Estate Maintenance Co., Inc., N.Y.C., 1969-71; mgr. reinsurance security World-wide, Am. Internat. Group, Inc., N.Y.C., 1978—. Mem. Mayor's Budget Adv. Com. Plainfield, 1980-81. C.P.A., N.J. Treas., Starr Found., 1970—. Served with U.S. Army, 1941-46; ETO. Mem. N.Y. State Bar Assn., Tax Execs. Inst. General corporate, Corporate taxation, Personal income taxation. Home: 17 Madison Ave #58 Madison NJ 07940 Office: 70 Pine St New York NY 10270

TENNEN, LESLIE IRWIN, lawyer; b. Toronto, Ont., Can., Aug. 26, 1952; came to U.S., 1961; s. Edward and Elsie (Liberbaum) T. B.A. with distinction, U. Ariz., 1973, J.D., 1976; Mount Scopus, Hebrew U., Jerusalem, 1975. Bar: Ariz. 1977, U.S. Dist. Ct. Ariz. 1979. Sole practice, Tucson, 1977-79; ptnr. Sterns and Tennen, Phoenix and Tucson, Ariz., 1979—; cons. internat. law and aerospace activities; lectr. Princeton U., U. Ariz., Am. Grad. Sch. Internat. Mgmt., also profl. aviation and aerospace congresses and seminars in N.Am., Europe, Asia; judge Jessup Internat. Moot Court Competition, 1982, 83, 85. Contbr. articles to profl. jours. Precinct committeeman State Democratic Com., 1972-73. Received highest score Ariz. Bar Examination, 1977. Mem. Internat. Inst. Space Law, Am. Soc. Internat. Law, AIAA, Aviation Space Writers Assn., Planetary Soc., Fedn. Aerospace Socs. in Tucson (exec. bd.). Private international, Aerospace and aviation, General corporate. Office: Sterns and Tennen 932 N Swan Rd Tucson AZ 85711

TENNESSEN, ROBERT JOSEPH, lawyer; b. Lismore, Minn., Aug. 24, 1939; s. Alphons J. and Helen C. (Klontz) T.; m. Christine J. Hestad; children: Natasha, Tonya, Christina. BA in Econs., U. Minn., 1965, JD, 1968. Bar: Minn. 1968, U.S. Dist. Ct. Minn. 1968, U.S. Ct. Appeals (8th cir.) 1968. Assoc. Helgeson, Peterson, Engberg & Spector, Mpls., 1968-75; ptnr. Gruse, Von Holtum, Sirben and Schmidt, Ltd., Mpls., 1975-81, Tennessen & Regan, Mpls., 1982—; fed. commr. Fed. Privacy Protection Study Commn., 1975-77. Senator Minn., 1971-83; chmn. fin. council Basilica of St. Mary's, Mpls., 1984—. Served with USAF, 1957-61. Mem. ABA (adv. to Nat. Conf. Commrs. on Uniform State Laws, 1978-80), Lawyers Alliance for Nuclear Arms Control, Minn. Supreme Ct. Adv. Com. on Privacy Rules. Banking, General corporate, Consumer commercial. Office: 625 4th Ave S Minneapolis MN 55415

TENNEY, PAUL ANTHONY, judge; b. Wakefield, Mass., Mar. 15, 1928; s. Patrick Hugh and Bertha Eva (Wenzel) T.; m. Marcia Constance Curley, Jan. 7, 1933. A.B., Harvard U., 1950; LL.B., Boston U., 1953; LL.M., Georgetown U., 1959. Bar: Conn. 1954, Mass. 1955, D.C. 1974. Chief adminstrv. law judge Occupational Safety and Health Rev. Com., 1978—. Mem. ABA. Administrative and regulatory, Health, Labor. Office: OSHA 1825 K St Washington DC 20006 *

TEPLER, SHELDON JOEL, lawyer; b. Montreal, Que., Can., July 25, 1954; came to U.S., 1956; s. Michael and Feiga (Rosenberg) T.; m. Denise Anne Schwartz, May 15, 1956; 1 child, Erika Alexandra. BA, SUNY, Binghamton, 1976; MA, Columbia U., 1978; JD, U. Pa., 1981. Bar: Pa. 1981, Maine 1983. Law clk. to presiding justice U.S. Ct. Appeals (8th cir.), Little Rock, 1981-83; asst. atty. gen. State of Maine, Augusta, 1983; assoc. Hardy, Wolf & Downing, Lewiston, Maine, 1984-86, ptnr., 1986—. Mem. Assn. Trial Lawyers Am., Maine Trial Lawyers Assn. Democrat. Jewish. Personal injury, Workers' compensation, Juvenile. Office: Hardy Wolf & Downing Box 3065 Lewiston ME 04240

TEPPER, ALAN MICHAEL, lawyer; b. Phila., Nov. 9, 1944; s. Rubin and Ida R. (Abrohms) T.; m. Diane L. Goldberg, Aug. 20, 1967; children: Brian Jay, Scott Andrew. BS, Temple U., 1966, JD, 1969. Bar: Pa. 1970, N.J. 1973, U.S. Dist. Ct. Pa. (ea. and mid. dists.) Pa. 1970, U.S. Dist. Ct. N.J. 1973, U.S. Supreme Ct. Assoc. Klovsky, Kuby & Harris, Phila., 1970-77; sole practice Phila. and Haddonfield, N.J., 1987—. Mem. Pa. Bar Assn., N.J. Bar Assn., Phila. Bar Assn. (treas. 1984-86), Phila. Bar Found. (treas. 1984-86), Phila. Trial Lawyers Assn. (treas. 1978—), Tau Epsilon Rho (nat. exec. dir. 1977—, labor award 1969), Tau Epsilon Phi. Club: Lake Sports Car (Medford, N.J.) (treas. 1980-85). Avocations: sporting events, road car rallies. Personal injury, Consumer commercial, State civil litigation. Home: 115 Gainsboro RD Cherry Hill NJ 08003 Office: 36 Kresson Rd Suite E Cherry Hill NJ 08034

TEPPER, ERIC ALAN, lawyer; b. Schenectady, N.Y., Feb. 5, 1957; s. Jason A. and Alice (Buff) T.; m. Patricia Lane, Jan. 15, 1984; 1 child, Jessica Lane. BA magna cum laude, Hamilton Coll., 1979; JD with honors, George Washington U., 1982. Bar: Mass. 1982, N.Y. 1983, U.S. Dist. Ct. (no. dist.) N.Y. 1983, U.S. Dist. Ct. Mass. 1986. Assoc. Parisi, De Lorenzo, Gordon, Pasquariello & Weiskopf P.C., Schenectady, 1982—. Mem. Schenectady County Jewish Community Ctr., 1985—, Schenectady Mus. Nature Preserve Com., 1985—. Mem. ABA (family law div.), N.Y. State Bar Assn. (family law div.), Schenectady County Bar Assn. Democrat. Avocations: skiing, tennis, ornithology. Family and matrimonial, Real property, Vehicle and traffic. Home: 411 Terrace Rd Schenectady NY 12306 Office: Parisi De Lorenzo Gordon et al 201 Nott Terr Schenectady NY 12307

TEPPER, R(OBERT) BRUCE, JR., lawyer; b. Long Branch, N.J., Apr. 1, 1949; s. Robert Bruce and Elaine (Ogus) T.; m. Belinda Wilkins, Nov. 26, 1971; children—Laura Katherine, Jacob Wilkins. A.B. in History, Dartmouth Coll., 1971; J.D. cum laude, St. Louis U., 1976, M.A. in Urban Affairs, 1976. Bar: Mo. 1976, Calif. 1977, Ill. 1978, U.S. Ct. Appeals (7th cir.) 1978, (8th cir.) 1976, (9th cir.) 1978, U.S. Dist. Ct. (cen., no. and so. dists.) Calif. 1978. Asst. gen. counsel St. Louis Redevel. Authority; 1976-77; assoc. Goldstein & Price, St. Louis, 1977-78, Loo, Merideth & McMillan, Los Angeles, 1978-82; sole practice, Los Angeles, 1982-84; ptnr., litigation supr. Weiser, Kane, Ballmer & Berkman, Los Angeles, 1984—; spl. counsel to Solano County, San Diego, Santa Barbara, Hermosa Beach, Anaheim, Oceanside, Moreno Valley, West Covina, Glendale and Hawthorne, Calif.; judge pro tempore Los Angeles County Mcpl. Ct., 1983—; grader State Bar Calif., 1980-84. Assoc. editor St. Louis U. Law Jour., 1974-76. Contbr. articles to legal jours. Grad fellow St. Louis U., 1973-76. Mem. Los Angeles County Bar Assn., Assn. Bus. Trial Lawyers, ABA. Republican. Jewish. Clubs: So. Calif. Dartmouth (bd. dirs. 1980-83), Los Angeles Athletic (Los Angeles). Real property, Local government, State civil litigation. Home: 10966 Wrightwood Ln Studio City CA 91604 Office: Weiser Kane Ballmer & Berkman 354 S Spring St Suite 420 Los Angeles CA 90013

TERANDO, G.H., lawyer; b. St. Louis, Mar. 31, 1945; s. Otto Henry and Lillian Nim (Derby) T.; m. Kathleen Lee Swetz, Sept. 29, 1967; children: Amy Catherine, Abby Lillian. BA, So. Ill. U., 1967; JD, Washington U., St. Louis, 1973, postdoctoral, 1973-74. Bar: Mo. 1974, U.S. Dist. Ct. (ea. and we. dists.) Mo. 1974, U.S. Tax Ct. 1983, U.S. Dist. Ct. (ea. and we dists.) Ark. 1984, U.S. Ct. Appeals (8th cir.) 1985. Assoc. Hyde, Purcell, Wilhoit & Edmundson, Poplar Bluff, Mo., 1974-76; ptnr. Little, Million & Terando, Poplar Bluff, 1977-85; asst. pros. atty. Butler County, Poplar Bluff, 1977-80; city atty. City of Poplar Bluff, 1977-84; ptnr. G.H. Terando & John Thomas Welch, Poplar Bluff, 1985—. Author: Missouri Taxation Law and Practice, 1980, Missouri Real Estate Practice, 1986. Chmn. Willhaven Residential Complex, Inc., Poplar Bluff, 1982—. Served to sgt. U.S. Army, 1969-71, Vietnam. Fellow Assn. Trial Lawyers Am.; mem. Mo. Bar Assn. (taxation and mcpl. law coms.), Mo. Trial Lawyers Assn. Lodge: Optimists. Avocations: athletics, refereeing. Contracts commercial, State civil litigation, Local government. Home: 2844 Lakeside Dr Poplar Bluff MO 63901 Office: G H Terando & John Thomas Welch 1980 State St Poplar Bluff MO 63901

TERC, JOSEPH ANTHONY, lawyer; b. Chgo., Aug. 27, 1947; s. Joseph F. and Mary A. (Trodden) T.; m. Patricia A. Madden, Aug. 8, 1970; children—Amanda P., Joseph E. B.A., St. Mary's Coll., Winona, Minn., 1969; J.D., John Marshall Law Sch., 1973. Bar: Ill. 1973, U.S. Dist. Ct. (no. dist.) Ill. 1973. U.S. Ct. Appeals (7th cir.) 1976. Inside salesman C.I.T. Corp., Chgo., 1969-71; salesman Addison-Wesley, Barrington, Ill., 1971-72; assoc. French & Rogers, Chgo., 1973-78; sole practice, Chgo., 1978—. Mem. ABA, Assn. Trial Lawyers Am., Ill. Trial Lawyers Assn., Ill. Bar Assn., Chgo. Bar Assn. (cert. of appreciation 1978-81, 83, 84, chmn. tort litigation com. 1979-80). State civil litigation, Personal injury, Federal civil litigation. Office: 180 N LaSalle St Chicago IL 60601

TERK, GLENN THOMAS, lawyer; b. Cobleskill, N.Y., Feb. 27, 1949; s. Raymond Arthur and Marguerite Ida (Nichols) T.; m. Mary Ann Michaud, Sept. 25, 1982. BSME, Clarkson Coll. Tech., 1971; JD, U. Conn., 1976. Bar: Conn. 1976, U.S. Dist. Ct. Conn. 1976. Engr. Combustion Engring. Co., Windsor, Conn., 1971-76; assoc. Francis, Kroopnick & O'Neil, Hartford, Conn., 1976-78; ptnr. Greene and Bloom, Hartford, 1978—. Mem. Dem. Town Com., Windsor, 1978-79, Windsor Inland Wetlands Commn., 1978-79; chmn. Trinity United Meth. Ch. adminstrv. bd., Windsor, 1982-83. Mem. Conn. Bar Assn. (lawyers and community subcom. 1981—). Contracts commercial, General practice, Real property. Home: 445 Old Reservoir Rd Wethersfield Ct 06109 Office: Greene and Bloom 60 Washington St Hartford CT 06106

TERNER, LINDA M. JOHNSON, lawyer; b. Newton, Mass., Oct. 14, 1955; d. Ellsworth L. and Emily A. (Defisher) Johnson; m. Michael John Johnson Terner, Oct. 11, 1980. AB, Princeton U., 1977; JD, U. Chgo., 1980. Bar: N.Y. 1981, U.S. Ct. Mil. Appeals 1981, Mass. 1984, U.S. Dist. Ct. (so. and ea. dists.) N.Y. 1985. Assoc. litigation dept. Reid & Priest, N.Y.C., 1984—. Served to capt. U.S. Army, 1981-84. Mem. ABA, Assn. of Bar of City of N.Y. Evangelical. Federal civil litigation, General corporate, Bankruptcy. Office: Reid & Priest 40 W 57th St New York NY 10019

TERRELL, HERBERT ARTHUR, lawyer; b. Phila., Aug. 5, 1951; s. William Cephas and Elizabeth (Kimble) T.; divorced June 1984; children: William, Anitra. BA in Polit. Sci., Widener U., 1973; JD, Temple U., 1976. Bar: Pa. 1977, U.S. Dist. Ct. (ea. dist.) Pa. 1978, U.S. Ct. Appeals (D.C. cir.) 1983. Assoc. McNeal & Colston, Phila., 1977-78; atty. to rep. Pa. Ho. of Reps., Phila., 1978-79; sole practice Phila., 1978-80, Balt., 1982—; ptnr. Michols & Givens, Chester, Pa., 1981-82. Served to capt. JAGC, U.S. Army, 1980-81. Federal civil litigation, General practice, Litigation support and appellate work. Office: 308 N Gay St 2d Floor Baltimore MD 21202

TERRELL, J. ANTHONY, lawyer; b. N.Y.C., Sept. 20, 1943; s. Claude M. and Kathleen L. (Prevost) T.; m. Karen E. Terrell, Aug. 8, 1969; 1 dau., Elizabeth S. B.A., NYU, 1965, LL.M. in Taxation, 1975; J.D., Villanova U., 1968. Bar: N.Y. Ptnr. Frueauff, Farrell, Sullivan & Bryan, N.Y.C., 1970-74, Reid & Priest, N.Y.C., 1974—. Mem. ABA (sect. corp., banking and bus. law, sect. taxation, sect. pub. utility law, vice chmn. corp. finance com., taxation and acctg. com.), Nat. Assn. Bond Lawyers. Clubs: Down Town Assn. (N.Y.C.), Coral Beach and Tennis (Paget, Bermuda), Belle Haven (Greenwich, Conn.). General corporate, Securities, Project and municipal finance. Home: Indian Harbor Greenwich CT 06830 Office: Reid & Priest 40 W 57th St New York NY 10019

TERRELL, JAMES THOMAS, lawyer; b. Jacksonville, Fla., Apr. 4, 1942; s. Vester James and Alice Omega (Hall) T.; m. Constance Fleischel Rooney, June 11, 1966 (div. May 1978); m. Dovie Ann Owens, June 30, 1982. BA, Stetson U., 1964, JD, 1967. Bar: Fla. 1967, U.S. Dist. Ct. (mid. dist.) Fla. 1970. Assoc. Howell, Kirby & Montgomery, Jacksonville, 1970-73; ptnr. Searcy, Brown & Terrell, Jacksonville, 1973-74, Brown, Terrell, Hogan & Ellis P.A. and predecessor firm Brown & Terrell, Jacksonville, 1974—; adj. prof. bus. law Jacksonville U., 1984-85. Bd. dirs. Fla. Muscular Dystrophy Assn., Jacksonville, 1978-80, Fla. Lung Assn., Jacksonville, 1980—, YMCA, Jacksonville, 1985—. Served to capt. U.S. Army, 1968-70. Charles Dana scholar Stetson U., 1966-67. Fellow Nat. Bd. Trial Advocacy; mem. Assn. Trial Lawyers Am., Acad. Fla. Trial Lawyers. Democrat. Avocations: triathlons, physical fitness. Personal injury, Federal civil litigation, State civil litigation. Home: 7751 Hollyridge Rd Jacksonville FL 32216 Office: Brown Terrell Hogan & Ellis PA 804 Blackstone Bldg Jacksonville FL 32202

TERRELL, PEGGY LEIGH, lawyer; b. Lexington, Ky., Jan. 21, 1959; s. Glendon and Ruby L. (Caudill) T. BA magna cum laude, Morehead (Ky.) State U., 1979; JD, U. Ky., 1982. Bar: Ky. 1982. Sole practice Morehead, 1982—; atty. Northeast Ky. Legal Aid, Morehead, 1984—, Dept. Pub. Adv., Morehead, 1984—; judge Law Enforcement Explorer's Conf., 1983; exam atty. Commonwealth Land Title Ins. Co., Louisville, 1986; lectr. Morehead State U., mem. adv. com. Paralegal Internships, 1987; examining atty. Lawyer's Title Corp. Active Cystic Fibrosis 1985 Walk-A-Thon and Auction; bd. dirs. Am. Cancer Soc., 1985, local Muscular Dystrophy Assn., 1985; judge parliamentary procedure competition Future Bus. Leaders Am. Mem. ABA, Ky. Bar Assn. (young lawyers div., family law sect.), Am. Judicature Soc., ACLU, Women's Law Assn., Louisville Lawyers Assn., Rowan County Bar Assn., NOW, AAUW (local legis. chmn., info. chmn., state legis. com., rec. sec.), Ky. Fedn. Bus. and Profl. Women (legis. chmn., state conv. del., mem. resolution com., Young Careerist award), NEA, Morehead State U. Alumni Assn., U. Ky. Alumni Assn., U. Ky. Law Sch. Alumni Assn., Phi Kappa Phi, Pi Gamma Mu, Psi Chi. Avocations: swimming, drawing, crafts, flute, horseback riding. Home: PO Box 25 Morehead KY 40351 Office: 151 E Main St Morehead KY 40351

TERRELL, RICHARD CLARK, lawyer; b. Tex., July 8, 1956; s. Robert D. and Mary Lou (Davis) T. BA, U. Tex., 1978; JD, St. Mary's U., San Antonio, 1980. Bar: Tex. 1981, U.S. Dist. Ct. (so. dist.) Tex. 1985. Law clk. Bexar County Legal Aid, San Antonio, 1979-80; assoc. Pat Maloney Law Offices, San Antonio, 1981-82, R.E. Lopez Law Offices, Alice, Tex., 1983; sole practice Alice, 1983—; asst. atty. Jim Wells County, 1984. Bd. dirs. Boy's Club, Alice, 1985—. Mem. ABA, Coastal Bend Bar Assn., Tex. Trial Lawyers Assn., Assn. Trial Lawyers Am. Democrat. Roman Catholic. Avocation: camping. Personal injury, Workers' compensation, State civil litigation. Home: 802 Jim Wells Dr Alice TX 78332 Office: 208 N Cameron Alice TX 78332

TERRY, BRIAN STEPHEN, law educator; b. Quincy, Mass., Apr. 11, 1944; s. Herbert LeRoy and Ruth Sarah (Silver) T.; m. Anne Balsam; children: Rebecca, Daniel. BA, U. Mass., Boston, 1977; JD, Suffolk U., 1980. Bar: Mass. 1980, U.S. Supreme Ct. 1984, U.S. Dist. Ct. Mass. 1985; registered physician's asst. Sole practice Taunton, Mass., 1980—; law prof. Johnson & Wales Coll., Providence, 1980—. Served with USAF, 1962-66. Mem. Mass. Bar Assn., Taunton Bar Assn. Legal education, Contracts commercial, General practice. Home: 230 Winthrop Ave Taunton MA 07280 Office: Johnson & Wales Coll Abbott Park Pl Providence RI 02903

TERRY, JACK CHATTERSON, lawyer; b. Monett, Mo., Nov. 23, 1919; s. Jacob E. and Florence V. (Chatterson) T.; m. Susan W. Terry, June 7, 1941; children—Susan L. Terry Galewaler, Philip C. B.A. in History and Govt., U. Mo. at Kansas City, 1949, J.D., 1952. Bar: Mo. 1952, U.S. Sup. Ct. 1961. Sole practice, Independence, Mo., 1952—; mem. Mo. Legislature, 1955-56; legis. liaison officer Jackson County (Mo.), 1967-68; atty. Inter-City Fire Protection Dist., 1955-74; city atty. City of Blue Summit (Mo.), 1971-76; atty. Jackson County (Mo.) Bd. Election Commrs., 1974-86. Pres. Independence Good Govt. League, 1961-63, Jackson County League Better Govt., 1962-66. Served as officer USAAF, 1941-46; PTO. Decorated Purple Heart, Air medal. Mem. ABA, Mo. Bar Assn., Kansas City Bar Assn. Democrat. Mem. Christian Ch. (Disciples of Christ). Club: Inter-City Kiwanis (pres. 1967), Masons, Shriners. General practice, State civil litigation, Family and matrimonial. Home: 614 Bellevista St Independence MO 64055 Office: 554 S Ash St PO Box 7800 Independence MO 64053

TERRY, JAMES JOSEPH, JR., lawyer; b. Yonkers, N.Y., July 2, 1952; s. James Joseph Sr. and Marie Catherine (O'Boyle) T.; m. Marguerite Mary O'Connor, Sept. 29, 1985. BA, NYU, 1974; JD, Columbia U., 1977. Bar: N.Y. 1978, U.S. Dist. Ct. (so. and ea. dists.) N.Y. 1978, U.S. Ct. Appeals (2d cir.) 1981. Assoc. Cole & Deitz, N.Y.C., 1977-86, ptnr., 1986—. Mem. ABA, N.Y. State Bar Assn., Assn. Trial Lawyers Am., N.Y. Trial Lawyers Assn., Maritime Law Assn. U.S., N.Y. County Lawyers Assn. Democrat. Roman Catholic. Avocations: fishing, reading. Federal civil litigation, State civil litigation, Contracts commercial. Home: 3622 Tibbett Ave Bronx NY 10463 Office: Cole & Deitz 175 Water St New York NY 10038

TERRY, JOHN ALFRED, judge; b. Utica, N.Y., May 6, 1933; s. Robert Samuel and Julia Berenice (Collins) T. B.A. magna cum laude, Yale U., 1954; J.D., Georgetown U., 1960. Bar: D.C. 1960. Asst. U.S. atty. for D.C. 1962-67; staff atty. Nat. Commn. Reform of Fed. Criminal Laws, Washington, 1967-68; pvt. practice law Washington, 1968-69; chief appellate div. U.S. Atty.'s Office for D.C., 1969-82; judge D.C. Ct. Appeals, 1982—. Mem. D.C. Bar (bd. govs. 1977-82), ABA, Phi Beta Kappa. Office: DC Ct Appeals 500 Indiana Ave NW Washington DC 20001

TERRY, JOHN HART, lawyer, utility company executive, former congressman; b. Syracuse, N.Y., Nov. 14, 1924; s. Frank and Saydee (Hart) T.; m. Catherine Jean Taylor Phelan, Apr. 15, 1950; children: Catherine Jean (Mrs. Richard Thompson), Lynn Marie (Mrs. Robert Tacher), Susan Louise (Mrs. Stanley Germain), Mary Carole (Mrs. Stephen Brady). B.A., U. Notre Dame, 1945; J.D., Syracuse U., 1948. Bar: N.Y. bar 1950, D.C. bar 1972. Asso. to partner Smith & Sovik, 1948-59; asst. sec. to Gov. State of N.Y., 1959-61; sr. partner firm Smith, Sovik, Terry, Kendrick, McAuliffe & Schwarzer, 1961-73; sr. v.p., gen. counsel, sec. Niagara Mohawk Power Corp., Syracuse, 1973—; mem. N.Y. State Assembly, 1962-70, 92d Congress from 34th Dist. N.Y., 1971-73; presdl. elector 1972. State chmn. United Services Orgn., 1964-73; past pres. John Timothy Smith Found.; Founder, dir. Bishop Foery Found., Inc.; dir. St. Joseph's Hosp. Council; past pres. Lourdes Camp; bd. dirs. N.Y. State Traffic Council; nat. bd. dirs. Am. Cancer Soc.; trustee Maria Regina Coll.; mem. adv. council Syracuse U. Sch. Mgmt.; past pres. Cath. Youth Orgn.; bd. dirs. Syracuse Community Baseball Club. Served to 1st lt. AUS, 1943-46. Decorated Purple Heart, Bronze Star; named Young Man of Year Syracuse Jr. C. of C., 1958, Young Man of Yr. N.Y. State Jr. C. of C., 1959, Young Man of Yr. U. Notre Dame Club Cen. N.Y., 1959. Mem. ABA (utility law sect.), N.Y. State Bar Assn. (chmn. com. on public utility law), Onondaga County Bar Assn. (chmn. membership and legis. coms.), D.C. Bar Assn., County Officers Assn., Citizens Found., U. Notre Dame, Syracuse U. law assns., Am. Legion, VFW, DAV, 40 and 8, Mil. Order of Purple Heart. Roman Catholic. Clubs: Century, Bellevue Country, Capitol Hill (Washington). General corporate, Public utilities, Contracts commercial. Home: 25 Erregger Terr Syracuse NY 13224 Office: Niagara Mohawk Power Corp 300 Erie Blvd W Syracuse NY 13202

TERRY, MARY SUE, state official, lawyer; b. Martinsville, Va., Sept. 28, 1947; d. N.C. and Nannie Ruth T. B.A., Westhampton Coll., 1969; M.A., U. Va., Charlottesville, 1970, J.D., 1973. Bar: Va., 1973. Asst. commonwealth's atty. Patrick County, Va., 1973-77, mem. house dels., 1977-85; ptnr. B.H. Cooper Farm, Inc., Stuart, Va., 1978—, Terry & Rogers, Stuart, Va., 1978—; atty. gen. State of Va., Richmond, Va., 1986—; dir. First Nat. Bank of Stuart. Mem. Piedmont Planning Dist. Crime Commn., 1974-77; bd. dirs. West Piedmont Health Planning Council, 1975-77; bd. dirs. Patrick Henry Mental Health Ctr., 1975-77; mem. Pres. Bd. Advisors Ferrun Coll., Va., 1978-83; bd. dirs. Va. YMCA, 1980—; trustee U. Richmond, Va., 1980—; chmn. Gov.'s Task Force to Combat Drunk Driving, 1982. Recipient Service to Youth award Va. YMCA, 1981, Disting. Alumna award U. Richmond, 1984. Mem. Va. Trial Lawyers Assn., ABA, Omicron Delta Kappa. Democrat. Baptist. Office: Atty Gen Va 101 N 8th St Richmond VA 23291 *

TERRY, PETER ANTHONY, lawyer; b. Sterling, Colo., Nov. 3, 1952; s. Fred Ward and Marian (Conroy) T. BA, U. Ariz., 1975, JD, 1978. Bar: Ariz. 1978, U.S. Dist. Ct. Ariz. 1978, Calif. 1979. Assoc. H.B. O'Brien, Scottsdale, Ariz., 1978-79; ptnr. Fannin, Terry, Hay & Lemberg, P.A., Phoenix, Ariz., 1979—. Mem. Fed. Bar Assn., Ariz. Bar Assn., Calif. Bar Assn. Real property, General corporate, Contracts commercial. Office: Fannin Terry Hay & Lemberg PA 100 W Washington St Suite 1465 Phoenix AZ 85003

TERRY, TAI CHANG, lawyer; b. Kaohsiung, Republic of China, Nov. 24, 1954; came to U.S., 1961; d. Nai Lin and Faye (Liu) C.; m. F. Davis Terry Jr., June 23, 1979. BA, Yale U., 1977; JD, U. Pa., 1980. Bar: N.Y. 1982. Assoc. Shearman & Sterling, N.Y.C., 1980-86, O'Sullivan, Graev & Karabell, N.Y.C., 1986—. Assoc. editor U. Pa. Law Jour., 1979-80. Banking, General corporate, Private international. Office: O'Sullivan Graev & Karabell 30 Rockefeller Plaza New York NY 10112

TERRY, T(AYLOR) RANKIN, JR., lawyer; b. Louisville, Ky., Sept. 17, 1946; s. T. Rankin and C. Ruth (Ochs) T.; m. Kristine Ann Luther, May 24, 1969; 1 child, Taylor Rankin III. BSME, U. Ky., 1968; JD, Washington U., 1971; LLM in Taxation, U. Fla., 1976. Bar: Fla. 1971, Ky. 1971. Assoc. Boehl, Stopher, Graves & Deindoerfer, Louisville and Paducah, Ky., 1971-72; from assoc. to ptnr. Roberts, Watson et al, Ft. Myers, Fla., 1972-77; ptnr. Terry, Adams & Corbin, Ft. Myers, 1977-81, Terry & Terry, Ft. Myers, 1981—. Mem. NSPE, Am. Soc. Trial Cons., Fla. Engring. Soc., Ky. Bar Assn., Fla. Bar (ethics com. 1976-78, civil rules com., drafting subcom. 1981—). Democrat. Presbyterian. Club: Royal Palm Yacht (Ft. Myers, chmn. by-laws com. 1985—). State civil litigation, Personal injury, Personal income taxation. Office: Terry & Terry 2115 Main St Fort Myers FL 33901

TERSCHAN, FRANK ROBERT, lawyer; b. Dec. 25, 1949; s. Frank Joseph and Margaret Anna (Heidt) T.; m. Barbara Elizabeth Keily, Dec. 28, 1974; 1 child, Frank Martin. BA, Syracuse U., 1972; JD, U. Wis., 1975. Bar: Wis. 1976, U.S. Dist. Ct. (ea. and we. dists.) Wis. 1976, U.S. Ct. Appeals (7th cir.) 1979. From assoc. to ptnr. Frisch, Dudek & Slattery Ltd., Milw., 1975—. Treas., sec. Ville du Park Homeowners Assn., Mequon, Wis., 1985-86. Served with USCG, 1972-73. Mem. ABA, Wis. Bar Assn., Assn. Trial Lawyers Am., Wis. Assn. Trial Lawyers, Ins. Trial Counsel Wis. Republican. Lutheran. Avocations: swimming, coin collecting, reading, outdoor activities. Insurance, Personal injury, Federal civil litigation. Office: Frisch Dudek & Slattery Ltd 825 N Jefferson St Milwaukee WI 53202

TERWILLIGER, GEORGE JAMES, III, lawyer; b. New Brunswick, N.J., June 5, 1950; s. George James Jr. and Ruth Nancy (Mellilo) T.; m. Carol Ann Hitchings, Dec. 18, 1976; children: Sara Katherine, George Zachary Grant. BA in Communications, Seton Hall U., 1973; JD, Antioch Law Sch., 1978. Bar: D.C. 1978, U.S. Dist. Ct. D.C. 1979, U.S. Ct. Appeals (D.C. cir.) 1979, U.S. Dist. Ct. (so. dist.) Fla. 1980, U.S. Dist. Ct. Vt. 1981, U.S. Ct. Appeals (2d cir.) 1982, Vt. 1983. Asst. U.S. atty. Office of U.S. Atty., Washington, 1978-81; asst. U.S. atty. U.S. Dist. Ct. Vt., Burlington, 1981-86, U.S. atty., 1986—. Mem. ABA, Vt. Bar Assn. Republican. Congregationalist. Avocations: skiing, tennis, fishing. Federal civil litigation, Criminal. Office: US Attys Office 11 Elmwood Ave PO Box 570 Burlington VT 05401

TERZICH, MILOS, lawyer; b. Portola, Calif., Oct. 25, 1934; s. Spaso and Saveta (Porobich) T.; m. Sylvia Peterson, Dec. 20, 1960 (div. Feb. 1980); children—Kimberly Ann, Sam. A.A., Stockton Jr. Coll., 1954; B.A., U. Calif.-Berkeley, 1959; LL.B., U. Calif.-San Francisco, 1962. Bar: Calif. 1963, Nev. 1969. Atty. Office Calif. Atty. Gen., Sacramento, 1963-68; bill drafter to legis. counsel, Carson City, Nev., 1968-69; assoc. Breen, Young, Whitehead, et al, Reno, 1969-74, Zephyr Cove, Nev., 1974-78; sole practice, Zephyr Cove, 1978-83, Gardnerville, Nev., 1982—. Profl. lobbyist in Nev. Legis., 1971-83; trustee Citizens for Justice Trust Fund, Nev., 1975—. Served with USMC, 1954-57. Mem. Nev. Trial Lawyers Assn. (bd. govs. 1971—, v.p. 1983—). Democrat. Club: Ducks Unltd. (area chmn. 1983-84, zone chmn. 1985-86). Lodge: Masons. State civil litigation, Personal injury, Real property. Home and office: Box 608 Gardnerville NV 89410

TESONE, ROBERT JOSEPH, lawyer; b. Youngstown, Ohio, Jan. 25, 1947; s. James Vincent and Ann Julia (Felicky) T.; m. L. Marlene Martin, Nov. 20, 1971. BA cum laude, Youngstown State U., 1970; JD, Duquesne U., 1975. Bar: Pa. 1975, U.S. Dist. Ct. (we. dist.) Pa. 1976. Sole practice Hermitage, Pa., 1975—; solicitor Pymatuning Township, Transfer, Pa., 1979—, Mercer (Pa.) County, 1984—, Farrell (Pa.) Zoning Bd., 1980—. Mem. ABA, Pa. Bar Assn. (former del. Mercer County Young Lawyers Div.), Mercer County Bar Assn., Pa. Trial Lawyers Assn., Italian Benevolent Soc. (auditor 1977—), Phi Alpha Delta. Democrat. Roman Catholic. Clubs: First Italian Social. Lodge: K.C. (advocate local club 1979—). General practice, Local government, Family and matrimonial. Office: 3366 E State St Hermitage PA 16148

TESORO, GEORGE ALFRED, lawyer; b. Rome, Feb. 6, 1904; s. Alfred and Anna (Russi) T.; m. Gilda De Mauro, Mar. 18, 1934; children: Alfred W., Alexandra L. Tesoro Miller. J.D., U. Rome, 1925, D. Polit. Sci., 1929, Ph.D. in Taxation, 1930. Bar: D.C. 1948, U.S. Supreme Ct. 1965. Corp. lawyer, Rome, 1927-38; instr., lectr. taxation U. Rome, 1930-35; assoc. prof. pub. fin. and taxation U. Bari (Italy), 1935-38; news editor Sta. WOV, N.Y.C., 1941-42; lectr. in econs. Lawrence Coll., 1942; vis. prof., lectr., adj. prof. econs. Am. U., 1942-55; cons. Bd. Econ. Warfare, 1943; econ. analyst, chief sect. Fgn. Econ. Adminstrn. and Office Fgn. Liquidation Commn., 1944-46; economist, dep. econ. adv. Div. Econ. Devel. and Office Western European Affairs, Dept. State, 1946-55; sr. econ. officer, counselor U.S. Mission, Geneva, 1956-65; counsel Cox, Langford & Brown, Washington, 1965-69, Coudert Bros., Washington, 1969-82, Dempsey and Bastianelli, Washington, 1982-83; ptnr. Bosco, Curry & Tesoro, 1984—, chmn. emeritus Am. U. of Rome, 1985—; dir. Ferrero U.S.A., Inc., Impregilo International U.S.A., Inc., Bencor Corp. Am., Inc., others. Decorated comdr. Merito della Repubblica, 1971. Author: La Psicologia a della Testimonianza, 1929; Le Penalità delle Imposte Dirette, 1930; Principii di Diritto Tributario, 1938; founder, editor Italian Jour. Fiscal Law, 1937-38. General practice. Address: 1220 19th St NW Washington DC 20036

TESS-MATTNER, KENT A., lawyer; b. Milw., Apr. 11, 1954; s. Alvin Harry and Donna Jean (Henske) M; m. Marna Marie Tess, May 30, 1975. BA, Carroll Coll., 1975; JD, Marquette U., 1980. Bar: Wis. 1980, U.S. Dist. Ct. (ea. dist.) Wis. 1980, U.S. Dist. Ct. (we. dist.) Wis. 1980. Jud. law clk. to presiding judge Wis. Ct. Appeals, Milw., 1980-82; assoc. Schoone, McManus, Hankel & Ware, S.C., Racine, Wis., 1982-83; sole practice Milw., 1983-84; assoc. Schmidt & Rupke, Milw., 1984—. Ruling elder W. Granville Presbyn. Ch., Milw., 1983—; head coach City of Lakes Cyclists, Mpls., 1982—, coach Brookfield (Wis.) Cycling Club, 1986—. Mem. ABA, Milw. Bar Assn. (chmn. litigation sect. 1982—, speakers bur. 1984—, joint bench and bar com. 1985—), Milw. Young Lawyers Assn. (vol. Lawyers Project award 1986), Assn. Trial Lawyers Am., Wis. Acad. Trial Lawyers, Bd. Profl. Responsibility (dist. com.). Avocation: bicycle racing. State civil litigation, Personal injury, Family and matrimonial. Home: 1542 Upper Pkwy S Wauwatosa WI 53213 Office: Schmidt & Rupke 2401 N Mayfair Rd Milwaukee WI 53226

TETHER, IVAN JOSEPH, lawyer, marketing director; b. Monticello, N.Y., Aug. 17, 1949; s. Ivan Joseph and Helen Louise (Jayne) T. BA in Polit. Sci., Union Coll., Schenectady, N.Y., 1971; JD, Georgetown U., 1975. Bar: D.C. 1975. Staff atty. Environ. Law Inst., Washington, 1975-78; assoc. Nat. Assn. Counties, Washington, 1978-79; sr. analyst Nat. Commn. Air Quality, Washington, 1979-81; sect. chief EPA, Washington, 1981-85; atty., mktg. dir. AER*X div. RMT Inc., Washington, 1985—; assoc. Environ. Law Inst., 1982—. Author: Government Operations and Procurement, 1977; also articles on environment and energy. Mem. ABA (air pollution com., natural resources sect.), Air Pollution Control Assn. (sec. legal sect.). Avocations: hiking, jogging, sailing, traveling. Environment, Administrative and regulatory, Contracts commercial. Home: 8518 Bradford Rd Silver Spring MD 20901 Office: RMT Inc AER*X Div 1901 Pennsylvania Ave NW Suite 907 Washington DC 20006

TE WINKLE, WILLIAM PETER, lawyer, senator; b. Sheboygan, Wis., June 30, 1954; s. Walter and Janet (Otte) Te W.; m. Jilda B. Berry, June 6, 1975; children: William Peter Jr., Katrina Joy. AB magna cum laude, Hope Coll., 1976; JD, U. Wis., 1979. Bar: Wis. 1979, U.S. Dist. Ct. (ea. and we. dists.) Wis. 1979, U.S. Ct. Appeals (7th cir.) 1979. Ptnr. Rohde, Neuses & Dales, Sheboygan, 1979—; instr. Lakeshore Tech. Inst., Cleve., 1979-83. Candidate Te Winkle for state senate 27th Assembly Dist., Wis., 1984, 9th Dist., Wis., 1987—; legacy adviser Am. Cancer Soc., Sheboygan, 1984-86; chairperson Sheboygan County Dems., 1980-85; bd. dirs. Mental Health Assn., Sheboygan, 1985-86, Phi Beta Kappa, Pi Sigma Alpha. Mem. ABA,

Wis. Bar Assn. Democrat. Avocations: reading, music, golf, tennis. State civil litigation, Family and matrimonial, Insurance. Home: 4165 S 14th St Sheboygan WI 53081 Office: Rohde Neuses & Dales 607 N 8th Suite 400 Sheboygan WI 53081

THADDEUS, ALOYSIUS PETER, JR., lawyer; b. Galveston, Tex., June 11, 1954; s. Aloysius Peter and Marhta Ann (Cox) T.; m. Anne Arundel Locker; B.A., St. Edwards U., 1976; J.D., 1982. Bar: Tex. 1982, U.S. Dist. Ct. (so. dist.) Tex. 1983. Briefing atty. Tex. Ct. Criminal Appeals, 1982-83; assoc. Judin, Barron & Seljos, McAllen, Tex., 1983—. Mem. State Bar Tex., ABA, Hidalgo County Bar Assn. (bd. dirs. 1986-87), Tex. Young Lawyers Assn., Hidalgo County Young Lawyers Assn., Tex. Trial Lawyers Assn., Am. Trial Lawyers Assn. Democrat. Roman Catholic. State civil litigation, Personal injury, Workers' compensation. Office: Judin Barron & Seljos Atty at Law 1400 McAllen State Bank Tower McAllen TX 78501

THALER, MARTIN S., lawyer; b. Bklyn., Mar. 22, 1932; s. Philip Paul and Mildred S. T.; m. Mary Kathleen O'Brien, June 30, 1973; 1 child, Megan; children by previous marriage: Diane, Paul, David, Amy. BBA, CCNY, 1953; LLB, Yale U., 1958. Bar: D.C. 1958. Ptnr. Martin, Whitfield, Thaler & Bebchick, Washington, 1961-78, Verner, Liipfert, Bernhard, McPherson & Hand, Washington, 1978—; lectr. in law and civil procedure George Washington U., 1959-60; adj. prof. uniform comml. code Georgetown U., 1971-78, 84-85, adj. prof. corp. fin., 1980-83, adj. prof. legal process, 1986—; bd. dirs. Signet Bank N.A., Abramson Assocs., Inc., CCX Inc. Trustee Glenelg (Md.) Country Sch., 1963-71; trustee Washington Theatre Club, 1966-73, v.p., 1966-69, pres., 1969-72. Served as cpl. Signal Corps, AUS, 1953-55. Mem. Am. Law Inst., ABA, Bar Assn. D.C. Clubs: Met. (Washington); Yale (N.Y.C.). Banking, General corporate, Public international. Office: 1660 L St NW Washington DC 20036

THALL, PETER MORGAN, lawyer; b. New London, Conn., Nov. 4, 1942; s. Morris and Phyllis Pearl (Cohen) T.; m. Dominique Anne Bazin, Dec. 20, 1980; children: Emily Megan, Vincent Laforet, Sophie Alexandra. BA, Columbia U., 1964; LLB, George Washington U., 1967. Bar: Conn. 1967, N.Y. 1968. Atty. ASCAP, N.Y.C., 1967-69; assoc. Orenstein, Arrow et al, N.Y.C., 1969-71; ptnr. Casper & Thall PC, N.Y.C., 1971-77, Levine & Thall PC, N.Y.C., 1977-84; pres. Thall & Plotkin PC, N.Y.C., 1984—; lectr. on copyright law, music industry. Mem. Assn. Bar City of N.Y. (entertainment and sports law com.). Entertainment. Home: 240 West End Ave New York NY 10023 Office: Thall & Plotkin PC 205 E 31st St New York NY 10016

THATCHER, DICKINSON, lawyer; b. Huntington Beach, Calif., May 26, 1919; s. Charles Harold and Gladys Belle (Dickinson) T.; m. Dale Nadine Mortensen, Feb. 2, 1952; children: Kirk R., Jeffrey L. BS, UCLA, 1941; postgrad. NYU, 1943-44, U. Paris, 1945-46; JD, Stanford U., 1948; LLM in Taxation, U. So. Calif., 1962. Bar: Calif. 1948, U.S. Ct. Claims 1956, U.S. Tax Ct. 1954, U.S. Supreme Ct. 1954. Dep. city atty. City of Los Angeles, 1948-51; credit atty. Union Oil Co., Calif., Los Angeles, 1951-54; trial atty. tax div. Dept. Justice, Washington, 1954-56; asst. U.S. atty. Los Angeles, 1956-57; sole practice Van Nuys, Calif., 1957-59, 72—, North Hollywood, Calif., 1959-72. Contbr. articles to legal jours. Served with AUS, 1942-46. Mem. ABA, State Bar Calif. (disciplinary bd. 1970-72, client security fund 1973-75), Los Angeles County Bar Assn. (chmn. council, affiliated bar pres. 1968-70, exec. com. probate and trust law sect. 1985—), San Fernando Valley Bar Assn. (pres. 1966). Estate planning, Probate, Estate taxation. Home: 15040 Hamlin St Van Nuys CA 91411 Office: 14540 Haynes St Suite 109 Van Nuys CA 91411

THAU, WILLIAM ALBERT, JR., lawyer; b. St. Louis, June 22, 1940; s. William Albert and Irene Elizabeth (Mundy) T.; m. Jane Hancock, Sept. 7, 1961; children—William Albert, Caroline Jane, Jennifer Elizabeth. B.S. in Indsl. Mgmt., Georgia Inst. Tech., 1962; J.D., U. Tex., 1965. Bar: Tex. 1965. Ptnr., head of real estate sect. Jenkens & Gilchrist, Dallas, 1965—; chmn. real estate developer/builder symposium Southwest Legal Found, 1975-79; lectr. Practicing Law Inst. Mem. ABA, Tex. State Bar Assn. (chmn real estate, probate, trust law sect.), Am. Coll. Real Estate Lawyers. Episcopalian. Author: Negotiating the Purchase and Sale of Real Estate, 1975; editor Tex. State Bar Assn. Newsletter on Real Estate, Probate & Trust Law, 1978-81; contbr. articles to Real Estate Rev. Real property, General corporate. Office: Jenkins & Gilchrist 3200 Allied Bank Tower 1445 Ross Ave Dallas TX 75202-2711

THAXTON, EVERETTE FREDERICK, lawyer; b. Charleston, W.Va., Jan. 11, 1938; s. Wilbur and Mildred F. (Gerwig) T.; m. Karen Caldwell, Dec. 29, 1967; children: James, LeeAnn, Emily. BA, U. Charleston; JD, W.Va. U. Cartographer, hwy. design technician W.Va. Dept. of Hwy., Charleston, 1941-63; dir. tax mapping W.Va. Tax Dept., Charleston, 1963-65; ptnr. Thaxton & Daniels, Charleston, 1970—. Served with USAF, 1955-61. Mem. ABA (various coms.), W.Va. Bar Assn., Assn. Trial Lawyers Am., W.VA. Trial Lawyers Assn., Am. Arbitration Assn. (panel arbitrators), Pi Gamma Mu, Aircraft Owners and Pilots Assn. Avocations: flying, sports cars, constrn. machinery and equipment. General corporate, General practice, Personal injury. Home: 502 Hillsdale Dr Charleston WV 25302 Office: Thaxton & Daniels 1115 Virginia St E Charleston WV 25301

THAYER, CHARLOTTE P., lawyer; b. Atchison, Kans., Sept. 22, 1927; d. Charles H. and Hazel V. (Belding) Thayer; B.A., U. Kans., 1948, M.A., 1950; J.D., U. Mo.-Kansas City, 1955. Bar: Mo. 1955, U.S. Dist. Ct. (we. dist.) Mo. 1955, U.S. Supreme Ct. 1971. Sole practice, Kansas City, Mo., 1956-60; pres. Thayer, Gum & Wickert, Grandview, Mo., 1961-82; pres. Thayer, Bernstein, Bass & Monaco P.C., Kansas City, 1983—; lectr. family law. Recipient Don Quixote award, U. Mo. Law Found., 1986. Bd. govs. Community Mental Health Ctr., 1982—. Mem. Am. Acad. Matrimonial Lawyers (gov. 1979-81, pres. Mo. chpt. 1978-81), Mo. Bar (chmn. family law com. 1973-75). Democrat. Unitarian. Contbg. author: Missouri Family Law Handbook, 1976, revised edit., 1978. Family and matrimonial. Office: Thayer Bernstein Bass & Monaco PC 8900 Ward Pkwy Suite 210 Kansas City MO 64114

THAYER, STUART WILSON WALKER, lawyer; b. Charleston, W.Va., May 4, 1926; s. Harry G. and Ethel (Wehrle) T.; m. Ann Hart, July 1, 1949; children: Janet Thayer Kiczek, Mark, David, Lucy Thayer Lucero, Peter. A.B., Princeton U., 1947; LL.B., Yale U., 1951. Bar: D.C. 1952, W.Va. 1954, N.Y. 1956. Law clk. to Justice Tom C. Clark U.S. Supreme Ct., Washington, 1951-52; assoc. Covington & Burling, Washington, 1952-54, Spilman, Thomas, Battle & Kolstermeyer, Charleston, W.Va., 1954-56; assoc. Sullivan & Cromwell, N.Y.C., 1956-60, ptnr., 1960—. Served to lt. (j.g.) USN, 1944-46. Mem. Assn. Bar City N.Y., N.Y. State Bar Assn., ABA, D.C. Bar Assn., W.Va. State Bar Assn. Clubs: India House; Sky (N.Y.C.). Home: 480 Park Ave New York NY 10022 Office: Sullivan & Cromwell 125 Broad St New York NY 10004

THAYER, W(ALTER) STEPHEN, III, lawyer; b. N.Y.C., Jan. 13, 1946; s. Walter S. and Dorothy (Pflum) T.; m. Judith O. O'Brien, Dec. 27, 1982. B.A. in Polit. Sci., Belmont Abbey Coll., 1968; J.D., John Marshall Law Sch., Chgo., 1974. Bar: N.H. 1975, U.S. Dist. Ct. N.H. 1975, U.S. Ct. Appeals (1st cir.) 1981. Sole practice Law Offices W. Stephen Thayer, III, Manchester, N.H., 1975-81; U.S. atty. Dist. N.H., Concord, 1981-84; assoc. justice N.H. Superior Ct., 1984-86, N.H. Supreme Ct., 1986—; legal counsel N.H. State Senate, 1978-80, N.H. Rep. State Com., 1977-80; cons. GSA, Washington, 1981. Alt. del. Rep. nat. conv., 1980; presdl. elector electoral coll., 1980. Served to 1st lt. U.S. Army, 1968-71. Decorated Bronze Star. Mem. N.H. Bar Assn., N.H. Trail Lawyers Assn. Roman Catholic. Home: 1943 Elm St Manchester NH 03101 Office: Supreme Ct Bldg Noble Dr Concord NH 03301

THEADO, THOMAS ROBERT, lawyer; b. Columbus, Ohio, Dec. 27, 1950; s. Albert John and Mary (Ansel) T.; m. Deborah Daphne Phillips, Aug. 30, 1971 (div. June 1980); children: Peter Saul, David Brooke; m. Stephanie Diane Sierra, July 1, 1983. BA in Econs. with honors, Oberlin Coll., 1974; JD, Case Western Res. U., 1979. Bar: Ohio 1979, U.S. Dist. Ct. (no. dist.) Ohio 1981. Law clk. U.S. Justice Dept. Organized Crime Strike Force, Cleve., 1978; instr. law Case Western Res. U. Sch. Law, Cleve., 1978-79; from. assoc. to ptnr. Ronald H. Gordon, Lorain, Ohio, 1979—. Trustee Oberlin (Ohio) Early Childhood Ctr.; candidate Oberlin Sch. Dist. Bd. Edn., 1986. Mem. Order of Coif. Roman Catholic. Avocations: reading, vacationing. State civil litigation, Federal civil litigation, Personal injury. Office: 309 Broadway Bldg Lorain OH 44052

THEBERGE, NORMAN BARTLETT, educator, lawyer; b. Norfolk, Va., Dec. 1, 1946; s. Norman Bartlett and Marjorie Delight (Malbon) T.; m. Louis Cobb Dibrell, Sept. 9, 1978; children—Mary Knight, Susan Dibrell. B.S. in Biology, Coll. William and Mary, 1969; J.D., Marshall-Wythe Law Sch., Williamsburg, Va., 1973; LL.M., U. Miami, Coral Gables, Fla., 1974. Bar: Va. 1974. prof. Coll. William & Mary, 1985—, acting assoc. dean Sch. Marine Sci., 1984-85, chmn. marine resource mgmt. subfaculty, 1976-86, chmn. dept. ocean and coastal law; lectr. Marshall Wythe Law Sch., 1974-83; asst. prof. dept. marine sci. U. Va., Gloucester Point, 1974-76; sr. marine scientist Va. Inst. Marine Sci., Gloucester Point, 1983-84; cons. Office of Tech. Assessment, Dept. Energy, U.S. Fish and Wildlife Service, other state and fed. agys.; mem. adv. bd. Inst. Law and Pub. Health Protection, Arlington, Va., 1984— . Contbr. numerous articles to profl. publs. Mem. ABA, Va. Bar Assn., AAUP. Presbyterian. Legal education, Environment, Law, science and resource management. Office: Va Inst Marine Sci Gloucester Point VA 23062

THEIS, DONALD EUGENE, lawyer; b. New Riegel, Ohio, Feb. 14, 1954; s. Raymond Edward and Teresa Mary (Vondenberg) T.; m. Ann Lynn Donahue, Apr. 11, 1981; 1 child, Adriane Rae. BA in Polit. Sci., Xavier U., 1976; JD, U. Mich., 1979. Bar: Ohio 1979, U.S. Dist. Ct. (so. dist.) Ohio 1980, U.S. Dist. Ct. (no. dist.) Ohio 1981. Assoc. Smith & Schnacke, Dayton, Ohio, 1979-80, Eastman & Smith, Toledo, Ohio, 1981—. Bd. dirs. Epilepsy Ctr. Northwest Ohio, Toledo, 1982—. Mem. ABA, Toledo Bar Assn., Ohio State Bar Assn., Def. Research Inst. Democrat. Roman Catholic. Lodge: KC. Avocations: running, tennis, biking. State civil litigation, Federal civil litigation, Insurance. Home: 3844 Lambert Dr Toledo OH 43623 Office: Eastman & Smith 240 Huron St Toledo OH 43604

THEIS, LINDA JANE, lawyer; b. New Hampton, Iowa, Jan. 5, 1955; d. Ralph Joseph and Mary Jane (Lynch) T. BA, Coll. St Catherine, 1977; JD, U. Minn., 1981. Bar: Minn. 1981, U.S. Dist. Ct. Minn. 1981, U.S. Ct. Appeals (8th cir.) 1981, U.S. Supreme Ct. 1985. Juvenile probation officer Dakota County Services, Hastings, Minn., 1977-78; assoc. Hvass, Weisman & King, Mpls., 1981-86, ptnr., 1986—, also bd. dirs. Mem. ABA, Minn. Bar Assn., Hennepin County Bar Assn., Assn. Trial Lawyers Am., Minn. Trial Lawyers Assn. (bd. govs. 1984—), Minn. Women Lawyers Assn. (bd. dir. 1983-86). Roman Catholic. Avocations: reading, gardening, canoeing. Personal injury, State civil litigation. Office: Hvass Weisman & King 100 S 5th St Suite 2100 Minneapolis MN 55402

THEIS, WILLIAM HAROLD, lawyer, educator; b. Chgo., Nov. 8, 1945; s. Clarence M. and Marion K. (McLendon) T.; m. Maria Luisa Belfiore, Dec. 5, 1973; children—Catherine, Elizabeth. A.B., Loyola U. Chgo., 1967; J.D., Northwestern U., 1970; LL.M., Columbia U., 1977, J.S.D., 1982. Bar: Ill. 1970, D.C. 1971, U.S. Ct. Appeals (7th cir.) 1971, U.S. Supreme Ct. 1974. Assoc. prof. La. State U. Law Ctr., 1972-78; assoc. prof. Loyola U. Law Sch., Chgo., 1978-81; sole practice, Chgo., 1981—; part-time lectr. admiralty Northwestern Sch. Law, Chgo. Served to lt. USNR, 1970-72. Mem. Am. Law Inst. Contbr. articles to legal jours. Criminal, Federal civil litigation, State civil litigation. Office: 19 LaSalle St Suite 800 Chicago IL 60603

THELEN, JOHN FREDERICK, lawyer; b. Des Moines, Oct. 27, 1949; s. Robert John and Mildred Kathryn (Gross) T.; m. Molly Kelly, Sept. 25, 1981; children: Christopher John, Matthew Robert, Michael Kelly. BS, U. Iowa, 1971, JD, 1974. Bar: Iowa 1974, U.S. Dist. Ct. (no. and so. dists.) Iowa 1984. Atty. IMT Ins. Co., Des Moines, 1974-77; claims atty. Continental Western Ins. Co., Des Moines, 1977-81, asst. v.p., 1981-86, legal counsel, 1983—, v.p., 1986—, also bd. dirs. Mem. Iowa State Bar Assn., Internat. Assn. of Ins. Counsel, Def. Research Inst. Club: Wakonda. Insurance, General corporate. Home: 4100 Muskogee Des Moines IA 50312 Office: Continental Western Ins Co PO Box 1594 Des Moines IA 50306

THEOBALD, EDWARD ROBERT, lawyer; b. Chgo., Feb. 10, 1947; s. Edward Robert Theobald Jr. and Marie (Turner) Logan; m. Bonnie J. Singer, July 18, 1970; children: Debra Marie, Kimberly Ann. BA, So. Ill. U., 1969; JD, Ill. Inst. Tech.-Chgo. Kent Coll. Law, 1974. Bar: Ill. 1974, U.S. Dist. Ct. (no. dist.) Ill. 1974. Asst. state's atty. Cook County, Chgo., 1974-77, 77-79, supr. felony trial div., 1980-81; assoc. firm Conklin, Leahy & Eisenberg, Chgo., 1977; ptnr. firm Boharic & Theobald, Chgo., 1981-83; sole practice, Chgo., 1983—; legal advisor Sheriff of Cook County, Ill., 1986—. Named Number One Trial Atty. in Felony Trial Div. of Office of Cook County State's Atty., Felony Trial Div. Suprs., 1979. Mem. Chgo. Bar Assn. (bd. mgrs. 1985—, labor and employment law com. 1983—), ABA (chmn. com. on sentencing alternatives young lawyers sect. 1982-83), Ill. Bar Assn., Assn. Trial Lawyers Am. Roman Catholic. Labor, Civil rights, Criminal. Home: 7104 Grand Ave Downers Grove IL 60516 Office: 29 S LaSalle St Suite 730 Chicago IL 60603

THEODORE, CAROL N., lawyer; b. Cleve., Feb. 12, 1943; d. John Matthew and Betty (Disko) Nagy; m. Eustace D. Theodore, June 13, 1964; children: Kyle James, Graham Clark. AB, Mt. Holyoke Coll., 1964; MS, Cornell U., 1966; JD, Yale U., 1977. Bar: Conn. 1977, U.S. Tax Ct. 1978. Cons. TAP, Inc., Roanoke, Va., 1966-68; assoc. Wiggin & Dana, New Haven, 1977-83; assoc. Brenner, Saltzman, Wallman & Goldman, New Haven, 1984-85, ptnr., 1986—; bd. dirs. NESSCO, Inc., Greenwich, Conn. Trustee Yale-New Haven Hosp., 1985—. Mem. Conn. Bar Assn. (treas., exec. com. on corps. 1982—), New Haven C. of C. (steering com. 1980—). Avocations: skiing, sailing. Real property, Contracts commercial, Private international. Home: 202 Prospect St New Haven CT 06511 Office: Brenner Saltzman Wallman & Goldman 271 Whitney Ave New Haven CT 06511

THERRIEN, VALERIE MONICA, lawyer; b. Hartford, Conn., Dec. 20, 1951; s. Jean Roger Therrien; m. Benny Edwards May 7, 1978 (div. Jan. 1983); m. Mark B. Mitchell Oct. 13, 1985 (div. June 1986). BS, Northeastern U., 1973, JD, 1976. Bar: Alaska 1976, U.S. Dist. Ct. Alaska 1977, U.S. Ct. Appeals (9th cir.) 1977, U.S. Supreme Ct. 1980. Assoc. Ed Niewohner, Fairbanks, Alaska, 1976-77; sole practice Fairbanks, 1977—. Dist. 20 Dem. committeewoman, Alaska, 1984—; councilwoman City of Fairbanks, 1982-85; borough assemblymember, 1986—; pres. Fairbanks chpt. NOW, 1986—; mem. celebration com. Martin Luther King, Jr., 1986-87. Mem. ABA, Alaska Bar Assn., Tanana Valley Bar Assn., Assn. Trial Lawyers Am., Am. Arbitration Assn., NOW (past treas., v.p., pres.), League of Women Voters, Bus. and Profl. Women's Club. Roman Catholic. Avocations: dancing, boating, camping, reading, art. Bankruptcy, Family and matrimonial, State civil litigation. Home and Office: 779 8th Ave Fairbanks AK 99701

THEUT, C(LARENCE) PETER, maritime lawyer; b. Center Line, Mich., July 24, 1938; s. Clarence William and Anna Marie (Martens) T.; m. Judith Fern Trombley, Aug. 4, 1962; children: Elizabeth Anne, Kristin Claire, Peter Christopher, Sarah Nicole. BA, U. Mich., 1960, LLB, 1963. Bar: Calif. 1964, Mich. 1964, U.S. Dist. Ct. (no. dist.) Ohio 1968, U.S. Dist. Ct. (ea. dist.) Mich. 1968. Assoc. Overton, Lyman & Prince, Los Angeles, 1963-67; ptnr. Foster, Meadows and Ballard, Detroit, 1968-72; ptnr. Theut & Schellig, Mt. Clemens, Mich., 1972-80; ptnr. Hill, Lewis, Adams, Goodrich & Tait, Mt. Clemens, 1980—; gen. counsel Nat. Marine Bankers Assn., Mich. Marine Dealers Assn.; twp. atty. Harrison Township. Lector St. Peter's Cath. Ch., Mt. Clemens. Mem: Calif. State Bar Assn., Mich. State Bar Assn., Macomb County Bar Assn., Maritime Law Assn., Nat. Marine Bankers Assn., Mich. Boating Industry Assn., ABA. Republican. Club: North Star Sail. Lodge: Kiwanis. Admiralty, Contracts commercial, Private international. Home: 38554 Hidden Ln Mount Clemens MI 48043 Office: Hill Lewis Adams Goodrich Tait 10 S Gratiot St Suite 201 Mount Clemens MI 48043

THEVENET, SUSAN MARIE, lawyer; b. San Antonio, Apr. 6, 1950; d. Stanley Edward and Marie Therese (Hulsebosch) Thevenet; m. Paul Steven Casamassimo, June 28, 1975 (div. 1981). B.A., Pa. State U., 1971; M.A., Georgetown U., 1973; J.D., U. Iowa, 1978. Bar: Colo. 1979, U.S. Dist. Ct. Colo. 1979. Legis. asst. Am. Assn. Dental Schs., Washington, 1973-74; civil rights investigator Cedar Rapids Human Rights Commn., 1974-75; assoc. Shoemaker & Wham, Denver, 1979; vis. prof. U. Colo. Coll. Law, Boulder, 1980; assoc. Smart, DeFurio & McClure, Denver, 1979-85, ptnr., 1985—. Co-author; Iowa Law Rev., 1977, editor-in-chief, 1977-78. Mem., officer Iowa Women's Polit. Caucus, 1974. Mem. ABA, Colo. Bar Assn. (mem. grievance policy com. 1982-84), Denver Bar Assn. Republican. Roman Catholic. Securities. Office: Smart DeFurio & McClure 1120 Lincoln St Suite 1600 Denver CO 80203

THIBAUT, CHAREST DELAUZON, JR., lawyer; b. Donaldsonville, La., Jan. 6, 1922; s. Charest deLauzon and Mildred (Winship) T.; m. Lillie M. Major, May 15, 1943; children—Natalie Major (Mrs. Clifford C. Comeaux, Jr.), Charest deLauzon III, Joseph Major, Cherie Adele (Mrs. Daniel L. Songy). B.A., La. State U., 1943, J.D., 1946. Bar: La. 1946. Mem. Thibaut, Thibaut, Garrett & Bacot and (predecessor firms), Baton Rouge, 1951—; gen. partner, counsel Tidewater Land Co. Ltd.; adj. asso. prof. law La. State U. Mem. La. State U. Found. Served with AUS, 1943. Decorated papal Knight comdr. Order Holy Sepulchre. Mem. Am., La., Baton Rouge bar assns., Omicron Delta Kappa, Delta Kappa Epsilon, Phi Delta Phi. Clubs: Baton Rouge Country (past pres.), Serra (past pres.), Kiwanis (past gov.). General corporate, General practice, Real property. Home: Pleasant View Plantation Oscar LA 70762 and: PO Box 36 Baton Rouge LA 70821 Office: 445 N Blvd Suite 601 City Plaza Baton Rouge LA 70802

THIBAUT, JOSEPH H. MAJOR, lawyer; b. Baton Rouge, Jan. 6, 1954; s. Charest D. and Lillie (Major) T.; m. Lynne Falcon, July 26, 1974; children: Joseph H. Major Jr., Ashley Eloise, Jonathan C. Winship. Student, Vanderbilt U., 1970-71; BA, La. State U., 1974, JD, 1976. Bar: La. 1976, U.S. Dist. Ct. (mid. dist.) La. 1976. Ptnr. Thibaut, Thibaut, Garrett & Bacot, Baton Rouge, 1976-82, Thibaut & Thibaut, New Roads, La., 1983-86; spl. counsel Parish of Pointe Coupee, New Roads, 1983—; asst. dist. atty. West Baton Rouge, Iberville and Pointe Coupee, 1985—; spl. asst. atty. gen. Dept. of Justice, 1983—; tchr. bus. law Cath. High Sch. of Pointe Coupee, New Roads, 1980—; bd. dirs. Peoples Bank and Trust Co., New Roads. Mem. bd. advisors Young Dems. of La., Baton Rouge, 1985—; pres. Indsl. Devel. Bd., New Roads, 1982—; trustee Pub. Affairs Research, Baton rouge, 1983—. Served with U.S. Army, 1977. Mem. Ho. of Dels. La. Bar Assn., 1985-86. Mem. 18th Jud. Dist. Ct. Bar Assn., La. Dist. Attys. Assn., La. Bankers Assn. (bank counsel sect.), Baton Rouge Bar Assn., La. Trial Lawyers Assn. Roman Catholic. Lodges: K.C. (3rd degree), Lions, Kiwanis (pres. Pointe Coupee club 1977). Avocations: horses, hunting. State civil litigation, Consumer commercial, Real property. Home: Box 75 Cherie Plantation Oscar LA 70762 Office: 148 E Main St New Roads LA 70760-0129

THIBEAULT, GEORGE WALTER, lawyer; b. Cambridge, Mass., Sept. 21, 1941; s. George Walter and Josephine (Maraggia) T.; m. Antoinette Miller Thibeault, June 30, 1963; children—Robin M., Holly Ann. B.S., Northeastern U., 1964; M.B.A., Boston Coll., 1966, J.D., 1969. Bar: Mass. 1969, Asso., Gaston, Snow & Ely Bartlett, Boston, 1969-73; ptnr. Testa, Hurwitz & Thibeault, Boston, 1973—. Mem. ABA, Mass. Bar Assn., Am. Arbitration Assn. General corporate, Securities, Private international. Home: 114 Indian Pipe Ln Concord MA 01742 Office: 53 State St Boston MA 02109

THIBODEAU, THOMAS RAYMOND, lawyer; b. St.Paul, Feb. 5, 1942; s. Raymond Anthony and Alice Marie (Parkos) T.; m. Mollie Nan Mylor, Sept. 24, 1966; 1 child, Matthew Raymond. BA in Polit. Sci., St. Thomas Coll., St. Paul, 1964; JD, U. Minn., 1967. Bar: Minn. 1967, U.S. Dist. Ct. Minn. 1967, U.S. Ct. Appeals (8th cir.) 1970, U.S. Supreme Ct. 1982, Wis. 1983, U.S. Dist. Ct. Wis. 1983; cert. civil trial specialist Nat. Bd. Trial Advocacy. Ptnr. Johnson, Killen, Thibodeau & Seiler, Duluth, Minn., 1967—, also bd. dirs.; pres. Legal Aid Service N.E. Minn., Inc., 1969-74. Chmn. Duluth City Charter Commn., 1976-78; vol. atty. St. Louis County Heritage and Arts Ctr., Duluth, 1980-87. Recipient Disting. Alumni award Coll. St. Thomas, 1985. Fellow: Am. Coll. Trial Lawyers; mem. Minn. Bar Assn. (chmn. specialization com. 1974-78, co-chmn. revision civil jury instrn. guide com. 1982-85), Minn. Def. Lawyers Assn. (pres. elect 1986-87, pres. 1987-88). Avocations: hunting, skiing, scuba diving and other water sports, reading, handball. Federal civil litigation, State civil litigation, Personal injury. Home: 407 Wallace Ave Duluth MN 55812 Office: Johnson Killen Thibodeau Seiler 811 Norwest Ctr Duluth MN 55802

THIELE, HERBERT WILLIAM ALBERT, lawyer; b. Gananoque, Ont., Can., Apr. 14, 1953; s. Herbert H.H. and Bertha (Shields) T.; m. Kathi M. Brown, May 29, 1982; children: Herbert R.R., Eric W.R. BA, U. Notre Dame, 1975; JD, U. Fla., 1978. Bar: Fla. 1978, U.S. Dist. Ct. (so. dist.) Fla. 1979, U.S. Ct. Appeals (5th and 11th cirs.) 1981, U.S. Supreme Ct. 1982, U.S. Tax Ct. 1983. Assoc. Law Offices of Roger G. Saberson, Delray Beach, Fla., 1979-81; asst. city atty. City of Delray Beach, 1979-81, city atty., 1981—. Bd. dirs. Delray Beach Mcpl. Employees Credit Union, 1985—. Named one of Outstanding Young Men Am., 1986. Mem. ABA, Fla. Bar Assn. (local govt. sect., exec. council 1985—, labor and employment law, trial, real property and gen. practice sects., bar com. on individual rights and responsibilities), Assn. Trial Lawyers Am., Fla. Mcpl. Attys. Assn. (steering com. 1985-86, bd. dirs. 1986—), Fla. Assn. Police Attys., Nat. Inst. Mcpl. Law Offices (personnel and labor law com.), Attys. Title Ins. Fund, Phi Delta Phi. Republican. Avocations: music, sports, philately. Local government, State civil litigation, Labor. Home: 420 Chapel Hill Blvd Boynton Beach FL 33435 Office: City Attys Office 100 NW 1st Ave Delray Beach FL 33444

THIERSTEIN, EMMA JOAN, lawyer, technical information specialist; b. Newton, Kans., Oct. 5, 1937; d. William and Emma Voth; m. Eldred A. Thierstein, Mar. 17, 1959; children—Joel, Gretchen. A.B. in Chemistry, Bethel Coll., North Newton, Kans., 1958; grad. Kans. U., 1958; J.D., U. Ky., 1976. Bar: Ky. 1976, D.C. 1979, Mich. 1979, U.S. Patent Office 1979. Pub. sch. tchr., Woodstock, Nfld., Can., 1960-61; lab. technician Procter & Gamble, Cin., 1966, tech. info. specialist, mgr., Cin. and Brussels, 1967-72, summer 1974; patent examiner U.S. Govt., Washington, 1976-78; patent atty. Upjohn Co., Kalamazoo, 1978-84, Parke Davis div. Warner Lambert, Ann Arbor, Mich., 1984—. Mem. Mich. bd. SSS. Mem. Ky. Bar Assn., D.C. Bar Assn., Mich. Bar Assn., Am. Patent Lawyers Assn., Women Lawyers Assn. S.W. Mich., Phi Alpha Delta Internat. (sec.-treas. 1973-74). Patent, Trademark and copyright, Private international. Home: 2636 Lakeshore Dr Hillsdale MI 49242 Office: Warner Lambert 2800 Plymouth Rd Ann Arbor MI 48105

THIES, DAVID CHARLES, lawyer; b. Urbana, Ill., Dec. 6, 1955; s. Richard L. and Marilyn (Webber) T.; m. Johanna B. Bokenkamp, May 21, 1977; children: Stephanie, Daniel. Degre' Semestriel, Cours de Civilisation Francaises Sorbonne, Paris, 1975; AB, U. Ill., 1977, JD, 1980. Bar: Ill. 1980, U.S. Dist. Ct. (cen. dist.) Ill. 1982. Assoc. Webber & Thies P.C., Urbana, 1980-84, ptnr., 1984—. V.p. Champaign-Urbana Symphony, 1985—. Mem. ABA, Champaign County Bar Assn., Ill. State Bar Assn. (sect. council young lawyers div. 1985—), Urbana C. of C. (chmn 1985—). Democrat. Lodge: Rotary (sec. 1986—). Avocations: music, sports. Labor, Banking. Home: 1109 W Charles Champaign IL 61821 Office: Webber & Thies PC PO Box 189 Urbana IL 61801

THIES, RICHARD LEON, lawyer; b. Scottsbluff, Nebr., Nov. 7, 1931; s. Arnold C. Thies and Wilma J. (Pattison) Player; m. Marilyn Lucille Webber, June 15, 1954; children—David, Nancy, Susan, John, Anne. B.A., U. Ill., 1953, J.D., 1955. Bar: Ill. 1955, U.S. Dist. Ct. (ea. dist.) Ill. 1958, U.S. Supreme Ct. 1986. Instr. engrng. law U. Ill., Urbana, 1955-56; ptnr. Webber & Thies, P.C., Urbana, 1958—; dir. 1st Illini Bank, 1st Galesburg Nat. Bank, Ill., Ill. past v.p. Champaign-Urbana Symphony; mem. Urbana Park Dist. Bd.; bd. dirs. Nat. Acad. Arts, Champaign-Urbana Urban League; bd. dirs., pres. Salvation Army, Champaign County. Served as 1st lt. USAF, 1956-58. Fellow Am. Bar Found. (Ill. chmn.); mem. ABA (ho. of dels. 1984-87), Ill. Bar Assn. (various offices, pres. 1986—), Champaign County Bar Assn. (v.p.), Urbana C. of C. (pres.). Democrat. Presbyterian. Club: Urbana Country. Lodge: Kiwanis (pres. Champaign-Urbana). General practice. Office: Webber & Thies PC 202 Lincoln S Urbana IL 61801

THIESS, KENNETH CHARLES, lawyer; b. Meadville, Pa., July 22, 1952; s. William George and Ruth M. (Dench) T.; m. Brooke A.W. Weiler, Sept. 9,

1978. BA, Coll. of Wooster, 1974; JD, U. Akron, 1978. Bar: Pa. 1978, U.S. Dist. Ct. (we. dist.) Pa. 1978, U.S. Supreme Ct. 1981. Ptnr. Ferguson & Thiess, Meadville, 1978-82; staff atty., asst. counsel Pennbancorp, Titusville, Pa., 1982—, counsel, sec., 1986—, v.p., counsel, sec., 1987—. Mem. Am. Corp. Counsel Assn. (charter Western Pa. chpt.). Banking, General corporate, Securities. Office: Pennbancorp Pennbank Ctr Titusville PA 16354

THIEWES, RONALD CHARLES, tax accountant, lawyer; b. Winona, Minn., July 14, 1946; s. Harold Frank and Marian Rose (Fisher) T.; m. Barbara Ann Erickson, Mar. 16, 1974; children—Joseph Gerard, Mary Elizabeth. B.A., St. Mary's Coll., 1968; J.D., St. Louis U., 1974; LL.M. in Tax, Washington U., St. Louis, 1975. Bar: Mo. 1974, Minn. 1975, U.S. Tax Ct. 1975, U.S. Ct. Claims 1982, U.S. Supreme Ct. 1979. Tax supr. Hurdman & Cranstoun, CPAs, Kansas City, Mo., 1978-79; asst. tax mgr. Kansas City Power & Light Co., 1979-83; tax. mgr. Troupe, Kehoe, Whiteaker & Kent, Kansas City, 1983—. Editor Mo. Taxation Law and Practice, 1981, 82, 85; contbr. articles to profl. jours. Mem. Kansas City Citizens Assn., Kansas City Consensus. Decorated Silver Star medal. Mem. ABA, Mo. Bar Assn., Kansas City Bar Assn., Kansas City Lawyers Assn., Kansas City Citizens Assn. Republican. Roman Catholic. Home: 1408 NW 67th St Kansas City MO 64118 Office: Troupe Kehoe Whiteaker & Kent 900 Penntower Office Ctr 3100 Broadway Kansas City MO 64111

THODE, ANNA CATHARINE, lawyer; b. Clemson, S.C., Mar. 6, 1956; d. Frederick Wilbur and Linda Crisp (Rhodes) T. BA magna cum laude, Furman U., 1978; JD cum laude, George Washington U., 1981. Bar: D.C. 1981, U.S. Dist. Ct. D.C. 1982, U.S. Ct. Appeals (D.C. and 4th cirs.) 1982. Assoc. Wilson, Elser, Moskawitz, Edelman & Dicken, Washington, 1981-85; enforcement atty. EPA, Washington, 1986—; cons. Booz-Allen & Hamilton Inc., Bethesda, Md., 1986. Mem. ABA, D.C. Bar Assn. (civil jury instruction com. young lawyers sect. 1984), D.C. Unified Bar Assn., Natural Resources Def. Council, Lawyers Alliance Nuclear Arms Control, Phi Beta Kappa. Democrat. Lutheran. Avocations: painting, dancing, swimming. Environment, Insurance, Professional liability. Home: 1400 S Joyce St Apt A-1503 Arlington VA 22202 Office: US EPA 401 M St SW Washington DC 20460

THOM, WILLIAM JOHN, judge; b. Ann Arbor, Mich., June 10, 1941; s. John Culbertson and Mary Margaret (Thomas) T. BA, Princeton U., 1963; JD, Yale U., 1966. Bar: N.Y., Conn., U.S. Dist. Ct. (so. and ea. dists.) N.Y., U.S. Ct. Appeals (2d cir.), U.S. Supreme Ct. Gen. counsel Breed, Abbott & Morgan, N.Y.C., 1968-69, Townley & Updike, N.Y.C., 1969-74; sole practice N.Y.C., 1974-76; ptnr. Boggan & Thom, N.Y.C., 1976-84; judge N.Y. Civil Ct., N.Y.C., 1984, 1985; judge N.Y. Criminal Ct., N.Y.C., 1986; instr. U. Md.; vol. New Haven Legal Aid; advisor Moot Ct. Program, Yale U. Founder Lamdba Legal Def. and Edn. Fund, Inc. pres., 1973-78, bd. dirs., 1973-82, bd. advisors, 1982-84. Served with U.S. Army, 1966-68. Mem. ABA (chmn. subcom. Rights of Gay People 1976-78), Bar Assn. for Human Rights, ACLU, Nat. Gay Task Force, NOW, Mus. of Modern Art. Democrat. Home: 342 E 49th St New York NY 10017 Office: NY Criminal Ct 100 Centre St New York NY 10013

THOMAS, ALBERT, JR., lawyer; b. Fayetteville, Ark., Aug. 27, 1937; s. Albert Janney and Evelyn Danner (Williams) T.; m. Frederica Rae Russell, Dec. 29, 1961; children—Jelyn Rae, Albert Janney III, Heather Hope. B.S. in Bus. Adminstrn., U. Ark., 1959, LL.B., 1962; Bar: Ark. 1963, U.S. Dist. Ct. (ea. dist.) Ark. 1963, U.S. Ct. Appeals (8th cir.) 1981, U.S. Supreme Ct. 1971. Sole practice, West Memphis, 1965—. Active Chickasaw council Boy Scouts Am. Mem. ABA, Ark. Bar Assn., N.E. Ark. Bar Assn., Crittenden County Bar Assn. Democrat. Methodist. General practice, Bankruptcy, Family and matrimonial. Office: 306 W Bond St West Memphis AR 72301

THOMAS, BASIL A., judge; b. Tripolis, Greece, Sept. 17, 1915; came to U.S., 1916.; s. Anargyros Thomas and Helen Koulias; m. Helen P. Thomas, May 18, 1941 (dec.); 1 child, Steven A.; m. Ernestine K. Thomas, Nov. 25, 1981. Degree, U. Balt., 1935; LLD, Coll. William and Mary, 1931-32. Adminstrv. asst. mayor's office Balt., 1948-49; asst. City Solicitor, Balt., 1949-54; supr. elections City of Balt., 1959-61; municipal ct. judge Balt., 1961-68, cir. ct. judge, 1968-83; of counsel Moore, Libowitz & Thomas; bd. trustees edn. found. U. Balt., 1985—. Served to 1st lt. U.S. Army, 1943-46. Mem. ABA, Md. Bar Assn., Balt. City Bar Assn. Democrat. Greek Orthodox. Club: Hillendale Country (pres. 1966-67). Lodges: Lions (pres. 1964-65), Masons. Avocation: modern painting.

THOMAS, BRIAN SEAN, lawyer; b. Passaic, N.J., Sept. 5, 1955; s. George F. and Eileen T. (Lyons) T. BA, Le Moyne Coll., 1977; JD, Rutgers U., 1980. Bar: N.J. 1980, U.S. Dist. Ct. N.J. 1980, Pa. 1984. Law clk. to presiding judge U.S. Bankruptcy Ct., Trenton, N.J., 1980-81; assoc. Megaragee, Youngblood, Franklin & Corcoran, Pleasantville, N.J., 1981—; adj. prof. Glassboro (N.J.) St. Coll., 1979-80, Atlantic Community Coll., Hamilton Twp., N.J., 1984. Mem. ABA, N.J. Bar Assn., Atlantic County Bar Assn. Democrat. Roman Catholic. Avocations: weight lifting, racquetball. Bankruptcy, Personal injury. Home: I-12 Ocean Heights Manor Somers Point NJ 08244 Office: Megargee Youngblood Franklin & Corcoran 600 Five Rd PO Box 850 Pleasantville NJ 08232

THOMAS, CHARLES CRABBE, lawyer; b. Camden, N.J., June 1, 1915; s. Malcolm Graham and Bernice (Crabbe) T.; m. Elizabeth Phillips Moses, June 21, 1947; children: Elizabeth Bogardus, Marjorie Phillips, Charles Jr., Charlotte Eves. Student, U. Pa., 1933-34; AB, Union Coll., 1935; JD, Temple U., 1938. Bar: N.J. 1940, U.S. Ct. Appeals (3d cir.) 1977, U.S. Supreme Ct. Assoc. Boyle & Archer, Camden, 1941-42; sole practice Camden and Woodbury, N.J., 1942-84; ptnr. Thomas & Cook, Woodbury, 1984—; Judge Gloucester County Small Claims Ct., 1938-45. Editor, founder American Squares, 1945-52; author poems under name Tom Barque. Chmn. Gloucester County Cultural and Heritage Commn., 1980—, Gloucester County Tercentenary Commn., 1982—. Served to sgt. N.J. State Guard. Mem. Gloucester County Bar Assn. (pres. 1976), Soc. of Poets for Southern N.J. Republican. Mem. Soc. of Friends. Lodge: Kiwanis (pres. Deptford). Avocations: semi-pro square dance caller and instructor. Home: 500 E Red Bank AVe Deptford NJ 08096 Office: Thomas & Cook 23 Newton Ave Woodbury NJ 08096

THOMAS, DAVID LLOYD, JR., lawyer; b. Lincoln, Nebr., Mar. 21, 1949; s. David L. Sr. and Mary Lou (Artman) T.; m. Kathryn Hayward, June 10, 1979; children: Jeremy Luke, Hillary Lynn. BA with honors, Haverford Coll., 1971; JD, Georgetown U., 1974. Bar: Pa. 1974, U.S. Ct. Appeals (3d cir.) 1974, Mass. 1975. Law clk. to judge Max Rosenn U.S. Ct. Appeals (3d cir.) Pa., Wilkes-Barre, 1974-75; assoc. Ropes & Gray, Boston, 1975-85; ptnr. Peabody & Brown, Boston, 1985—. Real property, Banking, General corporate. Office: Peabody & Brown 1 Boston Place Boston MA 02108

THOMAS, DAVID MICHAEL, lawyer; b. Allentown, Pa., Feb. 18, 1935; s. Harold Henry and Ruth (Wirtz) T.; m. Ann Marie Leh, June 8, 1957; children: David Jr., Charles, Gregory, Douglas, Christopher. BS, U.S. Naval Acad., 1957; MS, U.S. Naval Postgrad. Sch., 1965; JD, George Washington U., 1977. Bar: Md. 1977. Commd. ensign USN, 1957; engr. Sharp Corp., Washington, 1977-78; research dir. BD Dynamics, Rockville, Md., 1978—; of counsel William Skinner, Rockville, 1982—. Republican. Roman Catholic. Avocation: alumni recruiter. General practice. Home: 12413 Beall Spring Rd Potomac MD 20854

THOMAS, EUGENE C., lawyer; b. Idaho Falls, Idaho, Feb. 8, 1931; s. C.E. Thomas; m. Jody Raber; children—Michael E., Stephen R. A.B., Columbia U., 1952, J.D., 1954, LLD (hon.) Univ. Idaho, 1986. Bar: Idaho, 1954, U.S. Dist. Ct. Idaho 1957, US Ct. Appeals (9th cir.) 1958, U.S. Supreme Ct. 1970. Pros. atty. Ada County, Boise, Idaho, 1955-57; ptnr. Moffatt, Thomas, Barrett & Blanton, Boise, 1958—; dir. Shore Lodge, Inc., McCall, Idaho. Bd. editors ABA Jour., 1980-82; state editor Ins. Counsel Jour., 1977—. Bd. dirs. St. Luke's Regional Med. Ctr. and Mountain States Tumor Inst., Boise, 1963—, pres., chmn. bd. 1972-79; trustee Coll. of Idaho, 1980—, mem. exec. com., 1982—; bd. dirs. Boise Futures Found., 1981—, Univ./Community Health Scis. Assn., 1981—, Idaho Taxpayers Assn., 1983-85; chmn. Mayor's Select Com. on Downtown Devel., 1982-83. Named Exec. of Yr., Boise chpt. Nat. Secs. Assn., 1978. Fellow Internat. Acad. Trial Lawyers, Am. Bar Found.; mem. ABA (ho. of dels. 1971—, chmn. ho. of dels. 1980-82, bd. govs. 1980-82, pres. Idaho 1986-87), Idaho State Bar (pres. 1971-72), Def. Research Inst. (state chmn. Pacific region 1978—), Idaho Assn. Def. Counsel (trustee 1966-69, pres. 1967-68), Internat. Assn. Ins. Counsel, Am. Bd. Trial Advocates, Assn. Trial Lawyers Am., Fourth Dist. Bar Assn. (pres. 1962-63), Nat. Conf. Bar Pres. (trustee 1974-76), Rocky Mountain Oil and Gas Assn. (chmn. Idaho legal com. 1978—). Clubs: Arid (dir. 1977-79), Hillcrest Country (bd. dirs. 1969-72)(Boise). Lodge: Rotary. General corporate, Insurance, Workers' compensation. Office: Moffatt Thomas Barrett & Blanton Suite 300 First Security Bank Bldg 9th and Idaho Sts Boise ID 83702

THOMAS, FREDERICK BRADLEY, lawyer; b. Evanston, Ill., Aug. 13, 1949; s. Frederick Bradley and Katherine Kitter (Bingham) T.; m. Elizabeth Maxwell, Oct. 25, 1975; children: Bradley Bingham, Stephens Maxwell, Rosa Macaulay. Bar: Ill. 1974. Law clk. to presiding justice U.S. Ct. Appeals (5th cir.), Montgomery, Ala., 1974-75; assoc. Mayer, Brown & Platt, Chgo., 1975-80, ptnr., 1981—. Mem. allocations com. United Way, Chgo., 1983—. Mem. ABA, Chgo. Council Lawyers. Republican. Episcopalian. General corporate, Banking, Contracts commercial. Home: 44 Brier St Winnetka IL 60093 Office: Mayer Brown & Platt 231 S LaSalle St Chicago IL 60604

THOMAS, GERARD, lawyer, pharmaceutical company executive; b. 1925; married. Student Harvard U., 1951; LL.B., Cornell U., 1951. Bar: N.Y. 1951, Mich. 1957. Sole practice, N.Y.C., 1951-56; with legal div. Upjohn Co., Kalamazoo, 1956—, sec., 1962-64, v.p., gen. counsel, dir., 1964—. General corporate. Office: Upjohn Co 7000 Portage Rd Kalamazoo MI 49001 *

THOMAS, GERARD FRANCES, lawyer; b. Natchitoches, La., Jan. 20, 1923; s. Gerard Francis and Essie (Herminghaus) T.; m. Mary Jean Swift, Feb. 10, 1946; children: Richard, Jeffrey, Robert, Patrick, Stephen, Gerard F. III, Marcia (dec.). BA, Northwest La. State U., 1943; LLB, La. State U., 1948. Bar: La. 1948, U.S. Ct. Appeals (5th cir.) 1948, U.S. Dist. Ct. (ea. and we. dists.) La. 1948. Sole practice Natchitoches, La., 1946—. Mem. Judiciary Com. La., New Orleans, 1983—. Served to 1st lt. USMCR, 1942-46, PTO. Mem. ABA, La. State Bar Assn. (chmn. COPR 1985—), Assn. Trial Lawyers Am., La. Trial Lawyers Assn. (pres. 1965), Am. Coll. Trial Lawyers. Democrat. Baptist. Avocations: fishing, sports. State civil litigation, Probate, Workers' compensation. Office: Thomas & Dunahoe 137 Trudeau St Natchitoches LA 71457

THOMAS, HOWARD BERKELEY, lawyer; b. Berkeley, Calif., Apr. 26, 1912; s. Samuel David and Jessie Belle (Gartner) T.; m. Betty Macaulay, June 11, 1938; children—Elizabeth Thomas Burton, Jeanne Thomas Dickerson, Barbara Thomas Brereton. B.A., U. Calif., Berkeley, 1933, J.D., 1936. Bar: Calif., 1936, Fresno County, 1940, U.S. Supreme Ct., 1968. Assoc. McCutchen, Olney, Mannon & Greene, San Francisco, 1936-38; assoc. atty. Pub. Works Adminstrn., San Francisco, 1938-39; ptnr. Thomas, Snell, Jamison, Russell, Williamson & Asperger, Fresno, Calif., 1939—; vis. lectr. U. Calif.-Berkeley, 1956-58. Mem. Fresno County Bar Assn. (dir. 1958), Calif. State Bar (vice-chmn. com. taxation 1959-62), ABA, U. Calif.-Berkeley Alumni Assn. (trustee 1969-71), Phi Beta Kappa, Order of Coif, Delta Theta Phi, Pi Sigma Alpha. Christian Scientist. Clubs: Sunnyside Country, San Joaquin Country, Fresno Downtown. Assoc. editor California Law Rev., 1935-36. Estate planning, Estate taxation, Personal income taxation. Home: 4821 N Wishon St Fresno CA 93704 Office: PO Box 1461 Fresno CA 93716

THOMAS, JAMES GLADWYN, lawyer; b. Akron, N.Y., Oct. 5, 1901; s. James Robinson and Fannie (Wilder) T.; m. Helen H. Herrick, Aug. 19, 1925; children: Carol (Mrs. William Brigham), (dec.), Lott H. A.B., U. Ill., 1923, J.D., 1928. Bar: Ill. 1928. Asst. dean men U. Ill., 1923-28; since practiced in Champaign; of counsel Thomas, Mamer & Haughey and (predecessor firms), 1946—; part-time prof. law U. Ill. Coll. Law, 1947-65; past dir., v.p. Champaign Asphalt Co., Reliable Plumbing and Heating Co., Sandwells, Inc.; hon. dir. First Nat. Bank of Champaign. Past pres. YMCA, Community Chest, War Chest.; Past bd. dirs. Ill. Bar Found.; past dir., pres. U. Ill. Found.; past pres., bd. dirs. Carle Hosp. Found. Fellow Am. Bar Found.; mem. ABA (ho. dels. 1956), Ill. Bar Assn. (bd. govs. 1941-58, v.p. 1953-56, pres. 1956-57), Am. Law Inst., Am. Judicature Soc., Am. Coll. Probate Counsel, Sigma Chi. Republican. Episcopalian. Estate planning, Probate, Estate taxation. Home: 2015 Duncan Rd Champaign IL 61821 Office: Thomas Mamer & Haughey 30 Main St Champaign IL 61820

THOMAS, JAMES JOSEPH, II, lawyer; b. Allentown, Pa., May 17, 1951; s. James Joseph and Charlene Marie (Beiter) T. B.A., Coll. William and Mary, 1973, J.D., 1976. Bar: Ga. 1976, U.S. Dist. Ct. (no. dist.) Ga. 1976, U.S. Ct. Appeals (5th, 11th cirs.) 1976. Assoc. Long & Aldridge, Atlanta, 1976-81, ptnr., 1982—, mng. ptnr., 1984. Editor-in-chief William and Mary Law Rev., 1975-76. Recipient Weber Diploma for top law student, William and Mary Law Sch., 1976. Mem. Atlanta Council Younger Lawyers (chmn. juvenile ct. com. 1983-84), ABA, Assn. Trial Lawyers Am., Ga. Trial Lawyers Assn., Atlanta Bar Assn. Clubs: West Paces Racquet, Lawyers, Atlanta City (Atlanta). Federal civil litigation, State civil litigation. Home: 2392 DeFoors Ferry Rd Atlanta GA 30318 Office: Long Aldridge & Norman 134 Peachtree St Suite 1900 Atlanta GA 30043

THOMAS, JAMES TALBERT, IV, lawyer; b. Greenwood, Miss., Mar. 28, 1951; s. James Talbert III and Betty (Johnson) T.; m. Martha Ross, June 12, 1982; 1 child, Emily Herron. BBA, U. Miss., 1973, JD, 1976; LLM in Taxation, NYU, 1977. Bar: Miss. 1976, U.S. Dist. Ct. (no. dist.) Miss. 1976, U.S. Ct. Appeals (5th cir.) 1981. Sr. acct. Deloitte, Haskins & Sells, N.Y.C., 1977-78; assoc. Smith Barney, Harris Upham, N.Y.C., 1978-80; ptnr. Magruder, Montgomery, Brocato & Hosemann, Jackson, Miss., 1980—. Bd. dirs. Epilepsy Found. Miss., Jackson, 1982—. Mem. ABA, Miss. Bar Assn., Hinds County Bar Assn., Am. Inst. CPAs, Miss. Soc. CPAs. Republican. Episcopalian. Avocations: tennis, hunting, skiing. Corporate taxation, Real property, Probate. Office: Magruder Montgomery Brocato & Hosemann 1800 Deposit Guaranty Plaza Jackson MS 39201

THOMAS, JAMES WILLIAM, lawyer; b. N.Y.C., May 12, 1949; s. Howard and Alice (Brennan) T.; m. Cecilia Coleman Goad, July 7, 1973; children—James William Jr., Brennan McKinney. B.S., U. Dayton, 1971; J.D., Ohio No. U., 1974. Bar: Ohio 1974, U.S. Dist. Ct. Ohio 1976. Ptnr., Earley & Thomas, Eaton, Ohio, 1974—; village solicitor Village of Lewisburg (Ohio), 1977-81, Village of Verona (Ohio), 1979-81; asst. pros. atty. Preble County (Ohio), 1980-81. Mem. Community Improvement Corp., Eaton. Mem. Preble County Bar Assn. (pres. 1982-84). Republican. Roman Catholic. Club: Eaton Country. Lodge: Rotary (dir. 1980—). Avocations: boating; tennis. State civil litigation, Family and matrimonial, Personal injury. Home: 761 Vinland Cove Eaton OH 45300 Office: Earley & Thomas 112 N Barron St Eaton OH 45320

THOMAS, JOHN ARLYN, lawyer; b. Malad, Idaho, May 12, 1955; s. Frank Carson and Faye (Jones) T.; m. Vickie Servoss, Aug. 3, 1973 (div. Apr. 1983); children: Clinton John, Mary Jaclyn; m. Kimberly René Wallace, Jan. 21, 1984. BA summa cum laude with departmental honors, Coll. Idaho, 1977; JD, Brigham Young U., 1981. Bar: Utah 1981, U.S. Dist. Ct. Utah 1981, Wyo. 1982, U.S. Dist. Ct. Wyo. 1982. Assoc. Phillips & Lancaster P.C., Evanston, Wyo., 1981-84; ptnr. Phillips, Lancaster & Thomas P.C., Evanston, 1984—. Vice chmn. Bd. Adjustment, Evanston, 1984—; mem. planning and zoning commn., Evanston., 1985—. Mem. ABA, Utah Bar Assn., Wyo. Bar Assn. (3d jud. dist.), Uinta County Bar Assn., Wyo. Trial Lawyers Assn. Republican. Mormon. Avocations: racquetball, skiing, golf, softball. Consumer commercial, Family and matrimonial, Personal injury. Office: Phillips Lancaster & Thomas PC PO Drawer E Evanston WY 82930

THOMAS, JOHN CHARLES, state supreme court justice; b. Norfolk, Va., Sept. 18, 1950; s. John and Floretta V. (Sears) T.; m. Pearl Walden, Oct. 9, 1982; children: John Charles, Ruby Virginia. B.A. with distinction in Am. Govt., U. Va., 1972, J.D., 1975. Bar: Va. 1975, U.S. Dist. Ct. ea. and we. dists 1976, U.S. Ct. Appeals 4th cir. 1976, U.S. Supreme Ct. 1979, U.S. Ct. Appeals D.C. cir. 1980. Law clk. civil rights div. Dept. Justice, Washington, summer 1973; law clk. Gibson, Dunn & Crutcher, Los Angeles, summer 1974; mem. staff spl. council to pres. and legal advisor to rector and visitors U. Va., Charlottesville, 1973-74, 74-75; assoc. Hunton & Williams, Richmond, Va., 1975-82, ptnr., 1982-83; justice Supreme Ct. of Va., Richmond, 1983—. Mem. Gov.'s Commn. of Future of Va.; former mem. bd. dirs. Leadership Met. Richmond; operating bd. Met. Econ. Devel. Council, Richmond. Mem. Va. State Bar (former mem. 3d dist. com.), Va. Bar Assn. (law sch. liaison), Bar Assn. City of Richmond, Old Dominion Bar Assn. (former mem. exec. com.), U. Va. Alumni Assn., Omega Psi Phi. Judicial administration. Office: Supreme Ct Va PO Box 1315 Richmond VA 23210 *

THOMAS, JOHNNY WESLEY, lawyer, army reserve officer; b. Wichita, Kans., Aug. 15, 1952; s. John Wesley and Louise Elizabeth (Whitcomb) T.; m. Pamula Jean Williams, Aug. 7, 1976; 1 child, John. B.S., Pittsburg State U., 1974; J.D., U. Kans., 1977. Bar: Kans. 1977, Tex. 1980, U.S. Dist. Ct. Kans. 1977, U.S. Ct. Mil. Appeals 1977, U.S. Supreme Ct. 1984. Legal aid atty. U. Kans., 1977; commd. capt. U.S. Army, 1977; chief of legal assistance Korea, 1982-83; chief of claims, Ft. Bliss, Tex., 1984, USAR,. Named Disting. Mil. Grad., Pittsburg State U., 1974. Mem. ABA, Assn. Trial Lawyers, Tex. Bar Assn., Kans. Bar Assn., Alpha Phi Alpha, Omicron Delta Kappa, Phi Alpha Theta, Kappa Delta Pi. Democrat. Episcopalian. Criminal, Military, Personal injury.

THOMAS, JOSEPH EDWARD, lawyer; b. Atlantic City, N.J., June 4, 1955; s. George Lewis and Annabelle (Murphy) T.; m. Susan Marie Rutten, Oct. 2, 1982. BA, Lehigh U., 1977; LLB, Pepperdine U., 1981. Bar: Calif. 1981, U.S. Dist. Ct. (cen. dist.) Calif. 1981, U.S. Ct. Appeals (9th cir.) 1982. Jud. extern U.S. Dist. Ct. (cen. dist.), Los Angeles, 1980; assoc. Lawler, Felix & Hall, Los Angeles, 1981-85, Pettit & Martin, Costa Mesa, Calif., 1985—; gen. counsel Thomas Co., Atlantic City, 1981—; bd. dirs. Devinwood Corp., Los Angeles. Mem. ABA, Calif. Bar Assn., Orange County Bar Assn., Los Angeles County Bar Assn. Republican. Roman Catholic. Clubs: Lincoln (Orange County); Town Hall (Los Angeles). Banking, Federal civil litigation, Trademark and copyright. Home: 432 Nyes Pl Laguna Beach CA 92651 Office: Pettit & Martin 3200 Park Center Dr Suite 1110 Costa Mesa CA 92626

THOMAS, JOSEPH WINAND, lawyer; b. New Orleans, Aug. 2, 1940; s. Gerald H. and Edith Louise (Winand) T.; children: Jeffery J., Anthony W., Anne E.; m. Shawn B. Watkins, May 26, 1986. BS, Loyola U., Chgo., 1967; JD, Loyola U., New Orleans, 1973; MBA, Tulane U., 1984. Bar: La. 1973, D.C. 1980. Staff atty. New Orleans Legal Assistance Corp., 1973-74; asst. atty. gen. of La., 1974-80; sole practice, New Orleans, 1980—; dir. New Orleans Legal Assistance Corp. Mem. Louis Martinet Legal Soc., ABA, New Orleans Bar Assn., La. Bar Assn., NAACP. Democrat. Roman Catholic. Personal injury, Civil rights, State civil litigation. Office: 729 Camp St New Orleans LA 70130

THOMAS, LOWELL SHUMWAY, JR., lawyer; b. Phila., Aug. 9, 1931; s. Lowell Shumway and Josephine (McVey) T.; m. Judith Evans, Aug. 27, 1955; children: Megan E., Heather McVey, Lowell S., Taylor G. BA, Dartmouth Coll., 1953; JD, U. Pa., 1960. Bar: Pa. 1961, U.S. Tax Ct. 1961, U.S. Dist. Ct. (ea. dist.) Pa. 1961, U.S. Ct. Appeals (3d cir.) 1961. Assoc. Duane, Morris & Heckscher, Phila., 1960-64; assoc. Saul, Ewing, Remick & Saul, Phila., 1965-68, ptnr., 1968—; bd. dirs. Del. Valley-York, Inc. , Chestnut Hill Acad., Phila., 1978-86; bd. dirs. Southeastern Pa. ARC, 1975-82, chmn., 1983-86; trustee Beaver Coll. 1987—; mem. Eastern Ops. Office adv. council, 1980-83. Author: Taxation of Marriage, Separation and Divorce, 1986. Served to lt. USN, 1953-57. Fellow Am. Coll. Tax Counsel; mem. ABA, Pa. Bar Assn., Phila. Bar Assn., Phila. Bar Found. (trustee 1980-83), Am. Law Inst. Republican. Episcopalian. Clubs: Cricket, Union League (bd. dirs. 1979-82, treas. 1981-82). Corporate taxation, Personal income taxation, Pension, profit-sharing, and employee benefits. Address: 38th Floor Centre Sq W Tower Philadelphia PA 19102

THOMAS, MICHAEL ELI, lawyer; b. Indpls., Aug. 9, 1948; s. Lazarus Eli Thomas and Patricia Brodnax; m. Susan Renee Odegard, Aug. 5, 1972; children: Nicole Renee, Jack Odegard. BS in Indsl. Engring., Gen. Motors Inst., 1971; JD, Detroit Coll. Law, 1975. Bar: Mich. 1975, U.S. Dist. Ct. (ea. dist.) Mich. 1975, U.S. Tax Ct. 1986, U.S. Supreme Ct. 1986. Engr., supr. Buick Motor Div., Flint, Mich., 1966-76; sole practice Flint, 1976—. Bd. deacons South Bapt. Ch., Flint, 1977—; chmn. trustees Bapt. Children's Home, St. Louis, Mich., 1977-85. Mem. Mich. Assn. Christian Schs. (bd. dirs. 1983—). Republican. Probate, General corporate, Church - state. Office: G-3200 Beecher Rd Flint MI 48504

THOMAS, MICHAEL TRACY, lawyer; b. Atchison, Kans., Dec. 18, 1941; s. Richard Carl and Dorothy Olene (Tracy) T.; m. Barbara Englert, Jan. 26, 1974 (div. Dec. 1978); m. Sheridan Strickland, Mar. 19, 1983. Student, Cornell U., 1959-60; AB, U. Kans., 1963; LLB, Harvard U., 1966; LLM, Georgetown U., 1968. Bar: Va. 1966, Md. 1970, U.S. Supreme Ct. 1970, Alaska 1971, U.S. Dist. Ct. Alaska 1972, U.S. Ct. Appeals (9th cir.) 1974. Assoc. Robertson, Monagle, Eastaugh & Bradley, Juneau, Alaska, 1971-73; ptnr., dir. Robertson, Monagle & Eastaugh, Juneau and Anchorage, Alaska, 1973—. Mem. Draft Bd., Juneau, 1972-75; assemblyman Mcpl. Assembly, Juneau, 1974-76; bd. dirs. Juneau Arts and Humanities Council, 1977-79, Alaska Serving and Caring, Juneau, 1972-74; trustee Pacific Legal Found., 1986—. Served to maj. U.S. Army, 1966-71. Fellow Am. Bar Found.; mem. ABA, Alaska Bar Assn., Juneau Bar Assn. (pres. 1979-80). Democrat. Presbyterian. Clubs: Washington Athletic (Seattle), Petroleum (Anchorage, Alaska). Avocations: political biographies, model trains. Federal civil litigation, State civil litigation, Insurance. Office: Robertson Monagle & Eastaugh 550 W 7th Ave Suite 1200 Anchorage AK 99501

THOMAS, NORMAN ALLAN, lawyer; b. Norfolk, Va., Sept. 18, 1956; s. William Edward Jr. and Norma Elizabeth (Taylor) T.; m. Sandra Lee Peterson, Mar. 26, 1983; 1 child, Wesley Allan. BA in Govt. and Econs., U. Va., 1978; JD, Coll. William and Mary, 1981. Bar: Va. 1981, U.S. Dist. Ct. (ea. dist.) Va., U.S. Ct. Appeals (4th cir.). Assoc. Crenshaw, Ware & Johnson, Norfolk, 1981-83; asst. atty. Commonwealth of Va., Norfolk, 1983-85; research asst. Va. Ct. Appeals, Norfolk, 1985-86; asst. atty. City of Norfolk, 1986—. Methodist. Local government, Civil rights, State civil litigation. Office: Office of City Atty 908 City Hall Bldg Norfolk VA 23501

THOMAS, PATRICIA ANN, lawyer, artist; b. Burkesville, Ky., Oct. 11, 1952; d. Homer J. and Jewell (Williams) T. BA, Western Ky. U., 1974, BFA, 1975, MEd, 1978; JD, Chase Coll. Law, 1982. Bar: Ky. 1982. Sole practice Burkesville, 1982—. Works represented in pvt. art collections. Pres. Cumberland County Literacy Council, Burkesville, 1986—; mem. Dem. Club Cumberland County, 1970—. Mem. ABA, Ky. Bar Assn., Burkesville C. of C. (bd. dirs. 1983—, oil festival com. 1983—). Democrat. Mem. Ch. of Christ. Avocations: fishing, scuba diving, arts and creative scis., rose growing. Oil and gas leasing, General practice, State civil litigation. Office: Smith Sterns Bldg PO Box 37 Pub Sq Burkesville KY 42717

THOMAS, PATRICK POWERS, lawyer; b. Shreveport, La., Sept. 13, 1933; s. George Dewey and Marjorie Elizabeth (Powers) T.; m. Genevieve Fay Zahn, Dec. 28, 1958; 1 son, Patrick Andrew. B.S., Engr. Petroleum Geology, Colo. Sch. Mines, Golden, 1955; J.D., St. Mary's U., San Antonio, 1968. Bar: Tex. 1968, U.S. Dist. Ct. (we. dist.) Tex. 1970. Assoc. Dibrell, Gardner & Dotson, San Antonio, 1968-70, Masters, Gardner & Assocs., San Antonio, 1970-71; fed. estate and gift tax atty. IRS, 1971-72; staff atty. Tesoro Petroleum Corp., San Antonio, 1972-86; gen. counsel Taco Cabana Inc., 1986—; mem. environ. law com. Am. Petroleum Inst. Active boys clubs; lay minister Roman Catholic Ch. Served to 1st lt. C.E., AUS, 1959. Mem. ABA, Tex. Bar Assn., San Antonio Bar Assn. Amateur painter in watercolor and oil. Environment, Oil and gas leasing, General corporate. Home: 3309 San Pedro San Antonio TX 78212

THOMAS, RICHARD ENGLISH, lawyer; b. Macon, Ga., Jan. 18, 1951; s. Albert D. and Juanita (Crowe) T.; m. Yvonne Baker, Oct. 9, 1982; children: Richard Jr., Jennifer. BS, Auburn U., 1973; JD, Woodrow Wilson Coll., 1980; cert., Nat. Coll. Dist. Atty.'s, 1984. Bar: Ga. 1980, U.S. Dist. Ct. (no. dist.) Ga. 1980, U.S. Ct. Appeals (11th cir.) 1981, U.S. Dist. Ct. (mid. dist.)

Ga. 1982. Chief asst. dist. atty. Cordele (Ga.) Jud. Cir., 1981-85; sole practice Cordele, 1985—. Mem. ABA, Ga. Bar Assn., Cordele Cir. Bar Assn., Ga. Trial Lawyers Assn., Nat. Assn. Criminal Def. Lawyers, Ga. Assn. Criminal Def. Lawyers. Criminal, Personal injury, Workers' compensation. Home: PO Box 5101 Cordele GA 31015 Office: 213 S 7th ST Cordele GA 31015

THOMAS, RICHARD IRWIN, lawyer; b. Pitts., Jan. 28, 1944; s. Donald Martin and Mary Jane (Smith) T.; m. Karen Rose Sorg, July 31, 1966 (dec. Aug. 1979); children: Amy, Joe, Mike, Jim, Mauri, Mark, John. Student, Georgetown U., 1961-62; BA, W.Va. Wesleyan Coll., 1965; JD, Duquesne U., 1972. Bar: Pa. 1972, U.S. Dist. Ct. (we. dist.) Pa. 1972, U.S. Ct. Appeals (3d cir.) 1974, U.S. Dist. Ct. (ea. dist.) Pa. 1976, U.S. Supreme Ct. 1977, U.S. Ct. Appeals (6th cir.) 1981. Asst. personnel mgr. Continental Can Co., Pitts., 1966; mgr. labor relations U.S. Steel Corp., Pitts., 1966-72; ptnr. Thorp, Reed & Armstrong, Pitts., 1972—; adj. prof. Duquesne U., Pitts., 1974-76; jud. mgr. Allegheny County Common Pleas Ct., Pitts., 1985; bd. dirs. Gen. Roofing Co., Bridgeville, Pa. Coach Upper St. Clair (Pa.) Athletic Assn., 1977-85; firefighter Upper St. Clair (Pa.) Vol. Fire Co., 1977-84. Named one of Outstanding Young Men in Am., 1973. Mem. ABA, Pa. Bar Assn., Allegheny Bar Assn. Republican. Roman Catholic. Avocations: skiing, white water rafting, golf, athletics. Labor, Federal civil litigation, State civil litigation. Home: 287 McMurray Rd Upper Saint Clair PA 15241 Office: Thorp Reed & Armstrong 1 Riverfront Center Pittsburgh PA 15222

THOMAS, RICHARD VAN, state justice; b. Superior, Wyo., Oct. 11, 1932; s. John W. and Gertrude (McCloskey) T.; m. Lesley Arlene Ekman, June 23, 1956; children: Tara Lynn, Richard Ross, Laura Lee, Sidney Marie. B.S. in Bus. Adminstrn. with honors, U. Wyo., 1954, LL.B. with honors, 1956; LL.M., NYU, 1961. Bar: Wyo. 1956, U.S. Ct. Appeals (10th cir.) 1960, U.S. Supreme Ct. 1960. Law clk. to judge U.S. Ct. Appeals 10th Circuit, Cheyenne, 1960-63; asso. firm Hirst & Applegate, Cheyenne, 1963-64; partner firm Hirst, Applegate & Thomas, Cheyenne, 1964-69; U.S. atty. Dist. Wyo., Cheyenne, 1969-74; justice Wyo. Supreme Ct., Cheyenne, 1974-85, chief justice, 1985-86. Pres. Laramie County United Way, 1972, trustee, 1973-74, chmn. admissions and allocations com., 1968-69, chmn. exec. com., 1973, chmn. combined fed. campaign, 1974; bd. dirs. Goodwill Industries Wyo., Inc., 1974-77; exec. com. Cheyenne Crusade for Christ, 1974; v.p., exec. com. Wyo. Billy Graham Crusade, 1987; bd. dirs. Cheyenne Youth for Christ, 1978-81; chancellor Episcopal Diocese of Wyo., 1972—, lay dep. gen. conv., 1973—, chmn. search evaluation nomination com., 1976-77, lay reader, 1969—; bd. dirs. Community Action of Laramie County, 1977-82; chmn. Cheyenne dist. Boy Scouts Am., 1977-78, mem. nat. council, 1982—, mem. Longs Peak council, 1977—, v.p. membership relationships, 1979-81, pres., 1981-83; mem. North Cen. Region Exec. Bd., 1986—; chmn. Laramie County Health Planning Com., 1980-84. Served with JAGC USAF, 1957-60. Named Boss of Year, Indian Paintbrush chpt. Nat. Secs. Assn., 1974; Civil Servant of Year, Cheyenne Assn. Govt. Employees, 1973; Vol. of Yr., Cheyenne Office, Youth Alternatives, 1979; recipient St. George Episcopal award, 1982, Silver Beaver award Boy Scouts Am., 1985. Mem. Am., Laramie County bar assns., Wyo. State Bar, Phi Kappa Phi, Omicron Delta Kappa, Sigma Nu. Clubs: Kiwanis (Cheyenne) (program com. 1969-70, dir. 1970-72, chmn. key club com. 1973-76, disting. pres. 1980-81), Masons (Cheyenne) (33 deg., past master); Shriners; Nat. Sojourners (Cheyenne). Office: Supreme Ct Bldg Cheyenne WY 82001

THOMAS, RITCHIE TUCKER, lawyer; b. Cleve., Aug. 12, 1936; s. Myron F. and Marjorie (Ritchie) T.; m. Elizabeth Mary Melck, Jan. 31, 1964; children: Christopher, Andrew. BA, Cornell U., 1959; JD, Case-Western Res. U., 1964. Bar: Ohio 1964, U.S. Dist. Ct. (no. dist.) Ohio 1964, U.S. Ct. Appeals (D.C. 1971, U.S. Ct. Appeals (fed. cir.) 1973, U.S. Ct. Internat. Trade 1976, U.S. Ct. Appeals (9th cir.) 1985. Assoc. office of gen. counsel U.S. Tariff Commn., Washington, 1964-67; assoc. Squire, Sanders & Dempsey, Cleve., 1967-69, Cox, Langford & Brown, Washington, 1969-74; ptnr. Squire, Sanders & Dempsey, Washington, 1974—; mem. exec. com. Meridian House Internat., Washington, 1977—, bd. dirs. Contbr. articles to profl. jours. Recipient various book award West Pub. Co., 1964. Mem. Fed. Bar Assn., Ohio Bar Assn., D.C. Bar Assn., Order of Coif. Private international, General corporate, Banking. Home: 6629 Elgin Ln Bethesda MD 20817 Office: Squire Sanders & Dempsey 1201 Pennsylvania Ave NW Washington DC 20004

THOMAS, ROBERT ALLEN, lawyer, cons.; b. Balt., Feb. 11, 1951; s. Robert Willis and Mildred Mary (Dooms-Hargis) T. B.A., Allegheny Coll., 1973; M.Ed., Howard U., 1974; J.D., New Eng. U., 1977. Bar. Pa. 1977. Mem. staff U.S. Congress, 1973-75; legis. analyst taxation com. Mass. Ho. of Reps., 1975-77; sole practice, Meadville, Pa., 1977—; counsel Samuel T. Pees & Assocs., 1980—; dir. Amex Internat. Ltd., 1981—. Author: Ni Sekai Aida, 1986; contbr. articles to profl. publs. Bd. dirs. Martin Luther King, Jr. Scholarship Fund, 1982—; bd. dirs. Northwestern Legal Services Corp., 1980—, treas., 1982—, chmn. budget, personnel and fin. com., 1982—. Recipient Harry S. Truman Found. award, 1975. Mem. ABA, Pa. Bar Assn., Crawford County Bar Assn., NEA, Pa. State Edn. Assn., ACLU, NACCP. Democrat. Anglican. Oil and gas leasing, General corporate, General practice. Address: 310-312 Chestnut St Meadville PA 16335

THOMAS, ROBERT BOYCE, lawyer, military officer; b. Charlotte, N.C., Feb. 1, 1952; s. Robert Boyce and Jean Victoria (Gibbon) T.; m. Alice Ann Harding, June 15, 1974; children: Audrey Corbin, Jean Campbell. BS, U.S. Naval Acad., 1974; JD, Georgetown U., 1981. Bar: Va. 1981, U.S. Ct. Appeals (4th cir.) 1981, U.S. Ct. Mil. Appeals 1984. Commd. ensign USN, 1974, advanced through grades to lt. comdr., 1981; div. officer USS Lexington USN, Pensacola, Fla., 1974-77; plans and policy action officer, recruiting command USN, Alexandria, Va., 1977-78; counsel trial/def. naval legal service office USN, Jacksonville, Fla., 1981-83, officer in charge naval legal service trial def. activity, 1983-84, exec. officer naval legal trial def. activity, 1984-85; staff judge adv. naval air test ctr. and naval air sta. USN, Patuxent, Md., 1985—; bd. dirs. Cedar Point Fed. Credit Union, Lexington Park, Md. Mem. ABA, Va. Bar Assn. (criminal law sect.), U.S. Navy Acad. Alumni Assn. Democrat. Methodist. Avocations: running, sailing, canoeing. Criminal, Military, Jurisprudence. Home: Rt 3 112 Keith Ct Hollywood MD 20636 Office: Legal Office Naval Air Sta Patuxant River MD 20670-5409

THOMAS, ROBERT PAIGE, lawyer; b. Columbus, Ohio, July 31, 1941; s. Charles Marion and Elsie (Cavanaugh) T.; m. Sara Cason, Aug. 31, 1962; children—Paige Cason, Park Cavanaugh. B.A., Vanderbilt U., 1963, M.A., 1965, J.D., 1970. Bar: Tenn. 1970, U.S. Dist. Ct. (mid. dist.) Tenn. 1970, U.S. Ct. Appeals (6th cir.) 1977. Assoc. Boult, Cummings, Conners & Berry, Nashville, 1970-74, ptnr., 1974—, mng. ptnr., 1977-84. Mem. ABA, Tenn. Bar Assn., Nashville Bar Assn. Democrat. Episcopalian. Clubs: Yale of N.Y.C.; Belle Meade Country, Cumberland, Nashville City. Real property, Labor, General corporate. Office: 222 3d Ave N PO Box 198062 Nashville TN 37219

THOMAS, ROBERT WESTON, lawyer; b. Lapeer, Mich., May 11, 1950; s. Fillmore and Brunhilde (Schmidt) T.; m. Mary Ellen Meyers, Aug. 23, 1975; children—M. Ryan, Colleen A., Emily M. B.A., Albion Coll., 1971; J.D., Wayne State U., 1975. Bar: Mich. 1975, U.S. Dist. Ct. (ea. and we. dists.) Mich. 1976. Law clk. Mich. Ct. Appeals, Lansing, 1975-76; sole practice, Lapeer, 1976-83, 86—; mem. Thomas & Hable, Lapeer, 1983-86; v.p., sec., dir. Fillmore Thomas & Co., Inc., Lapeer, 1971—. Treas. Lapeer County Reps., 1983-86; mem. Lapeer unit Am. Cancer Soc., 1978-84; mem. Citizens Adv. Council, Oakdale Ctr., 1978-79. Mem. ABA, State Bar Mich., Lapeer County Bar Assn. (sec. 1978-86, pres. 1986-87). Episcopalian. Clubs: Lapeer Rotary (treas. 1984—), Lapeer County Players (treas. 1983-86). General practice, Consumer commercial, Family and matrimonial. Home: 310 Hickory Ln Lapeer MI 48446 Office: 396 Hickory Ln Lapeer MI 48446

THOMAS, RONALD JAMES, lawyer; b. Buffalo, Nov. 21, 1942; s. Edward and Genevieve (Kucia) T.; m. Joanne Rose Peloso, July 11, 1965; children: Ronald Jr., Elizabeth, David. BA, SUNY, Buffalo, 1964, JD, 1967. Bar: N.Y. 1967, Conn. 1973. Assoc. Jarvis & Pilz, N.Y.C., 1967-72; asst. gen. counsel Burndy Corp., Norwalk, Conn., 1972-81; gen. counsel Hattori (Seiko), N.Y.C., 1981—. Elected rep. Darien Town Meeting, 1974; bd. dirs. Norwalk Symphony, 1973; legal assistance program Norwalk Community Coll., 1979-81. Mem. ABA, Assn. of Bar of City of N.Y., N.Y. State Bar Assn., Conn. Bar Assn., Am. Corp. Counsel Assn. (bd. dirs. 1985—, founding pres. N.Y.C. chpt. 1984-86), Westchester Fairfield Corp. Counsel Assn. (pres. 1978). Clubs: N.Y. Athletic, Roton Point Sailing Assn. Avocations: sailing, tennis, amateur radio. General corporate, Private international. Home: 26 Red Rose Circle Darien CT 06820 Office: Hattori (Seiko) Corp Am 640 5th Ave New York NY 10019

THOMAS, SHERYL LYNN, lawyer; b. Birmingham, Ala., July 8, 1952; d. James Quinton and Sara Jo (Sherrill) T.; m. Henry Allen Leeper, May 20, 1986. BA in English, Trinity U., 1974; JD, St. Mary's U., 1980. Bar: Tex. 1981. Sole practice San Antonio, 1981—. Mem. ABA, Tex. Bar Assn., San Antonio Bar Assn. Real property, Contracts commercial. Office: 217 Alamo Plaza Suite 300 San Antonio TX 78205

THOMAS, STEPHEN ALLEN, lawyer; b. Harrisburg, Pa., Dec. 26, 1950; s. George William and Marian Estelle (McCarthy) T.; m. Margrit Else Cromwell, Jan. 1, 1979. BA, U. Pa., 1971; JD summa cum laude, U. Ariz., 1976. Bar: Ariz. 1976, U.S. Dist. Ct. Ariz. 1976, U.S. Ct. Appeals (9th cir.) 1976, U.S. Supreme Ct. 1979. Assoc. Bilby & Shoenhair P.C., Tucson, 1976-81, ptnr., 1982—; lectr. Nat. Bus. Inst., Eau Claire, Wis., 1985—. Fellow Ariz. Bar Found.; mem. ABA, Ariz. Bar Assn., Pima County Bar Assn., Order of Coif. Democrat. Bankruptcy. Office: Bilby & Shoenhair PC One S Church 15th Floor PO Box 871 Tucson AZ 85702-0871

THOMAS, WAYNE LEE, lawyer; b. Tampa, Sept. 22, 1945; s. Willard McSwain and June Frances (Jones) T.; m. Patricia H., Mar. 16, 1968; children—Brigitte Elisabeth, Kate Adelaide. B.A., U. Fla., 1967, J.D. cum laude, 1971. Bar: Fla., 1971, U.S. Supreme Ct., 1975, U.S. Ct. Appeals (5th cir.), 1975, U.S. Ct. Appeals (11th cir.), 1981, U.S. Ct. Claims 1976, U.S. Dist. Ct. (mid. dist.) Fla., 1973, U.S. Dist. Ct. (so. dist.) Fla., 1975. Law clk. U.S. Dist. Ct. (mid. dist.) Fla., 1971-73; assoc. Trenam, Simmons, Kemker, Scharf, Barkin, Frye & O'Neill, P.A., Tampa, 1973-77, ptnr., 1978-81; founder, mem. McKay & Thomas, P.A., Tampa, 1981—. Mem. Fla. Bar (chmn. sect. gen. practice, mem. ethics com., bd. bar examiners 1986—), ABA, Assn. Trial Lawyers Am., Am. Judicature Soc., Hillsborough County Bar Assn. (chmn. grievance com. 1985-86), Order of Coif, Fla. Blue Key, Phi Kappa Phi, Omicron Delta Kappa. Democrat. Federal civil litigation, State civil litigation, Contracts commercial. Office: One Harbour Place St #720 Tampa FL 33602

THOMAS, WILLIAM BRINKER, coast guard officer, lawyer; b. Thermopolis, Wyo., Oct. 22, 1947; s. William Charles and Virginia Ruth (Nyswander) T.; m. Barbara Tousley, June 5, 1976; children: Rachel Nyswander, Rebecca Tousley. B.S., USCG Acad., 1970; J.D. cum laude, U. Miami, Coral Gables, Fla., 1977; LL.M. in Admiralty, Tulane U., 1983. Bar: Fla. 1977, U.S. Ct. Mil. Appeals. Commd. ensign USCG, 1970, advanced through grades to comdr., 1985; deck watch officer USCGC Cutter RUSH, San Francisco/Vietnam, 1970-72; asst. readiness officer 13th Coast Guard Dist., Seattle, 1972-74; asst. legal officer 1st Coast Guard Dist., Boston, 1977-80; asst. chief investigations dept. Coast Guard Marine Insp. Office, New Orleans, 1980-83; sr. asst. legal officer 8th Coast Guard Dist., New Orleans, 1983-85; trial atty. Civil Div., Admiralty Sect., U.S. Dept. Justice, Washington, 1985-87; chief legal adminstrn. div. Coast Guard Hdqrs., Washington, 1987—. Trustee adminstrv. bd. Gretna United Meth. Ch., Gretna, La., 1984. Recipient Disting. Service award (mil. officer's category) Fed. Bus. Assn., 1983. Mem. ABA, Assn. Trial Lawyers Am., Maritime Law Assn. of U.S. (assoc.), Delta Theta Phi (pres. 1976-77). Admiralty, Administrative and regulatory, Military. Home: 10511 Acacia Ln Fairfax VA 22032 Office: Commandant G-LLA USCG 2100 2d St SW Washington DC 20593-0001

THOMAS, WILLIAM GRIFFITH, lawyer; b. Washington, Nov. 1, 1939; s. Henry Phineas and Margaret Wilson (Carr) T.; m. Suzanne Campbell Foster, June 7, 1960. Student Williams Coll., 1957-59, Richmond Coll., 1960; J.D., U. Richmond, 1963. Bar: Va. 1963. Mem., pres. Thomas & Fiske, P.C., Alexandria, Va., 1976—; dir. Perpetual Am. Fed. Savs. and Loan Assn., McLean, Va. Sec., Va. Democratic party, 1968-70, chmn., 1970-72. Mem. ABA, Am. Law Inst., Am. Coll. Real Estate Lawyers, Va. State Bar Assn., Alexandria Bar Assn. Legislative, Real property, Contracts commercial. Home: 217 S Fairfax St Alexandria VA 22313 Office: 510 King St Suite 200 Alexandria VA 22314

THOMAS, WILLIAM HARROLD, lawyer; b. Danville, Ill., Apr. 5, 1913; s. Thomas Joseph Jr. and Ethel Margaret (Turner) T.; m. Charlotte L. Harris, Jan. 20, 1947; children: Thomas J. III, William H. Jr., Elizabeth A. Thomas Sherwood, Robert H., James D. BA, Northwestern U., Evanston, Ill., 1933; JD, Northwestern U., Chgo., 1936. Bar: Ill. 1936, U.S. Dist. Ct. (so. dist.) Ill. 1939. Assoc. Thomas D. Huff, Chgo., 1936-37; ptnr. Chapman & Thomas, Alton, Ill., 1937-42; sole practice Alton, 1946-60; ptnr. Thomas, Mottaz & Eastman, Alton, 1960-84, Thomas, Mottaz, Eastman & Sherwood, Alton, 1984—. Vice pres. Boy Scout Council, Alton, 1942-86; pres. Alton Meml. Hosp., 1952-86; bd. dirs. Alton Community Unit Sch. Bd., 1961-71. Served to capt. U.S. Army, 1942-46, ETO. Decorated Purple Heart; recipient Silver Beaver award Boy Scouts Am., 1963, Health Care Leadership award St. Louis area Hosp. Assn., 1978, Citation of Achievement Am. Protestant Hosp. Assn., 1982. Mem. ABA, Ill. Bar Assn., Madison County Bar Assn., Alt-Wood Bar Assn. (pres. 1941-42). Republican. Methodist. Lodge: Kiwanis (lt. gov. 1947-48, pres. Alton chpt. 1940-41). General practice, Health, Probate. Home: 421 Belleview Ave Alton IL 62002 Office: Thomas Mottaz Eastman & Sherwood 307 Henry St PO Box 940 Alton IL 62002

THOMAS, WILLIAM SCOTT, lawyer; b. Joliet, Ill., Aug. 16, 1949; s. William Edward and Audrey Ann (Johnson) T.; m. Carolyn Smith Cotter, Aug. 10, 1974; children: Derek Cotter, Kimberley Cotter. AB, Stanford U., 1971; JD, U. Calif., San Francisco, 1974; LLM in Taxation, Golden Gate U., 1981. Bar: Calif. 1975, U.S. Dist. Ct. (no. dist.) Calif. 1975, U.S. Tax Ct. 1982. Tax editor Internat. Bur. Fiscal Documentation, Amsterdam, Holland, 1974-75; tax atty. Chevron Corp., San Francisco, 1975-77; from assoc. to ptnr. Brobeck, Phleger & Harrison, San Francisco, 1978—; bd. dirs. Value Line Inc., N.Y.C. Mem. ABA (taxation sect.), Calif. Bar Assn. (exec. com. 1984—, chmn. 1987—). Probate, Personal income taxation, State and local taxation. Office: Brobeck Phleger & Harrison Spear St Tower One Market Plaza San Francisco CA 94105

THOMASCH, ROGER PAUL, lawyer; b. N.Y.C., Nov. 7, 1942; s. Gordon J. and Margaret (Molloy) T. BA, Coll. William and Mary, 1964; LLB, Duke U., 1967. Bar: Conn. 1967, Colo. 1974. Assoc. atty. Cummings & Lockwood, Stamford, Conn., 1967-70; trial atty. U.S. Dept. Justice, Washington, 1970-73; ptnr. Roath & Brega, Denver, 1975-87, Ballard, Spahr, Andrews & Ingersoll, Denver, 1987—; vis. assoc. prof. of law Drake U. Sch. Law, Des Moines, 1973-74; frequent lectr. in field, U.S. and Can.; co-dean comml. litigation program of Atla Nat. Advanced Coll. of Advocacy, 1982-86; adj. faculty mem. U. Denver Coll. Law, 1976-80. Recipient Leland Forrest Outstanding Prof. award, Drake U. Sch. Law, 1973. Mem. ABA, Colo. Bar Assn., Assn. Trial Lawyers Am. (nat. chmn. comml. litigation sect. 1981-82), Colo. Trial Lawyers Assn. (bd. dirs. 1981-86, chmn. comml. litigation sect. 1978-79). Clubs: University, Denver Athletic, Tournament Players (Denver). Federal civil litigation, State civil litigation, Antitrust. Office: Ballard Spahr Andrews & Ingersoll 17th St Plaza Bldg 1225 17th St Suite 2300 Denver CO 80202

THOMASHOWER, WILLIAM JAY, lawyer; b. N.Y.C., Mar. 22, 1949; s. Sidney and Dorothy (Fisch) T.; m. Barbara Ann Liebig, Aug. 29, 1975; 1 child, Charles Franklin. BS in Mech. Engring., Columbia U., 1970, JD, 1973. Bar: N.Y. 1974, U.S. Dist. Ct. (ea. and so. dists.) N.Y. 1974, U.S. Ct. Appeals (2d cir.) 1975, U.S. Supreme Ct. 1977, U.S. Patent Office 1985. Assoc. Kaye, Scholer, Fierman, Hayes & Handler, N.Y.C., 1974-82, Fitzpatrick, Cella, Harper & Scinto, N.Y.C., 1982-85; ptnr. Kaplan, Thomashower & Landau, N.Y.C., 1985—. Bd. dirs. Lawyers Com. for Enforcement Animal Protection Law, N.Y.C., 1981—. Harlan Fiske Stone scholar Columbia U., 1972-73. Mem. ABA (various sects.), N.Y. State Bar Assn., Assn. of Bar of City of N.Y. (vice chmn. profl. and jud. ethics com. 1986-87), N.Y. Patent, Trademark & Copyright Law Assn., Trial Lawyers Assn. (U.S. internat. trade com.). Antitrust, Federal civil litigation, Patent. Office: Kaplan Thomashower & Landau 747 3d Ave New York NY 10017

THOMASON, CHARLES LEE, lawyer; b. Morganfield, Ky., Sept. 3, 1950; s. Ben Thomas and Lucy (Spalding) T.; m. Susan P., Aug. 30, 1980; 1 child, Charles Lee. BA, U. Ky., 1977, JD, 1980. Bar: Ky. 1980, N.J. 1982, U.S. Ct. Appeals (6th cir.) 1982, U.S. Patent Ct. 1984, U.S. Ct. Appeals (3rd cir.) 1984. Law clk. to chief judge U.S. Dist. Ct., Lexington, Ky., 1980-82; ptnr. Evans, Osborne & Kreizman, Red Bank, N.J., 1982—. Served to sgt. USMC, 1971-75. Democrat. Roman Catholic. Avocations: graphic arts, tennis. Federal civil litigation, Patent, Environment. Office: Evans Osborne & Kreizman One Harding Rd Red Bank NJ 07701

THOMASON, JOHN JOSEPH, lawyer; b. St. Louis, July 28, 1929; s. Joseph Jefferson and Clara (Galyean) T.; m. Sally Palmer, June 24, 1956; children: Jeffery, Palmer, Susan. LLB, U. Tenn., 1952. Bar: Tenn. 1952, U.S. Dist. Ct. (we. dist.) Tenn. 1952, U.S. Ct. Appeals (8th cir.) 1967, U.S. Supreme Ct. 1971, U.S. Ct. Appeals (6th cir.) 1952. Assoc. E.W. Hale, Jr., Memphis, 1955-56; ptnr. Nelson, Norvell, Wilson & Thomason, Memphis, 1956-67, Thomason, Hendrix, Harvey, Johnson, Mitchell, Blanchard & Adams, Memphis, 1967—. Pres. Boys' Clubs of Memphis, 1977, Memphis Arts Council, 1979. Served to capt. JAGC, U.S. Army, 1952-55. Recipient Ira Samuelson Jr. award Boys' Clubs of Memphis, 1980, Law Week award Memphis County and Shelby County Bar Assn., 1967, Teaching Excellence award U. Tenn., 1984. Fellow Am. Bar Found, Am. Coll. Trial Lawyers; mem. ABA (life, chmn. gen. practice sect. 1979), Internat. Assn. Def. Counsel. Republican. Presbyterian. Club: University (Memphis). Avocations: sailing, hiking, bicycling, tennis. Federal civil litigation, State civil litigation, Insurance. Home: 351 Riverbluff Pl Memphis TN 38103 Office: 1st Am Bank Bldg 44 N 2d St Memphis TN 38103

THOMPSON, ANNE ELISE, U.S. dist. judge; b. Phila., July 8, 1934; d. Leroy Henry and Mary Elise (Jackson) Jenkins; m. William H. Thompson, June 19, 1965; children: William H., Sharon A. B.A., Howard U., 1955, LL.B., 1964; M.A., Temple U., Phila., 1957. Bar: D.C. bar 1964, N.J. bar 1966. Staff atty. Office of Solicitor, Dept. Labor, Chgo., 1964-65; asst. dep. public defender Trenton, N.J., 1967-70; mcpl. prosecutor Lawrence Twp., Lawrenceville, N.J., 1970-72; mcpl. ct. judge Trenton, 1972-75; prosecutor Mercer County, Trenton, 1975-79; U.S. dist. judge Dist. of N.J., Trenton, 1979—; vice chmn. Mercer County Criminal Justice Planning Com., 1972; mem. com. criminal practice N.J. Supreme Ct., 1975-79, mem. com. mcpl. cts., 1972-75; v.p. N.J. County Prosecutors Assn., 1978-79; chmn. juvenile justice com. Nat. Dist. Attys. Assn., 1978-79. Del. Democratic Nat. Conv., 1972. Recipient Assn. Black Women Lawyers award, 1976, Disting. Service award Nat. Dist. Attys. Assn., 1979, Gene Carte Meml. award Am. Criminal Justice Assn., 1980, Outstanding Leadership award N.J. County Prosecutors Assn., 1980, John Mercer Langston Outstanding Alumnus award Howard U. Law Sch., 1981; also various service awards; certs. of appreciation. Mem. Am. Bar Assn., Fed. Bar Assn., N.J. Bar Assn., Mercer County Bar Assn. Democrat. Office: US Court House 402 E State St PO Box 401 Trenton NJ 08608 *

THOMPSON, BEVERLY KAY, lawyer; b. Mason City, W.Va., July 5, 1952; d. Elvin Eugene and Mary Eileen (Case) T.; 1 child, Andrew William. BA in English and Music, Ohio State U., 1974; postgrad., Capital U., 1974-76, Mich. State U., 1975; JD, Widener U., 1979. Bar: Pa. 1979, N.J. 1979, U.S. Dist. Ct. (ea. dist.) Pa. 1979, U.S. Dist. Ct. N.J. 1979, U.S. Ct. Appeals (3d cir.) 1979, U.S. Supreme Ct. 1979. Ptnr. Segal & Thompson P.A., Phila. and Haddonfield, Pa., 1980-82; sole practice Phila. and Cherry Hill, N.J., 1982-86; mng. ptnr. Thompson, Laureda & Bosch, Phila. and Haddonfield, 1986—; bd. dirs. 1st Fin. Corp., Phila. Mem. ABA, Pa. Trial Lawyers Assn., N.J. Bar Assn., Phila. Bar Assn. (civil rights com. 1981-84, profl. responsibility com. 1982-85, fee dispute com. 1982-85), Assn. Trial Lawyers Am., Pa. Trial Lawyers Assn. (fee dispute com. 1982—). Democrat. Presbyterian. Civil rights, Federal civil litigation, Labor. Office: Thompson Laureda & Bosch 100 N 17th St 5th Floor Philadelphia PA 19103

THOMPSON, CHARLES MURRAY, lawyer; b. Childress, Tex., Oct. 13, 1942; s. Walter Lee and Lois S. (Sheehan) T.; m. Charlotte Ann McKay, June 13, 1970; children: Murray McKay, McLean Ann. BS with honors, Colo. State U., 1965; JD cum laude, U. S.D., 1969. Bar: S.D., U.S. Ct. Appeals (8th cir.), U.S. Supreme Ct. Ptnr. May, Adam, Gerdes & Thompson, Pierre, S.D., 1969—; bd. dirs. Nat. Jud. Coll., Reno, Nev., 1984—, treas. 1986—; speaker at trial lawyer and state bar seminars. Editor S.D. Law Rev., 1969. Pres. S.D. Council Sch. Attys., 1984-86. Fellow Am. Bar Found.; mem. ABA (ho. of dels. 1978—, bd. govs. 1983-86, net adv. commn. 1984—, exec. com. of bd. govs. 1985-86, com. on rules and calendar 1986—, com. on meetings and travel 1986—), State Bar S.D. (pres. young lawyers sect. 1974-75, pres. 1986-87), Assn. Trial Lawyers Am., Am. Bd. Trial Advs., Am. Counsel Assn., S.D. Trial Lawyers Assn. (pres. 1980-81), Jackrabbit Bar Assn. (chancellor 1981-82), Am. Judicature Soc. (bd. dirs. 1981-85), Nat. Conf. of Bar Pres.'s (exec. council 1986—. Democrat. Lodges: Kiwanis (pres. local club 1977), Elks. Avocations: Flying; sailing; ranching. General practice, State civil litigation, Insurance. Home and Office: PO Box 160 Pierre SD 57501

THOMPSON, CLIFF F., lawyer, educator; b. Kansas City, Mo., Aug. 15, 1934; s. James Frederick and Grace Caroline T.; m. Judith Anne Phillips, June 23, 1957; children: James Frederick, Laura Marie, John Phillips, Hannah Caroline. A.B. magna cum laude, Harvard U., 1956, J.D., 1960; M.A. (Rhodes scholar), Oxford U., Eng., 1958. Bar: Kans. 1960. Asst. program officer Near East and Africa program Ford Found., N.Y.C., 1960-61; law lectr., dir. Sudan Law Project, U. Khartoum, Sudan, 1961-65; assoc. dir., co-founder Africa Law Center, Columbia U., 1965-66; co-founder, sr. lectr. law sch. U. Zambia, 1966-68; dean, prof. law Haile Selassie I U., Ethiopia, 1969-73; prof. law So. Meth. U., Dallas, 1973-77; prof. law, dean Law Sch., U. Hawaii, 1977-78, Coll. Law, U. Idaho, 1978-83, U. Wis. Law Sch., 1983—; cons. legal edn., Ethiopia, Sudan, Uganda, Tanzania, Kenya, Zambia. Author: Land Law of the Sudan, 3 vols., 2d edit, 1979; founder: Zambia Law Reports, 1969, African Law Digest, 1965; contbr. articles to law jours. Bd. dirs. Hawaii Legal Aid, 1977-78, Idaho Law Found., 1978-83, Four Lakes Council, Boy Scouts Am., 1984—. Fulbright grantee to Africa, 1983. Mem. ABA, Explorers Club, Phi Beta Kappa, Phi Kappa Phi. Democrat. Methodist. Clubs: Rotary, Signet. Office: U Wis Law Sch Office of Dean Madison WI 53706

THOMPSON, DAVID F., lawyer; b. Chgo., Oct. 19, 1942; s. Charles F. and Helen (Enright) T.; m. Monica McAleer, Dec. 15, 1973; children—Megan, Kristin. B.S., Loyola U., Chgo., 1965, M.S. in Indsl. Relations, 1966; J.D., Northwestern U., 1969. Bar: Ill. 1970, U.S. Dist. Ct. (no. dist.) Ill. 1970. Assoc., McDermott, Will & Emery, Chgo., 1969-72; asst. v.p. First Nat. Bank of Chgo., 1972-77; ptnr. Daleiden, Thompson & Tremaine, Ltd. and predecessors, Chgo., 1977—. Mem. ABA, Ill. State Bar Assn. Pension, profit-sharing, and employee benefits, General corporate, General practice. Home: 1529 E Course Dr Riverwoods IL 60015 Office: Daleiden Thompson & Tremaine Ltd 20 N Wacker Dr Chicago IL 60606

THOMPSON, EARL G(EORGE), lawyer; b. Chgo., Oct. 7, 1943; s. Earl Joseph and Mary Adeline (Tewksbury) T.; children: Richard Albert, Andrew Peter. BA, Yale U., 1964; JD, Harvard U., 1967. Bar: N.Y. 1969, U.S. Tax Ct. 1970. Sole practice N.Y.C. and Chgo., 1967—. Contbr. articles to profl. jours. Mem. Nat. Arts Club, Sno-Cat Ski Club. Club: Yale (Chgo.). International tax. Home: 121 Walton St Barrington IL 60010

THOMPSON, EDMONSTONE FIELD, lawyer; b. St. Louis, Mar. 15, 1912; s. Guy Atwood and Susan (Alexander) T.; m. Lida Lee Christy, June 1, 1940; children—Lida Lee Thompson Lloyd, Edmonstone Field, Tandy Christy Thompson Smith; m. Margaret Mathews Jenks, June 12, 1958; m. LaMay Capen, May 12, 1967; stepchildren—Laura Garesche Haffenreffer, Richard Louis Garesche. A.B., Yale U., 1934; LL.B., Harvard U., 1937. Bar: Mo. 1937, U.S. dist. ct. (ea. dist.) Mo. 1937, U.S. Sup. Ct. 1958. Assoc. Thompson, Mitchell, Thompson & Young, St. Louis, 1937-51, ptnr. 1951-60; ptnr. Thompson, Walther, Gaebe & Frank, St. Louis, 1960-81, Lewis & Rice, St. Louis, 1981—; dir. Childress Investment Co., St. Albans Farms, Inc. Bd. dirs. St. Louis Symphony Soc., 1946—, also mem. exec. com., sec. Served to lt. USN, 1942-46, to comdr. Res. (ret.). Mem. ABA, Met. St. Louis Bar Assn. Democrat. Presbyterian. Clubs: St. Louis Country, Noonday (St.

Louis). General corporate, Probate. Home: 939 Winterwood Ln Saint Louis MO 63124 Office: 611 Olive St Suite 1400 Saint Louis MO 63101

THOMPSON, EDWARD FRANCIS, lawyer, municipal judge; b. Yonkers, N.Y., Aug. 29, 1953; s. Edward Francis and Mary Francis (Keating) T. BA, Manhattanville Coll., 1975; JD, U. Puget Sound, 1978. Bar: Wis. 1978, U.S. Dist. Ct. (ea. and we. dists.) Wis. 1978, U.S. Ct. Claims 1980, U.S. Ct. Appeals (7th cir.) 1980, U.S. Supreme Ct. 1982. Legal intern Puget Sound Legal Assistance Found., Tacoma, Wash., 1976-78; assoc. Hammett, Williams, Riemer & Thompson and predecessor Hammett, Williams & Riemer, Delavan, Wis., 1978-80, ptnr., 1980-84; mcpl. judge Town of Delavan, 1983—; ptnr., v.p. Clair Law Offices, Delavan, 1984—; atty. chmn. Wis. Patients Compensation Panel, 1982-84. Bd. dirs. Delavan-Darien Sch. Dist. Found., 1982—, pres., 1983—. Mem. ABA, Assn. Trial Lawyers Am., Wis. Bar Assn., Walworth County Bar Assn. (v.p. 1984-85, pres. 1985-86), Wis. Acad. Trial Lawyers, Wis. Mcpl. Judges Assn., Walworth County Judges Assn. Personal injury, State civil litigation, General practice. Home: 311 Holig Ln Rt 4 Box 638 Delavan WI 53115 Office: Clair Law Offices SC 617 E Walworth Ave Delavan WI 53115

THOMPSON, EUGENE CEBRON, III, lawyer; b. Warsaw, N.C., Feb. 15, 1936; s. Eugene Cebron and Lydia (Briscoe) T.; m. Mary Sue Kennedy, Mar. 30, 1969; children: Eugene Cebron IV, Kennedy Lee. AB in Econs., U. N.C., 1959; JD, Wake Forest U., 1966. Bar: N.C. 1966. Ptnr. Thompson & Ludlum, Warsaw, 1966—. Served to capt. USMC, 1959-63. Mem. ABA, N.C. Bar Assn. (sec., treas. 1971-72), Duplin County Bar Assn. (v.p. 1969), Am. Trial Lawyers Assn., N.C. Trial Lawyers Assn., N.C. Mcpl. Attys. Assn. (bd. dirs. 1973-75, v.p. 1976, state pres. 1977). Democrat. Methodist. Avocations: snow skiing, handball, tennis, swimming, coaching. Personal injury, State civil litigation, Family and matrimonial. Home: 705 Forrest Rd Warsaw NC 28398 Office: Thompson & Ludlum 109 W Hill St Warsaw NC 28398

THOMPSON, FRANCES HOENE, lawyer; b. Emporia, Kans., Apr. 20, 1954; d. David D. and Joan P. (Lacey) Hoene; m. William W. Thompson Jr., May 24, 1980; children: Abraham E., Morgan P. BA in Lit. and Communication, Marquette U., 1976; JD, U. Idaho, 1981. Bar: Idaho 1981, U.S. Dist. Ct. Idaho 1981. Assoc. Rines & Thompson, Moscow, Idaho, 1981-83, Law Offices William W. Thompson Jr., Moscow, 1983—; hearing officer Health & Welfare Support Enforcement, Moscow, 1985. Mem. ABA, Idaho Bar Assn., Latah County Bar Assn. Episcopalian. Probate, Family and matrimonial, General practice. Office: Law Offices William W Thompson Jr 116 E 3d St Suite 201 Moscow ID 83843

THOMPSON, FRANK J(OSEPH), lawyer; b. N.Y.C., Feb. 2, 1932; s. Francis P. and Margaret (Burns) T.; m. Mary-Ellen Rand, Jan. 2, 1965; children—Elizabeth, Frank P., Patricia, Susan, Ruth. B.S.E.E., Loyola U., Los Angeles, 1954, J.D., Georgetown U., 1960. Bar: D.C. 1960, Conn. 1968, U.S. Ct. Appeals (D.C. cir.) 1960, U.S. Ct. Appeals (2d cir.) 1971, U.S. Ct. Appeals (4th cir.) 1978, U.S. Ct. Appeals (fed. cir.) 1984, U.S. Dist. Ct. Conn. 1971, U.S. Dist. Ct. (so. dist.) N.Y. 1971, U.S. Patent Office, U.S. Supreme Ct. 1973. Electronic engr. Nat. Security Agy., Washington, 1956-59; electric engr. ACF Industries, Alexandria, Va., 1959-60; patent atty. gen. Electric Co., Syracuse, 1960-63; RCA, Princeton, N.J., 1963-64; Sylvania Electric, 1964-65; Perkin Electric Co., Norwalk, 1966-71; sole practice, Stamford, Conn., 1971—; lectr. Conn. Bar Assn.; hearing commr. Conn. Superior Ct., 1978—; arbitration panelist Am. Arbitration Assn. Served with USAF, 1954-56. Recipient Certs. of Commendation, Jud. Dept. Conn., 1979, 80, 81, 82, 83, 84, 85. Mem. ABA, Conn. Bar Assn., Stamford Bar Assn., Conn. Patent Law Assn. Trademark and copyright, Federal civil litigation, Patent. Home: 1090 Galloping Hill Rd Fairfield CT 06430 Office: 111 Prospect St Stamford CT 06901

THOMPSON, GORDON, JR., judge; b. San Diego, Dec. 28, 1929; s. Gordon and Garnet (Meese) T.; m. Jean Peters, Mar. 17, 1951; children—John M., Peter Renwick, Gordon III. Grad., U. So. Calif., 1951, Southwestern U. Sch. Law, Los Angeles, 1956. Bar: Calif. bar 1956. With Dist. Atty.'s Office, County of San Diego, 1957-60; partner firm Thompson & Thompson, San Diego, 1960-70; U.S. dist. judge So. Dist. Calif., San Diego, 1970-84, chief judge, 1984—. Bd. visitors U. San Diego. Mem. Am. Bd. Trial Advocates (treas.), ABA, San Diego County Bar Assn. (v.p. 1970), Delta Chi. Club: San Diego Yacht. Office: 940 Front St San Diego CA 92189

THOMPSON, HAROLD LEE, lawyer; b. Dayton, Ohio, Feb. 17, 1945; s. Harold Edward Thompson and Johnita Dorothy (Cox) Metcalf; m. Kathryn Lynn Coleman, Aug. 3, 1968 (div. May 1983); children: Aishah T., Aliya S. BA in Acctg., Cen. State U., Wilberforce, Ohio, 1967; JD, U. Conn., 1972. Bar: Ohio 1975, U.S. Dist. Ct. (so. dist.) Ohio 1975, D.C. 1976. Acct. Communication Satellite Corp., 1968-69; atty. Ohio State Legal Service, Columbus, Ohio, 1972-74; lawyer Ohio Indsl. Commn., Columbus, 1974-76; sole practice Columbus, 1976-84; ptnr. Jones & Thompson, Columbus, 1984—. Legal counsel Franklin County Rep. Club, Columbus, 1986—; mem. Ohio Rep. Council, Columbus, 1986—. Reginald Heber Smith fellow U.S. Fed. Ct., 1972; named one of Outstanding Young Men of Am., 1974. Mem. Ohio Bar Assn., Columbus Bar Assn., Assn. Trial Lawyers Am., Cen. State U. Alumni Assn. (chmn. scholarships com. 1986—), Columbus Area C. of C. Roman Catholic. Lodge: Masons. Avocations: reading, music. Personal injury, Federal civil litigation, Real property. Office: 65 E State St Suite 306 Columbus OH 43215

THOMPSON, JAMES GRANT, III, lawyer, business executive, consultant; b. Jackson, Miss., Dec. 20, 1938; s. James Grant and Jewel Elizabeth (Russell) T., II; m. Jane Corolyn Dearing, Sept. 9, 1961; children—Edith Elizabeth, Ellen Douglas, James Grant IV, Elizabeth Eads; m. 2d, Jacqueline Leslie Hartmann, Oct. 20, 1979. B.A., Miss. Coll., 1966, B.S., 1967; J.D., U. Miss., 1973. Bar: Miss. 1973, U.S. Dist. Ct. Miss., 1973. Practice, Pass Christian, Miss., 1973-82, Jackson, 1982-83, Gulfport, 1983—; cons. oil and gas field; pres. T.R. Inc.; pres., chief exec. officer Southeastern Entertainment Enterprises, Inc. Mem. Miss. Bar Assn., Miss. Assn. Petroleum Landmen, Assn. Trial Lawyers Am. Phi Alpha Delta. Presbyterian. Real property, Oil and gas leasing, Family and matrimonial. Home: 301 W Main St Carthage MS 39051 Office: 115-A N Pearl Carthage MS 39051

THOMPSON, JAY ALAN, lawyer; b. San Antonio, July 17, 1948; s. Noel Edgar and Eron Anne (Gafford) T.; m. Marilynn C. Thompson, June 27, 1970 (div. Feb. 1984); children: Alyssa, Angela; m. Helene A. Alt, May 26, 1984. BBA in Acctg., Tex. Tech U., 1970; JD, U. Tex., 1972. Bar: U.S. Dist. Ct. (we. and no. dists.), U.S. Supreme Ct. Asst. staff judge adv. USAF, San Antonio, 1972-76; regional counsel Am. Ins. Assn., Dallas, 1976-79; assoc. Winstead, McGuire, Dallas, 1979-81; regional counsel INA, Dallas, 1981-82; assoc. Roan & Gullahorn, Austin, Tex., 1982-85, Clark, Thomas, Winters, Austin, 1985—. Served to maj. USAFR, 1972—. Mem. Travis County Bar, Austin Young Lawyers Assn. Democrat. Methodist. Avocations: tennis, piano. Insurance, Legislative. Office: Clark Thomas et al PO Box 1148 Austin TX 78767

THOMPSON, JAYNE AUDREY, lawyer; b. Albert Lea, Minn., Aug. 19, 1939; d. John Blain and Harriet Ordella (Blume) Roberts; m. Paul L. Kuennemeier, Feb. 14, 1987; children—Theresa Brown, Laura Thompson, Jennifer Thompson. B.A., Hamline U., 1961; M.Ed., U. Minn., 1965; J.D., No. Ky. U., 1979. Bar: Ohio 1979. Tchr., U.S. Army Mil. Schs., Wuerzburg, W.Ger., 1962-63, St. Paul Pub. Schs., 1961-62, 63-65, Parkway Sch. Dist., St. Louis, 1965-66; tchr.'s aide U. Cin., Cin. Pub. Schs.; tchr. Wyoming (Ohio) Pub. Schs., 1966-68; substitute tchr. Lockland, Greenhills and Finneytown, Ohio, 1968-70; corp. atty. Eagle Savs. Assn., Cin., 1979; sole practice, Cin., 1980—, ptnr. Thompson, Pierce & Bendycki, Cin. Author: Changing Attitudes through Literature, 1965; editor: (TV tape) Around the World with Literature, 1964. Reader, Clovernook Home for Blind; trustee No. Hills Unitarian Ch.; pres. Cin. Unitarian Universalist Council; v.p. UN Info. Com.; mem. Met. Area Religions Coalition Council; co-leader Girl Scouts U.S.A.; mem. Finneytown PTA; mem. Citizens Com. on Justice and Corrections; mem. allocations bd. children's services United Appeal; bd. dirs. Mental Health Services N.W. Mem. ABA, Ohio Bar Assn., Cin. Bar Assn., Assn. Trial Lawyers Am., LWV. Republican. Clubs: Singletons, Cingles (treas.), Zonta. Bankruptcy, Criminal, Family and matrimonial. Home: 8393 Sailboat Ln Maineville OH 45039

THOMPSON, JEFFREY DALE, lawyer; b. Palm Springs, Calif., Feb. 1, 1957; s. Dale H. and Ione C. (Gill) T. BS in Commerce, Santa Clara U., 1978; JD, U. So. Calif., 1981. Bar: Calif. 1981, U.S. Dist. Ct. (cen. dist.) Calif. 1981, U.S. Ct. Appeals (9th cir.) 1981. Corp. counsel Am. Med. Internat., Beverly Hills, Calif., 1981—, asst. v.p., 1985—. Mem. ABA (forum com. health law), Los Angeles County Bar Assn., Nat. Eagle Scout Assn., Beta Gamma Sigma. Republican. Health, General corporate. Office: Am Med Internat 414 N Camden Dr Beverly Hills CA 90210

THOMPSON, JOHN WILSON, JR., lawyer; b. Buffalo, Apr. 29, 1946; s. John Wilson Sr. and Hilda (Ruff) T.; m. Nancy A. Schwab, July 27, 1974; children: Jessica L. Greiman, Erin Sue, John Wilson III. BA, U. Pitts., 1968, JD, 1971. Bar: U.S. Ct. Appeals (3d cir.) 1973, U.S. Supreme Ct. 1980. Assoc. Office D.W. Shoemaker, York, Pa., 1971-73; ptnr. Shoemaker & Thompson, York, 1973-76, Shoemaker, Thompson & Ness, York, 1976-82; sole practice York, 1982—; 1st asst. dist. atty. York County, 1986—, solicitor treas., 1974-78, solicitor recorder deeds, 1978-86; solicitor York City, 1974-78. Mem. exec. com. York County Reps., 1978—. Mem. ABA, Pa. Bar Assn. (ho. dels. 1986—), York County Bar Assn. (bd. dirs. 1976-80), Assn. Trial Lawyers Am., Pa. Trial Lawyers Assn. Avocations: raising Hereford cattle, bridge. Bankruptcy, State civil litigation, Personal injury. Home: RD 2 PO Box 50 Felton PA 17322 Office: 111 E Market St York PA 17401

THOMPSON, KATHERINE GENEVIEVE, lawyer; b. Bklyn., May 11, 1945; d. George Otway and Marie (Burke) T. BS, Good Counsel Coll., 1966; JD, Bklyn. Law Sch., 1970; LLM, NYU, 1981. Bar: N.Y. 1971, U.S. Dist. Ct. (so. and ea. dists.) N.Y. 1978, U.S. Supreme Ct. 1981. Editor Matthew Bender Pub. Co., N.Y.C., 1970-71; atty. juvenile rights div. Legal Aid Soc., N.Y.C., 1971-76, asst. atty. in charge juvenile rights div. N.Y. County office, 1976-77; sole practice N.Y.C., 1977-78; ptnr. Rothenberg, Sherman, Thompson & Halpin, N.Y.C., 1978-84, Sherman, Thompson & Halpin, N.Y.C., 1984—; mem. appellate div. 1st Dept. Screening Panel, 1981-82, appellate div. 1st Dept. Family Ct. Adv. Com., 1983-86, chmn., 1986—. Contbg. editor: Bender's Federal Practice Forms, 1971, Bender's Forms of Discovery, 1971. Bd. dirs. August Aichorn Resdl. Ctr., N.Y.C., 1979—. Fellow Am. Bar Found., N.Y. State Bar Found.; mem. ABA (family law sect.) N.Y. State Bar Assn. (spl. com. on juvenile justice 1980—, family law sect. 1980—), Assn. of Bar of City of N.Y. (family ct. and family law com. 1977-80, chmn. 1980-83, lectures and continuing edn. com. 1984-85, matrimonial law com. 1985—), Womens Bar Assn., N.Y. County Lawyers Assn. (family ct. com. 1978-79). Family and matrimonial, Banking, General practice. Office: Sherman Thompson & Halpin 19 W 44th St New York NY 10036

THOMPSON, KERRY LEWIS, lawyer; b. Scottsburg, Ind., Aug. 27, 1949; s. Walter Kenneth and Phyllis Anne (Bailey) T.; m. Janice Frances McCammon, Aug. 29, 1969; 1 child, Angela Jean. BS, Ind. U., New Albany, 1971; JD, Ind. U., Indpls., 1975. Bar: Ind. 1975, Ky. 1975, U.S. Dist. Ct. (so. dist.) Ind. 1975. Ptnr. Bonsett & Thompson, Scottsburg, Ind., 1975-78, Everitt, Houston & Thompson, Scottsburg, 1979—; lectr. Ind. U., New Albany, 1982. Prosecutor Scott County, Scottsburg, 1978-82; speaker Meth. Ch., Scottsburg, 1981-83. Mem. ABA, Ky. Bar Assn., Ind. Bar Assn., Scott County Bar Assn., Assn. Trial Lawyers Am. Democrat. Lodge: Lions (pres. 1979). Avocations: golf, fishing. Criminal, State civil litigation, Real property. Home: PO Box 394 Scottsburg IN 47170 Office: Everitt Houston & Thompson 49 E Wardell St Scottsburg IN 47170

THOMPSON, LARRY ANGELO, lawyer, producer, personal manager; b. Clarksdale, Miss., Aug. 1, 1944; s. Angelo and Anne (Tuminello) T.; m. Pamela Edwards, Dec. 15, 1974 (div.). BBA, U. Miss., 1966, JD, 1968. Bar: Miss. 1968, Calif. 1970. In-house counsel Capitol Records, Hollywood, Calif., 1969-71; sr. ptnr. in entertainment law Thompson, Shankman and Bond, Beverly Hills, Calif., 1971-77; pres. Larry A. Thompson Orgn., Inc., 1977—; co-owner New World Pictures, 1983-85; lectr. entertainment bus. UCLA, U. So. Calif., Southwestern U. Law Sch. Co-chmn. Rep. Nat. Entertainment Com.; apptd. by Gov. of Calif. to Calif. Entertainment Commn. Recipient Show Bus. Atty. of Yr. award Capitol Records, 1971. Served with JAGC, U.S. Army, 1966-72. Mem. ABA, Miss. Bar Assn., Calif. Bar Assn., Inter-Am. Bar Assn., Hon. Order Ky. Colonels, Am. Film Inst., Nat. Acad. Recording Arts and Scis. Republican. Roman Catholic. Author: How to Make a Record Deal & Have Your Songs Recorded, 1975, Prime Time Crime, 1982; producer: Jim Nabors TV Show, 1977 (Emmy nominee), (series) Mickey Spillane's Mike Hammer, 1981, Bring 'Em Back Alive, 1982, Mickey Spillane's Murder Me, Murder You, 1982, (TV movies) The Other Lover, 1985, Convicted, 1986, Intimate Encounters, 1986, (motion picture) Crimes of Passion, 1984. Entertainment. Home: 9451 Hidden Valley Pl Beverly Hills CA 90210 Office: 1440 S Sepulveda Blvd Suite 118 Los Angeles CA 90025

THOMPSON, LARRY RICHARD, university administrator, law educator; b. Dayton, Ohio, Oct. 15, 1947; s. Theodore Roosevelt and Helen Ruth (Casey) T.; m. Francie Helen Hinson, July 10, 1971 (div.); 1 child, Eric Stephen; m. Patricia Lynn Rowe, Feb. 4, 1984. B.A., Wittenberg U., 1969; M.S., Calif. State U.-Los Angeles, 1973; J.D. summa cum laude, Ohio State U., 1976. Bar: Ohio 1976, U.S. Supreme Ct. 1980. Dir. fin. aid Wilmington Coll., Ohio, 1970-75; assoc. Vorys, Sater, Seymour & Pease, Columbus, Ohio, 1976-81; spl. asst. to pres., adj. prof. law Ohio State U., Columbus, 1981—. Vice chmn. editorial bd. Jour. Coll. and Univ. Law, 1986—. Mem. ex officio, bd. dirs. Friends of WOSU, Columbus, 1983—. Mem. Nat. Assn. Coll. and Univ. Attys. (rep. exec. bd. 1984—, chmn. sect. governance and accountability 1981-86, chmn. pubs. com. 1986—), Inst. Econ. and Social Dialogue (bd. dirs.), ABA, Ohio State Bar Assn., Columbus Bar Assn., C. of C. Central Ohio (task force for econ. devel. 1984), Order of Coif. Avocations: jogging, travel, reading. Home: 2533 Bryden Rd Columbus OH 43209 Office: Ohio State U 190 N Oval Mall Columbus OH 43210

THOMPSON, LAWRENCE BIGELOW, lawyer; b. N.Y.C., Mar. 29, 1936; s. D.G. Brinton and Anne (Bigelow) T.; m. Louise Blanchard, July 21, 1962; 1 dau., Elizabeth Barry. B.A., summa cum laude, Yale U., 1958; LL.B., Harvard, 1962. Bar: N.Y. 1963, Fla. 1980, U.S. Dist. Ct. (so. dist.) N.Y. 1965. Assoc. Emmet, Marvin & Martin, N.Y.C., 1962-69, ptnr., 1969—. Mem. ABA, N.Y. Bar Assn., N.Y.C. Bar Assn., Fla. Bar Assn., Phi Beta Kappa. Clubs: Union, Onteora, Downtown Assn. Probate, Estate taxation, Estate planning. Office: Emmet Marvin & Martin 48 Wall St New York NY 10005

THOMPSON, LEE BENNETT, lawyer; b. Miami, Indian Ter., Mar. 2, 1902; s. P.C. and Margerie Constance (Jackson) T.; m. Elaine Bizzell, Nov. 27, 1928; children: Lee Bennett, Ralph Gordon, Carolyn Elaine (Mrs. Don T. Zachritz). B.A., U. Okla., 1925, LL.B., 1927. Bar: Okla. 1927. Since practiced in Oklahoma City; spl. justice Okla. Supreme Ct., 1967-68; past sec., gen. counsel, dir. Mustang Fuel Corp. Past sec. Masonic Charity Found. Okla.; past pres. Okla. County chpt. ARC, past chmn. resolutions com. nat. conv.; founding mem. Dean's Council, Okla. U. Coll. Law. Served from capt. to col. AUS, 1940-46. Decorated Legion of Merit; recipient Distinguished Service citation U. Okla., 1971; Rotary Found. Paul Harris fellow. Fellow Am. Bar Found. (past Okla. chmn.), Okla. Bar Found., Am. Coll. Trial Lawyers (past Okla. chmn.); mem. Oklahoma City C. of C. (past bd. dirs.), Oklahoma City Jr. C. of C. (past pres.), U.S. Jr. C. of C. (past dir., v.p.), Oklahoma City Symphony Orch. (past dir.), Oklahoma City Community Fund (past dir.), ABA (del. 1972, past mem. com. law and nat. security, past mem. spl. com. on fed. ct. procedure), Okla. Bar Assn. (past mem. ho. dels., pres. 1972, Pres.'s award), Oklahoma County Bar Assn. (past pres. Jour. Record award), Okla. Bar Found. (trustee 1971-76, 81-84), U. Okla. Alumni Assn. (past mem. exec. com.), U. Okla. Meml. Student Union (past pres., Greek Alumnus of Yr. award 1982), Oklahoma City Zool. Soc. (past bd. dirs.), Am. Judicature Soc., Mil. Order World Wars, Mil. Order Carabao, Am. Legion, Phi Beta Kappa (Phi Beta Kappa of Yr. 1982), Beta Theta Pi (past v.p., trustee). Democrat. Mem. Christian Ch. (past deacon, life elder). Clubs: Mason (Shriner, Jester, 33 deg.), Rotary (past pres.), University, Men's Dinner (past mem. exec. com.), Oklahoma City Golf and Country, Beacon. Federal civil litigation, Oil and gas leasing, Probate. Home: 539 NW 38th St Oklahoma City OK 73118 Office: 2120 First Nat Bldg Oklahoma City OK 73102

THOMPSON, MARY ANNE, lawyer; b. Mobile, Ala., Sept. 23, 1955; d. Paul Rossa and Mary Jeannette (Harrison) T. Student, Universite de Clermont-Ferrand, France, 1975; BA in Internat. Bus., Auburn U., 1977; JD, Cumberland Sch. Law, 1981. Bar: Ala., D.C. Spl. asst. to dir., exec. secretariat office of sec. Dept. of Transp., Washington, 1983-84, spl. asst. to adminstr. Urban Mass Transp. Adminstrn., 1984-85, atty., advisor Urban Mass Transp. Adminstrn., 1985; asst. gen. counsel office admistrn. The White House, Washington, 1986—; European tour leader Osborne Travel Service, 1978-80; internat. travel cons. Southern Progress Corp., 1981, atty. Reagan Compliance Fund, 1983. Asst. to campaign mgr. Com. to Elect Seldon for U.S. Senate, 1980; campaign mgr. Com. to Elect Elliott for Congress, 1982-83; group dir. for personnel and vol. ops. Presdl. Inaugural Com., 1984-85, com. chmn. Jr. League Washington; legal counsel Taste-of-the-South; mem. Hist. Alexandria Docents, U.S. Ski Ball Host Com., Rep. Women's Fed. Forum. Office: The White House Office of Adminstrn Office of Gen Counsel Room 480-OEOB Washington DC 20500

THOMPSON, MICHAEL, lawyer, economist; b. Des Moines, Aug. 2, 1951; s. Harold L. and Carolyn Annette (Yacinich) T.; m. Barbara Ann Haafke, Oct. 29, 1977 (div. Oct. 1984). B.A., U. No. Iowa, 1973; M.A., U. Iowa, 1976, J.D., 1975. Bar: Mo. 1980, N.Y. 1978, Iowa 1976, U.S. Ct. Appeals (2d cir.) 1980, U.S. Ct. Appeals (7th cir.) 1982, U.S. Ct. Appeals (D.C. cir.) 1982, U.S. Supreme Ct. 1984. Asst. atty. gen. Iowa Dept. Justice, Des Moines, 1976; economist Iowa Commerce Commn., Des Moines, 1976-77; spl. asst. to N.Y. Pub. Service Commn., Albany, 1977-80; commerce counsel Mo. Pacific R.R., St. Louis, 1980-83; atty. Southwestern Bell Corp., St. Louis, 1983—; pres., gen. counsel Law & Econs., Inc., St. Louis, 1983—; adj. instr. corp. fin. Drake U., Des Moines, 1977. State chmn. Iowa Coll. Young Republican Fedn., 1973. Mem. ABA, Am. Econ. Assn., N.Y. State Bar Assn., Met. St. Louis Bar Assn., Phi Alpha Delta. Republican. Clubs: Mo. Athletic (St. Louis); U.S. Yacht Racing Union; Island Bay Yacht (Springfield, Ill.). Administrative and regulatory, Federal civil litigation, State civil litigation. Office: Law and Econs Inc PO Box 577 Saint Louis MO 63188

THOMPSON, MICHEL ALLEN, lawyer; b. Trenton, Mo., May 2, 1948; s. Carl Theodore and Jo Ann (Lirley) T.; m. Alexa Lani Jones, Aug. 11, 1973; children: Lindsay, Ellen. BA with distinction, U. Mo., Kansas City, 1970; JD, Harvard U., 1973. Bar: Mo. 1973. From assoc. to ptnr. Gage & Tucker, Kansas City, Mo., 1973—. Pres., bd. regents Northwest Mo. State U., Maryville, 1985—; sec. Midlands Med. Rev. Plan Inc., Kansas City, Mo., 1983—; bd. alternate Mid-Am. Coalition on Health Care Inc., Kansas City, Mo., 1982—. Mem. ABA (employee benefits subcom. tax sect.). Democrat. Pension, profit-sharing, and employee benefits. Home: 4219 Claymont Dr Kansas City MO 64116 Office: Gage & Tucker 2345 Grand Ave PO Box 23428 Kansas City MO 64141

THOMPSON, ORVAL NATHAN, lawyer; b. Shedd, Oreg., Nov. 29, 1914; s. Otto M. and Laura L. (Halverson) T.; m. Jessie Mila Jackson, Nov. 24, 1958 (dec. 1983); children—Kathleen Persons, Richard, Marion Wells. B.S., U. Oreg., 1935, J.D., 1937; LL.M., Northwestern U., 1939. Bar: Oreg., 1937, U.S. Ct. Appeals, 1949, U.S. Supreme Ct., 1945. Practiced, Albany, Oreg., 1938—, pres. firm Westherford, Thompson, Brickey & Quick, P.C., 1972—; dir. Citizens Valley Bank, 1956-86, Key Bank Oreg., 1986—; sec. Oreg. Metall. Corp., 1955—. Mem. Oreg. Ho. of Reps., 1941-42; mem. Oreg. Senate, 1947-50; legal advisor to gov. Oreg., 1957-58. Served to lt. USN, 1942-46. Mem. ABA, Oreg. Bar Assn., Linn County Bar Assn., Albany Area C. of C., Phi Beta Kappa. Democrat. Presbyterian. Clubs: Masons, Springhill Country, Elks. Probate, General corporate, Estate planning. Home: 605 Erin Crest NW Albany OR 97321 Office: Weatherford Thompson Brickey & Quick PC 130 W 1st Ave PO Box 667 Albany OR 97321

THOMPSON, PATRICK ALAN, lawyer; b. Danville, Ky., Jan. 31, 1949; s. Jasper Crowley and Dolly Clarke (Sanders) T.; m. Barbara Dee Poole, Aug. 15, 1970 (div. Jan. 1983); children: Chandler Poole, Hunter Clarke. BA, U. Ky., 1970, JD, 1973. Bar: Fla. 1973, Ga. 1976, U.S. Dist. Ct. (mid. dist.) Fla. 1974, U.S. Dist. Ct. (no. dist.) Ga. 1976, U.S. Ct. Appeals (3d and 4th cirs.) 1983, U.S. Ct. Appeals (5th and 11th cirs.) 1981. Assoc. Johnson, Motsinger, Trismen & Sharp, Orlando, Fla., 1973-75, Smith, Curris & Hancock, Atlanta, 1975—. Mem. ABA, Atlanta Bar Assn., Assn. Trial Lawyers Am., Order of Coif. Republican. Methodist. Club: Ansley Golf (Atlanta). Construction. Home: 3117 Vinings Ridge Dr Atlanta GA 30339 Office: Smith Curris & Hancock 233 Peachtree St NE Atlanta GA 30043

THOMPSON, PAUL BARKER, lawyer; b. Keene, N.H., Sept. 27, 1946; s. Theron Barker and Esther (Carr) T.; m. Elsa Jo Branch, Mar. 30, 1986. BA, Boston U., 1968; JD, U. Balt., 1976; LLM in Taxation, Georgetown U., 1979. Bar: Pa. 1976, D.C. 1977. Commd. lt. (j.g.) USN, 1969, advanced through grades to comdr., 1983; officer USN, Phila., 1970-76; judge advocate USN, Washington, 1976—. Mem. ABA, Fed. Bar Assn. Republican. Club: Army-Navy. Avocations: skiing, sailing. Military, Public international, Administrative and regulatory. Home: 120 6th St SE Washington DC 20003

THOMPSON, PETER RULE, lawyer; b. Cleve., Apr. 26, 1943; s. Allen Paul and Phyllis Gwendolyn (Clark) T.; m. Pamela Stufflebeme, Aug. 12, 1967; children—Christina, Peter Rule Jr. B.A., So. Meth. U., 1965, J.D., 1968. Bar: Tex. 1968, U.S. Dist. Ct. (no. dist.) Tex. 1972, U.S. Ct. Appeals (5th cir.) 1972, U.S. Supreme Ct. 1973. Asst. city atty. City of Dallas, 1970-74; sr. atty. Enserch Corp., Dallas, 1974-79; gen. atty. Dorchester Gas Corp., Dallas, 1979-82, gen counsel, chief legal officer, 1982-85; sole practice, Dallas, 1985—. Mem. Dallas Bar Assn., ABA. Presbyterian. Clubs: Brookhaven Country, DAC Country (Dallas). State civil litigation, General corporate, Oil and gas leasing. Office: 8300 Douglas Suite 800 Dallas TX 75225

THOMPSON, RALPH GORDON, judge; b. Oklahoma City, Dec. 15, 1934; s. Lee Bennett and Elaine (Bizzell) T.; m. Barbara Irene Hencke, Sept. 5, 1964; children: Lisa, Elaine, Maria. B.B.A., U. Okla., 1956, J.D., 1961. Bar: Okla. 1961. Ptnr. Thompson, Thompson, Harbour & Selph (and predecessors), Oklahoma City, 1961-75; judge U.S. Dist. Ct. (we. dist.) Okla., 1975—, chief judge, 1986—; mem. Okla. Ho. of Reps., 1966-70, asst. minority floor leader, 1969-70; spl. justice Supreme Ct. Okla., 1970-71; tchr. Harvard Law Sch. Trial Advocacy Workshop, 1983—; teaching judge U.S. Atty. Gen.'s Trial Advocacy Inst., 1981—. Republican nominee for lt. gov., Okla., 1970; chmn. bd. ARC, Oklahoma City, 1970-72; chmn. Midwestern area advisory council, 1973-74; pres. Okla. Young Lawyers Conf., 1965; mem. bd. visitors U. Okla., 1975-78; pres. bd. dirs. St. John's Episcopal Sch., Oklahoma City, 1977-79. Served to lt. USAF, 1957-60, col. Res. ret. Decorated Legion of Merit; named Oklahoma City's Outstanding Young Man, Oklahoma City Jaycees, 1967, Outstanding Young Oklahoman, Okla. Jaycees, 1968, Outstanding Fed. Trial Judge, Okla. Trial Lawyers Assn., 1980. Fellow Am. Bar. Found.; Mem. Nat. Conf. Fed. Trial Judges, Am. Bar Assn., Fed. Bar Assn., Okla. Bar Assn. (chmn. sect. internat. law and gen. practice 1974-75), Oklahoma County Bar Assn. (dir.), Jud. Conf. U.S. (com. on ct. adminstrn. 1981—), U. Okla. Dads' Assn. (pres. 1985-86), Order of Coif, Phi Beta Kappa (pres. Oklahoma City chpt. 1985-86), Beta Theta Pi, Phi Alpha Delta. Episcopalian. Club: Rotary (hon.). Jurisprudence. Office: US Courthouse Po Box 1996 Oklahoma City OK 73102

THOMPSON, RICHARD LEON, pharmaceutical company executive, lawyer; b. Rochester, N.Y., Dec. 5, 1944; s. Leslie L. and Marion (Cosad) T.; m. Catherine Jean Terry, July 6, 1974; children: Kristin Anne, Catherine Elizabeth. AB cum laude, SUNY, Albany, 1966; MA, Syracuse U., 1967; JD, Cath. U., 1975. Staff dir., counsel U.S. Ho. of Reps., Washington, 1973-78; dir. Abbott Labs., Washington, 1978-83; v.p. Squibb Corp., Washington, 1983—; chmn. legis. adv. com. Proprietary Assn., Washington, 1984. Mem. com. on changing enrollments Fairfax (Va.) County Pub. Sch., 1983-84, Supts. adv. com., 1984-85; chmn. legis. com. P.R. USA, 1985—. Served to capt. U.S. Army, 1969, Vietnam, with Res. 1968, 70. Named one of Outstanding Young Men of Am., Jaycees, 1976. Mem. ABA, D.C. Bar Assn. Club: Georgetown, City (Washington). Health, Trademark and copyright,

Legislative. Home: 1005 Woburn Ct McLean VA 22102 Office: Squibb Corp 655 15th St NW Suite 410 Washington DC 20005

THOMPSON, ROBERT THOMAS, lawyer; b. Pontiac, Ill., Jan. 25, 1930; s. McDuffie and Ivy (Slaughter) T.; m. Elaine Cheshire, Oct. 1, 1950; children: Robert Thomas, Randall C., David L. A.B., Emory U., 1950, J.D. with honors, 1952. Bar: Ga. 1951, S.C. 1964, D.C. 1973. Assoc., ptnr. Wilson, Branch, Barwick & Vandiver, Atlanta, 1952-64; sr. ptnr. Thompson, Mann & Hutson, Atlanta, Greenville, S.C., N.Y.C., Greensboro, N.C., Washington; lectr. Law Sch. Emory U.; mgmt. adv. U.S. Del. to Internat. Labor Orgn., 1970; mem., chmn. task force NLRB, 1974-77; mem. pub. Adminstrv. conf. U.S. Bd. vistors Emory U.; chmn. bd. advisors Furman U.; past trustee, past chmn. bd. advisors Buncombe St. United Methodist Ch. Contr. articles to profl. jours. Fellow Am. Bar Found.; mem. ABA, Fed. Bar Assn., U.S. C. of C. (past chmn. bd. dirs., past chmn. labor relations and bylaws coms.), State Bar Ga. (past pres. young lawyers sect., past bd. govs.), S.C. Bar Assn., S.C. State C. of C. (spl. counsel labor relations, adv. com. labor relations), Ga. State C. of C., Atlanta Bar Assn. (sec.-treas), Greenville Chamber Found (bd. dirs.). Clubs: Lawyer (Atlanta), Press (Atlanta), Commerce (Atlanta), Cherokee Town and Country (Atlanta); University (Washington), Metropolitan (Washington); Metropolitan (N.Y.C.); Bal Harbour (Fla.). Labor. Office: 2200 Daniel Bldg Greenville SC 29602

THOMPSON, STEPHEN DAVID, lawyer; b. Princeton, Ind., June 1, 1944; s. Donald John and Eva Jane (Davidson) T.; m. Maureen Brown, June 19, 1966; children: Andrew Brown, Ryan David, John Riley. AB, Hanover Coll., 1966; JD, Ind. U., 1971. Bar: Ohio 1972, U.S. Dist. Ct. (no. dist.) Ohio 1976, U.S. Ct. Appeals 1984. Assoc. Black, McCuskey, Souers & Arbaugh, Canton, Ohio, 1971-77, ptnr., 1977—. Pres., bd. dirs. Stark County Mental Health Clinic, Canton, 1975-80; trustee Downtown Canton YMCA, 1985-86. Served to capt. USMC, 1966-69, Vietnam. Mem. ABA, Ohio Bar Assn. (lectr. comml. law 1985), Stark County Bar Assn. (mem. exec. com. 1986—), Phi Alpha Delta, Phi Gamma Delta. Republican. Methodist. Avocations: ornithology, decoy carving, cycling. General corporate, State civil litigation, Bankruptcy. Home: 250 21st St NW Canton OH 44709 Office: Black McCuskey Souers & Arbaugh 220 Market Ave S Canton OH 44702

THOMPSON, STEPHEN LEE, lawyer; b. Charleston, Va., June 17, 1952; s. Kermit Lee and Wanda Lee (Carr) T.; m. Jean Beverly Namet, Nov. 22, 1980. BA, W.Va. U., 1973, postgrad., 1974-76, JD, 1977. Bar: W.Va. 1977, U.S. Dist. Ct. (so. dist.) W.Va. 1977, U.S. Dist. Ct. (no. dist.) W.Va. 1979, U.S. Dist. Ct. S.C. 1986. Ptnr. Worrell & Thompson, Pineville, W.Va., 1977-78, Loy, Shingleton & Caryl, Martinsburg, W.Va., 1978-81, Clark & Thompson, L.C., Charleston, 1981-85, Cecil, Barth & Thompson, Charleston, 1985—. Co-author: (with others) Duties and Functions of West Virginia County Courts, 1974. Trustee The Nature Conservancy, Charleston, 1984—. Mem. ABA, Assn. Trial Lawyers Am., W.Va. Bar Assn. Democrat. Presbyterian. Contracts commercial, Bankruptcy, Real property. Home: 3949 39th St E Nitro WV 25143 Office: Cecil Barth & Thompson Kanawha Blvd W at Berkeley St Charleston WV 25302

THOMPSON, STEPHEN MICHAEL, lawyer, educator; b. Monterey, Calif., Oct. 9, 1949; s. Joseph Ernest and Crystal Fern (Thode) T.; m. Ingrid Anne Hansen, Mar. 23, 1985; 1 child: Marta Anne. AB, Princeton U., 1971; JD, U. Denver, 1974, LLM, 1978. Bar: Colo. 1975, U.S. Dist. Ct. Colo. 1975, U.S. Ct. Appeals (10th cir.) 1975, U.S. Tax Ct. 1978. Assoc. Poulson, Odell & Peterson, Denver, 1975-79; ptnr. Poulson, Odell & Peterson, 1980—; adj. prof. law Denver U., 1982-85. Mem. ABA, Colo. Bar Assn., Denver Bar Assn. Republican. Episcopalian. Avocations: music, golf. Oil and gas leasing, Estate taxation, Probate. Office: Poulson Odell & Peterson 1775 Sherman #1400 Denver CO 80203

THOMPSON, T. JAY, lawyer; b. Ponca City, Okla., Aug. 10, 1947; s. Lurtis Howard and Frances (Wood) T. B.S., U. Okla., 1969; J.D., Washington U., St. Louis, 1972; LL.M. in Labor Law, George Washington U., 1976; LL.B. in Internat. Law, U. Cambridge (Eng.), 1979. Bar: Okla. 1972, D.C. 1976, U.S. Ct. Appeals (D.C. cir.) 1976, U.S. Supreme Ct. 1976, cir.) 1976, Colo. 1979, U.S. Ct. Appeals (10th cir.) 1979, U.S. Dist. Ct. (no., ea. and we. dists.) Okla. 1983, U.S. Dist. Ct. (so. dist.) Tex. 1984, U.S. Ct. Appeals (8th cir.) 1984, Tex. 1986, U.S. Ct. Appeals (7th and 5th cirs.) 1986. Assoc. Holland & Hart, Denver, 1979-82, dir., Nichols, Wolfe, Stamper, Nally & Fallis, Inc., Tulsa, 1982-86, assoc. gen. counsel, Burlington No. R.R. Co., Ft. Worth, Tex., 1986— . Contbr. articles to legal jours. Mem. allocation panel Tulsa United Way, 1984-86; bd. dirs. Four Mile Hist. Park, Denver, 1980-82. Served as capt. USAF, 1972-78, Turkey. Decorated USAF Commendation medal; Alfred P. Sloan Merit scholar Knox Coll., 1966. Mem. ABA, Okla. Bar Assn., Pi Mu Epsilon. Democrat. Clubs: Denver Athletic. Labor, Federal civil litigation, Civil rights. Office: Burlington Northern RR 777 Main St #3800 Fort Worth TX 76006

THOMPSON, TERENCE WILLIAM, lawyer; b. Moberly, Mo., July 3, 1952; s. Donald Gene and Carolyn (Stringer) T.; m. Caryn Elizabeth Hildebrand, Aug. 30, 1975; children: Cory Elizabeth, Christopher William. BA in Govt. with honors and high distinction, U. Ariz., 1974; JD, Harvard U., 1977. Bar: Ariz. 1977, U.S. Dist. Ct. Ariz. 1977, U.S. Tax Ct. 1979. Mem. Brown & Bain P.A., Phoenix, 1977—; legis. aide Rep. Richard Burgess, Ariz. Ho. of Reps., 1974; mem. bus. adv. bd. Great Western Bank & Trust, Phoenix, 1985-86. Contbr. articles to profl. jours. Mem. Phoenix Mayor's Youth Adv. Bd. 1968-70, Phoenix Internat. Active 20-30 Club, 1978-80, sec. 1979-80, Valley Leadership, Phoenix, 1983-84, citizens task force future financing needs City of Phoenix, 1985-86; deacon Shepherd of Hills Congl. Ch, Phoenix, 1984-85; pres. Maricopa County Young Dems., 1982-83, Ariz. Young Dems., 1983-84, sec. 1981-82, v.p. 1982-83; exec. dir. Young Dems. Am., 1985, mem. exec. com. 1983-85; sec. Ariz. Dem. Com., 1984-87. Mem. ABA, Ariz. Bar Assn. (vice chmn. internat. law sect. 1978), Maricopa County Bar Assn., Nat. Assn. Bond Lawyers, Am. Acad. Hosp. Attys., Blue Key, Phi Beta Kappa, Phi Kappa Phi, Phi Eta Sigma. Municipal bonds, Securities, General corporate. Home: 202 W Lawrence Rd Phoenix AZ 85013 Office: Brown & Bain PA PO Box 400 Phoenix AZ 85001

THOMPSON, THEODORE KVALE, lawyer; b. Fargo, N.D., Jan. 24, 1944; s. Kenneth Howard and Milred (Kvale) T.; m. Wanda Faye Benfer, July 25, 1964; children: Jeffrey, Jennifer, James. B.A., Tex. Lutheran Coll., 1967; J.D., U. Mont., 1970. Bar: Mont. 1970. Clk. Mont. Supreme Ct., 1970; asso. firm Hauge, Ober & Spangelo, Havre, Mont., 1970-75; partner firm Hauge, Ober & Thompson, 1975-83, Thompson & Swenson, 1983—; trustee State Bar Mont., 1970-78, chmn., 1975-77, pres., 1978-79. Bd. visitors U. Mont. Law Sch., 1976-83. Mem. Am. Judicature Soc., Mont. Bar Assn. (recipient Law Day award 1971, dir. 1974-75), 12th Jud. Dist. Bar Assn., Am. Bar Assn. Club: Havre Rotary. State civil litigation, Banking, Insurance. Home: 709 Sunset Dr Havre MT 59501 Office: Thompson & Swenson 419 4th Ave Havre MT 59501

THOMPSON, WILLIAM CARRINGTON, JR., judge advocate; b. Richmond, Va., Apr. 25, 1942; s. William Carrington and Margaret Sue (Colbert) T.; m. Diane M. Acuff, Mar. 25, 1983; children: Tracy Robyn, William Carrington III. BA with honors, Va. Mil. Inst., 1964; JD, U. Va., 1967; MS in Mgmt., U. Ark., 1974. Bar: Va. 1967, U.S. Ct. Mil. Appeals 1968, U.S. Supreme Ct. 1971. Commd. 2d lt. USAF, 1964, advanced through ranks to col., 1985; staff judge advocate 354 Tactical Fighter Wing USAF, Myrtle Beach, S.C., 1974-77; mil. judge Trial Judiciary USAF, Travis AFB, Calif., 1977-81; staff judge advocate USAF, Athens, Greece, 1981-83; dep. chief legis. liaison Office of Sec. USAF, Washington, 1983-85, chief, legis. div. Hdqrs., 1985-87; staff judge adv. 16th Air Force USAF, Torrejon Air Base, Spain, 1987—; bd. dirs. Pentagon Fed. Credit Union, Alexandria; chmn. bd. dirs. Myrtle Beach AFB Fed. Credit Union, 1975-77; chmn. supervisory commn. Travis (AFB) Fed. Credit Union, 1978-81. Editor: Comparative Analysis of ABA Standards and Military Practice and Procedure, 1978. Mem. Assn. Trial Lawyers Am. Baptist. Military, Criminal, Administrative and regulatory. Home: 7324 Glendower Ct Springfield VA 22153 Office: HQ USAF Room 5E 417 Pentagon DC 20330-5120

THOMPSON, WILLIAM SCOTT, patent lawyer; b. Grand Rapids, Mich., Feb. 6, 1930; s. William Scott Thompson and Mary Louise (Chatel) Kruse; m. Margaret Jane Favier, June 16, 1951; children: William, Michelle, Marta, Rebecca. BSME, U. Mich., 1952; JD, U. Notre Dame, 1959. Bar: Ind. 1959, U.S. Dist. Ct. (so. dist.) Ind. 1959, U.S. Ct. Appeals (Fed. cir.) 1963. Engr. Bendix Corp., South Bend, Ind., 1954-57, patent agt., 1957-59, patent atty., 1959-64, regional patent counsel, Utica, N.Y. and Detroit, 1964-74; patent dept. mgr. Caterpillar Inc., Peoria, Ill., 1974—. Served to 1st lt. USAF, 1952-54. Mem. Am. Intellectual Property Law Assn. (officer 1986—), Internat. Patent and Trademark Assn. (exec. com. 1982—), Assn. Corp. Patent Counsel, Pacific Indsl. Property Assn. (chmn. com. 1985—), ABA (com. chmn.). Patent, Legislative, Trademark and copyright. Office: Caterpillar Inc 100 NE Adams St Peoria IL 61629

THOMSON, HARRY PLEASANT, JR., lawyer; b. Kansas City, Mo., May 9, 1917; s. Harry Pleasant and Alice F. (DeWolff) T.; m. Martha Jean Martin, May 3, 1941 (dec. 1981); children: Jane Anne (Mrs. Edward G. McCarthy), Carol Lee Thomson, Lisa Clair, (Mrs. John Porter). A.B., U. Mo., 1937, J.D., 1939. Bar: Mo. bar 1939, also U.S. Supreme Ct. bar 1959. Practiced in Kansas City; now of counsel Shughart, Thomson & Kilroy (P.C.); lectr. Mo. Continuing Legal Edn. Programs, 1961-78; Mem. Mo. Supreme Ct. Com. on Jury Instrns., 1962-81, chmn., 1977-81; mem. Commn. on Retirement, Removal & Discipline of Judges, 1972-81, chmn., 1980-81. Author: (with others) Missouri Approved Jury Instructions, 1964, 69, 73, 76, 78, 80; Mem. bd. editors: Mo. Law Rev, 1938-39; editorial adv. bd. Antitrust Law & Econs. Rev.; contbr. articles to profl. jours. Trustee U. Mo. Law Sch. Found., 1975-87, pres., 1979-81. Served to lt. USNR, 1942-46. Recipient certificate of appreciation for disting. service Mo. Bar, 1964; Spurgeon Smithson award Mo. Bar Found., 1979; Charles E. Whittaker award Kansas City Lawyers Assn., 1984; Litigator Emeritus award Kansas City Met. Bar Assn., 1985. Fellow Am. Coll. Trial Lawyers (regent 1967-68), Am. Bar Found.; mem. Lawyers Assn. Kansas City (past pres.), Kansas City Claims Assn. (past pres.), Internat. Assn. Ins. Counsel, Mo. Bar Assn. (bd. govs. 1967-71, exec. com. 1970-71), ABA, Am. Judicature Soc., Internat. Soc. Barristers, Order DeMolay Legion of Honor, Phi Beta Kappa, Order of Coif, Psi Chi, Sigma Chi, Delta Theta Phi. Clubs: University (pres. 1977), Carriage, Kansas City. Lodge: Rotary. Antitrust, General corporate, General practice. Home: 1216 W 69th St Kansas City MO 64113 Office: 12 Wyandotte Plaza 120 W 12th St Kansas City MO 64105

THOMSON, PAUL RICE, JR., lawyer; b. Syracuse, N.Y., Dec. 28, 1941. B.A. in History, Va. Mil. Inst., 1963; J.D., Washington and Lee U., 1966. Bar: Va. 1966, U.S. Ct. Mil. Appeals 1967. Judge adv. USMC, 1966-69; assoc. Clement, Wheatley, Winston & Ingram, Danville, Va., 1969-71; asst. U.S. atty. Western Dist. Va., Roanoke, 1971-75, U.S. atty., 1975-79; gen. counsel natural resources The Pittston Co., Lebanon, Va., 1979—; pres. Roanoke Valley Law Enforcement Council, 1975-76; mem. Bd. Conciliation and Arbitration Panel, Richmond (Va.) Diocese; mem. Fed.-State Law Enforcement Council, 1975-79. Vice pres. Danville Jr. C. of C., 1971. Recipient Spl. Achievement award Dept. Justice, 1974. Mem. ABA, Va. Bar Assn., Assn. Trial Lawyers Am. General corporate, Labor, Coal and energy. Office: Pittston Co Coal Group PO Box 4000 Lebanon VA 24266

THOMSON, REBECCA WUNDER, lawyer; b. Chgo., Feb. 17, 1952; d. David Hart and Shirley (Dahlin) Wunder; m. K.C. Thomson, Oct. 6, 1978. Student, Wheaton Coll., 1970-72; BA magn cum laude, U. Denver, 1974, MS, LS, 1975, JD, 1978. Bar: Wyo. 1978, U.S. Dist. Ct. Wyo. 1978, U.S. Ct. Appeals (10th cir.) 1985, U.S. Claims Ct. 1986. Law clk. to presiding justice U.S. Dist. Ct. Wyo., Cheyenne, 1978-80; from assoc. to ptnr. Burgess & Davis, Sheridan, Wyo., 1980—. Del. Sheridan (Wyo.) County Rep. Party, 1980—; bd. dirs. Uptown Sheridan Assn. Mainstreet Devel., 1985-86; pres., bd. dirs. Wyo. Hist. Preservation Assn., 1981-84. Named one of Outstanding Young Women of Am. Bd. Outstanding Young Women, 1985. Mem. ABA (steering com. on solo and small law firms of econs. of law com.), Wyo. Bar Assn. (com. to cooperate with ABA), Sheridan County Bar Assn. (sec., treas.), Wyo. Trial Lawyers Assn., Rep. Women, Am. Judicature Soc., Sheridan C. of C. (econ. devel. com.), Phi Beta Kappa, Pi Gamma Mu. Lodge: DAR. Avocations: reading, hist. research and writing, walking, cooking. Federal civil litigation, State civil litigation, Administrative and regulatory. Home: 746 Arlington Blvd Sheridan WY 82801 Office: Burgess & Davis 40 S Main Sheridan WY 82801

THOMSON, WILLIAM HILLS, lawyer; b. Chgo., Nov. 6, 1942; s. Frank William and Margaret (Hills) T.; m. Gloria Sandra Thorp, June 12, 1965; children: Deborah, Karen. AB, U. Ill., 1964, JD, 1966. Bar: Ill. 1967, U.S. Dist. Ct. (no. dist.) Ill. 1967. Atty., trust officer 1st Nat. Bank Blue Island (Ill.), 1967—. Pres. United Way Blue Island-Calumet Park, 1986; bd. dirs. Blue Cap Sch., 1985. Mem. ABA, S. Suburban Bar Assn. Republican. Methodist. Avocations: jazz, painting, fishing. Probate, Estate planning, Pension, profit-sharing, and employee benefits. Office: 1st Nat Bank Blue Island 13057 S Western Blue Island IL 60406

THOMY, GEORGE ALBERT, lawyer, judge; b. Fayetteville, N.C., June 2, 1915; s. Najib and Careemy (Jacob) T.; m. Caronell Irene Jordan, Nov. 12, 1947; children: James. J., Gwendolyn Thomy Daniel, Gregory G. Student, Citadel, 1934-35; JD, U. S.C., 1952. Bar: S.C. 1952. Sole practice Lake City, S.C., 1952—; ptnr. Nettles, Thomy & Smith, Lake City, 1952-78; mcpl. judge City of Lake City, 1976—; pres. Stock Investments, Lake City, 1958-60. Councilman City of Lake City, 1954-70; chmn. Indsl. Loan and Devel. Commn. S.C., 1957-64. Served to 1st lt. U.S. Army, 1942-45, ETO. Decorated Bronze Star, 1944; named Lake City Young Man of Yr., Jaycees, 1941, one of Young Men of S.C., S.C. Jaycees, 1941, Man of Yr. Lake City, 1959. Mem. ABA, S.C. Bar Assn., Florence County Bar Assn., Assn. Trial Lawyers Am., Am. Legion (elected comdr. 1954), S.C. Jaycees (sec., v.p. 1941), Lake City Jr. C. of C. (pres. 1939-40). Democrat. Roman Catholic. Lodges: Rotary, KC. Judicial administration, Probate, Real property. Home and Office: 201 Magnolia Ave PO Box 1225 Lake City SC 29560

THON, WILLIAM MARVIN, lawyer; b. Long Beach, Calif., Aug. 16, 1938; s. Larry and Velva Thon; m. Cheryl Jean Abbott, Apr. 5, 1969. Student Pasadena City Coll., UCLA; J.D. cum laude Whittier Coll. Sch. Law, 1968. Bar: Calif. 1969. Dep. sheriff Los Angeles County, 1959-63; clk. Superior Ct., Los Angeles County, 1963-68; assoc. Magana & Cathcart, Los Angeles, 1969-76; ptnr. Thon & Matz, Encino, Calif., 1976-82, Thon & Beck, Encino, 1982-83, Pasadena, 1983—. Mem. State Bar Calif. (client trust fund commn.), Assn. Trial Lawyers Am., Calif. Trial Lawyers Assn. (legis. and med. malpractice coms. and speakers' bur.), Los Angeles County Trial Lawyers Assn. (bd. govs. 1977-78). Personal injury, Insurance, Admiralty. Home: 5 Deodor West Bradbury Estate CA 91010 Office: 1100 E Green St Pasadena CA 91106

THOREN-PEDEN, DEBORAH SUZANNE, lawyer; b. Rockford, Ill., Mar. 28, 1958; d. Robert Roy and Marguerite Natalie (Geoghegan) Thoren; m. Steven Elliot Peden, Aug. 10, 1985. BA in Philosophy, Psychology and Polit. Sci., U. Mich., 1978; JD, U. So. Calif., 1982. Bar: Calif. 1982, U.S. Dist. Ct. (cen. dist.) Calif. 1982. Assoc. Bushkin, Gaines & Gaims, Los Angeles, 1982-84, Rutan & Tucker, Costa Mesa, Calif., 1984-86; counsel First Interstate Bank of Calif., Los Angeles, 1986—. Mem. ABA, Calif. Bar Assn., Los Angeles County Bar Assn. Banking, Labor, State civil litigation. Home: 1800 Hermosa Ave Apt B Hermosa Beach CA 90254 Office: First Interstate Bank Calif 707 Wilshire 20th Floor Los Angeles CA 90017

THORNBERRY, WILLIAM HOMER, circuit judge, lawyer; b. Austin, Tex., Jan. 9, 1909; s. William Moore and Mary Lillian (Jones) T.; m. Eloise Engle, Feb. 24, 1945; children: Molly, David, Kate. B.B.A., U. Tex., 1932, LL.B., 1936; LL.D., Gallaudet Coll. Bar: Tex. 1936. Since practiced in Austin; dist. atty. 53d Jud. Dist., Travis County, Tex., 1941-42; Mem. city council Austin, 1946-48; mayor pro tem 1947-48; mem. Tex. Ho. of Reps., 1937-40, 81st-88th congresses, 10th Tex. Dist.; U.S. dist. judge Western Dist. Tex. 1963-65; U.S. judge Ct. Appeals, 5th Jud. Circuit, 1965—, sr. judge, 1979—. Served to lt. comdr. USNR, 1942-46. Recipient Silver Beaver award Boy Scouts Am.; Distinguished Alumnus award U. Tex., 1965; Hall of Honor Austin High Sch. Mem. Tex. State Bar, Travis County bar assns., Order of Coif (hon.). Democrat. Methodist. Lodges: Masons; Shriners; Kiwanis. Jurisprudence. Office: 108 US Courthouse 200 W 8th St Austin TX 78701

THORNBURG, FREDERICK FLETCHER, lawyer, bus. exec.; b. South Bend, Ind., Feb. 10, 1940; s. James F. and Margaret R. (Major) T.; children—James Brian, Charles Kevin, Christian Sean, Christopher Herndon; m. Patricia J. Malloy, Dec. 4, 1981. A.B., DePauw U., 1963; postgrad. U. Notre Dame, 1965; J.D. magna cum laude, Ind. U., 1968. Bar: Ind. 1968, U.S. Tax Ct. 1970, U.S. Supreme Ct. 1971. Tchr., coach U.S. Peace Corps, Colombia, 1963-65; law clk. to chief judge U.S. Ct. Appeals 7th Cir., 1968-69; assoc. Thornburg, McGill, Deahl, Harman, Carey & Murray, South Bend, 1969-75, ptnr., 1975-80; v.p. systems and services group, Wackenhut Corp., Coral Gables, Fla., 1981-82, sr. v.p. adminstrn., 1982-86; exec. v.p. 1986—; pres., bd. dirs. The Wackenhut Corp., Wackenhut Systems Corp., Wackenhut Internat. Inc., Coral Gables, 1982-83; sole practice, Coral Gables, 1983—; adj. prof. bus. law St. Mary's Coll., 1975-78. Bd. dirs. YMCA, Channel 34, Symphony Orch. Assn.; vice chmn., pvt.sec. adv. council Fla. Sec. of State; Mem. ABA, Ind. Bar Assn., Dade County Corp. Counsel Assn., Order of Coif, Coral Gables C. of C. (com. of 21), Greater Miami C. of C. (bd. dirs.), Phi Delta Phi, Alpha Delta Sigma. Clubs: Ind. Soc. Chgo., Doral Country, Calusa Country, Rotary. Assoc. editor in chief Ind. Law Jour., 1967-68; contbr. articles to legal jours. Clubs: City (Miami). General corporate, Labor, Taxation. Office: Wackenhut Corp 1500 San Remo Ave Coral Gables FL 33146

THORNBURG, LACY HERMAN, state attorney general; b. Charlotte, N.C., Dec. 20, 1929; s. Jesse Lafayette and Sarah Ann (Ziegler) T.; m. Dorothy Todd, Sept. 6, 1953; children—Sara Thornburg Evans, Lacy Eugene, Jesse Todd, Alan Ziegler. A.A., Mars. Hill Coll., 1950; B.A., U. N.C., 1951, J.D., 1954. Practice law Webster, N.C., 1954-67; superior ct. judge State of N.C., 1967-83; atty. gen State of N.C., Raleigh, 1985—; mem. staff Congressman Taylor, Sylva, N.C., 1960, Congressman David Hall, Sylva, 1959-60; mem. N.C. Ho. of Reps., 1961-65; mem. N.C. Cts. Commn., N.C. Criminal Code Commn., Capital Planning Commn., Raleigh; chmn. Law Enforcement Coordinating Com., Raleigh, 1985—. Chmn. Jackson County Bd. of Health, Sylva, 1965-84; commr. Tryon Palace, New Bern, N.C. Served with U.S. Army, 1947-48. Democrat. Lodges: Lions, Masons, Shriners. Avocations: fly fishing; skeet shooting. Criminal, State civil litigation. Office: Dept Justice PO Box 629 2 E Morgan St Raleigh NC 27602

THORNBURY, WILLIAM MITCHELL, lawyer, law educator; b. Kansas City, Mo., Feb. 11, 1944; s. Paul Cobb and Marguerite Madellaine (Schulz) T.; m. Joy Frances Barrett, Feb. 2, 1973; children: Barrett Mitchell, Adele Frances. B.A., UCLA, 1964; J.D., U. So. Calif., 1967, postgrad. 1967-69. Bar: Calif. 1968, U.S. Dist. Ct. (cen. dist.) Calif. 1968, U.S. Dist. Ct. (no. dist.) Calif. 1973, U.S. Dist. Ct. (so. dist.) Calif. 1980, U.S. Dist. Ct. (ea. dist.) Calif. 1980, U.S. Ct. Appeals (9th cir.) 1973, U.S. Ct. Claims 1980, U.S. Ct. Internat. Trade, 1981, U.S. Ct. Customs and Patent Appeals 1980, U.S. Ct. Mil. Appeals 1980, U.S. Supreme Ct. 1973, U.S. Ct. Appeals (Fed. cir.) 1984. Dep. pub. defender Los Angeles County Pub. Defender, 1969—, dep.-in-charge traffic ct., 1982-84, supervising atty. Juvenile Services div., 1984, dep. in charge, Inglewood, Calif., 1984-85; legal asst. prof. Calif. State U.-Los Angeles, 1983—; mem. adv. com. on alcohol determination State Dept. Health, 1984—; appointed to apprenticeship council by Gov. Deukmejian State of Calif., 1986—; chmn., vice chmn. Santa Monica Fair Election Practices Commn., Calif., 1981-85; advisor on drunk driving Calif. Pub. Defenders Assn., 1984—; alt. mem. Los Angeles County Commn. on Drunk Driving, 1983-84; mem. steering com. Santa Monica Coalition, nominations com., 1984—; bd. dirs. Westside Legal Services, 1984-86, v.p., 1986—. Columnist Calif. Defender; editor Drunk Driving Manual, 1984; contbr. article to Forum. Exec. bd. dirs. Santa Monica Young Rep., 1967-72, pres. 1972-73, treas. 1973-75, bd. dirs. 1968-72; delegate, precinct chmn., registration chmn. Los Angeles County Young Rep., 1968-70; chmn. legal com. Los Angeles County Rep. Cen. Com., 1977-81, 83-85; chmn. jud. evaluation com., 1978-80; pres. Santa Monica Rep. Club 1986—, bd. dirs., 1966—; bd. dirs. West Los Angeles Republican Club, 1986—; mem. Beverly Hills Rep. Club, Rep. State Cen. com., 1983-85, assoc. mem., 1980-83, 86—, Non-Partisan Candidate Evaluating Council, Inc. (bd. dirs. 1980-86, v.p. 1986—); bd. dirs. Santa Monicans Against Crime, 1979—; chmn. 44th Assembly Dist. Rep. Central Com. 1974-87; chmn. Western part of Los Angeles County for George Murphy for U.S. Senate, 1970, John T. LaFollette for Congress, 1970; campaign chmn. Donna A. Little for City Council, 1984; adv. Pat Geffner for City Council, 1979, 81; campaign mgr. Experienced Coll. Team, 1983. Recipient Outstanding Chmn. award Los Angeles County Rep. Party, 1974, sec.-treas. 1968-75, chmn. legal com. 1977-82, 83-85; named Outstanding Service to Rep. Party Legal Counsel, 1978; recipient award Am. Assn. UN, 1961. Mem. Los Angeles County Bar Assn. (vice chmn. indigent and criminal def. com., jud. qualification com. 1986, criminal justice com. 1986, criminal law and law enforcement com., 1986—), Santa Monica Bar Assn. (trustee 1976-77, 79—, chmn. legis. and publicity com., chmn. jud. evaluation com. 1982-84, pres.-elect 1984, pres. 1985-86, del. to state bar conv. 1974-86, liaison to Los Angeles County Bar Assn. 1986—), Los Angeles County Pub. Defenders Assn. (advisor, bd. dirs. 1980—), ABA, Calif. Pub. Defenders Assn. (advisor), Santa Monica Hist. Soc., San Fernando Valley Criminal Bar Assn. (membership chmn. 1986—, bd. trustees 1986—), Assn. Trial Lawyers Am., Supreme Ct. Hist. Soc., Nat. Legal Aid and Defenders Assn., Nat. Assn. Criminal Def. Attys., Acad. Criminal Justice Scis., U. So. Calif. Law Alumni Assn., UCLA Alumni Assn., N.Y. Acad. Scis., Am. Assn. Polit. Sci., Criminal Law sect. of State Bar of Calif., Am. Soc. Criminology (life), Western Region Criminal Law Educators, Santa Monica C. of C. (inebriate task force 1980), Calif. Hist. Soc., Santa Monica Coll. Patron's Assn., Nat. Assn. Criminal Def. Counsel, Navy League (life, bd. dirs. 1979—, legis. chmn. 1982, judge advocate 1983—), Nat. Rifle Assn. (life), Calif. Rifle and Pistol Assn. (life). Criminal.

THORNDIKE, DANIEL CARL, lawyer; b. Medford, Oreg., Oct. 15, 1955; s. William Downie and Carol Jeanne (Tengwald) T.; m. Joan Ewer, Aug. 25, 1984. BA magna cum laude, Colo. Coll., 1973-77; JD with honors, U. Wash., 1977-80. Bar: Oreg. 1980, U.S. Dist. Ct. Oreg., 1980. Assoc. Blackhurst, Hornecker, Hassen and Brian, Medford, Oreg., 1980-83, ptnr., 1983—. Pres. Peter Britt Music & Arts Festival Assoc., Medford, 1983-85, Medford Family YMCA, 1986—. Mem. ABA. Republican. Club: Rogue River Valley Univ. Club (Medford). Avocations: bicycling, cross-country skiing, climbing, running, photography. Contracts commercial, Real property, Local government. Office: Blackhurst Hornecker Hassen & Brian 129 N Oakdale Suite 1 Medford OR 97501

THORNDYKE, GORDON WILLIAM, lawyer; b. Cin., Mar. 25, 1906; s. John and Margaret (Fisk) T.; m. Ann Friese, Dec. 17, 1958. LL.B., U. Cin., 1932. Bar: Ohio 1951. Assoc. Gusweiler & Gusweiler, Cin., 1952-56; ptnr. Thorndyke & Thorndyke, 1956-69; sole practice, Cin., 1969—; prin. Fred. K. Schmidt Co. (real estate), Cin., 1956-57; former dir. Fisk Bros. Monument Co., Cin.; genealogist. Bd. dirs. Price Hill Republican Club, Cin., 1983-85; active United Appeal/Community Chest; precinct exec. Hamilton County Rep. Orgn., 1956, 58. Mem. Ohio Bar Assn., SAR, English Speaking Union, Cin. Hist. Soc., Hamilton County Geneal. Soc., Ohio Geneal. Soc., Kenton County Hist. Soc., Royal Astron. Soc., Scandinavian Soc. (charter), Pan-Am. Soc. Cin. Clubs: Travel (Cin.); Halo. Lodges: Shriners, Masons, KT, Caledonian Society. General practice. Office: PO Box 5061 Cincinnati OH 45205

THORNTON, D. WHITNEY, II, lawyer; b. Miami, Fla., Oct. 17, 1946; s. Dade Whitney and Hilda (Bryan) T.; m. Jane Collis, Nov. 27, 1971; children—Bryan Whitney, Elizabeth Jane, Virginaia Anne. B.A., Washington and Lee U., 1968, J.D., 1970. Bar: Va. 1970, D.C. 1976, U.S. Ct. Appeals (4th cir.) 1978, U.S. Sup. Ct. 1980. Atty., Naval Air Systems Command, Dept. Navy, Washington, 1970-73; asst. counsel to comptroller Dept. Navy, 1973-74, asst. to gen. counsel, 1974-76; assoc. Sullivan & Beauregard, Washington, 1976-77, ptnr., 1977-81; ptnr. Bowman, Conner, Touhey & Thornton, Washington, 1981-83; pres. Continental Maritime Industries, Inc., San Francisco, 1983—. Mem. ABA (public contract law sect.; chmn. suspension and debarment com. 1977), Fed. Bar Assn. (vice chmn. govt. contracts council; Disting. Service award 1981). Republican. Methodist. Club: Washington Golf and Country (Arlington, Va.). Contbr. articles to profl. jours. Government contracts and claims. Office: Continental Maritime Industries Inc Pier 50-54 San Francisco CA 94107

THORNTON, EDWARD ROBERT, JR., lawyer; b. Manchester, N.H., July 27, 1939; s. Edward Robert and Rita Marie (Kirby) T.; m. Jeanie

Cameron Raymond, Aug. 21, 1965 (div. June 1980); m. Kathleen Elizabeth Herod, Aug. 28, 1981; children: Kara, Tara, Meaghan, Maura, Shaunna. AB, Dartmouth Coll., 1961; JD, U. Maine, 1965. Bar: N.H. 1965, U.S. Dist. Ct. N.H. 1965, U.S. Tax. Ct. 1977, U.S. Supreme Ct. 1977. Ptnr. Thornton & Thornton, P.A., Manchester, 1965—; instr. bus. law Mt. St. Mary's Coll., Hooksett, N.H., 1966-67. State parliamentarian N.H. Jaycees, 1969; merit badge counselor Boy Scouts Am., Manchester, 1965—; fund raiser Cath. Charities of N.H., Manchester, 1965—; bd. dirs. Greater Manchester chpt. Nat. Council on Alcoholism, 1981—, Farnum Ctr. Rehab. Ctr, 1985—. Mem. ABA (com. on small firms 1980—, subcom. on assocs. 1980—, subcom. computers in small firms 1982—), N.H. Bar Assn. (participant various programs, mem. Hillsborough County case monitoring com. 1983—, com. on profl. continuity 1981—, com. coop. with cts. 1983—), Manchester Bar Assn. (dist. ct. system improvement com. 1978-79, Hillsborough county Law Library com. 1983-84), Assn. Trial Lawyers Am. (state del. 1985-87), N.H. Trial Lawyers Assn. (founding mem., treas. 1977-78, bd. govs. 1977-85, pres. 1983-84, various coms. 1977—), N.H. Conveyancers Council. State civil litigation, Personal injury, Real property. Home: 8 7th Ave Manchester NH 03104 Office: Thornton & Thornton PA 771 Chestnut St Manchester NH 03104

THORNTON, JOHN W., lawyer; b. Toledo, July 3, 1928; s. Cletus Bernard and Mary Victoria (Carey) T.; m. Mary Feeley, Mar. 10, 1951; children—John, Jane Thornton Mastrucci, Deborah Thornton Hasty, Michael; m. Sally Wolff, Jan. 9, 1982. A.B. magna cum laude, U. Notre Dame, 1950, LL.B., 1956, J.D., 1969. Bar: Fla. 1956, U.S. Dist. Ct. (so. dist.) Fla. 1956, U.S. Ct. Appeals (5th cir.) 1956, U.S. Ct. Appeals (11th cir.) 1982. Sole practice, Miami, Fla. Contbr. articles to legal jours. Served to lt. USN, 1950-53. Mem. Fla. Bar (chmn. continuing legal edn. program 1976-77, chmn. 1982-83), ABA (vice-chmn. practice and procedure com. 1969, 73, 76-81; vice-chmn. health ins. law com. 1972-73, chmn. 1974-76; chmn. Excess Surplus Lines and Re-ins. Law Commn., 1985-87; vice-chmn. program com. ann. meeting 1976; com. rules and procedure 1979-80), Internat. Assn. Ins. Counsel (chmn. med. malpractice com. 1975-76; def. counsel com. 1976-87; reins., excess and surplus lines com. 1980-87), Def. Research Inst. (chmn. practice and procedure com. 1972-76; industry-wide litigation com. 1978-87), So. Def. Lawyers Assn., Dade County Def. Bar Assn., Fedn. Ins. Counsel (casualty ins. law com. 1972-87; med. malpractice com. 1974-87; excess surplus and reins. com. 1976-85; publs. com. 1976-87), Maritime Law Assn. U.S., Fla. Def. Lawyers Assn. (dir., chmn. legis. com. 1974-77), Broward County Bar Assn., Am. Judicature Soc. Roman Catholic. Clubs: Coral Gables, Ocean Reef (Key Largo, Fla.) Country, Riviera Country; Sapphire Valley (N.C.) Country. Federal civil litigation, State civil litigation, Health. Office: Suite 720 Biscayne Bldg 19 W Flagler St Miami FL 33130

THORNTON, JOHN WILLIAM, JR., lawyer; b. Newport, R.I., Jan. 9, 1952; s. John William and Mary patricia (Feeley) T.; m. Melinda Tonnie Sterman, Apr. 21, 1979; children: David John, Ryan Thomas. BA, U. Notre Dame, 1974; JD, U. Miami, 1977. Bar: Fla. 1977, U.S. Dist. Ct. (so. dist.) Fla. 1978, U.S. Ct. Appeals (5th cir.) 1978, D.C. 1979, U.S. Ct. Appeals (11th cir.) 1981, U.S. Supreme Ct. 1981. Law clk. to presiding justice Miami, Fla., 1976-77; asst. state atty. Dade County, Miami, 1977-80; ptnr. Thornton & Rothman P.A. and predecessor firm, Miami, 1980—. Bd. dirs. Notre Dame Miami, 1980—. Mem. ABA, Dade County Bar Assn. (bd. dirs. young lawyers sect. 1980—, treas. 1986-87), Assn. Trial Lawyers Am., Fla. Criminal Def. Attys. Assn. (treas. 1985—), Nat. Assn. Criminal Def. Lawyers. Democrat. Roman Catholic. Club: City (Miami). Criminal. Home: 12490 Crescent Way Miami FL 33156 Office: Thornton & Rothman PA 2860 SE Financial Ctr Miami FL 33131

THORNTON, MICHAEL PAUL, lawyer; b. Lexington, Ky., May 13, 1948; s. Paul Alfred and Wilma Elsa (Hasekoester) T.; m. Deborah Phillips Davis, July 7, 1979; children—Barrett Parker, Katherine Davis. A.B., Dartmouth Coll., 1972; J.D., Vanderbilt U., 1975. Bar: N.H. 1975, U.S. Dist. Ct. N.H. 1975, Maine 1979, U.S. Dist. Ct. Maine 1979, Mass. 1982, U.S. Dist. Ct. Mass. 1982, U.S. Ct. Claims 1980. Assoc. Burns, Bryant, Hinchey, Cox & Shea, Dover, N.H., 1975-78; ptnr. Mulvey & Thornton, Portsmouth, N.H., 1978-80, Thornton & Early, Boston, 1980—. Served with USMC, 1966-68, Vietnam. Mem. ABA, Assn. Trial Lawyers Am. Democrat. Federal civil litigation, Environment. Home: 72 Woodcliff Rd Wellesley MA 02181 Office: Thornton & Early 200 Portland St Boston MA 02114

THORNTON, RICHARD JOSEPH, lawyer; b. Indpls., Dec. 24, 1922; s. Maurice Emerson and Helene Emelia (Biederman) T.; m. Edna Jean Thompson, Dec. 25, 1944; children—Charlotte Anne Thornton Julian, J. Thompson. B.S., Ind. U., 1943; J.D., U. Miami, 1949. Bar: Fla. 1949, U.S. Dist. Ct. (so. dist.) Fla. 1949, U.S. Dist. Ct. (mid. dist.) Fla. 1949, U.S. Ct. Appeals (5th cir.) 1952, U.S. Ct. Appeals (11th cir.) 1983, U.S. Supreme Ct., 1984 Assoc. Walton, Lantaff, Schroeder & Carson, Miami, Fla., 1949-54, ptnr., 1954-81; ptnr. Thornton, David & Murray, Miami, 1981-82; pres. Thornton, David & Murray, P.A., Miami, 1982—. Elder, Miami Shores Presbyterian Ch. Served to capt. AUS, 1946. Mem. ABA, Am. Judicature Soc., Internat. Assn. Defense Counsel, Am. Coll. Trial Lawyers, Phi Delta Phi. Club: Elks. Federal civil litigation, State civil litigation, Aviation and insurance law. Office: Thornton David Murray PA 2950 SW 27th Ave Suite 100 Miami FL 33133

THORNTON, ROBERT FLOYD, lawyer; b. Willard, Ohio, Jan. 27, 1932; s. Martin Floyd and Rosemary (Boehringer) T.; m. Joan Shanefelter, June 28, 1952; children—Rebecca, Kathryn, Alec, Andrew, Aaron. B.B.A., Ohio State U., 1955; LL.B., 1958. Bar: Ohio 1958, U.S. Dist. Ct. (no. dist.) Ohio 1966, U.S. Ct. Appeals (6th cir.) 1969. Ptnr. firm Thornton, Thornton & Harwood, Willard, Ohio, 1958—; law dir. City of Willard, 1960-68. Mem. bd. edn. Willard City Sch. Dist., 1971-79. Served to 1st lt. U.S. Army, 1955-57. Mem. Huron County Bar Assn. (pres. 1984), Ohio State Bar Assn. (del. 1978-82), ABA, Ohio Acad. Trial Lawyers (pres. 1975-76), Ohio State Bar Found., Order of Coif. Roman Catholic. Lodge: Elks. Personal injury, State civil litigation, General practice. Home: 46 Hillcrest St Willard OH 44890 Office: Thornton Thornton & Harwood 111 Myrtle Ave Willard OH 44890

THORNTON, ROBERT RICHARD, lawyer; b. Jersey City, Oct. 16, 1926; s. Arthur A. and Sabina V. (Williams) T.; m. Dorothy M. McGuire, Sept. 10, 1966; children: Matthew, Nicholas, Jennifer, Julia. AB, Georgetown U., 1950; LLB, Columbia U., 1953. Bar: N.Y. 1953, Ill. 1970. Assoc. Dorr, Hand & Dawson, N.Y.C., 1953-63, Mudge, Rose, Guthrie & Alexander, N.Y.C., 1963-70; gen. atty. Caterpillar Inc. (formerly Caterpillar Tractor Co.), Peoria, Ill., 1970-74, assoc. counsel, 1974-83, gen. counsel, sec., 1983—. Mem. ABA, Ill. State Bar Assn., Peoria County Bar Assn., Assn. Bar City of N.Y. Republican. Roman Catholic. Club: Country of Peoria. Antitrust, General corporate, Securities. Home: 3715 Linden Ln Peoria IL 61614 Office: Caterpillar Inc 100 NE Adams St Peoria IL 61629-7310

THORNTON, RUSSELL JAMES, lawyer; b. Lockney, Tex., Dec. 7, 1955; s. Herman B. and Mildred D. (Deavenport) T. B.B.A., Abilene Christian U., 1977; J.D., Tex. Tech U., 1980. Bar: Tex. 1980, U.S. Dist. Ct. (no. dist.) Tex. 1981. Sole practice, Plainview, Tex., 1981-82; county atty. Hale County, Plainview, 1982—. Revision co-editor: Texas Crimes and Punishment, 1983. Treas., adminstrv. v.p. Plainview Jaycees, 1982-84; bd. dirs. Plainview Symphony, 1982-83; adv. counsel Sr. Vol. Program, Plainview, 1983—. Mem. Hale County Bar Assn., Tex. Dist. and County Atty.'s Assn. (pub. relations com. 1983-84), ABA (criminal justice com. 1982-84), Nat. Dist. Atty.'s Assn., Tex. Trial Lawyers Assn. Democrat. Mem. Ch. of Christ. Criminal, Family and matrimonial, Local government. Home: 410 Mesa Circle Plainview TX 79072 Office: County Attys Office Hale County Cthouse Plainview TX 79072

THORON, GRAY, lawyer, educator; b. Danvers, Mass., July 14, 1916; s. Ward and Louisa Chapin (Hooper) T. AB, Harvard U., 1938, LLB, 1941; m. Pattie Porter Holmes, Dec. 30, 1971; children by previous marriage: Claire, Louisa, Grenville C., Molly D., Thomas G. Bar: N.Y. 1942. Assoc. Sullivan & Cromwell, N.Y.C., 1942, 45-48; assoc. prof. law U. Tex., 1948-50, prof., 1950-56; dean Law Sch., Cornell U., Ithaca, N.Y., 1956-63, prof. law, 1956—; vis. prof. law summers U. Mich., 1951, U. Tex., 1970; faculty Salzburg Seminar in Am. Studies, summer 1959; asst. to solicitor gen. Dept. Justice, Washington, 1954-56; mem. N.Y. State Laporte Legis. Ethics Com., 1964; spl. asst. atty. gen. N.Y. State, 1965. Del. Rep. Nat. Conv., 1952. Trustee Concord Acad., 1958-61. Served with inf. AUS, 1942-45. Decorated Silver Star, Bronze Star, Purple Heart with oak leaf cluster. Fellow Am. Bar Found.; mem. Am. Law Inst., Am. Judicature Soc., ABA, N.Y. State Bar Assn. (chmn. spl. com. to rev. code of profl. responsibility 1974-77, mem. com. profl. ethics 1965-87, vice chmn. 1973-83), Assn. Bar City N.Y., Lawyers Com. for Civil Rights Under Law (trustee 1965—), Phi Alpha Delta, Phi Kappa Phi. Clubs: Century Assn., Harvard (N.Y.C.). Legal education, Legal ethics and professional discipline. Office: Cornell U Law Sch Myron Taylor Hall Ithaca NY 14853

THORPE, CALVIN E., lawyer, legal educator; b. Springville, Utah, May 22, 1938; s. Ronald Eaton and Lillian (Thorn) T.; m. Patricia Warren, Feb. 2, 1961; children—Amber, Jill, Marc, Linda, Michael. B.S. in Physics, Brigham Young U., 1962; M.S. in Engring., U. Pa., 1963; J.D., Seton Hall U., 1969. Bar: N.J. 1969, Tex. 1971, Utah, 1974, U.S. Dist. Ct. Utah 1974, U.S. Ct. Customs and Patent Appeals 1975, U.S. Ct. Appeals (10th cir.) 1980. Assoc. Law Offices Giles C. Clegg, Dallas, 1971-73; ptnr. Thorpe, North & Western, Sandy, Utah, 1973—; adj. assoc. prof. U. Utah, Salt Lake City, 1975—; lectr. Brigham Young U., Provo, 1983—; dir. I.E. Sensors, Inc., Salt Lake City. Chmn., mem. Sandy City Planning Commn., 1975-84; mem. Sandy City Bd. Adjustment, 1980-81; chmn. Sandy Econ. Devel. Council, 1984. Mem. Am. Planning Assn. (Utah chpt., Citizen Planner award 1985), Utah C. of C. (Total Citizen award 1986), Sandy Area C. of C. (chmn. 1985), Am. intellectual Property Law Assn., Sigma Pi Sigma. Mormon. Patent, Trademark and copyright, Unfair competition. Office: Thorpe North & Western 9662 S State St Sandy UT 84070

THORPE, GEOFFREY LAWTON, lawyer; b. Oakland, Calif., Aug. 13, 1955; s. Maner L. and Michi Thorpe. BA, Claremont Men's Coll., 1977; JD, U. Calif., Berkeley, 1980. Bar: Calif. 1980, U.S. Dist. Ct. (no. dist.) Calif. 1980, U.S. Ct. Claims 1982, U.S. Tax Ct., U.S. Supreme Ct. 1986. Acct. tax dept. Arthur Young & Co., San Francisco, 1980-82; assoc. Dinkelspiel, Donovan & Reder, San Francisco, 1982-84; mgr. tax dept. U.S. Fleet Leasing Inc., San Mateo, Calif., 1984—. Mem. San Francisco Bar Assn., Tax Execs. Inst. Corporate taxation. Office: US Fleet Leasing Inc 2 Waters Park Dr San Mateo CA 94403

THORPE, WILLIAM LEE, lawyer; b. Phila., July 12, 1953; s. Sherman William and Bonnie (Lee) T.; m. Cynthia Louise Shupe; 1 child, Katherine Louise. BA, Stanford U., 1975; JD, Boston Coll., 1978. Bar: Ariz. 1978, U.S. Dist. Ct. Ariz. 1978. Ptnr. Fennemore, Craig, von Ammon, Udall & Powers P.C., Phoenix, 1978—. Mem. ABA, Ariz. Bar Assn., Maricopa County Bar Assn., Nat. Assn. R.R. Trial Counsel. Republican. Episcopalian. Federal civil litigation, State civil litigation, Personal injury. Home: 134 W Northview Phoenix AZ 95021 Office: Fennemore Craig von Ammon et al 100 W Washington Suite 1600 Phoenix AZ 85003

THORSON, DAVID MORRIS, lawyer; b. Schenectady, N.Y., July 31, 1950; s. Morris Herbert and Constance Jean (Wobig) T.; m. Karen Ruth Suoja, May 22, 1971; 1 child, Erica Karin. BA in Polit. Sci., Pacific Luth. U., 1972; JD cum laude, U. Puget Sound, 1977. Bar: Colo. 1977, U.S. Dist. Ct. Colo. 1977. Assoc. Itkin & Assocs. P.C., Breckenridge, Colo., 1977-81; ptnr. Thorson & Burns, Breckenridge, 1981-82; sole practice Breckenridge, 1982—; atty. Town of Fairplay, Colo., 1981-86, Alma, Colo., 1982—. Group leader Summit County Rescue Group, Inc., Frisco, Colo., 1979-81, mission coordinator, 1978—; v.p. Colo. Search and Rescue Bd., Inc., Golden, 1984-85, pres., 1986—, mission coordinator, 1984—; vol. Summit County Ambulance Service, Frisco, 1981—; trustee Town of Blue River, Colo., 1982-86; mem. Colo. Incident Command System Bd., 1986—. Mem. ABA, Colo. Bar Assn., Continental Divide Bar Assn., Summit County Bar Assn. Lutheran. Real property, General corporate, General practice. Home: 286 Blue River Rd PO Box 1877 Blue River CO 80424 Office: Box 1877 235 S Ridge St Breckenridge CO 80424

THORSON, JOHN ERIC, lawyer; b. Albuquerque, Sept. 28, 1946; s. E.J. and Margaret Rebecca (Crane) T.; m. Joyce Marie Gattas, Sept. 13, 1969 (div. 1977). BA, U. N.Mex., 1970; JD, U. Calif., Berkeley, 1973. Bar: N.Mex. 1973, Calif. 1973, U.S. Ct. Appeals (9th and 10th cirs.) 1974, U.S. Supreme Ct. 1981, Mont. 1986. Assoc. dir. Western Govs. Conf., San Francisco, 1980-83; dir. Conf. Western Atty. Gens., San Francisco, 1980-84; cons. in field Watershed West, Helena, Mont., 1984—; ptnr. Doney & Thorson, Helena, 1986—. Co-author: Salty Colorado, 1986; contbr. numerous articles on natural resources and water. Mem. ABA (water resources com.). Democrat. Club: Mont. (Helena). Water law, Environment. Office: Doney & Thorson PO Box 1185 Helena MT 59624

THORSON, LARRY JONATHAN, lawyer; b. Charles City, Iowa, Oct. 26, 1951; s. Oliver and Leone Belle (Gray) T.; m. Joan Alice Atherton, June 19, 1976. B in Gen. Studies, U. Iowa, 1973, JD, 1976. Bar: Iowa 1976, U.S. Dist. Ct. (no. dist.) Iowa 1977, U.S. Tax Ct. 1977. Law clk. to presiding justice Iowa Supreme Ct., Davenport, 1976-77; assoc. Goldberg, Mayne, Probasco & Berenstein, Sioux City, Iowa, 1977-80, White & Warbasse P.C., Cedar Rapids, Iowa, 1981-82; ptnr. Mundy & Thorson, Cedar Rapids, 1983, Mundy, Thorson & Meyer, Cedar Rapids, 1984—. Bd. dirs., v.p. Neighborhood Housing, Inc., Cedar Rapids, 1984—. Mem. ABA, Iowa Bar Assn. (corp. and bus. law com.), Linn County Bar Assn. Democrat. Mem. Unitarian Ch. Lodge: Lions (v.p. Cedar Rapids club 1986). General corporate, Personal income taxation, General practice. Office: Thorson & Meyer 118 Third Ave SE Cedar Rapids IA 52401

THRAILKILL, DANIEL B., lawyer; b. Fayetteville, Ark., Sept. 21, 1957. BSBA, U. Ark., 1979, J.D., 1981. Bar: Ark. 1982, U.S. Dist. Cts. (ea. and we. dists.) Ark. 1982, U.S. Ct. Appeals (8th cir.) 1983, U.S. Supreme Ct. 1985. Ptnr. Tucker & Thrailkill, Mena, Ark., 1981—; assoc. prof., lectr. Rich Mountain Community Coll. Recipient Appellate Advocacy award U. Ark. Sch. Law, 1981. Mem. Assn. Trial Lawyers Am., ABA, Nat. Dist. Attys. Assn., Ark. Bar Assn., Ark. Trial Lawyers Assn., Phi Alpha Delta. Methodist. Lodge: Lions. General practice, Personal injury, Oil and gas leasing. Home: 1717 W Church St Mena AR 71953 Office: Tucker & Thrailkill 311 De Queen St PO Drawer 30 Mena AR 71953

THRALL, GORDON FISH, lawyer; b. Jamestown, N.Y., July 28, 1923; s. Clyde Lowell and Beulah Mae (Fish) T.; m. Betty Jane Roberts, Sept. 24, 1964; 1 dau., Jenifer Jane. A.B. in History and Polit. Sci., Alfred U., 1949; J.D., Baylor U., 1953. Bar: Tex. 1953, U.S. Supreme Ct. 1957, D.C. 1958, U.S. Ct. Appeals (D.C. cir.) 1958, U.S. Ct. Mil. Appeals 1958, U.S. Dist. Ct. (ea. dist.) Tex. 1976, U.S. Ct. Appeals (5th cir.) 1986. Asst. prosecutor Dallas County Dist. Atty., 1954-55; assoc. firm Phinney & Hallman, Dallas, 1955-56; asst. atty. State of Tex. Atty. Gen., 1957; adviser, examiner ICC, Washington, 1957-59; asst. gen. counsel Tex. State Bar, Austin, 1959-61; county atty. Reagan County, Big Lake, Tex., 1961-72; ptnr. Norman, Spiers, Thrall, Angle & Rountree, Jacksonville, Tex., 1972—. Deacon, exec. com. Tex. Baptist Gen. Conv., 1965-70; chmn. Permian Basin dist. Concho Valley council Boy Scouts Am., Big Lake, 1965-66, Jacksonville United Fund Drive; pres. Cherokee County Health Facilities Devel. Corp., 1982—, Jacksonville United Fund Inc., 1986-87; bd. dirs. Travis Towers Retirement Facility, Jacksonville, 1980—. Mem. Tex. State Bar, Tex. Trial Lawyers Assn., Big Lake C. of C. (pres. 1963, 67), Jacksonville C. of C. (pres. 1979). Republican. Southern Baptist. Clubs: Cherokee Country (dir. 1981-83), Kiwanis (pres. 1978, disting. lt. gov. div. 34 1982) (Jacksonville), Lions (pres. 1969). Lodge: Masons. State civil litigation, Family and matrimonial, Probate. Home: 702 Fort Worth St Jacksonville TX 75766 Office: Norman Spiers Thrall Angle & Rountree 215 E Commerce St Jacksonville TX 75766

THRASH, THOMAS WOODROW, lawyer; b. Birmingham, Ala., May 8, 1951; s. Thomas Woodrow and Catherine (Pope) T.; m. Margaret Lines, June 20, 1981; children—Andrew Stiles, Margaret van Buren. B.A., U. Va., 1973; J.D. cum laude, Harvard U., 1976. Bar: Ga. 1976. Assoc. McClain, Mellen, Bowling & Hickman, Atlanta, 1976-77; asst. dist. atty. Atlanta Jud. Dist. 1977-81; assoc. Finch, McCranie, Brown & Thrash, Atlanta, 1981-85, ptnr. 1985—; adj. prof. litigation Ga. State U., 1986—; instr. Atlanta Law Sch., 1977, Atlanta Coll. Trial Advocacy, 1984-85. Active High Mus. Art, Atlanta, 1982—, Atlanta Hist. Soc., 1977—; bd. dirs. Current Historians, 1983—, Ga. Conservancy, 1982—. Mem. Ga. Bar Assn., Atlanta Bar Assn., Lawyers Club Atlanta. Democrat. Episcopalian. Contbr. articles to profl. jours. Personal injury. Home: 2850 Vinings Way SE Atlanta GA 30339 Office: Finch McCranie Brown & Thrash 1510 1st Atlanta Tower Atlanta GA 30383

THROWER, RANDOLPH WILLIAM, lawyer; b. Tampa, Fla., Sept. 5, 1913; s. Benjamin Key and Ora (Hammond) T.; m. Margaret Munroe, Feb. 2, 1939; children: Margaret (Mrs. W. Thomas MacCary), Patricia (Mrs. John R. Barmeyer), Laura (Mrs. David T. Harris, Jr.), Randolph William, Mary. Grad., Ga. Mil. Acad., 1930; Ph.B., Emory U., 1934, J.D., 1936. Bar: Ga. bar 1935, D.C. bar 1953. Partner Sutherland, Asbill & Brennan, Atlanta, Washington, 1947-69, 71—; commr. internal revenue, 1969-71; Lectr. bar, legal meetings; spl. agt. FBI, 1942-43; mem. Arthur Andersen & Co. Bd. of Rev., 1974-80, Nat. Council on Organized Crime, mem. exec. com., 1970-71. Past pres. Ga., Met. Atlanta mental health assns.; chmn. City of Atlanta Bd. Ethics; trustee Emory U., Clark Coll.; past chmn., trustee Wesleyan Coll.; bd. govs. Woodward Acad.; past chmn. bd. visitors Emory U. Served as capt. USMCR, 1944-45. Mem. Atlanta Legal Aid Soc. (past pres.), Emory U. Alumni Assn. (past pres.), ABA (chmn. spl. com. on survey local needs 1971-78, past chmn. sect. taxation, mem. ho. of dels. 1964-66, 74—), Ga. Bar Assn., Atlanta Bar Assn. (past pres.), Am. Bar Found. (dir. 1980—), Am. Law Inst., Atlanta Lawyers Club (past pres.), Phi Delta Phi. Republican. Methodist. Clubs: Commerce (Atlanta), Capital City (Atlanta), Piedmont Driving (Atlanta); Metropolitan (Washington), Chevy Chase (Washington). Home: 2240 Woodward Way NW Atlanta GA 30305 Office: 3100 First Nat Bank Tower Atlanta GA 30383 *

THUERMER, RICHARD JOSEPH, lawyer; b. Milw., June 28, 1935; s. Rudolph William and Viola Mary (Sloper) T.; m. Eleanor Caroline Schneider, June 8, 1957; children—Susan, Richard, Mary, Joseph. B.A., Marquette U., 1960, J.D., 1963. Bar: Wis. 1963. Sole practice, Reedsville, Wis., Mishicot, Wis.; village atty. Village of Reedsville. Served to cpl. USMC, 1953-55. Mem. State Bar Wis., Manitowoc County Bar Assn. Republican. Roman Catholic. Club: K.C. Estate planning, Probate, Personal income taxation. Home: Route 1 Box 94 Mishicot WI 54228 Office: 104 N 5th St Reedsville WI 54230 also: 407 Main St Mishicot WI 54228

THURBER, CLEVELAND, JR., trust banker; b. Detroit, Aug. 2, 1925; s. Cleveland and Marie Louise (Palms) T.; m. Elizabeth-Mary Hamilton, June 22, 1946; children: Cleveland III, Elizabeth King Thurber Crawford, David. Student, Purdue U.; B.A., Williams Coll., 1948. Asst. trust officer Comerica Bank-Detroit, 1958-61, trust officer, 1961-63, v.p., 1963-69, sr. v.p., 1969-81, exec. v.p., chief trust officer, 1981—. Pres. Friends of Grosse Pointe Pub. Library, 1971-72, Mich. Heart Assn., 1969-74; sec. United Community Services, 1968-70; Bd. dirs. Cottage Hosp., United Found., Mich. Humane Soc., Elmwood Cemetery, Ctr. for Creative Studies, Wm. L. Clements Library, Ann Arbor. Served with USMCR, 1943-46. Clubs: Detroit (Detroit) (past pres.), Yondotega (Detroit), Country (Detroit). Home: 34 Edgemere Rd Grosse Pointe Farms MI 48236 Office: Comerica Bank-Detroit 211 W Fort St Detroit MI 48226

THURBER, CLEVELAND, lawyer; b. Washington, Apr. 12, 1896; s. Henry Thomas and Elizabeth (Croul) T.; m. Marie Louise Palms, Sept. 20, 1924; children: Cleveland Jr., Peter Palms, Julie Thurber Sutherland, Marie Archibald. BA cum laude, Williams Coll., 1918; JD, Harvard U., 1922; LLD, Wayne State U., 1960. Bar: Mich. 1922, U.S. Dist. Ct. (so. dist.) Mich. 1923, U.S. Ct. Appeals (2d and 6th cirs.) 1934. Assoc. Miller, Canfield, Paddock & Stone, Detroit, 1922—; v.p., bd. dirs. Detroit Legal News. Trustee emeritus Williams Coll., Henry Ford Hosp., McGregor Fund; pres. Katherine Tuck Fund, David M. Whitney Fund; mem. Founders Soc. Detroit Inst. Arts; bd. dirs. Greater Detroit Area Hosp. Council, Marygrove Coll. Served to lt. U.S. Army, 1917-19. Mem. ABA, Mich. Bar Assn., Detroit Bar Assn., Am. Judicature Soc., Kappa Alpha. Presbyterian. Clubs: Yondotega, Detroit, Grosse Pointe, Country of Detroit. General corporate, Probate, Admiralty. Office: Miller Canfield Paddock & Stone 2500 Comerica Bldg Detroit MI 48226

THURMAN, ANDREW EDWARD, lawyer; b. Raleigh, N.C., May 11, 1954; s. William Gentry and Peggy Lou (Brown) T.; m. Patricia Stephens, May 19, 1979; 1 child, Gentry Brown. BA, Columbia U., 1976; JD, William & Mary Coll. of Law, 1979; MPH, U. Okla., 1984. Bar: Va. 1979, Okla. 1980, U.S. Ct. Appeals (10th cir.) 1981, U.S. Supreme Ct. 1985. Staff atty. Dept. of Human Services, Oklahoma City, 1979-80; counsel State of Okla. Teaching Hosps., Oklahoma City, 1980-84; mem. Miller, Dollarhide, Dawson & Shaw, Oklahoma City, 1984—; Pres. Council of Neighborhood Assns., Oklahoma City, 1984, Lincoln Terr. Neighborhood Assn., Oklahoma City, 1984; trustee Rader Trust, Oklahoma City, 1980—; treas., bd. dirs. SOTH Found., Oklahoma City, 1980—; bd. dirs. Newman Hosp., Shattuck, Okla., 1983—, Willowview Hosp., Spencer, Okla., 1984—. Fellow Am. Acad. Hosp. Atty.'s; mem. Nat. Health Lawyers Assn. Democrat. Methodist. Club: St. Anthony Hall (N.Y.C.) (pres. 1976). Avocation: reading detective novels. Health, Federal civil litigation, State civil litigation. Home: 607 NE 15th St Oklahoma City OK 73104 Office: Miller Dollarhide Dawson & Shaw 1200 Colcord Bldg Oklahoma City OK 73102

THURSTON, HAL, lawyer; b. Hartford, Conn., Apr. 16, 1948; s. Harold McBride Jr. and Helen (Peterson) T.; m. Mary F. Swenson, Mar. 26, 1981; children: Robin, Jesse. BA, Ohio State U., 1970; JD, Georgetown U., 1974. Bar: D.C. 1974, U.S. Dist. Ct. D.C. 1974, Wash. 1979, U.S. Dist. Ct. (we. dist.) Wash. 1979, U.S. Ct. Appeals (9th cir.) 1979. Staff atty. Neighborhood Legal Services, Washington, 1974-75; assoc. J. Joseph Barse, Washington, 1975-78; ptnr. Simonarson, Visser, Zender & Thurston, Bellingham, Wash., 1979—; instr. Nat. Inst. Trial Adv., Washington, 1978. Bd. dirs. Bellingham (Wash.) Food Bank, 1982—. Mem. ABA, Assn. Trial Lawyers Am., Wash. State Trial Lawyers Assn. Democrat. State civil litigation, Insurance, Personal injury. Office: Simonarson Visser Zender & Thurston 322 N Commercial St Suite 401 PO Box 5226 Bellingham WA 98227

THURSTON, MORRIS ASHCROFT, lawyer; b. Logan, Utah, May 25, 1943; s. Morris Alma and Barbara (Ashcroft) T.; m. Dawna Lyn Parrett, Sept. 10, 1966; children: Morris III, David, Ashley, Tyson. BA, Brigham Young U., 1967; JD, Harvard U., 1970. Bar: Calif. 1971, U.S. Dist. Ct. (cen. dist.) Calif. 1971, U.S. Supreme Ct. 1978. Assoc. Latham & Watkins, Los Angeles, 1970-77, ptnr., 1978—. Mem. Calif. Bar Assn., Orange County Bar Assn., Assn. Bus. Trial Lawyers. Republican. Mormon. Avocations: basketball, tennis, lit. Federal civil litigation, State civil litigation. Home: 9752 Crestview Circle Villa Park CA 92667 Office: Latham & Watkins 660 Newport Ctr Dr #1400 Newport Beach CA 92660

THURSWELL, GERALD ELLIOTT, lawyer; b. Detroit, Feb. 4, 1944; s. Harry and Lilyan (Zeitlin) T.; m. Lynn Satovsky, Sept. 17, 1967 (div. Aug. 1978); children—Jennifer, Lawrence; m. Judith Linda Bendix, Sept. 2, 1978; 1 son, Jeremy. LL.B. with distinction, Wayne State U., 1967. Bar: Mich. 1968, N.Y. 1984, D.C. 1986, Wis. 1986, U.S. Dist. Ct. (ea. dist.) Mich. 1968, U.S. Ct. Appeals (7th cir.) 1968. Student asst. to U.S. atty. Ea. Dist. Mich., Detroit, 1966; assoc. Zwerdling, Miller, Klimist & Maurer, Detroit, 1967-68; sr. ptnr. Thurswell, Chayet & Weiner, Southfield, Mich., 1968—; arbitrator Am. Arbitration Assn., Detroit, 1969—; mediator Wayne County Cir. Ct., Mich., 1983—, Oakland County Cir. Ct. Mich., 1984—; twp. atty. Royal Oak Twp., Mich., 1982—. Pres. Powder Horn Estates Subdiv. Assn., West Bloomfield, Mich., 1975, United Fund, West Bloomfield, 1976. Arthur F. Lederle scholar Wayne State U. Law Sch., Detroit, 1964, grad. profl. scholar Wayne State U. Law Sch., 1965, 66. Mem. Mich. Trial Lawyers Assn. (legis. com. on govtl. immunit, 1984, newsletter com. editor 1984), Assn. Trial Lawyers Am. (treas. Detroit met. chpt., 1986-87), Detroit Bar Assn. (lawyer referral com., panel pub. adv. com. judicial candidates), Oakland County Bar Assn. Jewish. Clubs: Wabeek Country (Bloomfield Hills), Boca Pointe Country (Boca Raton, Fla.). Personal injury, Local government, State civil litigation. Home: 1781 Golf Ridge Dr S Bloomfield Hills MI 48013 Office: Thurswell Chayet & Weiner 17117 W Nine Mile Rd Suite 500 Southfield MI 48075

TICE, RICHARD LEVERIDGE, lawyer; b. Plainfield, N.J., Oct. 21, 1950; s. Raymond Leroy and Audrey Alice (Morrison) T.; m. Deborah Jean Abbott, Aug. 14, 1971; children: Tyler, Ashley. BA, Gettysburg Coll., 1972; JD cum laude, Wake Forest U., 1976. Bar: N.J. 1976, U.S. Dist. Ct. N.J. 1976, U.S. Ct. Appeals (3d cir.) 1985. Law clk. to presiding justice N.J.

Superior Ct., Somerville, 1976-77; assoc. Large, Scamell & Danziger, Flemington, N.J., 1977-79, ptnr., 1979—. Assoc. editor Wake Forest U. Law Rev., 1975-76. Trustee Ctr. for Ednl. Advancement, 1986. Mem. ABA, N.J. Bar Assn., Hunterdon County Bar Assn. (sec. 1981), Civil Trial Atty. Com., Ethics Com. (presenter 1984-85). Republican. Club: Exchange (Flemington) (pres. 1985—, exchangite of yr. award 1984-85). State civil litigation, Bankruptcy, Personal injury. Home: RD 1 PO Box 482 D Stockton NJ 08559 Office: Large Scammell & Danziger 117 Main St Flemington NJ 08822

TICKNER, ELLEN MINDY, lawyer; b. Phila., May 30, 1951; d. Arnold Charles and Priscilla Frances (Wertlieb) Klomparens. B.S., Northwestern U., 1973; postgrad. U. Miami, Coral Gables, Fla., 1973-74; J.D., DePaul U., 1976. Bar: Ill. 1977, Mich. 1977, U.S. Dist. Ct. (ea. dist.) Mich. 1979, U.S. Ct. Appeals (6th cir.) 1986. Legal research and writing instr. U. Detroit Sch. Law, 1976-77; staff atty. Juvenile Defender Office, Detroit, 1977-79; litigation atty. U. Mich. Inst. Gerontology, Ann Arbor, 1980; clin. instr. law U. Mich. Law Sch., Ann Arbor, 1980-82, clin. asst. prof. law, 1982-83; assoc. Raymond, Rupp, Wienberg, Stone & Zuckerman, P.C., Troy, Mich., 1984-87, assoc. Miller, Canfield, Paddock & Stone, Detroit, 1987—. Bd. dirs. family law project, Ann Arbor, 1980-83, Mich. chpt. Nat. Com. for Prevention of Child Abuse, Lansing, 1980-82. Contbr. articles to legal jours. Mem. Women's Lawyers Assn. of Mich. (bd. dirs. 1981-82), 13th Nat. Conf. Women and the Law (steering com. 1981-82), Assn. Trial Lawyers Am., Fed. Bar Assn., Mich. Trial Lawyers Assn., ABA (litigation sect.), Oakland County Bar Assn. (vice chmn. continuing legal edn. com.), State Bar Mich. State civil litigation, Federal civil litigation, Environment. Office: Miller Canfield Paddock & Stone 2500 Comerica Bldg Detroit MI 48226

TIDWELL, DREW VIRGIL, III, lawyer; b. Miami, Fla., Aug. 12, 1948; s. Drew Virgil Jr. and Eleanor (Wiesner) T.; m. Marie Cecile Okoniewski, Aug. 28, 1971; children: Drew, Michael. BA in Pub. Affairs, George Washington U., 1970; JD, George Mason U., 1977. Bar: Va. 1977, D.C. 1978, U.S. Ct. Appeals (5th, 6th and 7th cirs.) 1979, U.S. Ct. Appeals (4th and D.C. cirs.) 1980, U.S. Supreme Ct. 1981, N.Y. 1985. Legis. and adminstrv. asst. to Congressman Ben B. Blackburn, Washington, 1966-74; v.p., gen. counsel Consumer Bankers Assn., Arlington, Va., 1974-84; sr. atty. Hiscock & Barclay, Buffalo, 1984—. Author: Most Common Violation, 1978, 3d. rev. edition, 1984; contbr. articles to profl. jours. Pres. Leewood Forest Homes Assn., Springfield, Va., 1977-81. Served with USAR, 1970-76. Mem. ABA (chmn. subcom. on relation to state law, com. on comml. fin. service), Consumer Bankers Assn. (lawyers com.). Republican. Lutheran. Banking, Consumer commercial, Federal civil litigation. Home: 156 Colony Ct Amherst NY 14226

TIDWELL, GEORGE ERNEST, U.S. district judge; b. Atlanta, Aug. 1, 1931; s. George Brown and Mary (Wooddall) T.; m. Carolyn White, July 1, 1961; children: Thomas George, Linda Carol, David Loran. LL.B., Emory U., 1954. Bar: Ga. 1954. Practiced in Atlanta, 1954-66, exec. asst. atty. gen., 1966-68; judge Civil Ct., Fulton County, Ga., 1968-71, Superior Ct., Atlanta Jud. Circuit, 1971-79, U.S. Dist. Ct. (no. dist.) Ga., Atlanta, 1979—. Mem. Am. Judicature Soc., Atlanta Bar Assn. Jurisprudence. Office: 1967 US Courthouse 75 Spring St SW Atlanta GA 30303

TIDWELL, MOODY R., III, judge; b. Kansas City, Mo., Feb. 15, 1939; s. Moody R., Jr. and Dorothy T.; m. Rena Alexandra, Jan. 28, 1966; children—Gregory, Jeremy. B.A., Ohio Wesleyan U., 1961; J.D., Am. U., 1964; LL.M., George Washington U., 1972. Bar: U.S. Ct. Appeals (D.C. cir.) 1964, U.S. Dist Ct. D.C. 1965, U.S. Ct. Claims 1972, U.S. Ct. Appeals (10th cir.) 1979. Assoc. solicitor gen. law div. Dept. Interior, Washington, 1972-75, assoc. solicitor Energy and Resources div., 1975-78, deputy solicitor, 1981-83; assoc. solicitor Mine Health and Safety div. Dept. Labor, Washington, 1978-80; judge U.S. Claims Ct., Washington, 1983—; dir., corporate sec. Keco, Inc., Cin. Pres. Pine Lake Recreation Bd., Glengary, W.Va., 1975—, Fairfax Farms Homeowners Assn., Va., 1980. Recipient Disting. Service award Sec. of Interior, 1983, Meritorious Service award Sec. of Labor, 1979. Mem. ABA, Fed. Bar Assn. Clubs: Army-Navy Country (Arlington, Va.); Fort Belvoir Officers (Alexandria, Va.). Avocations: photography; reading; writing; history. Office: US Claims Ct National Courts Bldg 717 Madison Pl NW Washington DC 20005

TIDWELL, WILLIAM C., III, lawyer; b. Haleyville, Ala., May 21, 1946; s. William C. and Lera (Jones) T.; m. Gloria Myrick, Jan. 24, 1970. B.S. in Chem. Engring., U. Ala., 1969, J.D., 1972. Bar: Ala. 1972, La. 1972, U.S. Dist. Ct. (so. dist.) Ala. 1975, U.S. Ct. Appeals (5th cir.) 1972, U.S. Ct. Appeals (11th cir.) 1979, U.S. Supreme Ct. 1979, U.S. Dist. Ct. (mid. dist.) Ala. 1982, U.S. Dist. Ct. (no. dist.) Ala. 1986. Assoc. firm Kullman, Lang, Inman & Bee, New Orleans, 1972-75; ptnr. firm Hand, Arendall, Bedsole, Greaves & Johnston, Mobile, Ala., 1975—; speaker Ala. Continuing Legal Edn. of Bar, Tuscaloosa, Ala. Mem. equal employment opportunity com. Def. Research Inst., 1979—; mem. com. on devel. of law Nat. Labor Relations Act, 1982—. Mem. Ala. State Bar (chmn. labor law sect. 1986-87), Fed. Bar Assn. (pres. Mobile chpt. 1986—), Mobile C. of C. Methodist. Clubs: Mobile Country, Athelstan (Mobile). Labor, Administrative and regulatory. Home: 169 S Georgia Ave Mobile AL 36604 Office: Hand Arendall Bedsole et al 2800 1st First Nat Bank Bldg Mobile AL 36602

TIERNEY, ALBERT GERARD, III, retail food executive; b. Boston, Mass., Dec. 24, 1953; s. Albert G. Jr. and Elizabeth (Colson) T.; m. Cathy Wheeler, Sept. 12, 1981; children: Caitlin A., Christopher W. AB, Dartmouth Coll., 1975; JD, Boston Coll., 1978. Bar: Mass. 1978. Law clk. Tierney and Manoil, Boston, 1976-78; assoc. Brickley, Sears & Cole, Boston, 1978-80, Bowker, Elmes, Perkins, Mecsas & Gerrard, Boston, 1981-83; of counsel DiCara, Selig, Sawyer & Holt, Boston, 1983-84; sr. v.p., gen. counsel J. Bildner & Sons Inc., Boston, 1984—. Mem. ABA, Mass. Bar Assn. Republican. Clubs: University (v.p. 1985-86), Harvard (Boston), The Country. Avocations: golf, squash. General corporate, Real property, Landlord-tenant. Home: 27 Stanford Rd Wellesley MA 02181 Office: J Bildner & Sons Inc 2 Oliver St Boston MA 02109

TIERNEY, JAMES EDWARD, state official; b. Bklyn., Apr. 12, 1947; s. Charles J. and Agnes V. (Quinn) T.; m. Susan Webster, Jan. 26, 1969; children: Adam, Josie, Matthew, Daniel. B.A. with highest honors, U. Maine, 1969, J.D., 1974. Bar: Maine bar 1974. Tchr. civics high sch. Auburn, Maine, 1969-71; mem. Maine State Ho. Reps., 1972-80, majority leader, 1976-80; atty. gen. State of Maine, 1981—. Criminal. Office: State House Augusta ME 04330 *

TIERNEY, PHILIP JAMES, lawyer; b. Bklyn., Nov. 13, 1936; s. Herbert Jerome and Reginia Mary (Conroy) T.; m. Carole Ann Campagna, July 15, 1961; children—Susan, Patrick, Mark; m. Rose Marie Hopper, Oct. 15, 1976. B.S., U. Notre Dame, 1958; postgrad. George Washington U., 1960-64; J.D., Cath. U. of Am., 1968. Bar: Md. 1968, U.S. Dist. Ct. Md. 1971, U.S. Ct. Appeals (4th cir.) 1972, U.S. Supreme Ct. 1972. Asst. county atty. Montgomery County, Md., 1968-71; gen. counsel Md. State Human Relations Commn., 1971-76; legis. counsel Montgomery County, 1976-79, dir. office of Zoning Adminstrv. Hearings 1979-85; dir. Office Zoning and Adminstrv. Hearings, 1985—; arbitration chmn. Md. Health Claims Arbitration; lectr. zoning Am. U. Law Sch., Cath. U. of Am. Chmn., mem. adv. council Coordination of Services to Handicapped, 1977-83; mem. bd. Village of Wilde Lake, 1985-87. Served with U.S. Army, 1959-62. Mem. ABA, Md. State Bar Assn. (chmn. adminstrv. law sect. 1982-83), Montgomery County Bar Assn. (chmn. adminstrv. law sect. 1979-80). Democrat. Roman Catholic. Clubs: Notre Dame of Md. (Balt.), K.C. (grand knight), St. Thomas More Soc. of Md. Co-author: Zoning and Land Use Practice in Md. 1981; contbr. articles to profl. jours. Administrative and regulatory, Local government, Real property. Home: 10025 The Mending Hall Columbia MD 21044

TIFFANY, JOSEPH RAYMOND, II, lawyer; b. Dayton, Ohio, Feb. 5, 1949; s. Forrest Fraser and Margaret Watson (Clark) T.; m. Terri Robbins, Dec. 1, 1984. AB magna cum laude, Harvard U., 1971; MS in Internat. Relations, London Sch. Econs., 1972; JD, U. Calif., Berkeley, 1975. Bar: U.S. Dist. Ct. (no. dist.) 1975, U.S. Dist. Ct. (ea. dist.) 1977, U.S. Ct. Appeals (9th cir.) 1982. Assoc. Pillsbury, Madison & Sutro, San Francisco, 1975-82, ptnr., 1983—. Patron Oreg. Shakespeare Festival Assn., Ashland, 1983, bd. dirs. Golden Gate Chpt. ARC, San Francisco, 1986—. Mem. ABA (antitrust, patent trademark and copyright, litigation sects.), Calif. Bar Assn. Club: Harvard (San Francisco). Federal civil litigation, State civil litigation, Libel. Office: Pillsbury Madison & Sutro 225 Bush St San Francisco CA 94104

TIFFORD, ARTHUR W., lawyer; b. Bklyn., July 7, 1943; s. Herman and Dorothy (Kessler) T.; m. Barbara J. Sinreich, Aug. 15, 1965; children: Melissa Beth, Alexandra Lynn. BA, CUNY, 1965; JD, Bklyn. Law Sch., 1966. Bar: N.Y. 1967, Fla. 1967, U.S. Dist. Ct. (so. dist.) Fla. 1968, U.S. Ct. Mil. Appeals 1968, U.S. Ct. Appeals (5th cir.) 1971, U.S. Dist. Ct. (mid. dist.) Fla. 1979, U.S. Ct. Appeals (10th cir.) 1979, U.S. Ct. Appeals (1st cir.) 1982, U.S. Ct. Appeals (9th cir.) 1982, U.S. Ct. Appeals (11th cir.) 1982, U.S. Ct. Appeals (fed. cir.) 1985. Researcher, mgr. clk. Cravath, Swaine & Moore, N.Y.C., 1967-69; asst. atty. U.S. Dept. Justice (so. dist.), Miami, 1971-72; sole practice Miami, 1972—. Served with JAGC, USMC, 1968-71, USMCR, 1978—. Mem. ABA, Am. Trial Lawyers Asns., Fla. Trial Lawyers Assn., Nat. Assn. Criminal Def. Lawyers, N.Y. Bar Assn., Fla. Bar Assn., Marine Corps Res. Officers Assn. (pres. Greater Miami chpt. 1978-79, 81-82, 84-85). Democrat. Avocations: writing, photography, parachuting, scuba diving, running. Federal civil litigation, Criminal, State civil litigation. Home: 9980 SW 128 St Miami FL 33176 Office: 1385 NW 15th St Miami FL 33125

TIGHE, DANIEL JOSEPH, lawyer; b. Oakland, Calif., Apr. 3, 1950; s. Peter Joseph and Rose Ellen (Keegan) T.; m. Antoinette Rafli Diab, Feb. 18, 1977; children: Justin K., Daniel Joseph. BS in History, Portland State U., 1972; JD, Gonzaga U., 1975. Bar: Wash. 1975. Atty. Poyhonen & Tighe, Inc., Montesano, Wash., 1975-81; sole practice Montesano, Wash., 1981—; v.p. DaPaul, Inc., Olympia, Wash., 1972—. Atty. City of Montesano Civil Service Commn., 1981—. Mem. ABA, Fed. Bar. Assn., Grays Harbor County Bar Assn., Wash. State Bar Assn., Wash. State Trial Lawyers., Am. Trial Lawyers Assn. Democrat. Roman Catholic. Lodge: Elks. Avocations: hunting, fishing, cars. Home: PO Box 567 Montesano WA 98563 Office: 120 Main Street S Montesano WA 98563

TILBURY, ROGER GRAYDON, lawyer; b. Guthrie, Okla., July 30, 1925; s. Graydon and Minnie (Lee) T.; m. Margaret Dear, June 24, 1952; 1 dau., Elizabeth Ann. B.S., U. So. Calif., 1945; J.D., U. Kans., 1949; LL.M., Columbia, 1950; postgrad., Oxford (Eng.) U., 1949. Bar: Mo. bar 1950, Oreg. bar 1953. Practiced in Kansas City, Mo., 1950-53, Portland, Oreg., 1953—; asso. firm Rogers, Field, Gentry, Kansas City, Mo., 1950-53, Stern, Reiter & Day, Portland, 1953-56; partner firm Roth & Tilbury, 1956-58, Tilbury & Kane, 1970-72, Haessler, Tilbury & Platten, 1978-81; individual practice law Portland, 1981—; circuit judge pro tem., Oreg., 1972—, arbitrator and fact finder, 1973—; tree farmer; sec. Barrington Properties; mem. nat. panel arbitrators U.S. Mediation and Conciliation Service; atty. Animal Defender League, 1969-73; dir. Consol. Cargos, Inc. Dep. election commr. Kansas City, Mo., 1952-53; bd. dirs. Multnomah Bar Found. Served to lt. (j.g.) USNR, 1943-45. Battenfeld scholar, 1943. Mem. Oreg. State Bar, Soc. Barristers, Am. Arbitration Assn., Save the Redwoods League, East African Wildlife League, Nat. Wildlife Found., Am. Trial Lawyers Assn., Delta Tau Delta, Phi Delta Phi. Antitrust, Federal civil litigation, Trial appellate negligence. Home: 9310 NW Cornell Rd Portland OR 97229 Office: 1123 SW Yamhill Portland OR 97205

TILGHMAN, CARL LEWIS, lawyer; b. Detroit, Aug. 3, 1944; s. Clifford Raymond and Alma (Gillikin) T.; m. Nancy Ann Huff, Aug. 21, 1965; children: Jason Andrew, Amanda Carol. BA, Wake Forest U., 1966, JD, 1969. Bar: N.C. 1969. Asst. U.S. atty. U.S. Dept. Justice, Raliegh, N.C., 1973-76; U.S. atty. U.S. Dist. Ct. (ea. dist.) N.C., Raleigh, 1976-77; sole practice Beaufort, N.C., 1977—. Vice chmn. Carteret County Commn., Beauford, 1984—. Served to capt. JAGC, U.S. Army, 1969-73. Mem. N.C. Bar Assn., Carteret County Bar Assn. (pres. 1983-84), N.S. Acad. Trial Lawyers. Republican. Baptist. Bankruptcy, State civil litigation, Criminal. Home: Rt #1 Box 214 Beaufort NC 28516 Office: PO Box 748 Beaufort NC 28516

TILGHMAN, RICHARD CARMICHAEL, JR., lawyer; b. Balt., July 6, 1947; s. Richard Carmichael and Mary Donnell (Singer) T.; m. Beverly Oliver Wheeler, Sept. 11, 1975; 1 child, Elizabeth Lloyd. BA, Union Coll., 1969; JD, U. Md., 1975. Bar: Md. 1975, U.S. Dist. Ct. Md. 1976. Law clk. to presiding justice Md. Ct. Appeals, Annapolis, 1975-76; assoc. Piper & Marbury, Balt., 1976-83, ptnr., 1983—. Asst. editor U. Md. Law Rev., 1975. Trustee Gilman Sch., Balt., 1980—, Balt. City Life Mus., 1983—. Served with USN, 1969-72. Mem. ABA, Md. Bar Assn., Order of Coif. Democrat. Episcopalian. Clubs: Md., Elkridge (Balt.). Avocations: golf, squash. Securities, General corporate, Health. Home: 1908 Ruxton Rd Baltimore MD 21204 Office: Piper & Marbury 36 S Charles St Suite 1100 Baltimore MD 21201

TILLAR, DARREL LONG, lawyer; b. Rockville Centre, N.Y., Oct. 19, 1950; d. Henry Richard and Mary Margaret (McKenna) L.; m. Thomas C. Tillar Jr., Dec. 9, 1972. BA in English, Va. Poly. Inst., 1971, MEd, 1973; JD, U. Va., 1981. Bar: Va. 1981, U.S. Dist. Ct. (ea. and we. dists.) Va. 1981, U.S. Ct. Appeals (4th cir.) 1986. Assoc. Long & Long, Blacksburg, Va., 1981-84; ptnr. Long, Long & Tillar, P.C., Blacksburg, 1984—. Chmn. Va. Commn. Status Women, 1984—. Mem. ABA, Va. Bar Assn., Assn. Trial Lawyers Am., Va. Trial Lawyers Assn., Va. Women Attys. Assn. (treas. 1983-84, pres.-elect 1986-87, pres. 1987—), AAUW (chmn. women's issues Blacksburg chpt. 1985—). Personal injury, General practice, Labor. Home: 3009 Stradford Ln Blacksburg VA 24060 Office: Long Long & Tillar PO Box 196 Blacksburg VA 24060

TILLER, EDWARD ALLAN, lawyer; b. Milton, Fla., Oct. 12, 1953; s. Edward John and Ruth Josephine (Allan) T. AA, Pensacola Jr. Coll., 1973; BA, U. W. Fla., 1975; JD, Vanderbilt U., Nashville, 1978; LLM in Tax, U. Fla., Gainesville, 1981. Bar: Fla. 1978, Tex. 1985. Assoc. Harrel, Wiltshire, Stone & Swearingen, Pensacola, 1978-80; tax advisor Gulf Oil Corp., Houston, 1981-84; assoc. Chamberlain, Hrdlicka, White, Johnson & Williams, Houston, 1984—. Contbr. articles to profl. jours. Mem. ABA, French-Am. C. of C., Inter-Am. C. of C., Japan Am. Soc., Asia Soc., Phi Kappa Phi. Democrat. Methodist. Corporate taxation, Personal income taxation, Tax, international. Home: 1718 Morse St Houston TX 77019 Office: Chamberlain Hrdlicka et al 1400 Citicorp Ctr Houston TX 77002

TILLERY, DWIGHT, educator, consultant; b. Cin., Mar. 10, 1948; s. Wesley and Doris Mae (Penman) T. BA, U. Cin., 1970; JD, U. Mich., 1972. Bar: Ohio 1973, U.S. Dist. Ct. (so. dist.) Ohio, U.S. Ct. Appeals (6th cir.). Asst. solicitor City of Cin., 1973-74; asst. exec. v.p. U. Cin., 1974-77; ptnr. Tillery & Assocs., Cin., 1977-83; sr. asst. atty. gen. State of Ohio, Columbus, 1983-85; asst. prof. bus. law Miami U., Oxford, Ohio, 1985—; adj. asst. prof. law U. Cin., 1975-77; cons. U. Cin. Law Sch., 1977-78, City of Cin., 1980-82, Office of Atty. Gen., Columbus, 1985—. Fellow mem. Cin. Scholarship Found., 1974-75; mem. Cin. City Council, 1975; vice chmn. Cin. Human Rights Commn., 1975-80, Cin. Bd. Health, 1976-80; del. 6th Cir. Jud. Conf., 1981-85. Named one of Outstanding Young Men Am., 1978. Fellow ABA, Nat. Bar Assn., Cin. Bar Assn., Assn. Trial Lawyers Am.; mem. Black Lawyers Assn. Cin. (founder). Democrat. Baptist. Avocations: jogging, basketball, tennis, football. General corporate, Legal education. Home: 3462 Trimble Ave Cincinnati OH 45207 Office: Miami U High St Oxford OH 45056

TILLMAN, DOUGLAS LEON, lawyer; b. Richmond, Va., Mar. 6, 1948; s. Lenwood Herbert and Isabelle Virginia (Montague) T. AB in Psychology, Franklin Coll., 1970; JD, Ind. U., 1977. Bar: Ind. 1977, U.S. Dist. Ct. (so. dist.) Ind. 1977. Personnel rep. Eli Lilly & Co., Indpls., 1972-75, dept. head, 1975-78, atty. securities, 1978-82, atty. regulatory, 1984—; atty. regulatory Elanco Products Co., Indpls., 1982-84; lectr. bus. law Ind. U., Indpls., 1978—. sec. bd. dirs. Jr. Achievement of Cen. Ind., Indpls.; mem. Indpls. Urban League. Served with U.S. Army, 1970-72. Mem. ABA, Ind. Bar Assn. Avocations: tennis, snow skiing. General corporate, Administrative and regulatory, Contracts commercial. Home: 6150 Afton Crest Indianapolis IN 46220 Office: Eli Lilly & Co Lilly Corp Ctr Indianapolis IN 46285

TILLMAN, MASSIE MONROE, lawyer; b. Corpus Christi, Tex., Aug. 15, 1937; s. Clarence and Artie Lee (Stewart) T.; m. Jerra Sue Comer, July 27, 1957; Jeffrey Monroe, Holly. BBA, Baylor U., 1959, LLB, 1961. Bar: Tex. 1961, U.S. Dist. Ct. (no. dist.) Tex. 1961, U.S. Ct. Appeals (5th cir.) 1969, U.S. Supreme Ct. 1969. Ptnr. Herrick & Tillman, Ft. Worth, 1961-66; sole practice Ft. Worth, 1966-70; ptnr. Brown, Herman et al., Ft. Worth, 1970-78, Street, Swift et al., Ft. Worth, 1978-79; sole practice Ft. Worth, 1979-87; bankruptcy judge U.S. Dist. Ct. (no. dist.) Tex., Ft. Worth, 1987. Author: Tillman's Trial Guide, 1970. Fellow Am. Bd. Trial Advocates, Tex. Bar Found.; mem. Ft. Worth/Tarrant County Bar (bd. dirs. 1969-70, v.p. 1970-71), Assn. Trial Lawyers Am. Democrat. Presbyterian. Avocations: cutting horses, competition shotgun shooting. Personal injury. Home: 4612 Briarhaven Rd Fort Worth TX 76109 Office: 206 US Courthouse Fort Worth TX 76102

TILSON, JOHN QUILLIN, lawyer; b. New Haven, Aug. 27, 1911; s. John Quillin and Marguerite (North) T.; m. Catherine E. Jackson, Sept. 14, 1934; children—John Quillin III, Thomas D., Rebecca E. Grad., Hotchkiss Sch., 1929; B.A., Yale, 1933, LL.B., 1936. Bar: Conn. bar 1936. Since practiced in New Haven; asso. Wiggin & Dana, 1936-48, partner, 1948—; lectr. hosp. law Yale Sch. Medicine, 1959—. Chmn. plan and zoning commn., Hamden, Conn., 1949-51; pres. Conn. Conf. Social Work, 1949-50; Bd. aldermen, New Haven, 1935-37; rep. Conn. Gen. Assembly, 1953; alternate Republican Nat. Conv., 1956, del., 1964; chmn. Hamden Rep. Town Com., 1964-68; Corporator Inst. Living, Hartford, 1959—; bd. dirs. New Haven Vis. Nurse Assn., New Haven United Fund; trustee Yale in China, 1936-62; bd. dirs. Yale New Haven Hosp., Yale Psychiat. Inst.; bd. dels. Am. Hosp. Assn. Served to lt. comdr. USNR, 1943-46, 51-53. Mem. ABA (del.), Conn. Bar Assn. (pres.), New Haven County Bar Assn. Clubs: Quinnipiack (New Haven), Graduate (New Haven); Morys. Legal education, Health. Home: 4 Marshall Rd Hamden CT 06517 Office: Wiggin & Dana 195 Church St PO Box 1832 New Haven CT 06508

TIMAEUS, DANA LEE, lawyer; b. Beaumont, Tex., Sept. 19, 1956; s. Lee Jefferson and Vernell (Lovin) T.; m. Kay Williams, Oct. 17, 1981. B.B.A. with highest honors, Lamar U., 1978; J.D., U. Tex., 1981. Bar: Tex. 1981, U.S. Ct. Appeals (5th and 11th cirs.) 1981, U.S. Dist. Ct. (ea. and so. dists.) Tex. 1982, U.S. Supreme Ct. 1985. Assoc., Benckenstein & Oxford, Beaumont, Tex., 1981-85, ptnr., 1986—. Editor, Am. Jour. Criminal Law, 1980-81; contbr. article in law jour. Bd. dirs., pres. Neighborhood Housing Services of Beaumont, 1984. Mem. Jefferson County Bar Assn., Tex. Young Lawyers Assn., Jefferson County Young Lawyers Assn. (mem. continuing legal edn. com. 1984—), ABA (mem. rules and procedures com., subcom. local rules), Blue Key, Phi Kappa Phi, Phi Eta Sigma (pres.). Democrat. Lutheran. Federal civil litigation, State civil litigation. Office: Beckenstein Oxford Radford & Johnson Allied Bank Bldg 3535 Calder 3d Floor Beaumont TX 77706

TIMBERG, SIGMUND, lawyer; b. Antwerp, Belgium, Mar. 5, 1911; came to U.S., 1916, naturalized, 1921; s. Arnold and Rose (Mahler) T.; m. Eleanor Ernst, Sept. 22, 1940; children—Thomas Arnold, Bernard Mahler, Rosamund and Richard Ernst (twins). A.B., Columbia U., 1930, A.M., 1930, LL.B., 1933. Bar: N.Y. 1935, U.S. Supreme Ct. 1940, D.C. 1954. Sr. atty., solicitors' office Dept. Agr., 1933-35, chief, soil conservation sect., 1935-38; staff mem. Temporary Nat. Econ. Com., 1938-39; sr. atty. SEC, 1938-42; chief, property relations and indsl. orgn. div., reoccupation br. Bd. Econ. Warfare and Fgn. Econ. Adminstrn., 1942-44; spl. asst. to atty. gen., antitrust div. Dept. Justice, 1944-45, chief judgment, judgment enforcement sect., 1946-52; sec. UN Com. on Restrictive Bus. Practices, 1952-53; cons. UN, 1953-55, 62-64; pvt. law practice 1954—; prof. law Georgetown U. Law School, 1952-54; faculty Parker Sch. Comparative Law, Columbia U., 1967-80; spl. counsel Senate Mil. Affairs Subcom. on Surplus Property Legislation, 1944; mem. Mission for Econ. Affairs, Am. Embassy, London, 1945; del. Anglo-Am. Telecommunications Conf., Bermuda, 1945, Geneva Copyright Conf., 1952; cons. Senate Patents Subcom., 1961, UN Patents Study, 1962-64, OAS, 1970; mem. adv. com. on fed. policy on indsl. innovation, patent and info. policy sub com., 1978-79, adv. com. on internat. investment, tech. and devel., 1979—. Contbr. articles on antitrust, intellectual property and internat. law to legal periodicals. Mem. Am., Internat., D.C. bar assns., Internat. Law Assn., Am. Soc. Internat. Law, Washington Fgn. Law Soc., Am. Law Inst., Assn. Bar City N.Y., Copyright Soc. Am. Clubs: Nat. Lawyers (Washington), Cosmos (Washington), Philosophy (Washington). Antitrust, Trademark and copyright, Private international. Home: 3519 Porter St NW Washington DC 20016 Office: 1700 K St NW Washington DC 20006

TIMBERLAKE, GEORGE WILLIAM, judge; b. Mt. Carmel, Ill., Nov. 17, 1948; s. Richard Woodrow Timberlake and Edith Helen (Beagley) Risley; m. Mary Jo Dunkel, Aug. 16, 1975. BA, U. Ill., 1970, MBA, JD, 1977. Bar: Ill. 1977. Clk. Office U.S. Magistrate, Benton, Ill., 1978; ptnr. Townsend, Townsend, Keenan & Timberlake, Mt. Carmel, 1979-81, Townsend, Timberlake, Price & Sawyer, Mt. Carmel, Ill., 1982-85; cir. ct. judge Edwards County, Albion, Ill., 1985-86; assoc. cir. judge 2d Jud. Cir. Ct., Mt. Vernon, Ill., 1987—. Pres. So. Ill. Arts, Carbondale, 1985-86. Mem. Ill. Bar Assn., Tri-County Bar Assn., Ill. Judges Assn. Democrat. Lodge: Lions. Avocations: sailing, acting. Judicial administration. Home: 239 N 6th St Albion IL 62806 Office: Jefferson County Cir Ct Jefferson County Courthouse Mount Vernon IL 62864

TIMBERLAKE, H. KENAN, lawyer; b. Stevenson, Ala., Oct. 9, 1935; s. Harold Kenan and Emma Evelyn (Wimberly) T.; m. Patricia Marquardt Henry, Aug. 12, 1961; children—Michael Kenan, Stephanie Arden. B.A., U. South, 1958; J.D., Vanderbilt U., 1961. Bar: Ala. 1962. With firm Page and Williams, 1962-63, Beck and Timberlake, 1963-68; sole practice, Huntsville, Ala., 1968-71, 73-78; partner Timberlake and Werdehoff, Huntsville, 1971-73; sr. ptnr. Timberlake and Gammons, Huntsville, 1978—; interim bankruptcy trustee, pilot program No. Dist. Ala. Served with USAF, 1961-65. Mem. Ala. Bar Assn., Assn. Trial Lawyers Am., Ala. Trial Lawyers Assn., Huntsville-Madison County Bar Assn., Huntsville Trial Lawyers Assn. Democrat. Methodist. Club: Sertoma (pres. 1969-70). Bankruptcy, General practice, Personal injury. Home: 5702 Tannahill Circle Huntsville AL 35802 Office: 106 South Side Sq Huntsville AL 35801

TIMMER, STEVEN JAMES, lawyer; b. LeMars, Iowa, Dec. 31, 1949; s. George and Clarraine A. (Vander Schaaf) T.; m. Lynn Carol McPheeters, Aug. 12, 1972; children: Andrew James, Phillip John. BS with honors, Iowa State U., 1972; JD cum laude, U. Minn., 1975. Bar: Minn. 1972, U.S. Dist. Ct. Minn. 1975, U.S. Ct. Appeals (8th cir.) 1972, U.S. Tax Ct. 1987. Assoc. Mastor & Mattson, Mpls., 1975-76, Baker & McKenzie, Mpls., 1976-79, O'Connor & Hannan, Mpls., 1980-85, Timmer & Van Vliet, Mpls., 1985—. Bd. dirs., chmn. elect Minn. World Trade Assn., Mpls., 1984—. Mem. ABA, Minn. Bar Assn. (chmn. internat. bus. law sect. 1985-86). Congregationalist. Avocations: fly fishing, music, bicycling, sailing. Federal civil litigation, State civil litigation, Private international. Home: 5348 Oaklawn Ave Edina MN 55424 Office: 5200 Willson Rd Minneapolis MN 55424

TIMMINS, EDWARD PATRICK, lawyer; b. Denver, June 8, 1955; s. M. Edward and Elizabeth Jean (Imhoff) T.; m. Mary Joanne Deziel, Dec. 27, 1985; 1 child, Edward Patrick Jr. BA with honors, Harvard U., 1977; JD magna cum laude, U. Mich., 1980. Bar: Colo. 1981, U.S. Ct. Appeals (D.C. and 9th cirs.) 1982, U.S. Dist. Ct. Colo. 1984, U.S. Ct. Appeals (10th cir.) 1984. Law clk. to cir. justice U.S. Ct. Appeals (7th cir.), Chgo., 1980-81; trial atty. U.S. Dept. Justice, Washington, 1981-84; asst. U.S. atty. Denver, 1984—; assoc. Otten, Johnson, Robinson, Neff & Ragonetti, Denver, 1985—. Sr. editor U. Mich. Law Rev., 1980. Harvard Nat. scholar, 1976. Mem. ABA, Colo. Bar Assn., Denver Bar Assn., Order of Coif. Avocations: reading, skiing, tennis, squash, bridge. Federal civil litigation, General corporate, Real property. Office: Otten Johnson Robinson Neff & Ragonetti 950 17th St Suite 1600 Denver CO 80202

TIMMONS, MARY SARAZIN, lawyer; b. Mpls., May 10, 1938; d. Norbert Delos and Alice Mary (Morrison) Sarazin; m. Martin John Timmons, Apr. 4, 1959; children: Daniel, Leo, Eileen, John, Kathleen. BS, Coll. St. Catherine, 1959; JD, William Mitchell Coll. Law, 1980. Bar: Minn. 1981, U.S. Dist. Ct. Minn. 1981, U.S. Ct. Appeals (8th cir.) 1985. VISTA atty. United Handicapped Fedn., Roseville, Minn., 1980-81; sole practice St. Paul, 1981; ptnr. Deretich & Timmons, St. Paul, 1982—. Mem. ABA, Minn. Bar Assn., Soc. Profls. in Dispute Resolution. Roman Catholic. General prac-

tice, Federal civil litigation, Public utilities. Home: 9125 Utica Ave Bloomington MN 55437 Office: Deretich and Timmons 375 Jackson Saint Paul MN 55101

TIMMONS, PATRICK FRANCIS, JR., lawyer; b. Houston, Nov. 4, 1947; s. Patrick Francis and Virginia (Penick) T.; m. Sharon Lynn West, Aug. 1, 1970; 1 child, Susan Emily. B.A., U. Tex.-Austin, 1969, J.D., 1972. Bar: Tex. 1972, U.S. Supreme Ct. 1978, D.C. 1973, U.S. Ct. Appeals (5th cir.) 1975, U.S. Ct. Appeals (D.C. cir.) 1974, U.S. Dist. Ct. D.C. 1974, U.S. Dist. Ct. (no. dist.) Tex. 1976, U.S. Dist. Ct. (so. dist.) Tex. 1975. Atty. U.S. Maritime Adminstrn., Dept. Commerce, Washington, 1972-75, Panhandle Eastern Corp., Houston, 1975-77; sole practice, Houston, 1977—; dir. Trunkline Credit Union, Houston, 1976-77; dir., chmn. Tex. Lawyers Credit Union, Austin, 1978-84; dir. Capitol Credit Union, Austin, 1984-86. Bd. dirs. Parents of Prematures, Houston, 1980—, pres., 1984-86; adv. dir. Parents of Prematures and High Risk Infants Internat., N.Y.C., 1982—; pres. Republican Men's Club West Harris County, Houston, 1976—. Served to maj. USAR, 1971—. Mem. Houston Young Lawyers Assn. (chmn., Outstanding Com. Chmn. award 1978-79), Houston Bar Assn., ABA. Presbyterian. Club: Exchange of Houston, University. State civil litigation, General corporate, Oil and gas leasing. Home: 1503 Buckmann Houston TX 77043 Office: 10200 Old Katy Rd Houston TX 77043

TIMMONS, PETER JOHN, lawyer; b. Madison, Wis., Jan. 23, 1954; s. Donald Ralph and Mary Jean (Boyd) T.; m. Michele Lynn Spolar, Dec. 17, 1977; children: Megan Ann, Andrew Peter. BA, Hamline U., 1976; JD, U. Minn., 1979. Bar: Minn. 1979, U.S. Dist. Ct. Minn. 1979, U.S. Ct. Appeals (9th cir.) 1979. Assoc. Bruce Douglas & Assocs., Mpls., 1979-80, Cousineau, McGuire et al, Mpls., 1980-82, Moss & Barnett, Mpls., 1982—; bd. dirs. Lawyers Credit Union, Mpls., pres. 1986—. Asst. scoutmaster Boy Scouts Am., Mpls., 1980-82; campaigner Dem. Farmer Labor candidates, Mpls., 1980—, chmn. local precinct, 1986—. Mem. ABA, Minn. Bar Assn., Hennepin County Bar Assn., Minn. Trial Lawyers Assn., Phi Beta Kappa, Pi Gamma Mu. Avocations: reading, politics, biking, golf. Personal injury, Criminal, State civil litigation. Home: 5035 Lyndale Ave S Minneapolis MN 55419 Office: Moss & Barnett 1200 Pillsbury Ctr Minneapolis MN 55402

TINARI, ANTHONY PHILIP, lawyer; b. Abington, Pa., Sept. 19, 1952; s. Frank A. and Anna F. (Palmer) T.; m. Mary Alice Classen, July 5, 1975; children: Philip Anthony, Matthew Classen, Celeste Marie. BS, Duke U., 1974; JD, Villanova U., 1977. Bar: Pa. 1977, U.S. Dist. Ct. (ea. dist.) Pa. 1980, U.S. Supreme Ct. 1982, U.S. Ct. Appeals (3d cir.) 1983. Law clk. to presiding justice Montgomery County Ct. Common Pleas, Norristown, Pa., 1977-78; trial atty. Marshall, Dennehey, Warner, Coleman & Goggin, Norristown, 1978-86; assoc. litigation counsel Squibb Corp., Princeton, N.J., 1986—. Commr. Lower Moreland Twp., Huntingdon Valley, Pa., 1983—. Mem. ABA, Pa. Bar Assn., Montgomery Bar Assn., Montgomery County Trial Lawyers Assn. (exec. bd. 1985—). Republican. Roman Catholic. Lodge: Rotary (bd. dirs. Huntingdon Valley 1984—). State civil litigation, Personal injury, Environment. Home: 2371 Terwood Dr Huntingdon Valley PA 19006 Office: Squibb Corp PO Box 4000 Princeton NJ 08543-4000

TINDEL, JOHN CURTIS, lawyer; b. Cabool, Mo., Nov. 19, 1935; s. Curtis Jordan and Nell Catherine (Johnson) T.; m. Shirley A. Haynes, Sept. 13, 1954; children—John M., Curtis J., Jeanne. B.A., U. Mo.-Columbia, 1956, M.A., 1957, J.D., 1963. Bar: Mo. 1963, Mich. 1977, U.S. Supreme Ct. 1980. Ptnr. Kennedy & Tindel, Nevada, Mo., 1963-68; real estate atty. Monsanto Co., 1968-75; asst. gen. counsel St. Paul Title Ins. Corp., 1975-76; sole practice, Cabool, 1976-82; pres. Hiett Abstract Co., Houston, Mo., 1980—; ptnr. Tindel & Ellsworth, Cabool, 1982-83; sole practice, Cabool and Houston, 1983—; judge Cabool and Licking mcpl. div. Tex. County Circuit Ct., 1979—. Mem. ABA, Mo. Bar, Mich. Bar, Mo. Assn. Assoc. and Municipal Ct. Judges, Bar Assn. Met. St. Louis, Tex. County Bar Assn. Republican. Baptist. Author: (with others) Missouri Family Law, 1967. Real property, Probate, Banking. Office: 104 W Main St Houston MO 65483

TINDER, JOHN DANIEL, lawyer; b. Indpls., Feb. 17, 1950; s. John Glendon and Eileen M. (Foley) T.; m. Jan M. Carroll, Mar. 17, 1984. B.S., Ind. U., 1972, J.D., 1975. Bar: Ind. 19, U.S. Dist. Ct. (so. dist.) Ind. 19, U.S. Ct. Appeals (7th cir.) 19, U.S. Supreme Ct. Asst. U.S. atty. Dept. of Justice, Indpls., 1975-77; pub. defender Marion County Criminal Ct., Indpls., 1977-78; chief trial dep. Marion County Pros. Office, Indpls., 1979-82; litigation counsel Harrisone Moberly, Indpls., 1982-84; U.S. atty. U.S. Dist. Ct. (so. dist.) Ind., Indpls., 1984—; adj. prof. Ind. U. Sch. of Law, Indpls., 1980—; mem. Supreme Ct. Character & Fitness Com., Ind., 1982—. Co-founder Turkey Trot Invitational Race, Indpls., 1980. Recipient Cert. of Appreciation award Bur. Alcohol, Tobacco & Firearms, Indpls., 1976; Service award Marion County Prosecutor, Indpls., 1981. Mem. ABA, Ind. State Bar Assn. (dir. criminal justice sect. 1984—), Indpls. Bar Assn., 7th Circuit Ct. Bar Assn., Fed. Bar Assn. Republican. Roman Catholic. Office: Office of U S Atty 46 E Ohio St Indianapolis IN 46204 *

TINGLE, JAMES O'MALLEY, lawyer; b. N.Y.C., June 12, 1928; s. Thomas Jefferson and Mercedes (O'Malley) T. B.S., U. Mont., 1950, B.A., 1952, LL.B., 1952; LL.M., U. Mich., 1953, S.J.D., 1958. Bar: Calif. 1959, Mont. 1952, N.Y. 1961. Assoc. prof. law U. Mont., Missoula, 1955-56; atty. Shell Oil Co., N.Y.C., 1957-62; assoc. Pillsbury, Madison & Sutro, San Francisco, 1962-68, ptnr., 1969—. Author: The Stockholder's Remedy of Corporate Dissolution, 1959; editor: State Antitrust Laws, 1974. Served to 1st lt. USAF, 1953-55. William W. Cook fellow U. Mich. Mem. Mont. Bar Assn., Calif. Bar Assn., ABA. Democrat. Club: Stock Exchange (San Francisco). Antitrust, Legislative, Intellectual property licensing. Office: Pillsbury Madison & Sutro 225 Bush St San Francisco CA 94104

TINNEY, RICHARD TOWNSEND, JR., lawyer consultant; b. Long Beach, Calif., Dec. 4, 1950; s. Richard Townsend and Mary Paul (DePasse) T. BA, UCLA, 1973; M Pub. Adminstrn., Pa. State U., 1974; JD, Georgetown U., 1977. Bar: D.C. 1977, U.S. Dist. Ct. D.C. 1977, U.S. Ct. Appeals (D.C. cir.) 1977, U.S. Ct. Appeals (10th cir.) 1978. Atty. U.S. Cts., Washington, 1978-79; supervisory cons. Coopers & Lybrand, Washington, 1978-81; counsel Ctr. for Environ. Edn., Washington, 1981—; lectr. Pa. State U., King of Prussia, 1978; mem. U.S. Del. North Pacific Fur Seal Commn., Washington and Moscow, 1983-84; cons. U.S. Marine Mammal Commn., Washington, 1982-86. Co-author: A Nation of Oceans, 1986; also articles. Research fellow Pa. State U., 1973, Law fellow, Georgetown U., 1976. Mem. ABA, AAAS, Ecol. Soc. Am., Soc. Marine Mammalogy, D.C. Bar Assn. Avocations: scuba diving, photography. Environment, Administrative and regulatory. Home: 1501 S George Mason Dr Apt 22 Arlington VA 22204 Office: Ctr for Environ Edn 1725 DeSales Washington DC 20036

TINSLEY, WALTON EUGENE, lawyer; b. Vanceburg, Ky., Jan. 22, 1921; s. Wilbur Walton and Sarah Edith (Frizzell) T.; m. Joy Mae Matthews, Aug. 31, 1952; children—Merry Walton Tinsley Moore, Troy Eugene, Paul Richard. E.E., U. Cin., 1943; M.S. in Aero. Engring, NYU, 1947; J.D., U. So. Calif., 1953. Bar: Calif. 1954, U.S. Supreme Ct. 1971. Practiced in Los Angeles, 1954—; mem. firm Harris, Kern, Wallen & Tinsley (patent attys.), 1958—. Signatory Roll of Disting. Philatelists, 1983. Fellow Royal Philatelic Soc. London; mem. IEEE (assoc.), Am. Inst. Aeros. and Astronautics, ABA, Los Angeles County Bar Assn., Am. Philatelic Soc. (v.p. 1965-69, Luff award 1986), S.R., English Speaking Union (dir. Los Angeles br.). Presbyterian (elder, trustee, chmn. trustees 1972). Patent, Trademark and copyright. Home: 2210 Moreno Dr Los Angeles CA 90039 Office: Harris Kern Wallen & Tinsley 650 S Grand Ave Los Angeles CA 90017

TIPPING, HARRY ANTHONY, lawyer; b. Bainbridge, Md., Nov. 2, 1944; s. William Richard and Ann Marie (Kelly) T.; m. Kathleen Ann Palmer, July 12, 1969; 1 child, Christopher A. B.A., Gannon U., 1966; J.D., U. Akron, 1970. Bar: Ohio. Asst. law dir. City of Akron, Ohio, 1971-72, chief asst. law dir., 1972-74; ptnr. Gillen, Miller & Tipping, Akron, 1974-77, Roderick, Myers & Linton, Akron, 1977-86; sole practice, Akron, 1987—. Chmn., Bd. of Tax Appeals, City of Fairlawn, Ohio, 1979-81, mem. merger com., 1980-82. Served with USCGR, 1966-72. Mem. Akron Bar Assn., Ohio Bar Assn., ABA, Ohio Acad. Trial Lawyers, Assn. Trial Lawyers Am., Defense Research Inst., Am. Arbitration Assn. Republican. Roman Catholic. Clubs: Fairlawn Country (Ohio); Cascade (Akron). State civil litigation, Labor, Federal civil litigation. Office: 600 CitiCtr Bldg Akron OH 44308

TIPPIT, JOHN HARLOW, lawyer; b. Marietta, Okla., July 22, 1916; s. Alva Ney and Edna Pearl (Harlow) T.; m. Ann Morse, Feb. 27, 1943; children—David H., Ann Maurine. B.A., U. Okla., 1940, LL.B., 1940. Bar: Okla., 1940, Colo., 1945, U.S. Supreme Ct., 1960. States atty. Love County, Okla., 1940; sole practice Denver, 1945-77, Boulder, Colo., 1978-83; ptnr. Tippit, Haskell & Welborn, Tippit & Haskell and Tippit & Whittington P.C., Boulder, 1947-48; dir. Buckingham Nat. Bank; pres., mng. ptnr. natural resources cos.; lectr. Rocky Mountain Mineral Law Found.; lectr. various legal confs. Co-author: American Law of Mining; contbr. articles to profl. jours. Vice pres. Denver council Boy Scouts Am.; pres. Red Rocks Assn.; bd. dirs., sec. Acad. Ind. Scholars. Served to lt. col. USAAF, 1940-44. Mem. ABA (chmn. sect. natural resources), Okla. Bar Assn., Colo. Bar Assn. (chmn. mineral law sect.), Denver Bar Assn. (trustee). Republican. Episcopalian. Clubs: Mile High Denver Country (Denver); Boulder Country. Oil and gas leasing, General practice, Private international. Home: 525 Aurora St Boulder CO 80302 Office: 305 Park West Bldg 250 Arapahoe St Boulder CO 80302

TISDALE, DOUGLAS MICHAEL, lawyer; b. Detroit, May 3, 1949; s. Charles Walker and Violet Lucille (Battani) T.; m. Patricia Claire Brennan, Dec. 29, 1972; children—Douglas Michael, Jr., Sara Elizabeth, Margaret Patricia, Victoria Claire. B.A. in Psychology with honors, U. Mich., 1971, J.D., 1975. Bar: Colo. 1975, U.S. Dist. Ct. Colo. 1975, U.S. Ct. Appeals (10th cir.) 1976, U.S. Supreme Ct. 1979. Law clk. to chief judge U.S. Dist. Ct. Colo., Denver, 1975-76; assoc. Brownstein, Hyatt, Farber & Madden, Denver, 1976-81, ptnr., 1981—; bd. dirs. Employer Services Program, Inc., Denver, Warner Devels., Inc., Vail, Colo.; lectr. Law Seminars, Inc., 1984—, Continuing Legal Edn. in Colo., Inc., 1984—, Nat. Bus. Insts., 1985—; Colo. Law-Related Edn. Coordinator, 1982—. Mem. ABA (mem. litigation sect. trial evidence com. 1981—, vice chmn. real property sect. com on creditors rights in real estate fin. 1984—, vice chmn. real property sect. com. on real property law and needs of public 1984-85, chmn. real property sect. sub-com. on foreclosures in bankruptcy 1982—), Colo. Bar Assn. (conv. com. 1979—), Denver Bar Assn. (jud. adminstrn. com. 1978—), Am. Judicature Soc., Assn. Trial Lawyers Am., Colo. Trial Lawyers Assn., Law Club of Denver (sec. 1984-85), Phi Alpha Delta, Phi Beta Kappa. Democrat. Roman Catholic. Federal civil litigation, State civil litigation, Real property. Home: 10986 West 77th Ave Arvada CO 80005 Office: Brownstein Hyatt Farber & Madden 410 17th St Denver CO 80202

TISDALE, JEFFREY ALAN, lawyer; b. Akron, Ohio, Feb. 10, 1949; s. Leon Winford and Elizabeth (Ritthaler) T. BA, U. Calif., Santa Barbara, 1974; JD, Calif. Western Sch. Law, 1977. Bar: Calif. 1978, Fla. 1979. Atty. Fed. Dept. Ins. Corp., Washington, 1977-79, Fed. Home Loan Bank Bd., Washington, 1979-80; assoc. Manatt, Phelps et al, Los Angeles, 1980-81, McKenna, Conner & Cuneo, Los Angeles, 1981-85; ptnr. Finley, Kumble, Wagner, Heine, Underberg, Manley, Myerson & Casey, Los Angeles, 1985—. Cons. campaign law Jerry Brown for Gov., Los Angeles, 1982. Mem. ABA. Democrat. Avocations: travel, skiing, reading. Banking, General corporate.

TISDALE, PATRICIA CLAIRE, lawyer; b. Detroit, Sept. 7, 1951; d. Joseph Terrence Jr. and Patricia Ann (Cottrell) Brennan; m. Douglas Michael Tisdale, Dec. 29, 1972; children: Douglas M., Sara E., Margaret P., Victoria C. BA, U. Detroit, 1971; JD, U. Denver, 1979. Bar: Colo. 1979, U.S. Dist. Ct. Colo. 1979. Dep. city atty. City of Arvada, Colo., 1979—. Mem. ABA, Colo. Bar Assn. (conv. com. chmn. 1984-86), First Jud. Dist. Bar Assn., Am. Judicature Soc., Metro City Attys. Assn., Phi Alpha Delta. Republican. Roman Catholic. Avocations: skiing, racquetball, reading, family activities. Local government, Condemnation, State civil litigation. Home: 10986 W 77th Ave Arvada CO 80005 Office: City of Arvada 8101 Ralston Rd Arvada CO 80002

TISHLER, NICHOLAS EUGENE, lawyer; b. N.Y.C., July 24, 1951; s. Victor Israel and Nina (Ginsburg) T.; m. Alison Dawn Curley, June 26, 1981. BA, SUNY, Stony Brook, 1975; JD, Northeastern U., 1980. Bar: N.Y. 1981, U.S. Dist. Ct. (so. and ea. dists.) N.Y. 1981, U.S. Ct. Appeals (2d cir.) 1983, U.S. Ct. Appeals (D.C. cir.) 1985, U.S. Supreme Ct. 1985, R.I. 1987. Asst. dist. atty. Suffolk County, Riverhead, N.Y., 1980-82; pvt. practice Wading River, N.Y., 1982—; cons. N.Y. State Archives, Albany, N.Y., 1984—. Mem. ABA, N.Y. State Bar Assn. (panelist appellate practice seminar 1987, Suffolk County Bar Assn. (profl. ethics com. 1984-85, chmn. appellate practice com. 1985-86, Spl. Award of Recognition 1986), Suffolk County Criminal Bar Assn. Appellate civil, criminal, state and fed. cts., General practice, Legal history. Home: 238 Wilbur Ave Cranston RI 02910 Office: 2400 N Ocean Ave Farmingville NY 11738 Office: 72 S Main St Providence RI 40127-4446

TITLE, PETER STEPHEN, lawyer; b. New Orleans, Nov. 24, 1950; s. Harold Benjamin and Beulah (Sterbcow) T.; m. Sheryl Gerber, June 14, 1981. B.A., Columbia U., 1972; J.D., Tulane U., 1975. Bar: La. 1975, U.S. Dist. Ct. (ea., we., mid. dists.) La., U.S. Ct. Appeals (5th cir.). Assoc. Sessions, Fishman, Rosenson, Boisfontaine, Nathan & Winn, New Orleans, 1975-81, ptnr., 1982—; instr. on property Tulane U., 1978; asst examiner com. on Admissions to Bar, 1980—; lectr. on real estate. Mem. ABA, La. Bar Assn. (chmn. sect. on trust estates, probate and immovable property law 1983-84), New Orleans Bar Assn., Rep. Am. Judicature Soc., Order of Coif, Phi Delta Phi. Jewish. Lodge: B'Nai Brith. Bankruptcy, General corporate, Real property. Home: 515 Hillary St New Orleans LA 70118 Office: Sessions Fishman Rosenson 201 St Charles Ave 35th Floor New Orleans LA 70170

TITTSWORTH, CLAYTON (MAGNESS), lawyer; b. Tampa, Fla., Nov. 8, 1920. Student U. Tampa, 1939-42; LL.B., Stetson Law Sch., 1951. Bar: Fla. 1951; ptnr. Tittsworth & Tittsworth, Tampa, 1951-65, Brandon, Fla., 1964-77; sole practice law, Brandon, 1973-83; Tittsworth and Curry P.A., Brandon, 1983—. Mem. ABA, Fla. Bar Assn., Hillsborough County Bar Assn. State civil litigation, Probate, Corps Relations, Domestic Relations. Office: 420 W Brandon Blvd Brandon FL 33511

TITTSWORTH, DAVID GREGORY, lawyer; b. Wichita, Kans., Apr. 3, 1953; s. George Herman and Wanda Lee (Grosvenor) T. BA, Kans. U., 1975, JD, 1978. Bar: Kans. 1978, U.S. Ct. Appeals (10th cir.) 1979. Research atty. Kans. Ct. Appeals, Topeka, 1978-81; spl. counsel on rail matters Kans. Dept. Transp., Topeka, 1981-82, chief of rail programs, 1982-83, chief counsel, 1983-85; assoc. Gaar & Bell, Overland Park, Kans., 1985—; spl. asst. atty. gen. State of Kans., Topeka, 1983-85. Recipient Pres. award Assn. Am. State Hwy. and Transp. Ofcls., 1983. Mem. ABA, Kans. Bar Assn., Nat. Assn. Bond Lawyers. Democrat. Avocations: theatre, music, sports. Municipal bonds, Local government, State and local taxation. Office: Gaar & Bell 8717 W 110th Suite 640 Overland Park KS 66210

TITUS, CHRISTINA MARIA, lawyer; b. Phila., Oct. 31, 1950; d. George Herman and Frieda Anna (Szuchy) T.; m. Richard Christopher Daddario, Jan. 19, 1980; 1 child, Alexandra Anna Daddario. BA, NYU, 1972; JD, Georgetown U., 1977. Bar: N.Y. 1978, U.S. Dist. Ct. N.Y. (so. and ea. dists.) 1979. Assoc. Trubin Sillcocks Edelman & Knapp, N.Y.C., 1977-80; v.p., co-gen. counsel Merrill Lynch, Hubbard, Inc., N.Y.C., 1980—. Recipient 1st prize Drexel Keyboard Competition, 1968. Mem. ABA, Assn. Bar City N.Y., N.Y. State Bar Assn. (com. on real estate financing and liens, real property law sect). Lutheran.

TITUS, JON ALAN, lawyer; b. Milw., Oct. 6, 1955; s. Mary (Irwin) Stephenson; m. Laura Jean Newman, Sept. 5, 1982. BA, U. Ariz., 1977; JD, Ariz. State U., 1980. Bar: Ariz. 1980, U.S. Dist. Ct. Ariz. 1980. Ptnr. Furth, Fahrner, Bluemle & Mason, Scottsdale, Ariz., 1980—. Sec. Ariz. Kidney Found., 1986—. Mem. ABA, Ariz. Bar Assn. (chmn. securities regulation sect. 1986—), Maricopa County Bar Assn., Scottsdale Bar Assn. Antitrust, Real property, Securities. Office: Furth Fahrner Bluemle & Mason 7373 N Scottsdale Rd Suite B252 Scottsdale AZ 85253

TJOFLAT, GERALD BARD, judge; b. Pitts., Dec. 6, 1929; s. Gerald Benjamin and Sarita (Romero-Hermoso) T.; m. Sarah Marie Pfohl, July 27, 1957; children: Gerald Bard, Marie Elizabeth Tjoflat McElligott. Student, U. Va., 1947-50, U. Cin., 1950-52; LL.B., Duke U., 1957; D.C.L. (hon.), Jacksonville U., 1978. Bar: Fla. 1957. Individual practice law Jacksonville, Fla., 1957-68; judge 4th Jud. Cir. Ct. Fla., 1968-70, U.S. Dist. Ct. for Middle Dist. Fla., Jacksonville, 1970-75, U.S. Ct. Appeals, 5th Cir., Jacksonville, 1975-81, U.S. Ct. Appeals, 11th Cir., Jacksonville, 1981—; mem. Adv. Corrections Council U.S., 1975—; mem. com. adminstrn. probation system Jud. Conf. U.S., 1972—, chmn., 1978—; U.S. del. 6th and 7th UN Congress for Prevention of Crime and Treatment of Offenders. Hon. life mem. bd. visitors Duke U. Law Sch.; pres. North Fla. council Boy Scouts Am., 1976-85, chmn., 1985—; trustee Jacksonville Marine Inst., 1976—, Episcopal High Sch. Jacksonville, 1983—; mem. vestry St. Johns Cathedral, 1985—. Served with AUS, 1953-55. Mem. ABA, Fla. Bar Assn., Am. Law Inst., Am. Judicature Soc. Episcopalian. Jurisprudence. Home: PO Box 960 Jacksonville FL 32201 Office: US Ct Appeals 11th Cir PO Box 960 Jacksonville FL 32201

TOBACK, ARTHUR MALCOLM, lawyer; b. N.Y.C., Dec. 18, 1944; s. Cecil and Lisa (Saltzman) T.; m. Patricia Anne Kruse, May 30, 1969; children—Sharon Tova, Sonya Celena, Lia Shoshana. B.A., U. Pa., 1966; J.D., Georgetown U., 1969; Bar: D.C. 1969, N.Y. 1973; U.S. Ct. Appeals (2nd cir.), U.S. Dist. Ct. (so. dist.) N.Y. U.S. Dist. Ct. (ea. dist.) N.Y. U.S. Supreme Ct. 1975, U.S. Tax Ct. 1982. Appellate atty. ICC, Washington, 1969-71; enforcement atty. EPA, N.Y.C., 1971-72; assoc. Kaye, Scholer, Fierman, Hays & Handler, N.Y.C., 1972-78; co-founder, sr. ptnr. Horwitz, Toback & Hyman, N.Y.C., 1978—. Contbg. editor: Georgetown Law Jour., 1968-69. Bd. dirs., mem. exec. com. Sutton Pl. Synagogue, N.Y.C., 1978—; bd. dirs. Tonetta Lake Park Assn., Brewster, N.Y., 1981—. Mem. Assn. of Bar of City of New York, Democrat. Federal civil litigation, State civil litigation, Contracts commercial. Home: 320 E 25th St New York NY 10010 Office: Horwitz Toback & Hyman 1114 Ave of Americas New York NY 10036

TOBER, STEPHEN LLOYD, lawyer; b. Boston, May 27, 1949; s. Benjamin Arthur Tober and Lee (Hymoff) Fruman; m. Susan V. Schwartz, Dec. 22, 1973; children: Cary, Jamie. Grad., Syracuse U., 1971, JD, 1974. Bar: N.H. 1974, U.S. Dist. Ct. N.H. 1974, U.S. Supreme Ct. 1978, N.Y. 1981. Assoc. Flynn, McGuirk & Blanchard, Portsmouth, N.H., 1974-79; sole practice Portsmouth, 1979-81; ptnr. Aeschliman & Tober, Portsmouth, 1981—; lectr. Franklin Pierce Law Ctr., Concord, N.H., 1978-80. Contbr. articles to law jours. Mem. Portsmouth Charter Commn., 1976, Portsmouth Planning Bd., 1977-81; del. N.H. Constl. Conv., Concord, 1984; city councilman, Portsmouth, 1977-81. Mem. Assn. Trial Lawyers Am. (gov. 1980-86), N.H. Bar Assn. (v.p. 1986-87, chair com. to redraft the code of profl. responsibility), N.H. Trial Lawyers Assn. (pres. 1977). Democrat. Jewish. Avocations: reading, tennis. State civil litigation, Personal injury, General practice. Home: 55 TJ Gamester Dr Portsmouth NH 03801 Office: Aeschliman & Tober 381 Middle St Portsmouth NH 03801

TOBIAS, ANDY MONROE, lawyer; b. Marlin, Tex., Dec. 4, 1939; s. Elmo Duane and Pauline Josephine (Hardeman) T.; m. Patricia Jean Musal; children: Teri, Casi, Misti. BA, SW Tex. State U., 1963; JD, S.Tex. Coll. Law, 1968. Bar: Tex. 1968. Dist. ct. div. chief felonies Dist. Atty.'s Office, Houston, 1969—; instr. Houston Police Acad., Harris County Sheriff's Acad., Pasadena Police Acad. Contbr. articles to legal jours.; author; producer tng. film: DWI Law and Video Taping Drunks, 1983. Mem. ABA, Houston Bar Assn. (dir. criminal law div. 1983-84), Tex. County and Dist. Atty.'s Assn., Traffic Safety Awareness Task Force, Houston Galveston Area Council. Methodist. Criminal. Home: 11923 Barrett Brae Houston TX 77072 Office: Dist Attys Office 210 Fannin St Houston TX 77002

TOBIAS, CHARLES HARRISON, JR., lawyer; b. Cin., Apr. 16, 1921; s. Charles Harrison and Charlotte (Westheimer) T.; m. Mary J. Kaufman, June 15, 1946; children—Jean M., Thomas Charles, Robert Charles. B.A. cum laude, Harvard U., 1943, LL.B., 1949. Bar: Ohio Bar 1949. Assoc. firm Steer, Strauss and Adair, Cin., 1949-56; ptnr. firm Steer, Strauss, White and Tobias, Cin., 1956—. Bd. dirs. Cin. City Charter Com., 1955-75; mem. Wyoming (Ohio) City Council, 1972-77, vice mayor, 1974-77; bd. govs., sec., Ch. Cin. Overseers, Hebrew Union Coll., Jewish Inst. Religion; pres. Met. Area Religious Coalition of Cin., 1977-80, Jewish Fedn. Cin., 1972-74; mem. nat. bd. govs. Am. Jewish Com., 1981—. Served with USN, 1943-46. Mem. Ohio State Bar Assn., Cin. Bar Assn. Club: Losantiville Country (Cin.). Contracts commercial, General corporate, Probate. Home: 21 Reily Rd Cincinnati OH 45215 Office: Steer Straus White & Tobias 2208 Central Trust Tower Cincinnati OH 45202

TOBIAS, JEFFREY, lawyer; b. N.Y.C., Feb. 12, 1956; s. Leon Paul and Fritzie (Itzkowitz) T.; m. Leanne Aronson, Oct. 23, 1983. BA, U. Rochester, 1977; JD, George Washington U., 1980. Bar: D.C. 1980, N.Y. 1983. Asst. dist. atty. Queens County, Kew Gardens, N.Y., 1982-86; legal editor Pike & Fischer, Inc., Bethesda, Md., 1986—. Communications. Office: Pike & Fischer Inc 4550 Montgomery Ave Bethesda MD 20814

TOBIAS, PAUL HENRY, lawyer; b. Cin., Jan. 5, 1930; s. Charles H. and Charlotte (Westheimer) T.; 1 child, Eliza L. A.B. magna cum laude, Harvard U., 1951, LL.B., 1958. Bar: Mass. 1958, Ohio 1962. Assoc. Stoneman & Chandler, Boston, 1958-61, Goldman & Putnick, Cin., 1962-75; ptnr. Tobias & Kraus, Cin., 1976—; instr. U. Cin. Law Sch., 1975-77. Author: Litigating Wrongful Discharge Claims, 1987; contbr. articles to profl. jours. Mem. Cin. Bd. of Park Commrs., 1973-81, Cin. Human Relations Commn., 1980-84. Served with U.S. Army, 1952-54. Mem. Cin. Bar Assn. (past chmn. legal aid com.), Ohio State Bar Assn., ABA, Plaintiff Employment Lawyers Assn. (pres.). Civil rights, Labor, Personal injury. Home: 15 Hill and Hollow Ln Cincinnati OH 45208 Office: Tobias & Kraus 911 Mercantile Library Bldg Cincinnati OH 45202

TOBIN, BENTLEY, lawyer; b. Bklyn., N.Y., Feb. 18, 1924; s. Nathan H. and Mildred E. (Aronoff) T.; m. Nancy Gurvitz, Sept. 13, 1947; children—Patricia E., Mitchell H.; m. 2d, Beverly Ann Mucciarone, Feb. 17, 1979. B.S., CCNY, 1943; LL.B., Harvard U., 1948. Bar: N.Y. 1948, Mass. 1951, R.I. 1952. Atty. N.Y.C. Housing Authority, 1948-49; ptnr. Titiev, Greenman & Tobin, Boston, 1949-52; sr. ptnr. Tobin & Silverstein, Inc., Providence, 1952-84; ptnr. Hinckley, Allen, Tobin & Silverstein, 1984— ; trustee Woonsocket Inst. Savs., Eastland Savs. Bank; dir. Woonsocket Inst. Trust Co., dir. Internat. Co., Eastland Bank; mem. R.I. Commn. on Jud. Tenure and Discipline. Trustee, v.p. Woonsocket Hosp. Served in USAR, 1943-46. Mem. ABA, R.I. Bar Assn., Woonsocket Bar Assn. Club: University (Providence). Contracts commercial, Probate, Real property. Address: 1500 Fleet Ctr Providence RI 02903

TOBIN, BRUCE HOWARD, lawyer; b. Detroit, July 17, 1955; s. Marshall Edward and Rhoda Maureen (Milman) T. BA in Social Sci., Mich. State U., 1978; JD, Detroit Coll. Law, 1982; LLM in Taxation, NYU, 1983. Bar: Mich. 1982, Fla. 1982, Nebr. 1983, U.S. Dist. Ct. (ea. dist.) Mich. 1982, U.S. Tax Ct. 1983. Assoc. Kutak, Rock & Campbell, Omaha, 1983-85; ptnr. Gropman, Lebow & Tobin, Birmingham, Mich., 1985—. Mem. ABA, Fla. Bar Assn., Mich. Bar Assn. (tax com. 1985—), Nebr. Bar Assn. Jewish. Club: Executive (Bloomfield Hills, Mich.). Corporate taxation, Estate taxation, Real property. Office: Gropman Lebow & Tobin 401 S Woodward Suite 306 Birmingham MI 48011

TOBIN, CRAIG DANIEL, lawyer; b. Chgo., Aug. 17, 1954; s. Thomas Arthur and Lois (O'Connor) T. BA with honors, U. Ill., 1976; JD with high honors, Ill. Inst. Tech., 1980. Bar: Ill. 1980, U.S. Dist. Ct. (no. dist.) Ill. 1980, U.S. Dist. Ct. (no. dist.) Ind. 1986, U.S. Ct. Appeals (7th cir.) 1986, U.S. Supreme Ct. 1987. Trial atty. Cook County Pub. Defender, Chgo., 1980-82; trial atty. homicide task force Pub. Defender, Chgo., 1982-84; ptnr. Craig P. Tobin and Assocs., Chgo., 1984—; lectr. Cook County Pub. Defender, Chgo., 1983, Ill. Pub. Defender Assn., 1987. Named One of Outstanding Young Men in Am., 1985. Mem. ABA, Chgo. Bar Assn., Nat. Assn. Criminal Def. Lawyers. Roman Catholic. Criminal, Personal injury. Office: Craig D Tobin and Assocs 79 W Monroe Chicago IL 60603

TOBIN, GERALD J., lawyer; b. Bklyn., Sept. 11, 1935; s. David and Dorothy (Gnatowsky) T.; m. Helene Pomerantz, June 24, 1956; children—Alyson Beth, Stacey Lynn, Adam Scott. B.A., U. Miami, 1959, J.D., 1962. Bar: Fla. 1962, N.Y. 1980, U.S. Supreme Ct. 1965, U.S. Ct. Appeals

(5th cir.) 1964, U.S. Ct. Appeals (11th cir.) 1981. Sole practice, Miami, Fla., 1962—; Judge Mcpl. Ct., City of Miami, 1965-72; chief judge, 1970-72; chmn. bd. Nat. Corrections Constrn. Inc., Nat. Corrections Mgmt. Inc. Bd. dirs. P.R.I.D.E.-Fla Prison Industries, 1982—, Big Bros., Miami, Congregation Bet Breira. State civil litigation, Criminal, Family and matrimonial. Home: 12005 SW 64th St Miami FL 33183 Office: 1414 Coral Way Miami FL 33145

TOBIN, HAROLD WILLIAM, lawyer; b. San Francisco, Apr. 7, 1922; s. Robert Douglass and Rita Mary (Lannon) T.; m. Julie DeLaveaga, Aug. 3, 1946; m. Shirley Ellen Traynor, Jan. 5, 1965; children: Douglass Michael, Kathleen, Harold William, Jr., Suzanne, Neil McKinley. Student U. San Francisco, 1940-42, U.S. Air Corp Aviation Cadet Sch., 1942-43; JD, U. San Francisco, 1946. Bar: Calif. 1949, U.S. Dist. Ct. (no. dist.) Calif. 1949, U.S. Ct. Apls. 1949. U.S. atty. War Crimes Trials, Manila, Phillipines, 1946-48; assoc. Hone & Lobree; assoc. Benjamin L. McKinely, 1951-53; ptnr. Jacobsen & Tobin, 1953-57, Tobin and Ransom, 1957-67; sole practice San Francisco, 1970-71, Antioch, Calif., 1971—. Mem. San Francisco Rep. County Central Com., 1949-51, 70-71; pres., VIP San Francisco Archdiocesan Council Cath. Men, 1958-59. chmn. Antioch Police Commn., 1977-81; sec. Bay Area Rapid Transit Citizens. Served with USAAF, 1942-43. Mem. ABA, Contra Costa County Bar Assn., State Bar Calif. (pres. conf. barristers 1957-58), Bar Assn. San Francisco (past dir.), Assn. Trial Lawyers Am. Club: Barristers of San Francisco (past pres.). Catholic. General practice, Personal injury, Probate. Home: 2100 Reseda Way Antioch CA 94509 Office: 2830 Lone Tree Way Antioch CA 94509

TOBIN, IRVING, lawyer; b. N.Y.C., Nov. 16, 1924; s. Samuel and Rose (Schreibman) T.; m. Lillian Nussbaum, Dec. 11, 1960 (div. 1964); m. Phyllis Onheiber, Dec. 14, 1975; 1 child, Rebecca. BS, Rutgers U., 1949, JD, 1957; MBA, NYU, 1953. Bar: N.J. 1857, U.S. Dist. Ct. N.J. 1957. Ptnr., owner Gluck & Tobin, Elizabeth, N.J., 1949—; adj. lectr. Rutgers U., Newark, N.J., 1958-61. Served with U.S. Army, 1942-46. Mem. Am. Assn. Attys., Am. Assn. CPA's. Jewish. Real property, Corporate taxation, Personal income taxation. Home: 61 Bauer Terrace Hillside NJ 07200 Office: Gluck & Tobin 570 N Broad St Elizabeth NJ 07208

TOCCI, DOMINICK P., lawyer; b. Utica, N.Y., July 1, 1934; s. Joseph and Rose (Louaglio) T.; m. Celia Zizzi, Aug. 16, 1958; children: Charmaine, Jennifer, Richard. BA, Hamilton Coll., 1956; JD, Syracuse U., 1959. Bar: N.Y. 1959. Ptnr. Pozefsky & Tocci, Albany, N.Y., 1960-78; sole practice Albany, 1978—; assoc. counsel N.Y. State Senate, Albany, 1965-67, N.Y. State Assembly. Albany, 1967-70, N.Y. State Legislature Task Force on Pari-Mutual Betting, Albany, 1978-83; lectr. labor law and arbitration courses Cornell U. Sch. Indsl. Relations, 1978-82. Recipient Award of Merit Union Label and Services Trades Council of the Capital Dist., Albany, 1977. Mem. Assn. Trial Lawyers Am., N.Y. State Bar Assn., Nat. Conf. of Unions and Employee Benefit Funds (adv. council 1978—), Indsl. Relations Research Assn. (adv. council 1983—). Democrat. Roman Catholic. Avocations: fishing, reading. Labor, Personal injury, Legislative. Office: 112 State St Albany NY 12207

TOCKMAN, GERALD, lawyer; b. St. Louis, Sept. 29, 1937. B.A., Washington U., St. Louis, 1958, J.D., 1960. Bar: Mo., Ill. 1960, D.C. 1971, Calif. 1984, U.S. Supreme Ct. 1976. Sole practice, St. Louis, 1960—. Mem. ABA, Mo. Bar Assn., Ill. Bar Assn., St. Louis Bar Assn., Assn. Trial Lawyers Am. Contbr. articles to profl. jours. Labor, Oil and gas leasing, Antitrust. Office: 319 N 4th St Suite 1001 Saint Louis MO 63102

TODARO, LAURA JEAN, lawyer; b. Neligh, Nebr., June 8, 1956; d. Andrew Robert and Mary Louise (Leenerts) T. BS, U. Ill., 1978; JD, Loyola U., New Orleans, 1981. Bar: La. 1981, U.S. Dist. Ct. (ea. and mid. dists.) La. 1981, U.S. Ct. Appeals (5th cir.) 1981, U.S. Supreme Ct. 1985. Assoc. Dutel & Dutel, New Orleans, 1981-85; ptnr. Todaro & Todaro, Kenner, La., 1985—; city atty. Kenner, 1985—. Bd. dirs. Kenner YMCA, Westwood Heights Civic Assn., Kenner; mem. Jefferson Parish Alliance for Good Govt. Mem. ABA, Fed. Bar Assn., Jefferson Parish Bar Assn., Kenner Bus. Women's Assn., U. Ill. Alumni Assn. (local organizer), Phi Delta Phi. Republican. Roman Catholic. Avocations: sailing, water and snow skiing. Local government, State civil litigation, Family and matrimonial. Home: 720 Vanderbilt Ln Kenner LA 70065 Office: Kenner City Atty's Office 1801 Williams Blvd Kenner LA 70065

TODD, ALBERT CRESWELL, III, lawyer; b. Greenwood, S.C., June 17, 1950; s. Albert Creswell and Marjorie (Byrd) T.; m. Deborah Moore, July 22, 1972; children: Andrew, Anna, David, John. BS in Indsl. Mgmt., Clemson U., 1972; JD, U. S.C., 1975; LLM in Estate Planning, U. Miami, 1976. Bar: S.C. 1975, U.S. Tax Ct. 1976, U.S. Ct. Appeals (4th cir.) 1976; cert. specialist in estate planning, probate and trust law. Assoc. Robert P. Wilkins, Colulmbia, S.C., 1976-79; ptnr. Todd & Johnson, Columbia, 1979—; instr. advanced estate planning The Am. Coll., 1980-81. Editorial asst. Drafting Wills and Trust Agreements in South Carolina, 1976; author booklet: A Diagrammatic Guide to Estate Planning, 1984. Bd. dirs. Children's Hosp. at Richland Meml., Columbia; tchr. Bethel Bible Series St. Martins-in-the-Fields Episcopal Ch., Columbia, 1983—; chmn. adv. bd. Columbia Bible Coll., 1985—; bd. dirs., sec.-treas. Episc. Ministry to the Aging, 1985-86. Mem. S.C. Bar Asssn. (chmn. estate planning, probate and trust law sect. 1981-82, lectr. 1975—), Richland City Bar Assn. (chmn. estate planning, probate and trust sect. 1979-80), ABA. Episcopalian. Club: Summit. Estate planning, Probate, Estate taxation. Home: 5842 Woodvine Rd Columbia SC 29206 Office: Todd & Johnson 1136 Washington St PO Box 11262 Columbia SC 29211

TODD, BEN, lawyer; b. Tupelo, Miss., Mar. 27, 1944; s. James B. Sr. and Carma Francis (Robinson) T.; m. Janice Grissom, 1963 (div. 1964); 1 child, Sulynn; m. Carolyn Victoria Meason, Sept. 18, 1971; children: Amy, Brad. BBA, U. Miss., 1967; JD, Memphis State U., 1970. Bar: Miss. 1970, Tenn. 1970, U.S. Dist. Ct. Miss. 1976, U.S. Dist. Ct. Tenn. 1976, U.S. Supreme Ct. 1976. Assoc. Walter Buford, Memphis, 1970-73; sole practice Memphis, 1973-76, 86—; sr. ptnr. Todd & Deal P.C., Memphis, 1976-86. Mem. men's com. Memphis Symphony, 1982-85; leadership mem. Boy Scouts Am., Memphis, 1984-86. Mem.Mem. ABA, Memphis Bar Assn., Shelby County Bar Assn., Assn. Trial Lawyers Am., N.Y. Trial Lawyers Assn., Tenn. Trial Lawyers Assn. (bd. of govs. 1974-84), Miss. Trial Lawyers Assn. Federal civil litigation, State civil litigation, Admiralty. Office: 294 Washington Ave Memphis TN 38103

TODD, CASEY IRA, seafood industry executive, lawyer; b. Crisfield, Md., July 22, 1954; s. Ira Thompson and Virginia (Tawes) T.; m. Kimberly Kaye Parsons, Mar. 28, 1980; children: Abigail Leah, Joshua Ira. BA in Econs., Coll. William and Mary, 1976; JD, U. Balt., 1978. Bar: Md. 1979. Pres. Metompkin Bay Oyster Co. Inc., Crisfield, Md., 1977—, also bd. dirs. Mem. ABA, Md. Bar Assn., Somerset County Bar Assn., Pi Lambda Phi. Democrat. Methodist. Business law as it relates to the seafood industry. Home: 30 Hall Highway Crisfield MD 21817 Office: Metompkin Bay Oyster Co Inc 11th and Dock St Crisfield MD 21817

TODD, JAMES D., federal judge; b. Scotts Hill, Tenn., May 20, 1943; m. Jeanie M. Todd; children: Michael, Julie. BS, Lambuth Coll., 1965; MS, U. Miss., 1968; JD, Memphis State U., 1972. Tchr. sci. Lyman High Sch., Longwood, Fla., 1965-68, Memphis U. Sch., 1968-72; ptnr. Waldrop, Farmer, Todd & Breen, Pa., 1972-83; judge U.S. Ct. Appeals div. II, Jackson, Tenn., 1983-85, U.S. Dist. Ct. (we. dist.) Tenn., Jackson, 1985—. Office: US Dist Ct 200 Federal Bldg Jackson TN 38302 *

TODD, JAMES MARION, lawyer; b. Paris, Ky., May 13, 1929; s. Thomas Marion and Ida Saxton (Estes) T.; m. Marjorie Ann Vance, Aug. 22, 1959; children: Thomas Melvin, James M. Jr. AB, U. Ky., Lexington, 1952, JD, 1956. Assoc. S.J. Stallings, Louisville, 1956-57; sole practice Lexington, Ky., 1957-65, 1982-86; ptnr. Todd & Compton, Lexington, 1965-73, Todd & Sherrow, Lexington, 1973-82, Todd & Todd, Lexington, 1986—. Vice mayor Lexington-Fayette Counties Govt., 1978-82. Served to maj. USAF, 1952-54. Mem. Assn. Trial Lawyers Am., Ky. Trial Lawyers Assn. Democrat. Lodge: Lions (pres. breakfast club 1965-66). State civil litigation, Collections, Real property. Home: 509 Clinton Rd Lexington KY 40502 Office: Todd & Todd 219 N Upper St Lexington KY 40507

TODD, JOHN JOSEPH, lawyer; b. St. Paul, Mar. 16, 1927; s. John Alfred and Martha Agnes (Jagoe) T.; m. Dolores Jean Shanahan, Sept. 9, 1950; children—Richard M., Jane E., John P. Student, St. Thomas Coll., 1944, 46-47; B.Sci. and Law, U. Minn., 1949, LL.B., 1950. Bar: Minn. bar 1951. Practice in South St. Paul, Minn., 1951-72; partner Thuet and Todd, 1953-72; asso. justice Minn. Supreme Ct., St. Paul, 1972-85; sole practice West St. Paul, 1985—. Served with USNR, 1945-46. Mem. Am. Bar Assn., state bar assns., Am. Legion, VFW. Jurisprudence. Home: 6659 Argenta Trail W Inver Grove Heights MN 55075 Office: 1535 Livingston Ave West Saint Paul MN 55118

TODD, ROBERT ALLEN, lawyer; b. Sweden, Eng., Nov. 13, 1957; came to U.S., 1958; s. Neal Kenneth and Martha (Mathis) T. BS, U. Tulsa, 1979, JD, 1982. Bar: Okla. 1982, U.S. Dist. Ct. (no. dist.) Okla. 1982. Asst. city prosecutor City of Tulsa, 1982-83; sole practice Tulsa, 1983-86; ptnr. Sharp, Todd & Patterson, Tulsa, 1986—; mediator Okla. Atty. Gen.'s Office, Oklahoma City, 1986—. Mem. com. Tulsans for Clean Air, Tulsa, 1985-86. Mem. Okla. Bar Assn. (advisor for mock trials 1984-85), Assn. Trial Lawyers Am., Okla. Trial Lawyers Assn. Republican. State civil litigation, Personal injury, Real property. Office: Sharp Todd & Patterson 2519 E 21st St Tulsa OK 74114

TODD, WILLIAM MICHAEL, lawyer; b. Cleve., Dec. 13, 1952; s. William Charles and Jennie Ann (Diana) T.; m. Sara Lynn, Jan. 4, 1986. BA, U. Notre Dame, 1973; JD, Ohio State U., 1976. Bar: Ohio 1976, U.S. Dist. Ct. (so. dist.) Ohio 1977. Assoc. Porter, Wright, Morris & Arthur, Columbus, Ohio, 1976-82, ptnr., 1983—. Mem. council St. Anthony's Med. Ctr., Columbus, 1985—; trustee Callvac Services, Columbus, 1985—. Mem. ABA, Ohio Bar Assn., Columbus Bar Assn., Def. Research Inst., Ohio Assn. Civil Trial Lawyers, Soc. Med. Assn. Counsel. Roman Catholic. Club: Columbus Athletic. Avocations: music, recreational sports. Federal civil litigation, State civil litigation, Health. Office: Porter Wright Morris & Arthur 41 S High St Columbus OH 43215

TODMAN, TERENCE ALPHONSO, JR., lawyer; b. Washington, July 30, 1953; s. Terence A. Todman, Sr. AB, Brown U., 1975; JD, Columbia U., 1978. Bar: N.Y. 1979. Atty. Office Legal Advisor Dept. of State, Washington, 1976; assoc. Curtis, Mallet et al, N.Y.C., 1977, Paul, Weiss, Rifkind, Wharton & Garrison, N.Y.C., 1978—. Trustee Nat. Urban League; term mem. Council on Fgn. Relations; bd. dirs. Black Filmaker Found. Mem. ABA, N.Y. State Bar Assn., Assn. Bar City of N.Y. Private international, General corporate, Public international. Home: 41 W 86th St New York NY 10024 Office: Paul Weiss Rifkind et al 1285 Ave of the Americas New York NY 10019

TODT, DANIEL THOMAS, lawyer; b. Cleve., Sept. 16, 1955; s. Simon Henry and Evelyn Marie (Bender) T.; m. Rebecca Louise Schultz, July 25, 1981; 1 child, Dominique Vanessa. BA in Polit. Sci. and Acctg., Cleve. State U., 1976; postgrad., U. Kiev and U. Moscow and Lenningrad U., USSR, 1977; JD, Cleve.-Marshall Coll. Law, 1980. Bar: Ohio 1982, U.S. Dist. Ct. (no. dist.) Ohio 1982. Sales constrn. mgr. Sqires Constrn., Macedonia, Ohio, 1976-78; assoc. Walter, Haverfield, Buesher & Chockley, Cleve., 1978-82; ptnr. Todt, Todt & Co. P.C., Cleve., 1982-86; dir. spl. services Hyatt Legal Services, Cleve., 1986—; bd. dirs. Valdez Inc., Cleve., Onthe Ave. Inc., Cleve., V-Tro Inc., Parma, Ohio. Author: The Deal, 1986. Councilman City of Independence, Ohio, 1978-81; exec. com. Cuyahoga County Rep. Orgn., Ohio, 1978—; pres. Independence Rep. Club, 1978. Fellow Phi Alpha Delta; mem. ABA, Jaycees (pres. 1982, Jaycee of Yr. 1982). Byzantine Catholic. Lodge: Kiwanis (membership chmn. Independence). Avocation: fencing. International finance, General practice, Banking. Office: Hyatt Legal Services 401 Euclid Ave Suite 227 Cleveland OH 44114

TOEDT, D(ELL) C(HARLES), III, lawyer; b. Maxwell AFB, Ala., Nov. 17, 1954; m. Maretta A. Comfort. BA with honors, U. Tex., 1973, JD, 1981. Bar: Tex. 1982, U.S. Dist. Ct. (so. dist.) Tex. 1984, U.S. Ct. Appeals (Fed. cir.) 1984. Atty. Schlanger, Cook, Cohn, Mills & Grossberg, Houston, 1982-83, Arnold, White & Durkee, Houston, 1983-86. Sr. assoc. editor Tex. Law Rev., 1981-82; contbr. articles to law jours. Served to lt. USN, 1974-79. Mem. ABA (chmn. subcom. computer litigation practices and tactics 1985—). Computer, Federal civil litigation, Patent. Office: Arnold White & Durkee PO Box 4433 Houston TX 77120

TOEPFER, THOMAS LYLE, lawyer; b. Hays, Kans., Oct. 4, 1950; s. Anthony Lyle and Mary Alice (Clark) T.; m. Karen L. Culley, May 20, 1972; 1 child, Russell Thomas. AB in Econs. summa cum laude, Ft. Hays State U., 1972; JD, Washburn U., 1975. Bar: Kans. 1975, U.S. Dist. Ct. Kans. 1975, U.S. Ct. Appeals (10th cir.) 1983. Assoc. Dreiling, Bieker & Kelley, Hays, 1975-83; prosecutor City of Hays, 1977—; sole practice Hays, 1984—. Mem. Hays Bd. Edn., 1985—; treas. Ellis County Dems., Hays, 1980; pres. St. Nicholas Ch. Parish Council, Hays, 1985-86. Mem. ABA, Kans. Bar Assn., Ellis County Bar Assn. (pres. 1984-85), Assn. Trial Lawyers Am., Kans. Trial Lawyers Assn. Roman Catholic. General practice, State civil litigation, General corporate. Home: 303 W 39th St Hays KS 67601 Office: 114 W 11th Hays KS 67601

TOFT, MARTIN JOHN, III, lawyer; b. St. Louis, June 21, 1936; s. Martin John Jr. and Edna Ann (Mortensen) T.; children—Diana Toft Engel, Tracy Lynn, Carolyn Quinn, Anneliese Marie. B.S.B.A., Washington U., St. Louis, 1963; J.D., St. Louis U., 1967. Bar: U.S. Dist. Ct. (ea. dist.) Mo. 1968, U.S. Ct. Appeals (8th cir.) 1972, U.S. Supreme Ct. 1979. Ptnr., mem. exec. com. Armstrong, Teasdale, Kramer, Vaughan & Schlafly and predecessor firm Schlafly, Griesedieck, Toft & Virtel, St. Louis, 1973—; lectr. Washington U. Sch. of Engring.; faculty Wash. U. Trial Practice Inst. Mem. ABA, Mo. Bar Assn., Met. St. Louis Bar Assn., Assn. Trial Lawyers Am., Am. Judicature Soc. Clubs: Algonquin Golf (Webster Groves, Mo.); Mo. Athletic, Noonday (St. Louis); University (Clayton, Mo.) General practice, General corporate, Personal injury. Office: Suite 1300 314 N Broadway Saint Louis MO 63102

TOFTNESS, CECIL GILLMAN, lawyer, consultant; b. Glasgow, Mont., Sept. 13, 1920; s. Anton Bernt and Nettie (Pedersen) T.; m. Chloe Catherine Vincent, Sept. 8, 1951. A.A., San Diego Jr. Coll., 1943; student Purdue U., Northwestern U.; B.S., UCLA, 1947; J.D., Southwestern U., 1953. Bar: Calif. 1954, U.S. Dist. Ct. (so. dist.) Calif. 1954, U.S. Supreme Ct. 1979. Sole practice, Palos Verdes Estates, Calif., 1954—; dir., pres., chmn. bd. Fisherman & Mchts. Bank, San Pedro, Calif., 1963-67; dir., v.p. Palos Verdes Estates Bd. Realtors, 1964-65. Chmn. Capital Campaign Fund, Richstone Charity, Hawthorne, Calif., 1983. Served to lt. (jg.) USN, 1938-46, ETO, PTO. Named Man of Yr., Glasgow, 1984. Mem. South Bay Bar Assn., Southwestern Law Sch. Alumni Assn. (class rep. 1980—), Internat. Physicians for the Prevention of Nuclear War (del. 7th World Congress, 1987), Themis Soc.-Southwestern Law Sch., Schumacher Founder's Circle-Southwestern Law Sch. (charter). Democrat. Lutheran. Lodges: Kiwanis (sec.-treas. 1955-83, v.p., pres., bd. dirs.), Masons, K.T. Antitrust, Contracts commercial, Probate. Home: 2229 Via Acalones Palos Verdes Estates CA 90274 Office: 2516 Via Tejon Palos Verdes Estates CA 90274

TOGNARELLI, RICHARD LEE, lawyer; b. Collinsville, Ill., Aug. 12, 1949; s. Albert John and Rosalie Frances (Brogliatto) T.; m. Gail Marie Culliton, June 11, 1971; children—Michael Anthony, Matthew Paul. A.B., St. Louis U., 1971, J.D., 1974. Bar: Ill. 1975, U.S. Dist. Ct. (so. dist.) Ill. 1975, U.S. Dist. Ct. (ea. dist.) Ill. 1975, U.S. Ct. Appeals (7th cir.) 1976. Clk., then assoc. firm Dunham, Boman, Leskera & Churchill, East St. Louis, Ill., 1973-78; ptnr. Cadagin, Cain & Tognarelli, Collinsville, 1978-84; ptnr. firm Tognarelli & Mattea, Collinsville, 1984—. Pres. parish council Sts. Peter and Paul Roman Cath. Ch., Collinsville, 1984-85. Named One of Outstanding Young Men of Am., Collinsville Jaycees, 1981, also recipient Disting. Service award, 1984. Mem. ABA (sect. of econs. of law practice com. on lawyer relations with pub. 1986-87), Ill. State Bar Assn. (chmn. jud. adv. polls com. 1986-87), Collinsville C. of C. (chmn. ambassadors 1984-87, v.p. orgn. affairs 1986—), Phi Beta Kappa. Democrat. Lodges: Rotary (pres. Collinsville 1983-84), K.C. General practice, Personal injury, Probate. Home: 303 Chesapeake Ln Collinsville IL 62234 Office: Tognarelli & Mattea 1605 Vandalia St Collinsville IL 62234

TOLAND, CLYDE WILLIAM, lawyer; b. Iola, Kans., Aug. 18, 1947; s. Stanley E. and June E. (Thompson) T.; m. Nancy Ellen Hummel, July 27, 1974; children: David Clyde, Andrew John, Elizabeth Kay. BA, U. Kans., 1969, JD, 1975; MA, U. Wis., 1971. Bar: Kans. 1975, U.S. Dist. Ct. Kans. 1975, U.S. Supreme Ct. 1980. Ptnr. Toland and Thompson, Iola, 1975—. Author: Samuel Franklin Hubbard and Permelia Caroline (Spencer) Hubbard: Pioneer Settlers in 1857 of Allen County, Kansas Territory, and their Descendants, 1985; (with others) Clark and Eliza (Wright) Toland: Their Ancestors and Descendants, 1984. Mem. exec. com. Friends of Library, U. Kans., 1977—, pres. elect, 1987—. Mem. ABA, Kans. Bar Assn., Allen County Bar Assn., U. Kans. Alumni Assn. (Strickland award 1969), Phi Beta Kappa, Order of Coif, Omicron Delta Kappa (presdl. plaque 1969). Republican. Presbyterian. Lodge: Rotary (pres. Iola club 1985-86). Avocations: speaking on estate planning and history; historical field trips. Probate, Estate planning, Estate taxation. Home: 211 S Colborn Iola KS 66749 Office: 103 E Madison Iola KS 66749

TOLAND, STANLEY E., lawyer; b. Galva, Kans., July 12, 1907; s. William E. and Angie Clarice (Severtson) T.; m. June Elizabeth Thompson, Mar. 8, 1942; children—John R., Clyde W. A.B. with honors, U. Kans., 1930, J.D., 1932. Bar: Kans. 1932, U.S. Dist. Ct. Kans. 1932, U.S. Ct. Appeals (10th cir.) 1935, U.S. Supreme Ct. 1960. Assoc. Oyler and Gard, Iola, Kans., 1932-33; ptnr. Gard and Toland, 1934-36; sole practice, Iola, 1936-57; sr. ptnr. Toland and Thompson, Iola, 1957—; mem. Kans. Supreme Ct. Nominating Com., 1963-72; commr. in land condemnation cases U.S. Dist. Ct. Kans., 1963-68; pres. Security Savs. Loan Assn., 1969-79; dir. Iola State Bank, 1947—; trustee Iola Pub. Library, 1946-57; mem. Kans. State Senate, 1941-45. Rotary Found. Paul Harris fellow, 1978. Mem. ABA, Kans. Bar Assn., Allen County Bar Assn. Republican. Presbyterian. Club: Iola Rotary. Probate, Real property, Oil and gas leasing. Office: Toland & Thompson 103 E Madison Iola KS 66749

TOLBERT, FRANK EDWARD, lawyer; b. Bloomington, Ind., Dec. 20, 1928; s. Lester Crews and Glodine Pearl (Bender) T.; m. Sarah Leigh Wynne; children—Sarah Tolbert Muehlhausen, Brooks W. A.B., Ind. U., 1952, LL.B., 1955. Bar: Ind. 1955, U.S. Dist. Ct. (no. and so. dists.) Ind. 1955, U.S. Ct. Appeals (7th cir.) 1975, U.S. Supreme Ct. 1982. Assoc., then ptnr. Miller, Tolbert, Wildman & Muehlhausen, Logansport, Ind., 1955—. Pres., Friends of Library, Inc.; bd. dirs. Cass County Hist. Soc. Served to 1st lt. AUS, 1946-49; served to lt. col. Ind. N.G., 1949-67. Mem. Cass County Bar Assn. (pres. 1961-62), Ind. State Bar Assn. (bd. mgrs. 1967-68), ABA, Ind. Trial Lawyers Assn., Assn. Trial Lawyers Am., Am. Coll. Trial Lawyers, Def. Research Inst., Assn. Ins. Attys. Republican. Methodist. Clubs: Logansport Country, Columbia, Elks. State civil litigation, Federal civil litigation, Probate. Home: 2600 E Broadway Logansport IN 46947 Office: 216 4th St Logansport IN 46947

TOLINS, ROGER ALAN, lawyer; b. Bklyn., Jan. 25, 1936; s. Albert and Claire (Rothstein) T.; m. Doris Levine, May 15, 1960; children—Fran, Jonathan. A.B. with distinction, Dartmouth Coll., 1956; LL.B., N.Y.U., 1959, LL.M. in Taxation, 1961. Bar: N.Y. 1959. Assoc. Brennan, London & Buttenwieser, N.Y.C., 1961-67; ptnr. Goldfeld, Charak, Tolins & Lowenfels, N.Y.C., 1967-74, Tolins & Lowenfels, N.Y.C., 1975—. Served with U.S. Army, 1959-60. Mem. ABA (sect. on taxation), N.Y. State Bar Assn. General corporate, Administrative and regulatory, Corporate taxation.

TOLL, CHARLES HANSEN, JR., lawyer; b. Springfield, Mass., June 24, 1916; s. Charles Hansen and Mayes (Martin) T.; m. Barbara Schorer, Mar. 28, 1942; children: Charles Hansen III, Richard Schorer, Barbara Caldwell. BA, Princeton U., 1938; LLB, Yale U., 1941. Bar: Mass. 1946, U.S. Dist. Ct. Mass. 1947, N.H. 1951, U.S. Dist. Ct. N.H. 1951. Assoc. Foley, Hoag & Eliot, Boston, 1945-51; from assoc. to ptnr. Orr & Reno P.A., Concord, N.H., 1951—; bd. dirs. EnergyNorth Inc., Manchester, N.H. bd. dirs. Concord Regional Devel. Corp., 1957-65, pres. 1963-65; trustee, Concord Hosp., 1958-78, pres. 1974-78, Phillips Exeter (N.H.) Acad., 1967-81, pres. 1978-81; chmn. Concord Housing Authority, 1961-64. Served to capt. U.S. Army, 1941-45, ETO. Decorated Bronze Star. Mem. ABA, N.H. Bar Assn. (bd. govs. 1971-72), Merrimack County Bar Assn. (pres. 1970), Sigma Xi. Republican. Club: Snowshoe Club (Concord). Public utilities, General corporate, Probate. Office: Orr and Reno PA 1 Eagle Sq PO Box 709 Concord NH 03301

TOLL, SEYMOUR I., lawyer, writer, educator; b. Phila., Feb. 19, 1925; s. Louis David and Rose (Eisenstein) T.; m. Jean Marie Barth, June 25, 1951; children: Emily Barth, Elizabeth Terry, Martha Anne, Constance Nora Frances. BA, Yale U., 1948, JD, 1951. Bar: N.Y. 1953, Pa. 1956, U.S. Dist. Ct. (ea. dist.) Pa., U.S. Ct. Appeals (3d and 5th cirs.) 1970, U.S. Supreme Ct. Law clk. U.S. Dist. Ct. (so. dist.) N.Y., N.Y.C., 1951-52; from assoc. to ptnr. Richter, Lord, Toll & Cavanaugh, Phila., 1955-65, 69; sole practice Phila., 1965-68, 69-74; ptnr. Toll, Ebby & Langer and predecessor firm Toll & Ebby, Phila., 1975—; vis. lectr. U. Pa. Law Sch., 1978—. Author: Zoned American, 1964; Editor jours. The Retainer, 1972-73, A Court's Heritage, 1984—; assoc. editor jour. The Shingle, 1970-78, editor 1979-80; contbr. numerous articles to profl. jours. Pres. Phila. Citizen's Council on City Planning, 1967-69; pub. dir., exec. com. Phila. Housing Devel. Corp., 1967-72. Served with U.S. Army, 1943-45, ETO. Grantee Am. Philos. Soc., 1968. Mem. ABA, Fed. Bar Assn., Pa. Bar Assn., Phila. Bar Assn. (Fidelity Bank award 1984), 3d Cir. Jud. Conf. (permanent del.), Jr. Legal Club. Democrat. Jewish. Clubs: The Franklin Inn (pres. 1981-84), Yale (Phila.). Avocations: music, sailing, travel. Federal civil litigation, Antitrust, Libel. Home: 453 Conshohocken State Rd Bala Cynwyd PA 19004 Office: Toll Ebby & Gough 1760 Market St 6th Floor Philadelphia PA 19103

TOLLEFSON, G. VAL, lawyer; b. Spokane, Wash., Apr. 29, 1942. BA, U. Wash., 1964, JD, 1973. Bar: Wash. 1973, U.S. Dist. Ct. (ea. and we. dist.) Wash., U.S. Ct. Appeals (9th cir.). Assoc. Lane, Powell, Moss & Miller, Seattle, 1973-80, ptnr., 1980-85; ptnr. Danielson, Harrigan, Smith & Tollefson, Seattle, 1986—. Pres., trustee Bainbridge Found., Bainbridge Island, Wash., 1984—; trustee Collins Acad., Seattle, 1982-83. Served to lt. commr. USN, 1964-74. Mem. ABA, Wash. Bar Assn., Maritime Law Assn., Lawyers Pilots Bar Assn. Admiralty, Federal civil litigation, Aviation. Office: Danielson Harrigan Smith & Tollefson 1st Interstate Ctr 44th Floor Seattle WA 98104

TOLLEN, ALLEN HAROLD, lawyer; b. Chester, Pa., July 4, 1947; s. Samuel M. and Miriam (Shapero) T.; m. Pamela Kennedy, June 15, 1969; children: Jason, Zachary, Julie. BA in Philosophy, Franklin and Marshall Coll., 1969; JD, Duke U., 1972. Bar: Pa. 1972, U.S. Dist. Ct. (ea. dist.) Pa. 1974, U.S. Supreme Ct. 1984. Assoc. Tollen & Tollen, Chester, 1972-1979; ptnr. Tollen, Seidman & Sherman, Media, Pa., 1979-84, Tollen & Proctor, Media, 1984—; chmn. bd. Del. County Legal Asst. Assoc., Chester, 1974-76. Bd. dirs. Lansdowne Symphony Orch., pres. 1981-82. Mem. Pa. Bar Assn., Del. County Bar Assn. (editor legal jour. 1978, sec. 1980). Avocations: trumpet player, handball, squash. General practice, Personal injury, General corporate. Home: 490 Riverview Rd Swarthmore PA 19081 Office: Tollen & Proctor 15 E Front St Media PA 19063

TOLLERIS, M(ARY) ANGELA, lawyer; b. Nassau County, N.Y., July 9, 1939; d. Harold Tolleris and Patricia Ruth Kurz; m. Theodore Schneider, Aug. 7, 1955 (div.); children: Adam, John, David, Nancy. AGS summa cum laude, Montgomery County Community Coll., Blue Bell, Pa., 1971; BA magna cum laude, Beaver Coll., Glenside, Pa., 1973; JD, Rutgers U., Camden, N.J., 1976; grad. teacher tng. program Nat. Inst. Trial Advocacy 1983. Bar: N.J. 1977, U.S. Dist. Ct. N.J. 1977. Nat. Reginald Heber Smith fellow in community law Camden Regional Legal Services, Gloucester County Office, Woodbury, N.J., 1976-78; asst. dep. pub. defender N.J. Office Pub. Defender, Vineland, N.J., 1978-81, sr. trial counsel, 1981-85; adj. prof. Cumberland County Coll., Vineland, 1980; guest lectr. N.J. criminal def. practice Del. Law Sch., Wilmington, 1982, 83; Moot Ct. judge Del. Law Sch. 1982, 83, Rutgers U., Camden, 1983, 84. Davison-Foreman Found. fellow, 1973-76. Mem. ABA (criminal justice sect.), N.J. State Bar Assn. (criminal justice sect.), Nat. Assn. Criminal Def. Lawyers (regional dir. speakers bur. 1984-85), Cumberland County Bar Assn. (trustee 1983-86), Assn. Criminal

Def. Lawyers N.J., Essex County Bar Assn. (del. from People to People, Inc. to Southeast Asia and China). Criminal, Personal injury. Office: Ronald Nelinson & Assocs 134 Evergreen Pl East Orange NJ 07018

TOLLERS, JEFFERY BARNET, law educator; b. Park Falls, Wis., Oct. 9, 1957; s. Rudolph and Opal (Jodell) T. BBA, U. Wis., JD. Bar: Wis. 1982, Tex. 1983, U.S. Doist. Ct. (we. dist.) Wis., 1982. Staff acct. Arthur Young & Co., Dallas, 1982-83; assoc. Anderson, Fisher, Stevens Point, Wis., 1983-85; asst. prof. U. Wis., Green Bay, 1985—. Mem. ABA, Wis. Bar Assn., Tex. Bar Assn., Am. Acctg. Assn. Probate, Estate taxation, Personal income taxation. Office: U Wis Green Bay 2420 Nicolet Dr Green Bay WI 54301

TOLLEY, EDWARD DONALD, lawyer; b. San Antonio, Jan. 31, 1950; s. Lyle Oren and Mary Theresa Tolley. BBA, U. Ga., 1971, MBA, 1974, JD, 1975. Bar: Ga. 1975, U.S. Dist. Ct. (5th cir.) 1976, U.S. Supreme Ct. 1978, U.S. Ct. Appeals (11th cir.) 1981. Ptnr. Cook, Noell, Tolley & Aldridge, Athens, Ga., 1975—; lectr. various colls., univs., civic and profl. groups. Active Family Counseling Assn. of Athens, Inc.; bd. dirs. Am. Cancer Soc. Served to capt. U.S. Army. 1971-75. Fellow Ga. Bar Found., Am. Bd. Criminal Lawyers (bd. dirs. 1987—); mem. State Bar Ga. (chmn. law office and econ. com.), Ga. Trial Lawyers Assn. (v.p. 1986—), Nat. Assn. Criminal Def. Lawyers, Ga. Assn. Criminal Def. Lawyers (pres. 1985, Indigent Def. award 1983), Athens Bar Assn. (past pres.), Am. Judicature Soc., Order of Barristers. Criminal, Federal civil litigation, State civil litigation. Home: PO Box 1927 Athens GA 30603 Office: Cook Noell Tolley & Aldridge 304 E Washington St Athens GA 30601

TOLMIE, DONALD MCEACHERN, lawyer; b. Moline, Ill., June 21, 1928; s. Ronald Charles and Margaret Blaine (Kerr) T.; m. Joann Phillis Swanson, Aug. 15, 1953; children: David M., John K., Paul N. AB, Augustana Coll., 1950; JD, U. Ill., 1953. Bar: Ill. 1953, Va. 1968. Atty. Pa. R.R., Chgo., 1953-60; asst. gen. soliciter Pa. R.R., Phila., 1961-67; gen. atty. Norfolk & Western, Roanoke, Va., 1968, gen. soliciter, 1968-75, gen. counsel, 1975-82; gen. counsel Norfolk (Va.) So. Corp., 1982, v.p., gen. counsel, 1983—; bd. dirs. Trailer Train Co., Chgo. Mem. ABA, Va. Bar Assn., Norfolk and Portsmouth Bar Assn., U.S. Supreme Ct. Bar Assn. Lutheran. Clubs: Harbor, Norfolk Yacht and Country, Cedar Point. General corporate. Home: 912 Hanover Ave Norfolk VA 23508 Office: Norfolk So Corp 1 Commercial Pl Norfolk VA 23510-2191

TOM, PING, trading company executive, lawyer; b. Chgo., Apr. 15, 1935; s. Y. Chan and Lillian (Goo) T.; m. Valerie Ching Oct. 11, 1958; children—Darryl, Curtis. B.A. in Econs., Northwestern U., 1956, J.D., 1958. Bar: Ill. 1958. Vice pres. Chinese Noodle Mfg., Chgo., 1958-66; v.p. Chinese Trading Co., Chgo., 1966-72, pres., 1972—; pres. Lekel Pail Co., Chgo., 1980—, Mah Chena Corp., Chgo., 1980—, Griesbaum Meat Co., Chgo., 1981—; bd. dirs. Madison Fin. Co. holding corp. Madison Nat. Bank, Niles, Ill., 1st Nat. Bank, Wheeling, Ill.; legal advisor Chinese Benevolent Assn., Chgo. Pres. Chinese Am. Civic Council, Chgo., 1973; trustee Hull House Assn., Chgo.; bd. dirs. South Side Planning Bd., Chgo.; mem. Chgo.'s World's Fair Corp., State of Ill. Devel. Fin. Authority; chmn. Chinatown Parking Corp.; pres. Chinese-Am. Devel. Corp. Mem. Chinatown C. of C. (pres. 1983). Club: Econ., Exec. (Chgo.); Park Ridge Country. General practice. Home: 6945 Lexington Ln Niles IL 60648 Office: Chinese Trading Co 2263 Wentworth Ave Chicago IL 60616

TOM, WILLARD KEN, lawyer; b. Honolulu, Aug. 11, 1952; s. Hing Yee and Marian (Chun) T.; m. Natalie G. Lichtenstein, June 10, 1979. AB cum laude, Harvard U., 1975, JD cum laude, 1979. Bar: D.C. 1979, U.S. Dist. Ct. D.C. 1979, U.S. Ct. Appeals (D.C. cir.) 1983, U.S. Supreme Ct. 1986. Trial atty. U.S. Dept. Justice, Washington, 1979-81; assoc. Sutherland, Asbill & Brennan, Washington, 1981-86, ptnr., 1986—. Mem. ABA (vice chmn. antitrust law devels. com., antitrust sect. 1986—), Asian-Pacific Am. Bar Assn. of Greater Washington (bd. dirs. 1983). Antitrust, Federal civil litigation. Office: Sutherland Asbill & Brennan 1666 K St NW Washington DC 20006

TOMAO, PETER JOSEPH, lawyer; b. Bklyn., Feb. 11, 1951; s. Joseph Louis Tomao and Marie A. (Buono) Hartmann; m. Kathryn Carter Reed, Oct. 15, 1978. BA, St. John's U., Queen's, N.Y., 1973; JD, Columbia U., 1976. Bar: N.Y. 1977, D.C. 1980, U.S. Dist. Ct. D.C.,1980, U.S. Ct. Appeals (2d cir.), 1983, U.S. Dist. Ct. (ea. dist.) N.Y. 1985. Trial atty. antitrust div. U.S. Dept. Justice, Washington, 1976-82; asst. U.S. atty. U.S. Dist. Ct. (ea. dist.) N.Y., Bklyn., Uniondale, N.Y., 1982—. Mem. ABA (antitrust, trial sects.), Nassau County Bar Assn., D.C. Bar Assn. Criminal, Antitrust. Office: US Attys Office Uniondale Ave at Hempstead Turnpike Uniondale NY 11553

TOMAR, RICHARD THOMAS, lawyer; b. Camden, N.J., Mar. 4, 1945; s. William and Bette (Brown) T.; m. Sherry Linsenmeyer, June 22, 1982; children: Dale Lindsay, Leanne Meryl. AB, Columbia U., 1967; JD, U. Pa., 1970. Bar: D.C. 1971, N.J. 1971, Md. 1976. Sole practice Washington, 1971-73; ptnr. Philipson, Mallios & Tomar, Washington, 1973—. Mem. D.C. Trial Lawyers Assn. (bd. dirs. 1980—). Banking, Federal civil litigation, State civil litigation. Office: Philipson Mallios & Tomar 1875 Eye St NW Suite 460 Washington DC 20006

TOMAR, WILLIAM, lawyer; b. Camden, N.J., Oct. 10, 1916; s. Morris and Katie (Sadinsky) T.; m. Bette Brown, Nov. 28, 1942; children—Richard T., Dean Jonathon. LL.B. cum laude, Rutgers U., 1939. Bar: N.J. 1940, Fla. 1975, D.C. 1978, U.S. Sup. Ct. 1953. Sr. ptnr. Tomar, Seliger, Simonoff, Adourian & O'Brien, Cherry Hill, N.J., 1958—;mem. faculty Ctr. Trial and Appellate Advocacy, Hastings Coll. Law, U. Calif., 1971-86, Nat. Coll. Advocacy, Harvard U. Law Sch., 1973-75. Mem. UN Speakers Bur., UNICEF, 1960—; mem. adv. bd. Inst. Med. Research, 1967—, Touro Law Sch., 1981; bd. dirs. South Jersey Assn. Performing Arts; mem. planning com. World Peace Through Law Center, 1970—; trustee Cooper Med. Center, 1979—. Fellow Am. Coll. Trial Lawyers; mem. ABA (com. on nuclear energy 1966), Assn. Trial Lawyers Am. (assoc. editor jour. 1966—, gov. 1963-64, nat. parliamentarian 1964-70, nat. exec. com. 1964-70, chmn. seminars 1965 lectr. student advocacy program 1968—), World Assn. Lawyers (founding mem. 1974—), N.J. Bar Assn. (fee arbitration com. 1972-74, 75-77), N.J. Assn. Trial Lawyers (recipient trial bar award 1977), N.J. Worker's Compensation Assn. (trustee 1958-83), N.Y. Trial Lawyers Assn., Phila. Trial Lawyers Assn., Camden County Bar Found. (bd. trustees 1986—), Camden County Bar Assn. (com. on relations of bench and bar 1964—, com. on worker's compensation 1956—, adult edn. com. 1975—). State civil litigation, Federal civil litigation, Personal injury. Office: 41 S Haddon Ave Haddonfield NJ 08033

TOMASZCZUK, ALEXANDER DANIEL, lawyer; b. St. Joseph, Mo., Dec. 4, 1955; s. Daniel and Katherine (Kivernagl) T.; m. Carol Arlene McDonald, Aug. 21, 1982. BA, Stanford U., 1977; JD, U. Mo., 1981. Bar: Mo. 1981, D.C. 1982, U.S. Dist. Ct. D.C. 1983, U.S. Ct. Claims 1982, U.S. Ct. Appeals (fed. cir.) 1982. Law clk. to presiding judge U.S. Ct. Claims, Washington, 1981-82; assoc. Shaw, Pittman, Potts & Trowbridge, Washington, 1982—. Mem. ABA (litigation sect.), Fed. Bar Assn., Mo. Bar Assn., D.C. Bar Assn. (litigation and govt. contracts sects.). Democrat. Roman Catholic. Avocations: tennis, golf. Federal civil litigation, Government contracts and claims, Private international. Home: 1414-A N 12th St Arlington VA 22209 Office: Shaw Pittman Potts & Trowbridge 2300 N St NW Washington DC 20037

TOMBERLIN, GEORGE E., JR., lawyer; b. Atlanta, Nov. 15, 1949; s. George E. Sr. and Sarah H. T.; m. Jennifer Hood, Aug. 4, 1973. AB, Princeton U., 1971; JD, U. Calif., Berkeley, 1976. Bar: Calif. 1976. Assoc. Cotton, Seligman & Ray, San Francisco, 1976-79, Dinkelspiel, Pelavin, Steefel & Levitt, San Francisco, 1979-80, Pelavin, Norberg, Harlick & Beck, San Francisco, 1980-82; counsel Kaiser Found. Health Plan, Inc., Oakland, Calif., 1983—. Bd. dirs. Berkeley (Calif.) Symphony Orch., 1979-83, v.p., 1980-83; bd. mgrs. Met. YMCA Oakland, 1986—. Nat. Merit scholar, 1967-71. Mem. ABA, Calif. Bar Assn., San Francisco Bar Assn., Nat. Health Lawyers Assn., Group Health Assn. Am. General corporate, General practice, Health. Office: Ordway Bldg One Kaiser Plaza Oakland CA 94612

TOMBRINK, RICHARD, JR., lawyer; b. Brooksville, Fla., Apr. 18, 1950; s. Richard and Margaret Louise (Rice) T.; m. Lynn Plecha. BS, Fla. State U., 1972; JD, U. Fla., 1977. Bar: Fla. 1977, U.S. Dist. Ct. (mid. dist.) Fla. 1978. Assoc. Law Offices of J.E. Johnston Jr., Brooksville, Fla., 1977-82; sole practice Brooksville, 1982—; bd. dirs. Withlacoochee Area Legal Services Inc., Ocala, Fla., 1982-86. Treas., bd. dirs. Downtown Devel. Corp. Brooksville Inc., 1985—, Hernando Area Seminole Boosters Club, Brooksville, 1984—, Red Male Runners, 1987—; bd. dirs. Hernando Hist. Mus. Served with U.S. Army, 1973-75. Mem. ABA, Fla. Bar Assn., Tri-County Bar Assn. (sec. 1982-83), Hernando County Bar Assn. (pres. 1980), Fla. Acad. Trial Lawyers, Am. Trial Lawyers Assn. Lodge: Kiwanis (Brooksville pres. 1986-87). Avocations: reading, rose gardening, sports. General practice, Family and matrimonial, Personal injury. Office: 200 W Fort Dale Ave Brooksville FL 33512

TOMCZAK, STARR LYN, lawyer; b. Gaylord, Minn., Mar. 7, 1947. BA, Carleton Coll., 1969; MA, Northwestern U., 1971; JD, NYU, 1975. Bar: N.Y. 1978, Ill. 1983. Law clk. U.S. Ct. Appeals (4th cir.), Richmond, Va., 1976-77; assoc. Cravath, Swaine & Moore, N.Y.C., 1977-82; ptnr. Sonnenschein Carlin Nath & Rosenthal, Chgo., 1982—; vis. asst. prof. law NYU, N.Y.C., 1981. Editor, contbg. author: Corporate and Commercial Finance Agreements, 1984; editor NYU Law Rev., 1973-75. Mem. ABA (chmn. subcom. on securitization of assets), Chgo. Bar Assn. (com. on corp. law), Ill. State Bar Assn., Order of Coif. General corporate, Securities.

TOMICH, LILLIAN, lawyer; b. Los Angeles, Mar. 28, 1935; d. Peter S. and Yovanka P. (Ivanovic) T. A.A., Pasadena City Coll., 1954; B.A. in Polit. Sci., UCLA, 1956, cert. secondary teaching, 1957, M.A., 1958; J.D., U. So. Calif., 1961. Bar: Calif. Sole practice, 1961-66; house counsel Mfrs. Bank, Los Angeles, 1966; ptnr. Hurley, Shaw & Tomich, San Marino, Calif., 1968-76, Driscoll & Tomich, San Marino, 1976—; dir. Continental Culture Specialists Inc., Glendale, Calif. Trustee, St. Sava Serbian Orthodox Ch., San Gabriel, Calif. Charles Fletcher Scott fellow, 1957; U. So. Calif. Law Sch. scholar, 1958. Mem. ABA, Calif. Bar Assn., Los Angeles County Bar Assn., Women Lawyers Assn., UCLA Alumni Assn., Order Mast and Dagger, Iota Tau Tau, Alpha Gamma Sigma. General corporate, General practice, Probate. Office: 2297 Huntington Dr San Marino CA 91108

TOMLINSON, HERBERT WESTON, lawyer; b. Upland, Pa., Feb. 11, 1930; s. Herbert Elmer and Hilda Josephine (Schlosbon) T.; m. Mary Jean Litwhiler, Oct. 27, 1961. B.S., Pa. State U., 1952, postgrad., 1956-57; J.D., Dickinson Sch. Law, 1960; postgrad. student Temple U. Law Sch., 1969-73. Bar: Pa. 1961, U.S. Supreme Ct. 1968. Law clk., pres. Delaware County Bar Assn., 1960-61; assoc. DeFuria Larkin DeFuria, Chester, Pa., 1960-62; assoc., Hodge & Balderston, Chester, 1962-65; assoc. Edward McLaughlin, Chester, 1965-67; exec. dir. Legal Services Program, Delaware County, 1967-69; sole practice, Media, Pa., 1969—; sr. staff atty. Delaware County Pub. Defender's Office, 1969—; prof. bus. law Pa. State U., 1969-75, Widener U., 1971-76, Delaware County Community Coll., 1971-75; arbitrator Am. Arbitration Assn.; prof. bus. law Widener U., 1978-80. Dir., Delaware County March of Dimes, 1966-71; Republican candidate U.S. Ho. Reps., 1976; Rep. committeeman, 1966—, treas. 168th Legis. Dist., 1975-81; chmn. Media Rep. Com., 1975-76; mem. Media Borough Auditor, 1975—. Served to capt. USMCR, 1952-56. Mem. Delaware County Bar Assn., ABA, Pa. Bar Assn., Pa. Trial Lawyers Assn., Am. Assn. Trial Lawyers, AAUP, Nat. Assn. Securities Dealers, Delaware County Real Estate Bd., Am. Arbitration Assn., Delaware County Med. Soc. (dir. pub. health fund 1967—). Republican. Presbyterian. Clubs: Kiwanis, Mason, Shrine, Rotary. Personal injury, Probate. Home: 320 N Providence Rd Media PA 19063 Office: 8 W Front St Media PA 19063

TOMLINSON, JOHN RANDOLPH, lawyer; b. Seattle, Jan. 11, 1931; s. Charles Lawrence and Irma (Schnauffer) T.; m. Susan Jo Weaver, June 15, 1953; children: John R. Jr., Lynn M., James L., Anne E. BBA, U. Wash., 1953, JD, 1955. Bar: Wash. 1955, U.S. Dist. Ct. (we. and ea. dists.) Wash. 1955, U.S. Ct. Appeals (9th cir.) 1957, U.S. Supreme Ct. 1975. Assoc. Jones, Grey & Bayley, Seattle, 1957-61, ptnr., 1962-78; ptnr. Lane, Powell, Moss & Miller, Seattle, 1979—; lectr. on continuing legal edn. Editorial bd. U. Wash. Law Rev., 1953. Served to 1st lt. USAFR, 1955-77. Fellow Am. Coll. Trial Lawyers; mem. ABA (chmn. litigation sect. 1986-87, vice chmn. 1984-85, chmn. elect 1985-86), Wash. State Bar Assn., Seattle Bar Assn., Phi Gamma Delta. Republican. Lodge: Rotary. Avocations: golf, skiing, fishing, hunting. Federal civil litigation, State civil litigation. Home: 8435 NE 21st Pl Bellevue WA 98004

TOMPKINS, JOSEPH BUFORD, JR., lawyer; b. Roanoke, Va., Apr. 4, 1950; s. Joseph Buford and Rebecca Louise (Johnston) T.; m. Stewart Hamilton Gamage, Feb. 28, 1976; children—Edward Graves, Claiborne Forbes. B.A. in Politics summa cum laude, Washington and Lee U., 1971; M.P.P. in Pub. Policy, Harvard U., 1975, J.D., 1975. Bar: Va. 1975, U.S. Dist. Ct. D.C. 1982, U.S. Ct. Appeals (D.C. cir.) 1976, U.S. Ct. Appeals (5th cir.) 1977, U.S. Ct. Appeals (11th cir.) 1982, U.S. Ct. Appeals (3d cir.) 1983, U.S. Ct. Appeals (6th cir.) 1985, U.S. Supreme Ct. 1977. Assoc. Sidley & Austin, Washington, 1975-79, ptnr., 1982—; assoc. dir. Office of Policy and Mgmt. Analysis, criminal div. U.S. Dept Justice, Washington, 1979-81, dep. chief fraud sect. criminal div., 1981-82. Contbr. articles to legal publs. Mem., vice chmn. Va. Commn. Health Regulatory Bds., Richmond, Va., 1984-86, chmn., 1986—. Recipient Spl. Commendation, U.S. Dept. Justice, 1981. Mem. ABA (criminal justice sect., mem. white collar crime com., 1980—, chmn. task force on computer crime; 1982—), Va. Bar Assn., D.C. Bar Assn., Fed. Bar Assn., Phi Beta Kappa. Democrat. Methodist. Federal civil litigation, State civil litigation, Criminal. Home: 6102 Woodmont Rd Alexandria VA 22307 Office: Sidley & Austin 1722 Eye St NW Washington DC 20006

TOMPKINS, RAYMOND EDGAR, lawyer; b. Oklahoma City, July 13, 1934; s. Charles Edgar and Eva Mae (Hodges) T.; m. Sue Anne Sharpe, June 10, 1963; children: Matthew Stephen, Christopher T., Katherine Anne. BS, Okla. State U., 1956; LLB, U. Okla., 1963. Bar: Okla. 1963, U.S. Dist. Ct. (no. dist.) Okla. 1963, U.S. Dist. Ct. (we. dist.) Okla. 1964, U.S. Ct. Appeals (10th cir.) 1965, U.S. Supreme Ct. 1968, U.S. Dist. Ct. (ea. dist.) Okla. 1969, U.S. Ct. Appeals (9th cir.) 1981. Ptnr. Hanson, Peterson & Tompkins, Oklahoma City, 1963-66, 68-80; adminstrv. asst. U.S. Congress, 1966-68; ptnr. Linn & Helms, Oklahoma City, 1980—. Chmn. bd. trustees Okla. Ann. Methodist Conf.; mem. Okla. State Rep. Exec. Com. Served to maj. USAR, 1956-71. Recipient award of Honor Oklahoma City Bi-Centennial Commn., 1976. Mem. ABA, Okla. County Bar Assn., Okla. Bar Assn. (Law Day award), Blue Key. Club: Lions (Oklahoma City). Federal civil litigation, State civil litigation, Personal injury. Home: 329 NW 40th Oklahoma City OK 73118 Office: Bank of Okla Bldg Suite 1200 Oklahoma City OK 73102

TOMPKINS, RICHARD NORTON, JR., lawyer; b. Forest City, Iowa, Nov. 7, 1946; s. Richard Norton Sr. and Helen Frances (Sheimo) T.; m. Cynthia Ann Hokenstad, June 3, 1984; children: Angela, Elizabeth, Van; stepchildren: Todd, Troy and Jonathan Feustel. BS, Iowa State U., 1969; JD, Drake U., 1975. Bar: Iowa 1976, U.S. Dist. Ct. (so. and no. dists.) Iowa 1976. Law clk. to presiding judge Polk County Dist. Ct., Iowa, 1976; assoc. Nelsen & Folkers, Mason City, Iowa, 1976-78; county atty. Cerro Gordo County, Iowa, 1979-82; sole practice Mason City, 1983—; instr. Iowa Supreme Ct. Commn. for Juvenile Probation Officers, Des Moines, 1979-80, 83, Area Community Coll., Mason City, 1983—. lectr. Gov.'s Conf. on Child Abuse, Des Moines, 1979, Child Abuse Resource and Edn. team, Mason City, 1978, also founder; founder County Atty.'s Victim Witness Program, Mason City, 1980, Dispute Resolution Ctr., Mason City, 1981. Mem. ABA, Iowa State Bar Assn., Dist. 2A Bar Assn., Cerro Gordo County Bar Assn. Republican. Lutheran. Avocation: bicycling. Personal injury, State civil litigation, General practice. Office: 536 Brick and Tile Bldg Mason City IA 50401

TOMPKINS, WILLIAM FINLEY, lawyer; b. Newark, Feb. 26, 1913; s. William Brydon and Lillian Elizabeth (Finley) T.; m. Jane Davis Bryant, Dec. 16, 1949; 1 child, William Finley, Jr. AB, Wesleyan U., 1935; LLB, Rutgers U., 1940. Bar: N.J. 1942, D.C. 1958. U.S. atty. Dist. N.J., 1953-54; asst. atty. gen. U.S., 1954-58; ptnr. Lum, Biunno & Tompkins, Newark, 1958-83, Tompkins, McGuire & Wachenfeld, Newark, 1984—; bd. dirs. Mut. Benefit Fund, MBL Growth Fund, MAP Govt. Fund. Mem. N.J. Ho. Assembly, 1951-53; chmn. Legis. Commn. to Study Narcotics, 1951-52; chmn. N.J. Commn. to Study Capital Punishment, 1964; del. Rep. Nat. Conv., 1964; pres. bd. trustees Newark Acad., Livingston, N.J., 1962-69, chmn. bd. trustees, 1969-75. Served to 1st lt. U.S. Army, 1943-46. Recipient First Americanism Citation for Meritorious Service South Mt. Lodge B'nai B'rith 1955; Ann. Award Soc. Former Spl. Agts. FBI, 1959. Mem. Fed. Bar Assn., ABA, N.J. State Bar Assn., Essex County Bar Assn., Am. Coll. Trial Lawyers, Am. Bar Found. Methodist. Clubs: Baltusrol Golf, Essex; Mid-Ocean (Bermuda). Author: (with Harry J. Anslinger) Traffic in Narcotics, 1953. General practice. Office: 550 Broad St Newark NJ 07102

TOMS, ROBERT LEE, lawyer; b. Asheville, N.C., May 12, 1935; s. M.F. and Joy (Wellford) T.; m. Valeria Franklin; children: Robert L., Sandra J., Clayton Yandle. BA, Bob Jones U., 1957; postgrad., U. So. Calif.; JD, Duke U., 1965. Bar: N.C. 1965, Calif. 1966. Commr. corps State of Calif., 1974-75; pres. Caldwell & Toms, Los Angeles, 1975—. Republican. Presbyterian. General corporate, Private international, Administrative and regulatory. Home: 50 Kewen Pl San Marino CA 90018 Office: Caldwell & Toms 700 S Flower St 15th Floor Los Angeles CA 90017

TONDEL, LAWRENCE CHAPMAN, lawyer; b. N.Y.C., Apr. 9, 1946; s. Lyman Mark and Jean (Basch) T.; m. Sharyn A. Smith, Aug. 3, 1974; children: Michael Lawrence, Kathryn Chapman. AB, Wesleyan U., 1968; JD, U. Mich., 1971. N.Y. 1972. Assoc. Brown & Wood, N.Y.C., 1971-79, ptnr., 1980—; chmn. PLI Inst. on Oil and Gas Financing, 1982. Mem. Am. Law Inst., Am. Bar Found., ABA, Assn. Bar City N.Y. Republican. Episcopalian. Club: Englewood (N.J.) Field. Securities, General corporate, Partnership Law. Office: Brown & Wood 1 World Trade Ctr New York NY 10048

TONETTI, LAWRENCE JOHN, judge; b. N.Y.C., Oct. 25, 1933; s. Giovanni Battista and Margherita (Borra) T.; m. Barbara Ann Giorgio, May 17, 1964; children: Rita Ann, Lawrence John Jr. AB, Iona U., 1955; LLB, NYU, 1958. Bar: N.Y. 1959, U.S. Dist. Ct. (so. dist.) N.Y. 1960. Assoc. atty. Legal Aid, N.Y.C., 1960-66; asst. dist. atty. Borough of Bronx, N.Y., 1966-71; judge criminal ct. City of N.Y., 1971-83; judge ct. claims State of N.Y., 1983—. Office: Bronx Supreme Ct 851 Grand Concourse New York NY 10451

TONGOUR, MICHAEL ALEXANDER, lawyer; b. Barnwell, S.C., July 29, 1956; s. Jack and Stella Helen (Tomsky) T. BA, U. S.C., 1978, JD, 1981. Bar: S.C. 1981, U.S. Dist. Ct. S.C. 1981. Assoc. King & Vernon, Columbia, S.C., 1981-82; sole practice Columbia, 1982-84; ptnr. Ellison, Quinn & Tongour, Columbia, 1984-85; counsel labor and human resources commn. U.S. Senate, Washington, 1985-86, legis. dir. to senator Strom Thurmond, 1986—; Pres. Sigma Housing Corp., Columbia, S.C., 1982-85, Top of Carolina, Columbia, 1984. Bd. dirs. Killingsworth Home, Columbia, 1984-85. Mem. S.C. Bar Assn., S.C. Trial Lawyers Assn. (treas. family law sect. 1984-85). Order of Coif, Order of Wig and Robe, Phi Beta Kappa. Episcopalian. Lodges: Optimists (bd. dirs. 1984), Masons. Avocation: squash. Legislative. Home: 1900 S Eads St #920 Arlington VA 22202 Office: US Senate Russell Bldg Room 218 Washington DC 20510

TONOZZI, THOMAS ALBERT, lawyer, educator; b. Spring Valley, Ill., Sept. 17, 1947; s. Albert and Rose (Partel) T.; m. Mary Jane Sabatini, June 27, 1970; children: Maria, Caroline, Angela, Daniel, Nicholas. BA, U. Notre Dame, 1969; JD, U. Ill., Champaign, 1972. Bar: Ill. 1972, U.S. Dist. Ct. (so. dist.) Ill. 1973, U.S. Dist. Ct. (no. dist.) Ill. 1979, U.S. Ct. Appeals (7th cir.) 1980, U.S. Tax Ct. 1985. Pub. defender Princeton County, Ill., 1973-82; sole practice Spring Valley, Ill., 1982—; instr. Ill. Valley Community Coll., Oglesby, 1975—. Bd. dirs. Sch. Dist. #99, Spring Valley, 1974—. General practice. Home: 511 W St Paul St Spring Valley IL 61362 Office: 222 E St Paul St Spring Valley IL 61362

TONSING, MICHAEL JOHN, lawyer, educator, arbitrator; b. Los Angeles, May 10, 1943; s. John Maurice and Mary Ellen (McMahon) T.; m. Cecilia Ann Degnan, Jan. 29, 1966; children—Catherine, Michael, Jr. B.A., St. Mary's Coll., 1965; M.A., Claremont Grad. Sch., 1970; J.D., U. San Francisco, 1975. Bar: Calif. 1976, U.S. Dist. Ct. (no. dist.) Calif. 1976, U.S. Supreme Ct. 1981, U.S. Ct. Mil. Appeals 1982, U.S. Ct. Appeals (9th cir.) 1982. Sole practice, Walnut Creek, Calif., 1976-77; adminstrv. law judge Pub. Employment Relations Bd., San Francisco, 1977-80; jud. fellow U.S. Supreme Ct., Washington, 1980-81; asst. U.S. atty. Dept. Justice, San Francisco, 1981-84; assoc. O'Gara & McGuire, San Francisco, 1984-85; ptnr. Pierucci & Tonsing, Oakland, Calif., 1985—; adj. prof. St. Mary's Coll. Paralegal Program, Moraga, Calif., 1977—, also dir.; dir. Calif. Admin. Law Coll., Sacramento. Vol. San Francisco Bay council Girl Scouts U.S., Oakland, 1966—; troop committeeman Piedmont (Calif.) Council Boy Scouts Am., 1986—. Weaver fellow Claremont Grad. Sch., Calif., 1966; recipient Tom C. Clark award U.S. Supreme Ct., Washington, 1981. Mem. ABA, Fed. Bar Assn. (pres. San Francisco chpt. 1985-86, nat. v.p. for 9th cir., 1986—), Am. Arbitration Assn. (labor arbitrator 1979—), Bar Assn. San Francisco, Alameda County Bar Assn., U. San Francisco Law Sch. Alumni Assn. (bd. govs. 1986—). Republican. Roman Catholic. Clubs: Commonwealth (San Francisco); Lakeview, Claremont Country (Oakland). Federal civil litigation, State civil litigation, Consumer commercial. Home: 911 Longridge Rd Oakland CA 94610 Office: Pierucci & Tonsing 1800 Harrison 11th Floor Oakland CA 94612

TOOKER, ROBERT LUCE, lawyer; b. Riverhead, N.Y., June 21, 1929; s. Clyde and Amy Leone (Luce) T.; m. Margaret Anne Wickham, Mar. 24, 1952; children—Pamela Anne, Mark Wickham, David Scott, Colin William, Robin Elizabeth. B.A., Amherst Coll., 1951, LL.B., Yale U., 1958. Bar: N.Y. 1958, U.S. Dist. Ct. (ea. and so. dists.) N.Y. 1965, U.S. Supreme Ct. 1967. Ptnr. Tooker and Tooker, 1958-65, Tooker, Tooker and Esseks, 1965-77, Tooker, Esseks, Hefter, Cuddy & Tohill, Riverhead, N.Y., 1977-79, ptnr. Tooker, Esseks, Hefter, Cuddy & Angel, Riverhead, 1979-81, Tooker and Smith, Riverhead, 1981-85; pres., bd. dirs. Equity Abstract, Inc., Peconic River Yacht Basin, Inc., Raynor-Michell Marine, Inc.; v.p., dir. Foremost Abstract, Inc. Served with USNR, 1952-56. Mem. Suffolk County Assn. (past dir.), Central Suffolk Hosp. Assn. (past pres., dir.). Congregationalist. Clubs: Riverhead Rotary, Masons. Probate, Real property, Banking. Home: 3 Waterview Ct Riverhead NY 11901 Office: 1380 Roanoke Ave Riverhead NY 11901

TOOMEY, RICHARD ANDREW, JR., lawyer; b. Portsmouth, N.H., Oct. 21, 1944; s. Richard Andrew and Elizabeth Neal (Rylander) T.; m. Jeanne Zurmuhlen. B.A., U. N.H., 1966; J.D., NYU, 1969. Bar: N.Y. 1969. Atty., VISTA, Mpls., 1969-71; assoc. Carter, Ledyard & Milburn, N.Y.C., 1971-77; v.p., sr. assoc. counsel Chase Manhattan Bank, N.Y.C., 1977—. Bd. dirs. Friends of the Hague Acad. Internat. Law, N.Y.C. Mem. Assn. Bar City N.Y. Banking, General corporate, Private international. Office: Chase Manhattan Bank 1 Chase Manhattan Plaza New York NY 10081

TOOTHMAN, JOHN WILLIAM, lawyer; b. Bryn Mawr, Pa., Dec. 6, 1954; s. Nolan Ernest Toothman and Caroline Nell (Reed) Pawl. BS ChemE with honors, U. Va., 1977, MS ChemE, 1979; JD cum laude, Harvard U., 1981. Bar: D.C. 1981, U.S. Dist. Ct. D.C. 1982, U.S. Ct. Appeals (D.C. cir.) 1982, U.S. Ct. Appeals (Fed. cir.) 1986. Assoc. Howrey & Simon, Washington, 1981-83, Akin, Gump, Strauss et al, Washington, 1983-84; trial atty. civil div. U.S. Dept. Justice, Washington, 1984-86; assoc. John Grad & Assocs., Alexandria, Va., 1986—. Vol. John Glenn for Pres. Campaign, Washington, 1984. NSF fellow, 1977. Mem. ABA, Assn. Trial Lawyers Am., Va. Trial Lawyers Assn., Sigma Xi, Tau Beta Pi. Democrat. Administrative and regulatory, Antitrust, Federal civil litigation. Home: 5860 Edgehill Dr Alexandria VA 22303

TOPLITZ, GEORGE NATHAN, lawyer; b. Winsted, Conn., June 13, 1936; s. Morris and Rose (Dolinsky) T.; m. Janet S. Strauss, July 30, 1961 (div.); children—Jill, Wendy, Anna; m. Kimilene A. Snead, Nov. 25, 1979. B.A., U. Conn., 1958; LL.B., Boston U., 1961. Bar: N.Y. 1964, U.S. Dist. Ct. (so. dist.) N.Y. 1968, U.S. Dist. Ct. (ea. dist.) N.Y. 1968, U.S. Ct. Appeals (2d cir.) 1986, U.S. Supreme Ct. 1987. Claims atty. Royal-Globe Ins. Co., surety

dept., N.Y.C., 1963-65; surety atty. Transam. Inst. Co., N.Y.C., 1965-67; assoc. Max E. Greenberg, Cantor, Reiss, N.Y.C., 1967—, ptnr., 1974—; lectr. Am. Mgmt. Assn., 1974-76, Am. Assn. Cost Engrs., 1974-75, Sch. Continuing Edn. NYU, 1975. Served with U.S. Army, 1961-63. Recipient Letter of Commendation for acting vol. spl. master Supreme Ct. N.Y., 1982, 84, 85, 86, 87. Mem. N.Y. State Bar Assn., N.Y. County Lawyers Assn., ABA, Assn. Trial Lawyers Am., Internat. Platform Assn. Federal civil litigation, State civil litigation, Government contracts and claims. Office: 100 Church St New York NY 10007

TOPOL, ALLAN JERRY, lawyer, author; b. Pitts., June 16, 1941; s. Morry and Selma (Weisman) T.; m. Barbara Rubenstein, July 27, 1963; children—David, Rebecca, Deborah, Daniella. B.S. in Chemistry, Carnegie-Mellon U., 1962; LL.B., Yale U., 1965. Bar: U.S. Dist. Ct. D.C. 1966, U.S. Ct. Appeals (D.C. cir.) 1966, U.S. Supreme Ct. 1968. Assoc. Covington & Burling, Washington, 1965-73, ptnr., 1973—. Author: The Fourth of July War, 1978; A Woman of Valor, 1980. Contbr. articles to profl. jours. and newspapers. Environment. Office: Covington & Burling 1201 Pennsylvania Ave NW Washington DC 20044

TOPPER, ROBERT CARLTON, lawyer; b. Tuscaloosa, Ala., May 23, 1949; s. Robert Carlton and Marguerite (Ekdahl) T.; m. Linda L. Stranathan, Apr. 12, 1980. B.A., So. Meth. U., 1970; J.D., 1973. Bar: Tex. 1973. Vice-pres. Am. Title Co. Dallas, 1975-80, v.p., 1983—; judge Dallas County Probate Ct., 1981-82; master Mental Illness Ct., Dallas, 1983. Vice pres. Dallas County Young Republicans, 1978-79; parliamentarian Dallas County Rep. Assembly, 1984—, v.p., 1985-86. Mem. Dallas Bar Assn., ABA, Dallas Young Lawyers Assn., Am. Judges Assn., Nat. Coll. Probate Judges, Tex. Coll. Probate Judges. Congregationalist. Real property, Probate. Home: 405 Shadow Bend Richardson TX 75081 Office: Am Title Co Dallas PO Box 538 Dallas TX 75221

TOPPINS, ROGER KEITH, lawyer; b. St. Louis, Feb. 12, 1956; s. Ralph Ward and Shirley Mavis (Lutes) T.; m. Kathleen McComb, Dec. 27, 1977; 1 child, Matthew Lee. BJ, U. Mo., 1977, JD, 1980. Bar: Mo. 1980, U.S. Dist. Ct. (we. dist.) Mo. 1980, U.S. Ct. Appeals (8th cir.) 1983. Law clk. to presiding justice Mo. Supreme Ct., Jefferson City, 1980-81; assoc. Bartlett, Venters & Pletz, Jefferson City, 1982-83; ptnr., dir. Bartlett, Venters, Pletz & Toppins, Jefferson City, 1983—. Mng. editor U. Mo. Law Rev., 1979-80. Mem. ABA, Cole County Bar Assn., Am. Judicature Soc. Republican. Federal civil litigation, State civil litigation, General practice. Home: 2617 Huntleigh Pl Jefferson City MO 65101 Office: Bartlett Venters Pletz & Toppins 325 Jefferson St Jefferson City MO 65101

TORBERT, CLEMENT CLAY, JR., state chief justice; b. Opelika, Ala., Aug. 31, 1929; s. Clement Clay Sr. and Lynda (Meadows) T.; m. Gene Hurt, May 2, 1952; children: Mary Dixon, Gene Shealy, Clement Clay III. Student, U.S. Naval Acad., 1948-49; B.S., Auburn U., 1951; postgrad., U. Md., 1952; LL.B., U. Ala., 1954. Bar: Ala. 1954. Practiced in Opelika, 1954-77, city judge, 1954-58; partner firm Samford, Torbert, Denson & Horsley, 1959-74; chief justice Ala. Supreme Ct., 1977—; chmn. Ala. Jud. Study Commn., Jud. Coordination Com.; pres. elect Conf. Chief Justices; supervisory bd. Ala. Law Enforcement Planning Agy., 1977-83; bd. dirs. Ala. Criminal Justice Info. Systems, Nat. Ctr. State Cts.; chmn. bd. dirs. State Justice Inst.; bd. dirs. First Nat. Bank Opelika, Opelika-Auburn Broadcasting Co. Mem. Ala. Ho. of Reps., 1958-62, Ala. Senate, 1966-70, 74-77. Served to capt. USAF, 1952-53. Elected to Ala. Acad. of Honor, 1979. Mem. Am. Judicature Soc. (bd. dirs.), Farrah Law Soc., Phi Delta Phi, Phi Kappa Phi, Alpha Tau Omega. Methodist. Lodge: Kiwanis. Judicial administration. Home: 611 Terracewood Dr Opelika AL 36801 Office: Supreme Ct Ala 445 Dexter Ave PO Box 218 Montgomery AL 36130

TORKILDSON, RAYMOND MAYNARD, lawyer; b. Lake City, S.D., Nov. 19, 1917; s. Gustav Adolph and Agnes (Opitz) T.; m. Sharman Elizabeth Vaughn, Sept. 8, 1956; children—Stephen, Thomas. S.B., U. S.D., 1946; J.D., Harvard U., 1948. Bar: Calif. 1949, Hawaii 1950. Assoc. James P. Blaisdell, Honolulu, 1949-52; ptnr. Moore, Torkildson & Rice and successors, Honolulu, 1955-64; exec. v.p. Hawaii Employers Council, Honolulu, 1964-67; ptnr. Torkildson, Katz, Jossem, Fonseca & Moore and predecessors, Honolulu, 1967-72, sr. ptnr., 1972—. Mem. mgmt. com. Armed Forces YMCA, Honolulu, 1971; treas. Hawaii Republican Com. 1977-83. Served with U.S. Army, 1941-46; lt. col. Res. ret. Mem. ABA, Hawaii Bar Assn. Roman Catholic. Clubs: Oahu Country, Pacific (Honolulu). Labor.

TORMEY, DOUGLAS JOSEPH, lawyer; b. Mineola, N.Y., Jan. 9, 1951; s. Joseph Edward Jr. and Charlotte Alice (Dluginsky) T.; m. Joyce Susan Williams, Nov. 25, 1978; children: Lauren, Christine. BA, Fordham U., 1972; JD, Hofstra U., 1975. Bar: N.Y. 1976, U.S. Dist. Ct. (so. and ea. dists.) N.Y. 1976, U.S. Dist. Ct. (ea. dist.) Wis. 1981. Sr. atty. Kimberly-Clark Corp., Neenah, Wis., 1978-84; asst. gen. counsel Colgate-Palmolive Co., N.Y.C., 1984—. Mem. ABA, Assn. of Bar of City of N.Y. Republican. Roman Catholic. General corporate, Securities, Pension, profit-sharing, and employee benefits. Office: Colgate-Palmolive Co 300 Park Ave New York NY 10022

TORMEY, JAMES ROLAND, JR., lawyer; b. San Jose, Calif., May 27, 1935; s. James Roland and Hope (Allario) T.; m. Mary Patricia O'Donnell, Oct. 16, 1957 (div. Oct. 1982); children—Anne, Erin, Christopher, Gregory, Marc; m. Mary Elizabeth Fenn, Feb. 28, 1985. Student San Jose State U., 1953-56; J.D., Santa Clara U., 1960. Bar: Calif. 1961, U.S. Supreme Ct. 1976. Sole practice, Burlingame and San Mateo, Calif., 1961-80; sr. ptnr. Tormey & Roesch, Inc., San Mateo, 1980—; dir. Borel Bank & Trust Co., San Mateo. Contbr. articles to state, nat. and local trustees' publs. Trustee, San Mateo County Community Coll. Dist., 1971—; nominee Calif. Senate, 1974; mem., former pres. San Mateo County Congress of Elected Ofcls., Redwood City, Calif., 1977—; mem. Govtl. Research Council, Redwood City, 1977—; bd. dirs. Republican Central Com., 1975-78. Served to capt. JAGC, U.S. Army, 1957-65. Recipient Disting. Service award San Mateo Jr. C. of C., 1969. Mem. Calif. State Bar Assn. (hearing referee), Calif. Trial Lawyers, San Mateo County Bar Assn. (treas., dir.), San Mateo County Barrister's Club (dir. 1963-68, former pres.). Club: Bombay Bicycle Riding (dir. 1975-78, 84—, pres. 1978) (Burlingame). Lodge: Elks. Contracts commercial, Banking, Real property. Office: Tormey & Roesch Inc 520 S El Camino Real Suite 520 San Mateo CA 94402

TORNSTROM, ROBERT ERNEST, lawyer; b. St. Paul, Jan. 17, 1946; s. Clifford H. and Janet (Hale) T.; m. Betty Jane Hermann, Aug. 5, 1978; children: Carter, Gunnar, Katherine. BA, U. Colo., 1968, JD, 1974. Bar: Colo. 1974, U.S. Dist. Ct. Colo. 1974, Calif. 1975, U.S. Dist. Ct. (cen. dist.) Calif. 1975. Atty. Union Oil Co. of Calif., Los Angeles, 1974-76, counsel internat. div., 1977-78; regional counsel Union Oil Co. of Calif., Singapore, 1976-77; sr. atty. Occidental Internat. Exploration and Prodn. Co., Bakersfield, Calif., 1978-81, mng. counsel, 1981-85, v.p., assoc. gen. counsel, 1985—; bd. dirs. Calif. Land and Cattle Co., King City, 602 Operating Corp., Bakersfield; China legal cons. Island Creek Coal Co., Lexington, Ky. Served to capt. U.S. Army, 1968-71, Vietnam. Decorated Bronze Star. Recipient Am. Jurisprudence award Bancroft-Whitney Co., 1974; named Eagle Scout, Boy Scouts Am. Mem. Am. Soc. Internat. Law, Am. Corp. Counsel Assn., Soc. Mayflower Descendants. Republican. Episcopalian. Club: Laurel Glen Tennis (Bakersfield). Avocations: skiing, tennis, golf, riding, collecting classic automobiles. Private international, Oil and gas leasing, General corporate. Home: 14812 Sunnybank Ave Bakersfield CA 93312 Office: Occidental Internat Exploration and Prodn Co 5000 Stockdale Hwy Bakersfield CA 93309

TORPY, RICHARD DONALD, lawyer; b. Denver, June 14, 1943; s. Alvin J. and Lois A. (Bamsey) T.; m. Janet S. Young, Sept. 3, 1966; children: Jennifer Lynn, Megan Christine. BS in Journalism, U. Colo., 1965; MA in History, JD, U. Denver, 1972. Bar: Colo. 1972, U.S. Dist. Ct. Colo. 1972, U.S. Ct. Appeals (10th cir.) 1975, U.S. Supreme Ct. 1980. Sole practice Englewood, Colo., 1972-75, 79-80; ptnr. Montgomery & Torpy, Denver, 1975-78, Torpy & Farrell, Englewood, 1981—. Editor RMR/Porsche mag., 1983-84. Mem. Greenwood Village (Colo.) City Council, 1981-83; bd. dirs. Met. Denver Legal Aid, 1985—. Served with USAR, 1967-73. Mem. Colo. Bar Assn., Arapahoe County Bar Assn., Sports Car Club of Am. (bd. dirs. Colo region 1986—), Porsche Club of Am. (bd. dirs. 1983-84). Democrat. Congregationalist. Avocation: creative writing. Consumer commercial, Bankruptcy, Real property. Home: 10 Brookside Dr Greenwood Village CO 80121 Office: Richard D Torpy and Assoc 3597 S Pearl #103 Englewood CO 80110

TORREY, N. MORRISON, lawyer; b. Aurora, Ill., Feb. 5, 1950; d. Francis Aldis and Margaret Elizabeth (Morrison) T.; m. David H. Hirschman, Apr. 3, 1981. AB, Wellesley Coll., 1972; JD with honors, Drake U., 1978. Bar: Iowa 1978, Ill. 1980, Ill. Trial Bar (no. dist.) 1983, U.S. Supreme Ct. 1984, U.S. Ct. Appeals (7th, 9th, and 10th cir.). Mgr. copyrights Harvard U. Press, Cambridge, Mass., 1972-73; editor-in-chief Armitage Press, Cambridge, 1973-74; asst. pub. Horticulture mag., Boston, 1974-75; labor relations examiner, hearing officer, mediator, atty. Iowa Pub. Employment Relations Bd., Des Moines, 1978-79; assoc. Vedder, Price et al., Chgo., 1979-84; trial atty. United Airlines, Chgo., 1984-86; asst. prof. law coll. law DePaul U., Chgo., 1986—. Federal civil litigation, State civil litigation, Labor. Home: 2144 N Lincoln Pk W Apt #16A Chicago IL 60614 Office: DePaul U 25 E Jackson Chicago IL 60603

TORRUELLA, JUAN R., federal judge. Judge U.S. Ct. Appeals, San Juan, P.R. Judicial administration. Office: US Ct Appeals PO Box 3205 Old San Juan Sta San Juan PR 00904 *

TORSHEN, JEROME HAROLD, lawyer; b. Chgo., Nov. 27, 1929; s. Jack and Lillian (Futterman) T.; m. Kay Pomerance, June 19, 1966; children: Jonathan, Jacqueline. BS, Northwestern U., 1951; JD, Harvard U., 1955. Bar: Ill. 1955, U.S. Dist. Ct. (no. dist.) Ill. 1955, U.S. Ct. Appeals (7th, 8th, 9th and D.C. cirs.) 1955, U.S. Supreme Ct. 1972. Assoc. Clausen, Hirsh & Miller, Chgo., 1955-62; pres. Jerome H. Torshen, Ltd., Chgo., 1963—; spl. asst. atty. gen. Ill., 1965-70; assoc. counsel Spl. Commn. Ill. Supreme Ct., 1969; counsel Ill. Legis. Redistricting Commn., 1971-72; spl. asst. corp. counsel City of Chgo., 1970-72; spl. state's atty. Cook County Ill., 1979-81, 83—; spl. counsel Met. Sanitary Dist. Greater Chgo., 1977-81, 84—. Counsel Cook County Dem. Cen. Com., Chgo., 1982—; bd. dirs. Jewish Family and Community Service. Served with U.S. Army, 1951-52. Recipient Torch of Learning award Am. Friends of Hebrew U., 1985, Outstanding Civic Duty award, Union League Club of Chgo., 1967. Mem. ABA, Ill. Bar Assn., Chgo. Bar Assn., Bar Assn. 7th Cir., Appellate Lawyers Assn. (founding mem., pres. 1976-77), Decalogue Soc. Clubs: Standard (Chgo.), Sixty (Chgo). Federal civil litigation, State civil litigation, Insurance. Office: 39 S LaSalle st Chicago IL 60603

TORTORIELLO, ROBERT LAURENCE, lawyer; b. Newark, Nov. 23, 1950; s. Frank and Leah L. (Megaro) T.; m. Margaret Ann F. Mullins, Sept. 29, 1979; children: Lauren Elyse, Christopher Robert. AB in History and Econs., St. Peter's Coll., 1971; JD, Harvard U., 1974. Bar: N.Y. 1975, N.J. 1975, U.S. Dist. Ct. (so. and ea. dists.) N.Y. 1975, U.S. Dist. Ct. N.J. 1975, U.S. Ct. Appeals (2d cir.) 1975, U.S. Supreme Ct. 1978. Assoc. Cleary Gottlieb Steen & Hamilton, N.Y.C., 1974-82, ptnr., 1982—. Contbr. articles to profl. jours. Mem. ABA, N.Y. State Bar Assn., Bar Assn. of City of N.Y. Republican. Roman Catholic. Banking, Securities, General corporate. Home: 91 Clarewill Ave Upper Montclair NJ 07043 Office: Cleary Gottlieb Steen & Hamilton 1 State St Plaza New York NY 10004

TOTENBERG, AMY MIL, lawyer; b. N.Y.C., Dec. 29, 1950; d. Roman and Melanie (Shroder) T.; m. Ralph Green, Sept. 27, 1980; stepchildren: Sonya, Naomi; 1 child, Emily. BA, Harvard U., 1974, JD, 1977. Bar: Ga. 1977, U.S. Dist. Ct. (no. and mid. dists.) Ga. 1977, U.S. Ct. Appeals (5th cir.) 1977, U.S. Ct. Appeals (11th cir.) 1982. Ptnr. Law Project R. Boult et al, Atlanta, 1977-82; sole practice Atlanta, 1982—; pro-hac mcpl. ct. judge City of Atlanta, 1986—; arbitrator Fulton County Superior Ct., State of Ga.; cons. in field. Legal advisor various community groups, Atlanta, 1984—; bd. dirs. Feminist Women's Health Ctr. Recipient Disting. Service award State Employees Rights Assn., 1980, 84. Mem. Ga. Bar Assn. (vice chmn. individual rights sect. 1985-85, sec. individual rights sect. 1985-86). Avocations: running, swimming. Civil rights, Labor, Federal civil litigation. Office: 44 Broad St Suite 218 Atlanta GA 30303

TOTH, CLAIRE E., lawyer; b. Evanston, Ill., Sept. 14, 1958; d. Richard C. and Marylou (Carl) T. AB, U. Chgo., 1980, JD, 1982; LLM, Georgetown U., 1987. Bar: Ill. 1982, U.S. Tax Ct. 1983. Assoc. Holleb & Coff Ltd., Chgo., 1982-84; atty. IRS Chief Counsel, Washington, 1984—. Contbr. articles to law jours. Mem. ABA (tax. sect., ptnrship. com.), Phi Beta Kappa. Corporate taxation, Personal income taxation. Office: IRS 1111 Constitution Ave NW Washington DC 20224

TOTH, ROBERT STEPHEN, lawyer; b. N.Y.C., Mar. 2, 1948; s. Ernest John and Faye (Apton) T. BA in Math., Hunter Coll., 1967; MD, Baylor Coll. Medicine, 1976; JD, South Tex. Coll. Law, 1981. Bar: Tex. 1982, U.S. Dist. Ct. (so. and ea. dists.) Tex. 1983, U.S. Ct. Appeals (5th cir.) 1983. Atty. Butler & Binion, Houston, 1981-84; sole practice Houston, 1984—; adj. prof. South Tex. Coll. Law, Houston, 1983-85. Contbr. articles to jours. Fellow Am. Coll. Legal Medicine; mem. ABA, Houston Med. Legal Soc. (pres. 1983—), Assn. Trial Lawyers Am., Tex. Bar Assn. (chmn. malpractice com. 1984—), Am. Bd. Law in Medcine (cert.), Phi Beta Kappa, Pi Mu Epsilon. Lodge: Masons. Personal injury, Health, Insurance. Office: 3000 Post Oak Blvd #1400 Houston TX 77056

TOTTENHAM, TERRY OLIVER, lawyer; b. Dallas, June 5, 1944; s. Edwin Pier and Ruth Elizabeth (Paris) T.; m. Carolyn Sue Lewis, July 7, 1967; children: Leslie Jo, Dana Elizabeth, Jessica Leigh. Student, Blinn Jr. Coll., 1962-67; B.S. in Pharmacy with high honors, U. Tex.-Austin, 1967, J.D. with honors, 1970; LL.M., George Washington U., 1973. Bar: Tex. 1970, U.S. Ct. Mil. Appeals 1971. Assoc. firm Fulbright, Crooker & Jaworski, Houston, 1970; ptnr. Fulbright & Jaworski, Houston, 1978—; mem. faculty South Tex. Coll. Law, U. Houston; vis. prof. med. jurisprudence Baylor U.; vis. prof. health law Tex. women's U.; speaker profl. groups. Editor: Patients Rights Handbook, 1980. Served to capt. USMC, 1971-75. Named Outstanding Young Lawyer Houston, 1981; named Outstanding Young Lawyer Tex., 1981. Fellow Tex. Bar Found. (life, trustee 1986—); mem. Tex. Assn. Def. Counsel, Am. Soc. Law and Medicine, Am. Soc. Pharmacy Law, Tex. Ex-Students Assn. (life), ABA, Nat. Health Lawyers Assn., Am. Soc. Hosp. Attys., State Bar Tex. (chmn. health law sect., chmn.-elect litigation sect, bd. dirs. 1985-86)), Houston Young Lawyers Assn. (dir. 1975-77), Tex. Young Lawyers Assn. (chmn. bd. 1979-80). Democrat. Episcopalian. Home: 25 Cicero Austin TX 78746 Office: Fulbright & Jaworski 600 Congress Ave Suite 2400 Austin TX 78701

TOUREK, STEVEN CHARLES, lawyer; b. Evanston, Ill., Apr. 28, 1948; s. Charles Frank and Gertrude Jean (Steiner) T., Jr.; m. Ann Elizabeth Elliott, Sept. 13, 1969; children—Peter S., Samuel C. B.A., Dartmouth Coll., 1970; M.A., Cambridge U., 1974, LL.B., 1975; postgrad. Yale U. Law Sch., 1970-71. Bar: Minn. 1976, Wis. 1981, U.S. Dist. Ct. Minn. 1976, U.S. Dist. Ct. (we. dist.) Wis. 1982, U.S. Ct. Appeals (8th cir.) 1981. Asst. dean Dartmouth Coll., Hanover, N.H., 1971-72; assoc. Oppenheimer, Wolff, Foster, Shepard & Donnelly, St. Paul, 1975-79; ptnr. Winthrop & Weinstine, St. Paul, 1979—. Dir Vol. Action Ctr., St. Paul, 1977-78; dir., treas. Bd. Edn. Ind. Sch. Dist. 197, West St. Paul, 1980-83; trustee, bd. dirs. Dodge Nature Ctr., West St. Paul, 1982—. Bd. dirs. Family Service Greater St. Paul, 1986—. Reynolds fellow, 1973-74; Hattie M. Strong Found. fellow, 1972-73; Rufus Choate scholar, Dartmouth Coll., 1966-70. Mem. Minn. Bar Assn., Wis. Bar Assn., Minn. Trial Lawyers Assn., Assn. Trial Lawyers Am., ABA, Phi Beta Kappa. Lutheran. Clubs: Cambridge U. Boat (pres. 1974-75), Cambridge Blues Com. (chmn. 1974-75). Lodge: Rotary (bd. dirs. Midway chpt. 1985—). Federal civil litigation, State civil litigation, Contracts commercial. Office: Winthrop & Weinstine 1800 Conwed Tower 444 Cedar St Saint Paul MN 55101

TOURKOW, JOSHUA ISAAC, lawyer; b. Fort Wayne, Ind., Mar. 5, 1947; s. Frederick Rhinehold and Leah Sarah (Schwartz) T.; m. Donna Susan Dubin, Aug. 30, 1970; children—Illana Joy, Lisa Michelle, Benjamin Ahron. Student Bar Ilan U., Israel, 1968; B.S. in Indsl. Mgmt., Purdue U., 1970; J.D., Ind. U.-Indpls., 1973. Bar: Ind. 1973, U.S. Dist. Cts. (no. and so. dists.) Ind. 1973, U.S. Ct. Appeals (7th cir.) 1973. Asst. dep. prosecutor Marion County, Indpls., 1972-73; ptnr. Tourkow, Crell, Rosenblatt & Johnston, Ft. Wayne, 1973—. Bd. dirs. Housing & Neighborhood Devel. Services, Inc., Ft. Wayne, 1980-84, Ft. Wayne Redevel. Com., 1983; atty. Ft. Wayne Housing Authority, 1983—; advisor, atty. Parents Without Partners, Ft. Wayne, 1981-85, Fathers United for Equal Rights, Ft. Wayne, 1980—. Mem. Ind. Trial Lawyers Assn., Assn. Trial Lawyers Am., ABA, Ind. Bar Assn., Allen County Bar Assn. Democrat. Family and matrimonial, Bankruptcy, General practice. Home: 7022 Winchester Rd Fort Wayne IN 46819 Office: Tourkow Crell Rosenblatt & Johnston 814 Anthony Wayne Bank Bldg Fort Wayne IN 46802

TOWE, THOMAS EDWARD, lawyer; b. Cherokee, Iowa, June 25, 1937; s. Edward and Florence (Tow) T.; m. Ruth James, Aug. 21, 1960; children: James Thomas, Kristofer Edward. Student, U. Paris, 1956; BA, Earlham Coll., 1959; LLB, U. Mont., 1962; LLM, Georgetown U., 1965. Ptnr. Towe, Ball, Enright & Mackey, Billings, Mont., 1967-71; legislator Mont. House of Rep., Billings, 1971-75, Mont. State Senate, Billings, 1975-87; served on various coms. Mont. Senate, 1973-87. Contbr. articles to law revs. Pres. Alternatives, Inc. Halfway House, Billings, 1985-86; mem. adv. com. Mont. Crime Control Bd. 1973-78, Youth Justice council, 1981-83; mem. State Dem. Exec. com., 1969-71, Yellowstone County Dem. Exec. Com., 1969-73; bd. dirs. Mont. Consumer Affairs Council, Regional Community Services for the Devel. Disabled, 1975-77, Rimrock Guidance Found., 1975-80, Vols. of Am., Billings, 1984—. Served to capt. U.S. Army, 1962-65. Mem. Mont. Bar Assn., Yellowstone County Bar Assn., Am. Hereford Assn., Billings C. of C. Mem. Soc. of Friends. Club: Billings Friends Meeting (clk. 1982-85). Lodge: Optimists. Avocation: outdoor recreation. Banking, Legislative, Federal civil litigation. Home: 2739 Gregory Dr S Billings MT 59102 Office: Mont State Senate 2525 Sixth Ave N Billings MT 59101

TOWERS, LAWRENCE ALAN, legal educator; b. Cleve., Mar. 11, 1952; s. Douglas William and Lillian Mary (Barnes) T.; m. Patricia Clare Bradford, Jan. 22, 1983. BA, Kenyon Coll., 1974; M Pub. Adminstrn., Calif. State U., Hayward, 1979; JD, U. Calif., San Francisco, 1981. Bar: Wis. 1981, U.S. Dist. Ct. (ea. and we. dists.) Wis. 1981, U.S. Ct. Appeals (7th cir.) 1981. Assoc. Whyte & Hirschboeck S.C., Milw., 1981-84; prof. law John Marshall Law Sch., Milw., 1984-85, Marquette U., Milw., 1985—; pres., owner Consumer Forms and Info. Service, Inc., Milw., 1985—. Co-inventor The Lemon Aid, 1985; contbr. articles to profl. jours. Mem. ABA, Assn. Trial Lawyers Am., Wis. Bar Assn. (reporter gen. practice sect. 1986—), Milw. Bar Assn. (cts. com.), Thurston Soc. Republican. Lutheran. Avocations: tennis, racquetball. Federal civil litigation, State civil litigation, Workers' compensation. Home: 1528 E Olive St Shorewood WI 53211 Office: Marquette U Law Sch 1103 W Wisconsin Ave Milwaukee WI 53233

TOWERY, CURTIS KENT, lawyer, director; b. Hugoton, Kans., Jan. 29, 1954; s. Clyde D. and Jo June (Curtis) T. BA, Trinity U., 1976; JD, U. Okla., 1979. Bar: Okla. 1980. Mem. Curtis & Blanton, Pauls Valley, Okla., 1980-81; lawyer land and legal dept. Trigg Drilling Co., Oklahoma City, 1981-82; adminstrv. law judge Okla. Corp. Commn., Oklahoma City, 1982-85; counsel Curtis & Blanton, Paul's Valley, Okla., 1985—; bd. dirs. First Nat. Bank of Pauls Valley, Okla., Clyde Towery Inc., Trinity Exploration Corp.; adminstrv. law judge Okla. Dept. Mines, 1985—. Assoc. Okla. Mus. Art, 1985—. Mem. ABA, Okla. Bar Assn., Am. Assn. Petroleum Landmen, Internat. Assn. Energy Economist, Okla. City Assn. Petroleum Landmen, Phi Alpha Delta. Democrat. Presbyterian. Clubs: Young Men's Dinner Club (Oklahoma City), Faculty House. Lodges: Rotary, Elks. Avocations: flying, golf, traveling, investment analysis. Oil and gas leasing, Probate, FERC practice. Home: 9009 N May Ave Sutton Pl 179 Oklahoma City OK 73120 Office: Curtis & Blanton 123 W Paul Pauls Valley OK 73075

TOWNER, FRANK SCHWABLE, JR., lawyer; b. San Diego, Apr. 10, 1951; s. Frank Schwable Sr. and Jean (Nordin) T.; m. Catherine Martin, June 17, 1980; 1 child, Marianne. BA, San Diego State U., 1973; JD, Loyola U., Los Angeles, 1979. Bar: Calif. 1980, Mass. 1986, U.S. Dist. Ct. Mass. 1986, U.S. Dist. Ct. (cen. dist.) Calif. 1982, U.S. Dist. Ct. (ea. dist.) Calif. 1982. Assoc. Kern & Wooley, Los Angeles, 1979-81; assoc. Robins, Zelle, Larson & Kaplan, Newport Beach, Calif., 1981-85, Wellesley, Mass., 1985—; of council Wausau Ins. Cos., Los Angeles. Mem. ABA (ins. law, tort and ins. practice, internat. practice and procedure, sci. and tech. sects.), Mass. Bar Assn., Calif. Bar Assn., Internat. Bar Assn. (ins. law and bus. law sects.), Lawyers Alliance for Nuclear Arms Control, World Affairs Council. Democrat. Roman Catholic. Club: French Library (Boston). Avocations: sailing, windsurfing, internat. cooking, scuba diving, French. Federal civil litigation, Insurance, Private international. Home: 48 Pealedale Rd Needham MA 02192 Office: Robins Zelle Larson & Kaplan 57 River St #100 Wellesley MA 02181

TOWNES, EDGAR EGGLESTON, JR., b. Beaumont, Tex., Dec. 16, 1906; s. Edgar Eggleston and Mary Elsie (Garrett) T.; m. Mary Louise Goss, Nov. 10, 1931; children—Mary Louise Townes Lee, Edgar Goss. Student Rice U., 1923-24; B.A., U. Tex., 1927. Bar: Tex. 1930, U.S. Dist. Ct. (so. dist.) Tex., U.S. Ct. Appeals (5th cir.), U.S. Supreme Ct. 1953. Assoc. John C. Townes, Jr., Houston, 1930-31, Vinson, Elkins, Weems and Francis, and predecessors, Houston, 1931-47; mem. Townes and Townes, Houston, 1947—; lectr. prof. med. jurisprudence Coll. Medicine, Baylor U., 1953-63; lectr. oil and gas S. Tex. Coll. Law, Houston; mem. com. bar candidates Harris County, Tex., 1961-63, chmn., 1962-63. Bd. regents, trustee S. Tex. Colls., 1956-66; trustee S. Tex. Coll. Law, 1966—, sec., 1966-82, chmn., 1982-86; trustee S. Tex. Law Jour., 1958—, pres., 1964; trustee S. Tex. Found., 1977, S. Tex. Jr. Coll., 1967-74. Served to brig. gen. Tex. State Guard, 1943-64. Mem. Tex. State Guard Assn. (life; pres. 1961-62), ABA, State Bar Tex. (spl. conf. com. with med. profession 1956-59, chmn. 1958-59), Houston Bar Assn., N.G. Assn. Tex. (assoc. life), Nat. Rifle Assn. (life), Tex. Rifle Assn. (life), Tex. Soc. SAR, Ex-Students Assn. U. Tex. (life), Beta Theta Pi, Delta Theta Phi (alumni). Baptist. Clubs: River Oaks Country, Inns of Court Commencement speaker S. Tex. Coll. Law, 1978. Probate, Oil and gas leasing, Real property. Office: Townes & Townes 603 San Jacinto Bldg Houston TX 77002

TOWNS, EMANUEL ALEXANDER, lawyer; b. N.Y.C., Dec. 3, 1947; s. William Herman and Ruth (Williams) T.; m. Brenda E. Ross, May 18, 1985. BA, Franklin & Marshall Coll., 1969; JD, Columbia U., 1972. Bar: N.Y. 1974, U.S. Dist. Ct. (ea. dist.) N.Y. 1979. Sole practice Bklyn., 1980—; arbitrator N.Y.C. Civil Ct., 1981—; hearing examiner Family Ct. N.Y.C., 1983-84; adimstrv. law judge Taxi & Limousine Commn. N.Y.C., 1984—. Mem. steering com. 21st Century Polit. Action Com., N.Y.C., 1985—; bd. deacons Cornerstone Bapt. Ch., Bklyn., 1986—. Mem. ABA, Nat. Bar Assn. (bd. govs. 1984—), Met. Black Bar Assn. (organizer, pres. 1985—). State civil litigation, Real property, Landlord-tenant. Home: 355 Clinton Ave Brooklyn NY 11238 Office: 308-310 Livingston St Suite 3R Brooklyn NY 11217

TOWNSEND, DIANE KATHLEEN, lawyer; b. Flushing, N.Y., July 6, 1951; d. James Alfred and Elsie Catherine (Lange) Smith; m. Joachim Rudiger Townsend, May 26, 1984. BA, Boston U., 1973; JD, New Eng. Sch. Law, 1977. Bar: N.Y. 1978. Atty. Dept. Treasury, Washington, 1978-80; atty. Naval Air Systems Command, Washington, 1980-84, assoc. counsel, 1985—; dep. counsel Joint Cruise Missiles Project, Washington, 1984-85. Mem. ABA, Fed. Bar Assn. Roman Catholic. Government contracts and claims. Home: 5205 Tamar Woods Ct Fairfax VA 22032 Office: Naval Air Systems Command Washington DC 20361

TOWNSEND, DONALD JOSEPH, lawyer; b. Chgo., Apr. 14, 1947; s. Edward Leo and Bernadine (Love) T.; m. Deborah Marie Haug, May 8, 1975 (div. Jan. 1980); 1 child, James Albert. AB, U. Ill., 1969, JD, 1972. Bar: Ill. 1972, U.S. Dist. Ct. (no. dist.) Ill. 1973, U.S. Ct. Appeals (7th cir.) 1973, U.S. Dist. Ct. (so. dist.) Ill. 1978. Vista atty. Legal Aid Found. Chgo., 1972-74; asst. atty. gen. State of Ill., Springfield, 1974-83; fin. assoc. Rudnick & Wolfe, Chgo., 1983—; mem. white collar crime task force U.S. Govt., 1982-83; spl. asst. to U.S. atty. U.S. Govt., 1982-83. Contbr. articles to profl. jours. Mem. ABA (franchise forum com.), Ill. Bar Assn., Chgo. Bar Assn., Springfield Chess Club (pres. 1981-82). Roman Catholic. Avocations: fgn. languages, chess, marathon running. Franchise law. Office: Rudnick & Wolfe 30 N LaSalle Suite 3500 Chicago IL 60602

TOWNSEND, EARL CUNNINGHAM, JR., lawyer, author, composer; b. Indpls., Nov. 9, 1914; s. Earl Cunningham and Besse (Kuhn) T.; m. Emily Macnab, Apr. 3, 1947; children: Starr (Mrs. John R. Laughlin), Vicki M. (Mrs. Christopher Katterjohn), Julia E. (Mrs. Edward Goodrich Dunn, Jr.), Earl Cunningham III, Clyde G. Student (Rector scholar), De Pauw U., 1932-34; A.B., U. Mich., 1936, J.D., 1939. Bar: Ind. 1939, Mich. 1973, U.S. Supreme Ct. 1973, U.S. Ct. Appeals (4th, 6th, 7th cirs.), U.S. Dist. Ct. (no. and so. dists.) Ind., U.S. Dist. Ct. (ea. dist.) Va., U.S. Dist. Ct. (ea. dist.) Mich. Sr. partner firm Townsend & Townsend, Indpls., 1940-69; sr. partner Townsend, Hovde & Townsend, Indpls., 1979-84, Townsend, Yosha & Cline, Indpls., 1985-86, 1986—; individual practice Roscommon, Mich., 1973—; dep. prosecutor, Marion County, Ind., 1942-44; radio-TV announcer WIRE, WFBM, WFBM-TV, Indpls., 1940-49, 1st TV announcer Indpls. 500 mile race, 1949, 50; Big Ten basketball referee, 1940-47; lectr. trial tactics U. Notre Dame, Ind. U., U. Mich., 1968-79; chmn. faculty seminar on personal injury trials Ind. U. Sch. Law, U. Notre Dame Sch. Law, Valparaiso Sch. Law, 1981; owner Tropical Isle Palm Tree Farms, Key Biscayne, Fla., Terney-Townsend Historic House, Roscommon, Mich.; founder, v.p., treas. Am. Underwriters, Inc., Am. Interinsurance Exchange, 1965-70; mem. Com. to Revise Ind. Supreme Ct. Pattern Jury Instructions, 1975-83; lectr. Trial Lawyers 30 Yrs. Inst., 1986. Author: Birdstones of the North American Indian, 1959, also articles in legal and archeol. fields; composer: Moon of Halloween. Founder, life fellow Roscoe Pound Am. Trial Lawyers Found., Cambridge, Mass.; co-founder, dir. Meridian St. Found.; mem. fin. and bldg. coms., bd. dirs., later life trustee Indpls. Mus. Art; life trustee Ind. State Mus.; trus Judge Cale J. Holder Meml. Scholarship Fund, Ind. U. Law Sch.; trustee Cathedral High Sch., Indpls., Starlight Musicials; mem. Ind. U. Found.; mem. Dean's Council, Ind. U.; life dir. Indpls./Marion County Hist. Soc.; fellow Meth. Hosp. Found. Recipient Ind. Univ. Writers Conf. award, 1960; Hanson H. Anderson medal of honor Arsenal Tech. Schs., Indpls., 1971; named to Council Sagamores of Wabash, 1969, Hon. Ky. Col., 1986; Ind. Basketball Hall of Fame; hon. chief Black River-Swan Creek Saginaw-Chippewa Indian tribe, 1971. Fellow Ind. Coll. Trial Lawyers (pres. 1984-86), Ind. Bar Found., Indpls. Bar. Found. (disting., charter), Internat. Acad. Trial Lawyers, Internat. Soc. Barristers; mem. Ind. Trial Lawyers Assn. (pres. 1963-64, life dir. 1981—), ABA (com. trial techniques 1964-76, com. aviation and space 1977—), Ind. State Bar Assn. (del. 1977-79), Indpls. Bar Assn., 34th Dist. (Mich.) Bar Assn., State Bar Mich., Assn. Am. Trial Lawyers (v.p. Ind. 1959-60, bd. govs. 7th jud. circuit 1966-68, assoc. editor Jour. 1964—), Am. Bd. Trial Advocates (diplomate, pres. Ind. chpt. 1982-85), Bar Assn. 7th Fed. Circuit, Roscommon County Bar Assn., Lawyers Assn. Indpls., Am. Judicature Soc., Am. Arbitration Assn. (panel), ASCAP, Ind. Archaeol. Soc. (founder, pres.), Indpls. C. of C., Ind. State C. of C., Genuine Indian Relic Soc. (co-founder, chmn. frauds com.), Ind. Hist. Soc., Trowel and Brush Soc. (hon.), U. Mich. Pres.'s Club, U. Mich. Victors Club (charter), Soc. Mayflower Descs. (gov. 1947-49), Key Biscayne C. of C., Delta Kappa Epsilon, Phi Kappa Phi. Republican. Methodist. Clubs: Mason (32 deg., Shriner), Players, U. Mich. (local pres. 1950), Columbia, Indpls. Athletic, Key Biscayne Yacht. Federal civil litigation, State civil litigation, Personal injury. Home: 5008 N Meridian St Indianapolis IN 46208

TOWNSEND, EDWIN CLAY, lawyer; b. Parsons, Tenn., Nov. 22, 1924; s. Mahlon Nathaniel Emma Annie (Odle) T.; m. Marjorie Lucille Duncan, Sept. 10, 1950; children: Edwin Townsend Jr., Karin Townsend. Student, Union U., Jackson, Tenn., 1942-43, 1946; LLB, Cumberland U., Lebanon, Tenn., 1947, BA, 1948; JD, Stamford U., Birmingham, Ala., 1969. Bar: Tenn. 1947, U.S. Dist. Ct. Tenn. 1949. Ptnr. Townsend & Townsend, Parsons; del. 1977 Tenn. Ltd. Const. Conv., 1977; mem. Bd. Profl. Responsibility of Supreme Ct. Tenn., Nashville, 1982—. Trustee Lambuth Coll., Jackson, 1980—; bd. dirs. Meth. Found., Memphis, 1980—; bd. dirs. Tenn. River Four County Port Authority, Parsons, 1980— (chmn. 1980-81, 85-86). Served with USN, 1943-45, PTO. Decorated Purple Heart. Mem. ABA, Am. Coll. Probate Counsel, Def. Research Inst., Tenn. Bar Assn. (bd. govs., com. on adminstrn. justice, ho. of dels.), Tenn. Bar Found., Tenn. Trial Lawyers Assn., Tenn. Def. Attys. Assn., Vets. of Fgn. Wars, Am. Disabled Vets., Am. Legion. Democrat. Methodist. Lodges: Lions (local pres. 1952-53, 76-77, dist. gov. 1961-62, bd. dirs. West Tenn. Lions Found. 1982—), Masons, Elks. Probate, Personal injury, General corporate. Office: Townsend & Townsend 121 Tennessee Ave S Parsons TN 38363

TOWNSEND, JOHN MICHAEL, lawyer; b. West Point, N.Y., Mar. 21, 1947; s. John D. and Vera (Nachman) T. BA, Yale U., 1968, JD, 1971. Bar: N.Y. 1972, U.S. Dist. Ct. (so. and ea. dists.) N.Y. 1975, U.S. Ct. Appeals (2d cir.) 1975, U.S. Supreme Ct. 1975, U.S. Ct. Appeals (8th cir.) 1982, U.S. Ct. Appeals (7th cir.) 1986. Assoc. Hughes Hubbard & Reed, N.Y.C., 1971-73, 1975-80, ptnr., 1980; assoc. Hughes Hubbard & Reed, Paris, France, 1973-74; arbitrator U.S. Dist. Ct. (ea. dist.) N.Y., Civil Ct. N.Y.C. Served as 1st lt. USAR, 1971-75. Mem. ABA, Internat. Bar Assn., Assn. of the Bar of the City of N.Y., Fed. Bar Council, Union Internat. des Avocats (regional sec.). Democrat. Episcopalian. Club: Yale (N.Y.C.). Antitrust, Federal civil litigation, Private international. Office: Hughes Hubbard & Reed One Wall St New York NY 10005

TOWNSEND, WILLIAM JACKSON, lawyer; b. Grayson, Ky., June 4, 1932; s. Robert Glenn and Lois Juanita (Jackson) T. B.S., Wake Forest U., 1954; Student U. Ky., 1957, U. Louisville, 1958, U. N.C., 1960. Bar: N.C. 1965. Claims adjuster State Farm Ins. Co., 1963; sole practice, Fayetteville, N.C., 1965—; pub. adminstr. Robeson County, N.C., 1966; dir., treas. Colonial Foods, Inc., St. Paul, N.C., 1959—. Served as 1st lt. U.S. Army, 1954-56. Mem. N.C. Bar Assn., N.C. State Bar. Presbyterian. Club: Kiwanis (treas. Fayetteville 1973-82). Personal injury, Family and matrimonial, General corporate. Address: PO Box 584 Fayetteville NC 28302

TOZER, FORREST LEIGH, lawyer; b. Morgantown, W.Va., Oct. 29, 1922; s. Aiden Wilson and Ada Cecelia (Pfautz) T.; m. Rosemary Peacock, June 16, 1947; children: Paul, Christine, Judith, Thomas. B.A., U. Chgo., 1947, J.D., 1948. Bar: Ill. 1948. Atty. anti-trust div. Dept. Justice, Detroit, 1948-50; mem. firm Lord, Bissell & Brook, Chgo., 1952—; partner firm Lord, Bissell & Brook, 1959—. Contbr. articles to profl. jours. Chmn. Cook County Sheriff's Police Dept. Merit Bd., 1963-69; chmn. Ill. State Police Merit Bd., 1969-73. Served with USMCR, 1943-46, 50-52. Decorated Purple Heart. Fellow Am. Coll. Trial Lawyers; mem. Am. Bar Assn., Fed. Bar Assn., Ill. State Bar Assn., Chgo. Bar Assn., Soc. Trial Lawyers. Republican. Presbyterian. Clubs: Mid-Am. (Chgo.), Attic (Chgo.); Flossmoor (Ill.) Country. Federal civil litigation, State civil litigation. Home: 843 Bruce St Flossmoor IL 60422 Office: Lord Bissell & Brook 115 S LaSalle St Chicago IL 60603

TRACEY, JAY WALTER, JR., lawyer; b. Rocky Ford, Colo., June 13, 1925; s. Jay Walter and Margaret Louise (Bish) T.; m. Elizabeth Longfellow Henry, Nov. 1, 1952; children: Jay Walter, William H., Anne E., John B. BS, Yale U., 1949; LLB, Harvard U., 1952. Bar: Colo. 1952, U.S. Dist. Ct. Colo. 1952, U.S. Ct. Appeals (10th cir.) 1958. Assoc. Holland & Hart, Denver, 1952-57, ptnr., 1957-71, 72—; pres. Von Frellick Assocs., Inc., Denver, 1971-72; dir. Ctr. for Dispute Resolution, Denver, 1984—. Councilman, City of Cherry Hills Village (Colo.), 1965-70, mayor pro tem, 1966-70, mem. Home Rule Charter Conv., 1966; trustee Denver Country Day Sch., 1967-70. Served with U.S. Army, 1943-46. Decorated Purple Heart. Mem. ABA, Colo. Bar Assn., Denver Bar Assn., Colo. Yale Assn. (pres. 1971-72), Assn. Yale Alumni (del. 1975-78), Harvard Law Sch. Assn. Colo. (pres. 1962-63), Harvard Law Sch. Assn. (v.p. 1963-64). Republican. Episcopalian. Clubs: University, Denver Country, Arapahoe Tennis. Lodge: Rotary (Denver chpt. bd. dirs. 1980-82, 1st v.p. 1981-82). Federal civil litigation, State civil litigation, Real property. Office: Holland & Hart PO Box 8749 Denver CO 80201

TRACHOK, RICHARD M(ATHEW), II, lawyer; b. Reno, Dec. 24, 1952; s. Richard Mathew and Frances (Sumner) T.; m. Cathleen Benna, Dec. 17, 1976. BS, U. Nev., 1974; JD summa cum laude, Calif. Western Sch. Law, 1980; LLM, U. Cambridge, Eng., 1984. Bar: Nev. 1980. Dep. dist. atty. Washoe County Dist. Atty.'s Office, Reno, 1980-81; assoc. Lionel Law Firm, Reno, 1981-84; ptnr. Bible, Santini, Hoy, Miller and Trachok, Reno, 1984%; adj. prof. Old Coll. Law Sch., Reno, 1981—. Served to 1st lt. USMC, 1974-77. Mem. ABA, Nev. Bar Assn., Washoe County Bar Assn. Avocations: squash, olympic class competitive sailing. Construction, Public international. Office: Bible Santini Hoy Miller Trachok 232 Court St Reno NV 89501

TRACT, HAROLD M., lawyer; b. N.Y.C., May 18, 1926; s. Meyer and Mary (Nadler) Trachtenberg; m. Natalie A. Meyerowitz, Nov. 16, 1958; children—Marc M., Laurence T. B.A., U. Wis., 1948; J.D., Harvard U., 1951. Bar: Mass. 1951, N.Y. 1953. Assoc. Rein, Mound & Cotton, N.Y.C., 1952-62, ptnr., 1962-85; sr. ptnr. Kroll & Tract, 1985—; dir. The Mercantile and Gen. Reins. Co. Am., N.Y. Surety Co., Cherry Valley Coop. Ins. Co., Gerling Am. Ins. Co., Navigators Ins. Co., Nasco Syndicate Mgrs., Inc., Windsor Life Ins. Co. Am., J.P. Woods (Bermuda) Ltd., Nasco N.Am. Inc., Toa-Re Ins. Co. Am., First United Am. LIfe Ins. Co., Preferred Life Ins. Co. of N.Y., Colonial Indemnity Ins. Co., Nordstern Ins. Co. Am., Ins. Fedn. N.Y. Inc.; bd. govs. Internat. Ins. Seminars Inc.; mem. arbitration panels Am. Arbitration Assn., N.Y. Ins. Exchange. Served with A.C., U.S. Army, 1944-46. Mem. ABA, City Bar Assn. N.Y., N.Y. County Lawyers, Nat. Assn. Ins. Commrs. (mem. adv. com. on reins., adv. com. on internat. insurer relations). Jewish. Clubs: Metropolitan, Harvard (N.Y.C.), Old Westbury Golf and Country. Editorial bd.: Ins. and Reins. Internat., Exec. Newsletter, Internat. Ins. Fin. Services newsletter. Insurance, General corporate. Home: 105 Fir Dr East Hills NY 11576 Office: 500 Fifth Ave New York NY 10110

TRACY, DAVID J., lawyer; b. Providence, Mar. 30, 1952; s. Paul E. Sr. and Constance P. (DelGiudice) T.; m. Jean M. Guerra, Dec. 1983. BA summa cum laude, Brandeis U., 1974; magna cum laude, Boston Coll., 1977. Bar: Mass. 1977, R.I. 1978. Assoc. Brown, Rudnick, Freed & Gesmer, Boston, 1977-80, Temkin, Merolla & Zurier, Providence, 1980-81, Hinckley, Allen, Tobin & Silverstein, Providence, 1981—. Mem. ABA (com. current lit. real property law 1980-83, real estate financing com. 1983-85), Mass. Bar Assn., R.I. Bar Assn. (com. on specialization 1983—), Order of Coif. Real property, Construction, Consumer commercial. Home: 8 Twins Ln North Providence RI 02904 Office: Hinckley Allen Tobin & Silverstein 1500 Fleet Ctr Providence RI 02903

TRACY, J. DAVID, lawyer; b. Ft. Worth, Jan. 1, 1946; s. Dennis Ford and Virginia Eloise (Hall) T.; m. Jeral Ann Wilson, June 3, 1967; children—Bradley Wilson, Jennifer Diann. B.A. with honors, U. Tex., Austin, 1968, J.D., 1970; LL.M., So. Meth. U., 1971. Bar: Tex. 1971, U.S. Tax Ct. 1971, U.S. Ct. Appeals (5th cir.) 1976, U.S. Supreme Ct. 1978; cert. in estate planning, probate and tax law Tex. Bd. Legal Specialization. Assoc. Shannon, Gracey, Ratliff & Miller, Ft. Worth, 1971-75, ptnr., 1975-76; ptnr. Bird & Appleman, Ft. Worth, 1976-80; sole practice, Ft. Worth, 1980-81; ptnr. Boswell & Tracy, Ft. Worth, 1981-85, Tracy, Crumley & Holland, 1985—; adj. prof. advanced corp. taxation So. Meth. U., 1975-77; lectr. continuing legal edn.; council mem. real estate, probate and trust law sects. State Bar Tex., 1983-87, newsletter editor 1987—; mem. Coll. State Bar Tex. Mem. adv. bd. dirs. Tarrant County Conv. Ctr., chmn. 1986-87. Named Outstanding Young Lawyer of Tarrant County, Tarrant County Young Lawyers Assn., 1982. Fellow Am. Coll. Probate Counsel; mem. ABA, Phi Delta Phi. Mem. Christian Ch. (Disciples of Christ). Clubs: Ft. Worth, Colonial Country (Ft. Worth). Contbr. articles to law jours. Probate, Corporate taxation, Pension, profit-sharing, and employee benefits. Office: 210 W 6th Suite 1050 Fort Worth TX 76102

TRACY, WILLIAM FRANCIS, II, lawyer; b. Decatur, Ill., Mar. 7, 1947; s. William Francis and Agnes Madonna (Ryan) T.; m. Elaine Baxter, Jan. 23, 1970; children: Katherine, Colleen, Ryan. AB, St. Louis U., 1969; JD, Northwestern U., 1972. Bar: Mo. 1972, Ill. 1977. Law clk. U.S. Dept. of Justice, Washington, summer 1971; jr. ptnr. Bryan, Cave, McPheeters & McRoberts, St. Louis, Mo., 1972-77; assoc. Doss, Simpson & Tracy, Monticello, Ill., 1977-78; ptnr., owner Miller, Tracy, Braun & Wilson, Ltd., Monticello, 1978—; spl. asst. atty. gen. State of Ill., Monticello, 1980-83, pub. adminstr., conservator, guardian, Piatt County, Ill., 1978—. Pres. Community Council, Bement, Ill., 1979. Mem. ABA, Mo. Bar Assn., Ill. Bar Assn., Piatt County Bar Assn., Estate Planning Council. Club: Monticello Golf (treas., bd. dirs. 1982-84). Lodges: Rotary (treas. 1983-84), Lions (pres. 1981), K.C. (adv. 1981-82). Probate, Estate planning, Estate taxation. Home: 807 N State St Monticello IL 61856

TRAFICANTI, TINA MICHELE, lawyer; b. Cleve., Feb. 6, 1956; d. Michael Angelo T. BA summa cum laude, U. Notre Dame, 1978; JD cum laude, Harvard U., 1981. Bar: Mass. 1981, U.S. Dist. Ct. Mass. 1982. Assoc. Sugarman Rogers Barshak & Cohen, Boston, 1981-86, ptnr., 1986. Contbr. articles to profl. jours. Mem. ABA, Mass. Bar Assn., Boston Bar Assn. Democrat. Avocations: running, swimming, tennis, reading, jazz. Federal civil litigation, State civil litigation, Personal injury. Office: Sugarman Rogers Barshak & Cohen 33 Union St Boston MA 02108

TRAGER, BERNARD H., lawyer; b. New Haven, July 18, 1906; s. Harry L. and Ida R. (Ruttenberg) T.; m. Mina R. Trager, Aug. 25, 1929; children—Roberta Trager Cohen, Philip. LL.B., NYU, 1928. Bar: Conn. 1929. Sole practice, 1929-60; sr. ptnr. Trager & Trager, Bridgeport, Conn., 1960-80, pres. Trager & Trager, P.C., 1980—; trustee Peoples Savs. Bank of Bridgeport, 1964-78, trustee emeritus, 1978—. Mem. Gov.'s Commn. Gambling, 1965-71; chmn. Conn. Bd. Pardons, 1959-73; life trustee U. Bridgeport; pres. Hundred Club Conn., 1976-77; mem. Bridgeport Mayor's Commn. Human Rights, 1958-62; chmn. Nat. Community Relations Adv. Council, 1953-55; pres. Conn. Conf. Social Work, 1948-49; mem. Bridgeport Fin. Adv. Commn., 1966-75; bd. dirs. Council Jewish Fedns. and Welfare Funds, 1954-61; trustee Nat. Health and Welfare Retirement Assn., 1955-68, Bridgeport Area Found., 1967-81; bd. dirs. Bridgeport Hosp., 1970—, also mem. profl. com. Mem. Bridgeport Bar Assn. (pres. 1959-61), Conn. Bar Assn. (pres. 1964-65), ABA (ho. dels. 1965-66), Fairfield Bar Assn. Jewish. Clubs: Algonquin of Bridgeport (pres. 1979-80). General corporate. Home: 25 Cartright St Apt 2G Bridgeport CT 06604 Office: Trager & Trager PC 1305 Post Rd Fairfield CT 06430

TRAGER, PHILIP, lawyer, photographer; b. Bridgeport, Conn., Feb. 27, 1935; s. Bernard Harold and Mina (Rubenstein) T.; m. Ina Louise Shulkin, Sept. 2, 1957; children: Michael, Julie. B.A., Wesleyan U., Middletown, Conn., 1956; J.D., Columbia U., 1960. Bar: Conn. 1960, N.Y. 1981, U.S. Supreme Ct. 1963. Ptnr. Trager & Trager, P.C., Fairfield, Conn., 1960—. Exhibited one man shows, Wesleyan U. Davison Art Ctr., 1970, 74, 81, 87, Balt. Mus. Art, 1977, Boston Ctr. for the Arts, 1979, Mus. of City of N.Y., 1980, The Witkin Gallery, 1973, 80, 86, Centre Internat. de Fotografia, Barcelona, Spain, 1981, Ufficio Dell-Arte, Paris, 1981; group shows include: Boston Ctr. Arts, 1982, Yale U. Art Gallery, 1979, Santa Barbara Mus. Art, Calif., 1979, N.Y. Hist. Soc., 1981, N.Y. State Mus., Albany, 1982, Creative Photography Gallery MIT, 1982, Bibliotheque Nationale, Paris, 1982, N.Y.U., 1985; represented in permanent collections, Balt. Mus. Art, Corcoran Gallery Art, Met. Mus. Art, Mus. Modern Art, New Orleans Mus. Art, Yale U. Gallery Art; author: Echoes of Silence, 1972, Photographs of Architecture (selected as Book of the Yr. Am. Inst. Graphic Arts), Philip Trager: New York, 1980, Wesleyan Photographs, 1982, The Villas of Palladio, 1986. Recipient Lay Person award Conn. Soc. Architects, 1980; recipient Disting. Alumnus award Wesleyan U., 1981. Mem. ABA, Conn. Bar Assn. Real property, Contracts commercial, Art. Home: 20 Rolling Ridge Rd Fairfield CT 06430 Office: Trager and Trager PC 1305 Post Rd Fairfield CT 06430

TRAINOR, PATRICIA HELEN, lawyer; b. N.Y.C., June 2, 1938; d. Charles Christopher and Helen Patricia (O'Donnell) T. AB, Coll. of New Rochelle, 1959; JD cum laude, NYU, 1975, LLM in Corp. Law, 1976. Bar: N.Y. 1976. Computer cons. Atlantic Richfield Co., N.Y.C., 1966-72; staff atty. SEC, Washington, 1976-77; assoc. counsel The Depository Trust Co., N.Y.C., 1977—. Mem. com. N.Y. County Dem. Party, 1985—. Fellow NYU, 1975. Mem. ABA (computer law div., sci. and tech. sect.), Assn. of Bar of City of N.Y. (internat. arms control and security affairs). Computer, Contracts commercial, General corporate. Home: 237 W 11th St New York NY 10014 Office: The Depository Trust Co 7 Hanover Sq New York NY 10004

TRAITZ, JAMES JOSEPH, JR., lawyer; b. Phila., May 2, 1950; s. James Joseph Sr. and Gloria Jeanette (Pezzillo) T.; m. Donna Joan Danto, Apr. 9, 1978 (div. Dec. 1979); m. J. Dana Stockton, Oct. 31, 1980; 1 child, James Joseph III. BA, Biscayne Coll., 1972; JD, U. Miami, 1975. Bar: Fla. 1975, U.S. Dist. Ct. (so. dist.) Fla., U.S. Ct. Appeals (5th cir.). Assoc. Adams, George, Wood, Lee & Schulte, Miami, Fla., 1975-76, Pyszka, Kessler & Adams, Miami, 1976-77, Nachwalter, Christie & Falk, Miami, 1977-79; ptnr. Vernis, Bowling, Montalto, Blank & Traitz, Miami, 1980-84, Ser, De Cardenas, Traitz & Freixas, Miami, 1984-86, Freshman, Freshman & Traitz, Miami, 1986—. Mem. ABA, Assn. Trial Lawyers Am., Acad. Fla. Trial Lawyers, MENSA. Democrat. State civil litigation, Insurance, Personal injury. Home: 13030 SW 104th Ct Miami FL 33176 Office: Freshman Freshman & Traitz 5975 Sunset Dr #701 Miami FL 33143

TRAMONTE, JAMES ALBERT, lawyer; b. New Orleans, Mar. 6, 1951; s. August Joseph and Genevieve (Tardiff) T.; m. Stephanie Thomas, Aug. 12, 1972; children—James Albert Jr., Karen Elizabeth, David August, Patrick Thomas. Student U. Miss., 1968-70; B.S. in Acctg., La. State U.-New Orleans, 1973; J.D., Tulane U., 1976; LL.M. in Taxation, NYU, 1977. Bar: La. 1976, U.S. Tax Ct. 1977, U.S. Ct. Claims 1978, U.S. Ct. Appeals (5th cir.) 1981, U.S. Ct. Appeals (11th cir.) 1981; cert. tax atty, La.; C.P.A., La. Assoc., then ptnr. firm Baldwin & Haspel, New Orleans, 1976-82; ptnr. firm Gauthier, Murphy, Sherman, McCabe & Chehardy, Kenner, La., 1982-83, Simon, Peragine, Smith & Redfearn, New Orleans, 1983—. Author: Estate Planning for Divorced and Remarried Persons, 1986. Mem. River Ridge Community Assn., La. Mem. New Orleans Estate Planning Council, ABA (sect. on taxation), La. State Bar Assn. (sect. on taxation, chmn. formulary com. 1981-82, chmn. liaison com. with dist. dir. IRS 1982-83), Am. Inst. C.P.A.s, La. State Soc. C.P.A.s. Roman Catholic. Club: Petroleum of New Orleans. Corporate taxation, Personal income taxation, Probate. Home: 9440 Calvary Ct River Ridge LA 70123 Office: Simon Peragine Smith & Redfearn 1100 Poydras St 30th Floor New Orleans LA 70163

TRANT, DOUGLAS ALLEN, lawyer; b. Pensacola, Fla., Nov. 14, 1951; s. David Amon and Annie Jacquetta (Sullivan) T.; m. Patty L. Cooper, Dec. 14, 1977. BA, Birmingham-So. Coll., 1973; MA, U. Toledo, 1974; JD, U. Tenn., 1977. Bar: Tenn. 1979, Ala. 1978, U.S. Dist. Ct. (so. dist.) Ala. 1978, U.S. Dist. Ct. (ea. dist.) Tenn. 1980, U.S. Supreme Ct. 1982, U.S. Ct. Appeals (6th cir.) 1984, U.S. Dist. Ct. (mid. dist.) Tenn. 1987. Staff atty. Legal Services, Selma, Ala., 1977-78; staff atty., instr.legal clinic U. Tenn., Knoxville, 1978-80; ptnr. Trant & Stephens, Knoxville, 1980—; cons. legal clinic U. Tenn., 1980-81. Author: Trial Manual for the Defense of Habitual Criminal Cases in Tennessee. Bd. dirs. Project First Offender, Knoxville, 1985—. Recipient Cert. Appreciation Tenn. Gov. Lamar Alexander, Nashville, 1982. Mem. Knoxville Bar Assn., Nat. Assn. Criminal Def. Lawyers (trial advisor death penalty com. 1986—), Tenn. Assn. Criminal Def. Lawyers (adv. bd. Death Penalty Def. Manual 1984—, bd. dirs. 1986—). Democrat. Avocations: shepherding, gardening. Criminal. Office: Trant & Stephens 707 Market St Knoxville TN 37902

TRATOS, MARK GEORGE, lawyer, educator; b. Price, Utah, Apr. 10, 1952; s. Mark and Marjory Luciell (Roberts) T.; m. Sandra Ruth Long, Aug. 1, 1981; 1 child, Markus Steven. BA, U. Nev., 1974; JD, Lewis & Clark Coll., Portland, Oreg., 1979. Bar: Nev. 1979, Calif. 1980, U.S. Dist. Ct. Nev. 1980, U.S. Dist. Ct. (so. dist.) Calif. 1980. Instr. polit. sci. U. Nev., Las Vegas, 1974-76; instr. legal research and writing Lewis and Clark Law Sch., Portland, Oreg., 1978-79; law clk. to trial judge 8th Jud. Dist. Ct., Las Vegas, Nev., 1979; assoc. Mills, Galliher, Lukens, Gibson & Schwartzer, Las Vegas, 1979-81; ptnr. Galliher & Tratos, Las Vegas, 1981-83, Seiler, Quirk & Tratos, Las Vegas, 1983—; instr. entertainment law U. Nev., 1982—, art law, 1985—; spl. counsel Sta. KNPR, Las Vegas, 1985—, Eastern Onion Singing Telegram Service, Las Vegas, 1985—. Author weekly legal news publ. In Re, 1977-78; also articles on art and the law. Pres., gen. counsel Allied Arts Council, Las Vegas, 1981—; bd. dirs. Suicide Prevention Ctr., Las Vegas, 1985—; gen. counsel, bd. dirs. Discovery the Children's Mus., Las Vegas, 1983—; pres. Las Vegas Zoo Soc., 1985—. Recipient cert. of merit Environ. Law Rev., Lewis and Clark Law Sch., Portland, 1977-78. Mem. ABA, Assn. Trial Lawyers Am., Clark County Assn., Bay Area Lawyers of the Arts, Nev. Intellectual Property Assn. (v.p. 1984—), U.S. Trademark Assn. (co-author Nev. chpt. State Trademark Law Handbook) Phi Alpha Delta, Pi Sigma Alpha. Democrat. Baptist. Trademark and copyright, Entertainment, Art Law. Office: 550 E Charleston Suite D Las Vegas NV 89104

TRAUBE, VICTORIA GILBERT, lawyer; b. Los Angeles, Sept. 3, 1946; d. Shepard and Mildred (Gilbert) T. BA, Radcliffe Coll., 1968; MA, Harvard U., 1970; JD, U. Pa., 1974. Bar: N.Y. 1975, U.S. Dist. Ct. (so. dist.) N.Y. 1975, U.S. Ct. Appeals (2d cir.) 1975. Assoc. Paul, Weiss, Rifkind, Wheaton & Garrison, N.Y.C., 1974-81; assoc. counsel Home Box Office Inc., N.Y.C., 1981-82, dir. bus. affairs, 1982-85; counsel Stults & Marshall, N.Y.C., 1985—; adj. prof. Cardozo Law Sch., N.Y.C., 1986. V.p. Dance Theater Workshop, N.Y.C., 1985—. Mem. ABA, Assn. of Bar of City of N.Y., Women in Communications. Entertainment, General corporate. Office: Stults & Marshall 1370 Ave of Americas New York NY 10019

TRAUTMAN, DONALD THEODORE, legal educator; b. Cleve., June 6, 1924; s. William Daniel and Florence Elizabeth (Zimmermann) T.; m. Susanah Conklin Bailie, Aug. 28, 1954; children: William, Ann, Benjamin. A.B., Harvard U., 1951, LL.B., 1951. Bar: D.C. 1953. Law clk. to Justice Frankfurter, Supreme Ct. U.S., 1952-53; asst. prof. law Harvard U., Cambridge, Mass., 1953-56; prof. Harvard U., 1956-80, Charles Stebbins Fairchild prof. law, 1980-81, Henry L. Shattuck prof. law, 1981—, co-chmn. div. grad. studies, 1969-75, pres. Ctr. for Computer-Assisted Legal Instrn., 1982-86, editorial chmn., 1986—; mem. adv. com. on pvt. internat. law U.S. Dept. State. Author: (with David R. Herwitz) Amory and Hardee, Materials on Accounting, 3d edit, 1959, (with Arthur T. von Mehren) von Mehren and Trautman, Law of Multistate Problems, 1965. Trustee, 2d v.p. Crittenton-Hastings House. Served with AUS, 1943-46. Guggenheim fellow, 1969. Mem. Am. Law Inst., Am. Soc. Internat. Law, Internat. Law Assn. (Am. br.), Phi Beta Kappa. Private international, Admiralty, Computer. Home: 20 Craigie St Cambridge MA 02138

TRAVER, ALFRED ELLIS, JR., law educator; b. N.Y.C., Dec. 17, 1939; s. Alfred E. and Stella (Clifton) T.; m. Carol Vivian Barnes, May 23, 1966; children: Margaret, Alfred III. BS, MIT, 1961, MS, 1962; PhD, U. Tex., 1968, JD, 1980. Bar: Tex. 1980. Engr. aero systems Gen. Dynamics, Ft. Worth, 1963-64; engr., scientist Tracor, Austin, 1965-70; prof. Tenn. Tech. U., Cookeville, 1970-78, U. Tex., Austin, 1978—; cons. in field. Mem. Tex. Bar Assn., Travis County Bar Assn., Am. Soc. Mech. Engrs., Tex. Soc. Profl. Engrs. Lodge: Rotary. Patent, Legal education, Computer. Home: 3209 Pickwick Austin TX 78746 Office: U Tex ETC 4154 Austin TX 78712

TRAVIS, JAY A., III, lawyer; b. McComb, Miss., June 8, 1940; s. John A. and Katharine (Brennan) T., Jr.; m. Judith Thompson, Sept. 8, 1965; children: Kathy, John E., William. BBA, U. Miss., 1962, JD, 1965. Bar: Miss. 1965, U.S. Dist. Ct. (so. dist.) Miss. 1967, U.S. Ct. Appeals (5th cir.) 1970. Assoc. Thompson, Alexander & Crews, Jackson, Miss., 1967-69; ptnr. Butler, Snow, O'Mara, Stevens & Cannada, Jackson, 1969—; chmn. Miss. Law Inst., 1974; pres. Estate Planning Council Miss., 1975-76. Mem. vestry, cathedral warden St. Andrew's Episc. Ch., 1983-87. Served to capt. JAGC, USAR, 1965-73. Fellow Am. Coll. Probate Counsel, Am. Bar Found.; mem. ABA (fellow young lawyers sect.), Miss. State Bar (pres. young lawyers sect. 1975-76), Miss. Bar Assn., Hinds County Bar Assn. (sec.-treas. 1986-87, pres.-elect 1987—), Phi Delta Phi. Clubs: University, River Hills (Jackson). Estate planning, Estate taxation, General corporate. Office: PO Box 22567 Jackson MS 39205

TRAVIS, JOAN FAYE SCHILLER, lawyer; b. Chgo., Mar. 15, 1939; d. Jack and Betty (From) Schiller; Ph.B. in Psychology, Northwestern U., 1969; J.D., John Marshall Law Sch., Chgo., 1981; children—Jeffrey Bernard, Leonard Edwin, Elizabeth Sue. Elem. sch. tchr., Chgo., 1970-72; admitted to Ill. bar, 1981, U.S. Ct. Appeals, 1981, U.S. Dist. Ct. bar, 1981, U.S. Ct. Mil. Appeals, 1982, Wis. bar, 1986, U.S. Supreme Ct. 1986; sole gen. practice, Park Ridge, Ill.; freelance writer, 1971-77; speaker, lectr. in field. Chmn. Consumer Affairs Commn., Skokie, Ill.; Niles Twp. collector. Mem. ABA, Ill. Bar Assn., Chgo. Bar Assn., Def. of Prisoners Com., N.W. Suburban Bar Assn. (parliamentarian), North Suburban Bar Assn. (1st v.p.), Women's Bar Assn., Assn. Trial Lawyers Am., Ill. Trial Lawyers Assn., Nat. Acad. TV Arts and Scis., Delta Theta Phi. Jewish. Author numerous articles in field.

Federal civil litigation, State civil litigation, Consumer commercial. Office: 1550 N Northwest Hwy Park Ridge IL 60068

TRAVIS, ROBERT FREDERICK, lawyer; b. Grand Rapids, Mich., Feb. 2, 1924. AB, Columbia U., 1948, MA, 1949; JD, U. Mich., 1972. Bar: Mich. 1973. Ptnr. Bauckham, Reed, Lang, Schaeffer & Travis, P.C., Kalamazoo, Mich., 1973-85; sole practice Kalamazoo, 1985-87. Contbr. articles to profl. jours. Mem. ABA, Kalamazoo County Bar Assn., Mich. Bar Assn., Mich. Trial Lawyers Assn., Assn. Trial Lawyers Am. Consumer commercial, Family and matrimonial, Local government. Office: 132 W South St Kalamazoo MI 49007

TRAVIS, SUSAN TOPPER, lawyer; b. Peekskill, N.Y., Sept. 10, 1951; d. Samuel H. and Ruth (Marks) Topper; m. Donald Travis; 1 child, Sarah Rachel. BS cum laude, Pa. State U., 1972; JD, Syracuse U., 1975. Bar: N.Y. 1976, U.S. Dist. Ct. (we., ea., so. and no. dists.) N.Y. 1978, U.S. Ct. Appeals (2d cir.) 1979, U.S. Supreme Ct. 1980, Pa. 1986. Staff atty. Rensselaer County, Troy, N.Y., 1976; assoc. counsel N.Y. State United Tchrs., Albany, 1976-79; counsel Xerox Corp., Rochester, N.Y., 1979-83; counsel N.E. region Xerox Corp., Greenwich and Stamford, Conn., 1984-87; counsel, spl. comml. and labor litigation Xerox Corp., Stamford, 1987—. Contracts commercial, General corporate, Labor. Office: Xerox Corp 1351 Washington Blvd Suite 7000 Stamford CT 06902

TRAXLER, WILLIAM BYRD, lawyer; b. Greenville, S.C., July 10, 1912; s. David Byrd and Mary Willey (Gatling) T. Student The Citadel, 1929-30, U. Tex., 1930-32; J.D., George Washington U., 1940. Bar: D.C. 1940, S.C. 1940, U.S. Ct. Appeals (4th cir.) 1960. Ptnr. Hinson, Traxler and Hamer, Greenville, 1950-58, Rainey, Fant, Traxler and Horton, 1958-60; sole practice, Greenville, 1960—. Bd. dirs. Phyllis Wheatly Assn., 1954, Vis. Nurse Assn., Greenville, 1957-59, United Way, Greenville, 1976; vice-chmn. bd. health City of Greenville, 1960-70; life mem. The Citadel Endowment Fund. Served to capt. U.S. Army, 1942-46. Recipient Alumni Achievement award George Washington U., 1946. Mem. S.C. Bar Assn., Greenville County Bar Assn. (pres. 1976), Greenville C. of C. (chmn. of yr. 1967, chmn. taxation com.), George Washington Law Assn. (life), Law Sci. Acad., George Washington U. Law Assn. (life), Phi Alpha Delta, Beta Theta Pi. Club: Torch (pres. 1956). Author: Military Government in Germany, 1960; Political Third Parties, 1968; History of the Fourteenth Amendment, 1974; The Jury Numbers Game, 1976; Medieval Harmony, 1982. Club: Greenville Country (bd. govs. 1982-85). General corporate, Estate planning, Estate taxation. Home: 100 Trails End Greenville SC 29607 Office: PO Box 10031 Greenville SC 29603 Office: 606 E North St Greenville SC 29603

TRAYNOR, J. MICHAEL, lawyer; b. Oakland, Calif., Oct. 25, 1934; s. Roger J. and Madeleine (Lackmann) T.; m. Shirley Williams, Feb. 11, 1956; children: Kathleen, Elizabeth, Thomas. B.A., U. Calif., Berkeley, 1955; J.D., Harvard U., 1960. Bar: Calif. 1961, U.S. Supreme Ct. 1966. Dep. atty. gen. State of Calif., San Francisco, 1961-63; spl. counsel Calif. Senate Com. on Local Govt., Sacramento, 1963; assoc. firm Cooley, Godward, Castro, Huddleson & Tatum, San Francisco, 1963-69, partner, 1969—; advisor 2d Restatement of Restitution, 1981-85, 3d Restatement of Unfair Competition, 1986—, 1986 revisions 2d Restatement of Conflict of Laws; mem. Joint Commn. on Fair Jud. Election Practices, 1976-79; lectr. Boalt Hall Sch. Law U. Calif.-Berkeley, 1982—; cons. Rand Corp., 1986—. Contbr. articles to legal jours. Trustee Head-Royce Sch., Oakland, 1974-83, chmn., 1980-82. Served to 1st lt. USMC, 1955-57. Fellow Am. Bar Found.; mem. Am. Law Inst. (pres. 1973, council 1985—), Bar Assn. San Francisco (pres. 1973), Sierra Club (treas. legal def. fund 1979—). Federal civil litigation, State civil litigation, Contracts commercial. Home: 3131 Eton Ave Berkeley CA 94705 Office: Cooley Godward Castro Huddleson Tatum One Maritime Plaza Alcoa Bldg Suite 2000 San Francisco CA 94111

TRAYNOR, WILLIAM PATRICK, lawyer; b. Laramie, Wyo., Jan. 19, 1947; s. William Clarence and Ruth (Shearer) T.; m. Sally Arnett, Apr. 8, 1971; children: Brian Patrick, Matthew Preston, William Frederick, Emily Ruth, Anne Marie. BA in Polit. Sci., Ariz. State U., 1969, JD, 1972. Bar: Ariz. 1972, U.S. Ct. Mil. Appeals 1972, U.S. Dist. Ct. Ariz. 1977. Assoc. Waterfall, Economidis, Caldwell & Hanshaw, P.C., Tucson, 1976-81; ptnr., bd. dirs. Waterfall, Economidis, Hanshaw & Villamana, P.C., Tucson, 1981—; judge pro tem Pima County Superior Ct., Tucson, 1985—. Bishop Ch. of Jesus Christ of Latter-Day Saints, Tucson, 1985—. Served to capt. JAGC, USAF, 1972-76. Fellow Am. Acad. Matrimonial Lawyers; mem. ABA (family law sect.), Ariz. Bar Assn. (family law sect.), Pima County Bar Assn. (family law sect.). Democrat. Club: Plaza (Tucson). Avocations: scouting, skiing, tennis, reading. Family and matrimonial, Juvenile. Home: 13330 E Camino la Cebadilla Tucson AZ 85749 Office: Waterfall Economidis Hanshaw & Villamana PC 5210 E Williams Circle Tucson AZ 85711

TREACY, VINCENT EDWARD, lawyer; b. Mass., Jan. 30, 1942; m. Edith Barnett, Feb. 9, 1980. AB, Boston Coll., 1964; JD, George Washington U., 1971. Bar: Va. 1972, D.C. 1973. Atty. Fed. Labor Relations Council, Washington, 1971-73; legis. atty. Am. law div. Congressional Research Service, Library of Congress, Washington, 1973—. Mem. ABA, Fed. Bar Assn., George Washington Law Alumni Assn. (pres. Capitol Hill chpt. 1986-87), Order of the Coif. Labor, Pension, profit-sharing, and employee benefits. Office: Library of Congress Am Law Div Congressional Research First & Independence SE Washington DC 20540

TREADAWAY, RANDELL EDWARD, lawyer; b. New Orleans, May 28, 1955; s. Lionel Walter and Dorothy Elizabeth (Huhner) T.; m. Stephanie Ann Cochran, June 24, 1978. BA in Psychology, Tulane U., 1977; JD, Loyola U., New Orleans, 1982. Bar: La. 1982, U.S. Dist. Ct. (ea. dist.) La. 1982, U.S. Ct. Appeals (5th cir.) 1982, U.S. Dist. Ct. (mid. dist.) La. 1983, U.S. Ct. Appeals (11th cir.) 1984, U.S. Dist. Ct. (we. dist.) La. 1985. Engr. Dresser Magcobar, Houston, 1978-79; engr. CNG Producing Co., New Orleans, 1979-80, petroleum cons.; law clk. to presiding justice U.S. Dist. Ct. (ea. dist.) La., New Orleans, 1981-82; assoc. Lemle, Kelleher et al., New Orleans, 1982-85, O'Neil, Eichin & Miller, New Orleans, 1985—. Mem. ABA, La. Bar Assn., New Orleans Bar Assn., Bar Assn. of the 5th Fed. Cir., Maritime Law Assn. U.S., La. Assn. Def. Counsel. Democrat. Avocations: fishing, hunting, boating. Admiralty, Insurance, Personal injury. Home: 3005 White St Metairie LA 70001 Office: O'Neil Eichin & Miller One Poydras Plaza New Orleans LA 70113

TREAKLE, JAMES EDWARD, JR., lawyer; b. Norfolk, Va., July 25, 1946; s. James Edward Sr. and Ida Louise (Reid) T.; m. Rebecca Louise Harden, Sept. 6, 1969; children: Graham Reid, Miles Sutton, Ross Edward. BA, U. Va., 1968, JD, 1974. Bar: Va. 1974, U.S. Dist. Ct. (we. dist.) Va. 1974. Assoc. Gilmer & Dezio, Charlottesville, Va., 1974-75; sole practice Charlottesville, 1975-79; ptnr. Haugh & Treakle, P.C., Charlottesville, 1979—; lectr. Criminal Justice Acad., Shenandoah, Va., 1975-78; asst. commonwealth atty., County of Albemarle, Va., 1975-78. Mem. Charlottesville Rep. Com., 1980—, ward study commn. for City of Charlottesville, 1982-83; chmn. Charlottesville Electoral Bd., 1984—. Served to 1st lt. U.S. Army, 1968-71, Vietnam. Mem. ABA, Va. Bar Assn., Charlottesville-Albemarle Bar Assn. Presbyterian. Lodge: Elks. Avocations: skiing, hunting, gardening, flying. General practice, Criminal, State civil litigation. Home: 611 Park St Charlottesville VA 22901 Office: Haugh & Treakle PC 435 Park St Charlottesville VA 22901

TREANOR, JOHN MCCORMACK, lawyer; b. Bronx, N.Y., Apr. 5, 1957; s. John Mortimer and Ann May (Fox) T. AB in History, Wofford Coll., 1979; JD, U. S.C., 1982. Bar: S.C. 1982, U.S. Dist. Ct. S.C. 1982, U.S. Ct. Mil. Appeals 1983, U.S. Ct. Appeals (4th cir.) 1982. Commd. 2d lt. U.S. Army, 1979, advanced through grades to capt., 1983; jr. assoc. Dowling, Sanders, Dukes, Novit & Svalina, P.A., Beaufort, S.C., 1982-83; trial counsel, pros. atty. 1st armored div. U.S. Army, Nuremberg, Fed. Republic Germany, 1983-84; counsel trial def. service U.S. Army, Erlangen, Fed. Republic Germany, 1984—. Mem. ABA, S.C. Bar Assn., Assn. Trial Lawyers Am., Nat. Assn. Criminal Def. Lawyers. Republican. Roman Catholic. Avocation: downhill skiing. Criminal, Military. Home: Dortmunder Strasse # 25, Nuremberg 8500, Fed Republic Germany Office: Erlangen TDS HHC 2d BDE (Judge Adv Gen) APO NY 09066

TREAT, WILLIAM WARDWELL, banker, former judge; b. Boston, May 23, 1918. AB, U. Maine, 1940; MBA, Harvard U., 1947. Bar: Maine 1945, N.H. 1949, U.S. Supreme Ct. 1955. Judge N.H. Probate Ct., Exeter, 1958-83; pres., chmn. bd. Bank Meridian N.A. (formerly Hampton Nat. Bank), 1958-84, chmn., 1984—; chmn. Towle Mfg. Co.; bd. dirs. Exeter & Hampton Electric Co., Unitil Co., Colonial Group, Inc., Amoskeag Bank Shares, Inc.; faculty Nat. Coll. for State Judiciary, Reno, 1975—; chmn. N.H. Jud. Council, 1976-83; adv. bd. Nat. Ctr. for State Cts., 1973-80; pres. Nat. Coll. Probate Judges, 1968-77, pres. emeritus, 1977—; mem. Nat. Fiduciary Acctg. Standards Project, 1975—, Am. Assembly on Death, Taxes and Family Property, 1976—. Author: Treat on Probate, 3 vols, 1968, Local Justice in the Granite State, 1961; contbr. articles to profl. jours.; editor: Probate Court Manual, 1976, Focus on the Bank Director: The Job, 1977. Mem. Rep. Nat. Com., 1954-58, 60-64; presdl. elector, sec. U.S. Electoral Coll., 1956, 60; del.-at-large Rep. Nat. Conv., 1960, program chmn., 1964; bd. dirs., v.p. Hundred Club of N.H.; trustee Franklin Pierce Coll., 1985—. Mem. Am. Law Inst., ABA, N.H. Bar Assn., Am. Bankers Assn. (exec. com. community bankers div. 1975-78, chmn. div. communications com. 1976, chmn. task force bank dirs. program 1976-77), N.H. Bankers Assn. (legis. com. 1975-77, fed. legis. com. 1977—), Am. Judicature Soc. (bd. dirs. 1971-77), New Eng. Law Inst. (adv. bd. 1969-76). Clubs: Harvard, Tavern, St. Botolph, Somerset (Boston); Royal Poinciana, Port Royal (Naples, Fla.); Bald Peak Colony (Melvin Village, N.H.). Probate. Home: PO Box 498 Hampton NH 03842 Office: 100 Winnacunnet Rd Hampton NH 03842

TREBISACCI, RAYMOND THOMAS, lawyer; b. Westerly, R.I., Feb. 4, 1957; s. Salvatore J. and Virginia P. (Christina) T. BS in Fgn. Studies, Georgetown U., 1979; JD, Seton Hall U., 1982. Bar: R.I. 1982, Conn. 1983. Assoc. Longolucco and Lenihan, Westerly, 1982-84, O'Brien, Shafner, Bartinik, Stuart and Kelly, Groton, Conn., 1984—. Assoc. editor: Seton Hall Law Rev., 1980-82; contbr. articles to profl. jours. Mem. Dem. Town Com., Westerly, 1984—. Mem. ABA, Assn. Trial Lawyers Am., Conn. Trial Lawyers Assn., R.I. Trial Lawyers Assn., R.I. Bar Assn. Lodge: Lions (sec. Pawcatuck, Conn. club 1984-86). Personal injury, Criminal, State civil litigation. Office: O'Brien et al PO Drawer 929 Groton CT 06340

TREBON, LAWRENCE ALAN, lawyer; b. Waterloo, Iowa, Mar. 28, 1949; s. Al C. and Ann (Ryan) T.; m. Lynn Kutsch, June 12, 1971; children: Scott, Luke. BA, Loras Coll., 1971; JD, Marquette U., 1974. Ptnr. Stepke & Trebon, Milw., 1974-76, Stepke, Kossow, Trebon & Stadtmueller, Milw., 1976-80, Stepke, Trebon & Schoenfeld, Milw., 1978-80, Trebon & Schoenfeld, Milw., 1980-85, Trebon & Polsky, Milw., 1985—. Coach basketball and t-ball, Milw., 1981—; active fin. com. St. Monica Parish, Whitefish Bay, Wis., 1984—; home and sch. com. St. Monica Sch., Whitefish Bay, 1986—. Republican. Roman Catholic. Club: Tripoli Country (Milw.). Avocations: golf, tennis. General corporate, Estate planning, Corporate taxation. Office: Trebon & Polsky 733 N Van Buren St Milwaukee WI 53202

TREEBY, WILLIAM DAVID, lawyer; b. Seattle, Jan. 3, 1942; s. Dwight Lowell and Mary Arlene (Peck) T.; m. Nancy Kaye Vollmert, Dec. 21, 1964; children—Jonathan Lowell, Patrick Lawrence. B.A. in Polit. Sci., U. Tex.-El Paso, 1963, J.D., 1966. Bar: La. 1966. Assoc. Stone Pigman, Walther, Wittmann & Hutchinson, New Orleans, 1966-69, ptnr., 1969—. Bd. dirs. Jimmy Swaggart Ministries, Lakeview Christian Ctr., La. Tenn Challenge, Inc., 1974-81. Mem. ABA, La. Bar Assn., Fed. Bar Assn., New Orleans Bar Assn., Am. Trial Lawyers Assn., La. Trial Lawyers Assn. (adv. council), Christian Legal Soc., Order of Coif. Mem. Assemblies of God. Contbr. case notes to Tulane Law Rev., 1964-66, articles to profl. jours. Federal civil litigation, State civil litigation, Admiralty. Office: 546 Carondelet St New Orleans LA 70130

TREECE, JAMES LYLE, lawyer; b. Colorado Springs, Colo., Feb. 6, 1925; s. Lee Oren and Ruth Ida (Smith) T.; m. Ruth Julie Treece, Aug. 7, 1949 (div. 1984); children—James (dec.), Karen, Teryl Wait, Jamilyn Snyser, Carol Crowder. Student Colo. State U., 1943, Colo. U., 1943, U.S. Naval Acad., 1944-46; B.S., Mesa Coll., 1946; J.D., U. Colo., 1950; postgrad. U. N.C., 1976-77. Bar: Colo. 1952, U.S. Dist. Ct. Colo. 1952, U.S. Ct. Appeals (10th cir.) 1952, U.S. Supreme Ct. 1967. Assoc., Yegge, Hall, Treece & Evans and predecessors, 1951-59, ptnr., 1959-69; U.S. atty., Colo., 1969-77; pres. Treece, Bahr & Arckey, P.C. and predecessor firms, Littleton, Colo., 1977—; mcpl. judge, 1967-68; mem. faculty Nat. Trial Advocacy Inst., 1973-76, Law-Sci. Acad., 1964; lectr. Chmn. Colo. Dept. Pub. Welfare, 1963-68; chmn. Colo. Dept. Social Services, 1968-69; mem. Littleton Bd. Edn., 1977-81. Served with USNR, 1944-46. Recipient awards Colo. Assn. Sch. Bds., 1981, IRS, 1977, FBI, 1977, DEA, 1977, Fed. Exec. Bd., 1977. Mem. Fed. Bar Assn. (pres. Colo. 1975), Colo. Bar Assn. (bd. govs.), Denver Bar Assn. (v.p., trustee). Republican. Lutheran. Federal civil litigation, State civil litigation, Insurance. Home: 7210 E Euclid Dr Englewood CO 80111 Office: 2596 W Alamo Ave Littleton CO 80120

TREES, PHILIP HUGH, lawyer; b. Greenfield, Ind., Mar. 23, 1953; s. Philip Lee and Lauretta May (Cummins) T.; m. Debra J. Tapanes, June 21, 1975 (div. May 1981); m. Diane Heller D'Amico, May 28, 1982; 1 child, Philip Thomas. BA, Fla. State U., 1974, JD with honors, 1977. Bar: Fla. 1978, U.S. Dist. Ct. (mid. dist.) Fla. 1978, U.S. Tax Ct. 1978, U.S. Ct. Appeals (5th and 11th cirs.) 1978, U.S. Supreme Ct. 1978. Assoc. Gray, Harris & Robinson, P.A., Orlando, Fla., 1977-81; ptnr. Gray, Harris & Robinson, P.A., Orlando, 1981—. Mem. exec. com. Task Force to Revitalize South Orange Blossom Trail, Orlando; mem. Orlando Crime Commn.; grad. Leadership Orlando program, 1985. Mem. ABA, Fla. Bar Assn., Orange County Bar Assn. (chmn. news media and pub. relations com. 1982-84, chmn. law and edn. com. 1984-87, Outstanding Chmn. award 1982-86, treas.), Am. Judicature Soc., Fla. C. of C. (edn. com.). Clubs: University (Orlando); Sabal Point Country (Longwood, Fla.). State civil litigation, Federal civil litigation, Consumer commercial. Home: 534 Sabal Trail Circle Longwood FL 32779

TREIMAN, DAVID MICHAEL, lawyer, legal editor; b. Glen Cove, N.Y., Oct. 30, 1955; s. Albert Hyman and Henrietta (Krafts) T.; m. Rachel Louise Hallford, Aug. 12, 1979; children: Jessica Grace, Andrew James. BA, SUNY, Stony Brook, 1977; JD, St. John's U., Jamaica, N.Y., 1980. Bar: N.Y. 1981, U.S. Dist. Ct. (ea. and so. dists.) N.Y. 1981. Assoc. Ralph M. Elbaum, Hollis, N.Y., 1979-81; sr. assoc. Charles S. Lazarus, Bronx, N.Y., 1981-82; ptnr. Balsam & Morris, Bronx, 1982-83; sole practice Forest Hills, N.Y., 1983-86; assoc. Koeppel & Koeppel, N.Y.C., 1986—. Author: A Passover Seder for Episcopalians, 1984; sr. editor Lamb's Flight Ltd., 1985—; editor: N.Y.C. Housing Court Reporter, 1983—, N.Y.C. Loft Board Reporter, 1985—. Mem. exec. com. Archdeaconry of Queens, N.Y., 1983—; steering com. Deanery of Southwest Queens, Jamaica, 1983. Mem. ABA, N.Y. State Bar Assn., Assn. Trial Lawyers Am., N.Y. County Lawyers Assn., N.Y.C. Protestant Lawyers Assn. (bd. dirs.), Forest Hills C. of C. Democrat. Episcopalian. Avocations: writing poetry and opera librettos, researching British history. Real property, Landlord-tenant. Home: 99-05 59th Ave Apt 2B Rego Park NY 11368 Office: Koeppel & Koeppel 30 E 42d St New York NY 10017

TREMAYNE, BERTRAM WILLIAM, JR., lawyer; b. St. Louis, Feb. 23, 1914; s. Bertram William and Pearl Inez (Flory) T.; m. Frances Lewis, July 6, 1940 (dec. Jan. 1964); children: Pamela L., Eric F.; m. Clara Tarling, Jan. 2, 1966. A.B., Washington U., St. Louis, 1935, J.D., 1938. Bar: Mo. 1938, U.S. Dist. Ct. (ea. dist.) Mo. 1938, U.S. Ct. Appeals (8th cir.) 1938. With firm Neuhoff & Millar, St. Louis, 1938-41; dist. rationing atty. OPA, 1941-43; partner firm Neuhoff, Millar, Tremayne & Schaefer, St. Louis, 1946-54, Tremayne, Lay, Carr, Bauer & Nouss (and predecessors), St. Louis, 1954—. Mem. St. Louis County Parks and Recreation Adv. Bd., 1956-63, chmn., 1959-63; Mem. met. bd. dirs. St. Louis and St. Louis County YMCA, 1960—, pres., 1970-73; mem. nat. council YMCAs, 1970-77; bd. dirs. Washington U., 1961-65; trustee Deaconess Hosp., St. Louis, 1973-82. Served to capt. AUS, 1943-46. Recipient Distinguished Eagle Scout award Boy Scouts Am., 1973. Fellow Am. Bar Found.; mem. ABA (Ho. of Dels. 1981-84), St. Louis County Bar Assn. (disting. service award 1982), Mo. Bar (bd. govs. 1973-80, pres. 1978-79), Bar Assn. Met. St. Louis, Am. Coll. Probate Counsel, Am. Judicature Soc., Judge Advs. Assn., Phi Delta Phi, Omicron Delta Kappa. Conglist. (pres. 1960-63). Club: Algonquin Golf. General practice, Probate, General corporate. Home: 58 Frederick Ln Glendale MO 63122 Office: Tremayne Lay Carr Bauer & Nouss 120 S Central Ave Clayton MO 63105

TREMAYNE, ERIC FLORY, lawyer; b. Washington, Nov. 29, 1945; s. Bertram William and Frances (Lewis) T.; m. Barbara Ann Williams, Sept. 18, 1982. B.A., Westminster Coll., 1967; J.D., Washington U., St. Louis, 1973. Bar: Mo. 1973, U.S. Dist. Ct. (ea. and we. dists.) Mo., 1973. Assoc. Tremayne, Lay, Carr, Bauer and Nouss, Clayton, Mo., 1973-77, ptnr., 1978—; dir. Vortex Engring. Inc., St. Louis. St. Louis. Campaign aide Citizens for Kit Bond, St. Louis, 1972. Served to sp. 4 U.S. Army, 1968-70. Mem. St. Louis County Bar Assn. (Outstanding Young Lawyer, 1981, pres. 1983-84), Bar Assn. Met. St. Louis. Republican. Anglican. Clubs: St. Louis Beta Theta Pi (v.p. 1978—), Sports Car Club Am. (instr. 1979—). General corporate, State civil litigation, Federal civil litigation. Home: 433 Eatherton Valley Rd Chesterfield MO 63017 Office: Tremayne Lay Carr Bauer & Nouss 120 S Central Suite 540 Clayton MO 63105

TREMBLAY, MICHAEL JEFFREY, lawyer; b. Marlboro, Mass., June 27, 1956; s. Leonard A. Sr. and Phyllis I (Fortin) T.; m. Loretta Collins, Sept. 1, 1979. BS in Criminal Justice, Northeastern U., Boston, 1979; JD, New Eng. Sch. Law, 1982. Bar: Mass 1982, U.S. Dist. Ct. Mass. 1983. Police officer Town of Concord, Mass., 1976-79; assoc. Law Office Armand Fernandes, New Bedford, Mass., 1982-84; sole practice Marlboro, 1984—. Bd. dirs. Office Cultural Affairs, Marlboro, 1985—. Served to 1st lt. USAR, 1973-85. Mem. Mass. Acad. Trial Lawyers, Mass. Bar Assn., Middlesex County Bar Assn., South Middlesex County Bar Assn. Democrat. Roman Catholic. Criminal, Family and matrimonial. Home: 8 Springhill Ave Marlboro MA 01752 Office: 32 Hosmer St Marlboro MA 01752

TRENDA, REGIS J(OHN), lawyer; b. New Prague, Minn., July 15, 1945; s. Joseph J. and Lydia M. (Sonka) T.; m. Donna C. Rowe, July 3, 1971; children: David, Carolyn, Daniel. BA magna cum laude, Loras Coll., 1966; JD, U. Notre Dame, 1969. Bar: Ill. 1969, Iowa 1969, U.S. Dist. Ct. (no. dist.) Ill. 1969, U.S. Ct. Appeals (7th cir.) 1969. Atty. Region 13 NLRB, Chgo., 1969-72; asst. gen. counsel Borg Warner Corp., Chgo., 1972—. Mem. ABA, Ill. State Bar Assn., Chgo. Bar Assn. Contbg. author: The Developing Labor Law Cumulative Supplement, 1971-75, 76, 83. Labor, Federal civil litigation, General corporate. Office: 200 S Michigan Ave Suite 2000 Chicago IL 60604

TRENNER, KATHRYN, lawyer; b. Westfield, N.J., Oct. 19, 1941; s. Nelson R. Sr. and Kathryn (Farrell) T. BS, Pa. State U., 1963; JD, Rutgers U., 1969. Bar: N.J. 1969, U.S. Ct. Appeals (3d cir.) 1980. Sole practice Princeton, N.J., 1972—. Mem. Princeton Bar Assn. (pres. 1980-81). Avocations: farming, writing, animal rights. Real property, Family and matrimonial, General practice. Home: 233 Carter Rd Princeton NJ 08540 Office: 245 Nassau St Princeton NJ 08540

TRENT, J(OHN) THOMAS, JR., lawyer; b. Munster, Ind., Mar. 11, 1954; s. John Thomas and Sally Dean (Ritter) T.; m. Laura Nelson, Aug. 5, 1978; children: Lauren, Valerie. AB magna cum laude, Wabash Coll., 1976; JD, Vanderbilt U., 1979. Bar: Tenn., 1979. Ptnr. Boult, Cummings, Conners & Berry, Nashville, 1979—; bd. dirs. Southeast Venture Cos., Nashville, 1984—. Mem. various coms. West End Meth. Ch., Nashville, 1984—; bd. dirs. Cumberland chpt. Nat. Hemophelia Found., Nashville, 1984-86, past chmn. Mens Merit scholar, 1972, Elliot E. Cheatham scholar, 1979. Mem. ABA, Tenn. Bar Assn., Nashville Bar Assn., Nat. Assn. Bond Lawyers, Phi Beta Kappa, Beta Theta Pi. Avocations: fishing, family. Real property, Landlord-tenant, Municipal bonds. Office: Boult Cummings Conners & Berry 222 3d Ave N Nashville TN 37201

TRESTER, JOSEPH EDWARD, lawyer; b. Linton, Ind., May 5, 1952; s. Faye E. and Helen Ruth (Inman) T.; m. Sandra L. Loveless, Sept. 20, 1973; children: Heather, Heath. BA, Ind. U., 1973, JD, 1979. Bar: Ohio 1979, U.S. Dist. Ct. (no. dist.) Ohio 1979, Ky. 1982, Ind. 1984, U.S. Dist. ct. (so. dist.) Ind. 1984. Archivist, historian USAF, Montgomery, Ala., 1973-76; assoc. Krugliak, Wilkins, Canton, Ohio, 1979-82, 86—; staff atty. Internat. Spike, Lexington, Ky., 1982-83; assoc. Charles W. Edwards, Spencer, Ind., 1983-86; panelist Ind. Continuing Legal Edn. Found. Seminar, 1984-85. De. Rep. State Conv., Indpla., 1985. Mem. Ky. Bar Assn., Ohio Bar Assn. Lutheran. Club: Exchange (Spencer). Avocations: camping, volleyball, coaching little league baseball and basketball. State civil litigation, Personal injury, Workers' compensation. Home: 2606 Northam Circle North Canton OH 44720 Office: Krugliak Wilkins Griffith & Dougherty 526 Citizens Savings Bldg Canton OH 44702

TREVETT, KENNETH PARKHURST, lawyer; b. Boston, Sept. 22, 1947; s. Laurence Davies and Naomi (Smith) T.; m. Barbara Kent, June 10, 1978; stepchildren: Kimberly, Dennison, Tanya. BA, Colgate U., 1969; JD cum laude, Suffolk U., 1979. Bar: Mass. 1980, U.S. Dist. Ct. Mass. 1980, Maine 1983. With office of pub. affairs Sec. of State, Commonwealth of Mass., Boston, 1978; asst. dean for adminstrn. Tufts U. Sch. Vet. Medicine, Boston, 1979-82; asst. to dir., house counsel The Jackson Lab., Bar Harbor, Maine, 1982—. Co-author: An Evaluation of the De-institutionalization of the Massachusetts Department of Youth Services, 1972; contbr. several invited papers on legal and ethical aspects of biotech. and medicine. Mem. Gov.'s Tech. Strategy Task Force, Augusta, Maine, 1983-84; trustee Mt. Desert Island Hosp., Bar Harbor, 1984—. Named one of Outstanding Young Men of Am., 1981. Mem. Maine Bar Assn. Democrat. Unitarian. Club: Kebo Valley (Bar Harbor) (bd. dirs.). Avocations: golf, writing. General corporate, Health. Home: 15 High St Bar Harbor ME 04609 Office: The Jackson Lab 600 Main St Bar Harbor ME 04609

TREVETT, THOMAS NEIL, lawyer; b. Rochester, N.Y., Mar. 14, 1942; s. Frank E. and Andrea (Kuhn) T.; m. Margaret H. Hepburn, July 29, 1967; children—Monica, Millicent, Thomas. B.S., St. John Fisher Coll., 1964; J.D., Albany Law Sch., 1967. Bar: N.Y. 1967, U.S. Dist. Ct. (we. dist.) N.Y. 1968. Assoc., Thomas J. Meagher, Rochester, Rochester, 1967-68; with Gough, Skipworth, Summers, Eves & Trevett and predecessor, Zurrett, Sullivin, Smith, Gough & Skipwork, Rochester, 1968—, ptnr., 1972—. N.Y. State Democratic committeeman; bd. dirs. Genesee region March of Dimes, Rochester Area Multiple Sclerosis Soc. Mem. ABA, N.Y. State Bar Assn. (ho. of dels. 1981, exec. com. ins. sect.), Monroe-Wayne County Bar Assn., Wayne County Bar Assn. (pres. 1979-80), Def. Research Inst., Fedn. Ins. Counsel. Roman Catholic. Insurance, Probate, Real property. Office: 1020 Reynolds Arcade Rochester NY 14608

TRIEBWASSER, JONAH IGNATIUS, lawyer, journalist; b. Bklyn., Feb. 8, 1950; s. Sidney and Tillie (Jacob) T.; m. Ellen Carol Kurtzman, Sept. 2, 1973; children: Thomas Charles, Alison Elizabeth. AA, John Jay Coll. Criminal Justice, 1971, BS, 1972; JD, New York Law Sch., 1979. Bar: N.Y. 1980, U.S. Dist. Ct. (no., so., ea. and we. dists.) N.Y. 1980, U.S. Ct. Internat. Trade 1981, U.S. Ct. Appeals (2d cir.) 1982, U.S. Tax Ct. 1984, U.S. Supreme Ct. 1984. Revenue officer U.S. Treasury Dept., Bklyn., 1972-73; spl. investigator prosecutors office State of N.Y., N.Y.C., 1973-75; atty. State of N.Y., Wingdale, 1979-81; asst. corp. counsel N.Y.C. Dept. Law, Kingston, 1981—; hearing officer N.Y. State Supreme Ct., Poughkeepsie, 1980—. Columnist Law Enforcement News, 1984—; host radio show Point of Law, 1985-86. Mem. ABA (vice chmn. govt. lawyers com.), N.Y. State Bar Assn. (membership chmn., recipient plaque 1986, media awards cert. merit 1986), Dutchess County Bar Assn. (sec. 1984-85, recipient cert. 1985), Ulster County Bar Assn. (sec. 1985-87, bd. dirs. 1987—), Phi Delta Phi. Condemnation, Real property, State civil litigation. Office: City of NY Office Corp Counsel 41 John St PO Box 3453 Kingston NY 12401

TRIEWEILER, TERRY NICHOLAS, lawyer; b. Dubuque, Iowa, Mar. 21, 1948; s. George Nicholas and Anne Marie (Oastern) T.; m. Carol M. Jacobson, Aug. 11, 1972; children: Kathryn Anne, Christina Marie, Anna Theresa. BA, Drake U., 1970, JD, 1972. Bar: Iowa 1973, Wash. 1973, U.S. Dist. Ct. (so. dist.) Iowa 1973, U.S. Dist. Ct. (we. dist.) Wash. 1973, Mont. 1975, U.S. Dist. Ct. Mont. 1977. Staff atty. Polk County Legal Services, Des Moines, 1973; assoc. Hullin, Roberts, Mines, Fite & Riveland, Seattle, 1973-75, Morrison & Hedman, Whitefish, Mont., 1975-77; sole practice, Whitefish, 1977—; lectr. U. Mont. Law Sch., 1981—; mem. com. to amend civil proc. rules Mont. Supreme Ct., Helena, 1984, commn. to draft pattern jury in-

strns., 1985; mem. Gov.'s Adv. Com. on Amendment to Work Compensation Act, 1981—, adv. com. Mont. Work Compensation Ct., 1982—. Mem. ABA, Mont. Bar Assn. (pres. 1986-87), Wash. Bar Assn., Iowa Bar Assn., Assn. Trial Lawyers Am., Mont. Trial Lawyers Assn. (dir., pres.). Democrat. Roman Catholic. Federal civil litigation, State civil litigation, Personal injury. Home: 305 Fairway Dr Whitefish MT 59937 Office: Trieweiler Law Firm 233 Second St Whitefish MT 59937

TRIFFIN, NICHOLAS, law librarian, law educator; b. Boston, May 30, 1942; s. Robert and Lois (Brandt) T.; m. Mary M. Bertolet, June 1, 1965 (div. June 1975); children: Amyk, A. Robert; m. Madeleine J. Wilken, May 30, 1981. BA cum laude, Yale U., 1965, JD, 1968; MLS, Rutgers U., 1978. Bar: N.Y. 1969, Conn. 1973, U.S. Dist. Ct. Conn. 1973, U.S. Ct. Appeals (2nd cir.) 1973, U.S. Tax Ct. 1974. Assoc. Willkie Farr & Gallagher, N.Y.C., 1968-70; dean students Johnson (Vt.) State Coll., 1970-72; assoc. Di Sesa & Evans, New Haven, 1972-76; head pub. services, instr. law U. Conn., W. Hartford, 1977-81; law library dir., assoc. prof. Hamline U., St. Paul, 1982-84; dir. law library, prof. Pace U., White Plains, N.Y., 1984—; adj. prof. Hartford (Conn.) Coll., 1978-80. Columnist Law Library Jour., 1983-84; author: Law Books Published, 1984—. Justice of the Peace, Conn., 1976-78. Mem. Am. Assn. Law Libraries (chmn. reader services spl. interest sect. 1982-83), Law Librarians New England (pres. 1981-82), Minn. Assn. Law Librarians (v.p. 1983-84), New Haven Young Lawyers Assn. (pres. 1976-77), Beta Phi Mu. Mem. Soc. of Friends. Club: Mory's (New Haven). Avocations: kayaking, rare books, opera. Librarianship, Legal education, Legal history. Office: Pace Univ Sch of Law 78 N Broadway White Plains NY 10603

TRIGG, DONALD CLARK, lawyer, insurance company executive; b. Flint, Mich., Aug. 22, 1949; s. Samuel Clark and Rose Mary (Solomen) T.; m. Carol L. Trigg, Oct. 28, 1978. AB in Polit. Sci., Ind. U., 1971, JD, 1974, MBA, 1987. Bar: Ind. 1974, U.S. Dist. Ct. Ind. 1974, U.S. Ct. Appeals (7th cir.) 1974, U.S. Supreme Ct. 1979. Dep. atty. gen. Ind. Attys. Gens. Office, Indpls., 1974-76; assoc. gen. counsel Blue Cross/Blue Shield Ind., Indpls., 1976-86, dir. health care ops. support, 1986—. Vice-precinct committeeman Ind. Reps., 1976. Mem. ABA, Ind. Bar Assn., Indpls. Bar Assn. Health, Antitrust, Federal civil litigation. Office: Blue Cross/Blue Shield Ind 120 W Market St Indianapolis IN 46204

TRILLING, HELEN REGINA, lawyer; b. Boston, May 13, 1950; d. Charles Alexander and A. Lillian Trilling. AB magna cum laude, Radcliffe Coll., 1973; JD, Harvard U., 1976. Bar: Mass. 1977, U.S. Dist. Ct. Mass. 1978, U.S. Supreme Ct. 1980, D.C. 1984, U.S. Ct. Appeals (10th cir.) 1984. Asst. gen. counsel Blue Cross/Blue Shield, Boston, 1976-79; sp. asst. to gen. counsel HHS, Washington, 1979-83; assoc. Hogan & Hartson, Washington, 1983-86, ptnr., 1987—. Mem. ABA (health law forum com.), Nat. Health Lawyers Assn., Women and Health Roundtable, Women's Legal Def. Fund, Wash. Council Lawyers. Administrative and regulatory, Health.

TRIMBLE, DALE LEE, lawyer; b. Houston, Nov. 15, 1954; s. Horace Lee and Eveline (Dunn) T.; m. Diane Arnold, June 25, 1977 (div. Mar. 1983); m. Jana Denman, May 25, 1985. BA, U. of the South, 1977; JD, Baylor U., 1981. Bar: Tex. 1981, U.S. Dist. Ct. (ea. and so. dists.) Tex. 1981. Assoc. Fulbright & Jaworski, Houston, 1981—. Assoc. editor Baylor U. Law Rev., 1979-81. Named one of Outstanding Young Men of Am., 1985. Mem. ABA, Tex. Bar Assn. (resolutions com.), Houston Bar Assn., Tex. Young Lawyers Assn. (bd. dirs. 1986—), Houston Young Lawyers Assn. (bd.dirs., sec. 1984—). Republican. Episcopalian. Avocations: racquet sports, travel, team sports. State civil litigation, Insurance, Personal injury. Home: 9407 Roos Houston TX 77036 Office: Fulbright & Jaworski 1301 McKinney Houston TX 77002

TRIMMIER, CHARLES STEPHEN, JR., lawyer; b. Chgo., June 25, 1943; s. Charles Stephen and Lucille E. (Anderson) T.; m. Rae Wade Trimmier, Aug. 19, 1966; children—Charles Stephen, Hallie Wade. B.A., U. Ala., Tuscaloosa, 1965, J.D., 1968. Bar: Ala. 1968. From assoc. to ptnr. Rives, Peterson, Pettus and Conway, Birmingham, Ala., 1968-77; pres. Trimmier and Assocs., P.C., Birmingham, 1977—. Mem. ABA (bus. and banking law sect., credit union com.), Ala. Bar Assn., Birmingham Bar Assn., Comml. Law League, Ala. Law Inst., Shades Valley Jaycees (sec. 1973). Episcopalian. Editor-in-chief: Ala. Law Rev. 1968. Contracts commercial, General corporate, Private international. Home: 3819 River View Circle Mountain Brook AL 35243 Office: Trimmier and Assocs PA PO Box 1885 Birmingham AL 35205

TRIMMIER, ROSCOE, JR., lawyer; b. Charlotte, N.C., July 22, 1944; s. Roscoe and Susie Elizabeth (Stitt) T.; divorced; 1 child, Leigh Snowden. AB, Harvard U., 1971, JD, 1974. Bar: Mass. 1974, U.S. Dist. Ct. Mass. 1975, U.S. Ct. Appeals (1st cir.) 1975, U.S. Supreme Ct. 1979, U.S. Claims Ct. 1983. Assoc. Ropes & Gray, Boston, 1974-83, ptnr., 1983—; mem. hearing com. Bd. Bar Overseers; bd. dirs., v.p. Family Counseling & Guidance Ctr., Inc., Boston, 1980—; v.p. Social Policy Research Group, 1982—; corp. mem. Mus. of Sci., 1981—. Served to 1st lt. U.S. Army, 1965-68. Fellow Mass. Bar Found.; mem. Mass. Bar Assn. (bd. dels., exec. com.), Mass. Soc. for Prevention of Cruelty to Children, Mass. Black Lawyers Assn. Federal civil litigation, State civil litigation, Administrative and regulatory. Home: 5 Spruce Ct Boston MA 02108 Office: Ropes & Gray 225 Franklin St Boston MA 02110

TRINKLEY, JANE WILROY, lawyer; b. Middletown, Ohio, Apr. 7, 1955; s. Robert David and Marian (Cocke) Wilroy; m. Michael Bolinger Trinkley, June 24, 1978. BA, U. N.C., 1976; JD, U. S.C., 1980. Bar: S.C. 1980, U.S. Dist. Ct. S.C. 1983, U.S. Ct. Appeals (4th cir.) 1983, U.S. Supreme Ct. 1986. Law clk. to presiding justice U.S. Dist. Ct., Florence, S.C., 1980-82; assoc. McNair Law Firm, Columbia, S.C., 1982-87, ptnr., 1987—. Bd. dirs. Birthright of Columbia, S.C., 1986. Mem. ABA (litigation sect., individual rights and responsibilities sect.), Christian Legal Soc. Roman Catholic. Club: Our Lady of the Hills Women's (Columbia) (pres. 1984). Federal civil litigation, Civil rights. Office: McNair Law Firm 1301 Gervais St 18th Floor Columbia SC 29201

TRIO, EDWARD ALAN, lawyer, accountant; b. Newark, N.J., Dec. 29, 1952; s. Edward B. and Dorothy J. (Salvia) T.; m. Patricia Ann Sherwood, June 19, 1982; 1 child, Edward Joseph. B.B.A., U. Notre Dame, 1974; J.D., Hamline U., St. Paul, 1977; LL.M. in Taxation with honors, Chgo.-Kent Coll. Law, 1984. Bar: Ill. 1977, U.S. Dist. Ct. (no. dist.) Ill. 1977, U.S. Tax Ct. 1979, U.S. Supreme Ct. 1984. C.P.A. Staff auditor Donald E. Bark, C.P.A., Arlington Heights, Ill., 1972-77; assoc. Graf & Gulbrandsen, Morton Grove, Ill., 1977-80; ptnr. Schneider, Graf & Trio, Morton Grove, 1980-82; tax specialist Deloitte Haskins & Sells, Chgo., 1982-85; assoc. Gould & Ratner, Chgo., 1985—. Mem. ABA, Ill. State Bar Assn., Am. Inst. C.P.A.s. Roman Catholic. Lodge: KC. Estate planning, Personal income taxation, Pension, profit-sharing, and employee benefits. Home: 909 N Derbyshire Arlington Heights IL 60004 Office: Gould & Ratner 222 N LaSalle Chicago IL 60601

TRIPP, DONALD WILLIAM, lawyer; b. Stronghurst, Ill., May 6, 1940; s. William Bernard and Mary Almarah (Beard) T.; m. Marjorie Frances Wake, Aug. 27, 1966; children: Kathleen Marjorie, Matthew Donald. BA cum laude, Bradley U., 1968; MPA, Tex. Christian U., 1976; JD, Washington U., St. Louis, 1979. Bar: Mo. 1979, Ill. 1980, U.S. Dist. Ct. (ea. dist.) Mo. 1980, U.S. Ct. Appeals (8th cir.) 1980, U.S. Supreme Ct. 1983. With Nat. Archives and Records Service, Washington, St. Louis and Ft. Worth, 1969-76; ptnr. Haller, Leonard & Tripp, P.C., St. Louis, 1982—. Served to airman 1st class USAF, 1958-62. Mem. ABA, Ill. Bar Assn., Mo. Bar Assn., Bar Assn. of Met. St. Louis. General corporate, Pension, profit-sharing, and employee benefits, Probate. Office: Haller Leonard & Tripp PC 7751 Carondelet Clayton MO 63105

TRIPP, NORMAN DENSMORE, lawyer; b. Binghamton, N.Y., Apr. 11, 1938; s. Merritt Frederick and Eleonore Graves (Satterley) T.; m. Jane Grace Mighton, June 15, 1962; children—Jennifer, Norman, Christine, Michael. B.A., U. Miami, 1962; J.D. magna cum laude, Cleve. State U., 1967. Bar: Ohio, Fla. Sr. ptnr. Tripp, Scott, Conklin & Smith, Fort Lauderdale, Fla.; gen. counsel, dir. Alamo Rent A Car Inc., Fort Lauderdale; gen. counsel Cert. Tours (Delta Dream Vacations). Mem. bd. adjustment City of Fort Lauderdale; bd. of trustees State of Fla. Community Coll. System. Mem. Am. Soc. Travel Agts., ABA, Am. Trial Lawyers Assn., Fla. Trial Lawyers Assn., Broward County Bar Assn., Fla. Bar Assn. Republican. Clubs: Ocean Reef (Key Largo); Fort Lauderdale Yacht, Fort Lauderdale Country. Contracts commercial, Real property. Office: Tripp Scott Conklin & Smith PO Box 11402 Fort Lauderdale FL 33339 *

TRITELL, RANDOLPH WAYNE, lawyer; b. Floral Park, N.Y., Apr. 18, 1953; s. Walter and Anita Tritell. Bar: N.Y. 1978, D.C. 1978. Staff atty. FTC, Washington, 1978-82, asst. to dir., 1982-83, exec. asst. to chmn., 1985-86, advisor to commr., 1983-85; assoc. Weil, Gotshal & Manges, N.Y.C., 1986—. Editor: U. Pa. Law Rev., 1976-77. Mem. ABA, N.Y. State Bar, D.C. Bar Assn., Phi Beta Kappa, Amnesty Internat. USA (regional corrdinator Washington 1983-86). Republican. Jewish. Administrative and regulatory, Antitrust. Home: 353 E 78th St 9A New York NY 10021 Office: Weil Gotshal & Manges 767 Fifth Ave New York NY 10153

TRITICO, RUSSELL THOMAS, lawyer; b. Franklin, La., June 1, 1928; s. Igmatius T. and Lena (Caro) T.; m. Thelma Dale Mallett, Oct. 21, 1950; children: Russell T., Kelley Ann. Bar: La. 1951. Sole practice Lake Charles, LA. Pres. St. Louis High Sch. Bd., Lake Charles, 1981; chmn. Task Force to Investigate Police, Lake Cahrles, 1985. Mem. ABA, La. Bar Assn., Southwest La. Bar Assn. (pres. 1985—), Assn. Trial Lawyers Am.; civil and criminal trial adv. Nat. Bd. of Trial Adv. Democrat. Roman Catholic. Club: Southwest La. Fishing (Lake Charles) (pres.). Avocations: fishing, wood working. State civil litigation, Federal civil litigation, Criminal. Office: 130 W Kirby St Lake Charles LA 70601

TROELSTRUP, JOHN FREDERICK, lawyer, consultant; b. Evanston, Ill., July 8, 1939; s. Arch William and Annabelle (Peterson) T.; m. Sandra Susan Lowry, Nov. 26, 1977; children—John Frederick, Levi Tate, Susan Paige, Jayne Holmberg, Anna Troolin, Samuel Archer. B.A., U. Mo., 1962; J.D., W. Va. U. Coll. Law, 1968. Bar: W. Va. 1968, U.S. Dist. Ct. (so. dist.) W. Va. 1968, U.S. Dist. Ct. (no. dist.) W. Va. 1969, U.S. Ct. Appeals (4th cir.) 1970, U.S. Supreme Ct. 1971, U.S. Dist. Ct. (ea. dist.) Wis. 1979, U.S. Dist. Ct. Trial Bar (no. dist.) Ill. 1979, U.S. Ct. Appeals (7th cir.) 1979, U.S. Dist. Ct. (we. dist.) Tenn. 1980, Ill. 1980. Gen. trial practice, Princeton, W. Va., 1968-69; asst. atty. gen. W. Va., Charleston, 1969-70; ptnr. Weaver & Troelstrup, Charleston, 1970-78; regional counsel Commodity Futures Trading Commn., Chgo., 1978-80; v.p. Chgo. Mercantile Exchange, Chgo., 1980-83; ptnr. Troelstrup, et al, Chgo., 1983-85, Gottlieb & Schwartz, Chgo., 1985—; assoc. prof. paralegal studies Marshall U., Huntington, W. Va., 1977—; planning com. Commodities Law Inst. Chgo. Bar Assn., 1978-79, sem. program participant, 1979; lectr. commodity futures regulation Ill. Inst. Tech. Kent Coll. Law, 1980. Active in Mayor's Youth Council, Princeton, 1968, Chgo. Counsel Fgn. Relations, 1980—; pres. Mercer County Community Action Program Princeton, 1968-72. Served to 1st lt. USAF, 1962-65. Benedum Found. grantee, 1965-68; bd. govs. W. Va. U. scholar, 1965-68. Mem. ABA, Assn. Trial Lawyers Am. (state committeeman 1974-75), W. Va. Trial Lawyers Assn. (v.p. 1976-77) Merit award, 1978), Ill. State Bar Assn., Chgo. Bar Assn., W.Va. State Bar, Futures Industry Assn. (exec. com. law and compliance div., 1981-83). Democrat. Episcopalian. Club: Metro (Chgo.). Federal civil litigation, Criminal, Commodity futures/securities. Office: Gottlieb & Schwartz 200 E Randolph Dr Suite 6900 Chicago IL 60601

TROFFKIN, HOWARD JULIAN, lawyer, diversified company executive; b. Port Chester, N.Y., Jan. 30, 1937; s. Irving and Frieda Troffkin; m. Rhea Dorothy, May 12, 1963; children—Stephen, Barbara. B.S. in Chemistry, St. Lawrence U., 1959; postgrad. Columbia U. Sch. Engring., 1959-60; J.D., Georgetown U., 1970. Bar: Va. 1971, D.C. 1972. Research chemist Am. Cyanamid Co., 1961-66, legal trainee, 1966-67, pat. agt., 1967-71; assoc. Pennie, Edmonds, Morton, Taylor & Adams, Washington, 1971-77; patent atty. W.R. Grace & Co., Columbia, Md., 1977-86; sr. patent counsel W.R. Grace & Co., 1987—. Patentee in chemistry field. Mem. Willerburn Civic Assn., 1971-75. Served with AUS, 1960-61. Mem. ABA, Va. Bar Assn., D.C. Bar Assn., Washington Pat. Lawyers Assn., Md. Pat. Law Assn. (pres. 1981-83), Am. Patent Law Assn., Am. Chem. Soc. Jewish. Patent. Home: 7808 Ivymount Terr Potomac MD 20854 Office: WR Grace & Co Washington Research Ctr 7379 Route 32 Columbia MD 21044

TROIA, ANTHONY SAMUEL, lawyer; b. Bakersfield, Calif., June 30, 1945; s. Joseph Anthony and Dorothy M. (Cimino) T.; m. Sandra K. Ferrara, June 8, 1968; children—Gina, Julie, Lisa, Laura, Maria. B.A., Creighton U., 1967; J.D., Tulsa U., 1971. Bar: Nebr. 1972, U.S. Dist. Ct. Nebr. 1972, U.S. Ct. Appeals (8th cir.) 1982, U.S. Supreme Ct., 1981. Mktg. exec. Golf Oil Co., Tulsa, 1968; law clk. Rucker & Tabor, Tulsa, 1969-71; atty. No. Natural Gas, Omaha, 1971-72; city prosecutor Omaha City Atty., 1972-74; trial atty. Troia Law Offices, Omaha, 1974—. Advisor St. Francis Cabrini Ch., Omaha, 1983-84. Mem. ABA, Assn. Trial Lawyers Am., Nebr. State Bar Assn., Nebr. Trial Lawyers Assn., Omaha Bar Assn. (mem. pub. relations com. 1983-84), Phi Alpha Delta Democrat. Roman Catholic. Club: Christ the King Men's (Omaha). Lodge: Order Sons of Italy (state pres. 1975—, outstanding Italian-Am. 1979, 84). Criminal, Family and matrimonial, Personal injury. Home: 848 S 93d St Omaha NE 68114 Office: 1905 Harmey St Suite 400 Omaha NE 68102

TROJACK, JOHN EDWARD, lawyer; b. St. Paul, Mar. 30, 1946; s. Albert G. and Eleanor (Mader) T.; m. Mary Jo LaNasa, Oct. 12, 1979; children—Anne Marie, Joseph, Elizabeth, Catherine. B.A., U. Minn., 1968; J.D., William Mitchell Coll. Law, St. Paul, 1976. Bar: Minn. 1976, U.S. Dist. Ct. Minn. 1976, U.S. Ct. Appeals (8th cir.) 1980, U.S. Supreme Ct. 1980. Assoc. John E. Daubney, St. Paul, 1976-78; ptnr. Wagner, Rutchick & Trojack, P.A., St. Paul, 1978-83; sole practice, St. Paul, 1983—; vol. atty. So. Minn. Legal Services Corp., St. Paul, 1982—; Conciliation Ct. referee Ramsey County Mcpl. Ct., St. Paul, 1979—. Served with USNR, 1968-72. Mem. ABA (mem. council state bar leaders 1983-85, task force on gen. practitioner and organized bar 1984-85), Minn. Bar Assn. (chairperson gen. practice sect. 1983-85), Assn. Trial Lawyers Am., Minn. Trial Lawyers Assn., Ramsey County Bar Assn. (mem. real property com., law office mgmt. and family law com. 1976—, dist. ethics com. 1985—), Naval Res. Assn., Res. Officers Assn., U.S. Naval Inst., Phi Alpha Delta. Club: The Harvesters. General practice, State civil litigation, Probate. Office: 46 E 4th St Minnesota Bldg Suite 900 Saint Paul MN 55101

TROMBADORE, RAYMOND ROBERT, lawyer; b. Easton, Pa., Jan. 5, 1930; s. John and Mary Trombadore; m. Ann Wilkin, July 10, 1954; children—J. William, R. Robert, David W., J. Thomas, Mary Ann, Matthew. B.A., Rutgers U., 1951; J.D., U. Mich., 1954. Bar: Mich. 1954, N.J. 1955. Ptnr. Trombadore & Trombadore, Manville, N.J., 1958-68; ptnr. Raymond R. & Ann W. Trombadore, P.C., Somerville, N.J., 1968—; asst. prosecutor, 1st asst. prosecutor County of Somerset, (N.J.), 1961-71; lectr. N.J. Inst. Continuing Legal Edn.; vice chmn. N.J. Supreme Ct. Com. on restructuring of disciplinary system; chmn. Supreme Ct. Ethics Com. for Somerset County; mem. Supreme Ct. Com. on Model Rules of Conduct, Com. on Rules of Criminal Practice, Com. on Civil Case Mgmt., Task Force on Gender Bias in Cts., Com. on Delay Reduction in Criminal Cases. Trustee, elder Bound Brook Presbyn. Ch. Served to 1st lt. JAG, USAR, 1955-58. Fellow Am. Bar Found.; mem. ABA, N.J. State Bar Assn. (chmn. spl. com. on proposed model rules of conduct, treas. 1981, sec. 1982 2d v.p. 1983, 1st v.p. 1984, pres.-elect 1985, pres., 1986—, chmn. hdqrs. com., chmn. travel and arrangements com., chmn. fin. com., chmn. long-range planning com.), Somerset County Bar Assn. (past pres.), Am. Judicature Soc., Fed. Bar Assn., Nat. Conf. Bar Pres.'s, Order of Coif. Democrat. Club: Raritan Valley Country. Bd. editors Mich. Law Rev., 1952-54. Criminal, State civil litigation, Real property. Home: 626 Watchung Rd Bound Brook NJ 08805 Office: 33 E High St Somerville NJ 08876

TROMBATORE, JANET MOULTON, lawyer; b. Lawton, Okla., July 2, 1949; d. John Fitzgerald and Helen Louise (Riskus) Moulton; m. Earl Capron, Jan. 1971 (div. Sept. 1977); m. Ben Trombatore, Mar. 22, 1978. BA, U. Conn., 1971; JD, Tulane U., 1976. Bar: La. Assoc. Trombatore & Vondenstein, Kenner, La., 1976-79; ptnr. Trombatore & Moulton, Kenner, 1979-86; sole practice Delta Law Ctr., Metairie, La., 1986—. Pres. Save Our Wetlands, New Orleans, 1976—. Mem. ABA, Assn. Trial Lawyers Am., Jefferson Bar Assn., La. Trial Lawyers Assn. Personal injury, Family and matrimonial, Bankruptcy. Office: Delta Law Ctr 3713 Airline Hwy Metairie LA 70001

TROMBLEY, MICHAEL JEROME, lawyer; b. Bay City, Mich., Dec. 10, 1933; s. Clare F. and Sarah I. (Ingersol) T.; m. Anna K. Simons (div. 1963); children—Peter, Tad; m. Sandra V. Bybee (dec. 1980); children—Christine, Jacques; m. Sherry V. Cribbs, June 10, 1981. A.A., Menlo Coll., 1953; B.A., Stanford U., 1955; LL.B., U. Mo., 1960. Bar: Mo. 1960, Fla. 1974. Sole practice, Columbia, Mo., 1960-68; ptnr. Alexander, Wayland, Trombley, Butcher, Columbia, Mo., 1964-68; sole practice, 1969-79; ptnr. Trombley, Matheny & Schommer, Sebring, Fla., 1980-84, Trombley, Lobozzo, Schommer & Disler, Sebring, 1984—. Charter pres. Estate Planning Council of Highlands County, Fla., 1979-80. Served to 1st lt. USMCR, 1955-57. Mem. Am. Judicature Soc., Acad. Fla. Trial Lawyers, Assn. Trial Lawyers of Am. Republican. Episcopalian. Clubs: Masons, Shriners, Elks. State civil litigation, Federal civil litigation, Estate planning. Office: 329 S Commerce Ave Sebring FL 33870

TROMPETA, JESUS IGLESIAS, lawyer, law educator; b. Banga, Aklan, Philippines, Dec. 24, 1928; s. Rafael and Andrea (Iglesias) T.; m. Bellaflor G. Villanueva, Aug. 12, 1978; 1 child, Andree V. AA, U. Philippines, Manila, 1950, BS in Edn., 1952, LLB, 1967; postdoctoral, Pepperdine U., 1975. Bar: Philippines 1967, N.Y. 1983, U.S. Dist. Ct. (no. and so. dists.) N.Y. 1983, U.S. Ct. Appeals (9th cir.) 1983. Instr. Manila City Schs., Philippines, 1952-62; supervising registar Philippines Dept. of Commerce, Manila, 1962-68; instr. law Philippine Coll. of Commerce, Manila, 1967-68; legal asst. McGarry Law Offices, Los Angeles, 1972-74; instr. Los Angeles Unified Sch. Dist., 1974-84; sole practice Los Angeles, 1983—; legal asst. Kwan Law Offices, Los Angeles, 1968-74. Pres. Filipino Am. Polit. Orgn., Los Angeles, 1969-82. Recipient Plaque of Honor Sulu Unltd., 1977, Plaque of Appreciation City of Los Angeles, 1981. Mem. ABA, Assn. Trial Lawyers Am., State Bar Calif. (cert. completion performance skills tng. program, 1987), Integrated Bar of Philippines, Filipino Am. Educators Assn. (v.p. 1975-76), Filipino Am. Council of So. Calif. (exec. sec. 1970-72, pres. 1986—), Philippine Lawyers Assn. (treas. 1980—, Plaque of Honor 1980), U. Philippine Alumni Assn. (cert. of honor 1973, Plaque of Spl. Recognition 1980, Outstanding Alumnus award 1987), Asian Am. Edn. Commn. (commr. 1974-83, Cert. of Appreciation 1980, 82), United Filipino Am. Assembly of So. Calif. (bd. dirs. 1972-76). Club: Filipino (pres.). Avocations: reading, bowling, dancing. Immigration, naturalization, and customs, Legal education, Personal income taxation. Office: 3580 Wilshire Blvd Suite 2080 Los Angeles CA 90010

TROMPETER, PHILIP, lawyer, judge; b. Roanoke, Va., Nov. 22, 1952; s. Samuel Albert and Ada Ella (Diamond) T.; m. Sarina Sara Liniado, Mar. 5, 1978; children: Jason Aaron, Jessica Tamar. BA, NYU, 1974; JD, U. Richmond, 1977. Bar: Va., U.S. Dist. Ct. (we. dist.) Va. Sole practice Roanoke, 1977-85; spl. justice City of Roanoke Gen. Dist. Ct., 1978-85; judge juvenile and domestic relations ct. State of Va. 23d Jud. Dist., Roanoke, 1985—; task force needs of mentally ill children, Va. Dept. Mental Health and Mental Retardation, Richmond, 1984, mem. adv. council to Office of Prevention, 1984—; jud. edn. com. Jud. Conf. Va., 1986—. Pres. Mental Health Assn. Roanoke Valley, Va., 1984, Child Abuse and Neglect Coordinating Council of Roanoke, 1985; bd. dirs., exec. com. Mental Health Assn. Va., 1984—. Recipient Medal of Honor Mental Health Assn. Roanoke Valley, 1985, Disting. Service award Mental Health Assn. Va., 1985. Mem. ABA, Va. Bar Assn. (mental health laws com. 1984—). Jewish. Lodge: Kiwanis. Avocations: aerobics, gardening, cooking. Family and matrimonial, Juvenile, Mental Health. Home: 6021 Saddleridge Rd SW Roanoke VA 24018 Office: Dist Ct Roanoke Juvenile and Domestic Relations PO Box 986 Roanoke VA 24018

TROPE, JACK FREDERICK, lawyer; b. Jersey City, Mar. 25, 1955; s. Anthony Joseph and Kit Mildred (Kopf) T.; m. Judith Wilson Voorhees, Oct. 14, 1984. AB, Rutgers U., 1977; JD, Harvard U., 1980. Bar: N.J. 1980. Law clk. to presiding justice N.J. Supreme Ct., Flemington, 1980-81; asst. counsel to Gov. State of N.J., Trenton, 1981-83; assoc. Rosen, Gelman & Weiss and successor firm, Newark, 1983-85; staff atty. Assn. on Am. Indian Affairs, Inc., N.Y.C., 1985—. Press dir. Union County (N.J.) Hart for Pres., 1984. Mem. N.J. Automobile Full Ins. Underwriting Assn. (bd. dirs. 1984—), N.J. Automobile Ins. Reform Study Commn. Democrat. Mem. Unitarian Ch. Avocations: travel, sports. Indian law. Home: 1151 Terrill Rd Scotch Plains NJ 07076 Office: Assn on Am Indian Affairs Inc 95 Madison Ave New York NY 10016

TROST, EILEEN BANNON, lawyer; b. Teaneck, N.J., Jan. 9, 1951; d. William Eugene and Marie Thelma (Finlayson) Bannon; m. Lawrence Peter Trost, Jr., Aug. 27, 1977; children: Lawrence Peter III, William Patrick, . BA with distinction, Shimer Coll., 1972; JD cum laude, U. Minn., 1976. Bar: Ill. 1976, U.S. Dist. Ct. (no. dist.) Ill. 1976, Minn. 1978, U.S. Tax Ct. 1978, U.S. Supreme Ct. 1981. Assoc. McDermott, Will & Emery, Chgo., 1976-82, ptnr., 1982—. Mem. Minn. Bar Assn., Chgo. Bar Assn. Roman Catholic. Estate planning, Probate, Estate taxation. Office: McDermott Will & Emery 111 W Monroe St Chicago IL 60603

TROSTEN, LEONARD MORSE, lawyer; b. Bklyn., Jan. 25, 1932; s. David and Anne Bertha (Belkin) T.; m. Arthea Howell Dickson, Aug. 21, 1954 (dec. Jan. 1978); children—Amanda Trosten Hagins, Jessica Trosten Forrest; m. Addie Jane Tyner Harris, Jan. 12, 1979; children—Hope Harris Freglette, Arthur F.M. Harris. A.B., Columbia U., 1953, LL.B., 1955. Bar: N.Y. 1955, D.C. 1965. Assoc. Dwight, Royall, Harris, Koegel & Caskey, N.Y.C., 1955-58; with Office of Gen. Counsel AEC, Washington, 1958-64; staff counsel Joint Congrl. Com. on Atomic Energy, Washington, 1964-67; ptnr. LeBoeuf, Lamb, Leiby & MacRae, Washington, 1968—. Contbr. articles to profl. jours.; editor Columbia Law Rev., 1953-55. Mem. ABA, Fed. Bar Assn., Assn. Transp. Practitioners, Am. Nuclear Soc., Izaak Walton League Am., Audubon Soc., Nature Conservancy, Nat. Cathedral Assn., English-Speaking Union, Nat. Trust for Hist. Preservation, Internat. Nuclear Law Assn., Phi Beta Kappa, Phi Alpha Delta. Republican. Episcopalian. Clubs: University (Washington); Columbia Country (Chevy Chase, Md.); Princeton (N.Y.C.). Lodge: Rotary. Avocations: bridge; gardening; bird watching; walking; bowling. Administrative and regulatory, Nuclear power, Transportation. Home: 7505 Arrowood Rd Bethesda MD 20817 Office: LeBoeuf Lamb Leiby & MacRae 1333 New Hampshire Ave NW Washington DC 20036

TROSTORFF, ALEX P., lawyer; b. Queens, N.Y., Apr. 6, 1951; s. Peter W. and Cecilia (Rott) T.; m. Danielle Lombardo, June 30, 1984. BA, Davidson Coll., 1973; JD, Washington U., 1976; LLM in Taxation, Georgetown U., 1981. Tax law specialist IRS, Washington, 1978-80; assoc. Jones, Walker, Waechter, Poitevant, Carrere & Denegre, New Orleans, 1980—, ptnr., 1984—. Lutheran. Avocations: tennis, basketball, golf. Corporate taxation, Personal income taxation, State and local taxation. Home: 4910 Baronne New Orleans LA 70115 Office: Jones Walker Waechter et al 201 Saint Charles Ave New Orleans LA 70170

TROSTORFF, DANIELLE LOMBARDO, lawyer; b. Dec. 31, 1951; married. BS, Cornell U., 1972; MSW, Washington U., St. Louis, 1976; JD, Washington U., 1977. Bar: N.Y. 1978, D.C. 1978, U.S. Dist. Ct. D.C. 1979, U.S. Ct. Appeals (D.C. cir.) 1980, La. 1981, U.S. Dist. Ct. (ea. dist.) La. 1981, U.S. Ct. Appeals (5th and 11th cirs.) 1981, U.S. Dist. Ct. (mid. dist.) La. 1983, U.S. Dist. Ct. (we. dist.) La. 1983. Mng. atty. family law unit Neighborhood Legal Services, Washington, 1978-80; trial atty. civil div. Govt. of D.C., 1980-81; ptnr. Donna D. Fraiche, 1981-84; ptnr., chmn. health law sect. Broadhurst, Brook, Mangham & Hardy, New Orleans, 1984—; lectr. various profl. assns. Mem. La. Soc. Hosp. Attys. (pres. 1983-85, 85—). Health. Home: 4910 Baronne New Orleans LA 70115 Office: Broadhurst Brook et al 400 Poydras St Suite 2500 New Orleans LA 70130

TROTT, DENNIS CHARLES, lawyer; b. Ft. Wayne, Ind., Oct. 31, 1946; s. Charles and Eileen (Collins) T.; m. Nancy J. Servis, Aug. 4, 1973; children: Eileen Susanne, Duncan Eric. AB, Ind. U., 1968; JD, U. Mich., 1973. Bar: N.Y. 1974, U.S. Dist. Ct. (so. dist.) N.Y. 1974, U.S. Ct. Appeals (2d cir.) 1974, U.S. Ct. Mil. Appeals 1985, U.S. Ct. Internat. Trade 1986, U.S. Tax Ct. 1986, U.S. Supreme Ct. 1986. Assoc. Haight, Gardner, N.Y.C., 1973-75,

Breed, Abbott, N.Y.C., 1975-77, Rathheim, Hoffman, N.Y.C., 1977-84; mem. Henderson & Koplik, N.Y.C., 1985—. Bd. dirs. Neighborhood Housing Services of N.Y.C., 1985—. Served with U.S. Army, 1968-78. Mem. Assn. of Bar of City of N.Y., N.Y. County Lawyers Assn., Maritme Law Assn. General corporate, Banking, Admiralty. Home: 304 Sherman St Brooklyn NY 11218 Office: Henderson & Koplik 950 3rd Ave New York NY 10022

TROTT, STEPHEN SPANGLER, lawyer, musician; b. Glen Ridge, N.J., Dec. 12, 1939; s. David Herman and Virginia (Spangler) T.; m. Sally Snow, Sept. 1, 1962; children: Christina, Shelley. B.A., Wesleyan U., 1962; LL.B., Harvard U., 1965. Bar: Calif. 1966, U.S. Dist. Ct. (cen. dist.) Calif. 1966, U.S. Ct. Appeals (9th cir.) 1983, U.S. Supreme Ct. 1984. Guitarist, mem. The Highwaymen, 1958-62; dep. dist. atty. Los Angeles County Dist. Atty.'s Office, Los Angeles, 1966-75; chief dep. dist. atty. Los Angeles County Dist. Atty.'s Office, 1975-79; U.S. dist. atty. Central Dist. Calif., Los Angeles, 1981-83; asst. atty. gen. Criminal div. Dept. Justice, Washington, 1983-86; mem. faculty Nat. Coll. Dist. Attys., Houston, 1973—; chmn. central dist. Calif. Law Enforcement Coordinating Com., Houston, 1981-83; coordinator Los Angeles-Nev. Drug Enforcement Task Force, 1982-83; Assoc. atty. gen. Justice Dept., Washington, 1986—. Recipient Gold record as singer-guitarist in Michael Row the Boat Ashore, 1961; recipient Disting. Faculty award Nat. Coll. Dist. Attys., 1977. Republican. Clubs: Wilderness Fly Fishers (Santa Monica) (pres 1975-77); Brentwood Racing Pigeon (Los Angeles) (pres. 1977-82). Criminal. Office: US Dept Justice Washington DC 20530 *

TROTTA, FRANK PAUL, lawyer, consultant; b. New Rochelle, N.Y., Jan. 19, 1955; s. Frank Anthony Trotta and Lorraine Burigo; m. Susan L. Piening, Nov. 10, 1981. BA, SUNY, Albany, 1975; JD, Union U., Albany, 1978; LLM, NYU, 1986. Bar: N.Y., U.S. Dist. Ct. (no. and we. dists.) N.Y. 1979, U.S. Ct. Mil. Appeals 1979, U.S. Dist. Ct. (so. and ea. dists.) N.Y. 1980, U.S. Ct. Internat. Trade 1980, U.S. Tax Ct. 1982, U.S. Supreme Ct. 1982, U.S. Ct. Appeals (D.C. cir.) 1983, U.S. Ct. Customs and Patent Appeals 1984. Assoc. Weil, Gotshal & Manges, N.Y.C., 1978-81; gen. counsel Lehrman for Gov., N.Y.C., 1981-82; sole practice Washington, N.Y.C. and New Rochelle, 1981-86; of counsel Aldo & Vitagliano, 1986—; bd. dirs. The 2000 Soc. Ltd., N.Y.C., Capitol Corp., New Rochelle, Max News Fin. Network, Inc., Darien, Conn. 1986; mng. dir. N.Y. Consultancy, New Rochelle, 1981—; gen. counsel L.E. Lehrman Corp., Washington, 1982—, sec., treas. 1983—, chief operating officer, 1986—; gen. counsel Citizens for Am., Washington, 1983—, sec., treas. 1985-87; sec., v.p., treas Monroe Corp., Mechanicsburg, Pa., 1985-86, pres., 1986—. Author: Lois Lane's On Hold: What a Lawyer Should Do if a Reporter Calls, 1987; (with others) Federal Regulation of Consumer Credit, 1979; editor: Finishing First: A Campaign Manual, 1983. Chmn. Statewide Inds., N.Y., 1982—; ops. dir. Fund to Keep Am. #1, Washington, 1983—; alt. del. Rep. Nat. Conv., Dallas, 1984; mem. Tricentennial Commn., New Rochelle, 1985—, planning commr., 1981-84, others. Named one of Outstanding Young Men Am., 1976. Mem. ABA (bd. govs. 1987—), N.Y. State Bar Assn. (exec. com. young lawyers sect.), Mensa Internat. Roman Catholic. Avocation: computers, politics. Legislative, Local government, Administrative and regulatory. Home: 27 Mt Etna Pl New Rochelle NY 10805-3598 Office: 24 North Ave New Rochelle NY 10805-3598

TROTTER, HAYNIE SEAY, lawyer; b. Clarksville, Va., Feb. 24, 1931; s. William Augustus and Frances (Seay) T.; m. Marguerite Stapleford, Feb. 6, 1958; (dec. Feb. 1981); children: Richard Haynie, Frances Patricia; m. Katrin Gunnarsdottir, May 31, 1986. AB, Coll. of William & Mary, 1952; LLB, U. Va., 1957. Bar: Va. 1957, U.S. Dist. Ct. (ea. dist.) Va. 1957, U.S. Ct. Appeals (4th cir.) 1963, U.S. Supreme Ct. 1963. Sole practice Vienna, Va., 1957-58; assoc. William C. Bauknight, Fairfax, Va., 1958-59; ptnr. Bauknight, Williams, Swann & Trotter, Fairfax, 1959-61, Bauknight, Prichard, McCandlish & Williams, Fairfax, 1961-71, Boothe, Prichard & Dudley, McLean, Va., 1971-87, McGuire, Woods, Battle & Boothe, 1987—; bd. trustees Nat. Hosp. Orthopaedics and Rehab., Alexandria, Va., 1981—; bd. dirs. Network Health Plan, Alexandria. Mem. ABA, Va. Bar Assn., Fairfax Bar Assn., Assn. Trial Lawyers Am. Republican. Episcopalian. Avocations: tennis, fishing. Federal civil litigation, State civil litigation, Condemnation. Home: 9185 Old Dominion Dr McLean VA 22102 Office: McGuire Woods Battle & Boothe 8280 Greensboro Dr Suite 900 McLean VA 22102

TROTTER, THOMAS ROBERT, lawyer; b. Akron, Ohio, Apr. 11, 1949; s. Fred and Josephine (Daley) T. BA, Ohio U., 1971; JD, Tulane U., 1975. Bar: Ohio 1975, U.S. Dist. Ct. (no. dist.) Ohio 1975. Assoc. Squire, Sanders & Dempsey, Cleve., 1975-80; mem. Buckingham, Doolittle & Burroughs, Akron, 1980—. Trustee Akron Symphony Orch., 1984—, MSP 503 Devel. Corp., Akron, 1983—. Mem. ABA, Ohio Bar Assn., Akron Bar Assn., Cleve. Bar Assn., Nat. Assn. Bond Lawyers. Democrat. Municipal bonds, Local government, Consumer commercial. Home: 589 Avalon Ave Akron OH 44309 Office: Buckingham Doolittle & Burroughs PO Box 1500 Akron OH 44309

TROTTER, WILLIAM PERRY, lawyer; b. Manchester, Ga., Nov. 2, 1919; s. McKie Massesburg and Tudor (Perry) T.; m. Julia Thomason, Aug. 5, 1950; children: Jefferson William, William Perry Jr. BA, Vanderbilt U., 1941; JD, U. Ga., 1948. Bar: Ga. 1947. Sole practice LaGrange, Ga., 1948—; senator State of Ga., 1951-52; mem. Ga. Ho. of Reps., 1959. Decorated Air medal USAF, 1944-45. Real property, Probate, Public utilities. Home: 1014 Country Club Rd LaGrange GA 30240 Office: 206 Battle St LaGrange GA 30241

TROUT, STRAN LIPPINCOTT, lawyer; b. Staunton, Va., Sept. 30, 1942; s. William Edgar and Harriet (McCurley) T. BA in Psychology, U. Richmond, 1971, JD, 1974. Bar: Va. 1974, U.S. Dist. Ct. Va. 1974, U.S. Ct. Appeals (4th cir.) 1974, U.S. Supreme 1977. Analyst labor market Va. Employment Commn., Richmond, Va., 1971-72; legis. asst. Va. Gen. Assembly, Richmond, 1974; atty. SBA, Richmond, 1974-80, dist. counsel, 1980—; nat. chmn. automation com. SBA, 1985—. Pres. WoodHaven (Va.) Property Owners Assn., 1981-84. Served with USN, 1966-70, PTO. Mem. Va. Bar Assn., Fed. Bar Assn., Richmond Bar Assn., Nat. Lawyers Club, Va. Jaycees (life, pres. Found. 1983-85, exec. nat. dir. 1976-77,senator Jaycees Internat. 1980, crew U.S. Jaycees 1982, pres. charitable found. conf. 1984—), Mensa. Republican. Presbyterian. Club: Ruritan (pres. 1986, zone gov. 1987). Consumer commercial, Bankruptcy, Government management. Home: 1393 Lakeshore Dr Quinton VA 23141 Office: SBA PO Box 10171 Richmond VA 23240

TROUTMAN, CHARLES HENRY, III, lawyer; b. Wooster, Ohio, Mar. 25, 1944; s. Charles Henry and Lois Margaret (Dickason) T. B.A., Wheaton Coll., 1966; J.D., Am. U., 1969; M.Comparative Law, So. Meth. U., 1970. Bar: Ill. 1969, D.C. 1969, Guam 1973, U.S. Ct. Appeals (9th cir.) 1973, Trust Territory Pacific Islands, 1973, U.S. Supreme Ct. 1976, Commonwealth of No. Mariana Islands 1978. Asst. atty. gen., Guam, 1970-74; assoc. Cronin, Troutman & Assocs., Guam, 1974-75; atty. gen., Guam, 1975-77; counsel Dept. Edn., Guam, 1977-78; compiler of laws Govt. of Guam, Agana, 1978—, acting atty. gen., 1987. Mem. ABA, Fed. Bar Assn. (sec. local chpt.), Am. Soc. Internat. Law, Christian Legal Soc., Guam Bar Assn. Democrat. Presbyterian. Legislative, Public international. Home: PO Box 455 Agana GU 96910 Office: 238 Archbishop FC Flores St PDN Bldg 7th Floor Agana GU 96910

TROVER, ELLEN LLOYD, lawyer; b. Richmond, Va., Nov. 23, 1947; d. Robert Van Buren and Hazel (Urban) Lloyd; m. Denis William Trover, June 12, 1971; 1 dau., Florence Emma. A.B., Vassar Coll., 1969; J.D., Coll. William and Mary, 1972. Asst. editor Bancroft-Whitney, San Francisco, 1973-74; owner Ellen Lloyd Trover Atty.-at-Law, Thousand Oaks, Calif., 1974-82; ptnr. Trover & Fisher, Thousand Oaks, 1982—; bd. dirs. Burco Mfg., Los Angeles. Editor: Handbooks of State Chronologies, 1972. Trustee, Conejo Future Found., Thousand Oaks, 1978—, vice chmn., 1982-84, chmn., 1984—; pres. Zonta Club Conejo Valley Area, 1978-79; trustee Hydro Help for the Handicapped, 1980-85. Mem. Conejo Simi Bar Assn. (pres. 1979-80, dir. 1983-85), Ventura County Bar Assn. (state del. 1984), State Bar Calif., Va. State Bar, Phi Alpha Delta. Democrat. Presbyterian. Probate, Estate taxation. Home: 11355 Presilla Rd Camarillo CA 93010 Office: Trover and Fisher 1107E Thousand Oaks Blvd Thousand Oaks CA 91362

TROXELL, JAMES DANE, petroleum company executive, lawyer; b. Akron, Ohio, Mar. 5, 1946; s. Delmont and Katherine T.; B.A., U. Akron, 1968, J.D., 1975; m. Sandra L. Coey, June 14, 1969. Trainee, Goodyear Aerospace Co., Akron, Ohio, 1969-70; legal counsel Babcock & Wilcox Co., Barberton, Ohio, 1970-76; admitted to Ohio bar, 1976, U.S. Supreme Ct. bar, 1979; asso. firm Hershey & Browne, Akron, 1976-78; corp. counsel Gen. Tire & Rubber Co., Akron, 1979-80; pres. Ohio Petroleum Energy Co., Cuyahoga Falls, Ohio, 1978-81; v.p. fin. Eddie Elias Enterprises and Elias Petroleum, 1981—; pres. Shafer & Elias Producers, Inc., 1982—; sec. Fuzzy & Hubert Golf Course Cons., Inc., 1984—; pres. Troxell Software Cons., 1984—. Past bd. dirs. United Cerebral Palsy of Summit County and Akron. Mem. Am. Bar Assn., Ohio Bar Assn., Akron Bar Assn., Ohio Oil and Gas Assn., Psi Chi. Republican. Club: Akron City. Entertainment, Computer, Personal income taxation. Home: PO Box 123 Cuyahoga Falls OH 44222-0123 Office: PO Box 266 Cuyahoga Falls OH 44222-0266

TRUBO, HERBERT ALAN, lawyer; b. Los Angeles, Oct. 9, 1948; s. Sam C. and Claire (Rozen) T. AB, U. Calif., Berkeley, 1970; JD, U. Mich., 1973. Bar: Oreg. 1973, Calif. 1974, U.S. Dist. Ct. Oreg. 1974. Atty. Multnomah County Legal Services, Portland, Oreg., 1973-74; ptnr. Friedman and Trubo, Portland, 1974-80, Sorensen-Jolink & Trubo, Portland, 1981—; adj. prof. Lewis & Clark Coll., Portland, 1984-85. Author: Marriage and Family Law in Oregon, 1982. Fellow Am. Acad Matrimonial Lawyers; mem. ABA. Family and matrimonial, Juvenile. Office: Sorensen Jolink & Trubo 1020 SW Taylor Suite 650 Portland OR 97205

TRUE, ROY JOE, lawyer; b. Shreveport, La., Feb. 20, 1938; s. Collins B. and Lula Mae (Cady) T.; m. Patsy Jean Hudsmith, Aug. 29, 1959; children: Andrea Alane, Alyssa Anne, Ashley Alisbeth. Student, Centenary Coll., 1957; B.S. (scholar), Tex. Christian U., 1961; LL.B. (scholar), So. Meth. U., 1963, postgrad., 1968-69. Bar: Tex. 1963. Practiced in Dallas, 1963—; pres. Invesco Internat. Corp., 1969-70, True & McLain, P.C. (formerly True & Zable, then The True Firm), 1975—; bus. adviser, counselor Mickey Mantle, 1969—. Editorial bd.: Southwestern Law Jour, 1962-63. Served with AUS, 1956. Mem. Am., Dallas bar assns., Tex. Assn. Bank Counsel, Phi Alpha Delta. Banking, Contracts commercial, General corporate. Home: 5601 Ursula Ln Dallas TX 75229 Office: 5601 Ursula Ln Dallas TX 75229

TRUETT, HAROLD JOSEPH, III, lawyer; b. Alameda, Calif., Feb. 13, 1946; s. Harold Joseph and Lois Lucille (Mellin) T.; m. Kathleen Truett, Dec. 5, 1970 (div. July 1982); 1 child, Harold Joseph IV; m. Anna V. Billante, Oct. 1, 1983; 1 child, James S. Carstensen. BA, U. San Francisco, 1968, JD, 1975. Bar: U.S. Dist. Ct. (no., so., cen. and ea. dists.) Calif. 1976, U.S. Ct. Appeals (9th cir.) 1980. Assoc. Hoberg, Finger et al, San Francisco, 1975-78, Bledsoe, Smith et al, San Francisco, 1979-80, Abramson & Bianco, San Francisco, 1980-83, Ingram & Dykman, San Rafael, Calif., 1983—. Mem. Marin Dem. Council, San Rafael, 1983—. Served to lt. USN, 1967-72. Mem. Calif. Bar Assn., San Francisco Bar Assn., Marin County Bar Assn., Calif. Trial Lawyers Assn., Lawyers Pilots Assn. Roman Catholic. State civil litigation, Aviation and space, Personal injury. Home: 1349 Vallejo St San Francisco CA 94109

TRUITT, PATRICIA PEYTON, lawyer; b. Lafayette, Ind., Apr. 26, 1939; d. Frank Wood and Mary Elizabeth (Fouse) Peyton; m. Robert B. Truitt, June 8, 1963; children: Randolph, Theodore, Elizabeth. BA, Duke U., 1961; MA, Purdue U., 1963; JD cum laude, Ind. U., 1979. Bar: Ind. 1979, U.S. Dist. Ct. (so. dist.) Ind. 1979, U.S. Dist. Ct. (no. dist.) Ind. 1980, U.S. Supreme Ct. 1982, U.S. Ct. Appeals (7th cir.) 1985. Tchr. Cudahy (Wis.) Pub. Schs., 1963-1964; info. ctr. dir. World Affairs Council, Boston, 1964-65; tchr. Lexington (Mass.) Pub. Schs., 1965-67; assoc. Stuart & Branigin, Lafayette, 1979-82, Ball, Eggleston, Bumbleburg & McBride, Lafayette, 1982—. Bd. dirs., founder Ind. Juvenile Justice Task Force, Indpls., 1973-75; bd. dirs. Ind. Com. for Humanities, Indpls., 1973-75, United Way of Tippecanoe County, Lafayette, 1983-86, Battle of Tippecanoe Outdoor Drama Inc., W. Lafayette, 1985—. Named one of Outstanding Young Women Am. Mem. ABA, Ind. Bar Assn., Tippecanoe Bar Assn. (treas. 1983-84), Assn. Trial Lawyers Am., Ind. Trial Lawyers Assn., Phi Delta Phi, Pi Beta Phi. Presbyterian. General practice, General corporate, Probate. Home: 613 Ridgewood West Lafayette IN 47906 Office: Ball Eggleston Bumbleburg & McBride 810 Banc One Bldg PO Box 1535 Lafayette IN 47902

TRUITT, ROBERT RALPH, JR., lawyer; b. Chaves County, N.Mex., Jan. 21, 1948; s. Robert Ralph and Dorothy (Butler) T.; m. Susan Donovan, Nov. 28, 1981. BA, BBA, Southwestern U., 1970; JD, U. Tex., 1973. Bar: Tex. 1973, U.S. Ct. Appelas (5th cir.) 1976, U.S. Dist. Ct. (we. dist.) Tex. 1977, U.S. Dist. Ct. (no. dist.) Tex. 1981, U.S. Dist. Ct. (ea. dist.) Tex. 1982. Assoc. Turpin, Smith & Dyer, Midland, Tex., 1973-77; sole practice Midland, 1977—. Chmn. planning and zoning com., City of Midland, 1979-80; chmn. and bd. dirs. Midland Downtown Lions Fire Prevention and Hist. Found., 1980—. Bar: ABA, Tex. Bar Assn. Banking, Bankruptcy, State civil litigation. Office: 901 W Texas Midland TX 79701

TRUMAN, ROLLAND A., judge; b. Loma Linda, Calif., Apr. 30, 1912; s. Archibald William and Daisy Ethel (Nary) T.; m. Iola LaVerne Gilbert, June 14, 1941 (div.); children—Rolland Gilbert, Norris Wesley; m. Laurel A. Weibel, Sept. 15, 1953; children—Tracy, Tammy, Trent, Tricia, Trina. B.A., U. So. Calif., 1940, J.D., 1943. Bar: Calif. 1942, U.S. Dist. Ct. (all dists.) Calif. 1942, U.S. Supreme Ct. 1957, U.S. Ct. Claims 1978, U.S. Tax Ct. 1978, U.S. Customs Ct. 1978, U.S. Ct. Customs and Patent Appeals 1978, U.S. Ct. Internat. Trade 1981. Atty., Pacific Electric Railway Co., Los Angeles, 1942-44; ptnr. Paap & Truman, Long Beach, Calif., 1944-48; sole practice, Long Beach, 1948-50; ptnr. Whitman & Truman, Southgate, Calif., 1950-58; sole practice, Southgate, 1958-63; superior ct. commnr. Los Angeles County, 1963-77, judge pro tem, 1980-81, 1982—; cons., referee, appeals hearing officer, arbitrator Los Angeles County, 1977—. Contbr. articles to profl. jours. Mem., Ch.-State Council, 1965—; trustee White Meml. Med. Ctr., Los Angeles, 1975-83; mem. Banjos-A-Plenty, El Monte, Calif., 1979—, Smithsonian Nat. Assocs., 1984—; performer Jerry Reilly and His Calif. Banjoleers, 1980—. Recipient numerous awards for community service and profl. excellence including Commendation, Congl. Record, 1983. Fellow Am. Acad. Matrimonial Lawyers; mem. ABA, Assn. Trial Lawyers Am., Calif. Bar Assn., Los Angeles County Bar Assn., Long Beach Bar Assn., Delta Theta Thi (Cert. of Honor). Democrat. Seventh-Day Adventist (elder). Clubs: Associated Radio Amateurs (Long Beach); Fretted Instrument Guild of Am.; Supreme Ct. Hist. Soc., Council on Religious Freedom (life, bd. dirs.). Federal civil litigation, General corporate, Personal injury. Home: 4522 Greenmeadow Rd Long Beach CA 90808

TRUMBO, GEORGE WILLIAM, judge; b. Newark, Ohio, Sept. 24, 1926; married; 5 children. B.S., Ohio State U., 1949; LL.B., Western Res. U., 1952. Bar: U.S. Tax Ct. 1954, U.S. Supreme Ct. 1976. Referee Ct. Common Pleas, 1977-82; judge Mcpl. Ct., City of Cleve., 1982—. Pres. bd. trustees Cleve. Pub. Library, 1984; chmn. Task Force House Corrections; past chmn., trustee, bd. dirs. Mt. Olive Bapt. Ch. Served with USN, 1944-46. Recipient Superior Jud. Service award Ohio Supreme Ct., 1982, 84, 85. Mem. Nat. Bar Assn., Cleve. Bar Assn., Ohio Bar Assn., Cuyahoga County Bar Assn. (award 1973), Norman S. Minor Bar Assn., Jud. Council Nat. Bar Assn. (bd. dirs.), NAACP, Kappa Alpha Psi. Lodges: Mason, Elks. Office: Cleve Mcpl Ct Justice Ctr Cleveland OH 44113

TRUSCH, NORMA LEVINE, lawyer; b. Point Pleasant, N.J., July 2, 1937; d. Max and Gertrude (Boyarsky) Levine; m. Howard Trusch; children: Marla Deborah, Matthew Rami. BFA, U. Okla., 1957; JD, South Tex. Coll., 1977. Bar: Tex. 1977. Continuity writer KTSM-TV, El Paso, Tex., 1957-59; prodn. asst. NBC TV, N.Y.C., 1959-62; researcher, writer Jules Power Prodns., N.Y.C., 1962-64; freelance writer, researcher various TV shows, N.Y.C., 1964-67; sole practice Houston, 1977—. Trustee South Tex. Law Jour. (Phil Burleson award). Bd. dirs. Houston Vol. Lawyers, 1983-85, Jewish Community Ctr., 1982-86, mem. pub. affairs com., 1981-85, also various coms., 1982—; bd. dirs. ACLU, 1982-83; bd. dirs. Jewish Fedn. Houston, 1984—, mem. community relations com., 1982—, also various coms. 1982—; bd. dirs. Am. Jewish Com., 1984-86, chmn. interreligious affairs com., 1985—. Mem. ABA (family sect.), Nat. Council Jewish Women (past pres. career br.), Tex. Bar Assn. (family law sects.), Houston Bar Assn. (trustee family law sect., bd. dirs. lawyers referral service 1982-84), South Tex. Coll. of Law Alumni Assn. (bd. dirs. 1982-84), Order of Lytae. Democrat. Family and matrimonial. Home: 6118 Rollingbrook Houston TX 77096 Office: 3816 W Alabama #200 Houston TX 77027

TSCHINKEL, ANDREW JOSEPH, JR., law librarian; b. Catskill, N.Y., Aug. 8, 1952; s. Andrew Joseph and Marie Frances (O'Connor) T. BA summa cum laude, St. John's Coll., Jamaica, N.Y., 1975, MLS, 1977; MBA, Fordham U., 1983. Grad. asst. div. library sci. St. John's Coll., Jamaica, 1975-77, asst. law librarian, 1977-79, adj. law librarian, 1983—; head librarian Christ the King High Sch., Middle Village, N.Y., 1979-80; sr. law librarian Bklyn. Supreme Ct., 1980-81; prin. law librarian N.Y. Supreme Ct., Jamaica, 1981—. Contbr. book revs. Queens Bar Bull. Recipient Pub. Service award Queens Borough Pres. and N.Y. Telephone Co., 1986. Mem. Am. Assn. Law Libraries, Beta Phi Mu. Republican. Roman Catholic. Librarianship. Office: NY Supreme Ct Library 88-11 Sutphin Blvd Jamaica NY 11435

TSCHIRN, DARRYL JUDE, lawyer; b. New Orleans, May 15, 1940; s. Edward and Lorraine Tschirn; divorce; children: Darryl J. Jr., Kathryn B., Jude J. BA, Loyola U., New Orleans, 1962, LLB, 1964. Bar: La. 1964, U.S. Dist. Ct. (ea. dist.) La. 1971, U.S. Ct. Appeals (5th cir.), U.S. Dist. Ct. (we. dist.) La. 1978, U.S. Supreme Ct. 1980. Law clk. to presiding U.S. dist. ct. justice La. State Ct., New Orleans, 1967-69; ptnr. Badeaux & Discon, New Orleans, 1969-71; sole practice Metairie, La., 1971—. Served to capt. U.S. Army, 1965-67. Mem. Assn. Trial Lawyers Am., La. Trial Lawyers Assn. (bd. of govs.), Blue Key, Scabbard and Blade. Republican. Roman Catholic. Avocations: tennis, racquetball, boating, marshall arts. Admiralty, Insurance, Personal injury. Home: #5 Miller Ln Metairie LA 70002 Office: 3850 N Causeway Blvd #1140 Metairie LA 70002

TSENIN, KSENIA, lawyer; b. Shanghai, Peoples Republic of China, Jan. 10, 1947; came to U.S., 1955; d. Konstantin and Iraida (Oparin) T. BA, San Francisco State U., 1970; JD, U. San Francisco, 1973. Bar: Calif. 1973, U.S. Ct. Appeals (9th cir) 1973. Sole practice San Francisco, 1973—. Cons. Marin Abused Women's Services, Calif., 1979—; chmn. women's caucus Calif. Dems., 1982-83; v.p. NOW., Calif., 1980-83, v.p. legal, 1976-78. Recipient numerous certs. appreciation. Mem. Calif. Bar Assn., San Francisco Bar Assn. (co-chmn. com. 1973-75), San Francisco Trial Lawyers Assn. (bd. dirs. 1981-83), Barristers Club. State civil litigation, Landlord-tenant, Personal injury. Office: 320 Clement St San Francisco CA 94118

TUBMAN, WILLIAM CHARLES, lawyer; b. N.Y.C., Mar. 16, 1932; s. William Thomas and Ellen Veronica (Griffin) T.; m. Dorothy Rita Krug, Aug. 15, 1964; children: William Charles Jr., Thomas Davison, Matthew Griffin. BS, Fordham U., 1953, JD, 1960; postdoctoral, NYU Sch. Law, 1960-61. Bar: N.Y. 1960, U.S. Ct. Appeals (2d cir.) 1966, U.S. Supreme Ct. 1967, U.S. Ct. Customs and Patent Appeals 1971. Auditor Peat, Marwick Mitchell & Co., N.Y.C., 1956-60; sr. counsel Kennecott Corp., N.Y.C., 1960-82; sr. counsel Phelps Dodge Corp., N.Y.C., 1982-85, sec., 1985-87, v.p., 1987—. Author: Exploiting the Ocean, 1966. Active, Big Bros. Inc., N.Y.C., 1963-73. Served with U.S. Army, 1953-55. Recipient Cert. Disting. Service, Big Brothers Inc., 1968. Mem. ABA, N.Y. State Bar Assn. Democrat. Roman Catholic. Club: Mining (N.Y.C.). Securities, General corporate, Antitrust. Home: 8008 N 66th St Paradise Valley AZ 85253 Office: Phelps Dodge Corp 2600 N Central Ave Phoenix AZ 85004

TUCHMAN, MORRIS, lawyer; b. Tel Aviv, June 4, 1950; came to U.S., 1952; s. Herbert and Magda (Maged) T.; m. Judith Gruss, June 25, 1972; children: Tova Rebecca, Sarah Rochelle. BS, CUNY, 1971; JD, N.Y. Law Sch., 1975. Bar: N.Y. 1976, U.S. Dist. Ct. (so. and ea. dists.) N.Y. 1976, N.J. 1977, U.S. Ct. Appeals (2d cir.) 1979, U.S. Ct. Appeals (3d cir.) 1982, Conn. 1984. Sole practice N.Y.C., 1975—. Mem. ABA, N.Y. State Bar Assn., N.Y. County Bar Assn. Democrat. Club: Stevenson (Queens. N.Y.). Labor. Office: 134 Lexington Ave New York NY 10016

TUCK, EDWARD HALLAM, lawyer; b. Brussels, June 27, 1927; s. William Hallam and Hilda (Bunge) T.; m. Liliane Solmsen, June 8, 1978; children by previous marriage—Edward, Jessica, Matthew. B.A., Princeton U., 1950; LL.B., Harvard Law Sch., 1953. Bar: N.Y. Assoc. Shearman & Sterling, N.Y.C., 1953-62, ptnr., 1962-86, of counsel, 1986—; dir. Corning Internat. Corp., Unimin Corp., Fromageries Bel; mem. internat. adv. bd. Lafarge Coppee. Bd. dirs. N.Y.C. Partnership, Belgian Am. Ednl. Found., Fgn. Policy Discussion Group, Assn. for Internat. Commn. of Jurists; trustee French Inst. Alliance Francaise; Pres., bd. dirs. French Am. Found.; chmn. bd. North Country Sch., Inc., 1974-78, The Drawing Ctr., Gateway Citizens Com., 1972-74; pres. The Parks Council, 1970-74; chmn. N.Y. State Parks and Recreation Commn., City of N.Y., 1971-76; pres. French-Am. Found. Served with USN, 1945-46. Mem. Assn. Bar City N.Y., Council on Fgn. Relations. Episcopalian. Clubs: Racquet and Tennis, The Brook, Down Town Assn., The Ivy, Pilgrims, Soc. of the Cin. Office: Shearman & Sterling 53 Wall St New York NY 10005

TUCKER, BILLIE ANNE, lawyer; b. Anniston, Ala., Aug. 11, 1936; d. L.B. and A.M. (Tatum) Crouch; m. Mose A. Tucker, Mar. 7, 1959; children: Allen, Joseph M., Stanley, John. BS, U. Ala., 1956, JD, 1959. Sole practice Lafayette, Ala., 1959—; city judge, Valley, Ala., 1982-83, Lanett, Ala., 1983. Mem. choir sunday sch. tchr. First Baptist Ch., LaFayette; drama dir., bd. dirs. Chamber Acad., LaFayette; bd. dirs. Valley Haven, LaFayette. Mem. ABA, Ala. Bar Assn., Chambers County Bar Assn. Republican. Family and matrimonial, Personal injury, General practice. Home: LaFayette St N LaFayette AL 36862 Office: 213 Ave A SE LaFayette AL 36862

TUCKER, BOWEN HAYWARD, lawyer; b. Providence, Apr. 13, 1938; s. Stuart Hayward and Ardelle Chase (Drabble) T.; m. Jan Louise Brown, Aug. 26, 1961; children: Stefan Kendric Slade, Catherine Kendra Gordon. A.B. in Math., Brown U., 1959; J.D., U. Mich., 1962. Bar: R.I. 1963, Ill. 1967, U.S. Supreme Ct. 1970. Assoc. Hinckley & Allen, Providence, 1962-66; sr. atty. Caterpillar Tractor Co., Peoria, Ill., 1966-72; counsel FMC Corp., Chgo., 1972-82, sr. litigation counsel, 1982—. Chmn. legal process task force Chgo. Residential Sch. Study Com., 1973-74, mem. Commn. on Children, 1983-85, Ill. Com. on Rights of Minors, 1974-77, Com. on Youth and the Law, 1977-79, Youth Employment Task Force; mem. White House Conf. on Children, ednl. services subcom., 1979-80; chairperson Youth Employment Task Force, 1982-83; mem. citizens com. on Juvenile Ct. (Cook County), 1978—, chmn. detention subcom., 1982—. Served to 1st lt. U.S. Army, 1962-69. Mem. ABA, Ill. State Bar Assn., R.I. Bar Assn., Chgo. (chmn. com. on juvenile law, 1976-77), Engine Mfrs. Assn. (chmn. legal com. 1972), Constrn. Industry Mfrs. Assn. (exec. com. of Lawyers' Council 1972, 1975-79, vice chmn. 1977, chmn. 1978-79), Machinery and Allied Product Inst. (products liability council 1974—, vice chmn. 1981-83, chmn. 1983-85), ACLU (bd. dirs. Ill. div. 1970-79, exec. com. 1973-79, sec. 1975-77), Phi Alph Delta. Club: Brown Univ. of Chgo. (nat. alunni schs. program 1973-85, v.p. 1980-81, pres. 1981-86). General corporate, Juvenile. Home: 107 W Noyes St Arlington Heights IL 60005 Office: 200 E Randolph St Suite 6700 Chicago IL 60601

TUCKER, JAMES DELZELL, lawyer; b. Springfield, Mo., Dec. 3, 1948; s. Donald James and Sara Marie (Delzell) T.; m. Nancy Miller, Jan 31, 1987; children from previous marriage: Donald James, Lu Ashley. BS, U. Mo., 1970, JD, 1973. Bar: Mo. 1973, U.S. Dist. Ct. (we. dist.) Mo. 1973. Instr. U. Mo., Columbia, 1973-74; assoc. Neale, Newman, Bradshaw & Freeman, Springfield, 1974-76; ptnr. Harrison, Tucker & Geisler, Springfield, 1976—; instr. law Southwest Mo. State U., Springfield, 1976—. Contbr. articles to profl. jours. Counsel Mo. Young Dems., 1977; chmn. Congl. Campaign 7th Dist. Mo., 1982; pres. Greene County Young Dems., Springfield, 1976, Ozark Empire Fair Adv. Bd., Springfield, 1983-84. Mem. Mo. Bar Assn., Mo. Defense Lawyers Assn. Democrat. Unitarian. Avocations: mountain climbing, photography, writing, farming. Real property, State civil litigation, General corporate. Home: Rt 1 Box 27B Willard MO 65781 Office: Harrison Tucker & Geisler 1121 Glenstone Springfield MO 65804

TUCKER, JAMES LETCHER, lawyer; b. Big Stone Gap, Va., July 1, 1941; s. Woodrow Wilson and Lillian Louise (Robinette) T.; m. Kendell Rene Quesenberry, Dec. 6, 1980; children—Mary, Jesika. B.A., Coll. William and Mary, 1963, B.C.L. and J.D., 1966. Bar: Va. 1966, U.S. Dist. Ct. (we. dist.)

Va. Assoc. Carneal, Smith & Athey, Williamsburg, Va., 1967-68, Gilmer, Sadler, Ingram, Thomas & Sutherland, Pulaski, Va., 1969-70; sole practice, Pulaski, 1970—. Mem. Va. State Bar, ABA, Pulaski County Bar Assn., Phi Beta Kappa. Contbr. articles to legal publs.; mem. editorial bd. William and Mary Law Rev. Family and matrimonial, Bankruptcy, Criminal. Office: 344 Jefferson Ave and 4th St NW PO Box 849 Pulaski VA 24301

TUCKER, JEFFREY THORNT, lawyer; b. Key West, Fla., Sept. 29, 1950; s. James Foster and Helen Nelson (Storms) T.; m. Carol Ann Ryan, May 26, 1973; children: Amanda, Sarah, Jeffrey. BS in Engring., U.S. Mil. Acad., 1972; JD, Dickinson Sch. Law, 1977. Bar: Pa. 1977, N.J. 1979, U.S. Dist. Ct. N.J. 1983, U.S. Dist. Ct. (ea. dist.) Pa. 1985. Commd. 2d lt. U.S. Army, 1972, advanced through grades to capt., 1974, resigned, 1981; assoc. Curtin & Heefner, Morrisville, Pa., 1981—. Bd. dirs. Pennsbury Scholarship Found., Fallsington, Pa., 1983—. Decorated D.M.S.M. Mem. ABA, Pa. Bar Assn. (treas. 1984-85, chmn. young lawyer div. 1986-87, bd. govs. 1985—), Bucks County Bar Assn. (chmn. young lawyers div. 1983-84). Lodge: Rotary. Avocation: running. Labor, Local government. Home: 11 E School Ln Yardley PA 19067 Office: Curtin & Heefner 250 N Pennsylvania Ave Morrisville PA 19067

TUCKER, ROBERT HENRY, lawyer; b. N.Y.C., Dec. 5, 1937; s. Al and Sylvia G. (Hoffman) T.; m. Linda B. Klein, July 4, 1963; children—Daniel Jay, Julie Carol, Ruth Leslie. B.A., Queens Coll., 1958; J.D., Georgetown U., 1961. Bar: N.Y. 1962, U.S Dist. Ct. (ea. and so. dists.) N.Y. 1964, U.S. Ct. Appeals (2d cir.) 1966, U.S. Supreme Ct. 1967. Assoc. Spitzbart & Hertan, Huntington, N.Y., 1962-63, Silverstein, Balin, Pares & Soloway, New Hyde Park, N.Y., 1963-64; sole practice, Forest Hills, N.Y., 1964-72; ptnr. Weiss, Tucker, Topper, Melville, N.Y., 1972-80; sole practice, Melville, 1980-83, 85—; ptnr. Tucker & Lacher, Melville, 1983-85. Mem. exec. bd. L.I. Regional Bd. Anti-Defamation League, Great Neck, N.Y.; mem. nat. law com. Anti-Defamation League of B'nai B'rith, N.Y.C. Served with U.S. Army, 1961-63. Mem. Assn. Trial Lawyers Am., N.Y. State Trial Lawyers Assn., Commercial Law League Am., N.Y. State Bar Assn., Suffolk County Bar Assn. (chmn. com. banking, corporate and bus. law 1982-84), Suffolk Acad. Law (merit recognition 1984). Democrat. Jewish. Lodge: B'nai B'rith (bd. govs. dist. 1). State civil litigation, Consumer commercial, Family and matrimonial. Office: 1 Huntington Quad Suite 2C04 Melville NY 11747

TUCKER, STEPHEN, lawyer; b. Coral Gables, Fla., Apr. 16, 1952; s. George R. Tucker and Maris Deborah (Hurt-Tucker) Wodrich. BS in Engring. with highest honors, U. Fla., 1975, JD, 1978. Bar: Ga. 1979, N.Y. 1981, U.S. Dist. Ct. N.Y. 1981. Assoc. Smith, Cohen et al, Atlanta, 1978-79; assoc. Mendes and Mount, N.Y.C., 1979-85, ptnr., 1985—; lectr. Stanford U. Communication Satellite Planning Ctr., 1985—. Mem. Internat. Assn. Space Law, Internat. Bar Assn. (space law com.), Lawyer/Pilots Bar Assn., Tau Beta Pi. Avocation: amateur radio. Space law, Insurance, Federal civil litigation. Office: Mendes and Mount 3 Park Ave New York NY 10016

TUCKER, THEODORE BRUSH, III, lawyer; b. Toledo, Jan. 11, 1951; s. Theodore Brush II and Norma Jean (Pollack) T.; m. Becky Sue Groch, Oct. 23, 1976; children: Theodore Brush IV, Matthew B., Kyle D. BE magna cum laude, U. Toledo, 1973, JD, 1976. Bar: Ohio 1976, U.S. Dist. Ct. (no. dist.) Ohio 1977, U.S. Ct. Appeals (6th cir.) 1981, U.S. Supreme Ct. 1985. Assoc. Jaffee, Jacobs & Tucker, Toledo, 1976—. Coach juvenile soccer Sylvania, Ohio; bd. dirs. Polish Roman Cath. Union Am., 1986. Mem. ABA, Ohio Bar Assn., Lucas County Bar Assn., Toledo Bar Assn. (mcpl. ct. com., pro bono), Assn. Trial Lawyers Am., Toledo Law Assn. Avocation: snowmobiling. Criminal, State civil litigation, Family and matrimonial. Home: 6024 Wakefield Dr Sylvania OH 43560 Office: Jaffee Jacobs & Tucker 924 Spitzer Bldg Toledo OH 43604

TUCKER, WILLIAM E., lawyer, cons.; b. Okla., Sept. 2, 1937; s. Owen and Dixie (Stiles) T.; m. Nancy L. Henkins, Nov. 25, 1956; children—Desiree, Gayle. B.S., S.D. Sch. Mines and Tech., 1956; J.D., Okla. U., 1962. Bar: Okla. 1962, Colo. 1962. With legal dept. J. M. Huber Corp. and Marathon Oil Co., Denver and Tulsa, 1962-65; asst. atty. gen. Colo., 1965-74; ptnr. Tucker & Brown, Denver, 1974-80, Denver and Washington, 1982—; White House counsel, 1980-81; chmn. drafting com. Am. Tort Reform Assn. 1986-87; mem. civil justice model legis. com. Am. Legis. Exchange Council, 1986; chief parliamentarian White House Conf. Small Bus., 1986; mem. internat. observing team to Phillipine elections, 1986; lectr. on civil justice reform. State chmn., nat. gen. counsel Young Republicans; active polit. campaigns; officer, bd. dirs. Edison Found.; bd. dirs. Air Force Acad. Found. Inc.; co-chmn. Am. Tort Reform Assn. Legal Commn., 1987—. Served to 2d lt. C.E., U.S. Army, 1958. Methodist. Clubs: Denver Athletic, Racquet World (Denver); Delphi (Washington); Regency Sport and Health (McLean, Va.). Author articles on govt. Oil and gas leasing, Administrative and regulatory. Office: Western Fed Savs Bldg Suite 1330 718 17th St Denver CO 80202

TUERKHEIMER, BARBARA WOLFSON, lawyer; b. N.Y.C., Dec. 4, 1945; d. Abraham Moshe and Ruth (Kranowitz) Wolfson; m. Frank Mitchel Tuerkheimer, Dec. 14, 1968; children—Deborah Beth, Alan Michael. B.A., Queens Coll., 1966; M.A., Columbia U., 1968; J.D., U. Wis.-Madison, 1977. Bar: Wis. 1977, U.S. Dist. Ct. (we. dist.) Wis. 1977, U.S. Ct. Appeals (7th cir.) 1977. Law clk. Ctr. for Study of Responsive Law, Washington, 1974-75; specialist, legal assistance to inmates project U. Wis. Law Sch., Madison, 1977-78; asst. atty. gen. Wis. Dept. Justice, Madison, 1978—. Mem. Wis. Bar Assn., Order of Coif, Phi Beta Kappa. Democrat. Jewish. Consumer protection, State civil litigation, Administrative and regulatory. Home: 122 Quarterdeck Dr Madison WI 53705 Office: Wis Dept Justice 123 W Washington Ave Madison WI 53702

TUFFLEY, FRANCIS DOUGLAS, lawyer; b. Lewistown, Mont., Feb. 10, 1946; s. Francis Darby and Norma Hermione (Arildson) T.; m. Mary Carolyn Dyar, June 27, 1970; children—Jessica Carolyn, Bradley Dyar. Student U. Wash., 1964-66; B.A. in Polit. Sci., U. Puget Sound, 1968; J.D. magna cum laude, Gonzaga U., 1976. Bar: Wash. 1976, U.S. Dist. Ct. (ea. dist.) Wash. 1976, U.S. Dist. Ct. (we. dist.) Wash. 1979, U.S. Ct. Appeals (9th cir.) 1979. Assoc. Paine, Lowe, Coffin, Herman & O'Kelley, Spokane, Wash., 1976-79; sole practice, Spokane, 1979-83; assoc. Burns & Ricketts, P.S., Seattle, 1983-84; ptnr. Tuffley & Assocs., P.S., Seattle, 1984—; counsel Vis. Nurses Assn., Spokane, 1979-81, Wash. State Psychol. Assn., 1985—. Mem. procurement com. Wampum, Spokane, 1979-81; mem. steering com. McDermott for Gov., Spokane, 1980, steering com. Donahue for Judge, 1982; co-chmn. Wasson for Judge Com., Spokane, 1981; active YMCA Indian Guides, 1984-87. Served to capt. USAF, 1968-73. Mem. ABA, Wash. State Bar Assn. (state tel-law task force 1978, lawyer referral com. 1978-83, legis. com. 1986—), Spokane County Bar Assn. (chmn. tel-law project 1977-80, trustee 1979-83, Ann. award of Merit 1981), Spokane Young Lawyer's Assn. (pres. 1979-81, trustee 1978-81), King County Bar Assn. (judiciary and courts com. 1985—), Wash. State Trial Lawyers Assn. (legis. steering com. 1985—, vice chmn. conv. com. 1986—), Assn. Trial Lawyers Am. Democrat. Methodist. Club: Bainbridge Island Sportsman's (Wash.); Wash. Athletic. Lodge: Elks. State civil litigation, Personal injury, Insurance. Home: 6550 NE Dapple Ct Bainbridge Island WA 98110 Office: Tuffley & Assocs PS 2501 First Interstate Ctr 999 Third Ave Seattle WA 98104

TULKOFF, MYER SIMON, lawyer; b. Ashland, Ky., Oct. 24, 1927; s. Robert and Sophie (Dubrow) T.; m. Esther J., Mar. 7, 1954; children—Donna Tulkoff Schwechter, Jonathan Mark. A.A., Ashland Jr. Coll., 1949; J.D., U. Ky., 1952. Bar: Ky. 1952, N.Y. 1957, U.S. Supreme Ct., 1961. Atty. FTC, N.Y. Regional Office, 1959-68, asst. regional dir., 1968-78; atty. (antitrust and privacy law) AT&T Communications, Inc., Basking Ridge, N.J., 1978—. Mem. Congressman Benjamin Gilman's Tech. Adv. Com., 1982. Served with AUS, 1946-48, 52-53, col. Res. ret. Recipient FTC Cert. of Commendation, 1966; decorated Meritorious Service medal. Mem. N.Y. State Bar Assn., (antitrust and corp. counsel sects., com. on antitrust legislation, chmn. subcom. on damages, mem. com. Robinson-Patman), ABA (mem. Sherman antitrust com.), Ky. Bar Assn., Res. Officers Assn., Jewish War Vets (Rockland County, N.Y.). Order of Coif. Republican. Jewish (bd. govs. Community Synagogue of Monsey, N.Y.). Club: The Kentuckians (N.Y.). Contbr. articles on antitrust law to profl. jours., chpt. to book. Antitrust, Administrative and regulatory. Home: 118 W Maple Ave Monsey NY 10952 Office: 295 N Maple Ave Berkeley Heights NJ 07920

TULLY, BRIAN BRENDAN, lawyer; b. Bklyn., Aug. 10, 1954; s. Edwin Raymond and Mary Teresa (McGready) T. Student, St. John's U., 1975; BA in Polit. Sci., U. N.Mex., 1976; JD, U. Tulsa, 1980. Bar: Okla. 1982, U.S. Dist. Ct. (no. dist.) Okla. 1982, U.S. Dist. Ct. (ea. dist.) Okla. 1984, U.S. Dist. Ct. (we. dist.) Okla. 1985, U.S. Ct. Appeals (10th cir.) 1985. Asst. dir. New Day Pre-Trial, Tulsa, 1979-81; contracts landman Cities Service Oil and Gas Corp., Tulsa, 1981—; sole practice Tulsa, 1982—; instr. oil and gas contracts Tulsa Jr. Coll., 1983—; prosecutor City of Coweta, Okla., 1983—; mcpl. judge Porter, Okla., 1986—. Named one of Outstanding Young Men in Am. U.S. Jaycees, 1984, 86. Mem. ABA, Okla. Bar Assn, Tulsa County Bar Assn. (vice chmn. mineral law sect. 1986—, sec. mineral law sect. 1985-86, budget officer mineral law sect. 1984-85), Wagoner County Bar Assn., Am. Assn. Petroleum Landmen, Tulsa Assn. Petroleum Landmen, U.S. Powersquadron. Democrat. Roman Catholic. Oil and gas leasing, Criminal, Local government. Home: 1712-C E 22d Pl Tulsa OK 74114 Office: Cities Service Oil and Gas Corp 110 W 7th St Tulsa OK 74102

TULLY, RICHARD T. C., lawyer, petroleum landman; b. Alliance, Nebr., Apr. 9, 1949; s. Thomas Bernard and Anna (Tully) Coupens; m. Deborah Elaine Williams, May 26, 1974 (div. 1977); m. Cecilia R. Buchanan, Feb. 16, 1980; children—Tanya Elizabeth, Rikki Allison, Anna Marie. B.A., N.Mex. State U., 1971; J.D., U. N.Mex., 1974. Bar: N.Mex. 1975, U.S. Dist. Ct. N.Mex. 1977, U.S. Ct. Appeals (10th cir.) 1978, U.S. Supreme Ct. 1982. Assoc. firm Darden, Sage & Darden, Las Cruces, N.M., 1974; landman El Paso Natural Gas Co., El Paso, 1974-76; gen. counsel, landman Dugan Prodn. Corp., Farmington, N.M., 1976-79; v.p. James B. Cooney, P.A., Farmington, N.Mex., 1979-81; sole practice, Farmington, 1981—; dir. Aztec Energy Corp., 1982; v.p., dir. Southwest Mud & Chem. Co., Farmington, 1982—. Mem. steering com. New Mexicans for Jobs & Energy, 1979-81; treas. Morgan for Senate Com., 1984; Morgan for Gov. com., 1986. Mem. ABA, Assn. Trial Lawyers Am., Am. Assn. Petroleum Landmen, Am. Petroleum Inst., Ind. Producers Assn., N.Mex. C. of C., Desk & Derrick (adv., bd. dirs. 1977-79), Delta Theta Phi. Republican. Presbyterian. Clubs: San Juan Country, N.Mex. Amigos. Lodge: Elks. Oil and gas leasing, FERC practice, Estate planning. Home: 935 E Navajo Farmington NM 87401 Office: 3001 Northridge Dr Farmington NM 87401

TULLY, ROBERT GERARD, lawyer; b. Dubuque, Iowa, Sept. 7, 1955; s. Thomas Alois and Marjorie May (Fosselman) T. BA, U. Notre Dame, 1977; postgrad., U. Notre Dame, London, summer 1979; JD, Drake U., 1981. Bar: Iowa 1981, U.S. Dist. Ct (no. and so. dists.) Iowa 1981, U.S. Ct. Appeals (8th cir.) 1981, U.S. Supreme Ct. 1986. Assoc. Verne Lawyer & Assocs., Des Moines, 1981—; bd. dirs. Dubuque Lumber Co., sec., treas. 1984—; lectr. Nat. Collegiate Mock Trial Drake U., Des Moines, 1984—. Contbr. articles to profl. jours. Mem. various coms. Dubuque County Dem. Party, 1976-78, Polk County Dem. Party, 1982-83, bd. counselors Drake Law Sch., 1986—; bd. dirs. Nat. Council on Alcoholism and Other Drug Dependencies for Des Moines Area (pres. 1985—). Mem. ABA, Assn. Trial Lawyers Am., Am. Judicature Soc., Lawyers Alliance for Nuclear Arms Control (treas. Iowa chpt. 1985—), Nat. Assn. Student Bar Assns. (v.p. 1980-81), Iowa Bar Assn. (young lawyers sect., com. legal services for elderly, chmn. fed. practice com.), Assn. Trial Lawyers Iowa (bd. govs. 1985—, Outstanding Key Person 1983-84, chmn. key person com. 1985-86), Iowa Acad. Trial Lawyers (compiler various prof. publs.), Polk County Bar Assn., Notre Dame Club of Des Moines (pres. 1981-83), Drake Student Bar Assn. (pres. 1980-81), Phi Alpha Delta. Roman Catholic. Club: Bohemian (Des Moines). Personal injury, State civil litigation, Federal civil litigation. Home: 4222 Grand Ave Des Moines IA 50312 Office: Verne Lawyer & Assocs 427 Fleming Bldg Des Moines IA 50309

TUMOLA, THOMAS JOSEPH, lawyer; b. Newtown Square, Pa., Jan. 18, 1941; s. Joseph Thomas and Vera P. Tumola; m. Sarabelle Hare, Aug. 19, 1972; children—Thomas Joseph, Jr., Cristabell Hill. B.S. in Econs., Villanova U., 1962, J.D., 1966; postgrad Temple U., 1970-72. Bar: Pa. 1967, U.S. Ct. Apls. (3d cir.) 1967, U.S. Dist. Ct. (ea. dist.) Pa. 1968, U.S. Tax Ct. 1971. Law clk. U.S. Ct. Apls. 3d cir., Phila., 1966-68; assoc. Clark, Ladner, Fortenbaugh & Young, Phila., 1968-73, ptnr., 1974—; mem. adv. task force on revision of Pa. Navigation Commn. Law, 1978. Mem. ABA, Pa. Bar Assn., Phila. Bar Assn., Gamma Phi. Clubs: Union League, Villanova (Phila.). Contbr. articles to legal jours. Corporate taxation, State and local taxation, General corporate. Home: 807 Bowman Ave Wynnewood PA 19106 Office: 1818 Market St 32d Floor Philadelphia PA 19103

TUMPSON, ALBERT JOSEPH, lawyer; b. Huntington, W.Va., Apr. 25, 1953; s. Sidney Lewis and Helen Jean (Bachrach) T. BJ, U. Calif., Berkeley, 1974; JD, U. Calif., San Francisco, 1977. Bar: Tenn. 1977, U.S. Dist. Ct. (ea. dist.) Tenn. 1978, U.S. Ct. Appeals (5th and 11th cirs.) 1981, Fla. 1984, Calif. 1986, U.S. Dist. Ct. (no. dist.) Calif. 1986, U.S. Ct. Appeals (9th cir.) 1986. Assoc. Meares & Meares, Maryville, Tenn., 1977-80; from staff atty. to regional counsel Fed. Deposit Ins. Corp., Washington and San Francisco, 1980—. Mem. ABA. Federal civil litigation, Consumer commercial, Banking. Office: Fed Deposit Ins Corp 25 Ecker St Suite 1400 San Francisco CA 94105

TUNE, JAMES FULCHER, lawyer; b. Danville, Va., May 13, 1942; s. William Orrin and Susan Agnes (Fulcher) T.; m. Katherine Del Mickey, Aug. 2, 1969; children: Katherine Winslow, Jeffrey Bricker. BA, U. Va., 1964; MA, Stanford U., 1970, JD, 1974. Bar: Wash. 1974, U.S. Dist. Ct. (we. dist.) Wash. 1974. Assoc. Bogle & Gates, Seattle, 1974-79, ptnr., 1980—, head comml./banking dept., 1985—, mng. ptnr., 1986—; chmn. bd. dirs. ASC Pacific Inc., Federal Way, Wash., BIEC Internat. Inc., Bethlemem, Pa. Bd. dirs. Found. for Group Health, Seattle, 1985—; bd, dirs. New Horizons Ministries, Seattle, 1984-85. Served to lt. USN, 1964-69, Vietnam. Woodrow Wilson fellow, 1964, Danforth Found. fellow, 1964. Mem. ABA, Wash. State Bar Assn. (lectr. continuing legal edn. 1976, 78, 84), Seattle-King County Bar Assn., Seattle C. of C. (vice chmn. City Budget Task Force 1980-82), Phi Beta Kappa. Presbyterian. Clubs: Ranier, Wash. Athletic, Seattle Tennis, Columbia Tower (Seattle). Lodge: Rotary (officer youth exchange Park-Hill club 1985—). Banking, Contracts commercial, General corporate. Office: Bogle & Gates 900 4th Ave Seattle WA 98164

TUNGATE, JAMES LESTER, lawyer; b. Columbus, Ohio, Sept. 27, 1947; s. Ernest O. Jr. and Diantha (Woltz) T.; m. Susan Sumner, Aug. 25, 1973; children: Edward Ernest, James Aaron. B.S., Ill. Wesleyan U., 1969; M.A., Northwestern U.-Ill., 1970, Ph.D., 1972; J.D., U. Ill.-Urbana, 1979; hon. D.H.L., London Sch. (Eng.), 1972. Bar: Ill. 1979, U.S. Supreme Ct. 1985. Spl. instr. Northwestern U., Evanston, Ill., 1971; prof., chmn. Loyola U., New Orleans, 1971-76; state dir. News Election Service, New Orleans, 1972-74; dir. Inst. Religious Communications, New Orleans, 1974-76; asst. to state's atty. Iroquois County, Watseka, Ill., 1978; ptnr. Tungate & Tungate, Watseka, 1979—; media cons. Inst. Politics, New Orleans, 1973-76; legal cons., lectr. Iroquois Mental Health Ctr., Watseka, 1980—; lectr. law Kankakee Community Coll., Ill., 1982. Author: Romantic Images in Popular Songs, 1972; Readings in Broadcast Law, 1975. Dir. Iroquois Mental Health Ctr., 1980—; chmn. Iroquois County chpt. ARC, 1982-84, 85—; dir. Iroquois Republican Council, 1983—. Recipient Internat. Radio and TV Found. award; Harnow scholar U. Ill., 1976. Mem. Ill. Bar Assn., Iroquois County Bar Assn. (Law Day chmn.), Chgo. Bar Assn., Assn. Trial Lawyers Am., Am. Film Inst., Pi Alpha Delta. Republican. Methodist. Lodges: Masons (master 1982-83), Elks. Banking, General practice, Probate. Home: PO Box 285 Milford IL 60953 Office: Tungate & Tungate 744 E Walnut St Watseka IL 60970

TUNGATE, SUSAN SUMNER, lawyer; b. Watseka, Ill., July 25, 1947; d. Edward Culver and Theresa Eagle Sumner; m. James L. Tungate, Aug. 25, 1973; children: Edward Earnest, James Aaron B.S., B.A., Ill. Wesleyan U., 1970; postgrad. John Marshall Law Sch., Chgo., 1970-73; J.D., Loyola Sch. Law, New Orleans, 1975. Bar: Ill. 1976, La. 1986, U.S. Supreme Ct. 1981. Asst. pub. defender Iroquois County, Ill., 1978-82; sole practice, Watseka, Ill., 1976-79; ptnr. Tungate & Tungate, Watseka, 1979—. Republican candidate States Atty., Iroquois County, Ill., 1984. Mem. Iroquois County Bar Assn. (v.p. 1981-82), Ill. Bar Assn., Chgo. Bar Assn., Women's Bar Assn., Bus. and Profl. Women (pres. 1983), Ill. Assn. Trial Lawyers, ABA, Ill. Pub. Defender Assn., La. Bar Assn., Women's Law Club, DAR, Phi Alpha Delta, Phi Kappa Delta. Episcopalian. Club: Home Extension Assn. (pres. 1983). Family and matrimonial, Personal injury, Probate. Home: PO Box 285 Milford IL 60953 Office: Tungate & Tungate PO Box 337 744 E Walnut Watseka IL 60970

TUPITZA, THOMAS ANTON, lawyer; b. Erie, Pa., Nov. 7, 1957; s. John and Geraldine Elizabeth (Girard) T.; m. Carol Jean Laird, Sept. 13, 1986. BA, Westminster Coll., 1979; JD, Harvard U., 1982. Bar: Pa. 1982, U.S. Dist. Ct. (we. dist.) Pa. 1982, U.S. Ct. Appeals (3d cir.) 1984. Assoc. Knox, Graham, McLaughlin, Gornall & Sennett, Inc., Erie, 1982—. Dir. Erie Summer Festival of Arts, 1983—; bd. dirs. Am. Baptist Chs. Pa. and Del., 1984—; mem. planning and allocations div. United Way of Erie County, 1984—. Mem. ABA, Nat. Health Lawyers Assn., Pa. Bar Assn., Erie County Bar Assn. Banking, Health, Municipal bonds. Office: Knox Graham et al 120 W Tenth St Erie PA 16501

TURBIN, RICHARD, lawyer; b. N.Y.C., Dec. 25, 1944; s. William and Ruth (Fiedler) T.; m. Rai Saint Chu-Turbin, June 12, 1976; children—Laurel Mei, Derek Andrew. B.A. magna cum laude, Cornell U., 1966; J.D., Harvard U., 1969. Bar: Hawaii 1971, U.S. Dist. Ct. Hawaii 1971. Asst. atty. gen. Western Samoa, Apia, 1969-70; dep. pub. defender Pub. Defender's Office, Honolulu, 1970-74; dir. Legal Aid Soc. Hawaii, Kaneohe, 1974-75; sr. atty., pres. Law Offices Richard Turbin, Honolulu, 1975—; legal counsel Hawaii Crime Commn., 1980-81. Editor Harvard Civil Rights-Civil Liberties Law Rev., 1969. Legal counsel Democratic Party, Honolulu County, 1981-82, precinct pres. Dist. 8, 1982-84; elected Neighborhood Bd., 1985; bd. dirs. Hawaii chpt. ACLU, 1974-78. East-West Ctr. grantee, 1971, 72. Mem. Hawaii Bar Assn., ABA (vice chairperson com. on internat. ins. law 1985), Am. Trial Lawyers Assn., Hawaii Jaycees (legal counsel 1981-82), Chinese Jaycees Honolulu (legal counsel 1980-81), Honolulu Tennis League (undefeated player 1983). Jewish. Club: Hawaii Harlequin Rugby (sec., legal counsel 1978-82), Pacific. Lodge: Elks. Personal injury, State civil litigation, Workers' compensation. Home: 4557 Kolohala St Honolulu HI 96816 Office: 165 S King St Suite 1101 Honolulu HI 96813

TURCOTTE, JOHN ARTHUR, JR., lawyer; b. Lowell, Mass., Mar. 27, 1950; s. John A. and Dorothy J. (Gillette) T.; m. Mary Catherine Willett, Nov. 12, 1976; 1 dau., Sarah Hamilton. B.S., Boston Coll., 1972; J.D., St. Louis U., 1976. Bar: Mo. 1977, U.S. Dist. Ct. (ea. dist.) Mo. 1979; U.S. Ct. Appeals (8th cir.) 1981. Law clk. to presiding justice Mo. Ct. Appeals (ea. dist.), St. Louis, 1976-78; assoc. Lashly, Caruthers, Baer & Hamel, St. Louis, 1978-81, ptnr., 1981-83; atty. Diekemper, Hammond & Shinners & Turcotte, St. Louis, 1983—. Mem. Assn. Trial Lawyers Am., ABA, Mo. Assn. Trial Attys., Bar Assn. Met. St. Louis (chmn. com. on cts., Merit award 1983). Democrat. Roman Catholic. Personal injury, Federal civil litigation, Family and matrimonial. Home: 139 Wildwood Kirkwood MO 63122 Office: Diekemper Hammond Shinners & Turcotte 7730 Carondelet Suite 222 Clayton MO 63105

TUREEN, THOMAS NORTON, lawyer; b. St. Louis, Dec. 15, 1943; s. Bernard Henry and Rose Lorraine (Dansker) T.; m. Susan Albright, June 15, 1968; children: Phoebe Albright, Rufus Louis. BA, Princeton U., 1966; JD, Goerge Washington U., 1969. Bar: Maine 1969, D.C. 1971, U.S. Dist. Ct. D.C. 1974, U.S. Dist. Ct. (we. dist.) N.Y. 1975, U.S. Ct. Appeals (1st cir.) 1975, U.S. Ct. Appeals (fed. cir.0 1976, U.S. Supreme Ct. 1980. Directing atty., Indian legal services unit Pine Tree Legal Assistance Inc., Calais, Maine, 1969-72; of counsel Native Americans Rights Fund, Calais, 1972-80; ptnr. Tureen & Margolin, Portland, Maine, 1981—; chmn. Tribal Assets Mgmt., Portland, 1983—. Trustee Susan Curtis Found., Portland, 1983. Club: Cumberland (Portland). Indian affairs law, Indian financial transaction. Home: Old Mill Box 216 Limerick ME 04048 Office: Tureen & Margolin 178 Middle St Portland ME 04101

TUREK, KENNETH CASPER, lawyer; b. Kenmore, N.Y., Sept. 16, 1955; s. Walter John and Ceilia Ann (Gryzwa) T.; m. Susan Von Bundschuh, July 25, 1981. BA cum laude, SUNY, Buffalo, 1977, JD with distinction, 1980. Bar: Calif. 1981, U.S. Dist. Ct. (so. dist.) Calif. 1981. Trial atty. Jennings, Engstrand & Henrikson, APLC, San Diego, 1981—. fund raiser Multiple Sclerosis Soc., San Diego, 1985. N.Y. State Regents scholar, 1973; recipient Schmieding Scholarship award Walter Schmieding Trust, 1977, Robert J. Connelly award SUNY Sch. Law and Erie County Trial Lawyers Assn., 1977. Mem. San Diego County Bar Assn. (chmn. eminent domain sect. 1986), Assn. Trial Lawyers Am., Calif. Trial Lawyers Assn., San Diego Trial Lawyers Assn., Barrister's Club (bd. dirs. 1985—). Roman Catholic. Stand-up comedian various clubs Calif. State civil litigation, Real property, Personal injury. Home: 12434 Oakfort Pl San Diego CA 92131 Office: Jennings Engstrand & Henrikson 2255 Camino del Rio S San Diego CA 92108

TURK, DAVID L., lawyer; b. Cleve., Nov. 20, 1945; s. Harold and Freida (Clay) T.; children: Jessica Holly, Tracy Beth. BA, U. Ariz., 1968; JD, UCLA, 1971. Bar: Hawaii 1972, U.S. Dist. Ct. Hawaii 1972, U.S. Ct. Appeals (9th cir.) 1980, U.S. Supreme Ct. 1980. Assoc. Law Offices of David Schutter, Honolulu, 1971-74; ptnr. Turk & Kuniyuki, Honolulu, 1974-77; sole practice Honolulu, 1978-85; ptnr., pres. Turk & Agena, Honolulu, 1985—; adj. prof. sch. law U. Hawaii, Honolulu, 1978. Mem. Assn. Trial Lawyers Am., Japan-Hawaii Bar Assn., Hawaii Bar Assn., Calif. Trial Lawyers Assn., Lawyer-Pilots Bar Assn. Avocation: aviation. Personal injury, Insurance, Aviation litigation. Office: Turk & Agena LC 220 S King St 2222 Central Pacific Plaza Honolulu HI 96813

TURK, JAMES CLINTON, chief judge; b. Roanoke, Va., May 3, 1923; s. James Alexander and Geneva (Richardson) T.; m. Barbara Duncan, Aug. 21, 1954; children—Ramona Leah, James Clinton, Robert Malcolm Duncan, Mary Elizabeth, David Michael. A.B., Roanoke Coll., 1949; L.L.B., Washington and Lee U., 1952. Bar: Va. bar 1952. Mem. firm Dalton, Poff & Turk, Radford, Va., from 1959; chief judge U.S. Dist. Ct., Western Dist. Va.; dir. 1st & Mchts. Nat. Bank of Radford. Mem. Va. Senate, from 1959, minority leader.; Trustee Radford Community Hosp., 1959—. Served with AUS, 1943-46. Mem. Order of Coif, Phi Beta Kappa, Omicron Delta Kappa. Baptist (deacon). Home: 1002 Walker Dr Radford VA 24141 Office: US Courthouse PO Box 2796 Roanoke VA 24001

TURK, S. MAYNARD, lawyer, business executive; b. Roanoke County, Va., Oct. 14, 1925; s. James Alexander and Geneva (Richardson) T.; m. Patricia A. Tucker, June 1, 1957; children—Heather F., William A., Thomas M.T. B.A. in Econs., Roanoke Coll., 1949; LL.B., Washington and Lee U., 1952. Bar: Va. 1951, Del. 1961, U.S. Patent and Trademark Office 1975. With Hercules Inc., 1954—; sr. counsel Hercules Inc., Wilmington, Del., 1966-70, sr. patent counsel, 1972, dir. patent dept., 1972-76, gen. counsel, 1976—, sec., 1980-82, v.p., 1982—. Bd. overseers Del. Law Sch., Widener U., 1977—. Mem. Assn. Gen. Counsel, ABA, Phila. Patent Law Assn., Mfg. Chemists Assn. (legal adv. com.), Mid-Atlantic Legal Found. (bd. dirs.), Southwestern Legal Found. (adv. bd.), Licensing Execs. Soc., N.A.M., Assn. Corp. Patent Counsel (emeritus), Nat. Security Indsl. Assn. (bd. bar examiners Del. chpt.). General corporate. Home: PO Box 3958 Heather Dr Greenville DE 19807 Office: Law Dept Hercules Inc Hercules Plaza Wilmington DE 19894

TURLEY, J. WILLIAM, lawyer; b. Van Nuys, Calif., Jan. 11, 1948; s. Billy Brown and Kathryn Ann (Kuniak) T.; children: Timothy Jay, Damon Andrew. BA, U. Mo., 1970, JD, 1974. Bar: Mo. 1974, U.S. Dist. Ct. (we. dist.) Mo. 1974, U.S. Dist. Ct. (ea. dist.) Mo. 1974. Stockholder Wesner, Turley & Kempton, Inc., Sedalia, Mo., 1975-84; ptnr. Carnahan, Carnahan & Turley, Rolla, Mo., 1984-87, Robinson, Turley, Turley & White, 1987—; atty. City of Sedalia, 1976; pros. atty. Pettis County, Sedalia, 1976; Author: Trial Handbook for Missouri Lawyers, 1984; contbr. articles to profl. jours. Chmn. Sedalia Dem. Com., 1982. Mem. Mo. Bar Assn. (bd. govs. 1986—), Assn. Trial Lawyers Am. (bd. govs. 1985—), Mo. Assn. Trial Attys. (dir. legis. activity 1982—, pres. 1985), Jaycees, Scribes. Democrat. Roman Catholic. Lodge: Optimists. Personal injury, State civil litigation, Federal civil litigation. Home: PO Box 206 Newburg MO 65555 Office: Robinson Turley Turley & White PO Box 47 Rolla MO 65401

TURLEY, ROBERT JOE, lawyer; b. Mt. Sterling, Ky., Dec. 6, 1926; s. R. Joe and Mavis Clare (Sternberg) T.; m. Mary Lynn Sanders, Dec. 17, 1948 (div.); children—Leighton Turley Isaacs, Lynn Turley McComas, R. Joe, Mavis Lee. Student Berea Coll., 1944-45, St. Mary's Coll. (Calif.), 1945-46;

LL.B., U. Ky., 1949. Bar: Ky. 1949, U.S. Dist. Ct. (ea. dist.) Ky. 1950, U.S. Ct. Appeals (6th cir.) 1958, U.S. Supreme Ct. 1959. Ptnr. Mooney & Turley and successor firms, Lexington, Ky., 1949-84, Turley & Moore, Lexington, 1984—; chmn. Fed. Jud. Selection Commn. Ky., 1985—; gen counsel Shriners Hosps. for Crippled Children, 1976-77, trustee, 1981—. Served with USNR, 1944-46. Diplomate Nat. Bd. Trial Advocacy, 1980. Fellow Am. Coll. Trial Lawyers; mem. Ky. Bar Assn., ABA, Assn. Trial Lawyers Am. Republican. Baptist. Clubs: Lafayette, St. Ives Journal. Lodges: Masons, Shriners. Contbr. articles to legal jours. Federal civil litigation, State civil litigation, Personal injury. Home: 643 W Short St Lexington KY 40508 Office: Turley & Moore 134 N Limestone St Lexington KY 40507

TURLEY, WINDLE, trial lawyer; b. Cheyenne, Okla., Jan. 25, 1939; s. O.C. and Virginia Lee (Taylor) T.; m. Shirley Ann Lacey, Dec. 8, 1957; children: Linda, Ronald. B.A., Oklahoma City U., 1962; J.D., So. Meth. U., 1965. Bar: Tex. 1965, U.S. Dist. Ct. (no., so., ea. and we. dists.) Tex. 1965, U.S. Dist. Ct. (so. dist.) Fla., U.S. Ct. Appeals (5th cir.) 1972, U.S. Ct. Appeals (7th and 8th cir.) 1974, U.S. Ct. Appeals (10th and 11th cirs.) 1981, U.S. Supreme Ct. 1972. Since practiced in Dalla; with firms Fritz, Vinson & Turley, 1965-68, McKool, Jones, Shoemaker, Turley & Vassallo, 1968-73; pres., chmn. bd. Windle Turley (P.C.), 1973—; lectr. in field. Author: Aviation Litigation, 1986; Contbr. articles on trial of product defect and aviation crash litigation to profl. jours. Mem. Dallas, Am. bar assns., State Bar Tex., Assn. Trial Lawyers Am., Dallas Trial Lawyers Assn. (pres. 1972-73), Tex. Trial Lawyers Assn. (dir.), Lawyers-Pilots Bar Assn. Personal injury, Federal civil litigation, State civil litigation. Office: 6440 N Central Expy 1000 University Tower Dallas TX 75206

TURNAGE, FRED DOUGLAS, lawyer; b. Ayden, N.C., Sept. 24, 1920; s. Fred C. and Lou (Johnson) T.; m. Margaret Futrell, Aug. 21, 1943 (div. Nov. 1980); children: Betty Lou Griffith, Douglas C.; m. Elizabeth Louisa Turnage, Jan. 23, 1981. Grad. Naval Sch. on Far Eastern Civil Affairs, Princeton U., 1945; LLB, Wake Forest U., 1948, LLD, 1970. Bar: N.C. 1948, U.S. Supreme Ct. 1953, U.S. Dist. Ct. D.C. 1965, U.S. Ct. Appeals (D.C. cir.) 1967, U.S. Ct. Appeals (4th and 7th cirs.) 1979. Trial atty. antitrust div. U.S. Dept. Justice, Kansas City, Mo., 1948-51; sr. trial atty. antitrust div. U.S. Dept. Justice, Washington, 1951-65, spl. asst. to atty. gen., 1965; sr. ptnr. Cleary, Gottlieb, Steen & Hamilton, Washington, 1968—; lectr. continuing legal edn. courses, 1973-77. Contbr. articles to profl. jours. Bd. Visitors Wake Forest U. Sch. Law, Winston-Salem, N.C., 1980—. Served to 1st lt. AUS, 1942-46. Recipient Disting. Service in Law citation Wake Forest U., 1979. Mem. ABA (antitrust and litigation sects.), Fed. Bar Assn., Adv. Bd. Antitrust Bulletin, Wake Forest U. Alumni Assn. (pres. 1977), Nat. Lawyers Clubs. Methodist. Avocations: fishing, golf, writing. Antitrust, Federal civil litigation, Criminal. Home: 209 N Liberty St Arlington VA 22203 Office: Cleary Gottlieb Steen & Hamilton 1752 N St NW Washington DC 20036

TURNAGE, JEAN A., state supreme court chief justice; b. St. Ignatius, Mont., Mar. 10, 1926. LL.B., Mont. State U., 1951. Bar: Mont. 1951, U.S. Dist. Ct. Mont. 1963. Formerly ptnr. Turnage & McNeil, Polson, Mont.; formerly Mont. State senator from 13th Dist.; pres. Mont. State Senate, 1981-85; chief justice Supreme Ct. Mont., 1986—. Mem. Mont. State Bar Assn., ABA. Judicial administration. Office: Mont Supreme Ct Justice Bldg Helena MT 59620

TURNBOW, WILLIAM RANDOLPH, lawyer; b. Eugene, Oreg., July 7, 1952; s. William E. and Joan (Dillon) T.; m. Martha L. Rice, Aug. 23, 1980; 1 child, Elizabeth Grace. BA in Urban Studies, Stanford U., 1974; JD, U. Oreg., 1980. Fireman, emergency med. technician City of Eugene Fire Dept., 1975-80; from assoc. to ptnr. Hershner, Hunter, Moulton, Andrews & Neill, Eugene, 1980—. Mem. ABA (litigation sect.), Oreg. Bar Assn., Lane County Bar Assn., Order of Coif. Democrat. Club: Downtown Athletic (Eugene). Avocations: mountaineering, skiing, kayaking, hiking, woodworking. Federal civil litigation, State civil litigation, Banking. Home: 2610 Highland Oaks Dr Eugene OR 97405 Office: Hershner Hunter Moulton Andrews & Neill 180 E 11th Ave Eugene OR 97401

TURNER, ANDREW ROLAND, lawyer; b. Tulsa, Feb. 4, 1956; s. Samuel Roland and Ethel Mae (Winborn) T.; m. Paula Elizabeth Pyron, May 20, 1978; children: Lauren Elizabeth, Sarah Ellen. BA with highest honors, U. Okla., 1978; JD, So. Meth. U., 1981. Bar: Okla. 1981, U.S. Dist. Ct. (no. dist.) Okla. 1981, U.S. Ct. Appeals (10th cir.) 1981, U.S. Dist. Ct. (we. and ea. dists.) Okla. 1982. Assoc. Conner & Winters, Tulsa, 1981—. Mem. nat. conf. Jr. Achievement, Inc., Bloomington, Ind., 1975—; bd. dirs. Parents Anonymous, Tulsa, 1984—. Mem. ABA, Okla. Bar Assn., Tulsa County Bar Assn. Republican. Mem. Christian Ch. (Disciples of Christ). Avocation: officiating sports. Bankruptcy, Contracts commercial, Oil and gas leasing. Office: Conner & Winters 2400 First Nat Tower Tulsa OK 74103

TURNER, BENNIE L., lawyer; b. West Point, Miss., Aug. 21, 1948; s. Robert and Ether (Hunter) T.; m. Edna Walker, Apr. 29, 1971; children—Angela, Carolyn, Leta. A.S., Mary Holmes Coll., 1968; B.A., Miss. State U., 1971; J.D., U. Miss., 1974. Bar: Miss. 1974, Miss. Supreme Ct. 1974, U.S. Dist. Ct. (no. dist.) Miss. 1974, U.S. Ct. Appeals (5th cir.) 1975. City prosecutor, West Point, Miss., 1977-79; county atty., Clay County, West Point, Miss., 1979—; ptnr. law firm Walker & Turner, West Point, Miss., 1975—; chmn. bd. dirs. North Miss. Rural Legal Service, Inc., Oxford, Miss., 1983—; mem. Miss. Bd. Bar Admissions, 1985—. Mem., Miss. Bar Complaints Com., Jackson, 1980-83. Chmn., Gov.'s Fleeing Felon Com., 1982; mem. Tenn-Tom Waterway Authority, 1980—, treas., 1985; mem. Sen. Stennis' Re-election Com., 1982. Named Outstanding Citizen, Clay County chpt. NAACP, 1983. Fellow Miss. Bar Found., mem. Magnolia Bar Assn., Assn. Trial Lawyers Am. Mem. African Methodist Episcopal Ch. Club: West Point Swim Assn. (pres. 1983-84). Personal injury, Federal civil litigation, Criminal. Home: Route 6 Box 113 West Point MS 39773 Office: Walker & Turner PO Box 312 West Point MS 39773

TURNER, BRUCE EDWARD, lawyer; b. Wichita Falls, Tex., Oct. 31, 1947; s. Charles William and Marie Jeanne (Masson) T.; m. Barbara Lu Oakes, Oct. 8, 1982; 1 child, Gradie. BA, Tex. Tech U., 1970, JD, 1973; LLM, NYU, 1974. Bar: Tex. 1974, U.S. Dist. Ct. (so. dist.) Tex. 1975, U.S. Tax Ct. 1975, U.S. Ct. Appeals (8th cir.) 1979. Assoc. Dillingham, Schleider & Marquelette, Houston, 1974-76, Johnston & Feather, Dallas, 1976-80; tax counsel Atlantic Richfield Co., Dallas, 1980-81; corp. counsel Lehndorff, Dallas, 1981-83; owner Turner & Assocs., Dallas, 1983—. Mem. Tex. Bar Assn., Dallas Bar Assn., ICC Practitioners. Republican. Methodist. Club: Downtown Mens (Dallas). Estate taxation, Real property. Home: 3228 Amherst Dallas TX 75225 Office: Turner & Assocs 15770 N Dallas Pkwy Suite 210 Dallas TX 75219

TURNER, CHARLES CARRE, association executive; b. Clarksburg, W.Va., May 20, 1944; s. Joseph Archer and Mary Donovan T.; m. Deborah Andrews, Jan. 28, 1968; children—Brian Curtis, David Carre, Michael Andrews. B.A., St. Lawrence U., 1966; J.D., U. Denver, 1971. Bar: Colo. 1971. Adminstrv. asst. U. Denver, 1971-72, dir. continuing legal edn., 1972-75, asst. dean, 1975-80; exec. dir. Colo./Denver Bar Assns., 1980—. Editor Ann. Survey of Colo. Law, 1978-84. Committeeman Denver Democratic Party, 1972-80; elder Central Presbyterian Ch., Denver, 1982-85. Served to 1st lt. U.S. Army, 1966-68. Mem. Denver Law Club (treas. 1980-81). Democrat. Clubs: Law, Denver Athletic, Skyline (Denver). Office: 1900 Grant St Suite 950 Denver CO 80203

TURNER, CHARLES HAMILTON, lawyer; b. Chgo., Jan. 14, 1936; s. Frederick William and Francis (Franklin) T.; m. Margot Mackmull, June 20, 1959; children: Cynthia Dale, Charles Scott. B.A., Brown U., 1958; LL.B., DePaul U., 1961. Bar: Ill. 1961, U.S. Dist. Ct. (no. dist.) Ill. 1961, U.S. Ct. Appeals (7th cir.) 1963, Oreg. 1966, U.S. Dist. Ct. Oreg. 1966, U.S. Dist. Ct. (so. dist.) Calif. 1970, U.S. Ct. Appeals (9th cir.) 1968, U.S. Supreme Ct. 1972. Contbr. articles to profl. publs. Active YMCA, Portland; active Jewish Community Ctr. Recipient Meritorious Service U.S. Dept. Justice, 1965; recipient Atty. Gen.'s Spl. Commendation, 1974, award for Outstanding Contbns. in field of Drug Enforcement Drug Enforcement Adminstrn., 1980, U.S. Dept. Justice spl. achievement, 1980. Mem. Ill. State Bar Assn., Oreg. State Bar Assn., Multnomah County Bar Assn., Oreg. Trial Lawyers Assn. Criminal, Federal civil litigation. Office: US Atty US Dept Justice 312 US Courthouse 620 SW Main St Portland OR 97205 *

TURNER, DANIEL CHARLES, lawyer; b. Denver, Oct. 21, 1950; s. Charles H. and Lois M. (Holland) T.; m. Barbara Jill Murphy, June 21, 1980. BA, U. Ariz., 1975, JD, 1979, MA, 1980; LLM, U. Fla., 1983. Bar: Ariz., U.S. Dist. Ct. Ariz. 1980, U.S. Ct. Appeals (9th cir.) 1980, U.S. Tax Ct. 1984, U.S. Supreme Ct. 1985. Lawyer Foley, Clark & Nye, Phoenix, 1979-82, Christoffel, Ross & Zickerman, Tucson, 1982, Waterfall, Economidis, Hanshaw & Villamana, Tucson, 1983—. Editor: Ariz. Law Rev., 1979; contbr. articles to profl. jours. Mem. ABA, Ariz. State Bar (rules of profl. conduct com.), So. Ariz. Estate Planners Council, Pima County Bar Assn. (editor-in-chief chpt. newsletter 1987—), Golden Key Nat. Honor Soc., Phi Kappa Phi, Phi Delta Phi, Alpha Kappa Delta. Corporate taxation, Pension, profit-sharing, and employee benefits, Probate. Office: Waterfall Economidis et al 5210 E Williams Circle 800 Tucson AZ 85711

TURNER, DONALD ALLEN, lawyer; b. Cleve., Aug. 14, 1938; s. Louis O. and Harriet B. (Keizer) T.; m. Amy Glicksberg, Dec. 16, 1962 (div. Oct. 1980); children—Matthew, Kelli; m. Vikki Holley, Sept. 30, 1984. B. Metall. Engring., Ohio State U., 1963; J.D., Detroit Coll. Law, 1967. Bar: Mich. 1967, U.S. Dist. Ct. (ea. dist.) Mich. 1967. Ptnr., Turner & Schaden, Detroit, 1967-69, Nelson, Gracey, Turner, Detroit, 1969-72; pres. Turner & Turner, P.C., Southfield, Mich., 1972—. Served with USNR, 1956-58. Mem. Assn. Trial Lawyers Am., Mich. Trial Lawyers Assn., State Bar Mich., Southfield Bar Assn., Oakland County Bar Assn. Jewish. Personal injury, Civil rights, Federal civil litigation. Home: 2261 Oakway Dr West Bloomfield MI 48033 Office: Turner & Turner PC 24901 Northwestern Hwy #417 Southfield MI 48075

TURNER, H. LEE, lawyer; b. Newton, Kans., July 26, 1927; s. Lester O. and Eva Mabel (Hampton) T.; m. Elizabeth Lura Dillon, Sept. 15, 1951; children: Deborah Turner Carney, Stephanie Turner Fleming, Shelley Turner Schlender, Cynthia Turner Latham, Chase, Fernanda. BA, U. Kans., 1950, JD, 1952. Bar: Kans. 1952, U.S. Dist. Ct. Kans. 1952, U.S. Ct. Appeals (10th cir.) 1952, U.S. Supreme Ct. 1952. Sr. ptnr. Turner & Boisseau C.A., Great Bend, Kans., 1952—. Contbr. numerous articles to profl. jours. Mem. ABA, Kans. Bar Assn., Southwest Bar Assn., Fedn. Ins. Counsel, Am. Law Firm Assn. (sr. mng. ptnr. numerous sects. and coms.). Insurance, State civil litigation, Federal civil litigation. Office: Turner & Boisseau CA 3900 Broadway Great Bend KS 67530

TURNER, JOHN MILLER, lawyer; b. Phoenix, Aug. 19, 1951; s. John Miller and Mary Elizabeth (O'Brien) T.; m. Lisa C. Unamuno, June 4, 1977; 1 child, Laurel L. BA, U. Ariz., 1974; JD, U. San Diego, 1977. Bar: Ariz. 1977, Calif. 1978, U.S. Dist. Ct. (so. dist.) Calif. 1978, U.S. Dist. Ct. (no. and cen.) Calif. 1984, U.S. Dist. Ct. (ea. dist.) Calif. 1986, U.S. Dist. Ct. Ariz. 19886, U.S. Ct. Appeals (9th cir.) 1986. Assoc. Cusick, Watkins, Stewart, Tucson, 1977-78, McDade & Treitler, 1978-80; assoc. Asaro & Keagy, San Diego, 1980-86, ptnr., 1986—. Mem. ABA, San Diego County Bar Assn. (real estate and real estate fin. coms.). Roman Catholic. Real property, Federal civil litigation, General corporate. Office: 3170 4th Ave 4th Floor San Diego CA 92103

TURNER, LESTER NATHAN, lawyer, consultant international trade; b. Colmar, Ky., July 11, 1933; s. Clifford G. and Minnie G. (Ensor) T.; m. Sandra B. Ward, July 3, 1976; children: children: Kimberly L., Michele M., Renee S., Mark L., Jeffrey S., Derek Kyle. BS, Lincoln Meml. U., 1955; JD, U. Mich., 1959. Bar: Mich. 1960, U.S. Dist. Ct. (ea. and we. dist.) Mich., U.S. Ct. Appeals (6th cir.), U.S. Supreme Ct. 1982. Law clk. to presiding justice, research atty. Mich. Supreme Ct., Lansing, 1960-62; ptnr. Sinas, Dramis, Brake & Turner, Lansing, 1960-78; sole practice East Lansing, Mich., 1978—; Mem. drafting com. standard jury instrns., Mich. Supreme Ct., Lansing, 1963-73. Mem. Mich. State Bar Assn., Mich. Trial Lawyers Assn. (bd. dirs. 1963-74, vice pres. 1974). Methodist. State civil litigation, Federal civil litigation, General practice. Home: 1005 Timber Pass Harbor Springs MI 49740 Office: 4970 Northwind Dr Suite 200 East Lansing MI 48823

TURNER, ROBERT FOSTER, lawyer, government official, writer; b. Atlanta, Feb. 14, 1944; s. Edwin Witcher and Martha Frances (Williams) T.; m. Debra Lou Herwig, Apr. 13, 1979. A.B., Ind. U., Bloomington, 1968; postgrad., Stanford U., 1972-73; J.D., U. Va., 1981. Bar: Va. 1982, U.S. Supreme Ct. 1986. Research assoc., pub. affairs fellow Hoover Instn. on War, Revolution and Peace, Stanford U., 1971-74; spl. asst., legis. asst. U.S. Sen. Robert P. Griffin, 1974-79; assoc. dir. Ctr. Law and Nat. Security, U. Va., Charlottesville, 1981, sr. fellow, 1985-86; spl. asst. undersec. for policy Dept. Def., 1981-82; counsel Pres.'s Intelligence Oversight Bd., White House, 1982-84; prin. dep. asst. sec. for legis. and intergovtl. affairs Dept. State, 1984-85; pres. U.S. Inst. Peace, Washington, 1986—. Author: Myths of the Vietnam War: The Pentagon Papers Reconsidered, 1972, Vietnamese Communism: Its Origins and Development, 1975, The War Powers Resolution: Its Implementation in Theory and Practice, 1983, Congress, the Constitution and Foreign Affairs, 1987, Nicaragua vs. United States: A Look at the Facts, 1987; (with John Norton Moore) The Legal Structure of Defense Organization, 1986, International Law and the Brezhnev Doctrine, 1987; contbr. articles to profl. jours. Pres. Endowment of U.S. Inst. of Peace, 1986—; trustee Intercollegiate Studies Inst., 1986—. Served to capt. U.S. Army, 1968-71, Vietnam. Grantee Hoover Press, 1972, Earhart Found., 1980, Inst. Ednl. Affairs, 1980, Carthage Found., 1980. Mem. ABA (chmn. com. on exec.-congl. relations, sect. internat. law and practice 1983-86, adv. com. on law and nat. security 1984-86, standing com. on law and nat. security, 1986—), Mensa, Va. State Bar Assn., Am. Soc. Internat. Law, Nat. Eagle Scout Assn. Public international, Legislative, National security law. Office: US Inst Peace 730 Jackson Pl NW Washington DC 20503

TURNER, TERRANCE NEIL, lawyer; b. Providence, Sept. 26, 1952; s. William Turner and Vivian (Procaccini) Auerbach; m. Deborah Ann Ferrario, June 16, 1985. BA, R.I. Coll., 1977; JD, Suffolk U., 1980. Bar: R.I. 1980, Mass. 1980, U.S. Dist. Ct. R.I. 1980, U.S. Dist. Ct. Mass. 1980, U.S. Ct. Appeals (1st cir.) 1980, U.S. Supreme Ct. 1986. Sole practice Smithfield, R.I., 1980-81, Providence, 1981-82, North Providence, R.I., 1982-83, Cranston, R.I., 1983-86, Providence, 1986—; law instr. Community Coll. R.I., Lincoln, 1981—; counsel Nat. Assn. Govt. Employees Internat. Brotherhood Police Officers, Cranston, 1984-87. Mem. R.I. Bar Assn., Mass. Bar Assn. Democrat. Roman Catholic. Avocations: athletics and sports related activities. Labor, State civil litigation, Federal civil litigation. Home: RR 3 Box 417 Chepachet RI 02814-9424

TURNER, WESLEY DALE, lawyer; b. Springfield, Ill., Aug. 3, 1952; s. Gene Warren and Charlotte Ann (Thigpen) T.; m. Vicki Leigh House, Sept. 16, 1978; children: Rebecca, Sarah, William. Student, U. Tenn., Martin, 1970-72; BA, U. Tenn., Knoxville, 1974; JD, Memphis State U., 1978. Bar: Tenn. 1978, U.S. Dist. Ct. (mid. dist.) Tenn. 1978, U.S. Ct. Appeals (6th cir.) 1978. Assoc. Gullett, Sanford, Robinson & Martin, Nashville, 1978-84, ptnr., 1984—. Mem. ABA, Tenn. Bar Assn., Nashville Bar Assn., Am. Coll. Mortgage Attys., Phi Delta Phi. Baptist. Real property, Contracts commercial, Banking. Office: Gullett Sanford Robinson & Martin 3d Floor 230 4th Ave N Nashville TN 37219

TURNER, WILLIAM HOWARD, lawyer; b. Troy, Ala., Dec. 16, 1940; s. Howard Lee and Gussie Dora (Williams) T.; m. Doris Jean Harris, June 1, 1968; children: Vanardo W., Sidney St. Paul. BBA, Tuskegee U., 1968; JD, So. U., 1978. Bar: Fla. 1982, Ala. 1982. Acct. J.E. Seagram and Sons, Lawrenceburg, Ind., 1968-69; acct. Tuskegee (Ala.) Inst., 1970-72, bus. developer, 1973-75; pilot So. Airways/ Rep. Airlines, Atlanta, 1972-73; legal research asst. Office of Atty. Gen., Montgomery, Ala., 1978-81; ptnr. Turner and Raby, Montgomery, 1982—. Served with U.S. Army, 1959-63. Mem. ABA, Nat. Bar Assn., Ala. State Bar Assn., Fla. State Bar Assn., Aircraft Owners & Pilots Assn. (participating lawyer 1984—). Aviation. Office: Turner and Raby 1311 S Court St Montgomery AL 36104

TURNER, WILLIAMSON BRANCH, lawyer; b. Houston, Aug. 22, 1938. BA, U. N.Mex., 1960; JD, Baylor U., 1965. Bar: N.Mex. 1966, U.S. Dist. Ct. N.Mex. 1968, U.S. Ct. Appeals (10th cir.) 1968, U.S. Ct. Appeals (5th cir.) 1972, U.S. Supreme Ct. 1972. Ptnr. The Branch Law Firm, Alququerque, 1965—; dir. liquor control State of N.Mex., 1966-68; atty. City of Gallup, 1970-72; mem. ho. judiciary com. and ho. corp. and banking com. N.Mex. Ho. of Reps., 1968-74. Sect. editor Baylor U. Law Rev., 1964-65; contbr. articles to jours. Served to 1st lt. USMC, 1960-63. Fellow N.Mex. Bar Found.; mem. ABA, Nat. Inst. Trial Advs., Am. Arbitration Assn. (negligence adv. com.), N.Mex. Bar Assn. (chmn. fee arbitration com. 1982—, legal med. rev. com.), Albuquerque (chmn. other professions com. 1969), N.Mex. Trial Lawyers Assn. (bd. dirs. 1969-73), Tex. Trial Lawyers Assn., Assn. Trial Lawyers Am. (state committeeman 1970-74, sustaining 1978—), Nat. Advance Coll. Trial Advs. (vice chmn. 1984-85 western states, The Best Lawyer in Am.), Am. Soc. Law and Medicine, Am. Judicature Soc., Am. Bd. Trial Advocates (pres. Albuquerque chpt. 1983-84), Pa. and N.Y. Trial Lawyers. Office: 2025 Rio Grande Blvd NW Albuquerque NM 87104

TURNEY, KENNETH WAYNE, lawyer; b. Huntsville, Ala., Apr. 9, 1952; s. William Ottis and Libbie (Legg) T. BS, Samford U., 1973; JD, U. Ala., 1976; LLM in Taxation, Georgetown U., 1986. Bar: Ala. 1976, Hawaii 1977, U.S. Dist. Ct. Hawaii 1978, Md. 1979, U.S. Supreme Ct. 1979. Sec., asst. gen. mgr. Paradise Cruise, Ltd., Honolulu, 1976-77; tax atty. Comml. Credit Co., Balt., 1978—. Vestryman Meml. Episcopal Ch., Balt., 1980-82, warden, 1983-85, cons. 1981-85. Mem. ABA, Md. Bar Assn., Ala. Bar Assn. Corporate taxation, State and local taxation. Home: 834 E Belvedere Ave Baltimore MD 21212 Office: Comml Credit Co 300 St Paul Pl Baltimore MD 21202

TURNIPSEED, SARA SADLER, lawyer; b. N.Y.C., Jan. 31, 1948; d. Rufus E. and Mary (Doherty) S.; m. William E. Turnipseed, Aug. 24, 1974; children: Mary Parker, Nancy Sadler, Kathleen Sadler. BA, Trinity Coll., 1969; JD, U. S.C., 1974. Bar: S.C. 1974, Ga. 1977, U.S. Dist. Ct. (no. dist.) Ga. 1977. Atty region IV U.S. EPA, Atlanta, 1974-81; sr. trial atty. Dickins & Irbin, Atlanta, 1981-84; sr. counsel Ga.-Pacific Corp., Atlanta, 1984—. Bd. dirs. Spina Bifida Assn. of Atlanta, 1980—, Leadership Atlanta, 1985-86. Mem. ABA, Ga. Bar Assn., S.C. Bar Assn., Atlanta Bar Assn., Def. Research Inst. Federal civil litigation, State civil litigation, Environment. Home: 260 Glendale Ave Decatur GA 30030 Office: Ga-Pacific Corp 133 Peachtree St NE Atlanta GA 30348

TUROFF, JACK NEWTON, lawyer, business consultant; b. Cleve., Dec. 8, 1933; s. Herman and Jean Y. (Pearlman) T.; m. Carole R., Aug. 19, 1961; children—Hyleri, Raechel, Elana, Avril. B.S. in Bus. Adminstrn., Ohio State U., 1955, J.D., 1960. Bar: Ohio 1960, U.S. Dist. Ct. (no. dist.) Ohio 1961, U.S. Supreme Ct. 1969. Asst. atty. gen. State of Ohio, 1960-62; sole practice, Cleve., 1960-62; assoc. Dudnik, Komito, Nurenberg, Plevin, Dempsey & Jacobson Assn., Cleve., 1963-64; ptnr. Turoff & Turoff, Cleve., 1965-81, 82—; ptnr. Koplow, Pomerantz, Turoff & Turoff Co., L.P.A., Cleve., 1981-82; cons. and lectr. in field of bus. Bd. dirs., sec. Jewish Children Group Homes, 1962-78; mem. Democratic Exec. Com., 1963-79; state steering rep. Senator Henry Jackson Presdl. campaign, 1980; active Dem. county congl. campaigns; chmn. bd. Neighborhood Counseling Service, 1980—; bd. dirs. West Side Community Mental Health Ctr. 1982—. Served with USAF, 1956-59, USAFR, 1959-70. Recipient Service award Big Bros. Am., 1975, Outstanding Service award Neighborhood Counseling Service, 1983. Mem. Ohio State Bar Assn., Am. Trial Lawyers Assn., Greater Cleve. Bar Assn., Cuyahoga County Bar Assn., Ohio Harness Horsemen's Assn. (bd. dirs. 1983—), Jewish. Lodge: KP. Personal injury, State civil litigation, General practice. Home: 2569 Snowberry Ln Pepper Pike OH 44124 Office: Nat City Bank Bldg 629 Euclid Ave Suite 420 Cleveland OH 44114

TURPEN, MICHAEL CRAIG, state official, lawyer; b. Tulsa, Nov. 10, 1949; s. Wallace Kendall and Marjorie Allyce (Kinkaid) T. BS in History Edn., U. Tulsa, 1972, JD, 1974. Bar: Okla. 1975. Legal advisor Muskogee Police Dept., Okla., 1975-76; asst. dist. atty. City of Muskogee, 1976, dist. atty., 1977-82; atty. gen. State of Okla., 1983-87; assoc. Chapel, Wilkinson, Riggs & Abney P.C., Oklahoma City, 1987—; conf. speaker; mem. Okla. Spl. Legis. Com. on Criminal Justice System, 1978-79; adj. prof. bus. law N.E. Okla. State U.-Tahlequah, 1977; adj. prof. criminal law Connors State Coll., 1977-79. Author: Police-Prosecutor Training Manuel, 1975. Mem. Gov.'s Alternatives to Incarceration Com., 1980-81; bd. dirs. Call Rape, Inc.; vice chmn. Okla. Crime Commn., 1980-81; commr. Okla. State Bur. Investigation, 1978—; bd. dirs., coach Muskogee Green Country Girls Softball Assn.; mem. Muskogee High Sch. Booster Club; mem., coach Muskogee Knothole League Boys Baseball Assn.; mem. Muskogee County Human Soc.; mem. Muskogee County Women's Dem. Club; hon. mem. Okla. Hwy. Patrol, 1980. Recipient Maurice Merrill Golden Quill award Okla. Bar Jour., 1981, Donald Santarelli award Nat. Orgn. Victim Assistance, Toronto, 1981, Mayor's commendation City of Muskogee, 1976, Mayor's commendation City of Owasso, 1975, $10,000 Cash award Found. for Improvement Justice, Inc., Achievement award Found. for Improvement Justice, Inc., 1986; named Outstanding Young Oklahoman, Okla. Jayeees, 1979, Outstanding Young Lawyer, Okla. Bar Assn., 1975, Outstanding Young Man, Muskogee Jaycees, 1979, One of Ten Outstanding Nat. Leaders in field of victim rights, Nat. Orgn. for Victim Assistance, 1986, One of Men and Women Under 40 Who are Changing Nation, Esquire Mag., 1985. Mem. ABA, Okla. Bar Assn., Muskogee County Bar Assn. (past sec.), Okla. Dist. Attys. Assn. (pres. 1980-81, now bd. dirs.), Tulsa U. Alumni Assn. Democrat. Presbyterian. Club: Tulsa U. Hurricane. Lodges: Fraternal Order of Police, Muskogee Rotary. Criminal. Office: Chapel Wilkinson Riggs & Abney 5801 N Broadway Suite 502 Oklahoma City OK 73118

TURRELL, JAMES JOEL, lawyer, consultant; b. Wilkes-Barre, Pa., Mar. 29, 1943; s. James Henry and Elizabeth Allen (Walter) T.; m. Susan Carter Williams, Oct. 5, 1968; children—James Fielding, Susan Carter. A.B., U. Pa., 1965, LL.B., 1968. Bar: Pa. 1968. Sole practice, Tunkhannock, Pa., 1969-75; ptnr. and mng. ptnr. Farr Davis Turrell & Fitze, Tunkhannock, 1976—; solicitor Tunkhannock Area Sch. Dist., 1970-80, Sullivan County (Pa.), 1972-76, Eaton, Falls, Lemon, Mehoopany twps., 1972—; assoc. dir. Wyo. Nat. Bank, 1973—; solicitor Grange Nat. Bank, 1980—, No. Tier Regional Planning and Devel. Commn., 1982—; asst. dist. atty. Wyoming County, 1976-78. Bd. dirs. Wyoming County (Pa.) United Fund, 1969-81, Wyoming County Cancer Soc., 1969-75; treas. Wyoming County Mental Health Assn., 1972-75; sec. Wyoming County Indsl. Found., 1982—. Mem. Wyoming County Bar Assn. (pres. 1983—), Pa. Bar Assn. (ho. of dels. 1980—), ABA. Episcopalian. General corporate, Local government, Banking. Address: 119 Warren St Tunkhannock PA 18657

TURRENTINE, JAMES DRAKE, lawyer; b. Louisville, Nov. 27, 1942; s. James Lewis and Elizabeth (McNerney) T.; m. JoAnn Butrico, Aug. 19, 1968; children: Elizabeth Ann, Daniel Calhoun, Katherine Drake. BA, U. Pa., 1969; JD, Yale U., 1972. Bar: D.C. 1973, Conn. 1975, U.S. Ct. Appeals (2d cir.) 1975, U.S. Ct. Appeals (D.C. cir.) 1976. Assoc. Leva, Hawes, Symington, Martin & Oppenheimer, Washington, 1972-74; assoc. Wiggin & Dana, New Haven, 1974-79, ptnr., 1979—; bd. dirs. Saab Systems Inc., Seattle. Bd. dirs. Internat. Ctr. Inc., New Haven, 1977—, pres., 1981-83. Served to sgt. USAF, 1962-66, Vietnam. Mem. ABA, Conn. Bar Assn. (chmn. internat. sect. 1982-84), Internat. Bar Assn., Union Internationale des Avocats, Phi Beta Kappa. Democrat. Clubs: New Haven Lawn, Quinnipiack (New Haven). General corporate, Private international, Trademark and copyright. Office: Wiggin & Dana 195 Church St PO Box 1832 New Haven CT 06508

TURSI, CARL THOMAS, lawyer; b. Mt. Vernon, N.Y., July 10, 1941; s. Frank Carl and Rose Lucy (Viggiano) T. AB, Colgate U., 1963; LLB, Harvard U., 1966. Bar: N.Y. 1967. Atty. Cahill Gordon, N.Y.C., 1967-71, Donovan Leisure, N.Y.C., 1971-76; v.p., sec. Amerada Hess Corp., N.Y.C., 1976—. Mem. N.Y. State Bar Assn. General corporate, Private international, Securities. Home: 20 Beekman Pl New York NY 10022 Office: Amerada Hess Corp 1185 Ave of the Americas New York NY 10036

TUSHLA, DENNIS MICHAEL, lawyer; b. Auburn, Nebr., Apr. 3, 1947; s. Francis Michael and Ruth Jeanette (Shelley) T.; m. Patricia Beth Adams, July 31, 1968; children: Lara Elizabeth, David Francis. BA, U. Notre Dame, 1969, JD, 1972. Bar: Mich. 1972, U.S. Dist. Ct. (we. dist.) Mich. 1977, U.S. Supreme Ct. 1977. Ptnr. O'Connor & Tushla, Cassopolis, Mich., 1975-81; sole practice Cassopolis, 1982-86; ptnr. O'Connor & Tushla, Cassopolis, 1986—; cons. Adams Farms Ltd., Peru, Nebr., 1978—. Atty. Vil-

lage of Cassopolis, 1973; bd. dirs. Cass County Council on Aging, Cassopolis, 1979-81. Served to capt. U.S. Army, 1969-77. Mem. Mich. State Bar Assn., Cass County Bar Assn. (pres. 1975-76), Internat. Bar Assn., Assn. Trial Lawyers Am., Mich. Trial Lawyers Assn. Club: Economic. Lodge: Elks. Personal injury, Probate, Criminal. Home: 516 Green St Dowagiac MI 49047 Office: O'Connor & Tushla 110 S Broadway Cassopolis MI 49031

TUTOLI, MICHELE ANN, lawyer, financial advisor; b. Teaneck, N.J., May 18, 1951; d. Octavius Rocco and Theresa Rosalia (Wouters) T.; m. Stephen M. Lord, Jan. 27, 1979; children: Stephanie, Michael, Christine, David. Student, George Washington U., 1969-70; AA, Am. Coll. in Paris, 1971; AB, Georgetown U., 1973; JD, Bklyn. Law Sch., 1978. Bar: N.J. 1978, N.Y. 1979, U.S. Dist. Ct. (ea. and so. dists.) N.Y., 1979, U.S. Tax Ct. 1986. Asst. prodn. mgr. Gerstin Advt. Agy., Washington, 1971-73; investment officer Morgan Guaranty Trust Co., N.Y.C., 1973-80; legal cons. office alcohol fuels U.S. Dept. Energy, Washington, 1980-81; asst. dir. trust div. Am. Bankers Assn., Washington, 1981-82; v.p., mgr. fin. planning Home Fed., San Diego, 1982—; ins. agt. Calif. Life and Disability, 1985—; active fin. instn. mgmt. adv. com. U. Calif., San Diego, 1985—; ambassador U. San Diego, 1982—. Sec. Olivenhain (Calif.) Town Council, 1985-86, pres. 1986—. Mem. ABA (spl. planning for execs. and profls. com., investments by fiduciaries com.), San Diego Soc. Fin. Analysts, Internat. Assn. Fin. Planners, Calif. Bankers Assn. (profl. devel. com.). Roman Catholic. Avocation: family. Financial consulting, Personal income taxation, Estate planning. Home: 157 Rancho Santa Fe Rd Olivenhain CA 92024 Office: IDS Am Express Tax Service 157 Rancho Santa Fe Rd Olivenhain CA 92024

TUTRONE, RONALD FRANCIS, lawyer; b. Bklyn., June 1, 1936; s. Frank D. and Amelia (Petrucci) T.; m. Catherine Villardi, Dec. 27, 1957; children: Joliann, Dwaine, Ronald Jr., Maris. BS, Holy Cross U., 1957; LLB, NYU, 1964, LLM, 1974. Bar: N.Y. 1965, U.S. Dist. Ct. (ea. and so. dists.) N.Y. 1966, U.S. Ct. Appeals (2d cir.) 1966, U.S. Dist. Ct. (no. dist.) N.Y. 1981. Assoc. Speiser, Shumate, Geoghan & Krause, N.Y.C., 1965-72; ptnr. Geoghan & Tutrone, N.Y.C., 1973—. Councilman Village of Ridgewood, N.J., 1984—. Served to lt. USNR, 1957-63. Mem. Am. Judges Assn., Assn. Trial Lawyers Am., N.Y. State Bar Assn., Am. Arbitration Assn., Columbian Lawyers Assn. (chmn. bd. dirs.), Nat. Italian-Am. Bar Assn. Roman Catholic. Avocations: coin collecting, music, gardening. Federal civil litigation, State civil litigation, Personal injury. Office: Geoghan & Tutrone 747 3d Ave New York NY 10017

TUTT, JOHN MARION, lawyer; b. Tyler, Tex., Oct. 8, 1942; s. Wilbur Walton and Marion Lexie (Dewberry) T.; m. Sally JoAnne Flournoy, Nov. 18, 1978. B.A., Baylor U., 1964; J.D., U. Tex., 1971. Bar: Tex. 1971, U.S. Dist. Ct. (we. dist.) Tex. 1973, U.S. Tax Ct. 1973, U.S. Ct. Appeals (5th cir.) 1975, U.S. Supreme Ct. 1976. Sole practice, San Antonio, 1971—. Served to lt. Army, N.G., 1964-70. Mem. ABA, San Antonio Bar Assn., Comml. Law League. Republican. Lutheran. Club: Lions (San Antonio). Bankruptcy, Consumer commercial, General corporate. Office: Suite 440 GPM South TWR San Antonio TX 78216

TUTT, LOUISE THOMPSON, lawyer; b. Centerville, Iowa, Nov. 10, 1937; d. Lawrence Eugene and Alice Helen (Thompson) T. B.A., U. Ariz., 1963, J.D., 1969. Bar: Calif. 1972, U.S. Dist. Ct. (so. dist.) Calif. 1972, Mo. 1976. Practice law, San Diego and LaJolla, Calif., 1972-75; appeals referee Div. Employment Security, Jefferson City, Mo., 1977-79; counsel Labor and Indsl. Relations Commn., Jefferson City, Mo., 1979-80; legal adviser Div. Workers Compensation, Jefferson City, 1980—. Bd. dirs. LaJolla Sinfonia, 1975. Mem. Mo. Assn. Trial Attys. Democrat. Mem. Pentecostal Ch. of God. Workers' compensation. Office: 722 Jefferson St Jefferson City MO 65201

TUTTLE, FRANLIN L., JR., lawyer; b. Austin, Tex., Jan. 27, 1953; s. Franklin L. and Maxine (Baty) T.; m. Nancy Gail Davis, Dec. 16, 1978; children: Norma Lisa, Trey. BBA, U. Tex., 1975, JD, 1977. Bar: Tex. 1978; CPA, Tex. Tax acct. Peat, Marwick, Mitchell and Co., Austin, 1978-79; assoc. Rinehart & Nugent, Austin, 1980-85; ptnr. McKeeman, Tuttle & Hein, Austin, 1985—. Mem. Tex. Bar Assn., Tex. Soc. CPA's. Republican. Baptist. Avocations: boating, flying. Corporate taxation, Personal income taxation, General corporate. Home: 11600 Santa Cruz Dr Austin TX 78759 Office: McKeeman Tuttle & Hein 5407 N IH-35 Suite 300 Austin TX 78723

TUTTLE, ROGER LEWIS, legal educator, lawyer; b. Wyandotte County, Kans., Nov. 9, 1930; s. Emmett Joseph and Freda Alberta (Lewis) T.; m. Beverly Jean Campbell, Aug. 3, 1957; children—Pamela Anne, Deborah Jean Tuttle Edwards. B.A., U. Kans., 1952; J.D., U. Miss., 1958. Bar: Miss. 1958, U.S. Dist. Ct. (so. dist.) Miss. 1958, U.S. Dist. Ct. (no. dist.) Miss. 1959, U.S. Dist. Ct. (ea. dist.) La. 1963, U.S. Ct. Appeals (4th cir.) 1964, Va. 1965, U.S. Dist. Ct. (ea. dist.) Va. 1971, U.S. Supreme Ct. 1971, U.S. Dist. Ct. (we. dist.) Va. 1976, Okla. 1982, U.S. Dist. Ct. (no. dist.) Okla. 1983, U.S. Ct. Appeals (10th cir.) 1983. Assoc. Neill, Clark & Townsend, Indianola, Miss., 1958-61, Heidelberg, Woodliff & Franks, Jackson, Miss., 1961-62; area atty. Exxon, New Orleans and Charlotte, N.C., 1962-65; asst. counsel Lawyers Title Ins. Corp., Richmond, Va., 1965-71; gen. atty. A.H. Robins Co., Richmond, 1971-76; asst. gen. counsel Dan River Inc., 1976-82; prof. law Oral Roberts U., Tulsa, 1982-85, dean, 1985—; v.p. law Oral Roberts Ministries, 1986—. Mem. Spl. Adv. Council to Mayor, Richmond, 1971-76; mem. Richmond Air Pollution Control Bd., 1972-73; bd. dirs. Richmond Met. Authority, 1973-76. Served to lt. col. M.I., USAR, 1952-73. Decorated Mil. Cross (Belgium), Bronze Star, Army Commendation Medal with oak leaf cluster; named Prof. of Yr., Oral Roberts U., 1984-85. Mem. ABA, Va. Bar Assn., Okla. Bar Assn. (civic program com., mem. continuing legal edn. com.), Assn. Trial Lawyers Am., Am. Coll. Legal Medicine, Assn. Former Intelligence Officers, Phi Alpha Delta, Pi Kappa Alpha. Republican. Presbyterian. Clubs: Masons, Scottish Rite, Shriners. Contbr. articles to legal publs. Legal education, Federal civil litigation, Workers' compensation. Home: 6111 E 67th Ct Tulsa OK 74136 Office: Oral Roberts Ministries 8181 S Lewis City of Faith 45th Floor Tulsa OK 74137

TWADDELL, MILES EDMISTON, lawyer; b. Lakehurst, N.J., Mar. 12, 1949; s. Miles Edmiston and Grace Rita (Rodgers) T.; m. Maurica Jane Doyle, Dec. 27, 1975; children: Beth, Miles Patrick, Kathryn, Nora. BA, Am. U., 1975; JD, George Mason U., 1979. Bar: Va. 1980, U.S. Dist. Ct. (ea. dist.) Va. 1982, U.S. Ct. Appeals (4th cir.) 1982, N.J. 1983, U.S. Dist. Ct. N.J. 1983. Assoc. Moody, Strople, Brahm & Lawrence, Portsmouth, Va., 1981-84, Harwood Lloyd, Hackensack, N.J., 1984—. Served with USN, 1967-71. Democrat. Roman Catholic. Avocations: military history, Russian literature. Insurance. Home: 3 Freeman St Roseland NJ 07068 Office: Harwood Lloyd 130 Main St Hackensack NJ 07601

TWARDY, STANLEY A., JR., lawyer; b. Trenton, N.J., Sept. 13, 1951; s. Stanley Albert Twardy and Dorothy M. Stonaker. BS with honors, Trinity Coll., 1973; JD, U. Va., 1976; LLM, Georgetown U., 1980. Assoc. Whitman & Ransom, Greenwich, Conn., 1976-77; counsel com. on small bus. U.S. Senate, 1977-79; counsel to Senator Lowell Weicker Jr., 1979-80; ptnr. Silver, Golub & Sandak, Stamford, Conn., 1980-85; U.S. atty. Dist. of Conn., New Haven, 1985—. Vestry St. John's Episc. Ch., Stamford, 1984—. Mem. ABA, Conn. Bar Assn., Assn. Trial Lawyers Am., Conn. Trial Lawyers Assn., Phi Beta Kappa. Office: US Attys Office PO Box 1824 New Haven CT 06508

TWEEDY, WILLIAM ELWYN, lawyer; b. Bklyn.; s. Joseph H. and Amy (Bogardus) T.; m. Elizabeth Coote Clark, June 20, 1936; children—Jeffrey Clark, Elizabeth Tweedy Morash. B.B.S., Syracuse U., 1924; J.D., Harvard U., 1927. Bar: N.Y. 1929. Sole practice, Bklyn., 1927-51, N.Y.C., 1951-58, Ft. Salonga, Northport, N.Y., 1950-76, East Chatham, N.Y., 1976—. Mem. ABA, N.Y. State Bar Assn., Suffolk County Bar Assn., Columbia Bar Assn., Phi Gamma Delta, Phi Delta Phi. Methodist. Clubs: Rotary (bd. dirs), Masons. Probate, Real property, Estate taxation. Address: PO Box 64 East Chatham NY 12060

TWIETMEYER, DON HENRY, lawyer; b. Rochester, N.Y., June 4, 1954; s. Frederick Herman and Norma Frances (Porter) T.; m. Victoria Mary Wolagiewicz, Sept. 24, 1983; 1 child, Laura Elizabeth. BA in Polit. Sci., Econs. with honors, SUNY, Buffalo, 1976; JD, Union U., 1979; LLM in Taxation, U. Miami, 1980; MBA in Acctg., Rochester Inst. Tech., 1983. Bar: N.Y. 1980, Fla. 1980, U.S. Dist. Ct. (so. and we. dists.) N.Y. 1980, U.S. Tax Ct. 1980, U.S. Ct. Appeals (5th and 11th cirs.) 1981; CPA, N.Y. Tax acct. Davie, Kaplan & Braverman, Rochester, 1980-82; assoc. DeHond-Stowe Law Office, Rochester, 1982-84, Lacy, Katzen, Ryen & Mittleman, Rochester, 1984-87; mng. atty. Deltond Law Office, Rochester, 1987—. Mem. ABA (tax sect.), Fla. Bar Assn. (tax sect.), N.Y. State Bar Assn. (tax sect.), Monroe County Bar Assn. (tax sect.), N.Y. State Soc. CPA's. Republican. Lutheran. Avocations: golf, tennis, racquetball, philately, softball. Probate, Pension, profit-sharing, and employee benefits, Personal income taxation. Office: Deltond Law Office 130 E Main St Rochester NY 14604

TWIFORD, H. HUNTER, III, lawyer; b. Memphis, Sept. 19, 1949; s. Horace Hunter and Elizabeth (Andrews) T.; m. Frances Dill, June 27, 1970; children—Elizabeth Smith, Horace Hunter IV. B.A., U. Miss., 1971, J.D., 1972. Bar: Miss. 1972, U.S. Dist. Ct. Miss. 1972, U.S. Ct. Appeals (5th cir.) 1977, U.S. Supreme Ct. 1977. Assoc., Holcomb, Dunbar, Connell, Merkel & Tollison, Clarksdale, Miss., 1972-75, H. Hunter Twiford III, Clarksdale, 1975-77; ptnr. Garmon, Wood & Twiford, Clarksdale, 1977-78, Wood & Twiford, P.A., Clarksdale, 1978-85, Twiford & Webster, P.A., Clarksdale, 1985—; adj. prof. Coahoma Jr. Coll., Clarksdale, 1976—; city atty. City of Clarksdale, 1977—, Town of Friars Point, Miss., 1981—; mcpl. judge pro tempore City of Clarksdale, 1974-76; city atty. City of Clarksdale, Miss., 1985—. Mem. vestry St. George's Episc. Ch., Clarksdale, 1974-76, 82-83, sr. warden, 1984-86; mem. Coahoma County C. of C., Clarksdale, 1975—; mem. Gov.'s Commn. on Drug Abuse, Jackson, Miss., 1976-80; sec. Clarksdale-Coahoma County Joint Airport Bd., Clarksdale, 1981—. Mem. Assn. Trial Lawyers Am., Miss. Trial Lawyers Assn., Nat. Assn. Criminal Def. Lawyers, Miss. Bar Assn., Miss. Prosecutors Assn., Am. Judicature Assn., Coahoma County Bar Assn. Lodge: Rotary (pres. 1984-85). General practice, General corporate, Real property. Home: 1420 Rose Circle Clarksdale MS 38614 Office: Twiford & Webster PA 148 Sunflower Ave Clarksdale MS 38614

TWILLEY, JOSHUA MARION, lawyer; b. Dover, Del., Mar. 23, 1928; s. Joshua Marion and Alice Hunn (Dunn) T.; m. Rebecca Jane Buchanan, Dec. 27, 1952; children—Stephanie, Jeffrey, Linda, Edgar, Joshua; m. 2d, Rosemary Miller, Dec. 1, 1972. B.A. cum laude, Harvard U., 1950, J.D., 1953. Bar: Del. 1953, U.S. dist. ct. Del. 1960, U.S. Sup. Ct. 1976. Sole practice, Dover, 1955-71; sr. ptnr. Twilley, Jones & Feliceangeli, Dover, 1971—; mem. Del. Pub. Service Commn., 1975—; pres. Kent County levy ct., 1970-75. Mem. exec. com. Del. Democratic Com., 1970—; pres. Elizabeth Murphey Sch., 1957—. Served with U.S. Army, 1953-55. Mem. ABA, Am. Judicature Soc., Del. Bar Assn., Kent County Bar Assn. Democrat. Lutheran. Banking, Public utilities, General corporate. Home: 124 Meadow Glen Dr Dover DE 19901 Office: 410 S State St Dover DE 19901

TWINING, ROLLIN LAVERNE, lawyer; b. Binghamton, N.Y., Dec. 22, 1916; s. Laverne Meeker and Violet (Woodley) T.; m. Helen Zelt, Nov. 23, 1939; children: Jacquelyn Twining Ffolliott, Marilyn Twining West. AB, Union Coll., Schenectady, N.Y., 1939; JD, LLB, Union U., Albany, N.Y., 1943. Bar: N.Y. 1943, U.S. Dist. Ct. (no. dist.) N.Y., 1949. Ptnr. Twining & Twining, Binghamton, 1943-44, 45-48, Twining & Fischer, Binghamton, 1948-71, Twining, Nemia, Hill & Griffin, Binghamton, 1971-79, Twining, Nemia & Hill, Binghamton, 1979-83, Twining, Nemia, Hill & Steflik, Binghamton, 1983—; asst. atty. Broome County, 1943-44. Past deacon West Presbyn. Ch.; pres. Roberson Meml. Ctr. for Arts and Scis., 1968-69, bd. dirs. emeritus, 1984; pres. New Industries for Broome, 1966-67, v.p., 1964-65, trustee; pres. Susquehanna Valley Home, 1955-57, bd. dirs., 1958-61; pres. Oquaga Lake Improvement Assn., 1953; trustee Glenwood Cemetary Assn.; bd. dirs., pres. SUNY Binghamton Found., past v.p.; mem. Binghamton City Council, 1947-49, pres. pro tem., 1950, majority leader, 1951, pres., 1952, various coms.; past mem. Council for SUNY Binghamton, Binghamton Bd. Edn., Binghamton Parking Authority, Broome County Indsl. Devel. Agy.; past chmn. City Planning Commn.; chmn. lawyers div. United Fund, 1955; past commr. Tri-Cities Airport; past bd. dirs. Binghamton Girls Club, Broadway Theater League; bd. dirs. Tri-Cities Opera, 1960-64. Served with U.S. Army, 1944-45, ETO. Decorated Bronze Star; recipient N.Y. State Conspicious Service award, 1985. Mem. ABA, N.Y. State Bar Assn., Broome County Bar Assn., Am. Legion, Broome County Hist. Soc. (pres. 1953-56, bd. dirs.), Broome County C. of C. (pres. 1958-59, bd. dirs. 1957-61, 75-81, various coms.), Am. Assn. Mus. (trustee mus. trustee com.). Republican. Clubs: Binghamton, Binghamton Country; Sky Top (Pa.); Live Wire. Lodges: Masons, Shriners. Probate, Real property, General practice. Home: 38 Front St Apt 7E Binghamton NY 13905 Office: Twining Nemia Hill & Steflik 53 Front St Binghamton NY 13902

TWITCHELL, ERVIN EUGENE, lawyer, corporation executive; b. Salt Lake City, Mar. 4, 1932; s. Irvin and Ethel Alberta (Davis) T.; m. Joyce A. Newey, Aug. 9, 1957; children: Laurie, Robert, David, Michael. Student Brigham Young U., 1954-55; BA, Calif. State U.-Long Beach, 1959; JD, UCLA, 1966. Bar: Mich. 1977, U.S. Dist. Ct. Mich. 1978, U.S. Supreme Ct. 1983. Contracts adminstr. Rockwell-N.Am. Aviation, Seal Beach, Calif., 1966-68; sr. contracts adminstr. McDonnell-Douglas Corp., Long Beach, 1968-73; in-house counsel Albert C. Martin & Assocs., Los Angeles, 1973-77; asst. corp. sec., corp. counsel Barton-Malow Co., Detroit, 1977—; instr. bus. law Golden West Coll., Huntington Beach, Calif., 1973-74; instr. seminars on constrn. and Mich. lien laws, 1982; trustee Barton-Malow Pension and Profit Sharing Plans, 1979—. Author: (with others) Michigan's New Construction Lien Act, 1982. Spl. trustee Econ. Devel. Corp., Troy, Mich., 1980; chmn. North Trails dist. Boy Scouts Am., 1978-80, vice chmn., 1980-81; mem. Detroit EEO Forum, 1979—; treas. Barton-Malow Polit. Action Com., 1981—. Served to sgt., USAF, 1950-52, Korea. Recipient cert. of recognition for EEO service Greater Detroit Round Table. Mem. ABA, Mich. Bar Assn., Assn. Trial Lawyers Am., Assoc. Gen. Contractors, Am. Corp. Counsel Assn. (bd dirs. Eastern Mich. chpt. 1983—), Am. Arbitration Assn. (mem. arbitrators panel). Republican. Mormon. General corporate, Contracts commercial, Construction. Home: 4069 Middlebury St Troy MI 48098 Office: 13155 Cloverdale St Oak Park MI 48237

TWITTY, HOWARD ALLEN, lawyer; b. Williams, Ariz., Sept. 6, 1909; s. Edgar Montrue and Emilie Marie (Kaiser) T.; m. Zoraida Stoddard, July 26, 1947; children: Hudson Barnes (dec.), Howard Allen, Mary Marie (dec.). A.B., U. So. Calif., 1931, LL.B., 1934. Bar: Calif. 1934, Ariz. 1935. Atty. Indsl. Commn. Ariz., 1935-42; pvt. practice law Phoenix, 1946—; specializing mining law 1950—; partner Twitty, Sievwright & Mills, 1962—. Author papers on mining law. Served to capt. Q.M.C., AUS, 1942-46. Mem. ABA (chmn. sect. natural resources law 1962-63), state bars Calif., Ariz. Republican. Methodist. Clubs: Arizona, Phoenix Country. Lodges: Masons, Rotary. Home: 520 W Lamar Rd Phoenix AZ 85013 Office: 2702 N 3d St Suite 4007 Phoenix AZ 85004

TWOMEY, JOSEPH GERALD, aircraft company executive; b. Boston, Sept. 9, 1926; s. Jeremiah James and Catherine (McPherson) T.; m. Eve Fatzinick, Nov. 3, 1956; children: Brendan, Denise, Lisa, Brian, Leslie. A.B cum laude, Boston Coll., 1948, LL.B., 1951. Bar: Mass. 1951, Calif. 1964. Atty. Office of Quartermaster Gen., Washington, 1951-61; chief trial atty. Def. Logistics Agy., Washington, 1961-62; counsel Def. Industry Supply Ctr., Phila., 1962-63; assoc. counsel, then chief counsel Lockheed Missiles & Space Co., Sunnyvale, Calif., 1963-77; v.p., chief counsel Lockheed Corp., Burbank, 1977-83, v.p., gen. counsel, 1983—. Served with AUS, 1944-46. Mem. ABA, Fed. Bar Assn., State Bar Calif., Los Angeles County Bar Assn. (exec. com., sec. corp. law dept. 1982-83), Nat. Contract Mgmt. Assn. Roman Catholic. Club: Woodland Hills Country (Calif.). General corporate, Government contracts and claims. Office: Lockheed Corp 4500 Park Granada Blvd Calabasas CA 91399

TWOMEY, THOMAS ALOYSIUS, JR., lawyer; b. N.Y.C., Dec. 8, 1945; s. Thomas A. and Mary (Maloney) Elizabeth (Curtain) T.; m. Judith Hope Twomey, Dec. 15, 1979; stepchildren—Erling Hope, Nisse Hope. B.A., Manhattan Coll., 1967; postgrad. U. Va., 1967-68; J.D., Columbia U., 1970. Bar: N.Y. 1972, U.S. Tax Ct. 1974. Asst. town atty. Town of Southampton N.Y., 1973-74; spl. asst. dist. atty. Suffolk County, N.Y., 1973-74; pvt. practice law, Riverhead, N.Y., 1974-75; ptnr. Hubbard & Twomey, Riverhead, 1976-79, Twomey, Latham, Shea & Kelley, Riverhead, 1980—; adj. prof. environ. law Southampton Coll., 1977-78. Mem., bd. dirs. East End Arts Council, Riverhead, 1983. Recipient Environ. award, U.S. EPA, 1980. Mem. ABA, Suffolk County Bar Assn., N.Y. State Energy Council, N.Y. State Fresh Water Wetlands Appeals Bd. Democrat. Roman Catholic. Real property, State civil litigation, Estate planning. Home: 68 Oyster Shores Rd East Hampton NY 11937 Office: Twomey Latham Shea & Kelley 33 W 2d St Riverhead NY 11901

TYACK, GEORGE GARY, lawyer; b. Columbus, Ohio, July 23, 1946; s. George Ernest and Elsie Naomi (Ballard) T.; m. Lori Marie Rowan, Aug. 20, 1983; children: Mathew John, Lauren Alexis, Reed Garrison, Christopher George. BA, Coll. of Wooster, 1968; JD, Ohio State U., 1974. Bar: Ohio 1975, U.S. Dist. Ct. (so. dist.) Ohio 1975, U.S. Ct. Appeals (6th cir.) 1978, U.S. Supreme Ct. 1980. Assoc. Tyack, Scott & Colley, Columbus, 1975-77; sole practice Columbus and Worthington, Ohio, 1977-80, 86—; ptnr. various ptnrships., Columbus, 1980-84, Tyack & Grubb, Columbus, 1984-86, Tyack, More & Grubb, Columbus, 1986; trustee Maryhaven, Inc., Columbus, 1979—; judge 10th dist. Ohio Ct. Appeals, 1986-87. Trustee United Cerebral Palsy, Columbus, 1978-80. Served to 1st lt. U.S. Army, Vietnam. Mem. ABA, Ohio Bar Assn., Columbus Bar Assn., Ohio Acad. Trial Lawyers (trustee 1983-86, Disting. Service award 1986), Am. Trial Lawyers Assn., Franklin County Trial Lawyers Assn. (trustee 1982-85, treas. 1986, sec. 1986-87). Democrat. Presbyterian. Criminal, Family and matrimonial, State civil litigation. Home: 365 Canyon Dr N Columbus OH 43214 Office: 7100 N High St Worthington OH 43085

TYGART, S. THOMPSON, JR., lawyer; b. Atlanta, Ga., May 17, 1941; m. Judi S. Tygart; children: Tyler, Travis, Lindsay. AB, U. N.C., 1962; JD, U. Fla., 1965. Bar: Fla. 1965, U.S. Dist. Ct. (mid. dist.) Fla. 1966, U.S. Ct. Appeals (11th cir.) 1966, U.S. Supreme Ct. 1972. Asst. atty. State of Fla., Jacksonville, 1966-69; sole practice Jacksonville, 1969—. Mem. Fla. Def. Lawyers Assn., Jacksonville Def. Counsel (pres. 1976-77), Acad. Fla. Trial Lawyers. Republican. Baptist. Personal injury, Insurance, Criminal. Office: 609 Barnett Regency Tower Jacksonville FL 32211

TYGRETT, HOWARD VOLNEY, JR., lawyer; b. Lake Charles, La., Jan. 12, 1940; s. Howard Volney and Hazel (Wheeler) T.; children: Carroll Diane, Howard V. III. B.A., Williams Coll., 1961; LL.B., So. Methodist U., 1964. Bar: Tex. 1964. Gen. atty. SEC, 1964-65; law clk. to chief judge U.S. Dist. Ct. No. Dist. Tex., 1965-67; partner Tygrett & Walker (and predecessors), Dallas, 1968—. Bd. dirs. Routh St. Center, 1976-83, Theatre Three, 1974-75, Shakespeare Festival, 1978-81, Suicide and Crisis Ctr., 1983-86. Mem. Am., Tex., Dallas bar assns., Delta Phi, Delta Theta Phi. Episcopalian. Clubs: Bent Tree, Civitan (lt. gov. Tex. dist. 1976-77, gov. 1979-80). Securities, Probate, Federal civil litigation. Home: 8530 Jourdan Way Dallas TX 75225 Office: Tygrett & Walker 8111 Preston Rd Suite 715 Dallas TX 75225-6375

TYLER, GEORGE JOSEPH, lawyer; b. Jersey City, Aug. 31, 1947; married;. BS in Mech. Enging., Manhattan Coll., 1969; JD cum laude, Seton Hall U., 1974. Bar: N.J. 1974, U.S. Dist. Ct. N.J. 1974. Sr. environ. engr. N.J. Dept. Environ. Protection, Trenton, 1969-74, legal analyst, spl. asst. to div. dir., 1974-78, dir. Div. Environ. Quality, 1978-80, asst. commr. for Environ. Mgmt. and Control, 1980-86; environ. atty., ptnr. Giordano, Halleran & Ciesla, Middletown, N.J., 1986—. Chmn. Garwood (N.J.) Zoning Bd. of Adjustment, 1973-75; active various govtl. environ. coms. Mem. ABA, N.J. Bar Assn. Environment, Administrative and regulatory, General corporate. Home: 721 Gull Wing Ct Smithville NJ 08201 Office: Giordano Halleran & Ciesla PO Box 190 Middletown NJ 07748

TYLER, HAROLD RUSSELL, JR., lawyer, former government official; b. Utica, N.Y., May 14, 1922; s. Harold Russell and Elizabeth (Glenn) T.; m. Barbara L. Eaton, Sept. 10, 1949; children—Bradley E., John R., Sheila B. Grad., Philips Exeter Acad., 1939; A.B., Princeton U., 1943; LL.B., Columbia U., 1949. Bar: N.Y. 1950. Pvt. practice N.Y.C., 1950-53, 55-60; mem. firm Gilbert & Segall, 1957-60, 61-62; asst. U.S. atty. 1953-55, asst. atty. gen. U.S. charge civil rights div., 1960-61; commr. N.Y.-N.J. Waterfront Commn., 1961-62; U.S. dist. judge So. Dist., N.Y., 1962-75; dep. atty. gen. U.S., 1975-77; mem. firm Patterson, Belknap, Webb & Tyler, N.Y.C., 1977—; adj. prof. law NYU Sch., 1966-75; vis. lectr. Inst. Criminology, Cambridge, 1968; vice chmn. Adminstrv. Conf. USA, 1975-77. Bd. dirs. Fed. Jud. Center, Washington, 1968-72; trustee Practising Law Inst., N.Y.C., William Nelson Cromwell Found., Law Center Found.; co-chmn. Lawyers Com. for Civil Rights Under Law. Federal civil litigation, General corporate. Home: Indian Hill Rd Bedford NY 10506 Office: 30 Rockefeller Plaza New York NY 10112

TYLER, RALPH SARGENT, III, lawyer; b. Cleve., Feb. 7, 1947; s. Ralph Sargent Jr. and Marion (Clark) T. BA, U. Ill., 1969; JD, Case Western Res. U., 1972; LLM, Harvard U., 1977. Bar: Mass. 1972, Mich. 1973, Ohio 1978, D.C. 1981, Md. 1982, U.S. Dist. Ct. Mass., U.S. Dist. Ct. (we. dist.) Mich., U.S. Dist. Ct. (no. dist.) Ohio, U.S. Dist. Ct. D.C., U.S. Dist. Ct. Md., U.S. Ct. Appeals (1st, 4th, 6th and D.C. cirs.), U.S. Supreme Ct. Atty. Greater Boston Legal Services, 1973-76, Mass. Law Reform Inc., Boston, 1977-78; asst. prof. law Cleve. State U., 1978-80; lectr. law Nat. U. Singapore, 1980-81; asst. atty. gen. State of Md., Balt., 1982-86, chief litigation, 1986—. Mem. ABA, Md. Bar Assn. Federal civil litigation, State civil litigation, Administrative and regulatory. Home: Summer Hill Farm West Friendship MD 21794 Office: Md Atty Gens Office 7 N Calvert St 2d Floor Baltimore MD 21202

TYRA, KENNETH THOMAS, lawyer; b. Bethesda, Md., Sept. 3, 1957; s. Thomas Norman and Suzanne (Sheldon) T.; m. Maureen Dolan, May 31, 1980; 1 child, Andrew. AB, U. Mich., 1979, JD, 1982. Bar: Minn. 1982, Mich. 1985. Assoc. Dorsey & Whitney, Mpls., 1982-85, Dykema, Gossett, Spencer, Goodnow & Trigg, Ann Arbor, Mich., 1985-87, Dorsey & Whitney, Ann Arbor, 1987—. James B. Angell scholar U. Mich., 1975-78. Mem. ABA, Phi Beta Kappa. Real property, Contracts commercial, General corporate. Office: Dorsey & Whitney 2200 First Bank Pl East Minneapolis MN 55402

TYSON, JOHN MARSH, lawyer; b. Fayetteville, N.C., July 14, 1953; s. Henry McMillan and Addie (Williams) T.; m. Kirby Thomason, July 19, 1975; children: Jason, Caroline, John Havens, Henry Culbreath. BA in English, U. N.C., 1974; postgrad., Notre Dame Law Sch., London, 1977; JD cum laude, Campbell U., 1979; psotgrad., Duke U., 1987—. Bar: N.C. 1980, U.S. Dist. Ct. (we. dist.) N.C. 1980, U.S. Ct. Appeals (4th cir.) 1981, Va. 1981, U.S. Supreme Ct. 1983. Counsel, real estate dir. Revco Drug Stores Inc., Twinsburg, Ohio, 1982—; adj. prof. Campbell U. Sch. Law, 1987. Author Fledgling, 1974 (Hoggard Medal, 1974); comments editor Campbell U. Law Rev., 1979. Bd. dirs. Firstsch., Fayetteville, 1984—. Mem. ABA, N.C. Bar Assn., Va. Bar Assn., Internat. Acad. Trial Lawyers (Trial Advocacy award 1979), Internat. Council Shopping Ctrs., Phi Kappa Phi. Democrat. Presbyterian. Avocations: antiques, autos, hunting, tennis, writing. Real property, Landlord-tenant, Contracts commercial. Home: Rt 9 Box 94 Dobbin Holmes Rd Fayetteville NC 28301 Office: 378 Eastern Blvd Cape Fear Plaza Fayetteville NC 28301

TYSON, ROY KNOX, lawyer, commercial and residential real estate broker; b. Houston, May 30, 1942; s. Alfred Knox and Katherine (Archer) T.; children—John Knox, Dorothy Katherine. A.B., Southwestern U., 1964; J.D., So. Meth. U., 1971. Bar: Tex. 1971, U.S. Dist. Ct. (no., so. and ea. dists.) Tex., U.S. Ct. Appeals (5th cir.), U.S. Tax Ct., U.S. Ct. Mil. Appeals, U.S. Supreme Ct. Assoc., Sorrell, Anderson & Sorrell, Corpus Christi, Tex., 1971-73, Touchstone, Bernays & Johnston, Dallas, 1973-76; atty. Southwestern Bell Telephone Co., Dallas, 1976-84; assoc. Burleson, Pate & Gibson, 1984—; comml. and residential real estate broker. Served to lt. (j.g.), USNR, 1965-68. Recipient Law Enforcement Assistance award Dept. of Justice, 1970. Mem. ABA, Dallas County Bar Assn., SAR, Sons. Republic of Tex. (pres. 1979-80). Episcopalian. General corporate, State civil litigation, Public utilities. Home: 3400 Normandy Ave Dallas TX 75205 Office: Burleson Pate & Gibson 2414 N Akard St Dallas TX 75201

UCHTMANN, DONALD LOUIS, legal educator, lawyer; b. East St. Louis, Ill., Sept. 18, 1946. BA in Agrl. Sci., U. Ill., 1968; MA in Econ. Devel., U.

Leeds, Eng., 1972; JD, Cleve. State U., 1974. Bar: Ohio 1974, Ill. 1975. Asst. prof. U. Ill., Urbana, 1974-79, assoc. prof., 1979-82, prof. agrl. law, 1982—, vice chair U. Ill. senate, 1986-87; legis. asst. Congressman Edward Madigan, Washington, 1982; participant internat. agrl. law programs. Author: (textbook) Agricultural Law: Principles and Cases; contbr. articles to profl. jours. Trustee McKinley Found., Champaign, Ill. Served to lt. USCGR, 1968-71. Fellow for internat. understanding Rotary Internat., Leeds, Eng., 1971. Mem. Am. Agrl. Law Assn. (pres. 1981-82), ABA (forum com. on rural lawyers and agribus.), Ill. Bar Assn., Ill. Inst. Continuing Legal Edn., Omicron Delta Kappa, Alpha Zeta, Gamma Sigma Delta. Lodge: Rotary. Public international, Estate taxation, Real property. Office: U Ill 151 Bevier Hall 905 S Goodwin St Urbana IL 61801

UCKER, DAVID A., lawyer, physician; b. Logan, Ohio, Mar. 8, 1926; s. Joseph William and Clara Helena (Shannon) U.; m. Mary Suzanne Gallagher, Sept. 21, 1954 (div. April 1969); children: Joseph William, Suzanne Marie, Claire Helene, Mary Louise. BA, Ohio State U., 1949, MS, 1950, MD, 1954; JD, Capital U., 1974. Bar: U.S. Dist. Ct. (so. dist.) Ohio 1976. Ptnr. Wristen & Ucker, LPA, Columbus, Ohio, 1976—. Served with USN, 1944-46, PTO. Mem. Ohio Bar Assn., Columbus Bar Assn., Ohio Med. Assn., Columbus OB/GYN Soc., Franklin City Acad. Med. Avocations: flying, tennis. Personal injury, State civil litigation, Medical-legal. Office: Wristen & Ucker LPA 181 E Livingston Ave Suite 1070 Columbus OH 43215

UDALL, CALVIN HUNT, lawyer; b. St. Johns, Ariz., Oct. 23, 1923; s. Grover C. and Dora (Sherwood) U.; m. Doris Fuss, Dec. 11, 1943; children: Fredric, Margaret Udall Learn, Julie (Mrs. Blair M. Nash), Lucinda (Mrs. Douglas Johnson), Tina (Mrs. Bret Petersen). LL.B., U. Ariz., 1948. Bar: Ariz. 1948. Practice in St Johns and Phoenix, Ariz., 1948—; partner Fennemore, Craig, von Ammon, Udall & Powers, 1953—; Ariz. spl. counsel Arizona v. California, 1954-62; mem. Council on Legal Edn. Opportunity, 1983—. Bd. dirs. Boys Clubs Phoenix, 1956-78; mem. Phoenix Musical Theatre, 1959-65. Recipient U. Ariz. Disting. Citizen award, 1984. Fellow Am. Bar Found., Ariz. Bar Found., Am. Coll. Trial Lawyers; mem. ABA (ho. dels. 1962—, bd. govs. 1981-84, exec. com. 1983-84, chmn. task force on minorities 1984-86), Maricopa County Bar Assn. (bd. dirs. 1954-58, pres. 1957, Disting. Pub. Service award 1986), State Bar Ariz. (bd. govs. 1960-65), U. Ariz. Alumni Assn. (bd. dirs. 1959-64), Ariz. Law Coll. Assn. (founding dir. 1967-80, pres. 1978-79). General practice. Office: One Renaissance Sq 2 N Central Ave Phoenix AZ 85004

UDDO, BASILE JOSEPH, law educator; b. New Orleans, Apr. 22, 1949; s. Joseph Frank and Camille Rose (Terranova) U.; m. Anne Carolyn Garlitz, Dec. 28, 1971; children—Joseph Patrick, Paul Basile, Gregory George, Marc Edward. BBA, Loyola U., New Orleans, 1970; JD, Tulane U., 1973; LLM, Harvard U., 1974. Bar: La. 1973, U.S. Dist. Ct. (ea. dist.) La. 1974, U.S. Supreme Ct. 1979, U.S. Ct. Appeals (5th cir.) La. 1985. Instr. law Boston U. Sch. Law, 1973-74; assoc. law firm Liskow & Lewis, New Orleans, 1974-75; asst. prof. Loyola U. Law Sch., 1975-78, assoc. prof., 1978-82, prof., 1982—; mem. nat. com. Human Life Found., N.Y.C., 1981—; bd. dirs. Legal Services Corp., Washington, 1984—. Contbr. articles to law jours., chpts. to books. Bd. dirs. New Orleans Right to Life, 1979—; mem. prolife adv. com. U.S. Catholic Conf.; bd. dirs. La. Mental Health Advocacy Service, 1977-81; former mem. adv. bds. Ridgewood Prep. also Xavier Prep. Schs. La. Legis. legis. grantee, 1982-84; mem. La. Bicentennial Commn. U.S. Constitution, 1986—. Mem. Order of Coif, Omicron Delta Kappa. Roman Catholic. Legal education, Personal injury, Jurisprudence. Home: 2211 Killdeer St New Orleans LA 70122 Office: Loyola Law Sch 6363 St Charles Ave New Orleans LA 70118

UDELL, MICHAEL BENNETT, lawyer; married. A.A., Miami Dade Jr. Coll., 1971; B.A., U. Fla., 1973; postgrad. Sch. Bus. and Mgmt., Fla. Internat. U., Miami, 1974; J.D., South Tex. Coll. Law, Houston, 1978. Bar admittee: Tex., Fla., U.S. Dist. Ct. (so. dist.) Fla., U.S. Ct. Claims, U.S. Ct. Internat. Trade, U.S. Tax Ct., U.S. Ct. Customs and Patent Appeals, U.S. Ct. Appeals (5th cir.), U.S. Supreme Ct. Chief operating officer Truco Med. Supplies, Inc., Miami, Fla., 1975; tchr. govt. and history Houston Ind. Sch. Dist., 1976-77; assoc. Stolbun & Shaw, P.A., Bellaire, Tex., 1978, Franklin, Ullman, Entin and Kimler, North Miami Beach, Fla., 1978; sole practice, Miami, 1979—; mem. Fla. Gov.'s Com. on Juvenile Justice. Bd. dirs. Cedarwoods Homeowners Assn.; mem. Pembroke Pines (Fla.) Code Enforcement Bd. Mem. ABA, Tex. Bar Assn., Fla. Bar Assn., Assn. Trial Lawyers Am., Broward County Bar Assn., Broward County Trial Lawyers Assn., North Dade Bar Assn., Dade County Trial Lawyers Assn., Am. Judicature Soc., Dade County Bar Assn., Acad. Fla. Trial Lawyers, Broward County Trial Lawyers Polit. Action Com., Phi Alpha Delta, Sigma Lambda Phi. Clubs: Kiwanis, B'nai B'rith, KP. Federal civil litigation, State civil litigation, Family and matrimonial. Address: 10281 Cypress Ct Pembroke Pines FL 33026 Office: 17240 NE 19th Ave Miami FL 33162

UEBLER, E(RNEST) ALAN, lawyer; b. Ottawa, Ill., Apr. 16, 1939; s. Ernest Robert and Frances M. (Lennie) U.; m. Barbara Fizzano, Oct. 22, 1966 (div. Aug. 1976); children: Julie A., John A., Jennifer L.; m. Marsh Wiltbank, July 2, 1977; 1 child, Thomas A. BS in Chem. Engring., U. Ill., 1962; MS in Chem. Engring., U. Del., 1964, PhD in Chem. Engring., 1966; JD, U. Md., 1974. Bar: Del. 1974, U.S. Dist. Ct. Del. 1974, U.S. Patent Office 1974, U.S. Ct. Appeals (3d cir.) 1980, U.S. Ct. Appeals (fed. cir.) 1982, U.S. Ct. Appeals (9th cir.) 1987. Sr. research engr. DuPont, Wilmington, Del., 1966-71, patent atty., 1975; engr. W. L. Gore & Assocs., Newark, Del., 1971-74, gen. counsel, 1974-77; ptnr. Mortenson & Uebler, P.A., Wilmington, 1978—; adj. prof. U. Del., Newark, 1978—; cons. W. L. Gore and Assocs., Newark, 1983—. Contbr. articles to profl. jours.; patentee filter pack. Pres. Del. chpt. Lawyers Alliance for Nuclear Arms Control, Wilmington, 1986-87; bd. dirs. Profls. for Nuclear Arms Control, Wilmington, 1986. Mem. ABA, Del. Bar Assn., Am. Intellectual Property Law Assn., Del. Trial Lawyers Assn., Am. Inst. Chem. Engrs., Tau Beta Pi, Phi Lambda Upsilon, Sigma Xi. Discoverer The Uebler Effect (fluid flow phenomenon). Avocations: tennis, swimming, reading. Patent, Trademark and copyright, General practice. Home: 38 The Horseshoe Newark DE 19711 Office: Mortenson & Uebler PA 1601 Milltown Rd Suite 4 Wilmington DE 19808

UEHLINGER, GERARD PAUL, lawyer; b. N.Y.C., July 30, 1949; s. Gerard Paul and Dorothy (Karthaus) U.; m. Julianne McGiffert, June 3, 1972; children—Kevin Gerard, Gregory James, Elizabeth Ann. A.B., Princeton U., 1971; J.D., U. Md., 1975. Bar: Md. 1975, U.S. Dist. Ct. Md. 1976, U.S. Ct. Appeals (4th cir.) 1979. Law clk. Ct. Appeals Md., 1975-76; assoc. Piper & Marbury, Balt., 1976-79, Gordon, Feinblatt et al, Balt., 1979-81, Law Office of Jerome Blum, Balt., 1981-83, Lentz, Hooper, Jacobs & Blevins, Balt., 1983—. Chmn. Balt. City Foster Care Rev. Bd., East Region 1, 1980-86; mem. State Foster Care Rev. Bd., 1983-86; bd. of trustees Fellowship of Lights, Inc., 1985—; pres. Md. Friends of Foster Children Found., Inc., 1987—; counsel several charitable religious and social orgns.. Mem. ABA, Md. State Bar Assn., Bar Assn. Balt. City (exec. com. young lawyers 1981-83, exec. com. 1982-83). Democrat. Roman Catholic. Federal civil litigation, State civil litigation, Personal injury. Home: 504 Anneslie Rd Baltimore MD 21212 Office: Lentz Hooper Jacobs & Blevins PA 222 St Paul 5th Floor Baltimore MD 21202

UELTSCHEY, WATTS CASPER, lawyer; b. Morton, Miss., Nov. 27, 1950; s. Charles Marion and Hilda Lee (Watts) U.; m. Martha Louise Malouf, May 17, 1975; children: Watts C. Jr., Michael Brien, Andrew Farrell. BS in Acctg., Miss. State U., 1972; JD, U. Miss., 1975. Bar: Miss. 1975, U.S. Dist. Ct. (no. and so. dists.) Miss. 1975. Adminstrv. asst. Sec. of State, Jackson, Miss., 1975; assoc. Carter & Robinson, Jackson, 1976; from assoc. to ptnr. Harper, Bellan, Ueltschey & McWhorter and predecessor firm Peterson, Harper & Bellan, Jackson, 1976-83; sole practice Jackson, 1983-85; ptnr. Jones & Ueltschey, Jackson, 1986—. Bd. dirs. Good Samaritan Ctr., Jackson, 1983—, Operation Shoestring, Jackson, 1985. Mem. ABA, Miss. Bar Assn., Hinds County Bar Assn., Miss. Oil and Gas Lawyers Assn., Miss. Assn. Petroleum Landmen, Beta Alpha Psi, Omicron Delta Kappa. Roman Catholic. Oil and gas leasing, Real property, Probate. Home: 1722 Brecon Dr Jackson MS 39211 Office: Jones & Ueltschey PO Box 55601 Jackson MS 39216

UFFORD, CHARLES WILBUR, JR., lawyer; b. Princeton, N.J., July 8, 1931; m. Isabel Letitia Wheeler, May 20, 1961; children: Eleanor Morris, Catherine Latourette, Alison Wistar. B.A. cum laude (Francis H. Burr scholar), Harvard U., 1953, LL.B., 1959; student (Lionel de Jersey Harvard studentship), Emmanuel Coll., Cambridge U., Eng., 1953-54. Bar: N.Y. 1961. Assoc. Riggs, Ferris & Geer, N.Y.C., 1959-61; assoc. Jackson, Nash, Brophy, Barringer & Brooks, 1961-69, ptnr., 1969-78; ptnr. Skadden, Arps, Slate, Meagher & Flom, N.Y.C., 1978—. Contbr. articles to legal jours. Trustee Nat. Squash Racquets Ednl. Found., N.Y.C., 1972-81, U.S. Squash Racquets Assn. Endowment Fund, 1984—. Fellow Am. Coll. Probate Counsel; mem. ABA, N.Y. Bar Assn. (chmn. trusts and estates law sect. 1984), Assn. Bar City N.Y., Internat. Acad. Trusts and Estates Law, U.S. Squash Racquets Assn. (hon. life.). Mem. NCAA All-Am. Soccer 1st Team, 1952: Nat. Intercollegiate squash racquets champion, 1952-53. Probate, Estate taxation, Estate planning. Home: 150 Mercer St Princeton NJ 08540 Office: Skadden Arps Slate Meagher & Flom 919 3d Ave New York NY 10022

UFHOLZ, PHILIP JOHN, lawyer; b. Hoboken, N.J., Dec. 26, 1947; s. Philip Adam and Elisabeth Sophie (Pfister) U.; m. Eugenia Andros, Aug. 19, 1972. BA, Tulane U., 1969; JD, Georgetown U., 1972, LLM, 1975. Bar: D.C. 1973, U.S. Dist. Ct. D.C. 1973, U.S. Ct. Mil. Appeals 1973, U.S. Ct. Appeals (D.C. cir.) 1976. Trial atty. FTC, Washington, 1972-74; assoc. Glassie, Pewett, Beebe & Shanks, Washington, 1974-77; tax counsel to senator Gaylord Nelson U.S. Senate, Washington, 1977-81, tax counsel to senator William V. Roth, 1981-83; v.p. Met. Life Ins. Co., Washington, 1983—. Served to capt. U.S. Army, 1972. Mem. ABA. Lutheran. Avocations: golf, skiing, tennis, sailing. Corporate taxation, Pension, profit-sharing, and employee benefits, Legislative. Home: 8611 Long Acre Ct Bethesda MD 20817 Office: Met Life Ins Co 1615 L St NW Washington DC 20036

UGHETTA, VALERIE JEANNE, lawyer; b. New Rochelle, N.Y., Sept. 18, 1951; d. Raoul Andre and Barbara (Berges) U. BA in English cum laude, Mt. Holyoke Coll., 1973; JD, Cath. U. Am., 1976. Bar: Md. 1976, D.C. 1977, U.S. Dist. Ct. Md. 1977, U.S. Dist. Ct. D.C. 1978. Law clk. to acting presiding justice D.C. Ct. Appeals, Washington, 1976-77; assoc. Carr, Jordan, Coyne & Savits, Washington, 1977-81; sr. atty. office of gen. counsel Am. Petroleum Inst., Washington, 1981—. Mem. ABA, Md. Bar Assn., D.C. Bar Assn., D.C. Women's Bar Assn., Women in Govt. Relations. Environment, Health, Personal injury. Home: 4849 Connecticut Ave NW Washington DC 20008 Office: Am Petroleum Inst Office of Gen Counsel 1220 L St NW Washington DC 20005

UGHETTA, WILLIAM CASPER, lawyer, manufacturing company executive; b. N.Y.C., Feb. 8, 1933; s. Casper and Frieda (Bohland) U.; m. Mary L. Lusk, Aug. 10, 1957; children: William C., Robert L., Edward F., Mark R. A.B., Princeton U, 1954; LL.B, Harvard U., 1959. Bar: N.Y. 1959. Assoc. Shearman & Sterling, N.Y.C., 1959-67; asst. sec. Corning Glass Works, N.Y., 1968-70, sec., counsel, 1971-72, v.p., gen. counsel, 1972-82, sr. v.p., gen. counsel, 1983—; dir. Corning Internat. Corp., Components Inc., MetPath, Inc., Siecor Corp., Corning Europe Inc., Corning Hilton Inn, Corning France, Chemung Canal Trust Co. Bd. dirs. Steuben Area Council Boy Scouts Am.; officer Corning Mus. Glass, Corning Glass Works Found. Served to lt. (j.g.) U.S. Navy, 1954-56. Mem. Assn. Bar. City N.Y., ABA, N.Y. State Bar Assn., Am. Corp. Counsel Assn. (trustee 1982-85). Clubs: Princeton (N.Y.C.), Univ. (N.Y.C.); Corning Country. General corporate. Home: 13 North Rd Corning NY 14830 Office: Corning Glass Works Houghton Park Corning NY 14831

UHL, SIMON KREBS, lawyer; b. Somerset, Pa., Feb. 22, 1903; s. Charles Franklin and Leah Katherine (Krebs) U.; m. Madge Boden, July 8, 1955. Grad. Princeton U., 1926; LL.B., U. Pitts., 1934. Bar: Pa. Sole practice, Somerset, Pa.; dir. Somerset Trust Co., 1947-87; dir. Rockwood Ins. Co. (now Rockwood Holding Co.), 1958—. Mem. Pa. Milk Control Commn., 1956-63, chmn., 1960-63; chmn. Somerset State Hosp., 1972-80; chmn. Somerset County Democratic Com., 1948-63, del. nat. conv., 1952, 60. Served to comdr. USNR, 1942-46. Decorated Bronze Star. Mem. Pa. State Bar Assn., Somerset County Bar Assn. Lutheran. Clubs: Princeton N.Y., Mason. General practice. Address: RFD 1 Somerset PA 15501 Office: 118 W Main St Somerset PA 15501

UHLENHOP, PAUL BUSCHER, lawyer; b. Litchfield, Ill., Oct. 22, 1936; s. Paul Christopher and Mary Elizabeth (Buscher) U.; m. Virginia Louise Zucks; children—Karin Elizabeth, Jon Paul. B.A., U. Ill., 1958, J.D., 1961. Bar: Ill. 1961, N.Y. 1962. Atty., SEC, Washington, 1961-63; staff law dept. Standard Oil Co., Chgo., 1963-69; assoc. gen. counsel Booz, Allen & Hamilton, Chgo., 1970; ptnr. Lawrence, Kamin, Saunders & Uhlenhop, Chgo., 1971—; lectr. in field. Pres. bd. visitors U. Ill. Law Sch.; bd. dirs. Wilmette (Ill.) Harbor Assn., 1975—, pres., 1980-81. Served with USN, 1954-58. Mem. Ill. Inst. Continuing Legal Edn. (award seminar teaching), ABA, Chgo. Bar Assn., Ill. Bar Assn. Democrat. Roman Catholic. Club: Sheridan Shores Yacht (Wilmette). Contbr. articles to profl. jours. Securities, Antitrust. Office: 208 S La Salle St Suite 1750 Chicago IL 60604

UHRIG, IRA JOHN, lawyer; b. Bellingham, Wash., May 16, 1957; s. Frank George and Marianne Patricia (Yeager) U. BA, Seattle Pacific U., 1978; JD, U. Wash., 1981. Bar: Wash. 1981, U.S. Dist. Ct. (we. dist.) Wash. 1981. Ptnr. Lee & Uhrig, Bellingham, 1982—. Rep. candidate for Wash. State Legislature, 1986; chmn. platform com. Whatcom County Rep. Party, 1986. Mem. Am. Trial Lawyers Assn., Wash. Trial Lawyers Assn., Wash. State Bar Assn., Nat. Rifle Assn., Nat. Assn. Music Mchts. Lutheran. Club: Custer Sportsman's. Family and matrimonial, Consumer commercial, Personal injury. Office: Lee & Uhrig 1200 Dupont Suite 2A Bellingham WA 98225

ULLMAN, LEO SOLOMON, lawyer; b. Amsterdam, Netherlands, July 14, 1939; s. Frank Leo and Emily (Konyn) U.; m. Katharine Laura Marbut, Aug. 27, 1960; children—Laura, Susan, Valerie, Frank. AB, Harvard U., 1961, JD, 1964, MBA, 1964. Bar: N.Y. 1966, U.S. Ct. Claims 1966, U.S. Tax Ct. 1969, U.S. Customs Ct. 1970. Assoc. Sullivan & Cromwell, N.Y.C., 1965-58; pres. and mem. Ullman, Miller & Wrubel and predecessors, N.Y.C., 1970-81; mem. Lane & Mittendorf and predecessor Casey, Lane & Mittendorf, 1981-84; mem. Reid & Priest, 1984—; adj. prof. internat. bus. NYU, 1972-77; lectr., panelist profl. organs. programs; pres. Amvest Properties, Inc. Pres. Port Washington (N.Y.) Bd. Edn., 1970-73, Found. for Jewish Hist. Mus. in Amsterdam, Inc., also bd. dirs. Served with USMCR, 1959-65. Co-recipient Community Service Award, Port Washington, 1981; Harlan Fiske Stone scholar, Columbia Law Sch., 1963. Mem. ABA (tax sect. com. U.S. taxation of fgn. persons), N.Y. State Bar Assn. (tax sect. com. internat. trade and investment). Clubs: Harvard, Netherlands, India House (N.Y.C.). Editor: European Taxation, Internat. Bur. Fiscal Documentation, Amsterdam, 1964-65; founding editor: Taxation of Private Investment Income in Europe; co-author Investeringen in Onroerend Goed in de Verenigde Staten, 1982; contbr. articles to profl. publs. Private international, Corporate taxation, General corporate. Home: Middle Road Sands Point NY 11050 Office: 40 W 57th St New York NY 10019

ULLSTROM, L. BERWYN, lawyer; b. Memphis, Nebr., Sept. 18, 1919; s. LeRoy and Myrtle Estella (Parrish) U.; m. Loine Evelyn Sloan, Sept. 11, 1942; children: Linda Louise Dixon, Jeanne Ann Cook, Bruce Richard. Student, Scottsbluff Coll., 1937-40; B.S., U. Mich., 1946; LL.B., U. Denver, 1948. Bar: Colo. 1948, U.S. Supreme Ct 1954; Licensed comml. pilot. Practice in Denver, 1948-51; instr. aviation law and legal subjects U. Denver, 1948-51; trial atty. CAA, 1951-54; asso. gen. counsel FCDA, 1954-56, dep. exec. asst. adminstr., 1956-58; observer Operation Redwing, Joint Task Force 7 Pacific Thermonuclear Bomb Drop Test, 1956; exec. asst. dir. Office Civil and Def. Mblzn., Exec. Office Pres., 1958-61; cons. Dept. Def., 1961; pvt. practice law Denver, 1961—. Served to comdr., aviation USNR, 1941-45; mem. Res. (ret.). Mem. ABA, Colo. Bar Assn., Denver Bar Assn., Lawyer-Pilots Bar Assn. (v.p. Rocky Mountain regional chpt. 1982-86), Am., Colo. Trial lawyers assns., Nat. Transp. Safety Bd. Bar Assn., Internat. Soc. Air Safety Investigators (pres. Rocky Mountain regional chpt. 1984-86), Aircraft Owners and Pilots Assn., Phi Delta Phi. Aviation law. Home: 13990 W 30th Ave Golden CO 80401 Office: Suite 400 601 Broadway Denver CO 80203

ULMER, NICOLAS COURTLAND, lawyer; b. Washington, Aug. 5, 1952; s. Alfred Conrad and Doris Lee (Bridges) U.; m. Stephanie Nebehay, Sept. 26, 1986. AB with honors, Brown U., 1974; JD, U. Calif., San Francisco, 1979. Bar: D.C. 1979, Calif. 1980, U.S. Dist. Ct. (D.C. dist.) 1980, U.S. Ct. Appeals (D.C. cir.) 1980. Assoc. Galland, Kharasch, Calkins & Short, Washington, 1979-81; assoc. Surrey & Morse, Washington, 1981-83, Paris, 1983-86; assoc. Jones, Day, Reavis & Pogue (merged with Surrey & Morse), Paris, 1986-87, Geneva, 1987—; asst. prof. advanced bus. law Schiller Internat. U., Paris, 1985; bd. dirs. Gander & White Inc., N.Y.C. Trial observer Amnesty Internat., Diyarbakir, Turkey, 1984, Elazig, Turkey, 1986, spokesman U.S. and France; mission del., Mauretania, 1987—. Mem. ABA (internat. law sect.). Episcopalian. Club: The Traveller's (Paris). Avocations: reading, running, cinema. International commercial arbitration, Private international, Public international. Office: Jones Day Reavis & Pogue, 43 Rue du Rhone, Geneva CH 1204, Switzerland Office: Jones Day Reavis & Pogue 599 Lexington Ave New York NY 10022

ULRICH, GREGORY LESLIE, lawyer; b. Detroit, June 22, 1952; m. Linda Ann Winter; 1 child, Todd Gregory. AB magna cum laude, U. Detroit, 1974, JD, 1977. Bar: Mich. 1977, U.S. Dist. Ct. (ea. dist.) Mich. 1977, U.S. Ct. Appeals (6th cir.) 1977, U.S. Supreme Ct. 1985. Law clk. to presiding judge 3d Jud. Cir., Detroit, 1976-77; sole practice St. Clair Shores, Mich., 1977—. Author: Small Claims, 1985. Mem. pub. safety justice com. New Detroit, Inc., 1977—. Mem. ABA (ho. of dels. 1984—), Mich. Bar Assn. (sec., treas. young lawyers sect. 1983-84, vice chmn. 1984-85, chmn.-elect 1985-86, chmn. 1986—, rep. assembly 1980, bd. of commrs. 1986—), U. Detroit Nat. Alumni Assn. (v.p. 1985—). Roman Catholic. General practice, General corporate, Judicial administration. Home: 1745 Stanhope Ave Grosse Pointe Woods MI 48236 Office: 21643 E 9 Mile Rd Saint Clair Shores MI 48080

ULRICH, PAUL GRAHAM, lawyer, author, editor; b. Spokane, Nov. 29, 1938; s. Donald Gunn and Kathryn (Vandercook) U.; m. Kathleen Nelson Smith, July 30, 1982; children—Kathleen Elizabeth, Marilee Rae, Michael Graham. B.A. with high honors, U. Mont., 1961; J.D., Stanford U., 1964. Bar: Calif. 1965, Ariz. 1966, U.S. Supreme Ct. 1969. Law clk. judge U.S. Ct. Appeals, 9th Circuit, San Francisco, 1964-65; assoc. firm Lewis and Roca, Phoenix, 1965-70; ptnr. Lewis and Roca, 1970-85; pres. Paul G. Ulrich PC, Phoenix, 1985—; owner Pathway Enterprises, 1985—; judge pro tem Ariz. Ct. Appeals Div. 1, Phoenix, 1986; instr. Thunderbird Grad. Sch. Internat. Mgmt., 1968-69, Ariz. State U., Coll. Law, 1970-73, 78, Scottsdale Community Coll., 1975-77, also continuing legal edn. seminars; owner Pathway Enterprises, 1985—. Author: Applying Management and Motivation Concepts to Law Offices, 1985; editor, contbr.: Working with Legal Assistants, 1980, 81; Future Directions for Law Office Management, 1982; People in the Law Office, 1985-86; contbr. numerous articles to profl. jours. Bd. visitors Stanford U. Law Sch., 1974-77. Served with U.S. Army, 1956. Recipient continuing legal edn. award State Bar Ariz., 1978, 86, Harrison Tweed Spl. Merit award Am. Law Inst./ABA, 1987. Mem. ABA (chmn. selection and utilization of staff personnel com., econs. of law sect. 1979-81, mem. standing com. legal assts. 1982-86, co-chmn. joint project on appellate handbooks 1983-85, co-chmn. fed. appellate handbook project 1985—, chmn. com. on liaison with non-lawyer orgns. Econs. of Law Practice sect. 1985-86), Ariz. Bar Assn. (chmn. econs. of law practice com. 1980-81, co-chmn. lower ct. improvement com. 1982-85, co-chmn. Ariz. Appellate handbook project 1976—), Maricopa County Bar Assn., Calif. Bar Assn., Am. Law Inst., Am. Judicature Soc. (Spl. Merit Citation 1987), Phi Kappa Phi, Phi Alpha Delta, Sigma Phi Epsilon. Republican. Presbyterian. Federal civil litigation, State civil litigation, Appellate practice. Home: 107 E El Caminito Rd Phoenix AZ 85020 Office: 3030 N Central Ave Suite 310 Phoenix AZ 85012

ULRICH, ROBERT GARDNER, retail food chain exec.; b. Evanston, Ill., May 6, 1935; s. Charles Clemens and Nell Clare (Stanley) U.; m. Diane Mary Granzin, June 6, 1964; children—Robert Jeffrey, Laura Elizabeth, Meredith Christine. LL.B. (Law Rev. key), Marquette U., Milw., 1960. Bar: Wis. bar 1960, Ill. bar 1960, N.Y. bar 1981. Law clk. to fed. dist. judge Milw., 1961-62; atty. S.C. Johnson & Son, Inc., Racine, Wis., 1962-65, Motorola, Inc., Franklin Park, Ill., 1965-68; atty., then asst. gen. counsel Jewel Cos., Inc., Melrose Park, Ill., 1968-75; v.p., gen. counsel Gt. Atlantic & Pacific Tea Co., Inc., Montvale, N.J., 1975—; sr. v.p., gen. counsel Gt. Atlantic & Pacific Tea Co., Inc., 1981—. Mem. Am. Bar Assn., N.Y. State Bar Assn. General corporate. Home: 500 Weymouth Dr Wyckoff NJ 07481 Office: The Great Atlantic and Pacific Tea Co 2 Paragon Dr Montvale NJ 07645

UNDERBERG, NEIL, lawyer; b. N.Y.C., May 16, 1928; s. Henry and Charlotte (Cohen) U.; m. Ruth Sondra, Jan. 23, 1957; children—James Adam, Amy Singer. B.A., Syracuse U., 1949; J.D., Cornell U., 1952; LL.M., NYU, 1957. Bar: N.Y. 1952, Republic of Korea 1953, U.S. Supreme Ct. 1969. Atty., advisor FHA, Washington, 1954-55; v.p., counsel Eastern Shopping Ctrs., Inc., N.Y.C., 1956-59; counsel Daitch Crystal Dairies, Inc., N.Y.C., 1959-61, Winston Muss Corp., N.Y.C., 1961-65; ptnr. Finley, Kumble, Wagner, Heine, Underberg, Manley, Myerson & Casey, N.Y.C., 1965—; dir. Security Title Co., N.Y.C., Alexander's, Inc., N.Y.C.; Contbr. articles to Practising Law Inst, Real Estate Rev., Shopping Ctr. World, N.Y. Law Jour., Syracuse Law Rev., Internat. Property Investment Jour. Vice chmn. bd. trustees Horace Mann Barnard Sch., N.Y.C., 1980. Mem. ABA, Am. Law Inst., Am. Arbitration Assn., Am. Coll. Real Estate Lawyers. Clubs: Harmonie, Beach Point N.Y.C. (commodore 1980-83, gov. 1978—). Real property, Legislative. Home: 480 Park Ave New York NY 10022 Office: Finley Kumble Wagner Heine Underberg Manley Myerson & Casey 425 Park Ave New York NY 10022

UNDERHILL, WILLIAM AMORY, lawyer; b. Basinger, Fla., Feb. 21, 1910; s. Wilford Perry and Martha Mabel (Alderman) U. LLB, John B. Stetson U., 1936, LLD (hon.), 1969; LHD (hon.), St. Leo Coll., 1980. Bar: Fla. 1936, U.S. Supreme Ct. 1946, D.C. 1952. Sole practice Deland, Fla., 1936-42; prosecuting atty. Volusia County, Fla., 1940-42; atty. various divs. U.S. Dept. Justice, Washington, 1946-52, asst. atty. gen., 1951-52; sole practice Washington and Deland, 1952—; spl. counsel to comptroller of Fla., Washington, 1967-70. Bd. overseers Stetson U. Coll. Law, St. Petersburg, Fla., chmn. 1977—; bd. dirs. Charles Dana Law Ctr Found., pres. 1971-77; trustee Stetson U., Deland, 1977—, St. Leo Coll., St. Leo, Fla., 1968—, Fla. House Washington D.C., Inc., treas. 1973—, Bert Fish Testamentary Trust, Deland, pres. 1977—, chmn. bd. 1986—. Served to lt. commr. USNR, 1942-46. Recipient George Washington Honor Medal Freedoms Found. at Valley Forge, 1970, C.H.I.E.F. award Ind. Colleges and Universities Fla., Inc., 1974, Key to City of Deland, 1980. Mem. ABA, Fed. Bar Assn., Fla. Bar Assn., D.C. Bar Assn., Volusia County Bar Assn., Stetson U. Lawyer's Assn. (Ben C. Willard award 1970), Fla. C. of C., Deland C. of C. (life), Deland Jaycees (life), Fla. State Soc. (Bob Sikes award 1977), Fla. Council of 100, Stetson U. Almni Assn. (pres. 1970-71, Disting. Alumni award 1974), Underhill Soc. Am., Mil. Order of World Wars, Am. Legion, Navy League, Phi Alpha Delta, Pi Kappa Phi, Theta Alpha Phi. Lodges: Elks, Masons. Home: 145 N Garfield Ave Deland FL 32720 Office: PO Box 66 Deland FL 32721-0066 also: 1700 K St NW Washington DC 20006-3817

UNDERWOOD, EDWIN HILL, lawyer; b. Bainbridge, Ga., Mar. 28, 1920; s. Edwin Hendon and Gladys (Legg) U.; m. Cynthia Ann Greiner, Feb. 1950 (div. 1967); children: Vance, Hill, Molly; m. Elizabeth Jane Morgan, Apr. 24, 1968; children: Michael, Samantha, Dorothy, Edith. AB, U. Fla., 1941; JD, U. Miami, Coral Gables, 1948. Bar: Fla. 1948. Sole practice Key Biscayne and Miami, Fla., 1948—; bd. dirs. Key Biscayne Bank and Trust Co., Fla., Guaranty Life Ins., Jacksonville, Fla. Pres. Marine Council Greater Miami, Fla., 1966. Served to capt. U.S. Army, 1940-46, ETO. Mem. ABA (tort and ins. practice sect., antitrust law sect.), Fla. Bar, Dade County Bar Assn. (bd. dirs. 1956-59), Internat. Assn. Ins. Counsel, Dade County Def. Bar Assn., Fla. Def. Lawyers Assn., Law Sci. Acad. Am., Maritime Law Assn. U.S., Am. Judicature Soc. Democrat. Episcopalian. Clubs: Key Biscayne (Fla.) Yacht (commodore 1964), Key Biscayne Beach (pres. 1960); Miami; Palm Bay (Fla.); Capital City Country (Tallahasse, Fla.), Coral Reef Yacht, Fishers Island. Avocations: golf, fishing. State civil litigation, Federal civil litigation, Admiralty. Home: 605 Ocean Dr Key Biscayne FL 33149

UNDERWOOD, SAMUEL BOBBITT, JR., lawyer; b. Durham, N.C., Feb. 2, 1911; s. Samuel Bobbitt and Eloise (Lister) U.; m. Alma Virginia Wyche,

July 13, 1940; children—Robert Marshall, Virginia Vincent Underwood Bass. A.B., Duke U., 1931; LL.B., Cumberland U., 1937. Bar: N.C. 1937, U.S. Dist. Ct. (ea. dist.) N.C. 1938. Practice, Greenville, N.C., 1937—; sr. ptnr. Underwood & Leech, Greenville. Trustee, Sheppard Meml. Library, Greenville, 1950-72; chmn. adminstrv. bd. Jarvis Meml. United Meth. Ch., Greenville, assoc. conf. lay leader N.C. Meth. Annual Conf., 1952-56. Mem. ABA, Am. Judicature Soc., N.C. Bar Assn. (v.p. 1967-68), Pitt County Bar Assn. Democrat. Methodist. Clubs: Rotary (pres. 1969-70), Golf and Country, Capital City (Raleigh, N.C.). Estate planning, Condemnation. Office: 201 Evans St Greenville NC 27834

UNDERWOOD, WILLIAM FLEMING, JR., lawyer; b. Atlanta, Oct. 29, 1944; s. William Fleming and Montine (Smith) U.; m. Brenda Marsha Fricks, Jan. 8, 1971; children—Charlotte Ashley, William Fleming III. A.A., Ga. Mil. Coll., 1964; A.B.J., U. Ga., 1967; LL.B., John Marshall Law Sch., 1974. Bar: Ga. 1975, U.S. Dist. Ct. (mid. dist.) Ga. 1975, U.S. Ct. Appeals (5th cir.) 1975, U.S. Ct. Appeals (11th cir.) 1981, U.S. Supreme Ct. 1981. Sole practice, Albany, Ga., 1975—. Mem. Dougherty County Bd. Commrs., Albany, 1979. Served to 1st lt. U.S. Army, 1967-69. Recipient Disting. Service award Life Dynamic Essentials. Dr. Sid Williams, 1981. Mem. ABA, Ga. Assn. Criminal Def. Lawyers (v.p. 1978-80), Ga. Bar Assn. (chmn. gen. practice and trial sect. 1983), Ga. Trial Lawyers Assn. (v.p. 1982—), Assn. Trial Lawyers of Am. Democrat. Episcopalian. Personal injury, Workers' compensation, Criminal. Home: 3302 Fulmer Dr Albany GA 31707 Office: Underwood Law Offices 419 W Oglethorpe Blvd Albany GA 31702

UNGER, ADRIENNE PENROD, lawyer; b. Bryan, Tex., Oct. 18, 1949; d. William Kenneth and Joyce (Pape) Penrod; m. Timothy John Unger, Nov. 23, 1974; children: Laurence, Lesley. BA with honors, U. Tex., 1973, JD with honors, 1974. Bar: Tex. 1974. Atty. Shell Oil Co., Houston, 1974-84, gen. atty. corp. and securities law, 1984—. Mem. ABA, Tex. Bar Assn., Houston Bar Assn. General corporate, Securities. Home: 1608 Banks Houston TX 77006 Office: Shell Oil Co Legal Orgn 900 Louisiana Houston TX 77002

UNGER, JOHN WILLIAM, JR., lawyer; b. Danville, Ill., June 11, 1954; s. John William and Lena R. (Roach) U.; m. Carolyn Ruth Welch, Sept. 17, 1982; children: Ashley, Adriana, John III. BA, U. Ark., 1977, JD, 1979. Bar: Ark. 1979, U.S. Dist. Ct. (ea. and we. dists.) Ark. 1979, U.S. Ct. Appeals (8th cir.) 1979, U.S. Tax Ct. 1980. Assoc. Jones & Segers, Fayetteville, Ark., 1978-81; assoc., ptnr. Crumpler, O'Connor & Wynne, El Dorado, Ark., 1981-84; ptnr. Unger & Hughes, El Dorado, 1984-86, Vickery & Unger, El Dorado, 1987—. Mem. ABA (com. on oil and gas 1985—), Ark. Bar Assn. (pres. natural resources sect. 1985—), Assn. Trial Lawyers Am. Republican. Presbyterian. Lodge: Rotary. Avocations: gardening, golf. Oil and gas leasing. Home: 2324 W Oak El Dorado AR 71730 Office: Vickey & Unger 470 N Washington El Dorado AR 71730

UNGER, ROBERTO M., law educator; b. 1947. Prof. law Harvard U., Cambridge, Mass. Office: Harvard U Law Sch Cambridge MA 02138 *

UNGERMAN, MAYNARD I., lawyer; b. Topeka, Dec. 5, 1929; s. Irvine E. and Hanna (Friedberg) U.; divorced; children: William Charles, Karla Beth, Rebecca Diane; m. Judith White, July 16, 1982; 1 child, Gregory. BA cum laude, Stanford U., 1951, JD, 1953. Ptnr. Ungerman, Conner & Little, Topeka, 1956—; spl. judge temp. div. 187, Okla. Ct. Appeals, 1982. Assoc. editor Comml. Law Jour., 1985—. Inaugural committeeman Pres. Johnson, 1965; chmn. Tulsa County Dems., 1967; pres. Community Service Council, Tulsa, 1986; past. pres., bd. dirs. Neighbor for Neighbor, Tulsa; bd. dirs. Oklahomans for Indian Opportunity, Norman, 1986; bd. dirs., chmn. community relations com. Tulsa Jewish Fedn., 1986. Named Citizen of the Yr. Okla. chpt. Nat. Assn. Social Workers, 1986. Mem. ABA, Comml. Law League, Okla. Bar Assn., Tulsa County Bar Assn. Democrat. Family and matrimonial, Labor, Consumer commercial. Home: 6203 S Jamestown Tulsa OK 74136 Office: Ungerman Conner & Little 1323 E 71st St Suite 300 Tulsa OK 74136

UNGLESBY, LEWIS O., lawyer; b. New Orleans, July 6, 1949; s. Lewis Huber and Mary Jane (Holloway) U.; m. Gail Hoy, Aug. 15, 1970; children—Lewis, Lance, Blake. B.S., U. Miss., 1971; J.D., La. State U., 1974. Bar: La. 1974, U.S. Dist. Ct. (ea., mid. and we. dists.) La. 1974, U.S. Ct. Appeals (5th cir.) 1974, U.S. Supreme Ct. 1980. Ptnr. Unglesby & Brown, Baton Rouge, 1985—; mem. Gov. La. Pardon Parole and Rehab. Commn., 1978; mem. judge's benchbook com. La. Supreme Ct., 1982—; lectr. La. Trial Lawyers Services. Fellow Am. Bd. Criminal Lawyers. Mem. Nat. Assn. Criminal Defense Lawyers, Am. Trial Lawyers Assn., ABA, La. Trial Lawyers Assn. (chmn. criminal law sect. 1983-85, bd. govs. 1983-87), La. State Bar Assn. (ho. of dels. 1979-87, lectr.). Criminal. Home: 14415 Highland Rd Baton Rouge LA 70810 Office: 246 Napoleon St Baton Rouge LA 70802

UNKOVIC, DENNIS, lawyer; b. Pitts., Mar. 28, 1948; s. Alexander and Joan (Callahan) U.; m. Diane Pfeifer, June 12, 1981; children: Alexis, Peter. BA, U. Va., 1970; JD, U. Pitts., 1973. Bar: Pa. 1973, D.C. 1974, U.S. Dist. Ct. D.C. 1974, U.S. Dist. Ct. (we. dist.) Pa. 1973, U.S. Ct. Appeals (D.C. cir.) 1974, U.S. Supreme Ct. 1978. Legis. counsel U.S. Senator Hugh D. Scott, Washington, 1973-75; asst. counsel U.S. Senate Judiciary Subcom. Patents, Trademarks, and Copyrights, Washington, 1973-75, 79; ptnr. Meyer, Unkovic & Scott, Pitts., 1975—; lectr. in field. Author: The Trade Secrets Handbook, 1985, Japanese translation 1986; contbr. articles to profl. jours. Bd. dirs. Alvernia Sch. Practical Nursing, Pitts., 1979—; candidate U.S. Congress 18th Congl. Dist., Pitts., 1976; mem. Pitts. Athletic Assn. Named One of Outstanding Young Men of Am., 1979, 83. Mem. ABA, Pa. Bar Assn., D.C. Bar Assn., Assn. Internationale Des Jeunes Advocats, Allegheny County Bar Assn., Licensing Execs. Soc., Am. Judicature Soc., Western Pa. Dist. Export Council, Corp. Counsel's Internat. Adviser. Republican. Presbyterian. Club: Duquesne (Pitts.). Avocations: writing, scuba diving, tennis. Federal civil litigation, General corporate, Private international. Home: 276 Kinvara Dr Pittsburgh PA 15237 Office: Meyer Unkovic & Scott 1300 Oliver Bldg Pittsburgh PA 15222

UNTERMEYER, SALLE PODOS, lawyer; b. Bklyn., Oct. 1, 1938; d. David Meyer and Rose (Ifshin) Garber; m. Steven Maurice Podos, June 20, 1959 (div. Dec. 1978); children—Richard Lance Podos, Lisa Beth Podos; m. Walter Untermeyer, Jr., May 2, 1982. B.A., Vassar Coll., 1959; M.A., Brandeis U., 1960; J.D., Columbia U., 1977. Bar: N.Y. 1978. Assoc., Paul, Weiss, Rifkind, Wharton & Garrison, N.Y.C., 1977-79; gen. counsel v.p., sec. MacAndrews & Forbes Group, Inc., N.Y.C., 1979-81; sr. assoc. Sage Gray Todd & Sims, N.Y.C., 1981-84, Proskauer Rose Goetz & Mendelsohn, N.Y.C., 1984—. Class fund-raising chmn. Vassar Coll., 1977-80; bd. dirs. Vassar Club N.Y., 1978-80; chmn. women's div. U.S. Senate Campaign, 1970; regional chmn. U.S. Presdl. Campaign, 1972; chmn. State Rep.'s Campaign, 1973; del.-elect Interim Democratic Conv., 1974, Lawyers Com. for Gov. Carey, 1978; chmn. Mo. state legis. Nat. Council Jewish Women, 1969-75, mem. nat. affairs com., 1969-77, chmn. Mo. juvenile justice project, 1970-75, mem. legis. coordinating com. Midwestern region, 1971-75, mem. nat. task force on constl. rights, 1974-77; v.p., bd. dirs. St. Louis Jewish Community Relations Council, 1970-75, chmn. ch.-state and Black Jack Amicus Curiae coms.; v.p., bd. dirs. St. Louis chpt. Am. Jewish Com., 1969-75, chmn. urban affairs and placement for ex-offenders coms., mem. com. on status of women, 1974-77; mem. legis. liaison Coalition for Environment, St. Louis, 1970-74; bd. dirs. St. Louis Jewish Community Ctrs. Assn., 1970-74, chmn. urban affairs and legis. affairs coms.; bd. dirs. St. Louis Jewish Family and Children's Service, 1972-74, chmn. welfare rights and health services coms.; bd. dirs. Glaucoma Found., 1986—; vol. coordinator Poor People's Campaign, 1968; founder, bd. dirs. Consumer's Assn., 1967-69; founder, chmn. Urban Corps program St. Louis Mayor's Com. on Youth, 1969-72; panelist White House Conf. on Children and Youth, 1970, 72, White House Conf. on Aging, 1974; founder, bd. dirs. Mo. chpt. PEARL (Pub. Edn. and Religious Liberty), 1972-75. Woodrow Wilson Found. fellow, 1959; NDEA fellow, 1959. Mem. Assn. Bar City N.Y. (mem. continuing legal edn. com.), ABA, N.Y. State Bar Assn. (com. on lectures and continuing legal edn.) General corporate, Securities. Home: 950 Park Ave New York NY 10028 Office: Proskauer Rose Goetz & Mendelsohn 300 Park Ave New York NY 10022

UNTHANK, G. WIX, U.S. dist. judge; b. Tway, Ky., June 14, 1923; s. Green Ward and Estell (Howard) U.; m. Marilyn Elizabeth Ward, Feb. 28, 1953. J.D., U. Miami, Fla., 1950. Bar: Ky. bar 1950. Judge Harlan County, 1950-57; asst. U.S. atty., Lexington, Ky., 1966-69; commonwealth atty. Harlan, 1970-80; judge U.S. Dist. Ct., Eastern Dist. Ky., Pikeville, 1980—. Served with AUS, 1940-45, ETO. Decorated Purple Heart, Bronze Star, Combat Inf. badge. Mem. Am. Bar Assn., Am. Judicature Soc., Ky. Bar Assn., Fla. Bar Assn. Democrat. Presbyterian. Jurisprudence. Office: District Court US Courthouse PO Box 278 Pikeville KY 41501 *

UPDEGROVE, ANDREW SCOTT, lawyer; b. Phila., Nov. 9, 1953; s. John Harvey and Ruby Fried (Hunsberger) U.; m. Katherine Lynn Dee, Aug. 6, 1983. BA, Yale U., 1975; JD, Cornell U., 1979. Bar: Mass. 1979. Assoc. Bingham, Dana & Gould, Boston, 1979-82, Testa, Hurwitz & Thibeault, Boston, 1982—. Bd. dirs., sec. nat. non-profit Council on Religion and Law, Atlanta, 1982—. Mem. ABA, Boston Bar Assn. Presbyterian. Club: Boston Racquet. Avocations: stained glass, sailing, backpacking. Computer, Securities, General corporate. Home: 41 Jersey St Marblehead MA 01945 Office: Testa Hurwitz & Thibeault 53 State St Exchange Pl Boston MA 01945

URAM, GERALD ROBERT, lawyer; b. Newark, July 11, 1941; s. Arthur George and Mildred (Stein) U.; m. Susan Wanderer, June 12, 1966; children—Michael, Alison. B.A., Dartmouth Coll., 1963; LL.B., Yale U., 1967. Bar: N.Y. 1967. Assoc. Paul, Weiss, Rifkind, Wharton & Garrison, N.Y.C., 1967-74; v.p., corp. counsel Prudential Bldg. Maintenance Corp., N.Y.C., 1974; ptnr. Davis & Gilbert, N.Y.C., 1974—. Bd. dirs. St. Francis Friends of Poor, Inc. Mem. ABA, N.Y. State Bar Assn., Assn. Bar City of N.Y. Contbr. to profl. publs. Landlord-tenant, Real property. Office: 16th Floor 850 3d Ave New York NY 10022

URBAN, EDMUND THEODORE, lawyer; b. Flushing, N.Y., Nov. 5, 1947; s. Edmund Joseph and Johanna Elizabeth (Schuster) U.; m. Brenda Gail Bolick, June 15, 1974; 1 child, Jonathan. BA, Wake Forest U., 1970, JD, 1972. Bar: N.C. 1972. Staff atty. Greensboro (N.C.) Legal Aid, 1972-73; staff atty. Jefferson Pilot Title Ins. Co., Greensboro, 1973-75, asst. gen. counsel, 1975-77; v.p., gen. counsel AMI Title Ins. Co., Raleigh, N.C., 1977-80; v.p., Southeast U.S. region counsel Safeco Title Ins. Co., Branden, Fla., 1980—; advisor N.C. Bar Real Property Com., 1975-76. Contbr. articles to jours. Guest lectr. Campbell U. Sch. Law, 1980. Mem. N.C. Bar Assn. (speaker real property sect. seminar 1979), N.C. Land Title Assn. (exec. com. 1977-80, pres. 1980, speaker continuing edn. seminars, 1978-80, 85), Am. Land Title Assn. (Wetlands com. 1979-80), Fla. Title Underwriters Bur. (sec., treas. 1983-85, chmn. liaison com. 1985—), Phi Alpha Delta, Sigma Pi. Republican. Roman Catholic. General corporate, Real property, Insurance. Home: 2105 Doefield Ct Valrico FL 33594 Office: Safeco Title Ins Co 1216 Oakfield Dr Brandon FL 33511

URBAN, LEE DONALD, lawyer; b. Portland, Maine, July 12, 1946; s. Donald Franklin and Mirriam Gertrude (Percy) U.; m. Anna Sanger Kirkpatrick, Feb. 15, 1975; children: Anna, Reid, Seth. BA, Colby Coll., 1968; JD, Georgetown U., 1974. Bar: Maine 1974, D.C. 1975. Atty. FTC, Washington, 1974-75; assoc. then ptnr. Perkins, Thompson, Hinckley & Keddy, Portland, 1975-84; ptnr. Pierce, Atwood, Scribner, Allen, Smith & Lancaster, Portland, 1985—; instr. real estate U. So. Maine, Portland, 1980—. Mem. adv. bd. Greater Portland Landmarks, Inc., 1975—, bd. advisors Nat. Trust for Hist. Preservation, Washington, 1984—; officer, bd. dirs. Intown Portland Exchange, 1982—; bd. dirs. Maine Real Estate Devel. Assn., 1985—, pres., 1986—. Served to lt. (j.g.) USN, 1968-71. Democrat. Avocations: bicycling, music. Real property, Landlord-tenant, Historic preservation. Office: Pierce Atwood Scribner et al One Monument Sq Portland MA 04101

URBIGKIT, WALTER C., state judge. Judge Wyo. Supreme Ct., Cheyenne, 1986—. Office: Wyo Supreme Court PO Box 1006 Cheyenne WY 82003 *

URBOM, DAVID WARD, lawyer; b. Oxford, Nebr., Oct. 4, 1952; s. Ward Clarence and Darien Jenette (Hermes) U.; m. Christine Ann Faw, July 17, 1976; children: Erin Michelle, Jonathan David. BS, U. Nebr., 1974; JD, Washburn U., 1977. Bar: Kans. 1977, Nebr. 1977, U.S. Dist. Ct. Kans. 1977, U.S. Dist. Ct. Nebr. 1977. Ptnr. Urbom Law Offices, P.C., Arapahoe, Nebr., 1977—; atty. Furnas County, Beaver City, Nebr., 1979—. Scoutmaster Boy Scouts Am., Arapahoe, 1978-80. Mem. Nat. Dist. Attys. Assn., 14th Jud. Dist. Bar Assn. (sec., treas. 1986—), Nebr. Bar Assn., Nebr. County Attys. Assn., Phi Delta Phi. Republican. Episcopalian. Club: Mid-County Country (Arapahoe) (pres. 1981-82). Avocations: golf, hunting, horses. General practice, Probate, Real property. Home: 1003 8th St Arapahoe NE 68922 Office: Urbom Law Offices PC 513 Nebraska Ave Arapahoe NE 68922

URBOM, RANDALL CRAWFORD, lawyer; b. Lincoln, Nebr., Sept. 20, 1955; s. Warren K. and Joyce C. (Crawford) U.; m. Kelli K. Wattles; children: Grant K., Alexander R. AB, Nebr. Wesleyan U., 1978; JD, U. Nebr., 1981. Bar: Neb. 1981. Assoc. Knapp, Mues, Beavers & Luther, Kearney, Nebr., 1981-84; atty. Nebr. Dept. Social Services, Lincoln, 1984-85; assoc. Mattson, Ricketts, Davies, Stewart & Calkins, Lincoln, 1985—; adj. prof. bus. law Kearney State U., 1983-84. Liaison, evaluator United Way, Lincoln, 1986—; bd. dirs. Alzheimers Disease and Related Disorders, Lincoln, 1986—. Mem. Assn. Trial Lawyers Am., Nebr. Trial Lawyers Assn., Nat. Assn. Coll. and Univ. Attys. Methodist. Avocation: tennis. Federal civil litigation, State civil litigation, Contracts commercial. Home: 2823 Shelley Circle Lincoln NE 68516 Office: Mattson Ricketts Davies et al 1401 Firstier Bldg Lincoln NE 68508

URBOM, WARREN KEITH, judge; b. Atlanta, Nebr., Dec. 17, 1925; s. Clarence Andrew and Anna Myrl (Irelan) U.; m. Joyce Marie Crawford, Aug. 19, 1951; children: Kim Marie, Randall Crawford, Allison Lee, Joy Renee. A.B. with highest distinction, Nebr. Wesleyan U., 1950, LL.D. (hon.), 1985; student, Iliff Sch. Theology, Denver, 1950; J.D. with distinction, U. Mich., 1953. Bar: Nebr. 1953. Mem. firm Baylor, Evnen, Baylor, Urbom, & Curtiss, Lincoln, Nebr., 1953-70; judge U.S. Dist. Ct. Dist. Nebr., 1970-72, chief judge, 1972-86; mem. com. on practice and procedure Nebr. Supreme Ct., 1965—; mem. subcom. on fed. jurisdiction Jud. Conf. U.S., 1975-83; adj. instr. trial advocacy U. Nebr. Coll. Law, 1979—; bd. dirs. Fed. Jud. Ctr., 1982-86; chmn. Fed. Judiciat Ctr. Com. on Orientation Newly Appointed Dist. Judges, 1986—. Contbr. articles to profl. jours. Trustee St. Paul Sch. Theology, Kansas City, Mo., 1986—; pres. Lincoln YMCA, 1965-67, bd. dirs., 1982-86; bd. govs. Nebr. Wesleyan U., chmn., 1975-80. Served with AUS, 1944-46. Recipient Medal of Honor, Nebr. Wesleyan U. Alumni Assn., 1983. Fellow Am. Coll. Trial Lawyers; mem. ABA, Nebr. Bar Assn. (ho. of dels. 1966-70), Lincoln Bar Assn. (pres. 1968-69). United Methodist (bd. mgrs., bd. global ministries 1972-76). Club: Masons (33 deg.). Jurisprudence. Home: 4510 Van Dorn Lincoln NE 68506 Office: 586 Federal Bldg Lincoln NE 68501

URDA, RICHARD BERNARD, JR., lawyer; b. Pitts., Apr. 24, 1950; s. Richard B. and Louise Frances (Zahratka) U.; m. Kathleen Alice McGuire, Aug. 10, 1974; children: Kathleen, Patrick, Anne, Elizabeth. BA, U. Notre Dame, 1972; JD, U. Mich., 1975. Bar: Ind. 1975, Mich. 1975, U.S. Dist. Ct. (no. dist.) Ind. 1975, U.S. Tax Ct. 1976, U.S. Ct. Appeals (7th cir.) 1976. Assoc. Thornburg, McGill, South Bend, Ind., 1975-79; sole practice South Bend, 1980-85; pres. Urda Profl. Corp., South Bend, 1985—; bd. dirs. St. Joseph County estate planning council South Bend. Pres. St. Joseph County Arthritis Soc., 1979, St. Joseph County United Health Services, 1982, St. Joseph County Mental Health Assn., 1984. Mem. Notre Dame Club (pres. 1986). Republican. Roman Catholic. Pension, profit-sharing, and employee benefits, Corporate taxation. Office: Urda Profl Corp 311 First Interstate Bank Bldg South Bend IN 46601

UREY, DAVID STAUFFER, lawyer; b. N.Y.C., Jan. 19, 1936; s. John Wesley and Elizabeth Ester (Stauffer) U.; m. Eleanor Donna Shea, Jan. 18, 1967; children: Brian John, Darby Christopher. BS in Indsl. Engring., Northwestern U., 1958; JD with honors, George Washington U., 1964. Bar: U.S. Dist. Ct. D.C. 1965, U.S. Supreme Ct. 1968, Pa. 1973. Assoc. Irons, Birch et al, Washington, 1965-68, Machine Tool Group Litton Industries, Hartford, Conn., 1968-72; corp. counsel Rust Engring. Co., Pitts., 1972-73; gen. atty. intellectual property law USX Corp., Pitts., 1973—. Author, co-editor: LES US/Eastern Europe Technology and Patents, 1977; contbr. articles to profl. jours. Served to lt. (j.g.) USN, 1958-60. Mem. Licensing Execs. Soc. (v.p. ea. region 1985—), Am. Intellectual Property Law Assn. (bd. dirs. 1981-84), Patent Law Assn. Pitts. (v.p. 1987-88). Republican. Avocations: golf, wood chopping. Licensing, technology transfer, Patent, Trademark and copyright. Office: USX Corp 600 Grant St Pittsburgh PA 15230

URICK, WALTER ALEKSY, lawyer; b. Evanston, Ill., June 3, 1939; s. Alesky and Eugenia (Bayer) U.; m. Karen M. Fick, Aug. 26, 1967; children: Anna, Alesky, Esther. AB magna cum laude, Albion Coll., 1961; JD with distinction, U. Mich., 1964. Bar: Mich. 1964, U.S. Supreme Ct. 1970. Pros. atty. Oceana County, Hart, Mich., 1965-70; atty. City of Hart, 1969—, Village of Pentwater, Mich., 1970-74; ptnr. Urick & Monton, Hart, 1977—; pres. Oceana-Muskegon Legal Aid, Inc., 1971-72. Asst. editor Mich. Law Rev., 1963; contbr. numerous articles to profl. jours. Chmn. adminstrv. bd. Hart United Meth. Ch., 1983-86; Oceana County chmn. Mich. Week Program, 1966; chmn. Oceana County Reps., 1972-74. Mem. Mich. Bar Assn., 27th Jud. Cir. Bar Assn. (past pres.), Oceana County Bar Assn. (pres. 1975-83), Hart C. of C. (pres. 1969-70). Clubs: Hart Rotary (pres. 1976-77, sec. 1971-76). Probate, Real property, General practice. Address: 214 Washington St Hart MI 49420

UROWSKY, RICHARD J., lawyer; b. N.Y.C., June 28, 1946; s. Jacob and Anne (Granick) U. BA, Yale U., 1967, JD, 1972; B Philosophy, Oxford U., Eng., 1970. Bar: N.Y. 1973, U.S. Dist. Ct. (so. dist.) N.Y. 1973, U.S. Ct. Appeals (2d cir.) 1973, U.S. Supreme Ct. 1977. Law clk. to Justice Reed U.S. Supreme Ct., Washington, 1972-73; assoc. Sullivan & Cromwell, N.Y.C., 1973-80, ptnr., 1980—. Mem. ABA, Assn. of the Bar of the City of N.Y., Fed. Bar Council. Clubs: Yale, Down Town Assn. (N.Y.C.). Federal civil litigation, Antitrust, Securities. Office: Sullivan & Cromwell 125 Broad St New York NY 10004

URQUHART, STEPHEN E., lawyer; b. Quincy, Mass., Mar. 2, 1949; s. Raymond Miles and M. Eileen (MacDonald) U.; m. Katherine Driscoll, Mar. 15, 1970; 1 child, Stephen M. AB, Boston Coll., 1976, JD, 1979. Bar: Mass. 1979, U.S. Dist. Ct. Mass. 1980. Legis. aide Mass. Ho. of Reps., Boston, 1976; counsel B.C. Legal Assistance Bur., Waltham, Mass., 1976-79; assoc. Law Offices of Robert J. Ladd (formerly Law Offices of Roland I. Wood), North Andover, Mass., 1980—. Precinct capt. Edward M. Kennedy for Senator, Mass. 1979-80; campaign worker various Dem. candidates. Recipient cert. of merit United World Federalists, 1974. Mem. ABA, Mass. Bar Assn., Mass. Acad. Trial Attys., Am. Arbitration Assn. Methodist. Club: Clan Urquhart (Va.). Avocations: model shipbuilding, Scottish history and music, reading, travel. State civil litigation, Insurance, Personal injury. Home: 429 Main St PO Box 637 Danville NH 03819 Office: 203 Turnpike St North Andover MA 01845

URSINI, JOSEPHINE LUCILLE, lawyer; b. N.Y.C., Sept. 17, 1952; d. Edilio R. and Lucille V. (Ciufo) U.; m. Kenneth A. Krantz. B.S., Boston Coll., 1974; J.D., NYU, 1977. Bar: Md. 1977, D.C. 1978, Va. 1987. Law clk. trial div. U.S. Ct. Claims, Washington, 1977-78; assoc. Fried, Frank, Harris, Shriver, Kampelman, Washington, 1978-83; prin. Dickstein, Shapiro & Morin, Washington, 1983-85; sole practice, 1985—. Contbr. articles to profl. jours. Mem. ABA, D.C. Bar Assn., Fed. Bar Assn. Roman Catholic. Georgetown Gilbert and Sullivan Soc. (dir.). Government contracts and claims, Construction. Home: 4523 Pickett Rd Fairfax VA 22032 Office: 4545 42d St NW Washington DC 20016

URWIN, GARY LEE, lawyer; b. Toledo, Jan. 6, 1955; s. Ray Ward and Evangeline Mae (Miller) U.; m. Barbara Lloyd, June 2, 1979 (div. July 1984). BA cum laude, Oberlin Coll., 1977; JD, UCLA, 1982. Bar: Calif. 1982, U.S. Dist. Ct. (cen. dist.) Calif. 1982, U.S. Dist. Ct. (no. and so. dists.) Calif. 1983, U.S. Dist. Ct. (ea. dist.) Calif. 1986, U.S. Supreme Ct. 1986. Assoc. Macdonald, Halsted & Laybourne, Los Angeles, 1982—; dep. dist. atty. Los Angeles County Bar Trial Atty. Program, 1984; atty. Los Angeles County Bar Pub. Counsel Program, 1983. Contbr. articles to law jours. Mem. ABA, Los Angeles County Bar Assn., State bar Assn. Calif., Assn. Bus. Trial Lawyers, Calif. Trial Lawyers Assn., ACLU, Los Angeles Jr. C. of C., Phi Beta Kappa. Democrat. Episcopalian. Club: Los Angeles Athletic. Avocations: playing trumpet, jazz arranging. Federal civil litigation, State civil litigation, Insurance. Office: Macdonald Halsted & Laybourne 725 S Figueroa St Suite 3600 Los Angeles CA 90017

URY, FREDERIC STEPHEN, lawyer; b. Zanesville, Ohio, Sept. 11, 1952; s. Perry S. and Lorraine (Greenstein) U.; m. Debby Hagopian, June 6, 1976; 1 child, Jennifer. BS, Babson Coll., 1974; JD, Suffolk U., 1977. Bar: Conn. 1977, U.S. Dist. Ct. Conn. 1978, U.S. Supreme Ct. 1982. Assoc., ptnr. Sherwood, Garlick & Cowell, Westport, Conn., 1977-84; ptnr. Rubenstein & Ury, Westport, Conn., 1984-87, Rutkin Rubenstein, Effron and Ury, Westport, 1987—; instr. Fairfield (Conn.) U., 1979—. Pres. Community Council, Westport, 1983-85; bd. dirs. Westport United Way, 1985—; corp. mem., trustee Babson Coll., Wellesley, Mass., 1974-84. Mem. Assn. Trial Lawyers Am., Conn. Bar Assn., Westport Bar Assn. Democrat. Jewish. Lodge: Kiwanis. Avocations: hiking, skiing. Federal civil litigation, State civil litigation, Real property. Home: 17 Dover Rd Westport CT 06880 Office: Rutkin Rubenstein Effron and Ury 121 Post Rd E Westport CT 06881

USSERY, ALBERT TRAVIS, lawyer, banker; b. Gulfport, Miss., Mar. 12, 1928; s. Walter Travis and Rosamond (Sears) U.; m. Margaret Grosvenor Paine, Nov. 22, 1950; children—Margaret Rosamond, John Travis, Marilyn Ann, Meredith Lee. A.B., Washington U., St. Louis, 1950; LL.B., U. N.Mex., 1951, J.D., 1968; LL.M., Georgetown U., 1955. Admitted to N.Mex. bar, 1951, since practiced in Albuquerque; mem. firm Gallagher and Ussery, 1951-53, Threet, Ussery & Threet, 1957-60; assoc. with Alfred H. McRae, 1961-63; ptnr. McRae, Ussery, Mims, Ortega & Kitts, 1964-65; chmn. Am. Bank Commerce, 1966-70, pres., 1967-70; ptnr. Ussery, Burciaga & Parrish, 1969-79; pres. Ussery & Parrish, P.A., 1980—; spl. counsel to Albuquerque on water law, 1956-66; chmn. Rio Grande Valley Bank, Albuquerque, 1972-83; pres. Albuquerque Small Bus. Investment Co., 1977—; dir. First City Investment Brokers, Inc., Lovelace Med. Systems & Techs., Inc.; lectr. mil. law U. N.Mex., 1956, instr. corp. fin., 1956-57, lectr. bus. law, 1960-61. Chmn. water adv. com. Albuquerque Indsl. Devel. Service, 1960-66; vice chmn. N.Mex. Council on Econ. Edn., 1969-74; mem. Region VI-Albuquerque adv. council SBA, 1982—; mem. N.Mex. Regional Export Expansion Council, 1969-74; mem. Albuquerque Armed Forces Adv. Assn., 1977— . Trustee Village Los Ranchos de Albuquerque, 1970-72; chmn. adv. bd. Lovelace-Bataan Med. Ctr., 1976-78; trustee Lovelace Med. Found., 1978—; bd. dirs. Goodwill Industries N.Mex., 1957-65, Albuquerque Travelers Assistance, 1956-66, Family Consultation Service, 1961-64, Albuquerque Symphony Assn., 1964-68, Hispanic Culture Found., 1983—, Lovelace Health Plan Inc., 1985—; bd. dirs. N.Mex. Arthritis Found., 1969-74, pres., 1971. Mem. Am., Fed., Albuquerque (treas. 1957-60) bar assns., State Bar N.Mex., Estate Planning Council Albuquerque (pres. 1962), N.Mex. Zool. Soc. (dir., pres. 1977-78), Am. Legion (comdr. 1962-63), Lawyers Club. (pres. 1983-84). Lodge: Kiwanis (dir. 1957-60). General corporate, Banking, Real property. Home: Rio Grande at Eakes Rd NW Albuquerque NM 87107 Office: 200 Rio Grande Valley Bldg PO Box 487 Tijeras Ave NW 501 Albuquerque NM 87103

UTERMOHLEN, WILLIAM JEROME, lawyer; b. Cottonwood, Idaho, Oct. 11, 1954; s. Charles Robert and Mary Lee (Cox) U. BA magna cum laude, Mankato State U., 1976; JD cum laude, U. Minn., 1980. Bar: Minn. 1980, U.S. Dist. Ct. Minn. 1981, D.C. 1984, U.S. Dist. Ct. D.C. 1985, U.S. Ct. Appeals (D.C. cir.) 1985. Assoc. Hessian, McKasy and Soderberg, Mpls., 1980-83, Stohlman, Beuchert, Egan and Smith, Washington, 1983—. Article editor U. Minn. Law Rev., 1979-80. Mem. ABA, D.C. Bar Assn., Minn. State Bar Assn., Hennepin County Bar Assn. Democrat. Avocation: genealogy. Federal civil litigation, State civil litigation, Real property. Home: 3901 Connecticut Ave NW Apt 212 Washington DC 20008 Office: Stohlman et al 1775 Pennsylvania Ave NW Washington DC 20006

UTEVSKY, DAVID, lawyer; b. Dayton, Ohio, Aug. 29, 1951; s. Fred and Shirley (Fishman) U.; m. Reba Allyn Shangrow, Apr. 22, 1983. BA in Communications, U. Wash., 1972; JD, U. Calif., Berkeley, 1977. Bar: Wash. 1977, U.S. Dist. Ct. (we. dist.) Wash. 1978, U.S. Ct. Appeals (9th cir.) 1979, U.S. Dist. Ct. (ea. dist.) Wash. 1982, U.S. Tax Ct. 1984, U.S. Supreme Ct., 1985. Law clk. to dist. judge U.S. Dist. Ct., Conn., 1977-78; assoc. Foster Pepper & Riviera, Seattle, 1978-84, ptnr., 1984—. Mem. ABA, Assn. Trial Lawyers Am., Am. Bankruptcy Inst., ACLU of Wash.(cooperating attys. legal com. 1980—, bd. dirs. 1983—), Order of Coif. Libel, Bankruptcy, Federal civil litigation. Office: Foster Pepper Riviera 1111 Third Ave 34th Floor Seattle WA 98101

UTRECHT, JAMES DAVID, lawyer; b. Camp Polk, Ia., May 23, 1952; s. James C. and Susan (McDevitt) U.; m. Karen Lee Kelly, Aug. 17, 1975; children: Ann Elizabeth, Claire Susan. B.B.A., U. Cin., 1974, J.D., 1977. Ptnr., Shipman, Utrecht & Dixon, Troy, Ohio, 1977—; asst. law dir. City of Troy, 1984—.Chmn. Miami County Reagan-Bush Com. (Ohio), 1984. Mem. Miami County Bar Assn., Ohio Bar Assn., ABA, 1/2 Republican. Roman Catholic. Clubs: Troy Jaycees (dir. 1983-84), Troy Rotary. Lodge: Elks. Banking, General practice, Personal injury. Home: 2299 Pleasantview Dr Troy OH 45373 Office: Shipman Utrecht & Dixon PA 12 S Plum St Troy OH 45373

UTTER, ROBERT FRENCH, judge; b. Seattle, June 19, 1930; s. John and Besse (French) U.; m. Elizabeth J. Stevenson, Dec. 28, 1953; children: Kimberly, Kirk, John. B.S., U. Wash., 1952; LL.B., 1954. Bar: Wash. 1954. Pros. atty. King County, Wash., 1955-57; individual practice law Seattle, 1957-59; ct. commr. King County Superior Ct., 1959-64, judge, 1964-69; judge Wash. State Ct. Appeals, 1969-71; judge Wash. State Supreme Ct., 1971—, chief justice, 1979-81; lectr. in field; leader comparative law tour Peoples Rep. in China, 86, 87. Editor books on real property and appellate practice. Pres., founder Big Brother Assn., Seattle, 1955-67; pres., founder Job Therapy Inc., 1963-71; mem. exec. com. Conf. of Chief Justices, 1979-80, 81-86; pres. Thurston County Big Bros./Big Sisters, 1984. Named Alumnus of the Year Linfield Coll., 1973, Disting. Jud. Scholar, U. Ind., 1987. Mem. ABA, Am. Judicature Soc. (Herbert Harley award 1983, sec. 1987—), Order of Coif. Baptist. Office: Temple of Justice Olympia WA 98504

UTZ, EDWARD JOSEPH, lawyer; b. Cin., Feb. 8, 1918; s. Edward Joseph and Frances (Kraemer) U. B.B.A., U. Cin., 1943; LL.B., Chase Law Sch., Cin., 1944. Bar: Ohio 1944, Ky. 1967. Design engr. Cin. Bickford Tool Co., 1942-44; practice with C.B. DesJardins, Cin., 1944-48; individual practice Cin., 1948—; instr. Chase Law Sch., 1960-71. Contbr. articles to legal jours. Fellow Am. Coll. Trial Lawyers; mem. Internat. Assn. Ins. Counsel, ABA, Am. Patent Law Assn., Ohio Bar Assn., Ky. Bar Assn., Cin. Bar Assn., Cin. Patent Law Assn. Republican. Clubs: Cincinnati, Bankers, Kenwood Country. State civil litigation, Patent, Insurance. Home: 4975 Councilrock Ln Indian Hill OH 45243 Office: 1306 4th and Walnut Bldg 36 E 4th St Cincinnati OH 45202

UVILLER, H. RICHARD, lawyer, educator; b. N.Y.C., July 3, 1929; m. Rena K. Uviller; 1 dau., Daphne R. B.A., Harvard U., 1951; LL.B., Yale U., 1953. Legal counsel U.S. Dept. Justice, 1953-54; asst. dist. atty. N.Y. County, 1954-68; prof. law Columbia U. Sch. of Law, N.Y.C., 1968—. Contbr. articles to profl. jours. Office: Columbia U Sch Law 435 W 116 St New York NY 10027 *

UYENO, THEODORE YOSHI, lawyer; b. Honolulu, Sept. 16, 1951; s. Ray Moriyoshi and Katherine Sachiye (Sasagawa) U. BA in Law and Society, U. Calif., Santa Barbara, 1973; JD, U. Hawaii, 1979. Bar: Hawaii 1979, U.S. Dist. Ct. Hawaii 1979, U.S. Ct. Appeals (9th cir.) 1979. Asst. specialist corrections Hawaii Law Enforcement Planning Agy., Honolulu, 1974-75; dep. pub. defender State of Hawaii, Honolulu, 1979-80; law clk. to presiding justice Hawaii Supreme Ct., Honolulu, 1980; ptnr. Reinwald, O'Connor & Marrack, Honolulu, 1980—. Mem. ABA, Hawaii Bar Assn. Construction, Real property, General practice. Home: 5334 Limu Pl Honolulu HI 96821 Office: Hoddick Reinwald O'Connor & Marrack PO Box 3199 Honolulu HI 96801

VACANTI, ALFRED CHARLES, JR., lawyer; b. Omaha, May 21, 1951; s. Alfred Charles Sr. and Louise M. (Spitella) V.; adopted s. Mary E. Holmes; m. Lorraine F. Bukowski, Apr. 19, 1980. BBA, Creighton U., 1973, JD, 1976. Bar: Nebr. 1976, U.S. Dist. Ct. Nebr. 1976. Bailiff, law clk. to presiding justice Nebr. Dist. Ct., Omaha, 1976-77; sole practice Omaha, 1977—. Vol., advisor Jr. Achievement Nat. Conf., Omaha and Bloomington, Ind., 1970—; chmn. auction Nat. Sno-Ball Softball Inc., Omaha, 1985—; mem. Santa Lucia Festival Com., Omaha, 1970-77. Named one of Outstanding Young Men Am., 1986. Mem. ABA, Nebr. Bar Assn., Omaha Bar Assn., Nebr. Assn. Trial Attys., Assn. Reps. Profl. Athletes. Roman Catholic. Avocations: sports, music, travel. Entertainment, Personal injury, General practice. Home: 323 S 151st Circle Omaha NE 68154 Office: 11414 W Center Rd Omaha NE 68144

VADNAIS, ALFRED WILLIAM, lawyer; b. Pawtucket, R.I., Nov. 25, 1935; s. Edmund L. and Hilda W. (Winn) V.; m. Joan Bernice Markowski, Feb. 1, 1959; children—Alison J., Arlene J., Elisabeth Ann. B.A., Hofstra U., 1958; LL.B., Syracuse U., 1961. Bar: R.I. 1961, Tenn. 1972, U.S. Ct. Appeals (6th cir.) 1973, U.S. Ct. Appeals (4th cir.) 1978, U.S. Ct. Appeals (2d cir.) 1980, U.S. Supreme Ct. 1980, Pa. 1981, U.S. Dist. Ct. (we. dist.) Pa. 1982, U.S. Ct. Appeals (3d cir.) 1984. Labor atty., chief counsel Westinghouse Electric Co., Pitts., 1965-72; ptnr. Humphreys, Hutcheson & Moseley, Chattanooga, Tenn., 1972-81; ptnr. Eckert, Seamans, Cherin & Mellott, Pitts., 1981—, chmn. labor-employment dept. Served to 1st lt. U.S. Army, 1961-63. Mem. ABA, Tenn. Bar Assn., Pa. Bar Assn., Allegheny County Bar Assn., Pitts. C. of C. Republican. Roman Catholic. Clubs: Pitts. Field, Pittsburgh. Labor. Address: 600 Grant St Pittsburgh PA 15219

VAGTS, DETLEV FREDERICK, lawyer, educator; b. Washington, Feb. 13, 1929; s. Alfred and Miriam (Beard) V.; m. Dorothy Larkin, Dec. 11, 1954; children—Karen, Lydia. Grad., Taft Sch., 1945; A.B., Harvard, 1948, LL.B., 1951. Bar: N.Y. 1952, Mass. 1961. Assoc. Cahill, Gordon, Reindel & Ohl, N.Y.C., 1951-53, 56-59; asst. prof. law Harvard Law Sch., 1959-62, prof., 1962—, Eli Goldston prof., 1981-86, Bemis prof., 1986—; counselor internat. law Dept. State, 1976-77. Author: (with others) Transnational Legal Problems, 1968, 2d edit., 1976, 3d edit., 1986, Basic Corporation Law, 1973, 2d edit., 1979; editor: (with others) Secured Transactions Under the Uniform Commercial Code, 1963-64; assoc. reporter: (with others) Restatement of Foreign Relations Law; book rev. editor Am. Jour. Internat., 1986—. Served to 1st lt. USAF, 1953-56. Mem. Am. Bar Assn., Am. Soc. Internat. Law, Phi Beta Kappa. General corporate, Private international, Public international. Home: 29 Follen St Cambridge MA 02138 Office: Harvard U Law Sch Cambridge MA 02138

VAIDIK, NANCY HARRIS, lawyer; b. West Lafayette, Ind., June 24, 1955; d. C. Thomas and Elaine S. (Guhl) Harris; m. Terry Vaidik, Aug. 1977 (div. 1979); m. James J. Stankiewicz, June 18, 1982; children: Kristin and Kelly (twins). BA in Polit. Sci. and Psychology with highest distinction, Valparaiso U., 1977, JD, 1980. Bar: Ind. 1980. Dep. prosecutor Porter County Prosecutor's Office, Valparaiso, 1980-83, chief dep. prosecutor, 1983-86; assoc. J.J. Stankiewicz and Assocs., Merrillville, Ind., 1986—; adj. prof. law trial practices Valparaiso U., 1987—; mem. community corrections adv. bd., 1981-86. Mem. Community Corrections Adv. Bd., Valparaiso, 1981—, Porter County Welfare Adminstrv. Rev. Panel, Valparaiso, 1985-87; founder, bd. dirs. Victim's Assistance Unit, Valparaiso, 1984—; founder, project dir. Sexual Assault Recovery Program, Valparaiso, 1986—. Mem. ABA, Ind. Bar Assn., Porter County Bar Assn., Lake County Bar Assn. Lutheran. Criminal. Home: 563 Ravine Valparaiso IN 46383 Office: J J Stankiewicz & Assocs 7870 Broadway Merrillville IN 46410

VALANTY, BURTON JOHN, lawyer consultant; b. Detroit, Sept. 18, 1949; s. John S. and Clara E. (Howe) V.; m. Leilani E. Wiesen, May 24, 1975 (div. Dec. 1984); children: Brandon John, Justin Scott. BS with honors, Mich. State U., 1971, MA, 1972; JD with honors, U. Detroit, 1976. Bar: Mich. 1977, U.S. Dist. Ct. (ea. dist.) Mich. 1977, U.S. Ct. Appeals (6th cir.) 1977. Labor relations staff Ford Motor Co., Dearborn, Mich., 1973-80; corp. labor relations mgr. Volkswagen of Am., Troy, Mich., 1980-86; personnel dir. mftg. plant Volkswagen of Am., Ft. Worth, 1986—; assoc. AMS, Inc., West Lafayette, Ind., 1986. Mem. U. Detroit Personnel Profls. Labor. Office: Volkswagen of Am 4401 Blue Mound Rd Fort Worth TX 76112

VALAUSKAS, CHARLES C., lawyer; b. Chgo., Nov. 14, 1952; s. Edward A. and Madeline V.; m. Linda S. Kawano, Nov. 6, 1977. BS, U. Ill., Chgo., 1977; JD, DePaul U., 1981; LLM, Northwestern U., 1985. Bar: Ill. 1981, U.S. Dist. Ct. (no. dist.) Ill. 1981, U.S. Patent Office, 1985. Research assoc. Schweppe Found., Chgo., 1981-85; assoc. Karon, Morrison & Savikas, Ltd., Chgo., 1984—. Contbr. articles to profl. jours. Nat. Wildlife Fedn. fellow, Washington, 1980; State Ill. fellow Gov.'s Com., 1979. Mem. Ill. Bar Assn., Fed. Cir. Bar Assn., Patent Office Bar Assn. Avocations: Bonsai, orchid propagation. Private international, Patent, Environment. Home: 205 Marengo Forest Park IL 60130 Office: Karon Morrison & Savikas Ltd 5700 Sears Tower 233 S Wacker Dr Chicago IL 60606

VALDES, RICHARD ALBERT, lawyer; b. Chgo., July 12, 1942; s. Mario and Juanita (San Martin) V.; m. Yolanda Torres, Sept. 12, 1964 (div. July 1984); children: Yolanda Maria, Richard Bartholomew; m. Rose Helen Arroyo, Sept. 26, 1985. AB, Princeton U., 1964; MA, Stanford U., 1966; PhD, U. Ill., 1975; JD, U. Mich., 1982. Bar: Tex. 1982, U.S. Dist. Ct. (no. dist.) Tex. 1983, U.S. Ct. Appeals (5th cir.) 1983. Prof. U. Okla., Norman, 1975-79; assoc. Thompson & Knight, Dallas, 1982-84, Boyd & DuBose, Dallas, 1984-86, Bedsole & Bird, Dallas, 1986—. Contbr. articles to profl. jours.; editor. Translator Bd. of elections, State of Okla., 1978-79; mem. Gov.'s Adv. Bd. Spanish-Am. Relations, State of Okla., 1977-79. NDEA fellow, 1965, 67, 70. Mem. ABA, Tex. Bar Assn., Dallas Bar Assn., Fed. Bar Assn., Assn. Trial Lawyers Am., Sigma Delta Pi. Federal civil litigation, State civil litigation, Trademark and copyright. Home: PO Box 214995 Dallas TX 75221 Office: Bedsole & Bird 5944 Luther Ln Dallas TX 75225

VALENTE, PETER CHARLES, lawyer; b. N.Y.C., July 3, 1940; s. Francis Louis and Aurelia Emily (Cella) V.; m. Judith Kay Nemeroff, Feb. 16, 1966; children: Susan Lynn, David Marc. BA, Bowdoin Coll., 1962; LLB, Columbia U., 1966; LL.M., N.Y.U., 1971. Bar: N.Y. 1967. Assoc. Tenzer, Greenblatt, Fallon & Kaplan, N.Y.C., 1967-73, ptnr., 1973—, ptnr. in charge trusts and estates dept., 1973—. Co-author column on wills, estates and surrogate's practice N.Y. Law Jour. Fellow Am. Coll. Probate Counsel; mem. ABA, N.Y. State Bar Assn. (lectr. on wills, trusts and estates), Assn. Bar City of N.Y., N.Y. County Lawyers' Assn. (dir., former chmn. com. on surrogates' ct., lectr. on wills, trusts and estates), Phi Beta Kappa. Probate. Office: Tenzer Greenblatt Fallon & Kaplan 405 Lexington Ave New York NY 10174

VALENTINE, ERIC WOODSON, judge; b. Los Angeles, Feb. 18, 1943; s. Richard G. and Ruth (Woodson) V.; m. Margaret A. Sutton, Sept. 2, 1967; children—Matthew, Michael. A.B., Stanford U., 1964, J.D., 1967; M.A.T., Eastern Oreg. State Coll., 1971. Bar: Oreg. 1972, U.S. Dist. Ct. Oreg. 1980. Adminstr. Eastern Oreg. State Coll., La Grande, 1971-72; dep. dist. atty. Union County, Oreg., 1972-79; ptnr. Helm, Valentine & Riedlinger, La Grande, 1979-83; judge Oreg. Dist. Ct. of Union/Wallowa Counties, La Grande, 1983—. Drive chmn., pres. United Way Union County, 1976-78; scoutmaster Blue Mountain council Boy Scouts Am., 1982—, commr. Mt. Emily dist., 1982-84. Recipient Others award Salvation Army, Union County, 1978, Dist. Merit award Boy Scouts Am., 1987. Mem. Oreg. State Bar, Union/Wallowa County Bar Assn. (pres. 1983-84), Oreg. Dist. Judges Assn. (sec., treas. 1985-86, v.p. 1986-87). Lodge: Rotary (pres. La Grande 1975-76, sec. 1976-86). Judicial administration. Home: 1712 Alder La Grande OR 97850 Office: Union County Dist Ct 1007 4th St La Grande OR 97850

VALENTINE, GARRISON NORTON, lawyer; b. N.Y.C., Apr. 7, 1929; s. Alan Chester and Lucia Garrison (Norton) V.; m. Margaret Brown Weeks, Mar. 15, 1952 (div. 1983); children: Peter, Stewart, Norah, Elizabeth; m. Inge Carola Froelich, Sept. 17, 1983; 1 stepchild, Carolyn A. Read. BA, Yale U., 1950, LLB, 1964. Bar: Conn. 1964, U.S. Dist. Ct. Conn. 1964. Assoc. Hoppin, Carey & Powell, Hartford, Conn., 1964-70, ptnr., 1970-86; ptnr. Ladwig & Valentine, Mystic, Conn., 1986—; sec., bd. dirs. Conn. Attys. Title Co., Rocky Hill, 1974—. Bd. dirs., sec. Mystic Marinelife Aquarium, Conn., 1984—; bd. dirs. Summer Music, Inc., New London, Conn., 1984—, Stonington (Conn.) Community Ctr., 1986—. Served to capt. USAF, 1952-61. Mem. ABA, Conn. Bar Assn., Hartford County Bar Assn., New London County Bar Assn. Republican. Episcopalian. Club: Wadawanuck. Real property, Probate, Land use and zoning. Home: RD 3 PO Box 84F Collins Rd Stonington CT 06378 Office: Ladwig & Valentine 12 Roosevelt Ave Mystic CT 06355

VALENTINE, JOHN WILLIAM, lawyer; b. Patchogue, N.Y., Aug. 27, 1949; s. Joseph Craft and Jeanette (Brandt) V.; m. Linda Laura Damuck, Dec. 11, 1977; children: Daniel Patrick, Degory Edward, Christopher John. BA in Econs. with distinction, Union Coll., 1971; JD cum laude, Syracuse U., 1974. Bar: N.Y. 1975, U.S. Dist. Ct. (so. dist.) N.Y. 1975, Conn. 1977. Asst. regional atty. AT & T Longs Lines, White Plains, N.Y., 1974-80; sr. atty. Lever Bros. Co., N.Y.C., 1980—; lectr. bus. law Westchester County Community Coll., White Plains, 1980. Chmn. Orange (Conn.) Congregation Ch. Stewardship Bd., 1985, 86. Mem. ABA, N.Y. State Bar Assn., Westchester-Fairfield Corp. Council Assn. (chmn. Equal Employment Opportunity/labor law com. 1982-83). Republican. Avocations: sailing, cross country skiing, woodworking, reading. Federal civil litigation, Civil rights, General corporate. Office: Lever Bros Co 390 Park Ave New York NY 10022

VALENTINE, STEPHEN KENNETH, JR., lawyer, broadcasting commentator; b. Detroit, Apr. 27, 1940; s. Stephen K. and Bernice M. (Falger) V.; m. Frances M. Craig, Oct. 20, 1967; children—Joanna, Victoria, Veronica. B.S., U. Detroit, 1962, J.D. (gen. scholar), 1966. Bar: Mich. 1967, Fla. 1970, U.S. Dist. Ct. (ea. dist.) Mich. 1967, U.S. Ct. Appeals (6th cir.) 1969, U.S. Supreme Ct. 1971. Appraiser, adminstrv. asst. Detroit Bd. Assessors, 1962-66; assoc. Colombo, Vermeulen & Colombo, Detroit, 1966-68; mem. Stephen K. Valentine, Jr. and Assocs., P.C., West Bloomfield, Mich., 1968—; mem. ct. rule revision com. Mich. Supreme Ct., 1975-80; mediator Oakland County Circuit Ct., 1979—; claims referee Oakland County Probate Ct., 1979—; participant Legal Forum, Sta. WOMC; commentator Sta. WJR; U.S. govt. appeal agt., 1970-71; seminar lectr. Fed. Bar Assn., 1978-79. Mem. pres.'s adv. council U. Detroit, 1961-62. Mem. ABA (litigation sect. bus. torts com.). Mich. Bar Assn. (rep. assembly 1973-76, 76-79, chmn. dist. ct. com. 1969-77, vice chmn. trial ct. com. 1979-83), State Bar Mich. (civil procedures com. 1971-78, econs. com. 1972-74, profl. liability ins. com. 1978-81), Fla. Bar Assn., Detroit Bar Assn. (pub. adv. com. 1979—), Nat. Advocates Soc., Am. Trial Lawyers Assn., Mich. Trial Lawyers Assn., Comml. Law League Am., Am. Arbitration Assn. (panel arbitrators 1969—). Roman Catholic. Federal civil litigation, General corporate, General practice. Home: 5850 Middlebelt Rd West Bloomfield MI 48033 Office: Valentine & Assocs PC 5767 W Maple Rd Suite 100 West Bloomfield MI 48033

VALLE, LAURENCE FRANCIS, lawyer; b. N.Y.C., Feb. 16, 1943; s. Mario John and Marian Josephine (Longinotti) V.; m. Joan Strachan, June 11, 1966; children: Christopher John, Stacia Lyn. BS, U. Miami, 1966, JD, 1969. Bar: Fla. 1969, U.S. Ct. Mil. Appeals 1970, U.S. Dist. Ct. (so. dist.) Fla. 1975, U.S. Ct. Appeals (D.C. cir.) 1975, U.S. Ct. Appeals (5th and 11th cirs.) 1981. Assoc. Underwood, Gillis & Karcher PA, Miami, Fla., 1973-77; ptnr. Underwood, Gillis, Karcher & Valle PA, Miami, 1977—; gen. counsel Greater Miami (Fla.) Marine Assn., 1983—. Contbr. articles to profl. jours. Served to capt. U.S. Army, 1970-74. Mem. ABA, Fla. Bar Assn. (chmn. grievance com., 1982-85), Assn. Trial Lawyers Am., SE Admiralty Law Inst., Maritime Law Assn. of US. Republican. Roman Catholic. Club: University (Miami). Avocations: tennis, running, water skiing, snow skiing. Admiralty, Personal injury, Workers' compensation. Office: Underwood Gillis Karcher et al 44 W Flagler St Penthouse Miami FL 33130

VALLENDER, CHARLES FRANCIS, III, lawyer; b. Boston, Oct. 1, 1939; s. Charles Francis and Evelyn Harlan (Weatherby) V.; m. Constance Emery Kellogg, Oct. 26, 1968 (dec. 1982); children—Prentiss Weatherby, Perrin Kellogg. B.A., Yale U., 1961, J.D., 1964. Bar: Conn. 1972, D.C. 1975, U.S. Supreme Ct. 1978. Exec. trainee Chase Manhattan Bank, N.Y.C., 1965-66; asst. to pres. Am. Express Co., N.Y.C., 1966-71; assoc. Gregory & Adams, Wilton, Conn., 1972-73; rep. West Pub. Co., St. Paul, 1973—. Advance man The White House, 1976. Served with U.S. Army, 1964-65. Mem. D.C. Bar Assn. Republican. Episcopalian. Clubs: Chevy Chase (Md.); Dunes (Narragansett, R.I.). Banking. Home and Office: 4301 Massachusetts Ave NW Washington DC 20016

VALLENS, BRENT EDWARD, lawyer; b. Los Angeles, Feb. 1, 1954; s. Jerome Henry and Myrna (Hoffman) V.; m. Carol Diane Brownstein, June 30, 1986; 1 child, Jacob william. BA in Polit. Sci., Calif. State U., Northridge, 1977; JD, Southwestern U., 1980. Bar: Calif. 1980, U.S. Dist. Ct. (cen. dist.) Calif. 1981, U.S. Tax Ct. 1981 U.S. Ct. Claims 1982, U.S. Ct. Mil. Appeals 1982, U.S. Ct. Appeals (9th cir.) 1982, U.S. Supreme Ct. 1984. Sole practice Granada Hills, Calif., 1981—; asst. prof. law Calif. State U., Northridge, 1982—. Pres. Calif. State U. Alumni Council, Long Beach, 1985-86, Calif. State U. Alumni Assn., Northridge, 1983-85 (Outstanding Alumnus of Year 1984). Mem. Blue Key. Republican. Jewish. Avocations: hunting, fishing, auto racing, carpentry, travel. Personal income taxation, Construction, Probate. Office: 17057 Chatsworth St Granada Hills CA 91344-5845

VALLERAND, PATRICIA ANN, lawyer; b. Lewiston, Maine, June 21, 1951; d. Romeo Gideon and Rita Blanche (Frechette) V. BA in Community Service and Pub. Affairs, U. Oreg., 1973, JD, 1979. Bar: Oreg. 1979, U.S. Dist. Ct. Oreg. 1979, U.S. Tax Ct. 1981. Counsel and job devel. Neighborhood Youth Corps, Salem, Oreg., 1972; social work assoc. VA Hosp., Roseburg, Oreg., 1973-76; trial asst. and research atty. Johnson, Harrang, Swanson & Long, Eugene, Oreg., 1979-81; ptnr. Leistner, Vallerand and Evans, Eugene, 1981—. Mem., chair Citizen Involvement Com., Eugene, 1981—; mem. Lane County Juvenile Ct. Consortium, Lane County Legal Aid Referral Panel; del. 5 yr. planning conf., Eugene, 1985; active Dem. precinct com., Eugene, 1985. Mem. ABA, Oreg. Trial Lawyers Assn., Nat. Lawyers Guild, Lane County Bar Assn. (family law sect.), Oreg. Bar Assn. (family law sect., profl. responsibility com., arbitration panel), Order of Coif. Avocations: hiking, camping, gardening, racketball, reading. State civil litigation, Family and matrimonial, Juvenile. Office: Leistner Vallerand Evans 767 Willamette St Suite 302 Eugene OR 97401

VALLEY, MARK R., lawyer; b. Prairie du Chien, Wis., Mar. 11, 1952; s. Robert George and Helen Lois (Wetzel) V.; m. Loral Ann Steinbarth, Nov. 24, 1978; 1 child, John Henry. BA, U. Wis., 1975; JD, Ill. Inst. Tech., 1978. Bar: Ill. 1978, U.S. Dist. Ct. (no. dist.) Ill. 1979, U.S. Ct. Appeals (7th cir.) 1980. Assoc. Murphy, Boyle & Banks, Chgo., 1978-79, Murphy & Boyle, Chgo., 1979-86; gen. counsel La Preferida, Inc., Chgo., 1986—. Mem. ABA, Ill. Bar Assn. Roman Catholic. Avocations: coin collecting, scripophily, basketball, golf. General corporate, Contracts commercial, Trademark and copyright. Office: La Preferida Inc 3400 W 35th St Chicago IL 60632

VALLONE, RALPH, JR., lawyer, cons.; b. Phila., Apr. 15, 1947; s. Ralph and Carmen Maria (Perez) V. B.A., Yale U., 1966, M. Phil. (Carnegie fellow), 1966; LL.D. Harvard U., 1972. Bar: P.R., 1972, U.S. dist. ct. P.R., 1972, U.S. Sup. Ct., 1972. Ptnr., Ralph Vallone Law Firm, San Juan, P.R., 1972—; prof. comml. law Interam. U. Law Sch., P.R., 1972—; mem. Interlaw, N.Y.C., London, Bogoté, Los Angeles, other locations; chief hearing examiner for Environ. Quality Bd. of P.R. Trustee Bronx Mus. Arts. Mem. P.R. Inst. Registry Law, Jud. Conf. of P.R. Roman Catholic. Clubs: N.Y. Athletic, Atrium of N.Y. Federal civil litigation, Banking, General corporate. Office: 165 Ponce de León Ave 3d Floor Hato Rey PR 00917

VALOIS, ROBERT ARTHUR, lawyer; b. N.Y.C., May 13, 1938; s. Frank Jacob and Harriet Frances (LaCroix) V.; m. Ruth Emilie Skacil, Dec. 23, 1961; children: Marguerite Jeannette, Robert Arthur Jr. BBA, U. Miami, 1962; JD, Wake Forest U., 1972. Bar: N.C. 1972, Fla. 1972, U.S. Ct. Appeals (4th cir.) 1973, U.S. Dist. Ct. (ea. and mid. dists.) 1974, U.S. Supreme Ct. 1975, U.S. Ct. Appeals (6th cir.) 1986. Field examiner NLRB, Winston-Salem, N.C., 1962-70; from assoc. to ptnr. Maupin. Taylor, Ellis & Adams P.A., Raleigh, N.C., 1972—; vice chmn. Legal Services Corp. Washington, 1984—, bd. dirs. Served with USN, 1956-59. Democrat. Presbyterian. Club: Capitol City (Raleigh). Labor. Office: Maupin Taylor Ellis & Adams PA 3201 Glenwood Ave Raleigh NC 27612

VALUKAS, ANTON RONALD, lawyer; b. Chgo., June 21, 1943; s. Anton J. and Mary Ann (Giusto) V.; m. Janice C. (separated); children—Amy Paige, Beth Catherine. B.A. in Polit. Sci., Art History, Lawrence U., 1965; J.D., Northwestern U., 1968. Bars: Ill. 1968, U.S. Dist. Ct. (no. dist.) Ill. 1968, U.S. Ct. Appeals (7th cir.) 1969, U.S. Ct. Appeals (10th cir.) 1977, U.S. Ct. Appeals (3d cir.) 1982. Dir. Nat. Defender Project, Chgo., 1968-70; asst. U.S. atty. U.S. Atty.'s Office, Chgo., 1970-76; ptnr. Jenner & Block, Chgo., 1976-85; U.S. atty. No. Dist. Ill., Dept. Justice, Chgo., 1985—; dir., treas. Met. Fair and Exposition Authority, Chgo., 1985. Mem. several commns. and coms. Evanston Housing Commn., Ill.; spl. asst. to Gov. James Thompson in various matters, Chgo. Recipient Spl. Commendation award Dept. Justice, Chgo., 1975, Disting. Grad. award Palatine High Sch., Ill., 1984, John Marshall Law Sch. Freedom award, Chgo., 1985; named one of Ten Outstanding Young Citizens of Chgo., Jr. C. of C., 1976. Mem. Chgo. Bar Assn. Club: Law of Chgo. Criminal. Home: 1462 Wesley St Evanston IL 60201 Office: US Atty's Office 219 S Dearborn St Chicago IL 60604

VAN, PETER, lawyer; b. Boston, Sept. 7, 1936; s. Frank Lewis and Ruth (Spevack) V.; m. Judith Ellen Hershman, June 9, 1958; children—Jami Lynne, Robert Charles. B.A., Dartmouth, 1958; LL.D., Boston Coll., 1961. Bar: Mass. 1962. Assoc. Brown, Rudnick, Freed and Gesmer, Boston, 1961-63; assoc. Fine and Ambrogne, Boston, 1963-65; ptnr., 1966-73, sr. ptnr., 1973—. Clubs: Pine Brook Country (Weston), Mason (Boston). Real property, Banking, Contracts commercial. Office: Exchange Pl 27th Floor Boston MA 02109

VAN ALLSBURG, JON AARON, lawyer, legal educator; b. San Diego, Aug. 2, 1955; s. Donald E. and Frances L. (Doornbos) Van A.; m. Susan D. Hiddinga, Aug. 25, 1984. BS, Cen. Mich. U., 1977; JD cum laude, Detroit Coll. of Law, 1981. Bar: Mich. 1981, U.S. Dist. Ct. (ea. and we. dists.) Mich. 1981. Assoc. Keller & Avadenka P.C., Bloomfield Hills, Mich., 1981-83; ptnr. Coupe & Van Allsburg P.C., Holland, Mich., 1983—; adj. prof. bus. law Grand Valley State Coll., Allendale, Mich., 1984—. Precinct del. Ottawa County Reps., Port Sheldon, 1984, 85, Holland, 1986, 87; Deacon Beechwood Reformed Ch., 1987—. Mem. ABA, Mich. Bar Assn., Ottawa County Bar Assn., Assn. Trial Lawyers Am., Holland Area C. of C. Republican. Lodge: Rotary. Avocations: history, internat. relations, downhill skiing, swimming. General corporate, Real property, State civil litigation. Office: Coupe & Van Allsburg PC 774 S Washington Ave Holland MI 49423

VAN ANTWERP, ROSEMARY DIRKIE, lawyer, executive; b. Detroit, Nov. 7, 1946; d. Anthony Gore and Colette Anne (Rothmeyer) Van A.; m. Peter Joseph Zacchilli, June 10, 1978. B.A. in History, Loyola U., New Orleans, 1969; M.A. in Sociology, Fordham U., 1971; J.D., U. Mich., 1974. Bar: R.I. 1975, Mass. 1978. Assoc. Tillinghast, Collins & Graham, Providence, 1975-77; v.p., asst. clerk, assoc. gen. counsel Keystone Group Inc., Boston, 1977-78, assoc gen. counsel, v.p., asst. sec., 1983—; counsel, asst. sec. Keystone Custodian Funds Inc., Boston, 1978—; v.p. Harbor Keystone Advisers Inc., 1984—; sec. Aggressive Stock Trust, Capital T Money Fund, Capital T Tax Free Fund, Cash Income Trust, Govt. Guaranteed Securities Trust, Govt. Securities Zero Coupon Trust, High Yield Bond Trust, Investment Bond Trust, Keystone Am. Govt. Securities Fund, Keystone Am. Tax-Free Income Fund, Keystone Am. Investment Grade Bond Fund, Keystone Am. Money Market Fund, Keystone Am. High Yield Bond Fund, Keystone Am. Tax Free Money Market Fund, Keystone Am. Equity Income Fund, Keystone Liquid Trust, Keystone Mass. Distbrs. Inc., Keystone Precious Metals Holdings, Inc., Keystone Tax Exempt Trust, Keystone Tax Free Fund, Managed Assets Trust, Managed Growth Stock Fund, Master Equity Trust, Master Income Trust, Master Mcpl. Trust, Master Res. Income Fund, Master Res. Tax Free Trust, Master Res. Trust, Money Market/Options Investments Inc., Mortgage Securities Income Trust, The Freedom Fund, The Salem Funds; clk. Fiduciary Investment Co., Inc.; asst. sec. TMC Realty Ptnrs., Keystone Fixed Income Advisors, Inc. Mem. ABA, Mass. Bar Assn. Securities, General corporate.

VAN ANTWERPEN, FRANKLIN STUART, judge; b. Passaic, N.J., Oct. 23, 1941; s. Franklin John and Dorothy (Hoedemaker) Van A.; m. Kathleen Veronica O'Brien, Sept. 12, 1970; children—Joy, Franklin W., Virginia. B.S. in Engring. Physics, U. Maine, 1964; J.D., Temple U., 1967; postgrad. Nat. Jud. Coll., 1980. Bar: Pa. 1969, U.S. Dist. Ct. (ea. dist.) Pa. 1971, U.S. Ct. Appeals (3d cir.) 1971, U.S. Supreme Ct. 1972. Corp. counsel Hazeltine, Corp., N.Y.C., 1967-70; chief counsel Northampton County Legal Aid Soc., Easton, Pa., 1970-71; assoc. Hemstreet & Smith, Easton, 1971-73; ptnr. Hemstreet & Van Antwerpen, Easton, 1973-79; judge Ct. Common Pleas of Northampton County (Pa.), 1979—; presiding judge Bradford County, 1983; adj. prof. Northampton County Area Community Coll., 1976-81; solicitor Palmer Twp., 1971-79; gen. counsel Fairview Savs. and Loan Assn., Easton, 1973-79. Recipient Booster award Bus. Indsl. and Profl. Assn., 1979; George Palmer award Palmer Twp., 1980; Man of Yr. award Atlantic Contractors Assn., 1981. Mem. ABA (com. on jud. edn.), Pa. Bar Assn., Northampton County Bar Assn., Am. Judicature Soc., Sigma Pi Sigma, Phi Alpha Delta. Republican. Club: Pomfret. Jurisprudence. Office: 100 N 3d St Easton PA 18042

VAN ATTA, DAVID MURRAY, lawyer; b. Berkeley, Calif., Oct. 20, 1944; s. Chester Murray and Rosalind (Eisenstein) Van A.; 1 child, Lauren Rachel. BA, U. Calif., Berkeley, 1966; JD, U. Calif., Hastings, 1969. Bar: Calif. 1970. Asst. gen. counsel Boise Cascade Corp., Palo Alto, Calif., 1970-73; ptnr. Miller, Starr & Regalio, San Francisco, 1973—; instr. Golden Gate U., San Francisco, 1984-85; U. Calif., Berkeley, 1976-84. Mem. ABA, Calif. Bar Assn. (vice chmn. exec. com. real property law sect. 1982-85, chmn. condominium and subdiv. com. real property law sect. 1981-83), Community Assn. Inst. Avocations: skiing, tennis, painting. Real property, Personal income taxation. Office: Miller Starr & Regalio 101 California St Suite 2200 San Francisco CA 94111

VANATTA, DEAN R., lawyer; b. Ellston, Iowa, Oct. 4, 1939; s. Mack L. and Mildred (Walters) V.; m. Jerilyn Compley, June 25, 1966; children: Eric, Ann. BS in Bus. Adminstrn., U. Colo., 1962, LLB, 1965. Bar: Colo. 1965, U.S. Dist. Ct. Colo. 1965, U.S. Ct. Appeals (10th cir.) 1965, U.S. Supreme Ct. 1981. Ptnr. Vanatta & Sullan, Denver, 1962—; lectr. litigation in field. Contbr. articles to profl. jours. Republican. Methodist. Federal civil litigation, Insurance, Personal injury. Office: Vanatta & Sullan 1873 S Bellaine #1400 Denver CO 80222

VAN BOKKELEN, JOSEPH SCOTT, lawyer; b. Chgo., June 7, 1943; s. Robert W. and W. Louise (Reynolds) Van B.; m. Sally Wardall Huey, Aug. 14, 1971; children—Brian, Kate. B.A., U. Ind., 1966, J.D., 1969. Bar: Ind. 1969, U.S. Dist. Ct. (so. dist.) Ind. 1969, U.S. Dist. Ct. (no. dist.) Ind. 1973, U.S. Ct. Appeals (7th cir.) 1973, U.S. Supreme Ct. 1973. Dep. atty. gen. State of Ind., Indpls., 1969-71, asst. atty. gen., 1971-72; asst. U.S. atty. No. Dist. Ind., Hammond, 1972-75; ptnr. Goldsmith, Goodman, Ball & Van Bokkelen, Highland, Ind., 1975—. Recipient Outstanding Asst. U.S. Atty. award U.S. Dept. Justice, 1974. Mem. ABA, Fed. Bar Assn., Ind. Bar Assn., Criminal Def. Lawyers Assn. Federal civil litigation, State civil litigation, Criminal. Home: 38 Glendale Pkwy Hammond IN 46320 Office: 3737 45th St Highland IN 46322

VAN BUREN, DAVID PAUL, criminal justice educator; b. Silver Springs, N.Y., Nov. 5, 1947; s. LaVerne Robert and Frances Elaine (Carney) V. B.A. magna cum laude, St. Bonaventure U., 1969; M.A., SUNY-Albany, 1971, Ph.D. with distinction, 1984. Instr., Genesse Community Coll., Batavia, N.Y., 1971-72; security coordinator Albany-Housing Authority, N.Y., 1975-76; prof. dept. criminal justice U. Wis.-Platteville, 1976—, chmn., 1986—; vis. scholar inst. criminology U. Cambridge, Eng.; cons. in field. Author: Rural Justice, 1984. Asst. editor Jour. Research in Crime and Delinquency, 1984-86. Contbr. articles to profl. jours., chpts. to books. Democratic candidate for sheriff, Wyoming County (N.Y.), 1972; mem. U. Wis. Regents Task Force on Status of Women, 1979-81. Grad. research fellow, U.S. Dept. Justice, 1969-71. Mem. Wis. Criminal Justice Edn. Assn. (pres. 1982). Am. Soc. Criminology, Acad. Crim. Justice Sci., Delta Epsilon Sigma. Democrat. Roman Catholic. Judicial administration, Legal education, Criminal. Home: 535 N 4th St Platteville WI 53818 Office: Univ Wisconsin 422 Warner Hall Platteville WI 53818

VAN CAMP, BRIAN RALPH, lawyer; b. Halstead, Kans., Aug. 23, 1940; s. Ralph A. and Mary Margaret (Bragg) Van C.; m. Mary Ann Gatewood, June 25, 1961; children: Marilyn M., Laurie E. A.B., U. Calif., Berkeley, 1962, LL.B., 1965. Bar: Calif. 1966. Dep. atty. gen. State Calif., 1965-67; agy. atty. Redevel. Agy., City of Sacramento, 1967-70; asst./acting sec. Bus. and Transp. Agy., State Calif., 1970-71; commr. of corps. State of Calif., Sacramento, 1971-74; partner firm Diepenbrock, Wulff, Plant & Hannegan, Sacramento, 1975-77, Van Camp & Johnson, Sacramento, 1978—; lectr. Continuing Edn. Bar, Practicing Law Inst.; lectr. C.P.A. Soc. Calif., others; mem. adv. bd. UCLA Securities Law Inst., 1978. Mem. Republican State Central Com. Calif., 1974-78, mem. exec. com., 1974-78; mem. Electoral Coll. State Calif., Presdl. Election, 1976; bd. dirs. Sacramento Symphony Assn., 1973—, mem. exec. com., 1978-79; bd. dirs. Republican Assos. Sacramento County, 1975-79; mem. govt. relations com. United Way Sacramento Area, 1977—, Sacramento Area Commerce & Trade Orgn. (pres. 1986—); elder Fremont Presbyn. Ch., 1968—. Recipient Sumner-Mering Meml. award Sacramento U. of Calif. Alumni Assn., 1962; named Outstanding Young Man of Year Sacramento Jaycees, 1970, Internat. Young Man of Year Active 20-30 Club Internat., 1973. Mem. Am. Bar Assn., Calif. State Bar (mem. com. on corps. 1977-80, partnerships and unincorporated bus. assns. 1983-87), Sacramento County Bar Assn., Los Angeles County Bar Assn., Calif. C. of C. (chmn. statewide energy task force 1979-85, dir. 1982—), Sacramento Met. C. of C. (co-chmn. econ. devel. com. 1979, bd. dirs. 1986—). Republican. Presbyterian. Clubs: Lincoln of Sacramento Valley (Sacramento) (dir., sec. 1975-82, v.p. 1982-84, pres. 1984-86), U. Calif. Men's (Sacramento) (pres. 1968); Sutter, El Rancho Racquet, Kandahar Ski, Marina Bay Yacht, Sacramento Jaguar. Lodge: Rotary (Sacramento) (co-chmn. program com. 1981-82, dir. 1982-84). General corporate, Securities, Franchising. Office: 555 Capitol Mall Suite 400 Sacramento CA 95814

VANCE, CYRUS ROBERTS, lawyer, former government official; b. Clarksburg, W.Va., Mar. 27, 1917; s. John Carl and Amy (Roberts) V.; m. Grace Elsie Sloane, Feb. 15, 1947; children: Elsie Nicoll, Amy Sloane, Grace Roberts, Camilla, Cyrus Roberts. Student, Kent Sch.; B.A., Yale U., 1939, LL.B., 1942, LL.D. (hon.), 1968; LL.D. (hon.), Marshall U., 1963, Trinity Coll., 1968, W.Va. U., 1969, Bowling Green U., 1969, Salem Coll., 1970, Brandeis U., 1971, Amherst Coll., 1974, W.Va. Wesleyan U., 1974, Harvard U., 1981, Colgate U., 1981, Gen. Theol. Sem., 1981, Williams Coll., 1981, Notre Dame U., 1982, Mt. Holyoke Coll., 1982. Bar: N.Y. State 1947, U.S. Supreme Ct. 1970. Asst. to pres. Mead Corp., 1946-47; assoc. firm Simpson Thacher & Bartlett, N.Y.C., 1947-56; partner firm Simpson Thacher & Bartlett, 1956-61, 67-77, 80—; gen. counsel Dept. Def., 1961-62; sec. of army 1962-63, dep. sec. def., 1964-67; spl. rep. of Pres. Cyprus, 1967, Korea, 1968; U.S. negotiator Paris Peace Conf. on Vietnam, 1968-69; sec. state 1977-80; spl. counsel preparedness investigating subcom. Senate Armed Services Com., 1957-60; cons. counsel Spl. Com. on Space and Astronautics, U.S. Senate, 1958; chmn. com. on adjudication of claims Adminstrv. Conf. U.S.; mem. Com. To Investigate Alleged Police Corruption in N.Y.C., 1970-72; chmn. UN Devel. Corp., 1976; mem. Ind. Com. on Disarmament and Security Issues; dir. Gen. Dynamics Corp., Mfrs. Hanover Trust Co., N.Y. Times. Trustee Yale Corp., 1968-78, 80—; Trustee Rockefeller Found., 1970-77, 80-82, chmn., 1975-77; Trustee Mayo Found., N.Y. Presbyn. Hosp., Aspen Inst. for Humanistic Studies; chmn. Am. Ditchley Found., 1981—. Served to lt. USNR, 1942-46. Recipient Medal of Freedom, 1969. Fellow Am. Coll. Trial Lawyers; mem. ABA, Assn. Bar City N.Y. (pres. 1974-76), Council on Fgn. Relations (dir., vice chmn. 1985—), Japan Soc. (chmn. 1985—). Office: Simpson Thacher & Bartlett 1 Battery Park Plaza New York NY 10004

VANCE, JAMES, manufacturing company executive; b. Cleve., May 20, 1930; m. Dolores Bernadette Doyle, July 6, 1957; 1 child, James J. B.A. cum laude, Baldwin Wallace Coll., 1955; J.D. magna cum laude, Cleve. Marshall Law Sch., 1960. Asst. treas., asst. to v.p. fin. and adminstrn., financial analyst Republic Steel Corp., 1956-68; treas. Addressograph & Multigraph Corp., Cleve., 1968-72; v.p. fin. Cin. Milacron Inc., 1972-77; vice chmn., dir. Dayton-Walther Corp., 1977-87; sr. v.p., sr. bus. advisor Varity Corp., 1987—; dir. Citation Cos., Amertool Corp., Gen. Automation, Min-Cer (S.A.), Mexico, Dwisa of Paris, Dayton-Est of Vesoul, Fiday of Asnieres, France; sr. v.p. Varity Corp.; lectr. bus. law Baldwin Wallace Coll., 1961-63. Vice chmn. United Appeal, 1959; mem. Citizens League Cleve., 1960—; mem. fin. com. YMCA, 1961—; mem. Greater Cleve. Growth Center, 1963—; Vice chmn. fin. com. Cuyahoga Republican Party, 1968-69. Served with inf. AUS, 1951-52. Decorated Bronze Star. Mem. Cleve. Soc. Security Analysts, Am., Ohio bar assns., Fin. Execs. Inst., Am. Ordnance Assn., Nat. Machine Tool Builders Assn., Machinery and Allied Products Inst., Am. Mgmt. Assn., Cin. Indsl. Inst., Ohio C. of C., Alpha Tau Omega, Delta Theta Phi. Club: Cleve. Treasurers (dir.). General corporate. Home: 6600 Wyman Ln Cincinnati OH 45243

VANCE, KENNETH ANTHONY, lawyer; b. Youngstown, Ohio, July 22, 1946; s. Louis Shannon and Dorothy May (Clark) V.; m. Sherry Maria Hill, Apr. 26, 1969; 1 child, Woodia Maria. Assoc., Am. U., 1972, B.S., 1975; J.D., Cath. U. Am., 1979. Bar: U.S. Supreme Ct. 1983, U.S. Ct. Mil. Appeals 1980, U.S. Ct. Appeals (fed. cir.) 1982, U.S. Ct. Appeals (D.C. cir.) 1980, U.S. Ct. Appeals (4th cir.) 1981, U.S. Ct. Customs and Patent Appeals 1981, D.C. 1980, Md. 1980, U.S. Ct. Claims 1980, U.S. Tax Ct. 1980, D.C. Ct. Appeals 1979. Police officer U.S. Capitol, Washington, 1967-69; patrol officer Metro Police Dept., Washington, 1969-71, vice investigator, 1971-72, detective, 1972-73, officer pilot, 1973-79, sgt., 1979-80; atty. Payton & Vance Law Offices, Washington, 1979—; del. 8th and 9th Jud. Conf., Washington, 1983-84. Served with USN, 1963-67. Mem. ABA (jud. selection, comp. and tenure com. 1980-82), D.C. Bar Assn., Nat. Bar Assn. (jud. selection and tenure com. 1983—) Fed. Bar Assn., Assn. Trial Lawyers Am., Washington Bar Assn. Democrat. Roman Catholic. Lodge: Masons. State civil litigation, Criminal, Probate. Home: 2139 Branch Ave SE Washington DC 20020 Office: Payton & Vance 601 13th St NW Suite 420 Washington DC 20005

VANCE, MICHAEL CHARLES, lawyer; b. Marshalltown, Iowa, May 31, 1951; s. Randall Scott and Irma Mae (Kneeland) V.; m. Brigid Rowan, June 3, 1972; children: Thomas Randall, Patrick Michael. BA in Polit. Sci. and Econs., U. Iowa, 1973, JD with distinction, 1976. Bar: Iowa 1976, U.S. Dist. Ct. (so. dist.) Iowa 1976. Sole practice Mt. Pleasant, Iowa, 1976—; atty. City of Wayland, Iowa, 1976—; instr. bus. law Iowa Wesleyan Coll., Mt. Pleasant, 1977-78; asst. atty. Henry County, Mt. Pleasant, 1979—. Mem., bd. dirs. Community Mental Health of Henry, Louisa and Jefferson Counties, Mt. Pleasant, 1977-82; chairperson Henry County Dems., Mt. Pleasant, 1978-83; pres. Mt. Pleasant Sesquicentennial Assn., 1984-86, St. Alphonsus Ch. Parish Council, Mt. Pleasant, 1985—. Mem. ABA, Iowa Bar Assn., Henry County Bar Assn. (sec., treas. 1977-78, v.p. 1978-79, pres. 1979-80), Iowa Conf. Bar Assn. Pres. (bd. dirs. 1979-81), Mt. Pleasant C. of C. (named Citizen of the Yr. 1985), Mt. Pleasant Jaycees (bd. dirs. 1978-83), Omicron Delta Kappa, Omicron Delta Epsilon. Roman Catholic. Lodges: Rotary, K.C. General practice. Home: 601 S Harrison Pl Mount Pleasant IA 52641 Office: 101 N Jefferson Mount Pleasant IA 52641

VANCE, ROBERT PATRICK, lawyer; b. Birmingham, Ala., Feb. 12, 1948; s. James Robert and Lucy Juanita (McMath) V.; m. Sarah Elizabeth Savoia, June 11, 1971; 1 son, Robert Patrick, Jr. B.A. with honors, La. State U., 1970, J.D., 1975. Bar: La. 1975, U.S. Dist. Ct. (ea. dist.) La. 1975, U.S. Dist. Ct. (mid. dist.) La. 1978, U.S. Dist. Ct. (we. dist.) La. 1979, U.S. Ct. Appeals (5th cir.) 1975, U.S. Ct. Appeals (11th cir.) 1981, U.S. Supreme Ct. 1981. Assoc. Jones, Walker, Waechter, Poitevent, Carrere & Denegre, New Orleans, 1975-80, ptnr., 1980—. Author, editor: Bankruptcy Rules: Parts I, II, VII, VIII and IX, 1983; Overview of the Bankruptcy Code and the Court, 1983. Co-author: Bankruptcy-Current Developments, 1983; Current Developments in Commercial Law, 1984. Contbr. articles to profl. jours. Mem. ABA (mem. creditors rights litigation com., bus. bankruptcy com., rules subcom. of bus. bankruptcy com.), comml. Law League Am. (mem. sect. bankruptcy and insolvency), Am. Bankruptcy Inst., Fed. Bar Assn. (mem. bankruptcy law com., polit. campaign and election law com., programs subcom.), La. State Bar Assn. (pres. consumer law sect.), New Orleans Bar Assn., La. Bankers Assn. (bank counsel com.), Pi Sigma Alpha, Phi Beta Kappa, Phi Kappa Phi. Democrat. Roman Catholic. Club: City, Blenville (New Orleans). Bankruptcy, Consumer commercial, Federal civil litigation. Home: 1670 Soniat St New Orleans LA 70115 Office: Jones Walker Waechter Poitevent Carrere & Denegre 201 St Charles Ave New Orleans LA 70170

VANCE, ROBERT SMITH, judge; b. Talladega, Ala., May 10, 1931; s. Harrell Taylor and Mae (Smith) V.; m. Helen Rainey, Oct. 4, 1953; children: Robert Smith, Charles R. B.S., U. Ala., 1950, J.D., 1952; LL.M., George Washington U., 1955. Partner, Vance, Thompson & Brown, Birmingham, Ala., 1956-77; judge U.S. Ct. Appeals 11th Circuit, Birmingham, 1978—; lectr. Cumberland Sch. Law, Samford U., 1967-69. Chmn., Ala. Democratic Com., 1966-67; pres. Nat. Assn. Dem. State Chairmen, 1973-75. Served to 1st lt. AUS, 1952-54. Fellow Internat. Soc. Barristers; mem. Am., Ala., Birmingham bar assns., Am. Judicature Soc., Newcomen Soc. N.Am., Omicron Delta Kappa, Beta Gamma Sigma, Delta Chi. Episcopalian. Clubs: Birmingham Kennel, Heart of Ala. Great Dane, Am. Saluki Assn. Jurisprudence. Office: US Court Appeals 234 Federal Courthouse Birmingham AL 35203 *

VANCE, ROY NEWTON, state supreme court justice; b. Paducah, Ky., Nov. 14, 1921; s. Roy Newton and Mary Louise (Bryan) V.; m. Euleen Hamilton, Oct. 20, 1949; children: Linda. Teresa, Roy Newton III. LL.B., U. Ky., 1942. Bar: Ky. 1942. County atty. McCracken County, (Ky.), 1949-53; commonwealth's atty. 2d Jud. Dist. Ky., 1953-57; mem. Vance, Grimes and Carlick, Paducah, 1957-70; commr. Ct. Appeals of Ky., Frankfort, 1970-76, judge, 1976-83; justice Ky. Supreme Ct., 1983—. Served with AUS, 1942-46. Mem. Order of Coif. Office: Ky Supreme Ct State Capitol Bldg Frankfort KY 40601

VANCE, SHELDON BAIRD, lawyer, former diplomat; b. Crookston, Minn., Jan. 18, 1917; s. Erskine Ward and Helen (Baird) V.; m. Jean Chambers, Dec. 28, 1939; children: Robert Clarke and Stephen Baird. A.B., Carleton Coll., 1939; J.D., Harvard U., 1942. Bar: Mass. 1942, D.C. 1977, U.S. Supreme Ct. 1977. Practiced in Boston, 1942; assoc. firm Ropes, Gray, Best, Coolidge & Rugg; joined Fgn. Service; econ. analyst, 3d sec. Am. embassy, Rio de Janeiro, Brazil, 1942-46; U.S. vice consul Nice, France and Monaco, 1946-49; U.S. consul Martinique, W.I., 1949-51; Belgium-Luxemburg desk officer Dept. State, Washington, 1951-54; 1st sec. Am. embassy, Brussels, Belgium, 1954-58; chief personnel placement br. Africa, Middle East and South Asia, 1958-60; student Sr. Seminar in Fgn. Relations, 1960-61; dir. Office Central African Affairs, 1961-62; dep. chief mission Am. embassy, Addis Ababa, Ethiopia, 1962-66; sr. fgn. service insp. 1966-67; U.S. ambassador to Republic of Chad, 1967-69, to Republic of Zaire, Kinshasa, 1969-74; promoted to rank of career minister 1971; sr. adviser to sec. state, coordinator internat. narcotics matters, also exec. dir. President's Cabinet Com. on Internat. Narcotics Control, Dept. State, 1974-77; ptnr. Vance, Joyce, Carbaugh, Fields and Cromelin, Washington, 1977—; bd. dirs. Sun Co., Inc., Radnor, Pa. Vice chmn. Mayor's Adv. Com. on Drug Abuse, Washington, 1980—; mem. com. of four internat. experts advising UN Conf. on Narcotic Drugs, 1987. Mem. Fgn. Service Assn. Presbyterian. Club: Columbia Country (Chevy Chase, Md.). General corporate, Private international, Estate planning. Home: 8510 Lynwood Pl Chevy Chase MD 20815 Office: Vance Joyce Carbaugh Fields & Crommelin 1701 Pennsylvania Ave NW Suite 940 Washington DC 20006

VANCE, VERNE WIDNEY, JR., lawyer; b. Omaha, Mar. 10, 1932; s. Verne Widney and June Caroline (Henckler) V.; m. Anita Paine, June 27, 1970; children—Lisa Joy, Charles Hebard Paine, Virginia Caroline. A.B., Harvard U., 1954, J.D., 1957. Bar: D.C. 1957, Mass. 1964. Law clk. U.S. Dist. Judge, Mass., 1957-58; assoc. Covington & Burling, Washington, 1958-60; atty. adv. Devel. Loan Fund, Washington, 1960-61; legal counsel AID, Washington, 1961-63; assoc. Foley, Hoag & Eliot, Boston, 1963-67, ptnr., 1967—; lectr. law Boston U., 1964-66; corp. clk. S.S. Pierce Co., 1971-72. Pres. UN Assn. Greater Boston, 1964-66, 77-78, treas., 1974-77; mem. Mass. Adv. Council on Edn., 1969-75, chmn., 1975; mem. Democratic City Com., Newton, Mass., 1972—, Gov.'s Local Govt. Adv. Commn., 1986—; alderman City of Newton, 1982—; bd. dirs. Newton Conservators, 1982—, Mass. Mcpl. Assn., 1986—. Mem. Boston Bar Assn. (bd. of editors bar jour. 1986—), Unitarian. Club: Longwood Cricket (Chestnut Hill, Mass.). Editor Harvard Law Rev., 1955-57; bd. editors Boston Bar Jour., 1986—; contbr. articles to profl. jours. Administrative and regulatory, Environment, Trademark and copyright. Home: 101 Old Orchard Rd Newton MA 02167 Office: 1 Post Office Sq Boston MA 02109

VANCE, VICTORIA LYNNE, lawyer; b. Cleve., Jan. 23, 1958; d. Thaddeus Joseph and Athalene (O'Donnell) Potelicki; m. Richard Allen Vance, May 21, 1983. AB in Econs. summa cum laude, John Carroll U., 1979; JD cum laude, Cornell U., 1982. Bar: Ohio 1982, U.S. Dist. Ct. (no. dist.) Ohio 1982. Assoc. Arter & Hadden, Cleve., 1982—. Mem. ABA, Ohio State Bar Assn., Cuyahoga County Bar Assn. Club: Cornell (Northeastern Ohio). State civil litigation, Health, Insurance. Home: 3661 Latimore Rd Shaker Heights OH 44122 Office: Arter & Hadden 1100 Huntington Bldg Cleveland OH 44115

VAN CLEVE, WILLIAM MOORE, lawyer; b. Mar. 17, 1929; s. William T and Catherine Baldwin (Moore) Van C.; m. Georgia Hess Dunbar, June 27, 1953; children—Peter Dunbar, Robert Baldwin II, Sarah Lewis, Emory Basford. Grad., Phillips Acad., 1946; A.B. in Econs., Princeton U., 1950; J.D., Washington U., St. Louis, 1953. Bar: Mo. 1953. Assoc. Dunbar and Gaddy, St. Louis, 1955-58; ptnr. Bryan, Cave, McPheeters & McRoberts, St. Louis, 1958—; chmn. Bryan, Cave, McPheeters & McRoberts, 1973—; dir. Emerson Electric Co., Station List Pub. Co. Chancellor, Episcopal Diocese of Mo., 1973—, former mem. diocesan standing com.; trustee St. Louis Children's Hosp., 1982—, sec., 1986, vice chmn. 1987— ; mem., v.p. exec. com. Andover Alumni Council, Phillips Acad., Mass., 1978-82; mem. alumni council com. to nominate alumni trustees Princeton U., 1976-78, chmn. com. 1978; trustee Washington U., 1983—, mem. exec. com. 1985—, pres. Eliot Soc. 1982-86, chmn. Law Sch. Nat. Council. Served as 1st lt. U.S. Army, 1953-55. Mem. Bar Assn. Met. St. Louis, ABA, St. Louis County Bar Assn., Order of Coif (hon.). Democrat. Episcopalian. Clubs: Princeton (exec. com., former pres.), Noonday (pres. 1985), St. Louis Country, Bogey (treas. 1986—), Round Table (St. Louis). General corporate, Estate planning, Banking. Home: 8 Dromara Rd Saint Louis MO 63124 Office: Bryan Cave et al 500 N Broadway Saint Louis MO 63102

VAN DE BUNT, DIRK WOUTER, lawyer; b. s'Gravenhage, The Netherlands, June 30, 1957; came to U.S., 1959; s. Wouter and Gerda (Bakker) van de B. BA, UCLA, 1978, JD, MA in History, 1982. Bar: Calif. 1982, U.S. Ct. Appeals (9th cir.) 1982, U.S. Dist. Ct. (cen. dist.) Calif. 1982, U.S. Dist. Ct. (so., no. and ea. dist.) Calif. 1983. Law clk. to sr. justice U.S. Dist. Ct., Los Angeles, 1981-83; assoc. Loeb & Loeb, Los Angeles, 1983-85; atty. bus. affairs, video distbn. Paramount Pictures Corp., Los Angeles, 1985-86, sr. atty. network television, 1986—. Editor in chief UCLA Alaska Law Rev., 1981-82. Mem. ABA, Los Angeles Bar Assn. (exec. bd. intellectual property sect. 1985—). Democrat. Club: Lawyers in Lust (Los Angeles). Avocations: backpacking, cartooning, history. Entertainment, General corporate, Libel. Home: 1541 Princeton Ave Santa Monica CA 90404 Office: Paramount Pictures Corp 5555 Melrose Ave Los Angeles CA 90038

VAN DE CAR, DIANA LEE, lawyer; b. Honolulu, Apr. 28, 1952; d. Robert Albert and Dolores (Souza) Pelletier; m. Lloyd Xavier Van De Car, Nov. 11, 1978; 1 child, Nicola E.K. BA, U. Hawaii, 1974, JD, 1977. Bar: Hawaii 1977, U.S. Dist. Ct. Hawaii 1977, U.S. Ct. Appeals (9th cir.) 1980. Assoc. Case, Kay & Lynch, Honolulu, 1977-79, ptnr., 1985-86; assoc. Case, Kay & Lynch, Hilo, Hawaii, 1981-85, ptnr., 1985—; sole practice Hilo, 1979-81. Mem. adv. council Am. Lung Assn., Honolulu, 1983—. Mem. Hawaii Bar Assn. (chmn. com. guardianships 1985—), Hawaii Island Bar Assn. (treas. 1980-81), Hawaii Island C. of C. (bd. dirs. 1984—). State civil litigation, Real property, Personal injury. Office: Case Kay & Lynch 275 Ponahawai St Honolulu HI 96720

VANDEGRIFT, LUCIAN B., lawyer, retired judge; b. Woodland, Calif., June 18, 1926; s. Rolland A. Vandegrift and Margaret (Bickford) Burket; m. Jacklyn Kay Montbriand, July 23, 1983; children by previous marriage—Rolland Stevens, Paul Lofton, Clarinda Jean, Scott McAmis. A.B., U. Calif.-Berkely, 1950, J.D., 1953. Bar: Calif. 1954. Dep. atty. gen. Calif. Dept. Justice, Sacramento, 1953-59; dep. dist. atty. Butte County, Oroville, Calif., 1959-60, asst. dist. atty., 1960-62, dist. atty., 1962-68; asst., then sec. Calif. Health and Welfare Agy., Sacramento, 1968-71; judge Superior Ct. Butte County, Oroville, 1971-84; sole practice, Oroville, 1984—. Served to lt. (j.g.) USNR, 1944-52. Mem. Calif. Bar Assn., Butte County Bar Assn. Republican. State civil litigation, Condemnation, Personal injury. Home: Meadowbrook Ranch De Sabla Stage Magalia CA 95954 Office: 1580 Bird St Oroville CA 95965

VAN DE KAMP, JOHN KALAR, state attorney general; b. Pasadena, Calif., Feb. 7, 1936; s. Harry and Georgie (Kalar) Van de K.; m. Andrea Fisher, Mar. 11, 1978; 1 dau., Diana. B.A., Dartmouth U., 1956; J.D., Stanford U., 1959. Bar: Calif. 1960. Asst. U.S. atty. Los Angeles, 1960-66, U.S. atty., 1966-67; spl. asst. Pres.'s Commn. on Campus Unrest, 1970; dep. dir. Exec. Office for U.S. Attys., Washington, 1967-68, dir., 1968-69; fed. pub. defender for Los Angeles 1971-75; dist. atty. Los Angeles County, 1975-83; atty. gen. State of Calif., 1983—; mem. Commn. on Jud. Appointments, Peace Officers Standards and Tng. Commn. Mem. Calif. Dist. Attys. Assn. (past pres.), Nat. Dist. Attys. Assn. (past v.p.), Peace Officers Assn. Los Angeles County (past pres.), Nat. Assn. Attys. Gen. (mem. exec. com.), Conf. Western Attys. Gen. (pres. 1986). Office: Office of Attorney General 3580 Wilshire Blvd Suite 800 Los Angeles CA 90010

VAN DE MARK, JULIE ANN, lawyer; b. San Antonio, June 6, 1957; d. Daniel Clay and Patricia Ann (Rahall) Van De M. BA, Miami U., Oxford, Ohio, 1978; JD, Ohio State U., 1982. Bar: Ohio 1982, U.S. Dist. Ct (so. and ea. dists.) Ohio 1983. Assoc. Wolske & Blue, Columbus, Ohio, 1982-84; ptnr. Alberty & Van De Mark, Columbus, 1984-85, Day & Van De Mark, Columbus, 1985—. Big sister Big Bros./Big Sisters, Columbus, 1984—. Mem. Ohio Bar Assn., Columbus Bar Assn., Assn. Trial Lawyers Am., Ohio Acad. Trial Lawyers, Franklin County Trial Lawyers. Democrat. Avocation: reading. Personal injury, State civil litigation, Criminal. Home: 481 E Sycamore St Columbus OH 43206 Office: Day & Van De Mark 492 City Park Ave Columbus OH 43215

VANDER ARK, STEVEN JOHN, lawyer; b. Grand Rapids, Mich., Aug. 21, 1949; s. John J. and Anne M. (Van Straten) V; m. M. Dawn Bedwell, Jan. 30, 1969; children: Heather Leigh, Adam Thomas. BA, Calvin Coll., 1971; MA, SUNY, Albany, 1974; JD magna cum laude, Thomas M. Cooley Law Sch., 1981. Bar: Mich. 1981, U.S. Dist. Ct. (we. dist.) Mich. 1981, U.S. Ct. Appeals (6th cir.) 1981. Chief probation officer Grandville (Mich.) Dist. Ct., 1975-78; assoc. Warner, Norcross & Judd, Grand Rapids, 1981—. Mem. Fed. Bar Assn., Mich. Bar Assn., Grand Rapids Bar Assn. Republican. Presbyterian. Club: University (Grand Rapids). Avocations: hunting, fishing, golfing. State civil litigation, Federal civil litigation, Insurance. Office: Warner Norcross & Judd 900 Old Kent Bank Grand Rapids MI 49503

VANDERBILT, ARTHUR T., II, lawyer; b. Summit, N.J., Feb. 20, 1950; s. William Runyon and Jean (White) V. BA, Wesleyan U., Middletown, Conn., 1972; JD, U. Va., 1975. Bar: N.J. 1975, U.S. Dist. Ct. N.J. 1975, U.S. Supreme Ct. 1978. Jud. clk. to presiding justice N.J. Superior Ct., 1975-76, dep. atty. gen., 1976-78, asst. counsel to gov., 1978-79; ptnr. Carella, Byrne, Bain & Gilfillan, Roseland, N.J., 1979—. Author: Changing Law 1976, Jersey Justice, 1978, Law School, 1981, Treasure Wreck, 1986. Mem. ABA (Scribes award 1976), N.J. Bar Assn., Am. Judicature Soc. Republican. Presbyterian. Avocation: writing. Municipal bonds, Administrative and regulatory, Securities. Office: Carella Byrne Bain & Gilfillan 6 Becker Farm Rd Roseland NJ 07068

VANDER BOEGH, DOUGLAS LEE, lawyer; b. Ontario, Oreg., Mar. 3, 1956; s. Robert George and Elizabeth Mae (Sampert) Van B.; m. Teri Lynn Keithly, Oct. 1, 1983. BA, Idaho State U., 1977; JD, U. Idaho, 1980. Bar: Idaho 1980, U.S. Dist. Ct. Idaho 1980, U.S. Ct. Appeals (9th cir.) 1985. Assoc. McDermott & McDermott, Pocatello, Idaho, 1980-82; ptnr. Churchill & Vander Boegh, Boise, Idaho, 1982—; adminstrv. judge Idaho Health and Welfare Dept., Boise, 1982—; contract atty. U.S. Govt., Boise, 1982—; dir.

Law Day USA, 1986—. Judge Forensic League Idaho Hich Sch., Boise and Pocatello, 1980—; dem. candidate state senate, Ada County, Idaho, 1984. Mem. ABA (Young Lawyers div.), Idaho Bar Assn., Idaho Trial Lawyers Assn. Lutheran. Avocations: skiing, camping, painting. Real property, State civil litigation, Civil rights. Office: Churchill & Vander Boegh 1221 W Hays Boise ID 83701

VANDERBURG, MICHAEL ROBERT, lawyer; b. Little Rock, Jan. 16, 1949; s. Robert Neal and Evelyn Ruth (Stocker) V.; m. Linda Ann Koons, Nov. 17, 1973; children: Robert William, Lauren Rebecca. BA, U. Ark., 1971, JD, 1975; cert., Nat. Law Inst./FBI Acad., 1985. Bar: Okla. 1975, U.S. Dist. Ct. (no. and ea. dists.) Okla. 1975, U.S. Ct. Appeals (10th cir.) 1983, U.S. Supreme Ct. 1983. Sole practice Tulsa, 1975-76; ptnr. Ellis Chenoweth and Vanderburg, Tulsa, 1976-77, Ellis, Vanderburg and Insabella, Tulsa, 1977-81; city atty. City of Broken Arrow, Okla., 1981—. Deacon John Knox Presbyn. Ch., Tulsa, 1979-82, elder, 1984-87; bd. dirs. Crosstown Day Care Ctr. 2d Presbyn. Ch., Tulsa, 1979-82; co-chmn. Constitution 200 Commn. of Broken Arrow, Okla. Mem. ABA, Okla. Bar Assn., Am. Trial Lawyers Assn., Okla. Trial Lawyers Assn., Nat. Assn. Mcpl. Legal Officers (com. mem. 1982-86), Okla. Assn. Mcpl. Attys. (bd. dirs. 1985-86). Republican. Club: Mariners (Tulsa) (skipper 1978-79, other officers 1976-82). Civil rights, Local government, Government contracts and claims. Home: 4105 S Lions Ave Broken Arrow OK 74011 Office: City of Broken Arrow 200 Municiipal Ctr Broken Arrow OK 74012

VANDERET, ROBERT CHARLES, lawyer; b. Bklyn., Apr. 12, 1947; s. James Gustav and Bernadette Cecelia (Heaney) V.; m. Sharon Kay Brewster, Oct 3, 1970; 1 child, Erin Anne Brewster. AB, UCLA, 1969; JD, Stanford U., 1973. Bar: Calif. 1973, U.S. Dist. Ct. (cen. and so. dists.) Calif. 1974, U.S. Ct. Appeals (9th cir.) 1976, U.S. Supreme Ct. 1978, U.S. Dist. Ct. (no. dist.) Calif. 1980, U.S. Dist. Ct. (ea. dist.) Calif. 1981, N.Y. 1986. Extern law clk. to judge Calif. Supreme Ct., 1972-73; assoc. O'Melveny & Myers, Los Angeles, 1973-80, ptnr., 1980—; transition aide Chief Justice Rose Bird, Calif. Supreme Ct., 1976. Del. Dem. Nat. Conv., 1968.; bd. dirs. Legal Aid Found. Los Angeles, 1974—. Mem. ABA, Los Angeles Bar Assn. Democrat. Libel, Federal civil litigation, State civil litigation. Home: 471 16th St Santa Monica CA 90402 Office: O'Melveny & Myers 400 S Hope St Los Angeles CA 90071

VANDERKLOOT, WILLIAM ROBERT, lawyer; b. Detroit, Apr. 6, 1937; s. Robert and Clara Augusta (Knudsen) V.; m. Keitha Vanderkloot; 4 children. A.B., U. Mich., 1958; LL.B., U. Va., 1961. Bar: Mich. 1961, Ill. 1963. Assoc. Hill, Lewis, Goodrich & Power, Detroit, 1964; Asst. pros. atty. Oakland County (Mich.), Pontiac, Mich., 1964-66; sole practice, Birmingham, Mich., 1966-82; ptnr. Vanderkloot, Haynes and Baxter, PC, Bloomfield Hills, 1982—. Trustee Oakland Law Library Found., pres., 1982-84; trustee Children's Hosp. of Mich., 1980—, audit com. 1983—; mem. Christ Church Cranbrook, Bloomfield Hills. Served to 1st lt. Intelligence Corps, U.S. Army, 1961-64. Mem. State Bar Mich. (trial counsel grievance bd. 1969-72, sec. civil procedure com. 1981-85, chmn. 1985-86), Ill. State Bar Assn., ABA (litigation, legal econs. sects.), Assn. Trial Lawyers Am. Democrat. Clubs: Rotary (bd. dirs. 1975-78); Village Players (Birmingham). Contbr. articles to profl. jours. Commercial litigation, corporate & business practice, Family and matrimonial, Personal injury. Office: Vanderkloot Haynes & Baxter PC 860 W Long Lake Rd Suite 200 PO Box 980 Bloomfield Hills MI 48013

VANDERLAAN, ROBERT D., lawyer; b. Grand Rapids, Mich., Aug. 22, 1952; s. Donald Gene and Elizabeth Jo (Stankiewicz) V.; m. Betty Jane Thomas, June 25, 1983. BA, U. Detroit, 1974, JD, 1977. Bar: Mich. 1977, U.S. Dist. Ct. (we. dist.) Mich. 1977, U.S. Ct. Appeals (3d cir.) 1983, U.S. Ct. Appeals (6th cir.) 1978, U.S. Supreme Ct. 1981. Ptnr., pres., dir. firm Mohney, Goodrich & Titta, P.C., Grand Rapids, Mich., 1977-86; with firm Miller, Canfield, Paddock & Stone, Grand Rapids, 1986—. Bd. dirs. St. John's Home, Grand Rapids, 1980—, Mercy Respite Care Corp., Grand Rapids, 1980-83, Grand Rapids Cath. Secondary Sch. Bd. Edn., 1982—. Mem. Nat. Inst. Trial Advocacy (faculty 1982—), Grand Rapids Bar Assn., Grand Rapids Jaycees (dir. 1979-80, legal counsel 1978-79, 82-83, v.p. 1985-86, pres. 1986-87, chmn. bd. 1987-88, Disting. Service award 1984). Roman Catholic. Federal civil litigation, State civil litigation. Office: Miller Canfield Paddock & Stone 1200 Campau Sq Plaza Bldg Grand Rapids MI 49503

VANDERLINDE, SUSAN KAY, lawyer; b. Balt., Nov. 28, 1951; d. Raymond Edward and Ruth Louise (Hansen) V.; m. Gary Kelley Bove, Aug. 23, 1975 (dec. July 1977); m. Albert Matthew Miller, June 19, 1981; 1 child, Molly Linden. BA, Coll. William and Mary, 1973; MA in Psychology, Vanderbilt U., 1975; JD, SUNY, Buffalo, 1979. Bar: Md. 1980, U.S. Dist. Ct. Md. 1980. Assoc. Miles & Stockbridge, Balt., 1979-80, Weinberg & Green, Balt., 1980-81; ptnr. Miller & Vanderlinde, Balt., 1982-83; sr. atty. U.S. Fidelity & Guaranty Co., Balt., 1983-84, counsel, 1984—. Counsellor, bd. dirs. Soc. of Mayflower Descendants in Md, 1981—. Mem. ABA, Md. Bar Assn.(program chmn. 1984-85), Women's Bar Assn. Md. (program chmn. 1981-83, sec. 1983-84, v.p. 1984-85). Democrat. Methodist. Contracts commercial, General corporate, Insurance. Home: 8-10 Charles Plaza Penthouse One Baltimore MD 21201 Office: US Fidelity & Guaranty Co 100 Light St Baltimore MD 21202

VANDERROEST, JAMES EDWARD, lawyer; b. Kalamazoo, Mich., June 29, 1956; s. John E. and Betty J. (Heath) V. BA with high honors, Mich. State U., 1978; JD cum laude, Brigham Young U., 1981. Bar: Mich. 1981, U.S. Dist. Ct. (we. dist.) Mich. 1982, U.S. Ct. Appeals (6th cir.) 1982. Assoc. Vlachos, Jerkins & Hurley, Kalamazoo, 1981—; mem. constl. law com. State Bar of Mich., 1985—, State Bar Mich. Rep. Assmebly 9th Jud. Cir., 1986—. Bd. dirs. Kalamazoo Community Concerts, Inc., 1981-86. Mem. ABA, Fed. Bar Assn., Kalamazoo County Bar Assn. Mormon. Avocations: history, classical music, religious service. General practice, Criminal, Probate. Home: 3530 N Drake Rd Kalamazoo MI 49007

VANDERSTAR, JOHN, lawyer; b. Jersey City, Sept. 17, 1933; s. John Vanderstar and Rosemarie (Torraco) Legette; m. Beth S. Vanderstar, Nov. 7, 1956 (div. Oct. 1984); children: Pippa, Alexandra, Thankful, Eliza; m. M. Elizabeth Culbreth, Mar. 16, 1985. BE, Princeton U., 1954; LLB, Harvard U., 1961. Assoc. Covington & Burling, Washington, 1961-70, ptnr., 1970—. Pres. ACLU Nat. Capital Area, Washington, 1976-78, bd. dirs., 1971-78; bd. dirs. NOW Legal Def. and Edn. Fund, N.Y.C., v.p. 1985—. Served to lt. USNR, 1954-58. Recipient Alan Barth award, ACLU Nat. Capital Area, 1984. Mem. ABA, D.C. Bar Assn. (bd. govs. 1985—). Episcopalian. Federal civil litigation, Antitrust, Civil rights. Home: 2319 N Glebe Rd Arlington VA 22207 Office: Covington & Burling 1201 Pennsylvania NW PO Box 7566 Washington DC 20044

VANDERVOORT, PETER, lawyer; b. Paterson, N.J., Dec. 15, 1929; s. Vincent and Jeannette Barbara (Scott) V.; m. Elena Drake, June 26, 1971. BA, Williams Coll., 1951; LLB, U. Va., 1954. Bar: Va. 1953, N.J. 1958. Assoc. Evans, Hand, Allabough & Amoresano, Paterson, 1958-62; ptnr. Evans, Hand, Allabough & Amoresano, West Paterson, N.J., 1963—; asst. sec. Essex Chem. Corp., Clifton, N.J., 1963-83, sec., 1983—. Trustee West Side Presbyn. Ch., Ridgewood, N.J., 1961-67, Family Counselling Service of Ridgewood, 1968-77, Soc. Valley Hosp., Ridgewood, 1976—; bd. dirs. Paterson YMCA, 1959-76, pres. 1967-74, trustee 1978-86, chmn. 1984—. Fellow Am. Coll. Probate Counsel; mem. ABA, N.J. Bar Assn., Va. Bar Assn., Order of Coif, Phi Beta Kappa. Clubs: Ridgewood Country, Upper Ridgewood Tennis (sec. 1960-61); Williams (N.Y.C.). Estate planning, Probate, Estate taxation. Home: 376 Beechwood Rd Ridgewood NJ 07450 Office: Evans Hand Allabough & Amoresand One Garret Mountain Plaza West Paterson NJ 07424

VAN DER WAL, JEANNE HUBER, lawyer, consultant; b. Flushing, N.Y., Feb. 7, 1954; d. William Joseph and Georgene (Lukes) Huber; m. Peter van der Wal, May 8, 1982. AB magna cum laude, Colgate U., 1975; JD, Suffolk U., 1978. Bar: D.C. 1979, U.S. Dist. Ct. D.C. 1979, U.S. Ct. Appeals (D.C. cir.) 1979, U.S. Supreme Ct. 1983. Regulatory atty. Kimberly-Clark Corp., Washington, 1978-83; corp. counsel Kimberly-Clark Corp., Roswell, Ga., 1983-86; pvt. practice cons. Northridge, Calif., 1986—; corp. rep. U.S. Mex. C. of C., Washington and Mex., 1979-83; corp. rep. ASTM, Phila., 1981-83; cons. Industry Sector Adv. Com. on Paper and Paper Products for Trade Policy Matters, Dept. of Commerce, Washington, 1982-85. Participant Women's Equality Day, The White House, 1984; mem. exec. women's briefing on commerce com. Rep. Nat. Com., Washington, 1985, Rep. Presdl. Task Force, Washington, 1985-87. N.Y. Regents scholar, 1971-75. Mem. ABA, Bar Assn. D.C., D.C. Bar Assn., Phi Beta Kappa. Republican. Roman Catholic. Clubs: Willow Springs Country (Roswell, Ga.) (bd. dirs., v.p. 1984-85, bd. dirs., sec. 1985-86). Avocations: real estate, sailing, golf, skiing. Administrative and regulatory, Contracts commercial, General corporate. Home and Office: 18930 Harnett St Northridge CA 91326

VANDER WOUDE, RICHARD JOHN, lawyer; b. Longview, Tex., Nov. 11, 1954; s. Jack Clarence and Jeanette Helen (Uddenberg) Vander W.; m. Jane Kay Robertson, June 7, 1975; children: Jeffrey Chad, Michael Craig, Kevin Clay. BBA, So. Meth. U., 1975, JD, 1978. Bar: Tex. 1978, U.S. Dist. Ct. (we. dist.) Tex. 1981, U.S. Ct. Appeals (5th cir.) 1982, U.S. Dist. Ct. (no. dist.) Tex. 1985. Assoc. Sheehy, Lovelace & Mayfield P.C., Waco, Tex., 1978-83, ptnr., 1983—; bd. dirs. Heart of Tex. Legal Services Inc., Waco, also pres. 1986—. Bd. dirs. Heart of Tex. Council on Alcoholism and Drug Abuse, Waco, 1983—, sec., 1985, v.p., 1986; adv. bd. Waco Rape Crisis Ctr., 1983—; mem. City of Woodway Planning and Zoning Commn., 1986—. Mem. ABA (various sects), Tex. Bar Assn. (various sects.), Waco-McLennan County Bar Assn., Waco-McLennan County Young Lawyers Assn., Tex. Assn. of Bank Counsel, Waco Jaycees (bd. dirs. 1979-84, sec. 1983). Methodist. Avocations: running, tennis. Banking, Contracts commercial, State civil litigation. Home: 609 Ivy Ann Waco TX 76710 Office: Sheehy Lovelace & Mayfield PC 1200 American-Amicable Bldg Waco TX 76701

VANDEVENTER, BRADEN, lawyer; b. Norfolk, Va., Sept. 27, 1921; s. Braden and Phelan (Ruffin) V.; m. Barbara Ann Lewis, June 10, 1954; children: Elizabeth, Thomas, William, Ann. BA, Va. Mil. Inst., 1943; LLB, U. Va., 1949. Bar: Va. 1949. Assoc. Vandeventer, Black, Meredith & Martin and predecessor Vandeventer & Black, Norfolk, 1949-52, ptnr., 1952—; bd. dirs. Life Fed. Savs. & Loan Assn., Bank of Va., Eastern; lectr. William and Mary Law Sch., Tulane U. Admiralty Law Inst. Bd. dirs. Hampton Rds. Maritime Assn., Norfolk, 1964-81, v.p., 1982—; trustee Mariners Mus., Newport News, Va. Served to maj. U.S. Army, 1943-46; ETO. Decorated Bronze Star. Mem. ABA, Va. Bar Assn., Norfolk and Portsmouth Bar Assn., Maritime Law Assn. U.S. (exec. com. 1976-79). Democrat. Episcopalian. Clubs: Va. (Norfolk); Princess Anne (Virginia Beach, Va.); Farmington (Charlottesville, Va.); India House (N.Y.C.). Contbr. articles to law jours. Admiralty, Banking, General corporate. Home: 1129 Chumley Rd Virginia Beach VA 23451 Office: 500 World Trade Ctr Norfolk VA 23510

VANDEVER, WILLIAM DIRK, lawyer; b. Chgo., Aug. 1, 1949; s. Lester J. and Elizabeth J. V.; m. Kathi J. Zellmer, Aug. 26, 1983; 1 child, Barton Dirk. BS, U. Mo., Kansas City, 1971, JD with distinction, 1974. Bar: Mo. 1975, U.S. Dist. Ct. (we. dist.) Mo. 1975. Dir. Popham Law Firm, Kansas City, Mo., 1975—; lectr. med. malpractice various hosps. and colls., Kansas City, Mo., 1979—. Issue editor U. Mo.-Kansas City Law Rev., 1974. Mem. Mo. Assn. Trial Attys., Kansas City Met. Bar Assn. (treas., sec., pres. exec. com. 1986—), Kansas City Bar Found. (treas. 1986—), Phi Delta Phi, Beta Theta Pi. Avocations: tennis, skiing, running, reading. Personal injury, Construction. Home: 11800 Central Kansas City MO 64114 Office: Popham Law Firm 1300 Commerce Trust Bldg Kansas City MO 64106

VANDEWALLE, GERALD WAYNE, justice state supreme court; b. Noonan, N.D., Aug. 15, 1933; s. Jules C. and Blanche Marie (Gits) VandeW. B.Sc., U. N.D., 1955, J.D., 1958. Bar: N.D. bar U.S. Dist. Ct. N.D 1959. Spl. asst. atty. gen. State of N.D., Bismarck, 1958-75; 1st asst. atty. gen. State of N.D., 1975-78; justice N.D. Supreme Ct., 1978—; mem. faculty Bismarck Jr. Coll., 1972-76; chmn. N.D. Jud. Conf. Editor-in-chief N.D. Law Rev, 1957-58. Active Bismarck Meals on Wheels; bd. dirs. Bismarck-Mandan Symphony. Mem. State Bar Assn. N.D., Burleigh County Bar Assn., Am. Bar Assn., Am. Contract Bridge League, Order of Coif, Phi Eta Sigma, Beta Alpha Psi, Beta Gamma Sigma, Phi Alpha Delta. Roman Catholic. Clubs: Elks, K.C. Office: Supreme Ct State Capitol Bismarck ND 58505

VANDIVIER, BLAIR ROBERT, lawyer; b. Rapid City, S.D., Dec. 24, 1955; s. Robert Eugene and Barbara Jean (Kidd) V.; m. Elizabeth Louise Watson, July 26, 1980; 1 child, Jessica Elizabeth. BS magna cum laude, Butler U., 1978; JD cum laude, Ind. U., 1981. Bar: Ind. 1981, U.S. Dist. Ct. (so. dist.) Ind. 1981, U.S. Tax Ct. 1985. Assoc. Henderson, Daily, Withrow, Johnson & Gross, Indpls., 1981-83; assoc., ptnr. Johnson, Gross, Densborn & Wright, Indpls., 1983-85; v.p. Benchmark Chem. Corp., Indpls., 1985—, also bd. dirs.; bd. dirs. Ecosoft, Inc., Indpls., Seleco, Inc., Indpls., Wiley Equipment Co., Inc.; of counsel Johnson, Gross, Densborn & Wright, Indpls., 1985—. Mem. com. Conner Prairie Settlement Fund Dr., Indpls., 1983-85, Riley Run, 1987—. Mem. ABA, Ind. Bar Assn., Indpls. Bar Assn., Am. Electroplaters Soc. (law com., sec. Indpls. br. 1986—), Metal Finishing Suppliers Assn. (spl. projects services com.). Republican. Episcopalian. Club: Highland Golf (Indpls.). Avocations: golf, reading. Contracts commercial, Real property, General corporate. Home: 8927 Woodcare Ln Indianapolis IN 46234 Office: Benchmark Chem Corp PO Box 68809 Indianapolis IN 46268

VAN DUERM, JAMES, lawyer; b. Berwyn, Ill., Apr. 19, 1951; s. Frank Stewart and Helen Cecilia (Mulvenna) Van D.; m. Mariapia Grano, Oct. 16, 1976; children: Frank Stewart, Christopher. BA, Loyola U., Chgo., 1973; JD, DePaul U., 1976, LLM in Taxation, 1985. Bar: Ill. 1976, U.S. Dist. Ct. (no. dist.) Ill. 1976. Trust officer 1st Chgo. Corp., 1978-81, asst. v.p., 1981-84, sr. atty., 1984—. Author: IICLE Basic Estate Planning, 1984. Mem. ABA, Ill. Bar Assn., Chgo. Bar Assn. (com. chmn. 1979-80, bd. dirs. 1981-82, treas. 1983-84, spl. project coordinator 1984-85 young lawyers sect.), Computer Law Assn., Chgo. Estate Planning Council. Avocations: golf, antique toys. Computer, Probate, Corporate taxation. Home: 659 Prospect St Elmhurst IL 60126 Office: 1st Chgo Corp Mail Suite 0292 Chicago IL 60670

VAN DUSEN, LEWIS HARLOW, JR., lawyer; b. Phila., Dec. 18, 1910; s. Lewis Harlow and Muriel (Lund) Van D.; m. Maria Pepper Whelen, Nov. 8, 1935; children: Duncan W., Lewis H. III, Michael H., Sally Johnson. BA, Princeton U., 1932; postgrad., Harvard U., 1932-33; B in Civil Law, New Coll., Oxford, Eng., 1935. Bar: Pa. 1935, U.S. Dist. Ct. (ea. dist.) Pa. 1936, U.S. Ct. Appeals (3d cir.) 1936, U.S. Supreme Ct. 1939. Assoc. Drinker Biddle & Reath, Phila., 1935-41, ptnr., 1941—, sr. ptnr., 1952—; bd. dirs. IU Internat. Contbr. articles to profl. jours. Served to lt. col. U.S. Army, 1942-45. Recipient Learned Hand award Am. Jewish Com., 1983. Mem. ABA (chmn. ethics com.), Pa. Bar Assn. (pres. 1974-75), Phila. Bar Assn. (chancellor 1968), Internat. Bar Assn., Am. Coll. Trial Lawyers. Republican. Episcopalian. Clubs: Union League, Philadelphia, Merion Cricket. Avocation: tennis. Federal civil litigation, State civil litigation, Estate planning. Home: 10 Righter's Ferry Rd Bala-Cynwyd PA 19004 Office: Drinker Biddle & Reath 1100 Philadelphia Nat Bank Bldg Philadelphia PA 19107

VAN DYKE, JON MARKHAM, lawyer, educator; b. Washington, Apr. 29, 1943; s. Stuart Hope and Eleonora (Markham) Van D.; m. Sherry Phyllis Broder, Feb. 12, 1978; children—Jesse Bernard, Eric Gabriel, Michelle Tiare. B.A., Yale U., 1964; J.D., Harvard U., 1967. Bar: D.C. 1968, Calif. 1970, Hawaii, 1976. Asst. prof. law Cath. U., Washington, 1967-69; law clk. Calif. Supreme Ct., San Francisco, 1969-70; vis. fellow Ctr. for Study of Democratic Instns., Santa Barbara, 1970-71; assoc. prof. law Hastings Law Sch., U. Calif.-San Francisco, 1971-75, prof., 1975-76; prof. law Law Sch., U. Hawaii, Honolulu, 1976—, assoc. dean, 1980-82; project dir., law of the sea Sea Grant Coll. Program, 1979—; research assoc. Environment and Policy Inst., East-West Ctr., Honolulu, 1982-84, adj. research assoc. Resource Systems Inst., 1986—; mem. exec. bd. Law of the Sea Inst., Honolulu, 1982—. Author: North Vietnam's Strategy for Survival, 1972; Jury Selection Procedures: Our Uncertain Commitment to Representative Panels, 1977; editor: Consensus and Confrontation: The United States and the Law of the Sea Convention, 1985. Mem. Reapportionment Commn., Honolulu, 1981-82, ACLU Litigation Com., Honolulu, 1986—, Hawaii Bicentennial Commn. of U.S. Constitution. Named Outstanding Prof. Hawaii Assn. of Plaintiffs Attys., 1984; recipient Presdl. Citation for Teaching Excellence, 1987. Mem. Am. Soc. Internat. Law, Hawaii State Bar Assn., Internat. Council Environ. Law, Amnesty Internat. USA Legal Adv. Council. Civil rights, Environment, Public international. Home: 41-911 Laumilo St Waimanalo HI 96795 Office: U Hawaii Law Sch 2515 Dole St Honolulu HI 96822

VAN ETTEN, LAURA, lawyer; b. Buchenbueren, Fed. Republic of Germany, Mar. 16, 1955; came to U.S., 1956; d. Chester Lumley and Marie Osada (Shinyue) Van E.; m. Thomas Michael Cannata, Jan. 21, 1984. BA, U. Fla., 1976; JD, George Washington U., 1980. Bar: D.C. 1980, U.S. Ct. Appeals (D.C. cir.) 1984. Legis. asst. congressman E.J. Markey, Washington, 1980-81; staff atty. congressman J.P.Hiler, Washington, 1981-83; legis. rep. Nat. Restaurant Assn., Washington, 1983-86; assoc. counsel The Equitable Life Assurance Soc., Washington, 1986—. Mem. The Tax Coalition, Washington, 1984—, Women in Govt. Relations, 1984—. Republican. Club: Arlington Women's Soccer League. Legislative, Real property, Corporate taxation. Home: 1206 W Abingdon Dr Alexandria VA 22314 Office: The Equitable Life Assurance Soc 1700 Pennsylvania Ave NW #525 Washington DC 20006

VAN FLEET, GEORGE ALLAN, lawyer; b. Monterey, Calif., Jan. 20, 1953; s. George Lawson and Wilma (Ruth) Van F.; m. Laurie Elise Koch, July 20, 1975; 1 child, Katia Elaine. BA, Rice U., 1976; JD, Columbia U., 1977. Bar: Tex. 1978, U.S. Dist. Ct. (so. dist.) Tex. 1978, U.S. Ct. Appeals (5th cir.) 1978, U.S. Ct. Appeals (11th cir.) 1981, U.S. Supreme Ct. 1981, U.S. Ct. Appeals (D.C. cir.) 1982. Law clk. U.S. Ct. Appeals (2d cir.), N.Y.C., 1977; assoc. Vinson & Elkins, Houston, 1977-84, ptnr., 1984—. Author: Pleadings: State and Federal; also articles; editor quarterly rev. Litigation News, 1983—. Adv. dir. Sheltering Arms, Houston, 1979—. Recipient Ordroneaux prize Columbia U., 1977. Mem. ABA, Tex. Bar Assn., Houston Bar Assn., Houston Young Lawyers Assn. (com. chmn. 1979-80). Democrat. Jewish. Antitrust, Federal civil litigation, State civil litigation. Home: 4323 N Roseneath Dr Houston TX 77021 Office: Vinson & Elkins 3000 1st City Tower Houston TX 77002

VAN GILDER, DEREK ROBERT, lawyer, engineer; b. San Antonio, Feb. 26, 1950; s. Robert Ellis and Genevieve Delphine (Hutter) Van G.; m. Charlene Frances Madison, Jan. 21, 1984. Student, U.S. Mil. Acad., 1969-71; BS in Civil Engring., U. Tex., 1974, JD, 1981; MBA, U. Houston, 1976. Bar: Tex. 1981, U.S. Ct. Appeals (5th cir.) 1981, Calif. 1982, U.S. Dist. Ct. (cen. dist.) Calif. 1982, U.S. Dist. Ct. (ea. and so. dists.) Tex. 1982, U.S. Ct. Appeals (9th cir.) 1982, U.S. Dist. Ct. (we. dist.) Tex. 1983; registered profl. engr. Tex., La., N.M., Calif. Engr. various engring cos., Houston, Longview and Austin, Tex., 1974-81; assoc. Thelen, Marrin, Johnson & Bridges, Los Angeles, 1981-82, Bean & Manning, Houston, 1982-85; sole practice Houston, 1985-86; prin. Van Gilder & Assocs., Houston, 1986—; instr. Houston Community Coll., 1981—. Mem. ABA, Houston Bar Assn., Tex. Young Lawyers Assn., Houston Young Lawyers Assn., Am. Arbitration Assn. (panel arbitrators), Houston Med.-Legal Soc., Nat. Soc. Profl. Engrs., Tex. Soc. Profl. Engrs. Republican. Roman Catholic. Club: Houston City. Avocations: racquetball, golf. Construction, Federal civil litigation, State civil litigation. Office: 11 Greenway Plaza Suite 2222 Houston TX 77046

VAN GRAAFEILAND, ELLSWORTH ALFRED, judge; b. Rochester, N.Y., May 11, 1915; s. Ivan and Elsie (Gohr) VanG.; m. Rosemary Vaeth, May 26, 1945; children—Gary, Suzanne, Joan, John, Anne. A.B., U. Rochester, 1937; LL.B., Cornell U., 1940. Bar: N.Y. bar 1940. Practiced in Rochester; now judge U.S. Ct. Appeals for 2d Circuit. Fellow Am., N.Y. bar founds.; mem. ABA (ho. dels. 1973-75), N.Y. State Bar Assn. (v.p. 1972-73, pres. 1973-74, chmn. negligence compensation and ins. sect. 1968-69), Monroe County Bar Assn. (past pres.), Am. Coll. Trial Lawyers., Mason. Clubs: Kent; Oak Hill Country (Rochester). Home: 76 Ramsey Park Rochester NY 14610 Office: Fed Bldg Room 423 Rochester NY 14614

VAN GRACK, STEVEN, lawyer; b. Memphis, Oct. 6, 1948; s. Irving and Edna (Schwartz) Van G.; m. Gail Beverly Lang, Nov. 18, 1972; children: Adam, Ryan, Brandon. BA, U. Md., 1970, JD, 1974. Bar: Md. 1974, D.C. 1976, U.S. Dist. Ct. Md. 1976, U.S. Dist. Ct. D.C. 1976, U.S. Ct. Appeals (4th cir.) 1977, U.S. Supreme Ct.1978. Law clk. to presiding justice Montgomery County Cir. Ct., Rockville, Md., 1974-75; assoc. Joseph Roesser Law OFfices, Silver Springs, Md., 1975-78; ptnr. Ebert & Bowytz, Washington, 1978-80, Van Grack, Axelson & Williamowsky, Rockville, 1980—; instr., lectr. Montgomery Coll., Germantown, Md., 1983-85. Campaign mgr. Com. to Elect the Sitting Judges, Rockville, 1982; mayor City of Rockville, 1985—; gen. counsel Montgomery County Dem. Cen. Com., Kensington, Md., 1978-82; bd. dirs. Washington Met. Council Govts. Serve with USAR, 1970-71. Named one of Outstanding Young Men of Am., Jaycess, 1978, 81. Mem. ABA, Md. Bar Assn., Montgomery County Bar Assn., Md. Trial Lawyers Assn., Am. Judicature Soc. Jewish. Avocations: running, swimming, exercising, coin collecting, polit. button collecting. Personal injury, State civil litigation, Criminal. Home: 1917 S Fallsmead Way Rockville MD 20854 Office: Van Grack Axelson & Williamowsky 110 N Washington St Suite 404 Rockville MD 20850

VAN HAGEY, WILLIAM, lawyer; b. Chgo., Sept. 30, 1946; s. William and Rama (Free) Van H.; m. Connie Wittenberg, Sept. 3, 1966; children: Catherine Elspeth, William Colin. AB, U. Ill., 1968, JD, 1972. Bar: Ill. 1972, U.S. Dist. Ct. (no. dist.) Ill. 1974, U.S. Ct. Appeals (7th cir.) 1976, U.S. Supreme Ct. 1978, U.S. Ct. Appeals (10th cir.) 1979, U.S. Ct. Appeals (11th cir.) 1985. Law clk. to chief justice Ill. Supreme Ct., 1972-73; assoc. Chadwell & Kayser Ltd., Chgo., 1973-79, ptnr., 1980-84; ptnr. Van Hagey & Bogan Ltd., Mundelein, Ill., 1984—; mem. Ill. Franchise Adv. Bd., 1981—, vice chmn., 1984—. Mem. U. Ill. Coll. Law Bd. Visitors, 1982—, pres.-elect, 1986—. Served with USAR, 1968-74. Mem. ABA, Ill. Bar Assn. (council sect. on patent-trademark-copyright law 1986—), Chgo Bar Assn., Phi Alpha Delta. Clubs: Union League, Legal of Chgo. Franchising, Federal civil litigation, Trademark and copyright. Office: Van Hagey & Bogan Ltd 700 N Lake St Mundelein IL 60060

VAN HEYDE, G. JAMES, lawyer; b. Columbus, Ohio, Oct. 21, 1944; s. George Adams and Helen Marie (Holzapfel) Van H.; m. Betsy Louise Bernert, Aug. 25, 1973; 1 child, J. Michael. BBA, Ohio State U., 1968; JD, Capital U., 1976. Bar: Ohio 1976, U.S. Dist. Ct. (so. dist.) Ohio 1976, U.S. Supreme Ct. 1980. Staff acct. D.C. Ritchey & Co., Columbus, 1968-69, Kirschner, Heimlich, Mulligan & Co., Columbus, 1971-75; atty. examiner Ohio Pub. Utility Commn., Columbus, 1976-83; sr. utility atty. Ohio Consumers' Counsel, Columbus, 1983—. Singing mem. Columbus Maennerchor, 1978—. Served to 1st lt., U.S. Army, 1969-71. Mem. ABA (pub. utilities sect., corp. law sect.). Democrat. Roman Catholic. Avocations: singing, tennis, sailing, computer programming. Administrative and regulatory, FERC practice, Public utilities. Home: 2574 Northwest Blvd Columbus OH 43221 Office: Ohio Consumer's Counsel 137 E State St Columbus OH 43215

VAN HOOK, CLAUDE ASHTON, III, lawyer, educator; b. Phoenix, May 28, 1945; s. Claude Ashton and Adele (Saba) Van H. B.A. in Econs., Belmont Abbey Coll., 1967; J.D., U. Fla., 1970. Bar: Fla. 1971. Asst. state's atty. 18th Jud. Cir., Seminole County, Fla., 1972-76, chief felony div., 1974, 75, 76; sole practice, Sanford, Fla., 1977-78, DeLand, Fla., 1978—; mem. faculty Seminole County Community Coll., Sanford, 1980-84. Recipient Am. Jurisprudence award, 1969; award. Sch. Bd. Seminole County, 1978; award. State of Fla., 1981. Mem. ABA, Fla. Bar Assn., Volusia County Bar Assn. Roman Catholic. Clubs: Kiwanis, KC, Jaycees. Criminal, Juvenile. Office: 536 W New York Ave DeLand FL 32720

VAN HORN, CAROL LYNN, lawyer; b. Roaring Spring, Pa., Aug. 26, 1958; d. Raymond Junior Eichelberger and Deloris Jean (Lundquist) Territo; m. John Marshall Van Horn, June 23, 1979; children: Lindsay Dee, Alison Jo. BS, Juniata Coll., Huntingdon, Pa., 1979; JD, Dickinson Sch. Law, 1982. Bar: Pa. 1982. Law clk. to presiding justice Ct. Common Pleas, 39th Jud. Dist. Pa., Chambersburg, 1981-84; assoc. Maxwell, Maxwell, Dick & Walsh, Waynesboro, Pa., 1984—; instr. paralegal program Pa. State U., Mont Alto, Pa., 1984—. Mem. Pa. Bar Assn., Franklin County Bar Assn. Republican. Mem. Ch. of Brethren. General practice, Family and matrimonial. Office: Maxwell Maxwell Dick & Walsh 92 W Main St Waynesboro PA 17268

VAN HORNE, PIETER HAMMOND, lawyer; b. Chgo., Dec. 26, 1941; s. David Eugene and Margerie (Nina) van H.; m. Priscilla Starr Kruse, Aug. 21, 1965; 1 child, Jennifer P. Student, Williams Coll., 1959-61; BA, Parsons Coll., 1963; JD, Northwestern U., 1966; LLM, Wayne State U., 1977. Bar: Mich. 1967, U.S. Dist. Ct. (ea. dist.) Mich. 1967. Atty. N.Y. Cen. R.R. and predecessor firm, Detroit, 1966-71; from assoc. to ptnr. McInally, Rockwell & Brucker, Detroit, 1971-77; sole practice Detroit, 1977-78; ptnr. English & van Horne P.C., Detroit, 1979—. Estate planning, General corporate. Office: English & van Horne PC 4472 Penobscot Bldg Detroit MI 48226

VANHOVE, LORRI KAY, lawyer, financial services executive; b. Madison, S.D., Dec. 10, 1956; d. Robert Harold Vanhove and Doris Darlene (Beck) Vanhove Strub. BS, S.D. State U., 1979; JD, U. Neb., 1982. Bar: S.D. 1982, U.S. Dist. Ct. S.D. 1982, Minn. 1985. Cons. fin. planning Fed. Land Bank of Omaha, 1982-85; mgr. advanced fin. planning IDS Fin. Services Inc., Mpls., 1985—. Speaker various civ. groups. William Holt scholar U. Neb., 1980, Yale C. Holland scholar U. Neb., 1981. Mem. ABA, S.D. Bar Assn. (contr. articles to jour.), Minn. Bar Assn., Hennipen County Bar Assn., Phi Delta Phi. Probate, Personal income taxation, Pension, profit-sharing, and employee benefits. Home: 7360 Gallager Dr #323A Edina MN 55435 Office: IDS Fin Services Inc IDS Tower Minneapolis MN 55474

VAN HOY, PHILIP MARSHALL, lawyer; b. Washington, Nov. 8, 1947; s. Joe Milton and Helen Virginia (Spangler) V.; m. Sylvia Kathryn Smith, Dec. 30, 1972; children—Marshall, Travis. A.B., Duke U., 1970; J.D., U. N.C., 1973. Bar: N.C. 1973, U.S. Dist. Ct. (ea., we. and mid. dists.) N.C. 1974, U.S. Ct. Appeals (4th cir.) 1974, U.S. Supreme Ct. 1978. Labor counsel Duke Power Co., Charlotte, N.C., 1973-80; assoc. firm Siegel, O'Connor & Kainen, Charlotte, 1980-83; ptnr. firm Mullins & Van Hoy, Charlotte, 1983—; mem. N.C. OSHA Rev. Bd., 1985—, Mecklenburg County, N.C. Personnel Commn., 1985—. Alt. del. Rep. Nat. Conv., Detroit, 1980; chmn. Mecklenburg County Young Rep., 1979-80; exec. bd. Mecklenburg County Rep. Com., 1979—, vice chmn., 1980-83. Served as 1st lt. U.S. Army, 1973-81. Mem. 4th Circuit Jud. Conf., ABA (OSHA com. 1981—), N.C. Bar Assn. (chmn. EEOC com. 1983—), N.C. State Bar. Republican. Methodist. Clubs: Charlotte Rotary, Charlotte Cotillion (pres. 1979-80). City. Labor, Federal civil litigation. Home: 2615 Hampton Ave Charlotte NC 28207 Office: Mullins & Van Hoy 1001 East Blvd Charlotte NC 28203

VAN LANDINGHAM, LEANDER SHELTON, JR., lawyer; b. Memphis, July 15, 1925; s. Leander Shelton Van L.; m. Henrietta Adena Stapf, July 5, 1959; children—Ann Henrietta, Leander Shelton III. B.S. in Chemistry, U. N.C., 1948, M.A. in Organic Chemistry, 1949; J.D., Georgetown U., 1955. Bar: D.C. 1955, Md. 1963, Va. 1976. Patent adviser Dept. Navy, Washington, 1953-55; sole practice comml. law and patent, trademark and copyright law, Washington met. area, 1955—. Served to lt. USNR, 1943-46, 51-53. Mem. Am. Chem. Soc., Sci. Assn., Fed. Bar Assn., ABA, D.C. Bar Assn., Va. Bar Assn., Md. Bar Assn., Am. Patent Law Assn., Am. Judicature Soc., Sigma Xi, Phi Alpha Delta. Consumer commercial, Patent, Trademark and copyright. Home: 10726 Stanmore Dr Potomac MD 20854 Office: 2001 Jefferson Davis Hwy Arlington VA 22202

VAN LEUVEN, ROBERT JOSEPH, lawyer; b. Detroit, Apr. 17, 1931; s. Joseph Francis and Olive (Stowell) Van L.; student Albion Coll., 1949-51; B.A. with distinction Wayne State U., 1953; J.D., U. Mich., 1957; m. Holly Goodhue Porter, Dec. 31, 1976; children—Joseph Michael, Douglas Robert, Julie Margaret. Bar: Mich. 1957. Since practiced in Muskegon, Mich.; ptnr. Hathaway, Latimer, Clink & Robb, 1957-68, McCroskey, Libner & Van Leuven, 1968-81, Libner, Van Leuven & Kortering, 1982—; past mem. council negligence law sect. State Bar Mich. Bd. dirs. Muskegon Children's Home, 1965-75. Served with AUS 1953-55. Fellow Am. Coll. Trial Lawyers; mem. Assn. Trial Lawyers Am., Mich. Assn. Professions, Am. Arbitration Assn., Delta Sigma Phi. Club: Muskegon Country. Personal injury, State civil litigation, Federal civil litigation. Home: 966 Mona Brook Muskegon MI 49445 Office: Hackley Bank Muskegon Mall Muskegon MI 49443

VANLIER, CHARLENE, lawyer; b. Grand Rapids, Mich., Feb. 26, 1958; d. James Wesley and Connie Jean (Richards) V.; m. Ted Allen Heydinger, May 4, 1985. BA, Mich. State U., 1978; JD, Wayne State U., 1981. Bar: Mich. 1981, D.C. 1982, U.S. Supreme Ct. 1985. Legis. asst. Congressman Harold S. Sawyer U.S. Congress, Washington, 1981-83, minority counsel subcom. on crime, judiciary com., 1983-87, assoc. minority counsel com. on energy and commerce, 1987—. Republican. Presbyterian. Legislative, Criminal, Judicial administration, Telecommunications. Office: Com Energy and Commerce 2322 Rayburn House Office Bldg Washington DC 20515

VAN METER, ABRAM DEBOIS, banker; b. Springfield, Ill., May 16, 1922; s. A.D. and Edith (Graham) Van M.; m. Margaret Schlipf, Dec. 1, 1956; children: Andy, Alice, Ann. B.S., Kings Point Coll., 1946; J.D., Northwestern U., 1948. Bar: Ill. 1949. Partner Van Meter, Oxtoby and Funk, Springfield, 1949—; adminstrv. asst. to treas. Ill., 1963; v.p. Ill. Nat. Bank, Springfield, 1964-65; pres. Ill. Nat. Bank, 1965—, also dir.; dir. Midwest Fin. Group, Inc. Bd. dirs. Ill. Housing Devel. Authority, 1977—; vice chmn. bd. trustees So. Ill. U., 1975—; bd. dirs., mem. exec. com. Meml. Med. Center. Banking. Home: 6 Fair Oaks St Springfield IL 62704 Office: Ill Nat Bank of Springfield 1 Old State Capitol Plaza N Springfield IL 62701

VAN METER, JOHN DAVID, lawyer; b. Owensboro, Ky., Oct. 30, 1951; s. Leslie Evan and Agnes Regina (Gropp) Van M.; m. Laura Ann Isbell, May 19, 1984. BA in Journalism, U. Ky., 1973, JD, 1978. Bar: Ky. 1978. Atty. Ashland (Ky.) Oil Inc., 1978-83, exec. asst. to chmn., 1983—; bd. dirs. Datacare Inc., Roanoke, Va. Mem. ABA, Ky. Bar Assn., Boyd County Bar Assn. Democrat. Roman Catholic. General corporate, Contracts commercial, Securities. Home: 1501 Ferguson St Ashland KY 41101 Office: Ashland Oil Inc PO Box 391 Ashland KY 41114

VAN METRE, PETER, judge; b. West Palm Beach, Fla., Dec. 28, 1926; s. Horace and Maybeth Susan (Mack) Van M.; m. Lucie Chapman, Aug. 10, 1951 (div. Aug. 1972); children: Joseph Mack, Peter Chapman; m. Jeanette Eunice Thede, June 29, 1974. BA, Trinity Coll., 1950, LLD (hon.), 1978; JD, U. Iowa, 1953. Bar: Iowa 1953. Law clk. to presiding justice U.S. Dist. Ct. (no. dist.) Iowa, 1953-54; judge 1st Judicial Dist. Iowa, Waterloo, 1959—; ptnr. Harris, Van Metre & Buckmaster, Waterloo, Iowa, 1954-59; vis. prof. U. Northern Iowa, Cedar Falls, 1965-70. served to sgt. U.S. Army, 1945-46 ETO. Mem. Iowa Bar Assn., Iowa Judges Assn. Democrat. Episcopalian. Judicial administration. Office: Courthouse Waterloo IA 50703

VANNEMAN, EDGAR, JR., lawyer; b. El Paso, Ill., Aug. 24, 1919; s. Edgar and Fern (Huffington) V.; m. Shirli Thomas, Apr. 28, 1951; children: Jill, Thomas. B.S., Northwestern U., 1941, J.D., 1947. Bar: Ill. 1947. Mem. firm Campbell, Clark & Miller, 1947-48; gen. atty. Chgo. and NorthWestern R.R. Co., 1949-62; gen. atty., asst. sec. Brunswick Corp., Skokie, Ill., 1962—; sec. Sherwood Med. Industries, Inc., 1976-82. Pres. Northeastern Ill. Planning Commn., 1978-82; dir. Suburban Health Systems Agy., 1976-82; mayor City of Evanston (Ill.), 1970-77; alt. del. Republican Nat. Conv., 1952, 56. Served with USAF, 1942-46. Decorated Bronze Star. Mem. ABA, Ill. Bar Assn. (past bd. govs.), Chgo. Bar Assn., Soc. Trial Lawyers. Presbyterian. Club: Law (Chgo.). General corporate, Contracts commercial, Real property. Home: 715 Monticello Pl Evanston IL 60201 Office: 1 Brunswick Plaza Skokie IL 60077

VAN NOPPEN, DONNELL, III, lawyer; b. Norfolk, Va., Sept. 24, 1952; s. Donnell Jr. and Nancy Jean (Smith) Van N.; m. Rivka Gordon, Nov. 28, 1981; 1 child, Eli Gordon-Van Noppen. BA cum laude, Yale U., 1975; JD with honors, U. N.C., 1980. Bar: N.C. 1980, U.S. Dist. Ct. (ea. dist.) N.C. 1980, U.S. Dist. Ct. (mid. and we. dists.) N.C. 1983, U.S. Ct. Appeals (4th cir.) 1983. Law clk. to presiding justice U.S. Dist. Ct. (ea. dist.) N.C., Raleigh, 1980-82; assoc. Smith, Patterson, Follin, Curtis, James & Harkavy, Raleigh, 1983-85, ptnr., 1986—. Morehead fellow, 1977-80. Mem. ABA, N.C. Bar Assn., Wake County Bar Assn., N.C. Acad. Trial Lawyers, ACLU, N.C. Civil Liberties Union. Federal civil litigation, Labor, Civil rights. Office: Smith Patterson Follin et al 206 New Bern Pl Raleigh NC 27601

VAN ORMAN, CHANDLER L., lawyer; b. Oak Park, Ill., Jan. 15, 1941; s. E.G. and Mary Elizabeth (Chandler) van O. A.B., U. N.C., 1963; LL.B., U. Va., 1966. Bar: Va. 1966, D.C. 1966. Mem. profl. staff anti-trust and monopoly subcom. Com. on the Judiciary, U.S. Senate, Washington, 1962-63; atty.-investigator FTC, Washington, 1966-67; ptnr. Wheeler & Wheeler, Washington, 1967-82, 84—; gen. counsel AID, Washington, 1982-83; dir. pvt. sector involvement, 1983, Summit of Industrialized Nations, 1983; exec. dir., commr. Legis. and Jud. Salaries, 1986—. Mem. vice presdl. staff-advance, 1974, presdl. staff-advance, 1976, 80, 84, 85; mem. Presdl. Inaugural Com., 1980, 84; exec. dir. Pres.'s Commn. on Exec., Legis., and Jud. Salaries, 1986. Mem. D.C. Bar Assn., Va. State Bar. Administrative and regulatory, Public international. Office: Wheeler & Wheeler 1729 H St NW Washington DC 20006

VANORSDEL, ROBERT ALAN, lawyer; b. Omaha, Nebr., Sept. 6, 1944; s. Virgil Samuel and Madeline Helen (Casart) V.; m. Susan Leslie Popple, Nov. 23, 1967; children: John Wesley, Sarah Kane. BBA in Acctg., U. Iowa, 1967; JD with honors, Drake U., 1974. Bar: Iowa 1975, U.S. Dist. Ct. (so. and no. dist.) Iowa 1975, U.S. Tax Ct. 1980. Assoc. Nyemaster, Goode, Mclaughlin, Emery & O'Brien, Des Moines, 1975—. Assoc. editor: Drake Law Review, 1974-75. Mem. Plymouth Congl. Ch., Des Moines, 1976—. Served with USN 1968-69, Vietnam. Named to Order of the Coif, 1975. Mem. Am. Inst. CPAs, Iowa Soc. CPAs, ABA, Iowa Bar Assn. (mem. tax com. 1980—), Polk County Bar Assn., Am. Coll. Probate Counsel. Clubs: Variety (Des Moines) (bd. dirs. 1975-84), Des Moines, Des Moines Golf and Country. Probate, Corporate taxation, Personal income taxation. Home: 304 29th St Des Moines IA 50312 Office: Nyemaster Law Firm 10th Floor Hubbell Bldg Des Moines IA 50309

VAN PERNIS, MARK, lawyer, land developer; b. Grand Rapids, Mich., Dec. 20, 1946; s. Paul Anton and Sarah Gertrude (Sterken) Van P.; m. Kristine Marie Vestal, Apr. 30, 1982. BA, Knox Coll., 1968; JD, U. Miami, 1972. Bar: Fla. 1974, Ill. 1974, Hawaii 1976, U.S. Dist. Ct. Hawaii 1978. Atty. Legal Services of Greater Miami, Fla., 1970-74; asst. atty. gen. State of Ill., Springfield, 1975; sr. ptnr. Gallup & Van Pernis, Kailua-Kona, Hawaii, 1976—. Author: (cookbook) Eating the Alligator Pear, 1986. Mem. ABA, Hawaii Bar Assn., W. Hawaii Bar Assn., Am. Arbitration Assn., Assn. Trial Lawyers Am. Avocations: land history research, avocado farming, marathon running. Personal injury, Real property, State civil litigation. Office: Gallup & Van Pernis PO Box 1837 Kailua-Kona HI 96745

VAN PRAAG, JANE CATHERINE, lawyer; b. La Jolla, Calif., June 12, 1953; d. Vincent A. and Margaret Ann (Grant) Van P.; m. John Edward Halter, Aug. 25, 1985. BA, U. Calif., Berkeley, 1971-75; JD, U. Calif., San Francisco, 1978. Bar: Calif. 1979, U.S. Ct. Appeals (9th cir.), U.S. Dist. Ct. (no., ea., so. dists.) Calif., United States Ct. of Claims. Assoc. Pillsbury, Madison & Sutro, San Francisco, 1979-80, Hancock, Rothert & Bunshoft, San Francisco, 1980-83; asst. counsel Signetics Corp., San Francisco, 1983—; speaker Boalt Hall Computer Law Group, U. Calif., Berkeley, 1985. Mem. ABA, Am. Corp. Counsel Assn., Santa Clara Bar Assn. Avocations: skiing, tennis, dance, photography. High technology, Computer, General corporate. Office: Signetics Corp 811 E Argues Ave PO Box 3409 Sunnyvale CA 94088-3409

VAN RENSSELAER, ROBERT MICKLE MILES, lawyer; b. Alexandria, Va., Apr. 5, 1941; s. Hendrik Barnard and Serena (Miles) Van R.; m. Hilary J. Prouty, Oct. 28, 1967; children—Serena, Richard Miles. B.A., Washington and Lee U., 1963; LL.B., 1966. Bar: N.J. 1969, U.S. Dist. Ct. N.J. 1969. Nat. div. rep. Chem. Bank, N.Y.C., 1969-72; assoc. Crummy, Del Deo, Dolan & Purcell, Newark, 1972-77; sr. ptnr., atty. in charge Bernardsville office Carter, Van Rensselaer, Swenson & Caldwell, Plainfield, N.J., Bernardsville, N.J., 1977—. Trustee Far Hills Country Day Sch. Served to capt. U.S. Army, 1966-68. Mem. N.J. State Bar Assn., ABA. Club: Somerset Lake and Game (Peapack, N.J.). General corporate, Real property. Home: Hilltop Rd Mendham NJ 07945 Office: 106 Mine Brook Rd Bernardsville NJ 07924

VAN RYE, KENNETH, lawyer; b. Passaic, N.J., Aug. 19, 1954; s. Kenneth C. and Joan (DiSalvo) Van R.; m. Barbara S. O'Rourke, Oct. 2, 1983; 1 child, Breama Taylor. BS, Seton Hall U., 1976; JD, Pepperdine U., 1979. Bar: N.J. 1979, U.S. Dist. Ct. N.J. 1979, U.S. Supreme Ct. 1983, U.S. Ct. Appeals (3d cir.) 1985. Assoc. Law Office of P.M. Saginario, Paterson, N.J., 1979-80; ptnr. Spinato & Van Rye, Elmwood Park, N.J., 1981—; atty. Violent Crimes Compensation Bd., Newark, 1984-85. Treas. Elmwood Park Rep. Club, 1979-80, trustee 1986; trustee Girls Softball Team, Elmwood Park, 1985-86; councilman Elmwood Park., 1980—; candidate N.J. Assembly. Mem. ABA, N.J. Bar Assn., Bergen County Bar Assn. Republican. Lodge: Elks. Personal injury, Probate, Criminal. Home: 23 Palsa Ave Elmwood Park NJ 07407 Office: Spinato & Van Rye 519 River Dr Elmwood Park NJ 07407

VAN SCHOONENBERG, ROBERT G., lawyer; b. Madison, Wis., Aug. 18, 1946; s. John W. and Ione (Henning) Schoonenberg. B.A., Marquette U., 1968; M.B.A., U. Wis., 1972; J.D., U. Mich., 1974. Bar: Calif. 1975, Fla. 1976. Atty. Gulf Oil Corp., Pitts., 1974-81; v.p., gen. counsel, sec. Avery Internat., Pasadena, Calif., 1981—; dir. Integrated Decision Systems, Inc., Los Angeles, 1982—. Bd. dirs. Pasadena Recreation and Parks Found., 1983—; mem. Pasadena Citizens Task Force on Crime Control, 1983—; vol. United Way, Pasadena, Calif., 1981. Served with U.S. Army, 1969-71. Mem. Am. Soc. Corp. Secs., ABA, Am. Corp. Counsel Assn., Calif. Bar, Fla. Bar, Los Angeles County Bar Assn. Clubs: Athletic (Pasadena); Wis. Union. General corporate, Securities, Private international. Office: Avery Internat Corp 150 N Orange Grove Blvd Pasadena CA 91103

VAN SETTER, GEORGE GERARD, lawyer; b. Bklyn., Dec. 11, 1940; s. George Gerard and Aimee Osborne (Keegan) van S.; m. Shirley Margaret Coan, Aug. 13, 1966; children: Margaret, George. BS, Holy Cross Coll., 1962; LLB, NYU, 1965. Bar: N.Y. 1965, U.S. Dist. Ct. (so. and ea. dists.) N.Y. 1965. Assoc. Martin, Clearwater & Bell, N.Y.C., 1965-75, ptnr., 1975—. State civil litigation. Office: Martin Clearwater & Bell 220 E 42nd St New York NY 10017

VAN SLYKE, PAUL CHRISTOPHER, lawyer; b. Dallas, Mar. 13, 1942; s. Anson Jr. and Winnell (Hill) Van S.; m. Lora Lynn Davis, July 18, 1964 (div. Apr. 1982); children: Christopher Paul, Scott Allen; m. Bonnie S. Dunbar, Jan. 2, 1987. BS in Elec. Engr., U. Tex., 1964; JD, So. Meth. U., 1968. Bar: Tex. 1968, D.C. 1969, U.S. Dist. Ct. (so. dist.) Tex. 1969, U.S. Supreme Ct. 1969, U.S. Ct. Appeals (Fed. cir.) 1984. Patent asst. Mobil Oil Corp., Dallas, 1964-69, patent atty., 1968-69; assoc. Arnold, White & Dirkee, Houston, 1969-72, mem., 1972-87; mem. Pravel, Gambrell, Hewitt & Kimball, Houston, 1987—. Deacon Meml. Dr. Presbyn. Ch., Houston, 1975-78. Mem. Tex. Bar Assn., Houston Bar Assn., Houston Intellectual Property Law Assn. (treas. 1971), U.S. Trademark Assn. Republican. Club: Houstonian. Trademark and copyright, Federal civil litigation, Patent. Home: 12507 Pinerock Ln Houston TX 77024 Office: Pravel Gambrell Hewitt & Kimball 1177 W Loop S Suite 1010 Houston TX 77027

VAN TASSEL, GEORGE MARTIN, JR., lawyer; b. Birmingham, Ala., June 7, 1947; s. George Martin and Selden Juarine (Berrey) Van T.; m. Dorothy Lee White, June 19, 1971; children: George Martin III, Susan Warren. BS, U. Ala., 1969, JD, 1972. Asst. atty. gen. State of Ala., Montgomery, 1972-74; ptnr. Sadler, Sullivan, Sharp & Stutts, Birmingham, Ala., 1974—. Mem. ABA, Ala. Bar Assn., Birmingham Bar Assn., Assn. Trial Lawyers Am., Ala. Def. Lawyers Assn., Def. Research Inst., Nat. Assn. R.R. Trial Counsel. Democrat. Baptist. Club: Country of Birmingham. Avocations: golf, reading. State civil litigation, Federal civil litigation, Personal injury. Home: 308 Cross Ridge Rd Birmingham AL 35213 Office: Sadler Sullivan Sharp & Stutts 1100 1st Nat S Natural Bldg Birmingham AL 35203

VAN VALER, JOE NED, lawyer, land developer; b. Gas City, Ind., Mar. 13, 1935; s. Richard Carl and Wilma Amy (Kelly) Van V.; m. Constance Joy Richardson, June 25, 1960; children—Kimberly Joy, Kelli June, Lynn Louise, Joseph Jeffrey. A.B., Franklin Coll., 1959; LL.B., Ind. U., 1963. Bar: Ind. 1963, U.S. Dist. Ct. (so. dist.) Ind. 1963. Assoc. Van Valer & Williams and predecessor firms, 1963-65, ptnr., 1965-75, sr. ptnr., 1975—; pres. Home Owners Warranty Corp. of Central Ind., Indpls., 1984—, also dir.; pros. atty. 8th Jud. Dist., Franklin, Ind., 1967-74. Served with AUS, 1957-58. Mem. ABA, Indpls. Bar Assn., 8th Jud. Circuit Bar Assn., Nat. Assn. Home Builders (bd. dirs.), Home Builders Assn. Ind. (dir.), Builders Assn. Greater Indpls. (dir.). Republican. Methodist. Administrative and regulatory, State civil litigation, Real property. Office: Van Valer & Williams 300 S Madison Ave PO Box 405 Greenwood IN 46142

VAN VALKENBURG, EDGAR WALTER, lawyer; b. Seattle, Jan. 8, 1953; s. Edgar Walter and Margaret Catherine (McKenna) Van V. BA, U. Wash., 1975; JD summa cum laude, Willamette Coll. of Law, 1978; LLM, Columbia U., 1984. Bar: Oreg. 1978, U.S. Dist. Ct. Oreg. 1979, U.S. Ct. Appeals (9th cir.) 1980. Law clk. to assoc. justice Oreg. Supreme Ct., Salem, 1978-79; assoc. Stoel, Rives, Boley, Fraser & Wyse, Portland, Oreg., 1979-82, 84-86, ptnr., 1986—; instr. Columbia U., N.Y.C., 1982-84. Editor-in-chief: Willamette Law Jour. 1977-78. Mem. ACLU. Antitrust, Libel, Trademark and copyright. Office: Stoel Rives Boley et al 900 SW Fifth Ave Portland OR 97204

VAN VOORHIS, HAROLD L., lawyer; b. Des Moines, Mar. 4, 1936; s. H.L. And Alice Mae (Jones) Van V.; m. Martha Mazuk; children: Krista, Coerte. BS in Bus. Adminstrn., Drake U., 1958, LLB, 1960. Bar: Iowa 1960, U.S. Dist. Ct. Iowa 1960, U.S. Supreme Ct. 1969. Atty. urban renewal City of Des Moines, 1965-68; sole practice Des Moines, 1968—. Served to col. USAR, 1986—. Mem. ABA, Iowa Bar Assn., Polk County Bar Assn., Holland Soc., Mayflower Descendents, S.R., SAR, Col. Order of Acorns, Mil. Order of World Wars, Descendents Col. Clergy. Republican. Episcopalian. Clubs: Social Register, Ch. Club of N.Y. Lodges: Soc. of Cin., St. Nicholas Soc., Ancient and Honorable Artillery Co. Consumer commercial, Family and matrimonial.

VAN WAGNER, ALBERT EDWIN, JR., lawyer; b. Bronxville, N.Y., Jan. 28, 1946; s. Albert Edwin and Margaret (Libby) Van W.; 1 child, Eric. BS, Ariz. State U., 1976, MBA, 1977, JD, 1978. Bar: Ariz. 1979, U.S. Dist. Ct. Ariz. 1979, U.S. Ct. Appeals (9th cir.) 1979. Assoc. Eldridge & Brown, Phoenix, 1979-80; ptnr. Eldridge & Van Wagner, Phoenix, 1981-84; sole practice Phoenix, 1984—. Served as cpl. USMC, 1966-68. Mem. ABA, Assoc. Trial Lawyers Am., Ariz. trial Lawyer's Assn., Ariz. State Coll. Law Alumni Assn. (bd. dirs. 1982, treas. 1983, v.p. 1984). Democrat. Avocations: bridge, golf, tennis, travel. Personal injury, Product liability, Medical malpractice. Office: 1001 N Central Ave Suite 501 Phoenix AZ 85004

VARAT, JONATHAN D., law educator; b. 1945. BA, U. Pa., Phila., 1967, JD, 1972. Law clk. to presiding justice U.S. Ct. Appeals (2d cir.), N.Y.C., 1972-73; law clk. to justice Byron White U.S. Supreme Ct., Washington, 1973-74; assoc. O'Melveny & Myers, Los Angeles, 1974-76; acting prof. UCLA, 1976-81, prof., 1981—. Office: U Calif Sch Law 405 Hilgard Ave Los Angeles CA 90024 *

VARELLAS, JAMES JOHN, JR., lawyer; b. Lexington, Ky., Dec. 12, 1939; s. James J. Sr. and Ruth Frances (Todd) V.; m. Sandra Motte, July 3, 1971; children: James J. III, David Todd. BA, U. Ky., 1963, JD, 1966. Bar: Ky. 1967, Fla. 1977, U.S. Supreme Ct. 1978. Sole practice Lexington, 1967-75; ptnr. Varellas & Varellas, Lexington, 1975-76, Varellas & Pratt, Lexington, 1976-81, Varellas, Pratt & Cooley, Lexington, 1981—. Mem. Fla. Bar Assn., Ky. Bar Assn., Assn. Trial Lawyers Am. Democrat. Presbyterian. State civil litigation, Federal civil litigation, Personal injury. Office: Varellas Pratt & Cooley 134 N Limestone St Lexington KY 40507

VARELLAS, SANDRA MOTTE, lawyer, judge; b. Anderson, S.C., Oct. 17, 1946; d. James E. and Helen Lucille (Gilliam) Motte; m. James John Varellas, July 3, 1971; children: James John III, David Todd. BA, Winthrop Coll., 1968; MA, U. Ky., 1970, JD, 1975. Bar: Ky. 1975, Fla. 1976, U.S. Dist. Ct. (ea. dist.) Ky. 1975, U.S. Ct. Appeals (6th cir.) 1976, U.S. Supreme Ct. 1978. Tchr. Midway Coll., Ky., 1970-72; adj. prof. U. Ky. Coll. Law, Lexington, 1976-78; instr. dept. bus. adminstrn. U. Ky., Lexington, 1976-78; atty. Varellas, Pratt & Cooley, Lexington, 1975—; Fayette County judge exec., Ky., 1980—; hearing officer Ky. Natural Resources and Environ. Protection Cabinet, Frankfort, 1984—. Committeewoman Ky. Young Dems., Frankfort, 1977-80; pres. Fayette County Young Dems., Lexington, 1977; bd. dirs. Ky. Dem. Women's Club, Frankfort, 1980-84; grad. Leadership Lexington, 1981; chairwoman Profl. Women's Forum, Lexington, Ky., 1985-86. Named Outstanding Young Dem. Woman, Ky. Young Dems., Frankfort, 1977, Outstanding Former Young Dem., Ky. Young Dems., 1983. Mem. ABA, Ky. Bar Assn. (treas. young lawyers div. 1978-79), Fla. Bar, Fayette County Bar Assn. (treas. 1977-78, bd. govs. 1978-80), LWV (nominating com 1984-85). Club: Philharm. Women's Guild (Lexington, Ky.) (bd. dirs. 1979-81, 86-87). Personal injury, Probate, Bankruptcy. Office: Varellas Pratt & Cooley 134 N Limestone St Lexington KY 40507

VARLEY, ROBERT JOHN, lawyer; b. Somerville, N.J., Dec. 21, 1948; s. Bernard William and Ruth Mary (Buchholz) V.; divorced; children: J.B., Jennifer; m. Patricia E. Ivie, Mar. 6, 1986. BS, Auburn U., 1970; JD, U. Ala., 1977. Bar: Ala. 1978, U.S. Dist. Ct. (mid. and no. dists.) Ala., U.S. Ct. Appeals (5th and 11th cirs.), U.S. Supreme Ct. Staff atty. Legal Service Corp. Ala., Montgomery, 1978-80, specialist atty. utilities, 1980-82, mng. atty., 1982—. Treas. Capri Community Film Soc., Montgomery, 1986—, bd. dirs., 1985—. Served to 1st lt. USMC, 1970-74. Mem. ABA, Fed. Bar Assn., Montgomery County Bar Assn., Assn. Trial Lawyers Am., Ala. Trial Lawyers Assn., Montgomery County Trial Lawyers Assn., Sierra Club. Democrat. Presbyterian. Club: Nature Conservancy (Montgomery). Avocations: backpacking, bicycling, running. Federal civil litigation, State civil litigation, Civil rights. Home: 3112 Lexington Montgomery AL 36106 Office: Legal Services Corp Ala Inc 207 Montgomery St Suite 900 Bell Bldg Montgomery AL 36104

VARNER, DAVID EUGENE, energy company executive, lawyer; b. Dallas, Oct. 9, 1937; s. E.C. and D. Evelyn (Bauguss) V.; m. Joan Paula Oransky, Aug. 13, 1963; children—Michael A., Kevin E., Cheryl L. B.A., So. Meth. U., Dallas, 1958, J.D., 1961. Bar: Tex. 1961, Fla. 1974, Okla., 1977, U.S. Supreme Ct. 1978. Assoc. Eldridge, Goggans, Davidson & Silverberg, Dallas, 1962-65; atty., asst. sec. Redman Industries, Inc., Dallas, 1965-66; assoc. gen. atty. Tex. Instruments, Inc., Dallas, 1966-73; sr. atty., asst. sec. Fla. Gas Co., Winter Park, 1973-76; v.p., gen. counsel, sec. Facet Enterprises, Inc., Tulsa, 1976-78, Summa Corp., Las Vegas, Nev., 1978-82; sr. v.p., gen. counsel, sec. Transco Energy Co., Houston, 1982—; dir. Transcontinental Gas Pipe Line Corp.; mem. royalty mgmt. adv. com. Minerals Mgmt. Service, Dept. Energy. Mng. editor Southwestern Law Jour., 1960-61. Mem. ABA, Fed. Energy Bar Assn., Houston Bar Assn., Tex. Bar Assn., Okla. Bar, Fla. Bar., Am. Soc. Corp. Secs. General corporate. Home: 13415 Perthshire Houston TX 77079 Office: Transco Energy Co 2800 Post Oak Blvd Houston TX 77056

VARNER, ROBERT EDWARD, judge; b. Montgomery, Ala., June 11, 1921; s. William and Georgia (Thomas) V.; children: Robert Edward, Carolyn Stuart.; m. Jane Dennis Hannah, Feb. 27, 1982. B.S., Auburn U., 1946; J.D., U. Ala., 1949. Bar: Ala. 1949. Atty. City of Tuskegee, 1951; asst. U.S. atty. Middle Dist. Ala., 1954-58; practice in Montgomery, 1958-71; partner firm Jones, Murray, Stewart & Varner, 1958-71; U.S. dist. judge Montgomery, 1971—; guest lectr. bus. law Huntingdon Coll. Pres. Montgomery Rotary Charity Found.; v.p., fin. chmn. Tukabatchee Area council Boy Scouts Am.; Mem. Macon County Bd. Edn., 1950-54. Served with USNR, 1942-46. Recipient Silver Beaver award Boy Scouts Am. Mem. ABA, Fed. Bar Assn., Montgomery Bar Assn. (pres. 1971), Macon County Bar Assn., Am. Trial Lawyers Assn., Jud. Conf. of U.S. (com. on operation of jury system), Phi Alpha Delta, Phi Delta Theta. Republican. Methodist. Club: Rotarian (pres. 1961). Office: PO Box 2046 Montgomery AL 36103

VAROUTSOS, GEORGE DOUGLAS, lawyer; b. Washington, Jan. 17, 1949; s. Paul George and Olga (Kaisell) V.; m. Alexandra Varoutsos; 1 child, Christine Georgia. BA, U. Richmond, 1970, JD, 1973. Bar: Va. 1973, D.C. 1976. Law clk. to presiding justice U.S. Ct., Alexandria, Va., 1973-74; ptnr. Varoutsos, Koutoulakos, Arthur & Dolan, Arlington, Va., 1974-76; sole practice Arlington, 1976—; bd. advisors Arlington Bank, 1984—; substitute judge Arlington County, 1986—. Mem. Va. Bar Assn., D.C. Bar Assn., Arlington County Bar Assn. (bd. dirs. 1980—), Assn. Trial Lawyers Am., Va. Trial Lawyers Assn. Criminal, Personal injury, Family and matrimonial.

Home: 2511 S Ives St Arlington VA 22202 Office: 2054 N 14th St Suite 200 Arlington VA 22201

VARY, GEORGE FOLK, lawyer; b. Fountain Hill, Pa., Aug. 17, 1948; s. George Crispin and Claire Elizabeth (Folk) V.; m. Elizabeth Mary Finley, Apr. 22, 1978; children: Elizabeth, Crispin. AB, Harvard U., 1970; JD, U. Pa., 1973. Bar: N.Y. 1974, U.S. Dist. Ct. (so. dist.) N.Y. 1975, U.S. Ct. Appeals (2d cir.) 1975, U.S. Dist. Ct. (ea. dist.) N.Y. 1977, Ohio 1981. Assoc. Breed, Abbott & Morgan, N.Y.C., 1973-79; assoc. counsel Armco, Inc., Middletown, Ohio, 1979-84; internat. trade counsel Armco, Inc., Washington, 1984—. Republican. Avocations: golf, bridge, cooking. Federal civil litigation, International trade, Legislative. Home: 5712 Newington Rd Bethesda MD 20816 Office: Armco Inc 1667 K St NW #650 Washington DC 20006

VAUGHAN, C. DAVID, lawyer; b. Birmingham, Ala., Sept. 20, 1945; s. Cornelius David and Mildred Greenwood (Redmond) V.; m. Nicki Ann Noel, Feb. 19, 1972; children—Patrick Taylor, Michael Hunter. B.A., Vanderbilt U., 1967; J.D. (first honor grad.), Emory U., 1970. Bar: Ga. 1970, U.S. Dist. Ct. (no. dist.) Ga. 1970, U.S. Ct. Appeals (5th cir.) 1971, U.S. Tax Ct. 1972, U.S. Ct. Appeals (11th cir.) 1982, U.S. Supreme Ct. 1982. Assoc., King & Spalding, Atlanta, 1970-77; ptnr. Vaughan & Butters, Atlanta, 1978-79, Vaughan, Roach, Davis, Birch, & Murphy, Atlanta, 1980—. Mem. ABA (antitrust law sect.), State Bar Ga. (chmn. antitrust sect 1981-82). Antitrust. Office: Suite 1500 One Ravinia Dr Atlanta GA 30346

VAUGHAN, DONALD RAY, lawyer; b. Greensboro, N.C., Sept. 13, 1952; s. Rowland G. and Catherine (Braswell) V. BA with highest honors, U. N.C., 1974; MA in Pub. Adminstrn., Am. U., 1976; JD, Wake Forest U., 1979. Bar: N.C., U.S. Dist. Ct. (mid. dist.) N.C., U.S. Ct. Appeals (4th cir.), D.C. Legis. aide U.S. Senator Robert Morgan, Washington, 1975-76; cons. R.J. Reynolds Industries, Winston-Salem, N.C., 1976-79; atty., econ. advisor Office of the Gov., Raleigh, N.C., 1979-81; v.p. govt. affairs Stedman Corp., Asheboro, N.C., 1981—; lectr. Am. U., Washington, 1975, 76. Mem. staff Wake Forest U. Law Review; contbr. articles to profl jours. Gen. counsel Nat. Found. for the Study of Religion and Econs., Greensboro, 1981—; legal counsel Govs. Efficiency Study Commn., Raleigh, 1985; treas. Freepac, Raleigh, 1986—. Mem. ABA, N.C. Bar Assn., N.C. Acad. of Trial Lawyers, Greensboro Bar Assn. Democrat. Legislative, Administrative and regulatory, General corporate. Home: 1118 Grayland Greensboro NC 27408 Office: Stedman Corp Asheboro NC 27203

VAUGHAN, HERBERT WILEY, lawyer; b. Brookline, Mass, June 1, 1920; s. David D. and Elzie G. (Wiley) V.; m. Ann Graustein, June 28, 1941. Student U. Chgo., 1937-38; SB cum laude, Harvard U., 1941, LLB, 1948. Bar: Mass. 1948. Assoc. Hale and Dorr, Boston, 1948-54, jr. ptnr., 1954-56, sr. ptnr., 1956-82, co-mng. ptnr. 1976-80, sr. ptnr., 1982—; pres. Herbert W. Vaugh, P.C. Fellow Am. Bar Found. (life); mem. Am. Coll. Mortgage Attys., Am. Coll. Real Estate Attys., ABA, Mass. Bar Assn., Boston Bar Assn., Internat. Bar Assn. (standing com. trustees of reservations). Clubs: Bay, Badminton and Tennis, Union (Boston), Boston Econ.; Longwood Cricket (Brookline, Mass.). Real property.

VAUGHAN, JAMES JOSEPH MICHAEL, lawyer; b. Newark, Mar. 19, 1942; s. James M. and Elizabeth (McDonnell) V.; m. Jeanette Rae Gerber, Aug. 5, 1967; children—Karen, Adrianne, Jennifer. B.S., U. Scranton, 1963; J.D., Cath. U., 1966. Bar: U.S. Dist. Ct. Md. 1979, U.S. Ct. Appeals (D.C. cir.) 1972, U.S. Ct. Claims 1973, U.S. Supreme Ct. 1977. Assoc. Dukes, Troese, et al, Chevy Chase, Md., 1969-72; atty. Assn. Am. Law Schs., Washington, 1972-76; mem. firm Giordano, Bush, Villareale & Vaughan, Upper Marlboro, Md., 1976—. Served to capt. U.S. Army, 1967-69. Mem. Assn. Trial Lawyers Am., Bar Assn. D.C., D.C. Bar Assn., Md. Bar Assn., Prince George's County Bar Assn. Democrat. Roman Catholic. State civil litigation, Personal injury, Workers' compensation. Office: Giordano Bush Villareale & Vaughan PA PO Box 520 Upper Marlboro MD 20772

VAUGHAN, MICHAEL RICHARD, lawyer; b. Chgo., Aug. 27, 1936; s. Michael Ambrose and Loretta M. (Parks) V.; m. Therese Marie Perri, Aug. 6, 1960; children—Charles Thomas, Susan Enger. Student U. Ill., 1954-59; LL.B., U. Wis., 1962. Bar: Wis. 1962. Chief atty. bill drafting sect. Wis. Legislature, 1962-68; dir. legis. attys., Wis., 1968-72; assoc. Murphy & Desmond, and predecessor, Madison, Wis., 1972-73, ptnr., 1974—; mem. Commn. Uniform State Laws, 1966-72; cons. Nat. Commn. on Marihuana and Drug Abuse, 1971-73; dir. State Bar Govtl. and Adminstrv. Law Sect., 1971-78, State Bar Interprofl. and Bus. Relations Com., 1976—; lectr. continuing legal edn. seminars. Sr. warden St. Dunstan's Episcopal Ch., 1975-78, vestryman, 1973-78, 1980-84, jr. warden, 1985-87; mem. Wis. Episc. Conf., 1972-76. Mem. ABA, Dane County Bar Assn., U. Wis. Law Sch. Bencher Soc., Delta Kappa Epsilon. Club: Madison. Contbr. articles to profl. jours. Legislative, Administrative and regulatory. Home: 4714 La Fayette Dr Madison WI 53705 Office: 150 E Gilman St PO Box 2038 Madison WI 53701

VAUGHN, DAVID BRENT, lawyer; b. Ogden, Utah, Mar. 15, 1942; s. George E. and Dorothy (Wheelwright) V.; m. Pamela Jeanne Murdoch; Cecily, Jordan, Regan, Melina. BA, Brigham Young U., 1965; JD, U. Calif., San Francisco, 1972. Bar: Idaho 1973, U.S. Dist. Ct. Idaho 1973, U.S. Ct. Appeals (9th cir.) 1981, U.S. Supreme Ct. 1983. Dep. U.S. marshall U.S. Marshall's Service, San Francisco, 1970-71; asst. atty. gen. State of Idaho, Boise, 1973-74; chief dep. ins. commr. Idaho Ins. Dept., Boise, 1974-79; sole practice Boise, 1979—. Served to capt. USMC, 1966-69, Vietnam. Insurance. Office: PO Box 5261 Boise ID 83705

VAUGHN, LESLEY MILLER MEHRAN, lawyer; b. Eng., Aug. 24, 1944; came to U.S., 1952; d. Victor Raymond and Daphne (Trecker) Miller; m. G.R.C. Mehran, June 29, 1966 (div. Jan. 1978); children: Diana, Mark, Rawley, Peter; m. John Spencer Vaughn, Aug. 6, 1983. Cert., U. Geneva, 1965, U. Paris, 1966; BS, U. Calif., Berkeley, 1967; JD, Loyola U., Los Angeles, 1982. Bar: Calif. 1982, U.S. Ct. Appeals (9th cir.) 1984. Assoc. Finley, Kumble, Wagner, Heine, Underberg, Manley & Casey, 1982-83, Smith & Holland, Los Angeles, 1983-86, Ross & Scott, Los Angeles, 1986—. Contbr. articles to profl. jours. Mem. ABA, Calif. Bar Assn., Phi Alpha Delta. Republican. Presbyterian. Federal civil litigation, State civil litigation, Real property. Home: 930 Afton Rd San Marino CA 91108 Office: Ross & Scott 601 W 5th St Los Angeles CA 90071

VAUGHN, NOEL WYANDT, lawyer; b. Chgo., Dec. 15, 1937; d. Owen Heaton and Harriet Christy (Smith) Wyandt; m. David Victor Koch, July 18, 1959 (div.); 1 child, John David; m. Charles George Vaughn, July 9, 1971. BA, DePauw U., 1959; MA, So. Ill. U., 1963; JD, U. Dayton, 1979. Bar: Ohio 1979, U.S. Dist. Ct. (so. dist.) Ohio 1979. Communications specialist Charles F. Kettering Found., Dayton, 1968-71; tchr. English Miami Valley Sch., Dayton, 1971-76; law clk. to judge Dayton Mcpl. Ct., 1978-79; coordinator Montgomery County Fair Housing Ctr., Dayton, 1979-81, 85—; atty. Henley Vaughn Becker & Wald, Dayton, 1981—; lectr. Wright State U., Dayton, 1965-67. Chmn. Dayton Playhouse, Inc., 1981—; pres. Freedom of Choice Miami Valley, Dayton, 1980-83, 86-87; bd. dirs. ACLU, Dayton, 1982-86; com. mem. Battered Woman Project-YWCA, Dayton, 1983-84; pres. Legal Aid Soc. Dayton, 1983-84; chmn. Artemis House, Inc., 1985—; bd. dirs. Miami Valley Arts Council, 1985-86. Recipient Order of Barristers award U. Dayton, 1979. Mem. ABA, Dayton Bar Assn. (chmn. delivery legal services com. 1983-84). General practice, Family and matrimonial, Civil rights. Home: 3700 Wales Dr Dayton OH 45405

VAUGHN, RAY W., lawyer; b. Olney, Ill., Oct. 15, 1957; s. Charles Robert and Elizabeth (Gassmann) V.; m. Marcia K., Dec. 27, 1980; children: Mitchell, Sarah. AS, Olney Cen. Coll.; BA, So. Ill. U., JD. Bar: Ill. 1982, U.S. Dist. Ct. (so. dist.) Ill. 1982. Ptnr. Vaughn & Vaughn, Olney, 1982—. Consumer commercial, Real property, Contracts commercial. Office: Vaughn & Vaughn 308 S Kitchell Olney IL 62450

VAUGHN, ROBERT CANDLER, JR., lawyer; b. Winston-Salem, N.C., Sept. 6, 1931; s. Robert Candler and Douglas Ellen (Arthur) V.; m. Carolyn Hartford, May 2, 1959; children: Patricia Anne, Robert Candler III. BS in Bus. Adminstrn., U. N.C., 1953, JD, 1955. Bar: N.C. 1955, U.S. Dist. Ct. (mid. dist.) 1959, U.S. Tax Ct. 1981. Assoc. Petree, Stockton & Robinson and predecessor firms, Winston-Salem, 1959-65, ptnr., 1965—; bd. dirs. So. Nat. Bank, and predecessor bank, Winston-Salem. Pres. United Way Forsyth County, Winston-Salem, 1970-71; chmn. Winston-Salem Coliseum Commn., Winston-Salem Conv. Ctr. Commn., 1974-78; bd. advs. U. N.C. Tax Inst., Chapel Hill; bd. dirs. Legal Services N.C., 1985-86, Leadership Winston-Salem. Served to lt. USN, 1955-58. Fellow Am. Bar Found., Am. Coll. Probate Counsel; mem. N.C. Bar Assn. (pres. 1985-86, bd. dirs.), U. N.C. Law Alumni Assn. (pres. 1974-75). Democrat. Methodist. Clubs: Old Town, Torch, Piedmont. Lodge: Rotary. General corporate, Probate, Estate taxation. Home: 2575 Club Park Rd Winston-Salem NC 27104 Office: Petree Stockton & Robinson 1001 W 4th St Winston-Salem NC 27101

VAUGHN, ROBERT GENE, law educator; b. Chickasha, Okla., Mar. 10, 1944; s. Owen and Ola Mae (Davis) V.; m. Nancy Gaye Breeden, June 28, 1969; children—Amanda Joy, Abigail Jane, Carolyn Elizabeth. B.A., U. Okla., 1966, J.D., 1969; LL.M., Harvard U., 1970. Bar: Okla. 1969, D.C. 1971. Assoc. atty. Pub. Interest Research Group, Washington, 1970-72; asst. prof. law Am. U., 1972-74, assoc. prof., 1974-77, prof., 1977-82, A. Allen King scholar and prof. law, 1982—, acting dep. dean, 1984-85; editorial cons. Prentice Hall. Recipient award for outstanding teaching Washington Coll. Law, Am. U., 1978, Outstanding Scholar/Tchr. award of Am. U., United Methodist Ch. Bd. Higher Edn., 1983. Democrat. Methodist. Author: The Spoiled System: A Call for Civil Service Reform, 1975; Principles of Civil Service Law, 1976; Conflict of Interest Regulation in the Federal Executive Branch, 1979; Merit Systems Protection Board: Rights and Remedies, 1984. Legal education, Administrative and regulatory, Legislative. Office: Am U Washington Coll Law 4400 Massachusetts Ave NW Washington DC 20016

VAZQUEZ, GILBERT FALCON, lawyer; b. Eagle Pass, Tex., Oct. 29, 1952; s. Catalina (Falcon) Vazquez; m. M. Lydia Martinez, Mar. 19, 1983. AB in Polit. Sci., Yale U., 1975; JD, Harvard U., 1978. Bar: Tex. 1978, U.S. Dist. Ct. (we. dist.) Tex. 1980, U.S. Ct. Appeals (5th and 11th cirs.) 1981. Ptnr. Matthews & Branscomb, San Antonio, Tex., 1978-85; ptnr. Akin, Gump, Strauss, Hauer & Feld, San Antonio, 1985-86, vice chmn., 1987—; mem. exec. com. Mayor's Target 90 Commn., San Antonio, 1986; mem. governing council internat. law sect. State Bar Tex. Co-chmn. issues com. H. Cisneros Mayoral Campaign, San Antonio, 1981; bd. dirs. Bexar County United Way, San Antonio, 1982-87, Mcpl. Legal Studies Ctr., Dallas, 1983—. Named Outstanding Young San Antonian, U.S. Jaycees, 1985, Outstanding Vol., J.C. Penny Co., 1984. Mem. ABA (internat. law sect., assoc. editor newsletter), Nat. Assn. Bond Lawyers, San Antonio Bar Assn., San Antonio Young Lawyers Assn. (Outstanding Young Lawyer 1987), San Antonio World Trade Assn. (bd. dirs.), Mexican C. of C. (bd. dirs.). Democrat. Roman Catholic. Club: Yale of S. Tex. (San Antonio) (pres. 1982-85). Avocations: community redevelopment, music, reading. General corporate, Private international, Municipal bonds. Office: Akin Gump et al 300 Convent St 1500 Intefirst Plaza San Antonio TX 78205

VAZQUEZ, MARTHA ALICIA, lawyer; b. Santa Barbara, Calif., Feb. 21, 1953; d. Remigio and Consuelo (Mendez) V.; m. Frank Mathew, Aug. 7, 1976; children: Cristina Vazquez Mathew, Nicholas Vazquez Mathew. BA in Govt., U. Notre Dame, 1975, JD, 1978. Bar: N.Mex. 1979, U.S. Dist. Ct. (we. dist.) N.Mex. 1979. Atty. Pub. Defender's Office, Santa Fe, 1979-81; ptnr. Jones, Gallegos, Snead & Wertheim, Santa Fe, 1981—. Chmn. City Santa Fe Grievance Bd. Mem. N.Mex. Bar Assn. (fee arbitration com., chmn. trial practice sect. 1984-85), Santa Fe Bar Assn. (jud. liasion com.), Nat. Assn. Criminal Def. Lawyers, Assn. Trial Lawyers Am., N.Mex. Trial Lawyers Assn. Democrat. Roman Catholic. Personal injury, Criminal, State civil litigation. Office: Jones Gallegos Snead & Wertheim 215 Lincoln Ave Santa Fe NM 87501

VAZQUEZ, PETER JOSEPH, lawyer; b. Newark, Apr. 28, 1949; s. Joseph and Marie (Cubelo) V.; m. Mary Margaret, June 13, 1971; children: Peter Jr., Steven, Cynthia. BA, Rutgers U., 1970; JD, Seton Hall U., 1973. Ptnr. Blume, Vazquez, Goldfaden et al, Newark, 1973—; arbitrator Am. Arbitration Assn., Essex County, N.J., 1976—, Essex County Mandatory Auto Arbitration Program, 1986. Avocation: boating. Personal injury. Home: 36 E McClellan Ave Livingston NJ 07039 Office: Blume Vazquez et al 5 Commerce St Newark NJ 07102

VEAL, REX R., lawyer; b. Lafayette, Ga., May 2, 1956; s. Boyd Herman and Barbara Ann (Sharp) V.; m. Vicky Elizabeth Wilkins, Dec. 13, 1980; children: Matthew Aaron and Richard Andrew (twins). BA, U. Tenn., 1978, JD, 1980. Bar: Tenn. 1981, U.S. Dist. Ct. (ea. dist.) Tenn. 1981, U.S. Ct. Appeals (10th cir. 1982), U.S. Ct. Appeals (6th cir.) 1984. Assoc. Finkelstein, Kern, Steinberg & Cunningham, Knoxville, Tenn., 1980-83; atty. Fed. Deposit Ins. Corp., Knoxville, 1983-84, sr. atty., 1984—. Mem. ABA, Tenn. Bar Assn., Knoxville Bar Assn., Assn. Trial Lawyers Am., Comml. Law League Am. Avocations: jogging, collecting books. Federal civil litigation, State civil litigation, Contracts commercial. Home: 5416 Dogwood Rd Knoxville TN 37918 Office: Fed Deposit Ins Corp PO Box 15154 800 S Gay St Knoxville TN 37901

VEATCH, WAYNE OTIS, SR., lawyer; b. Cottage Grove, Oreg., Mar. 2, 1905; s. Sylvester Curtis and Lena (Stockwell) V.; m. Miriam Audra Browder, June 21, 1936; children: Wayne Otis, Elizabeth Anne. BA, U. Oreg., 1929; LLB, U. Calif.-San Francisco, 1935. Bar: Calif. 1935. Ptnr. Veatch, Carlson, Grogan & Nelson (and numerous predecessor firms), Los Angeles, 1936—. Mem. editorial bd. Defense Law Jour., 1962—, Pacific regional editor, 1955-58. Mem. ABA, Los Angeles County Bar Assn., Wilshire Bar Assn., Internat. Assn. Ins. Counsel, So. Calif. Def. Counsel, So. Calif. Adjusters Assn., Am. Arbitration Assn., World Affairs Council, U. Oreg. Alumni Assn. (pres. So. Calif. div. 1948-49), Hastings Coll. Law Alumni Assn. (bd. dirs.). Republican. Presbyterian. Clubs: Los Angeles, Los Angeles Athletic. Lodges: Rotary (pres. internat. genealogy fellow 1986—), Masons. Insurance, Personal injury. Home: 4073 Chevy Chase Dr Flintridge CA 91011 Office: 3926 Wilshire Blvd Suite 200 Los Angeles CA 90010

VEENSTRA, YVES CORNELL, lawyer; b. Bruxelles, Brabant, Belgium, Feb. 9, 1943; came to U.S., 1951; s. Jacob Cornell and Gabrielle (Labin) V.; m. Francine E. Behenna, June 28, 1969; children: Chantale Danielle, Lianne Gabrielle. BA, Monmouth Coll., 1966; MA, SUNY, Binghamton, 1969; JD, Rutgers U., 1973. Bar: N.J. 1973, U.S. Dist. Ct. N.J. 1973. Assoc. Parker, McCay & Criscuolo, Marlton, N.J., 1973—. Served to 1st lt. U.S. Army, 1967-69, Vietnam. Mem. ABA, N.J. Bar Assn., N.J. Def. Assn., N.J. Trial Attys. Assn. (trustee 1986—), N.J. Health Care Risk Mgrs. Assn. (counsel), Am. Arbitration Assn. Lodge: Lions (Mt. Holly pres. 1982). Avocations: triathalons, ballroom dancing. State civil litigation, Federal civil litigation. Home: 33 Broad St Mount Holly NJ 08060 Office: Parker McCay & Criscuolo 3 Greentree Centre Marlton NJ 08053

VEGA, BENJAMIN URBIZO, retired judge; b. La Ceiba, Honduras, Jan. 18, 1916. AB, U. So. Calif., 1938, postgrad., 1939-40; LLB, Pacific Coast U. Law, 1941. Bar: Calif. 1947, U.S. Dist. Ct. (so. dist.) Calif. 1947, U.S. Supreme Ct. 1958. Assoc. Anderson, McPharlin & Connors, Los Angeles, 1947-48, Newman & Newman, Los Angeles, 1948-51; dep. dist. atty. County of Los Angeles, 1951-66; judge Los Angeles, County Mcpl. Ct., East Los Angeles Jud. Dist., 1966-86, retired, 1986; leader faculty seminar Calif. Jud. Coll. at Earl Warren Legal Inst., U. Calif-Berkeley, 1978. Mem. Calif. Gov.'s Adv. Com. on Children and Youth, 1968; del. Commn. of the Califs., 1978; bd. dirs. Los Angeles-Mexico City Sister City Com.; pres. Argentine Cultural Found., 1983. Recipient award for outstanding services from Mayor of Los Angeles, 1973, Disting. Pub. Service award Dist. Atty. Los Angeles County. Mem. Conf. Calif. Judges, Mcpl. Ct. Judges' Assn., Los Angeles County, Am. Judicature Soc., Pi Sigma Alpha. Judicial administration, Jurisprudence. Home: 101 California Ave Apt 1207 Santa Monica CA 90403

VEGA, MATIAS ALFONSO, lawyer; b. Paris, Feb. 2, 1952; s. Matias Guillermo and Colette (Lafosse) V.; m. Carmella Margarita Kurczewski, Nov. 20, 1982; 1 stepchild, Samantha Yvonne Fequiere. AB, Yale U., 1974; JD, Harvard U., 1977. Bar: N.Y. 1978, U.S. Dist. Ct. (so. and ea. dists.) N.Y. 1979, U.S. Supreme Ct. 1984, U.S. Ct. Appeals (6th and 9th cirs.) 1985, U.S. Dist. Ct. (no. dist.) Calif. 1985. Assoc. Curtis, Mallet-Prevost, Colt & Mosle, N.Y.C., 1977-85, ptnr., 1986—. Contbr. articles to profl. jours. Republican. Roman Catholic. Club: Yale (N.Y.C.). Private international, General corporate, Antitrust. Home: 809 Long Hill Rd W Briarcliff Manor NY 10510 Office: Curtis Mallet-Prevost Colt et al 101 Park Ave New York NY 10178

VELA, FILEMON B., U.S. district judge; b. Harlingen, Tex., May 1, 1935; s. Roberto and Maria Luisa Cardenas V.; m. Blanca Sanchez, Jan. 28, 1962; children: Filemon, Rafael Eduardo, Sylvia Adriana. Student, Tex. Southmost Coll., 1954-56, U. Tex., 1956-57; J.D., St. Mary's U., San Antonio, 1962. Bar: Tex. 1962. Mem. Vela & Vela, 1962-63; atty. Mexican-Am. Legal Def. Fund, 1962-75; pvt. practice law Brownsville, 1963-75; judge dist. 107, Tex. Dist. Ct., 1975-80; judge U.S. Dist. Ct., So. Dist. Tex., Brownsville, 1980—; instr. Law Enforcement Coll. City commr., Brownsville, 1971-73. Served with U.S. Army, 1957-59. Mem. State Bar Tex. Democrat. Jurisprudence. Office: PO Box 1072 Brownsville TX 78520

VELA, WILLIAM PAUL, lawyer; b. San Francisco, Mar. 16, 1953; s. Carlos Pineda Vela and Lucilla (Chavez) Zapata; m. Janice Elizabeth Toohey, Sept. 28, 1985; 1 child, Justin Francis. BA in Polit. Sci., Calif. State U., Sonoma, 1977; JD, U. Calif., San Francisco, 1980. Bar: N.D. 1983. Legis. atty., community organizer Com. United Against Immigration Attacks, San Francisco, 1981—; sole practice San Francisco, 1983—. Legal counsel Mexican. Am. Polit. Assn., San Francisco, 1985—; mem. Latino Dem. Club, San Francisco, 1983—. Mem. ABA, Nat. Lawyers Guild (immigration com.). Roman Catholic. Immigration, naturalization, and customs, Bankruptcy. Home: 261 Sussex St San Francisco CA 94131 Office: 2489 Mission St Francisco Bldg San Francisco CA 94110

VELASQUEZ, PATTI A., lawyer; b. Reno, Aug. 18, 1955; d. Nat Edward Velasquez and Shirley June Tombs. BA magna cum laude, Duke U., 1977; JD, Yale U., 1980. Bar: Ill. 1980, U.S. Dist. Ct. (no. dist.) Ill. 1980, U.S. Tax Ct. 1981, U.S. Ct. Appeals (7th cir.) 1981, Fla. 1984, U.S. Dist. Ct. (so. dist.) Fla. 1985, U.S. Ct. Appeals (11th cir.) 1985. Assoc. Sonnenschein, Carlin, Nath & Rosenthal, Chgo., 1980-83; sole practice Palm Beach, Fla., 1984-85; assoc. Honigman Miller Schwartz and Cohn, West Palm Beach, Fla., 1985-86; mem. Honigman Miller Schwartz and Cohn, West Palm Beach, 1987—. Mem. ABA, Palm Beach County Bar Assn., Phi Beta Kappa. Democrat. Avocations: choral singing, guitar, classical music, lit. Federal civil litigation, State civil litigation, Real estate tax appeals. Home: 3896 Begonia St Palm Beach Gardens FL 33410-5608 Office: Honigman Miller Schwartz & Cohn 1655 Palm Beach Lakes Blvd Suite 600 West Palm Beach FL 33401

VELAZQUEZ, HECTOR RADAMES, lawyer; b. Mayaguez, P.R.; came to U.S., 1952; s. Radames and Elba (Zabrana) V.; m. Naomi Martinez, Aug. 14, 1973; 1 child, Tanya. BA, Lehigh U., 1972; JD, SUNY, Buffalo, 1975. Bar: N.J. 1976, N.Y. 1976, U.S. Dist. Ct. N.J. 1976, U.S. Dist. Ct. (we. dist.) N.Y. 1976. Assoc. Petricca & Perfetto, Lackawamma, N.Y., 1976-79, Fuentes & Plant, Jersey City, 1979-82; ptnr. Plant & Velazquez, Jersey City, 1982—. Mem. N.J. Supreme Ct. Minority Affairs Task Force, 1986—; bd. dirs. Newark Legal Services, 1984. Mem. ABA, N.J. Bar Assn., Hudson County Bar Assn., Essex County Bar Assn., Assn. Trial Lawyers Am., Hispanic Bar Assn. (pres. N.J. 1984—). Lodge: Lions. Avocations: jogging, swimming, bicycling. Personal injury, Real property. Office: Plant & Velaquez 220 Newark Ave Jersey City NJ 07302

VELIE, FRANKLIN B., lawyer; b. N.Y.C., July 28, 1942; s. Lester and Frances (Rockmore) V.; m. Maureen Velie, July 2, 1966; children—Timothy Rockmore, Shian Melissa. A.B., Harvard U., 1965, LL.B., 1968. Bar: N.Y. 1969, U.S. Dist. Ct. (so. dist.) N.Y. 1970, (ea. dist.) 1970, U.S. Ct. Appeals (2d cir.) 1970, U.S. Sup. Ct. 1980. Assoc. Lord, Day & Lord, 1968-71; asst. U.S. atty. So. Dist. N.Y., 1971-75, asst. chief criminal div., 1974-75; ptnr. Gordon Hurwitz Butowsky Baker Weitzen & Shalov N.Y.C., 1975-84, Christy & Viener, N.Y.C., 1984—. Served with USMCR, 1960-66. Mem. N.Y. State Bar Assn., Assn. Bar City N.Y., New York County Lawyers Assn. Club: Harvard (N.Y.C.). Federal civil litigation, State civil litigation, Criminal. Home: 7 Locust Cove Ln Kings Point NY 11024 Office: 620 Fifth Ave New York NY 10020

VELTRI, STEPHEN CHARLES, lawyer, educator; b. Pitts., Mar. 29, 1955; s. Gabriel Alfred and Helen Louise (McConegly) V.; m. Melody Jo Mazzei, May 19, 1984. BA summa cum laude, U. Pitts., 1977; JD cum laude, Georgetown U., 1981; LLM, Columbia U., 1986. Info. specialist Library of Congress, Washington, 1978-80; assoc. Berkman Ruslander, Pitts., 1981-85; asst. prof. law Ohio No. U., Ada, 1986. Democrat. Roman Catholic. Contracts commercial, Legal education, Legal history. Home: 1315 S West St Findlay OH 45840 Office: Ohio Northern U Pettit Coll of Law Ada OH 45810

VELURE, LYLE CARL, lawyer; b. Coos Bay, Oreg., Jan. 2, 1941; s. John S. and Esther (Sahli) V.; m. Peggy H. McCleary, Aug. 7, 1967; 1 child, Matthew F. BS in Econs., U. Oreg., 1963, JD, 1966. Bar: Oreg. 1966, U.S. Dist. Ct. Oreg. 1967, U.S. Ct. Appeals (9th cir.) 1979. Assoc. Collins & Redden, Medford, Oreg., 1966-69; ptnr. Collins, Ferris & Velure and predecessor firm Collins, Redden, Ferris & Velure, Medford, 1969-77, Velure & Heysell, Medford, 1977-80, Velure & Bruce, Eugene, Oreg., 1980—; mem. Oreg. Bar Commn. on Fed. Practices and Procs., 1977-78, Oreg. Council on Ct. Procedures, 1980-83. Mem. Pub. Employees Relations Bd., Salem, Oreg., 1973-75, Medford Sch. Bd., 1978. Mem. Phi Delta Phi. Democrat. Lutheran. Personal injury, Workers' compensation. Home: 525 Fair Oaks Dr Eugene OR 97401 Office: Velure & Bruce PO Box 7275 Eugene OR 97401

VENA, DAVID HENRY, lawyer; b. Los Angeles, Dec. 21, 1938; s. David P. and Frances (Wilks) V.; m. Carolyn Willis, Jan. 20, 1961 (div. Dec. 1980); children: Gabrielle, Arianne; m. Carol A. Vena-Mondt, Sept. 30, 1984. AB, UCLA, 1961; LLB, Harvard U., 1964. Bar: Calif. 1965, U.S Dist. Ct. (so. dist.) Calif. 1965, U.S. Ct. Appeals (9th cir.) 1965. Assoc. Latham & Watkins, Los Angeles, ptnr.; legal cons. Concept Team Summa Corp., Marina del Ray, Calif., 1984—; bd. dirs. The Becket Group, Santa Monica, Calif. Founder Mus. Contemporary Art, Los Angeles; trustee Friends of Photography, Carmel, Calif., 1983—; bd. dirs. Otis/Parsons, Los Angeles, 1980—, Skystone Found. Inc., Flagstaff, Ariz., 1985—, UCLA Arts Council, 1986—. Mem. Los Angeles Bar Assn.,. Club: Los Angeles Country. Avocations: collecting contemporary art, golf. General practice, Real property. Home: 929 E 2d St #206 Los Angeles CA 90012 Office: Latham & Watkins 555 S Flower St Los Angeles CA 90071

VENA, JOSEPH ANTHONY, lawyer; b. Jersey City, Sept. 21, 1943; s. Carmine R. and Theresa V. (De Stefano) V.; m. Tanya Fesenko, Aug. 8, 1968; children—Damien, Alexis. A.B., Boston Coll., 1965; J.D., Seton Hall U., 1970. Bar: N.J. 1970, U.S. Dist. Ct. N.J. 1970. Assoc. Stephen N. Maskaleris, Newark, 1970-71; assoc. Rudd, Ackerman, Breitkopf, Leibowitz & Corradino, Esqs., Newark, 1971-73; sole practice, West Orange, N.J., 1973—; atty. Bd. of Adjustment, West Orange Twp., 1978—; trustee, chmn., West Orange Sr. Citizens Housing Assn., 1976-80; trustee, treas. Eagle Rock Sr. Citizens Housing Assn., 1979—. Mem. ABA, N.J. State Bar Assn., Essex County Bar Assn. (chmn. land use com. 1986-87, lectr.), Phi Alpha Delta. Club: Unico (Orange/West Orange) (pres. 1983-84.). State civil litigation, Land use and planning, Real property. Office: 20 Northfield Ave West Orange NJ 07052

VENERUSO, JAMES JOHN, lawyer; b. Bklyn., Feb. 4, 1951; s. Jack and Ann (Maugeri) V.; m. Lillian B. Curto, Aug. 16, 1975; children—Jacquelyn, James, Stephen. B.A., Iona Coll., 1972; J.D., Widener Coll., 1975. Bar: N.Y. 1976, Fla. 1980, U.S. Supreme Ct. 1979, U.S. Dist. Ct. (so. dist.) N.Y. 1979, U.S. Ct. Claims, 1977. Assoc. Griffin, Kane, Letsen & Coogan, Yonkers, N.Y., 1975-81; ptnr. Griffin, Letsen, Coogan & Veneruso, Bronxville, N.Y., 1981—. Bd. dirs. Big Bros.-Big Sisters, Yonkers, 1978-79, 83—. Assoc. editor Jour. Corp. Law, Widener Law Sch., 1973-74; bd. editors Pace Law Rev., 1979-80. Mem. N.Y. State Bar Assn., Westchester County Bar Assn. (features editor 1983), Yonkers Lawyers Assn. (sec. 1982-83, fin. sec. 1983-

84). Democrat. Roman Catholic. Contracts commercial, Real property, Banking. Home: 91 Longspur Rd Yonkers NY 10701 Office: Griffin Letsen Coogan & Veneruso 51 Pondfield Rd Bronxville NY 10708

VENTANTONIO, JAMES BARTHOLOMEW, lawyer; b. Orange, N.J., Jan. 5, 1940; s. Benjamin B. and Grace (D'Onofrio) V.; m. Anita L. Winkler, July 7, 1962; children: Peter, Lisa. BS, Seton Hall U., 1961, JD, 1964. Bar: N.J. 1965, U.S. Dist. Ct. N.J. 1965, U.S. Ct. Mil. Appeals 1965, U.S. Supreme Ct. 1969, N.Y. 1981. Dir. Somerset (N.J.) Sussex Legal Services Corp., 1969-74; assoc. prof. law Seton Hall U., Newark, 1974-78; atty. Bell Labs., Murray Hill, N.J., 1978-83; gen. atty. N.J. Bell Co., Newark, 1983—; pres. Sommerset-Sussex Legal Services Corp., 1978-85. Chmn. govs. adv. com. Legal Services, Trenton, N.J., 1979-83; pres. Community Health Law Project, East Orange, N.J., 1980-81. Served to maj. U.S. Army, 1965-69. Mem. ABA, N.J. Bar Assn. (chmn. standing com. on legal services 1979-80). State civil litigation, General corporate. Home: 747 W Foothill Rd Bridge Water NJ 08807 Office: NJ Bell Co 540 Broad St Newark NJ 07102

VENTO, JOHN SEBASTIAN, lawyer; b. Pitts., Apr. 23, 1949; s. John Joseph and Rose Ann (Bellante) V.; m. Jacqueline Lynnette Rex, Aug. 19, 1972. B.A. cum laude, U. Pitts., 1971; J.D. cum laude, Duquesne U., 1974; LL.M., U. Mich., 1979. Bar: U.S. Ct. Appeals (3d cir.) 1974, U.S. Dist. Ct. (we. dist.) Pa. 1974, U.S. Ct. Mil. Appeals 1975, Pa. 1974, U.S. Supreme Ct. 1980, Fla. 1981, U.S. Ct. Appeals (5th and 11th cirs.) 1981, U.S. Dist. Ct. (mid. dist.) Fla. 1981, U.S. Dist. Ct. (so. dist.) Fla. 1986, U.S. Ct. Internat. Trade, 1986. Law clk. U.S. Dist. Ct. (we. dist.) Pa., 1971-72; asst. staff judge advocate U.S. Air Force, MacDill AFB, Fla., 1974-76, chief internat law div., Clark AFB, Philippines, 1976-78; asst. prof. law U.S. Air Force Acad., Colo., 1979-81; atty. Trenam, Simmons Kemker, Scharf, Barkin, Frye and O'Neill, P.A., Tampa, Fla., 1981—. Assoc. editor: Duquesne Law Review, 1973-74. Co-author curriculum materials. Legal cons. Lake Forest Homeowners' Assn., Tampa, 1982—; bd. dirs. Hillsborough Community Mental Health Clinic, Tampa, 1984—; bd. dirs. Tampa Bay Area U. Mich. Alumni Club, Tampa, 1984—; Tampa Gasparilla Festival Krewe of Sant 'Yago, 1986; Served to capt. USAF, 1974-81. NEH fellow, 1980; Alcoa grantee, 1973-74. Mem. ABA, Inter-Am. Bar Assn., Am. Arbitrations Assn. (comml. arbitrator), Am. Soc. Internat. Law, Fla. Bar Assn., Hillsborough County Bar Assn., Nat. Order of Barristers, U. Mich. 4th Dist. Alumni Clubs Council (pres. 1986—), Phi Alpha Delta, Alpha Epsilon Pi. Republican. Roman Catholic. Club: Saddlebrook Golf and Country. Lodge: Kiwanis (bd. dirs). Federal civil litigation, State civil litigation, Private international. Office: Trenam Simmons Kemker Scharf et al 2600 First Florida Tower Tampa FL 33602

VER DUGHT, ELGENE CLARK, lawyer; b. Des Moines, Oct. 8, 1951; s. Elvyn Eugene and Betty Louise (Clark) Ver D.; m. Julie Esther Dieckmann, June 15, 1974; children: Janna, Jared. BA, U. Mo., 1973; JD cum laude, Hamline U., 1976. Bar: Mo. 1976, U.S. Dist. Ct. (we. dist.) Mo. 1976, U.S. Supreme Ct. 1979, U.S. Ct. Appeals (8th cir.) 1981. Sole practice Higginsville, Mo., 1976—; cons. Ver Dught Farms, Lexington and Winston, Mo., 1978—; atty. City of Corder, Mo., 1977-85, City of Wellington, Mo., 1978-85, City of Napoleon, Mo., 1979-85, City of Blackburn, Mo., 1982—; pros. atty. County of Lafayette and Lexington, Mo., 1979-80; city pros. Higginsville, 1986—. V.p. Lafayette County Dems., Mo., 1977. Democrat. Reorganized Ch. of Jesus Christ of Latter Day Saints. Lodge: Rotary (treas. Higginsville chpt. 1980, sec. 1981, dist. sec. 1983, v.p. 1982-83, pres. 1983-84, Paul Harris fellow, 1984). General practice, Family and matrimonial, State civil litigation. Home: 1904 Cypress Higginsville MO 64037 Office: 1814 Main St Box 174 Higginsville MO 64037

VERGARI, CARL ANTHONY, lawyer; b. Yonkers, N.Y., Dec. 7, 1921; s. Frank and Teresa (Molinari) V.; m. Genevieve Louise Lindermann, June 21, 1922; children—Bohn C., Jeanne Vergari Martinelli. Student Fordham U., 1938-40; LL.B., St. John's U., 1948; LL.M., N.Y. U., 1952. Bar: N.Y. 1948, U.S. Supreme Ct. Asst. dist. atty. N.Y. County, 1948-58; chief counsel N.Y. State Commn. of Investigation, 1958-68; dist. atty. Westchester County, White Plains, N.Y., 1968—; mem. joint strike force council on organized crime U.S. Justice Dept., 1972—, mem. exec. working group for fed.-state prosecutorial relations, 1978—. Bd. dirs. Am. Com. on Italian Migration, 1976—; bd. dirs. Enrico Fermi Ednl. Fund of Yonkers, 1972—, pres., 1973-75, mem. adv. bd. Nat. Obscenity Law Center, 1976—; mem. Westchester County Youth Services Adv. Com., 1968—, Westchester County Exec.'s Adv. Com. on Narcotics, 1968—; bd. dirs. Westchester Heart Assn., 1968-72. Served to capt. USMCR, 1941-45. Mem. Nat. Dist. Attys. Assn. (v.p. 1968, chmn. commn. on victim/witness assistance 1973-77, chmn. task force on ofcl. corruption 1978-80), N.Y. State Dist. Attys. Assn. (exec. com. 1968, pres. 1973-74), ABA, Westchester Bar Assn., Guild Cath. Lawyers. Criminal. Office: Courthouse 111 Grove St White Plains NY 10601

VERHAAREN, HAROLD CARL, lawyer; b. Salt Lake City, Apr. 11, 1938; m. Cynthia Mary Hughes, Nov. 25, 1964; children—Scott Harold, Steven Robert, Jill, Brent Carl, Brian Hughes. J.D., U. Utah, 1965. Bar: Utah 1965, U.S. Supreme Ct. 1978. Law clk. to chief justice Utah Supreme Ct., 1964-65; pres., bd. dirs. Mazuran, Verhaaren & Hayes, P.C., Salt Lake City; judge pro tem Small Claims Ct. Salt Lake County, 1978—. Chmn. Mt. Olympus Planning Dist., 1971-85; active Boy Scouts Am., 1967—. Recipient Silver Beaver award Boy Scouts Am. Mem. ABA, Utah Bar Assn., Salt Lake County Bar Assn., Am. Judicature Soc., Delta Theta Phi, Phi Kappa Phi, Phi Eta Sigma. Mormon. State civil litigation, Federal civil litigation, Probate. Office: 100 Boston Bldg 9 Exchange Pl Salt Lake City UT 84111

VERING, JOHN ALBERT, lawyer; b. Marysville, Kans., Feb. 6, 1951; s. John Albert and Bernadine E. (Kieffer) V.; m. Ann E. Arman, June 28, 1980; children: Julia Ann, Catherine Ann. BA summa cum laude, Harvard U., 1973; JD, U. Va., 1976. Bar: Mo. 1976, U.S. Dist Ct. (we. dist.) Mo. 1976, U.S. Dist. Ct. Kans. 1980, U.S. Ct. Appeals (8th cir.) 1977, U.S. Ct. Appeals (10th cirs.) 1980. Assoc. Dietrich, Davis, Dicus, Rowlands, Schmitt & Gorman, Kansas City, Mo., 1976-81, ptnr., 1982—. Editor: U. Va. Law Rev., 1974-76. Democrat. Roman Catholic. Club: Harvard (mem. exec. com. Kansas City chpt. 1977-86, v.p. 1981-82). Federal civil litigation, State civil litigation, Labor. Home: 1210 W 68th Terr Kansas City MO 64113 Office: Dietrich Davis Dicus et al 1700 City Ctr Sq 1100 Main St Kansas City MO 64105

VERITY, GEORGE LUTHER, lawyer; b. Oklahoma City, Jan. 3, 1914; s. George H. and Mae (Tibbals) V.; m. Ellen Van Hoesen, Mar. 18, 1939; children: George Luther II, Grover Steven, David Webster, Mark Sidney. LL.B., Okla. U., 1937. Bar: Tex. 1937, Okla. 1939, N.Mex. 1957. Practice in Wichita Falls, Tex., 1939-40, 46-48, Oklahoma City, 1948-57, Farmington, N.Mex., 1957-64, Oklahoma City, 1964—; partner Verity, Brown & Verity (and predecessor), 1964-77; of counsel Bay, Hamilton, Lee, Spears & Verity, 1978—; chmn. bd., dir. Big D Industries; pres., dir. Okla. Mgmt. Co., Okla. Ind. Exploration Co.; former chmn. bd., dir. Progress Life & Accident Ins. Co. Author: The Modern Oil and Gas Lease. Trustee Rocky Mountain Mineral Law Found. Served to capt. USAAF, 1941-46, PTO; prisoner of war. Decorated Purple Heart. Mem. ABA; Mem. Okla. Bar Assn., State Bar N.Mex. (chmn. mineral sect.), State Bar Tex., Assn. Trial Lawyers Am., Okla. Trial Lawyers Assn., Acacia. Lodges: Masons; Elks. Administrative and regulatory, Federal civil litigation, Oil and gas leasing. Home: Villa 55 3101 Castle Rock Road Oklahoma City OK 73120 Office: 320 NW 13th St Oklahoma City OK 73103

VERKAMP, JOHN, lawyer; b. Grand Canyon, Ariz., July 31, 1940; s. Jack and Mary (O'Leary) V.; m. Linda L. Meline, Sept. 14, 1965; children—Melanie, Jay, Gregory. B.S. in Bus. Adminstrn., U. Ariz., 1962, J.D., 1965. Bar: Ariz. 1965, U.S. Ct. Mil. Appeals 1965, U.S. Supreme Ct. 1973. Dep. county atty. Coconino County, Flagstaff, Ariz., 1970-71, county atty., 1980—; assoc. Mangum, Wall & Stoops, Flagstaff, 1972-74; ptnr. Verkamp & Verkamp, Flagstaff, 1974-80; mem. governing bd. Ariz. Pros. Attys. Adv. Council, Phoenix, 1981—, chmn. 1985—. Chmn. Coconino County Republican Com., Flagstaff, 1974-76, Coconino County Legal Aid, 1976-78; vice chmn. Calif. Social Services, 1982-83. Served as capt. JAGC, U.S. Army, 1965-70, Europe. Mem. Nat. Dist. Attys. Assn., Ariz. County Attys. and Sheriffs Assn. (pres. 1985-86), Ariz. Alliance Police Chiefs, Sheriffs and County Attys. (Ariz. County Atty. of Yr. 1985), Flagstaff C. of C., Am. Legion. Criminal, Environment, Legislative. Home: 2620 N Fremont Flagstaff AZ 86001 Office: Coconino County Atty Coconino County Courthouse San Francisco and Birch Sts Flagstaff AZ 86001

VERKUIL, PAUL ROBERT, college president; b. S.I., N.Y., Dec. 4, 1939; s. Marinus and Elsie Dorothy (Pohlmann) V.; m. Frances H. Gibson, Aug. 31, 1963; children—Tara Aldridge, John Gibson. B.A., Coll. William and Mary, 1961; LL.B., U. Va., 1967; LL.M., N.Y. U., 1969, J.S.D., 1972; M.A., New Sch. Social Research, 1971. Bar: N.Y. 1968. Asso. Cravath, Swaine & Moore, N.Y.C., 1967-69, Paul, Weiss, Rifkind, Wharton & Garrison, N.Y.C., 1969-71; asst. prof. U. N.C. Law Sch., Chapel Hill, 1971-74; asso. prof. U. N.C. Law Sch., 1974-76, prof., 1976-78; dean Tulane Law Sch., New Orleans, 1978-85; pres., prof. law Coll. William and Mary, 1985—; vis. prof. Duke U., 1973-74; cons. U.S. Dept. Energy, 1977-79; Kenan research prof., vis. scholar Columbia U., 1978; mem. Adminstrv. Conf. U.S., 1982—, White House Conf. on Small Bus., 1979-80. Author: Public Control of Business, 1977, Social Security Hearings and Appeals, 1978, Administrative Law and Process, 1985, Economic Regulation of Business, 2d edit., 1985. Served with U.S. Army, 1962-64. Mem. Raven Soc., Am. Law Inst., Am. Bar Assn., Maritime Law Assn., Order of Coif. Clubs: Army and Navy; University (N.Y.C.). Administrative and regulatory. Home: President's House Coll William and Mary Williamsburg VA 23185

VERMILLION, JOHN RICHARD, lawyer, consultant; b. San Antonio, June 18, 1952; s. James Richard and Patricia Ann (McMinn) V.; m. Patricia Dianne Wilhte, Oct. 9, 1976; children: John Regan, Jennifer Christine, Elizabeth Lauren. BA, Tex. Christian Coll., 1974; JD, La. State U., 1977. Bar: La. 1977. Contracts landman Exxon Co. USA, New Orleans, 1977-80; counsel Forman Exploration Co., New Orleans, 1980-81; regional land mgr. Sandefer Oil & Gas, Inc., Houston, 1981-83; v.p., Park Oil & Gas, Inc., Metairie, La., 1983—; also bd. dirs. Park Oil & Gas, Inc., Metairie, %. Treas. Spring Park Assn., Metairie, 1984—. Mem. ABA, La. Bar Assn., Independent Petroleum Assn. Am. (v.p. 1985—). Republican. Presbyterian. Oil and gas leasing, General corporate, Contracts commercial. Home: 5809 Flower Dr Metairie LA 70003 Office: Park Oil & Gas Inc 4415 Shores Dr Metairie LA 70006

VERNIS, FRANK CARL, JR., lawyer; b. McKeesport, Pa., Nov. 6, 1927; s. Frank C. and Nellie K. (Spiegel) V.; children—Nancy Vernis O'Brien, Barbara Vernis Cooper, Frank C., George J. J.D., U. Miami, 1953. Bar: Fla. 1953. Mem. Vernis & Bowling, P.A., Miami, Ft. Lauderdale, Fla. Keys, and New Orleans, sr. ptnr., 1970—. Served with USN, 1945-47; served to capt. U.S. Army, 1952-54. Mem. Fla. Bar Assn., Dade County Bar Assn., Broward County Bar Assn. Roman Catholic. State civil litigation, Personal injury, Insurance. Office: 301 SE 10th Ct Fort Lauderdale FL 33316 also: 2398 S Dixie Hwy Coconut Grove FL 33133 also: PO Box 611 Islamorada FL 33036 also: 10164 Jefferson Hwy River Ridge LA 70123

VERNON, DARRYL MITCHELL, lawyer; b. N.Y.C., May 4, 1956; s. Leonard and Joyce (Davidson) V.; m. Lauren Lynn Bernstein, Aug. 21, 1982. BA in Math., Tufts U., 1978; JD, Yeshiva U., 1981. Bar: N.Y. 1982, U.S. Dist. Ct. (so. and ea. dists.) N.Y. 1982. Assoc. Hochberg & Greenberg, N.Y.C., 1981-82; ptnr. Greenberg & Vernon, N.Y.C., 1982-83; pres. Law Offices of Darryl M. Vernon, N.Y.C., 1983—. Samuel Belkin scholar Yeshiva U., 1979. Mem. ABA (young lawyers div., tax sect., exec. com. animal rights sect. 1985—, animal law report, urban, state and local govt. law sect.), N.Y. State Bar Assn. (real property law sect.), Assn. of Bar of City of N.Y. (real property legis. com. 1985—), Am. Soc. for Prevention of Cruelty to Animals, Animal Legal Def. Fund, N.Y. Lawyers Basketball League. Jewish. Real property, Landlord-tenant, Animal rights. Home: 217 W 15th St New York NY 10003 Office: 261 Madison Ave New York NY 10016

VERNON, ROBERT GERARD, lawyer, oil company executive, consultant; b. N.Y.C., July 9, 1935; s. Weston, Jr., and Adelaide (Neilson) V.; m. Kathryn Barnes, Sept. 16, 1966; children: David Cannon, Linda, Richard Daniel. Student Columbia Coll., 1952-54; BA, U. Utah, 1956; postgrad. George Washington U. Law Sch., 1959; JD, Columbia U., 1963. Bar: Utah 1964, U.S. Dist. Ct. Utah 1964. Atty.-landman Skyline Oil Co., Salt Lake City, 1964-79, asst. sec., 1964-72, sec., 1972-77; sole practice, Salt Lake City, 1979-83; oil and gas lease investor and cons., Salt Lake City, 1979-83; v.p. Crossroads Oil Co., 1983—. Chmn. Rep. voting dist. 2644, Salt Lake City, 1970-71. Recipient E.B. Convers Prize, Columbia Law Sch., 1963. Mem. ABA, Utah State Bar (first chmn. oil and gas com. 1978-79), Utah Assn. Petroleum and Mining Landmen (pres. 1971), Am. Assn. Petroleum Landmen (cert. profl. landman). Mormon. Contbr. articles, papers to profl. publs. and confs. Oil and gas leasing, General corporate. Home: 1782 S 2500 E Salt Lake City UT 84108 Office: 530 Kennecott Bldg 10 East S Temple Salt Lake City UT 84133

VERON, EARL ERNEST, judge; b. Smoke Bend, La., Jan. 2, 1922; s. Dyer M. and Edna (Rodriguez) V.; m. Alverdy Heyd, Oct. 10, 1948; children: J. Michael, Douglas E. B.A., McNeese State U., 1958; J.D., La. State U., 1959. Bar: La. 1959. Pvt. practice law Lake Charles, La., 1959-67; judge 14th Jud. Dist., Lake Charles, La., 1967-77, U.S. Dist. Ct. Western Dist. La., Lake Charles, 1977—; mem. Orleans Parish Criminal Ct., 1972. Mem. ABA, La. State Bar Assn., Southwest La. Bar Assn., Am. Judicature Soc. Jurisprudence. Office: US District Ct PO Box 1404 Lake Charles LA 70602 *

VERON, J. MICHAEL, lawyer; b. Lake Charles, La., Aug. 24, 1950; s. Earl Ernest and Alverdy (Heyd) V.; m. Carolyn Sue Donaldson, Jan. 8, 1982; 1 child, John Heyd. BA, Tulane U., 1972, JD, 1974; LLM, Harvard U., 1976. Bar: La., U.S. Dist. Ct. (we., ea. and mid. dists.) La., U.S. Ct. Appeals (5th cir.). Law clk. to presiding justice La. Supreme Ct., New Orleans, 1974-75; sole practice Lake Charles, 1976-78; ptnr. Scofield, Bergstedt, Gerard, Mount & Veron, Lake Charles, 1978—; instr. legal method and research Boston U., 1975-76; lectr. environ. law McNeese State U., 1976-79; faculty Tulane Trial Adv. Inst., 1980. Mem. bd. editors Tulane Law Rev., 1972-73, assoc. editor, 1973-74. Mem. human rights com. Maison D'Arc, 1979-80, athletic adv. com. Tulane U., 1983-86; pres. Krewe of Barataria, 1980-86; bd. dirs. Friends of Gov.'s Program for Gifted Children, Inc., 1985. Mem. U.S. Golf Assn. (green sect. com.), La. Golf Assn. (bd. dirs.). Roman Catholic. Clubs: Lake Charles Country (pres. 1986), Tulane Green Wave (pres. Lake Charles chpt. 1984). Avocations: golf, gin rummy, athletics. State civil litigation, Personal injury, Federal civil litigation. Home: 4446 Prienterre Dr Lake Charles LA 70605 Office: Scofield Bergstedt Gerard Mount & Veron 1114 Ryan St Lake Charles LA 70601

VERRILL, CHARLES OWEN, JR., lawyer; b. Biddeford, Maine, Sept. 30, 1937; s. Charles Owen and Elizabeth (Handy) V.; m. Mary Ann Blanchard, Aug. 13, 1960; children: Martha Anne, Edward Blanchard, Ethan Christopher, Elizabeth Handy, Matthew Lawton, Peter Goldthwait. A.B., Tufts U., 1959; LL.B., Duke U., 1962. Bar: D.C. 1962. Practiced in Washington 1962—; assoc. Weaver & Glassie, 1962-64; assoc. Barco, Cook, Patton & Blow, 1964-66, ptnr., 1967; ptnr. Patton, Boggs & Blow, 1967-84, Wiley, Rein and Fielding, Washington, 1984—; lectr. Duke Law Sch., 1970-73; adj. prof. internat. trade law Georgetown U. Law Ctr., Washington, 1978—; conf. chmn. The Future of the Internat. Steel Industry, Bellogio, Italy, 1984, The U.S. Agenda for the Uruguay Round, Airlie House, Warenton, Va., 1986. Local dir. Tufts U. Ann. Fund, 1965-69; mem. Duke Law Alumni Council, 1972-75; trustee Internat. Law Inst., 1981—, chmn. bd. trustees, 1983—. Recipient Service citation Tufts U. Alumni Assn., 1968. Mem. ABA, D.C. Bar Assn., Order of Coif, Theta Delta Chi, Phi Delta Phi. Clubs: Metropolitan (Washington); Tarratine (Dark Harbor, Maine); Chevy Chase (Md.). Private international, Condemnation. Home: 8205 Dunsinane Ct McLean VA 22101 Office: 1776 K St NW Washington DC 20006

VERSFELT, DAVID SCOTT, lawyer; b. Mineola, N.Y., Feb. 17, 1951; s. William H. and Ruth (Gerland) V.; m. Mary Deborah Garber, Aug. 31, 1974; children: Christopher L., William S. AB, Princeton U., 1973; JD, Columbia U., 1976. Bar: N.Y. 1977, U.S. Dist. Ct. (so. and ea. dists.) N.Y. 1977, U.S. Ct. Appeals (D.C. cir.) 1979, U.S. Ct. Appeals (2d and 7th cirs.) 1980, U.S. Supreme Ct. 1980, U.S. Ct. Appeals (9th cir.) 1981, U.S. Ct. Appeals (3d cir.) 1982. Mem. Council of Community Law Office, vol. div. Legal Aid Soc., N.Y.C., 1985—. Mem. ABA, Assn. Bar City N.Y. (com. on state legislation 1983-85). Antitrust, General corporate, Securities. Office: Donovan Leisure Newton & Irvine 30 Rockefeller Plaza New York NY 10112

VERVILLE, RICHARD EMERY, lawyer; b. Haverhill, Mass., Mar. 21, 1939; s. Richard Laurier and Ruth Eames (Emery) V.; m. Marcia McCord, Oct. 23, 1982; 1 dau., Alexandria Laurier. B.A., Williams Coll., 1961; J.D., Columbia U., 1964. Bar: Mass. 1965, Washington, 1973. Assoc., Palmer & Dodge, Boston, 1964-69; asst. to sec. HEW, 1970-71, dep. asst. sec., 1971-72; ptnr. White Fine & Verville, Washington, 1973—, Fine & Ambrogne, Boston, 1973—. Mem. diabetes trial policy adv. com. NIH, bd. dirs. Coalition Health Funding; mem. Nat. Urban Coalition Adv. Council. Recipient Gold Key award Am. Congress Rehab. Medicine, 1979, Disting. Service award HEW, 1972, Assn. Rehab. Research Centers, 1979. Mem. ABA (chmn. health edn. com.), Fed. Bar Assn., Boston Bar Assn., Nat. Health Lawyers Assn. Contbr. articles to profl. jours. Health, Administrative and regulatory, Legislative. Home: 5301 Potomac Ave NW Washington DC 20016 Office: 1156 15th St NW #302 Washington DC 20005

VEST, DAVID GARDNER, county attorney; b. Lexington, Ky., Oct. 24, 1946; s. David Herschel and Nancy (Ward) V.; m. Sally Lee Foley, Aug. 3, 1968; children: David Hunter, Norrie Kristin. BA, U. Ky., 1968, JD, 1971. Bar: Ky. 1971, U.S. Dist. Ct. (ea. and we. dists.) Ky. 1972. Sr. atty. Commn. on Children State of Ky., 1971-72; ptnr. Wake and Vest, Lexington, 1972-79, Bradley, Emerson, Wake & Vest, Lexington, 1979-86; 1st asst. atty. Fayette County, Lexington, 1986—; trial commr. Fayette Quar. Ct., 1973-77; para-legal prof. Midway Coll., 1974-76; treas., trustee Fayette County Law Library, Lexington, 1976—. Author: Laws Concerning Youth, 1972. Mem. ABA, Ky. Bar Assn., Fayette County Bar Assn., Am. Trial Lawyers Assn., Ky. Assn. Trial Lawyers. Democrat. Presbyterian. Criminal. Home: 217 Culpepper Lexington KY 40502 Office: Fayette County Atty 207 N Upper Lexington KY 40507

VESTAL, TOMMY RAY, lawyer; b. Shreveport, La., Sept. 19, 1939; s. Louie Wallace and Margaret (Golden) V.; m. Patricia Marie Blackwell, Jan. 24, 1981; children: Virginia Ann Yancy, John Wallace Vestal, Douglas William Yancy. BSME, U. Houston, 1967, JD, 1971. Bar: Tex. 1970, U.S. Patent Office 1972, U.S. Ct. Appeals (D.C. cir.) 1975. Patent atty. Am. Enka Corp., Asheville, N.C., 1970-71, Akzona Inc., Asheville, 1971-84, Akzo Am., Inc., Asheville, 1985-86; sr. patent atty. Fibers div. BASF Corp., Enka, N.C., 1986—. Mem. ABA, Am. Intellectual Property Law Assn., Carolina Patent, Trademark and Copyright Law Assn. (bd. dirs. 1983-85, 2d v.p. 1985-86, 1st v.p. 1986-87, pres. 1987-88), Asheville C. of C. (chmn. legal affairs com.), Phi Alpha Delta. Republican. Lutheran. Lodge: Kiwanis (pres. 1982). Avocations: golf, fishing, hiking. Patent, Trademark and copyright, Antitrust. Home: 244 Bent Creek Ranch Rd Asheville NC 28806 Office: BASF Corp Div Fibers Sand Hill Rd Enka NC 28728

VESTNER, ELIOT N., JR., banker; b. Bronxville, N.Y., Aug. 4, 1935; s. Eliot N. and Priscilla Alden (Fuller) V.; m. Elizabeth Gwin, Jan. 1, 1966; children—Alice-Lee, Charles Fuller. B.A., Amherst Coll., 1957; M.A., U. Mich., 1958; LL.B., Columbia U., 1962. Bar: N.Y. 1963. Assoc. Debevoise, Plimpton, Lyons & Gates, N.Y.C., 1962-68; spl. counsel N.Y. State Bank Dept., 1968-70; spl. asst. to Gov. Nelson A. Rockefeller, 1970-72; 1st dep. supt. N.Y. State, 1972-75, supt. banking, 1974-75; sr. v.p., gen. counsel Irving Trust Co., 1975-82, exec. v.p., 1982-87; exec. counsel, office of chief exec. officer Bank of Boston, 1987—. Mem. Bd. Assessment Rev., Rye, N.Y., 1974-80. Republican. Episcopalian. Home: 30 Grace Church St Rye NY 10580 Office: Bank of Boston 100 Federal St Boston MA 02110

VETERE, ROBERT LOUIS, lawyer; b. Elizabeth, N.J., July 24, 1949; s. Robert and Pearl Elizabeth (Burlone) V.; m. Brenda Lee Viehweger, May 26, 1979; children: Robert Albert, Joshua Thomas. BS in Indsl. Mgmt., Rensselaer Poly. Inst., 1972, MBA in Fin., 1974; JD, Seton Hall Sch. of Law, Newark, 1980. Bar: Conn. 1982, N.J. 1983, U.S. Dist. Ct. N.J. 1983. Indsl. engr. Union Carbide Corp., Wayne, N.J., 1974-75, bus. mgr., 1975-77; product mgr. Union Carbide Corp., N.Y.C., 1977-78; dept. mgr. Union Carbide Corp., East Hartford, Conn., 1978-80, sr. indsl. engr., 1980-84; sole practice South Windsor, Conn., 1982—; sr. staff cons. First Brands Inc., East Hartford, 1984—; bd. dirs. PDQ-N.J., Inc., Woodbridge; bus. agt. More Assocs., Inc., Coventry, Conn., 1984—. Mem. ABA, N.J. Bar Assn., Conn. Bar Assn., Am., Mgmt. Assn. Avocations: golf, reading, hockey. Probate, General practice, Real property. Home: 171 Bourbon St South Windsor CT 06074 Office: First Brands Inc 88 Long Hill St East Hartford CT 06108

VETTER, JAMES GEORGE, JR., lawyer; b. Omaha, Apr. 8, 1934; s. James George and Helen Louise (Adams) V.; m. Mary Ellen Froelich, June 25, 1960; 1 child, James G. III. B.S., Georgetown U., 1954; J.D., Creighton U., 1960. Bar: Nebr. 1960, Tex. 1967. Counsel IRS, Washington, 1960-64, Dallas, 1964-67; practiced in Dallas, 1967—; sr. ptnr. Vetter, Bates, Tibbals, Lee & DeBusk (P.C.), 1979—; lectr. taxation seminars; dir. Pilgrim's Pride Corp., Inc., AFV Energy, Inc. Contbr. articles to profl. jours. Asst. sgt.-at-arms Tex. Democratic Conv., 1968; advisor selection com. Georgetown U., 1970-85; scoutmaster Boy Scouts Am., 1974-75. Served with USAF, 1954-57. Mem. Nebr. Bar Assn., State Bar Tex., Dallas Bar Assn. (chmn. fee disputes com. 1985), Real Estate Fin. Execs. Assn. (pres. 1982-83), Creighton U. Alumni Assn. (pres. Dallas-Ft. Worth 1969-70, v.p. Cash Alliance 1986—), Delta Theta Phi. Independent. Roman Catholic. Clubs: Lancers, Energy, City (Dallas). Corporate taxation, Estate taxation, Personal income taxation. Home: 11023 Rosser Rd Dallas TX 75229 Office: 2700 One Main Pl Dallas TX 75250

VETTER, JAN, legal educator; b. 1934. B.A., UCLA, 1956, LL.B., 1962. Bar: Calif. 1963. Assoc. Gibson, Dunn & Crutcher, Los Angeles, 1962-67; now. prof. law U. Calif.-Berkeley; vis. prof. Harvard U. Sch. Law, 1975-76. Former editor-in-chief UCLA Law Rev. Legal education. Office: U Calif Law Sch 225 Boalt Hall Berkeley CA 94720 *

VEVERKA, DONALD JOHN, lawyer; b. Chgo., July 20, 1935; s. John Edward and Irene Cecelia (Wasil) V.; m. Mary Almjeld, May 27, 1967; children—Tanya, Holly, Marc. B.S., Loyola U., Chgo., 1957; J.D., DePaul U., 1963. Bar: Ill. 1963, U.S. Dist. Ct. (no. dist.) Ill. 1963, U.S. Ct. Appeals (7th cir.) 1963, U.S. Supreme Ct. 1968. Asst. state's atty. civil appeals sect. Cook County State's Attys. Office, 1963-67; asst. atty. gen. appeals sect. Ill. Atty. Gen. Office, 1967-68; house counsel Kenilworth Ins. Co., 1968-69; ptnr. Bradshaw, Speranza, Veverka & Brumlik, 1969-72; spl. asst. atty. gen., 1970-72; ptnr. Speranza & Veverka, Chgo., 1972-73, 74—; officer Henehan Donovan Isaacson Speranza & Veverka, Ltd., Chgo., 1973-74; bd. dirs., officer DePaul Law Council, 1972-83; mem. Ill. Supreme Ct. Com. on Pattern Jury Instrns. Assoc. bd. dirs. LaGrange Community Meml. Hosp., 1979, officer, 1982-85, pres. 1986-87; bd. dirs. West Suburban YMCA, 1981—; trustee Village of LaGrange Park (Ill.), 1981—. Served to 1st lt. U.S. Army, 1967-69; capt. Res. Mem. ABA (faculty mem. Nat. Inst. Appellate Advocacy 1980, Ill. chmn. young lawyers com. on jud. selection 1971-72), Ill. State Bar Assn. (mem. com. on corrections reform 1974, also past mem. speakers bur., young mems. conf.), Bar Assn. Seventh Fed. Circuit (Ill. chmn. meetings com. 1976), DePaul Alumni Assn. (governing bd. 1975-82), Phi Alpha Delta, Blue Key. Roman Catholic. Clubs: YMCA Men's (LaGrange, Ill.); Athletic (Chgo.). Author: How To Buy or Sell Your Home Without a Lawyer, 1982; also articles. General corporate, General practice, Family and matrimonial. Home: 709 N Park Rd LaGrange Park IL 60525 Office: 180 N Michigan Ave Chicago IL 60601

VICE, ROBERT BRUCE, lawyer, investment banker; b. Mt. Sterling, Ky., Apr. 27, 1953; s. Bruce Leroy Vice and Evelyn Norris Rudder; m. M. Andrea Rabbeth, Aug. 19, 1972; 1 child, Robert Bruce Jr. BA, U. Ky., 1975; postgrad., Oxford U., Eng., 1975; JD, U. Ky., 1978. Bar: Ky. 1978, U.S. Dist. Ct. (we. dist.) Ky. 1978. Assoc. Wyatt, Tarrant & Combs, Louisville, 1978-80; pres. Hilliard Lyons Real Estate Fin., Inc., Louisville, 1980—. Mem. exec. com. Louisville Cen. Area, Inc., 1986—; program chmn. Young Leaders Inst., Louisville, 1983-86; chmn. Preservation Alliance, Inc., Louisville, 1983-87, chmn. Preservation Action, Inc., Washington, 1984—. Recipient Leadership of Louisville award Louisville C. of C., 1982, Ida Lee Willis award Ky. Heritage Council, 1986; named one of Outstanding Young Men of Am., 1985. Mem. ABA, Ky. Bar Assn., Louisville Bar Assn., U. Ky. Alumni Assn., Order of Coif. Democrat. Episcopalian. Avocations: tennis, cycling. Securities, Personal income taxation,

Real property. Office: Hilliard Lyons Real Estate Fin Inc 545 S 3d St Louisville KY 40202

VICIAN, GLENN STEVEN, lawyer; b. Camp Roberts, Calif., Aug. 29, 1953; s. Edward Steven and Dolores Mary (Palata) V.; m. Dawn Janine Jefferson, Dec. 12, 1956; children: Jessica M., Nicholas S. BA, Valparaiso U., 1975, JD, 1977. Bar: Ind. 1978, U.S. Dist. Ct. (no. dist.) Ind. Assoc. Borns & Quinn, P.C., Merrillville, Ind., 1978—. Mem. ABA, Ind. State Bar Assn., Lake County Bar Assn. Lutheran. Avocations: flying, water skiing, golf. Consumer commercial, Bankruptcy, Real property. Home: 467 Scarborough Rd Valparaiso IN 46383 Office: Borns & Quinn PC 1000 E 80th Pl Merrillville IN 46410

VICK, PAUL ASHTON, lawyer; b. Rochester, N.Y., Sept. 30, 1945; s. Robert A. and Dorothy Lou (Flanders) V.; m. Gail A. VanHouten, Dec. 17, 1966; children—Jennifer, Christopher, Benjamin. B.A., Kalamazoo Coll., 1967; M.Div., Colgate Rochester Div. Sch., 1971; postgrad. New Eng. Sch. Law, 1972-73; J.D., SUNY-Buffalo, 1975. Bar: N.Y. 1976, U.S. Dist. Ct. (we. dist.) N.Y. 1976. Dir. Southeast Area Coalition Family Counseling, Rochester, 1969-72; assoc. firm Sullivan, Peters, Burns and Holtzberg, Rochester, 1976-79; ptnr. firm Sullivan, Peters, Burns, Holtzberg & Stander, Rochester, 1980-81, firm Phillips, Lytle, Hitchcock, Blaine & Huber, Rochester, 1982—. Trustee Immanuel Bapt. Ch., Rochester, 1984—; bd. dirs. Cameron Community Ministries, Rochester, 1983—, Alternatives for Battered Women, Rochester, 1981—. Mem. Monroe County Bar Assn. (exec. council estate and trust sect. 1983—). Democrat. Lodge: Masons. Estate planning, Family and matrimonial. Home: 55 Monteroy Rd Rochester NY 14618 Office: Phillips Lytle Hitchcock Blaine & Huber 1400 First Fed Plaza Rochester NY 14614

VICK, PHILLIP ORAN, judge; b. Houston, Sept. 16, 1941; s. Orvil Travis and Ruby Belle (Utley) V.; m. Barbara K. Gupton, Dec. 23, 1963; children: Phillip Wayne, Casey Todd, Scott Alan. BBA, Sam Houston State U., 1963; JD, S. Tex. Coll. Law, 1971. Bar: Tex. 1971, U.S. Dist. Ct. (ea. dist.) Tex. 1977, U.S. Ct. Appeals (5th cir.) 1977. Asst. dist. atty. Denton County, Tex., 1971-73; pvt. practice Denton, Tex., 1973-86; judge 158th jud. dist. ct. Denton County, 1986—. Election atty. Denton County Reps., 1983. Served with USN, 1963-65. Mem. Tex. Bar Assn., Tex. Def. Lawyers Assn., Denton County Bar Assn. (pres. 1984-85). Avocation: boys' baseball. Criminal, Family and matrimonial, Juvenile. Home: 625 Magnolia Denton TX 76201 Office: Denton County Courthouse Denton TX 76201

VICKERSON, WILLIAM LEO, lawyer; b. Portland, Maine, Sept. 7, 1951; s. Frank Merrill and Dorothy Loretta (Foley) V.; m. Linda J. Kennedy, Dec. 30, 1977; 1 child, Amanda Jo. AB in History, Fairfield U., 1973; JD, Loyola U., 1977. Bar: Maine 1977, U.S. Dist. Ct. Maine 1978. Sole practice South Portland, Maine, 1977-80; ptnr. Kettle, Carter, Hannigan & Vickerson, Portland, 1980-83, Levenson & Vickerson, Portland, 1983—; counsel, legis. rep. Maine State Fedn. Firefighters, 1981—. Chmn. Cohen for Senator, South Portland, 1984, South Portland Republican Party, 1985, govt. relations com. Greater Portland United Way, 1986—. Mem. ABA, Assn. Trial Lawyers Am., Maine State Bar Assn., Maine Trial Lawyers Assn. Personal injury, Libel, Legislative. Office: Levenson & Vickerson 183 Middle St PO Box 465 Portland ME 04112

VICKERY, EUGENE BENTON, JR., lawyer; b. New Orleans, Nov. 23, 1936; s. Eugene Benton and Esther (Cleveland) V.; m. Anne Saunders Porteous, Aug. 25, 1961; children—Eugene Benton III, Saunders P., Ninette C., William A. A.B., Williams Coll., 1962; J.D., Loyola U., New Orleans, 1967. Bar: La. 1967, U.S. Dist. Ct. (ea. dist.) La. 1967, U.S. Ct. Appeals (5th cir.) 1967. Supr. computer systems, sr. tech. programmer Shell Oil Co., New Orleans Data Center, 1962-67; jr. ptnr. Porteous, Toledano, Hainkel & Johnson, New Orleans, 1968-73; ptnr. Sutterfield & Vickery, New Orleans, 1974-82; sole practice, New Orleans, 1982—; procurator-adv. Met. Tribunal for Archdiocese of New Orleans. Trustee, St. George's Epis. Sch., 1975-83, chmn., 1978-79; mem. La. Landmarks Soc., Met. Crime Commn., Uptown Neighborhood Improvement Assn. New Orleans and River Region C. of C. Served with U.S. Army, 1956-59. Mem. ABA, La. Bar Assn., New Orleans Bar Assn., La. Assn. Def. Counsel, New Orleans Assn. Def. Counsel, Def. Research Inst., Am. Judicature Soc., Am. Arbitration Assn. (panel of arbitrators 1968—), Notaries Assn. New Orleans, Delta Phi. Republican. Roman Catholic. Clubs: Boston, La., Pickwick, Lakeshore (New Orleans); Williams (N.Y.C.). General corporate, Insurance, Probate. Home: 5526 Chestnut St New Orleans LA 70115 Office: 600 Maritime Bldg 203 Carondelet St New Orleans LA 70130

VICKERY, GLENN, lawyer; b. Houston, Nov. 27, 1938; s. Barney Burren and Bonnie Beatrice (Wheeler) V.; m. Helen Roberta McMurrey, Aug. 18, 1947; children—Ronda, Teresa, Kay, Jessica. B.S. in Econs. U. Houston, 1963, J.D., South Tex. Coll. Law 1966. Bar: Tex. 1966. Sole practice, Houston, 1966—, Dallas, 1966—, Baytown, Tex., 1966—; justice of peace 1968-70. Mem. Tex. Ho. of Reps. 1966-68; active various civic assns. Mem. ABA, State Bar Tex., Houston Bar Assn., Assn. Trial Lawyers Am., Tex. Trial Lawyers Assn. Clubs: Ends of Court (Houston); Goose Creek Country (Baytown); Magnolia Ridge Country (Liberty). Admiralty, Personal injury. Home: Route 1 Box 143 M Hull TX 77521 Office: Citizens Bank Tower 6th Floor 1300 Rollingbrook Dr Baytown TX 77521

VICKREY, BARRY ROLAND, legal educator; b. Takoma Park, Md., Feb. 17, 1950; s. Roy A. and Katie (Terrell) V.; Mary L. Green, Aug. 21, 1971; children: David Terrell, Mark Franklin. BA magna cum laude, Vanderbilt U., 1971, JD, 1977. Bar: Tenn. 1977. Staff aide, policy planning staff govs. office State of Tenn., Nashville, 1971-74; asst. to pres. elect, asst. to pres. ABA, Chgo., 1977-79, dir. nat. insts., dir. div. of profl. edn., 1979-82; asst. prof. law U. N.D., Grand Forks, 1982-85, assoc. dean, 1984—, assoc. prof., 1985—, adj. prof. ctr. for peace studies, 1984—, coordinator ctr. for peace studies, 1986—; mem. various coms. N.D. Supreme Ct., 1983—. Elder 1st Presbyn. Ch., Grand Forks, 1984-87; pres. United Campus Ministry, Grand Forks, 1985—; del. Presbytery of No. Plains, 1985-87, N.D. Dem. Conv., Minot, 1986. Mem. ABA (standing com. on lawyer competence), Phi Beta Kappa. Avocations: various sports, travel. Legal education, Jurisprudence, Legislative. Home: 1002 Chestnut St Grand Forks ND 58201 Office: Univ ND Sch Law University Station Grand Forks ND 58202

VICKREY, JACK, lawyer; b. Hico, Tex., Dec. 5, 1915; s. Azel Alva and Irene (Higgins) V.; m. Anita English, Dec. 24, 1940; children—Jack, Nancy Vickrey Banks, Lori. LL.B., U. Tex., 1939. Bar: Tex. 1939, Ga. 1963. U.S. Supreme Ct. 1978, U.S. Dist. Ct. (5th cir.) 1981, (10th cir.) 1982, (D.C. cir.) 1983. Assoc., Beasley & Beasley, Beeville, Tex., 1939-40; spl. agt. FBI, 1940-43; atty. Mobil Oil Co., 1946-62; v.p., gen. counsel Colonial Pipeline, Co., Atlanta, 1962-73; ptnr. Andrews, Kurth, Campbell & Jones, 1973-76; sole practice Houston, 1976—; ptnr. Vickrey & Alsup and predecessor firms Vickrey & Doggett. Served to capt., USMC, 1943-45. Recipient Outstanding Service award Am. Petroleum Inst., 1971. Mem. ABA, Tex. Bar Assn., Ga. Bar Assn., Houston Bar Assn., Assn. Transp. Practitioners, Fed. Energy Bar Assn., Assn. Former FBI Agts., Tex. Utility Lawyers Assn. (pres. 1984), Assn. Oil Pipelines (adv.), Phi Delta Phi, Phi Delta Theta. Clubs: Houston Country, Peachtree Golf (Atlanta), Houston Petroleum. FERC practice, Federal civil litigation, State civil litigation. Office: Suite 3100 Interfirst Plaza Houston TX 77002

VICTOR, MICHAEL GARY, physician, lawyer; b. Detroit, Sept. 20, 1945; s. Simon H. and Helen (Litsky) V.; m. Karen Sue Hutson, June 20, 1975; children—Elise Nicole, Sara Lisabeth. Bars: Ill. 1980, U.S. Dist. Ct. (no. dist.) Ill. 1980, U.S. Ct. Appeals (7th cir.) 1981; diplomate Am. Bd. Law in Medicine. Pres., Advocate Adv. Assocs., Chgo., 1982—; assoc. in medicine Northwestern U. Med. Sch., Chgo., 1982—; sole practice law, Barrington, Ill., 1982—; dir. emergency medicine Loretto Hosp., Chgo., 1980-85 , chief. sect. of emergency medicine St. Josephs Hosp., Chgo., 1985—; v.p. Med. Emergency Services Assocs., Buffalo Grove, Ill; v.p. MESA Mgmt. Corp.; sec., treas. MESA Edn. and Research Found.; sec., treas. Mgmt. and Care Services Inc., bd. dirs., Vital Med. Labs. Inc. Author: Informed Consent, 1980; Brain Death, 1980; (with others) Due Process for Physicians, 1984, A Physicians Guide to the Illinois Living Will Act. Recipient Service awards Am. Coll. Emergency Medicine, 1973-83. Fellow Am. Coll. Legal Medicine, Chgo. Acad. Legal Medicine; mem. Am. Coll. Emergency Physicians (pres. 1980, med.-legal-ins. council 1980-81, 83-84), ABA, Ill. State Bar Assn., Am. Soc. Law and Medicine, Assn. Trial Lawyers Am., Chgo. Bar Assn. (med.-legal council 1981-83), AMA, Ill. State Med. Soc. (med.-legal council 1980-86), Chgo. Med. Soc. Jewish. State civil litigation, Legal education, Health. Home and Office: 1609 Guthrie Circle Barrington IL 60010

VICTOR, RICHARD STEVEN, lawyer; b. Detroit, Mich., Aug. 3, 1949; s. Simon H. and Helen (Litsky) V.; m. Denise L. Berman, Nov. 26, 1978; children: Daniel, Ronald, Sandra. Bar: Mich. 1975, U.S. Dist. Ct. (ea. dist.) Mich. 1975. Assoc. Law Offices of Albert Best, Detroit, 1975; ptnr. Best & Victor, Oak Park, Mich., 1976-80; sole practice Oak Park, 1981-85; ptnr. Law Offices of Victor & Robbins, Brimingham, Mich., 1986—; instr. Oakland U., 1976—. Columnist: Legally Speaking, 1983—. Mem. community adv. bd. Woodland Hills Med. Ctr., 1981—; v.p. Bloomfield (Mich.) Sq. Homeowners Assn., 1985—. Mem. Mich. Bar Assn., Oakland County Bar Assn. (chmn. lawyer's admission com. 1981, unauthorized practice of law 1982, oldtimer's night 1984-85, speakers bur. 1985), Family Law Council (chmn. legis. com. 1985-86, chmn. seminar series for continuing edn.), Oakland/Livingston Legal Aid Soc. (honor roll 1984), Stepfamily Assn. Am. Inc. (bd. dirs., legal counsel 1984—, bd. dirs. Southeast Mich. chpt. 1981—), Grandparents' Rights Org. (founder, bd. dirs. 1983—). Jewish. Lodge: B'nai B'rith Barristers. Avocation: playing piano. Family and matrimonial, Legal education, Personal injury. Office: Law Offices of Victor & Robbins 555 S Woodward Ave Suite 600 Birmingham MI 48011

VIDA, GLEN JOSEPH, lawyer; b. Elizabeth, N.J., Jan. 1, 1949; s. Alexander Theodore and Rose Margaret (McGarvey) V. A.B., Brown U., 1970; J.D. cum laude, Seton Hall Law Sch., 1974. Bar: N.J., U.S. Dist. Ct. (so. and ea. dists.) N.Y., U.S. Ct. Appeals (3d cir.), U.S. Supreme Ct. Assoc. Rinaldo & Rinaldo, 1974-78; sole practice, Union, N.J., 1978—; officer, dir. Creative Custom Builders, Inc., also 3 condominium conversion corps. Class agt. Brown U. Mem. ABA, N.J. Bar Assn., Union County Bar Assn., Brown U. Alumni Assn. (past pres.). Democrat. Roman Catholic. Contbr. numerous articles on law and edn., students rights to mags. Criminal, State civil litigation, Contracts commercial.

VIDAL-CORDERO, DAVID, lawyer; b. San Juan, Puerto Rico, July 5, 1955; s. David Vidal-Delgado and Ana Milagros Cordero Cardona; m. Carmen Irizarry-Diaz, Nov. 15, 1979. BA magna cum laude, U. Puerto Rico, San Juan, 1977, JD, 1982. Bar: D.C. 1982, U.S. Dist. Ct. D.C. 1983, U.S. Ct. Appeals (D.C. cir.), U.S. Tax Ct. 1983, U.S. Supreme Ct. 1985. Assoc. Haynes & Miller, Washington, 1983—. Mem. ABA, Nat. Assn. Bond Lawyers. Municipal bonds, Private international, Securities. Home: 903 Twin Oaks Dr Potomac MD 20854 Office: Haynes & Miller 1156 15th St NW 4th Floor Washington DC 20005

VIDAS, SCOTT QUINN, lawyer; b. Mpls., Feb. 7, 1953; s. Robert Odin and Donna Jean (Fernstrom) V.; m. Jodell Terese Mandel, Feb. 5, 1977; children: Julie, Brian. BS, U. Minn., 1975; JD, Hamline U., 1982. Bar: Minn. 1982, U.S. Patent Office 1982, U.S. Dist. Ct. Minn. 1983. Assoc. Schroeder, Siegfried, Vidas & Arrett, P.A., Mpls., 1982-85, Vidas & Arrett, P.A., Mpls., 1985—. Mem. ABA, Minn. Bar Assn., Fed. Bar Assn., Am. Intelletual Property Law Assn., Minn. Intellectual Property Law Assn., Order of Silver Gavel. Patent, Trademark and copyright. Home: 2335 Swan Dr Mendota Heights MN 55120 Office: Vidas & Arrett PA 2925 Multifoods Tower 33 S 6th St Minneapolis MN 55402

VIENER, JOHN DAVID, lawyer; b. Richmond, Va., Oct. 18, 1939; s. Reuben and Thelma (Kurtz) V.; m. Karin Erika Bauer, Apr. 7, 1969; children: John David Jr., Katherine Bauer. BA, Yale U., 1961; JD, Harvard U., 1964. Bar: N.Y. State 1965, U.S. Supreme Ct. 1970, U.S. Dist. Ct. (so. dist.) N.Y. 1974, U.S. Tax Ct. 1975. Assoc. Satterlee, Warfield & Stephens, N.Y.C., 1964-69; sole practice N.Y.C., 1969-76; founder, bd. dirs., gen. counsel Foxfire Fund Inc., 1968—; sr. ptnr. Christy & Viener, N.Y.C., 1976—; gen. counsel, bd. dirs. Landmark Communities, Inc., 1970—, Singer Fund, Inc., 1979—; gen. counsel Nat. Cancer Found. Cancer Care, 1982-85, Am. Continental Properties Group, 1978—, Troster, Singer & Co., 1970-77; bd. dirs. Gen. Financiere Immob. et Commer. S.A., 1985—; spl. counsel fin. instns., investment banking and securities concerns; real estate and tax advisor to fgn. instns. Mem. ABA, N.Y. State Bar Assn., Assn. Bar City N.Y. Clubs: Harmonie (N.Y.C.); Manursing Island (Rye, N.Y.). Real property, Securities, Corporations, Taxation. Home: 45 E 62d St New York NY 10021 Office: Christy & Viener 620 Fifth Ave New York NY 10020

VIENNA, KEVIN RICHARD, lawyer, military officer; b. Rochester, N.Y., June 7, 1951; s. Joh Edward and Barbara Ann (Bowers) V.; m. Kathleen Mary Reilly, June 16, 1974; children: Ryan Patrick, Sean Reilly. BS, U.S. Naval Acad., 1973; JD, Coll. William and Mary, 1981. Bar: Va. 1981. Commd. ensign USN, 1973, advanced through grades to lt. comdr., 1981; criminal litigation officer USN, San Diego, 1981-84, staff JAG, 1984-85; exec. officer legal dept. USN, Guam, 1985—. Mem. ABA, Order of the Coif. Roman Catholic. Avocation: triathlete. Military, Criminal. Office: US Naval Legal Service Office Guam Box 177 FPO San Francisco CA 96630-2400

VIEREGG, ROBERT TODD, lawyer; b. Woodstock, Ill., Oct. 3, 1934; s. Robert and Mae (Todd) V.; m. Darla Jean Ax, Dec. 12, 1959 (div. Oct. 1983); children: Dorian Jean Griffin, Robert Todd II; m. Carilane Newman Awalt, May 25, 1985. Student, U. Ill., 1952-53; BA, Mich. State U., 1955; postgrad., U. Chgo., 1968-69; JD cum laude, Northwestern u., 1970. Bar: Ill. 1970, U.S. Dist. Ct. (no. dist.) Ill. 1970. Mgr. Hogates Restaurant, Washington, 1959-60, Town and Country Restaurant, Chgo., 1960-62, Homestead Restaurant, Maywood, Ill., 1962-63; owner Concord Inn Restaurant, Glenview, Ill., 1963-65; registered rep. Dean Witter & Co., Chgo., 1966; from assoc. to ptnr. Sidley & Austin, Chgo., 1970—; constrn. project coordinator Town and Country Restaurant, Chgo., 1966-67. Mem. bd. edn. West Northfield Twp., Northbrook, Ill., 1971-75; bd. dirs. Northbrook Area United Fund, 1966-68, Lyric Opera Chgo. Guild Bd., 1984—. Served with USN, 1956-59. Mem. ABA, Ill. Bar Assn., Chgo. Bar Assn., Law Club Chgo. Republican. Clubs: Union League (Chgo.); Glen View (Ill.). Securities, General corporate. Office: Sidley & Austin One First Nat Plaza Suite 4300 Chicago IL 60603

VIETH, RICK, lawyer, law educator; b. Spartanburg, S.C., Aug. 27, 1947; s. Walter Richard and Evelyn (Lenz) V.; m. Mary Fagan, Nov. 15, 1981 (div. Aug. 1985). B.A., Methodist Coll., 1969; postgrad. Am. U., 1971-74; J.D., U. S.C., 1975. Bar: U.S. Dist. Ct. 1975, U.S. Ct. Appeals (4th cir.) 1976. Assoc., Vieth & Wilson, Spartanburg, 1975-76; tchr. Rutledge Coll., Spartanburg, part-time 1975-78; dep. solicitor, prosecutor Solicitor Office, Spartanburg, 1977-84; ptnr. Henderson, Brandt & Vieth, Spartanburg, 1984—; faculty Spartanburg Meth. Coll., 1984—. Served to E5 USN, 1971-74. Mem. S.C. Trial Lawyers Assn., Am. Trial Lawyers Assn., S.C. Bar Assn., Greenville Fedn. Musicians, ABA. Democrat. Methodist. Club: Pebble Creek Country (chmn. bd. dirs. 1978-80, bd. govs.). Lodge: Sertoma. Avocations: golf, tennis, swim, ski. Criminal, Personal injury, Family and matrimonial. Home: 6A Terrell St Spartanburg SC 29302 Office: Henderson Brandt & Vieth 360 E Henry St Spartanburg SC 29302

VIETOR, HAROLD DUANE, judge; b. Parkersburg, Iowa, Dec. 29, 1931; s. Harold Howard and Alma Johanna (Kreimeyer) V.; m. Dalia Artemisa Zamarripa Cadena, Mar. 24, 1973; children—Christine Elizabeth, John Richard, Greta Maria. B.A., U. Iowa, 1955, J.D., 1958. Bar: Iowa bar. Law clk. U.S. Ct. Appeals 8th Circuit, 1958-59; mem. firm Bleakley Law Offices, Cedar Rapids, Iowa, 1959-65; judge Iowa Dist. Ct., Cedar Rapids, 1965-79; chief judge Iowa Dist. Ct., 1970-79; U.S. dist. judge So. Dist. Iowa, Des Moines, 1979—; chief judge So. Dist. Iowa, 1985—. Contbr. articles to profl. jours. Served with USN, 1952-54. Mem. Iowa Bar Assn. (pres. jr. sect. 1966-67), Iowa Judges Assn. (pres. 1975-76), ABA, Am. Judicature Soc., Iowa Hist. Soc. Office: 211 US Courthouse Des Moines IA 50309

VIGDOR, JUSTIN LEONARD, lawyer; b. N.Y.C., July 13, 1929; s. Irving Barton and Ida (Devins) V.; m. Louise Martin, Mar. 8, 1952; children: Robert, Jill Vigdor-Feldman, Lisa Vigdor-Peck, Wendy. LL.B. magna cum laude, St. John's U., 1951; LL.M., N.Y. U., 1952. Bar: N.Y. 1951, U.S. Supreme Ct 1951, Fla. 1975. Partner firm Mousaw, Vigdor, Reeves Heilbronner and Kroll, Rochester, N.Y., 1958—; dir. adv. bd. Key Bank Cen. N.Y.; bd. dirs. Computer Consoles, Inc., IEC Electronics Corp., Monroe Prepaid Legal Service Plan, Automobile Club Rochester; former mem. faculty Nazareth Coll. Contbr. articles to profl. jours. Bd. dirs. Downtown Devel. Corp., Mary Cariola Children's Ctr., also panelist, Rochester Area Found., Al Sigl Ctr. for Rehab. Agys., also past pres.; chmn. N.Y. State 10LA Fund. Served with (JAGC) AUS, 1952-54. Recipient Community Service award, 1960, award for Service to Community and Legal Profession, 1983, Disting. Service award N.Y. State Assn. County Clks., 1985. Fellow Am. Bar Found., N.Y. Bar Found.; mem. ABA (Ho. of Dels.), Fla. Bar Assn., N.Y. State Bar Assn. (past pres., Ho. of Dels.), Monroe County Bar Assn. (past pres.), Am. Judicature Soc. (dir.), Estate Planning Council, Am. Arbitration Assn. (nat. panel 1962—), N.Y. State C. of C. (Distinguished Service award 1964). Democrat. Jewish religion. Clubs: Irondequoit Country, Ski Valley. General corporate, Securities, Real property. Home: 1880 Clover St Rochester NY 14618 Office: 6th Floor First Federal Plaza Rochester NY 14614

VIGIL, CAROL JEAN, lawyer; b. Santa Fe, Oct. 24, 1947; d. Martin Jr. and Evelyn (Abeita) V.; m. Philip D. Palmer, Dec. 16, 1977; 1 child, Erika L. BS, U. N.M., 1974, JD, 1978. Bar: N.M. 1979. Fellow in Indian law Indian Pueblo Legal Services, Santa Ana Pueblo, N.M., 1978-80; appellate div. clk. to atty. gen. State of N.Mex., Santa Fe, 1980-84; sole practice Santa Fe, 1984-87; tribal atty. Tesuque Pueblo, N.M., 1985—; tribal prosecutor Eight No. Indian Pueblo Council Child Abuse Prosecution Project, San Juan Pueblo, N.M. 1986—. Sec. No. N.M. Legal Services, Santa Fe, 1981—, chmn., 1982-83, vice chmn. 1984-85; bd. dirs. Santa Fe Mountain Ctr., 1985—; bd. dirs., sec., treas., Pueblo Ins. Agy., 1985—. Mem. ABA, N.M. Bar Assn., Indian Bar Assn., Delta Theta Phi. Democrat. Roman Catholic. Avocation: art: print and original drawings. Indian law, Family and matrimonial, General practice. Home and Office: 214 McKenzie Santa Fe NM 87501

VIGIL, CHARLES S., lawyer; b. Trinidad, Colo., June 9, 1912; s. J.U. and Andreita (Maes) V.; m. Kathleen A. Liebert, Jan. 2, 1943; children: David Charles Edward, Marcia Kathleen. LL.B., U. Colo., 1936. Bar: Colo. 1936. Dep. dist. atty. 3d Jud. Dist. Colo., 1937-42, asst. dist. atty., 1946-51; U.S. atty. Dist. Colo., 1951-53; pvt. practice law Denver.; Dir., sec. Las Animas Co. (Colo); ARC. Author: Saga of Casimiro Barela. Bd. dirs. Family and Children's Service Denver, Colo. Humane Soc.; dir. Auraria Community Center; mem. Bishop's com. on housing. Served as ensign to lt. (s.g.) USCG, 1942-46. Recipient award of civil merit Spain, 1960, award of civil merit Colo. Centennial Expn. Bd., 1976; award Colo. Chicano Bar Assn., 1979. Mem. Internat. Law Assn., ABA, Fed. Bar Assn., Colo. Bar Assn. (bd. govs.), So. Colo. Bar Assn., Hispanic Bar Colo. (bd. dirs.), Am. Judicature Soc., Internat. Bar Assn., Inter-Am. Bar, V.F.W. (comdr.), Am. Legion (comdr.), Nat. Assn. Def. Lawyers, Am. Trial Lawyers Assn., Lambda Chi Alpha, Elk, Eagle, Cootie. Clubs: Lions, Denver Athletic, Columbine Country, City of Denver, Trinidad Country. Home: 1085 Sherman St Denver CO 80203 Office: 485 Capitol Life Center 225 E 16th Ave Denver CO 80203

VIGIL, DAVID CHARLES, lawyer; b. Bklyn., Jan. 29, 1944; s. Charles S. and Kathleen A. (Liebert) V. B.A., U. Colo., 1966; J.D., U. N.Mex., 1969. Bar: Colo. 1969, U.S. Dist. Ct. Colo. 1969, U.S. Ct. Appeals (10th cir.) 1969, U.S. Supreme Ct. 1974. Sole practice, Denver, 1969-80; ptnr. Vigil & Vigil, Denver, 1980—. Nat. Inst for Trial Advocacy grantee, 1983. Mem. Colo. Bar Assn. (ethics com. 1973-79), Denver Bar Assn. (jud. selection and benefits com. 1975—), Assn. Trial Lawyers Am., Assn. Trial Lawyers Colo., Colo. Hispanic Bar Assn. Democrat. Roman Catholic. Clubs: City of Denver; Columbine County (Littleton, Colo.). Lodge: Elks. Federal civil litigation, State civil litigation, Personal injury. Office: Vigil & Vigil 485 Capitol Life Ctr Denver CO 80203

VIKTORA, RICHARD EMIL, lawyer; b. Chgo., July 1, 1943; s. Emil J. and Lillian B. (Smatlak) V.; m. Anne Marie Kus, Feb. 20, 1971. B.S., U. Ill., 1965; J.D., John Marshall Law Sch., 1969. Bar: Ill. 1969, U.S. Dist. Ct. (no. dist.) Ill. 1969, U.S. Ct. Appeals (7th cir.) 1970, U.S. Supreme Ct. 1975, N.Y. 1981, U.S. Dist. Ct. (so. and ea. dists.) N.Y. 1983. Assoc. Menk, Johnson, & Bishop, Chgo., 1969-73; instr. John Marshall Law Sch., Chgo., 1970-73; litigation group counsel, regulatory counsel, asst. sec. G.D. Searle & Co., Skokie, Ill., 1973-80; asst. sec., dir. gen. services Revlon, Inc., also asst. sec. Revlon Group, Inc., N.Y.C., 1980—. Zoning adminstr. Village of Bartlett (Ill.), 1974, chmn. Plan Commn., 1975, trustee, 1975-79. Mem. ABA, Ill. State Bar Assn., Chgo. Bar Assn., Def. Research Inst., Am. Corp. Counsel Assn., Assn. Trial Lawyers Am., Def. Assn. N.Y., Westchester-Fairfield Corp. Counsel Assn., Pharm. Mfrs. Assn. (product liability com.), Delta Theta Phi. Republican. Roman Catholic. Club: Anvil (East Dundee, Ill.). Lodge: Masons. Personal injury, State civil litigation, Federal civil litigation. Home: 11 Saddle Hill Ln Stamford CT 06903 Office: Revlon Inc 767 Fifth Ave New York NY 10153

VILARDO, LAWRENCE JOSEPH, lawyer, educator; b. Buffalo, June 6, 1955; s. Lawrence John and Dolores Marie (Catalano) V.; m. Jeanne Susan Gambino, Sept. 25, 1982; 1 child, Brigid Anne. BA summa cum laude, Canisius Coll., 1977; JD magna cum laude, Harvard U., 1980. Bar: N.Y. 1981, U.S. Dist. Ct. (we. dist.) N.Y. 1981, U.S. Ct. Appeals (3d, 5th and 11th cirs.) 1981, U.S. Ct. Appeals (2d cir.) 1983. Law clk. to presiding justice U.S. Ct. Appeals (5th cir.), Dallas, 1980-81; assoc. Damon & Morey, Buffalo, 1981-86; ptnr. Connors & Vilardo, Buffalo, 1986—; lectr. Canisius Coll., Buffalo, 1983—, appellate practice U. Buffalo, 1986—. Editor Litigation mag., 1986—. Mem. ABA, N.Y. State Bar Assn. (lectr.), Erie County Bar Assn., Western N.Y. Trial Lawyers Assn., Nat. Fedn. Paralegal Assns. (lectr.), Western N.Y. Paralegal Assn. (lectr.). Democrat. Roman Catholic. Federal civil litigation, State civil litigation, Criminal. Home: 265 Grimsby Rd Tonawanda NY 14223 Office: Connors & Vilardo 42 Delaware Ave Buffalo NY 14202

VILDERS, KURT RONALD, lawyer; b. Detroit, Oct. 17, 1953. B in Gen. Studies, U. Mich., 1975; JD, Wayne State U., 1979. Bar: Mich. 1979, U.S. Dist. Ct. (ea. dist.) Mich. 1981. Assoc. Dressell and Wright, Birmingham, Mich., 1979-80; staff atty. Met. Savs. Assn., Farmington Hills, Mich., 1980-82; sr. atty., asst. sec. Mich. Nat. Corp., Bloomfield, 1982-86; sr. atty. Volkswagen of Am. Inc., Troy, Mich., 1986—. Mem. ABA, Comml. Law League, Oakland City Bar Assn. Real property, General corporate, Banking. Office: Volkswagen of Am Inc PO Box 3951 Troy MI 48007

VILLAUME, PHILIP GORDON, lawyer; b. St. Paul, Sept. 9, 1949; s. Paul Eugene and Katherine Agnes (Kielty) V.; m. Kay Ann Hanratty, Sept. 30, 1979; children—Cory Philip, Allie Katharine. B.A. magna cum laude, Macalaster Coll., 1972, postgrad., 1972; M. Criminal Justice Program, Mankato State Coll., 1972; J.D., Hamline U., 1979. Bar: Minn. 1979, U.S. Dist. Ct. Minn. 1979, Wis. 1984, U.S. Supreme Ct. 1984. Probation and parole officer 2d jud. dist., Ramsey County Dept. Ct. Services, St. Paul, 1972-76; pres., owner Villaume Investigative Services, St. Paul, 1977-81; prin. Philip G. Villaume and Assocs., St. Paul and Mpls.; tchr. course Sibley Sr. High Sch., West St. Paul, 1972; instr. course Macalaster Coll., St. Paul, 1974, Maplewood Community Edn. Program, Minn., 1975; instr. legal asst. program Inver Hills Community Coll., Inver Grove Heights, Minn., 1980-82; lectr., vol. atty. Chrysalis Ctr. for Women; bd. mem. Ramsey County Atty. Referral System; bd. dirs. Families in Crisis, Lawyers Concerned for Lawyers, 1985—; apptd. Civil Commitment Def. Project, Fed. Pub. Def. Panel, Ramsey County Criminal Def. Project, Hennepin County Juvenile Def. Project. Named one of Outstanding Young Men in Am., 1985. Mem. ABA, Assn. Trial Lawyers Am., Minn. Trial Lawyers Assn. (ednl. coordinator criminal law sect. 1984—, lectr. affirmative bus. communication, continuing legal edn. 1983), Hennepin County Bar Assn., Ramsey County Bar Assn., Nat. Assn. Criminal Def. Lawyers, Hamline U. Sch. Law Alumni Assn. (pres.), Alpha Kappa Delta, Sigma Nu Phi. Home: 446 Mount Curve Blvd Saint Paul MN 55105 Office: Shepard Park Office Ctr Suite 180 2177 Youngman Ave Saint Paul MN 55116 Office: United Lbr Ctr Suite 592 312 Central Ave SE Minneapolis MN 55414

VILLAVASO, STEPHEN DONALD, lawyer; b. New Orleans, July 12, 1949; s. Donald Philip and Jacklyn (Tully) V.; m. Regina Smith, Apr. 17, 1971; children: Christine Regina, Stephen Warner. BS in Econs., U. New

Orleans, 1971, M in Urban and Regional Planning, 1976; JD, Loyola U., New Orleans, 1981. Bar: La. 1982. Urban and regional planner Barnard & Thomas, New Orleans, 1976-78; dir. analysis and planning City of New Orleans, 1978-81, counsel for planning and devel., 1983-84; dir. planning and environ. affairs Tecon Realty, New Orleans, 1981-83; v.p. Anthony Mumphrey & Assocs., New Orleans, 1984-86; v.p. for planning and project mgmt. Morphy, Makofsky, Mumphrey & Masson, New Orleans, 1986—; bd. dirs. New Orleans Traffic and Transp. Bur., 1981-86, Riverfront Awareness, New Orleans, 1984-86; guest lectr., adj. prof. Sch. Urban and Regional Studies, U. New Orleans, 1976—; spl. instr. grad. studies in urban planning So. U. New Orleans, 1987—. Served with USN, 1971-74. Named one of Outstanding Young Men of Am., 1980, 82. Mem. ABA, Am. Inst. of Cert. Planners, Am. Planning Assn. (pres. La. div. 1980-84, disting. service award 1985), Urban Land Inst., La. Bar Assn., Phi Kappa Phi, Delta Sigma Pi (pres. 1971). Democrat. Roman Catholic. Avocations: philately, camping, travel. Zoning land use, Local government, Real property. Home: 4671 Knight Dr New Orleans LA 70127

VIMONT, RICHARD ELGIN, lawyer; b. Lexington, Ky., Aug. 3, 1936; s. Richard Thompson and Christine Frazee (Anderson) V.; m. Louise Marie Salyer, Sept. 10, 1960; children—Richard Thompson II, Margaret Anderson; m. 2d, Martha Jane Murray, Nov. 13, 1982. B.S., U. Ky., 1958, J.D., 1960. Bar: Ky. 1960, U.S. Dist. Ct. (ea. dist.) Ky. 1960, U.S. Dist. Ct. (we. dist.) Ky. 1964, U.S. Ct. Appeals (6th cir.) 1964, U.S. Supreme Ct. 1966. Assoc., Brown, Sledd and McCann, 1960-64; ptnr. Core, Vimont and Combs, 1964-68, Breckinridge, Vimont and Amato, 1968-70, Anggelis, Vimont and Bunch, 1970-78, Vimont and Wills, Lexington, Ky., 1978—; city commr., Lexington, 1971-72; asst. commonwealth atty., 1973-75; vis. prof. Transylvania U., 1978-80. Mem. ABA, Am. Acad. Trial Attys., Ky. Bar Assn., Ky. Acad. Trial Attys., Fayette County Bar Assn., Lexington C. of C., Thoroughbred Club of Am. Democrat. Mem. Disciple of Christ Ch. Clubs: Lexington Polo, Lexington, Lafayette, Spindletop Hall. General practice. Office: 155 E Main St 3rd floor Lexington KY 40507-1317

VINCENT, ADRIAN ROGER, lawyer; b. Daggett, Mich., May 21, 1948; s. Adrian Donald and Dorothy (Heiden) V. BA, U. Mich., 1970; JD, Wayne State U., 1973. Bar: Mich. 1973, U.S. Dist. Ct. (we. dist.) Mich. 1974, U.S. Supreme Ct. 1979, U.S. Ct. Appeals (6th cir.) 1982, Ill. 1986. Ptnr. Anderson/Green/Vincent & Ingram P.C., Lansing, Mich., 1973-85; pvt. practice cons., Chgo., 1985—. Bd. dirs. Legal Aid Ctr. Mich., 1976-80, legal counsel Planned Parenthood Affilates of Mich., Lansing, 1984. Mem. ABA, Chgo. Bar Assn., Assn. Trial Lawyers Am., Ill. Bar Assn. Insurance, State civil litigation, Personal injury. Home: 2131 N Clark Chicago IL 60614

VINCENT, ORESTE, lawyer; b. Bklyn., May 7, 1924; s. Oreste F. and Mary (Fierro) Sicignamo; children—Thomas E., Richard C., Harry O., John M. Student, U. Rochester, 1943-44; St. John's U., 1946; LL.B., Albany Law Sch., 1949. Bar: N.Y. 1950, U.S. Dist. Ct. (no. and so. dist.) N.Y. 1960, U.S. Supreme Ct. 1958. Practice in Catskill, N.Y., 1950—; dir. Cairo br. State Bank of Albany, 1970-73. Bd. mgrs. Green County Meml. Hosp., 1976-80; mem. N.Y. State Park Commn., 1976-77. Served with USN, 1942-45. Mem. Greene County Bar Assn., N.Y. State Bar Assn., N.Y. Trial Lawyers Assn., Am. Trial Lawyers Assn., ABA, Am. Legion. Republican. Clubs: Elks, Masons. Personal injury, State civil litigation, Probate. Address: 329 Main St Catskill NY 12414

VINCENT, THOMAS PHILIP, lawyer; b. Greenfield, Mass., Mar. 22, 1951; s. Donald Wallace and Mary Lou (Lockhart) V. B.A. magna cum laude, U. Mass., 1974; J.D., So. Meth. U., 1977. Bar: Tex. 1977, Mass. 1978, U.S. Dist. Ct. Mass. 1978, U.S. Ct. Appeals (1st cir.) 1978, U.S. Supreme Ct. 1986. Sole practice, Northampton, Mass., 1978-79; assoc. firm Fogel & Fogel, P.C., Northampton, 1979-81; ptnr. firm Vincent & Green, Northampton, 1981—. Named in resolution of commendation Western Mass. Legal Services, 1983-86. Mem. Hampshire County Bar Assn., Mass. Bar Assn., ABA, Mass. Acad. Trial Attys., Assn. Trial Lawyers Am. Democrat. Methodist. Club: Northampton Lions (v.p. 1983-84, pres. 1984-85). State civil litigation, Criminal, Family and matrimonial. Office: Vincent & Green 5 Hampton Ave PO Box 210 Northampton MA 01060

VINCENTI, SHELDON ARNOLD, legal educator, lawyer; b. Ogden, Utah, Sept. 4, 1938; s. Arnold Joseph and Mae (Burch) V.; m. Elaine Cathryn Wacker, June 18, 1964; children—Matthew Lewis, Amanda Jo. A.B., Harvard U., 1960, J.D., 1963. Bar: Utah 1963. Sole practice law, Ogden, 1966-67; ptnr. Lowe and Vincenti, Ogden, 1968-70; legis. asst. to U.S. Rep. Gunn McKay, Washington, 1971-72, adminstrv. asst., 1973; prof., assoc. dean U. of Idaho Coll. of Law, Moscow, Idaho, 1973-83, dean, prof. law, 1983—. Legal education. Home: 2480 W Twin Rd Moscow ID 83843 Office: Coll Law U Idaho Moscow ID 83843

VINCI, MARTIN F.P., III, lawyer; b. McKees Rocks, Pa., Dec. 3, 1954; s. Michael Anthony and Helen V. (Divecchio) V.; m. Janice Cianchetti, Dec. 1, 1979. BA, U. Pitts, 1976; JD, Duquesne U., 1979. Bar: Pa. 1979, U.S. Dist. Ct. (we. dist.) Pa. 1979, U.S. Ct. Appeals (3d cir.) 1981. Law clerk L. Tarasi & Assocs., Pitts., 1977-79; assoc. Tarasi & Tighe, Pitts., 1979-81; ptnr. Law Offices of Martin F.P. Vinci III, Coraopolis, Pa., 1981—; mng. assoc. DuPlaga, Tocci, Coraopolis, Pa., 1985—; jud. law clk. Allegheny County Ct., Pitts., 1982—; gen. counsel Ohio River Land and Transp. Co., Pitts., 1986. Chmn. Stowe Twp. Dem. Party, 1985-86; mem. Italian Heritage Soc. Mem. ABA, Pa. Bar Assn., Pa. Trial Lawyers Assn., Assn. Trial Lawyers Am., Am. Law Enforcement Officers. Roman Catholic. Lodge: A.L.E.O. Avocations: drummer, building musical instruments, hockey, computers. Personal injury, Family and matrimonial, General corporate. Home and Office: 612 Main St McKees Rocks PA 15136 Office: 612 Main St McKees Rocks PA 15136

VINEBERG, PHILIP FISCHEL, lawyer; b. Mattawa, Ont., Can., July 21, 1914; s. Malcolm and Rebecca (Phillips) V.; m. Miriam S. Schachter, Dec. 19, 1939; children: Robert S., Michael D. B.A., McGill U., 1935, M.A., 1936, B.C.L., 1939; postgrad., Ecole Libre des Scis. Politiques, Paris, France, 1935-36; LL.D. (hon.), 1980. Bar: Called to bar, Que. 1939, appointed Queen's Counsel 1959. Since practiced in Montreal; mem. firm Phillips & Vineberg, 1939—; various lectureships and profesorships in econs., polit. sci., comml/ law and corp. law McGill U., 1939-68; chmn. consultative com. Que. Dept. Revenue. Author: The French Franc and the Gold Standard, 1936; Contbr.: chpts. to Money Credit and Banking, 1940, Studies in Canadian Company Law, 1968; contbg. editor: chpts. to Prentice Hall Income Taxation in Canada; Contbr. articles to profl. jours. Mem. Ry. Conciliation Bd., 1958, 60; v.p. Canadian Friends of Alliance Israelite Universelle; trustee Jewish Gen. Hosp., Canadian Inst. Research Pub. Policy, Inst. for Reseach on Pub. Policy; chmn. bd. govs. Canadian Tax Found., 1966-67; bd. govs. YMHA, McGill U., Cardoza Law Sch., Barilan U.; pres. fellows Found. for Legal Research in Can., 1973-76. Fellow Brandeis U., Bar-Ilan U., U.S. Coll. Trial Lawyers.; Apptd. officer Order of Canada, 1974. Mem. Canadian Bar Assn. (pres. Que. br. 1973-74, nat. exec. com. 1974-75), Bar Province Que. (vice chmn. 1969-70), Bar of Montreal (batonnier 1969-70), Internat. Fiscal Assn. (pres. Canadian br. 1974-76, internat. exec.). Corporate taxation, General corporate. Home: 32 Summit Crescent, Westmount, PQ Canada H3Y 1L3 Office: 5 Place Ville Marie, Montreal, PQ Canada H3B 2G2

VINES, LEONARD DEAN, lawyer; b. St. Louis, Nov. 29, 1946; s. Ben and Lillian Vines; m. Deborah Ellen Silver, Aug. 14, 1977; children—Stefanie, Jeffrey, Randall. B.S. with honors, U. Ill., 1969; J.D., Washington U., St. Louis, 1972. Bar: Mo. 1972, U.S. Dist. Ct. (ea. dist.) Mo. 1975, U.S. Tax Ct. 1975, U.S. Ct. Appeals (8th cir.) 1979. Ptnr., Ziercher and Hocker, St. Louis, 1972-78, Vines, Kreuter and Kruger, St. Louis, 1980-83, Vines, Jones, Ross, Kraner and Rubin and predecessor, St. Louis, 1983—; mcpl. judge City of Creve Coeur, Mo., 1986—. Mem. Mo. Bar Assn., Met. Bar Assn. St. Louis (chmn. bus. franchise law com.), Beta Gamma Sigma. Assoc. editor Urban Law Ann., 1971-72; contbr. articles to legal publs. General practice, General corporate, Franchise law. Office: 120 S Central Ave Saint Louis MO 63105

VINEYARD, C L, lawyer; b. Hale County, Tex., Nov. 9, 1927; s. Clarence Calvin and Louella Ruby (Ray) V.; m. Nora Lee Crawford, July 15, 1978; children from previous marriage: John, Paul, Anne. AA, Valley Coll., San Bernardino, Calif., 1953; BA in Admnstrn. and Acctg., Claremont Men's Coll., 1955; JD, U. Calif., Los Angeles, 1959. Bar: Calif. 1960. Ptnr. King & Mussell, San Bernardino, Calif., 1960-71; sole practice San Bernardino, Calif., 1971-74; ptnr. Eckhardt, Youmans & Vineyard, San Bernardino, Calif., 1974-75; assoc. Sprague, Milligan & Beswick, San Bernardino, Calif., 1975-76, sole practice, 1976—; judge pro tem San Bernardino County Mcpl. Ct., 1975-81; arbitrator personal injury panel San Bernardino Superior Ct., commr. 1975—; prin. referee Calif. State Bar, Los Angeles, 1979—. Served with USN, 1944-48. Mem. ABA, Am. Arbitration Assn. (arbitrator for claims, comml., constrn. and med. malpractice), San Bernardino County Bar Assn., Internat. Assn. for Ins. Counsel, Am. Bd. Trial Advocates, Calif. Trial Lawyers Assn., Calif. State Bar (prin. referee state bar ct.), Phi Delta Phi. Republican. Lodges: Lions, Elks, Masons, Shriners. State civil litigation, General practice, Insurance. Home: 808 E Avery San Bernardino CA 92404 Office: Pacific Savs Plaza 330 N D St Suite 430 San Bernardino CA 92401

VINICK, PHILIP BROD, lawyer; b. N.Y.C., Feb. 26, 1951; s. Milton and Marcia (Ranik) V.; m. Gina Magda Brod-Vinick, Dec. 19, 1976; children: Merisa, Benjamin. AB, Rutgers U., 1973, JD, 1976. Bar: N.J. 1976, U.S. Dist. Ct. N.J. 1976, N.Y. 1983, U.S. Ct. Appeals (3d cir.) 1983, U.S. Supreme Ct. 1985. Assoc. Weltchek, Prupis & Ritz, Elizabeth, N.J., 1977-83; assoc. Cohn & Lifland, Saddle Brook, N.J., 1983-85, ptnr., 1986—. Pres. Concerned Citizens for Chronic Psychiat. Adults, Piscataway, N.J., 1979-81, trustee, 1979-86. Mem. ABA, N.J. Bar Assn., Union County Bar Assn., Bergen County Bar Assn., Assn. Trial Lawyers Am., Internat. Assn. Jewish Lawyers and Jurists. Democrat. Avocation: running. State civil litigation, Federal civil litigation, Personal injury. Home: 27 Benjamin Dr Springfield NJ 07081 Office: Cohn & Lifland Park 80 Plaza West 1 Saddle Brook NJ 07662

VINING, (GEORGE) JOSEPH, law educator; b. Fulton, Mo., Mar. 3, 1938; s. D. Rutledge and Margaret (McClanahan) V.; m. Alice Marshall Williams, Sept. 18, 1965; children: George Joseph IV, Spencer Carter. B.A., Yale U., 1959, Cambridge U., 1961; M.A., Cambridge U., 1970; J.D., Harvard U., 1964. Bar: D.C. 1965. Atty. Office Dep. Atty. Gen., Dept. Justice, Washington, 1965; asst. to exec. dir. Nat. Crime Commn., 1966; assoc. firm Covington and Burling, Washington, 1966-69; asst. prof. law U. Mich., 1969-72; assoc. prof. U. Mich., Ann Arbor, 1972-74, prof., 1974-85; Hutchins prof. U. Mich., 1985—. Author: Legal Identity, 1978; The Authoritative and the Authoritarian, 1986. Bd. dirs., sec. Am. Friends of Cambridge U. NEH sr. fellow, 1982-83. Mem. ABA, D.C. Bar Assn., Am. Law Inst. Club: Century (N.Y.C.). Administrative and regulatory, General corporate, Jurisprudence. Office: U Mich 337 Hutchins Hall Ann Arbor MI 48109-1215

VINING, ROBERT LUKE, JR., judge; b. Chatsworth, Ga., Mar. 30, 1931; m. Martha Sue Cates; 1 child, Laura. A.B., J.D., U. Ga., 1959. Sole practice Dalton, Ga., 1958-69; dist. atty. Whitfield County, Dalton, 1958-69; judge Whitfield County Superior Ct., Dalton, 1969-79, U.S. Dist. Ct. Ga., 1979—. Judicial administration. Office: US Dist Ct 2167 US Courthouse 75 Spring St SW Atlanta GA 30303 *

VINSON, C. ROGER, federal judge; b. Cadiz, Ky., Feb. 19, 1940; m. Ellen Vinson; children: Matt, Todd, Kate, Patrick, Joey. BS, U.S. Naval Acad., 1962; JD, Vanderbilt U., 1971. Commd. 2d lt. USN, 1962, advanced through grades to lt., resigned, 1968; assoc. Beggs & Lane, Pensacola, Fla., 1971-83; judge U.S. Dist. Ct. (no. dist.) Fla., Pensacola, 1983—. Office: US Dist Courthouse 100 N Palafox St Pensacola FL 32501 *

VINSON, ROGER, federal judge. Judge, U.S. Dist. Ct. (no. dist.) Fla., Pensacola. Judicial administration. Office: US Courthouse 100 N Palafox St Room 105 Pensacola FL 32501 *

VIOLANTE, JOSEPH ANTHONY, lawyer, consultant; b. Jersey City, June 15, 1950; s. Carmine Joseph and Rosa (Cardillo) V.; m. Linda Lee Munn, July 5, 1972; children: Joseph Anthony II, Christy Anne, Gina Lee. Student, St. Peter's Coll., Jersey City, 1972-74; BA, U. N.Mex., 1975; JD, U. La., 1980. Bar: Calif. 1981, U.S. Dist. Ct. (cen. dist.) Calif. 1982. Sole practice Thousand Oaks, Calif., 1981-85; atty., cons. Bd. Vet. Appeals, Washington, 1985—. Asst. coach Am. Youth Soccer Orgn., Thousand Oaks, 1981-84, Little League, Thousand Oaks, 1981-84; del. John Glenn Calif. Dem. Presdl. Primary, Thousand Oaks, 1984; active campaign Combined Fed., Washington, 1985; vol. Nat. League Families of Prisoners of War/Missing in Action, Washington, 1986—. Served with USMC, 1969-72. Mem. ABA, Calif. Bar Assn., Conejo Valley Bar Assn., Italian-Am. Bar Assn., VFW (comdr. 1984-85), DAV (lifetime), Am. Legion, 3D Marine Div. Assn. Democrat. Roman Catholic. Avocations: collecting coins, soccer, softball, reading. Administrative and regulatory, Real property, Entertainment. Home: 15121 Narrows Ln Bowie MD 20716 Office: VA Bd Vet Appeals 811 Vermont NW Washington DC 20420

VIRELLI, LOUIS JAMES, JR., lawyer; b. Phila., Nov. 4, 1948; s. Louis James and Elsie Antoinette (Colombo) V.; m. Barbara Ann Rotella, Aug. 22, 1970; children: Louis J. III, Christopher F. B in Mech. Engring., Villanova U., 1970; JD, U. Tenn., 1972. Bar: Pa. 1973, U.S. Ct. Customs and Patent Appeals 1974, U.S. Dist. Ct. (we. dist.) Pa. 1976, U.S. Dist. Ct. (ea. dist.) Pa. 1977, U.S. Ct. Appeals (9th cir.) 1980, U.S. Ct. Appeals (D.C. cir.) 1982, U.S. Supreme Ct. 1982. Patent atty. Sperry New Holland Co., New Holland, Pa., 1973-74; assoc. counsel Westinghouse Co., Pitts., 1974-76; assoc. Paul & Paul, Phila., 1976-80, ptnr., 1980-84; patent counsel Nat. Starch and Chem. Corp., Bridgewater, N.J., 1984—; arbitrator U.S. Dist. Ct. (ea. dist.) Pa., Phila., 1982-84. Mem. ABA, N.J. Patent Law Assn., Phila. Patent Law Assn., Am. Soc. Mech. Engring. Roman Catholic. Clubs: Springhaven (Wallingford, Pa.); Seaview Country (Absecon, N.J.). Patent, Trademark and copyright, General corporate. Office: Nat Starch and Chem Corp 10 Finance Ave Bridgewater NJ 08807

VIRTUE, MAXINE BOORD, lawyer; b. Omaha, Oct. 1, 1909; d. Samuel Francis and Kathryn (Kerr) Boord; m. John B. Virtue, June 29, 1935; children—Veronica, Martha. B.A., Northwestern U., 1931; LL.B., Yale U., 1935. Bar: Kans. 1938, Mich. 1947. Asst. regional atty. Farm Security Adminstrn., Lincoln, Nebr. and Indpls., 1935-38; asst. atty. gen. Kans., 1945-46; research assoc. U. Mich., Ann Arbor, 1948-50; dir. study of basic structure children's services James Foster Found., Ann Arbor, 1950-52; lectr. law and social work U. Mich., 1953-61; assoc. firm Miller, Canfield, Paddock & Stone, Detroit, 1954-55; asst. atty. gen. State of Mich., 1955-57, head Div. Mun. Affairs and consumer Protection Div., 1960-64; lectr. law and social work Smith Coll., summer 1964-65; head Div. Mcpl. Affairs, Social, Mental Problems, Atty. Gen.'s Office, State of Mich., 1964-73; mem. firm Virtue and Carpenter, Ann Arbor, 1973-77; counsel Harris, Lax, Gregg & Guenzel, Ann Arbor, 1977—. Trustee, First Congregational Ch., Ypsilanti, Mich., 1968-69, United Way, Ypsilanti, 1969-70; founder, trustee Washtenaw County Coordinating Council for Children at Risk, 1976-80, 82—; trustee Center for Occupational and Personalized Edn., Inc., 1975-79, v.p., 1978-79; trustee Mich. Interprofl. Commn. on Marriage, Divorce and Family, Inc., 1979—; mem. Ypsilanti Mayor's Com. on Taxation, 1979-80; spl. investigator State of Mich. Grievance Commn., 1980; spl. counsel State of Mich. Grievance Commn., 1980—, others. Recipient Award of Merit, Atty. Gen. Frank J. Kelley, 1964, 1973, others. Fellow Am. Bar Found.; mem. ABA (dir. state com. 1953-55, chmn. family cts. and family judges com. 1979-82, mem. family law sect., mem. antitrust law com. 1960—), State Bar Mich. (treas. family law sect. 1974-75, chmn. 1976-77, chmn. family ct. com. 1965-81, co-chmn. 1983—, ex-officio mem. council 1981—). Democrat. Author: Laws Affecting Women in Kansas, 1946; Survey of Metropolitan Courts: Detroit Area, 1950; Public Services to Children in Michigan: A Study of Basic Structure, 1954; Judge Medina Speaks, 1954; Family Cases in Court, 1956; Metropolitan Court Survey: Final Report, 1962, others; contbr. articles to profl. jours. Local government, Librarianship, Family and matrimonial. Office: 320 City Center Bldg Ann Arbor MI 48104

VISH, DONALD H., lawyer, educator; b. Ft. Benning, Ga., Jan. 18, 1945; s. D.H. Jr. and Dorris (Parrish) V.; m. Catherine Hamilton, Aug. 20, 1966 (div. 1986); children: Donald Hamilton, Daphne Mershon. BA in English, Bellarmine Coll., 1968; JD cum laude, U. Louisville, 1971. Bar: Ky. 1971, Fla. 1972, U.S. Ct. Appeals (6th cir.) 1974. Sec., gen. counsel Gen. Energy Corp., Lexington, Ky., 1978-83; ptnr. firm Wyatt, Tarrant & Combs, Lexington, 1980—; assoc. prof. Coll. of Law, U. Ky., Lexington, part-time 1977-80, adj. assoc. prof. mineral law, 1979-85. Contbr. to legal ency. American Law of Mining, 2d edit., 1984; co-editor, contbr. Coal Law and Regulation, 1983. Trustee Sayre Sch., Lexington, 1980—, chmn. bd., 1986—. Fellow Am. Bar Found.; mem. Am. Law Inst., Eastern Mineral Law Found. (trustee 1979—, exec. com. 1979-82, chmn. coal subcom. 1984-85), Am. Judicature Soc., Fla. Bar Assn., Ky. Bar Assn. (ethics com. 1983-85), Am. Soc. Corp. Secs., English-Speaking Union., Bluegrass Charity Ball Assn. Republican. Episcopalian. Clubs: Pendennis (Louisville); Keeneland (Lexington). General corporate, Legal education, Oil and gas leasing. Home: 1146 Turkey Foot Rd Lexington KY 40502 Office: Wyatt Tarrant & Combs 1100 Kincaid Towers Lexington KY 40507

VISSER, KEVIN JAMES, lawyer; b. Warrensburg, Mo., Nov. 10, 1956; s. Harold E. and Irene T. (Tompkins) V.; m. Cynthia A. Christian, Sept. 1, 1979. BS in Econs., Cen. Mo. State U., 1977; JD, U. Iowa, 1980. Bar: Iowa 1980, U.S. Dist. Ct. (no. and so. dists.) Iowa 1980, U.S. Ct. Appeals (8th cir.) 1983, U.S. Supreme Ct. 1986. Ptnr. Moyer & Bergman, Cedar Rapids, Iowa, 1980—. Mem. ABA, Iowa Bar Assn., Linn County Bar Assn. Methodist. Labor, Federal civil litigation, Family and matrimonial. Office: Moyer & Bergman 2720 1st Ave Cedar Rapids IA 52402

VITIELLO, MICHAEL, lawyer, educator; b. N.Y.C., May 3, 1946; s. Michael and Ruth Frances (Weishaupt) V.; m. Erie Pearson, June 10, 1972; children: Elizabeth P., James M. BA, Swarthmore (Pa.) Coll., 1969; JD, U. Pa., 1974. Pa. 1974, N.J. 1975, U.S. Dist. Ct. (ea. dist.) Pa. 1976. Law clk. to judge Pa. Superior Ct., Phila., 1974-77; prof. law Loyola U., New Orleans, 1977—. Co-author: District Attorney's Trial Manual, 1980; contbr. articles to profl. jours. Cons. atty. ACLU, 1982—; bd. dirs. La. Capital Def. Project, 1985—. Democrat. Legal education, Criminal, Personal injury. Office: Loyola U Law Sch 7214 St Charles Ave New Orleans LA 70118

VITKO, JOHN PETER, lawyer; b. Virginia, Minn., Sept. 7, 1931; s. Leo and Frances Vitko; m. Mary Ann LePage, June 28, 1952; children: Jeffrey, Elizabeth, Susan, Jennifer, Stacy. AA, Va. Jr. Coll., 1951; LLB, U. Minn., 1953, JD, 1955. Bar: Minn. 1955, U.S. Dist. Ct. Minn. 1956, U.S. Ct. Appeals (8th cir.) 1958. Ptnr. Blomquist, Vitko, Niemeyer & Mooney, St. Paul, 1955-75, Dorsey and Whitney, St. Paul, 1975-85, John P. Vitko, P.A., Roseville, Minn., 1985—; bd. dirs. Boss Found., St. Paul, Splty. Mfg. Co., St. Paul, Sandy Mfg. Co., St. Paul, TMI Plastics, Inc. St. Paul. Editor law rev. U. Minn. Law Sch., 1953. Asst. chmn. St. Paul United Fund, 1960. Clubs: Internat. Torch (pres. 1969-70) (Buffalo); N. Oaks Country (St. Paul), Midland Hills Country, Pool and Yacht. Avocations: fishing, hunting, antique collecting. General corporate, Probate, Real property. Home: 45 Island Rd North Oaks MN 55110 Office: 1700 W Hwy 36 Suite 200 Roseville MN 55113-4082

VITKOWSKY, VINCENT JOSEPH, lawyer; b. Newark, Oct. 3, 1955; m. Mary Ann Gunzburg, May 16, 1981; 1 child, Vincent Jr. BA, Northwestern U., 1977; JD, Cornell U., 1980. Bar: N.Y. 1981, N.Y. Dist. Ct. (so. and ea. dists.) N.Y. 1981. Assoc. Hart and Hume, N.Y.C., 1980-84, Kroll, Tract, Harnett, Pomerantz & Cameron, N.Y.C., 1984-86, Finley, Kumble, Wagner, Heine, Underberg, Manley, Meyerson & Casey, N.Y.C., 1987—. Mem. ABA, Assn. Bar of City of N.Y. Democrat. Federal civil litigation, State civil litigation, Insurance. Home: 24 Radio Pl No 25 Stamford CT 06906 Office: Finley Kumble et al 425 Park Ave New York NY 10022

VITT, GEOFFREY JUDD, lawyer; b. N.Y.C., Oct. 30, 1946; s. Herbert Judd and Florence (Rossner) V.; m. Noelle Gorab; children: Geoffrey Barlow, Peter Judd. BA, George Washington U., 1969, JD with honors, 1972. Bar: U.S. Dist. Ct. (ea. dist.) Va. 1972, U.S. Supreme Ct. 1976, U.S. Dist. Ct. D.C. 1980. Assoc. Cohen & Rosenblum, Alexandria, Va., 1972-73; ptnr. Cohen, Vitt & Annand, Alexandria, 1973-79; assoc. Caplin & Drysdale, Chartered, Washington, 1979-84, ptnr., 1984—; lectr. George Washington U. Law Sch., Washington, 1979—. Mem. ABA, Assn. Trial Lawyers Am. Home: 4606 W St NW Washington DC 20007 Office: Caplin & Drysdale Chartered 1 Thomas Circle NW Washington DC 20005

VITTUM, DANIEL WEEKS, JR., lawyer; b. Lynch, Ky., Feb. 10, 1939; s. Daniel W. and Kathryn Margaret (Jones) V.; m. Stephanie Ann Empkie, Aug. 18, 1962 (sep.); children—Daniel W., III, Stephen F. B.S., U. Ill., 1961; J.D., U. Mich., 1964. Bar: Ill. 1964, U.S. Dist. Ct. (no. dist.) Ill. 1965, U.S. Supreme Ct. 1977, U.S. Ct. Appeals (7th cir.) 1976, U.S. Ct. Appeals (4th cir.) 1982, U.S. Ct. Appeals (9th cir.) 1978, U.S. Ct. Appeals (Fed. cir.) 1982. Assoc. Kirkland & Ellis, Chgo., 1964-69, ptnr., 1970—. Mem. ABA, Am. Intellectual Property Assn., Patent Law Assn. Chgo., Order of Coif, Phi Beta Kappa. Clubs: Mid-Am., East Bank (Chgo.). Patent, Trademark and copyright, Federal civil litigation. Home: 1625 Sheridan Rd Wilmette IL 60091 Office: Kirkland & Ellis 200 E Randolph Dr Chicago IL 60601

VLADECK, JUDITH POMARLEN, lawyer; b. Norfolk, Va., Aug. 1, 1923. BA, Hunter Coll., 1945; JD, Columbia U., 1947. Bar: N.Y. 1947, U.S. Supreme Ct. 1962. Assoc. Conrad & Smith, N.Y.C., 1947-51; sole practice N.Y.C., 1951-57; mem. Vladeck, Elias, Vladeck & Engelhard P.C., N.Y.C., 1957—; bd. dirs. Group Health Ins., Inc., Am. Arbitration Assn. Contbr. articles to profl. jours. mem. adv. bd. Inst. for Edn. and Research on Women and Work, Cornell U.; bd. dirs. N.Y. Civil Liberties Union, 1963-68; bd. dirs., counsel Tamiment Inst., Inc. Mem. ABA (co-chmn. various labor law and equal employment coms.), N.Y. State Bar Assn. (labor law com.), Assn. of Bar of City of N.Y., N.Y. County Lawyers Assn., Women's Bar Assn., Am. Arbitration Assn. (law com.), Columbia Law Sch. Alumni Assn. (bd. dirs.), Harlem Inst. Fashion Counsel (counsel, bd. dirs.). Home: 115 Central Park W New York NY 10023 Office: 1501 Broadway Ave New York NY 10036

VLCEK, JAN BENES, lawyer; b. Chgo., Nov. 16, 1943; s. Anton John and Alice (Benes) V.; m. Ann Lewis, Aug. 23, 1973; children: Elizabeth, Katharine. A.B., Princeton U., 1965; J.D., U. Pa., 1968; M.B.A., George Washington U., 1975. Bar: Fla. 1968, D.C. 1969. Trial atty. CAB, Washington, 1968-69; atty.-advisor Office of Legis., EPA, Washington, 1971-73; assoc. minority counsel Commerce Com. Ho. of Reps., Washington, 1973-76, regulatory programs counsel Energy Com., 1977-78; assoc., then ptnr. Gardner, Carton & Douglas, Washington, 1978-81; with Regan Energy Transition Team, Washington, 1980-81; ptnr. Sutherland, Asbill & Brennan, Washington, 1981—; chmn. Nat. Energy Resources Orgn. Served to sgt. U.S. Army, 1969-71. Mem. ABA (chmn. oil refining and mktg. com., chmn. energy policy com. of natural resources sect.), Fed. Energy Bar Assn. Club: Capitol Hill. Oil and gas general, Legislative, Environment. Office: 1666 K St NW Suite 800 Washington DC 20006

VLEISIDES, GREGORY WILLIAM, lawyer; b. Kansas City, Mo., June 17, 1950; s. William Chris and Irene Helen (Karos) V.; B.A., U. Kans., 1972; J.D., U. Mo.-Kansas City, 1976. Bar: Mo. 1977, U.S. Dist. Ct. (we. dist.) Mo. 1977, U.S. Ct. Appeals (8th cir.) 1977. Law clk. Cir. Ct. Jackson County, Mo., Kansas City, 1977-78; assoc. Tierney & Ernst, Kansas City, 1978-84; sr. ptnr. Gregory W. Vleisides, P.C., Kansas City, 1984—; of counsel F. Lee Bailey Law Offices, Boston, 1984-85, assoc. Turner & Boisseau, Kansas City, Mo., Overland Park, Wichita and Great Bend, Kans. 1985—; cons. Telecom. Corp., Overland Park, Kans., 1978—; guest lectr. Avila Coll., Kansas City, 1984; regional counsel Video Software Dealers Assn., 1985-87. Co-author: Challenges to Court Action in Child Abuse and Neglect Cases, 1976; contbg. author: Opening Statements, 1984; Closing Arguments, 1984. Host com. Republican Nat. Conv., Kansas City, Mo., 1976. Mem. ABA, Mo. Bar Assn., Kansas City Bar Assn. (bar-media com. 1978-84), Kansas City Met. Bar Assn. (press and pub. relations adv. bd. 1985—), Phi Beta Kappa, Delta Theta Pi. Greek Orthodox. Personal injury, Criminal, Federal civil litigation. Home: 3008 W 84th Pl Leawood KS 66206 Office: Law Offices Gregory W Vleisides PC 1001 E 101st Terr Kansas City MO 64131

VLIET, DANIEL GEORGE, lawyer; b. Chgo., Nov. 10, 1954; s. Roger G. and June S. (Hefferan) V.; m. Susan E. Borges, Dec. 10, 1983. BA, Wheaton Coll., 1976; JD, Marquette U., 1980; MS in Indsl. Relations, U. Wis., 1983. Bar: Mich. 1980, Wis. 1980, Ill. 1981. Assoc. Mika Meyers, Grand Rapids, Mich., 1980-81, Brynelson Herrick, Madison, Wis., 1982-85, Mulcahy & Wherry, Milw., 1985—. Mem. ABA, Wis. Bar Assn., Indsl. Relations

Research Assn. Labor, Workers' compensation, Health. Home: 895 E Birch Ave Whitefish Bay WI 53217 Office: Mulcahy & Wherry 815 E Mason St Milwaukee WI 53202

VOCHT, MICHELLE ELISE, lawyer; b. Detroit, Sept. 27, 1956. BA with honors, U. Mich., 1978; JD, Wayne State U., 1981. Bar: Mich., U.S. Dist. Ct. (ea. and we. dist.) Mich., U.S. Ct. Appeals (6th cir.), 1981. V.p., sec. Roy, Shecter & Vocht PC, Birmingham, Mich., 1981—. Mem. com. for re-election of current Mich. Supreme Ct. Justice, 1986. Mem. ABA, Assn. Trial Lawyers Am., Mich. Trial Lawyers Assn., Women Lawyers Assn. Mich., Oakland County Trial Lawyers Assn (exec. bd. dirs. 1982-84), State Bar Assn. Mich. (chmn. gen. practice section 1984-86, sec. 1982-83, vice-chmn. 1983-84, mem. civil procedure com. 1982-84)), Am. Inn of Ct. (barrister 1984—). Roman Catholic. Avocations: tennis, golf. Labor, Federal civil litigation, State civil litigation. Home: 901 N Adams Birmingham MI 48008 Office: Roy Shecter & Vocht PC 877 S Adams Suite 302 Birmingham MI 48011

VOCK, ROBERT DANIEL, lawyer; b. Paris, Nov. 14, 1933; s. Adolphe and Marguerite (Karyo) V.; m. Susan Maria Schuller, Dec. 24, 1957; children: Alexander, Jeffrey. BA, Dartmouth Coll., 1954; JD, Harvard U., 1957. Bar: N.Y. 1958, U.S. Dist. Ct. (ea. dist.) N.Y. 1958. Assoc. Shearman & Sterling, N.Y.C., 1961-64; with Mobil Oil Corp., N.Y.C., 1964-80, asst. gen. counsel, 1980—. Contbr. articles to profl. jours. Served to capt. U.S. Army, 1957-61. Mem. Internat. Bar Assn. (vice chmn. energy law sect. 1979-80), Am. Corp. Counsel Assn. Oil and gas leasing, Private international. Home: 14 Pierson Dr Greenwich CT 06831 Office: Mobil Oil Corp 150 E 42nd St New York NY 10017

VOEGELIN, HAROLD STANLEY, lawyer, financier; b. Summit, N.J., Sept. 10, 1919; s. Frederick Ernest and Clara Aestelle (Dorland) V.; m. Winifred Nemec Martin, Dec. 24, 1962; 1 son, Frederick P.; stepchildren: Jon F. Martin, Janis L. Kingaard. B.A., U. Mich., 1942, J.D., 1948. Bar: Calif. 1949. Teaching asst. constl. law, dept. polit. sci. U. Mich., 1947-48; assoc. firm McEntee, Willis & MacCracken, Los Angeles, 1948-52; asso., partner Brady & Nossaman, Los Angeles, 1952-57; partner Wood, Voegelin & Barton, 1957-60; sr. partner Voegelin, Barton, Harris & Callister, 1960-70, Voegelin & Barton, Los Angeles, 1970-84; ptnr. Finley, Kumble, Wagner, Heine, Underberg, Manley & Casey, Los Angeles, 1984—; Pres., dir. Five-Thirty Corp.; chmn. bd. West Coast Commodity Exchange, Inc., Nesbitt Food Products, Inc.; dir. Smith Internat., Inc., Newport Beach, Calif., A.J. Bayer Co., Los Angeles, Orange City Bank, Orange, Calif.; lectr. U. So. Calif. Inst. on Fed. Taxation, Title Ins. & Trust Co. Tax Forum, Internat. and Comparative Law Ctr., So. Meth. U. Vice pres., bd. dirs. United Cerebral Palsy Assn. of Los Angeles, Inc., 1958-62; bd. dirs. South Coast Child Guidance Clinic, Newport Beach; trustee Whittier (Calif.) Coll., Nesbitt Found., Los Angeles, Luella M. Murphey Found., So. Coast Repertory Theatre, Costa Mesa, Calif.; mem. exec. com. Pres.'s Club, U. Mich.; mem. adv. bd. Internat. and Comparative Law Center, Southwestern Legal Found., Dallas; mem. state adv. council World Trade Commn.; chmn. com. internat. trade devel. City of Los Angeles Econ. Devel. Council.; chmn., pres. Los Angeles Internat. Trade Devel. Corp. Served with USNR, 1943-45, PTO. Mem. ABA (lectr. Nat. Inst. on Current Legal Aspects of Doing Bus. in Europe), Internat. Bar Assn., Inter-Am. Bar Assn., Orange County Bar Assn., Los Angeles County Bar Assn. (chmn. com. on continuing edn. of bar 1961-62, 1st prize legal essay competition 1949), State Bar Calif. (lectr. Continuing Edn. of Bar Program), Los Angeles Area C. of C. (chmn. bd., chief exec. officer), Theta Delta Chi, Delta Theta Phi. Republican. Presbyterian. Clubs: California (Los Angeles); Newport Harbor Yacht (Newport Beach); Pacific; Balboa Bay (Newport Beach); Capitol Hill (Washington). Estate planning, Probate, Estate taxation. Home: 32 Harbor Island Newport Beach CA 92660 also: 121 S Hope St Los Angeles CA 90012 Office: 707 Wilshire Blvd 44th Floor Los Angeles CA 90017 also: 4400 MacArthur Blvd Newport Beach CA 92660

VOEGLER, DOUGLAS GENE, lawyer; b. Columbus, Nebr., Nov. 22, 1950; s. Dean William and Lillian Emily (Pinker) V.; m. Joanne K. Bejot, Nov. 25, 1978. BS, U. Nebr., 1973, JD cum laude, 1976. Bar: Nebr. 1976, N.Mex. 1979, U.S. Supreme Ct. 1979. Assoc. Leonard Pickering Law Offices, Albuquerque, 1979-80, Larry D. Beall P.A., Albuquerque, 1980-82; sole practice Albuquerque, 1982; assoc. Marchiondo & Berry P.A., Albuquerque, 1983-86; ptnr. Marchiondo, Vigil & Voegler, Albuquerque, 1986—. Republican. Unitarian. Avocations: art, antiques. Personal injury, State civil litigation, Federal civil litigation. Home: PO Box 11742 Albuquerque NM 87192 Office: Marchiondo Vigil & Voegler 315 5th Ave Albuquerque NM 87103

VOELPEL, MARK STEVEN, lawyer; b. St. Louis, Aug. 29, 1954; s. William Joseph and Phyllis Mae (Reichert) V.; m. Susan Therese Roos, Sept. 15, 1984. Student, U.S. Naval Acad., 1972-73; BA in History cum laude, U. Mo., 1976; JD, Washington U., St. Louis, 1979. Bar: Mo. 1979, U.S. Dist. Ct. (we. dist.) Mo. 1979, U.S. Dist. Ct. (ea. dist.) Mo. 1983, Ill. 1985. Law clk. to presiding chief justice Mo. Supreme Ct., Jefferson City, 1979-80; assoc. Shughart, Thomson & Kilroy, P.C., Kansas City, Mo., 1980-83, Greensfelder, Hemker, Wiese, Gale & Chappelow, P.C., St. Louis, 1983-84, Coburn, Croft & Putzell, St. Louis, 1984-87; atty. Southwestern Bell Corp., St. Louis, 1987—. Mem. Senator Frank Bild Re-election Campaign, St. Louis, 1976, Young Reps., St. Louis, 1976-78. Mem. ABA (litigation sect., young lawyers sect.), Ill. State Bar Assn., Mo. Bar Assn., St. Louis Met. Bar Assn., Phi Beta Kappa, Phi Kappa Phi, Phi Delta Phi (scholar 1978, clk. for Cooley Inn 1978-79). Roman Catholic. Corporate taxation, State and local taxation, Pension, profit-sharing, and employee benefits. Home: 1647 Dearborn Dr Saint Louis MO 63122 Office: Southwestern Bell Corp One Bell Ctr 40th Floor Saint Louis MO 63101-3099

VOGEL, CHARLES STIMMEL, lawyer; b. Los Angeles, Aug. 26, 1932; s. Charles Paul and Thurza Mae V.; m. Miriam Friedfeld, May 11, 1979; children by previous marriage: Steven, Beverly. B.A., Pomona Coll., 1955; LL.B., UCLA, 1959. Bar: Calif. 1959, U.S. Dist. Ct. for So. Dist. Calif 1959. Partner firm Allard, Shelton & O'Connor, Pomona, Calif., 1959-69; judge Mcpl. Ct., Pomona Jud. Dist., 1969-70, Los Angeles Superior Ct., 1970-77; partner firm Nossaman, Krueger & Marsh, Los Angeles, 1977-81, Sidley & Austin, Los Angeles, 1981—. Served with USN, 1955-56. Fellow Am. Bar Found.; mem. Los Angeles County Bar Assn. (trustee 1980-82, pres. 1985-86), UCLA Law Alumni Assn. (pres. 1977), Assn. Bus. Trial Lawyers (pres. 1984-85). Office: 2049 Century Park E Los Angeles CA 90067

VOGEL, HOWARD MICHAEL, lawyer; b. Phila., June 8, 1947; s. Edward Nathan and Sara C. (Harris) V. BS summa cum laude, U. Fla., 1970; postgrad., Stanford U., 1973-74, U. Geneva, Switzerland, 1974-75; JD, U. Calif., Berkeley, 1975. Bar: Fla. 1977, D.C. 1980, U.S. Supreme Ct. 1980. Legal officer Internat. Commn. on Jurists, Geneva, 1974-75; assoc. Brobeck, Phleger & Harrison, San Francisco, 1975-76; gen. counsel, fin. advisor Nationwide Chems., Ft. Lauderdale, Fla., 1978-82; sole practice Miami, Fla., 1982—. Author: Racial Discrimination and Repression in Southern Rhodesia, 1975, Universal Human Rights: Do They Exist in Rhodesia?, 1975. Ford Found. fellow, DuPont fellow; United Nations scholar, Dinkelspiel legal scholar. Mem. ABA, Internat. Bar Assn., Assn. Trial Lawyers Am., Internat. and Comparative Law Soc. (chmn.), Phi Beta Kappa, Kappa Tau Alpha, Tau Delta Tau. Avocations: writing, sailing, speleology, anthropology, skiing. Private international, General corporate, Criminal. Home: 2305 Lucaya Ln Suite J-4 Coconut Creek FL 33066

VOGEL, HOWARD STANLEY, lawyer; b. N.Y.C., Jan. 21, 1934; s. Moe and Sylvia (Miller) V.; m. Judith Anne Gelb, June 30, 1962; 1 son, Michael S. B.A., Bklyn. Coll., 1954; J.D., Columbia U., 1957; LL.M. in Corp. Law, NYU, 1969. Bar: N.Y. 1957, U.S. Supreme Ct. 1964. Assoc. Whitman & Ransom, N.Y.C., 1961-66; with Texaco Inc., 1966—, gen. atty., 1970-73, assoc. gen. counsel, 1973-81, gen. counsel Texaco Philanthropic Found. Inc., 1979-82, gen. counsel Jefferson Chem. Co., Texaco Chems. Can. Inc., 1973-82, assoc. gen. tax counsel, White Plains, N.Y., 1981—. Pres., dir. 169 E. 69th Corp., 1981—. Served to 1st lt. JAGC, U.S. Army, 1958-60. Mem. ABA, Assn. Bar City N.Y., Fed. Bar Council, Assn. Ex-Mems. of Squadron A (N.Y.C.). Club: Princeton (N.Y.C.). Corporate taxation, General corporate, Securities. Home: 169 E 69th St Apt 9-D New York NY 10021 Office: 2000 Westchester Ave White Plains NY 10650

VOGEL, JOHN HENRY, lawyer; b. Milw., Feb. 20, 1944; s. John Henry and Ione Marie (Tetting) V.; m. Virginia Reynolds, June 27, 1970; children: Christopher, Melissa. BA cum laude, Princeton U., 1965; JD, U. Mich., 1968. Bar: N.Y. 1970, U.S. Dist. Ct. D.C. 1971, D.C. 1972, U.S. Supreme Ct. 1973. Stagiaire European Econ. Community, Brussels, 1968-69; assoc. Lord, Day & Lord, N.Y.C., 1969-71; assoc. Patton, Boggs & Blow, Washington, 1971-77, ptnr., 1977—. Fulbright scholar, 1968. Mem. ABA, D.C. Bar Assn., Internat. Bar Assn., Union des Advs. Internat., Union des Stagiaires European Econ. Community, Phi Delta Phi. Episcopalian. Clubs: Metropolitan (washington); White Elephant (London). Private international, General corporate, Contracts commercial. Office: Patton Boggs & Blow 2550 M St NW Washington DC 20037

VOGEL, JOHN WALTER, lawyer; b. Dansville, N.Y., Sept. 19, 1948; s. Walter Earl and Betty (Elston) V.; m. Pamela Hill; children: Michael John, Jennifer Alexandra. BA, SUNY, Albany, 1970; JD, Syracuse U., 1976. Bar: N.Y. 1976, U.S. Dist. Ct. (we. dist.) N.Y. 1979, U.S. Tax Ct. 1980, U.S. Supreme Ct., 1980, U.S. Dist. Ct. (no. dist.) N.Y. 1985, U.S. Ct. Appeals (2d cir.) 1985. Assoc. Edward J. Degnan Law Offices, Caniesteo, N.Y., 1976-77; atty. N.Y. State Dept. Agrl. & Markets, Albany, 1977-78; sole practice law Dansville, 1978—; v.p., legal counsel Dansville Econ. Devel. Corp., 1983—; closing atty. Farmers Home Adminstrn., Dansville, 1982—. Dir. Livingston County (N.Y.) Drug Abuse Prevention Council, 1981-82. Served with U.S. Army, 1970-73. Mem. ABA, N.Y. State Bar Assn., Livingston County Bar Assn. (sec./treas. 1980-82, v.p. 1984-85, pres. 1985-86), Assn. Trial Lawyers Am., Dansville C. of C. (bd. dirs. 1985—). Republican. Presbyterian. General practice, Personal injury, State civil litigation. Home: 5 Livingston Blvd Dansville NY 14437 Office: 125 Main St Dansville NY 14437

VOGEL, LAWRENCE MARK, lawyer; b. N.Y.C., Jan. 26, 1953; s. Morton and Joyce (Sherman) V.; m. Holly Jean Felsinger, Nov. 29, 1985. BA, SUNY, Buffalo, 1973; JD, Boston Coll., 1977. Bar: Colo. 1977, U.S. Ct. Appeals (10th cir.) 1981. Assoc. Mancini, Humphrey & Curran, P.C., Denver, 1977-79; sole practice Aurora, Colo., 1979-85; ptnr. Sedlak & Vogel, P.C., Denver, 1985—; sec., dir. Met. Lawyer Referral Service, Denver, 1981-86. Mem. Nat. Assn. Entrepreneurs (bd. dirs. Denver chpt. 1986-87). Club: Toastmasters. Avocations: skiing, running. Workers' compensation, Personal injury, Real property. Office: Sedlak & Vogel PC 621 17th St Suite 710 Denver CO 80293

VOGEL, MARILYN BETH, lawyer; b. Duluth, Minn., July 12, 1949; d. Dick and Harriet (DeRoos) V.; m. Michael Grant Felton, Apr. 23, 1983. BA, Bemidji (Minn.) State U., 1971; JD, William Mitchell Coll. Law, 1978. Bar: Minn. 1978, Wash. 1981. Mgr. regulatory and bus. relations Continental Telephone, St. Paul, 1974-78, v.p. pub. affairs, 1978-80; assoc. gen. counsel Gen. Telephone of the N.W., Everett, Wash., 1980-82; sr. atty. GTE Service Corp., Stamford, Conn., 1982-85; v.p., gen. counsel GTE Telecom Inc., Stamford, 1986. Mem. ABA, Minn. Bar Assn., Wash. State Bar Assn., Alpha Phi Sigma. Republican. Avocations: antique collecting, piano. General corporate, Public utilities, Administrative and regulatory. Office: GTE Telecom Inc One Stamford Forum Stamford CT 06904

VOGEL, THEODORE JOHN, lawyer; b. Chgo., May 16, 1952; s. Cornelius and Rayda Ann (Dykstra) V.; m. Bethany Navis, Dec. 29, 1982. BA, Calvin, 1974; JD, U. Mich., 1979. Bar: Mich. 1979, U.S. Dist. Ct. (ea. dist.) Mich. 1979, U.S. Dist. Ct. (we. dist.) Mich. 1980, U.S. Ct. Appeals (6th cir.) 1981, U.S. Tax Ct. 1983, U.S. Supreme Ct. 1983. Acct. Vannatter, Howell & Co. CPA's, Grand Rapids, Mich., 1974-76; lawyer Consumers Power Co., Jackson, Mich., 1979—. Active Ann Arbor (Mich.) Republican Party, 1980-86, Campus Chapel, Ann Arbor, 1976-86; treas. bd. of dir. Christian Sch. Assn. of Ann Arbor, 1986—. Mem. State Bar Mich. (com. on corp. tax 1984—, corp. fin. and bus. law sect. 1981—), Jackson County Bar Assn., Washtenaw County Bar Assn. Republican. Mem. Christian Reformed Ch. Avocations: mountain climbing, skiing. Corporate taxation, Contracts commercial, General corporate. Home: 1316 Ravenwood Ann Arbor MI 48103 Office: Consumers Power Co 212 W Michigan Jackson MI 49201

VOGELS, DAVID SELLERS, JR., lawyer; b. Phila., May 2, 1925; s. David Sellers and Irene Ambler (Wallace) V.; m. Mary Stetson Prescott, Sept. 1, 1951 (div. Oct. 1977); children: David Sellers III, Robert Prescott, Edward Page, Jonathan Bryant. AB, Dartmouth Coll., 1949; postgrad, Harvard U., 1949-50; MBA, Syracuse U., 1957; JD, St. Mary's U., San Antonio, 1959; MA, U. Calif., Riverside, 1967; PhD, Mich. State U., 1973. Bar: Colo. 1974. Enlisted USAF, 1943, advanced through grades to col., 1970, ret., 1975; legal adminstr. Weller, Friedrich, et al, Denver, 1977-80; dir. legal adminstrn. Mountain Bell, Denver, 1981—. Sr. warden St. James Episcopal Ch., Wheat Ridge, Colo., 1985—. Decorated DFC, Legion of Merit, 31 other decorations and awards; recipient George E. Williams award Federation of Geneal. Socs., 1985. Mem. Denver Bar Assn. (chmn. law office mgmt. com. 1980-83), Colo. Bar Assn. (chmn. law office mgmt. com. 1981-83), Assn. Legal Adminstrs. (v.p. 1984-86, pres.-elect 1986-87, pres. 1987—). Avocation: genealogy. Legal administration. Office: Mountain States Telephone & Telegraph Co 1801 California St Denver CO 80202

VOGT, CARL WILLIAM, lawyer; b. Houston, Apr. 20, 1936; s. Carl Wilhelm and Myrtle Jesse (Jones) V.; m. Margrit Wulff, July 27, 1968; children—Erika, Bianca. B.A., Williams Coll., 1958; LL.B., U. Tex., 1965. Bar: Tex. 1965, U.S. Dist. Dist. (so. dist.) Tex. 1966, U.S. Dist. Ct. D.C., U.S. Ct. Appeals (5th cir. 1968, U.S. Ct. Appeals (D.C. cir.), U.S. Ct. Appeals (4th cir.), U.S. Ct. Appeals (3d cir.), U.S. Supreme Ct. 1980. Assoc., Fulbright, Crooker, Freeman, Bates & Jaworski, Houston, 1966-68; assoc., ptnr. Thompson, Ogletree, Deakins & Vogt, Atlanta and Washington, 1968-72; assoc., ptnr. Fulbright & Jaworski, Washington, 1972—. Chmn., bd. dirs. Chinquapin Sch., Highlands, Tex., 1968-73; mem., hon. mem. bd. trustee Boy and Girls Club of Washington, 1978—. Served to capt. USMC, 1958-62. Mem. ABA (mem. adminstn. law sect., chmn. equal employment opportunity com. 1976-80, chmn. mgmt. com. 1984, mem. labor and employment law sect., mem. litigation sect.), Nat. Assn. Coll. and Univ. Attys. (chmn. nat. office com. 1978-81, mem. exec. bd. 1981—), Am. Bar Found., State Bar Tex., Bar D.C. Republican. Club: Metropolitan (Washington). Civil rights, Federal civil litigation, Labor. Office: Fulbright & Jaworski 1150 Connecticut Ave NW Washington DC 20036

VOGT, JAMES WAYNE, lawyer; b. Cordell, Okla., Sept. 27, 1950; s. Marvin Roy and Elsie Sarah (Schmidt) V.; m. Deborah Davis Canon, Aug. 1, 1975; children: John William, Ashley Ruth. BA, Southwestern State U., 1972; JD, Oklahoma City U., 1975. Bar: Okla. 1975, U.S. Dist. Ct. (we. dist.) Okla. 1975, U.S. Ct. Appeals (10th cir.) 1975. Ptnr. Reynolds, Ridings & Hargis, Oklahoma City, 1975—; lectr. creditors rights various orgns. Mem. ABA, Comml. Law League Am., Okla. Bar Assn., Okla. County Bar Assn. (bench and bar com., unauthorized practice law com.), Phi Alpha Delta. Republican. Methodist. Club: Young Men's Dinner (Oklahoma City). Lodge: Kiwanis. Avocations: basketball, tennis, volleyball. Bankruptcy, Consumer commercial, Contracts commercial. Home: 12005 Camelot Ct Oklahoma City OK 73120 Office: Reynolds Ridings & Hargis 2808 First National Ctr Oklahoma City OK 73010

VOLCKHAUSEN, WILLIAM ALEXANDER, lawyer, bank executive; b. N.Y.C., Mar. 13, 1937; s. William Louis and Jessie (Rankin) V.; m. Grace Lyu, Aug. 2, 1968; children: Sharon, Alexander. AB, Princeton U., 1959; AM, U. Calif., Berkeley, 1963; JD, Harvard U., 1966. Bar: N.Y. 1967. Exec. v.p., gen. counsel, sec. Dime Savs. Bank of N.Y., FSB, Garden City, N.J., 1980—; adj. prof. Cardozo Yeshiva U., N.Y.C., 1980—. Mem. Berkeley Carroll St. Sch., Bklyn., 1974-82, pres., 1975-76. Mem. ABA, Assn. of Bar of City of N.Y., N.Y. County Bar Assn., Nassau County Bar Assn. Democrat. Club: Princeton (N.Y.C.). Avocations: swimming, skiing, gardening, reading, travel. Home: 262 President St Brooklyn NY 11231 Office: Dime Savings Bank of NY FSB 1225 Franklin Ave Garden City NY 11530

VOLENTINE, RICHARD J., JR., lawyer; b. Tampa, Fla., Apr. 2, 1955; s. Richard J. Sr. and Mary Frances (Shaw) V.; m. Susan Ruth Zimmerman, May 16, 1981; 1 child, Rachel Elizabeth. BS, Spring Hill Coll., 1977; JD, U. Ala., 1980. Bar: Ala. 1980, Mo. 1982, Fla. 1984. Staff atty. Ala. Jud. Coll., Tuscaloosa, 1980-81; staff counsel Citicorp Person-to-Person, Inc., St. Louis, 1982; regional counsel Citicorp Person-to-Person Corp., Tampa, 1982-84; asst. gen. counsel Citicorp Savs. Fla., Miami, 1984-85; assoc. counsel Nationwide Capital Corp., Atlanta, 1985-86; regional atty. FDIC, Atlanta, 1986—. Mem. ABA (fin. instns. regulation and consumer fin. subcom. young lawyers' div.), Atlanta Bar Assn., Ala. Jud. Coll. Faculty Assn. (hon.), Am. Judicature Soc. Republican. Roman Catholic. Avocations: golfing, sports, photography, writing. Banking, Real property, Administrative and regulatory. Home: 3499 Indian Ln Doraville GA 30340 Office: FDIC 245 Peachtree Ctr Ave Suite 1100 Atlanta GA 30303

VOLK, JEROME MILTON, JR., lawyer; b. New Orleans, July 14, 1947; s. Jerome M. Sr. and Francis Rita (Macaluso) V.; m. Antoinette L. Stewart, Sept. 6, 1975; children: Meredith A., Jerome M. III. BA in Journalism, La. State U., 1970; JD, Loyola U., New Orleans, 1973. Bar: La. 1973, U.S. Dist. Ct. (ea. dist.) La. 1973, U.S. Ct. Appeals (5th cir.) 1973, U.S. Dist. Ct. (we. dist.) La. 1975, U.S. Supreme Ct. 1977, U.S. Dist. Ct. (mid. dist.) La. 1986. Assoc. Windhorst, Heisler, deLaup & Wysocki, New Orleans, 1973-78; sole practice New Orleans, 1979; ptnr. McCann & Volk, New Orleans, 1980; of counsel DeMartini, LeBlanc & D'Aquila, Kenner, La., 1981-82; ptnr. DeMartini, LeBlanc, D'Aquila & Volk, Kenner, 1983—. Bd. dirs. Chateau Estates Civic Assn., Kenner, 1979-83, pres. 1982. Mem. La. Bar Assn., Jefferson Bar Assn., New Orleans Bar Assn. Club: Woodlake Tennis and Swim Club (Kenner) (bd. dirs. 1983-85). Insurance, Federal civil litigation, General corporate. Home: 4169 Loire Dr Kenner LA 70065 Office: DeMartini LeBlanc D'Aquila & Volk 3329 Florida Ave Kenner LA 70065

VOLK, MICHAEL DOUGLAS, lawyer; b. Grand Rapids, Mich., July 9, 1947; s. Karl William and Mary Elaine (Abbott) V.; m. Rosalina Ito, Aug. 12, 1977; children—Michael Douglas, David Alexander. B.A., U. Tex.-El Paso, 1974; J.D., U. Houston, 1977. Bar: Tex. 1977, U.S. Dist. Ct. (we. dist.) Tex. 1978, U.S. Ct. Appeals (5th cir.) 1980, U.S. Ct. Appeals (10th) cir. 1980, U.S. Supreme Ct. 1981. Ptnr., Marshall & Volk, El Paso, 1977-81, Volk & Morgan, El Paso, 1981—; speaker profl. meetings. Assoc. editor El Paso Trial Lawyers Rev., 1974-80; research editor U. Houston Law Rev., 1976-77; Author: Medical Malpractice: Handling Obstetric and Neonatal Cases, 1986; contbr. articles to legal publs. Mem. ABA, State Bar Tex., El Paso Bar Assn., Assn. Trial Lawyers Am. (internat. law and treaties com. 1980-82), Tex. Trial Lawyers Assn., El Paso Trial Lawyers Assn. (bd. dirs. 1979-81), Am. Soc. Law and Medicine, Am. Coll. Legal Medicine (assoc.-in-law, convocation com. 1984-85, edn. com. 1984-85), Melvin Belli Soc. (trustee). Democrat. Personal injury. Office: Volk & Morgan 1214 Montana El Paso TX 79902

VOLKMANN, ALFRED ARMISTEAD, lawyer; b. Bayshore, N.Y., Jan. 25, 1940; s. Alfred P. and Doris (Armistead) V.; m. Laurine T. Rothe, Aug. 16, 1964; children: Karen L., Tricia L. BA, Coll. of William and Mary, 1961; LLB, NYU, 1964. Bar: N.Y. 1965, U.S. Dist. Ct. N.Y. 1967, U.S. Tax Ct. 1969, U.S. Supreme Ct. 1970. Ptnr. Zwissler, Diedolf, Feuer & Volkmann and predecessor firms, Patchogue, N.Y., 1967—. Vice pres. Patchogue-Medford Bd. Edn., N.Y., 1976—; rear comdr., law officer U.S. Power Squadrons, Raleigh, N.C., 1986. Served to capt. U.S. Army, 1965-67, Vietnam. Mem. N.Y. State Bar Assn., Suffolk County Bar Assn. Republican. Lutheran. Lodges: Rotary, Masons. Administrative and regulatory, Real property, Probate. Home: 2 Autumn Ct East Patchogue NY 11772 Office: Zwissler Diedolf Feuer & Volkmann 292 Medford Ave Patchogue NY 11772

VOLLMANN, ALAN PETER, lawyer; b. Chgo., Mar. 27, 1948; s. Arthur Frank and Florence Marie (Speck) V.; m. Ann Blumenthal, July 1, 1978; children: Sarah Stefanie, Lydia Alison. BA, U. Calif., Irvine, 1970; MA, San Francisco State U., 1974; JD, Cath. U., 1980. Bar: D.C. 1980, U.S. Dist. Ct. D.C. 1981, U.S. Ct. Appeals (D.C. cir.) 1981. Assoc. Glassie, Pewett, Dudley, Beebe & Shanks, P.C., Washington, 1980-82, Lane and Edson, P.C., Washington, 1983—. Editor-in-chief Cath. U. Law Rev., Washington, 1979-80. Mem. ABA. Democrat. Contracts commercial. Office: Lane and Edson 2300 M St NW Washington DC 20037

VOLLMER, ANDREW N., lawyer; b. Madison, Wis., Aug. 14, 1953; m. Lynne E. Prymas, Jan. 21, 1984. BA, Miami U., Oxford, Ohio, 1975; JD, U. Va., 1978. Bar: D.C. 1978, U.S. Supreme Ct. 1982. From assoc. to ptnr. Wilmer, Cutler & Pickering, Washington, 1978—. Notes editor U. Va. Law Rev., 1977-78. Mem. ABA, Am. Arbitration Assn. (arbitrator). Private international, Antitrust, Securities. Office: Wilmer Cutler & Pickering 2445 M St NW Washington DC 20037-1420

VOLLMER, CHARLES JOSEPH, lawyer; b. Rochester, Pa., Aug. 14, 1946; s. Charles L. and Ellen Marie (Holleran) V.; m. mary Jeanette French, June 13, 1970; children: Heidi Rebecca, Devin Charles. BA in Polit. Sci., Adrian Coll., 1968; JD, U. Pitts., 1975. Bar: Pa. 1975, U.S. Dist. Ct. (we. dist.) Pa. 1975. Ptnr. Stonecipher, Cunningham, Beard & Schmitt, Pitts., 1975-87, Pollard, Walker & Vollmer, Pitts., 1987—. Treas., bd. dirs. Vintage, Inc., Pitts., 1980-86; bd. dirs. South Hills Area YMCA, Upper St. Clair, Pa., 1985-86. Served to capt. U.S. Army, 1968-72. Mem. ABA, Pa. Bar Assn., Allegheny County Bar Assn., Comml. Law League. Democrat. Roman Catholic. Avocations: sports, music. Contracts commercial, Bankruptcy. Home: 2352 Weston Dr Pittsburgh PA 15241 Office: Pollard Walker & Vollmer Grank Bldg Pittsburgh PA 15219

VOLLMER, STEVEN LYLE, lawyer, legal educator; b. Emporia, Kans., June 13, 1955; s. Gene Jante and Georgiann (McCoy) V.; m. Doris M. Ohland, June 23, 1984; 1 child, Jamison. BB in Adminstrn. magna cum laude, U. Wis., Whitewater, 1977; JD, Marquette U., 1981. Bar: Wis. 1981, U.S. Dist. Ct. (we. and ea. dists.) Wis. 1981, U.S. Tax Ct. 1981. Assoc. Grutzner, Byron & Holland, Beloit, Wis., 1981-82; ptnr. Grutzner, Byron, Holland & Vollmer, Beloit, 1982—; instr. bus. law Blackhawk Tech. Inst., Janesville, Wis., 1985—. Past council mem. Calvary Luth. Ch., Beloit, 1986—. Mem. ABA, Wis. Bar Assn., Rock County Bar Assn., Beloit Bar Assn. (pres. 1985), Beloit Jaycees, Phi Kappa Phi, Omicron Delta Epsilon. General corporate, Consumer commercial, State civil litigation. Office: Grutzner Bryon Holland & Vollmer 312 W Grand Ave Beloit WI 53511

VOLUCK, JEFFREY M., lawyer; b. Atlantic City, N.J., Sept. 14, 1943; s. Allan and Sylvia (Wallo) V.; m. Sonia Voluck, Dec. 18, 1968; children—Tammy, Justin. B.S., LaSalle Coll., 1966; J.D., U. Balt., 1974. Bar: Pa. 1975, U.S. Dist. Ct. (ea. dist.) Pa. 1975, U.S. Ct. Appeals (3d cir.) 1975, U.S. Dist. Ct. Md. 1980. Assoc., Robert F. Simone, Phila., 1975, Gross & Sklar, Phila., 1976; pres. Jeffrey M. Voluck, Phila., 1977—. Contbr. articles to profl. jours. Served with U.S. Army, 1966. Mem. ABA, Assn. Trial Lawyers Am., Pa. Bar Assn., Phila. Trial Lawyers Assn. Criminal, Personal injury. Office: Robinson Bldg 42 S 15th St 17th Floor Philadelphia PA 19102

VOLUCK, PHILIP RITTER, lawyer; b. N.Y.C., Apr. 22, 1954; s. Allan Stuart and Sondra (Ritter) V.; m. Nina Sue Kaplan, Oct. 17, 1983; children: Andrew Ritter. BS in Indsl. and Labor Relations, Cornell U., 1976; JD, Georgetown U., 1980—. Bar: Pa. 1980, U.S. Supreme Ct. 1985. Ptnr. Pechner, Dorfman, Wolffe, Rounick & Cabot, Phila., 1980—; instr. labor law Villanova U., Pa., 1985—. Vol. Phila. Vol. Lawyers for the Arts, 1980—; bd. advisors Phila. Eagles Fly for Leukemia, 1985—. Labor. Home: 2301 Cherry St Philadelphia PA 19103 Office: Pechner Dorfman Wolffe et al 3 Parkway Philadelphia PA 19102

VOLZ, JOHN PHILLIP, U.S. attorney; b. New Orleans, Apr. 2, 1935; s. John Ignatius and Mary Agnes (Ortolano) V.; m. Judy Billingsley, May 2, 1975; 1 son, John P. B.A., Tulane U., 1958, LL.B., 1959. Bar: La. Mem. U.S. Bd. Vets. Appeals, 1961-62; asst. dist. atty. New Orleans, 1963-68; spl. agt. Dept. Justice, 1968-69; chief asst. dist. atty. New Orleans, 1971-74; fed. public defender 1974-78; U.S. Atty. Eastern Dist. La., 1978—; faculty Tulane U. Law Sch., 1976-79. Mem. La., Fed. bar assns. Republican. Roman Catholic. Office: Officeof US Atty Eastern District of Louisiana 500 Camp St New Orleans LA 70130 *

VON DIOSZEGHY, ADAM GEORGE, lawyer; b. Budapest, Hungary, June 20, 1938; came to U.S., 1956, naturalized, 1962; s. George and Maria Jolan (Damokos) D. Student U. Budapest, 1956; A.A., Foothill Coll., 1962; A.B., Stanford U., 1964; J.D., 1970. Bar: Calif. 1971, U.S. Supreme Ct. Teaching fellow Stanford (Calif.) U., 1970-71; ptnr. Grogan, Vogelgesang &

von Dioszeghy, Campbell, Calif., 1971—. Served to lt. USNR, 1964-72. Mem. ABA, Santa Clara County Bar Assn., West Valley Bar Assn., Stanford Law Soc. Santa Clara County (pres. 1980-82). State civil litigation, Personal injury, Probate.

VON DREHLE, RAMON ARNOLD, lawyer; b. St. Louis, Mar. 12, 1930; s. Arnold Henry and Sylvia E. (Ahrens) Von D.; m. Gillian Margaret Turner, Sept. 13, 1980; children by previous marriage: Carin L., Lisa A., Courtney A. B.S., Washington U., St. Louis, 1952; LL.B., U. Tex., Austin, 1957; postgrad, Parker Sch. Internat. Law, Columbia U., 1965. Bar: Tex. 1956, Mich. 1957, U.S. Supreme Ct. 1981. Sr. atty. Ford Motor Co., Dearborn, Mich., 1957-67; assoc. counsel Ford of Europe, Inc., Brentwood, Essex, Eng., 1967-75; v.p., gen. counsel Ford of Europe, Inc., 1975-79; v.p. legal Ford Motor Credit Co., Dearborn, 1979—; v.p., gen. counsel Am. Road Ins. Co., Dearborn, 1979—. Article editor: Tex. Law Rev, 1956-57. Trustee Birmingham Unitarian Ch., 1966-67. Served to 1st lt. AUS, 1952-54, Korea. Mem. ABA, Mich. Bar Assn., Tex. Bar Assn., Internat. Bar Assn., Am. Fin. Services Assn. (dir. 1981—), Washington U. Alumni Club Detroit (past pres.), Order of Coif, Tau Beta Pi, Omicron Delta Kappa. Mem. Christ Ch. Clubs: Renaissance (Detroit); Les Ambassadeurs (London); Confrérie des Chevaliers du Tastevin (France). Contracts commercial, General corporate, Private international. Office: Ford Motor Credit Co Dearborn MI 48121

VON KALINOWSKI, JULIAN ONESIME, lawyer; b. St. Louis, May 19, 1916; s. Walter E. and Maybelle (Michaud) von K.; m. Penelope Jayne Dyer, June 29, 1981; children by previous marriage: Julian Onesime, Wendy Jean von Kalinowski Corzo. B.A., Miss. Coll., 1937; J.D. with honors, U. Va., 1940. Bar: Va. bar 1940, Calif. bar 1946. Asso. firm Gibson, Dunn and Crutcher, Los Angeles, 1946-52; partner Gibson, Dunn and Crutcher, 1953-62, mem. exec. com., 1962-82; dir. W. M. Keck Found.; mem. faculty Practising Law Inst. programs, 1971, 76, 78, 79, 80; instr. Columbia Law Sch., N.Y.C., summer 1981; mem. lawyer dels. com. to 9th Circuit Jud. Conf., 1953-73; UN expert Mission to People's Republic of China, 1982. Contbr. articles to legal jours.; author: Antitrust Laws and Trade Regulation, 1969, desk edit., 1981; gen. editor: World Law of Competition, 1978, Antitrust Counseling and Litigation Techniques, 1984. Mem. bd. regents So. Meth. U. Sch. Law. Served to lt. comdr. USN, 1941-46; capt. Res.; ret. Fellow Am. Bar Found., Am. Coll. Trial Lawyers; mem. ABA (ho. of dels. 1970), Am. Bar Assn. (chmn. antitrust law sect. 1972-73), State Bar of Calif., Los Angeles Bar Assn., U. Va. Law Sch. Alumni Assn., Phi Kappa Psi., Phi Alpha Delta. Republican. Episcopalian. Clubs: Calif, Los Angeles Country; Bohemian (san Francisco), Pacific-Union (san Francisco); Los Jolla Beach and Tennis; N.Y. Athletic (N.Y.C.), The Sky (N.Y.C.). Home: 12320 Ridge Circle Los Angeles CA 90049 Office: 333 S Grand Ave Los Angeles CA 90071

VON MEHREN, ARTHUR TAYLOR, educator, lawyer; b. Albert Lea, Minn., Aug. 10, 1922; s. Sigurd Anders and Eulalia Marion (Anderson) von M.; m. Joan Elizabeth Moore, Oct. 11, 1947; children—George Moore, Peter Anders, Philip Taylor. S.B., Harvard U., 1942, LL.B., 1945, Ph.D., 1946; Faculty of Law, U. Zurich, 1946-47; Faculte de Droit, U. Paris, 1948-49; Doctor iuris (h.c.), Katholeke U., Leuven, 1985. Bar: Mass. 1950; Bar: U.S. Dist. Ct. (Mass.) 1980. Law clk. U.S. Ct. Appeals (1st cir.), 1945-46; asst. prof. law Harvard U., 1946-53, prof., 1953-76, Story prof., 1976—, dir. East Asian legal studies program, 1981-83; acting chief legislation br., legal div. Occupation Mil. Govt. U.S.,Germany, 1947-48, cons. legal div., 1949; tchr. Salzburg Seminar in Am. Studies, summers 1953, 54; Fulbright research prof. U. Tokyo, Japan, 1956-57, Rome, Italy, 1968-69; cons. legal studies Ford Found., New Delhi, 1962-63; vis. prof. U. Frankfurt, summer 1967; Ford vis. prof. Inst. Advanced Legal Studies, U. London, 1976; professeur associé U. Paris, 1977; Goodhart prof. legal sci. U. Cambridge, 1983-84, fellow Downing Coll., 1983-84, hon. fellow, 1984—. Author: The Civil Law System, 1957, 2d edit. (with J. Gordley), 1977; co-author: The Law of Multistate Problems, 1965; bd. editors Am. Jour. Comparative Law, 1952-86; contbr. articles to profl. jours.; editor: Law in Japan-The Legal Order in a Changing Soc., 1963; mem. editorial com. Internat. Ency. Comparative Law, 1969—; mem. adv. bd. Internat. Ctr. for Settlement of Investment Disputes Rev.-Fgn. Investment Law Jour., 1985—. Mem. U.S. Del. Hague Conf. pvt. internat. law, 1966, 68, 76, 80, 85. Guggenheim fellow, 1968-69. Mem. Am. Acad. Arts and Scis., ABA, Am. Fgn. Law Assn., Internat. Acad. Comparative Law, Institut de Droit Internat., Japanese Am. Soc. Legal Studies, Am. Arbitration Assn. (mem. comml. panel), Am. Assn. Comparative Study Law (bd. dirs., v.p.), Am. Soc. Polit. and Legal Philosophy, Internat. Law Assn., Internat. C. of C. Inst. Internat. Bus. Law and Practice (mem. acad. council), Institut Grand-Ducal (corr.), Phi Beta Kappa. Legal education, Private international. Office: Harvard Law Sch Cambridge MA 02138

VOORHEES, DONALD SHIRLEY, judge; b. Leavenworth, Kans., July 30, 1916; s. Ephraim and Edna Mary (Oliphint) V.; m. Anne Elizabeth Spillers, June 21, 1946; children: Stephen Spillers, David Todd, John Lawrence, Diane Patricia, Richard Gordon. A.B., U. Kans., 1938; LL.B., Harvard U., 1946. Bar: Okla. 1947, Wash. State 1948. Practiced law Tulsa, 1946-47, Seattle, 1947-74; partner firm Riddell, Williams, Voorhees, Ivie, & Bullitt, Seattle, 1952-74; judge U.S. Dist. Ct., Western dist., Wash., 1974—; Bd. dirs. Fed. Jud. Center. Served with USN, 1942-46. Mem. Am., Washington State, Seattle-King County bar assns., Maritime Law Assn., Am. Judicature Soc., Phi Beta Kappa. Jurisprudence. Office: 502 US Courthouse Seattle WA 98104

VORENBERG, JAMES, lawyer, educator, univ. dean; b. Boston, Jan. 10, 1928; s. F. Frank and Ida (Muhlfelder) V.; m. Dorothy Greeley, Oct. 25, 1952; children: Jill, Amy, Eliza; m. Elizabeth Weiner Troubh, June 20, 1970. A.B., Harvard U., 1948, LL.B., 1951. Law clk. to Justice Frankfurter, 1953-54; with firm Ropes & Gray, 1954-62, partner, 1960-62; prof. law Harvard U., Cambridge, Mass., 1962—; dean Harvard U. (Law Sch.), 1981—; dir. Office of Criminal Justice, 1964-65; exec. dir. Pres.'s Commn. on Law Enforcement and Adminstrn Justice, 1965-67; asso. spl. prosecutor Watergate Spl. Prosecution Force, 1973-75. Trustee NAACP Legal Def. Fund. Served with USAF, 1951-53. Home: 9 Willard St Cambridge MA 02138

VORYS, ARTHUR ISAIAH, lawyer; b. Columbus, Ohio, June 16, 1923; s. Webb Isaiah and Adeline (Werner) V.; m. Lucia Rogers, July 16, 1949 (div. 1980); children: Caroline S., Adeline Vorys Cranson, Lucy Vorys Noll, Webb I.; m. Ann Harris, Dec. 13, 1980. BA, Williams Coll., 1945; LLB, Ohio State U., 1949. Bar: Ohio 1949. From assoc. to ptnr. Vorys, Sater, Seymour & Pease, Columbus, 1949—; sr. ptnr. Vorys, Sater, Seymour & Pease, 1982—; bd. dirs. Corroon & Black Corp., First Equity Life Ins. Co., N.Am. Nat. Corp., Ohio Casualty Corp., Ohio Casualty Ins. Co., Ohio Life Ins. Co., Ohio Security Ins. Co., Pan-Western Life Ins. Co., Shelby Ins. Co., Vorys Bros., Inc., Wendy's Internat., Inc., other corps.; Supt. of ins., Ohio, 1957-59. Del. Republican Nat. Conv., 1968, 72; trustee, past pres. Children's Hosp., Greenlawn Cemetery Assn., Griffith Found. for Ins. Edn., Internat. Ins. Soc.; trustee, chmn. Ohio State U. Hosps. Served as lt. USMCR, World War II. Decorated Purple Heart. Fellow Ohio State Bar, Columbus Bar Assns.; mem. ABA, Am. Judicature Soc., Phi Delta Phi., Chi Psi. Clubs: Rocky Fork Headley Hunt, Rocky Fork Hunt and Country (Gahanna); Columbus Athletic, Capital. General corporate, Insurance. Home: 5826 Havens Corners Rd Gahanna OH 43230 Office: 52 E Gay St PO Box 1008 Columbus OH 43216

VOSBURG, BRUCE DAVID, lawyer; b. Omaha, June 17, 1943; s. Noble Perrin and Dena V. (Ferrari) V.; m. Susan Simpson, May 27, 1972; children—Margaret Amy, Wendy Christine, Bruce David. B.A., U. Notre Dame, 1965, B.S.M.E., 1966; J.D., Harvard U., 1969. Bar: Nebr. 1969, Ill. 1970, U.S. Supreme Ct. 1974. Law clk. U.S. Dist. Ct. Nebr., 1969-70; assoc. Kirkland & Ellis, Chgo., 1970-72; ptnr. Fitzgerald & Brown, Omaha, 1972—. Pres. Children's Crisis Ctr., 1984-85, bd. dirs., 1981-85; pres. Child Sav. Inst., 1986—; pres. Omaha Tennis Assn., 1975-76, bd. dirs., 1973-84 ; pres. Nebr. Tennis Assn., 1976-77; chmn. grievance com. Missouri Valley Tennis Assn., 1978—, mem. exec. com., 1976—; mem. Leadership Omaha, 1979; adv. bd. City of Omaha Parks and Recreation, 1985—. Mem. ABA, Nebr. Bar Assn. (chmn. securities com.), Omaha Bar Assn. (exec. council 1983-86), Nat. Assn. Bond Attys., Tau Beta Pi. Republican. Roman Catholic. Club: Rotary. Author: Financing Small Businesses, 1981. Securities, General corporate, Trademark and copyright. Office: 1000 Woodmen Tower Omaha NE 68102

VOSBURGH, JOHN ADDISON, lawyer, educator; b. White Plains, N.Y., Aug. 23, 1933; s. Herbert Earl and Helen Frances (Benedict) V.; m. Emily Elizabeth Yerton, Dec. 30, 1968 (dec.); m. Mary Anthony Vlahopoulos, May 29, 1983. B.S. in Agr., U. Ariz., 1963, J.D., 1966, M.A., 1969, Ph.D., 1976; diploma Hague Acad., 1980; cert. with distinction in internat. law, U.S. Naval War Coll., 1981; diploma, Nat. Inst. for Trial Advocacy. Bar: Ariz. 1967, U.S. Supreme Ct. 1971, D.C. 1975, U.S. Dist. Ct. Ariz. 1967, U.S. Tax Ct. 1967, U.S. Ct. Claims 1967, U.S. Ct. Appeals (9th cir.) 1968, U.S. Ct. Appeals (5th cir.) 1969, U.S. Ct. Appeals (D.C. cir.) 1971, U.S. Customs Ct. 1972, U.S. Ct. Internat. Trade 1972, U.S. Ct. Mil. Appeals 1972, U.S. Ct. Customs and Patent Appeals 1974, U.S. Ct. Appeals (1st, 2d, 3d, 4th, 6th, 7th, 8th, 10th cirs.) 1975. Sole practice, Tucson, 1967-83, Phoenix, 1983—; mem. adj. faculty U. Ariz., So. Ariz. Law Enforcement Inst., 1977-78, vis. asst. prof. internat. law, 1981-82, vis. lectr. spring, 1981; civilian lectr. Ft. Huachuca, Ariz., 1980—, Davis Monthan AFB, Tucson, 1981—; Fulbright prof. internat. law and relations U. Suriname, 1978-80, alt. lectr. UNITAR course on conf. diplomacy, legal adv. Ministry Fgn. Affairs, 1978-80, asst. dept. chmn. dept. pub. internat. law, 1978-80; asst. prof. polit. sci. Tenn. Tech. U., Cookville, 1971-72. Ruth C. Ackerman Meml. scholar, 1966. Mem. State Bar Ariz., D.C. Bar, ABA (com. on marine resources, ad hoc com. on career opportunities in internat. law 1973—, com. on aerospace law 1968—, com. internat. control of atomic energy 1963-74, com. internat. aspects of natural resources 1974—), Inter-Am. Bar Assn. (com. inter-planetary space law 1968—, com. nuclear law 1968—), Internat. Law Assn., Maricopa County Bar Assn., East Valley Bar Assn., Lawyer to Lawyer Consultation Panel, Pi Sigma Alpha. Republican. Contbr. articles on internat. law to profl. jours. Public international, Immigration, naturalization, and customs, Legal education. Home and office: 4145 E Glenrosa Phoenix AZ 85018

VOSGUANIAN, RODNEY NERSES, lawyer; b. N.Y.C., Apr. 1, 1950; s. Charles and Mary (Lordigyan) V.; m. Armine Vosgueritchian, Apr. 5, 1986. BS in Acctg., Econs., Fordham U., 1972; JD, Pepperdine U., 1979. Bar: Calif. 1980, Ariz. 1981, U.S. Dist. Ct. (cen. dist.) Calif. 1981, U.S. Tax Ct. 1981, N.J. 1982, U.S. Dist. Ct. (so. and no. dists.) Calif. 1984, U.S. Ct. Appeals (9th cir.) 1984, U.S. Dist. Ct. (ea. dist.) Calif. 1985, U.S. Dist. Ct. N.J. 1981, U.S. Ct. Appeals (D.C. cir.) 1985, U.S. Supreme Ct. 1985, Tex. 1986. Acct. Charles Vosguanian, CPA, Yonkers, N.Y., 1972-74; prin. Rodney N. Vosguanian, CPA, Yonkers, 1974-77; sr. ptnr. Vosguanian & Vosguanian, Los Angeles, 1980—; adj. prof. bus. adminstrn. Pepperdine U., Malibu, Calif., 1981; arbitrator Los Angeles Superior Ct., 1986—. Served with USAR, 1973. N.Y. State Regents scholar, 1968-72; recipient Cert. of Commendation Bd. Regents N.Y. State, 1972. Fellow ABA, Am. Assn. Atty.-CPA's; mem. Calif. Bar Assn. (Voluntary Legal Services Commendation 1984). Armenian Orthodox. Lodge: Knights of Vartan. Avocations: bicycling, tennis, skiing, amateur photography. Probate, State civil litigation, Real property. Office: Vosguanian & Vosguanian 2040 Ave of the Stars #400 Los Angeles CA 90067

VOSS, DONALD HENRY, educator, psychologist; b. Grand Rapids, Mich., June 2, 1927; s. Henry D. and Grace (Smit) V.; m. Betty Ann Hart, July 3, 1953; Erica, Douglas, Kerry. AB, Calvin Coll., 1949; MDiv, Evang. Sem., 1955; MS, Northern Ill. U., 1957; PhD, Mich. State U., 1966; JD, Akron U., 1975. Bar: Pa. 1976. Prof. Lansing (Mich.) Community Coll., 1963-67, Slippery Rock (Pa.) U., 1967—. Chmn. Zoning Hearing Bd., Slippery Rock, 1981—. Served wtih USN, 1945-46, PTO. Mem. ABA, Am. Psychological Assn. Republican. Mem. United Ch. Christ. Probate, Health. Address: 248 Maple St Slippery Rock PA 16057

VOSS, JAMES VICTOR, lawyer; b. Pitts., Jan. 1, 1933; s. Victor E. and Gladys J. (James) V.; m. Nancy Ross, Feb. 13, 1960; children—Cathy A., Curtis J., Gregory J. A.B., Colgate U., 1954; J.D., U. Pitts., 1957. Bar: Pa. 1958, U.S. Dist. Ct. (we. dist.) Pa. 1958, U.S. Ct. Appeals (3d cir.) 1958, U.S. Supreme Ct. 1963. Ptnr. Voss & Voss, Pitts., 1958-65, Neely & Voss, Pitts., 1965-77, Meyer, Unkovic & Scott, Pitts., 1977—. Bd. dirs. Riverview (Pa.) Sch. Dist., 1968-73; mem. fin. com. Allegheny (Pa.) County Republican Party, 1974-78. Mem. Pa. Bar Assn. Allegheny County Bar Assn. (chmn. family law sect. 1982-83, mem. civil litigation council 1983—, chmn. 1987, judiciary com. 1983—), ABA, Acad. Trial Lawyers, Pa. Trial Lawyers, Am. Trial Lawyers, Am. Judicature Soc. Presbyterian. Clubs: Univ. (Pitts.), Duquesne; Oakmont Country (Pa.), Shriners, Jesters. State civil litigation, Federal civil litigation, Criminal. Home: 851 12th St Oakmont PA 15139 Office: Suite 1300 Oliver Bldg Pittsburgh PA 15222

VOVAKIS, LEWIS HARRY, lawyer, legal information management consultant; b. Carlisle, Pa., Jan. 31, 1934; s. Harry D. and Harriett H. (Gasparis) V. A.B., U. Pa., 1955; J.D., Dickinson Sch. Law, 1963. Bar: U.S. Dist. Ct. D.C. 1964, U.S. Ct. Appeals (D.C. cir.) 1964, U.S. Supreme Ct. 1968. Counsel, Am. Maritime Assn., Washington, 1964-66; legal asst. Govt. of D.C., 1966-67; ptnr. Rhyne & Rhyne, Washington, 1967-69; v.p. Autocomp, Inc., Washington, 1969-74, Aspen Systems Corp., N.Y.C., 1974-80, Informatics Gen. Corp., Rockville, Md., 1980-83; sr. v.p. Wells Internat., Washington, 1983-84; law firm mgmt. cons., Washington, 1984-86, v.p. Am. Legal Systems, 1986—. Served to lt. USNR, 1956-59. Mem. ABA, D.C. Bar Assn. Republican. Greek Orthodox. Club: Nat. Press (Washington). Computer. Home: 2545 Waterside Dr NW Washington DC 20008 Office: Suite 514 2000 L St NW Washington DC 20036

VOYLES, JAMES ROBERT, lawyer; b. Louisville, Ky., Apr. 6, 1940; s. Gerald W. Voyles and Edith V. (Geary) Nichter; m. Naomi Carter, Dec. 29, 1969. BS in Commerce, U. Louisville, 1961, MA, 1964, JD, 1968. Bar: Ky. 1968, U.S. Dist. Ct. (we. dist.) Ky. 1968, U.S. Supreme Ct. 1972, U.S. Ct. Appeals (3d cir.) 1973, U.S. Ct. Claims 1977, U.S. Tax Ct. 1977. Ptnr. Goldberg & Simpson, P.S.C., Louisville, 1984—; assoc. prof. wills and probate U. Louisville, 1979-80. Trustee Louisville Free Pub. Library, 1978-86, v.p., 1982-84, pres., 1984-86; mem. exec. bd. Urban Libraries Council, 1986—. Fellow Am. Coll. Tax Counsel, Am. Coll. Probate Counsel; mem. ABA (taxation sect., real property sect., probate and trust law sect.), Ky. Bar Assn. (chmn. taxation sect. 1980-81), Louisville Bar Assn. (chmn. taxation sect. 1980-83, vice chmn. probate 1984—, chmn. 1986—, Award Merit Outstanding Contribution 1981), Louisville Bar Found. (founder, bd. dirs. 1981-86, treas. 1984-86), Louisville Employee Benefit Council (pres. 1977-78), Nat. Assn. Estate Planning Councils (state chmn.). Estate taxation, Probate, Pension, profit-sharing, and employee benefits. Office: Goldberg & Simpson PSC 2800 1st Nat L Tower Louisville KY 40202

VOYLES, ROBB LAWRENCE, lawyer; b. Toledo, May 26, 1957; s. Lawrence E. and Marilyn L. (McQuade) V.; m. Loretta F. Herbert, July 19, 1980; 1 child, Lindsay Ann. BBA in Acctg. summa cum laude, U. Dayton, 1979; JD magna cum laude, U. Mich., 1982. Bar: Tex. 1982, U.S. Dist. Ct. (no. dist.) Tex. 1982, U.S. Ct. Appeals (5th cir.) 1983, U.S. Dist. Ct. (we. dist.) Tex. 1986. Assoc. Rain, Harrell, Emery, Young & Doke, Dallas, 1982—. Editor U. Mich. Law Rev., 1981-82. Mem. ABA (litigation sect., antitrust div.), State Bar of Tex., Dallas Bar Assn., Dallas Young Lawyers Assn., Order of Coif, Alpha Beta Psi. Democrat. Roman Catholic. Club: Towne (Dallas). Federal civil litigation, State civil litigation, Antitrust. Office: Rain Harrell Emery Young & Doke 4200 Republic Bank Tower Dallas TX 75201

VOYNICH, JOHN JOSEPH, educator, consultant; b. Washington, Pa.; s. Louis and Julia Voynich; m. June Brown, Feb. 6, 1946; children: John Michael, William Gregory, Steven Scott. BS in Gen. Sci., U. Md., 1953; MS in Mgmt., So. Ill. U., 1961, PhD in Econs., 1967; JD, John Marshall Sch. of Law, Atlanta, 1979. Bar: Ga. 1979, U.S. Dist. Ct. (no. dist.) Ga. 1980. Commd. 2d lt. USAF, 1948, advanced through grades to maj., 1963, ret., 1965; asst. prof. econs. So. Ill. U., Carbondale, 1965-67; assoc. prof. mgmt. U. Ga., Athens, 1967-70; chmn. sch. bus. Columbus (Ga.) Coll., 1970-73, prof. mgmt., law, 1973—; cons. econs., independent mgmt., law Columbus Coll., 1975—. Mem. ABA, Ga. Bar Assn., Am. Bus. Law Assn., So. Mgmt. Assn., So. Econ. Assn., U.S. Hang Glide Assn. Republican. Roman Catholic. Lodge: Kiwanis. Avocations: scuba diving, hang gliding, snow skiing, private flying. Legal education, Estate planning, Jurisprudence. Home: 4453 Smokey Mountain Trail Columbus GA 31907 Office: Columbus Coll Algonquin Dr Columbus GA 31993

VRADENBURG, GEORGE III, corporate lawyer. AB, Oberlin (Ohio) Coll.; LLB, Harvard U. V.p., gen. counsel CBS Inc., N.Y.C. Office: CBS Inc 51 W 52nd St New York NY 10019 *

VRANESH, GEORGE, lawyer; b. Hibbing, Minn., Oct. 26, 1925; s. Rade and Anna (Severovich) V.; m. Etta Jo Cleaver, Mar. 9, 1957; children: Rade, Anna, Perry. Engr. Mining, Colo. Sch. Mines, 1951; LLB, U. Colo., 1961. Bar: Colo. 1961; registered profl. engr., Colo. Mining engr. Ouray, Colo., 1952-53; mine owner and operator Moab, Utah, 1953-61; ptnr. Vranesh & Raisch, Boulder, Colo., 1961—, sr. ptnr.; counsel, project engr. Stearns-Rogers Inc., Denver, 1961-63; water referee Div. 1, Greeley, Colo., 1969-72. Author: Colorado Water Law; contbr. articles to profl. jours. Served with U.S. Army, 1943-46. Decorated Purple Heart. Mem. ABA (chmn. water resources com.), Colo. Bar Assn., Boulder County Bar Assn., AIME, Colo. Mining Assn. (bd. dirs.), Boulder County Metal Mining Assn. (past pres.), Clear Creek County Mining Assn. Lodge: Elks. Environment, Mining and minerals. Office: Vranesh & Raisch 2120 13th St PO Box 871 Boulder CO 80306

VREE, ROGER ALLEN, lawyer; b. Chgo., Oct. 2, 1943; s. Louis Gerard and Ruby June (Boersma) V.; m. Lauren Trumbull Gartside, Mar. 29, 1969; children: Jonathan Todd, Matthew David. BA, Wheaton Coll., 1965; MA, Stanford U., 1966, JD, 1969. Bar: Ill. 1969, U.S. Dist. Ct. (no. dist.) Ill. 1969. Assoc. Sidley & Austin, Chgo., 1969-75, ptnr., 1975—. Mem. ABA, Ill. Bar Assn., Chgo. Bar Assn., Law Club, Legal Club. Club: University (Chgo.). Construction, Landlord-tenant, Real property. Office: Sidley & Austin One First Nat Plaza Chicago IL 60603

VUKASIN, J. P., JR., federal judge; b. Oakland, Calif., May 25, 1928; s. John P. and Natalie V.; m. Sue D., July 1, 1956; children—John P., Kirk, Alexander G., Kim J., Karen L. A.B., U. Calif., 1950, J.D., 1956. Bar: Calif. 1956. Commr. Calif. Pub. Utilities Commn., 1969-74, chmn., 1971, 72; mem. Calif. Conf. of Pub. Utility Council; dir. Iowa State Conf. Pub. Utility Valuation and Ratemaking; judge Superior Ct. of Calif., Alameda County, 1974-83; judge U.S. Dist. Ct. (no. dist.) Calif., San Francisco, 1983—; vis. prof. bus. law Calif. State U.-Hayward, 1968; mem. Adminstrv. Conf. of U.S., 1972-75, Conf. Calif. Judges. Served with U.S. Army, 1951-53. Mem. ABA (mem. governing council sect. pub. utility law 1971-73, chmn. spl. com. to study state regulatory legislation pub. utility sect.). Republican. Contbr. articles to legal jours. Jurisprudence. Office: US Courthouse PO Box 36060 San Francisco CA 94102 *

WAAS, GEORGE LEE, lawyer; b. N.Y.C., July 12, 1943; s. George and Anne Waas; m. Harriet I. Waas, July 18, 1971; children—Elaine Beth, Amy Michelle. B.S. in Journalism, U. Fla., 1965; J.D., Fla. State U., 1970. Bar: Fla. 1970, U.S. Supreme Ct., 1973. Asst. atty. gen. State of Fla., 1970-71; staff atty. Fla. League of Cities, 1971; asst. to sec. and dir. labor Fla. Dept. Commerce, 1971-73; assoc. dir. continuing legal edn. Fla. Bar, 1973-74; asst. dean, instr. Coll. Law, Fla. State U., 1974-75; atty. Fla. Dept. Transp., 1975-77; asst. gen. counsel Fla. Dept. Health and Rehab. Services, 1977-80; ptnr. Slepin, Slepin, Lambert & Waas, 1981-86; counsel state elections Fla. Dept. of State, 1986—. Bd. dirs. Big Bend Muscular Dystrophy Assn., 1980-83, pres., 1983; mem. Leon County Cultural Resources Commn., 1985-87; asst. atty. gen. State of Fla., 1987— Mem. Fla. Govt. Bar Assn. (pres. 1976-77), Fla. Bar (exec. council adminstrv. law sect. 1981—, chmn. 1985-86). Democrat. Jewish. Clubs: Capital Tiger Bay (dir. 1974-80) (Tallahassee); Masons. Contbr. articles to profl. jours. State civil litigation, Administrative and regulatory, General practice. Home: 3797 Sally Ln Tallahassee FL 32312 Office: The Capitol Suite 1502 Tallahassee FL 32399

WACHTER, MICHAEL L., economics educator; b. N.Y.C., Mar. 12, 1943; s. Abraham and Florence W.; m. Susan M. Jaffe, June 23, 1968; children: Jessica, Jonathan. B.S., Cornell U., 1964; M.A., Harvard U., 1967, Ph.D., 1970. Asst. prof. econs. U. Pa., Phila., 1969-73, assoc. prof., 1973-76, prof., 1976—; sr. advisor Brookings Instr., Washington, 1976—; commr. Minimum Wage Study Commn., Washington, 1978-81; research assoc. NBER, Cambridge, Mass., 1978; mem. Nat. Council on Employment Policy, 1980—; cons. Joint Econ. Com., Washington, 1979-81, Council Econ. Advisors, 1976-78; bd. govs. FRS, 1976; cons. Congl. Budget Office, 1975-77. Editor: Removing Obstacles to Economic Growth, 1984, Toward a New U.S. Industrial Policy, 1982; contbr. articles to profl. jours. NIH grantee, 1981-83; NSF grantee, 1974-77; 20th Century Fund grantee, 1978-82; Gen. Electric Found. grantee, 1980-83. Mem. Am. Econ. Assn., Econometric Soc., Indsl. Relations Research Assn. Office: Dept Econ U Pa 3718 Locust Walk Philadelphia PA 19104 *

WACHTLER, SOL, state chief judge; b. N.Y.C., Apr. 29, 1930; s. Philip Henry and Fay (Sobel) W.; m. Joan Wolosoff, Feb. 23, 1952; children: Lauren Jane, Marjorie Dru, Alison Toni, Philip Henry. B.A., Washington and Lee U., 1951, LL.B., 1952, postgrad., 1980, LL.D. (hon.), 1981; LL.D. (hon.), Albany Law Sch., Union Coll., 1978, Bklyn. Law Sch., 1978, Hofstra U., 1980, SUNY, 1981, Syracuse U.; L.H.D. (hon.), LIU, Coll. of St. Rose. Bar: N.Y. 1956. Justice N.Y. State Supreme Ct., 1968-72; judge N.Y. State Ct. Appeals, Albany, 1972-84; chief judge N.Y. State Ct. Appeals, 1985—; guest lectr. Bklyn. Law Sch., Hofstra Law Sch., Yale U. Sch. Law, Albany Law Sch., St. John's Law Sch., 1968-77, USIS, Munich, Germany, 1973, Stuttgart, Germany, 1977; guest lectr. U. Leyden, Amsterdam; chmn. N.Y. State Fair Trial/Free Press Conf., N.Y. State Commn. on Bicentennial of U.S. Constitution. Contbr. articles to legal jours. Councilman Town of North Hempstead, N.Y., 1963-65, chief exec., 1965-67; mem. Nassau County Bd. Suprs., 1965-67, chmn. com. pub. safety, 1965-67; trustee L.I. Jewish-Hillside Med. Center, 1970—, L.I. U.; bd. overseers Nelson A. Rockefeller Inst. Govt.; dist. chmn. Boy Scouts Am., 1968-69; chmn. N.Y. State Commn. on Bicentennial of U.S. Constn.; trustee SUNY-Albany, Hofstra U. Sch. Law; trustee Cerebral Palsy Assn., Assn. for Help of Retarded Children, 1966-67; chmn. N.Y. State Commn. on the Bicentennial U.S. Constn. Mem. Am. Law Inst., Assn. N.Y. State Supreme Ct. Justices, Am., N.Y. State, Nassau County bar assns., Order of Coif, Phi Delta Phi. Jewish. Club: Masons. Jurisprudence. Home: 58 Fairway Dr Manhasset NY 11030 Office: Court of Appeals Hall Eagle St Albany NY 12207

WACKER, DANIEL JAMES, lawyer; b. Milw., Aug. 20, 1949; s. Joseph A. and Mary J. (McGettigan) W.; m. Yon-Hui Yim, Nov. 8, 1979. BS, USAF Acad., 1971; JD, Harvard U., 1974, postdoctoral, 1980-81. Bar: Wis. 1974, N.Y. 1981. Commd. USAF, 1971, advanced through grades to maj., 1980, resigned, 1980; counsel Mobil Oil Corp., N.Y.C., 1981—; judge adv. USAFR, Scott AFB, Ill., 1980—. Vol. adv. MFY Legal Services Inc., N.Y.C., 1985—. Mem. ABA, Assn. of Bar of City of N.Y. Private international, General corporate, Contracts commercial. Office: Mobil Oil Corp 150 E 42d St New York NY 10017

WADDELL, JOHN EMORY, lawyer; b. Dothan, Ala., Sept. 1, 1948; s. J.L. and Lillie Mae Waddell; m. Melanie Elizabeth Waddell, May 5, 1974; children: Kelli Elizabeth, Haley Drue. Student, George C. Wallace Community Coll.; BS in Mktg. and Bus. Adminstrn., Troy State U., 1970; JD, Samford U., 1973. Bar: Fla. 1973, U.S. Dist. Ct. (so. dist.) Fla. 1973, U.S. Tax Ct. 1973, Ala. 1974, Ga. 1974, U.S. Dist. Ct. (no. dist.) Fla. 1975, U.S. Dist. Ct. (mid. dist.) Ala. 1975. Sole practice Dothan, 1975—; pub. defender City of Dothan, 1975-80, mcpl. judge, 1980-86. Named one of Outstanding Young Men Am., 1985. Mem. Ala. Bar Assn., Fla. Bar Assn., Ga. Bar Assn., Assn. Trial Lawyers Am., Ala. Trial Lawyers Assn. (bd. govs. 1983-86). Methodist. Avocations: golf, boating. Personal injury, Probate, Family and matrimonial. Home: 3302 Cromwell Dr Dothan AL 36301 Office: 214 W Troy St PO Box 7024 Dothan AL 36302

WADDELL, PHILLIP DEAN, lawyer; b. Covington, Ky., Nov. 14, 1948; s. Ewell Edward and Sarah Isobel (Dean) W.; m. Jill Annette Tolson, Aug. 23, 1975; children: Nathan Ewell, James Seth. BA, Centre Coll. Ky., 1971; JD, No. Ky. U., 1982. Bar: Ky. 1982, Ohio 1983, Tenn. 1986. V.p., mgr. escrow Eagle Savings Assn., Cin., 1973-83; v.p., cons. Union Planters Nat. Bank, Memphis, 1983-84; v.p., liason First Nat. Bank & Trust Co., Oklahoma City, 1984-86; v.p., sec., gen. counsel First Mortgage Strategies Group, Inc.,

Memphis, 1986—. Mem. ABA, Am. Judicature Soc., Ky. Bar Assn. Republican. Presbyterian. Lodge: Kiwanis. Home: 2095 Allenby Rd Germantown TN 38138 Office: First Mortgage Strategies Group Inc 6060 Primary Pkwy Memphis TN 38119

WADDICK, WILLIAM ANTHONY, lawyer; b. Chgo., Dec. 7, 1931; s. William Anthony and Mary Elizabeth (Dolan) W.; m. Clara Maria Taylor, June 13, 1964; children: Maria B., Julia L., Patricia A., Brenda J., Linda J. BS in Commerce, U. Notre Dame, 1957; JD, Ind. U., 1961. Bar: Ind. 1961, U.S. Dist. Ct. (so. dist.) Ind. 1961, U.S. Ct. Appeals (7th cir.) 1972. Law clk. to presiding justice Ind. Supreme Ct., Indpls., 1961; assoc. Kunz & Kunz, Indpls., 1961-63, ptnr., 1963—. Contbg. author: Condemnation in Indiana, 1976; co-author: Eminent Domain in Indiana, 1976. Served with USAF, 1951-54. Mem. Ind. Bar Assn., Indpls. Bar Assn., Assn. Trial Lawyers Am., Ind. Trial Lawyers Assn., Am. Arbitration Assn. Republican. Roman Catholic. Club: St. Thomas More Soc. (Indpls.) (Ind. pres. 1970-71). Lodges: KC, Sertoma (pres. Carmel 1985-86). State civil litigation, General practice, General corporate. Home: 2 Songbird Ct Carmel IN 46032 Office: Kunz & Kunz 320 N Meridian #528 Indianapolis IN 46204

WADDLE, ROBERT GLEN, lawyer; b. Memphis, Aug. 8, 1955; s. William Clarence and Faye Waddle. BA in Pub. Adminstrn., U. Miss., 1977, JD, 1980. Bar: Miss. 1980, U.S. Dist Ct. (no. and so. dists.) Miss. 1980. Assoc. Beach, Luckett & Ross, Jackson, Miss., 1980—. Author: Ole Miss. Spirit and V.I.P. mags.; sportscaster WSLI, 1984-86, WJDX, 1986—. mem. various local civic groups, 1980—. Named as one of Nat. Jaycees Project of Yr. U.S. Jaycees, 1982-83. Mem. ABA, Miss. Bar Assn., Miss. Trial Lawyers Assn., Jackson Jaycees (legal advisor 1981—, pub. relations dir. 1983-85, Jackson Jaycee of Yr. 1982-83), Miss. Jaycees, Nat. Sportscasters and Sportswriters Assn., Miss. Sportswriters Assn. Club: Toastmasters (v.p. high noon chpt.). Avocation: sports. General practice. Home: 178 Travis Wood Jackson MS 39212 Office: Beach Luckett & Russ 499 S President St PO Box 1669 Jackson MS 39215-1669

WADE, DANIEL PLES, lawyer; b. Gainesville, Mo., Dec. 13, 1949; s. Howard Allen and LouAnna (Cupps) W.; m. Catherine Ann Walker, Aug. 16, 1969; children—Christopher, Matthew, Jeffrey. B.S., U. Mo.-Columbia, 1971; J.D., U. Mo.-Kansas City, 1974. Bar: Mo. 1975, U.S. Dist. Ct. (we. dist.) Mo. 1975. Sole practice law, Ava, Mo., 1975-79; sr. ptnr. Wade & Haden, Ava, 1979—; sec., bd. dirs. Douglas County Nat. Bank, 1982-84; pros. atty., Douglas County, Mo., 1977-78. Contbr. articles to law revs. Served with AUS, 1971-72. Mem. Douglas County Bar Assn. (pres. bd. dirs. 1981), Mo. Bar Assn., ABA, Mo. Assn. Trial Lawyers, Assn. Trial Lawyers Am. Republican. State civil litigation, Criminal, General practice. Office: Wade & Haden 100 W Public Sq Ava MO 65608

WADE, EDWIN LEE, lawyer; b. Yonkers, N.Y., Jan. 26, 1932; s. James and Helen Pierce (Kinne) W.; m. Nancy Lou Sells, Mar. 23, 1957; children—James Lee, Jeffrey K. B.S., Columbia U., 1954; M.A., U. Chgo., 1956; J.D., Georgetown U., 1965. Fgn. service officer U.S. Dept. State, 1956-57; mktg. analyst Chrysler Internat., S.A., Switzerland, 1957-61; intelligence officer CIA, 1961-63; industry analyst U.S. Internat. Trade Commn., 1963-65; gen. atty. Universal Oil Products Co., Des Plaines, Ill., 1965-72; atty. Amsted Industries, Inc., Chgo., 1972-73; chief counsel dept. gen. services State of Ill., Springfield, 1973-75; sr. atty. U.S. Gypsum Co., Chgo., 1975-84; gen. atty., USG Corp., 1985, corp. counsel, 1986, asst. gen. counsel, corp. sec., 1987—. Active Chgo. Symphony Soc. Mem. ABA, Ill. Bar Assn., Chgo. Bar Assn., Mid-Am. Arab C. of C., Am. Philatelic Soc., Royal Philatelic Soc. Can. General corporate, Antitrust, Private international. Home: 434 Mary Ln Crystal Lake IL 60014 Office: USG Corp 101 S Wacker Dr Chicago IL 60606

WADE, GEORGE JOSEPH, lawyer; b. N.Y.C., Mar. 3, 1938; s. George J. and Catherine V. (Sweeney) W.; m. Gwendolen Belmont Livermore, June 27, 1964; children: Barbara Caroline, George J. A.B., Fordham Coll., 1959; LL.B., Harvard U., 1962. Bar: N.Y. 1963, U.S. Supreme Ct., U.S. Dist. Ct. (so. and ea. dists.) N.Y., U.S. Dist. Ct. (we and no. dists.) Tex., U.S. Ct. Appeals (2d, 3d, 5th, 6th cir.). Assoc. Cravath, Swaine & Moore, N.Y.C., 1963-70; assoc. Shearman & Sterling, N.Y.C., 1970-72, ptnr., 1972—. Vestryman St. James Episcopal Ch., N.Y.C.; bd. dirs., sec., gen. counsel N.Y. Sch. Circus Arts, 1977—, Lamb's Theatre Co., N.Y.C., 1984—. Served with USNR, 1963-69. Mem. ABA, N.Y. State Bar Assn., Assn. Bar City of N.Y. Democrat. Episcopalian. Clubs: Union (N.Y.C.), West Side Tennis (gov.) (N.Y.C.). Federal civil litigation, Bankruptcy, Banking. Office: Shearman & Sterling 53 Wall St New York NY 10005

WADE, HUGH GERALD, lawyer; b. Juneau, Alaska, May 12, 1934; s. Hugh Joseph and Madge (Case) W.; m. Mary Elizabeth Pinter, Sept. 24, 1964 (div. 1979); m. Sylvia McCabe, Feb. 14, 1979; children: Hugh, Megan, Gretchen. BA, U. Notre Dame, 1956; LLB, Cath. U., 1959. Dist. magistrate State of Alaska, Anchorage, 1959-60; sole practice Anchorage, 1961—. Editor Cath. U., 1959. Mem. ABA (ho. dels. 1963-64), Alaska Bar Assn. (bd. govs. 1980-83), Anchorage Bar Assn. (pres. 1972-74), Associated Gen. Contractors. Democrat. Roman Catholic. Construction. Home: 5322 Shorecrest Anchorage AK 99515 Office: Wade & DeYoung 310 K St #410 Anchorage AK 99501

WADE, JAMES ALAN, lawyer; b. Duluth, Minn., May 18, 1950; s. Harry K. Wade and Elsie R. (Timm) Sauve; m. Sandra M. Santti, July 14, 1973; 1 child, Coleen L. BA, U. Minn., Duluth, 1975; JD, U. Minn., Mpls., 1978. Bar: Minn. 1978, U.S. Dist. Ct. Minn. 1978, U.S. Ct. Appeals (8th cir.) 1979, U.S. Supreme Ct. 1982, U.S. Dist. Ct. Wis. 1984, Wis. 1985. Trial atty. Johnson, Killen et al, Duluth, 1978—. Mem. Duluth City Charter Commn., 1984—; pres. YMCA Men's Club, Duluth, 1985-86; bd. dirs. YMCA, Duluth, 1986—. Served with U.S. Army, 1970-72, Vietnam, Minn. Nat. Guard, 1976-78. Mem. ABA, Minn. Bar Assn. Federal civil litigation, State civil litigation, Personal injury. Office: Johnson Killen et al 811 Norwest Ctr Duluth MN 55802

WADE, JOHN WEBSTER, law educator, lawyer; consultant; b. Little Rock, Mar. 2, 1911; s. John William and Sarah Vista (Webster) W.; m. Mary Moody Johnson, June 1, 1946; children—John Webster, Mary R. Wade Shanks, William J., Ruth E. Wade Grant. B.A., U. Miss., 1932, J.D. 1934; LL.M., Harvard U., 1935, S.J.D., 1942. Bar: Miss. 1934, Tenn. 1947. Asst. prof. law U. Miss., 1936-38, assoc. prof., 1938-40, prof., 1940-47; prof. Vanderbilt U. Sch. Law, 1947-71, dean, 1952-72, Disting. prof. law, 1971-81, dean and Disting. prof. emeritus, 1981—; vis. prof. U. Tex., 1946-47, Columbia U., 1964-65, U. Mo., 1976-77, Coll. William and Mary, 1981-82, Cornell U., fall 1972, U. Mich., Fall 1982, Pepperdine U., 1983-84, Memphis State U., 1986, U. Hawaii, 1987; uniform laws commr. from Tenn., 1961—, v.p. Nat. Conf. Commrs. Uniform State Laws, 1977-79; reporter Restatement (Second) of Torts, 1970-81; speaker in field. Trustee Rhodes Coll., Memphis. Served to capt. USMCR, 1943-45. Decorated Bronze Star; recipient William L. Prosser award for outstanding contbn. of devel. of tort law, 1980. Mem. ABA, Miss. Bar Assn., Tenn. Bar Assn., Nashville Bar Assn., Assn. Bar City N.Y., Order of Coif (nat. pres. 1973-76), Am. Law Inst. (council 1960-70, 82—). Author: Cases and Materials on Restitution, 2d edit., 1966; Cases and Materials on Torts, 7th edit., 1982; contbr. numerous articles on torts and restitution to law revs. and other law publs. Legal education, Personal injury, Libel. Office: Vanderbilt U Sch Law Nashville TN 37240

WADE, MILAM LEE ROY, lawyer; b. Sealy, Tex., Mar. 3, 1896; s. Jefferson Robert and Phoebe Nancy (Mahan) W.; m. Esther Marie Thompson, Sept. 11, 1924 (div. Mar. 1941); m. Helen Irene Starr, Apr. 29, 1942 (dec. Apr. 1980). Student, New S. Coll., Beaumont, Tex., 1915. Bar: Tex. 1933, Mo. 1947, U.S. Tax Ct. 1947, U.S. Dist. Ct. (no. dist.) Tex. 1958, U.S. Ct. Appeals (5th cir.) 1960. Div. acct. Santa Fe Ry. Co., Beaumont, 1918-20, spl. acct., Galveston, Tex., 1920-22; revenue agt. IRS, Dallas, 1922-27, appellate conferee, 1927-39, advisor in charge, Dallas, Oklahoma City, 1939-42; regional dir. U.S. Econ. Stblzn. Agy., Kansas City, Mo., 1942-47; sole practice, Kansas City, 1947-58, Dallas, 1958—. Mem. adminstrv. bd. 1st United Meth. Ch., Dallas, 1960—, Mem. Tex. Bar Assn., Dallas Bar Assn., Colophon Assocs. (So. Meth. U.), Dallas County Heritage Soc., Am. Legion (post comdr. 1963-64). Republican. Lodge: Lions (gen. group chmn. 1934). Probate, Estate taxation, Personal income taxation. Address: 4635 Sierra Madre Santa Barbara CA 93110

WADLER, ARNOLD L., lawyer; b. Bklyn., Aug. 15, 1943; s. Samuel and Anne (Lowenthal) W.; m. Elissa I. Devor, Sept. 17, 1967; children—Craig A., Todd J. B.A., Bklyn. Coll., 1964; J.D., NYU, 1967. Bar: N.Y. 1968, N.J. 1974. Asst. gen. counsel Metromedia, Inc., N.Y.C., 1968-82, assoc. gen. counsel, Los Angeles, 1982-85; v.p., gen. counsel, 1985-87, sr. v.p., sec. and gen. counsel, 1987—. Mem. Zoning Bd. Adjustment, Marlboro Twp., N.J., 1980-82; exec. v.p. Marlboro Jewish Ctr., 1980-82. Mem. ABA, N.Y. Bar Assn. Lodges: Conqueror (asst. sec. 1961-63), K.P. General corporate. Office: Metromedia Co 1 Harmon Plaza Secaucus NJ 07094

WADSWORTH, JAMES MARSHALL, lawyer; b. Buffalo, Sept. 1, 1939; s. John Vredenburgh and Gertrude (Murray) W.; m. Sarah Goodyear, Aug. 26, 1961; children—Mary, John, Kate, Eliza. A.B., Princeton U., 1961; LL.B., Stanford U., 1964. Bar: N.Y. 1965, Fla. 1977. Assoc. Hodgson, Russ, Andrews, Woods & Goodyear, Buffalo, 1964-69, ptnr., 1969—; dir. Empire of Am. FSA. Bd. dirs. Buffalo Waterfront Devel. Corp.; vice chmn. Erie County Republican Com., fin. chmn.; bd. dirs. Buffalo Fine Arts Acad.-Albright Knox Art Gallery; trustee Nichols Sch.; bd. commrs. Niagara Frontier Transp. Authority; bd. visitors Stanford U. Law Sch.; mem. adv. bd. CUNY Law Sch. Mem. N.Y. State Bar Assn., ABA, Bar Assn. Erie County, Fla. State Bar Assn. Estate planning, Probate, Estate taxation. Home: 40 Dana Rd Buffalo NY 14216 Office: 1800 One M & T Plaza Buffalo NY 14203

WADSWORTH, JOEL STUART, lawyer; b. Hartford, Conn., Jan. 26, 1946; s. James Thomas Sr. and Elizabeth Alice (Donahoe) W.; 1 child, Gable Marsh. BS, U. Fla., 1969, JD with honors, 1971. Bar: Ga. 1972, Fla. 1972, U.S. Supreme Ct. 1976, U.S. Dist. Ct. (no. dist.) Ga., 1976, U.S. Ct. Appeals (11th cir.) 1976. Assoc. Hansell Post, Brandon & Dorsey, Atlanta, 1971-74; ptnr. Carr, Wadsworth, Abney & Tabb, Atlanta, 1974-79; sole practice Atlanta, 1979—; assoc. prof. Mercer U., Atlanta, 1978; counsel, bd. dirs. Apt. Owners and Mgrs. Assn., Atlanta, 1978-82. Co-author Real Property Principles and Practises, 1987, (jour.) Apt. Owners and Mgrs. Assn. Contracts for Improvements and Ops. of Income Properties, 1981; legal editor Apartment Owners and Managers Association Property Management Handbook, 1981-82. Vol. adult leader Boy Scouts Am., West Palm Beach, Fla., 1964-66; instr. water safety and first aid ARC, Gainesville, Fla., 1969-71. Holland Law Ctr. scholar U. Fla., 1970-71. Mem. Atlanta Bar Assn. (chmn. real estate sect. 1978-80, bd. dirs. 1978-80, continuing legal edn. panelist 1977-79), Ga. Land Devel. Assn. (gen. counsel 1977-78), Ga. Mortgage Bankers Assn. (gen. counsel 1972-75), Lawyers Club Atlanta, Nat. Assn. Bond Counsel (continuing legal edn. panelist 1986, bd. dirs. 1977-79, Bond Lawyer's Workship and 1986 Tax Reform Act Implementation Workshop), Phi Alpha Delta. Club: Cherokee Town & Country (Atlanta). Avocations: music, woodworking, metal and stone sculpting, sports. Municipal bonds, Real property, Personal income taxation. Office: 3340 Peachtree Rd NE Suite 2220 Tower Pl Atlanta GA 30026

WADSWORTH, MURRAY MARVIN, lawyer; b. Tallahassee, Nov. 26, 1936; s. Newthon Howell and Alice (Collins) W.; m. Mary Matteson, April 30, 1966; children: Murray M. Jr., Mary Alice. BA, Washington & Lee U., 1959; LLB, U. Fla., 1962. Bar: Fla. 1963, U.S. Dist. Ct. (mid. dist.) Fla. 1963, U.S. Dist. Ct. (no. dist.) Fla. 1964, U.S. Ct. Appeals (5th cir.) 1964, U.S. Supreme Ct. 1979. Asst. U.S. atty. U.S. Dist. Ct. (no. dist.), Tallahassee, 1964-67; ptnr. Thompson, Wadsworth, Messer, Turner & Rhodes, Tallahassee, 1969-80, Wadsworth & Davis, Tallahassee, 1980—. Served to 2d lt. U.S. Army, 1959-60. Fellow Am. Coll. Trial Lawyers; mem. ABA, Tallahassee Bar Assn., Assn. Trial Lawyers Am., Acad. Fla. Trial Lawyers, Nat. Inst. Trial Adv. Methodist. Criminal, State civil litigation, Federal civil litigation. Home: 706 Piedmont Dr Tallahassee FL 32312 Office: Wadsworth & Davis 203 N Gadsen St PO Box 10529 Tallahassee FL 32302

WAECHTER, ARTHUR JOSEPH, JR., lawyer; b. New Orleans, Nov. 20, 1913; s. Arthur Joseph and Elinor (Reckner) W.; m. Peggy Weaver, Feb. 20, 1939; children: Susan Porter Waechter McClellan, Sally Ann Waechter McGehee, Robert. A.B., Tulane U., 1934, LL.B., 1936. Bar: La. 1936. Since practiced in New Orlean; partner Jones, Walker, Waechter, Poitevent, Carrere & Denegre, 1942—; prof. law Tulane U. Sch. Law, 1947-68; dir. Canal Barge Co., Inc., Central Marine Service, Inc., Eugenie and Joseph Jones Family Found. Bd. visitors Tulane U., 1959-64; bd. advisers to editors Tulane Law Rev. Assn., 1960—; bd. adminstrs. Tulane Ednl. Fund, 1968-83, adv. to bd. adminstrs., 1983—. Served to lt. (j.g.) USNR, 1943-46. Mem. ABA, La. Bar Assn. (gov. 1968- 70), New Orleans Bar Assn. (pres. 1961-62), Internat. Assn. Ins. Counsel, Tulane U. Alumni Assn. (pres. 1962-63), Maritime Law Assn. U.S., Am. Law Inst., Am. Judicature Soc., Am. Coll. Real Estate Lawyers (gov. 1983-86), Order of Coif, Phi Kappa Sigma, Phi Delta Phi. Clubs: Pickwick, Boston, Stratford, International House, Round Table, Southern Yacht , Louisiana, The Plimsoll (New Orleans); Pinnacle (N.Y.C.). General corporate, Contracts commercial, Real property. Home: 1210 Webster St New Orleans LA 70118 Office: Jones Walker WaechterPoitevent Carrere & Denegre 225 Baronne St New Orleans LA 70112

WAGERMAN, HOWARD LOUIS, lawyer; b. Memphis, Nov. 24, 1954; s. Benjamin and Sara Laverne (Tupper) W.; m. Martha Karen Lee, May 4, 1980; children: Stacy Lynne, Blake Matthew. BBA, Memphis State U., 1976, JD, 1979. Bar: Tenn. 1979, U.S. Dist. Ct. (we. dist.) Tenn. 1979. Assoc. Friedman and Sissman, Memphis, 1979-80; ptnr. Wagerman and Seligstein, Memphis, 1980—; bd. dirs., sec. H&W Cartage, Memphis, Macy Properties, Memphis. Mem. ABA, Tenn. Bar Assn. Memphis/Shelby County Bar Assn., Tenn. Trial Lawyers Assn., Memphis State U.-Cecil C. Humphreys Sch. Law Alumni Assn. Alpha Epsilon Pi (pres. 1975-76), Phi Alpha Delta. Criminal, Family and matrimonial, Consumer commercial. Home: 2036 Overhill Cove Germantown TN 38138 Office: Wagerman and Seligstein 100 N Main St Suite 2003 Memphis TN 38103

WAGGONER, LAWRENCE WILLIAM, legal educator; b. Sidney, Ohio, July 2, 1937; s. William J. and Gladys L. Waggoner; m. Lynne A., Aug. 27, 1963; children—Ellen, Diane. B.B.A., U. Cin., 1960; J.D., U. Mich., 1963; Ph.D., Oxford U. (England), 1966. Assoc. Cravath, Swaine & Moore, N.Y.C., 1963; prof. law U. Ill., Champaign, 1968-72; prof. law U. Va., Charlottesville, 1972-74; prof. law U. Mich., Ann Arbor, 1974-84, James V. Campbell prof. law, 1984—; dir. research joint editorial bd. Uniform Probate Code, 1986—. Served to capt. U.S. Army, 1966-68. Fulbright scholar Oxford U., 1963-65. Mem. Am. Law Inst., Am. Coll. Probate Counsel, Internat. Acad. Estate and Trust Law. Author: Future Interests in a Nutshell, 1981; Federal Taxation of Gifts, Trusts, and Estates (2d edit.), 1982; Trusts and Succession (4th edit.), 1983. Estate planning, Probate, Estate taxation. Office: U Mich Law Sch Ann Arbor MI 48109

WAGGONER, MICHAEL JAMES, lawyer; b. Evanston, Ill., Sept. 21, 1942; s. Alva Madison and Martha (Peacock) W.; m. Cynthia Lynn Goff, Mar. 17, 1984; 1 child, Julia Lauren. AB, Stanford U., 1964; LLB, Harvard U., 1967. Bar: D.C. 1968. Assoc. Wilmer, Cutler & Pickering, Washington, 1971-73; assoc. prof. law U. Colo., Boulder, 1973—. Served to capt. USAF, 1968-71. Federal civil litigation, Corporate taxation, Personal income taxation. Home: 930 Crestmoor Dr Boulder CO 80303 Office: U Colo Law Sch Campus Box 401 Boulder CO 80309-0401

WAGNER, CHARLES STEPHEN, lawyer; b. Reading, Pa., Mar. 23, 1950; s. John B. and Josephine A. (Corvaia) W.; m. Jane Adair Dansard, May 26. BA, U. S.C., 1972; M in Pub. Adminstrn., Golden Gate U., 1977; JD, Cumberland Law Sch., 1979. Bar: Ala. 1980, U.S. Dist. Ct. (no. dist.) Ala. 1980, U.S. Ct. Appeals (5th and 11th cirs.) 1980. Ptnr. Perhacs & Wagner, Birmingham, Ala., 1980-81; asst. county atty. Jefferson County, Birmingham, 1981—. Serves with USNR, 1972—. Mem. Ala. Bar Assn., Birmingham Bar Assn. (chmn adminstrv. law sect. 1986—). Avocation: sailing. Local government, State civil litigation, Administrative and regulatory. Home: 205 Shelterwood Circle Birmingham AL 35226 Office: County Atty's Office Rm 213 Jefferson County Ct House Birmingham AL 35263

WAGNER, CURTIS LEE, JR., judge; b. Kingsport, Tenn., Nov. 8, 1928; m. Jeanne E. Allen; children—Curtis L. III, Rex A. Student Tenn. Poly. Inst., 1947-49; LL.B., U. Tenn., 1951. Bar: Tenn. 1952. Assoc. Kramer, Dye, McNabb and Greenwood, Knoxville, Tenn., 1951-54; atty.-adv. gen. crimes and fraud sect. Criminal Div., Dept. Justice, Washington, 1954-56, trial atty. Dept. Justice, 1954-60, assigned to Ct. of Claims sect. Civil Div., 1956-60; spl. asst. to JAG for communications, transp. and utilities, Office JAG, Dept. Army, Washington, 1960-64, chief Regulatory Law Div., 1964-74, mem. civilian lawyer career com., 1960-74, chmn. JAG incentive awards com. 1960-74, mem. Army Staff Awards Bd., 1964-74, mem. Army Environ. Policy Council, 1972-74. Adminstrv. law judge FERC, Washington, 1974-79, chief adminstrv. law judge, 1979—. Dist. commr. Nat. Capital Area council Boy Scouts Am., 1967-69. Decorated Meritorious Civilian Service award, Exceptional Civilian Service award; recipient citation for outstanding performance Dept. Army, 1961-74; Scouter's Tng. award Boy Scouts Am., 1965, Scoutmaster's Key, 1966, Commr.'s Key, 1968, Commr.'s Arrowhead Honor, 1966, Silver Beaver award, 1969. Mem. ABA, Fed. Adminstrv. Law Judges Conf. (sec.), Nat. Lawyers Club, Order of Arrow. Methodist. Clubs: Annapolis Yacht (parliamentarian), Annapolis Power Squadron, U.S. Power Squadrons. FERC practice, Administrative and regulatory, General practice. Office: Fed Energy Regulatory Commn 825 N Capitol St NE Washington DC 20426

WAGNER, D. WILLIAM, lawyer; b. Dixon, Ill., Jan. 14, 1943; s. Earl L. and Lois Mae (Schrock) W.; m. Barbara J. Bogott, June 11, 1966; children—Peter Alan, Nicholas William. B.A., Northwestern U., 1965, J.D., 1968. Bar: Ill. 1968, U.S. Dist. Ct. (no. dist.) Ill. 1969, U.S. Ct. Appeals (7th cir.) 1971, Calif. 1982. Ptnr. firm Sidley & Austin, Chgo. and Los Angeles, 1969—. Co-author: Illinois Municipal Law—Subdivisions and Subdivisions in Controls, 1978, 81. Troop chmn. Crescent Bay Council Boy Scouts Am., Santa Monica, Calif., 1984-85. Mem. Los Angeles County Bar Assn., ABA, Ill. State Bar Assn., Chgo. Bar Assn. (chmn. real property land use com. 1980-81), Beverly Hills Bar Assn. (chmn. real estate sect. 1986—). Presbyterian. Clubs: Legal (Chgo.); Beach (Santa Monica). Real property, Environment, Construction. Home: 370 25th St Santa Monica CA 90402 Office: Sidley & Austin 2049 Century Park East Suite 3500 Los Angeles CA 90067

WAGNER, JOHN LEO, lawyer; b. Ithaca, N.Y., Mar. 12, 1954; s. Paul Francis and Doris Elizabeth (Hoffschneider) W. Student, U. Nebr., 1973-74; BA, U. Okla., 1976, JD, 1979. Bar: Okla. 1980, U.S. Dist. Ct. (we. dist.) Okla. 1980, U.S. Dist. Ct. (no. and ea. dists.) Okla. 1981, U.S. Ct. Appeals (10th cir.) 1982. Assoc. Franklin, Harmon & Satterfield Inc., Oklahoma City, 1980-82; ptnr. Franklin, Harman & Satterfield Inc., Oklahoma City, 1982; assoc. Kornfeld, Franklin & Phillips, Oklahoma City, 1982-85, ptnr., 1985; magistrate U.S. Dist. Ct. (no. dist.) Okla., Tulsa, 1985—. Mem. Okla. Bar Assn. Republican. Federal civil litigation, Judicial administration, Personal injury. Office: US Magistrate 333 W 4th St Room 4-528 Tulsa OK 74103

WAGNER, JON MARK, lawyer; b. N.Y.C., Dec. 16, 1949; s. Rudolph Theodore and Lucile Helene (Batchker) w.; m. Cathy Ann Raffkind, Aug. 9, 1975; children: Justin Philip, Robin Cari. AB, Oberlin Coll., 1972; JD, South Tex. Coll. Law, 1975; LLM in Taxation, NYU, 1979. Bar: Tex. 1975, U.S. Tax Ct. 1976, U.S. Dist. Ct. (so. dist.) Tex. 1977, U.S. Ct. Claims 1980, U.S. Ct. Appeals (5th cir.) 1980, U.S. Supreme Ct. 1980, U.S. Ct. Appeals (11th cir.) 1981. Assoc. Magids & White, Inc., Houston, 1976-77; asst. to corp. sec. Gen. Crude Oil Co., Houston, 1977-78; sole practice, Houston, 1979; assoc. Lackshin & Nathan, Houston, 1980-82, ptnr., 1983-85; ptnr. Lipstet, Singer, Hirsch & Wagner, Houston, 1985—; exec. v.p., sec., bd. dirs. Wagner Realty Co., Inc., Houston, 1983—; pres., dir. Four Sisters Oil and Gas Corp., Houston, 1983-86; adv. dir. Nat. Splty. Products, Houston, The Body Designer, Inc., Houston, 1987—; guest lectr. Exec. MBA Program U. Houston, 1984—. Mem. Rep. Nat. Com., Jewish Fedn. Greater Houston, Am. Jewish Com., Jewish Community Ctr. Houston. Mem. ABA (sects. taxation, bus. law, real property, probate and trust law, natural resources, forum com. on franchising), Houston Bar Assn., Internat. Assn. Fin. Planners, Houston Estate and Fin. Forum, Houston Young Lawyers Assn. Corporate taxation, Estate taxation, Personal income taxation. Home: 14672 C Perthshire Houston TX 77079 Office: Lipstet Singer Hirsch & Wagner 1980 Post Oak Blvd Suite 1780 Houston TX 77056

WAGNER, JOSEPH HAGEL, lawyer; b. Balt., June 4, 1947; s. Herman B. and Mary Louise (Hagel) W.; m. Hilary Reuss Becton, June 10, 1972; children: James Becton, Christopher Lowther. BA, Villanova U., 1969; JD, Syracuse U., 1972. Editor Bucks County Law Reporter, 1983-85, asst. editor, 85-86. Chmn. ch. com. ARC Bloodmobile, 1984—; v.p. Bucks County Estate Planning Council, 1984-87, pres., 1987—; former pres., v.p. New Britain Borough Civic Assn. Served to capt. USAR, 1972-81. Mem. Bucks County Bar Assn. (treas. 1983-85, bd. dirs. 1981-83). Republican. Roman Catholic. Probate, Estate planning, Real property. Home: 25 Linda Ln Warrington PA 18976 Office: 332 N Main St Doylestown PA 18901

WAGNER, LESLIE, academic director, lawyer; b. Houston, July 18, 1953; d. Jacob and Geraldine (Harris) W.; m. Stuart A. Kovar. BA cum laude, U. Tex., 1975; JD, U. Houston, 1980. Bar: Tex. 1980, U.S. Dist. Ct. (so. dist.) Tex. 1981. Trial atty. civil rights EEOC, Houston, 1981-84; sole practice Houston, 1984-85; dir. law placement U. Houston Law Ctr., 1985—; cons. EEOC, Houston, 1984—. Editor: U. Houston Law Rev., 1979, assoc. editor, 1980. Mem. health and edn. com. Jewish Community Ctr., Houston, 1983-85; polit. cons., Houston, 1984-85. Named Honors Day Honoree U. Tex., 1971; Arts and Sciences scholar U. Tex., 1971-74. Mem. ABA (com. on employee and labor relations 1983-85, employment rights com. gen. practice sect. 1986—), Houston Bar Assn., Assn. Trial Lawyers Am., Tex. Young Lawyers Assn. (job fair com.), Nat. Assn. Law Placement (careers com. 1986—), Am. Studies Assn., Houston Festival Dancers (treas. 1976-77), Eta Phi Sigma. Democrat. Avocations: creative writing, dance, reading. Labor, General practice, Law placement. Home: 5407 Wigton Dr Houston TX 77096 Office: U Houston Law Ctr Law Placement Office 4800 Calhoun Houston TX 77004

WAGNER, MICHAEL DUANE, lawyer; b. Shiner, Tex., July 4, 1948; s. Martin Matthew and Mary Margaret (Prasek) W.; m. Patricia Ann Miller, July 1, 1972; 1 child, Matthew Miller. BA, Tex. Christian U., 1970; JD, St. Mary's Sch. Law, San Antonio, 1973. Bar: Tex. 1973, U.S. Supreme Ct. 1977. Assoc. counsel United Services Automobile Assn., San Antonio, 1973-78, asst. v.p., counsel, 1978-80, v.p., counsel, 1980—; counsel investment mgmt. co. United Services Automobile Assn., San Antonio, 1980—, pres., chmn. bd. dirs. fed. credit union, 1981-84. Counsel United San Antonio Found., 1982; rep. Target 90/Goals for San Antonio, 1985; bd. dirs. De Paul Family Ctr., San Antonio, 1985. Named one of Outstanding Young Men in Am., U.S. Jr. C. of C., 1984. Mem. ABA, Fed. Bar Assn., San Antonio Bar Assn., Phi Delta Theta, Phi Alpha Delta. Roman Catholic. Avocations: running, home renovation. General corporate, Securities, Labor. Home: 260 Primera San Antonio TX 78212 Office: United Services Automobile Assn Bldg San Antonio TX 78288

WAGNER, MICHAEL G., lawyer; b. Bklyn., July 12, 1949; s. Irving and Vivian (Lederman) W.; m. Martha Rosario Estevez, Nov. 21, 1979; children—Roxanne, Eric, Jeannien, Nicole, Shawn B.S.B.A., Ithaca Coll., 1971; J.D., Bklyn. Law Sch., 1974. Bar: N.Y. 1975, U.S. Dist. Ct. (ea. dist.) N.Y., U.S. Dist. Ct. (so. dist.) N.Y., U.S. Ct. Appeals (2d cir.). Counselor Mental Health Info. Service, N.Y.C., 1974-76; ptnr. Klein, Wagner & Morris, N.Y.C., 1976—; lectr. on social security rights VA, 1984. Mem. N.Y. Social Security Bar Assn. (bd. dirs., treas., pres.), Bklyn. Bar Assn., Rockland Bar Assn., Queens Bar Assn., Nat. Orgn. Social Security Claimant's Reps. (pres., bd. dirs.), Delta Mu Delta (v.p. 1970-71). Democrat. Jewish. Pension, profit-sharing, and employee benefits, Workers' compensation, Federal civil litigation. Home: 3 Iroquois Trail Monsey NY 10952 Office: Klein Wagner & Morris 71 Murray St New York NY 10007

WAGNER, RICHARD HOPKINS, corporation lawyer; b. N.Y.C., Nov. 26, 1952; s. George Richard and Valda Florence (Hancock) W. BS, Cornell U., 1974; MBA, Iona Coll., 1978; postgrad., Cambridge U., Eng., 1979; JD, Pace U., 1981. Bar: N.Y. 1982, U.S. Dist. Ct. (so. dist.) N.Y. 1982, U.S. Ct. Appeals (D.C. cir.) 1982, U.S. Supreme Ct. 1985, U.S. Dist. Ct. (no. dist.) N.Y. 1986, U.S. Ct. Appeals (2d cir.) 1987. Assoc. AT&T, N.Y.C., 1981-83, N.Y. Telephone Co., N.Y.C., 1983—. Participating mem. Met. Mus. Art,

N.Y.C. Recipient James C. May award, Westchester County Bar Assn., 1981, Outstanding Lawyer award, N.Y. Telephone Co., 1986. Mem. ABA, Royal Oak Found., Smithsonian Assocs., Mass. Soc. Mayflower Descendants. Avocations: art, painting, history. Administrative and regulatory, Antitrust, Public utilities. Office: N Y Telephone Co 1095 Ave of Americas New York NY 10036

WAGNER, ROBERT F., lawyer, diplomat; b. N.Y.C., Apr. 20, 1910; s. Robert F. Wagner; m. Susan Edwards (dec. 1964); 2 sons; m. Barbara Joan Cavanagh, July 1965 (div. June 1971); m. Phyllis Fraser Cerf, Jan. 1975. A.B., Yale U., 1933, LL.B., 1937; postgrad., Harvard Sch. Bus. Adminstrn., 1934; LL.D., L.I. U., Fordham U., Bklyn. Law Sch., St. John's Law Sch., others. Mem. N.Y. State Assembly, 1938-41; city tax commn. N.Y.C., 1946; commr. housing and buildings 1947; chmn. City Planning Commn., 1948; pres. Borough of Manhattan, Greater N.Y.C., 1949-53; mayor N.Y.C., 1954-65; partner firm Finley, Kumble, Wagner, Heine, Underberg, Manley, Myerson & Casey, 1976—; U.S. ambassador to Spain, 1968-69; personal envoy of Pres. U.S. to Vatican, 1978-81; First v.p., del. N.Y. Constl. Conv., 1967; chmn. bd. United Neighborhood Houses; mem. Pres.'s Crime Commn., 1965-66. chmn. jud. nominating com. First Jud. Dept. N.Y. State, 1975-82; also mem. commn. on jud. nominations N.Y. State, 1978-83; vice chmn. Port Authority N.Y. and N.J. Served to lt. col. 9th Air Force, 1942-45; now col. ret. Address: Finley Kumble et al 425 Park Ave New York NY 10022

WAGNER, THOMAS JOSEPH, lawyer, insurance company executive; b. Jackson, Mich., June 29, 1939; s. O. Walter and Dorothy Ann (Hollinger) W.; m. Judith Louise Bogardue, Jan. 15, 1961; children—Ann Louise, Mark Robert, Rachel Miriam. B.A., Earlham Coll., 1957; J.D., U. Chgo., 1965. Bar: Ill. 1968, U.S. Supreme Ct. 1975. Asst. to gov. State of Ill., Springfield, 1966-67, legal counsel, adminstrv. asst. to treas., 1967-70; adminstrv. asst. to U.S. senator Adlai E. Stevenson, Washington, 1970-77; sr. v.p. govt. affairs div. Am. Ins. Assn., Washington, 1977-79; v.p., chief counsel Property Casualty Group, CIGNA Corp., Phila., 1982-86, v.p., assoc. gen. counsel property casualty group CIGNA Corp., Phila., 1986—. Dir. Phila. Crime Commn. Africa-Asia Pub. Service fellow Syracuse U., 1965-66. Mem. ABA (tort and ins. sect.), Am. Ins. Assn. (law and regulation com.). Insurance, Legislative. Office: CIGNA Corp 1600 Arch St Philadelphia PA 19103

WAGONER, DAVID EVERETT, lawyer; b. Pottstown, Pa., May 16, 1928; s. Claude Brower and Mary Kathryn (Groff) W.; m. Landon Jensen; children—Paul R., Colin H., Elon D., Peter B. B.A., Yale U., 1950; LL.B., U. Pa., 1953. Bar: D.C. 1953, Pa. 1953, Wash. 1953. Law clk. U.S. Ct. Appeals (3d cir.), Pa., 1955-56; law clk. U.S. Supreme Ct., Washington, 1956-57; ptnr. Perkins & Coie, Seattle, 1957—. Mem. sch. com. Mcpl. League Seattle and King County, 1958—, chmn., 1962-65; mem. Seattle schs. citizens coms. on equal ednl. opportunity and adult vocat. edn., 1963-64; mem. Nat. Com. Support Pub. Schs.; mem. adv. com. on community colls., to 1965, legislature interim com. on edn., 1964-65; mem. community coll. adv. com. to state supt. pub. instrn., 1965; chmn. edn. com. Forward Thrust, 1968; mem. Univ. Congl. Ch. Council Seattle, 1968-70; bd. dirs. Met. YMCA Seattle, 1968; bd. dirs. Seattle Pub. Schs., 1965-73, v.p., 1966-67, 72-73, pres., 1968, 73; trustee Evergreen State Coll. Found., chmn. 1986; trustee Pacific NW Ballet, v.p. 1986. Served to 1st lt. M.C., AUS, 1953-55. Fellow Am. Coll. Trial Lawyers; mem. English Speaking Union (v.p. Seattle 1961-62), ABA (chmn. appellate advocacy com.), Wash. State Bar Assn., Seattle-King County Bar Assn., Nat. Sch. Bds. Assn. (bd. dirs., chmn. Council Big City Bds. Edn. 1971-72), Chi Phi. General practice. Home: 1150 22d Ave E Seattle WA 98112 Office: Perkins and Coie Washington Bldg Seattle WA 98101

WAGONER, WALTER DRAY, JR., lawyer; b. New Haven, Dec. 25, 1942; s. Walter D. and Mariana (Parcells) W.; m. Rosa Nilda Morales, Jan. 22, 1980; children—David, William Carlos, Brenda, Lisa. B.A., Yale U., 1965, LL.B., 1970. Bar: Conn. 1971, U.S. Dist. Ct. Conn. 1971. Staff atty. New Haven Legal Assistance Assn., 1970-74, mng. atty., 1974-76, dir. legal edn., 1976-78; sole practice, New Haven, 1978—. Chmn., New Haven City Commn. Cultural Affairs, 1977-79; trustee Conn. Public TV, 1977-83; standing trustee U.S. Bankruptcy Ct. for Dist. of Conn. Mem. Conn. Bar Assn., New Haven County Bar Assn. Democrat. Club: Loizenos (hon.). Bankruptcy.

WAGSHAL, JEROME STANLEY, lawyer, philatelic consultant; b. Washington, June 20, 1928; s. Philip and May (Wolf) W. BA with distinction, George Washington U., 1950; LLB, Yale U., 1953. Bar: U.S. Dist. Ct. D.C. 1953, U.S. Ct. Appeals (D.C. cir.) 1953, U.S. Supreme Ct. 1958, N.Y. 1970. Instr. U.S. Naval Sch. of Naval Justice, 1953-57; sr. trial atty. Dept. of Justice Antitrust Div., 1957-68; v.p., gen. counsel Ecol. Sci. Corp., 1968-69; ptnr. Dickstein, Shapiro & Galigan and successor firms, 1970-73; founding ptnr. Pearce & Wagshal, Washington, 1973-75; sole practice, Washington, 1975. Contbr. articles to legal and philatelic jours. Bd. dirs., v.p. Georgetown Citizens Assn. Served to lt., USNR, 1953-57. Recipient Ashbrook Cup, U.S. Philatelic Classics Soc., 1970, Schreiber Cup, Am. Philatelic Soc., 1970. Mem. ABA, D.C. Bar, Order of Coif, Phi Beta Kappa, Omicron Delta Kappa, Pi Gamma Mu, Phi Eta Sigma, Delta Sigma Rho. Clubs: Yale (N.Y.C.); City Tavern (Washington). Antitrust, Federal civil litigation, State civil litigation. Office: 3256 N St NW Washington DC 20007

WAGSTAFF, ROBERT HALL, lawyer; b. Kansas City, Mo., Nov. 5, 1941; s. Robert Wilson and Katherine Motter (Hall) W. A.B., Dartmouth Coll., 1963; J.D., U. Kans., 1966. Bar: Kans., Alaska, U.S. Ct. Appeals (9th cir.), U.S. Supreme Ct. Asst. atty. gen State of Kans., 1966-67; asst. dist. atty. Fairbanks (Alaska), 1967-69; ptnr. Boyko & Walton, Anchorage, 1969-70; sr. ptnr. Wagstaff et. al., Anchorage, 1970—. Pres. U.S. Aerobatic Found., Oshkosh, Wis., 1986—. Mem. Alaska Bar Assn. (bd. govs. 1985—, pres.-elect 1987), Lawyer-Pilots Bar Assn., ACLU (nat. bd. dirs. 1972-78). Civil rights, State civil litigation, Personal injury. Home: 106 F St Anchorage AK 99501 Office: 912 W 6th Ave Anchorage AK 99501

WAHL, HAROLD BARKLEY, lawyer; b. Shawnee, Okla., Apr. 4, 1907. BA, U. Fla., 1932, JD with honors, 1932. Bar: Fla. 1932, U.S. Supreme Ct. 1936. Atty. Fla. East Coast Ry. Co., Jacksonville, 1932-50; ptnr. Loftin & Wahl, Jacksonville, 1948-75, Wahl & Gabel, Jacksonville, 1975—; asst. to trustee Fla. East Coast Ry. Co., 1940-71, gen. atty., 1950-69, gen. counsel, 1959-61; v.p., gen. counsel, Flagler System Inc., Palm Beach., Fla., 1948—, bd. dirs. Trustee Davidson Coll., 1956-60; elder Presbyn. Ch. Fellow Am. Bar Found.; mem. ABA, Fla. Bar Assn., Jacksonville Bar Assn., Fla. Jr. Bar Assn. (pres. 1940-41), Blue Key, Phi Beta Kappa. Home: 515 Ponte Vedra Blvd Ponte Vedra Beach FL 32082 Office: Wahl & Gabel 112 W Adams St 920 Barnett Bank Bldg Jacksonville FL 32202

WAHL, KARLA RAE, lawyer; b. Waterloo, Iowa, Sept. 12, 1951; d. Raymond Everett and Ethel Mae (Dawson) W. BA, St. Olaf Coll., 1973; JD, U. Iowa, 1976. Bar: Iowa 1976, Minn. 1976, U.S. Dist. Ct. Minn. 1976, U.S. Ct. Appeals (8th cir.), U.S. Supreme Ct. 1986. Assoc. Berman & Lazarus, Edina, Minn., 1976-79; sole practice Mpls., 1979-81; treas., bd. dirs. Minn. Mental Health Inst., Mpls., 1985—; lobbyist, 1982-83. Mem. JCC Community Orch., St. Louis Park, Minn., 1985—. Mem. ABA, Minn. Bar Assn., Hennepin County Bar Assn., Assn. Trial Lawyers Am., Minn. Trial Lawyers Assn. Avocations: tennis, music, aerobics. Federal civil litigation, State civil litigation, General corporate. Home: 2924 Webster Ave Saint Louis Park MN 55436 Office: 4717 IDS Ctr 80 S 8th St Minneapolis MN 55402

WAHL, ROSALIE E., judge; b. Gordon, Kans., Aug. 27, 1924; children: Christopher Roswell, Sara Emilie, Timothy Eldon, Mark Patterson, Jenny Caroline. B.A., U. Kans., 1946; J.D., William Mitchell Coll. Law, 1967. Bar: Minn. 1967. Asst. state pub. defender Mpls., 1967-73; clin. prof. law William Mitchell Coll. Law, 1973-77; assoc. justice Minn. Supreme Ct., St. Paul, 1977—; adj. prof. law U. Minn., 1972-73. Fellow Am. Bar Found; mem. ABA (chmn.-elect. sect. legal edn. and bar admissions, accreditation com., criminal justice sect., individual rights and responsibility sect.), Minn. State Bar Assn. (com. legal assistance to disadvantaged), Am. Judicature Soc., Nat. Assn. Women Judges, Nat. Assn. Woman Lawyers, Minn. Women Lawyers Assn. Judicial administration. Office: State Capitol Supreme Ct Saint Paul MN 55155

WAHOSKE, MICHAEL JAMES, lawyer; b. Ripon, Wis., June 4, 1953; m. Marcia Wilson; children: Jennifer, John. BA with highest honors, U. Notre Dame, 1975, JD summa cum laude, 1978. Bar: Minn. 1978, U.S. Dist. Ct. Minn. 1979, U.S. Ct. Appeals (7th cir.) 1979, U.S. Ct. Appeals (8th and 9th cirs.) 1980, U.S. Ct. Appeals (10th cir.) 1982, U.S. Supreme Ct. 1982. Law clk. to presiding justice U.S. Ct. Appeals (7th cir.), Chgo., 1978-79; law clk. to chief justice Warren E. Burger U.S. Supreme Ct., Washington, 1979-80; assoc. Dorsey & Whitney, Mpls., 1980-85, ptnr., 1986—; adj. prof. law U. Minn., Mpls., 1981-83. Exec. editor U. Notre Dame Law Rev., 1977-78; co-editor: Freedom & Education: Pierce v. Society of Sisters Reconsidered, 1978. Roger J. Kiley fellow U. Notre Dame, 1975. Mem. ABA, Minn. Bar Assn. (ct. rules com.), Hennepin County Bar Assn., Phi Beta Kappa. Federal civil litigation, State civil litigation. Office: Dorsey & Whitney 2200 1st Bank Pl E Minneapolis MN 55402

WAINBLAT, NEAL BRUCE, lawyer; b. Rochester, N.Y., Dec. 30, 1954; s. Ike and Marion (Tatleman) W. BA, U. Rochester, 1977; JD, Case Western Res. U., 1980. Bar: N.Y. 1981, Ohio 1981. Assoc. Duvin, Flinker & Cahn, Cleve., 1980—. Mem. ABA, Cleve. Bar Assn., Midwest Pension Conf., Order of Coif. Avocation: golf. Pension, profit-sharing, and employee benefits. Office: Duvin Flinker & Cahn 2000 E 9th St 1400 Citizens Fed Tower Cleveland OH 44115

WAINTROOB, ANDREA RUTH, lawyer; b. Chgo., Dec. 23, 1952; d. David Samuel and Lees (Carson) W. AB, Brown U., 1975; JD, U. Chgo., 1978. Bar: Ill. 1978, U.S. Dist. Ct. (no. dist.) Ill. 1978, U.S. Ct. Appeals (7th cir.) 1982. Assoc. Vedder, Price, Kaufman and Kammholz, Chgo., 1978-84; ptnr. Vedder, Price, Kaufman, Chgo., 1984—; lectr. indsl. relations Grad. Sch. Bus. U. Chgo. Mem. ABA, Chgo. Bar Assn., Nat. Council Sch. Attys. Labor, Federal civil litigation, State civil litigation. Home: 1560 N Sandburg Terr Apt 3915 Chicago IL 60610 Office: Vedder Price Kaufman and Kammholz 115 S LaSalle Chicago IL 60603

WAITE, BLAKELEY ROBINSON, lawyer; b. Boston, Apr. 16, 1932; d. William H. Jr. and Ann Blakeley (Watt) Robinson; m. Charles E. Waite, May 21, 1977. AB, Vassar Coll., 1953; MA, Yale U., 1955; JD, U. Fla., 1975. Bar: Fla. 1975, U.S. Dist. Ct. (mid. dist.) Fla. 1977. Analyst U.S. Govt., Washington, 1954-65; staff asst., mgr. Pan Am, N.Y.C., 1966-70; assoc. Smith & Hulsey, Jacksonville, Fla., 1975-78; sole practice Jacksonville and Jacksonville Beach, Fla., 1978—. Mem. Jacksonville Women's Network, 1982—, bd. dirs., 1984—; bd. dirs. Naval Continuing Care Retirement Found.d Inc., Jacksonville, 1985—. Mem. Fla. Bar Assn. (probate and guardianship rules com.), Jacksonville Bar Assn., Phi Beta Kappa. Probate, Estate planning. Office: 2320 S 3d St Suite 2 Jacksonville Beach FL 32250

WAITT, ROBERT KENNETH, lawyer; b. Seattle, Apr. 25, 1931; s. Charles Kenneth and Willa E. (Ryan) W.; m. Diane Dallam, Dec. 7, 1933; children: Mark Robert, Julie Lynn Reid. Student Wash. State Coll., 1949-50, 52-53; LLB, Gonzaga U., 1957, JD, 1967. Bar: Wash. 1957. Assoc. Morrissey, Hedrick & Dunham, Seattle, 1957-59; ptnr. Benson & Waitt, Seattle, 1959-60; assoc. Walsh & Margolis, Seattle, 1960-62; ptnr. Murray, Dunham & Waitt, Seattle, 1962-81; ptnr. Waitt, Johnson & Martens, Seattle, 1981—; judge King County Dist. Ct., Seattle, 1965-81, City of Issaquah Mcpl. Ct., 1961-81; chmn. City Issaquah Civil Service Commn., 1963-69; chmn. Gonzaga Law Council, Gonzaga U. Sch. Law, Spokane, Wash., 1983-85. Regent Gonzaga U., 1982—. Served with USMC, 1950-52. Mem. ABA, Wash. Bar Assn., Seattle-King County Bar Assn., Wash. Def. Trial Lawyers Assn. Clubs: Wash. Athletic, Tower (Seattle); Sahalee Country (Redmond, Wash.); Bermuda Dunes Country (Palm Springs, Calif.). Insurance, Federal civil litigation, State civil litigation. Home: 3815 E Lake Sammamish Shorelane SE Issaquah WA 98027 Office: 6100 Columbia Ctr Seattle WA 98104

WAIWOOD, MICHAEL FRANCIS, lawyer; b. Cleve., Jan. 14, 1943; s. Anthony J. and Elizabeth (Conlon) W.; m. Ann O'Reilly Oct. 14, 1977; children: Ellen, Mary, Kathleen, William, Richard. AB, John Carroll U., 1967; JD, Cleve. State U., 1971. Bar: Ohio Sup. Ct. 1971, U.S. Dist. Ct. (no. dist.) Ohio 1976, U.S. Ct. Appeals (6th cir.) 1984. Sole practice, Cleve., 1971—; assoc. gen. counsel Fraser Mortgage Investments, Cleve., 1971-73; gen. counsel Cleve. Trust Realty Investors, 1973-77, Midland Title Security, Inc., Cleve., 1977—, also bd. dirs. Author: Real Estate Title Examination, 1983; contbr. articles to legal jours. Mem. Cleve. Bar Assn., Ohio Land Title Assn., Lawyer-Pilots Bar Assn. Republican. Roman Catholic. Real property, Contracts commercial, Civil litigation. Home: 13090 W 130th St Strongsville OH 44136 Office: 113 St Clair E Cleveland OH 44114

WAKS, STEPHEN HARVEY, lawyer; b. Decatur, Ill., Apr. 9, 1947; s. Paul and Regina (Geisler) W. BA, U. Wis., 1969; JD, U. Calif., San Francisco, 1974. Bar: Calif. 1974, U.S. Ct. Appeals (9th cir.) 1977, U.S. Tax Ct. 1977. Assoc. Wohl, Cinnamon, Hagedorn, Dunbar & Johnson, Sacramento, 1978-79; mem. Stephen H. Waks, Inc., Sacramento, 1979—; instr. U. Calif.-Davis, 1982—, Golden Gate U., 1983—. bd. dirs. Am. River Bank, Sacramento. Mem. ABA, Calif. Bar Assn., Sacramento County Bar Assn., Real Estate Securities and Syndication Inst., Phi Delta Phi. Real property, Personal income taxation. Office: 555 Capitol Mall Suite 410 Sacramento CA 95814

WALBAUM, ROBERT C., lawyer; b. Springfield, Ill., Nov. 13, 1933; s. George Crum and Mary Emma (Taylor) W.; m. Anita P. Walbaum, Aug. 6, 1960; children—John Taylor, Charles Robert. Student Bradley U., Peoria, Ill., 1951-53; B.S. in Commerce, U. Ill.-Urbana, 1955; J.D., Washington U., St. Louis, 1960. Bar: Ill. 1961, U.S. Dist. Ct. (so. dist.) Ill. 1964, U.S. Ct. Apls. (7th cir.) 1973. With Chgo. Title & Trust Co., 1960-61; asst. states atty. County of Sangamon, Ill., Springfield, 1961-63; sole practice, Springfield, 1963—; atty. City Springfield, 1964-69, Village Pleasant Plains, Ill., 1970—; tech. advisor Ill. Dept. Law Enforcement, 1969-73; counsel Springfield Park Dist., 1984—; dir. Pleasant Plains State Bank. Mem. Sangamon County Bd. Suprs., 1962-75, chmn., 1974; bd. dirs. Washington St. Mission, Springfield, 1966—, pres., 1983-86. Served with U.S. Army, 1955-57. Mem. ABA, Ill. State Bar Assn., Sangamon County Bar Assn., Phi Alpha Delta. Republican. Episcopalian. Clubs: Illini Country, Sangamo, Am. Bus. (Springfield). Probate, General corporate, Banking. Address: 1049 Woodland Ave Springfield IL 62704

WALCHER, ALAN ERNEST, lawyer; b. Chgo., Oct. 2, 1949; s. Chester R. and Dorothy E. (Kullgren) W.; 1 son, Dustin Alan. B.S., U. Utah, 1971, cert. in internat. relations, 1971, J.D., 1974. Bar: Utah 1974, U.S. Dist. Ct. Utah 1974, U.S. Ct. Appeals (10th cir.) 1977, Calif. 1979, U.S. Dist. Ct. (cen. dist.) Calif. 1979, U.S. Ct. Appeals (9th cir.) 1983. Sole practice, Salt Lake City, 1974-79; ptnr. Costello & Walcher, Los Angeles, 1979-85, Walcher & Scheuer, 1985—; judge pro tem Los Angeles Mcpl. Ct., 1986—; dir. Citronia, Inc., Los Angeles, 1979-81. Trial counsel Utah chpt. Common Cause, Salt Lake City, 1978-79. Robert Mukai scholar U. Utah, 1971. Mem. Soc. Bar And Gavel (v.p. 1975-77), ABA, Los Angeles County Bar Assn., Century City Bar Assn., Beverly Hills Bar Assn., Assn. Bus. Trial Lawyers, Phi Delta Phi, Owl and Key. Club: Woodland Hills Country (Los Angeles). State civil litigation, Federal civil litigation, Government contracts and claims. Home: 17933 Sunburst St Northridge CA 91325 Office: Walcher & Scheuer 11300 W Olympic Blvd Los Angeles CA 90064

WALD, BERNARD JOSEPH, lawyer; b. Bklyn., Sept. 14, 1932; s. Max and Ruth (Wencher) W.; m. Francine Joy Weintraub, Feb. 2, 1964; children—David Evan, Kevin Mitchell. B.B.A. magna cum laude, CCNY; J.D. cum laude, NYU, 1955. Bar: N.Y. 1955, U.S. Dist. Ct. (so. dist.) N.Y. 1960, U.S. Dist. Ct. (ea. dist.) N.Y. 1960, U.S. Ct. Appeals (2d cir.) 1960, U.S. Supreme Ct. 1971. Mem. Herzfeld & Rubin, P.C. and predecessor firms, N.Y.C., 1955—. Mem. ABA, N.Y. State Bar Assn., Assn. Bar City N.Y., N.Y. County Lawyers Assn. Contracts commercial, General corporate, Private international. Office: 40 Wall St New York NY 10005

WALD, JOHN ROGER, lawyer; b. New Prague, Minn., June 19, 1954; s. Roger Leroy and Marguerite Ann (Christenson) W.; m. Marianne Theresa Remedios, Aug. 30, 1980. BA summa cum laude, Macalester Coll., 1976; JD, Columbia U., 1979. Bar: Minn. 1979, U.S. Dist. Ct. Minn. 1979, U.S. Ct. Appeals (8th cir.) 1979. Assoc. Leonard, Street & Deinard, Mpls., 1979-81; asst. div. counsel Litton Industries, Inc., Plymouth, Minn., 1981-84; atty. Super Valu Stores, Inc., Eden Prairie, Minn., 1984—. Mem. ABA, Minn. State Bar Assn., Hennepin County Bar Assn., Corp. Counsel Assn. of Minn., Phi Beta Kappa. Roman Catholic. General corporate, Real property, Contracts commercial. Home: 4503 Oak Dr Edina MN 55424 Office: Super Value Stores Inc 11840 Valley View Rd Eden Prairie MN 55344

WALD, MICHAEL H., lawyer, educator; b. Oceanside, N.Y., Feb. 11, 1953; s. Morton Lee Wald and Janice (Weinberg) Berger; m. Jacqueline O. Wald, May 25, 1980; children: Daniel, Rachel. Student, London Sch. Econs., 1973-74; BS, BA, U. Pa., 1974; JD, Duke U., 1977. Bar: Va. 1978, N.Y. 1978, D.C. 1978, U.S. Dist. Ct. (so. and ea. dists.) N.Y. 1978, U.S. Ct. Appeals (D.C. and 4th cirs.) 1978, U.S. Tax Ct. 1978, Fla. 1979, U.S. Dist. Ct. D.C. 1979, U.S. Dist. Ct. (ea. and we. dists.) Va. 1979, Tex. 1980, U.S. Ct. Appeals (5th cir.) 1981, U.S. Dist. Ct. (we. dist.) Tex. 1981, U.S. Dist. Ct. (no. dist.) Tex. 1982, U.S. Supreme Ct. 1983. Staff atty. FTC, Washington, 1977-78; assoc. Dunaway, McCarthy & Dye, Washington, 1979; assoc. gen. counsel Datapoint Corp., San Antonio, 1980-82, TGI Friday's, Dallas, 1982-83; owner M. Wald & Co. Law Offices, Dallas, 1983—; adv. dir. Purchasing and Materials Mgmt. Inst., Richardson, Tex., 1985—; mediator Dallas Mediation Ctr., 1984; arbitrator Am. Arbitration Assn., Dallas, 1984—. Columnist, The Legalizer, Richardson Daily News, 1986. Recipient Am. Jurisprudence award Lawyers Coop., 1975. Mem. ABA, Assn. Trial Lawyers Am., Dallas Bar Assn., Dallas Estate Planning Council. Lodge: Rotary. Contracts commercial, Family and matrimonial, Criminal. Office: 275 W Campbell #501 Richardson TX 75080

WALD, MICHAEL S., legal educator; b. 1941. A.B., Cornell U., 1963; LL.B., Yale U., 1967, M.A., 1967. Bar: Calif. 1970, D.C. 1970. Atty., Ctr. Law and Social Policy, D.C., 1970-71, Pub. Defender Service, Washington, 1970-71, Youth Law Ctr., San Francisco, 1971-72; nat. adv. commn. standards and goals LEAA, 1975-76; reporter juvenile justice standards project Inst. Jud. Adminstrn., 1971-77. Chmn. Calif. adv. com. on child abuse, 1977—. Mem. Soc. Research in Child Devel., Order of Coif. Legal education. Office: Stanford U Sch Law Stanford CA 94305 *

WALD, PATRICIA MCGOWAN, lawyer, government official; b. Torrington, Conn., Sept. 16, 1928; d. Joseph F. and Margaret (O'Keefe) McGowan; m. Robert L. Wald, June 22, 1952; children—Sarah, Douglas, Johanna, Frederica, Thomas. B.A. Conn. Coll, 1948; LL.B., Yale, 1951; H.H.D., Mt. Vernon Jr. Coll., 1980; LL.D., George Washington Law Sch., 1983; LLD, John Jay Sch. of Christ, 1984, Notre Dame U., 1985. Bar: D.C. 1952. Clk. U.S. Ct. of Appeals Judge Jerome Frank, 1951-52; asso. firm Arnold, Fortas & Porter, Washington, 1952-53; mem. D.C. Crime Commn., 1964-65; atty. Office of Criminal Justice, 1967-68, Neighborhood Legal Service, D.C., 1968-70; co-dir. Ford Found. Project on Drug Abuse, 1970, Center for Law and Social Policy, 1971-72, Mental Health Law Project, 1972-77; asst. atty. gen. for legis. affairs U.S. Dept. Justice, Washington, 1977-79; judge U.S. Ct. of Appeals, D.C. circuit, 1979-86, chief judge, 1986—. Author: Law and Poverty, 1965; co-author: Bail in the United States, 1964, Dealing with Drug Abuse, 1973; contbr. articles on legal topics. Trustee Ford Found., 1972-77, Phillips Exeter Acad., 1975-77, Agnes Meyer Found., 1976-77, Conn. Coll., 1976-77; mem. Carnegie Council on Children, 1972-77. Mem. ABA (bd. editors ABA Jour. 1978-84), D.C. Bar Assn. (dir.), Am. Law Inst. (council 1975—), Inst. Medicine, Phi Beta Kappa. Jurisprudence. Office: 3832 US Courthouse John Marshall Pl Washington DC 20001 Other Address: US Court of Appeals US Courthouse 3rd & Constitution Ave NW Washington DC 20001

WALD, ROBERT LEWIS, lawyer; b. Worcester, Mass., Sept. 9, 1926; s. Lewis and Freda Ann (Rosenfield) W.; m. Patricia Ann McGowan, June 22, 1952; children: Sarah Elizabeth, Douglas Robert, Johanna Margaret, Frederica Nora, Thomas Robert. AB, Harvard U., 1947; LLB, Yale U., 1951. Bar: Mass. 1951, U.S. Ct. Appeals (4th cir.) 1957, U.S. Supreme Ct. 1957, D.C. 1959, U.S. Ct. Appeals (D.C. cir.) 1959, U.S. Ct. Appeals (6th cir.) 1975. Asst. to gen. counsel FTC, Washington, 1954-56; assoc. and ptnr. Howrey, Simon, Baker & Murchison, Washington, 1956-61; ptnr. Wald, Harkrader, Ross and predecessors, Washington, 1961—. Served to lt. USNR, 1944-46, 52-53. Mem. ABA, Fed. Bar Assn., D.C. Bar Assn. Administrative and regulatory, Antitrust, General practice. Home: 2101 Connecticut Ave NW Washington DC 20008 Office: Wald Harkrader & Ross 1300-19th St NW Washington DC 20036

WALD, SANDRA LOUISE, lawyer; b. Riverside, N.J., Oct. 12, 1951; d. William and Mildred (Haabestad) W. Student, U. Mass., 1970; BA, U. Oreg., 1973, JD, 1981. Bar: Oreg. 1981, U.S. Ct. Appeals (9th cir.) 1981. Assoc. Stoel, Rives, Boley, Fraser & Wyse, Portland, Oreg., 1982-85, Ransom, Blackman & Simson, Portland, 1985—. Mem. ABA (corp., banking and bus. law sect.), Oreg. Bar Assn. (exec. com. debtor-creditor sect. 1986—), Order of Coif. Avocations: music, skiing, travel, reading. Contracts commercial, Bankruptcy, General corporate. Office: Ransom Blackman & Simson 621 SW Morrison Suite 900 Portland OR 97205

WALDER, ROBERT ALAN, lawyer; b. Peekskill, N.Y., Oct. 22, 1953; s. Burton and Naomi Estelle (Farber) W.; m. Joan Ellen Winerman; children: Jonathan, Adam. BS, Cornell U., 1975, JD cum laude, 1978. Bar: N.Y. 1979, U.S. Dist. Ct. (no., so. and ea. dists.) N.Y. 1979. Assoc. Seward & Kissel, N.Y.C., 1978-86, ptnr., 1986—. Mem. ABA, N.Y. State Bar Assn., ACLU. Securities, Contracts commercial, Real property. Home: 590 Monterey Ave Pelham Manor NY 10803 Office: Seward & Kissel Wall St Plaza New York NY 10005

WALDMAN, BART, lawyer; b. Stamford, Conn., Oct. 24, 1948; s. Murry Robert and Beatrice Carol (Goldstein) W.; m. Nancy Vivian Smith, Jan. 1, 1981; children: Marcy Nicole, Tracy Michelle. AB, Harvard U., 1970; JD, Georgetown U., 1978. Bar: Wash. 1978. Spl. asst. to pres. Assn. of Am. Med. Colls., Washington, 1971-78; ptnr. Perkins Coie, Seattle, 1978—. Mem. ABA, Wash. State Bar Assn., Seattle-King County Bar Assn., Am. Acad. Hosp. Attys. Club: Wash. Athletic (Seattle). Labor, Health. Office: Perkins Coie 1900 Washington Bldg Seattle WA 98101

WALDMAN, ROBERT ALLAN, lawyer; b. Boone, Iowa, July 18, 1952; s. William Howard and Francis Loraine (McGee) W.; m. Debra Marie Fitch, Dec. 27, 1980; children: Geoffrey Howard, Allison Chelsea. BA in Psychology, U. Iowa, 1975; JD, Drake U., 1978. Bar: Iowa 1979, Nebr. 1981. Staff atty. Iowa Beef Processors, Inc., Dakota City, Nebr., 1979-81; staff atty. Tex. Internat. Co., Oklahoma City, 1981-84, sr. staff atty., 1984-85, asst. gen. counsel, 1985; gen. counsel, sec. Red Eagle Oil Co., Oklahoma City, 1985—, also bd. dirs.; bd. dirs. Cimarron Helicopters, Inc., Oklahoma City, Cimarron Operating Co., Oklahoma City, Lakeshore Bank, N.A. Served with U.S. Army Air N. G., 1970-71. Mem. ABA, Am. Soc. Corp. Secs., Am. Corp. Counsel Assn. (treas. Okla. chpt.), Phi Alpha Delta. Presbyterian. Avocations: music, travel. Contracts commercial, General corporate, Securities. Home: 19916 Harness Ct Edmond OK 73034 Office: Red Eagle Oil Co 1601 NW Expressway Oklahoma City OK 73118

WALDMAN, ROBERT IRWIN, lawyer; b. Pitts., June 7, 1948; s. Leon and Ada (Singer) W.; m. Katherine Gibson, May 19, 1973; children: Andy, Elizabeth. BA, U. Pa., 1970; JD, Washington U., St. Louis, 1974. Bar: N.Mex. 1974, U.S. Dist. Ct. N.Mex. 1974. Assoc. Hunker, Fedric & Higginbotham, Roswell, N.Mex., 1974-77; sole practice Roswell, 1977-86; assoc. Francis & Arnold PA, Albuquerque, 1986—. Mem. ABA, N.Mex. Bar Assn., Chaves County Bar Assn. Bankruptcy, Personal injury, Workers' compensation. Home: PO Box 21572 Albuquerque NM 87154-1572 Office: Francis & Arland PA PO Box 25267 Albuquerque NM 87125-5267

WALDMAN, STEVE, lawyer; b. Beaumont, Tex., May 29, 1956; s. Carl and Sallye (Bagelman) W.; m. Gayle Lee Gittelson, Aug. 17, 1980. BA, U. Tex., 1977, JD, 1980. Bar: Tex. 1980, U.S. Dist. Ct. (ea. dist.) Tex. 1980, U.S. Dist. Ct. (so. dist.) Tex. 1981, U.S. Dist. Ct. (no. dist.) Tex. 1986. Assoc. Waldman & Smallwood, Houston, 1980-83; ptnr. Waldman, Smallwood & Grossman, Houston, 1984—. Mem. ABA, Assn. Trial Lawyers Am., Tex. Trial Lawyers Assn., Tex. Bd. Legal Specialization (bd. cert.). Democrat. Jewish. Personal injury, Libel, Admiralty. Office: Waldman Smallwood & Grossman 602 Sawyer Suite 600 Houston TX 77007

WALDO, JOSEPH THOMAS, lawyer; b. Roanoke, Va., Mar. 11, 1950; s. Harry Creekmur and Janet (Odom) W.; m. Patricia A. Goodman, July 2, 1983; 1 child, Joseph Patrick. AB, U. N.C., 1972; JD, Coll. of William & Mary, 1978. Bar: Va. 1978, U.S. Dist. Ct. (ea. dist.) Va. 1978, U.S. Bankruptcy Ct. 1978, U.S. Ct. Appeals (4th cir.) 1979, U.S. Tax Ct. 1981. Ptnr., founder Waldo & Tilhon, Virginia Beach, Va., 1978-84; ptnr. Pender & Coward, Virginia Beach, 1984—. Mem. Virginia Beach Dems.; bd. dirs. Virginia Beach SPCA, 1985—, Fred Heutte Found., 1986-87. Mem. ABA, Va. Bar Assn., Virginia Beach Bar Assn., William & Mary Law Sch. Alumni Assn. (bd. dirs., sec., treas. 1984—). Episcopalian. Club: Town Point (Norfolk, Va.). Contracts commercial, Real property, Construction. Home: 330 Raleigh Ave Norfolk VA 23507 Office: Pender & Coward 192 Ballard Ct Virginia Beach VA 23462

WALDOKS, PHILLIP HARRY, lawyer; b. St. Louis, Sept. 26, 1952; s. Earl and Bronis (Lipnicka) W.; m. Amy Zoe Persky, Aug. 27, 1972; children: Ehud, Noam, Briana. AB cum laude, Yale U., 1973; JD with honors, U. Chg., 1976. Bar: N.Y. 1977, U.S. Dist. Ct. (so. and ea. dists.) N.Y. 1977. Assoc. Paul, Weiss, Rifkind, Wharton & Garrison, N.Y.C., 1976-84, Fenwick, Davis & West, N.Y.C., 1984-85; v.p. corp. legal affairs Hasbro, Inc., N.Y.C., 1985—. Bd. dirs. Jewish Coalition Bd. of Am., N.Y.C., 1984—. Mem. ABA, Assn. of Bar of City of N.Y., Order of Coif. Democrat. Jewish. Securities, General corporate, Private international. Home: 17 E 97th St New York NY 10029 Office: Hasbro Inc 32 W 23d St New York NY 10010

WALDORF, GERALDINE POLACK, lawyer; b. N.Y.C., Jan. 10, 1942; d. Marcel and Pauline (Kornbluh) Polack; m. Donald S. Waldorf, June 22, 1963; children: Heidi A., Lawrence W., Mahlon R. AB magna cum laude, Vassar Coll., 1963; MA, Sarah Lawrence Coll., 1969; JD, Columbia U., 1979; LLM in Taxation, NYU, 1986. Bar: N.Y. 1979. Assoc. Kelley, Drye & Warren, N.Y.C., 1979-84; sole practice Nanuet, N.Y., 1984—. Co-author: New York Practice Guide: Probate and Estate Administration, 1985. Bd. dirs. Am. Cancer Soc., Rockland County, N.Y., 1971-77, 85—. Harlan Fiske Stone scholar Columbia U. Sch. Law, N.Y.C., 1976-78. Mem. ABA, Women's Bar Assn. of State of N.Y., N.Y. State Bar Assn., Assn. of Bar of City of N.Y., Rockland County Bar Assn., Rockland County Tax and Estate Planning Council (bd. dirs. 1986—). Estate planning, Probate, Estate taxation. Office: 57 N Middletown Rd Nanuet NY 10954

WALDRON, KENNETH LYNN, lawyer; b. Cape Girardeau, Mo., Oct. 18, 1941; s. Leonard Vernal and Edna Marion (Baskerville) W.; m. Norma K. Norwood, Mar. 25, 1967; children: Leonard, Matthew, Charles. Student, Westminster Coll., 1959-61; BS, U. Mo., 1963, JD, 1966. Bar: Mo. 1966, U.S. Dist. Ct. (ea. dist.) Mo. 1968, U.S. Ct. Appeals (8th cir.) 1971, U.S. Supreme Ct. 1975. Salesman Nat. Biscuit Co., various locations, 1963-66; assoc. Buerkle & Lowes, Jackson, Mo., 1966-71; ptnr. Waldron & Ponder, Jackson, 1971—. Served to capt. U.S. Army, 1966-68. Named one of Outstanding Young Men in Am., 1972, 74, 76. Mem. Mo. Bar Assn., Assn. Trial Lawyers Am., Mo. Assn. Trial Attys., Am. Soc. Law and Medicine, Nat. Inst. Mcpl. Law Officers, Jackson Jaycees (Mo. legal counsel 1972-74, disting. service award 1968, 74), Am. Legion. Baptist. Lodge: Rotary. Personal injury, State civil litigation, General practice. Home: 957 Shady Ln Jackson MO 63755 Office: Waldron & Ponder 417 N High Jackson MO 63755

WALDRUP, J(OHN) CHARLES, lawyer; b. Asheville, N.C., Mar. 28, 1951; s. R. Vester and Carole E. (Chandler) W.; m. Margaret Ann Robinson, Sept. 9, 1972. BS, U. Tenn., 1973; JD, U. N.C., 1976, MA, 1977, PhD, 1985. Bar: N.C. 1976, U.S. Dist. Ct. (mid. dist.) N.C. 1981, U.S. Dist. Ct. (ea. dist.) N.C. 1982, U.S. Ct. Appeals (4th cir.) 1982, U.S. Dist. Ct. (we. dist.) N.C. 1983. Assoc. Dalton H. Loftin, Hillsborough, N.C., 1980-81, Battle, Winslow, Scott & Wiley, P.A., Rocky Mount, N.C., 1981-85; assoc. atty. gen. N.C. Meml. Hosp., Chapel Hill, 1985-87, asst. atty. gen. N.C., 1987—; lectr. history Duke U. Continuing Edn. series, N.C., 1985-87; lectr. on AIDS and law, N.C. and S.C. chpts. of Risk and Ins. Mgmt. Soc. Inc. Conf., 1986. History lectr. N.C. Geneal. Soc. Conf., Raleigh, 1982, 85, 87, Duke U. Conf. Bicentennial U.S. Constitution, 1985, Am. Hist. Assn. History Teaching Alliance, Buncombe County, N.C., 1986. Mem. ABA (litigation, tort and ins. practice, labor and employment law sects., health law forum com., individual rights and responsibilities sect.), N.C. Bar Assn. (litigation and health law sects., editor health law sect. newsletter "Prognosis" 1986—), Nat. Health Lawyers Assn., N.C. Soc. Health Care Attys., Orange County Bar Assn., Am. Soc. Legal History, Orgn. Am. Historians, So. Hist. Assn., Soc. Historians of Early Am. Republic, Triangle d Base II Users, Phi Beta Kappa, Phi Kappa Phi, Phi Eta Sigma. Democrat. Presbyterian. Club: Raleigh Osborne Computer. Avocations: computers, history, tennis. Personal injury, Health, State civil litigation. Home: 1905 Fountain Ridge Rd Chapel Hill NC 27514 Office: NC Meml Hosp Legal Dept Chapel Hill NC 27514

WALDSMITH, MARY LOUISE, lawyer; b. Chgo., Feb. 22, 1956; d. Herman William Waldsmith. BS in Journalism, Ariz. State U., 1977, JD, 1980. Bar: Ariz. 1980, U.S. Dist. Ct. (so. dist.) Ariz. 1980. Asst. counsel USN Office of Gen. Counsel, San Diego, 1983-85, Long Beach, Calif., 1985; counsel USN Office of Gen. Counsel, China Lake, Calif., 1985-87; sr. atty., advisor U.S. Army Health Command, San Antonio, 1987—. Editor Teen Gazette, 1976-77, (law sch. newspaper) The Devil's Advocate, 1978-80. Served to capt. JAGC, U.S. Army, 1980-83. Named one of Outstanding Young Women of Am., 1983. Government contracts and claims, Administrative and regulatory, Military. Office: Office of Counsel Naval Weapons Ctr China Lake CA 93555

WALES, H. ELLIOT, lawyer; b. Providence, Feb 16, 1930; m. Fanee Wales, Aug. 12, 1956; children: Bruce, David. AB, Columbia U., 1951, LLB, 1954; LLM, NYU, 1965. Bar: N.Y. 1955, U.S. Dist. Ct. (ea. dist.) N.Y. 1960, U.S. Supreme Ct. 1960. Asst. U.S. atty. U.S. Dist. Ct. (ea. dist.) N.Y., Bklyn., 1955-56; sole practice N.Y.C., 1956—. Contbr. articles to profl. jours. Trustee Bklyn. Pub. Library, 1967-73. Mem. Fed. Bar Assn., N.Y. County Lawyers Assn. (fed. ct. com.). Criminal, Federal civil litigation. Home: 709 Stuart Ave Marmaroneck NY 10543 Office: 630 3d Ave New York NY 10017

WALINSKY, ADAM, lawyer; b. N.Y.C., Jan. 10, 1937; s. Louis J. Walinsky and Michele (Benson) Walinsky Wilt; m. Jane L. Rosenhirsch, Aug. 25, 1961; children—Peter, Cara. A.B., Cornell U., 1957; LL.B., Yale U., 1961. Bar: N.Y. 1962, U.S. Dist. Ct. (so. dist.) N.Y. 1971, U.S. Ct. Appeals (2d cir.) 1971, U.S. Supreme Ct. 1982. Law clk. U.S. Ct. Appeals for 2d Circuit, N.Y.C., 1961-62; assoc. Winthrop, Stimson, Putnam & Roberts, N.Y.C., 1962-63; atty. Dept. Justice, Washington, 1963-64; legis. asst. to Senator Robert F. Kennedy, Washington, 1964-68; ptnr. Kronish, Lieb, Shainswit, Weiner & Hellman, N.Y.C., 1971—; chmn. N.Y. State Commn. of Investigation, 1978-81. Mem. Yale Law Jour., 1960-61. Contbr. articles to profl. publs. Trustee Robert Kennedy Meml., 1969—. Served with USMCR, 1958. Ford Found. fellow, 1968. Mem. Assn. Bar City N.Y., Council Fgn. Relations. Democrat. Jewish. Federal civil litigation, State civil litigation, General practice. Office: Kronish Lieb Weiner & Hellman 1345 Ave of Americas New York NY 10105

WALK, DONALD WILLARD, lawyer; b. Milw., July 30, 1951; s. Willard P. and Blanche (Melby) W.; m. Susan Herrmann, Aug. 14, 1982. BSME, U. Wis., 1974; JD, Marquette U., 1977. Bar: Wis. 1977, U.S. Dist. Ct. (ea. and we. dists.) 1977, U.S. Patent Office 1978. Patent asst. Gen. Electric Co., Arlington, Va., 1977-78; patent atty. Gen. Electric Co., Evendale, Ohio, 1978-80, Lynn Engines div. Gen. Electric Co., Lynn, Mass., 1980-83; atty. internat. licensing Gen. Electric Co., N.Y.C., 1983-84; patent counsel internat. patent operation Gen. Electric Co., Bridgeport, Conn., 1986—; patent counsel Uniroyal Inc., Middlebury, Conn., 1984-86. Mem. ABA, Phi Delta Phi, Delta Upsilon (local chpt. pres. 1972-73). Congregationalist. Club: S-Kimos (Jackson, N.H.) (chmn. long-range planning 1981-83), Danbury (Conn.) Ski (racing chmn. 1986—). Avocations: Alpine ski racing, sailing. Patent, Private international, General corporate. Home: 853 Purchase Brook Rd Southbury CT 06488 Office: Gen Electric Co Internat Patent Operation 1285 Boston Ave Bridgeport CT 06601

WALK, STEVEN MARC, lawyer; b. Miami Beach, Fla., July 28, 1957; s. Edwin A. and Rhoda (Trattenberg) W.; m. Rochelle Friedman, June 23, 1985. BA, Emory U., 1979; JD, Ohio State U., 1982. Bar: Ohio 1982, U.S. Tax Ct. 1982. Tax assoc. Coopers & Lybrand, Columbus, Ohio, 1981-82; atty. office chief counsel IRS, Cleve., 1982—. Trustee Jewish Big Bros./Big Sisters Assn., Cleve., 1986—. Mem. ABA, Ohio Bar Assn. Corporate taxation, Estate taxation, Personal income taxation. Home: 24060 Shaker Blvd Shaker Heights OH 44122 Office: IRS Office Chief Counsel 1375 E 9th St Suite 810 Cleveland OH 44114

WALK, THOMAS PRESTON, lawyer; b. Bluefield, W.Va., May 4, 1956; s. Ernest Bruce and Grace Ramona (Stacy) W. BS in Fin., Va. Poly. Inst. and State U., 1978; JD, Wake Forest U., 1981. Bar: Va. 1981, U.S. Dist. Ct. (we. dist.) Va. 1982, U.S. Ct. Appeals (4th cir.) 1985. Assoc. Gillespie, Chambers & Combs, Tazewell, Va., 1981-84; ptnr. Gillespie, Chambers, Altizer, Givens, Walk & White, Tazewell, 1984—; hearing officer spl. edn. hearings Va. Supreme Ct., 1984—; spl. justice Gen. Dist. Ct., Tazewell, 1985—; mem. by-laws com. Tazewell Community Hosp., 1985—. Mem. ABA, Tazewell County Bar Assn. (gen practice sect.). Lodge: Lions (bd. dirs. Tazewell 1986—). Avocations: coaching youth basketball. Family and matrimonial, Real property, Consumer commercial. Office: Gillespie Chambers et al PO Box 30 Tazewell VA 24651

WALKE, GEARY LYNN, lawyer; b. Stephensville, Nfld., Can., Jan. 3, 1951; s. Emil Paul and Joyce (Proctor) W.; m. Barbara Ann Cain, Mar. 18, 1972; children—Justin Paul, Collin Robert. B.A., U. Okla., 1973; J.D., Oklahoma City U., 1975. Bar: Okla. 1976, U.S. Dist. Ct. (we. dist.) Okla. 1976, U.S. Ct. Appeals (10th cir.) 1980, U.S. Supreme Ct. 1981. Editorial asst. Okla. Hist. Soc., Oklahoma City, 1974-75; legal intern Legal Aid Western Okla., Oklahoma City, 1975-76; ptnr. Coleman, Walke & Briggs, Del City, Okla., 1976—. Chmn. bd. dirs. Hope Community Mental Health Ctr., Oklahoma City, 1980-82; mem. accreditation com. Rose State Coll., Midwest City, Okla., 1984—; chmn. Del City Bd. Adjustment, 1979—. Mem. ABA, Okla. Jaycees (state legal counsel 1980-81), Del City Area C. of C. (pres. 1984), Okla. Trial Lawyers Assn., Assn. Trial Lawyers Am., Okla. Bar Assn. Democrat. Presbyterian. General practice, Consumer commercial, Family and matrimonial. Home: 4413 SE 33rd St Del City OK 73115 Office: 3904 E Reno Oklahoma City OK 73117

WALKER, BRUCE LEROY, lawyer; b. Des Moines, July 18, 1946; s. Roy A. and Mesimeana (Aldini) W.; m. Marlys Schmidt, Aug. 23, 1969; children: Nicholas, Anthony, Sunday. BA, U. Iowa, 1968, JD with distinction, 1972. Bar: Iowa 1972. Assoc. Phelan, Tucker, Boyle & Mullen, Iowa City, 1972-77, ptnr., 1977—. Elder St. Andrew Presbyn. Ch., Iowa City, 1985—, deacon, 1981-84. Served with USAR, 1968-72. Mem. ABA (litigaton sect., trial evidence com.), Iowa Bar Assn. (young lawyers sect., speaker 1974, 79, 81—), Iowa Acad. Trial Lawyers, Iowa Assn. Trial Lawyers, Def. Research Inst. (mcpl. com., trial evidence com.), Delta Chi (treas. 1985—). Democrat. Avocation: coaching soccer and baseball. State civil litigation, Personal injury, Local government. Office: Phelan Tucker Boyle & Mullen 321 Market St Iowa City IA 52240-2150

WALKER, CHARLES HENRI, lawyer; b. Columbus, Nov. 11, 1951; s. Watson Hershel and Juanita Elizabeth (Webb) W.; m. Amanda Tressel Herndon, June 27, 1981; children: Katrina Della, Allison Lyles. BA magna cum laude, Tufts U., 1973; JD, Emory U., 1976. Bar: Ohio 1976. Assoc. Bricker & Eckler, and predecessors, Columbus, 1976-81, ptnr., 1982—. Bd. dirs. Salesian Boys Club, Columbus, 1983—, Planned Parenthood Central Ohio, Columbus, 1984-85. Mem. ABA, Nat. Bar Assn., Ohio Bar Assn., Columbus Bar Assn., Nat. Assn. R.R. Trial Counsel, Columbus Acad. Alumni Assn. (past pres.). Democrat. Roman Catholic. Clubs: Athletic, President's (Columbus). Real property. Home: 556 City Park Ave Columbus OH 43215 Office: Bricker & Eckler 100 S 3d St Columbus OH 43215

WALKER, DANIEL, JR., lawyer; b. Chgo., Jan. 29, 1949; s. Daniel and Roberta Marie (Dowse) W.; m. Loretta Graffort, May 27, 1979; children—Krista D., Daniel P. B.A., Santa Clara U., 1971; J.D., Northwestern U., 1974. Bar: Ill. 1974, U.S. Dist. Ct. (no. dist.) Ill. 1974. Assoc. Arvey, Hodes, Costello & Burman, Chgo., 1974-77; ptnr. Dan Walker Law Offices, Oak Brook, Ill., 1977—. Bd. dirs. Midwest Epilepsy Assn., 1980-82; precinct committeeman Democratic Party, DuPage County, Ill., 1978-83. Roman Catholic. General practice, Personal injury, Family and matrimonial. Home: 701 Mulberry Ct Naperville IL 60540 Office: Dan Walker Law Office 1211 W 22d Suite 616 Oak Brook IL 60521

WALKER, DANIEL JOSHUA, JR., lawyer; b. Gibson, N.C., Nov. 27, 1915; s. Daniel Joshua and Annie (Hurdle) W.; m. Sarah Elizabeth Nicholson, June 14, 1941. A.B., U. N.C., 1936, J.D., 1948. Bar: N.C. 1948, U.S. Dist. Ct. (mid. dist.) N.C. 1956, U.S. Ct. Appeals (4th cir.) 1956. Clk. of Superior Ct. of Alamance County, Graham, N.C., 1948-53; ptnr. firm Long, Ridge, Harris & Walker, Graham, 1953-67; county atty. Alamance County, 1964-77, county mgr., 1971-76; sr. mem. firm Walker Harris & Pierce, Graham, 1967-71; ptnr. firm. Allen & Walker and predecessor, Burlington, N.C., 1977—. Mem. Human Relations Council of Alamance County, 1963-71, chmn., 1970; mem. N.C. Environ. Mgmt. Commn., 1972-77; pres. Alamance County Young Democratic Club, 1950; chmn. Alamance County Dem. Exec. Com., 1956-58; mem. N.C. Dem. Exec. Com., 1958-66; trustee Tech. Inst. of Alamance, 1964-71, Presbyn. Found., Presbyn. Ch. of U.S., 1969-73; moderator Orange Presbytery, 1980, mem. council, 1972-74; bd. dirs. Alamance County United Fund, Cherokee council Boy Scouts Am., Burlington Community YMCA. Served to capt. AUS, 1942-46, ETO. Decorated Bronze Star. Mem. Alamance County C. of C. (pres. 1981), ABA, N.C. Bar Assn., Alamance County Bar Assn. (pres. 1977-78), N.C. Assn. County Attys. (pres. 1972, named County Att. of Yr. 1971), 15th Jud. Dist. Bar Assn. (pres. 1967-68), Phi Alpha Delta. Lodge: Burlington Kiwanis (pres. 1957, named Alamance County Citizen of Yr. 1969). Probate, Condemnation, Local government. Home: 215 Long Ave Graham NC 27253 Office: Allen and Walker PO Drawer 29 Burlington NC 27216

WALKER, DAVID TODD, lawyer; b. Norristown, Pa., Nov. 5, 1937; s. Albert Wetzel and Margaret (Todd) W.; m. Christa Ingrid Schroeter, July 27, 1963; children: David, Amanda. AB, Dickinson Coll., 1959; JD, Villanova U., 1964. Bar: Pa. 1965. Atty. Gen. Accident Group Ins Cos., Phila., 1964-68; asst. counsel Provident Mut. Life Ins. Co., Phila., 1969-71; asst. gen. counsel Ina Corp., Phila., 1971-73; asst. gen. counsel 1st Pa. Corp./1st Pa. Bank, Phila., 1973-82, v.p., assoc. gen. counsel, 1982-84, sr. v.p., gen. counsel, sec., 1985—; pres. Vestaur Securities Inc., Phila., 1983—. Bd. dirs. Pub. Interest Law Ctr., Phila. Mem. ABA, Pa. Bar Assn., Phila. Bar Assn., Phila. Bar Found. (trustee), Am. Soc. Corp. Secs., Am. Law Inst. General corporate, Banking. Home: 1048 General Allen Ln West Chester PA 19382 Office: 1st Pa Corp Centre Sq Philadelphia PA 19101

WALKER, DEE BROWN, lawyer; b. Royse City, Tex., Dec. 3, 1912; LL.B., So. Meth. U., 1935. Bar: Tex. 1935. Counsel to ins. cos., 1935-42; asst. to gen. counsel Southland Life Ins. Co., 1947-63, also mem. firm Dillard & Walker, 1949-63; judge 162d Jud. Dist. Ct. of Dallas County, 1963-84, ret. Mem. Dallas County Democratic Exec. Com., 1952-63; instnl. rep. Circle 10 council Boy Scouts Am., 1958-62, chmn. White Buffalo dist., 1956-68, exec. com., Silver Beaver award, 1965. Mem. ABA, Tex. Bar Assn., Dallas Bar Assn., Dallas County Bar Assn., Dallas County Criminal Bar Assn., Am. Judicature Soc., Southwestern Legal Found., Phi Alpha Delta. Jurisprudence, State civil litigation, Probate. Home: 5918 Vanderbilt Ave Dallas TX 75206 Office: 6220 Gastonare 606 Faulkner Tower Dallas TX 75214

WALKER, E. RALPH, lawyer; b. Cedar Rapids, Iowa, Dec. 7, 1942; s. Edgar E. and Alice Frances (Kolar) W.; m. Linda Marie Faber, Aug. 29, 1965; children: Jens, Damon, Trevor. AB cum laude, Harvard U., 1969; JD, U. Pa., 1972. Bar: Iowa 1972, U.S. Dist. Ct. (so. and no. dists.) 1973, Pa. 1986, U.S. Ct. Appeals (3d cir.) 1986. Ptnr. Davis, Hockenberg, Wine, Brown, Koehn & Shors and predecessor firm Thoma, Schoenthal, Davis, Hockenberg & Wine, Des Moines, Iowa, 1972—. Bd. dirs. Bidwell Riverside Community Ctr., Des Moines, 1982—, pres., 1983-86. Fellow Am. Judicature Soc.; mem. ABA, Iowa Bar Assn., Polk County Bar Assn., Def. Research Inst., Pa. Bar Assn., Des Moines C. of C. (health human and community services task force com. 1986—). Methodist. Clubs: Embassy, Echo Valley (Des Moines) (bd. govs. 1979-81). Product liability litigation, Federal civil litigation, State civil litigation. Home: 8832 Woodmayr Circle Norwalk IA 50211 Office: Davis Hockenberg Wine et al 2300 Financial Ctr Des Moines IA 50309

WALKER, FRANCIS JOSEPH, lawyer; b. Tacoma, Aug. 5, 1922; s. John McSweeney and Sarah Veronica (Meechan) W.; m. Julia Corinne O'Brien, Jan. 27, 1951; children—Vincent Paul, Monica Irene Hylton, Jill Marie Nudell, John Michael, Michael Joseph, Thomas More. B.A., St. Martin's Coll., 1947; J.D., U. Wash., 1950. Bar: Wash. Asst. atty. gen. State of Wash., 1950-51; sole practice, Olympia, Wash., 1951—; gen. counsel Wash. Cath. Conf., 1967-76. Served to lt. (j.g.) USNR, 1943-46; PTO. Probate. Home: 2723 Hillside Dr Olympia WA 98501 Office: 203 E 4th Ave Suite 301 Olympia WA 98501

WALKER, FRANK BRIGGS, lawyer; b. Houlton, Maine, Jan. 14, 1934; s. Donald and Gladys Iva (Briggs) W.; m. Pamela Sterling, June 16, 1962; children—Stanwood, Wilmot, Portia. B.A., Colby Coll., 1958; LL.B., Boston U., 1961. Bar: Maine, 1961, U.S. Dist. Ct. Maine 1963. Ptnr. Silsby, Silsby & Walker, Ellsworth, Maine, 1962-75; sole practice, 1975-81; ptnr. Walker & Ross, 1981—. Served with U.S. Army, 1954-56. Mem. ABA, Maine Bar Assn., Hancock Bar Assn., Aroostook Bar Assn. Republican. Admiralty, Probate, Real property. Office: Walker & Ross 204 Main St Ellsworth ME 04605

WALKER, GEORGE KONTZ, lawyer, educator; b. Tuscaloosa, Ala., July 8, 1938; s. Joseph Henry and Catherine Louise (Indorf) W.; m. Phyllis Ann Sherman, July 30, 1966; children: Charles Edward, Mary Neel. B.A., U. Ala., 1959; LL.B., Vanderbilt U., 1966; M.A., Duke U., 1968; LL.M., U. Va., 1972; postgrad. (Sterling fellow), Law Sch. Yale U., 1975-76. Bar: Va. 1967, N.C. 1976. Law clk. U.S. Dist. Ct., Richmond, Va., 1966-67; assoc. Hunton, Williams, Gay, Powell & Gibson, Richmond, 1967-70; practice law Charlottesville, Va., 1970-71; asst. prof. Wake Forest U. Law Sch., Winston-Salem, N.C., 1972-73, assoc. prof., 1974-77, prof., 1978—; vis. prof. Marshall-Wythe Sch. Law Coll. William and Mary, Williamsburg, Va., 1979-80, U. Ala. Law Sch., 1985; cons. Naval War Coll., 1976—. Author: International Law for the Naval Commander, 1985; contbr. articles to profl. jours. Served with USN, 1959-62; capt. USNR. Woodrow Wilson fellow, 1962-63. Mem. ABA, Va. Bar Assn., N.C. Bar Assn., Am. Soc. Internat. Law, Am. Judicature Soc., Maritime Law Assn., Order of Barristers, Phi Beta Kappa, Sigma Alpha Epsilon, Phi Delta Phi. Democrat. Episcopalian. Club: Piedmont. Legal education, Public international, Private international. Home: 3321 Pennington Ln Winston-Salem NC 27106-5439 Office: Wake Forest U Sch Law PO Box 7206 Winston-Salem NC 27109-7206

WALKER, GEORGE WILLIAM, lawyer; b. Boston, Apr. 22, 1929; s. George William and Mary A. (Moran) W.; m. Joanne T. Hersey; children—Sylvie T., Kathryn L. Student U. N.H., 1951; LL.B. cum laude, Boston U., 1954. Bar: N.H. 1954, Mass. 1954, U.S. Ct. Mil. Appeals 1955, U.S. Supreme Ct. 1960. Sole practice, Wolfeboro, N.H., 1959-60; ptnr. Cooper, Hall & Walker, Wolfeboro, 1961-81, Walker & Varney, Wolfeboro, 1982—; prosecutor Carroll County (N.H.), 1967-69; judge Wolfeboro Dist. Ct., 1973—; mem. N.H. Jud. Council, 1971—, chmn., 1984; chmn. bd., dir. Kingswood Trust & Savs. Bank, Wolfeboro, 1973-84. Moderator Gov. Wentworth Regional Sch. Dist., Wolfeboro; trustee Huggins Hosp., Wolfeboro. Mem. N.H. Trial Lawyers Assn. (pres. 1979), ABA, N.H. Bar Assn. (pres. county chpt. 1960), N.H. Judges Assn., Am. Judicature Soc. Republican. Personal injury, Probate, Real property. Office: Walker & Varney 12 N Main St Wolfeboro NH 03894

WALKER, G(LENN) PERRIN, lawyer; b. Rigby, Idaho, Sept. 24, 1939; s. Allen H. and Lora (Taylor) W.; m. Charlotte J. Johnson, Aug. 31, 1962; children—E. Allen, Perrin H., Aric I., Margaret (dec.), Brett Cory, Susan, Charlotte-Anne, Michael Joseph. B.A. in Polit. Sci. with high honors, Brigham Young U., 1963; J.D., U. Chgo., 1966. Bar: Wash. 1966, U.S. Dist. Ct. (we. dist.) Wash. 1966, U.S. Ct. Appeals (9th cir.) 1967, Alaska, 1981, U.S. Dist. Ct. (we. dist.) Tex. 1982, U.S. Claims Ct. 1983, U.S. Supreme Ct. 1984. Mem. law dept. Weyerhaeuser Co., Tacoma, 1966-69; ptnr. Kane, Vandeberg, Hartinger & Walker, Tacoma, 1969—. Co-founder, trustee, officer Pierce County Legal Assistance Found., 1968-76; exec. bd. Mt. Rainier council Boy Scouts Am., 1978-81; mem. Pierce County Citizens Ethics Rev. Commn., 1979-82, chmn., 1981; bishop Tacoma 1st ward Ch. of Jesus Christ of Latter-day Saints, 1967-69, pres. Tacoma stake, 1978-85, pres. Belgium Mission, Brussels, 1985—. Contbr. articles to profl. jours. General practice, General corporate, Federal civil litigation. Office: Suite 2100 First Interstate Plaza Bldg Tacoma WA 98402

WALKER, HARRY GREY, state judge; b. Ovett, Miss., Sept. 30, 1924; s. Chester A. and Ina (Mangum) W.; m. Carrie Thorne Lang, Apr. 4, 1953; 1 child, Harry Grey. LL.B., U. Miss., 1952. Bar: Miss. 1952. Practiced in Gulfport, Miss., 1952-64; judge Harrison County (Miss.) Ct., 1964-68, Circuit Ct., 2d Dist. Miss., 1968-72; presiding justice Miss. Supreme Ct., 1982-86, 1986, chief justice, 1986—. Mem. Miss. Ho. of Reps., 1964. Served with USCG, 1942-44. Mem. Am. Judicature Soc., Miss. State Bar, DAV, Paralyzed Vets. Am., Phi Alpha Delta, Kappa Alpha. Democrat. Methodist. Clubs: Am. Legion, Elks, Gulfport Yacht, Magnolia Hunting. Home: 23-53rd St Gulfport MS 39507 Office: Miss Supreme Ct Bldg Jackson MS 39205

WALKER, HENRY CLAY, IV, lawyer; b. Augusta, Ga., Sept. 13, 1942; s. Henry Clay Walker and Frances (Grey) Walker Jacobs; m. Jean Elizabeth Gallico, Aug. 26, 1966 (div. Dec. 1973); m. Laurie Wilkinson Lyons, May 25, 1985. BA, Tulane U., 1964, JD, 1968. Bar: La. 1968, U.S. Dist. Ct. (we. dist. La. 1968, U.S. Ct. Appeals (5th cir.) 1974, U.S. Supreme Ct. 1975, U.S. Dist. Ct. (mid. dist.) La. 1984. Assoc. Blanchard, Walker, O'Quin & Roberts, Shreveport, La., 1968-69; ptnr. Gerhardt & Walker, Shreveport, 1969-71, Walker, Feazel & Tooke, Shreveport, 1981-84, Walker, Tooke, Perlman & Lyons, Shreveport, 1984—; state bd. dirs. Odyssey House, Shreveport, New Orleans. Fellow Am. Trial Lawyers Found. (life, Roscoe Pound); mem., ABA, Am. Trial Lawyers Assn., Nat. Assn. of Criminal Def. Lawyers, La. Bar Assn., La. Criminal Def. Lawyers Assn. (bd. mem.), La. Trial Lawyers Assn. (past criminal sect. chmn.), Shreveport Bar Assn. Democrat. Unitarian. Clubs: Shreveport, Cambridge (Shreveport). Avocations: skiing, scuba, windsurfing. Civil rights, Criminal, Personal injury. Home: 815 Ontario St Shreveport LA 71106 Office: Walker Tooke Perlman & Lyons 1700 Irving Pl Shreveport LA 71101

WALKER, HENRY LAWSON, II, lawyer; b. Cin., Feb. 10, 1949; s. H. Lawson and Lucille (Kerr) W.; m. Peggy Lynn Behringer; children: Erin, Jonathan. BBA, U. Cin., 1972, JD, 1975. Bar: Ohio 1975, Ky. 1976, U.S. Ct. Appeals (6th cir.) 1975, U.S. Dist. Ct. (so. dist.) Ohio 1975, U.S. Dist. Ct. (ea. dist.) Ky. 1976. Assoc. Riggs & Riggs, Erlanger, Ky., 1975-80; ptnr. Riggs Riggs & Walker, Erlanger, 1981—; adj. asst. prof. aviation law No. Ky. U., Highland Heights, 1982—; atty. City of Villa Hills, Ky., 1981—; gen. counsel Community Bank, Erlanger, 1981—. Mem. Ky. Rep. Exec. Com., Frankfort, 1985—, Ky. Ho. of Reps. 66th dist., 1987— ; chmn. Kenton County Reps., Covington, Ky., 1980-84; deacon Lakeside Christian Ch., Ft. Mitchell, Ky., 1983—; atty. Erlanger-Elmere Bd. Edn., 1980—; bd. dirs. North Ky. Easter Seal Soc., Covington, 1979—. Mem. ABA, Ky. Bar Assn. (various coms.), Ohio Bar Assn., No. Ky. Bar Assn. (bd. dirs. 1985—), Kenton County Bar Assn. (treas. 1980-81, pres. 1982-83), Ky. Coincil Sch. Br. Attys., Ky. Mcpl. Attys. Assn. Lodges: Rotary (bd. dirs. Erlanger 1985—). General practice, Aviation, Federal civil litigation. Home: 729 Dry Creek Ct Villa Hills KY 41017 Office: Riggs Riggs & Walker 25 Erlanger Rd Erlanger KY 41018-0668

WALKER, HUFFMAN REED, lawyer; b. Kansas City, Mo., Dec. 3, 1952; s. Huffman Walker and Marjorie (McNees) Hallier; m. Jeanne R. Kettler, Aug. 16, 1975 (div. Dec. 1976); m. Paula P. Silvey, Sept. 16, 1978. BS in Bus. Adminstrn., William Jewell Coll., 1974; JD with honors, Washburn U., 1977. Bar: Kans. 1977, U.S. Dist. Ct. Kans. 1977, U.S. Supreme Ct. 1984. From assoc. to ptnr. Barnett & Ross, Kansas City, Kans., 1977—. Editor-in-chief Advocate newsletter, 1986—. Mem. ABA, Wyandotte County Bar Assn. (sec. 1984-85, pres.-elect 1987), Kans. Trial Lawyers Assn., Phi Delta Phi (cert. merit 1977). Republican. Presbyterian. Club: Kansas City. Personal injury, Family and matrimonial, Consumer commercial. Home:

4603 W 66th Terrace Prairie Village KS 66208 Office: Barnett & Ross 705 N 7th St Kansas City KS 66101

WALKER, JAMES DURWARD, JR., lawyer; b. Augusta, Ga., Aug. 8, 1948; s. J.D. and Hilda (Saggus) W.; m. Carole Leigh Weigle, May 8, 1970; children: James D. III, Ashley Meredith. BA, Augusta Coll., 1970; JD, U. S.C., 1974. Bar: Ga. 1974, U.S. Dist. Ct. (so. dist.) Ga. 1974. Ptnr. Surrett, Walker, Creson & Colley, Augusta, 1976—; trustee U.S. Bankruptcy Ct., 1976—. Mem. Augusta Coll. Alumni Assn. (pres. 1979), U.S.C. Law Sch. Assn. (bd. dirs. 1978—). Avocation: amateur radio. Bankruptcy, General corporate, Contracts commercial. Home: 753 Lancaster Rd Augusta GA 30909 Office: Surrett Walker Creson & Colley 800 Trust Co Bank Bldg Augusta GA 30902

WALKER, JAMES EDWARD, lawyer; b. Marion, N.C., Sept. 13, 1925; s. Ira Lee Walker and Queenie (Bowman) Walker Lockwood; m. Doris Reece, Aug. 16, 1953; children: James E. Jr., Nancy Elizabeth. BS, Wake Forest U., 1950, JD, 1951. Bar: N.C. 1954, U.S. Dist. Ct. (we. dist.) N.C. 1959, U.S. Dist. Ct. (mid. dist.) N.C. 1962, U.S. Ct. Appeals (4th cir.) 1974, U.S. Supreme Ct. 1978, U.S. Dist. Ct. (ea. dist.) N.C. 1984. Sole practice Charlotte, N.C., 1951-58; ptnr. Sanders, Walker & London, Charlotte, 1958-76, Walker, Palmer & Miller P.A., Charlotte, 1976-86, Kennedy, Covington, Lobdell & Hickman, Charlotte, 1986—; dist. atty. Mecklenburg County, 1959-60; pros. City of Charlotte, 1953-57. Served with USN, 1943-46. Fellow Am. Coll. Trial Lawyers; mem. N.C. Bar Assn. (pres. 1981-82), Mecklenburg County Bar Assn. (pres. 1966-67), 4th Jud. Cir. Conf. Democrat. Baptist. Clubs: City, Myers Park Country (Charlotte). Avocations: tennis, music, reading. Federal civil litigation, State civil litigation, Criminal. Home: 3900 Beresford Rd Charlotte NC 28211 Office: Kennedy Covington Lobdell & Hickman 3300 NCNB Plaza Charlotte NC 28280

WALKER, JAMES WILLIAM, JR., lawyer, business executive; b. Birmingham, Ala., Aug. 19, 1927; s. James William and Eva Victoria (Harris) W.; m. Eileen Newton, Apr. 30, 1949; children—James William III, Michael, Lee, Helen, Caroline. A.B., Birmingham So. Coll., 1949; J.D., Emory U., 1953. Bar: Ga. 1954, D.C. 1966. With Merrill Lynch, Fenner & Smith, N.Y.C., 1954-67; exec. v.p. Am. Stock Exchange, N.Y.C., 1968-74, Securities Industry Assn., Washington, 1974-77; exec. asst. to chmn. bd. INA Corp., Phila., 1977-78, sr. v.p., 1978-79, exec. v.p., 1979-80, exec. v.p., gen. counsel, 1980-82; exec. v.p., gen. counsel CIGNA Corp., Phila., 1982—. Mem. services policy com. of U.S. Trade Rep., policy com. of Pa. Bus. Roundtable, Emory U. Law Sch. Council. Served to capt. U.S. Army, 1946-48. Mem. ABA, Am. Law Inst., Ins. Fedn. Pa. (bd. dirs. Pa. Chamber of Bus. and Industry). Clubs: Union League (Phila.); Nat. Lawyers (Washington). Office: CIGNA Corp 1 Logan Square Philadelphia PA 19103

WALKER, JEAN ANN, lawyer; b. Cleve., July 23, 1939; d. LeRoy B. and Dolores G. (Schneider) W.; 1 child, Joshua Akin. BA cum laude, Am. U., 1971; JD cum laude, Howard U., 1978. Bar: D.C. 1979, U.S. Dist. Ct. D.C. 1979, U.S. Ct. Appeals (D.C. cir.) 1979, U.S. Supreme Ct. 1982. Asst. dir. Reginald Heber Smith Community Lawyer Fellowship Program, Washington, 1978-81; tax counsel com. on state taxation Council of State C. of C., Washington, 1981—; mem. adv. bd. Georgetown U. Law Ctr. Inst. State and Local Taxation, Washington, 1985-87. Contbr. articles to profl. jours. Bd. dirs. Rosemount Child Care Ctr., Washington, 1983—. Mem. ABA (tax sect., state and local tax com. 1982—), Fed. Bar Assn. (tax sect. 1980—, bd. dirs. D.C. chpt. 1979-84). State and local taxation. Home: 8101 Eastern Ave Apt 506 Silver Spring MD 20910 Office: Com on State Tax 122 C St NW Suite 200 Washington DC 20001

WALKER, JERRY VANZANT, lawyer; b. Casa Grande, Ariz., Dec. 12, 1925; s. Gerald Lee and Mildred (McMeans) W.; m. Virginia Lee Ridenhower, Dec. 18, 1948; children: Jerry Vanzant, Lucinda Lee. B.S., Tex. A&M U., 1949; LL.B., U. Tex., 1952. Bar: Tex. 1952. Since practiced in Houston; ptnr. Fulbright & Jaworski, 1952-86; vis. prof. med. jurisprudence Baylor Coll. Medicine; pres. Houston Jr. Bar Assn., 1960. Served with AUS, 1944-46. Fellow Am. Coll. Trial Lawyers; Mem. Am. Bar Assn. (com. admiralty and maritime law 1979-82, commn. med. profl. liability 1975-80, vice chmn. sect. ins., negligence and compensation 1976-79, vice chmn. sect. litigation 1979-80), State Bar Tex. (chmn. tort and compenation sect. 1966-67), Houston Bar Assn. (chmn. inter-profession relations with physicians com. 1970-74), Houston Assn. Def. Counsel (1st v.p. 1971), Tex. Assn. Def. Counsel, State Bar Tex. (dir. 1960-61), Internat. Assn. Ins. Counsel (pres. 1975-76), Def. Research Inst. (exec. com., dir. 1974-77, vice chmn. com. to improve adminstrn. civil justice 1976-77), Am. Bar Found., Tex. Bar Found., Houston Bar Found., Maritime Law Assn. U.S. (com. Comité Maritime Internat.), Houston C. of C. (life). Republican. Presbyterian. Clubs: Houston Country. Home: 101 Westcott St 1706 Houston TX 77007 Office: Houston Nat Bank Bldg 5757 Memorial Dr Suite 210 Houston TX 77007

WALKER, JOHN SUMPTER, JR., lawyer; b. Richmond, Ark., Oct. 13, 1921; s. John Sumpter, Mary Martha (Wilson) W.; m. Eljana M. duVall, Dec. 31, 1947; children—John Stephen, Barbara Monika Ann, Peter Mark Gregory. B.A., Tulane U., 1942; M.S., U. Denver, 1955, J.D., 1960; diploma Nat. Def. U., 1981. Bar: Colo. 1960, U.S. Dist. Ct. Colo. 1960, U.S. Supreme Ct., 1968, U.S. Ct. Appeals (10th cir.) 1960, U.S. Tax. Ct., 1981. With Denver & Rio Grande Western R.R. Co., 1951-61, gen. solicitor, 1961—; dir. Denver Union Terminal Ry. Co. Served with U.S. Army, 1942-46. Decorated Bronze Star. Mem. ABA, Colo. Bar Assn., Arapahoe County Bar Assn., Alliance Francaise (life), Order of St. Ives, U. Denver Chancellors' Soc., Cath. Lawyers Guild, Alpha Tau Omega. Republican. Roman Catholic. Club: Denver Athletic. Administrative and regulatory, Federal civil litigation, Public utilities. Home: 6185 S Columbine Way Littleton CO 80121 Office: 986 One Park Central PO Box 5482 Denver CO 80217

WALKER, JONATHAN LEE, lawyer; b. Kalamazoo, Mar. 8, 1948; s. Harvey E. and Olivia M. (Estrada) W. B.A., U. Mich., 1969; J.D., Wayne State U., 1977. Bar: Mich. 1977, U.S. Dist. Ct. (ea. dist.) Mich. 1982. Assoc. firm Moore, Barr & Kerwin, Detroit, 1977-79; ptnr. firm Barr & Walker, Detroit, 1979-82; assoc. firm Richard M. Goodman, P.C., Detroit, 1983—; hearing officer Mich. Civil Rights Commn., Detroit, 1983—; participant Detroit Bar Assn. Vol. Lawyer Program. Bd. dirs. Community Treatment Ctr.-Project Rehab., Detroit, 1983—; mem. scholarship com. Latino en Marcha Scholarship Fund, Detroit, 1984; contbr. Lawyers with Hart, Washington, 1984. Mem. State Bar Mich. Found., Wayne County Mediation Tribunal, Inc. (mediator), Am. Arbitration Assn. (arbitrator), Nat. Lawyers Guild, Mich. Trial Lawyers Assn., Assn. Trial Lawyers Am., State Bar Mich. (chmn. com. on underrepresented groups in law 1983-85, com. judicial qualifications 1985-86 , council mem. Latin-Am. sect. 1978—), Trial Lawyers for Pub. Justice (founder 1981, Amicus com. 1985-86), Ctr. for Auto Safety. Personal injury, State civil litigation. Office: Richard M Goodman PC 1394 E Jefferson St Detroit MI 48207

WALKER, JORDAN CLYDE, lawyer, shopping center executive, developer; b. Sacramento, July 18, 1927; s. Clarence Clyde and Verlina June (Jordan) W.; m. Viola Dale Stoner, Mar. 15, 1947 (div. Nov. 1964); children—Jordan Clyde Jr., Pamela Jean, Olivia June, Aaron Kim (dec.); m. Maxine M. Armstrong, Aug. 4, 1967; children—Karen Joann, Mark Allen, Leslie Susan. J.D., McGeorge Sch. Law, 1975. Bar: Calif. 1976. Sales mgr. Gen. Foods, Sacramento, 1949-58; sales rep. Smith-Klein & French, Sacramento, 1959-63; ind. real estate salesman and developer, Sacramento, 1963-75; ptnr. Walker & Crawford, Sacramento, 1976—; owner, operator Walker & Assocs. Sacramento, 1979—. Republican fundraiser, Sacramento, 1980—. Served with USN, 1945-46, PTO. Mem. Sacramento County Bar Assn., Calif. State Bar, ABA, Phi Alpha Delta. Mormon. Club: Sutter (Sacramento). Real property, Landlord-tenant, Construction. Office: Walker and Crawford 3600 American River Dr Suite 145 Sacramento CA 95864

WALKER, JOSEPH HILLARY, JR., lawyer, banker; b. Birmingham, Ala., Apr. 7, 1919; s. Joseph Hillary Sr. and Nora D. (Arnold) W.; m. Ann Tucker, Dec. 31, 1944; children—Joseph Hillary III, Harriet E., Mildred Katherin, Bonnie Jo. A.B., U. Ala., 1941, J.D., 1947. Bar: Ala. 1947, Tenn. 1947, U.S. Dist. Ct. (we. dist.) Tenn. 1947, U.S. Ct. Mil. Appeals 1956, U.S. Supreme Ct. 1956. Sole practice, Ripley, Tenn., 1947-76; sr. mem. Walker & Walker, Ripley, 1976—; mem. Tenn. Ho. of Reps., 1949-51, Tenn. Senate, 1951-53; chmn. bd. Farmers Union Bank, Ripley, 1964-86; dir. Lauderdale Devel. Corp., Ripley. Pres. Tenn. Constl. Conv., 1959, mem. 1965; chmn. Lauderdale County Bd. of Edn., 1964-67; trustee Lauderdale County Hosp., 1962; deacon Bapt. Ch., 1954—, treas., 1962—; trustee Union U., 1970—. Mem. Sigma Nu. Lodge: Rotary. State civil litigation, General practice, Estate planning. Home: 1 Lackey Ln Ripley TN 38063 Office: Walker Walker PO Box 287 Ripley TN 38063

WALKER, KENNETH LYNN, lawyer; b. New Haven, Nov. 22, 1948; s. John Charles and Virginia Clare (Lovett) W.; m. Suzanne Kay Thompson, Jan. 27, 1979; children: Katherine Leslie, Caroline Leigh. B.A., Coe Coll., 1969; M.A., New Sch. Social Research, 1973; J.D., U. Iowa, 1975. Bar: Ohio. Assoc. Baker & Hostetler, Cleve., 1975-79; atty. Cole Nat. Corp., Cleve., 1979-84; group counsel TRW, Inc., Cleve., 1984—. Editor Jour. Corp. Law, 1975. Mem. ABA, Ohio Bar Assn., Cleve. Bar Assn. General corporate, Private international. Office: TRW Inc 1900 Richmond Rd Cleveland OH 44124

WALKER, LYNDA KAY, lawyer; b. Orlando, Fla., Aug. 2, 1956; s. Leon David and Margaret Alice (McKay) W. BS in Indsl. Mgmt., Auburn U., 1978; JD cum laude, Samford U., 1981. Bar: Ala. 1981. Asst. counsel AmSouth Bank N.A., Birmingham, Ala., 1981-84; counsel Nat. Realty Com., Washington, 1985—. Assoc. editor Cumberland U. Law Rev., 1980-81; editor, writer Nat. Realty Com. newsletter,1985—. Mem. The Tax Coalition, Washington, 1986—, Women in Govt. Relations, Washington, 1986—, Joint Real Estate Tax Commn., Washington, 1985—, Urban Land Inst., Washington, 1985—, Potomac Group, Washington, 1986—, New Dem. Forum, Washington, 1985—. Named one of Outstanding Young Women in Am., 1980, 85. Mem. ABA (taxation law sect., real estate tax problems com., real property, probate and trust law sect., corp., banking and bus. law sect.), Ala. Bar Assn., Young Men's Bus. Club (sec. 1983-84), League of Women Voters (vice chmn. 1984), Ala. State Soc., Phi Delta Phi. Democrat. Methodist. Real property, Personal income taxation, Corporate taxation. Home: 2032 Belmont Rd NW 412 Valley Vista Washington DC 20009 Office: Nat Realty Com 1250 Connecticut Ave NW Suite 630 Washington DC 20036

WALKER, MARK ANTHONY, judge; b. Covington, Tenn., Sept. 3, 1908; s. Mark Anthony and Ella (Simonton) W.; m. Lulie Reynolds Eddins, Apr. 10, 1948 (dec. Oct. 1984); children: Mark A. III, Nathalie Eileen Hatfield, Lawrence. BS, U. Tenn., 1931; postgrad., U. Wis., 1934. Bar: Tenn. 1935. Sole practice Covington, 1935-46; judge Tenn. 16th Jud. Cir., 1946-67; judge Tenn. Ct. Criminal Appeals, Covington, 1967—, presiding judge, 1967-77, 79—. Mem. Tenn. Ho. of Reps., 1939-42, Tenn. State Dem. Exec. Com., 1940-43. Served to comdr. USN, 1942-46, PTO. Mem. ABA, Tenn. State Bar Assn., Am. Judicature Soc., Kappa Sigma. Lodges: Lions (pres. Covington club 1938), Masons. Home: 315 S Main St Covington TN 38019

WALKER, MARY ANN, lawyer; b. Anderson, S.C., Aug. 21, 1953; d. Ernest McCreary and Virginia (Selman) Glymph; m. Thomas M. Walker, Aug. 28, 1976. BS, U. Va., 1975; JD, U. Richmond, 1979. Bar: Va. 1979, U.S. Dist. Ct. (ea. dist.) Va. 1980, U.S. Ct. Appeals (4th cir.) 1980, U.S. Ct. Appeals (5th and 7th cirs.) 1984, U.S. Ct. Appeals (10th cir.) 1987. Assoc. Wickwire, Gavin & Gibbs, P.C., Washington and Vienna, Va., 1980-86; ptnr. Wickwire, Gavin & Gibbs, P.C., Washington, 1986—; bus. mgr. Energy Law Jour., Washington. 1986—; sec. Cogeneration Coalition Am. Inc., Washington, 1985—. Named Outstanding Atty. in Va. Met. Women's Bar Assn., Va. Womens Attys. Assn., 1986. Mem. ABA, Va. Bar Assn., Fairfax Bar Assn., Fed. Energy Bar Assn. (vice chmn. practice and procedures com. 1985-86). Presbyterian. Avocations: sailing, gardening, traveling. FERC practice, Administrative and regulatory, Energy, alternate energy practice. Office: Wickwire Gavin & Gibbs PC 1133 21st St NW Suite 500 Washington DC 20036

WALKER, MARY L., lawyer; b. Dayton, Ohio, Dec. 1, 1948; d. William Willard and Lady D. Walker. Student, U. Calif., Irvine, 1968; BA in Biology/Ecology, U. Calif., Berkeley, 1970; postgrad., UCLA, 1972-73; JD, Boston U., 1973. Bar: Calif. 1973, U.S. Supreme Ct. 1979. Atty. Southern Pacific Co., San Francisco, 1973-76; from assoc. to ptnr. Richards, Watson, & Gershon, Los Angeles, 1976-82; dep. asst. atty. gen. lands div. U.S. Dept. Justice, Washington, 1982-84; dep. solicitor U.S. Dept. Interior, Washington, 1984-85; asst. sec. of energy, environment, safety and health U.S. Dept. Energy, Washington, 1985—. Mem. Calif. Bar Assn., Nat. Fedn. Rep. Women, World Affairs Council, Renaissance Women. Environment, State civil litigation, Federal civil litigation. Office: US Dept Energy Environment Safety & Health 1000 Independence Ave SW Washington DC 20585

WALKER, PATRICIA ANN, lawyer; b. Latrobe, Pa., Nov. 13, 1953; d. William J. and Sylvia R. (Fradel) W.; m. Ralph E. Jocke, Oct. 8, 1982. A.B., Grove City Coll., 1975; J.D., Cleve.-Marshall Coll. Law, 1981. Bars: Ohio 1981, U.S. Dist. Ct. (no. dist.) Ohio 1981; U.S. Ct. Appeals (6th cir.) 1982; U.S. Supreme Ct. 1985. City clk. City of Broadview Heights, Ohio, 1975-77; claims rep. Soc. Security Adminstrn., Cleve., 1977-81; assoc. Law Offices of Ellis B. Brannon, Sharon Center, Ohio, 1981-85; sole practice, Medina, Ohio, 1985—. Advisor Divorce Equity, Inc., Cleve. Mem. ABA, Assn. Trial Lawyers Am., Fed. Bar Assn., Nat. Orgn. Soc. Security Claimants' Reps., Ohio State Bar Assn., Ohio Acad. Trial Lawyers, Medina County Bar Assn. (treas.), Akron Bar Assn., Cuyahoga County Bar Assn., Bar Assn. Greater Cleve., Cleve. Women Lawyers Assn., Medina County Law Library Assn. (v.p., bd. trustees). Democrat. Mem. United Ch. of Christ. Club: Slovenain Nat. Benefit Soc. Pension, profit-sharing, and employee benefits, Oil and gas leasing, State civil litigation. Office: 225 E Liberty St Medina OH 44256

WALKER, PATRICIA GAIL, lawyer; b. Ft. Knox, Ky., July 24, 1949; d. Luther Wesley and Zona (Robbins) W.; m. Thomas Joseph FitzGerald, Mar. 17, 1984; 1 child, Garrett Richard FitzGerald. BA, U. Ky., 1971; JD, U. Louisville, 1978. Bar: Ky. 1978, U.S. Dist. Ct. (ea. and we. dists.) Ky. 1980, U.S. Ct. Appeals (6th cir.) 1982. Staff atty. Ky. Dept. Justice, Frankfort, 1978-81; assoc. Gittleman & Barber, Louisville, 1981-84; ptnr. Walker & Radigan, Louisville, 1984-85, Walker, Radigan & Zeller, Louisville, 1985—; bd. dirs. Legal Aid Soc., Louisville, Cedar Lake Lodge Inc., LaGrange, Ky. Mem. Louisville Area Family Planning Council, 1982—. Mem. ABA, Ky. Bar Assn., Louisville Bar Assn. (chmn. mental health com. 1986—). Democrat. Civil rights, Probate, Family and matrimonial. Home: 1440 Christy Ave Louisville KY 40204 Office: Walker Radigan & Zeller 800 Republic Bldg 429 W Muhammad Ali Blvd Louisville KY 40202

WALKER, PAUL HOWARD, lawyer; b. Baldwyn, Miss., Feb. 10, 1923; s. Howard Earl and Frances Caroline (McElroy) W.; m. Gwendolyn Yvonne Loomis, June 17, 1950; children—Michael D., Melinda K. Student E. Miss. Jr. Coll., 1940-41, La. State U., 1941-43, U. Mo., 1943-44; J.D. with honors, George Washington U., 1948, LL.M., 1949; postgrad. Harvard U., 1975-82. Bar: D.C. 1948, Md., 1959, Mass. 1969. Atty.-editor U.S. Tax Ct., Washington, 1950-53; asst. gen. counsel Life Ins. Assn. Am. (now Am. Council of Life Ins.) Washington, 1953-68; tax counsel New Eng. Mut. Life Ins. Co., Boston, 1968-86; mem. tax policy adv. bd. Taxation with Representation Fund, Washington, 1975; adv. council Hartford Inst. on Ins. Taxation, Conn., 1981-83. Trustee New Eng. Coll., Henniker, N.H., 1978—; chancellor New Eng. Dist. Anglican Catholic Ch., 1981—. Served with AUS, 1943-45; to capt. USAFR, 1951-63. Decorated Silver Star. Fellow Am. Coll. Tax Counsel; Mem. ABA, Boston Bar Assn., Fed. Bar Assn., SAR (pres. Mass. Soc. 1981-83, nat. trustee 1983-85, chancellor gen. 1986—). Lodge: Masons. Republican. Contbr. articles to profl. jours.; mem. adv. bd. Estate Planning Mag., 1973-86, Compensation Planning Jour. Pension, profit-sharing, and employee benefits, Corporate taxation, Estate taxation. Home and Office: 21 Milton Rd Brookline MA 02146

WALKER, RICHARD BRUCE, judge; b. Newton, Kans., July 20, 1948; s. Thomas Franklin and Norma M. (Doell) W.; m. Martha Mangelsdorf, Nov. 26, 1977; children: Jacob, Benjamin. BA, Bethel Coll., 1970; JD, U. Kans., 1973. Bar: Kans. 1973, U.S. Dist. Ct. Kans. 1973, U.S. Supreme Ct. 1977, U.S. Ct. Appeals (10th cir.) 1982. Ptnr. Advian & Walker, Newton, 1973-77, Ice, Turner & Ice, Newton, 1982-84; chief legis. asst. to Senator James Pearson, Washington, 1977-78; mem. Kans. Parole Bd., Topeka, 1979-82; dist. judge Harvey County Ct., Newton, 1984—. State rep. Kans. Legislature, Topeka, 1972-77; bd. dirs. Bethel Coll., No. Newton, Kans., 1971-83. Mem. ABA, Kans. Bar Assn., Harvey County Bar Assn. Republican. Methodist. Judicial administration, Jurisprudence. Home: 309 E 3d Newton KS 67114 Office: Harvey County Dist Ct PO Box 665 Newton KS 67114

WALKER, ROBERT BENSON, lawyer; b. Wynne, Ark., Oct. 28, 1945; s. Stirling Russell and Betty Jean (Waldrep) W.; m. Peggy Josephine Wells, July 13, 1968; children: Robert Benson Jr., Robin Elizabeth. BS, Ark. State U., 1967; MS, U. Tenn., 1972; JD, Memphis State U., 1975. Bar: Tenn. 1976, D.C. 1977, U.S. Dist. Ct. D.C. 1977, U.S. Ct. Appeals (D.C. cir.) 1977, U.S. Ct. Appeals (3d cir.) 1980, U.S. Ct. Appeals (4th cir.) 1985, U.S. Ct. Claims 1986. Clin. chemist City of Memphis Hosp., 1967-75; assoc. Goff, Sims, Cloud & Stroud, Washington, 1976-83; ptnr. Sims, Walker & Steinfeld PC, Washington, 1983—. Mem. ABA, Fed. Bar Assn., Transp. Lawyers Assn. (chmn. practice and procedure com. 1983—). Avocations: running, sailing. Administrative and regulatory, General corporate, Immigration, naturalization, and customs. Home: 1621 Winterwood Pl Herndon VA 22070 Office: Sims Walker & Steinfeld PC 1275 K St NW Suite 875 Washington DC 20005

WALKER, ROBERT DONALD, lawyer; b. Sacramento, Calif., Dec. 4, 1937; s. Charles L. and Sylvia S. Walker; children: Michael C., Catherine D., William C. Student, Dartmouth Coll., 1955-58; B.S., U. So. Calif., 1959; J.D., UCLA, 1962. Bar: Calif. 1963, U.S. Dist. Ct. (so. and cen. dists.) Calif. Mem. firm Brill, Hunt, DeBuy & Burby, Los Angeles, 1963-68, Belcher, Henzie & Biegenzahn, 1968-74, Harney & Moore, 1974-78, Belcher, Henzie & Biegenzahn, 1978-85; sole practice, Los Angeles, 1985—. Mem. ABA, Calif. Bar Assn., Los Angeles County Bar Assn., Pasadena Bar Assn., Am. Bd. Trial Advs., Am. Bd. Profl. Liability Attys. Republican. State civil litigation, Personal injury.

WALKER, RONALD LYNN, lawyer; b. Enid, Okla., Dec. 10, 1953; s. Dayle E. and Hazel (Conner) W.; m. Ginger L. Jones, Aug. 27, 1955. BA in Philosophy magna cum laude, Phillips U., 1976; JD, U. Okla., 1979. Bar: Okla. 1979, U.S. Dist. Ct. (we. dist.) Okla. 1979, U.S. Ct. Appeals (10th cir.) 1980, U.S. Supreme Ct. 1980. Assoc. McKinney, Stringer & Webster, P.C., Oklahoma City, 1979-1984, ptnr., 1984—. Editor U. Okla. Law Rev., 1978-79. Mem. ABA, Okla. Bar Assn., Am. Trial Lawyers Assn., Okla. Trial Lawyers Assn., Okla. Assn. Def. Counsel, Def. Research Inst., Order of Coif. Avocations: racquetball, tennis, hunting, fishing. Personal injury, Securities, Insurance. Home: 13005 Red Eagle Pass Edmond OK 73013 Office: McKinney Stringer & Webster City Ctr Bldg 8th Floor Main & Broadway Oklahoma City OK 73102

WALKER, ROSS PAUL, lawyer; b. Chgo., Sept. 10, 1934; s. Ross Carl and Lucille Marie (Hock) W.; m. Elisabeth Charlotte Stein, Dec. 21, 1961. A.B., Earlham Coll., 1957; J.D., U. Chgo., 1960. Bar: Ind. 1960, U.S. Dist. Ct. (so. dist.) Ind. 1962, U.S. Dist. Ct. (no. dist.) Ind. 1972, U.S. Ct. Appeals (7th cir.) 1972. Practice law, Indpls., 1962—, ptnr. firm Dewester, Hall & Walker since 1963—; referee juvenile div. Superior Ct. Marion County, Indpls., 1964—. Served with U.S. Army, 1960-62. Mem. Ind. State Bar Assn. (chmn. labor law sect. 1980-81). Republican. Roman Catholic. Labor, Workers' compensation, Juvenile. Home: 10115 Indian Lake Blvd S Dr Indianapolis IN 46236 Office: Dewester Hall & Walker 315 Circle Tower Bldg Indianapolis IN 46204

WALKER, SUE SHERIDAN, history educator; b. Chgo., Aug. 11, 1935; d. J. Michael and Kathryn (Corrigan) Sheridan; m. Franklin A. Walker, May 30, 1959; 1 dau., Ann Sheridan Walker. B.S., Loyola U., 1958, M.A., 1961; Ph.D., U. Chgo., 1966. Asst. prof. history U. Windsor, (Ont., Can.), 1966-68; asst. prof. history Northeastern Ill. U., Chgo., 1968-72, assoc. prof., 1972-79, prof. history, 1979—. AAUW fellow, 1965-66; NEH fellow, 1982-83, fellow Royal Hist. Soc., 1986—. Mem. Am. Hist. Assn., Medieval Acad. Am., Selden Soc., Pipe Roll Soc., Am. Soc. Legal History (dir.). Club: University Women's (London). Author: The Court Rolls of the Manor of Wakefield from October 1331 to September 1333, 1983; contbr. articles to profl. jours.; mem. editorial bd. Am. Jour. Legal History, 1982—. Legal history. Address: 606 Lincoln Ave Winnetka IL 60093 Office: Dept History Northeastern Ill U 5500 N St Louis Ave Chicago IL 60625

WALKER, VERN ROBERT, lawyer; b. Atlantic City, Oct. 5, 1945; s. Vern Luke and Rosemary (Deanhofer) W.; m. Elizabeth Jean Arquin, June 21, 1969; children: Amanda Louise, Vern Edward. BA in Philosophy, U. Detroit, 1967; MA in Philosophy, U. Notre Dame, 1969, PhD, 1975; JD, Yale U., 1980. Bar: D.C. 1980, U.S. Dist. Ct. D.C., U.S. Ct. Appeals (D.C. and 5th cirs.). Asst. prof. Creighton U., Omaha, 1973-77; assoc. Leva, Hawes et al, Washington, 1980-82; assoc. Swidler & Berlin, Washington, 1982-86, ptnr., 1986—. Author: Product Risk Reduction in the Chemical Industry, 1985; contbr. articles to profl. jours. Served with U.S. Army, 1969-70, Vietnam. Decorated Bronze Star with bronze oak leaf cluster; Arthur J. Schmitt fellow, 1972-73, Nat. Def. Edn. Act fellow, 1967-69, 71-72; named one of Outstanding Young Men in Am. U.S. Jaycees, 1977. Mem. ABA. Democrat. Roman Catholic. Lodge: KC. Avocations: writing poetry, playing piano, tennis. Environment, Personal injury, Scientific evidence (administrative and court proceedings). Office: Swidler & Berlin 1000 Thomas Jefferson St NW Washington DC 20007

WALKER, WALLACE LEE, lawyer; b. Glen Allen, Ala., July 10, 1941; s. Odus Lee and Beulah Mae (Shaw) W.; m. Sylvia Lavonne Martin, July 8, 1967; children—Scott Christopher, Dana Renee. B.A., Calif. State U.-Los Angeles, 1966; J.D., UCLA, 1970. Bar: Pa. 1974, U.S. Dist. Ct. (ea. dist.) Pa. 1974, U.S. Supreme Ct. 1977, U.S. Ct. Appeals (3d cir.) 1982. Atty. Legal Aid, Compton, Calif., 1970-72; sr. cons. Calif. Legis., Sacramento, 1972-73; legal cons. Soc. Ednl. Leadership, Los Angeles, 1973-81; sole practice, Phila., 1981—. adj. prof. Calif. State U., Los Angeles, 1970-80. Served with U.S. Army, 1963-65. Mem. ABA, Barrister Assn., Sigma Delta Chi, Alpha Phi Alpha (nat. officer 1963-65). Criminal, Jurisprudence. Office: 1907 Two Mellon Bank Ctr Philadelphia PA 19102

WALKER, WALTER HERBERT, III, lawyer, writer; b. Quincy, Mass., Sept. 12, 1949; s. Walter H. Jr. and Irene M. (Horn) W.; m. Anne M. DiScuillo, June 17, 1982; children: Brett Daniel, Jeffrey St. John. BA, U. Pa., 1971; JD, U. Calif., San Francisco, 1974. Bar: Calif. 1974, Mass. 1981. Appellate atty. ICC, Washington, 1975-77; trial atty. Handler, Baker, Greene & Taylor, San Francisco, 1977-80; ptnr. Sterns, Smith, Walker & Grell, San Francisco, 1981—. Author: A Dime to Dance By, 1983 (Best 1st Novel by Calif. Author), The Two Dude Defense, 1985, Rules of The Knife Fight, 1986. Mem. Assn. Trial Lawyers Am., Calif. Trial Lawyers Assn., San Francisco Trial Lawyers Assn., Mystery Writers Am. Democrat. Club: Hastings Rugby. Personal injury, Insurance. Home: 211 Meda Ln Mill Valley CA 94941 Office: Sterns Smith Walker & Grell 280 Utah St San Francisco CA 94103

WALKER, WALTER LADARE, lawyer; b. Newton County, Mo., Oct. 6, 1927; s. Walter Joseph and Mae (Patterson) W.; m. Marilyn Louise Land, June 24, 1951; children—Marcia Lynn, Charlotte Ann. A.A., Joplin Jr. Coll., 1946; J.D., U. Mo.-Columbia, 1953. Bar: Mo. 1953, U.S. Dist. Ct. (we. dist.) Mo. 1955. Sole practice, Neosho, Mo., 1953—; municipal judge City of Neosho, 1957-66. Bd. dirs. Masonic Home of Mo., St. Louis, 1969-73, pres., 1972-73; pres. Neosho R5 Sch. Bd., 1985-86. Served with U.S. Army, 1946-47, 50-51. Decorated Purple Heart. Mem. Newton-McDonald Counties Bar Assn. (pres. 1957-59), Disabled Am. Veterans, Am. Legion (commander 1956), Delta Theta Phi. Republican. Lodges: Masons (Grand Master Mo. 1973-74, Shriners, Lions (pres. 1971-72). Probate, Real property, Transportation. Home: 1301 Benton Ave Neosho MO 64850 Office: PO Box 487 Neosho MO 64850

WALKER, WOODROW WILSON, lawyer; b. Greenville, Mich., Feb. 19, 1919; m. Janet K. Keiter, Oct. 7, 1950; children: Jonathan Woodrow, William Craig, Elaine Virginia. BA, U. Mich., 1943; LLB, Cath. U., 1950. Bar: D.C. 1950, U.S. Supreme Ct. 1958, Va. 1959. Atty. Am. law div. legis. reference Library of Congress, Washington, 1951-60; sole practice Arlington, Va., 1960—; counsel Calvary Found., Arlington, 1970-85, first pres., 1972; judge moot ct. George Mason Law Sch., 1986—. V.p. Jefferson Civic Assn., Arlington, 1955-61; pres. Nellie Custis PTA, Arlington, 1960-61; sec. Arlington County Bd. Equalization Real Estate Assessment, 1962, chmn.

1963; com. chmn. Arlington Troop 108 Boy Scouts Am., 1964-69; mem. Arlington County Pub. Utilities Commn., 1964-66, vice chmn., 1965-66; pres. Betschler Class Adult Sunday Sch., Calvary United Meth. Ch., Arlington, 1965. Served with U.S. Army, 1943-45, PTO. Mem. ABA, Arlington County Bar Assn. Methodist. Democrat. Consumer commercial, Contracts commercial, General practice. Home: 2822 Fort Scott Dr Arlington VA 22202 Office: Continental Fed Savings Bank Suite 202-203 Arlington VA 22201

WALKLEY, ROBERT EARLE, lawyer; b. Muskegon, Mich., Jan. 11, 1943; s. Arland R. and Phyllis M. (McIlveen) W.; m. Geraldine Salisbury, May 14, 1967; children: James E., Sarah A. BA in Econs., U. Mich., 1965, JD, 1968. Bar: Mich. 1969, U.S. Ct. Appeals (9th cir.) 1970, Wash. 1972, Oreg. 1973, Nebr. 1977, U.S. Dist. Ct. Nebr. 1978. Atty. Union Pacific R.R. Co., Portland, Oreg., 1972-77; gen. contract counsel Union Pacific R.R. Co., Omaha, 1977—. Treas. Am. Lung Assn. Nebr., Omaha, 1984—, bd. dirs. 1980—; bd. dirs. Combined Health Agys. Drive, Omaha, 1986—. Served as lt. USNR, 1968-72. Recipient fundraising merit award Combined Health Agys. Drive, 1984. Mem. ABA, Omaha Bar Assn., Phi Alpha Delta. General corporate, Real property, Contracts commercial. Office: Union Pacific RR Co Law Dept 1416 Dodge St Omaha NE 68179

WALKUP, CHARLOTTE LLOYD, lawyer; b. N.Y.C., Apr. 28, 1910; d. Charles Henry and Helene Louise (Wheeler) Tuttle; m. David D. Lloyd, Oct. 19, 1940 (dec. Dec. 1962); children—Andrew M. Lloyd, Louisa Lloyd Hurley; m. Homer Allen Walkup, Feb. 4, 1967. A.B., Vassar Coll., 1931; LL.B., Columbia U., 1934. Bar: N.Y. 1935, U.S. Supreme Ct. 1939, U.S. Dist. Ct. D.C. 1953, Va. 1954. Asst. solicitor Dept. Interior, Washington, 1934-45; asst. gen. counsel UNRRA, Washington and London, 1945-48; assoc. and cons. firms, Washington, 1953, 55, 60; atty., spl. asst. Office Treasury, Washington, 1961-65; asst. gen. counsel Dept. Treasury, Washington, 1965-73; cons. Rogers & Wells, Washington, 1975-86. Editor, Columbia Law Rev., 1934. Pres, Alexandria Community Welfare Council, 1950-52; bd dirs. Alexandria Council Human Relations, 1958-60, Womans Nat. Democratic Club, 1959-60, New Hope Found., 1977. Recipient Meritorious Service award Dept. Treasury, 1970, Exceptional Service award, 1973; Career Service award Nat. Civil Service League, 1973. Mem. Fed. Bar Assn., Columbia Law Sch. Alumni Assn. Democrat. Episcopalian. Administrative and regulatory, Public international, International trade. Home: 2501 Ridge Rd Alexandria VA 22302

WALKUP, HOMER ALLEN, lawyer, historian, writer; b. Dunloup, W.Va., Jan. 28, 1917; s. Homer Allen and Lillie Belle (Harris) W.; m. Edna Mae Tucker, Nov. 19, 1941 (dec. 1966); m. Charlotte M. Tuttle Lloyd, Feb. 4, 1967; children—Homer Allen, Randolph Michael, Pamela Susan. A.B., W.Va. U., 1935, LL.B., 1938; LL.M., Georgetown U., 1947. Bar: W.Va. 1938, U.S. Supreme Ct. 1946, U.S. Ct. Claims 1978, U.S. Ct. Appeals (fed. cir.) 1982, U.S. Claims Ct. 1982, U.S. Ct. Mil. Appeals 1984. Sole practice, W.Va., 1938-42; complaint atty. W.Va. Office OPA, Charleston, 1942; commd. ensign USNR, 1943, advanced through grades to capt., 1963; appellate judge Navy Ct. Mil. Rev., 1966-68; dep. asst., JAG of Navy, 1968-73; ret., 1973; sole practice, Summersville, W.Va., 1974—. Vice chmn. governing bd. Alexandria (Va.) Community Mental Health Ctr., 1981-82; mem. exec. bd. and social planning com. Alexandria United Way; mem. exec. bd. No. Va. Family Service, 1978-82. Mem. ABA, Fed. Bar Assn., W.Va. State Bar, W.Va. Bar Assn., Bar Assn. D.C., Fed. Cir. Bar Assn., Judge Advs. Assn., Navy-MarCorps Retired Judge Advs. Assn., Assn. Trial Lawyers Am., Am. Judicature Soc., Mil. Order World Wars, Res. Officers Assn., Ret. Officers Assn., Order of Coif. Democrat. Presbyterian. Club: Mil. Dist. Washington Officers. Contbr. in field. Military, Legal history, Administrative and regulatory. Office: PO Box 272 Summersville WV 26651

WALL, CHRISTOPHER READ, lawyer; b. Norfolk, Va., Oct. 6, 1952; s. Maurice E. Wall and Marilyn (Murrah) Hardin; m. Barbara L. Wartelle, June 21, 1980. BA, Yale U., 1974, Oxford U., 1976; JD, U. Va., 1979. Bar: N.Y. 1980, U.S. Dist. Ct. (so. dist.) N.Y. 1980, U.S. Ct. Internat. Trade 1985, D.C. 1986, U.S. Dist. Ct. D.C. 1986. Assoc. Winthrop, Stimson, Putnam & Roberts, N.Y.C., 1979—. Mem. ABA, Assn. Bar City N.Y., Council Fgn. Relations. Private international, General corporate. Office: Winthrop Stimson Putnam & Roberts 1155 Conneticut Ave NW Washington DC 20036

WALL, DONALD ARTHUR, lawyer; b. Lafayette, Ind., Mar. 17, 1946; s. Dwight Arthur and Myra Virgina (Peavey) W.; m. Cheryn Lynn Heinen, Aug. 30, 1970; children—Sarah Lynn, Michael Donald. B.A., Butler U., 1968; J.D., Northwestern U., 1971. Bar: Ohio 1971, U.S. Dist. Ct. (no. dist.) Ohio 1973, U.S. Ct. Appeals (6th cir.) 1982, U.S. Supreme Ct. 1980, Ariz. 1982, U.S. Dist. Ct. (no. dist.) W.Va. 1982, U.S. Dist. Ct. Ariz. 1983, U.S. Ct. Appeals (9th and 10th cir.) 1984. Assoc. Squire, Sanders & Dempsey, Cleve., 1971-80, ptnr., 1980-82, Phoenix, 1983—; speaker at profl. meetings; program moderator. Contbr. articles to profl. jours. Mem. adminstrv. bd. Ch. of Saviour, Cleve. Heights, Ohio, 1980-83; trustee Ch. of the Saviour Day Center, Cleve. Heights, 1979-82; fin. com. Paradise Valley (Ariz.) United Meth. Ch., 1986-87; bd. dirs., div. commr. North Scottsdale (Ariz.) Little League, sports coach, 1983-87; bd. dirs. Epilepsy Found. N.E. Ohio, 1976-82, pres., 1981-82. Mem. ABA (torts and ins. practice sect., past chmn. r.r. law com., litigation sect.), Nat. Assn. R.R. Trial Counsel, Def. Research Inst., Ariz. Bar Assn. (labor, trial practice, antitrust sects.), Maricopa County Bar Assn., Am. Judicature Soc. Methodist. Federal civil litigation, State civil litigation, Personal injury. Office: Valley Bank Center 201 N Central St Phoenix AZ 85073

WALL, JACK KNOX, lawyer; b. Abilene, Tex., Jan. 15, 1947; s. Jack Barnett and Ruth (Knox) W.; m. Maureen D. Wall, Dec. 8, 1979 (div. Dec. 1980); m. Erin M. Wall, Sept. 25, 1982; children: Mark Dotson, Toby Marcum. Grad., U. Tex., 1969, JD, 1972. Bar: Tex. 1973, U.S. Dist. Ct. (we. dist.) Tex. 1977; cert. specialist in family and criminal law, Tex. Asst. dist. atty. Midland County, Tex., 1973-76; assoc. Kerr, Fitz-Gerald & Kerr, Midland, 1977-80, J.A. Mashburn Law Office, Midland, 1980-82; sole practice Midland, 1982—; asst. judge Midland Mcpl. Ct., 1983—. Planning staff legal assts. Midland Coll., 1983—. Served to capt. USAR, 1972-80. Mem. ABA, Tex. Bar Assn., Assn. Trial Lawyers Am., Def. Lawyers Assn. Democrat. Baptist. Family and matrimonial, Criminal, General practice. Home: 3602 Oak Ridge Midland TX 79707

WALL, KENNETH E., JR., lawyer; b. Beaumont, Tex., Apr. 6, 1944; s. Kenneth E. and W. Geraldine (Peoples) W.; m. Marjorie Lee Hughes, Dec. 21, 1968; children—Barbara, Elizabeth, Kenneth. Grad. Lamar U., 1966, U. Tex.-Austin, 1969. Bar: Tex. 1969, U.S. Supreme Ct. 1979. Asst. city atty., Beaumont, 1969-73, city atty., 1973-84; with firm Olson & Olson, Houston, 1984—; dir. Tex. Mcpl. League Ins. Trust, 1979-84, vice chmn., 1983-84; counsel S.E. Tex. Regional Planning Commn., 1974, 76. Active Boy Scouts Am., Girl Scouts U.S.A. Mem. ABA, Nat. Inst. Mcpl. Law Officers (chmn. com. on local govt. personnel 1979-81, 82-84), State Bar Tex., Tex. City Attys. Assn. (pres. 1982-83), Jefferson County Bar Assn. (dir. 1975-77), Houston Bar Assn., Phi Delta Phi. Methodist. Office: MCorp Suite 3485 333 Clay Ave Houston TX 77002

WALL, LARRY WILLIAM, lawyer; b. Wichita, Kans., July 27, 1944; s. Larel William and Erma Beatrice (Bullene) W.; m. Kathy Diane Sadler, Feb. 25, 1967; children: Stacy Lynn, Jason William. BBA, North Tex. State U., 1969; JD, So. Meth. U., 1972. Bar: Kans. 1972, U.S. Dist. Ct. Kans. 1972, U.S. Ct. Appeals (10th cir.) 1982. Asst. dist. atty. 18th Jud. Dist., Wichita, 1972-74; assoc. Fleeson, Gooing, Coulson & Kitch, Wichita, 1974-78, ptnr., 1978-85; sole practice Wichita, 1985—. Mem. ABA, Kans. Bar Assn., Assn. Trial Lawyers Am., Kans. Assn. Def. Counsel, Kans. Trial Lawyers Assn., Am. Soc. Law and Medicine. Democrat. Avocations: golf, tennis. Federal civil litigation, Personal injury, Criminal. Home: 156 S Pinecrest Wichita KS 67214

WALL, SUSAN TAYLOR, lawyer; b. Washington, Nov. 27, 1947; d. Frank Dodd and Roberta (Stewart) Taylor; m. Robert Thorp Wall Jr., June 7, 1969; children: Spencer, Elizabeth. BA, Skidmore Coll., 1969; MA, U. Houston, 1974; postgrad., U. Puget Sound, 1976-78; JD cum laude, Stanford U., 1979. Bar: Calif. 1979, U.S. Dist. Ct. (no. dist.) Calif. 1979, U.S. Dist. Ct. S.C. 1982, U.S. Ct. Appeals (4th and 9th cirs.) 1982, S.C. 1983. Assoc. Long & Levit, San Francisco, 1979-82; assoc. Holmes & Thomson, Charleston, S.C., 1982-85, ptnr., 1986—. Mem. ABA, Calif. Bar Assn., S.C. Bar Assn., Def. Research Inst. Democrat. Insurance, Federal civil litigation, State civil litigation. Office: Holmes & Thomson 100 Broad St Charleston SC 29401

WALLACE, ANDERSON, JR., lawyer; b. Cleve., Sept. 24, 1939; s. Anderson and Agatha Lee (Culpepper) W.; 1 son, Anderson. Student Ga. Inst. Tech., 1957-58; B.A., George Washington U., 1962, J.D., 1964, LL.M., 1966. Bar: Tex. 1968, U.S. Dist. Ct. (no. dist.) Tex. 1968, U.S. Ct. Claims 1968, U.S. Tax Ct. 1968, U.S. Ct. Appeals (5th cir.) 1968, U.S. Supreme Ct. 1971, U.S. Ct. Appeals (11th cir.) 1981. Program mgmt. asst. NASA, Washington, 1962-64; atty. U.S. Dept. Treasury, Washington, 1964-66; tax atty. Price Waterhouse & Co., Atlanta, 1966-67; tax ptnr. Jackson, Walker, Winstead, Cantwell & Miller, Dallas, 1967-84; dir. in charge tax dept. Baker, Smith & Mills, P.C., Dallas, 1984—; instr. Sch. Law So. Meth. U. Trustee S.W. Mus. Sci. and Tech., Dallas, 1974—. Chmn. Inst. on Employee Benefits, Southwestern Legal Found., 1976. Mem. ABA. Corporate taxation, Personal income taxation, Estate taxation. Office: 500 LTV Center 2001 Ross Ave Dallas TX 75201

WALLACE, ARCH LEE, lawyer; b. New Orleans, Aug. 4, 1947; s. Arch Lee Jr. and Dorothy (Parnell) W.;. B in Indsl., Systems Engrng., Ga. Tech. U., 1970; JD, Tulane U., 1973. Bar: D.C., U.S. Ct. Appeals (D.C. cir.) 1973. With solicitor's office Fed. Power Commn., Washington, 1973-75; counsel House Sci. and Tech. Com., Washington, 1975-78, Senate Energy Com., Washington, 1978-81, House S&T Com., Washington, 1981-82; asst. dir., counsel Gas Research Inst., Washington, 1982—. Served to capt. USAFR, 1973-81. Mem. ABA, Fed. Energy Bar Assn. (chmn. subcommittee 1985). Administrative and regulatory, FERC practice, Legislative. Office: Gas Research Inst 1331 Pennsylvania #730N Washington DC 20004-1703

WALLACE, BARBARA WENDY, lawyer; b. Blue Island, Ill., June 9, 1951; d. James Carl and Dionysia Esther (Mackrie) W.; m. Kenneth Herbert Rinderknecht, Aug. 21, 1971. BA, Washington U., St. Louis, 1973, JD, 1976. Bar: Mo. 1976, U.S. Ct. Appeals (8th cir.) 1977, U.S. Dist. Ct. (ea. dist.) Mo. 1978. Law clk. to presiding justice Mo. Ct. Appeals, St. Louis, 1976-77; from assoc. to ptnr. Cupples, Cooper & Haller, St. Louis, 1977-81; sole practice St. Louis, 1981-82; ptnr. Mohme & Wallace, St. Louis, 1982-85; assoc. Stolar Partnership, St. Louis, 1985—; adj. prof. Washington U. Sch. Law, 1981-82. Mem. U.S. Merit Selection com., St. Louis, 1984; bd. dirs. Legal Services Eastern Mo., St. Louis, 1982-84. Mem. St. Louis County Bar Assn. (outstanding young lawyer award 1985), Bar Assn. of Met. St. Louis (chmn. bench and bar conf. 1986—), Women Lawyers Assn. (pres. 1980-81), Lawyers Assn. (exec. com. 1982-86, v.p. 1986—). Avocations: softball, volleyball, golf. Federal civil litigation, State civil litigation, Contracts commercial. Office: Stolar Partnership 911 Washington Ave 7th Floor Saint Louis MO 63101

WALLACE, CHRISTOPHER BAIRD, lawyer, land manager; b. Tachikawa, Japan, May 2, 1953; s. Robert Bruce and Flora E. (Baird) W.; m. Martha Capecelatro, June 8, 1974; children: Mary Clare, Emily Baird, William Dortch II. BA in Polit. Sci., U. Vt., 1976; JD, St. Mary's U., San Antonio, 1978. Bar: Tex. 1978, Colo. 1979, U.S. Dist. Ct. Colo. 1979, Pa. 1985. Atty., landman Pennzoil Co., Denver, 1978-79; staff atty., landman Anadarko Prodn. Co., Denver, 1979-84; regional atty., land mgr. Nat. Resource Mgmt. Corp., Pitts., 1984—. Bar: ABA, Tex. Bar Assn., Pa. Bar Assn., Eastern Mineral Law Found., Am. Assn. Petroleum Landmen, Can. Assn. Petroleum Landmen. Oil and gas leasing, Administrative and regulatory, General corporate. Home: 308 Maple Ln Sewickley PA 15143 Office: Nat Resource Mgmt Corp 681 Anderson Dr Pittsburgh PA 15220

WALLACE, ELAINE WENDY, lawyer; b. Worcester, Mass., Feb. 16, 1949; d. Louis S. and Ida (Zeiper) W. BA, Yeshiva U., 1971; JD, John F. Kennedy Sch. Law, 1976. Sole practice Oakland, Calif. Civil rights, Government contracts and claims, Labor. Home: 2430 Palmetto St #1 Oakland CA 94602 Office: 2430 Palmetto St #2 Oakland CA 94602

WALLACE, HERBERT NORMAN, lawyer; b. Syracuse, N.Y., Oct. 19, 1937; s. Louis H. and Betty (Wagner) W.; m. Frances Adele Groobman, June 1, 1963 (div. Sept. 1976); children: Craig, Julie; m. Frances Mae Souza, Nov. 15, 1977; 1 child, John. BA, Davis & Elkins Coll., 1959; JD, Syracuse U., 1962. Bar: N.Y. 1962, U.S. Dist. Ct. (no. dist.) N.Y. 1982. Asst. atty. gen. State of N.Y., Albany, 1963-66; asst. atty. gen in charge of Poughkeepsie (N.Y.) office State of N.Y., Poughkeepsie, 1966-79; counsel to banking com. N.Y. State Senate, Albany, 1979-84, counsel to Senator Rolison, 1984—; sole practice Poughkeepsie, N.Y., 1979-86; ptnr. Wallace & Moore, Poughkeepsie, 1986—. Mem. Poughkeepsie Rep. Com., 1977—;. Mem. N.Y. State Bar Assn., Dutchess County Bar Assn. Jewish. Condemnation, General practice, Real property. Home: 65 Cardinal Dr Poughkeepsie NY 12601 Office: 276 Main Mall Poughkeepsie NY 12601

WALLACE, J. CLIFFORD, judge; b. San Diego, Dec. 11, 1928; s. John Franklin and Lillie Isabel (Overing) W.; m. Virginia Lee Schlosser, Apr. 8, 1957; children: Paige, Laurie, Teri, John. B.A., San Diego State U., 1952; LL.B., U. Calif., Berkeley, 1955. Bar: Calif. 1955. With firm Gray, Cary, Ames & Frye, San Diego, 1955-70; judge U.S. Dist. Ct. So. Dist. Calif., 1970-72, U.S. Ct. Appeals 9th Circuit, 1972—. Contrbr. articles to profl. jours. Served with USN, 1946-49. Mem. ABA, Am. Bd. Trial Advocates, Inst. Jud. Adminstrn. Mormon (stake pres. San Diego East 1962-67, regional rep. 1967-74, 77-79). Jurisprudence. Address: US Courthouse Room 4N25 940 Front St San Diego CA 92189

WALLACE, JAMES P., Texas Suprme Court justice; b. Sidon, Ark., Apr. 8, 1928; s. Harvey J. and Belma G. W.; m. Martha J., Sept. 18, 1954; children—James, Jill. B.S. in Bus. Adminstrn, U. Ark., 1952; J.D., U. Houston, 1957. Bar: Tex. 1957. Ptnr. law firms 1958-75; mem. Tex. Senate, 1970-75; judge 215th Dist. Ct., Harris County, Tex., 1975-78; assoc. justice Ct. Civil Appeals, 1st Supreme Jud. Dist. Tex., 1978-81; justice Supreme Ct. Tex., 1981—. Served with USNR, 1946-49. Mem. Am. Bar Assn., Tex. Bar Assn., Houston Bar Assn. Democrat. Baptist.

WALLACE, JOHN R., lawyer; b. Miami, Okla., Nov. 24, 1913; s. Arthur C. and Grace (VanMatre) W.; m. Louise Bailey, Sept. 15, 1951; children—Ann Louise, John Robert. A.B., U. Okla., 1934; J.D., Harvard, 1937; LLD (hon.), Coll. Ozarks, 1969. Bar: Okla. 1937, U.S. Dist. Ct. (no. dist.) Okla. 1937, U.S. Dist. Ct. (ea. dist.) Okla. 1954, U.S. Ct. Appeals (10th cir.) 1955, U.S. Supreme Ct. 1960, U.S. Dist. Ct. (we. dist.) Okla 1965. Since practiced in Miami; partner firm Wallace & Wallace, 1937-41; sr. partner firm Wallace & Owens, 1946—; adv. dir. Security Bank & Trust Co., Green Country Fed. Savs. and Loan; dir. Exchange State Bank. Chmn. bd. trustees Coll. of Ozarks, 1966-68. Served with AUS, 1942-46, ETO. Decorated Legion of Merit; Paul Harris fellow Rotary, 1981. Fellow Am. Bar Found., Am. Coll. Trial Lawyers, Am. Coll. Probate Counsel; mem. ABA (bd. govs. 1976-77), Okla. Bar Assn. (pres. 1973), Miami C. of C. Presbyterian (elder). General practice, Probate, General corporate. Home: 2021 Yale Ave Miami OK 74354 Office: Wallace and Owens Inc 21 S Main PO Box 1168 Miami OK 74354

WALLACE, MILTON JAY, lawyer; b. Passaic, N.J., Dec. 17, 1935; s. Mark and Regina (Tenny) W.; m. Patricia Radin, July 7, 1963; children—Mark D., Hardy S. B.B.A., U. Miami, 1956, J.D., 1959. Bar: Fla. 1959, U.S. Dist. Ct. (so. dist.) Fla. 1963, U.S. Supreme Ct. 1969. Practice, Miami, 1959—; judge City of Miami, 1961-63; asst. atty. gen. State of Fla., 1965-70; ptnr. Wallace, Engels, Pertnoy & Martin, 1970—; dir. Internat. Asset Mgmt. Group, Inc., Biscayne Nat. Corp. Bd. dirs. Home Intensive Care, Inc., chmn. exec. com.; bd. dirs. Laser RK, Inc., Bank of Coral Gables, Fla.; chmn. Housing Fin. Authority of Dade County (Fla.), 1981—. Served with USAR, 1961-65. Mem. ABA, Dade County Bar Assn., Fla. Inst. C.P.A.s. Clubs: Bankers, Jockey, Palm Bay, City. Real property, General corporate, Banking. Office: 330 Biscayne Blvd Miami FL 33132

WALLACE, RICHARD POWELL, lawyer; b. Troy, N.Y., Apr. 28, 1941; s. Donald Foote and Jane Elizabeth (Powell) W.; m. Elizabeth Lee Allen, June 20, 1964; children—Stephen Allen, Lee Elizabeth, Scott Powell. A.B., Brown U., 1963; J.D. cum laude, Union U., 1967. Bar: N.Y. 1967, U.S. Dist. Ct. (no. dist.) N.Y. 1967. Confidential law asst. 3d dept., Appellate div. N.Y. Supreme Ct., 1967-68; asst. dist. atty. Rensselaer County, N.Y., 1970-71; ptnr. Martin, Shudt, Wallace, DiLorenzo & Copps, Albany and Troy, N.Y., 1968—; dir. capital regional bd. Marine Midland Bank, 1977-81, Eddy (LIC), Inc., 1986—; sec., dir. Blanchard Indsl. Supplies, Inc., Troy; trustee Herold Charitable Trust; trustee Albany Acad., 1974—; mem. faculty Emma Willard Sch., Troy. Vice pres. Gov. Clinton council Boy Scouts Am., 1974-78, pres., 1979-81; trustee, sec. Troy Cemetery Assn., 1974—; mem. exec. com., sec. Vis. Nurse Assn. of Capital Region, Inc., 1975-81, pres. 1982—; bd. dirs. United Way of Mohawk-Hudson Area, Inc., 1974—, allocations div., 1976; trustee Troy Pub. Library, 1974—, v.p., 1982—; bd. dirs. Troy Youth Hockey Assn., Inc., 1978—, pres., 1981—. Recipient Cardozo prize Albany Law Sch., 1967. Mem. ABA, N.Y. State Bar Assn. (mem. continuing legal edn. com., mem. trusts and estates sect., mem. estate litigation com.), Rensselaer County Bar Assn., Albany County Bar Assn., Albany Acad. Alumni Assn. (bd. dirs. 1972—, sec. 1974-75, pres. 1977-78), Brunswick Hills Assn., Inc. (pres. 1981-83). Clubs: Univ. (Albany); Troy Country, Rotary of Troy (pres. 1974-76). Author: Computer Print-Outs of Business and their Admissibility in New York, 1967. General corporate, Estate planning, Probate. Office: 146 Washington Ave Albany NY 12210

WALLACE, ROBERT E., lawyer, educator; b. N.Y.C., Mar. 1, 1956; s. Robert E. Sr. and Vivian A. (High) W. BA in Am. Studies, Yale U., 1978; JD, Georgetown U., 1981. Legal intern NFL, N.Y.C., 1980; assoc. Guilfoil, Petzall & Shoemake, St. Louis, 1981—; adj. prof. law St. Louis U., 1986—. Bd. govs. downton YMCA, St. Louis, 1985—; bd. dirs. Amateur Athletic Assn., St. Louis, 1985—. Recipient Dist. Service award St. Louis Pub. Schs., St. Louis, 1985, 86. Mem. ABA (sports lawyer div.), Met. Bar Assn. (exec. com. young lawyers sect., chmn. media com. 1983-86). Democrat. Avocations: sports, reading, bike riding. Sports law, Entertainment, Federal civil litigation. Home: 4303 E Laclude Saint Louis MO 63108 Office: Guilfoil Petzall & Shoemake 100 N Broadway Saint Louis MO 63101

WALLACE, SEAN DANIEL, lawyer; b. Walnut Creek, Calif., June 17, 1960; s. Daniel M. and Patricia Marie (Coyne) W. BA, Hampden-Sydney Coll., 1982; JD, U. Md., 1985. Bar: Md. 1985, U.S. Dist. Ct. Md. 1986, D.C. 1986, U.S. Dist. Ct. D.C. 1986, U.S. Ct. Appeals (4th, D.C. and Fed. cirs.) 1986. Spl. asst. to U.S. rep. Steny H. Hoyer, Washington, 1982; assoc. Knight, Manzi, Brennan & Ostrom, Upper Marlboro, Md., 1985—; bd. dirs. moot ct. U. Md. Law Sch., Balt., 1983-85. Mem. youth adv. com. City of Bowie, Md., 1976-78, security ops. staff Dem. Nat. Convention, N.Y.C., 1980; chmn. convention Young Dems. of Md., 1982. Named one of Outstanding Young Men in Am. U.S. Jaycees, 1982, 84. Mem. ABA, Prince George's County Bar Assn., Md. Bar Assn., Md. Trial Lawyers Assn., J. Dudley Digges Inn of Ct., Assn. Trial Lawyers Am., Nat. Eagle Scout Assn. Democrat. Roman Catholic. Federal civil litigation, State civil litigation, Criminal. Home: 15537 Norge Ct Bowie MD 20716 Office: Knight Manzi Brennan & Ostrom PA 14324 Old Marlboro Pike Upper Marlboro MD 20772

WALLACE, THOMAS ANDREW, lawyer; b. Sapulpa, Okla., Oct. 12, 1923; s. Thomas Hiram and Lucy Romig (Mauldin) W.; m. Geraldine Jones, July 22, 1946 (div. Jan. 1965); children: Pamela, Thomas Andrew, James Creekmore, William Stuart; m. Nelda Sharp, July 21, 1965. BS, Columbia U., 1951, JD, 1953. Bar: Okla. 1952. Sole practice, Oklahoma City; faculty lectr. O.B.A., Ctr. for Law and Edn. Served with USMC, 1942-46. Mem. Okla. Bar Assn. (Golden Gavel award 1984, subcom. Okla. evidence code, supreme ct. com., uniform jury instrns. com. 1979-81, Okla. Bus. Corp. Act, civil procedure com. 1981-84, chmn. legis. com. 1984-87), Okla. Trial Lawyers Assn. (pres. 1976, Meritorious Service award 1976), Assn. Trial Lawyers Am., Calif. Trial Lawyers Assn. Democrat. Personal injury, Condemnation, Federal civil litigation. Home: 12808 Deerfield Circle Oklahoma City OK 73149 Office: Fidelity Plaza 201 Robert S Kerr Ave Suite 1010 Oklahoma City OK 73102

WALLACE, WILLIAM FARRIER, JR., lawyer, banker; b. Dallas, Apr. 2, 1918; s. William Farrier and Mary Ethel (Pope) W.; m. Ruth Saunders, Aug. 2, 1956. Student U. Tex., 1935-41. Bar: Tex. 1941. Sole practice, Corpus Christi, Tex., 1941, 44—; chmn. bd. dirs. First State Bank, Bishop, Tex., 1964—; pres. WONDOB, Corpus Christi, 1965—. Founder, chmn. bd. dirs. Exec. Audial Rehab. Soc., Corpus Christi, 1966—. Served to 2d lt. AUS, 1941-44. Named Handicapped Texan of Yr., 1961; recipient Pres.'s Citation for Aid to Handicapped, 1961. Mem. Tex. Bar Assn., Corpus Christi C. of C., Tex. Bankers Assn., Independent Bankers Assn. Tex., Tex. Assn. Bank Counsel (charter mem.), Southwest Legal Found. Oil and Gas Inst. (founding mem.). Episcopalian. Clubs: Corpus Christi Town, Corpus Christi Country, Nueces; Dallas Petroleum. Lodge: Rotary. Banking, Oil and gas leasing. Home: 4767 Ocean Dr Corpus Christi TX 78412 Office: 500 American Bank Tower Corpus Christi TX 78403

WALLACE, WILTON LAWRENCE, government administrator, lawyer; b. Raleigh, N.C., Oct. 20, 1949; s. John and Margaret (Ransdell) W.; m. Lorena Long, 1979; children—Ronnie, Wilton, II. B.E., Vanderbilt U., 1972; J.D., Harvard U., 1975. Bar: Pa. 1975, N.C. 1977, D.C. 1980. Gen. counsel, dir. of enforcement N.C. Dept. Natural Resources, Raleigh, 1977-79; chief policy legislation and spl. litigation sect. U.S. Dept. Justice, Land and Natural Resources Div., Washington, 1982-84; dep. asst. atty. gen. for adminstrn Dept. Justice, Justice Mgmt. Div., Washington, 1984-85, asst. atty. gen. for adminstrn., 1985—. Recipient Merit award Boy Scouts Am., 1978, Atty. Gen.'s Commendation, Dept. Justice, 1983, Atty. Gen.'s Spl. Achievement award, 1985. Mem. ABA (vice chmn. environ. quality com. 1984—), Nat. Bar Assn., Vanderbilt Alumni Assn. (bd. dirs., named Disting. Alumnus 1983), Assn. Black Alumni of Vanderbilt (pres. 1984-85), Omega Psi Phi. Lodge: Elks. Avocations: golf; tennis; football. Environment, Government contracts and claims, Legislative. Home: 11505 Drop Forge Ln Reston VA 22091 Office: Dept Justice Justice Mgmt Div Room 1111 10th & Constitution Ave NW Washington DC 20530

WALLACH, EVAN JONATHAN, lawyer, international law educator; b. Superior, Ariz., Nov. 11, 1949; s. Albert A. and Sara Florence (Rothaus) W. B.A., U. Ariz., 1973; J.D., U. Calif.-Berkeley, 1976; LL.B. in Internat. Law, Cambridge U., Eng., 1981. Bar: Nev. 1977, U.S. Dist. Ct. Nev. 1977, U.S. Supreme Ct. 1984. Assoc. firm Lionel Sawyer & Collins, Las Vegas, 1976-82, ptnr., 1983-87; gen. counsel and pub. policy advisor to U.S. Sen. Harry M. Reid, Washington, 1987—; instr. internat. law U. Nev., Las Vegas, 1981—. Gen. counsel Nev. Democratic Party, 1980-84; coordinator Nevadans for Mondale, 1983-84; del. Dem. Nat. Conv., San Francisco, 1984. Served with U.S. Army, 1969-71; Vietnam. Decorated Bronze Star, Air medal. Mem. ABA, Phi Beta Kappa. Jewish. Club: Oxford-Cambridge (London). Libel, Pension, profit-sharing, and employee benefits, Public international. Office: 702 Hart Senate Office Bldg Washington DC 20015

WALLACH, MARK IRWIN, lawyer; b. Cleve., May 19, 1949; s. Ivan A. and Janice (Grossman) W.; m. Harriet Kinney, Aug. 11, 1974; children—Kerry Melissa, Philip Alexander. B.A. magna cum laude, Wesleyan U., 1971; J.D. cum laude, Harvard U., 1974. Bar: Ohio 1974, U.S. dist. ct. (no. dist.) Ohio 1974, U.S. Ct. Appeals (6th cir.) 1985, U.S. Supreme Ct. 1985. Law clk. U.S. Dist. Ct., Cleve., 1974-75; assoc. Baker & Hostetler, Cleve., 1975-79; chief trial counsel City of Cleve., 1979-81; assoc. Calfee, Halter & Griswold, Cleve., 1981-82; ptnr., 1982—. Author: Christopher Morley, 1976. Chmn. bd. trustees Ohio Group Against Smoking Pollution, 1986—; trustee Cleve. chpt. Am. Jewish Com., 1986—; bd. dirs. Citizens League of Greater Cleve., 1978-79; exec. com. mem. Van Aken Project Com., 1982—; pres. Wesleyan Alumni Club Cleve., 1983—. Mem. ABA, Ohio Bar Assn., Cuyahoga County Law Dirs. Assn., Greater Cleve. Bar Assn. Republican. Club: Commerce (Cleve.). Avocations: reading, space exploration, politics. Federal civil litigation, State civil litigation, Local government. Home: 23538 Duffield Rd Shaker Heights OH 44122 Office: Calfee Halter & Griswold 1800 Society Bldg Cleveland OH 44114

WALLE, JAMES PAUL, lawyer; b. Detroit, Sept. 4, 1956; s. Leonard Julius and Mary Frances (Baigent) W.; m. Joanne Marie Albert, Aug. 23, 1986; 1 child, Patrick Joseph. Honors BA summa cum laude, U. Detroit, 1977, JD- MBA cum laude, 1979; LLM, Wayne State U., 1986. Bar: Mich. 1980, U.S. Dist. Ct. (ea. and we. dists.) Mich. 1980, U.S. Ct. Appeals (6th

cir.) 1980, U.S. Ct. Appeals (D.C. cir.) 1982, U.S. Supreme Ct. 1983. Law clk. to assoc. justice Mich. Supreme Ct., Detroit, 1980-82; atty. environ. law Gen. Motors Corp., Detroit, 1982—; teaching fellow Detroit Coll. Law, 1980-81; adj. prof. law U. Detroit, 1981-82. Case and comment editor U. Detroit Law Rev., 1979-80; mem. editorial bd. Mich. Corp. Fin. and Bus. Law Jour. Vol. 3. Vol. legal services St. Benedict Cath. Ch., Highland Park, Mich., 1983-85. Mem. ABA, Mich. Bar Assn. (environ. and energy subcom. environ. law sect. 1983—, speaker young lawyers sect. 1983-86), Detroit Bar Assn. (pro bono atty. 1985—). Avocations: classical music, sci. fiction, sci., travel. Environment, General corporate, Labor. Office: Gen Motors Legal Staff 7-101 New Center One Bldg Detroit MI 48232

WALLENSTEIN, RAYMOND, lawyer; b. Chgo., Apr. 12, 1911; s. Jacob M. and Anna (Ager) W.; m. Edith Bell, May 28, 1953; children—David J., Joel M. B.S., U. Ill., 1932; J.D., U. Chgo., 1934. Bar: Ill. 1934, U.S. Dist. Ct. (no. dist.) Ill. 1934, Calif. 1947, U.S. Ct. Appeals (7th cir.) 1947, Calif. 1971, U.S. Supreme Ct. 1973, U.S. Ct. Appeals (9th cir.) 1971, U.S. Tax Ct. 1974. Mem. Rittenhouse, Marovitz & Wallenstein, Chgo., 1938-42, Wallenstein & Field, Los Angeles, 1957-71; of counsel Shapiro, Posell & Close, Los Angeles, 1982—; mem. panel arbitrators Am. Arbitration Assn., Superior Ct. of Calif., Los Angeles, Calif.; asst. atty. gen., 1934-38, spl. asst. to atty. gen., 1938-41, State of Ill. Mem. Nat. Alumni Cabinet U. Chgo., 1972-74. Mem. Los Angeles County Bar Assn., ABA, State Bar of Calif., U. Chgo. Nat. Law Sch. Alumni Assn. (v.p. 1976-77) pres. so. Calif. chpt. 1971-75), Nat. Counter Intelligence Corps Assn. (life mem. Chgo.), Soc. Calif. Counter Intelligence Corps Assn. (pres. 1955-58) (Los Angeles). Served to capt. AUS, 1942-46. Decorated Bronze Star. Democrat. Jewish. Real property, Probate, Entertainment. Home: 133 S Glenroy Ave Los Angeles CA 90049 Office: 2029 Century Park E Suite 2600 Los Angeles CA 90067

WALLER, EDWARD MARTIN, JR., lawyer; b. Memphis, July 2, 1942; s. Edward Martin and Freda (Lazarov) W.; m. Laura Jayne Rhodes, June 18, 1982; 1 dau., Lauren Elizabeth. B.A., Columbia U., 1964; J.D., U. Chgo., 1967. Bar: Fla. 1967. Assoc. Fowler, White, Gillen, Boggs, Villareal & Banker, P.A., Tampa, Fla., 1967-72, ptnr., 1972—. Active Big Bros. of Tampa, 1969-72. Mem. ABA (comml. banking and fin. transactions com., litigation sect. 1978-82, co-chmn. 1983—), Fla. Bar Assn., Hillsborough County Bar Assn., Acad. Fla. Trial Lawyers (chmn. comml. litigation sect. 1981-82). Democrat. Jewish. Club: Tower (Tampa). Federal civil litigation, Contracts commercial, Bankruptcy. Home: 3609 Watrous Ave Tampa FL 33629 Office: Fowler White Gillen Boggs et al PO Box 1438 Tampa FL 33601

WALLER, SETH, corporate lawyer; b. 1933. Student, CUNY, 1954, Harvard U. Law Sch., 1957. Sole practice 1957-61; house counsel Joe Lowe Corp., 1961-65; gen. counsel CPA Industries, 1965-70; v.p. sec., gen. counsel Matsushita Electric Co. of Am., Secaucus, N.J., 1970—. Office: Matsushita Electric Co of Am 1 Panasonic Way Secaucus NJ 07094 *

WALLIN, PAUL JEFFREY, lawyer; b. Los Angeles, Mar. 7, 1952; s. Jack and Bernice Wallin; m. Sharon Pardo, July 29, 1972; 3 children. BA, UCLA, 1974; JD cum laude, Pepperdine U., 1977. Bar: Calif. 1977. Sole practice Santa Ana, Calif., 1977-78; ptnr. Wallin & Lee, Santa Ana, 1978-79, Wallin & Roseman, Santa Ana, 1979-83, Wallin, Roseman & Talmo, Santa Ana, 1983-84, Wallin, Roseman & Klarich, Santa Ana, 1984—. Active Vols. in Parole, Tustin, Calif., 1984—. Mem. ABA, Calif. Bar Assn. (del. 1985-86), Orange County Bar Assn. (chmn. criminal law sect. 1985—), Newport Harbor Bar Assn., Cen. Orange County Criminal Bar Assn. (bd. dirs. 1982-84), North Orange County Criminal Bar Assn. Republican. Jewish. Criminal, Juvenile. Office: Wallin Roseman & Klarich 17291 Irvine Blvd #159 Tustin CA 92680

WALLIS, BEN ALTON, JR., lawyer, rancher; b. Llano County, Tex., Apr. 27, 1936; s. Ben A. and Jessie Ella (Longbotham) W.; children from previous marriage—Ben A. III, M. Jessica. B.B.A., U. Tex. 1961, J.D., 1966; postgrad. Law Sch. So. Meth. U., 1971. Bar: Tex. 1966, U.S. Dist. Ct. (no. dist.) Tex. 1971, U.S. Ct. Appeals D.C. 1974, U.S. Dist. Ct. D.C. 1975, U.S. Dist. Ct. (we. dist.) Tex. 1975, U.S. Dist. Ct. (no. dist.) Calif. 1983, U.S. Ct. Appeals (5th cir.) 1975, U.S. Ct. Appeals (8th cir.) 1980, U.S. Ct. Appeals (11th cir.) 1981, U.S. Dist. Ct. (ea. dist.) Wis. 1983. Sole practice, Llano, Tex., 1966-67; investigator, prosecutor State Securities Bd. Tex., 1967-71; sole practice, Dallas, 1971-73; v.p. of devel. Club Corp. Am., Dallas, 1973; assoc. counsel impeachment task force U.S. Ho. of Reps. Com. on Judiciary, Washington, 1974; prin. Ben A. Wallis, Jr., San Antonio, Tex., 1974—. Chmn. Nat. Land Use Conf., 1979-81; mem. Gov.'s Areawide Planning Adv. Com., 1975-78; pres. Inst. Human Rights Research, 1979-82. Mem. ABA, Tex. Bar Assn., D.C. Bar Assn., San Antonio Bar Assn., Dallas Bar Assn., Fed. Bar Assn., Assn. Trial Lawyers Am., Delta Theta Phi, Delta Sigma Pi. Republican. Baptist. Condemnation, Probate, State civil litigation. Office: 7550 IH-10 West Suite 680 San Antonio TX 78229

WALLIS, OLNEY GRAY, lawyer, educator; b. Llano, Tex., July 27, 1940; s. Ben Alton and Jessie Ella (Longbotham) W.; m. Linda Lee Johnson, June 29, 1963; children—Anne, Brett. B.A., U. Tex., 1962, J.D., 1965. Bar: Tex. 1965, U.S. Dist. Ct. (so. dist.) Tex. 1966, U.S. Ct. Mil. Appeals 1968, U.S. Supreme Ct. 1970, U.S. Dist. Ct. (we. dist.) Tex. 1976, U.S. Ct. Appeals (5th cir.) 1977, U.S. Tax Ct. 1980, U.S. Ct. Appeals (10th cir.) 1981, U.S. Ct. Appeals (11th cir.) 1983, U.S. Dist. Ct. (no. dist.) Tex. 1985, U.S. Dist. Ct. (ea. and we. dists.) Ark. 1985, U.S. Ct. Appeals (8th cir.) 1985. Assoc., Brown & Cecil, Houston, 1965-66; asst. U.S. atty. Dept. Justice, Houston, 1971-74; mem. Jefferson, Wallis & Sherman, Houston, 1975-81; mem. Wallis & Pruitt, Houston, 1981—; instr. U. Md., Keflauik, Iceland, 1968-69; mem. faculty continuing legal edn. U. Houston, 1981-84. Served to capt. USAF, 1966-70. Recipient Disting. Service award U.S. Dept. Justice, 1973. Mem. Assn. Trial Lawyers Am., Am Judicature Soc., Tex. Trial Lawyers Assn., Houston Trial Lawyers Assn., Houston Bar Assn., Houston Bar Found., Phi Delta Phi, Phi Kappa Tau. Democrat. Episcopalian. Criminal, Federal civil litigation, State civil litigation. Office: Wallis & Pruitt 2813 W T C Jester Blvd Houston TX 77018

WALLISON, FRIEDA K., lawyer; b. N.Y.C., Jan. 15, 1943; d. Ruvin H. and Edith (Landes) Koslow; m. Peter J. Wallison, Nov. 24, 1966; children—Ethan S., Jeremy L., Rebecca K. A.B., Smith Coll., 1963; LL.B., Harvard U., 1966. Bar: N.Y. 1967, DC 1982. Assoc. Carter, Ledyard & Milburn, N.Y.C., 1966-75; spl. counsel, div. market regulation Securities & Exchange Commn., Washington, 1975; exec. dir., gen. counsel Mcpl. Securities Rulemaking Bd., Washington, 1975-78; ptnr. Rogers & Wells, N.Y.C. and Washington, 1978-83, Jones, Day, Reavis & Pogue, Washington, 1983—; mem. Govtl. Acctg. Standards Adv. Council, Washington, Nat. Council on Pub. Works Improvement, Washington. Mem. Nat. Council Govtl. Acctg., Nat. Assn. Bond Lawyers, Fed. Bar Assn., ABA, N.Y.C. Bar Assn. Securities, Public finance. Office: Jones Day Reavis & Pogue 655 15th St NW Washington DC 20005

WALLMAN, LESTER, lawyer; b. N.Y.C., Apr. 18; m. Claudia Marcyle, June 1, 1971; children—James, Michael. LL.B., Bklyn. Law Sch., 1951; LL.M., NYU, 1954. Bar: N.Y. 1952. With Standard Oil Co. N.J., 1954-67; ptnr. Wallman and Kramer, N.Y.C., 1967—; panelist on divorce law TV networks. Chmn. Community Planning Bd., N.Y.C., 1981-83. Served with U.S. Army, 1949-51. Mem. N.Y. State Bar Assn. (chmn. com. on legis. family law sect. 1976—), Am. Acad. Matrimonial Lawyers, Nat. Art Club. Author: Complete Guide to Family Law; contbr. articles to N.Y. State Bar Jour., 1978—. Family and matrimonial. Office: 275 Madison Ave New York NY 10016

WALLMAN, STEVEN MARK HARTE, lawyer; b. N.Y.C., Nov. 14, 1953; s. Eugene and Doris (Lee) W.; m. Kathleen M. Harte, May 5, 1985. BS, MIT, 1975, MS, 1976; postgrad., Harvard U., 1976-77; JD, Columbia U., 1978. Bar: D.C. 1978, Va. 1986. Assoc. Covington & Burling, Washington, 1978-86, ptnr., 1986—. General corporate, Securities. Home: 4618 N 14th St Arlington VA 22207 Office: Covington & Burling Suite 1075 2000 Corporate Ridge McLean VA 22102

WALLS, ROBERT ERNEST, lawyer; b. Houston, Jan. 17, 1946; s. Ernest McCullough and Opal Kathleen (Sloan) W. B.A., Abilene Christian Coll., 1968; J.D., U. Tex., 1971. Bar: Tex. 1971, U.S. Dist. Ct. (so. dist.) Tex. 1972, U.S. Ct. Appeals (5th cir.) 1972, U.S. Ct. Appeals (10th cir.) 1977, U.S. Ct. Appeals (11th cir.) 1981. Assoc., Fulbright & Jaworski, Houston, 1971-77; staff atty. Coastal Corp., Houston, 1977-81, sr. atty., 1981-87; sole practice, Houston, 1987—. Patron Mus. Fine Arts, Houston, Served to 1st lt. USAR, 1970-78. Recipient Reagan Sayers award Tex. Law Review, 1970. Mem. ABA (antitrust and litigation sects.), Tex. Bar Assn., Houston Bar Assn. Democrat. Club: Houston City. Contbr. articles to legal review. Antitrust, Federal civil litigation, State civil litigation. Office: 3315 Marquart Suite 200 Houston TX 77027

WALMER, JAMES L., lawyer; b. Wabash, Ind., Oct. 18, 1948; s. Warren D. and Josephine (Clupper) W.; m. Carolyn Gwen Lackey, Apr. 23, 1977; children: Ryan, Christian, Jonathan, Geoffrey. BS, Ball State U., 1971; JD, U. Tulsa, 1973. Bar: Okla. 1974, Ind. 1974, U.S. Dist. Ct. (no. and ea. dists.) Okla. 1974, U.S. Dist. Ct. (so. dist.) Ind. 1974, U.S. Dist. Ct. (no. dist.) Ind. 1975. Sole practice Warsaw, Ind., 1974—; dep. prosecutor Kosciusko County, Warsaw, 1976—. Chmn., bd. dirs. Cardinal Ctr. Inc., Warsaw, 1978-84. Mem. ABA, Ind. Bar Assn., Kosciusko County Bar Assn. (treas. 1979—), Okla. Bar Assn., Ind. Mcpl. Lawyers Assn. Republican. Methodist. Lodges: Optimists (v.p. 1979-80), Shriners, Masons. General practice, Family and matrimonial, Local government. Home: 1705 E Springhill Rd Warsaw IN 46580 Office: PO Box 1056 Warsaw IN 46580

WALNER, ROBERT JOEL, lawyer; b. Chgo., Dec. 22, 1946; s. Wallace and Elsie W.; m. Charlene Walner; children: Marci, Lisa. BA, U. Ill., 1968; JD, DePaul U., 1972. Bar: Ill. 1972, U.S. Dist. Ct. (no. dist.) Ill. 1972, U.S. Ct. Appeals (7th cir.) 1972, Fla. 1973. Atty. SEC, Chgo., 1972-73; sole practice Chgo., 1973—; adminstrv. law judge Ill. Commerce Commn., Chgo., 1973-76; atty. Allied Van Lines, Inc., Broadview, Ill., 1976-79; sr. v.p., gen. counsel, sec. The Balcor Co., Skokie, Ill., 1979—; prin. fin. ops. Balcor Securities div. The Balcor Co., Skokie, 1984—; mem. securities adv. com. to Ill. Sec. of State. Mem. editorial bd. Real Estate Securities Jour. and Real Estate Syndicator; program chmn. Regulators and You seminar, Washington, 1983—; contbr. chpts. to books, articles on real estate and law to profl. jours. Served with USAR, 1968-73. Mem. ABA, Ill. Bar Assn., Chgo. Bar Assn., Am. Real Estate Commn. (pres. com. 1985—), Real Estate Syndication Commn., Inst. Continuing Legal Edn., North Am. Securities Adminstrs. Assn. Inc. (industry adv. com. to real estate com.), Nat. Assn. Realtors (chmn. regulatory and legis. com.), Real Estate Securities and Syndication Inst. of Nat. Assn. Realtors (specialist real estate securities, group v.p. exec. com.), Nat. Real Estate Investment Forum (vice chmn.), N.Am. Securities Adminstrs. Assn. (industry adv. com. to real estate com.), Nat. Real Estate Investment Forum (vice chmn.). Securities, Real property, Legislative. Office: The Balcor Co 4849 Golf Rd Skokie IL 60077

WALSH, CHRISTOPHER G., JR., lawyer; b. Binghamton, N.Y., Dec. 16, 1948; s. Christopher G. and Margaret M. (Ward) W.; m. Therese L. Hughes, Sept. 1, 1973; children: Megan, Christopher, Karen. AB in Classics, Honors magna cum laude, Loyola U., Chgo., 1970; MA, Sangamon State U., 1972; JD cum laude, NYU, 1976. Staff mem. Ill. State Senate, Springfield, 1970-73; law clk. to presiding justice U.S. Ct. Appeals (7th cir.), 1976-78; law clk. to chief justice Warren Burger U.S. Supreme Ct., 1978-79; ptnr. Rothschild, Barry & Myers, Chgo., 1979—. Mng. editor NYU Law Rev., 1975-76;. Chmn. Oak Park (Ill.) Citizens Com. for Handgun Control, 1984—; pres. Ascension Grammar Sch. Bd., Oak Park, 1986—; bd. dirs., v.p. Ill. Council Against Handgun Violence, Chgo., 1985—. Mem. ABA, Ill. State Bar Assn., Chgo. Bar Assn., NYU Law Rev. Alumni Assn. Roman Catholic. Federal civil litigation, Insurance. Office: Rothschild Barry & Myers Two First National Plaza Chicago IL 60603

WALSH, DONALD PETER, oil company executive, lawyer; b. Flushing, N.Y., Apr. 2, 1930; s. Harold S. and Geraldine V. (Shannon) W.; m. Joyce Marie Curtin, June 29, 1957; children: Donald Peter, Michael T., Patricia A., Richard T. B.S.S. in Econs., Georgetown U., 1952, LL.B., 1957. Bar: D.C. 1957, N.Y. 1957, Tex. 1971, Pa. 1981. Atty., Shell Oil Co., Houston, 1957-70, gen. atty., 1970-77, asst. gen. counsel, 1977-80; asst. gen. counsel Sun Co., Inc., Radnor, Pa., 1980, sr. v.p., gen. counsel, 1980—. Served to 1st lt. U.S. Army, 1952-54. Mem. Fed. Bar Assn., ABA, Pa. Bar Assn., Tex. Bar Assn. Roman Catholic. Club: Aronimink Golf (Newtown Square, Pa.). Antitrust, General corporate, Oil and gas leasing. Office: Sun Co Inc 100 Matsonford Rd Radnor PA 19087 *

WALSH, FRANCIS MICHAEL, lawyer; b. Bklyn., Nov. 3, 1923; s. Michael Francis and Catherine Marie (Dundon) W.; m. Frances H. Garvey; children: Mariane, Patrick. BS, Fordham U., 1949; JD, Columbia U., 1950. Bar: N.Y. 1950. Gen. claims atty. L.I. Lighting Co., Mineola, N.Y. Served as master sgt. USAF, 1943-46. Mem. ABA, Assn. Trial Lawyers Am., Nassau Bar Assn. Roman Catholic. State civil litigation. Home: 124 Seaman Rd Jericho NY 11753 Office: LI Lighting Co 220 Old Country Rd Mineola NY 11501

WALSH, GARY EUGENE, lawyer; b. N.Y.C., Jan. 31, 1949; s. James Michael Walsh and Jane Puerling (Hall) Noto; m. Bernadette Eileen Ross, Dec. 18, 1971; children: Kimberly Ann, James Ross. AB, Princeton U., 1971; JD, Fordham U., 1977. Bar: N.Y. 1978, N.J. 1981. Mgr. John Nuveen & Co., Inc., N.Y.C., 1971-76; assoc. Mudge, Rose, Guthrie, Alexander & Ferdon, N.Y.C., 1976-81; assoc. Riker, Danzig, Scherer, Hylan & Perretti, Morristown, N.J., 1981-83, ptnr., 1983—. Trustee Bayshore Community Hosp., Hazlet, N.J., 1986—. Mem. ABA, N.J. Bar Assn. Avocations: athletics, philately, reading. Municipal bonds, Securities. Office: Riker Danzig Scherer Hylan & Perretti 1 Speedwell Ave Hdqrs Plaza Morristown NJ 07960

WALSH, GERRY O'MALLEY, lawyer; b. Houston, Dec. 22, 1936; d. Frederick Harold and Blanche (O'Malley) W. BS., U. Houston, 1959; J.D., S. Tex. Coll. Law, 1966. Bar: Tex. 1966, U.S. Dist. Ct. (so. dist.) Tex. 1967, (we. dist.) Tex. 1976; cert. elem. tchr. Tex. Elem. tchr. Houston, 1959-65; instr. bus. law U. Houston, 1966-67; sole practice, Houston, 1966—; lectr. legal, jud. and civic orgns. Adviser, den mother Sam Houston council Boy Scouts Am.; mem. Mus. Fine Arts. Recipient den mother award Sam Houston council Boy Scouts Am. Mem. Houston Zool. Assn., Houston Archeol. Soc., Bus. and Profl. Women's Assn. (Woman of Yr. 1973), ABA, Am. Judicature Soc., Tex. Criminal Lawyers Assn., Harris County Criminal Lawyers Assn., Tex. Trial. Lawyers Assn., State Bar Tex., Houston Bar Assn., U. Houston Alumni Assn., So. Tex. Coll. Law Alumni Assn., Nat. Criminal Def. Lawyers Assn., Zeta Tau Alpha (best mem. and rec. sec. 1958), Sigma Chi (award 1958). Criminal, Family and matrimonial, General practice. Office: 5400 Memorial Dr Suite 210 Houston TX 77007

WALSH, JAMES HAMILTON, lawyer; b. Astoria, N.Y., May 20, 1947; s. Edward James and Helen Smith (Hamilton) W.; m. Janice Ausherman, Aug. 3, 1968; children—Tracy, Courtney, Eric. B.A. in Psychology, Bridgewater Coll., 1968; J.D., U. Va., 1975. Bar: Va. 1975, U.S. Dist. Ct. (ea. and we. dists.) Va. 1975, U.S. Ct. Appeals (4th cir.) 1976, U.S. Supreme Ct. 1982. Assoc. McGuire, Woods, Battle & Boothe (and predecessor firms), Richmond, Va., 1975-82, ptnr., 1982—; instr. Nat. Inst. Trial Adv.; spl. prosecutor U.S. Dist. Ct. (ea. dist.) Va., 1979, 84. Mem. staff Va. Law Rev. Served with U.S. Army, 1969-72. Mem. ABA (mem. antitrust sect. health care com., litigation sect.), Am. Trial Lawyers Assn., Va. State Bar (bd. govs. antitrust sect. 1984—, chmn. 1986—), Va. Bar Assn., Richmond Bar Assn., Order Coif, Phi Delta Phi. Episcopalian. Clubs: Willow Oaks, Bull and Bear (Richmond, Va.). Contbr. articles to profl. jours. Antitrust, Federal civil litigation, Health. Home: 3035 Stratford Rd Richmond VA 23225 Office: McGuire Woods Battle & Boothe 1 James Ctr Richmond VA 23219

WALSH, JOHN, lawyer; b. Madison, Wis., Mar. 16, 1950; s. William P. and Margaret (Kalschear) W.; m. Frankie Kirk, Sept. 11, 1982; 1 child, Taylor. Student, U. Wis., Eau Claire, 1978-79; BS, U. Wis., Madison, 1982; student, Grambling Coll., 1979-80. Bar: Wis. Assoc. Brynelson-Herrick, Madison, 1975—. Mem. State Bar Assn. Wis. (chmn. bd. dirs. 1985—). Personal injury, Insurance, State civil litigation. Home: 702 Oneida Pl Madison WI 53711 Office: Brynelson-Herrick PO Box 1767 Madison WI 53701

WALSH, JOHN BRONSON, lawyer; b. Buffalo, Feb. 20, 1927; s. John A. and Alice (Condon) W.; m. Barbara Ashford, May 20, 1966; 1 child, Martha. AB, Canisius Coll., 1950; JD, Georgetown U., 1952. Bar: N.Y. 1953, U.S. Supreme Ct. 1958, U.S. Ct. Internat. Trade 1969, U.S. Ct. Customs and Patent Appeals 1973. Law clk. Covington & Burling, Washington, 1950-52, Galley & Locker, N.Y.C., 1952-53; trial atty. Garvey & Conway, N.Y.C., 1953-54; vol. atty. Nativity Mission, N.Y.C., 1953-54; ptnr. Jaeckle, Fleischmann, Kelly, Swart & Augspurger, and successor Jaeckle, Fleischmann & Mugel, Buffalo, 1955-60, 1976-80; ptnr. Walsh & Cleary, P.C., 1980—; individual practice law, Buffalo, 1960-75; trial counsel Antitrust div. U.S. Dept. Justice, Washington, 1960-61; spl. counsel on disciplinary proc. N.Y. Supreme Ct., 1960-76; appointee legal disciplinary coordinating com. State of N.Y., 1971; legis. counsel, spl. counsel to mayor Buffalo, 1969-75; counsel to sheriff Erie County, 1969-72; legis. counsel Niagara Frontier Transp. Authority; cons. Norfolk So. R.R., Ecology and Environment on Govtl. Affairs; guest lectr. univ. and profl. groups. Author: (TV series) The Law and You (Freedom Found. award, ABA award, Internat. Police Assn. award). Past pres. Ashford Hollow Found. Visual and Performing Arts; past trustee Dollar Bills, Inc., charitable youth orgn.; past co-producer Grand Island Playhouse and Players. Served with U.S. Army, 1945-46. Recipient Buffalo Jr. C. of C. Gold Key award for efforts to revitalize Erie County Bar Assn., 1962, Freedom Found. award for Law Day editorial, 1966. Fellow Am. Bar Found.; mem. ABA (del. internat. confs. Brussels 1963, Mexico City 1964, Lausanne, Switzerland 1964; merit award com. 1961-68; crime prevention and control com. 1968-70), N.Y. Trial Lawyers Assn., Am. Immigration Lawyers Assn., Am. Judicature Soc., N.Y. State Bar Assn., Erie County Bar Assn. (past sec.), Buffalo Bar Assn., Nat. Public Employer Labor Relations Assn., Am. Legion, Capitol Hill Club of Buffalo, Am. Assn. Airport Execs., N.Y. State Bus. Council (environ. law subcom., chmn. subcom.). Roman Catholic. Clubs: Buffalo Irish (bd. dirs.), Buffalo Athletic (past dir. and 1st v.p.), Buffalo Canoe, Buffalo City, Ft. Orange of Albany. Lodge: KC, Knights of Equity, Leoknights. Lobbying, Antitrust, Environment. Home: 193 Depew Ave Buffalo NY 14214 Office: Walsh & Cleary 210 Ellicott Sq Bldg Buffalo NY 14203

WALSH, JOHN THOMAS, lawyer, construction company executive; b. Salt Lake City, May 17, 1950; s. William McLean and Alice (Olson) W.; m. Sharon Kay Walsh, Aug. 7, 1979; children: Michael J., Heather R., Diane M., Brooke A. BA, Brigham Young U.; JD, Calif. Western Sch. Law. Bar: Utah, 1977, U.S. Ct. Appeals (10th cir.), 1980, U.S. Supreme Ct., 1980. Sole practice, Salt Lake City, 1977—; pres. Butler, Crockett and Walsh Devel. Corp., Salt Lake City, Pinecrest Water Co., also bd. dirs.; bd. dirs. Butler Crockett and Walsh Devel. Corp. Pres. Monument Park 17th Ward Sunday Sch.; mem. athletic com. Monument Park Stake. Served with U.S. Army, until 1970. Mem. ABA, Utah Bar Assn., Salt Lake County Bar Assn., Assn. Trial Lawyers Am. Republican. Mormon. Club: Sports Mall. State civil litigation, Criminal, Personal injury. Home: 5195 Emigration Cyn Rd Salt Lake City UT 84108 Office: 3865 S Wasatch Blvd Suite 202 Salt Lake City UT 84109

WALSH, JOSEPH RICHARD, lawyer; b. Atlanta, May 10, 1951; s. Joseph Radamaker and Meta Lucille (Cole) W.; m. Elisabeth Clare Kane, July 27, 1980. B. Indsl. Engring., Ga. Inst. Tech., 1973; J.D., U. Ga., 1976; M.L. in Taxation, Georgetown Law Ctr., 1984. Bar: Ga. 1976, Va. 1978, D.C. 1979, Calif. 1984, U.S. Ct. Appeals (4th cir.) 1978, U.S. Ct. Appeals (5th cir.) 1976, U.S. Ct. Appeals (9th cir.) 1984, U.S. Ct. Appeals (11th cir.) 1982, U.S. Dist. Ct. (no. dist.) Ga. 1976, U.S. Dist. Ct. (no. dist.) Calif. 1984, U.S. Tax Ct. 1983, U.S. Claims Ct. 1983. Indsl. engr. So. Ry. System, Atlanta, 1973-74; atty. ICC, Washington, 1977-78, atty., asst. rail merger coordinator, 1979-84; assoc. Fulbright & Jaworski, Washington, 1978-79; counsel Bank of Am. Nat. Trust and Savs. Assn., San Francisco, 1984-85, sr. counsel, 1985—; counselor Athens Legal Aid and Defender Soc., Ga., 1976. Contbg. author Federal Regulatory Process: Practice and Procedure, 1981. Campaign volunteer Jimmy Carter Presdl. Campaign, New Hampshire, 1976. Recipient Spl. Achievement awards ICC, 1981, 82, 83, Chmn.'s Commendation award, ICC, 1982; named Outstanding Young Men Am. U.S. Jaycees, 1982. Ga. Inst. Tech. nat. merit scholar 1969; NSF grantee 1972. Mem. D.C. Bar Assn., Ga. Bar Assn., ABA, Fed. Bar Assn., Va. Bar Assn., Calif. Bar Assn., San Francisco Bar Assn., San Francisco Leasing Lawyers Forum, Am. Inst. Indsl. Engrs., Sierra Club, Phi Kappa Phi, Tau Beta Pi, Alpha Pi Mu. Methodist. Club: Lawyers (San Francisco). Contracts commercial, Administrative and regulatory, Private international. Home: 2711 Octavia St #201 San Francisco CA 94123 Office: Bank of Am NT&SA #3017 PO Box 37000 San Francisco CA 94137

WALSH, JOSEPH THOMAS, judge; b. Wilmington, Del., May 18, 1930; s. Joseph Patrick and Mary Agnes (Bolton) W.; m. Madeline Maria Lamb, Oct. 6, 1955; children: Kevin, Lois, Patrick, Daniel, Thomas, Nancy. BA, LaSalle Coll., 1952; LLB, Georgetown U., 1955. Bar: D.C. 1955, Del. 1955. Atty. Ho. of Reps., Dover, Del., 1961-62; chief counsel Pub. Service Commn., Dover, 1964-72; judge Del. Superior Ct., Wilmington, 1972-84; vice chancellor Ct. of Chancery, Wilmington, 1984-85; judge Del. Supreme Ct., Wilmington, 1985—. Served to capt. U.S. Army, 1955-58. Democrat. Roman Catholic. Judicial administration, State civil litigation, General corporate. Office: Supreme Ct Del 820 N French St PO Box 1997 Wilmington DE 19899

WALSH, LAWRENCE EDWARD, lawyer; b. Port Maitland, N.S., Can., Jan. 8, 1912; came to U.S., 1914, naturalized, 1922; s. Dr. Cornelius Edward and Lila May (Sanders) W.; m. Mary Alma Porter; children: Barbara Marie, Janet Maxine (Mrs. Alan Larson), Sara Porter (Mrs. Craig Miller), Dale Edward, Elizabeth Porter. A.B., Columbia, 1932, LL.B., 1935; LL.D., Union U., 1959, St. John's U., 1975, Suffolk U., 1975, Waynesburg Coll., 1976, Vt. Law Sch., 1976. Bar: N.Y. State 1936, D.C. 1981, Okla. 1981, U.S. Supreme Ct. 1951. Spl. asst. atty. gen. Drukman Investigation, 1936-38; dep. asst. dist. atty. N.Y. County, 1938-41; assoc. Davis Polk Wardwell Sunderland & Kiendl, 1941-43; asst. counsel to gov. N.Y. 1943-49, counsel to gov., 1950-51; counsel Pub. Service Commn., 1951-53; gen. counsel, exec. dir. Waterfront Commn. of N.Y. Harbor, 1953-54; U.S. judge So. Dist. N.Y., 1954-57; U.S. dep. atty. gen. 1957-60; partner firm Davis, Polk & Wardwell, 1961-81; counsel firm Crowe & Dunlevy, Oklahoma City, 1981—; dir. Kans. Gas and Electric Co., chmn. N.Y. State Moreland Commn. Alcoholic Beverage Control Law, 1963-64; pres. Columbia Alumni Fedn., 1968-69; dep. head with rank of ambassador U.S. delegation meetings on Vietnam, Paris, 1969; counsel to N.Y. State ct. on judiciary, 1971-72; 2d circuit mem. U.S. Circuit Judge Nominating Commn., 1978-80; independent counsel Iran-contra investigation, 1986—. Trustee emeritus Columbia U.; trustee William Nelson Cromwell Found. Fellow Am. Bar Found., Am. Coll. Trial Lawyers; mem. Am. Law Inst. (council), ABA (pres. 1975-76), N.Y. State Bar Assn. (pres. 1966-67), Oklahoma County Bar Assn., Okla. State Bar Assn., Internat. Bar Assn., Assn. Bar City of New York, N.Y. County Lawyers Assn.; hon. mem. Law Soc. Eng. and Wales, Can. Bar Assn., Mexican Bar Assn., Beta Theta Pi. Presbyterian. Clubs: N.Y. India House, The Century, Oklahoma City Golf and Country; Petroleum (Oklahoma City), Whitehall (Oklahoma City). Federal civil litigation, Antitrust, Administrative and regulatory. Home: 1902 Bedford St Oklahoma City OK 73116 Office: 1800 Mid-Am Tower Oklahoma City OK 73102

WALSH, MICHAEL RAYMOND, lawyer; b. Akron, Ohio, Mar. 26, 1936; s. Raymond M. and Catherine N. (Rodden) W.; m. Kathleen A. Couch, July 7, 1978; children by previous marriage—Michael Raymond, Amy Catherine. B.A., U. Akron, 1958; LL.B., Duke U., 1963, J.D., 1970. Bar: Fla., 1963, U.S. Ct. Appeals (11th cir.) 1982, Supreme Ct. U.S., 1973. Sole practice, Orlando, Fla., 1963—; city prosecutor City of Orlando, 1969-71; mcpl. judge City of Orlando, 1971-72; lectr. Mem. exec. com. Orange County Republican party, 1979-82. Named Most Outstanding Local Bar Pres., Fla. Bar, 1974. Mem. Fla. Bar (bd. govs. 1976-80), ABA, Orange County Bar Assn., Am. Acad. Matrimonial Lawyers. Republican. Roman Catholic. Club: University. Author: (with Stephen T. Dean) Tax Ideas for Professional Persons, 1965; contbg. author: Modification and Enforcement Proceedings After Dissolution of Marriage Manual, 1976; contbr. articles to profl. jours. Family and matrimonial. Office: 326 N Fern Creek Ave Orlando FL 32803

WALSH, ROBERT ANTHONY, lawyer; b. Boston, Aug. 26, 1938; s. Frank and Emily Angelica (Bissitt) W.; m. Angela Rosalie Barile, Aug. 3, 1966; children: Maria, Robert II, Amy. SB, MIT, 1960; MS, Fla. Inst.

Tech., 1967; JD, Suffolk U., 1971. Bar: Mass. 1971, Ill. 1976, U.S. Dist. Ct. Mass. 1972, U.S. Patent Office 1972, Can. Patent Office 1973, U.S. Supreme Ct. 1976, U.S. Ct. Appeals (Fed. cir.) 1982, U.S. Ct. Mil. Appeals 1983; registered profl. engr., Mass. Patent trainee, engr. Avco Research Lab., Everett, Mass., 1968-72; patent atty. GTE Labs., Waltham, Mass., 1972-73; group patent counsel Bell & Howell Co., Chgo., 1973-78; patent counsel ITT E. Coast Patents, Nutley, N.J., 1978-80; patent counsel internat. patent dept. ITT Corp., N.Y.C., 1980-82, sr. patent counsel internat., 1982-86, dir. internat. patents, 1986-87; gen. patent counsel ITT Corp., Nutley, 1987—; ednl. counselor admissions MIT, Northern, N.J., 1978—. Mem. Lakeland Hills YMCA, Mountain Lakes, N.J., Served to col. USAF, 1961-64, with Res. 1960—. Mem. ABA, Tri-State USAFR Lawyers Assn. (meritorious achievement award 1980), Internat. Patent Club, Am. Patent Law Assn., Internat. Patent Club, Chgo. Patent Law Assn., Air Force Assn., Res. Officers Assn., Sigma Xi. Roman Catholic. Lodge: K.C. Patent, Trademark and copyright, Military. Home: 39 Arden Rd Mountain Lakes NJ 07046 Office: ITT Def Tech Corp Patent Dept 500 Washington Ave Nutley NJ 07110

WALSH, RODGER JOHN, lawyer; b. Kansas City, Mo., Apr. 20, 1924; s. John Joseph and Margaret Mary (Halloran) W.; m. Patricia Ann O'Brien, Nov. 18, 1950; children—Regina, Martin, Eileen, Daniel, Veronica, Bernard, Kathleen. B.S., Rockhurst Coll., 1947; J.D., Georgetown U., 1950. Bar: Mo. 1950, D.C. 1950, U.S. Supreme Ct. 1960, U.S. Ct. Appeals (8th cir.) 1955. Spl. agt. FBI, Washington, 1950-53; ptnr. Linde-Thomson Van Dyke Fairchild, Kansas City, Mo., 1953-63, Biersmith & Walsh, 1963-69; v.p., asst. gen. counsel Riss Internat., 1969-83, exec. v.p., gen. counsel, 1983—; dir. Grandview Bank & Trust Co., Mo., chmn., mem. Mo. State Personnel Adv. Bd., Jefferson City, 1979-84; mem. Mo. State Environ. Improvement Authority, 1977-83. Bd. dirs. Mo. Bus and Truck Assn., Jefferson City, 1983—, Democracy Inc., Kansas City, Mo., 1960—; hon. dir. Rockhurst Coll., 1960—. Served with U.S. Army, 1942-45; ETO. Decorated Air Medal with 5 oak leaf clusters. Mem. Mo. Bar Assn., Fed. Bar Assn., Kansas City Bar Assn., Am. Legion, Soc. Former FBI Agts. Democrat. Roman Catholic. General corporate, Federal civil litigation, Banking. Home: 10512 Mersington St Kansas City MO 64137 Office: Riss Internat Corp 215 W Peshing Rd Kansas City MO 64108

WALSH, THOMAS JOHN, lawyer; b. Omaha, Aug. 6, 1927; s. John R. and Mary P. (Wokersien) W.; m. Virginia Frederick, June 10, 1950; children: Ellen, Thomas John, Jean, Dan, Jim, Pat, William. LLB, Creighton U., 1951. Bar: Nebr. 1951, U.S. Dist. Ct. Nebr. 1951, U.S. Ct. Appeals (8th cir.) 1954. Law clk. to judge U.S. Ct. Appeals (8th cir.), Omaha, 1951-54; dep. pub. defender Douglas County, Nebr., 1954-56; ptnr. Haney & Walsh, 1956-68; sr. ptnr. Walsh, Walentine, Miles, Fullenkamp & O'Toole, 1968-84, Walsh, Fullenkamp & Doyle, Omaha, 1984—. Pres. Nebr. Lawyers Trust Account Found., 1985. Fellow Am. Coll. Trial Lawyers; mem. Am. Bd. Trial Advs., Nebr. Bar Assn. (exec. com. 1977-83), Omaha Bar Assn. Federal civil litigation, State civil litigation, Insurance. Office: Walsh Fullenkamp & Doyle 11440 W Center Rd Omaha NE 68144

WALSH, THOMAS JOSEPH, lawyer; b. Kansas City, Mo., Oct. 3, 1932; s. Thomas E. and Clare E. (O'Leary) W.; m. Ellen B. Butler; children: Carolyn, David, Kathy. AB, U. Mo., 1953; JD, Georgetown U., 1958. Bar: D.C. 1958, Mo. 1958. Sole practice Lee's Summit, Mo., 1958—. Mem. 4th Congl. Dist. Youth Council, 1985—; vice chmn. Mo. Council on Criminal Justice, 1977-80. Served to 1st lt. U.S. Army, 1953-55. Mem. Mo. Bar Assn., Assn. Trial Lawyers Am., Met. Kansas City Bar Assn. Democrat. Roman Catholic. Lodge: Optimists (lt. gov. 1963-64, pres. 1960-61). General practice, State civil litigation, Family and matrimonial. Home: 210 Hillcrest Lees Summit MO 64063 Office: 528 W 3d St Lees Summit MO 64063

WALSH, WILLIAM, IV, lawyer; b. Los Angeles, Aug. 2, 1940; s. William and Marjorie Ann (Nesel) W.; m. Penny R. O'Reilly, Aug. 7, 1943; children—Kelli, Kori, Bill, Pat, Mike, Tim. B.A. in Polit. Sci., Loyola U., Los Angeles, 1962, LL.B., 1965. Bar: Calif. 1966, U.S. Dist. Ct. (cen. and so. dists.) Calif. 1965. Ptnr., Lewis, Varni, Ghirardelli, Lynch & Walsh, San Fernando, Calif. 1965-77; ptnr. Kestler & Walsh, Lancaster, Calif., 1977—. Mem. San Fernando Parks and Recreation Commn., Lancaster Planning Commn.; bd. dirs. Antelope Valley (Calif.) YMCA. Mem. Antelope Valley Bar Assn. (pres. 1984), ABA (mem. bus. law sect.). Republican. Roman Catholic. Clubs: KC Rotary (pres. San Fernando sect. 1975). Real property, Probate, General corporate. Address: 43770 W 15th St W Lancaster CA 93534

WALSHE, JOHN WILLIAM LEO, lawyer; b. Bridgeport, Conn., June 28, 1944; s. Arthur Hopkins and Margaret Mary (Finn) W. A.B., Sacred Heart U., 1968; J.D., NYU, 1980. Bar: N.Y. 1977, U.S. Dist. Ct. (so. and ea. dists.) N.Y. 1977, U.S. Dist. Ct. Conn. 1977, U.S. Dist. Ct. R.I. 1977, U.S. Ct. Appeals (2d cir.) 1977, U.S. Ct. Internat. Trade 1978, U.S. Ct. Appeals (3d cir.) 1979, U.S. Ct. Appeals (1st cir.) 1980, U.S. Supreme Ct. 1980. Assoc. James V. Joy, N.Y.C., 1975-76, Gibney, Anthony & Flaherty, N.Y.C., 1977-80; sole practice, N.Y.C., 1981—. Asst. mgr. May for U.S. Senate campaign, Hartford, Conn., 1968. Mem. N.Y. State Bar Assn. (com. cert. and specialization trial lawyers), ABA (com. comml. transactions), N.Y.C. Bar Assn. (litigation sect.), Maritime Law Assn. U.S., Am. Arbitration Assn., Fed. Bar Council, Assn. Trial Lawyers Am. Republican. Roman Catholic. Clubs: Canadian (gov. 1982), Metropolitan (N.Y.C.). Federal civil litigation, State civil litigation, General practice. Office: 230 Park Ave New York NY 10017

WALSTAD, PAUL J., lawyer; b. Great Falls, Mont., Aug. 27, 1944; s. Berner Murray Walstad and Elsie Vancil; m. Nancy Jo Thompson, Mar. 9, 1963; children: Kimberly Lynn, Paul J. Jr., Peter John, Phillip Joseph, Michael Andrew, Susan, Karen, Catherine, Kirsten, Sarah, David, Matthew. BA, Am. U., JD. Bar: Va., D.C., Utah, U.S. Claims Ct., U.S. Ct. Appeals (D.C., 4th and 11th cirs.), U.S. Supreme Ct. Assoc. Lewis, Mitchell & Moore, Vienna, Va.; sr. ptnr. Walstad & Babcock, Salt Lake City, 1974—; part-time faculty Brigham Young U., Provo, 1985—; lectr., cons. various orgns. Contbr. articles to profl. jours. Vice chmn. North Va. Planning Dist. Com., 1972-74; mem. com. Washington Counsel of Govt., 1973-74; Loudon County (Va.) Bd. Suprs., 1971-74. Named one of Outstanding Young Men in Am. U.S. Jaycees, 1973, Tchr. of Yr. Brigham Young U. Constrn. Mgmt. Program, 1986. Mem. ABA (litigation and pub. contract law sects., advocacy com.), Va. Bar Assn., D.C. Bar Assn. Republican. Mormon. State civil litigation, Construction. Office: Walstad & Babcock 185 S State Suite 1000 Salt Lake City UT 84111

WALSTON, BETH ELAINE, lawyer; b. Alton, Ill., Jan. 6, 1960; d. Keith Edwin and Betty Jane (Hill) W. BS in Psychology, Cen. Mo. State U., 1981; JD, St. Louis U., 1984. Bar: Ill. 1985, Mo. 1986, Nebr. 1987. Law librarian Guilfoil, Petzall & Shoemake, St. Louis, 1981-84; assoc. Lakin & Hernden, P.C., East Alton, Ill., 1984-85, Wiseman, Shaikewitz, McGivern, Wahl, Flavin, Hesi & Hale, P.C., Alton, Ill., 1986—. Coach speech team Roxana (Ill.) High Sch., 1985-86. Mem. ABA, Mo. Womens Bar Assn., Mo. Bar Assn. (tort and reform com.), Ill. Bar Assn., Madison County Bar Assn., Ill. Trial Lawyers Assn. Episcopalian. Avocation: travel. Admiralty, Personal injury, Federal civil litigation. Home: 409 E 8th #2 Alton IL 62002 Office: Wiseman Shaikewitz McGivern Wahl Flavin Hesi & Hale PC 620 E 3d Alton IL 62002

WALTA, JOHN GREGORY, lawyer; b. Volga, S.D., June 5, 1941; s. Jack and Betty (Kranz) W.; m. Vahona J. Fryar, Feb. 18, 1983; children: Mark, Jason, Michael; step children: Celeste Gerber, Nicole Gerber. BA, St. John's U., Collegeville, Minn., 1964; JD, Notre Dame U., 1967. Bar: Colo. 1967. Ptnr. Walta, Cross, Gaddis & Kin, Colorado Springs, Colo., 1970-78; chief counsel Colo. Pub. Defender System, Denver, 1978-82; mem. Supreme Ct. Nominating Commn., 1975-78, State Com. on Civil Rights, 1976-78, State Com. on Criminal Rules, 1978-82. State civil litigation, Criminal, Civil rights. Home: 30 Clubridge Place Colorado Springs CO 80906 Office: 620 S Cascade Colorado Springs CO 80903

WALTER, CHARLES FRANK, lawyer, scientist; b. Sarasota, Fla., June 19, 1936; s. Charles Francis and Louise Melanie (Godefrin) W. BS, Ga. Inst. Tech.; JD, U. Houston; MS, Fla. State U., PhD; postdoctoral, U. Calif., San Francisco. Bar: Tex. 1980, U.S. Dist. Ct. (so. dist.) Tex. 1980, U.S. Patent Office 1980, U.S. Ct. Appeals (5th cir.) 1982. Asst. prof. U. Tenn., Memphis, 1964-67, assoc. prof., 1967-69; assoc. biomathematician computer sci. staff M.D. Anderson Hosp. U. Tex. System Cancer Ctr., Houston, 1969-74; prof. chem. engring. U. Houston, 1974-79; sole practice Houston, 1980—; dir. program on law, science and tech. U. Houston Law Ctr., 1983-86; adj. prof. law U. Houston, 1986—; assoc. prof. biomath. and biochem., U. Tex., Houston, 1969-74; pres. Internat. Tech. Mgmt. Inc., Houston, 1979—; pres. Maisteller & Assocs. P.C., 1983—; lectr. in field. Author 7 books. U.S. Pub. Health Service predoctoral fellow, 1960-62, U.S. Pub. Health postdoctoral fellow, 1962-64; NSF research grantee, 1964-74, Robert A. Welch Found. research grantee, 1971-73; U.S. Pub. Health Service career devel. awardee, 1964-69. Mem. ABA (sci. and tech. sect.), Tex. Bar Assn., AAAS, Fedn. Am. Socs. for Experimental Biology, Am. Soc. Biological Chemists, Biophysical Soc., Soc. for Mathematical Biology, Sigma Xi. Avocations: camping, canoeing, hiking, piano, cooking. Computer, Patent, Trademark and copyright. Home: 9131 Timberside Dr Houston TX 77025 Office: U Houston Law Ctr 4800 Calhoun Houston TX 77004

WALTER, DONALD ELLSWORTH, federal judge; b. Jennings, La., Mar. 15, 1936; s. Robert R. and Ada (Lafleur) D'Aquin; m. Charlotte Sevier, Jan. 5, 1942; children: Laura Ney, Robert Wllsworth, Susannah Brooks. BA, La. State U., 1961, JD, 1964. Assoc. Cavanaugh, Brame, Holt et al, 1964-66, Holt & Woodley, Lake Charles, La., 1966-69; U.S. atty. U.S. Dept. Justice, Shreveport, La., 1969-77; lawyer Hargrove, Guyton, Ramey & Barlow, Shreveport, La., 1977-85; justice U.S. Dist. Ct. (mid. dist.) La., Monroe, 1985—. Served with AUS, 1957-58. Office: US Dist Ct PO Box 3107 Monroe LA 71210 *

WALTER, JOHN F., lawyer; b. Buffalo, Nov. 3, 1944; s. John M. and Bette (Cushing) W.; m. Joyce Langsdorf, June, 1967; children: Amy C., Jeffrey M. BA, Loyola U., Los Angeles, 1966; JD, Loyola U., 1969. Bar: Calif., U.S. Dist. Ct. (no., ea., so. and cen. dists.) Calif., U.S. Ct. Appeals (9th cir.), U.S. Supreme Ct. Assoc. Kindel & Anderson, Los Angeles, 1969-70, 72-76; atty. U.S. Dept. Justice, Los Angeles, 1970-72; ptnr. Walter, Finestone, Richter & Kane, Los Angeles, 1976—. Federal civil litigation, State civil litigation. Office: Walter Finestone Richter & Kane 10920 Wilshire Blvd Los Angeles CA 90024

WALTER, WILLIAM EUGENE, lawyer; b. Scranton, Pa., Feb. 22, 1947; s. William and Madelyn (Rockell) W.; m. Mary Lou Fuerst, Oct. 20, 1977; 1 son, Geoffrey. B.A., Villanova U., 1970; J.D., Duke U., 1973. Bar: N.Y. 1974, U.S. Dist. Ct. (ea. and so. dists.) N.Y. 1974. Assoc. Chadbourne, Parke, Whiteside & Wolff, N.Y.C., 1973-77; asst. sec. and asst. gen. counsel Williamhouse-Regency, Inc., N.Y.C., 1978-81, Athlone Industries, Inc., Parsippany, N.J., 1981-86; sr. counsel Baker Industries, Inc., Parsippany, 1987—. Mem. N.Y. State Bar Assn., Assn. of Bar of City of New York, Bar Assn. Nassau County. General corporate. Home: One Wilmar Pl Garden City NY 11530 Office: Baker Industries 1633 Littleton Rd Parsippany NJ 07054

WALTERS, AMY OTTINGER, lawyer; b. Lawrence, Kans., Jan. 2, 1952; d. Ray E. Jr. and Audrey M. (Kennedy) Ottinger; m. James F. Walters, Aug. 11, 1973; children: Mariah, Monica. Student, Lindenwood Coll., 1970-71; BA, U. Kans., 1974; JD, Washburn U., 1980. Bar: Kans. 1980, U.S. Dist. Ct. Kans. 1980. Trust officer, v.p. Rosedale State Bank, Kansas City, Kans., 1980-84; ptnr. Perry, Trent & Walters, Bonner Springs, Kans., 1984—; adv. bd. dirs. Salvation Army, Kansas City, 1984—. Mem. Bonner Springs City Council, 1985—, Bonner Beautiful Commn. Mem. ABA (real property, probate and trust sect., bus. and banking sect.), Kans. Bar Assn. (real property, probate and trust sect., bus. and banking sect.), Wyandotte County Bar Assn., Bus. and Profl. Womens Club. Episcopalian. Club: New Century (Bonner Springs, Kans.). Avocations: swimming, weaving. Probate, Personal income taxation, Family and matrimonial. Office: Perry Trent & Walters 144 N Nettleton Bonner Springs KS 66012

WALTERS, BETTE JEAN, lawyer; b. Norristown, Pa., Sept. 5, 1946; d. Albert Bradford and Elizabeth Moore (Daymon) W.; m. Allen H. Smith III, June 14, 1980. B.A., U. Pitts., 1967; J.D., Temple U., 1970, LL.M., 1974. Bar: Pa. 1970, U.S. Dist. Ct. (ea. dist.) Pa. 1971. Law clk., assoc. William R. Cooper, Lansdale, Pa., 1969-72; spl. asst. to pub. defender Montgomery County (Pa.), 1973; sole practice North Wales, Pa., 1972-73; assoc. counsel Alco Standard Corp., Valley Forge, Pa., 1973-79, group counsel mfg., 1979-83; v.p., gen. counsel, sec. Alco Industries, Inc., 1983—. Mem. DAR (chpt. rec. sec. 1982-83). Republican. Episcopalian. General corporate, Labor, Private international. Office: Alco Industries Inc PO Box 937 Valley Forge PA 19482

WALTERS, GOMER WINSTON, lawyer; b. Johnstown, Pa., Sept. 24, 1937; s. Philip Thomas and Margaret Elizabeth (Peat) W.; m. Jean Mary Jester, June 13, 1964; children—Bruce Joseph, Matthew Howel, Melinda Jean. B.E., Yale U., 1960; J.D., George Washington U., 1965. Bar: Ill. 1965, Pa. 1972, U.S. Dist. Ct. (no. dist.) Ill. 1965, U.S. Dist. Ct. (we. dist.) Pa. 1972, U.S. Dist. Ct. (no. dist.) Ohio 1973, U.S. Ct. Appeals (3 and 7th cirs.) 1981, U.S. Supreme Ct. 1982, U.S. Ct. Appeals (fed. cir.) 1982. Asso. Kirkland & Ellis, Chgo., 1965-70, ptnr., 1970-72; pat. atty. Westinghouse Electric Corp., Pitts., 1972-73; assoc. Walsh, Case & Coale, Chgo., 1973-74, Lee & Smith, Chgo., 1975; ptnr. Haight, Hofeldt, Davis & Jambor, Chgo., 1975—; dir. R2 Corp., 1981-84, Vast Research Co., 1981—. Mem. ABA, Chgo. Bar Assn., Am. Patent Law Assn., Patent Law Assn. Chgo., Pitts. Patent Law Assn., Am. Judicature Soc., Assn. Trial Lawyers Am. Republican. Club: Chicago Athletic Assn. Federal civil litigation, Patent, Trademark and copyright. Office: Haight & Hofeldt 55 E Monroe St 3614 Mid-Continental Plaza Chicago IL 60603

WALTERS, JUDY HARUE, lawyer; b. Columbus, Ohio, Mar. 1, 1953; d. Leon Kurtz and Sadae (Yamamoto) W. Student, Princeton U., 1971-73, 74-75; AB, U. Calif., Berkeley, 1977; JD, Harvard U., 1981. Bar: Calif. 1981, U.S. Dist. Ct. (cen. dist.) Calif. 1981. Assoc. Sheppard, Mullin, Richter & Hampton, Los Angeles, 1981—. Mem. ABA, Los Angeles County Bar Assn., Women Lawyers Assn. of Los Angeles, Princeton Profl. Women, Phi Beta Kappa. Democrat. Avocations: ballet, modern dance, ballroom dance, skiing. Real property. Office: Sheppard Mullin Richter & Hampton 333 S Hope St 48th Floor Los Angeles CA 90071

WALTERS, MARY COON, justice state supreme court; b. Baraga, Mich., Jan. 29, 1922; d. Marvin Leonard and Nancy C. (Conway) Coon; m. Asa Lane Walters, July 9, 1952 (dec. June 1974); 1 child, Mark Richard. J.D., U. N.Mex., 1962. Bar: N.Mex. 1962, U.S. Supreme Ct. Pvt. practice Albuquerque, 1962-71, 73-78; judge 2d Jud. Dist. N.Mex., Albuquerque, 1971-72; judge N.Mex. Ct. Appeals, Santa Fe, 1979-81, chief judge, 1981-83; justice N.Mex. Supreme Ct., Santa Fe, 1984—. Served with Women's Airforce Service Pilots, 1943-44, USAF, 1951-55. Mem. ABA, N.Mex. Bar Assn., Albuquerque Bar Assn., Santa Fe Bar Assn. Democrat. Roman Catholic. Judicial administration. Office: N Mex Supreme Ct PO Box 848 Santa Fe NM 87501

WALTERS, STEPHEN SCOTT, lawyer; b. Chgo., Mar. 20, 1945; s. Harold Stephen Walters and Thelma Rae (Scott) Carlyle; m. Mabel Barnett, Aug. 29, 1967; children: Sarah Elizabeth, Rebecca Strong. BS, Stanford U., 1967, JD, 1972. Bar: Calif. 1972, U.S. Dist. Ct. (no. dist.) Calif. 1972, U.S. Dist. Ct. (ea. dist.) Calif. 1978, U.S. Dist. Ct. Oreg. 1980, U.S. Ct. Appeals (9th cir.) 1980, U.S. Ct. Appeals (10th cir.) 1986. Law clk. to judge U.S. Ct. Appeals (9th cir.), San Francisco, 1972-73; assoc. Steinhart et al, San Francisco, 1973-74, 75-76; law clk. to chief justice U.S. Supreme Ct., Washington, 1974-75; dep. gen. counsel Legal Services Corp., Washington, 1976-79; assoc. Stoel, Rives, Boley, Fraser & Wyse, Portland, Oreg., 1979-81, ptnr., 1981—; instr. law U. Pa., Phila., 1978-79; chmn. MBA com. Legal Services, Portland, 1986—. Editor Stanford Law Rev. Counsel Nat. Abortion Rights Action League, Portland, 1980—; cooperating atty. ACLU, Portland, 1980—. Nat. Merit scholar, 1963; recipient Hilmer Oehlman Jr, prize Stanford U., 1968. Mem. ABA, Oreg. Bar Assn., Calif. Bar Assn., Multomah County Bar Assn. Democrat. Avocations: horse racing, fishing, music. Federal civil litigation, State civil litigation, Public utilities. Home: 2326 NE 17th Ave Portland OR 97212 Office: Stoel Rives Boley Fraser & Wyse 900 SW 5th Ave Portland OR 97204

WALTERS, SUMNER JUNIOR, judge; b. Van Wert, Ohio, Oct. 4, 1916; s. Sumner E. and Kittie (Allen) W.; m. Marjorie Acheson, May 22, 1948; 1 son, Sumner E. JD, Ohio No. U., 1940. Bar: Ohio 1940. Ptnr. Walters & Koch, 1941-42, Stroup & Walters, 1946-68; sole practice, Van Wert, 1969-71; ptnr. Walters, Young & Walters, 1971-80; judge Van Wert Mcpl. Ct., 1980-87; asst. pros. atty. Van Wert County, 1946-48, pros. atty., 1948-60; acting judge Van Wert Mcpl. Ct., also asst. city solicitor City of Van Wert, 1962; village solicitor Middle Point, 1960-80; pres. Van Wert Indsl. Devel. Corp., 1966-76. Pres. Humane Soc., 1963—, YMCA, 1962-63; mem. council Camp Fire Girls, 1965-72; pres. bd. trustees Van Wert County United Fund, 1959-60; trustee United Health Found., Van Wert County Hosp., Van Wert County Found., Marsh Found., Van Wert; chmn. ofcl. bd. Meth. ch., 1963-64, lay del. Ohio West Conf., 1967-79, conf. sec., 1970-71, mem. bd. hosps. and homes, trustee, 1983-86. Served with Mil. Police, C.I.C., AUS, 1942-45, ETO. Named Outstanding Citizen of Yr., Van Wert Jr. C. of C., 1965. Mem. Ohio Bar Assn., Northwestern Ohio Bar Assn. (pres. 1957-58), Van Wert County Bar Assn. (pres. 1953-55), Am. Legion, V.F.W., Sigma Phi Epsilon. Lodge: Masons (32 deg.), Shriners, K.T., Rotary (pres. 1966-67). Judicial administration. Home: Rt 2 Ohio City OH 45874 Office: Rt 2 Box 40 Ohio City OH 45874

WALTERS, WILLIAM PETER, lawyer, state legislator; b. Paris, Ark., Apr. 17, 1943; s. Peter Louis and Elizabeth Cecelia (Wilhelm) W.; m Shirley Ann Dixon, Aug. 20, 1971; children—Jamie Elizabeth, Sherry Ann. B.S., U. Ark., 1966, J.D., 1971. Bar: Ark. 1971, U.S. Dist. Ct. (we. dist.) Ark. 1971, U.S. Supreme Ct. 1976. Asst. prosecuting atty. State of Ark., Ft. Smith, 1971-74; ptnr. firm Walters Law Firm, P.A., Greenwood, Ark., 1975—; mem. Ark. State Senate, Little Rock, 1982—; dir. 1st Ark. Title Ins. Co., Pine Bluff; v.p., dir. Sebastian Co. Abstract & Title, Greenwood. Search pilot CAP, Ft. Smith, 1980—; committeeman Rep. Party of Ark., 1980. Recipient Silver medal of Valor, CAP, Ark., 1983; Cert. of Honor, Justice for Crimes Victims, Little Rock, 1983. Mem. ABA, Sebastian County Bar Assn., Profl. Landmen's Assn. (Speaker award 1983), Mineral Owners Collective Assn. (dir., sec.-treas. Greenwood chpt. 1973—). Republican. Roman Catholic. Federal civil litigation, Personal injury, Real property. Home: PO Box 700 Greenwood AR 72936 Office: PO Box 280 Greenwood AR 72936

WALTHER, DALE JAY, lawyer; b. Elko, Nev., Oct. 15, 1948; s. Harold V. and Beryl H. (Brand) W.; m. Kazue Mori, Sept. 25, 1975; children—Kent, Brian, Nolan, Lisa, Curtis. B.A., Northwestern U., 1972; postgrad., Notre Dame U. summer law program, Japan, 1974; J.D., Calif. Western Sch. Law, 1975. Bar: Alaska 1975. Assoc. Law Offices Murphy Clark, Anchorage, 1975-80; ptnr. Clark, Walther & Flanigan, Anchorage, 1980—. Mem. Anchorage Bar Assn., Alaska Bar Assn., ABA, Order of Barristers, Am. Arbitration Assn., Phi Alpha Delta. Lodge: Elks. Personal injury, State civil litigation, Insurance. Home: PO Box 100428 Anchorage AK 99510 Office: Clark Walther & Flanigan 807 G St Suite 300 Anchorage AK 99501

WALTHER, DAVID LOUIS, lawyer; b. Stevens Point, Wis., Oct. 31, 1936; married; children: Christopher, Elizabeth, Jonathan, Jennifer, Mark, Gretchen. BS, Marquette U., 1958, JD cum laude, 1961. Bar: Wis. 1961, U.S. Dist. Ct. (ea. and we. dists.) Wis. 1961, U.S. Ct. Appeals (7th cir.) 1974, U.S. Supreme Ct. 1979, N.Mex. 1986. Legal asst. Wis. Supreme Ct., Madison, 1961-63; asst. legal counsel to Gov. John W. Reynolds, Madison, 1963; assoc. Brady, Tyrell & Bruce, Milw., 1963-64; sole practice Milw., 1964-66; ptnr. Walther & Burns, Milw., 1966-70, Walther & Halling, S.C., Milw., 1970-86, Walther & Walther, S.C., Milw., 1986—; adj. prof. Marquette U. Sch. Law, Milw. Author: Wisconsin Appellate Practice, 1965, 2d rev. edition, 1986. Fellow Am. Acad. Matrimonial Lawyers (bd. dirs. Wis. chpt.); mem. ABA (family law sect.), Wis. Bar Assn. (vice chmn. family law sect.), Milw. Bar Assn. (chmn. family law sect., jud. selection com.), Woolsack Soc. Club: University (Milw.). Family and matrimonial, Federal civil litigation, State civil litigation. Home: 1127 N Edison Milwaukee WI 53202 Office: Walther & Walther SC 625 E St Paul Ave Milwaukee WI 53202

WALTON, EDMUND LEWIS, JR., lawyer; b. Salisbury, Md., Sept. 4, 1936; s. Edmund Lewis and Iris Tull (White) W.; m. Barbara Post, Sept. 18, 1965; children—Southy E., Kristen P. B.A., Coll. William and Mary, 1961, J.D. (Godwin scholar), 1963; postgrad. U. Md. 1957-59. Bar: Va. 1963, U.S. Dist. Ct. (ea. dist.) Va. 1964, U.S. Supreme Ct. 1971, U.S. Dist. Ct. (we. dist.) Va. 1972, U.S. Ct. Appeals (4th cir.) 1980, Grad. asst. Coll. William and Mary 1961-62; assoc. Simmonds, Coleburn, Towner & Carman, Arlington and Fairfax, Va., 1963-68, ptnr. 1968-74; ptnr. Putbrese and Walton, McLean, Va., 1975; mem. Edmund L. Walton, Jr., P.C., McLean, 1976-82, Walton and Adams, P.C., McLean, 1983—; judge pro tem Fairfax County Cir. Ct. 1977—; legis. com. Va. State Bar 1974-76, 10th dist. com. 1975-78, bus. law sect. exec. com. 1983, sec. 1984-85, vice chmn. 1985-86, chmn. 1986-87. Bd. dirs. Home Run Acres Civic Assn. 1968-70, v.p. 1969-70; bd. dirs. McLean Citizens Assns. 1976-79, 1st v.p. 1977-78; bd. dirs., pres. Rocky Run Citizens Assn. 1973-74; bd. dirs. Langley Sch., Inc. 1975-77, treas. 1976-77; mem. Fairfax County Rep. Com. 1966-82, chmn. 1970-72; del. Rep. Nat. Conv. 1972; mem. Va. Rep. Cen. Com. 1974-77, exec. com. 1976-77; chmn. Providence Dist. Rep. Com. 1968-70; mem. 10th Congl. Dist. Rep. Com. 1970-77, vice chmn. 1974-76, chmn. 1976-77; mem. 8th Congl. Dist. Rep. Com. 1967-70; v.p. Arlington County Young Reps. 1965-66; counsel Arlington County Rep. Com. 1965-66; bd. dirs. McLean Planning Com. 1975-79, chmn. 1976-77; bd. dirs. McLean Office Square Condominium Assn. 1979-83, pres. 1979-82; chmn. Tysons Corner Citizens Task Force 1977-78; mem. Fairfax County Council on Arts; bd. dirs. Fairfax YMCA 1974-75; bd. dirs. Friends of Turkey Run Farm 1981—, counsel, 1981—, mem. exec. com. 1981-83. Served with U.S. Army 1956-59. Mem. ABA, Va. Bar Assn. (spl. com. to study rules of ethics 1981-84, membership com. 1981-84, exec. com. 1982—, chmn. 1984-85, pres. elect 1985-86, pres., 1986-87), Arlington County Bar Assn., Fairfax County Bar Assn. (cts. com. 1975-77, dir. 1976-77), McLean Lawyers Assn. (dir. 1978-79, 80-83, sec. 1978-79, pres. 1980-82), Va. Trial Lawyers Assn., Am. Judicature Soc., William and Mary Law Sch. Assn. (dir. 1970-76), Fairfax County C. of C. (dir. ex officio 1981-83), McLean Bus. and Profl. Assn. (dir. 1976-85, pres. 1981-83, Phi Alpha Delta. Episcopalian. Clubs: Washington Golf and Country (Arlington, Va.); Gt. Falls Swim and Tennis (dir. 1971-74). Editor William and Mary Law Rev. 1961-63. State civil litigation, General corporate, Probate. Home: 914 Peacock Station Rd McLean VA 22102 Office: 1301 Vincent Pl McLean VA 22101

WALTON, HERBERT WILSON, judge; b. Anaconda, Mont., Apr. 9, 1929; s. George Myrick and Neola Josephine (Wilson) W.; m. Barbara Lavon Pratt, Aug. 4, 1949; children—Michael Eugene, Constance Lynn, Herbert Steven, Cynthia Diane. A.B., U. Mo.-Kansas City, 1955, J.D., 1957. Bar: Kans. 1957, U.S. Dist. Ct. Kans. 1957. Asst. county atty. Johnson County (Kans.), 1957-60; probate judge Johnson County, 1960-65; judge Div. 1 10th Jud. Dist. Ct., 1965—; instr. bus. law U. Kans. Extension, 1963-71. Founding pres. Johnson County Scholarship Found.; active Kaw council Boy Scouts Am. Served with USN, 1947-48, 51-52. Mem. ABA, Kans. Jud. Council (chmn. pattern instrns. 1975—, chmn. family law adv. com., mem. com. on publs. on parentage act, protection from abuse and new divorce code), Johnson County Bar Assn., Kans. Bar Assn., Am. Judicature Soc., Assn. Family and Conciliation Cts., Kans. Dist. Judges Assn. (pres. 1973), U. Mo.-Kansas City Law Alumni Assn. (pres. 1973). Republican. Club: Olathe (Kans.) Optimists. State civil litigation, Family and matrimonial. Home: 405 Normandy Dr Olathe KS 66061 Office: Courthouse Olathe KS 66061

WALTON, JOHN WAYNE, lawyer; b. Kingsport, Tenn., May 3, 1947; s. Willard J. and Katherine H. (Syrad) W.; m. Anna Marie Laws, Oct. 24, 1969; children: Natasha Lee, John Adam. BS, East Tenn. State U., 1970; JD, Memphis State U., 1975. Bar: Tenn. 1976, U.S. Dist. Ct. (ea. dist.) Tenn. 1977. Assoc. Dan M. Laws, Jr., Elizabethton, Tenn., 1976-80; ptnr. Laws & Walton P.C., Elizabethton, 1980—. City atty. City of Elizabethton, 1982—. Served to capt. U.S. Army, 1970-72. Mem. ABA, Tenn. Bar Assn., Carter County Bar Assn. (pres. 1978), Tenn. Trial Lawyers Assn., Tenn. Mcpl. Attys. Assn. Baptist. Lodge: Rotary (bd. dirs. Elizabethton club 1978). State civil litigation, Local government, Probate. Office: PO Box 709 Elizabethton TN 37643

WALTON, MORGAN LAUCK, lawyer; b. Woodstock, Va., July 30, 1932; s. Morgan Lauck and Frances (Allen) W.; m. Jeannette Freeman Minor,

Mar. 4, 1961; children: Morgan Lauck, Charles Lancelot Minor, Christoper Allen, Laura Cathlyn. BA, Randolph-Macon Coll., 1953; LLB, U. Va., 1959. Bar: Va. 1959, N.Y. 1959, U.S. Supreme Ct. 1963. Assoc. Donovan Leisure Newton & Irvine, N.Y.C., 1959-68, ptnr., 1968-84; sole practice Woodstock, Va., 1984-87; gen. counsel Applied Concepts Corp., Edinburg, Va., 1987—. Contbr. articles to legal jours. Chmn. bd. trustees All Souls Unitarian Ch., N.Y.C., 1974-76, chmn. investment com., 1978-80; bd. dirs. Shenandoah Valley Music Festival, 1984—, treas. 1986—. Mem. ABA (chmn. Clayton Act com. antitrust sect. 1976-78, vice chmn. exemptions com. 1978-79), N.Y. State Bar Assn., Va. Bar Assn., Assn. Bar City N.Y., Shenandoah County Bar Assn. (treas. 1987—), Order of Coif, Phi Beta Kappa. Unitarian. Clubs: Univ., Collectors (N.Y.). Lodge: Rotary. Federal civil litigation, Administrative and regulatory, Antitrust. Home: Rt 2 Box 225 Woodstock VA 22664 Office: 405 Stoney Creek Blvd Edinburg VA 22824

WALTON, ROBERT PRENTISS, lawyer; b. Cleve., Jan. 11, 1938; s. Robert Clark and Elizabeth (Bowman) W.; m. Rosalie S., May 29, 1965; children—Jenifer S., Robert D. B.A., Yale U., 1959; LL.B., U. Va., 1962. Bar: N.Y. 1963, Conn. 1962, Va. 1962, U.S. Supreme Ct. 1967. Assoc. gen. counsel NYU, 1977-83, sr. assoc. counsel, 1983—; asst. U.S. atty. So. Dist. N.Y., 1970-75; mem. McGarrahan & Heard, N.Y.C., 1975-77. Recipient Am. Jurisprudence prize Bancroft Whitney Co., 1962. Mem. N.Y. State Bar Assn., Assn. Bar City of N.Y. (com. on condemnation and tax certiorari 1983—), Va. State Bar Assn. Federal civil litigation, Contracts commercial, Real property. Home: 69 Midland St Huntington NY 11743 Office: 70 Washington Sq S New York NY 10012

WALTON, RODNEY EARL, lawyer; b. Corvallis, Oreg., Apr. 28, 1947; s. Ray Daniel Jr. and Carolyn Jane (Smith) W. BA, Coll. of Wooster, 1969; JD, Cornell U., 1976. Bar: Fla. 1976, U.S. Dist. Ct. (so. dist.) Fla. 1976, U.S. Dist. Ct. (mid. dist.) Fla. 1977, U.S. Supreme Ct. 1980, U.S. Ct. Appeals (11th cir.) 1981. From assoc. to jr. ptnr. Smathers & Thompson, Miami, Fla., 1976—. Sec. Kings Creek West Condominum Assn. Bd. Dirs., Miami, 1984—. Served to 1st lt. U.S. Army, 1969-73, Vietnam. Decorated Bronze Star. Mem. ABA, Fla. Bar Assn., Dade County Bar Assn., Nation Assn. R.R. Trial Counsel. Republican. Methodist. Club: Bankers (Miami). Avocations: travel, reading, sports. Admiralty, Federal civil litigation, State civil litigation. Home: 7985 SW 86th St Unit 430 Miami FL 33143 Office: Smathers & Thompson 1301 Alfred I Dupont Bldg Miami FL 33131

WALTON, STANLEY ANTHONY, III, lawyer; b. Chgo., Dec. 10, 1939; s. Stanley Anthony and Emily Ann (Pouzar) W.; m. Karen Kayser, Aug. 10, 1963; children: Katherine, Anne, Alex. BA, Washington and Lee U., 1962, LLB, 1965. Bar: Ill. 1965, U.S. Dist. Ct. (no. dist.) Ill. 1966, U.S. Ct. Appeals (7th cir.) 1966. Assoc. Winston & Strawn, Chgo., 1965-72, ptnr., 1972—. Trustee Village of Hinsdale (Ill.), 1985-89; bd. dirs. Washington and Lee Law Sch., Lexington, Va., 1975-78, bd. dirs. univ. alumni, 1983-87, pres. 1986-87; bd. dirs. UNICEF, Chgo., 1983; pres. Hinsdale Hist. Soc., 1979-81. Mem. Phi Alpha Delta. Republican. Roman Catholic. Club: Woods Bathe and Tennis (Burr Ridge, Ill.) (treas. 1984-85); Hinsdale Golf. Federal civil litigation, State civil litigation, Personal injury. Home: 321 S Elm St Hinsdale IL 60521 Office: Winston & Strawn Suite 5000 One First Nat Plaza Chicago IL 60603

WALTZ, JON RICHARD, lawyer, educator, author; b. Napoleon, O., Oct. 11, 1929; s. Richard R. and Lenore (Tharp) W. B.A. with honors in Polit. Sci, Coll. Wooster, 1951; J.D., Yale U., 1954. Bar: Ohio 1954, Ill. 1965. Assoc. Squire, Sanders & Dempsey, Cleve., 1954-64; chief prosecutor City of Willowick (Ohio), 1958-64; assoc. prof. law Northwestern U. Sch. Law, Chgo., 1964-65; prof. law Northwestern U. Sch. Law, 1965-78, Edna B. and Ednyfed H. Williams prof. law, 1978—; instr. med. jurisprudence Northwestern Med. Sch., 1969—; book critic Washington Post, Chgo. Tribune, others; Disting. vis. prof. law Ill. Inst. Tech.-Chgo.-Kent Coll. Law, 1974; lectr. Coauthor: The Trial of Jack Ruby, 1965, Cases and Materials on Evidence, 1968, Principles of Evidence and Proof, 1968, Medical Jurisprudence, 1971, Cases and Materials on Law and Medicine, 1980, Evidence: Making the Record, 1981; author: The Federal Rules of Evidence-An Analysis, 1973, Criminal Evidence, 1975, Evidence: A Summary Analysis, 1976, Introduction to Criminal Evidence, 1981; note and comment editor: Yale Law Jour., 1953-54; mem. editorial adv. bd., Harcourt Brace Jovanovich Law Group, 1978—; contbr. numerous articles to profl. jours. Mem. Ill. adv. com. U.S. Commn. on Civil Rights, 1971-74; mem. Ill. Criminal Justice System Policy and Planning Com., 1973-74, Ill. Jud. Inquiry Bd., 1980—; mem. com. med. edn. AMA, 1982-83; mem. Gov.'s Task Force on Med. Malpractice, 1985; Republican candidate Ill. Appellate Ct., 1978. Served to capt. AUS, 1955-58. Decorated Commendation medal; recipient Disting. Service award Soc. Midland Authors, 1972, Disting. Alumni award Coll. Wooster, 1987. Mem. Am. Arbitration Assn., Assn. Am. Law Schs., Judge Advs. Assn., Nat. Assn. Def. Lawyers in Criminal Cases, Bar Assn. 7th Jud. Circuit, ABA, Chgo. Bar Assn., Chgo. Council Lawyers, Law-Medicine Soc., Soc. Am. Law Tchrs., Order of Coif, Phi Alpha Delta, Pi Sigma Alpha. Presbyterian. Legal education. Home: 421 W Melrose St Chicago IL 60657 Address: Eagle's Nest 0-4005 Lakeridge Rd Holland MI 49424 Office: 357 E Chicago Ave Chicago IL 60611

WALWYN, STEPHEN JOHN, lawyer; b. Stoke-on-Trent, Staffordshire, Eng., Nov. 8, 1947; came to U.S., 1959; s. John and Lilian Mary (Baddeley) W. Cadet Royal Mil. Acad., Sandhurst, Eng., 1966-67; B.A. in History, U. Santa Clara, 1970, J.D. cum laude, 1973. Bar: Calif. 1973. Assoc. Boccardo, Lull, Niland, Teerlink & Bell, San Jose, Calif., 1973-81; ptnr. Boccardo Law Firm, San Jose, 1980—, mem. mgmt. com., 1983-85; judge pro tem Santa Clara County Superior Ct., 1976—; prof. law Peninsula U. Law Sch., Mountain View, Calif., 1977-79. Contbr. articles to profl. jours. Served with Brit. Army, 1966-67. Mem. State Bar Calif., Calif. Trial Lawyers Assn. (bd. of govs. 1986—), Santa Clara County Trial Lawyers Assn. (bd. govs. 1986—), Santa Clara County Bar Assn. (med.-legal liaison com. 1985), Santa Clara U. Alumni Assn., Phi Alpha Theta. Club: Bar L, Brit. Am. Personal injury, Insurance, State civil litigation. Office: Boccardo Law Firm 111 W St John St Suite 1100 San Jose CA 95115

WALZ, MARY BETH, lawyer; b. Spokane, Wash., Feb. 20, 1951; d. Robert LeRoy and Beverly Ardelle (Smith) Nefzger; m. Stewart Chaussee Walz, Aug. 15, 1973; 1 child, Ashley Marie. BA, U. S.D., 1973; postgrad., U. Tenn., 1975; JD, U. Utah, 1979. Bar: Utah 1980, U.S. Dist. Ct. Utah 1980, U.S. Tax Ct. 1980. Assoc. Parsons, Behle & Latimer, Salt Lake City, 1980-83; adminstrv. law judge Utah Dept. Employment Security, Salt Lake City, 1983; asst. atty. gen. State of Utah, Salt Lake City, 1983—; instr. legal asst. training program Westminster Coll., Salt Lake City, 1982—, mem. adv. bd., 1982—; mem. jud. nominating commn. Juvenile Ct. Named one of Outstanding Young Women of Am., 1976, 81, 84-85. Mem. ABA, Utah Bar Assn. (needs of children com.), Am. Contract Bridge League, Phi Beta Kappa, Pi Sigma Alpha, Phi Eta Sigma, Phi Sigma Iota. Republican. Episcopalian. Avocations: snow skiing, spectator sports, bicycle riding, reading. State and local taxation, Administrative and regulatory. Home: 380 D St Salt Lake City UT 84103 Office: Utah Atty Gen's Office State Capitol Room 130 Salt Lake City UT 84114

WALZ, STEWART CHAUSSEE, lawyer; b. Vermillion, S.D., Mar. 9, 1951; s. Robert Chaussee and Jean (DeHaven) W.; m. Mary Beth Nefzger, Aug. 15, 1973; 1 child, Ashley Marie. BA, U. S.D., 1973; JD, Vanderbilt U., 1976. Bar: S.D. 1976, Utah 1980, U.S. Dist. Ct. Utah 1980, U.S. Ct. Appeals (10th cir.) 1981. Atty. dist. counsel IRS, Salt Lake City, 1976-80; asst. U.S. atty. State of Utah, Salt Lake City, 1980-87, 1st asst. U.S. atty., 1987—; lectr., tchr. Westminster Coll. Paralegal Program, Salt Lake City, 1985—. Coach Utah Youth Soccer Assn., Salt Lake City, 1979-80. Mem. Cts. and Judges Com. Democrat. Club: Ft. Douglas Hidden Valley (Salt Lake City). Avocations: snow skiing, golf. Criminal, Personal income taxation. Office: US Attys Office 350 S Main Room 473 Salt Lake City UT 84101

WANCA, BRIAN JOHN, lawyer; b. N.J., Nov. 23, 1954; s. John F. and Helen Wanca; m. Marilyn Brasich, June 13, 1981. BA magna cum laude, Rutgers U., 1976; JD cum laude, Ind. U., 1979. Bar: Ind. 1979, U.S. Dist. Ct. (no. and so. dists.) Ind. 1979, Ill. 1980, U.S. Dist. Ct. (no. dist.) Ill. 1980. Assoc. Friedrich, Bomberger, Tweedle & Blackmun, Munster, Ind., 1979-82, Johnson, Cusack & Bell, Chgo., 1982—. Mem. ABA, Ill. Bar Assn., Chgo. Bar Assn. Federal civil litigation, Real property, Insurance. Office: Johnson Cusack & Bell 211 W Wacker Suite 1800 Chicago IL 60606

WANDERMAN, SUSAN MAE, lawyer; b. N.Y.C., Mar. 12, 1947; d. Leo and Muriel D. Wanderman. AB, Wheaton Coll., Norton, Mass., 1967; JD, St. John's U., 1970; LLM, NYU, 1976. Bar: N.Y. 1971, U.S. Dist. Ct. (ea. and so. dists.) N.Y. 1972, U.S. Ct. Appeals (2d cir.) 1973, U.S. Supreme Ct. 1974. Asst. legal officer, legal dept. Chem. Bank, N.Y.C., 1972-75; 2d v.p. legal dept. Chase Manhattan Bank N.A., N.Y.C., 1975-82; asst. gen. counsel Citicorp Services, Inc., N.Y.C., 1982-84, Citibank, N.A., 19842—; instr. bus. law and law for the layman LaGuardia Community Coll., 1976-77; lay day speaker Queens County Supreme Ct., 1979-83. Contbr. articles to legal publs. Vol. N.Y. State Bar Assn. Lawyers in the Classroom. Mem. ABA, N.Y. State Bar Assn., Assn. Bar City N.Y., Queens County Bar Assn. General corporate, Banking. Office: Citibank NA 330 Madison Ave 12th Floor New York NY 10017

WANG, CHARLESTON CHENG-KUNG, lawyer, engineer; b. Tainan, Republic of China, Oct. 17, 1956; came to U.S., 1972; s. Shan-Cheng and I-Tsen (Cheng) W.; m. Shirley Liao, Mar. 14, 1981; 1 child, Vivian. BS in Econs. and Chem. Engring., U. Del., 1977; MBA in Internat. Bus., Xavier U., 1979; JD, No. Ky. U., 1982. Bar: Ohio, U.S. Dist. Ct. (so. dist.) Ohio, U.S. Dist. Ct. (ea. dist.) Ky., U.S. Ct. Appeals (6th cir.); diplomate Am. Bd. Indsl. Hygiene; cert. indsl. hygienist. Chem. engr. Procter & Gamble, Cin., 1979-81, NIOSH, Cin., 1981-84; mng. ptnr. Groeber & Wang, Cin., 1982-85; compliance officer U.S. Dept. Labor, Cin., 1985—; adj. prof. No. Ky. U., 1983—, U. Cin., 1985—. Author: How to Manage Workplace Derived Hazards and Avoid Liability, 1987; contbr. articles to profl. jours. Mem. ABA, Assn. Trial Lawyers Am., Am. Acad. Indsl. Hygiene, Am. Inst. Chem. Engrs., Chinese Am. Assn. Cin. (v.p., pres. elect 1985-86). Avocation: swimming. Personal injury, Environment, Labor. Home: 5757 Gilmore Dr Cincinnati OH 45014 Office: US Dept Labor 550 Main St Room 4028 Cincinnati OH 45202

WANG, GEORGE HANSEN, lawyer; b. N.Y.C., Feb. 12, 1952; s. Thomas K. and En-Ming (Chen) W. BS, Cornell U., 1973; MS, MIT, 1975; JD, Cornell U., 1978. Bar: N.Y. 1979, U.S. Dist. Ct. (so. and ea. dist.) N.Y. 1979, U.S. Patent Office 1979. Assoc. Darby and Darby, N.Y.C., 1978-79, Vincenti and Schickler, N.Y.C., 1979-81, Breed Abbott and Morgan, N.Y.C., 1981-84, Ruffa and Hanover, N.Y.C., 1984—; ednl. counselor MIT, N.Y.C., 1984—. Mem. ABA, N.Y. State Bar Assn., Assn. of Bar City of N.Y., Asian Mgmt. & Bus. Assn. (bd. dirs. 1986). Republican. Securities, General corporate. Home: 315 E 69th St New York NY 10021 Office: Ruffa and Hanover 90 Park Ave New York NY 10021

WANNER, KATHLEEN ANN, lawyer; b. Cleve.; d. Anthony George and Michaline Agnes (Woloszyn) W.; m. Edward Robert Modzelewski, May 29, 1976; 1 child, Rochelle Helene. BA, Kent State U., 1975; JD, Case Western Res. U., 1978. Bar: Ohio 1978, U.S. Dist. Ct. (no. dist.) Ohio 1979; CPA, Ohio. Atty. EPP & Hamilton, Cleve., 1978-80; sole practice Cleve., 1980-81; sr. tax specialist Deloitte Haskins Sells, Cleve., 1981-84; sr. tax analyst TRW Inc., Cleve., 1984—. Mem. ABA (tax sect.), Ohio Soc. CPA's, Tax Club Cleve. Corporate taxation, Personal income taxation, State and local taxation. Home: 15930 Bennett Rd North Royalton OH 44133 Office: TRW Inc 1900 Richmond Rd 2N Cleveland OH 44124

WANVIG, JAMES LOUIS, lawyer; b. Mpls., Oct. 31, 1921; s. Merrill Louis and Florence Lydia (Truesdell) W.; m. Norma Jean Hall, Feb. 8, 1944 (div.); m. Jean Marilyn Darrow, Sept. 12, 1964 (div.); 1 dau., Katharine Darrow; m. Barbara Jean Williams, Sept. 2, 1984. B.S.L., U Minn., 1943; B.A., U. Minn., 1948; LL.B, U Minn., 1948. Bar: Calif. 1950, U.S. Ct. Appeals (9th cir.) 1951, U.S. Dist. Ct. (no. dist.) Calif. 1951. Instr. U. Minn. Law Sch., Mpls., 1948; lectr. Boalt Hall Law Sch. (U. Calif.-Berkeley), 1948-50; assoc. Pillsbury, Madison & Sutro, San Francisco, 1950-60, ptnr., 1961—; vice chmn. bd. Pacific Legal Found., Sacramento, 1973; bd. dirs. Human Dimensions in Med. Edn., La Jolla. Served to lt. (j.g.) USN, 1943-46. Mem. ABA, State Bar Calif., Bar Assn. San Francisco, Am. Judicature Soc., San Francisco C. of C. (govt. relations com. 1968-70), Calif. C. of C. (welfare com. 1971-72). Club: Commonwealth of Calif. (San Francisco). Home: 3046 Divisadero St San Francisco CA 94123 Office: Pillsbury Madison & Sutro 225 Bush St San Francisco CA 94104

WARBASSE, STEVEN KENNETH, lawyer; b. Cedar Rapids, Iowa, Mar. 23, 1947; s. Kenneth William and Velma Arlene (Scott) W.; m. Maria Jane Miltner, Nov. 18, 1966 (div. Feb. 1980); children: Lisa Anne, Wendy Knight; m. Mary Ellen Weiringer, July 3, 1980; children: Matthew Steven and Sarah Deliverance. BA, U. Iowa, 1969, JD with distiction, 1976. Bar: Iowa 1976, U.S Dist. Ct. (no. dist.) Iowa 1977, U.S. Dist. Ct. (so. dist.) Iowa 1979, U.S. Ct. Appeals (8th cir.) 1982. Assoc. Ball & Nagle, P.C., Waterloo, Iowa, 1976-80; ptnr., sec. White & Warbasse, P.C., Cedar Rapids, 1980—; atty. City of Central City, Iowa, 1982—. Author: (with others) Damages in Iowa, 1984, Iowa Product Liability, 1985; editor Practitioner's Corporate Reorganization Case Book, 1975. Bd. dirs. Com. of 1000 Reps., Cedar Rapids, 1985—. Served to capt. U.S. Army, 1969-73. Mem. ABA, Assn. Trial Lawyers Am., Iowa Bar Assn., Assn. Trial Lawyers Iowa (bd. dirs. 1981—, chmn. H.E.L.P. polit. action com. 1986—). Avocation: high performance automobiles. Federal civil litigation, State civil litigation, Personal injury. Home: 300 Tomahawk Trail SE Cedar Rapids IA 52403 Office: White & Warbasse PC 1715 1st Ave SE Box 607 Cedar Rapids IA 52406

WARBURTON, ROY DAVID, lawyer; b. Summit, N.J., Mar. 30, 1953; s. Reed Franklin and Ruth Miriam (Vreeland) W.; m. Cheri Lynn Austin; children: Reed Thomas, John Benjamin, Rebekkah Boyd, Daniel James, Christine Caroline. BA, Miami U., Oxford, Ohio, 1974; JD, Washington & Lee U., 1978. Bar: Va. 1978, U.S. Dist. Ct. (we. dist.) Va. 1978, U.S. Ct. Appeals (4th cir.) 1978. Law clk. to presiding justice Va. Supreme Ct., Richmond, Va., 1978-79; with Lookabill & Warburton, 1979-84; asst. commonwealth atty. Pulaski (Va.) County, 1979-80; sole practice Pulaski, 1984—. Mem. bd. of zoning appeals, Pulaski, 1980—. Mem. ABA (gov. 4th cir. law student div.), Va. State Bar Assn., Va. Trial Lawyers Assn., Assn. Trial Lawyers Am. Lodge: Kiwanis (pres. Pulaski chpt. 1985-86). State civil litigation, Criminal, Personal injury. Home: 104 Sixth St NE Pulaski VA 24301 Office: PO Box 1506 Pulaski VA 24301

WARD, ALAN S., lawyer; b. Wilmington, Del., Jan. 1, 1931; s. Gilbert Hughes and Sarah Anna (Sparks) W.; m. Mariette S. Schneider, Apr. 4, 1959; children: Kathryn Ann Ward Koch, Guy Gilbert, Carolyn Alice. A.B., Wesleyan U., 1952; J.D., U. Chgo., 1955. Law clk. to judge U.S. Dist. Ct., Wilmington, 1955-56; trial atty. Antitrust div. Dept. Justice, Washington, 1956-61, asst. chief spl. litigation sect., 1960-61; assoc. Breed, Abbott & Morgan, N.Y.C., 1961-63; ptnr. Hollabaugh & Jacobs, Washington, 1963-70; dir. Bur. Competition, FTC, Washington, 1970-73; ptnr. Baker & Hostetler, Washington, 1973—, mem. mng. com., 1977—; lectr. law George Washington U., 1967-70; lectr. profl. assns. Mem. bd. of trustees Wesleyan U., 1986—. Mem. Wesleyan U. Alumni Assn. (chmn. 1983-86). Clubs: Univ. (Washington); Union (N.Y.C.); Union (Cleve.); Columbia Country (Chevy Chase, Md.). Antitrust. Home: 5804 Cedar Pkwy Chevy Chase MD 20815 Office: Baker & Hostetler 1050 Connecticut Ave NW Suite 1100 Washington DC 20036

WARD, ANTHONY JOHN, lawyer; b. Los Angeles, Sept. 25, 1931; s. John P. and Helen C. (Harris) W.; A.B., U. So. Calif., 1953; LL.B., U. Calif. at Berkeley, 1956; m. Marianne Edle von Graeve, Feb. 20, 1960 (div. 1977); 1 son, Mark Joachim; m. 2d, Julia Norby Credell, Nov. 4, 1978. Admitted to Calif. bar, 1957; asso. firm Ives, Kirwan & Dibble, Los Angeles, 1958-61; partner firm Marapese and Ward, Hawthorne, Calif., 1961-69; individual practice law, Torrance, Calif., 1969-76; partner firm Ward, Gaunt & Raskin, 1976—. Mem. Los Angeles World Affairs Council. Served to 1st lt. USAF, 1956-58. Mem. Am., Los Angeles County bar assns., Blue Key, Lambda Chi Alpha. Democrat. State civil litigation, Personal injury, Probate. Home: 2136 Via Pacheco Palos Verdes Estates CA 90274 Office: Pavilion A 21525 Hawthorne Blvd Torrance CA 90503

WARD, CHARLES DANIEL, lawyer; b. Portland, Maine, Aug. 31, 1935; s. John Vincent and Nola Frances (Sours) W.; m. Mary Theresa Bohmer, Aug. 19, 1961; 1 child, Katherine Theresa. BA, Yale U., 1955; LLB, Harvard U., 1962. Bar: Maine 1962, U.S. Dist. Ct. Maine 1962, N.Y. 1968, U.S. Dist. Ct. (so. and ea. dists.) N.Y. 1969, U.S. Supreme Ct. 1971, Conn. 1974, U.S. Dist. Ct. Conn. 1974. Law clk. to judge U.S. Dist. Ct., Portland, Maine, 1962-63; assoc. Bernstein, Shur, Sawyer & Nelson, Portland, 1962-67, Dewey, Ballantine, Bushby, Palmer & Wood, N.Y.C., 1967-72; asst. gen. counsel GTE Service Corp., Stamford, Conn., 1972—. Bd. dirs. Norwalk Youth Symphony, Fairfield County, Conn., 1975—, chmn., 1978-79. Served to capt. USAR, 1955-59, ETO. Mem. ABA, Conn. Bar Assn., Westchester/Fairfield Corp. Counsel Assn. (bd. dirs. 1983—, sec. 1984, treas. 1985—). Avocations: sailing, rowing. Antitrust, Federal civil litigation, State civil litigation. Home: 42 Jonathan Rd New Canaan CT 06840 Office: GTE Service Corp One Stamford Forum Stamford CT 06904

WARD, DAVID LIVINGSTONE, JR., lawyer; b. New Bern, N.C., July 23, 1935; s. David Livingstone and Leah Duval (Jones) W.; m. Elizabeth Anderson Reese, Nov. 1, 1958; children—Margaret Neal, Leah Jones, David Livingstone, IV. B.S. in Acctg., U. N.C., 1957; J.D., Duke U., 1962. Bar: N.C. 1962, N.C. Supreme Ct. 1962, U.S. Dist. Ct. (ea. dist.) N.C. 1962, U.S. Ct. Appeals (4th cir.) 1975, U.S. Tax Ct. 1981. Ptnr., Ward and Tucker, New Bern, 1962-73; sr. ptnr., pres. Ward and Smith, P.A., New Bern, 1973—; lectr. in field; dir. Carolina Telephone & Telegraph Co., First-Citizens Bank & Trust Co., First Citizens BancShares. Chmn. U. N.C. Bd. Visitors, Chapel Hill; chmn. Craven County Morehead Scholarship Selection Com.; active Christ Episcopal Ch., New Bern, vestryman, 1982-85 , trustee Christ Ch. Trust, 1980—, chmn., 1983. Served to lt. USNR, 1957-59. Named New Bern-Craven County Young Man of Year, 1970. Mem. ABA, N.C. Bar Assn., Craven County Bar Assn., Am. Coll. Probate Counsel, Am. Bar Found., N.C. Assn. Def. Counsel, Craven County C. of C. (dir., past pres.). Banking, General practice, General corporate. Home: 3601 Country Club Rd Trent Woods New Bern NC 28560 Office: PO Box 867 New Bern NC 28560

WARD, DIANE A., lawyer; b. New Orleans, May 1, 1946; d. Charles Pierce and Dorothy (Walker) W.; m. James David Kronman, Apr. 5, 1983. BA, So. Meth. U., 1967, MA, 1968; postgrad., UCLA, 1970-74, JD, 1977. Bar: Calif. 1977. Assoc. Paul, Hastings, Janofsky & Walker, Los Angeles, 1977-79, Marshall, Bratter, Greene, Allison & Tucker, Los Angeles, 1979-82, Seyfarth, Shaw, Fairweather & Geraldson, Los Angeles, 1982-83, Skadden, Arps, Slate, Meagher & Flom, Los Angeles, 1983-84; corp. counsel Whittaker Corp., Los Angeles, 1985; sr. atty. ARCO, Los Angeles, 1986—. Author wine & food newsletter Taste, 1983—; editor The Informed Enophile, 1981—. Nat. Merit scholar, 1964. Mem. ABA, Calif. Bar Assn., Los Angeles County Bar Assn., Phi Beta Kappa. Avocations: gourmet cooking, wine and food, swimming, gardening. Securities, Corporate finance. Home: 2244 Bagley Ave Los Angeles CA 90034 Office: ARCO 515 S Flower St Los Angeles CA 90071

WARD, DIANE KOROSY, lawyer; b. Cleve., Oct. 17, 1939; d. Theodore Louis and Edith (Bogar) Korosy; m. S. Mortimer Ward IV, July 2, 1960 (div. 1978); children: Christopher LaBruce, Samantha Martha; m. R. Michael Walters, June 30, 1979. AB, Heidelberg Coll., 1961; JD, U. San Diego, 1975. Bar: Calif. 1977, U.S. Dist. Ct. (so. dist.) Calif. 1977. Ptnr. Ward & Howell, San Diego, 1978-79, Walters, Howell & Ward, A.P.C., San Diego, 1979-81; mng. ptnr. Walters & Ward, A.P.C., San Diego, 1981—; dir., v.p. Oak Broadcasting Systems, Inc., 1982-83; dir. Elisabeth Kubler-Ross Ctr., Inc., 1983-85; sheriff Ranchos del Norte Corral of Westerners, 1985—; trustee San Diego Community Defenders, Inc., 1986—. Pres. bd. dirs. Green Valley Civic Assn., 1979-80; trustee Palomar-Pomerado Hosp. Found., chmn., 1985—; trustee Episcopal Diocese of San Diego. Mem. ABA, Rancho Bernardo Bar Assn. (chmn. 1982-83), Lawyers Club San Diego, Profl. and Exec. Women of the Ranch (founder, pres. 1982—), San Diego Golden Eagle Club, Phi Delta Phi. Republican. Episcopalian. Club: Soroptimist Internat. (pres. chpt. 1979-80). Probate, Estate planning. Home: 16503 Avenida Florencia Poway CA 92064 Office: Walters & Ward 11665 Avena Pl Suite 203 San Diego CA 92128

WARD, ETTIE, legal educator, lawyer, consultant; b. N.Y.C., Oct. 10, 1951; d. Jacob Benjamin and Hilda (Meltzer) W.; m. Alexander Rosenzweig, Nov. 13, 1977; 1 child, Robert Harry. AB, Barnard Coll., 1971; JD, Columbia U., 1974. Bar: N.Y. 1975, U.S. Dist. Ct. (so. and ea. dists.) N.Y. 1975, U.S. Ct. Appeals (2d cir.) 1975, U.S. Supreme Ct. 1979. Assoc. Kaye, Scholer, Fierman, Hays & Handler, N.Y.C., 1974-82; asst. prof. law St. John's U., Jamaica, N.Y., 1983—; reporter U.S. Ct. Appeals (2d cir.) Com. Pretrial Phase Civil Litigation, N.Y.C., 1984-86, 2d cir. com. on Improvement of Civil Litigation, 1986—. Mem. Selective Service Bd., 1985—. Mem. ABA, Assn. Bar of City of N.Y., Fed. Bar Council. Democrat. Jewish. Avocations: reading, music. Legal education, Federal civil litigation, Securities. Office: St Johns U Law Sch Grand Central and Utopia Pkwys Jamaica NY 11439

WARD, GARY ARDUS, lawyer; b. Lubbock, Tex., May 19, 1950; s. Ardus John and Mary Etta (Miller) W.; m. Robbie Jean Lara, June 20, 1970 (div. 1979); children: Tiffany, Monty; m. Shana Renee Krebbs, May 27, 1983. BBA, Tex. Tech U., 1972, MBA, JD, 1975. Bar: Tex. 1976, U.S. Dist. Ct. (no. and we. dists.) Tex. 1976, U.S. Tax Ct. 1976. Tax staff Arthur Andersen & Co., Dallas, 1976-77; ptnr. McCleskey, Harriger, Brazill & Graf, Lubbock, 1977—. Contbr. articles to profl. jours. Mem. ABA, Tex. Bar Assn. (cert. in estate planning and probate 1984), Lubbock County Bar Assn. Republican. Methodist. Avocations: golf, skiing. Estate planning, Probate, Estate taxation. Office: McCleskey Harriger Brazill & Graf 5010 University Suite 500 Lubbock TX 79413

WARD, HIRAM HAMILTON, federal judge; b. Thomasville, N.C., Apr. 29, 1923; s. O.L. and Margaret A. W.; m. Evelyn M. McDaniel, June 1, 1947; children—William McDaniel, James Randolph. Student, Wake Forest Coll., 1945-47; J.D., Wake Forest U., 1950. Bar: N.C. bar 1950. Practiced law Denton, N.C., 1950-51; staff atty. Nat. Prodn. Authority, Washington, 1951-52; partner firm DeLapp, Ward & Hedrick, Lexington, N.C., 1952-72; U.S. dist. judge Middle Dist. N.C., 1972—, chief judge, 1982—. Contbr.: legal opinions to Fed. Reporter System, 1972—. Bd. visitors Wake Forest U. Sch. Law, 1973—; Mem. N.C. Bd. Elections, 1964-72; trustee Wingate Coll., 1969-72. Served with USAAF, 1940-45. Decorated Air medal, Purple Heart. Mem. Am., N.C. bar assns., Am. Judicature Soc., N.C. State Bar, Jud. Conf. Fourth Circuit, Phi Alpha Delta (hon. life). Republican. Baptist. Clubs: Lions (Denton), Masons (Denton). Jurisprudence. Home: Forest Park Dr Denton NC 27239 Office: Fed Bldg & U S Courthouse Suite 246 Winston-Salem NC 27101

WARD, HORACE TALIAFERRO, judge; b. LaGrange, Ga., July 29, 1927; m. Ruth LeFlore (dec.); 1 son. A.B., Morehouse Coll., 1949; M.A., Atlanta U., 1950; J.D., Northwestern U., 1959. Bar: Ga. 1960. Instr. polit. sci. Ark. A.M. and N. Coll., 1950-51, Ala. State Coll., 1951-53, 55-56; claims authorizer U.S. Social Security Adminstrn., 1959-60; assoc. firm Hollowell Ward Moore & Alexander (and successors), Atlanta, 1960-69; individual practice law Atlanta, 1971-74; judge Civil Ct. of Fulton County, 1974-77, Fulton Superior Ct., 1977-79; now U.S. Dist. Ct. judge No. Dist. Ga., Atlanta; lectr. bus. and sch. law Atlanta U., 1965-70; dep. city atty., Atlanta, 1969-70, asst. county atty., Fulton County, 1971-74. Former Trustee Friendship Baptist Ch., Atlanta; mem. Ga. adv. com. U.S. Civil Rights Commn., 1963-65; assisting lawyer NAACP Legal Def. and Edn. Fund, Inc., 1960-70; mem. Jud. Selection Commn., Atlanta, 1972-74, Charter Commn., 1971-72; mem. Ga. Senate, 1964-74, jud. com., rules com., county and urban affairs com.; mem. State Democratic Exec. com., 1966-74; former bd. dirs. Atlanta Legal Aid Soc.; bd. dirs. Atlanta Urban League, Fed. Defender Program, No. Dist. Ga.; trustee Met. Atlanta Commn. on Crime and Delinquency, Atlanta U., Fledgling Found. Mem. Am. Bar Assn., Nat. Bar Assn. (chmn. jud. council 1978-79), State Bar Ga., Atlanta Bar Assn., Gate City Bar Assn. (pres. 1972-74), Atlanta Lawyers Club, Phi Beta Kappa, Alpha Phi Alpha, Phi Alpha Delta, Sigma Pi Phi. Office: 2388 US Courthouse 75 Spring St SW Atlanta GA 30303

WARD, JACK DONALD, lawyer; b. Blue Island, Ill., Aug. 14, 1952; s. Sylvan Donald and Beatrice Dorrell (Stackhouse) W.; m. Sharmon Oaks,

Nov. 21, 1973; children—Spencer, Julianna, Christopher, Brent, Stefani. B.S. summa cum laude in Acctg., Brigham Young U., 1975, J.D. cum laude, 1978. Bars: Ill. 1978, U.S. Dist. Ct. (no. dist.) Ill. 1979, U.S. Ct. Appeals (7th cir.) 1982, U.S. Supreme Ct. 1983. Assoc. Reno Zahm Law Firm, Rockford, Ill., 1978-82, ptnr., 1982—. Research asst.: Bogert on Trusts, 5th edit., 1978. Vol. missionary Ch. of Jesus Christ of Latter-Day Saints, Italy, 1971-73; mem. com. for today and tomorrow Rockford Meml. Hosp., 1980—. Mem. ABA, Ill. Bar Assn., Winnebago County Bar Assn. (continuing legal edn. com.), Assn. Trial Lawyers Am., Fed. Trial Bar, Beta Gamma Sigma. Republican. Club: City of Rockford. General practice, Personal injury, Bankruptcy. Office: Reno Zahm Law Firm 1415 E State St Rockford IL 61108

WARD, JOE HENRY, JR., lawyer; b. Childress, Tex., Apr. 18, 1930; s. Joe Henry and Helen Ida (Chastain) W.; m. Carlotta Agnes Abreu, Feb. 7, 1959; children—James, Robert, William, John. B.S. in Acctg., Tex. Christian U., 1952; J.D., So. Meth. U., 1964. Bar: Tex. 1964, Va. 1972, D.C. 1972; C.P.A., Tex. Mgr. Alexander Grant & Co., C.P.A.s., Dallas, 1956-64; atty. U.S. Treasury, 1965-68; tax counsel U.S. Senate Fin. Com., 1968-72; sole practice, Washington, 1972-83; asst. gen. counsel, tax mgr. Epic Holdings, Ltd. and Crysopt Corp., 1983—. Served to lt. USNR, 1952-56. Mem. ABA, Am. Inst. C.P.A.s, Am. Assn. Atty.-C.P.A.s. Club: Univ. (Washington). Personal income taxation, Corporate taxation, Estate planning. Home: 2639 Mann Ct Falls Church VA 22046 Office: Crysopt Corp 3101 Park Ctr Dr Suite 1450 Alexandria VA 22302

WARD, JOHN THOMAS, lawyer; b. Virginia Beach, Va., Dec. 29, 1939; s. George Howard and Nell (Cropper) W.; m. Billye Shrieves, May 5, 1962; children: Elizabeth, Jonathan. BS, USCG Acad., 1961; LLB, U. Va., 1968. assoc. Ober, Kaler, Grimes & Shriver, Balt., 1968-75, ptnr., 1975-84; ptnr. Quinn, Ward & Kershaw P.A., Balt., 1984-86, v.p., 1986—. Served to lt. USCG, 1961-65. Mem. ABA, Md. Bar Assn., Va. Bar Assn., N.Y. State Bar Assn., D.C. Bar Assn. Avocations: fly fishing, scuba diving, dog breeding and judging. Admiralty, Federal civil litigation, Insurance. Home: 6279 W Rockburn Hill Elkridge MD 21227 Office: Quinn Ward & Kershaw PA 113 W Monument St Baltimore MD 21201

WARD, LESTER LOWE, JR., lawyer; b. Pueblo, Colo., Dec. 21, 1930; s. Lester Lowe and Alysmai (Pfeffer) W.; m. Rosalind H. Felps, Apr. 18, 1964; children—Ann Marie, Alison, Lester Lowe. A.B. cum laude, Harvard U., 1952, LL.B., 1955. Bar: Colo. 1955. Sole practice Pueblo, 1957—; ptnr. Predovich, Ward & Banner, Pueblo, 1974—. Trustee, Thatcher Found., Frank I. Lamb Found., Helen G. Bonfils Found., Denver Ctr. for Performing Arts; pres. bd. trustees Pueblo Pub. Library, 1960-66; trustee St. Mary-Corwin Hosp., 1972—, pres., 1979-80. Served with U.S. Army, 1955-57. Named Outstanding Young Man of Yr., Pueblo Jaycees, 1964. Fellow Am. Coll. Probate Counsel; mem. ABA (house of dels. 1986—), Colo. Bar Assn. (bd. govs. 1977-79, 82—, pres. 1983-84), Pueblo County Bar Assn. (Outstanding Young Lawyer award 1965, 67, pres. 1976-77), Harvard Law Sch. Assn. Colo. (pres. 1972). Democrat. Roman Catholic. Lodge: Kiwanis (pres. 1969). Banking, General corporate, Probate. Home: 118 Baylor St Pueblo CO 81005 Office: Predovich Ward & Banner 727 Thatcher Bldg Pueblo CO 81003

WARD, MICHAEL W., lawyer; b. Chgo., Aug. 16, 1950; s. John Francis and Mary Frances (Brophy) W.; m. Amy Louise Alsopiedy, June 29, 1974; children: Daniel Joseph, James Patrick. BA, U. Notre Dame, 1972; JD, Ill. Inst. Tech., 1976. Bar: Ill. 1976, U.S. Dist. Ct. (no. dist.) Ill. 1976, U.S. Ct. Appeals (7th cir.) 1976, U.S. Supreme Ct. 1980, U.S. Dist. Ct. (no. dist.) Ill. 1982, U.S. Ct. Appeals (6th cir.) 1985. Asst. state's atty. Cook County, Chgo., 1976-80; assoc. O'Keefe, Ashenden, Lyons & Ward, Chgo., 1980-85, ptnr., 1986—. v.p. Northshore Fellowship League, Evanston, Ill., 1982-84; mem. St. Nicholas Sch. Bd., Evanston, 1984-86; bd. dirs. New Horizons Youth Group, Evanston, 1979-85. Mem. ABA, Ill. Bar Assn., Chgo. Bar Assn., Evanston Bar Assn. Roman Catholic. Club: Midday (Chgo.). Telecommunications, Federal civil litigation, State civil litigation. Home: 1914 Keeney St Evanston IL 60202 Office: O'Keefe Ashenden Lyons & Ward 1 First Nat Plaza Suite 5100 Chicago IL 60603

WARD, NICHOLAS DONNELL, lawyer; b. N.Y.C., July 30, 1941; s. Francis Xavier and Sarah Delamater (Donnell) W.; m. Elizabeth Reed Lowman, Sept. 6, 1968 (dec. Dec. 22, 1984); m. Virginia Ann McArthur, June 7, 1985. B.A., Columbia Coll., 1963; LL.B., Georgetown U., 1966. Bar: D.C. 1967, U.S. Supreme Ct. 1977. Assoc. Hamilton & Hamilton, Washington, 1967-72, ptnr., 1973-85; ptnr. Muir & Ward, Chartered, 1986—; instr. paralegal progams U. Md., College Park, 1975-77, Georgetown U., Washington, 1977; mem. adv. com. on Superior Ct. rules of probate and fiduciary procedure, Superior Ct. of D.C., 1975—; mem. Jud. Conf., D.C., 1981—, D.C. Cir., 1981, 84, 85; mem. faculty Mus. Mgmt. Inst., Berkeley, Calif., 1979-86; adj. prof. Sch. Law Cath. U., 1986—. Editor legal form book: Will and Testamentary Trust Forms, 1974 (2d edit. 1982 ABA Spl. Recognition award 1982); state editor Drafting Wills and Trust Agreements, D.C. Supplement; contbr. articles to profl. jours.; performer and author phonograph record: The Roast Beef of Old England, Come Dance With Me In Ireland. Trustee Benjamin Franklin U., Washington, 1976-79; ann. corp. mem. Children's Hosp. of D.C., Washington, 1971-81; trustee Conf. Meml. Assn., Inc., Washington, 1975-77; comdr. Mil. and Hospitaller Order of Saint Lazarus of Jerusalem, 1977—; pres. gen. Soc. of War of 1812, 1984-87; gen. sec. Gen. Soc. SR, 1976-85; gov. gen. Hereditary Order of Descendants of Colonial Govs., 1983-85; gov. Soc. of Colonial Wars in D.C., 1982-84; mem. steering com. Friends of Music at Smithsonian, 1986—. Served to sgt. USAR, 1966-72. Fellow Am. Coll. Probate Counsel (state chmn. 1987—); mem. Bar Assn. of D.C. (bd. dirs. 1979-81, treas. 1982-85, Marvin E. Preis award 1980), Barrister Inn (pres. 1977-78), D.C. Estate Planning Council (dir. 1985-87, membership com. 1983-86), ABA (real property, probate and trust law sect., chmn. com. on charitable instns. 1985-87, chmn. 1985-87, state reporter on current probate and trust law decisions 1983—, planning com. and faculty continuing legal edn. program 1975—, real property probate and trust law sect.), Selden Soc., Am. Soc. for Legal History, Associated Musicians of Greater N.Y., Am. Fedn. Musicians, D.C. Jaycees (dir. Downtown chpt. 1971-72, legal counsel, 1972-74), D.C. Bar Assn. (trustee client's security fund 1981-1990, chmn. 1983-90, chmn. sect. 8, estates, trust and probate sect. 1984-86), Nat. Assn. of Coll. and Univ. Attys. (sec.-treas. 1979-86, chmn. sect. on univ. mus. and collections 1981-86), Phi Delta Phi. Episcopalian. Clubs: Cosmos (bd. mgmt. 1984-86, 87-90, sec. 1986-87), Met., City Tavern, Union (N.Y.C.), St. Nicholas Soc. of City of N.Y. (bd. mgrs. 1985—); Barristers. Avocation: golfing. Probate, Estate planning, Art. Home: 3040 O St NW Washington DC 20007-3107 Office: Muir & Ward Chartered Suite 902 Brawner Bldg 888 17th St NW Washington DC 20006

WARD, PAUL ANTHONY, lawyer; b. Grand Rapids, Mich., Dec. 13, 1929; s. Paul E. and Maude M. (Karreman) W.; m. Constance C. Coulter, Apr. 18, 1959; children—William L., David L., Susan L.; m. 2d, Mary Paula Smith, June 18, 1979. A.B., Calvin Coll., 1951; J.D., U. Mich., 1953. Bar: Mich. 1953, U.S. Ct. Appeals (6th cir.) 1964, U.S. Supreme Ct. 1964. House counsel Old Kent Bank & Trust Co., 1953-59; ptnr. Himelstein & Ward, Grand Rapids, 1959-69, Russell & Ward, Grand Rapids, 1969-80, Ward, Schenk & Boncher, Grand Rapids, 1980-87, sole practice, 1987—. Mem. ABA, Fed. Bar Assn., Am. Coll. Real Estate Lawyers (past chmn. corp., fin. and bus. law sect. and title standards com., council mem. real property law sect.), Mich. Bar Assn. (title standards com.), Grand Rapids Bar Assn. Clubs: Ambucs, Variety, Cascade Hills Country, Peninsular (Grand Rapids); Renaissance (Detroit); Commanders. Real property, Bankruptcy, State civil litigation. Home: 4161 Kings Row Ct NW Grand Rapids MI 49504 Office: The Law Ctr 60 Monroe Ctr NW Grand Rapids MI 49503

WARD, PHILIP HENRY, JR., lawyer; b. Sterling, Ill., Oct. 10, 1931; s. Philip Henry Sr. and Edith (Jamison) W.; m. Marilyn Sundquist, Aug. 15, 1953; children: Robert V., Philip H. III, Susan J. AB, U. Ill., 1953, JD, 1955. Bar: Ill. 1955. From assoc. to ptnr. Ward, Murray, Pace & Johnson, P.C., Sterling, 1957—, also chief exec. officer. Editor Ward on Title Examinations, 3d edit. 1975, 4th edit., 1986; contbr. articles to profl. jours. Sch. bd. mem. Dist. 134, Sterling, 1961-70; bd. dirs. Rock River Lumber & Grain Co., Prophetstown, Ill., 1967—. Served to 1st lt. JAGC, USAF, 1955-57. Fellow Am. Coll. Probate Counsel; mem. ABA, Ill. Bar Assn. (probate and trust council 1968-74, corp. and securities sect. 1974-78, real estate council 1961-68, 81—), Whiteside County Bar Assn., Chgo. Bar Assn., Am. Judicature Soc. Republican. Presbyterian. Estate planning, Probate, Real property. Home: 1505 Locust St Sterling IL 61081 Office: Ward Murray Pace & Johnson PC 202 E 5th St PO Box 400 Sterling IL 61081

WARD, RICHARD ALVORD, lawyer; b. San Bernardino, Calif., Oct. 21, 1922; s. John Stanley and Grace Lucile (Alvord) W.; m. Jean Ann Redick, Dec. 24, 1976; children—Normandie, Richard A., Heidi M. A.B. with distinction, George Washington U., 1961, J.D. with honors, 1965. Bar: Va. 1965, D.C. 1965, U.S. Supreme Ct. 1971. Sole practice, Washington, 1965-67; ptnr. Berliner and Ward, Washington, 1967-74; assoc. Rice, Carpenter & Carraway, Washington, 1974-76; ptnr., Washington and Arlington, Va., 1976-83; ret., 1985. Served with USMC, 1942-63. Decorated D.F.C., Air medal. Recipient Alumni Service award George Washington U., 1979. Mem. George Washington Law Assn. (pres. 1977-78, bd. dirs. 1970-78), Order of Coif, Phi Delta Phi, Phi Sigma Kappa. Assoc. editor George Washington Law Rev., 1964-65, bd. editors, 1963-65. Home: 1806 View Top Ct Annapolis MD 21401 Office: Second Nat Service Corp PO Box 1767 Annapolis MD 21404-1767

WARD, ROBERT ALAN, lawyer; b. East St. Louis, Ill., Sept. 2, 1957; s. Darrell Raymond and Lucille Gilda (Faletti) W.; m. Carol Lynn Grassi, Sept. 21, 1985. BS, So. Ill. U., Edwardsville, 1979; JD, Washington U., St. Louis, 1982. Bar: Mo. 1982, Ill. 1983, U.S. Dist. Ct. (ea. dist.) Mo. 1983. Assoc. Farrell, Heil, Long & St. Peters, Godfrey, Ill., 1982; tax adminstr. Centerre Trust Co. St. Louis, 1982-84; asst. gen. counsel Mo. Dept. of Revenue, Jefferson City, 1985—. Mem. ABA, Mo. Bar Assn., Ill. Bar Assn., Met. St. Louis Bar Assn., Sigma Phi Epsilon. State and local taxation, Administrative and regulatory. Office: Mo Dept of Revenue PO Box 475 Jefferson City MO 65105

WARD, ROBERT JOSEPH, judge; b. N.Y.C., Jan. 31, 1926; s. Joseph G. and Honor V. (Hess) W.; m. Florence C. Maisel, Apr. 15, 1951; children—Laura Alice, Carolyn. S.B., Harvard, 1945, LL.B., 1949. Bar: N.Y. State bar 1949. Practiced in N.Y.C., 1949-51, 61-72; asst. dist. atty. N.Y. County, 1951-55; asst. U.S. atty. So. Dist. N.Y., 1956-61; judge U.S. So. Dist. N.Y., 1972—. Served with USNR, 1944-46. Mem. Am., N.Y. State bar assns., Assn. of the Bar of City of N.Y. Jurisprudence. Office: US Courthouse Foley Sq New York NY 10007

WARD, ROBERT MORTON, lawyer, educator; b. Sullivan, Ind., Sept. 12, 1943; s. Robert Raymond and Rubylee (Tipton) W.; m. Amy Knox Hall, Aug. 17, 1974; children—Courtney Tipton, Justin Charles, Dana Livingston. B.S., Northwestern U., 1967; J.D., DePaul U., 1971. Bar: Ill. 1971, U.S. Dist. Ct. (no. dist.) Ill. 1971, U.S. Ct. Appeals (7th cir.) 1971. Assoc., Merriam, Marshall, Shapiro & Klose, Chgo., 1971-73, Cook, Wetzel & Egan, Ltd., Chgo., 1973—; lectr. trademarks and patents DePaul U., Chgo., 1980-82; dir. Corbern Corp., Chgo., Derma-Cure, Inc., Chgo., Delta Nameplate, Inc., Chgo. Editor-in-chief DePaul Law Rev., 1971. NIH grantee, 1962, 63. Mem. Chgo. Bar Assn., Patent Law Assn. Chgo., Am. Intellectual Property Assn., ABA. Clubs: Union League, Law. Patent, Trademark and copyright. Office: Cook Wetzel & Egan Ltd 135 S LaSalle St Chicago IL 60603

WARD, WILLIAM FRANCIS, lawyer; b. N.Y.C., Nov. 20, 1951; s. Edward Francis and Ruth Alice (Young) W.; m. Joan Louise Yanzek, Oct. 8, 1983. BA, Holy Cross Coll., Worcester, Mass., 1973; JD, Temple U., Phila., 1977. Bar: Pa. 1977, U.S. Dist. Ct. (ea. dist.) Pa. 1977, U.S. Dist. Ct. (we. dist.) Pa. 1979, D.C. 1979, U.S. Ct. Appeals (D.C. cir.) 1979, U.S. Ct. Appeals (3d cir.) 1983, U.S. Supreme Ct., 1982. Law clk. to presiding justice U.S. Dist. Ct. (ea. dist.) Pa., Phila., 1977-78; asst. U.S. atty. U.S. Atty's. Office, Pitts., 1979-85, chief econ. crime sect., 1983-85; assoc. Meyer, Unkovic and Scott, Pitts., 1986—; lectr. USNR, 1980, U.S. Postal Service, Pitts., 1981. Recipient Spl. Achievement award, U.S. Atty. Gen., 1980, Spl. Commendation award, 1984, FBI award White Collar Crime Squad, 1985. Mem. ABA, Pa. Bar Assn., Fed. Bar Assn., Allegheny County Bar Assn., Am. Judicature Soc. Roman Catholic. Criminal, Federal civil litigation, State civil litigation. Home: 266 Jefferson Dr Pittsburgh PA 15228 Office: Meyer Unkovic & Scott 1300 Oliver Bldg Pittsburgh PA 15222

WARDELL, JOHN WATSON, lawyer; b. Mt. Erie, Ill., Oct. 25, 1929; s. Charles R. and Rada (Travers) W.; m. Carol J. Gross, Aug. 6, 1955; (div. 1984); children—Michael, Amy, Laurie, Douglas. B.A., U. Ill., 1950, J.D., 1956. Bar: Ill. 1956, U.S. Dist. Ct. (no. dist.) Ill. 1967. Counsel law dept. Standard Oil Co. (Ind.), 1956-61, Motorola, Inc., Franklin Park, Ill., 1961-68; sole practice, 1968-69, 71-73, 74-75; ptnr. Franz, Franz, Wardell & Lindberg 1969-70, Wardell & Ungvarsky, 1970-71, Wardell & Meinhardt 1973-74, Wardell & Johnson Ltd. and predecessor, Crystal Lake, Ill., 1976—; gen. counsel, dir. Matsuo Electronics Am. Inc.; dir. other corps. Mem. Gov.'s Adv. Council 1969-73; bd. dirs. North Barrington (Ill.) Area Assn., 1970-84; mem. Lake County (Ill.) Taxpayers Com., 1970-73. Served with M.C., U.S. Army, 1951-53. Mem. ABA, Ill. Bar Assn. (chmn. younger mems. conf. 1965-66, council gen. practice sect. 1971-75, task force on publicity 1976-78, council internat. law sect. 1982-86), Chgo. Bar Assn. (internat. and fgn. law com. 1970-83), McHenry County Bar Assn., Am. Judicature Soc., Internat. Bus. Council MidAm., Mgmt. Forum, No. Ill. Indsl. Assn., Order of Coif, Phi Beta Kappa, Phi Delta Phi, Phi Kappa Phi. Republican. Club: Turnberry Country (Crystal Lake, Ill.). Contbr. articles to profl. jours. General corporate, Private international, Probate. Office: Schaumburg Corp Ctr 1515 E Woodfield Rd Suite 740 Schaumburg IL 60173 Office: 451 Coventry Green Crystal Lake IL 60014

WARDEN, JOHN L., lawyer; b. Evansville, Ind., Sept. 22, 1941; s. Walter Wilson and Juanita (Veatch) W.; m. Phillis Ann Rodgers, Oct. 27, 1960; children—Anne, John L., W. Carson. A.B., Harvard U., 1962; LL.B., U. Va., 1965. Bar: N.Y. 1966, U.S. Ct. Appeals (2d cir.) 1966, U.S. Dist. Ct. (so. and ea. dists.) N.Y. 1967, U.S. Ct. Appeals (10th cir.) 1971, U.S. Supreme Ct. 1972, U.S. Ct. Appeals (D.C. cir.) 1980. Assoc., Sullivan & Cromwell, N.Y.C., 1965-73, ptnr., 1973—. Fellow Am. Coll. Trial Lawyers; mem. Am. Law Inst., ABA, N.Y. State Bar Assn., Bar City N.Y., N.Y. County Lawyers Assn. Republican. Episcopalian. Clubs: Knickerbocker, Down Town Assn. (N.Y.C.); Bedford (N.Y.) Golf and Tennis. Editor-in-chief Va. Law Review, 1965. Antitrust, Federal civil litigation, State civil litigation. Office: 125 Broad St New York NY 10004

WARDEN, ROBERT ALLISON, lawyer; b. Washington, May 3, 1941; s. Robert L. and Mary Jane (Allison) W.; m. Carol Burchuk, Dec. 10, 1967; children: David Matthew, Michael Robert. BA, U. Mich., 1963; LLB, Harvard U., 1966; postdoctoral, London Sch. Econs., 1966-67. Bar: D.C. 1967, U.S. Ct. Claims 1967, U.S. Tax Ct. 1973, U.S. Ct. Appeals (D.C. cir.) 1967, U.S. Supreme Ct. 1971. Legis. atty. 1972-73, asst. legis. counsel, 1974-76, legis. counsel, 1976-77; asst. chief of staff Joint Com. on Taxation, Washington, 1978; ptnr. McDermott, Will & Emery, Washington, 1982—. Mem. Nat. Rep. Club Capitol Hill, Washington. Mem. D.C. Bar Assn. Lutheran. Corporate taxation, Personal income taxation, Estate taxation. Office: McDermott Will & Emery 1850 K St NW Washington DC 20006

WARE, GUILFORD DUDLEY, lawyer; b. Dunnsville, Va., Apr. 15, 1925; s. Catesby and Lila (Maddox) W.; m. Nancy Smith, Jan. 17, 1959 (dec. Dec. 1974); children: E. Latane, G. Dudley Jr., David B.; m. Gay Dantzler, Sept. 17, 1977. BS in Commerce, U. Va., 1949, LLB, 1952. Bar: Va. 1952, U.S. Dist. Ct. (ea. dist.) Va. 1952, U.S. Supreme Ct. 1956, U.S. Ct. Appeals (4th cir.) 1957. Ptnr. Crenshaw, Ware & Johnson, Norfolk, Va. Pres. YMCA, Norfolk, 1966-67, Symphony Orch., Norfolk, 1967-68. Mem. ABA, Norfolk/Portsmouth Bar Assn. (pres. elect 1987—), Maritime Law Assn., Southeast Admiralty Law Inst. (seminar chmn. 1983, gen. chmn. 1985), Assn. Trial Lawyers Am., Am. Judicature Soc. General practice, Admiralty, General corporate. Home: 7457 Saint Francis Ln Norfolk VA 23505 Office: Crenshaw Ware & Johnson 1640 Sovran Ctr Norfolk VA 23510

WARFORD, TOMMY GENE, lawyer; b. Gorman, Tex., June 16, 1941; s. Aubrey W. and Opal Jo (Fuller) W.; m. Mary G. Craven, May 28, 1983; stepchildren—Kelly Joiner, Kael Joiner. Grad. Ranger Jr. Coll., 1959-61; B.A., U. Tex., 1963, LL.B., 1966. Bar: Tex. 1966, U.S. Dist. Ct. 1975, U.S. Supreme Ct. 1985. Atty., Tex. Hwy. Dept., 1967-69; ptnr. Turner, Seaberry & Warford, Eastland, Tex., 1969—; dir. Eastland Nat. Bank, Ranger Savs. Trustee Eastland Meml. Hosp., 1982—; bd. dirs. Eastland County Water Supply Dist., 1984—. Served to 1st lt. JAG, USAR, 1966-72. Named Outstanding Alumni, Ranger Jr. Coll., 1982. Fellow Tex. Bar Found.; mem. Tex. Bar Assn., ABA. Presbyterian. Club: Lone Cedar Country (bd. dirs. 1983—). Probate, Real property, Oil and gas leasing. Home: 1103 S Seaman Eastland TX 76448 Office: Turner Seaberry & Warford PO Box 311 Eastland TX 76448

WARIN, EDWARD GEORGE, lawyer; b. Des Moines, Feb. 16, 1947; s. Roger F. and Mary A. (Gray) W.; m. Colleen Walsh, Aug. 6, 1971; children: Edward Walsh, Kathleen Hall, Mary Colleen. B.S., Creighton U., 1969; J.D., Georgetown U., 1973. Bar: D.C., Nebr. Dep. county atty. Douglas County, Omaha, 1973-77; U.S. atty. Omaha, 1978-80; ptnr. firm Gross, Welch, Vinardi, Kauffman & Day, Omaha, 1980—; instr. criminal law U. Nebr. at Omaha. Mem. Am., D.C., Nebr., Omaha bar assns., Nat. Dist. Attys. Assn. Democrat. Roman Catholic. Federal civil litigation, State civil litigation, Criminal. Home: 12426 Farnam St Omaha NE 68154 Office: 800 Commercial Federal Tower 2120 S 72d St Omaha NE 68124

WARMINGTON, ROBERT ANTHONY, court administrator; b. Newark, Dec. 9, 1949; s. Robert Anthony and Rhoda D. (Brand) W.; m. Linda Ann Schanbacher, June 17, 1972; children—Jennifer, David. B.A. in English magna cum laude, Seton Hall U., 1971, J.D. with honors, 1977. Bar: N.J. 1977, U.S. Dist. Ct. N.J. 1977. English tchr., Montvale, N.J., 1971-72; police officer, Newark, 1972-73; investigator/ct. liaison Hudson County Prosecutor's Office, Jersey City, 1973-76; sole practice, Lincoln Park, N.J., 1977-79; ct. adminstr. Newark Mcpl. Ct., 1976-79; asst. trial ct. adminstr. Passaic County Superior Ct., Paterson, N.J., 1979-85, 85—; adminstr. Morgan, Melhuish, Monaghan, Arvidson, Abrutyn and Lisowski, Livingston, N.J., 1985. dir. placement Seton Hall U. Law Sch., Newark, 1981—; paralegal instr., Pompton Plains, N.J., 1981-85; grader N.J. Inst. Continuing Legal Edn., Newark, 1981—. Author legal articles. Contbr. chpts. to books. Mem. Citizens Adv. Com. to Lincoln Park Planning Bd., 1976, to Sewer Authority, 1981. Recipient Acad. Excellence award Newark Police Benevolent Assn., 1972, Adminstrv. Merit award for Extraordinary Service Seton Hall U., 1986. Roman Catholic. Mem. Zeta Beta Tau (pres. 1969-70). Judicial administration, Legal education, Legal placement. Home: 1440 Alps Rd Wayne NJ 07470 Office: Pasaic County Ct 77 Hamilton St Paterson NJ 07505

WARNE, WILLIAM RAYMOND, lawyer; b. Orange, Calif., Apr. 28, 1948; s. Thomas Wesley and Miriam Mae (Green) W.; m. Sandra See, Dec. 28, 1985. B.S., Western State U., 1974, J.D., 1976. Bar: Calif. 1976, U.S. Dist. Ct. (cen. dist.) Calif. 1977. Sole practice, Orange, Calif., 1976—. Served with U.S. Army, 1969-70. Mem. Orange County Bar Assn. Democrat. Lutheran. Clubs: Exchange, Toastmasters. Landlord-tenant, Real property, Administrative and regulatory. Office: William R Warne 400 E Chapman Ave Orange CA 92666

WARNEMENT, PAMELA PEARSON, lawyer; b. Boston, June 1, 1957; d. Arthur David and Elizabeth (Kharasch) Pearson; m. Victor Alan Warnement, June 1, 1985. AB, Vassar Coll., 1975-79; JD cum laude, Cornell U., 1982. Bar: N.J. 1982, U.S. Dist. Ct. N.J. 1982. Assoc. Riker, Danzig, Scherer, Hyland & Perretti, Morristown, N.J., 1982—. Federal civil litigation, State civil litigation, Products liability. Office: Riker Danzig Scherer et al One Speedwell Ave Hdqrs Plaza Morristown NJ 07960

WARNER, CECIL RANDOLPH, JR., lawyer; b. Fort Smith, Ark., Jan. 13, 1929; s. Cecil Randolph and Reba (Cheeves) W.; m. Susan Curry, Dec. 10, 1955 (div. 1982); children—Susan Rutledge, Rebecca Jane, Cecil Randolph III, Matthew Holmes Preston, Katherine Mary; m. Barbara Ragsdale, May 26, 1983. B.A. magna cum laude, U. Ark., 1950; LL.B. magna cum laude, Harvard U., 1953, Sheldon fellow, 1953-54. Bar: Ark. bar 1953. Practiced in Fort Smith, 1954—; partner firm Warner & Smith (and predecessor), 1954—; pres., chief exec. officer Fairfield Communities, Inc., 1973-81, chmn., chief exec. officer, 1981-85, chmn., pres., chief exec. officer, 1985—; dir. Mid-Am. Industries, Inc., 214, Inc., Wortz Co., 1st Comml. Corp.; Instr. U. Ark. Sch. Law, 1954, 56; vice chmn. Ark. Constl. Revision Study Commn., 1967; v.p. 7th Ark. Constl. Conv., 1969-70. Scoutmaster troop 23 Boy Scouts Am., Fort Smith, 1955-58; commr. Ark. State Police Commn., 1970; bd. dirs. St. Vincent Infirmary Found., U. Ark. Found., Little Rock, Ark. Symphony. Fellow Am., Ark. bar founds.; mem. Fort Smith C. of C. (dir.), Little Rock C. of C., Am. Law Inst., ABA, Ark. Bar Assn. (past chmn. exec. com., past chmn. young lawyers sect.), Sebastian County Bar Assn., Fifty for the Future, Am. Trial Lawyers Assn., Phi Beta Kappa, Phi Eta Sigma, Omicron Delta Kappa, Sigma Alpha Epsilon. Methodist. Estate taxation, Real property. Office: Fairfield Communities Inc 2800 Cantrell Rd Little Rock AR 72203

WARNER, EDWARD WAIDE, JR., lawyer; b. St. Louis, Oct. 17, 1951; s. Edward Waide Sr. and Barbara (Hardy) W.; m. Cecilia Tso, Oct. 1, 1983; 1 child, Edward Waide. AB magna cum laude, Boston Coll., 1973; JD, Rutgers U., 1977; postgrad., U. Chgo., 1974. Bar: Mo. 1978, N.Y. 1980. Law clk. to presiding justice U.S. Ct. Appeals (8th cir.), St. Louis, 1977-78; assoc. Davis, Polk & Wardwell, N.Y.C., 1978-85, ptnr., 1986—. Mem. ABA, Assn. of Bar of City of N.Y., Mo. Bar Assn. Roman Catholic. General corporate, Banking, Securities. Home: 67 E 11th St New York NY 10003 Office: Davis Polk & Wardwell 1 Chase Manhattan Plaza New York NY 10005

WARNER, TEDDY FLEMING, lawyer; b. Findlay, Ohio, Jan. 3, 1932; s. Freeman Dininger and Marjorie (Fleming) W.; m. Carolyn Jean Warner, June 12, 1958; children—Wendy Ann, Randall Scott. A.A., Phoenix Coll., 1955; B.A. with distinction, Ariz. State U., 1956; J.D., U. Ariz., 1959. Bar: Ariz. 1959, U.S. Dist. Ct. Ariz. 1959, U.S. Supreme Ct. 1971. Ptnr. Warner Angle Roper & Hallam P.C. and predecessors, Phoenix, 1962—; sr. ptnr., pres., 1982—; lectr. legal econs. and pro bono legal services to poor programs. Bd. dirs. Phoenix and Valley of Sun YMCA, 1970-84, pres., 1977; bd. dirs. Sagauro-Grand Canyon chpt. March of Dimes/Birth Defects Found., 1968-82, chmn., 1972-73, state chmn., 1974-82, mem. nat. council chpt. vols., 1979-82; bd. dirs. Vol. Bur., 1975; life mem. Fiesta Bowl Com., 1979-84; chmn. bd. trustees Ariz. Perinatal Trust, 1980—; mem. Ariz. Acad.; state chmn. Reps. for re-election of Sen. Dennis DeConcini, 1982; mem. State-wide Com. Fairminded Arizonans for Integrity in Representation; bd. visitors Ariz. State U. Sch. Law, 1979—; mem Ariz. Supreme Ct. Com. on Fitness and Character, 1983—. Served with USAF, 1951-54. Fellow Am. Bar Found., Ariz. Bar Found. (founding); mem. Maricopa County Bar Assn. (pres., dir. 1981), State Bar Ariz. (chmn. com. on del. legal services com.), ABA (ho. of dels. 1981—, delivery legal services com.), Ariz. State Law Soc., Law Coll. Assn. U. Ariz., Phi Delta Phi, Delta Sigma Phi. Republican. Clubs: Ariz. Country, Ariz. (sec., dir. 1971-73), Pinetop Country, Phoenix Country. General corporate, Real property. Office: 3550 N Central Ave Suite 1700 Phoenix AZ 85012

WARNER, WILLIAM MILLARD, lawyer; b. West Point, Ga., Sept. 25, 1946; s. Jarrel Millard and Rochelle (Seagraves) W.; m. Carol Lynn Struble, Mar. 21, 1970; children: Stuart Ryan, Whitman Kent. BA in History, Emory U., 1968, JD, 1971. Bar: Ga. 1973, U.S. Dist. Ct. (no. and mid. dists.) Ga., U.S. Ct. Appeals (11th cir.). Trial lawyer DeKalb Pub. Defenders Office, Decatur, Ga., 1973-75; ptnr. Warner and Lloyd, Atlanta, 1975-78; assoc. Garland, Nichols et al, Atlanta, 1978-80; sole practice Atlanta, 1980—. Served with U.S. Army, 1968-74. Mem. Ga. Bar Assn., Atlanta Bar Assn., Am. Trial Lawyers Assn., Ga. Assn. Criminal Lawyers. Democrat. Methodist. Avocations: tennis, jogging, travel, reading, weight lifting. Criminal, Federal civil litigation, State civil litigation. Office: 504 Grant Bldg 44 Broad St Atlanta GA 30303

WARNLOF, JOHN SKINNER, lawyer; b. Fairmont, Minn., Aug. 5, 1945. Student, U. Glasgow, Scotland, 1965-66; AB, Claremont-McKenna Coll., 1967; JD, U. Calif., San Francisco, 1972. Assoc. Bledsoe, Smith, Cathcart, Boyd & Eliot, San Francisco, 1972-78; regional counsel Am. Arbitration Assn., San Francisco, 1978; assoc. Long & Levit, San Francisco, 1978-81; ptnr. Nelson & Warnlof, Danville, Calif., 1981—. Author: (with others) Practicing California Judicial Arbitration, 1983; contbr. articles to profl. jours. Served to capt. U.S. Army, 1967-69. Mem. ABA, Calif. Bar

Assn., Calif. Trial Lawyers Assn., Assn. Def. Counsel of Northern Calif., Am. Arbitration Assn. (adv. council Northern Calif.), Phi Delta Phi. Democrat. Club: St. Francis Yacht (San Francisco). Real property, State civil litigation, Personal injury. Office: Nelson & Warnlof 177 Front St Suite L Danville CA 94526

WARNOCK, CURTLON LEE, lawyer, consultant; b. Mpls., Nov. 30, 1954; s. Lowell Wayne and Peggy Joan (Teague) W.; m. DeAnn Douthit, Feb. 3, 1979; children: Curtlon Lee II, Joshua Douthit, Vanessa Ann. Student, Baylor U., 1973-77, JD, 1979. Bar: Tex. 1979, U.S. Dist. Ct. (so. dist.) Tex. 1981, U.S. Supreme Ct. 1986. Assoc. Culpepper & Conway, Houston, 1979-81; atty. Pogo Producing Co., Houston, 1981-86; sr. atty. Meridian Oil Inc., Houston, 1986—. Editor newspaper First Amendment, 1978. Mem. Com. for Pub. Info. Radio Show, Waco, Tex., 1978; bd. dirs., cons. Acad. Devel. Service, Inc., Houston, 1979—; counselor Baylor U. Law Sch., Waco, 1980; bd. dirs. Hugh O'Brien Youth Found., Houston, 1982-83. Nat. Merit scholar, Baylor U., 1973. Mem. ABA, Houston Bar Assn., Tex. Bar Assn., Houston Young Lawyers, Houston Jaycees (bd. dirs., legal counsel 1979-82). Republican. Baptist. Avocations: computers, swimming. State civil litigation, General corporate, Oil and gas leasing. Home: 8215 Town Creek Dr Houston TX 77095 Office: Meridian Oil Inc 2919 Allen Pkwy Suite 1000 Houston TX 77210

WARNOCK, WILLIAM REID, lawyer; b. Detroit, Mich., July 25, 1939; s. William G. and Margery E. (Ford) W.; m. Sanrda L. Klarich, Dec. 27, 1961; children: Cheryl Lynn, Laura Ellyn. BBA, U. Mich., 1961, JD with distinction, 1964. Bar: Ill. 1964, U.S. Dist. Ct. (no. dist.) Ill. 1965, U.S. Supreme Ct. 1972. With Ross & Hardies, Chgo., 1964-70; regional counsel U.S. Dept. HUD, Chgo., 1970-73; ptnr. Roan & Grossman, Chgo., 1973-82; sole practice Chgo., 1982-85; ptnr. Siegel & Warnock, Chgo., 1985—; cons. Ill. Dept. Bus. and Econ. Devel., Chgo., 1977-78, Ill. Housing Devel. Authority, Chgo., 1973-78, Council State Housing Financing Agys., Washington, 1975-78; pres., chmn. Atty.'s Title Guaranty Fund, Inc., Chgo., 1986—; also bd. dirs. Author: (legal references) Land Use and Zoning, 1974-86, Ward on Title Examination, 1975; editor Zoning Digest, 1968; assoc. editor U. Mich. Law Review, 1963-64. Mem. ABA, Ill. State Bar Assn., Chgo. Bar Assn., Am. Coll. Real Estate Lawyers. Republican. Methodist. Club: Union League (Chgo). Avocations: boating, woodworking. Real property, Local government, General corporate. Home: 165 Briarwood N Oak Brook IL 60521-8720

WARREN, ALVIN CLIFFORD, JR., lawyer, educator; b. Daytona Beach, Fla., May 14, 1944; s. Alvin Clifford and Barbara (Barnes) W.; m. Judith Blatt, Aug. 20, 1966; children—Allison, Matthew. B.A., Yale U., 1966; J.D., U. Chgo., 1969. Bar: Conn. 1970, Pa. 1975. Prof. law U. Conn.-West Hartford, 1969-73, Duke U., Durham, N.C., 1973-74, U. Pa., Phila., 1974-79, Harvard U. Law Sch., Cambridge, Mass., 1979—. Mem. ABA (tax sect.). Contbr. articles to law jours. Corporate taxation, Estate taxation, Personal income taxation. Office: Harvard U Law Sch Cambridge MA 02138 *

WARREN, BRUCE WILLARD, lawyer; b. Creighton, Nebr., Dec. 27, 1949; s. Merritt C. and Geraldine R. (Gillespie) W.; m. Susan L. Curtis, Nov. 26, 1971 (div. 1977); m. Susan L. Beck, Oct. 8, 1978; children: Randi S., Michael M. BA, U. Nebr., 1972, JD, 1974. Bar: Nebr. 1975, Colo. 1975, U.S. Dist. Ct. Colo. 1975, U.S. Ct. Appeals (10th cir.) 1975, U.S. Dist. Ct. Nebr. 1976. Ptnr. Sloat & Warren, Boulder, Colo., 1975; sole practice Niwot, Colo., 1975-78, 80-83; ptnr. Warren & Oliver, Niwot, 1978-80, Warren & Marek, Niwot, 1984-86, Warren & Carlson, Niwot, 1987—. Author: Town & Country Profiles, 1974. Officer Niwot Vol. Fire Dept., 1978-84, Nowot United Meth. Ch., 1975—, chmn. com.; precinct committeeman Boulder County Dems., Colo., 1983-85; com. chmn., organizer Niwot Community Assn., 1984—; bd. dirs. Niwot Baseball Inc., 1982—, Gunbarrell Lefthand Valley Recreation Assn., Niwot, 1982—. Mem. ABA, Colo. Bar Assn., Boulder County Bar Assn. Democrat. Avocation: baseball. Juvenile, Real property, General practice. Home: 7321 Dry Creek Rd Longmont CO 80501 Office: Warren & Carlson 210 Franklin PO Box 610 Niwot CO 80544

WARREN, HERBERT ALBERT, lawyer; b. Birmingham, Ala., Dec. 18, 1922; s. Herbert Allen and Virginia (Price) W.; m. Marjorie Mathis, June 6, 1953; children—Richard Alan, Pamela Jayne. B.S., U. Chgo., 1947; J.D., U. Miami, 1951. Bar: Fla. 1951, U.S. Dist. Ct. (so. dist.) Fla. 1951, U.S. Ct. Appeals (11th cir.) 1951, U.S. Supreme Ct. 1960. Ptnr., Carr & Warren, Miami, Fla., 1951-74; pres. Herbert A. Warren, P.A., Miami, 1974—; lectr. law U. Miami. Served to capt. AC, U.S. Army, 1943-46. Mem. ABA, Fla. Bar, Dade County Bar Assn., Assn. Trial Lawyers Am., Fla. Trial Lawyers Assn. Presbyterian. Clubs: Miami Shores Country (Miami); Bath, LaGorce Country, Com. of 100 (Miami Beach); Kiwanis, Lions (Miami Shores). General practice, Federal civil litigation, State civil litigation. Office: 1401 Brickell Ave Miami FL 33131

WARREN, JEFFREY WAYNE, lawyer; b. Jersey City, Jan. 7, 1948; s. Joseph D. and Betty E. (Dye) W.; m. Susan Piercy, Sept. 6, 1972; children: Matthew Justin, David Andrew, Laura Elizabeth. Bar: Fla. 1972, U.S. Dist. Ct. (mid. and so. dists.) Fla. 1972, U.S. Ct. Appeals (5th and 11th cirs.) 1972. From assoc. to ptnr. MacFarlane, Ferguson, Allison & Kelly, Tampa, Fla., 1972-81; ptnr. Bush, Ross, Gardner, Warren & Rudy, Tampa, 1981—. Bd. dirs. law ctr. council U. Fla., Gainesville, 1981-86. Mem. ABA, Fla. Bar Assn. (consumer protection com., chmn. 1979-80), Hillsborough County Bar Assn. (pres. young lawyers sect. 1979-80, chmn. corp., banking and bus. law sect. 1984-85). Democrat. Baptist. Club: Tampa (Fla.) Gator (pres. 1978). Bankruptcy, Commercial collections, Real property. Home: 124 Hickory Creek Blvd Brandon FL 33511 Office: Bush Ross Gardner Warren & Rudy 220 S Franklin St Tampa FL 33602

WARREN, JOHN PHILIP, JR., lawyer; b. Boulder, Colo., Feb. 8, 1946; s. John Philip and Eileen Patricia (Bolton) W.; m. Pamela Dianne Warren, Aug. 11, 1968; children—Scott, Melissa. Student U.S. Mcht. Marine Acad., 1963-64; B.A., Seton Hall U., 1967; postgrad. Sophia U., Tokyo, 1968-69; J.D., Stetson U., 1972. Bar: Fla. 1972, N.J. 1972, N.Y. 1976, Mich. 1984. Hearing examiner N.J. Pub. Utilities Commn., Newark, 1972-75; atty. AT&T Long Lines, Bedminster, N.J., 1975-78; legal adv. Parsons-Jurden Internat. Corp., Teheran, Iran, 1978-79, Saudi-Arabian Parsons Ltd., Jeddah, Saudi Arabia, 1979-81; prin. contract adminstr., atty. The Ralph M. Parsons Co., Pasadena, Calif., 1982-84; dir. contract adminstrn. Williams Internat. Corp., Walled Lake, Mich., 1984-86; sole practice, 1986—; guest lectr. Wayne State U. Law Sch, Pepperdine U., UCLA, U. Detroit Law Sch. Mem. Sparta Twp. (N.J.) Com. Comml. and Indsl. Devel., 1978. Served to maj. USAR, 1967—. Inst. Far Eastern Studies fellow, 1967. Mem. ABA, Fed. Bar Assn., Fla. Bar, Mich. Bar Assn., N.Y. State Bar Assn. Republican. Roman Catholic. Federal civil litigation, State civil litigation, Probate. Home: 29810 Deer Run Farmington Hills MI 48018 Office: 1520 N Woodward Ave Suite 106 Bloomfield Hills MI 48013

WARREN, LISBETH ANN, lawyer; b. Trenton, N.J., Feb. 26, 1953; d. George and Clarice (Kramer) W. BA, Wash. U., 1974; JD, NYU, 1978. Bar: N.J. 1979, U.S. Dist. Ct. N.J. 1979. Law clk. to judge State Supr. Ct. of N.J., Newark, 1978-79; assoc. Shanley & Fisher, P.C., Morristown, N.J., 1979-85, Johnson & Johnson, New Brunswick, N.J., 1985—. Contbr. articles to profl. jours. Mem. Supreme Ct. Jud. Coll. and Seminars Com., Trenton, N.J., 1984—. Mem. ABA, N.J. Bar Assn., Trial Attys. N.J. (trustee 1983-86). Avocations: theater, fiction, dance, travel, tennis. Personal injury, State civil litigation, Federal civil litigation. Office: Johnson & Johnson 1 Johnson & Johnson Plaza New Brunswick NJ 08933

WARREN, LOYDE HUGH, lawyer; b. Clinton, Okla., Apr. 18, 1939; s. Loyde Leon and Ruby Juanita (Hood) W.; m. Agnes Yolanda Galley, June 2, 1966; children: Lance, Wade. BS, Okla. State U., 1962; JD, U. Okla., 1969. Bar: Okla. 1969, U.S. Dist. Ct. (we. dist.) Okla. 1969, U.S. Ct. Appeals (10th cir.) 1980. Dep. sheriff Okla. County, 1967-69, asst. dist. atty., 1970-74; adminstrv. asst. dep. Okla. Dept. Pub. Safety, 1969-70; sole practice Oklahoma City, 1974—. Served to lt. USN, 1962-66. Mem. ABA, Okla. Bar Assn., Okla. County Bar, Am. Trial Lawyers Assn., Okla. Trial Lawyers Assn., Phi Alpha Delta. Democrat. Avocation: golf. Federal civil litigation, State civil litigation, Criminal. Home: 2917 Cedar Oak Dr Edmond OK 73034 Office: 719 N Shartel Oklahoma City OK 73102

WARREN, MANNING GILBERT, III, lawyer, legal educator; b. Dothan, Ala., Aug. 20, 1948; s. Linton Collins and Martha Jane (Faulkner) W.; m. Tanja Eikenboom; children: Catherine Lake, Bevelle Comer, Jennis Faulkner. BA, U. Ala., 1970; JD, George Washinton U., 1973. Bar: D.C. 1973, Ala. 1974, U.S. Supreme Ct. 1981. Law clk. to judge U.S. Dist. Ct., Birmingham, Ala., 1973-74; assoc. Bradley, Arant, Rose & White, Birmingham, 1974-76; ptnr. Ritchie, Rediker & Warren, Birmingham, 1976-83; prof. law U. Ala. Sch. of Law, Tuscaloosa, 1983—; vis. prof. George Washington U. Law Sch., Washington, 1984-85; reporter securities com. Ala. Law Inst., 1985—. Bd. dirs. Birmingham chpt. ARC, 1976-84; pres., bd. dirs. Birmingham Area Legal Services Corp., 1981-84; sr. advisor internat. services ARC, Washington, 1985—, bd. of govs., 1985—. Mem. ABA (state liaison com. on securities regulation). Avocation: poetry. Securities, Contracts commercial, Public international. Home: 27 Edwardian Pl Northport AL 35476 Office: U Ala Sch of Law PO Box 1435 Tuscaloosa AL 35487

WARREN, RICHARD DEXTER, lawyer; b. Washington, Aug. 15, 1941; s. Walter Dexter and Lillian (Stelzer) W.; m. Sharon MAe Blevins, Oct. 6, 1973 (div. Oct. 1981); 1 child, Jennifer. BA, U. of South, 1963; JD with honors, George Washington U., 1966. Asst. state's atty. Prince Georges County, Upper Marlboro, Md., 1971-72, Wicomico County, Salisbury, Md., 1972-74; state's atty. Wicomico County, 1975—; ptnr. Jacob & Warren, Salisbury, 1974-76. Served to capt. USAF, 1966-71. Mem. ABA, Md. State Bar Assn., Wicomico County Bar Assn., Nat. Dist. Attys. Assn., Md. State's Atty. Assn. (bd. dirs. 1975—, v.p. 1977-78). Episcopalian. Lodge: Lions (pres Allen, Md. club 1976). Criminal. Office: Wicomico County Courthouse Salisbury MD 21801

WARREN, RICHARD FENTON, JR., lawyer; b. Nashville, Sept. 24, 1951; s. Richard Fenton Sr. and Kathryn Lorene (Wilson) W.; m. Catherine Ashley Lawrence, June 3, 1974; children: John Richardson, Stephen Fenton. BA, Birmingham So. Coll., 1973; JD, Vanderbilt U., 1976. Bar: Tenn. 1976, U.S. Ct. Appeals (6th cir.) 1977, U.S. Dist. Ct. (mid. dist.) Tenn. 1978. Ptnr. Boult, Cummings, Conners & Berry, Nashville, 1976—. Mem. ABA, Tenn. Bar Assn., Nashville Bar Assn. Democrat. Presbyterian. Real property, Securities, General corporate. Office: Boult Cummings Conners & Berry 222 3d Ave N Nashville TN 37219

WARREN, ROBERT WILLIS, judge; b. Raton, N.M., Aug. 30, 1925; s. George R. and Clara (Jolliffe) W.; m. Laverne D. Voagen, Aug. 23, 1947; children: Cheryl Lynn, Iver Eric, Gregg Alan, Treiva Mae, Lyle David, Tara Rae. B.A. magna cum laude, Macalester Coll., 1950; M.A., U. Minn., 1951; J.D., U. Wis., 1956; postgrad., Fgn. Service Inst., 1951-52. Bar: Wis. 1956. Fgn. affairs officer U.S. Dept. State, 1951-53; mem. firm Godfrey, Godfrey & Warren, Elkhorn, 1956-57; ptnr. firm Warren & Boltz, Attys., Green Bay, 1957-59, Smith, Will & Warren, 1965-69; asst. dist. atty. Brown County, Wis., 1959-61; dist. atty. 1961-65; mem. Wis. Senate, 1965-69; atty. gen. Wis., 1969-74; U.S. dist. judge Milw., 1974—; Mem. Gt. Lakes Commn., Wis. Council on Criminal Justice, Wis. Bd. Commrs. Pub. Lands, Four Lakes council Boy Scouts Am., Wis. Controlled Substances Bd., Wis. Council on Drug Abuse, Wis. State Urban Affairs. Served with AUS, 1943-46, ETO. Decorated Purple Heart. Mem. ABA, Wis. Bar Assn., Nat. Assn. Attys. Gen. (pres. 1973-74), Midwestern Conf. Attys. Gen., Wis. Dist. Attys. Assn., VFW, DAV. Republican. Methodist. Club: Optimist. Jurisprudence. Office: U S Dist Ct 364 U S Courthouse 517 E Wisconsin Ave Milwaukee WI 53202 *

WARREN, WILLIAM CLEMENTS, lawyer, educator; b. Paris, Tex., Feb. 3, 1909; s. Archibald Levy and Elma (Clements) W.; m. Diana June Peel Willock, Jan. 13, 1945; children—Robert Peel, Larissa Eve, William Liversidge. A.B., U. Tex., 1930, A.M., 1931; LL.B., Harvard U., 1935; LL.D. (hon.), L.I. U., 1955, Columbia U., 1981; Dr. rer. pol., U. Basle, 1965. Bar: Ohio 1937, N.Y. 1952, D.C. 1959. Assoc. Davis, Polk & Wardwell, N.Y.C., 1935-37; assoc. Holiday, Grossman & McAfee, Cleve., 1937-42; assoc. Milbank, Tweed, Hadley & McCloy, N.Y.C., 1942-47; prof. law Western Res. U., Cleve., 1937-42; mem. faculty Columbia Law Sch., N.Y.C., 1946-82, Kent prof. law, 1959-77, Kent prof. emeritus, 1977—, dean, 1952-70, dean emeritus, 1970—; ptnr. Roberts & Holland, N.Y.C., 1957—; dir. Bankers Securities Corp., Guardian Life Ins. Co. Am., Sandoz, Inc., Sandoz United States, Inc., Sterling Nat. Bank & Trust Co. N.Y.C.; mem. N.Am. adv. bd. Swissair. Served as lt. col. U.S. Army, 1943-46. Decorated Bronze Star (2), Legion of Merit; comdr. Order of the Crown (Italy); recipient Medal for execellence Columbia Law Sch. Alumni Assn., 1969. Mem. ABA, Am. Judicature Soc., Am. Law Inst., Assn. Bar City N.Y., N.Y. County Lawyers Assn., N.Y. State Bar Assn., Inst. Internat. Edn. (trustee), Order Moral Scis. (fgn. corr.), Accademia delle Scienze dell' Instituto di Bologna (fgn. corr. mem.; Order Moral Scis. 1971). Presbyterian. Clubs: Broad Street, Century Assn., Cosmos, Links, Metropolitan, Univ. Co-author: U.S. Income Taxation of Foreign Corporations and Nonresident Aliens, 1966; Cases and Materials on Accounting and the Law, 1978; Cases and Materials on Federal Wealth Transfer Taxation, 1982; Cases and Materials on Federal Income Taxation, Vol. I, 1972, supplement, 1983, Vol. II, 1980. General corporate, Estate planning, Corporate taxation. Home: 325 Crest Rd Ridgewood NJ 07450 Office: 30 Rockefeller Plaza New York NY 10112

WARREN, WILLIAM DAVID, educator; b. Mt. Vernon, Ill., Nov. 13, 1924; s. Arthur and Dorothy Davis (Phillips) W.; m. Susan C. Audren, Nov. 15, 1965; children—John David, Sarah Hartwell. A.B., U. Ill., 1948, J.D., 1950; J.S.D., Yale U., 1957. Asst. prof. law Vanderbilt U., 1951-53, Ohio State U., 1953-54; asst. prof., then assoc. prof., prof. law U. Ill., 1954-59; prof. law UCLA, 1959-72, 75—; dean UCLA (Law Sch.), 1975-82; William Benjamin Scott and Luna M. Scott prof. law Stanford, 1972-75; Cons. Fed. Res. Bd. (chmn. consumer adv. council 1979-80), Nat. Commn. on Consumer Fin., Calif. Legislature, Calif. Law Revision Commn., Nat. Conf. Commrs. Uniform State Laws, 1964-74, 85—. Co-author: California Commercial Law III, 1966, Attorney's Guide to Truth in Lending, 1968, Cases and Materials on Debtor Creditor Law, 2d edit, 1981, Commercial Law, 1983, Bankruptcy, 1985. Served with USAAF, 1943-45. Mem. ABA, Order of Coif, Phi Beta Kappa, Phi Kappa Phi, Phi Delta Phi. Legal education. Office: U Calif Law Sch Los Angeles CA 90024

WARREN, WILLIAM GERALD, lawyer; b. Detroit, Apr. 22, 1930; s. William Grant and Margaret Kathryn (Matthews) W.; m. Martha Elsie Artz, Apr. 20, 1974; children—Mary Katharine, Elizabeth Barrett. A.B. with honors, U. Mich., 1952, LL.B. (Frederick L. Leckie scholar), 1955. Bar: Mich. bar 1956. Asso. firm Dickinson, Wright, Moon, Van Dusen & Freeman, Detroit, 1955-63, partner, 1964—; dir. Mackinac Corp., V.G. Nahrgang Co.; gen. counsel, sec. bd. Detroit Fed. Savs. and Loan Assn. Contbr. articles to profl. jours. Mem. Wayne County (Mich.) Grievance Com., 1966—; spl. counsel 4-H Found. Mich., 1966-68. Recipient Henry M. Campbell award, 1954, Roberts P. Hudson award State Bar Mich., 1978. Fellow Am. Coll. Trial Lawyers, Internat. Soc. Barristers, Am. Bar Found.; mem. Phi Beta Kappa, Phi Kappa Phi, Pi Sigma Alpha, Phi Alpha Delta. Republican. Roman Catholic. Clubs: Detroit, University, Otsego Ski. Federal civil litigation, State civil litigation, Banking. Office: Dickinson Wright Moon Van Dusen & Freeman 800 First Nat Bldg Detroit MI 48226

WARREN, WILLIAM ZIEGLER, lawyer, businessman, investor, consultant, engineer; b. Lebanon, Pa., Apr. 18, 1935; s. Lester Henry and Kathryn Sarah (Ziegler) W. B.S. in Engring. Sci., Pa. State U., 1963; M.S. in Mgmt. Sci. and Applied Physics, Cornell U., 1966; J.D., U. Md., 1971; cert. in acctg. U. Calif.-Berkeley, 1983. Bar: Pa. 1971, U.S. Dist. Ct. (ea. dist.) Pa. 1972, U.S. Patent Office 1973, U.S. Supreme Ct. 1975, U.S. Ct. Appeals (fed. cir.) 1982. Engr.-in-tng. Western Electric Co., Laureldale and Reading, Pa., 1962; research teaching asst. Cornell U., Ithaca, N.Y., 1963-65; sci. systems analyst Armstrong World Industries, Lancaster, Pa., 1966-68; engr. guided missile systems Vitro Labs, Silver Spring, Md., 1968-69; sole practice, Bethel, Pa., 1969—; cons., software developer, real estate broker; instr. bus. adminstrn. Pa. State U., Schuylkill Haven, 1973. Author software package: Comput-Appraise (TM), 1984. Served with U.S. Army, 1957. Recipient Carnegie scholarship, Pa. State U., 1960, Engring. award, 1961; Am. Jurisprudence award U. Md., 1969. Sr. mem. Am. Inst. Indsl. Engrs.; mem. Pa. Bar Assn., ABA, Fed. Bar Assn., Cornell Soc. Engrs., Inst. Mgmt. Scis., Ops. Research Soc. Am., Pi Mu Epsilon, Sigma Pi Sigma, Sigma Tau, Tau Beta Pi. Republican. Patent, Trademark and copyright, General corporate. Home: RD 1 Box 1091 Bethel PA 19507 Office: RD 1 Box 1091 Bethel PA 19507

WARRICK, RICHARD LLOYD, lawyer; b. Santa Rita, N.Mex. Nov. 10, 1940; s. Stuart Claire and Margaret Frances (Cross) W.; m. Veronica Collazo, Apr. 13, 1963 (div. Oct. 5, 1975); m. Marcia Lucille Ponas, Mar. 28, 1978 (dec. Jan. 1985). B.A. summa cum laude, U. Hawaii, 1967; J.D., Georgetown U., 1974; postgrad. McGill U., 1977-78. Bar: Va. 1975, Okla. 1982, U.S. Dist. Ct. (ea. dist.) Va. 1975, (we., no. and ea. dists.) Okla. 1982, U.S. Ct. Appeals (10th cir.) 1984, U.S. Supreme Ct. 1978. Mem. military intelligence Pentagon, Washington, 1967-74; sr. staff atty. Adminstrn. Office U.S. Cts., Washington, 1975-77; chief, aviation law sect. Hdqrs. Air Force Judge Advocate Gen., Washington, 1978-82; assoc. Looney, Nichols, Johnson & Hayes, Oklahoma City, Okla., 1982-86, v.p., gen. counsel Aviation Office Am., Inc., Dallas, 1986—. Served to staff sgt. USAF, 1959-63, Korea. Mem. ABA, Va. State Bar Assn., Internat. Bar Assn., Okla. State Bar Assn., Lawyer-Pilots Bar Assn., Internat. Law Assn., Internatl. Soc. Air Safety Investigators, Okla. Assn. Defense Counsel, Okla. County Bar Assn., Aircraft Owners and Pilots Assn., Okla. Pilots Assn., Nat. Transp. Safety Bd. Bar Assn., Am. Yankee Assn. Federal civil litigation, State civil litigation, Insurance. Home: 17409 Oakington Ct Dallas TX 75248 Office: Aviation Office of Am Love Field Terminal Bldg Dallas TX 75235

WARRINGTON, JOHN WESLEY, lawyer; b. Cin., June 6, 1914; s. George Howard and Eliza (Holmes) W.; m. Suzanne Mooney, May 5, 1951; children—Anne McGrath Warrington Wilson, George Howard, John Wesley, Mary Warrington Cassidy, Elizabeth Warrington Ott, Sarah Warrington Selnick, Rachel Gaff. A.B., Yale U., 1936; postgrad., Cambridge (Eng.) U., 1937; LL.B., Harvard U., 1940; D.F.A. (hon.), U. Cin., 1980. Bar: Ohio 1940. Since practiced in Cin.; ptnr. Graydon, Head & Ritchey, 1951—; dir. emeritus Fifth Third Bank. Chmn. planning commn., Indian Hill, Ohio, 1959-86; pres. emeritus Cin. Music Hall; chmn. Cin. Mus. Assn.; trustee emeritus Cin. Union Bethel, Am. Schs. Oriental Research, Seven Hills Schs., Cin. Natural History Mus.; trustee Cin. Inst. Fine Arts. Served to capt. Am. Field Service, 1942-45. Mentioned in dispatches Brit.). Mem. Am., Ohio, Cin. bar assns., Phi Beta Kappa. Republican. Episcopalian. Estate planning, Probate, Banking. Home: 8625 Camargo Dr Cincinnati OH 45243 Office: 1900 Fifth-Third Center PO Box 6464 Cincinnati OH 45201

WARSHAFSKY, TED M., lawyer; b. St. Louis, Dec. 6, 1926; s. Israel and Ida (Wacks) W.; m. Dolores Anne Weiss, July 10, 1971 (div. April 1983); children: Beth, Michael, Lynn, Lisabeth, William. BBA, U. Wis., 1949, JD, 1952. Bar: Wis. 1952, U.S. Dist. Ct. (we. and ea. dists.) Wis. 1952, U.S. Ct. Appeals (7th cir.) 1952, U.S. Supreme Ct. 1974. Sr. ptnr. Warshafsky Law Firm, Milw., 1952-72; pres. Warshafsky, Rotter, Tarnoff, Gesler, Reinhardt & Bloch, S.C., Milw., 1972—. Author: Trial Handbook for Wisconsin Lawyers; contbr. articles to profl. jours. Pres. Wis. Civil Liberties Union, Milw., 1964; bd. dirs. trial lawyers for pub. justice Citizens Legal Clinic, 1981—. Served to pvt. 1st class USMC, 1944-46, PTO. Fellow Internat. Soc. of Barristers, Internat. Acad. Trial Lawyers; mem. Am. Bd. of Profl. Liability Attys. (bd. dirs. 1980—), Inner Circle of Advs., Assn. Trial Lawyers Am. (past nat. sec.). Democrat. Jewish. State civil litigation, Personal injury. Office: Warshafsky Rotter Tarnoff Gesler Reinhardt & Bloch 839 N Jefferson St Milwaukee WI 53202-3796

WARSHAUER, IRENE CONRAD, lawyer; b. N.Y.C., May 4, 1942; d. A. Alfred and Sylvia (Bober) Conrad; m. Alan M. Warshauer, Nov. 27, 1966; 1 dau., Susan L. B.A. with distinction, U. Mich., 1963; LL.B. cum laude, Columbia U., 1966. Bar: N.Y. 1966, U.S. Supreme Ct. 1972. With First Jud. Dept., N.Y. State Mental Health Info. Service, 1966-68; assoc. Chadbourne Parke Whiteside & Wolff, 1968-75; mem. Anderson Russell Kill & Olick, P.C., N.Y.C., 1975—; lectr. Def. Research Inst., Aspen Inst. Humanistic Studies, ABA, Rocky Mountain Mineral Law Found., panelist Am. Arbitration Assn., 1973—. Contbr. articles, chpts. to profl. lit. Mem. Democratic County Com., 1968—. Mem. Assn. of Bar of City of N.Y. (judiciary com. 1982-84), N.Y. State Bar Assn. (chairperson subcom. mentally disabled and community 1978-82), ABA. Federal civil litigation, Product liability, Insurance. Office: 666 3d Ave New York NY 10017

WARSHAUER, IRVING JAY, lawyer; b. New Orleans, May 11, 1950; s. Sigmund and Anita Beatrice (Wolff) W. BA, U. N.C., 1972; JD, Tulane U., 1976. Bar: La. 1976, U.S. Dist. Ct. (ea. dist.) La. 1977, U.S. Ct. Appeals (5th cir.) 1978, U.S. Dist. Ct. (we. dist.) La. 1982, U.S. Dist. Ct. (mid. dist.) La. 1986. Asst. U.S. atty. Dept. of Justice, New Orleans, 1977-78; trial atty. U.S. Dept. of Justice, New Orleans, 1978-80; ptnr. Kierr, Gainsburgh et al, New Orleans, 1980—. Pres. East Riverside Neighborhood Assn., New Orleans, 1985—. Served with USCGR, 1972-78. Mem. La. Bar Assn. (award of Appreciation 1986), New Orleans Bar Assn., Assn. Trial Lawyers Am. (sustaining), La. Trial Lawyers Assn. (life), Phi Beta Kappa. Personal injury, Criminal. Office: Kierr Gainsburgh et al 210 Baronne St FNBC Bldg Suite 1718 New Orleans LA 70112

WARSHAVSKY, SUZANNE MAY, lawyer; b. N.Y.C., July 22, 1944; d. Charles Fincke and Charlotte (Ceaser) Goldman; m. Mordechai Warshavsky, June 7, 1964; children—Oren Jay, Adam Stuart, Claire Faye. A.B., Vassar Coll., 1965; J.D. NYU, 1968. Bar: N.Y. 1968, U.S. Dist. Ct. (so. and ea. dists.) 1972, U.S. Ct. Appeals (2d cir.) 1972, U.S. Supreme Ct. 1973. Assoc., Dewey, Ballantine, Bushby, Palmer & Wood, N.Y.C., 1968-73; assoc. Milgrim Thomajan Jacobs & Lee, P.C., N.Y.C., 1973-76; ptnr. Warshavsky, Hoffman & Cohen, P.C., N.Y.C., 1976—. Arbitrator, Civil Ct. of N.Y.C., 1975-86. Mem. ABA, N.Y. State Bar Assn. (pub. health com.), Assn. Bar City N.Y. (profl. and judicial ethics com.) N.Y. Women's Bar Assn. (chair com. on profl. ethics & discipline, mem. com. on bus. and tax laws), Am. Arbitration Assn. (panel comml. arbitrators), Mag. Pubs. Assn. (legal affairs com.). Contracts commercial, General corporate, Trademark and copyright. Home: 158 Gates Ave Montclair NJ 07042 Office: Warshavsky Hoffman & Cohen PC 500 Fifth Ave New York NY 10010

WARSHAW, MICHAEL THOMAS, lawyer; b. Jersey City, June 29, 1950; s. Thomas T. and June C. (Lancaster) W.; m. Mary Jane Egidio, July 12, 1986. BA in Sociology, Coll. of the Holy Cross, 1972; JD, Bklyn. Law Sch., 1975. Bar: N.J. 1976, U.S. Dist. Ct. N.J. 1976, U.S. Ct. Appeals (3d cir.) 1982, U.S. Supreme Ct. 1982. Law sec. to judge N.J. Supreme Ct., Jersey City, 1975-76; assoc. Drazin & Warshaw PC, Red Bank, N.J., 1976—; moderator, speaker Mock Trial Sem., Young Lawyers div. N.J. Bar Assn., 1984, Discovery Sem., 1986; speaker Home Buyer's Sem., 1986, Monmouth City Library Ask a Lawyer program, 1986; lectr. Am. Paralegal Inst.; mem. com. on mcpl. cts. N.J. Supreme Ct., 1984—. atty., advisor CBA mock trial team; trustee Long Branch (N.J.) Dem. Club, 1978-81; mem. St. Leo's Holy Name Soc., Lincroft, N.J., 1986—. Mem. ABA, Assn. Trial Lawyers Am., N.J. Bar Assn. (young lawyers div., exec. com. 1983-86), Monmouth County Bar Assn., Friendly Sons of St. Patrick of the Jersey Shore (trustee), Phi Delta Phi. Roman Catholic. Clubs: Beacon Hill Country (N.J.). Avocations: golf, skiing. State civil litigation, General practice, Real property. Home: 18 Quaker Rd Middletown NJ 07748 Office: 25 Reckless Pl Red Bank NJ 07701

WARTELLE, BARBARA LOUISA, lawyer; b. New Orleans, Sept. 30, 1954; d. Richard Cole and Ruth Druhan (Power) W.; m. Christopher Read Wall, June 21, 1980. BA, U. Va., 1976, JD, 1979. Bar: N.Y. 1980, U.S. Dist. Ct. (so. and ea. dists.) N.Y. 1980. Assoc. Satterlee & Stephens, N.Y.C., 1979-85; asst. gen. counsel Gannett Co., Inc., Arlington, Va., 1985—. Mem. ABA, N.Y. State Bar Assn., Assn. of Bar of City of N.Y. Republican. Roman Catholic. General corporate, Libel. Home: 5026 Tilden St NW Washington DC 20016 Office: Gannett Co Inc 1100 Wilson Blvd Arlington VA 22209

WARTMAN, CARL HENRY, lawyer; b. New Brunswick, N.J., Sept. 18, 1952; s. Lloyd Henry and Isabel (reynolds) W.; m. Vicky A. Slater, Oct. 9, 1983. BA, U. Chgo., 1974; JD, Loyola U., Chgo., 1979. Assoc. McDermott, Will & Emery, Chgo., 1979-85, ptnr., 1985—; bd. dirs. Quave Corp., Chgo. Mem. ABA, Chgo. Bar Assn. Club: Univ. (Chgo.). Contracts commercial, General corporate, Securities. Office: McDermott Will & Emery 111 W Monroe St Chicago IL 60603

WARWICK, CHARLES HENRY, III, lawyer; b. Nashville, June 4, 1924; s. Charles Henry and Elizabeth Clark (Culbert) W.; m. Elsie McCoy Cushman, Sept. 21, 1947; children—Charles Henry IV, Elizabeth Warwick Thebaut. Student U. N.C.-Chapel Hill, 1946-47; J.D., John B. Stetson U. Bar: Fla., U.S. Dist. Ct. (so. dist.) Fla., U.S. Tax Ct., U.S. Ct. Appeals (5th cir.), U.S. Supreme Ct. Ptnr. Warwick, Paul & Warwick, 1950-62; ptnr. Warwick, Paul & Herring, 1963-69; ptnr. Warwick Paul, Campbell & Shahady, 1970-73; ptnr. Warwick, Campbell & Hewitt, 1974-82; ptnr. Warwick & Campbell, 1982—; dir., chmn. trust com. Bank of Palm Beach & Trust Co. Mem. Palm Beach (Fla.) Town Council, 1977-84, pres., 1981-84; bd. govs. Good Samaritan Hosp., West Palm Beach, Fla., chmn., 1984; pres. West Palm Beach C. of C., 1979-80. Served to 2d lt. USAAC. Mem. ABA, Palm Beach County Bar Assn. (pres. 1956), Fla. Bar, Am. Judicature Soc. Clubs: Everglades, Sail Fish of Fla., Mayacoo Lakes Country, Tuscawilla, Elks, Masons, Shriners, Kiwanis (pres. club 1961). Estate planning, Probate, Estate taxation. Address: 218 Tangier Ave Palm Beach FL 33480

WARWICK, KATHLEEN ANN, corporate lawyer; b. Phila., Aug. 3, 1934; d. William and Mae Warwick. AB, Vassar Coll., 1956; LLB, Columbia U., 1963. Bar: N.Y. 1963, U.S. Dist. Ct. (ea. and so. dists.) N.Y. 1965, U.S. Ct. Appeals (2d cir.) 1966, U.S. Supreme Ct. 1973, U.S. Ct. Appeals (6th cir.) 1982. Atty. SEC, N.Y.C., 1965-69; assoc. Cadwalader, Wickersham & Taft, N.Y.C., 1969-75; corp. securities counsel Mobil Corp., N.Y.C., 1975-87; sole practice N.Y.C., 1986-87; regional adminstr. SEC, N.Y.C., 1987—; speaker Am. Law Inst., ABA, Fed. Bar Council, Harcourt Brace Jovanovich Publishing, others. Mem. adv. bd. Securities Regulation & Law Report, Bur. Nat. Affairs, Inc.; bd. contbg. editors and advisors Securities Regulation Law Journal. Mem. ABA (vice chmn. fed. reg. securities com. 1986—chmn. subcom. on reporting cos. under 1934 Act 1981-86, co-chmn. corp. counsel com. 1983-86, sect. coordinator for in-house counsel activities, numerous other coms., sects., exec. council, corp., banking and bus. law sect.), N.Y. State Bar Assn. (various coms.), Assn. Bar City N.Y. (adminstrv. law com. 1977-80, securities regulation com. 1982-85, chmn. subcom. on issuer regulation and periodic reporting 1984-85, corp. law com. 1985—, chmn. subcom. on programs 1986-87), Am. Law Inst., Fed. Bar Assn. (securities law com.), Fed. Bar Council (securities com.), Columbia U. Law Sch. Alumni Assn. (bd. dirs.). Republican. Clubs: India House, Vassar (N.Y.C.); Georgetown (Washington). General corporate, Securities. Home: 11 E 75th St New York NY 10021

WASCHER, JAMES DEGEN, lawyer, foundation executive; b. Chgo., Aug. 4, 1953; s. Gilbert Arthur and Virginia Ellen (Bowen) W. BA, Stanford U., 1975; JD, Northwestern U., 1978. Bar: Ill. 1983, U.S. Dist. Ct. (no. dist.) Ill. 1978, U.S. Ct. Appeals (7th cir.) 1981, U.S. Supreme Ct. 1981. Atty. James P. Chapman & Assocs., Ltd., Chgo., 1978-82, Phelan, Pope & John, Ltd., Chgo., 1982-85; exec. dir. Mayor Washington Fund, Chgo., 1985—; bd. dirs. Fund for Justice, Chgo., 1982—. Contbr. articles to law jours., 1978—. Mem. lawyers' adv. com. to housing unit Cook County Atty.'s Office, Chgo., 1981-82. Named one of the Outstanding Young Men of Am., 1982. Mem. ABA, Chgo. Bar Assn., Chgo. Council Lawyers (bd. govs. 1980-84, 85—, v.p. 1982-83). Democrat. Presbyterian. Club: Stanford (Kenilworth, Ill.)(pres. 1983-85). State civil litigation, Federal civil litigation. Home: 205 16th St Wilmette IL 60091 Office: Mayor Washington Fund 127 N Dearborn St Chicago IL 60602

WASHBURN, ROBERT BUCHANAN, patent lawyer; b. Syracuse, N.Y., Sept. 3, 1919; s. Louis Pierce and Lenore (Buchanan) W.; m. Nell Torrence, June 7, 1947; children—Robert Buchanan, Judith Ann. B.E.E., Kans. State U., 1941; student Georgetown U., 1946-48; J.D., Temple U., 1950. Bar: U.S. Dist. Ct. D.C. 1950, U.S. Ct. Appeals (D.C. cir.) 1950, U.S. Dist. Ct. (ea. dist.) Pa. 1950, U.S. Ct. Appeals (3d cir.) 1951, Pa. 1952, U.S. Supreme Ct. 1967, U.S. Ct. Appeals (Fed. cir.) 1982. Engr., Gen. Electric Co., Ft. Wayne, Ind., 1941-45, mem. patent dept. staff, 1946-48; patent lawyer Woodcock, Washburn, Kurtz, Mackiewicz & Norris, and predecessor firms, Phila., 1948-53 ptnr., 1953-70, sr. ptnr., 1970—; pres. Robert B. Washburn, P.C., 1979—. Mem. ABA, Phila. Bar Assn., Pa. Bar Assn., D.C. Bar Assn., Phila. Patent Law Assn., Am. Patent Law Assn., Delta Tau Delta, Delta Theta Phi, Eta Kappa Nu, Sigma Tau. Republican. Clubs: Union League, Waynesborough Country. Federal civil litigation, Patent, Trademark and copyright. Office: United Engring Bldg Suite 1800 Philadelphia PA 19103

WASHBURN, ROBERT MICHAEL, lawyer; b. Skowhegan, Maine, Jan. 15, 1955; s. Richard Charles Sr. and June Theresa (Beaulieu) W.; m. Pamela Jean York, Mar. 21, 1975; children: Gretchen, Seth. BA, U. Maine, 1977; JD, Vt. Law Sch., 1980. Bar: Maine 1980, U.S. Dist. Ct. Maine 1980. Assoc. Eames & Sterns, Skowhegan, 1980-84; ptnr. Eames, Sterns & Washburn, Skowhegan, 1984—. Bd. dirs., sec. Youth and Family Services, Inc., Skowhegan, 1982—. Mem. ABA, Maine Bar Assn., Somerset County Bar Assn. (sec. 1985—), Maine Trial Lawyers Assn., Jaycees. Republican. Roman Catholic. Club: Somerset County Stamp. Lodge: Elks. Avocations: sports, stamp collecting. Criminal, State civil litigation, Real property. Home: 5 1/2 Coburn Ave Skowhegan ME 04976 Office: Eames Sterns & Washburn PO Box 442 Skowhegan ME 04976

WASHINGTON, VALDEMAR LUTHER, judge; b. Balt., June 21, 1952; s. G. Luther and Vivian Irene (Edwards) W.; m. Ada C. Miller, Aug. 11, 1984; 1 child, Valdemar Luther II. BA, Mich. State U., 1974; JD, U. Mich., 1976. Bar: Mich. 1977. Assoc. Baker Law Firm, Bay City, Mich., 1977; dir. Acctg. Aid Soc., Flint, Mich., 1978; sole practice Flint, 1978-81, 81-86; ptnr. Robinson & Washington, Flint, 1981; judge cir. ct. Genesee County, Flint, 1986—. Pres. adv. bd. McCree Theatre, Flint, 1983; bd. dirs. Big Sisters Orgn., Flint, 1983; mem. legal redress com. NAACP, Flint, 1984-86. Mem. Mich. Bar Assn., Genesee County Bar Assn., Assn. Trial Lawyers Am., Mich. Trial Lawyers Assn., Genesee County Trial Lawyers Assn., Mensa. Episcopalian. Avocations: swimming, reading. State civil litigation, Personal injury, Federal civil litigation. Home: 1502 S Franklin Ave Flint MI 48503 Office: Genesee County Courthouse 900 S Saginaw St Room 107 Flint MI 48502

WASSERMAN, DAVID S., lawyer, business executive; b. N.Y.C., Nov. 17, 1942; s. Abraham and Lillian (Trupin) W.; m. Karin Frank, June 18, 1967; children: Laura A., Lisa A. BS in Acct., U. Md., 1965; JD, U. Balt., 1970; LLM in Taxation, Georgetown U., 1978; MBA, U. Pa., 1984. Bar: Md. 1980. Sr. v.p., dir. tax planning Midland-Ross Corp., Cleve., 1978—, dir. tax adminstrn., 1978-81, v.p. taxes, 1981-84. Mem. Tax Exec. Inst. (2d v.p., sec. 1985—), Fin. Exec. Inst. Inc. Jewish. Club: Beechmont Country (Beechwood, Ohio). Corporate taxation. Office: Midland Ross Corp 20600 Chagrin Blvd Cleveland OH 44122

WASSERMAN, EDWARD HENRY, lawyer; b. Bridgeport, Conn., Nov. 22, 1955; s. Heinrich August and Elizabeth Babette (Stippler) W.; m. Tina Krimmer, Jan. 31, 1982 (div. June 1983). BA, Fairfield U., 1977; JD, Syracuse U., 1980. Bar: N.Y. 1981, U.S. Dist. Ct. (no. dist.) Ill. 1983, U.S. Supreme Ct. 1986. Atty. Vista, Rochester, N.Y., 1980-81; staff atty. N.Y. State Defenders Assn., Albany, 1981-82, sr. atty., 1982-83, dep. dir., 1983—. Author: When Justice Prevails, 1981; contbr. articles to profl. jours.; composer: various piano productions, 1976—. Vol. Am. Cancer Soc., Jacksonville, Fla., 1978, Mondale Campaign, Albany, 1984; cons. Civil Rights Com., Albany, 1984, ACLU Legal Rights Pamphlet, Albany, 1984. Mem. Nat. Assn. Criminal Def. Lawyers, N.Y. State Defenders Assn. (editor jour. 1981—), Assn. Trial Lawyers Am., Am. Judicature Soc., Phi Alpha Theta. Democrat. Criminal, Legislative, Legal history. Office: NY State Defenders Assn 150 State St Albany NY 12207

WASSERMAN, MICHAEL ERIC, lawyer; b. Los Angeles, Jan. 8, 1953; s. David Marion and Janice (Heiman) W. BA magna cum laude, UCLA, 1975; MS in Ednl. Psychology, U. Oreg., 1978, JD, 1981. Bar: Oreg. 1981, U.S. Dist. Ct. Oreg. 1981, Calif. 1982, Wash. 1983, U.S. Dist. Ct. (cen. dist.) Calif. 1983. Assoc. Olson, Hittle & Gardner, Salem, Oreg., 1981-83, Veatch, Carlson, Grogan & Nelson, Los Angeles, 1983—. Mem. ABA, Los Angeles County Bar Assn., Assn. So. Calif. Def. Counsel, Phi Beta Kappa, Pi Gamma Mu. Democrat. Jewish. Avocations: film, skiing, fishing, psychology. Personal injury, Insurance, State civil litigation. Home: 1220 S Crescent Heights Los Angeles CA 90035

WASSERMAN, MICHAEL GARY, lawyer; b. Hartford, Conn., Mar. 14, 1946; s. Alexander and Loris Hope (Calegman) W.; m. Andrea Jane Weiner, June 25, 1967 (div. Oct. 1971); m. Harriet McGillivray King, Mar. 17, 1973; children: Harriet M., Rebecca F. BA summa cum laude, Williams Coll., 1968; PhD, MIT, 1971; JD magna cum laude, Harvard U., 1974. Bar: Ga. 1974. Assoc. Alston, Miller & Gaines, Atlanta, 1974-80, ptnr., 1980-82; ptnr. Alston & Bird, Atlanta, 1982-84, Holt, Ney, Zatcoff & Wasserman, Atlanta, 1984—; lectr. in math. Boston U., 1971-72, various other orgns. Contbr. articles to profl. jours. Chmn. legal issues com. Mental Health Assn. Met. Atlanta, 1975-77. Fellow Danforth Found., 1968-71. Mem. ABA (chmn. subcom. carryovers 1983-85, corp.-stockholder relations com. taxation sect.), Phi Beta Kappa, Sigma Xi. Jewish. Corporate taxation, General corporate, Real property. Home: 2455 Tanglewood Rd Decatur GA 30033 Office: Holt Ney Zatcoff & Wasserman 100 Galleria Pkwy Suite 600 Atlanta GA 30339

WATANABE, CORINNE KAORU AMEMIYA, lawyer, state official; b. Wahiawa, Hawaii, Aug. 1, 1950; d. Keiji and Setsuko (Matsumiya) Amemiya; m. Edwin Tsugio Watanabe, Mar. 8, 1975; children: Traciann Keiko, Brad Natsuo, Lance Yoneo. BA, U. Hawaii, 1971; JD, Baylor U., 1974. Bar: Hawaii 1974. Dep. atty. gen. State of Hawaii, Honolulu, 1974-84, 1st dep. atty. gen., 1984-85, 87—, atty. gen., 1985-87. Mem. ABA, Hawaii Bar Assn. Democrat. Office: Atty Gen 415 S Beretania St 405 State Capitol Honolulu HI 96813

WATANABE, ROY NOBORU, lawyer; b. Honolulu, July 23, 1947; s. Tadao I. and Clara Y. Watanabe; m. Myrna E. Watanabe, June 8, 1970 (div. Oct. 1983). AB, Columbia Coll., 1969; JD, Columbia U., 1973. Bar: N.Y. 1974, U.S. Dist. Ct. (so. and ea. dists.) N.Y. 1976, U.S. Ct. Appeals (2d cir.) 1976. Honors program atty. Office of Labor Relations, Office of Mayor, N.Y.C., 1973-76; assoc. Frankle and Greenwald, N.Y.C., 1976, Cohn, Glickstein, Lurie, Ostrin, Lubell & Lubell, N.Y.C., 1976-79; ptnr. Cohn, Glickstein and Lurie (formerly Cohn, Glickstein, Lurie, Ostrin, Lubell & Lubell, N.Y.C., 1979—; guest lectr. labor law Boston Coll. Law Sch., 1982, Albany (N.Y.) Law Sch., 1983, 85. Cooperating atty. Asian Am. Legal Def. & Edn. Fund., N.Y.C., 1982—. Nat. Def. Fgn. Language fellow, Columbia U., 1967. Mem. ABA (labor and employment law com. 1983—), N.Y. State Bar Assn. (labor arbitration com. 1983—), Assn. of Bar of City of N.Y. (labor and employment law com. 1980-83, 1986—, legal edn. and admission to bar com. 1984-85). Labor, Civil rights. Office: Cohn Glickstein & Lurie 1370 Ave of Americas New York NY 10019

WATERFALL, GORDON GARRETT, lawyer; b. Pasadena, Calif., Mar. 17, 1934; s. Louis N. and Marjorie (Imler) W.; m. Patricia Hewitt, June 15, 1960; children: Mark H., Gregory S., Karen R., Julia I. BS in Acctg., U. Calif., Berkeley, 1957; JD, U. Ariz., 1965. Bar: Ariz. 1965; CPA, Ariz., Calif. Ptnr. Waterfall, Economidis, Hanshaw & Villamana, P.C., Tucson; judge pro tem Pima County Superior Ct., Ariz., 1973-74; lectr. various orgns.; mem. faculty U. Ariz. Coll. Law, 1979-81. Past pres. So. Ariz. Estate Planning Council. Fellow Am. Coll. Probate Counsel (chmn. Ariz. chpt.); mem. ABA (estate and gift taxes com.), Ariz. Bar Assn. (chmn. taxation sect. 1984-85, co-chmn. updating and revising Ariz. Estate Tax Laws 1978), Ariz. Bar Found. (treas.), Pima County Bar Assn. (pres. 1976-77), Am. Assn. Atty.-CPA. General corporate, Estate planning, Corporate taxation. Office: Waterfall Economidis Hanshaw & Villamana PC 5210 E Williams Circle Suite 800 Tucson AZ 85711

WATERMAN, DAVID MOORE, lawyer; b. San Francisco, July 23, 1947; s. Joseph and Muriel Yvette (Moore) W.; children: Kimberley Anne, Kevin David; m. Denny L. Peck, Nov. 23, 1984. Student, U. Calif., San Diego, 1966-67; BA in Drama Theory, U. Ariz., 1970, JD, 1973; postdoctoral, U. Wash., 1978-80. Bar: Ariz. 1973, U.S. Dist. Ct. Ariz. 1973, U.S. Ct. Appeals (9th cir.) 1973. Assoc. Law Offices of William C. Berlat, Tucson, 1973-74; sole practice Tucson, 1974-76; assoc. Law Offices of David K. Wolfe, Tucson, 1976-78; staff asst. div. atty. gen. State of Washington, Seattle, 1978; instr. community services program Highline Community Coll., Midway, Wash., 1978-79; dir. opera theater Shoreline Community Coll., Seattle, 1979; staff assoc., undergrad. counselor U. Wash., Seattle, 1979-80; assoc. Rabinovitz, Dix & Rehling, Tucson, 1981-84; ptnr. Dix, Rehling & Waterman, Tucson, 1984-86, Dix & Waterman, Tucson, 1987—; instr. U. Phoenix; adj. prof. bus. law U. Puget Sound, Seattle, 1979-80. Mem. Ariz. Bar Assn. (co-chmn. worker's compensation com. 1986—), Southern Ariz. Worker's Compensation Counsel Assn., Ariz. Bd. Legal Specialization (cert. specialist), Phi Delta Phi. Democrat. Jewish. Personal injury, Workers' compensation, State civil litigation. Office: Dix & Waterman 120 W Broadway Box 70 Suite 260 Tucson AZ 85701

WATERS, CHARLES RICHARD, II, judge; b. Norfolk, Va., Oct. 20, 1935; s. Francis Baittle and Ethel (Parsons) W.; m. Anne Pultz, June 5, 1961 (div. Dec. 1979); 1 child, Barbara Anne. B.A., U. Va., 1958; LL.B., U. Richmond, 1961. Bar: Va. 1961, U.S. Dist. Ct. (ea. and we. dists.) Va. 1963, U.S. Ct. Claims 1968, U.S. Ct. Appeals (4th cir.) 1963. Asst. city atty. City of Norfolk, 1963-67; mem. firm Kaufman and Oberndorfer, Norfolk, 1967-71, ptnr., 1971-82; sr. ptnr., head litigation dept. Kaufman & Canoles, Norfolk, 1982-86; judge cir. ct. City of Norfolk, Va., 1986—. Chmn. Am. Cancer Soc., Norfolk, 1974-76; trustee U. Va. Student Aid Found., 1975-79. Served to 1st lt. U.S. Army, 1961-63. Mem. ABA, Am. Trial Lawyers Assn., Va. State Bar (mem. 2d dist. com. 1982-85), Va. Trial Lawyers Assn., Norfolk and Portsmouth Bar Assn. (pres. 1981-83). Methodist. Banking, Federal civil litigation, State civil litigation. Home: 356 Westover Ave Norfolk VA 23507 Office: Kaufman & Canoles Sovran Ctr Norfolk VA 23510

WATERS, H. FRANKLIN, federal judge; b. Hackett, Ark., July 20, 1932; s. William A. and Wilma W.; m. Janie C. Waters, May 31, 1958; children—Carolyn Denise, Melanie Jane, Melissa Ann. B.S., U. Ark., 1955; LL.B, St. Louis U., 1964. Engr., atty. Ralston-Purina Co., St. Louis, 1958-66; ptnr. Crouch, Blair, Cypert & Waters, 1967-81; judge U.S. Dist. Ct. (we. dist.) Ark., 1981—. Former bd. dirs. Springdale Schs.; former bd. govs. Washington Regional Med. Ctr. Mem. ABA, Ark. Bar Assn., Springdale C. of C. (bd. dirs.). Judicial administration. Office: PO Box 1908 Fayetteville AR 72702

WATHEN, DANIEL EVERETT, judge; b. Easton, Maine, Nov. 4, 1939; s. Joseph Jackson and Wilda Persis (Dow) W.; m. Judith Carol Foren, July 14, 1960; children: Julanne Carol, Daniel Arthur. A.B., Ricker Coll., 1962; J.D., U. Maine, 1965. Bar: Maine 1965. Atty. Wathen & Wathen, Augusta, Maine, 1965-77; trial judge Superior Ct. Maine, Augusta, 1977-81; appellate judge Supreme Jud. Ct. Maine, Augusta, 1981—. Office: Supreme Judicial Ct Maine Kennebec Courthouse Augusta ME 04330 *

WATKINS, JERRY WEST, oil company executive, lawyer; b. Vernon, Tex., Dec. 10, 1931; s. Terrell Clark and Daisy (West) W.; m. Elizabeth Jill Cole, Sept. 3, 1955; children: Jennifer Leigh, Jay West, Julie Elizabeth. Student, Hendrix Coll., 1949-50, La. Poly. Inst., 1950-51; LL.B., U. Ark., 1954. Bar: Ark. 1954. Law clk. Supreme Ct. Ark., 1954-55; with Murphy Oil Corp., El Dorado, Ark., 1955—; sec., gen. atty. Murphy Oil Corp., 1966-71, sec., gen. counsel, 1971—, v.p., 1975—, also dir.; mem. Ark. Bd. Law Examiners, 1969-74. Trustee Ark. State U., 1982-87, Barton Library Bd., El Dorado, Ark., 1966—; bd. dirs. South Ark. Arts Ctr., El Dorado, 1979-82, 85—, Warner Brown Hosp., El Dorado, 1984—. Mem. ABA, Ark., Union County bar assns., Am. Soc. Corp. Secs. General corporate, Private international, Corporate taxation. Home: 111 Watkins Dr El Dorado AR 71730 Office: Murphy Oil Corp 200 Peach St El Dorado AR 71730

WATSON, ANDREW SAMUEL, physician, law educator; b. Highland Park, Mich., May 2, 1920; s. Andrew Nicol and Eva Arvel (Barnes) W.; m. Catherine Mary Osborne, Sept. 1942; children: Andrew Nicol, John Lewis, David Winfield, Steven; m. Joyce Lyne Goldstein, July 21, 1967. BS in Zoology, U. Mich., 1942; MD, Temple U., 1950, M in Med. Sci., 1954. Intern, U. Pa. Grad. Hosp., 1950-51; resident in psychiatry Temple U., Phila., 1951-54; spl. lectr. Sch. Social Work, Bryn Mawr Coll., 1955-59; mem. med. faculty U. Pa., 1954-59, law faculty, 1955-59; prof. psychiatry U. Mich., Ann Arbor, 1959-80, mem. law faculty, 1959—; pvt. practice medicine, specializing in psychiatry, Ann Arbor, 1959—. Mem. Mich. Law Enforcement and Criminal Justice Commn., 1968-72. Served to capt. Med. Service Corps, AUS, 1942-46. Recipient Issac Ray award Am. Psychiat. Assn., 1978. Mem. Am. Psychiat. Assn., Am. Coll. Psychiatry, ABA (assoc.). Democrat. Unitarian. Author: Psychiatry for Lawyers, rev. edit., 1978; The Lawyer in the Interviewing and Counseling Process, 1976; others. Legal education. Home: 21 Ridgeway Ann Arbor MI 48104 Office: U Mich Law Sch 304 Hutchins Hall 621 S State St Ann Arbor MI 48109

WATSON, CARY STEPHEN, lawyer; b. Tyler, Tex., Apr. 4, 1952; s. Wellington Green and Peggy Sue (Smith) W.; m. Deborah Ann Grubbs, Aug. 11, 1984. BA in History, Tex. A&M U., 1974; JD, U. Tex., 1976. Bar: Tex. 1977, U.S. Dist. Ct. (so. dist.) Tex. 1977, U.S. Ct. Appeals (5th cir.) 1977, U.S. Supreme Ct. 1981, U.S. Ct. Appeals (11th cir.) 1983. Assoc. Rowland & Klein, Houston, 1977-80, ptnr., 1980-81; ptnr. Watson & Greiner, Houston, 1981-82; mem. Watson & Greiner, P.C., Houston, 1982-84, C.S. Watson & Assocs., P.C., Houston, 1984—; trustee, sec. Houston Lawyer Referral Service, Inc., 1984—. Mem. ABA, State Bar Tex. (grievance com. 1979-85), Houston Bar Assn. Republican. Baptist. Avocations: golf, tennis. Oil and gas leasing, General corporate, General practice. Home: 6422 Olympia Houston TX 77057 Office: 5151 San Felipe Suite 720 Houston TX 77056

WATSON, DANIEL CARVIN, lawyer; b. Coldwater, Mich., Aug. 15, 1952; s. Joseph Robert and Arleth (Carvin) W.; m. Anita Marie Fennessey, Feb. 25, 1977; children: Alesia Marie, David Joseph. BA, Mich. State U., 1974; JD, Wayne State U., 1977. Bar: Mich. 1977, U.S. Dist. Ct. (ea. dist.) Mich. 1977. Assoc. Joselyn, Rowe, Detroit, 1977; ptnr. Fitzgerald, Young, Detroit, 1978-84; assoc. counsel Standard Fed. Bank, Troy, Mich., 1984—. Mem. ABA. Contracts commercial, Real property, Banking. Home: 597 Peartree Grosse Pointe Woods MI 48236 Office: Standard Fed Bank 2401 W Big Beaver Rd Troy MI 48084

WATSON, FORREST ALBERT, lawyer, bank executive; b. Atlanta, May 5, 1951; s. Forrest Albert and Virginia Doris (Ritch) W.; m. Marlys Wise, Oct. 16, 1983. AB, Emory U., 1973; JD, U. Ga., 1975. Bar: Ga. 1975, U.S. Dist. Ct. (mid. dist.) Ga. 1976, U.S. Tax Ct. 1976, U.S. Ct. Appeals (5th cir.) 1977, U.S. Supreme Ct. 1980. Assoc. Banks, Smith & Lambdin, Barnesville, Ga., 1976-78; ptnr. Watson & Lindsey, Barnesville, 1978-82; gen. counsel United Bank Corp., Barnesville, 1981—, v.p., chief exec. officer, 1982—; gen. counsel Lamar State Bank, Barnesville, 1976-84; judge Small Claims Ct. Lamar County, Ga., 1976, City Ct. Milner, Ga., 1977; lectr. IBM, 1984-85; atty. City of Meansville, Ga., 1976, City of Milner, 1977. Assoc. editor Ga. Jour. Internat. Law, 1975. Gen. counsel Lamar County Devel. Authority, Barnesville, 1977; bd. dirs. Legaline Inc., Atlanta, 1983-85. Mem. ABA, Ga. Bar Assn., Cir. Ct. Bar Assn., Flint Circuit Bar Assn. Lutheran. Avocations: art, antiques, travel. Banking. Home: Po Box 347 Barnesville Rd Zebulon GA 30295 Office: United Bank Corp 314 Thomaston St Barnesville GA 30204

WATSON, GERARD PHILLIP, lawyer; b. Bklyn., July 28, 1931; s. Arthur Martin and Marie (Scholl) W.; m. Maureen Larkin, July 18, 1959; children—Mary P., Margaret Larkin, Tracey Martin, Maureen Cunniss. A.B. cum laude, St. Peter's Coll., 1953; J.D., Columbia U., 1959; LL.M., NYU, 1963. Bar: N.Y. 1959, U.S. Supreme Ct. 1963. Assoc. Mendes & Mount, N.Y.C., 1959-64; ptnr. LeBoeuf, Lamb, Leiby & MacRae, N.Y.C., 1965—. Trustee St. Ann's Sch., Bklyn., 1984—. Served to capt. USMC, 1953-56; ETO. Democrat. Roman Catholic. Home: 66-82 St Brooklyn NY 11209 Office: LeBoeuf Lamb Leiby & MacRae 520 Madison Ave New York NY 10022

WATSON, JACK CROZIER, judge; b. Jonesville, La., Sept. 17, 1928; s. Jesse Crozier and Gladys Lucille (Talbot) W.; m. Henrietta Sue Carter, Dec. 28, 1958; children: Carter Crozier (dec.), Wells Talbot. B.A., U. Southwestern La., 1949; J.D., La. State U., 1956; completed with honor, Appellate Judges Seminar, N.Y. U., 1974, Sr. Appellate Judges Seminar, 1980. Bar: La. bar 1956. Individual practice law Lake Charles, La., 1956; prosecutor City of Lake Charles, 1960; asst. dist. atty. Calcasieu Parish, La., 1961-64; assoc. firm Watson & Watson, Lake Charles, 1961-64; judge 14th Jud. Dist., La., 1964-72; judge ad hoc Ct. Appeals, 1st Circuit, Baton Rouge, 1972-73; judge Ct. Appeals, 3rd Circuit, Lake Charles, 1973-79; asso. justice La. Supreme Ct., New Orleans, 1979—; faculty Nat. Coll. State Judiciary, Reno, Nev., 1970, 73; del. Nat. Endowment for Humanities seminar, 1976; La. del. to Internat. Conf. Appellate Magistrates, Philippines, 1977. Served to 1st lt. USAF, 1950-54. Mem. ABA, La. Bar Assn., Southwest La. Bar Assn. (pres. 1973), Law Inst. State of La., La. Council Juvenile Ct. Judges (pres. 1969-70), Am. Judicature Soc., La. Jud. Council, Blue Key, Sigma Alpha Epsilon, Phi Delta Phi, Pi Kappa Delta. Democrat. Baptist. Clubs: Lake Charles Yacht (commodore 1974), Am. Legion (post comdr. 1963), SW La. Camellia Soc. (pres. 1973-74). Office: 301 Loyola Ave New Orleans LA 70112

WATSON, JAMES LOPEZ, U.S. judge; b. N.Y.C., May 21, 1922; s. James S. and Violet (Lopez) W.; m. D'Jaris Hinton Watson, July 14, 1956; children—Norman, Karen, Kris. B.A. in Govt, N.Y. U., 1947; LL.B., Bklyn. Law Sch., 1951. Bar: N.Y. bar 1951. Mem. N.Y. Senate from 21st Senatorial Dist. 1954-63; judge Civil Ct. N.Y., 1964-66; acting judge N.Y. State Supreme Ct., 1965; judge U.S. Customs Ct., 1966-80, U.S. Ct. Internat. Trade, 1980—. Bd. dirs. N.Y.C. Police Athletic League. Served with inf. AUS, World War II, ETO. Decorated Purple Heeart, Combat Inf. badge. Mem. Am., N.Y. State bar assns., Fed. Bar Council, World Peace Through Law. Administrative and regulatory, Federal civil litigation, Public international. Home: 676 Riverside Dr New York NY 10031 Office: 1 Federal Plaza New York NY 10007

WATSON, JAMES WILLIAM, lawyer; b. Memphis, Dec. 7, 1916; s. William and Willie (Weatherall) W.; m. Inez Clayton, Feb. 22, 1941; children: James William, Anne Watson Odom, Charles Clayton. Student, Southwestern U., 1934-35; JD, U. Tenn., 1940. Bar: Tenn. 1940, U.S. Dist. Ct. (we. dist.) Tenn. 1940, U.S. Ct. Appeals (6th cir.) 1955, U.S. Supreme Ct. 1965, U.S. Tax Ct. 1965. Ptnr. Taylor, Quick & Watson, Memphis, 1940-48; judge Probate Ct. Shelby County, 1948-50; ptnr. Laughlin, Watson, Creson, Garthright & Halle, Memphis, 1950-70, Watson & Knolton, Memphis, 1970-76, Watson, Arnoult & Quinn, Memphis, 1976—; judge Spl. Supreme Ct. Tenn., 1976; prof. So. Law. U., Memphis, 1948-50. Served with USAF, 1942-45. Decorated Air MEdal with five oak leaf clusters, DFC, Purple Heart medal. Mem. ABA, Tenn. Bar Assn., Memphis Bar Assn., Shelby County Bar Assn. Episcopalian. Federal civil litigation, State civil litigation, Estate planning. Office: Watson & Arnoult 100 N Main Bldg Memphis TN 38103

WATSON, JOHN HOWARD, lawyer; b. Atlanta, June 13, 1946; s. Howard B. and Mary Lou (Lynch) W.; 1 child from previous marriage, Julie; m. Jane E. Williams, Feb. 23, 1985; 1 child, John Vincent. BS, Ga. State U., 1969; JD, U. Ga., 1973. Bar: Ga. 1973, U.S. Dist. Ct. (no., mid., and so. dists.) Ga. 1986. Atty. Dist. Atty.'s Assn. Ga., Atlanta, 1973; ptnr. Stokes, Lazarus & Watson, Atlanta, 1973-86; sole practice Atlanta, 1986—. Mem. ABA, Ga. State Bar Assn., Atlanta Bar Assn., Assn. Trial Lawyers Am., Ga. Trial Lawyers Assn. Republican. Methodist. Avocations: hunting, travel. Federal civil litigation, State civil litigation, Contracts commercial. Office: Paper Mill Village 630 Village Terr Marietta GA 30067

WATSON, JOHN SLATER, lawyer; b. St. Paul, Aug. 22, 1952; s. Richard Edward and Lavonne Dorthea (Slater) W.; m. Ann Lockhart, Aug. 18, 1978; children: Elizabeth Ann, James Steven, Charles Lockhart. BA, U. Minn., 1975, JD cum laude, 1979. Bar: Minn. 1978, U.S. Dist. Ct. Minn. 1979. Assoc. Grossman, Karlins, Siegel, Brill & Greupner, Mpls., 1979-85, ptnr., 1986—; lectr. Community Assns. Inst., Mpls., 1980—; officer, bd. dirs. numerous corps. Served with U.S. Army, 1972-74. Mem. ABA, Minn. Bar Assn. (real estate sect.), Hennepin County Bar Assn., Phi Beta Kappa. Presbyterian. Club: Club 25 (Mpls.) (pres. 1984). Avocations: tennis, skiing, travel, bridge, woodworking. Real property, Contracts commercial, General corporate. Office: Grossman Karlins Siegel et al 100 Washington Sq Suite 1350 Minneapolis MN 55401

WATSON, KEITH, lawyer; b. Jacksonville, Fla., May 26, 1949; s. William A. and Tresser (Smoke) W. B.S. in Mktg., Jacksonville U., 1971; J.D., U. Fla., 1973. Bar: Fla. 1974, U.S. Dist. Ct. (mid. dist.) Fla. 1974. Assoc. Crider & Helwig, P.A., Jacksonville, 1973-75; ptnr. Newton, Watson, Morehead &

Allen, Jacksonville, 1975-85; sole practice, Jacksonville, 1985—; dir., officer Realty Title Services, Inc., Jacksonville, 1977—, Southeast Mortgage Life Ins. Agy., Inc., Jacksonville, 1978—; officer Watson Realty Corp., Jacksonville, 1974—. Named among Outstanding Coll. Athletes of Am. 1968, 74. Democrat. Methodist. Real property, Probate. Office: 6825 Lillian Rd Jacksonville FL 32211

WATSON, LON CHANDLER, JR., judge; b. Anniston, Ala., Aug. 3, 1922; s. Lon Chandler and Harriet Seraphine (Glover) W.; m. T. Marion Smith, Nov. 22, 1951; children—Lon Chandler, Marion Elizabeth Watson Murphree, William Robert, Harriet Glover Watson Lane. A.B., Emory U., 1944; LL.B., U. Ala., 1946; LL.M., Harvard U., 1947. Bar: Ala. 1947. Assoc., Emerson and Watson, Anniston, 1950-60, Emerson, Watson, Wilson and Propst, Anniston, 1961; U.S. bankruptcy judge No. Dist. Ala., Anniston, 1961—, chief judge, 1983-84. Mem. Nat. Conf. Bankruptcy Judges, ABA, Ala. State Bar, Calhoun County Bar Assn. Presbyterian. Club: Rotary (pres. 1961-62) (Anniston). Contbg. editor: Bankruptcy Law and Practice, 1981. Bankruptcy. Office: 117 US Courthouse Anniston AL 36201

WATSON, MARK HENRY, lawyer, bus. writer; b. Camden, N.J., Apr. 12, 1938; s. Donald Robert and Elizabeth Rozanne (Rowan) W.; m. Patricia A. Olsen, Aug. 27, 1960 (dec.); 1 son, Mark; m. 2d, Suzanne M. Young, Dec. 31, 1966; children—Matthew, Betsy, Daniel, William, Michael. B.A. with honors, Rutgers U., 1959, J.D., 1964; postgrad. U.Del., 1959-61. Bar: N.J. 1965. Assoc., Brown, Connery, Kulp & Wille, Camden, N.J., 1966-67; sole practice, Camden, 1967-69, Haddonfield, N.J., 1980—; house counsel S. Jersey Realty Abstract Co., Camden, 1969-70, N.Y.-N.J. div. Kaufman & Broad Homes, 1970-71; pres. C.F. Seabrook (N.J.) Co., 1971-76, Koster Nursery, Inc., 1976-80; bus. advisor, writer; arbitrator Am. Arbitration Assn., 1972—; adj. prof. bus. law Camden County Coll., Blackwood, N.J., 1979-80. Del. White House Conf. on Small Bus., 1980; organizer N.J. Small Bus. Unity Council. Named Small Bus. Media Adv. of Yr., U.S. Small Bus. Adminstrn., 1981, 82. Mem. ABA, N.J. Bar Assn., Camden County Bar Assn. Roman Catholic. Author: Succeeding in Your Own Business: Do It Right the First Time, 1982; contbr. articles on small bus. to newspapers. Contracts commercial, General corporate. Home: 12 2d Ave Haddon Heights NJ 08035 Office: 204 White Horse Pike PO Box 267 Haddon Heights NJ 08035

WATSON, PATRICIA SEETS, criminal justice educator, academic administrator; b. Sharples, W.Va., Nov. 29, 1930; s. James D. and Gladys Opal (Bias) Seets; m. Robert P. Watson, Jan. 11, 1957 (dec. May 1971); children: Elizabeth C. Meetze, Frances L. McGinn. BA in Psychology, U. S.C., 1977, M in Criminal Justice, 1979, JD, 1982. Bar: S.C. 1982. Reporter, editor Various S.C. newspapers, Greenville, Inman and Spartanburg, 1957-75; instr. criminal justice U. S.C., Columbia, 1981-84, asst. dean coll. criminal justice, 1984—. Author: South Carolina Criminal Law and Procedure, 1984; editor: The Retarded Offender, 1982. Bd. dirs. Inst. for Effective Citizenship Edn., Columbia, 1985—, Police Chaplaincy Training Program, Columbia, 1986. Mem. ABA, S.C. Bar Assn. (pub. affairs com. 1984—), Profl. Women on Campus Club, Phi Alpha Delta (state rep. for law related edn. 1986—). Democrat. Episcopalian. Avocations: music, piano, reading. Criminal, Legal education, Juvenile. Home: 1520 Senate St #22 Columbia SC 29201 Office: Univ SC Coll Criminal Justice Currell Coll Columbia SC 29208

WATSON, RICHARD A., lawyer; b. Oceanside, N.Y., Aug. 11, 1946; s. William Edgar and Grace (Brooks) W.; m. Mary Lee Brown, June 24, 1972; children: Rebecca, Sarah. BA, Hamilton Coll., 1967; JD, Columbia U., 1972. Bar: N.Y. 1973, U.S. Tax Ct. 1974, N.J. 1976. From assoc. to ptnr. Chamberlain, Willi & Ouchterloney, N.Y.C., 1972—. Mem. Morris Twp. Zoning Bd., N.J., 1981—; chmn. Morris Twp. Reps., 1985—. Served with U.S. Army, 1969-71, Vietnam. Mem. ABA, N.J. Bar Assn., Am. Assn. Hosp. Attys. Republican. Presbyterian. Estate planning, General practice, Health. Home: 5 Quaker Ridge Rd Morristown NJ 07960 Office: Chamberlain Willi & Ouchterloney 74 Trinity Pl New York NY 10006

WATSON, ROBERT ALLAN, lawyer; b. San Diego, Calif., Dec. 30, 1933; s. Albert Orville and Nadia Florence (Herman) W.; m. Elizabeth Ellen Payne, Apr. 7, 1956; children—Terri Elizabeth, Robert Allan, Leslie Margaret, Richard Payne. B.S.C., Tex. Christian U., 1955; J.D., So. Meth. U., 1958. Bar: Tex. 1958, D.C. 1981; cert. estate planning and probate law Tex. Bd. Legal Specializations, 1977, cert. tax law, 1983. With Office of Regional Counsel, IRS, Atlanta, 1958-59; atty. advisor Tax Ct. U.S., 1960; with Cantey, Hanger, Johnson, Scarborough & Gooch, and successor firms, 1961-79, Watson, Ice, McGee, Morgan, Hughes & Liles, Ft. Worth, 1979—; dir. Merc. Nat. Bank Arlington. Trustee, Tex. Christian U. Fellow Am. Coll. Probate Counsel; mem. Tex. Bar Assn., D.C. Bar Assn., Ft. Worth/Tarrant County Bar Assn., ABA, Fed. Bar Assn., Tex. Bar Found. Republican. Mem. Christian Ch. Clubs: Ft. Worth, Colonial Country, Masons. Corporate taxation, Estate taxation, Personal income taxation. Home: 4444 Overton Crest Fort Worth TX 76109 Office: 1212 Texas American Bank Bldg Fort Worth TX 76102

WATSON, ROBERT FRANCIS, lawyer; b. Houston, Jan. 9, 1936; s. Louis Leon and Lora Elizabeth (Hodges) W.; m. Marietta Kiser, Nov. 24, 1961; children—Julia, Melissa, Rebecca. B.A., Vanderbilt U., 1957; J.D., U. Denver, 1959. Bar: Colo. 1959, U.S. Dist. Ct. (no. dist.) Tex. 1967, U.S. Supreme Ct. 1968, Tex. 1973, U.S. Ct. Appeals (5th cir.) 1973, U.S. Dist. Ct. (so. dist.) Tex. 1980, U.S. Ct. Appeals (11th cir.) 1981. Law clk. U.S. Dist. Ct. Colo., 1960-61; trial atty. SEC, Denver, 1961-67, asst. regional adminstr., Ft. Worth, 1967-72, regional adminstr., 1972-75; ptnr. Law, Snakard & Gambill, P.C., Ft. Worth, 1975—; counsel City of Ft. Worth Police Investigation Commn., 1975; spl. counsel Office Atty. Gen. State Ariz., 1977-78. Mem. Ft. Worth Crime Commn., 1987—; pres. bd. trustees Trinity Valley Sch., Ft. Worth; adv. dir., pres. Lena Pope Home for Dependent and Neglected Children, Ft. Worth. Mem. ABA, State Bar Tex., Tarrant County Bar Assn., Colo. Bar Assn., Tex. Bar Found., Am. Counsel Assn., Fed. Bar Assn., Am. Judicature Soc., Phi Delta Phi. Republican. Presbyterian. Clubs: Ft. Worth, Shady Oaks Country (Ft. Worth). Contbr. articles to profl. jours. Securities, Federal civil litigation, General corporate. Office: Suite 3200 Tex Am Bank Bldg Fort Worth TX 76102

WATSON, ROBERT HARMON, JR., lawyer; b. Radford, Va., Nov. 22, 1945; s. Robert H. and Oma Lee (Hall) W.; m. Patricia Ann Fowler, Mar. 15, 1968; children—Elizabeth Lee, Mary Christin. B.S., U. Tenn., 1968, J.D., 1970. Bar: Tenn. 1971, U.S. Dist. Ct. (ea. dist.) Tenn. 1971, U.S. Ct. Appeals (6th cir.) 1982, U.S. Supreme Ct. 1975. Staff, U. Tenn. Legal Clinic, Knoxville, 1970-71; ptnr. Watson & Emert, Knoxville. Served to capt. USAR, 1968-75. Recipient Am. Jurisprudence Wills award, 1970. Mem. Knoxville Bar Assn., Tenn. Bar Assn., ABA, Tenn. Trial Lawyers Assn., Am. Trial Lawyers Assn. Democrat. Methodist. Author: U. Tenn. Legal Clinic Handbook of Forms, 1970. Federal civil litigation, State civil litigation, Civil rights. Address: PO Box 131 Knoxville TN 37901

WATSON, ROBERT JAMES, lawyer; b. Oceanside, N.Y., Mar. 30, 1955; s. Ralph Joseph and Mildred Adeline (Knapp) W.; 1 child, Emily Allyn. BA, Biscayne Coll., 1976; JD, U. Fla., 1979. Bar: Fla. 1979, U.S. Dist. Ct. (so. dist.) Fla. 1980, U.S. Dist. Ct. (no. dist.) Fla. 1981, U.S. Dist. Ct. (mid. dist.) Fla. 1982, U.S. Ct. Appeals (11th cir.) 1982. Asst. pub. defender Law Offices of Elton Schwarz, Ft. Pierce, Fla., 1979-81; ptnr. Wilkinson & Watson P.A., Stuart, Fla., 1981-86; sole practice Stuart, 1986—. Mem. Assn. Trial Lawyers Am., Fla. Bar Assn. (various coms.), Nat. Assn. Criminal Def. Lawyers, Fla. Oceanographic Soc. Democrat. Roman Catholic. Avocation: triathlon and marathon running. Criminal, Personal injury, Civil rights. Office: 221 E Osceola St Suite 120 Stuart FL 33494

WATSON, ROBERTA CASPER, lawyer; b. Boise, Idaho, July 11, 1949; s. John Blaine and Joyce Lucile (Mercer) C.; m. Robert George Watson, July 22, 1972; 1 child, Rebecca Joyce. BA cum laude, U. Idaho, 1971; JD, Harvard U., 1974. Bar: Mass. 1974, U.S. Dist. Ct. Mass. 1975, U.S. Supreme Ct. 1979, U.S. Ct. Appeals (1st cir.) 1979, U.S. Tax Ct. 1979, Fla. 1985, U.S. Dist. Ct. (mid. dist.) Fla. 1985. Assoc. Peabody & Brown, Boston, 1974-78, Mintz, Levin, Cohn, Ferris, Glovsky & Popeo, Boston, 1978-84; sr. dir. Wolper Ross & Co., Miami, 1983-85; assoc. Trenam, Simmons, Kemker, Scharf, Barkin, Frye & O'Neill P.A., Tampa, Fla., 1985—. Co-author articles in profl. jours. Pres. Performing Arts Ctr. of Greater Framingham, Mass., 1983; bd. dirs. Northside Community Mental Health Ctr., Tampa chpt. Am. Heart Assn.; mem. South Fla. Employee Benefits Council. Mem. ABA (tax sect.), Hillsborough County Bar Assn., Fla. West Coast Employee Benefits Council. Republican. Unitarian Universalist. Club: Tampa. Lodge: Order Eastern Star. Avocations: music, Lincoln historian. Pension, profit-sharing, and employee benefits, Health, Family and matrimonial. Home: 124 Adalia Ave Tampa FL 33606 Office: Trenam Simmons Kemker et al 111 Madison PO Box 1102 Tampa FL 33601

WATSON, THOMAS RILEY, lawyer; b. Mendin, La., Mar. 11, 1947; s. Lawrence Middleton Watson and Barbara Hazel (Moffat) Root; m. Suzanne Bryant, May 31, 1969; 1 child, Kate. BA in History, U. S.C., 1969; MA in Nat. Security Affairs, U.S. Naval Postgrad. Sch., 1975; JD, U. Maine, 1982. Bar: Maine 1982, U.S. Dist. Ct. Maine 1982. Commd. USN, 1969, advanced through grades to comdr., 1983; trans. USNR, 1979; assoc. McTeague, Higbee & Libner, Brunswick, Maine, 1982-85, ptnr., 1985—. Author: (play) Rules of Engagement, 1986; editor U. Maine Law Rev., 1981-82. Decorated Air medal. Mem. ABA, Maine Bar Assn., Assn. Trial Lawyers Am. Democrat. Avocation: acting and writing for the theater. Labor, Personal injury, Workers' compensation. Home: George Wright Rd Woolwich ME 04579 Office: McTeague Higbee & Libner 169 Park Row Brunswick ME 04011

WATSON, WILLIAM E., lawyer; b. Jane Lew, W.Va., July 31, 1936; s. Jefferson B. and Mary (Bush) W.; m. Mara Lindberger, Sept. 3, 1958; children: Lynn, Edward. BA, W.Va. Wesleyan Coll., 1958; JD, George Washington U., 1961. Bar: W.Va. 1961, U.S. Dist. Ct. (no. and so. dists.) W.Va., U.S. Supreme Ct. Assoc. Pinsky, Mahan & Barnes, Wellsburg, W.Va., 1961-65; ptnr. Pinsky, Mahan, Barnes & Watson, Wellsburg, 1965-83; prin. William E. Watson and Assocs., Wellsburg, 1983—. Dem. state chmn., W.Va., 1972-73; chmn. W.Va. Racing Commn., 1979-82; pres. W.Va. Bd. Regents, 1985-86. Mem. ABA, W.Va. Bar Assn. Methodist. Avocations: reading, fishing, skiing. Personal injury, General practice, Insurance. Home: 2000 Main St Wellsburg WV 26070 Office: 800 Main St Wellsburg WV 26070

WATTS, BARBARA GAYLE, academic administrator; b. Covington, Ky., Oct. 18, 1946; d. William Samuel and LaVerne Barbara (Ziegler) W. BA, Purdue U., 1968; MEd, U. Cin., 1969, JD, 1978. Bar: Ohio 1978, U.S. Dist. Ct. (so. dist.) Ohio 1978. Residence dir. Ohio State U., Columbus, 1969-71, asst. dean students, 1971-75; assoc. Frost & Jacobs, Cin., 1978-81; asst. dean U. Cin. Coll. Law, 1981-84, assoc. dean, 1984—. Trustee Summerfair Inc., Cin., 1982-85. Schleman fellow Purdue U., 1968, Castleberry fellow AAUW, 1977. Mem. ABA, Ohio State Bar Assn., Cin. Bar Assn., Nat. Assn. Women, Deans, Adminstrs. and Counselors, Order of Coif, Chi Omega. Democrat. Legal education. Office: U Cin Coll Law Clifton & Calhoun Sts Cincinnati OH 45221-0040

WATTS, DAVID E., lawyer; b. Fairfield, Iowa, June 13, 1921. B.A., U. Iowa, 1941, J.D., 1942; postgrad., Columbia Law Sch., 1946-47. Bar: Iowa 1942, Mass. 1950, N.Y. 1954. Instr. U. Iowa, Iowa City, 1947-48; asst. prof. U. Pa., 1948-49, Harvard Law Sch., 1949-52; adj. assoc. prof. NYU, 1952-55; mem. firm Dewey, Ballantine, Bushby, Palmer & Wood, N.Y.C., 1952-58, ptnr., 1958—; vis. lectr. Columbia U., 1954. Contbr. articles to legal jours. Mem. ABA, N.Y. State Bar Assn., Assn. Bar City N.Y., N.Y. County Lawyers Assn., Am. Law Inst. Home: 33 W 74th New York NY 10023 Office: 140 Broadway New York NY 10005

WATTS, DEY WADSWORTH, lawyer; b. Chgo., Jan. 8, 1923; s. Amos Holston and Lida Cremora (Hough) W.; m. Faith Whittemore Weis, June 28, 1951; children—William, D. Whittemore, John, Judson, Merideth. A.B., Princeton U., 1947; LL.B., Harvard U., 1949. Bar: Ill. 1950. Assoc. Chapman and Cutler, Chgo., 1949-63; ptnr. Chapman and Cutler, 1963—. Pres. Glencoe Community Chest, Ill., 1959-60; arbitrator Am. Arbitration Assn., Chgo., 1965—; treas. Little House of Glencoe, 1966-80; chmn. adv. council Glencoe Caucus Plan, 1985-87. Served to capt. AUS, 1943-46, PTO. Fellow Am. Coll. Investment Counsel; mem. Ill. Bar Assn. (chmn. corp. and securities law com. 1961-62), ABA, Chgo. Bar Assn. (chmn. ethics com. 1974-75, chmn. legal econs. com. 1978-79. Clubs: Legal of Chgo. (exec. com. 1978-79), Law of Chgo., University, Mid Day (Chgo.); Skokie Country (sec. 1980-82) (Glencoe). Securities, Contracts commercial, General corporate. Home: 684 Greenleaf Ave Glencoe IL 60022 Office: Chapman and Cutler 111 W Monroe St Chicago IL 60603

WATTS, STEVEN RICHARD, lawyer; b. Toledo, Oct. 5, 1955; s. James Hupp and Lona Jane Katherine (Miller) W.; m. Marcia Ann Jackson, Mar. 6, 1982. BA in History, Ohio State U., 1978; JD summa cum laude, U. Dayton, 1981. Bar: Ohio 1981, U.S. Dist. Ct. (so. dist.) Ohio 1981. Assoc. Smith & Schnacke, Dayton, Ohio, 1981-84, Porter, Wright, Morris & Arthur, Dayton, 1984—. Mem. ABA, Ohio State Bar Assn., Dayton Bar Assn. Lutheran. Avocation: golf. Antitrust, General corporate, Securities. Home: 810 Oakcreek Dr Dayton OH 45429 Office: Porter Wright Morris & Arthur 2100 1st Nat Bank Bldg Dayton OH 45402

WATTS-FITZGERALD, ABIGAIL CORY, lawyer; b. Summit, N.J., Mar. 23, 1952; d. Robert A. and Marilyn D. (Pierson) Watts; m. Thomas A. Watts-FitzGerald, Mar. 3, 1979; 1 child, Caitlin C. BA, Franklin and Marshall Coll., 1974; MA with high honors, U. Chgo., 1975; JD magna cum laude, U. Miami, 1979. Bar: D.C. 1979, Fla. 1985. Assoc. Arnold and Porter, Washington, 1979-85; ptnr. Steel, Hector & Davis, Miami, Fla., 1985—; Editor-in-chief U. Miami Law Rev., 1978-79; contbr. articles to profl. jours. Mem. ABA, D.C. Bar Assn., Fla. Bar Assn. Democrat. Clubs: Downtown Athletic, Bankers (Miami). General corporate, Banking, Securities. Home: 930 Valencia Ave Coral Gables FL 33134 Office: Steel Hector & Davis 4000 SE Fin Ctr 200 S Biscayne Blvd Miami FL 33131-2398

WAUGH (ZUCKER), KARIN WELLES, lawyer, army officer; B.A. Polit. Sci., Quincy (Ill.) Coll., 1966; M.A. in Philosophy, Boston Coll., 1967; J.D., U. Mo.-Kansas City, 1973; M.F.S., LL.M. in Law, Criminology and Psychiatry, George Washington U., 1976. Bar: Mo. 1973, U.S. Ct. Mil. Appeals 1974, U.S. Supreme Ct. 1976. Commd. capt. JAGC, U.S. Army, 1974, promoted to maj., 1981; criminal trial lawyer, Ft. Belvoir, Va., 1974-75; fellow in forensic medicine Armed Forces Inst. Pathology, Washington, 1975-76, legal counsel, 1981-86; action atty. tort br. litigation div. Office Judge Adv. Gen., Washington, 1976-78; command judge adv. 7th Med. Command, Heidelberg, W.Ger., 1978-81; sr. instr. mil. med. jurisprudence br. Acad. Health Scis., Ft. Sam Houston, Tex., 1986—; assoc. prof. health mgmt. U. Md., 1985; adj. assoc. prof. health sci. Tex. Wesleyan Coll., 1986—; asst. prof. health care adminstr. Baylor U., 1987; lectr. legal medicine. French hornist Vt. State Philharm. Orch., Montpelier, 1964-65; asst. dir. Mishawaum Choral Soc., Burlington, Mass., 1969-70; vestryman St. Hilda of Whitby Anglican Cath. Ch., Washington, 1984-86. Assoc. in law Am. Coll. Legal Medicine; mem. ABA (chmn. standing com. on mil. law 1985-86), Mo. Bar Assn., Am. Soc. Law and Medicine, Judge Advs. Assn. (bd. dirs 1984-86); DAR, Phi Alpha Delta. Health, Medical bioethics. Home: 5100 El Capitan San Antonio TX 78233

WAXLER, DAVID HARVEY, lawyer; b. New Bedford, Mass., May 25, 1950; s. Felix Benjamin and Helen (Fonfara) W.; Eileen V. Winterhalter, Aug. 23, 1986. BA, Brandeis U., 1972; JD, Boston Coll., 1977. Bar: Mass. 1977, U.S. Dist. Ct. Mass. 1978. Asst. dist. atty. County of Bristol, New Bedford, 1977-80, chief prosecutor major crimes unit, 1980-81; ptnr. Hamel, Waxler, Allen & Collins, New Bedford, 1981—; instr. Mass. Com. on Legal Edn., Boston, 1984—. Mem. New Bedford Bar Assn., Bristol County Bar Assn., Mass. Bar Assn., Acad. Trial Lawyers, ABA. Federal civil litigation, State civil litigation, Criminal. Home: 80 Cottage St New Bedford MA 02740

WAXMAN, NED WARREN, legal educator; b. Balt., Oct. 23, 1948; s. Melvin and Florine (Hornstein) W.; m. Edna Maman, Aug. 8, 1984. BS in Econs., Wharton Sch. Bus. U. Pa., 1970; attended, U. Miami, 1972-73; JD, Emory U., 1975; studied, Hebrew U., Jerusalem, 1983-84. Bar: Ga. 1975, D.C. 1976, U.S. Dist. Ct. (no. dist.) Ga. 1976, U.S. Supreme Ct. 1979, U.S. Ct. Appeals (11th cir.) 1981. Law clk. to presiding judge U.S. Dist. Ct. (no. dist.) Ga., Atlanta, 1975-79; law clk. to presiding judge U.S. Bankruptcy Ct., Atlanta, 1979-80, estate adminstr., 1981-82; assoc. Macey & Zusmann, Atlanta, 1980-81; asst. prof. sch. bus. adminstrn. Coll. William and Mary, Williamsburg, Va., 1982—; adj. prof. bus. law Mercer U., Atlanta, 1976, sch. bus. adminstrn. Emory U., Atlanta, 1976-78; speaker bankruptcy law various orgns. and instns., 1981—. Contbr. articles to profl. jours. Cantor various synagogues, 1972—. Served with USAR, 1970-76. Recipient Peabody prize City of Balt., 1966; named one of Outstanding Young Men Am., 1983; alumni fellow for outstanding teaching Coll. William and Mary, 1986. Mem. ABA, Am. Bus. Law Assn., Am. Profs. for Peace in Middle East. Jewish. Avocations: running, swimming. Bankruptcy, Contracts commercial. Home: 308-C Patriot Ln Williamsburg VA 23185 Office: Coll William and Mary Sch Bus Adminstrn Williamsburg VA 23185

WAYNE, RICHARD STUART, lawyer; b. Cin., June 5, 1952; s. David and Elaine Gloria (Schwartz) W.; m. Vanessa Victoria Whiteford-Boyle, May 30, 1976; children: Jared David, Nicolas Tristan. BA in Psychology, U. Cin., 1974; JD, U. Dayton, 1978. Bar: Ohio 1979, U.S. Dist. Ct. (so. dist.) Ohio 1979, U.S. Dist. Ct. (ea. dist.) Mich. 1979, U.S. Ct. Appeals (6th cir.) 1983, U.S. Ct. Appeals (4th cir.) 1984, U.S. Ct. Appeals (9th cir.) 1986, U.S. Ct. Appeals (5th cir.) 1987. Assoc. Gene Mesh Co. L.P.A., Cin., 1980-85; ptnr. Strauss & Troy, Cin., 1985—. Assoc. editor U. Dayton Law Rev., 1978. Vol. Legal Aid Soc., Cin., 1979, United Appeal, Cin., 1986—. Mem. ABA, Fed. Bar Assn., Ohio Bar Assn., Cin. Bar Assn., Assn. Trial Lawyers Am. Avocations: running, tennis, reading, music. General corporate, Litigation securities and complex commercial transaction, General buy-sells, organizations and reorganizations. Office: Strauss & Troy 2100 Central Trust Ctr Cincinnati OH 45202-4186

WAYNE, ROBERT ANDREW, lawyer; b. Newark, Oct. 4, 1938; s. David Michael and Charlotte (Chesler) W.; m. Charlotte Fainblatt, Aug. 14, 1969; children—Andrew Mark, Gary Howard, Deborah Jill. B.A., Princeton U., 1960; J.D., Columbia U. 1963. Bar: N.J. 1964, U.S. Dist. Ct. N.J. 1964, U.S. Dist. Ct. (ea. and so. dists.) N.Y. 1966, U.S. Ct. Apls. (3d cir.) 1967, N.Y. 1981, U.S. Ct. Apls. (2d cir.) 1984, U.S. Supreme Ct. 1984, U.S. Claims Ct., 1984, U.S. Tax Ct. 1984. Assoc., Shanley & Fisher, Newark, 1964-69, ptnr., 1969-71; ptnr. Robinson, Wayne, Levin, Riccio & LaSala, Newark, 1971—. Mem. Democratic County Com., Livingston, N.J., 1971-74. Served with AUS, 1963-69. Mem. ABA, N.J. Bar Assn., Essex County Bar Assn., Monmouth County Bar Assn., Fed. Bar Assn., Am. Coll. Real Estate Lawyers. Jewish. Real property, Contracts commercial, Federal civil litigation. Office: Robinson Wayne Levin Riccio & LaSala Gateway I Newark NJ 07102

WAYNE, ROBERT JONATHAN, lawyer, educator; b. Fresno, Calif., Apr. 4, 1951; s. William W. and Blanche (Freedman) W.; m. Dorothy A. Madden, Oct. 23, 1981; children: Daniel, Julia. BS, U. Oreg., 1971; JD, UCLA, 1974. Bar: Calif. 1974, Wash. 1975, U.S. Dist. Ct. (we. dist.) Wash. 1975, U.S. Ct. Appeals (9th and D.C. cirs.) 1975, U.S. Supreme Ct. 1979. Law clk. U.S. Ct. Appeals (D.C. cir.), 1974-75; assoc. Perkins, Coie, Stone, Olsen & Williams, Seattle, 1975-76; dep. prosecutor King County Prosecutor's Office, Seattle, 1976-78; sole practice Seattle, 1978—; instr. trail advocacy U. Wash., Seattle, 1977—, Nat. Inst. Trial Advocacy, Seattle, 1980—. Mem. Assn. Trial Lawyers Am., Wash. State Trial Lawyers Assn. (chmn. tort sect. 1983-85), Wash. State Bar Assn. (chmn. criminal law sect. 1982-83, 86-87), Nat. Assn. Criminal Def. Lawyers, Order of the Coif, Order of Barristers. Avocations: flying. Criminal, Personal injury. Office: 408 Pioneer Bldg Seattle WA 98104

WAZ, JOSEPH WALTER, JR., government relations consultant, author; b. Meriden, Conn., Jan. 13, 1953; s. Joseph Walter and Rose Marie (Barillaro) W.; m. Ann Stookey, Sept. 25, 1981. AB, Boston U., 1975; JD, U. Conn., 1978. Bar: Conn. 1978; D.C. 1979, U.S. Ct. Appeals D.C. 1980. Dep. dir. Telecommunications Research and Action Ctr., Washington, 1979-82; sr. assoc. govt. relations Wexler Reynolds Harrison & Schule, Inc., Washington, 1983-86, gen. counsel, 1986—. Author (with S. Simon) Reverse The Charges, 1983 (Book of the Month Club pro bono selection 1983); contbr. articles to communications trade publs. Mem. ABA, Fed. Communications Bar Assn. (chmn. continuing legal edn.), D.C. Bar Assn. Avocations: music, travel, team sports. Legislative, Communications, Trademark and copyright. Home: 9417 Russell Rd Silver Spring MD 20910 Office: Wexler Reynolds Harrison & Schule Inc 1317 F St NW #600 Washington DC 20004

WEAGANT, LANCE MAXWELL, lawyer; b. Lynwood, Calif., Mar. 13, 1950; s. Clifford Maxwell and Jean Edith (Harrup) W. BA magna cum laude, U. So. Calif., 1972, JD, 1976. Bar: Calif. 1976, U.S. Dist. Ct. (cen. dist.) Calif. 1977, U.S. Dist. Ct. (so. dist.) Calif. 1979, U.S. Tax Ct. 1980, U.S. Ct. Appeals (9th cir.) 1980. Ptnr. Fowler, Weagant & Loo, Los Angeles, 1976—; lectr. Calif. Continuing Edn. of Bar, Los Angeles, 1984—. Co-author: How to Live and Die with California Probate, 1984, California Decedent Estate Practice, 1986. Mem. ABA (taxation, real property, trust and probate law sect.), Beverly Hills Estate Planning Council (chmn. sub sect. legis., Beverly Hills probate, trust and estate planning sect. 1982-83), Phi Beta Kappa. Probate, Estate taxation, Corporate taxation. Home: 10465 Eastborne Ave Unit 306 Los Angeles CA 90024 Office: Fowler Weagant & Loo 1900 Ave of the Stars Suite 1900 Los Angeles CA 90067

WEARY, THOMAS SQUIRES, lawyer; b. Junction City, Kans., Feb. 15, 1925; s. Ulysses S. and Ina Belle (Kirkpatrick) W.; m. Helen Stephenson, Sept. 25, 1967. A.B. cum laude, Harvard U., 1946, J.D., 1950. Bar: Pa. 1951, U.S. Supreme Ct. 1963. prin. Saul, Ewing, Remick & Saul, Phila., 1967—; chief exec. officer Invisible Fence Co., Inc., Wayne, Pa., 1979—; arbitrator Am. Arbitration Assn. Bd. dirs., v.p., gen. counsel Acad. Vocal Arts, Phila.; bd. dirs. World Affairs Council Phila., mem. exec. com., treas.; bd. dirs. Diversified Community Services, Phila. Served to lt. (j.g.) USNR, 1943-49. Recipient Legion of Honor award Chapel of Four Chaplains, Phila., 1982. Mem. Interlex Group (founding ptnr.), Phila. Bar Assn., Pa. Bar Assn., Internat. Law Office Assn., ABA. Presbyterian. Clubs: Racquet, Harvard (dir.) (Phila.); Merion Cricket (Haverford, Pa.); Edgemere (Pike County, Pa.). General practice, Private international. Office: 3800 Centre Sq West Philadelphia PA 19102

WEATHERSBY, EARL EUGENE, lawyer; b. Gainesville, Tex., Mar. 27, 1925; s. Earl Eugene and Alex Evelyn (McCormick) W.; m. Minna McBee, Jan. 27, 1946 (dec. 1977); children—Jeanne, Alexis, Rebecca, Howard; m. Emma Jean Oslin, Nov. 21, 1979. A.A., Paris Jr. Coll., Tex., 1949; J.D., Baylor U., 1952. Bar: Tex. 1952, U.S. Supreme Ct. 1965, U.S. Ct. Mil. Appeals 1965, U.S. Ct. Claims 1970. Commd. officer U.S. Air Force, 1952; judge advocate U.S. Air Force, 1952-71; judge Air Force Bd. of Review, Washington, 1967-68, legis. atty., 1968-71; ret., 1971; mcpl. judge, San Angelo, Tex., 1971-75; lectr. Sul Ross U., Del Rio, Tex., 1977-79; sole practice, San Antonio, 1979—; realtor Lark-Weathersby Realtors, San Antonio, 1982—; lectr. in field. Recipient Outstanding Service award West. Tex. Therapy Ctr., 1967; Meritorious Service award USAF, 1970. Mem. Ret. Officers Assn., Ret. Air Force Judge Advocates Assn., Assn. Old Crows, Tex. Bar Assn., Phi Alpha Delta. Republican. Baptist. Club: San Angelo West. Lodge: Rotary (dir. 1974-75). General practice. Home: 115 Long Bow San Antonio TX 78231 Office: Earl E Weathersby 923 Vance Jackson #1509 San Antonio TX 78201

WEATHERSPOON, FLOYD DOUGLAS, b. High Point, N.C., Feb. 16, 1951; s. Carl R. and Ruth (Hamlin) Ingram; m. Stephanie Virginia Jones, Aug. 31, 1982; children: Autumn, Christopher. BS, N.C. A&T U., 1974; JD, Howard U., 1977. Bar: Ohio 1977. Law clk. Ohio Atty. Gen., Columbus, 1977-78; compliance officer Ohio Civil Rights Commn., Columbus, 1978-79; dir. fair practices Montgomery County, Dayton, Ohio, 1979-81; chief conciliation and mediation br. TVA, Knoxville, 1981—; cons. State of Ohio, Columbus, 1980-81; adj. prof. Knoxville Coll., 1983-87, Walters State Community Coll., 1983-87; lectr. nat. confs. of Soc. Dispute Resolution, Am. Affirmative Action Assn., Am. Soc. Pub. Administrn., others. Author: EEO/Affirmative Action, 1986. Active Membership sub-com. of Knoxville Urban League, Nat. Urban League Black Exec. Exchange Program. Named one of Outstanding Young Men Am., 1982, 84; recipient Arbitration award, Better Bus. Bur., Knoxville, 1985. Mem. ABA, Ohio Bar Assn., Nat. Acad. Conciliators, Nat. Panel Consumer Arbitrators, Soc. Dispute Resolution, Am. Arbitration Assn., Alpha Phi Alpha. Democrat. Baptist. Avocations: coin collecting, record collecting, tennis. Labor. Home: 8937 Moneymaker Rd Knoxville TN 37923

WEATHERUP, ROY GARFIELD, lawyer; b. Annapolis, Md., Apr. 20, 1947; s. Robert Alexander and Kathryn Crites (Hesser) W.; m. Wendy Gaines, Sept. 10, 1977; children: Jennifer, Christine. AB in Polit. Sci., Stanford U., 1968, JD, 1972. Bar: Calif. 1972, U.S. Dist. Ct. 1973, U.S. Ct. Appeals (9th cir.) 1975, U.S. Supreme Ct. 1980. Assoc. Haight, Dickson, Brown & Bonesteel, Los Angeles, Santa Monica and Santa Ana, Calif., 1972-78, ptnr., 1979—; Moot Ct. judge UCLA, Loyola U., Pepperdine U.; arbitrator Am. Arbitration Assn. Mem. Calif. Acad. Appellate Lawyers, ABA, Town Hall Calif., Los Angeles County Bar Assn. Republican. Methodist. State civil litigation, Insurance, Personal injury. Home: 17260 Rayen St Northridge CA 91325 Office: Haight Dickson Brown & Bonesteel 201 Santa Monica Blvd Santa Monica CA 90406

WEAVER, CYNTHIA MARIE, lawyer; b. Phila., Oct. 30, 1948; d. Lucien Russell and Antoinette Marie (Galizia) Favata; children—Tiffany Marie, Meredith Anne. B.A., Adelphi U., 1970; secondary edn. cert. Bloomsburg State Coll., 1972; J.D., SUNY-Buffalo, 1977. Bar: Pa. 1977, U.S. Dist. Ct. (ea. dist.) Pa. 1983, U.S. Supreme Ct. 1984, U.S. Ct. Appeals (3d cir.) 1987; Tchr. Bristol Jr./Sr. High Sch. (Pa.), 1970-72; law clk. Div. of Claims, State of N.Y., Buffalo, 1976; asst. pub. defender Bucks County, Doylestown, Pa., 1977-79, dep. pub. defender, 1979-81; sole practice, Newtown, Pa., 1982—; solicitor Children and Youth Agy., Bucks County, 1984—; speaker, panelist on various law related issues, Bucks County and Phila., 1977-81. Pres. bd. dirs. Preventative Rehab. Youth and Devel., Bristol, Pa., 1978-81; bd. dirs. Reaching-at-Problems Group Home, Chalfont, Pa., 1981-84, Three Arches, Inc., Falls Twp., Pa., 1985, Orgn. to Prevent Teenage Suicide, 1984—, Youth Services Assn., Bucks County, 1984—. Recipient Trial Lawyer's award Erie County Bar Assn., 1977. Mem. ABA, Assn. Trial Lawyers Am., Bucks County Bar Assn. (dir. 1983—). Democrat. Roman Catholic. Club: Soroptimists (pres.) (Indian Rock). Criminal, Personal injury, Juvenile. Home: 21 N Lancaster Ln Newtown PA 18940 Office: 110 S State St Newtown PA 18940

WEAVER, GEORGE MARVIN, lawyer; b. Atlanta, June 14, 1950; s. James Thomas and Ida (Elder) W.; m. Allison Cheatwood, July 28, 1984. BA, Ga. State U., 1972; JD, U. Ga., 1975; postgrad., Trinity Evang. Div. Sch., Lincolnshire, Ill., 1975-77. Bar: Ga., U.S. Dist. Ct. (no., mid. and so. dists.), U.S. Ct. Appeals (11th cir.), U.S. Supreme Ct. Asst. solicitor gen. Fulton County Solicitor's Office, Atlanta, 1977-81; asst. atty. gen. State of Ga., Atlanta, 1981-84; ptnr. and owner Sibley and Weaver, Atlanta, 1984—. Author: Handbook on the Prosecution of Obscenity Cases, 1985. Mem. exec. adv. com. 4th Congl. Dist. Ga., 1984—. Mem. ABA, Ga. Bar Assn., Christian Legal Soc. Republican. Presbyterian. Avocations: langs., home renovation, gardening, philosophy, tennis. Civil rights, Federal civil litigation, Personal injury. Office: Sibley & Weaver 1275 Peachtree St Suite 555 Atlanta GA 30367-1801

WEAVER, JACQUELINE LANG, educator; b. Westchester, Pa., Jan. 18, 1947; d. Hans J. and Ruth (Crowl) L.; m. Kirk Kenyon, Sept. 21, 1968; children: Kyle, Kenyon. BA, Harvard U., 1968; PhC in Econs., UCLA, 1971; JD, U. Houston, 1975. Bar: Tex. 1976. Economist Exxon Co., USA, Houston, 1971-76; prof. law U. Houston Law Ctr., 1977—. Author: Unitization of Oil and Gas Fields in Texas, 1986. Mem. ABA, Tex. Bar Assn. Oil and gas leasing, Environment. Home: 5033 Longmont Houston TX 77056 Office: U Houston Law Ctr 4800 Calhoun Houston TX 77056

WEAVER, JOHN HOSCH, lawyer; b. Great Falls, Mont., Sept. 4, 1914; s. James Albert and Bertha Katherine (Hosch) W.; m. Kay Shryne, Feb. 25, 1945; 1 child, Kristine Kay. AB, BS, U. Mont., 1936; JD, Harvard U., 1939. Bar: Mont. 1939. Ptnr. Jardine, Stephenson, Blewett, Weaver, Great Falls. Chmn. Supreme Ct.'s Commn. on Practice, Helena, Mont., 1970-75. Served to capt. JAGC, U.S. Army, 1943-46. Fellow ABA; mem. ABA, Mont. Bar Assn. (pres. 1965), Mont. Trial Lawyers Assn., Cascade County Bar Assn. (pres. 1962), Order of Barristers. Lodge: Rotary. State civil litigation, Condemnation, State and local taxation.

WEAVER, RONALD L., lawyer; b. Winston-Salem, N.C., June 8, 1949; s. Robert Lee and Laura (Reich) W.; m. Jacquelyn Kay Witt, June 12, 1971; children: Lara Alison, Ronald Lee. AB, U. N.C.-Chapel Hill, 1971; JD cum laude, Harvard U., 1974. Bar: Fla. Mem. Carlton, Fields, Ward, Emmanuel, Smith & Cutler, Tampa, Fla., 1974-79; ptnr. Stearns, Weaver Miller, Weissler, Alhadeff & Sitterson, Tampa, 1979—; dir. Founders Life Ins. Co., Majestic Towers, Pasadena, Fla. Chmn. Am. Heart Assn., Tampa, 1983. Served to 1st lst. USAF, 1971-81. Mem. ABA (chmn. real estate fin. subcom. comml. and fin. services com.), Hillsborough County Bar Assn. (program chmn. 1980), Tampa C. of C. (chmn. cultural affairs, bd. govs. 1983). Clubs: University, Palma Ceia Country (Tampa). Author: Florida and Federal Banking, 1981; Commercial Real Estate Acquisition, 1983. Real property. Home: 4304 W Azeele Tampa FL 33609 Office: Stearns Weaver Miller Alhadeff & Sitterson 3300 One Tampa City Ctr Tampa FL 33602

WEAVER, SUSAN M., lawyer, social worker; b. Cleve., Dec. 11, 1948; d. Edgar Walter and Shirley (Fagin) Miller. BS, Case Western Res. U., 1972, MS in Social Adminstrn., 1976; JD, Cleve. State U., 1980. Bar: Ohio 1980, U.S. Dist. Ct. (no. dist.) Ohio 1980. Dir. legal dept., adminstr. Domestic Relations Com., Cleve., 1980-82; exec. dir. Divorce Equity, Inc., Cleve., 1982-85; sole practice Cleve., 1985—; cons. GEAR Found., Cleve., 1985—. Pres. Ohio Women's Polit. Caucus, Columbus, 1984; sec., Cuyahoga Women's Polit. Caucus, Cleve., 1982-84; Dem. precinct committeeman, Cuyahoga County, 1982—; mem. adv. bd. JFSA Mediation, Cleve., 1984—, Cleve. Community Coll., 1980—. Named one of Cleve.'s 100 Most Influential Women Cleveland Mag., 1983. Mem. ABA, Greater Cleve. Bar Assn., Cuyahoga Bar Assn., Cleve. Women Lawyers Assn., Nat. Assn. Social Workers. Democrat. Jewish. Avocations: reading, cooking. Family and matrimonial, General practice, Civil rights. Home: 1065 Brandon Rd Cleveland Heights OH 44112 Office: 33595 Bainbridge Rd Suite 201 Solon OH 44139

WEAVER, WILLIAM CARROLL, lawyer; b. Grantsville, W.Va., Dec. 29, 1927; s. Arley E. and Grace Catherine (Davis) W.; m. Cary Spottstwood Breathed, Oct. 6, 1962; 1 dau., Laura Breathed. A.B., W.Va. U., 1950; J.D., George Washington U. and W.Va. U., 1953. Bar: W.Va., U.S. Dist. Ct. (no. dist.) W.Va., U.S. Dist. Ct. (so. dist.) W.Va., U.S. Supreme Ct., 1983. Assoc. Jackson, Kelly, Holt & O'Farrell, 1953-58; ptnr. Weaver & Hayes, and predecessors, Charleston, W.Va., 1958-76; sr. ptnr. Weaver, Hayes & Moredock, Charleston, from 1976; now in sole practice, Charleston. Active Boy Scouts Am., United Fund. Mem. W.Va. State Bar Assn. (bd. govs., exec. com. 1974-79, 2d v.p. 1978-79, 1st v.p. 1979-80, pres. 1980-81, chmn. bd. 1981, numerous coms.), Kanawha County Bar Assn. (pres. 1968-69), Inter-Am. Bar Assn., ABA, Internat. Bar Assn., W.Va. Trial Lawyers Assn., Assn. Trial Lawyers Am., Am. Judicature Soc., Union Internat. des Avocats, Am. Bd. Trial Advs. (advocate), Pitts. Inst. Legal Medicine, Am. Soc. Law and Medicine, World Peace Through Law Ctr., Phi Delta Phi, Phi Kappa Psi. Democrat. Clubs: Exchange, Edgewood Country (Charleston). Insurance, Personal injury, Workers' compensation. Office: Penthouse Kanawha Valley Bldg Charleston WV 25301

WEBB, DAN K., lawyer; b. Macomb, Ill., Sept. 5, 1945; s. Keith L. and Phyllis I. (Clow) W.; student Western Ill. U., 1963-66; J.D., Loyola U., 1970; m. Laura A. Buscemi, Mar. 15, 1973; children—Jeffrey, Maggie, Michael. Bar: Ill. 1970. Chief spl. prosecutions div. U.S. Atty.'s Office, Chgo., 1970-76; ptnr. firm Cummins, Decker & Webb, Chgo., 1976-79; dir. Ill. Dept. Law Enforcement, Chgo., 1979-80; ptnr. Pierce, Webb, Lydon & Griffin, Chgo., 1980-81; U.S. atty., Chgo., 1981-84; ptnr. Winston & Strawn, Chgo., 1984—; instr. John Marshall Law Sch., 1975—, Loyola U. Sch. Law, 1980—. Vice chmn. Met. Fair and Expn. Authority, 1978—; bd. advisers Mercy Hosp. and Med. Ctr.; mem. Chgo. Council on Arson. Recipient spl. commendation award U.S. Justice Dept., 1975; named 1 of 10 outstanding young Chicagoans, Chgo. Jaycees, 1979. Mem. ABA, Ill. Bar Assn., Chgo. Bar Assn., Fed. Bar Assn., Legal Club Chgo., Execs. Club Chgo. Republican. Home: 10020 S Damen Chicago IL 60643 Office: Winston & Strawn One First Nat Plaza Suite 5000 Chicago IL 60603

WEBB, DANIEL ANDREW, lawyer; b. Baton Rouge, Dec. 20, 1948; s. Harold Andrew and Lois Anne (Webre) W.; m. Elizabeth Verlander, Dec. 29, 1972; children: Craig Roth, Elizabeth Pearce, Preston Stafford. BS in Zoology, La. State U., 1971; JD, Loyola U., New Orleans, 1977. Bar: La. 1977, U.S. Dist. Ct. (ea. dist.) La. 1977, U.S. Dist. Ct. (mid. and we. dists.) La. 1978, U.S. Ct. Appeals (5th cir.) 1977. Law clk. U.S. Magistrate, New Orleans, 1976-77; assoc. Burke & Ballard, New Orleans, 1977-78, Herbert, Abbott & Horack, New Orleans, 1978-80; ptnr. Herbert & Abbott, New Orleans, 1980-84, Abbott, Webb, Best & Meeks, New Orleans, 1984—. Served to maj. USAR, 1971—. Mem. ABA, Maritime Law Assn. U.S. (procter), Southeast Admiralty Law Inst. Republican. Roman Catholic. Clubs: New Orleans Country, Bienville, Iris, Alpine, Cactus, Ambassador, Royal Soc. St. George. Avocations: golf, running. Admiralty, Federal civil litigation, Personal injury. Home: 322 Hector Metairie LA 70005 Office: Abbott Webb Best & Meeks 400 Lafayette Suite 200 New Orleans LA 70130

WEBB, HENLEY ROSS, lawyer; b. N.Y.C., June 21, 1940; m. Helen Osgood. BA, Yale U., 1963; JD, Harvard U., 1966. Bar: Mass. 1967. Corp. atty. Cabot Corp., Boston, 1967-73, group counsel, 1973-82, asst. gen. counsel, 1982-86, gen. counsel, 1986—. Mem. ABA, Boston Bar Assn. General corporate, Antitrust, Contracts commercial. Office: Cabot Corp 125 High St Boston MA 02110

WEBB, JERE M., lawyer; b. Portland, Oreg., July 28, 1944; s. Jesse F. Webb and Olive Rea (Coble) Chin; m. Judith A. Hartmann, Sept. 11, 1966. AB with distinction, Stanford U., 1966; JD, U. Chgo., 1969. Law clk. to justice Oreg. Supreme Ct., Salem, 1969-70; with Stoel, Rives, Boley, Portland, 1970—; trustee Oreg. Assn. of Def. Counsel, Portland, 1976-79; bd. dirs. Oreg. Law Inst., Eugene, Oreg. State Bar. Editor Civil Litigation Manual, 1982, Marketing and Trade Regulation Law News; bd. editors Computer Users Legal Reporter, 1985; contbr. articles to numerous profl. jours. Mem. Oreg. State Bar (chmn. continuing legal edn. com. 1984-85). Antitrust, Computer, General corporate. Home: 5433 SW Vacuna Portland OR 97219 Office: Stoel Rives & Boley 900 SW 5th Ave Portland OR 97204

WEBB, LLOYD JACKSON, lawyer; b. Twin Falls, Idaho, Oct. 6, 1931; s. Clarence Riley and Alta (Simmons) W.; m. Barbara Claire Birrell, Dec. 22, 1954; children: Kevan, Curtis, Carolea, Barry. Student, Brigham Young U., 1949-51, U. Idaho, 1951-52; LLB, U. Utah, 1955. Bar: Utah 1955, Idaho 1956, U.S. Dist. Ct. Idaho 1956, U.S. Dist. Ct. Utah 1956, U.S. Dist. Ct. Alaska 1956, U.S. Ct. Appeals (9th and 10th cirs.) 1956. Ptnr. Rayborn, Rayborn, Webb & Pike, Twin Falls, Idaho, 1957-62, 66-71, Webb, Burton, Carlson & Pedersen, Twin Falls, 1971—; judge 11th Dist., Burley, Idaho, 1962-66. Mem. Idaho Bar Assn., Utah Bar Assn., Alaska Bar Assn., Assn. Trial Lawyers Am., Idaho Trial Lawyers (pres. 1975), Am. Bd. Trial Advs. Republican. LDS. Avocations: travel, photography. Personal injury, State civil litigation, Federal civil litigation. Home: 1846 Alturas Dr Twin Falls ID 83301 Office: Webb Burton Carlson Pederson & Webb 155 2d Ave N Twin Falls ID 83301

WEBB, MICHAEL JOSEPH, lawyer; b. Oakland, Calif., Apr. 16, 1945; s. Sidney Joseph and Charlotte Frazer (Hartmann) W.; m. Joan Lynn Pigman, July 14, 1973; children: Gregory, Stephen, Kristin. BS, U. Calif., Davis, 1967, JD, 1970. Bar: Calif. 1971, U.S. Dist. Ct. (so. dist.) Calif. 1971, U.S. Dist. Ct. (ea. dist.) Calif. 1981. Dep. pub. defender Kern County, Bakersfield, Calif., 1971-81; assoc. Digiorgio, Davis, Klein et al, Bakersfield, 1981-83; sole practice Bakersfield, 1983—. Civil rights, Criminal. Office: 1430 Truxtun Ave #500 Bakersfield CA 93301

WEBB, MICHAEL STEVEN, lawyer, editor; b. Dallas, Apr. 18, 1954; s. Charles Edwin and Mary Ella (Jarrell) W.; m. Pamela Ann Smith, Dec. 27, 1980; children: Christopher Charles, Austin Matthew. AB in Anthropology cum laude, U. Ga., 1976; JD, Woodrow Wilson Sch. Law, 1979. Bar: Ga. 1979, U.S. Dist. Ct. (no. dist.) Ga. 1979, U.S. Ct. Appeals (11th cir.) 1981. Asst. legal editor The Harrison Co., Norcross, Ga., 1978-79; ptnr. Morris, Webb & Stinson, East Point, Ga., 1979-82; sole practice Lilburn, Ga., 1982-87; ptnr., editor Ga. Law Letter Pubs., Atlanta, 1985-86. Editor newsletter Ga. Law Letter, 1985, Ga. Law Letter Fed., 1986. Mem: Fed. Bar Assn., Ga. Bar Assn. (editorial bd. 1985—), Ga. Trial Lawyers Assn., Ga. Assn. Criminal Def. Lawyers, Gwinnett County Bar Assn., Delta Theta Phi, Woodrow Wilson Coll. Law Alumni Assn. (bd. dirs. 1982-84). Democrat. Roman Catholic. Lodges: KC (adv. Gwinnett County club 1985-86), Lions (lion tamer College Park club 1982-83). Avocations: singing, piano. State civil litigation, Criminal, Legal publishing. Home: 225 Windmill Pointe Lawrenceville GA 30245 Office: 3955 Lawrenceville Hwy Bruntley Hall Suite 200 Lilburn GA 30247

WEBB, MORRISON DESOTO, lawyer; b. Danbury, Conn., Dec. 25, 1947; s. Jean Francis III and Nancy (Bukeley) W.; m. Stacie Luise Jacob, May 27, 1979; children: Nicholas Beale, Nathaniel Rodman. BA, Amherst Coll., 1969; JD, Harvard U., 1976. Bar: N.Y. 1977, U.S. Dist. Ct. (ea. and so. dists.) N.Y. 1977, Mass. 1980. Assoc. Rogers & Wells, N.Y.C., 1976-80; atty. New England Telephone, Boston, 1980-83, gen. atty., 1983-84; v.p., gen. counsel NYNEX Bus. Info. Systems Co., White Plains, N.Y., 1984-86; corp. dir. NYNEX Corp. Strategic Mktg., White Plains, N.Y., 1986—. Served to lt. (j.g.) USNR, 1969-73. Mem. ABA, Boston Bar Assn., Westchester Fairfield Corp. Counsel Assn. Republican. Administrative and regulatory, Contracts commercial, General corporate. Home: 45 Glenwood Ln Katonah NY 10536 Office: NYNEX Corp 1113 Westchester Ave White Plains NY 10604

WEBB, ROBERT ALLEN, lawyer; b. Ann Arbor, Mich., Oct. 2, 1944; s. Edgar August and Harriet Wilda (Feetham) W.; m. Judith Travostino, Aug. 25, 1973; children—William Anthony, Christine Elizabeth. B.A., Amherst Coll., 1966; J.D., Yale U., 1969. Bar: Tex., 1970. Atty., OEO, 1969-70; ptnr. Baker & Botts, Houston, 1970—; adj. prof. U. Houston, 1973—; trustee Gulf Coast Legal Found., 1975—, pres., 1981-82, 1985; chmn. pub. utility law sect. State Bar Tex., 1981-82, chmn. com. legal aid to indigent, 1980-83. Recipient Houston Young Lawyers award of Achievement, 1981. Mem. Houston Young Lawyers (pres. 1975). Republican. Episcopalian. Club: Houston Athletic. Public utilities, FERC practice, Nuclear power. Home: 33 Carolane Trail Houston TX 77024 Office: 3000 One Shell Plaza Houston TX 77002

WEBB, RODNEY SCOTT, lawyer; b. Cavalier, N.D., June 21, 1935; s. Chester and Aylza (Martin) W.; m. Betty M. Lykken, Aug. 31, 1957; children: Sharon, Crystal, Todd, Wade, Susan. B.S., U. N.D., 1957, J.D., 1959. Bar: N.D. 1959, U.S. Dist. Ct. N.D. 1965, U.S. Ct. Appeals (8th cir.) 1981. Assoc. Ringsak & Webb, Grafton, N.D., 1959-81; state's atty. Walsh County, Grafton, N.D., 1966-74; mcpl. judge City of Grafton, 1975-81; spl. asst. atty. gen. State of N.D., 1970-81; U.S. atty. Dist. of N.D., Fargo, 1981—. Served to col. JAG, N.D. Army N.G. Republican. Lutheran. Criminal, Federal civil litigation. Office: Fed Courthouse Bldg Fargo ND 58108 *

WEBB, THOMAS IRWIN, JR., lawyer; b. Toledo, Ohio, Sept. 16, 1948; s. Thomas Irwin and Marcia Davis (Winters) W.; m. Polly S. DeWitt, Oct. 11, 1986; 1 child, Elisabeth Hurst. BA, Williams Coll., 1970; postgrad. Boston U., 1970-71; JD, Case Western Res. U., 1973. Bar: Ohio. Assoc. Shumaker, Loop & Kendrick, Toledo, 1973-79, ptnr., 1979—; dir. Comml. Aluminum Cookware Co., York Oldsmobile, Inc. Council mem. Village of Ottawa Hills, Ohio, 1978-85, planning commn., 1978-85; adv. bd. Ohio Div. Securities, 1979—; bd. dirs. Kiwanis Youth Found. of Toledo, Inc. Mem. ABA, Ohio Bar Assn., Toledo Bar Assn., Northwestern Ohio Alumni Assn. of Williams Coll. (pres. 1974-83), Nat. Assn. Bond Lawyers, Toledo-Rowing Found. (trustee 1985—), Order of Coif. Republican. Methodist. Clubs: Crystal Downs Country, Toledo Country, The Toledo (trustee 1984—); Williams Club of N.Y. General corporate, Municipal bonds, Securities. Office: Shumaker Loop & Kendrick 1000 Jackson Toledo OH 43624

WEBB, THOMAS LOWRY, lawyer; b. Meridian, Miss., July 16, 1948; s. Hunter C. Jr. and Nellah (Bailey) W.; m. Sarai Ann Canfield, June 21, 1968; children: Sarai Christian, Thomas L. Jr. BS, U. So. Miss., 1970; JD, U. Miss., 1973; cert. JAG sch., U. Va., 1973. Bar: Miss. 1973, U.S. Dist. Ct. (no. dist.) Miss. 1973, U.S. Ct. Mil. Appeals 1973, U.S. Ct. Claims 1977, U.S. Ct. Appeals (D.C. cir.) 1980, U.S. Ct. Appeals (5th cir.) 1983, U.S. Ct. Appeals (11th cir.) 1983. Asst. dist. atty. Miss. 11th Cir. Ct., various counties, 1976-77; from assoc. to ptnr. Bourdeaux & Jones, Meridian, 1977—; sec., treas. Miss. Bankruptcy Conf., Jackson, 1985-86. Served to capt. JAGC, U.S. Army, 1973-76. Mem. Lauderdale County Young Lawyers Assn. (pres.), Meridian C. of C. Presbyterian. Avocations: hunting, fishing, shooting, wood crafts. Bankruptcy, Consumer commercial, State civil litigation. Office: Bourdeaux & Jones 505 21st Ave PO Box 2009 Meridian MS 39302-2009

WEBB, WILLIAM HESS, lawyer; b. Scottdale, Pa., Sept. 10, 1905; s. Austin Allison and Gertrude (Hess) W.; m. Marian Elizabeth Wellings, Nov. 26, 1931; children: John M., Patricia Ann (Mrs. Terence S. Small). BS, U. Pitts, 1926, LLB, 1929. Bar: Pa. 1929. Since practiced in Pitts.; sr. ptnr. Webb, Burden, Robinson & Webb (and predecessor firm), Pitts., 1948—. Bd. dirs., v.p., treas. Pitts. Opera Soc.; mem. Pitts. Symphony Soc. Served to lst lt. U.S. Army Res., 1926-34. Mem. Am. Patent Law Assn. (bd. mgrs. 1953-62, pres. 1959-60), ABA (ho. of dels. 1961-65), Pa. Bar Assn., Inter-Am. Bar Assn., Allegheny County Bar. Assn., Am. Law Inst., Licensing Execs. Soc., Nat. Assn. Bar Pres.'s, Internat. Assn. Protection Indsl. Property, Civic Light Opera Soc., Delta Theta Phi., Theta Chi. Clubs: Duquesne, University (Pitts); Edgeworth (Sewickley, Pa.); Allegheny Country. Patent, Trademark and copyright, Federal civil litigation. Home: Apt 305 201 Grant St Sewickley PA 15143 Office: Oliver Bldg Pittsburgh PA 15222

WEBB, W(ILLIAM) Y(OUNG) ALEX, lawyer, financial planner; b. Newport News, Va., Feb. 6, 1948; s. Mason Young and Zelma Lee (Myers) W.; m. Rebecca McElroy, Sept. 2, 1966 (div. 1978); 1 child, Johanna Lee. BA magna cum laude, Western Carolina U., 1970; JD, U. N.C., 1973. Bar: N.C. 1973, U.S. Tax Ct. 1978. Mem. tax staff Arthur Andersen & Co., Charlotte, N.C., 1973-75; tax atty. Seawell, Pollock, Fullenwilder, Robbins & May, P.A., Southern Pines, N.C., 1975-79, Seawell, Robbins, May & Webb, Southern Pines, N.C., 1979-81; sole practice Pinehurst, N.C., 1981-85; ptnr. Van Camp, Gill, Bryan, Webb & Thompson, P.A., Pinehurst, 1985—; originator Moore County Tax Roundtable, Pinehurst, 1983-85; speaker estate planning Moore Meml Hosp., Pinehurst, 1981-85. Pres. Sandhills Estate Planning Council, Southern Pines, 1976, Moore County United Way, Southern Pines, 1981; treas. Friends of Weymouth, Southern Pines, 1978; chmn. Moore County adv. bd. Girl Scouts U.S.A., Southern Pines, 1980-82; co-legal counsel World Golf Hall of Fame, Pinehurst, 1980-83; legal counsel Harris D. Blake for Congress Com., Pinehurst, 1982, exec. com. Moore County Rep. Party, Southern Pines, 1982-83; vice-chmn. Sandhills Food Bank, Southern Pines, 1983. Named Man Yr. Southern Pines Jaycees, 1977, one of Outstanding Young Men Am., 1983, recipient Disting. Service award Southern Pines Jaycees, 1983. Mem. N.C. Bar Assn. (sec. tax council 1984-85), Internat. Assn. Fin. Planning (program dir. Triangle chpt. 1985-86), Am. Inst. CPA's, N.C. Assn. CPA's, N.C. Coll. Advocacy, Moore County LWV (chmn. land use com. 1985-86), Moore County Homebuilders Assn. (chmn. local govt. com. 1985-86),. Episcopalian. Lodges: Elks, Rotary. Pension, profit-sharing, and employee benefits, Probate, Personal income taxation. Office: Van Camp Gill Bryan Webb & Thompson Box 1389 Pinehurst NC 28374

WEBBER, CARL MADDRA, lawyer; b. Champaign, Ill., May 23, 1944; s. Charles Maddra and Lucille Ethelyn (Rankin) W.; m. Catherine Ann Johnson, June 21, 1975; children—Wendy Elizabeth, Christopher Maddra. B.S., Northwestern U., 1966; J.D., U. Ill., 1973. Bar: Ill. 1974, U.S. Dist. Ct. (cen. dist.) Ill. 1974, U.S. Ct. Appeals (2d cir.) 1979. Shareholder, dir. Webber & Thies, P.C., Urbana, Ill., 1974—. Contbr. article to profl. jour. Mem. Champaign County Jail Courts Tech. Adv. Com., 1978-79, Downtown Devel. & Redev. Commn., Urbana, 1978-79, U. Ill. Pres.'s Council, Urbana, 1984—; pres. Downtown Urbana Promotion Com., 1981-82; bd. dirs. Arrowhead Council Boy Scouts Am., 1974—, v.p., 1979-82, U. Ill. Library Friends, 1983—, v.p., 1984-86, pres. 1986—; bd. visitors. U. Ill. Coll. Law, 1980—. Served to lt. USN, 1966-70. Recipient Appreciation Award City of Urbana, 1980. Fellow Am. Bar Found., Ill. Bar Found.; mem. Urbana C. of C. (dir. 1978-81), ABA, Champaign County Bar Assn. (dir. 1980-83, pres. 1981-82), Ill. Bar Assn. (mem. Family Law Council 1978-79, Real Estate Council, 1983—). Lodge: Rotary (dir. 1980-82). Real property, Private international, Contracts commercial. Home: 1801 Moraine Dr Champaign IL 61821 Office: Webber & Thies PC 202 Lincoln Square PO Box 189 Urbana IL 61801

WEBER, ALBAN, association executive, lawyer; b. Chgo., Jan. 29, 1915; s. Joseph A. and Anna (von Plachecki) W.; AB, Harvard U., 1935, LLB, 1937; m. Margaret Kenny, Dec. 29, 1951; children: Alban III, Peggy Ann, Gloria, Brian. Bar: Ill. 1938, Mich. 1985. Ptnr. Weber & Weber, 1937-41; gen. counsel Fgn. Liquidation Commn., State Dept., 1946; trust officer Lake Shore Nat. Bank, Chgo., 1952-55; univ. counsel Northwestern U., Evanston, Ill., 1955-70; pres. Fedn. Ind. Ill. Colls. and Univs., Evanston, 1971-84; of counsel Schuyler, Roche & Zwirner, Evanston, 1984—. Bd. dirs. Benjamin Franklin Fund, Inc., 1965-75, Northwestern U. Press, Inc., 1965-70, pres., 1961-70; chmn. State Assn. Execs. Council, 1981. Pres. Northeast Ill. council Boy Scouts Am., 1970-71. Alderman, City of Chgo., 1947-51. Served to comdr. USNR, 1941-45, rear adm., 1974. Recipient Silver Beaver award Boy Scouts Am.; Meritorious Service award Loyola U., 1978; Edn. for Freedom award Roosevelt U., 1984. Mem. Nat. Assn. Coll. and Univ. Attys. (pres. 1962), Harvard Law Soc. Ill. (pres. 1984), Navy League (pres. Evanston council 1967-70, Univ. Risk Mgmt. Assn. (pres. 1965), Univ. Ins. Mgrs. (pres.). Clubs: Law, Economics, Harvard, Executives, Chicago Yacht; White Lake Golf, White Lake Yacht. Lodge: Kiwanis (lt. gov.). Estate planning, Probate, Legislative. Home: 1555 SE Sunshine Ave Port Sainte Lucie FL 33452 Office: Schuyler Roche & Zwirner State Bank Bldg Evanston IL 60201

WEBER, DAVID VICTOR, lawyer; b. Seattle, Feb. 2, 1951; s. James Gordon and Walda Patricia (Harbst) W.; m. Mary Frances Palmer, Aug. 4, 1973; children: Catherine Lynn, Lauren Patricia, Janet Rebecca, Elizabeth Anne. BA, Auburn U., 1972; JD, Mercer U., 1976. Bar: Ga. 1976, U.S. Dist. Ct. (no. and so. dists) Ga. 1976. Assoc. Lester, Lester & Flynt, Augusta, Ga., 1976-81; sole practice Augusta, 1981-82; ptnr. Thomas & Weber, Augusta, 1983—. Mem. ABA, Ga. Trial Lawyers Assn. Club: Optimist Of Augusta, Inc. (pres. 1985-86). Criminal, Real property, General practice. Home: 849 Brookfield Pkwy Augusta GA 30907 Office: Thomas & Weber Attys 2335 Lumpkin Rd Augusta GA 30906

WEBER, FRED J., justice Supreme Ct. Montana; b. Deer Lodge, Mont., Oct. 6, 1919; s. Victor N. and Dorothy A. (Roberts) W.; m. Phyllis M. Schell, June 2, 1951; children: Anna Marie, Donald J., Mark W., Paul V. B.A., U. Mont., 1943, J.D., 1947. Bar: Mont. 1947. Atty. Kuhr & Weber, Havre, Mont., 1947-55, Weber, Bosch & Kuhr, and successors, 1956-80; justice Supreme Ct. Mont., Helena, 1981—. Served to capt. inf. U.S. Army, 1943-46. Fellow Am. Bar Found., Am. Coll. Probate Counsel; mem. ABA, Am. Judicature Soc. Judicial administration. Office: Justice Bldg 215 N Sanders St Helena MT 59620

WEBER, GERALD JOSEPH, judge; b. Erie, Pa., Feb. 1, 1914; s. Joseph J. and Ruth M. (Sullivan) W.; m. Berta M. Drechsel, Aug. 21, 1947; children: Thomas, William, Mary. A.B., Harvard U., 1936; LL.B., U. Pa., 1939. Bar: Pa. 1940. Civilian with U.S. Forces, Austria, 1946-47; mem. firm Knox, Weber, Pearson & McLaughlin, Erie, 1957-64; city solicitor Erie, 1951-61; judge U.S. Dist. Ct. Western Dist. Pa., 1964—, now chief judge. Served with AUS, 1942-45. Decorated Bronze Star. Office: US Courthouse 2 Pittsburgh PA 15219 also: US Courthouse Erie PA 16501 *

WEBER, H. PATRICK, lawyer; b. Cin., Jan. 25, 1949; s. Harry P. and Peggy (Sebastiani) W.; m. Marilyn Bykowski, Nov. 30, 1974; children: Kevin, Carmen, Courtney. BBA, U. Notre Dame, 1971, JD, 1974. Bar: Ohio 1974, U.S. Dist. Ct. (so. dist.) Ohio 1974, U.S. Tax Ct. 1975. Ptnr. Strauss & Troy, Cin., 1974—; bd. dirs. All Parts Inc., Cin., Cin. Surg. Co. Trustee Med. Found. Cin., 1983—; mem. Cin. Estate Planning Council. Mem. ABA, Ohio Bar Assn., Cin. Bar Assn., Notre Dame Alumni Assn. (trustee Cin. 1976—). Probate, General corporate, Personal income taxation. Home: 773 Stonebridge Dr Cincinnati OH 45238 Office: Strauss & Troy 201 E 5th St Cincinnati OH 45202

WEBER, HERMAN JACOB, federal judge; b. Lima, Ohio, May 20, 1927; s. Herman Joacb and Ada Minola (Esterly) W.; m. Barbara L. Rice, May 22, 1948; children: Clayton, Deborah. BA, Otterbein Coll., 1949; JD summa

cum laude, Ohio State U., 1951. Bar: Ohio 1952. Assoc. Weber & Hogue, Fairborn, Ohio, 1952-56; judge Fairborn Mayor's Ct., 1956-58; acting judge Fairborn Mcpl. Ct., 1958-60; judge Greene County Common Pleas Ct., Xenia, Ohio, 1961-82, Ohio Ct. Appeals (2d dist.), Dayton, 1982-85, U.S. Dist. Ct. (so. dist.) Ohio, Cin., 1985—; chmn. Ohio Jud. Conf., Columbus, 1979-80; pres. Ohio Common Pleas Judges Assn., Columbus, 1975. Vice mayor City of Fairborn, 1955-57, council mem., 1955-59. Served with USNR, 1945-46. Mem. ABA, Fed. Bar Assn., Ohio Bar Assn., Cin. Bar Assn., Dayton Bar Assn., Greene County Bar Assn. (pres. 1961-62), Fed. Judges Assn., Am. Judicature Soc. Office: U S Dist Ct 808 US Courthouse & P O Bldg 5th & Walnut Sts Cincinnati OH 45202 *

WEBER, LOUIS JERRY, lawyer; b. St. Louis, Oct. 9, 1939; s. Walter Louis and Irma Anna (Precht) W.; m. Karen Lee Clifton, Oct. 3, 1980; 1 child, Rebecca Susan. AB, U. Mo., 1961, JD, 1965. Bar: Mo. 1965, U.S. Dist. Ct. (ea. dist.) Mo. 1965. Ptnr. Thurman, Smith, Howald, Weber & Bowles, Hillsboro, Mo., 1965—. Chmn. Charter Commn. Jefferson County, Hillsboro, 1972, 86. Served to 1st lt., U.S. Army, 1961-62. Mem. ABA, Jefferson County Bar Assn. (pres. 1974-75), Mo. Assn. Trial Lawyers, Council of Sch. Attys. Democrat. Mem. United Ch. Christ. Probate, State civil litigation, School law. Home: 114 Parkview Crystal City MO 63019 Office: Thurman Smith Howald Weber & Bowles 1 Thurman Ct Hillsboro MO 63050

WEBER, ROBERT CARL, lawyer; b. Chester, Pa., Dec. 18, 1950; s. Robert Francis and Lucille (Nobili) W.; m. Linda Brediger, June 30, 1972; children: Robert F., Mary Therese, David P. BA cum laude, Yale U., 1972; JD, Duke U., 1976. Bar: Ohio 1976, U.S. Dist. Ct. (no dist.) Ohio 1976, U.S. Ct. Claims 1980, U.S. Ct. Appeals (6th cir.) 1981. Assoc. Jones, Day, Reavis & Pogue, Cleve., 1976-83, ptnr., 1983—. Mem. ABA, Ohio Bar Assn., Cleve. Bar Assn. (chmn. jud. selection com. 1985—), Jud. Conf. for 8th Jud. Dist. Ohio (life), Order of Coif. Roman Catholic. Federal civil litigation, State civil litigation. Office: Jones Day Reavis & Pogue 1700 Huntington Bldg Cleveland OH 44115

WEBER, ROY PHILIP, lawyer; b. N.Y.C., Aug. 24, 1943; m. Laurie Bender, July 6, 1986; 1 child, Neela. BA, Bklyn. Coll., 1965; JD, NYU, 1968, LLM in Trade Regulation, 1973. Bar: N.Y. 1969, U.S. Dist. Ct. (so. and ea. dists.) N.Y. 1971, N.J. 1976, U.S. Dist. Ct. N.J. 1976. Assoc. Bass & Ullman, N.Y.C., 1969-71; atty. The Purdue Frederick Co., N.Y.C., 1971-73; from atty. to sr. atty. Becton Dickinson & Co., Franklin Lakes, N.J., 1973-85, assoc. gen. counsel, 1985—. Mem. ABA. Antitrust, Federal civil litigation, Administrative and regulatory. Office: Becton Dickinson & Co 1 Becton Dr Franklin Lakes NJ 07417-1880

WEBER, WALTER WINFIELD, JR., lawyer; b. Ramsey, N.J., Feb. 7, 1924; s. Walter W. and Mary Elizabeth (Collins) W.; m. Margaret Gardner Wilson, May 12, 1951; children—Ellen, Anne. B.S., Va. Mil. Inst., 1947; LL.B., Columbia U., 1950. Bar: N.J. 1949, N.Y. 1952, U.S. Supreme Ct. 1966. Assoc., Weber, Muth and Weber, Ramsey, N.J., 1949-52, ptnr., 1953—; dir. Citizens First Bancorp, Inc., Glen Rock, N.J., and subs.; judge Upper Saddle River Mcpl. Ct., 1955-56. Mem. bd. of mgrs. Bergen Pines County Hosp., 1972-76, v.p., 1976. Served in U.S. Army, 1943-45. Mem. Bergen County Bar Assn., N.J. State Bar Assn. (chmn. pub. utility law sect. 1972-74). Republican. Dutch Reformed. Clubs: Arcola Country (Paramus, N.J.), Joe Jefferson (Saddle River, N.J.), Masons. Banking, Public utilities, General corporate. Address: 1 Cherry Ln Ramsey NJ 07446

WEBER, WILLIAM RANDOLPH, lawyer, real estate developer; b. Columbia, Mo., Jan. 3, 1952; s. William Harry and Marie Antoinette (Fehlig) W.; m. Sondra Jean Gust, Aug. 12, 1972; children—Ashley Elizabeth, William Matthew. B.A., Vanderbilt U., 1974; J.D., St. Louis U., 1977. Bar: Mo. 1977, Ill. 1978, U.S. Dist. Ct. (ea. dist.) Mo. 1978, U.S. Ct. Appeals (8th cir.) 1978. Ptnr. Thompson & Mitchell, St. Louis, Mo., 1977—; dir. Centerre Bank of St. Peters, N.A., Mo. Mem. staff St. Louis U. Law Jour., 1975-76. Vice pres. St. Charles County Y's Men, Mo., 1979-80; chmn. bd. advisers Salvation Army, St. Charles, 1980-83; chmn. St. Charles County Rep. Com., 1978-84; mem. Mo. Rep. Com., Jefferson City, 1978-86; St. Charles County Counsellor, 1985-86; v.p., bd. govs., 1986— ; bd. govs. N.E. Mo. State U., 1981—; bd. dirs. St. Charles C. of C., 1984—; Eagle Scout Assn. 1977—. Recipient Disting. Community Service award St. Charles Jaycees, 1984. Mem. Am. Soc. Hosp. Attys., Mo. Bar Assn. (rep. young lawyers sect. 1982—), St. Charles County Bar Assn. (pres. 1984), Ill. Bar Assn., Assn. Trial Lawyers Am., ABA (del. to Ho. of Dels., 1987—). Roman Catholic. Health, Local government, Real property. Office: Thompson & Mitchell 200 N 3d St Saint Charles MO 63301

WEBSTER, BRUCE CHARLES, lawyer, accountant; b. Cin., Feb. 12, 1957; s. Harold Charles and Donna Lee (Cottrill) W.; m. Lee Ann Heaton, May 24, 1980. BBA, Bowling Green State U., 1977; MA in Acctg., U. Ala., 1979, JD, M in Tax Acctg., 1981. Bar: Ala. 1982. Mgr. Arthur Young and Co., Birmingham, Ala., 1982—; cons. The Entrepreneurship Forum, Columbus, Ohio, 1986; adj. faculty U. Ala., Tuscaloosa, 1978-81. Author: Starting and Operating a Business in Alabama, 1986. Mem. ABA (tax sect.), Am. Inst. CPA's, Ala. CPA Soc., Ohio CPA Soc., Birmingham Tax Club (events coordinator), Beta Gamma Sigma. Democrat. Methodist. Club: Cumberland Lake Country (Pinson. Ala.). Personal income taxation, State and local taxation, Estate planning. Home: 305 Malaga Ave Homewood AL 35209 Office: Arthur Young and Co 2100 FNSN Bldg Birmingham AL 35203

WEBSTER, C. EDWARD, II, lawyer, judge; b. Cody, Wyo., Mar. 27, 1944; s. Constant E. and Lucille (Moncur) W. B.A. in Bus. Administrn., U. Wyo., 1967, J.D., 1969. Bar: Wyo. 1969. Legis. asst. U.S. Senator Clifford P. Hansen, 1969-72; ptnr. Housel and Webster, Cody, Wyo., 1973-79; sole practice, Cody, 1979—; judge mcpl. ct.; justice of peace. Pres. Cody Stampede, 1980-84. Mem. ABA, Cody C. of C. (pres. 1974-75). Republican. Mormon. Club: Eagles (Cody). State civil litigation, Oil and gas leasing, Real property. Office: 1226 11th St Cody WY 82414

WEBSTER, DALE PHILIP, lawyer; b. Sayre, Pa., Feb. 23, 1948; s. Mortimer Clinton and Madge Edna (Parks) W.; divorced; 1 child, Nicole; m. Kim E. McClure, June 26, 1981: 1 child, Morgan. BA, Anderson Coll., 1970; JD, Ind. U., 1973. Bar: Ind. 1973, U.S. Dist. Ct. (so. dist.) Ind. 1973. Assoc. McCormick & McCormick, Vincennes, Ind., 1973-74; ptnr. McCormick & Webster, Vincennes, 1974-75; pros. atty. Ind. Cir. Ct. (12th cir.), Vincennes, 1975-82; assoc. Sturm, Smith & Webster, Vincennes, 1982-85, ptnr., 1985—. Served with USAFR, 1970-76. Mem. ABA, Ind. Bar Assn., Knox County Bar Assn. (pres. 1976), Assn. Trial Lawyers Am., Ind. Trial Lawyers Assn., Ind. Pub. Defenders Council. Democrat. Methodist. General practice, Criminal. Office: Sturm Smith & Webster 302 Main St PO Box 393 Vincennes IN 47591

WEBSTER, DANIEL ROBERT, lawyer; b. Wayne, Mich., June 23, 1945. B.A. with high distinction, Ind. U., 1967; J.D., Harvard U., 1970. Bar: Ind. 1971, U.S. Dist. Ct. (so. dist.) Ind. 1971, U.S. Ct. Appeals (7th cir.) 1972, U.S. Supreme Ct. 1982; assoc. Hogan and Hartson, Washington, 1970-1; assoc. Ice, Miller, Donadio & Ryan, Indpls., 1971-77, 84—; dir. research Ind. Lawyers Commn., Indpls., 1977-81; sr. atty. Cummins Engine Co., Columbus, Ind., 1981-83; of counsel Ice Miller Donadio & Ryan, Indpls., 1983-85, ptnr., 1986—; chmn. corrections com. Indpls. Lawyers Commn., 1979-80, chmn. pub. defender com., 1977-80, mem. community services com., 1973-74, bd. dirs., 1974-80; mem. Greater Indpls. Progress Com. Task Force on Criminal Justice; mem. Legal Def. Panel; adv. com. Interlink News Service, 1982—, Visions, Revisions, Inc., 1982—, The Carl Duisberg Soc., Ind. U. East Asian Studies Ctr.; mem. speakers bur. Indpls.; sec., bd. dirs. Moore-Langen Printing Co. Inc. Co-editor: An Anatomy of Criminal Justice, 1980, Juvenile Intervention, 1982; contbr. articles to profl. jours.; producer TV Spl. Violence and the Public Response, 1978. Mem. YMCA Task Force on Devel. Edn., Indpls.; vice committeeperson Democratic Party of Ind., 1976-80; Dem. nominee for Ind. Atty. Gen., 1980; campaign treas. for Rep. John Day, Indpls., 1976-80; Am. del. Internat. YMCA Conf. on Disarmament and Detente, 1981; counsel Ind. Dem. Policy Com., 1980-81; chmn. subcom. econ. devel. Ind. Dem. Party, 1983—; mem. culture com. Ind. Ptnrs. for the Americas, 1983—; bd. dirs. Am. Ctr. for Internat. Leadership, Indpls. Pan Am. Games Planning Com.; treas., bd. dirs. Indpls. Internat. Ctr. Served with U.S. Army, 1971. Ind. U. merit scholar, 1966-67; Wheeler scholar, 1966-67; Ford P. Hall scholar, 1967. Mem. Ind. State Assn. (internat. law sect.), Indpls. Bar Assn. NAACP, Ind. Hist. Soc., Ind. Lawyers Commn. (bd. dirs. 1982—), Ind. Council Fgn. Relations, Indpls. Lit. Club, Forum for Internat. Profl. Services, Inc. (bd. dirs., pres.) Blue Key, Phi Beta Kappa, Phi Eta Sigma. Club: Phoenix. General corporate, State civil litigation.

WEBSTER, JOHN CLYDE, lawyer; b. Springfield, Ill., June 4, 1944; s. Clyde L. and Margaret Mary (Murphy) W.; m. Donna Marie Young, May 28, 1977; children: Meghan Louise, Katherine Mary, Patrick Clyde. BS in acctg., econs., Holy Cross Coll., 1966; JD, St. Louis U., 1969. Bar: Ill. 1970, Mo. 1970. Tchr. dist. 189 East St. Louis, 1969-70; prosecutor Madison County State Attys. office State of Ill., Edwardsville, 1970-74; ptnr. Williamson, Webster, Groshong, Moorman & Falb, Alton, Ill. and St. Louis, 1974—; bd. dirs. Newco Enterprises Inc., St. Charles, Mo. Pres. adv. bd. dirs., Cath. Children's Home, Alton, 1981—. Mem. Assn. Trial Lawyer Am., Ill. Trial Lawyers Assn., Phi Delta Phi. Club: Lockhaven Country (Alton). Lodge: KC. Avocations: basketball, running, swimming, skiing. Personal injury, Workers' compensation, Family and matrimonial. Home: 3505 Riverview Ct Godfrey IL 62035 Office: Williamson Webster Groshong etal 601 E 3d St Alton IL 62002

WEBSTER, LUTHER IRA, lawyer; b. Kendall, N.Y., Nov. 18, 1905; s. William Farnsworth and Nellie (Bartlett) W.; m. Edna Hartsen, June 30, 1936; children—Lucinda Webster Schade, John Luther; m. Lorraine Telford, May 21, 1977. A.B., U. Rochester, 1926; LL.B., Union U., 1929, J.D., 1953. Bar: N.Y. 1929, U.S. Dist. Ct. (we. dist.) N.Y. 1930, U.S. Ct. Appeals (2d cir.) 1953. Assoc. O'Brien and McSweeney, (city) Rochester, N.Y., 1929-31; ptnr. Webster, Sullivan, Santero and Clifford and predecessor firms, Rochester, N.Y., 1931-86, spl. counsel Fulreader, Rosenthal, Sollioan, Clifford, Santoro & Krul, 1986—. Vice pres. Industries for Blind N.Y., Inc., 1981-86; Justinian Albany Law Sch., 1929. Mem. Internat. Assn. Shipman Counsel, Am. Coll. Trial Lawyers, Rochester Bar Assn., N.Y. State Bar Assn., ABA, Bar Found. N.Y., Phi Beta Kappa. Republican. Club: Oak Hill Country. Lodge: Masons. State civil litigation, Probate, Real property. Office: 1350 Midtown Tower Rochester NY 14604

WEBSTER, PETER BRIDGMAN, lawyer; b. Boston, Jan. 11, 1941; s. John Archibald and Mildred (Bridgman) W.; m. Elaine Gerber, Dec. 20, 1964; children—Amy Elizabeth, Peter Bridgman, Timothy James. A.B., Bowdoin Coll., 1962; LL.B., Cornell U., 1965. Bar: Maine 1965, U.S. Dist. Ct. Maine 1965. Assoc., then ptnr. Verrill & Dana, Portland, Maine, 1965—; mem. grievance commn. Maine Bd. Bar Overseers, Augusta, 1979—, chmn., 1984—, mem. 1986—; adj. prof. law U. Maine, Portland, 1981. Class agt. Bowdoin Coll, Brunswick, Maine, 1969—; bd. dirs. Portland United Way, 1973-79; bd. dirs. Portland Provident Assn., 1979—; bd. dirs. North Yarmouth (Maine) Acad., 1983—, pres., 1984-85. Mem. Cumberland County Bar Assn., ABA (corp. sect. 1971—), Maine State Bar Assn., Nat. Assn. Coll. and Univ. Attys. Republican. Congregationalist. General corporate, Banking, Legal education. Home: 81 W Main St Yarmouth ME 04096

WEBSTER, ROBERT BYRON, lawyer; b. Detroit, Mar. 9, 1932; s. Don B. and Glennie E. (Cole) W.; m. Marilyn Hey, July 18, 1959; children—Anne Elizabeth, Allison Dee, Peter Hey, James Byron. B.A., U. Mich., 1955, J.D., 1957. Bar: Mich. 1958, U.S. Dist. Ct. (ea. dist.) Mich., 1958, U.S. Dist. Ct. (we. dist.) Mich. 1972, U.S. Ct. Appeals (6th cir.) 1958, U.S. Supreme Ct. 1972. Law clk. U.S. Dist. Ct. 1957-59; assoc., ptnr. Hill, Lewis, Adams, Goodrich & Tait. 1959-73; judge Cir. Ct., Oakland County, 1973-82, chief judge, 1977; ptnr. Hill, Lewis, Adams, Goodrich & Tait, Birmingham, Mich., 1982—; chmn. Supreme Ct. Com. to Revise Ct. Rules, 1975-78; mem. Mich. Ct. Rule Adv. Com., 1984; trustee, chmn. Horizon Health Systems, 1983—. Chmn. Oakland Republican Com., 1970-71; trustee Family and Children Services Oakland County, 1976-84; mem. Oakland Community Mental Health Bd., 1971-73. Served with USAF, 1951-52. Fellow Am. Bar Found., State Bar Mich. Found.; mem. Fed. Bar Assn., ABA, State Bar Mich. (commr. 1983—), Oakland Bar Assn. Republican. Unitarian. Federal civil litigation, State civil litigation, General practice. Office: Suite 205 255 S Woodward Birmingham MI 48011

WEBSTER, RONALD B., lawyer; b. Cle Elum, Wash., June 11, 1942; s. Burnette O. and Lucille (Beck) W.; m. M. Gail Skinner, June 26, 1971; children: Noel, Michelle. BA, U. Wash., 1964; JD, Gonzaga U., 1969. Bar: Wash., U.S. Dist. Ct. (ea. and we. dists.) Wash. Dep. pros. atty. Cowlitz County, Kelso, Wash., 1970-73; ptnr. Hickman, Webster, Ensley & Carpenter, Colfax, Wash., 1970—. Mem. Whitman County Bd. Mental Health, Pullman, Wash., 1973-83; chmn. civil service commn. Whitman County Sheriffs Office, Colfax, 1973—; pres. Colfax and Community Fund, 1973-74. Mem. Whitman County Bar Assn. (pres. 1981-82). Club: Colfax Golf and Country. Lodge: Rotary (pres. Colfax club 1983-84). Personal injury, State civil litigation, Contracts commercial. Home: Rt 1 Box 29A Colfax WA 99111 Office: Hickman Webster et al N 302 Mill St Colfax WA 99111

WEBSTER, STUART ARTHUR, lawyer, nuclear engineer; b. Hartford, Conn., Jan. 28, 1941; s. Stuart Arthur and Lillian Agnes (Potter) W.; m. Dorothy Agnes Tarala, June 4, 1966; 1 child, Teresa Lillian. B in Chem. Engring., Rensselaer Poly. Inst., 1962; MBA, U. Hartford, 1970; JD, U. Conn., 1977. Bar: Conn. 1978, U.S. Patent Office 1980, U.S. Dist. Ct. Conn. 1981. Chem. engr. Am. Enka, Rocky Hill, Conn., 1962-65; prodn. supr. Brand Rex, Willimantic, Conn., 1965-67; nuclear engr. Combustion Engring., Windsor, Conn., 1967—; sole practice Rocky Hill, 1978—; chmn. Standard's Working Group, 1986. Contbr. articles to profl. jours. Mem. Rocky Hill Planning and Zoning Commn., 1986—; sec. Wetlands Commn., Rocky Hill, 1979-86. Served as cpl. USMCR, 1958-64. Mem. ABA, Conn. Bar Assn., Hartford County Bar Assn., Am. Nuclear Soc. Republican. Baptist. Lodge: Masons (master 1983). Real property, Patent, Probate. Office: Combustion Engring Inc 1000 Prospect Hill Rd Windsor CT 06095

WEBSTER, WALTER EARNEST, JR., judge; b. Ellensburg, Wash., Oct. 30, 1928; s. Walter Ernest Sr. and ELvangeline (Linder) W.; m. Frances T. Siemion, July 25, 1951; children: Debbie, Mark, Dan, Rita, Michael, Charles, Fran, Mary Jo. BS, Seattle U., 1950; JD, Georgetown U., 1953. Bar: Wash. 1953, U.S. Dist. Ct. D.C. 1953, U.S. Dist. Ct. (we. dist.) Wash. 1954, U.S. Supreme Ct. 1972. Atty. Wash. State Ct., Seattle, 1954-56, Wash. States Atty.'s Office, Olympia, 1956-57; sole practice Seattle, 1958-84; spl. asst. Wash. States Atty.'s Office, Seattle, 1970-84; judge Wash. Ct. Appeals, Seattle, 1984—; tchr. Seattle U., 1958-61; instr. Seattle Police Dept., 1961-66. Served to lt. col. USNG, 1976—. Mem. ABA, Wash. State Bar Assn., Assn. Trial Lawyers Am., Wash. State Trial Lawyers Assn., Am. Legion, VFW. Republican. Roman Catholic. Clubs: Wash. Athletic, Bellevue (Seattle). Judicial administration. Home: 401-100th Ave Bellevue WA 98104 Office: Wash State Ct Appeals 1 Union Sq Seattle WA 98101

WEBSTER, WILLIAM HEDGCOCK, govt. ofcl.; b. St. Louis, Mar. 6, 1924; s. Thomas M. and Katherine (Hedgcock) W.; m. Drusilla Lane, May 5, 1950; children—Drusilla Lane Busch, William Hedgcock, Katherine Hagee. A.B., Amherst Coll., 1947, LL.D., 1975; J.D., Washington U., 1949, LL.D., 1978; LL.D., William Wood Coll., 1978, DePauw U., 1978. Bar: Mo. bar 1949. With firm Armstrong, Teasdale, Kramer and Vaughan (and predecessors), St. Louis, 1949-50, 52-59; partner Armstrong, Teasdale, Kramer and Vaughan (and predecessors), 1956-59, 61-70; U.S. atty. Eastern Dist. Mo., 1960-61; mem. Mo. Bd. Law Examiners, 1964-69; judge U.S. Dist. Ct., Eastern Mo. dist., 1971-73, U.S. Ct. Appeals, 8th Circuit, 1973-78; dir. FBI, 1978-87, CIA, 1987—; Mem. adv. com. on criminal rules, 1971-78, mem. ct. adminstrs. com., 1975-78. Trustee Washington U., 1974—. Served as lt. (j.g.) USNR, 1943-46; lt. (s.g.) 1951-52. Recipient citation Washington U. Alumni, 1972; Disting. Alumnus award Washington U., 1977. Fellow Am. Bar Found.; mem. ABA (chmn. sect. on corp. banking and bus. law 1977-78), Fed. Bar Assn., Mo. Bar Assn., St. Louis Bar Assn., Am. Law Inst. (council 1978—), Washington U. Alumni Fedn. (pres. 1956-57), Washington U. Law Alumni (pres. 1961), Big Brother Orgn. St. Louis (dir. 1958-66, pres. 1965-66, hon. life pres.), Big Brothers of Am. (dir. 1966, hon. dir. 1978—), Mo. Assn. Republicans (pres. 1958), Order of Coif, Psi Upsilon., Delta Sigma Rho, Phi Delta Phi. Clubs: Rotary; St. Louis Country (St. Louis), Noonday (St. Louis); Alfalfa (Washington), St. Alban's Tennis (Washington). Office: CIA Washington DC 20505 *

WEBSTER, WILLIAM LAWRENCE, state attorney general; b. Carthage, Mo., Sept. 17, 1953; s. Richard Melton and Janet Posten (Whitehead) W.; m. Susan Kaye Tiemann, May 17, 1980; children: Jonathan Noel, Mark Andrew. Ed., U. Kans., 1975; J.D., U. Mo.-Kansas City, 1978. Bar: Mo. 1978. Assoc. Collins, Webster, Rouse, Joplin, Mo., 1978-84; mem. Mo. Ho. of Reps., Jefferson City, 1981-84; atty. gen. State of Mo., Jefferson City, 1985—. Criminal, State civil litigation. Office: Office Atty Gen PO Box 899 Jefferson City MO 65102 *

WECHT, ALAN CHARLES, accountant; b. Phila., July 11, 1957; s. Sol Wecht and Sylvia Weaner. BBA, Temple U., 1979, JD, 1982, LLM in Taxation, 1986. Bar: Pa. 1982, U.S. Dist. Ct. (ea. dist.) Pa. 1982, U.S. Tax Ct. 1982, U.S. Ct. Claims 1982, U.S. Ct. Appeals (3d cir.) 1982; CPA, Pa. Accountant Touche, Ross & Co., Phila., 1982-84, Gable, Peritz, Mishkin & Penfil, Blue Bell, Pa., 1985—. Committeeman Dems., Phila., 1975-80. Mem. ABA, Pa. Bar Assn., Phila. Bar Assn., Am. Inst. CPA's, Pa. Inst. CPA's, Am. Assn. CPA/Attys. Lodge: St. John's Masons (officer 1985—). Corporate taxation, Personal income taxation, State and local taxation. Home: 9364-B Hoff St Philadelphia PA 19115 Office: Gable Peritz Mishkin & Penfil 5 Sentry Pkwy E Blue Bell PA 19422

WECHT, CYRIL HARRISON, lawyer, educator, pathologist; b. Pitts., Mar. 20, 1931; s. Nathan and Fannie (Rubinstein) W.; m. Sigrid Ronsdal, Oct. 21, 1961; children: David N., Daniel A., Benjamin E., Ingrid A. BS cum laude, U. Pitts., 1952, MD, 1956, JD, 1962; postgrad., U. Buffalo Sch. Medicine, 1952-54; LLB, U. Md., 1962. Bar: Pa. 1963, U.S. Dist. Ct. (ea., mid. and we. dists.) Pa. 1963, U.S. Supreme Ct. 1969; diplomate Nat. Bd. Med. Examiners, Am. Bd. Pathology, Am. Bd. Forensic Pathology; lic. physician Pa., Calif., Md. Internship St. Francis Gen. Hosp. Rehabilitation Inst., Pitts., 1956-57; resident in pathology VA Hosp., Pitts., 1957-59; assoc. pathologist USAF, Maxwell AFB, ALa., 1959-61; pathologist North Charles Gen. Hosp., Balt., 1961-62; acting chief lab. service, pathologist Leech Farm VA Hosp., Pitts., 1962-64; dir. Pitts. Pathology and Toxicology Lab., 1964-78; chmn. dept. pathology, chief pathologist Cen. Med. Ctr. & Hosp., Pitts., 1973—; research prof. law, dir. Inst. Forensic Scis. Duquesne U., Pitts., 1964-78, adj. prof. law, 1984—; lectr. and clin. instr. various colls. and univs.; cons. various orgns.; appearances on TV show 20/20, 1976, 79; coroner Allegheny County, Pa., 1970-80, chief forensic pathologist, 1966-70; asst. dist. atty., med. legal advisor Allegheny County, 1964-65; mem. Allegheny Regional Planning Council Gov.'s Justice Commn., 1977-80, health adv. panel Sec.'s Med. Malpractice Commn. HEW, 1972, adv. bd. Milton Helpern Internat. Ctr. Forensic Scis., 1977—, adv. bd. Odyssey House Inst. for Law & Medicine, 1975—. Editor: Exploring the Medical Malpractice Dilemna, 1972, Scapel & Quill, 1966—, Microscopic Diagnosis in Forensic Pathology, 1980, Forensic Sciences, 1982, Legal Aspects of Medical Practice, 1978—, assoc. editor, 1977-78; mem. editorial bd. various publs.; contbr. numerous articles to profl. jours. Mem. Allegheny County Bd. Commrs., 1980-84, Allegheny County Bd. Health, 1971-76, community relations com. United Jewish Fedn., 1977—, suicide prevention com. Health and Welfare Assn. Allegheny County, 1967-85; med. legal cons. ARC Pitts.-Allegheny County chpt., 1977-82, exec. water safety com.; co-founder Pa. Guild Infant Survival Inc., Pitts., 1967-83; chmn. Allegheny County Council on Alcohol and Drug Abuse, 1975-80, Pitts. Conf. Soviet Jewry, 1975-80, nat. lawyers com.; trustee Am. Jewish Com. Pitts. chpt., 1963-67, 69-71; bd. dirs. Nat. Found. Ileitis and Colitis Inc., 1981—, United Cerebral Palsy Assn. Pitts. Dist., 1969-75, Jewish Community Ctr. Young Men & Women's Hebrew Assn., 1969-72, mem., 1965—, Jewish Family and Children's Service Pitts., 1965-67, Jewish Community Relations Council Pitts., 1962-68, Kollel Bais Yitzchok Inst. for Advanced Torah Studies, 1978—, Pitts. Zionist Orgn., 1976—, v.p., 1983—. Served to capt. USAFR, 1961-65. Recipient Man of Yr. award Am. Legion Allegheny County, 1977; named one of Outstanding Young Men of Am. U.S. Jaycees, 1965, Outstanding Alumnus U. Pitts., 1976. Fellow Am. Acad. Forensic Scis. (pres. 1971-72, exec. com. 1968-73, chmn. pathology and biology sect. 1968-69, chmn. legis. affairs com. 1966, chmn. internat. relations com. 1977—, various others), Am. Coll. Legal Medicine (pres. 1969-72, v.p. 1968-69, bd. govs. 1966-76, various coms.), Am. Soc. Clin. Pathologists; mem. ABA (vice chmn. com. law and medicine 1973-77, publs. vice chmn. com. law and medicine 1975-77, various others), Pa. Bar Assn. (various coms.), Allegheny County Bar Assn. (vice chmn. med. legal com. 1973, chmn. med. legal com. 1974-78, various others), Assn. Trial Lawyers Am. (chmn. com. on liaison with med. assns. 1969-73, various others), Am. Soc. Hosp. Attys., AMA, Pitts. Pathology Soc., Pa. Med. Soc., Allegheny County Med. Soc. (bd. dirs. 1968-71, various coms.), Pitts. Inst. Legal Medicine (bd. dirs., pres. 1963—), Internat. Acad. Legal Medicine (v.p. 1976-79), Internat. Assn. Accident and Traffic Medicine (v.p. 1970-73, sec. gen. 1966-69), Nat. Assn. Med. Examiners (bd. dirs. sty Internat. U.S.A. (adv. com. 1985—), Touro Law Sch. (nat. adv. bd. 1980-82), Phi Delta Epsilon, Omicron Delta Kappa. Democrat. Avocations: tennis, swimming, reading, skiing. Personal injury, Workers' compensation, Legal education. Home: 5420 Darlington Rd Pittsburgh PA 15217 Office: Cen Med Ctr & Hosp Dept Pathology 1200 Centre Ave Pittsburgh PA 15219

WECKSTEIN, CLIFFORD ROBERT, judge; b. Cin., Mar. 30, 1949; s. Norbert Leon and Gloria Sura (Buechler) W.; m. Mary Virginia Eure, Aug. 25, 1974; children: Virginia Minn, Margaret Claire. B.A., U. Va., 1971; J.D., Coll. William and Mary, 1974. Bar: Va. 1974, U.S. Dist. Ct. (we. and ea. dists.) Va., U.S. Ct. Appeals (4th cir.) 1975, U.S. Supreme Ct. 1979. Assoc. Barry N. Lichtenstein, Roanoke, Va., 1974-76; ptnr. Lichtenstein & Weckstein, Roanoke, 1976-79, Lichtenstein, Weckstein & Raney, Roanoke, 1979-83, Lichtenstein, Weckstein & Thomas, Roanoke, 1983-86, Lichtenstein, Weckstein, Thomas & Cleaveland, Roanoke, 1986-87; judge 23d Jud. Cir. Va., 1987—; substitute judge 23d Jud. Dist. Va., 1980-87; commr. in Chancery, 1982-87. Bd. dirs. Legal Aid Soc. Roanoke Valley, 1981-87, pres., 1984-87. Mem. ABA, Assn. Trial Lawyers Am., Va. Trial Lawyers Assn., Va. State Bar (6th dist. ethics com. chmn. 1984-86), Roanoke Bar Assn. (dir. 1982-84), Omicron Delta Kappa, Phi Alpha Delta. Jewish. Home: 2008 Mount Vernon Rd SW Roanoke VA 24015 Office: Roanoke City Courthouse 315 W Church Ave PO Box 211 Roanoke VA 24002-0211

WECLEW, ROBERT GEORGE, lawyer, educator; b. Chgo., Oct. 30, 1911; s. Victor T. and Mary (Tadrowski) W.; m. Jean Helen Vinson, Jan. 5, 1942; children: Harlene Villio, Robert Vinson Weclew. B.S. in Law, Northwestern U., 1932, J.D., 1935. Bar: Ill. 1934, U.S. Dist. Ct. (no. dist.) Ill. 1937, U.S. Supreme Ct. 1966. Assoc. Case and Lynn, Chgo., 1935-40; atty. Employers of Wausau, Chgo., 1940-42, VA, Chgo., 1945-57; prof. Law Sch., DePaul U., Chgo., 1957-78; acting dean Law Sch., DePaul U., 1968-71, prof. emeritus, 1978—; sole practice Chgo., 1978—; Mem. Am. Law Inst., 1968-71; counsel, co-founder Acad. of Gen. Dentistry, 1952-70. Contbr. articles on constl. law to profl. jours. Mem. Ill. Constl. Study Commn., Chgo., 1968-69. Fellow Acad. Continuing Edn. (counsel, co-founder 1974—); mem. Ill. Bar Assn. (council legal edn. 1969-71), Advocates Soc., Phi Kappa Theta, Delta Theta Phi. Civil rights, Probate, Real property.

WEDGE, VIRGIL HENRY, lawyer; b. Pioche, Nev., June 24, 1912; s. John William and Emma (Richards) W.; m. Charlotte Hekking, June 5, 1942; children: Suzanne Iola, Virgil Alan. BS, Brigham Young U., 1936; LLB, George Washington U., 1940. Bar: Nev. 1940, U.S. Supreme Ct. 1964. Ptnr. McCarran & Wedge, Reno, 1940-42; sp. agt. FBI, Washington, 1942-45; assoc. Griswold, Reinhardt & Vargas, Reno, 1945-47; atty. City of Reno, 1947-51; ptnr. Woodburn, Wedge, Blakey & Jeppson and predecessors, Reno, 1951—. Mem. adv. bd. Nev. div. Calif. Fed., Reno, 1983—; vice chmn. cen. com. Nev. Dems., 1952-54; chmn. cen. com. Washoe County Dems., Reno, 1974. Fellow Internat. Acad. Trial Lawyers (bd. dirs. 1954-62, 65-68); mem. ABA, Washoe County Bar Assn. (pres. 1968-69), Internat. Soc. Barristers, Am. Soc. Writers of Legal Subjects. Federal civil litigation, State civil litigation, Estate planning. Home: 320 Hillcrest Dr Reno NV 89509 Office: 1 E 1st St Reno NV 89505

WEDGLE, RICHARD JAY, lawyer; b. Denver, Dec. 2, 1951; s. Joseph M. and Lillian E. (Brown) W. BA, U. Calif., Berkeley, 1974; JD, U. Denver, 1978. Bar: Colo. 1978, U.S. Dist. Ct. Colo. 1978, U.S. Ct. Appeals (10th cir.) 1980. Ptnr. Cox, Wedgle & Padmore, P.C., Denver, 1978-85, Barnes, Wedgle & Shpall, P.C., Denver, 1986-87, Wedgle and Shpall, Denver,

1987—. Vol. coordinator Dick Lamm for Gov., 1974, citizen adv. office 1975; bd. dirs. Cherry Creek Improvement Assn., 1985—. Mem. ABA, Colo. Bar Assn., Colo. Women's Bar Assn., Denver Bar Assn. Club: Denver Athletic. Federal civil litigation, State civil litigation, Family and matrimonial. Home: 365 Marion St Denver CO 80218 Office: Wedgle and Shpall PC 730 17th St #230 Denver CO 80202

WEDGWOOD, RUTH GLUSHIEN, law educator; b. N.Y.C., Dec. 13, 1949; d. Morris P. and Anne (Williams) Glushien; m. Josiah Francis Wedgwood; May 29, 1982. BA magna cum laude, Harvard U., 1972; postgrad., London Sch. Econs., 1972-73; JD, Yale U., 1976. Bar: D.C. 1978. Law clk. to judge U.S. Ct. Appeals (2d cir.), N.Y.C., 1976-77; law clk. to justice Harry Blackmun U.S. Supreme Ct., Washington, 1977-78; spl. asst. to atty. gen. criminal div. U.S. Dept. Justice, Washington, 1978-80; asst. U.S. atty. U.S. Dist. Ct. (so. dist.) N.Y., N.Y.C., 1980-86; assoc. prof. law Yale U., New Haven, 1986—. Rockefeller fellow Aspen (Colo.) Inst. for Humanistic Studies, 1978-79; term mem. Council on Fgn. Relations, N.Y.C., 1980-85. Mem. ABA, D.C. Bar Assn., Am. Soc. Internat. Law, Assn. of Bar of City of N.Y. (internat. human rights com. 1980-83). Club: Elizabethan (New Haven), Yale (N.Y.C.). Criminal, Public international, Legal education. Office: Yale U Law Sch PO Box 401A Yale Sta New Haven CT 06520

WEDIG, HAROLD HARVEY, lawyer; b. New Orleans, Mar. 27, 1927; s. Walter G. and I. Lillian (Harvey) W.; m. Fay Beth Frey, July 29, 1950; children: Eric, Mark, Elisabeth, Brian. BA, Tulane U., 1947, LLB, 1950. Bar: La. 1950, U.S. Dist. Ct. (ea. and we. dists.) La. 1955, U.S. Supreme Ct. 1973, U.S. Ct. Appeals (5th cir.) 1981. Sr. ptnr. Wedig, Coman & Cooper, New Orleans, 1981—. Served to 1st lt. JAGC, U.S. Army, 1952-54. Mem. Phi Delta Phi. Roman Catholic. Club: Chess, Paul Morphy (New Orleans) (bd. dirs. 1968-80). Avocation: collecting coins. Estate planning, Probate, Estate taxation. Office: Wedig Coman & Cooper 1006 Hibernia Bank Bldg 812 Gravier St New Orleans LA 70112

WEDLOCK, ELDON DYMENT, JR., law educator; b. Providence, Oct. 29, 1942; s. Eldon Dyment and Madelyn Bernice (Daniels) W.; m. Janet Louise Nielsen, Aug. 1965; children: Stina Cole, Sara Nielsen. AB, Brown U., 1965; JD, Am. U., 1968; LLM, Yale U., 1969. Bar: D.C. 1969, U.S. Dist. Ct. D.C. 1968, U.S. Ct. Appeals (D.C. cir.) 1969. Asst. prof. law U. S.C., Columbia, 1969-72, assoc. prof., 1972-77, prof., 1977—. Author: (with others) The Emerging Rights of the Confined, 1972, The Tree of Liberty, 1986; editor The Jour. of Law and Edn., 1973—. Mem. D.C. Bar Assn., ACLU (pres. Columbia chpt. 1973-76). Democrat. Constitutional, Criminal, Legal education. Home: 200 S Edisto Ave Columbia SC 29205 Office: Univ SC Law Sch Columbia SC 29208

WEEDMAN, CHARLES EDWARD, JR., lawyer; b. St. Louis, Oct. 16, 1951; s. Charles E. Sr. and Molly A. (Gish) W.; m. Julie L. Whitton, June 4, 1983. BA in Econs. and Bus. Adminstrn., Westminster Coll., 1974; JD, U. Mo., 1978. Bar: Mo. 1978, U.S. Dist. Ct. (we. dist.) Mo. 1978, U.S. Ct. Appeals (8th cir.) 1978. From assoc. to ptnr. Crouch, Spangler & Douglas, Harrisonville, Mo., 1978—. Mem. ABA, Mo. Bar Assn., Kansas City Bar Assn., Cass County Bar Assn., Harrisonville C. of C. (sec. bd. dirs. 1986—). Methodist. Lodge: Rotary (pres. local club 1986—). Banking, State civil litigation, Insurance. Home: 155 N Price Harrisonville MO 64701 Office: Crouch Spangler & Douglas 117 S Lexington Harrisonville MO 64701

WEEKLEY, FREDERICK CLAY, JR., lawyer; b. San Antonio, Aug. 29, 1939; s. F. Clay and Topsy (Stevens) W.; m. Charlotte Lee Jones, Dec. 20, 1960; children—Amber Lee, Caroline Lee. B.B.A., Baylor U., 1962, J.D., 1963; LL.M., NYU, 1969. Bar: Tex. 1963. Ptnr. Bracewell & Patterson, Houston, 1969—. Editor: Texas Wills System, 1984. Mem. Commn. Probate Law Examiners, Tex. Bd. Legal Specialization, 1978-82. Fellow Am. Coll. Probate Counsel. Probate. Home: 2324 Bluebonnet St Houston TX 77030 Office: Bracewell & Patterson 711 Louisiana St Houston TX 77002

WEEKS, ARTHUR ANDREW, lawyer, educator; b. Hanceville, Ala., Dec. 2, 1914; s. A.A. and Anna S. (Seibert) W.; m. Carol P. Weeks; children: John David, Carol Christine, Nancy Anna. A.B., Samford U., 1936; LL.B., U. Ala., 1939, J.D., 1939; LL.M., Duke U., 1950; LL.D. (hon.), Widener U., 1980. Bar: Ala. 1939, Tenn. 1948. Sole practice law Birmingham, Ala., 1939-41, 1946-47, 1954-61; dean, prof. law Cumberland U. Sch. Law, 1947-54; dean, prof. Samford U., 1961-72, prof. law, 1972-74; prof. law Cumberland Sch. Law, Samford U., 1984—; prof. law Del. Sch. Law of Widener U., Wilmington, 1974-82, dean, 1974-80, interim dean, 1982-83, dean emeritus, prof., 1983—. Served to capt. AUS, 1944-46. Mem. ABA, Tenn. Bar Assn., Ala. Bar Assn., Birmingham Bar Assn., Del. Bar Assn. (assoc.), Phi Alpha Delta, Phi Kappa Phi, Delta Theta Phi. Legal education. Home: 1105 Water Edge Ct Birmingham AL 35244

WEEKS, JANET HEALY, judge; b. Quincy, Mass., Oct. 19, 1932; d. John Francis and Sheila Josephine (Jackson) Healy; A.B. in Chemistry, Emmanuel Coll., Boston, 1954; J.D., Boston Coll., 1958; LL.D. (hon.), U. Guam, 1984; m. George Weeks, Aug. 29, 1959; children—Susan, George. Admitted to Mass. bar, 1958, Guam bar, 1972; trial atty. Dept. Justice, Washington, 1958-60; trial atty. firm Trapp & Gayle, Agana, Guam, 1971-73; partner firm Trapp, Gayle, Teker, Weeks & Friedman, Agana, 1973-75; judge Superior Ct. Guam, Agana, 1975—; chmn. task force cts., prosecution and defense Terr. Crime Commn., 1973-76; mem. Terr. Crime Commn. Bd., 1975-76, Guam Law Revision Commn., 1981—; rep. Nat. Conf. State Trial Judges, 1982. Mem. Catholic Sch. Bd. Guam, 1973. Mem. Nat. Assn. Women Judges (charter), Am. Judges Assn., Am. Bar Assn., Fed. Bar Assn. (chpt. sec. 1974), Guam Bar Assn. Club: Internat. (Guam). Judicial administration. Office: Superior Ct Guam 110 W O'Brien Dr Agana GU 96910 *

WEEKS, ROBERT WALKER, lawyer, manufacturing company executive; b. Rock Island, Ill., Aug. 14, 1926; s. Harold Parker and Miriam (Walker) W.; m. Phyllis Anne Grams, July 24, 1948; children: Susan Carol, Katharine Ann, Nancy Jane. B.S. in Naval Sci, Purdue U., 1947, B.S. in Mech. Engring, 1948; J.D., Northwestern U., 1951. Bar: Ill. 1951. With law dept. Deere & Co., Moline, Ill., 1951—; gen. counsel Deere & Co., 1969—, v.p., 1977—; dir. John Deere Credit Co., John Deere Ins. Group, John Deere Leasing Co., Iowa-Ill. Gas and Electric Co., Rock River Ins. Co. Trustee Ill. Wesleyan U. Served with USNR, 1944-46. Mem. ABA, Ill. Bar Assn. General corporate. Home: 60 Hawthorne Rd Rock Island IL 61201 Office: John Deere Rd Moline IL 61265

WEEKS, WALTER WILLIAM, lawyer; b. Las Cruces, N.Mex., Oct. 18, 1953; s. Walter Leroy and Mary Shirley (Wheeler) W.; m. Mary Victoria Latham, Sept. 2, 1978; children: Joseph Daniel, John Brady. AB, Ind. U., 1975, JD magna cum laude, 1979. Bar: Ind. 1979, U.S. Ct. Appeals (7th cir.) 1981. Assoc. Sommer & Barnad, P.C., Indpls., 1979-82; state dir. Nature Conservancy, Indpls., 1982—; adj. assoc. prof. environ. law Butler U., Indpls., 1984, 86; panel mem. Gov's Conf. on Forestry, Indpls., 1985; mem. Outdoor Recreation Adv. Commn., Indpls., 1985, 86; chmn. subcom. on strategic planning for agr. Ind. Inst. Food and Nutrition, Inc. and Purdue U., 1985, 86; drafted Ind. Natural Heritage Protection Campaign statute enacted 1984. Recipient Outstanding Chpt. award Nature Conservancy, 1986. Mem. Ind. Acad. Sci., Natural Areas Assn., Order of Coif. Episcopalian. Club: Indpls. Athletic. Environment, Natural Area property and tax law. Home: 5336 Washington Blvd Indianapolis IN 46220 Office: The Nature Conservancy 4200 N Michigan Rd Indianapolis IN 46208

WEG, HOWARD J., lawyer; b. Los Angeles, Nov. 15, 1954; m. Karlene B., June 4, 1981; 1 child, Adam. BA, UCLA, 1976; JD, Southwestern U., 1979; LLM, Yale U., 1980. Bar: Calif. 1979, U.S. Dist. Ct. (cen., ea. and no. dists.) Calif. 1980, U.S. Tax Ct. 1980, U.S. Ct. Appeals (9th cir.) 1980. Assoc. Fine, Perzik & Friedman, Los Angeles, 1980-82, Dennis, Juarez, Reeser, Shafer & Young, Los Angeles, 1982-84, Gendel, Raskoff, Shapiro & Quittner, Los Angeles, 1984—. Mem. Fin. Lawyers Conf., L.A. County Bar Assn., Bankrupty Study Group. Contracts commercial, Bankruptcy, Banking. Office: Gendel Raskoff et al 1801 Century Park East Suite 600 Los Angeles CA 90067

WEGENER, MARK DOUGLAS, lawyer; b. Cedar Rapids, Iowa, Nov. 1, 1948; s. Virgil Albert and Jean Frances (Wilke) W.; m. Donna Chait, May 28, 1972; children—Tara, David, Marisa. B.A. cum laude, Central Coll., Pella, Iowa, 1970; J.D., Rutgers U., 1973. Bar: D.C. 1974, U.S. Dist. Ct. D.C. 1974, U.S. Ct. Appeals (D.C. cir.) 1974. Assoc. firm Howrey & Simon, Washington, 1973-79, ptnr., 1979—. Mem. Washington Mayor's Internat. Adv. Council, 1984—. Mem. ABA (anti-trust sect., litigation sect.), D.C. Bar Assn. Club: Army & Navy. Antitrust, Federal civil litigation, Private international. Home: 7257 Spring Side Way McLean VA 22101 Office: Howrey & Simon 1730 Pennsylvania Ave NW Washington DC 20006

WEGENER, RICHARD JAMES, lawyer; b. Lincoln, Nebr., June 7, 1948; s. Hubert James and Betty Ann (Bonebright) W.; m. Deborah Margerat Beal, Sept. 20, 1974; children: Richard James II, Elizabeth Piper. B.A., U. Nebr., 1970, J.D., 1973. Bar: Nebr. 1973, U.S. Dist. Ct. Nebr. 1973, U.S. Ct. Appeals (8th cir.) 1975, Minn. 1976, U.S. Ct. Appeals (7th cir.) 1984. Assoc. Swarr, May, Smith & Anderson, Omaha, 1973-76; sr. atty. Green Giant Co., Mpls., 1976-80; sr. atty., div. counsel frozen foods Pillsbury Co., Mpls., 1980-84, div. counsel grocery products, 1984-86, div. counsel U.S. foods sales, 1986—; mem. Industry Labor Law Com.; lectr. various continuing legal edn. programs. Mng. editor Nebr. Law Rev., 1972-73; author course materials Hamline Sch. Law, 1983. Mem. ABA, Minn. Bar Assn., Nebr. Bar Assn. Republican. Presbyterian. Club: Wayzata Country (Minn.). Antitrust, Labor, General corporate. Office: Pillsbury Co 3726 Pillsbury Ctr Minneapolis MN 55402

WEGING, JAMES EDWIN, lawyer; b. Chgo., Jan. 18, 1950; s. John Adolph and Caroline Bessie (Matzek) W.; m. Margaret Hasier, Aug. 3, 1974. B.S. in Chemistry, DePaul U., 1972, J.D., 1977. Bar: Ill. 1977, U.S. Dist. Ct. (no. dist.) Ill. 1977, U.S. Dist. Ct. (cen. dist.) Ill. 1981, U.S. Dist. Ct. (we. dist.) Tex. 1982, U.S. Ct. Appeals (7th cir.) 1978, U.S. Ct. Appeals (D.C. cir.) 1981. Asst. atty. gen. Ill., Chgo., 1977—. Mem. Chgo. Bar Assn. (subcom. chmn. in adminstrv. law com.), Chgo. Coalition for Law-Related Edn. Club: Royal History Soc. Am. (treas. 1978—) (Chgo.). Public utilities, Administrative and regulatory, State civil litigation. Office: Ill Commerce Commn 180 N Lasalle St Suite 810 Chicago IL 60601

WEGMANN, CYNTHIA ANNE, lawyer; b. New Orleans, July 12, 1949; d. Edward F. and Shirley (Caire) W.; m. James A. Babst, Nov. 17, 1973; children: C. Morgan, James A. Jr. BFA, Sophie Newcomb Coll., 1971; LLB, Tulane U., 1973. Bar: La. 1973, U.S. Dist. Ct. (ea., mid. and we. dists.) La. 1973, U.S. Ct. Appeals (5th cir.), 1974, U.S. Supreme Ct. 1975. Assoc. Leach, Paysse & Baldwin, New Orleans, 1973-77, mem., 1977-84; ptnr. Wegmann & Wegmann, New Orleans, 1984—. Alumni editor Tulane Maritime Lawyer, New Orleans. Bd. dirs. Travelers Aid Soc. New Orleans, 1974-85, pres., 1983-85; bd. dirs. vol. Info. Agy., Jr. League United Way Greater New Orleans; mem. Jr. League New Orleans; chmn. Second Careers. Mem. Fed. Bar Assn., Maritime Law Assn. (proctor), Southeastern Admiralty Assn., Average Adjusters Assn. of U.S. Democrat. Roman Catholic. Club: New Orleans Country. Office: 1047 1st National Bank Commerce Bldg New Orleans LA 70112

WEGNER, BRENT ALLEN, lawyer; b. San Diego, June 18, 1955; s. Allen D. and Joyce (Stuhr) W.; m. Anne R. Montague, April 9, 1983. Student, USAF Acad., 1973-75; BA, U. Va., 1977; JD with high honors, George Washington U., 1982. Bar: D.C. 1982. Assoc. Ginsburg, Feldman & Bress, Washington, 1982-84, Dunnells, Duvall, Bennett & Porter, Washington, 1984—. Mem. ABA, Order of Coif. Real property, Corporate taxation, Securities. Home: 1114 Moorefield Creek Rd Vienna VA 22180 Office: Dunnells Duvall Bennett & Porter 1220 19th St NW Suite 400 Washington DC 20036

WEGNER, HAROLD CLAUS, lawyer, educator, consultant; b. Evanston, Ill., Aug. 9, 1943; s. Helmuth A. and Cordelia E. (Claussen) W.; m. Barbara A. Mock, Dec. 18, 1975; children: Kirsten Birgit, Peter Christopher. BA, Northwestern U., 1965; JD, Georgetown U., 1969. Bar: Va. 1969, D.C. 1971, U.S. Ct. Appeals (fed. cir.) 1982, U.S. Supreme Ct. 1980. Patent examiner Dept. Commerce, Washington, 1965-69; assoc. Stevens, Davis, Miller & Mosher, Washington, 1969-71; ptnr. Armstrong & Wegner, Washington, 1971-74; vis. scholar Max Planck Inst. for Fgn. and Internat. Patent, Copyright and Competition Law, Munich, W.Ger., 1974-76; Kenshuin law faculty Kyoto (Japan) U., 1977; ptnr. Stevens, Davis, Miller & Mosher, Washington, 1977-80; mem. Wegner & Bretschneider, Washington, 1980—; adj. prof. law Georgetown U., 1983—; cons. Japan tech. transfer. Max Planck Inst. Fgn. and Internat. Author: Japanese Patent Law, 1979; contbr. articles to various pubis. Patent, Copyright and Competition Law fellow, 1974-76. Mem. ABA (chmn. sect. subcom. 1981-82, 86-87), Va. State Bar (chmn. sect. 1979-80), Am. Intellectual Property Law Assn. (chmn. internat. com. 1978-79, chmn. haas amicus com. 1978, chmn. chem. practice com. 1982-85, bd. dirs. 1985—), Internat. Patent and Trademark Assn. (chmn. employed inventors law 1982-85), Federation Internationale des Conseils en Propriété Industrielle, Intellectual Property Owners, Inc. Presbyterian. Patent, Trademark and copyright, Private international. Office: Wegner & Bretschneider 1233 20th St NW Washington DC 20036

WEGNER, JAMES DARWIN, lawyer; b. Fremont, Nebr., July 6, 1955; s. Darwin Erwin Wegner and Loean Fern (Kroenke) Feuerstein; m. Margaret Mary Greteman, June 10, 1977; children: Jonathan, Nicholas, Laura. BSBA summa cum laude, Creighton U., 1977, JD cum laude, 1980. Bar: Nebr. 1980, U.S. Dist. Ct. Nebr. 1980, U.S. Tax Ct. 1980, U.S. Ct. Appeals (8th cir.) 1980, U.S. Ct. Claims 1981. Ptnr. McGrath, North, O'Malley & Kratz, P.C., Omaha, Nebr., 1980—. Mem. ABA, Nebr. Bar Assn., Omaha Bar Assn., Am. Soc. CPA's, Nebr. Soc. CPA's, Alpha Sigma Nu, Beta Gamma Sigma, Beta Alpha Psi. Roman Catholic. Avocations: flying, skiing, all water activities. Personal income taxation, Corporate taxation, General corporate. Home: 659 Parkwood Ln Omaha NE 68132 Office: McGrath North O'Malley & Kratz PC 1 Central Park Plaza Suite 1100 Omaha NE 68102

WEHDE, ALBERT EDWARD, lawyer; b. Milw., Feb. 14, 1935; s. Albert Christian and Mary Hubbel (Dewey) W.; m. Joan M. Forney, Nov. 4, 1978; children: John C., Edward T. BS, Marquette U., 1956, JD, 1960. Bar: Wis. 1960, Calif. 1968. Atty. AEC, Albuquerque, 1963-66; counsel Lockheed Aircraft Co., Sunnyvale and Redlands, Calif., 1966-73; assoc. Schultz & Manfield, Palo Alto, Calif., 1973-74; sr. counsel FMC Corp., Santa Clara, Calif., 1974—; bd. dirs. Tech. Fed. Credit Union, San Jose, Calif. Pres. Mountain View (Calif.) Babe Ruth League, 1976; trustee Mid-Peninsula Family Services Assn., Palo Alto, 1973-74. Served to capt. U.S. Army, 1960-63. Mem. ABA (region VII chmn. 1977-81, pub. contracts sect.), Santa Clara County Bar (co-chmn. corp. counsels sect. 1983-84, mem. exec. com.), Am. Corp. Counsels Assn. (chpt. sec., bd. dirs. 1983—). Democrat. Roman Catholic. Club: Decathalon (Santa Clara). Avocations: gourmet cooking, music, sports. Private international, Government contracts and claims. Home: 1106 Lorne Way Sunnyvale CA 94087 Office: FMC Corp PO Box 58123 Santa Clara CA 95052

WEHNER, CHARLES VINCENT, lawyer; b. Chester, W.Va., Nov. 12, 1921; s. Elmer Vincent and Elma (Votaw) W.; m. Jerry Pickens, Mar. 15, 1946; children: Pamela, Charles C., Patricia J., Stephen V., Richard K., Paulette S. AB, W.Va. U., 1943, JD, 1946. Bar: W.Va. 1946, U.S. Supreme Ct. 1956, U.S. Ct. Appeals (4th cir.) 1962. Ptnr. Parrack, Snyder & Wehner, Kingwood, W.Va., 1946-50; sole practice Kingwood, 1950—; gen. receiver Cir. Ct., Preston County, Kingwood, 1966—; dep. commr. forfeited and delinquent lands advisor Valley br. Bruceton Bank, Reedsville, W.Va., 1967. Hon. mem. Kingwood Fire Dept.; chmn. Preston County chpt. ARC, 1950-55, Preston County Buckwheat Festival, 1955; lector St. Sebastian's Ch., Kingwood. Mem. ABA, W.Va. Bar Assn. (past bd. govs.), Preston County Bar Assn. (past pres.). Republican. Roman Catholic. General corporate, General practice, Real property. Office: 103 W Court Kingwood WV 26537

WEHNER, RICHARD KARL, lawyer; b. Kingwood, W.Va., Dec. 15, 1957; s. Charles Vincent and Geraldine (Pickens) W. BA, W.Va. U., 1979; JD, Cath. U. of Am., 1982. Bar: W.Va. 1982, U.S. Dist. Ct. (so. dist.) W.Va. 1982, Md. 1983, U.S. Dist. Ct. (no. dist.) W.Va. 1983, D.C. 1984, U.S. Dist. Ct. Md. 1984, U.S. Ct. Appeals (4th cir.) 1984. Sole practice Kingwood, W.Va., 1982-86; ptnr. Wehner Law Offices, Kingwood, W.Va., 1987—. Mem. ABA, Md. Bar Assn., W.Va. Bar Assn., Assn. Trial Lawyers Am., Am. Judicature Soc., Appalachian Trail Conf. Republican. Roman Catholic. Lodge: Moose. General practice, State civil litigation, Family and matrimonial. Office: Wehner Law Offices 103 W Court St Kingwood WV 26537-0428

WEHR, WILLIAM JAMES, lawyer; b. Covington, Ky., July 13, 1950; s. Robert F. and Margaret O. (Schmaeling) W.; m. Nancy Jean Harrison, Dec. 29, 1971; children—Laura Beth, Lindsay Ann. B.A., U. Ky., 1972; J.D., No. Ky. U., 1976. Bar: Ky. 1976, U.S. Dist. Ct. (ea. dist.) Ky., 1976, U.S. Supreme Ct., 1980. Assoc., Kaufman, Johnson and Blau, Newport, Ky., 1976-77; ptnr. Twehues, Verst & Wehr, Newport, 1978—; asst. county atty. Campbell County, Newport, 1978—; guest lectr. Chase Coll. Law, 1981, 83. Bd. dirs. Sr. Citizens No. Ky., Inc., Covington, 1980—, pres., 1984-85. Served with USCGR, 1968-74. Recipient Disting. Prosecutor award Citizens for Decency Through Law, Inc., 1981. Mem. Assn. Trial Lawyers Am., Ky. Bar Assn. (ho. of dels. 1985—), Cin. Bar Assn., Kenton County Bar Assn., Campbell County Bar Assn. (pres. 1984), No. Ky. Bar Assn. (pres. 1987). Democrat. Roman Catholic. Lodge: Elks. General practice, Personal injury, Workers' compensation. Home: 57 Memory Ln Fort Thomas KY 41075 Office: Twehues Verst & Wehr 331 York St Newport KY 41071

WEHRINGER, CAMERON KINGSLEY, lawyer; b. Glen Ridge, N.J., Nov. 21, 1924; s. H. Harry and Eleanor Marguerite (Heese) W.; div.; children—Craig Maxwell, Alison Diana. B.A., Amherst Coll., 1947; J.D., NYU, 1951, postgrad., 1953; postgrad. Columbia U., 1958. Bar: N.Y., 1952, N.H., 1967, U.S. Dist. Ct. (so., ea. dist.) N.Y., 1952, U.S. Dist. Ct. N.H. 1972, U.S. Ct. Appeals (1st cir.) 1952, U.S. Ct. Appeals (2d cir.) 1980, U.S. Supreme Ct. 1971. Sole practice, N.Y.C., 1970—; arbitrator Civil Ct., N.Y. County, 1978—; pres., dir. Council for Livestock Protection, Inc., 1980-82; v.p. Good Shepherd on-the-island Corp., N.Y.C., 1979-85, bd. dirs., 1979—; advisor IDEA Franklin Pierce Law Ctr., Concord, N.H., 1975-84. Served with USNR, 1942-46. Recipient N.Y. Law Dwight Inn award 1951. Mem. N.Y. State Bar Assn., N.H. State Bar Assn., Assn. Bar City N.Y., Mensa. Republican. Author: Arbitration: Precepts and Principles 1969; When and How to Chose an Attorney 1970; contbr. revs. and articles to legal jours. Probate, Trademark and copyright, Space. Home: 556 Main St Apt 110 New York NY 10044

WEICHSEL, JOHN LOUIS, lawyer; b. N.Y.C., Feb. 14, 1946; s. Manfred and Marja (Roettsen) W.; m. Susan Jane French, Apr. 25, 1976; children: Jonathan, Jeffrey. BA, Clark U., 1968; JD, NYU, 1971. Bar: N.Y. 1972, N.J. 1972, U.S. Dist. Ct. N.J. 1972, U.S. Dist. Ct. (so. dist.) N.Y. 1977, U.S. Dist. Ct. (ea. dist.) N.Y., 1977, U.S. Supreme Ct., 1978. Assoc. Parker, Chapin & Flattau, N.Y.C., 1971-73; asst. dep. pub. defender Office of Pub. Defender, Hackensack, N.J., 1973-76; sole practice Hackensack, 1976—. Mem. ABA, N.J. Bar Assn., Bergen County Bar Assn., Assn. Trial Lawyers Am., Nat. Assn. Criminal Def. Attys. Democrat. Jewish. Criminal, Civil rights, State civil litigation. Office: 79 Main St Hackensack NJ 07601

WEICK, PAUL ALFRED, II, lawyer; b. Akron, Ohio, Mar. 17, 1955; s. Paul Alfred and Lorraine (Brown) W.; m. Christine Jean Watson, Dec. 4, 1981; 1 child, Daniel P. BA, Yale U., 1976; JD, U. Akron, 1978. Bar: Ohio 1979, Conn. 1980. Ptnr. Weick & Gibson, Cuyahoga Falls, Ohio, 1979-81; trust officer Cen. Nat. Bank, Cleve., 1981-84; v.p., regional trust mgr. United Carolina Bank, Whitevillw, N.C., 1984—. Mem. ABA. Republican. Presbyterian. Lodge: Masons (jr. deacon 1982-83, sr. deacon 1983-84). Probate, Estate planning, Estate taxation. Home: Rt 1 Box H-56 Whiteville NC 28472 Office: United Carolina Bank PO Box 632 Whiteville NC 28472

WEIDEMEYER, CARLETON LLOYD, lawyer; b. Hebbville, Md., June 12, 1933. BA in Polit. Sci., U. Md., 1958; JD, Stetson U., 1961. Bar: Fla. 1961, D.C. 1971, U.S. Dist. Ct. (mid. dist.) Fla. 1963, U.S. Ct. Appeals (5th cir.) 1967, U.S. Ct. Appeals (D.C. cir.) 1976, U.S. Supreme Ct. 1966, U.S. Ct. Appeals (11th cir.) 1982. Research asst. Fla. 2d Dist Ct. Appeals, 1961-65; ptnr. Kalle and Weidemeyer, St. Petersburg, Fla., 1965-68; asst. pub. defender 6th Jud. Cir., Fla., 1966-69, 81-83; ptnr. Wightman, Weidemeyer, Jones, Turnbull and Cobb, Clearwater, Fla., 1968-82. Bd. advisors Musicians Ins. Trust. Served with USN, 1951-54. Mem. Musicians Assn. Clearwater (pres. 1976-81), Fla.-Ga. Conf. Musicians (sec., treas. 1974-76), ABA, Assn. Trial Lawyers Am., Fla. Acad. Trial Lawyers, Fla. State Hist. Soc., Am. Fedn. Musicians (internat. law com.; pres. so. conf. musicians 1979-80), Clearwater Genealogy Soc., Pa. Genealog. Soc., Am. Legion, D.A.V., Phi Delta Phi, Sigma Pi, Kappa Kappa Psi. Lodges: Masons, Egypt Temple Shrine, Moose, Sertoma (bd. dirs. Clearwater chpt. 1984-86). General practice, Estate planning. Home: 2261 Belleair Rd Clearwater FL 33546 Office: Legal Arts Bldg 501 S Ft Harrison Clearwater FL 33516

WEIDMAN, CHARLES RAY, lawyer; b. Harrisburg, Pa., May 13, 1922; s. Charles Ray and Carrie Fay (Walker) W.; m. Alice Paine Walsh, Feb. 2, 1946; children—Charles S., Christopher R., William W. B.S. in Fgn. Service, Georgetown U., 1948, J.B., 1950. Bar: Mass. 1976, U.S. Dist. Ct. Mass. 1976, U.S. Ct. Appeals (1st cir.) 1979, U.S. Supreme Ct. 1982. Indsl. relations dir. Underwood Corp., Bridgeport, Conn., 1950-57; account exec. John L. Schwab Assocs., Bridgeport, 1957-59; v.p., Eversharp, Inc., Milford, Conn., 1959-67, Rotron, Inc., Woodstock, N.Y., 1967-76; prin. Charles Ray Weidman Assocs., Chatham, Mass., 1976—; arbitrator Am. Arbitration Assn., Boston, 1958-84. Contbr. articles to profl. jours. Chmn. Bd. Edn., Stratford, Conn., 1965-67; chmn. Republican Town Com., Chatham, 1984; moderator Town of Chatham, 1985. Served to sgt. USMC, 1942-46, PTO. Mem. Mass. Bar Assn., Boston Bar Assn., IEEE, Nat. Marine Electronics Assn. (exec. v.p. 1979-84), Phi Delta Phi. Episcopalian. Lodge: Rotary Internat. (Chatham) (sec. 1982-84). Federal civil litigation, State civil litigation, General practice. Home: 21 Eliphamets Ln Chatham MA 02633 Office: 938 Main St Chatham MA 02633

WEIDNER, GARY RICHARD, lawyer; b. Mpls., Nov. 18, 1948; s. Edward William and Jean (Blomquist) W.; m. Ellen Rae Schell, June 21, 1980; 1 child, Peter E. BA, U. Wis., 1970, JD, 1974. Bar: Wis. 1974, U.S. Dist. Ct. (ea. dist.) Wis. 1975. Ptnr. Hanaway, Ross, Hanaway, Weidner, Garrity & Bachhuber, Green Bay, Wis., 1974—; ad-hoc instr. U. Wis., Green Bay, 1974—, Northeast Wis. Tech. Inst., Green Bay, 1974—. Bd. Harbor Commrs. Brown County, 1976—. Mem. Assn. Trial Lawyers Am., Wis. Acad. Trial Lawyers, Civil Trial Lawyers Wis., Wis. Bar Assn., Def. Research Inst. Personal injury, State civil litigation, Family and matrimonial. Home: 644 Saint James Circle Green Bay WI 54301 Office: Hanaway Ross Hanaway Weidner Garrity & Bachhuber 401 Crooks St Green Bay WI 54301

WEIGHT, MICHAEL A., lawyer, former judge; b. Hilo, Hawaii, Jan. 5, 1940; s. Leslie A. and Grace B. (Brown) W.; m. Dorothy B.; children—Rachael R., Elizabeth G. B.S. in History, U. Rochester, 1961; LL.B., Vanderbilt U., 1967. Bar: Hawaii 1967, U.S. Ct. Appeals (9th cir.) 1968, U.S. Supreme Ct. 1972. Sole practice, Honolulu; former judge Dist. Ct. (1st cir.) Hawaii. Bd. dirs. Bishop Mus. Assn. Served to 1st lt. USMC, 1961-63. Mem. ABA, Hawaii State Bar Assn. Criminal, Professional responsibility. Office: 735 Bishop St Suite 430 Honolulu HI 96813

WEIL, ANDREW L., lawyer; b. Pitts., July 19, 1920; s. Ferdinand T. and Allene (Guthman) W.; m. Margaret G. Thompson, Aug. 11, 1949; children—Wendy T., Peter A. A.B. cum laude, Princeton U., 1943; LL.B., U. Pitts., 1948, J.D., 1968. Bar: Pa. 1949, U.S. Ct. Appeals (3d cir.) 1955, U.S. Supreme Ct. 1965. Solicitor, Twp. of O'Hara (Pa.), 1956-64; spl. asst. atty. gen. Pa., Pitts., 1964-76; ptnr. Weil, Vatz & Weil, Pitts., 1958-68, Cleland, Hurtt, Witt & Weil, 1975-79, Rose, Schmidt, Chapman, Duff & Hasley, 1980—. Bd. dirs. Mary Hillman Jennings Found., 1970—. Served to lt. col. U.S. Army, 1943-46; ETO. Decorated Purple Heart, Bronze Star. Mem. ABA, Pa. Bar Assn., Allegheny County Bar Assn., Am. Counsel Assn. (pres. 1982-83), Assn. Mcpl. and Sch. Solicitors. Republican. Presbyterian. Clubs: Pitts. Athletic, Fox Chapel Racquet. Real property, Probate, Contracts commercial. Office: Rose Schmidt Chapman Duff & Hasley Suite 900 Oliver Bldg Pittsburgh PA 15222

WEIL, CASS SARGENT, lawyer; b. N.Y.C., Nov. 6, 1946; s. Theodore and Ruth (Sargent) W. BA, SUNY, Stony Brook, 1968; JD cum laude, William Mitchell Coll. Law, 1980. Bar: Minn. 1980, Wis. 1984, U.S. Dist. Ct. Minn.,

U.S. Dist. Ct. (we. dist.) Wis., U.S. Ct. Appeals (7th and 8th cirs.). Assoc. J.R. Kotts & Assocs., Mpls., 1980-81, Wagner, Rutchick & Trojack, St. Paul, 1981-83; ptnr. Zohlmann & Weil, Willmar, Minn., 1983, Peterson, Franke & Riach P.A., St. Paul, 1983—. Editor: Minnesota Legal Forms, Trial Bankruptcy, 1983, 87. Mem. Comml. Law League Am., Assn. Trial Lawyers Am., Minn. Trial Lawyers Assn., Minn. Bar Assn. (sec. bankruptcy sect. 1983-85, vice chmn. 1985—), Ramsey County Bar Assn., Am. Bankruptcy Inst., Order of Barristers. Mem. Democratic Farm Labor Party. Jewish. Bankruptcy, Consumer commercial, Contracts commercial. Office: Peterson Franke & Riach PA 300 Midwest Fed Bldg Saint Paul MN 55101

WEIL, GARY RONALD, lawyer; b. N.Y.C., Oct. 1, 1953; s. Leopold and Margarete (Offsijowitz) W. BS in Acctg., NYU, 1974, JD, 1978. Bar: N.Y. 1978, U.S. Dist. Ct. (so. dist.) N.Y. 1980. Asst. county atty. Westchester County Atty.'s Office, White Plains, N.Y., 1978-81; asst. dist. atty. Bronx (N.Y.) Dist. Atty.'s Office, 1981—, Spl. Narcotics Prosecutor's Office, N.Y.C., 1985—. Mem. ABA, N.Y. State Bar Asn. Democrat. Jewish. Avocations: philately, photography. Criminal. Office: Spl Narcotics Prosecutors Office 80 Centre St New York NY 10013

WEIL, GILBERT HARRY, lawyer; b. N.Y.C., Aug. 31, 1912; s. Alexis and Esther (Marks) W.; m. Louise Rhoda Cohen, Mar. 14, 1936; children: Allen Charles, Jeffrey Lee. B.S., NYU, 1933, J.D., 1937. Bar: N.Y. 1937, U.S. Dist. Ct. (so. dist.) N.Y. 1941, U.S. Ct. Appeals (2d cir.) 1949, U.S. Ct. Appeals (4th cir.) 1950, U.S. Dist. Ct. (ea. dist.) N.Y. 1952, U.S. Ct. Appeals (fed. cir.) 1954, U.S. Ct. Appeals (3d cir.) 1956, U.S. Dist. Ct. D.C. 1961, U.S. Supreme Ct. 1964, U.S. Ct. Appeals (9th cir.) 1968, U.S. Ct. Appeals (5th cir.) 1969, U.S. Ct. Appeals (7th cir.) 1976. Law clk. and assoc. to Isaac W. Digges, 1935-53; pvt. practice 1953-65; partner Weil and Lee, N.Y.C., 1966-69, Weil, Lee & Bergin, N.Y.C., 1969-76, Weil, Guttman & Davis, N.Y.C., 1976-82, Weil, Guttman, Davis & Malkin, N.Y.C., 1982-86, Weil, Guttman & Malkin, N.Y.C., 1986—; lectr. in field, 1952—. Contbr. articles to profl. jours. Served to lt (j.g.) USNR, 1943-45. Administrative and regulatory, General practice, Trade regulation. Office: Weil Guttman & Malkin 60 E 42d St New York NY 10165

WEIL, JEFFREY GEORGE, lawyer; b. Allentown, Pa., Apr. 28, 1951; s. Russel G.E. and Irene Marie (Kozlowski) W.; m. Deborah Lee Holt, Aug. 24, 1974; children: Michael, Stephen. AB, Princeton U., 1973; JD, Harvard U., 1976. Bar: Pa. 1976, U.S. Dist. Ct. (ea. dist.) Pa. 1976, U.S. Ct. Appeals (3d cir.) 1976. Assoc. Dechert, Price & Rhoads, Phila., 1976-84, ptnr., 1984—. Chmn. com. United Way Southeastern Pa., Phila., 1982-85, trustee, 1983—; participant Coummunity Leadership Seminar Program, Phila., 1986. Mem. ABA (vice chmn. adminstrn. law com. on pub. advs. and pub. representation 1985—), Pa. Bar Assn., Phila. Bar Assn. (fed. cts. com. 1985—), Princeton U. Alumni Schs. Com. Avocations: fly-fishing, reading, sports. Antitrust, Federal civil litigation, Securities. Home: 1440 Byrd Dr Berwyn PA 19312 Office: Dechert Price & Rhoads 1500 Market St 3400 Centre Sq W Philadelphia PA 19102

WEIL, PETER HENRY, lawyer; b. N.Y.C., Nov. 20, 1933; s. Frank L. and Henrietta Amelia (Simons) W.; m. Helen Fay Kolodkin, Dec. 18, 1960; children: Karen, Frank. B.A., Princeton U., 1954; LL.B., Harvard U., 1957. Bar: N.Y. 1957, U.S. Dist. Cts. (so. and ea. dists.) N.Y. 1972. Assoc. Weil, Gotshal & Manges, N.Y.C., 1958-62; assoc. Kaye Scholer, N.Y.C., 1962-67, ptnr., 1967—; chmn. panel Practicing Law Inst. Program, 1980—; lectr. SMU Inst. on Comml. Financing, 1985—. former chmn. N.Y. bd. overseers, former bd. govs. Hebrew Union Coll., Jewish Inst. Religion, Cin., N.Y.C., Los Angeles, Jerusalem. Served with U.S. Army 1957-58. Mem. Ringwood Golden Master Volleyball Team, U.S. Nat. Champions, 1983. Mem. ABA, Assn. Bar City N.Y. (banking law com. 1975-78). Banking, Contracts commercial, Bankruptcy. Office: Kaye Scholer Fierman Hays & Handler 425 Park Ave New York NY 10022

WEILER, PAUL CRONIN, law educator; b. Port Arthur, Ont., Can., Jan. 28, 1939; s. G. Bernard and Marcella (Cronin) W.; divorced; children: Virginia, John, Kathryn, Charles. B.A. with honors, U. Toronto, 1960, M.A. with honors, 1961; LL.B., Osgoode Hall Law Sch., 1964; postgrad. Law Sch., Harvard U., 1965; LL.D., U. Victoria, 1981. Bar: Ont. Prof. law Osgoode Hall Law Sch., 1965-72; chmn. Labour Relations Bd. B.C., 1973-78; Mackenzie King prof. Can. studies Harvard U. Law Sch., 1978-80, prof. law, 1980—; spl. counsel Govt. of Ont. Rev. of Worker's Compensation, 1980—; mem. pub. rev. bd. United Auto Workers. Author: Labor Arbitration and Industrial Change, 1970; In the Last Resort: A Critical Study of the Supreme Court of Canada, 1974; (with others) Labor Relations Law in Canada, rev. edit. 1974; (with others) Studies in Sentencing in Canada, 1974; Reconcilable Differences: New Directions in Canadian Labour Law, 1980; Reforming Workers Compensation, 1980; MEGA Projects: The Collective Bargaining Dimensions, 1981; Protecting the Worker From Disability, 1983. Contbr. articles to profl. jours. Mem. Nat. Acad. Arbitrators. Roman Catholic. Club: Cambridge Tennis (Cambridge, Mass.). Labor, Workers' compensation. Office: Harvard U Law Sch Cambridge MA 02138 *

WEIMER, PETER DWIGHT, mediator, lawyer; b. Grand Rapids, Mich., Oct. 14, 1938; s. Glen E. and Clarabel (Kauffman) W.; m. Judith Ann Minor; children: Melanie, Kim. BA, Bridgewater Coll., 1962; JD, Howard U., 1969. Bar: U.S. Ct. Appeals (D.C. cir.) 1971. Assoc. counsel Loporto & Weimer Ltd., Manassas, Va., 1970-75; chief counsel Weimer & Cheatle Ltd., Manassas, 1975-79, Peter D. Weimer, P.C., Manassas, 1979-82; pres., mediator Mediation Ltd., Manassas, 1981—; pres. Citation Properties, Inc., Manassas, 1971—; pres. Preferred Research of No. Va., Inc., 1985—. Family and matrimonial, Real property. Address: PO Box 1616 Manassas VA 22110

WEIN, BRUCE J., lawyer; b. N.Y.C., Jan. 15, 1944; s. Eber A. and Esther A. W.; m. Penny Kirsch, June 24, 1967; children: Joseph, Howard, Michael, Rebecca. AB, Clark U., 1966; JD cum laude, Boston U., 1969. Bar: N.Y. 1970, U.S. Tax Ct. 1970, U.S. Dist. Ct. (so. dist.) N.Y. 1970. Assoc., Marshall, Bratter, Greene, & Allison, & Tucker, N.Y.C., 1969-75, ptnr., 1975-76; ptnr. Gordon, Hurwitz, Butowsky, Weitzen, Shalov & Wein, N.Y.C., 1976—. Mem. ABA (taxation sect.), N.Y. State Bar Assn. (tax sect.). Corporate taxation, Personal income taxation, General corporate. Office: Gordon Hurwitz et al 101 Park Ave New York NY 10178

WEIN, JOSEPH ALEXANDER, lawyer; b. Montreal, Que., Can., June 4, 1931; s. Jacob and Eugenia (Szour) W.; m. Libby Wein, June 23, 1957; children—Michele G., Paul F. A.A., UCLA, 1950, B.A., 1952, J.D., 1955. Bar: Calif. 1956. Assoc. Buchalter Nemer Fields Chrystie & Younger, Los Angeles, 1962-68, ptnr., 1968—, also pres., chief fin. officer, mng. ptnr.; chmn. panel prejudgment remedies Western Regional Comml. Law League Am., 1976. Mem. ABA, Internat. Bar Assn., Fin. Lawyers Conf., Nat. Comml. Fin. Conf., Los Angeles County Bar Assn., Comml. Law League Am., UCLA Sch. Law Alumni Assn. (founder 1981). Bankruptcy, Contracts commercial. Office: 700 S Flower St Suite 700 Los Angeles CA 90017

WEIN, STEPHEN JOSHUA, lawyer; b. Bklyn., May 13, 1950; s. Max and Natalie (Messing) W.; m. Livia Monica Kahan, Jan 27, 1974; children: David Abraham, Matthew Jonathan. BA in Polit. Sci., Bklyn. Coll., 1972; JD, Stetson U., 1976. Bar: Fla. 1976, U.S. Dist. Ct. (mid. dist.) Fla. 1976, U.S. Ct. Appeals (D.C. cir.) 1979, U.S. Ct. Appeals (5th and 11th cirs.) 1981, U.S. Tax Ct. 1985, U.S. Supreme Ct. 1980. Assoc. Belcher & Fleece, St. Petersburg, Fla., 1976-78; sole practice St. Petersburg, 1978-79; assoc. Battaglia, Ross, Hastings, Dicus & Andrews, St. Petersburg, 1979-81, ptnr., 1981—. Bd. dirs., sec. Cong. Beth Chai, Seminole, Fla., 1978-84; bd. dirs. Pinellas City Jewish Day Sch., Seminole, 1980, 85—. Mem. ABA (corp., bus. and banking law sects.), Fla. Bar Assn. (criminal law and trial lawyers sects., fed. practice com.), St. Petersburg Bar Assn., Assn. Trial Lawyers Am., Nat. Assn. Criminal Def. Attys. Lodges: B'nai Brith, Seminole. Federal civil litigation, State civil litigation, Criminal. Office: Battaglia Ross Hastings et al 980 Tyrone Blvd PO Box 41100 Saint Petersburg FL 33743

WEINBERG, GARY SCOTT, lawyer; b. Los Angeles, Sept. 22, 1948; s. Daniel and Addie (Mishlove) W.; m. Gail Joan Gotzian, Aug. 8, 1971; children: Brian, Bradley, Blake. BS in Bus., U. Colo., 1970; JD with honors, U. Tex., 1973. Bar: Colo. 1973, U.S. Dist. Ct. Colo. 1973, Mo. 1976, U.S. Dist. Ct. (we. dist.) Mo. 1976; cert. real estate sales, Mo. Assoc. Issacson & Rosenbaun, Denver, 1973-75; house counsel Pachter & Tilzer, Kansas City, Mo., 1976-77; prin. Wardrobe Services, Kansas City, 1978-85, Ram Furs Co., Kansas City, 1981—. V.p. Child Advocacy Services Ctr., Kansas City, 1983—, bd. dirs.; bd. dirs. De La Salle Sch., Kansas City, 1984. Named hon. citizen, City of Austin, 1971. Mem. ABA, Colo. Bar Assn., Mo. Bar Assn., Colo. Real Estate Brokers Assn., Heart of Am. Fabricare Assn. (pres., founder), Internat. Acad. Merchandising and Design (bd. dirs. 1985—). Club: Plaza (Kansas City) (bd. dirs. 1983-84, 86-87). General corporate, Real property, Principal of corporation. Home: 2525 Tomahawk Mission Hills KS 66208 Office: Ram Fur Co 7211 W 97th Overland Park KS 66212

WEINBERG, MARTIN GETY, lawyer; b. N.Y.C., Mar. 8, 1946; s. Jerome and Sarah (Rothman) W.; m. Michele Brady, Sept. 6, 1985. BA, U. Wis., 1968; JD, Harvard U., 1971. Bar: Mass. 1971, N.Y. 1971. Assoc. Crane, Inker & Oteri, Boston, 1972-74, ptnr., 1974-75; ptnr. Oteri, Weinberg & Lawson, Boston, 1975—. Mem. ABA, Assn. Trial Lawyers Am., Nat. Assn. Criminal Def. Lawyers, Mass. Bar Assn., Mass. Assn. Criminal Def. Lawyers. Criminal.

WEINBERG, ROBERT LEONARD, lawyer; b. Balt., May 31, 1923; s. Leonard and Beatrice (Lansburgh) W. Student, Coll. William and Mary, 1940-43; B.S., Johns Hopkins, 1952; J.D., U. Md., 1949. Bar: Md. 1948. Assoc. Weinberg and Green (attys.), Balt., 1948-52; partner Weinberg and Green (attys.), 1952—; asst. atty. gen. Md., 1953; instr. labor law and contract law Eastern Coll., 1954-57. Pres. Comprehensive Housing for Aged, Inc., 1969-71, United Way Central Md., 1976-77; v.p. Levindale Hebrew Hosp. and Geriatric Center, 1971-75, Jewish Hist. Soc. Md., 1980-86; bd. dirs. Assoc. Jewish Charities Balt., Sinai Hosp., 1974-86, chmn. real property; nat. bd. dirs. NCCJ, co-chmn. Md. region, 1968-70; mem. Policy Studies Inst. com. Johns Hopkins U., 1984-86; mem. Md. Humanities Council, 1986—. Mem. ABA (mem. real property sect. coms.), Md. Bar Assn., Balt. Bar Assn., Am. Judicature Soc. (dir.), Am. Coll. Real Estate Lawyers, Md. Bar Found., Md. Hist. Soc. (v.p. 1973-76), Md. C. of C. (v.p. 1981-82), Am. Jewish Hist. Soc. (bd. dirs. 1980-86, v.p. 1984-86), Omicron Delta Kappa. Republican. Jewish. Clubs: Suburban of Baltimore County (Balt.) (pres. 1971-74), Center (Balt.) (bd. govs. sec., counsel 1962-72). Real property. Office: 100 S Charles St Baltimore MD 21201

WEINBERG, ROBERT LESTER, lawyer, educator; b. N.Y.C., May 23, 1931; s. Abraham Matthew and Beatrice (Kohn) W.; m. Patricia Wendy Yates, Aug. 19, 1956; children: Susan Clare, David Hal, Jeremy Michael. BA, Yale U., 1953, LLB, 1960; PhD in Econs., London Sch. Econs., U. London, 1960. Bar: D.C. 1961, Conn. 1960, U.S. Supreme Ct. 1963, U.S. Ct. Appeals (D.C. and 2d cirs.) 1961, U.S. Ct. Appeals (3d and 7th cirs.) 1965, U.S. Ct. Appeals (6th cir.) 1968, U.S. Ct. Appeals (9th cir.) 1976, U.S. Ct. Appeals (10th cir.) 1977, U.S. Ct. Appeals (5th cir.) 1978, U.S. Ct. Appeals (4th cir.) 1982. Assoc. Williams & Connolly and predecessors, Washington, 1960-66, ptnr., 1967—; vis. lectr. U. Va. Sch. Law, Charlottesville, 1965—; adj. prof. U. Tex. Sch. Law, summer 1986; chmn. standing com. on pro bono matters D.C. Cir. Jud. Conf., 1980—. Columnist No. Va. Sun, 1981—; contbr. articles to profl. jours. Pres. No. Va. Fair Housing, Inc., 1968-69; chmn. Arlington Pub. Utilities Commn. (Va.), 1968, Arlington County Dem. Com., 1969-71, 10th Congl. Dist. Dem. Com., No. Va., 1972-76; del. Dem. Nat. Conv., 1976; pres. Arlington County Civic Fedn., 1973-75; co-chmn. Am. Jewish Congress Nat. Capital Region Commn. on Law and Social Action, 1984—. Served with U.S. Army, 1957-59. Recipient Outstanding Citizen of Yr. award Washington Evening Star and Arlington County Civic Fedn., 1975. Mem. ABA (ho. of dels. 1977-79, 80-82), Conn. Bar Assn., D.C. Bar (pres. 1977-79), Conn. Bar Assn., D.C. Bar Assn. Federal civil litigation, Criminal. Home: 5171 N 37th Rd Arlington VA 22207 Office: Williams & Connolly 839 17th St NW Washington DC 20006

WEINBERG, STEVEN JAY, lawyer; b. Casa Grande, Ariz., July 3, 1950; s. Jerry and Suzanne (Fabricant) W.; m. Stephanie Allison Lund, Aug. 10, 1975; 1 son, Joshua Noah. B.A., UCLA, 1972; J.D., Pepperdine U., 1975. Bar: Calif. 1975. U.S. Dist. Ct. (cen. and no. dists.) Calif. 1975, U.S. Dist. Ct. (so. dist.) Calif. 1977. Assoc. Popelka, Allard, McCowan & Jones, San Jose, Calif., 1976-77, Law Offices of Thomas T. Anderson, Indio, Calif., 1977—; assoc. Anderson, Parkinson, Weinberg and Miller, Indio, Calif., 1977-85, ptnr., 86—; bd. govs. Calif. Trial Lawyers Polit. Action Com., 1981—; mem. faculty Nat. Coll. Advocacy, Assn. Trial Lawyers Am., 1984. Fellow Belli Soc.; mem. Assn. Trial Lawyers Am. (co-chmn. motorcycle crash worthiness litigation group), Am. Bd. Trial Advs. (assoc.), Calif. Trial Lawyers Assn. (bd. govs. 1981-87, sec. 1984—), cert. recognition of experience in field of personal injury 1979, editor Products Liability Forum 1984), Western Trial Lawyers Assn. (bd. govs. 1985). Democrat. Jewish. Personal injury. Home: 48-125 Adler Ln Palm Desert CA 92260 Office: Anderson Parkinson et al 45-926 Oasis St Indio CA 92201

WEINBERGER, STEVEN, lawyer, educator; b. Bklyn., Apr. 13, 1953; s. Robert Ira and Elaine (Lichtenthal) W.; m. Maureen Susan Horan, Oct. 15, 1978; children: John William, Matthew Lawrence. BA, SUNY, Binghamton, 1974; JD, U. Miami, 1977. Bar: N.Y. 1978, U.S. Dist. Ct. (no. dist.) N.Y. 1981. Legis. atty. N.Y. City Council, 1977-78; asst. county atty. Westchester County, White Plains, N.Y., 1978-79; sr. asst. county atty. Broome County, Binghamton, N.Y., 1979-81, dep. personnel officer, 1981-82; labor relations specialist State of Conn., Hartford, 1982-86, asst. dir. retirement, 1986—; adj. prof. Post Coll., Waterbury, Conn., 1984—. Mem. ABA, N.Y. State Bar Assn. Democrat. Jewish. Labor. Office: State Conn Retirement div 30 Trinity St Hartford CT 06106

WEINER, CHARLES R., U.S. judge; b. Phila., June 21, 1922; s. Max and Bessie (Chairney) W.; m. Edna Gerber, Aug. 24, 1947; children: William, Carole, Harvey. Grad., U. Pa., 1947, M.A., 1967, Ph.D., 1972; LL.B., Temple U., 1950. Bar: Pa. bar 1951. Asst. dist. atty. Philadelphia County, 1952-53; mem. Pa. Senate from Phila. County, 1952-67, minority floor leader, 1959-60, 63-64, majority floor leader, 1961-62; U.S. dist. judge Eastern Dist. Pa., 1967—; Mem. Phila. County Bd. Law Examiners, 1959—. Mem. Pres.'s Adv. Commn. Inter-Govtl. Relations, Phila. Pub. Policy Com., Phila. Crime Prevention Assn., Big Bros. Assn.; mem. Pa. Bd. Arts and Scis.; Trustee, exec. com. Fedn. Jewish Philanthropies Phila., Allied Jewish Appeal Phila.; bd. dirs. Mental Health Assn. Pa., Phila. Psychiat. Center, Phila. Tribune Charities, Phila. Wharton Center Parkside YMCA, Jewish Publ. Soc. Am., others; chmn. bd. govs. Dropsie U.; mem. nat. bd. advisers Practicing Law Inst. Served as officer USNR, World War II. Recipient Phila. Fellowship award; Founder's Day award Temple U.; Alumni award U. Pa.; Founder's award Berean Inst.; others. Mem. Am., Pa., Phila. bar assns., Am. Law Inst. Jurisprudence. Office: US District Court 6613 S US Courthouse Independence Mall West 601 Market St Philadelphia PA 19106 *

WEINER, EARL DAVID, lawyer; b. Balt., Aug. 21, 1939; s. Jacob Joseph and Sophia Gertrude (Rachanow) W.; m. Gina Helen Priestley Ingoglia, Mar. 30, 1962; children: Melissa Danis Balmain, John Barlow. A.B., Dickinson Coll., 1960; LL.B., Yale U., 1968. Bar: N.Y. 1969. Assoc. Sullivan & Cromwell, N.Y.C., 1968-76, ptnr., 1976—; bd. dirs. Hedwin Corp., Solvay Techs., Inc. Gov. Bklyn. Heights Assn., 1980—, v.p., 1983-85, pres. 1985—; gov. The Heights Casino, 1979-84, pres., 1981-84; trustee Green-Wood Cemetery, 1986—, Bklyn. Bot. Garden, 1985—; bd. advisors Dickinson Coll., Carlisle, Pa., 1986—. Served to lt. USN, 1961-65. Mem. ABA, N.Y. State Bar Assn., Bar Assn. City N.Y. General corporate, Private international. Office: Sullivan and Cromwell 125 Broad St New York NY 10004

WEINER, EDWARD A., lawyer; b. San Francisco, Aug. 3, 1940; s. Benjamin P. and Yetta L. (Spindel) W.; m. Joanne C. Rosenblatt, Aug. 26, 1962; children: Mark J., Joshua A., Andrew T. BS in Bus. Adminstrn., U. Calif., Berkeley, 1962; JD, U. Calif., San Francisco, 1965. Ptnr. Pillsbury, Madison & Sutro, San Francisco, 1970—; bd. dirs. Orchard Properties, San Jose, Calif. Author: California Mortgage and Deed of Trust Practice, 1985. V.p., bd. dirs. pacific div. Am. Jewish Congress, San Francisco, 1984—. Served to capt. U.S. Army, 1966-68. Mem. Calif. Bar Assn. (exec. com. real property law sect. 1984—), San Francisco Bar Assn., Am. Inst. CPAs. Democrat. Bankruptcy, Real property. Office: Pillsbury Madison & Sutro 235 Montgomery St PO Box 2880 San Francisco CA 94120

WEINER, JACK H., lawyer; b. Phila., Nov. 21, 1934; s. Samuel A. and Sophie S. (Snyderman) W.; m. Diana M. Wiess, June 12, 1960; children—Scott, Edward, Hope. A.B., U. Pa., 1956; LL.B., Yale U., 1959. Bar: D.C. 1959, Pa. 1960, N.Y. 1973. Trial atty. U.S. Dept. Labor, 1960-65, civil div., appellate sect. U.S. Dept. Justice, 1965-68, NLRB, 1970-72; assoc. gen. counsel litigation Bankers Trust Co., N.Y.C., 1973—. Mem. ABA, N.Y. State Bar Assn., Assn. Bar City of N.Y. Republican. Club: Yale (N.Y.C.). Banking, Federal civil litigation, State civil litigation. Home: 122 E 82d St Apt 3A New York NY 10028 Office: 280 Park Ave Suite 17W New York NY 10017

WEINER, MARCIA MYRA, lawyer; b. Chgo., Apr. 12, 1934; d. Adolph Carl and Esther (Kahan) Spitzer; m. Bernard Karl Weiner, Sept. 15, 1952; children—Audrey Weiner Scheinberg, Jodi Weiner Groff, Karen Weiner Miller. B.A., St. Mary's U., San Antonio, 1965, J.D., 1970. Bar: Tex. 1971. Atty.-advisor HUD, San Antonio, 1971-84, chief counsel, San Antonio, 1984—. Recipient Spl. Achievement awards HUD, 1972, 75, 77. Mem. ABA, Tex. Bar Assn., Fed. Bar Assn., Bexar County Women's Bar Assn. Jewish. Clubs: Hadassah, Mizrachi, ORT (San Antonio). Government contracts and claims, Landlord-tenant, Real property. Office: HUD 800 Dolorosa St San Antonio TX 78285

WEINER, MICHAEL LEWIS, lawyer; b. Mpls., Aug. 27, 1954; s. Nathan and Annette (Rudoy) W.; m. Paula Sue Orenstein, Sept. 4, 1982. B Elected Studies, U. Minn., 1977; JD cum laude, William Mitchell Coll. Law, 1981. Bar: Minn. 1981, U.S. Dist. Ct. Minn. 1981, U.S. Ct. Appeals (8th cir.) 1981, U.S. Ct. Appeals (4th cir.) 1983, U.S. Ct. Appeals (3d, 10th and 11th cirs.) 1984, U.S. Supreme Ct. 1984, U.S. Ct. Appeals (5th and 6th cirs.) 1985. Assoc. DeParcq, Hunegs, Stone, Koenig & Reid, Mpls., 1981—; instr. legal writing William Mitchell Coll. Law, St. Paul, 1986-87. Mem. ABA, Fed. Bar Assn., Hennepin County Bar Assn. (vol. legal advice clinic 1983—), Assn. Trial Lawyers Am., Minn. Trial Lawyers Assn., Am. Judicature Soc. Jewish. Avocations: pvt. pilot, skiing, tennis, hockey, photography. Personal injury, Federal civil litigation, State civil litigation. Office: DeParcq Hunegs Stone Koenig & Reid 608 2d Ave S Minneapolis MN 55402

WEINER, NEIL STEVEN, lawyer; b. Cin., June 27, 1950; s. Sam G. and Anita J. (Gottlieb) W.; m. Sandra F. Tuley; 1 child, Eric Tuley. BA in History with honors, U. Cin., 1972; JD, U. Louisville, 1975. Bar: Ky. 1975, U.S. Dist. Ct. (we. dist.) Ky. 1975, U.S. Ct. Appeals (6th cir.) 1975. Sole practice Louisville, 1975—. Mem. Ky. Bar Assn., Louisville Bar Assn., Assn. Trial Lawyers Am., Ky. Trial Lawyers Assn. Workers' compensation, Probate, Personal injury. Home: 1258 Bassett Ave Louisville KY 40204 Office: 429 Muhammad Ali Blvd 500 Republic Bldg Louisville KY 40202

WEINER, PAUL I., lawyer; b. Bklyn.. BA, Bklyn. Coll., 1964, JD, 1967. VISTA atty. N.J., 1967-68; assoc. Katz & Wolchok, N.Y.C., 1968-70; from atty. to sr. atty. GAF Corp., 1970-1973; assoc. counsel Certain-Teed Products Corp., 1973-74; labor counsel Nabisco, Inc., 1974-77, sr. atty., 1977-81, chief counsel employment practices, 1981—; chmn. employment litigation seminar Practicing Law Inst.; contract compliance seminar chmn. Georgetown U. Law Sch. at So. Meth. U.; lectr. various seminars and instns. Co-author: Wrongful Discharge: A Preventive Approach; contbr. articles to profl. jours. Trustee Med/Mark Corp. of St. Barnabas Hosp., Livingston, N.J. Mem. ABA (equal employment com.). Labor. Office: Nabisco Brands Inc PO Box 1937 East Hanover NJ 07936-1937

WEINER, RICHARD NORMAN, lawyer; b. Phila., Dec. 2, 1941; s. Morton Joseph and Elizabeth Harriet (Chachkin) W.; m. Barbara Mae Norwitz, July 28, 1966; children—Matthew Aaron, Andrew Michael. B.S., MIT, 1963; J.D. cum laude, U. Pa., 1966. Bar: Pa. 1966, U.S. Dist. Ct. (ea. dist.) Pa. 1975. Chief counsel Pa. Securities Commn., Harrisburg, 1971-73; ptnr. Bolger, Picker & Weiner; mem. Pa. State Bd. Accountancy, 1980-84; lectr. in field. Chmn. Sr. Citizen Judicare Project Phila., 1977—; bd. dirs. Pub. Interest Law Ctr. Phila., 1982-85, Community Legal Services, Inc., 1983-84; mem. Phila. Fellowship Commn. Franklin Inst.; treas. Phila. Bipartisan Com. Lawyers Qualified Judges. Mem. Phila. Bar Assn. (treas. 1978-80, bd. govs. 1971-72, 76-80, chmn. young lawyers sect. 1971-72, chmn. lawyer reference services 1975-78, chmn. bar placement com. 1979, vice chmn., sec. reg. subcom., corp. sec. 1971-73), ABA, Phila. Bar Found. (pres. 1986, trustee 1976—, chmn. grants com. 1982-84). General corporate, Real property, Securities. Office: Bolger Picker & Weiner 1800 Kennedy Blvd11th Floor Philadelphia PA 19103

WEINER, ROBERT NEIL, lawyer; b. San Antonio, May 20, 1952; s. Arthur and Sheila (Freedman) W.; m. Cheryl Toubin, May 29, 1977; children: Courtney, Lindsay. AB summa cum laude, Princeton U., 1974; JD, Yale U., 1977. Bar: D.C. 1979. Law clk. to presiding judge U.S. Ct. Appeals, 1977-78; law clk. to presiding justice U.S. Supreme Ct., Washington, 1978-79; from assoc. to ptnr. Arnold & Porter, Washington, 1979—; adj. prof. Georgetown U. Law Ctr., Washington, 1984-86. Mem. ABA, D.C. Bar Assn., Am. Judicature Soc., Nat. Assn. Criminal Def. Lawyers. Antitrust, Federal civil litigation, Criminal. Home: 5318 Wriley Rd Bethesda MD 20816 Office: Arnold & Porter 1200 New Hampshire Ave NW Washington DC 20036

WEINER, ROBIN WENDY, lawyer; b. N.Y.C., Aug. 9, 1950; s. Selig and Pauline (Dichter) W. BA, CUNY, Bronx, 1971; JD, Bklyn. Law Sch., 1974. Bar: N.Y. 1975, U.S. Dist. Ct. (so. and ea. dists.) 1975, U.S. Supreme Ct. 1978. Assoc. N.Y.C. Law Dept., 1974-86; asst. gen. counsel N.Y.C. Transit Authority, 1986—. Del. Dem. Nat. Conv., Miami, Fla., 1972. Mem. ABA, N.Y. State Bar Assn. Federal civil litigation, State civil litigation, Construction. Home: 30 Waterside Plaza 16H New York NY 10010

WEINFELD, DAVID M., lawyer; b. Phila., Jan. 11, 1955; s. Samuel Simon and Sylvia Lillian (Wexlar) W.; m. Regina Elizabeth Gerger, May 19, 1984. BA, U. Pitts., 1976, JD, 1979. Bar: Pa. 1979, U.S. Dist. Ct. (ea. dist.) Pa. 1982, U.S. Ct. Appeals (3d cir.) 1982. Assoc. Kaliner and Joseph, Phila., 1979-80, Boardman and Scherm, Phila., 1981-82; sr. assoc. Sacks, Basch, Edelson & Launer, Phila., 1982-83; sole practice Phila., 1983—; cons. to various trade unions, Phila. Committeeman Reps. of Cheltanham Twp., Montgomery County, Pa., 1981-84. Mem. ABA, Pa. Bar Assn., Phila. Bar Assn., Assn. Trial Lawyers Am., Pa. Trial Lawyers Assn., U. Pitts. Sch. Law Alumni Assn., Phi Delta Theta (bd. dirs. Phila. club 1983—). Federal civil litigation, State civil litigation, Personal injury. Office: Two Penn Ctr Plaza Suite 2025 Philadelphia PA 19102

WEINFELD, EDWARD, judge; b. N.Y.C., May 14, 1901; s. Abraham and Fanny (Singer) W.; m. Lillian Stoll, Dec. 22, 1929; children: Ann, Fern. LL.B., NYU, 1921, LL.M., 1922. Bar: N.Y. 1923. Judge U.S. Dist. Ct. So. Dist. N.Y., 1950—; commr. housing N.Y. State, 1939-42; chief counsel N.Y. State Legis. Com. investigating bondholders coms., 1935; del. N.Y. State Constl. Conv., 1938; pres. Nat. Assn. Housing Ofcls., 1941-42, Nat. Housing Conf., 1948-50; v.p., dir. Citizens Housing and Planning Council N.Y., 1945-50; exec. com. Citizens Union City N.Y., 1943-50; dir. War Housing N.Y. State War Council, 1940-42; mem. N.Y. State Post War Pub. Works Planning Commn., 1940-42. Chmn. bd. dirs. Citizens' Com. Children N.Y. City, 1950. Mem. ABA, N.Y. State Bar Assn., Am. Judicature Soc., Bar Assn. City N.Y., Phi Sigma Delta. Office: US Court House Foley Sq New York NY 10007

WEINGARTEN, MARC PHILIP, lawyer; b. Kingston, N.Y., Nov. 4, 1951; s. Jerome J. and Dorothy (Tannenbaum) W.; children: Neil Alan, Eric Robert. AB magna cum laude, Temple U., 1973; JD, Villanova U., 1976. Bar: Pa. 1976, U.S. Dist. Ct. (ea. dist.) Pa. 1979, U.S. Ct. Appeals (3d cir.) 1981, U.S. Supreme Ct. 1983. Law clk. to presiding judge Pa. Ct. Common Pleas, Chester County, 1976-78; assoc. Greitzer & Locks, Phila., 1978-83, ptnr., 1983—; lectr. Alvernia Coll., Reading, Pa., 1977-78, West Chester (Pa.) State Coll., 1977-78, Del. Law Sch., Wilmington, 1977-78, Glassboro (N.J.) State Coll., 1979. Mem. ABA, Pa. Bar Assn., Phila. Bar Assn., Assn. Trial Lawyers Am., Pa. Trial Lawyers Assn., Phila. Trial Lawyers Assn., Pi Sigma Alpha. Democrat. Jewish. Avocations: racket sports, music, travel. Personal injury, Federal civil litigation, State civil litigation. Office: Greitzer & Locks 1500 Walnut St 21st Floor Philadelphia PA 19102

WEINGARTEN, REID H., lawyer; b. Newark, Mar. 9, 1950. BS, Cornell U., 1971; cert., Hague Acad. Internat. Law, The Netherlands, 1974; JD, Dickinson Law Sch., 1975. Bar: Pa. 1975, D.C. 1981, U.S. Ct. Appeals (4th, 5th, 11th, and D.C. Cirs.) 1981. Dep. dist. atty. Dauphin County Dist. Atty., Harrisburg, Pa., 1975-77; trial atty. pub. integrity sect. U.S. Dept. Justice, Washington, 1977—; instr. FBI, Washington, 1978—. Mem. Fed. Bar Assn. (Young Fed. Lawyer award 1984), D.C. Bar Assn. Criminal, Public international. Office: US Dept Justice Washington DC 20003

WEINGARTEN, SAUL MYER, lawyer; b. Los Angeles, Dec. 19, 1921; s. Louis and Lillian Dorothy (Alter) W.; m. Miriam Ellen Moore, Jan. 21, 1949; children: David, Steven, Lawrence, Bruce. AA, Antelope Valley Coll., 1940; AB, UCLA, 1942; cert., Cornell U., 1943; JD, U. Southern Calif., 1949. Prin. Saul M. Weingarten, Inc., Seaside, Calif., 1954—; atty. City of Gonzales, Calif., 1954-74, City of Seaside, Calif., 1955-70; gen. counsel Redevelopment Agy., Seaside, 1955-76, Security Nat. Bank, Monterey, Calif., 1968-74; bd. dirs. Frontier Bank, Cheyenne, Wyo. Author: Practice Compendium, 1950; contbr. articles to profl. jours. Del. Internat. Union of Local Authorities, Brussels, Belgium, 1963, 73; candidate state legislature Dem. Com., Monterey County, 1958; counsel Monterey Peninsula Mus. of Art, Inc., 1972-80; gen. counsel Monterey County Symphony Assn., Carmel, Calif., 1974—, Mountain Plains Edn. Project, Glasgow, Mont., 1975-81; chmn. fund raising ARC, Monterey, 1964; chmn., bd. dirs. fund raising United Way, Monterey, 1962-63; pres., bd. dirs. Alliance on Aging, Monterey, 1968-82; bd. dirs. Family Service Agy., Monterey, 1958-66, Monterey County Cultural Council, 1986—. Served to commdr. USN, 1942-46, 50-54, Korea. Grad. fellow Coro Found., 1949-50. Mem. Calif. Bar Assn., Monterey County Bar Assn., Monterey County Trial Lawyers Assn. Jewish. Clubs: Commonwealth (San Francisco); Meadowbrook (Seaside, Calif.); Monterey Peninsula Sunrise. Lodge: Rotary (pres. 1982-83). Avocations: tennis, travel. General practice, State civil litigation, Family and matrimonial. Home: 4135 Crest Rd Pebble Beach CA 93953 Office: Saul M Weingarten Inc 1123 Fremont Blvd Seaside CA 93955

WEINGLASS, LEONARD IRVING, lawyer; b. Belleville, N.J., Aug. 27, 1933; s. Sol and Clara (Schwartz) W. B.A., George Washington U., 1955; LL.B., Yale U., 1958. Bar: N.J. 1959. Individual practice law Newark, 1961-71, Los Angeles, 1974—; of counsel Rabinowitz, Boudin, Standard, Krinsky & Lieberman, N.Y.C.; mem. Newark Law Collective, 1971-73; instr. on criminal advocacy U. So. Calif., People's Coll. Law; lectr. on criminal advocacy Practising Law Inst. Served with USAF, 1951-61. Recipient Clarence Darrow Found. award, 1977. Mem. Nat. Lawyers Guild, Calif. Bar Assn., Calif. Attys. for Criminal Justice (bd. govs. from 1976), Nat. Assn. Criminal Def. Lawyers, Californians for Econ. Democracy, Phi Beta Kappa. Jewish. Office: 304 S Broadway Los Angeles CA 90013 also: care Rabinowitz Boudin et al 740 Broadway at Astor Pl 5th Floor New York NY 10003 *

WEINHOLD, DONALD LEROY, JR., lawyer, engineer; b. Salisbury, N.C., Mar. 27, 1946; s. Donald Leroy and Merrea L. (Smith) W.; m. Patricia Lynn Heffner, May 15, 1966; children—Melena Lynn, Donald Brandt. B.S. in Engring., N.C. State U., 1969; J.D., Cath. U. Am., 1973. Bar: N.C., D.C.; cert. N.C. Bd. Engrs. and Land Surveyors. Patent examiner U.S. Dept. Commerce, Washington, 1970-74; mem. firm Davis Ford & Weinhold, Salisbury, 1974-76, Ford & Weinhold, Salisbury, 1976-80; pres. firm Donald L. Weinhold, P.A., Salisbury, 1980—; commr. N.C. Gen. Statutes Commn., 1977-81, N.C. Criminal Justice and Tng. Standards Council, 1979-81. Mayor, mayor pro tem City of Salisbury, 1977-81; pres. Nat. Sportscasters and Sportswriters Found., Ind., 1982—; chmn. Rowan County Democratic Party; dir. community orgns. including Salisbury Community Found., Citizens for Older Adults, Salisbury Community Service Council. Served with USAF, 1966. Recipient Superior Performance awards U.S. Dept. Commerce, 1971, 72, 73, Disting. Service awards Salisbury Jaycees, 1980. Mem. Am. Soc. Indsl. Engrs., ABA, N.C. Bar. D.C. Bar, Rowan County Bar Assn., N.C. Acad. Trial Lawyers, Assn. Trial Lawyers Am., Am. Legion, Salisbury Rowan C. of C. Lutheran. Clubs: Rotary, Sales Exec. Mktg. Club of Salisbury, KC. Author: Brief History of Politics, 1981. Home: 228 W Bank St Salisbury NC 28144 Office: 318 N Main St Salisbury NC 28144

WEINIG, RICHARD ARTHUR, lawyer; b. Durango, Colo., Mar. 23, 1940; s. Arthur John and Edna (Novella) W.; m. Barbara A. Westerland, June 16, 1964. B.A. in Polit. Sci., Stanford U., 1962, postgrad. in Soviet Studies, 1962-65; J.D., U. Calif.-San Francisco, 1971. Bar: Alaska, 1971, U.S. Dist. Ct. Alaska 1971, U.S. Ct. Appeals (9th cir.) 1978, U.S. Supreme Ct. 1979. Assoc. Burr, Pease & Kurtz, Anchorage, 1971-73; assoc. Greater Anchorage Area Borough, 1973-75, Municipality of Anchorage, 1975-82; ptnr. Pletcher & Slaybaugh, Anchorage, 1982—. Active, Stanford U. Young Republicans, 1961-65, Alaska Rep. Com., 1971-83, Sierra Club, Mountaineering Club, Knik Canoyers and Kayakers of Alaska, Alaska Ctr. for Environ. Mem. ABA, Alaska Bar Assn., Anchorage Bar Assn., Nat. Rifle Assn. Republican. Presbyterian. Mem. editorial bd. Hastings Law Jour. Condemnation, Personal injury, State civil litigation. Office: 480 W Tudor Rd Suite 101 Anchorage AK 99503

WEINMAN, ELLEN SHELTON, lawyer; b. New Orleans, Sept. 24, 1951; d. Jesse West and Fannie Louise (Cocke) Shelton; m. David George Weinman, June 18, 1977; 1 child, Matthew Christian. BA, Hollins Coll., 1973; JD, Coll. of William and Mary in Va., 1976. Bar: Va. 1977, U.S. Ct. Appeals (4th cir.) 1979, U.S. Dist. Ct. (we. dist.) Va. 1980. Asst. commonwealth atty. Roanoke County, Salem, Va., 1977-81; sole practice Salem, 1984—. Chmn. bd. dirs. TRUST, Roanoke Valley Trouble Ctr., 1982-84; bd. dirs. Legal Aid Roanoke Valley, 1985-86. Mem. Va. Bar Assn., Salem-Roanoke County Bar Assn., Va. Women's Attys. Assn. (bd. dirs. 1984-86). Democrat. Presbyterian. General practice, Family and matrimonial, Criminal. Home: 919 Peyton St NW Roanoke VA 24019 Office: 36C E Main St Salem VA 24153

WEINMAN, GLENN ALAN, lawyer; b. N.Y.C., Dec. 9, 1955; s. Seymour and Iris Rhoda (Bergman) W. BA in Polit. Sci., U. Calif., Los Angeles, 1978; JD, U. So. Calif., 1981. Bar: Calif. 1981. Assoc. counsel Mitsui Mfgs. Bank, Los Angeles, 1981-83; assoc. McKenna, Conner & Cuneo, Los Angeles, 1983-85, Stroock, Stroock & Lavan, Los Angeles, 1985-87, Buchalter, Nemer, Fields, Chrystie & Younger, Los Angeles, 1987—. Mem. ABA (corp., banking and bus. law sect.), Calif. Bar Assn. (bus. law sect.), Los Angeles County Bar Assn. (bus. and corps. law sect., subcom. on fin. insts.), Phi Alpha Delta, Legion Lex, U. So. Calif. Law Alumni Assn. Democrat. Avocations: travel, tennis, racquetball, softball. Banking, General corporate. Office: Buchalter Nemer Fields et al 700 S Flower St Suite 700 Los Angeles CA 90017

WEINMAN, HOWARD MARK, lawyer; b. N.Y.C., May 6, 1947; s. Joseph and Kate (Dorn) W.; m. Pamela Eve Brodie, Jan. 6, 1980. B.A. magna cum laude, Columbia U., 1969; M.P.P., Harvard U, 1973, J.D. cum laude, 1973; LL.M. with highest honors in Taxation, George Washington U., 1981. Assoc., Fried, Frank, Harris, Shriver & Kampelman, Washington and N.Y.C., 1973-78; legis. atty. Joint Com. on Taxation, U.S. Congress, Washington, 1978-80; assoc. Sachs, Greenebaum, & Tayler, Washington, 1980-82; assoc. Crowell & Moring, Washington, 1982-84, ptnr., 1984—. Contbr. articles to profl. jours. Mem. ABA (sect. on taxation). Corporate taxation. Home: 5404 Center St Chevy Chase MD 20815 Office: Crowell & Moring 1001 Pennsylvania Ave NW Washington DC 20004-2505

WEINMAN, RICHARD STEPHEN, lawyer, consultant; b. N.Y.C., June 21, 1943; s. Abraham Weinman; m. Laurie Hudes, Dec. 17, 1967; children: Jonathan, Jessica. BA, NYU, 1965, postgrad., 1966-67; MA, Brandeis U., 1966; JD, U. Puget Sound, 1978. Bar: Wash. 1979. Exec. dir. Land Use Research Council, Seattle, 1979-81; sole practice Mercer Island, Wash., 1981—85; cons. Land Use Cons., Mercer Island, 1981-85, Huckell/Weinman Assocs., Mercer Island, 1986—. Editor Northwest Land Use Rev., Mercer Island, 1984—. Bd. dirs. Mercer Island Schs. Found.; mem. Mercer Island Design Commn. Mem. Wash. State Bar Assn., Am. Planning Assn., Planning Assn. Wash. Avocations: running, tennis, biking. Real property, Environment, Local government. Home: 9350 SE 68th St Mercer Island WA 89040 Office: Huckell/Weinman Assocs. PO Box 1161 Mercer Island WA 98040

WEINMANN, JOHN GIFFEN, lawyer, oil company executive; b. New Orleans, Aug. 29, 1928; S. Rudolph John and Mary Victoria (Mills) W.; m. Virginia Lee Eason, June 11, 1955; children: Winston Eason, Robert St. George Tucker, John Giffen, Mary Virginia Lewis, George Gustaf. B.A., Tulane U., 1950, LL.B., 1952. Bar: La. 1952. Practice law New Orleans; mem. firm Phelps, Dunbar, Marks, Claverie & Sims, 1955-80, of counsel, 1981-83, 85—; gen. counsel Times-Picayune Pub. Corp., 1968-80; pres., dir. Waverly Oil Corp., 1981—; lectr. bills and notes New Orleans chpt. Am. Inst. Banking, 1958-59; dir. Eason Oil Co., 1961-81, chmn., 1977; dir. 1st Nat. Bank of Oklahoma City, 1978-84, Am. Life Ins. Co. of N.Y., 1981—, Allied Investment Corp., 1985—; asst. sec. Am. Bar Endowment, 1971-76, bd. dirs., sec., 1975-80. Mem. adv. bd.: Tulane Law Rev. Bd. govs. Tulane Med. Center, 1968-81; bd. adminstrs. Tulane Ednl. Fund, 1981—, chmn. devel. com., 1985—; bd. dirs. Tulane Children's Center, 1981-84, WYES Ednl. TV Sta., 1981-82; trustee Southwest Legal Found., 1978-80, trustee Metairie Park Country Day Sch., v.p., 1976-77, pres., 1978-80, U.S. commr. gen. for 1984 La. World Expn., 1983-85; U.S. del. Bur. Internat. Expns., 1984-85, chmn. del., 1984; nat. chmn. com. for giving The Campaign for Tulane, 1983-85. Named Outstanding Law Alumnus, Tulane U., 1985. Mem. ABA (chmn. jr. bar conf. 1963-64, mem. ho. dels. 1964-66, 70, 72-76, sec. com. ethics evaluation 1965, rep. to conv. Nat. des Jeunes Avocats de France 1964, chmn. sect. bar activities 1969-70), La. Bar Assn. (sec.-treas. 1965-67, Outstanding Young Lawyer award), La. Soc. Colonial Wars (gov. 1976), Phi Beta Kappa, Order of Coif, Delta Kappa Epsilon, Omicron Delta Kappa. Episcopalian. General practice, Libel. Home: 611 Hector Ave Metairie LA 70005 Office: 2690 Pan American Life Ctr New Orleans LA 70130

WEINMANN, RICHARD ADRIAN, lawyer, arbitrator; b. N.Y.C., Oct. 15, 1917; s. Randolph and Mae (Korber) W.; m. Bert Millicent Landes, Dec. 26, 1946; children—Harriet Joan, Elaine Anita. LL.B., Bklyn. Law Sch., 1948; LL.M., NYU, 1953. Bar: N.Y. 1958, U.S. Dist. Ct. (so. dist.) N.Y. 1960, U.S. Dist. Ct. (ea. dist.) N.Y. 1960, U.S. Ct. Appeals (2d cir.) 1965, U.S. Supreme Ct. 1964. Ptnr. Sipser, Weinstock & Weinmann, N.Y.C., 1953-71; sole practice, N.Y.C., 1972—: guest lectr. seminars; mem. staff Cornell U. Sch. Indsl. and Labor Relations; panel arbitrator Suffolk and Nassau Counties, Pub. Employment Relations Bds. N.Y. State; mem. panel N.Y. State Bd. Mediation. Committeeman Nassau County (N.Y.), 1965—. Served with AUS, 1943-46. Mem. N.Y. State Bar Assn., N.Y. County Lawyers Assn., Am. Trial Lawyers Assn., Bar Assn. Nassau County, Indsl. Relations Research Assn., Union Lawyers Ednl. Conf. (legal adv. bd.), ACLU. Club: B'nai B'rith. Labor, General practice. Office: 292 Madison Ave New York NY 10017

WEINREB, LLOYD LOBELL, educator; b. N.Y.C., Oct. 9, 1936; s. Victor and Ernestine (Lobell) W.; m. Ruth Plaut, May 5, 1963; children—Jennifer, Elizabeth, Nicholas. B.A., Dartmouth, 1957; B.A., U. Oxford, 1959, M.A., 1963; LL.B., Harvard, 1962. Bar: N.Y. bar 1963, Mass. bar 1969. Faculty Harvard Law Sch., Cambridge, Mass., 1965—; prof. law Harvard Law Sch., 1968—. Home: 119 Russell Ave Watertown MA 02172 Office: Harvard Law Sch Cambridge MA 02138

WEINREB, MICHAEL LEONARD, lawyer; b. Freeport, N.Y., June 14, 1955; s. Donald and Stephanie (Herman) W.; m. Sharon M. Stertz, May 20, 1982; 1 child, Jessica. BS, Syracuse U., 1976; JD, Miami U., 1979. Bar: Fla. 1979, N.Y. 1981. Sole practice 1981—; ptnr. Weinreb, Weinreb & Weinreb, 1986—; pres. Omni Abstract Corp., Babylon, N.Y., 1978—. Real property, Personal injury, Family and matrimonial. Office: 475 Sunrise Hwy PO Box 1579 West Babylon NY 11704

WEINRICH, JOHNATHAN EDWARD, lawyer; b. N.Y.C., Sept. 17, 1949; s. John Edward and Anne (Murray) W.; children—Joy Teresa, Johnathan Joseph. B.A., SUNY-Binghamton, 1974; J.D., Vt. Law Sch., 1978. Bar: N.Y. 1979, U.S. Dist. Ct. (ea. and so. dist.) N.Y. 1979, U.S. Tax Ct. 1981, U.S. Ct. Appeals (2d cir.) 1980. Staff atty. Legal Aid Soc., N.Y.C., 1979-81; ptnr. Rutberg & Weinrich, N.Y.C, 1981-83; owner Johnathan E. Weinrich Law Firm, N.Y.C., 1983—. Editor Vt. Law Rev., 1976-77. Counsel Luis Nine Dem. Assn., Bronx, 1984; mem. Gov.'s Metro Task Force on Correctional Services, N.Y.C., 1984; sec. Com. to Re-elect Ralph C. Colon, 1987; trustee Vt. Law Sch., 1975-76. Mem. ABA, N.Y. State Trial Lawyers Assn., Assn. Trial Lawyers Am., Bklyn. Bar Assn., Kings County Criminal Bar Assn., Legal Aid Alumni Assn. Democrat. Roman Catholic. Lodge: Masons. Legislative, Criminal. Address: 5 Beekman St Suite 801 New York NY 10038

WEINRIEB, STEVEN WILLIAM, patent lawyer; b. Bronx, N.Y., May 17, 1945; s. Charles Matthew and Ruth (Rosenthal) W.; m. Marla Ann Apatoff, Nov. 8, 1969; children—Jonathan Michael, Jill Melissa, Brett David. B.Aero. Engring., Rensselaer Poly. Inst., 1966; J.D., Bklyn. Law Sch., 1969; LL.M., George Washington U., 1973. Bar: N.Y. 1970, U.S. Ct. Customs and Patent Appeals 1971, Va. 1976, U.S. Supreme Ct. 1976, U.S. Ct. Appeals (fed. cir.) 1982. Patent examiner U.S. Patent Office, Washington, 1969-71; ptnr. Oblon, Fisher, Spivak, McClelland & Maier, Arlington, Va., 1971-76; ptnr. Schwartz & Weinrieb, Arlington, 1976—. Patentee adjustable instrument base; support apparatus for video game joystick control unit. Mem. ABA, Am. Intellectual Property Law Assn., Am. Trial Lawyers Assn., Va. Trial Lawyers Assn., U.S. Trademark Assn. Patent, Trademark and copyright. Home: 8717 Cold Spring Rd Potomac MD 20854 Office: Schwartz & Weinrieb 2001 Jefferson Davis Hwy Arlington VA 22202

WEINS, MICHAEL JAMES, lawyer; b. Ypsilanti, Mich., June 17, 1939; s. George Anthony and Juanita Francis (Higgins) W.; m. Janine Johnson, Oct. 5, 1986. BSME, U. Mich., 1962, MS in Metallurgy, 1963; PhD in Applied Physics, Harvard U., 1970; JD, Loyola U., Chgo., 1976. Bar: Ill. 1976, U.S. Dist. Ct. (no. dist.) Ill. 1976, U.S. Patent Office 1977, D.C. 1978, N.Y. 1979. Asst. prof. U. Ill., Chgo., 1970-76; assoc. Hopgood et al, N.Y.C., 1976-77; patent atty. IBM, Yorktown, N.Y., 1977-80; sr. patent atty. Allied Corp., Morristown, N.J., 1980-84; ptnr. Weins & Weins, Lebanon, N.H., 1984—; cons. Dept. Environ. Control, Chgo., 1971-76, Spencer & Kay, Washington, 1978-80; tech. expert Anesi, Ozmon & Assocs., Chgo., 1973-74. NSF grantee. Mem. ABA, Am. Intellectual Property Law Assn., Am. Soc. for Metals, Am. Foundryman's Soc. (exec. com. 1973-75). Club: Harvard (N.Y.C.). Patent, Trademark and copyright. Home and Office: Weins & Weins 6 Allen St Lebanon NH 03766

WEINSHANK, ARTHUR CHARLES, lawyer; b. N.Y.C., Nov. 14, 1950; s. Harry and Fannie (Dresher) W.; m. Deborah Jane Savage, Jan. 13, 1980; children: Joshua Aarron, Brett Taylor. AAA, Nassau Community Coll., 1970; BBA, Pace U., 1972; JD, U. Miami, Coral Gables, 1974; LLM in Taxation, NYU, 1980. Bar: Fla. 1975, N.Y. 1975, Conn. 1980. Acct. Arthur Young and Co., N.Y.C., 1974-75; tax acct. Gulf and Western Industry, N.Y.C., 1975-77, Touche Ross and Co., N.Y.C., 1977-79; assoc. Hutton & Solomon, N.Y.C., 1979-80; ptnr. Cramer & Anderson, New Milford, Conn., 1980—; instr. Adult Edn., Brookfield, Conn., 1984—; bd. dirs. Western Conn. Estate Planning Council. Mem. ABA, Fla. Bar Assn., Conn. Bar Assn. (exec. com. tax sect.), N.Y. State Bar Assn. Avocations: skiing, tennis. Corporate taxation, Estate taxation, Personal income taxation. Home: 14 Cove Rd Brookfield CT 06804

WEINSHIENK, ZITA LEESON, federal judge; b. St. Paul, Apr. 3, 1933; d. Louis and Ada (Dubov) Leeson; m. Hubert Troy Weinshienk, July 8, 1956 (dec. 1983); children: Edith Blair, Kay Anne, Darcy Jill; m. James N. Schaffner, Nov. 15, 1986. Student, U. Colo., 1952-53; B.A. magna cum laude, U. Ariz., 1955; J.D. cum laude, Harvard U., 1958; Fulbright grantee U. Copenhagen, Denmark, 1959. Bar: Colo. 1959. Probation counselor, legal adviser, referee Denver Juvenile Ct., 1959-64; judge Denver County Ct., 1964-71; Denver dist. judge 1972-79, U.S. dist. judge for dist. Colo., 1979—. Precinct com.-woman Denver Democratic Com., 1963-64; bd. dirs. Crime Stoppers. Named One of 100 Women in Touch with Our Time Harper's Bazaar Mag., 1971. Mem. ABA, Colo. Bar Assn., Denver Bar Assn., Nat. Conf. Fed. Trial Judges, Colo. Women's Bar Assn., Women's Forum of Colo., Harvard Law Sch. Assn., Denver League Women Voters, Soroptimist Club Denver, Bus. and Profl. Women's Club Denver (Woman of Yr. 1969), Order of Coif (hon. Colo. chpt.). Judiciary. Office: US District Court 1929 Stout St Rm C-246 Denver CO 80294

WEINSTEIN, ALAN ABRAHAM, editor; b. Bklyn., Sept. 26, 1948; s. Israel and Sylvia (Hoffman) W.; m. Eileen Gale Cohen, May 31, 1970; 1 child, Lauren Micol. BA, Queens Coll., 1969; JD, Rutgers U., 1972; MBA, Baruch Coll., 1984. Bar: N.Y. 1973. Editor West Pub. Co., Mineola, N.Y., 1975-82; mng. editor Clark Boardman Co., Ltd., N.Y.C., 1982—. Editor: Corpus Juris Secundum, 1975. Ops. supr. Channel 13, N.Y.C., 1975—. Mem. ABA, Nat. Assn. Criminal Def. Lawyers, Nat. Orgn. Reform Marijuana Laws, N.Y. County Lawyers Assn. General practice, Criminal, Civil rights. Home: 319 E 24th St New York NY 10010 Office: Clark Boardman Co Ltd 435 Hudson St New York NY 10014

WEINSTEIN, ARTHUR DAVID, lawyer; b. Hartford, Conn., Feb. 15, 1910; s. Morris J. and Dora (Pelzel) W.; m. Pearl Posmanter, June 7, 1938; children—David R., Peter M., Judith Weinstein Wheeler, Andrew S. A.B., Trinity Coll., 1931; J.D., Harvard U., 1934. Bar: Conn. 1934, U.S. Dist. Ct. Conn. 1935, U.S. Ct. Appeals (2d cir.) 1980. Successively ptnr. Schatz & Weinstein, Schatz, Weinstein & Seltzer, Schatz, Weinstein, Seltzer & DeNezzo, Weinstein, Seltzer, DeNezzo & Swirsky; sr. ptnr. Weinstein, Seltzer, DeNezzo, Swirsky & Kulick, 1980— (all Hartford, Conn.); mem. Conn. Bar Examining Com. Pres. Beth El Temple, 1954-56; v.p. Emanuel Synagogue, West Hartford, also bd. dirs.; co-chmn. Hartford Jewish Fedn. Campaign; pres. Hartford YMHA, 1936; pres. Brotherhood Emanuel Synagogue; co-chmn. com. on edn. Hartford Jewish Fedn. Recipient Merit award United Jewish Appeal, 1974; Cert. of Appreciation, Beth El Temple, 1954. Mem. Conn. Bar Assn., Hartford County Bar Assn. (chmn. commn. on adminstrn. civil justice), ABA, Am. Arbitration Assn. Clubs: Tumblebrook Country (Bloomfield, Conn.); Harvard No. Conn., Trinity, Trinity Coll. Half Century, U. Hartford Assocs. Probate, General corporate, General practice. Office: 639 Prospect Ave West Hartford CT 06105

WEINSTEIN, ARTHUR GARY, lawyer; b. N.Y.C., May 11, 1946; s. Jacob and Ada (Ambutter) W.; m. Judith Marilyn Rothstein, Dec. 24, 1969; children: Stephen, Marc. BA, Bklyn. Coll., 1967; JD, U. Pa., 1970. Bar: N.Y. 1971, N.J. 1977, U.S. Ct. Appeals (2d cir.) 1972, U.S. Supreme Ct. 1973, U.S. Dist. Ct. (so. dist.) N.Y. 1973, U.S. Dist. Ct. N.J. 1977. Asst. dist. atty. New York County, 1970-74; asst. counsel Office of Ct. Adminstrn., N.Y., 1974-76; spl. asst. atty. gen. Dep. Atty. Gen.'s Office, N.Y.C., 1976-81, counsel, 1981-85; dir. spl. litigation unit N.Y. County Dist. Atty., 1985-86; counsel, chief of criminal appeals N.Y. State Organized Crime Task Force, 1986—. Editor: U. Pa. Law Sch. Yearbook Report, 1969-70. Criminal.

WEINSTEIN, BURTON MARVIN, lawyer; b. N.Y.C., Mar. 15, 1929; s. George Weinstein and Anna (Flam) Haas; m. Arlyn Stein, Dec. 21, 1951; children: Gaye Hyre, Jordan. AB, Syracuse U., 1950; JD, Yale U., 1956. Bar: Conn. 1959, U.S. Supreme Ct. 1960, U.S. Tax Ct. 1970. Conn. regional mgr. Am. Arbitration Assn., Hartford, 1957-60; asst. gen. counsel New Haven Redevel. Agy., 1960-61; ptnr. Saltman, Weiss, Weinstein & Elson and predecessor firms, Bridgeport, Conn., 1961-70; pres. Weinstein, Weiner & Shapiro P.C., Bridgeport, 1970—; hearing examiner Conn. Commn. Human Rights and Opportunities, 1969-72; lectr. police response to domestic violence. Contbr. articles to profl. jours. Vol. atty. Conn. Civil Liberties Union, 1959—; mem. exec. bd. Fairfield County (Conn.) Civil Liberties Union, 1959-86; organizing mem. acad. standards com. Housatonic Community Coll., 1971-72; mem.Conn. Citizens for Jud. Modernization, 1973-74; vol. legal cons. Stratford (Conn.) Counseling Ctr., 1975-77. Mem. Fed. Bar Assn., Conn. Bar Assn., Comml. Law League Am. Office: 350 Fairfield Ave Bridgeport CT 06604

WEINSTEIN, DAVID HAYM, lawyer; b. Prescott, Ariz., Oct. 31, 1943; s. Selig B. and Betty (Galatzer) W.; m. Elli Burstein, 1963; children—Daniel M., Joshua I. B.A., U. Calif.-Berkeley, 1965, J.D., 1968. Bars: Calif. 1969, Pa. 1973, U.S. Supreme Ct. 1978, U.S. Ct. Appeals (3d cir.) 1973, U.S. Ct. Appeals (7th cir.) 1979, U.S. Ct. Appeals (9th cir.) 1969, U.S. Ct. Appeals (10th cir.) 1976, U.S. Dist Ct. (no. dist.) Calif. 1969, U.S. Dist. Ct. (so. dist.) Calif. 1977, U.S. Dist. Ct. (ea. dist.) Pa. 1973, U.S. Dist. Ct. (mid. dist.) Pa. 1982. Law. clk. to judges U.S. Ct. Appeals (9th cir.) 1968-69; with Kibbutz Yotvata, Israel, 1970-72; mem. firm Kohn, Savett, Klein & Graf, P.C., Phila., 1972—; guest lectr. antitrust Temple U., 1977. Bd. dirs. Temple Beth Hillel-Beth El, 1981—, v.p., 1982-85, chmn. bd., 1983-85, pres. 1985-87; treas. Pa. Valley Congregation, 1976-78; bd. dirs. Council on Soviet Jewry of Greater Phila., 1979-81. Mem. ABA, Pa. Bar Assn., Phila. Bar Assn., Nat. Health Lawyers Assn., Internat. Assn. Jewish Lawyers and Jurists. Democrat. Club: Lawyers. Co-author: Review of Selected 1967 Code Legislation (Calif.). Federal civil litigation, Antitrust, Securities. Office: 1101 Market St Suite 2400 Philadelphia PA 19107

WEINSTEIN, DAVID L., lawyer; b. Chgo., Oct. 1, 1951; m. Linda M. Horberg; children: Jeremy, Aaron. MA in Philosophy, Mich. State U., 1975; JD, Northwestern U., 1979. Bar: Ill. 1979, U.S. Dist. Ct. (no. dist.) Ill. 1979, U.S. Ct. Appeals (7th cir.) 1981, U.S. Tax Ct. 1982, U.S. Ct. Appeals (8th cir.) 1984, U.S. Supreme Ct. 1984. Mng. atty. Cook County Legal Assistance Fund, Evanston, Ill., 1979-81; assoc. Karon, Morrison & Savikas, Ltd., Chgo., 1981-85, ptnr., 1986—. Mem. ABA, Chgo. Bar Assn., Nat. Inst. Trial Adv. Federal civil litigation, Civil rights, Insurance. Home: 1720 Elmwood St Wilmette IL 60091 Office: Karon Morrison & Savikas Ltd 233 S Wacker Dr 5700 Sears Tower Chicago IL 60606

WEINSTEIN, HARRIS, lawyer; b. Providence; s. Joseph and Gertrude (Ruzitsky) W.; m. Rosa Grunberg, June 3, 1956; children: Teme Feldman, Joshua, Jacob. SB Math., MIT, 1956, SM in Math., 1958; LLB, Columbia U., 1961. Bar: D.C. 1962. Assoc. Covington & Burling, Washington, 1962-67, 69-71, ptnr., 1971—; asst. to soliciter gen. U.S. Dept. Justice, Washington, 1967-69; pub. mem. Adminstrv. Conf. of the U.S., 1982—. Chmn. MIT Alumni Fund Bd., Cambridge, Mass., 1986—. Home: 1836 Randolph St NW Washington DC 20011 Office: Covington & Burling 1201 Pennsylvania Ave NW PO Box 7566 Washington DC 20044

WEINSTEIN, JACK B., U.S. judge; b. Wichita, Kans., Aug. 10, 1921; s. Harry Louis and Bessie Helen (Brodach) W.; m. Evelyn Horowitz, Oct. 10, 1946; children—Seth George, Michael David, Howard Lewis. B.A., Bklyn. Coll., 1943; LL.B., Columbia, 1948; LL.D. (hon.), Bklyn. Law Sch. Bar: N.Y. bar 1949. Asso. Columbia Law Sch., 1948-49; law clk. N.Y. Ct. Appeals Judge Stanly H. Fuld, 1949-50; partner William Rosenfeld, N.Y.C., 1950-52; mem.faculty Columbia Law Sch., 1952-67, prof. law, 1956-67, adj. prof., 1967—; U.S. judge (Eastern Dist. N.Y.), 1967-80, chief judge, 1980—; vis. prof. U. Tex., 1957, U. Colo., 1961, Bklyn. Law Sch., 1977, Hebrew U., 1977, Harvard U., 1982; Counsel N.Y. Joint Legislative Com. Motor Vehicle Problems, 1952-54, State Senator Seymour Halpern, 1952-54; reporter adv. com. practice and procedure N.Y. State Temporary Commn. Cts., 1955-58; adv. com. practice N.Y. Judicial Conf., 1963-66; adv. com. rules of evidence U.S. Jud. Conf., 1965-75, mem. com. jurisdiction, 1969-75, mem., 1983-86; mem. 2d Circuit Jud. Council, 1982—, N.Y. State-Fed. Jud. Council, 1982-85, U.S. Jud. Council, 1983-86, N.Y. State Temporary Commn. Revision and Simplification Constn. and to prepare for Constl. Conv., 1966; atty., Nassau County, 1963-65; chmn. Nassau County Law Services Inc., 1966. Author: (with Morgan and Maquire) Cases and Materials on Evidence, 4th edit, 1965, (with Maguire, Chadbourne and Mansfield) 5th edit.), 1971, 6th edit., 1975, (with Rosenberg) Cases and Materials on Civil Procedure, 1961, rev. edit, (with Smit), 1971, (with Smit, Rosenberg and Korn), 1976, (with Korn and Miller) New York Civil Procedure, 9 vols., rev. edit, 1966, Manual of New York Civil Procedure, 1967, (with Berger) Basic Problems of State and Federal Evidence, 1976, Revising Rule Making Procedures, 1977, A New York Constitution Meeting Today's Needs and Tomorrow's Challenges, 1967, also reports, articles. Chmn. N.Y. Democratic adv. com. on Constl. Conv., 1966; Bd. dirs. N.Y. Civil Liberties Union, 1956-62, Cardozo Sch. Law, 1974—, Conf. on Jewish Social Studies, 1980—; nat. adv. bd. Am. Jewish Congress, 1960-67, CARE, 1985—, Fedn. Jewish Philanthropies, 1985—; chmn. lay bd. Riverside Hosp. Adolescent Drug Users, 1954-55. Served to lt. USNR, 1943-46. Mem. Inst. Jud. Adminstrn., AAUP, Am. Law Inst., ABA, N.Y. State Bar Assn., Assn. Bar City N.Y., Soc. Pub. Tchrs. Law (Eng.). Jewish religion. Home: 10 Romola Dr Kings Point NY 11024 Office: 225 Cadman Plaza East Brooklyn NY 11021

WEINSTEIN, LES, lawyer; b. Providence, R.I., June 19, 1938; s. Herman and Rose (Cohen) W.; 1 child, James. BA, Brown U., 1960; MPA, U.R.I., 1968; JD, George Mason U., 1980. Bar: D.C. 1981. Staff atty. FDA,

Rockville, Md., 1980—; sole practice Washington, 1981—; mediator div., Bethesda, Md., 1982—; adj. prof. Paralegal Inst., McLean, Va., 1983—, Montgomery Coll., Takoma Park, Md., 1985—. Mem. ABA. Jewish. Avocation: theater (acting and directing). Food and drug law, General practice. Home: 9201 Friars Rd Bethesda MD 20817 Office: 918 F St NW Suite 308 Washington DC 20004

WEINSTEIN, LEWIS H., lawyer; b. Vilna, Lithuania, Apr. 10, 1905; came to U.S., 1906; s. Jacob Menahem and Kuna (Romanow) W.; m. Selma Yeslawsky, Sept. 2, 1932; children: David J., Louise Weinstein Dozois. A.B. magna cum laude, Harvard U., 1927, J.D., 1930. Bar: Mass. 1930. Assoc., then ptnr. Rome & Weinstein, 1930-45; asst. corp. counsel Boston, 1934-45; ptnr. Foley, Hoag & Eliot, Boston, 1946-79; sr. ptnr. Foley, Hoag & Eliot, 1979—; lectr. law Harvard, 1960-75; sr. vis. lectr. dept. city and regional planning MIT, 1961-68; occasional lectr. Practising Law Inst., N.Y.C., New Eng. Law Inst., ABA, Am. Law Inst., Mass. Continuing Legal Edn.; past clk. Spencer Shoe Corp.; mem. faculty Nat. Inst. Trial Advocacy, Boulder, Colo.; mem. finance com., bd. dirs. B. & M. R.R., 1960-74; trustee Boston 5 Cent Savs. Bank, 1964-78; cons. U.S. Housing Authority, 1940-42. Contbr. articles to law and other jours.; author libretto, also chpts. in legal books. Chmn. Mass. Emergency Housing Commn., 1946-47; chmn. Mass. Bd. Housing, 1947-48, Mass. Housing Council, 1948-52; mem. rent control and housing coms. Nat. Def. Commn., 1941-42; chmn. Nat. Jewish Community Relations Adv. Council, 1960-64, Armed Forces Adv. Com. Greater Boston, 1946-48; pres., Combined Jewish Philanthropies Greater Boston, 1954-57, gen. campaign chmn., 1957, now mem. exec. com.; past pres. Jewish Community Relations Council Met. Boston, 1952-54; former mem. nat. council Jewish Welfare Bd.; chmn. Conf. Presidents Maj. Am. Jewish Orgns., 1964-66; chmn. Nat. Conf. Soviet Jewry, 1968-70; mem. nat. com. Harvard Center for Jewish Studies; past lay rep. Nat. Assembly for Social Policy and Devel.; former mem. exec. com. City of Boston Civic Unity Com.; former mem. adv. council Mass. Dept. Edn.; adv. council Mass. Dept. Mental Health; mem. human rights com. also housing and urban renewal com. World Peace Through Law Center; former mem. exec. com., bd. dirs. New Eng. region, nat. bd. dirs. NCCJ; exec. com. Pres.'s Com. Equal Opportunity Housing, 1961-68; past chmn. Gov.'s Task Force to Establish Mass. Dept. Community Affairs, now mem. adv. com.; pres., 1965-66, now mem. exec. com. Council Jewish Fedn.; former mem. nat. council Am. Jewish Joint Distbn. Com.; past v.p. Nat. Fedn. Jewish Men's Clubs.; former trustee United Israel Appeal; past trustee Social Law, Library Ct. House Boston; past v.p. Am. Jewish League for Israel; past trustee Mass. Fedn. Taxpayers' Assn.; past bd. overseers Hiatt Inst.; past mem. bd. overseers Lown Inst. Contemporary Jewish Affairs, Heller Grad. Sch. Pub. Welfare; fellow Brandeis U.; past mem. vis. com., bd. overseers Middle Eastern Ctr. and Near Eastern Langs. and Civilizations, Harvard U.; mem. steering com. capital fund campaign, past class agt. Law Sch. Class of 1930; mem. steering com. Divinity Sch. Fund for Christian-Jewish Relations; trustee Nat. Found. Jewish Culture, Meml. Found. Jewish Culture, Hebrew Rehab. Ctr. for Aged, Boston, Beth Israel Hosp., Inst. for Jewish Life; pres. Hebrew Coll., Boston, 1946-53, now trustee; mem. assembly Jewish Agy. for Israel; mem. exec. Seminar program Aspen (Colo.) Inst., 1978; mem. Spl. Mass. Commn. To Investigate Corruption and Malfeasance in State and County Constrn., 1978-80. Served to col. AUS, World War II. Decorated Legion of Merit, Bronze Star with 2 clusters; Legion of Honor; Croix de Guerre with palm (France); recipient nat. citation NCCJ, Heritage award Yeshiva U., Nat. Community Service award Jewish Theol. Sem., FDR Day award Ams. Democratic Action, Mass. Fellow Am. Coll. Trial Lawyers, Am. Bar Found., Am. Assn. Jewish Edn.; mem. Am. Jewish Hist. Soc. (past mem. exec. council), Assn. U.S. Army (dir. Bay State chpt.), Boston Bar Assn. (past mem. council, chmn. real estate com.), Mass. Bar Assn. (past chmn. grievance com.), ABA (past mem. standing com. fed. judiciary), Mil Govt. Assn. (past. pres. Mass. chpt.), Phi Beta Kappa. Jewish (former temple trustee). Clubs: Harvard, Union (Boston). Real property, State civil litigation, Legal education. Office: Foley Hoag & Eliot 1 Post Office Sq Boston MA 02109

WEINSTEIN, PAUL, patent lawyer, chemical and metals manufacturing company executive; b. Bklyn., Mar. 9, 1940; s. George and Eva (Silverstein) W.; m. Dorothy Goodman, Nov. 18, 1961; children: Peter D., Donald P., Marc K. B Metall. Engring., Poly. Inst. Bklyn., 1961, MS, 1965; JD, Georgetown U., 1969. Bar: Conn. 1970, Patent Office 1970. Engr. IBM, Poughkeepsie, N.Y., 1961-65; patent examiner U.S. Patent & Trademark Office, Washington, 1965-69; patent atty. Olin Corp., New Haven, 1969-73, group patent counsel, 1978—; patent atty. Xerox Corp., Rochester, N.Y., 1973-78. Mem. ABA, Conn. Bar Assn., Am. Intellectual Property Law Assn., Conn. Pat. Law Assn., Licensing Execs. Soc., Internat. Assn. for Protection Indsl. Property, Sigma Xi (asso.). Republican. Jewish. Patentee in field metall. engring. Patent, Trademark and copyright, Unfair competition. Home: 509 Carriage Dr Orange CT 06477 Office: Olin Corp 91 Shelton Ave New Haven CT 06511

WEINSTEIN, SEYMOUR, lawyer; b. Holyoke, Mass., Feb. 18, 1928; s. Moses and Rebecca (Brooks) W.; m. Janet Seligman, June 27, 1952; children—Jordan H., Susan Delaney. A.B. cum laude, Clark U., 1948; J.D., U. Mich., 1951. Bar: Mich. 1951, Mass. 1952. Chmn. bd. Weinstein, Bernstein & Burwick, P.C., Worcester, Mass.; mem. criminal rules project adv. com. Supreme Jud. Ct. Pres.' council Clark U. Served to 1st lt. USAF. Recipient Disting. Faculty Mem. award, Nat. Coll. Advocacy. Fellow Am. Coll. Trial Lawyers, Am. Bar Found.; mem. Assn. Trial Lawyers Am., Mass. Bar Assn. (v.p., chmn. com. jud. rev. Mass. and Boston Bar Assns., chmn. com. on specialization), Worcester County Bar Assn. (pres.), Mass. Acad. Trial Lawyers (bd. govs.), Am. Judicature Soc., Mass. Bar Found. Jewish. Clubs: Mt. Pleasant Country, Boca Greens Country. Banking, State civil litigation, General corporate. Office: Weinstein Bernstein & Burwick PC 370 Main St Suite 1150 Worcester MA 01608

WEINSTEIN, STEPHEN SAUL, lawyer; b. Newark, Jan. 13, 1939; s. Francis and Hanna (Posner) W.; m. Nancy Stein, June 27, 1962; children: Beth, Jill, Lisa, Michael. BS, Fairleigh Dickinson U., 1962; JD, American U., 1965. Bar: N.J. 1966, U.S. Dist. Ct. N.J. 1966, U.S. Supreme Ct. 1969, U.S. Ct. Appeals (D.C. cir.) 1977, U.S. Dist. Ct. (so. and ea. dist.) N.Y. 1980, U.S. Ct. Appeals (3d cir.) 1981, N.Y. 1981. Exec. asst. to Senator Harrison A. Williams Jr., U.S. Senate, 1963-65; law clk., 1965-66; asst. prosecutor County Morris, N.J., 1968-70; counsel Morris County Dem. Com., 1971, 73—; mem. Stevens & Mathias, Newark, 1966-68, A.I. Harkavy, East Orange, N.J., 1966-69; pres. Stephen S. Weinstein, P.C., Morristown, N.J., 1968—. Trustee Sammy Davis, Jr. Liver Found., Univ. Medicine and Dentistry N.J., 1976-84. Mem. Morris County Bar Assn. (trustee 1974-76, 79-82), Essex County Bar Assn., N.J. Bar Assn., Fed. Bar Assn., ABA, Assn. Trial Lawyers Am. (gov. 1981—), Pa. Trial Lawyers, Tex. Trial Lawyers Assn., Acad. Fla. Trial Lawyers, Nat. Dist. Attys. Assn., Trial Attys. N.J., Morris County 200 Club (trustee 1965-70), Practicing Law Inst. N.Y. (lectr.), Instn. Continuing Legal Edn. N.J. (lectr.), Scribes, Phi Alpha Delta. State civil litigation, Criminal, Insurance. Office: 20 Park Pl Morristown NJ 07960

WEINSTEIN, STEVEN DAVID, lawyer; b. Phila., May 3, 1946; s. Leon and Elizabeth (Evantash) W.; m. Karin Elkis, Feb. 16, 1986. BA, Rutgers U., 1968, JD, 1975. Bar: N.J. 1975, Pa. 1975, U.S. Dist. Ct. N.J. 1975, U.S. Dist. Ct. (ea. dist.) Pa. 1975, U.S. Supreme Ct. 1979, U.S. Ct. Appeals (3d cir.) 1981, U.S. Ct. Claims 1986. Assoc. Lewis Katz P.C., Cherry Hill, N.J., 1975-78; sole practice Collingswood, N.J., 1978-84; assoc. Blank, Rome, Comisky & McCauley, Cherry Hill, 1984—; atty. Camden (N.J.) County Counsel, 1982-84; v.p. N.J. County Counsels Assn. 1983. Trustee Camden County Coll., Blackwood, N.J. 1983, South N.J. Tech. Consortium, Glassboro, N.J., 1986—, West Jersey Hosp. Found., Camden, 1984—. Mem. ABA, N.J. Bar Assn., Camden County Bar Assn. Democrat. Jewish. State civil litigation, Municipal bonds. Office: Blank Rome Comisky & McCauley 1010 Kings Hwy S Bldg 2 Suite A Cherry Hill NJ 08034

WEINSTEIN, STEVEN LOUIS, lawyer; b. Portland, Oreg., Feb. 6, 1950; s. David and Rhea (Schneider) W. AB, U. Chgo., 1972; JD, U. Calif., San Francisco, 1975. Bar: Calif. 1975, U.S. Dist. Ct. (no. dist.) Calif. 1975. Trial atty. U.S. Dept. Justice, San Francisco, 1975-80; atty. Safeway Stores, Inc., Oakland, Calif., 1980-84, sr. atty., 1984—. Administrative and regulatory, Antitrust, General corporate. Office: Safeway Stores Inc Oakland CA 94660

WEINSTEIN, WILLIAM JOSEPH, lawyer; b. Detroit, Dec. 9, 1917; s. Joseph and Bessie (Abromovitch) W.; m. Evelyn Ross, Apr. 5, 1942 (dec.); children—Patricia, Michael; m. 2d, Rose Sokolsky, Oct. 25, 1972. LL.B., Wayne State U., 1940. Bar: Mich. 1940, U.S. Dist. Ct. (ea. and so. dists.) Mich. 1940, U.S. Ct. Appeals (6th cir.) 1951, U.S. Ct. Appeals (9th cir.) 1972. Ptnr. Charfoos, Gussin & Weinstein, Southfield, Mich., 1951-54, Charfoos, Gussin, Weinstein & Kroll, Detroit, 1955-59, Gussin, Weinstein & Kroll, Detroit, 1959-65, Weinstein & Kroll, P.C., Detroit, 1965-73, Weinstein, Kroll & Gordon, P.C., Detroit, 1973-85; sole practice, Southfield, 1985—; apptd. to standard jury instrn. com. Mich. Supreme Ct. 1965-72. Served to maj. gen. USMCR, 1941-75. Decorated Bronze Star with Combat V, Legion of Merit (2), Purple Heart (2). Recipient Disting. Alumnus award Wayne State U., 1973. Mem. Mich. Bar Assn. (chmn. negligence sect. 1962-63), Am. Coll. Trial Lawyers, Internat. Acad. Trial Lawyers. Club: Tam-o-Shanter (Orchard Lake, Mich.). Contbr. articles to legal jours. Federal civil litigation, State civil litigation, Personal injury. Home: 4140 Wabeek Lake Dr Bloomfield Hills MI 48013 Office: 18411 W 12 Mile Rd Suite 200 Southfield MI 48076

WEINSTOCK, BENJAMIN, lawyer; b. Bklyn., Mar. 16, 1953; s. Morris and Sara (Pinkiewicz) W.; m. Eileen Weinstock, Sept. 8, 1984; children: Daniel, Etan, Allon, Ariel. BA, Yeshiva U., 1975; JD, Bklyn. Law Sch., 1978. Bar: N.Y. 1979, U.S. Dist. Ct. (ea. and so. dists.) N.Y. 1980, U.S. Ct. Appeals (2d cir.) 1980, U.S. Supreme Ct. 1982. Assoc. Ruskin, Schlissel et al, Mineola, N.Y., 1978-82, ptnr., 1982—. Mem. ABA, N.Y. State Bar Assn. Republican. Jewish. Real property, Computer, Contracts commercial. Home: 505 Arbuckle Ave Cedarhurst NY 11516 Office: Ruskin Schlissel et al 170 Old Country Rd Mineola NY 11501-4366

WEINSTOCK, DAVID S(TANLEY), lawyer; b. N.Y.C., July 29, 1954; s. Werner and Sandra (Rigberg) W.; m. Cheryl Platzman, June 14, 1981. BA in Econs. with high honors, Hobart Coll., 1975; JD, Union U., 1978; LLM in Trade Regulation, NYU, 1982. Bar: N.Y. 1979, U.S. Dist. Ct. (so. and ea. dist.) N.Y. 1979, U.S. Ct. Appeals (2d cir.) 1982; cert.emergency med. technician State of N.Y., 1974. Assoc. Newman, Tannenbaum, Helpern, Syracuse and Hirschtritt, N.Y.C., 1979; editor antitrust trade regulation group Matthew Bender and Co., N.Y.C., 1980-81; staff specialist U.S. Dist. Ct. (so. dist.), N.Y.C., 1983-85; atty. Am. Home Products Corp., N.Y.C., 1985-86; gen. counsel Henry Schein, Inc., Port Washington, N.Y., 1987—; arbitrator Small Claims sect. Civil Ct. of City of N.Y., 1987—. Instr. trainer safety services div. ARC, N.Y.C., Albany, Nassau County, 1973—. Mem. ABA, Assn. of Bar of City of N.Y., N.Y. State Bar Assn. (mem. food, drug and cosmetic law sect. 1985—, mem. exec. bd. of sect. 1985—, editor sect. newsletter 1986—). Jewish. Avocations: cacti, stamp and coin collecting, swimming, tennis enthusiast. Food, drug and cosmetic law, Federal practice, Antitrust. Office: Henry Schein Inc 5 Harbor Park Dr Port Washington NY 11050

WEINSTOCK, LEONARD, lawyer; b. Bklyn., Aug. 18, 1935; s. Samuel Morris and Evelyn (Reiser) W.; m. Rita Lee Itkowitz, May 25, 1963; children—Gregg Douglas, Valerie Lisa, Tara Diane. B.S., Bklyn. Coll., 1956; J.D., St. John's U., Bklyn., 1959. Bar: N.Y. 1961, U.S. Supreme Ct. 1964, U.S. Ct. Appeals (2d cir.) 1963, U.S. Dist. Ct. (ea. and so. dists.) N.Y. 1963, U.S. Tax Ct. 1963. Assoc. Bernard Helfenstein law practice, Bklyn., 1962-63; supr. All State Ins. Co., Bklyn., 1963-64; atty. Hertz Corp., N.Y.C., 1964-65; ptnr. Nicholas & Weinstock, Flushing, N.Y., 1965-68; v.p., ptnr. Garbarini, Scher & DeCicco, P.C., N.Y.C., 1968—; lectr. Practicing Law Inst., N.Y.C., 1975—, N.Y. Trial Lawyers Assn., 1980—; arbitrator Nassau County Dist. Ct., Mineola, N.Y., 1979—, U.S. Dist. Ct. (ea. dist.) N.Y. 1986—; mem. Med. Malpractice Mediation Panel, Mineola, 1978—. Legal counsel Massapequa Soccer Club (N.Y.), 1981—; county committeeman Democratic Party, Massapequa Park, N.Y., 1979—. Served with U.S. Army, 1959-62. Mem. ABA, N.Y. State Bar Assn., Nassau County Bar Assn. (mem. med. jurisprudence ins. com. 1978), N.Y. Trial Lawyers Assn., Queens County Bar Assn. (mem. legal referral com. 1969). Democrat. Jewish. Lodge: K.P. (mem. admissions com. 1965-72). Avocations: stamp collecting, softball, racquetball. Personal injury, Federal civil litigation, State civil litigation. Home: 20 Massapequa Ave Massapequa NY 11758 Office: Garbarini Scher & Decico PC 500 Fifth Ave New York NY 10110

WEIR, HARLAN PATRICK, lawyer; b. Dickinson, N.D., Nov. 4, 1939; s. Harlan John and Cecelia Jane (McCabe) W.; m. Diane Taylor Lamb, Oct. 26, 1985; children—Paul F., Harlan P., Timothy W., Justin M. B.S. cum laude, St. John's U., 1961; J.D., U. Notre Dame, 1964. Bar: N.D. 1964, U.S. dist. ct. N.D., U.S. dist. ct. Minn. 1964, U.S. Ct. Appeals (8th cir.) 1964. Law clk. 8th Cir. Ct. Appeals, St. Louis, 1964-65; assoc. Wattam, Vogel, Bright & Peterson, Fargo, N.D., 1965-67; ptnr. Vogel Brantner Kelly Knutson Weir & Bye, Fargo, 1967—. Mem. Internat. Soc. Barristers, Can County Bar Assn. (pres. 1978-79), N.D. Bar Assn., ABA, Am. Judicature Soc., Am. Coll. Law and Medicine, Am. Soc. Hosp. Attys. Democrat. Roman Catholic. Club: Fargo Country. Editor Notre Dame Lawyer, 1961-64. Personal injury, Federal civil litigation, State civil litigation. Home: 2207 15th Ave S Fargo ND 58103 Office: PO Box 1389 502 1st Ave N Fargo ND 58102

WEIR, JOHN KEELEY, lawyer; b. New Haven, Jan. 27, 1947; s. John H. and Helen K. (Keeley) W.; m. Lucy P. Persico, May 21, 1977; children: John P., Keeley Anne. BA, Yale U., 1968; JD, Northwestern U., 1971. Bar: N.Y. 1972, U.S. Dist. Ct. (so. dist.) N.Y. 1973, U.S. Ct. Appeals (2d cir.) 1975, U.S. Supreme Ct. 1982. Assoc. Haight, Gardner, Poor & Havens, N.Y.C., 1971-80, ptnr., 1980—. Mem. ABA (del.), Internat. Bar Assn. (del.), Yale U. Alumni Assn. Democrat. Roman Catholic. Club: Yale (N.Y.C.). Avocations: tennis, squash, swimming, reading. Labor, Environment, Aviation. Home: 47 Winthrop Dr Riverside CT 06878 Office: Haight Gardner Poor & Havens 195 Broadway New York NY 10004

WEIR, PETER FRANK, lawyer; b. Stuttgart, Ger., Mar. 26, 1933; s. Robert Henry and Ruth Sophie W.; m. Jean M., Sept. 27, 1958; children—Bradford F., Elizabeth A. B.A., Williams Coll., 1955; LL.B., Harvard U., 1958; M.B.A., N.Y.U., 1967. Bar: N.Y. 1959, Ga. 1957. Assoc. Cole & Deitz, N.Y.C., 1959-66, ptnr., 1966—. Bd. dirs. Episcopal Ch. Found., 1982—, also treas., chmn. fin. com., mem. exec. com., mem. steering com. N.Y. Regional Council, 1975-81, chmn., 1979-81; bd. dirs., counsel Point O'Woods Assn., N.Y., 1976—, v.p., 1982—; alt. bd. dirs. Fire Island Assn., 1976-86; sec. and dir. Elderworks Found., 1982—. Served with Air N.G., 1958-63. Mem. ABA, N.Y. State Bar Assn., N.Y. County Bar Assn., Assn. Bar City N.Y. Republican. Clubs: Church, Down Town Assn., Williams (N.Y.C.); Club at Point O'Woods; Hillsboro (Pompano Beach, Fla.). Real property, Banking, General corporate. Home: 530 E 86th St Apt 11C New York NY 10028 Office: 175 Water St 10th Floor New York NY 10038-4924

WEIR, WALTER, JR., lawyer; b. Abington, Pa., June 17, 1947; s. Walter John Sr. and Kathryn (Turnan) W. BA, Temple U., 1973, JD, 1976. Bar: D.C. 1976, N.J. 1976, U.S. Dist. Ct. (ea. and no. dists.) Pa. 1976, U.S. Ct. Appeals (3d cir.) 1980, U.S. Supreme Ct. 1984. Atty. Defender Assn. Phila., 1976-77; assoc. Fellneimen, Eichen & Goodman, Phila., 1977-81, ptnr., 1981-85; mng. ptnr. Klehr, Harrison, Harvey, Branzburg, Ellers & Weir, Phila., 1985—. Served to sgt. USAF, 1966-70, Vietnam. Mem. ABA, Pa. Bar Assn., Phila. Bar Assn., N.J. Bar Assn., Nat. Inst. Trial Advocacy (faculty 1984—). Banking, Bankruptcy, Contracts commercial. Office: Klehr Harrison Harvey et al 1401 Walnut St Philadelphia PA 19102

WEIR, WILLIAM H., lawyer, educator; b. East Orange, N.J., Mar. 16, 1947; s. William F. and Nela (Stinnett) W.; m. Marilyn Fowler, Dec. 6, 1969; 1 child, William Bradley. B.S., Eastern Ill. U., 1969; J.D., John Marshall Law Sch., 1977. Bar: Ill. 1977, U.S. Dist. Ct. (no. dist.) Ill. 1977. Field rep. Aetna Casualty, Chgo., 1972-76; assoc. Tomlinson & Thomas, Arlington Heights, Ill., 1976-77; ptnr. Brittain, Ketcham, Strass, Terlizzi, Flanagan, Weir & Johnson, P.C., Elgin, Ill., 1977—; prof. bus. law Elgin Community Coll., 1980—. Author Tort Law Newsletter, 1981. Pres., Elgin YMCA, 1982-84. Served to capt. USMC, 1967-72. Mem. Assn. Trial Lawyers Am., Ill. Trial Lawyers Assn., ABA, Ill. State Bar Assn. (speaker, co-editor tort laws newsletter 1981-83), Kane County Bar Assn. (treas., civil practice com., speaker), Navy League, Am. Legion. Lodge: Kiwanis (Elgin). State civil litigation, Personal injury, Insurance. Home: 41W058 Kingston Ct Saint Charles IL 60174 Office: Brittain Ketcham Et Al 1695 Larkin Ave Elgin IL 60123

WEIR, WILLIAM JOHN ARNOLD, lawyer; b. Phoenix, June 22, 1939; s. Arnold Miller and Jane (Kimmel) W.; m. Diana McGee, June 20, 1959; children—Derek Anthony, Brandon Kimmel, Donovan John Alan; m. 2d, Susan Armstrong Smith, Oct. 6, 1977; 1 dau., Robin Smith. B.S., U. Calif.-Berkeley, 1965; J.D., U. Calif.-San Francisco, 1968. Bar: Calif. 1969, U.S. Dist. Ct. (no. dist.) Calif. 1969, U.S. Ct. Appeals (9th cir.) 1969, Dist. Ct. ct. (ea. dist.) Calif. 1971, U.S. Supreme Ct. 1980, U.S. Dist. Ct. (cen. dist.) Calif. 1982, U.S. Ct. Claims, 1975. Asst. gen. counsel Bank of Am., San Francisco, 1969-76; ptnr. Murphy, Weir & Butler, San Francisco, 1976—. Served in USMCR, 1957-65. Mem. Calif. Bar Assn., ABA, San Francisco Bar Assn. (chmn. comml. law and bankruptcy sect. 1980-82). Clubs: Stock Exchange, Commonwealth, Olympic (San Francisco). Bankruptcy, Federal civil litigation, State civil litigation. Office: 101 California St San Francisco CA 94111

WEIS, JOSEPH FRANCIS, JR., federal judge; b. Pitts., Mar. 12, 1923; s. Joseph Francis and Mary (Flaherty) W.; m. Margaret Horne, Dec. 27, 1958; children: Maureen, Joseph Francis, Christine. Student, Duquesne U., 1941-47; J.D., U. Pitts., 1950. Bar: Pa. 1950. Individual practice law Pitts., 1950-68; judge Ct. Common Pleas, Allegheny County, Pa., 1968-70, U.S. Dist. Ct. (we. dist.) Pa., 1970-73, U.S. Ct. Appeals (3d cir.), Pitts., 1973—; lectr. trial procedures, 1965—. Contbr. articles to legal jours. Mem. Mental Health and Mental Retardation Bd., Allegheny County, 1970-73; mem. Leukemia Soc., 1970-73; mem. bd. adminstrn. Catholic Diocese Pitts., 1971-83; trustee Forbes Hosp. System, Pitts., 1969-74. Served with AUS, 1943-48. Decorated Bronze Star, Purple Heart with oak leaf cluster; recipient St. Thomas More award, 1971. Hon. fellow Internat. Acad. Trial Lawyers; fellow Am. Bar Found.; mem. ABA (chmn. appellate judges' conf. 1981-83), Pa. Bar Assn., Allegheny Bar Assn. (past v.p.), Acad. Trial Lawyers Allegheny County (past pres.), Am. Judicature Soc., Jud. Conf. U.S. (chmn. civil rules com. 1986—, com. on adminstrn. bankruptcy system 1983—, subcom. on jud. improvements 1983—). Judicial administration. Home: 225 Hillcrest Rd Pittsburgh PA 15238 Office: 513 US Courthouse Pittsburgh PA 15219

WEISBARD, SAMUEL, lawyer; b. N.Y.C., Nov. 16, 1922; s. Morris William and Charlotte (Haber) W.; m. Ruth Ida Pfeiffer, Sept. 24, 1950; children: Victoria, Mark William, Carol Ellen, Jonathan Franklin. A.B. magna cum laude, NYU, 1942; LL.B., Harvard U., 1948; postgrad. fellow, Cornell U., 1942-43. Bar: N.Y. 1949, Ill. 1958. Assoc. Hartman, Sheridan, Tekulsky, Glass & Lynch, N.Y.C., 1948-50; atty. U.S. SEC, Washington, 1950-52; atty. antitrust div. U.S. Dept. Justice, Washington, 1952-57; assoc. Lederer, Livingston, Kahn & Adsit, Chgo., 1957-62; ptnr. McDermott, Will & Emery, Chgo., 1962—; dir. Hazeltine Research Inc., Chgo. Bd. govs. U. Chgo. Symphony Orch., 1985—, exec. com., dir. budget and fin., trustee., 1985—. Mem. ABA, Chgo. Bar Assn. (chmn. antitrust com. 1975-76). Jewish. Clubs: Standard, Mid-Day; Monroe (Chgo.). Home: 1160 Chatfield Rd Winnetka IL 60093 Office: McDermott Will & Emery 111 W Monroe St Chicago IL 60603

WEISBERG, ALAN LERNER, lawyer; b. Louisville, June 20, 1948; s. Charles L. and Marian (Bierman) W.; m. Bonnie Lerner, June 29, 1970; children: Brielle, Spencer, Quinton. BS in Acct., Ind. U., 1970; JD, Am. U., 1973; LLM in Taxation, U. Miami, 1974. Bar: U.S. Tax Ct. 1974, U.S. Dist. Ct. (so. dist.) Fla. 1975, U.S. Ct. Appeals (5th cir.) 1975, U.S. Supreme Ct. 1977, U.S. Ct. Appeals (11th cir.) 1981. Assoc. Cunningham & Weinstein, Miami, Fla., 1974-77; asst. U.S. atty. U.S. Dist. Ct. (so. dist.) Fla., Miami, 1977-81; sole practice Miami, 1981—. Chmn. Morningside Hist. Dist., Miami, 1984—; mem. Bayfront Park Adv. Com., Miami, 1986. Mem. Greater Miami Tax Inst. (sec. 1984—), Fla. Bar Assn. (vice chmn. criminal tax procedures, tax sect. 1986), Fed. Bar Assn. (exec. com. So. Fla. chpt., com. on standards for admission to fed. practice 1981-86). Criminal, Corporate taxation. Office: 1401 Brickell Ave #910 Miami FL 33131

WEISBERG, DAVID CHARLES, lawyer; b. N.Y.C., June 25, 1938; s. Leonard Joseph and Rae M. (Kimberg) W.; m. Linda G. Kerman, Aug. 27, 1975; children: Leonard J., Risa B. AB, U. Mich., 1958; LLB, Harvard U., 1961. Bar: N.Y. 1962, U.S. Dist. Ct. (so. and ea. dists.) N.Y. 1965, U.S. Supreme Ct. 1970. Assoc. firm Dreyer & Traub, Bklyn., 1962, Lee Franklin, Mineola, N.Y., 1962-65; sole practice, Patchogue, N.Y., 1965-67, 77-80; ptnr. Bass & Weisberg, Patchogue, 1967-77, Davidow, Davidow, Russo & Weisberg, Patchogue, 1981-82, Davidow, Davidow, Weisberg & Wismann, 1982—; assoc. justice and justice Village of Patchogue, 1968-70, village atty., 1970-85; spl. asst. dist. atty. Suffolk County, Patchogue, 1970-85; assoc. estate tax atty., appraiser N.Y. State Dept. Taxation and Fin., Hauppauge, N.Y., 1975-85. Law chmn. Suffolk County Democratic Com., N.Y., 1975-85; bd. dirs. Temple Beth El of Patchogue. Mem. Assn. Trial Lawyers Am., N.Y. State Trial Lawyers Assn., Nassau-Suffolk Trial Lawyers Sect., N.Y. State Bar Assn., Suffolk County Bar Assn. Lodges: Lions (pres. Medford 1978-79, 2d v.p. 1984-85), Masons. Personal injury, State civil litigation, General practice. Office: Davidow Davidow Weisberg & Wismann 110 N Ocean Ave Box 350 Patchogue NY 11772

WEISBERG, SHEILA ROSEANNE, lawyer; b. Burbank, Calif., Feb. 24, 1955; d. Charles H. and Estelle Weisberg. B in Spl. Studies magna cum laude, Cornell U., 1976; JD cum laude, Southwestern U., 1979. Bar: Calif. 1979, U.S. Dist. Ct. (cen. dist.) Calif. 1979. Dep. atty. City of Los Angeles, 1979-81; assoc. Omansky, Lyden & Lazarus, Encino, Calif., 1981-82, Federman, Gridley, Mogab & Gradwohl, Los Angeles, 1982-84; ptnr. Schmid & Weisberg, Los Angeles, 1984-86; asst. prof. sch. law Pepperdine U., Malibu, Calif., 1986—. Mem. ABA, Los Angeles County Bar Assn. (exec. bd. dirs. barristers sect. 1985—), Themis Soc. (sec., treas. 1985—). State civil litigation, Personal injury, Legal education. Office: Pepperdine U Sch Law 24255 Pacific Coast Hwy Malibu CA 90265

WEISBERG, STUART ELLIOT, federal department lawyer; b. Bklyn., Feb. 2, 1949; s. Julius and Esther Weisberg; m. Elizabeth Jane Krucoff, June 24, 1979. BA, Brandeis U., 1971; JD, U. Pa., 1974. Bar: N.Y. 1976, D.C. 1976, U.S. Ct. Appeals (9th cir.) 1976, U.S. Supreme Ct. 1979. Assoc. NLRB, Washington, 1975-84; staff dir., counsel employment and housing subcom. U.S. Ho. of Reps., Washington, 1984—. Democrat. Jewish. Avocations: basketball, tennis. Labor, Legislative. Office: Employment & Housing Subcom B-349A Rayburn Bldg Washington DC 20515

WEISBERGER, JOSEPH ROBERT, justice Rhode Island supreme court; b. Providence, Aug. 3, 1920; s. Samuel Joseph and Ann Elizabeth (Meighan) W.; m. Sylvia Blanche Pigeon, June 9, 1951; children: Joseph Robert, Paula Ann, Judith Marie. A.B., Brown U., 1942; J.D., Harvard U., 1949; LL.D., R.I. Coll., Suffolk U., Mt. St. Joseph Coll.; D.C.L., Providence Coll.; D.H.L., Bryant Coll. Bar: R.I. bar 1950. Practice with Quinn & Quinn, Providence, 1951-56; solicitor Glocester, R.I., 1953-56; judge R.I. Superior Ct., Providence, 1956—; presiding justice R.I. Superior Ct., 1972-78; mem. faculty Nat. Jud. Coll.; vis. lectr. Providence Coll., Suffolk Law Sch., Roger Williams Coll.; Chmn. New Eng. Regional Conf. Trial Judges, 1962, 63, 65; chmn. New Eng. Regional Commn. Disorderd Offender, 1968-71, R.I. Com. Adoption on Rules Criminal Procedure, 1968-72, Gov. of R.I. Adv. Com. Corrections, 1973, Nat. Conf. State Trial Judges, 1977-78; exec. com. Appelate Judges Conf., 1979—, vice chmn., 1983-85, chmn., 1985-86; bd. dirs. Nat. Center for State Cts., 1975—. Chmn. editorial bd.: Judges Jour, 1973-75. Pres. R.I. Health Facilities Planning Council, 1967-70; chmn. Gov. R.I. Council Mental Health, 1968-73; moderator Town of East Providence, 1954-56; mem. R.I. Senate, 1953-56, minority leader, 1955-56; vice chmn. bd. trustee R.I. Hosp., St. Joseph's Hosp. Served to lt. comdr. USNR, 1941-46. Inducted into R.I. Hall of Fame, 1980. Fellow Am. Bar Found.; Mem. ABA (mem. ho. of dels., task force on criminal justice standards 1977-79), R.I. Bar Assn., Am. Judges Assn. (gov.), Inst. Jud. Adminstrn., Am. Judicature Soc. (bd. dirs.), Am. Law Inst., Phi Beta Kappa. Clubs: K.C., Knight of St. Gregory. Jurisprudence. Home: 60 Winthrop St East Providence RI 02915 Office: Supreme Ct of RI Providence County Courthouse Providence RI 02903

WEISBROD, MARCY HELFAND, lawyer; b. Chgo., Sept. 2, 1954; d. Irwin and Pauline (Rosenthal) Helfand; m. Les Frank Weisbrod, Dec. 28, 1975; 1 child, Eric. Student, Pomona Coll., 1972-75; BS with high honors, So. Meth. U., 1976, JD cum laude, 1979. Bar: Tex. 1979, U.S. Dist. Ct. (no.

dist.) Tex. 1980; cert. comml. real estate Tex. Bd. Legal Specialization. Assoc. Freytag, Marshall et al, Dallas, 1979-83, Jones, Day, Reavis & Pogue, Dallas, 1983-84; of counsel Weisbrod & Weisbrod P.C., Dallas, 1984—. Chmn. Dem. Precinct, Dallas, 1980—. Mem. ABA (real property sect. comml. leasing com. 1985—), Dallas Bar Assn., Dallas Assn. Young Lawyers, Tex. Real Property Sect., Dallas Real Property Sect., Order of the Coif. Real property. Home: 7191 Kendallwood Dallas TX 75240 Office: Weisbrod & Weisbrod PC 10300 N Cen Expressway Bldg V Suite 470 Dallas TX 75231

WEISBURD, STEVEN I., patent lawyer; b. Bklyn., Sept. 18, 1949; s. Walter Bennett Weisburd and Sandra (Goldstein) Schmidt; m. Bonnie Ray Turner, Dec. 19, 1970; children—Bryan Joshua, Amy Rebecca. B.S.E.E., U. Hartford, 1971; J.D., Temple U., 1974. Bar: Pa. 1974, N.Y. 1977. Assoc. Seidel, Gonda & Goldhammer, Phila., 1974-76; assoc. Ostrolenk, Faber, Gerb & Soffen, N.Y.C., 1976-79, ptnr., 1980—. Mem. ABA, N.J. Patent Law Assn., N.Y. Patent, Trademark, and Copyright Law Assn., Inc. Patent, Trademark and copyright, Computer. Home: 1223 Dickinson Dr Yardley PA 11021

WEISEMAN, JAC BURTON, lawyer; b. Plainfield, N.J., Aug. 27, 1934; s. Albert and Gertrude (Gartenberg) W.; m. Constance R. Ahrons, June 17, 1956 (div. 1966); children: Geri Lynn, Amy Beth; m. Susan Miller, Nov. 29, 1969; children: Jennifer, Craig Barrett. AB, Lafayette Coll., 1956; JD, Rutgers U., Camden, 1967. Bar: N.J. 1967, U.S. Dist. Ct. N.J. 1967; cert civil trial lawyer N.J. Supreme Ct. Assoc. Blume & Kalb, Newark, 1968-69; ptnr. Blume, Kalb & Weiseman, 1970-74; mem. Blume & Weiseman, Newark, 1974-80, Blume, Weiseman & Vazquez, P.C., 1980-82; sole practice, Newark, 1982—; ptnr. Weiseman, Sherman & Mella, P.C., Mountainside, N.J., 1985-86, pres. Weiseman & Mella, P.A., 1986—; model jury charges Supreme Ct. Com., 1986—. Roscoe Pound Found. grantee, 1986. Jewish. Personal injury, State civil litigation, Workers' compensation. Home: 23 Briarcliffe Dr Scotch Plains NJ 07076 Office: Weiseman & Mella PA 1055 US Rt 22 E Mountainside NJ 07092

WEISENBURGER, TED, county judge; b. Tuttle, N.D., May 12, 1930; s. John and Emily (Rosenau) W.; children—Sam, Jennifer, Emily, Todd, Daniel, Dwight, Holly, Michael, Paul, Peter; m. Maylyne Chu, Sept. 19, 1985; 1 child, Irene. B.A., U. N.D., 1952, LL.B., 1956, J.D., 1969; B.F.T., Am. Grad. Sch. Internat. Mgmt., Phoenix, 1957. Bar: N.D. 1963, U.S. Dist. Ct. N.D. 1963. County judge Benson County, Minnewaukan, N.D., 1968-75, Walsh County, Grafton, N.D., 1975-87; tribal judge Devils Lake Sioux, Ft. Totten, N.D., 1968-84, Turtle Mountain Chippewa, Belcourt, N.D., 1974—; U.S. magistrate U.S. Dist. Ct., Minnewaukan, 1972-75. Served to 1st lt. U.S. Army, 1952-54. Recipient Humanitarian award U.S. Catholic Conf., 1978, 82, Right to Know award Sigma Delta Chi, 1980. Home: 441 Western Ave Grafton ND 58237 Office: Walsh County Courthouse Grafton ND 58237

WEISENFELS, JOHN ROBERT, lawyer; b. St. Louis, Feb. 10, 1949; s. Charles William Jr. and Marjorie Ann (Hughes) W.; m. Constance Jane Chronic, July 17, 1970; children: Kathryn Anne, Jon Michael. BS in Chem. Engring., U. Mo., 1971, JD, 1975. Bar: Mo. 1975, U.S. Dist. Ct. (we. dist.) Mo. 1975. Assoc. Shook, Hardy & Bacon, Kansas City, Mo., 1975-77, Jackson & Dillard, Kansas City, 1977-80; ptnr. Dillard & Weisenfels, Kansas City, 1980—. Mem. ABA, Mo. Bar Assn., Kansas City Bar Assn., Lawyers Assn. Kansas City. Clubs: Plaza (pres. 1980-81), Tiger (pres. 1986). Real property, Taxation of partnerships. Office: Dillard & Weisenfels 602 Westport Rd Kansas City MO 64111

WEISFELD, SHELDON, lawyer; b. McAllen, Tex., Feb. 20, 1946; s. Morris and Pauline (Horwitz) W.; B.B.A., U. Tex., 1967; postgrad. Nat. U.Mex., Mexico City, 1969; J.D., U. Houston, 1970. Bar: Tex. 1971, U.S. Dist. Ct. (so. dist.) Tex. 1978, U.S. Ct. Appeals (5th cir.) 1978, U.S. Ct. Appeals (11th cir.) 1981, U.S. Supreme Ct. 1982. Practice, Austin, Tex., 1973-77, sole practice, Brownsville, Tex., 1980—; asst. fed. pub. defender U.S. Dist. Ct. (so. dist.) Tex., Brownsville, 1977-80; dir., sec.-treas. Flying Nurses Inc.; sec.-treas. KVEO-TV, KTXF-FM Radio. Bd. dirs. Temple Beth El, Brownsville. Mem. Nat. Assn. Criminal Def. Lawyers, Tex. Criminal Def. Lawyers (dir.), ABA, Fed. Bar Assn., State Bar Tex., Cameron County (Tex.) Bar Assn. Democrat. Club: B'nai B'rith, Rotary (Brownsville). Criminal, Federal civil litigation. Office: PO Drawer 1231 864 Ridgewood Brownsville TX 78520

WEISFUSE, DAVID B., lawyer; b. Bklyn., May 11, 1949; s. George and Lucille (Garner) W.; m. Irene Wagner, Mar. 28, 1976; 1 child, Benjamin. B.A., U. Wis., 1970; J.D., Syracuse U., 1973. Bar: N.Y. 1974, U.S. Dist. Ct. (so. and ea. dist.) N.Y. 1976, U.S. Ct. Appeals (2d cir.) 1977, U.S. Supreme Ct. 1977. Assoc. counsel Legal Aid Soc. Westchester County, White Plains, N.Y., 1974-78, sr. counsel, 1978—; adj. lectr. Pace U., White Plains, 1980-81. Mem. ABA (criminal justice sect.), N.Y. State Bar Assn., Westchester County Bar Assn. (criminal justice sect.). Criminal. Office: Westchester County Legal Aid 1 N Broadway White Plains NY 10601

WEISGALL, JONATHAN MICHAEL, lawyer; b. Balt., Mar. 17, 1949; s. Hugo David and Nathalie (Shulman) W.; m. Ruth Macdonald, June 3, 1979; children: Alison, Andrew. BA, Columbia Coll., 1970; JD, Stanford U., 1973. Bar: D.C. 1974, N.Y. 1974, U.S. Supreme Ct. 1982, Marshall Islands 1983. Law clk. to judge U.S. Ct. Appeals (9th cir.), San Francisco, 1973-74; assoc. Covington & Burling, Washington, 1974-79; from assoc. to ptnr. Ginsburg, Feldman, Weil & Bress, Washington, 1980-83; sole practice Washington, 1983—; bd. dirs. Nat. Enterprise Bank, Washington. Pres. Crossroads 40, Oakland, Calif., 1985—. Mem. Phi Beta Kappa. Jewish. Federal civil litigation, Public international, Legislative. Home: 6109 Masachusetts Ave Bethesda MD 20816 Office: 1300 19th St NW Washington DC 20036

WEISLER, FAYE LESLIE, lawyer; b. New Orleans, Mar. 19, 1955; d. Morris Jacob and Ruth Natalie (Rosen) W. BA, U. Denver, 1977; JD, La. State U., 1982. Bar: La. 1982, U.S. Dist. Ct. (ea. dist.) La. 1984. Jud. law clk. to presiding justice La. Ct. Appeals (5th cir.), Gretna, 1982-83; assoc. Midlo & Lehmann, New Orleans, 1983-85, Gertler & Gertler, New Orleans, 1985-87, Herman, Herman, Katz & Cotlar, New Orleans, 1987—. Bd. dirs. New Orleans Legal Assistance Corp., 1986—. Mem. ABA, La. Bar Assn., Assn. Trial Lawyers Am., La. Trial Lawyers Assn., Assn. Women Attys. Personal injury, Family and matrimonial, Federal civil litigation. Office: Herman Herman Katz & Cotlar 820 O'Keefe Ave New Orleans LA 70113

WEISMAN, BARBARA, lawyer; b. Jersey City, N.J., Jan. 19, 1954; d. Albert and Estelle (Platt) W. B.A. magna cum laude, Douglass Coll., New Brunswick, N.J., 1975; J.D., Seton Hall Law Ctr., Newark, 1979. Bar: N.J. 1979, U.S. Dist. Ct. N.J. 1979, U.S. Supreme Ct. 1986. Law clk. Lamb Hartung Gallipoli & Coughlin, Jersey City, 1977-79; asst. prosecutor Hudson County Prosecutor's Office, Jersey City, 1980-82; atty. N.J. Solicitor's Office Port Authority of N.Y. & N.J., N.Y.C., 1982—. Mem. ABA, N.J. State Bar Assn., Hudson County Bar Assn. Contracts commercial, Landlord-tenant, Bankruptcy. Home: 75 W 55th St Bayonne NJ 07002 Office: Port Authority of NY and NJ 1 World Trade Ctr New York NY 10048

WEISMAN, FRED, lawyer; b. Cleve., Oct. 19, 1926; s. Max David and Sally (Miller) W.; m. Lois Jane Kutler, June 14, 1953; children—Marcy A.; Mark A., Mitchell A. B.A., Case Western Res. U., 1948, LL.B., 1951. Bar: Ohio 1951, U.S. Dist. Ct. (no. and ea. dists.) Ohio 1953, N.Y. 1983. Diplomate Nat. Bd. Trial Advocacy (Civil). Assoc., A. H. Dudnik, Cleve., 1951-61; sr. atty. Fred Weisman, Cleve., 1961-73, Weisman, Goldberg & Weisman Co., L.P.A., Cleve., 1973—; acting judge Shaker Heights Mcpl. Ct.; lectr. Case Western Res. U. Law Sch. and Law Medicine Ctr., Cleveland State Law Sch., 1970—. Trustee Cleve. Law Library, 1975—; chmn. lawyers div. United Appeal, 1970; chmn. alumni fund Case Western Res. U. Law Sch., 1974-75, 86-87, pres. bd. trustees, 1975-76. Mem. ABA, Am. Trial Lawyers Assn. (mem. faculty), Ill. Trial Lawyers Assn., Am. Arbitration Assn. (mem. panel arbitrators), Am. Soc. Profl. Liability Attys., Ohio State Bar Assn. (mem. council dels. 12th dist. 1968-70), Ohio Acad. Trial Attys. (trustee), Cuyahoga County Bar Assn. (pres. 1971-72), Cleve. Acad. Trial Attys. (pres. 1973-74), Cleve. Bar Assn., Soc. Benchers Case Western Res. U. Law Alumni. Personal injury, Federal civil litigation, State civil litigation. Home: 25018 Duffield Rd Beachwood OH 44122 Office: Leader Bldg Suite 540 Cleveland OH 44114

WEISMAN, HARRY JED, lawyer; b. Cleve., Feb. 4, 1933; s. Max David and Sally (Miller) W.; m. Harriet Friedman, Aug. 19, 1956; children: Shelley, Hope, David, Scott. BA, Ohio Wesleyan U., 1955; MA, Ohio State U., 1956; JD, Cleveland Marshall Law Sch., 1966. Bar: Ohio 1966, U.S. Dist. Ct. (no. dist.) Ohio 1968. Ptnr. Weisman, Goldberg, Weisman & Kaufman Co. L.P.A., Cleve., 1966—. Pres. Lyndhurst Dad's Club, Ohio, 1980-84. Served to 1st lt. USAF, 1956-58. Recipient Disting. Service award Lyndhurst Dad's Club, 1984, Winning Presentation award No. Coast Dental Assn., 1985. Mem. Ohio Bar Assn., Cleve. Bar Assn., Cuyahoga County Bar Assn. Jewish. Avocations: exercise, gardening. Personal injury, Probate. Home: 33045 Canon Rd Solon OH 44139 Office: Weisman Goldberg Weisman & Kaufman Co LPA 540 Leader Bldg Cleveland OH 44114

WEISMAN, LARRY EDWARD, lawyer; b. Chgo., May 11, 1949; s. Eugene Boyd Weisman and Miriam Wilks; m. Wendy Nathanson, Feb. 4, 1979; children: Scott, Ashley. BA, U. Ill., 1971; JD, DePaul U., 1973. Bar: Ill. 1974, U.S. Dist. Ct. (no. dist.) Ill. 1974. Assoc. Sweeney & Riman, Ltd., Chgo., 1974-78; ptnr. Goldberg, Fohrman & Weisman, Ltd., Chgo., 1978—. Mem. Ill. Trial Lawyers Assn. (lectr. 1984). Club: Twin Orchard Country (Long Grove, Ill.). Avocation: golf. Personal injury. Home: 385 Oakland Dr Highland Park IL 60035 Office: Goldberg Fohrman & Weisman Ltd 221 N LaSalle Chicago IL 60601

WEISMAN, PAUL HOWARD, lawyer; b. Los Angeles, Oct. 14, 1957; s. Albert L. and Rose J. (Zimman) W.; m. Allison L. Minas, Oct. 19, 1985. BA cum laude, U. Calif., Davis, 1979; JD, Loyola U., Los Angeles, 1982. Bar: Calif. 1982. Tax atty. legis. and regulations div. office of chief counsel Dept. of Treasury IRS, Washington, 1982-83; tax atty. dist. counsel/office of chief counsel Dept. of Treasury IRS, Los Angeles, 1983—. Mem. Jewish Fedn., Los Angeles, 1984-86, Concern II, Los Angeles, 1986—; participant Vol. Income Tax Assistance, Los Angeles, 1981-83. Mem. ABA, Fed. Bar Assn. Republican. Avocations: sports, running, art, music, politics. Federal civil litigation, Personal income taxation, Bankruptcy.

WEISS, ALVIN, lawyer; b. N.Y.C., Aug. 13, 1929; m. Hannah Weiss, July 3, 1958; 1 dau., Betsy. B.A., Rutgers U., 1951, LL.B., 1953; LL.M., N.Y.U., 1959. Bar: N.J. 1955, U.S. Dist. Ct. N.J. 1955, U.S. Ct. Appeals (3d cir.) 1967. Assoc. Whittemore, Porter & Pollis and Pollis, Williams & Pappas, 1955-56; assoc. Riker, Emery & Danzig, 1957-62; ptnr. Riker, Danzig, Scherer, & Perretti, Morristown, N.J., 1963-86; judge Superior Ct. N.J., 1987—; chmn. N.J. Supreme Ct. Bd. Trial Atty. Cert., 1979-86. Trustee, Rutgers U., 1978—. Served with U.S. Army, 1953-55. Fellow Am. Coll. Trial Lawyers, Am. Bar Found.; mem. ABA, N.J. State Bar Assn., Essex County Bar Assn. (sec. 1982-84, pres. 1985-86), Fed. Bar Assn., Trial Lawyers N.J. Jewish.

WEISS, ARNOLD HANS, lawyer; b. Nurnberg, Germany, July 25, 1924; m. Artemis Lychos, May 5, 1956; children: Daniel L., Andrew A. B.A., U. Wis., 1951, J.D., 1952. Bar: Wis. 1953, D.C. 1958. Atty. advisor Office Gen. Counsel U.S. Treasury, 1953-60; atty. Inter Am. Devel. Bank, 1960-61, dep. gen. counsel, 1961-70, gen. counsel, 1970-77; ptnr. Arent, Fox, Kintner, Plotkin & Kahn, Washington, 1977—; adj. prof. Am. U., Washington. Trustee Pan Am. Devel. Found. Served with U.S. Army, 1942-47; served to lt. col. JAGC USAR, 1948-62. Decorated Bronze Star. Mem. ABA, Am. Soc. Internat. Law, Inter-Am. Bar Assn., Internat. Bar Assn., D.C. Bar Assn., Wis. Bar Assn. Clubs: International (D.C.), Army-Navy (D.C.); Arts (London). Private international, Public international, Contracts commercial. Office: Arent Fox Kintner Plotkin & Kahn 1050 Connecticut Ave NW Washington DC 20036

WEISS, CAROL ANN, lawyer; b. Cleve., July 24, 1950; s. Raymond John and Lydia (Zappone) W. BA in English Lit., St. Mary's Coll., Notre Dame, Ind., 1972; MA in Journalism, Ohio State U., 1974; JD, Cleve. State U., 1977. Bar: Ohio 1977, U.S. Dist. Ct. (no. dist.) Ohio 1978, U.S. Dist. Ct. (so. dist.) Ohio 1979. Hearing examiner reclassifications appeals project Ohio Employee Compensation Bd., Columbus, 1977-78; atty. Ohio State Treas.'s Office, Columbus, 1978-79; asst. atty. gen. State of Ohio, Columbus, 1980-81; asst. counsel Huntington Nat. Bank, Columbus, 1981-82; legal counsel Ohio Dept. Commerce, Columbus, 1983—. Treas. Columbus Women's Polit. Caucus, 1981, bd. dirs. 1982-1983. Mem. ABA, Ohio Bar Assn., Columbus Bar Assn., Women Lawyers of Franklin County. Office: Ohio Dept Commerce 2 Nationwide Plaza Columbus OH 43206

WEISS, DONALD PAUL, lawyer; b. Bklyn., May 19, 1934; s. Louis J. and Sylvia (Horowitz) W.; m. Marion Wiener, Apr. 14, 1957; children: James, Eric, Jeffrey, Jennifer. BS in Econs., U. Pa., 1955; JD, Tulane U., 1961. Bar: La. 1961. Ptnr. Wiener, Weiss, Madison & Howell, Shreveport, La., 1963-85; pres. Wiener, Weiss, Madison & Howell, Shreveport, 1986—. Student editor Tulane U. Law Rev., 1959-61. Mem. deans adv. council Tulane U. Law Sch., New Orleans, 1986—; chmn. Community Found. of Shreveport-Bossier, La., 1986—; bd. dirs. Centenary Coll., Shreveport, 1986—. Fellow Am. Coll. Probate Counsel; mem. ABA, La. Bar Assn., Shreveport Bar Assn., Shreveport C. of C. (pres. 1979), Order of Coif, Beta Gamma Sigma, Omicron Delta Kappa. Clubs: Shreveport County Club, Shreveport (La.). General corporate, Oil and gas leasing, Probate. Home: 641 Longleaf Rd Shreveport LA 71106 Office: Wiener Weiss Madison & Howell 505 Travis St 3d Floor 1st Fed Plaza Shreveport LA 71101

WEISS, DUDLEY ALBERT, lawyer, trustee; b. Boston, May 17, 1912; s. William Jacob and Esther (Herman) W.; m. Thelma G. Akabas, June 9, 1940 (dec.); 1 child, Eleanor Weiss Angoff. BA, Harvard U., 1934, JD, 1937. Bar: Mass. 1937, U.S. Dist. Ct. 1938, U.S. Ct. Appeals 1939, U.S. Supreme Ct. 1979. Sr. ptnr. Weiss, Angoff, Coltin, Koski & Wolf P.C., Boston, 1937—; atty., economist Office Price Adminstrn., World War II, economist, Korean War; exec. dir., gen. counsel Library Binding Inst., 1950-82, exec. dir. emeritus, 1982—. Trustee Frank M. Barnard Found., Am. London Symphony Orch. Found.; nat. panelist Am. Arbitration Assn.; bd. dirs. Maurice F. Tauber Found. Lab. Dudley A. Weiss Book Testing Lab. at Rochester Inst. Tech. named in his honor, 1982. Mem. ABA, Mass. Bar Assn., Mass. Bar Found. (life), Boston Bar Assn., Norfolk County Bar Assn., Middlesex County Bar Assn., Am. Judicature Soc., Phi Beta Kappa. Club: Harvard of Boston. General corporate, Estate planning, Probate. Office: 50 Congress St Suite 630 Boston MA 02109

WEISS, EDWARD ABRAHAM, lawyer; b. Chgo., Jan. 26, 1931; s. Morris Isaac and Gizella (Zeiger) W.; m. Phyllis Seibel, Oct. 1, 1983; children—Jennifer, Nathan, Chris, Darin, Corey. B.S. in Bus. Adminstrn., U. Calif.-Berkeley, 1953; J.D. (Frank M. Angellotti scholar, John Norton Pomeroy scholar), Hastings Coll. Law, U. Calif.-San Francisco, 1959. Bar: Calif. 1960, U.S. Supreme Ct. 1971; C.P.A., Calif. Acct., Aitel & Aitel, C.P.A.s, San Francisco, 1953, 55-57; assoc. Dreher & Frankel, Oakland, Calif., 1959-61; sole practice, Oakland, 1961-71, Walnut Creek, Calif., 1973—; sr. ptnr. Weiss & Paul, Oakland, 1967-69, Weiss & Wald, Oakland, 1969-71; exec. v.p., gen. counsel Am. Plan Investment Corp., San Francisco, 1971-72; lectr., instr. J.F. Kennedy Law Sch., 1973-75. Mem. aviation adv. com. Bd. Suprs.; bd. dirs. Jewish Welfare Fedn. Alameda and Contra Costa Counties, 1963-69; founder, bd. dirs. Beth Olam Meml. Chapel, 1971-72; bd. dirs. Jewish Community Relations Council Alameda and Contra Costa Counties, 1963-65, 67-68; pres. Congregation B'nai Sholom, 1969-71. Mem. Comml. Law League, ABA, State Bar Calif., Alameda County Bar Assn., Contra Costa County Bar Assn., Lawyer-Pilots Bar Assn., Thurston Honor Soc., Order of Coif. State civil litigation, Real property, Consumer commercial. Home: 115 Bando Ct Walnut Creek CA 94595

WEISS, HARLAN LEE, lawyer; b. Washington, Dec. 6, 1941; s. Richard Stanley and Ethel (Shulman) W.; m. Elaine Sharon Schooler, Feb. 14, 1971; children—Rachel Shayna, Brian Adam. B.A., U. Md.-College Park, 1963; J.D. with honors, U. Md.-Balt., 1966. Bar: Md. 1967, D.C. 1967, U.S. Dist. Ct. Md., 1967, U.S. Dist. Ct. D.C., 1967, U.S. Ct. Appeals (D.C. cir.) 1968, U.S. Ct. Appeals (4th cir.) 1977, U.S. Supreme Ct. 1970. Law clk. Ct. Appeals of Md., 1966-67; assoc. Surrey & Morse and predecessors, Washington, 1967-72; assoc. Sachs, Greenebaum & Tayler, Washington, 1972-76, ptnr., 1976—; mem. Jud. Conf. D.C., 1978-79; arbitrator Am. Arbitration Assn. Mem. D.C. Bar, ABA, Md. State Bar Assn., Montgomery County Bar Assn. State civil litigation, Insurance, Federal civil litigation. Home: 12017 Cheyenne Rd Gaithersburg MD 20878 Office: 1140 Connecticut Ave NW Washington DC 20036

WEISS, IRWIN E., lawyer; b. Washington, Aug. 12, 1953; s. Peter J. and Lillian Louise (Deitch) W.; m. Cheryl Ruth Kaplowitz, June 5, 1983. BA, U. Md., 1975, JD, 1978. Bar: Md. 1978, U.S. Dist. Ct. Md. 1979, U.S. Ct. Appeals (4th cir.) 1979. Assoc. Ellin & Baker, Balt., 1978-80, Seidenman & Weiss PA, Balt., 1981-85, Rohd & Woranch PA, Balt., 1985; sole practice Towson, Md., 1985—. Co-author: Maryland Tort Damages, 1985. Mem. Md.State Bar Assn., Md. Trial Lawyers Assn., Am. Trial Lawyers Assn. Democrat. Jewish. Lodge: B'nai B'rith. Federal civil litigation, Personal injury, Workers' compensation. Home: 3213 Bancroft Rd Baltimore MD 21215 Office: 920 Providence Rd Suite 307 Towson MD 21215

WEISS, JEROME PAUL, lawyer; b. Binghamton, N.Y., May 16, 1934; s. Milton I. and Irene (Freeman) W.; m. Marion Levitt, June 30, 1963; children—Jonathan Peter, Andrew Stephen. A.B. magna cum laude, Princeton U., 1956; J.D., Harvard U., 1961. Bar: N.Y. 1962, D.C. 1975. Assoc., Hiscock, Cowie, Bruce, Lee & Mawhinney, Syracuse, N.Y., 1961-64; asst. gen. counsel Agway, Inc., Syracuse, 1964-72; dep. gov. and gen. counsel Farm Credit Adminstrn., Washington, 1972-73; assoc. Hamel, Park, McCabe & Saunders, Washington, 1974-76, ptnr., 1976-78, sr. ptnr., 1978—, mng. ptnr., 1983-86; mng. ptnr. Sonnenschein, Carlin, Nath & Rosenthal, Washington, 1986—; adj. prof. Syracue U. Sch. Law, 1970-74, Antioch Sch. Law, 1974-76. Trustee Landon Sch., Bethesda, Md. Served to lt. USNR, 1956-58. Mem. ABA, N.Y. State Bar Assn., D.C. Bar Assn. Clubs: Riverbend Country (Great Falls, Va.); Naples (Fla.) Bath and Tennis. Contbr. articles to legal jours. General corporate, Corporate taxation, Securities. Home: 488 Riverbend Rd Great Falls VA 22066 Office: 1330 Connecticut Ave Suite 1000 Washington DC 20036

WEISS, PHILIP DAVID, lawyer; b. Norristown, Pa., Oct. 8, 1934; s. Emmanuel and Esther (Jaffe) W.; m. Linda Horowitz, June 28, 1959; children—Cynthia Laura, Jeffrey Sherman. A.B., Lafayette Coll., 1955; LL.B., Yale U., 1960. Bar: Pa. 1961, U.S. Dist. Ct. (ea. dist.) Pa. 1961, U.S. Ct. Appeals (3d cir.) 1961, U.S. Supreme Ct. 1972. Assoc. Duffy, McTighe & McElhone, Norristown, Pa., 1960-66; ptnr. McTighe, Weiss, Stewart, Bacine & O'Rourke and predecessors, Norristown, 1966—; dir. Eagle Service Corp., Pilot Fin. Corp., Greater Norristown Corp. Pres. Montgomery County Emergency Service Bd., 1980-81; treas. Eagleville Hosp. Bd., 1975-82; mem. Norristown Jewish Community Bd., solicitor, 1965—. Served to capt. inf. U.S. Army, 1955-57, Res. Mem. ABA (chmn. profl. liability com. of gen. practice sect. 1978-79), Pa. Bar Assn., Montgomery County Bar Assn. (chmn. trials com. 1987), Am. Judicature Soc., Montgomery County Estate Planning Council (pres. 1972-73). Republican. Jewish. Club: American Business (Norristown). Contbr. articles to legal jours. State civil litigation, Federal civil litigation, Real property. Home: 10 Scarlet Oak Dr Lafayette Hill PA 19444 Office: 11 E Airy St PO Box 510 Norristown PA 19404

WEISS, SHERMAN DAVID, lawyer; b. Detroit, Dec. 26, 1929; s. Abraham and Eva (Lieberman) W.; m. Lorraine Gloria Moss, Apr. 5, 1952; children—Roger Kevin, Diane Leslie, Linda Beth. Student U. Ill., 1947-48; B.S.C., Roosevelt U., 1951; J.D., Chgo.-Kent Coll. Law, 1957. Bar: Ill. 1958, U.S. Dist. Ct. (no. dist.) Ill. 1958, U.S. Ct. Appeals (7th cir.) 1965. Mem. Deutsch & Kurlan, Chgo., 1959-60, Brody and Gore, Chgo., 1960-62, Arnstein, Gluck, Weitzenfeld and Minow, Chgo., 1963-65; asst. sec., asst. v.p. Walter E. Heller Internat. Corp., Chgo., 1965-75, Imperial Leather & Sportswear, Ltd., Los Angeles, 1975-76; exec. v.p. Roth Carpet Mills, Santa Monica, Calif., 1977-78; sole practice, Los Angeles, 1979—; sr. research rep. Greenwich Assocs., 1985—; cons. fin. and bus. mgmt.; adj. prof. law John Marshall Sch. Law, Chgo., 1976-77. Bd. dirs. Met. YMCA Chgo., 1961-64; gen. counsel Leukemia League Ill., 1960-70. Served with U.S. Army, 1952-54. Mem. Ill. Bar Assn., ABA. Jewish. Case editor Chgo.-Kent Law Rev., 1956-57. Private international, General corporate, Contracts commercial. Home: 5840 Etiwanda Ave Tarzana CA 91356

WEISS, STEPHEN JOEL, lawyer; b. N.Y.C., Sept. 12, 1938; s. Morris and Frances (Dinkin) W.; m. Madeline Adler, Aug. 12, 1962; children: Lowell Andrew, Valerie Elizabeth, Bradley Lawrence. B.S., Queens Coll., 1959; LL.B., Cornell U., 1962; LL.M., Georgetown U., 1966. Bar: N.Y. 1963, D.C. 1966, U.S. Supreme Ct. 1975. Atty. SEC, Washington, 1962-65; assoc. firm Arent, Fox, Kintner, Plotkin & Kahn, Washington, 1965-70; partner Arent, Fox, Kintner, Plotkin & Kahn, 1971—; lectr. securities and corporate law Am. Law Inst., Am., Fed. bar assns., Practicing Law Inst., Bur. Nat. Affairs, Exec. Enterprises, Orgn. Mgmt., Inc.; confs. Am. Land Devel. Assn. Mem. adv. bd.: Securities Regulation and Law Report, Bur. Nat. Affairs, 1980—; contbr. articles on securities and corp. law to legal jours. Mem. Am. Bar Assn. (fed. regulation securities com. 1970—, chmn. Rule 10b-5 subcom. 1976-78, chmn. civil liabilities subcom. 1978-81, chmn. ad hoc com. fgn. payments legislation 1976-77, devels. in bus. financing com. 1982—), Fed. Bar Assn. (chmn. securities law com. 1968-70, mem. exec. com. of securities law com. 1971—, chmn. council financing and taxation 1971-72, chmn. publs. bd. 1977-78, nat. council 1972-80, Leadership commendation 1973, Distinguished Service award 1970), D.C. Bar Assn., Am. Law Inst., Cornell Law Assn. (exec. com. 1981-84). Club: Cornell (Washington) (pres. 1971-79). General corporate, Securities. Office: Arent Fox Kintner Plotkin & Kahn 1050 Connecticut Ave NW Washington DC 20036

WEISSBARD, SAMUEL HELD, lawyer; b. N.Y.C., Mar. 3, 1947; m. Wendy L. Fields; children from a previous marriage: Andrew Joshua, David S. BA, Case Western Res. U., 1967; JD with highest honors, George Washington U., 1970. Bar: D.C. 1970, U.S. Supreme Ct. 1974. Assoc. Fried, Frank, Harris, Shriver & Kampelman, 1970-73, Arent, Fox, Kintner, Plotkin & Kahn, 1973-78; prin. Weissbard & Fields, P.C., 1978-83; shareholder, v.p. Wilkes, Artis, Hedrick & Lane, Washington, 1983-86; ptnr. Foley & Lardner, Washington, 1986—. Editor-in-chief George Washington U. Law Rev., 1969-70. Bd. dirs. Luther Rice Soc. George Washington U., 1985—. Recipient John Bell Larner medal, 1970. Mem. ABA, D.C. Bar Assn., Order of Coif. Real property. Office: Foley & Lardner 1775 Pennsylvania Ave NW Washington DC 20006

WEISSENBERGER, HARRY GEORGE, lawyer; b. Berlin, Fed. Republic of Germany, Aug. 20, 1928; s. George Wilhelm and Gabriele Anna (Hochberg) W.; m. Margaret Looper, Dec. 23, 1950; children: Carol Ann, Harry George Jr., Bruce Lee. Student, Swiss Inst. Tech., 1946-47; BEE, Ga. Tech. Inst., 1950; JD, Emory U., 1952; LLM, George Washington U., 1956. Bar: Ga. 1952, U.S. Dist. Ct. (no. dist.) Ga. 1952, U.S. Ct. Appeals (4th cir.) 1952, U.S. Supreme Ct. 1956, U.S. Ct. Customs and Patent Appeals 1956, Mo. 1957, U.S. Dist. Ct. (ea. dist.) Mo. 1957, U.S. Ct. Appeals (8th cir.) 1957, Mich. 1961, U.S. Dist. Ct. (we. dist.) Mich. 1961, U.S. Ct. Appeals (7th cir.) 1961, Calif. 1964, U.S. Dist. Ct. (no. and cen. dists.) Calif. 1964, U.S. Ct. Appeals (9th cir.) 1964, U.S. Dist. Ct. (ea. dist.) Calif. 1974, U.S. Dist. Ct. (we. dist.) Tex. 1976, U.S. Dist. ct. (so. dist.) Calif. 1982, U.S. Ct. Appeals (Fed. cir.) 1982. Examiner U.S. Patent Office, Washington, 1955-56; assoc. Bruninga & Sutherland, St. Louis, 1956-58, Sutherland, Polster & Taylor, St. Louis, 1958-89; assoc. Price & Heneveld, Grand Rapids, Mich., 1959-61, ptnr., 1961-63; ptnr. Mellin, Hanscom & Hursh, San Francisco, 1963-67, Mellin, Hursh, Moore & Weissenberger, 1967-74, Phillips, Moore, Weissenberger, Lempio & Strabala, San Francisco, 1974-76; ptnr. Phillips, Moore, Weissenberger, Lempio & Majestic, San Francisco, 1976-78, Newport Beach, Calif., 1978-81; ptnr. Weissenberger & Peterson, Newport Beach, 1982-86, Laguna Hills, Calif., 1986—. Bd. dirs. Movement Shorthand Soc.; mem. Indsl. League Orange County. Served tolst lt. USAF, 1953-55. Mem. ABA, Calif. Bar Assn., Orange County Bar Assn., Internat. Patent and Trademark Assn., Am. Patent Law Assn., Orange County Patent Law Assn. (sec. 1983, v.p. 1984, pres. 1985), Licensing Execs. Soc. (chmn. San Francisco Bay 1972-76, program chmn. 1980), IEEE. Republican. Presbyterian. Club: Newport-Balboa (Newport Beach, Calif.). Lodge: Rotary. Patent, Trademark and copyright. Office: Weissenberger & Peterson 24012 Calle de la Plata #470 Laguna Hills CA 92653-3621

WEISSENBORN, SHERIDAN KENDALL, lawyer; b. Trenton, N.J., Oct. 3, 1948; d. Howard and Shirleye Rose (Stanley) W.; m. Lee Edward, Mar.

19, 1977; stepchilden: Jim, Carol, Stephen. BA, U. Miami, 1970, JD, 1973. Bar: Fla. 1973, U.S. Dist. Ct. (so. dist.) Fla. 1974, U.S. Supreme Ct. 1980, U.S. Ct. Appeals (11th cir.) 1982, U.S. Dist. Ct. (mid. dist.) Fla. 1984. Ptnr. Papy, Poole, Weissenborn & Papy, Coral Gables, Fla., 1974—. Mem. ABA, Fla. Bar Assn., Fed. Bar Assn., Am. Acad. Trial Lawyers. Federal civil litigation, State civil litigation, Antitrust. Home: 14620 SW 82d Ave Miami FL 33158 Office: Papy Poole Weissenborn & Papy 201 Alhambra Circle Suite 502 Coral Gables FL 33134

WEISSMAN, BARRY LEIGH, lawyer; b. Los Angeles, May 30, 1948; s. Sidney and Eleanor (Siegel) W.; m. Beverly Jean Blumenfeld, Sept. 12, 1982. B.A., U. Calif.-Davis, 1970; J.D., U. Santa Clara, 1973. Bar: Calif. Supreme Ct. 1973, U.S. Dist. Ct. (cen. dist.) Calif. 1976, U.S. Supreme Ct. 1977, U.S. Ct. Appeals (D.C. cir.) 1978. Sole practice law, Beverly Hills, Calif., 1974-84; ptnr. Valentini, Fini, Ferraro, Gallavotti & Weissman, Brentwood, Calif., from 1984; now atty. Kroll, Tract, Harnett, Pomerantz & Cameron, Los Angeles; judge pro tem Los Angeles Mcpl. Ct., 1975—; arbitrator Am. Arbitration Assn.; examiner State Bar Calif., 1976-80. Mem. ABA (mem. spl. com. on prepaid legal services, co-chmn. editorial bd. gen. practice sect.'s publs.), Beverly Hills Bar Assn., Century City Bar Assn. (bd. govs., chmn., editor Century City Bar Jour.), Beverly Hills C. of C. (co-chmn. legal justice com.), Colorado River Assn., Western Los Angeles Regional C. of C. (dir., chmn. com. on energy prodn. and conservation). General corporate, Private international, General practice. Office: Kroll Pomerantz & Cameron 3435 Wilshire Blvd Los Angeles CA 90010

WEISSMAN, I. DONALD, lawyer; b. Maywood, Calif., Feb. 6, 1950; s. Herbert and Esther D. (Lunine) W.; m. Bonnie Jill Burns, May 3, 1980; children—Kimberleh Ariel, Russell Meir, Douglas Solomon. B.A., Calif. State U.-Northridge, 1972; J.D., Loyola U., 1975. Bar: Calif. 1975, U.S. Dist. Ct. (central dist.) Calif. 1976. With firm Morgan, Wenzel & McNicholas, Los Angeles, 1975-79, Simke, Chodos, Silberfeld & Soll Inc., Los Angeles, 1979-83, Pettler & Kantor, Los Angeles, 1983, Staitman & Snyder, Encino, Calif., 1984—. Mem. ABA, San Fernando Bar Assn., Los Angeles County Bar Assn., Los Angeles Trial Lawyers Assn., Assn. Trial Lawyers Assn. Jewish. Lodge: B'nai Brith. Personal injury, Insurance, State civil litigation. Office: Staitman & Snyder 15760 Ventura Blvd Suite 601 Encino CA 91436

WEISSMAN, JEFFREY MARK, lawyer; b. N.Y.C., Dec. 26, 1946; s. Samuel and Gertrude (Goldenberg) W.; m. Linda Claire Fleder, June 27, 1971; children—Karen, Erica. B.S., MIT, 1969, M.A., Harvard U., 1970; J.D., N.Y. U., 1974. Bar: N.Y. 1975, Fla. 1977, U.S. Dist. Ct. (so. and ea. dists.) N.Y. 1975, U.S. Dist. Ct. (so. dist.) Fla., 1977, U.S. Dist. Ct. (mid. dist.) Fla. 1979, U.S. Ct. Appeals (2d cir.) 1975, U.S. Ct. Appeals (5th cir.) 1977, U.S. Ct. Appeals (11th cir.) 1981, U.S. Supreme Ct. 1982, U.S. Dist. Ct. (no. dist.) Fla. 1985, U.S. Tax Ct. 1985. Tchr., coach, Brookline, Mass., 1970-71; assoc. Rogers & Wells, N.Y.C., 1974-77; assoc., then ptnr. Brown, Malman & Salmon, Miami, Fla., 1977-80; ptnr. Sparber, Shevin, Shapo & Heilbronner, P.A., Miami, 1980—, also bd. dirs. Counselor MIT Upward Bound, 1968-69; mem. staff appellate div. N.Y. State, 1st and 2d depts. coms. for ct. adminstrn., 1972-73; researcher Am. Bar Found., 1973-74. Recipient various awards W.T. Clarke High Sch., Westbury, N.Y., 1965, MIT, 1968, 69; N.Y. State Regents scholar, 1965, Gen. Motors scholar, 1966-69, Harvard U. scholar, 1969-70, Root-Tilden scholar, 1971-74. Federal civil litigation, State civil litigation. Home: 4000 N 41st Ct Hollywood FL 33021 Office: Sparber Shevin Shapo & Heilbronner P A 1 SE 3d Ave Miami FL 33131

WEISSMAN, ROBERT ALLEN, lawyer, real estate broker; b. Los Angeles, May 26, 1950; s. Joseph Jonas and Shirley Rhoda (Solitare) W.; m. Susan Renee Bashner, Apr. 5, 1975; children—Evan Gregory, Russell Joseph, Dustin Raymond. B.A., UCLA, 1972; J.D., Southwestern U., 1975. Bar: Calif. 1975, U.S. Dist. Ct. Calif. 1976, D.C. 1980, U.S. Supreme Ct. 1982, U.S. Ct. Appeals (9th cir.) 1982. Ptnr., Weissman & Weissman, Los Angeles, 1975-81, prin., 1981—; speaker to profl. and trade groups. Pres.'s adv. council City of Hope, 1981-86. Mem. ABA, State Bar Calif., Los Angeles County Bar Assn., Calif. Land Title Assn., Bus. Trial Lawyers Assn., Fin. Lawyers Conf., Comml. Law League Am., Assn. Real Estate Attys. Democrat. Jewish. Club: Acad. Magical Arts, Inc. Lodges: B'nai B'rith, Masons. Banking, Contracts commercial, State civil litigation. Office: 16130 Ventura Blvd Penthouse Suite 600 Encino CA 91436-2596

WEISSMAN, WILLIAM R., lawyer; b. N.Y.C., Aug. 16, 1940; s. Emanuel and Gertrude (Halpern) W.; m. Barbra Phylis Gershman, Jan. 14, 1944; 1 child, Adam; stepchildren: Eric, Jace, Julie Greenman. BA, Columbia U., 1962, JD cum laude, 1965. Bar: N.Y. 1965, D.C. 1969, U.S. Dist. Ct. (no. dist.) Tex. 1965, U.S. Dist. Ct. (so. and ea. dists.) N.Y. 1977, U.S. Ct. Appeals (5th cir.) 1966, U.S. Ct. Appeals (D.C. cir.) 1969, U.S. Ct. Appeals (9th cir.) 1973, U.S. Ct. Appeals (2d and 3d cirs.) 1974, U.S. Ct. Appeals (10th cir.) 1979, U.S. Ct. Appeals (11th cir.) 1981, U.S. Supreme Ct. 1968. News dir., program dir. WKCR-FM, N.Y.C., 1960-62; law clk. U.S. dist. judge, Dallas, 1965-66; trial atty. antitrust div. Dept. Justice, Washington, 1966-69; spl. asst. U.S. atty., Washington, 1967; assoc. Wald, Harkrader & Ross, Washington, 1969-72, ptnr., 1973-85; ptnr. Piper & Marbury, Washington, 1986—; instr. Georgetown U. Law Sch, D.C. Continuing Legal Edn. Program, 1980—, environ. regulation course Exec. Enterprises, Inc., 1985—. Mem. Arlington (Va.) County Tenant-Landlord Commn., 1973-77, chmn., 1975-77; parliamentarian Arlington County Dem. Com., 1971-75; sec. Columbia U. Law Sch. Alumni Assn. of Washington, 1982-84, pres., 1984-86, bd. dirs. 1984—. Recipient James Gordon Bennett prize Columbia U., 1962, E.B. Convers prize, 1965. Mem. ABA, Fed. Bar Assn., Fed. Communications Bar Assn., D.C. Bar Assn. Jewish. Administrative and regulatory, Antitrust, Environment. Home: 3802 Lakeview Terr Falls Church VA 22041 Office: 1200 19th St NW Washington DC 20036

WEISTART, JOHN C., law educator; b. 1943. BA, Ill. Wesleyan U., 1965; JD, Duke U., 1968. Law clk. to presiding justice Ill. Supreme Ct., Springfield, 1968-69; asst. prof. Duke U., Durham, N.C., 1969-72, assoc. prof., 1972-73, prof., 1973—. Office: Duke U Sch Law Durham NC 27706 *

WEISZ, FRANK BARRY, lawyer; b. Phila., Jan. 3, 1948; s. Richard Edward and Phyllis Weisz; m. Renee Susan Geboff, July 4, 1971 (div. Jan. 1983); children: Randy, Jason. BS in Math., Villanova U., 1969; JD, Temple U., 1973, LLM in Taxation, 1976. Advanced underwriting cons. Providence Mut. Ins., Phila., 1973-75, dir. advanced underwriting, 1975-80, acting v.p. advanced underwriting, 1980—; ptnr. Weisz and Assocs., Phila., 1976—. Author: Super Trust, 1978, (Best Seller), Estate Planners Guild, 1980, Super Trust II, 1982, Super Loan, 1982, Ultimate Tax Shelter (Super Trust III), 1985. Mem. ABA, Pa. Bar Assn., Phila. Bar Assn., Am. Assn. Life Underwriters, Nat. Assn. Life Underwriters. Estate taxation, Estate planning, Life Insurance/estate and business planning. Home and Office: 305 Tory Turn Radnor PA 19087

WEITZEL, WILLIAM CONRAD, JR., lawyer, oil company executive; b. Washington, Feb. 6, 1935; s. William Conrad and Pauline Lillian (Keeton) W.; m. Loretta LeVeck, Mar. 10, 1978; children: William Conrad III, Richard S., Sarah L. A.B., Harvard U., 1956, LL.B., 1959; postgrad., M.I.T., 1974. Bar: D.C. 1961. Law clk., chief judge U.S. Cts. Md., Balt., 1959-60; asst. U.S. atty., Washington, 1961-66; atty. Texaco, Inc., White Plains, N.Y., 1966-73; assoc. gen. counsel Texaco, Inc., 1973-76, gen. counsel, 1977-82, v.p., gen. counsel, 1982-84, sr. v.p., gen. counsel, 1984—; Pres. Texaco Philanthropic Found., Inc. Mem. adv. bd. Southwestern Legal Found., Parker Sch. Fgn. and Comparative Law at Columbia U. Served with USN, 1960-61. Mem. ABA, Conn. Bar Assn., Assn. Gen. Counsel, Westchester-Fairfield Corp. Counsel Assn. (pres. 1981, chmn., chief legal officers com.), Am. Petroleum Inst. (gen. com. on law, chmn. 1983-84). Republican. Episcopalian. Club: Country (Darien, Conn.). General corporate. Home: 1 Gracie Ln Darien CT 06820 Office: 2000 Westchester Ave White Plains NY 10650

WEITZMAN, DONALD MARTIN, lawyer; b. Newark, Apr. 16, 1939; s. Samuel and Esther (Lefkowitz) W.; m. Harriet Shames, Aug. 27, 1961; children: Jeffrey, Deborah, Lisa. BA, Dartmouth Coll., 1960; JD, Columbia U., 1963. Bar: N.J. 1963, U.S. Supreme Ct. 1969, U.S. Ct. Appeals (3d cir.) 1971. Assoc. Weitzman, Brady & Weitzman, Newark, 1964-68; ptnr. Glucksman & Weitzman, Morristown, N.J., 1968—; instr. Inst. for Continuing Legal Edn., Newark; instr. bus. law Fairleigh Dickinson U., Madison, N.J., 1967-70. Chmn. Morris Twp. Dems., 1971-72; pres. Morristown Jewish Community Ctr., 1976-78; v.p. N.J. region United Synagoue of Am., Hillside, 1981—. Named Man of Yr. State of Israel Bond Com., 1977. Mem. N.J. Bar Assn., Morris County Bar Assn. (pres. family law com. 1986—). Democrat. Jewish. Lodge: Lions (v.p. Morristown chpt. 1982-83). Avocations: skiing, tennis. Family and matrimonial, General practice, Criminal. Home: 53 Fieldstone Dr Morristown NJ 07960 Office: Glucksman & Weitzman 60 Maple Ave Morristown NJ 07960

WELBAUM, R. EARL, lawyer; b. Miami, Fla., Feb. 4, 1932; s. Rome Lewis and Helen Louise (Richter) W.; m. Joan M. Tubridy, May 16, 1959; children—Karl Patrick, Michael Frederick, Carrie Kathleen. B.B.A., U. Miami, LL.B., 1959. Bar: Fla. 1959, U.S. Dist. Ct. (so. dist.) Fla. 1959, U.S. Ct. Appeals (5th cir.) 1963, U.S. Ct. Appeals (11th cir.) 1983. Law clk. to chief judge 3d Dist. Ct. Appeals Fla., 1959-61; assoc., then ptnr. Welbaum, Zook, Jones & Williams, and predecessor firms, Miami, 1961—. Served to capt. USAFR, 1954-62. Mem. ABA (mem. fidelity and surety com. ins. sect.), Internat. Assn. Ins. Counsel (mem. fidelity and surety com.), Fla. Bar Assn., Dade County Bar Assn. Federal civil litigation, State civil litigation, Insurance. Office: 2701 S Bayshore Dr Miami FL 33133

WELBEL, MICHAEL GARY, lawyer; b. Chgo., Sept. 17, 1954; s. Aaron and Sarah Teltse (Rosenblit) W.; m. Janice Naomi Shapiro, Aug. 19, 1979; children: Jennifer, Rachel. BA, No. Ill. U., 1976; JD, John Marshall Law Sch., 1979. Bar: Ill. 1979, U.S. Dist. Ct. (no. dist.) Ill. 1979. Assoc. Melvin S. Dick & Assocs., Lincolnwood, Ill., 1980-81; claim atty. Shand-Morahan, Evanston, Ill., 1981-83, sr. claim atty., 1983-84, atty. in charge, 1984-85, claim mgr., 1985—. Dep. County Clk., Dekalb, Ill., 1972. Mem. ABA (LPN profl. liability editor Barrister), Ill. State Bar Assn., Phi Delta Phi. Democrat. Jewish. Avocations: sailing, photography, guitar. Insurance. Office: Shand Morahan Co Shand Morahan Plaza Evanston IL 60201

WELCH, CAROL MAE, lawyer; b. Rockford, Ill., Oct. 23, 1947; d. Leonard John and LaVerna Helen (Ang) Nyberg; m. Donald Peter Welch, Nov. 23, 1968 (dec. Sept. 1976). B.A. in Spanish, Wheaton Coll., 1968; J.D., U. Denver, 1976. Bar: Colo. 1977, U.S. Dist. Ct. Colo. 1977, U.S. Ct. Appeals (10th cir.) 1977, U.S. Supreme Ct. 1981. Tchr., State Hosp., Dixon, Ill., 1969, Polo Community Schs., Ill., 1969-70; registrar Sch. Nursing Hosp. of U. Pa., Phila., 1970; assoc. Hall & Evans, Denver, 1977-81, ptnr., 1981—; mem. Colo. Supreme Ct. Jury Inst., Denver, 1982—; vice chmn. com. on conduct U.S. Dist. Ct., Denver, 1982-83, chmn., 1983-84; lectr. in field; speaker Women and Bus. Conf., Denver, 1982. Named to Order St. Ives, U. Denver Coll. Law, 1977. Mem. Colo. Def. Lawyers Assn. (treas. 1982-83, v.p. 1983-84, pres. 1984-85), Denver Bar Assn., Colo. Bar Assn., ABA. Republican. Federal civil litigation, State civil litigation, Insurance. Office: Hall & Evans 1200 17th St Suite 1700 Denver CO 80202

WELCH, DAVID WILLIAM, lawyer; b. St. Louis, Feb. 26, 1941; s. Claude LeRoy Welch and Mary Eleanor (Peggs) Penney; m. Candace Lee Capages, June 5, 1971; children: Joseph Peggs, Heather Elizabeth, Katherine Laura. BSBA, Washington U., St. Louis, 1963; JD, U. Tulsa, 1971. Bar: Okla. 1972, Mo. 1973, U.S. Dist. Ct. (ea. dist.) Mo. 1974, U.S. Ct. Appeals(8th cir.) 1977. Contract adminstr. McDonnell Aircraft Corp., St. Louis, 1965-66; bus. analyst Dun & Bradstreet Inc., Los Angeles, 1967-68; atty. U.S. Dept. Labor, Washington, 1972-73; ptnr. Moller Talent, Kuelthau & Welch, St. Louis, 1973—. Author: (handbook) Missouri Employment Law, 1986; contbr. book chpt. Missouri Bar Employer-Employee Law, 1985. Mem. ABA, Fed. Bar Assn., Mo. Bar Assn., Okla. Bar Assn., St. Louis Bar Assn., Regional Commerce and Growth Assn., Mo. C. of C. Democrat. Mem. Christian Ch. Lodge: Kiwanis (bd. dirs. local chpt. 1979—, sec. 1982-83, v.p. 1983-84, named Man of Yr. 1985). Avocations: travel, landscaping, music. Labor. Home: 536 N Mosley Rd Saint Louis MO 63141 Office: Moller Talent Kuelthau & Welch 720 Olive Suite 2200 Saint Louis MO 63191

WELCH, DENISE MAJETTE, lawyer; b. Bklyn., May 18, 1955; d. Voyd Lee and Olivia Carolyn (Foster) Majette; m. David Anthony Welch. BA in History, Yale U., 1976; JD, Duke U., 1979. Bar: N.C. 1981, U.S. Dist. Ct. (mid. and we. dists.) N.C. 1981, Ga. 1983, U.S. Dist. Ct. (no. dist.) Ga. 1983. Staff atty. Legal Aid Soc. Northwestern N.C., Winston-Salem, 1979-83; law clk. to presiding judge DeKalb County Superior Ct., Decatur, Ga., 1983-84; law asst. Ga. Ct. Appeals, Atlanta, 1984—; adj. prof. Wake Forest Law Sch., Winston-Salem, 1982-83. Mem. ABA, Ga. Assn. Black Women Attys. (chmn. jud. legal positions com. 1985). Episcopalian. Avocation: running. Jurisprudence, Drafting appellate court opinions. Office: c/o Hon. Robert Benham Ga Ct Appeals 40 Capitol Sq Room 602 Atlanta GA 30334

WELCH, ERNEST WENDELL, lawyer; b. Cottondale, Fla., Oct. 5, 1917; s. Ernest Columbus and Edna Beatrice (Wallace) W.; m. Helen Phillips, Feb. 28, 1948; children: Kevin M., Lisa W. BSBA, U. Fla., 1939, JD, 1941. Bar: Fla. 1941, U.S. Dist. Ct. (no. dist.) Fla. 1941, U.S. Ct. Appeals (5th cir.) 1961. Asst. atty. gen. Fla., 1946-48; sole practice, Panama City, Fla., 1948-49; ptnr. Isler & Welch et al, 1949-73, Welch, Bennett, Logue, Burke & Blue, P.A., 1975-78, Welch & Munroe, P.A., Tallahassee, 1978-86, Welch, Munroe & Black, P.A., Tallahassee, 1986—; mem. Fla. Bd. Bar Examiners, 1960-67, chmn., 1965-66; mem. bd. govs. Fla. Bar, 1953-56. Served with USAAF, 1942-46. Fellow Am. Coll. Trial Lawyers, Am. Coll. Probate Counsel; mem. ABA. Club: Govs., Tallahassee Exchange. Lodge: Elks. Federal civil litigation, State civil litigation, General practice.

WELCH, GERALD THOMAS, lawyer, electrical engineer; b. Detroit, Aug. 2, 1949; s. Gerald John and Mary Eileen (Metty) W.; m. Lucia Ann Urso, Sept. 10, 1972; children: Gerald J., Anthony M., David T., Lucia M. BEE, U. Notre Dame, 1971; MBA, U. Utah, 1974; JD, U. Toledo, 1979. Bar: Ohio 1980, Tex. 1981, U.S. Patent Office 1981, U.S. Ct. Appeals (Fed. cir.) 1982. Assoc. John C. Purdue Co., L.P.A., Toledo, 1978-80; atty. Exxon Prodn. Research, Houston, 1980-81; legal counsel Owens-Ill., Toledo, 1981-85; v.p., gen. counsel, sec. M&SD Corp., Lyndhurst, N.J., 1985—; v.p. Welmet Inc., Flemington, N.J., 1980—. Served to capt. USAF, 1972-77. Mem. ABA, Ohio Bar Assn., Tex. Bar Assn., Am. Intellectual Property Law Assn., Am. Corp. Counsel Assn. Roman Catholic. Avocations: golf, tennis. Contracts commercial, General corporate, Patent. Home: 22 Forest Way Morris Plains NJ 07950 Office: M&SD Corp 1200 Wall St W Lyndhurst NJ 07071

WELCH, JAMES STEPHEN, lawyer; b. Lincoln, Nebr., Aug. 24, 1955; s. James Wesley and Hazel Glendyne (Bradley) W.; m. Susan Carol Thraikill, June 2, 1979; children: Jonathon, Jeremy. BA in English, Erskine Coll., 1979; JD, Oral Roberts U., 1982. Bar: Okla. 1982, U.S. Dist. Ct. (no. dist.) Okla. 1982. Assoc. Holliman, Langholz et al, Tulsa, 1982-83; ptnr. Albright & Welch, P.C. and predecessor firm Schuman and Welch, P.C., Tulsa, 1983—. Asst. editor law jour. Jour. of Christian Jurisprudence, 1982. Sustaining mem. Rep. Nat. Com., Washington, D.C., 1983—. Mem. ABA, Okla. Bar Assn., Tulsa County Bar Assn. Republican. Methodist. Avocations: reading, history. Personal injury, General corporate, Securities. Home: 6731 E 89th Tulsa OK 74133 Office: Albright and Welch PC 5110 S Yale Suite 205 Tulsa OK 74135

WELCH, JOHN EDWARD, lawyer; b. Gothenburg, Nebr., Dec. 23, 1954; s. John H. and Doris Louise (Peterson) W.; m. Suzanne Vaslef, Aug. 22, 1982. BA summa cum laude, U. Nebr., 1977; JD magna cum laude, Harvard U., 1982. Bar: U.S. Dist. Ct. (cen. dist.) Calif. 1982. Dep. dir. Whelan for Gov. Campaign, Lincoln, Nebr., 1978; legis. aide Nebr. Legislature, Lincoln, 1978-79; assoc. O'Melveny & Myers, Los Angeles, 1982—; mem. exec. and criminal justice coms. Los Angeles County Task Force on Drunk Driving, 1985-86. Mem. exec. com. Atty.'s for James K. Hahn, Los Angeles, 1985. Mem. ABA, Los Angeles County Bar Assn., Harvard Law Sch. Assn. General corporate, Securities, Private international. Home: 14069 Marquesas Way #111 Marina Del Rey CA 90292 Office: O'Melveny & Myers 400 S Hope St Los Angeles CA 90071

WELCH, ROBERT C., lawyer; b. Independence, Mo., Aug. 14, 1933; s. Arthur and Ova (Trimble) W.; m. Ellen Duncan, Sept. 2, 1955; children—Denise Louise Welch Masters, Andrea Marie. B.S., Kansas City Jr. Coll., 1955; J.D., U. Mo.-Kansas City, 1965. Bar: Mo. 1965. Ptnr. Paden, Welch, Martin, Albano & Graeff, P.C., Independence, 1965—; pros. atty. City of Blue Springs (Mo.), 1973—; pros. atty. City of Sugar Creek (Mo.), 1967—, city atty., 1981—. Author: Missouri Criminal Practice, 1977, 2d. edit., 1984. Mem. Kansas City Met. Bar Assn. (sec. 1981, 82, pres.-elect 1983, pres. 1984), Jackson County Legal Aid and Defenders Soc. (exec. bd. 1971-73, trustee 1975-77), U. Mo.-Kansas City Law Found. (sec. 1977-82, v.p. 1982-85 , pres. 1986-87), Eastern Jackson County Bar Assn. (pres. 1974-75 chmn. jud. recommendations com. 1983-84), Mo. Bar. Assn. (chmn. criminal law sect. 1975-76), Mo. Assn. Criminal Def. Lawyers (pres. 1980-81), Kansas City Bar Found. (v.p. 1985-86), Mo. Lawyers Trust Found. (bd. dirs. 1986—, 16th cir. judicial commn. 1986—) Sugar Creek Bus. and Profl. Club (past pres.). Club: Optimists (past pres.). Criminal. Home: 10703 Anderson Ct Sugar Creek MO 64054 Office: Paden Welch Martin Albano et al 311 W Kansas St Independence MO 64050

WELCH, ROBERT MORROW, JR., lawyer; b. Wichita Falls, Tex., Dec. 17, 1927; s. Robert Morrow and Sue (Hays) W.; m. Carol Cash, Dec. 21, 1951 (div. Oct., 1966); children: Catherine C., Robert Morrow III, Candice C.; m. Bernice Selma Weingarten, Apr. 22, 1967 (div. Mar. 1983); m. Annette Y. Apodaca, Dec. 17, 1985. LL.B., Baylor U., 1951. Bar: Tex. 1951. Briefing clk. Supreme Ct. Tex., Austin, 1951-52; assoc., then ptnr. Fulbright & Jaworski, Houston, 1952-83, sr. ptnr., 1983—. Served to sgt. USMC, 1946-48. Fellow Tex. Bar Found.; mem. ABA, Am. Acad. Matrimonial Lawyers (sec.-treas. 1978-79), Family Law Forum Houston (chmn. 1975-76), Houston Bar Assn. Home: 2701 Westheimer St Apt 11D Houston TX 77098 Office: Fulbright Jaworski 1301 McKinney 51st Fl Houston TX 77010

WELCH, THOMAS ANDREW, lawyer; b. Lincoln, Nebr., Dec. 22, 1936; s. Lawrence William and Edna Alberta (Tangeman) W.; m. Ann Reinecke, Sept. 12, 1959; children: Jonathan Thomas, Michael Andrew, Susan Jennifer. Student, Stanford U., 1955-56; BA, UCLA, 1959; LLB, Harvard U., 1965. Bar: Calif. 1966, U.S. Dist. Ct. (no. dist.) 1966, U.S. Ct. Appeals (9th cir.) 1966, U.S. Supreme Ct. 1976. Assoc. Brobeck, Phleger & Harrison, San Francisco, 1965-71, ptnr., 1972—; referee State Bar Ct., San Francisco, 1975—. Bd. dirs. Youth Law Ctr., San Fransisco, 1984—. Served to lt. USNR, 1959-62. Mem. ABA, Calif. Bar Assn., San Francisco Bar Assn., Am. Law Inst., An. Arbitration Assn. (arbitrator). Republican. Presbyterian. Club: World Trade (San Francisco). Federal civil litigation, State civil litigation, Private international. Home: 38 Irving Ln Orinda CA 94563 Office: Brobeck Phleger & Harrison 1 Market Plaza 2800 Spear Tower San Francisco CA 94105

WELCH, WALTER ANDREW, JR., lawyer; b. Dec. 13; s. Walter Andrew and Myrtle Marie (Kunzmann) W. BSAS, So. Ill. U., 1974; grad. U.S. Naval Justice Legal Edn. Inst., 1985; JD, Pepperdine U., 1980. Bar: Calif., N.J., U.S. Ct. Customs and Patent Appeals, U.S. Tax Ct., U.S. Ct. Mil. Appeals, U.S. Claims Ct., U.S. Ct. Appeals (3d, 4th, 5th and 9th cirs.), U.S. Dist. Ct. (so. and cen. dists.) Calif., U.S. Dist. Ct. N.J.; lic. comml. pilot FAA. Asst. dir. clin. law dept. Pepperdine U., Malibu, Calif., 1979; prosecutor, intern Child Abuse div. Los Angeles County Counsel, 1979-80; sole practice, Los Angeles and Washington, 1981—; adj. prof. aviation law So. Ill. U.; real estate broker, Calif., 1981—, Va. 1984—. Contbr. articles to legal revs. Served with USMC, 1974-77. Grantee and fellow Pepperdine U. Sch. Law, 1978-80. Mem. AIAA, Lawyer-Pilot's Bar Assn., Assn. Naval Aviation, Marine Corps Avaition Assn., Fed. Bar Assn., Assn. Trial Lawyers Am., ABA, Christian Legal Soc., Calif. State Bar (del. conv. 1981—). Aviation accident law, Admiralty, Federal civil litigation. Office: PO Box 9606 Marina Del Rey CA 90291

WELCH, WALTER SCOTT, III, lawyer; b. Jackson, Miss., Sept. 7, 1939; s. Walter Scott and Velma Lou (Hines) W.; children—Hermine, Walt from previous marriage; m. 2d, Mary Anne Kendrick, Dec. 6, 1981; children—Kasi, Dennis. B.A. cum laude, U. of the South, 1961; LL.B. with distinction, U. Miss., 1964. Bar: Miss. 1964, (U.S. Dist. Ct. (no. dist.) Miss. 1964, U.S. Dist. Ct. (so. dist.) Miss. 1967, U.S. Ct. Appeals (5th cir.) 1969, U.S. Supreme Ct. 1971, U.S. Dist. Ct. (ea. dist.) Ark. 1983. Assoc. Welch, Gibbes & Graves, Laurel, Miss., 1964; ptnr. Butler, Snow, O'Mara, Stevens & Cannada, Jackson, Miss., 1967—; past lectr. grad. realtors insts. Served to capt. JAGC, USAF, 1964-67. Mem. ABA, Miss. State Bar (chmn. task force on appellate judiciary 1985,chmn. standing com. on jud. liaison commn. 1986—, task force on tort reform 1986—), Hinds County Bar Assn. (pres. 1979-80, pres. elect 1978-79, sec.-treas. 1976-78), Internat. Assn. Ins. Counsel (vice chmn. standing com. auto liability ins. 1986), Miss. Def. Lawyers Assn. (dir. 1980-83, v.p. 1984), Am. Bd. Trial Advocates (v.p. Miss. chpt. 1986, pres. Miss. 1987) , Jackson C. of C. Episcopalian. Clubs: Capitol City Petroleum. Insurance, Personal injury, Libel. Home: 6223 Waterford Dr Jackson MS 39211 Office: Deposit Guaranty Plaza 17th Floor Jackson MS 39201

WELCH, WILLIAM F., lawyer; b. Logansport, Ind., June 17, 1918; s. George W. and Alyce (Fink) W.; m. Jean Louise Knauss, Mar. 5, 1949; children: Brian W., Sarah L. Welch McNaught. BA, DePauw U., 1940; JD, U. Mich., 1948. Bar: Ind. 1948, U.S. Dist. Ct. (so. dist.) Ind. 1948, U.S. Ct. Claims 1948, U.S. Ct. Appeals (7th cir.) 1952, U.S. Tax Ct. 1955, U.S. Supreme Ct. 1974. From assoc. to ptnr. McHale, Cook & Welch P.C., Indpls., 1948—, also chmn. bd.; trustee Citizens Gas and Coke, Indpls.; bd. dirs. First Nat. Bank Logansport, Kocolene Oil Corp., Seymour, Ind. Trustee Depauw U., Greencastle, Ind. Served to lt. comdr. USN, 1941-46, PTO. Fellow Am. Bar Found., Ind. Bar Found., Indpls. Bar Found.; mem. Seventh Cir. Bar Assn. (bd. govs.). Banking, Public utilities, Securities. Office: McHale Cook & Welch PC 320 N Meridian St Indianapolis IN 46204

WELD, WILLIAM FLOYD, lawyer; b. N.Y.C., July 31, 1945; s. David and Mary Blake (Nichols) W.; m. Susan Roosevelt, June 7, 1975; children: David Minot, Ethel Derby, Mary Blake, Quentin Roosevelt, Frances Wylie. A.B. summa cum laude, Harvard U., 1966, J.D. cum laude, 1970; diploma with distinction, Oxford (Eng.) U., 1967. Bar: Mass. 1970. Law clk. to Hon, R.A. Cutter, Supreme Jud. Ct. Mass., 1970-71; ptnr. firm Hill & Barlow, Boston, 1971-81; assoc. minority counsel U.S. Ho. of Reps. Judiciary Com. Impeachment Inquiry, 1973-74; U.S. Attorney for the District of Massachusetts 1981-86; asst. atty. general, criminal div. U.S. Justice Dept., Washington, 1986—. Republican nominee for atty. gen., Mass., 1978. Mem. Am. Law Inst., Boston Bar Assn., Am. Bar Assn. Clubs: Tavern, Brookline Country. Criminal, Federal civil litigation, State civil litigation. Office: US Dept Justice Rm 2107 Washington DC 20510

WELDON, C. MICHAEL, lawyer; b. Portsmouth, Va., Mar. 31, 1949; s. Claude E. and Garnett (Bernard) W.; m. Victoria Tesoro (div. 1975); 1 son, Christopher. B.S., U.S. Mil. Acad., 1971; J.D., Vanderbilt U., 1976. Bar: Ky. 1976, U.S. Dist. Ct. (we. dist.) 1979, U.S. Dist. Ct. (ea. dist.) Ky. 1982, U.S. Supreme Ct., 1985. Mem. Collier, Arnett & Coleman, Elizabethtown, Ky., 1978-81, Burnam & Thompson, Richmond, Ky., 1981—; adj. prof. paralegal studies Eastern Ky. U., 1982-84. Served to capt. U.S. Army, 1971-76. Recipient Profl. Merit award ABA, 1976; Judge Paul W. Brosman award U.S. Ct. Mil. Appeals, 1976. Mem. Ky. Bar Assn, Am. Legion (dept. judge advocate Ky. chpt., 1986-87). Republican. State civil litigation, Contracts commercial, Bankruptcy. Home: Route 1 Box 350 Paint Lick KY 40461 Office: Burnam & Thompson PO Box 726 Richmond KY 40475

WELIKSON, JEFFREY ALAN, lawyer; b. Bklyn., Jan. 8, 1957; s. Bennet Joseph and Cynthia Ann Welikson; m. Laura Sanders, Aug. 19, 1979; children: Gregory Andrew, Joshua Stuart. BS, U. Pa., 1976, MBA, 1977; JD, Harvard U., 1980. CPA, N.Y.; bar: N.Y. 1981. Assoc. Shearman & Sterling, N.Y.C., 1980-83; staff counsel Reliance Group Holdings Inc., N.Y.C., 1983-84, dir. legal dept., 1984-85, asst. v.p., corp. counsel, 1985—. Contbg. editor Harvard U. Internat. Law Jour., 1979-80. Mem. ABA, Am. Inst. CPAs. General corporate, Securities. Office: Reliance Group Holdings Inc Park Ave Plaza New York NY 10055

WELLBAUM, ROBERT WILLIAM, JR., lawyer; b. Waverly, Ohio, Oct. 3, 1943; s. Robert William and Della Frances (White) W.; m. Carolyn Sue Clemans, Ma. 20, 1966; children—Carrie, Lori, Robert William III. B.S., Ohio State U., 1966; J.D., Ohio No. U., 1973. Bar: Fla. 1974, U.S. Dist. Ct. (mid. dist.) Fla. 1977, U.S. Ct. Appeals (5th cir.) 1981, U.S. Ct. Appeals (11th cir.) 1981, U.S. Supreme Ct. 1980. Assoc. Wood, Karp, Wellbaum,

Miller & Seitl, P.A., Englewood, Fla., 1974-75, ptnr., 1975-85; ptnr. Wellbaum & McLennon P.A., Englewood, 1985—; adv. dir. NCNB Nat. Bank Fla. Mem. Englewood Civic Council. Named Jaycee of Yr., Englewood, 1975. Mem. Am. Coll. Mortgage Attys., ABA, Phi Alpha Delta. Clubs: Kiwanis, Elks (trustee), Quarterback, Sportsman's. Contracts commercial, Probate, Real property. Office: 350 S Indiana Ave Englewood FL 33533

WELLER, CHARLES DAVID, lawyer; b. Hartford, Conn., Oct. 19, 1944; s. Harry Deets and Betty Jane (Allenbaugh) W.; m. Susan Ann Carson, Feb. 28, 1982. BA, Yale U., 1966; JD, Case Western Res. U., 1973. Bar: Ohio 1973, U.S. Dist. Ct. (so. dist.) Ohio 1974, U.S. Dist. Ct. (no. dist.) Ohio 1976, U.S. Supreme Ct. 1978. Math tchr. U.S. Peace Corps, Johore Bahru, Malaysia, 1966-68; spl. asst. U.S. Peace Corps, Washington, 1969; dep. dir. so. region U.S. Peace Corps, Atlanta, 1969-70; asst. atty. gen. antitrust sect. Ohio Atty.'s Gen. Office, Columbus and Cleve., Ohio, 1973-82; of counsel Jones, Day, Reavis & Pogue, Cleve., 1982—; trustee Health Action Council, Cleve., 1982—, Health Systems Agy. of North, 1983—. Mem. Ohio Health Action Council, Columbus, 1983—. Mem. ABA (antitrust sect. and forum com. on health law). Antitrust, Health, Insurance. Home: 3346 Ingleside Rd Shaker Heights OH 44122 Office: Jones Day Reavis & Pogue 901 Lakeside Dr Cleveland OH 44114

WELLER, SUSAN NEUBERGER, lawyer; b. St. Albans, N.Y., July 19, 1956. BA, U. Miami, 1978; JD, George Washington U., 1981. Bar: Colo. 1981, U.S. Dist. Ct. Colo. 1982, U.S. Ct. Appelas (10th cir.) 1982, U.S. Tax Ct. 1983, D.C. 1984, U.S. Ct. Appeals (D.C. cir.) 1984, U.S. Dist. Ct. D.C. 1985. Assoc. Ireland, Stapleton, Pryor & Pascoe, Denver, 1981-84, Hamel & Park, Washington, 1984—. Vol. Kennedy Presdl. campaign, Washington, 1980; mem. Big Sisters Colo. Inc., Denver, 1982-83; lector St. John Neumann Parish, Gaithersburg, Md., 1986—. Mem. Colo. Bar Assn., D.C. Bar Assn., Women's Bar Assn. D.C., Omicron Delta Epsilon. Democrat. Roman Catholic. Avocations: weight training, photography, lit. Federal civil litigation, State civil litigation, Trademark and copyright. Home: 1 Morning Light Ct Gaithersburg MD 20878 Office: Hamel & Park 888 16th St NW Washington DC 20006

WELLES, MELVIN J., federal government official. Adminstrv. law judge Nat. Labor Relations Bd., Washington, 1985—. Office: Nat Labor Relations Bd Office of the Chmn 1717 Pennsylvania Ave NW Washington DC 20570 *

WELLFORD, HARRY WALKER, U.S. district judge; b. Memphis, Aug. 6, 1924; s. Harry Alexander and Roberta Thompson (Prothro) W.; m. Katherine E. Potts, Dec. 8, 1951; children: Harry Walker, James B. Buckner P., Katherine T., Allison R. B.A., Washington and Lee U., 1947; student, U. N.C., 1943-44; postgrad., U. Mich. Law Sch., 1947-48; LL.D., Vanderbilt U., 1950. Bar: Tenn. 1950. Atty. McCloy, Myar & Wellford, Memphis, 1950-60, McCloy, Wellford & Clark, Memphis, 1960-70; judge U.S. Dist. Ct., Memphis, 1970-82; U.S. circuit judge 6th Circuit Ct. Appeals, Cin., 1982—. Campaign chmn. Sen. Howard Baker campaigns, 1964, 66, Gov. Winfield Dunn, 1970; mem. Charter Drafting Com. City of Memphis, 1967; chmn. Tenn. Hist. Commn., Tenn. Constl. Bicentennial Commn., 1987—; mem. Tenn. Am. Revolution Bicentennial Commn., 1976, Com. on Adminstrn. of Fed. Magistrates System. Served as ensign USNR, 1944-45, PTO. Recipient Sam A. Myar award for service to profession and community Memphis State Law U., 1963; Tenn. Sr. Tennis Champion, 1974. Mem. Phi Beta Kappa, Omega Delta Kappa. Presbyterian (clk. of session, commr. Gen. Assembly, elder). Jurisprudence. Home: 91 N Perkins St Memphis TN 38117 Office: Court of Appeals 1176 Federal Bldg 167 N Main St Memphis TN 38103

WELLFORD, ROBIN SONNELAND, lawyer; b. Portland, Maine, Apr. 12, 1953; d. John Edward and Holly (Frost) Sonneland; m. Harry Walker Wellford Jr., Nov. 2, 1985. BA, Northwestern U., 1975; JD, Washington U., St. Louis, 1982. Bar: Ill. 1982, Mo. 1983, U.S. Dist. Ct. (ea. dist.) Mo. 1983. Law clk. to presiding justice U.S. Dist. Ct. (ea. dist.) Mo., St. Louis, 1982-83; assoc. Greensfelder, Hemker, Wiese, Gale & Chappelow, St. Louis, 1983-86, Suelthaus & Kaplan, St. Louis, 1987—. Mem. ABA, Mo. Bar Assn., St. Louis Bar Assn., Ill. Bar Assn., Order of Coif. Republican. Presbyterian. Avocations: tennis, music. Pension, profit-sharing, and employee benefits, Labor, Federal civil litigation. Office: Suelthaus & Kaplan 8000 Maryland 9th Floor Saint Louis MO 63105

WELLINGTON, HARRY HILLEL, lawyer, educator; b. New Haven, Aug. 13, 1926; s. Alex M. and Jean (Ripps) W.; m. Sheila Wacks, June 22, 1952; children: John, Thomas. A.B., U. Pa., 1947; LL.B., Harvard U., 1952; M.A. (hon.), Yale U., 1960. Bar: D.C. 1952. Law clk. to U.S. Judge Magruder, 1953-54, Supreme Ct. Justice Frankfurter, 1955-56; asst. prof. law Stanford U., 1954-56; mem. faculty Yale U., 1956—, prof. law, 1960—, Edward J. Phelps prof. law, 1967-83, Sterling prof. law, 1983—; dean Law Sch. Yale, 1975-85; Ford fellow London Sch. Econs., 1965; Guggenheim fellow; sr. fellow Brookings Instn., 1968-71; Rockefeller Found. fellow Bellagio Study and Conf. Ctr., 1984; faculty mem. Salzburg Seminar in Am. Studies, 1985; John M. Harlan disting. vis. prof. N.Y. Law Sch., 1985-86; review person ITT-SEC; moderator Asbestos-Wellington Group; cons. domestic and fgn. govtl. agys.; bd. overseers faculty arts and scis. U. Pa.; mem. jud. panel, exec. com. Ctr. Public Resources Legal Program. Author: (with Harold Shepherd) Contracts and Contract Remedies, 1957, Labor and the Legal Process, 1968, (with Clyde Summers) Labor Law, 1968, 2d edit., 1983, (with Ralph Winter) The Unions and the Cities, 1971; also articles. Mem. Am. Bar Assn., Bar Assn. Conn., Am. Law Inst., Am. Arbitration Assn., Am. Acad. Arts and Scis. Office: Yale Univ Law School New Haven CT 06520

WELLINS, SHELDON (SHEL) GARY, lawyer; b. Los Angeles, Mar. 21, 1944; s. Lawrence Arthur and Jeanette Jay W.; m. Lita Marie, Dec. 4, 1944; children—Cori Jay, Barry, Brian. A.A., Mt. San Antonio Coll., 1964; B.A. in Criminology, U. Calif., 1967; J.D., Hastings Coll. of Law, 1970. Bar: Calif. 1971. Assoc. Young Henrie, Humphries, Masons & Wellins and predecessors, Pomona, Calif., 1971-72, ptnr., 1972-78; sole practice, Claremont, Calif., 1978—; instr. community property and family law LaVerne Coll. Law, 1974-76; judge pro tem Los Angeles Superior Ct., 1975-77, 81—; family law mediator Los Angeles County and San Bernardino County. Mem. Claremont City Council, 1980-84. Served to capt. M.I., U.S. Army. Mem. Calif. Attys. for Criminal Justice, Los Angeles, Trial Lawyers Assn., Los Angeles County Bar Assn., ABA, Calif. Bar Assn., Am. Legion. Republican. Jewish. Club: Rotary (Claremont). Family and matrimonial, Personal injury, Criminal. Home: 222 W Lamar Claremont CA 91711 Office: 250 W 1st St Suite 312 Claremont CA 91711

WELLNITZ, CRAIG OTTO, lawyer, English educator; b. Elwood, Ind., Dec. 5, 1946; s. Frank Otto and Jeanne (Albright) W.; m. Karen Sue Thomas, Apr. 13, 1974; children—Jennifer Suzanne, Anne Katherine. B.A., Purdue U., 1969; M.A., Ind. U., 1972; J.D., Ind. U.-Indpls., 1978. Bar: Ind. 1978, U.S. Dist. Ct. (so. dist.) Ind. 1978, U.S. Supreme Ct. 1983, U.S. Ct. Appeals (7th and Fed. cirs.) 1984. Instr. Danville Jr. Coll., Ill., 1972-74, S.W. Mo. State U., Springfield, Mo., 1974-75; ptnr. Coates, Hatfield & Calkins, Indpls., 1978—; pub. defender Marion County, Ind., 1979—; instr. Ind. Central U., Indpls., 1981-82; mem. adj. faculty dept. English, Butler U., Indpls., 1983—; instr. Ind. U./Purdue U., Indpls., 1985—; pres. Ind. Account Mgmt., Indpls., 1985—. Columnist: A Jury of Your Peers, 1984—; lectr. The American Legal Justice System, 1984—; The Written Word: The Power of Effective Writing, 1985, A Way With Words, 1987. Vice committeeman Indpls. Rep. precinct, 1978. Postgrad. study grantee S.W. Mo. State U., Springfield, 1975. Mem. Indpls. Bar Assn., Ind. Bar Assn., ABA, Assn. Trial Lawyers Am., Ind. Trial Lawyers Assn. Methodist. Club: Riviera (Indpls.). Lodge: Elks. Personal injury, Criminal, State civil litigation. Home: PO Box 44162 Indianapolis IN 46204 Office: Coates Hatfield & Calkins 107 N Pennsylvania Suite 902 Indianapolis IN 46204

WELLON, ROBERT G., lawyer; b. Port Jervis, N.Y., Apr. 18, 1948; s. Frank Lewis and Alice (Stephens) W.; m. Jan Montgomery, Aug. 12, 1972; children: Robert F., Alice Wynn. AB, Emory U., 1970; JD, Stetson Coll. Law, 1974. Assoc. Turner, Turner & Turner, Atlanta, 1974-78; ptnr. Ridley, Wellon, Schwieger & Brazier, Atlanta, 1978-86, Wilson, Strickland & Benson, Atlanta, 1987—; adj. prof. Atlanta Law Sch., 1981—. Gov.'s task force chmn. Atlanta 2000, 1978; exec. com., treas., 2d v.p. Atlanta Easter Seals Soc., 1983-85; rep. Neighborhood Planning Unit, 1981-83. Served with USAR, 1970-76. Recipient Judge Joe Morris award Stetson Coll. Law, St. Petersburg, 1974. Mem. Fla. Bar, State Bar Ga., Atlanta Bar Assn. (bd. dirs. 1978-87, pres. 1986-87), Lawyers Club Atlanta. Methodist. Family and matrimonial, Personal injury, State civil litigation. Office: 5 Piedmont Center Suite 510 Atlanta GA 30305 Office: Five Piedmont Ctr Suite 510 339 Buckhead Ave NE Atlanta GA 30305-2396

WELLONS, WILLIAM LINDLEY, judge; b. Port Maria, Jamaica, Nov. 7, 1942; s. Harry Alvah and Esther A. (Lindley) W.; m. Jane Copley Dickerson, June 25, 1966; children: Sallie R., James B., Lindley, John S., Mary C. AB, Coll. William and Mary, 1965, JD, 1968. Bar: Va. 1968. Assoc. Richard E. Railey, Courtland, Va., 1969-71; sole practice, Victoria, Va., 1971-83; judge 10th Dist. Juvenile and Domestic Relations Dist. Ct., 1983—; mem. Va. State Bar Council, 1978-83. Baptist. Home: 1600 13th Ave Victoria VA 23974 Office: Courthouse Lunenberg VA 23952

WELLS, ANDREW NORMAN, lawyer; b. Staten Island, N.Y., July 25, 1953; s. Ira Merton and Mildred (Katz) W.; m. Melanie Resnick, Aug. 29, 1982; 1 child, Justine Amanda Miriam. BS in Psychology cum laude, Tulane U., 1974; JD cum laude, Cornell U., 1979. Bar: N.Y. 1980. Assoc. Shea & Gould, N.Y.C., 1979—. Mem. ABA, N.Y. State Bar Assn. General corporate, Securities. Office: Shea & Gould 330 Madison Ave New York NY 10017

WELLS, BILL CHARLES, lawyer; b. Portsmouth, Va., Nov. 9, 1956; s. William and Dorthey (McCreay) W.; m. Patricia Payne, June 6, 1981; children: Daniel Leonard, Cura Mae. BS in Secondary Edn., Old Dominion U., 1979; JD, Coll. William and Mary, 1982. Bar: Va. 1982, U.S. Ct. Mil. Appeals 1983. Commd. USAF, 1979; advanced through grades to capt. USAF, 1983; asst. staff JAG USAF, Oscoda, Mich., 1983-85, area def. counsel, 1985—; v.p., ptnr. TDC and Assocs., Virginia Beach, Va., 1980-83; atty. Scott, Cole, & Brown P.C., Newport News, Va., 1982-83. Mem. ABA, Assn. Trial Lawyers Am., Va. Trial Lawyers Assn. Criminal, Administrative and regulatory. Home: 8020 C S Alaska Wurtsmith AFB MI 48753 Office: Area Def Counsel Judge Adv Def Counsel Wurtsmith AFB MI 48753

WELLS, CHRISTOPHER BRIAN, lawyer; b. Belleview, Ill., Jan. 23, 1948; s. Frederick Meyers and Ethel Pauline (Morris) W.; m. Gaynelle Vansandt, June 6, 1970. BA in Econs., U. Kans., BS in Bus., 1972, JD. Enforcement atty. SEC, Seattle, 1977-82; ptnr. Lane, Powell, Moss & Miller, Seattle, 1982—. Served to capt. U.S. Army, 1974-77. Mem. ABA, Wash. State Bar Assn., King County Trial Lawyers Assn., Wash. Soc. CPA's., Kans. Bar Assn. Democrat. Federal civil litigation, Computer, General corporate. Office: Lane Powell Moss & Miller 3800 Rainier Bank Tower Seattle WA 98101

WELLS, CROSBY, lawyer; b. White Plains, N.Y., Jan. 25, 1922; s. Henry Hubbard and Caroline (Washburn) W.; m. Marianne Reed Conrad, Nov. 7, 1951 (div. June 1978); children—Reed, Conrad; m. Hedwig Porro, Aug. 6, 1978. B.A., Yale U., 1946; LL.B., U. Va., 1949. Bar: Va., N.Y. Assoc. Cadwalader Wickersham & Taft, N.Y.C., 1950-51; assoc. Reid & Priest, N.Y.C., 1951-61; gen. counsel Pub. Power Corp., Athens, Greece, 1951-55; legal officer Internat. Nickel Co., Inc., N.Y.C., 1961-73; v.p., gen. counsel, sec. Ebasco Services, Inc., N.Y.C., 1973-82, v.p., sr. counsel, 1982—; dir. Mt. Riga Inc. Salisbury Conn. Served with inf. U.S. Army, 1943-46, MTO. Decorated Bronze Star, Purple Heart. Republican. Club: Yale (N.Y.C.). General corporate, Construction. Home: 333 E 18th St New York NY 10003 Office: Ebasco Services Two World Trade Ctr New York NY 10048

WELLS, DAVID CONRAD, lawyer; b. Los Angeles, June 22, 1938; s. Glenn W. and Maxine B. Wells; m. D. Charlene Moore, Apr. 6, 1963; children—Karen A., Michael V. B.A., U. Colo., 1960, LL.B., 1963. Bar: Colo. 1963. Assoc., Mack, Johnson & Doty, Boulder, Colo., 1963-66; ptnr. Zook & Wells, Boulder, 1966-68; sole practice, Boulder, 1969-75; ptnr. Wells, Love & Scoby, Boulder, 1975—; lectr. Constable, Boulder County, 1960-63; fire chief Boulder Heights Fire Protection Dist., 1972-78. Mem. ABA, Colo. Bar Assn., Boulder County Bar Assn., Am. Arbitration Assn. Author legal articles. Construction, Government contracts and claims. Office: 225 Canyon Blvd Boulder CO 80302

WELLS, DAVID LEE, lawyer; b. Hooker, Mo., June 30, 1941; s. Sterling A. and Betty J. (Groover) W.; m. E. Annette Admire, June 13, 1965; children: Gretchen, Kyla. AB, William Jewell Coll., 1963; JD, U. Mo., 1967. Bar: U.S. Dist. Ct. (we. dist.) Mo. 1967, U.S. Ct. Appeals (8th cir.) 1967. Law clk. Mo. Ct. (6th cir.), Kansas City, 1966; assoc. William, Norton & Pollard, North Kansas City, Mo., 1967-77; sole practice North Kansas City, 1977—. Bd. dirs. Nat. Wildlife Art Show, Ducks Unltd., 1973-80; com. mem. Dem. Party, Fox Twp., Platt County, Mo., 1978-82; chmn. Rep. Dist. Dem. Party, Platt County, 1981, Senatorial Dist. Dem. Party, 1982; bd. govs. Citizens Assn., Kansas City, 1981—. Mem. ABA, Mo. Bar Assn., Kansas City Bar Assn., Clay County Bar Assn., Platt County Assn., Northland C. of C. (bd. dirs. 1982-85). Baptist. Clubs: Kansas City, Old Pike. Avocations: hunting, racquetball, cooking, gardening. General practice, Personal injury, Family and matrimonial. Office: 1910 Erie North Kansas City MO 64116

WELLS, FRANK MILTON, lawyer; b. Taunton, Mass., June 16, 1944; s. Hewett Steers and Janet (Scofield) W.; m. Pamela Jean Shaw, June 17, 1967 (div. Oct. 1979); children: Gretchen C., Katherine W. BA, Miami U., 1966; JD, Ohio State U., 1968. Bar: Ohio, 1969, Utah, 1975. Asst. atty. gen. Ohio Atty. Gen. Office, Columbus, 1969; sole practice Ogden, Utah, 1975—. bd. dirs. Ogden Valley Ski Edn. Found., Hill Afa, Utah, 1983—; elder 1st Presbyn. Ch., Ogden, 1980-82; mem. Utah Rep Govs. Club, 1985—. Served with USAF, 1969-74, res. 1975—. Mem. ABA, Fed. Bar Assn., Am. Trial Lawyers Assn., Res. Officers Assn. General practice, Consumer commercial, Administrative and regulatory. Home: 232 W 4900 S Ogden UT 84401 Office: 2485 Grant Suite 315-B Ogden UT 84401

WELLS, HUEY THOMAS, JR., lawyer; b. Gadsden, Ala., Mar. 22, 1950; s. Huey Thomas Sr. and Ruth (Allison) W.; m. Jan McKenzie, Dec. 29, 1972; children: Lynlee, Trey. BA with honors, U. Ala., 1972, JD, 1975. Bar: Ala. 1975, U.S. dist. Ct. (no. dist.) Ala. 1975, U.S. Ct. Appeals (D.C. and 5th cirs.) 1977, U.S. Supreme Ct. 1981, U.S. Ct. Appeals (11th cir.) 1982. Assoc. Cabaniss, Johnston, Gardner, Dumas & O'Neal, Birmingham, Ala., 1977-82; ptnr. Cabaniss, Johnston, Gardner, Damas & O'Neal, Birmingham, Ala., 1983-84, Maynard, Cooper, Frierson & Gale P.C., Birmingham, 1984—. Legal co-chmn. championship Profl. Golf Assn., Birmingham, 1984; legal chmn. U.S. Amateur Golf Championship, Birmingham, 1986. Served to capt. USAF, 1975-77. Mem. ABA (standing com. profl. discipline), Birmingham Bar Assn. (law day com., grievance com.), Ala. Bar Assn. (jud. liaison). Roman Catholic. Avocations: golf, softball, reading. Federal civil litigation, State civil litigation, Administrative and regulatory. Home: 4326 10th Ave S Birmingham AL 35222 Office: Maynard Cooper Fierson & Gale PC 2008 3d Ave N 12th Floor Watts Bldg Birmingham AL 35203

WELLS, LESLEY BROOKS, common pleas court judge; b. Muskegon, Mich., Oct. 6, 1937; d. James Franklin and Inez Simpson (Schallmo) W.; m. Arthur V.N. Brooks, June 20, 1959; (div.); children: Lauren Elizabeth, Caryn Alison, Anne Kristin, Thomas Eliot. BA, Chatham Coll., Pitts., 1959; JD cum laude, Cleve. State U., 1974; cert. Nat. Jud. Coll., Reno, 1983. Bar: Ohio 1975, U.S. Dist. Ct. (no. dist.) Ohio 1975. Sole practice, Cleve., 1975; ptnr. firm Brooks & Moffet, Cleve., 1975-79; dir., atty. ABAR Litigation Ctr., Cleve., 1979-80; assoc. firm Schneider, Smeltz, Huston & Ranney, Cleve., 1980-83; judge Ct. of Common Pleas. Cleve., 1983—; adj. prof. law and urban policy Cleve. State U., 1979-82. Editor, author: Litigation Manual, 1980. Past pres. Cleve. Legal Aid Soc.; legal chmn. Nat. Women's Polit. Caucus, 1981-82; chmn. Gov.'s Task Force on Family Violence, Ohio, 1983-87; Nat. Council Juvenile and Family Ct. Judges, 1985—, U.S. Constitution Bicentennial Commn.; mem. biomedical ethics com. Case Western Res. U. Med. Sch., 1985—; mem. com. of Ethics and Profl. Responsibility Jud. Adminstrn., 1986—, Northwest Ordinance U.S. Constitution Commn., Ohio, 1986—. Recipient Superior Jud. award Supreme Ct. of Ohio, 1983; J. Irwin award Womenspace, Ohio, 1984. Mem. ABA, Ohio Bar Assn., Cleve. Bar Assn. (Merit Service award 1983), Cleve. County Bar Assn., Nat. Conf. State Trial Judges (ethics and profl. responsibility com. 1986—), Nat. Assn. Women Judges. Judicial administration, Jurisprudence, Family and matrimonial. Home: 16926 E Park St Cleveland OH 44119 Office: Lakeside Ct Common Pleas 1 Lakeside St Cleveland OH 44113

WELLS, PETER BOYD, lawyer; b. Austin, Tex., Sept. 30, 1915; s. Peter Boyd and Eleanor (Henderson) W.; m. Betty Louise Perkins, May 26, 1951; children—Peter Boyd, Elizabeth Wells Howell. B.A., U. Tex., 1936; LL.B., Harvard U., 1940. Bar: Tex., 1941. Assoc., Benckenstein, Wells & Duncan, Beaumont, Tex., 1946-58; sole practice, Beaumont, 1958-61; ptnr. Wells, Duncan & Beard, Beaumont, 1961-70, Wells, Peyton, Beard, Greenberg, Hunt & Crawford, Beaumont, 1970—; speaker estate planning. Former treas. Tex. Hist. Found. Served to maj. inf., AUS, 1941-45; ETO. Decorated Bronze Star; cert. in estate planning and probate law. Mem. ABA, Tex. Bar Found., Tex. Philos. Soc., Phi Beta Kappa, Phi Kappa Psi. Presbyterian. Clubs: Tower, Beaumont, Beaumont Rotary, Knights of San Jacinto, Sons Republic of Tex. Probate, Corporate taxation, General corporate. Home: 2570 Long St Beaumont TX 77702 Office: Wells & Peyton 624 Petroleum Bldg PO Box 3708 Beaumont TX 77704

WELLS, PETER NATHANIEL, lawyer; b. Ogdensburg, N.Y., May 13, 1938; s. John Harris and Mary Theresa (Houlihan) W.; m. Diana Barry Wells, Apr. 8, 1967; children—Mary, Sarah, Matthew. B.S. in Polit. Sci., Manhattan Coll., 1960; LL.B., Boston Coll., 1963. Bar: N.Y. 1963, U.S. Dist. Ct. (no. dist.) N.Y. 1967, U.S. Dist. Ct. (we. dist.) N.Y. 1971, U.S. Ct. Appeals (2d cir.) 1974, U.S. Ct. Appeals (3d cir.) 1978, U.S. Supreme Ct. 1974. Asst. atty. gen. State of N.Y., 1964-68; assoc. Costello, Cooney & Fearon, Syracuse, N.Y., 1968-70, ptnr., 1970-76; ptnr. Williams, Micale & Wells, Syracuse, 1976—. Chmn. Dewitt Republican Com. Served with USAR, 1963-69. Mem. ABA, N.Y. State Bar Assn., Onondaga County Bar Assn., Def. Research Inst., Upstate Trial Lawyers Assn. Roman Catholic. Clubs: Cavalry, Manlius (N.Y.). State civil litigation, Federal civil litigation, Government contracts and claims. Home: 100 Downing Rd Dewitt NY 13214 Office: 250 Harrison St Syracuse NY 13202

WELLS, ROBERT STEVEN, lawyer; b. Pitts., July 7, 1951; s. Richard H. and Mary J. (Kimball) W. B.S., Purdue U., 1972; J.D., Ohio State U., 1976. Bar: Ohio 1977, U.S. Dist. Ct. (so. dist.) Ohio 1977, Ill. 1980, U.S. Dist. Ct. (no. dist.) Ill. 1981, U.S. Supreme Ct. 1983. Sole practice, Columbus, Ohio, 1977-78; research counsel ABA Ctr. for Profl. Responsibility, Chgo., 1979-84, ethics counsel, 1985; exec. dir. S.C. Bar, 1985—. Editor: ABA/BNA Lawyers' Manual on Professional Conduct, 1984; ABA Disciplinary Law and Procedure Research System, 1979. Mem. S.C. Bar Assn., ABA (torts and ins. practice sect., profl. independence and responsibility of lawyer com., econs. law practice sect., state and local bar liaison com.), Am. Judicature Soc., Nat. Assn. Bar Execs. (long-range planning com.). Jurisprudence, Professional responsibility. Office: SC Bar 1321 Bull St PO Box 11039 Columbia SC 29211

WELS, RICHARD HOFFMAN, lawyer; b. N.Y.C., May 3, 1913; s. Isidor and Belle (Hoffman) W.; m. Marguerite Samet, Dec. 12, 1954; children: Susan, Amy. A.B., Cornell, 1933; LL.B., Harvard U., 1936; postgrad., U. Ariz., 1944. Bar: N.Y. 1936. Spl. asst. dist. atty. N.Y. Co., 1936-37; asso. Handel & Panuch, N.Y.C., 1937-38; mem. legal staff, asst. to chmn. SEC, Washington, 1938-42; spl. asst. atty. gen. U.S. and spl. asst. U.S. atty., 1941-42; spl. counsel Com. Naval Affairs, U.S. Ho. of Reps., 1943, Sea-Air Commn., Nat. Fedn. Am. Shipping, 1946; trustee, sec. William Alanson White Inst. Psychiatry, N.Y.C., 1946—; vice. chmn., dir. Am. Parents Com.; mem. Moss & Wels, 1946-57, Moss, Wels & Marcus, 1957-68, Sulzberger, Wels & Marcus, 1968-72, Moss, Wels & Marcus, 1972-78, Sperry, Weinberg, Wels, Waldman & Rubenstein, 1979-84, Wels & Zerin, 1985—; gen. counsel Bowling Proprs. Assn. Am., 1956-67, N.Y. State Bowling Proprs. Assn., Am. Acad. Psychoanalysis; commr. Interprofl. Comn. on Marriage and Div.; lectr. Practising Law Inst.; dir. H-R Television, Inc., Belgrave Capital Corp., Broadcast Data Base, Inc., Belgrave Securities Corp.; chmn. bd. govs. Islands Research Found.; bd. govs., chmn., trustee Daytop Village, Inc.; chmn. bd. trustees Bleuler Psychotherapy Center; trustee N.Y. State Sch. Psychiatry, Margaret Chase Smith Library, Skowhegan, Maine. Co-author: Sexual Behavior and the Law; bd. editors Family Law Quar.; contbr. articles to profl. jours. Vice chmn. Am. Jewish Com., now mem. nat. exec. bd. Served from ensign to lt. USNR, 1942-46; mem. staff Under Sec. Forrestal, 1943-44; in 1944-46, P.T.O. Mem. ABA (fin. officer, mem. council Am. family law sect.), N.Y. State Bar Assn. (chmn. family law sect.), N.Y. City Bar Assn., Am. Acad. Matrimonial Lawyers (gov.), Am. Legion, Naval Order U.S., Mil. Order World Wars, Fed. Bar Assn., Res. Officers Assn., Assn. I.C.C. Practitioners, Fed. Communications Bar Assn., Pi Lambda Phi, Sphinx Head. Clubs: Harmonie (gov.), Harvard, Cornell (N.Y.C.); Nat. Lawyers (Washington); Sunningdale Country (Scarsdale, N.Y.), Statler (Ithaca, N.Y.). Family and matrimonial, Probate, Estate taxation. Home: 480 Park Ave New York NY 10022 Office: Wels & Zerin 55 E 59th St New York NY 10022

WELSH, ALFRED JOHN, lawyer, consultant; b. Louisville, May 10, 1947; s. Elvin Alfred and Carol (Kleymeyer) W.; m. Lee Mitchell, Aug. 1, 1970; children: Charles Kleymeyer, Kathryn Thomas. BA, Centre Coll., 1969; JD, U. Ky., 1972; LLM in Internat. Law, U. Brussels, 1973. Bar: Ky. 1972, U.S. Dist. Ct. (we. and ea. dists.) Ky. 1972, U.S. Ct. Appeals (6th cir.) 1972. Atty. Ky. Atty. Gen. Office, Frankfort, 1973-74; legis. counsel to congressman Ho. of Reps., Washington, 1974-77; ptnr. Nicolas, Welsh & Vandeventer, Louisville, 1977—; hon. counsel of Belgium, 1983—. Bd. dirs. Greater Louisville Swim Found., 1983—, Louisville Com. Fgn. Relations, 1983—, Jefferson County Alcohol and Drug Abuse Found., Louisville, 1986—. Named one of Outstanding Young Men Am., 1984. Mem. ABA, Ky. Bar Assn. (bd. dirs. 1981-82, pres. young lawyers div. 1981—), Am. Judicature Soc. Democrat. Presbyterian. Avocations: swimming, water polo. General practice, Personal injury, Workers' compensation. Office: Nicolas Welsh & Vandeventer 475 Starks Bldg Louisville KY 40204

WELSH, DONALD LEROY, lawyer; b. Macomb, Ill., Apr. 20, 1925; s. Olin Lloyd and Hazel Irene (Jury) W.; m. Betty Jeanne Myers, July 19, 1947; children—Sara Jury Welsh Colaianni, Julia Ann Welsh LeBosse. B.S. in Elec. Engring., Purdue U., 1946; J.D., U. Ill., 1948. Bar: Ill. 1949, U.S. Dist. Ct. (no. dist.) Ill. 1950, U.S. Ct. Appeals (7th cir.) 1965, U.S. Ct. Appeals (fed. cir.) 1983. Assoc. Carlson, Pitzner, Hubbard & Wolfe, Rockford, Ill., 1949-58; ptnr. Ooms, Welsh & Bradway, Chgo., 1958-63, Welsh & Bradway, Chgo., 1963-65, Fitch, Even, Tabin, Flannery & Welsh, Chgo., 1965-83; sr. ptnr. Welsh & Katz, Chgo., 1983—. Served with USMC, 1943-46, 51-52. Mem. ABA, Chgo. Bar Assn., Patent Law Assn. Chgo., Lincoln Park Zool. Soc., Tau Beta Pi, Eta Kappa Nu, Phi Delta Theta, Phi Delta Phi. Clubs: University, Attic (Chgo.). Patent, Trademark and copyright, Federal civil litigation. Office: 135 S LaSalle St Suite 1625 Chicago IL 60603

WELSH, JOHN BERESFORD, JR., lawyer; b. Seattle, Feb. 16, 1940; s. John B. and Rowena Morgan (Custer) W. Student U. Hawaii, 1960, Georgetown U., 1960; BA, U. Wash., 1962, LLB, 1965. Bar: Wash. 1965. Staff counsel Joint Com. on Govtl. Cooperation, 1965-66; asst. atty. gen. Dept. Labor and Industries, 1966-67; atty. Legis. Council, acting as counsel to Pub. Health Com., Labor Com., Pub. Employees Collective Bargaining Com., Com. on State Instns. and Youth Devel., State of Wash., 1967-73; sr. counsel Wash. Ho. of Reps., counsel to Ho. Com. on Social and Health Services, Olympia, 1973-86; counsel Ho. Com. Human Services and Ho. Com. Health Care, 1987—; legal cons. Gov.'s Planning Commn. Vocat. Rehab., 1968, Gov.'s Commn. on Youth Involvement, 1969; envoy from Gov. Wash. to investiture of Prince of Wales, London, 1969; faculty Nat. Conf. State Legislatures, Denver, 1977, New Orleans, 1977; faculty, chmn. legis. issues com., mem. steering com., long range planning com. Council of State Govts. Conf. on Licensure, Enforcement and Regulation, 1984, 86, 87. Hon. prof. health adminstrn. Eastern Wash. U., 1982. Mem. Wash. Bar Assn., Govtl. Lawyers Assn., Nat. Health Lawyers Assn., Société des Amis du Musée de l'Armée, Paris, English Speaking Union, Assn. Belge Napoleonienne, Souvenir Napoleonien (Paris), Napoleonic Soc., Phi Delta Phi. Legislative. Office: State of Washington House of Representatives Olympia WA 98504

WELSH, THOMAS HARRY, lawyer; b. Pitts., Sept. 19, 1922; s. Richard Joseph and Marie Elizabeth (Friday) W.; m. Kathleen Ann Manley, Nov. 29, 1950; children—Kathleen, Ann, Thomas Harry, Patricia, Rosemary, John.

B.A., U. Pitts., 1943, LL.B., 1950, J.D., 1968. Bar: Pa. 1950. Assoc., Beck McGinnis & Jarvis, 1952-53, Tobias & Weilersbacher, 1953-58; assoc., then ptnr. Metz, Cook, Hanna, Welsh, Bluestone & Beamer and predecessor Metz, Cook, Hanna & Kelly, Pitts., 1958—; asst. dist. atty. Allegheny County, Pa., 1958-63; del. Pa. Constl. Conv., 1968-69; dir. cos. Mem. Alumni Council, U. Pitts., 1975—, pres. CAS Alumni, 1975-80, mem. athletic com., 1980-81. Served to capt. U.S. Army, 1943-46, 51-52. Mem. Assn. Trial Lawyers Am., Am. Judicature Soc., Am. Arbitration Assn., U. Pitts. Gen. Alumni Assn. (pres. 1983-84), Phi Delta Phi (past pres.). Democrat. Roman Catholic. Clubs: Pitts. Athletic, Sertoma (past pres.) (Pitts.); Pittsburgh Field (Fox Chapel, Pa.). Federal civil litigation, General corporate, Probate. Home: 1003 Elmhurst Rd Pittsburgh PA 15215 Office: Grant Bldg 408 Grant St Pittsburgh PA 15219

WELTCHEK, PAUL RICHARD, lawyer; b. Elizabeth, N.J., Dec. 2, 1928; s. Lawrence L. and Fannie S. (Shor) W.; m. Edith Zanditon, July 11, 1954; children: Nancy Ellen, Ann Elizabeth, Peter Richard. B.A., U. Nebr., 1950; LL.B., Yale U., 1955. Bar: N.J. 1955, Calif. 1959, N.Y. 1962. Ptnr. Shearman & Sterling, N.Y.C., 1965—. Served to 1st lt. U.S. Army, 1951-52. Mem. Internat. Bar Assn., Internat. Fiscal Assn., ABA, N.Y. State Bar Assn., Assn. Bar City N.Y., Phi Beta Kappa. Clubs: Down Town Assn. Office: Shearman & Sterling 53 Wall St New York NY 10005

WELTCHEK, ROBERT JAY, lawyer; b. Elizabeth, N.J., July 28, 1955; s. Leslie Mayer and Patricia Marjorie (Schoenhaut) W.; m. Holly Prager; children: Nolan Joseph, Emily Rachel. BA, Rutgers U., 1977; JD with honors, U. Md., 1980. Bar: Md. 1980, U.S. Dist. Ct. Md. 1980, U.S. Ct. Appeals (4th cir.) 1981. Assoc. Bertram M. Goldstein P.A., Balt., 1980-82; ptnr. Goldstein, Weltchek & Assocs., Balt., 1983—. Mem. ABA, Md. State Bar Assn., Fed. Bar Assn., Balt. City Bar Assn., Assn. Trial Lawyers Am., Md. Trial Lawyers Assn. Democrat. Jewish. Avocations: tennis, racquetball. Personal injury, Federal civil litigation, State civil litigation. Home: 2313 Shaded Brook Dr Owings Mills MD 21117 Office: Goldstein Weltchek and Assocs 1 North Charles St Suite 222 Baltimore MD 21201

WELTMAN, JORDAN SCOTT, lawyer; b. N.Y.C., Mar. 25, 1953. BA, Yale U., 1975; JD, U. Pa., 1978. Bar: Pa. 1978, U.S. Supreme Ct. 1982, Calif. 1984. Assoc. Eckert, Seamans, Cherin & Mellott, Pitts., 1978-82; asst. counsel Republic Steel Corp., Cleve., 1982-84; counsel McDonnell Douglas Fin. Corp., Long Beach, Calif., 1984-86, sr. counsel, 1986—. General corporate, Contracts commercial. Home: 6507 Ocean Crest Dr Rancho Palos Verdes CA 90274 Office: McDonnell Douglas Fin Corp 340 Golden Shore Long Beach CA 90802

WELTNER, CHARLES LONGSTREET, state supreme court justice; b. Atlanta, Dec. 17, 1927; s. Philip W. and Sally (Cobb) Hull; m. Betty Jean Center, Sept. 16, 1950 (div. 1972); children: Elizabeth Shirley, Philip, Susan Martin, Charles L.; m. Anne Fitten Glenn, Mar. 22, 1978; children: June Spalding, Anne Glenn. AB, Oglethorpe U., 1948; LLB, Columbia U., 1950; LLD, Tufts U., 1967; MA, Columbia Theol. Sem., 1983; LLM, U. Va., 1986. Bar: Ga. 1949. Sole practice Atlanta, 1950—; mem. U.S. Congress from 5th dist. Ga., 1963-67; judge Superior Ct. Atlanta Jud. Cir., 1976-81; asssoc. justice Supreme Ct. Ga., Atlanta, 1981—; chmn. jud. council Ga., 1980-81. Author: Process of Service, 1962, Southerner, 1966, John Willie Reed, 1970, Heavens of Babylon, 1980. Dep. chmn. Dem. Nat. Com., Washington, 1967. Served to 1st lt. U.S. Army, 1955-57. Fellow Inst. of Politics, Harvard U. Fellow Am. Law Inst. Presbyterian. Jurisprudence. Home: 2642 Battle Overlook NW Atlanta GA 30327 Office: Supreme Ct Georgia State Jud Bldg Atlanta GA 30334

WELTON, CHARLES EPHRAIM, lawyer; b. Cloquet, Minn., June 23, 1947; s. Eugene Frances and Evelyn Esther (Koski) W.; m. Nancy Jean Sanda, July 19, 1969; children—Spencer Sanda, Marshall Eugene. B.A., Macalester Coll., 1969; postgrad. U. Minn., 1969-70; J.D., U. Denver, 1974. Bar: Colo. 1974, U.S. Dist. Ct. Colo. 1974, U.S. Supreme Ct. 1979, U.S. Ct. Appeals (10th cir.) 1980. Assoc., Davidovich & Assocs., and predecessor firm, Denver, 1974-77; Charles Welton and Assocs., Denver, 1978-80, 1984—; ptnr. Davidovich & Welton, Denver, 1981-84; ptnr. OSM Properties, Denver, 1982—. Contbr. articles to profl. jours. Co pres. PTSA, Denver, 1983-84; coach Colo. Jr. Soccer League, 1980-85; co-coach Odessey of the Mind (formerly Olympics of the Mind), 1986—. Served alt. mil. duty Denver Gen. Hosp., 1970-72. Mem. Denver Bar Assn., Colo. Bar Assn. (legal fee arbitration com.), Assn. Trial Lawyers Am., Colo. Trial Lawyers Assn. (bd. dirs. 1985—, chmn. seminar com. 1986—), Americans Building a Lasting Earth (founder), Exec. Ventures Group of Am. Leadership Forum (adv. bd.). Democrat. Lutheran. Club: Midtown Athletic. Personal injury, State civil litigation, Federal civil litigation. Home: 5020 Montview Blvd Denver CO 80207 Office: Old Smith Mansion 1751 Gilpin St Denver CO 80218

WELTY, JOHN RIDER, lawyer; b. Waynesboro, Pa., Nov. 5, 1948; s. Richard Samuel and Mary Catherine (Rider) W.; m. Susan Eileen Mescall, Aug. 7, 1970; children: John R. II, David Richard, Brian James. BA in Econs., Shippensburg State U., 1970; JD, Am. U., 1975. Bar: Pa. Economist bur. econ. analysis U.S. Dept. of Commerce, Washington, 1970-76; staff atty. to sr. atty. Carpenter Tech. Corp., Reading, Pa., 1976-82; assoc. gen. counsel Carpenter Tech. Corp., Reading, 1982—; sec. fed. polit. action com. Carpenter (Pa.) Tech. Corp., Reading, 1978—, sec. state polit. action com., 1978—. Founder Drexelwood Community Assn., Wyomissing, Pa., 1981-82; bd. dirs. Cornwall Terr. Community Assn., Sinking Spring, Pa., 1977-79,. Mem. ABA, Pa. Bar Assn., Am. Corp. Counsel Assn., Pa. Self Insurers Assn. (bd. dirs. 1978-81), Phi Alpha Delta, Alpha Phi Omega. Republican. Avocations: tennis, reading. Antitrust, Pension, profit-sharing, and employee benefits, Contracts commercial. Office: Carpenter Tech Corp 101 W Bern St Reading PA 19601

WELTZER, LOUIS ALBIN, lawyer; b. Moline, Ill., Mar. 12, 1948; s. Lucian M. and Lyna Rae (Coats) W.; m. Catherine Ann Lupton, Feb. 1, 1980; children: Michael Louis, Suzanne Catherine. BA, U. Colo., 1970, JD, 1974. Bar: Colo. 1974, U.S. Dist. Ct. Colo. 1974, U.S. Ct. Appeals (10th cir.) 1977, U.S. Supreme Ct. 1980. Assoc. Carroll, Bradley & Ciancio P.C., Denver, 1974-75; ptnr. Weltzer & Worstell, Denver, 1975-81; sole practice Denver, 1981—. Contbr. articles to profl. jours. Mem. ABA, Colo. Bar Assn., Denver Bar Assn. Roman Catholic. Avocations: running, skiing, reading. Personal injury, State civil litigation, General practice. Home: 4625 Teller St Wheat Ridge CO 80033 Office: 1626 Washington St Denver CO 80203

WENCE, GARY FRED, lawyer; b. Akron, Ohio, Mar. 20, 1957; s. George Edward and Phyllis Sue (Darnold) W.; m. Erin Pickard Leary, Aug. 18, 1984; 1 child, Charles Brian. BA, Colo. State U., 1979; JD, U. Ark., 1982. Bar: Ark. 1982, U.S. Dist. Ct. Ark. 1982, U.S. Dist. Ct. Okla. 1983, Nebr. 1984, U.S. Dist. Ct. Nebr. 1984, U.S. Ct. Appeals (8th cir.) 1986. Assoc. Wiggins, Christian & Garner, Fort Smith, Ark., 1982-83, Erickson-Sederstrom, Omaha, 1983-85, McGrath, North, O'Malley & Kratz, Omaha, 1985—. Mem. ABA, Nebr. Bar Assn., Ark. Bar Assn., Assn. Trial Lawyers Am. Republican. Presbyterian. Lodge: Masons. Contracts commercial, Federal civil litigation, State civil litigation. Office: McGrath North O'Malley & Kratz PC One Central Park Plaza Suite 1100 Omaha NE 68102

WENDEL, CHARLES ALLEN, lawyer; b. Lockport, N.Y., Aug. 13, 1942; s. Harold Henry and Doris Lillian (Gardner) W.; m. Helen W. Roberts, June 23, 1973; children—William Charles, Jonathan David. B.Chem. Engring., Rensselaer Poly. Inst., 1964; J.D., Am. U., 1968. Bar: N.Y. 1969, Va. 1971, D.C. 1980, U.S. Supreme Ct., U.S. Ct. Appeals (fed. and 4th cirs.), U.S. Dist. Ct. (ea. and we. dists.) Va. Patent examiner U.S. Patent and Trademark Office, Washington, 1964-66; patent trainee Union Carbide Corp, Washington, 1966-68, patent atty., N.Y.C., 1968-70; assoc., then ptnr. firm Stevens, Davis, Miller & Mosher, Arlington, Va., 1970-83; ptnr. firm Wegner & Bretschneider, Washington, 1983-85, assoc. solicitor U.S. Patent and Trademark Office, 1985—. Contbr. articles to profl. jours. Mem. ABA, Va. State Bar, (patent trademark copyright sect., chmn. 1977-78), Am. Internat. Patent Law Assn., Patent Lawyers Club Washington (pres. 1982-83), Delta Theta Phi. Republican. Patent. Office: Office of Solicitor PO Box 15667 Arlington VA 22215-4132

WENDEL, JOHN FREDRIC, lawyer, consultant; b. Newark, Nov. 8, 1936; s. John J. and Margaret D. (Mortimer) W.; m. Barbara Vaughn Smith, Dec. 17, 1960 (dec. July 1978); children: David I., Stephen F.; m. Carlene M. Arnoldini, 1 child, Carlene Margaret. BA, U. Fla., 1958; JD, Stetson U., 1963. Bar: Fla. 1963, U.S. Dist. Ct (so. and mid. dists.) 1964, U.S. Ct. Appeals (5th and 11th cirs.) 1964, U.S. Supreme Ct. 1968. Assoc. Troiano & Roberts, Lakeland, Fla., 1963-65, George C. Dayton, Dade City, Fla., 1965; sole practice John F. Wendel, Lakeland, 1965, 1970-73; ptnr. Wendel & Schott, Lakeland, 1965-70; ptnr., pres. Wendel & McArthur, P.A., Lakeland, 1973-75, Wendel & Chritton and predecessor firms, Lakeland, Fla., 1975—; town atty Town of St. Leo, Fla., 1964-78, town judge, 1968; asst. mcpl. judge Lakeland, Fla., 1966;, county atty. Citrus County, Fla., 1976-81; adj. faculty mem. Fla. So. Coll., Lakeland, 1963-65; faculty mem. St. Leo Coll., 1963-73; del. Second Internat. Conf. Ptnrs. for the Alliance for Progress; mem. Fla. Columbia Alliance Coms. and Subcoms. gen. counsel Nat. Assn. of Profl. Baseball Leagues, Inc., St. Petersburg, 1974-81, various profl. baseball leagues, 1969—. Active ARC. Served to 1st lt. USMC, 1957-59. Named one of Lakeland's Five Outstanding Young Men, Jaycees, 1967. Mem. Sports Lawyers Assn. (sec., v.p., bd. dirs., pres. 1986), ABA, Fla. Bar Assn., Lakeland Bar Assn., Canon Law Soc. of Am., Fla. Assn. County Attys. (pres. 1981). Democrat. Roman Catholic. Clubs: Lakeland Yacht and Country, U. Tampa. Lodges: Elks, Rotary, KC. Sports law, Administrative and regulatory, State civil litigation. Office: Wendel & Chritton 5300 S Florida Ave PO Box 5378 Lakeland FL 33807

WENDEL, MARTIN, lawyer; b. Elizabeth, N.J., Sept. 30, 1944; s. Henry H. and Catherine (McGovern) W.; m. Louise A. Damasiewicz, Oct. 19, 1968; children: Martin Jr., Andrew. BS with honors, Rutgers U., 1974; JD, N.Y. Law Sch., 1978. Bar: N.J. 1978, U.S. Dist. Ct. N.J. 1978, N.Y. 1979, U.S. Dist. Ct. (so. and ea. dists.) N.Y. 1979, U.S. Ct. Appeals (2d cir.) 1979. Assoc. Costello & Shea, N.Y.C., 1979-81; assoc. Curtis, Mallet, Prevost, Colt & Mosle, N.Y.C., 1981-87, ptnr. Atty. mcpl. planning bd., Rahway, N.J., 1979—; mem. com. Union County N.J., 1981—; bd. dirs. Make-a-Wish Found., N.J., 1983-85, med. malpractice mediation panel 1st Jud. Dept., 1980—. Served with USN, 1962-66. Mem. ABA, N.Y. State Bar Assn., (com. cert. specialization), N.J. State Bar Assn. (mem. civil bar sect.), N.Y. County Lawyers Assn. (mem. ins. com.), Assn. Trial Lawyers Am., N.Y. State Trial Lawyers Assn. Democrat. Lodge: Masons. Federal civil litigation, State civil litigation, Personal injury. Home: 1071 Midwood Dr Rahway NJ 07065 Office: Curtis Mallet Prevost Colt & Mosle 101 Park Ave New York NY 10178

WENDORF, HULEN DEE, law educator, author, lecturer; b. West, Tex., Oct. 29, 1916; s. Reinhardt and Laura (Blume) W.; m. Mary Jane Pfeffer, June 13, 1939; children: Robert Joseph, Donald Joseph, Florence Ann. B.S., U.S. Mil. Acad., 1939; J.D., Yale U., 1951. Bar: Conn. 1951, U.S. Ct. Mil. Appeals 1952, U.S. Supreme Ct. 1958, U.S. Dist. Ct. 1960, Tex. 1961. Commd. 2d lt. U.S. Army, 1939, advanced through grades to col., ret. as chief of adminstrv. law div. Office Judge Adv. Gen., 1959; practice El Paso, Tex., 1959-61; prof. law Baylor U. Law Sch., 1961-86, prof. emeritus, 1986—; former chmn. and long-time mem. Citizens Adv. Com. to Juvenile Judge; bd. dirs. Heart of Tex. Legal Aid Assn. Author: Texas Law of Evidence Manual, 1983, also 3 law sch. casebooks; contbr. various articles to law revs. Research dir. Texans War on Drugs, 1980-81; chmn. Food For People, 1981—; elder, trustee Westminster Presbyterian Ch. Decorated Legion of Merit, Bronze Star, Army Commendation medal. Mem. Assn. Trial Lawyers Am., Tex. Trial Lawyers, Tex. Criminal Def. Lawyers Assn., Waco-McLennan County Bar Assn. (dir., v.p.), Phi Delta Phi. Legal education, Pension, profit-sharing, and employee benefits, State civil litigation. Home: 2808 Cumberland Ave Waco TX 76707 Office: Baylor U Law Sch Waco TX 76798

WENDT, JOHN ARTHUR FREDERIC, JR., lawyer; b. Cleve.; s. John Arthur Frederic and Martha Ann (Hunter) W.; m. Marjorie Rickard Richardson, Oct. 2, 1962; children: Wendy Wendt Wood, Eric A., John A. F. III, Hilary H.; m. 2d Dorothy Fay Nuttall, Dec. 29, 1976. AB with honors, U. Mich., 1942; JD, U. Colo.-Boulder, 1951. Bar: Colo. 1951, U.S. Dist. Ct. Colo. 1951, U.S. Ct. Appeals (10th cir.) 1957, U.S. Sup. Ct. 1971. Assoc., Tippit, Haskell & Welborn, Denver, 1953-58; ptnr. Wendt & Kistler, Denver, 1958-62; ptnr. Clark & Wendt, Aspen, Colo., 1962-71; ptnr. Wendt Law Offices, Aspen, Colo., 1971-81, Delta, Colo., 1985—; dist. atty. 9th Jud. Dist. Colo., 1965-69; judge Pitkin County, Colo., 1971-78; dist. atty. 7th Jud. Dist. Colo., 1981-85; farmer. Served to maj. U.S. Army, 1942-46, 51-53. Decorated Silver Star, Bronze Star. Mem. Colo. Bar Assn. (gov. 1965-71, 82-85, 87—), Pitkin County Bar Assn. (pres. 1971-72), Delta County Bar Assn. (pres. 1986—), Am. Judicature Soc., Phi Kappa Psi, Phi Delta Phi, Phi Beta Kappa. Republican. Episcopalian. Clubs: U.S. Equestrian Team (chmn. Colo. chpt. 1976-86), Masters of Fox Hounds Assn., M.F.H. Roaring Fork Hounds. Criminal, General corporate, State civil litigation. Address: Lenado Farm Hotchkiss CO 81419 Office: PO Box 94 Delta CO 81416

WENDT, JOHN THOMAS, lawyer, educator; b. Chgo., Mar. 26, 1951; s. William Henry and Virginia (Hauf) W. B.A. summa cum laude in Humanities, U. Minn., 1973, M.A. in Am. Studies, 1981; J.D., William Mitchell, St. Paul, 1977. Bar: Minn., U.S. Dist. Ct. Minn., U.S. Ct. Appeals (8th cir.) 1978. Sole practice, Mpls., 1978—; Hennepin County Ct. arbitrator; instr. U. Minn., Mpls., 1984—, Coll. St. Thomas, St. Paul, 1983—, Lakewood Community Coll., St. Paul, 1983-84; dir. publ. Minn. Continuing Legal Edn., St. Paul, 1982-83. Contbr. articles to profl. jours. Counsel U.S. Aquatics, Inc., Colorado Springs, Colo., 1980—, Gov.'s Task Force on Minn. Sports Festival, Mpls., 1983—, U.S. Amateur Athletic Union, Indpls., 1978-80; bd. govs. U.S. Water Polo, 1983—. Recipient Gov.'s Cert. Commendation for Service, State of Minn., 1984. Mem. ABA (com. sports and entertainment law, chmn. spl. projects, 1982—), Hennepin County Bar Assn. (chmn. sports and entertainment law 1983-86), Minn. State Bar Assn. (legal edn. com.). Home: 1630 S 6th St Minneapolis MN 55454 Office: 219 Oliver Ave S Minneapolis MN 55405

WENTINK, MICHAEL JAMES, army officer, lawyer; b. Oak Park, Ill., Apr. 21, 1944; s. James Theodore and Geraldine Elizabeth (Baynes) W.; m. Frances Mary Basile, Sept. 12, 1970; children: Frank Christopher, Mark Alexander, Michael James. BS in Commerce, DePaul U., 1966, JD, 1969. Bar: Ill. 1969, U.S. Ct. Mil. Appeals 1970, U.S. Supreme Ct. 1976. Commd. Capt. U.S. Army, 1970, advanced through grades to lt. col., 1983; chief mil. affairs and procurement law Office Post Judge Adv., Fort Sam Houston, Tex., 1970-71; action officer Office Staff Judge Adv., Seoul, 1971-72; action officer Office of Judge Adv. Heidelberg, Fed. Republic Germany, 1972-75, dep. chief procurement law, 1975-76; litigation atty. Office Judge Adv. Gen., Washington, 1977-80; chief counsel U.S. Army Contracting Agy.-Europe, Frankfurt, Fed. Republic Germany, 1980-83, U.S. Army Info. Systems Software Support Command, Fort Belvoir, Va., 1983-86; chief Trial Team IV Contract Appeals Div. U.S. Army Legal Services Agy., Falls Church, Va., 1986—. Contbr. articles on standards of conduct to mil. publs. Mem. ABA, Ill. Bar Assn., Fed. Bar Assn. Roman Catholic. Government contracts and claims, Labor, Military. Office: USALSA (JALS-CA) Nassif Bldg 5611 Columbia Pike Falls Church VA 22041-5013

WENTLEY, RICHARD TAYLOR, lawyer; b. Pitts., July 31, 1930; s. Howard Magee and Beatrice (Taylor) W.; m. Jane Francis Garvey, Aug. 18, 1956; children: Richard Taylor, Anne Elizabeth, David William, Christopher James, Jane Margaret. B.A. in Polit. Sci., Bucknell U., 1953; J.D., U. Pitts., 1956. Bar: Pa. 1956, U.S. Ct. Appeals (3d cir.) 1956, U.S. Supreme Ct. 1967. Ptnr. Thorp, Reed & Armstrong, Pitts., 1956-68; judge Ct. Common Pleas of Allegheny County, Pitts., 1968-74; ptnr. firm Reed, Smith, Shaw & McClay, Pitts., 1974—; lectr. ednl. programs U. Pitts. Trustee Winchester Thurston Sch, Pitts.; vestry man Fox Chapel Episopal Ch. Mem. ABA, Pa. Bar Assn., Allegheny County Bar Assn. (lectr. ednl. programs), Acad. Trial Lawyers Allegheny County. Republican. Clubs: Pittsburgh, Pitts. Athletic Assn., Rivers. Home: 221 N Guyasuta Rd Pittsburgh PA 15215 Office: Reed Smith Shaw & McClay James H Reed Bldg 435 6th Ave Pittsburgh PA 15219

WENTWORTH, JOHN, lawyer; b. Albuquerque, Feb. 2, 1945; s. Jack and Manya (Norment) W.; m. Gretchen Dick, Sept. 17, 1977; 1 child, Nicholas. BS, Claremont Mens Coll., 1967; JD, U. N.Mex., 1970. Bar: N.Mex. 1970, U.S. Ct. Appeals (10th cir.) 1970. Law clk. to presiding justice N.Mex. Supreme Ct., Santa Fe, 1970-71; dep. dist. atty. State of N.Mex., Santa Fe, 1971-72; from assoc. to ptnr. Jones, Snead, Wertheim, Rodriguez & Wentworth, P.A., Santa Fe, 1972—. Author: Treatise on New Mexico Rules of Evidence, 1983. Mem. ABA, N.Mex. Bar Assn. (chmn. trial practice sect. 1983), N.Mex. Trial Lawyers Assn. (pres. 1979), Assn. Trial Lawyers Am., Am. Bd. Trial Advs. Federal civil litigation, State civil litigation, Personal injury. Home: 1841 Sun Mountain Dr Santa Fe NM 87505 Office: Jones Gallegos Snead & Wertheim PA 215 Lincoln Ave Santa Fe NM 87501

WENTWORTH, THEODORE SUMNER, lawyer; b. Bklyn., July 18, 1938; s. Theodore Sumner and Alice Ruth (Wortmann) W.; A.A., Am. River Coll., 1958; J.D., U. Calif., Hastings Coll. Law, 1962; m. Sharon Linelle Arkush, Mar. 26, 1965; children—Christina Linn, Kathryn Allison. Admitted to Calif. bar, 1963; asso. Adams, Hunt & Martin, Santa Ana, Calif., 1963-66; partner Hunt, Liljestrom & Wentworth, Santa Ana, 1967-77; pres. Solabs Corp.; chmn. bd., exec. v.p. Plant Warehouse, Inc., Hawaii, 1974-82; prin. Law Offices of Theodore S. Wentworth, specializing in personal injury, product liability and profl. malpractice litigation, Irvine, Calif. Pres., bd. dirs. Santa Ana-Tustin Community Chest, 1972; v.p., trustee South Orange County United Way, 1973-75; pres. Orange County Fedn. Funds, 1972-73; bd. dirs. Orange County Mental Health Assn. Diplomate Nat. Bd. Trial Advocacy. Mem. State Bar Calif., ABA, Orange County Bar Assn. (dir. 1972-76), Am. Trial Lawyers Assn. (judge pro tem superior ct. attys. panel), Calif. Trial Lawyers Assn. (bd. govs. 1968-70), Orange County Trial Lawyers Assn. (pres. 1967-68), Lawyer-Pilots Bar Assn., Am. Bd. Trial Advs., Aircraft Owners and Pilots Assn. Clubs: Bahia Corinthian Yacht, Balboa Bay (Newport Beach, Calif.); Lincoln (Orange County); Corsair Yacht (Catalina, Calif.). Research in vedic prins., natural law, metaphysics. Personal injury. Office: 2112 Business Center Dr Suite 220 Irvine CA 92715

WENZEL, LEE BEY, lawyer; b. Edgeley, N.D., July 1, 1930; s. Russell Henry and Dorothy Kay (Greene) W.; m. Barbara Knoll, Apr. 18, 1953; children—Teresa Zinn, Mark, Neil, Christy Bradford, Dean, Julie Cressman, Lisa Sumner, Kent, Todd. B.S., UCLA, 1952, LL.B., 1957. Calif. 1957, U.S. Dist. Ct. (no., cen. and so. dists.) Calif. 1957, U.S. Supreme Ct. 1966. Dep. city atty. Los Angeles City, 1957-59; assoc. firm Jarrett & Morgan, Los Angeles, 1959-61; ptnr. Morgan, Wenzel & McNicholas, Los Angeles, 1961—. Bd. regents U. Calif., 1979-80. Diplomate Am. Bd. Trial Attys., 1964. Fellow Internat. Acad. Trial Attys.; mem. Am. Coll. Trial Lawyers, UCLA Alumni Assn. (gen. counsel 1971-74, pres. 1978-80). Republican. Roman Catholic. Clubs: Jonathan Wilshire Country. State civil litigation, Federal civil litigation, Personal injury. Home: 9912 Melvin Ave Northridge CA 91324 Office: Morgan Wenzel & McNicholas Suite 800 1545 Wilshire Blvd Los Angeles CA 90017

WENZEL, STEVE EDWIN, lawyer; b. Moose Lake, Minn., Feb. 7, 1951; s. James Keith and Alice Florence (Ruschmeyer) W.; m. Mary Josephine Lee, Apr. 16., 1982; children: Jason, Melissa, Robin, James. Student, Minot (N.D.) State Coll., 1974-76; BS in Polit. Sci., U. Oreg., 1978, JD, 1982. Bar: Nev. 1983, U.S. Dist. Ct. Nev. 1983. Law clk. to presiding judge 2d Jud. Dist. Ct. Nev., Reno, 1982-83; assoc. Echeverria, Osborne & Jenkins, Chartered, Reno, 1984—. Served as sgt. USAF, 1970-73. Mem. ABA, Nev. Bar Assn., Assn. Trial Lawyers Am., Nev. Trial Lawyers Assn. Personal injury, Federal civil litigation, State civil litigation. Office: Echeverria Osborne & Jenkins 555 S Center St Reno NV 89501

WEPRIN, BARRY ALAN, lawyer; b. Bklyn., Sept. 29, 1952; s. Saul and Sylvia (Matz) W.; m. Patricia J. Langer, Sept. 16, 1979, 1 child, Alexander. AB, Harvard U., 1974; M Pub. Adminstrn., Princeton U., 1978; JD, NYU, 1978. Bar: N.Y. 1979, U.S. Dist. Ct. (so. and ea. dists.) N.Y. 1980, U.S. Supreme Ct. 1983. Law clk. to judge U.S. Dist. Ct., Bklyn., 1978-80; assoc. Wachtell, Lipton, Rosen & Katz, N.Y.C., 1980-85; counsel N.Y. State Housing Finance Agy., N.Y.C., 1985—, N.Y. State Med. Care Facilities Finance Agy., N.Y.C., 1985—. Editor NYU Law Rev., 1977-78. Nat. Merit scholar, 1974. Mem. N.Y. State Bar Assn., Assn. of Bar of City of N.Y. Democrat. Municipal bonds, Real property, Legislative. Home: 22 Dimitri Pl Larchmont NY 10538 Office: NY State Housing Fin Agy 3 Park Ave New York NY 10016

WERBER, STEPHEN JAY, counsel, educator; b. N.Y.C., Apr. 20, 1940; s. Murray H. and Teddie Werber; m. Mary Jo Weinberg (dec. June 1965); m. Joan C. Kirsh, June 30, 1968; children: David S., Lauren F. BA, Adelphi U., 1961; JD, Cornell U., 1964; LLM, NYU, 1970. Bar: N.Y. 1965, U.S. Dist. Ct (no. dist.) Ohio 1970, U.S. Supreme Ct. 1970, U.S. Dist. Ct. (so. dist.) Ohio 1980, U.S. Ct. Appeals (6th cir.) 1982. Atty. FCC, Washington, 1964-65; assoc. Sidney G. Hollander, N.Y.C., 1965-66, Herzfeld & Rubin, N.Y.C., 1966-70; asst. prof. law Cleve. State U., 1970-73, assoc. prof.law, 1973-76, prof. law, 1976—; of counsel Guren, Merritt, Feibel, Sogg & Cohen, 1979-84, Weston, Hurd, Fallon, Paisley & Howley, 1984—; asst. dean Cleve. State U., 1973-74. Contbr. numerous articles on product liability to profl jours. bd. dirs. NE Ohio Multiple Sclerosis Soc., Temple Emanu-El (v.p. 1983-85); Bur. Jewish Edn. (former bd. dirs.). Mem. ABA (litigation sect., com. on mfrs. liability), Fed. Bar Assn., Am. Arbitration Assn., Assn. Trial Lawyers Am., Am. Assn. Univ. Profs., N.Y. State Bar Assn., Ohio Bar Assn., Ohio Assn. Civil Trial Lawyers, Scribes. Democrat. Avocations: bridge, golf. Federal civil litigation, State civil litigation, Legal education. Home: 2560 Lafayette Dr University Heights OH 44118

WERNER, ROBERT GEORGE, lawyer; b. Burlington, Colo., June 29, 1944; s. Ronald Leslie and Opal Faye (Tinkum) W.; m. Lucia Henning Heldt, June 8, 1968 (div.); 1 son, Nicholas. A.B. cum laude, Harvard Coll., 1967; J.D., U. Calif., Berkeley, 1970. Bar: Calif. 1971. Assoc. Morrison & Foerster, San Francisco, 1971-74, Hersh & Hersh, San Francisco, 1974-76; sole practice, San Francisco, 1976-79; ptnr. Werner & Allen, San Francisco, 1979—. Mem. ABA, Am. Immigration Lawyers Assn., Calif. Trial Lawyers Assn., Bar Assn. San Francisco, Order of Coif. Editor, Calif. Law Rev., 1968-70; contbr. articles to profl. lit. Immigration, naturalization, and customs, Labor, Personal injury. Home: 1744 Mountain Blvd Oakland CA 94611 Office: 690 Market St Suite 1006 San Francisco CA 94104

WERNICK, KENNETH JONATHAN, lawyer; b. N.Y.C., Sept. 26, 1948; s. Nathaniel and Margaret (Lechner) W.; m. Sharyl Beth Hammer, Aug. 26, 1978. B.A., Bucknell U., 1970; J.D., Washington and Lee U., 1973. Bar: Va. 1973, D.C. 1976, U.S. Dist. Ct. (ea. dist.) Va. 1977, U.S. Dist. Ct. D.C. 1977. Assoc., Farley & Harrington, Fairfax, Va., 1977-79; atty., advisor Office of Info. and Privacy, U.S. Dept Justice, Washington, 1979-82; atty. Office of Gen. Counsel, U.S. Dept. Navy, Washington, 1982—. Elder, Fairlington Presbyn. Ch., 1984. Served to capt. JAGC, U.S. Army, 1973-77. Mem. Am. Soc. Access Profls. Administrative and regulatory, Federal civil litigation. Home: 6932 Essex Ave Springfield VA 22150 Office: Assoc Counsel Naval Sea Systems Command Dept of Navy Washington DC 20362

WERNLE, ROBERT FREDERICK, lawyer; b. Chgo., Nov. 15, 1914; s. Albert E. and Delia (McLeod) W.; m. Mary Griffith Curtis, Nov. 11, 1944; children—Bradford C., Helen A. B.A., Northwestern U., 1937, J.D., 1940. Bar: Ill. 1940, Ind. 1946. Sole practice, Mt. Carroll, Ill., 1941; ptnr. Wernle, Ristine and Ayers, and predecessors, Crawfordsville, Ind., 1946—; dir. emeritus Lincoln Fed. Savs. Bank. General practice. Office: Wernle Ristine et al 414 Ben Hur Bldg Crawfordsville IN 47933

WERTHEIM, JERRY, lawyer; b. Fort Sumner, N.Mex., Oct. 11, 1938; s. Max Wertheim and Helen Nanna; m. Mary Carole May, Aug. 20, 1960; children—Jerry Todd, John Vincent. B.A. with honors, U. N.Mex., 1960; LL.B., Georgetown U., 1964. Bar: N.Mex. 1964, U.S. Supreme Ct. 1981, U.S. Dist. Ct. N.Mex. 1964, U.S. Ct. Appeals (10th cir.) 1965. Asst. atty. gen. N.Mex. Atty. Gen. Office, Santa Fe, 1964-65; sr. ptnr. Jones, Snead, Rodriguez & Wentworth, P.A., Sante Fe, 1965—. Mem. N.Mex Supreme Ct.'s Rules of Evidence Com., 1976—. Recipient award for Outstanding Service to Teaching Profession, N.Mex. NEA, 1975; Cert. Appreciation for Outstanding Service to Judiciary, N.Mex. Supreme Ct., 1982. Mem. N.Mex. State Bar (chmn. adv. opinions com. 1968-76, outstanding service award 1971, 74, 83, 84), Assn. Trial Lawyers Am., N.Mex. Trial Lawyers Assn., ABA, First Jud. Dist. Bar Assn., Am. Bd. Trial Advocates. Democrat. Jewish. Federal civil litigation, State civil litigation. Office: Jones Snead

Wertheim Rodriguez & Wentworth PA PO Box 2228 215 Lincoln Ave Santa Fe NM 87501

WERTHEIM, RONALD P., judge; b. Phila., Sept. 7, 1933; s. Louis B. and Ruth (Gebelein) W.; m. Mitzi Dewey Mallina, Feb. 25, 1965; children—Carter, Christiana. B.S., U. Pa., 1954, J.D., 1957; diploma Hague Acad. Internat. Law, 1962. Bar: Pa. 1958, D.C. 1969. Assoc. Dechert, Price & Rhoads, Phila., 1957-59; pub. defender, Phila., 1959-61; assoc. prof. law U. Va. Sch. Law, Charlottesville, 1961-64; dep. gen. counsel Peace Corps, Washington, 1964-65, dir. Peace Corps, NE Brazil, 1966-68; assoc., then ptnr. Ginsburg, Feldman & Bress, Washington, 1969-79; assoc. judge Superior Ct. of D.C., Washington, 1982—; alt. rep. UN Conf. on Law of Sea, 1977; dir. Def. Dept. Task Force on Law of Sea, 1977; mem. U.S. Merit Systems Protection Bd., 1979-82. Editor-in-chief U. Pa. Law Rev., 1956-57. Trustee Arena Stage, Washington, 1971-81. Judicial administration. Home: 3230 Highland Pl NW Washington DC 20008 Office: Superior Ct 500 Indiana Ave NW Washington DC 20001

WERTHEIMER, SPENCER MILES, lawyer; b. N.Y.C., Oct. 5, 1943; s. Sidney Warren and Frances (Meyer) W.; 1 child, Joshua. BS, U. Pa., 1965; JD, Dickinson Coll., 1968. Bar: Pa. 1968, U.S. Ct. Appeals (3d cir.) 1970, U.S. Supreme Ct. 1973, N.Y. 1985. Ptnr. Bashnan & Wertheimer, Phila., 1972-76; sr. ptnr. Spencer M. Wertheimer & Assocs., Phila., 1977—; counsel Redevel. Authority, Phila., 1972-78, Pa. Senate, Phila., 1974-76. Pres. Phila. Dance Co., 1978—, Historic Rittenhouse, Phila., 1985—; v.p. Phila. Art Alliance, 1984—. Served to 1st lt. U.S. Army, 1970-71. Recipient Nathan Burkan award ASCAP, 1968. Mem. Pa. Bar Assn., Phila. Bar Assn., Assn. Trial Lawyers Am. Democrat. Jewish. Avocations: creative writing, tennis. Personal injury, Entertainment, Criminal. Office: 1324 Walnut St Philadelphia PA 19107

WERTHEIMER, SYDNEY BERNARD, lawyer; b. N.Y.C., Apr. 15, 1914; s. Sydney B. and Edna F. (Leimdorfer) W.; m. Jane B. Celler, Nov. 10, 1938; children: Sue Wertheimer Frank, Jill Wertheimer Rifkin. B.S. in Econs, U. Pa., 1935; LL.B., Harvard U., 1938. Bar: N.Y. 1938, U.S. Customs Ct 1970, U.S. Supreme Ct 1976, D.C. Ct. Appeals 1973. Mem. firm Glass & Lynch, N.Y.C., 1938-39; asst. U.S. atty. So. Dist. N.Y., 1939-42; exec. of subs. Schenley Distillers, N.Y.C., 1946-48; from assoc. to ptnr. Weisman, Celler, Spett, Modlin & Wertheimer, N.Y.C., 1947-83; former dir. Fedders Corp. Author: (with others) The Draft and You, 1940. Bd. dirs. Am. Red Magen David for Israel, 1951—, 1st v.p., 1980—. Served with USN, 1943-45. Mem. Assn. Bar City N.Y. Club: Quaker Ridge Golf (Scarsdale, N.Y.). Probate, Contracts commercial. Home: 5 Normandy Ln Scarsdale NY 10583 Office: 645 Fifth Ave Suite 715 New York NY 10022

WERTZ, JOHN R., lawyer; b. Washington, Jan. 17, 1946; s. John D. and Carol Jean (Manatt) W.; m. Susan Courter, Apr. 18, 1981; children: John Ross Jr., Jamie Lee, Margaret Julia. BS, U. Nebr., 1969, JD, 1972. Ptnr. Sullivan, Cummins, Wertz, McDade, Roberts & Wallace, San Diego, 1973—. Bd. dirs. San Diego Repertory Theatre, 1982—, sec. bd. dirs., 1983-86; bd. dirs. San Diego State U. Hearing and Speech Auxiliary, 1973, v.p., 1973-80; founding bd. dirs. Leadership Found. of San Diego, 1974, bd. dirs., treas., 1974-78, pres., 1976; nat. bd. dirs. Big Bros./Big Sisters Am., 1979-86, gen. counsel to nat. bd. dirs. of San Diego, 1982-84, active big brother, 1972-80, bd. dirs., 1974-83, pres., 1978, 79, v.p. agy. mgmt., 1975, 76; San Diego County Chair Gary Hart's Presdl. Campaign, 1984, 88. Served with U.S. Army, 1969. Mem. ABA, Calif. Bar Assn., Nebr. Bar Assn., San Diego Bar Assn. (chmn. lawyer referral and information service com. 1982, 83, chmn. legal ethics and unlawful practice com. 1979, chmn. advisor on ethics to sr. citizens ctr. com. 1976-77), Assn. Trial Lawyer Am., Calif. Trial Lawyers Assn., San Diego Trial Lawyers Assn. Democrat. Methodist. State civil litigation, Federal civil litigation, General practice. Office: Sullivan Cummins Wertz McDade Roberts & Wallace 1010 2d Ave Suite 2301 San Diego CA 92101

WESCH, CALVIN WALTER, lawyer; b. New Braunfels, Tex., Oct. 21, 1926; s. Hilmar A. and Rosa I. (Haecker) W.; m. Melba L. McCollough, Jan. 10, 1953; children—Sandra Kay Wesch Dare, Cynthia Ann, Katherine Rose; m. 2d, Judy D. Haney, Mar. 2, 1973; 1 dau., Angelia D'an. LL.B., U. Tex.-Austin, 1951. Bar: Tex. 1951, U.S. Dist. Ct. (we., no., and so. dists.) Tex. 1958, U.S. Ct. Appeals (5th cir.) 1958, U.S. Supreme Ct. 1973, N.Mex. 1985, U.S. Dist. Ct. N.Mex. 1985. Sole practice, San Antonio, 1951-55, Kermit, Tex., 1955-78; ptnr. Wesch, Trenchard & Davis, Kermit, 1978-86; sole practice Ruidoso, N.Mex., 1986—; city atty. Kermit, 1957-64; dist. atty. Andrews, Crane and Winkler counties, 1968-77. Served with USN, 1944-46. Mem. Tex. Bar Assn., N.Mex. Bar Assn., Tex. Trial Lawyers Assn., (dir. 1961-64), Winkler County Bar Assn. (pres. 1962-78), Trans Pecos Bar Assn., Am. Legion, VFW. Lutheran. General practice, State civil litigation, Federal civil litigation. Office: PO Box 3482 HS Ruidoso NM 88345

WESIERSKI, CHRISTOPHER PAUL, lawyer; b. Westchester, Calif., Oct. 20, 1953; s. Daniel Richard and Carmen Magdelena (Monge) W.; m. Maureen Dale Harsh, Oct. 22, 1976; children: Ryan, Kristin. AA, Long Beach Community Coll., 1972; BA cum laude, Calif. State U., 1974; JD, U. San Diego, 1978. Bar: Calif. 1979, U.S. Dist. Ct. (no., cen., ea. and so. dists.) 1979, U.S. Ct. Appeals (9th cir.) 1979, U.S. Supreme Ct. 1979. Assoc. Frank M. Moore, Long Beach, Calif., 1978-79, Spray, Gould & Bowers, Los Angeles, 1979-81; prin., assoc. Knapp, Peterson & Clarke, Universal City, Calif., 1981-83; mng. dir. Knapp, Peterson & Clarke, Newport Beach, Calif., 1983—; nat. counsel U.S. Swimming Team, Calif., 1985—. Leader Los Altos br. YMCA, Long Beach, 1975-78; coach little league baseball, Long Beach, 1984. Named one of Outstanding Young Men in Am., 1985. Mem. ABA, Orange County Bar Assn., Los Angeles Bar Assn., Def. Counsel Research Inst., Assn. So. Calif. Def. Counsels. Republican. Roman Catholic. Avocations: volleyball, reading, swimming. Personal injury, State civil litigation, Insurance. Home: 24552 Via Tonada El Toro CA 92630 Office: Knapp Peterson & Clarke 4000 MacArthur #900 Newport Beach CA 92660

WESLEY, HOWARD BARRY, lawyer; b. Murphysboro, Ill., Aug. 26, 1955; s. Samuel Howard and Billie Mae (Nehring) W.; m. Rebecca Anne Hartman, May 24, 1986. BA, So. Ill. U., 1976, JD, 1979; LLM in Tax, U. Fla., 1981. Bar: Ill. 1979, U.S. Tax Ct. 1980, U.S. Dist. Ct. (so. dist.) Ill. 1981. Assoc. Morris & Wesley, Lewistown, Ill., 1979-80; ptnr. Wesley & Erbes, Murphysboro, Ill., 1981—. Mem. ABA (tax sect., agrl. law subcom. 1981—), Ill. State Bar Assn. Democrat. Lutheran. Lodge: Kiwanis. Avocation: fishing. Consumer commercial, Workers' compensation, Personal injury. Office: 1000 Hanson St PO Box 461 Murphysboro IL 62966

WESSEL, PETER, lawyer; b. N.Y.C., Feb. 2, 1952; s. Harry Nathan Jr. and Charlene (Freimuth) W.; m. Bonnie Cohen, Dec. 1, 1985. BS, Syracuse U., 1974, M in Pub. Adminstrn., JD, 1980. Bar: N.Y. 1981, U.S. Dist. Ct. (no., so., ea. and we. dists.) N.Y. 1981, Fla. 1984. Confidential law clk. to presiding justice N.Y. Supreme Ct., Norwich, 1980-82; assoc. John Bonina & Assocs. P.C., N.Y.C., 1982-83; sr. atty. criminal def. div. The Legal Aid Soc., N.Y.C., 1982—; cons. Harcourt Brace Jovanovich Legal & Profl. Publs., Inc., N.Y.C., 1983-84. Notes and comments editor Syracuse Law Rev., 1979-80. Neal Brewster scholar, 1977-78, Syracuse U. Coll. Law scholar 1978-79, endowed scholar Louis Waters Meml., 1979-80, Hiscock, Cowie, Bruce & Lee, 1979-80. Mem. ABA, N.Y. State Bar Assn., Fla. Bar Assn. Criminal, State civil litigation, Federal civil litigation. Office: The Legal Aid Soc Criminal Def Div 15 Park Row New York NY 10038

WESSLING, DONALD MOORE, lawyer; b. Chgo., Nov. 26, 1936; s. Donald Moore and Helen Adele (Stueben) W.; m. Joan Marie Fiore, Sept. 19, 1959 (div. Feb. 1974); children: Elizabeth, Christopher. BS, Northwestern U., 1957, MA, 1958; JD, U. Chgo., 1961. Bar: Calif. 1962, U.S. Supreme Ct. 1965, U.S. Dist. Ct. (no., cen., ea. and so. dists.) Calif., U.S. Ct. Appeals (9th cir.). Assoc. O'Melveny & Myers, Los Angeles, 1961-69, ptnr., 1970—; mem. jud. nominees evaluation commn. Calif. State Bar, 1985, 87. Trustee Ctr. for Law in the Pub. Interest, Los Angeles, 1972—, Los Angeles County Bar Found., 1986—. Mem. State Bar Calif. (commn. judicial nominees evaluation 1987—), Los Angeles Bar Assn. (trustee 1985—). Democrat. Antitrust, Federal civil litigation, State civil litigation. Home: 590 Moreno Ave Los Angeles CA 90049 Office: O'Melveny & Myers 400 S Hope St Los Angeles CA 90071-2899

WESSLING, ROBERT BRUCE, lawyer; b. Chgo., Oct. 8, 1937; s. Robert Euans and Marguerite (Rickert) W.; m. Judith Ann Hanson, Aug. 26, 1961; children: Katherine, Jennifer, Carolyn. BA, DePauw U., 1959; JD, U. Mich., 1962. Bar: Calif. 1963, U.S. Dist. Ct. (cen. dist.) Calif. 1963, U.S. Ct. Appeals (9th cir.) 1965. Assoc. Latham & Watkins, Los Angeles, 1962-70, ptnr., 1970—; bd. govs. Fin. Lawyers Conf., Los Angeles, 1974—. Mem. World Affairs Council, Los Angeles, Town Hall, Los Angeles, Fraternity of Friends, Los Angeles. Mem. ABA, Calif. Bar Assn., Los Angeles Bar Assn., Phi Beta Kappa, Phi Delta Phi, Phi Eta Sigma, Order of Coif. Democrat. Methodist. Avocations: tennis, travel. Bankruptcy, Contracts commercial, Real property. Office: Latham & Watkins 555 S Flower St Los Angeles CA 90071

WEST, CAROL CATHERINE, law librarian, law educator; b. Phila., May 23, 1944; d. Scott G. and Helen (Young) West. B.A., Miss. U. for Women, 1966; M.L.S., U. So. Miss., 1984; J.D., U. Miss., 1970. Pub. services law librarian, U. Va., Charlottesville, 1966-67; catalog law librarian U. Miss., Oxford, 1967-70; legis. reference librarian Miss. Legislature, Jackson, 1970-75; law librarian, prof. law Miss. Coll., Jackson, 1975—. Mem. ABA, Am. Assn. Law Libraries (exec. bd. mem. 1980-82), Miss. State Bar, Miss. Library Assn., Miss. Assn. for Women in Higher Edn. Methodist. Legal education, Librarianship. Office: Miss Coll Sch of Law Law Library 151 E Griffith St Jackson MS 39201

WEST, DAVID CLAY, lawyer; b. Salt Lake City, Aug. 2, 1952; s. David E. and Dixie (Clay) W.; m. Holly Reynolds, Aug. 8, 1975; children: David D., William O., Michael B., Christopher R., Julie D. BS in Acctg., U. Utah, 1975, JD, 1978. Bar: Utah 1978. Assoc. Armstrong, Rawlings & West, Salt Lake City, 1978-84; sole practice Salt Lake City, 1984—; bar exam grader Utah State Bar, Salt Lake City, 1982—, cts. and judges com., 1983-84; mem. rules of practice Utah Jud. Com., Salt Lake City, 1984. County del. Salt Lake City Reps., 1984, voting dist. sec., 1986. Mem. ABA, Utah Bar Assn., Salt Lake County Bar Assn. Republican. Mormon. Avocation: Japanese lang. Real property, Personal injury, Probate. Home: 1156 Alton Way Salt Lake City UT 84108 Office: 1300 Walker Ctr Salt Lake City UT 84111

WEST, GEORGE F(ERDINAND), JR., lawyer; b. Natchez, Miss., Oct. 25, 1940; s. George F. and Artimese West (Morris) W.; m. Billie Guy, June 25, 1966; children—George F., Heath, Jarrod. B.A., Touglaloo Coll., 1962; J.D., So. U., Baton Rouge, 1966; J.D., U. Miss., 1968. Bar: Miss. 1968. Mem. faculty Natchez Jr. Coll., 1967, Alcorn State U., 1969; sole practice, Natchez, 1968—; moderator radio program Fact-Finding, 1969-79; lectr. speaker in field; atty. NAACP, Natchez, 1968—, also legal advisor; atty. Natchez Bus. and Civic League, 1968—, Southwestern Athletic Conf., 1981—; donation and fact finding proctor Natchez Coll.; legal advisor Jefferson County Sch. System; vice chmn. Natchez Pub. Sch. Bd.; pres. Men of Zion singing group; pres. sr. choir Zion A.M.E. Ch., also trustee, Sunday sch. tchr. Recipient lifetime T, Tougaloo Coll., 1962, Achievement award NAACP, 1980; Man of Yr. award Minority Bus. Award, 1981; Man of Yr. award Natchez Bus. and Civic League, 1981; Law award Council Negro Women League, 1982. Mem. Miss. State Bar, Magnolia Bar Assn., Adams County Bar, Assn. Trial Lawyers Am., Miss. Trial Lawyers Assn., Alpha Phi Alpha. Democrat. Methodist. General practice.

WEST, HAROLD, lawyer; b. Bklyn., June 26, 1929. B.A., U. Colo., 1951; LL.B., St. John's U., 1958. Bar: N.Y. 1958, Fla. 1960. Ptnr. West & Lindley (formerly Harold West & Assocs.), Miami, 1963—. Mem. ABA, Dade County Bar Assn., Fla. Bar, Assn. Trial Lawyers Am., Acad. Fla. Trial Lawyers. Insurance, Personal injury. Home: 5424 Jackson St Hollywood FL 33021 Office: 1011 Ives Dairy Rd Suite 210 North Miami Beach FL 33179

WEST, JAMES JOSEPH, lawyer; b. Tarentum, Pa., Nov. 26, 1945; s. Samuel Elwood and Rose (McIntyre) W.; m. Kathleen Geslak, Aug. 19, 1967; children: Joseph Allen, Yvonne Michelle. BS in Econs., St. Vincent Coll., 1967; JD, Duquesne U., 1970. Bar: Pa. 1971, U.S. Dist. Ct. (we. dist.) Pa. 1971, U.S. Ct. Appeals (3d cir.) 1971, U.S. Dist. Ct. (mid. dist.) Pa., 1980. Law clk. to presiding justice U.S. Dist. Ct., Pa., 1970-74; asst. U.S. atty. chief appellate sect. U.S. Atty.'s Office, Pitts., 1974-79; dep. dir. criminal law Pa. Atty. Gen.'s Office, Harrisburg, 1979-82; 1st asst. U.S. atty. U.S. Dist. Ct. (mid. dist.) Pa., Harrisburg, 1982-84, U.S. atty., 1984—. Recipient Outstanding Performance award U.S. Dept. Justice, 1974-78, Commendation Gov. of Pa., 1981. Mem. Pa. Bar Assn., Allegheny County Bar Assn., Dauphin County Bar Assn. Republican. Roman Catholic. Criminal, Government contracts and claims. Home: 519 Lamp Post Ln Camp Hill PA 17011 Office: US Attys Office 3d and Walnut Harrisburg PA 17108

WEST, LAURIE DIANE, lawyer; b. Denver, Aug. 8, 1957; d. David L. and Anita S. (Wolfe) W. Student, Colo. State U., 1974-75; BA, U. Denver, 1978, JD, 1981. Bar: Colo. 1981, U.S. Dist. Ct. Colo. 1981. Dep. pub. defender Colo. Pub. Defenders Office, Ft. Collins, 1981-84; sole practice Ft. Collins, 1984—; chairperson families involved in dependency and neglect cases task force resource devel. 8th Jud. Dist. Colo. Adv. bd. mem. student legal services Colo. State U., Ft. Collins, 1984—; liaison Ft. Collins United Way, 1985—. Mem. ABA, Colo. Bar Assn., Larimer County Bar Assn., Colo. Women's Bar Assn., Larimer County Women's Bar Assn. (program chmn. 1985), Larimer County Criminal Def. Bar Assn., Phi Alpha Delta. Avocation: fishing. Criminal, Family and matrimonial, Juvenile. Office: 416 W Oak St Fort Collins CO 80526

WEST, LEE ROY, judge; b. Clayton, Okla., Nov. 26, 1929; s. Calvin and Nicie (Hill) W.; m. MaryAnn Ellis, Aug. 29, 1952; children: Kimberly Ellis, Jennifer Lee. B.A., U. Okla., 1952, J.D., 1956; LL.M. (Ford Found. fellow), Harvard U., 1963. Bar: Okla. 1956. Individual practice law Ada, Okla., 1956-61, 63-65; faculty U. Okla. Coll. Law, 1961-62; judge 22d Jud. Dist. Okla., Ada, 1965-73; mem. CAB, Washington, 1973-78; acting chmn. CAB, 1977; sole practice law Tulsa, 1978-79; spl. justice Okla. Supreme Ct., 1965; judge U.S. Dist Ct. for Western Dist. Okla., 1979—. Editor: Okla. Law Rev. Served to capt. USMC, 1952-54. Mem. U. Okla. Alumni Assn. (dir.), Phi Delta Phi (pres. 1956), Phi Eta Sigma, Order of Coif. Jurisprudence. Home: 6500 E Danforth Edmond OK 73034 Office: 3001 U S Courthouse Oklahoma City OK 73102

WEST, RICHARD ANGUS, lawyer; b. Boston, Apr. 1, 1955; s. Richard Saltonstall and Ruth (Simonds) W.; m. Elizabeth Conway, Aug. 22, 1981. BA, Harvard U., 1977, JD, 1982. Bar: Mass. 1982. Investment analyst Morgan Guaranty Trust Co., N.Y.C., 1977-79; assoc. Ropes & Gray, Boston, 1982-87; v.p. Parker & West Mgmt., Inc., Boston, 1987—; mem. New Boston Venture Council, 1986—. State del. Mass. Repub. Party, Ipswich, 1986; trustees of the Reservation, Beverly, Mass., 1986. Mem. ABA, Mass. Bar Assn. Clubs: Somerset (Boston); Myopia Hunt (Hamilton, Mass.); Porcellian (Cambridge, Mass.); Harvard of N.Y. Avocations: skiing, windsurfing, sailing, tennis, literature. General corporate, Securities, Banking. Office: Parker & West Mgmt Inc 50 Federal Boston MA 02110

WEST, TOGO DENNIS, JR., lawyer, former government official; b. Winston-Salem, N.C., June 21, 1942; s. Togo Dennis and Evelyn (Carter) W.; m. Gail Estelle Berry, June 18, 1966; children—Tiffany Berry, Hilary Carter. BSEE, Howard U., 1965, JD cum laude, 1968. Bar: D.C. 1968, N.Y. 1969, U.S. Ct. Mil. Appeals 1969, U.S. Supreme Ct. 1978, U.S. Ct. Claims 1981. Elec. engr. Duquesne Light and Power Co., 1965; patent researcher Sughrue, Rothwell, Mion, Zinn and McPeak, 1966-67; legal intern U.S. EEOC, 1967; law clk. firm Covington & Burling, Washington, 1967-68; summer assoc. Covington & Burling, 1968, assoc., 1973-75, 76-77; law clk. to judge U.S. Dist. Ct. for So. Dist. N.Y., 1968-69; assoc. dep. atty. gen. U.S. Dept. Justice, Washington, 1975-76; gen. counsel Dept. Navy, Washington, 1977-79; spl. asst. to sec. and dep. sec. Dept. Def., Washington, 1979-80, gen. counsel, 1980-81; ptnr. Patterson, Belknap, Webb & Tyler, Washington, 1981—; adj. prof. Duke U. Sch. Law, 1980-81. Mng. editor: Howard Law Jour, 1968. Commr. D.C. Law Rev. Comm., 1982—, chmn., 1985—; mem. Nat. Council of Friends of Kennedy Ctr., 1984—, treas., 1987—; bd. govs. Antioch U. Sch. Law, 1983—, vice chmn., 1986-87; co-chmn. Greater Washington Bd. Trade Home Rule Task Force, 1986-87; vestry St. John's Ch., Lafayette Sq.; trustee The Aerospace Corp., 1983—, Ctr. for Strategic and Internat. Studies, 1987—; bd. dirs. D.C. Law Students in Ct. Program, 1986-87. Served to capt. Judge Adv. Gen. Corps U.S. Army, 1969-73. Decorated Legion of Merit; recipient Disting. Pub. Service medal Dept. Def., 1981, Eagle Scout award with Bronze Palm Boy Scouts Am. Mem. ABA, Nat. Bar Assn., Washington Council Lawyers (dir. 1973-75), Phi Alpha Delta, Omega Psi Psi, Alpha Omega. Democrat. Episcopalian. Clubs: Metropolitan, University (Washington). General corporate, Family and matrimonial, Criminal. Office: Patterson Belknap Webb & Tyler 1730 Pennsylvania Ave NW Washington DC 20006

WESTBERG, ROBERT MYERS, lawyer; b. Seattle, July 12, 1932; s. Alfred John and Jean Jackson (Myers) W.; m. Nancy Lyon, June 18, 1955; children: R. Britt, Jennifer J., Catherine C. Student, Princeton U., 1950-53; LL.B., U. Wash., 1956. Bar: Calif. 1957, Wash. 1957, D.C. 1981, N.Y. 1983. Ptnr. Pillsbury, Madison & Sutro, San Francisco, 1957—. Bd. dirs. Legal Aid Soc. San Francisco, 1972—. Mem. State Bar Calif., Wash. State Bar Assn., D.C. Bar Assn. Democrat. Episcopalian. Club: Princeton of N.Y. Office: Pillsbury Madison & Sutro 225 Bush St San Francisco CA 94104

WESTBROOK, GAYLE ROBINSON, lawyer; b. Wheeling, W.Va., May 19, 1947; d. William Francis and Elizabeth Marie (Naylor) Robinson; m. Robert Charles Westbrook, June 12, 1971; children: Shane, Liam, Brittany. BA, U. Denver, 1969; JD, U. Va., 1980. Bar: Ohio 1980, U.S. Dist. Ct. (so. dist.) Ohio 1981. Assoc. atty Vorys, Sater, Seymour & Pease, Columbus, Ohio, 1980-83; gen. counsel Advanced Drainage Systems, Inc., Columbus, 1983—. Mem. ABA, Ohio State Bar Assn., Columbus Bar Assn., Am. Corp. Counsel Assn. (cen. Ohio chpt. treas. 1985, pres. 1986). General corporate, Labor, Real property. Office: Advanced Drainage Systems Inc 3300 Riverside Dr Columbus OH 43221

WESTBROOK, JANE ELIZABETH, lawyer; b. Austin, Minn., June 29, 1952; d. James Curtis and Nancy Lee (Gillam) W. AA, Mesa Coll., 1972; BA, SUNY, Binghamton, 1974; JD, U. Calif., Davis, 1980. Bar: Calif. 1981, U.S. Dist. Ct. (ea. dist.) Calif. 1981, Colo. 1981, U.S. Dist. Ct. Colo. 1981, U.S. Ct. Appeals (10th cir.) 1987. Assoc. Blackmon et al, Sacramento, Calif., 1981; dep. dist. atty. State of Colo., Grand Junction, 1981-83, chief dep. dist. atty., 1983-85; atty. Cen. Bancorp. Inc., Grand Junction, 1985—. bd. dirs. Salvation Army, Grand Junction, 1983-85. Mem. ABA, Colo. Bar Assn., Mesa County Bar Assn., Calif. Bar Assn., Assn. Trial Lawyers Am. Avocations: skiing, sailboarding, reading, swimming, cooking. Banking, Criminal. Office: Cen Bancorp Inc PO Box 608 Grand Junction CO 81502

WESTBROOK, JOEL WHITSITT, III, lawyer; b. San Angelo, Tex., June 19, 1916; s. Lawrence Whittington and Minnie Frances (Millspaugh) W.; m. Elaine Frances Summers, Feb. 13, 1943; 1 son, Jay Lawrence. Student, U. Va., 1934-35; B.A., U. Tex., 1937, J.D., 1940. Bar: Tex. 1940. 1st asst. U.S. Atty., San Antonio, 1946-51; 1st asst. dist. atty. Bexar County, San Antonio, 1951-52; dist. atty. pro tem 1956; practice law San Antonio, 1952-54; partner Trueheart, McMillan, Russell & Westbrook, San Antonio, 1954-61, Jones, Boyd, Westbrook & Lovelace, Waco, Tex., 1962-68, Sheehy, Cureton, Westbrook, Lovelace & Nielsen, Waco, 1968-74, Trueheart, McMillan, Westbrook & Hoffman, San Antonio, 1974-80, Westbrook & Goldston, 1980-81, Westbrook Schroeder & Piker, San Antonio, 1981-84; sole practice San Antonio, 1984—; adj. prof. criminal law, legal ethics and evidence St. Mary's Sch. Law, San Antonio, 1957-61, 74-76; adj. prof. med. malpractice U. Tex. Law Sch., Austin, 1985, 86. Contbr. articles to legal and mil. jours. Chmn. San Antonio Crime Prevention Com., 1954-56; pres. Action Planning Council, Waco, 1966-68; chmn. Waco-McLennan County Mental Health-Mental Retardation Bd. Trustees, 1967-70; pres. adv. bd. Providence Hosp., Waco, 1969-70, Model City com., Waco, 1969-72, chmn., 1971-72. Served to maj., inf. AUS, 1940-46, ETO, MTO. Decorated Combat Inf. badge, Silver Star, Bronze Star, Purple Heart. Fellow Tex. Bar Found. (life sustaining, charter); mem. Waco-McLennan County Bar Assn. (dir. 1963-66), San Antonio Bar Assn. (pres. 1957-58), Tex. Bar Assn. (dir. 1965-68, chmn. com. for local bar services 1968-76, chm. com. for legal services to elderly 1976-79, mem. com. for ct. costs and delay 1980-81, mem. coll. bd. 1981-83, vice chmn. membership relations 1981-83, mem. history and traditions of bar 1983—, chmn. spl. projects), Tex. Assn. Def. Counsel (v.p. 1970-71), U. Tex. Law Sch. Alumni Assn. (dir. 1969-72), Mil. Order World Wars (comdr. San Antonio chpt. 1952-53), Delta Theta Phi, Sigma Alpha Epsilon. Anglican. Clubs: Giraud (San Antonio); Army-Navy (Washington). General practice, Litigation, Military. Home: 7709 Broadway Apt 208 San Antonio TX 78209 Office: One Alamo Ctr Suite 500 San Antonio TX 78205

WESTEN, PETER, legal educator; b. 1943. B.A., Harvard Coll., 1964; J.D., U. Calif.-Berkeley, 1968. Bar: Calif. 1970, D.C. 1971, Mich. 1973. Law clk. to Justice William O. Douglas, U.S. Supreme Ct., 1968-69; fellow Internat. Legal Ctr., 1969-71; assoc. Paul, Weiss, Rifkind, et al, 1971-73; asst. prof. U. Mich., 1973-76, assoc. prof., 1976-78, prof., 1978—. Guggenheim fellow, 1981-82. Mem. Order of Coif. Legal education. Office: U Mich Law Sch Ann Arbor MI 48109 *

WESTER, RURIC HERSCHEL, JR., lawyer; b. Ruskin, Fla., Aug. 9, 1930; s. Ruric Herschel and Mabel Olivia (Curry) W.; m. Joan Hisae Momohira, Oct. 12, 1951; children—Mary, John William, George Warham, Ruric Herschel, Mark, Luke. B.A. cum laude in Polit. Sci., St. Mary's U., San Antonio, 1973; J.D., 1976. Bar: Tex. 1976. Enlisted U.S. Air Force, 1948, served to maj., ret., 1970; owner, operator Fujiya Japanese Restaurant, San Antonio, 1970—; sole practice, Seguin, 1976-79; atty. Lippe & Wester, Seguin, 1979-84; asst. county atty. Guadalupe County, Tex., 1983-84; ptnr. Wester & Roush, Austin, 1984-85, Wester & Wester, Austin, 1985—; instr. polit. sci. St. Mary's U., San Antonio, 1978, bus. law Tex. Lutheran Coll., Seguin, 1980. County chmn. Guadalupe County Republican Party, 1980-84; mem. Seguin Planning Commn., 1983-84; del. Rep. State Conv., Tex., 1972-84, Nat. Conv., 1984. Mem. Tex. Bar Assn. (chmn. dist. subcom. on admissions 1979-85), Conservation Soc. Sequin (bd. dirs. 1965-85), Phi Delta Phi, Pi Gamma Mu. Methodist. Lodges: Lions (bd. dirs. 1976-78), Masons. General practice, Real property, State civil litigation. Home: 1811 E Court St Seguin TX 78155 Office: Wester & Wester 1001 S Interregional Suite 201 Austin TX 78741

WESTERFIELD, FRANK ORLEN, JR., lawyer; b. Albuquerque, Oct. 12, 1924; s. Frank Orlen and Maybelle (Lovelace) W.; m. Mary Louise Harkins, June 1, 1951; children: Kelly S., William R., David T., Mary L., Patrick L., John L. AB, Washington U., St. Louis, 1951; JD, U. N.Mex., 1952; postgrad. in taxation, NYU, 1952-53. Bar: N.Mex. 1953. Assoc. Law Office of John Dwyer, Albuquerque, 1953-59; sole practice Albuquerque, 1959-83; ptnr. Westerfield & Ehlert, Albuquerque, 1983—; mcpl. judge Village of Los Ranchos de Albuquerque, 1966-82. Mem. ABA, N.Mex. State Bar Assn. (bd. dirs. bar commrs. 1970-73, outstanding service award 1974), Albuquerque Bar Assn. (bd. dirs. 1965-67, outstanding service award 1978), Albuquerque Lawyers Club (pres. 1985-86). Corporate taxation, Personal income taxation, Probate. Home: 1300 Kentucky NE Albuquerque NM 87110 Office: Westerfield & Ehlert 733 San Mateo NE Albuquerque NM 87108

WESTERHAUS, DOUGLAS BERNARD, lawyer; b. Marion, Kans., Jan. 11, 1951; s. Edwin Gerard and Bernadine (Ullman) W.; m. Susan Elizabeth Scott, Aug. 20, 1973 (div. Jan. 1979); m. Karen Sue Giersh, Sept. 20, 1980; children: John Joseph, Jamie Lynn, Jeffrey Michael. BSBA, Kans. U., 1973, JD, 1976. Bar: Kans. 1976, U.S. Dist. Kans. 1976, U.S. SUpreme Ct. 1980. Assoc. Harper & Hornbaker, Junction City, Kans., 1976-78; ptnr. Harper & Hornbaker, Junction City, 1978-80; ptnr. Westerhaus Law Office, Marion, Kans., 1980-83, prin., 1983-86; pres. Hydrogen Energy Corp., 1986—, also bd. dirs.; atty. City of Grandview Plaza, Kans. 1977-80, City of Lehigh, Kans. 1980-86, Marion County, 1981-85; gen. counsel The Hydrogen Energy Corp., Kansas City, Mo. 1984-86, Marion Die & Fixture, 1980-86. Bd. dirs. St. Luke's Hosp., Marion, 1985-86. Mem. ABA, Kans. Bar Assn. (chmn. bd. 1979084, Outstanding Service award 1984), Cen. Kans. Bar Assn., Marion County Bar Assn. (pres. 1985), Kans. Trial Lawyers Assn. Republican. Roman Catholic. General practice, General corporate. Home: 11932 Goodman Overland Park KS 66213 Office: 6030 Connecticut Kansas City KS 67120

WESTERMAN, SUSAN S., lawyer; b. Lansing, Mich., Aug. 6, 1943; d. Howard C. and Cora A. (Walcutt) Swartz; m. Peter F. Westerman, Dec. 30, 1967. B.A. cum laude, Mich. State U., 1964; J.D., U. Mich., 1970. Bar: Mich. 1970, U.S. Dist. Ct., Mich. 1974, U.S. Tax Ct. 1978. Assoc. Hooper, Hathaway, Fichera, Price and Davis, Ann Arbor, Mich., 1970-74, Dykema,

Gossett, Spencer, Goodnow and Trigg, Detroit, 1974-79; ptnr. Dobson, Griffin and Westerman, P.C., Ann Arbor, 1979-85, Stein, Moran & Westerman, Ann Arbor, 1985—; past mem. taxation council State Bar Mich. Trustee, pres. Ann Arbor Area Found. Mem. State Bar Mich. (chmn. probate and estate planning sect. 1985-86), Mich. Bar Assn., Washtenaw County Bar Assn., Am. Coll. Probate Counsel, ABA, Washtenaw County Estate Planning Council (pres. 1979), Catherine McAuley Health Ctr. Devel. Council. Club: Barton Hills Country. Probate, Estate planning, General corporate. Office: Stein Moran and Westerman PC 320 N Main St Ann Arbor MI 48104

WESTERMEIER, JOHN THOMAS, JR., lawyer, educator; b. West Point, N.Y., Sept. 14, 1941; s. John Thomas and Louise (Melick) W.; m. Joddie Lynn Stephens, Feb. 8, 1964 (div. Dec. 1966); 1 child, Blake Lynn; m. Cynthia Ann Heins, Aug. 23, 1980. BS, U.S. Mil. Acad., 1963; MBA, George Washington U., 1969, LLM, 1978; JD, Am. U., 1974; cert. in data processing, Inst. for Cert. of Computer Profls., 1978. Bar: Va. 1974, D.C. 1975, U.S. Supreme Ct. 1978, Md. 1982, U.S. Dist. Ct. D.C. 1982, U.S. Dist. Ct. (ea. dist.) Va. 1983. Commd. 2d lt. U.S. Army, 1963; advanced through grades to maj. U.S. Army, Vietnam, 1966, 70; resigned U.S. Army, 1974; assoc. Arent, Fox, Kintner, Plotkin & Kahn, Washington, 1974-79; ptnr. Abrams, Westermeier & Goldberg P.C., Washington, 1980—; adj. prof. law Am. U., Washington, 1985—; bd. advisors Computer Negotiations, Orlando, Fla., 1982—, Computer Law Strategist, N.Y.C., 1985—. Author and editor: Data Processing and the Law, 1981, Computer Law Case Materials, 1985; articles editor Am. U. Law Rev., 1973; legal editor Information Strategy: The Executive's Jour., 1984— (bd. advisors 1984—); contbr. over 50 articles to profl. jours. Bd. advisors No. Va. Hotline, Arlington, 1975-78; del. Va. Rep. Conv., Virginia Beach, 1985. Served to col. USAR, 1974—. Decorated 2 Bronze Stars, Vietnamese Cross of Gallantry. Mem. ABA (chmn. com. of professionalism and malpractice of computer specialists computer law div. 1978—), D.C. Bar Assn. (instr. continuing legal edn., steering com. computer law div. 1986), Data Processing Mgmt. Assn. Washington (pres. 1982-82), D.C. Computer Law Forum (bd. dirs. 1984), Phi Alpha Delta. Republican. Episcopalian. Club: West Point Soc. (Washington) (bd. govs., sec. 1974-82). Avocations: tennis, golf, swimming, writing. Computer, General corporate. Home: 7525 Wilderness Way Fairfax Station VA 22039 Office: Abrams Westermeier & Goldberg PC 1828 L St NW Suite 660 Washington DC 20036

WESTFALL, DAVID, educator, lawyer; b. Columbia, Mo., Apr. 16, 1927; s. Wilhelmus David A. and Ruth (Rollins) W.; m. Elizabeth Putnam Beatty; children: Elizabeth Stewart, William Beatty, Thomas Curwen, Katharine Putnam. AB, U. Mo., 1947; LLB magna cum laude, Harvard U., 1950. Bar: Ill. 1950, Mass. 1956. Assoc. Bell, Boyd, Marshall & Lloyd, Chgo., 1950-55; asst. prof. law Harvard Law Sch., 1955-58, prof., 1958—, John L. Gray prof., 1983—. Author: Estate Planning Cases and Text, 1981, Estate Planning Law and Taxation, 1982; co-author: (part 21): American Law of Property, 1952, Every Woman's Guide to Financial Planning, 1984; co-editor: Readings in Federal Taxation, 1983. Served as 1st lt. JAGC, AUS, 1951-53. Fellow Am. Coll. Probate Counsel (acad.); mem. ABA, Mass. Bar Assn., Am. Law Inst., Phi Beta Kappa, Phi Delta Theta. Estate planning, Family and matrimonial, Labor. Home: 106 Kendall Rd Lexington MA 02173

WESTFALL, GEORGE MICHAEL, lawyer; b. Jerome, Idaho, July 11, 1954; s. George Edward and Barbara (Baker) W.; m. Karen Raye Bakken, June 29, 1979; children: Benjamin Michael, Amanda Kay. BS magna cum laude, Brigham Young U., 1978, JD, 1981. Bar: Utah 1981, U.S. Dist. Ct. Utah 1981. Assoc. Galliane & Westfall, St. George, Utah, 1981-84; ptnr. Gallian & Westfall, St. George, Utah, 1984—. Mem. ABA, Assn. Trial Lawyers Am., Utah Bar Assn., 5th Dist. Bar Assn., U.S. Amateur Dancers Assn. (Nat. Ballroom Champion 1985). Republican. Mormon. Avocations: dance, team sports. State civil litigation, Criminal, Personal injury. Home: 1605 W Village Rd A-10 Saint George UT 84770 Office: Gallian & Westfall 5 Main St PO Box 367 Saint George UT 84770

WESTHEIMER, STEPHEN JAMES, lawyer; b. Kansas City, May 27, 1941; s. Norman F. and Rhea R. Westheimer. BA, U. Mo., 1966; JD, Boston Coll., 1980. Bar: N.Mex. 1980, U.S. Dist. Ct. N.Mex., U.S. Ct. Appeals (10th cir.). Asst. atty. gen. State of N.Mex., Santa Fe, 1980-83, dep. atty. gen., 1984—; mem. rules of evidence com. N.Mex. Supreme Ct., Santa Fe, 1983—; spl. asst. U.S. Atty., N.Mex., 1985-86. Mem. ABA, N.Mex. Bar Assn. Criminal. Home: Rt 4 Box 57B Santa Fe NM 87501 Office: Office of Atty Gen PO Drawer 1508 Santa Fe NM 87504

WESTIN, DAVID LAWRENCE, lawyer; b. Flint, Mich., July 29, 1952; s. Lawrence Rae and Mary Louise (Holman) W.; m. Martha Ann Stubbins, Dec. 28, 1973; children: Victoria, Elizabeth. BA, U. Mich., 1974, JD, 1977. Bar: D.C. 1979. Law clk. to presiding justice U.S. Ct. Appeals (2d cir.), N.Y.C., 1977-78, U.S. Supreme Ct., Washington, 1979; assoc. Wilmer, Cutler & Pickering, Washington, 1979-84, ptnr., 1985—; lectr. Harvard U. Law Sch., Cambridge, Mass., 1986. Mem. visitors com. U. Mich. Law Sch., Ann Arbor, Mich., 1985—. Mem. ABA, Internat. Bar Assn. Democrat. Presbyterian. Club: Chevy Chase (Md.). Private international, Antitrust. Home: 6807 East Ave Chevy Chase MD 20815 Office: Wilmer Cutler & Pickering 2445 M St NW Washington DC 20037-1420

WESTLAND, JOHN ALDEN, lawyer; b. Spokane, Wash., Oct. 5, 1922; s. John A. and Lillian (Truscott) W.; m. Janet M. Lukaszeski, Mar. 2, 1944; children—Jania M., John Alden III, David M., James T., Daniel J. J.D., Gonzaga U., 1953. Bar: Wash. 1953, U.S. Dist. Ct. (ea. dist.) Wash. 1957, U.S. Ct. Appeals (9th cir.) 1958, U.S. Supreme Ct. 1983, U.S. Ct. Claims, 1985. Law clk. Wash. State Supreme Ct., 1953-54; ptnr. Day & Westland, Kennewick, Wash., 1954-57; Powell, Loney & Westland, Kennewick, 1957-59; Westland, Liebler, Ivey, Larsen & Quigley and predecessors, Kennewick, 1959—; dir. Tri-Cities Savs. & Loan Assn. Bd. dirs. Tri-Cities C. of C., 1983-85, Southeastern Wash. Devel. Assn., 1984—. Served to capt. USMC, 1942-46. Decorated Air medal. Mem. ABA, Wash. State Bar Assn., Benton-Franklin Counties Bar Assn. (pres. 1966-67). General practice, Personal injury, Probate. Office: PO Box 6125 Kennewick WA 99336

WESTMORELAND, KENT EWING, lawyer; b. Tulsa, May 17, 1949; s. Earl E. and Adeline (Burckhalter) W.; m. Mary Kathleen Price, June 14, 1981. B.B.A., So. Meth. U., 1971; J.D., U. Tex., 1975. Bar: Tex. 1975, U.S. Dist. Ct. (so. dist.) Tex. 1976, U.S. Dist. Ct. (ea. dist.) Tex. 1977, U.S. Ct. Appeals (5th cir.) 1977, U.S. Ct. Appeals (11th cir.) 1982, U.S. Dist. Ct. (no. dist.) Tex. 1984, U.S. Supreme Ct. 1985; cert. Tex. Bd. Legal Specialization, Civil Trial Law, Personal Injury Trial Law. Atty., Kronzer, Abraham & Watkins, Houston, 1975-76, Eastham, Watson, Dale & Forney, Houston, 1976-79, Ross, Griggs & Harrison, Houston, 1979—. Served with USNR, 1972-78. Mem. Maritime Law Assn. U.S. (proctor 1977), Tex. Assn. Def. Lawyers. Republican. Presbyterian. Clubs: Heritage, Metropolitan Racquet, Sweetwater Country (Houston). Admiralty, Federal civil litigation, State civil litigation. Home: 4 Town Oaks Pl Bellaire TX 77401 Office: Ross Griggs & Harrison 2800 Four Allen Ctr 1400 Smith St Houston TX 77002

WESTON, JOHN KERRY, lawyer; b. Dover-Foxcroft, Maine, July 31, 1952; s. John Colby and Jean Carol (Tourtillotte) W.; m. Marian Gambitsky, Apr. 7, 1979; 1 child, Katherine Dorothy. BA, Pa. State U., 1974; JD, Ohio State U., 1977. Bar: Pa. 1977, U.S. Dist. Ct. (ea. dist.) Pa. 1978. Sole practice Norristown, Pa., 1978-81; assoc. McCarthy & Hutchinson, Norristown, 1981-82; ptnr. McCarthy, Loughran, Hutchinson & Weston, Norristown, 1982-84; assoc. Sacks, Basch, Brodie & Sacks, Phila., 1984—. Mem. ABA, Pa. Bar Assn., Phila. Bar Assn. Avocations: firearms, sailing. Personal injury, State civil litigation, Federal civil litigation. Office: Sacks Basch Brodie & Sacks 210 W Washington Sq Philadelphia PA 19106

WESTON, KENNETH FREDERICK, lawyer; b. Chgo., Jan. 11, 1945; s. John Frederick and June (Sherman) W.; m. Elaina Santy, Mar. 31, 1973 (div. May 1978). BA, U. Calif., Santa Barbara, 1967, MA, 1972; JD, Southwestern U. Sch. Law, 1978. Bar: Calif. 1979, U.S. Dist. Ct. (cen. dist.) Calif. 1979, U.S. Dist. Ct. (so. dist.) Calif. 1984. Sole practice Los Angeles, 1979-82, 85—; assoc. Polston, Schwartz, Hamilton and Fenster, Los Angeles, 1982-85; instr. paralegal program Mission Coll., Los Angeles, 1983—; judge pro-tem Los Angeles Mcpl. Ct., 1985-86. Mem. ABA, Los Angeles County Bar Assn. (Bankruptcy sect., vice chmn. arbitration panel 1984-85), Assn. Trial Lawyers Am., Los Angeles Trial Lawyers Assn., Bankruptcy Study Group. Democrat. Avocations: guitar, poetry. State civil litigation, Bankruptcy, Family and matrimonial. Home: 230 Dimmick Ave Venice CA 90291 Office: 5455 Wilshire Blvd Suite 1012 Los Angeles CA 90036

WESTON, R. TIMOTHY, lawyer, government adminstrator; b. Los Angeles, Oct. 9, 1947; s. Robert Freidell and Thelma U. (Prince) W.; m. Mary T. Webber, May 3, 1986. BA, U. Calif., Santa Barbara, 1969; JD, Harvard U., 1972. Bar: Pa., U.S. Dist. Ct. (ea. dist.) Pa., U.S. Ct. Appeals (3d cir.), U.S. Supreme Ct. Asst. atty. gen. Pa. Dept. Environ. Resources, Harrisburg, 1972-79; bd. dirs. Interstate Conf. on Water Policy, Washington, chmn. 1984-85. Author: Public Rights in Pa. Waters, 1976, Ground Water Law in Pa., 1976; contbr. articles to profl. jours. Commr. Del. River Basin Commn., Trenton, N.J., 1979-87, Susquehanna River Basin commn., Harrisburg, Pa., 1980-87, Ohio River Basin Commn., Lexington, Ky., 1979-87, Great Lakes Commn., Ann Arbor, Mich., 1987—. Mem. ABA, Am. Water Resources Assn. Democrat. Avocations: bicycling, photography, model trains. Environment, Administrative and regulatory, FERC practice. Home: 2926 N Second St Harrisburg PA 17110 Office: Kirkpatrick & Lockhart 240 N 3d St Harrisburg PA 17101

WESTON, STEPHEN BURNS, lawyer; b. Yellow Springs, Ohio, May 4, 1904; s. Stephen F. and Nellie (Phinney) W.; m. Simonne Humphrey; children: Burns H., Monique Weston Clague. A.B., Antioch Coll., Yellow Springs, 1925; postgrad., Sorbonne U., Paris, 1925-26; LL.B., Yale U., 1929; LL.D. (hon.), Cleve. Marshall Law Sch., 1969. Bar: Ohio 1930, U.S. Supreme Ct. 1957, N.Y. State 1976, U.S. Dist. Ct. (no. dist.) Ohio, U.S. Ct. Appeals (6th cir.). Assoc. Thompson, Hine & Flory, Cleve., 1929-1935; Ohio adminstr. Nat. Youth Adminstrn., 1935-40; exec. dir., acting chmn. nat. adv. com. Nat. Youth Adminstrn., Washington, 1940-42; exec. sec. U.S. sect. Anglo-Am. Caribbean Commn., Dept. State, also acting chief Caribbean office, 1942-44; exec. dir. Postwar Planning Council, Met. Cleve. Devel. Council, 1944-46; sr. partner firm Weston, Hurd, Fallon, Paisley & Howley, Cleve., until 1976; now individual practice law Keene, N.Y.; mem. N.Y. State Gov's. Exec. Adv. Com. on Sentencing, 1977-79. Contbr. to: Trial Practice Manual of Ohio Legal Center, Ohio Bar Assn., 1965; also articles to profl. jours. Mem. citizens adv. com. Justice Center, Cleve., 1970-75; past trustee, chmn. bd. trustees Antioch Coll., mem. interim bd. govs.; trustee Keene Valley (N.Y.) Neighborhood Services, Inc.; mem. Keene Vol. Fire Dept.; chmn. Keene Fire Commn., 1984-86. Recipient award for outstanding pub. service League Young Democratic Clubs of Ohio, 1936-38, George W. Yancey Meml. award Internat. Assn. Ins. Counsel, 1963, Brother's Keeper award Jewish Community Fedn. Cleve., 1968. Fellow Am. Coll. Trial Lawyers (past com. chmn.); mem. Bar Assn. Greater Cleve. (Common Pleas Ct., Docket Conf. 1951-53, chmn. jud. candidates and campaign 1955-57, chmn. trial com. for disciplinary action 1956-60, fed. ct. com. 1957-58, 65-66, joint med. and legal com. 1966-67, hdqrs. location com. 1967-68, trustee 1961-64, pres. 1968-69, chmn. com. on sentencing procedures 1975), ABA (past chmn. legis. com., mem. products, gen. liability and consumer law com. sect. of ins., negligence and compensation law), N.Y. State Bar Assn., Ohio Bar Assn. (past mem. clients security fund com. 1974-75), Essex County (N.Y.) Bar Assn., Internat. Assn. Def. Counsel (past mem. exec. com., com. chmn.), Cleve. Def. Attys. Group (past chmn.), Sixth Circuit Jud. Conf. (life), Essex County Hist. Soc. (trustee, pres. 1976-79), Yale Law Sch. Assn. (alumni exec. com. 1975-80, bd. dirs. Yale Law Sch. Fund, mem. bequest com.). Democrat. Clubs: Adirondack Mountain; Philos. (Cleve.) (past pres.), Rowfant (Cleve.) (pres. 1973-74). Probate, Real property, General practice. Home and Office: West-on-East Keene NY 12942

WESTON, THEODORA WHITE, lawyer; b. Chgo., Dec. 31, 1955; d. Johnny Frank and Juanita Jane Ellen (Garth) White; m. M. Weston (div.); children: Qisha Marie, Jamel Roman. BS, Ill. State U., 1976; JD, St. Louis U., 1981. Bar: Ill. 1981, U.S. Ct. Appeals (7th cir.) 1981, Mo. 1982, U.S. Dist. Ct. (ea. dist.) Mo. 1982, U.S. Ct. Appeals, 8th cir.) 1982, U.S. Tax Ct. 1983. Sole practice St. Louis, 1982—. Mem. ABA, Am. Arbitration Assn., Chgo. Bar Assn., Mound City Bar Assn. (treas., co-chairperson joint com. of Met. Bar Assn. and Mound City Bar Assn.'s St. Louis courthand book com. 1985—), Phi Alpha Delta. Avocations: chess, cooking. Federal civil litigation, State and local taxation, Personal injury. Office: 1221 Locust Suite 1017 Saint Louis MO 63103

WESTPHAL, MARJORIE LORD, lawyer; b. Erie, Pa., July 24, 1940; d. Thomas and Dorothy (Hofft) Lord; m. David Melvin Zurn, Sept. 2, 1960 (div. Sept. 1970); children: Rena, Amelie Susan, Christopher F.; m. Lester Roy Westphal, May 26, 1971. Student, Brown U., 1958-60; BS, Gannon U., 1974; JD, Case Western Res. U., 1978. Bar: Ohio 1979. Assoc. Kohrman, Jackson, Weiss, Cleve., 1980-81; sole practice Cleve., 1981—. Trustee Emma Willard Sch., Troy, N.Y., 1978-80; dir. Ohioans for Merit Selection of Judges, Cuyahoga County, 1981; vol., mem. Lawyers for the Arts; mem. Citizen's League of Cleve., Women's City Club. Mem. ABA, Ohio Bar Assn., Cleve. Bar Assn., Cleve. Women's Bar Assn, Pi Gamma Mu. Club: Cleve. Skating. Avocations: swimming, the arts. Probate, Personal income taxation, General corporate. Office: 1604 Illuminating Bldg 55 Public Sq Cleveland OH 44113

WESTWOOD, JAMES NICHOLSON, lawyer; b. Portland, Oreg., Dec. 3, 1944; s. Frederick Alton and Catherine (Nicholson) W.; m. Janet Sue Butler, Feb. 23, 1980; children: Laura, David. BA, Portland State U., 1967; JD, Columbia U., 1974. Bar: Oreg. 1974, U.S. Dist. Ct. Oreg. 1974, U.S. Ct. Appeals (9th cir.) 1978, U.S. Supreme Ct. 1981, U.S. Ct. Appeals (fed. cir.) 1984. Assoc. Miller, Anderson, Nash, Yerke & Wiener, Portland, 1974-76, 78-81; asst. to pres. Portland State U., 1976-78; ptnr. Miller, Nash, Wiener, Hager & Carlsen, Portland, 1981—. Recipient Disting. Service award Portland State U. Found., 1984. Mem. ABA (vice chmn. forest resources com. 1985-87, chmn. 1987—), Oreg. Bar Assn. Republican. Unitarian. Clubs: University, City (Portland) (bd. govs. 1983-84). State civil litigation, Federal civil litigation, Government contracts and claims. Home: 3014 NE 32d Ave Portland OR 97212 Office: Miller Nash Wiener Hager & Carlsen 111 SW 5th Ave Portland OR 97204

WETHERELL, MIKE, lawyer; b. Redding, Calif., Mar. 2, 1945; s. Robert Miles and Rose Claire (Hart) W.; m. Karen Landsdown Mackenzie, Aug. 16, 1969; children: Kelly Mackenzie, Kristen Michelle, Katherine Marie. BS in Edn., U. Idaho, 1967; JD, George Washington U., 1972. Bar: Idaho 1972, U.S. Dist. Ct. Idaho 1978, U.S. Ct. Appeals (9th cir.) 1984. Legis. counsel Senator Frank Church, Washington, 1972-74, chief legal counsel, 1974-76, adminstrv. asst., 1974-76; assoc. Martin, Chapman & Hyde, Boise, Idaho, 1978-82; ptnr. Hyde & Wetherell, Boise, 1982-84, Hyde, Wetherell, Bray & Haff, Boise, 1984—. Editor Idaho Trial Lawyers mag., 1979-85. Candidate for Idaho atty. gen., 1978; mem. Boise City Council, 1986—; pres. Idaho Epilepsy League, 1978-80; regional dir. Epilepsy Found. Am., Washington, 1981-87. Mem. Idaho Bar Assn. (Outstanding Service to Handicapped award 1980), Boise Bar Assn., Idaho Trial Lawyers Assn. (regional dir. 1985). Democrat. Roman Catholic. Lodge: Kiwanis (pres. 1984-85). Avocations: fishing, sailing. Personal injury, State civil litigation, Family and matrimonial. Home: 1292 Candleridge Dr Boise ID 83705 Office: Hyde Wetherell Bray & Haff 1004 W Font St Boise ID 83701

WETMORE, KEITH CHIDESTER, lawyer; b. Valparaiso, Ind., Oct. 17, 1956; s. Leonard Leander and Dorisann (Chidester) W. BA, Northwestern U., 1977; JD magna cum laude, U. Mich., 1980. Bar: Calif. 1981, U.S. Dist. Ct. (no. dist.) Calif. 1981. Law clk. to presiding justice U.S. Ct. Appeals (2d cir.), 1980-81; assoc. Steinhart & Falconer, San Francisco, 1981-82; assoc. Morrison & Foerster, San Francisco, 1982-86, ptnr., 1986—. Articles editor U. Mich. Law Rev. 1980-81. Mem. ABA, Calif. Bar Assn., Bay Area Lawyers for Individual Freedom, San Francisco Bar Assn. Methodist. Contracts commercial, Bankruptcy, General corporate. Home: 17 Liberty St San Francisco CA 94110 Office: Morrison & Foerster 345 California St San Francisco CA 94104

WETTLAUFER, KARL FREDERICK, judge; b. Cleveland Heights, Ohio, May 31, 1936; s. George LeRoy and Jessie R. Wettlaufer; m. Eleanor B. Wettlaufer, Apr. 4, 1964. A.B., Colgate U., 1958; J.D., U. Mich., 1961. Bar: Ohio 1961. Sole practice, Fairborn, Ohio, 1965-66, Painesville, Ohio, 1966-67, Dayton Ohio, 1968-77; referee Montgomery County Ct. Domestic Relations, 1969-74; judge Fairborn (Ohio) Mcpl. Ct., 1978—. Mem. Community Mental Health Bd., Green County, Ohio. Served to capt. USAF, 1962-65. Mem. ABA, Ohio Bar Assn., Greene Country Bar Assn., Assn. Trial Lawyers Am., Am. Judges Assn., Ohio Mcpl. Judges Assn., Am. Legion. Clubs: Rotary, Eagles (Fairborn, Ohio). Family and matrimonial, Criminal, Personal injury. Home: 1564 Southlawn Dr Fairborn OH 45324 Office: 16 S Pleasant Ave Fairborn OH 45324

WETZEL, VOLKER KNOPPKE, judicial educator; B.A., Wayne State U., 1966; M.A., Goethe U., Franfurt, Fed. Republic Germany, 1967; LL.D., U. Wis.-Madison, 1971. Bar: Wis. 1971, U.S. Dist. Ct. Wis. 1971, U.S. Supreme Ct. 1971. Asst. prof. law U. Wis.-Madison, 1971-74; vis. prof. law Bielefeld U., Fed. Republic Germany, 1974-76; dir. criminal justice U. West Fla., Pensacola, 1976-77; assoc. prof. law Vt. Law Sch., Royalton, 1977-81; dir. jud. edn. Wis. Supreme Ct., Madison, 1981—; cons. German Ministry Justice, Bonn, 1977—. Author: Defense of Criminal Cases in Wisconsin, 1974. Co-editor: Wis. Jud. Benchbooks, 1982. Contbr. articles to profl. jours. Bd. dirs. Ctr. for Comparative Law and Social Scis., Madison, 1982—. Russell Sage fellow, 1967-69; NEH fellow, 1980. Mem. Wis. Bar Assn., Internat. Sociol. Assn., Sociology of Law Research Com. Legal education, Judicial administration, Public international. Address: Dir Judicial Edn Wis Supreme Ct 110 E Main St Madison WI 53703

WEWER, WILLIAM, lawyer; b. San Diego, May 27, 1947; s. William P. and Helen E. (Helm) Wewer. BA with honors, Pomona Coll., 1970; JD with high honors, George Washington U., 1977. Bar: D.C. 1977, U.S. Ct. Appeals (D.C. cir.) 1977, Calif. 1980, U.S. Ct. Appeals (9th cir.) 1980, U.S. Dist. Ct. D.C. 1981, U.S. Dist. Ct. (no. dist.) Calif. 1982, U.S. Supreme Ct. 1982. Legisl. asst. U.S. Senator Howard W. Cannon, Washington, 1970-74; profl. staff mem. Rules Com. U.S. Senate, Washington, 1974-77; assoc. Sutherland, Asbill & Brennan, Washington, 1977-79; ptnr. Wewer & Mann, P.C., Washington, 1979-83; sole practice Washington and Newport Beach, Calif., 1983—; cons. various candidates nationwide, 1966-76. Contbr. articles to profl. jours. Bd. dirs. Am. Tax Reduction Movement, Los Angeles, 1980—, various non-profit groups nationwide; bd. dirs., sec. Subscription TV Assn., Washington, 1979-83, Nat. Com. to preserve Social Security, Washington, 1982—. Mem. ABA. Democrat. Non-profit organizations, Administrative and regulatory, Legislative. Home: 11 E Irving St Chevy Chase MD 20815 Office: 1300 19th St NW Suite 501 Washington DC 20036 Office: 1900 Quail St Newport Beach CA 92660

WEXLER, BARBARA LYNNE, lawyer; b. Boston, Feb. 14, 1952; d. Sidney Abraham and Sylvia Dorothy (Finkelstein) W. BS, U. Mass., 1973; JD, Suffolk U., 1977. Bar: Mass. 1977, U.S. Dist. Ct. Mass. 1978, D.C. 1980, U.S. Ct. Appeals (1st cir.) 1982. Asst. dist. atty. Norfolk County, Dedham, Mass., 1977-78; asst. regional counsel Dept. Pub. Welfare, New Bedford, Mass., 1978-80; asst. gen. counsel Dept. Pub. Welfare, Boston, 1980—. Trustee Pond Ln. Condominium Trust, Arlington, Mass., 1984—. Mem. ABA, Mass. Bar Assn., Women's Bar Assn., Mass. Assn. Women Lawyers. Democrat. Jewish. Avocations: quilting, reading, softball. Administrative and regulatory, State civil litigation, Probate. Home: 12 Pond Ln 22 Arlington MA 02174 Office: Dept Pub Welfare 180 Tremont St Boston MA 02111

WEXLER, CHARLES W., JR., lawyer; b. Wildsville, La., Apr. 25, 1931; s. Charles W. Sr. and Addie (LeBlanc) W.; married, June 24, 1967; 1 child Laura Raquel. BA, Tex. So. U., 1950; JD, U. Mich., 1953; postgrad., Columbia U., 1978. Bar: Mich. 1954, N.Y. 1970, Tex. 1974. Assoc., ptnr. Taylor, Bailer, Patrick & Wexler, Detroit, 1956-64; atty. Chrysler Corp., Highland Park, Mich., 1965-69; asst. sec. Consol. Edison Co., N.Y.C., 1970-73; dir. counsel, sec. Exxon Gas System Inc., Houston, 1976-77; counsel Esso Eastern Inc., Houston, 1978-81, Exxon Co. U.S.A., Houston, 1974-76, 81—. Spl. asst. Atty. Gen. Mich., Detroit, 1962-64; arbitrator Civil Ct. N.Y., 1972. Served to cpl. U.S. Army, 1953-55. Mem. ABA, Mich. State Bar Assn., State Bar Tex., Houston Bar Assn., Tex. So. U. Alumni Assn. (nat. pres. 1978-81). Roman Catholic. Avocations: fishing, boating. Construction, Private international, Public utilities. Home: 1719 Prairie Mark Houston TX 77077

WEXLER, LEONARD D., judge; b. Bklyn., Nov. 11, 1924; s. Jacob and Bessie (Herman) W.; m. Barbara Blum, Mar., 1953; children: Allison Wexler Levine, Robert, William. B.S., Ind. U., 1947; J.D., NYU, 1950. Bar: N.Y. 1983, U.S. Dist. Ct. (ea. dist.) N.Y. 1983. Assoc. Siben & Siben Esqs., Bay Shore, N.Y., 1950-56; ptnr. Meyer & Wexler Esqs., Smithtown, N.Y., 1956-83; judge U.S. Dist. Ct. (eastern dist.) N.Y., Uniondale, 1983—; atty. Suffolk County Police Conf., 1956-83; 1st atty. Suffolk County Patrolmen's Benevolent Assn., 1960-75; 1st atty. Suffolk County Detectives Assn., 1964-70; temporary state chmn., legal counsel Com. for Rev. Juvenile Justice System, N.Y. State Bar Assn.; speaker, lectr.; 1st adminstr. Assigned Counsel Plan N.Y. State, 1966-83. Served with U.S. Army, 1943-45. Mem. Suffolk County Criminal Bar Assn. (founder 1965, dir. 1956-60). Republican. Jewish. Avocations: travelling; sailing. Home: 94 W Bayberry Rd Islip NY 11751 Office: U S Courthouse Hempstead Turnpike at Uniondale Ave Uniondale NY 11553 *

WEXLER, WARREN MARSHALL, lawyer; b. Chgo., Sept. 22, 1932; s. Max C. and Rose (Bawer) W.; m. Phyllis Klein, Aug. 7, 1960; children—Douglas, Michael. B.S., U. Ill., 1954; J.D., Northwestern U., 1956. Bar: Ill. 1956, U.S. Dist. Ct. (no. dist.) Ill. 1956. Sole practice, Chgo., 1956—; spl. asst. state's atty. Lake County, Ill., 1972-74; dir. Magic, Inc., Chgo. Contbr. articles to profl. jours. Chmn. Highland Park Traffic Commn., Ill., 1973-83; bd. dirs. Woodridge Homeowners' Assn., Highland Park, 1975—; v.p. Red Oak PTO, Highland Park, 1978-80. Recipient 25 yrs. of Merit award Northwestern U., 1981. Mem. ABA, Ill. Bar Assn. Republican. Clubs: Magic Circle (London) (assoc. inner magic circle 1977); IBM (Chgo.) (pres. 1974-75, 1978-79). Lodge: Mazda Mystic Ring (pres. 1973-77, 1980—). General corporate, Real property, Probate. Office: 1 N LaSalle St Chicago IL 60602

WEYHER, HARRY FREDERICK, lawyer; b. Wilson, N.C., Aug. 19, 1921; s. Harry Frederick and Laura Gray (Carter) W.; m. Barbara Dore McCusker, Sept. 9, 1950 (div. May 1971); children—Barbara Brandon, Harry Frederick III, Laura Carter; m. Laura Hyman Harvey, Oct. 17, 1971 (div. Sept. 1986). B.S., U. N.C., 1946; student, U. Glasgow, Scotland, 1946; LL.B. magna cum laude, Harvard U., 1949. Bar: N.Y., 1950. Assoc. Cravath, Swaine & Moore, N.Y.C., 1949-54; sr. assoc. counsel N.Y. State Crime Commn., 1950-52; ptnr. Olwine, Connelly, Chase, O'Donnell & Weyher, N.Y.C., 1954—; adj. assoc. prof. N.Y.U. Sch. Law, 1952-62; dir. AFA Protective Systems, Inc., Hollihold, Inc., The Pioneer Fund, Inc. Author: ESOP--Employee Stock Ownership Plan, 2d ed., 1985, (with Hiramn Knott) Hanging Out a Shingle, 1987; contbr. articles to profl. jours. Mem. ABA, N.Y. Bar Assn., N.Y.C. Bar Assn., Phi Beta Kappa, Beta Gamma Sigma, Zeta Psi. Clubs: Harvard, Racquet and Tennis (N.Y.C.), Lyford Cay (Nassau). Home: 211 E 70th St Apt 23F New York NY 10021 Office: Olwine Connelly Chase O'Donnell & Weyher 299 Park Ave New York NY 10171

WEZELMAN, JANICE ANNE, lawyer; b. Omaha, June 30, 1949; d. Norman and Mary (Wolfson) W.; m. David C. Bartlett, Feb. 11, 1979; children: Daniel, Elizabeth. BA, Stanford U., 1970; JD, U. Ariz., 1974. Bar: Ariz. 1974, U.S. Dist. Ct. Ariz. 1974, U.S. Ct. Appeals (9th cir.) 1976, U.S. Supreme Ct. 1981. Assoc. Miller & Pitt P.C., Tucson, 1974-78, ptnr., 1979—; lectr. U. Ariz., Tucson, 1976-85; bd. dirs. Ariz. Ctr. for Law in Pub. Interest. Bd. dirs. So. Ariz. Water Resources Assn., Tucson. Mem. Pima County Bar Assn., Assn. Trial Lawyers Am., Ariz. Trial Lawyers Assn. Democrat. Jewish. Federal civil litigation, State civil litigation, Personal injury. Home: 3236 Via Palos Verdes Tucson AZ 85716 Office: Miller & Pitt PC 111 S Church Ave Tucson AZ 85701

WHALEN, DANIEL ALOYSIUS, III, lawyer; b. Rensselaer, N.Y., Nov. 24, 1925; s. Daniel A. Jr. and Eleanor (Mitchell) W.; m. Ann M. Conway, June 18, 1955; children: Ellen, Eileen, Erin, Brigid, Mary, Daniel IV. BA, Siena Coll., 1950; LLB, Albany U., 1953, JD, 1968. Bar: N.Y. 1954, U.S. Dist. Ct. (no. dist.) N.Y. 1954, U.S. Supreme Ct. 1970, U.S. Ct. Appeals (2d cir.) 1975, U.S. Ct. Appeals (temporary emergency ct.) 1981. Assoc. Turner

and Murphy, Albany, N.Y., 1953-60, Brown and Gallagher, Albany, 1960-63, Hesson, Ford and Grogan, Albany, 1964-67, Bender, Hesson, Ford and Grogan, Albany, 1968-72; ptnr. Hesson, Ford, Grogan, Sherwood and Whalen, Albany, 1973, Hesson, Ford, Sherwood and Whalen, Albany, 1974-86, Hesson, Ford and Whalen, Albany, 1986—. Bd. dirs. Arbor House, Inc., Albany, 1975—, Families for Prayer, Inc., Albany, 1980—. Served with USMC, 1943-45, PTO. Fellow N.Y. State Bar Found.: mem. ABA, Am. Coll. Trial Lawyers, Def. Research Inse. of North East N.Y. (pres. 1967-69), Def. Research Inst. (regional chmn. 1973—), Am. Arbitration Assn. (mem. panel), ABA, Albany County Bar Assn. (grievance com. 1978-79, bd. dirs. 1978—, sec. 1981-82, treas. 1983, v.p. 1984, 1st v.p. 1985, pres. 1986), N.Y. State Bar Assn. (com. on supreme cts. 1974-77, com. on judicial adminstrn. 1974-79, chmn. 1977-79, mem. exec. com. INCL 1977—, house of dels. 1978—), Fedn. Ins. and Corp. Counsel (v.p. 1985—, chmn. aviation sect. 1985—, vice-chmn. publs. com. 1983—). Roman Catholic. Avocations: swimming, traveling, gardening. State civil litigation, Insurance, Probate. Home: 13 Fleetwood Ave Albany NY 12208 Office: Hesson Ford & Whalen 90 State St Rom 1522 Albany NY 12207

WHALEN, JAMES MICHAEL, lawyer; b. Springfield, Vt., Dec. 10, 1946; s. Francis Henry and Eileen Rose (Gosselin) W.; m. Susan Dorothy Shelly, May 9, 1969; children: Laura, Kimberly, Michael, Jill. AB, Coll. Holy Cross, 1968; JD, Boston Coll., 1975. Bar: Vt. 1976, U.S. Dist. Ct. Vt. 1976, Mass. 1977, U.S. Dist. Ct. Mass. 1977. Law clk. to presiding justice U.S. Dist. Ct. Vt., Rutland, 1975-76; assoc. Palmer & Dodge, Boston, 1976-82, ptnr., 1983—. Chmn. Foxborough (Mass.) Zoning Bd. of Appeal, 1978—. Served to lt. USNR, 1969-73, Vietnam. Mem. ABA, Mass. Bar Assn., Boston Bar Assn. Roman Catholic. Avocations: golf, skiing. Real property, Landlord-tenant, Construction. Office: Palmer & Dodge One Beacon St Boston MA 02108

WHALEN, MICHAEL PATRICK, lawyer; b. Waltham, Mass., Apr. 2, 1946; s. William Leo and Mary Alice (Allen) W.; 1 child, Michael Patrick. BA, U. Md., 1969; JD, U. Balt., 1973. Bar: Md. 1974, D.C. 1981. Asst. state's atty. civil div. State's Atty.'s Office Prince George's County, Md., 1974-75, dist. ct. div., 1975-76, sr. asst. state's atty. felony trials div., 1976-79, chief major offender unit, 1978-79; assoc. Baskin and Sears, Hyattsville, Md., 1979-80; sr. asst. state's atty. felony trials div. for Prince George's County, Upper Marlboro, Md., 1981-86; chief felony trials div., 1981-83, team leader felony trials div., 1982-83, dep. state's atty. for Prince George's County, 1983-86—; sr. atty. Am. Prosecutor's Research Inst. Nat. Dist. Attys. Assn., 1986—; of counsel Knight, Manzi, Brennan and Ostrom, Upper Marlboro, 1986—; instr. University Coll./Univ. of Md., 1979—, Prince George's County Police Acad., 1976—; mem. addictions adv. bd. PCP Task Force, 1985-86, DWI Task Force, 1985-86. Recipient John S. Holliday Scholarship award Nat. Coll. Dist. Attys., Md. State's Attys. Assn., 1981; named Arthur A. Marshall Jr. Prosecutor of Yr., 1986. Mem. Prince George's County Bar Assn., Nat. Dist. Attys. Assn., Md. State's Attys. Assn. (legislation com., assoc. bd. dirs.), Harvard Assocs. in Police Sci., Inc., Mcpl. Police Chiefs Assn., D.C. Bar Assn. Democrat. Roman Catholic. Criminal. Office: Am Prosecuters Research Inst 1033 N Fairfax St Suite 200 Alexandria VA 22314

WHALEN, PAUL LEWELLIN, lawyer; b. Lexington, Ky.; s. Elza Boz and Barbara Jean (Lewellin) W.; m. Teena Gail Tanner, Jan. 26, 1985; 1 child, Ashley. BA, U. Ky., 1978; JD, Northern Ky. U., 1982; cert., Bonn U., Fed. Republic Germany, 1981. Bar: W.Va. 1984, Ky. 1985, U.S. Ct. Appeals (6th cir.) 1984, U.S. Ct. Appeals (4th cir.) 1985. Interviewer Connonwealth of Ky., Covington, 1978-79; law clk. John J. Wagner, Covington, 1981-82; coordinator Bill Weinberg campaign, Hindman, Ky., 1982-83; employment counselor Ky. AFL-CIO, Florence, Ky., 1983-84; assoc. Geary Walker, Parkersburg, W.Va., 1984-85; Paul L. Whalen, Newport, Ky., 1985—. State sec. Ky. Young Democrats, 1981-82; mem. Campbell County Foster Care Rev. Bd., Newport, Ky., 1986, Leadership No. Ky.; bd. dirs. Ky. Council Child Abuse, Inc., No. Ky. Citizens Com.; elected to Ft. Thomas Bd. of Edn., 1986. Recipient Commendation No. Ky. Legal Aid, Covington, 1986. Mem. ABA, Assn. Trial Lawyers Am., No. Ky. Bar Assn., Cin. Bar Assn., Phi Alpha Delta. Democrat. Methodist. Lodge: Kiwanis. Avocations: freelance writing, stamp collecting, politics. Criminal, Family and matrimonial, Personal injury. Home: 208 Newman Ave Fort Thomas KY 41075 Office: 40 E 10th St Newport KY 41071

WHALEN, THOMAS J., lawyer; b. Jersey City, July 29, 1938; s. Arthur and Mae (Cavannagh) W.; m. Anne Marie Donovan, Sept. 5, 1970; 1 child, Honore. B.A., St. Peter's Coll., Jersey City, 1960; J.D., Georgetown U., 1963. Bar: N.J. 1964, D.C. 1964, N.Y. 1968. Law sec. to judge U.S. Ct. Appeals (3d cir.), Newark, 1963-64; assoc. firm Condon & Forsyth, N.Y.C. and Washington, 1967-75, ptnr., 1975—. Served to capt. JAGC, U.S. Army, 1964-67; Vietnam. Mem. ABA, Fed. Bar Assn. Democrat. Roman Catholic. Club: University (Washington). Federal civil litigation, Insurance, Antitrust. Office: Condon & Forsyth 1100 15th St NW Washington DC 20005

WHALEN, WAYNE W., lawyer; b. Savanna, Ill., Aug. 22, 1939; s. Leo R. and Esther M. (Yackley) W.; m. Paula Whalen, Apr. 22, 1970; children: Amanda, Clementine, Antonia, Nathaniel. BS, U.S. Air Force Acad., 1961; JD, Northwestern U., 1967. Bar: Ill., U.S. Ct. Appeals (7th cir.), U.S. Supreme Ct. Commd. 1st lt. USAF, 1961, ret., 1964; assoc. Mayer, Brown & Platt, Chgo., 1967-74, ptnr., 1974-84; ptnr. Skadden, Arps, Slate, Meagher & Flom, Chgo., 1984—; bd. dirs. Van Kampen Family Mut. Funds, Lisle, Ill. Author: Annotated Illinois Constitution, 1972. Del. 6th Ill. Constitutional Conv., 1969-70, chmn. style drafting and submission com. Mem. Chgo. Bar Found. (Outstanding Young Lawyers 1970). Club: Chgo. General corporate, Municipal bonds. Home: 4920 S Greenwood Chicago IL 60615 Office: Skadden Arps Slate et al 333 W Wacker Dr Chicago IL 60606

WHALEY, JOSEPH RANDALL, lawyer; b. Lafayette, Ind., Apr. 6, 1946; s. Randall McVey and Miriam (Weckesser) W.; m. Lois Elaine Orndorff, Sept. 10, 1983. BA, Antioch Coll., 1968; JD, Cath. U., 1975. Bar: Md. 1975, D.C. 1976, U.S. Dist. Ct. D.C. 1976, U.S. Ct. Appeals (4th cir.) 1977, U.S. Supreme Ct. 1980, U.S. Ct. Appeals (D.C. cir.) 1981. Sole practice Rockville, Md., 1976-79; ptnr. Chadwick & Whaley, Rockville, 1979-85, 86—. Mem. ABA, Md. Bar Assn., Bar Assn. Montgomery County. Democrat. Methodist. Avocations: camping, computers. General practice, State civil litigation, General corporate. Home: 11613 Pleasant Meadows Dr Gaithersburg MD 20878-4258 Office: Chadwick & Whaley 1688 E Gude Dr Suite 102 Rockville MD 20850-5306

WHARTON, JOHN MICHAEL, lawyer; b. Ames, Iowa, June 16, 1944; s. Michael M. and M. Myrna (Petersen) W.; m. Pamela M. Rafdal, June 28, 1986; 1 child, Lisa Elaine; B.S., Iowa State U., 1967; J.D., Drake U., 1970. Bar: Iowa 1970, Fla. 1972, U.S. Dist. Ct. (no. and so. dists.) Iowa 1974, U.S. Ct. Appeals (8th cir.) 1975, U.S. Ct. Mil. Appeals 1971. With Peddicord & Wharton, Des Moines, 1974—; mem. Iowa Bd. Law Examiners, Des Moines, 1983—. Case notes editor Drake U. Law Rev., 1970. Served as capt. JAGD, USAF, 1970-74. Recipient Disting. Service award Phi Alpha Delta, 1970. Mem. ABA, Iowa State Bar Assn., Lawyer-Pilots Bar Assn., Def. Research Inst., Iowa Def. Counsel Assn., Assn. Trial Lawyers Am. Republican. Presbyterian. Clubs: Des Moines Golf and Country. Federal civil litigation, State civil litigation, Insurance. Office: Peddicord & Wharton PC 218 6th Ave Fleming Bldg Suite 300 Des Moines IA 50309

WHARTON, THOMAS H(EARD), JR., lawyer; b. Houston, Dec. 18, 1930; s. Thomas Heard and Laura (Wellhausen) W. B.A., Rice U., 1952; LL.B., U. Tex., 1955. Bar: Tex. 1955, U.S. Dist. Ct. (so. dist.) Tex. 1966, U.S. Ct. Appeals (5th cir.) 1972. Assoc. firm Vinson & Elkins, Houston, 1959-70, ptnr., 1970—. Co-author: How to Live and Die with Texas Probate, 1969; Texas Estate Administration, 1975. Served with USN, 1956-59. Fellow Am. Coll. Probate Counsel; mem. ABA, Houston Bar Assn. Republican. Methodist. Clubs: Houston, Houston City, Governors, Met. Racquet (Houston). Probate, Estate taxation. Home: 2210 Welch St Houston TX 77019 Office: Vinson & Elkins 3400 1st City Tower Houston TX 77002

WHATLEY, JACQUELINE BELTRAM, lawyer; b. West Orange, N.J., Sept. 26, 1944; d. Quirino and Eliane (Gruet) Beltram; m. John W. Whatley, June 25, 1966. B.A., U. Tampa, 1966; J.D., Stetson U., 1969. Bar: Fla. 1969, Alaska 1971. Assoc. Gibbons, Tucker, McEwen Smith & Cofer, Tampa, Fla., 1969-71; sole practice, Anchorage, 1971-73; ptnr. Gibbons, Tucker, Miller, Whatley & Stein, P.A., Tampa, 1973-81, pres., 1981—. Bd. dirs. Travelers Aid Soc.; bd. dirs. Tenn. Walking Horse Breeders and Exhibitors Assn., v.p., 1984—. Mem. ABA, Fla. Bar Assn., Alaska Bar Assn. Republican. Methodist. Club: Athena (Tampa). Real property, Banking, Contracts commercial. Home: PO Box 17595 Tampa FL 33682 Office: 606 Madison St Tampa FL 33602

WHEALE, DUNCAN DOUGLAS, lawyer; b. Bridgeport, Conn., Apr. 14, 1947; s. Howard Douglas and Mary Elizabeth (Wallace) W.; m. Carolyn Ann Alexander, Sept. 7, 1974; children—Douglas Ryan, Patrick John. B.S., The Citadel, 1969; LL.B. magna cum laude, John Marshall Law Sch., 1976. Bar: Ga. 1976, U.S. Dist. Ct. (no., mid. and so. dists.) Ga., U.S. Ct. Appeals (5th and 11th cirs.). Ptnr. Fulcher Law Firm, Augusta, Ga., 1976—; chmn. Augusta Ports Authority, 1983—. Commr. Ga.-Carolina council Boy Scouts Am., 1979-82. Served to 1st lt. U.S. Army, 1970-71. Mem. State Bar Ga., Assn. Trial Lawyers Am., Ga. Def. Lawyers, The Citadel Alumni Assn. (bd. dirs. 1981—). Episcopalian. Federal civil litigation, State civil litigation. Home: 3720 Inverness Way W Lake Augusta GA 30907 Office: Fulcher Law Firm 520 Greene St Augusta GA 30913

WHEALEN, G. BYRON, corporate lawyer. JD, U. Calif, San Francisco, 1952. Gen. tax counsel Chevron Corp., San Francisco, 1981—. Office: Chevron Corp 225 Bush St San Francisco CA 94104 *

WHEAT, JOSIAH, lawyer; b. Tyler County, Tex., Dec. 21, 1928; s. James E. and Ruby R. Wheat; m. Glendale Richter, July 12, 1952; children—Julia Roberts, Elizabeth Seale, Josiah, Jennifer Wheat Pariseau. B.A., U. Tex., 1951, J.D., 1952. Bar: Tex. 1952, U.S. Dist. Ct. (ea. dist.) Tex. 1955, U.S. Supreme Ct. 1961, U.S. Ct. Appeals (5th cir.) 1969. Ptnr. Wheat & Wheat, Woodville, Tex., 1952-67; ptnr. Wheat & Stafford, Woodville, Tex., 1967-83, of counsel, 1983-86; counsel Wheat, Stafford & Allison, 1986—; legal counsel Tex. Water Quality Bd., 1971-73; gen. counsel Lower Neches Valley Authority, 1974—; city atty. City of Woodville, 1959—; ptnr. S-W Ranch, Chester, Tex., Wheat Abstract/Woodville Abstract and Title Combined Cos., Woodville, F,W & S and The Timber Co., Woodville; dir. August C. Richter, Inc., Laredo, Tex., Citizens State Bank, Woodville; trustee Goolsbee Mineral Trust, Wheat Mineral Trust. Contbr. articles to legal jours. Mem. Nat. Water Commn. U.S., 1969-73; life mem. bd. visitors, past mem. adv. council astronomy dept. and McDonald Obs., U. Tex., 1978-83; mem. exec. com. U. Tex. Centennial Commn.; mem. adminstrv. bd. Woodville United Methodist Ch.; mem. exec. com. Trinity Neches council Boy Scouts Am.; bd. dirs. Tyler County Indsl. Corp., Tyler County Devel. Corp.; pres. Tyler County Dogwood Festival Assn., Inc.; mem. Tex. med. disclosures panel Tex. Dept. Health; sec. Gov.'s Water Task Force, chmn. subcom. on water fin., 1980-83. Served with U.S. Army, 1953-54. Recipient Silver Beaver award Boy Scouts Am., 1976. Mem. ABA (state bar del. 1972-78, state del. 1978-83, bd. govs. 1983-86, ho. of dels., spl and standing coms. on environ. law 1969-76, 82-83, bd. edns. gen. practice sect., commn. on interest on lawyers trusts accounts 1986—), State Bar Tex. (pres. 1969-70, acting exec. dir. 1972-73, chmn. sect. environ. law 1973-74, Disting. Service award 1973), Tyler County Bar Assn., Jefferson County Bar Assn., Nat. Water Resources Assn., East Tex. C. of C. (bd. dirs. 1960-63), Beaumont C. of C. (waterways com.), Gulf Intercoastal Canal Assn. (bd. dirs.), Tex. Water Conservation Assn. (bd. dirs., pres. 1968-70, chmn. bd. dirs. 1970-72), Deep East Tex. Council Govts. (pres. 1970-72), Deep East Tex. Devel. Assn. (water resources com.), Tex. Ex-Students Assn. (life). Lodges: Masons (York and Scottish Rites, 32 deg., Red Cross of Constantine). Administrative and regulatory, Environment. Home: 509 Kelly Blvd Woodville TX 75979 Office: Wheat Stafford & Allison 300 W Bluff St Woodville TX 75979

WHEAT, THOMAS ALLEN, lawyer; b. Liberty, Tex., June 19, 1913; s. Allen and Kaleta (Smith) W.; m. Dora Arrendell, Nov. 25, 1941; children: Thomas A. Jr. (dec.), J. Nixon. AA, South Park Jr. Coll., 1933; LLB, U. Tex., 1936. Bar: Tex., U.S. Dist. Ct. (ea. and so. dists.) Tex., U.S. Ct. Appeals (5th cir.), U.S. Supreme Ct. Sole practice Liberty, 1936-38; atty. Liberty County, 1938-41; ptnr. Wheat & Wheat, Liberty, 1941—; judge Tex. 75th jud. dist., Liberty, 1968; mem. com. on admission to practice U.S. Dist. Ct. (ea. dist.) Tex., Beaumont, 1972—; bd. dirs. 1st Bank and Trust, Cleveland, Tex. Contbg. editor U. Tex. Law Rev., 1935. Bd. dirs. Chambers-Liberty Counties Navigation Dist., Anahauc, Tex., 1975—. Served to capt. JAGC, U.S. Army, 1943-46. Fellow Tex. Bar Found. (sustaining life), Tex. Bar Assn. (grievance com. 1965-68). Episcopalian. Lodge: Rotary. Personal injury, Real property, Oil and gas leasing. Home: 1704 Cos Liberty TX 77575 Office: Wheat & Wheat PC 714 Main PO Box 890 Liberty TX 77575-0890

WHEATLEY, FORD HARRY, IV, lawyer, elected official; b. Detroit, Oct. 26, 1953; s. F. Harry and Theresa (Mabarak) W. BA in Communications with honors, Mich. State U., 1976; JD cum laude, U. Mich., 1979. Colo. 1979, U.S. Dist. Ct. Colo. 1979, U.S. Ct. Appeals (10th cir.) 1980; lic. real estate sales agt., Mich., Colo. Assoc. Porterfield, Richtsmeier & Wheatley, Denver, 1979-82; ptnr. Porterfield & Wheatley, Denver, 1982-86; sec., treas. Registered Agts., Inc., Denver 1980-86, also bd. dirs. Councilman City of Glendale, Colo., 1984-86, mayor pro tem 1986. Mem. ABA, Colo. Bar Assn., Denver Bar Assn., Continental Divide Bar Assn., Cherry Creek Commerce Assn., Phi Kappa Phi. Home: 216 Gilbert Castle Rock CO 80104 Office: Porterfield & Wheatley 2005 E 20th Avenue Denver CO 80205

WHEATLEY, JEFF R., construction lawyer; b. Lawton, Okla., July 14, 1927; s. J. Carl and Dennis Belle (Roper) W.; m. Garline J. Johnson, Aug. 2, 1949; children—Michael Jeff, Kayci Garline, Kelly Donald. B.S.E.E., U. Okla., 1956; J.D. cum laude, Pepperdine U., 1970. Bar: Calif. 1971, U.S. Dist. Ct. (9th dist.) Calif. 1971. Sole practice, Long Beach, Calif., 1971-73, Placentia, Calif., 1973-77, Fullerton, Calif., 1977—; tchr. constrn. law 1981-82; mem. five atty. firm, Fullerton. Served with USN 1945-46. Recipient Charles R. Mower award Orange County Builders Assn., 1981. Mem. ABA (Constrn. Forum), Orange County Bar Assn., Am. Subcontractors Assn. (legal adv. com.), So. Calif. Builders Assn., USCG Aux. Producer audio tapes on constrn. law for Calif. contractors. Club: Dana Point Yacht. Federal civil litigation, State civil litigation, Construction. Office: 2600 E Nutwood Ave Suite 101 Fullerton CA 92631

WHEELER, ANNE MARIE, lawyer; b. Plainfield, N.J., Apr. 27, 1954; d. William Joseph and Joan Agnes (McCarthy) Stief; m. Gary Marvin Wheeler, Aug. 16, 1980; children: Gary, Stephen. BA, Cath. U., 1976; JD, George Washington U., 1980. Bar: D.C. 1981, U.S. Dist. Ct. D.C. 1981, U.S. Ct. Appeals (D.C. cir.) 1981. Law clk. to presiding justices FERC, Washington, 1980-81; atty. Kimberly-Clark Corp., Arlington, Va., 1982-83; assoc. Onek, Klein & Farr, Washington, 1983—. Ward rep. Takoma Park (Md.) Traffic Com., 1984-86. Mem. ABA, D.C. Bar Assn., Women's Bar Assn. D.C., Phi Beta Kappa. Democrat. Roman Catholic. Health, Administrative and regulatory. Home: 11501 Alma St Silver Spring MD 20902 Office: Onek Klein & Farr 2550 M St Suite 350 Washington DC 20037

WHEELER, JAMES JULIAN, lawyer; b. Independence, Mo., Mar. 20, 1921; s. Luther I. and Edith (Hesler) W.; m. Janet L. Esau, Apr. 28, 1951; children: Linnell Gretzinger, Robert W. LLB, U. Mo., 1948. Bar: Mo. 1948, U.S. Dist. Ct. (ea. dist.) Mo. 1956. Prosecuting atty. County of Chariton, Mo., 1950-54, probate judge, 1974-75; circuit judge 9th Judicial Circuit Court, Mo., 1976-82; sole practice Keytesville, Mo., 1948-74, 82—. Served as cpl. USMC, 1941-46, PTO. Mem. ABA, Mo. Bar Assn., Am. Judicature Soc., Assn. Trial Lawyers Am. Democrat. General practice, Criminal, State civil litigation. Home: 112 Kennedy Ave Keytesville MO 65261 Office: 304 S Walnut Keytesville MO 65261

WHEELER, JOHN WILLIAM, lawyer; b. N.Y.C.; s. John and Rosalie (Conroy) W.; m. Muriel Davis, Sept. 7, 1940; children—Richard J., Robert E. A.B., Columbia U., 1936, LL.B., 1939. Bar: N.Y. 1939, U.S. Dist. Ct. (so. and ea. dists.) N.Y., U.S. Ct. Appeals (2d cir.), U.S. Supreme Ct., U.S. Tax Ct. Assoc. Thacher, Proffitt & Wood, and predecessor firm, Barry Wainwright Thacher & Symmers, 1939-50, ptnr., 1950-74, sr. ptnr., 1974-84, counsel, 1984—. Pres. Alumni Fedn. Columbia U., 1962-64; chmn. bd. Columbia Coll. Fund, 1966-67. Served to lt., USNR, 1943-46. Recipient Alumni Fedn. medal for disting. service, Columbia U., 1947. Mem. ABA (ho. of dels. 1980-82), N.Y. State Bar Assn., Assn. Bar City of N.Y., Nat. Assn. Coll. and Univ. Attys. (pres. 1978-79, Disting. Service award 1982). Democrat. Roman Catholic. Clubs: Down Town Assn. (N.Y.C.); Plandome (N.Y.) Country; The Surf (Surfside, Fla.). Contbr. articles profl. jours. Banking, General corporate, Probate. Home: 11 Chelsea Dr Port Washington NY 11050 Office: 2 World Trade Ctr New York NY 10048

WHEELER, R(ICHARD) KENNETH, lawyer; b. Washington, July 25, 1934; s. Nathaniel Dudley and Ruth Lee (Matthews) W.; children: Jennifer L., Ruth E. B.A., U. Richmond, 1957, LL.B. (Williams scholar 1961-63), 1964. Bar: Va. 1963, D.C. 1977. Assoc. firm Hunton & Williams (and predecessor), Richmond, 1963-71; ptnr. Hunton & Williams (and predecessor), 1971—; adj. prof. law T.C. Williams Sch. Law, U. Richmond, 1966, 83, bd. dirs., 1977-79; adj. prof. Va. Commonwealth U., 1970. Served to capt. USMCR, 1957-61. Mem. ABA, Fed. Bar Assn., Nat. Assn. R.R. Trial Counsel, Am. Judicature Soc., Am. Law Inst., Va. State Bar (chmn. com. liaison with law schs. 1977-78, chmn. com. legal edn. and admission to bar 1978-80), Va. Bar Assn., Bar Assn. D.C., Richmond Trial Lawyers Assn., Va. Trial Lawyers Assn., Richmond Bar Assn., Chesterfield-Colonial Heights Bar Assn., Web Soc., McNeill Law Soc., Supreme Ct. Hist. Soc., Marine Corps League (life), Pi Sigma Alpha, Phi Delta Phi, Omicron Delta Kappa. Clubs: Rector's (U. Richmond); Downtown (Richmond). Federal civil litigation, State civil litigation, Personal injury. Office: 707 E Main St Richmond VA 23219

WHEELER, STANTON, law and social science educator; b. 1930. B.A., Pomona Coll., 1952; M.A., U. Wash., 1956, Ph.D., 1958. Instr. sociology U. Wash., 1956-58; instr. social relations Harvard U., 1958-60; Fulbright research fellow U. Oslo, Norway, 1960-61; asst. prof. social relations Harvard U, 1961-63; assoc. prof. sociology U. Wash., 1963-64; sociologist Russell Sage Found., 1964-68, cons., 1968—; adj. prof. Yale U., 1965-68, prof., 1968—, Ford Found. prof. law and social scis., 1985—; fellow Center Advanced Study in Behavioral Scis., Stanford U., 1970-71. Mem. Am. Sociol. Assn., Soc. Study of Social Problems, Law and Soc. Assn. Office: Yale Law Sch Drawer 401A Yale Sta New Haven CT 06520 *

WHEELER, SUSAN LYNN, lawyer, university counsel; b. Ft. Worth, Apr. 3, 1955; d. Raymond Louis and Dorothy Marie (Hutcherson) W.; m. Rodney G. Miner, July 5, 1986. BA, U. Tex., 1976, MA in English, 1978, JD, 1981. Briefing atty. 1st Ct. of Appeals, Houston, Tex., 1981-82; asst. atty. gen. State of Tex., Austin, 1982-83; research atty. 1st Ct. of Appeals, Houston, 1983-85; assoc. univ. counsel U. Houston, 1985—. Civil rights, Government contracts and claims, Labor. Office: Univ Houston 4600 Gulf Freeway #421 Houston TX 77023

WHEELOCK, EUGENE THOMAS, petroleum company executive, lawyer; b. Chgo., Apr. 9, 1947; s. Joseph Thomas and Marion (Richardson) W.; m. Ann Douglas Haehl, May 23, 1970; children—Sarah, Erica. B.S. in Chem. Engrig., U. Tex., 1970; J.D., U. Houston, 1973; LL.M., George Washington U., 1980. Bar: Tex. 1973, D.C. 1980, U.S. Dist. Ct. D.C. 1980, U.S. Supreme Ct. 1979. Patent examiner U.S. Patent & Trademark Office, Arlington, Va., 1973-78; tech. advisor to judge U.S. Ct. Customs and Patent Appeals, Washington, 1978-80; counsel Exxon Research and Engring. Co., Florham Park, N.J., 1980-86; counsel Exxon Chem. Co., 1985—. Mem. Am. Intellectual Property Law Assn., Am. Inst. Chem. Engrs., ABA. Patent, Antitrust, Labor. Office: Exxon Chem Co PO Box 5200 Baytown TX 77522

WHELAN, CHARLES DUPLESSIS, III, lawyer; b. Long Branch, N.J., Feb. 5, 1956; s. Charles D. and Patricia E. (Line) W.; m. Danette M. (Centuori), Sept. 29, 1984. BS, Rutgers U., 1974-78, JD, 1981. Bar: N.J. 1981, U.S. Dist. Ct. N.J. 1981, N.Y. 1984, U.S. Dist. Ct. (so. and ea. dists.) N.Y. 1984, U.S. Ct. Appeals (3d cir.) 1986, U.S. Supreme Ct. 1986. Sole practice Belleville, N.J., 1981-82; law clk. to presiding justice Appellate Div., Newark, 1982; assoc. Law Offices of Donald E. Sheil, Somerset, N.J., 1982—. Mem. Am. Trial Lawyers Assn., N.J. Bar Assn., N.Y. State Bar Assn., N.Y. County Lawyers Assn., Middlesex County Bar Assn., Somerset County Bar Assn. Personal injury, Contracts commercial, General corporate. Home: 440 Randolph Rd Plainfield NJ 07060

WHELAN, JOHN KENNETH, lawyer; b. N.Y.C., Sept. 18, 1941; s. John Joseph and Marion A. (McDonough) W.; m. Mary Agnes O'Neill, Nov. 27, 1965; children—Anne-Marie, Christopher John. B.S., Fordham U., 1962; J.D., U. Va., 1965. Bar: N.Y. 1965, U.S. Dist. Ct. (no. dist.) N.Y. 1966. Assoc. Dunnington, Bartholow & Miller, N.Y.C., 1967-73, ptnr., 1973—; dir. of several privately held corps. Served to capt. USAR, 1965-67. Decorated Joint Service Commendation medal. Mem. ABA, N.Y. State Bar Assn. Club: Sky (N.Y.C.). General corporate, Securities. Home: 848 Palmer Rd Bronxville NY 10708 Office: 666 3d Ave Suite 2700 New York NY 10017

WHELESS, ALBERT EUGENE, lawyer; b. Timmonsville, S.C., Feb. 15, 1935; s. A.B. and Marie M. Wheless; m. Celeste Graham, Sept. 6, 1958; children—Al, Art, Ann. B.A., Wofford Coll., 1959; J.D., U. S.C., 1969. Bar: S.C. 1969. Assoc. John W. Jenrette, North Myrtle Beach, S.C., 1969, ptnr. Jenrette & Wheless, North Myrtle Beach, 1970-75, Jenrette, Wheless, McInnis & Breeden, North Myrtle Beach, 1976-79, Wheless & McInnis, North Myrtle Beach, 1980—; city recorder North Myrtle Beach, 1970-71, city atty., 1972-79. Mem. ABA, S.C. Bar Assn., Horry County Bar Assn. (pres. 1982-84), Assn. Trial Lawyers Am., S.C. Trial Lawyers Assn., S.C. Def. Attys. Assn. General practice, Personal injury, Real property. Home: 11th Ave N North Myrtle Beach SC 29582 Office: 457 Main St North Myrtle Beach SC 29582

WHERRITT, ALAN FRANCISCO, lawyer; b. Pleasant Hill, Mo., June 15, 1895; s. Alonzo C. Wherritt and Cora Francisco; 1 child, Ann Wherritt Turpin. PhB, U. Chgo., 1917, JD, 1920. Bar: Mo. 1920. Ptnr. Wherritt and Turpin, Liberty, Mo., 1920—. Del. Dem. Conv., Phila., 1948; chmn. Clay County Dem. Cen. Commn., 1944-48; pres. Liberty C. of C., 1934-35; bd. regents Northwest Mo. State U., 1943-53. Served to capt. U.S. Army, 1917-19. Decorated Croix de Guerre (Italy). Mem. Mo. Bar Assn. (bd. govs. 1953-57, state exec. com. 1957), Clay County Bar Assn. (pres. 1940). Federal civil litigation, State civil litigation, Probate. Home: 626 College St Liberty MO 64068 Office: Wherritt and Turpin 106 N Main Liberty MO 64608

WHIGHAM, THOMAS EDMONDSON, attorney; b. Opp, Ala., Dec. 8, 1952; s. Julian Bertie and Mildred (Edmondson) W.; m. Sally Ann Oyler, Apr. 4, 1981; children: Thomas Edmondson Jr., Bert Michael. AA, U. Fla., 1974, BA, 1977; JD, Nova U., 1980. Bar: Fla. 1981, U.S. Dist. Ct. (mid. dist.) Fla. 1981, U.S. Ct. Claims 1981, U.S. Ct. Appeals (11th cir.) 1981, U.S. Supreme Ct., 1984. Ptnr. Stenstrom, McIntosh, Julian, Colbert & Whigham, P.A., Sanford, Fla., 1980—; designated atty. Personal Injury and Wrongful Death Fla., Bar Designation Program, 1985. Committeeman Seminole County Dem. Party, Sanford, 1978; del. Fla. Dem. Conv., Orlando, 1978. Mem. ABA, Fla. Bar Assn., Seminole County Bar Assn. (treas. 1985-86), Assn. Trial Lawyers of Am., Acad. Fla. Trial Lawyers, Ducks Unltd., Nat. Wildlife Fedn., Audubon Soc., Alpha Tau Omega, Phi Alpha Delta. Democrat. Baptist. Club: Cen. Fla. Gator Orlando. Lodge: Optimist (pres. Sanford club 1979-1980). Avocations: snow skiing, scuba diving, hunting, fishing. Personal injury, Insurance, State civil litigation. Office: Stenstrom McIntosh et al 200 W First St Suite 22 Sanford FL 32771

WHILDEN, ROBERT HARRAL, JR., lawyer; b. Houston, May 20, 1935; s. Robert Harral and Elizabeth (Hoyt) W.; m. Mary Preston, Aug. 24, 1957; children: Elizabeth, Margaret, Robert III. B.A., U. Tex., 1957, LL.B., 1960. Bar: Tex. Ptnr. Vinson & Elkins, Houston, 1960—. Mem. Tex. Bar Assn., Houston Bar Assn. Home: 1507 Briarmead Houston TX 77057 Office: Vinson & Elkins 3300 First City Tower 1001 Fannin Houston TX 77002-6760

WHIPPLE, CLYDE DAVID, lawyer; b. Kansas City, Mo., Oct. 3, 1927; s. Clyde Ward and Myrtle Launa (Smith) W.; m. Isabel Ann Wellington, Dec. 26, 1953. B.A., Baker U., 1950; J.D., U. Mo., 1952. Bar: Mo. 1952, U.S. Supreme Ct. 1960, U.S. Ct. Appeals (8th cir.) 1962, D.C. 1965, U.S. Ct. Appeals (10th cir.) 1979, U.S. Ct. Appeals (9th cir.) 1981. Ptnr., Gresham-Boughan & Whipple, 1952-59, Krings, Stewart, Whipple & Mauer, 1959-75,

Whipple, Eisler & Kraft, 1975-80, Whipple & Kraft, P.C., Kansas City, Mo., 1980—; adj. prof. U. Mo., Kansas City, 1970-78. Mayor, City of Parkville (Mo.), 1952-58, city atty., 1959-61; mayor-pro-tem City of Weatherby Lake, 1966-72, police judge, 1972-76, city atty., 1976-78; mem., pres. R-5 Sch. Dist. Bd. Edn., 1970-76. Served with U.S. Army, 1944-48. Mem. ABA, Mo. Bar Assn., Kansas City Bar Assn. Democrat. Presbyterian. Club: Masons, Order Eastern Star. Contbr. articles to profl. jours. Labor, Workers' compensation, Personal injury. Home: 10100 NW 74th St Lake Weatherby Parkville MO 64152 Office: 1111 Grand Ave Suite 200 Kansas City MO 64106

WHIPPLE, ROBERT JENKS, lawyer; b. Worcester, Mass., June 16, 1912; s. Robert Lee and Mildred Dean (Jenks) W.; m. Eleanor G. Thayer, Jan. 12, 1946 (div. 1958); children—Jeffrey, Wendy; m. Anne Coghlan, Nov. 3, 1960; children—Michael, Ellen. B.A., Princeton U., 1934; LL.B., Harvard U., 1937; hon. LL.D., Central New Eng. Coll., 1983. Bar: Mass. 1937, U.S. Dist. Ct. Mass. 1948, U.S. Supreme Ct. 1969. Assoc. Ropes Gray Boyden & Perkins, Boston, 1937-41, Gage Hamilton & June, Worcester, 1946-48; ptnr. June Fletcher & Whipple, Worcester, 1948-72; dir. Fletcher Tilton & Whipple, P.C., Worcester, 1972—; v.p., gen. counsel Warren Pumps, Inc., Mass., 1953-72; dir. Shawmut Worcester County Bank, N.A., Worcester, 1974—; asst. dist. atty. Office Dist. Atty., Worcester County, 1947. Served to maj. AUS, 1941-45. Fellow Am. Coll. Probate Counsel; mem. ABA, Mass. Bar Assn., Worcester County Bar Assn. Republican. Unitarian. Clubs: Tatnuck Country (pres. 1960-62); Worcester (pres. 1970-72). General corporate, Probate, Personal income taxation. Home: 4 Wheeler Ave Worcester MA 01609 Office: Fletcher Tilton & Whipple PC 370 Main St Worcester MA 01608

WHIPPS, EDWARD FRANKLIN, lawyer; b. Columbus, Ohio, Dec. 17, 1936; s. Rusk Henry and Agnes Lucille (Green) W.; children: Edward Scott, Rusk Huot, Sylvia Louise, Rudyard Christian. B.A., Ohio Wesleyan U., 1958; J.D., Ohio State U., 1961. Bar: Ohio 1961, U.S. Dist. Ct. (so. dist.) Ohio 1962, U.S. Dist. Ct. (no. dist.) Ohio 1964, U.S. Ct. Claims 1963, U.S. Supreme Ct. 1963, Miss. 1965, U.S. Ct. Appeals (6th cir.) 1980. Assoc. George, Greek, King & McMahon, Columbus, 1961-66; ptnr. George, Greek, King, McMahon & McConnaughey, Columbus, 1966-79, McConnaughey, Stradley, Mone & Moul, Columbus, 1979-81, Thompson, Hine & Flory, Columbus, 1981—. Host: TV programs Upper Arlington Plain Talk, 1979-82; TV program Briding Disability, 1981-82, Lawyers on Call, 1982—, U.A. Today, 1982—, The Ohio Wesleyan Experience, 1984—. Mem. Upper Arlington (Ohio) Bd. Edn., 1971-80, pres., 1978-79; mem. bd. alumni dirs. Ohio Wesleyan U., 1975-79. Mem. Columbus Bar Assn., Ohio State Bar Assn., ABA, Assn. Trial Lawyers Am., Ohio Acad. Trial Lawyers, Franklin County Trial Lawyers Assn., Am. Judicature Soc., Columbus Bar Found., Columbus C. of C., Upper Arlington Area C. of C. (trustee 1978—), Creative Living Inc. (founder, trustee 1969—), Delta Tau Delta (nat. v.p. 1976-78). Republican. Clubs: Lawyers, Barristers, Columbus Athletic, Columbus Touchdown, Ohio State U. Faculty (Columbus). Federal civil litigation, State civil litigation, Family and matrimonial. Home: 3771 Lyon Dr Columbus OH 43220 Office: 100 E Broad St Suite 1700 Columbus OH 43215

WHISONANT, MICHAEL WAYNE, lawyer; b. Leeds, Ala., Jan. 9, 1952; s. Charles Edward Whisonant and Peggy Ann (Bethune) Gore; m. Pamela Jean Estes, June 25, 1977; children: Ashley Brooke, Michael Wayne Jr. BS, Jacksonville State U., 1974, MBA, 1975; JD, Birmingham Sch. Law, 1979. Bar: Ala. 1980, U.S. Dist. Ct. Ala. 1980, U.S. Ct. Appeals (11th cir.) 1982. Dep. dist. atty. Jefferson County, Birmingham, 1980-84; asst. atty. Dept. Justice, Birmingham, 1984—. Named one of Outstanding Young Men Am., 1982. Mem. ABA, Birmingham Bar Assn. (co-chmn. criminal justice sect. 1984). Methodist. Lodge: Masons. Criminal, General corporate. Office: US Attys Office 200 Federal Ct House Birmingham AL 35226

WHISTON, RICHARD MICHAEL, lawyer; b. N.Y.C., Mar. 1, 1944; s. Michael W. and Dorothy M. (Kussman) W. BS in Econs. cum laude, U. Pa., 1964; JD, Harvard U., 1968. Bar: N.Y. 1968, U.S. Dist. Ct. (so. and ea. dists.) N.Y. 1977, U.S. Tax Ct. 1977, U.S. Supreme Ct. 1977, Conn. 1978, U.S. Dist. Ct. Conn. 1978, Fla., 1979, U.S. Ct. Claims 1979, U.S. Ct. Appeals (5th cir.) 1979. Assoc. Kelley, Drye, Warren, N.Y.C., 1970-77; dep. div. counsel Hamilton Standard, Windsor Locks, Conn., 1977-78; asst. gen. counsel United Techs. Corp., Hartford, Conn., 1980-82; div. counsel Latin Am. ops. Otis Elevator Co., West Palm Beach, Fla., 1978-80; div. counsel European ops. Otis Elevator Co., Paris, 1982-83; v.p., counsel No. Am. ops. Otis Elevator Co., Farmington, Conn., 1983-85, v.p., gen. counsel, sec., 1985—. Served to capt. U.S. Army, 1968-70. Mem. Alpha Beta Psi, Beta Gamma Sigma. Episcopalian. Avocations: comml. pilot. General corporate, Private international, Insurance. Office: Otis Elevator Co 10 Farm Springs Farmington CT 06032

WHITAKER, A(LBERT) DUNCAN, lawyer; b. Ft. Wayne, Ind., Jan. 3, 1932; s. Robert Lynn and Rhoda Irene (Duncan) W.; m. Adelaide B. Saccone, Aug. 13, 1955; children: Brent Robert, Alene G. Whitaker Lynch, Karen E. B.A., Yale U., 1954; J.D., U. Mich., 1957. Bar: Mich. 1957, U.S. Ct. Appeals D.C. 1959, U.S. Supreme Ct. 1961. Atty. antitrust div. U.S. Dept. Justice, 1957-59; assoc. Howrey & Simon, Washington, 1959-65, ptnr., 1965—; lectr. George Washington U., George Mason U. Law Sch. Contbr. articles to profl. jours. Mem. ABA, Fed. Bar Assn., D.C. Bar Assn., Order of Coif, Phi Beta Kappa. Clubs: Metropolitan, Nat. Lawyers (Washington). Antitrust, Federal civil litigation, General corporate. Office: Howrey & Simon Suite 900 1730 Pennsylvania Ave Washington DC 20006

WHITAKER, BENJAMIN PALMER, JR., lawyer; b. Hartford, Conn., July 4, 1937; s. Benjamin Palmer and Helen Frances (Johnson) W.; m. Susan Ann McIlwaine, Oct. 6, 1962 (div. 1983); children—Jeanne Ann, Benjamin Palmer III, Scott Theodore; m. 2d Janet Elizabeth Langley, June 4, 1983. B.S., Princeton U., 1958; J.D., Albany Law Sch., 1961. Bar: N.Y. 1962, adminstrv. asst. U.S. Ho. of Reps., Washington, 1961-63; ptnr. Allen and O'Brien, Rochester, N.Y., 1966-83; gen. counsel Pub. Enterprises, Inc., Rochester, 1983-85; sole practice, 1985—. Served to capt. USAF, 1963-65. Democrat. General corporate, Real property, Probate. Home: 303 Village Ln Rochester NY 14610 Office: 30 W Broad St Old City Hall Suite 505 Rochester NY 14614

WHITAKER, LEROY, lawyer; b. Marshall, Tex., Nov. 20, 1929; s. John W. and Effie Ruth (Allums) W.; m. Lu Broussard, May 24, 1952; children—John Steven, Catherine Anne. B.S., North Tex. State U., 1950, M.S., 1952; Ph.D., U. Ill., Urbana, 1955; J.D., U. Houston, 1967. Bar: Tex., 1967, Ind., 1968, U.S. dist. ct. (so. dist.) Ind. 1968, U.S. Ct. Cust. & Pat. Apls., 1969, U.S. Pat. Office, 1964. Research chemist Shell Chem. Co., Deer Park, Tex., 1955-57, Union, N.J., 1957; sr. research chemist Jefferson Chem. Co., Austin, Tex., 1957-59, market devel. man, Houston, 1959-62, pat. agt., 1962-67; with Eli Lilly and Co., Indpls., 1967—, asst. patent counsel, 1975-78, patent counsel chem. products, 1978-84, licensing counsel, asst. patent counsel, 1984-86, gen. patent counsel, asst. sec., 1986—. Mem. Am. Pat. Law Assn., ABA, Ind. Bar Assn. Methodist. Patent. Home: 6465 Kingswood Dr Indianapolis IN 46256 Office: Lilly Corp Ctr Indianapolis IN 46285

WHITAKER, LESLIE KENT, lawyer; b. Santa Monica, Calif., Aug. 10, 1938; s. Clarence Nelson and Dorothy (Stewart) W.; m. Elaine Croshier, Oct. 23, 1964 (div. Sept. 1975); children: Eric, Carol, Adrienne. AB, Stanford U., 1960; LLB, Yale U., 1965. Bar: Calif. 1966, U.S. Dist. Ct. (no., cen., ea. and so. dists.) Calif. 1966, U.S. Ct. Appeals (9th cir.) 1966, U.S. Supreme Ct. 1972. Law clk. Calif. Ct. Appeals (div. 2), Los Angeles, 1965-66; assoc. Chickering & Gregory, San Francisco, 1966-73; counsel Kaiser Industries Corp., Oakland, Calif., 1973-77; v.p., sr. counsel, sec. Kaiser Steel Corp., Fontana, Calif., 1977-85; prin. Verdon & Whitaker, Newport Beach, Calif., 1986—. Served to lt. USNR, 1960-62. Mem. ABA, Orange County Bar Assn., Western Pension Conf. Club: Center (Newport Beach). State civil litigation, General corporate, Pension, profit-sharing, and employee benefits. Home: 51 Lakeview Ave Irvine CA 92714 Office: Verdon & Whitaker 1600 Dove St Suite 313 Newport Beach CA 92660

WHITAKER, MEADE, federal judge; b. Washington, Mar. 22, 1919; s. Spier and Haidee (Meade) W.; m. Frances Dunn Baldwin, Feb. 10, 1945; children: Meade, Martin Baldwin (dec.), Frances Dunn Whitaker Schoonover; m. Carol Dekleva, Dec. 26, 1972. B.A., Yale U., 1940; LL.B., U. Va., 1948. Bar: Ala. 1948. Ptnr. Cabaniss, Johnston & Gardner, and predecessor, Birmingham, 1948-69, 70-73; tax legis. counsel Treasury Dept., Washington, 1969-70; chief counsel (IRS), Washington, 1973-76; ptnr. Arter & Hadden, Cleve., 1977-78; asst. gen. counsel Ford Motor Co., Dearborn, Mich., 1978-81; judge U.S. Tax Ct., Washington, 1982—. Served as officer USMCR, 1941-46. Mem. ABA, Ala. Bar Assn., Am. Law Inst. Episcopalian. Office: US Tax Court 400 2d St NW Washington DC 20217

WHITAKER, MICHAEL WRIGHT, lawyer; b. Memphis, June 30, 1945; s. John Aubrey and Marjorie (Wright) W.; m. Sharon North, Mar. 24, 1968; children—Aubrey Wright, Michael Cole. B.A. in Polit. Sci., Rhodes Coll., 1967; J.D., Vanderbilt Sch. Law, 1970. Bar: Tenn. 1970, U.S. Dist. Ct. (no. dist.) Miss. 1982, U.S. Ct. Appeals (5th cir.) 1983. Ptnr. Wilder & Whitaker, Somerville, Tenn., 1970-74, Gordon, Forrester & Whitaker, Covington, Tenn., 1982—; dist. atty. gen. Fayette, Harderman, Mc Nairy, Lauderdale & Tipton Counties, Somerville, 1974-82; mem. Tenn. Bd. Law Examiners, 1985—, state exec. com. Tenn. Dems., 1986—. Author: The Police Witness, 1985. Mem. Am. Trial Lawyers Assn., Tenn. Trial Lawyers Assn. Presbyterian. Civil rights, Criminal, State civil litigation. Office: Gordon Forrester & Whitaker 111 W Washington Covington TN 38019

WHITAKER, STEVEN KING, lawyer; b. Washington, Mar. 14, 1954; s. Edward Stephen and Norma Eveline (Waichulis) W.; m. Gayle Durloo, Aug. 15, 1975; children: Katherine Gayle, Michael Steven. BA in Econs. cum laude, Old Dominion U., 1975; JD, U. Dayton, 1979. Bar: Va. 1979, D.C. 1980. Assoc. Whitaker & Bushman, Arlington, Va., 1979-82; ptnr. Carter & Whitaker, Chesapeake, Va., 1982-85; sr. ptnr. Whitaker & McCormack, Chesapeake, 1985—; lectr. Tidewater Community Coll., Virginia Beach, Va., 1984—. Mem. ABA, Va. Bar, D.C. Bar, Chesapeake Bar Assn. Real property, Personal injury, General practice. Office: Whitaker & McCormack 1200 B Sparrow Rd Chesapeake VA 23325-3095

WHITAKER, THOMAS PATRICK, lawyer; b. Washington, Sept. 22, 1944; s. Thomas J. and Mary K. (Finn) W.; m. Donna Brenish, Feb. 16, 1974; children: Laura, Kevin. BA, George Washington U., 1966, MPA, 1973, JD, 1979; postgrad., Naval War Coll., 1984. Bar: Va. 1979. Staff asst. Adminstrn. Office of U.S. Cts., Washington, 1972-73, analyst, 1975-77; cons. Planning Research Corp., McLean, Va., 1973-75; mgmt. analyst CAB, Washington, 1977-82; case analyst HHS, Arlington, Va., 1982—. Served to lt. (j.g.) USNR, 1966-71, Vietnam, comdr. with Res. 1983—. Mem. ABA, Am. Soc. Pub. Adminstrn. (sect. chmn. 1974-76), U.S. Naval Inst., Naval Res. Assn., Res. Officers Assn. Administrative and regulatory, Pension, profit-sharing, and employee benefits, General corporate. Home: 9817 Days Farm Dr Vienna VA 22180

WHITBECK, JAMES ALLIS, lawyer; b. Greenfield, Mass., Jan. 21, 1944; m. Beverly Grace Grant, May 30, 1969; children: Matthew W., James A., Benjamin G. BA, U. Mass., 1969; JD, Western New Eng. Coll., 1979. Bar: Mass. 1979, U.S. Dist. Ct. Mass. 1979. Sole practice Shelburne Falls, Mass., 1979-85, Greenfield, 1985—; ptnr. Hammatt and Whitbeck, Chatham, Mass., 1986—. Bd. dirs. Girls Club of Greenfield, 1983—. Served with USN, 1961-65. Mem. Phi Beta Kappa. General practice, Family and matrimonial, Real property. Home: 44 Phillips St Greenfield MA 01301 Office: 278 Main St Greenfield MA 01301 also: 101 Depot Rd Box 649 Chatham MA 02633

WHITCOMB, MICHAEL ARTHUR ISAAC, lawyer; b. Milw., June 23, 1950; s. Arthur William and Julia Ruth (Crotty) W.; m. Debra Jean Lubotsky, Aug. 23, 1975; children: Erin Jean, Michael John. BS, U. Wis., 1973; JD, Marquette U., 1978. Bar: Wis. 1978, U.S. Dist. Ct. (ea. and we. dists.) Wis. 1978, U.S. Ct. Appeals (7th cir.) 1980. Asst. city atty. City of Milw., 1978-84, counsel to the Mayor, 1984—; mem. Cen. Bd. Purchases, Milw., 1984—, Deferred Compensation Bd., Milw., 1984—, Electronic Data Bd., Milw., 1984—. Named Outstanding Young Polit. Figure, Milw. Jaycees, 1986. Mem. Wis. Bar Assn. Avocation: triathlons. Local government, Legislative, State civil litigation. Home: 3324 N Shepard Ave Milwaukee WI 53211 Office: Office of Mayor 200 E Wells St Room 201 Milwaukee WI 53202

WHITCOMB, WILLIAM GRANDON, lawyer; b. Mt. Pleasant, Mich., Oct. 19, 1942; s. Charles Francis and Ruby Eileen (Grandon) W.; m. Janet Kathleen Paxton, Nov. 24, 1967; 1 child, Elizabeth Jane. BBA, Mich. State U., 1970; JD, Thomas M. Cooley Law Sch., 1979. Bar: Mich. 1980, U.S. Dist. Ct. (we. and ea. dist.) Mich. 1985, Fla. 1985, U.S. Dist. Ct. (mid. dist.) Fla. 1986. Owner, operator retail mdse. Whitcomb's, Lansing, Mich., 1971-80; sole practice Lansing and Okemos, Mich., 1980-85; prin. Whitcomb and Assocs., Okemos, 1985—; prin. ABC Legal Services, Ft. Myers, Fla., 1986—. Served with U.S. Army, 1964-65. Mem. ABA, Mich. Bar Assn., Fla. Bar Assn., Ingham County Bar Assn., Lee County Bar Assn., Mich. Trial Lawyers Assn. Methodist. Avocations: oil painting, sculpture. Bankruptcy, Criminal, Personal injury. Office: 1534 Hendry Suite 202 Fort Myers FL 33901

WHITE, ANDREA WALKER, lawyer; b. Corona, Calif., Dec. 14, 1953; d. William Floyd and Isabel (Couty) Walker; m. John Hubert White Jr., Mar. 21, 1982. BA, U. Calif., Irvine, 1975; JD, So. Meth. U., 1980. Bar: Tex. 1980, U.S. Dist. Ct. (no. dist.) Tex. 1983. In-house counsel Air-Marine Claims, Richardson, Tex., 1980-83; assoc. Ungerman, Hill et al, Dallas, 1983-84, Law Office of George S. Henry, Dallas, 1984—. Mem. ABA, Dallas Bar Assn (comml. and bankruptcy sect.). Republican. Roman Catholic. Bankruptcy, Consumer commercial. Office: Law Office of George S Henry 5000 Quorum Dr Suite 300 Dallas TX 75240

WHITE, ANDREW, III, lawyer; b. Winston-Salem, N.C., Dec. 11, 1957; s. Andrew Jr. and Gertrud Iris White. BS, Guilford Coll., 1977; JD, Case Western Res. U., 1982. Bar: Fla., Ga., U.S. Dist. Ct. (mid. dist.) Fla., U.S. Dist. Ct. (no. dist.) Ga., U.S. Ct. Appeals (11th cir.). Assoc. Smith, Currie & Hancock, Atlanta, 1982-84, Carlton, Fields, Ward, Emmanuel, Smith & Cutler P.A., Tampa, Fla., 1984—. Mem. Assn. Trial Lawyers Am., Am. Arbitration Assn. (nat. panel of arbitrators). Mem. Soc. of Friends. State civil litigation, Construction, Federal civil litigation. Home: 3311 W Sevilla Circle Tampa FL 33629 Office: Carlton Fields Ward et al One Harbour Place Tampa FL 33602

WHITE, ARNOLD S., lawyer; b. Columbus, Ohio, Oct. 7, 1944; s. Julius and Alice (Goldberg) W.; m. Susan R. Jay, July 4, 1971; children: Jeffrey, Eric, Lauren, Andrew. BA, Ohio State U., 1966; JD, Am. U., 1969. Bar: Ohio, 1969, U.S. Dist. Ct. (no. dist.) Ohio 1974, U.S. Supreme Ct. 1981. Chief legal services Ohio Dept. Urban Affairs, Columbus, 1971-72; chief legal affairs Ohio Dept. Econ. and Comml. Devel., Columbus, 1972-74; spl. counsel Office of Atty. Gen., State of Ohio, Columbus, 1975—; sole practice Columbus, 1975—. Dem. candidate for Franklin County commr., 1974; mem. exec. com. Franklin County Dem. Com. 1976. Mem. ABA, Columbus Bar Assn., Assn. Trial Lawyers Am. Jewish. State civil litigation, Real property, General corporate. Office: 700 E Broad St Columbus OH 43215

WHITE, BARRY BENNETT, lawyer; b. Boston, Feb. 13, 1943; s. Harold and Rosalyn (Schneider) W.; m. Eleanor Greenberg; Joshua S., Adam Jacob. A.B. magna cum laude, Harvard U., 1964; J.D. magna cum laude, Harvard U., 1967. Bar: Mass. 1967, U.S. Dist. Ct. Mass. 1967, U.S. Ct. Appeals, (1st cir.) 1967. Assoc. Foley Hoag & Eliot, Boston, 1969-74, ptnr., 1975—, exec. com., 1981—; corporator, Neworld Savs. Bank, 1981-83, mem. nominating and compensation com., 1982-83. Bd. dirs. Mass. affiliate Am. Diabetes Assn., 1975-82, Mass. Assn. Mental Health, 1985—, Mass. Elderly Equity Program Inc., 1986—; mem. Jewish Family and Children's Services, Boston, 1979—; bd. visitors Boston U. Grad. Sch. Dentistry, 1981—. Served with USPHS, 1967-69. Mem. ABA, Am. Soc. Hosp. Attys., Mass. Bar Assn., Fla. Assn. Hosp. Attys., Am. Hosp. Assn. (adj. task force on health planning, 1982-84), contbg. editor Hosp. Law Manual, 1981-84), Mass. Assn. for Mental Health (bd. dirs.). Democrat. Club: Harvard of Boston. Editor: Harvard Law Rev., 1965-67; Health, General corporate, Real property. Address: 1 Post Office Sq Boston MA 02109

WHITE, BENJAMIN TAYLOR, lawyer; b. Atlanta, Nov. 10, 1946; s. Edward Street and Jane Shannon (Taylor) W.; m. Ramona Taylor, Aug. 14, 1971; 1 child, Alexander Taylor. AB with honors, U. N.C., 1969; JD cum laude, Harvard U., 1973. Bar: Ga. 1973. Assoc. Alston & Bird, Atlanta, 1973-79, ptnr., 1979—. Trustee The Taft Sch., Watertown, Conn., 1978-81, Woodruff Arts Ctr., Atlanta, 1983—; pres., founder Ga. Vol. Lawyers for the Arts, 1979-82; chmn. Lee Harper and Dancers, Atlanta, 1979-83; pres. Alliance Theatre Co., Atlanta, 1985—. Fellow Am. Coll. Probate Counselors; mem. ABA, State Bar of Ga. (chmn. fiduciary law sect. 1986—), Atlanta Bar Assn., Internat. Bar Assn., Atlanta Tax Forum, Atlanta Estate Planning Council, Harvard Law Sch. Assn. Ga. (pres. 1981-82). Estate planning, Probate, Personal income taxation. Home: 3315 Valley Rd NW Atlanta GA 30305 Office: Alston & Bird 35 Broad St NW Suite 1200 Atlanta GA 30335

WHITE, BRINDA KAYE, lawyer; b. Shattuck, Okla., Sept. 18, 1951; d. Joe B. and Joy F. (Shelinbarger) W. BA in Edn. with high honors, Northwestern State Coll., Alva, Okla., 1973; MEd, U. Okla., 1974, PhD, 1978, JD, 1982. Bar: Okla. 1982, U.S. Dist. Ct. (we. dist.) Okla. 1982, U.S. Ct. Appeals (10th cir.) 1984. Law clk. to presiding justice U.S. Dist. Ct. (we. dist.) Okla., Oklahoma City, 1982-83, U.S. Ct. Appeals (10th cir.), Oklahoma City, 1983-85; assoc. Linn & Helms, Oklahoma City, 1985—. Mem. Order of Coif. Federal civil litigation. Office: Linn & Helms 1200 Fidelity Plaza Oklahoma City OK 73102

WHITE, BRYAN STANFORD, lawyer; b. Orange, Calif., Feb. 7, 1956; s. John Albert and Millie Christine (Parham) W. AB, U. Calif., Berkeley, 1978; JD, Duke U., 1981. Bar: Calif. 1981. Assoc. McKenna, Conner & Cuneo, Los Angeles, 1981-86; atty., asst. sec. MCO Holdings Inc., Los Angeles, 1986—. Mem. ABA, Los Angeles County Bar Assn., Phi Beta Kappa. Democrat. General corporate, Securities. Home: 11511 Rochester Ave #16 West Los Angeles CA 90025 Office: MCO Holdings Inc 10880 Wilshire Blvd 16th Floor Los Angeles CA 90024

WHITE, BYRON R., associate justice U.S. Supreme Court; b. Ft. Collins, Colo., June 8, 1917; m. Marion Stearns; children: Charles, Nancy. Grad., U. Colo., 1938; Rhodes scholar, Oxford (Eng.) U.; grad., Yale Law Sch. Clk. to chief justice U.S. 1946-47; atty. firm Lewis, Grant and Davis, Denver, 1947-60; dep. atty. gen. U.S., 1961-62; asso. justice Supreme Ct., U.S., 1962—. Served with USNR, World War II, Pacific. Mem. Phi Beta Kappa, Phi Gamma Delta, Order of Coif. Jurisprudence. Address: US Supreme Court Supreme Ct Bldg 1 First St NE Washington DC 20543 *

WHITE, C. THOMAS, justice Nebraska Supreme Court; b. Humphrey, Nebr., Oct. 5, 1928; s. John Ambrose and Margaret Elizabeth (Costello) W.; m. Joan White, Oct. 9, 1971; children: Michaela, Thomas, Patrick. J.D., Creighton U., 1952. Bar: Nebr. County atty. Platte County (Nebr.), Columbus, 1955-65; judge 21st Dist. Ct. Nebr., Columbus, 1965-77; justice Nebr. Supreme Ct., Lincoln, 1977—. Served with U.S. Army, 1946-47. Roman Catholic. Clubs: Elks, KC. Judicial administration. Office: Capitol Bldg Lincoln NE 68509 *

WHITE, CHARLES B., lawyer; b. Denver, July 22, 1953; m. Linda White, June 21, 1984; children: Alexander, Darcy. BA in Psychology, Stanford U., 1975, JD, 1978. Assoc. Hall & Evans, Denver, 1978-81; ptnr. Kirkland & Ellis, Denver, 1981—. Author: National Forest Management: A Handbook for Public Input and Review, 1978; contbr. articles to profl. jours. Mem. ABA (natural resources sect.), Colo. Bar Assn. (water and environ. law sect.), Colo. Lawyers Com. (bd. dirs.). Environment, Real property. Office: Kirkland & Ellis 1999 Broadway Suite 4000 Denver CO 80202

WHITE, CHERYL DENNEY, lawyer; b. Akron, Ohio, Aug. 23, 1949; d. Chester Vernon and Marjorie Jean (Kinsey) Denney; m. Christopher John White, May 22, 1976. BA, U. Mo., 1971; JD, U. Mo., Kansas City, 1976; MLT, Georgetown U., 1981. Bar: Mo. 1977, U.S. Dist. Ct. (we. dist.) Mo. 1977, U.S. Tax Ct. 1978, D.C. 1979, U.S. Claims Ct. 1981. Trial atty. IRS, Washington, 1977-81; assoc. Dickstein, Shapiro & Morin, Washington, 1981-86, Kaye, Scholer, Fierman, Hays & Handler, N.Y.C., 1986—. Mem. ABA (tax sect.), Mo. Bar Assn., D.C. Bar Assn., Women's Bar Assn. D.C., Women in Employee Benefits (membership chmn. 1986—). Pension, profit-sharing, and employee benefits, Corporate taxation. Office: Kaye Scholer Fierman Hays & Handler 425 Park Ave New York NY 10022

WHITE, CLAIR FOX, lawyer; b. Ft. Worth, Oct. 8, 1949; s. Joseph Andrew and Sally Blanche (Fox) W.; m. Linda Gage; 1 child, Gary Joseph. BA, Duke U., 1971, JD, 1974. Bar: Fla. 1974, Iowa 1980, La. 1985, U.S. Dist. Ct. (we. dist.) La., 1985, U.S. Supreme Ct. 1977, U.S. Ct. Appeals (5th cir.) 1980, U.S. Ct. of Claims 1980, U.S. Tax Ct. 1980, U.S. Customs Ct. 1980. Assoc. McCune, Hiaasen, Crum, Ferris & Gardner, Ft. Lauderdale, Fla., 1974-78; ptnr. McCune, Hiaasen, Crum, Ferris & Gardner, Ft. Lauderdale, 1979-80; contracts cons. Stanley Cons., Muscatine, Iowa, 1980-81, counsel, 1982-84; assoc. Hargrove, Guyton Ramey and Barlow, Shreveport, La., 1984-86, ptnr., 1987—. Mem. ABA, Fla. Bar Assn., La. Bar Assn., Iowa Bar Assn., Shreveport Bar Assn. State civil litigation, Federal civil litigation. Office: Hargrove Guyton Ramey and Barlow 505 Travis St Shreveport LA 71101

WHITE, CLAUDE ESLEY, lawyer; b. Bridgeton, N.J., Jan. 2, 1949; s. John Hosea and Viola (Sumrell) W.; m. Jane Denise Rice, Feb. 9, 1974; children: Claude Esley Jr., Stephanie Edith, Christopher Michael. BA, Rutgers U., 1971, JD, 1974. Bar: N.J. 1974, D.C. 1980, N.Y. 1986. Assoc. Pitney, Hardin, Kipp & Szuch, Morristown, N.J., 1974-76; corp. counsel Liggett Group, Inc., Montvale, N.J., 1976-83, GrandMet USA, Inc., Montvale, 1983-85; v.p., gen. counsel, sec. Quality Care, Inc., Rockville Centre, N.Y., 1985—. Chmn. community adv. bd. Rutgers U. Ednl. Opportunity, New Brunswick, N.J., 1980—; vice chmn., trustees Newark Community Sch. of Arts, 1980-85; trustees St. Paul Bapt. Ch., Montclair, 1974—; vice chmn. 1986—. Mem. ABA, Assn. of Bar of City of N.Y., Nat. Bar Assn., Home Health Services and Staffing Assn. (vice chmn. 1985-86), Nat. Assn. Home Care (bd. dirs. 1986—). Lodge: Masons (sr. warden 1984-85). General corporate, Health. Home: 725 River Vale Rd River Vale NJ 07675 Office: Quality Care Inc 100 N Centre Ave Rockville Centre NY 11570

WHITE, DANIEL BOWMAN, lawyer; b. Charlotte, N.C., Apr. 12, 1948; s. William Garner and Elizabeth (Bowman) W.; m. Sarah deSaussure Peterson, May 29, 1976; 1 child, Bentley Parker. A.B., Davidson Coll., 1970; J.D., U. S.C., 1976. Bar: S.C. 1976, U.S. Dist. Ct. S.C. 1976, U.S. Ct. Appeals (4th cir.) 1978. Ptnr. Rainey, Britton, Gibbes & Clarkson, P.A., Greenville, S.C., 1976—. Comments editor U. S.C. Law Rev., 1975-76. Commr. Greenville Zoning Commn., 1980—. Served to 1st lt. U.S. Army, 1971-73. Decorated Bronze Star; Dana scholar Davidson Coll., N.C., 1966-70. Mem. S.C. Bar Assn. (house dels. 1986—), Def. Research Inst., Nat. Assn. R.R. Trial Counsel, Greenville Young Lawyers Club (pres. 1981). Episcopalian. Federal civil litigation, State civil litigation, Insurance. Home: 104 Garden Trail Greenville SC 29605 Office: Rainey Britton Gibbes & Clarkson PA 330 E Coffee St Greenville SC 29601

WHITE, DANIEL JOSEPH, lawyer; b. Cleve., May 13, 1953; s. Melvin Marshall and Mary-Jane (Buckley) W. B.S., U. Cin., 1976; J.D. cum laude, Cleve.-Marshall Sch. Law, 1980. Bars: Ohio 1980, U.S. Dist. Ct. (no. dist.) Ohio 1980, U.S. Ct. Appeals (6th cir.) 1982, U.S. Dist. Ct. (so. dist.) Ohio 1983. Assoc. Nurenberg, Plevin, Jacobson, Heller & McCarthy Co., L.P.A., Cleve., 1980-82, Columbus, Ohio, 1983-85, Jacobson, Maynard, Tuschman & Kalur Co., L.P.A., Columbus, 1985—. Mem. Assn. Trial Lawyers Am., Ohio State Bar Assn., Columbus Bar Assn., Defense Research Inst. Roman Catholic. State civil litigation, Federal civil litigation, Personal injury. Home: 4770 Shire Ridge Rd W Columbus OH 43220 Office: Jacobson Maynard Tuschman & Kalur Co LPA 175 S 3d St #880 Columbus OH 43215

WHITE, DARRELL DEAN, judge; b. Baton Rouge, Dec. 8, 1946; s. Gordon M. and Geraldine (Hendrickson) W.; m. Fran Boudreaux; children: Ehren, Alexandra, Gordon, Winston. BA in Govt., La. State U., 1968, JD, 1971; postgrad., U.S. Army Command & Gen. Staff Coll., 1980, JAG Officers Advanced Course, 1984, Mil. Judges Course, 1985. Bar: La. 1971. Ptnr. White & May, Baton Rouge, 1973-77; first asst. U.S. atty. U.S. Dist. Ct. (mid. dist.) La., 1977-78; judge div. C Baton Rouge City Ct., 1978-79, sr.

judge, 1979—; adj. prof. La. State U. Law Ctr., 1979—; acting state district ct. judge by appointment of La. Supreme Ct., 1980-82; instr. La. Atty. Gen.'s Tng. Course for Justices Peace and Constables, 1984—. Bd. dirs. O'Brien House Alcohol Treatment Facility; mem. New Covenant, A Family Ch., La. Taskforce on Drinking and Driving, Baton Rouge Taskforce on Drinking and Driving. Served to maj. JAGC, La. N.G., 1980—. Inductee Baton Rouge High Sch. Hall of Fame, 1987. Mem. ABA (del. from La. to Nat. Conf. Spl. Ct. Judges, various coms.), Baton Rouge Bar Assn., Fed. Bar Assn., Am. Judges Assn., La. City Judges Assn. (pres. 1984-85, various coms.), Assn. Trial Lawyers Am., La. Trial Lawyers Assn., Am. Judicature Soc., Res. Officers Assn. U.S., N.G. Assn. U.S., N.G. Assn. La., Am. Legion, Baton Rouge C. of C., U.S. Tennis Assn., Phi Delta Phi, Alpha Tau Omega. Avocations: tennis, woodworking, gardening, reading. Office: Baton Rouge City Ct 1100 Laurel St Suite 201 Baton Rouge LA 70802

WHITE, DAVID LAWRENCE, lawyer, chief financial officer; b. Ft. Worth, Tex., Mar. 6, 1953; s. Lawrence Dale and Jean (Payne) W.; m. Kandy Hayes, June 1, 1980; children: Heather, Brandon. BBA, Tex. A&M U., 1974; JD, So. Meth. U., 1977. Bar: Tex. 1977, U.S. Dist. Ct. (no. dist.) Tex., U.S. Tax Ct. 1978, U.S. Ct. Appeals (5th cir.) 1978. Assoc. Tobolowsky & Schlinger, Dallas, 1977-78; ptnr. Young & White, Dallas, 1978-81; gen. counsel Hayes, Inc., Port Arthur, Tex., 1981-85; chief fin. officer Entronics Corp., Dallas, 1985—, also bd. dirs.; bd. dirs. Treble Investments, Dallas. Mem. arch com. Country Forest Homeowners Assn., Dallas, 1986; sponsor USA Film Festival, Dallas, 1986; treas. Chet Edwards for Congress, Dallas, 1978. Hatton W. Sumner scholar So. Meth. U., 1974-77. Mem. ABA, Dallas Bar Assn., Phi Delta Phi, Order of Coif. Republican. Presbyterian. Club: Brookhaven (Dallas). Avocation: tennis. Contracts commercial, Banking, General corporate. Home: 8 Duncannon Ct Dallas TX 75225 Office: Entronics Corp 10488 Markison Rd Dallas TX 75238

WHITE, DAVID WILLIAM, lawyer; b. Kansas City, Mo., Nov. 11, 1950; s. William Donnell and Shirley Ann (Scott) W.; m. Beverly Joyce Vanlerberg, May 20, 1972; 1 child, Robert. BA, Pitts. State U., 1972; MA, Kans. State U., 1973; JD, U. Mo., 1982. Bar: Mo. 1982, U.S. Dist. Ct. (we. dist.) Mo. 1982. Asst. mgr. Southwestern Bell, Moberly, Mo., 1977-79; assoc. Stoup & Thompson, Kansas City, 1982—; bd. dirs. Dancers Studios of Kansas City. Cases and statutes editor jour. Urban Lawyer, 1981-82. Coach Southwest United Soccer Club, Overland Park, Kans., 1983—; v.p., bd. dirs. Johnson County Child Care Assn., Kans., 1985—. Served to capt. U.S. Army, 1973-77, with Res. 1977—. Mem. Assn. Trial Lawyers Am., Mo. Bar Assn., Kansas City Met. Bar Assn., Lambda Chi Alpha Alumni Assn. Republican. Roman Catholic. Avocations: softball, reading, hist. novels. Workers' compensation, Personal injury, State civil litigation. Home: 9251 Moody Park Dr Overland Park KS 66212 Office: Stoup & Thompson 1006 Grand Suite 950 Kansas City MO 64106

WHITE, EDWARD ALFRED, lawyer; b. Elizabeth, N.J., Nov. 23, 1934. B.S. in Indsl. Engring., U. Mich., 1957, J.D., 1963. Bar: Fla. 1963, U.S. Ct. Appeals (5th cir.) 1971, U.S. Supreme Ct. 1976, U.S. Ct. Appeals (11th cir.) 1981; cert. civil trial lawyer Nat. Bd. Trial Advocacy. Jennings, Watts, Clarke & Hamilton, Jacksonville, Fla., 1963-66, ptnr., 1966-69; ptnr. Wayman & White, Jacksonville, 1969-72; sole practice, Jacksonville, 1972—; mem. clients security fund com. Fla. Bar, 1975-79, mem. aviation law com. Fla. Bar, 1976—, chmn., 1979-81, chmn. pub. relations comn., 1986—, bd. govs., 1984—. Mem. Jacksonville Bar Assn. (chmn. legal ethics com. 1975-76, gov. 1976-78, pres. 1979-80), ABA, Fla. Bar Assn. (bd. cert. civil trial lawyer), Assn. Trial Lawyers Am. (sustaining mem. 1984—), Acad. Fla. Trial Lawyers (diplomate), Fla. Council Bar Assn. Pres.'s, Lawyer-Pilots Bar Assn., Am. Judicature Soc., Maritime Law Assn. (proctor in admiralty), Southeastern Admiralty Law Inst. (dir. 1982—). Home: 1959 Largo Rd Jacksonville FL 32207 Office: 902 Barnett Bank Bldg Jacksonville FL 32202

WHITE, GEORGE W., federal judge; b. 1931. Student, Baldwin-Wallace Coll., 1948-51; J.D., Cleveland-Marshall Coll. Law, 1955. Sole practice law Cleve., 1956-68; judge Ct. Common Pleas, Ohio, 1968-80, U.S. Dist. Ct. (no. dist.) Ohio, 1980—. Mem. ABA, Fed. Bar Assn. Judicial administration. Office: U S Dist Ct 135 US Courthouse 201 Superior Ave NE Cleveland OH 44114 *

WHITE, HAROLD WAYNE, lawyer; b. Oak Ridge, Sept. 9, 1946; s. Clifford Lester and Grace Marie (Braddock) W.; m. Sallie Lorraine Dodson, Mar. 5, 1970; 1 child, Katherine Grace. BS, Tenn. Tech. U., 1970; MA, U. S.D., 1970; JD, U. Iowa, 1974. Bar: Iowa 1974, U.S. Dist. Ct. (so. dist.) Iowa 1974, U.S. Dist. Ct. (no. dist.) Iowa 1975, U.S. Ct. Appeals (8th cir.) 1978, U.S. Ct. Appeals (7th cir.) 1981, U.S. Supreme Ct. 1983. Asst. county atty. Lee County, Iowa, Ft. Madison, 1974; assoc. Fitzgibbons Bros., Estherville, Iowa, 1975—. Contbr. articles to Iowa Law Rev. Asst. chmn. Lee County Dem. Cen. Com., 1974. Served with AUS, 1965-67. Mem. Iowa State Bar Assn., Iowa Assn. Sch. Bd. Attys. Democrat. Roman Catholic. Lodges: Elks, Rotary. Banking, Local government, Personal injury. Home: W 802 N 7th St Estherville IA 51334 Office: Fitzgibbons Bros 108 N 7th St Estherville IA 51334

WHITE, HELENE NITA, judge; b. Jackson Heights, N.Y., Dec. 2, 1954; d. Frank William and Ruth (Gruber) W. AB, Columbia U., 1975; JD, U. Pa., 1978. Bar: Pa. 1979, Mich. 1979. Law clk. to justice Mich. Supreme Ct., Southfield, 1978-80; judge Common Pleas Ct., Detroit, 1981, 36th Dist Ct., Detroit, 1981-83, Wayne Cir. Ct., Detroit, 1983—. Bd. dirs. Met. Detroit YWCA, 1986—, Coalition Temporary Shelter, 1986—. Mem. ABA, Pa. Bar Assn., Detroit Bar Assn., Nat. Assn. Women Judges (chmn. publicity 1984, membership com. 1985—), Women Lawyers Assn. Mich. Jewish. Office: Wayne Cir Ct 433 Lafayette Bldg Detroit MI 48226

WHITE, IVAN VANCE, JR., lawyer; b. Paterson, N.J., July 5, 1946; s. I. Vance and Annie (Kate) Sells W.; m. Marlene H. Henderson, Nov. 20, 1982; children—Jason C., Darren E., Carlee L., Erik C. B.A., Rutgers U., 1968; J.D., George Washington U., 1971. Bar: N.J. 1971, U.S. Dist. Ct. N.J. 1971, D.C. 1973. Assoc., Mandon & White, Wayne, N.J., 1971-75; ptnr. Urbanick & White, Mendham, N.J., 1975-79; sole practice, Gladstone, N.J., 1980-82, Morristown, N.J., 1983—; mem. Hock, Silverlieb, White, DiConsiglio & Kramer, P.C., Livingston, N.J., 1982-83. Mem. N.J. Bar Assn. Democrat. Methodist. Family and matrimonial, Personal injury, Real property. Home: 37 Schooleys Mountain Rd Long Valley NJ 07853 Office: 90 Maple Ave Morristown NJ 07960

WHITE, JACK RAYMOND, lawyer; b. Lincoln, Nebr., Oct. 12, 1936; s. Raymond John and Twila Helen (Leonard) W.; children—Ann C., Raymond A., Arline C., Kathleen M., Colleen M. A.B., U. So. Calif., 1958, LL.B., 1961. Bar: Calif. 1962, U.S. Dist. Ct. (cen. dist.) Calif. 1962, U.S. Ct. Appeals (9th cir.) 1964, U.S. Ct. Claims 1967, U.S. Supreme Ct. 1982, U.S. Tax Ct. 1964. Assoc. Hill, Farrer and Burrill, Los Angeles, 1961-71, ptnr., 1971—. Mem. ABA, Calif. Bar Assn., Los Angeles County Bar Assn., Order Coif, Legion Lex. Federal civil litigation, State civil litigation, State and local taxation. Office: Hill Farrer and Burrill 34th Floor 445 S Figueroa St Los Angeles CA 90017

WHITE, JAMES ALFRED, lawyer; b. Bay City, Mich., Jan. 5, 1939; s. Gerald J. and Clara E. (Barnes) W.; m. Barbara J. White, Feb. 14, 1980. B.A. cum laude, Alma Coll., 1961; J.D., U. Mich., 1964. Bar: Mich., 1964. Assoc. Foster, Swift, Collins & Coey, Lansing, Mich., 1964-69, ptnr., 1969—. Csl. Mich. Edn. Assn., 1966—; labor arbitrator labor panel Am. Arbitration Assn. Bd. dirs. Big Bros. and Big Sisters of Greater Lansing, Inc., 1972-80. Mem. AMA, Mich. Bar Assn., Ingham County Bar Assn. Club: Met. Flying (pres.). Labor, Agricultural. Home: 1553 Epley Rd Williamston MI 48895 Office: 313 S Washington Sq Lansing MI 48933

WHITE, JAMES BOYD, law educator; b. Boston, July 28, 1938; s. Benjamin Vroom and Charlotte Green (Conover) W.; m. Mary Louise Fitch, Jan. 1, 1979; children: Emma Lillian, Henry Alfred; children by previous marriage: Catherine Conover, John Southworth. A.B., Amherst Coll., 1960; A.M., Harvard U., 1961, LL.B., 1964. Asso. firm Foley, Hoag & Eliot, Boston, 1964-67; asst. prof. law U. Colo., 1967-69, assoc. prof., 1969-73, prof., 1973-75; prof. law U. Chgo., 1975-83; prof. law and English U. Mich., Ann Arbor, 1983—; vis. assoc. prof. Stanford U., 1972. Author: The Legal Imagination, 1973; (with Scarboro) Constitutional Criminal Procedure, 1976; When Words Lose Their Meaning, 1984; Heracles' Bow, 1985. Sinclair Kennedy Traveling fellow, 1964-65; Nat. Endowment for Humanities fellow, 1979-80. Mem. Am. Law Inst., Chgo. Council of Lawyers. Legal education, Jurisprudence, Criminal. Office: U Mich Law Sch Ann Arbor MI 48109

WHITE, JAMES JUSTESEN, legal educator; b. Omaha, Feb. 19, 1934; s. Leland Cobb and Vernie Marie (Bisgard) W.; m. Nancy Ann Coleman, Dec. 23, 1956; children: James, Patricia, Christopher. B.A., Amherst Coll., 1956; J.D., U. Mich., 1962. Bar: Mich. 1967. Assoc. Latham & Watkins, Los Angeles, 1962-64; prof. law U. Mich., Ann Arbor, 1964-78, 81-82, assoc. dean, 1978-81, Robert A. Sullivan prof. law, 1982—; exec. dir. Nat. Inst. Consumer Justice, 1972-74; chmn. Gov.'s Adv. Commn. on Regulation of Fin. Instn., 1976; bd. dirs. Southeast Mich. Legal Services, 1978—; pres. U. Mich. Credit Union, 1983. Author: (with Speidel and Summers) Commercial and Consumer Law, 3d edit., 1981, (with Summer's) Handbook of the Law Under the Uniform Commercial Code, 2d edit., 1980, (with Symons) Banking Law Teaching Materials, 2d edit., 1984, (with Edwards) Negotiations Materials and Problems, 1976. Trustee Ann Arbor Bd. Edn., 1981-84. Served to 1st lt. USAF, 1956-59, 62. Mem. Am. Law Inst., Mich. Bar Assn., Order of Coif, Phi Beta Kappa. Republican. Congregationalist. Contracts commercial, Bankruptcy, Banking. Home: 1603 Granger Ann Arbor MI 48104 Office: Mich Law Sch Hutchins Hall Ann Arbor MI 48109 *

WHITE, JAMES PATRICK, lawyer, educator; b. Iowa City, Sept. 29, 1931; s. Raymond Patrick and Besse (Kanak) W.; m. Anna R. Seim, July 2, 1964. B.A., U. Iowa, 1953, J.D., 1956; LL.M., George Washington U., 1959; LL.D., U. of Pacific, 1984. Bar: Iowa 1956, D.C. 1959, U.S. Supreme Ct. 1959. Teaching fellow George Washington U. Law Sch., 1958-59; asst. prof. U. N.D. Law Sch., Grand Forks, 1959-62; asso. prof., acting dean U. N.D. Law Sch., 1962-63, asso. prof., asst. dean, 1963-67; dir. agrl. law research program; prof. law Ind. U. Law Sch., Indpls., 1967—; also dir. urban legal studies program Ind. U. Law Sch., 1971-74; univ. dean acad. devel. and planning, spl. asst. to the chancellor; cons. on legal edn. ABA, 1974—; mem. for N.D., Commn. on Uniform State Laws, 1961-66. Contbr. papers to tech. lit. Young Democratic nat. committeeman, Iowa, 1952-54. Served as 1st lt. JAGC, USAF, 1956-58. Carnegie postdoctoral fellow U. Mich. Center for Study Higher Edn., 1964-65. Fellow Am. Bar Found.; mem. Am., Ind., Indpls., N.D., Iowa bar assns., Am. Judicature Soc., Am. Law Inst., Order of Coif. Roman Catholic. Local government, Legal education. Home: 7707 N Meridian St Indianapolis IN 46260 Office: Ind Univ 355 N Lansing St Indianapolis IN 46202

WHITE, JERUSHA LYNN, lawyer; b. Kansas City, Mo., Nov. 30, 1950; d. Riley Vaughn and Edith Blynn (Ringen) White; m. Larry D. Hancock, Jan. 5, 1969 (div. 1973); m. 2d Stephen Perry Wasson, Nov. 30, 1978 (div. 1985). A.S., Mo. State Fair Community Coll., 1974; B.S., Central Mo. State U., 1978; J.D., U. Mo.-Kansas City, 1981. Bar: Mo. 1981. With Montgomery Ward & Co., Sedalia, Mo., 1968-69, Parkhurst Mfg. Co., Sedalia, 1969-71, United Farm Agy., Sedalia, 1972-73, Montgomery Ward & Co., 1973-74, Howard Truck & Equipment Co., Sedalia, 1974-75, McGraw-Edison Co., Sedalia, 1975-76, Rival Mfg. Co., Sedalia, 1977-78; buyer Hotel Equipment Co., Century City, Calif., 1978; law clk. Legal Aid of Western Mo., Kansas City, 1979-80, Horowitz & Shurin, P.C., Kansas City, 1980-81; assoc. firm Steve Borel/Steve Streen, Kansas City, 1982-83; sole practice law, Sedalia, Mo., 1983-85; ptnr. Cope, Schuber & White, 1985-86; with Hyatt Legal Services, 1986—. Mem. ABA, Mo. Bar Assn., Kansas City Bar Assn., Pettis County Bar Assn. Democrat. Presbyterian. Clubs: American Business Women's Assn., Bus. and Profl. Women's Orgn. General practice. Home: 5500 NE Scandia Ln, Kansas City 65301 Office: Hyatt Legal Services 5522 NE Antioch Rd Kansas City MO 64119

WHITE, JOHN AARON, JR., lawyer; b. St. Louis, Oct. 20, 1943; s. John Aaron and Helen Inez (Stewart) W.; m. Georgia Kenyon, Mar. 22, 1980; children—Dorian, Cameron, Lauren. B.A., U. Nev., 1965; J.D., George Washington U., 1968. Bar: D.C. 1969, Nev. 1969, U.S. Dist. Ct. (D.C. dist.) 1969, U.S. Supreme Ct. 1979. Atty. City Atty.'s Office, Reno, 1969-74, chief dep. city atty., 1972-74; sole practice Reno, 1974-78; ptnr. White Law Chartered, Reno, 1978—; tchr. contracts, agy. law Reno Bd. Realtors, 1979-81; adj. prof. in bankruptcy Old Coll. Nev. Sch. of Law, 1986—; lectr. computers and law Nev. State Bar Conv., 1986. Author (with others) Nevada Civil Practice Manual, 1986. Organizer, Consumer Action No. Nev., 1975-76, Citizens for Responsible Growth, 1976-77, Secret Witness Program Reno, Sparks and Washoe County, 1977-81, Friends of Pyramid Lake, 1982-84; mem. Reno Mayor's Ad Hoc Adv. Com., 1979-81, Gov.'s Commn. on Status of People, 1975-78, honor award com. Am. Lung Assn. of Nev., 1982—. Served with USMCR, 1961-68. Mem. ABA, Washoe County Bar Assn. Democrat. Mormon. Club: Reno Host Lions. Contbr. article to legal jour. Bankruptcy, State civil litigation, Local government. Office: White Law Chartered 50 W Liberty St Suite 940 Reno NV 89501

WHITE, JOHN LINDSEY, lawyer; b. Camden, N.J., Apr. 1, 1930; s. John R. and Jean L. (Lord) W.; m. Jane E. White, Dec. 27, 1952; children: Linda White McFadden, John L. Jr., Douglas A., Karen R. AB, Franklin & Marshall Coll., 1952; LLB, Temple U., 1955. Bar: N.J. 1955, U.S. Dist. Ct. N.J. 1955, U.S. Supreme Ct. 1960, U.S. Ct. Appeals (3d cir.) 1984. Sr. ptnr. LaBrum & Doak, Woodbury, N.J.; bd. dirs. 1st Fidelity Bank, Woodbury. Mem. N.J. Assembly, Trenton, 1964-68, N.J. State Senate, Trenton, 1968-72; trustee Underwood-Meml. Hosp., Woodbury. Fellow Am. Bar Found., Am. Coll. Trial Lawyers; mem. ABA, N.J. Bar Assn. (pres. 1985-86), Internat. Assn. Def. Counsel, Woodbury Jaycees (disting. service award 1966). Republican. Presbyterian. Lodges: Shriners, Masons. Avocations: hunting, fishing, boating. Federal civil litigation, State civil litigation, Insurance. Home: 193 Briar Hill Ln Woodbury NJ 08096 Office: LaBrum & Doak 66 Euclid St Woodbury NJ 08096

WHITE, JOHN PATRICK, lawyer; b. Boston, Oct. 14, 1946; s. John Marion and Margaret Patricia (Gannon) W.; m. Gemma Mary Flattly, Feb. 9, 1980; 1 son, John Myles. B.S. in Chem. Engring., Columbia U., 1968, M.A. in Biochemistry, 1971, M.Ph. in Molecular Biology, 1975; J.D., Fordham U., 1977. Bar: N.Y. 1978, U.S. dist. ct. (ea. and so. dists.) N.Y. 1978, U.S. Ct. Customs and Patent Appeals 1979, U.S. Ct. Appeals (Fed. cir.) 1982. Legis. dir. Community Council Greater N.Y., 1971-77; assoc. Cooper, Dunham, Clark, Griffin & Moran, N.Y.C., 1977-82, ptnr., 1983—. Mem. Biosafety com. Columbia U., 1969-71; dir. Oncogene Sci., Inc. Democratic dist. leader, 1975-81; vice chmn. Dem. Com. N.Y. County, 1977-81; jud. del. 1st jud. dept., 1975, 76, 77, 79; adminstr. screening panel 2d Mcpl. Ct. Dist.; pub. mem. Columbia U. Recombinant DNA Biosafety Com. Columbia U. faculty fellow, 1969-71; NIH grantee, 1969-71. Mem. ABA, Am. Chem. Soc., Am. Patent Law Assn., N.Y. Patent Law Assn., Assn. Bar City N.Y. Club: Columbia of N.Y.C. Contbr. articles to sci. and legal jours. Patent, Trademark and copyright, Federal civil litigation. Office: 30 Rockefeller Plaza New York NY 10112

WHITE, KATHERINE PATRICIA, lawyer; b. N.Y.C., Feb. 1, 1948; d. Edward Christopher and Catherine Elizabeth (Walsh) W. BA in English, Molloy Coll., 1969; JD, St. John's U., 1971. Bar: N.Y. 1972, U.S. Dist. Ct. (ea. and so. dists.) N.Y., 1973, U.S. Supreme Ct. 1976. Atty. Western Electric Co., Inc., N.Y.C., 1971-79, AT&T Co., Inc., N.Y.C., 1979-83, AT&T Communications, Inc., N.Y.C., 1984—. Vol. Sloan Kettering Inst., 1973, North Shore U. Hosp., 1975, various fed., state and local polit. campaigns; judge N.Y. State Bicentennial Writing Competition, N.Y.C., 1977-78; chmn. Com. to Elect Supreme Ct. Judge, N.Y.C., 1982. Mem. ABA (pub. utility law sect. 1978—), Am. Corp. Counsel Assn., Women's Nat. Republic Club, N.Y. State Bar Assn. (young lawyers com., bus. and banking law com. real estate law sect., corp. counsel sect.), N.Y. County Lawyers Assn. (adminstrv. law com. 1986—), Nassau County Bar Assn. (membership com., environ. law com., real estate sect., young lawyers sect.), Assn. of Bar of City of N.Y. (adminstrv. law com. 1982-85, young lawyers com. 1976-79, judge nat. moot ct. competition 1979—), Cath. Lawyers Guild for Diocese of Rockville Ctr. (pres. 1980-81), St. John's U. Sch. Law Alumni Assn. (pres. L.I. chpt. 1986—), Wharton Bus. Sch. Club of N.Y. Club: Metropolitan (N.Y.C.). Avocations: racing sailboats, figure skating, golf, tennis. Administrative and regulatory, Contracts commercial, Public utilities. Home: 5 Starlight Ct Babylon NY 11704 Office: AT&T Communications Inc 32 Ave of the Americas New York NY 10013

WHITE, KENNETH JAMES, lawyer; b. Bryan, Ohio, Apr. 16, 1948; s. James Foster and Doris E. (Hatfield) W.; m. Diane G. Frechette, Sept. 20, 1969. B.S. cum laude in Journalism, Bowling Green State U., 1970; J.D. cum laude, U. Toledo, 1974. Bar: Ohio 1974, U.S. Dist. Ct. (no. dist.) Ohio 1974, U.S. Ct. Appeals (6th cir.) 1983. Law clk. to pres. judge U.S. Dist. Ct., Toledo, Ohio, 1974-76; ptnr. Spengler, Nathanson, McCarthy & Durfee, Toledo, 1976-84; ptnr. Jacobson, Maynard, Tuschman & Kalur, 1985—. Articles editor U. Toledo Law Rev. 1973-74. Author: (with others) Appellate Practice, Ohio Legal Center Institute, 1981. Mem. ABA, Ohio Bar Assn., Toledo Bar Assn. Federal civil litigation, State civil litigation, Personal injury. Home: 560 Wilkshire Dr Waterville OH 43566 Office: Jacobson Maynard Tuschman & Kalur 9th Floor Four Seagate Toledo OH 43604

WHITE, LAWRENCE RICHARD, lawyer; b. Barksdale AFB, La., June 6, 1948; s. Herbert Richard and Muriel Elaine (Worrel) W.; m. Phala Sue Payne, Oct. 7, 1978; 1 child, Ian Richard. BS in Advt., Ariz. State U., 1970, postgrad., 1971-73; JD, Pepperdine U., 1976. Bar: Calif. 1976, U.S. Dist. Ct. (no. dist.) Calif. 1976, Hawaii 1978, U.S. Dist. Ct. Hawaii 1978, U.S. Ct. Appeals (9th cir.) 1983. Dep. pros. atty. City and County of Honolulu, 1979-82, dep. corp. counsel, 1982-85; assoc. Libkuman, Ventura, Ayabe & Hughes, Honolulu, 1985—. Mem. ABA, Hawaii Bar Assn., Calif. Bar Assn., Assn. Trial Lawyers Am. Republican. Avocations: soccer, stained glass work, woodworking. Civil rights, Federal civil litigation, Personal injury. Home: 47-672-4 Hui Kelu St Kaneohe HI 96744 Office: Libkuman Ventura Ayabe & Hughes 737 Bishop St Mauka Tower Honolulu HI 96813

WHITE, MARK WELLS, JR., governor of Tex.; b. Henderson, Tex., Mar. 17, 1940; s. Mark Wells and Sarah Elizabeth W.; m. Linda Gale Thompson, Oct. 1, 1966; children: Mark Wells III, Andrew, Elizabeth Marie. B.B.A., Baylor U., 1962, J.D., 1965. Bar: Tex. 1965. Asst. atty. gen. ins., banking and securities div. State of Tex. Austin, 1966-69; asso. firm Reynolds, White, Allen & Cook, Houston, 1969-71; partner Reynolds, White, Allen & Cook, 1971-73; sec. of state State of Tex., Austin, 1973-79; atty. gen. 1979-82; gov. State of Tex., Austin, 1983—. Chmn. So. States Energy Bd.; mem. Interstate Oil Compact Comm.; sponsor Nat. Conf. on Ednl. Excellence and Econ. Growth; mem. adv. council Southwestern Baptist Theol. Sem.; mem. Christian Edn. Coordinating Bd., S.W. Regional Energy Council, So. Regional Edn. Bd., Edn. Commn. of States. Served with Tex. N.G., 1966-69. Named Lawyer of Year Baylor U. chpt. Phi Alpha Delta, 1975. Mem. Nat. Assn. Secs. State (pres. 1977-79), Nat. Govs. Assn., So. Govs. Assn. Democrat. Baptist. Legislative. Office: Box 12428 Capitol Station State Capitol Austin TX 78711

WHITE, MICHAEL DOUGLAS, lawyer; b. Ft. Leavenworth, Kans., Nov. 8, 1941; s. William Bradford and Elizabeth (Montgomery) White; m. Mary Danforth Ray, July 20, 1963; children: Matthew Bradford, Mary Elizabeth, Montgomery Lee. BS, U.S. Mil. Acad., 1963; MS, U. So. Calif., 1967; JD, Cornell U., 1970. Bar: Colo., Wyo., U.S. Ct. Appeals (10th cir.), U.S. Supreme Ct. Assoc. Holland & Hart, Denver, 1970-72, Nelson, Hoskin, Groves & Prinster, Grand Junction, Colo., 1972-73; ptnr. Bermingham, White, Burke & Ipsen, Denver, 1973-78, Hall & Evans, Denver, 1978-80, Nossaman, Guthner, Knox & Elliott, Denver, 1980-84, White & Jankowski, Denver, 1984—. Contbr. articles to profl. jours. Chmn. dist. com. and exec. bd. Denver Area council Boy Scouts Am., 1986—; pres. bd. trustees Thorne Ecol. Inst., Boulder, 1978-80. Served to capt. USAF, 1963-67. Mem. ABA (vice chmn. water resources com. natural resources law sect. 1985-86), Colo. Bar Assn. (chmn. environ. sect. 1977-78, chmn. water law sect. 1976-77). Club: Denver. Avocations: hunting, fishing. Water, Real property, Environment. Office: White & Jankowski 511 16th St Suite 500 Denver CO 80202

WHITE, PAMELA JANICE, lawyer; b. Elizabeth, N.J., July 13, 1952; s. Emmet Talmadge and June (Howlett) W. BA with honors, Mary Washington Coll., 1974; JD, Washington and Lee U., 1977. Bar: Md. 1977, U.S. Dist. Ct. Md. 1978, D.C. 1979, U.S. Dist. Ct. D.C. 1979, U.S. Ct. Appeals (4th cir.) 1979, U.S. Ct. Appeals (D.C. cir.) 1981, U.S. Ct. Claims 1981, U.S. Ct. Appeals (2d cir.) 1983, N.Y. 1983, U.S. Dist. Ct. (so. dist.) N.Y. 1983, U.S. Supreme Ct. 1981. Assoc. Ober, Kaler, Grimes & Shriver, Balt., 1977-84, ptnr., 1985—; mem. Md. Bd. Bar Examiners, 1986—. Note and comment editor Washington and Lee Law Rev. 1976-77, Washington and Lee Law Council 1983-87. Mem. ABA, N.Y. State Bar Assn., Md. State Bar Assn., D.C. Bar Assn., Balt. City Bar Assn., Fed. Bar Assn., Women's Bar Assn. Md. (treas. 1986-87, v.p. 1987—, bd. dirs. 1984-86), Md. Assn. Def. Counsel. Presbyterian. Avocations: hiking, softball, baseball. Federal civil litigation, Labor, Environment. Office: Ober Kaler Grimes & Shriver 10 Light St Baltimore MD 21202

WHITE, PAUL STEPHEN, lawyer; b. Louisville, July 7, 1951; s. Carlton Francis and Alpha Ann (Shely) W.; m. Rachel Ryan White, Dec. 22, 1972; children: Stephanie, Cassandra. BA, U. Ky., 1974, JD, 1981. Bar: Ky. 1982, U.S. Dist. Ct. (ea. dist.) Ky. 1983. Assoc. Forcht & Trimble, P.S.C., Corbin, Ky., 1982-83; sole practice Danville, Ky., 1983—; asst. county atty. Boyle County, Ky., 1984—. Editor Amanuensis (lit. jour.), 1972-74. Rep. Preservation Alliance, Louisville, 1975; bd. dirs. Shelby Park Neighborhood Assn., Louisville, 1975-76. Mem. ABA, Ky. Bar Assn., Boyle County Bar Assn. (sec., treas. 1984-85). Democrat. Roman Catholic. Lodge: Lions (treas. Danville 1985-86). General practice. Home: 407 E Main St Danville KY 40422 Office: PO Box 1161 326 W Main St Danville KY 40422

WHITE, PENNY J., lawyer; b. Kingsport, Tenn., May 3, 1956; d. C.A. and Alvira Euogene (Bush) W.; m. Gary C. Shockley, Sept. 24, 1983. BS, East Tenn. State U., 1978; JD, U. Tenn., 1981; postdoctoral, Georgetown U., 1983. Bar: Tenn. 1981, Md. 1983. Assoc. Richard Pectol & Assocs., Johnson City, Tenn., 1981-83; sole practice Johnson City, Tenn., 1985—; bd. dirs. Comprehensive Community Service, Johnson City. E. Barrett Prettyman fellow Georgetown Law Ctr., Washington, 1983-85. Mem. ABA, Assn. Trial Lawyers Am., Tenn. Bar Assn., East Tenn. State U. Nat. Alumni Assn. (pres. 1985-86). Democrat. Avocations: crafts, travel. Criminal, Personal injury, Civil rights. Home: 106 E Woodrow Jonesborough TN 37615 Office: 100 W Unaka Johnson City TN 37601

WHITE, PETER ALLEN, lawyer; b. Toledo, Nov. 11, 1944; s. Charles Allen and Nancy Carolyn (Turner) W.; m. Anne Heather Fullagar, Dec. 21, 1974; children—John Charles, Michael Allen. A.B. cum laude with high honors in Eng. Lit., Kenyon Coll., 1966; J.D., Duke U., 1969. Bar: Ohio 1969, U.S. Dist. Ct. (no. dist.) Ohio 1971, D.C. 1973, U.S. Dist. Ct. D.C. 1973, U.S. Ct. Claims 1975, U.S. Ct. Appeals (D.C. cir.) 1976, U.S. Supreme Ct. 1977. Law clk. to Chief Justice, Ohio Supreme Ct., 1969-70; assoc. Thompson, Hine & Flory, Cleve., 1970-72; assoc. Hogan & Hartson, Washington, 1972-73; sr. atty. FTC, Washington, 1973-75; ptnr. Fulbright & Jaworski, Washington, 1975-86, of counsel, 1986—; pres. Internat. Skye Assocs., Inc., 1986—; dep. spl. counsel Com. on Standards of Ofcl. Conduct, U.S. Ho. of Reps., 1977-78; dir. Fountain House, Eagle Mgmt. Co.; mem. panel of arbitrators Am. Arbitration Assn. Recipient FTC award for superior service, 1975. Mem. ABA, Fed. Bar Assn., Internat. Bar Assn., Inter-Am. Bar Assn., Internat. Law Inst., U.S. C. of C., Am. Textile Mfrs. Inst. Contbr. writings to profl. legal pubs. Private international, General corporate, Federal civil litigation. Office: 1150 Connecticut Ave NW Suite 400 Washington DC 20036

WHITE, R. QUINCY, lawyer; b. Chgo., Jan. 16, 1933; s. Roger Q. and Carolyn Jane (Everett) W.; m. Joyce Caldwell, Aug. 4, 1962; children: Cleaver Dorothea, Annelia Everett. B.A., Yale U., 1954; J.D., Harvard U., 1960. Bar: Ill. 1960, U.S. Dist. Ct. (no. dist.) Ill. 1960. Assoc. Leibman, Williams, Bennett, Baird & Minow, Chgo., 1960-67, ptnr., 1967-73; ptnr. Sidley & Austin, Chgo., 1973—; hon. consul. gen. Islamic Rep. Pakistan, Chgo., 1978—; sec., dir. W.F. McLaughlin Co., Chgo., 1964-68; designated mem. U.S. Trademark Assn., 1985—. Dir., counsel Off The Street Club, Chgo., 1974-84; sec. nat. governing bd. The Ripon Soc., 1971-72; mem. exec. com. 43d-44th ward regional Republican orgn., 1970-73; mem. Council Fgn. and Domestic Affaris, 1970-76; v.p., bd. dirs. Juvenile Protective Assn., 1965-87. Recipient Sitara-i-Quaid-i-Azam Pakistan, 1982. Mem. Chgo. Council Lawyers, Chgo. Bar Assn., ABA. Home: 316 W Willow St Chicago IL 60614 Office: Sidley & Austin 1 First National Plaza Chicago IL 60603

WHITE, RENEE ALLYN, judge; b. Bronx, N.Y., Sept. 22, 1945; d. Lawrence and Ann (Kaufman) W. B.A., Hofstra U., 1966, J.D., Bklyn. Law Sch., 1969. Bar: N.Y. 1969, U.S. Dist. Ct. (ea. and so. dists.) N.Y. 1977, U.S. Supreme Ct. 1978. Trial atty. Criminal Def. div. The Legal Aid Soc. N.Y.C., 1969-74; atty. in charge Criminal Justice sect. Office of Projects Devel. Appeal div. First Dept., N.Y.C., 1974-78; adminstrv. law judge City N.Y. Office Adminstrv. Trials and Hearings, 1978-84; judge N.Y.C. Civil Ct., 1984, Criminal Ct. City of N.Y., 1985—; lectr. in field. Mem. ABA, N.Y. State Bar Assn. (chmn. criminal justice sect. 1985—), Assn. of Bar of City of N.Y., N.Y. Women's Bar Assn. Contbr. in field. Criminal, Administrative and regulatory, Legal education. Home: 256 Henry St #4 Brooklyn NY 11201

WHITE, RICHARD BELL, lawyer; b. San Mateo, Calif., June 18, 1951; s. Richard White Jr. and Beverly (Bell) W.; m. Frankie Lee Gage, Nov. 8, 1952; children: Richard, Stephen, Brian. BA, Gonzaga U., 1975, JD, 1980. Bar: Wash. 1980, U.S. Dist. Ct. (ea. dist.) Wash. 1980. Probation officer juvenile div. Spokane (Wash.) County, 1974-77; legal intern U.S. Atty. Office, Spokane, 1978-80; assoc. Layman, Mullen & Etter, Spokane, 1980-83, Evans, Craven & Lackie, Spokane, 1983—. Bd. dirs. Legal Services Corp., Spokane, 1980-83, Alcoholism Outpatient Services, Spokane, 1980—. Mem. Spokane County Bar Assn. (trustee), Wash. State Trial Lawyers Assn., Assn. Trial Lawyers Am. Democrat. Roman Catholic. Home: 8201 N Antietam Dr Spokane WA 99208 Office: Evans Craven & Lackie 1170 Seafirst Fin Ctr 501 W Riverside Ave Spokane WA 99201

WHITE, RICHARD CLARENCE, lawyer; b. Sioux City, Iowa, Oct. 31, 1933; s. William David and Gwendolyn Rena McGlauflin; m. Beverly Frances Fitzpatrick, Feb. 22, 1955; children—Anne, Richard, William, Christopher. B.A.; LL.B., Stanford U., 1962. Bar: Calif. 1963, U.S. Supreme Ct. 1970, N.Y. 1983. Assoc. O'Melveny & Myers, Los Angeles, 1962-70, ptnr., 1970—. Lectr. in field. Bd. dirs. Equal Employment Adv. Council, Washington, 1976-80, 83, Performing Arts Ctr. of Orange County. Served with USMC, 1954-59; capt. USMC Res. Mem. ABA (co-chmn. com. on practice and procedure labor and employment law sect. 1977-80, mem. equal opportunity law com. 1980-85, co-chmn. com. on insts. and meetings 1985—), Los Angeles County Bar Assn., Orange County Bar Assn. Republican. Club: Lincoln (Orange County). Contbr. articles to profl. publs. Labor, Administrative and regulatory.

WHITE, ROBERT ELLSWORTH, lawyer; b. Ottawa, Ill., Feb. 18, 1933; s. Lawrence James and Lura Mae (Ellsworth) W.; m. Elinore Eileen Corrigan, Sept. 16, 1961; children—Leslie Marie, Michael Robert, Kathleen Marie, Brendan Michael. B.S., U. Notre Dame, 1955, J.D., 1961. Bar: Ill. 1961. Sole practice, Ottawa, 1961-65; ptnr. White & Marsh, 1965-81, White & Marsh, 1981—. Served to capt. USAF, 1955-59. Mem. Ill. Bar Assn., LaSalle County Bar Assn. Roman Catholic. Clubs: Elks, KC. Probate, Banking, State civil litigation. Office: White Marsh & Mueller Ottawa National Bank Bldg Ottawa IL 61350 *

WHITE, RUSSELL ALAN, lawyer; b. Long Beach, Calif., Sept. 2, 1951; s. Robert Lanon and Betty June (Nelson) W.; m. Sandy Austin, Apr. 23, 1982; 1 child, Matthew. AB, U. Chgo., 1973; JD, U. Md., 1976. Bar: Fla. 1978, U.S. Dist. Ct. (so. dist.) Fla., 1980. Assoc. Rogers, Morris & Ziegler, Ft. Lauderdale, Fla., 1984—. Advocate for Archdiocese of Miami, 1983—. Recipient Fundraising Leadership award U. Chgo., 1981. Mem. Broward County Bar Assn. (law day com.), Christian Bus. Men's Com. (bd. dirs. Ft. Lauderdale chpt.), Broward County Christian Lawyers Assn. (pres. 1986—). Republican. Roman Catholic. Lodge: Rotary (bd. dirs.). Avocations: bible study, basketball, reading. Real property, Banking, State civil litigation. Office: 800 E Broward Blvd Fort Lauderdale FL 33301

WHITE, SHARON ELIZABETH, lawyer; b. Galveston, Tex., July 5, 1955; d. Edward and Clara Adelia (Haden) W. BA, Baylor U., 1977; JD, So. Meth. U., 1981. Bar: Tex. 1981, U.S. Dist. Ct. (no. dist.) Tex. 1983, U.S. Ct. Appeals (5th cir.) 1985. Assoc. Underwood, Wilson, Berry, Stein & Johnson, Amarillo, Tex., 1981-86, ptnr., 1987—. Asst. editor-in-chief Southwestern Law Rev., Dallas, 1980-81. Bd. dirs., sec. council Amarillo Girl Scout U.S., 1983-85, 3d v.p., 1985, 1st v.p. 1985—; bd. dirs. Amarillo Little Theatre, 1984-86, treas., 1985—; grants chmn. Don Harrington Discovery Ctr., 1984-86, future planning and devel. chmn., 1986—; active Amarillo Symphony Guild, Amarillo Art Alliance, Panhandle Plains Hist. Soc. Mem. ABA, Amarillo Bar Assn., Phi Delta Phi, Delta Delta Delta. Republican. Presbyterian. Real property, Consumer commercial, General corporate. Office: Underwood Wilson et al PO Box 9158 Amarillo TX 79105

WHITE, STEPHEN ALAN, lawyer; b. Little Rock, Ark., Aug. 23, 1949; s. Eugene Edwin and Laura Elizabeth (O'Bryan) W.; m. Tad Warren, Dec. 30, 1970; Seth Aaron. Student, U. Ark., 1972, JD, 1975. Bar: Ark. 1975, U.S. Dist. Ct. (ea. and we. dists.) Ark. 1975, U.S. Ct. Appeals (8th cir.) 1980, U.S. Supreme Ct. 1981. Sole practice Charleston, Ark., 1975—; judge Charleston Mcpl. Ct., 1977—. Adv. trustee Sparks Regional Med. Ctr., Ft. Smith, Ark., 1976-78; chmn. bd. dirs. Charleston 1st United Meth. Ch., 1978-80, 82; chmn. Charleston Econ. Devel. com., 1980—. Served as cpl. USMC, 1967-69. Mem. ABA, Ark. Bar Assn. (Lawyer Citizen award 1982), Franklin County Bar Assn., Ark. Mcpl. Judge's Assn., Charleston C. of C. (pres. 1977, Citizen of Yr. 1981, Community Service award 1983). Democrat. Methodist. State civil litigation, Banking, Real property. Home and Office: PO Box 85 Charleston AR 72933

WHITE, STEPHEN RICHARD, lawyer, educator; b. Pensacola, Fla., Apr. 14, 1948; s. Edward Timothy and Jane Helen (Zaruba) W.; m. Veronica DiBenedetto, Mar. 19, 1972; children—Christopher Stephen, John Patrick. B.A., Fla. State U., 1970, J.D., 1972; M.A., Yale U., 1974, M.Philosophy, 1975. Bar: Fla. 1973, U.S. Dist. Ct. (mid. dist.) Fla. 1980, U.S. Ct. Appeals (5th cir.) 1980, U.S. Ct. Appeals (11th cir.) 1983, U.S. Supreme Ct. 1980. Intake counselor Juvenile Ct. of Record, Pensacola, Fla., 1970; legal intern Office Atty Gen. Fla., Tallahassee, 1972, Legal Aid, Tallahassee, 1972; hot-line asst. Office Atty. Gen. Fla., Tallahassee, 1972-73; asst. state atty., Jacksonville, Fla., 1976—, tng. officer for State Atty.'s Office, 1984-86; spl. asst. atty gen., 1983-84; instr. Police Acad., Jacksonville, 1982—; substitute instr. U. No. Fla., Jacksonville, 1983-84; lectr. on drugs Duval County Schs., Jacksonville, 1983-85, to statewide seminar of prosecutors regarding workload mgmt., 1986, for police in-service tng., 1986—, on role of prosecutor Fla. Jr. Coll., 1986, research on prosecutorial decision making. Editor Fla. State U. Law Rev., 1972, Newsletter of Law, State Atty.'s Office, Jacksonville, 1983-84; contbr. to book and profl. jours. Served to capt., legal officer USAF, 1973. Mem. Am. Judicature Soc., Law and Soc. Assn., Jacksonville Bar Assn., Fla. Pros. Attys. Assn. (mem. edn. com.), Alpha Kappa Delta, Pi Sigma Alpha. Democrat. Roman Catholic. Criminal, Legal education, Prosecution management. Home: 12516 Shady Creek Dr Jacksonville FL 32223 Office: State Attorney's Office Duval County Courthouse Jacksonville FL 32202

WHITE, STEVEN GREGORY, lawyer; b. Dallas, July 11, 1957; s. Kenneth and Merle Allene (Johnston) W.; m. Ellen McGregor, Sept. 4, 1984; children: Cora Ellen, Shelby Jean. Student, Baylor U., 1976-79, JD, 1982. Bar: Tex. 1982, U.S. Dist. Ct. (we. dist.) Tex. 1984, U.S. Ct. Appeals (5th cir.) 1985, U.S. Dist. Ct. (no. dist.) Tex. 1986. Assoc. McGregor & White, Waco, Tex., 1982—; bd. dirs., sec. Bankers Protective Life, Dallas. Active United Way, Waco, 1984. Mem. Waco Young Lawyers Assn. (bd. dirs.), Phi Delta Phi. Baptist. Federal civil litigation, State civil litigation, Contracts commercial. Office: McGregor White et al 1700 Alico Center Waco TX 76701

WHITE, THOMAS OWEN, law educator, university dean, lawyer; b. Pitts., Sept. 4, 1940; A.B., Cornell U., 1962; J.D., U. Pitts., 1965. Bar: Pa. 1965. Assoc. Dickie McCamey & Chilcote, Pitts., 1965; assoc. dean, prof. U. Pitts. Sch. Law, 1965—; dir. law programs div. Ednl. Testing Service, Princeton, N.J., 1976, v.p., 1979; pres., chief operating officer Law Sch. Admission Services/Council. Pres. Neighborhood Legal Services of Pitts. and Allegheny County, 1970-73; chmn. Forest Hills Planning Commn., 1970-76. Mem. Am. Law Inst., Am. Judicature Soc., Pa. Bar Assn. Author: (with Murray) Commercial Transactions, 1972; (with Sell) Pennsylvania Keystone, 5 vols., 1970-77. Legal education. Home: 33 Montague Ave West Trenton NJ 08628 Office: PO Box 40 Newtown PA 18940

WHITE, TRUDY MELITA, lawyer; b. Baton Rouge, July 5, 1956; d. Gilbert A. and Avis (Baker) W. BBA, Howard U., 1978; JD, La. State U., 1981. Bar: La. 1981. Staff atty. La. Dept. Revenue, Baton Rouge, 1981-85; sole practice Baton Rouge, 1981—; gen. counsel La. Child Support Enforcement Program, Baton Rouge, 1985—. Mem. Leadership Greater Baton Rouge, 1985. Mem. Nat. Bar Assn., Baton Rouge Bar Assn., Black Women Lawyers of Baton Rouge Area, Southwest Child Support Attys. Assn. (pres. 1986—), Louis Martinet Legal Soc., Delta Sigma Theta. Democrat. Roman Catholic. Family and matrimonial, Juvenile, General practice. Home: 9827 Siegen Ln Baton Rouge LA 70810 Office: La Child Support Enforcement Program PO Box 94065 Baton Rouge LA 70804

WHITE, WALTER HIAWATHA, JR., lawyer; b. Milw., Aug. 21, 1954; s. Walter H. and Winifred (Parker) W.; m. Sonja Athene Rein, Dec. 30, 1977. Student, Leningrad Pedagogical Inst., USSR, 1976; BA, Amherst Coll., 1977; JD, U. Calif., Berleley, 1980. Bar: Wis. 1980, U.S. Dist. Ct. (ea. dist.) Wis. 1980, U.S. Ct. Appeals (7th cir.) 1980, U.S. Supreme Ct. 1983. Assoc. Michael, Best & Friedrich, Milw., 1980—; vice-chmn. dist. com. Bd. Attys. Profl. Responsibility, Milw., 1984-87; bd. dirs. Wis. Trust Found., Madison, 1986—. Editor Black Law Jour., 1978-80; also articles. Mem. Cardinal Stritch Coll. Bus. Adv. Bd., Milw., 1982-85, health law com. Wis. Civil Liberties Union, Milw., 1985—, Gov.'s Adv. Bd. to Legal Services Corp., Madison, 1982-87; sec. Milw. Forum Inc., 1982—; pres. Milw. Urban League, 1985; bd. dirs. WUWM Pub. Radio Sta., Milw., 1983-86, Family Service Milw., Inc., 1987—, Neighborhood House of Milw., Inc., 1987—. John Woodruff Simpson fellow, 1977; Named one of the 86 most interesting people in Milw., Milw. Mag., 1986. Mem. ABA (dir. young lawyers div. 1985-86, commn. on opportunities for minorities in the profession, assn. of Soviet lawyers del.), Nat. Bar Assn., Internat. Bar Assn. (bus. law sect.), Milw. Bar Assn., Wis. Black Lawyers Assn. (bd. dirs. 1982-83), Milw. Young Lawyers Assn. (pres. 1984-85, pres.'s award 1985), Bd. Attys. Profl. Competence. Avocations: Russian and Soviet lit., rowing, squash. Health, General corporate, Private international. Home: 904 E Pleasant St Milwaukee WI 53202 Office: Michael Best & Friedrich 250 E Wisconsin Ave Milwaukee WI 53202

WHITE, WILLIAM RICHARD, lawyer; b. Newton, Iowa, Nov. 24, 1946; s. William Robert and Eva Erlene (Trout) W.; m. Ann Maurine Onnen, Dec. 15, 1979; children: Joshua, Judd, Dustin. Bar: Iowa 1976, U.S. Dist. Ct. (so. dist.) Iowa 1976, U.S. Dist. Ct. (no. dist.) Iowa 1976, U.S. Ct. Appeals (8th cir.) 1976, U.S. Supreme Ct. 1979. Asst. atty. gen. dept. justice State of Iowa, Des Moines, 1976-78; spl. prosecutor child support recovery unit State of Iowa, Decorah, 1978-83; ptnr. Morrow & White, Waukon, Iowa, 1983—. Mem. cen. com. Winneshiek County (Iowa) Reps., 1982—; chmn. bd. dirs. Winneshiek County Cancer Soc., 1982; bd. dirs. Northeast Iowa Devel. Ctr., Waukon, 1985—. Served with USN, 1967-71. Mem. ABA, Iowa Bar Assn., Allamakee County Bar Assn. (pres. 1986—). Republican. Lutheran. Lodge: Lions. Avocations: fishing, hunting, golf. General practice. Home: Rt 6 Box 71 Decorah IA 52101 Office: Morrow & White 18 3d Ave SW Waukon IA 52172

WHITEAKER, RAYMOND COMBS, lawyer; b. Nashville, Apr. 20, 1927; s. Raymond C. and Dorothy (Naylor) W.; m. Janice Malsberger, Jan. 3, 1957; children: Dorothy L. Whiteaker Malloy, Kent D., Lon N. BA, Vanderbilt U., 1951, JD, 1952; LLM, NYU, 1953. Bar: Tenn. 1953, U.S. Dist. Ct. (mid. dist.) Tenn. 1953, Ga. 1958, U.S. Ct. Appeals (6th cir.) 1970. Assoc. Barksdale & Hodgins, Nashville, 1953-54; sr. trial atty. IRS, Atlanta, 1955-59; atty. So. Bell Tel.&Tel. Co., Atlanta, 1959-68; gen. atty. So. Cen. Bell Telephone Co., Nashville, 1968—. Served with USN, 1945-46. Mem. ABA, Fed. Bar Assn. (pres. local chpt. 1976), Tenn. Bar Assn., Nashville Bar Assn. Methodist. Club: Hillwood Country (Nashville). Administrative and regulatory, Public utilities. Home: 5926 Post Rd Nashville TN 37205 Office: So Cen Bell Telephone Co 356 Greenhills Bldg Nashville TN 37215

WHITEHEAD, JOHN W., lawyer, organization administrator; b. Pulaski, Tenn., July 14, 1946; s. John M. and Alatha (Wiser) W.; m. Virginia Carolyn Nichols, Aug. 26, 1967; children: Jayson Reau, Jonathan Mathew, Elisabeth Anne, Joel Christofer, Joshua Benjamen. BA, U. Ark., 1969, JD, 1974. Bar: Ark. 1974, U.S. Dist. Ct. (ea. and we. dists.) Ark. 1974, U.S. Supreme Ct. 1977, U.S. Ct. Appeals (9th cir.) 1980, Va. 1981, U.S. Ct. Appeals (7th cir.) 1981. Spl. counsel Christian Legal Soc., Oak Park, Ill., 1977-78; assoc. Gibbs & Craze, Cleve., 1978-79; sole practice law Manassas, Va., 1979-82; pres. The Rutherford Inst., Manassas, Va., 1982—, also bd. dirs.; frequent lectr. colls., law schs.; past adj. prof. O.W. Coburn Sch. Law. Author: The Separation Illusion, 1977, Schools on Fire, 1980, The New Tyranny, 1982, The Second American Revolution, 1982, The Stealing of America, 1983, The Freedom of Religious Expression in Public High Schools, 1983, The End of Man, 1986, several others; contbr. numerous articles to profl. jours.; contbr. numerous chpts. to books. Served to 1st lt. U.S. Army, 1969-71. Named Christian Leader of Yr. Christian World Affairs Conf., Washington, 1986. Mem. ABA, Ark. Bar Assn., Va. Bar Assn. Civil rights, Federal civil litigation, Criminal. Office: The Rutherford Inst 9411 Battle St Manassas VA 22110

WHITEHILL, CHARLES ALLEN, lawyer; b. Cin., July 24, 1952; s. Thelma Alleyne (Robbins) W. BA summa cum laude, Marian Coll., 1974; JD magna cum laude, Ind. U., 1979. Bar: Ind. 1979, U.S. Dist. Ct. Ind. 1979, U.S. Tax Ct. 1979. Adminstrv. asst. Marian Coll. office of admissions, Indpls., 1971-74; sole practice Indpls., 1979—; gen. counsel Garington Properties, Indpls., 1981—, Yohler Realty Co., Indpls., 1982—. Editor: (book) The Indiana Tax Practitioner's Directory, 1980. Recipient Am. Jurisprudence award Lawyers Coop. Pub. Co. and Bancroft-Whitney Co., 1975, excellence in bus. taxation, 1978. Mem. ABA (taxation sect.), Ind. State Bar Assn. (taxation sect.), Ind. U. Sch. Law Alumni Assn., Delta Epsilon Sigma. Roman Catholic. Avocations: auto racing, aviation, bodysurfing, travel. Corporate taxation, Personal income taxation, Real property. Home and Office: 521 N Emerson Ave Indianapolis IN 46219

WHITEHILL, CLIFFORD LANE, lawyer, food company executive; b. Houston, Apr. 14, 1931; s. Clifford R. and Catalina Borega (Yarza) W.; m. Daisy Mae Woodruff, Apr. 18, 1959; children—Clifford Scott, Alicia Anne, Stephen Lane. B.A., Rice U., 1954; LL.B., U. Tex.-Austin, 1957; LL.M., Harvard U., 1958. Bar: Tex. 1957, Minn. 1970. Assoc., Childress, Port & Crady, 1957-59; atty. Haskins & Sells, 1959, Tex. Butadiene & Chem. Co., N.Y.C., 1959-62; with Gen. Mills, Inc., Mpls., 1962—, sr. v.p., gen. counsel, 1975—. Bd. dirs. Minn.-Uruguay Ptnrs.; past pres. Mpls. People To People; bd. dirs. Minn. Opera Co.; commr. Chanhassen Housing and Redevel. Authority; bd. dirs. Nat. Hispanic Scholarship Fund; bd. trustees Food and Drug Law Inst. Mem. Am. Judicature Soc., Bus. Roundtable (lawyers steering com.), Minn. Assn. Commerce and Industry (bd. dirs.), GMA (legal exec. com.), Am. Soc. Internat. Law, Am. Arbitration Assn., ABA, Tex. Bar Assn., Minn. Bar Assn. Roman Catholic. Clubs: Harvard (N.Y.C.); Lafayette (Mpls.). Editor Tex. Law Rev., 1954-57. General corporate, Private international, Corporate taxation. Office: Gen Mills Inc 9200 Wayzata Blvd Minneapolis MN 55440

WHITEHORN, JO-ANN H., lawyer; b. N.Y.C., Aug. 11, 1948; d. Jules and Blanche Whitehorn. B.A. in History, U. Pa., 1969; J.D., Columbia U., 1972. Bar: N.Y. 1973, U.S. Dist. Ct. (so. and ea. dists.) N.Y. 1973, U.S. Ct. Appeals (2d cir.) 1975, U.S. Supreme Ct. 1976. Asst. counsel Office Gen. Counsel, N.Y. Life Ins. Co., N.Y.C., 1972-77; assoc. Wien, Malkin & Bettex, N.Y.C., 1977-82; dep. gen. counsel Battery Park City Authority, N.Y.C., 1982, N.Y. State Urban Devel. Corp., N.Y.C., 1982—. Assoc. mem. Real Estate Bd. N.Y. Mem. ABA (sect. real property, probate and trust law, young lawyers' sect.), N.Y. State Bar Assn. (real property law sect.), Assn. Bar City N.Y. (com. on sex and law 1973-82, chmn. 1978-82, sec. 1973-74; mem. com. on mil. justice and mil. affairs 1980-81, com. on real property law 1982-85); Council N.Y. Law Assocs., N.Y. County Lawyers' Assn., Assn. Real Estate Women, Mortar Bd., Sphinx and Key. Real property, Construction, General corporate.

WHITEHURST, CHARLES ELWOOD, JR., lawyer; b. Columbus, Ohio, Apr. 5, 1952; s. Charles E. Sr. and Roberta (Stuart) W. AA, Wesley Coll., 1972; BS, Lycoming Coll., 1975; JD, George Washington U., 1978. Bar: D.C. 1978, Del. 1981. Assoc. Schmittinger & Rodriguez P.A., Dover, Del., 1981—. Mem. ABA, Del. Bar Assn., Del. Trial Lawyers Assn., Assn. Trial Lawyers Am., Nat. Assn. Criminal Def. Attys., Order of Coif. Criminal, Personal injury, Toxic tort. Office: Schmittinger & Rodriguez PA 414 S State St Dover DE 19901

WHITEHURST, WILLIAM O., lawyer; b. Ardmore, Okla., Oct. 23, 1945; s. William Oscar and Freddie Leizabeth (Ormsby) W.; m. Stephanie Anne Evans, June 22, 1968; children: Emilee Dawn, Rebecca Danielle. BS in Pharmacy, U. Okla., 1968; JD, U. Tex., 1970. Bar: Tex. 1971, U.S. Dist. Ct. (we. amd so. dists.) Tex. 1971, U.S. Ct. Mil. Appeals 1971, U.S. Ct. Appeals (5th cir.) 1971, U.S. Supreme Ct. 1971. Assoc. Fulbright & Jaworski, Houston, 1971; counsel, staff dir. jud. affairs com. Tex. Ho. Reps., Austin, 1975; ptnr. Kidd, Whitehurst, Harkness & Watson, Austin, 1975—; mem. Senate-House Select Com. on the Judiciary, 1983—, subcom. on Service Delivery, subcom. on Jurisdicition; faculty law U. Tex., 1979—, Tex. Coll. Trial Adv., 1984. Fellow Am. Bar Found., Tex. Bar Found.; mem. ABA, Tex. Bar Assn. (pres. 1986—, exec. com. 1981-83, 85—, bd. dirs. 1981-84, active various coms.), Travis County Bar Assn. (sec. 1980-81, bd. dirs. 1979-81), Tex. Young Lawyers Assn. (pres. 1982-83, bd. dirs. 1979-84), Austin Young Lawyers Assn. (pres. 1978-79), Assn. Trial Lawyers Am., Tex. Trial Lawyers Assn., Am. Soc. Pharmacy Law, Am. Soc. Law and Medicine, Order of Barristers. Democrat. Presbyterian. Clubs: University, Austin Country. Avocations: flying, snow and water skiing, travel. Personal injury, Federal civil litigation, State civil litigation. Home: 2703 Westlake Dr Austin TX 78746 Office: Kidd Whitehurst Harkness & Watson 1122 Colorado Austin TX 78701

WHITELAW, BRIAN WILLIAM, lawyer; b. Lakewood, Ohio, Feb. 22, 1954; s. William Murray and Pepper (Brianzoni) W. BS cum laude, Mich. State U., 1977; JD, Detroit Coll. Law, 1981. Bar: Mich. 1981, U.S. Dist. Ct. (ea. dist.) Mich. 1981. Staff atty. City of Troy, Mich., 1981-83; sr. assoc. Kitch, Saurbier, Drutchas, Wagner & Kenney, Detroit, 1983—. Mem. Detroit Bar Assn., Macomb County Bar Assn., Oakland County Bar Assn. Republican. Club: St. John Hosp. Guild (Detroit). Avocations: scuba diving, running, handball, chess. Personal injury. Home: 16147 Hauss East Detroit MI 48021 Office: Kitch Saurbier Drutchas et al 1 Woodward Ave 10th Fl Detroit MI 48226

WHITEMAN, ROBERT GORDON, lawyer; b. N.Y.C., Feb. 12, 1951; s. Robert Joseph and Bettye Rollins (Durrence) W.; m. Cynthia Vail White, Dec. 30, 1978; children: Alexander St. Julian, Elizabeth Ravenel. BA, Alfred U., 1973; JD, Drake U., 1976. Bar: N.Y. 1977, D.C. 1978, U.S. Ct. Appeals (2d cir.) 1983, U.S. Dist. Ct. (ea. and so. dists.) N.Y. 1983. Middle East mgr. Brady Internat., Kuwait, 1977-79; assoc. Howard Davis, N.Y.C., 1979-80, Mirabel, Wortman & Freidel, Huntington, N.Y., 1980-84, Whiteman & Gorray, Westbury, N.Y., 1984—; atty. cons. Jaime Palmer, Palma de Mallorca, Spain, 1979—. Mem. ABA, N.Y. State Bar Assn., Suffolk County Bar Assn., Assn. Trial Lawyers Am., Nassau-Suffolk Trial Lawyers Assn., Def. Research Inst. Club: Westchester Country (Rye, N.Y.). Private international, Insurance, Personal injury. Home: 115 Hampton Rd Garden City NY 11530 Office: Whiteman & Gorray 1600 Stewart Ave Westbury NY 11590

WHITENTON, DEWEY CRAFT, judge; b. Bolivar, Tenn., June 4, 1934; s. Dewey and Lorena (Craft) W.; m. Marne Davis, Apr. 30, 1960; children: Carol, David, Joel. BA, Vanderbilt U., 1956, JD, 1959. Bar: Tenn. 1959. Sole practice Bolivar, 1959-76; judge chancery ct. 25th jud. dist. State of Tenn., 1976—; atty. Hardeman County, Bolivar, 1970-76; mem. jud. council Tenn. Supreme Ct., Nashville, 1980—; mem. Tenn. Jud. Conf.; bd. dirs. Home Fed. Savs. & Loan Assn., Memphis. Chmn. adminstrv. bd. 1st United Meth. Ch., Bolivar. Served with U.S. Army, 1960-65. Mem. ABA, Tenn. Bar Assn. (ho. dels. 1972-76), Tenn. Trial Judges Assn. Club: Hardeman County Country (Bolivar) (pres.). Lodge: Rotary (pres. Bolivar). Office: 116 Warren St PO Box 303 Bolivar TN 38008

WHITESIDE, DAVID POWERS, JR., lawyer; b. Tupelo, Miss., Jan. 1, 1950; s. David Powers and Delores Dean (Gerkin) W. m. Roseanna McCoy, June 2, 1972; children—David III, Lauren. B.A., Samford U., 1972; cert. Exeter Coll., Oxford U., England, 1974; J.D., Duke U., 1975; LL.M., U. Ala.-Tuscaloosa, 1980. Bar: Ala. 1975, U.S. Dist. Ct. (no. dist.) Ala. 1975, U.S. Ct. Appeals (5th cir.) 1975, U.S. Ct. Appeals (11th cir.) 1981, U.S. Supreme Ct. 1978. Assoc. Johnston, Barton, Proctor et al., Birmingham, Ala., 1975-81, ptnr., 1981—; gen. counsel, Personnel Bd. Jefferson County, Birmingham, 1981-86; legal counsel Jefferson County Citizens Supervisory Commn., Birmingham, 1982-85; lectr. Ala. Jud. Coll., 1985—. First. v.p. Birmingham Music Club, 1979-81; mem. Com. for a Better Ala., Birmingham, 1981-82. Recipient Mark Donahue Meml. award Ala. Sports Car Club, 1981-82; Memorable Quotes award Birmingham Post-Herald, 1981; named to Outstanding Young Men of Am., 1982; Winner Palm Beach Hist. Races, 1984. Mem. U.S. Ct. of Appeals Fifth Cir. Judicial Conf. (Host com. 1977), U.S. Ct. Fifth Cir. Judicial Conf., (del. 1978); U.S. Ct. Appeals 11th Cir. Judicial Conf. (del. 1982, 86), Newcomen Soc. N.Am., Birmingham Bar Assn. (editorial staff 1980-81), ABA (sect. on employment relations), Phi Alpha Theta, Omicron Delta Kappa. Episcopalian. Civil rights, Labor, State civil litigation. Home: 2840 Overton Rd Birmingham AL 35223 Office: Johnston Barton Proctor Swedlaw & Naff 1100 Park Place Tower Birmingham AL 35203

WHITESIDE, FIFE MORRIS, lawyer; b. Holly Springs, Miss., Sept. 23, 1952; s. Robert Morris and Kathleen (Alexander) W.; m. Emily Vann Luttrell, Aug. 25, 1979; 1 child, Anna Elizabeth. BA in English, Miss. State U., 1974; JD, U. Miss., 1976. Bar: Miss. 1977, Ga. 1982. Sole practice Holly Springs, Miss., 1977-81, Columbus, Ga., 1983—; law clk. to presiding justice U.S. Bankers Ct. (mid. dist.), Columbus, Ga., 1981-83. Mem. ABA, Assn. Trial Lawyers Am., Comml. Law League, Am. Judicature Soc., Columbus Lawyers Club. Bankruptcy, Federal civil litigation, State civil litigation. Home: 1440 Cherokee Columbus GA 31906 Office: PO Box 5383 Columbus GA 31906

WHITESIDE, WILLIAM ANTHONY, JR., lawyer; b. Phila. Feb. 23, 1929; s. William Anthony and Ellen T. (Hensler) W.; m. Eileen Ann Ferrick, Feb. 27, 1954; children—William Anthony III, Michael P., Eileen A., Richard F., Christopher J., Mary P. B.S. Notre Dame U., 1951; LL.B. U. Pa., 1954. Bar: Pa. 1955. Assoc. Speiser, Satinsky, Gilliland & Packel, Phila., 1956-58, ptnr., 1958-61; ptnr. Fox, Rothschild, O'Brien & Frankel, Phila., 1961—; Trustee, Germantown Acad., also past pres. Served to 1st lt. USAF, 1954-56. Named Man of Yr., Notre Dame Club Phila., 1967. Mem. ABA, Pa. Bar Assn., Phila. Bar Assn. Republican. Roman Catholic. Clubs: Union League, Wissahickon Skating, Pa. Soc. (Phila.); North Hills (Pa.) Country. Private international, Pension, profit-sharing, and employee benefits, Labor. Home: 7808 Cobden Rd Laverock Philadelphia PA 19118 Office: Fox Rothschild O'Brien & Frankel 2000 Market St 10th Floor Philadelphia PA 19103

WHITESMAN, GUY EDWARD, lawyer; b. Chambersburg, Pa., Sept. 1, 1956; s. Norman Irvin and Gloria June (Rothstein) W. AB, U. Mich., 1978, JD, 1981; LLM in Taxation, U. Fla., Gainesville, 1985. Bar: Fla. 1981, U.S. Dist. Ct. (so. dist.) Fla. 1981, U.S. Ct. Appeals (11th cir.) 1981, D.C. 1985, U.S. Tax Ct. 1985, U.S. Dist. Ct. (mid. dist.) Fla. 1986. Assoc. Paul & Thomson, Miami, Fla., 1981-82, Henderson, Franklin, Starnes & Holt P.A., Ft. Myers, Fla., 1986—. Served to capt. JAGC U.S. Army, 1982-84. Mem. ABA (tax sect.). Democrat. Jewish. Corporate taxation, Estate taxation, Personal income taxation. Office: Henderson Franklin Starnes & Holt PA 2100 2d St PO Box 280 Fort Myers FL 33902-0280

WHITFIELD, MILTON BAILEY, lawyer; b. Norfolk, Va., Mar. 10, 1951; s. George Milton Whitfield and Rosa Mae (Owen) Halblieb; m. Lorraine Walker, June 1, 1974. BS, U. Va., 1974; JD, Georgetown U., 1979; MBA, George Washington U., 1983. Bar: D.C. 1979, Va. 1980, U.S. Dist. Ct. (ea. dist.) Va., U.S. Ct. Appeals (D.C. and 4th cirs.), U.S. Supreme Ct. Staff asst. div. Naval Reactors U.S. Dept. of Energy, Washington, 1974-79; assoc. Dickstein, Shapiro & Morin, Washington, 1979—. Bd. dirs. ARC, Fairfax, Va., 1983-84. Served to lt. cmdr. USNR, 1974—. Mem. ABA (litigation sect.), D.C. Bar Assn., Beta Gamma Sigma, Tau Beta Pi, Omicron Delta Kappa. Methodist. Avocation: Athletics. Federal civil litigation, Administrative and regulatory, Oil and gas leasing. Home: 5811 Queens Gate Ct

Alexandria VA 22303 Office: Dickstein Shapiro & Morin 2101 L St NW Washington DC 20037

WHITFIELD, WILLIAM ERNEST, lawyer; b. Cherry Point, N.C., Oct. 30, 1955; s. William Ernest and Nelda (Pugh) W.; m. Anita Kay Robertson, Jan. 5, 1979. BA, Mobile Coll., 1977; JD, Miss. Coll., 1980. Bar: Ala. 1981, Miss. 1983, U.S. Dist. Ct. (so. dist.) Miss. 1983. Legal asst. S. Nicholas, Jackson, Miss., 1979-81; law clk. to U.S. magistrate U.S. Dist. Ct. (so. dist.), Biloxi, Miss., 1981-83; assoc. Bryant, Stennis & Colingo, Gulfport, Miss., 1983—. Recipient Am. Jurisprudence award Am. Jurisprudence Soc., Jackson, Miss., 1979. Mem. Harrison County Bar Assn. Baptist. Avocations: golf, racquetball, tennis, swimming. Personal injury, Insurance, Federal civil litigation. Home: 2449 Summerwood Circle Gulfport MS 39507

WHITING, RICHARD ALBERT, lawyer; b. Cambridge, Mass., Dec. 2, 1922; s. Albert S. and Jessie (Coleman) W.; m. Marvelene Nash, Feb. 22, 1948 (div. 1984); children—Richard A. Jr., Stephen C., Jeffrey D., Gary S., Kimberly G.; m. Joanne Sherry, Oct. 14, 1984. A.B., Dartmouth Coll., 1944; J.D., Yale U., 1949. Bar: D.C. 1949. Assoc. Steptoe & Johnson, Washington, 1949-55, ptnr, 1956—; adj. prof. Vt. Law Sch., South Royalton, 1985—; mem. exec. com. Yale Law Sch. Assn., New Haven, 1985—; mem. adv. bd. The Antitrust Bull., N.Y.C., 1975—. Contbr. articles to profl. jours. Served to 1st lt. U.S. Army, 1945-46. Mem. ABA (council mem. Antitrust Law sect. 1977-85, del. to Ho. Dels. 1982-83, chmn. 1984-85). Presbyterian. Antitrust. Home: 5901 Mt Eagle Dr #1-1008 Alexandria VA 22303 Office: Steptoe & Johnson 1330 Connecticut Ave Washington DC 20036

WHITING, RICHARD MATTHEW, lawyer; b. Binghamton, N.Y., Oct. 17, 1948; s. Harold Irving and Joanne Marie (Salasky) W.; m. Cornelia Sue Early, July 30, 1972; children: Corinne Elizabeth, Matthew Robert. BA, SUNY, Binghamton, 1970; JD, Boston Coll., 1973; banking cert., Rutgers U., 1985. Bar: Va. 1974, D.C. 1977, U.S. Ct. Appeals (4th cir.) 1976, U.S. Supreme Ct. 1979. Atty. Fed. Reserve Bd., Washington, 1973-75, sr. atty., 1977-83; law clk. to presiding justice U.S. Ct. Appeals (4th cir.), Richmond, Va., 1976; chief regulatory council Assn. bank Holding Cos., Washington, 1984-85, gen. council, sec., 1985—; mem. adv. bd. CLE Com., Georgetown U., Washington, 1986; faculty mem. Am. Inst. Banking, Washington, 1986. Author: Bank Holding Co. Ins. Activities, 1985; editor articles Boston Coll. Law Review, 1972-73. Recipient Outstanding Accomplishment award Fed. Examination Council, 1983. Mem. Fed. Bar Assn. (banking com., exec. com. 1985—), Va. Bar Assn., D.C. Bar Assn. Roman Catholic. Banking, Administrative and regulatory, General corporate. Home: 5004 Linette Ln Annandale VA 22003 Office: Assn Bank Holding Cos 730 15th St NW Washington DC 20005

WHITLING, TERRANCE LEROY, lawyer; b. Oil City, Pa., Jan. 20, 1948; s. Merrill L. and Roselyn A. (Gdanitz) W.; m. Rhesha A. Erickson, Oct. 23, 1976; children: Tracy, Nicholas. BA in Math., Natural Scis., Clarion State U., 1969; JD, U. Toledo, 1975. Bar: U.S. Dist. Ct. (we. dist.) Pa. 1983. Sole practice Oil City, 1976—; pub. defender Venango County, Franklin, Pa., 1976-81, solicitor, hearing officer domestic relations div., 1981—; solicitor Venango County Housing Authority, 1981—; councilman Oil City, 1984—. Served to 1st lt. U.S. Army, 1969-72, Vietnam. Mem. ABA, Pa. Bar Assn., Venango County Bar Assn. Republican. Episcopalian. Club: Franklin. Lodge: Masons. Avocations: distance running, sports, reading. Real property, Family and matrimonial, Personal injury. Home: 710 North St Oil City PA 16301 Office: 3 Drake Sq Drake Bldg 1st Floor Oil City PA 16301

WHITLOCK, BRIAN THOMAS, lawyer; b. Chgo., Oct. 5, 1954; s. James Joseph Jr. and Marjorie (Riordan) W.; m. Nancy Ellen Prendergast, May 16, 1981; 1 child, Mallory. BA, Northwestern U., 1976; JD with honors, Ill. Inst. Tech., 1979. Bar: Ill. 1979, U.S. Tax Ct. 1982, U.S. Dist. Ct. (no. dist.) Ill. 1983; CPA, Ill. Tax mgr. Stein, Larmon & Co., CPAs, Oak Brook, Ill., 1979-84; assoc. Bellows and Bellows, P.C., Chgo., 1984—. Mem. ABA, Ill. Bar Assn. (young lawyers div. sect. council), Am. Inst. CPA's, Ill. Soc. CPA's (fed. income tax com.). Personal income taxation, General corporate, Estate taxation. Office: Bellows and Bellows 79 W Monroe St Suite 800 Chicago IL 60603

WHITLOCK, WILLIE WALKER, lawyer; b. Mineral, Va., Nov. 16, 1925; s. Edward Jackson and Lottie Alma (Talley) W.; m. Eula Madeline Dymacek, July 15, 1950; children—John D., Jane Whitlock Sisk. B.S. in Bus., Coll. William and Mary, 1950, LL.B., Va. Coll. Law, 1953. Bar: Va. 1955, U.S. Dist. Ct. Va. 1957. Atty. Town of Mineral, 1965—, County of Louisa, 1976-79; mem. adv. bd. Nat. Bank and Trust, Mineral, 1972—. Chmn. Louisa County Democratic Com., Louisa, Va., 1978-82, 32d Legis. Dist. Va., 1978-82. Served to sgt. U.S. Army, 1945-46. Mem. Va. State Bar, Piedmont Bar Assn. (pres. 1976), Louisa County Bar Assn. (pres. 1981—), Am. Legion. Baptist. Lodges: Lions, Masons. Personal injury, Real property, Probate. Home and Office: PO Box 128 Mineral VA 23117

WHITMAN, CHRISTINA BROOKS, law educator; b. 1949. BA, U. Mich., 1968, MA, 1970, JD, 1974. Law clk. to justice Harold Leventhal U.S. Supreme Ct., Washington, 1974-75, law clk. to justice Powell, 1975-76; asst. prof. U. Mich., Ann Arbor, 1976-79, assoc. prof., 1979-82, prof., 1982—. Office: U Mich Law Sch Ann Arbor MI 48109 *

WHITMAN, DALE ALAN, law school dean; b. Charleston, W.Va., Feb. 18, 1939; m. Marjorie Miller; 8 children. Student, Ohio State U., 1956-59; BEE, Brigham Young U., 1963; LLB, Duke U., 1966. Bar: Calif. 1967, Utah 1974. Assoc. O'Melveny & Myers, Los Angeles, 1966-67; asst. prof., then assoc. prof. Sch. Law, U. N.C., Chapel Hill, 1967-70; vis. prof. law N.C. Central U., Durham, 1968, 69; vis. assoc. prof. law UCLA, 1970-71; dep. dir. Office Housing and Urban Affairs, Fed. Home Loan Bank Bd., Washington, 1971-72; sr. program analyst FHA, HUD, Washington, 1972-73; prof. law Brigham Young U., 1973-78, 79; vis. prof. law U. Tulsa, 1976, U. Mo., Columbia, 1976; prof. law U. Wash., Seattle, 1978-82, assoc. dean, 1978-79, 81-82; dean U. Mo. Sch. Law, Columbia, 1982—; cons., lectr. in field. Coauthor: Cases and Materials on Real Estate Finance and Development, 1976, Real Estate Finance Law, 1979, Cases and Materials on Real Estate Transfer, Finance and Development, 1981, Land Transactions and Finance, 1983, The Law of Property, 1984. Contbr. articles to profl. jours. Real property. Home: 1005 Audubon Dr Columbia MO 65201 Office: U Mo Columbia Tate Hall Columbia MO 65211

WHITMAN, DOUGLAS FRANK, legal educator; b. Kansas City, Mo., Mar. 30, 1948; s. Doyle Collins and Anna Mary (White) W. BA, Knox Coll., 1970; JD, U. Mo., 1973; LLM, U. Mo., Kansas City, 1982; MBA, U. Kans., 1975. Bar: Mo. 1973, U.S. Dist. Ct. (we. dist.) Mo. 1973, Kans. 1974, U.S. Dist. Ct. Kans. 1974. Prof. sch. bus. U. Kans., Lawrence, 1975—; sole practice Lawrence, 1974—. Author: Commercial Law, 1985, Modern Business Law, 1984, Legal & Social Environment Business, 1985, Law and Business, 1987; contbr. articles to profl. jours. Mem. ABA, Am. Bus. Law Assn. (staff editor jour. 1979-82, 85—), Mid-West Bus. Law Assn. (pres. 1978-79). Episcopalian. General corporate. Home: 2534 Cedarwood Lawrence KS 66046 Office: U Kans Sch Bus Lawrence KS 66045

WHITMAN, JULES I., lawyer; b. N.Y.C., Apr. 30, 1923; s. Louis and Jenny (Mednitzky) W.; divorced; children: David, Douglas. BBA, CCNY, 1943; LLB, NYU, 1948, LLM in Taxation, 1950. Bar: N.Y. 1948, Pa. 1950. Assoc. Otto A. Samuels, N.Y.C., 1948-50; trial atty. IRS, Phila., 1950-56; mng. ptnr., sr. ptnr., head tax dept. Dilworth, Paxson, Kalish & Kauffman, Phila., 1956—; dir. U. Pa. Tax Conf., Phila.; lectr. Villanova U. Law Sch., Pa., 1980-81, NYU. Contbr. articles to profl. jours. Pres. Phila. chpt. Am. Jewish Com., 1977-79, chmn. bd., 1980-81, nat. gov., N.Y.C., 1981-84; bd. dirs. Citizens Crime Commn., Phila., 1980-86; trustee Rodeph Shalom Synagogue, Phila., 1980-86. Recipient Human Relations award Am. Jewish Com., 1983. Mem. ABA, Fed. Bar Assn., Pa. Bar Assn., Phila. Bar Assn. Jewish. Club: Locust (Phila.). Corporate taxation, Personal income taxation. Office: Dilworth Paxson Kalish & Kauffman 123 S Broad St Philadelphia PA 19109

WHITMER, FREDERICK LEE, lawyer; b. Terre Haute, Ind., Nov. 5, 1947; s. Lee Arthur and Ella (Diekhoff) W.; m. Margaret Verbist Connors, June 15, 1969; children—Caitlin Margaret, Meghan Connors. B.A., Wabash Coll., 1969; J.D., Columbia U., 1973. Bar: N.Y. 1975, U.S. Dist. Ct. (so. dist.) N.Y. 1975, N.J. 1976, U.S. Dist. Ct. N.J. 1976, U.S. Ct. Appeals (3d cir.) 1977, U.S. Ct. Appeals (fed. cir.) 1983. Assoc. Kaye, Scholer, Fierman, Hays & Handler, N.Y.C., 1973-76, Pitney, Hardin & Kipp, Morristown, 1976-78; ptnr. Pitney, Hardin, Kipp & Szuch, Morristown, 1979—. Mem. ABA, N.J. Bar Assn., Phi Beta Kappa. Republican. Lutheran. Club: Morristown. Antitrust, Trademark and copyright, Federal civil litigation. Home: 326 Brook Vale Rd Kinnelon NJ 07405 Office: Pitney Hardin Kipp & Szuch 163 Madison Ave Morristown NJ 07960

WHITMER, LESLIE GAY, lawyer, federal official; b. Lexington, Ky., July 31, 1941; s. Leslie Allen and Gaynelle Kimbrell (McPherson) W.; m. Patricia Ann Welch, July 5, 1969; 1 child, Mary Gay. BS, U. Ky., 1963, JD, 1965. Bar: Ky. 1966, U.S. Dist. Ct. Ky. 1972, U.S. Ct. Appeals (D.C. cir.) 1972, U.S. Supreme Ct. 1972. Atty. advisor gen. Office of Gen. Counsel, U.S. Dept. Agr., Chgo., 1966-69; asst. dir., bar counsel Ky. Bar Assn., asst. editor Ky. Bar Jour., 1974-83, registrar Supreme Ct. Ky., 1975-83; clk. U.S. Dist. Ct. (ea. dist.) Ky., 1983—; adj. prof. law U. Ky. Coll. Law, 1980, 82. Contbr. articles to legal jours. Mem. Gov.'s Task Force on Office Public Advocacy, 1982; exec. dir. Ky. Bar Ctr., 1979-83; bd. dirs., sec., treas. Ky. Bar Title Ins. Agy. Inc., 1973-83; asst. sec.-treas. Ky. Bar. Found., 1979-83; exec. dir. Ky. Fed. Jud. Selection Commn., 1978-83; bd. dirs., sec.-treas. Ky. Legal Services Plan, Inc., 1978-83. Recipient Recognition of Merit award U. Ky. Coll. Law Alumni Assn., 1983. Mem. Ky. Bar Assn. (bd. dirs., bar counsel, treas. 1973-83, Continuing Legal Edn. Recognition award 1980—), Fed. Clks. Assn., Psi Chi, Phi Alpha Delta. Club: Spindletop Hall. Administrative and regulatory, Jurisprudence. Office: Federal Courthouse Lexington KY 40507

WHITMORE, SHARP, lawyer; b. Price, Utah, Apr. 26, 1918; s. Leland and Anne (Sharp) W.; m. Frances Dorr, Aug. 15, 1940; children: Richard, William, Ann. A.B., Stanford U., 1939; J.D., U. Calif.-Berkeley, 1942; LL.D., U. Pacific, 1982. Bar: Calif. 1944. Asso. Gibson, Dunn & Crutcher, Los Angeles, 1946-50; partner Gibson, Dunn & Crutcher, 1951—; chmn. Calif. Com. Bar Examiners, 1956-58. Pres. Bd. Mcpl. Auditorium Commrs. City of Los Angeles, 1974-75. Served with USNR, 1942-46. Fellow Am. Bar Found. (chmn. 1982-83); mem. Los Angeles County Bar Assn. (pres. 1970-71), Nat. Conf. Bar Examiners (chmn. 1957-58), State Bar Calif. (bd. govs. 1962-65, v.p. treas. 1964-65), ABA (ho. of dels. 1957-58, 68—, bd. govs. 1985—), Order of Coif (hon.). Republican. Clubs: Bohemian, Sunset, Chancery (pres. 1962-63). Labor. Home: 2005 Gird Rd Fallbrook CA 92028 Office: 600 B St Suite 2300 San Diego CA 92101

WHITNEY, CHARLES LEROY, lawyer; b. Aurora, Nebr., Oct. 1, 1918; s. Charles Leroy and Alta Leona (Entriken) W.; m. Emily Louise Rothman, Nov. 17, 1942; children: Charles Leroy III, Anne Rothman, Mary Elizabeth, William Shafer. AB, York Coll.; LLB, U. Nebr. Bar: Nebr. 1946. Sole practice Aurora, 1946-59; ptnr. Whitney and Newman, Aurora, 1959-73; sr. ptnr. Whitney, Newman, Mersch, Otto & Warren, Aurora, 1974—. Bd. dirs., v.p. Hamilton Community Found., Aurora; bd. dirs. Prairie Plains Inst., Aurora. Served to lt. USNR, 1942-46, PTO. Mem. ABA, Nebr. State Bar Assn., Aurora C. of C., Am. Legion (past comdr. local post). Democrat. United Methodist. Avocations: fishing, woodworking, photography. General practice, Probate, Real property. Home: 40 Rosewood Dr Aurora NE 68818 Office: Whitney Newman Mersch Otto & Warren Profl Bldg Box 228 Aurora NE 68818

WHITNEY, DOUGLAS E., SR., lawyer; b. Malden, Mass., May 1, 1939; s. Edgar Gordon and Jennie (Johnson) W.; m. Carol Annette Moore, July 31, 1965; children—Douglas, Jr., James A., Charles B. B.Chem. Engring., Cornell U., 1962; J.D., Columbia U., 1965. Bar: N.Y. 1965, Mass. 1970, Del. 1973, U.S. Dist. Ct. (so. dist.) N.Y. 1966, U.S. Dist. Ct. Mass. 1969, U.S. Dist. Ct. Del. 1973, U.S. Ct. Appeals (fed., 1st, 2d and 3d cirs.), U.S. Supreme Ct. 1972. Patent agt. Mobil Oil Corp., N.Y.C., 1963-65; assoc. Davis, Hoxie, Faithfull & Hapgood, N.Y.C., 1965-69; ptnr. Russell & Nields, Boston, 1969-72; ptnr. Morris, Nichols, Arsht & Tunnell, Wilmington, Del., 1972—. Bd. dirs. U.S. Orienteering Fedn., St. Louis, 1981-84. Mem. ABA, Am. Intellectual Property Assn., Del. Bar Assn. Democrat. Congregationalist. Federal civil litigation, Patent, Trademark and copyright. Home: Box 168 Rockland Mills Rockland DE 19732 Office: PO Box 1347 1105 N Market St Wilmington DE 19899

WHITNEY, GEORGE WARD, lawyer; b. N.Y.C., June 30, 1924; s. Reginald and Muriel Janet (Hall) W.; m. C. Patricia Thayer, June 18, 1949; children: Lynn T., George W., Jonathan, Mark. B.E.E., Rensselaer Poly. Inst., 1949; J.D., George Washington U., 1952. Bar: D.C. 1952, N.Y. 1954, U.S. Ct. Claims 1965, U.S. Ct. Appeals (2d cir.) 1969, U.S. Ct. Appeals (fed. cir.) 1982, U.S. Supreme Ct. 1980. Asst. examiner U.S. Patent Office, Washington, 1948-50; law clk. Gen. Motors Corp., Washington, 1950-52; assoc. Brumbaugh, Graves, Donohue & Raymond, N.Y.C., 1952-60, ptnr., 1960—. U.S. del. Law of Sea Conf., 1981-82; dep. mayor, village trustee, Garden City, N.Y., 1969-72; pres. Citizens Adv. Com. on Edn., Garden City, 1967; pres. Garden City Central Property Owners Assn., 1968-69; chmn., trustee Garden City Library, 1974-80; mem. council Cathedral of the Incarnation, 1983—. Served with Signal Corps, AUS, 1943-46. Fellow Am Bar Found.; mem. N.Y. Patent Law Assn. (bd. govs. 1973-76), Am. Patent Law Assn. (pres. 1980-81, bd. mgrs. 1972-75, dir. 1977-82), Am. Intellectual Property Law Assn. (chmn. pub. appointments com. 1983-85), ABA (litigation sect., chmn. patent litigation 1977-81, spl. commn. punitive damages 1983—, chmn. inequitable conduct, misuse and antitrust matter 1983-85, patent, trademark and copyright sect. chmn. Div. IV, 1985—, chmn. com. patent legis. 1986—), Am. Arbitration Assn. (nat. panel arbitrators), Assn. Bar City of N.Y. (patents com. 1979-82), Fed. Bar Council, Fed. Cir. Bar Assn. (jud. selection com. 1985—), ITC Trial Lawyers Assn., Rensselaer Alumni Council (chmn. 1962-64), Delta Tau Delta, Phi Alpha Delta. Republican. Episcopalian. Clubs: Downtown Athletic (bd. govs. 1970-75), N.Y. Athletic; Cherry Valley (Garden City). Federal civil litigation, Patent, Trademark and copyright. Address: 4 Cedar Pl Garden City NY 11530 also: House By The Lake Route 10 Lyme NH 03768

WHITNEY, JOHN ADAIR, lawyer; b. Cin., Jan. 25, 1932; s. Nathaniel Ruggles and Helen Blanchard (Loos) W.; m. Linda Hollis Leary, Dec. 22, 1956; children: William Nathaniel, Jane Whitney McGreevy, Anne Dickson. BA cum laude, Williams Coll., 1953; LLB, Harvard U., 1956. Bar: Ohio 1956, D.C. 1960, U.S. Supreme Ct. 1961, Md. 1965. Assoc. Pope, Ballard & Loos, Washington, 1959-63, ptnr., 1964-69, 73-81; mem. Md. Ho. of Dels., 1967-69; asst. gen. counsel NASA, Washington, 1969-73; ptnr. Holland & Knight, Washington, 1982-84, Whitney & Greif, Washington, 1984—. Chmn. fin. adv. com., Montgomery County, Md., 1970; chmn. County Com. on Coms., Rockville, Md., 1977-78; mem. County Ethics Com., Rockville, 1985-86;. Recipient Exceptional Service medal NASA, 1972, Resolution of Commendation Md. Ho. of Dels., 1970. Mem. ABA, Bar Assn. D.C. (chmn. adminstrv. law 1979-80), Md. State Bar Assn., Montgomery County Bar Assn., Phi Beta Kappa. Republican. Presbyterian. Clubs: Edgemoor (Bethesda, Md.) (pres. 1981-83); University (Washington). Avocations: tennis, squash, sailing. Government contracts and claims, Construction, Probate. Home: 8007 Aberdeen Rd Bethesda MD 20814 Office: 2101 L St NW Washington DC 20037

WHITNEY, JOHN FRANKLIN, lawyer; b. Green Bay, Wis., Aug. 10, 1953; s. John Clarence and Helen (Mayer) W. BA, Tulane U., 1975; JD, Georgetown U., 1978. Bar: La. 1978. Assoc. Phelps, Dunbar, New Orleans, 1978-82; assoc. Barham & Churchill, New Orleans, 1983-85, ptnr., 1985—. Fellow La. Bar Found. (life); mem. ABA, Fed. Bar Assn., Fed. Energy Bar Assn. Republican. Roman Catholic. Avocations: golf, racquetball. Federal civil litigation, State civil litigation, Securities. Home: 4007 Saint Charles Ave #305 New Orleans LA 70115 Office: Barham & Churchill 400 Lafayette St New Orleans LA 70130

WHITNEY, RICHARD B., lawyer; b. Corpus Christi, Tex., Mar. 1, 1948; s. Franklyn Loren and Elizabeth Wolcott (Fish) W.; m. Chantal Marie Gindt, Aug. 18, 1972; children: Jennifer L., James R., Katherine E. BA in Polit. Sci., Union Coll., 1970; JD, Case Western Res. U., 1973. Bar: Ohio 1973, U.S. Dist. Ct. (no. dist.) Ohio 1973. From assoc. to ptnr. Jones, Day, Reavis & Pogue, Cleve., 1973—. Mem. ABA, Ohio Bar Assn., Cuyahoga County Bar Assn., Cleve. Bar Assn. (grievance com., unauthorized practice of law com.). Federal civil litigation, State civil litigation, Insurance. Home: 2750 Southington Rd Shaker Heights OH 44120 Office: Jones Day Reavis & Pogue 1700 Huntington Bldg Cleveland OH 44115

WHITNEY, ROBERT MICHAEL, lawyer; b. Green Bay, Wis., Jan. 29, 1949; s. John Clarence and Helen (Mayer) W.; m. Carol L. Becker, Sept. 23, 1977. Student, U. Wis., 1967-70, JD, 1974. Bar: Wis. 1974, U.S. Dist. Ct. (we. dist.) Wis. 1979, U.S. Dist. Ct. (ea. dist.) Wis. 1984, U.S. Ct. Appeals (7th cir.) 1980. Law clk. to presiding justice Dane County Cir. Ct., Madison, Wis., 1970-76; legal counsel Wis. State Election Bd., Madison, 1976-78; ptnr. Walsh, Walsh, Sweeney & Whitney, S.C., Madison, 1979—; counsel Advocacy Assn. for Retarded Citizens, Madison, 1977-79. bd. dirs. Community TV, Inc., Madison, 1984—; vol. Wis. Assn. for Retarded Citizens, Madison, 1984—, Abbot Pennings Found., 1985—. Mem. Assn. Trial Lawyers Am., Wis. Bar Assn. (citation for service to continuing legal edn. 1978), Dane County Bar Assn. Club: Rugby (Madison). Federal civil litigation, State civil litigation, Personal injury. Home: 2352 Monroe St Madison WI 53711 Office: Foley & Lardner 1 S Pickney St 1st Wis Plaza Madison WI 53701

WHITSON, LISH, lawyer; b. Washington, Oct. 13, 1942; s. I. Lish and Clytie B. (Collier) W.; m. Barbara Lee Sullivan, Sept. 16, 1965; children—L. Richard, Kimberly S. B.A. in Philosophy, Pa. State U., 1965; J.D., U. Wash., 1972. Bar: Wash. 1973, U.S. Dist. Ct. (we. dist.) 1973, U.S. Supreme Ct. 1977. Assoc. Seattle-King County Pub. Defender Assn., 1972-76; assoc. Helsell, Fetterman, Martin, Todd & Hokanson, Seattle, 1976-81, ptnr., 1981—; dir. Am. Judicature Soc., Chgo., Seattle Pub. Def. Assn., 1982-86. Bd. mem., chmn. Downtown Emergency Service Ctr., Seattle, 1981-86. Mem. ABA, Seattle-King County Bar Assn. (pro bono com. chmn. 1981—), Fed. Bar Assn., Assn. Trial Lawyers Am. Am. Judicature Soc. Club: Wash. Athletic. Federal civil litigation, State civil litigation, Personal injury. Office: Helsell Fetterman Martin Todd & Hokanson 1500 Washington Bldg Seattle WA 98101

WHITT, JANE REBECCA, lawyer; b. Richmond, Va., Nov. 16, 1953; d. John Burton Tuck and Rebecca Evelyn (Williams) W. BA, Hollins Coll., 1975; MS, Va. Poly. Inst. and State U., 1977; JD, U. Va., 1980. Bar: Va. 1980, U.S. Dist. Ct. (ea. dist.) Va. 1980, U.S. Bankruptcy Ct. 1980, U.S. Ct. Appeals (4th cir.) 1980. Assoc. McGuire, Woods, Battle & Boothe, Richmond, 1980—. V.p., bd. dirs. Meals on Wheels Greater Richmond, 1983-86. Mem. ABA (dist. rep. exec. council young lawyers div. 1985-87), Va. bar Assn. (sec., pres. elect, pres. young lawyers conf. 1985-88), Order of Coif, Phi Beta Kappa. Episcopalian. General corporate, Securities. Home: 4608 Hanover Ave Richmond VA 23226 Office: McGuire Woods Battle & Boothe 1 James Ctr Richmond VA 23219

WHITT, ROBERT HOLT, JR., lawyer; b. Danville, Va., Dec. 21, 1955; s. Robert Holt Sr. and Faye (Dixon) W.; m. Sharon Marie Hines, Aug. 4, 1984. BA cum laude, Hampden-Sydney Coll., 1978; JD, U. Richmond, 1981. Bar: Va. 1981, U.S. Dist. Ct. (we. dist.) Va. 1981. Assoc. Carter & Wilson, Danville, 1981-83, John W. Carter Law Offices, Danville, 1983-85; sole practice Danville, 1985—. Pres. Danville Estate Planning Council, 1984—; vice chmn. Danville Reps., 1986. Mem. ABA, Va. Bar Assn. (com. for legal services to public 1984—), Danville Bar Assn. (treas. 1985-86), Va. Trial Lawyers Assn., Hampden-Sydney Coll. Alumni Club (pres. 1984—). Presbyterian. Clubs: Danville Golf, Dan River Rugby (Caswell County, N.C.) (sec. 1985—). Lodge: Optimists. Avocations: gardening, fishing, rugby, golf. Personal injury, Criminal, General practice. Home: 136 Chestnut St Danville VA 24541 Office: 410 Patton St Suite B Danville VA 24541

WHITTAKER, MARION ALMA, lawyer; b. Springfield, Ohio, Nov. 2, 1947; d. George and Ollie B. (Mackin) Bentley; m. Anderson Whittaker, Mar. 29, 1969 (div. Mar. 1974); m. Keith Hall, Jan. 6, 1982; children: Shawnda, Askia. AA, SUNY, Buffalo, 1975; BA in Journalism, San Jose State U., 1977; JD, U. Calif., San Francisco, 1980. Law clk. then assoc. Pub. Defenders Office, San Jose, Calif., 1978-82; assoc. Mackey & Friedland, San Jose, Calif., 1982-85; ptnr. Baker, Johnson, Stallworth & Whittaker, San Jose, Calif., 1985—. Mem. ABA, Assn. Trial Lawyers Am., Calif. Assn. Criminal Trial Lawyers, Calif. Bar Assn., Santa Clara County Bar Assn., Santa Clara County Women Lawyers Assn. (exec. officer 1985—), Black Lawyers Assn. (sec. 1984—), Sigma Delta Chi. Administrative and regulatory, Criminal, Juvenile. Office: Baker Johnson Stallworth & Whittaker 738 N 1st St San Jose CA 95112

WHITTED, BROOKE ROSS, lawyer; b. Los Angeles, Sept. 2, 1946; s. James Bartram and Betty Jean (Chappell) W.; m. Linda Joyce Murakishi, Jan. 14, 1985. BS in Psychology, Okla. State U., 1969; JD, John Marshall Sch. of Law, 1978. Bar: Ill. 1978, U.S. Dist. Ct. (no. dist.) Ill. 1978, U.S. Supreme Ct. 1982, Wis. 1983, U.S. Dist. Ct. (ea. dist.) Wis. 1983, U.S. Ct. Appeals (7th cir.) 1986. Ptnr., pres. Whitted & Spain, Chgo., 1980—. Office: Whitted & Spain 1 N LaSalle St Suite 1750 Chicago IL 60602 also: 21 N Old Skokie Lake Bluff IL 60044

WHITTEMORE, F(RANK) CASE, lawyer; b. Lockport, N.Y., Jan. 7, 1945; s. Allan Pendleton and Catherine Cushing (Pevear) W.; m. Anne Marie Grimes, June 22, 1968; 1 child, Robert Pendleton. BS, Yale U., 1966; JD, U. Va., 1974. Bar: Va. 1974, D.C. 1977. Assoc. Hunton & Williams, Richmond, Va., 1974-79; asst. counsel Ethyl Corp., Richmond, 1979—; mem. Joint Bar Commn. Va. Stock Corp. Act, Richmond, 1984-85. Pres. Yale Fund Va., Richmond, 1985—; bd. dirs. Family and Children's Services Agy., Richmond, 1985—, Housing Opportunities Made Equal, Richmond, 1985—. Served to lt. USN, 1966-71. Mem. ABA, Va. Bar Assn., Richmond Bar Assn. (chmn. corp. counsel sect. 1984-85, exec. com. 1983-86), 4th Cir. Jud. Conf., Internat. Mobjack Assn. (sec. 1985—, treas. 1983-84, Nat. Sailing Champion 1975). Clubs: Fishing Bay Yacht (Deltaville, Va.) (rear commodore 1985-86, vice commodore 1986—); Country Club Va. (Richmond). General corporate, Personal injury, Energy, coal. Home: 1 Huntly Rd Richmond VA 23226 Office: Ethyl Corp 330 S 4th St Richmond VA 23219

WHITTEN, C. G., lawyer; b. Abilene, Tex., Apr. 1, 1925; s. C.G. and Eugenia (St. Clair) W.; m. Alene Henley, Nov. 25, 1945; children—Julie, Jennifer, Blake; m. 2d, Carol Owen, Apr. 22, 1977. B.S., U. Tex.-Austin, 1943, J.D., 1949. Bar: Tex. 1949, U.S. Dist. Ct. (no. dist.) Tex. 1950, U.S. Supreme Ct. 1955. Assoc. Grisham & King, Abilene, Tex., 1949-52; ptnr. Jameson & Whitten, 1952-54, Jameson, Whitten, Harrell & Wilcox, 1954-58, Whitten, Harrell, Erwin & Jameson, 1958-68, Whitten, Sprain, Wagner, Price & Edwards, 1968-79, Whitten, Haag, Cobb & Hacker, 1979-82; sr. ptnr. Whitten, Haag, Hacker, Hagin & Cutbirth, 1983—. Served with USAAF, 1943-45, to 1st lt., 1950-54. Decorated Air medal with 6 oak leaf clusters. Fellow Am. Bar Found.; mem. Abilene Bar Assn. (pres. 1968), State Bar Tex. (dir. 1977-80), ABA, Tex. Bar Found. (chmn. 1982, chmn. fellows 1985). Democrat. Presbyterian. Clubs: Rotary (pres. 1960), Abilene Country (pres. 1964). Oil and gas leasing, Contracts commercial, General corporate. Office: Box 208 Abilene TX 79604 *

WHITTEN, REGGIE NEIL, lawyer; b. Seminole, Okla., May 23, 1955; s. Robert L. and Agatha (Pickett) W.; m. Peggy Ann Gandy, May 21, 1986; 1 child from previous marriage, Brandon Neil. BA, U. Okla., 1977, JD, 1980. Bar: U.S. Dist. Ct. (no., ea. and we. dists.) Okla., U.S. Ct. Appeals (10th cir.). Ptnr. Mills, Whitten, Mills, Mills & Hinkle, Oklahoma City, 1980—. Mem. ABA, Okla. Bar Assn., Okla. County Bar Assn., Okla. Assn. Def. Counsel, Order of Barristers. Democrat. Civil rights, Insurance, Personal injury. Home: 1009 SW 112th Oklahoma City OK 73170 Office: Mills Whitten Mills Mills Hinkle 211 N Robinson Oklahoma City OK 73102

WHITTINGTON, MARVIN EDWARD, lawyer; b. El Paso, Tex., Aug. 11, 1915; s. Charles Clements and Harriet (Rowe) W.; m. Lavina Childs Hand, Oct. 27, 1943; children—Marvin II, Jeanne R. LL.B., U. Tex., 1938. Bar: Tex. 1938, U.S. Dist. Ct. (we. dist.) Tex. 1940, U.S. Supreme Ct. 1946. Sole practice law, El Paso, 1938-40; asst. county atty. El Paso County, 1940-42; atty. U.S. Bur. Reclamation, Amarillo, Tex., 1946-54; atty. U.S. section Internat. Boundary & Water Commn., U.S. and Mex., El Paso, 1954-58,

chief counsel, 1958-75; sole practice, El Paso and Euless, Tex., 1975—. Served to capt. U.S. Army and USAAF, 1942-47. Decorated Army Commendation medal; recipient wall plaque from govts. U.S. and Mex., with letter from Pres. U.S., 1967. Methodist. Club: 20-30 (pres. 1942) (El Paso). Lodge: Masons. General practice.

WHITTINGTON, THOMAS LEE, lawyer; b. Waukesha, Wis., July 14, 1943; s. Floyd Leon and Winifred Carol (McDonald) W.; m. Rachel Foy, June 12, 1971; children—Erin Elizabeth, Hilary Ann. B.A., Coll. of Wooster, 1965; J.D., U. Mich., 1967. Bar: Trust Ter. of Pacific Islands 1967, Mich. 1969, Wash. 1974, U.S. Dist. Ct. (we. dist.) Wash. 1974. Vol. Peace Corps, Micronesia, 1967-69; staff asst. legis. office Dept. Interior, Washington, 1969-74; ptnr. Thomas, Whittington, Anderson & Bergan, Issaquah, Wash., 1974—. Co-editor: Trust Territory Reports, vols. 1-3, 1969. Mem. Wash. State Bar Assn., Seattle-King County Bar Assn., East King County Bar Assn. (bd. dirs. 1979-81, pres. 1983), Issaquah C. of C. (bd. dirs. 1978-79). Republican. Club: Rotary (pres. 1979-80). Real property, Contracts commercial, Family and matrimonial. Home: 23720 SE 18th St Issaquah WA 98027 Office: Thomas Whittington Anderson & Bergan 970 5th NW PO Box 1304 Issaquah WA 98027

WHITTLE, JOSEPH M., lawyer. U.S. atty. we. dist. State of Ky., Louisville. Office: US PO and Courthouse Room 211 601 W Broadway Louisville KY 40202 *

WHITWELL, ROBERT Q., lawyer; b. 1946. BS, Delta State Coll.; JD, U. Miss. Bar: Miss. 1972. U.S. atty. no. dist. State of Miss., Oxford. Office: US Attys Office PO Drawer 886 Oxford MS 38655 *

WHITWORTH, H. PHILIP, JR., lawyer; b. Smithville, Tex., Feb. 25, 1947; s. Harry P. and Edna (Widen) W.; children: Gary Scott, Anne Ashley. BA with honors, U. Tex., 1969, JD with honors, 1972. Bar: Tex. 1972, Temporary Emergency Ct. Appeals 1975, U.S. Ct. Appeals (5th cir.) 1975, U.S. Dist. Ct. (we. dist.) Tex. Assoc. Clark, Thomas, Winters & Shapiro, Austin, Tex., 1972-77; ptnr. Scott, Douglass & Luton, Austin, Tex., 1977—. Contbr. articles to profl. jours. Vestry St. David's Episcopal Ch., Austin, 1983—. Fellow Tex. Bar Found.; mem. ABA, Tex. Bar Assn. (treas. elect oil gas and mineral council 1986—), Travis County Bar Assn. (chmn. oil gas and mineral law sect. 1986—, vice chmn. oil gas and mineral law sect. 1985-86, bd. dirs. 1986—), U. Tex. Ex-Students Assn. (bd. dirs. Travis County chpt. 1982-83). Avocations: golf, hunting, sports. Oil and gas leasing, Administrative and regulatory, Environment. Office: Scott Douglass & Luton 1200 1st City Bank Bldg Austin TX 78701

WHORISKEY, ROBERT DONALD, lawyer; b. Cambridge, Mass., May 9, 1929; s. John Joseph and Katherine Euphemia (MacDonald) W.; m. Martha Beebe Poutas, Apr. 16, 1966; children: Alexandra, Jonathan, Eliza. A.B., Harvard U., 1952; J.D., Boston Coll., 1958; LL.M., NYU, 1960. Bar: Mass. 1958, N.Y. 1963, U.S. Tax Ct. 1961, U.S. Ct. Claims 1969, U.S. Dist. Ct. (so. dist.) N.Y. 1969, U.S. Ct. Customs 1971, U.S. Ct. Appeals (2d cir.) 1972, U.S. Supreme Ct. 1974. Sr. trial atty. Office Chief Counsel, IRS, N.Y.C., 1960-67; assoc. Curtis, Mallet-Prevost, Colt & Mosle, N.Y.C., 1967-70, ptnr., 1970—, mem. exec. com., 1978-82, chmn. tax dept., 1982—; dir., v.p., lectr. Internat. Tax Inst., 1980-84, chmn. bd., pres., lectr., 1985—; lectr. Practicing Law Inst., World Trade Inst., Tax Execs. Inst., Am. Mgmt. Assn., bd. dirs. McMillen, Inc., 1987—. Author: Foreign Trusts, 1977, Annual Institute on International Taxation, 1966, 80, 81, (with Sidney Pine, Ralph Seligman) Tax and Business Benefits of the Bahamas, 1986. Trustee, treas. Montessori Sch. Westchester, 1974-77. Served with U.S. Army, 1952-54. Mem. ABA, N.Y. State Bar Assn., Assn. Bar City N.Y. Democrat. Roman Catholic. Clubs: Harvard (N.Y.C.); Larchmont (N.Y.) Yacht. Corporate taxation, Personal income taxation, State and local taxation. Office: Curtis Mallet-Prevost Colt & Mosle 101 Park Ave New York NY 10178

WHYNOTT, PHILIP PERCY, lawyer; b. Waltham, Mass., Jan. 11, 1944; s. Percy Arthur and Grace Gordon (King) W.; children—Ray, Malcolm. B.A. in History, U. Wyo., 1966, M.A. in Polit. Sci., 1971, J.D., 1971; cert. advanced internat. studies U. Pacific McGeorge Sch. Law, Salzburg, Austria, 1980; cert. study in socialist law and legal problems of East-West trade Warsaw U., 1982; diplomate Paris Inst. on Internat. and Comparative Law, 1982, Russia-Poland Inst. on Internat. and Comparative Law, 1982. Bar: Wyo. 1972, U.S. Dist. Ct. Wyo. 1972, U.S. Ct. Appeals (10th cir.) 1973, U.S. Supreme Ct. 1976. Sole practice, Cheyenne, Wyo. Recipient Internat. Trial Lawyers award, 1971. Mem. Wyo. State Bar Assn., Internat. Bar Assn., Laramie County Bar Assn., Omicron Delta Epsilon, Pi Sigma Alpha. State civil litigation, Private international, Immigration, naturalization, and customs. Office: PO Box 1654 Cheyenne WY 82001

WIACEK, BRUCE EDWARD, lawyer; b. N.Y.C., Aug. 3, 1943; s. A. Edward and Ann Catherine (Miller) W.; m. Dianne Gail Masumian, Aug. 26, 1984. BA, Fordham U., 1965, MA, 1971, JD, 1978; MS in Edn., Iona Grad. Sch., 1974; LLM, NYU, 1981. Bar: N.Y. 1979, U.S. Dist. Ct. (so. and ea. dists.) N.Y. 1979. Tchr. Cardinal Spellman High Sch., N.Y.C., 1967-73, Tarrytown (N.Y.) Pub. Sch., 1973-79; supervisor labor relations Sperry Corp., Great Neck, N.Y., 1979-84; ptnr. Wiacek & Corcoran, White Plains, N.Y., 1984—; arbitrator small claims City Ct. White Plains, 1985—. Legal columnist The Advocate, 1978—. Dir. legal assistant program Seton Coll., Yonkers, N.Y., 1985—. Mem. N.Y. State Bar Assn., Westchester County Bar Assn., Am. Assn. Univ. Profs., Am. Arbitration Assn. (arbitrator 1985—), Yonkers Lawyers Assn., Soc. Profls. in Dispute Resolution. Roman Catholic. Labor, General practice, Legal education. Home: 1180 Midland Ave Bronxville NY 10708 Office: Wiacek & Corcoran 175 Main St Suite 505 White Plains NY 10601

WICH, DONALD ANTHONY, JR., lawyer; b. Detroit, Apr. 13, 1947; s. Donald Anthony and Margaret Louise (Blatz) W. B.A. with honors, Notre Dame U., Ind., 1969, J.D., 1972. Bar: Fla. 1972, U.S. Dist. Ct. (so. dist.) Fla. 1972; U.S. Ct. Appeals (5th and 11th cirs.) 1982, U.S. Supreme Ct. 1976. Assoc. VISTA, Miami, Fla., 1972-74; atty. Legal Services, Miami, 1973-75; adj. prof. law U. Miami, Fla., 1974-75; ptnr. Sullivan, Bailey, Wich & Stockman, P.A., Pompano, and Ft. Lauderdale, Fla., 1976—; pres., dir. Legal Aid of Broward, Ft. Lauderdale, 1976-82. Mem. ABA, Lawyers Title Guaranty Fund (spl. bar counsel to Fla. Bar Grievance com., bro. chmn. Fla. Bar UPL com.), Am. Arbitration Assn., North Broward Bar Assn. (pres. 1983-84), Acad. Fla. Trial Lawyers Assn. (sustaining mem.), Broward County Trial Lawyers Assn. (pres.-elect 1987—), Broward Bar Assn. (chmn. legis. com. 1984-85, exec. com. 1986—, vice-chmn. bench-bar com.), Assn. Trial Lawyers Am., Pompano Beach C. of C. (v.p. 1986-87, dir. 1984-87, Govtl. Affairs Chmn. 1983-84, Art Show chmn. 1984-85, Seafood festival chmn. 1986—). Lodge: Rotary (bd. dirs. 1987—). Personal injury, Labor, Constitutional. Office: Glendale Fed Bldg Sullivan Bailey Wich & Stockman PA 2335 E Atlantic Blvd Suite 301 Pompano Beach FL 33062

WICKA, RICHARD VINCENT, lawyer; b. Beach, N.D., Apr. 3, 1930; s. Daniel John and Alice (Groskup) W.; m. Sunny Bach, Sept. 3, 1955; children: Richard Jr., James, William, Kristin, John, Thomas. BA, St. John's U., Collegeville, Minn.; JD, U. N.D. Bar: N.D. 1955, Minn. 1956, U.S. Dist. Ct. Minn., U.S. Dist. Ct. N.D., U.S. Dist. Ct. S.D., U.S. Dist. Ct. Iowa, U.S. Ct. Appeals (8th cir.), U.S. Supreme Ct. Assoc. Meagher, Geer, Markham & Anderson, Mpls., 1956-57; asst. gen. counsel Great No. R.R. Co., St. Paul, 1957-70; assoc. gen. counsel Burlington No. R.R. Co., St. Paul, 1970-86, gen. counsel, 1986—; mem. Minn. Supreme Ct. Com. Ct. Appeals, St. Paul, 1983-85. Chmn. Minn. Pvt. Detective and Protective Agts. Bd., St. Paul, 1979—. Mem. ABA, Minn. Bar Assn., Minn. Def. Lawyers Assn., Minn. R.R. Trial Lawyers Assn. (chmn.), Ramsey County Bar Assn. (ethics com. 1983—). Republican. Roman Catholic. Federal civil litigation, State civil litigation, Personal injury. Home: 427 Woodlawn Saint Paul MN 55105 Office: Burlington No RR Co 3800 Continental Plaza Fort Worth TX 76102

WICKER, VERONICA DICARLO, judge; b. Monessen, Pa., Nov. 26, 1930; s. Vincent James and Rose Margaret DiCarlo; m. Thomas Carey Wicker, Jr.; children: Cathy, Carey. B.F.A., Syracuse U., 1952; J.D., Loyola U. of the South, 1966. Bar: La. 1966. U.S. magistrate New Orleans, 1977-79; judge U.S. Dist. Ct. (ea. dist.) La., New Orleans, 1979—. Mem. vis. com. Loyola U. Law Sch. Mem. ABA, Fed. Bar. Assn., La. Bar Assn., New Orleans Bar Assn., Jefferson Parish Bar Aux., Fed. Dist. Judges Assn., Assn. Women Judges, Maritime Law Assn., Assn. Women Attys., Justinian Soc. Jurists, Phi Alpha Delta, Alpha Xi Alpha, Phi Mu. Jurisprudence. Office: US Courthouse 500 Camp St Room C-406 New Orleans LA 70130

WICKER, WALTER CHRIS, lawyer; b. Casper, Wyo., Nov. 21, 1952; s. Walter Lee and Mary Wanda (Pults) W.; m. Andrea Leigh Fox, Nov. 17, 1976; children: Justin Dane, Brianne Marie. BS in Polit. Sci. with highest honors, U. Wyo., 1975, JD with honors, 1979. Bar: Utah 1979, U.S. Dist. Ct. Utah 1979, Nev. 1983, U.S. Dist. Ct. Nev. 1983. Assoc. Watkins & Faber, Salt Lake City, 1979-83, Woodburn, Wedge, Blakey & Jeppson, Reno, 1983—; researcher Water Resource Research Inst., Laramie, Wyo., 1978-79. Chief "Y" Indian Guides, Reno, 1986—. Mem. ABA, Washoe County Bar Assn., Assn. Trial Lawyers Am. Democrat. Avocations: hiking, skiing, reading, history. State civil litigation, Federal civil litigation, General corporate. Office: Woodburn Wedge Blakey & Jeppson 1 E First St Reno NV 89501

WICKERSHAM, RALPH READ, lawyer, b. Pensacola, Fla., Mar. 26, 1937; s. Ralph Clyne and Margaret (Read) W.; m. Ann Duprez Gardner, Apr. 30, 1982; m. Margo Read, Karen Elizabeth, Craig Finley. Student, East Tenn. State Coll., 1955-56; A.B., Duke U., 1959, LL.B., 1962. Bar: Fla. 1962. Assoc. Freeman, Richardson & Watson, Jacksonville, 1962-69, Milam, Martin & Ade, Jacksonville, 1969-74, Milam & Wilbur, Jacksonville, 1974-82; ptnr. Mahoney Hadlow & Adams, P.A., Jacksonville, 1982—. Active Fla. Wildlife Fedn., Audubon Soc. Nature Conservancy; mem. adv. council Child Guidance Clinic of Duval County, 1974—, bd. dirs., 1966-74, treas., 1968-69, pres., 1970, 71, 72; pres. N.E. Fla. Dist. Mental Health Bd., 1972; bd. dirs. Jacksonville chpt. Urban League, 1968-72, Jacksonville Urban Ministries Program; pres. Jacksonville United Methodist Met. Mission Bd., 1969. Mem. Fla. Bar, Jacksonville Bar Assn., ABA. Democrat. Methodist. General corporate. Home: 4850 Ortega Forest Dr Jacksonville FL 32210 Office: 100 Laura St PO Box 4099 Jacksonville FL 32201

WICKHAM, DENNIS J., lawyer; b. San Diego, Mar. 21, 1954; s. Jack and Josephine (Grant) W.; m. Debra M. Harrison, June 5, 1977; children: Amanda Marie, Adam Michael. BA, San Diego State U., 1976; JD, U. Calif., Davis, 1979. Bar: Calif. 1979, U.S. Dist. Ct. (so. dist.) Calif. 1979, U.S. Ct. Appeals (9th cir.) 1984, U.S. Dist. Ct. (ea. dist.) Calif. 1985. Ptnr. Seltzer, Caplan, Wilkins & McMahon, San Diego, 1979—. Mem. ABA, San Diego Trial Lawyers Assn., Am. Trial Lawyers Assn., Order of the Coif. Democrat. Roman Catholic. Bankruptcy, Federal civil litigation, State civil litigation. Office: Seltzer Caplan Wilkins McMahon 3003 Fourth Ave San Diego CA 92103

WICKLAND, DAVID EDWIN, lawyer; b. Chgo., Aug. 4, 1950; s. Albert Edwin Jr. and Patricia Louise (Hammond) W.; m. Jacqueline Anne Frantz, Aug. 12, 1972; children: Elizabeth Louise, Kathryn Anne. AB in Polit. Sci., Ind. U., 1972, JD cum laude, 1975. Bar: Ind. 1975, U.S. Dist. Ct. (so. dist.) Ind. 1975, U.S. Dist. Ct. (no. dist.) Ind. 1977, U.S. Supreme Ct. 1984. Assoc. Law Office R.F. Benne, Munster, Ind., 1975-79; ptnr. Benne & Wickland, Munster, 1979-83; sole practice Munster, 1983—; town atty. Town of St. John, Ind., 1984—; pres. Villa Southwood Condominium Assn., Munster, 1978-84. Chmn. nominating com. Town of Munster, 1978—; bd. dirs. Hammond (Ind.) Area YMCA, 1980—; v.p. Calumet (Ind.) Council Boy Scout Am., Munster, 1982—. Recipient Dist. Merit award Calumet Council Boy Scouts Am., 1981. Mem. ABA, Ind. State Bar Assn., Lake County Bar Assn., Ind. Trial Lawyers Assn., Ind. Mcpl. Lawyers Assn. Club: Briar Ridge Country (Dyer). Lodge: Masons, Shriners. Avocations: golf, handball, hunting. State civil litigation, General practice, Real property. Home: 1326 Camellia Dr Munster IN 46321 Office: 8146 Calumet Ave Munster IN 46321

WICKS, CHARLES CARTER, lawyer; b. Goshen, Ind., May 28, 1945; s. Charles Sterling and Christine (Carter) W.; m. Penny Rae Krull, Oct. 31, 1970; children—Jay, Kristin, Scott. B.A., Tulane U., 1967; J.D., Ind. U., 1970. Bar: Ind. 1970, U.S. Ct. Mil. Appeals 1971. Ptnr., Matthews-Petsche-Wicks, South Bend, Ind., 1974-78; ptnr. Virgil, Cawley, Platt & Wicks, Elkhart, Ind., 1978; sole practice, Elkhart, 1978—; dep. pros. atty., Elkhart, 1978—. lectr. forensic medicine Goshen Coll. Sch. Nursing. Mem. Republican Central Com., Goshen, 1978—; mem. vestry St. James Episcopal Ch., 1977-79, 1981-84, 86—. Served to capt. USAF, 1970-74. Mem. ABA, Ind. Bar Assn., Assn. Trial Lawyers Am., Ind. Trial Lawyers Assn., Elkhart County Estate Planning Council (pres. 1982-83), Elkhart County Past Masters' Assn. (pres. 1984), Am. Legion. Lodges: Masons (master 1980, trustee 1983-85, pres. 1984, bd. dirs. 1985—), Shriners, Moose, Elkhart Kiwanis (bd. dirs.). Clubs: Christiana Creek Country. Personal injury, Family and matrimonial, State civil litigation. Home: 26207 Hilly Ln Elkhart IN 46517 Office: 215 S 2d St PO Box 1884 Elkhart IN 46515

WIDDEL, JOHN EARL, JR., lawyer; b. Minot, N.D., Nov. 17, 1936; s. John Earl Sr. and Angela Victoria (Gefroh) W.; m. Yvonne J. Haugen, Dec. 21, 1973; children: John P., James M., Susan N., Andrea K. B in Philosophy, BS in Bus. Adminstrn., U. N.D., 1966, JD, 1971. Ptnr. Thorsen & Widdel, Grand Forks, N.D., 1971—; mcpl. judge City of Grand Forks, 1972—; ct. magistrate Grand Forks County, 1975. Mem. N.D. Foster Parent Program, 1974—; del. N.D. Rep. Conv., Fargo, 1985; bd. dirs. YMCA, Grand Forks, 1982; dist. chmn. Boy Scouts Am., 1987—. Served with U.S. Army, 1960-62. Mem. N.D. Bar Assn. (bd. govs. 1983—, pres. 1986-87), Greater Grand Forks County Bar Assn. (pres. 1982), N.E. Cen. Jud. Dist. (pres. 1983), N.D. State Bd. Govs. (pres. 1986-87), Grand Forks Cemetary Assn. (bd. dirs. 1984—), Grand Forks Hist. Soc. (pres. 1983), Grand Forks Jaycees, N.D. Region Club Am. Antique Automobile (pres. 1977, 78, 83, 84), Club Am. Antique Automobile (nat. dir. 1984-85, v.p. 1985-86-87), Club Am. (v.p. 1985-86). Roman Catholic. Lodges: Elks (exhaulted ruler 1986-87), Masons, Sertoma (bd. dirs. 1984—, dist. chmn. 1987—). General practice, Probate, Real property. Home: 3209 Belmont Rd Grand Forks ND 58201 Office: Thorsen & Widdel 114 Belmont Rd Grand Forks ND 58201

WIDENER, HIRAM EMORY, JR., judge; b. Abingdon, Va., Apr. 30, 1923; s. Hiram Emory and Nita Douglas (Peck) W.; m. Jo Smith O'Donnell; children: Molly Berentd, Hiram Emory III. Student, Va. Poly. Inst., 1940-41; B.S., U.S. Naval Acad., 1944; LL.B., Washington and Lee U., 1953, LL.D., 1977. Bar: Va. 1951. Pvt. practice law Bristol, Va., 1953-69; judge U.S. Dist. Ct. Western Dist. Va., Abingdon, 1969-71; chief judge U.S. Dist. Ct. Western Dist. Va., 1971-72; judge U.S. Ct. Appeals 4th Circuit, Abingdon, 1972—; U.S. commr. Western Dist. Va., 1963-66; mem. Va. Election Laws Study Commn., 1968-69. Chmn. Republican party 9th Dist. Va., 1966-69; mem. Va. Rep. State Central Com., 1966-69, state exec. com., 1966-69; trustee Va. Intermont Coll. Served to lt. (j.g.) USN, 1944-49; to lt. USNR, 1951-52. Decorated Bronze Star with combat V. Mem. Am. Law Inst., Va. Bar Assn., Va. State Bar, Am. Legion, Phi Alpha Delta. Republican. Presbyterian. Jurisprudence. Home: Box 868 Abingdon VA 24210 Office: US Ct Appeals Abingdon VA 24210

WIDENER, JO S., lawyer; b. Detroit, Dec. 27, 1945; d. Roy Charles and Shirley Rita (Dronkowski) Smith; m. H. Emory Widener Jr., Aug. 12, 1977; children: Molly Beretd, H. Emory III. BA, U. Mich., 1967; MA, Oakland U., Rochester, Mich., 1972; JD cum laude, U. Detroit, 1976. Bar: Va. 1976, U.S. Dist. Ct. (we. dist.) Va. 1977, U.S. Ct. Appeals (4th cir.) 1977, U.S. Supreme Ct. 1984. Law clk. to judge U.S. Ct. Appeals (4th cir.), Richmond, Va., 1976-77; assoc. Hunton & Williams, Richmond, 1977, Widener & Frackelton, Bristol, Va., 1983-84; sole practice Bristol, 1984—. Assoc. editor U. Detroit Law Rev., 1976. Bankruptcy. Home: Rt 1 PO Box 485 AA Abingdon VA 24210 Office: 54 Piedmont Bristol VA 24201

WIDETT, IRVING, lawyer; b. Chelsea, Mass., May 21, 1913; s. Phillip and Annie Widetzky; m. Rose Rubenstein; children—Neal, Arleen; m. 2d, Joanne S. McCarthy, Dec. 28, 1980. J.D., Northeastern U., 1937. Bar: Mass. 1938. Sr. ptnr. Widett, Glazier & McCarthy, Boston, 1979—. Served in U.S. Army, 1943. Decorated Bronze Star. Mem. ABA, Boston Bar Assn., Mass. Bar Assn. Democrat. Jewish. Bankruptcy, Consumer commercial, General corporate. Office: 111 Devonshire St Boston MA 02109

WIDING, CAROL SCHARFE, lawyer; b. South Orange, N.J., Dec. 18, 1941; d. Howard Carman and Marjorie (McConaghy) Scharfe; m. C. Jon Widing, July 2, 1966; 1 child, Daniel McClure. BA, Wellesley Coll., 1964; MEd, Harvard U., 1965; JD, Widener U., 1980. Bar: Del. 1981, Pa. 1981, U.S. Dist. Ct. Del. 1981, U.S. Ct. Appeals (3d. cir.) 1983, Conn. 1984. Tchr. elem. schs. Lexington, Mass. and Bryn Mawr, Pa., 1964-68; pvt. tutor Ibadan, Nigeria, 1965; tchr. Phila. Adult Basic Edn. Acad., 1970-72; dep. atty. gen. child protection services Del. Dept. Justice, Wilmington, 1981-83; staff atty. UAW Legal Services, Newark, Del., 1983; assoc. Hebb & Gitlin, P.C., Hartford, Conn., 1985-86, Steinberg & Louden, P.C., Hartford, 1987—. V.p. program AAUW, Middletown, Del. 1974; chmn. pub. relations and fundraising Lower New Castle County Med. Ctr., Middletown, 1980. Mem. ABA, Pa. Bar Assn., Del. Bar Assn., Conn. Bar Assn., Hartford County Bar Assn., Hartford Assn. Women Attys., Assn. Trial Lawyers Am., Jr. League (program chmn. Phila. 1972). Avocations: piano, gardening, skiing. Family and matrimonial. Home: 6 September Way Avon CT 06001 Office: Steinberg & Louden 99 Pratt St Hartford CT 06103

WIDISS, ALAN I., lawyer, educator; b. Los Angeles, Sept. 28, 1938; s. Al and Rose H. (Sobole) W.; m. Ellen Louise Magaziner, June 28, 1964; children: Benjamin L., Deborah Anne, Rebecca Elizabeth. B.S., U. So. Calif., 1960, LL.B., 1963; LL.M., Harvard U., 1964. Bar: Calif. 1963. Teaching fellow Harvard U., 1964-65; asst. prof. law U. Iowa, Iowa City, 1965-68; asso. prof. U. Iowa, 1968-69, prof., 1969-78, Josephine R. Witte prof., 1978—; vis. prof. U. So. Calif., U. San Diego; dir. CLRS Mass. No-Fault Automobile Ins. Study, 1971-76. Author, editor: (with others) Arbitration: Commercial Disputes, Insurance and Tort Claims, 1979; author: A Guide to Uninsured Motorist Coverage, 1969, (with others) No-Fault Automobile Insurance in Action: The Experiences in Massachusetts, Florida, Delaware and New York, 1977; author Uninsured and Underinsured Motorist Insurance, Vol. 1, 1985, Vol. 2, 1987; author: (with Judge Robert E. Keeton) Insurance Law, 1988; contbr. articles to law jours. Bd. trustees U. Iowa Sch. Religion, 1976—; chair Johnson County Citizens Adv. Com. for Regional Transp. Study, 1971-75; chair U. Iowa Com. on Ins. & Funded Retirement, 1978-82, 86-87. Mem. Am. Law Inst., ABA, Calif. Bar Assn., Am. Assn. Law Schs., Order of Coif, Phi Kappa Phi, Delta Sigma Rho. Avocations: tennis, squash. Insurance, Contracts commercial, Legal education. Home: 316 Kimball Rd Iowa City IA 52240 Office: U Iowa Coll Law Iowa City IA 52242

WIDMAN, DOUGLAS JACK, lawyer; b. Neptune, N.J., Feb. 28, 1949; s. Leonard and Phyllis (Rose) W.; m. Jill Rosenblad; children: Phyllis, Jared Leonard, Sarah. BA in Polit. Sci. cum laude, Syracuse U., 1971, JD, 1973. Bar: N.J. 1973, U.S. Dist. Ct. N.J. 1973, U.S. Supreme Ct. 1979, D.C. 1981, N.Y. 1981. Research assistant Syracuse (N.Y.) U., 1972; legal planner Syracuse-Onondaga (N.Y.) County Planning Agy., 1971-73; law sec. to presiding judges N.J. Dist. Ct. and N.J. Superior Ct., 1973-74; dep. atty gen. State Enforcement Bur. Div. Criminal Justice, Trenton, N.J., 1974-76; ptnr. Widman and Cooney, Ocean, N.J., 1976—; instr. Monmouth Coll., West Long Branch, N.J. Assoc. editor Syracuse Jour. Internat. Law & Commerce. Student tchr. Martin Luther King Jr. Elem. Sch., Syracuse. Syracuse U. Coll. Law scholar, 1971-73; Syracuse U. Grad. Reasearch fellow, 1972. Mem. Phi Alpha Delta, Alpha Phi Omega, Pi Sigma Alpha. Personal injury, Insurance, Criminal. Office: Widman and Cooney 1300 Hwy 35 Monmouth Exec Plaza II Ocean NJ 07712

WIDMANN, HARRY THOMAS, lawyer; b. Phila., Nov. 5, 1952; s. Frank J. and Nellie M. (Sheehy) W.; Mary Linda Beck, Oct. 25, 1980; children: Michelle Catherine, Julia Denise. BA, LaSalle Coll., 1974; JD, Loyola U., New Orleans, 1977. Assoc. Alford & Caruso, New Orleans, 1977-79; ptnr. Alford & Widmann, New Orleans, 1979-82; pres. Harry T. Widmann & Assocs. P.L.C., New Orleans, 1982—; instr. criminal law Tulane U., New Orleans, 1981, U. New Orleans Paralegal Inst., 1982-85. Mem. Assn. Trial Lawyers Am., La. Trial Lawyers Assn., La. State Bar Assn. Democrat. Roman Catholic. Club: Lakewood Country (New Orleans). Personal injury, State civil litigation. Home: 3813 Metairie Heights Ave Metairie LA 70001 Office: Harry T Widmann & Assocs PLC 2610 Esplanade Ave New Orleans LA 70126

WIDTFELDT, JAMES ALBERT, lawyer; b. O'Neill, Nebr., Nov. 18, 1947; s. Albert Theodore and Gusteva Emma (Peterson) W. BS., MIT, 1970, M.S., 1970; postgrad. Rensselaer Poly. Inst., 1970-75, Ph.D., 1977; J.D., U. Nebr.-Lincoln, 1978. Bar: Nebr. 1978, U.S. Dist. Ct. Nebr. 1978. Civilian employee Office Naval Research, Troy, N.Y., 1973-75; assoc. Cronin & Hannon, O'Neill, Nebr., 1978-79; sole practice law, Atkinson, Nebr., 1979—. Coauthor articles in Jour. Acoustical Soc., 1973-75. Mem. Nebr. Bar Assn., Sigma Xi, Delta Theta Phi, Sigma Pi Sigma. Republican. Methodist. Club: Toastmasters. Lodges: Masons, Shriners. State civil litigation, Probate, Real property. Home: Anncar Rt O'Neill NE 68763 Office: 103 State St Atkinson NE 68713

WIEBUSCH, RICHARD VERNON, lawyer, author; b. Schenectady, N.Y., Dec. 4, 1946; s. Vernon Ralph and Marjorie (Hush) W.; m. Margaret Alice Meacham, May 6, 1967; children—Kimberley Ann, Alice Christina, Katrina Elizabeth. A.B., Dartmouth Coll., 1968; J.D., Cornell U., 1973. Bar: N.H. 1973, U.S. Dist. Ct. N.H. 1973, U.S. Ct. Appeals (1st cir.) 1976. Chief consumer protection div. N.H. Atty. Gen., Concord, 1973-76, chief div. legal counsel, 1976-77; assoc. firm Sheehan, Phinney, Bass & Green, Manchester, N.H., 1977-78, ptnr, 1979-85; U.S. atty. U.S. Dist. Ct. N.H., Concord, 1985—; adj. prof. Franklin Pierce Law Ctr., Concord, 1985. Author: New Hampshire Civil Practice and Procedure, 3 vols., 1984. Dist. enrollment dir. Dartmouth Coll., Manchester, 1976-85; mem. Downtown Concord Revitalization Commn., 1978-79; commr. N.H. Ballot Law Commn., 1981-85; mem. adv. com. State Law Library, 1982-85; pres. N.H. Estate Planning Council, 1983-84. Mem. ABA, Hillsborough County Bar Assn., N.H. Bar Assn., Am. Judicature Soc. Republican. General corporate, State civil litigation, Administrative and regulatory. Home: 125 School St Concord NH 03301 Office: 55 Pleasant St Concord NH 03301

WIECHMANN, ERIC WATT, lawyer; b. Schenectady, N.Y., June 12, 1948; s. Richard Jerdone and Ann (Watt) W.; m. Merrill Metzger, May 22, 1971. B.A., Hamilton Coll., 1970; J.D., Cornell U., 1974. Bar: Conn. 1975, D.C. 1981, U.S. Dist. Ct. (so. and ea. dists.) N.Y. 1975, U.S. Dist. Ct. Conn. 1975, U.S. Dist. Ct. D.C. 1981, U.S. Ct. Appeals (2d cir.) 1975, U.S. Ct. Appeals (9th cir.) 1980, U.S. Ct. Appeals D.C. 1982, U.S. Supreme Ct. 1978, U.S. Ct. Appeals (5th cir.) 1986. Assoc., Cummings & Lockwood, Stamford, 1974-82, ptnr., 1982—; spl. pretrial master U.S. Dist. Ct. Conn. 1984; state atty. trial referee, 1986. Contbr. articles to profl. jours. Mem. Zoning Bd. Appeals, New Canaan, Conn., 1984-85. Mem. Def. Research Inst., Conn. Bar Assn., ABA (exec. com. antitrust sect. 1982—), Fed. Bar Council. Republican. Episcopalian. Club: Hartford, Golf Club Avon. Federal civil litigation, State civil litigation, Antitrust. Home: 21 Foxcroft Run Avon CT 06001

WIECK, PAUL HANS, II, lawyer; b. Waterloo, Iowa, Sept. 7, 1952; s. Paul Hans and Catharine (Weaver) W.; m. Jenine Kristine Owen, June 1, 1971; children: Owen Leigh, Jennifer Kathleen. BS, Iowa State U., 1973; JD, Drake U., 1982. Bar: Iowa 1982, U.S. Dist. Ct. (so. dist.) Iowa 1982, U.S. Tax Ct. 1982. Exec. asst. to chief justice Iowa Supreme Ct., Des Moines, 1982-83; assoc. Reynoldson, Van Werden, Kimes, Reynoldson and Lloyd, Osceola, Iowa, 1983-84; ptnr. Reynoldson, Van Werden, Kimes, Reynoldson, Lloyd and Wieck, Osceola, 1985—. Served to capt. USAR, 1973-79, to maj. USNG, 1980—. Mem. Order of Coif, Order of Barristers. General practice. Office: 200 W Jefferson St Osceola IA 50213

WIEGAND, BRUCE, lawyer; b. Dallas, Nov. 27, 1947; s. Frank Louis and Undine (Phillips) W.; m. Barbara Louise McKenna, July 18, 1970; children: Christy C., Laura C., Bruce Phillips. AB cum laude, Harvard U., 1969; JD, U. Pitts., 1973. Bar: Pa. 1973, U.S. Dist. Ct. (we. dist.) Pa. 1973, U.S. Ct. Appeals (3d cir.) 1973. Assoc. Kirkpatrick & Lockhart, Pitts., 1973-80, ptnr., 1980—; bd. dirs., pres. T.W. Phillips Gas and Oil Co., Butler, Pa.; bd. dirs., gen. counsel, sec. Phillips Resources, Inc., Butler, 1984—. Mem. ABA, Pa. Bar Assn., Allegheny County Bar Assn., Pa. Oil, Gas and Minerals. Republican. Clubs: Duquesne, St. Clair Country Rivers, Harvard, Yale, Princeton (Pitts.). Oil and gas leasing, FERC practice, General corporate. Home: 1425 Navahoe Dr Pittsburgh PA 15228 Office: Kirkpatrick & Lockhart Oliver Bldg Suite 1500 Pittsburgh PA 15222

WIEGAND, ROBERT, II, lawyer; b. New Orleans, Feb. 11, 1947; s. Robert Nelson and Olivia Eustis (Eaves) W.; m. Pamela Danos, Apr. 23, 1976; children: Stephen B., Kelly M., Julianna. BA in History, Tulane U., 1970, JD, 1972; LLM, U. Denver, 1977. Bar: La. 1972, U.S. Dist. Ct. (ea. dist.) La. 1972, U.S. Ct. Appeals (5th cir.) 1975, Colo. 1976, U.S. Dist. Ct. Colo. 1976. Assoc. Deutsch & Kerrigan, New Orleans, 1972-76, Banta & Hoyt, Englewood, Colo., 1977-78; ptnr. Allspach & Wiegand, Denver, 1978-80; prin. Wiegand and Assocs. P.C., Denver, 1980-83; prin. O'Connor & Hannan, Denver, 1983-86, of counsel, 1986—; pres., chief exec. officer SPM Group Inc., Denver, 1986—; corp. counsel SPM Group, Inc., Denver, 1980-86, Information Solutions, Inc., Denver, 1984-86. councilman City of Greenwood Village, Colo., 1985—. Mem. Colo. Bar Assn. (bus.and banking coms. on Colo. corp. code and uniform ltd. partnership act). Republican. Episcopalian. Club: University (Denver). General corporate, Securities, Corporate taxation. Office: O'Connor & Hannan 1700 Lincoln St Denver CO 80203

WIELAND, ROBERT RICHARD, lawyer, recreation and leisure time products manufacturing executive; b. Columbus, Ohio, Jan. 30, 1937; s. Robert Milton and Evelyn Marion (Turner) W.; m. Sara J. Gerhart, Dec. 17, 1966; 1 child, Christopher David. B.A., Ohio State U., Columbus, 1958, J.D., 1960. Bar: Ohio 1960, Ill. 1966. Atty. Ohio Bell Telephone Co., Cleve., 1960-65, United Air Lines, Inc., Chgo., 1965-67; asst. gen. counsel, asst. sec. Youngstown Sheet and Tube Co., Ohio, 1967-73, Mead Corp., Dayton, Ohio, 1974-76; v.p., gen. counsel, sec. Huffy Corp., Dayton, 1976—; dir., officer Huffman Mfg. Co., H.C.A., Inc., YLC Enterprises, Inc., Raleigh Cycle Co. Am., Gerico, Inc., Snugli, Inc.; sec. Huffy Found., Inc.; mng. dir. Huffy Internat. Finance N.V. Trustee Byron R. Lewis Edn. Fund, 1976-80; pres. Miami Valley council Boy Scouts Am.; pres. assoc. bd., trustee Dayton Art Inst., 1979-83, 87—; v.p., mem. Friends of Aullwood Ctr., 1981-84; trustee Miami Valley Sch., 1985-86. Served with USAF, 1961-62. Mem. ABA, Ohio Bar Assn., Dayton Bar Assn., Am. Arbitration Assn. (arbitration panel), Am. Soc. Corp. Secs. (v.p. SW Ohio chpt. 1986-87), Sigma Pi (pres. 1972-74). General corporate, State civil litigation, Patent. Address: Huffy Corp 7701 Byers Rd Miamisburg OH 45342

WIEMAN, TERRY LYNN, lawyer; b. Montrose, Colo., Oct. 9, 1951; s. Simon William and Martha Elizabeth (Bell) W.; m. Diane DeBekker, May 27, 1983 (div. May 1984). BS, Wichita State U., 1974; JD, Washburn U., 1981. Bar: Colo. 1982, U.S. Dist. Ct. Colo. 1982. Field supr. Smith and Co., Inc., Wichita, Kans., 1974-75; owner Thousand Oaks, Inc., Wichita, 1975-78; assoc. Colo. Law Ctns. Co., Colorado Springs, 1981-85; ptnr. Alexander & Weiman, Colorado Springs, 1985—; co-owner, corp. counsel R & K Enterprises, Inc., Colorado Springs, 1985—, also bd. dirs.; pres., co-owner White Cliffs, Inc., Colorado Springs, 1985—, also bd. dirs.; owner Century Centre Mall; co-owner, fin. advisor Gordon Ready-Mix and Construction; cons., bd. dirs. Pro Lawn, Inc., Colorado Springs. Mem. ABA, Colo. Bar Assn., Am. Trial Lawyers Assn., Colo. Trial Lawyers Assn., El Paso County Bar Assn. Republican. Methodist. Avocations: golf, fishing, skiing, hunting, working with deprived children. Personal injury, Insurance, State civil litigation. Office: Alexander & Weiman 740 Citadel Dr E # 406 Colorado Springs CO 80909

WIENER, HOWARD ALAN, lawyer, realtor; b. Paterson, N.J., Apr. 14, 1932; s. Louis and Mary (Mendelsohn) W.; m. Barbara Lavin, Aug. 28, 1955; children—Joel, Stephen, Suzanne. B.S. in Econs., U. Pa., 1953, LL.B., 1956. Bar: Pa. 1956, U.S. Dist. Ct. (ea. dist.) Pa. 1957, U.S. Supreme Ct. 1971, U.S. Tax Ct. 1982. Sole practice, Allentown, Pa., 1956-66, 70-81; ptnr. Wiener & Young, and successor firm Wiener, Young & Hayes, Allentown, 1966-70; sr. ptnr. Wiener & Wiener, Allentown, 1981—. Bd. dirs. Jewish Community Ctr. of Allentown, 1961—, sec., 1969-73, fin. sec., 1973-75, 3d v.p., 1975-77, 1st v.p., 1977-79, pres. 1979-81; bd. dirs. Lehigh United Way, 1978-81, mem. exec. com., 1979-82. Mem. ABA, Pa. Bar Assn., Lehigh County Bar Assn. (dir. 1977—, v.p. 1981, pres. 1983). General corporate, Estate taxation, Probate. Office: Wiener & Wiener 400 Commonwealth Bldg Allentown PA 18101

WIENER, IRA EDWARD, lawyer; b. Bklyn., Sept. 25, 1950; s. Elliot and Neoma (Cohen) W.; m. Myra Phyllis Zang, Aug. 21, 1977; 1 child, Lauren Anne. BA, SUNY, Buffalo, 1972; JD, Bklyn. Law Sch., 1976. Bar: N.Y. 1977, U.S. Dist. Ct. (so. and ea. dists.) N.Y. 1977. Asst. to mng. clk. Cravath, Swaine and Moore, N.Y.C., 1973-77; mng. atty. Ballon, Stoll and Itzler, N.Y.C., 1977-78, Golenbock & Barell, N.Y.C., 1978-81, Hawkins, Delafield & Wood, N.Y.C., 1981—. Mem. Jewish Community Ctr. Middlesex County. Mem. ABA, N.Y. State Bar Assn., N.Y. County Lawyers Assn., Assn. Mng. Attys. and Clks. Federal civil litigation, State civil litigation. Home: 12 Monica Dr Edison NJ 08820 Office: Hawkins Delafield & Wood 67 Wall St New York NY 10005

WIENNER, S. THOMAS, lawyer; b. Detroit, July 23, 1953; s. James Monroe and Marilyn Lee (Sandorf) W.; m. Jane Irene Spokes, July 26, 1975; children: Adam Joseph, Carolyn Gail. AB, Harvard U., 1975; JD, U. Mich., 1978. Bar: Mich. 1978, U.S. Dist. Ct. (ea. dist.) Mich. 1978, U.S. Dist. Ct. (we. dist.) Mich. 1981, U.S. Ct. Appeals (6th cir.) 1984. Assoc. Dykema, Gossett, Spencer, Goodnow & Trigg, Detroit, 1978-86, ptnr., 1986—. Mem. ABA (litigation sect., trial practice com.), Mich. Bar Assn., Detroit Bar Assn. Federal civil litigation, State civil litigation, Personal injury. Home: 3696 Forest Hill Rd Bloomfield Hills MI 48013 Office: Dykema Gossett et al 400 Renaissance Ctr 35th Floor Detroit MI 48243

WIER, RICHARD ROYAL, JR., lawyer; b. Wilmington, Del., May 19, 1941; s. Richard Royal and Anne (Kurtz) W.; m. Anne E. Wier, Nov. 25, 1978; children—Melissa Royal, Emma Kurtz; children from previous marriage: Richard Royal, III, Mimi Poole. B.A. in English, Hamilton Coll., 1963; LL.B., U. Pa., 1963; cert., Temple U. Law Sch., 1982. Bar: D.C. 1967, Del. 1967, Pa. 1980. Assoc. Connolly, Bove & Lodge, Wilmington, 1966-68; atty. gen. Del., 1975-79; dep. atty. gen. 1968-70; state prosecutor Del. Dept. Justice, 1970-74; ptnr. firm Prickett, Jones, Elliott, Kristol & Schnee, Wilmington, 1979—; lectr. criminal law various instns., 1970-75. Active United Way campaign, 1976, 77; mem. supervisory bd. Gov.'s Commn. on Criminal Justice.; Bd. dirs. Del. Council Crime and Justice, 1982—. Recipient Law Enforcement award Newark Police Dept., 1974; Law Enforcement Commendation medal Nat. Soc. SAR, 1976; Ideal Citizen award Am. Found. for Sci. Creative Intelligence, 1976; commendation Del. Gen. Assembly Senate, 1976, 77, 80; Outstanding Achievement award, 1976. Mem. Nat. Dist. Attys. Assn. (state dir.), ABA, Del., Pa., D.C. bar assns., Nat. Assn. Attys. Gen. (exec. com.), Am. Judicature Soc., Am., Del. trial lawyers assns., Nat. Assn. Extradition Ofcls. (hon. life mem., regional v.p., exec. dir.), Italian Radio TV Assn. (hon.), Pi Delta Epsilon. Office: Prickett Jones et al 1310 King St Box 1328 Wilmington DE 19899

WIERSMA, DAVID CHARLES, lawyer; b. Lakewood, Ohio, May 11, 1947; s. Milton Edward and Violet (Tinker) W.; m. Martha Denning, June 14, 1969 (div. Sept. 1976); 1 son, Andrew David; m. Eileen Marguerite Novello, July 21, 1978 (div. 1984); 1 child, Holly Elizabeth. BA in Econs./Math., U. Pitts., 1969; JD cum laude, Cleveland Marshall Coll. Law, 1976. Bar: Ohio 1976, U.S. Dist. Ct. (no. dist.) Ohio 1977. Tchr. high sch. Lorain City Schs., Ohio, 1969-72; trust officer Lorain County Savs. & Trust Co., Elyria, Ohio, 1972-76; assoc. Cook and Batista Co. L.P.A., Lorain, 1976-81, ptnr., 1981—. Trustees Lorain County Law Library Assn., Elyria, 1982—, pres. bd. trustees, 1986; trustee St. Joseph Urgent Care Ctr., Elyria, 1983—, sec.-treas. bd. trustees, 1985-86; trustee Firelands council Boy Scouts Am., Vermilion, Ohio, 1983-85. Mem. Ohio State Bar Assn., Lorain County Bar Assn., Greater Cleve. Bar Assn., Greater Lorain C. of C., Am. Mensa. Democrat. Lutheran. Lodge: Rotary. Probate, Banking, Real property. Home: 5211 Hillgrove Dr Lorain OH 44053 Office: Cook and Batista Co LPA 209 6th St Lorain OH 44052

WIESE, JOHN PAUL, federal judge; b. Brooklyn, Apr. 19, 1934; s. Gustav and Margaretha W.; m. Alice Mary Donoghue, June 1961; 1 child,John Patrick. B.A., Hobart College, Geneva, NY, 1962; L.L.B., Univ. of Virginia, Charlottesville, 1965. Private practice Washington, DC, 1967-1974; trial judge U.S. Claims Court, Washington, DC, 1974-1982, judge, 1982—. Judicial administration. Office: US Claims Ct Nat Courts Bldg 717 Madison Ave NW Washington DC 20005 *

WIESE, LARRY CLEVENGER, lawyer; b. Huntsville, Tex., May 30, 1949; s. Arthur Edward and Lola Irene (Clevenger) W.; m. Patricia Petty Barr, Aug. 12, 1972; 1 son, Hugh Clevenger. B.S., Sam Houston State U., 1971; J.D., Tex. Tech. U., 1974; M.B.A., George Washington U., 1978. Bar: Tex. 1974, U.S. Ct. Mil. Appeals 1975, U.S. Supreme Ct. 1976, U.S. Dist. Ct. (so. dist.) Tex. 1979, U.S. Dist. Ct. (ea. dist.) Tex. 1980, U.S. Ct. Appeals (5th cir.) 1982. Staff atty. Shell Oil Co., Houston, 1978-80; atty. Houston div. Marathon Oil Co., 1980-84, Marathon Internat. Oil Co., London, 1984—. Contbr. article to profl. jour. State coordinator Nebr. George Bush for Pres. campaign, Houston, 1980; precinct chmn. Mayor Kathy Whitmire campaign, Houston, 1982; mem. Western Harris County Republican Men's Club, 1980-84, Gulf Coast Council Fgn. Affairs, Galveston, 1980-84. Served to lt. comdr. USCG, 1974-78. Named one of Outstanding Young Men in Am., 1981. Mem. Tex. Bar Assn., Houston Bar Assn. (chmn. corp. counsel sect. 1983-84), Houston Young Lawyers Assn. (program chmn. 1982-83), Maritime Law Assn., Res. Officers Assn., Navy League. Lutheran. Club: Luth. Men. Oil and gas leasing, General corporate, State civil litigation. Home: 4 Randolph Crescent, London England Office: Marathon Internat Petroleum Co Ltd, 174 Marylebone Rd, Marathon House, London NWI-5AT, England

WIETMARSCHEN, DONALD ALAN, lawyer; b. Cin., Sept. 7, 1954; s. Henry Clarence and Ruth Mabel (Rogers) W.; m. Nancy Carol Huber, May 27, 1978; children: Gretchen MacRae, Erich Carl. BA, Ohio Dominican Coll., 1977; JD, Ohio No. U., 1981. Bar: Ohio 1981, U.S. Dist. Ct. (so. dist.) Ohio 1981, U.S. Tax Ct. 1982. Ptnr. Jessee & Wietmarschen, Fairborn, Ohio, 1981-82; tax specialist Mesarvey, Russell & Co., Springfield, Ohio, 1982-84; assoc. Calhoun, Benzin et al, Mansfield, Ohio, 1984-85, Gottlieb, Johnston, Beam & Joseph, Zanesville, Ohio, 1985—. Named on of Outstanding Young Men of Am., 1984, 85. Mem. ABA, Ohio State Bar Assn., Cleve. Bar Assn., Muskingum County Bar Assn., Jaycees(treas. Zanesville chpt. 1986—), Delta Theta Phi. Roman Catholic. General corporate, Corporate taxation, Personal income taxation. Home: 1067 Terrace Ct Zanesville OH 43701 Office: Gottlieb Johnston Beam & Joseph 320 Main St PO Box 190 Zanesville OH 43701

WIGGINS, CHARLES EDWARD, federal judge; b. El Monte, Calif., Dec. 3, 1927; s. Louis J. and Margaret E. (Fanning) W.; m. Yvonne L. Boots, Dec. 30, 1946 (dec. Sept. 1971); children: Steven L., Scott D.; m. Betty J. Koontz, July 12, 1972. B.S., U. So. Calif., 1953, LL.B., 1956; LL.B. (hon.) Ohio Wesleyan, 1975, Han Yang. U., Seoul, Korea, 1976. Bar: Calif. 1957, D.C. 1978. Lawyer, Woods & Wiggins, El Monte, Calif., 1956-66, Musick, Peeler & Garrett, Los Angeles, 1979-81, Pierson, Ball & Dowd, Washington, 1982-84, Pillsbury, Madison & Sutro, San Francisco, 1984; mem. 90-95th congresses from 25th and 39th Calif. Dists.; judge U.S. Ct. Appeals 9th Circuit, 1984—. Mayor City of El Monte, Calif., 1964-66; mem. Planning Commn. City of El Monte, 1956-60. Served to 1st lt. U.S. Army, 1945-48, 50-52, Korea. Mem. ABA, State Bar Calif., D.C. Bar Assn. Republican. Lodge: Lions. Office: US Ct Appeals PO Box 547 San Francisco CA 94104

WIGGINS, KIP ACKER, lawyer; b. Springfield, Mo., Mar. 17, 1950; s. Edward R. and Frances E. (Acker) W.; m. Mary E. Peacock, Oct. 29, 1977; children: Molly E., Matthew E.. BBA, U. Mo., Columbia, 1972; JD, U. Mo., Kansas City, 1975. Bar: Mo. 1975, U.S. Dist. Ct. (we. dist.) Mo. 1975. Ptnr. Hoskins, King, McGannon & Hahn, Kansas City, 1975-84; of counsel Shook, Hardy & Bacon, Kansas City, 1985—. Mem. ABA, Lawyers Assn. Kansas City, Kansas City Met. Bar Assn. Republican. General corporate, Venture capital, Mergers and acquisitions. Home: 12333 High Dr Leawood KS 66209 Office: Shook Hardy & Bacon 120 W 12th St Suite 600 Kansas City MO 64105

WIGHT, LES D., II, lawyer; b. Independence, Mo., July 11, 1951; s. Les D. and Darlene (Van Biber) W.; 1 child, Les D. III. BA, Graceland Coll., Lamoni, Iowa, 1973; JD, U. Mo., Kansas City, 1976. Bar: Mo. 1977. Sole practice Independence, 1977-86; prin. Les D. Wight, P.C., Independence, 1986—. Fundraiser Independence YMCA, 1986. Mem. ABA, Mo. Bar Assn., Kansas City Bar Assn., Eastern Jackson County Bar Assn., Independence C. of C. (com. chmn. 1984-86). General practice, Family and matrimonial, Real property. Office: 530 E 23d St Independence MO 64055

WIKLE, KENNETH CLINTON, JR., lawyer; b. Los Angeles, Dec. 4, 1935; s. Kenneth Clinton and Lorene (Botkin) W.; m. Victoria Tankersley, Feb. 20, 1971; children—Leslie Ann, Lorene Alison. B.S., Columbia U., 1967, J.D., 1969. Bar: Calif. 1970, U.S. Dist. Cts. (cen. and ea. dists.) Calif. 1970. Assoc. William G. Tucker, Los Angeles, 1970-76, Kern, Wooley & Maloney, Los Angeles, 1976-81; mem. Jackson & Wikle, Santa Monica, 1981—; judge pro tem Los Angeles Mcpl. Ct.; mem. panel arbitrators Los Angeles Superior Ct., Am. Arbitration Assn. Pres. Las Virgenes (Calif.) Democratic Club. Served to maj. USAFR, 1956-72. Mem. Aviation Ins. Assn. (past pres. Los Angeles chpt.), Los Angeles County Bar Assn. (jud. evaluation com.), ABA (aviation and space law com.). Federal civil litigation, State civil litigation, Insurance. Home: 25053 Mulholland Hwy Calabasas CA 91302 Office: 2800 28th St Suite 305 Santa Monica CA 90405

WILBORN, WOODY STEPHEN, lawyer; b. Cin., Apr. 20, 1947; s. R. Walter and Viola (Eades) W.; m. Kay Anne Frazier, May 29, 1971; 1 child, Christopher B. BA, Eastern Ky. U., 1969; JD, U. Ky., 1973. Bar: Ky. 1973, U.S. Dist. Ct. (ea. dist.) Ky. 1976, U.S. Supreme Ct. 1978, U.S. Dist. Ct. (we. dist.) Ky. 1982. Sole practice Shelbyville, Ky., 1973—; gen. council ho. leadership Ky. Gen. Assembly, Frankfort, 1985—. State rep. 58th legis. dist. Ky. Gen. Assembly, 1978-82. Served with U.S. Army, 1970-71. Mem. ABA, Ky. Bar Assn. (pres. young lawyers sect.), Assn. Trial Lawyers Am. Democrat. Baptist. State civil litigation, Criminal, General practice. Home: Rt 3 Box 11 Shelbyville KY 40065 Office: PO Box 545 Shelbyville KY 40065

WILBUR, PETER DAVIS, lawyer; b. Palo Alto, Calif., Sept. 14, 1954; s. Richard S. and Betty Lou (Fannin) W.; m. Mary E. Eastman, Sept. 14, 1983. BA in Econs., Stanford U., 1975; JD, U. Chgo., 1978. Bar: Ill. 1978, N.Y. 1980. Sr. counsel The Carburundum Co., Niagara Falls, N.Y., 1979-82; atty. Standard Oil of Ohio, Cleve., 1982—. Mem. ABA, Ill. Bar Assn., N.Y. Bar Assn. Contracts commercial, Private international, General corporate. Office: The Standard Oil Co 200 Public Square Standard Oil Bldg 39B S300 Cleveland OH 44122

WILCOX, BRUCE ANDREW, lawyer; b. Berkeley, Calif., Oct. 8, 1948; s. William Bruce and Barbara (Chase) W.; m. Nancy Joan Youngs, June 6, 1977; children: Katrin, Jonathan, Henry, Andrew. AB in History, U. Calif., Berkeley, 1970; JD, Golden Gate U., 1981. Bar: Calif. 1981, Va. 1984, U.S. Ct. Mil. Appeals 1983, U.S. Dist. Ct (ea. dist.) Va 1985. Atty. Naval Legal Service Office, Norfolk Naval Base, Va., 1982-85; assoc. Tavss, Fletcher & Earley P.C., Norfolk, 1985—. Mem. Rep. City Com., Norfolk, 1985, Heritage Found., 1985. Served as lt. USNR, 1981-85. Mem. ABA, Fed. Bar Assn., Calif. Bar Assn., Va. Bar Assn., Norfolk-Portsmouth Bar Assn., Assn. Trial Lawyers Am., Judge Advs. Assn. Club: Civitan (Norfolk, Va.). Avocations: running, golf, tennis. State civil litigation, Military, Real property. Office: Tavss Fletcher & Earley PC 2 Commercial Place Royster Bldg Suite 100 Norfolk VA 23510

WILCOX, DONALD ALAN, lawyer; b. Grantsburg, Wis., July 18, 1951; s. John Charles and Lois Margaret (Finch) W.; m. Rachel Ann Johnson, Dec. 28, 1973; children: Benjamin Ray, Joseph Charles, Sara Johanna. BS, USAF Acad., 1973; JD, Georgetown U., 1979. Bar: Minn. 1979. Commd. 2d lt. USAF, 1973, advanced through grades to capt., resigned, 1979; assoc Holmquist & Holmquist, Benson, Minn., 1979-81; ptnr. Holmquist & Wilcox, 1981—; gen. counsel Swift County-Benson Hosp., 1981—, Farmer's Mut. Coop., Bellingham, Minn., 1986—, Agralite Coop., Benson, 1986—; atty. City of Benson, 1985—; examiner of titles, Swift County, Benson, 1986—. Mem. Benson Planning Commn., 1975-85; pres. Our Redeemer's Luth. Ch., Benson, 1985-86; pres., bd. dirs. Swift County Homes, Inc., Benson, 1984—. Recipient Lawyers Coop. Pub. award Lawyers Coop. Pub. Co., 1979. Mem. ABA, Minn. Bar Assn., Minn. Assn. Hosp. Attys., Benson C. of C. (bd. dirs. 1981-84). Lodge: Kiwanis (treas. Benson 1982-84). Avocations: reading, golf, skiing. Contracts commercial, Probate, Real property. Home: 604 13th St S Benson MN 56215 Office: Holmquist & Wilcox PA 1150 Wisconsin Ave Benson MN 56215

WILCOX, EVERETT HAMMOCK, JR., lawyer; b. Clearwater, Fla., Apr. 25, 1944; s. Everett Hammock Sr. and Alice (Wilson) W.; m. Janet Elaine Springman, June 7, 1967; children: Alexis Shields Wilcox, Merrill Morrow Wilcox. BA, Duke U., 1966; MA, U. Fla., 1969, JD with honors, 1971. Bar: Fla. 1972, D.C. 1972, Ga. 1980. Law clk. to presiding justice U.S. Ct. Appeals (5th cir.), Jacksonville, Fla., 1971-72; assoc. Alston, Miller & Gaines, Washington, 1972-78, ptnr., 1978; ptnr. Alston & Bird, Atlanta, 1979—; speaker various orgns. and schs. Exec. editor U. Fla. Law Rev., 1971. Mem. econ. devel. adv. bd. Fulton County, Atlanta, 1986—; asst. counsel campaign Carter for Pres., 1976; co-counsel Va. Carter Campaign, 1976; mem. steering com. Cobb Internat. Ctr., Atlanta, 1982-86; chmn. Trade Devel. com. 1982-85; vice chmn., chmn. exec. com. Southeastern regional adv. bd. Inst. of Internat. Edn., 1985—. Fellow Internat. Bus. Fellows (bd. dirs. 1985-86, v.p. 1986—); mem. ABA (internat. law), Internat. Bar Assn., D.C. Bar Assn., Fla. Bar Assn., Ga. Bar Assn., Atlanta Bar Assn., Cobb C. of C. (chmn. East Asia task force 1985), Order of Coif. Clubs: World Trade Atlanta (bd. dirs. 1983-85), Georgian, The Atlanta City. Private international. Office: Alston & Bird 35 Broad St 1200 C&S Nat Bank Bldg Atlanta GA 30335

WILCOX, FRANCIS JOHN, lawyer; b. Eau Claire, Wis., June 27, 1908; s. Roy Porter and Maria Louisa (de Fryre) W.; married; children: John F., Roy S., Christopher J., Katharine E. BA, Yale U., 1930; LLB, U. Wis., 1932. Bar: Wis. 1932. Ptnr. Wilcox & Wilcox, Eau Claire, 1933—; chmn. Wis. Jud. Council, Madison, 1956-62. Chmn. program Union Internationale Contra Cancer, 1970-78; sec. bd. dirs. Eau Claire Pub. Library, 1967-72; chmn. bd. dirs. Am. Cancer Soc., 1961-66. Recipient Presdl. citation Wis. Med. Soc., 1966, Disting. Alumni award Wis. Law Sch., 1985, Nat. award Am. Cancer Soc., 1969; named Knight of St. Gregory, 1965. Fellow Am. Coll. Trial Lawyers; mem. ABA, Wis. Bar Assn. (pres. 1963-64), Wis. Bar Found. (bd. dirs. 1965—), Am. Judicature Soc. Republican. Roman Catholic. Club: County (Eau Claire). State civil litigation, Personal injury, Probate. Office: Wilcox & Wilcox 131 S Barstow St Eau Claire WI 54701

WILCOX, JAMISON VAN VOORHEES, lawyer, legal educator; b. Nashville, Oct. 5, 1946; s. John Harvey and Martha Florence (Smith) W.; m. Eileen Kennelly, May 19, 1973. AB, Amherst Coll., 1970; JD, Columbia U., 1973. Bar: N.Y. 1974, N.J. 1976, U.S. Dist. Ct. (so. and ea. dists.) N.Y., U.S. Dist. Ct. N.J., U.S. Ct. Appeals (2d and 3d cirs.). Assoc. Lovejoy, Wasson, Lundgren & Ashton, N.Y.C., 1973-75; law clk. to judge U.S. Dist. Ct. N.J., Newark, 1975-76; assoc. Casey, Lane & Mittendorf, N.Y.C., 1976-80; from asst. to assoc. prof. U. Bridgeport (Conn.) Sch. of Law, 1980—. Mem. ABA, Assn. of Bar of City of N.Y., N.Y. State Bar Assn., N.J. Bar Assn., N.Y. County Lawyers Assn. Democrat. Federal civil litigation, State civil litigation, Legal education. Home: 68 Romanock Pl Fairfield CT 06430 Office: U Bridgeport Sch of Law 303 University Ave Bridgeport CT 06601

WILCOX, JEAN EVELYN, lawyer; b. Ft. Collins, Colo., Oct. 11, 1950; d. Earl C. and Doris (Hentschel) Kettler; m. David W. Wilcox, May 15, 1977; 1 child, Keegan D. BA, U. Colo., 1973; MA, U. Mont., 1976, JD, 1980. Bar: U.S. Dist. Ct. Mont. 1980, Wis. 1986. Dep. county atty. Missoula (Mont.) County, 1980-86; staff atty. Beloit (Wis.) Coll., 1986—; faculty affiliate U. Mont., Missoula, 1982-86. Bd. dirs. Childstart, Inc., Missoula, 1982-83. Mem. ABA, Mont. Bar Assn., Wis. Bar Assn., Am. Planning Assn., LWV. Congregationalist. Lodge: Soroptimists. Avocations: hiking, canoeing, golf. Probate, Government contracts and claims, Labor. Home: 2647 Austin Pl Beloit WI 53511 Office: Beloit Coll 400 E Grand Suite 308 Beloit WI 53511

WILCOX, JOHN CAVEN, lawyer, corporate consultant; b. N.Y.C., Nov. 12, 1942; s. Daniel A. and Jessie A. (Caven) W.; m. Vanessa Guerrini-Maraldi, Sept. 30, 1983; 1 child Daniel D.G. B.A. magna cum laude, Harvard U., 1964; M.A., U. Calif., Berkeley, 1965; J.D., Harvard U., 1968; LL.M., N.Y. U., 1981. With Georgeson & Co. Inc., N.Y.C., 1973—, mng. dir., 1979—; trustee Family Dynamics, Inc. Served with U.S. Army, 1968-70. Woodrow Wilson fellow. Mem. N.Y. State Bar Assn., Am. Soc. Corp. Secs., Phi Beta Kappa. Club: Broad Street. General corporate, Securities. Home: 190 Riverside Dr New York NY 10024 Office: Wall Street Plaza New York NY 10005

WILCOX, MARK DEAN, lawyer; b. Chgo., May 25, 1952; s. Fabian Joseph and Zeryle Lucille (Tase) W.; m. Catherine J. Wertjes, Mar. 12, 1983; 1 child, Glenna Lynn. B.B.A., Notre Dame U., 1973; J.D., Northwestern U., 1976. Bar: Ill. 1976, U.S. Dist. Ct. (no. dist.) Ill. 1976, U.S. Ct. Appeals (7th cir.) 1987. Staff asst. Nat. Dist. Attys. Assn., Chgo., 1974-75; trial asst. Cook County States Atty., Chgo., 1975; intern U.S. Atty. No. Dist. Ill., Chgo., 1975-76; assoc. Lord, Bissell & Brook, Chgo., 1976-85, ptnr., 1986—. Active YMCA. Mem. ABA, Am. Coll. Life Underwriters, Chgo. Bar Assn. (ins. law com.), Trial Lawyers Chgo. Club. Episcopalian. Clubs: Union League (Chgo.), Exec. Sportsmen (Chgo.). Insurance, Personal injury, State civil litigation. Office: Lord Bissell & Brook 115 S LaSalle St Chicago IL 60603

WILCOX, MARTHA ANNE, lawyer; b. Miami, Fla., Jan. 13, 1948; d. Thomas Wesley and Martha Caroline (Bechdolt) Forshee; m. Ralph Ogden, Jan. 31, 1981; children: Helen Marie Wilcox, Christopher Thomas Wilcox. BA summa cum laude, Ind. U. Purdue U. Indpls., 1976; JD, Ind. U., Indpls., 1976. Bar: Ind. 1976, U.S. Dist. Ct. (so. dist.) Ind. 1976, U.S. Ct. Apeals (7th cir.) 1976, Colo. 1984, U.S. Supreme Ct. 1983, U.S. Dist. Ct. Colo. 1984, U.S. Ct. Appeals (10th cir.) 1984. Assoc. faculty speech dept. Ind. U. Purdue U. Indpls., 1974-81; ptnr. Wilson, Coleman & Roberts, Indpls., 1976-77, Eldridge, Lindstom, Wilcox & Ogden, Denver; adj. faculty law Ind. U., Inpls., 1976-77. Bd. dirs. Network Women in Bus., Indpls., 1978-82, YWCA, Indpls., 1982. Named Alumni of Yr., Ind. U., Indpls., 1981; named one of Outstanding Young Women of Am., 1982. Fellow Ind. Bar Found; mem. ABA, Colo. Bar Assn., Ind. Bar Assn., Assn. Trial Lawyers Am., Am. Arbitration Assn. Avocation: horseback riding. Personal injury, Federal civil litigation, Professional disciplinary defense. Home: 21579 Cabrini Blvd Golden CO 80401 Office: Wilcox & Ogden 1120 Lincoln Suite 809 Denver CO 80203

WILCOX, MAURICE KIRBY C., lawyer; b. Bronxville, N.Y., Mar. 4, 1948. Labor. Office: Morrison & Foerster 345 California St San Francisco CA 94104

WILCOX, ROBIN BACHRACH, lawyer; b. Redlands, Calif., July 7, 1954; d. Robert Allen and Ellen (Nilsson) Bachrach. AB, Standard U., 1976; JD cum laude, U. Idaho, 1981. Bar: Idaho 1981, U.S. Dist. Ct. Idaho 1981, Oreg. 1984. Counsel Boise Cascade Corp., Portland, Oreg., 1981-84; assoc. gen. counsel Boise Cascade Corp., Portland, 1985-87; assoc. Spears, Lubersky, Campbell, Bledsoe, Anderson & Young, Portland, 1987—. Vol. Washington Park Zoo, Portland, 1986—. Idaho Law Found. grantee, 1981. Mem. ABA, Oreg. Bar Assn., Idaho Bar Assn. (affiliate, bar exam grader 1982, 83), Multnomah Bar Assn., Am. Corp. Counsel Assn., U. Idaho Alumni Assn (award excellance 1981). Avocations: biking, swimming, hiking, gardening. Antitrust, Contracts commercial, General corporate. Office: Spears Lubersky Campbell Bledsoe Anderson & Young 520 SW Yamhill Portland OR 97204

WILCOX, STEVEN ALAN, lawyer; b. Providence, Mar. 26, 1955; s. Donald W. Wilcox and Edna Mae Firth; m. Nancy Solari, Aug. 24, 1980. BA, Boston Coll., 1977, JD, 1980. Bar: Mass. 1980. Assoc. Ropes & Gray, Boston, 1980—. Mem. ABA, Mass. Bar Assn., Boston Bar Assn., Nat. Assn. Bond Lawyers. General corporate, Banking, Municipal bonds. Home: 36 Canterbury Dr Sudbury MA 01776 Office: Ropes & Gray 225 Franklin St Boston MA 02110

WILD, CLAUDE CHARLES, III, federal agency counselor; b. Austin, Tex., Sept. 18, 1949; s. Claude Charles Jr. and Nadine (King) W.; m. Mary Ann Voress, June 30, 1984. AB, Duke U., 1972; JD, Georgetown U., 1975. Bar: Colo. 1976, DC 1979. Intern U.S. Dept. Justice, Washington, 1973; ptnr. Makaroff & Wild, PC, Denver, 1976-78; assoc. Wiggins & Smith PC, Denver, 1978-83; regional dir. FTC, Denver, 1983—. Pres. Cinnimon Down the Street Homeowners Assn., Denver, 1978-82. Mem. ABA (antitrust sect.), Colo. Bar Assn., Denver Bar Assn., Siberian Husky Club Am. Republican. Baptist. Club: Lone Tree Country (bd. govs. 1986). Avoca-

tions: breeding and exhibiting dogs, sled dog racing. Antitrust. Office: FTC 1405 Curtis St #2900 Denver CO 80202

WILD, NORMAN RICHARD, lawyer; b. Antigo, Wis., Aug. 5, 1944; s. Frank Joseph Wild and Hilda Mae (Servi) Wolter; m. Patricia Anne Novy, Oct. 17, 1965; children: Michele, Laurie, Norman Jr., Christopher. BS, U. Wis., Stevens Point, 1973; JD, U. Wis., Madison, 1976. Bar: Wis. 1976, U.S. Dist. Ct. (we. dist.) Wis. 1976. Assoc. Winter & Winter, Antigo, 1976-79, ptnr., 1980—; asst. atty. City of Antigo, 1977—. Chmn. Langlade County chpt. ARC, Antigo, 1979—; bd. dirs. Wis. Judicare, Wausau, 1984—. Served to sgt. USAF, 1962-70. Mem. ABA, Wis. Bar Assn., Langlade County Bar Assn. (pres.1981—), Antigo Area C. of C. (bd. dirs. 1985—). Roman Catholic. Lodges: Elks, KC. Avocations: hunting, fishing, golf. General practice, Family and matrimonial, Bankruptcy. Home: 313 Hudson St Antigo WI 54409 Office: Winter Winter & Wild 835 5th Ave Antigo WI 54409

WILD, VICTOR ALLYN, lawyer, educator; b. Logansport, Ind., May 7, 1946; s. Clifford Otto and Mary E. (Helvey) W.; m. Wesley Hobbs, July 26, 1975; 1 child, Rachel. BS in Pub. Adminstrn., U. Ariz., 1968, JD, 1974. Bar: Ariz. 1975, U.S. Dist. Ct. Ariz. 1975, Mass. 1984, U.S. Dist. Ct. Mass. 1984. Escrow officer Lawyers Title Co., Tucson, 1970-71, chief escrow officer, Denver, 1971-72; law clk. Pima County Atty., Tucson, 1973-75, dep. county atty., 1975-81, chief criminal dep., 1981-84; asst. U.S. Atty., Dist. of Mass., Boston, 1984-86; chief gen. crimes unit U.S. Atty.'s Office, Boston, 1986—; seminar instr. State Bar Ariz., Tucson and Phoenix, 1981-84; instr. U. Ariz., Tucson, 1981-84, Pima Community Coll., Tucson, 1981-84. Mem. vestry St. Michael's Episc. Ch., Marblehead, Mass., 1986—; bd. dirs. Crime Resistors, Inc., Tucson, 1983, CODAC, Tucson, 1983, 88-Crime, Inc., Tucson, 1983. Served with USAF, 1968-70. Mem. ABA, Ariz. Bar Assn., Mass. Bar Assn., Tau Kappa Epsilon, Delta Sigma Pi. Criminal, Trademark and copyright, Real property. Office: US Attys Office Suite 1107 McCormack US PO and Courthouse Boston MA 02109

WILDENSTEINER, OTTO MELVIN, lawyer; b. Louisville, July 27, 1939; s. Otto and Elizabeth (Wagner) W. B.S. with honors in Mech. Engring., New Mex. State U., 1961; J.D., U. Conn., 1970. Bar: D.C. 1971, U.S. Ct. Appeals (D.C. cir.) 1972, U.S. Ct. Claims 1976, U.S. Ct. Appeals (fed. cir.) 1982. Patent atty. Colton & Stone, Arlington, Va., 1970-72, Schellin & Hoffman, Arlington, 1972, Naval Ship Research and Devel. Ctr., Carderock, Md., 1972-75, U.S. Dept. Transp., Washington, 1975—. Patentee drip meters, 1974. Mem. Govt. Patent Lawyers Assn. (program and events chmn. 1979-81), Domestic Policy Rev. of Indsl. Innovation, Pi Tau Sigma, Sigma Tau. Republican. Lutheran. Patent. Home: 5909 Cheshire Dr Bethesda MD 20814 Office: US Dept Transp 400 7th St SW Washington DC 20590

WILDER, FRED JENNINGS, lawyer; b. Clearwater, Fla., Dec. 28, 1926; s. Guss and Freddie Leigh (Jennings) W.; m. Dorothy Marie Houghton, Aug. 15, 1953; children: Gregory Fred, Stephen Mark, Diane Gayle W. Burrell. Student, U. N.C., 1944, Vanderbilt U., 1944-45; BS, U.S. Naval Acad., 1949; postgrad., U. Md., 1954-55; JD, Stetson U., 1957. Bar: Fla. 1957, U.S. Dist. Ct. (so. dist.) Fla. 1958. Commd. ensign USN, 1951, advanced through grades to lt. comdr., 1962, resigned, 1954, pilot with all weather night carrier squadrons, 1949-52; instr. in celestial navigation U.S. Naval Acad., Annapolis, Md., 1952-53; ptnr. Wilder & Wilder, Clearwater, 1957-58, Wilder & White, Clearwater, 1958-60; sr. ptnr. Wilder & Thacker, Clearwater, 1960—. Mayor City of Belleair, Fla., 1971-73; v.p., bd. dirs. Clearwater Concert Assn. Inc., 1978—; pres., bd. dirs. Footlight Theatre Inc., 1975. Served with USNR, 1955-77. Recipient Meml. Bronze plaque City of Belleair, 1973. Mem. Fla. Bar Assn., Clearwater Bar Assn. (pres. 1967-68), Aircraft Owners and Pilots Assn. Republican. Baptist. Avocations: pilot, boating. Probate, Real property, General corporate. Home: 1 S Pine Circle Belleair FL 33516 Office: Wilder & Thacker 407 S Ewing Ave PO Box 1808 Clearwater FL 33517-1808

WILDER, JOYCE ANN, lawyer; b. Keene, N.H., Mar. 10, 1950; d. Russell Roland and Theresa Marie (Beauregard) W. Student Bryn Mawr Coll., 1967-69; m. Joseph M. Anderson, May 5, 1984. B.A. magna cum laude, Yale U., 1971; J.D., Cornell U., 1974; LL.M. in Taxation, Boston U., 1977. Bar: N.H. 1974, U.S. Dist. Ct. N.H. 1974, U.S. Tax Ct. 1975, U.S. Ct. Appeals (1st cir.) 1979. Assoc. Bell & Kennedy, Keene, 1974-76; ptnr. Smith, Connor & Wilder, P.C. and predecessor firm Smith, Connor & Wilder, P.C., Nashua, N.H., 1976—, also dir.; dir. Clement Indsl. Park of Hudson, Inc. (N.H.). Bd. dirs. Big Bros./Big Sisters of Nashua, 1982-84. Mem. ABA, N.H. Bar Assn., Assn. Trial Lawyers Am., N.H. Trial Lawyers Assn. Episcopalian. Real property, Probate, Personal injury. Office: 47 Factory St Nashua NH 03061

WILDER, RAYMOND EDWARD, lawyer; b. Muskegon, Mich., Oct. 7, 1931; s. Raymond Frederick and Alma Elizabeth (Wenger) W.; m. Patricia Ann Erickson, Sept. 10, 1955; children—Ann Marie, John Raymond, Nancy Beth, Janet Lee, Sandra Rochelle, James Richard. B.A., Mich. State U., 1957; LL.B., U. Colo., 1960. Bar: Colo. 1960, U.S. Dist. Ct. Colo. 1960. Sole practice law, Colorado Springs, Colo., 1960-63; dep. dist. atty. 4th Jud. Dist., Colorado Springs, 1961-63; ptnr. firm Quigley, Wilder & Palermo, Colorado Springs, 1963-76; sr. mem. firm Wilder, Wells & Larimer, P.C., Colorado Springs, 1976—; county atty. El Paso County, Colorado Springs, 1976-77. Served with USMC, 1950-53, Korea. Mem. Colo. Ho. of Reps., 1967-69; exec. asst. to gov. of Colo., 1973-75; pres. Broadmoor Improvement Soc., Colorado Springs, 1978-86; mem. Sch. Dist. 12 Bd. Edn., Colorado Springs, 1981—; chmn. State Bd. Community Colls., 1982—. Mem. ABA, Colo. Bar Assn., El Paso County Bar Assn. Republican. Clubs: El Paso (trustee 1973-76), Cheyenne Mountain Country (Colorado Springs.) General corporate, Probate, Real property. Home: 16 Lake Ave Colorado Springs CO 80906 Office: Wilder Wells & Larimer PC 524 S Cascade St Suite # Colorado Springs CO 80903

WILDER, ROLAND PERCIVAL, JR., lawyer; b. Malden, Mass., June 21, 1940; s. Roland Percival and Clarissa (Hunting) W.; m. Susan McAra Randell, Sept. 3, 1965; children: Roland Percival III, William Randell. BA, Washington and Jefferson Coll., 1963; JD, Vanderbilt U., 1966. Bar: D.C. 1967, U.S. Dist. Ct. D.C. 1967, U.S. Ct. Appeals (D.C. cir.) 1967, U.S. Supreme Ct. 1972, U.S. Ct. Appeals (4th, 5th and 6th cirs.) 1976, U.S. Ct. Appeals (8th and 9th cirs.) 1977, U.S. Ct. Appeals (2d cir.) 1978, U.S. Ct. Appeals (11th cir.) 1981. Atty. Office of Solicitor U.S. Dept. Labor, Washington, 1967-69; asst. counsel civil rights office of solicitor U.S. Dept. Labor, Washington, 1969-70, counsel civil rights office of solicitor, 1970-71; supr. atty. office gen. counsel NLRB, Washington, 1972-74; assoc. gen. counsel Internat. Brotherhood Teamsters, Washington, 1974-85; sr. ptnr. Baptiste & Wilder P.C., Washington, 1985—; lectr. numerous continuing legal edn. programs various states, 1970—. Mng. editor Vanderbilt U. Law Rev., 1965-66; contbr. articles to profl. jours. V.p. Arlington (Va.) Cubs Youth Club, Inc., 1975-81; coach Fairfax (Va.) Hockey Club, 1979-83. Mem. D.C. Bar Assn., Fed. Bar Assn., Assn. Trial Lawyers Am., Assn. Transp. Practitioners, Phi Delta Phi, Pi Sigma Alpha, Phi Alpha Theta, Roosevelt Soc., Joint Council Flight Attendant Unions (hon. flight attendent 1985). Democrat. Avocations: history, tennis. Labor, Federal civil litigation, Administrative and regulatory. Home: 4623 N Carlin Springs Rd Arlington VA 22203 Office: Baptiste & Wilder PC 1919 Pennsylvania Ave NW #505 Washington DC 20006

WILDER, WILLIAM KEITH, lawyer; b. Medford, Oreg., Oct. 31, 1942; s. William Briscoe and JoAnn (England) W.; m. Jane Gautier; children: Amanda Jean, Tiffany Reneé. Student, Trinity U., 1961-63; BA in Econs., U. Tex., 1965; JD, South. Tex. Coll. Law, 1971. Bar: Tex. 1971. Sole practice Edna, Tex., 1971-80, 82—; ptnr. Orr & Wilder, 1981-82. Pres. Mens Group 1st United Meth. Ch., 1984. Served to 1st lt. U.S. Army, 1968-71. Mem. Tex. Bar Assn., Assn. Trial Lawyers Am., Tex. Trial Lawyers Assn. Democrat. Lodge: Kiwanis (pres. Bay City club 1985-86). Avocations: swimming, traveling, reading, crafts. Personal injury, Workers' compensation. Office: 2127 Ave G Bay City TX 77414

WILDES, LEON, lawyer, educator; b. Scranton, Pa., Mar. 4, 1933. BA magna cum laude, Yeshiva U., 1954; JD, NYU, 1957, LLM, 1959. Bar: N.Y. 1958, U.S. Dist. Ct. (so. dist.) N.Y. 1960, U.S. Supreme Ct. 1961. Ptnr. Wildes and Weinberg, N.Y.C., 1960—; adj. prof. law Benjamin N. Cardozo Sch. Law, N.Y.C., 1981—. Contbr. numerous articles to law revs. Mem. ABA, Assn. Bar City of N.Y. (com. immigration and nationality law 1975-78), Am. Immigration Lawyers Assn. (nat. pres. 1970-71, bd. govs. 1971—, editor Immigration and Nationality Law symposium 1983). Immigration, naturalization, and customs, Family and matrimonial, Criminal. Office: 515 Madison Ave New York NY 10022

WILDEY, SHARON ANN, lawyer; b. North Vernon, Ind., June 21, 1943; d. Murrell Edward and Virginia Lorane (Beach) W.; m. Edward Victer Mikesell, Feb. 23, 1975 (div. Apr. 1980); children—Tim, Heather, Brooke, Meredith. B.S., Ind. U., 1972, J.D., 1975. Bar: Ind. Assoc., Luber, Sakaguchi & Wildey, South Bend, 1976-78, Wildey & Forsman, South Bend, 1978-81; founder, pres. Women's Legal Clinic, Inc., South Bend, 1980—. Editor Justicia, 1976. Recipient Roses award Ind. U. Women's Studies, 1979. Mem. Ind. Bar Assn., ABA, Assn. Trial Lawyers Am., Ind. Bar Found., Ind. Women's Polit. Caucus. Democrat. Mem. Soc. Friends. Family and matrimonial, State civil litigation, Civil rights.

WILDHACK, WILLIAM AUGUST, JR., lawyer; b. Takoma Park, Md., Nov. 28, 1935; s. William August and Martha Elizabeth (Parks) W.; m. Martha Moore Allston, Aug. 1, 1959; children: William A. III, Elizabeth L. B.S., Miami U., Oxford, Ohio, 1957; J.D., George Washington U., 1963. Bar: Va. 1963, D.C. 1965, Md. 1983, U.S. Supreme Ct. 1967. Agt. IRS, No. Va., 1957-65; assoc. Morris, Pearce, Gardner & Beitel, Washington, 1965-69; sole practice Washington, 1969; v.p., corp. counsel B.F. Saul Co. and affiliates, Chevy Chase, Md., 1969-87, Chevy Chase Savs. Bank and affiliates, 1987—; sec. B.F. Saul Real Estate Investment Trust, Chevy Chase, 1972-87. Mem. Arlington Tenant Landlord Commn., 1976—; pres. Am. Cancer Soc., Arlington unit, 1970-71. Mem. Am. Soc. Corp. Secs., ABA, D.C. Bar Assn., Md. Bar Assn., Va. Bar Assn., Arlington County Bar Assn., D.C. Assn. Realtors, Phi Alpha Delta. Presbyterian. General corporate, Securities. Office: BF Saul Mortgage Co 8401 Connecticut Ave Chevy Chase MD 20815

WILDMAN, MAX EDWARD, lawyer; b. Terre Haute, Ind., Dec. 4, 1919; s. Roscoe Ellsworth and Lena (Shaw) W.; m. Joyce Lenore Smith, Sept. 25, 1948; children: Leslie, Kim, William. B.S., Butler U., 1941; J.D., U. Mich., 1947; M.B.A., U. Chgo., 1952. Bar: Ill. Mng. ptnr. Kirkland & Ellis, Chgo., 1947-67; mng. ptnr. Wildman, Harrold, Allen & Dixon, Chgo., 1967—; dir. Colt Industries, N.Y., Nat. Blvd. Bank, Ill. Contbr. articles to profl. jours. Trustee Butler U., Indpls., Lake Forest Hosp., Ill., Lake Bluff Library Bd., Ill.; chmn. Lake Bluff Zoning Bd. Served to lt. col. USAF, 1943-46; PTO. Fellow Am. Coll. Trial Lawyers; mem. Soc. Trial Lawyers, Law Club, Legal Club, Trial Lawyers Club of Chgo. Presbyterian. Clubs: Anglers (Chgo.), Pere Marquette Rod and Gun (Baldwin, Mich.), Shoreacres (Lake Bluff), Univ. of Chgo. Antitrust, Federal civil litigation, State civil litigation. Office: Wildman Harrold Allen & Dixon One IBM Plaza Chicago IL 60611

WILDSTEIN, DAVID M., lawyer; b. Irvington, N.J., May 20, 1944; s. Julius and Frances (Mermin) W.; m. Bonita Wildstein; children: Jessica, Erik. BA, Lafayette Coll., 1966; JD, Seton Hall U., 1969. Bar: N.J. 1970. Ptnr. Wildstein & Wildstein P.A., Newark, 1970-72; assoc. Wilentz, Goldman & Spitzer, Woodbridge, N.J., 1972-77, sr. ptnr., 1977—; lectr. N.J. Inst. Continuing Legal Edn., 1980—; mem. Pashman II com. N.J. Supreme Ct., 1983-84, family part practice com. N.J. Supreme Ct., 1985-86, liaison com. N.J. Supreme Ct., 1985-86. Mem. N.J. Bar Assn. (chmn. legis. sect. of family law sect. 1981-82, chmn. equitable distbr. sect. 1982-83, chmn. family law sect. 1984-85), Middlesex County Bar Assn. (family law sect.), Monmouth County Bar Assn., Acad. Matrimonial Lawyers Assn. (chmn. family law sect.), Assn. Family Conciliation Cts. Jewish. Avocations: skiing, racquetball, boating. Family and matrimonial. Office: Wilentz Goldman & Spitzer PC 900 Rt 9 PO Box 10 Woodbridge NJ 07095

WILENSKY, SAUL, lawyer; b. Bklyn., Dec. 9, 1941; s. Morris and Pearl (Wagman) W.; m. Sandra J. Brunault, Nov. 11, 1979; 1 child, Margot. BA, Hunter Coll., 1963; LLB, St. John's U., Bklyn., 1966; LLM, NYU, 1976. Bar: N.Y. 1967, U.S. Dist. Ct. (ea. and so. dists.) N.Y. 1970, U.S. Supreme Ct. 1971, U.S. Ct. Appeals (2d cir.) 1973, U.S. Dist. Ct. (no. dist.) N.Y. 1974. Ptnr. Lester, Schwab, Katz & Dwyer, N.Y.C., 1966—. Personal injury, State civil litigation, Admiralty. Office: Lester Schwab Katz & Dwyer 120 Broadway New York NY 10271

WILENTZ, ROBERT N., state supreme court justice; b. Perth Amboy, N.J., Feb. 17, 1927; m. Jacqueline Malino, 1949; children: James Robert, Amy, Thomas Malino. Student, Princeton U.; A.B., Harvard U., 1949; grad., Columbia U. Law Sch., 1952. Bar: N.J. bar 1952. Partner firm Wilentz, Goldman and Spitzer, Perth Amboy, from 1952; mem. N.J. legislature, 1966-69; chief justice N.J. Supreme Ct., 1979—. Served with USN, 1945-46. Jurisprudence. Office: Supreme Ct 313 State St Perth Amboy NJ 08861 also: NJ Supreme Ct Trenton NJ 08625 *

WILES, WILLIAM DIXON, JR., lawyer; b. Wellington, Tex., Apr. 1, 1949; s. William Dixon Wiles Sr. and Metha (Bacon) Chapman; m. Betsy Flowers, Mar. 21, 1971; children: Dixon, Robert. BA magna cum laude, U. Houston, 1971; JD, So. Meth. U., 1974. Bar: Tex. 1974, U.S. Dist. Ct. (no., so., ea. and we. dists.) Tex., U.S. Dist. Ct. Ark., U.S. Ct. Appeals (5th and 11th cirs.). Ptnr. Bailey & Williams, Dallas, 1974—. Mem. ABA, Am. Bd. Trial Advocates, Am. Soc. Law and Medicine, Nat. Health Lawyers Assn., Tex. Assn. Def. Counsel, Dallas Assn. Def. Counsel. Democrat. Episcopalian. Club: Lakewood Country (Dallas). Federal civil litigation, State civil litigation, Personal injury. Home: 5527 Swiss Ave Dallas TX 75214 Office: Bailey & Williams 3500 Interfirst Plaza 901 Main St Dallas TX 75202

WILEY, EDWIN PACKARD, lawyer; b. Chgo., Dec. 10, 1929; s. Edwin Garnet and Marjorie Chastina (Packard) W.; m. Barbara Jean Miller, May 21, 1949; children: Edwin Miller, Clayton Alexander, Stephen Packard. BA, U. Chgo., 1949, JD, 1952. Bar: Wis. 1952, U.S. Dist. Ct. (ea. dist.) Wis. 1953, U.S. Supreme Ct. 1978. Assoc. Foley & Lardner, Milw., 1952-60, ptnr., 1960—; bd. dirs. Badger Meter, Inc., Genetic Testing, Inc., Nat. Rivet and Mfg. Co., Shaler Co., Waukesha Cutting Tools, other corps. and founds. Co-author: Bank Holding Companies: A Practical Guide to Bank Acquisitions and Mergers, 1985, Wisconsin Uniform Commercial Code Handbook, 1971; author: Promotional Arrangements: Discrimination in Advertising and Promotional Allowances, 1976; contbr. articles to legal jours. Pres. bd. dirs. Blood Ctr. of Southeastern Wis., Blood Ctr. Research Found., Inc.; v.p. Friends of Schlitz Audubon Ctr., Inc., 1975—; active United Performing Arts Fund of Milw.; pres. Wis. Conservatory of Music, 1968-74; pres. First Unitarian Soc. Milw., 1961-63; v.p. Mid-Am. Ballet Co., 1971-73, Milw. Ballet Co., 1973-74; pres. Florentine Opera Co., 1983-86; mem. vis. com. Coll. of U. Chgo., 1976—. Mem. Am. Law Inst., ABA, State Bar of Wis., Milw. Bar Assn., Assn. Bank Holding Cos. (lawyers com., chmn. 1979-80), Order of Coif, Phi Beta Kappa (pres. Greater Milw. assn. 1962-63). Unitarian-Universalist. Clubs: Milw., University. Antitrust, General corporate, Private international. Home: 3017 N Marietta St Milwaukee WI 53211 Office: Foley & Lardner 1st Wisconsin Center 777 E Wisconsin Ave Milwaukee WI 53202-5367

WILEY, H. SEYMOUR, lawyer; b. Sault Ste. Marie, Mich., Aug. 24, 1912; s. Merlin and Helen (Seymour) W.; m. Mary Shepard, June 26, 1937 (dec. Mar. 1957); m. Ruth Kearns, Oct. 26, 1957. BS, Harvard U., 1934, LLB, 1937. Bar: R.I. 1939, U.S. Dist. Ct. R.I. 1940. Assoc., then ptnr. Swan, Keeney (and successor firm names), Providence, 1938-77; ptnr. Asquith, Merolla, Anderson, Riley & Wiley, Providence, 1977—. Pres. R.I. Philharmonic Orch., 1955-58. Mem. ABA, R.I. Bar Assn. (title standards com. 1976—). Democrat. Avocations: shoemaking, running 4th of July parades. Real property, Advising Developers. Home: RD 6 Louise Luther Dr Cumberland RI 02864 Office: Asquith Merolla Wiley et al 155 S Main St Providence RI 02903-2963

WILEY, JAN M., lawyer; b. Dillsburg, Pa., Feb. 19, 1938; s. Lester E. and Catherine L. (Harbold) W.; m. Joan W. Wetzel, Nov. 28, 1941; children—James, Jan, Justin. A.B. Dickinson Coll. 1960, J.D. 1963. Assoc. Anstine & Griest, York, Pa., 1963; ptnr. Griest & Wiley, York, 1964-67; ptnr. Wiley & Benn, Dillsburg, 1967—; mem. regional bd. Commonwealth Nat. Bank, chmn. bd. Dillsburg br. Trustee Messiah Coll. Mem. Adams County Bar Assn., York County Bar Assn. (bd. dirs. 1983—, trustee, 2d v.p. 1987), Cumberland County Bar Assn. Methodist. Clubs: Lafayette (York); Dillsburg Lions (past pres.), Masons. Probate, Corporations, Real property. Home: 1 Hall Dr Dillsburg PA 17019 Office: 204 Mumper Ln Dillsburg PA 17019

WILEY, RICHARD EMERSON, lawyer; b. Peoria, Ill., July 20, 1934; s. Joseph Henry and Jean W. (Farrell) W.; m. Elizabeth J. Edwards, Aug. 6, 1960; children: Douglas S., Pamela L. B.S. with distinction, Northwestern U., 1955, J.D., 1958; LL.M., Georgetown U., 1962. Bar: Ill. 1958, D.C. 1972. Mem. law firm Chadwell, Keck, Kayser, Ruggles & McLaren, Chgo., 1962-68; asst. gen. counsel Bell & Howell Co., Chgo., 1968-70; partner law firm Burditt, Calkins & Wiley, Chgo., 1970; gen. counsel FCC, Washington, 1970-72; mem. FCC, 1972-74, chmn., 1974—; mng. ptnr. Wiley, Rein & Fielding, Washington, 1986—; prof. law John Marshall Law Sch., U. Chgo., 1963-70. Editor-in-chief: Law Notes, 1963-65; chmn. bd. editors: Jour. of ABA; Contbr. articles to profl. jours. Served to capt. AUS, 1959-62. Mem. ABA (mem. ho. of dels. 1969-71, mem. commn. campus govt. and student dissent 1969-70, chmn. lawyers in govt. com., Forum com. on communications), Fed. Bar Assn. (pres.), Fed. Communications Bar Assn. (pres.), Ill. Bar Assn., Chgo. Bar Assn., Phi Delta Phi, Phi Delta Kappa. Methodist. Communications. Home: 3818 N Woodrow St Arlington VA 22207 Office: Wiley Rein & Fielding 1776 K St NW Suite 1100 Washington DC 20006

WILEY, ROBERT WAYNE, lawyer; b. Los Angeles, July 15, 1933; s. Ruby Marie (Scott) W.; m. Juanita Ruth Sawrey, July 26, 1970; children: William Gene, Donna Kaye. AA, Riverside Coll., 1962; BSL, Glendale Coll., 1972, LLB, 1974. Bar: Calif. 1975, U.S. Dist. Ct. (cen. dist.) Calif. 1975, U.S. Ct. Appeals (9th cir.) 1975. Sole practice Pasadena, Calif., 1975—; judge pro tem Pasadena Mcpl. Cts., 1980—. Mem. Glendora (Calif.) Reps. Served with U.S. Army, 1955-58. Mem. Pasadena Bar Assn., Juvenile Criminal Bar Assn., Assn. Trial Lawyers Am., Calif. Attys. for Criminal Justice. Lodge: Masons. Bankruptcy, State civil litigation, Contracts commercial. Office: 151 S Molino Suite 300 Pasadena CA 91101

WILHELM, JACK MORTON, lawyer; b. Little Rock, May 3, 1953; s. Alfred Donovan and Margaret Ann (Morton) W.; m. Ann S. Lindsey, Sept. 26, 1981; 1 child, Edward Morton. BA, Rhodes Coll., 1975; JD, U. Ark., Little Rock, 1978; LLM, Tulane U., 1984. Bar: Ark. 1978, U.S. Dist. Ct. (ea. dist.) Ark., U.S. Dist. Ct. (ea. dist.) La., U.S. Ct. Appeals (5th, 7th and 11th cirs.), La. 1981, U.S. Dist. Ct. (mid. dist.) La. 1982. Atty. Ark. Pub. Service Commn., Little Rock, 1978-80, Amoco Production Co., New Orleans, 1980—. Elder St. Charles Ave. Presbyn. Ch., New Orleans, 1982—; trustee Uptown Neighborhood Improvement Assn., New Orleans, 1985—. Mem. ABA, La. State Bar Assn., Ark. State Bar Assn., Rhodes Coll. Alumni Assn., Tulane Alumni Assn. Republican. FERC practice, Oil and gas leasing, Public utilities. Home: 821 State St New Orleans LA 70118 Office: Amoco Prodn Co PO Box 50879 New Orleans LA 70150

WILHELM, ROBERT OSCAR, lawyer, civil engineer; b. Balt., July 7, 1918; s. Clarence Oscar and Agnes Virginia (Grimm) W.; m. Grace L. Sanborn Luckie, Apr. 4, 1919. B.S. in Civil Engring., Ga. Tech. Inst., 1947, M.S.I.M., 1948; J.D., Stanford U., 1951. Bar: Calif. 1952, U.S. Sup. Ct. Mem. Wilhelm, Thompson, Wentholt and Gibbs, Redwood City, Calif., 1952—; gen. counsel Bay Counties Gen. Contractors; pvt. practice civil engring., Redwood City, 1952—; pres. Bay Counties Builders Escrow, Inc., 1972—. Served with C.E., AUS, 1942-46. Mem. Bay Counties Civil Engrs. (pres. 1957), Peninsula Builders Exchange (pres. 1958-71, dir.), Calif. State Builders Exchange (tres. 1971). Clubs: Mason, Odd Fellows, Eagle, Elks. Author: The Manual of Procedures for the Construction Industry, 1971; columnist Law and You in Daily Pacific Builder, 1955—; author: Construction Law for Contractors, Architects and Engineers. Construction, Government contracts and claims. Home: 463 Raymondo Dr Woodside CA 94062 Office: 600 Allerton Redwood City CA 94063

WILHELM, THOMAS VINCENT, lawyer; b. Schenectady, N.Y., Dec. 6, 1950; s. Clarence Joseph and Alice Louise (Bradley) W.; m. Eileen Annette Mason, Aug. 10, 1974; children: Kathleen Carol, Colin James. BA, U. Notre Dame, 1973; JD, U. Detroit, 1978. Bar: Mich. 1978, U.S. Dist. Ct. (ea. dist.) Mich. 1978, U.S. Ct. Appeals (6th cir.) 1978. Appellate atty. Fed. Defenders Office, Detroit, 1978-79, trial atty., 1979-84; assoc. Lustig & Lustig P.C., Southfield, Mich., 1984-85, Louis Demas P.C., Southfield, 1985—. Mem. ABA, Mich. Bar Assn., Mich. Criminal Def. Attys. Assn. Criminal, Federal civil litigation, State civil litigation. Office: Louis Demas PC 16000 W 9 Mile Southfield MI 48075

WILK, DAVID I., lawyer, consultant; b. Lubbock, Tex., Feb. 1, 1957. BS magna cum laude, U. Tex., 1977; JD, U. Okla., 1981. Bar: Tex. 1981, U.S. Dist. Ct. (no. dist.) Tex. 1981, U.S. Tax Ct. 1982, U.S. Ct. Appeals (5th cir.) 1983. Assoc. Remmel & Rubin, Dallas, 1981-82; gen. cousel Entec Products Corp., Dallas, 1982-83; ptnr. Wilk & Flint, Dallas, 1983—; cons. Intermode Inc., Dallas, 1985—; instr. bus. law El Centro Coll., Dallas, 1983; bd. dirs. The Reservation Desk Inc., Dallas, Accessories Unltd., Hong Kong and Dallas. Mem. ABA, Tex. Bar Assn., Assn. Trial Lawyers Am., Tex. Young Lawyers Assn., Tax Lawyer Assn. (articles editor 1983-85). Club: Cipango (Dallas). Avocations: running, weight lifting. Personal injury, Workers' compensation. Office: Wilk & Flint 3710 Rawlins LB22 Suite 911 Dallas TX 75219

WILKA, WILLIAM CHARLES, lawyer; b. Sioux Falls, S.D., Dec. 11, 1949; s. William C. and Kathleen Marie (Kelly) W.; m. Theresa Anne Willke, Aug. 6, 1977; 1 child, Matthew William. BA, U. Notre Dame, 1972; JD, Georgetown U., 1975. Bar: D.C. 1976, Calif. 1978, U.S. Dist. Ct. (no. dist.) Calif. 1979, U.S. Ct. Appeals (9th cir.) 1979. Assoc. counsel judiciary com. U.S. Senate, Washington, 1975-77; lectr. faculty law U. Singapore, 1977-78; assoc. Fenwick, Stone, Davis & West, Palo Alto, Calif., 1979-83; ptnr. Gordon & Rees, San Francisco, 1983—. Henry Luce Found. scholar, 1977. Mem. ABA, Phi Beta Kappa. Federal civil litigation, Contracts commercial, Insurance. Home: 28 La Cuesta Dr Greenbrae CA 94904 Office: Gordon & Rees 601 Montgomery St San Francisco CA 94111

WILKE, JOHN WILLIAM, lawyer; b. Denision, Iowa, Feb. 24, 1951; s. Joseph Anthony and Mary Lorraine (Murphy) W.; m. Marlyn Kae Hawkes, Jan. 13, 1973; children: Jake, Jacque. BBA in Criminal Justice, U. Nebr., Omaha, 1975; JD, Creighton U., 1978; cert., Trial Technique Inst., Chgo., 1981. Bar: Nebr. 1979, U.S. Dist. Ct. Nebr. 1979, U.S. Ct. Appeals (8th cir.) 1982. Law clk. to presiding justice Nebr. Dist. Ct., Omaha, 1977-78; bailiff Judge Pat Lynch, Nebr. State Dist. Ct. (4th dist.), Omaha, 1979, Judge Keith Howard, Nebr. State Dist. Ct. (4th dist.), Omaha, 1980; dep. county atty. City of Fremont, Nebr., 1981. Poll worker election com., City of Omaha, 1979—. Mem. ABA (chmn. state young lawyers div. 1983—, career planning and pacement com., 1986—), Nebr. Bar Assn., Omaha Bar Assn. (co-editor newsletter), Assn. Trial Lawyers Am., Nat. Assn. Criminal Def. Attys., Order of Barristers (v.p. 1985-86, pres. 1986—). Republican. Roman Catholic. Avocation: golf. State civil litigation, Personal injury, Criminal. Home: 12511 Crawford Rd Omaha NE 68144 Office: Sodoro Daly & Sodoro 7000 Spring St Omaha NE 68106

WILKENS, BETH ELA, lawyer; b. Grand Junction, Colo., June 22, 1949. BA magna cum laude, Pomona Coll., 1971; JD with distinction, Cornell U., 1974. Bar: N.Y. 1975, U.S. Dist. Ct. (we. dist.) N.Y., U.S. Tax Ct. Ptnr. Harris, Beach, Wilcox, Rubin & Levey, Rochester, N.Y., 1974—; mem. adv. bd. Ctr. Dispute Settlement, Inc.; bd. dirs. Found. Monroe County Bar, Pre-Trial Services Corp. Contbr. articles to profl. jours. Mem. bd. govs. Genesee Hosp., Rochester; bd. dirs., vice chmn., various activities YMCA Greater Rochester; bd. dirs. United Way, Rochester, Campfire Girls Rochester; bd. dirs., coms. Rochester Downtown Devel. Corp.; commr. Rochester Housing Authority, Rochester Civil Service Commn. Mem. ABA (bar leaders conf.), N.Y. State Bar Assn. (ho. of dels., bar leaders conf., various coms. banking, corp. and bus. law sect.), Monroe County Bar Assn. (pres. 1985—, bd. trustees, chairperson various coms., others), Greater Rochester Assn. Women Attys. Democrat. Baptist. Banking, Municipal bonds, Contracts commercial. Office: Harris Beach Wilcox Rubin & Levey 130 E Main St Rochester NY 14604

WILKENS, JEFFREY MARTIN, lawyer; b. Rochester, N.Y., Dec. 8, 1946; s. Frederick J. and Frances S. (Schrader) W.; m. Beth Ela, May 18, 1974; 1 child, Dennett J. BA, Yale U., 1968; JD, Cornell U., 1974. Bar: N.Y. 1975, U.S. Dist. Ct. (we. dist.) N.Y. 1975, U.S. Ct. Appeals (4th cir.) 1981. Assoc. Osborn, Reed, Van de Vate & Burke, Rochester, 1974-78, ptnr., 1978-82, mng. ptnr., 1982—. Served to capt. U.S. Army, 1968-71, Vietnam. Mem. Am. Soc. Law and Medicine, Def. Research Inst. Republican. Club: University (Rochester). Personal injury, Federal civil litigation, State civil litigation. Office: Osborn Reed Van de Vate & Burke 47 S Fitzhugh St Rochester NY 14614

WILKERSON, JAMES NEILL, lawyer; b. Tyler, Tex., Dec. 17, 1939; s. Hubert Cecil and Vida (Alexander) W.; children—Cody, Ike. A.A., Tyler Jr. Coll., 1960; B.B.A., U. Tex., 1966, LL.B., 1968. Bar: Tex. 1968, U.S. Dist. Ct. (we. dist.) Tex. 1974, U.S. Supreme Ct. 1973. Sole practice, Georgetown, Tex., 1977—; intr. Central Tex. Coll., Copperas Cove, Tex., 1973-74; asst prof. law U.S. Mil. Acad., West Point, N.Y., 1971-73; pres. Ind. Living and Security Co., 1986—. Pres., Beautify Georgetown Assn., 1977-80, 81-82; pres. U. Tex. Young Reps., 1964-65; conty chmn. Bush for Pres., later Reagan-Bush campaign, 1980; mem. Williamson County Rep. Com., 1977-81; chmn. Hist. Preservation Com., 1979-85. Served to col. JAGC AUS, 1968-77. Decorated Bronze Star, Air medal. Mem. Williamson County Bar Assn. Methodist. Lodges: Sertoma (v.p. 1981-83, 87—), Lions (pres. 1982-83). Family and matrimonial, State civil litigation, General practice. Office: PO Box 1090 Georgetown TX 78627

WILKERSON, LEO CARL, lawyer; b. Mebane, N.C., Sept. 9, 1933; s. Banks H. and Cynthia M. (Hinshaw) W.; m. Patricia R. Crotts, June 18, 1961; children: Carl, Caroline. BSBA, U. N.C., 1955; LLB, U. Va., 1965. Bar: Ohio 1965, Va. 1965. Acctg. supr. Thomasville (N.C.) Furniture, 1957-62; assoc. Frost & Jacobs, Cin., 1965-69; corp. securities counsel RJR Nabisco Inc., Winston-Salem, N.C., 1969-86, v.p., counsel law, corp. fin. and securities, 1986—. Mem. ABA, Ohio Bar Assn., Va. Bar Assn., Phi Beta Kappa. General corporate, Securities. Home: 2934 Buena Vista Rd Winston-Salem NC 27106 Office: RJR Nabisco Inc Reynolds Blvd Winston-Salem NC 27102

WILKES, BEVERLY LAKE, lawyer; b. Boston, Apr. 25, 1949; d. Thomas E. and Ann W. Lake; m. Lawrence R. Wilkes, Oct. 9, 1976. BA, Wheaton Coll., 1970; JD, Fordham U., 1976. Bar: N.Y. 1977, U.S. Tax Ct. 1978, U.S. Dist. Ct. (so. and ea. dist.) N.Y. 1978. Stockbroker E.F. Hutton & Co. Inc., N.Y.C., 1972-74; estate planner U.S. Trust Co. of N.Y., N.Y.C., 1974-76; assoc. Davis Polk & Wardwell, N.Y.C., 1976-82; fin. counsel Union Carbide Corp., Danbury, Conn., 1983-86; counsel Phibro Energy, Inc., Greenwich, Conn., 1986—. Mem. ABA, Nat. Assn. Women Lawyers, Westchester Fairfield County Corp. Counsel Assn. Avocation: horseback riding. Securities, General corporate, Banking. Office: Phibro Energy Inc 600 Steamboat Rd Greenwich CT 06830

WILKES, JOHN MICHAEL, lawyer; b. Detroit, July 26, 1949; s. John Lewis and Margaret Elnora (Anderson) W.; m. Ruth Newcomer; children: Melissa, Jennifer, John. BA, U. Cin., 1972; JD, Baylor U., 1975; LLM in Taxation, NYU, 1977. Bar: Tex. 1975; Tex. Bd. Legal Specialization (cert.). Part. Cox & Smith Inc., San Antonio, 1977—. Articles editor Baylor U. Law Rev., 1972. Bd. dirs. Victoria Cts., San Antonio, 1981-83, YMCA, San Antonio, 1983—, Boysville, San Antonio, 1986—. Republican. Presbyterian. Estate planning, Probate, Estate taxation. Home: 403 Lazy Bluff San Antonio TX 78216 Office: Cox & Smith Inc 600 NBC Bldg San Antonio TX 78205

WILKES, RICHARD CLARENCE, lawyer; b. Fargo, N.D., Jan. 28, 1944; s. Clarence Herman and Elsie Jean (McGillivray) W. BA, Minot State Coll., 1966; JD, U. N.D., 1976. Bar: N.D. 1976, U.S. Dist. Ct. N.D. 1976. Asst. states atty. War County, Minot, N.D., 1976-83; ptnr. Peterson & Wilkes, Bowbells, N.D., 1984—; asst. states atty. Barke County, Bowbells, 1984—. Mem. N.D. Bar Assn., Nat. Bar Assn. Methodist. Avocation: hunting. Probate, Estate taxation, Oil and gas leasing. Home: Rural Rt #1 Box 122 Bowbells ND 58721 Office: Peterson & Wilkes Main St PO Box 39 Bowbells ND 58721

WILKIE, BARRY LYNN, lawyer; b. Cherokee, Iowa, Dec. 2, 1954; s. John Ora and Dorothy Ann (Rasmussen) W. BS, Iowa State U., 1977; JD, Drake U., 1980. Assoc. Shaw, Spangler & Roth, Denver, 1980-85, ptnr., 1986—. Editor Drake U. Law Rev., 1979-80. Mem. Colo. Bar Assn., Denver Bar Assn., Order of Coif, Phi Kappa Phi. Avocations: basketball, running, skiing. Bankruptcy, Oil and gas leasing, Contracts commercial. Office: Shaw Spangler & Roth 1700 Broadway Suite 1400 Denver CO 80290

WILKIE, ROBERT ARTHUR, lawyer; b. N.Y.C., Mar. 9, 1951; s. Robert Arthur and Dolores (Mack) W.; m. Christine Theresa Lacouara, Nov. 3, 1973; children: Robert, Victoria, Christopher. BA in Math., Hofstra U., 1973; MS in Taxation, Pace U., 1978; JD, Bklyn. Law Sch., 1982; postdoctoral, NYU, 1984—. Bar: N.Y. 1982, U.S. Dist. Ct. (ea. and so. dists.) N.Y. 1985. Asst. v.p. U.S. Trust Co., N.Y.C., 1973-84; mgr. Touche Ross, N.Y.C., 1984-85; ptnr. Wilkie & Wilkie, Great Neck, N.Y., 1985—; prof. Adelphi U., Garden City, N.Y., 1984—. Legal counsel soc. for fin. planning Adelphi U., 1984—, bd. advs. Sch. Bus., 1985. Mem. ABA, N.Y. State Bar Assn., Assn. of Bar of City of N.Y., N.Y. Estate Planning Council, L.I. Estate Planning Council. Republican. Roman Catholic. Estate taxation, Personal income taxation, Probate. Home: 809 Highview Ave Westbury NY 11590 Office: Wilkie & Wilkie 185 Great Neck Rd Great Neck NY 11021

WILKINS, HERBERT PUTNAM, state judge; b. Cambridge, Mass., Jan. 10, 1930; s. Raymond Sanger and Mary Louisa (Aldrich) W.; m. Angela Joy Middleton, June 21, 1952; children: Douglas H., Stephen M., Christopher P., Kate T. A.B., Harvard U., 1951, LL.B. magna cum laude, 1954; LL.D., Suffolk U., 1976; J.D., New Eng. Sch. Law, 1979. Bar: Mass. 1954. Assoc. firm Palmer & Dodge, Boston, 1954-59; ptnr. Palmer & Dodge, 1960-72; assoc. justice Mass. Supreme Jud. Ct., 1972—. Editor: Harvard Law Rev., 1953-54. Bd. overseers Harvard Coll., 1977-83, pres. bd., 1981-83; trustee Milton Acad., 1971-76, Phillips Exeter Acad., 1972-78; mem. Concord (Mass.) Planning Bd., 1957-60; selectman Town of Concord, 1960-66, town counsel, 1969-72; town counsel Town of Acton, Mass., 1966-72. Mem. Am. Law Inst. (council), Am. Coll. Trial Lawyers (jud. fellow). Republican. Unitarian-Universalist. Office: 1300 Court House Boston MA 02108

WILKINS, JERRY LYNN, lawyer, oil producing company executive, clergyman; b. Big Spring, Tex., June 1, 1936; s. Claude F. and Grace L. (Jones) W.; children by previous marriage—Gregory, Tammy, Scott, Brett; m. Valerie Ann Nuanez, Aug. 1, 1986. B.A., Baylor U., 1958, LL.B., 1960. Bar: Tex. 1960, U.S. Dist. Ct. (no. dist.) Tex. 1960, U.S. Ct. Appeals (5th cir.); ordained to ministry, 1977. Sole practice, Dallas, 1960—; capt. Air America, Vietnam, 1967-68, Joint Church Aid, Biafra, 1969-70, TransInternat. Airlines, Oakland, Calif., 1977-79; gen. counsel First Tex. Petroleum, Dallas, 1982; owner Wooltex, Inc., Dallas, 1983—; owner, dir., legal counsel Intermountain Gas Inc., Dallas, 1983-84; dir. Engineered Roof Cons., Continental Tex. Corp., Arlington, Acklin Pain Research Inst., Inc., Irving, Tex.; dir., co-founder R.O.A.S., Inc., Maritime Internat., Inc., Maritime Oil Recovery, Inc., Moriah Oil Recovery Barges, Inc., Megas Homes Internat., Urex Internat.; cons. in field. Author: Gods Prosperity, 1980; So You Think You Have Prayed, 1980. Editor numerous books. Contbr. articles to profl. jours. Bd. dirs., pres. Beasley For Children Found. Inc., Dallas, 1978—; mem. Republican Presdl. Task Force, Washington, 1984—; bd. dirs., pilot Wings for Christians, Dallas, 1976—, Wings for Christ, Waco, Tex., 1976—. Recipient Cert. of Appreciation Parachute Club of Am., 1966; cert. of record holder for high altitude sky diving State of Tex., 1966, 67; Cert. of Achievement, Tex. State Guard, 1968. Mem. Parachute Assn. Am., Tex. Trial Attys. Assn., Assn. Trial Lawyers Am., Quiet Birdmen, Phi Alpha Delta. Club: U.S. Parachute (Monterrey, Calif.). Achievements: atty. (2 Tex. landmark cases) securing custody of female child for stepfather against natural parents, securing outside jail work program for convicted man. Federal civil litigation, State civil litigation, Oil and gas leasing. Office: PO Box 59462 Dallas TX 75229

WILKINSON, DAVID LAWRENCE, state government official; b. Washington, Dec. 6, 1936; s. Ernest LeRoy and Alice Valera (Ludlow) W.; m. Patricia Anne Thomas, Dec. 30, 1976; children: David Andrew, Samuel Thomas, Margaret Alice. B.A. cum laude in History, Brigham Young U., 1961; B.A. in Jurisprudence, Oxford U., Eng., 1964, M.A., 1969; J.D., U. Calif.-Berkeley, 1966. Bar: Calif. 1966, Utah 1972. Assoc. Lawler, Felix & Hall, Los Angeles, 1966-71; ptnr. Cook & Wilkinson, Los Angeles, 1971-72; asst. atty. gen. State of Utah, Salt Lake City, 1972-76, 77-79; chief dep. to Salt Lake County Atty., 1979-80; atty. gen. State of Utah, Salt Lake City, 1981—; spl. instr. Brigham Young U. Sch. Law, 1976-77, bd. visitors Sch. of Law, 1983-85; panelist Robert A. Taft Inst. Of Govt., Salt Lake City, 1974-76, 83-84; founder, mgr. Utah Bar. Rev. Course, 1973-76. Mem. Utah Council Criminal Justice Adminstrn., 1974-76, 77, Council Criminal and Juvenile Justice, 1984—. Served with U.S. Army, 1961-62. Rhodes scholar, 1961-64. Mem. Utah Bar Assn. (chmn. eminent domain sect. 1979-80); mem.. Nat. Assn. Attys. Gen. (exec. com. 1984-85); mem. Statewide Assn. Prosecutors (chmn. bd. 1983-84). Republican. Mormon. Government contracts and claims. Office: Utah State Attorney General 236 State Capitol Salt Lake City UT 84114

WILKINSON, DONALD MICHAEL, JR., lawyer; b. Detroit, Apr. 22, 1931; s. Donald Michael and Martha Mary (Dursek) W.; m. Minette Yoshimoto, Oct. 26, 1963; children: Phoebe, Donald, Heidi, Genevieve. B.A., U. Mich., 1951, J.D., 1954. Bar: Mich. 1954, N.Y. 1957. Assoc. White & Case, N.Y.C., 1957-68, ptnr., 1968—; resident ptnr. White & Case, London, 1979-83. Editor: Mich. Law Rev., 1954; contbr. articles to legal periodicals. Trustee Village of Laurel Hollow, N.Y., 1969-79, dep. mayor, 1976-79. Served to 1st lt. U.S. Army, 1955-57. Mem. ABA, N.Y. State Bar Assn., Assn. Bar City N.Y., Order of Coif. Democrat. Roman Catholic. Clubs: Huntington Country (N.Y.); Princeton (N.Y.C.); Wentworth (Virginia Lake, Eng.). Office: White & Case 1155 Ave of Americas New York NY 10036

WILKINSON, GEORGE ALBERT, JR., lawyer; b. Washington, Sept. 9, 1933; s. George A. and Grace Lillian (Hayden) W.; m. Mary Anne Reilly, Aug. 31, 1957; Anne, Jean, Thomas, Kathleen, Rose, Bernadette, George III, James, Rebecca, John, Daniel, Megan. BS, Georgetown U., 1957; JD, Cath. U., 1963. Bar: Md. 1964, D.C. 1966, U.S. Supreme Ct. 1969. Sole practice Hyattsville, Md., 1963-70; ptnr. Wilkinson & Zapp, Hyattsville, 1970—. Served to 1st lt. U.S. Army, 1957-59. Democrat. Roman Catholic. Lodge: Rotary. General corporate, General practice.

WILKINSON, HOMER FAWCETT, judge; b. Cedar City, Utah, Jan. 27, 1926; s. Harold Herbert and Luella (Fawcett) W.; m. Lorraine Ashton, June 21, 1950; children: Robyn, Sherman, Georgia, Clark, Wade. BS, U. Utah, 1950, JD, 1955. Bar: Utah 1955, U.S. Dist. Ct. Utah 1955, U.S. Ct. Appeals (10th cir.) 1955. Asst. atty. gen. State of Utah, Salt Lake City, 1956-62; sole practice Salt Lake City, 1962- 78; judge 3d jud. dist. Utah Dist. Ct., Salt Lake City, 1979—; tchr. bus. law Stevens-Henager Bus. Coll., Salt Lake City, 1966-71, Utah Tech. Coll., Salt Lake City, 1972-74, Brigham Young U., Salt Lake City, 1975—. Chmn. voting dist. Salt Lake City Reps., 1962-64; mem. ho. of reps. Utah State Legislature, 1967-76, Rep. Cen. Com., Utah, 1970-74; judge Nat. Mother of Yr., Salt Lake City, 1982. Mormon. General practice, Personal injury, Real property. Office: Utah Dist Ct 3d Jud Dist 240 E 400 S Salt Lake City UT 84111

WILKINSON, JAMES ALLAN, lawyer; b. Cumberland, Md., Feb. 10, 1945; s. John Robinson and Dorothy Jane (Kelley) W.; m. Elizabeth Susanne Quinlan, Apr. 14, 1973; 1 child, Kathryn Barrett. BS in Fgn. Service, Georgetown U., 1967; JD, Duquesne U., 1978. Bar: Pa., U.S. Dist. Ct. (we. dist.) Pa. Legis. analyst Office of Mgmt. and Budget, Washington, 1972-73; dep. exec. sec. Cost of Living Council, Washington, 1973-74; sr. fin. analyst U.S. Steel Corp., Pitts., 1974-82; ptnr. Buchanan Ingersoll, Pitts., 1982—; pres. Parental Stress Ctr., Pitts., 1983—; bd. dirs. Med. Eye Bank, Pitts., Comprehensive Safety Compliance, Pitts. Author: Financing and Refinancing Under Prospective Payment, 1985; contbr. articles to profl. jours. Counsel Oversight Com. on Organ Transplantation, Pitts., 1986; bd. dirs. Pitts. Symphony Soc., 1986—. Served with USN, 1968-71. Mem. ABA, Am. Acad. Hosp. Attys., Am. Soc. of Law and Medicine, Nat. Assn. of Bond Lawyers, Nat. Health Lawyers Assn. Republican. Episcopalian. Health, Real property, Municipal bonds. Home: 1201 Macon Ave Pittsburgh PA 15218 Office: Buchanan Ingersoll Profl Corp 600 Grant St 57th Floor Pittsburgh PA 15219

WILKINSON, JAMES HARVIE, III, federal judge; b. N.Y.C., Sept. 29, 1944; s. James Harvie and Letitia (Nelson) W.; m. Lossie Grist Noell, June 30, 1973; children: James Nelson, Porter Noell. B.A., Yale U., 1963-67; J.D., U. Va., 1972. Bar: Va. 1972. Law clk. to U.S. Supreme Ct. Justice Lewis F. Powell, Jr., Washington, 1972-73; asst. prof. law U. Va., 1973-75, assoc. prof., 1975-78; editor Norfolk (Va.) Virginian-Pilot, 1978-81; prof. law U. Va., 1981-82, 83—; dep. asst. atty. gen. Civil Rights div. Dept. Justice, 1982-83; judge U.S. Ct. Appeals (4th cir.), 1984—. Author: Harry Byrd and the Changing Face of Virginia Politics, 1968, Serving Justice: A Supreme Court Clerk's View, 1974, From Brown to Bakke: The Supreme Court and School Integration, 1979. Bd. visitors U. Va., 1970-73; Republican candidate for Congress from 3d Dist. Va., 1970. Served with U.S. Army, 1968-69. Mem. Va. State Bar, Va. Bar Assn. Episcopalian. Home: 1713 Yorktown Dr Charlottesville VA 22901 Office: US Court Appeals 255 W Main St Room 230 Charlottesville VA 22901

WILKINSON, JANE RAE, lawyer; b. Kalamazoo, Mar. 6, 1946; d. Clarence C. and Alice G. (Schoonmaker) Hotneier; m. William Malcolm Wilkinson, Jan. 28, 1978; children—Jay William, Clark Malcolm. A.B., U. Mich., 1968; J.D. summa cum laude, Gonzaga U., 1974; Bar: Wash. 1974, U.S. Dist. Ct. (we. dist.) Wash. 1976. Facility dir. U.S.A. Spl. Services Europe, Fed. Republic Germany, 1968-71; law clk. to presiding judge U.S. Ct. Appeals, Tacoma, 1974-76; atty. Weyerhaeuser Co., Tacoma, 1976-85; sole practice, Tacoma, 1985— . Bd. editors Gonzaga U. Law Rev., 1972-74. Subcom. chmn. King County Juvenile Ct. Conf. Com. (Wash.), 1976-77; chmn. Wash. Pub. Employment Relations Comm., Olympia, 1980—. Mem. Wash. State Bar Assn., Wash. Women Lawyers, Am. Arbitration Assn. Environment, Labor, Administrative and regulatory. Office: 1411 Scenic Dr NE Tacoma WA 98422 Office: 500 Union St Suite 1047 Seattle WA 98109

WILKINSON, JOHN BRUCE, lawyer; b. Orange, N.J., Nov. 13, 1942; s. Chester Bruce and Kathleen Margaret (Ellis) W.; m. Martha Noyes, June 14, 1969 (div. Oct. 1981). Student, U. Va., 1960-62, U. Paris, 1962-63; BA cum laude, Yale U., 1965; JD, Stanford U., 1968. Bar: N.Y. 1968, U.S. Dist. Ct. (no. dist.) Calif. 1984, Ill. 1985. Fgn. service officer U.S. Dept. State, Washington, 1968; assoc. Dunnington, Bartholow & Miller, N.Y.C., 1968-73; internat. atty. The Upjohn Co., Kalamazoo, 1973-77; regional counsel Latin Am. and Can. Abbott Labs., North Chicago, Ill., 1977-78; group counsel internat. ops. Container Corp. of Am., Chgo., 1978—; supervisory dir. Mercurius Golfkartonindustrie, B.V., The Netherlands, 1981—; bd. dirs. Mobil S.A., Spain, Carton y Papel de Mexico, S.A. de C.V., Mex., Carton de Venezuela, Venezuela Fibras Internat. de P.R. Inc. Mem. com. on fgn. affairs Chgo. Council on Fgn. Relations, 1978—. Mem. ABA, Chgo. Bar Assn., Am. Corp. Counsel Assn. Republican. Public international, General corporate. Office: Container Corp Am 1 First National Plaza Chicago IL 60603

WILKINSON, ROBERT WARREN, lawyer; b. Oak Ridge, Dec. 7, 1950; s. Michael Kennerly and Virginia (Sleap) W.; m. Patsy Ann McFall, Jan. 3, 1980; 1 son, Michael McFall. B.A. cum laude, Emory U., 1975; J.D., U. Tenn., 1975; LL.M. in Taxation, Georgetown U., 1978. Bar: Tenn. 1975, U.S. Tax Ct. 1977, U.S. Ct. Claims 1977, U.S. Supreme Ct. 1978, U.S. Dist. Ct. (ea. dist.) Tenn. 1980. Assoc. Buxton, Lain & Buxton, Oak Ridge, 1979-83; ptnr. Buxton, Layton, Webster & Wilkinson, Oak Ridge, 1983—; city atty. City of Oakdale, Tenn., 1981—; atty. Morgan County Sch. Bd., Tenn., 1982—. Officer Arts Council Oak Ridge, 1983; bd. dirs. Hope of Oak Ridge, 1982, Daniel Arthur Rehab. Ctr., Oak Ridge, 1984. Served to capt. U.S. Army, 1976-79. Decorated Army Commendation medal. Mem. ABA, Tenn. Bar Assn., Anderson County Bar Assn. Lodge: Rotary. Estate planning, Estate taxation, General practice. Home: 100 Carson Ln Oak Ridge TN 37830 Office: Suite 1000 Buxton Layton Webster & Wilkinson 800 Oak Ridge Turnpike Jackson Plaza Tower Oak Ridge TN 37831

WILKINSON, TOBY CHARLES, lawyer; b. Galveston, Tex., Nov. 26, 1955; s. Covy Beard and Frances Katherine (Anselmo) W.; m. Andrea Parks, June 4, 1983; 1 child, Matthew Clark. BA, E. Tex. State U., 1977; JD, Pepperdine U., 1980. Bar: Tex. 1980, U.S. Dist.Ct. (so. dist.) Tex. 1981, U.S. Supreme Ct. 1986. Assoc. Sharpe and Kajander, Houston, 1981-82, Law Offices of Ronald Haddox, Baytown, Tex., 1982-84; sole practice Baytown, 1984-87; atty. Hunt County, Greenville, Tex., 1987—. Vol. Bay Area Dems., 1984-86, Project Bus., Baytown, 1986. Mem. ABA, Tex. Bar Assn. (continuing profl. competence com., 1985—), Delta Theta Phi, Baytown C. of C. Roman Catholic. State civil litigation, Family and matrimonial, Criminal. Home: 4312 Bois D'Arc Greenville TX 75401 Office: 4406 N Main Baytown TX 77521

WILL, ALFRED JOSEPH, lawyer, engineer; b. Jamaica, N.Y., Mar. 11, 1950; s. James George and Catherine Rose (Steinmuller) W.; m. Therese Catherine Buttner, Nov. 23, 1972; children—Peter Simon, Daniel Alfred, Meredith Marie. B.S. in Engring., U.S. Merchant Marine Acad., 1972; J.D., St. John's Law Sch., 1975. Bar: N.Y. 1976, U.S. Dist. Cts. (so. and ea. dists.) N.Y. 1976, U.S. Ct. Appeals (2d cir.) 1982, U.S. Supreme Ct. 1982. Assoc. Tabak, Ezratty & Mellusi, N.Y.C., 1975-76; assoc., sr. Vincent, Berg, Russo, Marcigliano & Zawacki, N.Y.C., 1976-81; sr. ptnr. Badiak & Will, N.Y.C., 1981—; past pres., founder Admiralty Law Sch. of St. John's Law Sch., N.Y.C., 1974-75. Served to lt. USNR, 1969-78. Recipient Gov.'s Scholastic award N.Y. State, 1967-68; named Athlete of Yr. (track) U.S. Merchant Marine Acad., 1972. Mem. Maritime Law Assn. of U.S., Average Adjusters Assn. of U.S., N.Y. County Bar Assn. Roman Catholic. Admiralty, Federal civil litigation, Insurance. Home: 207 Mayflower Ave Williston Park NY 11596 Office: Badiak & Will 90 John St New York NY 10038

WILL, JOSEPH HENRY MICHAEL, lawyer, military officer; b. Erie, Pa., Aug. 2, 1945; s. Joseph Henry Michael and Mary Ann (Hilbert) W.; m. Margaret Cotter, July 13, 1968 (div. Apr. 1986); children: Joseph Henry Michael, Christopher Patrick; m. Dorothy M. Quitoriano, Oct. 17, 1986. BS, SUNY, Buffalo, 1967; MBA, U. Tenn., 1975; JD, SUNY, Buffalo, 1980. Bar: N.Y. 1981. Commd. USAF, 1967, advanced through grades to maj.; asst. staff judge advocate USAF, Chanute AFB, Ill., 1980-82, Clark Air Base, Phillipines, 1982-85, Keesler AFB, Miss., 1985—. Republican. Roman Catholic. Civil rights, Environment, Immigration, naturalization, and customs. Home: 9405 Red Bluff Dr Ocean Springs MS 39564

WILL, TREVOR JONATHAN, lawyer; b. Ashland, Wis., Aug. 11, 1953; s. William Taylor and Geraldine Sue (Trevor) W.; m. Margaret Ann Johnson, Aug. 28, 1976; children: Tyler William, Alexandra Marie, Jennifer Catherine. BA summa cum laude, Augustana Coll., 1975; JD cum laude, Harvard U., 1978. Bar: Wis. 1978, U.S. Dist. Ct. (ea. dist.) Wis. 1978, U.S. DIst. Ct. (we. dist.) Wis. 1980, U.S. Ct. Appeals (7th cir.) 1983, U.S. Supreme Ct. 1984, U.S. Dist. Ct. (ea. dist.) Mich. 1985. Assoc. Foley & Lardner, Milw., 1978-87, ptnr., 1987—. Mem. ABA, State Bar Wis., Milw. Bar Assn., Milw. Young Lawyers Assn. Federal civil litigation, State civil litigation, Administrative and regulatory. Home: 10011 Waterleaf Mequon WI 53092 Office: Foley & Lardner 777 E Wisconsin Ave Milwaukee WI 53202

WILLARD, DONNA CAROL MORRIS, lawyer; b. Calgary, Alta., Can., Jan. 19, 1944; came to U.S., 1965, naturalized, 1970; d. Donald Arthur and Margaret Cavell (Snook) Morris. B.A. with 2d class honors, U. B.C., 1965, student law, 1965-66; J.D., U. Oreg., 1970. Bar: Alaska 1970. Assoc. Boyko & Walton, 1970-71, Walton & Willard, 1971-73; ptnr. Gruenberg, Willard & Smith, 1974-75, Richmond, Willoughby & Willard, Anchorage, 1976-81, Willoughby & Willard, Anchorage, 1981—; bd. dirs. Alaska Legal Services Corp., 1979-80; mem. Anchorage adv. council Am. Arbitration Assn., 1978—; mem. Alaska Comml. Arbitration Panel, 1975—; vice chmn. Alaska Code Revision Commn., 1976-78; mem. Anchorage Transp. Commn., 1983-87, chmn., 1986-87; chmn. Alaska State Officers' Compensation Commn., 1986—. Copy editor: Alaska Bar Rag, 1979-83; ann. reviser: Probate Counsel, 1972-87. Trustee Alaska Indian Arts, Inc., 1970—, Chilkat Dancer of Alaska, 1965—; mem. Anchorage Port Commn., 1987—. Mem. Alaska Bar Assn. (pres. 1979-80, gov. 1977-80), ABA (Alaska Bar del. to ho. of dels., standing com. renationalized practice of law 1980-83, chmn. 1982-83, standing com. on bar activities and services 1983—), Nat. Conf. Bar Presidents (exec. council 1986—), Western States Bar Conf. (v.p. 1981-82, pres. 1983-84), Am. Judicature Soc., Assn. Trial Lawyers Am., Nat. Conf. Bar Found. (bd. trustees). Presbyterian. Bankruptcy, Federal civil litigation, State civil litigation. Office: Willoughby & Willard 124 E 7th Ave Anchorage AK 99501

WILLARD, JAMES ROBERT, lawyer; b. Camdenton, Mo., Jan. 29, 1934; s. Timothy Detweiler and Thelma Irene (Chandler) W.; m. Elizabeth Hess Buffe, Aug. 1, 1963; children—Kathryn Chandler, David Matthew, Elizabeth Anne, James Robert, Timothy Detweiler. B.S. in Bus. Adminstrn., U. Mo., 1955, J.D., 1960. Bar: Mo. 1960, U.S. dist. Ct. (we. dist.) Mo. 1961, U.S. Ct. Apls. (8th cir.) 1962, U.S. Ct. Apls. (10th cir.) 1963, U.S. Ct. Apls. (D.C. cir.) 1967, U.S. Sup. Ct. 1967. Assoc. Spencer, Fane, Britt & Browne, Kansas City, Mo., 1960-65, ptnr., 1966—; asst. instr. indsl. mgmt. U. Mo., Columbia, 1958-60; professorial lectr. labor law U. Mo., Kansas City, 1967. Mem. Reapportionment Commn., Mo. Ho. of Reps., 1966, Jackson County Charter Commn., 1970, Jackson County Apportionment Com., 1971, Jackson County Republican Com., 1966-70. Served to 1st lt. USAF, 1955-57. Mem. ABA (labor law sect.), Mo. Bar Assn., Lawyers Assn. Kansas City, Order of Coif, Omicron Delta Kappa, Phi Delta Phi. Club: Masons. Mem. Law Rev. U. Mo., 1958-60; contbr. to The Developing Labor Law, supplements, 1974—. Labor. Home: 600 W 113th St Kansas City MO 64114 Office: 1400 Commerce Bank Bldg 1000 Walnut Kansas City MO 64106

WILLARD, JAMES STUART, lawyer; b. Topeka, Sept. 22, 1952; s. Dean Eldon and Phyllis Lee (Tindell) W.; m. RoJene Ella Conwell, Feb. 14, 1979; children: Christopher Edward, Eric Lee. BA in Journalism, Washburn U., 1973, JD cum laude, 1976. Bar: Kans. 1976, U.S. Dist. Kans. 1976. From assoc. to ptnr. Scott, Quinlan & Hecht, Topeka, 1976—; sec. Auburn (Kans.) Discount Foods, Inc., 1983—. Mem. ABA, Kans. Bar Assn., Topeka Bar Assn., Kans. Trial Lawyers Assn., Phi Kappa Phi. Republican. Lodges: Masons (master 1980-81, 84-85); Shriners. Avocations: farming, gardening, travel. Banking, Bankruptcy, Real property. Home: 8231 SW 29th Topeka KS 66614 Office: Scott Quinlan & Hecht 3301 Van Buren Topeka KS 66611

WILLARD, JOHN MARTIN, lawyer; b. Wilmington, Del., Jan. 21, 1946; s. H. Ernest and Catherine (Martin) W.; m. Mary Laurent Gibon, Aug. 7, 1971 (div. Nov. 1973); m. Eugenia A. DelleDonne, Nov. 12, 1976 (div. Feb. 1982); 1 child, Ernest John Martin. BS, U. Del., 1969; JD, U. Louisville, 1976. Bar: Del. 1975, U.S. Dist. Ct. Del., U.S. Ct. Appeals (3d cir.). Dep. atty. gen. State of Del., Wilmington, 1974-76; ptnr. Baumeister, Willard & Rago, Wilmington, 1976-80; dir. litigation Levin, Goldlust & Clark, Wilmington, 1980-83; chief dep. Kent County Del. Dept. Justice, Dover, 1983-85; sole practice Wilmington, 1985—. Bd. dirs. Cath. Youth Orgn., Wilmington, 1975-85, v.p. 1980; instr. Confraternity of Christian Doctrine, Wilmington, 1985—. Mem. ABA, Assn. Trial Lawyers Am., Del. Bar Assn., Del. Trial Lawyers Assn. Democrat. Roman Catholic. Club: Rodney Square (Wilmington). Lodges: Masons, Elks. Avocations: power boating, antique car restoration. Criminal, Family and matrimonial, State civil litigation. Home: 224 Plymouth Rd Wilmington DE 19803 Office: 803 Shipley St Wilmington DE 19801

WILLARD, RICHARD KENNON, government official, lawyer; b. Houston, Sept. 1, 1948; s. Fair McDaniel Willard and Elsbeth Rowe (Kennon) Willard Armistead; m. Leslie Harral Hopkins, July 10, 1976; children: Stephen Hopkins, Lauren Suzanne. B.A., Emory U., 1969; J.D., Harvard U., 1975. Bar: Tex. 1978, Ga. 1975. Law clk. U.S. Ct. Appeals, San Francisco, 1975-76, U.S. Supreme Ct., Washington, 1976-77; atty. Baker & Botts, Houston, 1977-81; counsel for intelligence policy U.S. Dept. Justice, Washington, 1981-82, dep. asst. atty. gen. civil div., 1982-83, asst. atty. gen., 1983—. Note editor: Harvard Law Rev., 1974-75. Gen. counsel Republican Party of Tex., Austin, 1980-81. Served to 1st lt. U.S. Army, 1969-72. Mem. ABA, Phi Gamma Delta. Episcopalian. Office: Dept Justice 10th and Constitution Aves NW Washington DC 20530

WILLARD, ROBERT EDGAR, lawyer; b. Bronxville, N.Y., Dec. 13, 1929; s. William Edgar and Ethel Marie (Van Ness) W.; m. Shirley Fay Cooper,

May 29, 1954; children: Laura Marie, Linda Ann, John Judson. B.A. in Econs., Wash. State U., 1954; J.D., Harvard U., 1958. Bar: Calif. 1959. Law clk. to U.S. dist. judge 1958-59; practiced in Los Angeles, 1959—; asso. firm Flint & Mackay, 1959-61; individual practice 1962-64; mem. firm Willard & Baltaxe, 1964-65, Baird, Holley, Baird & Galen, 1966-69, Baird, Holley, Galen & Willard, 1970-74, Holley, Galen & Willard, 1975-82, Galvin & Willard, Newport Beach, Calif., 1982—; Dir. various corps. Served with AUS, 1946-48, 50-51. Mem. Am., Los Angeles County bar assns., State Bar Calif., Assn. Trial Lawyers Am., Am. Judicature Soc., Acacia Frat. Congregationalist. Club: Calcutta Saddle and Cycle. Federal civil litigation, State civil litigation, Real property. Home: 1840 Oriole Costa Mesa CA 92626 Office: Galen & Willard 610 Newport Ctr Dr Suite 1530 Newport Beach CA 92660

WILLARD, WILLIAM WELLS, lawyer; b. Springfield, Mass., Mar. 9, 1941; s. William Wells and Betty Ruth (Thomas) W.; m. Martha Furnans, June 12, 1965; children: Nathaniel Wells, Matthew Jay. AB, Tufts Coll., 1963; JD, Boston U., 1966. Bar: Mass. 1966, Maine 1967. Law clk. to presiding justice Mass. Superior Ct., 1966-67; assoc., ptnr. Bernstein, Shur, Sawyer & Nelson, Portland, Maine, 1967—. Contbr. articles to profl. jours. Bd. dirs. Wilbraham Acad., Big Bros./Big Sisters of So. Maine; past bd. dirs. United Way of Portland, Maine Health Systems Agy., So. Maine Comprehensive Health Agy. Mem. ABA, Assn. Trial Lawyers Am., Am. Judicature Soc., Maine Bar Assn., Maine Trial LAwyers Assn., Cumberland County Bar Assn. Democrat. Personal injury, Insurance, State civil litigation. Office: One Monument Sq Portland ME 04101

WILLCOX, BRECKINRIDGE LONG, lawyer; b. San Diego, Aug. 2, 1944; s. Arnold Augur and Christine Graham (Long) W.; m. Laura Henderson, Nov. 21, 1973; 1 child, Blair Breckinridge. BA, Yale U., 1966; JD, Duke U., 1969. Bar: Ma. 1969, U.S. Dist. Ct. (D.C. dist.) 1969, Hawaii 1972. Criminal dir. U.S. Dept. Justice, Washington, 1975-81, sr. litigation cousnel, 1981-84; U.S. atty. U.S. Dept. Justice, Balt., 1986—; ptnr. McKenna, Conner & Cuneo, Washington, 1984-86. Served to capt. USMC, 1970-73. Mem. ABA, Md. Bar Assn., D.C. Bar Assn., Hawaii Bar Assn. Criminal, Government contracts and claims. Office: US Courthouse 101 W Lombard St 8th Floor Baltimore MD 21201

WILLEMSSEN, MAC RONALD, lawyer; b. Estherville, Iowa, Oct. 9, 1947; s. Raymond McKinlay and Betty Ann (McMillan) W.; m. Judith Ann Shoup, June 5, 1971. BS, Iowa State U., 1969; MA, Bowling Green State U., 1971; JD, U. Minn., 1977. Bar: Minn. 1977, U.S. Dist. Ct. Minn. 1978. Ptnr. Melchert, Hubert, Sjodin & Willemssen, Chaska, Minn., 1977—; bd. dirs. Dist. Ethics Commn., Shakopee, Minn. Chmn. Waconia (Minn.) Devel. Commn., 1978-82; dir. Carver County Dems., Chaska, 1980-82. Mem. Minn. Bar Assn. (long range planning com.). Democrat. Methodist. Lodges: Rotary, Lions. Avocations: mountain climbing, hiking, cross country skiing, basketball, reading. State civil litigation, Insurance, Banking. Home: 317 W First St Chaska MN 55318 Office: Melchert Hubert Sjodin & Willemssen 112 2d St W PO Box 67 Chaska MN 55318

WILLENBROCK, RONALD CHRISTOPHER, lawyer; b. St. Louis, Apr. 22, 1939; s. Christopher Oscar and Margare Lena (Suttner) W.; m. Madeleine Anne Zuehlke, Dec. 20, 1975. B.S. in Bus. Adminstrn., St. Benedicts Coll., 1961; J.D., St. Louis U., 1967. Bar: Mo. 1967, U.S. Dist. Ct. (ea. dist.) Mo. 1968, U.S. Ct. Appeals (8th cir.) 1972, U.S. Supreme Ct. 1971. With claims dept. INA, St. Louis, 1961-68; assoc. Holtkamp & Amelung, St. Louis, 1968-70, ptnr., 1970-73; sr. ptnr. Amelung, Wulff & Willenbrock, 1973—. Served with USAR, 1961-67. Mem. Mo. Bar Assn., Bar Assn. Met. St. Louis (award of merit 1978, mem. faculty Trial Practice Inst.), Assn. Trial Lawyers Am., Assn. Def. Counsel (pres. 1973-74), Def. Research Inst., Am. Judicature Soc. Roman Catholic. General practice, Insurance, State civil litigation. Office: 14th Floor 705 Olive St Saint Louis MO 63101

WILLEY, BENJAMIN TUCKER, JR., lawyer; b. Richmond, Va., Feb. 23, 1946; s. Benjamin Tucker and Virginia (Bradshaw) W.; m. Beverly Jane Buscanics, Jan. 21, 1984; children by previous marriage: Benjamin Tucker III, Theresa. BA, U. Tex.-Arlington, 1973; JD, Oklahoma City U., 1976. Bar: Okla. 1976, Tex. 1985, U.S. Dist. Ct. (we. dist.) Okla. 1976. Ptnr. Evans & Willey, Oklahoma City, 1976-80; sr. ptnr. Willey & Kilpatrick, Oklahoma City, 1980—; chmn. continuing legal edn. program-title exam. basics and oil and gas title exam. U. Tulsa, 1984. Coach North Oklahoma City Soccer Club, 1980-83. Served to capt. U.S. Army, 1966-72, Vietnam. Decorated Bronze Star medal, Combat Infantryman's Badge. Mem. Okla. Bar Assn. (chmn. continuing legal edn. program-Indian land titles 1983, mem. faculty oil and gas continuing legal edn. program 1983), Phi Delta Phi. Episcopalian. Oil and gas, Civil litigation, Real property. Home: 6640 Avondale Dr Oklahoma City OK 73116 Office: Willey & Kilpatrick 501 Northwest Expressway Suite 525 Oklahoma City OK 73118

WILLEY, CHARLES WAYNE, lawyer; b. Dillon, Mont., Oct. 7, 1932; s. Asa Charles and Elizabeth Ellen (Leonard) W.; m. Helene D., July 21, 1962 (div.); children: Stephen Charles, Heather Helene, Brent David, Scott D; m. Alexis W. Grant, Jan. 26, 1986. BS with honors, Mont. State U., 1954; JD with high honors, U. Mont., 1959. Bar: Mont. 1959, Calif. 1960, U.S. Ct. Claims 1975, U.S. Tax Ct. 1975, U.S. Ct. Appeals (9th cir.) 1959, U.S. Ct. Appeals (Fed. cir.) 1983, U.S. Supreme Ct. 1972. Law clk. to presiding judge U.S. Ct. Appeals (9th cir.), 1959-60; ptnr. Price, Postel & Parma, Santa Barbara, Calif., 1960-77; sole practice Santa Barbara, 1977—; instr. Santa Barbara City Coll., 1961-63, U. Calif., Santa Barbara, 1963-64. Chief editor Mont. Law Rev., 1958-59. Pres. Legal Aid Found. Santa Barbara, 1970; mem. Laguna Blanca Sch. Bd., pres. 1980-81; v.p. Phoenix of Santa Barbara. Served to capt. USAF, 1954-56. Mem. Santa Barbara County Bar Assn. (pres. 1972-73), Phi Kappa Phi, Phi Eta Sigma, Phi Delta Phi. Republican. Episcopalian. Lodge: Kiwanis. Avocations: reading, writing, skiing. Probate, Real property, State civil litigation. Office: 812 Presidio Ave Santa Barbara CA 93101

WILLEY, N. LAURENCE, JR., municipal official; b. Biddeford, Maine, Sept. 11, 1949; s. Nelson L. Sr. and Barbara J. (Leighton) W.; m. Lorna H. Rand, Dec. 19, 1970; children: Ezra A.R., Josiah L.R., Monica J. BS in Econs., U. Maine, 1971, M in Community Devel., 1973; JD, Suffolk U., 1976; SL, Harvard U., 1984. Bar: Maine 1976, U.S. Dist. Ct. D.C. 1976, U.S. Supreme Ct. 1984. Mayor City of Bangor, Maine, 1983-84, 86-87, city councilman, 1981—; Named Outstanding Young Man of Yr. Maine Jaycees, 1982. Republican. Roman Catholic. Personal injury, Criminal, Workers' compensation. Home: 27 Howard St Bangor ME 04401

WILLIAMS, ALLEN KENNETH, lawyer; b. Carlisle, Pa., Dec. 2, 1950; s. James B. Williams and Blanche (Rocha) Hughes; m. Paulette Wong, Sept. 14, 1974 (div. Dec. 1983). BBA, Chaminade U., Honolulu, 1975; JD, Loyola U., Los Angeles, 1979. Bar: Calif. 1980, U.S. Dist. Ct. (no., so., ea. and cen. dists.) Calif. 1980, Hawaii 1981, U.S. Dist. Ct. Hawaii 1981, U.S. Ct. Appeals (9th cir.) 1981. Assoc. Kern & Wooley, Los Angeles, 1980-81; sole practice Honolulu and Los Angeles, 1981-82, Cronin, Fried, Sekiya, Kekina & Fairbanks, Honolulu, 1982—. Liaison to bd. dirs. State of Hawaii Orgn. of Police Officers, Honolulu, 1973-74. Mem. ABA, Fed. Bar Assn., Lawyers-Pilots Bar Assn., Assn. Trial Lawyers Am., Calif. Trial Lawyers Assn., Assn. Aircraft Owners and Pilots, Phi Alpha Delta. Democrat. Roman Catholic. Lodges: Rotary, Elks. Avocation: flying. Insurance, Personal injury. Home: 55 S Judd St #401 Honolulu HI 96817 Office: Cronin Fried Sekiya Kekina & Fairbanks 841 Bishop St Suite 1900 Honolulu HI 96813

WILLIAMS, ANN C., federal judge; b. 1949; M. David J. Stewart. BS, Wayne State U., 1970; MA, U. Mich., 1972; JD, U. Notre Dame, 1975. Asst. U.S. atty. U.S. Dist. Ct. (no. dist.) Ill., Chgo., 1976-85, judge, 1985—; adj. prof., lectr. Northwestern U. Law Sch., Chgo., 1979—. Mem. Fed. Bar Assn. Office: U S Dist Ct 219 S Dearborn St Chicago IL 60604 *

WILLIAMS, AVERILL MARSHALL, lawyer; b. New York, Aug. 16, 1931; s. Sydney L. and Beatrice B. (Berger) W.; m. Greta E. Weil, July 15, 1962; children: Jennifer Alison, Karen Barbara. AB, NYU, 1951; JD, Ind. U., 1956. Bar: N.Y. 1957, U.S. Dist. Ct. (so. and ea. dist.) N.Y. 1960, U.S. Ct. Appeals (2d cir.) 1960, U.S. Supreme Ct. 1967. Trial atty. anti-trust div. Dept. of Justice, N.Y.C., 1957-58; asst. U.S. atty. U.S. Dist. Ct. (ea. dist.) N.Y., N.Y., 1958-61; assoc. Bleakley, Platt, Schmidt, Hart & Fritz, N.Y.C., 1961-71; assoc., gen. counsel Amerada Hess Corp., N.Y.C., 1971—. Chmn. Zoning Bd. Appeals, Lewisboro, N.Y., 1970-80. Served to 1st lt. U.S. Army, 1951-53, Korea. Mem. N.Y. State Bar Assn., Maritime Law Assn. Antitrust, Federal civil litigation, Admiralty. Home: RD 2 Box 110 South Salem NY 10590 Office: Amerada Hess Corp 1185 Ave of Americas New York NY 10036

WILLIAMS, BARBARA JUNE, lawyer, consultant; b. Lansing, Mich., Jan. 6, 1948; d. Ben Allan and Virginia Jane (Searing) W.; m. John Paul Halvorsen, Oct. 21, 1971. A.A., Stephens Coll., 1968; B.A., U. Ill.-Champaign, 1970; J.D., Rutgers U., 1974. Bar: N.J. 1974, N.Y. 1981. Assoc., Bookbinder, Coulagori & Bookbinder, Burlington, N.J., 1974-76, Law Offices of Cyrus Bloom, Newark, 1976-78, Warren, Goldberg, Berman & Lubitz, Princeton, N.J., 1978-84; with Rutgers U. Sch. Law, Newark, 1984-85; now assoc. Strauss & Hall, Princeton. Assoc. editor Rutgers Camden Law Jour., 1973-74. Contbr. articles to profl. jours. Mem. N.J. Citizens for Better Schs. Mem. Nat. Sch. Bds. Assn. (dir. nat. council sch. attys. 1981-86), ABA, N.J. Bar Assn. (dir. govt. law sect. 1981—), Mercer County Bar Assn., Princeton Bar Assn., N.J. Trial Lawyers Assn., NOW, Lawrence Arts Assn., Lawrence Twp. Republican Club. Federal civil litigation, State civil litigation, General practice. Home: 90 Denow Rd Lawrenceville NJ 08648 Office: Strauss & Hall 32 Nassau St Princeton NJ 08542

WILLIAMS, BETTY OUTHIER, lawyer; b. Woodward, Okla., Sept. 11, 1947; d. Robert E. and Ethel M. (Castiller) Outhier; m. Ted S. Williams, Apr. 26, 1975; children: Amanda J., Emily Rebecca. BA, Oklahoma City U., 1969; JD, Vanderbilt U., 1972. Bar: Okla. 1972, U.S. Dist. Ct. (no. dist.) Okla. 1972, U.S. Ct. Appeals (10th cir.) 1973, U.S. Dist. Ct. (ea. dist.) Okla. 1973, U.S. Supreme Ct. 1980. Atty. Reginald Heber Smith Community Lawyer Fellowship, Tulsa, 1972-73; asst. U.S. atty. U.S. Dept. Justice, Muskogee, Okla., 1973-81, U.S. atty., 1981-82; ptnr. Robinson, Locke, Gage, Fife & Williams, Muskogee, 1982—. Pres. Bus. and Profl. Womens Found., Muskogee, 1975-77, 83; pres., bd. dirs. YWCA, Muskogee, 1975-82; bd. dirs. Green Country Mental Health, Muskogee, 1986—. Named one of Outstanding Young Career Women Bus. and Profl. Womens Found., 1974. Mem. ABA, Okla. Bar Assn., Muskogee County Bar Assn. (pres. 1984-85), Gamma Phi Beta. Republican. Methodist. Lodge: Soroptimists (pres. 1986—). Federal civil litigation, Bankruptcy, State civil litigation. Home: PO Box 355 Muskogee OK 74402 Office: Robinson Locke Gage Fife & Williams PO Box 87 Muskogee OK 74402-0087

WILLIAMS, BRADFORD J., JR., lawyer, restaurant co. exec.; b. Denver, Dec. 10, 1944; s. Bradford J. and Mary Elinor (Grubb) W.; m. Nanci K. Mullendore, Jan. 21, 1966; children—Bradford J. III, Brent. B.A., Okla. U., 1966; J.D., U. Tulsa, 1969. Bar: Okla. 1970, U.S. Dist. Ct. (no. dist.) Okla. 1970. Asst. dist. atty. Tulsa County (Okla.), 1970-72; assoc. Hall, Estill, Hardwick, Gable, Collingsworth & Nelson, Tulsa, 1973-79; gen. counsel, sr. v.p. franchising Ken's Restaurant Systems, Inc. (formerly Ken's Pizza Parlors, Inc.), Tulsa, 1979—. Served to sgt. Air N.G., 1966-72. Mem. ABA, Okla. Bar Assn., Tulsa County Bar Assn. (jud. com.), Delta Theta Phi. Democrat. Episcopalian. Contracts commercial, General corporate, Labor. Home: 5905 S New Haven Tulsa OK 74135 Office: 4441 S 72d E Ave Tulsa OK 74145

WILLIAMS, BRADLEY LOUIS, lawyer; b. Dayton, Ohio, July 20, 1950; s. Henry Louis and Julia Lois (Raderstorf) W.; m. Anne Farlow Uyesugi, Aug. 12, 1972; children: Elizabeth Anne, Sarah Anne. AB with honors, Ind. U., 1972, JD cum laude, 1975. Bar: Ind. 1975, U.S. Dist. Ct. (so. dist.) Ind. 1975, U.S. Ct. Appeals (7th cir.) 1976, Ohio 1978, U.S. Supreme Ct. 1978. Asst. U.S. atty. U.S. Dept. Justice, Indpls., 1975-82, 1st asst. U.S. atty., 1984—; assoc. Sommer & Barnard P.C., Indpls., 1982-84; instr. justice Atty. Gen.'s Adv. Inst., Washington, 1980—. Pres. Scarborough Village Civic Assn., Indpls., 1982; bd. dirs. Castleton East Civic Orgn., Indpls., 1984. Mem. ABA (standing com. on Gavel awards 1978—), Ind. Bar Assn., Indpls. Bar Assn., Fed. Bar Assn., 7th Cir. Bar Assn. Republican. Roman Catholic. Club: Indpls. Athletic. Federal civil litigation, Condemnation, Environment. Home: 7416 Marla Dr Indianapolis IN 46256 Office: US Attys Office 46 E Ohio St Room 274 Indianapolis IN 46204

WILLIAMS, CHARLES HIRAM, lawyer; b. Orangeburg, S.C., Mar. 18, 1950; s. Marshall Burns and Margret (Shecut) W.; m. Karen Johnson, Dec. 27, 1968; children: Marian, Ashley, Charles III, David. BS, U. S.C., 1972, JD, 1975. Bar: S.C. 1975, U.S. Dist. Ct. S.C. 1975, U.S. Ct. Appeals (4th cir.) 1976, U.S. Supreme Ct. 1981. Ptnr. Williams & Williams, Orangeburg, 1975—; mem. 4th cir. jud. conf., Richmond, Va., 1981—. Chmn. Orangeburg chpt. ARC, 1980-82; trustee S.C. State Coll., Orangeburg, 1986—. Mem. ABA, S.C. Bar Assn., Orangeburg County Bar Assn., Assn. Trial Lawyers Am., S.C. Trial Lawyers Assn., Beta Gamma Sigma, Omicrom Delta Epsilon. Democrat. Baptist. Avocations: hunting, fishing, snowskiing. Personal injury, Federal civil litigation, State civil litigation. Office: Williams & Williams PO Box 1084 Orangeburg SC 29116-1084

WILLIAMS, CHARLES JUDSON, lawyer; b. Sam Mateo, Calif., Nov. 23, 1930; s. John Augustus and Edith (Babcock) W.; children: Patrick, Victoria, Apphia. AB, U. Calif.-Berkeley, 1952, LLB, 1955. Bar: Calif. 1955, U.S. Supreme Ct. 1970. Assoc. Kirkbride, Wilson, Harzfeld & Wallace San Mateo County, Calif. 1956-59; sole practice Solano County, Calif., 1959-64, Martinez, Calif., 1964-81, Benicia, Calif. 1981—; city atty. Pleasant Hill, Calif., 1962-80, Yountville, Calif., 1965-68, Benicia, 1968-76, 80-82, Lafayette, Calif. 1968—, Moraga, Calif., 1974—, Danville, Calif., 1982—, Pittsburg, Calif., 1984—, Orinda, Calif., 1985—; lectr. Calif. Continuing Edn. Bar 1964-65, U. Calif. Extension 1974-76, John F. Kennedy U. Sch. Law 1966-69; spl. counsel to various Calif. cities; legal advisor Alaska Legis. Council 1959-61; advisor Alaska sup. ct. 1960-61; advisor on revision Alaska statues 1960-62; atty. Pleasant Hill Redevel. Agy. 1978-82; sec., bd. dirs. Vintage Savs. & Loan Assn., Napa County, Calif., 1974-82; bd. dirs. 23d Agrl. Dist. Assn., Contra Costa County, 1968-70. Author: California Code Comments to West's Annotated California Codes, 3 vols. 1965, West's California Code Forms, Commercial, 2 vols., 1965, West's California Government Code Forms, 3 vols., 1971, supplement to California Zoning Practice, 1978, 80, 82, 84, 85; contbr. articles to legal jours. Mem. ABA, Calif. Bar Assn., Contra Costa County Bar Assn., Mt. Diablo Bar Assn. Administrative and regulatory, State civil litigation, Local government. Office: 1060 Grant St Benicia CA 94510

WILLIAMS, CHARLES MICHAEL, human resources manager; b. Norman, Okla., Sept. 17, 1955; s. George Thomas and Dolores Mae (Barrick) W.; m. Linda Diane Wright, June 4, 1977; children: Christopher Michael, Lindsay Diane. BBA, Okla. State U., 1977; JD, U. Ark., 1980. Bar: Ark. 1980. Mgr. personnel Wolverinr Worldwide, Jonesboro, Ark., 1980-82; mgr. employment Frito-Lay, Pulaski, Tenn., 1982-83; mgr. personnel Frito-Lay, Irving, Tex., 1983-85; mgr. human resources Laidlaw Waste Systems, Inc., Hurst, Tex., 1985-86, Laidlaw Waste Systems, Hurst, 1986—; mem. Tenn. Private Industry Council, Columbia, Tenn., 1982-84. Mem. ABA, Ark. Bar Assn., Am. Soc. Personnel Adminstrs. Labor, Workers' compensation, Environment. Home: 614 Plumlee Pl Coppell TX 75019 Office: Laidlaw Waste Systems 669 Airport Freeway #400 Hurst TX 76053

WILLIAMS, CHRIS E, lawyer; b. Malvern, Ark.; s. Tom E. and Thalma (Van Dusen) W.; m. Janice Marie Morrison, Nov. 1984. BA, Henderson State U., 1978; JD, U. Ark., 1981. Bar: Ark. 1981, U.S. Dist. Ct. (we. dist.) Ark. 1982. Sole practice Malvern, 1981—; city atty. Malvern, 1986—. Mem. Ark. Bar Assn., Hot Spring County Bar Assn., Garland County Bar Assn., Malvern C. of C. Lodge: Lions. Avocation: golf. Office: 829 Halbert Ave Malvern AR 72104

WILLIAMS, D. LEE, lawyer; b. Warren, Ohio, July 4, 1931; s. Fredric Douglas and Freddie Lee (Hester) W.; m. Evelyn Clark, Aug. 22, 1956 (div. Nov. 1979); m. Theresa E. Hubbard, May 21, 1980; children: Douglas R., Dawn R., Darlene R., Daryl R., Lori, Lisa, Mellissa, Sonya. BS, Youngstown State U., 1971; JD, U. Akron, 1974. Bar: Mich. 1974. Detective Warren (Ohio) Police Dept., 1954-56; engr. Gen. Motors Corp., Warren, 1956-74; legal intern State of Ohio, 1973; ptnr. Adams, Goler & Williams, Jackson, Mich., 1974—. Referee Mich. State Civil Rights. Served with U.S. Navy, 1949-50, served to capt. U.S. Army, 1950. Mem. Jackson Fraternal Order Police. Methodist. Lodge: Lions. Avocations: scuba diving, hunting, fishing. Civil rights, Criminal, Family and matrimonial. Home: 309 Meadow Ln Jackson MI 49203 Office: 501 W Prospect Jackson MI 49203

WILLIAMS, DAVID HUNTINGTON, lawyer; b. Chgo., Sept. 14, 1946; s. David Benton and Edith Chapin (Huntington) W.; m. Diana Pritchard, Aug. 23, 1969 (div. May 1979); children: David D.P., Benjamin F.; m. Carol Lynn Eoannou, Jan. 1, 1983. AB, Harvard U., 1969; JD, Stanford U., 1972. Bar: Calif. 1973, D.C. 1973. Atty. FTC, Washington, 1972-74, program dir., 1974-83; pres. Litten & Williams, Richmond, Va., 1983-85; ptnr. Williams & Eoannov, Washington, 1985—; bd. dirs. ACI, Inc., Wheaton, Md. Mem. ABA, Fed. Bar Assn., Nat. Lawyers Club. Club: Raffles (London). Administrative and regulatory, Federal civil litigation, General corporate. Home: 6913 Oakridge Ave Chevy Chase MD 20815 Office: Williams & Eoannou 1915 Eye St NW Washington DC 20006

WILLIAMS, DAVID ROY, tax attorney, accountant; b. London, Nov. 7, 1954; came to U.S., 1956; s. Roy O. and Catherine B. (Herd) W. BS, Stanford U., 1976, MS, 1977; JD, U. of the Pacific, 1980. Bar: Nev. 1980; CPA, Calif. Sr. tax mgr. Arthur Young & Co., Sacramento, Calif., 1980-84; dir. tax Arthur Young & Co., Reno, 1985—. Mem. Congl. Action Com. Reno C. of C., 1986. Mem. ABA (tax acctg. com. 1983—), Am. Inst. CPA's, Calif. Soc. CPA's. Republican. Presbyterian. Club: Stanford (Reno) (treas. 1986-87). Avocations: skiing, tennis. Corporate taxation, Personal income taxation, Estate taxation. Home: PO Box 3380 Incline Village NV 89450 Office: Arthur Young & Co 200 S Virginia Suite #250 Reno NV 89501

WILLIAMS, DAVID WESLEY, law librarian; b. Providence, R.I., Aug. 1, 1947; s. Warrenton Archibald and Claire (Burdick) W.; m. Barbara Ruth Donelan, Jan. 23, 1975. B of Applied Sci. cum laude, Boston U., 1972; JD cum laude, Suffolk U., 1976; MS, Simmons Coll., 1985. Bar: Mass. 1977, U.S. Dist. Ct. No. Mariana Islands 1978, U.S. Ct. Claims 1979, U.S. Ct. Appeals (9th cir.) 1979, U.S. Dist. Ct. Mass. 1982, U.S. Ct. Appeals (1st cir.) 1983. Atty. Govt. of Guam, Agana, Guam, 1977-81; asst. gen. counsel Mass. Dept. of Welfare, Boston, 1982-83; asst. tech. services librarian Social Law Library, Boston, 1983-85; librarian, reader services Assn. of Bar of City of N.Y., N.Y.C., 1985—. Mem. ABA, Mass. Bar Assn., Am. Assn. Law Librarians, Law Librarians of Greater N.Y., Am. Soc. Info. Sci., Am. Radio Relay League, Beta Phi Mu. Avocations: computers, amateur radio, calligraphy. Librarianship. Home: 13 Maurice Ave Ossining NY 10562 Office: Assn Bar City NY 42 W 44th St New York NY 10036

WILLIAMS, DEIRDRÉ LAJEAN, association executive, speech pathologist; b. Detroit, July 13, 1956; d. Juanita (Douglas) James; m. Larry Charles Williams, Mar. 31, 1979 (div. Feb. 1982): 1 child, Jameel Karl. AB with distinction, U. Mich., 1978; MA, U. Calif., Santa Barbara, 1980; MHuman Resources and Adminstrn., Cen. Mich. U. Speech-lang. pathologist G.J. Cooper & Assocs., Grosse Pointe, Mich., 1980-85, Detroit Hearing and Speech Ctr., 1981-83; exec. asst. to exec. dir. Legal Aid and Defender Assn. Detroit, 1983-84, exec. dir., 1984—. Mem. NAACP, Nat. Assn. Female Execs. Democrat. Baptist. Avocations: swimming, reading, music, theatre. Administrative and regulatory. Home: 16885 Lesure Detroit MI 48235 Office: Legal Aid and Defender Assn Detroit 1 Kennedy Sq Suite 1910 Detroit MI 48235

WILLIAMS, EDDIE ERWIN, III, lawyer; b. Rocky Mount, N.C., Feb. 6, 1948; s. Eddie Erwin and Eula Meredith (Garland) W.; m. Frances Ann Jackson, July 15, 1972; children—Jackson Hill, James Barnett. B.A., Wofford Coll., 1970; J.D., Vanderbilt U., 1973. Bar: Tenn. 1973, U.S. Dist. Ct. Tenn. 1974, U.S. Supreme Ct. 1979. Atty.-ptnr. Bryant, Price, Brandt, Jordan & Williams, Johnson City, Tenn., 1973-79; cir. ct. judge 1st Jud. Dist., Tenn., 1979-84; atty.-ptnr. Baker, Worthington, Crossley, Stansberry & Woolf, Johnson City, 1984—; faculty Tenn. Jud. Acad., 1982—; bd. of regents State of Tenn. Bd. dirs. Sequoyah Council Boy Scouts Am., United Way; regional chmn. Am. Cancer Crusade for Tenn.; exec. com., bd. dirs. East Tenn. State U. Found. Recipient Hon. Alumnus award East Tenn. State U. Mem. ABA, Tenn. Bar Assn. (Liberty Through Law award 1981), Internat. Acad. Trial Judges (fellow), Assn. Am. Trial Lawyers, Assn. Tenn. Trial Lawyers, Johnson City C. of C. (v.p., bd. dirs.), Rocky Mt. Hist. Assn. (trustee, v.p.). Republican. Episcopalian. Environment. Home: 811 Cloudland Dr Johnson City TN 37601 Office: Baker Worthington et al 207 Mockingbird Ln PO Box 3038 CRS Johnson City TN 37602

WILLIAMS, EDWARD BENNETT, lawyer; b. Hartford, Conn., May 31, 1920; s. Joseph Barnard and Mary (Bennett) W.; m. Dorothy Adair Guider, May 3, 1946 (dec. 1959); children—Joseph Barnard, Ellen Adair, Peter Bennett; m. Agnes Anne Neill, June 11, 1960; children—Edward Neill, Dana Bennett, Anthony Tyler, Kimberly Anne. A.B. summa cum laude, Coll. Holy Cross, 1941, S.J.D., 1963; LL.B., Georgetown U., 1945, LL.D., 1968; LL.D., Loyola Coll., 1967, Fairfield U., 1968, Loyola U., Chgo., 1970, Albert Magnus Coll., 1971, St. Joseph's Coll., Phila., 1971, Lincoln (Ill.) Coll., 1972, Suffolk U., 1974, U. Detroit Sch. Law, 1976, Mount St. Mary's Coll., 1977, U. Md., 1983, Scranton U., 1986, Barry U., 1986. Bar: D.C. bar 1944. Since practiced in Washington; sr. partner firm Williams & Connolly (and predecessor firms), 1967—; prof. criminal law and evidence Georgetown U. Law Sch., 1946-58, gen. counsel univ., 1949—; guest prof. U. Frankfurt, Germany, 1954; vis. lectr. Yale Law Sch., 1971; chmn. bd., pres., owner Balt. Orioles Baseball Club.; Mem. U.S. Jud. Conf. Adv. Com. on Fed. Rules of Evidence, 1965-74, Chief Justice's Com. on Court Facilities and Design, 1971-74; chmn. Md. Jud. Nominating Commn. 6th Jud. Dist., 1971-78; mem. President's Fgn. Intelligence Adv. Bd., 1976-77, 82-85, gen. counsel, 1985—. Author: One Man's Freedom, 1962; contbr. articles to profl. publs. Treas. Dem. Nat. Com., 1974-77; trustee Coll. Holy Cross, 1976—, chmn., 1982—. Served with USAAF, 1941-43. Mem. ABA (com. minimum standards for adminstrn. criminal justice 1965-67, chmn. spl. com. crime prevention and control 1970-72), D.C. Bar, Bar Assn. D.C. (v.p. 1950, 55-56, Lawyer of Yr. award 1966), Am. Coll. Trial Lawyers (bd. regents 1968-72), Internat. Acad. Trial Lawyers. Democrat. Roman Catholic. Clubs: University, Federal City, Vinson, Nat. Lawyers, Metropolitan, Barristers, Alfalfa, Nat. Press (Washington), Knights of Malta, Fed. Assn. (pres. 1984—). Office: 839 17th St NW Washington DC 20006

WILLIAMS, FRANK J., lawyer, judge; b. Providence, Aug. 24, 1940; s. Frank and Natalie L. (Corelli) W.; m. Virginia E. Miller, Aug. 24, 1966. BA, Boston U., 1962, JD, 1970, MS in Taxation, Bryant Coll., 1986, LHD Lincoln Coll., 1987. Bar: R.I. 1970, U.S. Dist. Ct. R.I. 1970, U.S. Supreme Ct. 1976. Assoc. Tillinghast, Collins & Graham, Providence, 1970-75, Leonard Decof Ltd., Providence, 1976-78; law clk. Graham, Reid, Ewing & Stapleton, Providence, 1969; law clk., adminstrv. asst. R.I. atty. gen., Providence, 1967-68; pres. Frank J. Williams Ltd., attys.-at-law, Providence, 1978—; judge of probate Town of Hopkinton (R.I.), 1978-82, 84-87, solicitor, 1978-82, 84—; judge of probate Town of West Greenwich, R.I., 1984—, solicitor, 1984-86; dep. judge of probate, 1987—; solicitor Town of Coventry, R.I., 1972-74, 76-78; vis. lectr. bus. and legal practices R.I. Sch. Design, Providence, 1976-80; mem. panel of arbitrators Am. Arbitration Assn.; mem. R.I. Bd. of Bar Examiners. Pres., Lincoln Group of Boston; pres. Abraham Lincoln Assn., Springfield, Ill.; del. R.I. Constitutional Conv., 1986; bd. dirs., sec. John E. Fogarty Found. for Mentally Retarded; mem. corp. Roger Williams Coll.; bd. dirs. Narragansett council Boy Scouts Am., 1969-80; chmn. Lincoln adv. com. Brown U.; mem. Lincoln planning group Gettysburg Coll.; mem. Lincoln adv. com. Endicott Coll. Served to capt. U.S. Army, 1962-67; Vietnam. Decorated Bronze Star medal, Air medal (3), Army Commendation medal; Vietnam Gallantry Cross with silver star. Mem. ABA, R.I. Bar Assn. (house of dels., chmn. new lawyers adv. com.), Am. Judicature Soc., Nat. Coll. Probate Judges. Roman Catholic. General corporate, Legislative, Local government.

WILLIAMS, FRANK JOHN, JR., lawyer; b. Albany, N.Y., Jan. 12, 1922; s. Frank John and Mary Louise (Wood) W.; m. Marjorie Susan White, Apr. 12, 1950; children: Jrank John III, Carrie Louise, Frederick Jesse. BA, Princeton U., 1946; LLB, Albany Law Sch., 1949. Bar: N.Y. 1951, U.S. Dist. Ct. (no. dist.) N.Y. 1952, U.S. Tax Ct. 1977, U.S. Ct. Claims 1977. Assoc. W.W. Bullis, Lake George, 1949-50, Wiswall and Wood, Albany,

1950-60; sole practice Albany, 1960-84; ptnr. Williams and DuBrin, Albany, 1984—; atty. Town Guilderland, N.Y., 1960-83. Active Town of Guilderland Rep. Com., 1955-83, chmn., 1962-64; of counsel Town of Guilderland Indsl. Devl. Agy., 1973-83. Served to cpl. U.S. Army, 1943-45, MTO. Mem. ABA, N.Y. Bar Assn., Albany County Bar Assn. Republican. Lutheran. Club: Ft. Orange (Albany) (sec. 1976—); Lake George. Lodge: Masons. Avocations: history, sailing, squash, skiing. General practice, Probate, Federal civil litigation. Office: Williams and DuBrin 96 S Swan St Albany NY 12210

WILLIAMS, GEORGE HOWARD, lawyer, association executive; b. Hempstead, N.Y., Feb. 12, 1918; s. George R. and Marcella (Hogan) W.; m. Mary Celeste Madden, Nov. 23, 1946; children—Mary Beth Williams Barritt, Stephen, Kevin, Jeanne Marie. A.B., Hofstra Coll., 1939, LL.D. (hon.), 1969; J.D., N.Y. U., 1946, LL.D. (hon.), 1969; postgrad., Inst. Advanced Legal Studies, U. London, 1959. Bar: N.Y. bar 1946. Adminstrv. asst. to dean NYU Law Sch., N.Y.C., 1946-48, instr. law, 1948-50, asst. prof., 1950-52, assoc. prof., 1952-55, prof., 1956-62, v.p. univ. devel., 1962-66, exec. v.p. planning and devel., 1966-68; pres. Am. U., Washington, 1968-75; exec. v.p., dir. Am. Judicature Soc., Chgo., 1976-87. Author: (with A.T. Vanderbilt and L.L. Pelletier) Report on Liberal Adult Education, 1955; (with K. Sampson) Handbook for Judges, 1984. Bd. dirs. Nat. Center Edn. Politics, 1948-58, trustee, 1958-65; trustee Hofstra U., 1961-64; chmn. bd. trustees Trinity Coll., Vt., 1978-86. Served to lt. col., inf. AUS, World War II. Decorated Legion of Merit, Silver Star. Mem. Am. Polit. Sci. Assn., ABA Assn. Bar City N.Y., Alpha Kappa Delta, Phi Delta Phi. Clubs: N.Y. U. (N.Y.C.); Nat. Lawyers (Washington). Jurisprudence, Judicial administration. Home: 1322 Judson Ave Evanston IL 60201 Office: 25 East Washington Chicago IL 60602

WILLIAMS, GERALD JOSEPH, lawyer; b. Chadds Ford, Pa., Aug. 21, 1951; s. Henry Anthony Sr. and Theres Marie (Marenco) W.; m. Susan Marie Kean, May 7, 1973 (div. Sept. 1976). BS in Sociology, St. Joseph's Coll., 1973; MA in Sociology, U. Pitts., 1976; JD, Temple U., 1982. Bar: Pa. 1982, U.S. Dist. Ct. (ea. dist.) Pa. 1982, U.S. Ct. Appeals (3d dist.) 1983, U.S. Supreme Ct. 1986. Psychol. tester Diagnostic and Rehab. Ctr., Phila., 1973-74; evaluation analyst St. Luke's and Children's Med. Ctr., Phila., 1975-77; dir. research and evaluation Brnjamin Rush Mental Health/Mental Research Ctr., Phila., 1977-80; law clk. Wapner, Newman & Assocs., Phila., 1980-82, atty., 1982-83; ptnr. Slap, Williams & Cuker, Phila., 1984—; bd. dirs., Feltonville Bldg. and Loan Assn., Phila. Mem. ABA (environ. and toxic tort litigation sect.), Pa. and Phila. Bar Assns., Assn. Trial Lawyers Am., Pa. Trial Lawyers Assn. (sustaining), Phila. Trial Lawyers Assn. Democrat. Roman Catholic. Avocation: baseball. Environment, Civil rights, Federal civil litigation. Office: Slap Williams & Cuker One Franklin Plaza Suite 960 Philadelphia PA 19102

WILLIAMS, GLEN MORGAN, U.S. district judge; b. Jonesville, Va., Feb. 17, 1920; s. Hughy May and Hattie Mae W.; m. Jane Slemp, Nov. 17, 1962; children: Susan, Judy, Rebecca, Melinda. A.B. magna cum laude, Milligan Coll., 1940; J.D., U. Va., 1948. Bar: Va. 1947. Practiced law Jonesville, 1948-76; judge U.S. Dist. Ct. for Western Va., 1976—; commonwealth's atty. Lee County, Va., 1948-51; Mem. Va. Senate, 1953-55. Editorial bd.: Va. Law Rev, 1946-47. Mem. Lee County Sch. Bd., 1972-76; trustee, elder First Christian Ch., Pennington Gap, Va. Served to lt. USN, 1942-46, MTO. Recipient Citation of Merit Va. Def. Lawyers Assn. Mem. ABA, Va. State Bar (citation of merit), Va. Bar Assn. (citation of merit), Fed. Bar Assn., Va. Trial Lawyers Assn. (Meritorious Service award 1986), Am. Legion, 40 and 8. Republican. Clubs: Lions, Lee Players, Masons, Shriners. General practice, Criminal, Federal civil litigation. Office: Fed Bldg PO Box 339 Abingdon VA 24210

WILLIAMS, HENRY JOSEPH, lawyer; b. Carteret, N.J., Feb. 2, 1926; s. Walter and Stephanie (Kaminski) W.; m. Rose Frances Caruso, May 11, 1957; 1 child, Lesley Elizabeth. BA, Lafayette Coll., 1951; JD, Rutgers U., 1956. Bar: N.J. 1956, U.S. Dist. Ct. N.J. 1956, U.S. Supreme Ct. 1969. Assoc. Seaman & Seaman, Perth Amboy, N.J., 1956-58; ptnr. Seaman, Williams & Seaman, Perth Amboy, 1958-77; pres. Scotch Plains, N.J., 1977—. Served with USN, 1944-46. Mem. ABA, Middlesex Bar Assn. (trustee 1958-60), Assn. Trial Lawyers Am., Trial Lawyers Assn. Middlesex County (pres. 1969-70), Phi Delta Theta (reporter 1955-56). Roman Catholic. Lodge: Lions (Fanwood N.J. pres. 1978-79). Avocations: tennis, golf, swimming. State civil litigation, Personal injury, Probate. Office: 1100 South Ave PO Box 2246 Westfield NJ 07091-2246

WILLIAMS, HENRY WARD, JR., lawyer; b. Rochester, N.Y., Jan. 12, 1930; s. Henry Ward and Margaret Elizabeth (Simpson) W.; children—Edith French, Margaret Williams Warren, Sarah Williams Muzikar, Ann Ward, Elizabeth DeLancey, Victoria Maureen. A.B., Darmouth Coll., 1952; LL.B., U.Va., 1958. Bar: N.Y. 1959, U.S. Dist. Ct. (we. dist.) N.Y. 1959, U.S. Dist. Ct. (so. dist.) Mich. 1982, U.S. Ct. Appeals (2d cir.) 1963, U.S. Tax Ct. 1960, U.S. Supreme Ct. 1968. Ptnr., Harris, Beach Wilcox, Rubin & Levey, Rochester, N.Y., 1958-78, Robinson, Williams, Angeloff & Frank, Rochester, 1978-82, Weidman, Williams, Jordon, Angeloff & Frank, Rochester, 1982-83; dir. Voplex Corp. Bd. dirs. Presbyn. Residence Ctr. Corp., Ctr. for Environ. Info.; mem. Genesee Finger/Lakes Regional Planning Council, 1973—, past chmn.; mem. Monroe County Legislature, 1967-79. Served to lt. j.g. USN, 1952-55. Mem. ABA, N.Y. State Bar Assn., Monroe County Bar Assn. (trustee 1982-85), Raven Soc., Va. Law Rev., Order of Coif, Omicron Delta Kappa. Clubs: Rochester Yacht, Royal Can. Yacht, (Toronto, Ont., Can.), Royal Ocean Racing (London). General practice. Home: 6 Village Grove Pittsford NY 14534 Office: 47 S Fitzhugh St Rochester NY 14614

WILLIAMS, HOUSTON GARVIN, lawyer; b. Estancia, N.Mex., Nov. 27, 1922; s. Jason Christian and Katherine (Garvin) W.; m. Martha Germon, Apr. 1, 1945; children—Barry G., Richard L. B.S.C.E., U. Colo.-Boulder, 1947, J.D., 1950. Bar: Colo. 1950, Wyo. 1950, U.S. Dist. Ct. Wyo. 1950, U.S. Ct. Appeals (10th cir.) 1956, U.S. Supreme Ct. 1971. Assoc. W.J. Wehrli, Casper, Wyo., 1950-64; ptnr. Wehrli and Williams, Casper, 1964-78, Williams, Porter, Day and Neville, Casper, 1978-79; pres. Williams, Porter, Day and Neville, P.C., 1979—. Bd. dirs. United Fund, Blue Envelope Health Fund. Served to capt. C.E., USAF, 1943-46. Fellow Am. Bar Found.; mem. ABA (ho. of dels. 1975-77), Wyo. State Bar (pres. 1972-73), Natrona County Bar Assn. (pres. 1960), Internat. Soc. Barristers (bd. govs.), Am. Coll. Trial Lawyers, Am. Bd. Trial Advocates, Am. Coll. Probate Counsel, Am. Judicature Soc. Republican. Roman Catholic. Clubs: Rotary (pres. 1969-70), K.C. (Casper). Probate, State civil litigation, Oil and gas leasing. Office: Williams Porter Day Neville PC 145 S Durbin St Suite 300 Casper WY 82601

WILLIAMS, J. BRYAN, lawyer; b. Detroit, July 23, 1947; s. Walter J. and Maureen June (Kay) W.; m. Jane Elizabeth Eisele, Aug. 24, 1974; children: Kyle Joseph, Ryan Patrick. AB, U. Notre Dame, 1969; JD, U. Mich., 1972. Bar: Mich. 1972, U.S. Dist. Ct. (ea. dist.) Mich. 1972. Ptnr. Dickinson, Wright, Moon, Van Dusen & Freeman, Detroit, 1972—. Mem. ABA, Mich. Bar Assn., Detroit Bar Assn. Roman Catholic. Club: Notre Dame (Detroit)(pres. 1984); Oakland Hills Country (Birmingham, Mich.). Banking, Securities, General corporate. Home: 444 Pilgrim Birmingham MI 48009 Office: Dickinson Wright et al 800 1st National Bldg Detroit MI 48226

WILLIAMS, JACQUES RALPH ANDRÉ, lawyer; b. Morgantown, W.Va., Dec. 19, 1953; s. John Ryan and Madeleine (Cremilliac) W.; m. Janet Nelson, Sept. 15, 1979; children: Stephanie Marie, Maureen Lynn. Student, London Sch. of Econs. and Polit. Scis., 1975; BA, W.Va. U., 1975. Bar: W.Va. 1975, U.S. Dist. Ct. (no. dist) W.Va. 1978, U.S. Dist.Ct. (so. dist.) W.Va. 1975, U.S. Ct. Appeals (4th cir.) 1983, U.S. Supreme Ct. 1986. Ptnr. Hamstead, Hamstead & Williams, Morgantown, W.Va., 1978—. Mem. Policemen's Civil Service Com., Westover, W.Va., 1979—; assoc. mem. Monongalia County Rep. Exec. Com., 1982—, ballot commr., 1984—; treas. Bartlett House Shelter for Homeless, Morgantown, 1985—. Named one of Outstanding Young Men Am., 1980. Mem. ABA, Order of Barrister, Phi Beta Kappa. Roman Catholic. Lodge: KC. Insurance, Labor, Workers' compensation. Home: 58 Tyler St Westover WV 26505 Office: Hamstead Hamstead & Williams LC 170 Chancery Row Morgantown WV 26505

WILLIAMS, J(AMES) D(ENNIS), lawyer, mayor; b. Malad, Idaho, June 3, 1942; James Bland and Ardelle (Evans) W.; m. Rosemary Zaugg, Aug. 18, 1967; children: Leslie, Jennifer, Rebecca, Amanda. BS, Brigham Young U., 1966, MS, 1967; JD, Am. U., 1971. Bar: Idaho 1971, U.S. Dist. Ct. Idaho 1971, U.S. Ct. Appeals (9th cir.) 1971, U.S. Tax Ct., U.S. Ct. Claims, D.C. 1979. Dep. Idaho Atty. Gen., Boise, 1971-73; pros. atty. Franklin County, Preston, Idaho, 1974-83; ptnr. Williams & Castleton, Preston, 1975-83; sole practice Preston, 1983—; mayor City of Preston, 1984—. Mem. Idaho Water Resources Bd., 1983—. Mem. ABA, Idaho Bar Assn., Idaho Pros. Atty. Assn. (pres. 1981), Idaho Juvenile Justice (chmn. 1980-83). Democrat. Mormon. Lodge: Rotary (local pres. 1980-81). Home: 194 E Valley View Dr Preston ID 83263 Office: PO Box 191 Preston ID 83263

WILLIAMS, JAMES EDWARD, lawyer; b. Alexandria, La., Jan. 2, 1955; s. Jerrell Elbert and Doris (Jefferson) W.; m. Sharon Valencia, Dec. 28, 1979; 1 child, Tenisha Nicole. BA, N.Mex. State U., 1976, MA, 1977; JD, Georgetown U., 1980; cert., Columbia U., 1986. Bar: Minn. 1981. Contract mgr. avionics div., mem. EEO adv. council, v.p. focus div. Honeywell Inc., Mpls., 1980-81, gen. corp. atty., 1981-86, sr. counsel internat. law, 1986—. Advisor Jr. Achievement, Minnetonka, Minn., 1981-83; mem. solicitations com. United Way, Mpls., 1980-81; advisor United Way Allocations Com., Mpls., 1981-82; chmn. West Suburban Black History Month Program Com., 1982—; mem. City of Golden Valley Human Rights Commn., 1982-85. Named one of the Outstanding Young Men of Am., U.S. Jaycess, 1981, 84; recipient Black History Month Appreciation award, City of Golden Valley, 1985. Mem. ABA, Minn. Bar Assn., Minn. Minority Lawyers Assn., Delta Theta Phi Law Frat. Baptist. Lodge: Rotary (chmn. Golden Valley chpt. 1984—). Avocations: music, sports. General corporate, Private international. Office: 117 Turnpike Rd Golden Valley MN 55416

WILLIAMS, JAMES JOSEPH, lawyer; b. Detroit, Feb. 1, 1947; s. John Matthew and June Rose (Shappee) W.; m. Pamela Jeanne Boyle, July 30, 1982. BME, U. Detroit, 1970, JD, 1976. Bar: Mich., U.S. Dist. Ct. Mich. Application engr. Vickers, Inc., Troy, Mich., 1968-70; with alumni relations dept. U. Detroit, 1971-72; with tech. and corp. pub. relations dept. Ford Motor Co., Dearborn, Mich., 1972-77; assoc. Harvey, Kruse & Westen, Detroit, 1977-79, Monaghan, Campbell, LoPrete & McDonald, Bloomfield Hills, Mich., 1979—. Mem. ABA, Detroit Bar Assn., Oakland County Bar Assn. Federal civil litigation, State civil litigation, Probate. Home: 4600 Kirkcaldy Bloomfield Hills MI 48013 Office: Monaghan Campbell LoPrete McDonald 1700 N Woodward Suite A Bloomfield Hills MI 48013

WILLIAMS, JAMES WILLIAM, lawyer; b. McKenzie, Tenn., Feb. 26, 1936; s. Levi Joe and Lillie Angela (Medlin) W.; m. Shirley Jean Crawford, Dec. 23, 1956; children—Doris, Charles, John, Catherine, Michael. B.S.E.E. cum laude, Vanderbilt U., 1957; J.D. with honors, George Wash. U., 1961. Bar: Okla. 1961, U.S. Patent Office 1961, U.S. Ct. Customs and Patent Appeals 1970, U.S. Ct. Appeals (fed. cir.) 1982. Patent examiner U.S. Patent Office, Washington, 1957-60; patent solicitor Phillips Petroleum Co., Washington, 1960-61, patent atty., Bartlesville, Okla., 1961-71, sr. atty., 1971-84, assoc. gen. patent counsel, 1984-85, gen. patent counsel, 1985. Co-inventor, container and closure therefor, 1972. Mem. Little Theater Guild, Bartlesville, 1962-63; deacon Highland Park Bapt. Ch., Bartlesville, 1965—; treas. Boy Scouts Am., Bartlesville, 1970. Recipient of Merit Toastmasters, 1964; Highest Grade in Evidence Bancroft-Whitney Co., 1960. Mem. Am Intellectual Property Law Assn., Assn. Corp. Patent Counsels, Licensing Execs. Soc., Order of Coif, Delta Theta Phi (Outstanding Service award 1961). Republican. Clubs: Toastmasters, Hamilton Investment (treas.). Lodge: Masons. Patent, General corporate, Federal civil litigation. Office: Phillips Petroleum Co 208A Patent Library Bldg Bartlesville OK 74004

WILLIAMS, JERRE STOCKTON, judge; b. Denver, Aug. 21, 1916; s. Wayne Cullen and Lena (Day) W.; m. Mary Pearl Hall, May 28, 1950; children: Jerre Stockton, Shelley Hall, Stephanie Kethley. A.B., U. Denver, 1938; J.D., Columbia, 1941. Bar: Colo. 1941, Tex. 1950, U.S. Supreme Ct. 1944. Instr. U. Iowa Law Sch., 1941-42; asst. prof. U. Denver Law Sch., 1946; mem. faculty U. Tex. Law Sch., Austin, 1946-80; John B. Connally prof. civil jurisprudence U. Tex. Law Sch., 1970-80; judge U.S. Ct. Appeals Fifth Circuit, 1980—; mem. faculty Inst. Internat. and Comparative Law San Diego U., Merton Coll. Oxford (Eng.) U., 1977, Magdalen Coll., 1979, Kings Coll., London, Eng., 1981; chmn. Adminstrv. Conf. U.S., 1967-70, pub. mem., 1972-78, sr. conf. fellow, 1980—; Labor arbitrator, bd. govs. Nat. Acad. Arbitrators, 1964-67, v.p., 1974-75; chmn. Southwestern Regional Manpower Adv. Com., 1964-66; cons. Bur. Budget, 1966-67. Author: Cases and Materials on Employees Rights, 1952, The Supreme Court Speaks, 1956; Editor-in-chief: Labor Relations and the Law, 3d edit, 1965, Constitutional Analysis, 1979. Served to capt. USAF, 1942-46. Mem. Internat. Soc. Labor Law and Social Legis., ABA (winner Ross Essay contest 1963, chmn. sect. adminstrv. law 1975-76), Fed.Bar Assn., Tex. Bar Assn., Assn. Am. Law Schs. (pres. 1980). Methodist. Judicial administration. Home: 3503 Mt Barker Dr Austin TX 78731 Office: US Court Appeals 1620 M Bank Tower 221 W 6th St Austin TX 78701

WILLIAMS, JERRY JOHN, law educator, arbitrator; b. Midland, Pa., Dec. 8, 1931; s. Benjamin Harrison and Evelyn Edith (Clark) W.; m. Nola Ruth Craig, June 8, 1982; m. Adele R. Hynek, Dec. 15, 1963; children—Gina, Kelly, Mark, Danica. A.B., UCLA, 1953, J.D., 1961. Bar: Calif. 1962, U.S. Dist. Ct., U.S. Ct. Apls. (9th cir.), U.S. Supreme Ct. Sr. ptnr. Brundage, Williams & Zellmann, 1962-78; prof. law U. San Diego Law Sch., 1978—, dir. Labor Mgmt. Relations Ctr., 1978-83; arbitrator FMCS, 1978—; factfinder, arbitrator Employment Relations Bd., City of Los Angeles; mem. panel of neutrals Public Employee Relations Bd. State Calif.; mem. neutral appellate authority Employee Relations Bd. San Diego County. Mem. Am. Arbitration Assn. (arbitrator), ABA, State Bar Calif., San Diego County Bar Assn., Indsl. Relations Research Assn. (past pres. San Diego). Legal education, Labor, Labor arbitration and third party despute resolution. Home and Office: PO Box 33246 San Diego CA 92103-0420

WILLIAMS, JOHN COBB, lawyer; b. Chgo., June 11, 1930; s. Ralph Milton and Mary Mason (Cobb) W.; m. Helen Gilbert, Aug. 19, 1955; children: Holly Montague, Nancy Morrison, Sarah M. B.A., Wesleyan U., 1951; LL.B., Yale U., 1954. Bar: Ill. 1955, Fla. 1974. Assoc. firm. Sidley & Austin, Chgo., 1954-63; ptnr. Sidley & Austin, 1964—. Trustee Village of Northbrook, Ill., 1965-69, village pres., 1969-73, mem. plan commn. zoning bd. appeals, 1965-69; mem. police pension fund bd. Village of Glencoe, Ill., 1980-82; chmn. pub. safety commn. Village of Gencoe, 1982—; bd. dirs. North Suburban Assn. Health Resources, 1973, pres., 1974-75; bd. dirs. North Suburban Blood Ctr., 1973-75. Fellow Am. Coll. Probate Counsel; mem. ABA, Ill. Bar Assn. (chmn. on legis. 1975-76, chmn. estate planning, probate and trust sec. council 1984-85), Chgo. Bar Assn. (chmn. legis. com. 1969-71, chmn. com. on probate practice 1972-73). Clubs: Skokie Country (Glencoe); University, Econ, Law, Legal (Chgo.). Home: 486 Greenleaf Ave Glencoe IL 60022 Office: 1 First National Plaza Chicago IL 60603

WILLIAMS, JOHNNY JACKSON, lawyer; b. Houston, Dec. 24, 1954; s. Johnny Jackson Sr. and Frances (Mulson) W. BS, U. Houston, 1976; JD, South Tex. Coll. Law, 1980; LLM in Taxation, Boston U., 1981. Bar: Tex. 1980, U.S. Dist. Ct. (so. dist.) Tex.1981, U.S. Tax Ct. 1981, U.S. Ct. Appeals (5th cir.) 1981. Assoc. Groom. Miglicco & Gibson, Houston, 1981-82; sole practice Houston, 1982-85; ptnr. Atkinson & Williams P.C., Houston, 1985—. Mem. deed restriction com. Meml. Plaza Civic Assn., Houston, 1986—. Mem. Tex. Bar Assn. (small tax payers com. 1981—, tax sect.). Republican. Methodist. Avocations: softball, tennis, running. Personal income taxation, Corporate taxation, Consumer commercial. Office: Atkinson & Williams PC 1818 Memorial Dr Houston TX 77079

WILLIAMS, KAREN JOHNSON, lawyer; b. Orangeburg, S.C., Aug. 4, 1951; d. James G. Johnson and Marcia (Reynolds) Johnson Dantzler; m. Charles H. Williams, Dec. 27, 1968; children: Marian, Ashley, Charlie, David. BA, Columbia Coll., 1972; postgrad., U. S.C., 1973, JD cum laude, 1980. Bar: S.C. 1980, U.S. Dist. Ct. S.C. 1980, U.S. Ct. Appeals (4th cir.) 1981. Tchr. Irmo (S.C.) Mid. Sch., 1972-74, O-W High Sch., Orangeburg, 1974-76; assoc. Charles H. Williams P.A., Orangeburg, 1980—; mem. uniform simplified jury com. S.C. Bar, 1981-82, med.-legal com., 1985; mem. exec. bd. grievance commn. S.C. Supreme Ct., Columbia, 1983—, corp. law rev. com. S.C. State Senate, Columbia, 1985—. Mem. child devel. bd. First Baptist Ch., Orangeburg, planning commn.; bd. dirs. Orangeburg Area Resource Ctr., 1986—. Mem. ABA, S.C. Bar Assn., Orangeburg County Bar Assn. (co-chairperson Law Day 1981), Assn. Trial Lawyers Am., S.C. Trial Lawyers Assn., Bus. and Profl. Women Assn. (v.p., chairperson com.), Order of Wig and Robe, Order of Coif, Jr. Service League (Career Woman Yr. award 1979, 81 82). State civil litigation, Personal injury, Real property. Home: Rt 2 Box 110 Orangeburg SC 29115 Office: Charles H Williams PA 370 Saint Paul St NE Orangeburg SC 29115

WILLIAMS, KATHRYN DIGGS, lawyer; b. Alexandria, Va., Jan. 22, 1930; d. John Thurman and Sarah Virginia (Nicklin) Diggs; m. Francis Aloysius Williams, Jr., Mar. 10, 1972. B.A., Am. U., 1951; M.S., Simmons Coll., 1953; J.D. cum laude, Washington Coll. Law, 1961. Bar: Md., 1961, U.S. Dist. Ct. Md., 1969, U.S. Supreme Ct. 1969. Law clk. Circuit Ct. Montgomery County (Md.), 1960-62; ptnr. Bowen & Diggs, Wheaton, Md., 1962—. Mem. County Council for Montgomery County, 1962-66, pres., 1965-66. Mem. ABA, Bar Assn. Md., Bar Assn. Montgomery County. Republican. Episcopalian. Club: Manor. Family and matrimonial, Personal injury, Probate. Home: 14701 Carrolton Rd Rockville MD 20853 Office: Wheaton Plaza Office Bldg 703 Wheaton MD 20902

WILLIAMS, LAWRENCE DWIGHT, lawyer; b. Los Angeles, May 11, 1938; s. Dwight Nicolas and Maxine Alymyra (Webb) W.; m. Shera Jean Gazay, June 22, 1963; children—Laura, Mary, Elizabeth, Matthew. Student U. Redlands, 1956-57; B.A., Calif. State U.-Long Beach, 1960; LL.B., UCLA, 1963. Bar: Calif. 1964, U.S. Dist. Ct. (cent. dist.) Calif. 1964. With Williams Walsh & Sullivan and predecessor firms, Los Angeles, 1964—, ptnr., 1969—. Alpha Kappa Psi scholar, 1960. Mem. Los Angeles County Bar Assn., Santa Monica Bay Bar Assn., Blue Key, Sigma Pi. Republican. Presbyterian. Club: Marina City (Marina del Rey, Calif.). Estate planning, Probate, General corporate. Office: Williams Walsh and Sullivan 10960 Wilshire Blvd Suite 1808 Los Angeles CA 90024

WILLIAMS, LEE DWAIN, lawyer; b. Enid, Okla., Sept. 2, 1950; s. Lawrence and Wilma Jean (Richards) W. BA Polit. Sci., U. Calif., Santa Barbara, 1974; JD, UCLA, 1977. Bar: Calif. 1977, U.S. Dist. Ct. (cen. dist.) Calif. 1977. Assoc. Irell & Manella, Los Angeles, 1973-79, Riordan, Caps, Carbone McKinzie, Los Angeles, 1979-84; sole practice Law Offices of Lee D. Williams, Los Angeles, 1984—; bd. dirs. CCR Video Corp., Los Angeles. Trustee Children's Inst. Internat., Los Angeles, 1979-84. Avocations: skiing, reading, theatre. General corporate, Federal civil litigation, State civil litigation. Office: 12100 Wilshire Blvd Suite 1550 Los Angeles CA 90403

WILLIAMS, LON RAYBURN, JR., lawyer; b. Dallas, Apr. 29, 1947; s. Lon Rayburn and Virginia Ruth (Vaughan) W. BA, So. Meth. U., 1970; MS in Fgn. Service, Georgetown U., 1976, JD, 1977. Bar: Tex. 1977, D.C. 1978. Sr. counsel The Southland Corp., Dallas, 1980—. Mem. ABA, Tex. Bar Assn., Dallas Bar Assn. Labor, General practice. Home: 5106 Junius Dallas TX 75214 Office: The Southland Corp 2828 N Haskell Ave Dallas TX 75204

WILLIAMS, LYMAN NEIL, JR., lawyer; b. Charlotte, N.C., Mar. 22, 1936; s. Lyman Neil and Thelma (Peterson) W.; m. Sue Sigmon, Aug. 23, 1958; children—Fred R., Susan S. A.B., Duke U., 1958, J.D., 1961. Bar: Ga. 1962, U.S. Dist. Ct. (no. dist.) Ga. 1977, U.S. Ct. Appeals (11th cir.) 1977. Assoc. Alston & Bird (and predecessor firm), Atlanta, 1961-65, ptnr., 1966—, mng. ptnr., 1984—; dir. Nat. Data Corp., Atlanta, Printpack, Inc., Atlanta. Chmn. bd. trustees Duke U., 1983—, trustee, 1980—; chmn. bd. trustees Vasser Woolley Found., Atlanta, 1975—, Leadership Atlanta, 1976-80; trustee Brevard Music Ctr., 1977-86, Presbyn. Ch. USA Found., N.Y. and Charlotte, 1983—. Research Triangle Inst., 1983—; bd. dirs. Atlanta Symphony Orch., 1970-76, 84—, vice pres., 1986—; Central Atlanta Progress, 1984—. Mem. Am. Law Inst., ABA, State Bar Ga., Lawyers Club Atlanta, Phi Beta Kappa, Omicron Delta Kappa. Clubs: Piedmont Driving, Commerce (Atlanta); University (N.Y.C.). Contracts commercial, General corporate, Securities. Home: 3 Nacoochee Pl NW Atlanta GA 30305 Office: Alston & Bird 35 Broad St Atlanta GA 30335

WILLIAMS, MARCUS DOYLE, judge, lawyer; b. Nashville, Oct. 24, 1952; s. John Freelander and Pansy (Doyle) W.; m. Carmen Myrie, May 21, 1983; 1 child, Aaron Doyle. BA with honors, Fisk U., 1973; JD, Cath. U. of Am., 1977. Bar: Va. 1977, D.C. 1978. Asst. commonwealth's atty. County of Fairfax, Fairfax, Va., 1978-80, asst. county atty., 1980-87; dist. ct. judge County of Fairfax, Va., 1987—; lectr. bus. and legal studies, George Mason U., Fairfax, 1980—; instr. pvt. investigators, N.Va. Community Coll., Fairfax, 1979; mem. Fairfax Criminal Justice Adv. Bd., 1980-81. Book reviewer for ABA Jour., 1981-84. Thomas J. Watson Found. fellow, 1977. Mem. ABA, Fairfax Bar Assn. (CLE com., vice-chmn. 1986—), Am. Bus. Law Assn., Brit. Inst. Internat. and Comparative Law, Phi Alpha Delta, Beta Kappa Chi. Lutheran. Government contracts and claims, Public utilities, Legal education. Home: 9005 Stoneleigh Ct Fairfax VA 22031 Office: Office of County Atty 4110 Chain Bridge Rd Fairfax VA 22030

WILLIAMS, MICHAEL EDWARD, lawyer; b. Ft. Worth, Aug. 10, 1955; s. Jerrol Evans and Helen Louise (Hoffner) W.; m. Jackie Ann Gordiner, Dec. 30, 1978; children: Margaret Eileen, James Andrew. BA, U. Calif., Riverside, 1977; JD, U. San Diego, 1980. Bar: Calif. 1980, U.S. Dist. Ct. (so. dist.) Calif. 1980, U.S. Tax Ct. 1981, U.S. Dist. Ct. (ea. and cen. dists.) Calif. 1982, U.S. Dist. Ct. (no. dist.) Calif. 1985. Assoc. Jamison & McFadden, Solana Beach, Calif., 1980-86, Dorazio, Barnhorst & Bonar, San Diego, 1986; sole practice Encinitas, Calif., 1987—. Atty. pro bono Community Resource Ctr., Encinitas, Calif., 1984—. Mem. ABA, San Diego County Bar Assn. Democrat. Presbyterian. State civil litigation, Bankruptcy, Contracts commercial. Office: 610 2d St Encinitas CA 92024

WILLIAMS, MICHAEL PETER ANTHONY, lawyer; b. Bridgeport, Conn., Sept. 1, 1945; s. Francis P.A. and Elsie Millicent (Blight) W.; m. Ethel Anderson Hoffman, Apr. 18, 1970; children—Greyson P., Trevor H., Meredith S., Tristan àBeckett. A.B. in English, Boston U., 1968; J.D., Cumberland Law Sch., 1974. Bar: Conn. 1974, U.S. Dist. Ct. Conn. 1974, U.S. Ct. Appeals (2d cir.) 1979. Assoc., Marsh, Day & Calhoun, Bridgeport, 1974-79, ptnr., 1980—; counsel Pinewood Lake Assn., Trumbull, Conn., 1982—. Mem. Trumbull Town Council, 1981-83, Trumbull Bd. Edn., 1983—, chmn., 1986—; bd. dirs. Coop. Ednl. Services, Norwalk, Conn., 1984-86 . Mem. ABA, Conn. Bar Assn., Bridgeport Bar Assn. Republican. Contracts commercial, Real property, Probate. Home: 362 Putting Green Rd Trumbull CT 06611 Office: Marsh Day & Calhoun 2507 Post Rd Southport CT 06490 also: 955 Main St Bridgeport CT 06604

WILLIAMS, MICHAEL STEPHEN, lawyer; b. St. Louis, Nov. 9, 1948; s. Francis Herbert and Minta Louise (Johnson) W.; m. Margaret Barbara Leicht, Jan. 7, 1981; children: Michael Jr., Elizabeth , Allison. BA, St. Louis U., 1977, JD, 1980. Bar: Mo. 1980, Ill. 1980, U.S. Ct. Appeals (8th cir.) 1980. Police officer St. Louis Police Dept., 1971-80; assoc. Haley, Fredrickson & Walsh, St. Louis, 1980-85; ptnr. Cueto, Daley, Williams & Moore, Belleville, Ill., 1985—. Served as cpl. USMC, 1967-69, Vietnam. Mem. Mo. Bar Assn., Ill. Bar Assn., Assn. Trial Lawyers Am. Democrat. Roman Catholic. Personal injury. Office: Cueto Daley Williams & Moore 123 W Main Belleville IL 62220

WILLIAMS, NANCY ONDROVIK, lawyer; b. Weaver, S.D., Nov. 1, 1952; d. Frank and Jane (Akin) Ondrovik; m. Paul K. Williams, Aug. 4, 1979; children: Jennifer Morgan, Brittany Jane. BS in Psychology, Tex. A&M U., 1974; JD, U. Tex., 1977. Bar: Tex. 1977, U.S. Dist. Ct. (no. dist.) Tex. 1977. Assoc. Stark, Barnhart & Moore, Gainesville, Tex., 1978-79; asst. dist. atty. Cooke, Jack & Wise Co., Gainesville, 1979-80; assoc. Henry & Hatcher, Gainesville, 1980-81; sole practice Gainesville, 1981-85; ptnr. Williams, Ledbetter & Ledbetter, Gainesville, 1985-86; prin. Williams & Assocs., Gainesville, 1986—; atty. City of Gainesville, 1986—; bd. dirs. Group 5, Inc., Gainesville. Mem. Tex. Bar Assn. (quality of life com.), Cooke County Bar Assn. (pres. 1980-82), Tex. Young Lawyers Assn. (co-chmn. legal rigts of battered women com, affiliates com.), Young Lawyers Assn. Cooke County (pres. 1986—), Tex. City Atty. Assn. (bd. v.p. friends of family-victim assistance 1986—), League of Women Voters (pres. 1983-85), Bus. and Profl. Womens Club (pres. 1982-83), Nat. Inst. Mcpl. Legal Officers, C.

of C. (ambassador Gold Coat 1985—). Democrat. Methodist. Avocations: gardening, target shooting. Family and matrimonial, Local government, State civil litigation. Home: 306 Fairfield Dr Gainesville TX 76240 Office: Williams & Assocs PO Drawer 510 Gainesville TX 76240

WILLIAMS, NORMAN CHARLES, lawyer; b. Shirley, Mass., July 20, 1952; s. Charles William and Barbara Lucille (James) W.; m. Lucy Totten, May 28, 1985. BA, U. Colo., 1974; JD, Yale U., 1979. Bar: Vt. 1981, U.S. Dist. Ct. Vt. 1981, U.S. Ct. Appeals (2d cir.) 1983, U.S. Supreme Ct. 1985. Assoc. Coudert Freres, Paris, 1980-81, Gravel & Shea, Burlington, Vt., 1981—. Author: The Unlovely Child, 1985. Mem. Common Cause, Vt., 1982—. Lowell fellow, 1979-80. Mem. Vt. Bar Assn. Federal civil litigation, State civil litigation. Home: PO Box 309 North Ferrisburgh VT 05473 Office: Gravel & Shea PO Box 1049 Burlington VT 05402

WILLIAMS, PERCY DON, lawyer; b. Dallas, Sept. 19, 1922; s. Percy Don and Frances (Worrill) W.; m. Helen Lucille Brunsdale, Aug. 4, 1954; children—Anne Lucy, Margaret Frances, Elizabeth Helen. B.A. with honors, So. Methodist U., 1942, M.A., 1943; LL.B. magna cum laude, Harvard, 1946. Bar: Tex. 1951. Instr. So. Meth. U. Law Sch., 1946-47; asst. prof., then assoc. prof. U. Tex. Law Sch., Austin, 1947-49; lectr. U. Va. Law Sch., 1951; law clk. to justice Tom C. Clark U.S. Supreme Ct., 1949-51; pvt. practice Houston, 1952—; master dist. ct. Harris County, Tex., 1980—. Contbr. articles to legal jours. Mem. Am., Fed., Houston bar assns., Am. Law Inst., Am. Judicature Soc., State Bar Tex., Houston Bar. Assn., Phi Beta Kappa, Order of Coif, Pi Sigma Alpha, Tau Kappa Alpha, Kappa Sigma. Clubs: Houston (Houston), Plaza. General corporate, Contracts commercial, General practice. Home: 31 Briar Hollow Ln Houston TX 77027 Office: 5685 Allied Bank Plaza Houston TX 77002

WILLIAMS, QUINN PATRICK, lawyer; b. Evergreen Park, Ill., May 6, 1949; s. William Albert and Jeanne Marie (Quinlan) W.; m. Linda Irene Prather, Apr. 21, 1979; children—Michael Ryan, Mark Reed. B.B.A., U. Wis., 1972; J.D., U. Ariz., 1974. Bar: Ariz. 1975, N.Y. 1984, U.S. Dist. Ct. Ariz. 1976. Vice pres., sec., gen. counsel Combined Communications Corp., Phoenix, 1975-80; v.p., sec., gen. counsel Swensen's Ice Cream Co., Phoenix, 1980-83; sr. v.p. legal and adminstrn. Swensen's Inc., Phoenix, 1983-86; of counsel Winston & Strawn, Phoenix, 1985-87, ptnr., 1987—. Vice chmn., treas. Combined Communications Polit. Action Com., Phoenix, 1976-80. Served with USAR, 1967-73. Mem. ABA, Maricopa County Bar Assn., N.Y. Bar Assn., State Bar Ariz., Internat. Franchise Assn., Phi Alpha Delta. Republican. Roman Catholic. General corporate, Real property, Securities. Home: 8547 Woodland Ct Scottsdale AZ 85258 Office: Winston & Strawn 3200 N Central Suite 2300 Phoenix AZ 85012

WILLIAMS, RALPH ROGER, lawyer; b. Phenix City, Ala., Nov. 21, 1918; s. Cary Arthur and Elizabeth (Formby) W.; m. Beatrice Hill, June 14, 1942; children: Roger, Cary, Craig, Locke. AB in Journalism, U. Ga., 1941, LLB, 1947; MA, Syracuse U., 1945; LLM, Stanford U., 1948; LLD (hon.), Atlanta Law Sch., 1960. Bar: Ga. 1946, Ala. 1952. Prof. law U. Ala., Tuscaloosa, 1949-52; ptnr. Williams & Williams P.C., Tuscaloosa, 1953—; dir. industrial relations State of Ala., Montgomery, 1959-63. Author: Standerd Ga. Practice, 1955, Tenn. Workmen;s Compensation, 1952, Williams Ala. Workmen's Compensation, 1962, Williams Ala. Evidence, 1967. Del. Nat. Dem. Conv., Chgo., 1956. Served to lt. USMC, 1940-45. Mem. Nat. Acad. Arbitrators (v.p., bd. dirs.), Nat. Labor Mgmt. Found. (pres., bd. dirs. 1965—). Presbyterian. Lodge: Kiwanis (pres., lt. gov. Tuscaloosa). Office: Williams & Williams PC 2628 8th St Tuscaloosa AL 35403

WILLIAMS, RICHARD D., lawyer; b. Los Angeles, Aug. 30, 1946; s. Alfred Curry and Joanne (Dessert) W.; m. Brenda Spriggs, July 25, 1983; children: Alison, Christine, Darren. BA, Wash. State U., 1969; JD, UCLA, 1973. Bar: Calif., U.S. Dist. Ct. (cen. dist.) Calif., U.S. Ct. Appeals (9th cir.). Ptnr. Finley, Kumble, Wagner, Manatt, Phelps, Rothenberg & Tunney, Los Angeles, 1974-83, 1984—. Bd. editors UCLA Law Rev., 1972-73. Mem. ABA (co-chmn. environ. com. litigation sect. 1986—), Calif. Bar Assn., Los Angeles County Bar Assn., Assn. Bus. Trial Lawyers, Practicing Law Inst. (chmn. bad faith litigation program 1986—). Republican. Federal civil litigation, Insurance, Environment. Office: Finley Kumble Wagner et al 9100 Wilshire Blvd East Tower Beverly Hills CA 90212

WILLIAMS, RICHARD LEROY, federal judge; b. Morrisville, Va., Apr. 6, 1923; s. Wilcie Edward and Minnie Mae (Brinkley) W.; m. Eugenia Kellogg, Sept. 11, 1948; children—Nancy Williams Davies, R. Gregory, Walter L., Gwendolyn. LLB, U. Va., 1951. Bar: Va. 1951. Ptnr. McGuire, Woods & Battle and predecessor firms, 1951-72; judge Cir. Ct. City of Richmond, 1972-76; ptnr. McGuire, Woods & Battle, 1976-80; judge U.S. Dist. Ct., Richmond, Va., 1980—. Served to 2d lt., USAAF, 1940-45. Fellow Am. Coll. Trial Lawyers; mem. Va. State Bar, Va. Bar Assn., Richmond Bar Assn. Office: US Dist Ct PO Box 2-AD Richmond VA 23205

WILLIAMS, ROBERT JENE, leasing company executive; b. Darby, Pa., Oct. 30, 1931; s. Joslyn Justus and Dolores Marie (Dugan) W.; m. Shirley Geraldine Fiedler, Aug. 8, 1953; children: Robin Jeanne, Sara Ann. B.S., Ursinus Coll., 1953; J.D., U. Pa., 1956. Bar: N.J. 1957, Pa. 1959, Ill. 1973. Asso. firm Bleakly, Stockwell & Zink, Camden, N.J., 1956-58; atty., asst. gen. atty. Reading Co., Phila., 1958-69; gen. counsel, sec. Trailer Train Co., Phila., 1969-71, Chgo., 1971—; v.p. Trailer Train Co., 1975—. Mem. ABA, Ill. Bar Assn., Chgo. Bar Assn., Assn. Transp. Practitioners, SAR, Nat. Social Scis. Honors Soc., Mayflower Soc., Soc. of Friends. Club: Metropolitan (Chgo.). General corporate. Home: 1349 Woodland Dr Deerfield IL 60015 Office: 101 N Wacker Dr Chicago IL 60606

WILLIAMS, ROGER PAUL, lawyer; b. Buffalo, June 30, 1939; s. Rowland Phillip and Martha (Borscharding) W.; m. Patricia Anne Ingavo; children: Erika Kristen, Greta Leigh. BA, SUNY, Buffalo, 1962, JD, 1965. Ptnr. Stein & Dittman, Buffalo, 1968-72; asst. U.S. atty. Dept. Justice (we. dist. N.Y.), Buffalo, 1972-78, chief criminal div., 1978-81, 1st asst. U.S. atty., 1981, 82-86, U.S. atty., 1981-82, 86—. Pres. Nardin Council, Buffalo, 1984. Mem. Erie County Bar Assn. Republican. Club: Buffalo Yacht (bd. dirs. 1982-83). Avocations: tennis, racquetball. Office: We Dist NY US Atty's Office 502 US Courthouse 68 Court St Buffalo NY 14202 *

WILLIAMS, RONALD DOHERTY, lawyer; b. New Haven, Apr. 6, 1927; s. Richard Hugh and Ethel W. (Nelson) W.; m. Laura Costarelli, Aug. 25, 1951; children—Craig F., Ronald D., Ellen A., Jane E. B.A., U. Va., 1951, LL.B., 1954. Bar: Conn. 1954. Assoc., Pullman, Comley, Bradley & Reeves, Bridgeport, Conn., 1954-60, ptnr., 1960—; atty. state trial referee, 1984—; Selectman, Town of Easton (Conn.), 1975-85, justice of the peace, 1977—, town atty., 1985—. v.p. Bridgeport Area Found.; mem. adv. com. U. Bridgeport Law Sch., 1982—; mem. statewide Grievance Com., 1985—. Served with AC, U.S. Army, 1945-46. Fellow Am. Coll. Trial Lawyers; mem. ABA, Conn. Bar Assn. (bd. govs. 1975-78), Bridgeport Bar Assn. (pres. 1975), Conn. Def. Lawyers Assn. (pres. 1984-85), Am. Bd. Trial Advs. Republican. Roman Catholic. Club: Algonquin (Bridgeport). Personal injury, Federal civil litigation, State civil litigation. Home: 14 Newman Dr Easton CT 06612 Office: 855 Main St Bridgeport CT 06604

WILLIAMS, RONALD PAUL, lawyer; b. Tulsa, June 28, 1947; s. Donald Paul and Reon Bessie (Thomason) W.; m. Judy Ann Seivers, May 25, 1968 (div. Apr. 1984); children: Heather Ann, Brian Paul; m. Barbara Susan Wehby, Nov. 9, 1984; children: Amy Katherine Paul, Marianne Christine Paul. BA in Polit. Sci., Southwestern Coll., Winfield, Kans., 1974; JD, Washburn U., 1977. Bar: Kans. 1977, U.S. Dist. Ct. Kans. 1977, U.S. Dist. Ct. (we dist.) Mo. 1986, U.S. Ct. Appeals (10th cir.) 1980. Assoc. Shaw, Hergenreter, Quarnstrom & Wright, Topeka, 1977-80, McDonald, Tinker, Skaer, Quinn & Herrington, Wichita, Kans., 1980-84, Morrison, Hecker, Curtis, Kuder & Parrish, Wichita, 1984—; instr. Nat. Inst. for Trial Advocacy, 1982—, Kans. Coll. Advocacy, Topeka, 1980—. Served with USAF, 1965-69. Mem. Nat. Transp. and Safety Bd. Bar Assn. (regional v.p. 1986-87), Def. Research Inst., Kans. Bar Assn. (pres. aviation sect. 1984, 85), Kans. Assn. Def. Counsel (sec., treas. 1986-87). Democrat. Avocations: flying, golf, baseball coaching. Personal injury, Insurance, Federal civil litigation. Home: 1644 Mars Wichita KS 67212 Office: Morrison Hecker et al 150 N Main St Suite 600 Wichita KS 67202

WILLIAMS, RONALD WAYNE, SR., lawyer; b. Danville, Va., Aug. 27, 1936; s. Ebbie H. and Lillia S. (Shuping) W.; m. LuRae Baker, Sept. 1, 1958; children: Ronald Wayne Jr., Mark T., David M., Stacey R., Andrea L. LLB, U. Richmond, 1962. Bar: Va. 1962. Ptnr. Warren, Parker, Williams, Stilwell & Morrison, Danville, 1962—. Mayor City of Danville, 1970-72; mem. City Council, Danville, 1970-77, sch. bd. Pittsylvania County, Chathan, Va., 1984—; atty. Pittsylvania County, 1977-79;. Mem. ABA, Va. Bar Assn., Am. Judicature Soc., Va. Trial Lawyers Assn. Methodist. Avocation: farming. Criminal, Family and matrimonial, Personal injury. Home: Rt 1 Box 1525 Cascade VA 24069 Office: Warren Parker Williams Stilwell & Morrison 317 Patton St Danville VA 24541

WILLIAMS, SPENCER M., dist. judge; b. Reading, Mass., Feb. 24, 1922; s. Theodore Ryder and Anabel (Hutchison) W.; m. Kathryn Bramlage, Aug. 20, 1943; children—Carol Marcia (Mrs. James B. Garvey), Peter, Spencer, Clark, Janice, Diane. A.B., U. Calif. at Los Angeles, 1943; postgrad., Hastings Coll. Law, 1946; J.D., U. Calif. at Berkeley, 1948. Bar: Calif. bar 1949, U.S. Supreme Ct. bar 1952. Asso. firm Beresford & Adams, San Jose, Calif., 1949, Rankin, O'Neal, Center, Luckhardt, Bonney, Marlais & Lund, San Jose, Evans, Jackson & Kennedy, Sacramento; atty. office county counsel Santa Clara County, 1949-50, 52-55; county counsel 1955-67; adminstr. Calif. Health and Welfare Agy., Sacramento, 1967-69; judge U.S. Dist. Ct. No. Dist. Calif., San Francisco, 1969—; County exec. pro tem, Santa Clara County; adminstr. Calif. Youth and Adult Corrections Agy., Sacramento; sec. Calif. Human Relations Agy., Sacramento, 1967-70. Chmn. San Jose Christmas Seals Drive, 1953, San Jose Muscular Dystrophy Drive, 1953, 54; team capt. fund raising drive San Jose YMCA, 1960; co-chmn. indsl. sect. fund raising drive Alexian Bros. Hosp., San Jose, 1964; team capt. fund raising drive San Jose Hosp.; mem. com. on youth and govt. YMCA, 1967-68; Candidate for Calif. Assembly, 1954, Calif. Atty. Gen., 1966, 70; Bd. dirs. San Jose Better Bus. Bur., 1955-66, Boys City Boys' Club, San Jose, 1965-67; pres. trustees Santa Clara County Law Library, 1955-66. Served with USNR, 1943-46; to lt. comdr. JAG Corps USNR, 1950-52, PTO. Named San Jose Man of Year, 1954. Mem. ABA, Calif. Bar Assn. (vice chmn. com. on publicly employed attys. 1962-63), Santa Clara County Bar Assn., Sacramento Bar Assn., Calif. Dist. Attys. Assn. (pres. 1963-64), Nat. Assn. County Civil Attys. (pres. 1963-64), Ninth Circuit Dist. Judges Assn. (pres. 1981-83), Fed. Judges Assn. (pres. 1982—), Theta Delta Chi. Club: Kiwanian. Jurisprudence. Office: 280 S 1st St Suite 5150 San Jose CA 95113

WILLIAMS, STEPHEN FAIN, federal judge; b. N.Y.C., Sept. 23, 1936; s. Charles Dickerman and Virginia (Fain) W.; m. Faith Morrow, June 11, 1966; children: Susan, Geoffrey Fain, Sarah Margot Nu, Timothy Dwight, Nicholas Morrow. B.A., Yale U., 1958; J.D., Harvard U., 1961. Bar: N.Y. 1962, Colo. 1977. Assoc. Debevoise, Plimpton, Lyons & Gates, N.Y.C., 1962-66; asst. U.S. atty. So. Dist. N.Y., 1966-69; asst. prof. law U. Colo., Boulder, 1969-77; prof. U. Colo., 1977-86; judge U.S. Ct. Appeals (D.C. cir.), Washington, 1986—; vis. prof. UCLA, 1975-76; vis. prof., fellow in law and econs. U. Chgo., 1979-80; vis. William L. Hutchison prof. energy law So. Meth. U., 1983-84; cons. Adminstrv. Conf. U.S., 1974-76, FTC, 1983-85; mem. Boulder Area Growth Study Commn., 1972-73. Contbr. articles to law revs., mags. Served with U.S. Army, 1961-62. Mem. Am. Law Inst., ABA. Administrative and regulatory, Nuclear power, Oil and gas leasing. Office: US Courthouse Washington DC 20001

WILLIAMS, STEPHEN LEE, lawyer; b. Terre Haute, Ind., Jan. 10, 1949; s. Jess Madison and Donna Lee (Milner) W.; m. Carole Lynn Jones, June 7, 1971; children—Jason, Zachary. B.S., Ind. State U., 1971; J.D. magna cum laude, Ind. U.-Indpls., 1974. Bar: Ind. 1974, U.S. Dist. Ct. (no. and so. dists.) Ind. 1974, U.S. Ct. Appeals (7th cir.) 1983; cert. civil trial adv. Nat. Bd. Trial Advocacy, 1984. Ptnr. Snouffer, Haller & Colvin, Fort Wayne, Ind., 1974-82, Mann, Chaney, Johnson, Goodwin & Williams, Terre Haute, 1984—. Instr., Ind. U.-Purdue U., Fort Wayne, 1978-81. Mem. Leadership Terre Haute, 1984; pres. bd. dirs. MLK Montessori Sch., 1980-81, United Way Allen County, 1980-81. Corpus Juris Secundum scholar Ind. U. Law Sch., 1974. Mem. Assn. Trial Lawyers Am., Ind. Trial Lawyers, Ind. Bar Assn., Vigo County Bar Assn., Sigma Pi Alpha. Methodist. Club: Wabash Valley Roadrunners. Lodges: Sertoma, Elks. State civil litigation, Federal civil litigation. Home: 180 Deming Ln Terre Haute IN 47803 Office: Mann Chaney Johnson Goodwin & Williams PO Box 1643 Terre Haute IN 47808

WILLIAMS, STEVEN HENRY, lawyer; b. Parris Island, S.C., Apr. 19, 1947; s. Herman Ray and Helen Louise (Cryts) W.; m. Johannah Cornell, Aug. 4, 1971; children—Ryan Alexander, Joseph Cornell, Michael Andrew. B.A. in Polit. Sci., Ariz. State U., 1968, J.D., 1971. Bar: Ariz. 1971, U.S. Ct. Mil. Appeals, 1971, U.S. Supreme Ct. 1975, U.S. Tax Ct., 1982. Assoc. Norling, Rolle, King & Oeser, Phoenix, 1975-78, ptnr. Norling, Rolle, Oeser, Williams, 1979—; chmn. fee arbitration panel State Bar Ariz., 1981, counsel to local adminstrv. com., 1982. Served to capt. JAGC, U.S. Army, 1971-75. Decorated Meritorious Service medal. Mem. ABA, Maricopa County Bar Assn., Assn. Trial Lawyers Am. Republican. Roman Catholic. State civil litigation, Federal civil litigation, General corporate. Office: 7101 N 1st ST Phoenix AZ 85020-4801

WILLIAMS, STEWART DORIAN, lawyer; b. Lima, Peru, Feb. 7, 1954; came to U.S., 1964.; s. Owen Foster and Gloria (Sangines) W.; m. Mary Stirling, June 9, 1984 (div. Apr. 1986). Student, U. S.C., 1974; BS, Fla. Internat. U., 1979; JD, Calif. Western Sch. Law, 1982. Bar: Fla. 1982, U.S. Dist. Ct. (so. dist.) Fla. 1984, U.S. Ct. Appeals (11th cir.) 1984. Asst. pub. defender Dade County, Miami, Fla., 1982-85; assoc. Adams, Hunter, Angones et al, Miami, 1985—. Mem. Assn. Trial Lawyer Am., Acad. Fla. Trial Lawyers, Dade County Bar Assn. Democrat. Roman Catholic. Personal injury, State civil litigation, Criminal. Home: 4151 Park Ave Coconut Grove FL 33133 Office: Adams Hunter Angones et al 66 W Flagler Miami FL 33130

WILLIAMS, STUART ALAN, lawyer; b. Brownsville, Pa., Nov. 18, 1953; s. Max J. and Sylvia S. Williams; m. Francine W. Williams; 1 child, Louis Samuel; B.A. with highest distinction, Pa. State U., 1975; J.D., Georgetown U., 1978. Bar: Pa. 1978, U.S. Dist. Ct. (we. dist.) Pa. 1978. Ptnr. Eckert, Seamans, Cherin & Mellott, Pitts., 1978—; adj. prof. labor law Duquesne U. Sch. Law, Pitts., 1980—. pres. Meadows Real Estate, Inc., 1986—. Mem. Pa. Bar Assn. (sec.-treas. labor law sect. 1981, vice chairperson 1982), ABA (com. on devel. law under Nat. Labor Relations Act), Phi Delta Phi, Phi Beta Kappa, Phi Kappa Phi, Omicron Delta Kappa. Assoc. editor The Tax Lawyer; contbr. articles to legal jours. Club: Washington Trotting Assn. (pres. 1986—). Labor, General corporate. Office: Eckert Seamans Cherin & Mellott 600 Grant St 42d Floor Pittsburgh PA 15219

WILLIAMS, THOMAS ARTHUR, lawyer; b. Wilmington, N.C., Sept. 26, 1943; s. Louis C. and Mary Alice (Elmore) W.; m. Karen Barbara Hoster, Feb. 2, 1978; children—Morgan, Duncan; stepchildren—Quentin, Marady. B.S. In Journalism, Okla. State U., 1966; J.D.S., U. Okla., 1972. Bar: Okla. 1972, U.S. Dist. Ct. (we. dist.) Okla. 1972, U.S. Dist. Ct. (ea. and no. dists.) Okla. 1973, U.S. Ct. Appeals (10th cir.) 1973. Assoc. Jones, Atkinson, Williams, Bane & Klingenberg, Oklahoma City, 1972-73, Jones, Williams, Bane, Ray & Klingenberg, Oklahoma City, 1973-74; owner Bane & Williams, Oklahoma City, 1974-76; ptnr. Kratz, Thomas, Williams & Patton, Oklahoma City, 1976-78; ptnr. Drummond, Patton, Williams & Tullius, Oklahoma City, 1978-79; ptnr. Williams, Patton, Patton & Hyde, Oklahoma City, 1981-83; prof. corrections law Oscar Rose Jr. Coll., 1976-78; judge Temporary Ct. Appeals 124, Okla., 1982. Mem. Okla. Bar Assn. (exec. bd. family law sect. 1987), Oklahoma County Bar Assn., Okla. Criminal Def. Lawyers Assn., ABA, Phi Delta Phi. Family and matrimonial, Probate, Personal injury. Office: 6242 N Western Suite 200 Oklahoma City OK 73118

WILLIAMS, THOMAS ASHURST, lawyer; b. Chattanooga, Dec. 9, 1939; s. Eugene Wismond and Ann (Ashurst) W.; m. Connie Marie McDaniel, Dec. 26, 1970; children: Tom Jr., Mary. BS, U. Chattanooga, 1961; JD, U. Tenn., 1963. Bar: Tenn. 1964, U.S. Dist. Ct. (ea. dist.) Tenn. 1966, U.S. Ct. Mil. Appeals 1966, U.S. Ct. Appeals (6th cir.) 1966. Asst. U.S. atty. U.S. Dept. of Justice, 1966-69, atty., 1969—; ptnr. Leitner, Warner, Moffitt, Williams, Dooley, Carpenter & Napolitan, Chattanooga, 1973—. Deacon 1st Bapt. Ch., Chattanooga, 1983. Served to 1st lt. U.S. Army S.C., 1964-66; lt. col. USAR JAGC, 1983. Mem. Tenn. Bar Assn., Chattanooga Bar Assn. (pres. elect 1985-86, pres. 1986-87), Fed. Ins. and Corp. Counsel, Tenn. Def. Lawyers Assn., U. Tenn. Nat. Alumni Assn. (v.p. 1974). Democrat. Club: Civitan. Federal civil litigation, State civil litigation, Insurance. Home: 4748 Sussex Ln Chattanooga TN 37421 Office: 801 Broad St 3d Floor Pioneer Bank Chattanooga TN 37402

WILLIAMS, THOMAS SCOTT, lawyer; b. Cadillac, Mich., Aug. 15, 1957; s. Albert Arthur and Frances Margaret (Rekeny) W. BA, Kalamazoo Coll., 1979; JD, Am. U., 1982. Bar: D.C. 1982. Asst. counsel to insp. gen. U.S. Small Bus. Adminstrn., Washington, 1982-85, atty. advisor office of gen. counsel, 1985—. Mem. ABA, D.C. Bar Assn., Phi Delta Phi. Republican. Roman Catholic. Avocation: tennis. Administrative and regulatory, Government contracts and claims. Home: 5503 Northfield Rd Bethesda MD 20817 Office: US Small Bus Adminstrn 1441 L St NW Room 706 Washington DC 20416

WILLIAMS, W. CLARK, JR., law educator; b. Nov. 10, 1949; married; 2 children. BA in Polit. Sci. cum laude, Brown U., 1971; JD, Vanderbilt U., 1974. Bar: Tex. 1974, U.S. Dist. Ct. (no. dist.) Tex. 1975, U.S. Ct. Appeals (5th cir.) 1976, Va. 1983. Assoc. Strasburger & Price, Dallas, 1974-79; prof. law T.C. Williams Sch. Law, U. Richmond (Va.), 1979—. Assoc. editor Vanderbilt Law Rev., 1974. Chmn., reporter Supreme Ct. Com. to Draft Rules of Procedure for Ct. Appeals Va., 1981-84, Supreme Ct. Com. to Study Appeal by Trial de Novo in Va., 1985; mem. Henrico County Mental Health and Retardation Community Services Bd., 1982-86, chmn. 1984; adminstrv. bd. dirs. Reveille United Meth. Ch.; counsel to com. on legal relations Va. Conf. United Meth. Ch. Named one of Outstanding Young Men Am. Nat. Jaycees, 1980, 82; recipient Disting. Educator award U. Richmond, 1982. Mem. ABA, Va. Bar Assn., Va. Assn. Def. Attys. (exec. dir., editor quarterly 1982—). Lodge: Rotary. Home: 4709 N Lakefront Dr Glen Allen VA 23060 Office: Univ Richmond TC Williams Sch Law Richmond VA 23173

WILLIAMS, WALTER WAYLON, lawyer, pecan grower; b. Gause, Tex., Nov. 12, 1933; s. Jesse Nathaniel and Lola Fay (Matthews) W.; m. Velmalene Von Gonten, Mar. 6, 1953; children—Diana Lee, Virginia Marie. B.B.A. with honors, U. Tex., 1959, J.D. with honors, 1960. Bar: Tex. bar 1960. Since practiced in Houston; mem. firm Fulbright, Crooker, Freeman, Bates & Jaworski, 1960-63, Bates & Brock, 1964-66, Brock, Williams & Boyd, 1966-79, Williams & Boyd, 1979—; Pres. Tex. Pecan Growers Assn., Federated Pecan Growers Assn., 1976-78. Served with AUS, 1953-55. Named Outstanding Soldier of Second Army, 1955. Mem. Am., Houston bar assns., State Bar Tex., Tex. Trial Lawyers Assn. (dir. 1972-76), Houston Trial Lawyers Assn. (dir. 1969), Assn. Trial Lawyers Am., Chancellors, Beta Gamma Sigma, Phi Delta Phi. State civil litigation, Personal injury, Workers' compensation. Home: 9607 Meadowglen St Houston TX 77063 Office: 1212 Main St Houston TX 77002

WILLIAMS, WESLEY SAMUEL, JR., lawyer; b. Phila., Nov. 13, 1942; s. Wesley Samuel and Bathrus Amanda (Bailey) W.; m. Karen Roberta Hastie, Aug. 17, 1968; children: Amanda Pedersen, Wesley Hastie, Bailey Lockhart. B.A. in French Lit. magna cum laude, Harvard U., 1963, J.D., 1967; M.A. (Woodrow Wilson fellow), Fletcher Sch. Law and Diplomacy, Medford, Mass., 1964; LL.M., Columbia U., 1969. Bar: D.C., U.S. Supreme Ct., N.Y. Spl. counsel D.C. City Council, 1967-69; assoc.-in-law Columbia U. Law Sch., 1968-69; legal counsel com. on D.C. U.S. Senate, 1969-70; asso. firm Covington & Burling, Washington, 1970-75; partner Covington & Burling, 1975—; trustee Penn Mut. Life Ins. Co., Phila., 1978—; bd. dirs. Broadcast Capital, Inc., 1979—, Broadcast Capital Fund, Inc., 1979—; mem. Pres.'s U.S. Circuit Judge Nominating Commn., 1977-80; mem. com. on admissions and grievances U.S. Ct. Appeals (D.C. cir.), 1980—; gen. counsel D.C. Bar, 1979-81; adj. prof. Georgetown U. Law Sch., 1971-73; mem. exec. com. Washington Lawyers Com. Civil Rights Under Law, 1972—; mem. editorial bd. D.C. Real Estate Reporter. Author legal articles; contbr. chpts. to legal edn. course texts. Pres. bd. trustee Nat. Child Research Center, 1980-82; mem. exec. com. Harvard Law Sch. Assoc. Council, 1985—, bd. dirs., 1979-82, bd. overseers Harvard U., 1985—, chmn. vis. com. Harvard U. Divinity Sch., 1986—; bd. dirs. World Affairs Council of Washington, D.C., Inc., 1980—, Nat. Symphony Orch. Assn., 1977—; bd. dirs. Family and Child Services Washington, 1970—, pres., 1973-76; exec. com. community adv. com. Jr. League Washington, 1977-86 ; adv. bd. D.C. Salvation Army, 1978-86 ; pres. standing com. Episcopal Diocese of Washington, 1983—; sec. chpt. governing bd. Protestant Episc. Cathedral Found. Fellow Am. Bar Found.; mem. Am. Bar Assn., Nat. Bar Assn., Fed. Bar Assn., D.C. Bar Assn., Washington Bar Assn., Alpha Phi Alpha., Sigma Pi Phi. Clubs: Harvard (Boston, N.Y.C. and Washington), City Tavern (N.Y.C. and Washington); Met. (Washington), Univ. (Washington). Banking, Contracts commercial, General corporate. Office: Covington & Burling 1201 Pennsylvania Ave NW PO Box 7566 Washington DC 20044

WILLIAMS, YVONNE LAVERNE, educational executive, lawyer; b. Washington, Jan. 7, 1938; d. Smallwood Edmund and Verna Lucille (Rapley) W. B.A., Barnard Coll., 1959; M.A., Boston U., 1961; J.D., Georgetown U., 1977. Bar: D.C. 1980. Fgn. service officer USIA, Washington and abroad, 1961-65; dir. women's Africa commn. African-Am. Inst., N.Y.C., 1966-68; assoc. prof. African studies Benedict Coll., Columbia, S.C., 1968-70; press sec. Hon. Walter Fauntroy, U.S. Congress, Washington, 1970-72; dir. African-Am. Scholars Council, Washington, 1972-73; assoc. Leva, Hawes, Symington, Martin, Washington, 1977-79; asst. v.p. Brimmer & Co., Washington, 1980-82; assoc. dir. fed. relations, legal counsel Tuskegee U., Washington, 1982-83, v.p. fed. and internat. relations, legal counsel, 1983—. Vol., mem. Operation Crossroads Africa, N.Y.C. and Washington, 1960—; mem. Mayor's Internat. Task Force, Washington, 1982-83. African Research and Studies Program fellow, Boston U., 1960; Barnard Coll. scholar, 1955-57. Mem. ABA, Nat. Bar Assn., Nat. Assn. Coll. and Univ. Attys., Nat. Assn. State Univ. and Land Grant Colls., Assn. Univ. Dirs. Internat. Agrl. Programs, Democrat. Club: Barnard (Washington)(bd. dirs. 1986—). Legislative, Administrative and regulatory. Office: Tuskegee U Washington Office Suite 490 11 DuPont Circle NW Washington DC 20036

WILLIAMSON, CARLTON FORREST, lawyer; b. Whiteville, N.C., June 5, 1954; s. Edward L. and Sara (Benton) W.; m. Anne Torbert, Sept. 6, 1980; children: Emily James, John Forrest. BBA, U. N.C., 1976; JD, Wake Forest U., 1980. Bar: N.C. 1980, U.S. Dist. Ct. (ea. dist.) N.C. 1980. Mem. comml. banking sect. Atlantic Bancorp., Jacksonville, Fla., 1976-77; assoc. Williamson & Walton, Whiteville, 1980-82, ptnr., 1982—; bd. dirs. 1st Investors Savs. and Loan Inc., Whiteville, Columbus House Inc., Whiteville. Mem. N.C. Bar Assn., Columbus County Bar Assn. (pres. 1985—), N.C. Acad. Trial Lawyers, Ducks Unltd. (chmn. Whiteville chpt. 1985—), Phi Delta Phi. Democrat. Methodist. General practice. Home: 129 Fuller St Whiteville NC 28472 Office: Williamson & Walton 136 Washington St Whiteville NC 28472

WILLIAMSON, CHARLES GURLEY, JR., lawyer; b. Detroit, Feb. 25, 1925; s. Charles Gurley Sr. and Lillian (Wedel) W.; m. Gwenda Rollins Pryse, June 21, 1948; children: Cynthia Williamson Johnson, Lynda Williamson Selby, Charles Gurley III, Morgan Pryse, Gwenda Rollins. BS, U.S. Mil. Acad., 1946; JD with honors, U. Mich., 1956; LLM, Georgetown U., 1961. Bar: D.C. 1957, U.S. Supreme Ct. 1960, Md. 1963, Ky. 1964, U.S. Dist. Ct. (ea. dist.) Ky. 1964. Commd. 2d lt. U.S. Army, advanced through grades to capt., 1950, resigned, 1954; assoc. Steptoe & Johnson, Washington, 1957-64; sole practice Lexington, Ky., 1964-66, 76-78; asst. prof. U. Ky. Coll. Law, Lexington, 1966-69, asst. dean, 1970-72; ptnr. Clay, Williamson & Robe, Lexington and Mt. Sterling, Ky., 1978-84, Clay, Williamson & Lane, Lexington and Mt. Sterling, Ky., 1984—; judge 22d jud. dist. Fayette Cir. Ct., Lexington, 1969-70; bd. dirs. Exchange Bank of Ky., Mt. Sterling, Blue Grass Rural Electric Coop., Nicholasville. Mem. Ky. Crime Commn., Frankfort, 1968-80, Ky. Parole Bd., Frankfort, 1972-76; chmn. eastern appeal bd. SSS, Lexington, 1970-75; curator Transylvania U., Lexington, 1980—. Fellow Am. Coll. Probate Counsel; mem. ABA, Ky. Bar Assn., Fayette County Bar Assn., D.C. Bar Assn. Republican. Episcopalian. Lodge: Kiwanis (pres. Lexington club 1973-74, gov. Ky.-Tenn. dist. 1983-84). Avocations: photography, history. Probate, Estate taxation, General corporate. Home: 1325 Delong Rd Lexington KY 40515 Office: Clay Williamson & Lane 50 Broadway Mount Sterling KY 40353

WILLIAMSON, CHARLES READY, lawyer; b. Boston, Jan. 2, 1944; s. Charles Ready and Anne Margaret (Livingstone) W.; m. Julie Anne Williamson, Nov. 6, 1971; 1 dau., Anne Lucinda. B.A., Colgate U., 1965; LL.B., Suffolk U., 1968. Bar: Mass. 1968, Oreg. 1970. Law clk. to Judge Joseph B. Silverio, Mass. land ct., Boston 1968-69; VISTA atty., dep. dir. Multnomah County Legal Aid Service, Portland, 1970-74; assoc. Kell, Alterman & Runstein, Portland, 1974-78; sole practice, Portland, 1978—; pres. Oreg. Legal Service Corp., 1976-77; mem. Oreg. Bd. Psychologist Examiners, 1973-74; vice chmn. Oreg. Grad. Sch. Profl. Psychology, Pacific U. Pres. Oreg. Consumer League, 1972-74; councilor Met. Service Dist. 1978-84; treas. Democratic Bus. Forum 1982-84. Mem. ABA, Oreg. Bar Assn., Multnomah County Bar Assn. Club: Portland City. Contbr. in field. State civil litigation, General practice, Legislative. Home: 2530 NW Westover Rd Portland OR 97210 Office: 520 SW Yamhill St Suite 1001 Portland OR 97204

WILLIAMSON, GREGORY LOPEZ, lawyer; b. Cleve., Dec. 1, 1951; s. Leonard Lopez and Gwendolyn (Fortson) W.; divorced; 1 child, Kenneth Gerard; m. Lisa Ann Reitz, July 26, 1985. BA, Cleve. State U., 1976, JD, 1981. Bar: Ohio 1982, U.S. Dist. Ct. (no. dist.) Ohio 1982. Dep. dir. child support enforcement Common Pleas Court Cuyahoga County, Cleve., 1982-83; asst. pros. atty. Pros. Atty.'s Office Cuyahoga County, Cleve., 1983-86; assoc. Brown, Bartunek & Worthing, Cleve., 1986; pro bono counsel Legal Aid Soc., Cleve., 1982-85; arbitrator Common Pleas Ct. Cuyahoga County, Cleve., 1986—. Mem. Citizens League Cleve., 1983-85. Mem. ABA, Ohio State Bar Assn., Cleve. Bar Assn., Ohio Pros. Attys. Assn., Cuyahoga County Bar Assn., Assn. Trial Lawyers Am. Democrat. Lutheran. Avocations: weightlifting, mystery novels, horror and science fiction movies, general sports. State civil litigation, Insurance, Personal injury. Home: 3136 Warrington Rd Shaker Heights OH 44120 Office: Brown Bartunek & Worthing 118 St Clair Ave NE 708 Mall Bldg Cleveland OH 44114

WILLIAMSON, HAROLD EDWARD, legal educator, university administrator; b. Huntsville, Tex., Apr. 15, 1947; s. Clifford Odell and Willie Elzora (Peacock) W.; m. Sharon Ann Clark, Dec. 20, 1969; children: Crystal Ann, Jason Eric, Travis Aaron. BS, Sam Houston State U., 1974, MA, 1975, PhD, 1980. Correctional employee Tex. Dept. Corrections, Huntsville, 1970-76, instr. training, 1976-77, research analyst, 1977-79, adminstr., 1979-80, dir. ops. research, 1980-81; acad. program dir. Northeast La. U., Monroe, 1981—; cons. North Delta Police Acad., Monroe, 1981—; chmn. Ouachita Parish Jail Com., Monroe, 1984-86. Contbr. articles to profl. jours. Lectr. numerous civic orgns. and founds., 1980—. Served with USAF, 1966-70. Mem. Acad. Criminal Justice Scis., Am. Correctional Assn., Am. Soc. Criminology, La. Assn. Criminal Justice Educators (pres. 1984-85). Democrat. Methodist. Criminal justice education. Office: Northeast La U 700 University Ave Monroe LA 71209

WILLIAMSON, JULIE ANN STULCE, lawyer; b. Los Angeles, Apr. 19, 1944; d. Fred Jefferson and Mary Helen (Bein) Stulce; m. Robert F. Williamson Jr.; children: Robert F. III, Jeffery B. BS, Stanford U., 1966; JD, Fordham U., 1977. Bar: Fla. 1978. Assoc. Kimbrell & Hamann P.A., Miami, Fla., 1977-80, Greenberg, Traurig, Askew, Hoffman Lipoff, Rosen & Quentel, P.A., Miami, 1980-84; ptnr. Fine Jacobson Schwartz Nash Block & England P.A., Miami, 1984—. Mem. Stanford U. Assocs., 1980—; past chmn., mem. code enforcement bd. Village of Miami Shores, 1981—; mem. adv. citizens bd. sch. social service Barry U., Miami, 1985—; Fla. co-chmn. Stanford U. Annual Fund, 1979—. Mem. Fla. Bar Assn. (exec. council real property, probate and trust law sect., chmn. mortgage law com.). Democrat. Roman Catholic. Real property, Contracts commercial. Office: Fine Jacobson et al PA 100 SE 2d St 1 Central Trust Fin Ctr Miami FL 33131

WILLIAMSON, MICHAEL GEORGE, lawyer; b. West Point, N.Y., Feb. 22, 1951; s. John and Alice (MacAniff) W.; m. Linda Ann Cappelli, June 27, 1980. Student U.S. Mil. Acad., 1969-71; B.S. magna cum laude, Duke U., 1973; J.D., Georgetown U., 1976. Bar: Fla. 1976, U.S. Dist. Ct. (mid. dist.) Fla. 1977, U.S. Dist. Ct. (so. dist.) Fla. 1981. Instr. legal research and writing Georgetown U. Law Ctr., Washington, 1975-76; assoc. Johnson, Motsinger, Trisman & Sharp, Orlando, Fla., 1976-78; assoc. Maguire, Voorhis & Wells, Orlando, 1978-82, ptnr., 1982—; instr. bus. law Valencia Community Coll., Orange County, Fla., 1978-80; lectr. seminars. Editor: Internat. Jour. Georgetown Law Ctr., 1975-76. Contbr. articles to profl. publs. Mem. steering com. 1984 Nat. Conf. Bankruptcy Judges, Orlando, 1984; chmn. com. on middle dist. bankruptcy rules, 1985. Mem. Fla. Bar Assn. (UCC/Bankruptcy com. 1978—, chmn. 1986-87), Orange County Bar Assn. (corp. and bus. law sect. chmn. 1984-85, chmn. bankruptcy law com. 1983-84). Republican. Roman Catholic. Bankruptcy. Home: 757 Terra Pl Maitland FL 32751 Office: Maguire Voorhis & Wells PA 2 S Orange Plaza Orlando FL 32801

WILLIAMSON, NILE JAY, lawyer; b. Iowa City, Iowa, Jan. 24, 1947; s. Douglas Robert and Beverly Earl (Draper) W.; m. Deborah Williamson, Aug. 9, 1969 (div. 1975); m. Mary Ann Williamson, Jan. 24, 1976 (div. 1985); 1 child, Stephen Douglas. BA, U. Iowa, 1969; JD, Drake U., 1972. Assoc. Cassidy, Cassidy & Mueller, Peoria, Ill., 1973-74; ptnr. Lindholm & Williamson, Peoria, 1974-81; sole practice Peoria, 1981—. Mem. Am. Trial Lawyers Assn., Ill. Trial Lawyers Assn., Iowa Bar Assn., Peoria County Bar Assn., Ill. Bar Assn. (various coms.). Republican. Methodist. Personal injury. Home: 1812 W Moss Ave Peoria IL 61614 Office: 1120 Savings Center Tower Peoria IL 61602

WILLIAMSON, OLIVER EATON, economist, educator; b. Superior, Wis., Sept. 27, 1932; s. Scott Gilbert and Lucille S. (Dunn) W.; m. Dolores Jean Celeni, Sept. 28, 1957; children: Scott, Tamara, Karen, Oliver, Dean. SB, Mass. Inst. Tech., 1955; MBA, Stanford U., 1960; PhD, Carnegie-Mellon U., 1963; PhD (hon.), Norwegian Sch. Econs. and Bus. Adminstrn., 1986; PhD in Econ. Sci. (hon.), Hochschulest Gallen, 1987. Project. engr. U.S. Govt., 1955-58; asst. prof. econs. U. Calif., Berkeley, 1963-65; assoc. prof. U. Pa., Phila., 1965-68; prof. U. Pa., 1968-83, Charles and William L. Day prof. econs. and social sci., 1977-83; spl. econ. asst. to asst. atty. gen. for antitrust Dept. Justice, 1966-67; dir. Center for Study of Organizational Innovation, U. Pa., 1976-83; Gordon B. Tweedy prof. econs. of law and orgn. Yale U., 1983—; cons. in field. Author: The Economics of Discretionary Behavior, 1964, Corporate Control and Business Behavior, 1970, Markets and Hierarchies, 1975, The Economic Institutions of Capitalism, 1985, Economic Organization, 1986, Antitrust Economics, 1987; assoc. editor: Bell Jour. Econs., 1973-74, editor, 1975-82; co-editor: Jour. Law, Econs., and Orgn., 1983—. Fellow Center for Advanced Study in Behavioral Scis., 1977-78; Guggenheim fellow, 1977-78; Am. Acad. Arts and Scis. fellow, 1983; Recipient Alexander Henderson award Carnegie-Mellon U., 1962. Fellow Econometric Soc.; mem. Am. Econ. Assn. Office: Yale Sch Orgn and Mgmt New Haven CT 06520

WILLIAMSON, PETER DAVID, lawyer; b. Houston, Oct. 13, 1944; s. Sam and Sophie Ann (Kaplan) W.; m. Carol Jane Ivy, Aug. 1, 1972; children: Heather, Amber, Asia, Ginger. B.A., U. Ill., 1966; J.D., U. Tex., 1969. Bar: Tex. 1969, U.S. Ct. Appeals (5th, 8th, 10th, 11th and D.C. cirs.); lic. comml. pilot. Sole practice Houston, 1971-79; ptnr. Williamson & Gardner, 1979-84, Williamson, Gardner, Hall & Wiesenthal, 1984—; adj. prof. Tex. So. U. Law Sch., 1980. Mem. Am. Immigration Lawyers Assn. (v.p. Tex. chpt. 1978-79, pres. 1979-80, nat. bd. govs. 1982—). Immigration, naturalization, and customs. Home: 4130 Martinshire Houston TX 77025 Office: MBank Plaza 333 Clay St Suite 2300 Houston TX 77002

WILLIAMSON, STEVEN LLOYD, lawyer; b. San Diego, June 26, 1953; s. Wesley Byrom and Adena Adelene Brown) W.; m. Laura Maria De Myer, Sept. 29, 1979; 1 child, Michael Wesley. Bar: N.Y. 1979, U.S. Dist. Ct. (ea. and so. dists.) N.Y. 1979. Assoc. Chadbourne, Parke, Whiteside & Wolff, N.Y.C., 1978-81, Chadbourne, Parke & Afrida, United Arab Emirates, 1981-84; assoc. Chadbourne & Parke, N.Y.C., 1984-86, ptnr., 1986—. Contbr. articles to profl jours. Mem. ABA, N.Y. State Bar Assn., Assn. of Bar of City of N.Y. Avocations: scuba diving, volleyball. Contracts commercial, General corporate, Private international. Office: Chadbourne & Parke 30 Rockefeller Plaza New York NY 10112

WILLIAMSON, THOMAS SAMUEL, JR., lawyer; b. Plainfield, N.J., July 14, 1946; s. Thomas Samuel and Winifred (Hall) W.; divorced. BA, Harvard U., 1968; postgrad., Oxford U., Eng., 1968-69; JD, U. Calif., Berkeley, 1974. Bar: D.C. 1975, Calif. 1975, U.S. Dist. Ct. D.C. 1977. Dir. tng. div. Alem Pub. Relations, Addis Ababa, Ethiopia, 1970-71; assoc. Covington & Burling, Washington, 1974-78, 81-82, ptnr., 1982—; dep. inspector gen. U.S. Dept. Energy, Washington, 1978-81; mem. exec. com. Lawyers for Civil Rights Under Law, 1983—. Mem. vis. com. to dept. of athletics Harvard U., 1985—. Rhodes scholar, 1968. Mem. ABA, Nat. Bar Assn., Council on Fgn. Relations, Washington Council Lawyers (bd. dirs. 1975—). Avocations: touch football, cycling. Administrative and regulatory, Health, General corporate. Home: 1663 Primrose Rd NW Washington DC 20012 Office: Covington & Burling 1201 Pennsylvania Ave NW PO Box 7566 Washington DC 20044

WILLIAMSON, THOMAS W., JR., lawyer; b. Miami, Fla., July 22, 1950; s. Thomas W. Sr. and Elizabeth (Worthington) W. BA, Va. Mil. Inst., 1972; JD, U. Richmond, 1976. Bar: Va., U.S. Dist. Ct. (ea. and we. dists.) Va., U.S. Ct. Appeals (4th cir.). Assoc. Emanual Emroch & Assocs., Richmond, Va., 1976-82; ptnr. Emroch & Williamson, Richmond, 1982—. Served to capt. USAR. Mem. Va. State Bar, Va. Trial Lawyers Assn. (gov. at large), ABA, Assn. Trial Lawyers Am., Richmond Bar Assn., Richmond Trial Lawyers Assn. (pres. 1986-87). Federal civil litigation, State civil litigation, Personal injury. Home: 3009 Floyd Ave Richmond VA 23221 Office: Emroch & Williamson PO Box 8692 Richmond VA 23226

WILLIAMSON, WALTER, lawyer; b. N.Y.C., Apr. 23, 1939; s. Zarah and Leah (Golding) W.; m. Barbara Alice Fisher, Sept. 9, 1973; children—Douglas Fisher, Andrew Fisher. B.A., Cornell U., 1960; M.D., NYU, 1964; J.D., Columbia U., 1973. Bar: N.Y. 1974, U.S. Dist. Ct. (ea. and so. dists.) N.Y. 1974, U.S. Ct. Appeals (2d cir.) 1975, U.S. Supreme Ct. 1977. Intern Mt. Sinai Hosp., N.Y.C., 1964-65; resident Hillside Hosp., Queens, N.Y., 1965-66; resident Mt. Sinai Hosp., N.Y.C., 1968-70; ptnr. Williamson & Williamson, N.Y.C., 1974-78; prin. Williamson & Williamson, P.C., N.Y.C., 1978—. Served as capt. M.C., USAF, 1966-68. Editor Columbia Law Rev., 1972-73. Fellow Am. Coll. Legal Medicine; mem. ABA, N.Y. State Bar Assn., Assn. Bar City of N.Y., N.Y. County Lawyers Assn., Phi Beta Kappa, Phi Kappa Phi. Personal injury, Insurance, Civil litigation. Home: 322 Central Park W New York NY 10025 Office: Williamson & Williamson PC 305 Broadway New York NY 10007

WILLIAMSON, WALTER BLAND, lawyer; b. Selma, Ala., Apr. 6, 1938; s. Walter Bland and Tina (Matheny) W.; m. Betty Ann Sherrod, Dec. 4, 1940; children—Michael Davis, Amy Caroline. B.S., Stetson U., 1959; J.D., Emory U., 1963. Bar: Okla. 1969, Ga. 1963, U.S. Ct. Mil. Appeals 1963, U.S. Supreme Ct. 1969. Atty. Office of Gen. Counsel Fed. Deposit Ins. Corp., Washington, 1967; atty. Office of Standards Policy, U.S. Dept. Commerce, 1968-69; ptnr. Pray, Walker, Jackman, Williamson & Marlar, and predecessors, Tulsa, 1969—. Mem. steering com. Conf. on Nuclear Power Generation, Nat. Energy Law and Policy Inst., 1981; mem. adv. com. on natural gas allowables Okla. Corp. Commn., 1983. Served to capt. U.S. Army, 1963-67. Mem. Okla. Bar Assn. (chmn. mineral law sect. 1982), Tulsa County Bar Assn. (chmn. mineral law sect. 1979) ABA (vice chmn. natural gas mktg. and transp. com., natural resource sect. 1986—), Fed. Energy Bar Assn., Okla. Ind. Petroleum Assn. (chmn. legal com. 1979-83, gen. counsel 1983—), Phi Delta Phi. Club: Summit. Oil and gas leasing, FERC practice, Administrative and regulatory. Home: 2240 E 25th Pl Tulsa OK 74114 Office: 900 Oneok Plaza Tulsa OK 74103

WILLIAN, CLYDE FRANKLIN, lawyer; b. Indpls., Sept. 20, 1930; s. Clyde W. and Ruth L. (Robinson) W.; m. Patricia Strong, Aug. 16, 1953; children—James, Jeffrey, John, Mary, Michael. B.S., Rose-Hulman Inst. Tech., 1952; postgrad. Ind. U., 1953-54; LL.B., George Washington U., 1957; postgrad. Chgo. Kent Coll. Law, 1957. Bar: Ill. 1957, U.S. Supreme Ct. 1970, U.S. Dist. Ct. (no. dist.) Ill. 1957, U.S. Ct. Appeals (7th cir.) 1958. With Willian Brinks Olds Hofer Gilson & Lione Ltd. and predecessors, Chgo., 1957—, pres., 1978—. Bd. dirs. Hadley Sch. for Blind, Rose-Hulman Inst. Tech. Mem. ABA, Chgo. Bar Assn., Ill. Bar Assn., Bar Assn. 7th Fed. Circuit, Am. Judicature Soc., Am. Patent Law Assn., Phi Alpha Delta. Republican. Episcopalian. Clubs: Union League (Chgo.); Skokie Country. Patent, Antitrust, Federal civil litigation. Office: One IBM Plaza Suite 4100 Chicago IL 60611

WILLICK, MARSHAL SHAWN, lawyer; b. St. Louis, Aug. 1, 1958; s. Jerry S. and Birdie Faye (Glazer) W. BA in English, U. Nev., 1979; JD, Georgetown U., 1982. Bar: Nev. 1982, U.S. Dist. Ct. Nev. 1982, Calif. 1983, U.S. Ct. Appeals (9th cir.) 1984. Atty. cen. legal staff Nev. Supreme Ct., Carson City, 1982-84; assoc. Thorndal, Backus, Maupin & Manoukian, Las Vegas, 1984-85; ptnr. LePome & Willick, Las Vegas, 1985—; lectr. various orgns. Author: Professional Malpractice and the Unauthorized Practice of Professions: Some Legal and Ethical Aspects of the Use of Computers as Decision-Aids, 1985. Pres. Young Dems. Nev., Carson City, 1982-84, nat. committeeman, Las Vegas, 1984-85. Mem. ABA (sci. and tech. sect.), Clark County Bar Assn., Assn. Trial Lawyers Am., MENSA Las Vegas (pres. 1975-79, 85-86, Nexus award 1979), World Future Soc. Club: Intertel (Las Vegas). Avocations: computers, tech., martial arts, writing, speaking. Computer, State civil litigation, Trademark and copyright. Office: LePome & Willick 330 S 3d St Suite 960 Las Vegas NV 89101

WILLIFORD, JOHN LEA, lawyer, oil company executive; b. Kingsland, Ark., Sept. 18, 1936; s. John H. and Archer F. (Lea) W.; m. Margaret C. Barton, Apr. 4, 1964; 1 son, John B. Student Tex. Tech. Coll., 1954-55; B.A., U. Okla., 1958; J.D., U. Tex., 1960. Bar: Tex. 1960, U.S. Ct. Mil. Appeals 1962, U.S. Dist. Ct. (so. dist.) Tex. 1964, Okla. 1969, U.S. Supreme Ct. 1971, U.S. Ct. Appeals (5th cir.) 1971, U.S. Ct. Appeals (10th cir.) 1971, U.S. Ct. Appeals (D.C. cir.) 1972, U.S. Ct. Appeals (11th cir.) 1981. Sr. v.p., gen. counsel Phillips Petroleum Europe-Africa, London, 1981-85, assoc. gen. counsel Phillips Petroleum Co., Bartlesville, 1985—. Served to capt., AUS, 1960-63. Mem. Tex. Bar Assn., Okla. Bar Assn., ABA, Phi Alpha Delta. General corporate, Private international, Oil and gas leasing. Office: Phillips Petroleum Co 1266 Adams Bldg Bartlesville OK 74004

WILLIG, WILLIAM PAUL, lawyer; b. Schenectady, N.Y., Mar. 29, 1936; s. James R. and Mildred (Nock) W.; m. Renee A. Rosch, Nov. 4, 1984. AB in Liberal Arts, St. Michael's Coll., Winooski Park, Vt., 1958; JD, Union U., 1962. Ptnr. Higgins, Roberts, Beyerl & Coan, P.C., Schenectady, 1962—; panelist on Med. malpractice and arbitration N.Y. Supreme Ct.; lectr., chmn. inter-profl. com. Schenectady County Bar Assn. Mem. Schenectady County Cancer Golf Day Crusade; candidate N.Y. Supreme Ct. 4th Jud. Dist., 1981. Mem. N.Y. State Bar Assn., Am. Trial Lawyers Assn., Federated Bar Assn., Med. Malpractice Panel of N.Y. Democrat. Clubs: Mohawk Golf (Schenectady), Saratoga Golf and Polo (Saratoga Springs, N.Y.). Avocations: antique and classic power boats, golf, skiing. State civil litigation, Environment, Personal injury. Home: The Hill Top Rt 67 Amsterdam Rd Ballston Spa NY 12020 Office: Higgins Roberts Beyerl & Coan PC 502 State St Schenectady NY 12305

WILLIHNGANZ, PAUL W., lawyer; b. Bklyn., May 19, 1937; s. Eugene A. and Lorna Rea W.; m. Nancy K. Willihnganz, Dec. 1, 1962; children—Joseph, Heather. B.S. in M.E., U. Notre Dame, 1959; J.D., Georgetown U., 1968. Bar: Calif. 1969, U.S. Supreme Ct. 1972, Maine 1979. Program mgr. Hydrotronics div. Data Design Labs., Inc., Falls Church, Va., 1967-68; assoc. Higgs, Jennings Fletcher & Mack, San Diego, 1969-71; ptnr. Brundage, Williams & Zellman, San Diego, 1971-74; ptnr. Willihnganz, Manning & Sudman, San Diego, 1975-77; asst. counsel UNUM Life Ins. Co., Portland, Maine, 1977-80; 2d v.p., csl. Union Mut. Life Ins. Co., 1980—; instr. Law Sch. U. Maine, 1981-82. Bd. dirs. Portland Lyric Theatre, 1981-84; pres. Windham Community Theater, 1980-81; mem. Waterboro Charter Commn., 1981-82. Served with USN, 1959-67. Mem. ABA, Calif. Bar Assn., Maine Bar Assn., Maine Trial Lawyers Assn., Phi Delta Phi. Club: Notre Dame San Diego (pres. 1975-76). Insurance, General corporate, Federal civil litigation. Home: 36 Foreside Common Dr Falmouth ME 04105 Office: 2211 Congress ST Portland ME 04122

WILLINGER, WARREN JAY, lawyer; b. N.Y.C., June 24, 1937; s. Louis and Viola (Friedman) W.; m. Sandra Willinger, June 7, 1962; children: Douglas, Lisa, Lauren, Byron. BA, George Washington U., 1959, LLB, 1961. Bar: N.Y. 1962, U.S. Dist. Ct. (so. dist.) N.Y. 1963, U.S. Dist. Ct. (ea. dist.) N.Y. 1967, U.S. Supreme Ct. 1973. Assoc. Law Offices of Sidney M. Wittner, N.Y.C., 1964-68, Law Offices of Joseph L. Rudell, N.Y.C., 1968-71, Gair, Gair & Conason, N.Y.C., 1971—; Mem. panel med. malpractice Westchester County Supreme Ct., 2d dept. appellate div. Panel Assigned Counsel Indigent Defendents, panel arbitrators U.S. Dist. Ct. (ea. dist.) N.Y., 1986. Served with USCG, 1961-62. Mem. N.Y. State Bar Assn., Westchester County Bar Assn., Assn. Trial Lawyers Am., N.Y. State Trial Lawyers Assn. Avocations: stamps, coins, golf. Personal injury, Products liability, Medical malpractice. Home: 537 Stratton Rd New Rochelle NY 10804 Office: Gair Gair & Conason 80 Pine St New York NY 10001

WILLIS, RICHARD ALLAN, lawyer; b. Brownsville, Tex., Dec. 7, 1956; s. Charles Leon and Mary (Bastenello) W.; m. Leslie Kay Gautreau; children: Rikki Kay, Reid Michael. BS in Edn., La. State U., 1978, JD, 1982. Bar: La. 1982. Assoc. Percy & Percy, Gonzales, La., 1982-84; ptnr. Percy, Holdridge & Willis, Gonzales, 1984—. Mem. Assn. Trial Lawyers Am., La. Bar Assn., La. Trial Lawyers Assn. Democrat. Roman Catholic. Lodges: Lions (v.p. local chpt. 1985—). Avocations: travel, sports. Consumer commercial, Criminal. Home: PO Box 1172 Gonzales LA 70737 Office: Percy Holdridge & Willis PO Box 1096 Gonzales LA 70737

WILLIS, RUSSELL ANTHONY, III, lawyer; b. Peoria, Ill., June 2, 1953; s. Russell A. and Martha Lois (Wilson) W.; m. Debra R. Austin, July 27, 1975; children: Sarah E. Austin-Willis, Benjamin D. Austin-Willis. BA in English with honors, Ind. U., 1975; MA, U. Chgo., 1976; JD, St. Louis U., 1979. Bar: Mo. 1979, U.S. Dist. Ct. (ea. and we. dists.) Mo. 1979, U.S. Ct. Appeals (8th cir.) 1980, U.S. Tax Ct. 1982. Sole practice St. Louis, 1981, 83-84; assoc. Tremayne, Lay, Carr & Bauer, St. Louis, 1981-83; of counsel Wolff & Frankel, St. Louis, 1983-84; asst. trust counsel Mercantile Trust Co., St. Louis, 1984-85; assoc. Guilfoil, Petzall & Shoemake, St. Louis, 1985-87; sole practice St. Louis, 1987—. Contbr. articles to profl. jours. Mem. ABA (various coms. and sects.), Mo. Bar Assn. (various coms. and sects.), Bar Assn. Met. St. Louis (legis. com.). General corporate, Estate planning, Estate taxation. Office: Guilfoil Petzall & Shoemake 120 S Centtal Ave Suite 1505 Saint Louis MO 63105

WILLIS, WAYNE GEORGE, lawyer; b. Oakland, Calif., May 1, 1947; s. Albert Harrison and Catherine Mae (Craney) W.; m. Stephanie Kittredge, July 17, 1971 (div. Sept. 1979); children: Caleb, Molly; m. Debi Kay Linhardt, Aug. 4, 1984; 1 child, Tyler. BS, Yale U., 1969, MA, 1974, JD, 1975. Bar: Calif. 1976, Ohio 1978, U.S. Dist. Ct. (no. dist.) Calif. 1976, U.S. Dist. Ct. (so. dist.) Ohio 1978. Law clk. to presiding justice U.S. Ct. Appeals (9th cir.), San Francisco, 1975-76; assoc. Brobeck, Phleger & Harrison, Los Angeles, 1976-77; sr. ptnr. Hyatt Legal Services, Kansas City, Mo., 1977—; advisor tng. task force Legal Services Corp., Washington, 1986—; bd. dirs. Block Mgmt. Co., Kansas City, 1980—. Mem. ABA, Calif. Bar Assn., Ohio Bar Assn., Am. Legal Clinic Assn. (pres. 1979-80). General practice, Family and matrimonial, Administrative and regulatory. Home: 8533 High Dr Leawood KS 66206 Office: Hyatt Legal Services 4410 Main St Kansas City MO 64111

WILLKIE, WENDELL LEWIS, II, lawyer; b. Indpls., Oct. 29, 1951; s. Philip Herman Willkie and Rosalie (Heffelfinger) Hall. AB, Harvard U., 1973; BA, Oxford (Eng.) U., 1975, MA, 1983; JD, U. Chgo., 1978. Bar: N.Y. 1979. Assoc. Simpson Thacher and Bartlett, N.Y.C., 1978-82; gen. counsel NEH, Washington, 1982-84; assoc. counsel to Pres. The White House, Washington, 1984-85; chief of staff, counselor to Sec. U.S. Dept. Edn., Washington, 1985, gen. counsel, 1985—. Harvard U. scholar, 1969-73, Rhodes scholar, 1973. Republican. Episcopalian. Home: 1613-30th St NW Washington DC 20007 Office: US Dept of Education Office Gen Counsel 400 Maryland Ave SW Room 4091 Washington DC 20202

WILLMAN, PHILIP LOUIS, lawyer; b. St. Louis, Mar. 31, 1953; s. Vallee Louis and Melba Lorraine (Carr) W. BA magna cum laude, Duke U., 1975; JD, Vanderbilt U., 1978. Bar: Mo. 1978, Ill. 1979, U.S. Dist. Ct. (no. dist) Ill. 1980, U.S. Dist. Ct. (ea. dist.) Mo. 1984. Research fellow in environ. law U. Ill., Urbana, 1978-79; asst. atty. gen. environ. control div. State of Ill., Chgo., 1979-84; assoc. Moser, Marsalek, et al, St. Louis, 1984—. Bd. dirs. Soulard Restoration Group, St. Louis, 1985. Named one of Outstanding Young Men in Am., U.S. Jaycees, 1979. Mem. ABA, Mo. Bar Assn., Ill. State Bar Assn., Bar Assn. Met. St. Louis, Mo. Orgn. Def. Lawyers. Roman Catholic. Avocations: skiing, hiking, gardening. Personal injury, Insurance, Environment. Home: 2219 S 12th St Saint Louis MO 63104 Office: Moser Marsalek et al 314 N Broadway Suite 360 Saint Louis MO 63102

WILLMETH, ROGER EARL, lawyer; b. Atchison, Kans., Apr. 24, 1946; s. Marion Clair and Virginia Rosemary (Bryant) W.; m. Janice Hazel Matthews, Apr. 14, 1973; children: Jennifer Lynn, Melissa Anne. Student No. Ill. U., 1964-65, DePaul U., 1965-67; J.D., John Marshall Law Sch., Chgo., 1970. Bar: Ill. 1970, U.S. Ct. Mil. Appeals 1971, U.S. Ct. Appeals (9th cir.) 1978, Guam 1979, U.S. Dist. Ct. Guam, 1979, U.S. Supreme Ct. 1979, U.S. Dist. Ct. (cen. dist.) Ill. 1979. Asst. atty. gen. Territory of Guam, Agana, 1977-79, State of Ill., Springfield, 1979-81; gen. atty. 375th Air Base Group, U.S. Air Force, Scott AFB, Ill., 1981-84, atty., adviser communications command, 1984—; spl. asst. U.S. atty. So. Dist. Ill., 1983-84. Bd. dirs. Country Lake Estates Owners Assn. Served to capt. JAGC, USAF, 1970-77, lt. col. with Res. 1977—. Decorated Air Force Commendation medal; recipient Am. Jurisprudence award, 1970; Award of Excellence for Civil Litigation, Guam Atty. Gen., 1979; Outstanding Civilian Atty. of Yr. award Mil. Airlift Command, 1982, Air Force Civilian Meritorious Service Medal, 1984. Mem. Guam Bar Assn., Res. Officers Assn., U.S. Tennis Assn. Methodist. Club: St. Clair Tennis (O'Fallon, Ill.). Government contracts and claims, Public utilities, Telecommunications. Home: Rural Route 4 4 S Mulberry St Collinsville IL 62234 Office: HQ Air Force Communications/JA Scott AFB IL 62225

WILLS, DON PAUL, lawyer; b. Miami, Okla., Sept. 13, 1935; s. Richard Franklin and Jane (Worley) W.; m. Donna Willet, Nov. 24, 1956; children: Lillian Elizabeth Wills Williams, Gregory Eugene. BA, Baylor U., 1957, JD, 1959. Bar: U.S. Dist. Ct. (ea. and no. dists.) Tex. 1959. Lawyer USAF, Cheyenne, Wyo., 1959-62, Dallas County Dist. Atty's Office, Dallas, 1962-65, Bean, Francis, Wills & Street, Dallas, 1965-86; sole practice Dallas, 1986—. Served to capt. USAF, 1962-65. Mem. ABA, Dallas Bar Assn., Tex. Trial Lawyers Assn. Personal injury, Workers' compensation. Home: 10015 Trailpine Dallas TX 75238 Office: 9221 LBJ Freeway #209 LBJ N Bldg Dallas TX 75243-3428

WILLS, ROBERT ROY, lawyer, legal instructor; b. Mpls., Sept. 15, 1950; s. Stanley Milton and June Winifred (Anderson) W. BA, U. Minn., 1972; JD, Stetson U., 1976. Bar: Fla. 1976, U.S. Dist. Ct. (so. dist.) Fla. 1977, U.S. Supreme Ct. 1980. Legal intern 6th Jud. Ct., St. Petersburg, Fla., 1976; asst. pub. defender 17th Jud. Ct., Ft. Lauderdale, Fla., 1976-80, chief asst. pub. defender, 1980—; guest lectr. Nova U. Law Sch., Ft. Lauderdale, 1980—; instr. Broward Community Coll., Ft. Lauderdale, 1983—, Broward Police Acad., Ft. Lauderdale, 1984—. Mem. Concerned Dems., Hollywood, Fla., 1984—, Hills Dem. Club, Hollywood; vol. Ft. Lauderdale Dems., 1984—; alt. del. Rep. Nat. Convention, Miami, Fla., 1972; youth chmn. Flenzel for Congress, Mpls., 1972. Mem. ABA, Fla. Bar Assn., Broward Bar Assn., Criminal Justice Planning Counsel, Criminal Justice Coordinating Com. Democrat. Lutheran. Avocations: travel, jogging, weight lifting, sports. Criminal. Home: PO Box 2356 Fort Lauderdale FL 33303 Office: Pub Defender 201 SE 6th Suite 740 Fort Lauderdale FL 33301

WILLSEY, F. PATTERSON, lawyer; b. Tucson, July 24, 1955; s. Frank Evan and Adele (Patterson) W.; m. Kathleen Louise Pitts, Aug. 14, 1982; 1 child, Tyler Patterson. Bar: Calif. 1982. Assoc. Dorazio, Barnhorst, Goldsmith & Bonar, San Diego, 1981-85; gen. counsel Arnold-Pacific Properties, Inc., AHL Constn., Arnold-Pacific Mgmt., Inc., Tustin, Calif., 1985—. Kratter Family scholar, 1979-81, Irvin J. Kahn scholar, 1982. Mem. ABA, Calif. Bar Assn., San Diego Bar Assn., Orange County Bar Assn. Avocations: golf, skiing, basketball. Real property, General corporate, Landlord-tenant. Home: 401 Camino Alondra San Clemente CA 92672 Office: Arnold Pacific Properties Inc 1254 Irvine Blvd Suite 210 Tustin CA 92680

WILLY, THOMAS RALPH, lawyer; b. Phila., Sept. 30, 1943; s. Albert Ralph and Dorothy Rose (Driver) W.; m. Kay Harris, Jan. 12, 1968; children—Elyn Alexandria Jon Charles. B.A. in History, U. Mo.-Kansas City, 1966, J.D. with distinction, 1974. Bar: Mo. 1974, U.S. Tax Ct. 1982. Assoc. Deacy & Deacy, Kansas City, Mo., 1974-75, Logan, Hentzen, Haitbrink & Moore, Kansas City, 1975; ptnr. Hentzen, Haitbrink & Moore, Kansas City, 1976-78, Hentzen, Moore & Willy, Kansas City, 1978-80, Moore and Willy, Kansas City, 1980—. Mem. Friends of Art, Kansas City, Kansas City Consensus, Hist. Kansas City Found., People to People, Friends of Zoo, Kansas City. Served to capt. USAF, 1966-70. Mem. ABA, (sect. corp., banking and bus. law), Kansas City Bar Assn., Mo. Bar Assn. Lodge: Lions (bd. dirs. Leawood). General corporate, Contracts commercial, General practice. Home: 10314 Lee Blvd Leawood KS 66206 Office: 408 Seville Sq Country Club Plaza Kansas City MO 64112

WILMOTH, WILLIAM DAVID, lawyer; b. Elkins, W.Va., July 11, 1950; s. Stark Amasa and Goldie (Johnson) W.; m. Rebecca Weaver, Aug. 21, 1971; children: Charles, Anne, Samuel, Peter. BS in Fin. cum laude, W.Va. U., 1972, JD, 1975. Bar: W.Va. 1975, U.S. Dist. Ct. (so. dist.) W.Va. 1976, U.S. Dist. Ct. (no. dist.) W.Va. 1977, U.S. Ct. Appeals (4th cir.) 1977, U.S. Supreme Ct. 1981, Pa. 1986. Law clk. to presiding judge U.S. Dist. Ct. (no. dist.) W.Va., Elkins, 1975-76; assoc. Bachmann, Hess, Bachmann & Garden, Wheeling, W.Va., 1976-77; asst. U.S. atty. U.S. Dept. Justice, Wheeling, 1977-80; ptnr. Schrader, Stamp, Byrd, Byrum & Companion, Wheeling, 1980—. V.p. nat. trial council Boy Scouts Am., Wheeling; bd. dirs. Big Bros. & Big Sisters, Wheeling, 1986—; trustee Christ United Meth. Ch. Mem. ABA, Am. Bankruptcy Inst., Def. Research Inst., Def. Trial Lawyers W.Va. Democrat. Lodge: Rotary. State civil litigation, Federal civil litigation, Bankruptcy. Home: 4 Highland Pk Wheeling WV 26003 Office: Schrader Stamp Byrd Byrum & Companion 1000 Hawley Bldg Wheeling WV 26003

WILSON, ABRAHAM, lawyer; b. Zhitomir, Ukraine, Nov. 19, 1922; came to U.S., 1923; s. Isaac and Katie (Garshoig) W.; m. Gloria Bachman, July 26, 1949 (div. Dec. 1965); 1 child, Chana; m. Christine Haftkowycz, July 23, 1966; children—Marko A., Raissa. B.S., Rutgers U., 1947, M.S. in Chemistry, 1950; Ph.D. in Chemistry, 1951; J.D. cum laude, Seton Hall U., 1974. Bar: N.J. 1974, U.S. Dist. Ct. N.J. 1974, U.S. Patent Office 1975, U.S. Supreme Ct. 1984. Sr. scientist Colgate Palmolive Co., Jersey City, 1951-55; group leader phys. chem. research Am. Cyanamid Co., Bound Brook, N.J., 1955-74; counsel, asst. to pres. TPCO, Inc., South Brunswick, N.J., 1974-76; sole practice, Piscataway, N.J., 1976-86; ptnr., Sherman, Kuhn, Justin & Wilson, 1986—; gen. counsel Enzon, Inc., South Plainfield, N.J., 1981—. Patentee in field. Councilman Borough Govt., Millstone, N.J., 1959-61, mayor, 1962-64; trustee N.J. Council of Orgns. and Schs. for Autistic Children and Adults, Inc., Princeton, N.J., 1979—; chmn., bd. dirs. Piscataway Community TV Authority, 1986—; bd. dirs. Raritan Valley ARC, 1986—. Served as 2d lt. USAF, 1943-46, PTO. Recipient Sr. Research award Am. Cyanamid Co.; fellow Imperial Coll. Sci. Tech., London, 1961-62. Mem. Am. Chem. Soc., N.J. Bar, Middlesex County Bar Assn. Democrat. Jewish. General corporate, Patent, General practice. Office: Sherman Kuhn Justin & Wilson Raritan Ctr Plaza 1 Box 6315 Edison NJ 08818

WILSON, ALMA D., state supreme court justice; b. Pauls Valley, Okla., May 25, 1917; d. William R. and Anna L. (Schuppert) Bell; m. William A. Wilson, May 30, 1948; 1 child, Lee Anne. A.B., U. Okla., 1939, LL.B., 1941, J.D., 1970. Bar: Okla. 1941. Sole practice Muskegee, Okla., 1941-43; sole practice Oklahoma City, 1943-47, Pauls Valley, 1948-69; judge Pauls Valley Mcpl. Ct., 1967-68; apptd. spl. judge Dist. Ct. 21, Norman, Okla., 1969-75, dist. judge, 1975-79; assoc. justice Okla. Supreme Ct., Oklahoma City, 1983—. Mem. bd. visitors U. Okla., mem. alumni bd. dirs.; mem. Assistance League; trustee Okla. Meml. Union. Recipient Guy Brown award, 1974, Woman of Yr. award Norman Bus. and Profl. Women, 1975; elected to U. Okla. Hall of Fame, 1975. Mem. Garvin County Bar Assn. (past pres.), Okla. Bar Assn. (co-chmn. law and citizenship edn. com.), AAUW, Altrusa, Am. Legion Aux. Judicial administration. Office: Supreme Ct Okla 1 State Capitol Oklahoma City OK 73105 *

WILSON, BRENDA COKER, lawyer; b. El Dorado, Ark., June 25, 1952; d. Paul Henderson and Virginia Helen (Everett) Coker; m. George Allen Wilson II, Apr. 23, 1983; 1 child, Brenton Tyler. BA, U. No. Iowa, 1974; JD, U. Tulsa, 1977. Bar: Fla. 1978, U.S. Dist. Ct. (so. dist.) Fla. 1978. Assoc. Rhodes & Tucker, Marco Island, Fla., 1978-80; sole practice Naples, Fla., 1981-1983, 1986—; ptnr. Faerber & Wilson, Naples, 1983-85; apptd. spl. master Cir. Ct., Naples, 1986. Chmn. county Graham for U.S. Senate, 1986. Named one of Outstanding Young Women of Marco Island, Marco Island Jaycettes, 1980; recipient Exec. Dirs. award Cath. Service Bur., 1981, Woman Achiever of Collier County award Salute to Women Orgn., 1983. Mem. ABA, Fla. Bar Assn. (merit awards 1985), Collier County Bar Assn. (pres. 1984-85), Naples Profl. Women's Network (co-founder 1980). Democrat. Presbyterian. Avocations: tennis, reading, collecting books, needlepoint. Family and matrimonial, General practice, State civil litigation. Office: 2500 Airport Rd Suite 309 Naples FL 33962

WILSON, BRENT LAWRENCE, lawyer, legal educator; b. New Orleans, Jan. 9, 1952; s. Commodore Waddell and Mildred Louise (Quave) W.; m. Trojanell Theresa Bordenave, June 22, 1974. BA, Morehouse Coll., 1973; postgrad., U. Ga., 1973-74; JD, SUNY, Buffalo, 1976. Bar: La. 1976, Ga. 1979, U.S. Dist. Ct. (no. dist.) Ga. 1979, U.S. Ct. Appeals (5th and 11th cirs.) 1979, U.S. Ct. Appeals (3d cir.) 1982, U.S. Ct. Appeals (6th cir.) 1986. Field atty. NLRB, Atlanta, 1976-80; assoc. Elarbee, Thompson & Trapnell, Atlanta, 1980—; lectr. Atlanta U., 1984; adj. prof. law Emory U., Atlanta, 1984-85. Mem. Urban League, Atlanta, 1985-86. Mem. ABA (labor and employment law, mgmt. com.), Atlanta Bar Assn. (labor law sect., sec., treas. 1985, vice chmn. 1986—), Gate City Bar Assn. (asst. sec. 1984-85, Dist. Service award 1985), Nat. Bar Assn., NAACP, Omega Psi Phi. Democrat. Club: Atlanta Morehouse. Avocations: spectator sports, racquetball. Labor. Home: 5574 Fox Glen Circle Lithonia GA 30058 Office: Elarbee Thompson & Trapnell 229 Peachtree St NE Suite 800 Atlanta GA 30043

WILSON, BRUCE BRIGHTON, transportation executive; b. Boston, Feb. 6, 1936; s. Robert Lee and Jane (Schlotterer) W.; m. Elizabeth Ann MacFarland, Dec. 31, 1958; children: Mabeth, Mary, Bruce Robert, Caroline Daly. A.B., Princeton U., 1958; LL.B., U. Pa., 1961. Bar: Pa. 1962. Assoc. Montgomery, McCracken, Walker & Rhoads, Phila., 1962-69; atty. U.S. Dept. Justice, Washington, 1969-79; dep. asst. atty. gen. antitrust div. U.S. Dept. Justice, 1971-76; spl. counsel Consol. Rail Corp., Phila., 1979-81, gen. counsel litigation and antitrust, 1981-82, v.p., gen. counsel, 1982-84, v.p. law, 1984-87, sr. v.p. law, 1987—; dir. Trailer Train Co., Chgo., 1980-82, Penn Car Leasing, Wynnewood, Pa., 1983. Fellow Salzburg Seminar in Am. Studies (Austria), 1965; fellow Felz Inst. State and Local Govt., 1967. Mem. ABA, Phila. Bar Assn. Club: Corinthian Yacht. Antitrust. Home: 224 Chamounix Rd Saint Davids PA 19087 Office: Consol Rail Corp 1842 Six Penn Center Philadelphia PA 19103

WILSON, CHARLES JULIAN, lawyer; b. Freeport, Tex., July 26, 1934; s. Charles J. and Martha E. (Hall) W.; m. N. June Dominy, Oct. 19, 1963. BBA, U. Tex., 1958, LLB, 1960. Bar: Tex. 1960, U.S. Dist. Ct. (so. dist.) Tex. 1962, U.S. Ct. Appeals (5th cir.) 1973, U.S. Ct. Appeals (D.C. cir.) 1974, U.S. Supreme Ct. 1974. Assoc. Stone & Davis, Freeport, Tex., 1960-62; asst. county atty. County Atty.'s Office, Harris County, Tex., 1962-74; assoc. Barrow, Bland & Rehmet, Houston, 1974-77, ptnr., 1977-84; sole practice, Houston, 1984-86, ptnr. Wilson & Swanner, 1986—. Mem. Tex. Bar Assn. (past dir. environ. law sect.). Democrat. Clubs: University, Texas. State civil litigation, Condemnation, State and local taxation. Office: 1600 Smith St Suite 3790 Houston TX 77002

WILSON, CHARLES MICHAEL, lawyer; b. Winston-Salem, N.C., Mar. 3, 1951; s. Charles Homer and Hazel Anne (Enscore) W.; m. Mary Pollard Brigman, Sept. 16, 1978; 1 child, Andrew Charles. BS in Indsl. Engring. magna cum laude, N.C. State U., 1973; JD, Duke U., 1976. Bar: N.C. 1976, U.S. Dist. Ct. (we. dist.) N.C. 1976, U.S. Ct. Appeals (4th cir.) 1982, U.S. Supreme Ct. 1983. Assoc. Griffin, Gerdes, Harris, Mason & Brunson, Charlotte, N.C., 1976-79; ptnr. Gerdes, Mason, Wilson & Tolbert and predecessor firm, Charlotte, 1979—; mem. profl. advisory group Quality Care, Inc., Charlotte, 1984-85. Vol. various polit. campaigns, N.C., 1974—; vol. law clk. Legal Aid Soc. of Durham County, N.C., 1975; vol. asst. dist. atty. Wake County, Raleigh, N.C., 1976; emergency room vol. Charlotte Meml. Hosp. and Med. Ctr., 1977, 83. Mem. N.C. Bar Assn., Assn. Trial Lawyers Am., N.C. Acad. Trial Lawyers, U.S. Tennis Assn., Phi Kappa Phi, Phi Eta Sigma, Alpha Pi Mu (pres. local chpt.). Democrat. Federal civil litigation, General corporate, Personal injury. Home: 4106 Tapperty Circle Charlotte NC 28226 Office: Gerdes Mason Wilson & Tolbert 216 N McDowell St Suite 110 Charlotte NC 28204

WILSON, CHRISTIAN BURHENN, lawyer; b. Balt., Feb. 24, 1946; s. Christian Columbus and Ruth Louise Frieda (Burhenn) W.; m. Kay Spencer Lewis, June 20, 1974. BA, Towson State U., 1968; JD, U. Balt., 1975. Bar: Md. 1976, U.S. Dist. Ct. Md. 1976, U.S. Supreme Ct. 1980. Staff atty. Monumental Properties, Inc., Balt., 1977-79; counsel Mall Mgmt. and Assocs., Balt., 1979-85; sole practice Bel Air, Md., 1986—; asst. prof. Towson (Md.) State U., 1982—. Served to 2d lt., Md. N.G., 1969-70. Mem. ABA, Md. State Bar Assn., Bar Assn. City Balt., Sigma Delta Kappa. Republican. Lutheran. Real property, Landlord-tenant, Consumer commercial. Home: 257 Victory Ln Bel Air MD 21014 Office: 5 S Main St Suite 102 Bel Air MD 21014

WILSON, CLAUDE RAYMOND, JR., lawyer; b. Dallas, Feb. 22, 1933; s. Claude Raymond and Lottie (Watts) W.; m. Barbara Jean Cowherd, Apr. 30, 1960; 1 dau., Deidra Nicole. B.B.A., So. Meth. U., 1954, LL.B., 1956. C.P.A., Calif., Tex. Asso. firm Cervin & Melton, Dallas, 1956-58; atty. Tex. & Pacific R.R. Co., Dallas, 1958-60; atty. office regional counsel IRS, San Francisco, 1960-63; sr. trial atty. office chief counsel IRS, Washington, 1963-65; partner firm Golden, Potts, Boeckman & Wilson, Dallas, 1965—. Mem. Dallas, Am. bar assns., State Bar Tex., Tex. Soc. C.P.A.s (dir. 1973—, sec. 1978-79, mem. exec. com. 1980-81, v.p. 1985-86, pres. Dallas Chpt. 1983-84), Delta Sigma Phi, Delta Theta Phi. Republican. Episcopalian. Clubs: Dallas Gun, Willow Bend Hunt and Polo, Crescent. Lodges: Masons, Shriners, Jesters. Corporate taxation, Estate taxation, Personal income taxation. Home: 4069 Hanover St Dallas TX 75225 Office: 2300 Republic Bank Tower Dallas TX 75201

WILSON, CLIFFORD H., lawyer; b. Bklyn., June 10, 1952; s. Clifford H. and Catherine M. (Ward) W.; m. Mary Ann Francher, June 2, 1979; children: Anna, Michael, Christopher. BA, Yale U., 1975; JD, Syracuse U., 1980. Bar: N.Y. 1981, U.S. Dist. Ct. (no. dist.) N.Y. 1983. Sr. law clk. to presiding justice N.Y. State Supreme Ct., St. Lawrence County, 1980-83; assoc. Hiscock & Barclay, Syracuse, N.Y., 1983—. Mem. Onondaga County Planning Fedn., Syracuse, 1986—. Mem. ABA (natural resource law and state and local govts. sects.), N.Y. State Bar Assn. (environ. and mcpl. law coms. 1980), Onondaga County Bar Assn. (chmn. mcpl. law com. 1986—). Roman Catholic. Avocations: running, racquetball. Environment, Local government, Real property. Office: Hiscock & Barclay PO Box 4878 Syracuse NY 13221

WILSON, CLIFFORD RALPH, lawyer; b. Torrance, Calif., Aug. 12, 1946; s. Oscar Ralph and Dorothy Edna (McCready) W.; m. Abigail Scarlett Biggs, Sept. 10, 1966 (div. 1971); 1 child, Lara Gabrielle; m. Sheryl Lee Stevens, April 14, 1974; 1 child, Clifford Bond. BA, U. Nebr., 1971; JD, U. Iowa, 1974. Bar: Calif. 1974, U.S. Dist. Ct. (no., cen. and ea. dists.) Calif. 1974, Nev. 1975, U.S. Dist. Ct. Nev. 1975, U.S. Ct. Appeals 1976. Asst. dir. acad. dept. Nat. Jud. Coll., Reno, Nev., 1974-76; asst. U.S. atty. Dept. of Justice, Los Angeles, 1976-78; ptnr. Sherbourne, Stevens, Wilson & Reid, Pleasant Hill, Calif., 1978-80, C. Wilson and Assocs., Walnut Creek, Calif., 1980-82, Andersen & Bonnifield, Concord, Calif., 1982-85, C. Wilson and Assocs., Pleasant Hill, 1985—. Served to capt. USAF, 1966-70. Mem. ABA, Contra Costa County Bar Assn., Pleasant Hill C. of C. (pres. 1979-81). Democrat. Club: Corinthian Yacht (Tiburon, Calif.). Avocation: sailing. Federal civil litigation, State civil litigation, Contracts commercial. Home: 1744 Reliez Valley Rd Lafayette CA 94549 Office: Clifford R Wilson and Assocs 3478 Buskirk Ave Pleasant Hill CA 94523

WILSON, CRAIG ALAN, lawyer; b. Washington, Feb. 12, 1956; s. Samuel William and Clara B. (Shannon) W. BA, Yale U., 1978; JD, Harvard U. Bar: D.C., Tex., U.S. Dist. Ct. D.C., U.S. Ct. Appeals (D.C. and 5th cirs.). Law clk. to chief judge U.S. Ct. Appeals (5th cir.), Houston, 1981-82; assoc. White & Case, Washington, 1982—. Contbr. articles to profl. jours. Class agent Yale Alumni Fund, New Haven, Conn., 1981—. Mem. ABA, Bar Assn. D.C., Tex. Bar Assn. Republican. Episcopalian. Avocations: language, skiing. Private international, General corporate, Banking. Home: 4902 Cloister Dr Rockville MD 20852 Office: White & Case 1747 Pennsylvania Ave NW Washington DC 20006

WILSON, DAVID KEITH, lawyer; b. Cheyenne, Wyo., May 1, 1954; s. Robert Keith and Elizabeth Grace (Carnes) W.; m. Patsy Sue Hobbs, June 3, 1978; children: Darbie Renee, Aaron Keith. BS in Banking and Fin., Abilene Christian U., 1976; JD, Baylor U., 1980. Bar: Tex. 1980, U.S. Dist. Ct. (ea. dist.) Tex. 1985, U.S. Dist. Ct. (no. dist.) Tex. 1986, U.S. Ct. Appeals (5th cir.) 1986. Prosecutor justice ctr. Grayson County, Sherman, Tex., 1980-84; assoc. Nance & Caston, Sherman, 1984—. Deacon Travis St. Ch. Christ, Sherman, 1985. Mem. ABA, Tex. Bar Assn., Grayson County Bar Assn. Lodge: Lions. Avocations: fishing, basketball. Federal civil litigation, State civil litigation, Criminal. Office: Nance & Caston 421 N Crockett Sherman TX 75090

WILSON, DONALD L., lawyer; b. Eufaula, Okla., Dec. 10, 1932; s. Arthur J. and Opal Evelyn (Bullard) W.; m. Nancy Caroline Harris, Aug. 15, 1954; children: Wade Harris, Julie Ann, Mary Caroline. BA in Govt., U. Okla., 1955, LLB, 1957; LLM, So. Meth. U., 1964. Assoc. Embry, Crowe, et al, Oklahoma City, 1959-60; pntr. Brooks, Tarlton, Wilson, Ft. Worth, 1960-69; pres. Wilson, & Pierson, Ft. Worth, 1969—. Contbr. articles to profl. jours. Served to capt. USAF, 1957-59. Fellow Tex. Bar Found.; mem. ABA, Okla. Bar Assn., Am. Coll. Probate Council, State Bar Tex. (grievance com. chmn. dist. 7A 1973-74), Ft. Worth Bus. and Estate Planning Council, Ft. Worth-Tarrant County Bar Assn., Phi Beta Kappa. Lodge: Rotary. Estate planning, Probate, Estate taxation. Office: Wilson & Pierson 1100 Tex Am Bank Bldg 500 Throckmorton St Fort Worth TX 76102

WILSON, DONALD RUSSELL, lawyer; b. Birmingham, Ala., Oct. 20, 1947; s. Richard P. and Nelle (O'Mara) W.; m. Clare Robin, Aug. 7, 1971; children: Nell O'Mara, Cydney Robin. BA in History, La. State U., 1971, JD, 1974. Bar: La. 1974, U.S. Dist. Ct. (ea., we. and mid. dists.) La. 1974, U.S. Ct. Appeals (5th cir.) 1974. Assoc. B.C. Bennet Jr., Marksville, La., 1974-75; ptnr. Bennett & Wilson, Marksville, 1975-78; sole practice Marksville, 1978-80; ptnr. Gaharan & Wilson, Jena, La., 1980—. Del. La. Dem. Party, 1985. Mem. ABA, La. Bar Assn. (del. 1978-80, exec. council young lawyers sect. 1976-79), Assn. Trial Lawyers Am., La. Trial Lawyers Assn., LaSalle Parish Bar Assn. Democrat. Roman Catholic. Oil and gas leasing, State civil litigation, Contracts commercial. Office: Gaharan & Wilson PO Box 1356 Jena LA 71342

WILSON, DOUGLAS DOWNES, lawyer; b. Astoria, N.Y., Jan. 20, 1947; s. Douglas and Mildred P. (Payne) W.; m. Joan Bottorf, Feb. 1, 1969; children—Douglas S., Debra J. A.B., Grove City Coll., 1968; J.D., Am. U., 1970; LL.M., George Washington U., 1974. Bar: Md. 1971, D.C. 1971, U.S. Ct. Appeals (D.C. cir.) 1972, U.S. Ct. Mil. Appeals 1972, U.S. Supreme Ct. 1975, Va. 1978, U.S. Tax Ct., U.S. Ct. Claims, U.S. Ct. Appeals (4th cir.), U.S. Dist. Ct. (we. dist.) Va. 1978, U.S. Dist. Ct. (ea. dist.) Va. 1979, U.S. Dist. Ct. (ea. dist.) Ky. 1981. Staff judge advocate Air Force Office Sci. Research, Arlington, Va., 1971-74; trial atty. Office Chief Trial Atty., Dept. Air Force, Wright Patterson AFB, Ohio, 1974-77; assoc. Martin, Hopkins & Lemon, P.C., Roanoke, Va., 1977-78; ptnr. Gardner, Moss & Brown, Washington and Roanoke, 1978-83; ptnr. Parvin & Wilson, P.C., 1984—; guest lectr. Old Dominion U., Norfolk, U. Wis., Madison, Alaska Pacific U., Anchorage. Deacon, chmn. fin. com. First Presbyn. Ch., Roanoke, 1979-82; mem. Roanoke Valley Estate Planning Council, 1979-82; dir. Legal Aid Soc., Roanoke Valley, 1982-84; chmn. long range planning commn. Roanoke City Sch. Bd., 1986-87. Served to capt. USAF, 1971-77. Decorated Air Force Commendation medal with oak leaf cluster. Mem. ABA (pub. contract law sect.), Md. Bar Assn., D.C. Bar Assn., Fed. Bar Assn., Am. Trial Lawyers Assn., Va. Trial Lawyers Assn., Va. Bar Assn., Nat. Assn. Bond Lawyers. Presbyterian. Clubs: Elks (exalted ruler 1973-74), Forest Ridge Civic Assn. (dir. 1974-77). Government contracts and claims, Labor, Construction. Home: 3030 Bancroft Dr SW Roanoke VA 24014 Office: Dominion Bank Bldg 213 S Jefferson St Roanoke VA 24011

WILSON, DUANE ALBERT, lawyer; b. Huntsville, Ala., Oct. 9, 1959; s. William Albert and Velma Elwanda (Ammons) W.; m. Paula Dionis Blankenship, Aug. 29, 1981. BA, U. Ala., 1979; JD, Vanderbilt U., 1982. Bar: Ala. 1982, U.S. Dist. Ct. (so. dist.) Ala. 1972, U.S. Ct. Appeals (11th cir.) 1985. Assoc. Coale, Helmsing, Lyons & Sims, Mobile, Ala., 1982—. Mem. ABA, Mobile Bar Assn. (pres. young lawyers sect. 1986—). Club: Athelstan (Mobile). Federal civil litigation, State civil litigation, Insurance. Home: 1602 Monterey Pl Mobile AL 36604 Office: Coale Helmsing Lyons & Sims 150 Government St Mobile AL 36602

WILSON, EDWARD CHURCHILL, lawyer; b. Chgo., Oct. 15, 1940; s. Max Elroy and Margaret (Tufts) W.; m. Patricia Daley, Sept. 2, 1961; children—Edward Wallace, David Maxwell. B.S. with honors, Lewis U., 1974, J.D., 1978. Bars: Ill. 1978, U.S. Dist. Ct. (no. dist.) Ill. 1978, U.S. Ct. Appeals (7th cir.) 1978, U.S. Supreme Ct. 1982. Assoc. Conklin and Adler, Chgo., 1978-81; sole practice, LaGrange, Ill., 1981—; pres. Edward C. Wilson & Assocs., Aviation Accident Investigators. Named mem. Barional Order of Magna Charta, 1970. Mem. Chgo. Bar Assn., Ill. State Bar Assn., ABA, Lawyer/Pilots Bar Assn., Internat. Soc. Air Safety Investigators, Aircraft Owners and Pilots Assn. (legis. liaison com. 1980—). Aviation, Personal injury. Home: 724 N LaGrange Rd LaGrange Park IL 60525 Office: 521 S LaGrange Rd LaGrange IL 60525

WILSON, EDWARD MILLER, lawyer; b. Fort Dodge, Iowa, July 30, 1954; s. Charles Robert and Viola Arvella (Miller) W.; m. Joanna Marie Bohn, Aug. 21, 1976; children: Joanna Lynn, Emily Katherine. A.B., Princeton U., 1977; J.D., U. Iowa, 1980. Bar: Iowa 1980, U.S. Dist. Ct. (no. dist.) Iowa 1983. Assoc. Birdwell Law Office, Corydon, Iowa, 1980-82; asst. county atty. Wayne County, Iowa, Corydon, 1980-82, Clinton County, Iowa, 1982; county atty., Calhoun County, Iowa, Manson, 1983-85, asst. county atty., 1985-86; proprietor Wilson Law Office, Manson, 1983-86. Mem. ABA, Iowa State Bar Assn., Iowa County Attys. Assn., Calhoun County Bar Assn., Dist. 2 Bar Assn., Manson C. of C. (v.p.). Republican. General practice, Criminal, Probate. Home: 1714 Tesla Dr Colorado Springs CO 80909

WILSON, FRED PALMER, lawyer; b. Amory, Miss., Dec. 7, 1922; s. Jesse Clarence and Leta Belle (Palmer) W.; m. Jean Carter Wilson, Aug. 27, 1948; children—Fred P., Stuart A. B.S., Memphis State U., 1947; J.D., Vanderbilt U., 1950. Bar: Tenn. 1951. Ptnr. Wilson, McRae, Ivy, Sevier, McTyier & Strain, Memphis. Served with U.S. Navy, 1943-46. Fellow Am. Coll. Trial Lawyers, Tenn. Bar Found.; mem. ABA, Tenn. Bar Assn., Memphis and Shelby County Bar Assn., Fedn. Ins. Counsel, Tenn. Def. Lawyers Assn., Phi Alpha Delta. Republican. Methodist. Clubs: Tenn., Petroleum, Racquet (Memphis). Federal civil litigation, State civil litigation, Insurance. Home: 6523 Corsica Dr Memphis TN 38119 Office: 100 N Main Bldg Suite 3130 Memphis TN 38103

WILSON, GARY KEITH, lawyer; b. Erie, Pa., Oct. 10, 1951; s. Ned S. and Anna Jane (Borger) W.; m. Sharon Lindblad; July 2, 1977; children: Michael Ned, Erika Seelbach. BA, Fla. State U., 1973, MS, 1974; JD, Loyola U., New Orleans, 1980. Bar: Fla. 1980. Assoc. Carroll & Bolesky, Naples, Fla., 1980-85, Bolesky & Wilson, Naples, 1985—; bd dirs. Milestone Youth Home, Naples. Deacon First Presbyn. Ch., Naples, 1982-85. Mem. Collier County Bar Assn., ABA. Republican. Lodge: Kiwanis (bd. dirs. Naples club 1985-86). Avocations: tennis, racquetball, stained glass. General corporate, General practice, Real property. Home: 54 32nd Ave S Naples FL 33940 Office: Bolesky & Wilson 1169 Eighth St S Naples FL 33940

WILSON, GEORGE ALLEN, lawyer; b. Pitts., Jan. 22, 1955; s. George Allen and Shirley Reagan (Parker) W.; m. Brenda Kay Coker, Apr. 23, 1983; 1 child, Brenton Tyler. BA in Econs., U. Cin., 1977; JD, U. Toledo, 1980; LLM in Estate Planning, U. Miami, 1981. Bar: Ohio 1980, Fla. 1981. Assoc. Cummings & Lockwood, Naples, Fla., 1981—; lectr. various edni. seminars. Bd. dirs. Tng. and Ednl. Ctr. for Handicapped, Naples, 1984—, Moorings Park, Naples, 1986—, Found. Mental Health, Naples, 1986—. Mem. ABA, Fla. Bar Assn. (real property and probate sects.). Republican. Presbyterian. Estate planning, Probate, Estate taxation. Home: 2821 66th St SW Naples FL 33999 Office: Cummings & Lockwood 3001 Tamiami Trail N Suite 400 Naples FL 33940

WILSON, GEORGE SIMPSON, III, lawyer; b. Owensboro, N.Y., Aug. 9, 1932; s. George Simpson Jr. and Virginia (Queen) W.; m. Marian Williams, Feb. 16, 1957; children: Jennifer, Berry. BA magna cum laude, Washington and Lee U., 1954, JD magna cum laude, 1956. Bar: Ky. 1956, U.S. Dist. Ct. (we. dist.) Ky. 1956, U.S. Ct. Mil. Appeals, U.S. Ct. Appeals (6th cir.) 1970, U.S. Supreme Ct. 1973. Atty. Wilson, Wilson & Plain, Owensboro, Ky., 1956—. Deacon First Bapt. Ch., Owensboro, 1957—; bd. dirs. Jr. Achievement of Owensboro (past pres. 1975), Owensboro Symphony Orch. (past pres. 1978), Am. Radio Relay League, Newington, Conn., 1984—; mem. Ky. Bd. Bar Examiners, 1985—, sec., 1987—. Mem. ABA, Ky. Bar Assn. (bd. govs. 1971-77, committeeman unauthorized practices 1977—, joint committeeman rev. code of conduct), Owensboro-Daviess County Bar Assn. Democrat. Baptist. Probate, Insurance, General practice. Office: 414 Masonic Bldg 227 St Ann St Owensboro KY 42301

WILSON, HARRISON BENJAMIN, III, lawyer; b. Jackson, Miss., Nov. 9, 1955; s. Harrison Benjamin Jr. and Lucy Reed W.; m. Tammy Devar Turner, June 20, 1981; children: Harrison Benjamin IV. BA in History, Dartmouth Coll., 1977; JD, U. Va., 1980. Bar: Ohio 1982. Counsel Procter & Gamble, Cin., 1980—. V.I.P. Cin. Easter Seal Telathon, 1984-86; sec., bd. dirs. People Working Cooperatively, Cin., 1985-86; bd. dirs. Lytle Park Child Devel. Ctr., Cin., 1985-86, Reggie Williams Scholarship Fund, Cin., 1986. Mem. ABA, Cin. Black Lawyers Assn. Workers' compensation, Product liability. Home: 432 Whitestone Ct Cincinnati OH 45231 Office: Procter & Gamble Co. 1 Procter & Gamble Plaza Cincinnati OH 45202

WILSON, HUGH STEVEN, lawyer; b. Paducah, Ky., Nov. 27, 1947; s. Hugh Gipson and Rebekah (Dunn) W.; m. Clare Maloney, Apr. 28, 1973; children: Morgan Elizabeth, Zachary Hunter. BS, Ind. U., 1968; JD, U. Chgo., 1971; LLM, Harvard U., 1972. Bar: Calif. 1972, U.S. Dist. Ct. (cen. dist.) Calif. 1972, U.S. Dist. Ct. (so. dist.) Calif. 1973, U.S. Ct. Appeals (9th cir.) 1975, U.S. Dist. Ct. (no. dist.) Calif. 1977, U.S. Dist. Ct. (ea. dist.) 1980. Assoc. Latham & Watkins, Los Angeles, 1972-78, ptnr., 1978—, chmn. litigation dept., 1986—. Recipient Jerome N. Frank prize U. Chgo. Law Sch., 1971. Mem. ABA, Los Angeles County Bar Assn., Order of Coif. Republican. Club: Jonathan (Los Angeles). Avocations: lit., zoology. Federal civil litigation, General corporate, Criminal.

WILSON, JACK, lawyer; b. Melbourne, Pa., Oct. 26, 1926; s. Bryan and Idell (Brown) W.; m. Bobbie Jenkins, Dec. 7, 1952; children: Jane, John, Julia. BS, U. Ala., 1950, JD, 1953. Bar: Ala. 1955, U.S. Ct. Appeals (11th cir.), U.S. Supreme Ct. Ptnr. Wilson, Pumroy, Rice & Adams, Anniston, Ala. Chmn. Calhoun County Rep. Party, 1972, Boys Club of Anniston, 1980, Donahoe Sch., 1984-85; mem. Ala. Rep. Com., 1964—. Mem. ABA, Ala. State Bar Assn., Calhoun County Bar Assn. (pres. 1962), Jaycees (pres. 1962). Lodge: Kiwanis (pres. 1965). Avocation: golf. State civil litigation, Contracts commercial, Real property. Home: 7 Timothy Trace Anniston AL 36201 Office: Wilson Pumroy Rice & Adams 1431 Leighton Ave Anniston AL 36201

WILSON, JAMES BARKER, lawyer, writer; b. Visalia, Calif., Jan. 29, 1926; s. John Fleming and Helen Mae (Barker) W.; m. Joanne Bailey, Apr. 27, 1956. B.A., U. Wash., 1948, J.D., 1950. Bar: Wash. 1950, U.S. Supreme Ct. 1955. Asst. atty. gen. Wash. State Atty. Gen., Seattle, 1951-52; prin. Harlow, Ringold & Wilson, Seattle, 1953-63; asst. atty. gen. U. Wash., Seattle, 1963-67, sr. asst. atty. gen., 1967—; gen. counsel U. Wash., 1967—. Contbr. chpts. to books, articles to profl. jours. Democrat candidate for U.S.

Congress, 1st Dist., Wash., 1956; del. Dem. Nat. Conv., 1952, 60; pres. bd. trustees Group Health Credit Union, 1954-61; v.p. Group Health Co-op, Seattle, 1963-64; bd. dirs. Henry Gallery, U. Wash., 1972-80, Allied Arts of Seattle, 1973-75. Served with USAAF, 1944-45. Mem. ABA, Wash. State Bar Assn., Seattle-King County Bar Assn., Nat. Assn. Coll. and Univ. Attys. (bd. dirs. 1972-73, pres. 1979-80, cert. of merit 1980), Phi Alpha Delta, Theta Chi. Administrative and regulatory, Civil rights, General practice. Office: U Wash AF-50 Seattle WA 98195

WILSON, JAMES DONEHOO, lawyer; b. Royal Oak, Mich., Nov. 7, 1950; s. William Donehoo and Anne (Willis) W.; m. Pamela Ange, Aug. 4, 1973; children: Elizabth Tazewell, Tyler James. BS, Oreg. State U., 1973; JD, Ill. Inst. Tech., 1978. Bar: Ill. 1978, U.S. Dist. Ct. (no. dist.) Ill. 1978. Law clk. to presiding justice Ill. Ct. Appeals, Waukegan, 1978-79; mgr. ct. systems Cook County Cir. Ct., Chgo., 1979-84, dir. ct. systems, 1984—. Coauthor: Civil Practice Before Trial, 1978, Civil Practice, 1983, rev. edit., 1985; also articles. Mem. ABA (del. young lawyers div. 1983-86), Ill. Bar Assn., Chgo. Bar Assn. (project dir. young lawyers sect. 1984—, chmn. 1986—), Nat. Assn. Ct. Mgmt. Episcopalian. Judicial administration. Home: 625 Ivy Ct Kenilworth IL 60043 Office: Cook County Cir Ct 2600 RJ Daley Ctr Chicago IL 60602

WILSON, JAMES WILLIAM, lawyer; b. Spartanburg, S.C., June 19, 1928; s. James William and Ruth (Greenwaldt) W.; m. Elizabeth Clair Pickett, May 23, 1952; children: Susan Alexandra, James William. Student, Tulane U., 1945-46; B.A., U. Tex., Austin, 1950, LL.B., 1951. Bar: Tex. bar 1951. Practiced in Austin, 1951-79; partner McGinnis, Lochridge & Kilgore (and predecessors), 1960-76; counsel Stubbeman, McRae, Sealy, Laughlin & Browder, 1976-79; sr. v.p. and gen. counsel Brown & Root, Inc., Houston, 1980—, also dir.; asst. atty. gen., 1957-58; counsel Senate Democratic Policy Com.; legis. asst. to senate majority leader Lyndon B. Johnson, 1959-60; lectr. U. Tex. Law Sch., 1962-63; dir. Continental Air Lines, Tex. Air Corp., Ea. Airlines, Inc., Highlands Ins. Co. Served from ensign to lt. (j.g.) USNR, 1952-55. Fellow Tex. Bar Found.; mem. Am., Tex., Harris County bar assns., Am. Law Inst., Order of Coif, Phi Beta Kappa. General corporate, State civil litigation, Antitrust. Home: 3218 Reba Dr Houston TX 77019 Office: PO Box 3 4100 Clinton Dr Houston TX 77001

WILSON, JOSEPH MORRIS, III, lawyer, law educator; b. Milw., July 26, 1945; s. Joseph Morris Jr. and Phyllis Elizabeth (Cresson) W.; m. Margaret McClure, July 28, 1973 (div. Oct. 1983); children: Elizabeth J., Eric M.; m. Dixie Lee Brock, Mar. 23, 1984. BA, Calif. State U., Chico, 1967; MA, U. Washington, 1968; JD, Ohio State U., 1976. Bar: Alaska 1976, U.S. Dist. Ct. Alaska 1976, U.S. Ct. Appeals (9th cir.) 1986. Recruiter and vol. U.S. Peace Corps, People Republic of Benin, 1969-73; legal intern U.S. Ho. of Reps., Washington, 1975; ptnr. Guess & Rudd P.C., Anchorage, 1976—, chmn. comml. dept., 1981-82, ptnr. compensation com., 1982—; bus. law instr. U. Alaska, Anchorage, 1977-78. Counsel Tanaina Child Devel. Ctr., Anchorage, 1982—, Alaska Child Passenger Safety Assn., Anchorage, 1983—; bd. dirs. Alaska Alcohol Safety Action Program, Anchorage, 1977—. Mem. ABA, Alaska Bar Assn. (taxation sect.), Anchorage Bar Assn., Anchorage Jazz Soc., Anchorage C. of C. Democrat. Club: UAA BAsketball Boosters. Avocations: music, sports, investments, traveling, languages (fluent in French and Dendi). State and local taxation, General corporate, Contracts commercial. Home: 1779 Morningtide Ct Anchorage AK 99501 Office: Guess & Rudd PC 510 L St Suite 700 Anchorage AK 99501

WILSON, KENNETH BELTON, lawyer; b. Dickens, Tex., Feb. 23, 1938; s. Ben E. and Jo Helen (French) W.; m. Laura J. Stewart, (div.); children—Helena A., Patricia C.; m. Philia L. Purcella, Jan. 14, 1966; 1 son, Wendell Ray. B.B.A., Baylor U., 1972, J.D., 1974. Bar: Tex. 1974, N. Mex. 1975, U.S. Dist. Ct. N. Mex. 1976, U.S. Dist. Ct. (we. dist.) Tex. 1977. Assoc. Brown & Assocs., Roswell, N.Mex., 1975-79; sole practice, Roswell, 1980—. Mem. ABA, Tex. Bar Assn., N.Mex. Bar Assn., N. Mex. Trial Lawyers Assn. Republican. Baptist. State civil litigation, Criminal, Personal injury. Home: Route 3 Box 214-D Roswell NM 88201 Office: PO Box 849 215 W 6th St Roswell NM 88201

WILSON, LAURA JANE, lawyer; b. Kansas City, Mo., Feb. 21, 1937; d. Samuel B. and Jr. and Dorothy (Cunningham) Haskin; Lauren R. Wilson, Jan. 25, 1959; children: Lance, Keela. BA, Baker U., 1958; MS, U. Kans., 1959; JD, Capital U., 1982. Bar: 1982, U.S. Dist. Ct. (so. dist.) Ohio 1983. Sole practice Delaware, Ohio, 1982—. Pres. Council on Alcoholism, Delaware County, 1985. Mem. ABA, Ohio Bar Assn., Delaware County Bar Assn., Delaware County Trial Lawyers Assn. Family and matrimonial, Juvenile, General practice. Home: 196 W Lincoln Ave Delaware OH 43015 Office: 2 W Winter St Suite 3 Delaware OH 43015

WILSON, LEONARD HENRY (L.H.), lawyer; b. Poplar Bluff, Mo., Nov. 12, 1950; s. Vencil Willard and Helen Jane (Scheerer) W.; m. Carolyn Elizabeth Nix, June 1, 1974; 1 child, Jack Louis. B.S. with highest honors, U. So. Miss., 1972, M.S., 1973; J.D., U. Mo.-Kansas City, 1975; grad. Miss. Sch. Banking, U. Miss., 1981, Sch. of Banking of South, La. State U., 1986. Bar: Mo. 1976, U.S. Dist. Ct. (we. dist.) Mo. 1976, Miss. 1979, U.S. Dist. Ct. (so. dist.) Miss. 1979. Asst. dist. counsel U.S. Army C.E., Kansas City, Mo., 1976-78; gen. counsel Miss. Bankers Assn., Jackson, Miss., 1978—; lectr. Miss. Sch. Banking, Oxford, 1981—; speaker bank attys. com. sessions Miss. State Bar convs., Biloxi, 1982—. Editor: Selected Mississippi Banking Laws, 1979, 80, 82, 84, 86. Congl. intern U.S. Congress, Washington, 1972; mem., sec. Gov.'s Com. to Mitigate Flood Damage, Jackson, Miss., 1979; treas., organizer Miss. Bankers Assn. Polit. Action Com., Jackson, 1979—. U. So. Miss. grad. fellow, Hattiesburg, 1972-73. Mem. ABA, Mo. Bar Assn., Miss. State Bar (bank attys. com. 1982-83, 85—), Hinds County Bar Assn., Phi Kappa Phi, Phi Alpha Delta. Presbyterian. Club: Colonial Country (Jackson, Miss.). Banking, Consumer commercial, Legislative. Home: 5346 Red Fox Rd Jackson MS 39211 Office: Miss Bankers Assn PO Box 37 640 N State St Jackson MS 39205

WILSON, LEROY, JR., lawyer; b. Savannah, Ga., June 16, 1939; s. Leroy and Mary Louise (Frazier) W.; m. Helen Odum (div.); 1 child, Andrea Lynette; m. Jane Marie Beaver, Nov. 18, 1967; children: Jason Garrett, Christopher Harlan. Student, U. Vienna, Austria, 1959-60; BS, Morehouse Coll., 1962; MS, U. Calif., Berkeley, 1965, JD, 1968. Bar: N.Y. 1969, U.S. Dist. Ct. (so. dist.) N.Y. 1974, U.S. Supreme Ct. 1981, U.S. Dist. Ct. (ea. dist.) N.Y. 1982, U.S. Ct. Internat. Trade 1984, U.S. Dist. Ct. (no. dist.) N.Y. 1985, U.S. Tax Ct. 1985, U.S. Ct. Appeals (2d cir.) 1985. Atty. IBM Corp., Armonk, N.Y., 1968-74; asst. div. counsel Union Carbide, Danbury, Conn., 1974-82; sole practice White Plains, N.Y., 1982—; mem. N.Y. State Banking Bd., N.Y.C., 1983—. Mem. ABA, N.Y. State Bar Assn., Nat. Bar Assn. (v.p. bd. govs. 1984-85), N.Y. State Trial Lawyers Assn., Am. Trial Lawyers Assn. Avocations: movies, travel, music, spectator sports. Civil rights, Federal civil litigation, General corporate. Home: 350 Stratton Rd New Rochelle NY 10804 Office: 149 Grand St White Plains NY 10601

WILSON, LEVON EDWARD, lawyer, law educator; b. Charlotte, N.C., Apr. 2, 1954; s. James A. and Thomasina Wilson. BSBA, Western Carolina U., 1976; JD, N.C. Cen. U., 1979. Bar: N.C. 1981, U.S. Dist. Ct. (mid. dist.) N.C. 1981, U.S. Tax Ct. 1981, U.S. Ct. Appeals (4th cir.) 1982. Sole practice Greensboro, N.C., 1981-85; asst. county atty. Guilford County, Greensboro, 1985—; instr. N.C. A & T State U., Greensboro, 1979-85; legal counsel, bd. dirs. Rhodes Assocs., Inc., Greensboro, 1982—; legal counsel Guilford County Sheriff's Dept., Greensboro, 1985—. bd. dirs. Post Advocacy Detention Program. Recipient Service award Blacks in Mgmt., 1980. Mem. ABA, N.C. Bar Assn., Am. Bus. Law Assn., N.C. Assn. Police Attys., Greensboro Jaycees, Phi Delta Phi. Democrat. Methodist. Local government, State civil litigation, Legal education. Home: PO Box 21664 Greensboro NC 27420 Office: Guilford County Legal Dept PO Box 3427 Greensboro NC 27402

WILSON, MARTIN BRYANT, lawyer; b. Saginaw, Mich., July 29, 1951; s. Bryant S. and Ella Mae (DePrekel) W.; m. Deborah Lynn Reid, Sept. 13, 1986. BA with high honor, Mich. State U., 1973; JD, Detroit Coll. Law, 1976. Bar: Mich. 1976, U.S. Dist. Ct. Mich. (ea. and no. dists.) 1980. Assoc. LeFevre & Swartz, Saginaw, 1976-79, ptnr., 1979—. Bd. dirs. Abortion Alternatives, Saginaw, 1986—. Mem. Mich. Bar Assn. (negligence law sect.), Saginaw County Bar Assn. (treas. 1978-80, Cert. Meritory Service 1979), Assn. Trial Lawyers Am., Mich. Trial Lawyers Assn., ACLU. Democrat. Roman Catholic. Lodge: KC. Avocations: reading, travel, chess. Personal injury, State civil litigation, General practice. Home: 1842 Glendale Saginaw MI 48603 Office: LeFevre Swartz & Wilson 908 Court St Saginaw MI 48602

WILSON, MARTIN S., JR., lawyer; b. Atlantic City, Apr. 9, 1946; s. Martin S. Sr. and Anna M. (Chialastri) W.; m. Kathryn E. Molinari, Dec. 20, 1969; children: Kathryn A., Martin L., Meredith M. BS in Acctg., St. Joseph's Coll., Phila., 1968; JD, Villanova U., 1973; LLM in Taxation, Temple U., 1979. Bar: N.J. 1974, U.S. Dist. Ct. N.J. 1974, U.S. Tax Ct. 1975. Assoc. Blatt & Mairone, Atlantic City, 1974-78; ptnr. Blatt, Mairone, Biel et al, Atlantic City, 1978-81, Luciani & Wilson, Atlantic City, 1982-83, Wilson & Scerni, Atlantic City, 1983-84, Wilson, Fusco & Scerni P.A., Atlantic City, 1985—; mem. com. N.J. Casino Law. Chmn. Columbus Day Com., Atlantic City; bd. dirs. Atlantic County Boy Scouts Am., Atlantic City, Miss Am. Pageant, Atlantic City, 1985—. Recipient Appreciation award Boys' Town Italy, Rome, 1985, Coop. Vocat. Edn., Atlantic City, 1985, Am. Heart Assn., Atlantic City, 1985, Inter-racial award Federated Charities, Atlantic City, 1986. Mem. ABA (mcpl. and taxation sects.), N.J. Bar Assn., Atlantic County Bar Assn., Am. Arbitration Assn. (panel), Internat. Assn. Gaming Attys. (gen. counsel). Administrative and regulatory, Local government, Real property. Office: Wilson Fusco & Scerni PA PO Box 567 Atlantic City NJ 08404

WILSON, MICHAEL B(RUCE), lawyer; b. Boise, Idaho, Aug. 5, 1943; s. George E. and Helen E. (Hughes) W.; m. Sarah J. Copeland, June 18, 1966; children: David B., Janet L. BS in Math., Oreg. State U., 1965, MS in Gen. Sci., 1966; JD, Northwestern U., 1978. Bar: Oreg. 1978, U.S. Ct. Mil. Appeals 1978. Commd. 2d lt. USAF, 1966, advanced through grades to maj., 1978, served in Vietnam, 1968; chief of logistics 3d Weather Wing, Offut AFB, Nebr., 1969-71; chief maintenance 2d Weather Wing, Wiesbaden AFB, Fed. Republic Germany, 1971-75; chief civil law HQ Chanute TTC, Chanute AFB, Ill., 1978-80; chief civil and mil. affairs HQ 17th Air Force, Sembach AFB, Fed. Republic Germany, 1980-83; dir. communications and computer systems law Air Force Communications Command, Scott AFB, Ill., 1983—; chmn. Joint Services Telephone Working Group, 1983—, Air Force Comml. Communications Working Group, Scott AFB, 1985—, AFCC Comml. Communications Working Group, Scott AFB, 1985—, DOD Comml. Telecommunications Com. Liason Officer Boy Scouts Am., Sembach AFB, 1981-83. Recipient Mgmt./Adminstrv. Excellence award Interagy. Com. on Info. Resources Mgmt., 1987. Mem. ABA, Fed. Communications Bar Assn., Armed Forces Communications Electronics Assn. Telecommunications, Public utilities, Computer. Home: 808 W Lakeshore Dr OFallon IL 62269 Office: HQ AFCC/JAS Scott AFB IL 62225

WILSON, OSCAR, JR., lawyer, army reserve officer; b. Jasper, Fla., May 10, 1935; s. Oscar and Susie Mae (Brown) W.; m. Lola Will Carter, Aug. 17, 1956; m. Tu-I Yim, May 22, 1970; children—Curtis Lee, Hank, Joseph, Maria. B.S., Fla. A&M U., 1958, J.D., U. Akron, 1978; B.S., U. Md., 1981; M.S., U. So. Calif., 1983. Bar: Ohio 1978, Fla. 1985. Commd. 2d lt. U.S. Army, 1959, advanced through grades to maj., 1973, active duty USAR, 1958—, commd. lt. col., 1978; served in various positions in U.S., Germany, 1961-63; adviser, Vietnam, 1965; insp. gen. Ft. Hood, Tex. and 8th U.S. Army, Korea, 1969-73; edn. counselor U.S. Army, Camp Casey, Korea, 1973-75; dir. edn. Camp Ames, then Camp Carroll, Korea, 1981-83; edn. specialist Army Res. Readiness Tng. Ctr., 1983—; law clk. Parms, Parnell & Williams, Akron, Ohio, 1976-78; sole practice, Seoul and Taegu, Korea, 1978-83. Decorated Legion of Merit. Mem. ABA, Akron Bar Assn., Akron U. Alumni Assn., Am. Personnel and Guidance Assn., Assn. of U.S. Army, Nat. Fedn. Fed. Employers, Res. Officers Assn. of U.S., Phi Alpha Delta, Phi Beta Sigma. Democrat. Criminal, Family and matrimonial, Probate. Office: 406 NL St Sparta WI 54656

WILSON, PAUL DENNIS, lawyer; b. Milw., Apr. 23, 1953; s. Robert D. and Dorothy (Fischer) W.; m. Mary B. Donchez, June 15, 1985. AB cum laude, Princeton U., 1975; JD cum laude, NYU, 1981. Bar: Mass. 1982, U.S. Dist. Ct. Mass. 1983, U.S. Ct. Appeals (1st cir.) 1983. Law clk. to judge U.S. Dist. Ct., Atlanta, 1981-82; assoc. Mintz, Levin, Cohn, Ferris, Glovsky and Popeo, Boston, 1982—; adj. lectr. Boston U., 1985—. Mem. ABA, Mass. Bar. Assn., Boston Bar Assn. Lodge: Order of Coif. Avocations: hiking, canoeing, skiing. Federal civil litigation, State civil litigation. Home: 19 Follen St Boston MA 02116 Office: Mintz et al One Fin Ctr Boston MA 02111

WILSON, PAUL LOWELL, lawyer; b. Rockingham County, Va., May 12, 1951; s. James Joseph and Edna Vivian (Halterman) W.; m. Thea Elaine Hermit, June 21, 1975; children: Meredith Elaine, Taylor Halterman. AB, W.Va. U., 1973; JD, Coll. of William and Mary, 1976. Bar: W.Va. 1976, U.S. Dist. Ct. (so. dist.) W.Va. 1976, Va. 1979. Assoc. Brown & Peyton, Charleston, W.Va., 1976-78; title atty. Lawyers Title Ins. Corp., Williamsburg, Va., 1978-80; assoc. S.J. Baker, Williamsburg, 1981-83; counsel edn. com. W.Va. Legislature, Charleston, 1977-78; gen counsel A.J. & L. Corp., Washington, 1983-85, v.p., gen. counsel, Williamsburg, 1985—; bd. dirs. First Va. Bank-Commonwealth, Grafton, 503 Cert. Devel. Co., Richmond, Sta. WHRO-TV.Mem. York County Sch. Bd. 1986—, trustee Nat. Housing Corp., 1986—. Mem. ABA, Va. Bar Assn., Va. State Bar, W.Va. State Bar, Williamsburg Bar Assn., EconoLodges Am. Franchisee Assn. (bd. dirs. 1986—), Sigma Phi Epsilon. Methodist. Lodge: Kiwanis (Williamsburg). General corporate, Contracts commercial, Real property. Home: 130 Holcomb Dr Williamsburg VA 23185 Office: A J & L Corp 1408 Richmond Rd Williamsburg VA 23185

WILSON, PETE, senator; b. Lake Forest, Ill., Aug. 23, 1933; s. James Boone and Margaret (Callaghan) W.; m. Betty Robertson (div.); m. Gayle Edlund, May 29, 1983. B.A. in English Lit., Yale U., 1955; J.D., U. Calif.-Berkeley, 1962; LL.D., Grove City Coll., 1983, U. Calif.-San Diego, 1983, U. San Diego, 1984. Bar: Calif. 1962. Mem. Calif. Legislature, Sacramento, 1966-71; mayor City of San Diego, 1971-83; U.S. Senator from Calif. 1983—. Trustee Conservation Found.; mem. exec. bd. San Diego County council Boy Scouts Am.; hon. trustee So. Calif. Council Soviet Jews; adv. mem. Urban Land Inst., 1985-86; founding dir. Retinitis Pigmentosa Internat.; hon. dir. Alzheimer's Family Ctr., Inc., 1985; hon. bd. dirs. Shakespeare-San Francisco, 1985. Recipient Golden Bulldog award, 1984, 85, 86, Guardian of Small Bus. award, 1984; ROTC scholar Yale U., 1951-55; named Legislator of Yr., League Calif. Cities, 1985; Man of Yr. award Nat. Guard Assn. Calif., 1986, Man of Yr. citation U. Calif. Boalt Hall, 1986. Mem. Nat. Mil. Family Assn. (adv. bd.), Phi Delta Phi, Zeta Psi. Republican. Episcopalian. Office: US Senate 720 Hart Senate Bldg Washington DC 20510

WILSON, REID CARROLL, lawyer; b. San Antonio, Oct. 14, 1954; s. Ray Clarence and Lucy (Reid) W.; m. Kim Rogers, Sept. 6, 1980. BBA, U. Tex., 1975, JD, 1979, postgrad., 1976. Bar: Tex. 1979, U.S. Dist. Ct. (so. dist.) Tex. 1981, cert. in comml. real estate law, Tex. Assoc. Saccomanno, Clegg, Martin & Kipple, Houston, 1979-84; mng. ptnr. Reese, Meyer & Cribbs P.C., Houston, 1984—. Mem. charter commn. City of W. Univ. Place, 1983, nomination com. W. Univ. Place Party, 1985; chmn. planning and zoning commn. W. Univ. Place, 1985—. Mem. ABA, Tex. Bar Assn., Houston Bar Assn., Tex. Assn. of Bank Counsel. Club: University (Houston). Banking, Real property. Home: 6107 Lake Houston TX 77005 Office: Reese Meyer & Cribbs PC 1700 West Loop S #1100 Houston TX 77027

WILSON, RHYS THADDEUS, lawyer; b. Albany, Ga., May 9, 1955; s. Joseph Farr Jr. and Betty Ann (WilKins) W.; m. Carolyn Reid Saffold, June 2, 1984. AB, Duke U., 1976; JD, U. Ga., 1979; LLM, Emory U., 1985. Bar: Ga. 1979. Assoc. Henkel & Lamon, P.C., Atlanta, 1979-81, Lamon, Elrod & Harkleroad, Atlanta, 1981-84; ptnr. Harkleroad & Hermance, P.C., Atlanta, 1984—, also bd. dirs.; speaker continuing legal edn. seminars. Contbr. articles to profl. jours. Mem. ABA, Ga. Bar Assn. (chmn. internat. law com. Ga. Younger Lawyers sect. 1985-86, vice chmn. internat. law sect. 1986-87, Ga. State Bar Jour.), Atlanta Bar Assn. (editor newsletter 1984-86, Outstanding Service award 1986). Episcopalian.Clubs: World Trade (Atlanta), Lawyers (Atlanta). Personal income taxation, Private international, General corporate. Office: Harkleroad & Hermance PC 2500 Cain Tower 229 Peachstree St NE Atlanta GA 30043

WILSON, ROBERT FOSTER, lawyer; b. Windsor, Colo., Apr. 6, 1926; s. Foster W. and Anne Lucille (Svedman) W.; m. Mary Elizabeth Clark, Mar. 4, 1951 (div. Feb. 1972); children—Robert F., Katharine A.; m. Sally Anne Nemec, June 8, 1982. B.A. in Econs., U. Iowa, 1950, J.D., 1951. Bar: Iowa 1951, U.S. Dist. Ct. (no. and so. dists.) Iowa 1956, U.S. Ct. Appeals (8th cir.) 1967. Atty., FTC, Chgo., 1951-55; sole practice, Cedar Rapids, Iowa, 1955—; dir. Appollo Computer Tech., Veterans Pub. Safety. Democratic state rep. Iowa Legislature, Linn County, 1959-60; mem. Iowa Reapportionment Com., 1968; pres. Linn County Day Care, Cedar Repids, 1968-70. Served to sgt. U.S. Army, 1944-46. Mem. Am. Legion (judge advocate 1970-75), Iowa Trial Lawyers Assn., Assn. Trial Lawyers Am., Iowa Bar Assn., Linn County Bar Assn., Delta Theta Phi. Club: Cedar View Country. Lodges: Elks, Eagles. Personal injury, Labor, Workers' compensation. Home: 100-1st Ave NE Cedar Rapids IA 52401 Office: 810 Dows Bldg Cedar Rapids IA 52401

WILSON, ROBERT M., accountant, lawyer; b. St. Louis, Aug. 10, 1952; s. William H. and Mary E. (Sacksteder) W.; m. Joli Schneeberger, Oct. 7, 1978. B.S., Miami U. Oxford, Ohio, 1974; J.D. magna cum laude, Cleve. State U., 1977. Bar: Ohio 1977; C.P.A., Ohio. With Touche Ross & Co., Dayton, Ohio, 1972—, tax ptnr., 1983—; sec., treas. Inst. for Study of Corp. Responsibility. Past pres. Friends of Dayton Ballet Inc.; treas. Dayton Ballet Assn.; treas. Downtown Dayton Assn., Leadership Dayton; Montgomery County Rep. Party. Mem. ABA (chmn. com.), Ohio Bar Assn., Dayton Bar Assn., Ohio Soc. CPA's (past pres.). Republican. Clubs: Dayton Racquet, Dayton Country. Corporate taxation, Estate taxation, Personal income taxation. Home: 6 Lookout Dr Dayton OH 45409 Office: Touche Ross & Co 1700 Courthouse Plaza NE Dayton OH 45402

WILSON, ROBERT MARTIN, JR., lawyer; b. Little Rock, Apr. 28, 1952; s. Robert Martin and Jan (Herrick) W.; m. Jennifer Watkins, Sept. 8, 1984. Student, Am. U., 1971-72; BA, U. Ark., 1972, JD, 1977. Bar: Ark. 1978, U.S. Dist. Ct. (ea. and we. dists.) Ark. 1978, U.S. Ct. Appeals (8th cir.) 1978. Ptnr. Wilson, Wood & Harris, Little Rock, 1978—. Served to sgt. USAF, 1970-76. Mem. ABA, Ark. Bar Assn. (vice chmn. real estate sect, 1982-86, chmn. 1986—)Assn. Trial Lawyers Am., Ark Trial Lawyers Assn., Mortgage Bankers Assn. (lawyers sect.). Episcopalian. Real property, General corporate, Condemnation. Home: 15 Ranch Valley Little Rock AR 72207

WILSON, RODGER LEE, lawyer; b. Gallipolis, Ohio, Oct. 24, 1946; s. John V. and Donna D. (Danner) W. BA, Ohio State U., 1968; MS, IIT, 1971; JD, Capital U., 1975. Bar: Ohio 1975, U.S. Dist. Ct. (so. dist.) Ohio 1975, Colo. 1983, U.S. Dist. Ct. Colo. 1983, Va. 1985, U.S. Dist. Ct. (ea. dist.) Va. 1985, U.S. Claims Ct. 1985, U.S. Ct. Appeals (4th cir.) 1985. Asst. pros. atty. Franklin County, Columbus, Ohio, 1974-76; assoc. Crabbe, Brown, Jones, Potts & Schmidt, Columbus, 1976-78; sr. counsel Manville County, Denver, 1978-84; asst. gen. counsel A. H. Robins, Richmond, Va., 1984—. Served to lt. col. U.S. Army, 1968—. Personal injury, Federal civil litigation, State civil litigation. Home: 13803 Watch Harbour Ct Midlothian VA 23113

WILSON, ROGER GOODWIN, lawyer; b. Evanston, Ill., Sept. 3, 1950; s. G. Turner Jr. and Lois (Shay) W.; m. Giovinella Gonthier, Mar. 7, 1975. AB, Dartmouth Coll., 1972; JD, Harvard U., 1975. Bar: Ill. 1975, U.S. Dist. Ct. (no. dist.) Ill. 1976, U.S. Ct. Appeals (7th cir.) 1977, U.S. Dist. Ct. (no. dist.) Ind. 1985. Assoc. Kirkland & Ellis, Chgo., 1975-81, ptnr., 1981-86; sr. v.p., gen. counsel, corp. sec. Blue Cross/Blue Shield, 1986—. Advisor Constitutional Rights Found., Chgo., 1982—; mem. So. Poverty Law Ctr., Montgomery, Ala., 1981—. Mem. ABA, Chgo. Bar Assn., Nat. Health Lawyers Assn. (speaker 1984), Chgo. Council Lawyers, Phi Beta Kappa. Club: Univ. (Chgo.). Avocations: french lang. and culture. Health, General corporate, Insurance. Home: 2800 N Lake Shore Dr Unit 1917 Chicago IL 60657 Office: Blue Cross/Blue Shield 676 N St Clair St Chicago IL 60611

WILSON, SAMUEL ALEXANDER, III, lawyer; b. Charlotte, N.C., Apr. 12, 1951; s. Samuel Alexander Jr. and Julia (Hill) W.; m. Harriett Heard, Sept. 28, 1985; children: James W. Knight, Katherine E. Knight, Patricia, Joan, Caroline. BA, U. N.C., 1972, JD, 1975. Bar: U.S. Dist. Ct. (we. dist.) N.C. 1975, U.S. Dist. Ct. (ea. dist.) N.C. 1984. Assoc. Welling and Miller, Charlotte, 1975-77; sole practice Charlotte, 1977-79; ptnr. Jordan, Durham & Wilson, Charlotte, 1979-84, Walker, Palmer & Miller, Charlotte, 1985; legal counsel Gov. Martin, Raleigh, N.C., 1985—. Chmn. Mecklenburg Rep., Charlotte, 1984-84. Mem. ABA, N.C. Bar Assn., Wake County Bar Assn. Presbyterian. Club: Myers Pk. Country, Lake Norman Yacht (Charlotte). Judicial and recruitment; commutations and pardons; extraditions, Legislative. Home: 619 Brooks Ave Raleigh NC 27607 Office: 116 W Jones St Raleigh NC 27611

WILSON, STANLEY P., lawyer, electric utility holding company executive; b. Hamlin, Tex., Sept. 1, 1922; s. Milton Young and Ethel M. (Patterson) W.; m. Claudie Park, Sept. 23, 1944; children: Stanley P., Russell Park, Marianne. B.S., North Tex. State U., Denton, 1943; LL.B., U. Tex., Austin, 1948. Bar: Tex. 1948. Ptnr. McMahon, Smart, Wilson, Surovik & Suttle, Abilene, Tex., 1948-81; exec. v.p., gen. counsel Central and S.W. Corp., Dallas, 1981-86, 1986—; dir. First Abilene Bankshares, First Nat. Bank, Abilene. Served to lt. (j.g.) USN, 1943-46, PTO. Mem. ABA, Dallas Bar Assn., State Bar Tex., Am. Coll. Trial Lawyers, Abilene Bar Assn. Methodist. Club: Abilene Country, Northwood, Preston Trails, Gleneagles. Home: 1921 Elmwood St Abilene TX 79605 Office: Central and South West Corp 2121 San Jacinto St Suite 2500 PO Box 660164 Dallas TX 75266-0164

WILSON, STEPHEN VICTOR, lawyer; b. N.Y.C., Mar. 26, 1941; s. Harry and Rae (Ross) W. B.A. in Econs., Lehigh U., 1962; J.D., Bklyn. Law Sch., 1966; LL.M., George Washington U., 1973. Bars: N.Y. 1967, D.C. 1971, Calif. 1973, U.S. Ct. Appeals (9th cir.) U.S. Dist. Ct. (so., cen. and no. dists.) Calif. Trial atty. Tax div. U.S. Dept. Justice, 1968-71; asst. U.S. atty., Los Angeles, 1971-77, chief spl. prosecutions, 1973-77; ptnr. Hochman, Salkin & Deroy, Beverly Hills, Calif., 1977—; adj. prof. law Loyola U. Law Sch., 1976-79; U.S. Dept. State rep. to govt. W.Ger. on 20th anniversary of Marshall Plan, 1967; del. jud. conf. U.S. Ct. Appeals (9th cir.), 1982—. Recipient Spl. Commendation award U.S. Dept. Justice, 1977. Mem. ABA, Los Angeles County Bar Assn., Beverly Hills Bar Assn. (chmn. criminal law com.), Fed. Bar Assn. Jewish. Contbr. articles to profl. jours. Criminal. Address: 9100 Wilshire Blvd Beverly Hills CA 90212 *

WILSON, STEVEN (WHITE), lawyer; b. Phila., Feb. 24, 1943; s. Robert North and Virginia Ruth (Spurlock) W.; m. Marjorie Christine Warden, Feb. 17, 1973; children: Robert Warden, Catherine MacLeod. AB in English, Princeton U., 1965; MFA in Cinema, U. So. Calif., 1971; JD, Villanova U., 1976. Bar: Pa. 1976, U.S. Dist. Ct. (ea. dist.) Pa. 1977, U.S. Supreme Ct. 1979, U.S. Ct. Appeals (3d cir.) 1981. Film editor, screenwriter Independent Film Producers, Los Angeles, 1967-73; asst. dist. atty. Montgomery County, Norristown, Pa., 1976-79; assoc. Murphy & Slota, Bryn Mawr, Pa., 1979-86, Greitzer & Locks, Phila., 1986—; solicitor Zoning Hearing Bd., Narberth, Pa., 1984—. Councilman Narberth Borough Council, 1979-84, chmn. pub. safety com., 1982-84. Recipient Harvard Club of Phila. award, 1961; Silverberg scholar U. So. Calif. cinema dept., 1968. Mem. ABA, Pa. Bar Assn., Assn. Trial Lawyers Am., Phila. Bar Assn., Pa. Trial Lawyers Assn., Haverford (Pa.) Sch. Alumni Assn. (sec.-treas. 1984—), DKA hon. fraternity, Mensa, Merion Cricket Club, Princeton Club of Phila. Republican. Presbyterian. Avocations: photography, sports cars, Japanese art. Personal injury, Federal civil litigation, State civil litigation. Home: 680 Mill Rd Villanova PA 19085 Office: Greitzer & Locks 1500 Walnut St Philadelphia PA 19102

WILSON, THOMAS JOHNSTON, lawyer; b. Winston-Salem, N.C., Feb. 5, 1914; s. William T. and Alice Franklin W.; m. Jane Myers, Nov. 25, 1948; children—Thomas Johnston, Ann Lindsay. student Davidson Coll. 1931-34, LL.B. U. N.C. 1949. Bar: N.C. 1949. Ptnr. Wilson & Wilson, P.A., Lincolnton, N.C., 1949— ; judge Lincoln County Ct., 1952-56; dir. Heritage Savs. & Loan Co., Monroe, N.C., Heafner Tire Co., Lincolnton. Served to capt. AUS, 1942-46. Mem. ABA, N.C. Bar Assn. Democrat. Methodist. Author: McIntosh North Carolina Practice and Procedure, 1956. Pension,

profit-sharing, and employee benefits, Probate, Real property. Office: 228 E Main Lincolnton NC 28092

WILSON, THOMAS MATTHEW, III, lawyer; b. Ware, Mass., Feb. 22, 1936; s. Thomas Matthew Jr. and Ann Veronica (Shea) W.; m. Deborah Ord Lockhart, Feb. 10, 1962; children: Deborah Veronica, Leslie Lockhart, Thomas Matthew IV. BA, Brown U., 1958; JD, U. Md., 1971. Bar: Md. 1972, U.S. Ct. Appeals (4th cir.) 1976, U.S. Supreme Ct. 1977. Sales mgr. Mid-Eastern Box Mfg. Co., Balt., 1966-74; asst. atty. gen. and chief antitrust div. State of Md., Balt., 1974-79; ptnr. Tydings & Rosenberg, Balt., 1979—. Mem. editorial adv. bd. Bur. of Nat. Affairs Antitrust and Trade Regulation Report, 1979—; patentee in field. Mem. ABA (sect. on Antitrust Law 1974—, chmn. State Antitrust Enforcement com. 1986—), Md. State Bar Assn. (Antitrust subcom. 1975-78), Internat. Bar Assn. (sect. on Bus. Law, Antitrust Law and Monopolies com. 1983—). Republican. Clubs: Merchants, Towson Chess. Antitrust, Franchise Litigation. Home: Baobab Farm Hampstead MD 21074 Office: Tydings & Rosenberg 201 N Charles St Baltimore MD 21201

WILSON, THOMAS WILLIAM, lawyer; b. Bklyn., Sept. 14, 1935; s. Matthew and Alice (McCrory) W.; m. Eileen Marie McGann, June 4, 1960; children—Jeanne Alice, Thomas William, David Matthew, A.B., Columbia U., 1957, LL.B., 1960. Bar: N.Y. 1962, U.S. Dist. Ct. (so. and ea. dists.) N.Y. 1962, D.C. 1972. Assoc. Mendes and Mount, N.Y.C., 1961-65, Haller & Small, N.Y.C., 1965-66; gen. counsel Prudential of Gt. Brit., N.Y.C., 1966-68; ptnr. Wilson, Elser, Edelman & Dicker, N.Y.C., 1968—. Contbr. articles to profl. jours. Served with U.S. Army, 1960-65. Mem. ABA, N.Y. Bar Assn., Def. Research Inst. (editorial bd. profl. liability reporter). Insurance. Office: Wilson Elser Moskowitz Edelman & Dicker 420 Lexington Ave New York NY 10170

WILSON, VIRGIL JAMES, III, lawyer; b. San Jose, Calif., July 25, 1953; s. Virgil James Wilson Jr. and Phyllis Emily (Mothorn) Brasser. BA, U. Calif., Santa Cruz, 1975; JD, U. Santa Clara, 1981. Bar: Calif. 1981, Hawaii 1982, U.S. Dist.Ct. (no. dist.) Calif. 1981, U.S. Dist. Ct. Hawaii 1982, U.S. Supreme Ct., 1987; licensed pvt. investigator, Calif. Atty. James Krueger P.C., Wailuku, Maui, 1981-83; resident counsel Sterns & Ingram, Honolulu, 1983—; owner Wilson Investigations, Santa Cruz, 1978-81, Honolulu, 1981—. Mem. ABA, Hawaii Bar Assn., Calif. State Bar Assn., Am. Trial Lawyers Assn., Calif. Trial Lawyers Assn. Avocation: profl. magician. Personal injury, Insurance, Federal civil litigation. Office: Sterns & Ingram 733 Bishop St Suite 2300 Honolulu HI 96813

WILSON, WALTER WILLIAM, lawyer; b. Newton, Kans., Dec. 8, 1947; s. Walter Garnet and Mary Elizabeth (Lynsky) W.; m. Judy Marie Anne Destouet, Jan. 26, 1976; children—Melissa Marie, Walter William. B.S., Woodbury Coll., 1972; J.D., Am. U., 1975. Bar: Mo. 1976, U.S. Dist. Ct. (we. dist.) Mo. 1976. Sole practice, St. Louis, 1976—. Bd. dirs. Ctr. for POW/MIA Accountability, Washington, 1982—, Orgn. for Americans Missing Abroad, St. Louis, 1976—; Counsel St. Charles County Bd. Edn., 1978-79, Mo. Parents and Children, St. Louis, 1982-83. Served with U.S. Army, 1967-68. Mem. ABA, Bar Assn. Met. St. Louis, Am. Soc. Internat. Law Inst., Inter-Am. Bar Assn., Internat. Bar Assn., Internat. Antitrust Soc., Union Internat. des Avocats, English Speaking Union (bd. dirs. St. Louis br.), Com. Fgn. Relations. Republican. Episcopalian. Club: Discussion (St. Louis) (bd. dirs.), Univ. Private international, Contracts commercial, Antitrust. Home: 1126 Basswood Ln Saint Louis MO 63132 Office: 1126 Basswood Ln Saint Louis MO 63132

WILSON, WILLIAM ANDREW, lawyer; b. N.Y.C., Jan. 3, 1934; s. Robert Blakeley and Sarah (Cruise) W.; m. Patricia Bent Ramson, Aug. 4, 1962; children: Robert Ramson, William Andrew Jr., Rebecca Allbright. BA, Syracuse U., 1960; JD, Boston U., 1965. Bar: Colo. 1965, Maine 1965, U.S. Dist. Ct. Colo. 1965, U.S. Ct. Appeals (10th cir.) 1966, U.S. Supreme Ct. 1970. Assoc. Isaacson, Rosenbaum, Goldberg & Miller, Denver, 1965-66; sole practice Denver, 1966—. Dir., legal counsel Citizen's Scholarship Found., Denver, 1967-71. Served with USAF, 1952-56. Mem. ABA, Colo. Bar Assn., Denver Bar Assn. Lutheran. Avocations: mountain climbing, skiing, running, hist. studies. Federal civil litigation, State civil litigation, Administrative and regulatory. Office: 1700 Lincoln Suite 2530 Denver CO 80203

WILSON, WILLIAM BERRY, lawyer; b. Cape Girardeau, Mo., June 17, 1947; s. Charles F. and Anita (Bartlum) W.; m. Suzanne T. Wilson; children: Matthew James, Sarah Talbot. BA summa cum laude, Westminster Coll., 1969; JD, U. Mich., 1972. Bar: Fla. 1972, U.S. Dist. Ct. (mid. dist.) Fla. 1972, U.S. Ct. Appeals (11th cir.) 1972. Ptnr. Maguire, Voorhis & Wells P.A., Orlando, Fla., 1977—; mng. dir. Maguire, Voorhis & Wells P.A., Orlando, 1982-84, pres., 1984—. Mem. Indsl. Devel. Authority, Orlando, 1982—, subcom. chmn. Project 2000, Orlando, 1985—; bd. dirs. The Fla. Symphony, Orlando, 1985—. Mem. ABA, Fla. Bar Assn. (chmn. code and rules of evidence com. 1986—), Orange County Bar Assn. (chmn. fed. and state practice sect. 1982-84), Def. Research Inst., Fla. Def. Lawyers Assn. Republican. Presbyterian. Club: University (Orlando). Lodge: Rotary. Avocations: tennis, scuba diving. Federal civil litigation, State civil litigation, Construction. Office: Maguire Voorhis & Wells PA 2 S Orange Ave PO Box 633 Orlando FL 32802

WILSON, WILLIAM EDWARD, lawyer; b. Long Branch, N.J., June 9, 1944; s. Everett R. and Dolores J. (Meehan) W.; m. Jane Cook, July 7, 1964; children: William, Catherine, Michael, Holly. BA, Tulane U.; JD, Wake Forest U. Bar: N.J. 1969, U.S. Dist. Ct. N.J. 1969, U.S. Supreme Ct. 1977. Atty. Oceanport (N.J.) Bd. Edn., 1976-80, Twp. of Middletown, N.J., 1978-79; prosecutor Borough of Highlands (N.J.), 1983-84, atty., 1985, 86—; atty. Atlantic Highlands Harbour Com., Highlands, 1985; ptnr. Wilson & Fasano, Navesink, N.J.; atty. Port-Au-Peck Chem. Hose Co., 1979—, Borough of Highlands, 1985, 86—; spl. counsel Horseman's Protective Benevolent Assn., 1985-86; Vol. probation, 1979; mem. Juvenile Conf. Com., 1980—. atty. Keyport Little League; mem. Monmouth County Dems. Mem. Assn. Trial Lawyers Am., Nat. Inst. Mcpl. Legal Officers, N.J. Bar Assn., Monmouth County Bar Assn., Assn. Sch. Bd. Attys., Am. Horse Council, Thoroughbred Breeders Assn., ACLU, NRA, Nat. Assn. Clock and Watch Collectors, Am. Judicature Soc. Methodist. Lodges: Lions (atty. Oceanport Swim Club 1977—), Elks. Avocations: clock, print and book collecting. Real property, Local government, Adminstrv. law, horse racing. Home: 89 Sagamore Ave Oceanport NJ 07757 Office: Wilson & Fasano 500 State Hwy PO Drawer 389 Navesink NJ 07752

WILSON, WILLIAM HAROLD, JR., lawyer; b. Princess Anne, Md., Jan. 24, 1947; s. William Harold Sr. and Mary Lee (Hayman) W. BA, Washington Coll., 1969; postgrad., U. Va., 1970; JD, Franklin Pierce Coll., 1979. Bar: N.H. 1978, U.S. Ct. Appeals (1st cir.) 1978, U.S. Supreme Ct. 1986. Sole practice Concord, N.H., 1978-79; atty. Energy Law Inst., Concord, 1979-82; atty., v.p. Eli Corp., Concord, 1982-84; ptnr. Brown, Olson & Wilson, Concord, 1984—. Author: Financing Hydroelectric Projects, 1982, 85, Financing Cogeneration, 1984. Served to 1st lt. USAF, 1971-75. Mem. ABA (tax sect., utility sect., corp. sect.), N.H. Bar Assn., Aircraft Owners and Pilots Assn. Republican. Episcopalian. Avocations: skiing, flying, tennis. Administrative and regulatory, Public utilities, General corporate. Office: Brown Olson & Wilson 21 Green St Concord NH 03301

WILTSE, JAMES BURDICK, lawyer; b. St. Paul, Nov. 7, 1927; s. Verne Hazen and Frances J. (Carlson) W.; m. Lois J. Ashton, July 5, 1945 (dec. May 1961); children—James Burdick, Lois J., Kathryn E., Douglas V.; m. Yvonne Amoroso, Mar. 31, 1972; children—Jamie Jo, Julie Loiuse. B.A., Calif. State U.-Los Angeles, 1962; J.D., Southwestern U., Los Angeles, 1969. Bar: Pa. 1972, D.C. 1980, U.S. Dist. Ct. (we. dist.) Pa. 1972, U.S. Ct. Appeals (3d cir.) 1974, U.S. Supreme Ct. 1977. Law library cons. West Pub. Co., St. Paul, 1969-81; sr. ptnr. Wiltse & Nene, Pitts., 1981-84; assoc. Zoffer, Wiltse, Hackney & Lestitian, Pitts., 1984—. Treas. campaign to elect common pleas judge, 1979, commonwealth ct. judge, 1983, state rep., 1984. Served with U.S. Army, 1946-47; PTO. Mem. Pa. Bar Assn., D.C. Bar Assn., Allegheny County Bar Assn. (bd. dirs. credit union 1984), Assn. Trial Lawyers Am., Pa. Trial Lawyers Assn. Republican. Presbyterian. Club: Amen Corner (Pitts). Librarianship. Office: West Pub Co PO Box 486 Herudon VA 22070

WILTSHIRE, ASHLEY TURMAN, JR., lawyer; b. Richmond, Va., Nov. 16, 1941; s. Ashley Turman and Sarah Henderson (Proctor) W.; m. Susan Chappell Ford, June 7, 1969; children: Matthew Ashley, Carrie Chappell. BA, Washington and Lee U., 1963; BD, Union Theol. Sem., 1967; JD, Vanderbilt U., 1972. Bar: Tenn. 1972, U.S. Dist. Ct. (mid. dist.) Tenn. 1972, U.S. Ct. Appeals (6th cir.) 1972. Atty. Legal Services of Mid. Tenn., Nashville, 1972-76, exec. dir., 1976—. Mem. Leadership Nashville, 1981. Recipient Reginald Heber Smith award, 1981, Disting. Service Council of Community Services, 1986. Fellow Tenn. Bar Found.; mem. ABA, Tenn. Bar Assn. (various coms.), Nashville Bar Assn. (various coms.), Nashville Barristers (Nat. Legal Aid and Defenders Assn. Legal services/legal aid, Family and matrimonial. Home: 1900 Blair Blvd Nashville TN 37212 Office: Legal Services Mid Tenn 800 Stahlman Bldg Nashville TN 37201

WILTSHIRE, WILLIAM HARRISON FLICK, lawyer; b. Martinsburg, W.Va., Dec. 29, 1930; s. Harrison Flick and Virginia Faulkner (White) W.; m. Edith Hayward, Nov. 13, 1954; children—Ashley Wiltshire Spotswood, Winn Faulkner, William Harrison Flick, Jr., Ashton Hayward. B.A., Shepherd Coll., 1952; J.D., U. Fla., 1960. Bar: Fla. 1960, U.S. Ct. Appeals (5th cir.) 1960, U.S. Dist. Ct. (no. dist.) Fla. 1960, U.S. Dist. Ct. (so. dist.) La. 1975, U.S. Dist. Ct. (so. dist.) Ala. 1978, U.S. Dist. Ct. (so. dist.) Fla. 1980, U.S. Ct. Appeals (11th cir.) 1982; cert. in civil trial Nat. Bd. Trial Advocacy and Fla. Bar. Assoc., Jones & Harrell, Pensacola, Fla., 1960-62; ptnr. Harrell, Wiltshire, Stone & Swearingen, and predecessor firms, Pensacola, 1962—; Pres. Bayou Tex. Assn., 1967-71; dir. Fiesta Five Flags, 1968-82, pres. 1976-77. Trustee Episcopal Day Sch., 1965-69; bd. dirs. Pensacola Acad. Arts and Scis., 1970-75, pres., 1973-74; bd. dirs. Gul Coast Council Boy Scouts Am., 1982—. Served with USN, 1952-57. Fellow Am. Coll. Trial Lawyers, Nat. Bd. Trial Advocacy; mem. ABA, Fla. Bar Assn., Am. Trial Lawyers Assn., Acad. Fla. Trial Lawyers, State Bar Fla. (chmn. trial lawyers sect. 1973-74, chmn. appellate rules com. 1974-78), Def. Research Inst., Am. Judicature Soc. Republican. Club: Rotary. Contbr. articles to profl. jours. Federal civil litigation, Personal injury, Admiralty. Address: PO Box 1832 Pensacola FL 32598

WIMBISH, ROBERT ALLAN, lawyer; b. Winston-Salem, N.C., Oct. 4, 1928; s. Joseph H. and Mary Armes (Noel) W.; m. Joan Schoen Bortnik, Aug. 19, 1983; children: Robin Wimbish Cale, Nancy Grant, Jane Noel, Lawrence Schoen, David Schoen. BA, U. Va., 1951, LLB, 1955. Bar: Va. 1952, D.C. 1962. Law clk. to presiding judge U.S. Ct. Appeals (4th cir.), 1955-56; assoc. Hunton, Williams, Gay, Powell & Gibson, Richmond, Va., 1956-58; various positions Southern Ry. System, Washington, 1958-82; sr. gen. solicitor Norfolk (Va.) Southern Corp., 1982—. Served with U.S. Army, 1952-54. Mem. ABA, Va. Bar Assn., D.C. Bar Assn., Bar of Republic South Korea, Assn. Transp. Practitioners, Va. C. of C., Phi Delta Phi, Delta Upsilon. Clubs: Hunting Hills Country, Cavalier Golf and Yacht (Virginia Beach). Transportation, Railroad-commerce law. Home: 504 Susan Constant Dr Virginia Beach VA 23451 Office: Norfolk So Corp One Comml Pl Norfolk VA 23510-2101

WIMBROW, PETER AYERS, III, lawyer; b. Salisbury, Md., Apr. 11, 1947; s. Peter Ayers Jr. and Margaret (Johnson) W. B.S., East Tenn. State U., 1970; J.D., Washington and Lee U., 1973. Bar: Md. 1973, U.S. Dist. Ct. Md. 1974, U.S. Ct. Appeals (4th cir.) 1979, U.S. Supreme Ct. 1979, U.S. Tax Ct. 1981, U.S. Ct. Appeals (D.C. cir.) 1981, U.S. Ct. Appeals (3d cir.) 1985. Sole practice, Ocean City, Md., 1974—. Mem. ABA, Md. Bar Assn., Worcester County Bar Assn. (sec., v.p.), Am. Trial Lawyers Assn., Md. Criminal Def. Attys. Assn. (appellate jud. nominating commn. 1983—), Md. Trial Lawyers Assn. Republican. Civil rights, Federal civil litigation, State civil litigation. Home: Seatime Apts 136th St #502-N Ocean City MD 21842 Office: PO Box 56 4100 Coastal Hwy Ocean City MD 21842

WIMBUSH, FREDERICK BLAIR, lawyer; b. Halifax, Va., July 24, 1955; s. Freddie Blair and Sue Carol (Lovelace) W.; m. Jane B. Seay, Aug. 15, 1981. BA, U. Rochester, 1977; JD, U. Va., 1980. Bar: Va. 1980. Atty. N&W Railway Co., Roanoke, Va., 1980-83; solicitor NS Corp., Roanoke, 1983-85, asst. gen. solicitor, 1985—; bd. dirs. exec. com. Legal Aid Soc. of Roanoke Valley, 1982-86. Mem. Roanoke (Va.) County Transp. and Safety Commn., 1984-85, Roanoke City Arts Commn., 1984—, adv. panel Va. Commn. for the Arts, 1985—, United Way Spl. Study of Agys., 1983; trustee Roanoke Mus. of Fine Arts, 1981—, sec., 1982-84, v.p., 1984-86, pres. 1986—; nat. bd. dirs. Big Bros./Big Sisters Am., 1986—. Named one of Outstanding Young Men in Am., 1985. Mem. ABA, Va. Bar Assn., Nat. Bar Assn., Roanoke Bar Assn., Old Dominion Bar Assn. (exec. com.). Administrative and regulatory, Contracts commercial, Antitrust. Home: 3433 Londonderry Ct SW Roanoke VA 24018 Office: Norfolk So Corp 204 S Jefferson St Roanoke VA 24042-0069

WIMS, MICHAEL DAVID, lawyer, air force officer; b. Norwich, Eng., Dec. 11, 1944 (father Am. citizen); s. James Clifford Wims and Rosemarie (Walker) Deffler; m. Pamela Jeanne Page, July 21, 1967. B.A., N. Tex. State U., 1967; J.D., U. Tex., 1970; grad. with distinction Air Command and Staff Coll., 1980. Bar: Tex. 1970, U.S. Ct. Mil. Appeals 1971, U.S. Supreme Ct. 1973, Utah 1986, Colo. 1986. Commd. 2d lt. U.S. Air Force, 1967, advanced through grades to col., 1987; asst. staff judge advocate, Little Rock AFB, 1970-73; cir. def. counsel 1st cir. USAF, Bolling AFB, Washington, 1973-74, cir. prosecutor, 1974-75; cir. prosecutor 7th cir. USAF, Clark AB, Philippines, 1975-77; staff judge advocate 416th Bomb Wing, Griffiss AFB, N.Y., 1977-79, 51st Combat Support Group, Osan AB, Korea, 1982-84; U.S. mil. judge 2d cir. USAF, Maxwell AFB, Ala., 1980-82; appellate def. counsel Hdqrs. USAF, Washington, 1984-86; chief mil. personnel litigation, 1986—; lectr. on trial tactics. Del. Tex. Republican State Conv., 1966. Decorated Air Force Commendation medal, 4 Meritorious Service medals. Mem. Nat. Assn. Parliamentarians (registered), Am. Inst. Parliamentarians (cert. 1970), Delta Theta Phi, Delta Sigma Phi, Delta Phi Epsilon (hon.). Military. Home: 12513 MacDuff Dr Fort Washington MD 20744 Office: HG USAF/JACL Pentagon 5E425 Washington DC 20330-5120

WINCHELL, MICHAEL GEORGE, lawyer; b. Ardmore, Okla., Oct. 30, 1949; s. George Stockwell and Willis Marion (Woolery) W.; divorced; children—Merridith Elaine, Candace Michelle, Brent Wayne. B.B.A., Central State U., 1974; J.D., U. Okla., 1976. Bar: Okla. 1977, U.S. Dist. Ct. (no. dist.) Tex. Assoc. Sokolosky & Becker, Oklahoma City, 1977; atty. GSA, Fort Worth, Tex., 1977—, pres. employee's assn., 1982-84. Recipient Outstanding Service awards GSA, 1982, 83. Mem. Fed. Bus. Assn. (pres. 1984-85), Fed. Bar Assn. (pres. Fort Worth chpt. 1981-82, bd. dirs. younger lawyers' div. 1981-85, 2d v.p. 5th cir. 1982-83, v.p. 83-84, sec. cir. officers 1983-84, dep. chmn. cir. officers 1984-85, chmn. rules com. 1985-86, sustaining). Democrat. Methodist. Government contracts and claims, Real property, Construction. Home: 6416 Meadow Glen Arlington TX 76018 Office: Office Region Counsel 7L GSA Region 7 819 Taylor St Fort Worth TX 76102

WINCHELL, WILLIAM OLIN, lawyer, consultant; b. Rochester, N.Y., Dec. 31, 1933; s. Leslie Olin and Hazel Agnes (Apker) W.; m. Doris Jane Martenson, Jan. 19, 1957; children: Jason, Darrell, Kirk. BME, GMI Engring. and Mgmt. Inst., 1956; MSc, Ohio State U., 1970; MBA, U. Detroit, 1976; JD, Detroit Coll. Law, 1980. Bar: Mich. 1981, U.S. Dist. Ct. (ea. dist.) Mich. 1981, U.S. Ct. Appeals (6th cir.) 1982, U.S. Supreme Ct. 1985. Cons. Gen. Motors Corp., Warren Mich., Detroit and Lockport, N.Y., 1951—; sole practice Royal Oak, Mich., 1981—. Mem. Royal Oak Long Range Planning Commn., 1980. Served to lt. commdr. USNR, 1956-76. Burton fellow Detroit Coll. Law, 1978. Fellow Am. Soc. Quality Control (v.p. 1985-87); mem. ABA, Mich. Bar Assn., Soc. Mfg. Engrs., Inst. Indsl. Engrs., Tau Beta Pi, Beta Gamma Sigma. Roman Catholic. Club: North Star Sail. Avocations: sailing, woodworking. General practice, Probate, General corporate. Home and Office: 1729 Sycamore Royal Oak MI 48073

WINCKLER, JAMES LEE, lawyer, educator; b. Avon, S.D., May 18, 1948; s. Edwin and Hazel Dorothy Winckler; 1 child, Diana. BA, U. S.D., 1970; MA, Cen. Mich. U., 1971; JD, U. Tex., 1973. Bar: Mich. 1973, U.S. Dist. Ct. Ohio 1976, U.S. Dist. Ct. (ea. dist.) 1976, U.S. Dist. Ct. (we. dist.) Ct. 1976. Ptnr. Brown & Winckler, Lansing, Mich., 1973-86; prof. T.M. Cooley Law Sch., Lansing, 1977—; prin. Winckler & Cunningham, Lansing, 1986—. Pres. North Lansing Community Ctr., 1975-76; chmn. Waterfront Devel. Bd., Lansing, 1983—. Home: 1581 N Genesee Lansing MI 48915 Office: Winckler & Assocs 109 W Michigan Ave Suite 700 Lansing MI 48933

WIND, CAROL MARLENE, lawyer; b. Tampa, Fla., Aug. 17, 1953; d. Henry and Jennie (Shapiro) W.; m. Michael Leslie Einstein, Apr. 4, 1982; 1 child, Mark Harris Einstein. BA, U. South Fla., 1974; JD, U. Houston, 1978. Bar: U.S. Dist. Ct. (so. dist.) Tex. 1978, U.S. Ct. Appeals (5th cir.) 1978, U.S. Dist. Ct. (mid. dist.) Fla. 1979, U.S. Ct. Appeals (11th cir.) 1981. Counsel child support enforcement Harris County, Houston, 1978-82; asst. dist. counsel Fla. Dept. Health and Rehabilitative Services, Clearwater, Fla., 1982—. Chmn. honor roll Women's Am. Orgn. Rehab. Through Tng., St. Petersburg, Fla., 1983; mem. Hadassah, St. Petersburg, 1984. Mem. ABA, Tex. Bar Assn., Fla., Bar Assn., Nat. Assn. Counsel Children, Delta Theta Phi. Democrat. Jewish. Avocations: boating, reading. Administrative and regulatory, Government contracts and claims, Juvenile. Home: 16122 4th St E Redington Beach FL 33708-1614 Office: Fla Dept Health and Rehabilitative Services 2255 E Bay Dr Clearwater FL 33546

WINDELS, PAUL, JR., lawyer; b. Bklyn., Nov. 13, 1921; s. Paul and Louise E. (Gross) W.; m. Patricia Ripley, Sept. 10, 1955; children: Paul III, Mary H., James H.R., Patrick D. A.B., Princeton U., 1943; LL.B., Harvard U., 1948. Bar: N.Y. 1949. Spl asst. counsel N.Y. State Crime Commn., 1951; asst. U.S. atty. Eastern Dist. N.Y., 1953-56; N.Y. regional adminstr. SEC, 1956-61, also spl. asst. U.S. atty. for prosecution securities frauds, 1956-58; lectr. law Am. Inst. Banking, 1950-57; ptnr. Windels, Marx, Davies & Ives (and predecessor firms), 1961—. Author: Our Securities Markets-Some SEC Problems and Techniques, 1962. Trustee, pres. Bklyn. Law Sch.; trustee, past pres. Fed. Bar Council; trustee, treas. French Inst./Alliance Française; chmn. French-Am. Monument Found.; mem. adv. bd. NYU Inst. French Studies; mem. Woods Hole Oceanographic Inst. Served from pvt. to capt. F.A. AUS, 1943-46, ETO; maj. Arty. Res. Recipient Flemming award for fed. service; decorated chevalier Order French Acad. Palms; officer Nat. Order Merit France. Fellow Am. Bar Found.; mem. Am., N.Y. State bar assns., Assn. Bar City N.Y.; Assn. N.Y. County Lawyers Assn. Republican. Presbyterian. Federal civil litigation, General corporate. Office: 51 W 51st St New York NY 10019

WINDER, DAVID KENT, U.S. dist. judge; b. Salt Lake City, June 8, 1932; s. Edwin Kent and Alma Eliza (Cannon) W.; m. Pamela Martin, June 24, 1955; children: Ann, Kay, James. B.A., U. Utah, 1955; LL.B., Stanford U., 1958. Bar: Utah bar 1958, Calif. bar 1958. Asso. firm Clyde, Mecham & Pratt Salt Lake City, 1958-66; law clk. to chief justice Utah Supreme Ct., 1958-59; dep. county atty. Salt Lake County, 1959-63; chief dep. dist. atty. 1965-66; asst. U.S. atty. Salt Lake City, 1963-65; partner firm Strong & Hanni, Salt Lake City, 1966-77; judge Utah Dist. Ct., 1977-79, U.S. Dist. Ct., Dist. Utah, Salt Lake City, 1979—; examiner Utah Bar Examiners, 1975-79, chmn., 1977-79. Served with USAF, 1951-52. Mem. Am. Bd. Trial Advocates, Utah State Bar (Judge of Yr. award 1978), Salt Lake County Bar Assn., Calif. State Bar. Democrat. Jurisprudence. Office: 235 US Courthouse 350 S Main St Salt Lake City UT 84101 *

WINDHAM, JOHN FRANKLIN, lawyer; b. Fayette, Ala., Jan. 21, 1948; s. Grover B. Windham Jr. and Nancy Katherine (McAdams) Haynie; m. Patricia Strain, Dec. 31, 1969; 1 child, John Franklin. BA, U. West Fla., 1970; JD, U. N.C., 1975. Bar: Fla. 1975, U.S. Dist. Ct. (no. dist.) Fla. 1976, U.S. Ct. Appeals (11th cir.) 1983, U.S. Supreme Ct. 1984. Acctg. supr. Monsanto Co., Research Triangle Park, N.C., 1970-72; law clk. to U.S. Atty Pensacola, Fla., 1974; assoc. Beggs & Lane, Pensacola, 1975-79, ptnr., 1979—; adj. instr. bus. law Troy State U., Pensacola, 1983—. Active Am. Cancer Soc. Escambia County Unit, Pensacola, 1977—, mem. com. Fla. div., Tampa, 1982—; chmn. bd. Escambia Christian Sch., Pensacola, 1976—; bd. dirs. ARC, Pensacola, 1984—. Mem. Fla. Bar Assn. (comml. litigation com.), Fla. Def. Lawyers Assn., Southeastern Admiralty Law Inst. (bd. dirs. 1986—). Democrat. Mem. Ch. of Christ. Lodge: Kiwanis (pres. Pensacola 1978-79). Avocations: golf, tennis, jogging, ch. activites. Federal civil litigation, State civil litigation, Banking. Office: Beggs & Lane PO Box 12950 Pensacola FL 32576-2950

WINDMAN, JOEL A., trade association executive, lawyer; b. N.Y.C., May 11, 1934; s. Nathan and Rose (Glauberman) W.; m. Eleanor Iris Mandler, Feb. 14, 1957; children—Vicki Sue Windman Semoff, Michael Jay, Jessica Leigh. A.B., NYU, 1956, LL.M. in Trade Regulation, 1969; J.D., Fordham U., 1959. Bar: N.Y. 1960, U.S. Dist. Ct. (so. and ea. dists.) N.Y. 1969. Assoc., Weisman, Celler, Allan, Spett & Sheinberg, N.Y.C., 1959-62; ptnr. Feiden, Gilman & Windman, Inc., Nassau, N.Y., 1962-65; asst. atty. gen. State of N.Y., 1965-69; exec. v.p., gen. counsel Jewelers Vigilance Com., Inc., N.Y.C., 1969—. Recipient Edward Thompson Co. award Fordham U., 1959. Mem. ABA, N.Y. State Bar Assn., Assn. Bar City N.Y. Administrative and regulatory, Antitrust, Trade Regulation. Office: 1180 Ave of Americas New York NY 10036

WINDMEYER, JOSEPH EDWIN, lawyer; b. New Orleans, Apr. 9, 1946; s. Amador George and Evelyne Sybil (Cambre) W.; m. Jamie Anne Moreau, Aug. 17, 1968; children—Joseph Edwin, Lauren Anne. B.S., U. New Orleans, 1968; J.D., Loyola U. of the South, New Orleans, 1971. Bar: La. 1971, U.S. Dist. Ct. (ea. dist.) La. 1971, U.S. Ct. Appeals (5th cir.) 1973, U.S. Dist. Ct. (we. dist.) La. 1978, U.S. Supreme Ct. 1978. Assoc. Ungar, Dulitz, Jacobs & Manuel, New Orleans, 1971-77; ptnr. Windmeyer & Dinwiddie, Metairie, La., 1977-81; sole practice, Metairie, 1981—. Active St. Catherine Siena Sch. Bd. Mem. ABA, Assn. Trial Lawyers Am., La. Trial Lawyers Assn. (bd. govs.), Henri Capitant Assn. Republican. Roman Catholic. Club: Airline Lions. Admiralty, Federal civil litigation, Personal injury. Home: 3629 Metairie Heights Ave Metairie LA 70002

WINE, DONALD ARTHUR, lawyer; b. Oelwein, Iowa, Oct. 8, 1922; s. George A. and Gladys E. (Lisle) W.; m. Mary L. Schneider, Dec. 27, 1947; children: Mark, Marcia, James. B.A., Drake U., 1946; JD, State U. Iowa, 1949. Bar: Iowa 1949, D.C. 1968. Pvt. practice in Newport and Wine, 1949-61; U.S. atty. So. Dist. Iowa, 1961-65; now partner firm Davis, Hockenberg, Wine, Brown, Koehn & Shors. Bd. dirs. Des Moines YMCA, 1963-75; bd. dirs. Salvation Army, 1969—, chmn. , 1971; bd. dirs. Davenport YMCA, 1961; bd. dirs. Internat. Assn. Y's Men, 1957-59, area v.p., 1961; Mem. internat. com. YMCA's U.S. and Can., 1961-75; v.p. Iowa Council Chs.; pres. Des Moines Area Religious Council, 1975; chmn. bd. trustees First Bapt. Ch., 1975; trustee U. Osteo. Medicine and Health Scis., 1980—; Organizer Young Dems., Iowa, 1946; co-chmn. Scott County Citizens for Kennedy, 1960. Served to capt., navigator USAAF, 1943-45. Decorated D.F.C. Mem. ABA (chmn. com. jud. adminstrn. jr. bar sect. 1958), Iowa Bar Assn. (pres. jr. bar sect. 1957), Polk County Bar Assn. (sec. 1973-74), Des Moines C. of C. (chmn. city-state tax com. 1978-79, chmn. legis. com. 1979-84, bd. dirs. 1981), Order of Coif, Sigma Alpha Epsilon. Clubs: Des Moines, Wakonda. Lodges: Masons, Kiwanis (pres. Downtown club 1969). Federal civil litigation, State civil litigation. Office: 2300 Financial Center 666 Walnut St Des Moines IA 50309

WINE, MARK PHILIP, lawyer; b. Iowa City, Jan. 6, 1949; s. Donald Arthur and Mary Lepha (Schneider) W.; children from previous marriage: Nicholas, Meredith Kathryn; m. Kathryn Bouquet Arneson, May 31, 1986. AB, Princeton U., 1971; JD, U. Iowa, 1974. Bar: Iowa 1974, Minn. 1976, U.S. Dist. Ct. Minn., U.S. Ct. Appeals (4th and 8th cirs.), U.S. Supreme Ct. Law clk. to presiding judge U.S. Ct. Appeals (8th cir.), St. Louis, 1974-76; ptnr. Oppenheimer Wolff & Donnelly, Mpls., 1976—. Mem. ABA, Minn. Bar Assn. (governing council, civil litigation). Democrat. Congregationalist. Clubs: Mpls. Athletic, Princeton of N.W. Avocations: cooking, reading, biking, tennis. Federal civil litigation, State civil litigation, Computer. Home: 5321-15th Ave S Minneapolis MN 55417 Office: Oppenheimer Wolff & Donnelly 4800 IDS Ctr Minneapolis MN 55402

WINER, JONATHAN HERMAN, lawyer; b. Abington, Pa., Nov. 30, 1951; s. David Arthur and Janet Mae (Ratner) W.; m. Carolyn Doris Winters, Aug. 25, 1974; children: Steven Morris, Rachel Louise. AB, Dartmouth Coll., 1973; JD, NYU, 1976. Bar: N.Y. 1977, U.S. Dist. Ct. (we. dist.) N.Y. 1977, Vt. 1983. Assoc. Nixon, Hargrave, Devans & Doyle, Rochester, N.Y., 1976-83; corp. atty Green Mountain Power Corp., South Burlington, Vt., 1983-85, sr. atty, 1985—. Chmn. Brighton (N.Y.) Dem. Com., 1982-83. Mem. ABA, N.Y. Bar Assn., Vt. Bar Assn. Democrat. Jewish. Clubs:

Dartmouth (Burlington, Vt.) (pres. 1984—). General corporate, Pension, profit-sharing, and employee benefits, Public utilities. Home: 183 Van Patten Pkwy Burlington VT 05401 Office: Green Mountain Power Corp PO Box 850 Burlington VT 05402

WING, DAVID LESLIE, lawyer; b. Kansas City, Kans., Sept. 21, 1949; m. Annette Eslick, May 2, 1981; children: Sarah Elizabeth, Rebecca Dianne. BS in Edn., U. Kans., 1971, JD, 1978. Bar: Kans. 1978, U.S. Dist. Ct. Kans. 1978, Mo. 1982, U.S. Ct. Appeals (10th cir.) 1982. Law clk. U.S. Dist. Ct. Kans., Kansas City, 1978-81, U.S. Ct. Appeals (10th cir.), Olathe, Kans., 1981-82; assoc. Spencer, Fane, Britt & Browne, Kansas City, Mo., 1982—. Mem. ABA, Kans. Bar Assn., Mo. Bar Assn. Labor, Federal civil litigation, Health. Office: Spencer Fane Britt & Browne 1000 Walnut Kansas City KS 64106

WING, STEPHEN PRENTICE, lawyer; b. Milw., June 14, 1956; s. Merrick Stanton and Elizabeth Bowles (Block) W.; m. Marilyn Martha Link, Oct. 9, 1982. AB, Ripon Coll., 1977; JD, U. Iowa, 1980. Bar: Iowa 1981, U.S. Dist. Ct. (so. and no. dists.) Iowa 1981, U.S. Ct. Appeals (8th cir.) 1981, Ill. 1986. Assoc. Walter, Newport & Assocs., Davenport, Iowa, 1981-85; ptnr. Dwyer & Wing P.C., Davenport, 1985—. Mem. ABA, Iowa Bar Assn., Ill. Bar Assn., Scott County Bar Assn., Assn. Trial Lawyers Am., Assn. Trial Lawyers Iowa. Avocations: radio engring., computers, skiing, golf, tennis. Personal injury, Contracts commercial, Criminal. Office: Dwyer & Wing PC 1503 Brady St Davenport IA 52803

WINGATE, C(HARLES) DOUGLAS, lawyer; b. Wilmington, Del., Apr. 11, 1953; s. Phillip Jerome and Katharine S. (Smith) W. BA in Chemistry magna cum laude, Duke U., 1975; JD with honors, U. Fla., 1980. Bar: Fla. 1980, N.Y. 1983, U.S. Dist. Ct. (ea. and so. dists.) N.Y. 1983, U.S. Ct. Appeals (6th cir.) 1985. Atty. E.I. DuPont Co., Wilmington, 1980-82; assoc. Kenyon & Kenyon, N.Y.C., 1982—. Bd. U. Fla. Law Rev., 1978. Bd. govs. N.Y.C. Capital Age of Enlightenment, 1985—. Mem. ABA, N.Y. County Lawyers Assn., N.Y. Patent Trademark and Copyright Law Assn., Am. Chem. Soc. Republican. Episcopalian. Club: Downtown Athletic (N.Y.C.). Avocation: swimming. Federal civil litigation, Patent, Trademark and copyright. Home: 201 E 25th St 11-L New York NY 10010 Office: Kenyon & Kenyon 1 Broadway New York NY 10004

WINGATE, HENRY TRAVILLION, judge; b. Jackson, Miss., Jan. 6, 1947; s. J.T. and Eloise (Anderson(W.; m. Turner Arnita Ward, Aug. 10, 1984. BA, 1969; JD, Yale U., 1972; LLD (hon.), Grinnell Coll., 1986. Bar: Miss. 1973, U.S. Dist. Ct. (so. dist.) Miss. 1973, U.S. Ct. Appeals (5th cir.) 1973, U.S. Mil. Ct. 1973. Law clk. New Haven (Conn.) Legal Assistance, 1971-72, Community Legal Aid, Jackson, 1972-73; spl. asst. atty. gen. State of Miss., Jackson, 1976-80; asst. dist. atty. U.S. Ct. Appeals (7th cir.), Jackson, 1980-84; asst. U.S. atty. U.S. Dist. Ct. (so. dist.), Jackson, 1984-85; judge U.S. Dist. Ct. (so. dist.) Miss., Jackson, Ms., 1985—; lectr. Miss. Prosecutors Coll., 1980—, Law Enforcement Tng. Acad., Pearl, Miss., 1980—, Miss. Jud. Coll., 1980—, Nat. Coll. Dist. Attys., 1984-86; adj. prof. law subjects Golden Gate U., Norfolk, Va., 1975-76, Tidewater Community Coll., 1976, Miss. Coll. Sch. of Law, 1978—. Mem. adv. bd. City of Jackson Parks and Recreation; bd. dirs. SCAN Am. of Miss., Inc., Jackson Arts Alliance, Drug Research and Edn. Assn. in Miss., Inc., United Way of Jackson. Served to lt. USN (JAGC), 1973-76; USNR, 1983—. Recipient State Singles Champion Jr. Vets. Div., 1981, State Singles Champion Srs. Div., 1981, Outstanding Legal Service award NAACP (Jackson br. and Miss. br.), 1982, Civil Liberties award Elks, 1983, Community Service award Women for Progress Orgn., 1984. Mem. ABA, Miss. Bar Assn., Hinds County Bar Assn., Internat. Assn. of Arson Investigators, Inc., Nat. Dist. Atty.'s Assn., Miss. Prosecutors Assn. (bd. dirs. 1980-81, 83—), Fed. Bar Assn., YMCA (chmn. bd. dirs. 1978-80). Club: Yale (Miss.). Avocations: reading, theater, racquetball, jogging, bowling. Home: 6018 Huntview Dr Jackson MS 39206 Office: James D Eastland Courthouse 245 E Capitol St Jackson MS 39205

WINGATE, RICHARD CHARLES, lawyer; b. Salisbury, Md., Oct. 15, 1954; s. Isaac Armwell and Doris (Grunsten) W.; m. Susan Gale Duncan, May 16, 1982. BA, Rutgers U., 1976; JD, Tulane U., 1979. Bar: La. 1979, N.Y. 1982, U.S. Dist. Ct. (so. dist.) N.Y. 1984. Land atty. Chevron USA Inc., New Orleans, 1979-80; atty. Chevron USA Inc., Perth Amboy, N.J., 1980-83; counsel Pan Atlantic Group Inc., White Plains, N.Y., 1983-85; atty. Sony Corp. Am., Park Ridge, N.J., 1985—. Mem. ABA, N.Y. State Bar Assn. (corp. counsel com. 1985—), La. Bar Assn., Westchester County Bar Assn. Contracts commercial, General corporate, Antitrust. Office: Sony Corp Am One Sony Dr Park Ridge NJ 07656

WINGER, RALPH O., lawyer; b. Keokuk, Iowa, July 8, 1919; s. Ralph O. and Mary Ellen (Lee) W.; m. Irene L. Sutton, Apr. 5, 1941; children: Ralph O., Allen, Louise, Robert. B.A., State U. Iowa, 1940; LL.B., Harvard U., 1947. Bar: N.Y. 1948. Assoc. Cahill Gordon & Reindel and predecessor firms, N.Y.C., 1947-60, ptnr., 1960—. Served to lt. USNR, 1942-46, PTO. Mem. ABA, N.Y. State Bar Assn. (chmn. tax sec. 1973-74, ho. of dels. 1974-75). Republican. Methodist. Club: Bayside (N.Y.) Yacht. Pension, profit-sharing, and employee benefits, Corporate taxation, Personal income taxation. Home: 209-08 28th Rd Bayside NY 11360 Office: Cahill Gordon & Reindel 80 Pine St New York NY 10005

WINGERTER, JOHN RAYMOND, lawyer; b. Erie, Pa., June 30, 1942; s. Raymond J. and Magdalene (Pfeil) W.; m. Susan Tracy Smith, Aug. 5, 1967; children: Julie, Kara, Lori, Darcie, Daryle. BA, Norwich U., 1964; JD, U. Notre Dame, 1968. Bar: Pa. 1967, U.S. Dist. Ct. (we. dist.) Pa. 1967, U.S. Ct. Appeals (3d cir.) 1971, U.S. Supreme Ct. 1973. Assoc. Carney, Palmisano & Walsh, Erie, Pa., 1967-69; ptnr. Carney & Good, Erie, 1969—; spl. litigation solicitor City of Erie, 1980—. Mem. ABA, Pa. Bar Assn. (ho. dels. 1983—), Erie Bar Assn. (exec. com.), Assn. Trial Lawyers Am., Pa. Trial Lawyers Assn. Democrat. Roman Catholic. Clubs: Erie, Erie Yacht. Federal civil litigation, State civil litigation, Personal injury. Home: 1540 S Shore Dr Erie PA 16505 Office: Carney & Good 254 W 6th St Erie PA 16507

WINGET, WALTER WINFIELD, lawyer; b. Peoria, Ill., Sept. 12, 1936; s. Walter W. Winget and Arabella (Robinson) Richardson; m. Ann Robert, July 12, 1969; children: Marie, Marshall. AB cum laude, Princeton U., 1958; JD, U. Mich., 1961. Bar: R.I. 1962, Ill. 1962, U.S. Supreme Ct. 1971. Assoc. Edwards & Angell, Providence, 1961-64; sole practice Peoria, 1964-77; ptnr. Winget & Kane, Peoria, 1977—; asst. pub. defender Peoria, 1969-70; bd. dirs. various corps. Atty., bd. dirs. Better Bus. Bur. Cen. Ill., Inc. 1973—, chmn., 1979-81. Served to sgt. U.S. Army, 1961-62. Mem. ABA, Assn. Trial Lawyers Am., Ill. Bar Assn., Ill. Trial Lawyers Assn., Peoria County Bar Assn. Republican. Episcopalian. Club: Peoria Country. Avocations: competetive target shooting, big game and duck hunting. Federal civil litigation, State civil litigation, General corporate. Home: 135 W Forrest Hill Peoria IL 61604 Office: Winget & Kane 416 Main St Peoria IL 61602

WINICK, MITCHEL LANE, lawyer, consultant; b. Muncie, Ind., Apr. 23, 1955; s. Darvin M. and Veta L. (Edelstein) W. BA, U. Pacific, 1976; JD, U. Houston, 1978. Bar: Tex. 1979, U.S. Dist. Ct. (so., no. and we. dists.) Tex. 1980, U.S. Ct. Appeals (5th cir.) 1980. Mgmt. cons. LWFW, Inc., Houston, 1976-78; lectr. bus. law U. Houston, 1978-80; asst. atty. gen. State of Tex., Austin, 1980-81; pvt. practice Winick & Assocs., Inc., Houston, 1981—; v.p. corp. devel. Houstonian, Inc., Houston, 1983-84; lectr. contract law U. St. Thomas, Houston, 1982; bd. dirs. devel. bd. InterFirst Bank-Fannin. Named one of Outstanding Young Men Am., 1983. Mem. ABA, Tex. State Bar Assn., Houston Young Lawyers Assn., South Freeway Corridor Assn. (econs. devel. com.), Phi Alpha Delta. Club: The Athletics Congress. Avocations: running, snow skiing, softball. Mergers and acquisitions, Real property, Management consulting. Office: Winick and Assocs Inc 3223 Smith #212 Houston TX 77006

WINICKI, ROBERT JOHN, lawyer; b. Chgo., Mar. 12, 1954; s. Robert John and Colette Marie (McGrane) W. BA, U. Chgo., 1976; JD, U. Miami, 1979. Bar: Ill. 1979, Fla. 1981. Law clk. to presiding justice U.S. Ct. Appeals, Kansas City, Mo., 1979-81; assoc. Mahoney Adams Milam Surface & Grimsley, Jacksonville, Fla., 1981—, ptnr., 1985—. Antitrust, Banking. Home: 5451 Robert Scott Dr Jacksonville FL 32207 Office: Mahoney Adams Milam et al 100 Laura St Jacksonville FL 32202

WINIKOFF, ROBERT LEE, lawyer; b. N.Y.C., May 17, 1946; s. Abraham and Anne (Brawer) W.; m. Enid L. Rabinowitz, July 13, 1969; children: Meredith, Brian, Deborah. BA, Ithaca Coll., 1968; JD, William & Mary Coll. of Law, 1973. Bar: N.Y. 1974, U.S. Dist. Ct. (ea. and so. dists.) N.Y. 1974, U.S. Tax Ct. 1974, U.S. Ct. Appeals (2d cir.) 1974. Assoc. Dewey, Ballantine, Bushby, Palmer & Wood, N.Y.C., 1973-76, Goldman Cooperman & Levitt, N.Y.C., 1977-79; ptnr. Cooperman, Levitt & Winikoff P.C., N.Y.C., 1980—. Comments editor William & Mary Law Rev., 1972-73. Coach Clarkstown Recreation Program, New City, N.Y., 1982-85, New City Little League, 1983-84, Rockland County Temple Basketball League, New City, 1985-86; coach, dir. New City Babe Ruth League. Mem. ABA, N.Y. Bar Assn., Assn. of Bar of City of N.Y., Omicron Delta Kappa. Democrat. Jewish. General corporate, Real property, Securities. Home: 4 Hemptor Rd New City NY 10956 Office: Cooperman Levitt & Winikoff PC 800 3d Ave New York NY 10022

WINKELMAN, ROGER EDWARD, lawyer; b. Detroit, Sept. 30, 1954; s. Stanley Jay and Margaret Jane (Wallace) W.; m. Linda Elizabeth Schwartz. BA with distinction, U. Mich., 1976; JD, Wayne State U., 1979; student, U. San Diego, Paris, summers 1974, 76, 78. Bar: Mich. 1980, U.S. Dist. Ct. (ea. dist.) Mich. 1980. Sole practice Bloomfield Hills, Mich., 1980-86; estate adminstr. Nat. Bank of Detroit, 1986-87, personal trust adminstr., 1987—; spl. asst. atty. gen. State of Mich., Detroit, 1983-86; proctor, grader State Bar Exam., Mich., 1984—; mediator small claims 46th and 48th Dist. Ct., Mich., 1984-86; arbitrator Mich. Employment Relations Commn., 1984-86. Mem. exec. com. Oakland County Dems., 1980-84; past chmn., vice-chmn., trustee Dem. Club; bd. dirs. citizens adv. com. U. Mich., Dearborn, 1983—, Met. Detroit Youth Found., 1984—, citizens adv. com. Wayne County Juvenile Ct., Detroit, 1985—, Jewish Community Council, 1985-86, assoc. chmn. community relations com. 1984-86. Named one of Outstanding Young Men in Am., U.S. Jaycees, 1983; recipient Commendation Oakland Div. United Community Services Met. 1985, SEMFCO-Urban Hunger Workcamp, 1986. Mem. ABA, Mich. Bar Assn., Oakland County Bar Assn., Am. Judicature Soc. (probate sect.). Club: Birmingham (West Bloomfield). Probate. Home: 5185 Cold Spring Ln West Bloomfield MI 48033 Office: Nat Bank Detroit Trust Div 1116 W Long Lake Rd Bloomfield Hills MI 48013

WINKJER, DEAN, lawyer; b. Wildrose, N.D., Jan. 19, 1923; m. Betty Joanne Septon, Aug. 24, 1950; children: DeAnn Allen, Andrea, Collin, Kirsten Eppinger Winkjer, Jonathan. PhD, U. N.D., 1944, JD, 1947. Bar: N.D. 1947, U.S. Dist. Ct. N.D. 1952, U.S. Supreme Ct. 1964, U.S. Dist. Ct. Mont. 1967, U.S. Ct. Customs 1969. Assoc. Arley R. Bjella, Williston, N.D., 1947; ptnr. Rolfstad, Winkjer, McKennett, Kaiser & Stenehjem P.C., Williston; legal counsel Northwest Mut. Aid Telephone Corp., Ray, N.D. Mem. N.D. Ho. of Reps., 1973-81; chmn. Ho. Judiciary Com., Ho. and Senate Interim Com.; appointed State Social Service Bd., chmn. 1980; bd. of regents Wartburg Luth. Coll., Waverly, Iowa; lay rep. Nat. Ch. Council of Am. Luth. Ch.; chmn. United Fund Dr., Salvation Army, Community Concert Assn.; parliamentarian Nat. Convention Am. Luth. Ch., San Diego, 1982. Recipient Silver Beaver award Boy Scouts Am., Lamb award Nat. Luth. Council U.S. Mem. Williams County Bar Assn. (pres.), Northwest Bar Assn. (pres.), N.D. Bar Assn. (chmn. ethics com., law sch. liaison com., mem. exec. com.), C. of C. Republican. Office: Rolfstad Winkjer McKennett & Stenehjem PC 314 1st Ave E PO Box 1366 Williston ND 56801-1366

WINKLER, ANDREA JOANNE, lawyer; b. Jersey City, Apr. 13, 1953; married;. BA in Spanish, BA in Latin Am. Studies, Hiram Coll., 1974; JD, Am. U., 1978. Bar: D.C. 1978, U.S. Dist. Ct. D.C. 1979, U.S. Supreme Ct. 1984. Atty., advisor Office of Privacy and Info. Appeals U.S. Dept. Justice, Washington, 1978-81, dep. dir. U.S. Trustee Program, 1982—; acting asst. U.S. Trustee (no. dist.) Ill. U.S. Dept. Justice, 1981-82, acting asst. U.S. Trustee dist. D.C., (ea. dist.) Va., 1982, acting U.S. Trustee (no. dist.) Tex., 1985; bd. dirs. JDS Design, Inc., Washington. Articles editor Am. U. Law Rev., 1977-78. Mem. ABA, D.C. Bar Assn., Womens Bar Assn., Phi Beta Kappa. Bankruptcy, Administrative and regulatory, Legislative. Office: US Trustee Program Exec Office 320 1st St NW Room 812 Washington DC 20530

WINKLER, DANA JOHN, lawyer; b. Wichita, Kans., Jan. 2, 1944; s. Donald Emil and Hazel Claire (Schmitter) W.; m. Mary Ann Seiwert, Oct. 14, 1967; 1 child, Jonathan. BA, Wichita State U., 1967; JD, Washburn Law Sch., 1971. Staff writer Wichita Eagle & Beacon, Kans., 1961-67; ptnr. Davis, Bruce, Davis & Winkler, Wichita, 1972-77; asst city atty. City of Wichita, 1977—; dir. Wichita Mcpl. Fed. Credit Union, 1980—, pres., 1982; dir. Deaf and Hard of Hearing Counseling Service, 1979-80. Vol. Sedgwick County United Way, Wichita, 1973-74; mem. Wichita Pub. Schs. Spl. Edn. Adv. Council, 1984—. Served to 1st lt. U.S. Army, 1967-69. Mem. Kans. Bar Assn., Wichita Bar Assn. Republican. Roman Catholic. Lodge: Masons. Government contracts and claims, Local government, Pension, profit-sharing, and employee benefits. Home: 1621 Harlan St Wichita KS 67212 Office: City of Wichita Dept Law 455 N Main St 13th Floor Wichita KS 67202

WINN, DAVID BURTON, lawyer; b. Dallas, Feb. 6, 1953; s. Edward Burton and Conchita (Hassell) W.; m. Becky Oberthier, Apr. 30, 1982. BA in History, So. Meth. U., 1975; JD, U. Tex., 1978. Bar: Tex. 1978, U.S. Dist. Ct. (no. dist.) Tex. 1978, U.S. Ct. Appeals (5th cir.) 1979, U.S. Dist. Ct. (so. dist.) Tex. 1986. Assoc. Kasmir, Willingham & Krage, Dallas, 1978-84; assoc. Winn, Beaudry & Virden, Dallas, 1985-86, ptnr., 1986—. Editor (newsletter) Amundsen Inst. U.S.-Mex. Studies, 1985—. Del. US-USSR Emerging Leaders Conf., 1986—. Named one of Outstanding Young Men Am., 1982; Amundsen Inst. U.S.-Mex. Studies fellow, 1982—. Mem. ABA, Dallas Bar Assn. (pro bono atty. legal clinic, recipient disting. pro bono service award 1986), Tex. Bar Assn. Federal civil litigation, State civil litigation. Home: 5419 Morningside Ave Dallas TX 75206 Office: Winn Beaudry & Virden 3330 Republic Bank Bldg Dallas TX 75201

WINN, MARSHALL, lawyer; b. Anderson, S.C., Nov. 24, 1952; s. Ralph Marshall and Hazel Lou (Isehower) W.; m. Jeannette Anderson, Aug. 16, 1975; 1 child, Richard. BA summa cum laude, U. S.C., 1974; JD, Harvard U., 1982. Bar: S.C. 1982, U.S. Dist. Ct. S.C. 1983, U.S. Ct. Claims 1983, U.S. Ct. Appeals (4th cir.) 1983. Assoc. Buist, Moore, Smythe & McGee, Charleston, S.C., 1982-85, Wyche, Burgess, Freeman & Parham P.A., Greenville, S.C., 1985—. Chmn. bd. student advisors Harvard U. Law Sch., Cambridge, Mass., 1980-82; mem., treas. Charleston Symphony Singers Guild, 1982-85; mem. Greenville Civic Chorale, 1985—. Mem. S.C. Bar Assn., Greenville County Bar Assn., Greenville Commerce Club, Phi Beta Kappa. Democrat. General corporate, Contracts commercial, Federal civil litigation. Home: 200 Tindal Ave Greenville SC 29605 Office: Wyche Burgess Freeman & Parham 44 E Camperdown Way PO Box 10207 Greenville SC 29603

WINNER, JOHN DENNETT, lawyer; b. Port Washington, Wis., Sept. 10, 1921; s. Paul Chester and Jeanne (Dennett) W.; m. Marcelaine Hobson, Sept. 10, 1949; children: John Randall, Gary Hobson, Scott Paul. BA, U. Wis., 1943, JD, 1949. Bar: Wis. 1949, U.S. Dist. Ct. (we. dist.) Wis. 1950, U.S. Ct. Appeals (7th cir.) 1957, U.S. Supreme Ct. 1957, U.S. Dist. Ct. D.C. 1958, U.S. Tax Ct. 1978, U.S. Dist. Ct. (ea. dist.) Wis. 1983. Assoc. Roberts, Roe & Boardman, Madison, Wis., 1949-56; dist. atty. Dane County, Wis., 1956-57; dep. atty. gen. State of Wis., Madison, 1957-59; ptnr. Winner, McCallum, Wixson & Pernitz, Madison, 1959—; lectr. law U. Wis., Madison, 1953-56. Served to lt. col. U.S. Army, 1943-46, JAG, 1961-62. Decorated Bronze Star. Fellow Am. Coll. Trial Lawyers; mem. ABA, State Bar Assn. Wis., Civil Trail Counsel Wis., Dane County Bar Assn. (pres. 1975-76), Def. Research Inst. State civil litigation, Insurance, Personal injury. Home: 1222 Gilbert Rd Madison WI 53711 Office: Winner McCallum Wixson & Pernitz 121 E Wilson St Box 2626 Madison WI 53701

WINNER, RUSSELL LEE, lawyer; b. Oil City, Pa., June 1, 1948; s. Lee Burton and Jean Louise (Smillie) W.; m. Sharon Morrissey, Jan. 7, 1978; children: Brooke Allison, Adam Lee. BA, Stanford U., 1970; JD, U. Chgo., 1975. Bar: Wash. 1977, Alaska 1978, U.S. Dist. Ct. Alaska 1979, U.S. Ct. Appeals (9th cir.) 1981. Atty. regional solicitor's office U.S. Dept. Interior, Anchorage, 1978-79; assoc. Graham & James, Anchorage, 1979-82, McGrath & Assocs., Anchorage, 1982-85; prin. Winner & Assocs., Anchorage, 1986—; vis. asst. prof. law Lewis and Clark Law Sch., Portland, Oreg., 1976-77. Contbr. articles to profl. jours. Research fellow marine policy and ocean mgmt., Woods Hole (Mass.) Oceanographic Instn., 1975-76, Nat. Resources Law Inst., Lewis and Clark Law Sch., 1976-78. Mem. Alaska Bar Assn. (mem. bar examiners com.), Assn. Trial Lawyers Am., Alaska Acad. Trial Lawyers. Avocation: fishing. General practice, Real property, Personal injury. Office: 900 W 5th Ave Suite 700 Anchorage AK 99501

WINNICK, HELENE ANN, lawyer; b. Sacramento, Sept. 21, 1956; d. Byron Monroe and Estelle (Feinberg) W. A.A., Am. River Coll., Sacramento, 1975; B.A., UCLA, 1977; J.D., Southwestern U., Los Angeles, 1980. Bar: Calif. 1981, U.S. Tax Ct. 1982. Staff mem. U.S. Ho. of Reps., Los Angeles, 1976, Los Angeles Dept. Consumer Affairs, 1977; law clk. Rosenstock & Rosenstock, Los Angeles, 1979, Goller, Gillin & Menes, Los Angeles, 1979-80; v.p. Winns Sales Inc., Citrus Heights, Calif., 1977—; exec. dir. Quantum Ednl. Devel., Sacramento, 1981-82; assoc. Wohl Cinnamon & Hagedorn, Sacramento, 1980-82; sole practice, Sacramento, 1982-86; atty. U.S. Small Bus. Adminstrn., Sacramento, 1986—; prof. Pacific Coll. Legal Careers, Sacramento, 1983, Barclay Coll., 1983—; lectr. in field U. Calif.-Davis, 1983. Mem. task force cable TV Council of Jewish Fedn., N.Y.C., 1982—; mem. Sacramento Regional Arts Council; bd. dirs. Religious Coalition for Cable TV, Sacramento, 1984-86, Los Rios Community Coll. Found., Sacramento, 1984, Sacramento Community Cable Found. Mem. ABA, Calif. State Bar, Sacramento County Bar Assn., Women Lawyers Sacramento, Calif. Young Lawyers Assn. Democrat. Entertainment, Trademark and copyright, General corporate. Office: 77 Cadillac Dr Sacramento CA 95825

WINNING, JOHN PATRICK, lawyer; b. Murphysboro, Ill., Oct. 29, 1952; s. William T. Jr. and Lillian (Albers) W.; m. Jessica Anne Yoder, June 17, 1978; children: Erika, Brian, Derek. BA, Mo. Bapt. Coll., 1974; JD, St. Louis U., 1979. Bar: Mo. 1979, U.S. Dist. Ct. (ea. dist.) Mo. 1979, U.S. Ct. Appeals (8th cir.) 1979, U.S. Dist. Ct. (so. dist.) Tex. 1985. Assoc. Chused, Strauss et al, St. Louis, 1979-81; assoc. counsel Mfrs. Hanover Fin. Services, Phila., 1981-83; corp. counsel Cessna Fin. Corp., Wichita, Kans., 1983-85; atty. Southwestern Bell Publs., Inc., St. Louis, 1985—. Mem. ABA (comml. fin. services com., creditor's rights subcom., interest and usury subcom.), Met. St. Louis Bar Assn. Republican. Baptist. Avocation: sports. Home: 604 Forest Leaf Dr Ballwin MO 63011 Office: Southwestern Bell Publs Inc 12800 Publications Dr Saint Louis MO 63131

WINQUIST, THOMAS RICHARD, lawyer; b. Grand Rapids, Mich., Mar. 16, 1933; s. Harold George and Martha (Bos) W.; m. Shirley Ellen Bye; children—Tomison Elizabeth, Brett Thomas, Blake Harold. A.A. with high honors, Grand Rapids Jr. Coll., 1953; B.A. with high distinction, U. Mich., 1955, J.D. with distinction, 1958. Bar: Mich. 1958, U.S. Dist. Ct. (we. dist.) Mich. 1958, U.S. Supreme Ct. 1985. Assoc., Warner, Norcross & Judd, Grand Rapids, 1958-63, ptnr., 1963—, mng. ptnr., 1982—; v.p., dir. Grand Hotel Co., Mackinac Island, Mich., 1968—; sec./treas., dir. Gen. Aluminum Products, Inc., Charlotte, Mich. Sec./treas. Vomberg Found., Charlotte; adv. bd. YWCA, 1980—. Mem. ABA, Mich. State Bar Assn. (sect. taxation and corp. law), Grand Rapids Bar Assn., Grand Rapids C. of C. (legis. liaison com. 1976-80), Order of Coif, Phi Beta Kappa, Phi Kappa Phi, Delta Pi Alpha. Republican. Methodist. Clubs: Peninsular, University (Grand Rapids). Asst. editor Mich. U. Law Rev., 1957-58. General corporate, Estate planning, Corporate taxation. Office: Warner Norcross & Judd Suite 900 Old Kent Bank Bldg Grand Rapids MI 49502

WINSHIP, PETER, law educator; b. Pensacola, Fla., Jan. 5, 1944; s. Stephen and Frances Norinne (Hayford) W.; m. Marion Christina Nelson, June 18, 1966; children: Verity Elizabeth, Adam Edward. BA, Harvard U., 1965, LLB, 1968; LLM, London Sch. of Econs., 1973; postdoctoral, Yale U., 1973-74. Bar: Tex. 1975, U.S. Dist. Ct. (no. dist.) Tex. 1981, U.S. Ct. Appeals (5th and 11th cirs.) 1981. Legal advisor Ethiopian Ministry of Commerce, Addis Ababa, 1968-70; lectr. Haile Selassie I U., Addis Ababa, 1970-72; prof. So. Meth. U. Sch. Law, Dallas, 1974—; vis. prof. U. Calif., Berkeley, 1979-80, UCLA Sch. Law, 1986—. Co-author: Texas Litigation Guide, Vols. 7-10, 1979, Commercial Transactions, 1985; editor: Background Documents of the Ethiopian Commercial Code, 1974. Mem. Internat. Inst. for Unification Private Law (corr. collaborator 1983—). Contracts commercial, General corporate, Legal history. Home: 3448 Amherst St Dallas TX 75225 Office: So Meth U Sch Law Dallas TX 75275

WINSLOW, DONALD ARTHUR, lawyer, legal educator; b. Lincoln, Nebr., Mar. 12, 1953; s. Worth Richard and Barbara Jane (Beal) W.; m. Mary Wavelette Shaw, May 18, 1980; 1 child, Edward Arthur Charles. BA, UCLA, 1975; MBA, Cornell U., 1979, JD, 1980. Bar: Ga. 1981, U.S. Dist. Ct. (no. dist.) Ga. 1981, U.S. Ct. Appeals (11th cir.) 1981, U.S. Tax Ct. 1984. Law clk. to judge U.S. Ct. Appeals (5th cir.), Atlanta, 1980-81; assoc. Sutherland, Asbill & Brennan, Atlanta, 1981-86; asst. prof. law U. Ky., Lexington, 1986—; instr. law Emory U., Atlanta, 1984. Editor Cornell U. Law Rev., 1979-80; contbr. articles to legal jours. Mem. com. Cornell Alumni Secondary Schs., Atlanta, 1983-86, bd. advisors Legal Prep, Inc., Atlanta, 1986—. Regents scholar U. Calif., 1971. Mem. ABA (taxation sect.), Ga. Bar Assn., Atlanta Bar Assn., Cornell Alumni Assn., Order of Coif, Phi Beta Kappa, Omicron Delta Epsilon. Democrat. Episcopalian. Avocations: tennis, reading. Corporate taxation, General corporate, Insurance. Office: U Ky Coll Law Lexington KY 40506-0048

WINSLOW, HELEN LITTELL, lawyer; b. Wilmington, Del., May 11, 1952; d. Julian Dallas and Jean (Littell) W.; m. Jonathan David Jaffe, Nov. 8, 1980; 1 child, Kenan Winslow Jaffe. AB, Bryn Mawr Coll., 1974; JD, U. N.C., 1977. Bar: Del. 1977, U.S. Dist. Ct. Del. 1977, U.S. Ct. Appeals (3d cir.) 1980, U.S. Supreme Ct.1980. Law clk. to presiding judge U.S. Dist. Ct. Del., Wilmington, 1977-79; assoc. Richards, Layton & Finger, Wilmington, 1979—. Mem. ABA, Fed. Bar Assn. (v.p. Del. chpt. 1985-86, pres. Del. chpt. 1987—), Del. Bar Assn., Am. Judicature Soc. Democrat. Jewish. Club: Bryn Mawr Del (Wilmington). Avocation: singing. Trademark and copyright, Contracts commercial. Office: Richards Layton & Finger 1 Rodney Sq PO Box 551 Wilmington DE 19899

WINSLOW, JOHN FRANKLIN, lawyer; b. Houston, Nov. 15, 1933; s. Franklin Jarnigan and Jane (Shipley) W. BA, U. Tex., 1957, LLB, 1960. Bar: Tex. 1959, D.C. 1961. Atty., Hispanic law div. Library Congress, Washington, 1965-68; counsel, com. on the judiciary Ho. of Reps., Washington, 1968-71; atty., editor Matthew Bender & Co., Washington, 1973-79; atty. FERC, Washington, 1979-84; sole practice Washington, 1984—; researcher Hispanic Law Research, Washington, 1979—. Author: Conglomerates Unlimited: The Failure of Regulation, 1974; editor: Fed. Power Service, 1974-79; contbr. articles to Washington Monthly, Nation, 1975—. Mem. vestry St. Thomas's Episc. Ch., 1976—. Mem. Tex. Bar Assn., D.C. Bar Assn. Administrative and regulatory, Antitrust, Public international. Office: 1255 New Hampshire Ave NW Washington DC 20036

WINSLOW, JULIAN DALLAS, lawyer; b. Elizabeth City, N.C., Oct. 10, 1914; s. Joseph D. and Mary Anne (Cooper) W.; m. Jean Littell, Dec. 27, 1941; children—Julian Dallas, Mary P. Winslow Reddick, Helen L. B.S. in Commerce, U. N.C., 1935, J.D., 1941. Bar: N.C. 1941, Del. 1949, U.S. Dist. Ct. Del. 1952, U.S. Ct. Appeals (3d cir.) 1982. Assoc. J.H. LeRoy Jr., Elizabeth City, 1941-42; sole practice, Elizabeth City 1945-48, Wilmington, Del., 1949—; solicitor Currituck County (N.C.) Ct. 1946-47; chief of enforcement heavy machinery and indsl. materials sect. Office Price Stablzn., Del. dist. 1952; arbitrator Am. Arbitration Assn. Served to lt. USCG, 1942-45. Decorated Philippine Liberation medal. Mem. Del. State Bar Assn. (com. labor and employment law). Republican. Quaker. Workers' compensation, Real property, General practice.

WINSTEIN, STEWART ROBERT, lawyer; b. Viola, Ill., May 28, 1914; s. Abraham and Esther (Meyer) W.; m. Dorothy Shock, Nov. 2, 1961; 1 son, Arthur R. A.B., Augustana Coll., 1935; J.D., U. Chgo., 1938. Bar: Ill. Ptnr. Winstein, Kavensky, Wallace & Doughty, Rock Island, Ill., 1939—. Trustee Marycrest Coll., Davenport, Iowa, 1980—; fin. officer State of Ill., 1963-70; del. Democratic Nat. Conv., 1968, 72 and mid-term conf., 1974, 78; 17th

Dist. Dem. State Central committeeman, 1970—; vice chmn. State of Ill. Dem. State Central Com., 1970-82; pub. adminstr. Rock Island County, 1974-78; commr. Met. Airport Authority, 1972—, chmn. bd., 1986—. Mem. ABA, Ill. Bar Assn., Rock Island County Bar Assn., Chgo. Bar Assn., Assn. Trial Lawyers of Am. Jewish. Contbr. articles to profl. jours. General practice, Family and matrimonial, Criminal.

WINSTEN, I.W., lawyer, law educator; b. Flint, Mich., Sept. 10, 1952; s. Stanley Dean and Harriet (Solomon) W.; m. Beth Tanenhaus, Dec. 18, 1982. BA with honors, Wayne State U., 1976, JD magna cum laude, 1979. Bar: Mich. 1979, U.S. Dist. Ct. (ea. dist.) Mich. 1979, U.S. Dist. Ct. (we. dist.) Mich. 1980, U.S. Ct. Appeals (6th cir.) 1980, U.S. Ct. Appeals (9th cir.) 1984, U.S. Ct. Appeals (11th, D.C. and 4th cirs.) 1985. Assoc. Honigman, Miller, Schwartz & Cohn, Detroit, 1979-83, ptnr., 1984—. Landlord-tenant advisor Palmer Park Citizens Action Com., Detroit, 1977-80. Bronze Key scholar Wayne State U., 1977-79. Mem. ABA (instr. trial advocacy Am. Law Inst. 1986—), Fed. Bar Assn. (instr. trial advocacy 1985—, chmn. membership com. 1985—), Mich. Bar Assn., Detroit Bar Assn., Assn. Trial Lawyers Am., ACLU (cooperating atty. 1983—), Detroit Inst. of Arts Founders Soc., Wayne State Alumni Assn., Jaycees (named one of Outstanding Young Men of Am. 1984). Democrat. Jewish. Club: Detroit Press. Federal civil litigation, State civil litigation, Libel. Office: Honigman Miller Schwartz & Cohn 2290 1st National Bldg Detroit MI 48226

WINSTON, HAROLD RONALD, b. Atlantic, Iowa, Feb. 7, 1932; s. Louis D. and Leta B. (Carter) W.; m. Carol J. Sundeen, June 11, 1955 (divorced); children—Leslie Winston Yannetti, Laura L.; m. Lisa Winston Barbour. B.A., U. Iowa, 1954, J.D., 1958. Bar: Iowa 1958, U.S. District Ct. (no. and so. dists.) Iowa 1962, U.S. Tax Ct. 1962, U.S. Ct. Appeals (8th cir.) 1970, U.S. Supreme Ct. 1969. Trust Officer United Home Bank & Trust Co., Mason City, Iowa, 1958-59; mem. Breese & Cornwell, 1960-62, Breese Cornwell Winston & Reuber, 1963-73, Winston Schroeder & Reuber, 1974-79, Winston, Reuber & Swanson, P.C., Mason City, 1980—. police judge, Mason City, 1961-73. Author profl. publs. Past pres. Family YMCA, Mason City, Cerro Gordo County Estate Planning Council; active numerous local charitable orgns. Served to capt. USAF, 1955-57. Fellow Am. Coll. Probate Counsel; mem. ABA, Iowa Bar Assn. (gov., lectr. ann. meeting 1977, 78, 79), 2d Jud. Dist. Ba r Assn. (lectr. meeting 1981, 82), Cerro Gordo County Bar Assn. (past pres.), Am. Judicature Soc., Assn. Trial Lawyers Am. Republican. Presbyterian (elder). Clubs: Euchre and Cycle, Mason City County, Masons, Kiwanis. Probate, General corporate, General practice.

WINSTON, JACQUELINE BERRIER, lawyer; b. Columbia, S.C., Oct. 25, 1952; d. William Jackson and Elma (Welch) Berrier; m. Thomas Edward Winston III, Mar. 16, 1974; 1 child, Christopher Jackson. BA, U. S.C., 1974, JD, 1978. Bar: S.C. 1978, U.S. Dist. Ct. S.C. 1979, U.S. Ct. Appeals (4th cir.) 1979. Asst. counsel Colonial Life and Acccident Ins. Co., Columbia, 1978—. Treas. Colonial Life Polit. Action Com., Columbia, 1984—; bd. dirs. Southeastern Children's Home, 1987—. Fellow Life Mgmt. Inst. 1985; mem. ABA, Phi Beta Kappa. General corporate, Corporate taxation, Securities. Office: Colonial Life & Accident Ins Co 1200 Colonial Life Blvd Columbia SC 29210

WINSTON, ROBERT TUNSTALL, JR., lawyer; b. Hanover, Va., July 25, 1919; s. Robert Tunstall and Grace Ellen (McKey) W.; m. Elisabeth Joyce Robinson, Feb. 12, 1949; children—Julia, Frances, Martha. B.A., Randolph-Macon Coll., 1940; LL.B., Duke U., 1947. Bar: Va. 1947, U.S. Ct. Appeals (4th and 6th cirs.) 1953, U.S. Supreme Ct. 1959. Assoc. Fred B. Greear, Norton, Va., 1947-48; ptnr. Greear, Bowen, Mullins & Winston, Norton, 1948-65, 68-74; ptnr. Mullins, Winston, Stout & Thomason, Norton, 1974-86; judge 30th Jud. Cir., 1986—. assoc. and ptnr. Kime, Jolly, Winston & Clemens, Salem, Va., 1965-67. Chmn. Norton Democratic Com., 1954, 55. Served to capt. U.S. Army, 1941-46. Decorated Bronze Star. Mem. ABA, Va. Bar Assn., Assn. Trial Lawyers Am., Va. Trial Lawyers Assn. Episcopalian. Clubs: Res. Officers Assn., Kiwanis, Lonesome Pine Country. Federal civil litigation, State civil litigation, Personal injury. Office: Law Bldg Norton VA 24273

WINSTON, ROGER DEAN, lawyer; b. Washington, June 10, 1954; s. Sidney and Elizabeth (Stepanik) W.; m. Karen Lynn Lovell, Jan. 10, 1954; children: Amanda Christine, Emily Rebecca. BA, U. Md., 1976, JD, 1979; ML in Taxation, Georgetown U., 1983. Bar: U.S. Ct. Appeals Md., D.C. 1980. Assoc. Nylen and Gilmore, Hyattsville, Md., 1979-80; assoc. Linowes and Blocher, Silver Spring, Md., 1980-85, ptnr., 1985—; drafter Md. Homeowners Assn. Act; bd. dirs., chmn. legis. com., speaker Community Assns. Inst. (Washington chpt.); gov. appointee Md. Governors Commn. on Condomimums, Coops. and Homeowners Assns., Annapolis, Md., 1982-86; speaker Community Assns. Inst. Mem. membership com. Montgomery (Md.) Edn. Connection, 1985-86. Recipient William Cunningham award. Mem. ABA (real property trusts and probate sect., subcom. on condominiums), Md. State Bar Assn. (speaker), D.C. Bar Assn., Bar Assn. of D.C., Community Assns. Inst. (speaker), Md. Inst. for Continuing Profl. Edn. (speaker), Montgomery County C. of C. Democrat. Episcopalian. Real property, Community Association Development. Office: 8720 Georgia Ave 5th Floor Silver Spring MD 20910 also: 655 15th St NW Washington DC 20005

WINSTON, RUSSELL CLAY, lawyer; b. Memphis, May 29, 1951; s. Thomas Daniel and Gladys (Coleman) W. BBA, Memphis State U., 1972, JD, 1975. Bar: Tenn. 1976, U.S. Dist. Ct. Tenn. 1979, U.S. Supreme Ct. 1981, U.S. Ct. Appeals (6th cir.) 1985. Sole practice Memphis, 1976—. Mem. ABA, Tenn. Bar Assn., Memphis and Shelby County Bar Assn. (bd. dirs. family law sect. 1986—), Assn. Trial Lawyers Am., Tenn. Assn. Criminal Def. Lawyers., Delta Theta Phi. State civil litigation, Contracts commercial, Family and matrimonial. Office: 44 N 2d St Suite 701 Memphis TN 38103

WINTER, AUDREY STACEY, lawyer; b. Long Beach, Calif., Feb. 2, 1956; d. Sidney Joseph and Mary Dorothy (Tomsykoski) W. BS summa cum laude, U. Ga., 1977, JD cum laude, 1980; Licence Speciale grande distinction, Free U. Brussels, 1980-81. Bar: D.C. 1980, Ga. 1980, D.C. 1982.. Atty. Com. of European Communities, Brussels, 1981-82; atty. office gen. counsel for import adminstrn. Dept. Commerce, Washington, 1983-84; assoc. Boden, Oppenhoff & Schneider, Cologne, Fed. Republic Germany, 1985, Dewey, Ballantine, Bushby, Palmer & Wood, Washington, 1985—. Fellow Belgian-Am. Ednl. Found., 1980-81. Mem. ABA, West German Young Lawyers Program (dept. of justice, German acad. exchange service 1984-85), Internat. Bar Assn., Young Lawyers Internat. Bar Assn., Kappa Delta Phi. Private international. Home: 2804 Dumbarton St NW Washington DC 20007 Office: Dewey Ballantine Bushby et al 1775 Pennsylvania Ave NW Washington DC 20006

WINTER, FRANK LOUIS, lawyer; b. Vienna, Austria, May 12, 1928; came to U.S., 1938; s. Paul and Clara (Payor) W.; m. Aureen Ladiosca Mayne, Sept. 21, 1968; children: Stephen, Donna, Terence. B.S., Northwestern U., 1949, J.D., 1952. Bar: Ill. 1954. Ptnr. Kirkland & Ellis, Chgo., 1954—; arbitrator Am. Arbitration Assn., Chgo., 1976—. Dir. and v.p. Calvert Found., Chgo., 1978—. Served with U.S. Army, 1952-54. Mem. Ill. Bar Assn., Chgo. Bar. Assn. (chmn. real property law com. 1981-82). Democrat. Roman Catholic. Club: University (Chgo.). Landlord-tenant, Real property, Environment. Home: 4914 S Ellis Ave Chicago IL 60605 Office: Kirkland and Ellis 200 E Randolph Dr Chicago IL 60601

WINTER, HARRISON L., judge; b. Balt., Apr. 18, 1921; s. J. George and Bessie (Biden) W.; m. Gladys Woolford, June 28, 1947; children—Barbara B., Anne B. A.B., Johns Hopkins U., 1942; LL.B., U. Md., 1944. Bar: Md. bar 1945. Asso. firm Miles, Walsh, O'Brien & Morris, 1946-51, partner, 1951-53; partner Miles & Stockbridge, 1953-59; asst. atty. gen. Md., 1948-51, dep. atty. gen., 1954-55; city solicitor Balt., 1959-61; judge U.S. Dist. Ct. of Md., Balt., 1961-66; U.S. circuit judge U.S. Ct. of Appeals, 4th Circuit, Richmond, Va., 1966—; chief judge U.S. Ct. of Appeals, 4th Circuit, 1981—. Trustee Johns Hopkins U., vice chmn. bd., 1968-81; trustee Peabody Inst., 1959-85, chmn. bd. 1967-77; bd. dirs. Evergreen House Found. Fellow Am. Bar Found.; mem. Am. Law Inst., Inst. Jud. Adminstrn., Am., Md., bar assns., Am. Coll. Trial Lawyers, Am. Judicature Soc. (bd. dirs.), Order of Coif, Omicron Delta Kappa. Episcopalian. Clubs: Md. (Balt.), 14 W. Hamilton St. (Balt.), Elkridge (Balt.). Home: 16 Roland Mews Baltimore MD 21210 Office: 101 W Lombard St Baltimore MD 21201

WINTER, RALPH KARL, judge; b. Waterbury, Conn., July 30, 1935; married. B.A., Yale U., 1957, J.D., 1960. Bar: Conn. 1973. Research assoc., lectr. Yale U., 1962-64, asst. prof. to assoc. prof. law, 1964-68, prof. law, 1968-82; judge U.S. Ct. Appeals (2d cir.), New Haven, 1982—; spl. cons. subcom. on separation of powers U.S. Senate Com. on Judiciary, from 1982; adj. prof. law U. Chgo., 1966; sr. fellow Brookings Inst., 1968-70; adj. scholar Am. Enterprise Inst., 1972-82. Contbr. articles to profl. jours. Legal education. Office: US Court of Appeals 142 Orange St 3d Floor Box 802 New Haven CT 06510 *

WINTER, STEVEN LAWRENCE, lawyer, educator; b. Bronx, N.Y., Apr. 13, 1953; s. Joseph and Paula (DeVorzon) W.; m. Margaret Lynn Snuffer, May 4, 1986. BA, Yeshiva U., 1974; JD, Columbia U., 1977. Bar: N.Y. 1978, U.S. Supreme Ct. 1982, U.S. Ct. Appeals (5th and 6th cirs.) 1979, U.S. Dist. Ct. (so. and ea. dists.) N.Y. 1980, U.S. Ct. Appeals (11th cir.) 1981, U.S. Ct. Appeals (2d cir.) 1985. Law clk. to presiding judge U.S. Ct. Appeals (2d cir.), N.Y.C., 1977-78; asst. counsel NAACP Legal Def. and Ednl. Fund Inc., N.Y.C., 1978-86; assoc. prof. law U. Miami, Coral Gables, Fla., 1986—; lectr. in law Rutgers U. Law Sch., Newark, 1984-86, Cardozo Law Sch., N.Y.C., 1985; cons. Helsinki Watch, N.Y.C., 1980, 85; witness Ho. Subcom. on Criminal Justice, Washington, 1979, 85. Contbr. articles to profl. jours. and newspapers. Mem. ABA. Democrat. Avocations: bicycling, jazz. Civil rights, Criminal, Legal education. Office: U Miami Law Sch PO Box 248087 Coral Gables FL 33124-8087

WINTERSHEIMER, DONALD CARL, judge; b. Covington, Ky., Apr. 21, 1932; s. Carl E. and Marie A. (Kohl) W.; m. Alice T. Rabe, June 24, 1961; children: Mark D., Lisa Ann, Craig P., Amy T., Blaise Q. B.A., Thomas More Coll., 1953; M.A., Xavier U., 1956; J.D., U. Cin., 1959. Bar: Ky 1960, Ohio 1960. Practice Covington, Ky., 1960—; city solicitor City of Covington, 1962-76; judge Ky. Ct. Appeals, Frankfort, 1976-83; justice Ky. Supreme Ct., Frankfort, 1983—. Recipient Community Service award Thomas More Coll., 1968; recipient Disting. Alumnus award Thomas More Coll., 1982; named Disting. Jurist Chase Coll. Law, 1983. Mem. ABA, Am. Judicature Soc., Ky. Bar Assn., Ohio Bar Assn., Cin. Bar Assn. Democrat. Roman Catholic. Judicial administration. Home: 224 Adams Ave Covington KY 41014 Office: Ky Supreme Ct State Capitol Frankfort KY 40601

WINTHROP, LAWRENCE FREDRICK, lawyer; b. Los Angeles, Apr. 18, 1952; s. Murray and Vauneta (Cardwell) W.; B.A. with honors, Whittier Coll., 1974; J.D. magna cum laude, Calif. Western Sch., 1977. Bar: Ariz. 1977, Calif. 1977, U.S. Dist. Ct. Ariz. 1977, U.S. Dist. Ct. (so. dist.) Calif. 1981, U.S. Ct. Appeals (9th cir.) 1981, U.S. Dist. Ct. (cen. dist.) Calif. 1983, U.S. Supreme Ct. 1983. Assoc. Snell and Wilmer, Phoenix, 1977-83, ptnr., 1984—. lectr. Ariz. personal injury law and practice Profl. Edn. Systems, Inc. Mem. ABA Ariz. Bar Assn. (uniform laws com.), Calif. Bar Assn., Maricopa County Bar Assn., Phoenix Assn. Def. Counsel (bd. dirs.). Club: Phoenix Country. Editor-in-chief Calif. Western Law Rev., 1976-77. Personal injury, Federal civil litigation, State civil litigation. Home: 7033 N 6th Ave Phoenix AZ 85021 Office: Snell & Wilmer 3100 Valley Bank Ctr Phoenix AZ 85073

WINTON, WARD WILLIAM, lawyer; b. Ft. Lewis, Wash., July 2, 1945; s. Warren E. and Mary C. (Robinson) W.; m. Kay Brown, MAy 1, 1971; children; Anna Flora Trepania, Angeline Eva Katherine. BA in History, Wis. State U., 1967; MA in History, U. Wis., River Falls, 1976; JD cum laude, Hamline U., 1976. Bar: Minn. 1977, Wis. 1977, U.S. Dist. Ct. (we. dist.) Wis. 1977. Assoc. Winton & Fischer, Shall Lake, Wis., 1977-81; sole practice Hayward, Wis., 1981—. Vice chmn. Sawyer County Dem. Party, 1984—. Served with U.S. Army, 1967-69. Mem. ABA, Wis. Bar Assn., Vietnam Vets. Am. (pres. local 1986—), Washburn County Hist. Soc. (life mem. 1981). Democrat. General practice. Home: Rt 8 Box 8436 Hayward WI 54843 Office: 104 W 2d St PO Box 796 Hayward WI 54843

WINWARD, LAMAR J., lawyer; b. Preston, Idaho, Dec. 23, 1955; s. Thane Dalley Sr. and Evelyn Julia (Larsen) W.; m. Kathleen Bridget Merrell, Aug. 21, 1979; children: Jay Thane, Bryce LaMar. BS, Utah State U., 1979; JD, Brigham Young U., 1981. Bar: Utah 1981, U.S. Dist. Ct. Utah 1981. Assoc. Snow & Nuffer, P.C., St. George, Utah, 1981—; instr. bus. law Henegars Bus. Coll., Provo, Utah, 1980-81. Scout master Boy Scouts Am., St. George, Utah, 1983-86. Mem. ABA, Utah Bar Assn., Souther Utah Bar Assn. Democrat. Mormon. Avocations: outdoor recreation, hunting, fishing. General practice, Family and matrimonial, State civil litigation. Home: 630 N 400 W Saint George UT 84770 Office: Snow & Nuffer PC 50 E 100 S PO Box 386 Suite 302 Saint George UT 84770

WIRKEN, CHARLES WILLIAM, lawyer; b. Moline, Ill., Aug. 29, 1951; s. Walter William and Elizabeth Claire (Mallory) W.; m. Melissa Louise Day, May 24, 1975; children: Nicole, Michelle. BS, U. Ariz., 1972, JD, 1975. Bar: Ariz. 1975, U.S. Dist. Ct. Ariz. 1976, U.S. Ct. Appeals (9th cir.) 1980, U.S. Supreme Ct. 1980, U.S. Ct. Appeals (Fed. cir.) 1985. Assoc. Killian, Legg & Nicholas, Mesa, Ariz., 1975-79; ptnr. Killian, Legg, Nicholas, Fischer, Wirken, Cook & Pew, Mesa, 1980—; pres. Vol. Lawyers Project, Phoenix, 1981-83; judge pro tem Ariz. Ct. Appeals, 1985, Maricopa County Superior Ct., 1986—; mem. civil study com. Maricopa County Superior Ct., 1984—; dir. Community Legal Services, Phoenix, 1979-82. Exec. v.p. East Valley Partnership, Mesa, 1984; pres. Tri-City Cath. Social Service, Mesa, 1983-84; bd. dirs. East Valley Cultural Alliance, Mesa, 1984. Mem. Maricopa County Bar Assn. (bd. dirs. 1983—, v.p. 1987—), East Valley Bar Assn. (pres. 1979-80), Assn. Trial Lawyers of Am., Nat. Assn. Coll. and Univ. Attys., Mesa C. of C. (dir. 1980-83), Am. Arbitration Assn. (arbitrator). Democrat. Roman Catholic. Lodge: Rotary (bd. dirs. 1980-87, pres. 1987-88). Federal civil litigation, State civil litigation. Home: 1811 E Hackamore Mesa AZ 85203 Office: Killian Legg Nicholas et al PO Box 1467 Mesa AZ 85201

WIRKEN, JAMES CHARLES, lawyer; b. Lansing, Mich., July 3, 1944; s. Frank Joseph and Mary Catherine (Brosnahan) W.; m. Mary Teresa Morse, June 12, 1971; children: Christopher Burke, Erika Elizabeth, Kurt Joseph, Gretchen Marie. B in English Philosophy, Theology and Speech, Rockhurst Coll., 1967; JD, St. Louis U., 1970. Bar: Mo. 1970, U.S. Dist. Ct. (we. dist.) Mo. 1970. Asst. prosecuter Jackson County Pros. Atty., Kansas City, 1970-72; assoc. Morris, Larson, King, Stamper & Bold, Kansas City, 1972-75, Welch & Austin, Kansas City, 1975-76; ptnr. Spradley, Wirken & Reismeyer, Kansas City, 1976—; adj. prof. law U. Mo., Kansas City, 1984—. Co-author Missouri Civil Procedure Form Book, 1984. Bd. dirs. Easter Seals Soc., Mo., 1979-83, 1st v.p., 1982-83. Recipient Spl. Appreciation award Easter Seals Soc., 1980, Outstanding Service award Easter Seals Soc., 1981. Mem. Mo. Bar Assn. (bd. govs. 1976-78, chmn. econs. and methods practice com. 1982—, sec. young lawyers sect. 1975-76), Kansas City Bar Assn. (pres. young lawyers sect. 1975, active various com.), Assn. Trial Lawyers Am., Mo.. Assn. Trial Lawyer (bd. govs. 1983—). Federal civil litigation, State civil litigation, Personal injury. Home: 6011 Main Kansas City MO 64113 Office: Spradley Wirken & Riesmeyer 120 W 12th St Suite 1410 Kansas City MO 64105

WIRT, ALEXANDER WELLS, lawyer; b. Edinburgh, Scotland, Nov. 25, 1946; came to U.S., 1951; s. Sherwood Eliot and Helen Winola (McCain) W.; m. Eugenia Clair Cook, Oct. 3, 1970; children: Tyler Eliot, Bree Anna. BA, Whitworth Coll., 1972; JD, Gonzaga U., 1977. Bar: Wash. 1977, U.S. Dist. Ct. (we. dist.) Wash. 1977, U.S. Ct. Appeals (9th cir.) 1978, U.S. Supreme Ct. 1983, U.S. Dist. Ct. (ea. dist.) Wash. 1984. Asst. regional counsel Region X U.S. Dept. Housing and Urban Devel., 1977-78; assoc. Moriarity, Mikkelborg, Broz, Wells & Fryer, Seattle, 1978-83; sole practice Seattle, 1983-84; ptnr. Matsen, Cory, Sprague, Layman & Wirt, Bellevue, Wash., 1984—. Served to sgt. USMC, 1964-69. Mem. Seattle-King County Bar Assn., Wash. State Bar Assn., ABA, Fed. Bar Assn., Assn. Trial Lawyers Am., Wash. State Trial Lawyers Am. Democrat. Presbyterian. Avocations: golf, fishing, racquetball, hunting. General practice, Consumer commercial, Personal injury. Home: 3455 E Lake Sammamish Pky N Redmond WA 98053 Office: Matsen Cory Sprague et al 1000 ONB Plaza 10800 NE 8th Bellevue WA 98004

WIRT, WILLIAM STEPHEN, lawyer; b. Palestine, Ill., Feb. 7, 1953; s. William Z. and Dorothy Evelyn (Sheets) W.; m. Deborah Ann Jorgenson, Sept. 6, 1975; children: Matthew, Caitlin. BA, U. Ill., 1975; JD, Ohio State U., 1977. Bar: Ohio 1978, U.S. Dist. Ct. (so. dist.) 1980. Assoc. Federico, Myers & Enz, Columbus, Ohio, 1978-80; ptnr. Samuels & Wirt, Columbus, 1980-82; staff atty. Wendy's Internat. Inc., Dublin, Ohio, 1982-84, real estate counsel, 1984—. Fund raising Cystic Fibrosis, Columbus, 1984-85, Children's Hosp., Columbus, 1981986-87. Mem. ABA (real property and corps. and banking and bus. law sects.), Phi Beta Kappa. Methodist. Real property, Contracts commercial. Office: Wendy's Internat Inc 4288 W Dublin-Granville Rd Dublin OH 43017

WIRTZ, GREGG LEE, lawyer; b. Pitts., Jan. 30, 1953; s. James Henry and Betty Lee (Pelissier) W.; m. Martha McMahon, Oct. 29, 1977. BA in Econs., Denison U., 1974; JD, Stetson U., 1977. Bar: Fla. 1977, U.S. Dist. Ct. (mid. dist.) Fla. 1977. Asst. chief justice USAF, Shaw AFB, S.C., 1978-80, area def. counsel, 1980-81, staff judge adv., 1981-82; ptnr. Boyd, Jenerette, Staas, Joos, Williams, Felton & Wirtz, Jacksonville, Fla., 1982—; speaker seminar on civil trial practice Fla. CLE, med. malpractice U. Hosp. Served to capt. (judge adv.) USAF, 1977-82. Mem. ABA, Fla. Bar Assn., Jacksonville Bar Assn., Assn. Trial Lawyers Am., Def. Counsel Assn., Omicron Delta Kappa, Omicron Delta Epsilan. Democrat. Methodist. Avocation: sports. State civil litigation, Insurance, Personal injury. Office: Boyd Jenerette Staas et al 231 E Adams St Jacksonville FL 32202

WISE, AARON NOAH, lawyer; b. Hartford, Conn., Feb. 14, 1940; s. Joseph J. and Ethel (Sklar) W.; m. Genevieve Ehrlich, Dec. 17, 1966; children—Haywood Martin, Paul Russell, Renee Alicia. A.B., Boston U., 1962; J.D., Boston Coll., 1965; LL.M. in Comparative/Internat. Law, NYU, 1971; certificat de Doctorate d'Université en Droit, U. Paris Law Sch., 1970. Bar: N.Y., U.S. Dist. Ct. (so. dist.) N.Y. Internat. atty. Schering-Plough Corp., Kenilworth, N.J., 1969-74; ptnr. Conboy Hewitt O'Brien & Boardman, N.Y.C., 1974-80, Rosenbaum Wise Lerman & Katz, N.Y.C., 1981—; lectr. bus. and legal groups U.S., Europe, Latin Am. Mem. ABA, N.Y. State Bar Assn. Author: Trade Secrets and Know-How Throughout the World, 5 vols.; co-author: Foreign Businessman's Guide to U.S. Law-Practice-Taxation; contbr. articles to publs. in U.S. and Europe. Avocations: multi-lingual including French, Spanish, Italian, Russian, Japanese and German. Private international, General corporate, Contracts commercial. Home: 105 Stonebridge Rd Montclair NJ 07042 Office: 300 Madison Ave New York NY 10017

WISE, JOSEPH POWELL, lawyer; b. Jackson, Miss., June 19, 1946; s. Sherwood Willing and Elizabeth Carter (Powell) W.; m. Charlene Idell Carter, Mar. 30, 1980; children: Carter Willing, Elizabeth Ramsey. B.A., Yale U., 1968; J.D., Washington and Lee U., 1974. Bar: Miss. 1975; U.S. Dist. Ct. (no. and so. dists.) Miss. 1975, U.S. Ct. Appeals (5th cir.) 1975. Assoc., Wise Carter Child Steen & Caraway, Jackson, 1974-78, ptnr., 1978-79; prin. Wise, Carter, Child & Caraway, P.A., Jackson, 1979—. Served to lt. USN, 1968-71. Mem. ABA, Order of Coif. Federal civil litigation, Public utilities, State civil litigation. Home: 4526 Brook Dr Jackson MS 39206

WISE, NANCY JOAN, lawyer; b. Oak Park, Ill., Aug. 5, 1950; s. Robert S. and Grace Ann (Ackerman) W. B.S., Wittenberg U., 1973; J.D., U. of Dayton, 1977. Bar: Ill. 1977, U.S. Dist. Ct. (no. dist.) Ill. 1977. Atty., Ceco Corp., Oak Brook, Ill., 1977-84, asst. sec., 1977—; atty. Ceco Industries, Inc., Oak Brook, 1984—, asst. sec., 1984—. Mem. ABA, Chgo. Bar Assn. General corporate. Office: Ceco Industries Inc 1400 Kensington Rd Oak Brook IL 60521

WISE, PHILIP J., lawyer; b. Dallas, Feb. 4, 1957; s. Marvin Jay and Gloria Marion (Johnson) W. BA, BBA, So. Meth. U., 1978, JD, 1981; postgrad., Oxford U., Eng., 1981. Bar: Tex. 1981. Ptnr. Wise & Stuhl, Dallas, 1981-83; v.p., gen. counsel Cambridge Cos., Inc., Dallas, 1983-86; cons. Trammell Crow Co., Dallas, 1987—. Legal counsel Am. Heart Ball, Dallas, 1981-83; bd. dirs. Plaza Theater Assocs., Dallas, 1981-83; Dallas Bonds Election, 1984; mem. City Bonds 1985, Dallas; mem. selection com. Nat. Alumni Scholarship, So. Meth. U. Named one of Outstanding Young Men of Am., U.S. Jaycees, 1981. Mem. Am. Judicature Soc., Tex. Bar Assn., Dallas Bar Assn. (real estate sect.), Dallas Young Lawyers Assn. (corp., banking and real estate sect.), Future Dallas (founding mem.), Urban Land Inst., Hist. Preservation League. Avocations: reading, snow and water skiing, football, basketball, tennis. General corporate, Real property, Entertainment.

WISE, ROBERT KENNETH, lawyer; b. Cleve., May 10, 1952; s. Rudy and Josephine (Schwartz) W. BA, Marietta Coll., 1974; JD, Coll. William and Mary, 1977. Bar: Ohio 1977, D.C. 1978, Tex. 1980, U.S. Dist. Ct. (no., we. and ea. dists.) Tex., U.S. Dist. Ct. (no. dist.) Ohio, U.S. Ct. Appeals (5th, 6th and 9th cirs.). Law clk. to presiding judge U.S. Ct. Appeals (6th cir.), Akron, Ohio, 1977-78; assoc. Hughes & Luce, Dallas, 1978-83, Worsham, Forsythe, Sampels & Woodridge, Dallas, 1983—; lectr. Southern Meth. Sch. Law, Dallas, 1982-86. Editor William and Mary Law rev. 1976-77. Mem. ABA, Tex. Bar Assn., Dallas Bar Assn., D.C. Bar Assn. Avocations: sports, reading, cycling. Federal civil litigation, State civil litigation. Home: 2834 Lawtherwood Pl Dallas TX 75214 Office: Worsham Forsythe Sampels Woodridge 2001 Bryan Tower Suite 3200 Dallas TX 75201

WISE, ROBERT POWELL, lawyer; b. Jackson, Miss., Nov. 13, 1951; s. Sherwood Willing and Elizabeth (Powell) W. AB, Colgate U., 1973; MA, U. Va., 1975; JD, Washington & Lee U., 1979. Bar: Miss. 1979, U.S. Dist. Ct. Miss. 1979. Ptnr. Wise, Carter, Child & Caraway, Jackson, 1979—. Lic. lay reader St. Andrews Episc. Cathedral, Jackson, 1984—; pres. Caledonian Soc. Miss., Jackson, 1987—; bd. dirs. English Speaking Union of Miss., Jackson, 1985—. Mem. ABA, Miss. Bar Assn. Construction, Administrative and regulatory, Consumer commercial. Home: 1602 Linden Pl Jackson MS 39202 Office: Wise Carter Child & Caraway 600 Heritage Bldg Jackson MS 39205

WISE, SANDRA ELIZABETH, lawyer; b. Williamsport, Pa., Oct. 3, 1957; d. Robert Campbell and Margaret Louise (Browne) W. BA, Franklin & Marshall Coll., 1979; JD, Dickinson Sch. Law, 1982. Bar: Pa. 1982, U.S. Dist. Ct. (mid. dist.) Pa. 1983, U.S. Ct. Appeals (3d cir.) 1983, U.S. Ct. Appeals (6th, 9th and D.C. cirs.) 1984, U.S. Supreme Ct. 1985. Assoc. Ball, Skelly, Murren & Connell, Harrisburg, Pa., 1982—. Mem. Jr. League, Harrisburg. Named one of Outstanding Young Women Am., 1980. Mem. ABA, Pa. Bar Assn., Dauphin County Bar Assn., Assn. Trial Lawyers Am., Am. Immigration Lawyers Assn., Christian Legal Soc., Phi Alpha Delta. Federal civil litigation, Constitutional law, Nonprofit organizations. Office: Ball Skelly Murren & Connell 511 N 2d St Harrisburg PA 17101

WISE, SHERWOOD WILLING, lawyer; b. Hazelhurst, Miss., Aug. 13, 1910; s. Joseph Sherwood and Myra (Willing) W.; m. Elizabeth Carter Powell, July 28, 1937; children: Elizabeth Wise Copeland, Sherwood Willing, Joseph Powell, Robert Powell and Louise Wise Hardy (twins). B.A., Washington and Lee U., 1932, J.D., 1934. Bar: Miss. 1934. Practiced law Jackson; partner Wise Carter Child & Caraway, 1941—; commr. Miss. Bar, 1958-60; gen. counsel Miss. Power & Light Co., 1961-80. Co-founder Jackson Symphony Orch., 1944; pres. Jackson Community Chest, 1950; Miss. chmn. Ducks Unlimited, Inc., 1961-71; mem. exec. com. Episcopal Diocese Miss., 1941, past mem. dept. missions and standing com., also trustee, 1959—; del. Episc. Gen. Conv., 1952, 64, 67, 69, 70, 79; mem. joint commn. ecumenical relations Episc. Ch., 1967-73; co-founder, chmn. St. Mark's Ednl. Day Care Ctr., 1967; a founder, organizer St. Andrews Episc. Day Sch., Jackson, 1947, trustee, 1947-72, 78-82; trustee Nat. Cathedral Assn., 1975-77; del. Democratic Nat. Conv., 1940; trustee State Dept. Archives and History, 1964—. Served to lt. comdr. USNR, 1942-46. Recipient Disting. Alumnus award Washington and Lee U., 1983. Fellow Am. Coll. Trial Lawyers; mem. ABA (com. on civil rights and racial unrest 1962, standing com. fed. judiciary 1969-75, chmn. Nat. Conf. Lawyers and Environ. Design Profls. 1979-85, Miss. state del. to ho. of dels. 1981—), Miss. Bar Assn. (pres. 1961-62), Hinds County Bar Assn. (pres. 1958-59), Edison Electric Inst. (legal com. 1962-80), Nat. Assn. R.R. Trial Counsel, Am. Judicature Soc., Scribes, Jackson C. of C. (past v.p., dir.), Newcomen Soc., Kappa Sigma, Omicron Delta Kappa, Phi Delta Phi. Clubs: Rotary (past dir.), Jackson Country (past bd. govs.), Capital City Petroleum, Jackson Yacht (past gov.). Federal civil litigation, General corporate, Public

utilities. Home: 3839 Eastover Dr Jackson MS 39211 Office: PO Box 651 Jackson MS 39205

WISE, STEPHEN RULE, lawyer; b. Maryville, Tenn., Dec. 5, 1953; s. Norman Kenneth and Addie (Rule) W.; m. Linda Kaye Temple, Sept. 12, 1981; children: Anne Temple, Jane Catherine. BA, U. Tenn., 1975, JD, 1978; LLM, Cambridge U., Eng., 1982. Bar: U.S. Dist. Ct. (no. dist.) Tenn. 1978. Assoc. Ridenour Law Firm, Clinton, Tenn., 1978-81, Knoxville, Tenn., 1982-83; assoc. Wilson Ritchie, P.C., Knoxville, 1983-84; ptnr. Ritchie & Wise, P.C., Knoxville, 1984—. Mem. Knoxville Arts Council, 1984—, Knoxville Heritage, 1984—, Dulin Art Gallery, 1987—, East Tenn. Hist. Soc., 1984—, Knoxville-Knox County Literacy Council, 1987—. Mem. ABA, Tenn. Bar Assn., Knox County Bar Assn., Assn. Trial Lawyers Am., Cranworth Law Soc., Jaycees (sec. Clinton 1980). Democrat. Methodist. Avocation: basketball. General corporate, Contracts commercial, General practice. Home: 6015 Grove Park Dr Knoxville TN 37918 Office: Ritchie & Wise PC 2301 Plaza Tower PO Box 987 Knoxville TN 37901

WISE, STEVEN LANIER, lawyer; b. Eufaula, Ala., Oct. 3, 1956; s. Edward Lanier and Cathryn (Ryals) W.; m. Eloise Massey, July 30, 1983. BA in English, U. Ala., 1978, MA in Counselling, 1979, JD, 1982. Bar: Ala. 1982, U.S. Dist. Ct. (no. dist.) Ala. 1982. Staff atty. Ala. Ct. Civil Appeals, Montgomery, 1982-83; ptnr. Hardin & Wise, Tuscaloosa, Ala., 1983—. Sec., bd. editors The Ala. Lawyer, Montgomery, 1983—. Sponsor Cen. High Sch. Key Club, Tuscaloosa, 1984—; judge citizen lock-up March of Dimes, Tuscaloosa, 1986. Mem. ABA, Tuscaloosa County Bar Assn. (chmn. subcom. 1985—), Ala. Trial Lawyers Assn., Tuscaloosa Trial Lawyers Assn., Farrah Law Soc., Kappa Delta Pi, Pi Tau Chi. Democrat. Baptist. Lodge: Kiwanis (2d v.p. Tuscaloosa club 1986-87). Avocations: woodworking, golf, softball, music. General practice, Family and matrimonial, Consumer commercial. Home: 1413 48th Ct E Tuscaloosa AL 35404 Office: Hardin & Wise 720 Energy Ctr Blvd Suite 503 Northport AL 35476

WISE, TONI PRYOR, lawyer; b. Santa Monica, Calif., Aug. 13, 1948; d. G.H. and Alice Harriet (Tilden) P.; m. Dale Wise, June 8, 1972; children: Christopher, Graham, Joshua. AB magna cum laude, magna cum distinctione, Mt. Holyoke, 1971, AM, 1973; JD, Stanford U., 1978. Bar: Calif. 1978, U.S. Dist. Ct. (no. dist.) Calif. 1978. Asst. project dir. Mt. Holyoke Coll., South Hadley, Mass., 1973-75; research asst. Stanford U., Palo Alto, Calif., 1976-77; assoc. Steinhardt et al, San Francisco, 1977-81, Pillsbury, Madison and Sutro, San Jose, Calif., 1981—. Past pres. Mission West Homeowners Assn. Mem. ABA, Calif. Bar Assn., Santa Clara County Bar Assn. (chmn. bus. law sect. 1986—), Phi Beta Kappa, Sigma Xi. Avocations: skiing, gardening, travel. Contracts commercial, General corporate, Real property. Home: 38614 Oliver Way Fremont CA 94536 Office: Pillsbury Madison & Sutro 333 W Santa Clara Suite 800 San Jose CA 95113

WISE, WILLIAM JERRARD, lawyer; b. Chgo., May 27, 1934; s. Gerald Paul and Harriet Muriel (Rosenblum) W.; m. Peggy Spero, Sept. 3, 1959; children: Deborah, Stephen, Betsy, Lynne. B.B.A., U. Mich., 1955, M.B.A., 1958, J.D. with distinction, 1958. Bar: Ill. 1959. Spl. atty. Office Regional Counsel, IRS, Milw., 1959-63; with firm McDermott, Will & Emery, Chgo., 1963-70, Coles & Wise, Ltd., 1971-81, Wise & Stracks, Ltd., 1982—; Lectr., contbr. Ill. Inst. Continuing Legal Edn.; bd. dirs. Park Ave. Distbrs. Ltd. Mem. Village of Winnetka (Ill.) Caucus, 1974-75; Bd. dirs. Blind Service Assn., Chgo., 1964-74; dir., treas. Suzuki Orff Sch. for Young Musicians, Chgo. Served with AUS, 1958-59. Mem. Chgo. Bar Assn. Corporate taxation, Personal income taxation, Pension, profit-sharing, and employee benefits. Home: 1401 Tower Rd Winnetka IL 60093 Office: Wise & Stacks Ltd 20 N Clark St Suite 1000 Chicago IL 60602

WISE, WILLIAM T., corporate lawyer. LLB, La. State U. V.p., gen. counsel Shell Oil Co., Houston. Office: Shell Oil Co 1 Shell Plaza Houston TX 77001 *

WISEHEART, MALCOLM BOYD, JR., lawyer; b. Miami, Fla., Sept. 18, 1942; s. Malcolm B. and Dorothy E. (Allen) W.; m. Michele I. Romanens, Dec. 11, 1976. B.A., Yale U., 1965; M.A. in English Jurisprudence, Cambridge U., 1973; J.D. with honors, U. Fla., 1970. Bar: Fla. 1970, Eng. and Wales 1970, Jamaica 1970, Trinidad and Tobago 1971, D.C. 1980. Assoc. Helliwell, Melrose & DeWolf, Miami, 1970-72; sr. ptnr. Wiseheart & Joyce, P.A., Miami, 1973—; sec., gen. counsel Wiseheart Found.; spl. master Dade County Property Appraisal Adjustment Bd., 1977-87; pres. Fla. Law Inst., 1980-87. trustee, mem. exec. com. Players State Theater, 1982-84; bd. dirs. Sta. WLRN Pub. Radio, 1982, Council for Internat. Visitors. Named Most Outstanding, U. Fla. Law Rev. Alumnus, 1981. Mem. Fla Bar (chmn. grievance com. 1978-81), Dade County Bar Assn. (dir. 1971-74, 86—, treas. 1974-75, sec. 1975-77), Order of Coif. Clubs: Yale (Miami pres. 1976-77); United Oxford and Cambridge U. (London). Real property, State civil litigation, Landlord-tenant. Office: Wiseheart Bldg 2840 SW 3d Ave Miami FL 33129

WISEMAN, THOMAS ANDERTON, JR., U.S. district judge; b. Tullahoma, Tenn., Nov. 3, 1930; s. Thomas Anderson and Vera Seleta (Poe) W.; m. Emily Barbara Matlack, Mar. 30, 1957; children: Thomas Anderton III, Mary Alice, Sarah Emily. B.A., Vanderbilt U., 1952, LL.B., 1954. Bar: Tenn. Practice law Tullahoma, 1956-63; partner Haynes, Wiseman & Hull, Tullahoma and Winchester, Tenn., 1963-71; treas. State of Tenn., 1971-74; partner Chambers & Wiseman, 1974-78; judge U.S. Dist. Ct. Middle Dist. Tenn., Nashville, 1978—; now chief judge U.S. Dist. Ct. Middle Dist. Tenn.; mem. Tenn. Ho. of Reps., 1964-68. Assoc. editor: Vanderbilt Law Rev, 1953-54. Democratic candidate for gov., Tenn., 1974; Chmn. Tenn. Heart Fund, 1973, Middle Tenn. Heart Fund, 1972. Served with U.S. Army, 1954-56. Mem. Am. Bar Assn., Tenn. Bar Assn. Presbyterian. Club: Amateur Chefs Am. Lodges: Masons; Shriners. Office: US District Court 824 US Courthouse Nashville TN 37203 *

WISER, NICHOLAS VAN, lawyer; b. Memphis, July 8, 1953; s. Winfred L. and Nell Hauser (Funderbunk) W. BA, Vanderbilt U., 1975; JD, Miss. Coll., 1982. Bar: Miss. 1982, U.S. Dist. Ct. (so. dist.) Miss. 1983, U.S. Ct. Appeals (5th cir.) 1983, U.S. Supreme Ct. 1987. Law clk. to presiding justice Miss. Supreme Ct., Jackson, 1982-83; assoc. Rushing & Guice, Biloxi, Miss., 1983-87, Robert Alan Byrd & Assocs., Biloxi, 1987—. Articles editor Miss. Coll. Law Rev., 1981-82. Mem. ABA, Miss. bar Assn., Fed. Bar Assn., Miss. Trial Lawyers Assn. Republican. Avocation: golf. Contracts commercial, Federal civil litigation, Bankruptcy. Home: 1601 Golfing Green Ocean Springs MS 39564 Office: Robert Alan Byrd & Assocs 391 Reynoir St Biloxi MS 39531

WISHINGRAD, JAY MARC, lawyer; b. Bklyn., Apr. 19, 1949; s. Irving Wishingrad and Phyllis (Leibowitz) Wishingrad Mendelson; m. Susan Leshe, Aug. 9, 1980. B.A., NYU, 1971; J.D. cum laude, SUNY-Buffalo, 1975. Bar: N.Y. 1976, U.S. Dist. Ct. (so. and ea. dists.) N.Y. 1977, U.S. Sup. Ct. 1979. Law clk. appellate div., 4th dept. N.Y. State Supreme Ct., Rochester, 1975-77; litigation assoc. Kaye, Scholer, Fierman, Hays & Handler, N.Y.C., 1977-84; litigation ptnr. Shapiro, Spiegel, Garfunkel & Driggin, N.Y.C., 1984-86, Frankfurt, Garbus, Klein & Selz, P.C., N.Y.C., 1986—; adj. instr. Benjamin N. Cardozo Sch. Law, Yeshiva U., N.Y.C., 1978-80. Contbr. book revs., articles to profl. jours. Mem. N.Y. Lawyers Against The Death Penalty (founding mem.), Assn. of Bar of City of N.Y., Phi Beta Kappa. Federal civil litigation, Securities, Legal history. Office: Frankfurt Garbus Klein & Selz PC 485 Madison Ave New York NY 10022

WISNIEWSKI, MARSHALL DONALD, lawyer; b. Toledo, July 26, 1951; s. Donald A. and Margaret (Fry) W.; m. Marlene Ann Pawelec, Sept. 11, 1971; 1 child, Laura Ann. BA, U. Toledo, 1975, JD, 1980. Bar: Ohio 1981, U.S. Dist. Ct. (no. dist.) Ohio 1982. Mem. personnel dept. Chrysler Corp., Toledo, 1977-80; assoc. Czerniakowski & Errington, Toledo, 1980-82; sr. ptnr. David R. Pheils Jr. and Assocs., Perrysburgh, Ohio, 1982—. Mem. ABA, Ohio Bar Assn., Wood County Bar Assn. (com. on mcpl. ct. liason), Toledo Bar Assn. General corporate, Personal injury, Real property. Office: David R Pheils Jr & Assocs 410 Louisiana Ave Perrysburg OH 43551

WISNIEWSKI, ROBERT EDWARD, lawyer; b. N.Y.C., Apr. 3, 1946; s. Theodore Edward and Rose Irene (O'Rourke) W.; m. Jean Shirlaw, Aug. 2, 1970; children: James, Robyn. BA, Upsala Coll., 1969; M in Pub. Adminstrn., U. Okla., Norman, 1973; JD, U. Toledo, 1976. Bar: Ariz. 1976, U.S. Dist. Ct. Ariz. 1976, U.S. Ct. Appeals (9th cir.) 1984, U.S. Supreme Ct. 1984. Law clk. to presiding judge Ariz. Ct. Appeals (div. 1), Phoenix, 1976-77; assoc. Robbins, Green, O'Grady & Abbuhl, Phoenix, 1977-79; ptnr. Crampton, Woods, Broening & Oberg, P.C., Phoenix, 1979-83, Conklin & Adler, Phoenix, 1983-85, Wisniewski, Surrano & Fendon P.C., Phoenix, 1985—; instr. litigation Sterling Sch. Legal Assts., Phoenix; adj. faculty aviation law Embry-Riddle Aero. U., Phoenix. Notes and comment editor U. Toledo Law Rev. Mem. Pres.'s forum Upsala Coll., N.J., ch. council All Sts. Luth. Ch., Phoenix, exec. com. Theodore Roosevelt council Boy Scout Am., Phoenix. Served as maj. USAR (jag), 1973—. Mem. ABA (litigation sect.), Ariz. Bar Assn. (workers compensation sect., pub. relations com.), Maricopa County Bar Assn., Def. Research Inst., Assn. Trial Lawyers Am., Ariz. Trial Lawyers Assn., Phoenix Assn. Def. Counsel. Republican. Lodge: Elks. Avocation: long distance running. Insurance, Workers' compensation, Personal injury. Office: 3200 N Central #1550 Phoenix AZ 85012

WISWALL, FRANK LAWRENCE, JR., admiralty lawyer; b. Albany, N.Y., Sept. 21, 1939; s. Frank Lawrence and Clara Elizabeth (Chapman) W.; m. Elizabeth Curtiss Nelson, Aug. 9, 1975; children by previous marriage: Anne W. Larson, Frank Lawrence III. B.A., Colby Coll., 1962; J.D., Cornell U., 1965; Ph.D. in Jurisprudence, Cambridge U., 1967. Bar: Maine 1965, N.Y. 1968, U.S. Supreme Ct. 1968, D.C. 1975, Va. 1978; lic. master small ocean passenger vessels, 1960—. Mem. firm Wiswall & Wiswall, Castine, Maine, 1965-72; atty. Burlingham, Underwood, Barron, Wright & White, N.Y.C., 1967-73; maritime legal adviser Republic of Liberia, 1968—, admiralty counsel, 1974-85; gen. counsel Liberian Services, Inc., N.Y.C. and Reston, Va., 1973-77; pres. Liberian Services, Inc., 1974-85, chief counsel, 1977-86; legal adviser Internat. Bank, Washington, 1972—; ptnr. firm Martin & Smith, Washington, 1975-78; counsel Martin & Smith, 1979-80; mem. legal com. Internat. Maritime Orgn., London, 1972-74, vice chmn. 1974-79, chmn., 1980-84; vis. lectr. Cornell Law Sch., 1969-76, 82; lectr. U. Va. Law Sch. and Center for Oceans Law and Policy, 1978-82; prof. law Cornell U., 1984; Johnsen prof. maritime law Tulane U., 1985; prof. law World Maritime U., Malmo, Sweden, 1986; tutorial supr. internat. law Clare Coll., Cambridge, Eng., 1966, 67; del. Internat. Conf. Marine Pollution, London, 1973; del., chmn. drafting com. Internat. Conf. Carriage of Passengers and Luggage by Sea, Athens, 1974; del. Internat. Conf. on Safety of Life at Sea, London, 1974, 3d UN Conf. on Law of Sea, Caracas, Venezuela, 1974, 3d UN Conf. on Law of Sea (all subsequent sessions); del., chmn. com. final clauses Internat. Conf. on Limitation of Liability for Maritime Claims, London, 1976; del. UN Conf. Carriage of Goods by Sea, Hamburg, 1978, XIII Diplomatic Conf. on Maritime Law, Brussels, 1979; chmn. com. of the whole Internat. Conf. Carriage of Certain Substances by Sea, 1984; counsel various marine casualty bds. of investigation, 1970—, harbormaster, Port of Castine, 1960-62. Author: The Development of Admiralty Jurisdiction and Practice Since 1800, 1970; contbr. articles to profl. jours. Recipient Yorke prize U. Cambridge, 1968-69. Fellow Royal Hist. Soc.; mem. Titulaire, Comite Maritime Internat., Maritime Law Assn. U.S. (chmn. com. on intergovtl. orgns. 1983—), Selden Soc., Am. Socs. Legal History and Internat. Law, U.K., U.S. assns. average adjusters, ABA, Maine Bar Assn., Bar Assn. City N.Y. (admiralty com. 1971-79), Alpha Delta Phi, Phi Delta Phi. Clubs: United Oxford and Cambridge U, London; Century Assn. (N.Y.C.); Cosmos (Washington). Admiralty, Public international, Legal history. Office: 11870-D Sunrise Valley Dr Reston VA 22091

WITCHER, ROGER KENNETH, JR., lawyer; b. Lafayette, Tenn., Sept. 12, 1952; s. Roger Kenneth Sr. and Maitred Yates (Neel) W.; m. Susan Clark, Nov. 2, 1970; children: Teresa Diane, Kenneth Andrew. BS in Polit. Sci., Tenn. Tech. U., 1973; JD, U. Tenn., 1975. Bar: Tenn. 1976, U.S. Dist. Ct. (mid. dist.) Tenn. 1976. Sole practice Lafayette, 1976—; atty. City of Red Boiling Springs, Tenn., 1977—; referee juvenile ct. Macon County, Lafayette, 1978—; gen. counsel Tri-County Electric Membership Corp., Lafayette, 1982—. Chmn. Macon County Reps., 1982-85. Mem. Tenn. Bar Assn., Tenn. Mcpl. Attys. Assn. Republican. Baptist. Lodge: Masons (worshipful master 1985, sec. 1986—). Probate, State civil litigation, Family and matrimonial. Home: Rt 2 Red Boiling Springs TN 37150 Office: 100 Public Sq Lafayette TN 37083

WITHEREL, MICHAEL JOSEPH, lawyer; b. Pitts., Nov. 18, 1953; s. Thomas G. and Phyllis J. (Perka) W.; m. Brenda G. Miller, Oct. 2, 1982; children: Matthew A., Michael P. BA, U. Pitts., 1974, JD, 1978. Bar: Pa. 1978, U.S. Dist. Ct. (we. dist.) Pa. 1978, U.S. Supreme Ct. 1986. Asst. dist. atty. Allegheny County Dist. Atty., Pitts., 1978-82; assoc. Gondelman, Baxter, McVerry, Smith, Yatch & Trimm P.C., Pitts., 1982-85, ptnr., 1986-87; ptnr. Brucker & Witherel, Pitts., 1987—. Mem. CSC West View Borough, Pitts., 1977-82; bd. dirs. North Hills Sch. Dist., 1981, solicitor, 1983—. Mem. ABA, Pa. Bar Assn., Allegheny County Bar Assn., Pa. Trial Lawyers Assn., Allegheny County Criminal Trial Lawyers. General practice, Criminal, Local government. Office: Brucker & Witherel 930 Grant Bldg Pittsburgh PA 15219

WITHERELL, DENNIS PATRICK, lawyer; b. Toledo, Ohio, Dec. 15, 1951; s. Thomas William and Kathryn Marie (Savage) W.; m. Leslie Buckholtz, Dec. 15, 1979; children—Natalie and Jay. A.B. with highest honors, U. Mich., 1973; J.D. summa cum laude, Ohio State U., 1977. Bar: Ohio, U.S. Dist. Ct. (no. dist.) Ohio, U.S. Ct. Appeals (6th cir.). Law clk. U.S. Ct. Appeals (6th cir.), Cin., 1977-78; assoc. Shumaker, Loop & Kendrick Toledo, 1978-83, ptnr., 1983—. Mem. exec. bd. March of Dimes Birth Defects Found., N.W. Ohio Chpt., Toledo, 1978—, chmn. N.W. Ohio chpt., 1982-84. Mem. Am. Acad. of Hosp. Attys., Nat. Health Lawyers Assn., ABA, Ohio State Bar Assn., Toledo Bar Assn., Ohio Soc. of Hosp. Attys. Roman Catholic. Health, Administrative and regulatory, Antitrust. Home: 2644 Meadowwood Dr Toledo OH 43606 Office: Shumaker Loop & Kendrick 1000 Jackson Toledo OH 43624

WITHERSPOON, JAMES WINFRED, lawyer; b. Indianola, Okla., Sept. 20, 1906; s. Ernest and Mary Etta (Stafford) W.; m. Margaret Gilliland, July 25, 1930 (dec.); children—Eleanor Irene Witherspoon Couch, Gerald Winfrey (dec.); m. 2d, Elizabeth Spradley Womble, Feb. 14, 1959; 1 dau., Janie Smith. B.A., Montezuma Coll. (N.Mex.), 1926; postgrad. U. Tex., 1926-27; LL.B., U. Okla., 1929. Bar: Tex. 1929, Okla. 1929, U.S. Ct. Claims 1957, U.S. Ct. Appeals (5th, 10th and 11th cirs.) 1949, U.S. Supreme Ct. 1958. Practiced Hereford, Tex., 1929—; sr. ptnr. Witherspoon, Aikin, Langley, 1950—; dist. atty. 69th Jud. Dist. of Tex., 1933-40, dist. judge, 1940-44; chmn. bd. dirs. First Nat. Bank Hereford; founder First Nat. Bank Dumas (Tex.). Bd. regents Tex. A&M U., 1951-57; del. Tex. State Dem. Conv., 1948, 52, 56, 60. Named Deaf Smith County Citizen of Yr., 1961, Hereford Citizen of Yr., 1961. Mem. 69th Jud. Dist. Bar Assn., Tex. Bar Assn., ABA, Am. Judicature Soc., Tex. Assn. Plaintiffs Attys., Nat. Plaintiffs Attys. Assn., Am. Coll. Probate Counsel, Am. Trial Lawyers Assn., Tex. Criminal Def. Lawyers Assn., Deaf Smith County C. of C., West Tex. C. of C., SCV, SAR. Clubs: Hereford Country, Amarillo Country, Sugar of N.Y., Hereford Riders, Amarillo Knife and Fork. Lodges: Elks, Masons, Shriners, Rotary, Lions. Antitrust, General practice, Personal injury. Office: Witherspoon Aikin & Langley 140 E 3d St Hereford TX 79045

WITKIN, ERIC DOUGLAS, lawyer; b. Trenton, N.J., May 14, 1948; s. Nathan and Norma Shirley (Stein) W.; m. Regina Ann Bilotta, June 8, 1980; 1 child, Daniel Robert. AB magna cum laude, Columbia U., 1969; JD, Harvard U., 1972. Bar: N.Y. 1973, U.S. Dist. Ct. (so. and ea. dists.) N.Y. 1974, U.S. Ct. Appeals (2d and D.C. cirs.) 1974, U.S. Supreme Ct. 1977. Assoc. Poletti, Freidin, Prashker & Gartner, N.Y.C., 1972-80, ptnr., 1980-85; sr. atty. labor Kaye, Scholer, Fierman, Hays & Handler, N.Y.C., 1985—. treas., founder Property Owners Against Unfair Taxation, N.Y.C., 1983—. Lawrence Chamberlain scholar Columbia U., N.Y.C., 1968. Mem. ABA (labor and employment law sects.), N.Y. State Bar Assn. (labor and employment law sects.), Assn. of Bar of City of N.Y. (spl. com. on sex and law, com. on labor and employment law), Columbia Coll. Alumni Assn. (1st v.p., recipient Robert Lincoln Carey prize, Alumni prize 1969). Club: Harvard (N.Y.C.). Avocations: sailing, skiing. Labor, Federal civil litigation, State civil litigation. Home: 29 W 87th St New York NY 10024 Office: Kaye Scholer et al 425 Park Ave New York NY 10022

WITKIN, SUSAN PECKETT, lawyer; b. N.Y.C., Aug. 31, 1957; d. Joseph Charles and Ingeborg Peckett; m. Ned H. Witkin, May 15, 1983. BA, CUNY, Queens, 1978; JD, St. John's U., Jamaica, N.Y., 1981; LLM in Taxation, NYU, 1986. Bar: N.Y. 1982, N.J. 1982, U.S. Dist. Ct. N.J. 1982. Assoc. Fox & Fox, Newark, 1981—. Mem. ABA (real property, probate and trust law com.), N.Y. State Bar Assn. (pension com., probate and trust law com,). Democrat. Avocations: swimming, diving, deep sea fishing, films and theatre, travel. Probate, Estate taxation, Personal income taxation. Home: 1 Carol Pl Plainview NY 11803

WITLIN, BARRY ETHAN, lawyer; b. Chgo., Nov. 18, 1953; s. Morton William and Fern (Lazarus) W.; m. Mindy Susan Trossman, Dec. 2, 1979 (dissolved); m. Ina Sue Mecklenburg, Apr. 20, 1986. BA, U. Ill., 1975; JD, Loyola U., Chgo., 1978. Bar: Ill. 1978, U.S. Dist. Ct. (no. dist.) Ill. 1978, Fla. 1980, U.S. Dist. Ct. (so. dist.) Fla. 1980, U.S. Supreme Ct. 1981. Assoc. James W. Reilley & Assocs., Chgo., 1978-84; sole practice North Miami, Fla., 1984—. Democrat. Jewish. Criminal, Entertainment, Sports. Office: 1100 NE 125th St Suite 109 North Miami Beach FL 33161

WITT, ALAN MICHAEL, lawyer, accountant; b. Chgo., Apr. 13, 1952; s. Robert Lee and Lois (Kaye) W.; m. Pamela Beth Ander, Dec. 29, 1976; children—Caryn, Kenneth, Amy. B.S. in Acctg., B.S. in Fin., U. Ill.-Chgo., 1974; J.D., U. Ill.-Champaign, 1977. Bar: Ill. 1977. Tax and audit cons. Weisbard, Strauss & Snider, Chgo., 1971-75; tax cons. Touche Ross & Co., Chgo., 1977-81; tax mgr. Laventhol & Horwath, Chgo., 1981-83; tax ptnr. Ostrow, Reisin, Berk & Abrams, Ltd., 1983—; lectr. law Lewis Coll. Law, Glen Ellyn, Ill., 1980, Kent Coll. Law, Chgo., 1981—; sole practice, Wheeling, Ill., 1977—. Mem. ABA, Ill. State Bar Assn., Chgo. Bar Assn., Am. Inst. C.P.A.s, Ill. C.P.A.s Soc., Am. Israel Chamber Commerce and Industry/Midwest, Chgo. Estate Planning Council, Beta Gamma Sigma, Tau Kappa Epsilon. Co-author: Year End Tax Planning, 1982; co-editor: Callaghan's Legal Checklists, 1985, 86. Estate taxation, Corporate taxation, Estate planning. Home: 1603 Blackhawk Trail Wheeling IL 60090 Office: 676 St Clair St Suite 2100 Chicago IL 60611

WITT, CAROL ANN, lawyer; b. Fremont, Ohio, Nov. 27, 1947; Student, Bowling Green State U., 1965-68; B.S., Suffolk U., 1973, J.D. cum laude, 1977. Bar: Mass. 1977, U.S. Dist. Ct. Mass. 1978, U.S. Tax Ct. 1978, U.S. Dist. Ct. Vt. 1982. Assoc., Louison & Cohen, P.C., Brockton, Mass., 1977-79; ptnr. Louison, Witt & Hensley, P.C., Brockton, 1979-83; mng. ptnr. Louison & Witt, P.C., Brockton, 1983—. Mem. ABA, Assn. Trial Lawyers Am., Mass. Bar Assn. (civil litigation sect. council 1984—), Plymouth County Bar Assn., Mass. Acad. Trial Attys., Women's Bar Assn. Federal civil litigation, State civil litigation, Family and matrimonial. Home: 30 Valley Spring Rd Newton MA 02158 Office: Louison & Witt PC 495 Westgate Dr Brockton MA 02401

WITTE, GORDON MICHAEL, judge; b. Batesville, Ind., Jan. 14, 1957; s. Carl Owen and Joyce Yukiko (Kanzawa) W. BA in Forensic Studies, Ind. U., 1979, JD, 1982. Atty. U.S. Dist. Ct., Ind., 1982; dep. pros. atty. Ind. Cir. Ct., Dearborn County, 1983-84; atty. U.S. Ct. of Appeals (7th cir.), Dearborn County, Ind., 1984; judge Dearborn County Ct., Lawrenceburg, Ind., 1985—. Dist. vice chmn. Boy Scouts Am., Dearborn, Ind., 1986; area chmn. TKE Ednl. Found., Cin., 1986. Mem. ABA, Ind. State Bar Assn., Dearborn County Bar Assn., Ind. Judges Assn., Dearborn County Men's Rep. Club, Ind. U. Alumni Club of Dearborn County. Dearborn Jaycee's. Republican. Roman Catholic. Lodge: KC. Criminal, Judicial administration, State civil litigation. Home: PO Box 521 Lawrenceburg IN 47025 Office: Dearborn County Ct Courthouse 3rd Fl Lawrenceburg IN 47025

WITTEBORT, ROBERT JOHN, JR., lawyer; b. Chgo., Dec. 29, 1947; s. Robert John and Marguerite (Shaughnessy) W. B.A., Yale U., 1969; J.D., Notre Dame U., 1974. Bar: Ill. 1974, U.S. Dist. Ct. (no. dist.) Ill. 1974, U.S. Ct. Appeals (7th cir.) 1975, U.S. Tax Ct. 1977, U.S. Ct. Mil. Appeals 1982. Assoc. Hopkins & Sutter, Chgo., 1974-77; gen. counsel, asst. dir. Ill. Housing Devel. Authority, Chgo., 1977-82; ptnr. Chapman and Cutler, Chgo., 1982—. Contbg. editor: Business Law, 4th edit., 1977. Contbr. Notre Dame Lawyer, 1974. Bd. dirs. Orch. Ill. Assn., Chgo. Served to comdr. USNR, 1969-71. Mem. Nat. Assn. Bond Lawyers, Naval Order U.S. (vice comdr.-gen.), Ill. Commandery Naval Order U.S. (comdr. 1987), Lambda Alpha. Republican. Clubs: Chicago, Saddle & Cycle (Chgo.). Municipal bonds, Securities, Real property.

WITTENBERG, PHILIP, lawyer; b. Cleve., Feb. 4, 1928; s. Samuel Monroe and Rhea (Shapiro) W.; m. Mary Berry Rion, April 16, 1963; stepchildren: Madelyn B. Butts, James Rion Bourgeois, John E. Bourgeois; 1 child, Mindy Rochelle Wittenberg Lawandales. AB, U. Mich., 1948, JD, 1950. Bar: S.C. 1950. Sole practice Columbia, S.C., 1953-62; ptnr. Levi & Wittenberg, Sumter, S.C., 1962-78, Levi, Wittenberg, Harritt, Hoefer & Davis, Sumter, 1978—. Served to 1st lt. U.S. Army, 1951-53. Mem. ABA, S.C. Bar Assn., Sumter County Bar Assn., Richland County Bar Assn., Am. Judicature Soc., S.C. Trial Attys. Assn., S.C. Def. Bar Assn., Comml. Law League Am., Sumter C. of C. Democrat. Jewish. Lodge: Kiwanis. Federal civil litigation, State civil litigation, Insurance. Home: 7 Paisley Park Sumter SC 29150 Office: Levi Wittenberg Harritt Hoefer & Davis PA PO Drawer 730 Sumter SC 29150

WITTENSTEIN, ARTHUR, lawyer; b. Bklyn., Feb. 14, 1926; s. Martin and Esther (Katz) W.; m. Aileen Classon, June 29, 1950; children: Andrew, Kate, Jessica. A.B., Columbia U., 1948; J.D., Harvard U., 1951; M.B.A., NYU, 1957. Bar: N.Y.; C.P.A., N.Y. Assoc. Coopers & Lybrand, N.Y.C., 1951-58, Stroock & Stroock & Lavan, N.Y.C., 1958-60; ptnr. Stroock & Stroock & Lavan, 1961—. Contbr. various profl. jours. Served with U.S. Army, 1945-46. Mem. ABA, N.Y. State Bar Assn., Assn. Bar City N.Y., Am. Inst. C.P.A.s, N.Y. State Soc. C.P.A.s, Authors Guild. Democrat. Clubs: Heights Casino (Bklyn.); Broad St. (N.Y.C.). Corporate taxation, Personal income taxation. Office: Stroock & Stroock & Lavan 7 Hanover Sq New York NY 10004

WITTIG, RAYMOND SHAFFER, lawyer; b. Allentown, Pa., Dec. 13, 1944; s. Raymond Baety and Alice (Shaffer) W.; m. Beth Glover, June 21, 1975; children—Meaghan G., Allison G. B.A., Pa. State U., 1966, M.Ed., 1968; J.D., Dickinson Sch. Law, 1974. Bar: Pa. 1974, D.C. Ct. Apls. 1978. Research psychologist Intext Corp., Scranton, Pa., 1968; minority counsel, procurement subcom. and gen. oversight subcom. Small Bus. Com., U.S. Ho. of Reps., Washington, 1975-76, 77-78, counsel full Ho. Small Bus. Com. 1979-84; atty. Lipsen, Hamberger, Whitten & Hamberger, Washington, 1984—. Served to capt. U.S. Army, 1969-71. Mem. Nat. Fedn. Ind. Bus., U.S. C. of C. (small bus. council), Nat. Order Barristers. Club: Capitol Hill. Legislative, Administrative and regulatory, Government contracts and claims. Home: 4618 Holly Ridge Rd Rockville MD 20853 Office: Lipsen Hamberger Whitten & Hamberger 1725 DeSales St Suite 800 Washington DC 20036

WITTLINGER, TIMOTHY DAVID, lawyer; b. Dayton, Ohio, Oct. 12, 1940; s. Charles Frederick and Dorothy Elizabeth (Golden) W.; m. Diane Cleo Dominy, May 20, 1967; children—Kristine Elizabeth, David Matthew. B.S. in Math., Purdue U., 1962; J.D. with distinction, U. Mich., 1965. Bar: Mich. 1966, U.S. Dist. Ct. (ea. dist.) Mich. 1966, U.S. Ct. Appeals (6th cir.) 1968, U.S. Supreme Ct. 1971. Assoc. Hill, Lewis, Adams, Goodrich & Tait, Detroit, 1965-72, ptnr., 1973—, head litigation dept., 1976—; mem. profl. assistance com. U.S. Dist. Ct. (ea. dist.) Mich., 1981-82. Mem. house of deps. Episcopal Ch., N.Y.C., 1979—; sec. bd. trustees Episcopal Ch., Diocese of Mich., Detroit, 1983—; bd. dirs., sec. Grubb Inst. Behavioral Studies Ltd., Washington. Mem. State Bar Mich., ABA, Nat. Bd. Trial Advocacy (cert.), Engring. Soc. Detroit. Federal civil litigation, State civil litigation, Construction. Home: 736 N Glenhurst Birmingham MI 48009 Office: Hill Lewis Adams Goodrich & Tait 100 Renaissance Ctr 32d Floor Detroit MI 48243

WITTMAN, MICHAEL LEE, lawyer. Student, Northwestern U.w, 1971-72; BA, St. John's U., 1976; JD, Yeshiva U., 1980. Bar: N.Y. 1980, U.S. Dist. Ct. (so. and ea. dists.) N.Y. 1980. Ptnr. Wittman & Klempner, N.Y.C., 1980-86; sole practice N.Y.C., 1987—. General practice, Criminal, State civil litigation. Home and Office: 150 Fifth Ave New York NY 10011

WITTNER, DEREK A., lawyer; b. N.Y.C., July 1, 1943; s. Henry W. and Miriam (Antonow) W.; m. Barbara L. Handler, Aug. 21, 1965; 1 child, Lisa. BA, Columbia U., 1965, JD, 1968. Bar: N.Y. 1968. Atty. Robinson & Silverman, N.Y.C., 1968-70, Delson & Gordon, N.Y.C., 1970-72, Green & Sharpless, N.Y.C., 1972-74; ptnr. Carro & Spanbock, N.Y.C., 1974—. Author: Blue Sky Practice, 1986. Mem. N.Y. State Bar Assn. Securities, General corporate, Contracts commercial. Home: 29 Pond Hill Rd Chappaqua NY 10514 Office: Carro Spanbock 1345 Ave of the Americas New York NY 10105

WITUS, DAVID GORDON, lawyer; b. Kansas City, Kans., Dec. 25, 1956; s. Warren S. and Esther Florence (Shaye) W. BA, U. Fla., 1979, JD, 1982. Bar: Fla. 1982, Calif. 1984. Assoc. Barnett, Bolt & Russo, Tampa, Fla., 1982-84; assoc. litigation Wyman, Bautzer et al, Los Angeles, 1984-85; counsel litigation 20th Century Fox Film Corp., Los Angeles, 1985—. Mem. Los Angeles County Bar Assn., Beverly Hills Bar Assn., Order of Coif, Phi Kappa Phi. Democrat. Jewish. Antitrust, Federal civil litigation, General corporate. Office: 20th Century Fox Film Corp PO Box 900 Beverly Hills CA 90213

WITWER, SAMUEL WEILER, JR., lawyer; b. Chgo., Aug. 5, 1941; s. Samuel Weiler and Ethyl Loraine (Wilkins) W.; m. Susan P. Stewart, Sept. 18, 1971; children—Samuel Stewart, Michael Douglas. A.B. with honors, Dickinson Coll., 1963; J.D., U. Mich., 1966. Bar: Ill. 1967, U.S. Dist. Ct. (no. dist.) Ill. 1967, U.S. Ct. Appeals (7th cir.) 1972, U.S. Supreme Ct. 1973, U.S. Ct. Appeals (6th cir.) 1985, U.S. Dist. Ct. (ea. dist.) Mich., 1987. Assoc. Witwer, Moran, Burlage & Atkinson, Chgo., 1967-74, ptnr., 1974—; mem. Fed. Trial Bar Admissions Com. No. Dist. Ill., 1982—. Governing mem. Chgo. Zool. Soc., 1986—; trustee United Meth. Homes and Services, Chgo., 1974—, Dickinson Coll., Carlisle, Pa., 1976—; mem. Cook County Home Rule Commn., Chgo., 1974-75; chmn. Agy. Appeals Com. Chgo., 1975—; gov. United Republican Fund of Ill., Chgo., 1982—; atty. Glenview Park Dist., 1982—; spl. asst. atty. gen. Auditor Gen. Ill., 1984— . Mem. Meth. Bar Assn. (pres. 1972-73), ABA, Chgo. Bar Assn., Ill. Bar Assn., Law Club of Chgo., Sigma Chi, Phi Delta Phi. Republican. Methodist. Club: Union League. Federal civil litigation, State civil litigation. Home: 1330 Overlook Dr Glenview IL 60025 Office: Witwer Moran Burlage & Witwer 125 S Wacker Dr Chicago IL 60606

WITZ, ALLEN BARRY, lawyer; b. Chgo., Mar. 12, 1941; s. Melvin and Faye (Galsky) W.; m. Carol Maurer, July 30, 1975. BBA, Roosevelt U., 1962; JD, Loyola U., Chgo., 1966. Bar: Ill. 1966, N.Y. 1972. Staff atty. SEC, Washington, 1966-71; atty. N.Y. Stock Exchange, N.Y.C., 1971-75; sr. ptnr. Arvey, Hodes, Costello & Burman, Chgo., 1975-86; sr. ptnr. Wood, Lucksinger & Epstein, Chgo., 1987—; bd. dirs. Bayswater Realty Investment Corp., Golden State Broadcasting Corp., Polaris Entertainment, Inc. ; chmn. Rosebud Entertainment, Inc., 1986—, Fun Foods, Inc., 1986—. Bd. dirs. Am. Jewish Com., 1974-75; asst. campaign dir. for Congl. candidate, 1974-75, 1975. Mem. Internat. Bar Assn., ABA. Clubs: Downtown Athletic (N.Y.C.); Carlton (Chgo.). Securities, Private international, Communications. Office: Wood Lucksinger & Epstein 333 W Wacker Dr Chicago IL 60606

WOCHNER, WILLIAM JAMES, lawyer; b. Falls City, Nebr., July 21, 1947; s. William James and Marjorie Lee (Herbster) W.; m. Jo E. Pierce, Sept. 1, 1984; children: Jennifer, Joanna.. BBA, U. Nebr., 1969, JD, 1971. Bar: Nebr. 1972, Mo. 1974. Atty. Kansas City (Mo.) So. Industries. Mem. ABA, Mo. Bar Assn., Nebr. Bar Assn., Kansas City Met. Bar Assn., Assn. Tranps. Practitioners. Avocations: wood carving, tennis. Administrative and regulatory, Antitrust, General corporate. Office: Kansas City So Industries 301 W 11th St Kansas City MO 64105

WOGLOM, ERIC COOKE, lawyer; b. Bklyn., Mar. 14, 1943; s. Joseph F. and Rita Mary (Cooke) W.; m. Joshan Robin Levitsky, May 11, 1968; children—Peter Douglas, Brian Stewart. B.A., Yale U., 1964; LL.B., U. Pa. 1967. Bar: N.Y. 1968, U.S. Patent Office 1970, U.S. Ct. Appeals (9th cir.) 1972, U.S. Ct. Appeals (2d cir.) 1973, U.S. Dist. Ct. (so. and ea. dist.) N.Y. 1974, U.S. Supreme Ct. 1974, U.S. Ct. Appeals (7th cir.) 1980, U.S. Ct. Appeals (Fed. cir.) 1982. With Fish & Neave, N.Y.C., 1967—, sr. ptnr., 1976—. Served with U.S. Army, 1967. Mem. ABA, Am. Intellectual Property Law Assn., Assn. Bar City N.Y., Licensing Execs. Soc., N.Y. Law Inst., N.Y. Patent, Trademark and Copyright Law Assn., N.Y. State Bar Assn. Republican. Roman Catholic. Clubs: Yale of N.Y.C.; Shelter Island Yacht. Federal civil litigation, Patent, Trademark and copyright. Home: 430 North St Harrison NY 10528 Office: Fish & Neave 875 3d Ave New York NY 10022

WOHL, JAMES PAUL, lawyer, educator, author; b. N.Y.C., Oct. 3, 1937; s. Joseph and Mae (Kreshover) W.; m. Sigrid Elenor Sletteland, June 6, 1969 (div. Feb. 1979); children—Frederic, Kristin, Jenifer. Student Princeton U., 1955-57; A.B., Stanford U., 1962, J.D., 1963. Bar: Calif. 1963, Hawaii 1964, N.Y. 1969. Assoc. Carlsmith, Carlsmith, Wichman & Case, Honolulu, 1963-68, Fried, Frank, Harris, Shriver & Jacobson, N.Y.C., 1968-70; pres. Hawaii Land Corp., Honolulu, 1970-78; prof. law Laverne San Fernando Law Ctr., Sepulveda, Calif., 1978—; bd. dirs. Original N.Y. Seltzer Can., Ltd.; chmn. bd. European Original N.Y. Seltzer Ltd., 1986—. Author novels: The Nirvana Contracts, 1977; Talon, 1978; The Blind Trust Kills, 1979. Bd. dirs. Salvation Army, Hilo, Hawaii, 1964-67; pres. Hawaii Media Adv. Council, 1975-76. Mem. Mystery Writers Am., West Hollywood C. of C. (dir. 1983—). Clubs: Princeton (N.Y.C.); Hilo Yacht. Real property, General corporate, Legal education. Home: 1539 Griagos Rd Albuquerque NM 87107 Home: 21 Old Barrack Yard, London SW1, England Office: Golderown House, Saint Albans Mews, London W218Y, England

WOHL, KENNETH ALLAN, lawyer; b. Denver, May 26, 1950; s. Milton and Leah (Liss) W. BA with honors, U. Calif., Berkeley, 1972; JD, U. Denver, 1975. Bar: Calif. 1975, U.S. Dist. Ct. (cen. dist.) Calif. 1975, Colo. 1976, U.S. Dist. Ct. Colo. 1976. Trial atty. U.S. Equal Employment Oportunity Commn., Denver, 1976-79; regional counsel Mexican-Am. Legal Def. and Ednl. Fund, Denver, 1979-81; employment litigation cons. Denver, 1981-82; adminstrv. law judge State of Ariz., Tucson, 1982-83; sr. trial atty. U.S. Equal Employment Opportunity Commn., Phoenix, 1983—; cons. Rocky Mountain Assn. Indsl. Psychologists, Denver, 1977-79. Del. Colo. Dem. Conv., Denver, 1976. Mem. ABA, Colo. Bar Assn., Denver Bar Assn., Ariz. Fair Employment Practices Com. Avocations: hiking, short story writing. Civil rights, Federal civil litigation, Labor. Office: US Equal Employment Oportunity Commn 135 N 2d Ave Phoenix AZ 85003

WOHLFEIL, JOEL R., lawyer; b. San Diego, Jan. 28, 1956; s. Lorraine Pearl (Guttormson) W.; m. Rachel Ruth Widmann, June 20, 1981; children: Benjamin Carl, Jacob Richard. BA, No. Ariz. U., 1978; JD, Western State U., 1980. Bar: Calif. 1981, U.S. Dist. Ct. (so. dist.) Calif. 1983. Supr. Calif. Youth Authority, San Diego, 1980-82; assoc. Hozmann, Imhoff & Stone, San Diego, 1983-84; sole practice San Diego, 1984-85; assoc. Patrick R. Frega, San Diego, 1985—. pres. Our Savior Luth. Ch., San Diego, 1983-84, Fellowship Christian Athletes, San Diego, 1984; bd. dirs. Greater San Diego Indsl. Edn., 1984-85, San Diego Ecumenical Conf., 1986—. Mem. ABA, San Diego County Bar Assn., Assn. Trial Lawyers Am., Calif. Trial Lawyers Assn., San Diego Trial Lawyers Assn. Democrat. Avocations: recreational activities. State civil litigation, Personal injury. Office: Law Offices Patrick R. Frega 1010 2d Ave 1906 San Diego CA 92101

WOHLFORTH, ERIC EVANS, lawyer; b. N.Y.C., Apr. 17, 1932; s. Robert Martin and Mildred Campbell (Evans) W.; m. Caroline Penniman, Aug. 3, 1957; children—Eric Evans, Charles Penniman. A.B., Princeton U., 1954; LL.B., U. Va., 1957. Bar: N.Y. 1958, Alaska 1967. Assoc. Hawkins, Delafield & Wood, N.Y.C., 1957-66; ptnr. McGrath & Wohlforth, Anchorage, 1966-70; commr. revenue State of Alaska, Anchorage, 1970-72; ptnr. McGrath, Wohlforth & Flint, Anchorage, 1972-74, Wohlforth & Flint, Anchorage, 1974—; mem. Alaska Investment Adv. Com., 1973-80. Chancellor Episcopal Diocese of Alaska, 1972—. Mem. Alaska Bar Assn., Assn. Bar City N.Y. Home: 2226 Arbor Circle Anchorage AK 99503 Office: 900 W 5th Ave Anchorage AK 99501

WOHLREICH, JACK JAY, lawyer; b. Newark, Feb. 8, 1946; s. Charles Carl and Erna D. (Epstein) W.; Jane Friedlander, June 28, 1969; children: Erin Michelle, Caleb Joshua. BA in Polit. Sci., Am. U., 1968, JD, 1971; postdoctoral, George Washington U., 1972. Bar: Md. 1972, D.C. 1972, U.S. Dist. Ct. Md. 1972, U.S. Dist. Ct. D.C. 1972, U.S. Ct. Appeals (4th cir.) 1973, U.S. Supreme Ct. 1975, Ill. 1976, U.S. Dist. Ct. (no. dist.) Ill. 1976. Assoc. chief counsel FDA div. HHS, Washington, 1971-75; corp. counsel, chief litigation Baxter Travenol Labs., Inc., Deerfield, Ill., 1975-86, assoc. gen. counsel, 1986—; lectr. various insts. Contbg. editor Am. U. Law Rev., 1969-71. Asst. to candidate/advanceman Dem. Nat. Com., 1968, Kennedy for Pres. Com., Washington, 1968; chief of advance R. Sargent Shriver, 1970-71; staff asst. congl. leadership for future com., 1971; founding mem. Gaithersburg (Md.) Hebrew Congregation, 1974. Mem. ABA, Ill. Bar Assn., D.C. Bar Assn., Md. Bar Assn., Food and Drug Inst., Pharm. Mfgs. Assn., Health Industries Mfgs. Assn., Tau Epsilon Phi. Avocations: collecting and restoring antique cars, collecting wines. Personal injury, Health, Federal civil litigation. Home: 175 Belle Ave Highland Park IL 60035 Office: Baxter Travenol Labs Inc One Baxter Pkwy Deerfield IL 60015

WOJAHN, DENNIS GILBERT, lawyer; b. Oshkosh, Wis., June 19, 1945; s. Carl Herman and Marilyn (Weissert) W.; m. Karen Louise Langsten, June 15, 1968; children: Laura, Patrick. BBA, U. Wis., 1967, JD, 1972. Bar: Wis. 1972, U.S. Dist. Ct. (ea. dist.) Wis. 1972. Sr. tax acct. Touche Ross & Co., Milw., 1972-75; supr. tax Touche Ross & Co., Buffalo, 1975-78; tax mgr. Deloitte Haskins & Sells, Appleton, Wis., 1978-84; pres. Wojahn & Fisher, Appleton, 1984-85; ptnr. Schumaker, Romenesko & Assocs., Green Bay, Wis., 1985—. Mem. Appleton Estate Planning Council. Served with U.S. Army, 1968-70. Mem. ABA (tax acctg. problems com. 1975—), Wis. Bar Assn., Am. Inst. CPA's, Wis. Inst. CPA's, Green Bay Area Pension Profls. Soc (pres. 1985—). Methodist. Clubs: Riverview Country (Appleton) (treas. 1983-86), Oneida Country. Lodge: Rotary. Corporate taxation, Personal income taxation, Estate taxation. Office: Schumaker Romenesko & Assocs 1551 Park Pl Green Bay WI 54304

WOLAVER, STEPHEN ARTHUR, lawyer; b. Springfield, Ill., Sept. 4, 1950; s. Lynn Ellsworth and Arah Dean Phyllis (Scheele) W.; m. Gayla Sue Howard, Feb. 28, 1987. B.S., Miami U., Oxford, Ohio, 1972; J.D., Valparaiso U., 1975. Bar: Ohio 1975, U.S. Dist. Ct. (so. dist.) Ohio 1976, U.S. Supreme Ct. 1979. Ptnr., Gill, Wolaver & Welch, Fairborn, Ohio, 1975—; asst. pros. atty. Greene County (Ohio), Xenia, 1976—; ptnr. Wolaver Welch Graf & Gill, Fairborn, 1981—; instr. Fairborn Bd. Edn., 1978—; adj. prof. Clark Tech. Coll., 1979—, lectr., 1982—, mem. law enforcement adv. com., 1983-86. Greene County campaign chmn. gov. Rhodes re-election com., 1978, 86. mem. Greene County Rep. Cen. Com., 1978—; youth counselor Bethlehem Luth. Ch., Fairborn, 1980—, head usher com. pres. Rona Village Homeowners Assn., 1981. Named one of Outstanding Young Men Am., Jaycees, 1981, Greene County Legal Secs. Boss of Year, 1985. Mem. Greene County Bar Assn., Ohio Bar Assn., Assn. Trial Lawyers Am., Nat. Dist. Attys. Assn., Miami U. Alumni Assn., Delta Tau Delta. Club: Sertoma (pres. 1982-83). Criminal, Family and matrimonial, Probate. Home: 1112 Charleston Ct Fairborn OH 45324 Office: Wolaver Welch Graf & Gill Attys 1 1/2 S Central Ave Fairborn OH 45324

WOLCOTT, EDWARD WALLACE, lawyer; b. Norfolk, Va., Apr. 27, 1921; s. James Mounts and Nannie (Baylor) W.; m. Clara Elizabeth Mitchell, Sept. 9, 1949; children: Anne Garnett, Edward W. Jr., Elizabeth Brooke. BA, Hampden-Sydney Coll., 1943; LLB, U. Va., 1949. Bar: Va. 1949, U.S. Dist. Ct., U.S. Ct. Appeals (4th cir.) 1949. Chmn. Norfolk Rent Control Bd., 1951-52; commr. in chancery Norfolk Cir. Ct., 1952—; divorce commr. U.S. Ct. Appeals (4th cir.), Norfolk, 1954—; substitute judge Norfolk Gen. Ct., Norfolk, 1957—; pres. Wolcott, Rivers, Wheary, Basnight & Kelly, Norfolk and Virginia Beach, 1979—; regional dir. Sovran Bank N.A., Norfolk, 1970—; pres. Eastern Carolina Farming Corp., Norfolk and Currituck County, N.C., 1976—; v.p., gen. counsel Hampton Roads Naval Mus., Norfolk, 1983—. Served to comdr. USNR, 1942-82. Mem. ABA, Va. Bar Assn., Va. Beach Bar Assn., Norfolk and Portsmouth Bar Assn., Omicron Delta Kappa. Episcopalian. Clubs: Norfolk Yacht and Country (bd. dirs. 1968-74), Harbor (Norfolk). Avocations: sailing, gardening, maritime history. Probate, General corporate, Real property. Office: Wolcott Rivers et al 1010 United Virginia Bank Bldg Norfolk VA 23510 Office: 110 Sovran Bank Bldg Columbus Ctr Virginia Beach VA 23462

WOLDY, KRISTINE CAROL, lawyer; b. Decatur, Ill., Feb. 5, 1948; d. Orvle J. and Ruth E. (Knute) Robison; m. Paul N. Woldy, Sept. 20, 1969; children: Katherine L., Diana L. BA, Knox Coll., 1969; JD, U. Houston, 1978. Bar: Tex. 1978, U.S. Ct. Appeals (5th cir.) 1982, U.S. Supreme Ct. 1982. Asst. dist. atty. Harris County, Houston, 1978-82; assoc. Shults, Hetherington & Linder, Houston, 1982; sole practice Houston, 1982—. Coleader Girl Scout Troop 4044, Houston, 1980-85; bd. dirs. Westland YMCA, Houston, 1985—, Young Children's Choir Westbury Meth. Ch., Houston, 1978-80, 85. Mem. ABA, Tex. Bar Assn. (cert. criminal law specialist 1982), Houston Bar Assn. (criminal and family sects.), Tex. Criminal Def. Lawyers Assn., Nat. Criminal Def. Lawyers Assn., Houston C. of C. (crime control com.), Harris County Criminal Lawyers Assn. (bd. dirs. 1986—). Avocations: needlecraft, music, photography. Criminal, Family and matrimonial, Juvenile. Office: 10103 Fondren Suite 450 Houston TX 77096

WOLF, CHARLES BENNO, lawyer; b. Chgo., Apr. 16, 1950; s. Ludwig and Hilde (Mandelbaum) W.; m. Sarah Lloyd, Sept. 1, 1973; children: Walter Ludwig, Peter Barton. AB, Brown U., 1972; JD, U. Chgo., 1975. Bar: Ill. 1975, U.S. Dist. Ct. (no. dist.) Ill. 1975, U.S. Ct. Appeals (7th and 11th cirs.) 1985, U.S. Supreme Ct. 1985. Ptnr. Vedder, Price, Kaufman & Kammholz, Chgo., 1975—. Contbr. articles to profl. jours. Mem. ABA, Chgo. Bar Assn., Internat. Found. Employee Benefit Plans. Pension, profit-sharing, and employee benefits, Labor. Office: Vedder Price Kaufman & Kammholz 115 S LaSalle St Suite 3000 Chicago IL 60603

WOLF, CHRISTOPHER, lawyer; b. Washington, Feb. 8, 1954; s. Alexander Jr. and Miriam (Auerbach) W. Student, London Sch. Econs., 1974-75; AB cum laude, Bowdoin Coll, 1976; JD magna cum laude, Washington and Lee U., 1980. Bar: D.C. 1980, U.S. Dist. Ct. D.C. 1980, U.S. Ct. Appeals (D.C. cir.) 1980, U.S. Dist. Ct. (ea. dist.) Wis. 1985, U.S. Ct. Claims 1985. Law clk. to presiding justice U.S. Dist. Ct. D.C., Washington, 1980-82; assoc. Arnold & Porter, Washington, 1982-86, Ballard, Spahr, Andrews & Ingersoll, Washington, 1986—. Bd. dirs. Nat. Symphony Orch., Washington, Friends Assisting Nat. Symphony Orch., Washington, 1986—, also pres., 1986—. Mem. ABA, Fed. Bar Assn., Am. Soc. Internat. Law, Washington Council Lawyers, Order of Coif. Democrat. Avocations: music, running. Federal civil litigation, Antitrust, Civil rights. Home: 1311 30th St NW Washington DC 20007 Office: Ballard Spahr Andrews & Ingersoll 555-13th St NW Washington DC 20004

WOLF, DAVID, lawyer; b. Boston, July 11, 1927; s. Ezekiel and Ray (Cohen) W.; m. Maxine Laura Bunin, June 29, 1963; children—Eric E., Douglas R., James A. Grad., Boston Latin Sch., 1945; B.A., U. Mass., 1949; LL.B., Harvard U., 1952; postgrad., Northeastern U., 1952-55. Bar: Mass. 1952, U.S. Patent Office 1952, U.S. Ct. Customs and Patent Appeals 1955, U.S. Supreme Ct. 1958, U.S. Ct. Appeals (fed. cir.) 1983. Ptnr. Wolf, Greenfield & Sacks (P.C.), Boston, 1952—; dir. Emile Bernat & Sons Co. Watercolor artist; exhibited various local shows. Bd. dirs. Killington East Homeowners Assn., 1986, Newton Country Players, 1964-67. Recipient various awards for art. Mem. ABA (lectr. trademark trial adv. program 1986), Am. Patent Law Assn., Lic. Execs. Soc., U.S. Trademark Assn., Mass. Bar Assn., Boston Bar Assn., Boston Patent Law Assn. (pres. 1976), New Eng.-Israel C. of C. (v.p., bd. dirs. 1984-87), Alpha Epsilon Pi. Lodge: B'nai B'rith, Free Sons Israel. Patent, Trademark and copyright, Federal civil litigation. Office: Wolf Greenfield & Sacks PC 201 Devonshire St Boston MA 02110

WOLF, EDWARD LEONARD, lawyer; b. Phila., Oct. 21, 1930; s. Jacob and Blanche (Grass) W.; m. Arleen, May 1, 1973; children—Michael, Allison, Craig. B.S., Villanova U., 1952; J.D., Temple U., 1958. Bar: Pa. 1957, U.S. Dist. Ct. (ea. dist.) Pa. 1957, U.S. Ct. Appeals (3d cir.) 1957, U.S. Supreme Ct. 1960. Assoc. Richter, Lord, Levy, Phila., 1958-68, Kolsby & Wolf, 1968-76, Kolsby, Wolf, & Gordon, 1976-81; sr. ptnr. Segal, Wolf, Berk & Gaines, 1981—. Served to lt. (j.g.) USN, 1952-54. Mem. ABA, Pa. Bar Assn., Phila. Bar Assn. Jewish. Contbr. articles to profl. jours. Federal civil litigation, State civil litigation, Personal injury. Home: 124 Spruce St Philadelphia PA 19106 Office: Segal Wolf Berk & Gaines 1700 Benjamin Franklin Pkwy Windsor Philadelphia PA 19103

WOLF, G. VAN VELSOR, JR., lawyer; b. Balt., Feb. 19, 1944; s. G. Van Velsor and Alice Roberts (Kimberly) W.; m. Ann Holmes Kavanagh, May 19, 1984; 1 child, Casey. B.A., Yale U., 1966; J.D., Vanderbilt U., 1973. Bar: N.Y. 1974, Ariz. 1982, U.S. Dist. Ct. (so. dist.) N.Y. 1974, U.S. Dist. Ct. Ariz. 1982, U.S. Ct. Appeals (2d cir.) 1974, U.S. Ct. Appeals (9th cir.) 1982. Agrl. advisor U.S. Peace Corps, Tanzania and Kenya, 1966-70; assoc. Milbank, Tweed, Hadley & McCloy, N.Y.C., 1973-75; vis. lectr. law Airlangga U., Surabaya, Indonesia, 1975-76; editor in chief Environ. Law Reporter, Washington, 1976-81; cons. Nat. Trust for Historic Preservation, Washington, 1981; assoc. Lewis & Roca, Phoenix, 1981-84, ptnr., 1984—. Bd. dirs. Ariz. div. Am. Cancer Soc., 1985—. Editor: Toxic Substances Control, 1980. Contbr. articles to profl. jours. Bd. dirs. Phoenix Little Theater, 1983—. Mem. ABA, Assn. Bar City N.Y., Ariz. Bar Assn. (com. on environ. and natural resources law), Maricopa County Bar Assn. (legis. com.), Ariz. Acad. Clubs: Union (N.Y.C.); University (Phoenix). Environment, Legislative, Zoning. Office: Lewis and Roca 100 W Washington St Phoenix AZ 85003

WOLF, GUY WALKER, III, lawyer; b. Albany, Oreg., July 7, 1943; s. Guy Walker and Myrtle Leona (Rehrends) W.; m. Grayce Lynn Cerino, Aug. 8, 1965; children: Nancy, Sandra, Janice. BS, U.S. Merchant Marine Acad., 1965; JD, U. Conn., 1971. Bar: Conn. 1971, U.S. Dist. Ct. Conn. 1971, U.S. Ct. Appeals (2d cir.) 1972. Assoc. Siegal & O'Connor, Hartford, Conn., 1971-72; asst. chief pros. atty. Cir. Ct. Conn., 1972-73; asst. pros. atty. Cir. Ct. Common Pleas, Windsor, Conn., 1973-78; asst. state's atty. New Haven (Conn.) Superior Ct., 1978—, unit supr. career criminal div. Home: 219 Laurelbrook Dr Guilford CT 06437 Office: Asst States Atty 246 Church St Suite 106 New Haven CT 06510

WOLF, JAMES PAUL, lawyer; b. Ft. Lauderdale, Fla., July 31, 1955; s. Paul H. and Alice M. (Adams) W.; m. Kathleen R. Robinson, June 27, 1981; children: Stephen James, Katelyn Marie. BA with honors, U. Fla., 1977; JD, Duke U., 1980. Bar: Fla. 1980, U.S. Dist. Ct. (mid. and no. dists.) Fla. 1980, U.S. Ct. Appeals (11th cir.) 1980. Assoc. Mathews, Osborne, McNatt, Gobelman & Cobb, Jacksonville, Fla., 1980; bd. dirs. Jacksonville Area Legal Aid, Inc. Mem. ABA, Fla. Bar Assn., Jacksonville Bar Assn. Democrat. Roman Catholic. Avocations: music, guitar. State civil litigation, Real property, Contracts commercial. Home: 736 Grove Park Blvd Jacksonville FL 32216 Office: Mathews Osborne McNatt Gobelman & Cobb 1500 Am Heritage Life Bldg Jacksonville FL 32216

WOLF, JEROME THOMAS, lawyer; b. Austin, Minn., June 13, 1937; s. William B. and Charlotte Elaine (Rosenstock) W.; m. Ellen L., Jan. 9, 1965; children: Margo Ann, Gregory Thomas. BA, Yale U., 1959; JD, Harvard U., 1962. Bar: Minn. 1962, Mo. 1966, Kans. 1984 Ptnr., Spencer Fane Britt & Browne, Kansas City, Mo., 1966—. Bd. dirs. Jewish Community Center, v.p., 1984—; chmn. legal com. Temple B'Nai Jehudah; chmn. Jewish Community Relations Bur. of Kansas City, 1973-79; trustee Kansas City Mus., 1984—. Served to capt. JAGC, U.S. Army, 1962-66. Mem. Kansas City Bar Assn. (pres. 1979), Kansas City Bar Found. (pres. 1979-80), Mo. Bar, ABA, Phi Beta Kappa. Democrat. Federal civil litigation, State civil litigation. Home: 2411 W 70th Terr Shawnee Mission KS 66208 Office: 1000 Power and Light Bldg Kansas City MO 64105

WOLF, JOHN BARTON, lawyer; b. N.Y.C., Jan. 13, 1952; s. Barnet and Harriet (Malina) W.; m. LouAnne Michaels, May 27, 1984; 2 children. AB, Vassar Coll., 1974; JD, Emory U., 1978. Bar: N.J., 1979, Ga., 1978, U.S. Dist. Ct. N.J., 1979, U.S. Dist. Ct. (no. dist.) Ga., 1978, U.S. Ct. Appeals (5th cir.) 1978, U.S Ct. Appeals (11th cir.) 1981. Assoc. Golden, Shore, Zahn & Richmond, South River, N.J., 1980-84; employment and labor counsel Rutgers U., New Brunswick, N.J., 1984—. Nominating com. Alumnae and Alumni Vassar Coll., Poughkeepsie, N.Y., 1984—. Mem. ABA, N.J. Bar Assn., Ga. Bar Assn., Nat. Assn. Coll. and Univ. Attys., N.J. Assn. Sch. Attys. Avocations: athletics, basketball, photography. Labor, Civil rights, College and university law. Home: 66 Oakey Dr Kendall Park NJ 08824 Office: Employment and Labor Counsel 60 College Ave New Brunswick NJ 08903

WOLF, LAWRENCE, lawyer; b. Los Angeles. BA, Calif. U., Northridge, 1972; JD, U. Calif., Santa Clara, 1975. Bar: Calif. 1975. Atty. City of Santa Monica, Calif., 1975-77, Los Angeles County Pub. Defender, 1977-79; sole practice Los Angeles, 1979—; coordinator law confs. Calif. Juvenile Cts., Inglewood, 1983. Mem. Los Angeles County Bar Assn., Juvenile Cts. Bar Assn. Criminal, Juvenile, Alternative sentencing specialist. Office: 2049 Century Park E 18th Floor Los Angeles CA 90067

WOLF, LEWIS ISIDORE, lawyer; b. Bklyn, June 8, 1933; s. Ephraim and Rachel (Dunajevsky) W.; m. Ruth Ullmann; children: Sara S., Joseph J. BA, Bklyn. Coll., 1954; JD cum laude, Bklyn. Law Sch., 1957; LLM, NYU, 1967. Bar: N.Y. 1958, U.S. Dist. Ct. (so. and ea. dists.) N.Y. 1961, U.S. Ct. Appeals (2d cir.) 1964, U.S. Supreme Ct. 1964. Sole practice, N.Y.C., 1958—; atty. of record Cosmopolitan Mut. Ins. Co., 1977-81; assoc. Smith, Mazure, Director & Wilkins, N.Y.C., 1981—. Served with Army NG, 1957-63. Mem. ABA, N.Y. State Bar Assn., N.Y. County Lawyers Assn. Personal injury, Insurance, Appeals. Office: 277 Broadway Ave New York NY 10007 *

WOLF, MARK CHARLES, lawyer; b. Washington, Apr. 25, 1952; s. Seymour and Hannah (Biscow) W.; m. Patricia Lynn Sandler, Aug. 26, 1984. AB, U. So. Calif., 1974; JD, Okla. City U., 1977; ML in Taxation, Georgetown U., 1986. Bar: Okla. 1977, D.C. 1977, U.S. Dist. Ct. D.C. 1977, U.S. Ct. Appeals (D.C. cir.) 1977, Md. 1985. Gen. atty. U.S. Customs Service, Washington, 1977-79, FCC, Washington, 1979—. Sec., bd. dirs. Dupont West Condominium Assn., Washington, 1981-83. Recipient Spl. Achievement award FCC, Washington, 1984. Mem. ABA. Jewish. Avocations: physical fitness, golf, travel, reading. Administrative and regulatory, Pension, profit-sharing, and employee benefits, Estate taxation. Home: 5032 Cloister Dr Rockville MD 20852 Office: FCC Common Carrier Bur 1919 M St NW Washington DC 20554

WOLF, MARK LAWRENCE, lawyer; b. Boston, Nov. 23, 1946; s. Jason Harold and Beatrice (Meltzer) W.; m. Lynne Lichterman, Apr. 4, 1971; children: Jonathan, Matthew. BA cum laude, Yale U., 1968; JD cum laude, Harvard U., 1971. Bar: Mass. 1971, D.C. 1972, U.S. Supreme Ct. 1976. Assoc. Surrey, Karasik & Morse, Washington, 1971-74; spl. asst. to dep. atty. gen. U.S. Dept. Justice, Washington, 1974-75, spl. asst. to atty. gen., 1975-76; dep. U.S. atty. U.S. Dept. Justice, Boston, 1981-85; from assoc. to ptnr. Sullivan & Worcester, Boston, 1977-81; judge U.S. Dist. Ct.Mass., Boston, 1985—. V.p. Albert Schweitzer Fellowship, N.Y.C., 1974—; trustee Hebrew Rehab. Ctr., Boston, 1985—; chmn. John William Ward Fellowship, Boston, 1986—. Recipient cert. appreciation U.S. Pres., 1975, Disting. Service award U.S. Atty. Gen., 1985. Mem. ABA, Boston Bar Assn. (council 1982-85), Am. Law Inst. Office: US Dist Ct 1201 U S Courthouse Boston MA 02109

WOLF, MAURICE, lawyer; b. London, Oct. 15, 1931; came to U.S., 1947; s. D.I. and Esther (de Miranda) W.; m. Yolanda Pazmino, May 4, 1963; children: J. David, Monica Maria. Cert., Universidad Nacional Autonoma de Mexico, Mexico City, 1957; BA, UCLA, 1959; LLB, Columbia U., 1962. Bar: N.Y. 1962, D.C. 1964, U.S. Supreme Ct. 1980. Atty., advisor Office Satellite Communications, FCC, Washington, 1962-66, counsel, 1966-72; sr. counsel Inter-Am. Devel. Bank, Washington, 1972-77; sr. ptnr. Wolf, Arnold & Cardoso P.C., Washington, 1977-85, Wolf, Arnold & Monroig P.C., Washington, 1985—. Contbr. articles to profl. jours. Pres. Riverside Civic Assn., Fairfax, Ct., 1967, co-chmn. Mt. Vernon council, Fairfax, 1967. Mem. Am. Soc. Internat. Law, Inter-Am. Bar Assn. Avocations: racquetball, cooking, carpentry. Private international, Public international, General corporate. Home: 8354 Wagon Wheel Rd Alexandria VA 22309 Office: Wolf Arnold & Monroig PC 1850 M St NW Washington DC 20036

WOLF, MICHAEL JAY, lawyer; b. Buffalo, Feb. 12, 1955; s. Ernest and Vivienne Francis (Hotz) W.; m. Elizabeth Alice Munro, July 15, 1978. BA

with distinction, U. Wis., 1977; JD, Washington U., St. Louis, 1982. Bar: Mo. 1982, Tex. 1986. Exec. dir. Community Youth Services, Sun Prairie, Wis., 1976-79; asst. counsel Nat. Treasury Employees Union, Washington and Austin, Tex., 1982—. Contbr. articles to profl. jours.; co-author: (radio drama) Museum of Consumer Horrors, 1980. Cons. People Against Violent Crime, Austin, 1982-84, C.R.I.M.E., Austin, 1982-84; exec. dir. High Sch. Law Project, St. Louis, 1980-82; mediator Dispute Resolution Ctr., Austin, 1985—. Recipient Tribute to Outstanding Achievement award Star Countryman, 1978, Community Service award Rotary Club, 1979; grantee Wis. Council on Criminal Justice, 1977-78, United Way of Dane County, 1978-79; fellow U.S. Ho. of Reps, 1982. Mem. ABA (vice chmn. young lawyers div. crime services com. 1985-87, vice chmn. affiliate outreach project subcom. 1986—, exec. com. alternative dispute resolution young lawyers div. 1985-87, nat. confs. 1987—, publs. 1987—, citizenship edn. 1985-87, labor law 1985-87, author Voter Participation Project, 1986), Mo. Bar Assn., St. Louis Bar Assn. (chmn. subcom. 1981), Soc. Fed. Labor Relations Profls. Democrat. Jewish. Avocations: raquetball, guitar, music, travel, theater. Administrative and regulatory, Labor. Home: 6104 Bull Creek Rd Austin TX 78757 Office: Nat Treasury Employees Union 3636 Exec Ctr Dr Suite 101 Austin TX 78731

WOLF, SUSAN M., lawyer; b. Washington, Aug. 5, 1953; d. William B. Jr. and Edna (Jacobs) W. AB summa cum laude, Princeton U., 1975; postgrad.in Psychology, Harvard U., 1977-78; JD, Yale U., 1980. Bar: N.Y. 1982, U.S. Dist. Ct. (so. dist.) N.Y. 1983. Law clk. to judge U.S. Dist. Ct. (so. dist.), N.Y.C., 1980-81; assoc. Paul, Weiss, Rifkind, Wharton & Garrison, N.Y.C., 1981-84; NEH fellow The Hastings (N.Y.) Ctr., 1984-85, assoc. for law, 1985—; adj. assoc. prof. law NYU, 1986—. Contbr. articles to profl. jours. Mem. ethics com. Meml. Sloan-Kettering Cancer Ctr., 1985—, Bronx Mcpl. Hosp. Ctr., 1984-86. Mem. ABA, Am. Soc. Law and Medicine, N.Y.C. Bar Assn. (medicine and law com. 1985—). Health, Jurisprudence. Office: The Hastings Ctr 255 Elm Rd Briarcliff Manor NY 10510

WOLF, WILLIAM B., JR., lawyer; b. Washington, Sept. 11, 1927; s. William B. and Ruth (Pack) W.; m. Edna Russell Jacobs, Aug. 8, 1952 (div. Oct. 1976); children: Susan Marcia, William B. III, Victoria Katharine; m. Audrey Ann Riven, Nov. 29, 1980. AB, Princeton, 1948; postgrad., Oxford U., 1950; LLB, Yale U., 1951. Bar: D.C. 1951, U.S. Supreme Ct. 1954, Md. 1963. Ptnr. Wolf & Wolf, Washington, 1951-64, 82—; sole practice Washington, 1964-72, 75-81; ptnr. Wolf & Rosenblatt, Washington, 1972-75, Wolf, Amram & Hahn, P.C., Washington, 1981-82; vice chmn. Security Nat. Bank, Washington, 1984-85. Pres. Nat. Capital USO, 1966-67, Brotherhood Washington Hebrew Congregation, 1967-68, Jewish Hist. Soc. Greater Washington, 1977-78. Served to sgt. U.S. Army, 1946-48. Mem. ABA, Bar Assn. D.C., Am. Judicature Soc. Republican. Jewish. Clubs: Woodmont Country (Rockville, Md.); Edgartown (Mass.) Yacht; Nassau (Princeton, N.J.). General practice, Real property, Banking. Home: Watergate East Washington DC 20037 Office: Wolf & Wolf 1001 Connecticut Ave Washington DC 20036

WOLFE, BARDIE CLINTON, JR., law librarian, educator; b. Kingsport, Tenn., Oct. 21, 1942; s. Bardie Clinton and Joy (Gillenwater) W.; J.D., U. Ky., 1967, M.S.L.S., 1972. Bar: Ky. 1967. Circulation librarian, dir. reader services U. Tex., 1968-71; acquisition librarian, asst. prof. U. Va., 1971-73; law librarian, asst. prof. Cleve. State U., 1973-76, librarian, assoc. prof., 1976-77; librarian, assoc. prof. law U. Tenn., Knoxville, 1977-80; librarian, prof. law Pace U., White Plains, N.Y., 1980-84; librarian, prof. law St. Thomas U., Miami, Fla., 1984—. accreditation insp. ABA, Assn. Am. Law Schs.; cons. Queens Coll. Sch. Law, 1981-82. Mem. ABA, Ky. Bar Assn., Am. Judicature Soc., Am. Assn. Law Libraries, Assn. Am. Law Schs., Nat. Micrographics Assn. Librarianship, Legal education. Office: St Thomas U Law Library 16400 NW 32d Ave Miami FL 33054

WOLFE, DAVID K., lawyer; b. Lafayette, Ind., Feb. 6, 1922; s. Simon and Nora I. (Connaroe) W.; m. Charity Phillips, Aug. 19, 1958. Student, Purdue U.; JD, U. Ariz., 1950. Bar: Ariz. 1950, U.S. Dist. Ct. Ariz. 1957, U.S. Ct. Appeals (9th cir.), U.S. Supreme Ct. Since practiced in Tucson, 1950—; sr. ptnr. Wolfe & Ostapuk; judge pro tem domestic relation div. Pima County Superior Ct., Tucson, 1986—. Served with USAAF, 1943-45, USAF, 1950-52; maj. USAFR ret. Decorated D.F.C. with oak leaf cluster, Air medal with 4 oak leaf clusters. Fellow Am. Acad. Trial Lawyers, Ariz. Bar Found.; mem. ABA (family law sect., pub. utility law sect., litigation sect.), State Bar Ariz. (com. profl. ethics 1960-72, bd. govs. 1961-64, com. on exams. and admissions 1961-72, chmn. 1968-72, 78-80, family law sect.), Inter.-Am. Bar Assn., Pima County Bar Assn. (pres. 1958), Judge Advs. Assn., Order of Coif, Alpha Delta, Phi Kappa Phi, Theta Xi. Democrat. Family and matrimonial, Federal civil litigation, State civil litigation. Home: 3407 Arroyo Chico Tucson AZ 85716 Office: Pima Bldg 149 N Stone Ave Tucson AZ 85701

WOLFE, DAVID LOUIS, lawyer; b. Kankakee, Ill., July 24, 1951; s. August Christian and Irma Marie (Nordmeyer) W.; m. Gail Lauret Fritz, Aug. 25, 1972; children—Laura Beth, Brian David, Kaitlin Ann. B.S., U. Ill., 1973; J.D., U. Mich. 1976. Bar: Ill. 1976, U.S. Dist. Ct. (no. dist.) Ill. 1976. Assoc., Gardner, Carton & Douglas, Chgo., 1976-82, ptnr., 1983—. Contbr. articles to legal publs.; lectr. estate planning Aid Assn. for Lutherans SMART Program, Chgo., 1980—; lectr. Ill. Inst. Continuing Legal Edn., Chgo. Bar Assn., Lake Shore Nat. Bank. Recipient Recognition award Ill. Inst. Continuing Legal Edn., 1981-84. Mem. ABA (sects. on taxation, corp. banking and bus. law, forum com. on entertainment and sports industries, 1981—), Chgo. Bar Assn. (employee benefits com., sports law com., fed. tax com.), Chgo. Assn. Commerce and Industry (employee benefit subcommittee 1983—), Ill. State Bar Assn. (employee benefits sect. council, 1986—, recognition award 1983), Phi Kappa Phi, Beta Alpha Psi, Beta Gamma Sigma, Sigma Iota Lambda, Phi Eta Sigma, NFL Players' Assn. (cert. contract advisor). Republican. Mem. Evangelical Free Ch. Pension, profit-sharing, and employee benefits, Corporate taxation, General corporate. Office: Gardner Carton & Douglas One First Nat Plaza Suite 3300 Chicago IL 60603

WOLFE, HARRIET MUNRETT, lawyer; b. Mt. Vernon, N.Y., Aug. 18, 1953; d. Lester John Francis Jr. and Olga Harriet (Miller) Munrett; m. Charles Briant Wolfe, Sept. 10, 1983. B.A., U. Conn., 1975; postgrad., Oxford U. (Eng.), 1976; J.D., Pepperdine U., 1978. Bar: Conn. 1979. Assoc. legal counsel, asst. sec. Citytrust, Bridgeport, Conn., 1979—; mem. govt. relations com. Electronic Funds Transfer Assn., Washington, 1983—. Mem. Conn. Bar Assn. (mem. legis. com. banking law sect.), ABA, Conn. Bankers Assn. (trust legis. com.), Guilford Flotilla Coast Guard Aux., U.S. Yacht Racing Union, Phi Alpha Delta Internat. (Frank E. Gray award 1978, Shepherd chpt. Outstanding Student award 1977-78). Banking, General corporate, Securities. Home: 26 FarmView Dr Madison CT 06443 Office: Legal Dept Citytrust 961 Main St Bridgeport CT 06601

WOLFE, J. THOMAS, lawyer; b. Balt., Mar. 27, 1947; s. T. Robey Jr. and Antoinette Cecelia (Teano) W.; m. Maria C. Lameiro, Feb. 14, 1975; children: Paul Michael, Rebeca Elizebeth. BS in Aerospace Engring., U. Md., College Park, 1969; JD, U. Md., Balt., 1973; M of Laws, George Washington U., 1977. Bar: Md. 1973, D.C. 1975, U.S. Supreme Ct. 1979, U.S. Ct. Appeals (D.C. cir.) 1985, U.S. Ct. Appeals (4th cir.) 1986. Enforcement counsel EPA, Washington, 1973-77; dep. asst. gen. counsel U.S. Dept. Energy, Washington, 1977-83; regulatory counsel Balt. Gas and Electric Co., 1983—. Mem. ABA, Fed. Energy Bar Assn., Md. Bar Assn. Democrat. Roman Catholic. Avocations: astronomy, photography, skin diving. Environment, FERC practice, Nuclear power. Home: 4519 Q St NW Washington DC 20007 Office: Balt Gas Electric Co Legal Dept PO Box 1475 Baltimore MD 21203

WOLFE, JAMES RONALD, lawyer; b. Pitts., Dec. 10, 1932; s. James Thaddeus and Helen Matilda (Corey) W.; m. Anne Lisbeth Dahle Eriksen, May 28, 1960; children: Ronald, Christopher, Geoffrey. B.A. summa cum laude, Duquesne U., 1954; LL.B. cum laude, NYU, 1959. Bar: N.Y. 1959. Assoc. Simpson Thacher & Bartlett, N.Y.C., 1959-69, ptnr., 1969—. Co-editor: West's McKinney's Forms, Uniform Commercial Code, 1965. Served to 1st lt. U.S. Army, 1955-57. Mem. ABA, N.Y. State Bar Assn., Am. Judicature Soc., N.Y. Law Inst. Republican. Roman Catholic. Home: 641 King St Chappaqua NY 10514

WOLFE, JOHN GEORGE, III, lawyer; b. Winston-Salem, N.C., Sept. 23, 1945; s. John G. Jr. and Polly (Donnell) W.; m. Roberta Bryson; children: J.G. IV, Cary. BA, Maryville Coll., 1967; JD, Wake Forest U., 1970. Bar: N.C. 1970, U.S. Dist. Ct. (mid. dist.) N.C. 1970, U.S. Supreme Ct. 1978. Assoc. Hatfield, Allman & Hall, Kernersville, N.C., 1970-73; sole practice Kernersville, 1973-74, 1979-84; sr. ptnr. Wolfe and Prince, Kernersville, 1974-79; sr. partner Wolfe and Collins, P.A., Kernersville, 1984—; town counsel Kernersville, 1976—; pres. Triad Motion Pictures, Inc., Kernersville; bd. dirs. First Citizens Bank Kernersville. Mem. local bd. Selective Service System, N.C., 1985—. Mem. ABA, N.C. Bar Assn., N.C. Mcpl. Attys. Assn. (bd. dirs. 1984—, v.p.), Forsyth Bar Assn., C. of C. (pres. 1973, v.p. 1986—). Republican. Moravian. Lodge: Lions (pres. Kernersville 1974-75). Local government. Home: 312 S Main St Kernersville NC 27284 Office: 101 S Main St Kernersville NC 27284

WOLFE, JOHN LESLIE, lawyer; b. Cuyahoga Falls, Ohio, Dec. 6, 1926; s. Leslie George and Phyllis (Bond) W.; m. Barbara Lou Carle, Dec. 27, 1950 (div.); children—David, Karla. A.B., U. Akron, 1950; J.D., U. Mich., 1953. Bar: Ohio 1953, U.S. Dist. Ct. (no. dist.) Ohio 1955, U.S. Ct. Appeals (6th cir.) 1966, U.S. Supreme Ct. 1970. Sole practice, Akron, 1953-56; asst. pros. atty. Summit County, Ohio, 1956-57; assoc. Hershey & Browne, Akron, 1957-61, ptnr. 1961-85; ptnr. Wolfe, Axner, Williams & Gallagher, 1986—, pres. Akron Centre Title Agy., Inc., 1986—; asst. atty. gen. State of Ohio, 1971-74; adj. prof. trial practice U. Akron, 1975-80; counsel Tri County Regional Planning Commn. of Portage, Summit and Medina Counties, 1960-74. Trustee Akron Law Library, 1961—. Served with U.S. Army, 1945-47. Recipient Ohio Legal Ctr. Inst. Award of Merit, 1966. Mem. ABA, Ohio State Bar Assn., Akron Bar Assn., Assn. Trial Lawyers Am., Ohio Acad. Trial Lawyers. Democrat. Club: City (Akron). Civil litigation, Insurance. Home: 45 Mayfield Ave Akron OH 44313 Office: Akron Ctr Plaza Suite 505 50 S Main St Akron OH 44308

WOLFE, RICHARD BARRY MICHAEL, lawyer; b. N.Y.C., Dec. 25, 1932; s. Herman E. and Florence (Cohen) W.; m. Lilyan Aren, June 8, 1957; children—Brian, Stacey. B.A., Alfred U. (N.Y.), 1954; J.D., Bklyn. Law Sch., 1957; postgrad. Practicing Law Inst., N.Y.C. Bar: N.Y. 1960. gen. counsel to Katz, Leidman, Grossman, Wolfe & Freund, N.Y.C., 1970—. Tchr. high sch. (nights) various Jersey Temples; lectr. various synagogues, N.Y., N.J. councilman Matawan Twp. (N.J.), 1974-78, Aberdeen Twp. (N.J.), 1984—; pres. Aberdeen Twp. Democratic Club, 1981-82, Matawan Twp. Dem. Club, 1973-74; editor county newspaper of Dem. Party, 1972-73. Served with USAR, 1959-65. Recipient U.S. Naval Base Care award, 1981; Kiwanis award, 1979. Mem. N.Y. Workers Compensation Bar Assn. (trustee), N.Y. County Bar Assn. (labor com. 1979), Assn. Bar City N.Y. (young lawyers com. 1973), ABA (young lawyers com. 1965), Assn. Trial Lawyers Am. (young lawyers com.). Jewish. Lodge: Elks. Administrative and regulatory, Workers' compensation, Securities. Home: 120 Warren Dr Aberdeen Township NJ 07747 Office: 921 46th St Brooklyn NY 11219

WOLFE, RICHARD FREDERICK, lawyer; b. National City, Calif., Sept. 4, 1952; s. Maurice Dale and Jean Roberta (Miller) W. BA in Polit. Sci., Calif. Poly. U., 1974; JD, Western State U., 1977. Bar: Calif. 1979, U.S. Dist. Ct. (so. dist.) Calif. 1979, U.S. Supreme Ct. 1984. Assoc. Millsberg, Dickstein & McKee, San Diego, 1979-83, McCormick & Mitchell, San Diego, 1984—. Mem. Calif. Bar Assn., San Diego County Bar Assn., San Diego Def. Lawyers. State civil litigation, Construction, Personal injury. Office: McCormick & Mitchell 110 W A St Suite 1110 San Diego CA 92101-3780

WOLFE, ROBERT J., lawyer; b. New Haven, Mar. 13, 1936; s. Aaron J. and Selma (Ash) W.; m. Joan Tarle, Jan. 15, 1961; children: Elizabeth, Deborah, Carolyn. BS in Commerce and Econ., U. Vt., 1957; JD, U. Va., 1960. Assoc. Spiro & Levine, Danbury, Conn., 1960, A.W. Spiro, Danbury, 1960-66; ptnr. Davis, Cheney, Tyler & Wolfe, Danbury, 1966-78, Pinney, Payne, VanLenten, Burrell, Wolfe & Dillman, Danbury, 1978—. Bd. dirs. Northern Fairfield County United Way, Danbury, 1975—, planning commn. Danbury Hosp., 1980—. Mem. Conn. Bar Assn. (numerous coms., bd. of govs. 1978—), Danbury Bar Assn. (pres. 1980-81). Club: Ridgewood County (Danbury) (bd. dirs. 1980—, treas. 1985—). General corporate, Real property, Contracts commercial. Office: Pinney Payne VanLenten Burrell Wolfe & Dillman 26 West St Danbury CT 06813-0650

WOLFE, ROBERT SHENKER, retired lawyer; b. Quanah, Tex., May 29, 1945; s. William Shenker and Hortense (Goldbas) Asher; m. Ellyn Helene Peska, Nov. 3, 1979. B.A., Hamilton Coll., 1967; postgrad. MIT, 1969-70; J.D., Boston U., 1970. Bar: N.Y. 1970, U.S. Dist. Ct. (no. and ea. dists.) N.Y. 1970, U.S. Ct. Appeals (1st cir.) 1970, Mass. 1971, U.S. Dist. Ct. Mass. 1971. Assoc. firm Kaplan, Latti & Flannery, Boston, 1970-73; prin. Sriberg, Berman & Wolfe, Boston, 1973-76; propr. Wolfe Assocs., Boston, 1976—; trial counsel Ricklefs & Uehlein, Boston, 1976-85, Ricklefs & Uchlein, 1976-85; pres., dir. Meditor Systems, Inc., Boston; vis. prof. admiralty law Suffolk U. Sch. Law, Boston, 1972-73. Bd. dirs. Alchemic Art Gallery, Ipswich River Watershed Assn.; mem. growth planning subcom. Manchester Planning Bd.; pro bono vol. environ. issues Lawyers Referral Service, 1975—. pres., bd. dirs. Heritage Preservation, Inc., Boston, 1983—. Author: Power, Pollution and Public Policy, 1971. Mem. Assn. Trial Lawyers Am., Mass. Boston Bar Assn., Boston Bar Assn. Club: University. Jewish. Admiralty, Insurance, Personal injury. Office: Wolfe Assocs PO Box 1424 Manchester MA 01944

WOLFE, STEVEN EDWARD, lawyer; b. Phila., July 31, 1954; s. David Wolfe and Marilyn Lipson; m. Sandra Lynn Freedman, Sept. 20, 1979. BA, Temple U., 1976, JD, 1979. Bar: Pa. 1979, U.S. Dist. Ct. (ea. dist.) Pa. 1980, U.S. Ct. Appeals (3d cir.) 1980. Sole practice Holland, Pa., 1980-84, 87—, Feasterville, Pa., 1984-87. Mem. ABA, Am. Arbitration Assn., Pa. Bar Assn., Bucks County Bar Assn., Feasterville Bus. Assn. Republican. Jewish. Club: Nat. Exchange. Lodge: Masons. Avocations: photography, skiing, golf, softball, travel. Personal injury, Criminal, State civil litigation. Home: 19 Jasmine Ct Newtown PA 18940 Office: 295 Buck Rd Suite 202 Holland PA 18966

WOLFE, WARREN DWIGHT, lawyer; b. Boston, July 30, 1926; s. Louis Julius and Rose (Daniels) W.; m. Caroline M. DuMont, Dec. 29, 1973. B.S. in Journalism, Northwestern U., 1949; M. Internat. Affairs, Columbia U., 1951; J.D. with high honors, U. Toledo, 1959. Bar: Ohio 1959, Mich. 1960. Reporter Wilmington Record, Del., 1951-52; Sunday editor, asst. news editor Middletown Jour., Ohio, 1952-55; copy reader, sect. editor Toledo Blade, 1955-60; assoc. Bugbee & Conkle, Toledo, 1960-64; ptnr. 1964—. Pres., Health Planning Assn. Northwest Ohio, 1970-73; mem. Comprehensive Health Planning Adv. Council to Ohio Dept. Health, 1972-75; mem. Ohio Gov.'s Task Force on Health, 1973-74; mem. Lucas County Health Planning Study Com., 1984—; trustee Toledo Legal Aid Soc., 1968—, pres., 1973-75; trustee Toledo Animal Shelter Assn., 1962-75; trustee Lucas County unit Am. Cancer Soc., 1964—, v.p., 1976-81, pres., 1981-83; trustee Ohio div., 1969-70, 85—. Served with USNR, 1944-46. Mem. Am. Trial Lawyers Assn., ABA, Ohio Bar Assn., Lucas County Bar Assn. (pres. 1966), Toledo Bar Assn. (exec. com. 1969-75), State Bar Mich., Law Alumni Assn. U. Toledo Coll. Law (pres. 1965), Sigma Delta Chi. Club: Toledo Ski (treas. 1972-75, pres. 1975-76). Lodge: Masons. Home: 5617 Dianne Ct Toledo OH 43623 Office: Bugbee & Conkle 1301 Toledo Trust Bldg Toledo OH 43604

WOLFE, WILLIAM MILTON, lawyer; b. Alexandria, La., Dec. 16, 1954; s. Horace Milton and Joan Kay (Barron) W.; m. Janet D'Amico, Aug. 11, 1982; children: William James, Kiley Cullen. BBA, La. State U., 1976; JD, Loyola U., New Orleans, 1980. Bar: La., U.S. Dist. Ct. (we. and ea. dists.) La., U.S. Ct. Appeals (5th cir.) 1981. Assoc. Law Offices of Charles F. Wagner, Pineville, La., 1980-83; house counsel AMI, Shreveport, La., 1983-85; sole practice Pineville, 1986—; v.p. Gulf Coast Mineral Mgmt., Lafayette, La., 1985—. Sec. Full Gospel Businessmens Fellowship Internat., Alexandria, La., 1986—. Democrat. Oil and gas leasing, General practice, Consumer commercial. Office: 818 D Main Pineville LA 71361-0252

WOLFF, ALAN WILLIAM, lawyer; b. Malden, Mass., June 12, 1942; s. Louis K. and Etta (Bernstein) W.; m. Helene N. Wolff, Mar. 3, 1965; children: Anna, Jeremy, Ewan. AB, Harvard U., 1963; LLB, Columbia U., 1966. Bar: Mass. 1967, N.Y. 1966, U.S. Supreme Ct. 1971, D.C. 1972, U.S. Ct. Appeals (fed. cir.) 1984. Atty., office of gen. counsel U.S. Treasury Dept., Washington, 1968-73; dep. gen. counsel Spl. Trade Rep. (now U.S. Trade Rep.), Washington, 1973-74, gen. counsel, 1974-76, dep. spl. trade rep., 1977-79; ptnr. Verner, Liipfert et al, Washington, 1979-85, Dewey, Ballantine, Bushby, Palmer & Wood, Washington, 1985—; counsel Labor-Industry Coalition for Internat. Trade, Washington, 1979—, Semiconductor Industry Assn., Washington, 1980—; mem. U.S. Coalition for Lumber Fair Can. Imports, Pres.'s Adv. Com. for Trade Negotiations, Washington, 1980-82, U.S. Trade Rep.'s Services Policy Adv. Com., Washington, 1980-86. Contbr. articles to profl. jours. Mem. Inst. for Internat. Econs. (bd. advisors 1981—), Council on Fgn. Relations, Nat. Planning Assn. (changing internat. realities com. 1982—), Japan-Am. Soc. Washington (trustee 1983—), Atlantic Council (adv. trade panel 1979—). Democrat. Unitarian. Private international, Public international, Legislative. Office: Dewey Ballantine Bushby Palmer & Wood 1775 Pennsylvania Ave NW Suite 500 Washington DC 20006

WOLFF, DEBORAH H(OROWITZ), lawyer; b. Phila., Apr. 6, 1940; d. Samuel and Anne (Manstein) Horowitz; m. Morris H. Wolff, May 15, 1966 (divorced); children—Michelle Lynn, Lesley Anne; m. Walter Alan Levy, June 7, 1987. B.S., U. Pa., 1962, M.S., 1966; postgrad., Sophia U., Tokyo, 1968; J.D., Villanova U., 1979. Tchr. Overbrook High Sch., Phila., 1962-68; homebound tchr. Lower Merior Twp., Montgomery County, 1968-71; asst. dean U. Pa., Phila., 1975-76; law clk. firm Stassen, Kostos and Mason, Phila., 1977-78; assoc. firm Spencer, Sherr, Moses and Zuckerman, Norristown, Pa., 1980-81; ptnr. Wolff Assocs., 1981—; lectr. law and estate planning, Phila., 1980—; Recipient 3d ann. Community Service award Phila. Mayor's Com. for Women, 1984; named Pa. Heroine of Month, Ladies Home Jour., July 1984. Founder Take a Brother Program; bd. dirs. Germantown Jewish Ctr.; high sch. sponsor World Affairs Club, Phila., 1962-68; mem. exec. com. Crime Prevention Assn., Phila., 1965—; bd. dirs. U. Pa. Alumnae Bd., Phila., 1965—; dir. organized classes. Mem. ABA, Pa. Bar Assn., Phila. Bar Assn., Montgomery County Bar Assn., Phila. Women's Network, Bus. Women's Network (v.p.). Club: Cosmopolitan (membership com. Phila.). General corporate, Probate, Real property. Home and Office: 422 W Mermaid Ln Philadelphia PA 19118

WOLFF, ELROY HARRIS, lawyer; b. N.Y.C., May 20, 1935; s. Samuel and Rose Marian (Katz) W.; children: Ethan, Anna Louise. A.B., Columbia U., 1957, LL.B., 1963. Bar: N.Y. 1963, D.C. 1969. Assoc. Kaye, Scholer, Fierman, Hays & Handler, N.Y.C., 1963-65; atty.-adviser to commr. FTC, Washington, 1965-67; sr. trial atty. Dept. Transp., 1967-69; assoc. Leibman, Williams, Bennett, Baird & Minow, Washington, 1969-70, ptnr., 1970-72; ptnr. Sidley & Austin, Washington, 1972—; mem. adv. com. on practice and procedure FTC, 1969-71; chmn. adv. com. on procedural reform CAB, 1975. Served to 1st lt. USAF, 1957-60. Mem. ABA, Assn. Bar City N.Y. Clubs: Monroe, Fed. City, Nat. Lawyers. Antitrust, Administrative and regulatory, Federal civil litigation. Office: Sidley & Austin 1722 Eye St NW Washington DC 20006

WOLFF, JESSE DAVID, lawyer; b. Mpls., Aug. 26, 1913; s. Maurice I. and Annalee (Weiskopf) W.; m. Elizabeth Hess, Nov. 22, 1939; children: Nancy Nicholas, Paula, Daniel Jesse. B.A. summa cum laude, Dartmouth Coll., 1935; J.D., Harvard U., 1938. Bar: N.Y. 1938. Since practiced in N.Y.C.; asso., then partner firm Weil, Gotshal & Manges, 1938-68, sr. mng. partner, 1968—; past dir., dep. chmn. Sotheby Parke Bernet Group (Eng.); dir. Sotheby's Holdings Inc.; dir. also others; bd. dirs. Am. Arbitration Assn. Exec. bd. Greater N.Y. ARC; past mem. exec. com. Salvation Army N.Y.C. Served as officer AUS, 1942-45. Mem. ABA, Judge Adv. Gen. Assn. General practice, Probate. Office: 767 Fifth Ave New York NY 10153

WOLFF, KURT JAKOB, lawyer; b. Mannheim, Ger., Mar. 7, 1936; s. Ernest and Florence (Marx) W.; m. Sanda Lynn Dobrick, Dec. 28, 1958; children—Tracy Ellin, Brett Harris. A.B., NYU, 1955; J.D., U. Mich., 1958. Bar: N.Y. 1958, U.S. Supreme Ct. 1974, Hawaii 1985. Practice, N.Y.C., 1958—; assoc. Hays, Sklar & Herzberg, 1958-60; sr. assoc. Nathan, Mannheimer, Asche, Winer and Friedman, 1960-65; sr. assoc. Otterbourg, Steindler, Houston & Rosen, 1965-68, sr. ptnr., 1968-70, dir., treas. 1970—, chmn. bd., 1978-82, chief exec. officer, 1982—; spl. master N.Y. Supreme Ct., 1977-85; vol. master U.S. Dist. Ct. (so. dist.) N.Y., 1978-82. Lectr., U. Mich. Law Sch. Mem. N.Y. State Bar Assn. (lectr.), Am. Arbitration Assn. (arbitrator), N.Y.C. Bar Assn. (arbitration com. 1979-83, state cts. of superior jurisdiction com. 1983—), ABA (chmn. ins. com. econs. sect. 1980-82, editor arbitration newsletter, arbitration com. sect. of litigation), Gen. Arbitration Council Textile Industry N.Y.C., Fed. Bar Council. Contbr. articles to legal jours. Federal civil litigation, State civil litigation, Contracts commercial. Home: 9 Sunset Dr N Chappaqua NY 10514 also: 48-641 Torrito Ct Palm Desert CA 92260 Office: 230 Park Ave New York NY 10017

WOLFGANG, MARVIN EUGENE, sociologist, criminologist, educator; b. Millersburg, Pa., Nov. 14, 1924; s. Charles T. and Pauline (Sweigard) W.; m. Lenora D. Poden, June 1, 1957; children: Karen Eleanor, Nina Victoria. B.A., Dickinson Coll., Carlisle, Pa., 1948; M.A., U. Pa., 1950, Ph.D., 1955. Instr., asst. prof. Lebanon Valley Coll., 1948-52; instr. to prof. sociology U. Pa., Phila., 1952—; chmn. dept. U. Pa., 1968-72, prof. sociology and law, 1972—; also dir. Sellin Center for Studies in Criminology and Criminal Law; vis. prof., fellow Churchill Coll., U. Cambridge, Eng., 1968-69; cons. Rand Corp.; Chmn. rev. com. on crime and delinquency NIMH, 1971-73; research dir. Nat. Commn. on Causes and Prevention of Violence, 1968-69; commr. Nat. Commn. on Obscenity and Pornography, 1968-70. Author: Patterns in Criminal Homicide, 1958, Crime and Race, 1964, (with T. Sellin) The Measurement of Delinquency, 1964, (with F. Ferracuti) The Subculture of Violence, 1967, Crime and Culture, 1968, (with L. Radzinowicz) Crime and Justice, 3 vols, 1971, rev. edit., 1977, (with T. Sellin, R. Figlio) Delinquency in a Birth Cohort, 1972, (with R. Figlio, T. Thornberry) Criminology Index, 2 vols, 1975, Evaluating Criminology, 1978, (with N. Weiner) Criminal Violence. Bd. dirs. Thomas Skelton Harrison Found. Served with AUS, 1943-45, ETO. Recipient Fulbright Research award, 1957-58, Research award Am. Soc. Criminology, 1960; Guggenheim fellow, 1957-58, 68-69. Mem. Am. Philos. Soc., Am. Acad. Arts and Scis., Internat. Soc. Criminology, Am. Soc. Criminology (past pres.), Am. Acad. Polit. and Social Sci. (pres.), Pa. Prison Soc. (dir., past pres.). Home: 4106 Locust St Philadelphia PA 19104

WOLFMAN, BERNARD, lawyer, educator; b. Phila., July 8, 1924; s. Nathan and Elizabeth (Coff) W.; m. Zelda Bernstein, Dec. 25, 1948 (dec. Oct. 1973); children: Jonathan L., Brian S., Dina A.; m. Toni A. Grotta, June 12, 1977. A.B., U. Pa., 1946, J.D., 1948; LL.D. (hon.), Jewish Theol. Sem., 1971. Bar: Pa. 1949, Mass. 1976. Mem. law firm Wolf, Block, Schorr & Solis-Cohen, Phila., 1948-63; prof. law U. Pa. Law Sch., 1963-76, dean, 1970-75, Kenneth W. Gemmill prof. tax law and tax policy, 1973-76, chmn. Faculty Senate, 1969-70; Fessenden prof. law Harvard U., 1976—; vis. prof. Stanford Law Sch., summer 1966, U. Mich. Law Sch., summer 1982, NYU Law Sch., 1987—; Irvine lectr. Cornell U. Law Sch., 1980; Halle lectr. Case Western Res. U. Law Sch., 1983, Cleve. State U. Sch. Law, 1983; mem. editorial bds. law div. Little, Brown & Co., Jour. Corp. Taxation, CCH Trans. Tax Library; gen. counsel AAUP, 1966-68, mem. council, 1979-82; mem. adv. group to commr. internal revenue, 1966-67; cons. tax policy U.S. Treasury Dept., 1963-68, 77-80; chmn. Task Force Univ. Governance, U. Pa., 1968-70; mem. steering com. IRS project Adminstrv. Conf. U.S., 1974-80; vice chmn. bd. advs. NYU/IRS Continuing Profl. Edn. Project, 1981-85; mem. legal activities policy bd. Tax Analysts, 1974—; exec. com. Fed. Tax Inst. New Eng., 1976—. Author: Federal Income Taxation of Business Enterprise, 1971, 2d edit., 1982, Supplement, 1987; (with J. Holden) Ethical Problems in Federal Tax Practice, 1981, 2d edit., 1985; sr. author: Dissent Without Opinion: The Behavior of Justice William O. Douglas in Federal Tax Cases, 1975; contbr. articles to profl. jours. Adv. com. Commn. Philanthropy and Pub. Needs, 1973-75; mem. Phila. regional council Pa. Gov.'s Justice Commn., 1973-75; trustee Found. Center, N.Y.C., 1970-76, Fedn. Jewish Agys. Greater Phila., 1968-74; bd. dirs. Phila. Lawyers Com. Civil Rights Under Law, 1970-74, Phila. Defender Assn., 1955-69; mem. Nat.

Lawyers Adv. Council of Earl Warren Legal Tng. Program. Served with AUS, 1943-45. Fellow Center Advanced Study in Behavioral Scis. (1975-76), Am. Bar Found., Am. Coll. Tax Counsel; mem. ABA (former chmn. com. on taxation, council sect. individual rights and responsibilities 1978-82, council sect. taxation 1982-85), Am. Law Inst. (cons. fed. income tax project 1974—), ACLU (nat. dir. 1973-75, dir. Phila. chpt. 1964-76, pres. 1972-75), Phi Beta Kappa, Order of Coif (exec. com. 1982—, v.p. 1986—). Legal education, Corporate taxation, Personal income taxation. Home: 229 Brattle St Cambridge MA 02138 Office: Harvard Law Sch Cambridge MA 02138

WOLFMAN, PAUL IRWIN, lawyer; b. Racine, Wis., Apr. 30, 1949; s. Seymour and Marion Shirley (Krieger) W.; m. Judith Anne Cremer, Aug. 17, 1974; children: Rebekah Erin, Laura Beth. BA with distinction, U. Wis., 1971; JD with distinction, John Marshall Law Sch., 1975. Bar: Fla. 1975, Ill. 1976, U.S. Dist. Ct. (no. dist.) Ill. 1976, U.S. Supreme Ct. 1979. Trust adminstr. Sears Bank and Trust Co., Chgo., 1975-76; counsel CNA Ins. Co., Chgo., 1976-84; v.p., gen. counsel, sec. N.Am. Co., Chgo., 1984—. Mem. ABA (life ins. com.), Fla. Bar Assn., Ill. Bar Assn., Chgo. Bar Assn., Assn. Life Ins. Counsel, Am. Council Life Ins. (legal sect.), Am. Corp. Counsel Assn. (vice chmn. fin. services com.), Decalogue Soc. Lawyers. Insurance, General corporate. Office: North Am Co for L&H Ins 222 S Riverside Plaza Chicago IL 60606

WOLFSON, HERBERT MILTON, lawyer; b. N.Y.C., June 12, 1923; s. Benjamin and Rebecca (Shapiro) W.; m. Harriet Krantz, Sept. 10, 1950; children: Eugenie, David, Martin. BA in Chemistry, Bklyn. Coll., 1942; BS in Chem. Engring., U. Mich., 1943, MS in Chem. Engring., 1947, JD, 1951. Bar: Mich. 1951, D.C. 1954, U.S. Supreme Ct. 1964, Del. 1985. Corp. counsel Du Pont De Nemours & Co., Wilmington, Del. Mem. ABA, Am. Intellectual Property Assn. (bd. dirs.), Phila. Patent Law Assn. (pres. 1980-81). Patent, Antitrust. Home: 1213 Brook Dr Wilmington DE 19803 Office: Du Pont De Nemours & Co 2608 Montchanin Wilmington DE 19898

WOLFSON, JACK LEONARD, lawyer; b. Worcester, Mass., Oct. 28, 1924; s. Morris and Cora (Krock) W.; m. Marcia Paul, Mar. 23, 1952; children—Jeffrey S., Geri S. B.B.A. with honors, Clark U., 1948; LL.B., Boston U., 1951. Bar: Mass. 1951, U.S. Supreme Ct. 1975, U.S. Tax Ct. 1980. Assoc. Seder and Seder, Worcester, 1951-56; ptnr. Conlin and Wolfson, Worcester, 1956-73; sr. ptnr. Wolfson, Moynihan, Dodson and O'Connor, Worcester, 1973-78, Wolfson, Moynihan, Dodson and Keenan, 1978—; corporator Worcester County Instn. for Savs. Pub. adminstr. Worcester County; distbn. com. Greater Worcester Community Found.; trustee Temple Emanuel (past pres. brotherhood; Man of Year award 1965). Recipient Boston U. Law Sch. Centennial award, Ecumenical award St. Thomas More Soc., 1986. Mem. ABA, Mass. Bar Assn., Worcester County Bar Assn. (exec. bd., chmn. coms. bus. law, practice and bankruptcy law), Clark U. Alumni Council (chmn. alumni fund.). Club: Masons (Worcester). Contbr. Boston U. Law Rev. Bankruptcy, Consumer commercial, General corporate.

WOLFSON, JEFFREY STEVEN, lawyer; b. Worcester, Mass., Jan. 9, 1954; s. Jack L. and Marcia (Paul) W.; m. Judy Rosen, Oct. 25, 1981. AB summa cum laude, Tufts U., 1976; JD, Yale U., 1979. Bar: Mass. 1979, U.S. Dist. Ct. Mass. 1980, U.S. Ct. Appeals (1st cir.) 1980. Assoc. Goulston & Storrs, P.C., Boston, 1979-86, ptnr., 1986—; clk. Malden Mills Industries, Inc., Lawrence, Mass., 1981—. Bd. dirs. Performers Ensemble, Inc., Boston, 1985—. Mem. ABA, Boston Bar Assn., Phi Beta Kappa. General corporate, General practice, Entertainment. Home: 166 Lindbergh Ave Needham MA 02194 Office: Goulston & Storrs PC 400 Atlantic Ave Boston MA 02210

WOLFSON, SUSAN WARTUR, lawyer; b. Bklyn., May 2, 1938; d. Marcus Harry and Pertha (Stern) Wartur; m. Steven Wolfson, April 10, 1960; children: Ellen Paula, Roger Samuel. BA, Barnard Coll., 1959; JD, U. Conn., 1976. Bar: Conn. 1976, U.S. Dist. Ct. Conn. 1977. Assoc. Lieberman & Segaloff, New Haven, 1976-80; ptnr. Lieberman, Segaloff & Wolfson, New Haven, 1980-87, Susman, Duffy & Segaloff, P.C., New Haven, 1987—. Bd. dirs. Legal Assistance Assn. of New Haven, 1983—. Mem. Conn. Bar Assn. (ho. of dels. 1983-87, counsel of pres. 1983-84, bd. govs. 1983-87, sec. 1987—), New Haven County Bar Assn. (exec. bd. 1978—, pres. 1983-84). Family and matrimonial, Real property, General practice. Home: 571 Muirfield Ln New Haven CT 06515 Office: Susman Duffy & Segaloff PC 234 Church St New Haven CT 06510

WOLFSON, WILLIAM STEVEN, lawyer; b. Bronx, N.Y., Dec. 6, 1951; s. Irving and Harriet (Levine) W.; m. Barbara L Libensperger, Aug. 19, 1979. B.A. in English Lit., Temple U., 1973; J.D., Del. Law Sch., 1976. Bar: N.J. 1976, U.S. Dist. Ct. N.J. 1976, U.S. Ct. Appeals (3rd cir.) 1979, U.S. Tax Ct. 1981, U.S. Supreme Ct. 1986. Assoc., John E. Weinhofer, Flemington, N.J., 1976-78; sole practice, Flemington, 1978-81; ptnr. Wolfson & Knee, Flemington, 1981—; mem. N.J. Supreme Ct. Com. on County Dist. Ct. Practice, 1980-82; adj. faculty real estate law Somerset Community Coll. Mem. environ. commn. Raritan Twp. Environ. Commn., 1976-79; mem. exec. com. Hunterdac County Reps.; bd. dirs. Hunterdon County Legal Services, Flemington, 1978-83; mem. Hunterdon Central High Sch. Bd. Edn. Mem. Hunterdon County Bar Assn. (legis. chmn. 1979-81), Assn. Trial Lawyers Am., N.J. State Bar (governing council Young Lawyers div. 1981-83), N.J. Trial Lawyers Assn. Republican. Lodge: Flemington Lions (past pres.), Elks. Bankruptcy, Personal injury, Real property. Home: 12 Hackberry Pl Sun Ridge Flemington NJ 08822 Office: Wolfson & Knee 79 Main St Flemington NJ 08822

WOLGEL, HAROLD HORACE, lawyer; b. N.Y.C., Apr. 17, 1920; s. Abraham and Clara (Sumner) W.; m. Betty Goldman, Aug. 28, 1951; children: Susan, Barbara, Amy. BSS, City Coll. N.Y., 1940; postgrad., Harvard U., 1940-41; JD, Columbia U., 1943. Bar: N.Y. 1943, U.S. Supreme Ct. 1948, U.S. Ct. Internat. Trade 1982. Ptnr. Gottesman, Wolgel, Smith & Secunda, P.C., N.Y.C., 1968—. Mem. Nassau County Commn. Human Rights, 1970-74. Served with U.S. Army, 1943-45, ETO. Mem. ABA, N.Y. State Bar Assn., Am. Arbitration Assn. (nat. panel), N.Y. County Lawyers Assn., Union Internationale des Advocats, Internat. Assn. Ins. Counsel. Democrat. Jewish. Federal civil litigation, Insurance. Office: Gottesman Wolgel Smith & Secunda PC 29 John St New York NY 10038

WOLHAR, ROBERT CHARLES, JR., lawyer; b. Wilmington, Del., Mar. 20, 1948; s. Robert Charles Sr. and Helen Ann (Kwiatkowski) W.; m. Bonnie Hayden, Aug. 11, 1979; 1 child, Robert Charles III. BA, U. Del., 1970; JD cum laude, Detroit Coll. Law, 1973; LLM in Urban Affairs, U. Mo., 1974. Bar: Mo. 1974, U.S. Dist. Ct. (we. dist.) Mo. 1974, Del. 1974, U.S. Dist. Ct. Del. 1974, U.S. Supreme Ct. 1979. Assoc. Paul R. Reed, Georgetown, Del., 1974-76; sole practice Georgetown, 1976-77; ptnr. Wolhar & Moore, Georgetown, 1977-84; ptnr., pres. Wolhar & Assocs., Georgetown, 1984—; instr. law Del Tech. and Community Coll., Georgetown, 1984—. Dem. committeeman, Lewes, Del., 1972—; parliamentarian Sussex County (Del.) Dem. Exec. Com., Georgetown, 1984; asst. parliamentarian Del. State Dem. Conv., Dover, 1984; legal counsel Miss Del. Pageant, Rehoboth, 1977-78, pres. 1979—. Recipient Presdl. Award of Honor, Georgetown Jaycees, 1977; John Gage B. fellow, 1974; Mich. Consol. Gas. Co. scholar, 1970-71. Mem. ABA, Del. Bar Assn., Assn. Trial Lawyers Am., Del. Trial Lawyers Assn., Comml. Law League Am., Sussex County Bar Assn., Del. Jaycees (legal counsel 1974-79, 81-82, key man award 1976-77, 79-81), Rehoboth Jaycees (pres. 1974). Roman Catholic. State civil litigation, Consumer commercial, Personal injury. Home: 4 Elm Ln Lewes DE 19958 Office: 107 S Race St PO Box 364 Georgetown DE 19947

WOLIN, DEBRA RUTH, lawyer; b. Bklyn., Mar. 7, 1947; d. Milton B. and Harriet (Mollick) W. BA, U. Chgo., 1967; JD, Bklyn. Law Sch., 1979. Bar: N.Y. 1980, N.J. 1980, U.S. Dist. Ct. (ea. and so. dists.) N.Y. 1980, U.S. Dist. Ct. N.J. 1980, U.S. Ct. Appeals (3d cir.) 1986. Law asst. N.Y. County Supreme Ct., N.Y.C., 1979-81; staff atty. U.S. Dist. Ct. (so. dist.) N.Y., N.Y.C., 1981-85; assoc. Altieri, Kushner, Miuccio & Frind, P.C., N.Y.C., 1986—; bd. dirs. Animal Legal Defense Fund, N.Y.C., 1982—. Avocations: music, art. Federal civil litigation, State civil litigation, Labor. Office: Altieri Kushner et al 60 E 42nd St New York City NY 10165

WOLK, ALAN MURRAY, lawyer, labor arbitrator; b. Cleve., Mar. 17, 1932; s. Samuel Louis and Jean (Mintz) W.; m. Phyllis Grossberg, Dec. 1, 1957; children—Martin, Jeff, Scott. B.B.A., Cleve. State Coll., 1953; J.D., Ohio State U., 1955; postgrad. Case Western Res. Sch. Law, 1959-62; postgrad. student Ohio State Bar Assn. Coll., 1983-84, 86-87. Bar: Ohio 1955, U.S. Supreme Ct., 1965. Asst. atty. gen. State of Ohio, 1958-62, 70-81; acting judge Mcpl. Ct., Shaker Heights, Ohio, 1969-77; dir. of law City of University Heights, Ohio, 1980—; seminar chmn., program chmn. Cuyahoga County Law Dirs., Cleve., 1981—, labor panel mem. Am. Arbitration Assn., Cleve., 1974—, Fed. Mediation and Conciliation Service, Washington, 1979—; mem. panel Ohio State Employment Relations Bd., 1985—. del. 8th Jud. Conf., Ohio. Editor mag. Cuyahoga County Bar Bull., 1958-63. Contbr. articles to profl. jours. Pres. University Heights Democratic Club, Ohio, 1968-74; jud. scanning com. Citizens League Cleve., 1977; bd. dirs. Temple Emanu El, University Heights, 1982-84; trustee Handgun Fedn. Ohio, 1985—. Fellow Cleve. Acad. Trial Lawyers; mem. Cuyahoga County Bar Assn. (sec. 1963-70, pres. 1984-85, exec. dir. 1963-70) (award of Special Merit 1970), ABA, Ohio Assn. Civil Trial Attys., Ohio State Bar Assn. (ho. of dels. 1974—), Ohio Jud. Conf. of 8th Jud. Dist., Tau Epsilon Rho (chancellor, 1963). Lodges: Masons (master 1974-75), B'nai B'rith (fin. sec. 1958-63). Office: 1525 Leader Bldg Cleveland OH 44114

WOLK, STUART RODNEY, lawyer, educator, author; b. N.Y.C., May 15, 1938; s. Charles and Cressie (Bresky) W.; m. Priscilla Wahl, Feb. 3, 1968; 1 dau., Melissa Cressie. B.A., Queens Coll., 1958; M.A., New Sch. Social Research, 1960; J.D., Bklyn. Law Sch., 1961; Ph.D., St. Andrews Coll. (Eng.), 1964, D.H.L., 1973. Bar: N.Y. 1961, D.C. 1961, U.S. Supreme Ct. 1964, N.J. 1975, U.S. dist. ct. (ea. and so. dists.) N.Y., U.S. dist. ct. N.J., U.S. dist. ct. D.C., U.S. Tax Ct., U.S. Ct. Mil. Appeals, U.S. Claims Ct., U.S. Ct. Appeals (D.C. cir.), U.S. Ct. Appeals (2d and 5th cirs.), Conn. 1984. Asst. staff judge adv. for procurement law USAF, 1961-65; asst. div. counsel Litton Systems, Inc. div. Litton Industries, Inc., New Rochelle, N.Y., 1965-66; contract counsel Kollsman Instrument Corp., Syosset, N.Y., 1966-67; assoc. gen. counsel, dir. govt. contracts Bulova Watch Co., N.Y.C., 1967-69; sr. ptnr. Wolk Neuman & Bakshi, and predecessors, Washington, N.Y.C., Hartford, Conn., Trenton and Montville, N.J., 1969—, Wolk, Neuman & Maziarz; adj. prof. mgmt. and law Roth Grad. Sch., Bus., LIU, academic dir. exec. degree program; prof. Hartford Grad. Ctr. Sch. Mgmt. Served to col. JAGC, USAFR, 1958-85; res. designee to dir. Sec. USAF Personnel Council. Alvin-Johnson Prize scholar, 1958-61; Bancroft-Whitney scholar, 1961. Mem. N.J. Bar Assn., N.Y. State Bar Assn., D.C. Bar Assn., Conn. Bar Assn., Houston Bar Assn., Res. Officers Assn. (bd. govs.). Nat. Council Fin. Edn. (bd. govs.), Soc. Fin. Analysts (bd. govs.). Contbg. author: Your Book of Financial Planning; author: Legal Aspects of Computer Use; contbr. numerous articles to legal jours. Administrative and regulatory, General corporate, Labor. Office: One Craig Ct Montville NJ 07045 Office: 4801 Massachusetts Ave Washington DC 20037 also: 30 E 40th St New York NY 10016 Office: 275 Windsor St Hartford CT 06120

WOLKE, MILTON SPENCER, JR., lawyer; b. Chgo., June 28, 1939; s. Milton Spencer and Ruth Marie (McKenna) W.; m. Loretta Cecilia Primeau, July 16, 1966; children: James, Joanne. BA, Cornell Coll., Mt. Vernon, Iowa, 1961; JD, U. Chgo., 1964. Bar: Ill. 1964, U.S. Dist. Ct. (no. dist.) Ill. 1964, Ind. 1974, Pa. 1978. Asst. gen. counsel Kemper Ins. Group, Long Grove, Ill., 1964-73, Assocs. Ins. Group, South Bend, Ind., 1973-75; gen. counsel United Equitable Ins. Group, Skokie, Ill., 1975-78; sr. counsel CIGNA Corp., Phila., 1978—. Bankruptcy, Insurance, Financial. Home: 29 Candy Tuft Levittown PA 19056 Office: CIGNA Corp 1600 Arch St Philadelphia PA 19103

WOLKIN, PAUL ALEXANDER, lawyer, institute executive; b. Phila., Oct. 14, 1917; s. Alex and Anna (Friedman) W.; stepson Rebecca (Likalter) W.; m. Martha Kessler, June 25, 1944; children: Rachel, Adam. B.A., U. Pa., 1937, M.A., 1938, J.D., 1941. Bar: Pa. 1942, U.S. Supreme Ct. 1947. Law clk. U.S. Ct. Appeals (3d Cir.), Phila., 1942-44; atty. Fgn. Econ. Adminstrn., Washington, 1944-45; asso. gen. counsel French Supply Council, Washington, 1945-46; asst. legal adviser Dept. State, 1946-47; legis. draftsman Phila. Charter Commn., 1948-51; spl. asst. to Phila. Solicitor, 1951; partner firm Wolkin, Sarner & Cooper, Phila., 1951-66; counsel Sarner, Cooper & Stein, Phila., 1966-69, Hudson, Wilf & Kronfeld, Phila., 1971-78, Rawle & Henderson, 1980-81; asst. dir. Am. Law Inst., Phila., 1947-77; exec. v.p. Am. Law Inst., 1977—, sec., 1979—; exec. dir. com. on continuing profl. edn. Am. Law Inst.-ABA, 1963—; sec. permanent editorial bd. Uniform Comml. Code, 1962—; mem. com. specialized personnel Dept. Labor, 1964-69; dir. Public Service Satellite Consortium, 1980-84. Editor: The Practical Lawyer, 1955—; contbr. articles to profl. jours. Pres. Phila. Child Guidance Center, 1966-72. Fellow Am. Bar Found.; mem. Am. Law Inst., Jud. Conf. Third Cir. U.S., ABA (spl. com. on standards and codes 1974-80), Pa. Bar Assn., Phila. Bar Assn., Pa. Bar Inst. (bd. dirs. 1967-75), Order of Coif, Lawyers Club, Scribes (past pres.). General practice, Continuing legal education. Home: 1610 N 72d St Philadelphia PA 19151 Office: Am Law Inst 4025 Chestnut St Philadelphia PA 19104

WOLLAN, EUGENE, lawyer; b. N.Y.C., Nov. 2, 1928; s. Isidor and Mollie (Elterman) W.; m. Jean B. Sack, June 6, 1954 (div. 1974); children—Eric G., Jennifer J.; m. Marjorie Cama, Nov. 25, 1977; stepchildren—Valerie M. Rosenwasser, Jon J. Rosenwasser. B.A. cum laude, Harvard U., 1948, J.D., 1950. Bar: N.Y., 1950, U.S. Dist. Ct. (so. and ea. dists.) N.Y. 1953. U.S. Ct. Appeals (2d cir.) 1955, U.S. Ct. Mil. Appeals 1951, U.S. Supreme Ct. 1960. Assoc. Rein Mound & Cotton, N.Y.C., 1953-62, ptnr., 1963-87, Mound, Cotton & Wollan, 1987—. Mem. Joint Conf. Com. on Ct. Congestion. Served to col. USAR, 1951-81. Mem. Internat. Assn. Ins. Counsel, Defense Research Inst., Internat. Soc. Barristers, Assn. Internationale De Droit Des Assurances, N.Y.C. Bar Assn., N.Y. County Lawyers, Judge Advocates Assn. Clubs: Harvard (N.Y.C.), Met. Opera Guild (N.Y.C.), City Midday Drug and Chem. (N.Y.C.). Insurance, Federal civil litigation, State civil litigation. Home: 200 E 71st St New York NY 10021 Office: Mound Cotton & Wollan 125 Maiden Ln New York NY 10038

WOLLE, CHARLES ROBERT, state supreme court justice; b. Sioux City, Iowa, Oct. 16, 1935; s. William Carl and Vivian (Down) W.; m. Kerstin Birgitta Wennerstrom, June 20, 1961; children: Karl Johan Knut, Erik Vernon, Thomas Dag, Aaron Charles. AB, Harvard U., 1959; JD, Iowa Law Sch., 1961. Bar: Iowa 1961. Assoc. Shull, Marshall & Marks, Sioux City, 1961-67, ptnr., 1968-80; judge U.S. Dist. Ct. Iowa, Sioux City, 1981-83; justice Iowa Supreme Ct., Sioux City, 1983—; faculty Nat. Jud. Coll., Reno, 1983—. Editor Iowa Law Rev., 1960-61. Vice pres. bd. dirs. Sioux City Symphony, 1972-77; sec., bd. dirs. Morningside Coll., Sioux City, 1977-81. Fellow Am. Coll. Trial Lawyers; mem. ABA, Iowa Bar Assn., Sioux City C. of C. (bd. dirs. 1977-78). Methodist. Avocations: sports; music. State civil litigation, Labor, Judicial administration. Home: 2727 Glenwood Dr Des Moines IA 50321 Office: Iowa Supreme Ct Statehouse Des Moines IA 50319

WOLLER, JAMES ALAN, lawyer; b. Adrian, Mich., Dec. 27, 1946; s. Robert Arthur and Florence Emma (Jacob) W.; m. Jill Ann Samis, Aug. 18, 1968 (div. Aug. 1978); 1 child, Emily Erin; m. Elizabeth Julia Frey, May 22, 1982. BA, U. Mich., 1969; JD, Columbia U., 1974. Bar: N.J. 1974, U.S. Dist. Ct. N.J. 1974, U.S. Tax Ct. 1976. Assoc. McCarter & English, Newark, 1974-79; v.p. Pfaltz & Woller, P.A., Summit, N.J., 1979—; bd. dirs. Royal Engring. Co., Trenton, N.J. Editor Columbia U. Human Rights Law Rev., 1973-74. Mem. ABA, N.J. Bar Assn., Union County Bar Assn., Summit Bar Assn. Republican. Methodist. Clubs: Downtown (Summit); Raritan Yacht (Perth Amboy, N.J.). Avocation: sailing. General corporate, Banking, Real property. Home: 207 Springfield Ave Summit NJ 07901 Office: Pfaltz & Woller PA 382 Springfield Ave Summit NJ 07901

WOLLMAN, ROGER LELAND, federal judge; b. Frankfort, S.D., May 29, 1934; s. Edwin and Katherine Wollman; m. Diane Marie Schroeder, June 21, 1959; children: Steven James, John Mark, Thomas Roger. BA, Tabor Coll., Hillsboro, Kans., 1957; JD magna cum laude, U. S.D., 1962; LLM, Harvard U., 1964. Bar: S.D. 1964. Sole practice, Aberdeen, 1964-71; justice S.D. Supreme Ct., 1971-85, chief justice, 1978-82; judge U.S. Ct. Appeals (8th cir.), 1985—; states atty. Brown County, Aberdeen, 1967-71. Served with AUS, 1957-59. Jurisprudence. Office: 212 Federal Bldg Pierre SD 57501

WOLLMAN, STEVEN LANCE, lawyer; b. Boston, June 24, 1953; s. Gabriel and Shirley (Sussman) W.; m. Nora S. Feldman, Nov. 16, 1985. BA, Salem (Mass.) State Coll., 1975; JD, Suffolk U., 1978. Assoc. Law Office of Jerril J. Krowen, Boston, 1979-80; ptnr. Davids & Wollman, Swampscott, Mass., 1980—. Mem. ABA, Mass. Bar Assn., Boston Bar Assn., Salem Bar Assn., Essex Bar Assn. Lodge: Lions (treas. Lynn chpt. 1986—, 2d v.p. 1987—). Consumer commercial, Contracts commercial, Construction. Office: Davids & Wollman 25 Rail Road Ave Suite 6 Swampscott MA 01907

WOLLOCH, RICHARD DAVID, lawyer; b. N.Y.C., July 4, 1953; s. Zygfryd Berthold and Helene (Wander) W.; m. Nora Gail Klion, Mar. 18, 1978; children: Samuel Abraham, Jonathan Bart. BA in Am. Lit., George Washington U., 1975; JD, Fordham U., 1978. Bar: N.Y. 1979. Gen. counsel Sloan's Supermarkets, N.Y.C., 1979-82; atty. real estate Supermarkets Gen. Corp., Woodbridge, N.J., 1982—. Mem. N.Y. State Bar Assn. (real property and probate sect.). Real property. Home: 52 Gaby Ln New Rochelle NY 10804 Office: Supermarket Gen Corp 301 Blair Rd Woodridge NJ 07095

WOLNITZEK, STEPHEN DALE, lawyer; b. Covington, Ky., Mar. 13, 1949; s. Frederick William Jr. and Mary Ruth (Meiners) W.; m. Katherine Anita Bishop, Dec. 15, 1972; children: Marcus Stephen, Justin Bishop. BA, U. Notre Dame, 1970; JD, U. Cin., 1974. Bar: Ky. 1975, U.S. Dist. Ct. (ea. dist.) Ky. 1976, U.S. Supreme Ct. 1978, U.S. Dist. Ct. (we. dist.) Ky. 1981. Dep. sheriff Kenton County, Covington, 1971-75; assoc. Taliaferro & Smith, Covington, 1975-80; ptnr. Taliaferro, Smith, Mann, Wolnitzek & Schachter, Covington, 1980-86; officer Smith, Wolnitzek, Schachter & Rowekamp, Covington, 1986—; bd. dirs. Ky. Def. Counsel Inc., 1984—, Ky. Legal Services Plan Inc., 1986—. Mem. exec. com. Kenton County Boys/Girls Club, 1981—, Ky. Law Enforcement Council, Frankfort, 1984—; councilperson City of Ft. Wright, Ky., 1984-85; pres. No. Ky. Community Ctr., Covington, 1985—. Recipient Roy Taylor award No. Ky. Legal Aid Soc., 1985; named Vol. of Yr., Community Chest United Appeal, Cin., 1986. Fellow Ky. Bar Found.; mem. Ky. Bar Assn. (bd. govs. 1984-86, chmn. ho. of dels. 1985—), Council Sch. Bd. Attys., Notre Dame Club of Cin. Democrat. Roman Catholic. Lodges: Elks, Fraternal Order Police. Avocation: sports. Insurance, Personal injury, State civil litigation. Home: 61 Rivard Dr Fort Wright KY 41011 Office: Smith Wolnitzek Schachter & Rowekamp 502 Greenup St PO Box 352 Covington KY 41012-0352

WOLSON, CRAIG ALAN, lawyer; b. Toledo, Feb. 20, 1949; s. Max A. and Elaine B. (Cohn) W.; m. Janis Nan Braun, July 30, 1972 (div. Mar. 1986); m. Ellen Carol Schulgasser, Oct. 26, 1986. BA, U. Mich., 1971, JD, 1974. Bar: N.Y. 1975, U.S. Dist. Ct. (so. and ea. dists.) N.Y. 1975, U.S. Ct. Appeals (2d cir.) 1975, U.S. Supreme Ct. 1978. Assoc. Shearman & Sterling, N.Y.C., 1974-81; v.p., asst. gen. counsel Thomson McKinnon Securities Inc., N.Y.C., 1981-85; v.p., sec., gen. counsel J.D. Mattus Co., Inc., Greenwich, Conn., 1985—; also bd. dirs. J.D. Mattus Co., Inc., Greenwich; dep. clk. Lucas County Courthouse, Toledo, 1968-69, 71-72. Articles and administrv. editor U. Mich. Law Rev., 1973-74. Mem. ABA, N.Y. State Bar Assn., Assn. of Bar of City of N.Y., Phi Beta Kappa, Phi Eta Sigma, Pi Sigma Alpha. Avocations: reading, playing piano, fine dining, theater. Securities, General corporate. Home: 36 Sutton Place S New York NY 10022 Office: JD Mattus Co Inc 22 Greenwich Plaza Greenwich CT 06830

WOMMACK, JR. GEORGE TOBIN, lawyer; b. Freeport, Tex., July 11, 1945; s. George Tobin and Hester (Guthrie) W.; m. Julia Fay Kluge, June 10, 1967; children: Julia Christina, Monica Faye, George T. III. BBA, U. Tex., 1967, JD, 1969. Bar: Tex. 1969. Assoc. Davis, Stovall & Wommack, Freeport, 1969-71; ptnr. Brown & Wommack, Lake Jackson, Tex., 1971-74; pres., sr. ptnr. Wommack, Denman & Mauro, P.C., Lake Jackson, 1974—; sec., bd. dirs. Houston Bancorp., Inc. 1985—; bd. dirs. First City Bank, Lake Jackson, Associated Builders and Contractors, Lake Jackson, Citizens Nat. Bank, Houston. Sec. bd. dirs. 100 Club of Brazoria County, Tex.; bd. dirs. Crime Stoppers of Brazosport, Lake Jackson, Lake Jackson Hist. Assn. Fellow Tex. Bar Found.; mem. ABA, State Bar Tex., Tex. Assn. Bank Counsel. Methodist. Banking, General corporate, Real property. Home: PO Box 420 Lake Jackson TX 77566 Office: Wommack Denman & Mauro PC PO Drawer 828 Lake Jackson TX 77566

WONG, ALFRED MUN KONG, lawyer; b. Honolulu, Sept. 12, 1930; s. Inn and Mew Kung (Choy) W.; m. Laureen Hong, Nov. 20, 1965; children—Peter Marn On, Julie Li Sharn. Student U. Hawaii, 1948-50; B.S., Marquette U., 1953; J.D., U. Calif., 1964. Bar: Hawaii 1964. With Thomas Lee, C.P.A., 1961-62, firm Scott and Balacco, San Francisco, 1962-64; contract atty. Honolulu Redevel. Agy., 1968-71; mng. dir. Okumura, Takushi, Funaki & Wee, Attys. at Law, A Law Corp., Honolulu, 1964—; adj. prof. U. Hawaii Law Sch., 1980-82; mem. bd. bar examiners State of Hawaii, 1968-79; mem. Hawaii Jud. Selection Commn., 1979-85, chmn., 1983-85. Bd. dirs. Pacific council Girl Scouts U.S.A., 1973-78 (Outstanding Service award 1978); pres. Niu Valley Community Assn., 1975, bd. dirs., 1974, 76, 77. Served to capt. C.E., U.S. Army, 1953-61. Recipient Chicago Tribune medal, 1952, 83. Mem. ABA Hawaii Bar Assn. (dir., chmn. unauthorized practice of law com., nominating com.), Hastings Coll. Law Alumni Assn. (bd. govs., Disting. Service award 1987), Am. Judicature Soc., Friends of U. Hawaii Law Sch. (bd. dirs.), Am. Soc. Engrs. Clubs: Waialae Country (Honolulu), Honolulu (founding dir.), Beverly Hills Country. Real property, Banking, Landlord-tenant. Office: Okumura Takushi Funaki Wee 733 Bishop St Honolulu HI 96813

WONG, DANTON SUNMUN, lawyer, real estate company executive; b. Lihue, Hawaii, Feb. 2, 1957; s. Daniel Wellington and Lucille (Lee) W.; m. Helen Yee, Aug. 10, 1985. AB, Stanford U., 1979; JD, U. Calif., San Francisco, 1982. Bar: Hawaii 1982, U.S. Dist. Ct. Hawaii 1982. Assoc. Case, Kay & Lynch, Honolulu, 1982—; real estate agt. Joan Wong Realtor, Honolulu, 1985—. Mem. Chinatown Adv. Com., Honolulu, 1985—, Hawaiian History Ctr. 200th Anniversary of Chinese in Hawaii, Honolulu, 1985—. Recipient Outstanding Achievement award FAA, 1980. Mem. Hawaii Bar Assn. (fin. services and real property sects.), Honolulu Bd. Realtors, Hawaii C. of C. (land and water use planning commn.), Jaycees. Lutheran. Avocations: tennis, travelling, Chinese physical edn. Banking, Contracts commercial, Real property. Office: Case Kay & Lynch 737 Bishop St 26th Floor Honolulu HI 96813

WONG, HAP YEE, lawyer; b. Canton, Peoples Republic of China, Nov. 29, 1948; came to U.S., 1961; s. Bing Kee and Chun Chu (Ng) W.; m. Juliana Wong. BA, Reed Coll., 1971; JD, U. Oreg., 1976. Bar: Oreg. 1976, U.S. Dist. Ct. Oreg. 1977, U.S. Ct. Appeals (9th cir.) 1977. Sole practice Portland, Oreg., 1976—. Mem. Assn. Trial Lawyers Am., Oreg. Trial Lawyers Assn., Multnomah Bar Assn., Am. Contract Bridge League (life master). Democrat. Avocations: philosophy, religious studies, bridge. Criminal, Personal injury. Office: 510 SW 3d #417 Portland OR 97204

WONG, JACKSON D., lawyer; b. San Francisco, Mar. 17, 1952; s. Thyn G. and Bik N. (Ma) W.; m. Anna Louie, July 11, 1978 (div. Dec. 1982); m. Jenny P. Chan. BS in Polit. Sci. and Speech, San Francisco State U., 1975; JD, Golden Gate U., 1979, postgrad. Bar: Calif. 1980, U.S. Dist. Ct. (no. dist.) Calif. 1980, U.S. Ct. Appeals (9th cir.) 1980. Sole practice San Francisco, 1980—; adj. prof. law New Coll. Calif., 1981—; active San Francisco Neighborhood Legal Assistance Found., 1976-78; rep. Bd. of Immigration Appeals, 1978-80; hearing officer San Francisco Rent Stabilization and Arbitration Bd., 1980-81; lectr. various civic and profl. groups. Bd. dirs. Charity Cultural Services Ctr., 1986—, Immigrant Legal Resource Ctr., 1980—, Nihomachi Legal Outreach Ctr., 1982—, Chinese Am. Dem. Club, 1984—; chmn. bd. Chinatown Resources Devel. Ctr., 1984—. Mem. Asian Am. Bar Assn. (chmn. mem. com. 1982, bd. dirs. 1983-84), Wong Yan Yen Benevolent Assn. (gen. counsel 1986—). Immigration, naturalization, and customs, Contracts commercial. Office: 465 California St Suite 400 San Francisco CA 94104

WONG, JAMES THOMAS, lawyer; b. N.Y.C., Sept. 15, 1955; s. Swee Chee and Dorothy Chuan-Ying (Yang) W.; m. Patricia Uyehara, Aug. 15, 1981; 1 child, Thomas Jon. BA cum laude, U. Pa., 1976; JD, Case Western Res. U., 1979. Bar: Pa. 1979, U.S. Dist. Ct. (ea. dist.) Pa. 1979, Hi. 1982, U.S. Ct. Appeals (9th cir.) 1982. Dep. atty. gen., asst. gen. counsel Commonwealth of Pa., 1980-82; assoc. Law Offices Richard K. Quinn, Honolulu,

1982-85, Libkuman, Ventura, Ayabe & Hughes, Honolulu, 1985—. Bd. dir. Asian Am. Council Greater Phila., 1980-82. Mem. ABA, Pa. Bar Assn., Hi. Bar Assn., Am. Arbitration Assn. Democrat. Episcopalian. Construction, Personal injury, State civil litigation. Home: 1717 Mott-Smith Dr Apt 2602 Honolulu HI 96822 Office: Libkuman Ventura Ayabe & Hughes 737 Bishop St Suite 3000 Honolulu HI 96813

WONG, MICHAEL JUNG-YEN, lawyer; b. Honolulu, Mar. 13, 1950; s. Mun Charn and Mew Choy (Chock) W.; m. Terrina Gail Wong, Sept. 2, 1979; 1 child, Randall Gin. Student U. Hawaii, 1968-70; B.S. in Bus. Adminstrn., U. Calif.-Berkeley, 1972; J.D., U. So. Calif., 1976. Bar: Hawaii 1976, U.S. Dist. Ct. Hawaii 1976. Assoc. John S. Edmunds, Honolulu, 1976-77; sole practice, Honolulu, 1977-82, 82—; assoc. O'Brien & Char, Honolulu, 1982; panelist Hawaii permanency planning conf. Nat. Council Juvenile and Family Ct. Judges, Honolulu, 1982; mediator Neighborhood Justice Ctr. Honolulu, Inc., 1982—; mem. Medical Claim Conciliation Panel, Honolulu, 1982—; arbitrator panel of arbitrators 1st Jud. Cir. State of Hawaii, 1986—. Contbr. articles to profl. jours. NEH grantee, 1980. Mem. ABA (Young Lawyers div. child adv. and protection com. 1984—, state chairperson 1986, presenter/panelist Nat. Pub. Service Conf. 1983, 85, 86, Sole Practitioners 1987), Hawaii State Bar Assn. (bd. dirs. 1986—, dir. Young Lawyers div. 1986—, treas. 1984, v.p. 1985, pres. 1986). Juvenile Ad Hoc Com. Family Ct. (chmn. 1981—), Nat. Assn. Counsel for Children, Assn. Trial Lawyers Am., Hawaii Inst. Continuing Legal Edn. (dir. 1985—, panelist and faculty Guardian Ad Litem Tng. Program, 1983, 86). Family and matrimonial, Juvenile, Personal injury. Office: 1500 Pacific Tower 1001 Bishop St Honolulu HI 96813

WONG, PATRICIA UYEHARA, lawyer; b. Dec. 1, 1956; d. Thomas T. and Eiko (Haraguchi) Uyehara; m. James Thomas Wong, Aug. 15, 1981; 1 child, Thomas Jon Uyehara. Student, U. Hawaii, 1974-76; BA, Yale U., 1978; JD, U. Pa., 1981. Bar: Hawaii 1981, U.S. Dist. Ct. (ea. dist.) Pa. 1981, Pa. 1982, U.S. Dist. Ct. Hawaii 1982. Law clk. to judge Phila. Common Pleas Ct., 1981-82; adminstrv. law clk. to chief justice Hawaii Supreme Ct., Honolulu, 1982-83; assoc. Cades, Schutte, Fleming & Wright, Honolulu, 1983—. Mem. ABA, Hawaii Bar Assn., Pa. Bar Assn., Am. Inn of Cts., Hawaii Women Lawyers Assn. State civil litigation, Federal civil litigation. Office: Cades Schutte Fleming & Wright 1000 Bishop St Honolulu HI 96813

WONG, REUBEN SUN FAI, lawyer; b. Honolulu, Mar. 12, 1936; s. Lin and Ella Mew Quon (Ching) W.; m. Vera Hui, Dec. 4, 1966; children: Delwyn, Irwyn. BSCE, U. Hawaii, 1958; JD, U. Ill., 1964. Bar: Hawaii 1964, U.S. Dist. Ct. Hawaii 1964, U.S. Ct. Appeals (9th cir.) 1967, U.S. Supreme Ct. 1974. Law clk. Supreme Ct. of Hawaii, Honolulu, 1964-65; dep. corp. counsel City and County of Honolulu, 1965-67; adminstrv. asst. Hawaii Ho. of Reps., Honolulu, 1967; ptnr. Chuck & Fujiyama, Honolulu, 1967-76; sole practice Honolulu, 1976—; lectr. U. Hawaii, 1967-70; legal advisor Hoo Cho Sch., Honolulu. Vice chairperson Legislature's Adv. Study Commn. on Water Resources, Honolulu, 1982-85. Served to capt. USAF, 1959-62. Mem. ABA, Am. Judicature Soc., Assn. Trial Lawyers Am., Am. Arbitration Assn. (mem. panel of arbitrators), Hawaii C. of C. (bd. dirs. 1976-80, v.p. 1977-78), Chinese C. of C.(Honolulu chpt.), Phi Alpha Delta. Lodge: Aloha Temple. Real property, State civil litigation, Banking. Home: 15 Homelani Pl Honolulu HI 96817 Office: 1001 Bishop St Suite 1630 Pacific Tower Honolulu HI 96813

WONG, WAYSON WAI SUN, lawyer; b. Honolulu, Sept. 16, 1949; s. Victor Buck Choy and Mildred Bow Jun (Lai) W.; m. Pamela Jill Santos, Oct. 25, 1969; children: Kimberley, Kelly, Kathleen. BS in Civil Engring., U. Hawaii, 1973, JD, 1976. Bar: Hawaii 1976, U.S. Dist. Ct. Hawaii 1976, U.S. Ct. Appeals (9th cir.) 1978. Law clk. to presiding chief judge Hawaii Supreme Ct., Honolulu, 1976-77; assoc., dir. Lee, Henderson, Chipchase & Wong and predecessor firm Rice, Lee & Wong, Honolulu, 1977—. Served to lt. col., Hawaii NG, 1968—. Mem. ABA, Hawaii Bar Assn., Assn. Trial Lawyers Am. Democrat. Federal civil litigation, Insurance, Personal injury. Office: Lee Henderson Chipchase & Wong 345 Queen St Suite 700 Honolulu HI 96813

WOO, VERNON YING-TSAI, lawyer, judge; b. Honolulu, Aug. 7, 1942; s. William Shu-Bin and Hilda (Kamaura) W.; m. Arlene Gay Ischar, Feb. 14, 1971; children—Christopher, Lia Gay. B.A., U. Hawaii, 1964, M.A., 1966; J.D., Harvard U., 1969. Bar: Hawaii 1969, U.S. Dist. Ct. Hawaii, 1969. Pres., Woo, Kessner & Duca, Honolulu, 1974—; per diem judge Dist. Ct. (1st dist.) Hawaii, Honolulu, 1979-85. Active Hawaii Commn. on Yr. 2000. Mem. ABA, Hawaii Bar Assn. (dir. 1982—). Episcopalian. Clubs: Wakiki Yacht, Pacific (Honolulu). Civil litigation, Real property, Contracts commercial. Office: 19th Floor Central Pacific Plaza 220 S King St Honolulu HI 96813

WOOCHER, FREDRIC DEAN, lawyer; b. N.Y.C., Jan. 13, 1951; s. Howard and Ruth Liberty (Rosenberg) W.; m. Wendy Harriet Dozoretz, June 19, 1983. BA magna cum laude, Yale U., 1972; PhD in Psychology, Stanford U., 1976, JD, 1978. Bar: Calif. 1980, U.S. Dist. Ct. (cen. dist.) Calif. 1981, U.S. Ct. Appeals (9th cir.) 1981, U.S. Supreme Ct. 1983. Law clk. to chief judge U.S. Ct. Appeals (D.C. cir.), Washington, 1978-79; law clk. to justice William Brennan U.S. Supreme Ct., Washington, 1979-80; spl. asst. to sec. Dept. Defense, Washington, 1980-81; staff atty. Ctr. for Law in Pub. Interest, Los Angeles, 1981—. Exec. bd. dirs. Marin Ednl. Found., San Francisco, 1981. Mem. ABA, Calif. Bar Assn. (chmn. com. on human rights 1982-86, chmn. environment com. 1986-87), Angeles County Bar Assn. (jud. evaluation com.), Law and Soc. Assn., Order of Coif, Phi Beta Kappa. Democrat. Jewish. Civil rights, Environment, State civil litigation. Home: 10532 Ayres Ave Los Angeles CA 90064 Office: Ctr for Law in Pub Interest 10951 W Pico Blvd Los Angeles CA 90064

WOOD, CLEMENT BIDDLE, III, lawyer; b. Washington, Apr. 23, 1952; s. Clement Biddle Wood Jr. and Jane Wood Harvey; m. Sally Sandberg, June 4, 1983. AB magna cum laude, Harvard U., 1974; JD, Northwestern U., 1978. Bar: U.S. Dist. Ct. (no. dist.) Ill. 1978, N.Y. 1979. Law clk. to sr. judge U.S. Ct. Appeals, Chgo., 1978-79; assoc. Cravath, Swaine, Moore, N.Y.C., 1979-81, Morgan, Lewis & Bockius, N.Y.C., 1981-85; assoc. Eaton & Van Winkle, N.Y.C., 1985-86, ptnr., 1986—. Notes and comments editor Northwestern U. Law Review, 1977-78. Mem. ABA, N.Y. State Bar Assn. Avocation: sailing. General corporate, Contracts commercial. Home: 128 Central Park South New York NY 10019 Office: Eaton & Van Winkle 600 Third Ave New York NY 10016

WOOD, DAVID LESLIE, lawyer; b. Ft. Collins, Colo., Sept. 11, 1938; s. Paul E. and Claire B. (SHirley)w.; m. Carol L. Bales, Aug. 31, 1958; children: Jeff, Julie. BA, Colo. U., 1960, LLB, 1962. Bar: Colo. 1962, U.S. Dist. Ct. Colo. 1962, U.S. Ct. Appeals (10th cir.) 1963, U.S. Supreme Ct. 1973. Pres. Wood, Herzog, Osborn & Bloom, P.C., Ft. Collins, 1965—; dist. atty. 8th Jud. Dist., Colo., 1970-73; bd. dirs. First Interstate Bank of Ft. Collins. Pres., chmn. bd. Poudre Valley Hosp. Dist., Ft. Collins, 1976—, Colo. State U. Found., 1983-87. Fellow ABA, Colo. Bar Found.; mem. Colo. Bar Assn. (pres. 1981-82), Ft. Collins C. of C. (pres. 1967), Colo. U. Alumni Bd. State civil litigation, General corporate, Real property. Home: 17 Forest Hills Ln Fort Collins CO 80524 Office: Wood Herzog Osborn & Bloom PO Box 2003 Fort Collins CO 80522

WOOD, DAVID THOMAS, U.S. atty.; b. Deadwood, S.D., Oct. 23, 1941; s. Clarence Arthur and Agnes Anna (Ringlbauer) W.; m. Ellen Faye Perrine, June 17, 1962; children: Amanda Leigh, Jason Thomas. B.A. in English, Walla Walla (Wash.) Coll., 1963; J.D., Willamette U., 1969. Bar: Wash. bar, Guam bar. Tchr. English Columbia Acad., Battleground, Wash., 1963-66; jr. partner firm Jones & Wood, Walla Walla, 1969-70; dep. pros. atty. Spokane County, 1971-74; asst. atty. gen. Guam, 1974-75, dep. pub. defender, 1976, asst. U.S. atty., 1976-77; U.S. atty. 1977—, Commonwealth of No. Mariana Islands, 1978—. Mem. Fed., Guam, Wash. bar assns. Democrat. Office: Office of US Attorney Suite 502-A Pacific Daily News Bldg Martyr and O'Hara Sts Agana GU 96910 *

WOOD, DIANE PAMELA, legal educator; b. Plainfield, N.J., July 4, 1950; d. Kenneth Reed and Lucille (Padmore) Wood; m. Dennis James Hutchinson, Sept. 2, 1978; children—Kathryn, David, Jane. B.A., U. Tex.-Austin, 1971, J.D., 1975. Bar: Tex. 1975, D.C. 1978. Law clk. U.S. Ct. Appeals, 5th Cir., 1975-76, U.S. Supreme Ct., 1976-77; atty.-advisor U.S. Dept. State, Washington, 1977-78; assoc. law firm Covington & Burling, Washington, 1978-80; asst. prof. law Georgetown U. Law Ctr., Washington, 1980-81, U. Chgo., 1981—; spl. cons. antitrust div. internat. guide U.S. Dept. Justice, 1986—. Bd. dirs. Hyde-Park-Kenwood Community Health Ctr., 1983-85. Mem. ABA (sec. antitrust and internat. law, chmn. internat. law sect. BIT com.), Am. Soc. Internat. Law. Democrat. Antitrust, Federal civil litigation, Private international. Office: U Chgo Law Sch 1111 E 60th St Chicago IL 60637

WOOD, HARLINGTON, JR., judge; b. Springfield, Ill., Apr. 17, 1920; s. Harlington and Marie (Green) W. A.B., U. Ill., 1942, J.D., 1948. Bar: Ill. 1948. Practiced in Springfield, 1948-69; U.S. atty. So. Dist. Ill., 1958-61; partner firm Wood & Wood, 1961-69; asso. dep. atty. gen. for U.S. attys. U.S. dept. Justice, 1969-70; asso. dep. atty. gen. Justice Dept., Washington, 1970-72; asst. atty. gen. civil div. Justice Dept., 1972-73; U.S. dist. judge So. Dist. Ill., Springfield, 1973-76; judge U.S. Ct. Appeals for 7th Circuit, 1976—. Address: U S Ct of Appeals 600 E Monroe St PO Box 299 Springfield IL 62705-0299

WOOD, HUGH LEE, lawyer; b. Miami, Fla., Dec. 28, 1928; s. Hayes Stearns and Helene Bernice (Brandt) W.; m. Molly Roberts Norton, May 23, 1953 (div. June 1976); children: Kitty Wood Edison, Hugh, Lynn Wood Hart, Laura Lee. BBA, U. Miami, Coral Gables, Fla., 1953, JD, 1956. Bar: Fla. 1956. Ptnr. Wood and Wood, Miami, 1956-58; asst. states atty. State of Fla., Miami, 1958-62; sr. ptnr. Adams, George and Wood, Miami, 1962-76; sole practice Miami and Coral Gables, 1976-85, Miami, 1985—; bd. dirs., officer Gemstone Security, Miami, 1983—, G. Gordon Liddy & Assocs., 1985—; mem. Law Revision Commn., State of Fla, 1974-76. Served to capt. USNR, 1952-84. Mem. Acad. Trial Lawyers Am., Fla. Trial Lawyers Assn., Navy League U.S. (Miami chpt. pres., nat. dir. 1974-78). Republican. Episcopalian. Club: Univ. (Miami) (pres. 1966). Avocations: golf, fishing. State civil litigation, Military, General practice. Home: 260 Crandon Blvd Box 32-386 Key Biscayne FL 33149

WOOD, JAMES ALLEN, lawyer; b. McMinnville, Tenn., Jan. 14, 1906; s. Ira and Emma (Calhoun) W.; m. Eva Beth Sellers, Dec. 28, 1941; 1 son, Eben Calhoun. A.B., U. Tenn., 1929; LL.B., U. Tex., 1934. Bar: Tex. 1934. Tchr. Bolton High Sch., Alexandria, La., 1929-32; since practiced in Corpus Christi; mem. firm Wood & Burney, 1971—; state dist. judge, Corpus Christi, 1941-43; mem. rules adv. com. Supreme Ct. Tex., 1949-86. Contbr. articles to profl. jours. Bd. dirs. Nueces River Authority, pres., 1981. Served to lt. USNR, 1943-45. Fellow Am. Coll. Trial Lawyers; mem. ABA, Tex. Bar Assn., Nueces County Bar Assn. (pres. 1941). General practice. Home: 458 Dolphin St Corpus Christi TX 78411 Office: 1700 First City Tower II Corpus Christi TX 78478

WOOD, JAMES CLARENCE, lawyer; b. Cameron, Mo., Oct. 1, 1923; s. Clarence L. and Florina F. (Crall) W.; m. Mary Bennett, Sept. 17, 1946; children: Jody Lee, Betty Jean, James Bennett, Mary Jo. BS in Civil Engring., U. Ill., Urbana, 1945, LLB, 1948. Bar: Ill. 1949, U.S. Dist. Ct. (no. dist.) Ill. 1950, U.S. Ct. Appeals (7th cir.) 1954, U.S. Supreme Ct. 1966, U.S. Ct. Appeals (Fed. cir.) 1982. Ptnr. Wood, Dalton, Philips, Mason & Rowe, Chgo., 1955—. Mem. Dist. #110 Sch. Bd., Lake County, Ill., 1960-66, pres., 1966. Mem. ABA, Fed. Cir. Bar Assn., 7th Cir. Bar Assn. (pres. 1978-79), Am. Intellectual Property Bar Assn., Chgo. Patent Law Assn. Club: Thorngate Country Club (Deerfield, Ill.) (pres. 1971-72, 84-86). Patent, Trademark and copyright. Office: Wood Dlaton Phillips Mason & Rowe 20 N Wacker Dr Chicago IL 60606

WOOD, JAMES JERRY, lawyer; b. Rockford, Ala., Aug. 13, 1940; s. James Ronald and Ada Love (Shaw) W.; m. Earline Luckie, Aug. 9, 1959; children—James Jerry, William Gregory, Diana Lynn. A.B. Samford U. 1964, J.D. 1969. Bar: Ala. 1969, U.S. Supreme Ct. 1976. Dir. legal affairs Med. Assn. State of Ala., 1969-70; asst. atty. gen. State of Ala., 1970-72; asst. U.S. atty. Middle Dist. Ala., 1972-76; ptnr. Segrest, Pilgrim & Wood, 1976-77; sole practice, 1977-78; pres. Wood & Parnell, P.A., Montgomery, Ala., 1979—; chmn. character and fitness com. Ala. State Bar, 1981-84, 86—. Served to capt. USAR, 1974-79. Mem. ABA, Fed. Bar Assn. (pres. Montgomery chpt. 1974-75), Ala. Bar Assn., Montgomery Bar Assn., Assn. Trial Lawyers Am. Republican. Baptist. Lodge: Montgomery Capital Rotary (pres. 1986-87). Federal civil litigation, State civil litigation, Criminal. Office: 641 S Lawrence St Montgomery AL 36104

WOOD, JOHN BUSEY, lawyer; b. Belleville, Ill., July 6, 1950. BBA, Washburn U., 1973, JD, 1977; MBA, U. Kans., 1975. CPA, Kans.; lic. real estate broker, N.Y.; bar: Kans. 1978, U.S. Dist. Ct. Kans. 1978, U.S. Ct. Appeals (10th cir.) 1978, N.Y. 1979, U.S. Dist. Ct. (so. dist.) N.Y. 1979. Asst. atty. gen. State of Kans., 1977-78; ptnr. Cole & Deitz, N.Y.C., 1984—. Mem. Rep. Nat. Com., Rep. Senatorial Club, Rep. Presdl. Task Force, Bronxville Rep. Club; mem. legal adv. com. Village of Bronxville, 1985—, spl. counsel to bd. zoning appeals, 1984-85, spl. counsel to planning bd., 1985—. Mem. ABA (comml. leasing com. real property probate and trust law sect.), N.Y. State Bar Assn., Assn. of Bar of City of N.Y., Am. Inst. CPAs, Am. Assn. Atty-CPAs, Associated Builders and Owners (bd. legal advisors), Real Estate Bd. N.Y.C. Real property, Construction, Contracts commercial. Office: Cole & Deitz 175 Water St New York NY 10038

WOOD, JOHN MARTIN, lawyer; b. Detroit, Mich., Mar. 29, 1944; s. John Francis and Margaret Kathleen (Lynch) W.; m. Judith Anne Messer; children—Timothy Peter, Meagan Anne. B.A., Boston Coll., 1966; J.D., Cath. U. Am., 1969. Bar: D.C. 1970, U.S. Dist. D.C. 1970, U.S. Ct. Appeals (D.C. cir., 3d cir., 4th cir.), U.S. Supreme Ct. 1973. Trial atty. tax div. Dept. Justice, Washington, 1969-73; assoc. Reed Smith Shaw & McClay, Washington, 1973-80, ptnr., 1980—. Mem. D.C. Bar, ABA, Phi Alpha Delta, Delta Sigma Pi. Club: Barristers (Washington). Federal civil litigation, Administrative and regulatory, Banking. Home: 9490 Oak Falls Ct Great Falls VA 22066

WOOD, JUDSON RAWLINGS, lawyer; b. Washington, May 30, 1934; s. Sumner and Mary (Rawlings) W.; m. Sarah Venable, June 29, 1957; children: Mary Katherine, Judith Lynn. BA, Emory and Henry Coll., Emory, Va., 1956; LLB, U. Md., 1959. Bar: Md. 1959, U.S. Supreme Ct. 1963, U.S. Dist. Ct. Md. 1966. Sole practice Rockville, Md., 1959—; asst. states atty. Montgomery County, Md., 1963-66. Mem. Montgomery County Bar Assn. Democrat. Episcopalian. Lodges: Elks, Moose, Eagles. Criminal, Personal injury, General practice. Office: 932 Hungerford Dr Rockville MD 20850

WOOD, JULIAN EMORY, lawyer; b. LaGrange, Ga., Jan. 27, 1953; s. Thomas Jackson Sr. and Sarah Lucrette (Crenshaw) W.; m. Margaret Crist, Aug. 30, 1975; children: Mary Catherine, Julian Emory Jr., Warren Crenshaw. Student, U. Ga., 1971-72; BA, LaGrange Coll., 1976; JD, Stetson U., 1979. Bar: Fla. 1979, U.S. Dist. Ct. (mid. dist.) Fla. 1980, U.S. Ct. Appeals (11th cir.) 1981. Assoc. Harris, Barrett & Dew, St. Petersburg, Fla., 1979-81, Butler & Burnett, Tampa, Fla., 1981-84; ptnr. Butler Burnett Wood & Freeman, Tampa, Fla., 1985; sole practice law Tampa, 1985—; bd. dirs. St. Petersburg Toy Shop, Inc. Democrat. Methodist. Club: St. Petersburg Yacht. Avocations: golf, basketball, tennis. Insurance, State civil litigation, Personal injury. Home: 3151 Maple St NE Saint Petersburg FL 33704 Office: 600 N Florida Ave Suite 1900 Tampa FL 33602

WOOD, L. LIN, JR., lawyer; b. Raleigh, N.C., Oct. 19, 1952; s. Lucian Lincoln and Josephine (Currin) W.; son, Matthew Carlton; m. Linda Evett McAlister, Feb. 10, 1984; 1 child, Elizabeth Ashley. B.A. cum laude Mercer U., 1974, J.D. cum laude, 1977. Bar: Ga. 1977, U.S. Dist. Ct. (no. and mid. dist.) Ga. 1977, U.S. Ct. Appeals (5th cir.) 1977, U.S. Ct. Appeals (11th cir.) 1981. Assoc. firm Jones, Cork, Miller & Benton, Macon, Ga., 1977-80, Freeman & Hawkins, Atlanta, 1980-83; ptnr. Wood, Moore & Grant, Atlanta, 1983—. Mem. staff Mercer Law Rev., 1975-77. Recipient Am. Jurisprudence award 1976, 77; U.S. Law Week award, 1977. Mem. ABA, Assn. Trial Lawyers Am., State Bar Ga., Atlanta Bar Assn., Lawyers Club Atlanta, Ga. Trial Lawyers Assn. Republican. Methodist. Club: Atlanta City. Personal injury, Insurance, State civil litigation. Home: 595 Windsor Pkwy Atlanta GA 30342 Office: Wood & Grant 620 Carnegie Bldg Atlanta GA 30303

WOOD, LARRY DEAN, lawyer; b. Anchorage, July 29, 1950; s. Sidney J. and Allie E. (Tantilla) W.; m. Ellen M. Madsen, Oct. 15, 1975; children: Matthew, Jeremy, Adam, Suzanne. BA in Polit. Sci., Wash. State U., 1972; JD, Willamette U., 1975. Bar: Wash. 1975, Alaska 1975, U.S. Dist. Ct. Alaska 1975. Law clk. Alaska Superior Ct., Fairbanks, Alaska, 1975-76; asst. pub. defender State of Alaska, Fairbanks, 1976-77, asst. atty. gen., 1977-80, chief asst. atty. gen., 1980-85; chief counsel Alaska R.R. Corp., Anchorage, 1985—. Brook scholar, 1974. Mem. ABA, Alaska Bar Assn., Nat. Assn. Assocs. of R.R. Trial Counsel. Avocations: fishing, hunting, camping. Home: 19640 Montague Loop Eagle River AK 99577

WOOD, LEONARD JAMES, lawyer; b. Camden, N.J., Dec. 21, 1949; s. Leonard and Virginia (Ferraro) W.; m. Catherine Mary Dugan, June 29, 1979; children: Leonard James III, Tara Kathleen. BA, Manhattan Coll., 1972; JD, Rutgers U., 1976. Bar: N.J. 1976, U.S. Ct. Appeals (3d cir.) 1977, U.S. Supreme Ct. 1980. Law clk. to presiding judge Chancery div. Superior Ct. of N.J., Camden, 1976-77; ptnr. Console, Marmero, Li Volsi, Wood, Curcio, Berlin, N.J., 1977—. Mem. ABA (family law sect.), N.J. State Bar Assn. (family law sect.), Camden County Bar Assn., (trustee). Family and matrimonial, Real property, Personal injury. Home: 203 Station Ave Haddon Heights NJ 08035 Office: Console Marmero Li Volsi Wood & Curcio 264 Route 73 Berlin NJ 08009

WOOD, MARY CATHERINE, lawyer; b. Jacksonville, Fla., Apr. 16, 1957; d. Joseph Gladstone and Clarice Annette (Thomas) W. BA, U. Fla., 1978, JD, 1980. Bar: Fla. 1981, U.S. Dist. Ct. (no. and mid. dists.) Fla. 1981, U.S. Dist. Ct. (so. dist.) Fla. 1983, U.S. Ct. Appeals (11th cir.) 1982. Law clk. U.S. Dist. Ct. (mid. dist.) Fla., Jacksonville, 1981-82; assoc. Marks, Gray, Conroy & Gibbs P.A., Jacksonville, 1982-86; sr. house counsel Blue Cross/Blue Shield Fla., Inc., Jacksonville, 1987—. Mem. Hendricks Ave. Bapt. Ch., Jacksonville, 1981—, deacon 1986—; mem. Willing Hands, Inc., Jacksonville, 1985; vol. Legal Aid, Inc., Jacksonville, 1982; bd. dirs. Theatre Jacksonville, Inc., 1987—. Named one of Outstanding Young Women of Am., 1985. Mem. Fed. Bar Assn. (pres. Jacksonville chpt. 1986-87), Jacksonville Bar Assn., Jacksonville Womens Lawyers Assn., Order of Coif. Democrat. Baptist. Avocations: reading, gardening, entertaining, music. Bankruptcy, Federal civil litigation, Banking. Office: Blue Cross/Blue Shield Inc PO Box 1798 Jacksonville FL 32231

WOOD, NICHOLAS JOSEPH, lawyer; b. Milw., Apr. 23, 1951; s. Marvin Henry and Angela (Ranieri) W.; m. Sandra Susan Fordon, Dec. 29, 1977; children: Robert, Wendy, Nicholas II, Cristina. BS, U. Wis., Milw., 1973; JD, Marquette U., 1982; LLM in Taxation, DePaul U., 1985. Bar: Wis. 1982, U.S. Dist. Ct. (we. and ea. dists.) Wis. 1982, Ariz., 1986, U.S. Dist. Ct. Ariz. 1986. Assoc. Greenberg & Assocs., Milw., 1982-85, Beus, Gilbert, Wake & Morrill, Phoenix, 1985—; adj. prof. property law, Marquette U. Law Sch., Milw., 1985. Author: Wisconsin Land Contract, 1985, Wisconsin Marital Property Reform, 1985, Arizona Real Estate Taxation, 1986. St. Thomas More scholar Marquette U., 1980-82, Justice E. Harold Hallows scholar, Marquette U. Law Sch., 1982, Quarles & Brady scholar Marquette U. Law Sch., 1982; recipient Amjur award Marquette U. Law Sch., 1981. Mem. ABA, Wis. Bar Assn., Ariz. Bar Assn. Real property, Landlord-tenant, Corporate taxation. Office: Beus Gilbert Wake & Morrill 3300 N Central Suite 1000 Phoenix AZ 85012

WOOD, RANDAL LEE, legal educator; b. Columbia, S.C., Aug. 25, 1952; s. George Eugene and Sara Belle (Sutley) W.; m. Elizabeth Gayle McAnally, June 20, 1982. BS in Acctg., Jacksonville State U., 1975; JD, Cumberland Sch. Law, 1980. Bar: Ala. 1980, U.S. Dist. Ct. (no. dist.) Ala. 1981. Sole practice Jacksonville, Ala., 1981; ptnr. Wood & Maloney, Jacksonville, 1981-83; faculty Jacksonville State U., 1981—. Mem. Phi Alpha Delta, Pi Kappa Phi. Legal education. Home: PO Box 113 Jacksonville AL 36265 Office: Jacksonville State U N Pelham Rd Jacksonville AL 36265

WOOD, ROBERT WARREN, lawyer; b. Des Moines, July 5, 1955; s. Merle Warren and Cecily Ann (Sherk) W.; m. Beatrice Wood, Aug. 4, 1979; 1 child, Bryce Mercedes. Student, U. Sheffield, Eng., 1975-76; AB, Humboldt State U., 1976; JD, U. Chgo., 1979. Bar: Ariz. 1979, Calif. 1980, U.S. Tax Ct. 1980. Assoc. Jennings, Strouss, Phoenix, 1979-80, McCutchen, Doyle, San Francisco, 1980-82, Broad, Khourie, San Francisco, 1982-85, Steefel, Levitt & Weiss, San Francisco, 1985—; instr. in law U. Calif. San Francisco, 1981-82. Author: Taxation of Corporate Liquidations: A Complete Planning Guide, 1987; mem. editorial bd. Jour. Corporate Taxation, Taxation for Lawyers, Jour. Real Estate Taxation; contbr. articles to profl. jours. Republican. Corporate taxation, Personal income taxation, State and local taxation. Office: Steefel Levitt & Weiss One Embarcadero Ctr 29th Floor San Francisco CA 94111

WOOD, TERI WILFORD, lawyer; b. Ames, Iowa, June 28, 1950; d. Joseph B. and Margaret J. (Anderson) W.; m. John Busey Wood, July 19, 1977; children: Alexander Wilford, Emily Wilford. BA, U. Mo., 1972; JD, Washburn U., 1978; postgrad., NYU Sch. Law. Bar: N.Y. 1979, Kans. 1979, U.S. Dist. Ct. N.Y. 1979, U.S. Dist. Ct. Kans. 1979, U.S. Ct. Appeals (10th cir.) 1979. Assoc. Stroock, Stroock & Lavan, N.Y.C., 1979; adminstrv. judge gen. counsels office EEOC, N.Y.C., 1979-81; counsel Am. Express Co., N.Y.C., 1981—; mem., sec. supervisory com. Bd. Dirs. Am. Express Fed. Credit Union, N.Y.C., 1986—. Chmn. Children's Library of The Reformed Ch., Bronxville, N.Y., 1984—, mem. Christian edn. com., 1983—. Mem. ABA (litigation sect. 1985—, employment and labor law com. 1984—), Assn. of the Bar of the City of N.Y. Republican. Clubs: The Bronxville Women's, Siwanoy Country (Bronxville). Avocations: horseback riding, jumping. Labor, Pension, profit-sharing, and employee benefits. Office: Am Express Co World Fin Ctr New York NY 10285

WOOD, WALTER EDWARDS, lawyer; b. Cleveland, Miss., July 22, 1954; s. Walter Frank and Alice Calmes (Dorroh) W.; m. Charlotte Ann Thayer, Oct. 22, 1983. BA, Belhaven Coll., 1976; JD, Miss. Coll., 1981. Bar: Miss. 1981. Staff atty. Miss. State Hwy. Dept., Jackson, 1981-83; sole practice Ridgeland, Miss., 1983—. Mem. Miss. Trial Lawyers Assn. Mem. Evangelical Orthodox Ch. Avocation: triathalon. Office: 855 Pear Orchard Rd Orleans Sq Suite 402 Ridgeland MS 39157

WOOD, WELDON SANFORD, lawyer; b. Boise, Idaho, June 7, 1938; s. Weldon Asbury and Ida Mae (Sanford) W.; m. Ruth Irene Dickey, Dec. 15, 1973; children: Dianne Lynn, Laura Ann. Student U. Idaho, Moscow, 1956-59; BA, N.W. Nazarene Coll., Nampa, Idaho, 1960; JD, Willamette U., Salem, Oreg., 1963. Bar: Calif. 1964, Idaho 1964, U.S. Dist. Ct. Idaho 1964, U.S. Dist. Ct. (no. dist.) Calif. 1964, U.S. Ct. Appeals (9th cir.) 1964, U.S. Supreme Ct. Law clk. Idaho Supreme Ct., 1963-64; asst. atty. gen. State of Idaho, 1964-66; judge Boise Mcpl. Ct., 1966-67; assoc. McClennahan & Greenfield, Boise, 1967-68; ptnr. Robinson & Wood, Inc., San Jose, Calif., 1968—; lectr. Calif. Continuing Edn. of Bar, 1979-84; instr. Acad. Appellate and Trial Practice, Hastings Coll. of Law, 1983. Mem. Internat. Assn. Def. Counsel, Am. Bd. Trial Advs., Assn. Def. Counsel No. Calif. (dir. 1978-81), Def. REsearch Inst. (chmn. northern Calif.). Club: San Jose Athletic, Commonwealth Calif. State civil litigation, Federal civil litigation, Insurance. Office: 227 N 1st St Suite 300 San Jose CA 95113

WOOD, WENDY ANN, lawyer; b. Columbus, Ohio, Sept. 20, 1954; s. Richard Clark and Betty Lee (Culp) W. AA, Stephens Coll., 1974; BA, Ohio Wesleyan U., Delaware, 1976; JD, Ohio No. U., 1981. Bar: Ohio 1981, U.S. Dist. Ct. (no. dist.) Ohio 1982, U.S. Supreme Ct. 1984. Asst. prosecutor Ottawa County, Ohio, 1981-82; sole practice Port Clinton, 1982—. Bd. dirs. Children's Outreach, Sandusky, Ohio, 1982-83. Mem. ABA, Ohio Bar Assn., Ottawa Bar Assn. (pres. 1984). Republican. Methodist. Club: Port Clinton Jr. Women's (northwest dist. pres. 1986—). Avocations: golf, boating, reading, needlepoint. Criminal, Family and matrimonial, Probate. Office: PO Box 118 Port Clinton OH 43452

WOOD, WILLIAM JEROME, lawyer; b. Indpls., Feb. 14, 1928; s. Joseph Gilmore and Anne Cecilia (Morris) W.; m. Joann Janet Jones, Jan. 23, 1954; children: Steven, Matthew, Kathleen, Michael, Joseph, James, Julie,

David. Student, Butler U., 1945-46; A.B. with honors, Ind. U., 1950, J.D. with distinction, 1952. Bar: Ind. bar 1952. Mem. firm Wood, Tuohy, Gleason, Mercer & Herrin (and predecessor), Indpls., 1952—; dir. Grain Dealers Mut. Ins. Co., Indpls.; gen. counsel Ind. Realtors Assn., Ind. Cath. Conf., Ind. Assn. Osteo. Physicians and Surgeons; city atty., Indpls., part-time, 1959-60; instr. Ind. U. Sch. Law, part-time, 1960-62. Mem. Ind. Corp. Survey Commn., 1963—, chmn., 1977—; mem. Ind. Corp. Law Study Commn., 1985-86; Past bd. dirs. Alcoholic Rehab. Center, Indpls., Indpls. Lawyers' Commn., Community Service Council Indpls., Indpls. Bar Found. Served with AUS, 1946-48. Recipient Brotherhood award Ind. region NCCJ, 1973. Mem. ABA, Ind. Bar Assn. (award 1968, sec. 1977-78), Indpls. Bar Assn. (pres. 1972-73), St. Thomas More Legal Soc. (pres. 1970). Democrat. Roman Catholic. Clubs: Indianapolis Literary (pres. 1973-74), K.C, Indianapolis Athletic. Insurance, General corporate, Probate. Home: 3619 E 75th Pl Indianapolis IN 46240 Office: 1930 Indiana Tower 1 Indiana Sq Indianapolis IN 46204

WOOD, WILLIAM LAURENCE, JR., lawyer; b. Cleve., Dec. 4, 1940; s. William Laurence and Bernice Silverine (Williams) W.; m. Patricia Mixon, July 14, 1965; children: Robin, Melissa. BA, Brown U., 1962; LLB, Yale U., 1965. Bar: Tex. 1965, U.S. Dist. Ct. (so. dist.) Tex. 1966, U.S. Ct. Appeals (5th cir.) 1966, N.Y. 1969. Assoc. Mandell & Wright, Houston, 1965-68; atty. Pfizer, Inc., N.Y.C., 1971-74, The Internat. Nickel Co., N.Y.C., 1970-71, Union Carbide Corp., N.Y.C., 1971-74; gen. counsel Comptroller City of N.Y., 1974-79; chief edn. bur. Office of N.Y. State Atty. Gen., N.Y.C., 1979-80; exec. dir. N.Y. State office Profl. Discipline, N.Y.C., 1981-85; ptnr. Wood & Scher, N.Y.C., 1985—; mem. N.Y. State Task Force on Pharmacy Practice, Albany, 1983-84, Nat. Clearinghouse Licensure, Enforcement and Regulation, Lexington, Ky. 1981—; chmn. adv. com. on State Credentialing of Health Personnel, Lexington, 1984—. Contbg. editor jour. Discipline, Chgo., 1982—; contbr. articles to profl. jours. Mem. bd. edn. Union Free Sch. dist. 13, Greenburgh, N.Y., 1975-80; mem. counsel Black Dems. Westchester County, White Plains, N.Y., 1978; co-founder, chmn. Alliance of Minority Bus. Orgns., N.Y.C., 1980-83; counsel Hudson Valley Minority Regional Congress, White Plains, 1982-84. Recipient Black Achievers in Industry award Harlem YMCA, N.Y.C., 1974. Mem. N.Y. State Bar Assn., Tex. Bar Assn., Black Lawyers Westchester County, Retired Detectives N.Y.C. (award 1984). Mem. African Methodist Episcopal Ch. Administrative and regulatory. Home: 39 Sunset Dr Croton on Hudson NY 10520 Office: Wood & Scher One Chase Rd Scarsdale NY 10583

WOOD, WILLIAM MCBRAYER, lawyer; b. Greenville, S.C., Jan. 27, 1942; s. Oliver Gillan and Grace (McBrayer) W.; m. Nancy Cooper, Feb. 17, 1973; children: Margaret, Walter, Lewis. BS in Acctg., U. S.C., 1964, JD cum laude, 1972; LLM in Estate Planning (scholar), U. Miami, 1980. Bar: S.C. 1972, Fla. 1979, D.C. 1973, U.S. Tax Ct. 1972, U.S. Ct. Claims 1972, U.S. Supreme Ct. 1977. Intern ct. of claims sect., tax div. U.S. Dept. Justice, 1971; law clk. to chief judge U.S. Ct. Claims, Washington, 1972-74; ptnr. firm Edwards Wood, Duggan & Reese, Greer and Greenville, 1974-78; asst. prof. law Cumberland Law Sch., Samford U., Birmingham, Ala., 1978-79; faculty Nat. Inst. Trial Advocacy, N.E. Regional Inst., Hofstra U., 1979, 83-85, teaching team 5th intensive trial techniques course, 1983; ptnr. firm Shutts & Bowen, Miami, 1980-85; sole practice, Miami, 1985—. Contbg. editor: The Lawyers PC; Fla. editor: Drafting Wills and Trust Agreements; substantive com. editor ABA: The Tax Lawyers, Income Taxation of Trusts and Estates, 1983-85, Estate and Gift Taxation, 1986—; ann. report editor The Tax Lawyer, ABA sect. on taxation, 1985, 86, 87. Mem. Pres. Piedmont Heritage Fund., Inc. 1975-78. Served with USAF, 1965-69, Vietnam. Decorated Air Force Commendation medal; recipient Am. Jurisprudence award in real propery and tax I, 1971; winner Grand prize So. Living Mag. travel photo contest, 1969. Mem. ABA, S.C. Bar Assn., Fla. Bar Assn., D.C. Bar Assn., Greer C. of C. (pres. 1977, Outstanding leadership award 1976), Greater Greenville C. of C. (dir. 1977), Order Wig and Robe, Estate Planing Council South Fla., Omicron Delta Kappa. Episcopalian. Club: Bankers. Lodge: Masons, Rotary. Estate planning, Estate taxation, Probate. Office: One Biscayne Tower Suite 1616 Miami FL 33131

WOOD, WILLIAM PHILLER, lawyer; b. Bryn Mawr, Pa., Oct. 3, 1927; s. Clement Biddle and Emily (Philler) W.; m. Maud Isabel Atherton, Dec. 30, 1950 (dec. 1976); children: William P., Maude H., Louisa B.; m. 2d Sara Elizabeth Wadsworth, Mar. 19, 1977; stepchildren: Jeremy B. Grace Eric W. Grace. A.B., Harvard U., 1949, J.D., 1955. Bar: Pa. 1956. Assoc. firm Morgan, Lewis & Bockius, Phila., 1955-64; ptnr. Morgan, Lewis & Bockius, 1964—; dir. McArdle Desco Corp., New Castle, Del., Church & Dwight Co. Inc., Princeton, N.J. Trustee Grundy Found., Bristol, Pa., 1980—, Louis L. Stott Found., Phila., 1969—; pres. Phila. Mus. of Art, 1976-80, chmn. exec. com., 1980—, v.p., 1972-76, treas., 1968-72; trustee Fairmount Park Art Assn., 1972—, v.p., 1985—; trustee Bryn Mawr Hosp., 1962-76, Phila. Lyric Opera Co., 1960-70; treas. Phila. Art Alliance, 1960-66; pres. La Napoule Art Found. of Henry Clews Meml., La Napoule, France, 1984-86; chmn. 1986—. Served to 1st lt. U.S. Army, 1950-52. Mem. ABA, Phila. Bar Assn., Pa. Bar Assn. Clubs: Phila., Union League, Knickerbocker, Manchester Yacht. Probate, Estate taxation, Estate planning. Home: Woodbine Farm 457 E London Grove Rd West Grove PA 19390 Office: 2000 One Logan Sq Philadelphia PA 19103

WOODARD, BILLIE ELAYNE COLOMBARO, lawyer; b. Bklyn., May 29, 1945; d. Joseph and Nelle Colombaro; m. Charles B. Woodard, Aug. 28, 1976. BA in Pschology, William & Mary Coll. of Law, 1967; cert. in drama, Am. Acad. Dramatic Arts, 1970; M, Med. Coll. Va., 1976; JD, Loyola U., New Orleans, 1981. Bar: La. 1981. Cooradinator St. Luke's Episcopal Hosp., Houston, 1972-78; sole practice 1981—; instr. bus. law McNeese State U., Lake Charles, La., 1981—. Producer, broadcaster Sta. KPLC TV, 1981—. Mem. ABA, La. Bar Assn., Southwest La. Bar Assn. (ethics and grievance com. 1984), Nat. Assn. Criminal Def. Lawyers, Assn. Women Attys., Assn. Trial Lawyers Am., La. Trial Lawyers Assn. Avocations: teaching, tennis, painting, ballet, outdoor activities. Family and matrimonial, Personal injury, Criminal. Office: 212 S Ryan Lake Charles LA 70601

WOODARD, DUANE, attorney general of Colorado; b. Kansas City, Mo., Jan. 12, 1938; s. Duane and Maxine (Reed) W.; m. Thelma Hanser, Apr. 11, 1964; children—Elizabeth, Mary. B.A., U. Wyo., 1963; J.D., U. Okla., 1967. Bar: Okla. 1967, Colo. 1968, U.S. Dist. Ct. Colo. 1968, U.S. Supreme Ct. 1972, U.S. Ct. Appeals (10th cir.) 1986. Practice law Fort Collins, Colo., 1967—, dep. dist. atty., 1970-72; mem. Colo. State Senate Denver, 1977-80; pub. utility commr. State of Colo., 1980-82, atty. gen., 1982—. Mem. Fort Collins Planning and Zoning Commn., 1974-76. Lodge: Rotary. Criminal. Home: 1749 Grape St Denver CO 80220 Office: Office of Colo Atty Gen 1525 Sherman St Denver CO 80203

WOODARD, HAROLD RAYMOND, patent lawyer; b. Orient, Iowa, Mar. 13, 1911; s. Abram Sylvanus and Grace Lenora (Brown) W.; children: Walter J., Turner J., Laurel C. B.S., Harvard U., 1933, LL.B., 1936. Bar: Ind. 1936. Since practiced in Indpls.; mem. firm Woodard, Weikart, Emhardt & Naughton.; Adj. prof. patent law Ind. U. Sch. Law, Indpls. Served as lt. USNR, 1942-46. Fellow, Am. Coll. Trial Lawyers; mem. ABA, Ind. 7th Circuit Bar Assn. (past pres.), Am. Patent Law Assn., Lawyers Assn. Indpls. (past pres.). Methodist. Clubs: Columbia (past pres.), Woodstock (past pres.), University (past pres.). Patent, Legal education. Office: One Indiana Sq Suite 2600 Indianapolis IN 46204

WOODARD, LINDA STRITE, lawyer; b. East Orange, N.J., Feb. 3, 1952; d. Norman George and Anna Mae (Holscher) Strite; children: Christina Michelle Veillon, Rachel Lyn Veillon. AA, Thomas Nelson Community Coll., 1975; BA, Coll. William and Mary, 1976; postgraduate, Loyola U., New Orleans, 1977-78; JD, U. Cin., 1980. Bar: Ohio 1981, U.S. Ct. Mil. Appeals 1981. Commd. 2d lt. USAF, 1976, advanced through grades to maj., 1987; asst. staff judge adv. USAF, Travis AFB, Calif., 1981-82, area def. counsel, 1982-84; chief mil. justice USAF, Wright-Patterson AFB, Ohio, 1984-86; dep. staff judge adv. USAF, Randolph AFB, Tex., 1986—. Charter mem. Huffman Prairie League, Dayton, Ohio, 1985—; bd. dirs. Greene County Domestic Violence Project, Dayton, 1985—. Recipient Nat. Honor Cert. Valley Forge Freedoms Found., 1981, Am. Jurisprudence award, 1978, Urban Morgan Inst. Internat. Human Rights fellow, 1980. Mem. ABA, Ohio Bar Assn., Assn. Trial Lawyers Am. Avocation: classical ballet. Military, Criminal, Federal civil litigation. Home: 3521 Wimbledon Cibolo TX 78108 Office: USAF 12FTW/JA Randolph AFB TX 78150

WOODBRIDGE, RICHARD CARVETH, patent lawyer; b. Niagara Falls, N.Y., Nov. 15, 1943; s. Richard G. and Marie Josephine (Carveth) W.; m. Karen L. Moore, Dec. 3, 1971; children—Jennifer, Richard, Janie. B.S.E.E., Princeton U., 1965; J.D., George Washington U., 1971. Bar: Va. 1971, D.C. 1972, N.J. 1974. Project engr. Proctor & Gamble Co., Cin., 1965-67; patent examiner U.S. Patent Office, Washington, 1968-72; assoc. Baker & McKenzie, Washington, 1972-73; ptnr. Behr & Woodbridge, Princeton, N.J., 1973-77; sole practice, Princeton, 1977-80; sr. ptnr. Mathews, Woodbridge, Goebel, Pugh & Collins, Princeton and Morristown, N.J., 1980—; lectr. in field; also pub. TV appearances. Mem. Princeton Borough Council, 1977-79, 80-82, 83-85, 86—, pres., 1983, 84, 85; pres. Republican Assn. Princeton, 1982. Mem. N.J. Bar Assn., Va. Bar Assn., D.C. Bar Assn., Am. Patent Law Assn., N.J. Patent Law Assn., IEEE, Washington Soc. Engrs. Republican. Clubs: Nassau, Pretty Brook Tennis. Contbr. articles to profl. jours.; patentee in field. Patent, Trademark and copyright, General corporate. Home: 56 William St Princeton NJ 08540 Office: 100 Thanet Circle Suite 306 Princeton NJ 08542-3662

WOODBURY, MARIE SPENCER, lawyer; b. Washington, Aug. 3, 1951; d. Richard Aloysius Jr. and Helen Theresa (O'Conor) Spencer; m. David P. Woodbury, Aug. 10, 1974 (div. Apr. 1985); children: Brendan Spencer, Christopher Padfield. BS in Fgn. Studies, Georgetown U., 1973; JD, Kans. U., 1979. Bar: Kans. 1979, U.S. Dist. Ct. Kans. 1979, Mo. 1981. Assoc. Payne & Jones, Olathe, Kans., 1979-81; assoc. Shook, Hardy & Bacon, Kansas City, Mo., 1981-85, ptnr., 1986—. Mem. ABA, Mo. Bar Assn., Kans. Bar Assn., Def. Research Inst., Order of Coif. Personal injury. Office: Shook Hardy & Bacon 1101 Walnut Kansas City MO 64106

WOODERSON, JAMES MICHAEL, lawyer, educator; b. Jasper, Tex., Oct. 10, 1944; s. Robert Clyde and Mary Virginia (Ashley) W.; m. Charlotte Loving, Nov. 23, 1968; children—Robert Clyde, Jennifer Kate. B.A., U. Southwestern La., 1967, M.A., 1985; A.A., Ins. Inst. Am., 1972; J.D., La. State U., 1975. Bar: La. 1975, U.S. Dist. Ct. (we. dist.) La. 1977, U.S. Dist. Ct. (ea. dist.) La. 1979. Claims rep. Aetna Life & Casualty Co., New Orleans, 1968-72; claims adjuster Pat Brown Claims Service, Baton Rouge, La., also spl. dep. East Baton Rouge (La) Parish Sheriff's Office, part-time 1972-75; sole practice, Lafayette, La., 1975—; asst. city atty. Lafayette, 1979-81; atty. Lafayette Parish Sch. Bd., 1981—. Scoutmaster Evangeline Area council Boy Scouts Am., 1979-82; candidate Lafayette Parish Police Jury, 1979, Lafayette Parish Sch. Bd., 1980. Served with USMCR, 1962-77, 85—. Mem. ABA, La. Bar Assn., Lafayette Parish Bar Assn., Nat. Sch. Bd. Assn. Legal Advisers. Republican. Episcopalian. Local government, Insurance, State and local taxation. Office: PO Box 53516 Lafayette LA 70505

WOODHEAD, FRANK WOMACK, lawyer; b. Houston, Sept. 29, 1909; s. Harold and Lillah (Winne) W.; m. Mary Katherine Gelbach; children—Nancy Woodhead McMullen, James G. B.S. in Bus., U. Kans., 1930; J.D., Loyola U., Los Angeles, 1936. Bar: Calif. 1936. Counsel, Pacific Employers Ins. Co., Los Angeles, 1936-61; ptnr. Jarrett, Woodhead & Brandt, Los Angeles, Calif., 1961-81; of counsel John Nouskajian Jr., P.C., South Pasadena, Calif., 1981—. Served to comdr. USNR, 1944-46. Mem. Ins. Counsel Assn. (editor Calif. jour.). Republican. Clubs: University (Pasadena); Shriners. State civil litigation, Insurance, Personal injury. Home and office: 1799 Homewood Dr Altadena CA 91001

WOODHOUSE, EDWARD JAMES, JR., lawyer; b. Durham, N.C., June 11, 1953; s. Edward James Sr. and Margaret Eleanor (Kinsman) W.; m. Cynthia Ellen Dodge, Nov. 29, 1980; 1 child, Victoria. AB magna cum laude, Harvard U., 1975; JD, U. Va., 1978. Bar: Va. Assoc. Goldsmith & Anderson, Radford, Va., 1978-79; ptnr. Goldsmith, Anderson & Woodhouse, Radford, 1979-82, Terwilliger & Woodhouse, Pulaski, Va., 1982-84, Terwilliger, Woodhouse & Dodge, Radford and Pulaski, 1984, Woodhouse & Dodge, Radford, 1984—. Pres. Radford Dems., 1986, New River Valley Young Dems., 1986; escheator City or Radford, 1987—. Mem. ABA, Va. Bar Assn., Assn. Trial Lawyers, Va. Trial Lawyers Assn. Episcopalian. Lodge: Rotary (pres.-elect Radford club). Avocations: endurance athletics, writing. General practice, General corporate, Real property. Home: 207 Fairway Dr Radford VA 24141 Office: Woodhouse & Dodge 206 1st St Radford VA 24141

WOODHOUSE, GAY VANDERPOEL, lawyer; b. Torrington, Wyo., Jan. 8, 1950; d. Wayne Gaylord and Sally (Rouse) Vanderpoel; m. Randy Leon Woodhouse, Nov. 26, 1983. B.A. with honors, U. Wyo., 1972. J.D., 1977. Bar: Wyo. 1978, U.S. Dist. Ct. Wyo., U.S. Supreme Ct. Dir. student Legal Services, Laramie, Wyo., 1976-77; assoc. Jones Law Offices, Torrington, Wyo., 1977-78; asst. atty. gen. State of Wyo., Cheyenne, 1978—; chmn. Wyo. Telephone Consumer Panel, Casper, 1982—. Bd. dirs. Pathfinder, Cheyenne, Wyo., 1983—. Republican. Unitarian. Administrative and regulatory, Consumer commercial, Securities. Home: 13432 Stewart Rd Cheyenne WY 82009 Office: Atty Gen's Office 123 Capitol Bldg Cheyenne WY 82002

WOODHOUSE, THOMAS EDWIN, lawyer; b. Cedar Rapids, Iowa, Apr. 30, 1940; s. Keith Wallace and Elinor Julia (Cherny) W.; m. Kiyoko Fujie, May 29, 1965; children—Miya, Keith, Leighton. A.B. cum laude, Amherst Coll., 1962; J.D., Harvard U., 1965. Bar: N.Y. 1966, U.S. Supreme Ct. 1969, Calif. 1975. Assoc. Chadbourne, Parke, Whiteside & Wolff, N.Y.C., 1965-68; atty./adviser AID, Washington, 1968-69; counsel Pvt. Investment Co. for Asia S.A., Tokyo, 1969-72; ptnr. Woodhouse Lee & Davis, Singapore, 1972-74; assoc. Graham & James, San Francisco, 1974-75; asst. gen. counsel Natomas Co., San Francisco, 1975-81; mem. Lasky, Haas, Cohler & Munter, San Francisco, 1982—; part-time instr. U. Singapore Law Faculty, 1972-74. chmn. Police Rev. Com. of Berkeley (Calif.), 1980-84; mem. Berkeley Police Res., 1986—; bd. dirs. Friends Assn. of Services for Elderly, 1979-84; clk. fin. com. Am. Friends Service Com. of No. Calif., 1979-83; pres. Zyzzyva Inc., lit. quar., 1985-87 . Served with U.S. Army, 1958. Mem. ABA, Calif. Bar Assn. Democrat. Quaker. Clubs: Harvard (N.Y.C.); University (San Francisco); Tanglin, Cricket (Singapore); Book of California; Roxburghe. General corporate, Private international, Securities. Home: 1800 San Antonio Berkeley CA 94707 Office: 505 Sansome St San Francisco CA 94111

WOODLEY, JOHN PAUL, lawyer; b. Shreveport, La., July 27, 1926; s. John Earnest and Katherine (Kelly) W.; m. Hazel Eugenia (Iles) May 5, 1951; children—John Paul, Anita, Joseph, Thomas, David, Cecilia, Keith. J.D., La. State U., 1948. Bar: La. 1948, U.S. Dist. Ct. (we. dist.) La. 1950, U.S. Ct. Appeals (5th Cir.) 1958. Sole practice, Shreveport, 1948—. Served with USAAF, 1944-45. Mem. La. Bar Assn., Shrevport Bar Assn., Phi Delta Phi. Republican. Roman Catholic. Clubs: Kiwanis, Petroleum of Shreveport. General practice. Office: 1019 Slattery Bldg Shreveport LA 71101

WOODLEY, JOHN PAUL, JR., lawyer; b. Shreveport, La., Sept. 28, 1953; s. John Paul and Hazel Eugenia (Iles) W.; m. Priscilla Anne Ingersoll, June 6, 1981; 1 child, Elizabeth Ingersoll. BA, Washington & Lee U., 1974, JD, 1977. Bar: Va. 1977, U.S. Ct. Appeals (4th cir.) 1978, U.S. Dist. Ct. (ea. dist.) Va. 1979, U.S. Ct. Mil. Appeals 1979, U.S. Supreme Ct. 1982, U.S. Ct. Appeals (5th cir.) 1984, U.S. Ct. Appeals (11th and fed. cirs.) 1985. Law clk. to judge U.S. Dist., Richmond, Va., 1977-79; sole practice Richmond, 1985-86; ptnr. Woodley & Simon, Richmond, 1986—. Ward chmn. Richmond Rep. Com., 1985. Served to capt. JAGC, U.S. Army, 1979-85. Mem. ABA, Va. Bar Assn., Richmond Bar Assn., Assn. Trial Lawyers Am., Phi Beta Kappa, Assn. Va. Hearing Officers, Va. Trial Lawyers Assn. Roman Catholic. Avocation: skiing. Federal civil litigation, Labor, Military. Home: 21 North Blvd Richmond VA 23220 Office: 1 N Fifth St Suite 301 Richmond VA 23219

WOODLOCK, DOUGLAS PRESTON, fed. judge; b. Hartford, Conn., Feb. 27, 1947; s. Preston and Kathryn (Ropp) W.; m. Patricia Mathilde Powers, Aug. 30, 1969; children—Pamela, Benjamin. B.A., Yale U., 1969; J.D., Georgetown U., 1975. Bar: Mass. 1975. Reporter Chgo. Sun-Times, 1969-73; staff mem. SEC, Washington, 1973-75; law clk. to Judge F.J. Murray, U.S. Dist. Ct. Mass., Boston, 1975-76; assoc. Goodwin, Procter & Hoar, Boston, 1976-79, 83-84, ptnr., 1984-86; asst. U.S. atty., Boston, 1979-83; judge U.S. Dist. Ct., Boston, 1986—; instr. Harvard U. Law Sch., 1981, 82. Contbr. articles to profl. jours. Articles editor Georgetown Law Jour., 1973-75. Chmn. Commonwealth of Mass. Com. for Pub. Counsel Services, 1984-86; chmn. Town of Hamilton Bd. Appeals, 1978-79. Recipient Dir.'s award U.S. Dept. Justice, 1982. Mem. ABA, Mass. Bar Assn., Boston Bar Assn., Am. Law Inst., Am. Judicature Soc. Judicial administration. Office: J W McCormack POCH Boston MA 02109

WOODROW, RANDALL MARK, lawyer; b. Anniston, Ala., June 17, 1956; s. Herbert Milisam and Rose (Marshall) W.; m. Carolyn Ann Jackson, Jan. 7, 1977; children: Amanda Lauren, Emily Claire, Taylor Jackson. BS in Polit. Sci., Jacksonville (Ala.) State U., 1978; JD, Samford U., 1981. Bar: Ala. 1981. Law clk. to presiding judge U.S. Dist. Ct. (no. dist.) Ala., 1981-82; ptnr. Merrill, Porch, Doster & Dillon P.A., Anniston, Ala., 1983—; asst. dist. atty. 7th Jud. Cir., Anniston, 1983; spl. asst. atty. gen. State of Ala., Anniston, 1984—; adj. prof. Jacksonville State U., Ala., 1985—. Chmn. crusade Calhoun County Cancer Soc., Anniston, 1983; adminstrv. bd. dirs. 1st United Meth. Ch., Anniston, 1984—; pres. Boys Clubs of Anniston, Inc., 1985. Mem. ABA, Ala. Bar Assn., Calhoun County Bar Assn., Calhoun County C. of C., Greater Anniston Bus. and Profl. Assn. Lodges: Kiwanis (bd. dirs. 1983-84), Rotary. Federal civil litigation, State civil litigation, General corporate. Home: 621 Crestview Rd Anniston AL 36201 Office: Merrill Porch Doster & Dillon PA South Trust Bank Suite 500 Anniston AL 36202

WOODRUFF, CHARLES NORMAN, lawyer; b. Mason City, Wash., Sept. 10, 1941; s. Norman C. and Catherine L. (Snow) W.; m. Patricia M. Masson, Dec. 27, 1964; children—Michael, Megan, Charles. B.A., U. Colo., 1964, J.D., 1967. Bar: Colo. 1967. Law clk. U.S. Dist. Ct. Colo., 1967-68; atty. appellate sect., land and natural resources div. U.S. Dept. Justice, Washington, 1968-70; legis. asst. to U.S. Senator Peter H. Dominick, Washington, 1970-72; assoc. minority counsel U.S. Senate Com. Labor and Pub. Welfare, 1972-73; prin. Moses, Wittemyer, Harrison and Woodruff, P.C., Boulder, Colo., 1974—; adj. prof. of water resources law, Univ. Colo. Law Sch., 1986. Recipient cert. of appreciation Rocky Mountain Mineral Law Found., 1976, Colo. Div. Wildlife, 1982. Mem. ABA, Colo. Bar Assn., Boulder County Bar Assn., Rocky Mountain Mineral Law Found. Republican. Presbyterian. Clubs: Trout Unlimited (v.p. and dir. chpt. 1979-82), Boulder. Water rights, Environment, Real property.

WOODRUM, CLIFTON A., III, lawyer, state legislator; b. Washington, July 23, 1938; s. Clifton A. Jr. and Margaret (Lanier) W.; m. Emily Abbitt, Aug. 10, 1963; children—Robert, Meredith, Anne. A.B., U. N.C., 1961; LL.B., U. Va., 1964. Bar: Va. 1964, U.S. Dist. Ct. (we. dist.) Va. 1964, U.S. Ct. Appeals (4th cir.) 1968, U.S. Supreme Ct. 1970. Assoc. Dodson, Pence & Coulter, Roanoke, Va., 1964-68; ptnr. Dodson, Pence, Viar, Young & Woodrum, Roanoke, 1968—; mem. Va. Ho. of Dels., 1980—. Chmn. 6th Dist. Democratic Com., Va., 1972-76; mem. State Water Commn., 1981—; State Crime Commn., 1982—; chmn. Med. Malpractice Study, Va., 1984-85. Mem. ABA, Assn. Trial Lawyers Am., Trial Lawyers Assn., Roanoke Bar Assn. Episcopalian. State civil litigation, Federal civil litigation, General practice. Home: 2641 Cornwallis Ave Roanoke VA 24014 Office: Dodson Pence Viar Young & Woodrum PO Box 1371 Roanoke VA 24007

WOODRUM, MILTON LANIER, lawyer; b. Quantico, Va., July 7, 1942; s. Clifton Alexander and Margaret (Lanier) W.; m. Marged Griffith, May 6, 1966 (div. 1976); children: Milton Lanier Jr., Melissa Griffith; m. Beverly Tretter, Oct. 18, 1980. BS in Commerce, Washington & Lee U., 1965, JD cum laude, 1980; MBA, U. Va., 1969. Bar: Va. 1980, U.S. Dist. Ct. (we. dist.) Va. 1980, U.S. Ct. Appeals (4th cir.) 1981. From trainee to br. mgr. First Nat. Exchange Bank Va., Roanoke, 1965-67; auditor Price, Waterhouse & Co., Washington, 1969-71; dir. internal audit Chesapeake Corp. Va., West Point, 1971-76; assoc. Woodward, Fox, Wooten & Hart, Roanoke, 1980-85; ptnr. Fox, Wooten & Hart, Roanoke, 1985—. Mem. ABA, Va. Bar Assn., Def. Research Inst., Va. Assn. Def. Attys. Club: Shenandoah. Avocations: fly-fishing, hunting. Insurance, Personal injury, Workers' compensation. Office: Fox Wooten & Hart PC PO Box 12247 Roanoke VA 24024

WOODS, CURTIS E(UGENE), lawyer; b. Ft. Leavenworth, Kans., May 29, 1950; s. Cecil Eugene and Velma Marie (Storms) W.; m. Kathleen L. Kopach, June 8, 1985; children: Colin Eric, Alexandra Marie. BA, U. Mo., Kansas City, 1972; JD, Northwestern U., Chgo., 1975. Bar: Ill. 1975, Mo. 1976, U.S. Dist. Ct. (no. dist.) Ill., U.S. Dist. Ct. (we. dist.) Mo., US. Dist. Ct. Kans., U.S. Ct. Appeals (7th, 8th and 10th cirs.). Law clk. U.S. Ct. Appeals (7th cir.), Chgo., 1975-76; assoc. Spencer Fane Britt & Browne, Kansas City, 1976-81; ptnr. Spencer Fane Britt & Browne, Kansas City, Mo., 1982—. Contbr. articles to profl. jours. Recipient William Jennings Bryan award Northwestern U., 1974. Mem. ABA, The Mo. Bar, Kansas City Bar Assn., Order of Coif. Antitrust, Federal civil litigation, Trademark and copyright. Office: Spencer Fane Britt & Browne 1000 Walnut Suite 1000 Kansas City MO 64106-2140

WOODS, GERALD MARION IRWIN, lawyer; b. New Orleans, Dec. 18, 1947; s. Marion and Cecilia Fredericka (Durr) W. BBA, Loyola U., 1971, JD, 1976; postgrad. acctg., tax, U. New Orleans, 1986—. Bar: La. 1976, D.C. 1982, U.S. Dist. Ct. (ea. dist.) La. 1977, U.S. Ct. Appeals (5th cir.) 1978, U.S. Ct. Appeals (11th cir.) 1983, U.S. Supreme Ct. 1982, U.S. Tax Ct. 1982, U.S. Mil. Ct. 1983. Comptroller ARC, New Orleans, 1971-79; assoc., acct. McGovern and Assocs., New Orleans, 1975-78; asst. dist. atty. New Orleans Dist. Atty.'s Office, 1979-80; in-house counsel Dormal Corp., New Orleans, 1982-83, A. Copeland Enterprises, Inc., New Orleans, 1983-85; sole practice New Orleans, 1985—; assoc., asst. adminstr. United Consumers Health Care Assn., New Orleans, 1985-86; atty. Richard Reynolds & Assocs., La., 1987—, Record Data, Inc. subs. TRW, Inc., La., 1987—; vice pres. Alliance Good Gov., Jefferson, La., 1982—; in-house counsel My Favorite Year, Inc., New Orleans, 1983-85. Recipient Silver Key award (2) ABA, 1974-76; named one of Outstanding Young Men of Am. Mem. New Orleans Bar Assn., Fed. Bar Assn., Jefferson Bar Assn., Loyola U. Alumni Assn., Delta Theta Phi (dist. chancellor 1976—), Blue Key (v.p. 1976). Democrat. Roman Catholic. Avocations: hunting, fishing, camping, car ralleys. Real property. Home: 2108 Roosevelt Blvd Kenner LA 70062 Office: 3127 Harvard Ave Suite 101 Metairie LA 70006

WOODS, HENRY, judge; b. Abbeville, Miss., Mar. 17, 1918; s. Joseph Neal and Mary Jett (Wooldridge) W.; m. Kathleen Mary McCaffrey, Jan. 1, 1943; children—Mary Sue, Thomas Henry, Eileen Anne, James Michael. B.A., U. Ark., 1938, J.D. cum laude, 1940. Bar: Ark. bar 1940. Spl. agt. FBI, 1941-46; mem. firm Alston & Woods, Texarkana, Ark., 1946-48; exec. sec. to Gov. Ark., 1949-53; mem. firm McMath, Leatherman & Woods, Little Rock, 1953-80; U.S. dist. judge Eastern Dist. Ark., 1980—; referee in bankruptcy U.S. Dist. Ct., Texarkana, 1947-48; spl. asso. justice Ark. Supreme Ct., 1967-74, chmn. com. model jury instrns., 1973-80; chmn. bd. Center Trial and Appellate Advocacy, Hastings Coll. Law, San Francisco, 1975-76; mem. joint conf. com. Am. Bar Assn.-AMA, 1973-78, Ark. Constl. Revision Study Commn., 1967-68. Author treatise comparative fault.; Contbr. articles to legal jours. Pres. Young Democrats Ark., 1946-48; mem. Gubernatorial Com. Study Death Penalty, 1971-73. Mem. ABA, Ark. Bar Assn. (pres. 1972-73, Outstanding Lawyer award 1975), Pulaski County Bar Assn., Assn. Trial Lawyers Am. (gov. 1965-67), Ark. Trial Lawyers Assn. (pres. 1965-67), Internat. Acad. Trial Lawyers, Internat. Soc. Barristers, Am. Coll. Trial Lawyers, Am. Bd. Trial Advocates, Phi Alpha Delta. Methodist. Jurisprudence. Home: 42 Wingate Dr Little Rock AR 72205 Office: PO Box 3683 Little Rock AR 72203

WOODS, JEFF CHANDLER, lawyer; b. Lewisburg, W.Va., Mar. 28, 1954; s. Frank William and Catherine (Brown) W.; children: Christi, Jennifer. BA in Sociology, W.Va. State Coll., 1975; postgrad., W.Va. Coll. Grad. Studies, 1976; JD, Howard U., 1979. Bar: W.Va. 1979, U.S. Dist. Ct. (so. dist.) W.Va. 1979, U.S. Ct. Appeals (4th cir.) 1980, U.S. Ct. Mil. Appeals, 1982. Law clk. W.Va. Supreme Ct. Appeals, Charleston, 1979-80; prosecutor U.S. Army, Ft. Polk, La., 1980-83; assoc. Jackson, Kelly, Holt & O'Farrell, Charleston, W.Va., 1988—; chmn. workers compensation com. W.Va. State Bar, 1985—. Judge adv. W.Va. N.G., Charleston, 1983-86; bd. dirs. Mattie V. Lee Home, Charleston, 1985—, Charleston Legal Aid Soc. Served to capt. U.S. Army, 1980-83. Mem. ABA, Phi Delta Phi, Alpha Phi Alpha. Democrat. Baptist. Avocation: golf. Workers' compensation, Criminal,

Military. Office: Jackson Kelly Holt & Farrell 1600 Laidley Tower Charleston WV 25322

WOODS, JOSEPH REID, lawyer, arbitrator; b. Milroy, Ind., Oct. 11, 1929; s. John Melvin and Mary Lorenda (Johnston) W.; m. Avis Lorene Woods, June 14, 1958; children—John P., Edward W., Ann L. B.S., Ind. U., 1952, J.D., 1963. Bar: Ind. 1963. Practice law, Indpls., 1963—; ins. claims adjuster State Farm Ins. Co., 1958-62; spl. agt. Office Naval Intelligence, resident agt. in charge, Des Moines, 1954-57. Mem. Bd. Edn. Franklin Twp. Community Sch. Corp., 1970-82, pres., 1972-74, 76, 78, 81; Served as cpl. AUS, 1952-54. Recipient Service award Am. Arbitration Assn., Bd. Edn., 1982. Mem. ABA, Indpls. Bar Assn., Ind. Trial Lawyers Assn. Presbyterian (elder). Family and matrimonial, General practice, Personal injury. Home: 6305 Fairlane Dr Indianapolis IN 46259 Office: 130 E Washington St Suite 800 Indianapolis IN 46204

WOODS, KAY, lawyer; b. Van Wert, Ohio, May 14, 1952; d. Elmer True Woods and Miriam Olive (Wilson) Schwaberow; m. Gregory J. Hankins, June 10, 1973 (div. Dec. 1979); m. Garry B. DeWitt, Oct. 17, 1981; 1 child, Michael True. BS in Edn., Bowling Green State U., 1973; JD, Ohio State U., 1981. Bar: Ohio 1981, U.S. Dist. Ct. (no. dist.) Ohio 1981. Assoc. Jones, Day, Reavis & Pogue, Cleve., 1981-85; litigation atty, LTV Corp., Cleve., 1986—. Mem. ABA, Ohio Bar Assn., Cleve. Bar Assn. Federal civil litigation, State civil litigation. Office: LTV Corp 25 Prospect Ave NW PO Box 6778 Cleveland OH 44101

WOODS, LARRY DAVID, lawyer, educator; b. Martinsburg, WV, Sept. 10, 1944; s. Allen Noel and Loyce L. (Dillingham) W.; m. Jinx S. Woods, Jan. 17, 1981; children—Rachel, Allen, Sarah. B.A., Emory U., 1966; J.D., Northwestern U., 1969. Bar: Tenn. 1969, Ga. 1970. Dir. litigation Atlanta Legal Aid Soc., Inc., 1969-71; assoc. dir. Atlanta Mcpl. Defender Project, 1970; ptnr. Woods & Woods, Nashville, 1971—; assoc. prof. Tenn. State U., 1972-84, prof., 1984—; lectr. Taft Ins., 1974-79, Am. Criminology Soc., 1984; chmn. bd. Southeastern Inst. Paralegal Tng. Nat. bd. editors' Matthew Benders, 1984—. Del., Tenn. Democratic Conv., 1972, 76, 80. Mem. Tenn. Bar Assn. (ho. of dels. 1979-85), Ga. State Bar Assn., ABA, Fed. Bar Assn., Tenn. Assn. Criminal Def. Lawyers (dir. 1975-78). Methodist. Author: (with Fowler) Crime and Investigation, 1967; Compulsory Service and the Alternatives, 1968; The Strategy of Intervention, 1969; Pollution: Problems and Proposals, 1970. General practice, General corporate, Federal civil litigation. Office: 121 17th Ave S Nashville TN 37203

WOODS, RICHARD DALE, lawyer; b. Kansas City, Mo., May 20, 1950; s. Willard Dale and Betty Sue (Duncan) W.; m. Cecelia Ann Thompson, Aug. 11, 1973; children: Duncan Warren, Shannon Cecelia. BA, U. Kans., 1972; JD, U. Mo., 1975. Bar: Mo. 1975, U.S. Dist. Ct. (we. dist.) Mo. 1975. Assoc. Shook, Hardy & Bacon, Kansas City, Mo., 1975-79, ptnr., 1980—; gen. chmn. Estate Planning Symposium, Kansas City, 1985-86. Chmn. fin. com. North Woods Ch., Kansas City, 1986—. Mem. ABA, Mo. Bar Assn., Kansas City Met. Bar Assn., Clay County Bar Assn., Lawyer's Assn. Kansas City (sec., v.p., then pres. Young Lawyer's sect. 1981-84), Kansas City Estate Planning Assn. (bd. dirs. 1985-86), Kansas City Estate Planning Soc. (bd. dirs. 1986—). Democrat. Lodge: KC. Probate, Real property, Estate taxation. Office: Shook Hardy & Bacon 120 W 12th St Suite 600 Kansas City MO 64105

WOODS, ROBERT EDWARD, lawyer; b. Albert Lea, Minn., Mar. 27, 1952; s. William Fabian and Maxine Elizabeth (Schmit) W.; m. Cynthia Anne Pratt, Dec. 26, 1975; children: Laura Marie Woods, Amy Elizabeth Woods. BA, U. Minn., 1974, JD, 1977; MBA, U. Pa., 1983. Bar: Minn. 1977, U.S. Dist. Ct. Minn. 1980, U.S. Ct. Appeals (8th cir.) 1980. Assoc. Moriarty & Janzen, Mpls., 1977-81, Berger & Montague, Phila., 1982-83; assoc. Briggs and Morgan, St. Paul and Mpls., 1983-84, ptnr., 1984—; adj. prof. law William Mitchell Coll. of Law, St. Paul, 1985. Mem. ABA, Minn. State Bar Assn., Hennepin County Bar Assn., Ramsey County Bar Assn. (chmn. corp., banking and bus. law sect. 1985—), Am. Trial Lawyers Assn., Wharton Club of Minn., Phi Beta Kappa. Federal civil litigation, Securities, General corporate. Home: 13646 Hannibal Circle Saint Paul MN 55124 Office: Briggs and Morgan 2200 First National Bank Saint Paul MN 55101

WOODWARD, CHARLES CARROLL M., lawyer, businessman; b. Nice, France, Feb. 21, 1929 (parents Am. citizens); s. Harold Chase and Izetta May (Humphreys) W.; m. Patricia Karin Robinson, Sept. 13, 1952; children—Karin Chase Dalton, Ann Elizabeth Lang. B.S. in Civil Engring., Va. Mil. Inst., 1951; J.D., George Washington U., 1960. Bar: U.S. Ct. Customs and Patent Appeals 1960, U.S. Dist. Ct. D.C. 1960, U.S. Ct. Appeals (D.C. cir.) 1960, U.S. Patent Office 1961, U.S. Supreme Ct. 1965. Examiner U.S. Patent Office, Washington, 1956-61; patent atty. NASA, Huntsville, Ala. and Cape Canaveral, Fla., 1961-63; patent counsel Gen. Dynamics Corp., Ft. Worth, 1963-73, corp. counsel Process Systems Internat., Inc., Tyler, Tex., 1973—, asst. sec., 1974—; asst. sec., counsel Howe-Baker Engrs., Inc., Tyler, 1974—; sec., counsel Process Mgmt. Internat., Tyler, 1976—, White Chem. Internat., Inc., Houston, 1976—, Quest Research & Engring., Inc., Tyler, 1976—, Improtec, Inc., Tyler, 1979—, Constructors Internat., Inc., Tyler, 1974—, Longview Custom Fabricating, Inc., Tex., 1975—, Superior Air Products Co., Sayreville, N.J., 1976—. Mem. planning bd. and zoning commn. City of Benbrook, Tex., 1968-73, mem. bd. equalization, 1970-73; pres. Gen. Dynamics Mgmt. Assn., Ft. Worth, 1971. Served to capt. USMC, 1951-56, Korea. Decorated Purple Heart; recipient award of honor Gen. Dynamics Mgmt. Assn., 1971. Mem. ASCE, Am. Astron. Soc., Fed. Bar Assn., Va. Mil. Inst. Alumni Assn. (pres. North Tex. chpt. 1969-72), DAV (comdr. Huntsville chpt. 1963-64), VFW, Am. Legion, Delta Theta Phi. Republican. Episcopalian. General corporate, Private international, Patent. Home: Route 25 Box 692 Tyler TX 75707 Office: Process Systems Internat Inc 3102 E 5th St Tyler TX 75701

WOODWARD, HALBERT OWEN, judge; b. Coleman, Tex., Apr. 8, 1918; s. Garland A. and Helen (Halbert) W.; m. Dawn Blair, Sept. 28, 1940; children: Halbert Owen, Garland Benton. B.B.A., U. Tex., 1940, LL.B., 1946. Bar: Tex. 1941. Mem. Woodward & Johnson, Coleman, 1949-68; mem. Tex. Hwy. Commn., 1959-68, chmn., 1967-68; judge U.S. Dist. Ct. No. Dist. Tex., 1968—, now chief judge; dir. S.W. State Bank, Brownwood, Tex. Bd. dirs. Overall Meml. Hosp., Coleman. Served with USNR, 1942-45. Mem. Am., Tex. bar assns., Am. Judicature Soc., Beta Theta Pi. Office: C-210 US Courthouse 1205 Texas Ave Lubbock TX 79401 *

WOODWARD, MADISON TRUMAN, JR., lawyer; b. New Orleans, Feb. 15, 1908; s. Madison Truman and Maude W.; m. Elvina Bernard, June 30, 1937 (dec. Sept. 26, 1964); children: Anne Carol Woodward Baker, Elizabeth H. Woodward Ryan, Lucie B. Woodward Cavaroc, Margaret E., Madison Truman III; m. Ethel Dameron, June 24, 1977. LL.B., Tulane U., 1927; postgrad., U. Mich., 1927-28. Bar: La. 1929. Since practiced in New Orleans; asso. firm Milling, Benson, Woodward, Hillyer, Pierson & Miller (and predecessors), 1929-36, mem. firm, 1937—. Author: Louisiana Notarial Manual, 1952, 2d edit., 1962, Supplement, 1973; contbr. articles to legal jours. Trustee Trinity Episcopal Sch., New Orleans, 1965-71; chmn. Victor Bernard Found., 1965—. Fellow Am. Bar Found., Am. Coll. Trial Lawyers, Am. Coll. Probate Counsel; mem. ABA (state del. 1982—, ho. of dels. 1979—), La. Bar Assn. (pres. 1973-74), New Orleans Bar Assn., Am. Law Inst., La. State Law Inst. (council 1957—, v.p. 1969-80, pres. 1980-81, vice chmn. 1982—), Nat. Conf. Bar Presidents (exec. council 1973-75), 5th Circuit Jud. Conf. (del. 1966, lawyers adv. com. 1982-84), Am. Judicature Soc. (dir. 1973-76), La. Bar Found. (chmn. 1980-85), Valencia Inc. (gov. 1960-78, pres. 1963-64), U.S. Supreme Ct. Hist. Soc. (trustee 1985—), New Orleans C. of C., Garden Dist. Assn. (pres. 1964-65), Soc. Colonial Wars in La. (council 1973—, gov. 1983-85), Order St. Lazarus (comdr. so. comandery 1986—), Pi Kappa Phi. Clubs: Pickwick (New Orleans), New Orleans Country (New Orleans), Plimsoll (New Orleans), Stratford (New Orleans), International House (New Orleans); City (Baton Rouge). Federal civil litigation, General practice, Probate. Home: 1234 6th St New Orleans LA 70115 Office: Whitney Bldg New Orleans LA 70130

WOODWARD, MARION KENNETH, lawyer; b. Amarillo, Tex., Apr. 15, 1912; B.A., U. Tex., 1933, LL.B., 1943; M.A., W. Tex. State U., 1940. Bar: Tex. 1942. Sole practice, Amarillo, 1945; staff atty. Phillips Petroleum Co., Amarillo, 1945-46; assoc. prof. law U. Tex., 1946-49, prof., 1950-65, Robert F. Windfohr prof. law, 1965-82; Robert F. Windfohr & Anne Burnet Windfohr prof. emeritus of oil, gas and mineral law, 1982—; Tex. mem. Nat. Conf. Commrs. on Uniform State Laws, 1956-62; mem. legal com. Interstate Oil Compact Commn., 1962-73. Fellow Am. Bar Found.; mem. ABA, Tex. Bar Assn., Travis County Bar Assn., Am. Coll. Probate Counsel (acad. fellow), Order of Coif. Author: (with Huie and Smith) Cases and Materials on Oil and Gas Law, 1972; (with Smith) Probate and Decedent's Estates, 1971; Probate and Administration of Estates, 1980; contbr. articles to legal jours. Oil and gas leasing, Probate. Home: 3408 Shinoak Dr Austin TX 78731 Office: 727 E 26th St Austin TX 78705

WOODWARD, ROLAND CAREY, lawyer; b. Roanoke, Va., Dec. 17, 1926; s. Raymond Wickliffe and Lella Loraine (Huckstep) W.; m. Virginia Hart Tyree, July 8, 1960; children—Roland Carey, Allin Loraine, John Wickliffe. B.S., Wake Forest Coll., 1950; J.D., U. Va., 1956. Bar: Va. 1956, Ga. 1969, U.S. Dist. Ct. D.C. 1969, U.S. Supreme Ct. 1971. Assoc. McGuire Eggleston, Bocock & Woods, Richmond, 1956-60; ptnr. McGuire, Woods & Battle, Richmond, 1960-69, Sutherland, Asbill & Brennan, Atlanta, 1969-70; sole practice, Richmond, 1971-78; mem. Woodward, Fox, Wooten & Hart, P.C., Richmond, 1979-84, Woodward & Lacy, P.C., 1985, Sands, Anderson, Marks & Miller, 1986—; commr. in chancery. Bd. dirs. Buford Acad., Richmond, 1980—. Fellow Am. Coll. Probate Csl.; mem. ABA, Va. Bar Assn., Richmond Bar Assn. (chmn. jr. bar sect. 1960-61), Raven Soc., Phi Beta Kappa, Omicron Delta Kappa. Episcopalian. Clubs: Commonwealth, Bull & Bear (Richmond). Probate, Estate taxation, General corporate. Home: 7 Banbury Rd Richmond VA 23221 Office: 1400 Ross Bldg Richmond VA 23216

WOODWARD, WILLIAM EDWARD, lawyer; b. Port Arthur, Tex., Jan. 13, 1927; s. Fred Wall and Emma Mary (Wolf) W.; m. Hattie Bell Whittington, Aug. 22, 1964; stepchildren: Willie L. Sullivan, Robert Lee Sullivan. Student Balboa Jr. Coll., 1949; BA, La. State U., 1956, JD, 1959. Bar: La. 1961. Assoc. Lean A. Picou, Jr., 1961, Richard H. Kilbourne, 1961-66; sole practice, Clinton, La., 1966-77; pub. defender 20th Jud. Dist., 1973-77, 1st asst. dist. atty., 1977-85. Contbr. poems to anthologies, 1976-82. Co-founder Silliman Inst., Clinton, La., bd. dirs., sec., 1967-74; consul comdr. Woodmen of World Camp 20, Clinton, 1969, sec., 1970-85. Served with U.S. Army, 1948-54. Decorated Companion of Honor Order St. John of Jerusalem Knights Hospitaller; recipient Mr. Woodman award Camp 20 Woodmen of World, 1969, Golden Poet award, 1985-86. Mem. La. Bar Assn., Feliciana Bar Assn., Am. Legion, Am. Coll. Heraldry. Democrat. Criminal, Real property, Probate. Home: 4025 Market St Jackson LA 70748

WOODWARD, WILLIAM JOHN, JR., legal educator, consultant; b. N.Y.C., Apr. 9, 1947; s. William John Sr. and Madeline Marie (Kiechlin) W.; m. Suzanne Mary Vojak, Oct. 22, 1978; 1 child, Molly. BA, U. Pa., 1968; JD, Rutgers U., 1975. Bar: Pa. 1975, U.S. Dist. Ct. (ea. dist.) Pa. 1975, U.S. Ct. Appeals (3d cir.) 1975. Assoc. Dechert, Price & Rhoads, Phila., 1975-1980; asst. prof. law Ind. U., Indpls., 1980-83, assoc. prof. law, 1983-84; assoc. prof. law Temple U. Sch. of Law, Phila., 1984—. Contbr. articles to profl. jours. Served to lt. (j.g.) USN, 1969-72, PTO. Mem. ABA, Phila. Bar Assn., Assn. Trial Lawyers Am., ACLU. Avocations: sailing, furniture making. Bankruptcy, Contracts commercial, Legal education. Office: Temple U Sch of Law 1719 N Broad St Philadelphia PA 19122

WOODWORTH, JAMES NELSON, lawyer; b. Bad Axe, Mich., Sept. 3, 1947; s. Philip and Florence (Russ) W.; m. Lisa B. Bloom, Oct. 19, 1979. BA, Mich. State U., 1973; JD, Thomas M. Cooley Law Sch., 1976. Bar: Mich. 1976, U.S. Dist. Ct. (ea. dist.) Mich. 1976, U.S. Ct. Appeals (6th cir.) 1977. Ptnr. Woodworth & Woodworth, Bad Axe, 1976-79; sr. ptnr. Woodworth & Neeb P.C., Bad Axe, 1979-81; sole practice Bad Axe, 1981—; bd. dirs., sec. Bad Axe Indsl. Devel. Corp., 1981—. Sec., mem. City of Bad Axe Charter Commn., 1979; bd. dirs. Cath. Family Services of Thumb Area, Caro, Mich., 1978—. Fellow Mich. Bar Found.; mem. Mich. Bar Assn. (assembly rep., com. on hearings 1978-84), Huron County Bar Assn. (pres. 1985—), Assn. Trial Lawyers Am., Mich. Trial Lawyers Assn., Am. Agrl. Law Assn., Am. Arbitration Assn., Comml. Law League, Mich. State U. Alumni Club (bd. dirs., treas. 1986—), Phi Alpha Delta. Club: Verona Hills Golf (bd. dirs.) (Bad Axe). Lodge: Elks. General practice, State civil litigation. Office: 125 N Heisterman St Bad Axe MI 48413

WOODY, CLYDE WOODROW, lawyer; b. Princeton, Tex., Oct. 3, 1920; s. James W. and Emma Mae (Heard) W.; m. Paula Fay Mullen, Aug. 23, 1969; children—Todd, Joe. B.S., U. Houston, 1951, J.D., 1951; postgrad. St. Mary's U., San Antonio, 1952, U. Colo., 1953. Bar: Tex. 1952, U.S. Ct. Appeals (5th, 6th and 11th cirs.), U.S. Supreme Ct.; cert. specialist in criminal law and family law Tex. Bd. Legal Specialization. Sole practice Houston, 1952-66; ptnr., then sr. ptnr. Woody & Rosen, Houston, 1966-80; sole practice, Houston, 1980—; city atty. Southside Place, Houston, 1955-57; dir. Unitedbank-Houston, Cen. Bank Holding Co., Miami, Fla.; lectr. Bd. dirs. Mossler Found., 1966-70; sect. chmn. State Bar Tex., 1964-65. Served to capt. U.S. Army, 1941-45, to capt. USAF, 1951-53; PTO, CBI. Mem. Am. Judicature Soc., Nat. Assn. Criminal Def. Lawyers, Tex. Trial Lawyers Assn., Assn. Trial Lawyers Am., ABA, Houston Bar Assn., Tex. Criminal Def. Lawyers Assn., Nat. Transp. Safety Bd. Bar Assn., Phi Delta Phi. Democrat. Methodist. Clubs: University, Texas, (Houston). Contbr. articles to legal jours. Criminal, Family and matrimonial, Federal civil litigation. Home: 731 Brogden Houston TX 77024 Office: 1500 United Bank Plaza 1415 Louisiana Houston TX 77002

WOODY, DONALD EUGENE, lawyer; b. Springfield, Mo., Mar. 10, 1948; s. Raymond D. and Elizabeth Ellen (Bushnell) W.; m. Ann Louise Ruhl, June 5, 1971; children: Marshall Wittmann, Catherine Elizabeth. BA in Polit. Sci. with honors, U. Mo., 1970, JD, 1973. Bar: Mo. 1973, U.S. Dist. Ct. (we. dist.) Mo. 1973, U.S. Ct. Appeals (8th cir.) 1973. Assoc. Neale, Newman & Bradshaw, Springfield, 1973-74; ptnr. Taylor, Stafford & Woody, Springfield, 1974-82, Taylor, Stafford, Woody, Cowherd & Clithero, Springfield, 1983—. Editor U. Mo. Law Rev., 1973. Chmn. county campaign U.S. senator Thomas Eagleton, Springfield, 1980; committeeman Greene County Dem. Party, Springfield, 1984—; cons. Children's Home Mayors commn., Springfield, 1985. Mem. ABA, Greene County Bar Assn. (sec. 1977-80, procedure com. 1986—), Assn. Trial Lawyers Am., Springfield C. of C. (chmn. performing arts com. 1980-84), Order of Coif, Phi Delta Phi. Club: Hickory Hills Country (Springfield). Avocations: fishing, growing roses, golf, running. Federal civil litigation, State civil litigation, Personal injury. Home: 3124 E Seminole Springfield MO 65804 Office: Taylor Stafford Woody Cowherd & Clithero Plaza Towers 10th Fl Springfield MO 65804

WOODY, ROBERT JAMES, lawyer; b. Bartlesville, Okla., Jan. 23, 1944; s. Monte Claud and Vivian Patricia (Fry) W.; m. Nancy Lou Harrington, June 10, 1967; children—Kristin, John, Karen, James. B.A., U. Kans., 1966, J.D., 1969. Bar: Kans. 1969, D.C. 1975. Legis. asst. U.S. Senator James B. Pearson of Kans., Washington, 1969-71; counsel Com. on Commerce, U.S. Senate, Washington, 1971-73; assoc. Breyfogle, Gardner, Martin, Davis & Kreamer, Olathe, Kans., 1973-75; assoc., ptnr. Lane & Mittendorf, Washington, 1975—, mng. ptnr., 1980—; spl. counsel UN, Red Cross, UNESCO; mem.-at-large U.S. Nat. Commn. on UNESCO, 1983—. Counsel permanent orgn. com. Republican Nat. Conv., 1980; vice-chmn., trustee's council, bd. dirs. YMCA of Met. Washington, 1980—; vestryman, sr. warden St. Peter's Episcopal Ch., Arlington, Va., 1980-83. Served to capt. USAR, 1969-76. Recipient George & Agnes Strickland award U. Kans., 1966, Spl. Law Faculty award, 1969; Outstanding Service award YMCA Met. Washington, 1984. Mem. ABA (sect. natural resources), Fed. Energy Bar Assn., D.C. Bar Assn. Republican. Episcopalian. General corporate. Home: 3420 N Albemarle St Arlington VA 22207 Office: Lane & Mittendorf 1750 K St Suite 1200 Washington DC 20006

WOOLDRIDGE, WILLIAM CHARLES, lawyer; b. Miami, Fla., Feb. 24, 1943; s. Clarence Edward and Easter Marguerite (Souders) W.; m. Joyce L. Norton, June 15, 1968; children—William Charles, John Michael. B.A., Harvard U., 1965, LL.B., U. Va., 1969. Bar: Va. 1969. Atty., Norfolk and Western Ry. Co., Roanoke, Va., 1973-82; sr. gen. atty. Norfolk So. Corp., 1982-86, gen. solicitor, 1986—. Treas., v.p. Roanoke Valley Hist. Soc., 1979-82. Served to capt. JAGC, U.S. Army, 1969-73. Mem. ABA, Va. Bar Assn. Republican. General corporate, Administrative and regulatory, Antitrust. Office: Norfolk So Corp 1 Commercial Pl Norfolk VA 23510

WOOLEY, KENNETH VIRGIL, lawyer; b. San Gabriel, Calif., July 20, 1938; s. Virgil Franklin and Isabel Naomi (Cuber) W.; m. Pamela Gaye Patruno, Aug. 19, 1968; children: Christopher, Alison, Priscilla. A.A., Pasadena City Coll., 1964; J.D., Southwestern U., 1969. Bar: Calif. 1969. Sole practice, Alhambra, Calif., 1969—; judge pro tem Alhambra Mcpl. Cts. Past pres. Alhambra Jaycees; bd. dirs. Christian Counseling Assn. Served with USNR, 1956-60. Mem. San Gabriel Valley Bar Assn. (past pres.), San Marino C. of C. (past pres.). Republican. Clubs: San Marino City; Alhambra Exchange (bd. dirs. 1985—). Real property, Family and matrimonial, General practice. Office: 940 E Main St Alhambra CA 91801

WOOLF, JEFFREY DAVID, lawyer; b. Youngstown, Ohio, Mar. 5, 1946; s. Ben R. and Mildred I. (Friedman) W.; m. Mary P. Dollard, Oct. 8, 1983. BA, Yale U., 1968; MA, Boston U., 1969, postgrad., 1969-71, JD, 1974. Bar: Mass. 1974, U.S. Dist. Ct. Mass. 1975, U.S. Ct. Appeals (1st and 9th cirs.) 1976, D.C. 1978, U.S. Ct. Appeals (4th cir.) 1979, U.S. Supreme Ct. 1980. Teaching fellow Boston U., 1968-71; research assoc. Ctr. for Criminal Justice, Boston, 1969-74; assoc. Swartz & Swartz, Boston, 1974-79, Shapiro, Israel & Weiner, Boston, 1979-81; ptnr. Knoll & Woolf, Boston, 1981-83, 1986—; sole practice, Boston, 1983-86; ptnr. Woolf, Keane & Klein, Boston, 1986—; adj. prof. New Eng. Sch. Law, Boston, 1982-83. Author: (with others) Preparation, Negotiation and Trial of a 93A Case, 1982. Recorder White House Conf. on Children and Youth, 1981. Mem. ABA, Mass. Bar Assn., Boston Bar Assn. (chmn. consumer protection sect. 1980-83), Mass. Trial Lawyers Ednl. Found., Inc. (bd. dirs. 1984-86), D.C. Bar Assn., Assn. Trial Lawyers Am., Am. Soc. Law and Medicine, Woburn Sportsmen's Assn. Democrat. Personal injury, Federal civil litigation, State civil litigation. Home: 46-A Dana St Cambridge MA 02138 Office: 55 Union St Boston MA 02108-2409

WOOLF, JOHN PAUL, lawyer; b. Bloomington, Ind., Apr. 21, 1943; s. Frank Edward and Martha Ann (Barrett) W.; m. Mary L. Waller, Aug. 20, 1967; children—Thomas, Matthew, David, Susan. B.S. in Bus., Kans. State U., 1965; J.D., U. Kans., 1968; postgrad. Nat. Coll. Advocacy Suffolk U. Law Sch., 1976. Bar: Kans. 1968, U.S. Ct. Apls. (10th cir.) 1968, U.S. Ct. Apls. (5th cir.) 1977. Ptnr., Martin, Porter, Pringle, Schell & Fair, Wichita, Kans., 1970-82, Martin, Pringle, Oliver, Triplett & Wallace, Wichita, 1982-85, Triplett, Woolf & Garretson, 1985—. Bd. dirs. Big Bros. Sedgwick County, Kans., 1973-77, pres., 1976-77; bd. dirs. Big Bros./Big Sisters of Sedgwick County, 1977—; bd. dirs. Big Bros./Big Sisters of Am., 1978-85, mem. exec. com., 1980-85, pres. Region IX, 1979-83; bd. dirs. Kans. Vietnam Veterans Leadership Program, 1982—. Served to capt. U.S. Army, 1968-70. Decorated Bronze stars (2), Nat. Def. medal, USARV Vietnam medal. Mem. ABA, Kans. Bar Assn., Wichita Bar Assn., Assn. Trial Lawyers Am., Kans. Trial Lawyers Assn. Congregationalist. Federal civil litigation, State civil litigation, Contracts commercial. Office: 151 N Main Suite 800 Wichita KS 67202-1409

WOOLLEY, EDWARD ALEXANDER, lawyer; b. Brookline, Mass., Mar. 15, 1929; s. Paul and Helen (von der Pahlen) W.; m. Nancy Jane Kerr, June 20, 1963; children—Paul, David, Mary Alexandra. A.B., Princeton U., 1951; J.D., U. Pa., 1954; postgrad. U. Bonn (W.Ger.), 1954-55, Free U. Berlin, 1955. Bar: U.S. Dist. Ct. (D.C. dist.) 1955, N.Y. 1957, U.S. Dist. Ct. (so. and ea. dists.) N.Y. 1959, U.S. Ct. Appeals (2d cir.) 1959, U.S. Ct. Appeals (5th cir.) 1970, U.S. Supreme Ct. 1970, U.S. Ct. Appeals (3d cir.) 1981. Assoc. dir. Jud. Adminstrn. Project, U. Pa. Law Sch., 1955-56; assoc. Cleary, Gottlieb, Steen & Hamilton, N.Y.C., 1956-66, Heald, Hobson & Assocs., N.Y.C., 1966-67; assoc. Malcolm A. Hoffmann, N.Y.C., 1967-70, ptnr., 1970-79; of counsel Jones, Hirsch & Bull, N.Y.C., 1981; ptnr. Lawless and Woolley, N.Y.C., 1981-82; sole practice, Bedford, N.Y., 1982—; sec. Inst. Internat. Container Lessors. Elder, Manhattan Christian Reformed Ch., N.Y.C., 1964-66; deacon Stanwich Congl. Ch., Greenwich, Conn., 1970-73; trustee Evangelical Presbyn. Ch., Stamford, Conn., 1975-81; deacon Long Ridge Congl. Ch., Stamford, 1982-85. Mem. ABA, N.Y. State Bar Assn., Assn. Bar City N.Y., Assn. ICC Practitioners. Author articles. Containers, Antitrust, Private international. Home: Rt 1 Box 63 Pound Ridge NY 10576 Office: Bedford Cons Bldg Box 605 Bedford NY 10506

WOOLLS, PAUL, lawyer; b. Bloomington, Ind., Dec. 19, 1954. AB, Wabash Coll., 1975; JD, U. Pitts., 1979. Bar: Pa. 1979, Calif. 1983, U.S. Dist. Ct. (ea., cen. and we.) Pa. 1980, U.S. Dist. Ct. (cen.) 1983, U.S. Dist. Ct. (no., so. and ea.) Calif. 1985, U.S. Ct. Appeals (3d cir.) 1982, U.S. Ct. Appeals (9th cir.) 1985. Law clk. to presiding justice Pa. State Supreme Ct., Erie, Pa., 1979-80; assoc. Pepper, Hamilton & Scheetz, Phila., 1980-83, Buchalter, Newer, Fields, Chsystie & Younger, Los Angeles, 1983—; lectr. Paralegal Inst., Phila., 1981-83, atty. asst. tng. program UCLA, 1984—, Ins. Edn. Assn., 1986—. Mem. ABA, Pa. Bar Assn., Calif. Bar Assn., Phila. Bar Assn., Los Angeles County Bar Assn. Insurance, Reinsurance litigation and arbitration. Office: Buchalter Newer et al 700 S Flower Suite 700 Los Angeles CA 90017-4183

WOOLSTON, V.L., lawyer; b. Syracuse, N.Y., May 10, 1954; s. Vernon Lee Woolston and Elizabeth Mae (Kohler) Milanette; m. Robyn L. Ramsey, Feb. 1, 1985. BA, Amherst Coll., 1976; JD, Duke U., 1979. Bar: Wash. 1979, U.S. Dist. Ct. (we. dist.) Wash. 1979, U.S. Ct. Appeals (9th cir.) 1983, U.S. Supreme Ct. 1985. Assoc. Perkins Coie, Seattle, 1979-85, ptnr., 1985—. Mem. ABA, Wash. Bar Assn. Clubs: Rainier, Wash. Athletic (Seattle). Avocation: squash. Federal civil litigation, Insurance, Products liability litigation. Home: 2518 Crestmont Pl W Seattle WA 98199 Office: Perkins Coie 1900 Washington Bldg Seattle WA 98101

WOOSNAM, RICHARD EDWARD, venture capitalist, lawyer; b. Anderson, Ind., June 27, 1942; s. Richard Wendell and Ruth (Cleveland) W.; m. Susan L. Mangel, Aug. 21, 1965; children: Cynthia S., Elizabeth C. BS, Ind. U., 1964, JD, 1967, MBA, 1968. Bar: Ind. 1967, U.S. Dist. Ct. (so. dist.) Ind. 1967. Instr. bus. law Ind. U., Bloomington, 1966-68; assoc. Ferguson, Ferguson & Lloyd, Bloomington, 1967-68; dep. prosecutor Monroe County (Ind.), Bloomington, 1967-68; tax acct. Price Waterhouse, Phila., 1968-69; v.p., treas. Innovest Group, Inc., Phila., 1969-82, chmn., pres., 1983—, also dir.; guest lectr. Wharton Sch. Bus., U. Pa., Ind. U., Bloomington, 1975—; bd. dirs. Capital Mgmt. Corp., Modern Video Prodns., Inc., Skyworks, Inc., No. Lites Ltd., Visionaire Communications, Inc.; adv. council Nat. Entrepreneurship Found. Mem. ABA, Ind. Bar Assn., World Affairs Council. Republican. Methodist. Club: Union League of Phila. Corporate taxation, Personal income taxation, General corporate. Home: 429 Leopard Rd Berwyn PA 19312 Office: 1700 Market St Suite 1228 Philadelphia PA 19103

WORD, TERRY MULLINS, lawyer; b. Corpus Christi, Tex., Dec. 30, 1943; s. Terrence Stuart and Leila Elba (Mullins) W.; m. Alice G. Hector, Jan. 27, 1971 (div. 1977); children—Morgan Anna, Zachary Hector; m. Mary Ann L. Rios Garcia, May 28, 1983; 1 child, Jettie Laure, 1 stepson, John Jarrett Garcia. B.A. in Econs., Math., U. Tex., 1966, J.D., 1973. Bar: Tex. 1973, N.Mex. 1973, U.S. Dist. Ct. N.Mex. 1973. Ptnr. Stribling, Anderson, Read & Word, Albuquerque, 1973-74; atty. N.Mex. Pub. Defender, Albuquerque, 1974-76; sole practice, Albuquerque, 1976-77; assoc. Richard E. Ransom, P.A., Albuquerque, 1977-83; pres. Terry M. Word, P.C., Albuquerque, 1983—. Workmen's compensation editor The N.Mex. Trial Lawyer, Albuquerque, 1982-84 . Bd. dirs. Big Bros./Big Sisters Albuquerque, 1983—. Served to lt. USN, 1966-70, Vietnam. Mem. Assn. Trial Lawyers Am., N.Mex. Trial Lawyers Assn. (chmn. continuing legal edn. com. 1984-85, treas. 1984-85, bd. dirs. 1984—, pres. elect 1985-86, pres. 1986-87). Democrat. Episcopalian. Personal injury, Workers' compensation, Civil rights. Home: PO Box 1105 Corrales NM 87048 Office: PO Box 25686 Albuquerque NM 87125

WORENKLEIN, JACOB J., lawyer; b. N.Y.C., Oct. 1, 1948; s. Abraham and Cela (Zyskind) W.; m. Marion Knopf, June 27, 1967; children: David, Daniel, Laura. BA, Columbia U., 1969; MBA, JD, NYU, 1973. Bar: N.Y. 1974. Assoc. Milbank, Tweed, Hadley & McCloy, N.Y.C., 1973-81, ptnr., 1982—, also firm exec. com., 1984-86. Contbr. articles to profl. jours. Pres. Old Broadway Synagogue, N.Y.C., 1978—; trustee Fedn. Jewish Philanthropies, N.Y.C., 1984-86; bd. of overseers, USA-Fedn. Jewish Philanthro-

pies, 1987—. Mem. ABA (electricity and utility financing com.), N.Y. State Bar Assn. (sec. action unit toward more effective legislature 1975), Assn. of Bar of City of N.Y., Fed. Energy Bar Assn., Down Town Assn., Phi Beta Kappa. Banking, General corporate, Public utilities. Office: Milbank Tweed Hadley & McCloy 1 Chase Manhattan Plaza New York NY 10005

WORHATCH, S. DAVID, lawyer; b. Pitts., Nov. 19, 1954; m. Paula Marian Plummer, May 26, 1979; children: Mark David, Richard James. BA, Duquesne U., 1976; JD, U. Notre Dame, 1979. Bar: Mich. 1979, U.S. Dist. Ct. (we. dist.) Mich. 1979, U.S. Ct. Appeals (6th cir.) 1980, Ohio 1981, U.S. Dist. Ct. (no. dist.) Ohio 1981, U.S. Dist. Ct. (no. dist.) Calif. 1986. Assoc. Schmidt, Howlett, Van't Hof, Snell & Vana, Grand Rapids, Mich., 1979-80; law clk. to presiding judge U.S. Dist. Ct. (we. dist.) Mich., Grand Rapids, 1980-81; assoc. Calfee, Halter & Griswold, Cleve., 1981-82; corp. atty. Picker Internat. Inc., Cleve., 1982-85, sr. corp. counsel, 1985-86; corp. counsel, div. counsel The B.F. Goodrich Co., Akron, Ohio, 1986—; adj. prof. bus. law Grand Valley State Colls., Grand Rapids, 1980-81. Mem. ABA, Ohio Bar Assn. Democrat. Roman Catholic. General corporate, Federal civil litigation, Contracts commercial. Home: PO Box 2220 Hudson OH 44236 Office: BF Goodrich Co 500 S Main St Akron OH 44311

WORLEY, DONALD ROBERT, lawyer; b. Detroit, Nov. 17, 1938; s. John Kyle and Virginia Alice (Fox) W.; m. Patricia Ann Craven, Dec. 22, 1973. B.A., Yale U., 1960; postgrad. U. Mich., 1960-61; J.D. magna cum laude, U. San Diego, 1970; LL.M., U. of Pacific McGeorge Sch. Law, 1982. Bar: Calif. 1971, U.S. Dist. Ct. (so. dist.) Calif. 1971, U.S. Ct. Appeals (9th cir.) 1982. Assoc. Seltzer Caplan Wilkins and McMahon, San Diego, 1969-72, ptnr., 1972-75; ptnr. McDonald, Hecht, Worley and Solberg, San Diego, 1975-83; ptnr. Hahn & Cazier, San Diego, 1983-86, Worley, Schwartz, Garfield & Rice, 1986—; adj. prof. law Calif. Western Sch. Law, U. San Diego Sch. Law; arbitrator San Diego Mcpl. and Superior Cts.; seminar panelist and moderator; pres. PortaSport Ocean Ventures and San Diego Sailing Ctr., 1977-81. Mem. property dept. adv. bd. City San Diego; mem. art acceptance and loan com. San Diego Mus. Art. Served to lt. USNR, 1962-66. Mem. Internat. Bar Assn., ABA, Calif. Bar Assn., San Diego Bar Assn., World Trade Assn. of San Diego, Internat. Trade Commn. County San Diego. Republican. Author, pub.: Guide to Constitutional Law, 1976. Real property, Private international, State civil litigation. Office: 110 W A St Suite 1365 San Diego CA 92101

WORLEY, L. GLENN, lawyer; b. Louisville, Ky., Dec. 2, 1952; s. Emmett Leo and Ruby Marie (Tuell) W.; m. Barbara Mae Dube, Apr. 5, 1975; children: Katrina, Briana, Mark Dakota. BA, U. Fla., 1975, LLM, 1983; JD, NYU, 1978. Bar: Mich. 1978, Fla. 1980, Tenn. 1983. Assoc. Jaffe, Snider, Raitt, Garrett & Heuer, Detroit, 1978-80; ptnr. Leckrone & Holton, Nashville, 1983—. Bd. dirs. Bill Wilkerson Hearing and Speech Ctr., Nashville, 1985—. Mem. ABA, Tenn. Bar Assn., Mich. Bar Assn., Fla. Bar Assn. Democrat. Club: The City (Nashville). Corporate taxation, Estate planning, Personal income taxation.

WORLEY, ROBERT WILLIAM, JR., lawyer; b. Anderson, Ind., June 13, 1935; s. Robert William and Dorothy Mayhew (Hayler) W.; m. Diana Lynn Matthews, Aug. 22, 1959; children—Nathanael, Hope. B.S. in Chem. Engring., Lehigh U., 1956; LL.B., Harvard U., 1960. Bar: Conn. 1960, Fla. 1977, U.S. Supreme Ct. 1966. Assoc. Cummings & Lockwood, Stamford, Conn., 1960—, now ptnr. Mem. trustees com. on bequests and trusts Lehigh U., 1979—; chmn. Greenwich Arts Council, 1981-82; v.p., bd. dirs. Greenwich Choral Soc., 1962-77, 80, mem., 1960—; bd. dirs. Greenwich Ctr. for Chamber Music, 1981-85, Greenwich Symphony, 1986—; commr. Greenwich Housing Authority, 1972-77; past mem. Republican Town Com. Greenwich; mem. bldg. com. for sr. ctr. Greenwich Bd. Selectmen, 1980-81. Served to capt. JAGC, AUS, 1965. Mem. ABA, Conn. Bar Assn. (exec. com. probate sect. 1980), Fla. Bar Assn., Stamford Bar Assn. (sec.), Greenwich Bar Assn., Palm Beach County Bar Assn., Am. Arbitration Assn. Republican. Christian Scientist. Club: Landmark. Banking, Probate, Contracts commercial. Home: 258 Riverside Ave Riverside CT 06878 Office: 10 Stamford Forum Box 120 Stamford CT 06904

WORONOFF, DAVID SMULYAN, lawyer; b. Balt., June 20, 1937; s. Samuel Murray and Ella Sarah (Smulyan) W.; m. Karen Gail Scholz, Apr. 18, 1978; children—Jamie, Keith, Robin; children by previous marriage—Stefan, Bonnie. B.S. in Elec. Engring., M.I.T., 1959; J.D. (scholar), Boston Coll., 1962; postgrad. Utica Coll., 1965-66, Rutgers U., 1968-69. Bar: Conn. 1962 U.S. Dist. Ct. Conn. 1963, U.S. Patent Office 1965, N.J. 1972, U.S. Dist. Ct. N.J. 1972, R.I. 1979, U.S Dist Ct. R.I. 1979. U.S. Ct. Customs and Patent Appeals 1980, U.S. Ct. Appeals (Fed. cir.) 1981. Mem. patent dept. Western Electric Co., Washington, 1961-62; law clk. Conn. Supreme Ct., 1962-63; sole practice, Bridgeport, Conn., 1972-75; patent atty. Bendix Corp., 1964-66; patent counsel Vitramon, Inc., 1966-68; line, staff mgmt. positions Singer Co., 1968-70, Xerox Corp., 1970-72; exec. v.p. Servco Leasing Corp., N.Y.C., 1972-74; sole practice, Bridgewater, N.J., 1972-77, Ormond Beach, Fla., Windsor, Colo., 1977—; of counsel Wood, Herzog, Osborn & Bloom, Ft. Collins, Colo., 1986—; ptnr. Colo. land devel.; cons. to industry on tech. devel.; lectr., tchr. profl. seminars various schs., univs., and govt. agys. Vol., United Jewish Appeal, 1974-76 M.I.T. Alumni Assn., 1975-78, Am. Cancer Soc., 1978-82; dir. N. Colo. Med. Ctr. Found., Inc.; mem. accountability com. RE-4 Sch. Dist.. Mem. ABA (litigation, patent sects., ethics com. patent sect.) N.J. Bar Assn., R.I. Bar Assn. Editor: Boston Coll. Bus. and Comml. Law Rev., 1961-62. Lodge: Rotary (local officer and dir.). Patent, Trademark and copyright, Unfair Competition.

WORRELL, LEE ANTHONY, lawyer; b. Providence, Nov. 12, 1907; s. Charles Tylden and Atala Lee Worrell; m. Edith Read DeWitt, Oct. 8, 1932; children—Richard DeWitt, Elizabeth Lee, Anne Randall. Student Boston U., 1925-27, LL.B., 1930. Bar: R.I. 1931, U.S. Dist. Ct. R.I. 1932, U.S. Ct. Appeals (1st cir.) 1955, U.S. Supreme Ct. 1955. With Gardner, Moss & Haslam, Providence, 1930-32, Shepard and Worrell, Providence, 1932, Sisson and Fletcher, Providence, 1940, Sisson, Fletcher, Worrell and Hodge, 1941-43, Worrell and Hodge, Providence, 1943-76; sole practitioner, Providence, 1933-40, 76—; officer, dir. various corps. Mem. Providence City Council, 1947-61, minority leader, 1947-61; mem. Providence Bur. Licenses, 1961-65. Served to lt. USN, 1944-46. Fellow Am. Coll. Trial Lawyers; mem. R.I. Bar Assn. (sec. 1939-44, pres. 1966-67). Republican. Episcopalian. Clubs: University (Providence). Lodge: Masons. Probate, Estate taxation, Personal income taxation. Office: 1021 Hospital Trust Bldg Providence RI 02903

WORTHAM, ROBERT JOHN, lawyer; b. Beaumont, Tex., Sept. 8, 1947; s. Albert Glenn and Lauretta (Kujawa) W.; m. Karen Guzardo, Apr. 20, 1985; children: Robert John, Jr., Baylor Glenn. B.S. in Govt., Lamar U., 1971; J.D., Baylor U., 1974. Bar: Tex. 1974. Asst. criminal dist. atty. Jefferson County, Beaumont, Tex., 1974-75; ptnr. Waldman & Smallwood, Beaumont, 1975-80; state dist. judge 60th Dist Ct., Beaumont, 1980-81; U.S. atty ea. dist. Tex. Dept. Justice, Beaumont, 1981—. Bd. dirs. Baylor Law Sch., Waco, Tex., 1979—; sec., treas. Jefferson County Young Lawyers, Beaumont Tex., 1975-76; mem. Atty. Gen's Adv. Subcom. Debt. Collection, 1981—; ofcl. Southwest Football Ofcls., Beaumont, 1976—; trustee Fireman Pension Fund, 1977-82; bd. dirs. Cerebral Palsy Found., 1977—. Named Outstanding Young Lawyer Jefferson County Bar Assn., 1981. Mem. State Bar Tex., Tex. Trial Lawyers. Republican. Episcopalian. Federal civil litigation, Criminal, Personal injury. Home: 1405 Futura Beaumont TX 77706 Office: Dept of Justice 700 North Beaumont TX 77701 *

WORTHINGTON, LEONARD A., lawyer; b. San Francisco, Feb. 4, 1908; s. William Frank and Caroline (Schmelz) W. AB, U. Calif., Berkeley, 1929; JD, U. Calif., San Francisco, 1932. Bar: Calif. 1932. Ptnr. Worthington & Worthington, San Francisco, 1932-38, Worthington, Fields & Worthington, San Francisco, 1938—; atty. div. hwys. State of Calif., 1934; past gen. counsel Apt. Ho. Assn. San Francisco, Surety Underwriters Assn. No. Calif. Pres. Great Western U., 1957-63; past pres., bd. dirs., Young Voters League San Francisco, 1936; past bd. dirs., San Francisco Dem. Club, 1938-48, Dem. Confederation Calif., 1938-49; past pres. St. Francis Heights Convalescent Hosp., St. Francis Pavilion Hosp.; past pres., bd. dirs. AUM Found.; past bd. dirs. Young Dems. San Francisco, Children's Agy. San Francisco, Valley Med. Convalescent Hosp., Am. Acad. Asian Studies; bd. dirs. San Andreas Health Council, 1976-77. Served with inf., AUS, 1942-45. Mem. ABA, Calif. Bar Assn. (past chmn. no. Calif. com. on discovery procedures, past chmn. com. to confer with banks and title cos., adminstrn. justice and unlawful practice coms.), San Francisco Bar Assn. (past bd. dirs., legal ethics and medico-legal interprofl. coms., pres., bd. dirs. 1942-43), Lawyers Club (jud., ins. and minimum fee coms., past pres., past bd. dirs.), San Francisco Barristers Club, Assn. Trial Lawyers Am., Am. Judicature Soc., Am. Legion (comdr. 1947—), Mil. Order World Wars, Legion of Guardsmen, Native Sons Golden West (pres. Castro parlor 1937), Phi Alpha Delta, Alpha Chi Rho. Clubs: Press (2d v.p.), Golden Gate Tennis (pres. 1940-41). Personal injury, Probate. Home: 1015 Lakeview Way Redwood City CA 94062 Office: Worthington Fields & Worthington 111 Pine St Suite 1501 San Francisco CA 94111

WORTHINGTON, WILLIAM ALBERT, III, lawyer; b. Pitts., June 26, 1950; s. William Albert Jr. and Patricia Lou (Reynolds) W.; m. Candace Ann Clark, Apr. 8, 1978; children: Elizabeth Clark, Emily Robin. B.S., U. Utah, 1972; J.D., Washington and Lee U., 1976. Bar: Tex. 1976, U.S. Dist. Ct. (so. dist.) Tex. 1977, U.S. Ct. Appeals (5th cir.) 1977, U.S. Ct. Appeals (11th cir.) 1981, U.S. Supreme Ct. 1981, U.S. Dist. Ct. (we. dist.) Tex. 1982, U.S. Dist. Ct. (ea. dist) Tex. 1986. Assoc. firm Sewell & Riggs, Houston, 1976-82, ptnr., 1982—. Exec. editor Washington and Lee Law Rev., 1976. Mem. Tex. Assn. Def. Counsel, Def. Research Inst., Nat. Assn. R.R. Trial Counsel, Product Liability Adv. Council, Houston Bar Found., Tex. Bd. Legal Specialization (cert. civil trial lawyer, personal injury trial lawyer), Houston YMCA. Federal civil litigation, State civil litigation, Personal injury. Home: 2614 Carolina Way Houston TX 77005 Office: Sewell & Riggs 333 Clay St McCorp Plaza Suite 800 Houston TX 77002

WORTHY, K(ENNETH) MARTIN, lawyer; b. Dawson, Ga., Sept. 24, 1920; s. Kenneth Spencer and Jeffrie Pruett (Martin) W.; m. Eleanor Blewett, Feb. 15, 1947 (dec. July 1981); children: Jeffrie Martin, William Blewett; m. Katherine Teasley Jackson, June 17, 1983. Student, The Citadel, 1937-39; B.Ph., Emory U., 1941, J.D. with honors, 1947; M.B.A. cum laude, Harvard U., 1943. Bar: Ga. 1947, D.C. 1948. Assoc. mem. firm Hamel & Park, Washington, 1948-52; partner Hamel & Park, 1952-69, 72—; chief counsel IRS, 1969-72; also asst. gen. counsel Treasury Dept., 1969-72; dir. Beneficial Corp., 1978—; mem. Nat. Council Organized Crime, 1970-72; cons. Justice Dept., 1972-74. Author: (with John M. Appleman) Basic Estate Planning, 1957; contbr. articles to profl. jours. Del. Montgomery County Civic Fedn., 1951-61, D.C. Area Health and Welfare Council, 1960-61; mem. Emory Law Sch. Council, 1976—; trustee Chelsea Sch., 1981—. Served to capt. AUS, 1943-46, 51-52. Recipient Treasury Exceptional Service award and medal, 1972, IRS Commrs. award, 1972. Fellow Aspen Inst., Am. Bar Found., Am. Coll. Tax Counsel (bd. regents 1980—, vice chmn. 1983-85, chmn. 1985-87); mem. Ga. Bar Assn., D.C. Bar Assn., Fed. Bar Assn. (nat. council 1969-72, 77-79), ABA (council taxation sect. 1965-68, vice chmn. 1968-69, 72-73, chmn. 1973-74 Ho. of Dels. 1983—, chmn. audit com. 1985—), Nat. Conf. Lawyers and C.P.A.s (del. 1981-87), Am. Law Inst., Nat. Tax Assn., Phi Delta Theta, Phi Delta Phi, Omicron Delta Kappa. Episcopalian (chmn. dept. finance Washington Diocese 1969-70). Clubs: Chevy Chase (Washington), Metropolitan (Washington), National Lawyers (Washington), City Tavern (Washington); Harvard (N.Y.C.); James River Country (Newport News, Va.). Corporate taxation, Personal income taxation, Government contracts and claims. Home: 5305 Portsmouth Rd Bethesda MD 20016 Office: 7th Floor 888 16th St NW Washington DC 20006

WOULFE, MARGARET FRANCES, lawyer; b. Chgo., Feb. 14, 1957; d. James Joseph and Yvonne Elizabeth (Kenney) W.; m. Steven C. Arens, Oct. 12, 1986. BS, Ill. State U., 1979; JD, U. Ill., 1982. Bar: Ill. 1982, U.S. Dist. Ct. (no. dist.) Ill. 1982, U.S. Ct. Appeals (7th cir.) 1983, U.S. Dist. Ct. (ea. dist.) Wis. 1985. Assoc. Chadwell & Kayser Ltd., Chgo., 1982-85; atty. Hartmarx Corp., Chgo., 1985-86; sole practice Chgo., 1986—; instr. Chgo. Lawyers Com. for Civil Rights Under Law, 1983. Bd. dirs. Ill. State U. Found., Normal, 1986—; adv. bd. Queen of Peace High Sch., Burbank, Ill., 1986—. Mem. ABA, Ill. Bar Assn., Chgo. Bar Assn. (co-chmn. community law week 1986, neighborhood outreach com. of young lawyers sect.), Chgo. Council of Lawyers, Women's Bar Assn. of Ill., Sierra Club. Roman Catholic. Clubs: River (Chgo.). Federal civil litigation, State civil litigation, General corporate. Office: 600 S Federal St Suite 201 Chicago IL 60605

WOZENCRAFT, FRANK MCREYNOLDS, lawyer; b. Dallas, Apr. 25, 1923; s. Frank Wilson and Mary Victoria (McReynolds) W.; m. Shirley Ann Cooper, Nov. 25, 1960; children: Frank McReynolds, Ann Lacey, George Wilson. B.A. summa cum laude, Williams Coll., 1946; LL.B., Yale U., 1949. Bar: Tex. 1950. Law clk. to Justice Hugo L. Black, U.S. Supreme Ct., Washington, 1949-50; mem. firm Baker & Botts, Houston, 1950-60; partner Baker & Botts, 1960-66, 69—; dir. Rusk Corp.; asst. atty. gen. charge Office Legal Counsel, Dept. Justice, Washington, 1966-69; mem. legal adv. com. N.Y. Stock Exchange, 1978-83; Mem. Commn. Polit. Activity Govt. Employees, 1967; mem. Pres.'s Adv. Panel on Ins., 1967-68; vice chmn. Adminstrv. Conf. U.S., 1968-71, sr. fellow, 1982—; U.S. rep. Vienna Conf. on Law of Treaties, 1968. Mem. exec. bd. Sam Houston Area council Boy Scouts Am., 1959-66, 69—, v.p., 1974-79; past mem. adv. bd. Houston Mus. Fine Arts; past chmn. bd. Assn. Community TV; past mem. bd. govs. Public Broadcasting Service; trustee Hedgecroft Hosp., 1964-66, St. John's Sch., Houston, 1972-79; bd. dirs. Alley Theatre, 1961-66, 73-80. Served to capt. U.S. Army, 1943-46. Decorated Bronze Star. Mem. Am. Law Inst. (council), ABA (chmn. sect. adminstrv. law 1973-74, spl. com. open meetings legislation 1974-75), Houston Bar Assn., State Bar Tex. (chmn. sect. corp. banking and bus. law 1962-63), Order of Coif, Gargoyle, Phi Beta Kappa, Phi Delta Theta, Phi Delta Phi. Episcopalian. Clubs: Houston (pres. 1984-85), Houston Country; Chevy Chase (Md.); Univ. (Washington). Administrative and regulatory, General corporate. Home: 51 E Broad Oaks St Houston TX 77056 Office: 3000 One Shell Plaza Houston TX 77002

WRAGG, LAISHLEY PALMER, JR., lawyer; b. Pitts., Oct. 11, 1933; s. Laishley Palmer and Irma Grace (Hill) W.; m. Marilyn Jean Smith, Apr. 26, 1957; children: Laishley P., Peter M.B. BBA, U. Mich., 1955; LLB cum laude, Harvard U., 1960; diploma in comparative legal studies Trinity Hall Coll., Cambridge U. (Eng.), 1961. Bar: N.Y. 1962, U.S. Supreme Ct. 1974, Conseil Juridique, France 1977. Assoc. Cravath, Swaine & Moore, N.Y.C., 1961-62, 1965-69, Paris, 1963-65; assoc. Curtis, Mallet-Prevost, Colt & Mosle, N.Y.C., 1969-70, ptnr., 1970—. Mem. U.S. Dept. State ad hoc com. on large constrn. projects; U.S. del. to 15th session of UNCITRAL. Mem. Assn. Bar City N.Y., U. S. Council of Internat. C. of C. (com. on restrictive bus. practices), Inter-Am. Bar Assn., French Am. C. of C., France Am. Soc. (N.Y.C.). Clubs: Am. Yacht (Rye, N.Y.); Hawks (Cambridge, Eng.), Ekwanok County (Manchester, Vt.); Automobile de France (Paris); Harvard of N.Y., Duquesne (Pitts.). Contbr. articles on law to profl. jours. Private international. Home: 123 E 75th St New York NY 10021 Office: 101 Park Ave New York NY 10178

WRAPP, EMILIE D., lawyer; b. Bologna, Italy, Nov. 13, 1955; came to U.S., 1955; d. Henry William and Emma Davoli; m. Gregory Dennis Wrapp, Aug. 17, 1975; 1 child, Paul. AB, Georgetown U., 1976; JD, Loyola U., Chgo., 1979; MBA, U. Chgo., 1984. Bar: Ill. 1979, U.S. Dist. Ct. (no. dist.) Ill. 1979. Assoc. Braun, Lynch, Smith & Strohel, Chgo., 1980-83, Stein Roe & Farnham, Chgo., 1983-85; v.p. Kidder, Peabody and Co. Inc., N.Y.C., 1985—. Mem. ABA, Ill. Bar Assn., U. of Chgo. Bus. Club. General corporate, Securities. Home: 27 Morton Dr Ramsey NJ 07446 Office: Kidder Peabody and Co Inc 20 Exchange Place New York NY 10005

WRAY, CECIL, JR., lawyer; b. Memphis, Nov. 19, 1934; s. Thomas Cecil and Margaret (Malone) W.; m. Gilda Gates, Sept. 11, 1964; children—Christopher A., Kathleen M. Student, U. Va., 1952-53; B.A. magna cum laude, Vanderbilt U., 1956; LL.B., Yale U., 1959. Bar: Tenn. 1959, N.Y. 1961, U.S. Supreme Ct. 1964. Registered conseil juridique, France, 1978-82. Law clk. to justice Tom C. Clark U.S. Supreme Ct., Washington, 1959-60; assoc. Debevoise & Plimpton, N.Y.C., 1960-67, ptnr., 1967—; resident ptnr. Debevoise & Plimpton, Paris, 1976-79. Co-author: Innovative Corporate Financing Techniques, 1986. Pres., Search & Care, Inc., N.Y.C., 1981—; vestryman St. James' Ch., N.Y.C., 1982—; trustees Fondation des Etats-Unis, Paris, 1976-79. Fellow Am. Coll. Investment Counsel (pres. 1983-84, trustee 1981-86); mem. Am. Law Inst., Assn. Bar City N.Y., ABA, N.Y. State Bar Assn., Internat. Bar Assn., Union Internat. des Avocats, Am. Soc. Internat. Law, Order of Coif, Phi Beta Kappa. Episcopalian. Clubs: Yale (N.Y.C.); Ausable (St. Huberts, N.Y.); Quantuck Beach (Westhampton, N.Y.), Century. Home: 47 E 88th St New York NY 10128 Office: Debevoise & Plimpton 875 3d Ave New York NY 10022

WRAY, DONN HAYES, lawyer; b. Gary, Ind., May 12, 1955; s. Donald Robert and Violet (Hayes) W.; m. Lori L. Klein, June 15, 1985. Student Ind. U., 1975-76; B.A., Valparaiso U., 1977, J.D., 1980. Bar: Ind. 1980, Ill. 1980, U.S. Dist. Ct. (so. dist.) Ind. 1980. Law clk. Ind. Ct. Appeals, 1980-82; assoc. Stewart, Irwin, Gilliom, Meyer & Guthrie, Indpls., 1982—. Mem. ABA, Ind. State Bar Assn., Ill. State Bar Assn., Indpls. Bar Assn. Republican. Club: Columbia (Indpls.). State civil litigation, Automotive retail defense. Home: 2450 E 86th St Indianapolis IN 46240 Office: Stewart Irwin Gilliom Meyer & Guthrie 2 Market Sq Ctr Suite 1100 251 E Ohio St Indianapolis IN 46204

WRAY, THOMAS JEFFERSON, lawyer; b. Nashville, July 17, 1949; s. William Esker and Imigene (Cushman) W.; m. Susan Elizabeth Wells, Aug. 19, 1972; children: William Clark, Caroline Kell. BA, Emory U., 1971; JD, U. Va., 1974. Bar: Tex. 1974, U.S. Dist. Ct. (so., no. and ea. dists.) Tex. 1974, U.S. Ct. Appeals (5th and 11th cirs.) 1974. Assoc. Fulbright & Jaworski, Houston, 1974-82, ptnr., 1982—. Mem. ABA, Houston Bar Assn., Houston Mgmt. Lawyer Forum (chmn. 1981-82), Phi Beta Kappa. Republican. Episcopalian. Clubs: Houston, Houston City. Labor, Civil rights, Federal civil litigation. Home: 3776 Garnet Houston TX 77005 Office: Fulbright & Jaworski 1301 McKinney St Houston TX 77010

WREN, CHRISTOPHER GOVE, lawyer; b. Rochester, N.Y., Jan. 9, 1950; s. Carl Ulmer and Barbara Jean (Nichols) W.; m. Jill Darline Robinson, June 12, 1976. Student Brown U., 1968-69; B.A., George Washington U., 1976; J.D., Harvard U., 1979. Bar: Mass. 1979, U.S. Ct. Mil. Appeals 1979, Wis. 1980, U.S. Dist. Ct. Mass. 1980, U.S. Dist. Ct. (we. and ea. dists.) Wis. 1980, U.S. Ct. Appeals (1st and 7th cirs.) 1980. Research assoc. Atty. Douglas Danner, Boston, 1979-80; law clk. U.S. Dist. Ct. (we. dist.) Wis., Madison, 1980-81; assoc. Michael, Best & Friedrich, Madison, 1981-84; asst. atty. gen. Wis. Dept. Justice, Madison, 1984—; dir. statewide pros. Edn. and Tng. Program, 1985—; bd. dirs. legal writing inst. U. Puget Sound Sch. Law, 1987—. Co-Author: The Legal Research Manual: A Game Plan for Legal Research and Analysis, 1983, 2d edition, 1986. Mem. Dane County Democratic Exec. Bd., Madison, 1981-86 ; mem. Wis. Law Enforcement Standards Bd., 1986—, mem. Wis. Dem. Platform Com., Madison, 1982-86 . Served with U.S. Army, 1969-71, Army N.G. 1973-76, 77-85, USAR, 1985—. Mem. ABA, State Bar Wis., Dane County Bar Assn., Assn. Trial Lawyers Am., Soc. Profl. Journalists (Nat. Mark of Excellence award 1974). Criminal law, appellate. Home: 702 Emerson St Madison WI 53715-1718 Office: Wis Dept Justice PO Box 7857 Madison WI 53707-7857

WREN, JAMES ERIC, III, lawyer; b. Longview, Tex., Oct. 6, 1956; s. James Eric Jr. and Peggy Jean (Culp) W. Student, Baylor U., 1975-77, JD cum laude, 1980; MA, U. Canterbury, 1982. Bar: Tex. 1980, U.S. Dist. Ct. (we. dist.) 1982, U.S. Ct. Appeals (5th cir.) 1984. Assoc. Haley & Davis, Waco, Tex., 1981-84; ptnr. Haley, Davis, Wren, Bristow & Rasner, Waco, 1984—; lectr. Baylor U. Sch. Law, Waco, 1986; sec. bd. dirs. Cryo-Genetics, Inc., Tyler, Tex., 1982—; bd. dirs. Cryo-Genetics Internat., Inc., Waco, 1984—. Editor Baylor Law Rev., 1979-80. Bd. dirs. Waco Leadership Assn., 1985-86; treas. Celebrate Waco Commn., 1986; fin. chmn. Boy Scouts of Am., Waco, 1985. Rotary fellow, 1980-81. Mem. Waco-McLennan County Young Lawyers Assn. (bd. dirs. 1983—), Greater Waco C. of C. Baptist. Clubs: Ridgewood, Brazos (Waco). Avocations: snow skiing, scuba diving. Health, Banking, State civil litigation. Home: 2913 Fort Waco TX 76707 Office: 510 N Valley Mills Suite 310 Waco TX 76710

WREN, JILL ROBINSON, lawyer, author, editor; b. Summit, N.J., Apr. 30, 1954; d. William and Mrytle Irene (Bennett) Robinson; m. Christopher Gove Wren, June 12, 1976. Student, U. Del., 1972-74; BA, George Washington U., 1976; JD, Boston U., 1980. Bar: Wis. 1980, U.S. Dist. Ct. (ea. and we. dists.) Wis. 1980, U.S. Ct. Appeals (7th cir.) 1980. Jud. law clk. Dane County Cir. Ct., Madison, 1981-83; editor continuing edn. State Bar of Wis., Madison, 1984-86; editor Am. Acad. Press, Madison, 1986—. Coauthor: The Legal Research Manual: A Game Plan for Legal Research and Analysis, 1983, 2d edit., 1986; also articles. Mem. ABA, Wis. State Bar Assn., Soc. Profl. Journalists, ACLU, Wis. Civil Liberties Union. Democrat. Librarianship. Office: Am Acad Press PO Box 9684 Madison WI 53715

WRIGHT, BENJAMIN TAPPAN, lawyer; b. Berkeley, Calif., Aug. 24, 1922; s. Austin Tappan and Margaret (Stone) W.; m. Mary Louise Premer, Mar. 13, 1953. B.S., Harvard U., 1943; J.D., Boston U., 1950. Bar: Mass. 1952, Fed. 1953. Sr. v.p., sec., gen. counsel The Badger Co., Inc., Cambridge, Mass., 1950-85; trustee Cambridge Savs. Bank, 1974—. Pres. U.S. Figure Skating Assn., 1973-76; mem. tech. com. Internat. Skating Union, 1973—; Mem. adv. bd. Cambridge Citadel, Salvation Army, 1978—; corporator Mt. Auburn Hosp., 1980—. Served to 1st lt. AUS, 1943-46, lt. col. res. Mem. Mass. Bar Assn., S.R. (sec. 1977—). Clubs: Winchester Country (Boston) (dir. 1971-74), Harvard (Boston), Masons (Boston), Cambridge Rotary (Boston) (dir. 1977-80, pres. 1982-83), Skating (Boston) (gov. 1952-65). General corporate, Pension, profit-sharing, and employee benefits. Home: 65 Foster Rd Belmont MA 02178 Office: 1 Broadway Cambridge MA 02142

WRIGHT, BLANDIN JAMES, lawyer; b. Detroit, Nov. 29, 1947; s. Robert Thomas and Jane Ellen (Blandin) W.; m. Kay Emons Heideman, Aug. 28, 1969; children—Steven Blandin, Martha Kay. B.A., U. Mich., 1969; J.D., Dickinson Law Sch., 1972; LL.M. in Taxation, NYU., 1973. Bar: Pa. 1973, Fla. 1976, U.S. TAx Ct. 1977, U.S. Supreme Ct. 1979, Va. 1984, D.C. C.P.A., Tex., Va. Atty. IRS, Washington, 1973-76; tax dir. Intairdril Ltd., London, 1976-78; tax atty. Allied Chem. Corp., Houston, 1978-79; v.p., gen. counsel Assoc. Oiltools, Inc., London, 1979-82, J. Lauritzen (USA), Inc., Charlottesville, Va., 1982-85; sole practice, Charlottesville, 1986—; officer JL Offshore Drilling, Inc., Houston, 1985—, Hot Springs Auto Wash Corp. Am., Panaco Partnership Mgmt. Corp., Va., 1986—; dir. JL Heavyweight Transport, Inc., 1983—; arbitrator Am. ARB Assn., N.Y.C., 1985—. Contbr. articles to profl. jours. Coach Charlottesville Youth Soccer, Baseball and Basketball, 1984—; coach London Youth Baseball, 1982. Mem. ABA, Albemarle County Bar Assn., Am. Inst. C.P.A.s, Tex. Soc. C.P.A's, Va. Soc. C.P.A's, Blue Ridge Soc. CPAs, Charlottesville-Albemarle C. of C. Roman Catholic. Clubs: Farmington Country, Charlottesville, Rormy. Corporate taxation, Private international, Oil and gas leasing. Home: 6 Farmington Dr Charlottesville VA 22901 Office: 2568 B Ivy Rd Charlottesville VA 22903

WRIGHT, BOB FORREST, lawyer; b. Monticello, Ky., Feb. 7, 1932; s. Cyrus and Dora Wright; m. Mary Holt, Sept. 18, 1954 (div. Mar. 1978); children: Forrest Holt, Emily Ellen; m. Gaynell LeGorgne, July 29, 1978. BA, Cenlenary Coll., 1954; JD, Tulane U., 1957. Bar: La. 1957, U.S. Dist. Ct. (we. dist.) La. 1957, U.S. Ct. Appeals (5th cir.) 1957. Ptnr. Domengeaux & Wright, Lafayette, La., 1957—. Mem. ABA, La. Bar Assn. (pres. 1978-79), Assn. Trial Lawyers Am., La. Trial Lawyers Assn. (pres. 1970). Democrat. Admiralty, Personal injury. Home: 318 Beverly Dr Lafayette LA 70502 Office: Domengeaux & Wright 556 Jefferson St Lafayette LA 70501

WRIGHT, CHARLES ALAN, law educator, author; b. Phila., Sept. 3, 1927; s. Charles Adshead and Helen (McCormack) W.; m. Mary Joan Herriott, July 8, 1950 (div. Jan. 1955); children—Charles Edward; m. Eleanor Custis Broyles Clarke, Dec. 17, 1955; children—Henrietta, Cecily; stepchildren—Eleanor Custis Clarke, Margot Clarke. A.B., Wesleyan U., Middletown, Conn., 1947; LL.B., Yale U., 1949. Bar: Minn. 1951, Tex. 1959. Law clk. U.S. Circuit Judge Clark, New Haven, 1949-50; asst. prof. law U. Minn., 1950- 53, assoc. prof., 1953-55; asso. prof. law U. Tex., Austin, 1955-58; prof. U. Tex., 1958-65, McCormick prof., 1965-80, Bates chair, 1980—; Vis. prof. U. Pa., Phila., 1959-60, Harvard U., 1964-65, Yale, 1968-69; vis. fellow Wolfson Coll., Cambridge U., 1984; reporter study div. of jurisdiction between state and fed. cts. Am. Law Inst., 1963-69; mem. adv. com. on civil rules Jud. Conf. U.S., 1961-64, mem. standing com. on rules of practice and proc., 1964-76; cons., counsel for Pres., 1973-74; mem. com. on infractions NCAA, 1973-83, chmn., 1978-83; mem. permanent com. for Oliver Wendell Holmes Devise, 1975-83; mem. Commn. on Bicentennial of U.S. Constn., 1985—. Author: Wright's Minnesota Rules, 1954, Cases on Remedies, 1955, (with C.T. McCormick and J.H. Chadbourn) Cases on Federal Courts, 7th

edit., 1982, Handbook of the Law of Federal Courts, 4th edit., 1983, (with H.M. Reasoner) Procedure-The Handmaid of Justice, 1965, Federal Practice and Procedure: Criminal, 2d edit., 1982, (with A.R. Miller) Federal Practice and Procedure: Civil, 1969-73, 2d edit. (with A.R. Miller and M.K. Kane), 1983—, (with A.R. Miller and E.H. Cooper) Federal Practice and Procedure: Jurisdiction and Related Matters, 1975-82, 2d edit., 1986—, (with K.W. Graham) Federal Practice and Procedure: Evidence, 1977—. Trustee St. Stephen's Episcopal Sch., Austin, Tex., 1962-66; trustee St. Andrew's Episcopal Sch., Austin, 1971-74, 77-80, 81-84, chmn. bd., 1973-74, 79-80; trustee Capitol Broadcasting Assn., Austin, 1966—, chmn. bd., 1969—; trustee Austin Symphony Orch. Soc., 1966—, mem. exec. com., 1966-70, 72-83, 86—; trustee Austin Choral Union, 1984—, Austin Lyric Opera Soc., 1986—. Hon. fellow Wolfson Coll., Cambridge U., 1986—. Mem. Am. Law Inst. (mem. council 1969—), Am. Bar Assn. (mem. commn. on standards jud. adminstrn. 1970-77), Am. Bar Found., Inst. Jud. Adminstrn., Am. Judicature Soc., Am. Acad. Arts and Scis., Philos. Soc. Tex., Order of Coif, Phi Kappa Phi, Omicron Delta Kappa. Republican. Episcopalian (sr. warden). Clubs: Country, Tarry House, Headliners, Metropolitan (Austin); Century, Yale (N.Y.C.). Federal civil litigation, Criminal, Legal education. Home: 5304 Western Hills Dr Austin TX 78731

WRIGHT, DAVID SCOTT, lawyer; b. Parsons, Tenn., Dec. 23, 1950; s. Jesse Paul and Maxine (Scott) W.; m. Sarah Catherine Bliss, Aug. 5, 1978; children: Alice, Catherine. BA, Samford U., 1974; JD, Cumberland U., 1978. Bar: Ala. 1978, U.S. Dist. Ct. (no. dist.) Ala. 1978, U.S. Dist. Ct. (so. dist.) Ala. 1980, U.S. Ct. Appeals (5th cir.) 1980, U.S. Ct. Appeals (11th cir.) 1981, U.S. Supreme Ct. 1981. Sole practice Talladega, Ala., 1978-79; assoc. Brown, Hudgens Richardson PC, Mobile, Ala., 1980-82, ptnr., 1982—. Contbr. articles to profl. jours. Chorus mem. Mobile Opera, 1980—; active Mobile Art Assn., 1982—; deacon Cen. Presbyn. Ch., 1981-83. Named one of Outstanding Young Men of Am., 1985. Mem. ABA, Ala. State Bar Assn., Mobile Bar Assn., Def. Research Inst., Ala. Arson Investigators Assn., Ala. Def. Lawyers Assn., Ala. Ins. Claim Assn., Mobile Ins. Claim Assn. Avocations: reading, woodworking, camping, hiking. Insurance, Personal injury, Workers' compensation. Home: 5100 Karlan Dr Mobile AL 36609 Office: Brown Hudgens Richardson PC 1495 University Blvd Mobile AL 36609

WRIGHT, DOUGLAS RICH, lawyer, educator; b. Provo, Utah, Oct. 17, 1951; s. Earle Coulsen and Marjorie Ada (Kasky) W.; m. Karen Faye Best, Dec. 3, 1971; children: Scott, Heather, Jennifer, Briton, Seth, Melissa, Rachel, Angela. BA, Brigham Young U., 1976, JD, 1981; postgrad. in law, The Judge Adv. Gen.'s Sch., Charlottesville, Va., 1985-86. Bar: Utah 1981, U.S. Ct. Mil. Rev. 1982, U.S. Supreme Ct. 1986. Enlisted U.S. Army, 1972, advanced through grades to capt.; comdr. 30th fin. sect. U.S. Army, Ft. Sill, Okla., 1976-78; prosecutor U.S. Field Artillery Ctr., U.S. Army, Ft. Sill, Okla., 1981-84, chief legal asst., 1984-85; instr. law U.S. Mil. Acad., West Point, N.Y., 1986—. Contbr. articles to profl. jours. Troop committteman Boy Scouts Am., Charlottesville, 1985-86, Webelos Den leader, Lawton, Okla., 1982-85. Recipient George S. Patton Leadership award U.S. Army, 1974, Prof. Mil. Sci. Leadership award U.S. Army, 1976. Mem. ABA, Utah Bar Assn., Phi Delta Phi, Phi Kappa Phi. Republican. Mormon. Avocation: running. Legal education, Military. Home: 378 Howze Pl West Point NY 10996 Office: US Mil Acad Dept Law 230 Thayer Hall West Point NY 10996

WRIGHT, EUGENE BOX, lawyer, business executive; b. Fulton, Ky., Feb. 21, 1943; s. Hugh French and Madeline (Box) W.; m. Deborah Ann Reed; children— Alan Fulton, Julia Anne, Elliot Brandon, Elizabeth Alphia Lowry. BBA, So. Meth. U., 1965; JD, U. Houston, 1968. Bar: Tex. 1968, U.S. Supreme Ct. 1975, U.S. Ct. Appeals (5th cir.) 1975, U.S. Dist. Ct. (ea. dist.) Tex. Sole practice, Cleveland, Tex.; former pres., chmn. bd. Wright Energy Corp.; approved atty. U.S. Life Title Ins. Co. Dallas, Southwest Title Ins. Co., Title Ins. Co. Minn., Pioneer Nat. Title Ins. Co., Lawyers Title Ins. Corp., Chgo. Title Ins. Co., Stewart Title Guaranty Co.; founder, sec., dir. Splendora Lumber Co., Cleveland Pub. Co., Inc., Triangle Press, Inc., Greater Beaumont Pub. Co., Olympic, Inc. Chmn. Bicentennial Com., City of Cleveland ; chmn. UN Day, Cleveland, 1977-78. Mem. Tex. Bar Assn., Liberty County Bar Assn. (pres.), Assn. Trial Lawyers Am., Am. Judicature Soc., Greater Cleveland C. of C. (bd. dirs.), Phi Mu Alpha, Delta Sigma Pi, Beta Gamma Sigma, Phi Delta Phi. Clubs: Cleveland Rotary (pres.), Cleveland Country (sec.). General corporate, Probate, Real property. Office: PO Box 192 Cleveland TX 77327

WRIGHT, FRANCES MINA JOHNSON, lawyer; b. Warsaw, Ind., Sept. 18, 1950; d. James Edgar Johnson and Frances (Fitts) Johnson Scovill; m. John Parke Wright, Dec. 11, 1983. B.A., Duke U., 1972; postgrad. in law Oxford U.; J.D., U. Fla., 1975. Bar: Fla. 1975, U.S. Ct. Appeals (5th cir.) 1975. Trial counsel Fla. Power Corp., St. Petersburg, 1975-78; sole practice, Tampa, Fla., 1979—; pres. Da-Lite, Inc., Frances M. Johnson, P.A.; owner, operator Allied Interiors, 1980; ptnr. Allied Investments. Candidate for Pinellas County Judge, St. Petersburg, 1976; active St. Petersburg Leadership, 1978, Leadership Tampa, 1980, Leadership Fla., 1982. Mem. Pinellas County Trial Lawyers Assn. (bd. dirs. 1977), ABA (jud. adminstrn. div.), Fla. Bar, Dallas Bar Assn., Hillsborough County Bar Assn., Hillsborough Assn. Women Lawyers, Bus. and Profl. Women (St. Petersburg Young Career Woman of Yr. award 1978). Republican. Presbyterian. Clubs: Tampa, Centre (bd. govs.), Tower (Tampa). State civil litigation, General corporate, Oil and gas leasing.

WRIGHT, FRANK CLARENCE, JR., lawyer; b. Eagle Butte, S.D., Dec. 5, 1942; s. Frank Clarence Sr. and Evelyn Ruth (Bailey) W.; m. Barbara Ruth Shepard, Mar. 20, 1968; 1 child, Ross. BA in Polit. Sci., Calif. State U., Fullerton, 1968; JD, U. So. Calif., 1975. Bar: Calif. 1976, Wash. 1976, U.S. Dist. Ct. (so. dist.) Calif. 1977, U.S. Dist. Ct. (cen. dist.) Calif. 1978, U.S. Ct. Appeals (9th cir.) 1978, U.S. Dist. Ct. (no. and ea. dists.) Calif. 1979, U.S. Dist. Ct. (we. dist.) Wash. 1979, U.S. Ct. Claims 1979, U.S. Tax Ct. 1979, U.S. Ct. Customs and Patent Appeals 1979, U.S. Ct. Mil. Appeals 1979, U.S. Supreme Ct. 1979, U.S. Dist. Ct. (ea. dist.) Wash. 1981, U.S. Ct. Appeals (fed. cir.) 1983. Ptnr. Reed & Wright, Laguna Beach, Calif., 1976—; judge pro-tem, 1982—. Served to col. Confederate Air Force. Mem. ABA, Assn. Trial Lawyers Am., Orange County Trial Lawyers Assn. (sustaining). Republican. Personal injury, Criminal, Family and matrimonial. Office: Reed & Wright 800 Glenneyre Southwest Bank Bldg Laguna Beach CA 92651

WRIGHT, FREDERICK LEWIS, II, lawyer; b. Roanoke, Va., Sept. 17, 1951; s. Frederick Lewis and Dorothy Marie (Trent) W.; m. Margaret Suzanne Rey, Oct. 16, 1982; children: Lauren Elizabeth, Emily Trent. BA, Ga. State U., 1978; JD, U. Ga., 1981. Bar: Ga. 1982, U.S. Dist. Ct. (no. dist.) Ga. 1984, U.S. Ct. Appeals (11th and 8th cirs.) 1984. Law clk. to presiding justice U.S. Ct. Appeals, Atlanta, 1981-82; assoc. Smith, Currie and Hancock, Atlanta, 1982—. Articles editor Ga. Law Rev., 1980-81. Mem. ABA (forum com. constrn. industry), Assn. Trial Lawyers Am., Fed. Bar Assn., Order of Coif. Methodist. Construction, Government contracts and claims, Federal civil litigation. Office: Smith Currie and Hancock 2600 Peachtree Ctr Harris Tower Atlanta GA 30043-6601

WRIGHT, GROVER CLEVELAND, JR., lawyer; b. Portsmouth, Va., May 15, 1933; s. Grover C. Sr. and Annie (Elliott) W.; m. Linn Lash, Apr. 13, 1957 (div. Nov. 1975); children: Laura, Corbitt; m. Ann Laughter, Dec. 17, 1975; 1 child, Hannon; stepchildren: James, Laura. BS in Commerce, U. Va., 1956, JD, 1961. Bar: Va. 1961, U.S. Dist. Ct. (ea. dist.) Va. 1964, U.S. Ct. Appeals (4th cir.). Asst. to counsel Fed. Res. Bank, Richmond, Va., 1961-64; sole practice Virginia Beach, Va., 1964—. Gen. counsel Virginia Beach Gen. Hosp., 1969-79. Served to capt. USMC, 1956-58. Mem. Va. Bar Assn. (1st and 2d dist. coms.), Virginia Beach Bar Assn. (pres. 1975-76). Episcopalian. Family and matrimonial, State civil litigation, Administrative and regulatory. Home: 220 79th St Virginia Beach VA 23451 Office: 3330 Pacific Ave Virginia Beach VA 23451

WRIGHT, HARRY RALPH, JR., lawyer, educator; b. Atlanta, May 8, 1954; s. Harry Ralph and Frances Elizabeth (Cannon) W.; m. Melinda Irene Bunton, July 28, 1979, 1 child, Leigh Ann. BA, Mercer U., 1976, JD, 1979. Bar: Ga. 1979. Atty. Allen, Brown Wright & Edenfield, Statesboro, Ga., 1979-83; asst. prof. law Ga. So. Coll., Statesboro, 1983—; tax cons. various firms, Statesboro, 1983—. Bd. dirs. Statesboro Humane Soc., Inc. 1984-86, Ogeechee Home Health, Inc., Statesboro, 1986—; treas., bd. dirs. Wesley Found., Statesboro, 1986—. Mem. ABA, Ga. Bar Assn., Southeastern Bus. Law Assn., Am. Bus. Law Assn. Republican.. Methodist. Lodge: Optimists (pres. Statesboro club 1981-82, lt. gov. Ga. dist. 1982-83). Avocations: computers, dancing, travel, woodworking, racketball. Estate planning, Probate, Estate taxation. Home: 309 Wendwood Dr Statesboro GA 30458 Office: 51 E Main St Statesboro GA 30458

WRIGHT, JACK, JR., lawyer; b. Monroe, La., July 21, 1933; s. Jack and Sadie Mae (Joffrion) W.; m. Bonnie Overcast, 1958 (div. 1970); m. Jackie Brand (div. 1976); children: Roxie Lynn, Sherry Ann; m. Margaret Bernice Worley, July 27, 1979; 1 child, Michael Boyd. BA in History, Northwest Nazarene Coll., 1960; MA in Sociology, La. State U., 1963, PhD in Sociology, 1969; JD, Loyola U., New Orleans, 1981. Bar: La. 1982, U.S. Dist. Ct. (we. and ea. dists.) La., U.S. Ct. Appeals (5th cir.). Asst. prof. criminology Fla. State U., Tallahassee, 1967-70; assoc. prof. sociology Miss. State U., Starkville, 1971-73; assoc. prof. criminal justice Loyola U., New Orleans, 1974-81; sole practice Monroe, 1981—. Co-author: Introduction to Criminology, 1974, Preventing Delinquency, 1974, Social Problems in America, 1976, Modern Criminal Justice, 1978. Served as cpl. U.S. Army, 1953-55. Mem. ABA, Assn. Trial Lawyers Am., La. Trial Lawyers Assn., La. Bar Assn. Democrat. Episcopalian. Club: Toastmasters (Monroe) (pres. 1985). Personal injury, Family and matrimonial, Criminal. Home: 3103 W Deborah Dr Monroe LA 71201 Office: 1011 S Grand Monroe LA 71201

WRIGHT, JAMES CHARLES, lawyer; b. Murtreesboro, Tenn., May 29, 1956; s. William Charles and Wilma Orr (Adams) W.; m. Kathy Denise Hartsook, Dec. 10, 1983; 1 child, Sarah Katherine. BS magna cum laude, Mid. Ten. State U., 1977; JD, U. Tenn., 1980. Bar: Tenn. 1981, U.S. Dist. Ct. (ea. dist.) Tenn. 1981, U. Ct. Appeals (6th cir.) 1984. Assoc. Butler and Vines, Knoxville, 1981-85, ptnr., 1986. Mem. ABA, Knoxville Bar Assn., Tenn. Bar Assn., Order of Coif. Democrat. Baptist. Federal civil litigation, State civil litigation, Personal injury. Office: 1st American Ctr Suite 810 Knoxville TN 37902

WRIGHT, JAMES SKELLY, federal judge; b. New Orleans, Jan. 14, 1911; s. James Edward and Margaret (Skelly) W.; m. Helen Mitchell Patton, Feb. 1, 1945; 1 son, James Skelly. Ph.B., Loyola U., 1931, LL.B., 1934; LL.D., Yale U., 1961, U. Notre Dame, 1962, Howard U., 1964, U. So. Calif., 1975, Loyola U., New Orleans, 1981, Georgetown U., 1981, N.Y. Law Sch., 1981, U. D.C., 1983, U. Vt., 1986. Bar: U.S. Supreme Ct. High sch. tchr. 1931-35; lectr. English history Loyola U., 1936-37; asst. U.S. atty. New Orleans, 1937-42, 45-46; U.S. atty. E. Dist. La., 1948-49, U.S. dist. judge, 1949-62; U.S. circuit judge D.C., 1962—; chief judge U.S. Ct. Appeals D.C. Circuit, 1978-81, Temporary Emergency Ct. Appeals of U.S., 1982—; faculty Loyola U. Sch. Law, 1950-62; James Madison lectr. N.Y. U., 1965; Robert L. Jackson lectr. Nat. Coll. State Trial Judges, 1966; lectr. U. Tex., 1967; Irvine lectr. Cornell U., 1968; Brainerd Currie lectr. Duke U., 1970; lectr. Notre Dame in London, 1974; Meiklejohn lectr. Brown U., 1976; lectr. adminstrv. law Tulane U. in Grenoble, 1979; Francis Biddle lectr. Harvard Law Sch., 1979; George Dreyfous lectr. Tulane U., 1981; Samuel Rubin lectr. Columbia U. Sch. Law, 1982; Mathew Tobriner lectr. Hastings Coll. Law, U. Calif., Berkeley, 1983; Observer U.S. State Dept. Internat. Fisheries Conf., London, 1943. Served as lt. comdr. USCG, 1942-46. Mem. La. Bar Assn. (bd. govs.), Fed. Bar Assn. (pres. New Orleans chpt.), D.C. Bar Assn., ABA, New Orleans Bar Assn., Blue Key, Phi Delta Phi, Alpha Delta Gamma (nat. pres.). Democrat. Roman Catholic. Jurisprudence. Home: 5317 Blackistone Rd Bethesda MD 20816 Office: US Courthouse Washington DC 20001

WRIGHT, JEFFERSON VAUGHAN, lawyer; b. Washington, Aug. 24, 1955; s. William Marshall and Mable J. (Johnson) W.; m. Susan L. Messick, Apr. 21, 1984. BA, Tufts U., 1977; JD, Georgetown U., 1980. Bar: Md., U.S. Dist. Ct. Md., U.S. Ct. Appeals (4th cir.). Law clk. to presiding jugde U.S. Ct. Appeals Md., Annapolis, 1979-81; assoc. Miles and Stockbridge, Balt., 1981—. Mem. ABA, Md. State Bar Assn. (com. on ethics 1982-86, chmn. 85-86), Balt. City Bar Assn. Democrat. Clubs: Merchant's, Center (Balt.). Corporate and commercial litigation, Personal injury. Home: 726 E Lake Ave Baltimore MD 21212 Office: Miles and Stockbridge 10 Light St Baltimore MD 21202

WRIGHT, JOHN HOMER, lawyer; b. Hot Springs, Ark., Nov. 13, 1950; s. Jack and Mary Clementine (Baldwin) W.; m. Cynthia Jean Edwards, May 28, 1973; 1 child, Susannah Justine. BA, Hendrix Coll., 1972; JD, U. Ark., 1975. Bar: Ark. 1975. Sole practice Hot Springs, 1975-81, 85—; ptnr. Callahan, Wright, Crow, Bachelor & Lax, Hot Springs, 1981-85; dep. pros. atty. City of Hot Springs, 1980-81, mcpl. judge, 1985—. Trustee Garland County Library, Hot Springs, 1976-85. Democrat. Methodist. Personal injury, Probate. Home: 211 Bellaire Dr Hot Springs AR 71901 Office: 304 Ovachita Hot Springs AR 71901

WRIGHT, LAWRENCE A., federal judge; b. Stratton, Maine, Dec. 25, 1927; m. Avis Leahy, 1953; children: Michael, David, Stephen, Douglas. BA, U. Maine, 1953; JD, Georgetown U., 1956; LLM, Boston U., 1962. Ptnr. Gravel, Shea & Wright Ltd., Vt.; sr. trial counsel chief counsel office IRS, Boston, 1958-69; tax commr. State of Vt., 1969-71; judge U.S. Tax Ct., Washington, 1984—. Served to 2d lt. U.S. Army, 1945-48. Office: US Tax Court 400 Second St NW Washington DC 20217 *

WRIGHT, LUKE WILLIAMS, lawyer; b. Pasquotank County, N.C., June 3, 1914; s. Silas G. and Ina (Williams) W.; m. Sue Polson, Feb. 4, 1941; children—John G., Sarah N., Susan F. B.A., U. Ala., 1937, LL.B., 1939. Bar: N.C. 1939. With Jefferson Standard Life Ins. Co., Greensboro, N.C., 1939-43; assoc. Smith, Wharton, Sapp & Moore and predecessor, 1943-49, Welch Jordan, 1949-52; ptnr. Jordan, Wright, Nichols, Caffrey & Hill and predecessor, 1952-78; sole practice, Greensboro, 1978—. Mem. ABA, N.C. State Bar, Greensboro Bar Assn. (pres. 1975-76), N.C. Bar Assn., Am. Judicature Soc., Assn. Trial Lawyers Am. Democrat. Methodist. Club: Greensboro City. General practice. Home: 2515 Lakeshore Dr Greensboro NC 27407 Office: 430 W Friendly Ave Suite 207 Greensboro NC 27401

WRIGHT, MICHAEL EUGENE, lawyer; b. Anchorage, May 13, 1958; s. James Carroll and Frances (Evans) W.; m. Glenda D. Brown, June 16, 1984. BBA, U. So. Miss., 1979; JD, U. Miss., 1982. Bar: Miss. 1982. Sole practice Lucedale, Miss., 1982-83; asst. counsel So. Farm Bur. Life Ins. Co., Jackson, Miss., 1983—. Mem. ABA, Miss. Bar Assn. Southern Baptist. Club: Deacons (Lucedale). Avocations: hunting, fishing, reading, landscaping. Real property, Bankruptcy. Home: 107 Beaver Brook Ct Ridgeland MS 39157 Office: So Farm Bur Life Ins Co 1401 Livingstone Ln PO Box 78 Jackson MS 39205

WRIGHT, PAUL WILLIAM, oil company executive; b. Jamestown, N.Y., July 7, 1944; s. Julian M. and Ruth (Blake) W.; m. Elizabeth O'Rourke Wright, Nov. 22, 1975; children—Jeffrey, Stephen. B.S. in Bus. Adminstrn., Georgetown U., 1966, J.D., 1969. Bar: Va. 1969, D.C. 1972, Tex. 1973, U.S. Supreme Ct. 1972, La. 1985. Staff atty. Fed. Power Commn. 1969-70; assoc. Wolf & Case, Washington 1970-72; atty. Exxon Co. U.S.A., Houston, 1973—, now area gen. atty., litigation, New Orleans, bd. dirs. of La. Pro Bono-Project, 1986-88, bd. dirs. Mem. ABA, Tex. Bar Assn., La. Bar Assn., Va. Bar Assn., D.C. Bar Assn., La. Bar Found. (bd.dirs., sec., treas. 1986—), Am. Petroleum Inst., N.Mex. Oil and Gas Assn., Midcontinent Oil and Gas Assn. Republican. Roman Catholic. General corporate, FERC practice. Office: PO Box 60626 New Orleans LA 70161

WRIGHT, RICHARD JAY, lawyer; b. Ogdensburg, N.Y., Sept. 20, 1944; s. Leo and Gene Marion (Graham) W.; m. Laura Esther Snow, Aug. 5, 1978 (div.); 1 child, Richard Parker; m. Carol Lee Coburn, Apr. 19, 1986. BA, U. Vt., 1966; JD, Boston U., 1972. Bar: Vt. 1972, U.S. Dist. Ct. Vt. 1974, U.S. Ct. Appeals (2d cir.) 1976, U.S. Supreme Ct. 1979. Dep. state's atty. Rutland (Vt.) County, 1972-73; assoc. Law Office Joseph A. DeBonis, Poultney, Vt., 1973-76; ptnr. DeBonis & Wright, P.C., Poultney, 1976—. Served to 1st lt. U.S. Army, 1966-68, Vietnam. Mem. ABA, Vt. Bar Assn., Rutland County Bar Assn., Assn. Trial Lawyers Am., Vt. Trial Lawyers Assn. Lodge: Rotary (pres. Poultney 1976-77, 1985—). Avocations: photography, golf, skiing. Personal injury, Real property, Family and matrimonial. Home: PO Box 154 Wells VT 05774 Office: DeBonis & Wright PC 25 Main St Poultney VT 05764

WRIGHT, ROBERT ROSS, III, lawyer, educator; b. Fort Worth, Nov. 20, 1931; children: Robert Ross IV, John, David, Robin. BA cum laude, U. Ark., 1953, JD, 1956; MA (grad. fellow), Duke U., 1954; SJD (law fellow), U. Wis., 1967. Bar: Ark. 1956, U.S. Supreme Ct. 1968, Okla. 1970. Instr. polit. sci. U. Ark., 1955-56; mem. firm Forrest City, Ark., 1956-58; partner firm Norton, Norton & Wright, Forrest City, 1959; asst. gen. counsel, asst. sec. Crossett Co., Ark.; atty. Crossett div. Ga.-Pacific Corp., 1960-63; asst. sec. Pub. Utilities Co., Crossett, Triangle Bag Co., Covington, Ky., 1960-62; mem. faculty law sch. U. Ark., 1963-70; asst. prof., dir. continuing legal edn. and research, then asst. dean U. Ark. (Little Rock div.), 1965-66, prof. law, 1967-70; vis. prof. law, spl. asst. to provost and pres. U. Iowa, 1969-70; prof. U. Okla., 1970-77; dean U. Okla. (Coll. Law); dir. U. Okla. (Law Center), 1970-76; vis. prof. U. Ark., Little Rock, 1976-77; Donaghey Disting. prof. U. Ark, 1977—; Ark. commr. Nat. Conf. Commrs. Uniform State Laws, 1967-70; past chmn. Com. Uniform Eminent Domain Code; past mem. Com. Uniform Probate Code, Ark. Gov.'s Ins. Study Commn.; chmn. Gov. Commn. on Uniform Probate Code; chmn. task force joint devel. Hwy. Research Bd.; vice chmn. Okla. Jud. Council, 1970-72, chmn., 1972-75; chmn. Okla. Center Criminal Justice, 1971-76. Author: Arkansas Eminent Domain Digest, 1964, Arkansas Probate Practice System, 1965, The Law of Airspace, 1968, Emerging Concepts in the Law of Airspace, 1969, Cases and Materials on Land Use, 3d edit., 1982, supp. 1987, Uniform Probate Code Practice Manual, 1972, Model Airspace Code, 1973, Land Use in a Nutshell, 1978, 2d edit. 1985, The Arkansas Form Book, 1979, Zoning Law in Arkansas: A Comparative Analysis, 1980; contbr. numerous articles to legal jours. Mem. Little Rock Planning Commn., 1978-82, chmn., 1982. Named Ark. Man of Year Kappa Sigma, 1958. Fellow Am. Law Inst., acad. fellow Am. Coll. Probate Assn.; mem. Ark. Bar Assn. (ho. of dels. 1978-81, 82-85, chmn. eminent domain code com., past mem. com. new bar center; past chmn. preceptorship com.; exec. com. young lawyers sect.), Okla. Bar Assn. (past vice-chmn. legal internship com.; former vice chmn. gen. practice sect.), ABA (exec. council gen. practice sect., chmn. legal edn., sect. gen. practice, new pubs. editorial bd.; standing com. on profl. career devel.), Pulaski County Bar Assn., Ark. Bar Found., U. Wis., U. Ark., Duke alumni assns., Order Coif, Phi Beta Kappa, Phi Alpha Delta, Omicron Delta Kappa. Episcopalian. Real property, Probate, Legal education. Home: 1409 N Hughes Little Rock AR 72207 Office: 400 W Markham St Little Rock AR 72201

WRIGHT, ROBERT WILLIAMS, lawyer; b. Elgin, Ill., May 31, 1928; s. Robert Williams and Caroline Elizabeth (Chapman) W.; m. Nancy Campbell Tucker, Oct. 30, 1954; children—Patricia, Katherine, Robert. S.B., MIT, 1950; LL.B., Harvard U., 1954. Bar: Ill. 1954, U.S. Dist. Ct. (no. dist.) Ill. 1955. Assoc., then ptnr. Keck, Mahin & Cate and predecessors, Chgo., 1954—; chmn. mgmt. com. Pres., Village of Kenilworth (Ill.). Mem. ABA, Ill. State Bar, Chgo. Bar Assn., Law Club Chgo., Legal Club Chgo. Republican. Episcopalian. Clubs: Chicago, Mid-Day. General corporate, Banking, General practice. Office: Keck Mahin Cate 8300 Sears Tower 233 S Wacker Dr Chicago IL 60606

WRIGHT, SCOTT OLIN, federal judge; b. Haigler, Nebr., Jan. 15, 1923; s. Jesse H. and Martha I. W.; m. Shirley Frances Young, Aug. 25, 1972. Student, Central Coll., Fayette, Mo., 1940-42; LL.B., U. Mo., Columbia, 1950. Bar: Mo. 1950. City atty. Columbia, 1951-53; pros. atty. Boone County, Mo., 1954-58; practice of law Columbia, 1958-79; U.S. dist. judge Western Dist. Mo., Kansas City, 1979—. Pres. Young Democrats Boone County, 1950, United Fund Columbia, 1965. Served with USN, 1942-43; as aviator USMC, 1943-46. Decorated Air medal. Mem. ABA, Am. Trial Lawyers Assn., Mo. Bar Assn., Mo. Trial Lawyers Assn., Boone County Bar Assn. Unitarian. Clubs: Rockhill Tennis, Woodside Racquet. Lodge: Rotary (pres. Columbia 1965). Jurisprudence. Office: U S Dist Ct U S Courthouse 811 Grand Ave Room 613 Kansas City MO 64106

WRIGHT, SUSAN WEBBER, law educator; b. Texarkana, Ark., Aug. 22, 1948; d. Thomas Edward and Betty Jane (Gary) Webber; m. Robert Ross Wright, III, May 21, 1983; 1 child, Robin Elizabeth. BA, Randolph-Macon Woman's Coll., 1970; MPA, U. Ark., 1972, JD with high honors, 1975. Bar: Ark. 1975. Law clk. U.S. Ct. Appeals 8th Circuit, 1975-76; asst. prof. law U. Ark.-Little Rock, 1976-78, assoc. prof., 1978-83, prof., 1983—, asst. dean, 1976-78; vis. assoc. prof. Ohio State U., Columbus, 1981, La. State U., Baton Rouge, 1982-83; mem. adv. com. U.S. Ct. Appeals 8th Circuit, St. Louis, 1983—. Author: (with R. Wright) Land Use in a Nutshell, 1978, 2d edit., 1985; editor-in-chief Ark. Law Rev., 1975; contbr. articles to profl. jours. Mem. Ark. Bar Assn., Pulaski County Bar Assn., Ark. Assn. Women Lawyers (v.p. 1977-78). Episcopalian. Oil and gas leasing, Real property. Office: U Ark Sch Law 400 W Markham St Little Rock AR 72201

WRIGHT, THOMAS PRESTON, lawyer; b. Reno, June 2, 1949; s. Hesden Leo and Lois (Chamberlain) W.; m. Sarah Howell Woodburn, Dec. 18, 1971 (div. May 1977). BA in Journalism, U. Nev., Reno, 1972; cert. in Comparative Law, Austro-Am. Inst., Vienna, Austria, 1974; JD, U. of Pacific, 1978; postdoctoral, Georgetown U., 1980. Bar: Hawaii 1979, Nev. 1979, U.S. Dist. Ct. Nev. 1979, U.S. Dist. Ct. Hawaii 1979, U.S. Ct. Internat. Trade 1979, U.S. Ct. Appeals (9th cir.) 1980, U.S. Supreme Ct. 1982. Dep. atty. gen. State of Nev., Carson City, 1980-83; sole practice Reno, 1982-83; dist. atty. Storey County, Nev., Virginia City, 1984—; mem. law council Nev. Sch. Law, Reno, 1985—; legal advisor Josh Inc., Reno, 1985—. Bd. dirs. Nev. Humane Soc., Reno, 1985—, Am. Heart Assn., Reno, 1985—. Recipient Disting. Service award, Northern Nev. March Dimes, Reno, 1985. Mem. ABA, Assn. Trial Lawyers Am. Nat. Dist. Attys. Assn. (bd. dirs., state dir. 1985—), Nev. Bar Assn. (alcohol and substance abuse com. 1985—), Nev. Dist. Atty. Assn., Phi Delta Phi. Republican. Club: Lakeridge Tennis (Reno). Avocations: tennis, writing, travel, wildlife photography, running. Local government, Criminal, Personal injury. Office: PO Box 496 Virginia City NV 89440

WRIGHT, WALLACE MATHIAS, lawyer; b. Johnston, S.C., Sept. 29, 1928; s. Luther Sloan and Kathleen (Barre) W.; m. Sally Ann Nelson, May 2, 1959; children: Wendy, Russell, Todd. A.B., Wofford Coll., 1949; LL.B., U. S.C., 1955. Bar: S.C. 1955, Ohio 1962, Tex. 1981. Trial atty. Dept. Justice, Washington, 1955-56; sr. tax trial atty. Office of Regional Counsel IRS, Atlanta, 1956-61; assoc. Jones, Day, Reavis & Pogue, Cleve., 1961-64, ptnr., 1965-81; ptnr. Jones, Day, Reavis & Pogue, Dallas, 1981—. Served to 2d lt. USAF, 1950-53, Korea. Mem. ABA, State Bar Tex., Dallas Bar Assn. Presbyterian. Estate planning, Probate, Estate taxation. Home: 6848 Midcrest Dr Dallas TX 75240 Office: Jones Day Reavis & Pogue 2001 Ross Ave Suite 2300 Dallas TX 75201

WRIGHT, WILLARD JUREY, lawyer; b. Seattle, Feb. 25, 1914; s. Raymond Garfield and Elizabeth (McPherson) W.; m. Alice Ostrander, Dec. 27, 1939 (dec. Dec. 1969); children: Susan, Alice, Rosemary, Raymond Garfield II; m. Katharyn Stubbs Little, July 18, 1970; children: Anne, Gwendolyn, Kathy. A.B. with honors, Princeton, 1936; certificate, Woodrow Wilson Sch. Pub. and Internat. Affairs, 1936; J.D. with honors, U. Wash., 1939; grad., Navy. Lang. Sch., U. Colo., 1944. Bar: Wash. 1939, U.S. Dist. Ct. 1939, Supreme Ct. 1954, Ct. Appeals 1958. Editor Wash. Law Rev., 1937-39; practice of law Wash., 1939—; partner Wright, Innis, Simon & Todd, Seattle, 1939-69, Davis, Wright, Todd, Riese & Jones, 1969-85; counsel Davis Wright & Jones, 1986—; spl. asst. atty. gen., Wash., 1953; acting prof. fed. income taxation U. Wash. Law Sch., 1956; pres. Assoc. Vintners, Inc., 1979-81, officer, dir. or gen. counsel various bus. corps. U.S. Chmn. King County Republican Rules Com., 1950-58; chmn. 37th Dist Rep. Orgn. (precinct committeeman), 1936-74; del. Rep. Nat. Conv. Chgo., 1952. Contbr. articles to profl. jours. Trustee Seattle Found., 1954-63, pres., 1961-63; trustee Seattle Com. Fgn. Relations, 1959-62; trustee Lakeside Sch., 1938-67, pres., 1951-55, hon. trustee, 1967—; vis. com. U. Wash. Coll. Bus. Adminstrn., 1963-70, U. Wash. Law Sch., 1974-78; pres. U. Wash. Ann. Fund, 1973-74, U. Wash. Law Sch. Found., 1974-75; trustee Helen Bush Parkside Sch., 1946-63, pres., 1959-62; trustee Princeton U., 1957-61; mem. governing bd. Univ. Hosp., Seattle, 1978-87, chmn., 1980-82; sec., trustee Seattle Art Mus., 1958—, R.D. Merrill Found., Hauberg Found.; pres. Spring Street Owners' Assn., 1986—, Served to lt. USNR, 1943-46.

Recipient Vivian Carkeek prize; Disting. Service award Lakeside Sch., 1964; Disting. Alumnus award, 1980. Fellow Am. Bar Found., Am. Coll. Probate Counsel; mem. ABA, Wash. State Bar Assn. (chmn. real estate, probate and trusts sect. 1958-61), Seattle-King County Bar Assn. (trustee 1955-58, 64-67, pres. 1966-67), Am. Judicature Soc., Nat. Assn. Estate Planning Councils (dir. 1969-71), Estate Planning Council Seattle (pres. 1968-69, dir.), Alumni Assn. U. Wash. Law Sch. (pres. 1957-58), Seattle World Affairs Council (charter trustee, sec. 1949-57), Urban League Seattle (trustee 1956-60, 68-70, pres. bd. trustees 1956-58), Phi Delta Phi, Order of Coif. Episcopalian (vestryman 1959-64, 68-70, 73-76, sr. warden 1970, 74-76, chancellor 1976-87, trustee ch. pension fund, N.Y. 1970-76, Bishop's Cross 1977). Clubs: Princeton Quadrangle (pres. 1935-36), Princeton of N.Y., University (sec. and trustee 1950-51, 62-64, pres. 1968-70), Seattle Golf (sec., trustee 1968-71); Royal and Ancient Golf (St. Andrews, Scotland). Probate, Estate taxation, General corporate. Home: 1223 Spring St Apt 601 Seattle WA 98104 Office: Century Sq Seattle WA 98101

WRIGHT, WILLIAM EVERAR, JR., lawyer; b. New Orleans, Dec. 4, 1949; s. William E. and Claire (Carter) W.; m. Alice Marquez, May 26, 1972; children: Matthew, Caroline. BA, Tulane U., 1971, JD, 1974. Bar: La. 1974. Assoc. Little, Schwartz & Dussom, New Orleans, 1974-76; ptnr. Baldwin & Haspel, New Orleans, 1976—. Mem. La. Bd. Examiners, 1981-84. Mem. ABA, Fed. Bar Assn., La. Bar Assn. (bd. dels. 1985—), New Orleans Bar Assn. (exec. com. 1980-86, officer 1983-86), New Orleans C. of C. State civil litigation, Construction, Bankruptcy. Home: 700 Eleonore St New Orleans LA 70115 Office: Baldwin & Haspel 225 Baronne St New Orleans LA 70112

WRIGLEY, ALBERT BLAKEMORE, lawyer; b. Phila., Mar. 22, 1934; s. Clarence Blakemore and Helen Marie (Tinti) W.; m. Marlene Pearl Chase, Mar. 16, 1956; children: Albert, Kurt, Jill, Lara. BA, Pa. State U., 1955; JD, Temple U., 1960. Bar: Pa. 1961, U.S. Dist. Ct. (ea. dist.) Pa. 1961. Ptnr. Wrigley, Yergey, Daylor & Scheffey, Pottstown, Pa., 1968—. Chmn. civil service commn. Lower Pottsgrove, Pottstown, 1970—. Served wo 1st lt. U.S. Army, 1955-57, Korea. Avocations: aviation, pvt. piloting, photography. Family and matrimonial, Probate, Real property. Home: 980 Valley Rd Pottstown PA 19464 Office: Wrigley Yergey Daylor & Scheffey 1129 High St Pottstown PA 19464

WRIGLEY, JULIE ANN, lawyer; b. Buffalo, May 23, 1948; d. Donald Snow and Lucy (Keating) B.; m. William Wrigley, Nov. 28, 1981. BA in Anthropology, Stanford U., 1971; JD, U. Denver, 1975. Bar: Colo. 1975, Ill. 1978. Assoc. Holme, Roberts & Owen, Denver, 1975-76, Banta & Eason, Denver, 1976-77; atty. Wrigley Estates, Chgo., 1977—. Editor U. Denver Law Jour. Trustee Orme Sch., Phoenix, 1980-84; pres. Tersk Found., 1985—; bd. dirs. Chgo. City Ballet, 1981—, Northwestern Hosp., Chgo., 1986—. Mem. Order of St. Ives. Avocation: breeding horses. Estate planning, Probate, Equine law. Office: Wrigley Estates 1600 Wrigley Bldg Chicago IL 60611

WROBEL, ROBERT FRANKLIN, lawyer, business executive; b. Chgo., Dec. 24, 1944; s. Frank and Julia (Szili) W.; m. Patricia L. Nixon, Aug. 11, 1968; children: Jeffrey, Stephen. B.S. in Fin., U. Ill.-Urbana, 1967, J.D., 1970. Bar: Mo. 1970, Kans. 1973. Atty. Stinson, Mag & Fizzell, Kansas City, Mo., 1970-73; sr. v.p., gen. counsel, chief adminstrv. officer The Marley Co., Mission Woods, Kans., 1973—, dir.; vice chancellor for health affairs, dean U Calif. Coll. Medicine, Irvine, 1986—. General corporate. Home: 24 Urey Ct Irvine CA 92715 Office: U Calif Coll of Medicine Irvine CA 92717

WROBLE, ARTHUR G., lawyer; b. Taylor, Pa., Jan. 21, 1948; s. Arthur S. and Sophia P. Wroble; m. Mary Ellen Sheehan, Nov. 19, 1977; 2 daus., Sophia Ann, Sarah Jean. B.S. in Bus. Adminstrn. with honors, U. Fla., 1970, M.B.A., 1971, J.D., 1973. Bar: Fla. 1973, U.S. Ct. Appeals (5th cir.) 1974, U.S. Supreme Ct. 1976, U.S. Ct. Appeals (11th cir.) 1981, U.S. Dist. Ct. (so. dist.) Fla. 1974, U.S. Dist. Ct. (mid. dist.) Fla. 1982, U.S. Dist. Ct. (no. dist.) Fla. 1986. Ptnr., Burns, Middleton, Farrell & Faust (now Steel, Hector, Davis, Burns & Middleton), Palm Beach, Fla., 1973-82; ptnr. Wolf, Block, Schorr & Solis-Cohen, Phila. and West Palm Beach, Fla., 1982-87, Scott, Royce, Harris & Bryan, P.A., Palm Beach, 1987—; mem. 15th Jud. Cir. Ct. Nominating Commn., 1979-83; mem. U. Fla. Law Center Council, 1981-84; mem. adv. bd. alternative sentencing program Palm Beach County. Served to maj. JAG, U.S. Army Res., 1984. Eagle Scout, 1962. Mem. ABA, Fla. Bar (bd. govs. young lawyers sect. 1979-83, bd. govs. 1985—), Palm Beach County Bar Assn. (pres. young lawyers sect. 1978-79, dir. 1979-81, sec.-treas. 1981-83, pres.-elect 1983-84, pres. 1984-85), Fla. Assn. Women Lawyers, Fla. Council Bar Assn. Pres. (bd. dirs. 1986—), Guild Cath. Lawyers Palm Beach County, Inc. (pres. 1980-81, dir. 1981—), Legal Aid Soc. Palm Beach County, Inc. (dir. 1981—), Fla. Council Bar Assn. Pres.'s (bd. dirs. 1986—), Univ. Fla. Alumni Assn. Palm Beach County (pres. 1983-84). Roman Catholic. Clubs: Kiwanis (pres. 1980-81), Palm Beach County Gator (pres. 1982-83), KC (grand knight 1978-79). Contbr. articles to profl. jours. Consumer commercial, Federal civil litigation, State civil litigation. Home: 7645 Clarke Rd West Palm Beach FL 33406 Office: 450 Royal Palm Way Palm Beach FL 33480

WROBLEY, RALPH GENE, lawyer; b. Denver, Sept. 19, 1935; s. Matthew B. and Hedvig (Lyon) W.; m. Madeline C. Kearney, June 13, 1959; children: Kirk Lyon, Eric Lyon, Ann Lyon. BA, Yale U., 1957; JD, U. Chgo., 1962. Bar: Mo. 1962. With Bell Telephone Co., Phila., 1957-59; mem. Stinson, Mag & Fizzell, Kansas City, Mo., 1962—, ptnr., 1965—; bd. dirs. Sosland Pub. Co. Bd. dirs. Human Resources Corp., 1971; mem. civic council Kansas City, 1986—; chmn. Pub. Housing Authority of Kansas City, 1971-74; vice chmn. Mayor's Adv. Commn. on Housing, Kansas City, 1971-74; bd. govs. Citizens Assn., 1965—, exec. commn., 1969-75, 78-81, 85—, vice chmn., 1971-75, chmn., 1978-79; bd. dirs. Council on Edn., 1975-81, v.p., 1977-79; bd. dirs., pres. Sam E. and Mary F. Roberts Found., 1974—; bd. dirs. Helzberg Found., 1982—; trustee, chmn. Clearinghouse for Mid Continent Founds., 1977—; bd. dirs. Bus. Innovation Center, 1984—. Mem. ABA, Mo. Bar. Republican. Presbyterian (elder). Club: Yale (pres. 1969-71, outstanding mem. award 1967). Contracts commercial, General corporate, Private international. Home: 1015 W 67th Terr Kansas City MO 64113 Office: 2100 Boatmen's Ctr Kansas City MO 64105

WSZOLEK, DENNIS FRANCIS, lawyer; b. Trenton, N.J., Nov. 19, 1951; s. Doris Barbara (Keenan) W.; m. Marion I. Maniewicz, June 22, 1974; children: Dennis Francis Jr., Stephen Dennis. BA, Trenton State Coll., 1973; JD, Capital U., 1976. Bar: U.S. Ct. Appeals (3d cir.), U.S. Supreme Ct. Law clk. to presiding justice N.J. Superior Ct., Trenton, 1976-77; assoc. Wherry & Casale, Trenton, 1977-78; ptnr. Wherry & Wszolek, Trenton, 1978-82; sole practice Hamilton Twp., N.J., 1982—; advising atty. Nat. Alzheimer's Assn., Trenton, 1980—. Producer, broadcaster legal program The Law and You, Sta. 1260 WBUD, 1984—. Lawyer Mercer County Vol. Lawyers Project, Trenton, 1985—. Mem. ABA, N.J. Bar Assn., Mercer County Bar Assn. Roman Catholic. Avocation: music. Insurance, Family and matrimonial, Jurisprudence. Office: 3629 Nottingham Way Hamilton Square NJ 08690

WUEST, GEORGE W., state judge; b. Lake Andes, S.D., Feb. 3, 1925; m. Sandra Wuest, June 25, 1956; children: Linda, Douglas. LLB, U. S.D., 1949. Atty. State of S.D., Lake Andes; asst. atty. gen. State of S.D.; judge U.S. Ct. Appeals (4th cir.), S.D., 1965-87, S.D. Supreme Ct., Pierre, 1987—. Office: Supreme Court Office Capitol Building Pierre SD 57501 *

WUESTNER, LINDA DOUGLAS, lawyer; b. Evnasville, Ind., Dec. 9, 1955; d. Union and Mary (Swanback) Douglas; m. Joseph A. Wuestner Jr., May 16, 1981. BJ, U. Mo., 1977; JD, Washington U., 1981. Bar: Mo. 1981, U.S. Dist. Ct. (we. dists.) Mo. 1981, U.S. Dist. Ct. (ea. dist.) Mo. 1983. Assoc. Blackwell, Sanders, Matheny, Weary & Lmobardi, Kansas City, Mo., 1981-83, Kohn, Shands, St. Louis, 1983-84; sr. atty. Emerson Electric Co., St. Louis, 1984—. Notes and comments editor Washington U. Law Rev., 1981. Mem. ABA, Mo. Bar Assn., St. Louis Bar Assn. Product liability litigation, Environment, Litigation. Office: Emerson Electric Co PO Box 4100 Saint Louis MO 63136

WUKITSCH, DAVID JOHN, lawyer; b. Schenectady, N.Y., June 7, 1955; s. Julius and Laura (Isabel) W. BA, SUNY, Albany, 1977; MA, Sch. Criminal Justice, 1978; JD, Union U., 1981. Bar: N.Y. 1982, U.S. Dist. Ct. (no. dist.) N.Y. 1982, U.S. Ct. Appeals (2d cir.) 1986. Law assistant Appellate div. N.Y. Supreme Ct., Albany, 1981-83; law clk. to assoc. judge N.Y. Ct. Appeals, Albany, 1983-85; assoc. McNamee, Lochner, Titus & Willaims P.C., Albany, 1985—; cons. Police Found., Washington, 1980-81. Mem. ABA, N.Y. State Bar Assn., Assn. Trial Lawyers Am., Justinian Soc. Democrat. Roman Catholic. Avocations: skiing, jogging. State civil litigation, Contracts commercial, Criminal. Office: McNamee Lochner Titus & Williams PC 75 State St PO Box 459 Albany NY 12201

WULFERS, JOHN MANNING, lawyer; b. Morristown, N.J., Apr. 28, 1947; s. John Wilbur and Dorothy Virginia (Wood) W.; m. Nancy Gay Bauch, June 19, 1971; 1 child, Theodore Manning. BA with distinction, U. Wis., 1972; JD, So. Meth. U., 1975. Bar: N.Y. 1976, Ill. 1978, U.S. Dist. Ct. (we. dist.) N.Y. 1978, U.S. Dist. Ct. (no. dist.) Ill. 1978. Asst. dist. atty. Monroe County, Rochester, N.Y., 1976-78; assoc. Hinshaw, Culbertson et al, Chgo., 1978-80; ptnr. Lord, Bissell & Brook, Chgo., 1981—. Served with USNR, 1968-70. Mem. ABA, Ill. Bar Assn., Chgo. Bar Assn., Am. Arbitration Assn. (arbitrator), Nat. Assn. Dist. Attys. (lectr. 1983—). Avocations: golf, travel, fishing, youth sports. Reinsurance, Insurance, Environment. Home: Arlington Heights IL 60005 Office: Lord Bissell & Brook 115 S LaSalle St Chicago IL 60603

WULFSBERG, HAROLD JAMES, lawyer; b. Long Beach, Calif., May 24, 1944; s. Rudolph E. and Grace M. Wulfsberg; m. Janet K. Bergesen, Aug. 19, 1967; children—Analisa Kristina, Richard Tyler, James Todd. A.B., U. So. Calif., 1966; J.D., U. Calif., 1969. Bar: U.S. Dist. Ct. (no. dist.) Calif. 1970, U.S. Ct. Appeals (9th cir.) 1970, U.S. Dist. Ct. (ea. dist.) Calif. 1975, U.S. Dist. Ct. (cen. dist.) Calif. 1982. Ptnr. Lempres & Wulfsberg, Oakland, Calif., 1970—. Recipient Am. Jurisprudence award, 1968; Internat. Acad. Trial Lawyers commendation, 1969. Mem. ABA (fidelity and surety law com., constrn. industry forum com.), Calif. Bar Assn., Alameda County Bar Assn., San Francisco Bar Assn. Co-author: The Deskbook of Construction Contract Law--With Forms, 1981; Avoiding Liability in Architecture, Design and Construction, 1983. Construction, State civil litigation, Federal civil litigation. Office: Lempres and Wulfsberg Kaiser Ctr 300 Lakeside Dr 18th Floor Oakland CA 94612

WULLER, ROBERT GEORGE, JR., lawyer; b. East St. Louis, Ill., Sept. 24, 1947; s. Robert George and Helen Ann (English) W.; m. Jan Ellyn Wittlich, Feb. 4, 1977. BA, U. Notre Dame, 1969; JD, St. Louis U., 1972. Bar: Ill. 1972, U.S. Dist. Ct. (so. dist.) Ill. 1972, Mo. 1983. Assoc. Gundlach, Lee, Eggmann, Boyle & Roessler, Belleville, Ill., 1971-84, ptnr., 1985—. Served to capt. U.S. Army, 1969-75. Mem. ABA, Ill. Bar Assn. (com. unauthorized practice of law 1981-86), Nat. Assn. R.R. Trial Counsel, Ill. Def. Counsel, St. Clair County Bar Assn., Mo. Bar Assn., Bar Assn. Met. St. Louis. State civil litigation, General practice, Federal civil litigation. Home: #2 Teakwood Dr Belleville IL 62221 Office: Gundlach Lee Eggmann Boyle & Roessler 5000 W Main St Belleville IL 62222

WURMS, MARCEL RONALD, lawyer, accountant; b. Queens, N.Y., Jan. 19, 1958; s. Harry and Stella (Hamerslag) W.; m. Marlene Anne Salerno, June 14, 1980; 1 child, Michelle Andrea. BS, Syracuse U., 1979; JD, Rutgers U., 1982. Bar: N.J. 1982, U.S. Dist. Ct N.J. 1982, U.S. Tax Ct. 1983. Sr. tax cons. Arthur Young and Co., N.Y.C., 1982-84, Saddlebrook, N.J., 1984-86; sr. tax cons. Price Waterhouse, Hackensack, N.J., 1986—; tax atty. in field. Chmn. Lodi (N.J.) Citizens Adv. Com., 1985-86. Mem. ABA (tax sect.), N.J. Bar Assn. (tax sect.), Bergen County Bar Assn. (tax sect.), Phi Alpha Delta. Avocations: photography, skiing, motorcycle touring. Personal income taxation, Corporate taxation, Probate. Home: 56 Midland Ave Garfield NJ 07026 Office: Price Waterhouse 411 Hackensack Ave Hackensack NJ 07601

WUTT, ROBERT ANTHONY, lawyer; b. Milw., Oct. 19, 1924; s. Henry J. and Dorothy F. (Koelsch) W.; married; children: Mark R., Mary E. BBA, Marquette U., 1946, JD, 1948. Bar: Wis. 1948, Fla. 1956. Asst. dist. atty. Milw. County, 1959-62, asst. commr. family ct., 1962-64; assoc. Law Firm of Houghton, Bullinger & News, Milw., 1964-66; ptnr. Law Firm of Clarke, O'Brien & Wutt, Deerfield Beach, Fla., 1966-86; sole practice Pompano Beach, Fla., 1986—; bd. govs. Broward County (Wis.) Estate Planning Counsel, 1972-74. Vice pres. Broward County Mental Health Assn., 1970-74. Served with USAF, 1942. Mem. Wis. Bar Assn., Fla. Bar Assn., Broward County Bar Assn., North Broward Bar Assn. (pres. 1974-75). Republican. Episcopalian. Avocations: reading, gardening. Estate planning, Probate, Real property. Office: 2335 E Atlantic Blvd Pompano Beach FL 33064

WYATT, CHARLES HERBERT, JR., lawyer; b. Birmingham, Ala., Aug. 18, 1937; s. Charles Herbert and Elizabeth Florida (Farrell) W.; m. Lane Laverne Bradley, Mar. 18, 1966. B.S. in Bus., Jacksonville State U., 1960; J.D., Cumberland U., 1964. Bar: Ala. 1964, U.S. Dist. Ct. (no. dist.) Ala. 1964, U.S. Ct. Appeals (5th cir.) 1975, U.S. Ct. Appeals (11th cir.) 1981, U.S. Supreme Ct. 1984. Ptnr. Cole, Wyatt & Bradshaw, Birmingham, 1964-73; prin. atty. City of Birmingham, 1973—. Pres. Nat. Guard, 1973-74; chaplin Vulcan Power Squad, U.S. Power Squad, Birmingham, 1983, asst. sec., 1984, adminstrv. officer, 1985, exec. officer, 1987; commdr., Vulcan Power Squadron, 1987—. Mem. Nat. Inst. Mcpl. Law Officers, Sigma Delta Kappa (nat. grand pres. 1973-74). Local government, Labor, Federal civil litigation. Home: 1300 Beacon Pkwy E Birmingham AL 35209 Office: City of Birmingham Law Dept 600 City Hall-710 N 20th St Birmingham AL 35203

WYATT, DONALD L., JR., lawyer; b. Berkeley, Calif., Apr. 24, 1957; s. Donald L. and Louise B. (Barnhill) W.; m. Patty M., June 23, 1979. BA cum laude, U. N.H., 1979; JD cum laude, Suffolk U., Boston, 1982. Bar: N.H., U.S. Dist. Ct. N.H. Assoc. Bossie, Kelly & Hodes, Manchester, N.H., 1982-83; sole practice Wolfeboro, N.H., 1983—. Bd. dirs. Wolfeboro Area Children Ctr., 1984—. Mem. N.H. Bar Assn., Carroll County Bar Assn. (pres. 1984-85). Lodge: Rotary. General corporate, Contracts commercial, Probate. Home: 2 Libby St Wolfeboro NH 03894 Office: Depot St PO Box 1450 Wolfeboro NH 03894

WYATT, HARRY MILLER, III, lawyer; b. Stillwater, Okla., Jan. 26, 1949; s. Harry Miller Jr. and Billie Ruth (Bear) W.; m. Nancy Sue Griffin, Aug. 20, 1971; children: Colby Bryan, Kelly Ruth, Shelby Lynn, Stacy Lee. BBA, So. Meth. U., 1971; JD, U. Tulsa, 1980. Bar: U.S. Dist. Ct. (no. dist.) Okla. 1982. Assoc. Logan, Lowry, Johnston, Switzer, West, Wyatt & McGeady, Vinita, Okla., 1980-83, ptnr., 1983-85; sole practice Stillwater, 1985—; 1985—. Served to maj. Okla. Air N.G., 1977—. Mem. ABA, Assn. Trial Lawyers Am., Okla. Bar Assn., Okla. Trial Lawyers Assn., Payne County Bar Assn. Republican. Methodist. Club: Stillwater Country. Lodge: Rotary (officer 1980-85). Avocations: golf, tennis, coll. athletics. General practice, Contracts commercial, Personal injury. Home: 824 Oakridge Stillwater OK 74074 Office: PO Box 2707 Stillwater OK 74076

WYATT, THOMAS C., lawyer, arbitrator; b. Toronto, Ont., Can., Mar. 19, 1952; came to U.S., 1979; s. Charles and Marietta (Marcinka) Wojatsek; m. Helen A. Johnson, Dec. 24, 1979; 1 child, John Paul Maximilian. BA, Bishop's U., 1975; BCL, McGill U., Montreal, Que., Can., 1974; LLM, U. Montreal, 1980; JD, U. San Francisco, 1981. Bar: Que. 1975, Calif. 1982, U.S. Dist. Ct. (no. dist.) Calif. 1982, U.S. Ct. Appeals (9th cir.) 1982. Assoc. McMaster, Meighen, Montreal, 1975; assoc. counsel Can. Gen. Electric, Lachine, Que., 1975-77; solicitor Du Pont Can. Inc., Montreal, 1977-79; assoc. Blum, Kay & Merkle, Oakland, Calif., 1981-82; internat. counsel Computerland Corp., Hayward, Calif., 1982-85; sr. counsel Bank of Am., San Francisco, 1985—; arbitrator Am. Arbitration Assn., N.Y.C., 1984—; adj. prof. Nat. U., Oakland, 1985—. Author: Joint Ventures in the Province of Quebec, 1980. Mem. Internat. Bar Assn., ABA, Can. Bar Assn., Computer Law Assn. Avocations: tennis, fitness training. Home: 8 Millwood Ct San Rafael CA 94901 Office: Bank of Am NT & SA 555 California St 8th Floor San Francisco CA 94104

WYCHE, BRADFORD WHEELER, lawyer; b. Greenville, S.C., Feb. 22, 1950; s. C. Thomas and Harriet Durham (Smith) W.; m. Carolyn Diane Smock, July 1, 1978; children: Charle Denby Smock, Jessica Kaye. AB in Environ. Sci., Princeton U., 1972; MS in Natural Resource Mgmt., Yale U., 1974; JD, U. Va., 1978. Bar: S.C. 1978, U.S. Dist. Ct. S.C. 1978, U.S. Ct. Appeals (4th cir.) 1978. Assoc. Wald, Harkrader & Ross, Washington, 1978-79; ptnr. Wyche, Burgess, Freeman & Parham, Greenville, 1979—; cons. Nat. Govs. Assn., Washington, 1980; lectr. Exec. Enterprises Confs. on Environ. Regulation, Washington, 1979-84. Contbr. articles to profl. jours. Mem. Gov.'s Council on Natural Resources, Columbia, S.C., 1983-84; pres. Warehouse Theatre, Greenville, 1982-83; bd. dirs. Greenville Symphony Assn., 1984—, Pendleton Place, Greenville, 1984—; mem. S.C. Coastal Council, 1986—. Mem. ABA (vice chmn. environ. quality com. natural resources div. 1980-84), S.C. Bar Assn. Democrat. Avocations: tennis, piano, whitewater kayaking. Environment, General corporate. Home: 312 Raven Rd Greenville SC 29615 Office: Wyche Burgess Freeman & Parham 44 E Camperdown Way PO Box 10207 Greenville SC 29603

WYCHE, CYRIL THOMAS, lawyer; b. Greenville, S.C., Jan. 28, 1926; C. Granville and Mary (Wheeler) W.; m. Harriet Smith, June 19, 1948; children: Sara McCall, Bradford Wheeler, Mary Frances. BE, Yale U., 1946; LLB, U. Va., 1949. Bar: S.C. 1948, U.S. Dist. Ct. S.C. 1950, U.S. Ct. Appeals (4th cir.) 1952, U.S. Ct. Claims 1964, U.S. Supreme Ct. 1970. Ptnr. Wyche, Burgess, Freeman & Parham, P.A., Greenville, S.C., 1948—; bd. dirs. Citizens & So. Nat. Bank S.C., Columbia; bd. dirs., sec. RSI Corp., Greenville. Pres., bd. dirs. YMCA, Greenville, 1960; pres. Greenville Little Theatre, 1965, Arts Festival Assn., Greenville, 1970, Greenville Community Corp., 1976—; bd. dirs. Greater Greenville C. of C., 1980. Served with USN, 1943-46. Named Environmentalist of Yr., State of S.C., 1979; recipient Conservation award Gulf Oil Corp., 1983. Mem. ABA, S.C. Bar Assn., Greenville County Bar Assn., Am. Judicature Soc. Presbyterian. Avocations: skiing, scuba diving, piano, tennis, white water canoeing. General corporate, Probate, Corporate taxation. Office: Wyche Burgess Freeman & Parham 44 E Camperdown Way PO Box 10207 Greenville SC 29603

WYCHE, MADISON BAKER, III, lawyer; b. Albany, Ga., Aug. 11, 1947; s. Madison Baker Jr. and Merle (McKemie) W.; m. Marguerite Jernigan Ramage, Aug. 7, 1971; children: Madison Baker IV, James Ramage. BA, Vanderbilt U., 1969, JD, 1972. Bar: Ga. 1972, U.S. Dist. Ct. (mid. dist.) Ga. 1972, U.S. Ct. Appeals (5th cir.) 1973, S.C. 1976, U.S. Dist. Ct. S.C. 1977, U.S. Ct. Appeals (4th cir.) 1977, U.S. Supreme Ct. 1980, U.S. Ct. Appeals (11th cir.) 1981. Assoc. Perry, Walters, Lippitt & Custer, Albany, 1972-76, Thompson, Ogletree & Deakins, Greenville, S.C., 1976-77, Ogletree, Deakins, Smoak & Stewart, Greenville, 1977-80; ptnr. Ogletree, Deakins, Nash, Smoak & Stewart, Greenville, 1980—; bd. dirs. Wyche Oil Co., Inc., Elberton, Ga., Happy Ho., Inc., Albany. Co-incorporator, sec. of State Tenn. Intercollegiate State Legis., Nashville, 1967-69; state sec.-treas. Coll. Young Dems., Nashville, 1968; mem. employer and employee relations com. N.C. Citizens for Bus. and Industry, Raleigh, 1984-86; vestry Christ Episc. Ch., Greenville, 1981-85. Served to capt. U.S. Army, 1969-77. Recipient Eagle Scouts award Boy Scouts Am., 1961. Mem. ABA, S.C. Bar Assn. (unauthorized practice of law com., 1977—, 1982-86), Ga. Bar Assn., Atlanta Bar Assn. (chmn.), Phi Delta Phi. Club: St. Andrews Soc. Upper S.C. (bd. dirs. 1982-84, v.p. 1986—). Lodge: Rotary (bd. dirs. 1982-84, Paul Harris fellow 1986). Labor, Workers' compensation, Environment. Office: Ogletree Deakins Nash Smoak & Stewart PO Box 2757 Greenville SC 29602

WYCHE, N(ORMAN) HUNTER, JR., lawyer; b. Raleigh, N.C., May 12, 1951; s. Norman H. and Nannie (York) W.; m. Jacquelyn Hill, Apr. 12, 1976; children: Cameron, Hunt. BBA, Campbell U., Buies Creek, N.C., 1976, JD, 1980. Bar: N.C. 1980, U.S. Dist. Ct. (ea. dist.) 1980, U.S. Dist. Ct. (mid. dist.) N.C. 1982, U.S. Dist. Ct. (we. dist.) N.C. 1984, U.S. Supreme Ct. 1985. Ptnr. Smith, Debnam, Hibbert & Pahl, Raleigh, 1980—. Mem. ABA, N.C. Bar Assn., Wake County Bar Assn., Comml. Law League Am. Republican. Episcopalian. Bankruptcy. Office: Smith Debnam et al PO Drawer 26268 Raleigh NC 27611

WYER, JAMES INGERSOLL, lawyer; b. Denver, June 9, 1923; s. William and Katherine (Rolfe) W.; m. Joan Best Connelly, Aug. 13, 1960; children: Joan Connelly Tatnall, Peter Ford, June Wyer Nugent. B.A., Yale U., 1945, LL.B., 1949. Bar: N.Y. 1950. Assoc. Dewey, Ballantine, Bushby, Palmer & Wood, N.Y.C., 1949-56, Am. Cyanamid Co., Wayne, N.J., 1956; v.p., gen. counsel Am. Cyanamid Co., 1973-86; of counsel Robinson, Wayne, Levin, Riccio & LaSala, Newark, 1986—. Served with USNR, 1943-46. Mem. Assn. Gen. Counsel (1st v.p. 1982-84, pres. 1985-86), ABA, Assn. Bar City N.Y. Republican. Clubs: Jupiter Island (Hobe Sound, Fla.); Beach, Lawn and Tennis (Seabright, N.J.); Met. Opera (N.Y.C.); Coral Beach and Tennis (Bermuda). Office: Robinson Wayne Levin Riccio & LaSala One Gateway Ctr Newark NJ 07102

WYKOFF, JOHN ROBERT, lawyer; b. Erie, Pa., Sept. 17, 1951; s. Robert George and Dorothy Jean (Conrad) W.; m. Jean Marie Vincent, Aug. 17, 1973; children—Bradford Conrad, Juli Marie, Brett William. Student in bus. Ohio U., 1970-73; B.B.A. cum laude, U. Cin., 1974; J.D. cum laude, U. Dayton, 1979. Bar: Ohio 1979, U.S. Dist. ct. (so. dist.) Ohio 1979. Assoc. Brannon & Cox, Dayton, 1979-80, Lang, Horenstein & Dunlevey, Dayton, 1980-84, White, Getgey & Meyer, Cin., 1984—; law dir. Village of New Lebanon, Ohio, 1982—, city of Forest Park, Ohio, 1987—; legal adviser KDI, Inc., handicapped workshop, Dayton, 1983-84; legal counsel, trustee Miami Valley Golf Club, Dayton, 1984. Mem. Madeira Schs. Planning Commn., 1986—, central com. and jud. screening com. Montgomery County Republican Party, Dayton, 1983-84; bd. dirs. Montgomery County unit Am. Cancer Soc., 1983-84, Daybreak, Inc., Dayton, 1984. Mem. ABA, Ohio State Bar Assn. (aviation law com.), Cin. Bar Assn. (negligence law com.), Dayton Bar Assn., Assn. Trial Lawyers Am., Ohio Assn. Trial Lawyers. Roman Catholic. Clubs: Miami Valley Golf (trustee); Kenwood Country. Federal civil litigation, State civil litigation, Personal injury. Home: 6552 Madeira Hills Dr Madeira OH 45243 Office: White Getgey & Meyer Co LPA 2021 Auburn Ave Adam Riddle House Cincinnati OH 45219

WYKOWSKI, HENRY GEORGE, lawyer; b. Mineola, N.Y., Oct. 18, 1948; s. Henry T. and Stephanie (Kruk) W.; m. Sara A. Keller, Mar. 10, 1984. BS, U. Bridgeport, 1970; JD, Tulane U., 1974. Bar: La. 1974, U.S. Ct. Appeals (5th cir.) 1975, Calif. 1976, U.S. Ct. Appeals (9th cir.) 1980, U.S. Dist. Ct. D.C. 1981, U.S. Tax Ct. 1984. Polit. coordinator Jimmy Carter Presdl. Campaign, 1976; trial atty. tax div. U.S. Dept. Justice, 1977-80; asst. U.S. atty. U.S. Dist. Ct. (no. dist.) Calif., San Francisco, 1980-82; assoc. Mosher, Pooley, Sullivan & Hultquist, Palo Alto, Calif., 1982-86; sole practice San Francisco, 1986—; faculty Atty. Gen.'s Advocacy Inst.; instr. bus. litigation Hastings Coll. Trial Advocacy, San Francisco, 1985—; guest lectr. criminal practice seminar Boalt Hall, U. Calif.; active Fed. Pub. Defender's Panel. Bd. dirs. Boyer House Found., San Francisco, 1984—. Mem. ABA, Assn. Trial Lawyers Am., Calif. Atty.'s for Criminal Justice. Democrat. Roman Catholic. Criminal, Federal civil litigation, State civil litigation. Home: 1890 Broadway Apt 107 San Francisco CA 94109 Office: 240 Stockton St Suite 500 San Francisco CA 94108

WYLIE, PAUL RICHTER, JR., lawyer; b. Livingston, Mont., Dec. 25, 1936; s. Paul Richter and Alice (Hazel) Dredge; m. Arlene Marie Klem, Mar. 6, 1982; children—Lynne Catherine, John Michael, Thomas Robert. B.S. in Chem. Engring., Mont. State U., 1959; J.D., Am. U., 1965. Bar: Calif. 1970, Utah 1967, U.S. Supreme Ct. 1971. Patent examiner U.S. Patent and Trademark Office, Washington, 1962-64; asst. gen. patent counsel Dart Industries Inc., Los Angeles, 1967-81; sole practice, Los Angeles, 1981-86, Pacific Palisades, Calif., 1986—. Mem. ABA, Los Angeles County Bar Assn., Am. Patent Law Assn., Patent Law Assn. Los Angeles, Am. Inst. Chem. Engrs., Am. Chem. Soc., Licensing Execs. Soc., Inter-Am. Assn. Indsl. Property, U.S. Trademark Assn. Patent, Trademark and copyright, Antitrust. Home: 1012 Las Pulgas Rd Pacific Palisades CA 90272 Office: 15200 Sunset Blvd Suite 210 Pacific Palisades CA 90272

WYLIE, RICHARD JOHN, lawyer; b. Fresno, Calif., Dec. 13, 1933; s. John M. and Ruth (Williams) W.; Karen Sue Cress, May 7, 1960; children—Pamela Jean, Michael John. A.B., Stanford U., 1955, J.D., 1958. Bar: Calif. 1959, U.S. Supreme Ct. 1979, U.S. Ct. Appeals (9th cir.) 1959, U.S.

Ct. Appeals (5th cir.) 1967. Partner Morgan, Beauzay, Wylie, Ferrari & Leahy, San Jose, Calif., 1960-68; dep. legislative counsel State of Calif., 1959; dep. dist. atty. Contra Costa County, Calif., 1959-60; mem. firm Wylie, Leahy, Blunt, McBride, San Jose, 1968-76; partner Wylie, Blunt & McBride, San Jose, 1977-82, Wylie, Blunt, McBride & Jesuiger, 1982—; lectr. Calif. State Bar continuing edn. of the bar courses. Chmn., Assemblyman John Vasconcellos, 1966; mem. Santa Clara County Dem. Central Com., 1964-68, chmn., 1966-68; chmn. Robert F. Kennedy county campaign, 1968; del. Dem. Conv., 1968; mem. Dem. State Central Com., 1966-68. Recipient Service award Community Legal Services of Santa Clara County, 1976. Mem. Santa Clara County Bar Assn. (pres. 1970), Am. Trial Lawyers Assn., Calif. Trial Lawyers Assn. (bd. dirs. 1987—), Los Angeles Trial Lawyers Assn., ABA, Calif. Bar Assn. (mem. judicial council, joint commn. on civil discovery, mem. exec. com. conf. of dels. 1978-81). State civil litigation, Personal injury, Condemnation. Address: Suite 1001 101 Park Center Plaza San Jose CA 95115

WYMAN, WILLIAM ALAN, lawyer; b. Denver, Jan. 1, 1931; s. John Corbett Wyman and Marry (Wood) George; m. Barbara Lu Hough, Dec. 17, 1955 (div.); children—Alan Ross Wyman Smith, Robert Frank Wyman Smith. B.A. in Chemistry, U. Wash., 1960; J.D., Gonzaga U., 1966. Bar: S.D. 1972, U.S. Dist. Ct. (we. dist.) S.D. 1972. Practice law, Rapid City, S.D., since 1972—, sole practice, 1974—. Served to sgt. USMC, 1951-54; Korea. Mem. Assn. Trial Lawyers Am., S.D. Trial Lawyers Assn., S.D. Bar Assn., ABA. Personal injury, Environment, Criminal. Home: 1110 Oriole St Rapid City SD 57701 Office: 624 6th St Suite 212 Rapid City SD 57701

WYMER, JOHN FRANCIS, III, lawyer; b. West Palm Beach, Fla., July 26, 1949; s. John Francis Jr. and Thelma Virginia (Smith) W.; 1 child, Mason. BA, U. Ala., 1971; JD, U. Va., 1974. Bar: Ala. 1974, Ga. 1975, U.S. Dist. Ct. (no. dist.) Ga. 1975, U.S. Ct. Appeals (5th and 11th cirs.) 1975. Ptnr. Smith, Currie & Hancock, Atlanta, 1974-84, Paul, Hastings, Janofsky & Walker, Atlanta, 1984—; mem. adv. bd. Inst. for Applied Mgmt. and Law, Newport Beach, Calif., 1983—; bd. dirs. Ga. Employment Law Council, Atlanta, 1986—. Mem. ABA (labor and employment law), Ala. Bar Assn., Ga. Bar Assn., Nat. Labor Relations Assn. (devel. law com.), Bus. Council of Ga. (jud. com.). Club: Cherokee Country (Atlanta). Labor, Federal civil litigation, Administrative and regulatory. Home: 4235 Glengary Ct Atlanta GA 30342 Office: Paul Hastings Janofsky & Walker 133 Peachtree St NE 42d Floor Atlanta GA 30303

WYNN, CHARLES MILTON, lawyer; b. Marianna, Fla., Jan. 21, 1953; s. Milton Gerard and Joanne (Wandeck) W.; m. Roberta Lyn Hovanec, Jan. 28, 1977; 1 child, Charles Philip Wynn. AA, Chipola Jr. Coll., 1972; BA, U. Fla., 1974; JD, Nova U., 1977. Bar: Fla. 1977, U.S. Dist. Ct. (no. dist.) Fla. 1978, U.S. Ct. Appeals (11th cir.) 1981, U.S. Dist. Ct. (mid. dist.) Fla. 1985. Assoc. Herman Laramore Law Offices, Marianna, 1977-78; sole practice Marianna, 1978—; assoc. pub. defender, Marianna, 1977—; sec. Fla. Audio Research, Inc., Marianna, 1986. Bd. dirs. Jackson County Guidance Clinic, Mairanna, 1978-83; pres. Bright Start Learning Ctr., Inc., Marianna, 1984; deacon First Presbyn. Ch., Marianna, 1983; mem. Marianna Gideon Camp, 1984—, Marianna Christian Cen. Ch., 1985; chmn. Jackson County Freedom Council, Marianna, 1986. Mem. ABA, Fla. Bar Assn. (cert. of appreciation 1979), Panhandle Bar Assn. (pres. 1984), Pub. Defender's Assn., Comml. Law League of Am., Marianna Jaycee's (membership award 1979), Phi Alpha Delta (v.p. 1985—). Democrat. Lodge: Rotary (treas. Marianna 1985). Avocations: canoeing, fishing. Bankruptcy, Contracts commercial, General corporate. Home: 163 Watson Dr Marianna FL 32446 Office: PO Box 793 Marianna FL 32446

WYNN, MARY ELLEN, lawyer; b. Cleve., Nov. 25, 1946; d. William B. and Margaret E. (Ludwig) W.; m. Leonard M. Sussman, May 29, 1977; 1 child, Emily Wynn Sussman. Student, Western Coll. for Women, 1964-66; BA, Ohio State U., 1968, JD, 1973. Bar: Conn. 1973, D.C. 1974, U.S. Ct. Appeals (2d cir.) 1975, U.S. Supreme Ct. 1980. Assoc. Magill, Badger, Fisher, Cohen & Barnett, Greenwich, Conn., 1973-74; ptnr. Williams, Avery & Wynn, New Haven, 1974-77, Williams, Wynn & Wise, New Haven, 1977-79; sole practice Stamford, Conn., 1979-86; ptnr. Wynn, Casper & de Toledo, Stamford, Conn., 1987—; mem. Gov.'s Commn. on Child Support, 1985-86. Mem. editorial bd. Conn. Law Tribune, 1986—. Bd. dirs. Stamford YWCA, 1985—, Tower Sch., Stamford, 1982-85. Mem. Conn. Bar Assn. (chmn. family law sect. 1984-86, exec. com. women and the law sect. 1982—, com. on jud. selection and evaluation 1986—), Stamford-Darien Bar Assn. (bd. dirs. 1986—). Democrat. Avocations: gardening, swimming, tennis. Family and matrimonial. Office: Wynn Casper & de Toledo 22 5th St Stamford CT 06905

WYNNE, WILLIAM JOSEPH, lawyer; b. Little Rock, July 17, 1927. Student Little Rock U., 1946-48; J.D., U. Ark., 1951. Bar: Ark. 1951, U.S. Dist. Ct. Ark. 1951, U.S. Supreme Ct. 1958; ordained to ministry Presbyterian Ch. Sr. counsel Murphy Oil Corp., El Dorado, 1951-68; ptnr. Crumpler, O'Connor & Wynne, El Dorado, 1963—; gen. counsel and hearing officer Ark. Oil and Gas Commn.; pastor St. Andrew Cumberland Presbyterian Ch. Mem. ABA, Ark. Bar Assn., Union County Bar Assn., Assn. Trial Lawyers Am., Ark. Trial Lawyers Assn., El Dorado C. of C. (Outstanding Young Man 1961-62). General practice, Oil and gas leasing. Home: 1501 W Block El Dorado AR 71730 Office: NBC Plaza Suite 308 El Dorado AR 71730

WYNSTRA, NANCY ANN, lawyer; b. Seattle, June 25, 1941; d. Walter S. and Gaile E. (Cogley) W. B.A. cum laude, Whitman Coll., 1963; LL.B. cum laude, Columbia U., 1966. Bar: Wash. 1966, D.C. 1969, Ill. 1979, Pa. 1984. With appellate sect., civil div. U.S. Dept. Justice, Washington, 1966-67; TV corr.-legal news Sta. WRC, NBC and Sta. WTOP, CBS, Washington, 1967-68; spl. asst. Corp. Counsel, D.C., Washington, 1968-70; dir. planning and research D.C. Superior Ct., Washington, 1970-78; spl. advisor White House Spl. Action Office for Drug Abuse Prevention, Washington, 1973-74; fellow Drug Abuse Council, 1974-75; gen. counsel Michael Reese Hosp. and Med. Center, Chgo., 1978-83; sr. v.p., gen. counsel Allegheny Health Services, Inc., Pitts., 1983—; cons. to various drug abuse programs, 1971-78. Mem. ABA, Nat. Health Lawyers Assn. (bd. dirs. 1985—), Am. Soc. Hosp. Attys., others. Presbyterian. Contbr. articles to profl. jours. Health, Personal injury, General corporate. Office: Allegheny Gen Hosp 320 E North Ave Pittsburgh PA 15208

WYRSCH, JAMES ROBERT, lawyer, educator; b. Springfield, Mo., Feb. 23, 1942; s. Louis Joseph and Jane Elizabeth (Welsh) W.; m. B. Darlene Wyrsch, Oct. 18, 1975; children—Scott, Keith, Mark, Brian, Marcia. B.A., U. Notre Dame, 1963; J.D., Georgetown U., 1966; LL.M., U. Mo., Kansas City, 1972. Bar: Mo. 1966, U.S. Ct. Appeals (8th cir.) 1971, U.S. Supreme Ct. 1972, U.S. Ct. Appeals (10th cir.) 1974, U.S. Ct. Appeals (5th cir.) 1974, U.S. Ct. Mil. & Appeals 1978, U.S. Ct. Appeals (6th cir.) 1982, U.S. Ct. Appeals (11th cir.) 1984, U.S. Ct. Appeals (7th cir.) 1986. Assoc., Koenigsdorf, Kusnetzky Wyrsch, and predecessors, Kansas City, Mo., 1970-71, of counsel, 1972-77, ptnr., 1978—; adj. prof. U. Mo., 1981—; mem. com. instrns. Mo. Supreme Ct., 1983—. Served as capt. U.S. Army, 1966-69. Mem. Am. Arbitration Assn. (panel arbitrators), ABA, Mo. Bar Assn. (vice chmn. criminal law com. 1978-79), Kansas City Bar Assn. (chmn. anti-trust com. 1981), Assn. Trial Lawyers Am., Nat. Assn. Criminal Def. Attys., Mo. Assn. Criminal Def. Attys. (sec. 1982), Phi Delta Phi. Democrat. Roman Catholic. Contbr. in field. Criminal, Antitrust, Legal education. Home: 811 Hearnes St Blue Springs MO 64015 Office: Koenigsdorf Kusnetzky & Wyrsch 1006 Grand Ave Suite 1050 Kansas City MO 64106

WYSE, SCOTT CAMPBELL, lawyer; b. Portland, Oreg., July 20, 1948; s. William W. and Janet E. (Oswalt) W.; m. Karen Berry, Aug. 10, 1974 (div.); children: Kyoko K., Jessica J. BA, U. Pa., 1970; postgrad., UCLA, 1970-74; JD, U. Oreg., 1974. Bar: Oreg. 1974. Assoc. Meyer, Habernigg & Wyse and predecessor firms, Portland, 1974-80, ptnr., 1980—. Bd. dirs. Oreg. Downtown Devel. Assn., Portland, 1986—. Mem. ABA, Oreg. Bar Assn., Multnomah Bar Assn. Democrat. Club: Portland City. General practice, Real property, State civil litigation. Home: 4309 SW Twombly Ave Portland OR 97201 Office: Meyer Habernigg & Wyse 900 SW 5th Ave Suite 1900 Portland OR 97204

WYSE, WILLIAM WALKER, lawyer; b. Spokane, Wash., July 20, 1919; s. James and Hattie (Walker) W.; m. Janet E. Oswalt, Jan. 30, 1944; children: Wendy L., Scott E., Duncan C. A.B., U. Wash., 1941; LL.B., Harvard U., 1948. Bar: Oreg. 1948. Since practiced in Portland; ptnr. Stoel, Rives, Boley, Fraser and Wyse, 1953—; dir. Treasureland Savs. and Loan Assn.; past trustee, sec. Pacific Realty Trust; trustee Holladay Park Plaza. Bd. dirs. Community Child Guidance Clinic, 1951-57, pres., 1956-57; chmn. cen. budget com. United Fund, 1958-60; 1st v.p. United Good Neighbors; chmn. dir. Portland Sch. Bd., 1959-66; pres. Oreg. Symphony Soc., Tri-County Community Council, 1971-73; bd. dirs. Portland Mental Health Assn.; bd. dirs., sec. Oreg. Parks Found. Served to lt. USNR, 1942-46. Mem. ABA, Oreg. Bar Assn., Multnomah County Bar Assns., Am. Coll. Real Estate Lawyers, Delta Upsilon. Republican. Presbyterian (trustee 1955-58, chmn. 1958). Clubs: University (Portland), Arlington (Portland), City (Portland) (sec. 1957). Real property, Private international, Contracts commercial. Home: 3332 S W Fairmount Ln Portland OR 97204 Office: 900 S W 5th Ave Portland OR 97201

WYSOCKI, HENRY VICTOR, lawyer; b. N.Y.C., Mar. 10, 1950; s. Victor and Anna (Brzozowski) W.; m. Alisa Maria Capozzi, June 12, 1976. BBA, Siena Coll., 1971; MBA, Adelphi U., 1975; JD, N.Y. Law Sch., 1980. Bar: N.Y. 1981. Asst. treas. Chase Manhattan Bank, N.Y.C., 1975-80, asst. counsel, 1980-85; counsel N.Y. Clearing House, N.Y.C., 1985—. Served to lt. USAR, 1971-75, maj. JAGC Res. Mem. ABA, N.Y. Bar Assn., Assn. Corp. Counsel. Democrat. Roman Catholic. Avocations: running, weight lifting, Am. history. Banking, Military. Home: 1848 E 32d St Brooklyn NY 11234 Office: NY Clearing House 90 Broad St New York NY 10004

WYSOCKI, JAMES ANTHONY, lawyer; b. Chgo., Oct. 31, 1938; s. Felix B. and Virginia Marie (Konopa) W.; m. M. Cristina Longoria, Dec. 7, 1974; B.B.A. cum laude, U. Notre Dame, 1960, B.Laws (scholar), 1963; J.D., Loyola Sch. Law, New Orleans, 1965. Bar: Ind. 1963, La. 1964, U.S. Dist. Ct. (ea. dist.) La. 1964, U.S. Ct. Appeals (5th cir.) 1966, U.S. Supreme Ct. 1968. U. Notre Dame teaching fellow, 1961-63; law clk. to Frank B. Ellis, U.S. Dist. Judge, Eastern Dist. La., 1963-65; trial atty. Ungar, Dulitz & Martzell, New Orleans, 1965-69; trial atty., sr. ptnr. Heisler & Wysocki and predecessor firms, New Orleans, 1969—; mem. internat. com. to select greatest 100 courses in world Golf mag. Active New Orleans City Ballet, New Orleans Mus. Art (fellow), Preservation Resource Ctr., Lakewood Property Owners Assn., Boy Scouts Am. Contbr. articles to profl. jours. Mem. Fed. Bar Assn. (chpt. pres. 1964-65), New Orleans Acad. Trial Lawyers (pres. 1975-76, co-chmn. legis. com.), Assn. Trial Lawyers Am. (La. state del. 1984-86), Maritime Law Assn. (1984 conv. com.), Lawyer Pilots Bar Assn. (dir. 1974-82), CAP (squadron comdr. and search pilot), La. Trial Lawyers Assn. (gov. 1973-75, 80-86), ABA, La. Bar Assn. (ho. of dels. 1985-87), Greater New Orleans Trial Lawyers Assn., New Orleans Bar Assn., Jefferson Parish Bar Assn., Ind. Bar Assn., Aircraft Owners and Pilots Assn. Roman Catholic. Clubs: Metairie Country, Century, Notre Dame of New Orleans, Freret Carnival. Personal injury, Admiralty, Federal civil litigation. Home: 5638 Evelyn Ct New Orleans LA 70124 Office: 844 Baronne St New Orleans LA 70113

WYSOLMERSKI, SIGISMUND JOHN ALBERT, lawyer; b. Proctor, Vt., Mar. 22, 1953; s. Sigismund Simon and Jane Lucille (Wasik) W.; m. Donna Marie Shappy, Apr. 26, 1986. A.B., Loyola Coll., Montreal, 1977; J.D., U. Balt., 1980. Bar: Vt. 1980, U.S. Dist. Ct. Vt. 1980, Md. 1981. Atty., Abatiell & Abatiell, Rutland, Vt., 1977—. Sch. commr. City of Rutland, 1982-85, alderman, 1986—; mem. City Republican Com., Rutland, 1984-85; alderman City of Rutland. Mem. ABA (dist. rep. young lawyers div., exec. council), Vt. Trial Lawyers Assn., Am. Trial Lawyers Assn., Md. Trial Lawyers Assn., Vt. Bar Assn. (bd. mgrs., chmn. young lawyers sect.), Nat. Assn. Criminal Def. Lawyers, Polish Am. Soc. Republican. Roman Catholic. Lodges: K.C., Moose, Elks. Personal injury, State civil litigation, Family and matrimonial. Office: Abatiell and Abatiell 56 1/2 Merchants Row Rutland VT 05701

WYSS, JOHN BENEDICT, lawyer; b. Evanston, Ill., Nov. 23, 1947; s. Walther Erwin and Caroline Nettie (Benedict) W.; m. Dianne Dunlop, Aug. 12, 1978; children: John Christian, Kirsten Dunlop. BS in Physics summa cum laude, Stanford U., 1969; JD, Yale U., 1972. Bar: Calif. 1972, D.C. 1974, U.S. Supreme Ct. 1976. Trial atty. antitrust sect. U.S. Dept. Justice, Washington, 1972-74; assoc. Kirkland & Ellis, Washington, 1974-78, ptnr., 1978-83; ptnr. Wiley, Rein & Fielding, Washington, 1983—. Mem. ABA, Phi Beta Kappa. Antitrust, Federal civil litigation, Administrative and regulatory. Office: Wiley Rein & Fielding 1776 K St NW Washington DC 20006

YABLON, BABETTE, lawyer; b. N.Y.C.. BA, NYU, 1950, JD, 1953. Bar: N.Y. 1953, U.S. Dist. Ct. (so. and ea. dists.) N.Y. 1953. Sole practice N.Y.C., 1955-74; ho. counsel Lion Ins. Co., Lynbrook, N.Y., 1976-78; assoc. Shayne, Dachs, Stanisci & Corker, Mineola, N.Y., 1978—; lectr. C.W. Post Univ. U.S. Mil. Acad. Author: (with others) Discovery in Personal Injury Actions, 1980, Women Trial Lawyers: How They Succeed in Practice and in the Courtroom, 1987. Mem. Nassau Bar Assn. Personal injury, Family and matrimonial, General practice. Home: 941 Glenwood Rd West Hempstead NY 11552 Office: Shayne Dachs Stanisci & Corker 1501 Franklin Ave Mineola NY 11501

YACHMETZ, PHILIP KEITH, lawyer; b. Jersey City, Feb. 20, 1957; s. Peter and Margaret (Marko) Y.; m. Maria Anne Fiorentino, Oct. 10, 1981 (div. Apr. 1984); m. Marusia Szczupak, Nov. 28, 1986. BA, George Washington U., 1978; JD, Calif. Western Law Sch., 1981. Bar: N.J. 1981, U.S. Dist. Ct. N.J. 1981, U.S. Dist. Ct. (so. and ea. dists.) N.Y. 1982, U.S. Ct. Internat. Trade 1985, U.S. Supreme Ct. 1985. Assoc. Hill, Rivkins, Carey, Loesberg, O'Brien & Mulroy, N.Y.C., 1981-84, Haight, Gardner, Poor & Havens, N.Y.C., 1984-85; asst. gen. counsel shipping div. Burmah Oil Shipping Inc., N.Y.C., 1985-86; counsel, corp. sec. shipping div. Burmah LNG Shipping, Inc./ Burmah Gas Transp. Ltd., Greenwich, Conn., 1986—. Counsel, bd. dirs. Bayonne (N.J.) Community Day Care Ctr., 1986-87. Mem. ABA, Internat. Law Assn. (Am. br.), Inter-Am. Bar Assn., Maritime Law Assn., Assn. Trial Lawyers Am., Ukrainian Am. Bar Assn. (chmn. membership 1985—). Republican. Mem. Ukrainian Catholic Ch. Avocations: antiques, photography, sailing, skiing, woodworking. Admiralty, General corporate, Private international. Home: 1308 Stillson Rd Fairfield CT 06430-3052 Office: Burmah LNG Shipping Inc 3 Pickwick Plaza Suite 400 Greenwich CT 06830-5592

YAGER, JOHN WARREN, lawyer, banker; b. Toledo, Sept. 16, 1920; s. Joseph A. and Edna Gertrude (Pratt) Y.; m. Dorothy W. Merki, July 25, 1942; children: Julie M., John M. AB, U. Mich., 1942, JD, 1948. Bar: Ohio 1948. Sole practice Toledo, 1948-64; trust officer Toledo Trust Co., 1964-69; v.p., trust officer First Nat. Bank, Toledo, 1969—; sec. First Ohio Bancshares, Inc., 1980-85. Pres. Toledo Met. Park Dist., 1971-85, Neighborhood Health Assn., 1974-75, councilman, Toledo, 1955-57, 60-61, mayor, 1958-59; bd. dirs. Toledo-Lucas County Library, 1968-70, Riverside Hosp., Downtown Toledo Assn.; past pres. Toledo Legal Aid Soc., Toledo Council Chs., Toledo Mcpl. League, Econ. Opportunity Planning Assn., Toledo, Com. on Relations with Toledo, Spain. Served to maj. USMC, 1942-46, 50-52. Decorated Bronze Star; named one of 10 outstanding young men Toledo, 1952, 54, 55. Mem. Ohio Bar Assn., Toledo Bar Assn., Toledo Estate Planning Council, Delta Tau Delta. Club: Belmont Country (Toledo). Estate planning, Probate, Estate taxation. Home: 29301 Bates Rd Perrysburg OH 43551-3808 Office: First Nat Bank Toledo 606 Madison Ave Toledo OH 43604

YAGERMAN, HOWARD W., lawyer; b. Bklyn., Feb. 23, 1949; s. Jack L. and Lila J. (Sugarman) Y.; m. Hillary Anne Horwitz, Aug. 29, 1971; children—Justin, Zachary. B.A., Harpur Coll., 1970; M.A., U. Del., 1972; J.D., Bklyn. Law Sch., 1977. Bar: N.Y. 1978, U.S. Dist. Ct. (so. dist.) N.Y. 1979, U.S. Dist. Ct. (ea. dist.) N.Y. 1979. Researcher, Temporary State Commn. on Child Welfare, N.Y. Senate, 1975-77, counsel Subcom. Juvenile Justice, 1977; dir. juvenile justice div. Criminal Justice Services, N.Y.C., 1978-79; gen. counsel N.Y.C. Dept. Probation, 1979-87, 1st dep. commr., 1987—; adj. prof. John Jay Coll. Criminal Justice, N.Y.C., 1977-80; lectr. Bklyn. Coll., 1981—; lectr. Forensic Psychiat. Clinic, N.Y.C., 1983-84; mem. adv. bd. Family Ct. Appellate div. 1st Dept., N.Y.C., 1983-84. N.Y. State Regents scholar, 1966-70. Mem. N.Y. County Lawyers Assn. (sec. family ct. 1979-83, chmn. family ct. 1984-85), N.Y. State Bar Assn. (com. on juvenile justice) Democrat. Jewish. Family and matrimonial, Legislative, Criminal. Home: 574 E 16th St Brooklyn NY 11226 Office: New York City Dept Probation 115 Leonard St New York NY 10013

YALE-LOEHR, STEPHEN WILLIAM, lawyer, editor; b. Newport News, Va., June 10, 1954; s. Raymond Charles and Joan Mary (Briggs) Loehr; m. Amy Janet Yale, July 16, 1977; 1 child, Elizabeth. BA, Cornell U., 1977, JD cum laude, 1981. Bar: D.C. 1981, U.S. Dist. Ct. (D.C. dist.) 1982, U.S. Ct. Appeals (D.C. cir.) 1983. Law clk. to chief judge U.S. Dist. Ct. (no. dist.) N.Y., Syracuse, 1981-82; assoc. Sutherland, Asbill & Brennan, Washington, 1982-86; assoc. editor Interpreter Releases, Washington, 1986—. Cofounder, editor Imagework mag., 1977; contbr. articles to profl. jours. Coordinator Amnesty Internat., 1983—, mem. Turkey Co-Group, 1985—. Mem. ABA, D.C. Bar Assn., Am. Immigration Lawyers Assn., Phi Beta Kappa. Democrat. Avocations: photography, hiking. Immigration, naturalization, and customs, Private international, Public international. Home: 7453 Broken Staff Columbia MD 21045 Office: Interpreter Releases 1120 20th St NW Suite 500 S Washington DC 20036

YALOWITZ, KENNETH GREGG, lawyer; b. Moline, Ill., Apr. 9, 1954; s. Jerome M. and Esther F. (Falkoff) Y.; m. Jan A. Albright, Jan. 4, 1976; children: Kevan, James T. BS, Ill. State U., 1976; JD, So. Ill. U., 1979. Bar: Ill. 1979, Mo. 1980, Wash. 1982, U.S. Dist. Ct. (ea. and we. dists.) Wash. 1982, U.S. Ct. Appeals (9th cir.) 1985. Assoc. Peper, Martin, Jensen, Maichel & Hetlage, St. Louis, 1979-82, Nourse & Assocs., Seattle, 1982-86, Hight & Green, Seattle, 1986—; instr. Bellevue Community Coll., Wash., 1985. Commr. Issaquah (Wash.) Planning Commn., 1986—. Mem. ABA, Wash. State Bar Assn., King County Bar Assn., Associated Gen. Contractors. Avocations: hiking, skiing, running. Federal civil litigation, Contracts commercial, Construction. Office: Hight & Green 3230 First Interstate Ctr Seattle WA 98104

YAMADA, STEPHEN KINICHI, lawyer; b. Honolulu, July 19, 1946; s. Harold Kiyoshi and Frances Sadako (Uchida) Y.; m. Amy M. Chiemi, Apr. 23, 1965 (div.); 1 child, Tammy Lynn; m. Kwi Nam Kim, Nov. 19, 1984. BA, U. Hawaii, 1968; JD, U. Calif., San Francisco, 1971. Bar: Hawaii 1972, U.S. Dist. Ct. Hawaii 1972. Dep. atty. gen. State of Hawaii, Honolulu, 1971-74; sole practice Honolulu, 1974—. Mem. ABA, Assn. Trial Lawyers Am., Hawaii Jaycees (state legal counsel 1976). Democrat. Lodge: Rotary. Avocations: reading, swimming. Federal civil litigation, State civil litigation, Personal injury. Office: 820 Mililani St #612 Honolulu HI 96813

YAMAKAWA, DAVID KIYOSHI, JR., lawyer; b. San Francisco, Jan. 25, 1936; s. David Kiyoshi and Shizu (Negishi) Y. B.S., U. Calif.-Berkeley, 1958, J.D., 1963. Bar: Calif. 1964, U.S. Supreme Ct. 1970. Prin. Law Offices of David K. Yamakawa Jr., San Francisco, 1964—. Dep. dir. Community Action Agy., San Francisco, 1968-69; dir. City Demonstration Agy., San Francisco, 1969-70; mem. adv. council Calif. Senate Subcom. on the Disabled, 1982-83; chmn. community residential treatment system adv. com. Calif. Dept. Mental Health, 1980-85; bd. dirs. Family Survival Project, 1981—; mem. San Francisco Human Rights Commn., 1975—; sr. v.p. Japanese Cultural and Community Ctr. of No. Calif., 1981-86; pres. Legal Assistance to the Elderly, 1981-83, Council of Internat. Programs, San Francisco, 1987—; 2d v.p. Nat. Conf. Social Welfare, 1983—; sec. Rescue Now, 1979—; v.p. Region IX, Nat. Mental Health Assn., 1981-83; bd. dirs. Mt. Zion Hosp. and Med. Ctr., 1983—; bd. dirs. United Neighborhood Ctrs. of Am., 1977-83; chmn. bd. trustees United Way Bay area, 1983-85; bd. dirs. Children's Home Soc. Calif., 1985—; v.p. Friends of Legal Assistance to the Elderly, 1984—; vice chmn. Friends of the San Francisco Human Rights Commn., 1985—; bd. dirs. Ind. Sector, 1986—, Keep Libraries Alive, 1986—, La Madre de los Pobres, 1982—, Nat. Concilio of Am., 1987—; pres. Council Internat. Programs, San Francisco, 1987—. Recipient John S. Williams Outstanding Planning and Agy. Relations vol. award United Way of the Bay Area, 1980, Mortimer Fleishhacker Jr. Outstanding Vol. award, United Way, 1985; Spl. Recognition award Legal Assistance to the Elderly, 1983, commendation Bd. Suprs. City and County of San Francisco, 1983, cert. Honor, Bd. Suprs. City and County San Fracnsico, 1985; San Francisco Found. award, 1985; October 10, 1985 proclaimed as David Yamakawa Day in San Francisco, 1985. Mem. ABA (Liberty Bell award 1986). General practice. Office: 582 Market St Suite 410 San Francisco CA 94104

YAMAMOTO, JEREL IKMO, lawyer; b. Hilo, Hawaii, Feb. 4, 1955; s. Akira and Margaret (Kawano) Y. BA, U. So. Calif., 1977; JD, Georgetown U., 1980. Bar: Hawaii 1980, U.S. Dist. Ct. Hawaii 1980. Law clk. to presiding justice Hawaii Supreme Ct., Honolulu, 1980-82; assoc. Nakamoto, Yoshioka & Okamoto, Hilo, 1982-84, ptnr., 1985—. Mem. ABA, Hawaii Bar Assn., Hawaii County Bar Assn. (officer, bd. dirs.), Lehua Jaycees (C. William Brownfield Meml. award 1986, Officer of the Yr. 1986), Phi Beta Kappa, Phi Kappa Phi. Avocations: golf, tennis, softball, football, baseball. General practice, Probate, State civil litigation. Office: Nakamoto Yoshioka & Okamoto 187 Kapiolani St Hilo HI 96720

YAMBRUSIC, EDWARD SLAVKO, lawyer, consultant; b. Conway, Pa., Mar. 9, 1933; s. Michael Misko and Slavica Sylvia (Yambrusic) Y. B.A., Duquesne U., 1957; postgrad. Georgetown U. Law Ctr., 1959-61; J.D., U. Balt., 1966; cert. The Hague (Netherlands) Acad. Internat. Law, 1967, 69, diploma Ctr. Study and Research of Internat. Law and Internat. Relations, 1970; Ph.D. in Pub. Internat. Law, Cath. U. Am., 1984. Bar: Md. 1969, U.S. Ct. Customs and Patent Appeals 1972, U.S. Supreme Ct. 1972. Copyright examiner U.S. Copyright Office, Library of Congress, Washington, 1960-69, atty. adviser Office Register of Copyrights, 1969—; pvt. practice internat. and immigration law, 1969—; legal counsel Nat. Ethnic Studies Assembly, 1976—, Soc. Fed. Linguists, 1980. Pres. Nat. Confedn. Am. Ethnic Groups, Washington; nat. chmn. Croatian-Am. Bicentennial Com.; nat. chmn. Nat. Pilgrimage of Croatian-Ams. to Nat. Shrine of Immaculate Conception, Washington; v.p. Croatian Acad. Am. Served to capt. U.S. Army, 1957-59. Duquesne U. Tamburitzans scholar, 1953-57; Hague Acad. Internat. Law fellow, 1970. Mem. ABA, Md. Bar Assn., Internat. Law Assn., Internat. Fiscal Assn., Am. Soc. Internat. Law, Croatian Cath. Union Am., Croatian Frat. Union Am. Republican. Roman Catholic. Author: Treaty Interpretation: Theory and Reality, 1987; contbr. articles to ofcl. newsletter Nat. Confedn. Am. Ethnic Groups, also legal jours. Trademark and copyright, Public international, Immigration, naturalization, and customs. Home and Office: 4720 Massachusetts Ave NW Washington DC 20016

YAMIN, MICHAEL GEOFFREY, lawyer; b. N.Y.C., Nov. 10, 1931; s. Michael and Ethel Y.; m. Martina Schaap, Apr. 16, 1961; children—Michael Jeremy, Katrina. A.B. magna cum laude, Harvard U., 1953, LL.B., 1958. Bar: N.Y. 1959, U.S. Dist. Ct. (so. dist.) N.Y., U.S. Dist. Ct. (ea. dist.) N.Y., U.S. Ct. Appeals (2d cir.) 1966, U.S. Supreme Ct. 1967. Assoc. Weil, Gotshal & Manges, N.Y.C., 1958-65; sr. ptnr. Colton, Hartnick, Yamin & Sheresky, N.Y.C., 1966—. Bd. trustees Gov.'s Comm. Scholastic Achievement, 1976-86; chmn. Manhattan Community Bd. 6, 1986-87, mem., 1974—; bd. trustees Rockland County Soc. Prevention of Cruelty to Children, 1979—. Served as lt. USNR, 1953-55, Korea. Mem. ABA, N.Y. State Bar Assn., Assn. Bar City N.Y., Fed. Bar Counsel, Am. Fgn. Law Assn., Internat. Law Assn., Societe de Legislation Compare, Internat. Bar Assn. Clubs: Harvard Faculty (Cambridge, Mass.); Harmonie, Harvard (N.Y.C.) (trustee N.Y. Found. 1981—, sub-chmn. schs. and scholarships com. 1972—, bd. mgrs. 1985—). Contracts commercial, General corporate, Private international. Home: 206 E 30th St New York NY 10016 Office: 79 Madison Ave New York NY 10016

YAMIN, ROBERT JOSEPH, lawyer; b. Waterbury, Conn., May 31, 1949; s. Joseph George and Elizabeth Mary (Bouharoun) Y.; children: Rebecca Anne, Samantha Blythe. Student, Yale U., 1978; AB in Polit. Sci. and History summa cum laude, Western Conn. State U., 1979; JD, Harvard U., 1982. Bar: Conn. 1982, U.S. Dist. Ct. Conn. 1983, U.S. Tax Ct. 1983, N.Y. 1984, U.S. Supreme Ct. 1986. Assoc. Day, Berry & Howard, Hartford, Conn., 1982-85, Reid and Riege, P.C., Hartford, 1985-87, Cohen and Wolf, P.C., Bridgeport, Conn., 1987—. Sr. exec. editor Harvard Jour. Law and Pub. Policy, 1981-82. Mem. Jaycees, Danbury, Conn., 1970-75; mem., ward chmn. Danbury Rep. Town Com., 1973; pres. Greater Danbury Young Rep. Club, 1974; del. to White House/State House Conf. on Library and Info.

Services, Conn., 1978. Mem. ABA, N.Y. State Bar Assn., Conn. Bar Assn. (fellow acad. of continuing legal edn. 1985, chmn. corp. banking and bus. law com. young lawyers div. 1986, profl. discipline com.), Fed. Bar Assn., Hartford County Bar Assn., Danbury Bar Assn., Bridgeport Bar Assn., Alliance Francaise Internat. (conferee), Am. Soc. Writers on Legal Subjects, Phi Alpha Delta, Pi Gamma Mu, Phi Alpha Theta. Roman Catholic. Club: Hartford. Lodges: Elks, Moose. Avocations: internat. and foreign affairs, strategic studies and nat. security matters, outdoor activites. General corporate, General practice, Health. Home: 21 Morris St Danbury CT 06810 Office: Cohen and Wolf PC 1115 Broad St Bridgeport CT 06604

YANAS, JOHN JOSEPH, lawyer; b. Albany, N.Y., July 18, 1929; m. Mary Faith Casey; children—John J., Joseph J., Kathleen Ann, Mary Patricia. Student Russell Sage Coll., 1947-50; LL.B., Albany Law Sch., 1953. Bar: N.Y. 1954, U.S. Ct. Appeals (2d cir.) 1962. Assoc. Casey, Honikel and Wisely, Albany, 1954-60; ptnr. Dugan, Casey, Burke & Lyons, Albany, 1960-69; ptnr. Casey, Yanas, Mitchell & Amerling, Albany, 1969-84, Casey, Yanas, Clyne, Mitchell & Amerling, Albany, 1984—; counsel Albany County Pub. Welfare Dist., 1959-60; mem. Albany City CSC, 1970-73, Albany County CSC, 1970-73; justice Albany City Ct., 1973-77; trustee Home and City Savs. Bank; dir. Monroe Abstract & Title Corp., Rochester, N.Y. Trustee Christian Bros. Acad., Albany, 1972—, Albany Law Sch., 1975—. Fellow Am. Bar Found., N.Y. Bar Found., ABA; mem. Am. Coll. Real Estate Lawyers, N.Y. State Bar Assn. (chmn. real property law sect. 1974-75, (chmn. com. to confer with N.Y. State Realty Bd. 1975-77, chmn. com. continuing legal edn. 1977-80, treas. 1980—), Albany County Bar Assn. (pres. 1978). Banking, Probate, Real property. Office: 100 State St Albany NY 12207

YANCEY, DAVID WALLACE, lawyer, finance company executive; b. Lamar, Mo., Nov. 5, 1948; s. Chester Wallace and Elzene Maria Yancey. BA in Psychology, Stanford U., 1970, JD, 1974. Assoc. Brobeck, Phleger & Harrison, San Francisco, 1974-77; ptnr. Ream, Train, Horning, Maxwell & Yancey, Palo Alto, Calif., 1977-79; pres., gen. counsel Crown Capital Corp., San Jose, Calif., 1979—; pres. Safeguard Escrow Services, Inc., 1984—; mem. Nat. Def. Exec. Res. for the Fed. Emergency Agency, 1975—; referee Calif. State Probate, 1978—. Mem. Calif. Bar Assn. Club: Commonwealth Calif. Lodge: Rotary (bd. dirs. Palo Alto, pres. endowment fund). Avocation: rugby. Real property, Mortgage law, Banking. Office: Crown Capital Corp 690 Saratoga Ave Suite 1 San Jose CA 95129

YANDLE, STEPHEN THOMAS, law school administrator; b. Oakland, Calif., Mar. 7, 1947; s. Clyde Thomas and Jane Walker (Hess) Y.; m. Martha Anne Welch, June 26, 1971. BA, U. Va., 1969, JD, 1972. Bar: Va. 1972. Asst. dir. admissions U. Va. Law Sch., Charlottesville, 1972-76; from asst. to assoc. dean Northwestern U. Sch. Law, Evanston, Ill., 1976-85; assoc. dean Yale U. Law Sch., New Haven, 1985—. Served to capt. U.S. Army, 1972. Mem. Law Sch. Admission Council (programs, edn. and prelaw com. 1978-84), Assn. Am. Law Schs. (chmn. legal edn. and admissions sect. 1979), Nat. Assn. for Law Placement (pres. 1984-85, co-chairperson Joint Nat. Assn. com. on placement 1986—). Legal education. Office: Yale U. Law Sch Drawer 401A Yale Sta New Haven CT 06511

YANITY, GERALD JOSEPH, lawyer; b. Crabtree, Pa., Nov. 8, 1945; s. Harry T. and Minnie (Sorice) Y.; m. Kathleen Palko, Aug. 10, 1968, children: Gerald W., Jeralyn Lee. BS, St. Vincent Coll., 1967; JD, Duquesne U., 1975. Bar: Pa. 1975, U.S. Dist. Ct. (we. dist.) Pa. 1975. Assoc. Stewart, Belden and Belden, Latrobe, Pa., 1976—; solicitor New Alexandria (Pa.) Borough Council, 1980—, Youngwood (Pa.) Borough Council, 1986—; of counsel Latrobe Area Hosp., 1978—. Pres., chmn. bd. Latrobe Youth Commn., 1979—. Served with USAR, 1968-74. Mem. ABA, Pa. Bar Assn., Westmoreland County Bar Assn., Soc. Hosp. Attys. Western Pa., Hosp. Assn. Pa. (hosp. counsel). Democrat. Roman Catholic. Lodges: Lions (trustee Latrobe club), Elks. Probate, Health, Local government. Office: Stewart Belden Belden 305 Mellon Bank Bldg Latrobe PA 15650

YANKOWITZ, JACK ALAN, lawyer; b. N.Y.C., Apr. 20, 1954; s. Murray and Roslyn (Balaban) Y.; m. Cheryl M. Schulberg, Dec. 19, 1976; 1 child, Brandon Ross. B.A. cum laude, Queens Coll., 1975; J.D., Albany Law Sch., Union U., 1978. Bar: N.Y. 1979, U.S. Dist. Ct. (so. and ea. dists.) N.Y. 1979, U.S. Supreme Ct. 1984. Assoc. Bruckman, Bernstone & Goldman, N.Y.C., 1978-81, Lipsig, Sullivan & Liapakis, N.Y.C., 1981-83; sr. assoc. and product liability dept. head of firm Morris J. Eisen, P.C., N.Y.C., 1983-85; sr. ptnr. Shapiro & Yankowitz, P.C., N.Y.C., 1985—; products liability and personal injury cons. in pvt. practice, N.Y.C., 1982—; guest lectr. St. John's Law Sch., N.Y.C., 1985. Legis. asst. N.Y. State Assemblyman Saul Weprin, Queens, N.Y., 1973-75; founding mem. ct. watcher program Queens Dem. Orgn., 1972-74. Mem. Assn. Trial Lawyers Am., ABA, N.Y. County Lawyers Assn., Queens Bar Assn., N.Y. State Bar Assn., N.Y. Trial Lawyers Assn. Jewish. Personal injury, Federal civil litigation. Office: Empire State Bldg 350 5th Ave Suite 601 New York NY 10118

YANNELLO, JUDITH ANN, judge; b. Buffalo, Mar. 27, 1943; d. Guy Raymond and Grace (Barone) Y. B.A., Barnard Coll., 1964; J.D., Cornell U., 1967. Bar: N.Y. 1967, D.C. 1970, U.S. Supreme Ct 1971. Law clk. U.S. Ct. Claims, Washington, 1967-68; trial atty. civil div. Dept. Justice, Washington, 1968-73; asso. firm Hudson, Creyke, Koehler & Tacke, Washington, 1973-76; adminstrv. judge Armed Services Bd. Contract Appeals, Washington, 1976-77; trial judge U.S. Ct. Claims, Washington, 1977-82; judge U.S. Claims Ct., Washington, 1982—; speaker, lectr. Contbr. articles to profl. jours.; co-editor, contbg. author: Manual for Practice in U.S. Court of Claims, 1976. Recipient Disting. Service award Fed. Bar Assn., 1975; Meritorious Service award Dept. Justice, 1972. Mem. ABA (mem. Jud. Adminstrn. Div., chmn. continuing legal edn. com. Public Contract Law Sect. 1981-82), Fed. Bar Assn. (chmn. Ct. Claims com. 1974-76), D.C. Bar Assn. (cert. of appreciation 1976), N.Y. State Bar Assn., D.C. Bar, Exec. Women in Govt., Nat. Assn. Women Judges (v.p. dist. 4 1979-81). Club: Zonta. Jurisprudence. Office: US Claims Court 717 Madison Pl NW Washington DC 20005

YANNUCCI, THOMAS DAVID, lawyer; b. Springfield, Ohio, Mar. 30, 1950; s. David Marion and Patricia (Wilson) Y.; m. Lisa Marie Copeland, June 30, 1972; children: Teresa, Andrea, Thomas D. Jr. AB, U. Notre Dame, 1972, JD, 1976. Bar: Ohio 1977, U.S. Ct. Appeals (1st and 8th cirs.) 1980, U.S. Supreme Ct. 1980, D.C. 1981. Law clk. to presiding justice U.S. Ct. Appeals (D.C. cir.), Washington, 1976-77; trial atty. U.S. Dept. Justice, Washington, 1977-80; ptnr. Kirkland & Ellis, Washington, 1980—. Editor-in-chief U. Notre Dame Law Rev., 1975-76. Roman Catholic. Federal civil litigation, Antitrust, State civil litigation. Office: Kirkland & Ellis 655 15th St NW Suite 1200 Washington DC 20005

YANO, FRANCIS HISAO, lawyer; b. Waltham, Mass., Sept. 17, 1947; s. Vincent Hisaki and Eloise Yoshie (Takiguchi) Y.; m. Shelley Yan Hoo Yung, May 25, 1970; children: Jennifer, Christopher, Kymberly. BA, U. Hawaii, 1970; JD, U. Colo., 1972. Bar: Hawaii 1973, U.S. Dist. Ct. Hawaii 1973. Sole practice Honolulu, 1973-74, 79-83; ptnr. Ing, Lebb & Yano, Honolulu, 1974-79, Yano & Matsumoto, Honolulu, 1983-86; sole practice Honolulu, 1987—; pres. TVF Inc., Honolulu, 1982—. Bd. dirs. Protection and Advocacy, Honolulu, 1986—. Served to capt. USAR, 1970-78. Mem. Assn. Trial Lawyers Am. Real property, Probate, Personal injury. Office: Yano & Matsumoto 333 Queen St Suite 601 Honolulu HI 96813

YARBROUGH, EDWARD MEACHAM, lawyer; b. Nashville, Dec. 17, 1943; s. Gurley McTyeire and Miriam (Mefford) Y. BA, Rhodes Coll., 1967; JD, Vanderbilt U., 1973. Bar: Tenn. 1973. Asst. dist. atty. Davidson County, Nashville, 1973-76; ptnr. Hollins, Wagster & Yarbrough, Nashville, 1976—. Chmn. com. Crime Commn., Nashville, 1981-82; mem. task force House Judiciary Com., Nashville, 1984; chmn. Crimestoppers Inc., Nashville, 1983—; trustee United Way, Nashville, 1983—; bd. dirs. Big Bros. Inc., Nashville, 1983-85. Served to 1st lt. U.S. Army, 1969-71, Vietnam. Decorated Bronze Star, 1971. Fellow Nat. Speleological Soc (bd. dirs. 1960—); mem. ABA (bd. dirs. 1985), Tenn. Bar Assn., Nashville Bar Assn. (pres. 1983), Tenn. Criminal Def. Lawyers. Democrat. Baptist. Club: Richland Country, City (Nashville). Avocations: cave exploration, photography, skiing, golf, running. Criminal, State civil litigation, Domestic relations litigation. Home: 5230 Granny White Pike Nashville TN 37220 Office: Hollins Wagster & Yarbrough 201 4th Ave N Nashville TN 37219

YARBROUGH, MARILYN VIRGINIA, law educator, university administrator; b. Bowling Green, Ky., Aug. 31, 1945; d. William Ottoway Yarbrough and Merca Lee (Hardin) Toole; m. Walter James Ainsworth, Sept. 3, 1967 (div. Oct. 1980); children: Carmen Virginia, Carla Renee. BA, Va. State U., 1966; JD, UCLA, 1973. Bar: Calif. 1973, Kans. 1982. Instr. Boston Coll. Law Sch., Newton, Mass., 1975-76; prof. law U. Kans., Lawrence, 1976—, assoc. vice chancellor, 1983—; chmn. bd. Law Sch. Admission Services Inc., Newtown, Pa.; pres. bd. trustees Law Sch. Admission Council, Newtown, 1986—. Editor-in-chief Black Law Jour. 1972-73; contbr. articles to profl. jours. Pres. Lawrence United Way, 1985—, Lawrence Housing Authority, 1986—. Mem. ABA (reporter Am. Law Inst.-ABA com. continuing edn. 1985—), Nat. Collegiate Athletic Assn. (com. on infractions 1986—). Democrat. Congregationalist. Personal injury, Civil rights. Home: 926 Indiana St Lawrence KS 66044 Office: U Kans 226 Strong Hall Lawrence KS 66045

YARED, PAUL DAVID, lawyer; b. Grand Rapids, Mich., Aug. 10, 1949; s. Woodrow Alexander and Jane (Coury) Y.; m. Kristine Elizabeth Bruce, July 17, 1971; 1 child, Elizabeth. BA, Mich. State U., 1971; JD, U. Denver, 1974. Bar: Mich. 1975, U.S. Dist. Ct. (we. dist.) Mich. 1975. Corp. atty. Foremost Ins. Co., Grand Rapids, 1974—, v.p., sec., 1984—; v.p., sec., gen. counsel Foremost Corp. Am., Grand Rapids, 1985—; bd. dirs. Centennial Park Hotel Corp., Grand Rapids. Bd. dirs. Centennial Park Devel. Rev. Bd., Grand Rapids, 1978—. Mem. ABA, Mich. Bar Assn., Grand Rapids Bar Assn. Clubs: Charlevoix, Meadowood (Grand Rapids). Securities, General corporate, Contracts commercial. Office: Foremost Corp Am 5800 Foremost Dr SE PO Box 2450 Grand Rapids MI 49501

YAREMA, GEOFFREY STEVEN, lawyer; b. Orlando, Fla., Sept. 21, 1953; s. Steven and Doris Marie (Erb) Y. BS, U. Fla., 1975; JD, U. Va., 1978. Bar: Calif. 1978, U.S. Dist. Ct. (cen. dist.) Calif. 1978. Assoc. Nossaman, Guthner, Knox & Elliott, Los Angeles, 1978-84, ptnr., 1984—; lectr. U. So. Calif. Grad. Sch. Urban and Regional Planning, Los Angeles, 1980-81. Articles editor Va. Jour. Internat. Law, 1977-78; contbr. articles to profl. jours. Chmn. Calif. chpt. Job Opportunities Program U.S. Olympic Com., 1984—; bd. dirs. Los Angeles Ctr. Photog. Studies, 1983-86, chmn. 1984-86, Manhattan Beach Sr. Housing Found., 1983—. Mem. ABA, Calif. Bar Assn., Phi Beta Kappa. Oil and gas leasing, Real property, Environment. Office: Nossaman Guthner Knox & Elliott 445 S Figueroa St 31st Floor Los Angeles CA 90071-1672

YARES, HOWARD SCOTT, lawyer; b. N.Y.C., May 2, 1947; s. Abraham David and Charlotte (Cohen) Y.; m. Bonnie E. Kalmus, Nov. 21, 1971; children: Ari, Ami, Gravri. BA, Case Western Reserve U., 1969, JD, 1972; postgrad., LaSalle Coll., 1981, U. Pa., 1981-82. Bar: Pa. 1972, N.J. 1972, U.S. Dist. Ct. (ea. dist.) Pa. 1972, U.S. Dist. Ct. N.J. 1972, U.S. Ct. Appeals (3d cir.) 1981. Sole practice Phila., 1972-76; asst. dir. Victim Counseling Service, Phila., 1976, dir., 1976-78; dir. legal services Phila. Bar Assn., 1978—; cons. ABA, Chgo., 1986—. Pres. Young Assocs., Congregational Beth'El, Cherry Hill, N.J., 1981; bd. dirs. Kelman Acad., Cherry Hill, 1983, Bur. Jewish Edn., Cherry Hill, 1984. Mem. ABA (com. on crime victims, lawyer referral service gen. practice sect.), Assn. Trial Lawyers Am., Nat. Orgn. Victim Assistance. Delivery of legal services. Office: Lawyer Referral and Info Service 1 Reading Ctr 11th Floor 1101 Market St Philadelphia PA 19107

YARMEY, RICHARD ANDREW, lawyer, financial consultant; b. Kingston, Pa., Aug. 23, 1948; s. Stanley Richard and Rose Mary (Rees) Y.; m. Jeanne Marie Cappelli, Aug. 5, 1972; children: Lynn Rees, Jessica Brett, Kristen Alexandra. BS, U. Scranton, 1970; JD, Cath. U., 1975. Bar: Pa. 1975, D.C. 1976, U.S. Ct. Appeals (5th cir.) 1976, U.S. Tax Ct. 1978, U.S. Ct. Appeals (D.C. cir.) 1980. Contract adjudicator GAO, Washington, 1970-73; program asst. EPA, Washington, 1973; assoc. Sharon, Pierson, et al, Washington, 1975-82; of counsel Pierson, Semmes et al, Washington, 1982—, Winkler, Danoff et al, Wilkes-Barre, Pa., 1982—; fin. cons. various individuals and bus. concerns, 1976—; TV panelist, speaker on energy law. Contbr. articles to newspapers; editor EPA publs. Sordoni Found. grantee, Wilkes-Barre, Pa., 1971. Mem. ABA, D.C. Bar Assn., Pa. Bar Assn., ACLU, Common Cause, Aircraft Owners and Pilots Assn., Alpha Sigma Nu. Democrat. Avocation: flying. FERC practice, Contracts commercial, General corporate. Office: 304 Wilkes Barre Ctr Wilkes Barre PA 18711

YATES, ALFRED GLENN, JR., lawyer; b. Sarver, Pa., June 17, 1946; s. Alfred Glenn and Mary Etta (Best) Y.; m. Barbara Jean Lang, June 12, 1982; children: Jennifer Christine, Elizabeth Ann. BA in Philosophy, Coll. William and Mary, 1968; JD, U. Pitts., 1973. Bar: Pa. 1973, U.S. Dist. Ct. (we. dist.) Pa. 1973, U.S. Ct. Appeals (3d cir.) 1984, W.Va. 1987. Asst. v.p. trust dept. Pitts. Nat. Bank, 1973-79; assoc. Wayman, Irvin & McAuley, Pitts., 1979-80; sole practice, Pitts., 1981—; instr. taxation Robert Morris Coll., Pitts., 1982. Developer (book) Pocket Tax Calculators, 1976—; assoc. editor The Quiz Book, 1986. Legal counsel, founding mem. West Pa. chpt. Lupus Found. Am., Pitts., 1982—. Served with U.S. Army, 1968-70. Decorated Joint Service Commendation medal. Mem. Pa. Bar Assn., Assn. Trial Lawyers Am. (Ethics Exam award 1987), William Penn Assn. Lodge: Masons. Probate, Personal injury, Estate planning. Office: Yates & Caplan Attys at Law 519 Allegheny Bldg 429 Forbes Ave Pittsburgh PA 15219

YATES, CARL EUGENE, lawyer; b. Long Lane, Mo., Nov. 11, 1940; s. Roma Earnest and Mary Artimissi (Wing) Y.; m. Joy Lauranna Evertz, July 16, 1965; children: Steven B., Juli C., Nicole M. BA, S.W. Mo. State U., 1962; JD, Washington U., St. Louis, 1965. Bar: Mo. 1965, U.S. Dist. Ct. (we. dist.) Mo. 1965, U.S. Ct. Appeals (8th cir.) 1968. Assoc. Lincoln, Haseltine, Keet, Forehand & Springer, Springfield, Mo., 1965-69; ptnr. Lincoln, Forehand & Yates, Springfield, 1969-71, Yates, Mauck, Bohrer & Elliff, P.C. and predecessor firms, Springfield, 1971—. Treas. Mo. State Dem. Com., Jefferson City, 1977-79; chmn. Springfield Regional Airport Bd., 1979; co-chmn. Gov.'s Econ. Devel. Adv. Com., Springfield, 1979-80; vice chmn. Mo. Hwy. and Transp. Bd., Jefferson City, 1984; dir. emeritus Greater Ozarks Zool. Soc. Served with U.S. Army, 1960-66. Mem. ABA, Mo. Bar Assn., Green County Bar Assn. (treas. 1968-69), Nat. Assn. Bond Lawyers, Springfield C. of C. (pres. 1982). Avocations: fishing, gardening. Municipal bonds. Home: 1954 Meadowview Springfield MO 65804 Office: Yates Mauck Bohrer & Elliff PC 1736 E Sunshine Springfield MO 65804

YATES, DAVID FLOYD, lawyer; b. St. Louis, Mar. 27, 1944; s. Ballard Alton and Vandora (Evans) Y.; m. Linda Zambakian, June 30, 1966; children—Brian David, Mark Christopher. B.A., Ohio Wesleyan U., 1966; J.D., U. Mo., Columbia, 1969. Bar: Mo. 1969, U.S. Dist. Ct. (ea. dist.) Mo. 1971, U.S. Ct. Appeals (8th cir.) 1973, U.S. Supreme Ct. 1983. Atty., NLRB, St. Louis, 1969-71; ptnr. Rassieur, Long, Yawitz & Schneider, St. Louis, 1971-76; prin. Suelthaus & Kaplan, P.C., St. Louis, 1976—. Ruling elder Webster Groves Presbyterian Ch.; trustee Webster Groves Library Dist., 1979-82; chmn. troop com. Boy Scouts Am., 1982. Mem. ABA, Bar Assn. Met. St. Louis, Mo. Bar Assn., Midwest Pension Conf., Assn. For Corp. Growth. Republican. Clubs: Algonquin Golf, Masons. Labor, Pension, profit-sharing, and employee benefits, General corporate. Home: 371 Gray Ave Webster Groves MO 63119 Office: 8000 Maryland Ave 9th Floor Saint Louis MO 63105

YATES, LAWDEN HENRY, criminalist, lawyer; b. Gadsden, Ala., Mar. 2, 1947; s. Lawden Henry and Bessie Louise (Cooper) Y.; m. Kathleen Smelley, Sept. 5, 1970 (div. July 1976); 1 child, Lawden Christopher; m. Judy Ann Lott, Aug. 2, 1980; 1 child, Amanda Lauren. BS, Auburn U., 1974; JD, Birmingham Sch. Law, 1982. Bar: Ala. 1982, U.S. Dist. Ct. (no. dist.) Ala. 1983. Criminalist II, lab. dir. Ala. Dept. Forensic Scis., Birmingham, 1972—. Mem. Assn. Firearms and Toolmark Examiners, So. Assn. of Forensic Scis., Birmingham Bar Assn. Democrat. Episcopalian. Avocations: canoeing, kayaking, camping, fishing, hunting. Local government, General practice, Firearms expert. Home: 2533 Carmel Rd Birmingham AL 35235 Office: Ala Dept Forensic Scis 1001 13th St S Birmingham AL 35205

YATRON, GEORGE CONSTANTINE, lawyer; b. Jan. 9, 1951; m. Shirlee D. Sabalski. BA in Econs., U. Pitts., 1973; JD, Georgetown U., 1976. Bar: Pa. 1976, U.S. Dist. Ct. (ea. dist.) Pa. 1977. Sole practice Reading, Pa., 1976-80; mem. Berk's County Pub. Defenders Office, Reading, 1976-79; dist. atty. Berks County, 1979—. Mem. task force com. Berks County Prison Soc.; advisor Berks County Law Explorer Post. Recipient Appreciation award Crime Victims Ctr., 1984, Richard Eshelman award Berks County Prison Soc., 1984. Mem. Berks County Bar Assn. (criminal law com.), Pa. Dist. Attys. Assn. (exec. com., resolutions com.), Am. Legion (appreciation award 1980). Home: 19 Birdie Ln Reading PA 19607 Office: Dist Atty County of Berks Reading PA 19601

YEAGER, DENNIS RANDALL, lawyer; b. Dallas, Jan. 10, 1941; s. William C. and Katherine (Bell) Y.; m. Jere Jones, Aug. 31, 1963; children—Stephanie Ann, Karen Elizabeth, Brenda Marie. B.S.S., Loyola U. of South, 1964; LL.B., Columbia U., 1967. Bar: N.Y. 1967, D.C. 1979, U.S. Supreme Ct. 1971, U.S. Ct. Appeals (2d cir.) 1972, U.S. Ct. Appeals (4th cir.) 1971, U.S. Ct. Appeals (5th cir.) 1970, U.S. Dist. Ct. (so. dist.) N.Y. 1969, U.S. Dist. Ct. Md. 1974, U.S. Dist. Ct. (we. dist.) N.Y. 1975. Dir. law intern program Columbia U., summer 1967; assoc. Willkie Farr & Gallagher, N.Y.C., 1967-69; dir., chief exec. officer Nat. Employment Law Project, N.Y.C., 1969-75; from assoc. to ptnr. Tufo, Johnston & Allegaert, N.Y.C., 1975-81; ptnr. Yeager & Lang, N.Y.C., 1980—; chmn. program on bus. errors and omissions ins. Practising Law Inst., 1983, program on role of outside counsel in bus. investigation, 1985 Program v.p. U.S. Nat. Student Assn., 1962-63. Mem. ABA, N.Y. State Bar Assn., Assn. Bar City N.Y., Blue Key, Alpha Sigma Nu. Roman Catholic. Federal civil litigation, State civil litigation, Insurance. Home: 70 W 95th St New York NY 10025 Office: Yeager & Lang 888 7th Ave New York NY 10106

YEE, KENNETH M.P., lawyer; b. Canton, Republic of China, Feb. 5, 1946; s. Kin Hon and Wai Ching (Lee) Y.; m. May Chan, May 3, 1970; children: Susana, Ann Marie, Betty Kay, Angela Cathy, Kevin Robert. BA, Sir George Williams U., Montreal, Can., 1968; MS, Northeastern U., 1971; JD, Suffolk U., 1978. CPA, Mass. Tax acct. Deloitte, Haskins & Sells, Boston, 1970-76; sole practice law, pvt. practice acctg. Boston, 1976—. Mem. ABA, Am. Inst. CPA's, Am. Immigration Lawyers Assn. Immigration, naturalization, and customs, Real property, Corporate taxation. Office: 30 Kneeland St Boston MA 02111

YELENICK, MARY THERESE, lawyer; b. Denver, May 17, 1954; d. John Andrew and Maesel Joyce (Reed) Y. B.A. magna cum laude, Colo. Coll., 1976; J.D. cum laude, Georgetown U., 1979. Bar: D.C. 1979, U.S. Dist. Ct. D.C. 1980, U.S. Ct. Appeals (D.C. cir.) 1981, N.Y. 1982, U.S. Dist. Ct. (so. and ea. dists.) N.Y. 1982. Law clk. to presiding justices Superior Ct. D.C., 1979-81; assoc. Chadborne & Parke, N.Y.C., 1981—. Editor Jour. of Law and Policy Internat. Bus., 1978-79. Mem. Phi Beta Kappa. Democrat. Roman Catholic. Federal civil litigation, State civil litigation. Home: 310 E 46th St New York NY 10017 Office: Chadbourne & Parke 30 Rockefeller Plaza New York NY 10112

YELLIN, STANLEY JAY, lawyer; b. N.Y.C., Mar. 30, 1948; s. Irving and Lea (Schnitzer) Y. BA in Econs., Queens Coll., 1969; JD, U. Conn., 1972; LLM in Taxation, NYU, 1976. Bar: Conn. 1973, N.Y. 1973, N.J. 1978. Legal editor Prentice Hall, Inc., Englewood Cliffs, N.J., 1973-74, Matthew Bender & Co., N.Y.C., 1974-75, Inst. for Bus. Planning, Port Washington, N.Y., 1975-76; tax atty. M. Sternlieb & Co., Hackensack, N.J., 1976-82; sole practice Hackensack, 1982—; adj. prof. Farleigh Dickinson U., Teaneck and Rutherford, N.J., 1984—; writer bank tax report, Warren Gorham & Lamont, N.Y.C., 1976—. Com. mem. atty. div. United Jewish Community Bergen County, River Edge, N.J., 1983—. Mem. ABA (tax, probate and real property law sects.), N.J. Bar Assn., Bergen County Bar Assn., Greater N.J. Estate Planning Council. Pension, profit-sharing, and employee benefits, Probate, Personal income taxation. Home: 555 North Ave Fort Lee NJ 07024 Office: One University Plaza Hackensack NJ 07601

YELLOTT JR., JOHN BOSLEY, lawyer, writer; b. Balt., Aug. 14, 1954; s. John Bosley and Ann (James) Y. BA, Kenyon Coll., 1977; JD, Washington and Lee U., 1980. Bar: D.C. 1981, U.S. Dist. Ct. D.C. 1981, U.S. Ct. Claims 1981, U.S. Ct. Appeals (D.C. and fed. cirs.) 1981. Assoc. Bowman, Conner et al, Washington, 1980-84; of counsel Howard & Law, Washington, 1986—. Law columnist Value Digest, 1985—; contbr. articles to profl. jours. Mem. ABA, D.C. Bar Assn., Contract Mgmt. Assn., Soc. Am. Value Engrs., Phi Beta Kappa. Avocations: classical guitar, cycling, martial arts, painting. Administrative and regulatory, Federal civil litigation, Government contracts and claims. Office: 1701 Pennsylvania Ave NW Suite 350 Washington DC 20006

YELNICK, MARC M(AURICE), lawyer; b. N.Y.C., Jan. 30, 1947; s. Louis and Jeanne (Friedman) Y.; m. Linda Sherwin, Dec. 20, 1973; children: Sandy, Shauna. BA, Bklyn. Coll., 1967; postgrad., NYU, 1967-70; JD, St. John's U., 1976. Bar: N.Y. 1977, U.S. Dist. Ct. (ea. and so. dists.) N.Y. 1977, U.S. Dist. Ct. (no. dist.) Calif. 1985. Assoc. Billet, Billet & Avirom, N.Y.C., 1977-79, Whitman & Ransom, N.Y.C., 1979-84; sole practice San Mateo, Calif., 1984—. Mem. ABA, Am. Immigration Lawyers Assn. (no. Calif. and N.Y. chpts.). Immigration, naturalization, and customs. Office: 66 Bovet Rd Suite 353 San Mateo CA 94402

YEN, DAVID SHU-FANG, lawyer; b. Schenectady, N.Y., Dec. 25, 1950; s. Chih-Min and Ping (Pei) Y. BA, Yale U., 1971; JD, U. Pa., 1975. Bar: Pa. 1976, N.Y. 1976, N.J. 1976, Ala. 1978, U.S. Dist. Ct. (mid. dist.) Ala. 1978, U.S. Ct. Appeals (11th cir.) 1981. Law clk. to presiding justice Superior & County Cts, Cape May, N.J., 1975-76; atty. Mid-Hudson Legal Services Project, Monticello, N.Y., 1976-77, Legal Services Corp. Ala., Montgomery, 1977-80; sr. atty. Legal Services Corp. Ala., Montgomery and Opelika, 1980—. Mem. ACLU (bd. dirs. 1981—). Poverty law. Office: Legal Services Corp Ala 403 2d Ave Suite 400 Opelika AL 36801

YEN, ELIZABETH CHIH-SHENG, lawyer; b. Chgo., Feb. 22, 1957; s. Ti. and Esther K.T. (Tan) Y.; m. Seth M. Powsner, Aug. 18, 1985. BA, Yale U., 1976; JD, U. Mich., 1980. Bar: Conn. 1980, U.S. Dist. Ct. Conn. 1980. Assoc. Tyler, Cooper & Alcorn, New Haven, 1980-83; assoc. Gager, Henry & Narkis, Waterbury, Conn., 1983-87, ptnr., 1987—. Bd. dirs. New Haven chpt. Conn. Civil Liberties Union, 1985—, Conn. Women's Ednl. and Legal Fund, Hartford, 1985—, Conn. Atty.'s for a Progressive Legis., 1982—, treas. 1986—. Mem. Conn. Bar Assn. (chmn. consumer law sect. 1984—, exec. com. banking law sect. 1984—). Banking, Consumer commercial, General corporate. Office: Gager Henry & Narkis One Exchange Pl Waterbury CT 06722

YERBICH, JOSEPH THOMAS, lawyer; b. Roslyn, Wash., Feb. 21, 1938; s. Rudolph Andrew and Juanita (Thomas) Deming; m. Sharon Katherine Miller, Nov. 22, 1963; children: Denise, April, Katherine, Michelle. JD with distinction, U. Pacific, 1971. Bar: Calif. 1972, U.S. Dist. Ct. (cen. dist.) Calif. 1973, Calif., U.S. Ct. Appeals (9th cir.) 1973, Alaska 1977, U.S. Tax Ct. 1977, U.S. Supreme Ct. 1978. Enlisted USN, 1955, advanced through grades to lt. (j.g.), resigned, 1965; legal research atty. Orange County (Calif.) Superior Ct., Santa Ana, 1971-73; assoc. Duryea, Randolph, Malcolm, Newport Beach, Calif., 1973-76, F.K. Friedeman, Orange, Calif., 1976-77; ptnr. Wadsworth, Stanley & Yerbich, Anchorage, 1977-82; sr. ptnr. Yerbich & Stanley, Anchorage, 1982-84, Yerbich & Assocs., Anchorage, 1984—. Mem. Am. Arbitration Assn. (comml. and const. panels). Republican. Avocations: reading, home remodeling. Bankruptcy, General corporate, Corporate taxation. Home: 13240 Mountain Pl Anchorage AK 99516 Office: Yerbich & Assocs 329 F St STE 210 Anchorage AK 99501

YERBICH, THOMAS JOSEPH, lawyer; b. Roslyn, Wash., Feb. 21, 1938; s. Rudolph Andrew and Juanita (Thomas) Y.; m. Sharon Katherine Miller, Nov. 22, 1963; children: Denise, April, Katherine, Michelle. JD with distinction, U. of Pacific, 1971. Bar: Calif. 1972, U.S. Dist. Ct. (cen. dist.) Calif. 1973, U.S. Ct. Appeals (9th cir.) 1973, Alaska 1977, U.S. Dist. Ct. Alaska 1977, U.S. Tax Ct. 1977, U.S. Supreme Ct. 1978. Legal research atty. Orange County (Calif.) Superior Ct., 1971-73; assoc. Duryea, Randolph, Malcolm & Daly, Newport Beach, Calif., 1973-76; mem. F. K. Friedemann, Orange, Calif., 1976-77 Wadsworth, Stanley & Yerbich, P.C., Anchorage, 1977-82; sr.

ptnr. Yerbich & Stanley, Anchorage, 1982-84; prin. Yerbich & Assocs., Anchorage, 1984—; prof. law Western State U., 1972-77; lectr. U. Alaska, Anchorage, 1980—, Anchorage Community Coll., 1982—; mem. comml. and constrn. panels Am. Arbitration Assn. Trustee, sec. Debenham-Alaska Scholarships, Inc., 1979—; bd. dirs. Armed Forces YMCA, Anchorage, 1982—, vice chmn., 1983-84, chmn. 1987—. Served to lt. (j.g.) USN, 1955-65. Mem. Navy League (pres. Council 151 1981-83, Alaska state pres., nat. dir. 1983-86). Bankruptcy, Corporate taxation, General corporate. Office: 329 F St Suite 210 Anchorage AK 99501

YERRID, C. STEVEN, lawyer; b. Charleston, W.Va., Sept. 30, 1949; s. Charles George and Audrey Faye Y.; m. Vee West, Aug. 23, 1985. BA in History and Polit. Sci., La. State U., 1971; JD, Georgetown U., 1975. Bar: Fla. 1975, Va. 1975, U.S. Supreme Ct. 1979, D.C. 1984. Aide U.S. Senator Ellender, Washington, 1971-73; lobbyist Am. Hosp. Assn., Washington, 1973-75; ptnr. Holland & Knight, Tampa, Fla., 1975-86, Stagg, Hardy & Yerrid, Tampa, 1986—. Mem. Acad. Fla. Trial Lawyers, Fla. Bar Assn., Southeastern Admiralty Law Inst., Am. Judicature Soc., Assn. Trial Lawyers Am., Maritime Law Assn. U.S., Nat. Bd. Trial Advocacy. Democrat. Clubs: Tampa, University, Centre, Harbour Island Athletic (Tampa). Avocations: tennis, scuba diving, skiing, swimming, fishing. Admiralty, Personal injury. Office: Stagg Hardy & Yerrid One Tampa City Ctr Suite 2600 Tampa FL 33602

YETKA, LAWRENCE ROBERT, state supreme ct. justice; b. Cloquet, Minn., Oct. 1, 1924; s. Frank and Martha (Norkowski) Y.; m. Ellen Marie Fuller, Nov. 11, 1950; children: Frank Barry, Lawrence George, Christopher Hubert. B.S., U. Minn., 1947, J.D., 1948. Bar: Minn. bar 1949. Founder, partner firm Yetka & Newby, Cloquet, 1949-73; spl. municipal judge 1960-64; city atty. Cloquet, 1964-73; atty. Duluth Port Authority, 1957-60, Western Lake Superior San. Dist., 1970-73; asso. justice Minn. Supreme Ct., St. Paul, 1973—; atty., dir. Carlton County Fed. Savs. & Loan Assn., 1958-73; chmn. State Jud. Council, 1974-82, Select Com. on State Jud. System, 1974-77, State Jud. Planning Agy., 1976-84; Del., 12 state Democratic convs., 1948-72, Dem. Nat. Conv., 1956, 64, 68; chmn. Students for Humphrey for Mayor, 1947; Democratic Farmer Labor county officer, 1948-72, (8th Dist.), 1962-66; state Dem. vice chmn., 1966-70; mem. Minn. Ho. of Reps., 1951-61; chmn. Ho. Jud. Com., 1955-61, asst. majority leader, 1959-61; Grad. Appellate Judges Seminar sponsored by Inst. Jud. Adminstrn. at N.Y. U. Law Sch., 1976. Mem. ABA, Minn. Bar Assn., Carlton County Bar Assn. (pres. 1963-73), Am. Judicature Soc., Inst. Jud. Adminstrn. Lutheran. Jurisprudence. Office: Minn Supreme Ct State Capitol Saint Paul MN 55155 *

YETT, CHARLES WILLIAM, lawyer; b. Austin, Tex., June 4, 1941; s. James William and Rose Fenwick (Greenwood) Y.; m. Naomi June Spencer, Oct. 23, 1968; children—April, Jennifer, Charles. B.B.A., U. Tex., 1965, LL.B., 1966. Bar: Tex. 1966, U.S. Dist. Ct. (no. dist.) Tex. 1970, Colo. 1976, U.S. Dist. Ct. Colo. 1976, U.S. Supreme Ct. 1976, U.S. Ct. Appeals (10th cir.) 1976, U.S. Dist. Ct. (so. and we. dists.), Tex. 1980, U.S. Ct. Appeals (5th cir.) 1981, U.S. Dist. Ct. (ea. dist.) Tex. 1982. Asst. atty. gen. State of Tex., Austin, 1966-68, 83—; asst. city atty. City of Dallas, 1969; asst. dist. atty. Dallas County, 1969-76; dep. dist. atty. El Paso County, (Colo.), Colo. Springs, 1976-79; asst. gen. counsel State Bar of Tex., Austin, 1980-83; instr. Abilene Christian Coll., Dallas, 1971-76, Nat. Coll. of Bus., Colorado Springs, 1976-79, Univ. Colo.-Colorado Springs, 1976. Co-author: Texas Civil Litigation Handbook, 1984; Criminal Prosecution Course, 1976. Recipient Cert. of Appreciation, Dallas Jr. Bar Assn., 1974, Justice of Peace Tng. Ctr., San Maroos, Tex., 1975. Named an Outstanding Young Man of Am., 1978. Mem. Nat. Dist. Attys. Assn., Nat. Assn. of Bar Counsels, Tex. Dist. and County Attys. Assn., Nat. Assn. of Medicaid Fraud Control Units. Club: Longhorn. Criminal, Civil rights, Health. Home: 1207 Quail Run Austin TX 78746 Office: Office of Atty Gen 1101 Camino LaCosta Suite 257 Austin TX 78752

YIM, B(URGESS) CASEY, lawyer; b. Honolulu, Sept. 10, 1948; s. Albert S.U. and Ruth N. (Burgess) Y. A.B., San Diego State U., 1971; J.D. cum laude, Cleve. State U., 1975. Bar: Ohio 1975, Calif. 1982. profl. assoc. Squire, Sanders & Dempsey, Cleve., 1975-83; ptnr.Lewis, D'Amato, Brisbois & Bisgaard, Los Angeles, 1983—; ann. seminar lectr. Assoc. Industries of Cleve., 1979-82; Editor-in-chief Cleve. State U. Law Rev., 1974-75. Recipient Am. Jurisprudence Book award Lawyers Coop. Pub. Co., 1974; Corpus Juris Secundum award, 1973. Mem. ABA (litigation sect.), Ohio Bar Assn., Cleve. Bar Assn., Los Angeles County Bar Assn., Calif. Bar Assn., Assn. Bus. Trial Lawyers. Federal civil litigation, State civil litigation, Personal injury. Office: Lewis D'Amato Brisbois & Bisgaard 261 S Figueroa St Suite 300 Los Angeles CA 90012

YOCHES, EDWARD ROBERT, lawyer; b. Denver, Jan. 23, 1953; s. Marvin and Ruth Devorah (Spiegleman) Y.; m. Karen Ruth Droller, Aug. 20, 1978; children: Aaron Stuart, Meryl Laura. BEE in Computer Sci., U. Colo., 1974; JD, U. Pa., 1980. Bar: D.C. 1980. Engr. Goddard Space Flight Ctr. NASA, Greenbelt, Md., 1974-77; assoc. Finnegan, Henderson, Farabow, Garrett & Dunner, Washington, 1980—. Mem. ABA (chmn. computer law subcom. on trade secrets and internat. protection 1982—), D.C. Bar Assn. (vice chmn. computer law div. 1985—), Am. Intellectual Property Assn. Computer, Patent, Trademark and copyright. Office: Finnegan Henderson Farabow et al 1775 K St NW Washington DC 20006

YOCK, ROBERT JOHN, judge; b. St. James, Minn., Jan. 11, 1938; s. William Julius and Erma Idella (Fritz) Y.; m. Carla Marie Moen, June 13, 1964; children: Signe Kara, Torunn Ingrid. B.A., St. Olaf Coll., 1959; J.D., U. Mich., 1962; postgrad., U. Strasbourg, France, 1961, Old Dominion Coll., 1964-65, U. Minn., 1966-67. Bar: Minn. 1962, U.S. Supreme Ct. 1965, D.C. 1972. Asso. Thomas, King, Swenson & Collatz, St. Paul, 1966-69; chief counsel Nat. Archives, Office Gen Counsel, GSA, Washington, 1969-70, exec. asst. to adminstr., 1970-72; asst. gen. counsel GSA, 1972-77; trial judge U.S. Ct. Claims, Washington, 1977-82; judge U.S. Claims Ct., Washington, 1982—. Served with JAGC USN, 1962-66. Mem. Am., Minn., Fed., D.C. bar assns. Jurisprudence. Home: 4200 Webster Ct Annandale VA 22003 Office: US Claims Ct 717 Madison Pl NW Washington DC 20005 *

YOCKEY, KURT DAVID, lawyer; b. Detroit, Jan. 7, 1955; s. Fred Leo and Marion Elain (Parr) Y.; m. Cheryl L. Chandler, May 11, 1985. BA, Mich. State U., 1977; JD, Detroit Coll. Law, 1981. Bar: Mich. 1981, U.S. Dist. Ct. (ea. dist.) Mich. 1981. Assoc. Kitch, Suhrheinrich, Smith, Shurbier & Drutchas, Detroit, 1981-82, Taub, Still, Nemier & Winter, Detroit, 1982-86; ptnr. Still, Nemier, Winter & Yockey, Detroit, 1986—. Vol. Hospice of Southeast Mich., Southfield, 1986. Named to Academic All-Big 10 Baseball Team, 1975. Mem. Mich. Bar Assn., Detroit Bar Assn. Avocations: skiing, football, coaching sports, sailing. Personal injury, Federal civil litigation, State civil litigation. Office: Still Nemier Winter & Yockey 37000 Grand River Metro Bank Bldg Suite 300 Farmington Hills MI 48024

YODER, JOHN CHRISTIAN, business executive, lawyer; b. Newton, Kans., Jan. 9, 1951; s. Gideon G. and Stella H. Yoder; B.A., Chapman Coll., 1972; J.D., U. Kans., 1975; M.B.A., U. Chgo., 1976. Bar: Kans. 1975, Ind. 1976, U.S. Supreme Ct. 1981, D.C. 1985. Asst. prof. bus. Goshen Coll. (Ind.), 1975-76; pvt. practice law, Hesston, Kans., 1976-77; assoc. dist. judge 9th Jud. Dist., Newton, Kans., 1977-80; chmn. bd., v.p., dir. Jay Energy Devel. Co., 1978-81; chmn. bd. Stone Mill Wichita, Inc., 1977-80, Stone Mill Bakeries, Inc., 1977-81; jud. fellow U.S. Supreme Ct., Washington, 1980-81; spl. asst. to chief justice U.S. Supreme Ct., Washington, 1981-83; dir. Asset Forfeiture Office, Dept. Justice, Washington, 1983-84; gen. counsel Sterling Investment Resources Inc., Wichita, Kans., 1987—; chmn. bd., pres. Eon Resources, Inc., 1981—; pres. Bus. Resources Group, Inc., Washington, 1984—; exec. v.p., dir. Patriot Life Ins. Co., 1985; chmn. Gattlin Inc., Albuquerque, 1986—; dir. Kinderhook Oil & Gas, Inc., Sanders & Co., U.S. Petroleum Corp. Bd. dirs. Showalter Villa, Hesston, 1977-80, Substance Abuse Bd. Harvey County, 1977-80. Mem. ABA, Kans. Bar Assn., Ind. Bar Assn., Harvey County Bar Assn., D.C. Bar Assn., Fed. Bar Assn., U.S. C. of C. (council on trends and perspectives 1981—). Republican. Mennonite. Bankruptcy, Federal civil litigation, General corporate. Home: Rt 3 Box 109 Harpers Ferry WV 25425 Office: 1667 K St NW Suite 801 Washington DC 20006

YODER, THOMAS WOODROW, lawyer; b. Pullman, Wash., Apr. 23, 1927; s. Fredrick Roy and Wilma Eylene (Porter) Y.; m. Marian D. McCoy, Aug. 20, 1950; children—Thomas P., Katherine Ann, Kristine D. A.B., Wash. State U., 1949; J.D., U. Chgo., 1952. Bar: Ind. 1953, U.S. Dist. Ct. (so. dist.) Ind. 1953, U.S. Dist. Ct. (no. dist.) Ind. 1955, U.S. Dist. Ct. (no. dist.) Ohio 1958, U.S. Ct. Appeals (7th cir.) 1963, U.S. Supreme Ct. 1970. Assoc. Campbell, Livingston, Dildine & Haynie, Ft. Wayne, Ind., 1952-59, ptnr., 1959-65; ptnr. Livingston, Dildine, Haynie & Yoder, Ft. Wayne, 1965—. Served with USAAF, 1944-46. Diplomate Ind. Def. Trial Counsel. Fellow Ind. Bar Found.; mem. ABA (pub. utilities, litigation and torts and ins. practice sects.), Bar Assn. 7th Fed. Cir. (Ind. chmn. com. on rules and practice 1978—, steering com. and contbg. author Fed. Appellate Handbook project 1985-87, exec. com. 1976—), Ind. Def. Lawyers Assn. (dir. 1972—, pres. 1974) Am. Judicature Soc., Ind. State Bar Assn. (bd. mgrs. 1971-73, chmn. automobile accident reparations com. 1974-76, mem. trial lawyers sect.), Allen County Bar Assn. Republican. Methodist. Clubs: Rotary, Summit, Olympia Athletic (Ft. Wayne), Masons, Shriners. Co-author: Condemnation in Indiana, 1966, rev. edit., 1976; Damages, 1975; Settlements, 1978; Personal Injury Trials in Indiana, 1981, Integration of Trial Preparation and Discovery: The Defendant's Viewpoint, 1982; Strategic Considerations for the Advocate under Comparative Negligence: The Defendant's Point of View, 1984, Land Condemnation: Trial Tactics from the Condemnor's Viewpoint, 1984; The Duty of a Primary Carrier to the Excess Carrier, 1986; also contbr. articles to law jours. Insurance, Public utilities, Antitrust. Home: 3530 Rosewood Dr Fort Wayne IN 46804 Office: Livingstone Dildine Haynie Yoder 1400 One Summit Sq Fort Wayne IN 46802

YOERG, NORMAN, JR., lawyer; b. N.Y.C., Jan. 27, 1944; s. Norman Sr. and Elizabeth Winston (Peyton) Y.; m. Donna Dorogoff, Aug. 21, 1971; children: Peter, Virginia, Anastasia. BBA, Washington and Lee U., 1965; JD, Fordham U., 1970; LLM, NYU, 1978. Bar: N.Y. 1971. Law clk. to presiding justice U.S. Dist. (so. dist.) N.Y., N.Y.C., 1970-72; assoc. White & Case, N.Y.C., 1972-81; atty. Am. Cyanamid Co., Wayne, N.J., 1981—; lectr. Practicing Law Inst. Contbr. articles to legal jours. Served to 1st lt. U.S. Army, 1965-67, Vietnam. Mem. ABA (chmn. econ. com., antitrust sect., mem. conf. bd.), N.Y. State Bar Assn. (chmn. merger com., antitrust sect.). Episcopalian. Private international, General corporate, Antitrust. Office: Am Cyanamid Co Wayne NJ 07470

YOGI, NOLAN KIMEI, lawyer; b. Honolulu, Sept. 20, 1947; s. Henry K. and Gertrude T. (Enafuku) Y.; m. Dorothy Rose Setian, Sept. 3, 1983; 1 child, David Kimei. BBA, U. Hawaii, 1972; JD, Drake U., 1975. Bar: Hawaii 1977, U.S. Dist. Ct. Hawaii 1977, Ohio 1980, U.S. Dist. Ct. (no. dist.) Ohio 1980, U.S. Tax Ct. 1982, U.S. Dist. Ct. (so. dist.) Ohio 1984, Calif. 1986. Sole practice Honolulu, 1977-79; asst. gen. counsel The Way Internat., New Knoxville, Ohio, 1979-84, gen. counsel, 1985—; sec., gen. counsel The Way Credit Union Inc., New Knoxville, 1982—; lectr. Word in Bus. & Profession Confs., St. Louis, 1981, Columbus, Ohio, 1982, Kansas City, Mo., 1983. Served with USAR, 1966-72. Mem. ABA, Ohio Bar Assn., Shelby County Bar Assn., Assn. Trial Lawyers Am. General corporate, Contracts commercial, Consumer commercial. Office: The Way Internat Legal Dept 5555 Wierwille Rd PO Box 328 New Knoxville OH 45871

YOHE, SUSAN ANN, lawyer; b. Tarentum, Pa., July 28, 1948; d. William Clark and Dorthy Agnus (Bucknell) Y.; m. Robert Sidney Hoover, Nov. 23, 1973; children: Margaret Fluellen, Elizabeth Dally, Dorothy Claire. BA, Pa. State U., 1970; JD, U. Pitts., 1979. Bar: Pa. 1980, U.S. Dist. Ct. (we. dist.) Pa. 1983, U.S. Ct. Appeals (3d cir.) 1983. Law clk. to presiding judge Pitts., 1969-72; assoc. Strassburger, McKenna et al, Pitts., 1983-86, ptnr., 1986—; vis. teacher Carnegie Mellon U., Pitts., 1985—; speaker in field, 1985—. Mem. Pa. Bar Assn., Allegheny County Bar Assn. Democrat. Antitrust, Federal civil litigation, Civil rights. Home: 1519 Buena Vista St Pittsburgh PA 15212 Office: Strassburger McKenna et al 322 Boulevard of the Allies Pittsburgh PA 15222

YOHLIN, JOSEPH MICHAEL, lawyer; b. Phila., Oct. 3, 1954; s. Harry and Jeanette Rose (Hoffman) Y.; m. Pamela Jane Goren, June 18, 1978; children: Hilary Paige, Elizabeth Emily. BA, U. Pa., 1972-76; JD, Temple U., 1979, LLM, 1982. Bar: Pa. 1979, U.S. Tax Ct. 1980. Assoc. Krekstein, Wolfson & Krekstein, P.C., Phila., 1979—; bd. dirs. Phila. Estate Planning Council, MS Initiative, Inc., Phila.; lectr. various confs. and seminars. Bd. dirs. Adath Jeshurun Men's Assn., Elkins Park, Pa., 1987—. Mem. ABA (real property, probate, and trust law sects.), Phila. Bar Assn. (tax sect.), Pa. Bar Assn. (probate sect.). Democrat. Jewish. Avocations: art collecting, all sports. Probate, Estate taxation, General corporate. Office: Krekstein Wolfson & Krekstein PC 1760 Market St Philadelphia PA 19103

YONTS, STEWARTS H., lawyer; b. San Diego, Dec. 6, 1945; s. Homer V. and Kathleen (Buhl) Y. BS, U. Ky., 1967; JD, U. Louisville, 1976; postgrad., Coll. William and Mary, 1977-78, U. Houston, 1985. Bar: Ky. 1976. Mgr. tax and auditing Branco Inc., Louisville, 1972-76; mgr. taxes and benefits acctg. Newport News (Va.) Shipbuilding and Dry Deck Co., 1976-78; tax counsel Tenneco Inc., Houston, 1978-80; tax mgr. Home Petroleum Corp., Houston, 1980-82; dir. taxes MCO Resources Inc., Houston, 1982-85; assoc. Goldberg & Simpson PSC, Louisville, 1986—. Served to capt. USAR, 1968-81. Mem. ABA, Ky. Bar Assn., Louisville Bar Assn. Corporate taxation, Personal income taxation, State and local taxation. Office: Goldberg & Simpson 2800 1st Nat Tower Louisville KY 40202

YONTZ, RANDALL EUGENE, lawyer; b. Columbus, Ohio, July 28, 1951; s. E. Eugene and Dorothy L. Keller Y.; m. Deborah Richards, Sept. 29, 1979; children: Brian Randall, Daniel Forrest. BA, Wittenberg U., 1973; JD, Ohio Northern U., 1977. Adminstrv. judge Pub. Utilities Commn., Columbus, 1977-80; asst. pros. atty. Franklin County Prosecuting Attys. Office, Columbus, 1980-84; sole practice Columbus, 1984—; mem. Evans, St. Clair & Kelsey, Columbus, 1986. Mem. ABA, Ohio Bar Assn., Columbus Bar Assn., Assn. Trial Lawyers Am. State civil litigation, Criminal, Personal injury. Office: Evans St Clair & Kelsey 480 S High St Columbus OH 43215

YOON, HOIL, lawyer; b. Tokyo, Nov. 22, 1943; came to U.S. from Korea, 1970; s. Hakwon and Hoik (Lee) Y.; m. Giyun Kim, June 1, 1968; children—Shinwon E., Eunice J., Grace J., James S. LL.B., Seoul Nat. U., 1965, LL.M., 1967; J.D., Notre Dame U., 1973. Bar: Korea 1967, Ill. 1973, D.C. 1981, U.S. Supreme Ct. 1977. Judge, Seoul Civil Dist., Korea, 1970; assoc. Baker & McKenzie, Chgo., 1973-79, ptnr., 1979—; panelist Am. Arbitration Assn., N.Y.C., 1982—; mem. Korean Comml. Arbitration Bd., 1982—; lectr. Columbia U. Sch. of Law, N.Y.C., 1985—. Contbr. articles to legal jours. Bd. dirs. Korean-Am. Community Services, Inc., 1982—, U.S.-Korea Soc., Inc., 1984—. Served to capt. Korean Air Force, 1967-69. Recipient Presdl. decoration Republic of Korea, 1984. Mem. ABA (chmn. subcom. on Korea 1983-84), Bar Assn. D.C., Chgo. Bar Assn., Seoul Bar Assn., Korean Bar Assn. Private international, Contracts commercial, Banking. Home: 3633 Torrey Pines Pkwy Northbrook IL 60062 Office: Baker & McKenzie 2800 Prudential Plaza Chicago IL 60601

YORK, JOHN C., lawyer, investment banker; b. Evansville, Ind., Apr. 27, 1946; s. James Edward and Madge (Weas) Y.; m. Judith Anne Carmack, Aug. 24, 1968; children—George Edward Carmack, Charlotte Bayley, Alice Mercer. B.A., Vanderbilt U., 1968; J.D., Harvard U., 1971. Bar: Ill. 1971, U.S. Dist. Ct. (no. dist.) Ill. 1971. Assoc. firm Mayer Brown & Platt, Chgo., 1971-74; sr. v.p., sec., prin. JMB Realty Corp., Chgo., 1974-84; pres. Robert E. Lend Co. Inc., 1984—, Packard Properties Inc., 1984—; counsel Bell, Boyd & Lloyd, Chgo., 1986—; bd. dirs. Riverside Corp., Chgo., McKeever Electric Supply Co., Columbus, Ohio. Bd. dirs. Landmarks Preservation Council of Ill., 1972—, Streeterville Corp., 1986—, Washington Sq. Health Found., 1985—, Henrotin Hosp., 1976—; mem. vestry St. Chrysostom's Ch., 1980—. Mem. ABA, Chgo. Bar Assn., Lambda Alpha Internat. Republican. Episcopalian. Clubs: Chgo., Casino, Racquet, Saddle and Cycle. Real property, Securities, General corporate. Home: 1242 Lake Shore Dr Chicago IL 60610 Office: One N LaSalle Chicago IL 60602

YORK, LOUIS B., lawyer; b. N.Y.C., June 3, 1938; s. Julius and Pearl (Lopatkin) Y.; m. Judith Harriet Bader, Dec. 17, 1967; 1 dau., Elizabeth. BBA, CCNY, 1960; JD, Cornell U., 1963; LLM, NYU, 1973. Bar: N.Y. 1964, U.S. Dist. Ct. (so. dist.) N.Y. 1966, U.S. Ct. Appeals (2d cir.) 1971, U.S. Supreme Ct. 1972. Staff atty. FCC, Washington, 1963-65; staff atty. Legal Aid Soc., N.Y.C., 1965-67; assoc. Max E. Greenberg, Trayman, Harris, Cantor, Reiss & Blaskey, N.Y.C., 1967-68; assoc. Golenbock & Barrell, N.Y.C., 1968-69; sole practice, N.Y.C., 1969-71; staff atty., dir. litigation, chief counsel Manhattan Legal Services, N.Y.C., 1971-85; ptnr. York & Prosnitz, N.Y.C., 1985-86; judge Civil Ct. of City of N.Y., 1987—; counsel N.Y.C. Fair Housing Task Force; arbitrator Small Claims Ct., 1977—. Vice chmn. N.Y. State New Dem. Coalition, 1981—, chmn. platform com., 1982—; del. N.Y. State Jud. Conv., 1981. Mem. ABA, N.Y. County Lawyers Assn. (com. on civil ct. 1982-85, lectr. program for new lawyers 1983—), Assn. Bar City N.Y., Citizens Union (com. on legis.). Landlord-tenant, Welfare, State civil litigation. Office: 170 E 116th St New York NY 10029

YORRA, MYRON SETH, lawyer; b. Cambridge, Mass., June 24, 1945; s. Henry and Eve (Atkins) Y.; m. Diane Harrison, May 3, 1980; children: Ashley Marie, Alexandra Michelle. BA, Reed Coll., 1967; MA, U. Iowa, 1972; JD, Golden Gate U., 1981; postdoctoral, Tech. U., Braunschweig, Fed. Republic of Germany. Bar: Mass. 1982, U.S. Dist. Ct. Mass. 1982, Nev. 1985, U.S. Dist. Ct. Nev. 1985. Wine purchaser Pastene Wines, Somerville, Mass., 1974-77; dir. mktg. Geyser Peak (Calif.) Park Winery, 1977-82; sole practice Gloucester, Mass., 1982—, Lamoille, Nev., 1985—. Rep. alumni admissions Reed Coll., Portland, Oreg. Mem. Mass. Bar Assn., Essex County Bar Assn., Gloucester Bar Assn., Elko County Bar Assn., Am. Fedn. TV and Radio Artists, Screen Actors Guild, Actors Equity Assn. Lodge: Masons. Avocations: sailing, theater. General practice, Jurisprudence, Probate.

YOSHA, LOUIS BUDDY, lawyer; b. Indpls., Aug. 25, 1937; m. Janet Esterline, Jan. 25, 1963; children—Cynthia A., Laura Sue, Alan Bradley. Student, U. Ala., B.A., Ind. U., 1960, J.D., 1963; postgrad. U. So. Calif., 1961. Bar: Ind. 1963. Ptnr. Townsend, Yosha & Cline, 1963—. Contbr. articles to legal jours. Fellow Ind. Trial Lawyers Assn. (bd. dirs.), Internat. Soc. Barristers; mem. ABA, Ind. Bar Assn. (Res Gestae lit. award 1984), Indpls. Bar Assn., Am. Trial Lawyers Assn., Am. Bd. Trial Advocates. Jewish. Personal injury, State civil litigation. Office: Townsend Yosha & Cline 2220 N Meridian St Indianapolis IN 46208

YOSKOWITZ, IRVING BENJAMIN, manufacturing company executive, lawyer; b. Bklyn., Dec. 2, 1945; s. Rubin and Jennie Y.; m. Carol L. Magil, Feb. 11, 1973; children: Stephen M., Robert J. B.B.A., CCNY, 1966; J.D., Harvard U., 1969; postgrad., London Sch. Econs., 1971-72. Bar: D.C., N.Y., Conn. Programmer IBM, East Fishkill, N.Y., 1966; systems analyst Office Sec. Def., Washington, 1969-71; asso. firm Arnold & Porter, Washington, 1972-73; atty. IBM, 1973-79; regional counsel IBM, Bethesda, Md., to 1979; dep. gen. counsel United Technologies Corp., Hartford, Conn., 1979-81; v.p. and gen. counsel United Technologies Corp., 1981-86; sr. v.p., gen. counsel United Techs. Corp., 1986—. Mem. editorial bd. Harvard Law Rev., 1968-69. Trustee Sci. Mus. of Conn., 1982—, Mt. Sinai Hosp. Served with U.S. Army, 1969-71. Knox fellow, 1971-72. Mem. ABA, D.C. Bar Assn., Am. Corp. Counsel Assn. (bd. dirs. 1982-85). Contracts commercial, General corporate, Antitrust. Office: United Technologies Corp Hartford CT 06101

YOSOWITZ, SANFORD, aluminum company executive, lawyer; b. Cleve., July 26, 1939; s. Joseph and Esther (Moss) Y.; m. Ruth A. Goodman, June 24, 1962; children: Jeffrey Seth, Mark Robert, Chari Beth. B.S., Ohio State U., 1961; J.D., Case Western Res. U., 1964. Bar: Ohio 1964. Assoc. Lane, Krotinger & Santora, Cleve., 1964-66; law practice Cleve., 1966-69; corp. atty., asst. sec. Alcan Aluminum Corp., Cleve., 1969-73, sr. atty., asst. sec., 1979-80, v.p., gen. counsel, sec., 1980—; also dir. Alcan Aluminum Corp.; div. counsel Alcan Bldg. Products, Cleve., 1973-79; lectr. Ohio Legal Ctr. Inst., 1969-70, Greater Cleve. Bar Assn., 1972—. Editor-in-chief: Western Res. Law Rev., 1963-64; pub., editor: Industrial Concentration, 1979; editorial chmn.: Antitrust Law Jour., 1977-84. Ann. show producer Boy Scouts Am., 1982; auctioneer pub. TV auction, 1974-81, community theatre actor, producer and lyricist. Recipient of merit Ohio Legal Ctr. Inst., 1969. Mem. ABA (council mem. antitrust law sect.). Bar Assn. Greater Cleve. (chmn. corp. law dept. sect. 1973), Ohio Bar Assn., Cuyahoga County Bar Assn., Sigma Alpha Mu. Clubs: Clevelander (Cleveland) (sec.), Mid-Day (Cleveland), 13th St. Racquet (Cleveland). Home: 2585 Larchmont Dr Beachwood OH 44122 Office: Alcan Aluminum Corp 100 Erieview Plaza 29th Floor Cleveland OH 44114

YOSPIN, RICHARD LAWRENCE, lawyer; b. Bklyn., Oct. 17, 1948; s. Tobias and Audrey (Kreinik) Y.; m. Joan E. Marcus; children: Matthew, Gabriel, Sarina. AB, Columbia U., 1970; JD, Boston U., 1973. Bar: Mass. 1973, Alaska 1974, U.S. Dist. Ct. Alaska 1978, U.S. Supreme Ct. 1979. With VISTA Alaska Legal Services, Ketchikan, 1973-74, staff atty., 1974-75; atty. Alaska Pub. Defender Agy., Juneau and Ketchikan, 1975-84; assoc. Keene & Currall, Ketchikan, 1985—. Founder, past chmn. Rainbird Community Broadcasting, Ketchikan, 1976-81; bd. dirs. Southeast Symphony Assn., Ketchikan, 1985—. Mem. ABA, Assn. Trial Lawyers Am. Avocation: clarinet. State civil litigation, Criminal, Federal civil litigation. Office: Keene & Currall 540 Water St Ketchikan AK 99901

YOST, GERALD B., lawyer; b. Harvey, Ill., Dec. 21, 1954; s. Richard Dennis and Marilyn Patricia (Moore) Y.; m. Kay Lynn Benton, Apr. 16, 1977; 1 child, Matthew Brian. BA in Journalsim, Drake U., 1973-76; student, Purdue U., 1975; JD, Hamline U., 1980. Bar: Minn. 1980, U.S. Dist. Ct. Minn. 1980, Wis. 1987. Assoc. Bergman, Street & Ulmen, Mpls., 1980-84; ptnr. Wasserman and Baill, Mpls., 1984—. Editor: Student Osteo. Med. Assn. Publ. mag., 1976; mem. Law Review Hamline U., 1978-80. Recipient Am. Jurisprudence award, Lawyers Coop. Pub. Co., St. Paul, 1979. Mem. ABA, Minn. State Bar Assn., YMCA, St. Paul Bar Assn., Wis. Bar Assn. Avocations: tennis, racquetball, boating and water skiing, jogging. General corporate, Contracts commercial, Consumer commercial. Home: 277 Mount Curve Blvd Saint Paul MN 55105 Office: Wasserman and Baill 2200 1st Bank Place W 120 S Sixth St Minneapolis MN 55402

YOST, WILLIAM ARTHUR, III, corporation lawyer; b. Greensburg, Pa., Apr. 7, 1935; s. William Arthur Jr. and Virginia (Penny) Y.; m. Katherine Luedke, Apr. 20, 1963; children: Virginia, Alexander. AB, Haverford Coll., 1957; LLB, Yale U., 1960. Bar: Wis. 1960, Tex 1984. Assoc. Erbstoeszer, Cleary & Zabel, Milw., 1960-61; atty. Allis-Chalmers Co., Milw., 1961-68, Pabst Brewing Co., Milw., 1968-70, Ft. Howard Paper Co., Green Bay, Wis., 1970-72; corp. counsel, sec., v.p. adminstrn. Will Ross Inc., Milw., 1972-78; pres. Yost, Krombach & Schmitt, S.C., Cedarsburg, Wis., 1978-83; v.p. legal and sec. Pearle Health Services Inc., Dallas, 1983—. Sec., bd. dirs. Wis. Arthritis Found., Milw., 1978-83; bd. dirs. St. John's Home, Milw., 1975-83, pres. 1983; bd. dirs. Milw. chpt. ARC, 1963-70, 72-78. Mem. ABA, Tex. Bar Assn., Wis. Bar Assn., Dallas Bar Assn. Republican. Episcopalian. Clubs: Yale (N.Y.C.); Town (Milw.); T-Bar Racquet (Dallas). Private international, General corporate, Real property. Office: Pearle Health Services Inc 2534 Royal Ln Dallas TX 75266

YOST, WILLIAM KENT, lawyer; b. Massillon, Ohio, June 27, 1912; s. William Kent and Anna Laura (Silk) Y.; m. Marguerite Trimble, Apr. 21, 1937; children—Stephen T., Ann Yost Binge. Student, Ohio Wesleyan U., 1930-31; LL.B., Ohio No. U., 1936; LL.M., Case Western Res. U., 1966; Bar: Ohio 1966, U.S. Ct. Mil. Appeals, 1956. Sole practice, Massillon, Ohio, 1936—; gen. counsel First Nat. Bank, Massillon, 1966—, Peoples Fed. Savs. & Loan Assn., Massillon, 1946—; dir. First Nat. Bank of Massillon, chmn. bd. dirs., 1983—. Served to capt. JAGC, U.S. Army, 1943-46. Mem. Stark County Bar Assn., Ohio Bar Assn., ABA, Am. Judicature Soc., Ohio State Bar Found. Republican. Episcopalian. Clubs: Massillon, Masons (Massillon); Brookside Country (Canton). Real property, General corporate, Probate. Office: 108 3d St NE Massillon OH 44646

YOSTE, CHARLES TODD, lawyer; b. Vicksburg, Miss., Nov. 11, 1948; s. Harry M. and Charlene (Todd) Y. B.S., Miss. State U., 1971; J.D., U. Miss., 1976. Bar: Miss. 1976, U.S. Dist. Ct. Miss. 1976, U.S. Ct. Appeals, 1982. Sole practice, Starkville, Miss., 1976—; city atty. Starkville, Miss., 1979-85, pros. atty., 1977-79, city judge, 1981-82. Candidate for Congress 2d dist. Miss., 1980. Served to capt. U.S. Army, 1971-73. Recipient Outstanding Young Man award Starkville Jaycees, 1980. Mem. ABA, Miss. Bar Assn., Am. Trial Lawyers Assn., Miss. Trial Lawyers Assn., Starkville C. of C.

(pres. 1982), Am. Legion. Republican. Roman Catholic. Lodge: Rotary. General practice, Personal injury, Bankruptcy. Home: 902 S Montgomerery St Starkville MS 39759 Office: PO Box 488 Starkville MS 39759

YOUNEY, JOHN WILLIAM, state judge; b. Manchester, N.H., May 10, 1954; s. William John and Christine (Zoulias) Y.; m. Karol A. Kish. BS in Resource Devel., Mich. State U., 1975; JD, Western New Eng. Coll., 1980; LLM in Taxation, Boston U., 1981. Bar: Maine 1980, Mass. 1980. Sole practice Boston and Skowhegan, Maine, 1980-81; sr. tax specialist Laventhol & Horwath, Tucson, 1981-83; mgr. Tax Computer Systems, Inc., Tucson, 1984; adminstrv. law judge dept. econ. security, Office of Appeals State of Ariz., Tucson, 1984—; bus. and tax cons. 1980—. Rep. campaign coordinator, Augusta, Maine, 1976; campaign mgr. Laos for Congress Com., Tucson, 1982; Rep. Com. mem. Skowhegan, 1972-80; chmn. assembly St. Demetrios Greek Orthodox Ch., 1986. Recipient Eagle Scout award Boy Scouts Am., 1969. Mem. ABA (adminstrv. law sect., taxation sect.), Maine Bar Assn., Ariz. Adminstrs. Assn. (organizing com. Tucson chpt.), Mich. State U. Alumni Club (advisor Tucson chpt.), Am. Hellenic Ednl. Progressive Assn. (warden 1985-86, bd. govs. 1986—), Alpha Zeta. Lodges: Lions, Masons. Administrative and regulatory, Business and tax planning, Personal income taxation. Home: 2505 N Dodge Blvd Apt #E-2 Tucson AZ 85716 Office: Office of Appeals Dept of Econ Security 2555 E First St Suite 104 Tucson AZ 85716

YOUNG, ARDELL MOODY, former judge, lawyer; b. Ringgold, Tex., Oct. 11, 1911; s. Horace G. and Emma (Garvin) Y.; m. Marjorie Maschal, July 27, 1934; children-Mardelle Fay (Mrs. S.E. Moyers), John Hurschel. A.B., U. Okla., 1932, LL.B., 1936. Bar: Okla. and Tex. bars 1936. 1st asst. dist. atty. Tarrant County, Tex., 1946; partner firm Brown, Herman Scott, Young & Dean, Ft. Worth, 1947-71; judge 153d Dist. Ct., Tarrant County, Tex., 1971-81; of counsel firm Brown, Herman, Scott, Dean and Miles, 1981—. Served to lt. col. Judge Adv. Gen.'s Dept. AUS, 1941-46. Mem. Am., Tarrant County bar assns., State Bar Tex. (bd. dirs. 1959-62), Am., Tex. bar founds., Am. Coll. Trial Lawyers, Phi Alpha Delta. Democrat. Presbyterian. Club: Mason (33 deg, K.T., Shriner). State civil litigation, Condemnation, Probate. Home: 4064 Hidden View Circle Fort Worth TX 76109 Office: 203 Ft Worth Club Bldg Fort Worth TX 76102

YOUNG, BARBARA ANN, lawyer; b. Pontiac, Mich., Nov. 4, 1949; d. William Stewart and Mary Augusta (Bennett) Y. BA, U. Colo., 1971; JD, Valparaiso U., 1976. Bar: Ind. 1976, U.S. Dist. Ct. (no. and so. dists.) Ind. 1976. Ptnr. Hoeppner, Wagner & Evans, Valparaiso, Ind., 1976—. Bd. dirs. United Way, 1986, also past pres. Mem. ABA, Ind. Bar Assn., Porter County Bar Assn., Valparaiso U. Law Sch. Alumni Assn. (pres. 1985—). General corporate, Estate taxation, Probate. Office: Hoeppner Wagner & Evans 103 Lincolnway PO Box 2357 Valparaiso IN 46384

YOUNG, BLESS STRITAR, lawyer; b. Mar. 17, 1947. Student, Marietta Coll., 1965-68; BA, Temple U., 1969, JD, 1973. Bar: Pa., N.Y., Calif., D.C., U.S. Dist. Ct. (ea. dist.) Pa., U.S. Dist. Ct. (no. and cen. dists.) Calif., U.S. Supreme Ct. Assoc. Arthur S. Kafrissen & Assocs., Phila., 1973-74; atty. Bell of Pa., Phila., 1974-77, AT&T, N.Y.C., 1977-83; gen. atty. AT&T, San Francisco, 1983—; judge pro tem Contra Costa County Superior Ct., Martinez, Calif., 1985—. Atty. Vol. Lawyers for Arts, N.Y.C., 1977-83. Named one of Outstanding Young Women Am., 1977. Mem. ABA, Fed. Communications Bar Assn., Pa. Bar Assn., N.Y. State Bar Assn., Calif. Bar Assn., San Francisco Bar Assn., Queen's Bench and Bar Assn., Am. Corp. Counsel Assn., Pi Kappa Delta. Federal civil litigation, State civil litigation, Labor. Office: AT&T 795 Folsom St Suite #690 San Francisco CA 94565

YOUNG, BRYANT LLEWELLYN, businessman, lawyer; b. Rockford, Ill., Mar. 9, 1948; s. Llewellyn Anker and Florence Ruth Y. A.B., Cornell U., 1970; J.D., Stanford U., 1974. Bar: Calif. 1974, Nev. 1975, D.C. 1979. Law clk. U.S. Dist. Ct. No. Dist. Calif., San Francisco, 1974-75; mem. firm Dinkelspiel, Pelavin, Steefel & Levitt, San Francisco, 1975-77; White House fellow, spl. asst. to sec. HUD, Washington, 1977-78; spl. asst. to sec. HUD, 1978-79; acting dep. exec. asst. for ops. HUD (Office of Sec.), 1979; dep. gen. mgr. New Community Devel. Corp., 1979, acting gen. mgr., 1979-80; mgmt. cons. AVCO Corp., 1980; spl. asst. to chmn. bd. and chief exec. officer U.S. Synthetic Fuels Corp. Washington, 1980-81; project dir. 1981; pres. Trident Mgmt. Corp., San Francisco, 1981—; of counsel Pelavin, Norberg, Harlick & Beck, San Francisco, 1981-82, mem. firm, 1982—. Mem. pub. affairs com. San Francisco Aid Retarded Citizens, Inc., 1977; U.S. co-chmn. New Towns Working Group, U.S.-USSR Agreement on Cooperation in Field of Housing and Other Constrn., 1979-80; treas., bd. dirs. White House Fellows Found., 1980-84; prin. Ctr. Excellence in Govt., Washington, 1986—. Mem. Am. Bar Assn., White House Fellows Assn. (chmn. annual meeting 1979, del. People's Republic of China 1980), Am. Field Service Returnees Assn. Real property, General corporate, Private international. Office: Two Embarcadero Center 23d Floor San Francisco CA 94111

YOUNG, C. CLIFTON, state supreme court justice; b. Nov. 7, 1922. B.A., U. Nev., 1943; LL.B., Harvard U., 1949; justice Nev. Supreme Ct., Carson City, 1985—. Judicial administration. Office: Nev Supreme Ct Supreme Ct Bldg Carson City NV 89710 *

YOUNG, CHARLES FLOYD, lawyer; b. Newark, Ohio, Aug. 30, 1921; s. Bert Edward and Helen Louise (Cole) Y.; m. Carolyn Rose Kearns, Sept. 20, 1947; children: Patricia Elaine, John Charles, Kathryn Ann. Student, Denison U.; LLB, U. Cin., 1948. Bar: Ohio 1949. Ptnr. Young, Pryor, Lynn & Jerardi predecessor firms, Dayton, Ohio, 1949—; bd. dirs. Brookville (Ohio) Nat. Bank. Served to lt. (j.g.) USNR, 1942-46. Mem. ABA, Ohio Bar Assn., Dayton Bar Assn. (pres. 1976-77). Clubs: Dayton Bicycle, Dayton Country (Ohio). Contracts commercial, General corporate, General practice. Home: 4700 Tait Rd Dayton OH 45429 Office: Young Pryor Lynn & Jerardi 120 W 3d St Suite 350 PO Box 910 Dayton OH 45402

YOUNG, DAVID HAYWOOD, lawyer; b. San Antonio, Feb. 6, 1943; s. Haywood V. Jr. and Mary Sue (Whitehead) Y.; m. Sharon L. Seals, Nov. 24, 1967; children: David H. Jr., Darrow F., Kelley L. BA, U. Tex., 1965, JD, 1972. Bar: Tex. 1968, U.S. Dist. Ct. (we. dist.) Tex. 1974, U.S. Ct. Appeals (5th cir.) 1976, U.S. Supreme Ct. 1977, U.S. Ct. Appeals (11th cir.) 1981, U.S. Dist. Ct. (so. dist.) Tex. 1982. Atty. Tex. Dept. Human Resources, 1968-73; chief counsel Tex. Dept. Human Resources, Austin, 1973-76; asst. atty. gen. State of Tex., Austin, 1976-81; sole practice San Antonio, 1981—; sec. San Antonio Alliance of Bus., 1985-87; pres. San Antonio Bus. Forum, 1985-86. Mem. Tex. Bar Assn., San Antonio Bar Assn., Bus. and Profl. Club San Antonio (pres. 1986). Clubs: Plaza (San Antonio), San Antonio. General practice, General corporate, Health. Home: 6506 River Hills San Antonio TX 78239 Office: 106 S St Mary's Suite 500 One Alamo Center San Antonio TX 78205

YOUNG, DOUGLAS REA, lawyer; b. Los Angeles, July 21, 1948; s. James Douglas and Dorothy Belle (Rea) Y.; m. Terry Forrest, Jan. 19, 1974; 1 dau., Megann Forrest. B.A. cum laude, Yale U., 1971; J.D., U. Calif.-Berkeley, 1976. Bar: Calif. 1976, U.S. Dist. Ct. (no. dist.) Calif. 1976, U.S. Ct. Appeals (6th and 9th cirs.) 1977, U.S. Dist. Ct. (cen. dist.) Calif. 1979, U.S. Supreme Ct. 1982. Law clk. U.S. Dist. Ct. (no. dist.) Calif., San Francisco, 1976-77; assoc. Farella, Braun & Martel, San Francisco, 1977-82, ptnr., 1983—; spl. master U.S. Dist. Ct. (no. dist.) Calif., 1977-78; mem. faculty Calif. Continuing Edn. of Bar, Berkeley, 1982—, Nat. Inst. Trial Advocacy, Berkeley, 1984—, Hastings Coll. of Advocacy, 1985— ; vis. lectr. law Boalt Hall/U. Calif., Berkeley, 1986; judge pro tem San Francisco Mcpl. Ct. 1984—. Author: (with Purver and Davis) California Trial Handbook, 2d ed.; contbr. articles to profl. jours. Bd. dirs. Berkeley Law Found., 1977-79, chmn., 1978-79; bd. dirs. San Francisco Legal Aid Soc., Pub. Interest Clearinghouse, San Francisco, chmn., 1987—. Recipient award of appreciation Berkeley Law Found., 1983. Mem. ABA, San Francisco Bar Assn., Lawyers Club San Francisco. Democrat. Federal civil litigation, State civil litigation, Criminal. Office: Farella Braun & Martel 235 Montgomery St Suite 3000 San Francisco CA 94104

YOUNG, HUBERT HOWELL, JR., lawyer, real estate investor and developer; b. Franklin, Va., May 30, 1945; s. Hubert Howell and Elizabeth Ann (Davidson) Y.; m. Christine P. Brooks, Dec. 31, 1964; 1 son, Hubert Howell, III. B.A., Washington Lee U., 1967, LL.B., Magna Cum laude, 1969. Bar: Va. 1969, U.S. Supreme Ct. 1972, Tex. 1974, U.S. Dist. Ct. Tex. 1974, U.S. Dist. Ct. (ea. dist.) Va. 1980. Assoc., Johnson, Bromberg, Leeds and Riggs, Dallas, 1973-75; gen. counsel Trammel Crow Co., Dallas, 1975-79; sole practice, Suffolk, Va., 1979—; gen. counsel Young Properties, Suffolk, 1979—; dir. Young Properties Devel. Corp., Trammel Crow Investment Corp., Suffolk Broadcasting Corp. Pres. Suffolk (Va.) Found. Trust, 1982-83; vice chmn. Suffolk Coalition for Sr. Citizen Housing, Inc., 1982-83; mem. Suffolk Substance and Abuse and Youth Council, 1982-84; chmn. Suffolk Republican Party, 1982-85. Served as lt. JAG, USN, 1969-73. Designated col. Confederate Army The Lee-Jackson Meml. Inc., 1981. Mem. ABA, Va. Trial Lawyers Assn., Suffolk Bar Assn. Club: Cedar Point, Town Point, Sports, Ducks Unlimited (Suffolk). General practice, General corporate, Real property. Office: PO Box 3020 Suffolk VA 23434

YOUNG, JASON OBER, JR., lawyer; b. Jeffersonville, Vt., Aug. 18, 1951; s. Jason Ober and Mary Frances (Green) Y. BS in ChemE, U. Tenn., 1973, JD, 1977. Bar: Tenn. 1977. Ptnr. Maness, Young & Maness, Union City, Tenn., 1978-81, Holt, Batchelor, Spicer, Ryan, Flynn, Maness & Young, Union City and Memphis, 1981-84, Shuttleworth, Smith, Young & Webb, Memphis and Tupelo, Miss., 1984—; judge City of Union City, 1980-84. Sec. Obion County Election Commn., Union City, 1977-80. Mem. ABA, Tenn. Bar Assn. (ho. dels. 1979-81), Memphis Shelby County Bar Assn., Union City-Obion County Bar Assn. (pres. 1981), Tenn. Def. Lawyers Assn. Republican. Methodist. Avocation: golf. Insurance, State civil litigation, Federal civil litigation. Home: 641 N Trezevant Memphis TN 38112 Office: Shuttleworth Smith Young & Webb 8 S Third St Suite 300 Memphis TN 38103

YOUNG, JEANNE CATHERINE, lawyer; b. St. Cloud, Minn., June 1, 1954; d. Frederic George and Florence Drusilla (Jones) Y. BA, St. Cloud State U., 1976; JD, U. Minn., 1980. Bar: Ariz. 1980, U.S. Dist. Ct. Ariz. 1980, Minn. 1981. Assoc. Wentworth & Lundin, Phoenix, 1980-84, Lancy, Scult & McVey, PA, Phoenix, 1984-86; ptnr. Lancy, Scult & Ryan, Phoenix, 1986—. Mem. Phoenix Symphony Council, 1986—; v.p., bd. dirs. The New Found., Phoenix, 1983—. Mem. ABA, Women in Comml. Real Estate, Ariz. Bar Assn., Ariz. Women Lawyers Assn., Maricopa Bar Assn. Club: University (Phoenix). Real property, Contracts commercial. Office: Lancy Scult & McVey PA 3003 N Central #2601 Phoenix AZ 85012

YOUNG, JESS WOLLETT, lawyer; b. San Antonio, Sept. 16, 1926; s. James L. and Zetta (Alonso) Y.; m. Mary Alma Keeter, Apr. 17, 1954; children—Zetta, Imogen. B.A., Trinity U., San Antonio, 1957; LL.B., St. Mary's U., 1958. Bar: Tex. 1957, U.S. Dist. Ct. (we. dist.) Tex. 1960, U.S. Dist. Ct. (so. dist.) Tex. 1961, U.S. Tax Ct. 1970, U.S. Ct. Appeals (5th cir.) 1981, U.S. Supreme Ct. 1981. Ptnr. Thompson, Thompson, Young & Jones, San Antonio, 1958-63, Mousund, Ball & Young, San Antonio, 1965-73; v.p., dir. Moursund, Ball & Young, Inc., San Antonio, 1973-78; pres., dir. Young & Richards, Inc., San Antonio, 1978-81, Young, Murray & Richards, Inc., San Antonio, 1981-82, Young & Murray, Inc., 1983—; county judge, Bexar County (Tex.), 1964; city atty. City of Olmos Park (Tex.), 1965-70, City of Poteet (Tex.), 1975-76; spl. county judge, Bexar County, 1967; mem. Tex. State Dem. Exec. Com., 1970-72, Tex. State Rep. Exec. Com., 1984—. Served with USNR, 1944-46. Mem. ABA, Tex. Assn. Def. Counsel, Tex. Assn. Bank Counsel, San Antonio Bar Assn., Delta Theta Phi. Episcopalian. Real property, Banking, Administrative and regulatory. Home: 321 Thelma Dr San Antonio TX 78212 Office: 111 W Olmos Dr PO Box 15948 San Antonio TX 78212

YOUNG, JOHN ANDREW, lawyer; b. Corpus Christi, Tex., Nov. 10, 1916; s. Phillip Marvin and Katherine Julia Y.; m. Jane Fife Gallier, Jan. 21, 1950 (dec. 1977); children—Gaffney, Nancy, John, Robert, Patty. B.A., St. Edward's U., Austin, Tex., 1938, LL.D., 1961; student Tex. U. Sch. Law, 1939-41. Bar: Tex. 1940, U.S. Supreme Ct. 1955, U.S. Ct. Appeals (D.C. cir.) 1979, U. D.C. 1978. Chief prosecutor Dist. Atty's. Office, Corpus Christi, 1946-50; county atty. Nueces County (Tex.), Corpus Christi, 1950-51, county judge, 1952-56; mem. 1957-79 Congresses from 14th Tex. dist.; sole practice Washington, 1979—; legal and legis. cons. The Coastal Corp., Houston, 1979—. Contbr. numerous articles and treatises to newspapers and legal jours. Served to lt. cmdr. USN, 1941-45. Recipient Distinguished Service award City of Corpus Christi, 1971, Distinguished Service medal U.S. Fish & Wildlife Service, 1967; numerous plaques of appreciation, 1965-77. Mem. ABA, D.C. Bar Assn., Tex. Bar Assn., Maritime Law Assn. of U.S., Corpus Christi C. of C. (plaques 1965, 76), Delta Theta Phi. Clubs: Chesapeake Country, (Lusby, Md.), Old Dominion Yacht (Alexandria, Va.), Nat. Democratic (Washington). Lodges: K.C., Elks, Eagles, Moose, VFW, DAV, Am. Legion. Admiralty. Home: 1705 N Albemarle St McLean VA 22101 Office: 1899 L St Suite 500 Washington DC 20036

YOUNG, JOHN HARDIN, lawyer; b. Washington, Apr. 25, 1948; s. John D. and Laura Virginia (Gwathmey) Y. A.B., Colgate U., 1970; J.D., U. Va., 1973; postgrad., Hague Acad. Internat. Law, Netherlands, 1973; B.C.L., Oxford U., (Eng.), 1976. Bar: Va. 1973, D.C. 1974, Pa. 1979, U.S. Dist. Ct. (ea. dist.) Va. 1974, U.S. Dist. Ct. (ea. dist.) Pa. 1978, U.S. Dist. Ct. D.C. 1974, Internat. Trade Ct. 1974, U.S. Ct. Appeals (4th, Fed. and D.C. cirs.), U.S. Supreme Ct. 1977. Intern U.S. Senator William B. Spong, Jr., Washington, 1968; asst. atty. gen. complex litigation Commonwealth of Va., Richmond, 1976-78; trial counsel U.S. Dept. Labor, Washington, 1981-82; ptnr. Delaney & Young, Washington, 1982—; U.S. rep. UN Internat. Law Seminar, Geneva, 1974; mem. adv. bd. Antitrust Bull., Jour. Reprints Antitrust and Econs.; mem. U.S. Sec. State's Adv. Com. Pvt. Internat. Law, 1987—; lectr. continuing legal edn. Contbr. articles to profl. jours. Mem. ABA (council 1986—, adminstrv. law sect. 1986—, chmn. antitrust, trade regulation and competition com.), Am. Law Inst., Hon. Soc. Middle Temple, Phi Alpha Theta, Phi Delta Phi. Episcopalian. Administrative and regulatory, Federal civil litigation, Private international. Home: 5146 Woodmire Ln Alexandria VA 22311 Office: 1629 K St NW Washington DC 20006

YOUNG, JOHN MARK, lawyer; b. Tulsa, Sept. 10, 1950; s. John W. and Claudeen (Humes) Y.;m. Deborah Sue Young, Aug. 20, 1971; children: Evan, Kristi, Mike, Jeni, Lyndi, J.J., Wendy. BBA, U. Okla., 1972, JD, 1974. Bar: Okla., U.S. Dist. Ct. (no. dist.) Okla., U.S. Ct. Appeals (10th cir.), U.S. Ct. Mil. Appeals, U.S. Supreme Ct. Ptnr. Young and Young, Sapulpa, Okla. Served to maj. USMCR, 1975-79. Mem. Okla. Bar Assn., Christian Legal Soc. (state membership chmn. 1985-86), Am. Legion, Sapulpa C. of C., Kappa Sigma. Democrat. Club: Full Gospel Businessmen's (Sapulpa) (pres. 1983-85). Lodge: Lions. Avocations: pvt. pilot, freelance writing, hunting, shooting, fishing. General practice, Oil and gas leasing, Tort litigation. Home: 1533 E McKinley Sapulpa OK 74066 Office: Young and Young Bldg PO Box 1364 Sapulpa OK 74067

YOUNG, JOSEPH H., federal judge; b. Hagerstown, Md., July 18, 1922; s. J. Edgar and Mabel K. (Koser) Y.; m. Doris Oliver, Sept. 6, 1947; children: Stephen A., William O., J. Harrison. A.B., Dartmouth Coll., 1948; LL.B., U. Va., 1951. Bar: Md. 1951. Assoc. firm Marbury Miller & Evans, Balt., 1951-52, Piper & Marbury, Balt., 1952-58; ptnr. Piper & Marbury, 1958-68, mng. ptnr., 1968-71; judge U.S. Dist. Ct. Md., 1971—; instr. Johns Hopkins U. (McCoy Coll.), 1954-62. Bd. dirs. Legal Aid Soc. Balt., 1958-71, CICHA (Health Appeal), 1964-71; bd. dirs. exec. com. Md. div. Am. Cancer Soc., 1958—, chmn. div. bd. dirs. 1969-71, bd. dirs. 1966—, chmn. nat. services com. 1970-73, chmn. exec. com. 1976-77, dir.-at-large 1973-83, vice-chmn. nat. bd. dirs. 1975-77, chmn. nat. bd. 1977-80, chmn. public issues com. 1981-83, past officer dir. 1983—, chmn. world-wide fight com. 1987—, also mem. trust adv. bd.; mem. oncology adv. council Johns Hopkins U.; mem. exec. com., program chmn. Internat. Union Against Cancer, Geneva, 1981—; mem. Dartmouth Coll. Alumni Council. Served with inf. U.S. Army, 1942-46. Decorated Bronze Star, Purple Heart. Recipient Disting. Service Award Am. Cancer Soc., 1983; Dartmouth Coll. Alumni award, 1983; James Ewing Soc. award, 1983. Mem. 4th Circuit Jud. Conf., Assn. Alumni Dartmouth Coll. (pres. 1984-85). Republican. Presbyterian (elder, deacon, trustee). Clubs: Hamilton Street, Rule Day, Lawyers Round Table. Jurisprudence. Office: US District Court 740 US Court House Baltimore MD 21201 *

YOUNG, MARLENE ANNETTE, lawyer, consultant; b. Portland, Oreg., Mar. 3, 1946; d. Hardy Shelby and Eunice Jean (Gregory) Y.; m. Abdullah Samir Rifai, June 3, 1973 (div. May 1981); m. John Hollister Stein, Jan. 1, 1986. BS, Portland State U., 1967; PhD, Georgetown U., 1973; JD, Willamette U., 1975. Bar: Oreg. 1975. Dir. research Multnouah County Sheriff's Office, Portland, 1975-77; sole practice Wilsonville, Oreg., 1975-81; exec. dir. Applied Systems Research & Data, Wilsonville, 1976-81, Nat. Orgn. Victim Assistance, Washington, 1981—; instr. Essex Community Coll., 1971-73, U. Utah, 1976-78, Portland State U., 1979; cons. U. Research Corp., Washington, 1979-83, ABT Assocs., Boston, 1984—. Author: Victim Service System, 1983; (manuals) Patrol Officers and Crime Victims, 1984, Prosecutors: Attorneys for the People, Advocates for the Victims, 1984; editor: Justice and Older Americans, 1977; contbr. articles to profl. jours. Mem. Ways and Means Com., Wilsonville City, 1977-79, planning commn., 1979-81; Bd. visitors Willamette Coll. Law, Salem, Oreg., 1981-83; bd. dirs. Chemeketa Community Coll., Salem, 1979. Recipient Presdl. award Nat. Orgn. Victim Assistance, Washington, 1981, Pub. Policy award World Fedn. Mental Health, Washington, 1983. Mem. ABA (criminal justice sect., adv. bd. 1981—), Nat. Criminal Justice Assn., Soc. Traumatic Stress Studies (bd. dirs. 1985—), World Soc. Victimology (adv. bd. 1979—, Hans Von Hentig award 1985), Gerontol. Soc. Democrat. Methodist. Avocations: piano, running, gardening, pets. Criminal, Real property, Family and matrimonial. Office: Nat Orgn Victim Assistance 717 D St NW Washington DC 20004

YOUNG, MARY GARR, lawyer; b. Kansas City, Mo., June 7, 1954; d. Reginald Jr. and Catherine Ann (Bonderer) Garr; m. John Allen Young, June 19, 1982; children: Elizabeth, Rebecca. BA, Rockhurst Coll., 1976; JD, U. Mo., Kansas City, 1979. Bar: Mo. 1979, U.S. Dist. Ct. (we. dist.) Mo. 1979. Assoc. Law Offices R. Jay Ingraham, Kansas City, 1979-80; asst. gen. counsel Mo. Pub. Service Commn., Jefferson City, 1981-84, dep. gen. counsel, 1985—; dep. dir. Mo. Dept. Econ. Devel., Jefferson City, 1984-85. Mem. ABA, Mo. Bar Assn. (adminstrv. law com. council 1984-86, adminstrv. law vice chmn. 1986—). Roman Catholic. Public utilities, Administrative and regulatory, Nuclear power. Office: Mo Pub Service Commn 301 W High St Jefferson City MO 65101

YOUNG, MICHAEL RICHARD, lawyer; b. Wiesbaden, Fed. Republic Germany, May 12, 1956; came to U.S., 1957; s. Richard Barton and Janet (Crawford) Y.; m. Leslie Anne Carroll, Aug. 11, 1984. BA magna cum laude, Allegheny Coll., 1978—; JD, Duke U., 1981—. Bar: N.Y. 1982, U.S. Dist. Ct. (so. and ea. dists.) 1982. Assoc. Willkie Farr & Gallagher, N.Y.C., 1981—. Research and mng. editor Duke U. Law Rev., 1980-81. Mem. N.Y.C. Bar Assn. (com. on legal edn. and admission to bar 1983—), Phi Beta Kappa. Federal civil litigation, Securities, Mergers and acquisitions. Home: 390 First Ave Apt MH New York NY 10010 Office: Willkie Farr & Gallagher One Citicorp Ctr 153 E 53rd St New York NY 10022

YOUNG, RALPH EDWARD, JR., lawyer; b. Meridian, Miss., May 19, 1943; s. Ralph Edward and Nell (Ison) Y.; m. Martha Gay Moffett, Dec. 21, 1974; 1 child, Ralph Edward III. BBA, U. Miss., 1965, JD, 1967. Bar: Miss. 1967, U.S. Dist. Ct. (so. dist.) Miss. 1968, U.S. Ct. Appeals (5th cir.) 1969, U.S. Supreme Ct. 1977. Law clk. to presiding justice Supreme Ct. Miss., Jackson, 1967-68; ptnr. Deen, Cameron, Prichard, Young, Kittrell & Loeb, Meridian, 1968—. Chmn. ARC, Meridian, 1977-78, Salvation Army Adv. Bd., Meridian, 1985-86; pres. Meridian Jr. Coll. Found., 1976-79; mem. Jud. Nominating Com., Miss., 1981-84; trustee Meridian Jr. Coll. Dist., 1984—; bd. dirs. law alumni Chpt. U. miss., 1980-83. Recipient Top Hat award Meridian Jr. Coll., 1982. Mem. ABA, Miss. Bar Assn., Landendale County Bar Assn. (pres. 1977-78). Episcopalian. Avocations: tennis. Banking, Contracts commercial, General practice. Home: 4341 18th Ave Meridian MS 39305 Office: Deen Cameron Prichard Young et al 1122 22d Ave Meridian MS 39302

YOUNG, RANDY WILLIAM, lawyer; b. Ft. Wayne, Ind., Oct. 19, 1949; s. Robert Arnold and Genevieve Mary (Obert) Y.; m. Julie Maree Brunson, June 16, 1984; children: Maree Elizabeth, Ann Elaine. BBA, U. Notre Dame, 1972; JD, Ind. U., 1975. Bar: Ind. 1975, U.S. Dist. Ct. (no. dist.) Ind. 1976. Law clk. to judge Ind. Ct. Appeals, Indpls., 1975-76; ptnr. Christoff, Cornelius & Young, Ft. Wayne, 1976-80; sole practice Ft. Wayne, 1980—. Recipient Silver Beaver award Boy Scouts Am., 1981, dist. award of Merit, 1985. Mem. Allen County Bar Assn. (treas. 1983-85), Allen County Law Library Assn. (treas. 1980—), St. Thomas Moore Soc. Roman Catholic. Clubs: St. Vincent Men's (Ft. Wayne), Notre Dame of Ft. Wayne (award of the year 1985). Avocations: scouting, skiing, camping, backpacking. Probate, Family and matrimonial, Personal injury. Home: 2115 W Carroll Rd Fort Wayne IN 46818 Office: 550 Metro Bldg Fort Wayne IN 46802

YOUNG, ROBERT EARL, lawyer; b. St. Louis, July 28, 1948; s. Earl Pitt and Hazel Charlene (Taylor) Y.; m. Patricia Lou Isle, Sept. 30, 1972; children: Derek, Jaime Beth, Robert P. BA, U. Mo., 1970, JD, 1976. Bar: Mo. 1976, Ark. 1976, U.S. Dist. Ct. (ea. dist.) Ark. 1976, U.S. Ct. Appeals (8th cir.) 1976. Ptnr. Rhine, Rhine & Young, Paragould, Ark., 1976—; prin. Greene County Abstract Co., Paragould, 1985—. Bd. dirs. Mission Outreach Inc., Paragould; mem. Greene County Fine Arts Council. Served with U.S. Army, 1970-72, Vietnam. Mem. ABA, Ark. Bar Assn., Mo. Bar Assn., Greene County Bar Assn. (pres.), Ark. Trial Lawyers Assn. Democrat. Methodist. Lodge: Kiwanis. Avocations: square dancing, bridge. General practice, Real property, Family and matrimonial. Home: 510 S 7th St Paragould AR 72450 Office: Rhine Rhine & Young 120 N 2d St Paragould AR 72451

YOUNG, ROBERT GEORGE, lawyer; b. Atlanta, Mar. 9, 1923; s. Samuel Rollo and Cidney A. (Young) Y.; m. Martha Latimer, Dec. 10, 1949; children—John Latimer, R. Carlisle, S. Scott. Grad. Ga. Mil. Acad., 1940; A.B., Emory U., 1943; LL.B., U. Ga., 1949. Bar: Ga. 1949. Assoc. Heyman, Howell and Heyman, Atlanta, 1949-51, Heyman and Abram, 1951-53, Marshall, Greene and Neely, Atlanta, 1953-55; ptnr. Heyman, Abram and Young, Atlanta, 1955-63, Edenfield, Heyman and Sizemore, Atlanta, 1963-69, Webb, Parker, Young and Ferguson, Atlanta, 1970-81, Young & Murphy, 1982—; asst. county atty. Fulton County (Ga.), 1966-71, county atty., 1971-87, sr. atty., 1987—. Mem. exec. com. Nat. Assn. R.R. Trial Counsel, 1965-68; treas. Fulton County Republican Exec. Com., 1962-64; bd. dirs. Atlanta Union Mission. Served to lt. (j.g.) USNR, 1944-46; PTO. Mem. ABA, Scotch-Irish Soc. U.S., Alpha Tau Omega. Presbyterian. Clubs: Lawyers of Atlanta, University Yacht, Capital City, Kiwanis. Federal civil litigation, State civil litigation, Local government. Home: 3561 Ridgewood Rd Atlanta GA 30327 Office: Young & Murphy 229 Peachtree St NE Suite 1902 Cain Tower Atlanta GA 30303

YOUNG, ROBERT H., lawyer; b. Pitts., Mar. 31, 1921; s. Robert and Ann Zella (Jordan) Y.; m. Jean K. Laros, Oct. 25, 1944; children: Susan L. Young Davis, Cynthia A. Young Mardis, Robert H., Judith L. Young Savage, Stacey J. A.B., Princeton U., 1942; J.D., Harvard U., 1945. Bar: Pa., U.S. Supreme Ct. Sr. ptnr. Morgan, Lewis & Bockius, Phila., 1948—; bd. dirs. Blue Cross of Greater Phila.; chmn. exec. com., chmn. mgmt. com. Active Adminstrv. Conf. U.S., Washington, 1975-78. Served to capt. U.S. Army, 1943-46. Mem. ABA (chmn. Pub. Utility sect. 1972). Republican. Presbyterian. Clubs: Gulph Mills Golf (Bryn Mawr, Pa.) (sec. 1983); Courts (Wynnewood, Pa.) (pres. 1981-84); Woodstock Country (Vt.); Merion Cricket (Haverford, Pa.). Home: 111 Righters Mill Rd Narberth PA 19072 Office: Morgan Lewis & Bockius 2000 One Logan Sq Philadelphia PA 19103

YOUNG, RODGER DOUGLAS, lawyer; b. Gt. Falls, Mont., June 10, 1946; s. Rodger D. Dorthey (Hogan) Y.; m. Linda S. Young, Nov. 29, 1974. BA, U. Mont., 1968; JD, U. Minn., 1972. Bar: Mich. 1973. Ptnr. Moll Desenberg Bayer et al, Detroit, 1976—; vice-chmn. Mich. Transp. Commn., 1978—. Mem. Mich. Environ Rev. Bd., 1974-78; chmn. fin. com. Oakland County Reps., Birmingham, Mich., 1975; chmn. St. Joseph Hosp. Pediatric Fund, Pontiac, Mich., 1985. Served with USAF, 1968-73. Mem. Mich. Bar Assn., Oakland County Bar Assn. Republican. Baptist. State civil litigation, Federal civil litigation. Home: 1336 Deerhurst Ln Rochester Hills MI 48063 Office: Moll Desenberg Bayer et al 666 American Ctr Southfield MI 48034

YOUNG, ROWLAND LEE, lawyer, writer; b. Galesburg, Ill., Aug. 19, 1922; s. Harry Lee and Doris (Rowland) Y. A.B., Bradley U., 1944; J.D., U. Chgo., 1948. Bar: Ill. 1949, U.S. Supreme Ct. 1960. Mem. staff ABA Jour., Chgo., 1948-66, assoc. editor, 1966-80; sole practice, Chgo., 1980—. Served

with AUS, 1942-46; to lt. col. USAR, 1946-82. Mem. ABA, Chgo. Bar Assn. Democrat. Episcopalian. Legal history, Jurisprudence. Address: 6007 N Sheridan Rd Chicago IL 60660

YOUNG, SIDNEY DAVID, lawyer; b. N.Y.C., Jan. 10, 1916; s. Benjamin and Pauline (Simmons) Y.; married, Dec. 10, 1939; children: Alan H., Estelle, Robert, Wendy. BS, Bklyn. Coll., 1937, LLB, 1939. Bar: N.Y. 1939, U.S. Dist. Ct. (ea. and so. dists.) N.Y. 1966. Ptnr. Dreyer and Traub, Bklyn., 1937-49; sr. ptnr. Lindenbaum and Young, Bklyn., 1949—. Pres. U.S. Com. Sports for Israel, N.Y.C., 1972-76. Mem. Bklyn. Bar Assn. (bd. dirs. real estate tax 1980-82), Rev. Bar Assn. Lodge: B'nai Brith. Real property, Landlord-tenant, State and local taxation. Office: 16 Court St Brooklyn NY 11241

YOUNG, STEPHEN BONSAL, law school dean, educator; b. Washington, Nov. 2, 1945; s. Kenneth Todd and Patricia (Morris) Y.; m. Hoa Thi Pham, Mar. 22, 1970; children—Ian, Warren, Antonia. A.B., Harvard U., 1967, J.D., 1974. Bar: N.Y. Chief village devel. AID, Saigon, Vietnam, 1968-71; assoc. Simpson, Thatcher & Bartlett, N.Y.C., 1974-78; asst. dean Harvard U. Law Sch., Cambridge, Mass., 1978-80, research assoc., 1978-81; dean Hamline U. Law Sch., St. Paul, 1981—. Author: Virtue and Law: Human Rights in Traditional China and Vietnam; Understanding Vietnam. Contbr. articles to profl. jours. Sec. Mpls.-St. Paul Com. on Fgn. Relations; mem., Citizens Commn. for Indochinese Refugees, N.Y.C., 1978—; v.p. and dir. Vietnam Women's Meml. Project, 1985—; dir. Hmong Farming Coop., Minn., 1983—; v.p. and dir. Resources for Child Caring, Minn., 1984—. Fellow Am. Bar Found.; mem. Council on Fgn. Relations, ABA, Minn. State Bar Assn. (bd. govs. 1981—), SAR, St. Paul C. of C. (co-chmn. task force on edn., 1986—). Clubs: University, Minnesota, Skylight, Informal (St. Paul). Lodge: Rotary. Avocation: archaeological discovery. General corporate, Private international, Jurisprudence. Office: Hamline U Law Sch 1536 Hewitt Ave Saint Paul MN 55104

YOUNG, TERRY CRESSLER, lawyer; b. Orlando, Fla., Aug. 8, 1951; s. Robert William and Claire Aileen (Carney) Y.; m. Linda Dismuke, Aug. 18, 1973; children: Logan Jay, Lawson James. BS in Advt., U. Fla., 1973, JD, 1975. Bar: Fla. 1976, U.S. Dist. Ct. (mid dist.) Fla. 1977, U.S. Ct. Appeals (11th cir.) 1983, U.S. Supreme Ct. 1984. Assoc. Giles, Hedrick & Robinson P.A., Orlando, 1975-80, ptnr., 1980-86; of counsel Lowndes, Drosdick, Doster, Kantor & Reed P.A., Orlando, 1986—. Mem. ABA, Fla. Bar Assn., Orange County Bar Assn. (chmn. state and fed. trial practice sect.), Nat. Bd. of Trial Adv., Acad. of Fla. Trial Lawyers. Republican. Methodist. Clubs: Univ., Country (Orlando). Lodge: Toastmasters (Orlando). Personal injury, Family and matrimonial, State civil litigation. Home: 2417 Pershing Oaks Place Orlando FL 32806 Office: Lowndes Drosdick Doster Kantor & ReedPA 215 N Eola Dr PO Box 2809 Orlando FL 32802

YOUNG, THOMAS JORDAN, lawyer; b. Bloomington, Ind., Oct. 10, 1935; s. Howard Sloan Young and Jean (Jordan) Maclay; m. Lila Jean Lee, June 15, 1962 (div. June 1978); m. Barbara Browne, Mar. 21, 1980. BA, Northwestern U., 1957, JD, 1960. Bar: Ind. 1060, U.S. Dist. Ct. (so. dist.) Ind. 1960, U.S. Ct. Appeals (7th cir.) 1960. Trial atty. Regional Counsel, Dept. Treasury, Cin. and Cleve., 1960-64; dep. prosecutor Marion County Prosecutor's Office, Indpls., 1965-75, 80-82; mem. Young & Young, Indpls., 1964—; civil trial adv. Nat. Bd. Trial Advocacy, 1985. Author: Wrongful Death in Indiana, 1986. Served with U.S. Army, 1961. Fellow Ind. Coll. of Fellows; mem. Ind. Trial Lawyers Assn. (past pres., bd. dirs.), Indpls. Bar Assn. (bd. mgrs.), Assn. Trial Lawyers Am. (state committeeman), Lawyers Club. Republican. Club: Toastmasters (Indpls. and Greenfield, Ind.) (pres. both clubs 1985). Federal civil litigation, State civil litigation, Personal injury. Home: Rt 8 Box 78 Greenfield IN 46140 Office: Young & Young 118 N Delaware St Indianapolis IN 46204

YOUNG, WILLIAM FIELDING, lawyer; b. N.Y.C., Jan. 6, 1948; s. Charles Fielding and Josephine Cope (Roig) Y.; m. Mary Anne Silver, June 13, 1970. BA, U. Va., 1970; JD, Harvard U., 1977. Bar: Va. 1977, U.S. dist. Ct. (ea. and we. dists.) Va. 1977, U.S. Ct. Appeals (4th cir.) 1977. Assoc. Hunton & Williams, Richmond, Va., 1977-85; ptnr. Hunton & Williams, Washington, 1985—, Fairfax, Va., 1985—. Mem. Va. Dist. Export Council, Richmond, 1983—. Served to lt. USN, 1970-74. Mem. Va. Bar Assn. (bd. govs. antitrust sect. 1985—, internat. law sect. 1985—), Phi Beta Kappa. Democrat. Episcopalian. Club: Downtown (Richmond). Antitrust, Private international, Federal civil litigation. Home: 1215 Mottrom Dr McLean VA 22101 Office: Hunton & Williams 2000 Pennsylvania Ave Washington DC 20036

YOUNG, WILLIAM GLOVER, federal judge; b. Huntington, N.Y., Sept. 23, 1940; s. Woodhull Benjamin and Margaret Jean (Wilkes) Y.; m. Beverly June Bigelow, Aug. 5, 1967; children: Mark Edward, Jeffrey Woodhull, Todd Russell. A.B., Harvard U., 1962, LL.B., 1967. Bar: Mass. 1967, U.S. Supreme Ct. 1970. Law clk. to chief justice Supreme Jud. Ct., Mass., 1967-68; spl. asst. atty. gen. Mass., 1969-72, chief legal counsel to gov., 1972-74; asso. firm Bingham, Dana and Gould, Boston, 1968-72; ptnr. Bingham, Dana and Gould, 1975-78; assoc. justice Superior Ct., Commonwealth of Mass., Boston, 1978-85; judge U.S. Dist. Ct. Mass., Boston, 1985—; lectr. part time Harvard Law Sch., Boston Coll. Law Sch., Boston U. Law Sch. Served to capt. U.S. Army, 1962-64. Mem. Am. Law Inst., Mass. Bar Assn., Boston Bar Assn., Harvard Alumni (pres. 1976-77). Office: US Dist Ct 1403 US Courthouse Boston MA 02109

YOUNGBLOOD, ELAINE MICHELE, lawyer; b. Schenectady, N.Y., Jan. 9, 1944; d. Roy W. and Mary Louise (Read) Ortoleva; m. William Gerald Youngblood, Feb. 14, 1970; children—Flagg Khristian, Megan Michele. B.A., Wake Forest Coll., 1965; J.D., Albany Law Sch., 1969. Bar: Tex. 1970, U.S. Dist. Ct. (no. dist.) Tex. 1971, U.S. Dist. Ct. (so. dist.) Tex. 1972, Tenn. 1978, U.S. Dist. Ct. (mid. dist.) Tenn. 1978. Assoc., Fanning & Harper, Dallas, 1969, Crocker & Murphy, Dallas, 1970-71, McClure & Burch, Houston, 1972-75, Brown, Bradshaw & Plummer, Houston, 1975-76; ptnr. Seligmann & Youngblood, Nashville, 1977—. Mem. Com. for Women in Govt., Dallas, 1969-71, Law Day com. of Dallas Bar Assn., 1970-71. Mem. ABA, Tex. Bar Assn., Tenn. Bar Assn., Nashville Bar Assn., Tenn. Trial Lawyers Assn., Nat. Assn. Women Lawyers. Republican. Episcopalian. Club: Cable of Nashville (charter). Federal civil litigation, Workers' compensation. Address: PO Box 17283 Nashville TN 37217

YOUNGER, ALEXANDER, judge; b. N.Y.C., Oct. 5, 1943; s. Douglas Erskine and Evelyn Sarah (Brown) Y. A.B., U. Pa., 1965; J.D., George Washington U., 1969. Bar: D.C. 1970. Assoc. Rhyne & Rhyne, Washington, 1969-70, Cole and Groner, Washington, 1970-71; trial atty., frauds sect. Dept. Justice, Washington, 1971-76, asst. chief, frauds sect., 1976-78, asst. dir. comml. litigation br., 1978-82, sr. trial counsel, 1982-84; adminstrv. judge Bd. of Contract Appeals, Corps Engrs., Washington, 1984—. mem. arbitration panel constrn. industry; lectr. coll. law Washington U., Am. U. Contbr. to books. Mem. Mayor's Com. on Handicapped Individuals, Washington, 1983—; v.p. Epilepsy Found. for Nat. Capital Area, 1983—; pres. D.C. Ctr. for Independent Living, Inc., 1986—, Capcom, Inc., Washington, 1983—. Recipient Spl. Achievement award Dept. Justice 1980, Meritorious award Dept. Justice, 1974. Mem. Fed. Bar Assn. (fed. circuit claims ct. com. 1982—), Am. Arbitration Assn., ABA. Government contracts and claims, Public international, Federal civil litigation. Home: 420 Seward Sq SE Washington DC 20003 Office: Bd of Contract Appeals Corps of Engrs 20 Massachusetts Ave NW Washington DC 20314

YOUNGER, JUDITH TESS, lawyer, educator; b. N.Y.C., Dec. 20, 1933; d. Sidney and Kate (Greenbaum) Weintraub; m. Irving Younger, Jan. 21, 1955; children: Rebecca, Abigail M. B.S., Cornell U., 1954; J.D., NYU, 1958; LL.D. (hon.), Hofstra U., 1974. Bar: N.Y. 1958, U.S. Supreme Ct. 1962, D.C. 1983, Minn. 1985. Law clk. to judge U.S. Dist. Ct., 1958-60; asso. firm Chadbourne, Parke, Whiteside & Wolff, N.Y.C., 1960-62; mem. firm Younger and Younger, and (successors), 1962-67; adj. asst. prof. N.Y. U. Sch. Law, 1967-69; asst. atty. gen. State of N.Y., 1969-70; assoc. prof. Hofstra U. Sch. Law, 1970-72, prof., assoc. dean, 1972-74; dean, prof. Syracuse Coll. Law, 1974-75; dep. dean, prof. law Cornell Law Sch., 1975-78, prof. law, 1978-85; vis. prof. U. Minn. Law Sch., Mpls., 1984-85; prof. law U. Minn. Law Sch., 1985—; Trustee Cornell U., 1974-78; cons. NOW, 1972-74, Suffolk County for Revision of Its Real Property Tax Act, 1972-73; mem. Gov. Rockefeller's Panel to Screen Candidates of Ct. of Claims Judges, 1973-74. Contbr. articles to profl. jours. Mem. ABA (council legal edn. 1975-79), Am. Law Inst. (adv. restatement property), AAUP (v.p. Cornell U. chpt. 1978-79), N.Y. State Bar Assn., Assn. of Bar of City of N.Y., Minn. Bar Assn. Probate, Real property, Family and matrimonial. Home: 3520 W Calhoun Pkwy Minneapolis MN 55416 Office: U Minn Law Sch Minneapolis MN 55455

YOUNGER, WILLIAM CARL, state law librarian; b. Sulligent, Ala., Nov. 5, 1919; s. Clarence William and Mary Avice (Jackson) Y.; m. Ronnie Belle Coggins, July 7, 1943; children—Myra Nell Younger Finley, William Daniel, Brenda Alice Younger Hill. B.S., U. Ala., 1954, M.L.S., 1973, J.D., 1956. Bar: Ala. 1956, U.S. Dist. Ct. (mid. dist.) Ala. 1957, U.S. Ct. Appeals (5th cir.) 1957, U.S. Ct. Appeals (11th cir.) 1982, U.S. Supreme Ct. 1959. Law clk. Ala. Supreme Ct., 1956; asst. atty. gen. State of Ala., 1957-59, 64-65; asst. dir. Ala. Dept. Indsl. Relations, 1959; dir. Ala. Dept. Conservation, 1959-63; pvt. practice, Montgomery, Ala., 1962-64; state law librarian, marshal Ala. Supreme Ct., Montgomery, 1965—, librarian, 1965—. Pres. East Montgomery Exchange Club, 1967. Served with AUS, 1940-51. Decorated Purple Heart with one bronze oak leaf cluster, Combat Infantryman Badge, Silver Star, Bronze Star; Brit. Mil. medal; named Sesquicentennial Hon. Prof., U. Ala., 1981. Mem. Ala. Bar Assn., Montgomery County Bar Assn., Am. Assn. Law Libraries (pres. S.E. chpt. 1974-76), Ala. Peace Officers Assn., Ala. Library Assn., Montgomery County Library Assn., Am. Legion. Baptist. Editor: Alabama Appellate Courts, 1968, 3d edit., 1973, (with others) 7th edit., 1983. Librarianship. Office: Supreme Court and State Law Library Judicial Bldg 445 Dexter Ave Montgomery AL 36130

YOUNGLOVE, EDWARD EARL, III, lawyer; b. Seattle, Feb. 10, 1949; s. Edward Earl Jr. and Shirley Jannette (Engholm) Y.; m. Celeste J. Kardonsky; 1 child, Alexis. BA, U. Wash., 1971; JD, Gonzaga U., 1974. Bar: Wash. 1974, U.S. Dist. Ct. (we. and ea. dists.) Wash. 1974, U.S. Ct. Appeals (9th cir.) 1979. Ptnr. Swanson, Parr, Cordes, Younglove, Peeples & Wyckoff, P.S., Olympia, Wash., 1974—. Mem. Assn. Trial Lawyers Am., Wash. State Trial Lawyers Assn. State civil litigation, Labor, Administrative and regulatory. Office: Swanson Parr et al 924 E 7th Suite A Olympia WA 98501

YOUNGMAN, JOHN CRAWFORD, lawyer; b. Williamsport, Pa., Jan. 25, 1903; s. Charles Worman and Margaret Maud (Porter) Y.; m. Ruth Young Allen, Feb. 7, 1933 (dec. July 1976); children—John Crawford Jr., C. Van, Margaret Youngman Holman. B.S. in Econs., U. Pa., 1924; LL.B., Harvard U., 1927, J.D., 1969. Bar: Pa. 1928, U.S. Ct. Appeals (3d cir.), U.S. Dist. Ct. (mid. dist.) Pa., U.S. Supreme Ct. Dist. atty. Lycoming County (Pa.), 1932-35; sr. ptnr. Candor, Youngman, Gibson & Gault, Williamsport, Pa., 1943—; dir. Williamsport Hotels Co. Nat. assoc. Boys Clubs Am., 1952—; chmn. Williamsport San. Authority, 1952—; vice chmn. Williamsport Water Authority, 1966—. Recipient Kemper Disting. Service award, 1983. Mem. World Assn. Lawyers (vice-chmn.), Jud. Conf. 3d Cir. Ct. Apls., ABA, Pa. Bar Assn., Lycoming County Law Assn. (pres. 1939), Am. Judicature Soc. Recipient Grit award, 1956; Conservation award Pa. Game Commn. 1975. Federal civil litigation, State civil litigation, Probate. Home: 54 Roderick Rd Williamsport PA 17701 Office: 23 W 3d St Williamsport PA 17701

YOUNGS, CHRISTOPHER JAY, lawyer; b. Stuttgart, Fed. Republic Germany, Dec. 20, 1956; came to U.S., 1958; s. Jay Rotigel and Nancy (Hazen) Y.; m. Lisa Pepicelli, May 14, 1983. BA cum laude, U. Pitts., 1978, JD, 1982. Bar: Pa. 1982, U.S. Dist. Ct. (we. dist.) Pa. 1982. Assoc. RosenzWeig & Burton, Pitts., 1982-83, Pepicelli, Pepicelli, Watts & Youngs PC, Meadville, Pa., 1983-85; ptnr. Watts, Pepicelli, Youngs & Youngs PC, Meadville, Pa., 1985—. Advisor Crawford County (Pa.) Law Exploring Post, 1986. Mem. Assn. Trial Lawyers Am., ABA, Pa. Bar Assn., Allegheny County Bar Assn., Crawford County Bar Assn., Meadville Area C. of C. (bd. dirs.). Democrat. Presbyterian. Lodge: Kiwanis (v.p. 1986). Avocations: canoeing, fishing, hunting, cross-country skiing, working with children and young adults. Workers' compensation, Local government, State civil litigation. Home: PO Box 647 Cochranton PA 16314-0647 Office: Watts Pepicelli Youngs & Youngs 363 Chestnut St Meadville PA 16335

YOUNGS, JOHN CURTIS, lawyer; b. N.Y.C., Mar. 18, 1944; s. Eugene Ward and Laura (Iglauer) Y. AB, Harvard U., 1968; JD, Georgetown U., 1974. Bar: Va. 1976, U.S. Dist. Ct. (ea. dist.) Va. 1978, U.S. Ct. Appeals (4th cir.) 1978, U.S. Dist. Ct. (D.C. cir.) 1978, U.S. Ct. Mil. Appeals 1978, U.S. Ct. Appeals (D.C. cir.) 1979. Youth counselor Ohio Youth Commn., Cin., 1967-68; research asst. Georgetown Law Ctr., Washington, 1969-70; chief ops. D.C. Pretrial Agy., Washington, 1973-78; sole practice Arlington, Va., 1978—. Mem. ABA, D.C. Bar Assn., Arlington County Bar Assn. (treas. 1983-85, pres.-elect 1986-87), Assn. Trial Lawyers Am., Va. Trial Lawyers Assn., Nat. Assn. Criminal Def. Lawyers, Delta Upsilon. Club: Hasty Pudding. Criminal, State civil litigation, Personal injury. Office: 2009 N 14th St Suite 307 Arlington VA 22201 also: 129 E St NW Washington DC 20001

YOUNGS, LINDA MILLER, lawyer; b. Worcester, Mass., May 13, 1942; d. James Wesley Miller and Hope (Norman) Connell; m. J. William T. Youngs, Jr., June 24, 1967; children—J. William Theodore III, Hope Eleanor. A.B., Wellesley Coll., 1963; M.Sc., U. Pa., 1966; J.D., Gonzaga U., 1975. Bar: Wash. 1975. City atty. City of Bellevue, Wash., 1981-84; of counsel Davis Wright & Jones, Bellevue, 1984—. Mem. ABA, Seattle-King County Bar Assn., Wash. Women Lawyers (dir. 1982). Democrat. Environment, Local government, Real property. Home: 10014 SE 16th St Bellevue WA 98004 Office: Davis Wright & Jones 110 110th Ave NE Suite 700 Bellevue WA 98004

YOW, CICERO PRESTON, lawyer; b. Randolph County, N.C., Dec. 24, 1914; s. Amos and Cassie (Langley) Y.; m. Mary Elizabeth Hardwicke, June 5, 1948; 1 child, Elizabeth Nixon. LLB, Wake Forest U., 1942. Bar: N.C. 1942. Ptnr. Yow, Yow, Culbreth & Fox, Wilmington, 1943—; solicitor New Hanover County, Wilmington, N.C., 1948-52, atty., 1954-55; 1st asst. U.S. atty. U.S. Dist. Ct. (ea. dist.) N.C., 1952-54, City of Wilmington, 1955-79. State Senator N.C., Raleigh, 1955-63; chmn. Dems. New Hanover County, Wilmington, 1962. Served with USAF 1942-43. Episcopalian. Lodges: Optimists, Masons. Avocation: fishing. Municipal bonds, Probate, Legislative. Home: 329 W Renovah Circle Wilmington NC 28403 Office: Yow Yow Culbreth & Fox Attys 102 N 5th Ave Wilmington NC 28401

YSLAS, STEPHEN DANIEL, lawyer; b. Los Angeles, Mar. 28, 1947; m. Alice Troy. BA, UCLA, 1969, JD, 1972. Bar: Calif. 1973. Atty. NLRB, Los Angeles, 1972-73, Atlantic Richfield, Los Angeles, 1973-75; div. counsel Northrop Corp., Los Angeles, 1975—. Commr. City of Los Angeles Police Dept., 1980—; bd. dirs. Youth Opportunities Found., Los Angeles. Mem. ABA, Mexican Am.-Bar Assn. (Benito Juarez award for community service), Calif. Bar Assn. General corporate, Labor. Office: Northrop Corp 1 Northrop Ave Hawthorne CA 90250

YUCEL, EDGAR KENT, lawyer, consultant; b. Ankara, Turkey, Aug. 18, 1927; came to U.S., 1948, naturalized, 1958; s. Mustafa Muammer and Refika (Sunkitay) Y.; m. Martha Ellen Diggs, Sept. 8, 1954; 1 child, Edgar Kent. B.S., Galatasaray Lyceum, Istanbul, Turkey, 1948; M.A., U. Ala., 1953, postgrad., 1953-56; J.D., U. Minn., 1962. Bar: Minn. 1962, U.S. Dist. Ct. Minn. 1969. Instr. polit. sci. and econs. U. Ala., Tuscaloosa and Huntsville, 1953-56; project engr. So. Assoc. Engrs., Huntsville, 1956-59, supervising engr. Sperry Univac Co., St. Paul, 1959-62; sr. atty. 3M Co., St. Paul, 1962-69, asst. gen counsel, 1969-81, spl. counsel, 1981—; seminar lectr. St. John's U., Collegeville, Minn., 1976; adj. faculty grad. sch. Coll. St. Thomas, St. Paul, 1986; pro bono atty. So. Minn. Regional Legal Services, St. Paul, 1983—. Patentee marking tape. Trustee, gov. Health Central Inc., Mpls., 1972-78; v.p., sec., bd. dirs. Life Scis. Found., Mpls., 1973—; pres. Turkish Cultural Soc., Mpls., 1965-67; vice consul ad honorem Republic of Costa Rica, Mpls., 1964—. Mem. ABA, Minn. Bar Assn., Corp. Counsel Assn. (bd. dirs. 1964-67, pres. 1967-68), Licensing Execs. Soc., Soc. Univ. Patent Adminstrs., Minn. Patent and Trademark Law Assn., Am. Arbitration Assn. (arbitrator 1984—). Clubs: Minneapolis, Minn. Alumni (Mpls). General corporate, Private international, Intellectual property licensing. Home: 4712 Merilane Minneapolis MN 55436 Office: 3M Co Patent Counsel 3M Ctr 220-11W-01 Saint Paul MN 55144

YUDES, JAMES PEYTON, lawyer; b. N.Y.C., July 5, 1950; s. Alfred Edward and Mary (Peyton) Y.; m. Bebbins Rahmeyer, Aug. 11, 1973; children—Meghan, Jeannette. B.S./B.A., Villanova U., 1972, J.D., 1975. Bar: N.J. 1975, U.S. Dist. Ct. N.J. 1975, U.S. Tax Ct. 1979, U.S. Ct. Appeals (3d cir.) 1981, U.S. Supreme Ct. 1981. Jud. law clk. Superior Ct. N.J., 1975-76; assoc. atty. Skoloff & Wolfe, Newark, 1976-78; ptnr. Newman, Yudes & Carey, Cranford, N.J., 1978-79; sr. atty. James P. Yudes, P.C., Counsellors at Law, Mountainside, N.J., 1979—; mem. Morris county Matrimonial Early Settlement Panel, 1978-80, Middlesex County Matrimonial Early Settlement Panel, 1982, Essex County Matrimonial Early Settlement Panel, 1980-84; mem. Union County Matrimonial Early Settlement Panel, 1978-84, chmn., 1981-84; exec. mem. Inst. for Continuing Legal Edn. N.J., 1982-85; Author: Pre-Nuptial Agreements in New Jersey, 1985. Trustee Family Law Inst. N.J., 1984-85. Fellow Am. Acad. Matrimonial Lawyers (editor newsletter N.J. chpt. 1982-83); mem. Am. Judicature Soc., ABA (family law com. 1976—, exec. mem. mediation com. 1981-84, merit cert. 1980, 81), N.J. State Bar Assn. (legis. coordinator family law sect. 1983-84, exec. com. family law sect. 1981-84, exec. mem. specialization com. 1983-84, family law co-ordinator Supreme Ct. com. of family part 1984-85, Supreme Ct. com. on supervised visitation, awards 1983, cert. recognition for disting. service 1981, 82, 83, 84), Assn. Trial Lawyers N.J. (legis. adv. bd. 1981-84). Republican. Roman Catholic. Family and matrimonial. Office: 1243 Rt 22E Mountainside NJ 07092

YUILL, WILLIAM DUANE, lawyer; b. Williston, N.D., Nov. 29, 1935; s. William G. and Gladys T. (Husbey) Y.; m. Madonna M. Younggren, Aug. 12, 1955; children: Timothy, Todd, Anthony, Jennifer. PHB, LLB, U. N.D., 1959. Bar: N.D. 1959, U.S. Dist. Ct. N.D. 1962, U.S. Ct. Appeals (8th cir.) 1962. Sole practice Fargo, N.D., 1959—. Mem. N.D. Bar Assn., Cass County Bar Assn. (pres. 1974-75), N.D. Trial Lawyers Assn. (bd. dirs.). Avocation: auto racing. Federal civil litigation, State civil litigation, Insurance. Home: PO Box 1637 Fargo ND 58102

YUNG, CARROLL JOHN, lawyer; b. Washington, Nov. 26, 1956. SB in Math., MIT, 1979; JD, Cornell U., 1982. Bar: D.C. 1982, U.S. Dist. Ct. D.C. 1983, U.S. Ct. Appeals (D.C. cir.) 1983, U.S. Supreme Ct. 1986. Assoc. Chadbourne, Parke, Whiteside & Wolff, Washington, 1982-84, Fisher, Wayland, Cooper & Leader, Washington, 1984—. Mem. ABA, Fed. Communications Bar Assn., D.C. Bar Assn., Sigma Xi. Avocations: chess, jogging, tennis. Administrative and regulatory, General corporate, Communications. Office: Fisher Wayland Cooper & Leader 1255 23rd St NW Suite 800 Washington DC 20037

YURASKO, FRANK NOEL, lawyer, judge; b. Rahway, N.J., Dec. 22, 1938; s. Frank H. and Estelle (Trudeau) Y.; m. Mary Byrd, July 23, 1966; children—Elizabeth Anne, Suzanne, Frank. B.A., Brown U., 1960; cert. London Sch. Econs., 1961; student Gray's Inn, London, 1960-61; J.D., Yale U., 1964. Bar: N.J. 1964, Fla. 1979, U.S. Dist. Ct. N.J. 1965, U.S. Ct. Appeals (3d cir.) 1980, U.S. Supreme Ct. 1969; cert. civil trial atty., N.J. Judge's law clk. N.J. Dept. Judiciary, Trenton, 1964-66; ptnr. Graham, Yurasko, Golden, Lintner & Rothchild, Somerville, N.J., 1966-80; sole practice, Somerville, 1980—; judge Montgomery Twp. (N.J.) Mcpl. Ct., 1973-84; twp. atty. Hillsborough Twp. (N.J.), 1973—; atty. Green Brook (N.J.) Bd. Adjustment, 1973—. Trustee Gill/St. Bernard Sch., Bernardsville, N.J.; mem. alumni bd. trustees Peddie Sch., Hightstown, N.J. Mem. Am. Judicature Soc., N.J. Bar Assn., Fla. Bar Assn., ABA, Somerset County Bar Assn., Mercer County Bar Assn., Assn. Trial Lawyers Am., Trial Attys. N.J., N.J. Fedn. Planning Ofcls., Nat. Inst. Mcpl. Legal Officers, Middlesex County Trial Lawyers Assn. State civil litigation, General practice, Local government. Office: 63 Route 206 S PO Box 1041 Somerville NJ 08876

YUSPEH, ALAN RALPH, lawyer; b. New Orleans, June 13, 1949; s. Michel and Rose Fay (Rabenovitz) Y.; m. Janet Horn, June 8, 1975. B.A., Yale U., 1971; M.B.A., Harvard U., 1973; J.D., Georgetown U., 1978. Bar: D.C. 1978. Mgmt. cons. McKinsey & Co., Washington, 1973-74; adminstrv. asst., legis. asst. Office of U.S. Senator J. Bennett Johnston, Washington, 1974-78; atty. Shaw, Pittman, Potts & Trowbridge, Washington, 1978-79, Ginsburg, Feldman, Weil and Bress, Washington, 1979-82; gen. counsel Com. on Armed Services-U.S. Senate, Washington, 1982-85; ptnr. Preston, Thorgrimson, Ellis & Holman, 1985—. Editor Law and Policy in Internat. Business jour., 1978-79. Served to 1st lt. USAR, 1971-77. Mem. ABA (vice chmn. com. major systems, com. acctg., cost and pricing, sect. pub. contract law 1984—). Club: Fed. City, Army and Navy (Washington). Government contracts and claims, Legislative. Home: 2332 Bright Leaf Way Baltimore MD 21209 Office: Preston Thorgrimson Ellis & Holman 1735 New York Ave NW Suite 500 Washington DC 20006

ZAANDER, MARK CHARLES, lawyer; b. Chgo., Jan. 24, 1951; s. Carl J. and Marion E. (Penshorn) Z.; m. Linda S. Rabin, Dec. 15, 1974; children: Brian C., Paula F. BS in Math., U. Ill., 1973; JD, U. Chgo., 1976. Bar: Ill. 1976. Assoc. Schiff, Hardin & Waite, Chgo., 1976-83, ptnr., 1983—. Mem. ABA, Chgo. Bar Assn. Securities, General corporate, Contracts commercial. Office: Schiff Hardin & Waite 7200 Sears Tower Chicago IL 60606

ZABEL, WILLIAM DAVID, lawyer; b. Omaha, Dec. 14, 1936; s. Louis J. and Annie I. Z.; m. Deborah M. Miller, Oct. 31, 1979; children by previous marriage: Richard, David. A.B. summa cum laude, Princeton U., 1958; LL.B. cum laude, Harvard U., 1961. Bar: N.Y. 1961, U.S. Supreme Ct. 1966, Fla. 1975. Ptnr. firm Schulte Roth & Zabel, N.Y.C., 1969—, Palm Beach, Fla., 1975—; lectr. Cornell Law Sch., So. Fed. Tax Inst., U. Miami Inst. Estate Planning, Great Plains Tax Inst., profl. orgns.; N.Y. State adv. com. U.S. Civil Rights Commn., 1969-73; vol. civil rights litigator Lawyers Constnl. Def. Com., Miss., summer 1965. Author: Estate Planning for the Large Estate, 1976, Domicile, Wills and Tax Problems of Migrating Clients Transplanted to Florida, 1976, Income, Estate and Gift Tax Consequences of Marital Settlements, 1979, Estate Planning for Interests in a Closely Held Business, 1981, Use of Trusts in Connection with Marital Dissolutions, 1983; Am. editor: The Lawyer, Eng., 1963-66; mem. editorial adv. bd. (Trusts & Estates mag.); contbr. articles to periodicals. Pres. Merlin Found.; mem. Lymphona Found., Open Soc. Fund, Inc., Soros Found., Ottinger Found., David H. Cogan Found., Samuel Waxman Cancer Research Found., ALTRO, Fund for Reform and Opening of China Inc.; legal counsel Internat. Confedn. Art Dealers. Recipient Disting. Community Service award Brandeis U., 1986; fellow Brandeis U., 1987. Fellow Am. Coll. Probate Counsel, Internat. Acad. Estate and Trust Law, Brandeis U. Alumni Assn.; mem. Am. Law Inst., ABA, N.Y. State Bar Assn., Assn. of Bar of City of N.Y. (internat. human rights com.), Lawyers Com. for Human Rights (bd. dirs.), Estate Planning Council N.Y.C. (bd. dirs. 1975-79), Fla. Bar Assn., Phi Beta Kappa. Clubs: Harmonie (bd. govs.) (N.Y.C.); Century Country. Probate, Estate taxation, Family and matrimonial. Home: 850 Park Ave New York NY 10021 Office: 900 3d Ave New York NY 10022 also: 249 Royal Palm Way Palm Beach FL 33480

ZABROSKY, ALEX WALTER, lawyer; b. Chgo., Aug. 18, 1953; s. Alex J. and Olga Zabrosky. BA, U. Chgo., 1975; JD, George Washington U., 1978. Bar: Ill. 1978, U.S. Dist. Ct. (no. dist.) Ill. 1978. Assoc. Abramson & Fox, Chgo., 1978-80; assoc. counsel Trailer Train Co., Chgo., 1980-82; asst. legal counsel, asst. sec. Heizer Corp., Chgo., 1982-84; gen. counsel, sec. Alexander Proudfoot Co., Chgo., 1984—. Mem. ABA, Chgo. Bar Assn. General corporate, Securities. Home: 2464 N Orchard St Chicago IL 60614 Office: Alexander Proudfoot Co Three Illinois Ctr Chicago IL 60601

ZACHARY, WILLIAM EDMOND, JR., lawyer; b. Atlanta, Feb. 26, 1943; s. William Edmond Sr. and Sue (Miller) Z.; m. Gayle Jackson, 1964 (div. 1974); children: Tori, Trenee'; m. Katherine Carriere, Apr. 10, 1976; 1 child, Kristen. BA, Emory U., 1964, JD, 1967. Bar: Ga. 1966, U.S. Dist. Ct. (no. and mid. dists.) Ga. 1966, U.S. Ct. Appeals (5th and 11th cirs.) 1971, U.S. Supreme Ct. 1971. Ptnr. Zachary & Segraves, Decatur, Ga., 1969—; chmn. bd. dirs. Bank Atlanta. Mem. exec. com. DeKalb County (Ga.) Dems., 1972; bd. dirs. Pat Galloway Ministries Prison Fellowship, 1982—. Mem. Ga. Bar Assn. (grievance tribunal 1974-76, legal edn. and admission to bar com., clin. edn. com. young lawyers sect.), Decatur-DeKalb Bar Assn., Assn. Trial Lawyers Am., Ga. Trial Lawyers Assn., Christian Legal Soc., Atlanta Lawyers Christian Fellowship. General practice. Home: 197 Roe Hampton Stone Mountain GA 30087 Office: Zachary & Segraves PA 1000 Commerce Dr Decatur GA 30030

ZACHARY, WILLIAM EDMUND, lawyer; b. Cordele, Ga., Nov. 29, 1913; s. James Edmund and Luta Mae (Elliott) Z.; m. Sue Miller, Feb. 4, 1939 (dec. Nov. 1980); children: Mary Elizabeth Zachary Wilson, William Edmund Jr., Susan Zachary Cornwell; m. Amelia McLean, June 4, 1981. LLB, Woodrow Wilson Coll. of Law, Atlanta, 1945. Bar: U.S. Dist. Ct. (no. dist.) Ga. 1947, U.S. Ct. Appeals (5th cir.) 1950, U.S. Supreme Ct. 1950, U.S. Ct. Appeals (11th cir.) 1981. Sole practice Decatur, Ga., 1946-54; ptnr. Zachary & Hunter, Decatur, 1954-72; pres. Zachary & Segraves, P.A., Decatur, 1972—; pres. Decatur Bar Assn., 1952, Stone Mt. Bar Assn., Decatur, 1954; bd. govs. Ga. Bar Assn., 1961-62; instr. Inst. Continuing Legal Edn., 1964; atty. City of Decatur, 1964-68. Commr. City of Decatur, 1952, recorder, 1954-57. Mem. State Bar Ga. (bd. govs. 1962—, dean 1985). Methodist. Club: Decatur-Clairmont (pres. 1952-53). Lodge: Civitan, Masons. Family and matrimonial, General practice, Personal injury. Home: 804 Pinetree Dr Decatur GA 30030 Office: Zachary & Segraves PA 1000 Commerce Dr Decatur GA 30030

ZACK, DAVID, lawyer; b. N.Y.C., Sept. 16, 1917; s. Harry and Beckie (Lang) Z.; m. Beatrice Bodin, July 4, 1940; children: Brian Bary, Donald Jeffrey. BBA, CUNY, 1937; JD, St. John's U., 1939. Bar: N.Y. 1939, CPA, N.Y. Sr. ptnr. David Berdan & Co., N.Y.C., 1944—. contbr. articles to profl. jours. Mem. N.Y. State Soc. CPA's (pres.). Estate planning, Corporate taxation, Estate taxation. Home: 25 Central Park W Apt 115 New York NY 10023 Office: David Berdan & Co 415 Madison Ave New York NY 10017

ZACKAROFF, PETER TIMOTHY, lawyer, educator; b. Yonkers, N.Y., Aug. 23, 1955; s. Alexander George and Bernadette Ann (Gateley) Z.; m. Ilene Gay Cohen, July 31, 1982; 1 child, Scott Andrew. B.A., Fairleigh Dickinson U., 1977; J.D., U. Akron, 1980; student Coll. Fin. Planning, Denver, 1984—. Bar: Ohio 1980, U.S. Dist. Ct. (no. dist.) Ohio 1980, D.C. 1982. Assoc. Schwab, Grosenbaugh, Fort & Seamon Co., L.P.A., Akron, Ohio, 1980-83, ptnr. Schwab, Grosenbaugh, Fort, Seamon & Zackaroff, 1984—; instr. Ohio Paralegal, Cleve., 1980-83, Career Studies Inst., Canton, Ohio, 1983—. Panel atty. Vol. Legal Services Project, Akron, 1984; bd. dirs. Big Bros. & Sisters Greater Akron. Mem. ABA, Ohio State Bar Assn. (bd. govs. young lawyer div.), Akron Bar Assn., D.C. Bar Assn., Ohio Bar Coll., Assn. Trial Lawyers Am., Ohio Acad. Trial Lawyers, Akron Jaycees (legal counsel 1980-85, v.p. 1986, Jaycee of Month 1983, 84, Silver Key award 1983, 84, Presdl. award of Honor 1983-84). Republican. Roman Catholic. State civil litigation, General practice, Personal injury. Home: 249 Sand Run Rd Akron OH 44313 Office: Schwab Grosenbaugh Fort et al 40 E Mill St Akron OH 44308

ZACUR, RICHARD AARON, lawyer; b. Miami, Fla., Nov. 19, 1949; s. Howard Aaron and Helen (Pizzuti) Z. BA, Fla. State U., 1971; JD, Stetson Coll. of Law, St. Petersburg, Fla., 1974. Bars: Fla. 1974, U.S. Dist. Ct. (mid. dist.) Fla. 1974, U.S. Ct. Appeals (5th cir.) 1974, U.S. Supreme Ct. 1977, D.C. 1982. Ptnr. Mensh, Zacur & Graham, P.A., St. Petersburg, 1974—. Mem. Big Bros./Big Sisters, St. Petersburg, 1981; mem. Fla. Lawyer's Action Group, St. Petersburg, 1978. Named one of Outstanding Young Men of Am., U.S. Jaycees, 1977. Mem. ABA, Am. Judicature Soc., Assn. Trial Lawyers Am., Acad. Fla. Trial Lawyers, Pinellas County Trial Lawyers Assn., Lawyer's Title Guaranty Fund, Gold Key Soc., Omicron Delta Kappa. Presbyterian. Avocations: alpine skiing, golf. Family and matrimonial, Real property, State civil litigation. Office: Mensh Zacur & Graham PA 5200 Central Ave Saint Petersburg FL 33707

ZAFIS, ANDREW JAMES, hotel executive, lawyer; b. Milw., May 23, 1925; s. James John and Josephine (Przybylowski) Z.; m. Jean Marie Kalscheur, Nov. 10, 1951; children: Lynn Ann, Constance Lee, John James, Mary Jo. BS, U. Wis., 1948, JD, 1950; MPA, Harvard U., 1951; postgrad. U. Calif.-San Diego, 1979-80. Bar: Wis. 1950, Calif. 1978, U.S. Dist. Ct. (ea. dist.) Wis. 1954, U.S. Supreme Ct. 1965, U.S. Dist. Ct. (so. dist.) Calif. 1980, U.S. Ct. Appeals (9th cir.) 1985. Mem. Wis. Atty. Gen.'s staff, 1950; U.S. atty.-advisor Wage Stabilization Bd., Richmond, Va., 1951-52; practice, Oconomowoc, Wis., 1953-76; city atty., Oconomowoc, 1958-63; mcpl. atty., cons. Oconomowoc, Merton, Eagle, Summit and Lac La Belle, Wis., 1953-76; sr. mem. Zafis Rummel, Caldwell & Calhill, 1967-76; prof. law, head dept. civil procedure Western State U. Coll. Law, San Diego, 1976-81; sole practice, San Diego and Coronado, Calif., 1980-83; v.p., litigation counsel Hotel del Coronado (Calif.), 1981—; adj. prof. law Nat. U. Law Sch., San Diego, 1981—; guest lectr. Wis. Law Sch., 1969-75; sec., bd. dirs., gen. counsel Enrichment Reading Co. Am., 1970—; judge pro tem El Cajon Mcpl. Ct., 1983—. Author: (with A. Schaffer) California Courtroom Practice and Procedure, rev. edit., 1980. Pres. Library Bd., 1965-76; mem. City Bd. Appeals, Oconomowoc, 1964; founder NW unit Dem. party, 1954, chmn., 1954-56; pres. YMCA, Oconomowoc, 1974-76. Served with Signal Corps, U.S. Army, 1943-46. Adminstrv. fellow Littauer Sch. Govt., Harvard U., 1950-51; recipient Wis. Alumni Testimonial award, 1982. Mem. Assn. Trial Lawyers Am., Wis. State Bar (com. on legal edn. and bar standards 1976, 83-84), Wis. Acad. Trial Lawyers (bd. govs. 1970), Calif. State Bar, Calif. Trial Lawyers Assn., San Diego County Bar, San Diego Trial Lawyers Assn., U. Wis. Alumni Assn. (local pres., nat. dir.), Coronado C. of C. (bd. dirs. 1984-86), Phi Alpha Delta, Beta Theta Pi. Roman Catholic. Clubs: Mission Bay Yacht (judge adv. 1983, 85-86, bd. dirs. 1985), Harvard (San Diego); Coronado Yacht, La Belle Yacht (Oconomowoc, Wis.), San Diego Crew Classic (bd. dirs.). Lodge: Kiwanis (sec. local club). State civil litigation, Federal civil litigation, Local government. Office: Hotel Del Coronado 1500 Orange Ave Coronado CA 92118

ZAGAMI, ANTHONY JAMES, lawyer; b. Washington, Jan. 19, 1951; s. Placidino and Rosemary Zagami; m. Natalie Ann Manganello, July 19, 1980; 1 child, Brian. AA, Prince Georges Community Coll., 1971; BS in Bus. and Pub. Adminstrn., U. Md., 1973, postgrad., 1974; JD, George Mason U., 1977. Bar: D.C. 1978, U.S. Dist. Ct. D.C. 1979, U.S. Ct. Appeals (D.C. cir.) 1979, U.S. Supreme Ct. 1983. Asst. to sec. of majority U.S. Senate, Washington, 1977-78, staff asst. to Sec. of Senate, 1978-81; gen. counsel joint com. on printing U.S. Congress, Washington, 1981—. Chmn. legal adv. com. U.S. Senate Employees Fed. Credit Union Bd. Dirs.; counsel U.S. Senate Staff Club. Mem. ABA, Phi Alpha Phi. Legislative, Government contracts and claims, Federal government in general. Home: 9021 Adelphi Rd Adelphi MD 20783 Office: US Congress Joint Com Printing Hart Senate Office Bldg Room SH-818 Washington DC 20510

ZAGORSKY, PETER JOSEPH, lawyer; b. New Britain, Conn., Oct. 27, 1950; s. Edward Joseph and Genevieve Mary (Bogdanski) Z.; m. Jane Elizabeth Bremner, July 14, 1979; children: Kathryn Elizabeth, Kristin Mary. BA, Hofstra U., 1972; JD, Georgetown U., 1975. Bar: Conn. 1975, U.S. Dist. Ct. Conn. 1976, N.Y. 1986. Assoc. Glazer, Wechsler & Seelig, Stamford, Conn., 1975-77; ptnr. Poulos & Zagorsky, Plainville, Conn., 1977—. Pres., bd. dirs. United Way of Plainville, Conn., 1984; treas., bd. dirs. Visiting Nurse Home Care Service of Central Conn., Inc., New Britain, Conn., 1984. Mem. ABA, Am. Trial Lawyers Assn., Conn. Bar Assn., Conn. Trial Lawyers Assn., Hartford County Bar Assn. General practice, State civil litigation, Criminal. Home: 90 N Mountain Rd Canton CT 06019 Office: 100 E Main St Plainville CT 06062

ZAHARAKO, LEW DALEURE, lawyer; b. Columbus, Ind., Dec. 21, 1947; s. Lewie J. and May (Daleure) Z. B.S., Ind. U.-Bloomington, 1971, J.D., 1974. Bar: Ind. 1974. Investigator, asst. dir. consumer protection div. Ind. Atty. Gen.'s Office, Indpls., 1974-75, dir., 1975-76, chief antitrust sect. 1976, dep. atty. gen. environ. sect. 1976-78; atty. Curry & Zaharako, Columbus, 1978—. Mem. allocation com. United Way, 1981-86. Mem. Ind. Bar Assn., Bartholomew County Bar Assn. (sec.-treas. 1979). Republican. Lodge: Kiwanis (dir. Columbus club 1981-83). General corporate, Contracts commercial, Consumer commercial. Home: Curry and Zaharako 2530 Sandcrest Blvd Columbus IN 47203

ZAHN, DONALD JACK, lawyer; b. Albany, N.Y., Oct. 24, 1941; s. Jerome and Clara (Zinsher) Z.; m. Laurie R. Hyman, Aug. 19, 1966; children—Lawrence, Melissa. A.B., NYU, 1963; LL.B., Union U., 1966; LL.M. in Taxation, NYU, 1967. Bar: N.Y. 1966, U.S. Dist. Ct. (no. dist.) N.Y. 1966, U.S. Tax Ct. 1969, U.S. Ct. Appeals (2d cir.) 1970, Tex. 1972, U.S. Ct. Appeals (5th and 11th cirs.). Assoc., Bond, Schoeneck and King, Syracuse, N.Y., 1967-71; ptnr. Haynes and Boone, Dallas, 1971-82, Akin, Gump, Strauss, Hauer & Feld, Dallas, 1982—; adj. prof. Sch. Law, So. Meth. U., Dallas, 1972—. Trustee, sec. mem. exec. and fin. com. Greenhill Sch., Addison, Tex., 1980—; trustee, chmn. budget com., mem. fin. com. Jewish Fedn. Greater Dallas, 1978—; trustee, chmn. Found. Jewish Fedn., Dallas, 1980—; trustee, v.p., pres. Dallas chpt. Am. Jewish Com., 1980—; appointed to Tex. World Trade Council, 1986—. Mem. State Bar Tex. (sec. 1982-83, chmn. tax sect. 1984-85, newsletter taxation sect. editor 1980-81), Internat. Comte (N. Tex. commn.). Jewish. Corporate taxation, Private international, Securities. Office: Akin Gump Strauss Hauer & Feld 4100 First City Center 1700 Pacific Ave Dallas TX 75201

ZAHND, LLOYD GLEN, lawyer; b. Savannah, Mo., Aug. 19, 1931; s. Lloyd Rolland and Mary Nadine (Gore) Z.; m. Melissa Linda Hardy, June 1, 1953; children: Brian, Melissa, Eric. AB, William Jewell Coll., Liberty, Mo., 1953; JD, Washington U., St. Louis, 1958. Bar: Mo. 1958, U.S. Dist. Ct. (we. dist.) Mo. 1958. Sole practice, Savannah, 1958—. Trustee Rolling Hills Regional Library, pres., 1963-70; trustee St. Joseph Hosp. (Mo.), 1973-84, chmn., 1979-82; trustee Heartland Health System, 1983—, chmn., 1987—. Served with U.S. Army, 1953-55. Recipient Meritorious Achievement citation Mo. Library Assn., 1968. Mem. ABA, Mo. Bar Assn. (bd. govs. 1981-85), William Jewell Coll. Nat. Alumni Assn. (pres. 1973-75). Republican. Baptist. Lodge: Masons. General practice, Probate, Real property. Office: Box 281 Savannah MO 64485

ZAHRT, WILLIAM DIETRICH, II, lawyer; b. Dayton, Ohio, July 12, 1944; s. Kenton William and Orpha Catharine (Wagner) Z.; m. Patricia Ann Marek, June 10, 1969; children—Justin William, Alitheia Patricia. B.S. in Physics, J.D., Yale U. Bar: N.Y. 1970, Ohio 1972, Tex. 1982, U.S. Ct. Appeals (Fed. cir.) 1977. Assoc. Kenyon & Kenyon, N.Y.C., 1969-71; assoc. Biebel, French & Nauman, Dayton, Ohio, 1971-80; sr. patent atty. Schlumberger Well Services, Houston, 1980-82; sole practice, Kingwood, Tex., 1982-85; patent atty., Shell Oil Co., Houston, 1985— . Mem. ABA, Am. Intellectual Property Law Assn., Tex. Bar Assn., Houston Intellectual Property Law Assn. Anglican. Clubs: Kingwood Country; Dayton Racquet, Masons (Dayton). Patent, Trademark and copyright. Address: 8 Kings Creek Kingwood TX 77339

ZAISER, KENT AMES, lawyer; b. St. Petersburg, Fla., June 10, 1945; s. Robert Alan and Marion (Brown) Z. A.B. Duke U., 1967; postgrad. U. Calif.-Berkeley, 1971; J.D., U. Fla., 1972. Bar: Fla. 1973, U.S. Dist. Ct. (no. dist.) Fla. 1974, U.S. Dist. Ct. (so. dist.) Fla. 1980. U.S. Dist. Ct. (mid. dist.) Fla. 1981, U.S. Ct. Appeals (11th cir.) 1981, U.S. Supreme Ct. 1978. Research aide Fla. Supreme Ct., Tallahassee, 1973-75, adminstrv. asst. to chief justice, 1975-76; asst. gen. counsel Fla. Dept. Natural Resources, Tallahassee, 1976-80; asst. atty. gen. Fla. Dept. Legal Affairs, Tallahassee, 1980-85; dep. gen. counsel Southwest Fla. Water Mgmt. Dist., Brooksville, 1985—; cons. Fla. State Cts. Adminstr., Tallahassee, 1975. Contbg. author: Environmental Regulation and Litigation in Florida, 1980-84. Campaign chmn. Vince Fechtel for State Rep., Leesburg, 1972. Mem. Fla. Bar Assn., Tallahassee Bar Assn., Fla. Govt. Bar Assn., Fla. Council Crime and Delinquency. Democrat. Episcopalian. Club: Governors. Federal civil litigation, State civil litigation, Environment. Home: 3286 Longleaf Rd Tallahassee FL 32304 Office: SW Fla Water Mgmt Dist 2379 Broad St Brooksville FL 33512

ZAKARIAN, ALBERT, lawyer; b. Pawtucket, R.I., May 3, 1940; m. Barbara Ann Zakarian, May 28, 1967; children: Adam, Dana. BA, Trinity Coll., 1962; LLB, Columbia U., 1965. Bar: Conn. 1965, U.S. Dist. Ct. Conn. 1965, U.S. Ct. Appeals (2d cir.) 1971. Assoc. Day, Berry & Howard, Hartford, Conn., 1968-75, ptnr., 1975—. Contbr. articles to profl. jours. Mem. town com. Simsbury (Conn.) Dems., 1974—; chmn. Simsbury Human Relations Commn., 1985. Served to capt. JAGC USAF, 1965-68, Vietnam. Decorated Bronze Star. Mem. Conn. Bar Assn. (chmn. civil justice sect. 1979-82, fed. judiciary com.), Hartford County Bar Assn. (pres. 1985-86), Nat. Bd. Trial Advocacy, Am. Bd. Trial Advs. (adv.). Democrat. Labor, Personal injury, Federal civil litigation. Office: Day Berry & Howard City Place Hartford CT 06103-3499

ZAKRZEWSKI, CHRISTOPHER THADDEUS, lawyer; b. Chgo., May 30, 1951; s. Thaddeus J. and Wanda (Merek) Z. BA, U. Ill., 1974; JD, DePaul U., 1978. Bar: Ill. 1978, Tex. 1982. Gen. corp. counsel Handle Techs., Houston, 1981-86; sec., dir. legal services Granada Corp., Houston, 1986—.

ZALASKY, JEFF M., lawyer; b. Mpls., Jan. 2, 1953; s. Saul and June (Dikel) Z. B in Elective Studies magna cum laude, U. Minn., 1975; JD, Hamline U., 1977. Bar: Minn. 1978, U.S. Dist. Ct. Minn. 1978, U.S. Ct. Appeals (8th cir.) 1981. Assoc. Harry N. Ray Ltd., Mpls., 1978-81; atty. Home Ins. Co., Mpls., 1981-84; assoc. Chadwick, Johnson & Condon, P.A., Mpls., 1984—. Mem. Minn. Bar Assn., Hennepin County Bar Assn., Minn. Def. Lawyers Assn. Avocations: racquetball, scuba diving, photography, travel. Personal injury, Employment law, Workers' compensation. Office: Chadwick Johnson & Condon PA 7235 Ohms Ln Minneapolis MN 55435

ZALECKI, PAUL HENRY, lawyer, automotive executive; b. Toledo, Oct. 14, 1931; s. Walter D. and Hattie S. (Oniszko) Z.; m. Mary Louise Sakowski, Sept. 29, 1956; 1 child, Karen Ann. A.B. magna cum laude, U. Notre Dame, 1953; LL.B. magna cum laude, Harvard U., 1956. Bar: Mich. 1957, Ohio 1960. Atty. Kaiser Jeep Corp., Toledo, 1961-66; atty. Gen. Motors Corp., Detroit, 1966—; v.p. Gen. Motors Corp., assoc. gen. counsel. Served with U.S. Army, 1956-58. Mem. ABA, Ohio and Mich. Bar Assns. Republican. Roman Catholic. Clubs: Bloomfield Hills Country, Renaissance (Detroit), Inverness (Toledo). Avocations: gardening; golf. General corporate, Corporate taxation. Home: 1371 Cedar Bend Dr Bloomfield Hills MI 48013

ZALEWSKI, JAMES CONRAD, lawyer; b. Omaha, Dec. 22, 1953; s. Conrad Marion and Eugenia Anne (Toczylowski) Z.; m. Carol Patricia Dendinger, Aug. 12, 1978; children: Kimberly, Zachary, Nicholas. BA, U. Nebr., Lincoln, 1976; JD, Creighton U., 1979. Bar: Neb. 1979, U.S. Dist. Ct. Neb. 1979, U.S. Ct. Appeals (8th cir.) 1979, U.S. Ct. Appeals (9th and 10th cirs.) 1980, U.S. Supreme Ct. 1982. Law clk to presiding justice Nebr. Supreme Ct., Lincoln, 1979-80; atty. Alaniz, Bruckner & Sykes, Lincoln, 1980-85, Erickson & Sederstrom, Lincoln, 1985—; sec., bd. dirs. Woods Tennis Corp., Lincoln, 1985—. Recipient Service award Midwest Labor Law Conf. Ohio Bar Assn., Columbus, 1983. Mem. ABA (com. on individual rights in the workplace, 1983—), Nebr. Bar Assn. Democrat. Roman Catholic. Club: Hillcrest Country. Avocations: tennis, reading, softball. Labor, Federal civil litigation, Pension, profit-sharing, and employee benefits. Office: Erickson & Sederstrom Suite 400 301 S 13th Lincoln NE 68508

ZALOOM, JOHN B(ASIL), lawyer; b. Paterson, N.J., Mar. 31, 1941; s. James B. and Mary A. (Habeeb) Z.; m. Karen L. Klingberg, Sept. 3, 1966; children: Sara A., Laura A., Kara A. BA, Rutgers U., 1963, LLB, 1963. Bar: N.J. 1966. Law clk. to presiding justice N.J. Superior Ct., Paterson, 1966-67; assoc. Jeffer, Walter & Tierney, Paterson, 1967-68; asst. counsel Becton, Dickinson & Co., Rutherford, N.J., 1968-70; counsel Rapidata, Inc., Fairfield, N.J., 1970-82; div. counsel Nat. Data Corp., Fairfield, 1982-84; v.p., sec. Optimal Solutions, Inc., Hoboken, N.J., 1984—. Assoc. editor Rutgers Law Rev., 1965-66. Avocations: tennis, racquetball, music, gardening. Computer, General corporate, Intellectual property. Home: 30 Birch Run Ave Denville NJ 07834 Office: Optimal Solutions Inc 80 River St Hoboken NJ 07030

ZALUTSKY, MORTON HERMAN, lawyer; b. Schenectady, Mar. 8, 1935; s. Albert and Gertrude (Daffner) Z.; m. Audrey Englebardt, June 16, 1957; children—Jane, Diane, Samuel. B.A., Yale U., 1957; J.D., U. Chgo., 1960. Bar: Oreg. 1961. Law clk. Oreg. Supreme Ct., 1960-61; assoc. Hart, Davidson, Veazie & Hanlon, 1961-63, Veatch & Lovett, 1963-64, Morrison, Bailey, Dunn, Cohen & Miller, 1964-69; prin. Morton H. Zalutsky, P.C., 1970-76; ptnr. Dahl, Zalutsky, Nichols & Hinson, 1977-79, Zalutsky & Klarquist, P.C., Portland, Oreg., 1980-85, Zalutsky, Klarquist & Johnson, P.C., Portland, 1985—; instr. Portland State U., 1961-64, Northwestern Sch. Law, 1969-70; assoc. prof. U. Miami Law Sch.; lectr. Practicing Law Inst., 1971—, Oreg. State Bar Continuing Legal Edn. Program, 1970, Am. Law Inst.-ABA Continuing Legal Edn. Program, 1973—, 34th, 37th NYU ann. insts. fed. taxation, So. Fed. Tax Inst., U. Miami Inst. Estate Planning, Southwestern Legal Found., Internat. Found. Employee Benefit Plans, numerous other profl. orgns. Author: (with others) The Professional Corporation in Oregon, 1970, 82; contbg. author: The Dentist and the Law, 3d edit.; contbr. to numerous publs. in field. Mem. ABA (vice chairperson profl. services 1987—, mem. council tax sect. 1985—, spl. coordinator 1980-85, vice chair profl. services 1987—), Multnomah County Bar Assn., Oreg. State Bar Assn., Oreg. Estate Planning Council. Jewish. Corporate taxation, Pension, profit-sharing, and employee benefits, Estate taxation. Home: 3118 SW Fairmount Blvd Portland OR 97201 Office: 215 SW Washington St 3d Floor Portland OR 97204

ZAMARIN, RONALD GEORGE, lawyer; b. N.Y.C., May 2, 1946; s. Leonard Leon and Laura Aileen (Gargus) z.; m. Kathleen Veronica Durkin, July 20, 1968; children—Ryan, Chad, Jennifer. B.A., UCLA, 1969, J.D., 1972. Bar: Ill. 1972, U.S. Dist. Ct. (no. dist.) Ill. 1972, U.S. Ct. Appeals (7th cir.) 1972. Assoc. Isham, Lincoln & Beale, Chgo., 1972-79, ptnr., 1980—; coop. atty. ACLU, Chgo., 1982—; litigating mem. Lawyers Com. for Civil Rights under Law, Chgo., 1974-78. Co-author: Media Law Handbook, 1982. Trustee, treas. Palatine Pub. Library Dist. (Ill.), 1980—; mem. Palatine Adv. Bd., 1978-79; mem. bd. commrs. Palatine Boys' Baseball, 1983—, sec. 1986—. Mem. ABA (forum com. on communications law). Republican. Libel, Federal civil litigation, State civil litigation. Home: 553 Juniper Dr Palatine IL 60067 Office: Isham Lincoln & Beale Three First Nat Plaza Chicago IL 60602

ZAMBO, RICHARD ALAN, lawyer, counsellor, energy and regulatory consultant; b. Chgo., July 1, 1945; s. Steven Paul and Anna Jane Zambo; m. Susan Kay Nemeth, Apr. 15, 1972; children—Nicholas Steven, Matthew Joseph. B.S. in Mech. Engring., Purdue U., 1969; J.D., Franklin Pierce Coll., 1980. Bar: Fla. 1980, U.S. Patent Office 1978. Design engr. United Tech., West Palm Beach, Fla., 1969-73; project mgr. Consulting Firm, West Palm Beach, 1973-77; prin. Richard A. Zambo, P.E., Concord, N.H. and West Palm Beach, 1977-80; sole practice, Tampa, Fla., 1980-82, Brandon, Fla., 1982—; energy cons.; lectr. in field. Coach, Youth Soccer League, Brandon, Fla., 1983-86; chief YMCA Indian Guides, Brandon, 1983—; dir. YMCA, Brandon, 1984—; chmn. Fla. Cogeneration Assn. Recipient Acad. Achievement award Purdue U., 1969. Mem. Fla. Bar Assn. (chmn. energy com.), Fed. Energy Bar Assn., Fla. Engring. Soc. (energy com.). Roman Catholic. Administrative and regulatory, FERC practice, Patent. Home: 2214 Wildwood Hollow Dr Valrico FL 33594 Office: 205 N Parsons Ave Brandon FL 33511 also: 1017 Thomasville Rd Tallahassee FL 32303

ZAMECK, HARVEY JASON, lawyer; b. Detroit, Oct. 19, 1943; s. Aaron and Mary (Silverstein) Z.; m. Diane Roslyn Smaller, Aug. 30, 1970; children—Allison Nicole, Stephanie Dawn. B.S.Ed., Wayne State U., 1964; J.D. (Clyde DeWitt scholar), U. Mich., 1968. Bar: Mich. 1968. Assoc. Keywell and Rosenfeld, Detroit, 1968-70; sole practice, Southfield, Mich., 1970—. Mem. ABA, Detroit Bar Assn., Am. Trial Lawyers Assn., Comml. Law League, Oakland Couty Bar Assn. Jewish. General corporate, Family and matrimonial, State civil litigation. Home: 30740 Woodstream Ct Farmington Hills MI 48018 Office: 24100 Southfield Rd Southfield MI 48075

ZAMORA, ANTONIO RAFAEL, lawyer; b. Havana, Cuba, Jan. 18, 1941; came to U.S., 1960; s. Juan Clemente and Rosario (Munne) Z.; m. Nelly Reggio, Nov. 28, 1963; children—Maria G., Antonio Rafael. License in Diplomatic and Consular Law, U. Havana, 1960; B.A., U. Fla.-Gainesville, 1965, J.D., 1973; M.A., U. Miami, Fla., 1969. Bar: Fla. 1973. Assoc. Shutts & Bowen, Miami, Fla., 1973-78, ptnr., head internat. dept., 1978-82; ptnr. McDermott, Will & Emery, Miami, 1982-83, mng. ptnr., 1983-84; sr. ptnr. Barnett, Alagia, Zamora & Suarez, Miami, 1984—; pres. Terra Nostrum, Inc., Miami, 1982—; v.p. Corporate Services Inc., Miami, 1984—; dir. Fla. Internat. Bank, Miami, 1983-84; dir. Internat. Law Conf. for Lawyers of the Americas, 1978, 80. Legal counsel Cuban Am. Nat. Found., Miami, Washington, 1982—; mem. council advisors Hispanic Coalition, Washington, 1984; pres. Hispanic Am. Voters Edn. Inc., Miami, 1984; sec. Brigada 2506, Miami, 1984. Served to lt. USNR, 1963-65. Mem. Interam. Bar Assn., ABA, Cuban Am. Bar Assn. (v.p. 1976-79, disting. service award 1980, dir. emeritus 1982), Fla. Bar. Republican. Roman Catholic. Clubs: Big Five, American (Miami, Fla.); Ocean Reef (Key Largo, Fla.); Miami Rowing. Private international, Real property, General corporate. Home: 7500 SW 82d Ct Miami FL 33143 Office: Barnett Alagia Zamora & Suarez 799 Brickell Plaza Suite 606 Miami FL 33131

ZAMORE, PETER HOKANSON, lawyer; b. Glen Ridge, N.J., Apr. 25, 1952; s. David Potter and Alice (Bisbee) Z.; m. Rosemary Siragusa, Oct. 12, 1975; children: Frederick Bisbee, Turner Joseph. BA, Marlboro Coll., 1974; JD, Vt. Law Sch., 1979. Bar: Vt. 1979, U.S. Dist. Ct. Vt. 1983. Spl. counsel Vt. Pub. Service Bd., Montpelier, 1979-81, Vt. Pub. Service Dept., Montpelier, 1981-84; assoc. Sheehey, Brue & Gray, Burlington, Vt., 1984-85, ptnr., 1986—. Mem. ABA, Vt. Bar Assn., Chittenden County Bar Assn. Administrative and regulatory, Public utilities. Office: Sheehey Brue & Gray PO Box 66 119 S Winooski Ave Burlington VT 05402

ZANDER, JANET HOLTER, lawyer; b. Williston, N.D., Feb. 19, 1955; d. James Norman and Myrtle Barbara (Howen) Holter; m. David Joseph Zander, June 17, 1978; children: Nathan David, Adam Joseph, Heidi Jayne. BS, U. N.D., 1977, JD, 1980. Bar: N.D. 1980. Assoc. Anseth & Zander, Williston, 1980—; asst. states atty. Williams County, Williston, 1980-82. Mem. N.D. Commn. on Child Support, Bismarck, 1985-86. Mem. ABA, N.D. State Bar Assn., Upper Mo. Bar Assn. Club: Ladies Petroleum (Williston). Avocations: cross-stitch, boating, golf. General practice, Consumer commercial, Probate. Home: 1718 28th St W Williston ND 58801 Office: Anseth & Zander 417 1st Ave E PO Box 2536 Williston ND 58801

ZANDROW, LEONARD FLORIAN, lawyer; b. Chgo., Aug. 14, 1955; s. Leonard Florian Sr. and Gladiann (Urbanski) Z. BJ, Northwestern U., 1976, MJ, 1977; JD, Boston Coll., 1981. Bar: Mass. 1982, U.S. Dist. Ct. Mass. 1982, U.S. Ct. Appeals (1st cir.) 1982. Law clk. to presiding justice Mass. Superior Ct., Boston, 1981-82, chief law clk., 1982-83; assoc. Parker, Coulter, Daley & White, Boston, 1983—. Assoc. editor Uniform Comml. Code Reporter Digest, 1981. Mem. ABA, Mass. Bar Assn., Boston Bar Assn., Phi Alpha Delta, Kappa Tau Alpha, Sigma Delta Chi. Roman Catholic. Avocations: sports. State civil litigation, Libel, Personal injury. Office: Parker Coulter Daley & White 1 Beacon St Boston MA 02108

ZANKEL, JEFFREY ALAN, lawyer; b. N.Y.C., Mar. 5, 1952; s. Herbert Morton and Lucille (Feuerstein) Z.; m. Lori Metnick, Dec. 26, 1976; children: Julie, Bradley. BA in Econs., SUNY, 1974; MS in Acctg., JD magna cum laude, Syracuse U., 1977; LLM in Taxation, NYU, 1981. Bar: N.Y. 1978, U.S. Tax Ct. 1979. Mem. tax staff Touche Ross and Co., N.Y.C., 1977-78; assoc. Parker, Chapin, Flattau & Klimpl, N.Y.C., 1978-83, Estroff, Waldman & Poretsky, N.Y.C., 1983-86, Herrick, Feinstein, N.Y.C., 1986—. Mem. ABA, N.Y. State Bar Assn., N.Y. County Lawyers Assn., Am. Inst. CPA's, Order of Coif, Omicron Delta Epsilon. Estate taxation, Probate, Personal income taxation. Office: Herrick Feinstein 2 Park Ave New York NY 10016

ZANOLLI, STEVE (WILLIAM), lawyer, industrial relations executive, educator; b. Fredericktown, Pa., Feb. 6, 1922; s. Fortunato and Anna (Dalla Santa) Z.; m. Lenora Paler, Nov. 8, 1947; children: William S., Jane Zanolli Lowell, Ann M. Zanolli Lettin, Mary Zanolli Natkin, Michael. AB cum laude, Washington and Jefferson Coll., 1943; MA, U. Pitts., 1948; JD, 1953. Bar: Pa. 1954, D.C. 1972, U.S. Supreme Ct. 1969. Supr. labor relations and personnel Island Creek Coal Co., Holden, W.Va., 1948-51; personnel dir. heavy products ops. U.S. Steel Corp., Pitts., 1953-67; exec. v.p. Bituminous Coal Operators Assn., Washington, 1968-72; ptnr. Webster and Kilcullen, Washington, 1973-74; v.p. indsl. relations Kaiser Steel Corp. and Kaiser Industries Corp., Oakland, Calif., 1974-80; ptnr. Smith Heenan Althen & Zanolli, Washington, 1980-84; adj. prof. econs. and bus. Washington and Jefferson Coll., 1984—. Served to capt. U.S. Army, 1943-46, ETO. Decorated Bronze Star with cluster, Purple Heart with 2 clusters. Mem. ABA (labor law sect.), Pa. Bar Assn., D.C. Bar Assn., Am. Arbitration Assn. Republican. Roman Catholic. Legal education. Home: PO Box 8 Washington PA 15301 Office: Washington and Jefferson Coll Bus and Econs Dept Washington PA 15301

ZANOT, CRAIG ALLEN, lawyer; b. Wyandotte, Mich., Nov. 15, 1955; s. Thomas and Faye Blanch (Sperry) Z. AB with distinction, U. Mich., 1977; JD cum laude, Ind. U., 1980. Bar: Ind. 1980, U.S. Dist. Ct. (so. dist.) Ind. 1980, U.S. Dist. Ct. (no. dist.) Ind. 1981, U.S. Ct. Appeals (6th cir.) 1985, U.S. Dist. Ct. (ea. dist.) Mich. 1987. Law clk. to presiding justice Allen County Superior Ct, Ft. Wayne, 1980-81; assoc. Davidson, Breen & Doud P.C., Saginaw, Mich., 1981—. Mem. ABA, Mich. Bar Assn., Ind. Bar Assn., Saginaw County Bar Assn. Roman Catholic. Workers' compensation, Insurance, Personal injury. Home: 2085 Marlou Ct Saginaw MI 48603 Office: Davidson Breen & Doud PC 1121 N Michigan Ave Saginaw MI 48602

ZAPHIRIOU, GEORGE ARISTOTLE, lawyer, educator; b. Athens, Greece, July 10, 1919; came to U.S., 1973, naturalized, 1977; s. Aristotle George and Calli Constantine (Economos) Z.; m. Peaches J. Griffin, June 1, 1973; children—Ari, Marie. J.D., U. Athens, 1940; LL.M., U. London, 1950. Bar: Supreme Ct. Greece 1946, Eng. 1956, Ill. 1975, Va. 1983. Gen. counsel Counties Ship Mgmt. and R & K Ltd., London, 1951-61; lectr. City of London Poly., barrister, 1961-73; joint editor Jour. Bus. Law, London, 1962-73; vis. prof. Ill. Inst. Tech.-Chgo. Kent Coll. Law, 1973-76; sole practice, Northbrook, Ill., 1976-78; prof. law George Mason U. Sch. Law, 1978—. Mem. Am. Assn. Study of Comparative Law (dir.), Am. Arbitration Assn. (mem. panel arbitrators), Am. Soc. Internat. Law, Internat. Law Assn., U.S. Maritime Law Assn., Internat. Third World Legal Studies Assn. Author: Transfer of Chattels in Private International Law, 1956, 1st rev. edit., 1981, European Business Law, 1970; bd. editors Am. Jour. Comparative Law; contbr. articles to law revs. and profl. jours. Admiralty, Private international, Public international. Home: 400 Green Pasture Dr Rockville MD 20852 Office: 3401 N Fairfax Dr Arlington VA 22201

ZAPPALA, STEPHEN A., state supreme court justice; b. 1932; s. Frank and Josephine Z. B.A., Duquesne U.; LL.B., Georgetown U., 1958. Bar: Pa. 1958. Solicitor Allegheny County, Pitts., 1974-76; judge Ct. of Common Pleas-Allegheny County, 1980-82; assoc. justice Pa. Supreme Ct., 1982—. Served with U.S. Army. Judicial administration. Office: Supreme Ct Supreme Ct Grant Bldg Pittsburgh PA 15219 *

ZAPRUDER, HENRY G., lawyer; b. N.Y.C., Mar. 28, 1938; s. Abraham and Lillian Zapruder; m. Marjorie Seiger, Oct. 13, 1963; children: Matthew, Michael, Alexandra. BBA, Okla. U.; LLB, Harvard U.; postdoctoral, Oxford U. Bar: Tex. 1962, D.C. 1967, U.S. Ct. Appeals (D.C. cir.). Atty. U.S. Dept. Justice, Washington, 1963-67; atty., advisor U.S. Treasury Dept., Washington, 1967-69; ptnr. Cohen & Uretz, Washington, 1969-85, Morgan, Lewis & Bockius, Washington, 1985—. Corporate taxation, Federal civil litigation. Home: 10 E Lenox St Chevy Chase MD 20815 Office: Morgan Lewis & Bockius 1800 M St NW Washington DC 20036

ZAREMBA, THOMAS S., lawyer; b. Warren, Ohio, Dec. 20, 1951; s. Joseph Stanley and Gertrude Alice (Restemeier) Z.; m. Patty Ann Lilly, June 10, 1978; children: Shannon, Sierra, Amanda, Thomas Jeremiah. BA, Hillsdale Coll., 1974; JD, Case Western Res. U., 1977. Bar: Ohio 1977, U.S. Dist. Ct. (no. dist.) Ohio 1977, U.S. Ct. Appeals (6th cir.) 1985. From assoc. to ptnr. Fuller & Henry, Toledo, 1977—. Supporter campaign to elect D. Lewandowski, Lucas County, Ohio, 1985. Mem. ABA, Ohio Bar Assn., Toledo Bar Assn. (grievance investigator 1985—, sec. bankruptcy com. 1985—). Roman Catholic. Bankruptcy, Federal civil litigation, State civil litigation. Office: Fuller & Henry 300 Madison Ave 1200 Edison Plaza Toledo OH 43603

ZARETSKY, BARRY LEWIS, law educator; b. Bklyn., May 4, 1950; s. Harold and Edythe Zaretsky; m. Joan S. Glatman, Nov. 16, 1980; 1 child, Arielle. BA, NYU, 1971; JD, U. Mich., 1974. Bar: Mich. 1974, N.Y. 1980, U.S. Dist. Ct. (so. and ea. dists.) N.Y. 1980. Asst. prof. Wayne State U., Detroit, 1974-78; prof. Bklyn. Law Sch., 1978—; cons. N.Y. State Law Revision Commn., Albany, 1984—. Author: Debtors and Creditors Rights, 1984; also articles. Mem. ABA, Phi Beta Kappa. Bankruptcy, Contracts commercial, Legal education. Office: Bklyn law Sch 250 Joralemon St Brooklyn NY 11201

ZARETSKY, ESTHER ANNE, lawyer; b. Bklyn., Sept. 6, 1951; d. Chareles Edward and Sophia (Davidowitz) Friedgood; m. Richard Paul Zaretsky, Sept. 6, 1970; children: Sophia Helen, Abraham Max. BS, Syracuse U., 1972; JD, Widener U., 1975. Bar: Fla. 1976, U.S. Dist. Ct. (so. dist.) Fla. 1981. Research asst. Fla. Ct. Appeals (4th dist.), West Palm Beach, 1976; sole practice West Palm Beach, 1977—; v.p. Med. Ednl. Corp., West Palm Beach, 1974—, East Coast Title Ins. Agy., West Palm Beach, 1985—; mem. Attys. Title Ins. Fund, Orlando, Fla., 1978—. Author: Osteopathic Medical School Bulletin, 1976. Legal counsel Palm Beach (Fla.) Planned Parenthood Guild, 1983—. Mem. Fla. Bar Assn., Palm Beach County Bar Assn. (chmn. jour. 1983—), Assn. Trial Lawyers Am., Fla. Trial Lawyers Assn. State civil litigation, General practice, Personal injury. Home: 2119 Embassy Dr West Palm Beach FL 33401 Office: 1655 Palm Beach Lakes Blvd Forum III Suite 900 West Palm Beach FL 33401

ZARNOWSKI, JAMES DAVID, lawyer, insurance specialist; b. Freehold, N.J., Feb. 22, 1950; s. Andrew G. and Joan M. (Voltz) Z. B.S., Monmouth Coll., 1972; J.D., Rutgers U., 1977. Bar: N.J. 1977. Prin. research analyst N.J. Dept. Ins., Trenton, 1977-78, project specialist, 1978-79, dir. regulatory affairs, 1987—; sr. actuarial asst. Chubb & Son, Inc., Short Hills, N.J., 1979-82; sr. research assoc. Am. Ins. Assn., N.Y.C., 1982-84; research mgr., counsel Ind. Ins. Agts. Am., N.Y.C., 1984-87. Active, Rutgers Legal Aid Clinic, 1976-77. N.J. State scholar, 1968-72; Monmouth Bar Found. scholar, 1974, 75, 76. Mem. N.J. Bar Assn., ABA. Insurance, Legislative, Workers' compensation. Home: 107 Bimbler Blvd Ocean NJ 07712 Office: 201 E State St Trenton NJ 08625

ZAUDERER, MARK CARL, lawyer; b. N.Y.C., Jan. 26, 1946. B.A., Union Coll., 1967; J.D., NYU, 1971. Bar: N.Y. 1972. Law clk. U.S. Dist. Ct., Newark, 1971-72; assoc. Kaye, Scholer, Fierman, Hays & Handler, N.Y.C., 1972-81; ptnr. Stein, Zauderer, Ellenhorn, Frischer & Sharp, N.Y.C., 1981—; faculty chmn. Practicing Law Inst. Program., Litigating Comml. Cases up to Trial, N.Y.C. and San Francisco, 1986, faculty mem. Deposition Skills Tng. Program, N.Y., 1986. Co-author: Deposition Strategy, Law and Forms, rev. edit. 1987. Mem. ABA, Assn. Bar City N.Y. (com. state cts. superior jurisdiction), Fed. Bar Council, Phi Epsilon Pi. Federal civil litigation, State civil litigation. Home: 185 E 85th St New York NY 10028 Office: 45 Rockefeller Plaza New York NY 10111

ZAVATSKY, MICHAEL JOSEPH, lawyer; b. Wheeling, W.Va., Dec. 15, 1948; s. Mike and Mary (Mirich) Z.; m. Kathleen Hanson, May 28, 1983; children: David, Emily. BA in Internat. Studies, Ohio State U., 1970; MA in Polit. Sci., U. Hawaii, 1972; JD, U. Cin., 1980. Bar: Ohio 1980, U.S. Dist. Ct. (so. dist.) Ohio 1981, U.S. Ct. Appeals (6th cir.) 1985. Assoc. Taft, Stettinius & Hollister, Cin., 1980—; lectr. in trial practice U. Cin., 1986—. Trustee Internat. Visitors Ctr., Cin., 1984—. Served to capt. USAF, 1973-77. William Graham fellow U. Cin., 1979, East West Ctr. fellow U. Hawaii, 1970. Mem. ABA, Cin. Bar Assn., Ohio Bar Assn., Am. Immigration Lawyers Assn., Potter Stewart Inn of Ct., Order of Coif. Federal civil litigation, State civil litigation, Immigration, naturalization, and customs. Home: 3820 Eileen Dr Cincinnati OH 45209

ZAX, LEONARD A., lawyer; b. Paterson, N.J., July 16, 1950; s. Harry and Shirley Jeanne (Hollander) Z.; m. Helen Kemp, May 25, 1980; 1 child, David Hollander. B.A., U. Chgo., 1971; M. City Planning, Harvard U., 1975, J.D., 1975. Bar: N.J. 1978, D.C. 1978. Spl. asst. to gen. counsel HUD, 1975-76, spl. asst. to sec. HUD, 1976-77; lectr., mem. faculty Harvard U., 1977-78; assoc. Fried, Frank, Harris, Shriver & Jacobson, Washington, 1977-82, ptnr. Fried, Frank, Harris, Shriver & Jacobson, 1982—; co-chmn. Mayor's Downtown Housing Commn., Washington, 1986—. Mem. Jerusalem Com., Mcpl. Art. Soc., D.C. Preservation League, Nat. Trust for Hist. Preservation; exec. bd. Am. Jewish Com., Washington; co-chmn. Mayor's Downtown Housing Commn., Washington, 1986—; mem. mcpl. Arts Soc., D.C. Prevention League, Nat. Trust for Hist. Preservation; trustee Greater Washington Research Ctr. Mem. ABA (chmn. housing and urban devel. law com.), D.C. Bar Assn., Fed. Bar Assn., Mcpl. Soc., Am. Planning Assn., Nat. Assn. Housing and Redevel. Ofcls., Nat. Housing Conf., Urban Land Inst. Real property. Home: 2555 Pennsylvania Ave NW Apt 809 Washington DC 20037 Office: 1001 Pennsylvania Ave NW Suite 800 Washington DC 20004-2505

ZAZAS, GEORGE JOHN, lawyer; b. Indpls., Feb. 17, 1926; s. John George and Rhoda John (Giovanni) Z.; m. Sylvia Levinson, May 16, 1963; 1 stepson, Eric S. Edelson; m. Hope Chandler, Feb. 21, 1947; children: James B., Robert C. AB, Harvard U., 1947, JD, 1949. Bar: Ind., 1949, U.S. Ct. Appeals (5th, 6th, 7th cirs.). Assoc. Barnes & Thornburg and predecessor firm, Indpls., 1949-56, ptnr., 1957—. Mem. Ind. Dem. Cent. Com., 1972-76; bd. dirs. Ensemble Music Soc. Indpls. Served to lt. USNR, 1943-58. Mem. ABA (co-chmn. com. on practice and procedure under Nat. Labor Relations Act, labor and employment law sect. 1974-77, council mem. 1985—), U.S. C. of C. (labor relations council). Clubs: Woodstock, Lawyers. Labor. Home: 6105 Shawnee Trail Indianapolis IN 46220 Office: 1313 Merchants Bank Bldg Indianapolis IN 46204

ZEARFOSS, HERBERT KEYSER, lawyer; b. Montandon, Pa., Oct. 13, 1929; s. Dean Wilson Susan Lesher (Keyser) Z.; m. Thelma Mary McCarthy, Dec. 19, 1953 (dec. 1984); children—Timothy McCarthy, Jonathan Andrew, Sarah Creighton; m. Carolyn Mary Howell, Nov. 4, 1985. A.B., Bucknell U., 1951; postgrad. Yale U., 1951-53; J.D., Am. U., 1958. Bar: Pa. 1959, U.S. Dist. Ct. (mid. dist.) Pa. 1959, U.S. Dist. Ct. (ea. dist.) Pa. 1975, U.S. Supreme Ct. 1975. Ptnr. Fetter & Zearfoss, Lewisburg, Pa., 1959-60; asst. counsel Fidelity Mut. Life Ins. Co., Phila., 1960-67, sr. v.p., gen. counsel, 1978-82; sec., mgr. Ins. Fedn. of Pa., Inc., 1967-68; ptnr. Zearfoss & Campbell, 1968-78; sr. v.p., sec., gen. counsel Provident Indemnity Life Ins. Co. and parent co. Provident Am. Corp., Norristown, Pa., 1982—. Rep. Pa. Gen. Assembly from 167th dist., 1968-78; justice of the Peace, Radnor Twp., Delaware County, Pa., 1966-67; v.p. Valley Forge council Boy Scouts Am., 1982-86 ; treas. Netherlands-Am. Amity Trust, Inc., 1981-86. Served to lt. comdr. USNR, 1954-58. Decorated officer Order of Orange-Nassau (Netherlands). Mem. ABA, Pa. Bar Assn., Phila. Bar Assn., Am. Council Life Ins., Assn. Life Ins. Counsel, Netherlands Soc. Phila. (pres. 1979-83), SAR (pres. Phila. Continental chpt. 1986—), Omicron Delta Kappa, Phi Alpha Delta, Phi Alpha Theta, Tau Kappa Alpha, Pi Sigma Alpha. Republican. Episcopalian. Clubs: Yale of Phila., Rittenhouse, Penn; Martin's Dam Swim and Tennis. Author: The Life Insurance Law of Pennsylvania, 1983; book rev. editor Am. U. Law Rev., 1956-58. Insurance, General corporate, Pension, profit-sharing, and employee benefits. Home: 210 Orchard Way Saint Davids PA 19807 Office: Provident Idemnity Life Ins Co 2500 DeKalb Pike Morristown PA 19401

ZECHER, ALBERT MICHAEL, lawyer; b. San Francisco, July 3, 1930; s. Albert Gustav and Mary Madaline (Hayes) Z.; children: Vanessa A., Albert M., Eryth Z. BS, U. San Francisco, 1953; JD, U. Calif., 1956. Bar: Calif. 1956, U.S. Dist. Ct. (no. dist.) Calif., U.S. Ct. Appeals 1956, U.S. Tax Ct. 1978. Dep. county counsel San Joaquin County (Calif.), 1957-60, Santa Clara County (Calif.), 1960-62; ptnr. Zecher & Pestarino, San Jose, Calif., 1962-75; sole practice, San Jose, 1975—; ptnr. Zecher, DeKlotz and Melino, 1987; lectr. Calif. Continuing Edn. Bar. Served with U.S. Army, 1948-49. Mem. ABA, Calif. Bar Assn., Santa Clara County Bar Assn. (chmn. bus. litigation sect.), Bus. Trial Lawyers Assn. Democrat. Club: Olympic (San Francisco). Federal civil litigation, State civil litigation, Real property. Office: 4 N Second St 13th Floor San Jose CA 95113

ZEDROSSER, JOSEPH JOHN, lawyer; b. Milw., Jan. 24, 1938; s. Joseph and Rose (Zollner) Z. AB, Marquette U., 1959; LLB, Harvard U., 1963. Bar: N.Y. 1964, U.S. Dist. Ct. (so. dist.) N.Y. 1966, U.S. Dist. Ct. (ea. dist.) N.Y. 1971, U.S. Ct. Appeals (2d cir.) 1971, U.S. Ct. Appeals (D.C. Cir.) 1975, U.S. Supreme Ct. 1975. Assoc. William G. Mulligan, N.Y.C., 1964-67, Christy, Bauman, Frey and Christy and successors, N.Y.C., 1967-71; dir. community devel. unit Bedford-Stuyvesant Community Legal Services Corp., N.Y.C., 1971-73; assoc. atty. fed. defender services unit Legal Aid Soc., N.Y.C., 1973-74; asst. atty. gen. Environ. Protection Bur., N.Y. State Dept. Law, N.Y.C., 1974-80; regional counsel EPA, N.Y.C., 1980-82; assoc. prof. law St. John's U. Sch. Law, N.Y.C., 1982-86; ptnr. Rivkin, Radler, Dunne & Bayh, Uniondale, N.Y., 1986—. Served to lt. USNR, 1965-74, with USAR, 1963-65. Mem. Assn. Bar City N.Y., N.Y. State Bar Assn. (editor Environ. Law Sect. Jour.), ABA, Alpha Sigma Nu. Roman Catholic. Lectr., contbr. to course handbooks for courses sponsored by Practicing Law Inst. and other assns. Federal civil litigation, State civil litigation, Environment. Home: 511 E 78th St New York NY 10021 Office: Rivkin Radler Dunne & Bayh EAB Plaza Uniondale NY 11556

ZEEHANDELAAR, DAVID NICO, lawyer; b. N.Y.C., Sept. 27, 1954; s. Frederik J. and Gertrude B. (Bette) Z.; m. Mona R. Gusoff, June 26, 1977; children: Rachel, Daniel. BA in Polit. Sci., U. Pa., 1976; JD, Villanova U., 1979. Bar: U.S. Ct. Appeals (3d cir.) 1979, N.J. 1982, U.S. Dist. Ct. N.J. 1982, Pa. 1980, U.S. Dist. Ct. (ea. and mid. dists.) Pa. 1982. Law clk. to presiding justice Ct. Common Pleas, Phila., 1979-81; assoc. Bolger, Picker & Weiner, Phila., 1981-86, ptnr., 1987—. Co-author: Manual for Practice in the Court of Common Pleas, 1983. Dir. fin. mayoral campaign Friends of Bill Green, Phila., 1979. Mem. ABA, Pa. Bar Assn., N.J. Bar Assn., Phila. Bar Assn., Camden County Bar Assn., Def. Research Inst., Phila. Assn. Def. Counsel, N.J. Assn. Def. Lawyers. Democrat. Jewish. Federal civil litigation, State civil litigation, Insurance. Home: 244 Harrogate Rd Penn Wynne PA 19151 Office: Bolger Picker & Weiner 1800 JFK Blvd Philadelphia PA 19103 Office: 120 Fairview Ave Voorhees Township NJ 08043

ZEESE, KEVIN BRUCE, lawyer; b. N.Y.C., Oct. 28, 1955; s. Charles Alfred and Barbara Karen (Brudenell-Bruce) Z.; m. Dina Ruth Smith, Sept. 5, 1976; 1 child, Alexander Bruce. BS, U. Buffalo, 1976; JD, George Washington U., 1979. Bar: D.C. 1980, U.S. Dist. Ct. D.C. 1980, U.S. Ct. Appeals (D.C. cir.) 1980. Chief counsel Nat. Orgn. for Reform Marijuana Laws, Washington, 1980-86, nat. dir., 1983-86; assoc. Zwerling, Mark, Ginsberg & Lieberman, Alexandria, Va., 1986—; adj. prof. Am. U., Washington, 1985—; legal advisor, mem. nat. legal com. Nat. Orgn. Reform Marijuana Laws, 1986—. Editor drug law report Clark Boardman Co., Washington, 1982—. Mem. ABA, D.C. Bar Assn., Nat. Assn. Criminal Def. Lawyers. Administrative and regulatory, Civil rights, Criminal. Home: 890 N Lexington Arlington VA 22205 Office: Zwerling Mark Ginsberg & Lieberman 1001 Duke St Alexandria VA 22313

ZEGAS, ALAN LEE, lawyer; b. Newark, Oct. 28, 1952; s. Norman and Harriet (Lava) Z.; m. Tina Hannah Burk, Aug. 22, 1976; 1 child, Rachel Sarah. BS, U. Pa., 1974; MBA, Harvard U., 1978; JD, Rutgers U., 1981. Bar: N.J. 1981, U.S. Dist. Ct. N.J. 1981, N.Y. 1982, U.S. Ct. Appeals (3d cir.) 1982. Law clk. to presiding justice U.S. Dist. Ct. N.J., Newark, 1981-83; assoc. Robinson, Wayne, Levin, Riccio & La Sala, Newark, 1983-84; sole practice West Orange, N.J., 1984—; adj. prof. law Rutgers U., Newark, 1983—; reader N.J. Bd. Bar Examiners, Trenton, 1985. Editor-in-chief Rutgers U. Law Rev., 1980-81; editor (pamphlet) Law Tips for the Elderly, 1983. Mem. N.J. Bar Assn. (dist. rep. young lawyers div. 1983-85, vice chmn. 1985-86, trustee 1986—), Essex County Bar Assn. (chmn. lawyers referral service 1986—), Rutgers U. Law Sch. Alumni Assn. (rep. 1983—), U. Pa. Alumni Assn. (sec. 1986—), Harvard U. Bus. Sch. Alumni Assn. Federal civil litigation, Criminal, Contracts commercial. Home: 121 Chaucer Dr Berkeley Heights NJ 07922 Office: 20 Northfield Ave West Orange NJ 07052

ZEGLEN, JOHN MICHAEL, lawyer; b. Connellsville, Pa., Mar. 4, 1956; s. John F. and Margaret (Carlock) Z.; m. Diane L. Constable, Nov. 17, 1984. BA, Pa. State U., 1978; JD, U. Pitts., 1981. Bar: Pa. 1981, U.S. Dist. Ct. (we. dist.) Pa. 1982. Law clk. to presiding judge Ct. of Common Pleas Fayette County, Uniontown, Pa., 1981-82; assoc. Cook & Leskinen, Uniontown, 1982-84; asst. dist. atty. Fayette County, Uniontown, 1983—; sole practice Uniontown, 1984—; law instr. Pa. State U., Uniontown, 1986—. Mem. ABA, Pa. Bar Assn., Fayette County Bar Assn., Phi Alpha Delta. Democrat. Roman Catholic. Club: Colonial 3 Athletic (Grindstone, Pa.). Personal injury, Real property, Probate. Office: 107 E Main St Uniontown PA 15401

ZEICHNER, MARK, lawyer; b. N.Y.C., June 6, 1949; s. Lester and Rosalind (Schulman) Z.; m. Judy Ann Koenig; 1 child, Eric Benjamin. AB, Hamilton Coll., 1971; JD, Syracuse U., 1974. Bar: N.Y. 1975, U.S. Dist. Ct. (so. and ea. dists.) N.Y. 1976, U.S. Ct. Appeals (2d cir.) 1976, U.S. Ct. Appeals (5th cir.) 1978. Assoc. Shearman & Sterling, N.Y.C., 1974-78, Harvis, Pomerantz & Rosenbluth, N.Y.C., 1978-79; ptnr. Harvis & Zeichner, N.Y.C., 1979—. Banking, Contracts commercial, General practice. Office: Harvis & Zeichner 757 3d Ave New York NY 10017

ZEIDMAN, PHILIP FISHER, lawyer; b. Birmingham, Ala., May 2, 1934; s. Eugene Morris and Ida (Fisher) Z.; m. Nancy Levy, Aug. 19, 1956; children: Elizabeth Miriam, John Fisher (dec.), Jennifer Kahn. B.A. cum laude, Yale U., 1955; LL.B., Harvard U., 1958; postgrad., Grad. Sch. Bus. Adminstrn., 1957-58. Bar: Ala. 1958, Fla. 1960, U.S. Supreme Ct. 1961, D.C. 1968, N.Y. 1981. Trial atty. FTC, 1960-61; staff asst. White House Com. Small Bus., 1961-63; spl. asst. to adminstr. Small Bus. Adminstrn., 1961-63, asst. gen. counsel, 1963-65, gen. counsel, 1965-68; spl. asst. to Vice Pres. of U.S., 1968; govt. relations mgr. Nat. Alliance Businessmen, 1968; now partner firm Brownstein Zeidman and Schomer; chmn. grants and benefits com. Adminstrv. Conf. U.S., 1968; chmn. food industry adv. com. Dept. Energy, 1979-81; chmn. distbn. and food merchandising subcom. Alliance to Save Energy, 1978; vice chmn. Pres.'s Commn. on Exec. Exchange, 1978-81; mem. adv. bd. antitrust and trade regulation report Bur. Nat. Affairs, 1978-85; gen. counsel Internat. Franchise Assn.; Wash. counsel Am. Bus. Conf. Editor/author: Survey of Laws and Regulations Affecting International Franchising, 1982, Regulation of Buying and Selling a Franchise, 1983, Legal Aspects of Selling and Buying, 1983; assoc. editor Jour. of International Franchising Law and Distribution; contbg. ediotr Legal Times of Washington. Mem. young leadership council Democratic Nat. Com.; exec. dir. Dem. platform com., 1972; adviser Nat. Presdl. Campaign of Jimmy Carter, 1976; mem. pres.'s adv. com. John F. Kennedy Center for Performing Arts, 1981; chmn. class council Yale Class of 1955.; mem. adv. bd. Yale U. Sch. Mgmt.; trustee Yale-China Assn. Served with USAF, 1958-60. Recipient Younger Fed. Lawyer award Fed. Bar Assn., 1965; Jonathan Davenport Oratorical award, 1954; William Houston McKim award, 1955. Mem. ABA (chmn. com. on franchising 1977-81), D.C. Bar Assn., Ala. Bar Assn., Fla. Bar Assn., Fed. Bar Assn., Bar Assn. D.C., Internat. Bar Assn. (chmn. internat. franchising com. 1986—), N.Y. State Bar Assn., Am. Intellectual Property Law Assn. Antitrust, Franchising. Office: 1401 New York Ave NW Suite 900 Washington DC 20005

ZEIDWIG, HOWARD MICHAEL, lawyer; b. Elizabeth, N.J., Nov. 6, 1943; m. Carol Zeidwerg; children: Gary, Melissa. BS, U. Fla., 1967; JD, Stetson U., 1970. Bar: Fla. 1970, U.S. Dist. Ct. (so. dist.) Fla. 1971, U.S. Supreme Ct. 1977, U.S. Dist. Ct. (so. dist.) Ala. 1979, U.S. Ct. Appeals (5th cir.) 1979. Asst. county solicitor Ft. Lauderdale, Fla., 1970-71; legal advisor police City of Davie, Fla., 1972-75; pub. defender City of Lauderhill, Fla., 1974-76; sole practice Ft. Lauderdale, 1976—; chmn. unauthorized practice of law com., jud. nominating com., 1986—, mem. grievance com., Fla. 17th Jud. Cir. Mem. Fla. Bar Assn., Broward County Bar Assn., Acad. Fla. Trial Lawyers, Nat. Assn. Criminal Def. Lawyers, Fla. Criminal Def. Atty.'s Assn. Criminal. Home and Office: Trial Lawyers Bldg 4-F 633 SE 3d Ave Fort Lauderdale FL 33301

ZEISEL, LAURA, lawyer, educator law; b. Bklyn., June 9, 1948; d. Melvin and Shirley Martha (Weinstein) Z.; m. David Seymour Strong, Nov. 20, 1970; children—Sara Zeisel, Elizabeth Pearl. Student Smith Coll., 1966-68; B.A., Washington Sq. Coll., NYU, 1970, postgrad., 1970-72; J.D., SUNY-Buffalo, 1975. Bar: N.Y. 1976, U.S. Dist. Ct. (so. dist.) N.Y. 1976, U.S. Ct. Appeals (2d cir.) 1977, U.S. Dist. Ct. (no. dist.) N.Y. 1979. Atty. Mid-Hudson Legal Services, Poughkeepsie, N.Y., 1975-80; ptnr. Lazar & Zeisel, Poughkeepsie, 1980-82; regional atty. N.Y. State Dept. Environ. Conservation, New Paltz, 1982-85; resident counsel Mid-Hudson br. office Sive, Pagest & Riesel, P.C., 1985— ; adj. prof. Marist Coll., Poughkeepsie, 1976—; mem. Gov.'s Commn. Domestic Violence, Albany, N.Y., 1983—. Recipient Bennett award Faculty Law and Jurisprudence SUNY, Buffalo, 1975. Mem. N.Y. State Bar Assn., Ulster County Bar Assn., Mid-Hudson Women's Bar Assn. (pres. 1983-84). Democrat. Jewish. Environment. Office: 169 Main St New Paltz NY 12561

ZEITER, WILLIAM EMMET, lawyer; b. Harrisburg, Pa., Dec. 1, 1934; s. Jacob David and Maude Elizabeth (Hamm) Z.; m. Jean Palmer Greer, May 22, 1965. B.A., Lehigh U., 1955, B.S.E.E., 1956; J.D. (Root-Tilden scholar 1956-59), N.Y. U., 1959. Bar: Pa. 1960, D.C. bar 1962, U.S. Supreme Ct. bar 1963. Acting mgr. Moving the EE-Z Way, Harrisburg, 1956-63; mem. patent staff Bell Telephone Labs., Inc., 1956, 57, 58; asso. firm Morgan, Lewis & Bockius, Phila., 1959-66; mem. firm Morgan, Lewis & Bockius, 1967—, sr. partner, 1975—, mem. exec. com., 1980-82; legal cons. to Ct. Adminstr. Pa., 1972-79; exec. dir. Adv. Com. on Appellate Ct. Rules, 1973-81; mem. Pa. Joint Com. on Documents, 1968—; bd. dirs. Am. Nat. Metric Council, Washington, 1973-78, vice chmn., 1975-78; reporter Uniform Metric System Procedure Act; mem. legal adv. panel metric study U.S. Metric Bd., 1979-80; mem. exec. com. Nat. Metric Adv. Panel, U.S. Dept. Commerce, 1969-71; cons. Office Invention and Innovation, Nat. Bur. Standards, 1967-72; mem. ad hoc energy panel Office Tech. Assessment, U.S. Congress, 1975-76. Contbr. various articles on legal codification, corp. law, adminstrv. law and metric conversion. Pres. Friends of Logan Sq. Found., 1985—, bd. dirs., 1984—; trustee Franklin Inst., 1981—. Recipient Gov.'s citation for drafting Appellate Ct. Jurisdiction Act, 1970, awards for drafting Pa. Jud. Code Allegheny County Bar Assn., 1978. Fellow Am. Bar Found.; mem. Am. Bar Assn. (chmn. sect. sci. and tech. 1977-78, chmn. conf. sect. chairmen 1978-79, mem. ho. of dels. 1980—, mem. nominating com. 1986—), Pa. Bar Assn., Phila. Bar Assn. (Fidelity award 1979), IEEE, Am. Law Inst. Federal civil litigation, General corporate, Legislative. Home: 8917 Crefeld St Philadelphia PA 19118 Office: Morgan Lewis & Bockius 2000 One Logan Sq Philadelphia PA 19103

ZEITLAN, MARILYN L., lawyer; b. N.Y.C., Sept. 17, 1938; d. Charles and Florence (Geller) Labb; m. Barrett Mandel Zeitlan, Apr. 14, 1957; children: Adam Scott, Daniel Craig. BA, Queens Coll., 1958, MS, 1970; JD, Hofstra U., 1978. Bar: N.Y. 1979, U.S. Dist. Ct. (ea. and so. dists.) N.Y. 1979. Tchr. N.Y.C., 1958-61, sole practice, 1979—. Assoc. editor Hofstra U. Law Rev., 1976-78. Mem. East Hills (N.Y.) Environ. Commn., 1971-75, chairperson, 1974-75; co-founder Roslyn (N.Y.) Environ. Assn., 1970; v.p. Roslyn League Women Voters, 1974-75. Hofstra U. Law fellow, 1976. Mem. ABA, N.Y. State Bar Assn. (family law sect.), Nassau County Bar Assn. (family law sect.), Nassau-Suffolk Women's Bar Assn., Phi Beta Kappa. Avocation: horseback riding. Family and matrimonial. Office: 1025 Northern Blvd Roslyn NY 11576

ZELENKA, DONALD JOHN, lawyer; b. Akron, Ohio, Feb. 16, 1952; s. Donald Banser and Jane (Cunningham) Z.; m. Leslie Rock, May 24, 1975. BA in Arts and Scis., Ohio State U., 1974; JD, U. S.C., 1977. Bar: S.C. 1977, U.S. Ct. Appeals (4th cir.) 1978, Va. 1980, U.S. Dist. Ct. S.C. 1981, U.S. Supreme Ct. 1983, U.S. Ct. Appeals (11th cir.) 1985. Law clk., research asst. U.S. Ct. Appeals (4th cir.), Richmond, Va., 1977-79; from asst. to chief dep. atty. gen. S.C. Atty. Gen., Columbia, 1979—; tchr., instr. clin. programs U. S.C. Law Sch., Columbia, 1983-84. Mem. Sentencing Guidelines Commn., Columbia, 1983—. Mem. ABA, Richland County Bar Assn., Assn. Govt. Attys. in Capital Litigation (exec. bd. dirs. 1985-86). Democrat. Methodist. Criminal, Federal civil litigation. Home: 118 Chadford Circle Irmo SC 29063 Office: SC Atty Gen PO Box 11549 Columbia SC 29211

ZELLER, PAUL WILLIAM, lawyer; b. Eunice, La., Sept. 17, 1948; s. Andrew Albert and Margaret Lucille (Fontenot) Z.; m. Marlene Linda Parrillo, Dec. 17, 1966; children—Paul William, Jr., Jonathan Randolph, Amanda Louise, Joshua Andrew. B.A., La. State U., 1969; J.D., U. Va., 1972. Bar: N.Y. 1973, U.S. Dist. Ct. (so. dist.) N.Y. 1974, U.S. Ct. Appeals (2nd cir.) 1974. Assoc., Debevoise and Plimpton, N.Y.C., 1972-81; asst. corp. counsel Reliance Group, Inc., N.Y.C., 1981-83; asst. v.p. Reliance Group Holdings, Inc., N.Y.C., 1982, v.p., asst. gen. counsel, 1983, v.p., dep. gen. counsel, 1984—; bd. dirs. Empire Gas Corp. Bd. of editors, U. Va. Law Review, 1970-72. Mem. Assn. Bar City of N.Y., Phi Delta Phi. Democrat. Roman Catholic. General corporate, Contracts commercial, Securities. Home: 30 Lincoln Ave Clifton NJ 07011 Office: Reliance Group Holdings Inc 55 East 52d St New York NY 10055

ZELLNER, ROBERT JOHN, corporate lawyer, business administrator; b. Green Bay, Wis., Jan. 16, 1922; s. Charles and Eva (Klaus) Z.; m. Mary M. Kitslaar, Feb. 12, 1944; children: Margaret, John, Mary Ann, Paul, Ann. BA, St. Norbert Coll., 1943; JD, IIT, 1967. Bar: U.S. Patent Office 1959, Ill. 1967, U.S. Dist. Ct. (no. dist.) Ill. 1967, Ohio 1983, U.S. Ct. Appeals (fed. cir.) 1983. Sr. v.p., counsel McGean-Rohco, Inc., Cleve., 1979—. Holds several U.S. patents. Served to lt. (j.g.) USN, 1944-46. Mem. Am. Intellectual Property Law Assn., Ill. State Bar Assn., Ohio Bar Assn., Chgo. Bar Assn., Cleve. Bar Assn., Patent Law Assn. Chgo., Cleve. World Trade Assn., Licensing Exec. Soc. Roman Catholic. General corporate, Patent, Trademark and copyright. Office: McGean-Rohco Inc 1250 Terminal Tower Cleveland OH 44113

ZELMAN, ANDREW ERNEST, lawyer; b. N.Y.C., Dec. 3, 1941; s. Benjamin M. and Beatrice (Feldman) Z.; m. Marjorie Ann Sussman, June 21, 1964; children—Lorraine Amy, Elissa Karen. B.A., Colgate U., 1963; LL.B., Columbia U., 1966. Bar: D.C. 1967, U.S. Ct. Appeals (D.C. cir.) 1967, U.S. Dist. Ct. (so. and ea. dists.) N.Y. 1970, U.S. Ct. Appeals (2d cir.) 1970, U.S. Supreme Ct. 1976. Assoc., Collier, Shannon, Rill, Edwards & Scott, Washington, 1966-67; asst. to chmn. NLRB, 1967-69; assoc. Polletti, Freidin, Prashker, Feldman & Gartner, N.Y.C., 1969-71, Surrey & Morse, N.Y.C., 1971-73; ptnr. Surrey & Morse, N.Y.C., 1974-79, Seham, Klein & Zelman, N.Y.C., 1979—; lectr. Cornell Sch. Indsl. and Labor Relations. Labor relations columnist N.Y.C. Bus. Mag. Mem. ABA (labor law sect. com. NLRB practice and procedure), N.Y. Bar Assn. (sec. com. labor and employment law 1982-85), Phi Beta Kappa. Labor. Office: Seham Klein & Zelman 15th Floor 485 Madison Ave New York NY 10022

ZELMANOVITZ, MENACHEM OSHER, lawyer; b. Bklyn., Mar. 29, 1951; s. Morris and Fay (Rosenberg) Z.; m. Simy S. Slamovits, Nov. 24, 1974; children: Jacob, Raizy, Judah Alan, Rebecca. BS in Chemistry magna cum laude, Bklyn. Coll., 1973; JD magna cum laude, Bklyn. Law Sch., 1977. Bar: N.Y. 1978, U.S. Dist. Ct. (so. and ea. dists.) N.Y. 1978, U.S. Ct. Appeals (2d cir.) 1979; ordained rabbi, 1973. Asst. corp. counsel N.Y.C., 1977-79; assoc. Zalkin, Radin & Goodman, N.Y.C., 1979-84, ptnr., 1985—. Mem. ABA, Assn. of Bar of City of N.Y. Democrat. Bankruptcy, Federal civil litigation, Consumer commercial. Office: Zalkin Rodin & Goodman 750 Third Ave New York NY 10017

ZELTONOGA, WILLIAM LEO, lawyer, consultant; b. Chgo., May 13, 1941; s. Leo John and Jean (Kereluk) Z. BA, UCLA, 1962; MA, Oxford U., 1965; JD, Harvard U., 1968. Bar: Calif. 1969, U.S. Dist. Ct. (cen. dist.) Calif. 1969, U.S. Ct. Appeals (9th cir.) 1984, U.S. Supreme Ct. 1984, D.C. 1985, U.S. Ct. Appeals (D.C. cir.) 1987. Assoc. Wyman, Bautzer, Rothman & Kuchel, Los Angeles, 1968-72; sole practice Los Angeles, 1972—. Served as 1st lt. Armored Corps, U.S. Army, 1969-70, Vietnam. Decorated Bronze Star; Rhodes scholar, 1962. Mem. ABA, Calif. Bar Assn., Los Angeles Bar Assn., Assn. Trial Lawyers Am., Calif. Trial Lawyers Assn., Am. Juridical Soc., Nat. Trust for Hist. Preservation, ACLU, Nat. Rifle Assn. Club: Les Amis du Vin. Lodge: Masons. Federal civil litigation, State civil litigation, Personal injury.

ZEMAITIS, THOMAS EDWARD, lawyer; b. York, Pa., Oct. 16, 1951; s. Leonard Brobst and Ruth Eleanor (Day) Z.; m. Jacqueline Ann Staley, Aug. 18, 1973; 1 child, Daniel Staley. BA magna cum laude, U. Pa., 1973, JD magna cum laude, 1976. Bar: Pa. 1976, U.S. Dist. Ct. (ea dist.) Pa. 1976, U.S. Ct. Appeals (3d cir.) 1977, U.S. Supreme Ct. 1980, U.S. Ct. Appeals (5th and 11th cirs.) 1981, U.S. Dist. Ct. (ea. dist.) Mich. 1986. Assoc. Pepper, Hamilton & Scheetz, Phila., 1976-84, ptnr., 1984—. Bd. dirs. Support Ctr. for Child Advs., Phila., 1978—, v.p., 1980-83, pres., 1983-85; trustee Women's Law Project, Phila., 1980—, treas., 1984—. Mem. ABA, Pa. Bar Assn., Phila. Bar Assn., Order of Coif, Phi Beta Kappa. Democrat. Avocations: theater, reading. Antitrust, Federal civil litigation, Administrative and regulatory. Home: 8326 Bryn Mawr Ave Pennsanken NJ 08109 Office: Pepper Hamilton & Scheetz 123 S Broad St Philadelphia PA 19109

ZENK, ANN MARIE, lawyer, educator; b. LeMars, Iowa, May 26, 1955; d. Cyril Michael and Corrine Stella (Staver) Z.; m. Jerry Evan Bliss, June 7, 1980. BA, Coll. St. Teresa, Winona, Minn., 1977; MRE, Seattle U., 1981; JD, Creighton U., 1982. Bar: Iowa 1982, Nebr. 1982, U.S. Dist. Ct. (no. and so. dists.) Iowa 1983, U.S. Ct. Appeals (8th cir.) 1984. Atty. Legal Services Corp. Iowa, Council Bluffs, 1982-87, The Maytag Corp., Newton, Iowa, 1987—; adj. prof. Council Bluffs br. Buena Vista Coll., 1982-87. Mem. editorial staff Creighton U. Law Rev., 1982. Mem. parish council Queen of Apostles, Council Bluffs, 1982-85. Mem. ABA, AAUW, Iowa Bar Assn., Pottawattamie County Bar Assn. (chairperson law day 1986), Nebr. Bar Assn. Democrat. Roman Catholic. Avocations: softball, tennis, golf, soccer, reading. General corporate, Environment, Real property. Home: 1549 S 12th Ave W Newton IA 50208 Office: The Maytag Corp One Dependability Sq Newton IA 50208

ZENOFF, ELYCE HOPE, legal educator; b. Milw., Feb. 2, 1930; d. Ben and Gertrude (Rothstein) Z.; m. Charles B. Ferster, May 17, 1964; children—William, Andrea, Sam, Warren. B.S., U. Wis., 1951; J.D., Northwestern U., 1954. Bar: Ill. 1954, D.C. 1968, U.S. Supreme Ct. 1961. Research atty. Bar Found. Chgo., 1956-59; atty. AMA, Chgo., 1959-61; counsel U.S. Senate Subcom. on Constl. Rights, Washington, 1961-62; atty. U.S. Commn. on Civil Rights, Washington, 1962-64; faculty George Washington U., Washington, 1964—, prof. law, 1969—. Mem. ABA, D.C. Bar Assn. Democrat. Author: Mental Impairment and Legal Incompetaency, 1968, Readings in Law and Psychiatry, 2d edit., 1975, Sanctions, Sentencing and Corrections, 1982. Contbr. numerous articles to profl. jours. Legal education, Criminal, Mental health. Office: George Washington Law Sch 2000 H St NW Washington DC 20052

ZERGER, KIRSTEN LOUISE, lawyer; b. Newton, Kans., Oct. 15, 1950; d. Homer Joshua and Karolyn Louise (Kaufman) Z.; m. Edward Peters Dick, Mar. 28, 1969 (div. 1978); 1 child, Daagya Shanti; m. Sanford Norman Nathan, June 14, 1980; children: Jesse Zerger, Jonathan Kaufman. BA with highest distinction, Bethel Coll., 1973; JD, U. Calif.-Berkeley, 1977. Bar: Calif. 1977, U.S. Dist. Ct. (no. dist.) Calif. 1977, U.S. Supreme Ct. 1985. Staff atty. United Farm Workers, AFL-CIO, Salinas, Calif., 1977-79; staff atty. Calif. Tchrs. Assn., Burlingame, 1979-85, dep. chief counsel, 1985, chief counsel, 1985—; speaker ednl., profl. confs. Writer on public sector labor law issues. Mem. ABA (labor and litigation sect.), Calif. Bar Assn. (chmn. labor and employment law sect. 1983-85, membership com. 1982-83, exec. com., 1985—, treas. 1986—), Nat. Assn. Tchr. Attys. Mennonite. Labor, State civil litigation, Administrative and regulatory. Office: Calif Tchrs Assn 1705 Murchison Dr Burlingame CA 94010

ZERIN, STEVEN DAVID, lawyer; b. N.Y.C., Oct. 1, 1953; s. Stanley Robert and Cecilie Paula (Goldberg) Z.; m. Susan Marilyn Wershba, Oct. 13, 1984; 1 child, Alexander James. BS, Syracuse U., 1974; JD, St. Johns U., 1977. Bar: N.Y. 1978, U.S. Dist. Ct. (so. dist.) N.Y. 1986. Assoc. Longhi & Loscalzo, N.Y.C., 1978-81, Gladstein & Isaac, N.Y.C., 1981-82, Sperry, Weinberg, Wels, Waldman & Rubenstein, N.Y.C., 1982-85; ptnr. Wels & Zerin, N.Y.C., 1985—. Mem. bd. govs. Daytop Village. Mem. ABA (exec. mem. and lectr. family law sect.), N.Y. State Bar Assn. (exec. com. family law sect.), Assn. Bar of City of N.Y. Democrat. Jewish. Avocations: tennis, traveling. Family and matrimonial, Probate, State civil litigation. Home: 96 Fifth Ave New York NY 10011 Office: Wels & Zerin 55 E 59 St New York NY 10022

ZERKIN, GERALD THOMAS, lawyer; b. Queens, N.Y., Mar. 1, 1949; s. Max and Rhoda (Sigel) Z.; m. Catherine Ann Aldrich, Sept. 23, 1978; children: Errol, Jeremy, Sasha. BA, Brandeis U., 1971; MA, U. Va., 1975; JD, Boston Coll., 1976. Bar: Va. 1976, U.S. Dist. Ct. (ea. dist.) Va. 1976, U.S. Dist. Ct. (we. dist.) Va. 1978, U.S. Ct. Appeals (4th cir.) 1978, U.S. Tax Ct. 1984, U.S. Supreme Ct. 1985. Staff atty. Neighborhood Legal Aid, Richmond, Va., 1976-78; ptnr. Bricker & Zerkin, Richmond, 1978-80; sole practice Richmond, 1980-82; ptnr. Zerkin, Wright & Heard, Richmond, 1982-84, Zerkin, Heard & Kozak, Richmond, 1984—. Bd. dirs. Va. Coalition on Jails and Prisons, Richmond, 1984—, Virginians Against Death Penalty, Richmond, 1986—. Mem. Va. Trial Lawyers Assn., ACLU (legal panel, bd. dirs. 1986—). Avocation: sports. Civil rights, Federal civil litigation, Criminal. Home: 4226 Seminary Ave Richmond VA 23227 Office: Zerkin Heard & Kozak 4 N First St Richmond VA 23219

ZERNER, RICHARD EGON, lawyer; b. Toledo, Aug. 27, 1947; s. Carl Egon and Erma K. (Klein) Z.; m. Nancy L. Goodman, Apr. 6, 1972; children—Loryn Brooke, Robert Egon. B.A., Hillsdale Coll., 1969; J.D., U. Toledo, 1972. Bar: Ohio 1973. Sole practice law, Toledo, 1973—; assoc. Associated Legal Group, Toledo, 1982—; bd. dirs. Westgate br. Mid-Am. Nat. Bank & Trust Co.; legal counsel Northwestern Ohio Gasoline Dealers Assn. Mem. pres.'s council Toledo Mus. Art; past trustee Maumee Valley Country Day Sch. Mem. ABA, Ohio Bar Assn., Toledo Bar Assn., Jewish Community Ctr., Maumee Valley Country Day Sch. Alumni Assn. (past pres.). Clubs: Belmont Country, Carranor Hunt & Polo, Toledo Tennis, Masons. General corporate, Probate, Corporate taxation. Home: 5045 Cartagena Dr Toledo OH 43623 Office: 3223 Sylvania Ave Toledo OH 43613

ZERR, RICHARD KEVIN, lawyer; b. St. Charles, Mo., Apr. 10, 1949; s. Elmer George and Lillian Grace (Gross) Z.; m. Martha Jo Zerr, Mar. 19, 1969 (div. June 1976); m. Judy Ann Yeager, Aug. 8, 1978; 1 child, Richard Kevin Jr. AB in Polit. Sci., U. Mo., 1971; JD, U. Ark., 1974. Bar: Mo. 1974, U.S. Dist. Ct. (we. dist.) Mo. 1974, U.S. Dist. Ct. (ea. dist.) Mo. 1983, U.S. Ct. Appeals (8th cir.) 1985, U.S. Supreme Ct. 1985. Asst. to pros. atty. City of St. Charles, 1974, magistrate judge, 1975-78; assoc. judge Cir. Ct., St. Charles, 1979-82; ptnr. Beck, Tiemeyer & Zerr, St. Charles, 1983—; bd. dirs. St. Charles County Police Acad., 1978—. Mem. ABA (state chmn. small claims ct. com. 1978-82), Mo. Bar Assn., St. Charles County Bar Assn. Democrat. Roman Catholic. Lodge: Kiwanis. Avocation: high sch. and coll. football official. Criminal, Personal injury, Family and matrimonial. Home: 509 S Duchesne Saint Charles MO 63301 Office: Beck Tiemeyer & Zerr 2777 W Clay Saint Charles MO 63301

ZEUGHAUSER, PETER DOUGLAS, lawyer; b. N.Y.C., June 2, 1950; s. Milton and Phyllis (Deutsch) Z. BA, U. Wis., 1972; JD, St. Louis U., 1975. Assoc. Green & Hennings, St. Louis, 1975-77, Duryea, Malcolm, Randolph and Daly, Newport Beach, Calif., 1977-79; pres. Procal, Newport Beach, 1979-81; gen. counsel The Irvine Co., Newport Beach, 1981—; bd. dirs. Davcon, Inc. Vice chmn. area campaign Orange County Ctr. for Performing Arts, 1986—, bd. dirs., founder, 1985—, Local Elected Officials of Am., 1983—; bd. dirs. Child Care Advs. Am., 1984-87. Mem. ABA, Bar Assn. Met. St. Louis, Orange County Bar Assn. (bd. dirs. corp. law dept. sect., chmn. 1984-86, newsletter editor 1983), Am. Corp. Counsel Assn. (bd. dirs. 1984—, chmn. young lawyers sect. 1984, founder, bd. dirs. So. Calif. chpt. 1984). Home: 1312 Santanella Terr Corona del Mar CA 92625 Office: The Irvine Co 500 Newport Ctr Dr PO Box I Newport Beach CA 92660

ZIEGLER, ARNOLD GERARD, lawyer, former marine corps officer; b. Boston, Feb. 16, 1926; s. Arnold Ulerich and Mary Sylvia (Day) Z.; m. Mae Aline, Oct. 8, 1949; 1 son, Arnold Dennis. B.B.A. (1st in grad. class), George Washington U., 1966, M.B.A., 1966; J.D., U. Md., 1978. Bar: Md. 1978, Fla. 1978, D.C. 1978, U.S. Dist. Ct. D.C. 1978, U.S. Dist. Ct. Md. 1979, U.S. Ct. Appeals, D.C. cir. 1979, U.S. Ct. Appeals (4th cir.) 1982. Joined U.S. Marine Corps, 1943 advanced through grades to col.; 7 years sr. policy exec., 16 yrs. sr. adminstr. and communications ops. exec., Pacific, Washington, Korea, Europe, Viet Nam; prin. tech. adviser to communications dir. UN Mediator for Palestine, 1st and 2d truce, 1948; ret., 1974; assoc. Blooston and Mordkofsky and predecessors, Washington, 1978-79; ptnr. Ziegler and Burman, Odenton, Md., 1979-80; ptnr. Katz and Ziegler, Laurel, Md., 1980-82; sole practice, Riverdale Md., 1982-83; of counsel Lipshultz & Hone, Chartered, Silver Spring, Md., 1983—. Decorated 2 Legion of Merit, Navy Commendation Medal, Meritorious Service Medal. Mem. ABA, Md. Bar Assn., Fed. Communications Bar Assn., Alpha Sigma Lambda (charter pres. chpt.). Republican. Roman Catholic. General practice, Personal injury, Family and matrimonial. Home: 11501 Lamberton Ct Silver Spring MD 20902 Office: 8630 Fenton St Suite 108 Spring MD 20910

ZIEGLER, CRAIG E., lawyer; b. Lebanon, Pa., May 14, 1954; s. Elam H. and Kathryn K. (Dubble) Z. BA, Dickinson Coll., 1976; JD, U. Va., 1980. Bar: Pa. 1980, U.S. Dist. Ct. (ea. dist.) Pa. 1980, U.S. Ct. Internat. Trade 1982, U.S. Ct. Appeals (3d cir.) 1983, U.S. Ct. Appeals (fed. cir.) 1985. Assoc. Montgomery, McCracken, Walker & Rhoads, Phila., 1980—. Mem. ABA, Pa. Bar Assn., Phila. Bar Assn., Phi Beta Kappa. Republican. Federal civil litigation, State civil litigation. Home: 7185 Lafayette Ave Fort Washington PA 19034 Office: Montgomery McCracken Walker & Rhoads 3 Pkwy 20th Floor Philadelphia PA 19102

ZIEGLER, DONALD EMIL, judge; b. Pitts., Oct. 1, 1936; s. Emil Nicholas and Elizabeth (Barclay) Z.; m. Claudia J. Chermak, May 1, 1965; 1 son, Scott Emil. B.A., Duquesne U., 1958; LL.B., Georgetown U., 1961. Bar: Pa. bar 1962, U.S. Supreme Ct. bar 1967. Practice law Pitts., 1962-74; judge Ct. of Common Pleas of Allegheny County, Pa., 1974-78, U.S. Dist. Ct. for Western Dist. of Pa., Pitts., 1978—. Treas. Big Bros. of Allegheny County, 1969-71. Mem. Am. Bar Assn., Pa. Bar Assn., Allegheny County Bar Assn., Am. Judicature Soc., St. Thomas More Soc. Democrat. Roman Catholic. Club: Oakmont Country. Jurisprudence. Office: 10th Floor US Post Office and Courthouse 7th and Grant Sts Pittsburgh PA 15219

ZIEGLER, EDWARD HOWARD, JR., legal educator, consultant; b. Dayton, Ky., May 31, 1948; s. Edward Harold Sr. and Rita Catherine (Steil) Z.; m. Mary Nick, Nov. 26, 1985. BA, U. Notre Dame, 1970; JD, U. Ky., 1973; LLM, George Washington U., 1975. Atty. U.S. Atomic Energy Commn., Washington, 1974-75; prof. law No. Ky. U., Highland Heights, 1975-80, U. Dayton, Ohio, 1980—; cons., lectr. local govt. Zoning and Planning Commn. Contbr. articles to profl. jours. Local government, Real property, Environment. Office: U Dayton Sch of Law 300 College Park Dayton OH 45469

ZIEGLER, WILLIAM JOSEPH, lawyer; b. Balt., Mar. 24, 1933; s. John Charles and Marie Elizabeth (Franz) Z.; m. Jacqueline Joyce Dees, Apr. 11, 1959; 1 child, William J. B.S. summa cum laude, Loyola Coll., Balt., 1958; J.D. magna cum laude, U. Balt., 1965; M.A.C. in Pub. Adminstrn., U. Va., 1971. Bar: Md. 1966, U.S. Dist. Ct. Md. 1967. Atty., Social Security Adminstrn., Balt., 1966—. Served with USN, 1952-54. Mem. Md. Bar Assn., Alpha Sigma Nu. Administrative and regulatory, Federal civil litigation, Pension, profit-sharing, and employee benefits. Home: 4038 Pebble Branch Rd Ellicott City MD 21043 Office: Social Security Adminstrn 6401 Security Blvd Baltimore MD 21235

ZIERING, WILLIAM MARK, lawyer; b. New Britain, Conn., Feb. 4, 1931; s. Jacob Max and Esther (Freedman) Z.; m. Harriet Koskoff, Aug. 20, 1958; 1 son, Benjamin. B.A., Yale U., 1952; J.D., Harvard U., 1955. Bar: Conn. 1955, Calif. 1962. Assoc. firm Koskoff & McMahon, Plainville, Conn., 1959-60; sr. trial atty. SEC, San Francisco, 1960-65; pvt. practice San Francisco, 1965—; partner firm Bremer & Ziering, 1972-77; instr. Golden Gate U. Law Sch., San Francisco, 1968-75. Vice pres., bd. dirs. Calif. League Handicapped, 1972—. Served to comdr. USNR, 1955-58. Mem. ABA, Calif. Bar Assn., San Francisco Bar Assn. (past chmn. securities, corps. and banking), Navy League (dir.). Club: Commonwealth. General corporate, Securities. Home: 2027 Lyon St San Francisco CA 94115 Office: 4 Embarcadero Ctr Suite 3400 San Francisco CA 94111-4187

ZIFF, LLOYD RICHARD, lawyer; b. N.Y.C., Mar. 9, 1942; s. George and Lillian (Gisnet) Z.; m. M. Morrow Cox, Jan. 28, 1967; children: Tina Marie, M. Courtney, Robert G. Grad., Peekskill Mil. Acad.; B.A., U. Pa., 1968, J.D. magna cum laude (Warwick Found. scholar), 1971. Bar: Pa. 1971, U.S. Supreme Ct. 1975. Assoc. Pepper, Hamilton & Scheetz, Phila., 1971-77, ptnr., 1977—; teaching fellow U. Pa. Sch. Law, 1971, lectr., 1981-82; faculty Acad. Advocacy, 1980—; mem. Devitt implementation com. U.S. Dist. Ct. (ea. dist.) Pa., 1980-84, mem. continuing legal edn. com., 1985—; co-chmn. Seminar on Complex Litigation, 1983. Contbr. articles to legal jours. Mem. Kent State U. Task Force, Pres.'s Commn. on Campus Unrest, (Ohio), 1970; mem. Inter-disciplinary Com. on Child Abuse S.E. Pa., 1973-75; mem. adv. com. Family Resources Ctr., St. Christopher's Hosp. for Children, Phila., 1976; chmn. Phila. Bail Project, 1969. Served with U.S. Army, 1965-67. Fellow Salzburg Seminar Am. Studies-Am. Law and Legal Instns., (Austria), 1978. Mem. ABA, Pa. Bar Assn., Phila. Bar Assn. (chmn. election procedures com. 1976, chmn. spl. com. on admission attys. to fed. practice 1986), Order of Coif. Federal civil litigation. Office: Pepper Hamilton & Scheetz 123 S Broad St Philadelphia PA 19109

ZIFFREN, LESTER, international public relations consultant; b. Rock Island, Ill., Apr. 30, 1906; s. Davis J. and Rose Ziffren; m. Edythe Wurtzel, May 21, 1937 (dec. 1977); 1 dau. B.J., U. Mo., 1927. Various positions UPI, 1927-37; writer, prodn. exec. 20th Century Fox Studios, Beverly Hills, Calif., 1937-42; dir. Office of Coordinator Inter-Am. Affairs, Santiago, Chile, 1942-45; 1st sec., pub. affairs officer USIA, Am. Embassy, Bogota, Colombia, Santiago, Chile, 1951-54; dir. pub. relations Braden Copper Co. subs. Kennecott Copper Corp., Chile, 1954-60; dir. pub. relations, advt. Kennecott Copper Corp., N.Y., 1961-71; internat. pub. relations cons., N.Y., 1971—; cons. Kennecott, Peabody Coal Co., Minerec Corp., Cerro Corp. Decorated comdr. Order Merit, Bernardo O'Higgins, Republic of Chile, 1946. Mem. Am. Fgn. Service Assn., Americas Found. (v.p., treas.), Pub. Relations Soc. Am., Diplomatic and Ret. Officers, Soc. Silurians, Bolivarian Soc. U.S. (treas., v.p.), Pan Am. Soc. U.S. (treas.), N.Am.-Chilean C. of C. (exec. dir.). Clubs: Nat. Press, Army, Navy (Washington); Overseas Press (N.Y.C.). Home and Office: 220 E 81st St New York NY 10028

ZIKER, BARRY GENE, lawyer; b. Pitts., Jan. 19, 1955; s. Melvin and Norma (Wise) Z.; m. Margaret Chillingworth, Dec. 28, 1986. BA, U. Mich., 1976, JD, 1980. Bar: Wash. 1980, U.S. Dist. Ct. (we. dist.) Wash. 1980, U.S. Ct. Appeals (9th cir.) 1983. Assoc. Cable, Barrett, Langenbach & McInerney, Seattle, 1980-86; sole practice Seattle, 1986-87; assoc. Smolenski & Wooddell, Honolulu, 1987—; mem. Joint Legal Task Force, Seattle, 1984-85. Staff atty. Cen. City Legal Clinic, Seattle, 1982-86. Mem. ABA, Wash. State Bar Assn., Seattle-King County Bar Assn. Club: Sierra (legal cons. 1984—). Avocations: bicycling, hiking, sailing, photography. Federal civil litigation, State civil litigation, Environment.

ZILLY, THOMAS SAMUEL, lawyer; b. Detroit, Jan. 1, 1935; s. George Samuel and Bernice M. (McWhinney) Z.; m. Ruth Flanders, Oct. 24, 1957; children: John, Peter, Paul, Luke. BA, U. Mich., 1956; LLD, Cornell U., 1962. Bar: Wash. 1962, U.S. Ct. Appeals (9th cir.) 1962, U.S. Supreme Ct. 1976. Ptnr. Lane, Powell, Moss & Miller, Seattle, 1962—; judge pro tem Seattle Mcpl. Ct., 1972-80. Contbr. articles to profl. jours. Mem. Cen. Area Sch. Council, Seattle, 1969-70; scoutmaster Thunderbird Dist. council Boy Scouts Am. Seattle, 1976-84; bd. dirs. East Madison YMCA. Served to lt. (j.g.) USN, 1956-59. Recipient Tuahku Dist. Service to Youth award Boy Scouts Am., 1983. Mem. ABA, Wash. State Bar Assn., Seattle-King County Bar Assn. (treas. 1979-80, trustee 1980-83, sec. 1983-84, 2d v.p. 1984-85, 1st v.p. 1985-86, pres. 1986—). Contracts commercial, Federal civil litigation, State civil litigation. Home: 541 McGilvra Blvd Seattle WA 98112 Office: Lane Powell Moss & Miller 3800 Rainier Bank Tower Seattle WA 98101

ZIMMER, BRUCE IRWIN, educational organization executive, lawyer; b. N.Y.C., Oct. 3, 1944; s. Murray M. and Bea (Gottlieb) Z.; m. Debra Judith Dorfman, Mar. 22, 1975; children: Claudia Elizabeth, Andrew David. BA, Columbia U., 1965; JD, NYU, 1968; postgrad. Columbia U. Sch. of Law, 1973-75. Bar: N.Y. 1969. Asst. dean Columbia Coll., Columbia U., N.Y.C., 1970-75; assoc. dean Coll. Law, U. Utah, 1975-78; exec. dir. Law Sch. Admission Council, Washington, 1978-83; exec. v.p. Law Sch. Admission Services, Law Sch. Admission Council, 1983—; liaison to numerous coms. and task forces of legal edn. orgns. Bd. dirs. Manhattanville Community Ctrs., 1974-75. Mem. ABA, Am. Mgmt. Assoc., Order of Coif. Assoc. editor NYU Jour. Internat. Law and Politics, 1967-68; editor Legal Affairs Manual, Assn. Am. Law Schs., 1978—, Financing Your Law School Education, The Right Law School for You; sr. editor Law Sch. Admission Council Prelaw Handbook, 1978—; author various publs. on legal edn., fin., demographics and mgmt. Legal education, Legislative, Administrative and regulatory. Office: Law Sch Admission Council/Services PO Box 40 Newtown PA 18940

ZIMMER, JANET ROSE, lawyer; b. Lancaster, Pa., Apr. 14, 1949; d. Robert Clare and Rose Evelyn (Williams) Zimmer; m. Gene D'Agostino. AB magna cum laude, Duke U., 1971; JD, Georgetown U., 1975. Bar: D.C. 1975, N.Y. 1986. Tchr. English, Ea. Lancaster County Sch. Dist., Pa., 1971-72; atty./advisor Div. Corp. Fin. U.S. SEC, Washington, 1975-78, spl. counsel and br. chief Div. Market Regulation, 1978-80; assoc. Rogers & Wells, Washington, 1980-82; assoc. Seward & Kissel, Washington, 1982-85, ptnr., 1986—. D.C. chmn. Robert L. Burch for (Ohio) State Senate, 1984. Mem. ABA (sect. corp., banking and bus. law, com. on fed. regulation of securities), D.C. Bar Assn., Women's Bar Assn. D.C., Kappa Delta Pi. Club: Sierra (No. Va. conservation com. mem. 1980). Securities, Banking, General corporate. Office: Seward & Kissel 818 Connecticut Ave NW Suite 800 Washington DC 20006

ZIMMER, JOHN HERMAN, lawyer; b. Sioux Falls, S.D., Dec. 30, 1922; s. John Francis and Veronica (Berke) Z.; student Augustana Coll., Sioux Falls, 1941-42, Mont. State Coll., 1943; LL.B., U. S.D., 1948; m. Deanna Langner, 1976; children by previous marriage—June, Mary Zimmer Levene, Robert Joseph, Judith Maureen Zimmer Rose. Bar: S.D. 1948. Practice law, Turner County, S.D., 1948—; ptnr. Zimmer & Duncan, Parker, S.D.; states atty. Turner County, 1955-58, 62-64; asst. prof. med. jurisprudence U. S.D.; minority counsel S.D. Senate Armed Services Com. on Strategic and Critical Materials Investigation, 1962-63; chmn. Southeastern Council Govts., 1973-75; mem. U. S.D. Law Sch. adv. council, 1973-74. Chmn. Turner County Rep. Com., 1955-56; mem. S.D. Rep. adv. com., 1959-60; alt. del. Rep. Nat. Conv., 1968; pres. S.D. Easter Seal Soc., 1986-87. Served with AUS, 1943-46; PTO. Decorated Bronze Star, Philippine Liberation ribbon. Mem. Am., Fed., S.D. (commr. 1954-57) bar assns., Am. Trial Lawyers Assn., S.D. Trial Lawyers Assn. (pres. 1967-68), VFW, Am. Legion, Phi Delta Phi. Lodges: Elks, Shriners. State civil litigation, Administrative and regulatory, Probate. Home: Rural Rt Parker SD 57053 Office: Zimmer & Duncan Law Bldg PO Box 547 Parker SD 57053

ZIMMER, RICHARD ALAN, lawyer; b. Newark, Aug. 16, 1944; s. William and Evelyn (Schlank Rader) Z.; m. Marfy Goodspeed, Dec. 27, 1965; children: Carl William, Benjamin Goodspeed. BA, Yale U., 1966, LLB, 1969. Bar: N.Y. 1971, U.S. Dist. Ct. (so. and ea. dists.) N.Y. 1974, N.J. 1975, U.S. Dist. Ct. N.J. 1975, U.S. Supreme Ct. 1980. Assoc. Cravath, Swaine and Moore, N.Y.C., 1969-75; gen. atty. Johnson & Johnson, New Brunswick, N.J., 1976—; mem. N.J. Gen. Assembly, 1982—, chmn. state govt. com., 1986-87; mem. N.J. Senate, 1987—. Chmn. March of Dimes WalkAmerica, Hunterdon County, N.J., 1984-86; treas. Hunterdon Hospice, Flemington, N.J., 1984-86; chmn. Nat. Council for Clean Indoor Air, Flemington, N.J., 1986—. Mem. ABA, N.J. State Bar Assn., Hunterdon County Bar Assn. Republican. General corporate. Home: RD 2 Box 391 Flemington NJ 08822 Office: Johnson & Johnson 1 Johnson & Johnson Plaza New Brunswick NJ 08933

ZIMMERLY, JAMES GREGORY, lawyer, physician; b. Longview, Tex., Mar. 25, 1941; s. George James and Irene Gertrude (Kohler) Z.; m. Nancy Carol Zimmerly, June 11, 1966; children—Mark, Scott, Robin. B.A., Gannon Coll., 1962; M.D., U. Md., 1966, J.D., 1969; M.P.H., Johns Hopkins U., 1968. Bar: Md. 1970, D.C. 1972, U.S. Ct. Mil. Appeals 1973, U.S. Supreme Ct. 1973. Ptnr. Acquisto, Asplen & Morstein, Ellicott City, Md., 1970—. Chief dept. legal medicine Armed Forces Inst. Pathology, 1971—; prof. George Washington U., 1972-80; adj. prof. law Georgetown U. Law Ctr., 1972—, Antioch Sch. Law, 1977-80; assoc. prof. U. Md. Sch. Medicine, 1973—; cons. Dept. Def., Dept. Justice, HHS, VA, 1971—. Fellow Am. Acad. Forensic Scis., Am. Coll. Legal Medicine, (pres. 1980-81), Am. Coll Preventive Medicine; mem. ABA, Md. Bar Assn., Am. Soc. on Law and Medicine, Am. Coll. Legal Medicine, Am. Coll. Emergency Physicians, Md. Med. Soc. Editor: Legal Aspects of Medical Practice, 1978—, Jour. Legal Medicine, 1975-78, Md. Med. Jour., 1977—, Lawyers' Med. Ency., 1980—. Personal injury, Health, Legal education. Home: Bluestone Sanctuary General Delivery Cooksville MD 21723 Office: Dept Legal Medicine Armed Forces Inst Pathology Washington DC 20306

ZIMMERMAN, AARON MARK, lawyer; b. Syracuse, N.Y., Jan. 28, 1953; s. Julius and Sara (Lavine) Z. B.S., Syracuse U., 1974, J.D., 1976. Bar: N.Y. 1977, Pa. 1977, D.C. 1978, S.C. 1978, Fla. 1978, U.S. Dist. Ct. S.C. 1978,

U.S. Dist. Ct. (no. dist.) N.Y. Corp. atty., asst. sec. Daniel Internat. Corp., Greenville, S.C., 1977-79; ptnr. Abend, Driscoll & Zimmerman, 1979-81; sole practice, Syracuse, 1981—. Bd. dirs. Syracuse Friends Ametuer Boxing, 1982—. Mem. Am. Arbitration Assn. (arbitrator), Workers Compensation Com. N.Y. State Bar (exec. com.), Workers Compensation Assn. of Cen. N.Y. (charter, dir., treas.), N.Y. State Bar, S.C. State Bar, D.C. State Bar, Fla. State Bar, ABA. Lodge: Masons. Personal injury, Workers' compensation, General practice. Home: 602 Standish Dr Dewitt NY 13214 Office: Zimmerman Law Offices 117 S State St Syracuse NY 13202-1175

ZIMMERMAN, AUSTIN MANLOVE, lawyer, business executive; b. Chgo., Dec. 28, 1909; s. Edward A. and Isabel (Chave) Z.; m. Elizabeth Thayer, Dec. 26, 1934; children: Edward Austin, John Jeffrey. A.B., Amherst Coll., 1931; postgrad., Nat. U. Mexico, 1931; J.D., Northwestern Law Sch., 1934. Bar: Ill. bar 1934. Practice in Chgo., 1934-67, Barrington Hills, Ill., 1967—; partner Norman, Engelhardt, Zimmerman, Franke & Lauritzen (and predecessor firms), 1937-67, Austin M. Zimmerman, 1967—; Sec., gen. counsel All Am. Aviation (now U.S. Air and All Am. Engring.), Wilmington, Del., 1942-46; sec., dir. Allied Tractor Equipment Co., 1938-42, Gust Corp., Flex-O-Lace, Inc., 1940-42, Anela Distbrs., Inc., 1945-67, Wacker-Dearborn Corp., 1945-66, Midwest Electric Mfg. Corp., 1945-72, 1647 W. Walnut Bldg. Corp., 1952-72; sec., treas. Chgo. Exhibitions Corp., 1955-67; v.p., sec., gen. counsel, dir. Randall Bearings, Inc., Lima, Ohio, 1946—; spl. counsel Chgo. and So. Airlines, 1946-50, United Airlines, 1947; sec.-treas., dir. Vancouver Ritz Properties, Ltd., B.C., Can., 1960-67, RBI, Inc., Springfield, Tenn., 1977—, Bearing & Bronze Warehousing, Inc., Greenbriar, Tenn., 1977—; atty. for zoning hearing Countryside Assn., 1948; chmn. annexation com. McHenry County property Village of Barrington Hills, 1957; chmn. law com., mem. finance and health coms. Village Bd., 1958-69. V.p. Barrington chpt. Lyric Opera Guild of Chgo.; alumni adviser admissions Amherst Coll., 1951—, mem. alumni council, 1964-69, 1931, 50th reunion gift chmn. class of 1931, 1966-73, chmn. 53d and 55th reunions; treas., bd. dirs. Contemporary Concerts, Inc., Chgo. Mem. Am. Bar Assn. (chmn. Midwest area, sect. of pub. contract law 1965-68, council 1968-70), Ill. State Bar Assn., McHenry Bar Assn., Chgo. Bar Assn., Fed. Bar Assn., Los Rancheros Vistadores, Chi Psi, Phi Alpha Delta. Clubs: Lion, Law, Legal, Literary, University, Mid-Day, Amherst (Chgo.) (past pres.); Barrington Hills Country, Lake Geneva (Wis.) Yacht. General practice. Address: Brae Burn Farm Barrington Hills Algonquin IL 60102

ZIMMERMAN, BERNARD, lawyer; b. Munich, Bavaria, Fed. Republic Germany, May 31, 1946; came to U.S., 1949; s. Sam and Roza (Spodek) Z.; m. Grace L. Suarez, OCt. 23, 1976; children: Elizabeth, Adam, David, Dara Bylah. AB, U. Rochester, 1967; JD, U. Chgo., 1970. Bar: Calif. 1971, La. 1971, U.S. Supreme Ct. 1975, U.S. Dist. Ct. (no., ea., cen. and so. dists.) Calif., U.S. Dist. Ct. (ea. dist.) La., U.S. Ct. Appeals (9th cir.). Law. clk. chief judge U.S. Dist. Ct. (ea. dist.) La., New Orleans, 1970-71; asst. prof. law La. State U., Baton Rouge, 1971-72; ptnr. Pillsbury, Madison & Sutro, San Francisco, 1972—; dep. pub. defender City of San Francisco, 1975; arbitrator U.S. Dist. Ct., San Francisco. bd. dirs., exec.com. San Francisco Lawyers' Com. on Urban Affairs, 1984—. Mem. Phi Beta Kappa. Democrat. Jewish. Club: Olympic (San Francisco). Federal civil litigation, State civil litigation, Libel. Office: Pillsbury Madison & Sutro 235 Montgomery St San Francisco CA 94104

ZIMMERMAN, DON ALAN, lawyer, municipal association executive; b. Little Rock, Aug. 10, 1942; s. Glenn George and Louise Eleanor (Moorman) Z.; m. Debra Jane Gray, June 12, 1970 (div. Jan. 1981); 1 child, Glenda Gray; m. Janet Lea, Nov. 23, 1984. BSBA, U. Ark., 1964, JD, 1972. Bar: Ark. 1974, U.S. Dist. Ct. (ea. dist.) Ark. 1979. Exec. dir. Ark. Mcpl. League, North Little Rock, 1974—. Presbyterian. Avocations: tennis, boating. Home: 11306 Shenandoah Valley Dr Little Rock AR 72115 Office: Ark Mcpl League PO Box 38 North Little Rock AR 72115

ZIMMERMAN, DONA HOPE, lawyer, bar review program co-owner; b. Pitts., Feb. 9, 1949; d. John Florian and Hope Lenore (Gephart) Wolsko; m. David Allan Zimmerman, Oct. 30, 1976; children: Scott David, Danielle Hope. BA, U. Pitts., 1971; JD, Del. Law Sch., 1976. Bar: Pa. 1976, U.S. Dist. Ct. (ea. dist.) Pa., 1978. V.p., exec. dir. PMBR/Multistate Legal Studies, Inc., Phila., 1977—, also bd. dirs. Bd. elections ofcl. Stowe Twp., Pa., 1972-73. Mem. ABA, Pa. Bar Assn., Cousteau Soc., Am. Montessori Soc., Phi Alpha Delta. Republican. Avocations: water sports, traveling, arts and crafts. Legal education, General corporate, Bar review program. Home: 2203 Valley Ave Wilmington DE 19810 Office: PMBR 211 Bainbridge St Philadelphia PA 19147

ZIMMERMAN, D(ONALD) PATRICK, lawyer; b. Albany, N.Y., Mar. 20, 1942; s. Bernard M. and Helen M. (Eshelman) Z.; m. D.C. Gila, June 30, 1979. B.A., Rollins Coll., 1964; J.D., Dickinson Sch. Law, 1967. Bars: Pa. 1968, U.S. Supreme Ct. 1971. Atty., Legal Aid, 1968-69; pub. defender, Lancaster County, Pa., 1969-72; sole practice, Lancaster, Pa., 1974—; instr. Ct. Common Pleas for Constables, 1976—; solicitor Lancaster County Dep. Sheriff Assn., 1977—, Lancaster County Constable Assn., 1975—; instr. sheriff's dept. Lancaster County for Dep. Sheriffs, 1978—; of counsel to Dep. Sheriff Assn. Pa., 1979-81; spl. counsel Pa. State Constables Assn., 1981; chmn. Bd. Arbitrators Lancaster County, 1975-81; spl. counsel Legislative Com. to Constable Assn. Pa., 1982. Recipient Ofcl. Commendation of Merit, Lancaster County Sheriff's Dept., 1979, Ofcl. Commendation of Merit Fraternal Order Police State Lodge 66, 1985. Mem. ABA, Am. Trial Lawyers Assn., Pa. Bar Assn., Lancaster County Bar Assn. Author: The Pennsylvania Landlord and Tenant Handbook, 1982; contbr. articles to profl. jours. Family and matrimonial, Landlord-tenant, Personal injury. Office: 214 E King St Lancaster PA 17602

ZIMMERMAN, GOLDA, lawyer, educator; b. Syracuse, N.Y., Sept. 25, 1949; d. Julius and Sara (Lavine) Z.; m. David C. Kapell, Sept. 16, 1977; children: Jeremy S., Bethany R. B.S. in Edn., Boston U., 1971; M.S. in Ednl. Adminstrn., U. Kans., 1974; J.D., Syracuse U., 1980. Bar: N.Y. 1984, U.S. Tax Ct. 1984, U.S. Dist. Ct. (no. dist.) N.Y. 1984. Elem. tchr. St. John's Sch., Lawrence, Kans., 1971-73; adminstrv. asst. U. Kans., Lawrence, 1973-75; sr. system analyst student data systems Syracuse U., 1975-77; law clk. Onondaga County Ct., Syracuse, summers 1978, 79; prof. law Simmons Sch. Mortuary Sci., Syracuse, 1982-85; atty. Zimmerman Law Office, Syracuse, 1980—; dir. N.Y. State Law Exam for Funeral Dirs. review course, Syracuse; speaker various groups on family and mortuary law. Author: (with Sandra Crowther) Five Career Education Module for Pre-Service and In Service Teachers, 1974. Mem. Syracuse Opera Guild, 1975—, St. Joseph Hosp. Aux., Syracuse, 1975—, Dewitt Welcome Wagon, N.Y., 1982—, Crouse-Irving Meml. Hosp. Aux. Mem. ABA, N.Y. Women's Bar Assn. (corr. sec. cen. N.Y. chpt. 1986—), N.Y. Bar Assn., Onondaga County Bar Assn., N.Y. State Trial Lawyers Assn., Boston U. Alumni Assn. Democrat. Family and matrimonial, Real property, Adoptions. Home: 401 Standish Dr Dewitt NY 13224 Office: Zimmerman Law Office 117 South State St Syracuse NY 13202

ZIMMERMAN, JEAN, lawyer; b. Berkeley, Calif., Dec. 3, 1947; d. Donald Scheel Zimmerman and Phebe Jean (Reed) Doan; m. Gilson Berryman Gray III, Nov. 25, 1982; children—Charles Donald Buffum, Catherine Elisabeth Phebe (twins); stepchildren—Alison Travis, Laura Rebecca, Gilson Berryman. B.S. in Bus. Adminstrn., U. Md., 1970; J.D., Emory U., 1975. Bar: Ga. 1975, D.C. 1976, N.Y. 1980. Asst. mgr. investments FNMA, Washington, D.C., 1970-73; assoc. counsel Fuqua Industries Inc., Atlanta, 1976-79; assoc. Sage Gray Todd & Sims, N.Y.C., 1979-84; assoc. counsel J. Henry Schroder Bank & Trust Co., N.Y.C., 1984-85, asst. gen. counsel, 1985-86; assoc. gen. counsel IBJ Schroder Bank & Trust Co., N.Y.C., 1987—. Founder, officer ERA Ga., Atlanta, 1977-79. Mem. ABA, N.Y. State Bar Assn., Ga. Assn. Women Lawyers (bd. dirs. 1977-79), LWV, DAR. Democrat. Banking, Contracts commercial, General corporate. Office: IBJ Schroder Bank & Trust Co 1 State St New York NY 10004

ZIMMERMAN, LEROY S., state official; b. Harrisburg, Pa., Dec. 22, 1934; s. LeRoy and Amelia (Magaro) Z.; m. Mary Augusta Jaymes, Feb. 9; children: Susan A., Mark J., Amy A. B.S. in Econs., Villanova (Pa.) U., 1956; J.D., Dickinson Sch. Law, Calisle, Pa., 1959. Bar: Pa. Practiced law 1960-81; partner firm Hepford, Zimmerman & Swartz, 1970-81; asst. dist. atty., then dist. atty. Dauphin County, 1963-80; atty. gen. Commonwealth Pa., 1981—; past pres. Pa. Dist. Attys. Assn. Trustee Dickinson Sch. Law; mem. devel. council Villanova U. Served with USAF. Recipient Man of Yr. award Police Chiefs Assn. Southeastern Pa., 1982, Achievement award Nat. Italian-Am. Found., 1983, Pres.'s award Pa. Chiefs Police Assn., 1986. Mem. Nat. Assn. Attys. Gen. (chmn. criminal law subcom., chmn. exec. working group 1983), Sons Italy in Am., Phi Alpha Delta. Republican. Roman Catholic. Club: K.C. Criminal, State civil litigation. Office: 16th Floor Strawberry Sq Harrisburg PA 17120

ZIMMERMAN, NORMAN, lawyer, toxicology consultant; b. N.Y.C., May 6, 1941; s. Samuel and Leah (Epstein) Z.; m. Rena Gross, Nov. 13, 1964; 1 child, Leah. BA in Biology and Chemistry, U. Rochester, 1963; ScM in Biology, Brown U., 1966; PhD in Biochemistry, U. Hawaii, 1971; JD, Am. U., 1980. Bar: Mich. 1982, U.S. Dist. Ct. (ea. and we. dists.) Mich., U.S. Ct. Appeals (6th cir.). Postdoctoral fellow NIH-Nat. Cancer Inst., Honolulu, 1971-72; dir. Scientist Coop. Industries, Colebrook, N.H., 1972-75; tech. staff Mitre, McLean, Va., 1975-78; sr. regulatory analyst Am. Petroleum Inst., Washington, 1978-80; sr. toxicologist Toxic Substance Control Commn., Lansing, Mich., 1980-82; atty., cons. toxicology Toxic Substance Control Commn., Lansing, 1982—; research dir. Upper CT Valley Hosp., Colebrook, 1973-75; adj. faculty mem. Catholic U., Washington, 1975, Georgetown U., 1976-77. Contbr. articles to sci. and law pubs. Recipient Ratigan-third prize Am. Soc. Law and Medicine, 1979; Silver medal Am. Chem. Soc., 1962; Canciro fellow L'Institut de Radium, Paris, 1962; Charlton Cancer scholar Am. Cancer Soc., 1959. Mem. ABA, Assn. Trial Lawyers Am., Mich. Trial Lawyers Assn., Am. Chem. Soc., Mich. Soc. of Toxicology, Soc. Environ. Toxicology and Chem., Sigma Xi. Jewish. Avocations: swimming, fishing, philately, drama. Environment, Personal injury, State civil litigation. Home: 4607 Barnes Rd Mason MI 48854 Office: 530 S Capitol Ave Lansing MI 48933

ZIMMERMAN, SANDRA L., lawyer; b. Pitts., Aug. 3, 1956; d. Irwin T. and Sylvia Dorothy (Davis) Z. BS, U. Ill., 1978, JD cum laude, 1981. Bar: Ill. 1981, U.S. Dist. Ct. (no. dist.) Ill. 1981, N.Y. 1985, U.S. Dist. Ct. (ea. and so. dists.) N.Y. 1985. Assoc. Vedder, Price, Kaufman & Kammholz, Chgo., 1981-84, Roberts & Finger, N.Y.C., 1984—. Editor U. Ill. Law Rev., 1980-81. Recipient Rickert award Rickert Trust, Urbana-Champaign, Ill., 1980. Mem. ABA, N.Y. State Bar Assn., Assn. Bar City N.Y., Chgo. Bar Assn., Ill. Bar Assn. Democrat. Jewish. Labor, Pension, profit-sharing, and employee benefits, Federal civil litigation. Office: Roberts & Finger 767 Third Ave New York NY 10017

ZIMMERMAN, STEVEN LOUIS, lawyer; b. Woonsocket, R.I., Sept. 14, 1945; s. Irving Israel and Eleanor Murial (Elovich) Z.; m. Barbara Toby Prostkoff, Apr. 28, 1968; children: Robin, Michael, Martin. BA, Columbia U., 1967; JD, Boston U., 1971. Bar: Colo. 1971, U.S. Dist. Ct. Colo. 1971, U.S. Ct. Appeals (10th cir.) 1971. Assoc. Sterling & Simon, Denver, 1971-74; founder, supervising atty. Legal Ctr. for Handicapped Citizens, Denver, 1974-76; ptnr. Zimmerman & Schwartz P.C., Denver, 1977—; adv. dir. Citizens Bank Glendale, Colo., 1985—. Pres. Congregation Rodef Shalom, Denver, 1986—. Mem. ABA, Colo. Bar Assn., Denver Bar Assn., Denver Assn. for Retarded Citizens (pres. 1983-84). Democrat. Bankruptcy, Banking, Contracts commercial. Home: 653 S Oneida Way Denver CO 80224 Office: Zimmerman & Schwartz PC 1625 Broadway Suite 1800 Denver CO 80202

ZIMMERMANN, JOHN FREDERICK, lawyer; b. Milw., Jan. 17, 1921; s. Adolph John and Huldena (Zechinato) Z.; m. Rosemarie Ruess Sexmith, Apr. 26, 1952 (dec. Feb. 24, 1965); children: John E., Peter C., David D., Ann M., Robert J.; m. Maryann Lewandowski Dalpe, Sept. 7, 1965. AB, U. Mich., 1943; JD, Marquette U., 1948. Bar: Wis. 1948, Hawaii, 1970, U.S. Ct. Appeals (7th cir.), 1953, U.S. Supreme Ct. 1955, U.S. Ct. Appeals (9th cir.) 1970. Ptnr. Prosser, Zimmermann, Wiedabach, Koppa & Lane, and predecessors, Milw., 1955-69, Fong, Miho, Robinson, Zimmermann & McComish, Honolulu, 1970-73; sole practice, Honolulu, 1973-81; ptnr. Zimmermann & Kiang, Honolulu, 1980; counsel to Goodsill, Anderson Quinn & Stifel, Honolulu, 1982-83; preceptor Marquette U. Law Sch., 1956-58. Contbr. chpts. to books. Served to capt. AUS, 1943-46. Decorated Army Commendation medal. Fellow Am. Coll. Trial Lawyers; mem. ABA. Insurance, Personal injury, Public utilities. Home: 941 Archer St San Diego CA 92109

ZIMMERMANN, JOHN JOSEPH, lawyer; b. Chgo., Apr. 30, 1939; s. John Joseph and Ernestine Elizabeth (Leuver) Z.; m. Alice Rose Farrell, July 4, 1964; children—John, Michael, Thomas, Margaret, Kathleen. A.B., DePaul U., 1962, J.D., 1967. Bar: Ill. 1967, U.S. Dist. Ct. (no. dist.) Ill. 1967, U.S. Ct. Appeals (7th cir. 1967. Ptnr. Bradtke & Zimmermann, Mt. Prospect, Ill., 1979—; village atty. Village of Mt. Prospect, 1968-79, acting village mgr., 1969, 70-71; city atty. City of Wood Dale, Ill., 1975—; spl. corp. counsel City of Highland Park, Ill., 1979—; atty. Mt. Prospect Pub. Library, 1982—; village atty. Village of Mettawa, Ill., 1983—; dir. Joe Mitchell Buick, Inc., Mt. Prospect, 1979—; lectr. Ill. Inst. for Continuing Legal Edn., 1979—. Mem. St. Paul of the Cross Sch. Bd. of Edn., Park Ridge, 1972-75, pres., 1974-75; mem. sponsoring com. Ann. Men's Prayer Breakfast, Park Ridge, 1979—. Recipient ofcl. commendation Village of Mt. Prospect, 1971, named hon. citizens, 1974; recipient certs. of appreciation Ill. Inst. Continuing Legal Edn., 1980, Chgo. Bar Assn., 1984. Mem. Nat. Inst. Mcpl. Law Officers (del., lectr., regional v.p.), Ill. State Bar Assn. (sec. 1983, mem. local govt. sect. council 1981—), Ill. Home Rule Attys. Com. (charter mem., chmn. 1979), Chgo. Bar Assn. (chmn. local govt. com. 1983-84). Roman Catholic. Local government, Government contracts and claims, Real property. Home: 524 S Vine Ave Park Ridge IL 60068 Office: Bradtke & Zimmermann 1190 S Elmhurst Rd Mount Prospect IL 60056

ZIMMETT, MARK PAUL, lawyer; b. Waukegan, Ill., July 4, 1950; s. Nelson H. Zimmett and Roslyn (Yastrow) Zimmett Grodzin; m. Joan Robin Urken, June 11, 1972; children—Nora Helene, Lili Eleanor. B.A., Johns Hopkins U., 1972; J.D., NYU, 1975. Bar: N.Y. 1976, U.S. Dist. Ct. (so. and ea. dists.) N.Y. 1976, U.S. Dist. Ct. (no. dist.) Calif. 1980, U.S. Ct. Appeals (2d cir.) 1980, U.S. Supreme Ct. 1981, U.S. Ct. Appeals (5th cir.) 1986. Assoc. Shearman & Sterling, N.Y.C., 1975-83, ptnr., 1984—; adj. assoc. prof. internat. law NYU Law Sch., 1986-87. Contbr. articles to profl. jours. Mem. ABA, N.Y. State Bar Assn., Assn. Bar City N.Y., Citizens Union. Democrat. Jewish. Federal civil litigation, State civil litigation, Private international. Office: Shearman & Sterling 153 E 53d St New York NY 10022 also: 53 Wall St New York NY 10005

ZIMRING, FRANKLIN E., legal educator, lawyer; b. 1942. B.A., Wayne State U., 1963; J.D., U. Chgo., 1967. Bar: Calif. 1968. Asst. prof. U. Chgo., 1967-69, assoc. prof., 1969-72, assoc. dir. Center for Studies in Criminal Justice, 1971-73, prof., 1972-85, co-dir. Ctr. for Studies in Criminal Justice, 1973-75, dir., 1975-86; dir., prof. law Earl Warren Legal Inst., Univ. Calif., Berkeley, 1985—. Author: Confronting Youth Crime, 1978; (with Newton) Firearms and Violence in American Life, 1969; (with Hawkins) Deterrence, 1973, 76, (with Frase) Criminal Justice System, 1979, The Changing Legal World of Adolescence, 1982, (with Hawkins) Capital Punishment and the American Agenda, 1986. Mem. Phi Beta Kappa, Order of Coif. Office: Earl Warren Legal Inst Boalt Hall U Calif Berkeley CA 94720

ZINK, DEBORAH BURKS, lawyer; b. Richmond, Va., May 18, 1954; d. Sidney Edward and Willie Mae (Tatum) Burks; m. Charles Talbott Zink, Nov. 26, 1983. BA in Govt., Pub. Adminstrn., U. S.C., 1975; JD, Emory U., 1981. Bar: Ga. 1981, U.S. Dist. Ct. (no. dist.) Ga. 1981, U.S. Ct. Appeals (11th cir.) 1981. Assoc. Smith, Gambrell & Russell, Atlanta, Ga., 1981—. Mem. Ga. Bar Assn., Atlanta Bar Assn. (editor newsletter 1986-87), Atlanta Council of Younger Lawyers (bd. dirs. 1983-87, editor newsletter 1983-86, treas. 1986-87), Atlanta Women's C. of C. Avocations: tennis, cooking. Bankruptcy, General corporate. Office: Smith Gambrell & Russell 2400 First Atlanta Tower Atlanta GA 30383

ZINMAN, ROBERT MARSHALL, ins. co. legal exec.; b. N.Y.C., Apr. 23, 1931; s. Arthur H. and Ruth (Rosenberg) Z.; m. Marion B. Janel, July 1, 1965. B.A., Tufts U., 1953; J.D., Harvard U., 1960; LL.M., NYU, 1965. Bar: N.Y. 1961. With Met. Life Ins. Co., N.Y.C., 1960—, v.p., investment counsel, 1975—; adj. prof. law Fordham U., 1974—, NYU, 1987—; advisor Drafting Com. to Rev. Uniform Fraudulent Conveyance Act, Nat. Conf. Commrs. on Uniform State Laws, 1983-85. Bd. dirs. Greater Westchester Youth Orch. Assn., Conf. on Jewish Social Studies; bd. dirs., treas. Camp Rainbow. Served to capt. USNR. Recipient Arthur A. May award Am. Inst. Real Estate Appraisers, 1972. Mem. ABA (chmn. ad hoc com. to study the fed. priority in insolvency, council real property probate and trust sect.), Assn. Life Ins. Counsel (chmn. investment sect. 1980-83), Am. Council Life Ins. (chmn. bankruptcy legis. com.), Am. Law Inst., Am. Coll. Real Estate Lawyers (gov.), Am. Bankruptcy Inst. (bd. dirs.), Navy Marine Res. Lawyers Assn. (pres. 1976). Contbr. articles to profl. jours. Real property, Bankruptcy, Contracts commercial. Address: 1 Madison Ave New York NY 10010

ZINN, HENRY JACKSON, lawyer; b. Amarillo, Tex., Oct. 29, 1943; s. Houston Jackson and Teresa Henrietta (Frass) Z.; m. Joy Borromeo Rotairo, Dec. 12, 1980; 1 child, Esther Bee. B.A., U. Kans., 1965; J.D., So. Meth. U., 1968; B.E., U. Kans., 1976. Bar: Kans. 1969, U.S. Dist. Ct. Kans. 1969, U.S. Ct. Appeals (10th cir.) 1969, Calif. 1981, U.S. Dist. Ct. (no. dist.) Calif. 1981. Asst. instr. U. Kans., Lawrence, 1969-70, student tchr., 1974-76; sole practice, Shawnee Mission, Kans., 1969-74, Lawrence, Kans., 1977-81, San Francisco, 1981—; arbitrator San Francisco Domestic Relations Ct. Author: The War Against The War, 1973. Pres. Philippine Statehood Com., San Francisco, 1981—; local campaign coordinator Hart For Pres., San Francisco, 1984. Mem. San Francisco Bar Assn. (cert. for pro bono work 1982), Phi Alpha Delta. Democrat. Mem. Soc. of Friends. Clubs: Calif. Collectors, San Francisco Lawyers. Administrative and regulatory, Family and matrimonial, Military. Home: 1029 Geary #48 San Francisco CA 94109 Office: 870 Market #368 San Francisco CA 94102

ZIONTS, HARRIETTE ABRAMS, lawyer; b. Pitts., Feb. 26, 1941; d. Isadore H. and Florence (Merwitzer) Abrams; m. Stanley Zionts, June 5, 1960; children: David, Michael, Becca, Andrew. BA, Chatham Coll., 1962; postgrad., U. Pitts., 1962-65; JD, SUNY, Buffalo, 1981. Bar: N.Y. 1982, Fla. 1982. Assoc. Magavern & Magavern, Buffalo, 1981-83; sole practice Buffalo, 1983—. Mem. N.Y. State Bar Assn., Fla. Bar Assn., Erie County Bar Assn. Democrat. Jewish. Family and matrimonial, Real property, General practice. Office: 775 Main St Suite 230 Buffalo NY 14203

ZIONTZ, MARTIN LOWELL, lawyer; b. Mather AFB, Calif., Feb. 16, 1954; s. Alvin J. and Lenore Marion (Guralnick) Z.; m. Susan Marti Silverman, May 25, 1986. BA with honors, U. Chgo., 1976; JD, Northwestern U., 1980. Bar: Wash. 1980. Assoc. Bassett, Gemson & Morrison, Seattle, 1980-83; assoc. Bassett & Morrison, P.S., Seattle, 1983-85, ptnr., 1985—. Bd. dirs. Am. Jewish Com., Seattle, 1986. Mem. ABA, Wash. State Bar Assn., Seattle-King County Bar Assn. (legis. com. 1984—). Democrat. Avocations: lit., intergroup relations, conditioning. Insurance, Personal injury, Antitrust. Office: Bassett & Morrison PS 2001 Market Place One #600 Seattle WA 98121

ZIPFINGER, FRANK PETER, lawyer; b. Sydney, Australia, Feb. 27, 1953; s. Franz Johann and Annie Thea (Van Kooij) Z.; m. Susan Elizabeth Culliver, Jan. 6, 1979; 1 child, Sarah Elizabeth. BA in Econs., Macquarie U., Sydney, 1974; LLB, Sydney U., 1977, LLM, 1986. Bar: Australia 1977, High Ct. Australia 1977, N.Y. 1981. Assoc. Stephen, Jaques & Stephen, Sydney, 1977-80, Winthrop, Stimson, Putnam & Roberts, N.Y.C., 1980-81; assoc. Jaques, Stone and James, Sydney, 1982-83, ptnr., 1983—. Author: Australian Revenue Duties-Stamp Duties, 1982, Stamp Duty Aspects of Trusts Settlements and Gifts in Australia, 1984. Mem. Law Soc. New South Wales (stamp duties liaison com.), Taxation Inst. Australia, ABA. Club: Rugby (Sydney). Avocations: philately, tennis. Real property, Securities, State and local taxation. Home: 63 Bradfield Rd, West Lindfield Australia NSW2070 Office: Stephen Jaques Stone & James 30 Rockfeller Plaza Suite 1929 New York NY 10012

ZIPP, RONALD DUANE, judge; b. New Braunfels, Tex., Dec. 7, 1946; s. Nolan William and Irene Alyce (Stiba) Z.; m. Diane Martin, Aug. 16, 1969; children—Robert Andrew, Kristi Nicole; m. 2d, Paulette Boring, Jan. 14, 1983. B.B.A., Tex. A&M U., 1968; J.D. St. Mary U., San Antonio, 1971. Bar: Tex. 1971, U.S. Dist. Ct. (so. dist.) Tex. 1972, U.S. Dist. Ct. (we. dist.) Tex. 1974, U.S. Ct. Appeals (5th cir.) 1973, U.S. Supreme Ct. 1974. Assoc. Kelley, Looney, Alexander & Hiester, Edinburg, Tex., 1971-73; ptnr. Pena, McDonald, Prestia & Zipp, Edinburg, 1973-81; sole practice, New Braunfels, 1981-82; judge Comal County (Tex.) Ct.-at-Law, New Braunfels, 1983—. Bd. dirs. New Braunfels Community Services, pres. 1981-83; bd. dirs. Child Welfare, vice-chmn., 1981-82, chmn. 1982-83. Mem. ABA, Tex. State Jr. Bar (criminal law com. 1975-76), Tex. Criminal Def. Lawyers' Assn. (bd. dirs. 1976-77, mem. various coms.), Tex. Aggie Bar Assn. (charter), Comal County Bar Assn. (past pres.), Comal County A&M Club (pres.), Hidalgo County Bar Assn. (treas. 1972-75), Hidalgo County A&M Club (pres.), Phi Delta Phi. Methodist. Clubs: Elks, Kiwanis, Lions. Author local newspaper column; contbr. articles to profl. jours. Jurisprudence. Office: PO Box 667 New Braunfels TX 78130

ZIPPRICH, JOHN L., II, lawyer; b. Port Arthur, Tex., May 8, 1948; s. Sylvester Joseph and Beatrice (Hollier) Z. AB, U. Notre Dame, 1971, JD, 1972. Bar: Tex. 1972. Assoc. Butter, Binion, Rice, Cook & Knapp, Houston, 1972-81; gen. counsel Sisters of Charity of Incarnate Word, Houston, 1981—, also bd. dirs.; faculty Combined Program for Med. Tech., Houston, 1975-84. Author: Bond Manual, 1983. V.p. Neartown Assn., Houston, 1981; judge fed. and state elections, Harris County, Tex., 1974-84; mem. Harris County Dem. Exec. Com., 1974-84; counsel Harris Galveston Coastal Subsidence Dist., Harris and Galveston Counties, 1975-81; commr. Housing Authority City of Houston, 1982—; chmn. Montrose Civic Coalition, 1979-80; bd. dirs. St. Elizabeth Hosp. and Found., Houston, 1982—. Served to 2d lt. U.S. Army, 1973. Recipient commendation Harris Galveston Coastal Subsidence Dist., 1981; John Zipprich Day proclaimed by City of Houston, 1985. Mem. Am. Acad. Hosp. Attys., Nat. Health Lawyers Assn., Notre Dame Club. Roman Catholic. Health, General corporate, Religious congregations. Office: Sisters Charity Incarnate Word 6400 Lawndale Houston TX 77023

ZISSER, STEVEN LAWRENCE, lawyer; b. Bklyn., Mar. 12, 1953; s. Roy L. and Thelma (Nirenberg) Z.; m. Mindie Pam Stern, June 3, 1979; 1 child, Rachel Heather. BA in Polit. Sci. and Econs., U. Rochester, 1975; JD, Union U., 1978; LLM in Taxation, Georgetown U., 1982. Bar: N.Y. 1979, U.S. Tax Ct. 1980, U.S. Dist. Ct. (ea. dist.) N.Y. 1981, Ohio 1983. Assoc. Brent, Phillips, Dranoff & Davis, Nanuet, N.Y., 1978-79; atty. estate tax IRS, Washington, 1979-83; assoc. Schottenstein, Zox & Dunn, Columbus, Ohio, 1083—; lectr. Ohio Legal Ctr. inst., Columbus, 1985—. Author: Ohio Taxation, 1985; contbr. articles to profl. jours. Mem. ABA, Ohio Bar Assn., Columbus Bar Assn., Nat. Assn. Bond Lawyers. Democrat. Jewish. Lodge: B'nai B'rith. Estate taxation, Personal income taxation, Municipal bonds. Home: 147 N Merkle Columbus OH 43209 Office: Schottenstein Zox & Dunn 41 S High St Columbus OH 43215

ZISSU, ROGER LLOYD, lawyer; b. Oceanside, N.Y., Feb. 16, 1939; s. Leonard Zissu and Ruth (Katz) Zissu Kahn; divorced; children—Nicole, Alexandra. Student Sorbonne, U. Paris, 1958-59, Institut d'Etudes Politiques, Paris, 1958-59; A.B. summa cum laude, Dartmouth Coll., 1960; LL.B. cum laude, Harvard U., 1963. Bar: N.Y. 1963, U.S. Dist. Ct. (ea. and so. dists.) N.Y. 1965, U.S. Tax Ct. 1972, U.S. Ct. Appeals (2d cir.) 1965, U.S. Supreme Ct. 1974. Law clk. U.S. Dist. Ct. (ea. dist.) N.Y., Bklyn., 1963-65; assoc. Davis Polk & Wardwell, N.Y.C., 1965-70; corp. counsel Vornado, Inc., Garfield, N.J., 1970-73; assoc. Cowan Liebowitz & Latman, P.C., N.Y.C., 1973, ptnr., 1974—; lectr. in copyright field. Class agt. Dartmouth Coll. Alumni Fund, Hanover, N.H., 1960—. Mem. Assn. Bar City N.Y., ABA, N.Y. State Bar Assn., Copyright Soc. U.S.A. (trustee 1981, 83-86), Phi Beta Kappa, Alpha Delta Phi. Trademark and copyright, Federal civil litigation. Office: Cowan Liebowitz & Latman PC 605 Third Ave New York NY 10158

ZITO, FRANK R., lawyer, accountant; b. Haverhill, Mass., Mar. 14, 1946; s. Dan and Anne (Grieco) Z.; m. Carol S. Tandy, Sept. 19, 1976. BS, U. Mass., 1969; JD, Suffolk Law Sch., 1972; LL.M., NYU, 1973. Bar: Mass. 1972, U.S. Supreme Ct. 1982, U.S. Tax Ct. 1984. Gen. mgr. Sun Ray Baking Co., 1973-79; atty., mem. Tofias Fleishman Shapiro & Co. P.C., Cambridge, Mass., 1979—. Contbr. articles to law jour. Mem. ABA (mem. forum com. 1982-84), Mass. Bar Assn., Am. Inst. CPA's, Mass Soc. CPA's. Fidelity and

surety bond investigations, Construction, Family and matrimonial. Home: 6 Edgecliff Rd Watertown MA 02172

ZITO, JEFFREY RAYMOND, insurance broker, lawyer; b. Hartford, Conn., July 16, 1950; s. Joseph Rudolph and Adele Iva (LaVoie) Z.; m. L. Ann Gibson, Aug. 19, 1972 (div. Jan. 1986); children: Joseph R., Allison M. BS cum laude, Embry Riddle Aero. U., 1974; MA in Personnel Mgmt., Cen. Mich. U., 1977; JD, Woodrow Wilson U., Atlanta, 1980. Bar: Ga. 1980. Underwriter Assn. Aviation Underwriters, Atlanta, 1978-80; ins. broker Bayly Martin Fay, Phila., 1980-81; v.p. aviation Fred S. James & Co. of Ga., Inc., Atlanta, 1981—. Served with U.S. Army, 1970-76, Vietnam. Mem. Internat. Assn. Approved Basketball Ofcls. (constn. com. 1986—), Met. Basketball Ofcls. Assn. (bd. dirs. 1984—), Am. Legion (judge adv. 1981-83). Republican. Roman Catholic. Avocations: aviation, basketball officiating. Aviation, Insurance, General corporate. Home: 12080 Brookmill Point Alpharetta GA 30201 Office: Fred S James & Co of Ga Inc 3333 Peachtree Rd NE Suite 500 Atlanta GA 30326

ZIVE, GREGG WILLIAM, lawyer; b. Chgo., Aug. 9, 1945; s. Simon Louis and Betty Jane (Hansen) Z.; m. Franny Alice Forsman, Sept. 3, 1966; children—Joshua Carleton; m. 2d, Lu Ann Zive, June 9, 1974; 1 dau., Dana Mary. B.A. in Journalism, U. Nev., 1967; J.D. magna cum laude, U. Notre Dame, 1973. Bar: Calif. 1973, Nev. 1976, U.S. Ct. Appeals (9th cir.). Asso. Gray, Cary, Ames & Frye, San Diego, 1973-75; asso. Breen, Young, Whitehead & Hoy, Reno, 1975-76; ptnr. Hale Lane, Peek, Dennison & Howard, Reno, 1977—; lectr. bus. law U. Nev. Bd. dirs. Washoe Youth Found., Jr. Achievement. Served to 1st lt. U.S. Army, 1968-70. Mem. ABA, Calif. Bar Assn., State of Nev. Bar Assn. (chmn. publs. com., law related ed. com.), San Diego County Bar Assn., Washoe County Bar Assn., Am. Judicature Soc., Assn. Trial Lawyers Am., Nev. Trial Lawyers Assn., Soc. Profl. Journalists, U. Nev. Reno Alumni Assn. (dir., v.p. 1983—, legis. relations com., pres. 1986), Common Cause, U. N.C. Alumni Assn. (pres. 1986). Democrat. Club: University (dir., past pres.) (U. Nev., Reno, past pres.). Note and comment editor Notre Dame Lawyer, 1972-73; contbr. articles to profl. jours. Federal civil litigation, State civil litigation, Real property. Home: 1001 Sherwood Dr Reno NV 89509 Office: 50 W Liberty St Suite 650 Reno NV 89501

ZIVIN, NORMAN H., lawyer; b. Chgo., Aug. 10, 1944; s. Alfred E. and Irene (Scher) Z.; m. Lynn F., Dec. 27, 1967; children—Allison, Stephen, Michael. E.M., Colo. Sch. Mines, 1965; J.D. cum laude, Columbia U., 1968. Bar: N.Y. 1968, Ill. 1970, U.S. Supreme Ct. 1975. Assoc. Cooper, Dunham, Griffin & Moran, N.Y.C., 1968-70, 71-76, ptnr., 1976—. Mem. Bd. Ethics New Castle (N.Y.), 1974-79. Mem. ABA, Assn. Bar City N.Y., Am. Patent Law Assn., N.Y. Patent Law Assn., U.S. Trademark Assn., Copyright Soc., AIME. Clubs: Town of New Castle (pres. 1982-84); Birchwood (Chappaqua, N.Y.). Trademark and copyright, Patent, Federal civil litigation. Home: 3 Valley Ln Chappaqua NY 10514 Office: Cooper Dunham Griffin & Moran 30 Rockefeller Pl New York NY 10112

ZLATOS, STEVE EDWARD, lawyer; b. Chgo., Oct. 25, 1951; s. William Frank and Hope (McKesson) Z.; m. Elizabeth Ann Miller, May 9, 1981; 1child, Megan Elizabeth. BS in Engring., Purdue U., 1973; postgrad., Gonzaga U., 1974-75; JD, Indiana U., 1977. Bar: Ind. 1977, U.S. Dist. Ct. (so. dist.) Ind. 1977, U.S. Patent Office, U.S. Ct. Appeals 1986. Dep. atty. State of Ind., Indpls., 1977-81; product engr. Sheller-Globe Corp., Union City, Ind., 1973-74; ptnr. Woodard, Emhardt, Naughton, Moriarty & McNett, Indpls., 1981—. Mem. ABA, Assn. Trial Lawyers Am., Ind. Bar Assn., Indpls. Bar Assn., Alpha Kappa Lambda (alumni bd.). Roman Catholic. Club: Indpls. Athletic. Avocations: tennis, squash, golf. Patent, Trademark and copyright. Office: Woodard Weikart et al One Indiana Sq #2600 Indianapolis IN 46204

ZLOCH, WILLIAM J., federal judge; b. 1944. BA, U. Notre Dame, 1966, JD, 1974. Sole practice Saunders, Curtis, Ginestra & Core, Ft. Lauderdale, Fla., 1974-75, Kelley, Tompkins, Frazier & Kelley, Ft. Lauderdale, 1975-81, Patterson & Maloney, Ft. Lauderdale, 1981-85; judge U.S. Dist. Ct. (so. dist.) Fla., Ft. Lauderdale, 1985—; pro bono atty. Broward Lawyers Care, Ft. Lauderdale, 1983-85. Served to lt. USN, 1966-69. Mem. ABA, Fla. Bar Assn. (unauthorized practice of law com., health law com.) Acad. Fla. Trial Lawyers, Broward County Bar Assn. (fee arbitration com., legis. com., exec. com., Pres.'s award 1982-84), Atty.'s Title Ins. Fund. Office: 202 B US Courthouse 299 E Broward Blvd Fort Lauderdale FL 33301 *

ZLOTNICK, NORMAN LEE, lawyer; b. Bklyn., Nov. 2, 1947; s. Harry S. and Frances Zlotnick; m. JoAnn L. Zlotnick, Nov. 26, 1976. B.A. in History, CCNY, 1969; J.D., Rutgers U., 1972. Bar: N.J. 1972, U.S. Dist. Ct. N.J. 1972, U.S. Ct. Appeals (3d cir.), 1974, U.S. Supreme Ct. 1976. Assoc. Perskie & Callinan, 1972-77; ptnr. Perskie, Bloom & Zlotnick, P.A., 1977-79, Bloom & Zlotnick, 1979-82, Blatt, Mairone, Biel, Zlotnick, Feinberg & Griffith, P.A., Atlantic City, 1982—. Mem. ABA, N.J. Bar Assn., Cape May County Bar Assn., Atlantic County Bar Assn., Trial Attys. N.J., Assn. Trial Lawyers Am. Jewish. Contbr. Rutgers-Camden Law Jour. Federal civil litigation, Contracts commercial, Local government. Office: 3201 Atlantic Ave Atlantic City NJ 08401

ZOBEL, RYA W., judge; b. Germany, Dec. 18, 1931. A.B., Radcliffe Coll., 1953; LL.B., Harvard U., 1956. Bar: Mass. bar 1956, U.S. Dist. Ct., Mass., 1956, U.S. Ct. Appeals (1st cir.) 1967. Mem. Hill & Barlow, Boston, 1967-73; mem. Goodwin, Procter & Hoar, Boston, 1973-79; U.S. dist. judge of Mass. Boston, 1979—. Mem. ABA, Boston Bar Assn., Am. Bar Found., Mass. Bar Assn., Am. Law Inst. Jurisprudence. Office: US Dist Ct McCormack Post Office & Courthouse Bldg Boston MA 02109

ZOBELL, KARL, lawyer; b. La Jolla, Calif., Jan. 9, 1932; s. Claude E. and Margaret (Harding) ZoB.; m. Barbara Arth, Nov. 22, 1968; children: Bonnie, Elizabeth, Karen, Claude, Mary. Student, Utah State U., 1949-51, Columbia U., 1951-52; AB, Columbia U., 1953, student of law, 1952-54; JD, Stanford U., 1958. Bar: Calif., 1959. Assoc., lawyer Gray, Cary, Ames and Frye, San Diego, 1959-64, ptnr., lawyer, 1964—; bd. dirs. La Jolla (Calif.) Bank and Trust Co. Trustee La Jolla Town Council, 1962—, chmn. bd. dirs., 1967-68, pres. 1976-77, 80-81, v.p., 1986—; trustee La Jollans Inc., 1974-77, founder, 1964, 78-80, pres. 1965-68, 73-76, 78-89; mem. charter rev. com. City San Diego, 1968-73; trustee La Jolla Mus. Art, 1964-72, pres. 1967-70, bd. dirs Scripps Meml. Hosp. Found., 1980-84, bd. overseers, Stanford Law Sch., 1977-80, U. Calif., San Diego, 1974-76. Served to lt. USCG, 1954-57. Fellow Am. Coll. Probate Counsel; mem. ABA, Calif. Bar. Republican. Clubs: La Jolla Beach and Volleyball (pres. 1982—), La Jolla Beach and Tennis. Real property, Estate taxation, Estate planning. Home: 1555 Coast Walk PO Box 1 La Jolla CA 92037 Office: Gray Cary Ames & Frye 1200 Prospect St La Jolla CA 92037

ZOBRIST, KARL, lawyer; b. Evanston, Ill., Nov. 2, 1949; s. Benedict Karl and Donna Mae (Anderson) Z.; m. Elizabeth Jane Roush, July 9, 1983; 1 child, Andrew Karl. AB, Augustana Coll., Rock Island, Ill., 1971; JD, U. Iowa, 1974. Bar: Iowa 1974, U.S. Ct. Mil. Appeals 1975, Mo. 1977, U.S. Dist. Ct. (we. dist.) Mo. 1980, U.S. Ct. Appeals (8th cir.) 1982. Assoc. Blackwell, Sanders, Matheny, Weary & Lombardi, Kansas City, Mo., 1977-82, ptnr., 1982—; lectr. in law U. Kansas Law Sch., Lawrence, 1982—. Pres. Kansas City Civic Orch., 1983—; mem. exec. com., trustee Conservatory of Music, U. Mo. Kansas City, 1985—; bd. dirs. Com. for County Progress, Kansas City, 1985—, Harry S. Truman Good Neighbor Award Found., 1986—. Served to lt. USN, 1974-77. Mem. ABA (product liability com., litigation sect.), Mo. Bar Assn., Kansas City Met. Bar Assn., Lawyers Alliance for Nuclear Arms Control. Democrat. Mem. United Ch. Christ. Federal civil litigation, Labor, Military. Home: 36 W Winthrope Rd Kansas City MO 64113 Office: Blackwell Sanders Matheny et al 2300 Main Suite 1100 Kansas City MO 64108

ZOGHBY, GUY ANTHONY, lawyer; b. Mobile, Ala., Sept. 30, 1934; s. Herbert Michael and Laureice (Haik) Z.; m. Verna Madelyn Antoine, Mar. 2, 1957 (dissolved); children: Guy Anthony, Madelyn A., Gregory M.; m. Judy-ann Eckberg, Jan. 2, 1976. AB in English, Spring Hill Coll., 1955; JD, U. Cin., 1963; cert., U.S. Army JAG Sch., 1964. Bar: Ohio 1963, Ala. 1965, Calif. 1978. Commd. 2d lt. U.S. Army, 1955, advanced through grades to capt., 1963, various assignments, 1955-63; dep. staff JAG 11th Air Assault Div., Ft. Benning, Ga., 1963-64, 1st Cav. Div., 1964-65; atty. office of v.p. and gen. counsel IBM, Armonk, N.Y., 1965-67, staff atty., 1967-69, sr. atty., 1969-71, div. counsel, 1977-80, mng. atty., 1980-83, group counsel, 1983—; regional counsel IBM, Bethesda, Md., 1972-73; corp. staff counsel IBM, London, 1973-77; adj. faculty Corp. Counsel Inst., Northwestern U.; lectr. profl. seminars. Editor U. Cin. Law Rev., 1962-63. Active Westchester Assn. Retarded Citizens, 1981—; mem. adv. council Pace U. Sch. Law; bd. visitors U. Cin. Coll. Law, 1986. Decorated Commendation medal with one oak leaf cluster; recipient Lawrence Maxwell prize U. Cin. Mem. ABA, Am. Corp. Counsel Assn. (dir., exec. com. 1982-86, chmn. 1987—), Order of Coif. Roman Catholic. Antitrust, General corporate. Office: IBM Old Orchard Rd Armonk NY 10504

ZOLA, MICHAEL S., lawyer; b. Madison, Wis., Dec. 15, 1942; s. Emanuel and Harriet (Sher) Z.; 1 son, Emanuel David. B.S. cum laude, U. Wis., 1964; LL.B., Columbia U., 1967. Bar: D.C. 1968, Wis. 1968, Calif. 1969, Hawaii 1981, U.S. Dist. Ct. Hawaii 1981, U.S. Dist. Ct. (we. dist.) Wis. 1968, U.S. Dist. Ct. (no. dist.) Calif. 1969, U.S. Ct. Appeals (9th cir.) 1969. Law clk. to judge U.S. Dist. Ct. (we. dist.) Wis., 1967-68; mng. atty. San Francisco Neighborhood Legal Assistance Found., San Francisco, 1968-70; sole practice, Calistoga, Calif., 1970-73; directing atty. Mendocino Legal Services, Ukiah, Calif., 1973-76; state chief of legal services State of Calif., Sacramento, 1976-78, dep. state pub. defender, State of Calif., 1978-79; sole practice, Kailua-Kona, Hawaii, 1980—. Chmn. Mendocino County Dem. Cen. Com., Ukiah, 1975-76; pres. Sacramento Waldorf Sch. Parent Council, Sacramento, 1976-77; v.p. Kailua Village Assn., 1983-84. Reginald Heber Smith Poverty Law fellowship, 1968-70. Mem. Nat. Assn. Criminal Def. Lawyers, Legal Aid Soc. Hawaii (bd. dirs.). Criminal, General practice. Office: 223 Kona Inn Village 75-5744 Alii Dr Kailua-Kona HI 96740

ZOLKE, SCOTT BRYAN, lawyer; b. Chgo., Feb. 21, 1954; s. Sy and Sarah (Burroughs) Z.; m. Stacy L., Beddingfield, Aug. 23, 1986. BS in Indsl. Mgt., Ga. Inst. Tech., 1976; JD, U. Miami, 1979. Bar: Ill. 1980, U.S. Dist. Ct. (no. dist.) Ill. 1980, U.S. Ct. Appeals (7th cir.) 1980, U.S. Ct. Appeals (11th cir.) 1983, U.S. Dist. Ct. (no. dist.) Ga. 1984, U.S. Ct. Appeals (9th cir.) 1984, U.S. Supreme Ct. 1985. Assoc. Belmonte, Kagan, Hibbler & DePalma, Chgo., 1979-82; counsel Ga. Inst. Tech. Athletic Assn., Atlanta, 1982-86, counsel, asst. dir. athletics, 1986—; lectr. on drugs and agts. Nat. Col. Athletic Assn., 1984—. Mem. ABA (patent copyright, trademark section, forum com. sports and entertainment sect.), Assn. Trial Lawyers Am., Ill. Bar Assn., Ga. Bar Assn. Presbyterian. Entertainment, State civil litigation, Federal civil litigation. Office: Ga Inst Tech Athletic Assn 150 3d St NW Atlanta GA 30332

ZOLL, DAVID WESLEY, lawyer; b. Findlay, Ohio, Jan. 9, 1952; s. David Joy Jr. and Lois Nan (Good) Z.; m. Myra Sue Gerber, May 13, 1973; children: Benjamin David, Sarah Joy. MusB, U. Cin., 1974; JD, U. Toledo, 1976. Bar: Ohio 1977, U.S. Dist. Ct. (no. dist.) Ohio 1977, U.S. Tax Ct. 1979, U.S. Dist. Ct. (no. dist.) Mich. 1981, U.S. Ct. Appeals (6th cir.) 1982, U.S. Dist. Ct. (no. dist.) Ind. 1985, U.S. Ct. Appeals (7th cir.) 1986. Ptnr. Gallon, Kalniz & Iorio Co., LPA, Toledo, 1976-84, 1984—. v.p., bd. dirs. Beach House, Toledo, 1980—; pres., bd. deacons Christ Presbyn. Ch., Toledo, 1984-85. Performance scholarship Coll. Conservatory Music, U. Cin., 1970-74. Mem. Assn. Trial Lawyers Am., Ohio Acad. Trial Lawyers, Toledo Bar Assn. Democrat. Avocations: raquetball, basketball, music. State civil litigation, Pension, profit-sharing, and employee benefits, Personal injury. Home: 6800 Kristi Lynne Ln Toledo OH 43617 Office: Gallon Kalniz & Iorio LPA PO Box 7417 Toledo OH 43615

ZOLL, JEFFERY MARK, lawyer; b. Evergreen Park, Ill., Sept. 25, 1954; s. Frank Earl and Earline Ruth (Abadie) Z. AB cum laude, U. Ill., 1975, JD, 1978. Bar: Ill. 1978; CPA, Ill. Tax mgr. Touche Ross and Co., Chgo., 1978-85, Arthur Andersen and Co., Chgo., 1985—. Mem. ABA, Chgo. Bar Assn., Am. Inst. CPA's, Phi Beta Kappa. Personal income taxation, Pension, profit-sharing, and employee benefits, Corporate taxation. Office: Arthur Andersen and Co 33 W Monroe Chicago IL 60603

ZOLLINGER, THOMAS TENNANT, lawyer; b. Louisville, Feb. 13, 1945; s. Robert William and Betty Beatrice (Benkert) Z.; m. Sandra Renee File, Dec. 26, 1976 (div. Aug. 1984). B.S., Murray State U., 1969; J.D., U. Wyo., 1972. Bar: Wyo. 1972, U.S. Dist. Ct. Wyo. 1972, U.S. Ct. Appeals (10th cir.) 1979. Sole practice, Lander, Wyo., 1972-74, Rock Springs, Wyo., 1975—; prosecuting atty. Sweetwater County, 1987—; commr. Wyo. State Bar, Cheyenne, 1983—. Chmn., Sweetwater County central com. Republican party, 1975-76, state committeeman, 1977—; bd. dirs. S.W. Wyo. Alcohol Rehab. Assn., 1981. Mem. Assn. Trial Lawyers Am., ABA, Am. Judicature Soc. Methodist. Lodges: Elks, Eagles. Criminal, Personal injury, Civil rights. Home: 817 Valley Rock Springs WY 82901 Office: PO Box 2064 Rock Springs WY 82901

ZOLOT, NORMAN, lawyer; b. New Haven, Aug. 20, 1920; s. Jacob Zolot and Mamie Lehrer; m. Marilyn McKenna, June 6, 1934. BS, Yale U., 1941, JD, 1947. Bar: Conn. 1947, U.S. Dist. Ct. Conn. 1949, U.S. Supreme Ct. 1958, U.S. Ct. Appeals (2d cir.) 1964. Counsel AFL-CIO, Hamden, Conn., 1947—, Community Health Ctr. Plan, New Haven, 1961—; asst. prosecutor State of Conn., New Haven, 1961-63. Served to sgt. USAF, 1943-46. Mem. ABA, Conn. Bar Assn., New Haven County Bar Assn., Am. Trial Lawyers Assn. Club: Graduates (New Haven). Labor. Office: 9 Washington Ave Hamden CT 06510

ZOOK, DAVID LLOYD, lawyer; b. Curryville, Pa., Aug. 25, 1922; s. Simon F. and Mary Grace (Brown) Z.; m. Dorothy Jean Dunkle, July 15, 1944; children—Ann Louise, James David, Susan Lynn. B.A., Juniata Coll., 1947, LL.B., Dickinson Sch. Law, 1948, J.D., 1968. Bar: Pa., 1949, Fla., 1963, U.S. Supreme Ct., 1971. Sole practice, Johnstown, Pa., 1949-54; counsel Old Republic Ins. Co., Greensburg, Pa., 1956-59; sec. Allegheny Nat. Life Ins. Co., Erie, Pa., 1959-60; ptnr. Welbaum, Zook, Jones & Williams (and predecessor firms), Miami and Orlando, Fla., from 1964, now of counsel. Mem. ABA (vice chmn. fidelity and surety law com., torts and ins. practice sect. 1975-83), Internat. Assn. Ins. Counsel, Fla. Bar, Pa. Bar Assn. Served with AUS, 1943-46. Clubs: Masons. Real property, Insurance, Probate. Office: 1091 W Morse Blvd Winter Park FL 32789

ZORIE, STEPHANIE MARIE, lawyer; b. Walla Walla, Wash., Mar. 18, 1951; d. Albert Robert and L. Ruth (Land) Z.; m. Francis Benedict Buda, Apr. 18, 1981 (div. 1985). BA, U. Fla., 1974, JD, 1978. Bar: U.S. Dist. Ct. (so. and mid. dists.) Fla. 1979, U.S. Ct. Appeals (5th cir.) 1979, U.S. Tax Ct. 1980, U.S. Ct. Customs and Patent Appeals 1980, U.S. Customs Ct. 1980, U.S. Ct. Mil. Appeals 1980, U.S. Ct. Claims 1981, U.S. Ct. Internat. Trade 1981, U.S. Ct. Appeals (11th cir.) 1981, U.S. Ct. Appeals (fed. cir.) 1982. Assoc. Richard Hardwich, Coral Gables, Fla., 1978-79, Brown, Terrell & Hogan P.A., Jacksonville, Fla., 1979-80, Dorsey, Arnold & Nichols, Jacksonville, 1980-81; sole practice Jacksonville, 1981-84; ptnr. Blakeley & Zorie P.A., Orlando, Fla., 1985-86; sole practice Orlando, 1986—. Recipient Rep. Claude Pepper award, 1978. Mem. ABA, Orange County Bar Assn., Assn. Trial Lawyers Am., John Marxhall Bar Assn., Spanish-Am. Law Students Assn., Exec. Assn. Gtr. Orlando, Phi Alpha Delta (local sec.-treas. 1978-79). Avocations: water sports, needlework, cooking. Family and matrimonial, Personal injury, State civil litigation. Office: PO Box 1468 Orlando FL 32801

ZOSS, PAUL ARTHUR, lawyer; b. South Bend, Ind., June 8, 1947; s. Abraham and Mildred Irene (Warner) Z.; m. Jeannette Rouse Powers, July 5, 1969 (div. Dec. 1982); children: Nathan Jerome, Amy Mae, Nicholas Adam, Benjamin Owen. BS, Ind. U., 1969; JD with honors, U. Tex., 1972. Bar: Tex. 1972, D.C. 1973, U.S. Dist. Ct. (no. and so. dists.) Iowa 1974, Iowa 1975, U.S. Ct. Appeals (8th cir.) 1975. Trial atty. U.S. Dept. Justice, Washington, 1972-74; asst. U.S. atty. Des Moines, 1974-77, U.S. atty., 1977; assoc. Dull, Keith & Beaver, Ottumwa, Iowa, 1977-78; ptnr. Myers, Knox & Hart, Des Moines, 1978-84; ptnr., owner Adams, Howe & Zoss P.C., Des Moines, 1984—. Mem. ABA, Iowa Bar Assn., Polk County Bar Assn., Order of Coif. Club: Embassy (Des Moines). Banking, Federal civil litigation, State civil litigation. Office: Adams Howe & Zoss PC 620 Hubbell Bldg Des Moines IA 50309

ZOTALEY, BYRON L., lawyer; b. Mpls., Mar. 18, 1944; s. Leo John and Tula (Koupis) Z.; m. Theresa L., Sept. 7, 1969; children: Nicole, Jason, Krisanthy,. BA in Psychology, U. Minn., 1966; MA, Coll. St. Thomas, St. Paul, 1968; JD, William Mitchell Coll. of Law, 1970. Bar: Minn. 1970, U.S. Dist. Ct. Minn. 1971, U.S. Ct. Appeals (8th cir.) 1972, U.S. Supreme Ct. 1976. Ptnr., v.p. LeVander, Zotaley, Vander Linden & Rydland, Mpls., 1970—; arbitrator Minn. Supreme Ct., St. Paul, 1975—. Mem. ABA, Fed. Bar Assn., Minn. Bar Assn., Hennepin County Bar Assn., Am. Judicature Soc., Assn. Trial Lawyers Am., Minn. Trial Lawyers Assn. (chmn. Amicus Curiae com. 1980—, bd. govs. 1983—). State civil litigation, Contracts commercial, General corporate. Home: 5504 Parkwood Ln Edina MN 55436 Office: LeVander Zotaley Vander Linden & Rydland 720 Northstar Ctr Minneapolis MN 55402

ZOUHARY, KATHLEEN MAHER, lawyer; b. Greenville, Ohio, June 28, 1951; d. Thomas Richard and Mary (Brown) Maher; b. Jack Zouhary, Oct. 21, 1978; children—Kathleen Marie, Alexis Jacqueline. B.A. in Polit. Sci. cum laude, Miami U., Oxford, Ohio, 1973; J.D. cum laude, U. Notre Dame, 1976. Bar: Ohio 1976. Assoc., Fuller & Henry, Toledo, 1976-81, ptnr., 1981-85; v.p., gen. counsel St. Luke's Hosp., Maumee, Ohio, 1985—. Gen. chmn. Tribute to Women and Industry, Toledo, 1984, honoree, 1982; bd. dirs. Women Involved in Toledo, 1981-83; trustee Toledo Legal Aid Soc., 1977—. Mem. Am. Soc. Hosp. Attys., ABA, Ohio Bar Assn., Toledo Bar Assn., Miami Presidents Club, St. Luke's Hosp. Pacesetter Club, Phi Beta Kappa. Health. Office: St Luke's Hosp 5901 Monclava Rd Maumee OH 43537

ZOUKIS, STEPHEN JAMES, lawyer; b. Montpelier, Vt., July 2, 1949; s. Christo S. and Alice Rose (McCormish) Z.; m. Suzan Hardy Moore, Jan. 30, 1971; children—Abigail Moriah, Christopher Hardy. B.S. in M.E. with honors, U. Va., 1971; J.D., Columbia U., 1974. Bar: Ga. 1974. Assoc. atty. Powell, Goldstein, Frazer & Murphy, Atlanta, 1974-76; assoc. atty. Hansell, Post, Brandon & Dorsey, Atlanta, 1976-79; ptnr. Wildman, Harrold, Allen, Dixon & Branch, Atlanta, 1979—. Bd. dirs. Lullwater Estate Homeowners Assn., Atlanta, 1986—. Mem. ABA, Atlanta Bar Assn. (bd. dirs. real estate sect. 1984), Ga. Bar Assn., Atlanta C. of C. (mgmt. assistance task force, small bus. group). Democrat. Episcopalian. Club: Ansley Golf. Avocations: fly fishing, tennis. Real property, Private international. Home: 34 Lullwater Estate Rd NE Atlanta GA 30307 Office: Wildman Harrold Allen Dixon & Branch Two Midtown Plaza 15th Floor 1360 Peachtree St NE Atlanta GA 30309-3209

ZOX, BENJAMIN LOUIS, lawyer; b. Des Moines, May 18, 1937; s. Joseph Frankel and Leah (Kiefer) Z.; m. Julie Pailet, June 27, 1959; children: Holly, Melissa, William. AB, Williams Coll., 1959; JD, Ohio State U., 1962. Bar: Ohio 1962. Exec. v.p. Schottenstein, Zox & Dunn Co. LPA, Columbus, Ohio, 1962—. Vice-chair, trustee United Way of Franklin County, Columbus, 1981—; chmn., trustee St. Ann's Hosp. Columbus Inc., Columbus, 1986—. Fellow Columbus Bar Assn. (pres. 1986-87), Ohio Bar Assn.; mem. ABA. Clubs: Winding Hollow Country (Columbus), Capital, Athletic, Univ., Boca Lago Country. General corporate, Health, Real property. Home: 44 S Parkview Columbus OH 43209 Office: 41 S High St Columbus OH 43215

ZSCHAU, JULIUS JAMES, lawyer; b. Peoria, Ill., Apr. 1, 1940; s. Raymond Johann Ernst and Rosamond Lillian (Malicoat) Z.; m. Leila Joan Krueger, Aug. 7, 1971; children—Kristen Elisabeth, Kimberly Erna, Kira Jamie, Karla Johanna. B.S., U. Ill., Champaign, 1964, J.D., 1966; LL.M., John Marshall Law Sch., 1978. Bar: Ill. 1966, Fla. 1975. Atty., Ill. Central Gulf R.R. Co., Chgo., 1966-68; assoc. Coin & Sheerin, Chgo., 1968-70, Snyder, Clarke, Dalziel, Holmquist & Johnson, Waukegan, Ill., 1970-72; csl. Ill. Center Corp., Chgo., 1972-74; v.p., gen. csl., sec. Am. Agronomics Corp., Tampa, Fla., 1974-76; pres. Sorota & Zschau, Clearwater, Fla., 1976—; dir. Pinellas Review, Inc., Attys. Title Services, Inc.; chmn. com. on land trusts, exec. com. real property sect., mem. grievance com. Fla. Bar, chair leadership conf. 1987. Bd. dirs. Fla. Gulf Coast Symphony; mem. Pinellas County Exec. Com.; bd. dirs. Attys. Title Ins. Fund; mem. bd. St. Mark Christian Sch. Served to capt. USNR, 1962-64. Mem. ABA (vice chmn. condo com., editor newsletter, co-chmn. com. on role of lawyers in real estate transactions), Ill. Bar Assn., Chgo. Bar Assn., Clearwater Bar Assn. (past pres.), Fla. Council Bar Pres. (bd. dirs.), Clearwater C. of C. (bd. govs., exec. com.). Republican. Lutheran. Clubs: Harborview, Countryside Country (Clearwater, Fla.); Masons, Scottish Rite, Shriners. Editor Res Ipsa Loquitur, 1982-84. Real property, General corporate, Probate. Home: 1910 Saddlehill Rd N Dunedin FL 33528

ZUBEL, ERIC LOUIS, lawyer; b. Detroit, Nov. 14, 1943; s. Stanley and Virginia (Poplawski) Z.; m. Catherine Hodges, Oct. 6, 1973; children—Conrad, Roland, Kristin. A.B., U. Mich., 1966; J.D., Golden Gate U., 1971. Bar: Nev. 1973, U.S. Dist. Ct. Nev. 1973, U.S. Ct. Appeals (9th cir.) 1973, U.S. Supreme Ct. 1976. Law clk. to 8th Jud. Ct., Las Vegas, Nev., 1971-73; sole practice, Las Vegas, 1973—. Mem. Nev. Trial Lawyers (bd. govs. 1981-83), Am. Trial Lawyers. Federal civil litigation, State civil litigation, Civil rights. Home: 2825 Santa Margarita Las Vegas NV 89102 Office: 101 Convention Ctr Dr Las Vegas NV 89109

ZUCKER, DAVID CLARK, lawyer, army officer; b. St. Louis, July 29, 1946; s. Clark S. and Georgia L. (Sellers) Z.; m. Karin Wells Waugh, July 10, 1971 (div. Sept. 1985); 1 child, William Waugh; m. Charlotte Denton, Feb. 8, 1986. B.A., U. Mo., 1968, J.D., 1971; postgrad. Judge Advocate Gen.'s Sch., Charlottesville, Va., 1977-78, Armed Forces Staff Coll., 1981-82. Bar: Mo. 1971, U.S. Ct. Mil. Appeals 1971, U.S. Ct. Appeals (fed. cir.) 1983, U.S. Supreme Ct, 1974. Commd. 2d lt. U.S. Army, 1968, advanced through grades to lt. col., 1983; chief mil. justice, Ft. Leavenworth, Kans., 1971-74; trial atty. Office of Army Chief Trial Atty., Falls Church, Va., 1974-77; dep. chief adminstrv. law Hdqrs. U.S. Army Europe, Heidelberg, W. Ger., 1978-80, internat. logistics atty. contract law, U.S. Army, Heidelberg, Fed. Rep. of Germany, 1980-81; litigation atty. Office of Judge Advocate Gen., Washington, 1982; chief trial team III, Office of Chief Trial Atty. Hdqrs. Dept. Army, Falls Church, 1982-86; chief, contract law div., Gilbert A. Cuneo prof. govt. contract law, U.S. Army JAG Sch., Charlottesville, Va., 1986—. Mem. ABA, Am. Trial Lawyers Assn., Assn. U.S. Army, Judge Advocates Assn. (bd. dirs. 1983—), Mo. Bar Assn., Phi Alpha Delta (chpt. vice justice 1969-70). Government contracts and claims, Military, Federal civil litigation. Home: 2116 Morris Rd Charlottesville VA 22903 Office: JAG Sch Contract Law Div 600 Massie Rd Charlottesville VA 22903

ZUCKER, HOWARD, lawyer; b. N.Y.C., June 21, 1952; s. Morris Milton and Sarah Shirley (Spector) Z.; m. Lynn Carol Bierschenk; children: Lauren Heather; Erica Rachael. Student, London Sch. Econs., 1973; BS in Econs. summa cum laude, U. Pa., 1973, JD, 1977. Bar: N.Y. 1978. Ptnr. Hawkins, Delafield & Wood, N.Y.C., 1977—. Author: ABC's of Housing Bonds, 1985. Mem. Moot Ct. Bd. U. Pa., Phila., 1977. Mem. ABA (com. tax. exempt obligations 1983—), N.Y. State Bar Assn., Nat. Assn. Bond Lawyer, Omicron Delta Epsilon. Municipal bonds, State and local taxation, Securities. Office: Hawkins Delafield & Wood 67 Wall St New York NY 10005

ZUCKERMAN, ALAN RANDY, lawyer; b. L.I., N.Y., Aug. 1, 1951; s. Walter and Dorothy Z.; m. Karen J. Tourtillotte, June 22, 1981. BA, U. So. Calif., 1973; JD, Loyola U., Los Angeles, 1977. Bar: Calif. 1977, U.S. Dist. Ct. (cen. dist.) Calif. 1978, U.S. Ct. Appeals (9th cir.) 1978, U.S. Supreme Ct. 1984. Assoc. Frederick J. Lawson, Sherman Oaks, Calif., 1977-79; assoc. Hagenbaugh & Murphy, Los Angeles, 1979-83, ptnr., 1984—. Mem. ABA, Los Angeles County Bar Assn. (litigation sect., tort and ins. practice sect), Def. Research Inst., Supreme Ct. Hist. Soc., So. Calif. Def. Counsel. Insurance, Federal civil litigation, State civil litigation. Office: Hagenbaugh & Murphy 3701 Wilshire Blvd Suite 400 Los Angeles CA 90010

ZUCKERMAN, MITCHELL, art auction firm executive, lawyer; b. N.Y.C., Apr. 13, 1946; s. Morton and Minna (Miller) Z.; m. Joanne Zuckerman, May 21, 1973; children—Robert, Suzanne. B.A., U. Rochester, 1968; M.A., Harvard U., 1971; J.D., Columbia U., 1974. Assoc. Weil Gotshal & Manges, N.Y.C., 1974-79; sr. v.p., dir. Sotheby's Inc., N.Y.C., 1979—; sr. v.p. corp. devel. Sotheby's Holdings, Inc., 1986—. Avocation: running. Contracts commercial, General corporate, Securities. Office: Sotheby's Inc 1334 York Ave New York NY 10021

ZUCKERMAN, PAUL HERBERT, lawyer; b. Bklyn., Mar. 7, 1935; s. Max B. and Minnie (Mendelson) Z.; m. Sara Shiffman, Aug. 25, 1963; children—David Isaac, Daniel Mark. B.S. in Econs., Wharton Sch., U. Pa., 1957; M.B.A. in Corp. Fin., NYU, 1964; J.D., Bklyn. Law Sch., 1967. Bar: N.Y. 1968, U.S. Dist. Ct. (so. and ea. dists.) N.Y. 1975, U.S. Tax Ct. 1977, U.S. Ct. Appeals (2d cir.) 1972, U.S. Supreme Ct. 1973. Security analyst U.S. Trust Co., N.Y.C., 1962-66; sr. security analyst CNA Mgmt. Research Corp., N.Y.C., 1966-71, mgr. dept. investment research, 1971-73; sole practice, N.Y.C., 1973—; mem. faculty New Sch. for Social Research, N.Y.C., 1983—; speaker and writer in field; radio, TV appearances; publisher Tax Planning and Estate Planning Concepts for Individuals and Corporations newsletter. Served to lt. (j.g.) USN, 1957-60. Mem. Assn. Bar City N.Y. Club: Wharton Bus. Sch. (N.Y.C.). Estate planning, Corporate taxation, Estate taxation. Office: 19 W 44th St Suite 1616 New York NY 10036

ZUCKERMAN, RICHARD ENGLE, lawyer, educator; b. Yonkers, N.Y., Aug. 2, 1945; s. Julius and Roslyn (Ehrlich) Z.; m. Denise Ellen Spoon, July 14, 1968; children: Julie Ann, Lindsay Beth. BA, U. Mich., 1967; JD cum laude, Southwestern U., 1974; LLM in Taxation, Wayne State U., 1979. Bar: Calif. 1974, U.S. Dist. Ct. (ea. dist.) Mich. 1977, U.S. Ct. Appeals (6th cir.) 1977, Mich. 1980, U.S. Ct. Appeals (9th cir.) 1982, U.S. Supreme Ct. 1985, Nev. 1986. Spl. atty. organized crime and racketeering sect. U.S. Dept. Justice, Detroit, 1974-77; sr. ptnr. Raymond, Rupp, Wienberg, Stone & Zuckerman, P.C., Troy, Mich., 1977—; adj. prof. Detroit Coll. Law, 1978—. Served to lt. USN, 1967-71, Vietnam. Mem. ABA (grand jury com. criminal justice sect.), Fed. Bar Assn. (chmn. criminal law sect. Detroit chpt. 1985—, bd. dirs. Detroit chpt. 1985—). Republican. Jewish. Clubs: Knollwood Country (West Bloomfield, Mich.); Standard (Detroit). Criminal, Federal civil litigation. Office: Raymond Rupp Wienberg Stone & Zuckerman PC 755 W Big Beaver Rd Suite 1900 Troy MI 48084

ZUGER, WILLIAM PETER, lawyer; b. Bismarck, N.D., Sept. 16, 1946; s. John A. and Irene (Kolb) Z.; m. Mary Haunson, June 3, 1977; 2 sons, Peter William, Jack Everett. B.A., U. Minn., 1969, J.D., 1972. Bar: N.D. 1972, U.S. Dist. Ct. N.D. 1972, U.S. Ct. Appeals (8th cir.) 1972, Minn. 1985. Ptnr. Zuger & Bucklin, Bismarck, 1972-84, sr. ptnr. Zuger Zuger Kapsner & Blazer, 1984—; lectr. various med. groups, nursing schs., physician groups. Mem. ABA (nat. affiliate rep. young lawyers sect. 1975-76), N.D. Bar Assn. (chmn. law office mgmt. and procedures com. 1974-77, young lawyers sect. 1975-76, sec.-treas. 1975-76), Burleigh County Bar Assn., 4th Dist. Bar Assn. (v.p. 1976). Contbr. articles to legal jours. State civil litigation, Federal civil litigation, Personal injury. Home: 604 West Blvd Bismarck ND 58501 Office: 2800 N Washington St Bismarck ND 58502

ZUKERMAN, MICHAEL, lawyer; b. Bklyn., Oct. 3, 1940; s. Charles Morris and Gertrude Ethel Z.; m. Claire J. Goldsmith, June 25, 1961 (div. 1986); children—Steven, Amy; m. Elaine DeMasi, Nov. 21, 1986. BBA, U. Fla., 1961; LLB, St. John's U., 1964; LLM, NYU, 1966. Bar: N.Y. 1965. Credit analyst, loan officer Franklin Nat. Bank, 1964-66; assoc. Jaffin, Schneider, Kimmel & Galpeer, N.Y.C., 1966-67; ptnr. Zukerman, Licht & Friedman, and predecessors, N.Y.C., 1967-79; ptnr. Baskin & Sears, P.C., N.Y.C., 1979-85, Graubard, Moskowitz, Dannett, Horowitz & Mollen, 1985-86, Gersten, Savage, Kaplowitz & Zukerman, 1986—; bd. dirs. ACTV, Dayton Mgmt. Corp.; exec. v.p. and mng. dir. Brookhill Group, 1986—. Active Temple Beth Torah, Melville, N.Y., 1972-80, Jewish Communal Planning Council, 1982-85; trustee Suffolk YM-YWHA, 1980-85, treas., 1983-85. Mem. ABA. Real property, General corporate. Office: 10 E 53d St New York NY 10022

ZUKOWSKI, MARK DANIEL, lawyer; b. Grosse Pointe, Mich., June 22, 1957; s. Melvin T. and Eleanore (Paschke) Z.; m. Raeann Palumbo, June 9, 1984; 1 child, Kristen Ann. BS in Acctg., Wayne State U., 1978; JD, U. Ariz., 1980. Bar: Ariz. 1981, U.S. Dist. Ct. Ariz. 1981, U.S. Ct. Appeals (9th cir.) 1983. Assoc. Phillips & Lyon, Phoenix, 1981, Jones, Skelton & Hochuli, Phoenix, 1983—; law clk. to presiding justice Ariz. Ct. Appeals, Phoenix, 1982-83; cons. Fireman's Ins. Co., Phoenix, 1983—, St. Paul Ins. Co., Phoenix, 1983—, Aetna Ins. Co., Phoenix, 1983—, Sentry Ins. Co., Phoenix, 1983—. Mem. ABA, Ariz. Bar Assn., Assn. Trial LAwyers Am., Ariz. Trial Lawyers Assn., Phoenix Assn. Def. Counsel, Beta Alpha, Phi Alpha Delta. Republican. Roman Catholic. Avocations: golf, tennis, sailing. Insurance, Personal injury, Federal civil litigation. Office: Jones Skelton & Hochuli 2702 N 3d St #3000 Phoenix AR 85004

ZUKOWSKI, MICHAEL CHESTER, lawyer; b. Bremerton, Wash., Apr. 14, 1952; s. Chester Michael and Margaret Leoni (Qualheim) Z. BA, Stanford U., 1974; JD, U. Chgo., 1977. Bar: Ariz. 1977, U.S. Dist. Ct. Ariz. 1977. Assoc. McLoone, Theoblad & Galbut, Phoenix, 1977-83, Tower, Byrne & Beaugureau P.C., Phoenix, 1983—; instr. edn. panel State Supreme Ct., Phoenix, 1986—; bd. dirs. bus. adv. bd. Citibank (Ariz.), Phoenix. Avocations: running, weight training, outdoor sports. Banking, Landlord-tenant, Consumer commercial. Office: Tower Byrne & Beaugureau PC 2111 E Highland Ave #255 Phoenix AZ 85016

ZUMBRUN, RONALD ARTHUR, lawyer; b. Oak Park, Ill., Dec. 12, 1934; s. Arthur Raymond and Jean (Crandall) Z.; m. Ann Hartley, July 14, 1957; children: Kevin Ronald, Richard Douglas, Heidi Ann. BA in Econs., Pomona Coll., 1957; LLB, U. Calif., Berkeley, 1961. Bar: Calif. 1962, U.S. Dist. Ct. (no. dist.) Calif. 1962, U.S. Ct. Appeals (9th cir.) 1962, U.S. Dist. Ct. (cen. dist.) Calif. 1963, U.S. Supreme Ct. 1974, U.S. Dist. Ct. (ea. dist.) Calif. 1974, U.S. Ct. Appeals (D.C. cir.) 1975, U.S. Dist. Ct. (so. dist.) Calif. 1978, U.S. Ct. Appeals (3d, 5th, 7th, 8th, 9th and 11th cirs.) 1981, D.C. 1985. Sr. trial atty. Calif. State Dept. Pub. Works, Sacramento, 1961-71; dep. dir. legal affairs Calif. State Dept. Social Welfare, Sacramento, 1971-73; spl. counsel HEW, Washington, 1973; legal dir., pres. Pacific Legal Found., Sacramento, 1973—. Mem. Gov. Reagan's Task Force on Pub. Assistance, Sacramento, 1970, exec. office of Pres. Welfare Reform Study Team, 1972, Gov. Reagan's Task Force Project: Safer Calif., 1974, Carmichael (Calif.) adv. commn. on Parks and Recreation, 1969—. Served to capt. U.S. Army, 1957-70.9. Mem. Calif. Bar Assn., Sacramento Bar Assn., Phi Alpha Delta. Republican. Episcopalian. Lodge: Rotary. Public interest law. Office: Pacific Legal Found 555 Capitol Mall Suite 350 Sacramento CA 95814

ZURAV, DAVID BERNARD, lawyer; b. N.Y.C., Apr. 21, 1926; s. Irwin and Ida (Levine) Z.; m. Frances Stalford, Mar. 18, 1951; children—Ilene, Edward. B.S. in Econs., U. Pa., 1950; LL.B., Rutgers U., 1953. Bar: N.J. 1953, N.Y. 1984, U.S. Supreme Ct. 1957. Practiced in Union, N.J., 1953-70, 71—; partner firm Zurav & Myers, Union, 1970-71; atty. Springfield Twp. Planning Bd., 1961-79, Union Twp. Planning Bd., 1975-81; spl. counsel N.J. Dept. Transp., 1970; dir., gen. counsel Brunswick Capital Corp., Hillside, N.J., 1966-70; gen. counsel Met. N.J. Home Builders Assn., 1980—; asst. county counsel Union County, N.J., 1982—. Mem. adv. bd. 1st N.J. Bank Union, 1966-73. Union County Freeholder, 1968-71. Served with USNR, 1944-46. Republican mcpl. chmn., Springfield, N.J., 1967-68. Fellow Am. Acad. Matrimonial Lawyers (mem. N.J. state bd. mgrs. 1985—); mem. Am. State Bd. Mgrs., Union County, Essex County bar assns., N.J. Inst. Mcpl. Attys., N.J. Home Builders Assn. (dir. 1982—), Union Twp. C. of C. (dir. 1980—, v.p. 1983-87, pres. 1987—), Am. Arbitration Assn. (nat. panel arbitrators), Lawyers Club Union (past pres.). Family and matrimonial, Real property, Local government. Home: 1 Archbridge Ln Springfield NJ 07081 Office: 1460 Morris Ave Union NJ 07083

ZWACK, HENRY FRANCIS, lawyer; b. Bronx, N.Y., Dec. 5, 1952; s. Frank and Maria (Mohos) Z.; m. Laura M. Giumarra, Oct. 28, 1984. BA, Siena Coll., 1975; JD, ALbany Law Sch., 1978. Bar: N.Y. 1979, U.S. Dist. Ct. (no. dist.) N.Y. 1979. Sole practice Stephentown, N.Y., 1979—. Fireman Stephentown Vol. Fire Dept., 1972—, emergency med. technician, 1980—; counsel to Senator Owen H. Johnson civil services N.Y. State Senate, Albany, 1979-80, social services, Albany, 1980—; scoutmaster Troop 518 Boy Scouts Am., Stephentown, 1983-85; legislator Rensselaer County, N.Y., 1986—. Named Gus Johnson Fireman of Yr., Stephentown Vol. Fire Dept., 1984. Mem. ABA, N.Y. State Bar Assn., Rensselaer County Bar Assn. Republican. Roman Catholic. Club: Stephentown Rod and Gun. Avocation: hunting. General practice, Legislative, Real property. Home: Madden Rd Stephentown NY 12168 Office: 272 Main St Stephentown NY 12168

ZWAYER, TED, lawyer; b. Columbus, Ohio, Dec. 23, 1950; s. Eldon R. and Betty I. (Busby) Z.; m. Kay Elaine Kohler, Mar. 27, 1982; 1 child, Carrie Patricia. BSc in Bus. Adminstrn., Ohio State U., 1973, JD, 1976. Bar: Tenn. 1976, Ohio 1977, U.S. Dist. Ct. (no. dist.) Ohio 1980. Assoc. Law Office of Paul Clark, Marysville, Tenn., 1976-77; hearing officer State of Ohio, Columbus, 1977; city prosecutor City of Athens, Ohio, 1977-79; city atty. City of Whitehall, Ohio, 1980—. Mem. ABA (exec. com. town hall com. 1986, crime victims services com. 1986), Columbus Bar Assn., Ohio Bar Assn. Republican. Methodist. Avocations: photography, historical reading, politics, golf. Municipal law, Criminal, Probate. Home: 979 Pierce Ave Whitehall OH 43227-1254

ZWEIG, MICHAEL K., lawyer; b. Altoona, Pa., Dec. 2, 1952; s. Robert and Estelle Zweig; m. Marie Diane Kinsella, Apr. 5, 1986. BA, SUNY, Buffalo, 1974; JD, Georgetown U., 1977. Bar: Calif. 1977, U.S. Dist. Ct. (cen. dist.) Calif. 1977, U.S. Dist. Ct. (so. dist.) Calif. 1983, U.S. Ct. Appeals (9th cir.) 1984, U.S. Dist. Ct. (ea. dist.) Calif. 1986. Assoc. Reavis & McGrath, Calif., 1977-81, Drummy, Garrett, King & Harrison, Costa Mesa, Calif., 1981-82; ptnr. Sacks & Zweig, Los Angeles, 1983—; judge protem Los Angeles Mcpl. Ct., 1984-86. Editor Georgetown Law Jour., 1976-77. Organizer Community Action Group, Buffalo, 1972. Mem. ABA, Assn. Bus. Trial Lawyers, Los Angeles County Bar Assn., Beverly Hills Bar Assn., Am. Arbitration Assn. (arbitrator 1986), Lawyers Coalition Arms Control, Phi Beta Kappa. Jewish. State civil litigation, Federal civil litigation. Office: Sacks & Zweig 9255 Sunset Blvd Suite 620 Los Angeles CA 90069

ZWERLING, JOHN KENNETH, lawyer; b. Bklyn., May 14, 1943; s. Eric Carl and Ruth Ann (Hoffman) Z.; m. Patricia Ann West, Oct. 20, 1973. B.S., Tufts U., 1965; J.D., Am. U., 1970. Bar: Va. 1970, D.C. 1971, N.Y. 1981. Mem. Zwerling, Mark, Ginsberg & Lieberman, P.C., Alexandria, Va., 1970—. Bd. dirs. Nat. Orgn. for Reform of Marijuana Laws. Served to lt. USN, 1965-67. Mem. Nat. Assn. Criminal Def. Attys. (chmn. Brief Bank com.), ABA (criminal justice sect. com. on rules of evidence and procedure), Va. Bar Assn., Va. Coll. Criminal Def. Attys. (pres.), Alexandria Bar Assn. Jewish. Office: Zwerling Mark Ginsberg & Lieberman PC 1001 Duke St PO Box 1929 Alexandria VA 22313

ZWICK, KENNETH LOWELL, lawyer; b. Cleve., Oct. 30, 1945; s. Alvin Albert Zwick and Selma (Mack) Durbin; m. Ruth Winifred Epstein, June 21, 1969; children: Tara, Monica. BSME,BS in Mgmt., MIT, 1969; JD, Temple U., 1976. Bar: Pa. 1976. Engr. Raytheon Corp., Norwood, Mass., 1969-71; tech. mgr. On-Line Systems, Inc., Phila., 1971-76; staff atty. Mead Data Cen., Washington, 1976-83; dir. litigation support office U.S. Dept. Justice, Washington, 1983—. Mem. ABA, D.C. Computer Law Forum, ASME (assoc.). Democrat. Jewish. Federal civil litigation, Computer, Automated litigation support. Home: 2 Elmwood Ct Rockville MD 20850 Office: US Dept Justice 520 Todd Bldg Washington DC 20530

ZYCHICK, JOEL DAVID, lawyer; b. Cleve., June 23, 1954; s. Eugene K. and Myra (Rotblatt) Z. BBA, George Washington U., 1976; JD, Case Western Res. U., 1979; LLM in Taxation, NYU, 1979. Bar: Ohio 1979, N.Y. 1985, D.C. 1985, U.S. Tax Ct. 1980, U.S. Ct. Claims 1980, U.S. Ct. Appeals (fed. cir.) 1982. Assoc. Jones, Day, Reavis & Pogue, Cleve., 1980-83, Milbank, Tweed, Hadley & McCloy, N.Y.C., 1983-85, Gelberg & Agrams, N.Y.C., 1985-86; ptnr. Hertzog, Calamari & Gleason, N.Y.C., 1986—. Mem. ABA (tax sect., chmn. sales and fin. transactions com.), N.Y. State Bar Assn., Assn. of Bar of City of N.Y., Cleve. Bar Assn. Club: City (Cleve.). Avocations: hiking, music, traveling. Corporate taxation, Personal income taxation. Home: 233 E 86th St New York NY 10028 Office: Hertzog Calamari & Gleason 100 Park Ave New York NY 10017

ZYCHOWICZ, RALPH CHARLES, lawyer; b. Toledo, Mar. 22, 1948; s. Ralph Stanley and Sophia Imelda (Sliwinski) Z.; m. Beverly Ann King, Aug. 6, 1983. BS, U.S. Mil. Acad., 1970; JD, U. Toledo, 1978. Bar: Ohio 1979, U.S. Dist. Ct. (no. dist.) Ohio. Commd. 2d lt. U.S. Army, 1970, advanced through grades to capt., 1973, resigned, 1975, maj. with Res., 1975—; criminal prosecutor Lucas County, Ohio, 1980-82; civil law staff atty., prosecutor's office Lucas County, 1982-86; assoc. Batt & Zychowicz, Toledo, 1983-86; asst. law dir. City of Oregon, Ohio, 1983—; in-house counsel Zychowicz Sausage Factory, Inc. Maumee, Ohio, 1980—. Mem. steering com. Dem. Roundtable, Toledo, 1986. Mem. ABA, Ohio Bar assn., Toledo Bar Assn., Reserve Officers Assn., La Grange Bus. and Profl. Assn. (v.p. 1981-84), West Toledo Exchange (bd. dirs. 1981-82). Roman Catholic. Avocations: jogging, softball, golf. Local government, Government contracts and claims, General practice. Home: 2735 Sagamore Rd Toledo OH 43606 Office: Lucas County Prosecutor County Courthouse Toledo OH 43624

ZYSK, ROBERT JOSEPH, lawyer; b. Mineola, N.Y., Jan. 6, 1944. BA cum laude, Ithaca Coll., 1967; JD, Hofstra U., 1973. Bar: N.Y. 1974, U.S. Dist. Ct. (ea. dist.) N.Y. 1974, U.S. Supreme Ct. 1979. Assoc. Edmund J. Waldron Sr., New Hyde Park, N.Y., 1974-76, John H. Hultman, Rockville Ctr., N.Y., 1976-77, Siben & Siben, Bay Shore, N.Y., 1977-78, Pace & Pace, West Islip, N.Y., 1978-86, Lawrence H. Hahn, Melville, N.Y., 1986—. Mem. ABA, N.Y. State Bar Assn., Suffolk County Bar Assn. Republican. Lodge: Elks. General practice, Real property, State civil litigation. Home: 155 Bellport Rd Medford NY 11763 Office: Lawrence H Hahn 568 Walt Whitman Rd Melville NY 11747

Index
Fields of Practice or Interest

Tether, Ivan Joseph
Thomas, William Brinker
Thompson, Paul Barker
Thompson, William Carrington, Jr.
Tinney, Richard Townsend, Jr.
Trosten, Leonard Morse
Van Orman, Chandler L.
Vaughn, Robert Gene
Verville, Richard Emery
Violante, Joseph Anthony
Wagner, Curtis Lee, Jr.
Wald, Robert Lewis
Walker, Mary Ann
Walker, Robert Benson
Wallace, Arch Lee
Weissman, William R.
Wernick, Kenneth Jonathan
Wewer, William
Wheeler, Anne Marie
Whitfield, Milton Bailey
Whiting, Richard Matthew
Wilder, Roland Percival, Jr.
Williams, David Huntington
Williams, Stephen Fain
Williams, Thomas Scott
Williams, Yvonne LaVerne
Williamson, Thomas Samuel, Jr.
Winkler, Andrea Joanne
Winslow, John Franklin
Wittig, Raymond Shaffer
Wolf, Mark Charles
Wolff, Elroy Harris
Wyss, John Benedict
Yellott Jr., John Bosley
Young, John Hardin
Yung, Carroll John

Florida

Alper, Harvey Martin
Aurell, John Karl
Bartolone, Frank Salvatore
Billingsley, Curtis Ashley
Booth, Edgar Charles
Bracete, Juan Manuel
Brightman, Richard Stephen
Brooks, Roy Howard, Jr.
Burris, Johnny Clark
Canter, Bram D. E.
Cardwell, David Earl
Chumbris, Stephen Claude
Dady, Robert Edward
Dee, David Scott
Delancett, John Gerald
Denker, Randall Elizabeth
Dye, Dewey Albert, Jr.
Fleming, Joseph Z.
Fry, Stephen
Gaddy, Rodney Edwin
Geiger, William Harold
Glass, Roy Leonard
Goldsmith, Karen Lee
Hadlow, Earl Bryce
Hart, Deborah Diane
Hurtgen, Peter Joseph
Katz, Allan Jack
Kerns, David Vincent
Kibler, Rhoda Smith
Kiefner, John Robert, Jr.
Kohl, Donald Phillip
Kreutzer, Franklin David
Kuehne, Benedict P.
Kuersteiner, Jonathan Daniel Boone
LaBoda, Barry Charles
Leibowitz, Matthew Leon
Leonhardt, Frederick Wayne
Lopacki, Edward Joseph, Jr.
Lurie, Jeanne Flora
Mang, Douglas A.
Mathews, Byron B., Jr.
Mofsky, James Steffan
Nimmons, Ralph Wilson, Jr.
Parker, Whilden Sessions
Petrey, Roderick Norman
Pevsner, Beverly Limmer
Rappaport, Richard Warren
Royce, Raymond Watson
Rubinstein, Louis Baruch
Rutledge, Gary Ray
Salem, Richard Joseph
Sandler, Gilbert Lee
Scott, Janice Gail
Sechen, Robert Nicholas
Sharfman, Herbert
Spriggs, Kent
Steele, Robert Michael
Stein, Leslie Reicin
Strickland, Delphene Coverston
Waas, George Lee
Wendel, John Fredric
Wind, Carol Marlene
Zambo, Richard Alan

Georgia

Baker, Anita Diane
Boynton, Frederick George
Branch, John Ellison
Casto, Keith Michael
Flynt, John James, Jr.
Foulke, Edwin Gerhart, Jr.
Giffin, Gordon D.
Huszagh, Fredrick Wickett
Marvin, Charles Arthur
Menkin, Lita Sue
Prince, David Cannon
Russell, Harold Louis
Rutledge, Ivan Cate
Sbaratta, Richard Mark
Scavo, James J.
Volentine, Richard J., Jr.
Wymer, John Francis, III

Hawaii

Fujiyama, Rodney Michio
Kaneshige, Melvin Yoshio
Takayama, Ken Hideshi

Idaho

Ellsworth, Maurice Owens
Jones, James Thomas
Madsen, Roger Bryan
Russell, Robie George

Illinois

Allen, John Trevett, Jr.
Andrin, Albert Antal

Artman, Eric Alan
Baer, John Richard Frederick
Baird, Russell Miller
Baker, Bruce Jay
Barr, John Robert
Bernstein, John Thomas
Bierig, Jack R.
Blaszak, Michael William
Bleiweiss, Shell J.
Blume, Paul Chiappe
Bragg, Michael Ellis
Breen, James Joseph
Brown, Steven Spencer
Burditt, George Miller, Jr.
Burns, Kenneth Jones, Jr.
Coffee, Richard Jerome, II
Currie, David Park
Dechene, James Charles
Delp, Wilbur Charles, Jr.
DeVries, James Howard
Dilling, Kirkpatrick Wallwick
Dodegge, Thomas Roland
Fawcett, Dwight Winter
Fellows, Jerry Kenneth
Fewell, Terry Glenn
Fleps, John Joseph
Frick, Robert Hathaway
Garrison, Ray Harlan
Gavin, John Neal
Godfrey, Richard Cartier
Gordon, James S.
Gottlieb, Paul Mitchel
Groenke, Theodore A.
Guthman, Jack
Head, Patrick James
Herman, Stephen Charles
Hilliard, David Craig
Hoffman, S. David
Howe, Jonathan Thomas
Hunt, Lawrence Halley, Jr.
Kuczwara, Thomas Paul
Lythcott, Stephen Xavier
Maher, David Willard
McConnell, Jack Lewis
Miller, Ralph William, Jr.
Mintel, Judith King
Mitchell, Lee Mark
Morse, Saul Julian
Orloff, Ronald Leonard
Perlberg, Jules Martin
Podlewski, Joseph Roman, Jr.
Polaski, Anne Spencer
Raymond, David Walker
Rosso, Christine Hehmeyer
Rosso, David John
Rubinowitz, Leonard S.
Russell, Tomas Morgan
Saunders, George Lawton, Jr.
Sechen, Glenn Charles
Senescu, Stuart
Shannon, Peter Michael, Jr.
Stack, Paul Francis
Stassen, John Henry
Weging, James Edwin

Indiana

Allen, David James
Beckwith, Lewis Daniel
Capshaw, Tom Dean
Collier-Magar, Kenneth Anthony
Cracraft, Bruce Noel
Evans, Daniel Fraley, Jr.
Kennedy, Sheila Suess
Palmer, Judith Grace
Price, Phillip Vincent
Robisch, Robert Karl
Rubright, Charles Russell
Smith, Theodore Frederick, Jr.
Tillman, Douglas Leon
Van Valer, Joe Ned

Iowa

Dahl, Harry Waldemar
Davis, James Casey
Fox, Terry Roy
Hutchison, Robert Alan
Johnson, John Paul
Low, Susan A.
Luchtel, Keith Edward
Lyford, F. Richard
Nowadzky, Roger Alan
Rhodes, Ann Marie
Shane, Peter Milo
Smith, William Herbert, Jr

Kansas

Dimmitt, Lawrence Andrew
Hecht, Robert D.
Lang, Joe Allen
Lefebvre, David Marshall
Mudrick, David Phillip
Reeves, Jean Brooks
Sears, Ruth Ann
Speer, Wilson Edward

Kentucky

Cocklin, Kim Roland
Dowell, Douglas Melvin
Dozier, Rush Watkins, Jr.
Edelen, Francis Hennessy, Jr.
Miller, Carl Theodore
Moore, Charles Dudley, Jr.
Murphy, Richard Vanderburgh
Powell, Karen Ann Pitts
Whitmer, Leslie Gay

Louisiana

Cicet, Donald James
Colbert, Kathryn Hendon
Fraiche, Donna DiMartino
Hardy, Ashton Richard
Haygood, John Warren
Marcello, David Anthony
Mmahat, John Anthony
Osakwe, Christopher
Riddick, Winston Wade, Sr.
Ross, Bobbie Jean
Ryan, Gary Lee
Stewart, Melinda Jane

Maine

Curtis, Kenneth M.
Douglas, Wayne Rodger

Maryland

Armold, Judith Ann
Bliss, Donald Tiffany, Jr.
Brugger, George Albert
Buchanan, Phillip Gerald
Cashour, Mary Catherine
Chaplin, Peggy Fannon
Davidson, Daniel Joseph
Dulany, William Bevard
Geldon, Fred Wolman
Gnocchi-Franco, Claudio
Gonya, Donald Alan
Grange, George Robert, II
Greenstein, Ruth Louise
Harris, Janine Diane
Hitchcock, Paul Richard
Jenkins, Robert Rowe
Katz, Barry Edward
Keplinger, Helen Bunten
Kimball, Sherman Paul
Levinson, Daniel Ronald
Nystrom, Harold Charles
Papkin, Robert David
Paul, Carl Frederick
Pensinger, John Lynn
Rachanow, Gerald Marvin
Redden, Roger Duffey
Rheinstein, Peter Howard
Rhodes, Thurman Haywood
Ryan, David Charles
Schwartz, Joseph Anthony, III
Sfekas, Stephen James
Skoler, Daniel Lawrence
Tierney, Philip James
Tyler, Ralph Sargent, III
Ziegler, William Joseph

Massachusetts

Atkinson, James Peter
Auerbach, Joseph
Baker, Horace Ross, Jr.
Dacey, Kathleen Ryan
Ferriter, Maurice Joseph
Fischer, Thomas Covell
Fluker, Brenda Ann
Gargiulo, Andrea Weiner
Hoefling, Virginia Ann
Hoover, David Carlson
Kanin, Dennis Roy
Keuthen, Catherine J. Norman
Larson, Allen Robert
Latham, Oliver Bradley
Lyons, Nance
Mc Cormack, Edward Joseph, Jr.
Meyer, Michael Broeker
Moschos, Demitrios Mina
Pepyne, Edward Walter
Phillipes, Peter Michael
Rabinowitz, Alan James
Rich, Christopher Charles
Rockefeller, Regina Strazzulla
Scott, David Oscar
Shapiro, David Louis
Trimmier, Roscoe, Jr.
Vance, Verne Widney, Jr.
Wexler, Barbara Lynne

Michigan

Basso, Ronald Matthew
Burns, Marshall Shelby, Jr.
Carlin, John Bernard, Jr.
Cwirko, Claris Kaye
Dunne, Francis Hugh
Feikens, John
Garcia, Joseph Antonio
Huss, Allan Michael
Kurtz, James P.
Leavitt, Martin Jack
Lobenherz, William Ernest
Marvin, David Edward Shreve
Melia, James Patrick
Murphy, Joseph Albert, Jr.
Nern, Christopher Carl
Peirce, Kenneth B., Jr.
Polito, Joseph Michael
Raven, Jonathan Ezra
Rossen, Jordan
Schultz, Stephen Otto
Skipper, Nathan Richard, Jr.
Spence, Howard Tee Devon
Stasson, Shelley Andrea
Steinberg, Harvey Laurance
Stoetzer, Gerald Louis
Sullivan, Alfred A.
Swift, Theodore Wells
Vining, (George) Joseph
Wells, Bill Charles
Williams, Deirdré LaJean

Minnesota

Broeker, John Milton
Engle, Donald Edward
French, John Dwyer
Grindal, Harald Theodore
Habicht, James Robert
Jensen, Patricia Ann
Keppel, William James
Knapp, John Anthony
Luis, Juanita Bolland
Martin, Mary Kay
Nettles, Alan Ross

Mississippi

Barber, Frank David
Fenton, Howard Nathan, III
Garrity, Thomas Anthony, Jr.
Hatcher, John Leslie
Smith, Stanley Quinten
Wise, Robert Powell

Missouri

Atwood, Hollye Stolz
Banks, Eric Kendall
Barkofske, Francis Lee
Bartlett, Alex
Barvick, William Michael
Brooks, Douglas Michael
Christiansen, Steven Allan
Dement, Sandra Helene
Derque, Joseph Alexander, III
Deutsch, James Bernard
English, Mark Gregory
Ferry, Joseph Dean
Fritz, Tobias Bodwell
Gardner, Paul Hendricks

Gilhousen, Brent James
Hoffman, John Raymond
Kleine, Richard Allen
Lorenz, Jack Chapin
Mayfield, Edgar
Monaco, Nicholas M.
Moore, Jean Bante
O'Donnell, Thomas Patrick
Palmer, Randall Bruce
Thompson, Michael
Ward, Robert Alan
Willis, Wayne George
Wochner, William James
Young, Mary Garr

Montana

Alke, John
Mitchell, Jayne Francis
Seiffert, Terry L.

Nebraska

Davlin, Michael Charles
Kratz, Paul David
Krutter, Forrest Nathan
Lee, Dennis Patrick
Rinn, Louise Anne

Nevada

Ashleman, Ivan Reno, II
Brown, Joseph Wentling
Cavin, Rhonda Lynn
Faiss, Robert Dean
Gallagher, Dennis Vincent
Giordano, Paul Gregory
Golden, Michael Patrick
Hoppe, Craig Allen
Jost, Richard Frederic, III
Kirkman, Robert Akeridge, Jr.
Nelson, Jane Wandel
O'Brien, Daniel Louis

New Hampshire

Arnold, Wynn Edmund
Cronmiller, Thomas Bernard
Smith, Gregory Hayes
Wiebusch, Richard Vernon
Wilson, William Harold, Jr.

New Jersey

Babineau, Anne Serzan
Banse, Robert Lee
Blumrosen, Alfred William
Blumrosen, Ruth Gerber
Cangelosi, Carl J.
Casiello, Nicholas, Jr.
DeBois, James Adolphus
Dowd, Dennis Owen
Eichler, Burton Lawrence
Fleming, Russell, Jr.
Gindin, William Howard
Halpern, Samuel Joseph
Harris, David B.
Hill, Henry Albert
Hyland, William Francis
Isele, William Paul
Jacobs, Joseph James
Lewis, Albert Michael
Maurer, Henry Stephen, Jr.
Milton, Gabriel
Molloy, Brian Joseph
Oliver, Raymond A.
Pickus, Robert Mark
Porter, John Issac
Rockwell, Mark Paul
St. Landau, Norman
Salibello, Salvatore Joseph
Spinrad, Max
Sterns, Joel H.
Sweeney, Gerald Bingham
Teitler, Paul Hugh
Tulkoff, Myer Simon
Tyler, George Joseph
Vanderbilt, Arthur T., II
Weber, Roy Philip
Wilson, Martin S., Jr.
Wolk, Stuart Rodney

New Mexico

Apodaca, Patrick Vincent
Salazar, John Paul

New York

Adler, Alan Michael
Agatstein, David Joseph
Allen, Leon Arthur, Jr.
Ashe, Bernard Flemming
Augello, William Joseph
Bagge, Michael Charles
Baker, David Remember
Bankston, Archie Moore, Jr.
Bartlett, Cody Blake
Bearak, Corey B(ecker)
Berg, Alan
Berg, Gale Diane
Bermann, George Alan
Bialkin, Kenneth J.
Blanc, Roger David
Borgese, John A.
Bress, Joseph Michael
Brewer, Curtis
Brickwedde, Richard James
Broady, Tolly Rupert
Buldrini, George James
Cantor, Samuel C.
Condon, John William, Jr.
Cooney, Michael Francis
Cooper, R. John, III
Davis, Steven H.
Davison, Irwin Stuart
Douchkess, George
Dunham, Corydon Bushnell
Earle, Victor Montagne, III
Earley, Anthony Francis, Jr.
Eldridge, Douglas Alan
Estreicher, Samuel
Faison, William Franklin, II
Farrell, Thomas Dinan
Figueora, Nicholas
Fitt, Benjamin Jones
Foley, Patrick Joseph
Forte, Wesley Elbert
Franciscovich, George
Freeman, Robert John
Ginsberg, Ernest

Goldbrenner, Ronald Steven
Green, Jeffrey Steven
Greenman, Frederick Francis
Gulino, Frank
Hall, Robert Turnbull, III
Harkins, Francis Joseph, Jr.
Harrigan, Nancy Stafford
Healy, Joseph Robert
Hecht, Charles Joel
Hoffman, John Ernest, Jr.
Hoffman, Marvin
Hudson, Paul Stephen
Jacobson, Jerold Dennis
Janney, Oliver James
Jibilian, Gerald Arsen
Juceam, Robert E.
Kandel, William Lloyd
Kempler, Cecelia
Kent, James Ewart
Knigin, Kenneth Sheldon
Koeltl, John George
Korman, Iris J.
Kostelny, Albert Joseph, Jr.
Kreutzer, S. Stanley
Landa, Howard Martin
Lebowitz, Jack Richard
Lifland, William Thomas
Lovallo, Timothy Robin
Malawsky, Donald N.
Marlatt, Jerry Ronald
Matias, Thomas Redmond
McSorley, Bernard Thomas
Meader, John Daniel
Mendez, William, Jr.
Miller, Richard Allan
Miller, Sam Scott
Miller, Wesley A. Looney
Most, Jack Lawrence
Murphy, Joseph F.
Myerson, Harvey Daniel
Neville, Martin John
Nolan, Terrance Joseph, Jr.
Northrop, Cynthia Ellen
Oliensis, Sheldon
Peaslee, Maurice Keenan
Piedmont, Richard Stuart
Pogrebin, Bertrand B.
Raff, David
Rago, Daniel Anthony
Raisler, Kenneth Mark
Rose, Michael Edward
Ruzow, Daniel Arthur
Sack, Edward J.
Schlinger, Alexander Peter
Schoeneck, Charles A., Jr.
Schumacher, Harry Richard
Schwartz, Marvin
Schwed, Michael J.
Shadley, Kay Lee
Shaw, Arnold H(arold)
Shinkle, John Thomas
Smith, Brian Joseph
Sorensen, Theodore Chaikin
Straub, Chester John
Strauss, Peter L(ester)
Szwalbenest, Benedykt Jan
Teitelbaum, Steven Usher
Tritell, Randolph Wayne
Trotta, Frank Paul
Volkmann, Alfred Armistead
Wagner, Richard Hopkins
Watson, James Lopez
Webb, Morrison DeSoto
Weil, Gilbert Harry
White, Katherine Patricia
White, Renee Allyn
Windman, Joel A.
Wolfe, Richard Barry Michael
Wood, William Laurence, Jr.

North Carolina

Carmichael, Carson, III
Case, Charles Dixon
Conway, Robert George, Jr.
Currin, Samuel Thomas
Derrick, Jack Holley
Flowers, Kent Gordon, Jr.
Goodrum, Wayne Louis
Hubbard, Thomas Edwin (Tim)
Kane, Terry Richard
Kapp, Michael Keith
Koonce, Neil Wright
Kripner, George Martin
Lansche, John Elmer
Loeb, Ben Fohl, Jr.
Manthei, Gayl Marie
Markham, Charles Buchanan
Perschetz, Arthur Driban
Rusher, Derwood H., II
Taylor, Vaughan Edward
Vaughan, Donald Ray

North Dakota

Sandstrom, Dale Vernon

Ohio

Acomb, James Richard, II
Adams, Lee Stephen
Angel-Shaffer, Arlene Beth
Aukland, Duncan Dayton
Baxter, Randolph
Bonaventura, Mark Gabriel
Buehler, Thomas Lee
Burlingame, John Hunter
Casper, Paul William, Jr.
Christensen, Jon Alexander
Davis, Frederick Benjamin
Donohoe, James D.
Edwards, John White
Farrell, Clifford Michael
Feheley, Lawrence Francis
Garvey, Mary Anne
Gibson, Rankin MacDougal
Gippin, Robert Malcolm
Graney, Michael Proctor
Grundstein, Nathan David
Haddox, Jerome B.
Hardy, Michael Lynn
Harrison, William K.
Hitchcock, J. Gareth
Jackson, Robert Howard
Jacobs, Leslie William
Kacir, Barbara Brattin
Lee, William Johnson
Levering, Robert Bruce
Libert, Donald Joseph

Mann, Richard Lynn
Masek, Raymond John
Maurer, John William
McClain, William Andrew
McCuen, John Francis, Jr.
Morgan, Dennis Richard
O'Reilly, James Thomas
Paleudis, John George
Perry, George Williamson
Racine, Kathleen Celeste
Rennick, Kyme Elizabeth Wall
Roscoe, George Dennis
Ruxin, Paul Theodore
Schermer, Marsha Rockey
Schneider, Karl Herbert
Sobecki, Thomas Alva
Speros, James Mandamadiotis
Stanton, Elizabeth McCool
Tell, A. Charles
Van Heyde, G. James
Witherell, Dennis Patrick

Oklahoma
Arrington, John Leslie, Jr.
Carson, Michael Jay
Cates, Jennifer Ann
Decker, Michael Lynn
Dowd, William Timothy
Enis, Thomas Joseph
Hacker, Jerry William
Huffman, William Hicks
McElroy, Bert Colyar
Specht, Randolph Stephen
Spencer, Thomas Lee
Steelman, Jacob DeHart
Swimley, Gary Wallace
Verity, George Luther
Walsh, Lawrence Edward
Williamson, Walter Bland

Oregon
Baxendale, James Charles Lewis
Brenneman, Delbert Jay
Frohnmayer, David Braden
Funk, William F.
Girard, Leonard Arthur
Glick, Richard Myron
Johnston, David Frederick
Kane, Henry Smith
Lindsay, Dennis John
Marks, J(ohn) Barrett
Riemer, George Arthur
Rutzick, Mark Charles
Smith, Kim Ridgely
Sullivan, Edward Joseph

Pennsylvania
Bambrick, Joseph Thomas, Jr.
Beren, Daniel Edward
Blenko, Don Balman
Bradshaw, William Elbert
Bressman, Marc Ira
Conley, Martha Richards
Elman, Gerry Jay
Engler, W. Joseph, Jr.
Feld, Arthur Michael
Feldmann, Louis George
Freeman, Antoinette Rosefeldt
Gerjuoy, Edward
Gornish, Gerald
Heim, Robert Charles
Hender, George Snowden
Hunter, Keith Alan
Kelly, Robert Edward, Jr.
Killian, John Doran, III
Kury, Franklin Leo
Martin, Charles Howard
McKeever, John Eugene
Milkman, Murray
Murphy, Joseph Edward
Ogden, W. Edwin
Oplinger, Jon Carl
Pang, Peter Chiusing
Phillips, Almarin
Pillai, K. G. Jan
Porach, Richard Andrew
Richardson, Joseph Ablett, Jr.
Rose, Andrew James Evans
Sarno, Daniel Anthony
Schulz, William Frederick, Jr.
Skelly, Joseph Gordon
Sosnov, Steven Robert
Stewart, Allen Warren
Stiller, Jennifer Anne
Teklits, Joseph Anthony
Wallace, Christopher Baird
Weston, R. Timothy
Zemaitis, Thomas Edward
Zimmer, Bruce Irwin

Rhode Island
Fogarty, Edward Michael
Isaacs, Michael Burton
Smith, Edward Philip

South Carolina
Devereux, Anthony Quentin
Fusco, Arthur Geiger
Harleston, John
Harvey, William Brantley, Jr.
Jedziniak, Lee Peter
Knowlton, Robert Yates
Medlock, Thomas Travis
Pollard, William Albert
Powell, Osborne Eugene, Jr.
Schweitzer, Eric Campbell
Scott, Ronald Charles
Spencer, Mary Elizabeth

South Dakota
Eichstadt, Craig Martin
Zimmer, John Herman

Tennessee
Akers, Charles David
Bush, Wendell Earl
Cherry, Mack Henry
Epps, James Haws, III
Gerrish, Jeffrey C.
Harrington, Penny Nancy
Jaqua, David Palmer
Jolly, Charles Nelson
Jones, Kenneth Ray, Jr.
Penny, William Lewis

Ramsaur, Allan Fields
Samuels, Seymour, Jr.
Whiteaker, Raymond Combs

Texas
Ackerman, John Edward
Adams, Harold Gene
Allen, Joan Howard
Balough, Richard Charles
Barlow, W. P., Jr.
Beard, Glenda Rainwater
Berndt, Karen Ann
Black, William Earl
Boles, David LaVelle
Bridges, Russell Brian
Brim, Jefferson Kearney, III
Caldwell, James Wiley
Calhoun, Frank Wayne
Cantilo, Patrick Herrera
Cassin, William Bourke
Cochran, George Calloway, III
Coffield, Conrad Eugene
Cosgrove, Ritamae Gober
Ehrle, William Lawrence
Ericson, Roger Delwin
Eubank, Christina
Forbes, Thomas Allen
Frisby, Thomas Newton
Geiger, Richard Stuart
Gilberg, Howard Larry
Gosselink, Margaret Lavidge
Hallman, Leroy
Hargis, James Richard
Harkey, Paul
Hathcox, VaLinda
Heffron, Jonathon Kenneth
Jacobo, Paulina Moreno
James, Ann Nixon
Johnstone, Debbi Merriman
Judice, C(harles) Raymond
Kawaguchi, Meredith Ferguson
Kendall, David Matthew
King, C. Glyn
Legendre, John Peter
McCreary, Frank E., III
McDaniel, Myra Atwell
McGinnis, Robert Campbell
Meer, Julian Milton
Moros, Nicholas Peter
Ochs, Robert Francis
Odiorne, James Thomas
Otto, Byron Leonard
Patman, Philip Franklin
Payne, James Parker
Pierce, Richard James, Jr.
Pollan, Thomas Miller
Pope, David Bruce
Pope, Joseph Ronald
Rendon, Josefina Muniz
Ricciardelli, Thomas Patrick
Richter, Alfred Grammar, Jr.
Richter, Martin Edward
Roan, Forrest Calvin, Jr.
Robinett, Mark Webster
Rothermel, John Fisher, III
Ruhl, John Benjamin
Salch, Steven Charles
Sanders, Thelma E.
Schenkkan, Pieter (Pete) Meade
Schwartz, Leonard Jay
Seeman, Robert Foster
Steen, John Thomas, Jr.
Steimel, Walter Earl, Jr.
Stevens, Jeron Lynn
Strawn, James Roy
Taylor, Kerns Bowman
Temple, Larry Eugene
Wheat, Josiah
Whitworth, H. Philip, Jr.
Wolf, Michael Jay
Wozencraft, Frank McReynolds
Young, Jess Wollett

Utah
Anderson, Reese C.
Cassity, James Junior
Jensen, Dallin W.
Melich, Mitchell
Stirba, Anne Melinda Morr
Walz, Mary Beth
Wells, Frank Milton

Vermont
Cheney, Kimberly Bunce
Glinka, Gleb
Jarrett, Glenn Alan
Marshall, John Henry
Nichols, Elaine Kilburn
Zamore, Peter Hokanson

Virginia
Angulo, Charles Bonin
Arey, Stephen Edward
Aronin, Louis
Bishop, Alfred Chilton, Jr.
Bridewell, Sherry Hazelwood
Briney, Roger Albert
Bussewitz, Roy Jon
Calkins, Gary Nathan
Chelen, John Cas
Dewey, Anne Elizabeth Marie
Donlan, Martin Andrew, Jr.
Donovan, William Jeremiah
English, William deShay
Fisher, Catherine Ambrosiano
Freeman, George Clemon, Jr.
Gales, Robert Robinson
Gary, Richard David
Goforth, William Clements
Grant, Charles Randall, Jr.
Gresham, Timothy Ward
Hall, Franklin Perkins
Herge, J. Curtis
Holland, William Louis
Hulvey, Craig Wallace
Jackson, William Paul, Jr.
Kanovsky, Helen Renee
Kleiler, James Robert
LaGow, John Christopher
Lanphear, Martha Jean
Layton, Garland Mason
Levy, Richard
Lewis, Walter Laughn
Light, Alfred Robert
Merrill, Richard Austin
Miller, Charles Joseph

Morrison, James Lawrence
Payne, J(oe) Stanley
Peters, David Frankman
Price, Ilene Rosenberg
Pugh, William Wallace
Rasmus, John Charles
Rau, Lee Arthur
Regirer, Walter Wlodzimierz
Robie, William Randolph
Smoots, Carol Anne
Stephens, William Theodore
Talarek, Walter Glenn
Toothman, John William
Verkuil, Paul Robert
Walkup, Charlotte Lloyd
Walton, Morgan Lauck
Whitaker, Thomas Patrick
Wimbush, Frederick Blair
Wood, John Martin
Wooldridge, William Charles
Wright, Grover Cleveland, Jr.
Zeese, Kevin Bruce

Washington
Backstein, Robert Joseph
Blais, Jan David
Crane, Stephen Joel
Dempsey, Thomas Lawrence
Dowdy, Robert Alan
Eadie, Richard Douglas
Edmondson, Frank Kelley, Jr.
Kilbane, Thomas Martin, Jr.
McCorkle, Linda Ann
Moniz, Donna Maria
Phillips, Catherine
Ransom, Clark Taylor
Redman, Eric
Rosen, Jon Howard
Wilkinson, Jane Rae
Wilson, James Barker
Younglove, Edward Earl, III

West Virginia
Barnette, David Allen
Flannery, David Michael
Markey, E. Lowell
Walkup, Homer Allen

Wisconsin
Brant, Kirby Ensign
Dalton, LeRoy LaVerne
Gorske, Robert Herman
Hesslink, Robert Melvin, Jr.
Miran, Claudia Berry
Mukamal, Stuart Sassoon
Perez, David William
Ryan, Thomas Joseph
Tuerkheimer, Barbara Wolfson
Vaughan, Michael Richard
Will, Trevor Jonathan

Wyoming
Hathaway, Stanley Knapp
Senkewicz, Mary E.
Thomson, Rebecca Wunder
Woodhouse, Gay Vanderpoel

ADDRESS UNPUBLISHED
Aronsohn, Richard Frank
Bernard, Pamela Jenks
Bolch, Susan Bass
Comer, Vivian Adelia
Crandell, John Smith
Culver, Sue Ann Ray
Eastin, Keith E.
Ellis, Neil Richard
Fainter, John Wells, Jr.
Heise, John Irvin, Jr.
Helms, David Alonzo
Holbrook, Donald Benson
Lapidus, Steven Richard
Learned, James Roy
Mattson, James Stewart
McFarland, Robert Edwin
Midkiff, Charles Franklin
Milbrath, Dennis Henry
Neese, Sandra Anne
O'Leary, Marilyn C.
Pendergrass, John Ambrose
Rubinkowski, Conrad Sigmund
Taylor, Reese Hale, Jr.
Tolins, Roger Alan
Trilling, Helen Regina
White, Richard Clarence

ADMIRALTY

UNITED STATES

Alabama
Chambers, K.W. Michael
Hamilton, Palmer Clarkson
Hoff, Timothy
Lattof, Mitchell George, Jr.
Meigs, Walter Ralph
Pittman, Craig Sorrell

Alaska
Bradbury, John Howard
Conway, John Martin
Richmond, Robert Lawrence
Smith, John Anthony

Arkansas
Ralls, Rawleigh Hazen, III

California
Denniston, Thomas Robert
Einhorn, Lawrence Martin
Flynn, John Allen
Hoey, James Douglas, III
Leonard, Arthur Alan
LiMandri, Charles Salvatore
Meadows, John Frederick
Moomjian, Cary Avedis, Jr.
Pierry, Thomas James
Rosenthal, Kenneth Wolfgang
Staring, Graydon Shaw
Stolpman, Thomas Gerard
Suter, Bernard Reynold
Thon, William Marvin

Welch, Walter Andrew, Jr.

Connecticut
Becker-Lewke, Laura Virginia
Black, Charles Lund, Jr.
Stone, Dennis J.
Yachmetz, Philip Keith

District of Columbia
Bastek, John Anthony
Casey, Geraldine Holland
Flowe, Benjamin Hugh, Jr.
Gaughan, John Anthony
Hoppel, Robert Gerald, Jr.
Macleay, Donald
Mayer, Neal Michael
Miller, Damon Craddock
Thomas, William Brinker
Young, John Andrew

Florida
Anderson, Cromwell Adair
Cacciatore, S. Sammy, Jr.
Cole, Robert Allen
Douglas, Hubert Gene, II
Gabel, George DeSaussure, Jr.
Gaines, Robert Pendleton
Gonzalez-Pita, J. Alberto
Hastings, Lawrence Vaeth
Hester, Christopher Scott
Kennedy, Marc J.
Lipcon, Charles R.
McCoy, Francis Tyrone
McDonald, Julia Carol
McGill, Gerald Allen
Merting, John Webster
Moseley, James Francis
Poole, Sharon Alexandra
Rumrell, Richard Gary
Shea, J. Michael
Underwood, Edwin Hill
Valle, Laurence Francis
Walton, Rodney Earl
Wiltshire, William Harrison Flick
Yerrid, C. Steven

Hawaii
Frey, Philip Sigmund

Illinois
Baffes, Thomas Gus
Bauer, Joseph Louis
Boyle, Patrick Otto
Godfrey, Richard Cartier
Gundlach, Norman Joseph
Johnson, Richard Fred
Walston, Beth Elaine

Indiana
Gleason, Charles Sappington

Louisiana
Anzelmo, Donald Joseph
Ates, J. Robert
Bains, David Paul
Barry, Francis Julian, Jr.
Bassett, Jeffrey Michael
Bengtson, Karl Wayne
Booksh, Robert William, Jr.
Broussard, Richard C.
Chapman, Alex David, Jr.
David, Robert Jefferson
Dinwiddie, Bruce Wayland
Ensenat, Donald Burnham
Evans, Robert Collin
Fowler, George J., III
Fuhrer, Leonard
Godofsky, Harvey Joseph
Guilliot, Paul Jerome
Hanemann, James, Jr.
Healy, George William, III
Holmes, James Richard
Hurley, Grady Schell
Johnson, Ronald Adams
Lane, Charles Ray
Leefe, Richard K.
Leger, Walter John, Jr.
Lestelle, Andrea Sucherman
Lirette, Danny Joseph
Lombard, Michael Albert
Milly, Raymond Anthony
Nungesser, Nancy Ann
Price, Lionel Franklin
Robinson, Michael
Ryan, James, III
Salas, Camilo Kossy, III
Schoemann, Rudolph Robert
Seabolt, Charles Frederick
Siegel, Robert Irwin
Story, Clement, III
Stout, A(rthur) Wendel, III
Swift, John Goulding
Treadaway, Randell Edward
Treeby, William David
Tschirn, Darryl Jude
Webb, Daniel Andrew
Windmeyer, Joseph Edwin
Wright, Bob Forrest
Wysocki, James Anthony

Maine
Walker, Frank Briggs

Maryland
Bartlett, James Wilson, III
Bekman, Paul D.
Ferris, William Michael
Hopkins, Samuel
Rosenthal, Lawrence Gerald
Ward, John Thomas

Massachusetts
Calabro, Michael James
Costello, Walter Anthony, Jr.
Dahlen, Richard Lester
Dokurno, Anthony David
O'Connell, Henry Francis
Rose, Leonard
Trautman, Donald Theodore
Wolfe, Robert Shenker

Michigan
Jaques, Leonard C.
Kramer, LeRoy, III
Meyer, Philip Gilbert
Mundell, John Andrew, Jr.
Proffitt, Roy Franklin
Theut, C(larence) Peter
Thurber, Cleveland

Minnesota
Keenan, Kevin Patrick
Koskinen, David John
Loper, Stewart Collins

Mississippi
Breland, Norman Leroy
Chapman, John Wendell
Dornan, Donald C., Jr.
Dukes, James Otis
Ferrell, Wayne Edward, Jr.
Netterville, Robert Lavelle
Rood, Ralph Edward

Missouri
Bay, William Robert
Kortenhof, Joseph Michael
Lee, James Roger
Rush, Douglas Kevin

Nevada
Schutt, William Eldon

New Jersey
Carr, Hubert Franklin
Cohen, Lawrence Gene
Stalker, Timothy Wayne

New York
Barcelo, John James, III
Beltz, Paul William
Burrell, Lizabeth Lorie
Calamari, Joseph August
Calkins, Steven Potter
Callahan, Nancy Kay
Colmant, Andrew Robert
Dune, Steve Charles
Edelman, Paul Sterling
Gotimer, Harry Albert
Hayden, Raymond Paul
Healy, Nicholas Joseph
Kenny, James Michael
Kimball, John Devereux
Koelzer, George Joseph
Ligelis, Gregory John
Lyons, Kirk Matthew
Maitland, Guy Edison Clay
Martowski, David William
McConnell, John Hay
Mirone, Robert C(armelo)
Nixon, Elliott Bodley
O'Brien, Francis Joseph
Rassner, Alan Carl
Rosow, Malcolm Bertram
Ryan, James Vincent
Schmidt, Charles Edward
Semel, Martin Ira
Sequeira, Manuel Alexandre, Jr.
Sesser, Gary Douglas
Sheehan, Kenneth Edward
Shirley, James Theo, Jr.
Stratakis, Christ
Symmers, William Garth
Trott, Dennis Charles
Wilensky, Saul
Will, Alfred Joseph
Williams, Averill Marshall

Oregon
Johnston, David Frederick
Lindsay, Dennis John
Nye, Daniel Alan

Pennsylvania
Hochberg, Robert Boaz
Kane, John Joseph
Levin, Arnold
Mattioni, John

Tennessee
Folmar, Oliver Wiley
Goldin, Arnold B.
Todd, Ben

Texas
Cheavens, Joseph D.
Clann, Michael Kammer
Creeden, Carl Francis
Davis, Martha Algenita Scott
Dimitry, Theodore George
Eckhardt, William Rudolf, III
Engerrand, Kenneth Gabriel
Kline, Allen Haber, Jr.
Konopisos, Konstantine A.
Latham, B. Mills
Lewis, Kenneth Wayne
Pickle, George Edward
Porto, Joseph Anthony
Schechter, Arthur Louis
Silva, Eugene Joseph
Steele, Richard Parks
Sydow, Michael David
Vickery, Glenn
Waldman, Steve
Westmoreland, Kent Ewing

Virginia
Hoffman, Walter Edward
Indest, George Felix, III
Metcalfe, James Ashford
Plaetzer, Ross Frederick
Schwartz, Steven Gary
Vandeventer, Braden
Ware, Guilford Dudley
Wiswall, Frank Lawrence, Jr.
Zaphiriou, George Aristotle

Washington
Anderson, David Bowen
Budlong, John
Gustafson, Albert Katsuaki
Henderson, Dan Fenno

Kilbane, Thomas Martin, Jr.
Russell, Steven Turner
Scowcroft, Jerome Chilwell
Tollefson, G. Val

West Virginia
Hayhurst, Richard Allen

Wisconsin
Baldwin, Gordon Brewster

TERRITORIES OF THE UNITED STATES

Puerto Rico
Ezratty, Harry Aaron

JAPAN
Shannon, William James

SAUDI ARABIA
Chang, Leo

ADDRESS UNPUBLISHED
Carrington, Morris Clifford
Maher, John A.
Mattson, James Stewart

ANTITRUST

UNITED STATES

Alabama
Page, Lewis Wendell, Jr.
Ruegsegger, Martin Craig
Shoulders, Bobby Harris
Somerville, William Glassell, Jr.
Spransy, Joseph William
Stabler, Lewis Vastine, Jr.

Arizona
Allen, Robert Eugene Barton
Bluemle, Robert Louis
Burke, Timothy John
Galbut, Martin Richard
Harrison, Mark I.
Henderson, David Allen
Lieb, John Stevens
Peck, Deana S.
Price, Charles Steven
Spritzer, Ralph Simon
Titus, Jon Alan
Tubman, William Charles

Arkansas
Creasman, William Paul
Jennings, Alston
Simpson, James Marlon, Jr.

California
Adams, Cary Meredith
Adams, Marcia Howe
Alexander, George Jonathon
Baker, Robert Kenneth
Barza, Harold A.
Baxter, William Francis
Belleville, Philip Frederick
Bernhard, Herbert Ashley
Bertain, G(eorge) Joseph, Jr.
Bower, Paul George
Boyd, William Sprott
Brick, Ann Veta
Callan, Terrence A.
Cameron, Mark Alan
Chilvers, Robert Merritt
Clark, Alan Benjamin
Cohen, Nancy M.
Cox, Stephen Troyce
Cumming, George Anderson, Jr.
Curry, Daniel Arthur
Daggett, Robert Sherman
Denman, Alexandra
Dixon, William Cornelius
Donnici, Peter Joseph
Doyle, Morris McKnight
Dungan, Malcolm Thon
Dunne, Stephen Lewis
Duvall, Paul Hamilton
Eisenstat, Albert A.
Epstein, Judith Ann
Ericson, Bruce Alan
Fine, Richard Isaac
Fine, Timothy Herbert
Flick, John Edmond
Fredericks, Dale E.
Gelhaus, Robert Joseph
Getto, Ernest J.
Gowdy, Franklin Brockway
Haas, Richard
Hackmann, Kathy Alene
Hallisey, Jeremiah Francis
Handschuh, G. Gregory
Hanger, Charles Ernest
Harris, Richard Eugene Vassau
Hensley, William Michael
Jackson, Michele Chickerella
Jaffe, Stephen R.
Judson, Philip Livingston
Keenan, Richard
Kirchheimer, Arthur E(dward)
Kwalwasser, Harold Joseph
Libott, Robert Yale
Maddux, Parker Ahrens
Marshall, Douglas Anton
Martin, Joseph, Jr.
Mattson, Marcus
McBurney, George William
McDermott, John Aloysius, II
Merring, Robert Alan
Michaels, Sheldon
Miller, Steven Jeffrey
Miller, William Napier Cripps
Minich, Mark Andrew
Mussman, William Edward, III
Mussman, William Edward
Oggel, Stephen Peter
Olson, Ronald Leroy
Pasahow, Lynn Harold
Powers, Marcus Eugene
Reeves, Barbara Ann
Salomon, Darrell Joseph
Samson, Anthony Donald
Sanders, Joel S.
Schuck, Carl J.
Selman, Roland Wooten, III
Sherman, Martin Peter
Sherrer, Charles William
Sherwood, Arthur Lawrence
Sherwood, Richard Edwin
Sinnott, Randolph Paul
Skol, Armand George
Sparks, John Edward
Spencer, Gregory Scott
Steer, Reginald David
Stone, Richard James
Sullivan, Patrick James
Taylor, William James
Tingle, James O'Malley
Toftness, Cecil Gillman
Weinstein, Steven Louis
Wessling, Donald Moore
Witus, David Gordon
Wylie, Paul Richter, Jr.

Colorado
Cramer, R. Norman, Jr.
Devine, Sharon Jean
Featherstone, Bruce Alan
Figa, Phillip Sam
Hanley, Robert Francis
Harris, Dale Ray
Hautzinger, James Edward
Hjelmfelt, David Charles
Kobayashi, John M.
Kullby, Roy Sigurd
Maginness, Craig Richard
Meiklejohn, Alvin J., Jr.
Miller, Gale Timothy
Sanford, Kendall Thaine
Setter, David Mark
Thomasch, Roger Paul
Wild, Claude Charles, III

Connecticut
Amschler, James Ralph
Bamford, David Ellery
Carten, Francis Noel
Corthell, Jon Randolph
Frank, Mark Kennith, III
Gray, Chester L., Jr.
Langer, Robert Mark
McCobb, John Bradford, Jr.
McGuire, Eugene Guenard
Murphy, William Robert
Neigher, Alan
Owen, H. Martyn
Reynolds, Richard Morgan
Russell, Allan David
Sherer, Frank Audemars, Jr.
Siverd, Robert Joseph
Ward, Charles Daniel
Wiechmann, Eric Watt
Yoskowitz, Irving Benjamin

Delaware
Carroll, John Hawkins
Partnoy, Ronald Allen
Sanson, Barbara Elizabeth
Sheridan, John Robert
Staves, Marion Cole
Wolfson, Herbert Milton

District of Columbia
Abrams, Samuel K.
Alprin, Brian Dean
Andrews, Dale Carter
Atwood, James R.
Bachrach, Eve Elizabeth
Barnard, Robert C.
Barnes, Donald Michael
Bassman, Robert Stuart
Beerman, Bernard Marvin
Berger, Melvin Gerald
Berner, Frederic George, Jr.
Bernstein, Lewis
Bersoff, Donald Neil
Blankenheimer, Susan Leslie
Bono, Gaspare Joseph
Boudin, Michael
Buffon, Charles Edward
Calderwood, James Albert
Carr, Ronald Gene
Carroll, Thomas Phillip
Carter, Barry Edward
Casson, Joseph Edward
Chapman, Dudley Harry
Clarkson, Stephen Batchelder
Coburn, David H.
Cotter, Frank James
Dameron, Del Stiltner
deKieffer, Donald Eulette
DeMuth, Christopher Clay
Denvir, James Peter, III
Dolin, Mitchell F.
Dubuc, Carroll Edward
Efros, Ellen Ann
Ewing, Ky Pepper, Jr.
Flagg, Ronald Simon
Flynn, Richard James
Fortenberry, Joseph Edwin
Fryer, Hugh Nevin
Gellhorn, Ernest Albert Eugene
Goodman, Alfred Nelson
Gorinson, Stanley M.
Green, Robert Lamar, Jr.
Gribbon, Daniel McNamara
Grossman, Joanne Barbara
Grundfest, Joseph Alexander
Halle, Peter Edward
Henry, Roxann Elizabeth
Hills, Carla Anderson
Hobbs, Caswell O., III
Hochberg, Jerome A.
Hoegle, Robert Louis
Howard, Jeffrey Hjalmar
Jacobsen, Raymond Alfred, Jr.
Katz, Hadrian Ronald
Kelly, John James
Kennedy, Cornelius Bryant
Kilcarr, Andrew Joseph
Kiley, Edward John
Kintner, Earl Wilson
Klawiter, Donald Casimir
Kolasky, William Joseph, Jr.
Kurtz, James Louis
Leary, Thomas Barrett
Lerner, Richard David
Lichtenberg, J(oan) Cathy
Lipstein, Robert A.
Loevinger, Lee
Mallory, Charles King, III
Manly, Marc Edward
Matt, Peter Kent
McAvoy, John Joseph
McDavid, Janet Louise
McDiarmid, Robert Campbell
McGrew, Thomas James
McMillan, Richard, Jr.
Melamed, Arthur Douglas
Meyer, Lawrence George
Miller, John T., Jr.
Moates, G. Paul
Mobille, George Thomas
Murchison, David Claudius
Muris, Timothy Joseph
Murphy, James Paul
Murphy, Richard Patrick
Nateman, Gary M.
Nordlinger, Douglas Edward
O'Brien, Denise Marie
O'Sullivan, James Paul
Owen, Roberts Bishop
Palmer, Alan Kenneth
Patton, Thomas Earl
Payne, Kenneth Eugene
Pearce, Cary Jack
Pitofsky, Robert
Podberesky, Samuel
Pollard, Michael Ross
Reidl, Paul William
Richman, Sheldon Barnett
Roach, Patrick Joseph
Rose, Jonathan Chapman
Rubin, Stephen
Rupp, John Peter
Scammel, Harry Glenn
Scocozza, Matthew Vincent
Shaffer, Jay Christopher
Shea, Francis Michael
Shenefield, John Hale
Sims, Joe
Smith, Brian William
Sneed, James H.
Spiegel, George
Spina, George Charles
Sternstein, Alan Barry
Stewart, David Pentland
Stromberg, Clifford Douglas
Stuntz, Reid Pendleton Fitzhugh
Tapley, James Leroy
Tasker, Joseph
Timberg, Sigmund
Tom, Willard Ken
Turnage, Fred Douglas
Vanderstar, John
Vollmer, Andrew N.
Wagshal, Jerome Stanley
Wald, Robert Lewis
Ward, Alan S.
Wegener, Mark Douglas
Weiner, Robert Neil
Weissman, William R.
Westin, David Lawrence
Whalen, Thomas J.
Whitaker, A(lbert) Duncan
Whiting, Richard Albert
Winslow, John Franklin
Wolf, Christopher
Wolff, Elroy Harris
Wyss, John Benedict
Yannucci, Thomas David
Young, William Fielding
Zeidman, Philip Fisher

Florida
Adkins, Edward Cleland
Babler, Wayne E.
Bellak, Richard Charles
Garlick, Michael
Gifford, Donald Arthur
Greer, Alan Graham
Hart, Karl Vance
Kauffman, Alan Charles
Kearns, John W.
Luskin, Paul Bansech
Maurer, Virginia Gallaher
Nachwalter, Michael
Nagin, Stephen E.
Ruggles, Rudy Lamont
Smith, William Reece, Jr.
Weissenborn, Sheridan Kendall
Winicki, Robert John

Georgia
Beringer, William Ernst
Bratton, James Henry, Jr.
Doyle, Michael Anthony
Johnson, Daniel Patrick
Kirkland, June Ann
Langstaff, James Pope
Lester, Charles Turner, Jr.
Marquis, Harold Lionel
Merdek, Andrew Austin
Murphy, Charles Conrow, Jr.
Ponsoldt, James Farmer
Russell, Harold Louis
Vaughan, C. David

Hawaii
Char, Vernon Fook Leong
Sumida, Gerald Aquinas

Idaho
Helvie, Kirk Randall
Hurlbutt, Daniel Chater, Jr

Illinois
Aldrich, Thomas Lawrence
Allen, Henry Sermones, Jr.
Allen, John Trevett, Jr.
Arlow, Allan Joseph
Baker, James Edward Sproul
Banks, Theodore Lee
Barnhill, Charles J., Jr.
Barrett, Roger Watson
Baumgartner, William Hans, Jr.
Bergstrom, Robert William
Beschle, Donald L.
Bierig, Jack R.
Bodenstein, Ira
Bouma, Robert Edwin
Bowman, Phillip Boynton
Boyd, David Parker
Braun, William David
Brezina, David Charles
Britton, Clarold Lawrence
Brock, Charles Marquis
Bunge, Jonathan Gunn
Campbell, Christian Larsen
Carpenter, David William
Cherney, James Alan
Conison, Jay
Costigan, John Mark
Crane, Mark
Dechene, James Charles
Dell, Robert Michael
Easterbrook, Frank Hoover
Eaton, Larry Ralph
Edelman, Daniel Amos
Edgell, George Paul
Elwin, James William, Jr.
Ettinger, Albert Franklin
Fahner, Tyrone Clarence
Finke, Robert Forge
Freeborn, Michael D.
Fritz Cohn, Loreli
Fuson, Douglas Finley
Futterman, Ronald L.
Gordon, James S.
Groenke, Theodore A.
Hahn, Richard Ferdinand
Hanson, Kenneth Hamilton
Hardgrove, James Alan
Harris, D. Alan
Haubold, Samuel Allen
Heininger, Erwin Carl
Hetke, Richard L.
Hiering, James G.
Hoskins, Richard Jerold
Howe, Jonathan Thomas
Hull, J(ames) Richard
Hunter, James Galbraith, Jr.
Johnson, Douglas Wells
Kanner, Steven Alan
Keck, Robert Clifton
Kempf, Donald G., Jr.
King, Michael Howard
Kotz, Richard Frederick
LaRue, Paul Hubert
Lee, Mark Richard
Lee, William Marshall
Leopold, Mark Freudenthal
Levi, Edward Hirsch
Levine, Laurence Harvey
Linklater, William Joseph
Lynch, John Peter
Mason, Henry Lowell, III
McConnell, Jack Lewis
McLaughlin, T. Mark
McNamara, Barry Thomas
Michaels, Richard Edward
Mills, John Welch
Mitchell, Lee Mark
Morrison, John Horton
Morsch, Thomas Harvey
Netsch, Dawn Clark
Nord, Robert Eamor
Nygren, Karl Francis
Perlberg, Jules Martin
Poe, Douglas Allan
Potter, Richard Clifford
Pratt, Robert Windsor
Rahl, James Andrew
Rankin, James Winton
Roos, Robert Carl, Jr.
Rosenfield, Andrew M.
Roti, Thomas David
Rovner, Jack Alan
Saunders, George Lawton, Jr.
Sawyier, Michael Tod
Schink, James Harvey
Schramm, Marilyn Jean
Schultz, Allen H.
Scott, Robert Kent
Shapiro, Stephen M.
Skinner, Samuel Knox
Snell, Thaddeus Stevens, III
Staubitz, Arthur Frederick
Thornton, Robert Richard
Uhlenhop, Paul Buscher
Wade, Edwin Lee
Wildman, Max Edward
Willian, Clyde Franklin
Wood, Diane Pamela

Indiana
Jackson, Andrew Dudley
Ponader, Wayne Carl
Pytynia, Thomas Lee
Trigg, Donald Clark
Yoder, Thomas Woodrow

Iowa
Byers, Donald Charles
Clark, Beverly Ann
Davison, George Frederick, Jr.
Ehlers, Michael Gene

Kentucky
Moremen, John S.
Reed, John Squires, II

Louisiana
Feldman, Martin L. C.
Fraiche, Donna DiMartino
Lipsich, Jerome K.
Stetter, Roger Alan

Maryland
Deerson, Bruce Alan
Hitchcock, Paul Richard
Rettberg, Charles Clayland, Jr.
Wilson, Thomas Matthew, III

Massachusetts
Areeda, Phillip
Beeby, Kenneth Jack
Bennett, Richard Edward
Comegys, Walker Brockton
Dickie, Robert Benjamin
Fitzpatrick, Lawrence Scott
Gannon, Christopher Richard
Goldman, Robert Huron
Larson, Allen Robert
Meserve, Robert William
Messing, Arnold Philip
Mugler, Molly Scott
Phillipes, Peter Michael
Russell, Robert Bernard
Webb, Henley Ross

Michigan
Avant, Grady, Jr.
Calkins, Stephen
Campbell, Scott Robert
Cooper, Edward Hayes
Davis, Roger Edwin
Dunne, Francis Hugh
Goldberg, Fredric Norman
Huss, Allan Michael
Jordan, Michael Jay
Kennedy, Kael Behan
Miela, Deborah Lynn
Nehra, Gerald Peter
Petersen, O. Keith
Ronquillo, Allan Louis
Saylor, Larry James
Steiner, Peter Otto
Tallerico, Thomas Joseph

Minnesota
French, John Dwyer
Heckt, Paul Norman
Loper, Stewart Collins
Maclin, Alan Hall
Marquardt, Merritt Reno
Mays, Charles Andrew
Mundt, Daniel Henry
Oates, Kathleen Marie
Palmer, Deborah Jean
Palmer, John Marshall
Sippel, William Leroy
Sullivan, Michael Patrick
Wegener, Richard James

Mississippi
Henegan, John Clark

Missouri
Bowman, Pasco Middleton, II
Clear, John Michael
Conran, Joseph Palmer
Gardner, Paul Hendricks
Halpern, Burton
Kleine, Richard Allen
Lysaught, Patrick
Miller, Stephen
O'Donnell, Thomas Patrick
Pickle, Robert Douglas
Roedel, John Kennedy, Jr.
Schwartz, Theodore Frank
Thomson, Harry Pleasant, Jr.
Tockman, Gerald
Wilson, Walter William
Wochner, William James
Woods, Curtis E(ugene)
Wyrsch, James Robert

Nebraska
Bartle, Robert Franklin
Krutter, Forrest Nathan
Rinn, Louise Anne

Nevada
Giordano, Paul Gregory

New Jersey
Banse, Robert Lee
Bongiorno, Andrew William
Bovaird, Brendan Peter
Clapp, Alfred C.
Coben, Carl Gerald
Corbett, Peter Gerald
Croft, John W.
Dornbusch, Arthur A., II
Eakeley, Douglas Scott
Einhorn, Harold
Fredericks, Wesley Charles, Jr.
Gimmy, Daniel Patrick
Gleit, Ernest Aaron
Harris, Micalyn Shafer
Kagan, Irving
Lambert, Richard Justin, Jr.
McDonald, James Douglas
Michaelson, Peter Lee
Poyourow, Robert Lee
Rosen, Norman Edward
Sheldon, Scott Jeffrey
Simon, David Robert
Slifkin, Irving
Sperber, Mark David
Stern, John Jules
Storms, Clifford Beekman
Tauber, Frederic J.
Tulkoff, Myer Simon
Weber, Roy Philip
Whitmer, Frederick Lee
Wingate, Richard Charles
Yoerg, Norman, Jr.

New Mexico
Burton, John Paul

New York
Alcorn, Wendell Bertram, Jr.
Altieri, Peter Louis
Andrew, Leonard DeLessio
Angland, Joseph
Arps, Leslie Hansen
Ashley, Daniel Joseph
Axinn, Stephen Mack
Barron, Francis Patrick
Benjamin, Jeffrey
Bernstein, Robert Bruce
Bezikos, Lynne A.
Birrell, George Andrew
Blake, Harlan Morse
Blumkin, Linda Ruth
Boes, Lawrence William
Brendzel, Michael L.
Briggs, Taylor Rastrick
Burkard, Peter Hubert
Cartenuto, David J.
Carter, James Hal, Jr.
Cavanagh, Edward Dean
Charen, Steven Craig
Cirillo, Richard Allan
Clark, John Holley, III

Collins, Wayne Dale
Cooper, Michael Anthony
Cooper, R. John, III
Cornelison, Albert Otto, Jr.
Cotton, James Alexandre
Cox, Marshall
Critchlow, Charles Howard
Dallas, William Moffit, Jr.
Daniels, James Eliot
Davidow, Joel
Davis, Richard Ralph
Debo, Vincent Joseph
Donovan, Richard Edward
Edel, Martin David
Eiszner, James Richard, Jr.
Ekern, George Patrick
Epstein, Michael A.
Evans, Martin Frederic
Faison, William Franklin, II
Falls, Raymond Leonard, Jr
Ferguson, Tracy Heiman
Finkelstein, Ira Allen
Fischel, Shelley Duckstein
Fleming, John C.
Forte, Wesley Elbert
Foster, David Lee
Freeman, David John
French, John, III
Freund, Fred A.
Friedman, Victor Stanley
Gaffney, Mark William
Gaines, Weaver Henderson, Jr.
Gallantz, George Gerald
Garcia, Maria Elias
Gillespie, Alexander Joseph, Jr.
Givens, Richard Ayres
Glickstein, Steven
Gold, Stuart Walter
Goldschmid, Harvey Jerome
Greenawalt, William Sloan
Greenberg, Ira George
Greenfield, Jay
Greenspan, Leon Joseph
Halpern, Ralph Lawrence
Handler, Milton
Harbison, James Wesley, Jr.
Hardin, Adlai S., Jr.
Hartzell, Andrew Cornelius, Jr.
Hay, George Alan
Himes, Jay L(eslie)
Hoffman, John Flethcer
Hoffmann, Malcolm Arthur
Hope, Theodore Sherwood, Jr.
Horkovich, Robert Michael
Horowitz, Harold A.
Hudspeth, Stephen Mason
Jackson, Thomas Gene
Jackson, William Eldred
Jacobson, Jonathan M.
Jaglom, Andre Richard
Joffe, Robert David
Jones, Lucian Cox
Joseph, Leonard
Kane, David Schilling
Kaplan, Lewis A.
Katz, Robert James
Kaufmann, Jack
Kessler, Jeffrey L.
Keyko, David George
Kocher, Walter William
Koob, Charles Edward
Krane, Steven Charles
Larkin, Leo Paul, Jr.
Levy, Herbert Monte
Lewis, Grant Stephen
Lieberman, Steven Paul
Lifland, William Thomas
Lindley, David Morrison
Lira, David M.
Lynn, Robert Patrick, Jr.
MacCrate, Robert
Machlowitz, David Steven
MacWhorter, Robert Bruce
Maidman, Stephen Paul
Malina, Michael
Marames, William Etheme
Maxeiner, James Randolph
McBaine, John Neylan
McCarthy, Robert Emmett
Mc Donald, William J.
McGuire, Harold Frederick
McKinney, James Bernard, Jr.
Meiklejohn, Donald Stuart
Melican, James Patrick, Jr.
Mitchell, Robert Everitt
Mohen, Thomas Patrick
Moyer, Jay Edward
Murray, Conal Eugene
Neville, Martin John
O'Reilly, Kevin Thomas
Orr, Dennis Patrick
Osgood, Robert Mansfield
Paul, James William
Payment, Kenneth Arnold
Pearlman, Michael Allen
Pegram, John Braxton
Pelster, William C.
Pepper, Allan Michael
Petito, Christopher Salvatore
Pfeffer, David H.
Piliero, Robert Donald
Pinzler, William Michael
Plottel, Roland
Poth, Harry Augustus, Jr.
Primps, William G.
Prince, Kenneth Stephen
Prutzman, Lewis Donald, Jr.
Quinlan, Guy Christian
Quinn, Yvonne Susan
Reinthaler, Richard Walter
Rich, R(obert) Bruce
Rifkind, Robert Singer
Robinowitz, Stuart
Rosdeitcher, Sidney S.
Rudoff, Surie
Ryan, Michael Edmond
Sacks, Ira Stephen
Safer, Jay Gerald
Saunders, Paul Christopher
Schirmeister, Charles F.
Segall, Mark Edward
Serota, James Ian
Sesser, Gary Douglas
Sexton, Richard
Shannon, Michael George
Shapiro, Jerome Gerson
Silverman, Moses
Simonton, Robert Bennet
Smith, George Emmett
Smith, John Stuart
Soden, Paul A.
Sokolow, Asa D.
Sorkin, Laurence Truman
Spivack, Gordon Bernard
Springer, Paul David
Stengel, James Lamont
Steuer, Richard Marc
Stewart, Charles Evan
Stoll, Neal Richard
Stratton, Walter Love
Struve, Guy Miller
Swanson, Richard Paul
Sweet, Joseph Church, Jr.
Taffet, Richard S.
Takashima, Hideo
Targoff, Michael Bart
Taylor, Job, III
Thomashower, William Jay
Tomao, Peter Joseph
Townsend, John Michael
Tritell, Randolph Wayne
Urowsky, Richard J.
Vega, Matias Alfonso
Versfelt, David Scott
Wagner, Richard Hopkins
Walsh, John Bronson
Warden, John L.
Weinstock, David S(tanley)
Williams, Averill Marshall
Windman, Joel A.
Woolley, Edward Alexander
Zoghby, Guy Anthony

North Carolina

Bambury, Joseph Anthony, Jr.
Clodfelter, Daniel Gary
Enns, Rodrick John
Guterman, James Hans
Remsburg, F(rank) Raine
Vestal, Tommy Ray

Ohio

Borowitz, Albert Ira
Faruki, Charles Joseph
Fisher, Stanley Morton
Ford, Ashley Lloyd
Franz, Paul Allen
Gary, Robert Dale
Gerhart, Peter Milton
Graney, Michael Proctor
Hardy, William Robinson
Harrison, William K.
Hartman, George Edward
Hoerner, Robert Jack
Hornbostel, John F., Jr.
Jacobs, Leslie William
Kahrl, Robert Conley
Karch, George Frederick, Jr
Kubiak, Jon Stanley
Libert, Donald Joseph
McCuen, John Francis, Jr.
McNew, Robert A.
Piraino, Thomas Anthony
Pogue, Richard Welch
Rapp, Gerald Duane
Sandrock, Scott Paul
Saul, Irving Isaac
Stancati, Joseph Anthony
Steinhouse, Carl Lewis
Watts, Steven Richard
Weller, Charles David
Witherell, Dennis Patrick

Oklahoma

Fischer, John Frederick
Jarboe, John Bruce
Lewis, John Furman
Nelon, Robert Dale
Scott, Willard Philip
Walsh, Lawrence Edward

Oregon

Bonyhadi, Ernest
Fechtel, Edward Ray
Hurd, Paul Gemmill
Kane, Henry Smith
LaBarre, Jerome Edward
Tilbury, Roger Graydon
Van Valkenburg, Edgar Walter
Webb, Jere M.
Wilcox, Robin Bachrach

Pennsylvania

Armstrong, Stephen Wales
Berger, David
Blenko, Don Balman
Bogus, Carl Thomas
Brown, Donald
Busch, H. Donald
Chamberlain, James Robert
Curran, William James, III
Demers, Timothy Francis
Dougherty, James Thomas
Elliott, John Michael
Elliott, William Homer, Jr.
Fox, Michael David
Fox, Reeder Rodman
Granoff, Gail Patricia
Grant, M. Duncan
Gutnick, H. Yale
Hershey, Dale
Kauffman, Bruce William
Kessler, Alan Craig
King, Dominic Benson
Kohn, Harold Elias
Levin, Arnold
Lipson, Barry J.
Mannino, Edward Francis
Mills, Kathleen Anne Merry
Mullinix, Edward Wingate
Murphy, Joseph Edward
Nalle, Horace Disston, Jr.
Newberg, Herbert Barkan
O'Connor, Edward Gearing
Phillips, Almarin
Poul, Franklin
Quay, Thomas Emery
Reich, Abraham Charles
Rome, Edwin Phillips
Schmidt, Edward Craig
Schmidt, Gordon Williams
Schmidt, Harold Robert
Shestack, Jerome Joseph
Smith, Judy Goldstein
Specter, Howard Alan
Spiegel, Robert Joseph
Toll, Seymour I.
Walsh, Donald Peter
Weil, Jeffrey George
Weinstein, David Haym
Welty, John Rider
Wilson, Bruce Brighton
Yohe, Susan Ann
Zemaitis, Thomas Edward

Rhode Island

Maneckji, Bhikhaji Maneck
Medeiros, Matthew Francis

South Carolina

Day, Richard Earl
McKnew, Natalma M.
Phillips, Joseph Brantley, Jr.
Robinson, David Wallace
Swagart, Harry Augustus, III

Tennessee

McQuiston, John Ward, II
Raines, Jim Neal
Riley, Steven Allen
Standel, Richard Reynold, Jr.

Texas

Alexander, Neil Kenton, Jr.
Allison, John Robert
Atlas, Scott Jerome
Austin, Page Insley
Beane, Jerry Lynn
Bircher, Edgar Allen
Bonesio, Woodrow Michael
Buether, Eric W.
Carmody, James Albert
Casterline, Cecil W.
Degenhardt, Harold F.
Dieter, James George
Dillon, Clifford Brien
Ericson, Roger Delwin
Folse, Parker C(amile), III
Freeman, Philip Dayne
Furgeson, William Royal
Glickman, Julius
Harrison, Orrin Lea, III
Harrison, Reese Lenwood, Jr.
Harvin, David Tarleton
Hinshaw, Chester John
Hoag, Mary Moore
Huffman, Gregory Scott Combest
Leatherbury, Thomas Shawn
Lents, Ann
Lezar, Tex
Lippe, Emil, Jr.
Mack, Theodore
Marks, Gary Lee
Marquardt, Robert Richard
Matthews, Wilbur Lee
McAtee, David Ray
McClure, Donald John
McGowan, Gary V.
McGowan, Patrick Francis
Moros, Nicholas Peter
Morton, Thomas Edward, Jr.
Moss, Joe Albaugh
Petersen, Gale Roy
Peterson, Gale Roy
Pfunder, Curtis Clark
Poehner, George Richard
Price, John Aley
Reasoner, Harry Max
Reed, Harry Lowe
Schwartz, Charles Walter
Smith, Phillip Nolan, Jr.
Stephens, John F., Jr.
Tanner, Sheryl Malick
Van Fleet, George Allan
Voyles, Robb Lawrence
Walls, Robert Ernest
Wheelock, Eugene Thomas
Wilson, James William
Witherspoon, James Winfred

Utah

Dallimore, Suzanne Meredith
Gardiner, Lester Raymond, Jr.

Vermont

Jarrett, Glenn Alan

Virginia

Briney, Roger Albert
Calvetti, Frederick F.
Carrell, Daniel Allan
Clinard, Robert Noel
Feidler, Robert Ernest
Hugin, Adolph Charles
Kovacic, William Evan
Levy, Richard
Patterson, Robert Hobson, Jr.
Peters, David Frankman
Rau, Lee Arthur
Schwaab, Richard Lewis
Toothman, John William
Walsh, James Hamilton
Walton, Morgan Lauck
Wimbush, Frederick Blair
Wooldridge, William Charles

Washington

Alsdorf, Robert Hermann
Berry, Douglas Clayton
Bishin, William Robert
Brenner, David (Merle)
Burman, David John
Foreman, Dale Melvin
Gandara, Daniel
Gardner, Alan Joel
Greenan, Thomas J.
Hereford, Earle J., Jr.
Langlie, Arthur Sheridan
Sandler, Michael David
Ziontz, Martin Lowell

West Virginia

Barnette, David Allen
Fusco, Andrew G.
Shepherd, Richard Earnshaw

Wisconsin

Bolger, T(homas) Michael
Burroughs, Charles Edward
Cross, David R.
Fairbanks, Roberta R(onya)
Fischer, Michael Davin
Holz, Harry George
Schramm, Bernard Hall
Wiley, Edwin Packard

CANADA

Ontario

Roberts, Richard Jack

ENGLAND

Jackman, Robert L.

SWITZERLAND

Goldstein, E. Ernest

ADDRESS UNPUBLISHED

Alexander, James Patrick
Avery, James Thomas, III
Braun, Jerome Irwin
Dratler, Jay, Jr.
Ellis, Neil Richard
Glober, George Edward, Jr.
Goldman, Barbara Lynn
Gusman, Robert Carl
Hafner, Thomas Mark
Holbrook, Donald Benson
Maher, John A.
Marx, Gary Samuel
McCarthy, J. Thomas
Newman, Carol L.
Reycraft, George Dewey
Shaffert, Kurt

APPELLATE. *See* Civil Litigation.

BANKING. *See also* Commercial.

UNITED STATES

Alabama

Barnes, Louie Burton, III
Bell, Thomas Reuben
Borg, Joseph Philip
Byram, James Asberry, Jr.
Campbell, Maria Bouchelle
Childs, Larry Brittain
Clark, John Foster
Garner, Robert Edward Lee
Hamilton, Palmer Clarkson
Hardegree, Arthur Lee, III
Holland, Lyman Faith, Jr.
McKinley, Edmon Howard
Page, Lewis Wendell, Jr.
Riegert, Robert Adolf
Sims, Ronald Louis
Taylor, George Malcolm, III

Alaska

Ostrovsky, Lawrence Zelig
Sneed, Spencer Craig

Arizona

Beggs, Harry Mark
Clarke, Marilee Miller
Dunipace, Ian Douglas
Epling, Richard Louis
Rivoir, William Henry, III
Zukowski, Michael Chester

Arkansas

Bailey, Frank Henry
Brady, Lawrence Joseph
Campbell, George Emerson
Friday, Herschel Hugar
Hughes, Thomas Morgan, III
Lance, James Winslow
White, Stephen Alan

California

Abbott, Barry A.
Adams, Dirk Standley
Baudler, David Evan
Bear, Henry Louis
Black, Donald Bruce
Burrill, Janice Hilary
Callender, William Lacey
Castro, Leonard Edward
Chilleri, Gino Amerigo
Chong, Debra Ann
Clark, R(ufus) Bradbury
Coleman, Thomas Young
Cologne, Knox Mason, III
Demko, Joseph Nicholas, Jr.
Downer, Michael Josef
Eckardt, Richard William
Engel, George Larry
Fabian, JoAnne Frances
Fields, Henry Michael
Garcia, Terry Donato
Goldstein, Richard Jay
Greenberg, Maxwell Elfred
Haines, Michael Anthony
Harley, Halvor Larson
Harwood, Dennis Westcott
Houck, John Burton
Jordan, Lawrence Whiting, Jr.
Kelly, Daniel Grady, Jr.
Klafter, Cary Ira
Lerrigo, Frank C.
Leventhal, Frederic Daniel
Link, George Hamilton
Marker, Marc Linthacum
Marshall, Ellen Ruth
McLane, Frederick Berg
Meyer, Donald Robert
Millard, Neal Steven
Miller, Mona Joy Deutsch
Minnick, Malcolm David
Musacchio, Kirk Anthony
Nelson, David Edward
Nichols, Alan Hammond
Olson, James Calvin
Preble, Laurence George
Quenneville, Kathleen
Reeves, Barbara Ann
Richard, Monte Dwight
Roster, Michael
Ryan, Reade Haines, Jr.
Santandrea, Mary Frances
Saroyan, Suren Michael
Scott, Kenneth Eugene
Sheehan, Lawrence James
Shortz, Richard Alan
Silbaugh, Preston Norwood
Smith, Milan Dale, Jr.
Smith, Scott Ormond
Spatz, Alan Brent
Sterrett, James Kelley, II
Sullivan, William Francis
Thomas, Joseph Edward
Thoren-Peden, Deborah Suzanne
Tormey, James Roland, Jr.
Tumpson, Albert Joseph
Weg, Howard J.
Weinman, Glenn Alan
Weissman, Robert Allen
Yancey, David Wallace

Colorado

Benjamin, James Gilbert
Cahan, Judith E.
Dauer, Edward Arnold
DeMuth, Alan Cornelius
Durfee, Amy Lee McElheny
Gabriel, Eberhard John
Gast, Richard Shaeffer
Haake, Catharine Ann
Hanrahan, Kathleen Susan
Jacobs, Ronald Hedstrom
Keely, George Clayton
Knudsen, Curtis Edwin
Maas, John Edward
Martin, Ronald M.
McCray, Sandra Broomfield
Owen, James Churchill
Padilla, James Earl
Pluss, Stewart Jay
Smethills, Harold Reginald
Ward, Lester Lowe, Jr.
Westbrook, Jane Elizabeth
Zimmerman, Steven Louis

Connecticut

Arturi, Peter A., II
Fignar, Eugene Michael
Fineberg, David L(eman)
Finn, Harold Bolton, III
Gold, Steven Michael
Hawkins, Barry Curtis
Jensen, Frode, III
Rome, Donald Lee
Rose, Richard Loomis
Schroth, Peter W(illiam)
Schwartz, Lawrence B.
Seiger, Mark Brian
Wilkes, Beverly Lake
Wolfe, Harriet Munrett
Worley, Robert William, Jr.
Yen, Elizabeth Chih-Sheng

Delaware

Blancato, Lydia Cox
Moran, Joseph Milbert
O'Toole, John James
Twilley, Joshua Marion

District of Columbia

Alprin, Brian Dean
Bachman, Kenneth Leroy, Jr.
Ballen, Robert Gerald
Bates, Lawrence Fulcher
Bell, James Frederick
Bernhard, Berl
Blankenheimer, Susan Leslie
Bruemmer, Russell John
Carmel, Frank Joseph
Clark, Larry Allen
Crotty, Michael F.
Cushing, Robert Hunter
Eccard, Walter Thomas
Fleischer, James Sidney
Gell, Carl Leddin
Gibson, Joseph Lee
Gilberg, David Jay
Gingold, Dennis Marc
Gleason, Jean Wilbur
Golden, Gregg Hannan Stewart
Griffin, L. Robert
Hill, Rufus Sadler, Jr.
Hunt, David Wallingford
Kelly, Anastasia Donovan
Koffler, Warren William
Kramer, Franklin David
Kramer, William David
Kroener, William Frederick, III
Lawton, Bettina Mary
Leedy, William H.
Leibold, Arthur William, Jr.
Levenson, Alan Bradley
Lipton, Frederick Steven
Long, Charles Thomas
Lucas, Steven Mitchell
Lynn, James Bruce
Madden, Jerome Anthony
Maguire, Margaret Louise
Maiwurm, James John
Marans, J. Eugene
Marinaccio, Charles Lindbergh
Marshall, Sylvan Mitchell
Muckenfuss, Cantwell Faulkner, III
Okun, Todd Alan
Pilecki, Paul Steven
Policy, Vincent Mark
Raimi, Burton Louis
Rath, Francis Steven
Rowe, Robert Gammell, III
Rubin, Stephen
Sczudlo, Raymond Stanley
Shepherd, John Michael
Smith, Brian William
Smith, Jack David
Steingold, Stuart Geoffrey
Tanaka, Akihiko
Thaler, Martin S.
Thomas, Ritchie Tucker
Tomar, Richard Thomas
Vallender, Charles Francis, III

Whiting, Richard Matthew
Williams, Wesley Samuel, Jr.
Wilson, Craig Alan
Wolf, William B., Jr.
Zimmer, Janet Rose

Florida

Abrams, Lehn Edward
Allen, Jospeh Bernard
Ames, Stuart D.
Anderson, Cromwell Adair
Andrews, Dean
Astigarraga, Jose Ignacio
Atlas, Allan Jay
Berley, David Richard
Bogue, Russell S.
Book, Ronald Lee
Borgognoni, Gregory Paul
Buck, Thomas Randolph
Cane, Marilyn Blumberg
Christian, Gary Irvin
Cronig, Steven Carlyle
Cunningham, Ralph Eugene, Jr.
del Valle, Ignacio Gonzalez
Hadlow, Earl Bryce
Hall, David Wayne
Hodge, James Edward
Holliday, Ronald Sturgis
Hornsby, Cyrus Edward, III
Hume, John
Johnston, Shepherd Davis
Jones, John Arthur
Klein, Marina Shank
Krinzman, Richard Neil
Landy, Burton Aaron
Lester, Edgel Celsus
Marcus, Jonathan Seth
McCormick, John Hoyle
McEwan, Oswald Beverley
Moran, James Michael
Moreno, M. Cristina
Orlin, Karen J.
Pajon, Eduardo Rodriguez
Paul, Robert
Petrey, Roderick Norman
Remsen, John Lockwood
Roess, Martin John
Sacasas, Rene
Soble, James Barry
Teblum, Gary Ira
Wallace, Milton Jay
Watts-FitzGerald, Abigail Cory
Whatley, Jacqueline Beltram
White, Russell Alan
Windham, John Franklin
Winicki, Robert John
Wood, Mary Catherine

Georgia

Austin, Thomas Nelson
Baker, David S.
Clarke, Thomas Hal
Dettmering, William O'Neal, Jr.
Dowling, Roderick Anthony
Eubanks, Gary Franklin
Gilbert, John Jordan
Jeffries, McChesney Hill, Jr.
Jordan, Hilary Peter
Kessler, Richard Paul, Jr.
Langway, Richard Merritt
Lester, James Luther
Lower, Robert Cassel
McLemore, Gilbert Carmichael, Jr.
Pennington, Brooks Maddox, III
Searcy, William Nelson
Sibley, James Malcolm
Volentine, Richard J., Jr.
Watson, Forrest Albert

Hawaii

Chung, Harrison Paul
Dyer, George Lewis, Jr.
Fujiyama, Wallace Sachio
Lau, Jeffrey Daniel
Leas, Philip Joseph
Matsushige, Cary Shigeru
Moon, John Paul
Okinaga, Lawrence Shoji
Wong, Alfred Mun Kong
Wong, Danton Sunmun
Wong, Reuben Sun Fai

Illinois

Adair, Wendell Hinton, Jr.
Anderson, J. Trent
Baker, Bruce Jay
Brennan, James Joseph
Burke, Richard William
Carter, Melanie Sue
Chandler, Kent, Jr.
Clay, John Ernest
Coughlan, Kenneth Lewis
Drymalski, Raymond Hibner
Elmore, Elbert Francis
Ermentrout, John Curtis
Fawcett, Dwight Winter
Fein, Roger G.
Field, Robert Edward
Finch, Ronald Corydon
Fisher, Ned Lawrence
Fishman, Robert Michael
Franks, Herbert Hoover
Gaines, Peter Mathew
Gieseke, Corinne Joyce
Golden, Bruce Paul
Greenblatt, Ray Harris
Hablutzel, Philip Norman
Hajek, Robert J.
Hanson, Fred B.
Hantla, George Bradley
Hartigan, John M.
Hartmann, Kenneth
Hartzell, Franklin MacVeagh
Harwood, Bruce Alan
Hennessey, Gilbert Hall, Jr.
Herzel, Leo
Howard, Timothy John
Jersild, Thomas Nielsen
Jock, Paul F., II
Kamin, Kay Hodes
Kapnick, Richard Bradshaw
Karaba, Frank Andrew
Kravitt, Jason Harris Paperno
Lapelle, William J.
Liebling, Norman Robert
Malkin, Cary Jay
McDermott, John Henry
McMenamin, John Robert
Meador, James Lewis
Moline, Gary L.
Moltz, Marshall Jerome
Morrow, John Ellsworth
Mulcahy, Daniel Joseph, Jr.
Norden, Dennis Arthur
O'Rourke, Daniel
Prather, William Chalmers
Ras, Robert A.
Reum, James Michael
Ritchie, William Paul
Rosso, David John
Schwartz, Donald Lee
Schwartz, Thomas D.
Seyfarth, Henry Edward
Shapiro, Stephen M.
Southern, Robert Allen
Swanson, Warren Lloyd
Tabis, Bruno Walter, Jr.
Tallant, David, Jr.
Thies, David Charles
Thomas, Frederick Bradley
Tungate, James Lester
Van Meter, Abram DeBois
Walbaum, Robert C.
White, Robert Ellsworth
Wright, Robert Williams
Yoon, Hoil

Indiana

Ancel, Sorelle Jean Lewis
Ancel, Steven Harlan
Austgen, David Michael
Bever, Robert Lynn
Brames, Arnold Henry
Guy, John Martin
Mazur, Lawrence Joseph
Millard, David B.
Miller, Peter David
Modesitt, Fritzy Dal
Neff, R. Matthew
Schultess, LeRoy Kenneth
Smith, Bruce Arthur
Starkes, Dale Joseph
Welch, William F.

Iowa

Eidsmoe, Robert Russell
Hinton, Charles Franklin
Morrison, Edmund Dunham, Jr.
Noyes, Michael Lance
Pechacek, Frank Warren, Jr.
Reasoner, Carroll Jane
Taylor, Richard Lee
White, Harold Wayne
Zoss, Paul Arthur

Kansas

Clinkscales, J(ames) Randall
Cornish, Lebbeus M.
Fursman, Nancy Johanna
Guy, James Matheus
Lasater, Thomas John
Logan, Carl M.
Matlack, Don(ald) (Clyde)
Powell, Craig Steven
Willard, James Stuart

Kentucky

Fannin, David Cecil
Feazell, Thomas Lee
Hogg, Stephen Leslie
Miller, Herbert Allan, Jr.
Schaeffer, Edwin Frank, Jr.

Louisiana

Charboneau, Brian Paige
Chastain, Merritt Banning, Jr.
Cheatham, Robin Bryan
Cutshaw, James Michael
Dwyer, Stephen Irwin
Johnson, Delos Rozelus, Jr.
Larke, George Joseph, Jr.
Lilley, Roy Stuart
McMillan, Lee Richards, II
Morgan, Louis Linton
Richards, Marta Alison
Rubin, David Samuel
Ryan, Gary Lee
Schewe, Bruce Victor
Simmons, Kermit Mixon
Sklamba, Stephen Gerard
Stiel, David Harold, III
Stuart, Walter Bynum, IV

Maine

Neagle, Christopher Scott
Taintor, Frederick Giles
Webster, Peter Bridgman

Maryland

Batoff, Steven Irving
Gershberg, Richard Louis
Godey, Laurence Ringgold
Hopkins, Samuel
Keir, Duncan Wray
Kochanski, David Majlech
Loewy, Steven A.
Mathias, Joseph Marshall
Michaelson, Benjamin, Jr.
Olander, Christopher Dean
Patz, Edward Frank
Stalfort, John Arthur
Taylor, Dane Edward

Massachusetts

Bacon, Douglas Arms
Bryson, David C.
Fischer, Eric Robert
Hall, Susan Medbury
Keshian, Richard
Loria, Martin Alan
Malley, Robert John
McDaniel, James Alan
Mercer, Richard James
Minot, Winthrop Gardner
Paran, Mark Lloyd
Polebaum, Mark Neal
Rosenthal, Gerald Allen
Rubens, James I.
Scott, Hal S.
Sheils, James Bernard
Simons, Steven J(ay)
Thomas, David Lloyd, Jr.
Van, Peter
Weinstein, Seymour
West, Richard Angus
Wilcox, Steven Alan

Michigan

Allen, James Lee
Boltz, Russ Edward
Byington, Robert Lee
Callahan, John William
Fauri, Eric Joseph
Good, Carl Soren
Gordon, Edgar George
Graves, Ray Reynolds
Hertzberg, Robert Steven
Massie, Joel Lee
Olson, M(elvin) Richard
Rabidoux, Mark Kenneth
Rolf, Ramon Frederick, Jr.
Sharp, John
Shoop, Deborah
Skora, Susan Sundman
Spreitzer, John Richard
Steffel, Vern John, Jr.
Vilders, Kurt Ronald
Warren, William Gerald
Watson, Daniel Carvin
White, James Justesen
Williams, J. Bryan

Minnesota

Anderson, Laurence Alexis
Beattie, Charles Robert, III
Florence, Dorothy M.
Fulton, Robert Wright
Heckt, Paul Norman
Jarboe, Mark Alan
Kantor, David
Leonard, Brian Francis
Marrinan, Timothy David
Moland, Bruce
Nys, John Nikki
Savelkoul, Donald Charles
Seymour, McNeil Vernam, Jr.
Stroup, Stanley Stephenson
Tennessen, Robert Joseph
Willemssen, Mac Ronald

Mississippi

Chaffin, William Michael
Harral, John Menteith
Lalor, Owen Patrick
Powell, Roy Durward
Shiyou, Orvis A., Jr.
Snowden, Elton Gregory
Wilson, Leonard Henry (L.H.)
Young, Ralph Edward, Jr.

Missouri

Baer, David, Jr.
Blackwell, Menefee Davis
Bodker, Stuart Eliot
Breckenridge, Bryan Craig
Cooper, Corinne
Ellebrecht, Mark Gerard
Ewing, Lynn Moore, Jr.
Fallon, John Joseph
Fretwell, Norman Elliott
Gallop, Donald Philip
Goldstein, Steven
Graham, Robert Clare, III
Jenkins, James M(ichael)
Johnson, William Ashton
Klamen, Marvin
Minogue, Thomas John
Neill, Robert
Proost, Robert Lee
Reefer, Elizabeth Dross
Schlecht, William Rogers
Starnes, James Wright
Stierberger, Edward Albert
Tindel, John Curtis
Van Cleve, William Moore
Walsh, Rodger John
Weedman, Charles Edward, Jr.

Montana

Jardine, John Hawley
Pedersen, Lance Alden
Robinson, Calvin Stanford
Schaplow, Terry Frederick
Thompson, Theodore Kvale
Towe, Thomas Edward

Nebraska

Domina, David Alan
Haggart, Virgil James, Jr.
Hutfless, Frank James
Katskee, Melvin Robert
Papik, James Elvin

Nevada

Gourley, Robert Vaughn
Pike, George Russell

New Hampshire

Cloutier, Raymond Arthur
Gottesman, David Mark
Hood, James Calton

New Jersey

Alexander, Robert Louis
Blumberg, Leonard Richard
Fasolo, William Alexander
Finestein, Russell Mark
Freis, James Henry
Jaffe, Sheldon E.
Jeffer, Herman
Karp, Donald Mathew
Katz, Richard W.
Lavey, Stewart Evan
Lawatsch, Frank Emil, Jr.
Linett, David
McMahon, Edward Richard
Pfaltz, Hugo Menzel, Jr.
Weber, Walter Winfield, Jr.
Woller, James Alan

New Mexico

Monroe, Jerald Jacob
Pederson, Robert David
Reagan, Gary Don
Skarda, Lynell Griffith
Smith, Leslie Clark
Templeman, James Edwin
Ussery, Albert Travis

New York

Ackerman, Kenneth Edward
Armstrong, James Sinclair
Aswad, Richard Nejm
Baker, Bruce J.
Ballot, Alissa E.
Bean, Bruce Winfield
Bell, Jonathan Robert
Beller, Barry
Benton, Donald Stewart
Berner, Thomas Franklyn
Bialkin, Kenneth J.
Bishar, John Joseph, Jr.
Bleich, David Lloyd
Bornmann, Carl M(alcolm)
Breckenridge, James Richard
Callahan, Nancy Kay
Campbell, Woodrow Wilson
Carswell, Robert
Cashel, Thomas William
Caywood, Warren Gustave, Jr.
Chamberlin, Michael Meade
Cohen, Henry Rodgin
Cohen, Marcy Sharon
Cohen, Richard Barton
Daingerfield, Richard Paul
Daitz, Ronald Frederick
DeKoven, Ronald
Dorado, Marianne Gaertner
Douglas-Hamilton, Margaret Hambrecht
Doyle, Joseph Anthony
Dubin, James Michael
Duffy, James Henry
Eaton, William Mellon
Elicker, Gordon Leonard
Feldman, Edward Steven
Fernandez, Jose Walfredo
Fishman, Mitchell Steven
Flatley, Daniel Kevin
Franklin, Blake Timothy
Garber, Robert Edward
Gaylord, Bruce Michael
Geitz, Michael M(eyer)
Gelatt, Timothy Arthur
Gewirtz, Elliot
Gillespie, David Arthur
Ginsberg, Ernest
Giusti, William Roger
Golden, Christopher Anthony
Goldstein, Marcia Landweber
Gooch, Anthony Cushing
Gordon, Jeffrey Neil
Greene, Herman Fortescue
Grew, Robert Ralph
Handwerker, Kevin
Haroldson, Jeffrey David
Hauser, Rita Eleanore Abrams
Hayes, Norman Robert, Jr.
Hellman, Charles David
Hirsch, Melvin L.
Hopkins, Thomas Arscott
Humphreys, Noel Dutton
Iovenko, Michael
Jones, Jeffrey Russell
Jones, Lucian Cox
Juterbock, Richard Edwin
Kamarck, Martin Alexander
Kanter, Carl Irwin
Katzenstein, Charles Bernard
Kelly, William Wright
Kornstein, Michael Allen
Kullen, Richard Charles, Jr.
Lane, Arthur Alan
Lee, Robert Edward, Jr.
Levie, Joseph Henry
Lindskog, David Richard
Lovejoy, Allen Fraser
MacRae, Cameron Farquhar, III
Malloy, Michael Patrick
Maney, Michael Mason
Marcus, Eric Peter
Marcus, Myron
Marlatt, Jerry Ronald
Martin, Allan A.
Masinter, Edgar Martin
McLaughlin, Joseph Thomas
Meislahn, Harry Post
Millard, John Alden
Miller, Arthur Madden
Mitchell, Richard Austin
Moore, Harold Francis
Mudge, George Alfred
Musselman, Francis Haas
Myerson, Toby Salter
Nadkarni, Girish Vishwanath
Nelson, Joni Lysett
Newcomb, Danforth
Nimkin, Bernard William
Nussbaum, Paul Allan
O'Connor, William Jennings, Jr.
O'Connor, William Matthew
O'Hara, Robert Sydney, Jr.
Pacious, Shaun Francis
Parry, William Henry
Peet, Charles D., Jr.
Peterson, James Richard
Pike, Laurence Bruce
Pisar, Samuel
Plum, Stephen Haines, IV
Plump, Leslie Z.
Pollack, Stanley P.
Pollan, Stephen Michael
Potter, Hamilton Fish, Jr.
Prentice, Eugene Miles, III
Puleo, Frank Charles
Rabb, Bruce
Radon, Jenik Richard
Reitman, Jeffrey B.
Rinaldi, Frank Robert
Roach, Peter Tatian
Robinson, Irwin Jay
Rocklen, Kathy Hellenbrand
Root, Stuart Dowling
Rosenblith, Robert Manuel
Ross, Michael Aaron
Ruda, Howard
Satrom, Robert Charles
Schaefer, David Stuart
Schechter, Daniel Philip
Schecter, Sandra Jan
Scheibe, Robert Henry
Schnall, Flora
Schwarcz, Steven Lance
Seader, Paul Alan
Serchuk, Ivan
Shapiro, George M.
Shea, William Alfred
Silverman, William Michael
Sims, Garland Dwight
Spollen, John W.
Stack, Daniel
Stevenson, Justin Jason, III
Stuart, Alice Melissa
Sussman, Edna Rubin
Szwalbenest, Benedykt Jan
Taverni, Linda Troy
Taylor, Gregory Frederick
Taylor, Richard Trelore
Tehan, John Bashir
Terry, Tai Chang
Thompson, Katherine Genevieve
Tidwell, Drew Virgil, III
Tooker, Robert Luce
Toomey, Richard Andrew, Jr.
Tortoriello, Robert Laurence
Trott, Dennis Charles
Veneruso, James John
Wade, George Joseph
Wanderman, Susan Mae
Warner, Edward Waide, Jr.
Weil, Peter Henry
Weiner, Jack H.
Weir, Peter Frank
Wheeler, John William
Wilkens, Beth Ela
Worenklein, Jacob J.
Wysocki, Henry Victor
Yanas, John Joseph
Zeichner, Mark
Zimmerman, Jean

North Carolina

Adams, Alfred Gray
Bata, Rudolph Andrew, Jr.
Craven, David Leigh
Dunn, Jackson Thomas, Jr.
Eads, Wayne Buchanan
Gallant, Wade Miller, Jr.
Loughridge, John Halsted, Jr.
Strayhorn, Ralph Nichols, Jr.
Ward, David Livingstone, Jr.

North Dakota

Kelsch, William Charles

Ohio

Adams, Lee Stephen
Biars, Mark Martin
Bridgeland, James Ralph, Jr.
Burgess, Julia Edith
Campbell, Anita Peli
Campbell, Paul Barton
Cavendish, Thomas Edgar
Christensen, Jon Alexander
Coen, George Weber
Coquillette, William Hollis
Csank, Paul Lewis
DeRousie, Charles Stuart
Detec, David Alan
Dixon, Carl Franklin
Farrar, Elizabeth Grace Turrell
Finn, Chester Evans
Fox, Mary Ellen
Frasier, Ralph Kennedy
Gherlein, John Harlan
Haines, Richard McKinney
John, Sidney Charles
Johnston, Lorene Gayle
Lang, Francis Harover
Lenn, Stephen Andrew
Peltier, Linda Jeanne
Roj, William Henry
Rubin, Robert Samuel
Savage, Barry Emery
Todt, Daniel Thomas
Utrecht, James David
Warrington, John Wesley
Wiersma, David Charles

Oklahoma

Andrews, John Charles
Banker, Barbara L.
Beech, Johnny Gale
Britton, James Edward
Dean, Bill Verlin, Jr.
Drake, David Allen
Ford, Michael Raye
McCollam, M. E.
McElroy, Bert Colyar
Pray, Donald Eugene
Pringle, Lynn Allan
Robinson, Adelbert Carl
Sparks, John O.
Swinford, John Walker

Oregon

Bailey, Henry John, III
Bauer, Henry Leland
Byczynski, Edward Frank
Chapman, Matthew William
Fulsher, Allan Arthur
Greenwood, Myrtle Rae
Muhlheim, Wilson C.
Nye, Daniel Alan
Philpott, Steven Lee
Rasmussen, Richard Robert
Turnbow, William Randolph

Pennsylvania

Auerbach, Sheryl Lynn
Barrett, Karen Moore
Beckman, Donald
Berger, Lawrence Howard
Brown, Edward George
Brown, Robert Wayne
Chamberlain, Gerard Alfred
Coldren, Ira Burdette, Jr.
Dell, Ernest Robert
Demers, Timothy Francis
Denby, Peter
Dilks, Park Bankert, Jr.
Farley, Andrew Newell
Fernsler, John Paul
Grace, Eugene Peter
Hammond, Mark Bashline
Hershman, Morris Paul
Holland, Fred Anthony

Holloway, Hiliary Hamilton
Hunter, James Austen, Jr.
Jacobson, Miriam Nechamah
Johnson, Rena
Kline, Sidney DeLong, Jr.
Krawitz, Sidney L.
Laberee, Peter Walter
Lees, Steven Thomas
Mannino, Edward Francis
Monteverde, Tom Peter
Mundheim, Robert Harry
Nicholson, Bruce Allen
Page, Clemson North, Jr.
Phillips, Almarin
Picker, Millicent Ann
Posner, David S.
Preate, Ernest D.
Richardson, Joseph Ablett, Jr.
Rogers, Thomas Charles
Schoyer, David Kennedy
Schroeder, William Francis
Shagin, Craig Randall
Singer, Paul Meyer
Sloane, William Martin
Speers, Thomas James
Stone, Laura Williams
Thiess, Kenneth Charles
Tupitza, Thomas Anton
Turrell, James Joel
Walker, David Todd
Weir, Walter, Jr.

Rhode Island

Cohen, Linda Marks
Dowling, Sarah T.
Schoenfeld, Barbara Braun

South Carolina

Barnes, Rudolph Counts
Bethea, William Lamar, Jr.
Clement, Robert Lebby, Jr.
DeLoach, Harris E(ugene), Jr.
Foster, John Witherspoon
Johnson, Lawrence Wilbur, Jr.
King, George Savage, Jr.
Lake, Robert Campbell, Jr.

South Dakota

Prendergast, Terry Neill
Taylor, James Danforth

Tennessee

Bruce, William Roland
Butler, Edward Franklyn
Camp, Randy Coleman
Donelson, Lewis Randolph, III
Evans, Thomas Martin
Farris, Frank Mitchell, Jr.
Fowler, John Ballard
Gerrish, Jeffrey C.
Henry, Arthur Wayne
Kizer, John Fuqua
Langevoort, Donald Carl
Patrick, Gary Ray
Shelton, David Cochran
Siciliano, Gerard Michael
Stringham, Jack Fred, II
Tate, James Solomon, Jr.
Turner, Wesley Dale

Texas

Ainbinder, Michael Cooper
Anders, Milton Howard
Baggett, W. Mike
Barlow, W. P., Jr.
Beasley, Norma Lea
Benson, Larry John
Berry, John Fredrick
Beuttenmuller, Rudolf William
Bishop, Bryan Edwards
Block, Nelson Richard
Block, Steven Robert
Burney, Cecil Edward
Burney, Frank Burleson
Casseb, Robert Michael
Castle, John Raymond, Jr.
Chalk, John Allen
Chaney, William Calvin
Cobb, Charles Louis
Cobb, Chester Lee
Cochran, George Calloway, III
Conner, Warren Wesley
Cox, Sanford Curtis, Jr.
Craft, George Sullivan
Davidson, Charles E.
de la Garza, Luis Adolfo
Dowd, Steven Milton
Estle, Mark David
Finkelstein, William Berndt
Fisher, J(ohn) Robert
Ginsburg, Marcus
Goldberg, Charles Ned
Gorman, Joseph Thomas, Jr.
Hagerman, John David
Harrington, Bruce Michael
Harris, Charles Dick
Harrison, Clarence Buford, Jr.
Heffron, Jonathon Kenneth
Henderson, George Ervin
Higgins, Robert Gerard
Hunter, Todd Ames
Jameson, Gene Lanier
Jeffers, William A., Jr.
Jones, Billy Ray
Jones, Lindy Don
Jones, Russell C.
Kaufman, Andrew Michael
Kelly, Francis Thomas
Kneipper, Richard Keith
Langley, Earnest Lee
Lippman, Kyle David
Lobert, James Edward
Manley, Larry Paul
McKay, Robert Connally
McNamara, John Bolivar, Jr.
Moehlman, Michael Scott
Morrison, Jeanne Lunsford
Nassberg, Richard T.
Neal, A. Curtis
Neblett, Stewart Lawrence
Nelson, Jack Odell, Jr.
Newsom, Neil Edward
Oates, Carl Everette
Olson, George Albert
Paden, Lyman Rushton
Pettigrew, Karen Beth
Pollan, Thomas Miller
Porter, Charles Raleigh, Jr.
Powers, Timothy Eugene
Rainey, John David
Ratliff, William D., III
Riddle, Michael Lee
Sanders, John Moncrief
Sharp, Christopher Glenn
Sheinfeld, Myron M.
Slaydon, Kathleen Amelia
Smith, Steven Lee
Steele, Glenn Horace, Jr.
Steen, John Thomas, Jr.
Stoffer, James Myron, Jr.
Strauss, Robert Schwarz
Taylor, Joseph William
Taylor, Mark Edward
Taylor, Thomas Alan
Temple, Larry Eugene
True, Roy Joe
Truitt, Robert Ralph, Jr.
Vander Woude, Richard John
Wallace, William Farrier, Jr.
White, David Lawrence
Wilson, Reid Carroll
Wommack, Jr. George Tobin
Wren, James Eric, III
Young, Jess Wollett

Utah

Carlile, Craig
Gallian, Russell Joseph
Harding, Ray Murray, Jr.
Kent, Dale R.
Lewis, Kay Michie
Mackey, Randall Aubrey
Moore, Larry G.
Pleshe, Dorothy Clare
Ross, Yan Michael

Vermont

Capel, Guy B.
Lang, Richard Arnold, Jr.
Prentice, Frederick Sheldon

Virginia

Blair, Richard Eugene
Buford, Robert Pegram
Cabaniss, Thomas Edward
Carter, Joseph Carlyle, Jr.
Dewey, Anne Elizabeth Marie
Donovan, William Jeremiah
Downey, William Gerald, Jr.
Faggert, David Young
Kanovsky, Helen Renee
Kay, William Richard, Jr.
McCauley, Cleyburn Lycurgus
Morris, Dewey Blanton
Pearson, Henry Clyde
Rasmus, John Charles
Stegeman, Thomas Albert
Vandeventer, Braden
Waters, Charles Richard, II
Wood, John Martin

Washington

Bonesteel, Richard David
Gibbs, Nancy Patricia
Gingerich, Florine Rose
Graham, Stephen Michael
Johnson, Theodore Marvin, Jr.
Kuhrau, Edward W.
Pelandini, William Albert
Tune, James Fulcher

West Virginia

Blair, Andrew Lane
Bunner, Patricia Andrea
Hayhurst, Richard Allen
Phillips, John Davisson
Simmons, Alan Russell

Wisconsin

Bosshard, John
Dye, William Ellsworth
Flynn, William Frederick
Gehringer, John G.
Hallett, Kenneth Victor
Klos, Jerome John
Kobriger, Richard Roman, Jr.
Sikora, Ted Robert, II
Stutt, John Barry

Wyoming

Dyekman, Gregory Chris
Guetz, Burton Walter
Lowe, Robert Stanley
McLaughlin, Douglas Ray
Norman, Cherie Shelton

TERRITORIES OF THE UNITED STATES

Puerto Rico

Flax-Davidson, Ron Hunter
Rodriguez-Diaz, Juan E.
Vallone, Ralph, Jr.

ENGLAND

Mecz, Jane Beltzer

FRANCE

Riggs, John Hutton, Jr.

JAPAN

Dickson, Thomas Page

MEXICO

Ritch, James Earle, Jr.
Rogers, John Ellsworth

SAUDI ARABIA

Chang, Leo

SINGAPORE

Siegfried, David Charles

ADDRESS UNPUBLISHED

Baris, Jay G.
Beck, Robert Edward
Cohen, Robert Yale, II
Dickey, Sam S.
Dimon, John E.
Friedman, Lawrence Andrew
Goldman, Matthew Ralph
Hemmer, James P.
Jensen, Gail Kathleen
Lewellyn, Bruce
Moore, Elizabeth Reitz
Murphy, Thomas Hugh
Nash, James Harry
Orlins, Peter Irwin
Schley, Michael D.
Shambaugh, Stephen Ward
Sherrard, Alexander Conn
Simon, Richard Hege
Snider, Ronald Albert
Tisdale, Jeffrey Alan

BANKRUPTCY. *See also* Commercial.

UNITED STATES

Alabama

Alidor, Gary Paul, Sr.
Allen, Robert A.
Bailey, Robert Theodore Russ
Brown, Earl Terry
Conwell, Joseph Thomas
Cotton, Gregory Dale
Crownover, Walter Parker
Davis, Mallory Donald, Jr.
Friedman, Barry Allen
Frierson, Sarah Stewart
Irons, William Lee
Kelly, Leon Fred, Jr.
Kloess, Lawrence H., Jr.
McWhorter, Robert Dale, Jr.
Price, Walter Jasper, Jr.
Scott, Romaine Samples, III
Shepard, Tazewell Taylor, III
Shields, Robert Lloyd, III
Silver, Irving
Sledge, James Scott
Teague, Dewey Wayne
Timberlake, H. Kenan
Watson, Lon Chandler, Jr.

Alaska

Davies, Bruce Owen
Ostrovsky, Jan Samuel
Ostrovsky, Lawrence Zelig
Sneed, Spencer Craig
Therrien, Valerie Monica
Willard, Donna Carol Morris
Yerbich, Joseph Thomas
Yerbich, Thomas Joseph

Arizona

Charles, Robert Marshall, Jr.
Cowser, Danny Lee
Epling, Richard Louis
Forrester, Stephen Cary
Furnish, Dale Beck
Hoog, Patrick Edward
Lee, Richard H(arlo)
Salerno, Thomas James
Stanley, Brian Keith
Thomas, Stephen Allen

Arkansas

Eaton, Jimmy Don
Grace, David Allen
Lee, John Terry
Scott, Isaac Alexander, Jr.
Thomas, Albert, Jr.

California

Allen, Jeffrey Michael
Bennett, Bruce Scott
Borell, Karen Lorraine
Bramley, William Alexander, III
Broude, Richard Frederick
Cecchini, Garrett Lee
Coats, William Sloan, III
Cross, Sandra Lee
Engel, George Larry
Fein, Ronald Lawrence
Goldstein, Richard Jay
Gordon, Robert P.
Hirsch, Morris Wayne
Holden, Frederick Douglass, Jr.
Hotchkiss, Nancy
Jackson, Pamela Curulewski
Jordan, Robert Leon
Kraft, Henry R.
Krahelski, Michael Anthony
Kump, Kary Ronald
Lewis, Adam Aiken
Luppi, Michael Dennis
McCrary, Toni Maree
Mednick, Richard
Meyers, James William
Minnick, Malcolm David
Newmark, Milton Maxwell
Parker, Jeffrey Lionel
Philo, DuWayne Allen
Rabin, Jane Hurwitz
Riesenfeld, Stefan Albrecht
Sallus, Marc Leonard
Schulner, Lawrence Mayer
Share, Richard Hudson
Smith, Scott Ormond
Stenfeldt, Lillian Gerda
Stinnett, Terrance Lloyd
Sussman, Mitchell Reed
Vela, William Paul
Weg, Howard J.
Wein, Joseph Alexander
Weiner, Edward A.
Weir, William John Arnold
Wessling, Robert Bruce
Weston, Kenneth Frederick
Wetmore, Keith Chidester
Wickham, Dennis J.
Wiley, Robert Wayne
Williams, Michael Edward

Colorado

Appel, Garry Richard
Brown, James Elliott
Chapman, Karen Louise
Cleveland, Leslie Click
Cohen, Jeffrey
Cook, Kenneth Totman
DeLaney, Herbert Wade, Jr.
DeMuth, Alan Cornelius
Dowdle, Patrick Dennis
Eklund, Carl Andrew
Falcone, Richard Edward
Gunn, Rebecca Louise
Haake, Catharine Ann
Haskins, Thomas Marston
Inman, Robert Dale
Kimmell, Thomas J.
Kogovsek, Daniel Charles
Maas, John Edward
Markel, Robert Edwin
Martin, Ronald M.
McDowell, Karen Ann
Merrick, Glenn Warren
Moss, Victor
Nunn, Leslie Edgar
Padilla, James Earl
Parker, George Earl
Robinson, Wayne E.
Seifert, Stephen Wayne
Slavin, Howard Leslie
Torpy, Richard Donald
Wilkie, Barry Lynn
Zimmerman, Steven Louis

Connecticut

Coan, Richard Morton
DiPietro, Andrew Michael, Jr.
Fineberg, David L(eman)
Freccia, Vincent John, III
Gitlin, Richard Alan
Grafstein, Joel M.
Lupica, Joseph Richard
Rome, Donald Lee
Royston, Christopher Michael
Shiff, Alan Howard William

District of Columbia

Bardwell, Stanford O., Jr.
Channon, Patricia Sugrue
FitzSimon, Jean Kathleen
Flax, Samuel Allan
Focht, Theodore Harold
Gell, Carl Leddin
Green, Paul Andrew
Hennessy, Ellen Anne
Lamb, Kevin Thomas
Loewinger, Kenneth Jeffery
Mackiewicz, Edward Robert
Micheel, Richard Arthur
Moskof, Howard Richard
Tarkenton, Jeffrey L.
Winkler, Andrea Joanne
Yoder, John Christian

Florida

Bemis, Lawrence Perry
Bogue, Russell S.
Cohen, Jules Simon
Eggen, Eric Carl
Gerlin, William Lance
Hodge, Wilson Eugene
Murrell, Sam Edwin, Jr.
Neiwirth, Ronald George
Rosenfeld, Alexander M.
Schneider, Michael Louis
Shields, William Henry
Stein, Allan Mark
Waller, Edward Martin, Jr.
Warren, Jeffrey Wayne
Whitcomb, William Grandon
Williamson, Michael George
Wood, Mary Catherine
Wynn, Charles Milton

Georgia

Bisbee, David George
Chapman, Barry Ryan
Claxton, Edward Burton, III
Crockett, David Gideon
Gibbs, Stephen Mark
Gifford, William David
Greenblatt, Edward Lande
Head, William Carl
Herzog, Richard Blum, Jr.
Johnson, Walter Frank, Jr.
Kelley, Jeffrey Wendell
Kessler, Richard Paul, Jr.
Lamberth, J. Michael
Lee, Carol Elizabeth
Pennington, Brooks Maddox, III
Scroggins, Frank W.
Stamps, Thomas Paty
Stone, Ralph Kenny
Walker, James Durward, Jr.
Whiteside, Fife Morris
Zink, Deborah Burks

Hawaii

Barbin, Ryther Lynn
Chung, Harrison Paul
Chung, Steven Kamsein
Dodd, William Horace
Gelber, Don Jeffrey
Iczkovitz, Leslie Keith
Kemper, Edward Crawford
Lau, Jeffrey Daniel
Lawson, William Homer

Idaho

Beard, David Benjamin
Blaser, Stephen Jeffery
Eisele, R. Joseph
Sorensen, Murray Jim

Illinois

Ahlenius, William Matheson
Baird, Douglas Gordon
Bates, R. Edward
Bender, Paul Edward
Beu, William Raymond
Blaszak, Michael William
Boies, Wilber H.
Cascino, Anthony Elmo, Jr.
Cohen, Allan Richard
Collen, John Olaf
Coughlan, Kenneth Lewis
Deer, William Henry
Fenton, Marc Ira
Fishman, Robert Michael
Fleischli, Franz K., III
Gaffney, Terrence John
Greenberg, Lorraine M.
Hallock, Robert Wayne
Hanson, Ronald William
Harris, D. Alan
Harvitt, Adrianne Stanley
Harwood, Bruce Alan
Hoseman, Daniel
Kawitt, Alan
Kohn, Shalom L.
Mayerson, Sandra Elaine
McDunn, Susan Jeanine
Nissen, William Forbes
Patricoski, Paul Thomas
Rabinowitz, Mark Allan
Rein, Eric Steven
Richardson, William F.
Schimberg, A. Bruce
Schwartz, Donald Lee
Schwartz, Stuart Randall
Schwartz, Thomas D.
Squires, John Henry
Tabb, Charles Jordan
Tanenbaum, Brian Ira
Ward, Jack Donald

Indiana

Abels, Jonathan Berle
Ancel, Jerald Irwin
Ancel, Sorelle Jean Lewis
Ancel, Steven Harlan
Baker, Ronald Lee
Blomquist, Robert Frank
Hendrickson, Thomas Atherton
Jaffe, Jay
Johnson, Shelli Wright
Jordan, Denver Christian
McNeely, Mark Wright
Miller, Peter David
Moore, James Dalton
Motsinger, Carl Daniel
Ponader, Wayne Carl
Powlen, David Michael
Tourkow, Joshua Isaac
Vician, Glenn Steven

Iowa

Dumbaugh, Robert Frederick
Giles, William Jefferson, III
Karr, Lloyd
Lam, Eric Wing-sum

Kansas

Altenhofen, Craig Joseph
Arnhold, Thomas Dean
Braun, Glenn Robert
Carver, Kevin Scott
Depew, Harry Luther
Guy, James Matheus
Hay, Charles Richard
Johnson, Kevin Blaine
Justus, Jo Lynne
Lowe, Jon Kent
McGee, John Francis
Morton, Robert Ball
Stover, Kathy Ann
Willard, James Stuart

Kentucky

Ames, John William
Apperson, Jeffrey Allen
Atherton, Bruce Dwain
Aulenbach, W(illiam) Craig
Bradshaw, Alice Linda
Bucalos, Dean Walter
Goldberg, James S.
Snyder, Paul Stewart
Spalding, Michael Fredrick
Spalding, Wallace Hugh, Jr.
Varellas, Sandra Motte
Weldon, C. Michael

Louisiana

Anderson, Lawrence Robert, Jr.
Arceneaux, M. Thomas
Begoun, Michael Jay
Bernheim, Sadye Kern
Bezet, Gary Anthony
Burck, Cyril B., Jr.
Cheatham, Robin Bryan
Davis, S. P.
Eatman, Robert Emerson
Friend, Joseph Ernest
Hargrove, Joseph Leonard, Jr.
Johnson, Patrick, Jr.
Leefe, Richard K.
Reed, Bruce Gilbert
Rubin, David Samuel
Steen, Wesley Wilson
Title, Peter Stephen
Trombatore, Janet Moulton
Vance, Robert Patrick
Wright, William Everar, Jr.

Maine

Humpert, Samuel Jay
Patterson, Dennis Michael

Maryland

Barkley, Brian Evan
Brooks, Sheila Durant
Frankel, Roger L.
Harwick, Robert Dean, Jr.
Keir, Duncan Wray
Patz, Edward Frank
Rosen, Gary Alan
Schneider, James Frederick

Massachusetts

Bailey, Frank Joseph, Jr.
Belford, Lloyd Earl
Berliner, L. Jed
Berman, Mark Niles
Cheek, Jo Frances
Countryman, Vern
Czerwonka, Joseph John
Gabovitch, William
Glosband, Daniel Martin

Jackson, Thomas Humphrey
Krulewich, Leonard M.
Marullo, Steven Jeffrey
Parker, Christopher William
Pittas, Sydelle
Polebaum, Mark Neal
Portnoy, Barry Michael
Rosensaft, Lester Jay
Salter, Leonard Melvin
Widett, Irving

Michigan

Batchelor, James Wiley
Bolton, Robert Saul
Callahan, John William
Cline, Daniel James
Cornelius, Ellen Audrey
Ellmann, Douglas Stanley
Ferrier, Jon Todd
Graves, Ray Reynolds
Harris, Stephen James
Hertzberg, Robert Steven
Johnson, Clark Cumings
Lint, Louis Raymond
Mears, Patrick Edward
Panek, Michael John
Riemersma, Jeffrey Kurt
Rochkind, Louis Philipp
Sarb, Thomas Patrick
Taunt, Charles Joseph
Ward, Paul Anthony
White, James Justesen

Minnesota

Johnston, Donald Robert
Keate, Kenneth Earl
Leonard, Brian Francis
Nadler, Richard Gregory
Nora, Wendy Alison
Nys, John Nikki
Saeks, Allen Irving
Weil, Cass Sargent

Mississippi

Abbott, William W., Jr.
Brown, William Houston
Hafter, Jerome Charles
Harral, John Menteith
Holbrook, Frank Malvin
King, Robert Wilson
Olack, Neil Peter
Presson, William Russell
Rosenblatt, Stephen Woodburn
Shaw, Susan Boyce
Smith, Stanley Quinten
Steadman, Susan Kirkpatrick
Webb, Thomas Lowry
Wiser, Nicholas Van
Wright, Michael Eugene
Yoste, Charles Todd

Missouri

Cole, James Silas, Jr.
Cooper, Richard Alan
Cruse, Fredrich James
Enslein, Jerald Stephen
Goldstein, Steven
Hendin, Roy Allen
Lander, David Allan
McCubbin, Garry
O'Loughlin, John Patrick
Pelofsky, Joel
Roser, Michael R.
Rund, William Drake
Shaffer, Herman Morris
Standridge, Richard E.

Montana

Caughlan, Deirdre
Graham, William Arthur
Guthals, Joel Eric
Matovich, Carey E.
Murphy, Gregory G.
Nye, Jerrold Linden
Smartt, Michael Stewart

Nebraska

Benak, James Donald
Cada, James Alden
Cuypers, Charles James
Frank, Julie Ann
Jones, Ida Mae
Loftis, Nancy Lynn

Nevada

Allf, Nancy L.
Beesley, Bruce Thomas
Burns, Thomas Martin
Carter, George Richard
Golden, Michael Patrick
Gourley, Robert Vaughn
Jimmerson, James Joseph
Leverty, Vernon Eugene
Richards, Paul A.
Smith, Stephanie Marie
Sumpter, Rodney Evert
White, John Aaron, Jr.

New Hampshire

Jones, Franklin Charles
Marts, Anthony Charles
Michels, John Rudolf
Rakowsky, Connie Lee

New Jersey

Chaitman, Helen Davis
Chobot, John Charles
Cohen, Mitchell Robert
Corash, Richard
Gindin, William Howard
Harris, Allan Michael
Holt, Jason
Horton, William Harrison
Jacobson, Gary Steven
Kuller, Jonathan Mark
Lihotz, Marie Elaine
Miller, Arthur Harold
Naar, Alan S.
Orr, Thomas John
Robinson, Sandra Ann
Schenkler, Bernard
Smith, Hayden, Jr.
Stanger, Douglas Scott
Thomas, Brian Sean
Tice, Richard Leveridge
Wolfson, William Steven

New Mexico

Bartholomew, James Ira
Curtis, Stephen Paul
Dahl, Jeffrey A(lan)
Fish, Paul Mathew
Hall, Rex Andrew
Hilgendorf, Robert Nelson
Myers, Edward Doran
Waldman, Robert Irwin

New York

Ackerman, Kenneth Edward
Ackerman, Neil Harris
Allen, Richard Marlow
Bader, Howard David
Balaber-Strauss, Barbara
Berzow, Harold Steven
Bienenstock, Martin J.
Blachor, Isaac
Blackman, Kenneth Robert
Bleich, David Lloyd
Block, Lester H.
Booth, Edgar Hirsch
Borowitz, Peter
Brown, Lawrence Charles
Bruno, Richard Thomas
Bryan, Thomas Lynn
Capell, Walter Richard
Cook, Michael Lewis
Cowen, Edward S.
Curran, John Gerard
DeKoven, Ronald
De Natale, Andrew Peter
Dichter, Barry Joel
Drebsky, Dennis Jay
Dresner, Byron
Duberstein, Conrad B.
Eisenberg, Theodore
Emrich, Edmund Michael
Fortgang, Chaim Jacob
Genova, Joseph Steven
Goldberg, Harold P.
Goldstein, Marcia Landweber
Gropper, Allan Louis
Gross, Jack
Gross, Steven Ross
Hahn, Paul Bernard
Halper, Emanuel Barry
Halpern, Kenneth Jay, N
Handelsman, Lawrence Marc
Hatt, Donald Gregory
Hershcopf, Gerald Thea
Heyer, John Henry, II
Hirshon, Sheldon Ira
Howard, Robert Lawrence
Karotkin, Stephen K.
Keller, Robin Elizabeth
King, Lawrence Philip
Kriger, Brian Elliott
Lacy, Robinson Burrell
Laughlin, James Patrick
Levie, Joseph Henry
Lichtenstein, Sarah Carol
Lipton, Robert Steven
Lumbard, Eliot Howland
Maney, Michael Mason
Mann, Philip Roy
Marinstein, Elliott F.
Mayer, Thomas Moers
Mayka, Stephen P.
McDonald, Willis, IV
Mendales, Richard Ephraim
Miller, Richard Steven
Miller, Robert M.
Minkel, Herbert Philip, Jr.
Mitchell, Richard Austin
Moloney, Thomas Joseph
Musselman, Francis Haas
Nissan, Randy S.
Olick, Arthur Seymour
Perkiel, Mitchel H.
Potter, Hamilton Fish, Jr.
Rothman, Robert Pierson
Ruda, Howard
Samet, Joseph
Scheibe, Robert Henry
Scheler, Brad Eric
Schwarcz, Steven Lance
Schwed, Peter Gregory
Siegel, Lewis Wolfe
Silverberg, Sheldon
Silverman, William Michael
Spivack, Edith Irene
Strickon, Harvey Alan
Sussman, Edna Rubin
Taverni, Linda Troy
Terner, Linda M. Johnson
Wade, George Joseph
Weil, Peter Henry
Weisman, Barbara
Zaretsky, Barry Lewis
Zelmanovitz, Menachem Osher
Zinman, Robert Marshall

North Carolina

Badger, David Russell
Brisson, Lloyd Clifford, Jr.
Clodfelter, Daniel Gary
Conti, Sara Angela
Elliott, Joseph Bryan
Farver, Harry Craig
Frassineti, Jordan Joseph
Hopkins, Grover Prevatte
Johnson, Robert Keith
Kirby, Mark Clayton
Schwenn, William Lee
Tilghman, Carl Lewis
Wyche, N(orman) Hunter, Jr.

North Dakota

Minch, Roger James
Price, Robert Quentin

Ohio

Barrett, David Carroll
Baumgart, Richard Alan
Beck, James Hayes
Bertrand, Louis Robertson
Bonaventura, Mark Gabriel
Burns, Donald Andrew
Coombs, Frederick Stanley, III
Cunningham, James Joseph
Fine, Michael William
George, Donald Elias
Haines, Richard McKinney
Heintz, Jeffrey Theodore
Jacobs, Ann Elizabeth
Kopit, Alan Stuart
Lukey, Paul Emeran
Menninger, Henry Edward, Jr.
Meyer, Charles Mulvihill
Mickley, Richard Stroud
O'Brien, William Scott
Petersen, Lee
Pikna, Raymond John, Jr.
Rabin, Mary Ann
Reed, Tyrone Edward
Savage, Barry Emery
Sayler, John Liston
Snow, David Forrest
Strozdas, Jerome Mark
Thompson, Jayne Audrey
Thompson, Stephen David
Zaremba, Thomas S.

Oklahoma

Abrahamson, A. Craig
Banker, Barbara L.
Bohanon, Richard L.
Carson, Michael Jay
Conner, Leslie Lynn, Jr.
Cowdery, Allen Craig
Cunningham, M.C., II
Fitzgerald, Tami Lynn
Graves, Herbert Mac
Henneke, David Charles
Jarboe, John Bruce
Johnson, H. Allen
Kline, David Adam
Kline, Timothy Deal
Miner, Joseph Brian
Moss, Raymond Gene, II
Pringle, Lynn Allan
Rife, Gary Alan
Swinford, John Walker
Turner, Andrew Roland
Vogt, James Wayne
Williams, Betty Outhier

Oregon

Bailey, Henry John, III
Chapman, Matthew William
Deguc, Vincent Anthony
Goldstein, Bennett Howard
Levine, Howard Michael
Snyder, Kent Victor
Spencer, Jesse Neal
Wald, Sandra Louise

Pennsylvania

Adler, Theodore Arthur
Aronstein, Martin Joseph
Bernstein, Robert Steven
Carnecchia, Baldo M., Jr
Cheever, George Martin
Conti, Joy Flowers
Coyne, Charles Cole
Faucher, John Dennis
Gaertner, Gary J.
Galie, Lawrence Pius
Greenfield, James Milton
Gruenstein, Debra Lynne
Hollinshead, Earl Darnell, Jr.
James, Keith Alan
Kaminsky, Ira Samuel
Kemp, K(enneth) Lawrence
Knupp, Robert Louis
Lampl, Sanford Mark
Malady, Eugene Joseph
Mansori, Zubair S.
Meyers, Jeffrey
Morrissey, Philip Patrick
Murdoch, David Armor
Nowak, Darlene M.
Peluso, Gino Francis
Perlman, Richard Brian
Rayman, Robert Craig
Ristau, Mark Moody
Ristau, Mark Moody
Sanders, Russell Ronald
Schorling, William Harrison
Siedzikowski, Henry Francis
Siegel, Marlena
Siegel, Neil Yahr
Singer, Paul Meyer
Tabas, Lawrence Jeffrey
Thompson, John Wilson, Jr.
Vollmer, Charles Joseph
Weir, Walter, Jr.
Wolke, Milton Spencer, Jr.
Woodward, William John, Jr.

Rhode Island

Oster, Robert Daniel

South Carolina

Harvey, James Martin, Jr.
Henry, Angela Louise
Johnson, Lawrence Wilbur, Jr.
Jones, Marvin Coleman
Licata, Steven Barry
Mc Cullough, Ralph Clayton, II
Smith, Thorn McClellan

South Dakota

Sveen, Jeffrey T.

Tennessee

Bandy, Thomas Rochelle, III
Boswell, George Harvey
Cosner, Charles Kinian, Jr.
Grisham, Arthur C., Jr.
Jones, John Thomas, Jr.
Kennedy, Richard Carl
Koontz, George Edward
McIntosh, James Arthur
Merkel, Albert Benton
Okrasinski, Mary Ann
Ragan, Charles Oliver, Jr.
Rothschild, Edgar Meyer, III
Tarpy, Thomas Lynn

Texas

Anton, Richard Henry
Bateman, Hal Marion
Berenson, William Keith
Bernard, Donald Ray
Berry, John Fredrick
Boze, Uriele L.
Brister, Bill H.
Burgchardt, Kathryn Dee
Burke, William Temple, Jr.
Carmody, James Albert
Chaney, William Calvin
Charles, Beverly M.M.
Conner, George Manion, III
Constant, Patricia Reed
Creel, Luther Edward, III
Davidson, Charles E.
Davis, Harrel Leon, III
Eisenbraun, Eric Charles
Ellis, David Dale
Evans, Roger
Farr, Sidney Lavelle
Finkelstein, William Berndt
Gandy, Dean Murray
Gilles, Herbert Jeffrey
Goldberg, Charles Ned
Gover, Alan Shore
Hampton, Charles Edwin
Harris, Charles Dick
Henderson, George Ervin
Hunt, Richard Martin
Hytken, Franklin Harris
Jeffers, William A., Jr.
Jones, Edith Hollan
King, Ronald Baker
Lacey, David Morgan
Leslie, John Edward
Lobert, James Edward
Mack, Theodore
MacNaughton, William Alexander
Maddox, Charles J., Jr.
May, David P.
Mora, David Baudilio
Morgan, Thomas Sidney
Morgenstern, Jonathan David
Neblett, Stewart Lawrence
Noel, David Bobbitt, Jr.
Nolan, John Michael
Oliver, J. Van
Orleans, Neil Jeffrey
Ory, Charles Nathan
Palmer, Philip Isham, Jr.
Patterson, Donald Ross
Peck, David Hill
Pinnell, Gary Ray
Portman, Glenn Arthur
Prestridge, Pamela Adair
Pulliam, Karen Ann
Ray, Hugh Massey, Jr.
Rochelle, Williams Jennings, Jr.
Sessions, William Lewis
Sheetz, William Dean
Sheinfeld, Myron M.
Shipp, H(amilton) Thomas
Silver, Louis Edgar
Slaydon, Kathleen Amelia
Truitt, Robert Ralph, Jr.
Tutt, John Marion
White, Andrea Walker

Utah

Lochhead, Robert Bruce
Mabey, Ralph Rampton
Ockey, Ronald J.

Vermont

Glinka, Gleb

Virginia

Abreu, Luis Alberto
Ackerly, Benjamin Clarkson
Bromm, Frederick Whittemore
Brown, Henry Otis
Cabaniss, Thomas Edward
Clark, Bruce Arlington, Jr.
Conlon, Debera Frick
Eason, Carl Edward, Jr.
Feidler, Robert Ernest
Marzloff, George Ernest
Mulligan, Jennifer
Musselman, Robert Metcalfe
Palmer, William Ralph
Pearson, Henry Clyde
Peyton, Gordon Pickett
Trout, Stran Lippincott
Tucker, James Letcher
Waxman, Ned Warren
Widener, Jo S.

Washington

Carlson, Timothy John
Crandall, Patricia Irene
Feinstein, Larry Burton
Hames, William Lester
Hulse, Brian Douglas
Mathieu, Richard Louis
Mitchell, John Joseph
Sandman, Irvin Willis
Shogan, Alexander Joe, Jr.
Simburg, Melvyn Jay
Utevsky, David

West Virginia

Chaney, Michael Thomas
Kagler, Robert Wayne
Markey, E. Lowell
Richardson, Randolf Emrys
Thompson, Stephen Lee
Wilmoth, William David

Wisconsin

Arnold, Bruce George
Doran, Kenneth John
Eustice, Francis Joseph
Gass, David
Harrington, Arthur John
Howarth, Kim A.
Israel, Scott Michael
Kelly, Mark Daniel
Ludwig, R. Arthur
Mann, Douglas Floyd
Moore, David Charles
Rameker, William John
Russell, David Brent
Sturm, William Charles
Wild, Norman Richard

Wyoming

Girard, Nettabell
Norman, Cherie Shelton

ADDRESS UNPUBLISHED

Bentley, Anthony Miles
Brown, Manny S.
Chesnutt, Charles Raphael
Comer, Vivian Adelia
Drabkin, Murray
Englebrecht, Bruce
Eovaldi, Thomas L.
Fisher, Joseph Freiler
Goldman, Matthew Ralph
Jensen, Gail Kathleen
McIntyre, Anita Grace
Montee-Charest, Karen Ann
Nash, James Harry
Roberts, Larry F.
Rosen, Alex L.
Stout, George McBride
Wagoner, Walter Dray, Jr.
Weisman, Paul Howard
Wolfson, Jack Leonard

CIVIL LITIGATION, FEDERAL

UNITED STATES

Alabama

Bains, Lee Edmundson
Barnard, Hollinger Farmer
Boardman, Mark Seymour
Brown, Earl Terry
Burns, Peter Francis
Byram, James Asberry, Jr.
Byrne, Bradley Roberts
Centeno, Douglas Joseph
Chambers, K.W. Michael
Crouch, James Michael
Davenport, George William
De Ment, Ira
Embry, Thomas Eric
Flowers, Francis Asbury, III
Fuller, William Sidney
Gillis, Lucian, Jr.
Goldstein, Debra Holly
Granade, Callie Virginia Smith
Hanson, Frank Oscar, Jr.
Hellums, Clarence Theo
Hollis, Louie Andrew
Howell, Allen Windsor
Hull, Daniel Talmadge
Huskey, Dow Thobern
Jackson, Micheal Stewart
Jones, Patrick Allen
Kloess, Lawrence H., Jr.
Lawson, Thomas Seay, Jr.
Lyles, Harry Arthur
Lyons, George Sage
Max, Rodney Andrew
McPhillipps, Julian Lenwood, Jr.
Mills, William Hayes
Moorer, Mac Mitchell
Morgan, Wendell Richmond
Moss, Robert William
Munsey, Stanley Edward
Newton, Alexander Worthy
Noojin, Ray Oscar, Jr.
Norman, Robert Daniel
Owens, James Bentley, III
Page, Lewis Wendell, Jr.
Patrick, J. Vernon, Jr.
Pennington, Al
Philips, James Albert
Pierce, Donald Fay
Porter, James Wallace, II
Potts, Robert Leslie
Powell, Scott Ashley
Prestwood, Alvin Tennyson
Quillen, Michael Clay
Ray, Thomas Morgan
Redden, Lawrence Drew
Richardson, Schuyler Harris, III
Rogers, Ernest Mabry
Sapp, Ernestine S.
Sheehan, Charles Winston, Jr.
Shields, Robert Lloyd, III
Shoulders, Bobby Harris
Sledge, James Scott
Smith, Carol Ann
Smith, Robert McDavid
Smith, Rufus Randolph, Jr.
Somerville, William Glassell, Jr.
Stabler, Lewis Vastine, Jr.
Stephens, Ferris W.
Stephens, (Holman) Harold
Stewart, Julia Smeds
Still, Edward
Van Tassel, George Martin, Jr.
Varley, Robert John
Wells, Huey Thomas, Jr.
Wilson, Duane Albert
Wood, James Jerry
Woodrow, Randall Mark
Wyatt, Charles Herbert, Jr.

Alaska

Conway, John Martin
De Lisio, Stephen Scott
Dickson, Robert Jay
Feldman, Jeffrey Marc
Fortier, Samuel John
Hayes, George Nicholas
Hedland, John Sigurd
Pfiffner, Frank Albert
Richmond, Robert Lawrence
Sedwick, John Weeter
Smith, John Anthony
Thomas, Michael Tracy
Willard, Donna Carol Morris
Yospin, Richard Lawrence

Arizona

Bakker, Thomas Gordon
Barron, Caroline Joan
Barry, Edward Louis
Bartos, John Bury
Begam, Robert George
Beggs, Harry Mark
Bivens, Donald Wayne
Bodney, David Jeremy
Charles, Robert Marshall, Jr.

Ching, Anthony Bartholomew
Crenshaw, Richard N.
D'Antonio, Gregory Douglas
Daughton, Donald
Dickey, Harrison Gaslin
Ehinger, James Oakleaf
Galbut, Martin Richard
Gomez, David Frederick
Grant, Merwin Darwin
Harrison, Mark I.
Henderson, David Allen
Hendricks, Edwin Francis
Hyams, Harold
Kelly, Joseph Sylvester, Jr.
Kennedy, Michael Kevin
Kimble, William Earl
Korn, Gary Clifford
Lemberg, Frederic Gary
Myers, Robert David
Novak, Peter John
Paige, David Alwin
Parker, Jeffrey Robert
Paupore, Jeffrey George
Peck, Deana S.
Peters, Donald Mullen
Placenti, Frank Michael
Rusing, Michael John
Ryan, Timothy Leo
Salerno, Thomas James
Seidenfeld, Glenn Kenneth, Jr.
Sims, Terrance Lee
Thorpe, William Lee
Ulrich, Paul Graham
Wall, Donald Arthur
Wezelman, Janice Anne
Williams, Steven Henry
Winthrop, Lawrence Fredrick
Wirken, Charles William
Wohl, Kenneth Allan
Wolfe, David K.

Arkansas

Allen, H. William
Baker, Darryl Ellis
Bristow, Bill Wayne
Carpenter, Thomas Milton
Dillahunty, Wilbur Harris
Drummond, Winslow
Dudley, Timothy Oliver
Dunn, James Melvin
Ellis, George Dawlin
Fleming, Victor Anson
Griffin, Richard Earl
Hall, Betsy
Hargis, David Michael
Harkey, John Norman
Hopkins, Randolph Byrd
Jennings, Alston
Lee, John Terry
Mayes, S. Hubert, Jr.
McClurg, Andrew Jay
Perroni, Samuel Arnold
Ralls, Rawleigh Hazen, III
Roachell, Richard Wilson
Ross, Robert Dwain
Scott, Isaac Alexander, Jr.
Simpson, James Marlon, Jr.
Skinner, Jack Merle
Smith, Michael Glen
Spencer, Frederick S.
Talley-Morris, Neva Bennett
Walters, William Peter
Zukowski, Mark Daniel

California

Adler, Erwin Ellery
Aguirre, Michael Jules
Alexander, Richard
Allan, Walter Robert
Amidon, Robert Bruce
Armstrong, Orville A.
Askew, James Albert
Axelrad, David M.
Babcock, Barbara Allen
Bakaly, Charles George, Jr.
Baker, Robert Kenneth
Balestracci, Paul Noel
Bancroft, David Phillips
Barbabelata, Robert D.
Barnhorst, Howard Joseph, II
Baron, Frederick David
Barrett, Dennis Christopher
Barrett, Jane H.
Barza, Harold A.
Baskin, David Green
Behrendt, John Thomas
Belcher, John Arthur
Bell, Frank Ouray, Jr.
Belleville, Philip Frederick
Bender, Charles William
Bennett, James Patrick
Bennett, Lawrence Arthur
Bentley, John Martin
Bergman, Gregory Mark
Bernhard, Herbert Ashley
Berry, Samuel Harper, Jr.
Bertain, G(eorge) Joseph, Jr.
Bingman, Terrence L.
Bjork, Robert David, Jr.
Bodkin, Henry Grattan, Jr.
Bomberger, Russell Branson
Bonesteel, Michael John
Booher, Lawrence J., Jr.
Borowsky, Philip
Bottger, William Carl, Jr.
Bower, Paul George
Boyd, William Sprott
Brenner, Anita Susan
Bressan, Paul Louis
Brick, Ann Veta
Bridges, B. Ried
Broderick, Daniel Thomas, III
Brooks, Roy Lavon
Brosnahan, James Jerome
Brown, Donald Wesley
Brown, John Clark, Jr.
Bryan, Robert Russell
Burgess, John All
Busch, Peter Jonathan
Bushnell, Roderick P.
Callan, Terrence A.
Candland, D. Stuart
Caples, Michael Edward
Carella, Eugene John
Carrow, Robert Duane
Cathcart, Patrick Alan
Chilvers, Robert Merritt
Chu, Morgan
Clark, Alan Benjamin
Coats, William Sloan, III
Cobey, Christopher Earle
Cochran-Bond, Walter C.
Colley, Nathaniel S(extus), Jr.
Connally, Michael W.
Corrales, Manuel, Jr.
Costello, Edward J., Jr.
Cotchett, Joseph Winters
Cumming, George Anderson, Jr.
Currer, William John, Jr.
Daar, David
Daggett, Robert Sherman
Dalton, Douglas
Daniels, John Peter
Dazé, David Timothy
Dempsey, Michael Douglas
Denniston, Thomas Robert
Derin, Greg David
Diedrich, Peter Joseph
Dolan, Peter Brown
Donnici, Peter Joseph
Dorit, J Niley
Dorr, Roderick Akin
Downing, James Christie
Doyle, Morris McKnight
Drummond, Donald Francis
Dryovage, Mary Margaret
Dungan, Malcolm Thon
Dunlavey, Dean Carl
Dunne, Stephen Lewis
Duvall, Paul Hamilton
Dyer, Charles Arnold
Elion, Gary Douglas
Engstrand, Paul David, Jr.
Ericson, Bruce Alan
Eule, Julian N.
Fairbank, Robert Harold
Farley, Barbara Suzanne
Feller, David E.
Field, Richard Clark
Finch, David Samuel
Fine, Richard Isaac
Fine, Timothy Herbert
Fink, Robert Stanley
Fink, Scott Alan
Fischer, Dale Susan
Fisher, Barry Alan
Fitzgerald, William Brendan, Jr.
Flanders, Gilbert Lee
Flanders, Gilbert Lee
Fredericks, Dale E.
Freiser, Lawrence M.
Fromholz, Haley James
Galton, Stephen Harold
Garay, Erica Blythe
Gauntlett, David Allan
Gelhaus, Robert Joseph
Getto, Ernest J.
Glaser, Patricia L.
Gold, Michael Allan
Golper, John Bruce
Goodwin, James Jeffries
Gordon, Robert Allen
Gowdy, Franklin Brockway
Gray, Veronica Meryl
Greenfield, Larry Stuart
Gregg, Richard
Groman, Arthur
Grossman, Richard Alan
Guilford, Andrew John
Haas, Richard
Hale, Candace
Hale, Charles Russell
Hanger, Charles Ernest
Hanley, Daniel E.
Harris, James Michael
Harris, Richard Eugene Vassau
Harris, Robert Thomas
Hart, Larry Calvin
Harutunian, Albert Theodore, III
Hasson, Kirke Michael
Hausmann, Edwin David
Heafey, Edwin Austin, Jr.
Heilbron, David M(ichael)
Heller, Donald Herbert
Heller, Philip
Hendrickson, Robert Charles
Henke, Raymond Lange
Hensley, William Michael
Herbert, James Keller
Herlihy, Thomas Mortimer
Hetland, John Robert
Heyck, Theodore Daly
Hicks, James B(radley)
Higgins, Willis Edward
Higgs, Craig DeWitt
Highberger, William Foster
Hite, Randall Lee
Hobbs, Franklin Dean, III
Hoey, James Douglas, III
Hofstadter, Sarah Katherine
Holmes, Kenneth Howard
Holzmann, James Charles
House, Calvin Richard
Howard, Kenyon B.
Huebner, Kurt Benoit
Ingram, Robert Bruce
Jackson, Michele Chickerella
Jacobson, Richard Lee
Jaffe, Stephen R.
Johnson, Robert Howard
Johnson, Terry Turner
Jordan, Lawrence Whiting, Jr.
Judson, Philip Livingston
Kaiser, Erik Michael
Kallberg, Kenneth J(oseph)
Kaplin, Gale P. Sonnenberg
Keenan, Richard
Keker, John Watkins
Kerrigan, Thomas Sherman
Kimberling, John Farrell
Kitchen, Jonathan Saville
Klinedinst, John David
Kolkey, Daniel Miles
Kozinski, Alex
Kravitz, Jeffrey Stephen
Ladar, Jerrold Morton
Lageson, Ernest Benjamin
Langer, Simon Hrimes
Lascher, Edward Leonard
Lascher, Wendy Jean Cole
Lathrop, Mitchell Lee
Lauchengco, Jose Yujuico, Jr.
Lawless, William Burns
Lazo, Ignacio Jesus
Levine, David Israel
Levine, Jerome Lester
Levit, Victor Bert
Levit, William Harold
Libott, Robert Yale
Link, George Hamilton
Lloyd, William Emmons, Jr.
Lobner, Kneeland Harkness
Lombardi, David Ennis, Jr.
Lundquist, Weyman I.
Lyon, R. Douglas
Maddux, Parker Ahrens
Mannerino, John David
Marshall, Douglas Anton
Mattson, Marcus
McBurney, George William
Mc Donough, John Richard
McGinley, Nancy Elizabeth
McGuire, E. James
McPherson, Edwin Francis
Meadows, John Frederick
Melbye, Richard Brenton
Merring, Robert Alan
Michaels, Michael Daniel
Millar, Richard William, Jr.
Miller, James L.
Miller, Jules Frederick
Miller, Milton Allen
Miller, Mona Joy Deutsch
Miller, Steven Jeffrey
Miller, William Napier Cripps
Mishkin, Paul J.
Mobley, Gary Steven
Mocciaro, Perry D.
Mogin, Daniel Jay
Mohr, Anthony James
Moore, Douglas Matthew, Jr.
Morgan, Robert Hall
Morgan, William Robert
Mosk, Richard Mitchell
Muhlbach, Robert Arthur
Muller, Edward Robert
Mussman, William Edward, III
Mussman, William Edward
Neumeyer, Richard Albert
Newell, Thomas Peter
Newman, Michael Rodney
Niles, John Gilbert
Nissly, Kenneth L.
Nocas, Andrew James
Nordin, John Eric, II
Oder, Kenneth William
Oggel, Stephen Peter
Olson, Ronald Leroy
Palffy, Thomas
Parish, William Henry
Parker, Jeffrey Lionel
Pasahow, Lynn Harold
Pasternak, David Joel
Pavitt, William Hesser, Jr.
Pearlman, Lisa Ann
Peck, Aaron Martin
Pereyra-Suarez, Charles Albert
Perez, Richard Lee
Perlis, Michael Fredrick
Pizzulli, Francis Cosmo Joseph
Pleiss, Larry Thomas
Plishner, Michael Jon
Pollock, John Phleger
Pooley, James Henry Anderson
Poster, Jeffrey Charles
Pulliam, Mark Stephen
Ramsey, Owen Jasper, Jr.
Reed, William James
Reeves, Barbara Ann
Regalia, Edmund Louis
Regnier, Richard Adrian
Reuben, Timothy D.
Rice, Randolf James
Riffer, Jeffrey Kent
Rinck, Gary M.
Ritter, G. Christopher
Robertson, David Govan
Roche, Thomas Garrett
Roethe, James Norton
Rogan, Patrick Goode
Rosenberg, Arnold Steven
Rosenthal, Kenneth Wolfgang
Rosenthal, Robert Michael
Rothwell, Thomas Henry
Rudolph, George Cooper
Ruston, Donald Allen
Salzberg, Arthur Jonathan
Sanders, Joel S.
Sayad, Pamela Miriam
Schachter, Alesa Rose
Schack, David Paul
Schisler, George Milford, Jr.
Schleicher, Estelle Ann
Schreiber, James Phillip
Schuck, Carl J.
Scoular, Robert Frank
Seal, James Lee
Selman, Roland Wooten, III
Sherwood, Arthur Lawrence
Sherwood, Richard Edwin
Silberberg, Henry J.
Simmons, Robert Michael
Simon, Bruce Lee
Simons, Bernard Philip
Sinnott, Randolph Paul
Sitkin, Peter Edward
Slater, Jill Sherry
Smith, Steven Ira
Snow, Tower Charles, Jr.
Solis, Carlos
Sparks, John Edward
Specter, Richard Bruce
Spencer, Gregory Scott
Steer, Reginald David
Stolpman, Thomas Gerard
Stone, Richard James
Stout, Gregory Stansbury
Stratton, Richard James
Strong, George Gordon, Jr.
Sturdevant, Patricia Tenoso
Sugarman, Paul William
Sullivan, Patrick James
Sullivan, William Francis
Sutro, John Alfred
Taylor, William James
Thomas, Joseph Edward
Thurston, Morris Ashcroft
Tiffany, Joseph Raymond, II
Tonsing, Michael John
Traynor, J. Michael
Truman, Rolland A.
Tumpson, Albert Joseph
Turner, John Miller
Urwin, Gary Lee
Vanderet, Robert Charles
Vaughn, Lesley Miller Mehran
Walcher, Alan Ernest
Walter, John F.
Weir, William John Arnold
Welch, Thomas Andrew
Welch, Walter Andrew, Jr.
Wenzel, Lee Bey
Wertz, John R.
Wessling, Donald Moore
Wheatley, Jeff R.
White, Jack Raymond
Wickham, Dennis J.
Wikle, Kenneth Clinton, Jr.
Wilka, William Charles
Willard, Robert Edgar
Williams, Lee Dwain
Williams, Richard D.
Wilson, Clifford Ralph
Witus, David Gordon
Wood, Weldon Sanford
Wulfsberg, Harold James
Wykowski, Henry George
Yim, B(urgess) Casey
Young, Bless Stritar
Young, Douglas Rea
Zafis, Andrew James
Zecher, Albert Michael
Zimmerman, Bernard
Zuckerman, Alan Randy
Zweig, Michael K.

Colorado

Appel, Garry Richard
Barnthouse, William Joseph
Bayer, Richard Stewart
Bernstein, Jeremy Marshall
Blakey, Milton Keith
Branney, Joseph John
Brown, Ian Alexander
Browne, C. Willing, III
Campbell, Richard Bruce
Caplan, Gerald A.
Carlson, Robert James
Carney, Deborah Leah Turner
Carney, Thomas T.J.
Carr, James Francis
Chalat, James Harold
Cortez, Miles Cogley, Jr.
Cramer, R. Norman, Jr.
Demuth, Lael Saunders
Donnelly, Frederick James
Downey, Arthur Harold, Jr.
Downsbrough, Bruce Owen
Duncan, Stephen Mack
Englander, Paula Tyo
Epstein, Joseph Marc
Featherstone, Bruce Alan
Feder, Harold Abram
Figa, Phillip Sam
Figuli, David John
Friedberg, Alan Charles
Gallegos, Larry Duayne
Goldberg, Charles
Green, Philip Burton
Halpern, Alexander
Halpern, Joseph W.
Hanley, Robert Francis
Harris, Dale Ray
Haskins, Thomas Marston
Hjelmfelt, David Charles
Hoffman, Daniel Steven
Horowitz, Jay Stanley
Inman, Robert Dale
Jablonski, James Arthur
Jackson, Richard Brooke
Johnson, Philip Edward
Judd, Joel Stanton
Judd, Richard D(onald)
Keithley, Roger Lee
Keller, Alex Stephen
Kobayashi, John M.
Kraft, C. William, III
Kullby, Roy Sigurd
LaFond, Richard Charles
Law, John Manning
LeHouillier, Patric Jaymes
Leiser, Harvey Wayne
Luce, Charles F., Jr.
Lutz, John Shafroth
Maginness, Craig Richard
Magoon, Brian A(lan)
Mark, Denis Hugh
Marquess, Lawrence Wade
Marsh, William Robert
Martin, E. Gregory
Martin, J. Landis
Maywhort, William Walter
McConnell, Michael T.
McCotter, James Rawson
McLain, William Allen
Merker, Steven Joseph
Merrick, Glenn Warren
Meyer, William Dale
Michaels, Jane
Miller, David William
Miller, Gale Timothy
Minahan, Daniel F., Jr.
Morris, Marc
Netzorg, Gordon Wemple
Noall, L. Scott
Nottingham, Edward Willis, Jr.
O'Donnell, Michael Lawrence
Olson, Ronald Keith
Pack, Stuart Harris
Palmer, David Gilbert
Peck, Kenneth Eldon
Purvis, John Anderson
Raymond, Douglas J.
Rector, Leo Daniel
Rodgers, Ralph Emerson
Roth, Robert Charles
Rudy, Peter Harris
Salcito, Donald
Sandman, James Joseph
Sands, Jon F(rederick)
Satter, Raymond Nathan
Serini, John Peter
Skelton, Darrell Jean
Spangler, Edwin Leroy
Spelts, Richard John
Starrs, Elizabeth Anne
Suthers, John William
Thomasch, Roger Paul
Timmins, Edward Patrick
Tisdale, Douglas Michael
Tracey, Jay Walter, Jr.
Treece, James Lyle
Vanatta, Dean R.
Vigil, David Charles
Waggoner, Michael James
Walker, John Sumpter, Jr.
Wedgle, Richard Jay
Welch, Carol Mae
Welton, Charles Ephraim
Wilcox, Martha Anne
Wilson, William Andrew

Connecticut

Adelman, Robert Bardwell
Alesevich, Walter Charles
Amschler, James Ralph
Bonee, John Leon, III
Borod, Donald Lee
Brady, Matthew Joseph
Casagrande, Daniel Eugene
Chinitz, Stephen Solomon
Cifelli, Armand
Clendenen, William Herbert, Jr.
Coles, Kevin Andrew
Comley, Frederick Luquiens
Dalton, Victoria Clayman
De Lio, Anthony Peter
Dempsey, Edward Joseph
Dowling, Michael Anthony
Dowling, Vincent John
Duke, Steven Barry
Dwyer, Gerald Parker
Elliot, Ralph Gregory
Elliott, Edwin Donald, Jr.
Fain, Joel Maurice
Feldman, Samuel Botwinik
Fitzgerald, Thomas Raymond
Friar, Martha Jane
Gewirtz, Paul D.
Goetsch, Charles Carnahan
Green, Raymond Bert
Greenspon, Robert Alan
Haviland, James Thomas, II
Heiman, Maxwell
Holth, Fredrik Davidson
Kanaga, Lawrence Wesley
Katz, Melvin Seymour
Koh, Harold Hongju
Lombardo, Michael John
Lowry, Houston Putnam
Luby, Thomas Stewart
Lupica, Joseph Richard
Lynn, Robert John
Mason, Margaret Pendleton Pearson
McKinney, Ivy Thomas
Medzie, Kenneth Stephen
Mirsky, Ellis Richard
Morris, Jeffrey Lyons
Morrison, Francis Henry
Murphy, William Robert
Murtha, Thomas Michael
Neigher, Alan
Noonan, Patrick Matthew
Orth, Paul William
Pepe, Louis Robert
Ponzini, John Lino
Razzano, Pasquale Angelo
Ribicoff, Irving S.
Rohrer, Dean Cougill
Rosenberg, Burton Stuart
Russ, Lawrence
Sanetti, Stephen Louis
Schaefer, Daniel Robert
Seiger, Mark Brian
Shipman, Mark Samuel
Siverd, Robert Joseph
Slez, Anthony Francis, Jr.
Smith, Spencer Thomas
Sobol, Alan J.
Sparks, William James Ashley
Sussman, Mark Richard
Tanski, James Michael
Thompson, Frank J(oseph)
Ury, Frederic Stephen
Ward, Charles Daniel
Wiechmann, Eric Watt
Wilcox, Jamison Van Voorhees
Williams, Ronald Doherty
Zakarian, Albert

Delaware

Balick, Steven Jeffrey
Carpenter, Edmund Nelson, II
Crompton, Charles Sentman, Jr.
Davis, James Francis
Del Pesco, Susan Marie Carr
Gallagher, Henry Edmond, Jr.
Green, James Samuel
Harrington, Rick Alan
Holzman, James L(ouis)
Johnston, William David
Manley, Marshall
Marin, Bayard
Marvel, Wayne Andrew
Pepperman, Walter Leon, II
Rothschild, Steven James
Whitney, Douglas E., Sr.

District of Columbia

Abelson, Michael Allen
Adams, John Jillson
Allen, William Hayes
Alushin, Michael Stephen
Ambrose, Myles Joseph
Anderson, David Lawrence
Anikeeff, Anthony Hotchkiss
Attridge, Daniel F.
Axelrod, Jonathan Gans
Bader, Michael Haley
Baran, Jan Witold
Barnes, Donald Michael
Barnes, Mark James
Bates, Lawrence Fulcher
Bayly, John Henry
Beach, Chester Paul, Jr.
Beckler, Richard William
Beers, Donald Osborne
Bell, Robert Brooks
Bennett, Marion Tinsley
Berkin, Jeffrey Jack
Bernstein, Edwin S.
Bersoff, Donald Neil
Bierbower, Mark Butler
Bokat, Stephen A.
Bolden, Melvin Wilberforce, Jr.
Bonner, Walter Joseph
Bono, Gaspare Joseph

Boudin, Michael
Breneman, William Dudley
Brenner, Edgar H.
Brilliant, Shalom
Broida, Peter Barry
Brooten, Kenneth Edward, Jr.
Brower, Charles Nelson
Bruce, E(stel) Edward
Burnim, Ira Abraham
Burt, Jeffrey Amsterdam
Calderwood, James Albert
Campbell, Frank Andrew Scott
Caron, Wilfred Rene
Carr, Lawrence Edward, Jr.
Carr, Ronald Gene
Carroll, Thomas Phillip
Casey, Geraldine Holland
Chabot, Philip Louis, Jr.
Chafetz, Marc Edward
Chapman, Dudley Harry
Chierichella, John W.
Clagett, Brice McAdoo
Coburn, David H.
Cohen, Jay Loring
Cook, Michael Harry
Cooper, Jean Saralee
Cooter, Dale A.
Corber, Robert Jack
Covington, Alice Lucille
Crotty, Michael F.
Cullen, Thomas Francis, Jr.
Cummings, Frank
Czarra, Edgar F., Jr.
Daniel, Aubrey Marshall, III
Darling, Charles M., IV
DeBerardinis, Robert Andrew, Jr.
Denvir, James Peter, III
Deutsch, David
Dickieson, David H.
Dickson, Peter Dean
Dinan, Donald Robert
Disheroon, Fred Russell
Doherty, Ashley
Dolin, Mitchell F.
Douglas, John Woolman
Doyle, Austin Joseph, Jr.
Drennan, Joseph Peter
Dubuc, Carroll Edward
Duvall, Richard Osgood
Efros, Ellen Ann
Einhorn, Bruce Jeffrey
Emmett, Robert Addis, III
Epstein, David
Etters, Ronald Milton
Ewing, Ky Pepper, Jr.
Farley, John Joseph, III
Faron, Robert Steven
Fegan, David Albert
Fegan, David Coyle
Feldman, Clarice Rochelle
Feldman, Mark B.
Feldman, Michael Harris
Fitzhugh, David Michael
Fitzpatrick, John Michael
Flagg, Ronald Simon
Fleischer, Sarah Perry
Flynn, David Kevin
Flynn, Richard James
Fortenberry, Joseph Edwin
Foscarinis, Maria
Fox, Hamilton Phillips, III
Friedman, Daniel Mortimer
Friedman, Paul Lawrence
Fryer, Hugh Nevin
Fryman, Virgil Thomas, Jr.
Gardiner, Richard Ernest
Garland, Merrick Brian
Garrett, Theodore Louis
Ginsburg, Charles David
Gittens, James P.
Glosser, Jeffrey Mark
Gold, Laurence Stephen
Golden, Gregg Hannan Stewart
Goodson, Robert Wade
Gorelick, Jamie Shona
Gorinson, Stanley M.
Graubert, John David
Green, Robert Lamar, Jr.
Greenberger, I. Michael
Greenebaum, Leonard Charles
Gribbon, Daniel McNamara
Grier, Phillip Michael
Griffin, L. Robert
Griswold, Erwin Nathaniel
Groner, Isaac Nathan
Grossman, Joanne Barbara
Halle, Peter Edward
Halpern, Linda Ann
Halvorson, Newman Thorbus, Jr.
Hamilton, James
Handleman, Aaron L.
Harbottle, Ann Woodley
Harris, Scott Blake
Heenan, Michael Terence
Hefter, Laurence Roy
Henderson, Harold Richard
Hennemuth, Jeffrey Alan
Henry, Roxann Elizabeth
Hess, Michael Anthony
Highsaw, James Leonard, Jr.
Hochberg, Jerome A.
Hodgson, Morgan Day
Hoegle, Robert Louis
Hogan, Thomas Francis
Hollingsworth, Joe Gregory
Horn, Stephen
Hoscheit, Dale Herbert
Hubschman, Henry Allan
Huge, Harry
Hughes, Dennis Michael
Hundt, Reed Eric
Ifshin, David Michael
Isbell, David Bradford
Jacobsen, Raymond Alfred, Jr.
Jaffe, Robert A.
Janis, N. Richard
Jones, Aidan Drexel
Jones, Keith Alden
Jordan, James Francis
Joseph, Daniel Mordecai
Junkin, Timothy Deforest
Juster, Kenneth Ian
Karp, Ronald Alvin
Katz, Hadrian Ronald
Keeney, John Christopher, Jr.
Kelly, John James
Kennedy, Cornelius Bryant
Kerrine, Theodore Michael

Kharasch, Robert Nelson
Kieve, Loren
Kilcarr, Andrew Joseph
King, James Forrest, Jr.
King, Rufus
Kirk, Dennis Dean
Kirsch, Laurence Stephen
Kissel, Peter Charles
Klawiter, Donald Casimir
Klonoff, Robert Howard
Knauer, Leon Thomas
Knudson, Scott Gregory
Kolasky, William Joseph, Jr.
Kovacs, William Lawrence
Kramer, Andrew Michael
Kramer, Noël Anketell
Kurrelmeyer, Louis Hayner
Kurtz, James Louis
Lacovara, Philip Allen
Lamb, Kevin Thomas
Lamm, Carolyn Beth
Lange, William Michael
Larroca, Raymond G.
Lawton, Bettina Mary
Lazarus, Arthur, Jr.
Leary, Thomas Barrett
Lenhart, James Thomas
Leonard, Jerris
Lerman, Lisa Gabrielle
Lerner, Richard David
Lettow, Charles Frederick
Levine, Henry David
Lewis, William Henry, Jr.
Lichtenberg, J(oan) Cathy
Lide, Vinton DeVane
Liebman, Ronald Stanley
Lillard, John Franklin, III
Lippo, Tom A.
Lister, Charles
Loeffler, Robert Hugh
Loftus, Carroll Michael
Longstreth, Robert Christy
Macleod, John Amend
Madden, Jerome Anthony
Madole, Donald Wilson
Manly, Marc Edward
Markham, Jerry Wayne
Martoche, Salvatore Richard
Mathers, Peter Robert
Mathis, John Prentiss
McAvoy, John Joseph
McBride, Michael Flynn
McDavid, Janet Louise
McDiarmid, Robert Campbell
McMillan, Richard, Jr.
McNamara, Roger Thomas
McReynolds, Mary Armilda
Means, Thomas Cornell
Medaglia, Mary-Elizabeth
Medalie, Richard James
Melamed, Arthur Douglas
Meserve, Richard Andrew
Metcalfe, Robert Davis, III
Meyer, Lawrence George
Michaels, Gary David
Miller, Damon Craddock
Mitchell, Gerard Ellsworth
Mobille, George Thomas
Morant, Blake Dominic
Morgan, William Caswell
Morris, Frank Charles, Jr.
Morrison, Alexia
Mullenix, Linda Susan
Muller, Scott William
Murchison, David Claudius
Murphy, James Paul
Murphy, Richard Patrick
Murry, Harold David, Jr.
Nace, Barry John
Nelson, William Eugene
Newberger, Stuart Henry
Noone, Michael F., Jr.
Nordlinger, Douglas Edward
Norwind, Edward Lee
O'Brien, Denise Marie
Oliver, Dale Hugh
Onek, Joseph Nathan
O'Toole, Francis J.
Owen, Roberts Bishop
Palmer, Alan Kenneth
Panzer, Irving Reller Myron
Parkinson, Kenneth Wells
Patton, Thomas Earl
Peck, Jeffrey Jay
Peters, Frederick Whitten
Pickering, John Harold
Pierson, W. DeVier
Pilger, Karl William
Pitofsky, Robert
Pohl, Mark Ronald
Pomeroy, Harlan
Postol, Lawrence Philip
Povich, David
Powell, Robert Dominick
Preston, Charles George
Quarles, James Linwood, III
Quarles, William Daniel
Railton, William Scott
Raim, David Matthew
Ramsey, Stephen Douglas
Raul, Alan Charles
Razzano, Frank Charles
Reback, Joyce Ellen
Reback, Richard Neal
Reichler, Paul Stuart
Reidl, Paul William
Rephan, Jack
Repper, George Robert
Reynolds, William Bradford
Roach, Arvid Edward, II
Roach, Patrick Joseph
Robertson, Joseph Martin
Rogers, Edward Lee
Rogovin, Mitchell
Rommel, John Marshall
Rosenthal, Steven Siegmund
Rothenberg, Steven Alan
Rowe, James Henry, III
Rubin, Janet Beth
Ruff, Charles F.C.
Ruggeri, Robert Edward
Rupp, John Peter
Sallet, Jonathan Bruce
Sayler, Robert Nelson
Scammel, Harry Glenn
Schaefer, William Goerman, Jr.
Scheer, Peter Edward
Schneebaum, Steven Marc

Schropp, James Howard
Schwartz, David
Schwarzbart, Robert Morton
Scullen, James Roche
Sedky, Cherif
Seidman, Paul Joseph
Shanks, Hershel
Shea, Francis Michael
Shean, Owen Joseph
Sheehan, Richard Jere
Shenefield, John Hale
Sherk, George William
Shibley, Raymond Nadeem
Siemer, Deanne C.
Silver, Harry R.
Skinner, William Polk
Smith, Arthur Lee
Smith, Jack David
Smith, Walter Joseph, Jr.
Sneed, James H.
Snider, Jerome Guy
Snyder, Allen Roger
Sonde, Theodore Irwin
Sowles, Marcia Kay
Spaeder, Roger Campbell
Spriggs, William James
Stabbe, Mitchell Howard
Statland, Edward Morris
Stein, William Robert
Stewart, Eugene Lawrence
Straser, Richard Alan
Stromberg, Clifford Douglas
Stuart, Pamela Bruce
Sturtevant, Brereton
Sullivan, Eugene Raymond
Swartz, Dean Elliot
Swift, Stephen Jensen
Sykes, Thomas Dale
Szybala, Renee Leslie
Tansill, Frederick Riker
Tasker, Joseph
Taylor, Carl Larsen
Tom, Willard Ken
Tomar, Richard Thomas
Tomaszczuk, Alexander Daniel
Tompkins, Joseph Buford, Jr.
Turnage, Fred Douglas
Utermohlen, William Jerome
Vanderstar, John
Vary, George Folk
Vogt, Carl William
Wagshal, Jerome Stanley
Walker, Mary L.
Wegener, Mark Douglas
Weinberg, Robert Lester
Weiner, Robert Neil
Weisgall, Jonathan Michael
Weiss, Harlan Lee
Weld, William Floyd
Weller, Susan Neuberger
Wernick, Kenneth Jonathan
Whalen, Thomas J.
Whitaker, A(lbert) Duncan
White, Peter Allen
Whitfield, Milton Bailey
Wilder, Roland Percival, Jr.
Williams, David Huntington
Wolf, Christopher
Wolff, Elroy Harris
Wyss, John Benedict
Yannucci, Thomas David
Yellott Jr., John Bosley
Yoder, John Christian
Young, John Hardin
Young, William Fielding
Younger, Alexander
Zapruder, Henry G.
Zwick, Kenneth Lowell

Florida

Adkins, Edward Cleland
Allen, Richard Lewis
Allen, W. Riley
Alpert, Jonathan Louis
Anderson, Cromwell Adair
Anderson, Terence James
Aragon, Rudolph Fermin
Arencibia, Raul A.
Armstrong, Suzanne Rae
Ashby, Kimberly A.
Astigarraga, Jose Ignacio
Aurell, John Karl
Babler, Wayne E.
Barnhart, Forrest Gregory
Bartlett, Charles John
Bemis, Lawrence Perry
Berger, C. William
Bernstein, Michael Alan
Betts, James Robert
Biggs, Thomas Sanford, Jr.
Blackwell, William Leggett
Blank, Nelson Douglas
Blumberg, Edward Robert
Booth, Edgar Charles
Borgognoni, Gregory Paul
Bosse, Richard Edward
Boyd, Joseph Arthur, Jr.
Brett-Major, Lin
Briggs, Randy Robert
Brumbaugh, John Moore
Buesing, Karen Meyer
Burnbaum, Michael William
Burton, Richard Jay
Butler, Paul B.
Cagney, William Patrick, III
Callender, John Francis
Carstetter, David Wilson
Chandler, John Brandon, Jr.
Cheffy, Edward Kefgen
Clarkson, Julian Derieux
Coe, Jack Martin
Cohen, Jeffrey Michael
Cole, Robert Allen
Coleman, C. Randolph
Connor, Terence Gregory
Corcoran, C. Timothy, III
Crabtree, Robert Crosby
Cunningham, James Reynolds
Davis, Barry Lee
Davis, William Howard
Day, George Everette
Deehl, David Lee
Del Russo, Alexander D.
Dempsey, Bernard Hayden, Jr.
DeWitt, Sherri Kandel
Diaz, Benito Humberto
Dominik, Jack Edward
Eagan, William Leon

Earle, William George
Eaton, Joel Douglas
Edelstein, Steven A(llen)
Ehrlich, Raymond
Ervin, Robert Marvin
Evans, George Michael
Evans, John F.
Farese, Lawrence Anthony
Feder, Scott Jay
Ferrell, Milton Morgan, Jr.
Fox, Gary Devenow
Fridkin, Jeffrey David
Fromberg, Malcolm Hubert
Fuller, Diana L.
Gabel, George DeSaussure, Jr.
Gaines, Robert Pendleton
Galamaga, Robert John
Garbis, Gary Edward
Gassler, Frank Henry
Gerlin, William Lance
Gievers, Karen A.
Gifford, Donald Arthur
Gilbert, Richard Allen
Goldman, Joel L.
Goldstein, Harvey M.
Gorman, Robert James
Graham, Donald Lynn
Greer, Alan Graham
Grilli, Peter John
Gurney, James Thomas
Hart, Karl Vance
Hastings, Lawrence Vaeth
Hester, Christopher Scott
Hickey, John Heyward
Hill, Brian Donovan
Hingston, Robert Allen
Hinkle, Robert Lewis
Hoey, William Edward
Hogg, Jesse Stephen
Holland, William Meredith
Holliday, Ronald Sturgis
Hooper, Joel Randall
Hootman, Gregory Wayne
Horan, John Patrick
Jacobo, Winston Wendle
Johnson, Paul Bryan
Johnston, Charles Motley
Joy, Daniel Foster
Justice, Thomas Hardwick, III
Kaimowitz, Gabe Hillel
Kauffman, Alan Charles
Kelly, John Patrick
Kelly, Thomas Paine, Jr.
Kiefner, John Robert, Jr.
Korchin, Judith Miriam
Lance, Miles A.
Levenstein, Richard Harry
Lewis, Neal Randolph
Lipcon, Charles R.
MacDonald, Thomas Cook, Jr.
Makowski, Raymond Edmund
Mang, Douglas A.
Martin, James Addison, Jr.
Martinez, Mel R.
Masterson, Bernard Joseph
Mayans, Steven Anthony
McAliley, Thomas Watson
McIntosh, Douglas Malcolm
McKeown, Frank James
McLemore, Michael Kerr
McQuigg, John Dolph
Meade, Russell Arthur
Mehrtens, William Osborne, Jr.
Miller, Raymond Vincent, Jr.
Mitrani, Isaac Jaime
Montgomery, Robert Morel, Jr.
Moody, James Shelton, Jr.
Moore, John Henry, II
Moran, James Michael
Moseley, James Francis
Motes, Carl Dalton
Muratides, John Nicholas
Nachwalter, Michael
Nagin, Stephen E.
Nifong, J. Michael
Novack, Catherine Gail
Nutzhorn, Carl Robbins
O'Neal, Michael Scott, Sr.
Ormond, Gregg Joseph
Owen, Richard Knowles
Palahach, Michael
Parker, Julius Frederick, Jr.
Parker, Whilden Sessions
Parrish, Sidney Howard
Pawluc, Sonia M.
Pertnoy, Leonard David
Phillips, Gary Stephen
Pierce, Francis Edmund, III
Reid, R(alph) Benjamine
Reiter, Joseph John
Richardson, Sally M.
Rogovin, Lawrence H.
Rosen, Michael James
Rumrell, Richard Gary
Rydberg, Marsha Griffin
Sadowski, William Edward
Salem, Richard Joseph
Sarkis, Frederick Derr
Scarola, John
Schember, Steven George
Schmidt, Whitney Lawrence
Searcy, Christian Deitrich, Sr.
Sharett, Alan Richard
Shields, William Henry
Singer, Stuart H.
Siplin, Gary Anthony
Smith, Harold Delane
Smith, William Reece, Jr.
Solomon, Douglas Paul
Spector, Brian F.
Sprowls, Paul Alan
Stack, Charles Rickman
Stankee, Glen Allen
Stanley, Bruce McLaren
Stein, Craig Edward
Stewart, Larry S.
Stieglitz, Albert Blackwell
Strawn, David Updegraff
Stubbs, Sidney Alton
Taitz, Steven Carter
Terrell, James Thomas
Thomas, Wayne Lee
Thornton, John W.
Thornton, Richard Joseph
Tifford, Arthur W.
Trees, Philip Hugh
Trombley, Michael Jerome
Udell, Michael Bennett

Underwood, Edwin Hill
Velasquez, Patti A.
Vento, John Sebastian
Wadsworth, Murray Marvin
Waller, Edward Martin, Jr.
Walton, Rodney Earl
Warren, Herbert Albert
Wein, Stephen Joshua
Weissenborn, Sheridan Kendall
Weissman, Jeffrey Mark
Welbaum, R. Earl
White, Andrew, III
Wilson, William Berry
Wiltshire, William Harrison Flick
Windham, John Franklin
Wood, Mary Catherine
Wroble, Arthur G.
Zaiser, Kent Ames

Georgia

Anderson, Peter Joseph
Artis, Gregory Dwight
Ashe, Robert Lawrence, Jr.
Baverman, Alan Jerold
Biggins, Franklin N.
Billington, Barry E.
Bird, Terry Cornelius
Blackstock, Jerry Byron
Blank, A(ndrew) Russell
Boynton, Frederick George
Branch, Thomas Broughton, III
Bratton, James Henry, Jr.
Brewer, Edward Cage, III
Canfield, Peter Crane
Christy, Gary Christopher
Connelly, Lewis Branch Sutton
Cooney, William J.
Crockett, David Gideon
Curry, Stephen Euree
Dailey, Michael Alan
Dalziel, Charles Meredith, Jr.
Davis, George Thomas
Denham, Vernon Robert, Jr.
Dickert, Neal Workman
Doyle, Michael Anthony
Draughon, John Albert
Drescher, Ann Marie
DuBose, Charles Wilson
Duffey, William Simon, Jr.
Eastwood, Myles Eric
Elmore, Marvin Jerome
Emmons, Peter Ribeiro
Felton, Jule Wimberly, Jr.
Finnell, Robert Kirtley
Fleming, Julian Denver, Jr.
Forbes, Morton Gerald
Foulke, Edwin Gerhart, Jr.
Freed, Gary Stuart
Frey, Monroe Lynn, III
Gadrix, Edward Wallace, Jr.
Gleaton, Frederick Neal
Glucksman, Joyce Francine
Gray, Herbert Harold, III
Greenblatt, Edward Lande
Gunn, Robert Russell
Halle, Mollie Johnson
Harness, William Walter
Hayes, Dewey Norman, Jr.
Hinchey, John William
Ingram, George Conley
Jenkins, Thomas A(llan)
Johnson, Daniel Patrick
Jones, Glower Whitehead
Kadish, Mark J.
Kelley, Jeffrey Wendell
Kessler, Kathleen
Killorin, Edward Wylly
Kirkland, June Ann
Knox, Wyckliffe Austin, Jr.
Lachance, James Martin
Lackland, Theodore Howard
Lamberth, J. Michael
Langstaff, James Pope
Lewis, H(enry) Worthington
Liston, Paul Sperry
Lokey, Hamilton
Lore, Stephen Melvin
Maines, James Allen
Malone, Thomas William
Martin, Charles Lee
Mass, Allen Robert
Mayoue, John Charles
Menendez, Kenneth Gary
Miles, Dana Brent
Miller, Alfred Montague
Murphy, Charles Conrow, Jr.
Nash, Thomas Acton, Jr.
Ordover, Abraham Philip
Ortiz, Jay Richard Gentry
Ossick, John Joseph, Jr.
Owens, L(awrence) Dale
Pannell, James Loughridge
Patton, Matthew H.
Pendergast, John Francis, Jr.
Perry, Alan Rogers, Jr.
Ponsoldt, James Farmer
Powell, Douglas Richard
Powell, Richard Lynn
Prince, David Cannon
Purdom, Wayne Miller
Reemsnyder, Ronald David
Reinhardt, Daniel Sargent
Reinhart, Richard Paul
Riggs, Gregory Lynn
Roberson, Lynn Marie
Ross, Robert T.
Russell, Harold Louis
Satcher, James Alton, Jr.
Savell, Edward Lupo
Seacrest, Gary Lee
Slawsky, Norman Joel
Smith, Malcolm Percy
Stone, Freddie Ray Josh
Sweeney, Neal James
Thomas, James Joseph, II
Tolley, Edward Donald
Totenberg, Amy Mil
Turnipseed, Sara Sadler
Warner, William Millard
Watson, John Howard
Weaver, George Marvin
Wheale, Duncan Douglas
Whiteside, Fife Morris
Wright, Frederick Lewis, II
Wymer, John Francis, III
Young, Robert George
Zolke, Scott Bryan

Hawaii

Akiba, Lorraine Hiroko
Beaman, Andrew Varnum
Brown, Boyce Reid, Jr.
Burke, Edmund
Chuck, Walter G(oonsun)
Chung, Steven Kamsein
Clifton, Richard Randall
Crumpton, Charles Whitmarsh
Deaver, Phillip Lester
Devens, Paul
Dodd, William Horace
Duffy, James Earl, Jr.
Floyd, Shelby Anne
Fried, L. Richard, Jr.
Fujiyama, Wallace Sachio
Fukumoto, Leslie Satsuki
Gelber, Don Jeffrey
Hall, David Winston
Hastert, Diane Deskins
Kemper, Edward Crawford
Kim, Edward Y.N.
Lawson, William Homer
Morse, Jack Craig
Murakami, Alan Tomoo
Potts, Dennis Walker
Sattler, James Michael
Schraff, Paul Albert
White, Lawrence Richard
Wilson, Virgil James, III
Wong, Patricia Uyehara
Wong, Wayson Wai Sun
Yamada, Stephen Kinichi

Idaho

Banducci, Thomas Anthony
Christenson, Jeffrey Robert
Clark, Merlyn Wesley
Davis, James Julian
Dryden, William George
Johnson, L. Charles
Miller, Patrick Eugene
Read, Michael John
Risch, James E.
Schlender, E. Lee
Webb, Lloyd Jackson

Illinois

Africk, Joel Jay
Aldrich, Thomas Lawrence
Alesia, James H(enry)
Alexander, Richard Elmont
Allen, Henry Sermones, Jr.
Allen, Ronald Jay
Allen, Thomas D.
Allison, Thomas D., Jr.
Amend, James Michael
Angst, Gerald L.
Anspach, Kenneth Gordon
Apcel, Melissa Anne
Artwick, Frederick John
Badel, Julie
Baker, James Edward Sproul
Barnett, William A.
Barrett, Roger Watson
Barron, Howard Robert
Bashwiner, Steven Lacelle
Bator, Paul Michael
Baugher, Peter V.
Bell, Ronald Lee
Bellah, Kenneth David
Bellows, Laurel Gordon
Berenzweig, Jack Charles
Berghoff, Paul Henry
Bergstrom, Robert William
Berner, Robert Lee, Jr.
Bernstein, Stuart
Birmingham, William Joseph
Blan, Kennith William, Jr.
Boand, Charles Wilbur
Bodenstein, Ira
Boehnen, Daniel A.
Bohlen, Christopher Wayne
Boies, Wilber H.
Boodell, Thomas Joseph, Jr.
Bortman, David
Bose, Thomas Lewnau
Botti, Aldo E.
Bouma, Robert Edwin
Boyd, David Parker
Bradner, James Holland, Jr.
Bramnik, Robert Paul
Branding, Frederick H.
Brennan, James Joseph
Bresnahan, Arthur Stephen
Bridgman, Thomas Francis
Britton, Clarold Lawrence
Brown, Robert Howard
Brown, Steven Spencer
Bunge, Jonathan Gunn
Burditt, George Miller, Jr.
Burke, Dennis J.
Burke, John Michael
Burke, Thomas Joseph, Jr.
Campbell, Christian Larsen
Canel, James Harrison
Carey, Richard Peter
Carlson, Stephen Curtis
Carpenter, David William
Carponelli, Stephen Peter
Carroll, William Kenneth
Carton, Laurence Alfred
Cheely, Daniel Joseph
Chemers, Robert Marc
Cherney, James Alan
Cherry, Daniel Ronald
Chester, Mark Vincent
Churchill, Allen Delos
Cicero, Frank, Jr.
Cipolla, Vincent Charles
Coccia, Michel Andre
Coghill, William Thomas, Jr.
Cohen, Edward A.
Colantoni, Anthony Michael
Coleman, William T(homas)
Collen, John Olaf
Collen, Sheldon Orrin
Conison, Jay
Connelly, P. Kevin
Cook, James Christopher
Coulson, William Roy
Courtney, Thomas Frances
Crane, Mark
Crawford, Sandra Kay
Crowley, Wilbert Francis
Cummins, Robert Patrick
Danekas, Steven Ernest
Davis, Scott Jonathan
Dell, Robert Michael
Demetrio, Thomas A.
DeSanto, James John
Devience, Alex, Jr.
DeWolfe, John Chauncey, Jr.
Dilling, Kirkpatrick Wallwick
Ditkowsky, Kenneth K.
Domanskis, Alexander Rimas
Donohue, Richard Harney
Eaton, Larry Ralph
Eckols, Thomas Aud
Edelman, Daniel Amos
Edlund, Curtis Eric
Egan, Kevin James
Ehrlich, Jeff Paschal
Eisenberg, Stephen Paul
Emerson, William Harry
Epstein, Edna Selan
Erlebacher, Arlene Cernik
Erlich, Barry Arnold
Ettinger, Albert Franklin
Ettinger, Joseph Alan
Fahner, Tyrone Clarence
Farnell, Alan Stuart
Farrug, Eugene Joseph
Feagley, Michael Rowe
Feirich, John Cottrill
Ferguson, Stanley Lewis
Filler, Ronald Howard
Finke, Robert Forge
Fleps, John Joseph
Forde, Kevin Michael
Fowle, Frank Fuller
Fowler, Don Wall
Fox, Shayle Phillip
Franklin, Richard Mark
Freed, Mayer Goodman
Freehling, Paul Edward
Fuson, Douglas Finley
Futterman, Ronald L.
Fylstra, Raymond Alan
Galatz, Henry Francis
Gallagher, Thomas Jordan, Jr.
Garley, Barry Ernest
Garvey, Margaret S.
Gavin, William Patrick
Gekas, Constantine John
George, John Martin, Jr.
Gerstman, George Henry
Gevers, Marcia Bonita
Giampietro, Wayne Bruce
Gibbons, William John
Gifford, Geoffrey L.
Gilbert, Daniel Thomas
Gilford, Steven Ross
Gladden, James Walter, Jr.
Gordon, James S.
Goslawski, Leonard Stephen
Grabemann, Karl W.
Greenough, Walter Croan
Griffith, D. Kendall
Groenke, Theodore A.
Gundlach, Norman Joseph
Haight, Edward Allen
Hall, Joan M.
Hallock, Robert Wayne
Hamblet, Michael Jon
Hanson, Kenneth Hamilton
Hanson, Ronald William
Hardgrove, James Alan
Harmon, Robert Lon
Harper, Steven James
Harris, D. Alan
Harris, Daniel Mark
Harris, Donald Ray
Harrold, Bernard
Harvitt, Adrianne Stanley
Harwood, Bruce Alan
Haubold, Samuel Allen
Hay, Peter Heinrich
Hayes, Richard Johnson
Haynes, Jean Reed
Head, Patrick James
Hecht, Frank Thomas
Hefter, Daniel S.
Heininger, Erwin Carl
Heinz, William Denby
Heitland, Ann Rae
Hepplewhite, David Wilson
Herald, John Patrick
Herman, Stephen Charles
Hess, Frederick J.
Hiering, James G.
Hilliard, David Craig
Hoff, William Bruce, Jr.
Hoffman, Richard Bruce
Hoffman, S. David
Hoover, Russell James
Hoskins, Richard Jerold
Howe, Jonathan Thomas
Hunter, James Galbraith, Jr.
Hupert, Jeffrey David
Jackson, Charles C.
Jacover, Jerold Alan
Jager, Melvin Francis
Johnson, Douglas Wells
Kaminsky, Richard Alan
Kanner, Steven Alan
Kapnick, Richard Bradshaw
Karaba, Frank Andrew
Kathrein, Reed Richard
Katz, Avrum Sidney
Katz, Harold Ambrose
Kempf, Donald G., Jr.
Kennelly, John Jerome
Kimball, Franklyn Davis
King, Michael Howard
Klaff, Ramsay Laing
Knight, William D., Jr.
Kohn, Shalom L.
Komie, Stephen Mark
Kornichuk, Ellen S.
Kozak, John W.
Krieger, Frederic Michael
Krupka, Robert George
Kuczwara, Thomas Paul
Kurland, Philip B.
Lane, William Edward
LaRue, Paul Hubert
Latshaw, K. Michael
Leahy, Daniel James
Leech, Michael John
Lefkow, Michael Francis
Leopold, Mark Freudenthal
Leopold, Valerie Ann
Levine, Laurence Harvey
Lewis, James Brooke
Lieberman, Eugene
Linder, Rex Kenneth
Lindstedt, Norman Edward
Linklater, William Joseph
Lipton, Mark Daniel
List, David Patton
Livingston, Bradford Lee
Lousberg, Peter Herman
Lucas, John Kenneth
Lynch, James Daniel
Lynch, John Peter
Malone, James Laurence, III
Marcus, Richard Leon
Marick, Michael Miron
Marmer, Ronald Louis
Mason, Henry Lowell, III
Matchett, Hugh Moore
Mateer, Don Metz
McClure, Thomas Edward
McConnell, James Guy
McDonald, Thomas Alexander
McDunn, Susan Jeanine
McGonegle, Timothy J.
McLaughlin, T. Mark
McNamara, Barry Thomas
McRae, Donald James
Menges, Eugene Clifford
Miller, Barry Alan
Mone, Peter John
Moorehead, Timothy Lucas
Moran, Donald J.
Morrison, John Horton
Mueller, Richard Edward
Mulack, Donald G.
Mulcahy, Daniel Joseph, Jr.
Mulroy, Thomas Robert, Jr.
Munson, James Calfee
Murray, Lorene Frances
Nichols, Robert Hastings
Nicklin, Emily
Nixon, Lewis Michael
Nogal, Richard John
Nord, Robert Eamor
Norek, Frances Therese
North, Kenneth Earl
Nowacki, James Nelson
Nyeste, James Thomas
O'Brien, Patrick W.
Oldfield, E. Lawrence
Osann, Edward William, Jr.
Palm, Gary Howard
Palmer, Michael Paul
Palmer, Robert Towne
Parkhurst, Beverly Susler
Patterson, Robert Bruce, Jr.
Pattishall, Beverly Wyckliffe
Patton, Stephen Ray
Pavalon, Eugene I.
Pelton, Russell Meredith, Jr.
Pelz, Joel Thomas
Peterson, Donald George
Phebus, Joseph W.
Phillips, Michael James
Platz, George Arthur, III
Poe, Douglas Allan
Polaski, Anne Spencer
Pope, Daniel James
Potter, Richard Clifford
Pusch, Herbert Barringer
Rabinowitz, Mark Allan
Radler, Warren S.
Raney, Donald Raymond
Rank, John Thomas
Rankin, James Winton
Rappaport, Earle Samuel, Jr.
Ras, Robert A.
Rawles, Edward Hugh
Record, Richard Franklin, Jr.
Redish, Martin Harris
Redman, Clarence Owen
Redmond, Richard Anthony
Rein, Eric Steven
Rhode, Shari René
Richmond, William Patrick
Richter, Tobin Marais
Rieger, Mitchell Sheridan
Ring, Leonard M.
Robins, Lawrence Richard
Romanyak, James Andrew
Rooney, Matthew A.
Roper, Harry Joseph
Ropiequet, John L.
Ropski, Gary Melchior
Roth, Ronald Anthony
Roustan, Yvon D.
Rovner, Jack Alan
Rudd, Donnie
Rundio, Louis Michael, Jr.
Rupert, Donald William
Russell, Tomas Morgan
Rutkoff, Alan Stuart
Sale, Edwin Wells
Salomon, Richard Adley
Schaefer, Nancy
Schink, James Harvey
Schoumacher, Bruce Herbert
Schroeder, Carl Frederick, Jr.
Schuckit, Robert Jay
Schultz, Allen H.
Schuman, William Paul
Schwab, Stephen Wayne
Scott, Theodore R.
Scudder, Theodore Townsend, III
Sechen, Glenn Charles
Seiden, Glenn
Serritella, William David
Serwer, Alan Michael
Sfasciotti, Mary L.
Shapiro, Stephen M.
Sheldon, Harvey M.
Sido, Kevin Richard
Skinner, Samuel Knox
Smith, Arthur B(everly), Jr.
Sneckenberg, William John
Spears, Ronald Dean
Stack, Paul Francis
Starkman, Gary Lee
Stassen, John Henry
Steinman, Joan Ellen
Stevens, Douglas Robert
Stone, Victor J.
Stout, James Dudley
Streeter, Benjamin Arrington, III
Strodel, Robert Carl
Strom, Michael A.
Sullivan, Barry
Szczepanski, Slawomir Zbigniew Steven
Tarun, Robert Walter
Terc, Joseph Anthony
Theis, William Harold
Torrey, N. Morrison
Torshen, Jerome Harold
Tozer, Forrest Leigh
Travis, Joan Faye Schiller
Trenda, Regis J(ohn)
Troelstrup, John Frederick
Van Hagey, William
Vittum, Daniel Weeks, Jr.
Waintroob, Andrea Ruth
Walsh, Christopher G., Jr.
Walston, Beth Elaine
Walters, Gomer Winston
Walton, Stanley Anthony, III
Wanca, Brian John
Ward, Michael W.
Wascher, James Degen
Weinstein, David L.
Welsh, Donald LeRoy
Wildman, Max Edward
Willian, Clyde Franklin
Winget, Walter Winfield
Witwer, Samuel Weiler, Jr.
Wohlreich, Jack Jay
Wood, Diane Pamela
Woulfe, Margaret Frances
Wuller, Robert George, Jr.
Zamarin, Ronald George

Indiana

Anast, Nick James
Ancel, Jerald Irwin
Becher, Paul Eugene
Belknap, Jerry P.
Bennett, Roger William
Berger, Charles Lee
Berger, Sydney L.
Bodkin, Robert Thomas
Bodle, John Frederick
Brown, Richard Lawrence
Byrne, Maurice Andrew, Jr.
Choplin, John Max, II
Cleveland, Peter Devine
Conour, William Frederick
Dahling, Gerald Vernon
Deveau, Francis Joseph
Dieterly, Douglas Kevin
Drummy, William Wallace, III
Dywan, Jeffery Joseph
Elberger, Ronald Edward
Emhardt, Charles David
Evans, Daniel Fraley, Jr.
Fairchild, Raymond Francis
Flannery, James Lloyd
Frey, Eric Alan
Fuller, Samuel Ashby
Gikas, Rick Christopher
Greer, Charles Eugene
Guy, John Martin
Haynie, Gilmore Smith, Jr.
Hendrickson, Thomas Atherton
Hoffman, John Frederick
Hovde, F. Boyd
Jackson, Andrew Dudley
Jeffers, Albert Lavern
Jennings, Charles Thomas
Jones, David L.
Katich, Nick
Keen, Robert Thomas, Jr.
King, Douglas Bruce
Kinney, Richard Gordon
Layden, Charles Max
Lee, William Charles
Leeman, William Kelly
Levy, Joel C.
Linnemeier, Philip
Loftman, Guy Rickard
McDermott, Renée R(assler)
Meacham, Jerald Samuel
Montross, W. Scott
Moody, James T(yne)
Moss, Kirby Glenn
Motsinger, Carl Daniel
Muller, John
Murphy, Lester F(uller)
Myers, James Woodrow, III
Palmer, Robert Joseph
Pardieck, Roger L.
Pennell, Stephen Richard
Plouff, Thomas O'Connor
Ponader, Wayne Carl
Pope, Mark Andrew
Reinke, William John
Reuben, Lawrence Mark
Rittner, Kathleen Ardell
Robisch, Robert Karl
Roby, Daniel Arthur
Ruman, Saul I.
Shoulders, Patrick Alan
Shreve, Gene Russell
Skolnik, Bradley William
Stalmack, Joseph
Steger, Evan Evans
Stommel, R. Robert
Suedhoff, Carl John, Jr.
Taylor, Brent Douglas
Tolbert, Frank Edward
Townsend, Earl Cunningham, Jr.
Trigg, Donald Clark
Van Bokkelen, Joseph Scott
Williams, Bradley Louis
Williams, Stephen Lee
Young, Thomas Jordan

Iowa

Belin, David William
Blackburn, Milford Gene
Conlin, Roxanne Barton
Crook, Charles Samuel, III
Davis, James Casey
Davison, George Frederick, Jr.
Eidsmoe, Robert Russell
Ellefson, James C.
Farr, Thomas Carey
Foxhoven, Jerry Ray
Frederici, C. Carleton
Gibb, William Stewart
Grace, David Joseph
Hammer, David Lindley
Hileman, Richard Glenn, Jr.
Hutchison, Robert Alan
Johnson, John Paul
Karr, Lloyd
Kelly, Edwin Frost
Kersten, Donald Norbert
Koehn, William James
Langdon, Herschel Garrett
Langdon, Richard Garrett
Lathrop, Roger Alan
Lawyer, Verne
Leitner, David Larry
Liabo, Mark Elliot
Logan, Thomas Joseph
Lyford, F. Richard
Malm, Richard Allan
McNeil, Jean Anne
Noyes, Michael Lance
Peddicord, Roland Dale
Quinn, Kirke Craven
Rhodes, Keith Stewart
Rosenberg, Paul Herschel
Samuelson, Jacqueline K.
Sanders, Doyle Dee
Scism, Robert Bruce
Smith, William Sidney
Stefani, Randall H.
Taylor, Wallace L.
Tully, Robert Gerard
Visser, Kevin James
Walker, E. Ralph
Warbasse, Steven Kenneth
Wharton, John Michael
Wine, Donald Arthur
Zoss, Paul Arthur

Kansas

Badgerow, John Nicholas
Boyle, Edward Michael
Burgess, Benjamin L., Jr.
Concannon, Don Owen
Davis, Charles Leroy
Delhotal, Van Russell
Dimmitt, Lawrence Andrew
Erickson, George Everett, Jr.
Fisher, Randall Eugene
Grace, Brian Guiles
Gross, Edmund Samuel
Hamilton, John Richard
Harbur, Nathan Clayton
Hathaway, Gary Ray
Hecht, Robert D.
Herrington, Alvin D.
Justus, Jo Lynne
Keplinger, (Donald) Bruce
Marshall, Herbert A.
Metzger, Alan Glen
Mitchell, Alexander Baldwin
Mudrick, David Phillip
Nelson, Bryan Eugene
Nygaard, Diane Acker
Ochs, Robert Duane
Patterson, Donald
Reeves, Jean Brooks
Rogers, Terry Lee
Ruse, Steven Douglas
Sanborn, Richard John Jay
Schroer, Gene Eldon
Sevart, Daniel Joseph
Shull, William Edgar, Jr.
Smithyman, Lee Miller
Solon, James Davis
Stanton, Roger D.
Sullivan, Thomas Eugene
Turner, H. Lee
Wall, Larry William
Williams, Ronald Paul
Wing, David Leslie
Woolf, John Paul

Kentucky

Adams, Wesley Price, Jr.
Atherton, Bruce Dwain
Barr, James Houston, Jr.
Barrickman, Uhel Overton
Bishop, Robert Whitsitt
Boylan, Michael Lee
Brandon, Douglas Colliver
Bratton, Robert Milton
Brill, David Alan
Carey, Marcus Stephen
Chambers, Dorothy J.
Chauvin, Leonard Stanley, Jr.
Cowan, Frederic Joseph, Jr.
Davis, Russell H.
DeFalaise, Louis
Dolt, Frederick Corrance
Ely, Hiram, III
Feather, Mark Randolph
Friedman, David Alan
Greene, James S., Jr.
Herren, Thomas Kelly
Kerrick, Thomas Neal
King, Nicholas Neal
Masters, Richard L.
Mathison, Harry Lee
Meredith, Ronald Edward
Mulloy, William Patrick, II
Nelson, Richard S.
Neuber, Frank William, Jr.
Ogden, Len Willis, Jr.
Parker, William Jerry
Penick, Michael Preston
Perkinson, Michael Leon
Philipps, Kurt A.
Pitt, Dorothy Moore
Ratterman, David Burger
Reed, John Squires, II
Roark, Jimmy Lee
Robinson, William T., III
Rudloff, William J.
Seiller, Bill Victor
Sexton, David Andrew
Shuffett, James Avery
Spalding, Michael Fredrick
Stopher, Robert Estes
Sullivan, Richard Morrissey
Turley, Robert Joe
Varellas, James John, Jr.
Walker, Henry Lawson, II

Louisiana

Alsobrook, Henry Bernis, Jr.
Anderson, Lawrence Robert, Jr.
Angelle, Robert
Anzelmo, Donald Joseph
Ates, J. Robert
Bains, David Paul
Barry, Michael Francis
Beckner, Donald Lee
Bengtson, Karl Wayne
Bezet, Gary Anthony
Blackman, Gordon N., Jr.

Booksh, Robert William, Jr.
Broussard, Richard C.
Buckley, Samuel Olliphant, III
Burns, William Glenn
Burt, Earl Daniel, Jr.
Butcher, Bruce Cameron
Centola, Lawrence Joseph
Cheatwood, Roy Clifton
Cheramie, Carlton Joseph
Daigle, Patrick Keith
Darden, Marshall Taylor
Davidson, Van Michael, Jr.
Dugas, David Roy
Dwyer, Ralph Daniel, Jr.
Eatman, Robert Emerson
Ensenat, Donald Burnham
Evans, Robert Collin
Everett, Stephen Edward
Feldman, Martin L. C.
Friend, Joseph Ernest
Garcia, Patricia A.
Gauthier, Wendell Haynes
Gertler, Meyer H.
Godofsky, Harvey Joseph
Guidry, Hervin A.
Halliburton, John Robert
Hanemann, James, Jr.
Hargrove, Robert Clyde
Harris, Thorne D., III
Haygood, John Warren
Henican, Caswell Ellis
Herbert, John Campbell
Herman, Russ Michel
Hillyer, Haywood Hansell, III
Hoskins, David LeRoy
Johnson, Patrick, Jr.
Johnson, Ronald Adams
Jones, Johnnie Anderson
Kuhn, James E.
Lamonica, P(aul) Raymond
Leger, Walter John, Jr.
Lestelle, Andrea Sucherman
Levy, Adolph J.
Little, Michael Frederick
Looney, James Holland
Lyons, Laurie Wilkinson
Madison, James Robinson
Madison, Vivian L.
Manard, Robert Lynn, III
McCall, Harry
McGlinchey, Dermot Sheehan
McGovern, Glenn Charles
McMichael, James David
Milligan, Edward Joseph, Jr.
Mitchell, Robert Burdette
Molony, Michael Janssens, Jr.
Nungesser, Nancy Ann
Payne, Roy Steven
Perez, Luis Alberto
Provosty, LeDoux Roger, Jr.
Raymond, Charles Michael
Riccio, Marie Olympia
Robinson, Michael
Roddy, Virginia Niehaus
Rosen, William Warren
Rowley, Horace Perez, III
Ryan, James, III
St. John, James Berry, Jr.
Schewe, Bruce Victor
Scott, L. Havard, III
Seabolt, Charles Frederick
Shields, Lloyd Noble
Siegel, Robert Irwin
Smith, Brian David
Smith, Charles Sterling
Smith, J. Arthur, III
Stetter, Roger Alan
Stockwell, Oliver Perkins
Stout, A(rthur) Wendel, III
Stuart, Walter Bynum, IV
Treeby, William David
Tritico, Russell Thomas
Vance, Robert Patrick
Veron, J. Michael
Volk, Jerome Milton, Jr.
Webb, Daniel Andrew
Weisler, Faye Leslie
White, Clair Fox
Whitney, John Franklin
Windmeyer, Joseph Edwin
Woodward, Madison Truman, Jr.
Wysocki, James Anthony

Maine

Ballou, John Waldo
Bohan, Thomas Lynch
Hartwell, Jane Barry
Harvey, Charles Albert, Jr.
Hirshon, Robert Edward
Horton, Andrew Marcus
Hunt, Merrill Roberts
Johnson, Phillip Edward
Lanham, Samuel Wilbur, Jr.
Moss, Logan Vansen
Smith, Jeffrey Allen
Willihnganz, Paul W.

Maryland

Anderson, Lee Berger
Ayres, Jeffrey Peabody
Baker, William Parr
Bartlett, James Wilson, III
Berman, Michael David
Bliss, Donald Tiffany, Jr.
Boone, Harold Thomas
Bresnahan, Pamela Anne
Burke, Raymond Daniel
Clarke, William Anthony Lee, III
Cobb, Ty
Comeau, Michael Gerard
Crocker, Michael Pue
Crowe, Thomas Leonard
Digges, Edward S(imms), Jr.
Dubé, Lawrence Edward, Jr.
Eisenberg, Harvey Ellis
Freeman, Martin Henry
Furrer, David Eugene
Gadhia, Lalit Harilal
Geldon, Fred Wolman
Golomb, George Edwin
Grattan, S. Amy
Hanley, Robert Lee, Jr.
Hansen, Christopher Agnew
Hare, Glenn Patrick
Harris, Janine Diane
Hill, Milton King, Jr.
Howell, Harley Thomas
Hughes, Leo A., Jr.
Jayson, Lester Samuel
Joseph, Fredric Robert
Junghans, Paula Marie
Kayson, David
King, John Frances
Kramer, Paul R.
Little, William Scott
Loker, F(rank) Ford, Jr.
Lulie, Edward, III
McLain, Susan Lynn
Miles, Gerard Frances
Moorhead, James Barr
Morrow, Thomas Campbell
Mullenbach, Linda Herman
Nolan, Paul William
Ohly, D. Christopher
Orman, Leonard Arnold
Pappas, George Frank
Pensinger, John Lynn
Powell, Michael Calvin
Price, Howard Jack, Jr.
Radding, Andrew
Reid, Richard Ayres
Risik, Philip Maurice
Schatzow, Michael
Schochor, Jonathan
Schwartz, Joseph Anthony, III
Sfekas, Stephen James
Shar, Marcus Z.
Shepard, Adam Hoffman
Sherer, Ronald Brian
Shore, Elbert Russell
Smouse, H(ervey) Russell
Snyder, Stuart Jay
Souder, Susan
Strandberg, Rebecca Newman
Sweeney, Eileen Cecilia
Terrell, Herbert Arthur
Tyler, Ralph Sargent, III
Uehlinger, Gerard Paul
Wallace, Sean Daniel
Ward, John Thomas
Weiss, Irwin E.
Weltchek, Robert Jay
White, Pamela Janice
Wimbrow, Peter Ayers, III
Ziegler, William Joseph

Massachusetts

Adomeit, Peter Loring
Andrews, David Joseph
Apjohn, Nelson George
Asher, Robert Michael
Auerbach, Joseph
Bailey, Frank Joseph, Jr.
Barber, Robert Cushman
Bennett, Richard Edward
Berliner, L. Jed
Berman, David
Campbell, Richard P.
Carpenter, Robert Brent
Cheek, Jo Frances
Costello, Walter Anthony, Jr.
Curley, Robert Ambrose, Jr.
Dahlen, Richard Lester
Danner, Douglas
Davis, Christopher Patrick
Devlin, Paul Anthony
Dignan, Thomas Gregory, Jr.
Dillon, James Joseph
Dimare, Charles Joseph
Doherty, Joseph Leo, Jr.
Donahue, Michael Christopher
Donahue, Richard King
Doniger, Anthony M.
Estrine, Andrew Bradley
Felter, John Kenneth
Field, Martha Amanda
Fine, Phil David
Finn, John Joseph
Fox, Francis Haney
Frieden, James Anthony
Friedmann, Jonathon David
Furman, Mark Steven
Gad, Robert K., III
Geiger, David R.
Gelb, Richard Mark
Gibson, Daniel Peter
Gilmore, John Allen Dehn
Glovsky, Susan G. L.
Golder, Frederick Thomas
Goldman, Robert Huron
Gordon, Richard Warren
Gordon, Stephen Jacob
Greco, Michael S.
Griffin, J. Kenneth
Gross, Susan Larky
Herrick, Stewart Thurston
Hieken, Charles
Houlihan, F(rancis) Robert, Jr.
Hunt, William John
Kavanaugh, James Francis, Jr.
Keeton, Robert Ernest
Knight, Peter Carter
Kociubes, Joseph Leib
Krasnoo, James B.
Kuzinevich, John Jacob
Lacek, Michael Joseph
Lamson, David Hinkley
Legasey, John Samuel
Levine, Julius Byron
Linek, Ernest Vincent
Looney, William Francis, Jr.
Lovins, Nelson Preston
Madan, Anil
Manfreda, Michael Joseph
Margolis, Jonathan J.
McNamara, Frank Luke, Jr.
Meehan, James Francis
Mercer, Richard James
Meserve, Robert William
Messing, Arnold Philip
Meyer, Andrew C., Jr.
Michelson, Mark A.
Mugler, Molly Scott
Newton, Francis Chandler, Jr.
Owens, Henry Freeman, III
Parker, Christopher William
Perry, Edward Needham
Petrucelly, Jeffrey Paul
Pittas, Sydelle
Polk, Victor H., Jr.
Redlich, Marc
Repetti, James Randolph
Rose, Leonard
Rosenthal, Gerald Allen
Ryan, Allan Andrew, Jr.
Saltzberg, Edward Charles
Schafer, Steven Harris
Schiller, Robert James
Schwartz, William
Segal, Terry Philip
Semerjian, Evan Yervant
Shapiro, David Louis
Simonds, Marshall
Starrett, Loyd Milford
Straus, William Marc
Thornton, Michael Paul
Towner, Frank Schwable, Jr.
Traficanti, Tina Michele
Trimmier, Roscoe, Jr.
Waxler, David Harvey
Weidman, Charles Ray
Wilson, Paul Dennis
Witt, Carol Ann
Wolf, David
Woolf, Jeffrey David

Michigan

Alatalo, Richard
Alber, Phillip George
Amsden, Ted Thomas
Andreoff, Christopher Andon
Baker, Frederick Milton, Jr.
Baxter, Richard Brian
Berry, Steven Craig
Bishop, Lawrence Ray
Blaske, Thomas Hugh
Blum, Irving Ronald
Boltz, Russ Edward
Boyle, Patricia Jean
Brady, Edmund Matthew, Jr.
Brander, Reynolds A., Jr.
Bransdorfer, Stephen Christie
Bregman, Judy Ellen
Brenneman, Hugh Warren, Jr.
Brooks, Keefe Alan
Browning, Charles W.
Buchanan, John Cowan
Buchanan, William D.
Bullard, Rockwood Wilde, III
Bushnell, George Edward, Jr.
Callahan, John William
Carson, Robert William
Christopher, William Garth
Cinabro, Robert Henry
Cloon, William Graham, Jr.
Cooke, Marcia Gail
Cooper, David Joseph
Cooper, Edward Hayes
Cothorn, John Arthur
Crehan, Joseph Edward
Dahm, Peter Franklin
Darling, Robert Howard
Decker, Harold James
Devlin, Eugene Joseph
Drummond, Donald Francis
Drutchas, Gregory G.
Dunne, Francis Hugh
Fallon, William Hume
Feringa, Scott Douglas
Forrest, Robert Edwin
Fosmire, Michael Sean
Geary, James H.
Gifford, Ernest Irving
Goodman, William Harry
Googasian, George Ara
Gootee, Jane Marie
Gorland, Scott Lance
Grate, Marshall Warren
Gustafson, Richard B.
Haisch, Anthony Albert
Haliw, Andrew Jerome, III
Harris, Patricia Skalny
Harvey, Barbara
Hay, Thomas Harold
Heinen, Mark Lee
Heldt, Jeffrey Alan
Hertzberg, Robert Steven
Hines, Paul William
Joseph, Raymond
Kalec, Robert Michael
Kara, Paul Mark
Kennedy, Kael Behan
Kienbaum, Karen Smith
Koernke, Thomas Frederick
Kramer, LeRoy, III
Kritselis, William Nicholas
Leavitt, Martin Jack
Lebow, Michael Jeffrey
Lenihan, Robert Joseph, II
Lilly, Terence Joseph
Longhofer, Ronald Stephen
Lopatin, Albert
Lubben, Craig Henry
Lucow, Milton
Malone, Daniel Patrick
Mann, John Raymond, III
Maxwell, Robert Alexander
McGlory, Willie Edward
Mears, Patrick Edward
Messmer, Kirk Daniel
Miela, Deborah Lynn
Miller, Sheldon Lee
Moch, Joseph William
Morganroth, Fred
Morganroth, Mayer
Mosher, Richard Underhill
Murg, Gary Earl
Murray, Gregory Vincent
Nichols, Charles Leonard
Nizio, Frank
Novak, Michael Alan
Pappas, Edward Harvey
Parish, Tat
Parker, Dona Scott
Plaszczak, Roman Thaddeus
Ponitz, John Allan
Pylman, Norman Herbert, II
Rader, Ralph Terrance
Rauss, Dennis Michael
Robb, Dean Allan
Rowe, Jack Douglas
Roy, William Alan
Saylor, Larry James
Schefman, Leslie Craig
Schroer, J. Michael
Scudi, Morgan John Clift
Secrest, Stephen Frederick
Sills, John Dennis
Smietanka, John Allen
Smith, Arthur Allan
Snyder, George Edward
Soet, Henry David
Souter, Don Vern
Spreitzer, John Richard
Steiner, Sanford Lee
Steingold, Fred Saul
Stella, Daniel Francis
Sumpter, Jerry Lee
Tallerico, Thomas Joseph
Tartt, Tyrone Chris
Taunt, Charles Joseph
Tickner, Ellen Mindy
Turner, Donald Allen
Turner, Lester Nathan
Valentine, Stephen Kenneth, Jr.
Vander Ark, Steven John
VanderLaan, Robert D.
Van Leuven, Robert Joseph
Vocht, Michelle Elise
Warren, John Philip, Jr.
Warren, William Gerald
Washington, Valdemar Luther
Webster, Robert Byron
Weinstein, William Joseph
Wienner, S. Thomas
Wilhelm, Thomas Vincent
Williams, James Joseph
Winsten, I.W.
Wittlinger, Timothy David
Yockey, Kurt David
Young, Rodger Douglas
Zuckerman, Richard Engle

Minnesota

Allgeyer, David Alan
Balmer, James W.
Bassford, Charles Addison
Beens, Richard Albert
Bennett, Robert
Bleck, Michael John
Brosnahan, Roger Paul
Bruner, Philip Lane
Bujold, Tyrone Patrick
Bulinski, Gregory Paul
Cattanach, Robert Edward, Jr.
Ciresi, Michael Vincent
Colacci, Irving Roger
Devney, John Leo
Dosland, Chester Allen
Eisenberg, Jonathan Lee
Eustis, Warren Penhall
Finch, Frederick Earl
Finzen, Bruce Arthur
Frauenshuh, Ronald Ray, Sr.
French, John Dwyer
Friederichs, Norman Paul
Gislason, Daniel Adam
Gordon, John Bennett
Hagglund, Clarance Edward
Hanson, Bruce Eugene
Hanson, Kent Bryan
Hunter, Donald Forrest
Jamar, Steven Dwight
Johnson, Donald E.
Johnson, Richard Walter
Jones, Bradley Mitchell
Karan, Bradlee
Keppel, William James
Keyes, Leonard John
Kirsch, Steven Jay
Lange, Frederick Emil
Lindberg, Michael Charles
Maclin, Alan Hall
Magnuson, Roger James
Mansfield, Seymour J.
Marquart, Steven Leonard
Mays, Charles Andrew
McKenna, David William
McReynolds, Michael Patrick
Mills, Anthony Belden
Murphy, Diana E.
Nelson, Peggy Ann
Nelson, Susan Richard
Oates, Kathleen Marie
Palmer, Deborah Jean
Pentelovitch, Willian Zane
Reite, Charles Douglas
Remele, Lewis Albert, Jr.
Reuter, James William
Rowlette, Roger Lee
Saeks, Allen Irving
Seaburg, Jean
Seykora, David Gerard
Shaw, A. Reid
Short, Marianne Dolores
Shroyer, Thomas Jerome
Sippel, William Leroy
Skaar, Harvey Engaard
Tanick, Marshall Howard
Thibodeau, Thomas Raymond
Timmer, Steven James
Timmons, Mary Sarazin
Tourek, Steven Charles
Wade, James Alan
Wahl, Karla Rae
Wahoske, Michael James
Weiner, Michael Lewis
Wine, Mark Philip
Woods, Robert Edward

Mississippi

Abbott, William W., Jr.
Barton, William Harvey
Breland, Norman Leroy
Brown, William Houston
Bullock, Jim
Clark, Charles
Currie, Edward Jones, Jr.
Denham, Earl Lamar
Dent, George E.
Dornan, Donald C., Jr.
Fondren, Louis
Goodman, Herbert Raymond
Goodman, William Flournoy, III
Griffith, Benjamin Elmo
Grower, John Marshall
Hafter, Jerome Charles
Hannan, Edwin York
Harkins, Patrick Nicholas, III
Henegan, John Clark
Holbrook, Frank Malvin
Hopkins, Alben Norris
Howell, Joel Walter, III
Kirkland, Thomas Lee, Jr.
Lancaster, William Robert
Mitchell, Cynthia Inis
Montjoy, Richard Wilson, II
Morrison, Harvey Lee, Jr.
Olack, Neil Peter
Perry, Lee Nace
Pyle, Luther Arnold
Smith, James Edwin, Jr.
Sumners, Lester Furr
Turner, Bennie L.
Whitfield, William Ernest
Wise, Joseph Powell
Wise, Sherwood Willing
Wiser, Nicholas Van

Missouri

Adams, Philip James, Jr.
Atwood, Hollye Stolz
Aylward, Timothy Michael
Bartlett, Alex
Bay, William Robert
Beard, Charles Richard
Beckett, Theodore Charles
Berendt, Robert T.
Bevan, Kent Morgan
Blakeslee, Julia Fay
Braun, N. Barrett
Breen, Jean Marie
Brown, Paul Sherman
Bruening, Richard Patrick
Carlson, Mary Susan
Chackes, Kenneth Michael
Chassaing, J. Patrick
Cipolla, Thomas Alphonse
Claggett, Daniel Elliot
Clarke, Milton Charles
Clear, John Michael
Colagiovanni, Joseph Alfred, Jr.
Cole, James Silas, Jr.
Collins, James Slade, II
Conran, Joseph Palmer
Cooper, Richard Alan
Cronan, John Michael
Deacy, Thomas Edward, Jr.
DeCuyper, Joseph Ysidore
Delaney, Michael Francis
Dempsey, David Gerard
DeWoskin, Alan Ellis
Feder, Gary Harold
Fritz, Tobias Bodwell
Gamm, Gordon Julius
Gilhousen, Brent James
Gilster, Peter Stuart
Gordon, Michael David
Greiman, Gerald Phillip
Growe, Gary Alan
Hart, Michael David
Higgins, Stephen Boyd
Hipsh, Harlene Janet
Horgan, John Joseph
Hubbell, Ernest
Hullverson, James Everett, Jr.
Humphrey, James William, Jr.
Johnson, Leonard James
Johnson, Mark Eugene
Jones, David Christopher
Kennedy, Walter Jeff, Jr.
Kilroy, John Muir
Kleine, Richard Allen
Kohn, Alan Charles
Kortenhof, Joseph Michael
Lolli, Don R(ay)
Lucchesi, Lionel Louis
Lysaught, Patrick
Martucci, William Christopher
Mattern, Keith Edward
McCalpin, Francis William
McCubbin, Garry
McDonald, William Henry
Michener, John Athol
Moore, McPherson Dorsett
Mueller, Joseph Henry
Myers, Ronald Lynn
Newman, Charles A.
Nichols, Stephen Wayne
Noel, Edwin Lawrence
Nutter, Thomas Edward
Oliver, David Field
Oliver, John Leachman
Owens, Dennis James Campbell
Parker, Linda Louise
Popham, Arthur Cobb, Jr.
Proctor, George Edwin, Jr.
Rabbitt, Daniel Thomas, Jr.
Reed, David Q.
Reeg, Kurtis Bradford
Remley, David Mark
Reynolds, Jerry Lee
Rice, Canice Timothy, Jr.
Ritter, Robert Forcier
Roberts, Patrick Kent
Rush, Douglas Kevin
Ryder, Bruce David
Sableman, Mark Stephen
Schermerhorn, Sandra Leigh
Schult, Thomas Peter
Schwartz, Theodore Frank
See, Andrew Bruce
Sestric, Anthony James
Shapiro, Alvin Dale
Sher, Richard Philip
Sherman, Joseph Allen
Simon, Roy D., Jr.
Sneeringer, Stephen Geddes
Sowers, David Eric
Spalty, Edward
Sparks, Billy Schley
Stoup, Arthur Harry
Stribling, Gray Carroll, Jr.
Strong, Thomas Gorman
Sugg, Reed Waller
Tatlow, Gary Arthur
Thompson, Michael
Toppins, Roger Keith
Tremayne, Eric Flory
Turcotte, John Arthur, Jr.
Turley, J. William
Vering, John Albert
Vleisides, Gregory William
Wallace, Barbara Wendy
Wallace, Robert E.
Walsh, Rodger John
Wellford, Robin Sonneland
Weston, Theodora White
Wherritt, Alan Francisco
Wirken, James Charles
Wolf, Jerome Thomas
Woods, Curtis E(ugene)
Woody, Donald Eugene
Zobrist, Karl

Montana

Best, George Bullock, Jr.
Clarke, Dennis Person
Dalthorp, George Carrol
Guthals, Joel Eric
Johnson, Margaret Mary Joyce
Jones, James Leonard
Matovich, Carey E.
Matteucci, Sherry Scheel
Morrison, Frank Brenner, Jr.
Morrison, Sharon McDonald
Mouat, William Gavin
Murphy, Gregory G.
Nye, Jerrold Linden
Ogg, Robert Kelley
Towe, Thomas Edward
Trieweiler, Terry Nicholas

Nebraska

Bartle, Robert Franklin
Baumann, Larry R(oger)
Benak, James Donald
Bradford, Charles Steven
Busick, Denzel Rex
Caporale, D. Nick
Colleran, Kevin
Dahlk, Thomas Harlan
Dolan, James Vincent
Gewacke, John Clifford
Hutfless, Frank James
Inserra, John Phillip
Jensen, Sam
Kay, Stephen William
Lang, James Edward
Lauritsen, Thomas Christian
Mueller, William Jeffrey
Pohren, Edward Francis
Snowden, James Arthur
Urbom, Randall Crawford
Walsh, Thomas John
Warin, Edward George
Wence, Gary Fred
Zalewski, James Conrad

Nevada

Barkley, Thierry Vincent
Claassen, Sharon Elaine
Galane, Morton Robert
Guild, Clark Joseph, Jr.
Jimmerson, James Joseph
Kelesis, George Peter
Koch, Jan Paul
Murphy, Patrick James
Perry, Robert Harry
Pinkerton, C(harles) Frederick
Richards, Paul A.
Smith, Stephanie Marie
Sourwine, Julien Gillen
Wedge, Virgil Henry
Wenzel, Steve Edwin
Wicker, Walter Chris
Zive, Gregg William
Zubel, Eric Louis

New Hampshire

Brown, Stanley Melvin
Conboy, Carol Ann
Damon, Claudia Cords
Danenbarger, W. Wright
Engel, David Chapin
Hanna, Katherine Merritt
Johnson, Robert Veiling, II
Kitchen, John Scott
McNamara, Richard Bedle
Shaines, Robert Arthur
Snierson, Richard S.

New Jersey

Abut, Charles C.
Adlerstein, Jo Anne Chernev
Banks, Cecil James
Beidler, John Nathan
Cerny, Edward Charles, III
Chiumento, Gary C.
Clemen, John Douglas
Connell, William Terrence
Cooper, Richard Craig
Corbett, Peter Gerald
Curran, Catherine Moore
Dughi, Louis John, Jr.
Eakeley, Douglas Scott
Eder, Todd Brandon
Egan, Robert T.
Eittreim, Richard MacNutt
Ellenport, Robert Saul
Friedman, Richard Lloyd
Garrigle, William Aloysius
Gordon, Harrison J.
Gordon, Michael
Greenbaum, William I.
Haberbusch, Carl Arthur
Harris, Brian Craig
Harrison, Charles Maurice
Haskins, Guy Halifax, Jr.
Hayes, Lewis Mifflin, Jr.
Hector, Bruce John
Hewit, Russell Lyle
Hoens, Charles Henry, Jr.
Horan, John Donohoe
Horton, William Harrison
Humick, Thomas Charles Campbell
Jacobs, Andrew Robert
Jacobson, Gary Steven
Jeffers, Albert Brown
Joel, Jack Bowers
Kallmann, Stanley Walter
Kelsky, Richard Brian
Kent, Thomas Day
Klein, Paul Ira
Knoblauch, Leo N.
Korin, Joel Benjamin
Kott, David Russell
Kozyra, Barry Alan
Kronman, Carol Jane
Kuttner, Bernard A.
Lavigne, Lawrence Neil
Maraziti, Joseph James, Jr.
McClear, Nicholas Willard
McDonough, Joseph Richard
McGuire, William B(enedict)
McKenna, Michael Francis
McMahon, Edward Richard
Medvin, Alan York
Mintz, Jeffry Alan
Montana, Janice
Moore, Thomas Michael
Muscato, Andrew
Naar, Alan S.
O'Connell, Hans James
O'Leary, Richard Patrick
Oliver, Raymond A.
Ozer, Lisa Goldberg
Pearlman, Peter Steven
Peckar, Robert S.
Pentony, Kenneth Richard
Platkin, Lawrence Peter
Puffer, Leonard Bruce, Jr.
Rabinowitz, Daniel Lawrence
Raveson, Louis Sheppard
Reid, Charles Adams, III
Reiken, Samuel N.
Reitman, Sidney
Risinger, D. Michael
Robertson, William Withers
Roth, Kenneth David
Rowe, Paul Andrew
Saffer, Judith M.
Samay, Z. Lance
Santoli, Joseph Ralph
Schwartz, David Elving
Shackleton, Richard James
Sheldon, Scott Jeffrey
Silver, Cole Brian
Simon, David Robert
Slifkin, Irving
Smith, Hayden, Jr.
Smith, Peter John
Sponzilli, Edward George
Steedle, Roger Craig
Stern, John Jules
Stewart, James
Sullivan, Eugene John
Teicher, Martin
Thomason, Charles Lee
Tomar, William
Veenstra, Yves Cornell
Vinick, Philip Brod
Warnement, Pamela Pearson
Warren, Lisbeth Ann
Wayne, Robert Andrew
Weber, Roy Philip
White, John Lindsey
Whitmer, Frederick Lee
Williams, Barbara June
Zegas, Alan Lee
Zlotnick, Norman Lee

New Mexico

Berardinelli, David Joseph
Branch, James Alexander, Jr.
Branch, Turner Williamson
Burton, John Paul
Caldwell, Paul Raymond
Casey, Patrick Anthony
Chavez, Rudolph Ben
Crider, Charles Joseph
Dahl, Jeffrey A(lan)
Fish, Paul Mathew
Gibson, Louise
Hall, Rex Andrew
Howell, Mark Franklin
Huffaker, Gregory Dorian, Jr.
Konrad, Alan Karl
Madrid, Patricia Ann
Matthews, Marian
McClaugherty, Joe L.
Monroe, Jerald Jacob
Myers, Edward Doran
Paskind, Martin Benjamin
Ricco, Edward Robert
Roehl, Jerrald J(oseph)
Schwarz, Michael Howard
Singleton, Sarah Michael
Stuckey, Charles Edward
Voegler, Douglas Gene
Wentworth, John
Wertheim, Jerry
Wesch, Calvin Walter

New York

Abady, Samuel Aaron
Abramowitz, Elkan
Ackman, Milton Roy
Adler, Alan Michael
Aksen, Gerald
Albans, Gabrielle Victoria
Alice, Ronald William
Allen, Ronald Roger, Jr.
Allison, Richard Clark
Alonso, Andrea Maria
Altieri, Peter Louis
Amabile, John Louis
Amsterdam, Mark Lemle
Angland, Joseph
Arenson, Gregory K.
Arps, Leslie Hansen
Ausubel, Marvin Victor
Avery, Patricia I.
Axinn, Stephen Mack
Bader, Albert Xavier, Jr.
Bader, Howard David
Baechtold, Robert Louis
Bagge, Michael Charles
Baird, Bruce Allen
Baker, Lloyd Harvey
Barist, Jeffrey
Barron, Francis Patrick
Barry, Desmond Thomas, Jr.
Bauer, George A., III
Bauman, Arnold
Bazerman, Steven Howard
Beach, Charles Addison
Beatie, Russel Harrison, Jr.
Becker, John Ernest, Jr.
Beckerman, Ray
Beckey, Sylvia Louise
Beha, James Alexius, II
Behrle, Sandra Gale
Belnick, Mark Alan
Benedict, James Nelson
Berney, Lonn E.
Bernstein, Richard Forbes
Bernstein, Robert Bruce
Berry, Charles Gordon
Beshar, Robert Peter
Bienstock, Joshua Elliott
Birnbaum, Edward L.
Bizar, Irving
Bloom, Jeffrey Brian
Blumkin, Linda Ruth
Boes, Lawrence William
Booth, Edgar Hirsch
Bosses, Stevan J.
Bowen, John Wesley Edward, IV
Bragar, Raymond Aaron
Braid, Frederick Donald
Bramwell, Henry
Braun, Jeffrey Louis
Brenner, Mark B.
Briggs, Taylor Rastrick
Brizel, Michael Alan
Brody, Neil
Brokate, Brian William
Bronner, William Roche
Brooks, Russell Edwin
Brown, David Edward
Brown, Jerrold Stanley
Brown, Paul M.
Brown, Peter Megargee
Brown, Ronald Wellington
Bschorr, Paul Joseph
Buchwald, Don David
Burgman, Dierdre Ann
Burns, John MacDougal, III
Burrell, Lizabeth Lorie
Burrows, Kenneth David
Busner, Philip H.
Cahn, Richard Caleb
Callahan, Joseph Patrick
Calvaruso, Joseph A.
Capra, Daniel Joseph
Carlisle, Jay Charles, II
Carnegie, Christa Lew
Carter, James Hal, Jr.
Cashman, Gideon
Castel, P. Kevin
Cavanagh, Edward Dean
Cayea, Donald Joseph
Cedarbaum, Miriam Goldman
Chapin, Edward Whiting
Charen, Steven Craig
Cherundolo, John Charles
Chizmadia, Stephen Mark
Cirillo, Richard Allan
Clarey, Robert Louis
Clark, Cameron
Clary, Richard Wayland
Clermont, Kevin Michael
Cohen, Richard Barton
Cohen, Robert Stephan
Cole, Charles Dewey, Jr.
Cole, Richard Charles
Cook, Michael Lewis
Cornelison, Albert Otto, Jr.
Costello, Robert Joseph
Cox, Marshall
Crain, William Earl
Creel, Thomas Leonard
Critchlow, Charles Howard
Cunha, Mark Geoffrey
Curnin, Thomas Francis
Curran, Maurice Francis
Currey, Charles Thomas
Curvin, Steven P.
Dallas, William Moffit, Jr.
Dalton, Kenneth M.
Daniels, George Benjamin
Daniels, James Eliot
Dankner, Jay Warren
Davidson, George Allan
Davidson, Robert Bruce
Davis, Richard Joel
Deffina, Thomas Victor
Delehanty, John McDonald
Del Gadio, Robert G.
Dell, Michael John
De Luca, Thomas George
DeMarco, Anthony J., Jr.
DeMarie, Joseph
Dershowitz, Nathan Zev
Derzaw, Richard Lawrence
De Vivo, Edward Charles
DiBlasi, John Peter
Dickerson, Thomas Arthur
DiNardo, Joseph
Dixon, Harry Thomas
Dolin, Lonny H.
Donley, Joseph Francis
Donohue, John Patrick
Donovan, Richard Edward
Dowling, Thomas Patrick
Dubbs, Thomas Allan
Dunham, Dan Steven
Dunne, Gerard Francis
Dweck, Jack S.
Dwyer, Robert Jeffrey
Dwyer, Susan Tate
Earle, Victor Montagne, III
Edel, Martin David
Edelson, Gilbert Seymour
Edgerton, Lynne Todd
Eilen, Howard Scott
Eiszner, James Richard, Jr.
Ellenberg, Michael Aron
Elsen, Sheldon Howard
Engel, Richard Lee
Eno, Lawrence Raphael
Erim, Ahmet Martin
Estreicher, Samuel
Evans, Martin Frederic
Evans, Richard Joseph
Evans, Thomas William
Fagen, Leslie Gordon
Fahey, Joseph Edmund
Falls, Raymond Leonard, Jr
Farley, William Patrick
Fein, Scott Norris
Feldberg, Michael Svetkey
Felfe, Peter Franz
Fensterstock, Blair Courtney
Fern, Frederick Harold
Fersko, Raymond Stuart
Fialkoff, Jay R.
Fiddler, Robert William
Fink, Rosalind Sue
Finkelstein, Ira Allen
Finnegan, George Bernard, Jr.
Fisher, Cheryl Smith
Fiske, Robert Bishop, Jr.
Fitt, Benjamin Jones
Fitzpatrick, Joseph Mark
Flamm, Leonard N(athan)
Fleming, John C.
Fleming, Peter Emmet, Jr.
Fletcher, Anthony L.
Flynn, Michael
Forstadt, Joseph Lawrence
Foster, David Lee
Frankel, Sandor
Freedman, Monroe Henry
Freeman, David John
Freund, Fred A.
Freyer, Dana Hartman
Friedberg, Harry Jacob
Friedland, Paul Daniel
Friedman, John Maxwell, Jr.
Friedman, Jon George
Friedman, Victor Stanley
Frumento, Aegis Joseph
Fryd, Robert
Furgang, Philip
Futterman, Stanley Norman
Gaffney, Mark William
Gallantz, George Gerald
Garfinkel, Barry Herbert
Garley, R. Scott
Geiger, Alexander
Geisler, Thomas Milton, Jr.
Genova, Joseph Steven
Gerber, Edward F.
Gerber, Robert Evan
Gerrard, Michael Burr
Getlan, Norman
Getnick, Neil Victor
Giacomo, Paul Joseph, Jr.
Gilman, Charles Alan
Gitter, Max
Givens, Richard Ayres
Glanville, Robert Edward
Glekel, Jeffrey Ives
Glickstein, Steven
Gold, Stuart Walter
Goldhirsch, Lawrence Bertram
Goldschmid, Harvey Jerome
Goldstein, Howard Warren
Golomb, David Bela
Gordon, Michael Mackin
Gorman, Gerald Patrick
Greenawalt, William Sloan
Greenbaum, Sheldon Marc
Greenberg, Ira George
Greene, Barry Todd
Greenfield, Jay
Greenspan, Leon Joseph
Greilsheimer, James Gans
Grill, Steven Eric
Gruen, Michael Stephan
Guttlein, Jorge de Jesus
Habian, Bruce George
Hagelin, Michael Thomas
Halberstam, Malvina Guggenheim
Hall, Christopher Patrick
Halpern, Philip Morgan
Halpern, Ralph Lawrence
Hamm, David Bernard
Handelsman, Lawrence Marc
Handler, Milton
Harbison, James Wesley, Jr.
Hardin, Adlai S., Jr.
Harris, Allen
Harris, Joel B(ruce)
Hartzell, Andrew Cornelius, Jr.
Hathaway, Gerald Thomas
Hauhart, Robert Charles
Hauser, Gregory Francis
Hazen, James Michael
Hellerstein, Alvin Kenneth
Hellman, Charles David
Hemingway, Alfred Henry, Jr.
Henderson, Erskine Dale
Herzog, Ronald Steven
Higginson, James Jackson
Hill, Alfred
Himes, Jay L(eslie)
Hirsch, Jerome Seth
Hoffman, John Ernest, Jr.
Hoffman, John Fletcher
Hoffman, Mathew
Hoffmann, Malcolm Arthur
Hollyer, A(rthur) Rene
Horkovich, Robert Michael
Horowitz, Louise Schwartz
Howorth, David Bishop
Hoynes, Louis LeNoir, Jr.
Hritz, George F.
Hudspeth, Stephen Mason
Huettner, Richard Alfred
Hunziker, Robert McKee
Hurnyak, Christina Kaiser
Hyde, David Rowley
Hyman, Montague Allan
Iannuzzi, John Nicholas
Isaacs, Robert Charles
Iselin, Josephine Lea
Isquith, Fred Taylor
Itzkoff, Norman Jay
Jackson, Thomas Gene
Jackson, William Eldred
Jacob, Edwin J.
Jacobs, Randall Scott David
Jacobson, Jeffrey Eli
Jacobson, Jonathan M.
Jauvtis, Robert Lloyd
Jehu, John Paul
Jensen, J. Christopher
Joffe, Robert David
Jones, E. Stewart, Jr.
Jordan, David Francis, Jr.
Joseph, Gregory Paul
Joseph, Leonard
Juceam, Robert E.
Kadet, Samuel
Kalow, David Arthur
Kamin, Lawrence O.
Kaminer, Peter H.
Kandel, William Lloyd
Kaplan, Eugene Neal
Kaplan, Joseph Charles
Kaplan, Lewis A.
Karger, Arthur
Kasold, Bruce Edward
Kassebaum, John Philip
Katona, Gabriel Paul
Katz, Michael Albert
Katz, Robert James
Kaufman, Rosalind Fuchsberg
Kaufman, Stephen E.
Kaufmann, Jack
Kavaler, Thomas J.
Kaye, Richard Paul
Keen, Andrew Nick
Kelly, Raymond Aloysius, Jr.
Kelner, Robert Steven
Kelton, John Tremain
Kempler, Cecelia
Kenney, John Joseph
Kenny, James Michael
Kessler, Jeffrey L.
Keyko, David George
Kidd, John Edward
Killeen, Henry Walter
Kimball, John Devereux
King, Margaret Gram
King, Robert Lucien
Kinzler, Thomas Benjamin
Kirschbaum, Myron
Klein, Arnold Spencer
Klinger, Alan Mark
Klingsberg, David
Kocher, Walter William
Koegel, William Fisher
Koeltl, John George
Koelzer, George Joseph
Koevary, A. George
Kolbrener, Peter D.
Konove, Ronald L.
Koob, Charles Edward
Koster, Eric David
Kraft, Melvin D.
Krane, Steven Charles
Krause, Charles Frederick
Kraver, Richard Matthew
Kreutzer, S. Stanley
Krinsky, Andrew Neal
Kuh, Richard Henry
Kunstadt, Robert M.
Kurland, Paul C.
Kurzweil, Harvey
Lack, Robert Joel
Lacy, Robinson Burrell
Land, David Potts
Lange, Paul Kruse
Langer, Bruce Alden
Lans, Deborah Eisner
Larkin, Leo Paul, Jr.
Lauer, Eliot
Laughlin, James Patrick
Law, Michael R.
Lawton, Jeff
Lee, Christopher Peter
Lee, Jerome G.
Lester, Howard
Levi, Mark David
Levin, Robert Daniel
Levin, Roger Michael
Levine, Alan
Levine, Ronald Jay
Levinson, Paul Howard
Levitt, Daniel Philip
Levy, George Michael
Levy, Herbert Monte
Levy, Julius
Lewis, David L.
Lewis, Grant Stephen
Lichtenstein, Sarah Carol
Licker, Jeffrey Alan
Lifland, William Thomas
Liggio, Carl Donald
Lindley, David Morrison
Lippe, Richard Allen
Lipsitz, Randy
Lipton, Robert Steven
Litman, Jack Theodore
Lombardi, Joseph Edward
Lowe, John Anthony
Lumbard, Eliot Howland
Lunney, J. Robert
Lupert, Leslie Allan
Lustig, David Carl, III
Lynch, Thomas Halpin
Lynn, Robert Patrick, Jr.
MacCrate, Robert
Machlowitz, David Steven
Madsen, Stephen Stewart
Maglaras, Nicholas George
Malina, Michael
Maney, Michael Mason
Mangone, Louis A.
Marcellino, Stephen Michael
Martin, Allan A.
Martirano, John Joseph
Martone, Patricia Ann
Mattar, Lawrence Joseph
Mattiaccio, Richard L.
Maulsby, Allen Farish
Maurer, Ira Mark
Maxeiner, James Randolph
Mayesh, Jay Philip
McAmis, Edwin Earl
McBaine, John Neylan
McCabe, Stephen M.
McCarthy, Catherine Frances
McCarthy, Robert Emmett
McClaskey, Norman Dean
Mc Donald, William J.
McGraw, Charlene Evertz
McGuire, Harold Frederick
McKinney, James Bernard, Jr.
McLaughlin, Joseph Thomas
McLean, David Lyle
McMahon, Colleen
McShane, Bruce Winthrop
McSherry, William John, Jr.
Medina, Standish Forde, Jr.
Meiklejohn, Donald Stuart
Meiklejohn, Paul Thomas
Meister, Ronald William
Menton, Francis James, Jr.
Milberg, Lawrence
Miller, Richard Allan
Miller, Steven Scott
Miller-Wachtel, Ellen
Minuse, Catherine Jean
Mirone, Robert C(armelo)
Mirsky, Moshe Z.
Mirvis, Theodore Neal
Moerdler, Charles Gerard
Mohen, Thomas Patrick
Moloney, Thomas Joseph
Monaghan, Peter Gerard
Mone, Mathias Edward
Morris, John E.
Morrison, Peter Henry
Moxley, Charles Joseph, Jr.
Muccia, Joseph William
Muka, Betty Loraine Oakes
Mullaney, Thomas Joseph
Mulligan, William G(eorge)
Murphy, Daniel Hayes, II
Murphy, Robert Anthony, Jr.
Murphy, Samuel Wilson, Jr.
Mushkin, Martin
Muskin, Victor Philip
Myerson, Harvey Daniel
Naftalis, Gary Philip
Nearing, Vivienne W.
Nelson, Norman Roy

Neville, Martin John
Newcomb, Danforth
Newcombe, George Michael
Newman, Lawrence Walker
Nolan, Kenneth Paul
Norton, Gerard Francis, Jr.
Novotny, F. Douglas
Null, Douglas Peter
Obermaier, Otto George
O'Brien, Christopher Edward
O'Connor, William Matthew
O'Donnell, Paul Eugene, Jr.
O'Dwyer, Brian
O'Gara, James Vincent
Olick, Arthur Seymour
Oliensis, Sheldon
Olmstead, Clarence Walter, Jr.
Ordman, Howard Francis
O'Reilly, Kevin Thomas
O'Sullivan, Thomas J.
Page, Alfred Emil, Jr.
Palermo, Anthony Robert
Parker, Douglas Martin
Paul, James William
Payment, Kenneth Arnold
Pelton, Russell Gilbert
Pennell, William Brooke
Penney, Freeland N.F.T. Christian
Pepper, Allan Michael
Perrin, Gregory J.
Persons, John Wade
Peskin, Stephan Haskel
Petito, Christopher Salvatore
Phillips, Anthony F.
Piel, Eleanor Jackson
Pietrzak, Alfred Robert
Pikus, David Heller
Piliero, Robert Donald
Pinsky, Michele Dougherty
Pinzler, William Michael
Piziali, Michael H.
Plastaras, Thomas Edward
Platto, Charles
Podell, Albert N.
Pohorelsky, Viktor Vaclav
Polak, Werner L.
Poss, Stephen Daniel
Powers, John Kieran
Prodsky, Edward
Profeta, Fred Robert, Jr.
Prutzman, Lewis Donald, Jr.
Pulos, William Whitaker
Purcell, Edward Aloysius, Jr.
Quinlan, Guy Christian
Quinn, James W.
Quinn, Yvonne Susan
Raab, Sheldon
Raisler, Kenneth Mark
Rakoff, Jed Saul
Raylesberg, Alan Ira
Raymond, Dana Merriam
Reed, James Alexander, Jr.
Reibstein, Richard Jay
Reich, Perry Seth
Reid, Ross
Reilly, Conor Desmond
Reiner, John Paul
Reinthaler, Richard Walter
Rembar, Charles (Isaiah)
Rich, R(obert) Bruce
Rifkind, Robert Singer
Ringel, Dean (I.)
Ringer, James Milton
Robertson, Edwin David
Robinowitz, Stuart
Rogers, Laurence Steven
Rolfe, Ronald Stuart
Rosen, Ted Manus
Rosenbaum, Eli M.
Rosenberg, Gerald Alan
Rosenberg, Maurice
Rosenblith, Robert Manuel
Rosensaft, Menachem Zwi
Rosenzweig, Charles Leonard
Rosner, Jonathan Levi
Ross, Gerald Elliott
Ross, Otho B., III
Rountree, Asa
Rovine, Arthur William
Rovins, Jeffrey Seth
Rubenstein, Allen Ira
Rubinstein, Aaron
Ryan, James Vincent
Ryan, Leonard Eames
Sacks, Ira Stephen
Safer, Jay Gerald
Saltzman, Barry Neal
Saltzman, Michael I.
Salvan, Sherwood Allen
Samels, Stephen Cooper
Samet, Joseph
Samuel, Raphael
Santucci, John J.
Saunders, Paul Christopher
Savit, Joel B.
Savitt, Susan Schenkel
Sawyer, James
Scardilli, Frank Joseph
Scarzafava, John Francis
Scharf, Jared J.
Scheck, Frank Foetisch
Schiffman, Daniel
Schirmeister, Charles F.
Schlau, Philip
Schmidt, Charles Edward
Schneider, Kenneth Paul
Schulman, Steven Gary
Schulz, David Alan
Schumacher, Harry Richard
Schwartz, Marvin
Schwed, Peter Gregory
Segall, Mark Edward
Seidel, Selvyn
Seidler, B(ernard) Alan
Senn, Laurence Vaughn, Jr.
Serota, James Ian
Sesser, Gary Douglas
Shanahan, James Patrick
Shanman, James Alan
Shannon, Michael George
Shapiro, Jerome Gerson
Shea, William Alfred
Shear, Stephen Barrett
Sherwood, James Cruze
Shollenberger, Elizabeth Ann
Short, Skip
Siffert, John Sand
Silverman, Elliot
Silverman, Karen Fay
Silverman, Leon
Silverman, Moses
Slade, Jeffrey Christopher
Sladkus, Harvey Ira
Smiley, Guy Ian
Smith, Briscoe R.
Smith, Janet Diane
Smith, Jeffrey G.
Smith, John Stuart
Smith, Lisa Margaret
Smith, Robert Everett
Smith, Robert Sherlock
Smyk, Stephen Douglass
Snow, Charles
Socol, Melinda
Sonberg, Michael Robert
Sorkin, Laurence Truman
Sovern, Jeff
Soyster, Margaret Blair
Sparkes, James Edward
Sparks, Robert W.
Speiser, Stuart Marshall
Springer, Paul David
Steer, Richard Lane
Steinbrecher, William John
Steinthal, Kenneth L.
Stengel, James Lamont
Stephan, H. Peskin
Stern, Gerald Daniel
Stern, Peter R.
Stern, Warren Roger
Steuer, Richard Marc
Stewart, Charles Evan
Steyer, Roy Henry
Stoll, Neal Richard
Stone, Paula Lenore
Stratton, Walter Love
Straub, Chester John
Struve, Guy Miller
Sugarman, Robert Gary
Summit, Paul Eliot
Summit, Stuart A.
Susser, Stuart J.
Sussman, Alexander R.
Sussman, Edna Rubin
Sussman, Howard S(ivin)
Sutton, Paul J.
Swanson, Richard Paul
Sweeney, John Francis
Sword, Carl H(arry)
Symmers, William Garth
Tanenbaum, William Alan
Tarangelo, Richard Michael
Tarnoff, Jerome
Taussig, Eric Alfred
Taylor, Job, III
Terner, Linda M. Johnson
Terry, James Joseph, Jr.
Thomashower, William Jay
Tidwell, Drew Virgil, III
Toback, Arthur Malcolm
Toplitz, George Nathan
Townsend, John Michael
Tucker, Stephen
Tutrone, Ronald Francis
Tyler, Harold Russell, Jr.
Urowsky, Richard J.
Valentine, John William
Velie, Franklin B.
Viktora, Richard Emil
Vilardo, Lawrence Joseph
Vitkowsky, Vincent Joseph
Wade, George Joseph
Wagner, Michael G.
Wales, H.Elliot
Walinsky, Adam
Walshe, John William Leo
Walton, Robert Prentiss
Ward, Ettie
Warden, John L.
Warshauer, Irene Conrad
Watson, James Lopez
Weiner, Jack H.
Weiner, Robin Wendy
Weinstock, Leonard
Wells, Peter Nathaniel
Wendel, Martin
Wessel, Peter
White, John Patrick
Whitney, George Ward
Wiener, Ira Edward
Wilkens, Jeffrey Martin
Will, Alfred Joseph
Williams, Averill Marshall
Williams, Frank John, Jr.
Wilson, Leroy, Jr.
Windels, Paul, Jr.
Wingate, C(harles) Douglas
Wishingrad, Jay Marc
Witkin, Eric Douglas
Woglom, Eric Cooke
Wolff, Kurt Jakob
Wolgel, Harold Horace
Wolin, Debra Ruth
Wollan, Eugene
Yankowitz, Jack Alan
Yeager, Dennis Randall
Yelenick, Mary Therese
Young, Michael Richard
Zauderer, Mark Carl
Zedrosser, Joseph John
Zelmanovitz, Menachem Osher
Zimmerman, Sandra L.
Zimmett, Mark Paul
Zissu, Roger Lloyd
Zivin, Norman H.

North Carolina

Abrams, Douglas Breen
Ayscue, Edwin Osborne, Jr.
Bell, Paul Buckner
Bennett, Harold Kimsey
Bradshaw, Penni Pearson
Coenen, Dan Thomas
Cogburn, Max Oliver
Comerford, Walter Thompson, Jr.
Currin, Samuel Thomas
Dahl, Tyrus Vance, Jr.
Davis, Jeffrey J.
Davis, Roy Walton, Jr.
Ellis, Lester Neal, Jr.
Enns, Rodrick John
Foster, Charles Allen
Garlitz, Thomas Drake
Gates, James Edward
Gitter, Allan Reinhold
Grier, Joseph Williamson, Jr.
Hirsch, Alan Seth
Huffstetler, Noah Haywood, III
Jones, Henry W., Jr.
Jorgensen, Ralph Gubler
Joyce, Dennis Robert
Kapp, Michael Keith
Maxwell, James Beckett
McCotter, Charles Kennedy, Jr.
McIver, Robert Gilmour
Michael, Mark A.
Mills, William S.
Mineo, Robert Anthony
Newby, Paul Martin
Phillips, Randel Eugene
Poling, Richard Duane
Porter, Leon Eugene, Jr.
Randolph, Clyde Clifton, Jr.
Raper, William Cranford
Remsburg, F(rank) Raine
Reynolds, Mark Floyd, II
Riddle, Robert Edward
Rowe, Thomas Dudley, Jr.
Rusher, Derwood H., II
Sasser, Jonathan Drew
Sentelle, David Bryan
Smith, Norman Barrett
Starnes, Oscar Edwin, Jr.
Stockton, Ralph Madison, Jr.
Strayhorn, Ralph Nichols, Jr.
Van Hoy, Philip Marshall
Van Noppen, Donnell, III
Walker, James Edward
Wilson, Charles Michael

North Dakota

Bucklin, Leonard Herbert
Gilbertson, Joel Warren
Sortland, Paul Allan
Webb, Rodney Scott
Weir, Harlan Patrick
Yuill, William Duane
Zuger, William Peter

Ohio

Adams, John Marshall
Alkire, Richard Charles
Allotta, Joseph John
Ashmus, Keith Allen
Ashworth, John Lawrence
Bacon, Brett Kermit
Baker, Richard Southworth
Baranowkski, Edwin Michael
Baxter, Randolph
Beckwith, Karen Lu
Bennett, Marshall Alton Jr.
Bixenstine, Kim Fenton
Boggs, Ralph Stuart
Boles, Edgar Howard, II
Boone, Timothy J.
Bouscaren, Timothy Lincoln
Bradigan, Brian Jay
Brant, Charles Ensign
Briggs, Marjorie Crowder
Brinkman, Herbert Charles
Britain, James Edward
Buchmann, Alan Paul
Budish, Armond David
Bunda, Robert Alan
Burke, Kim Kenneth
Burns, Donald Andrew
Burth, John Hamrick
Carlin, Clair Myron
Cassidy, William Anthony
Cherpas, Christopher Theodore
Chester, John Jonas
Chockley, Frederick Wilson, Jr.
Cooper, Hal Dean
Creech, Herbert
Crist, Paul Grant
Cvetanovich, Danny Lee
DeLong, Deborah
Dornette, W(illiam) Stuart
Duff, Gerald Patrick
Edwards, John Wesley, II
Ely, Albert Love, Jr.
Eynon, Ernest Alfred, II
Fadel, William Isaac
Faigin, Arnold Jeffrey
Faruki, Charles Joseph
Ferguson, Gerald Paul
Fisher, John Edwin
Fisher, Stanley Morton
Garvey, Mary Anne
Gippin, Robert Malcolm
Gold, Gerald Seymour
Goldfarb, Bernard Sanford
Graney, Michael Proctor
Greer, David Carr
Hamilton, Richard Abbott
Hardy, Michael Lynn
Hardy, William Robinson
Harshman, Michael Stuart
Hart, Douglas Edward
Hermann, Philip J.
Hermann, Thomas George
Hoffheimer, Daniel Joseph
Hutson, Jeffrey Woodward
Jackson, Reginald Sherman, Jr.
Jordan, Joseph Patrick, Jr.
Kacir, Barbara Brattin
Kampinski, Charles
Kancler, Edward
Karch, George Frederick, Jr
Kilbane, Thomas Stanton
Knapp, A. Michael
Knepper, William Edward
Kramer, Edward George
Krembs, Peter Joseph
Kulewicz, John Joseph
Lancione, Nelson
Lane, Matthew Jay
Leksan, Thomas John
Levering, Robert Bruce
Lewis, John Bruce
Lieberman, Dennis Alan
Long, Thomas Leslie
Lowe, James Allison
Madsen, H(enry) Stephen
Manley, Robert Edward
Marco, Richard Joseph, Jr.
Marx, Dianne Frances
Maxwell, Robert Wallace, II
McClain, William Andrew
McCoy, John Joseph
Mc Elhaney, James Willson
McLaren, Richard Wellington, Jr.
McLaughlin, Patrick Michael
McMenamin, Michael Terrence
Mc Neal, Harley John
Merz, Michael
Metz, Jerome Joseph, Jr.
Minamyer, William Eric
Moore, Kenneth Cameron
Morris, Earl Franklin
Murtaugh, John Patrick
Naegele, Jori Bloom
Namanworth, Eli
Nelson, Steven Sibley
Nissl, Colleen Kaye
O'Brien, Ronald Joseph
O'Reilly, Timothy Patrick
Palmer, Thomas Earl
Petro, James Michael
Pheils, David R., Jr.
Phillips, Patrick Paul
Reminger, Richard Thomas
Rieser, John Paul
Rockel, John Edward
Roscoe, George Dennis
Rossi, Michael Dudley
Roush, Bradley Craig
Saul, Irving Isaac
Sawyer, Theodore D(aniel)
Serraino, Stephen R.
Shaw, Nancy Ann
Shea, Joseph William, III
Silverman, Peter Ray
Skulina, Thomas Raymond
Slough, J(osephine) Helen
Sobecki, Thomas Alva
Somrak, David Joseph
Speros, James Mandamadiotis
Spurgeon, Roberta Kaye
Stancati, Joseph Anthony
Steinhouse, Carl Lewis
Stewart, Lawrence Edward
Stillpass, John Edward
Strauch, John L.
Stuhldreher, George William
Swartzbaugh, Marc L.
Sweebe, Richard Dale
Sydlow, Holly Taft
Theado, Thomas Robert
Theis, Donald Eugene
Thompson, Harold Lee
Tipping, Harry Anthony
Todd, William Michael
Wallach, Mark Irwin
Weber, Robert Carl
Weisman, Fred
Werber, Stephen Jay
Whipps, Edward Franklin
White, Daniel Joseph
White, Kenneth James
Whitney, Richard B.
Woods, Kay
Worhatch, S. David
Wykoff, John Robert
Zaremba, Thomas S.
Zavatsky, Michael Joseph

Oklahoma

Abrahamson, A. Craig
Alexander, Linda Diane (Graham)
Angel, Arthur Ronald
Ashton, Mark Alfred
Barnes, Robert Norton
Bergner, William Joseph
Berry, James Wilson
Biolchini, Robert Fredrick
Brett, Thomas Rutherford
Brewster, Clark Otto
Catron, Gary Wayne
Collins, Leon Frederick
Crawford, B(urnett) Hayden
Davis, Charles Bishop
Dawson, Jack Sterling
Eagleton, Edward John
Eldridge, Richard Mark
Elias, William Keith
Featherly, Henry Frederick
Fellers, James Davison
Fenton, Elliott Clayton
Fischer, John Frederick
Gurich, Noma Diane
Hacker, Jerry William
Haskins, Walter Dewey
Haught, Robert Steven
Heggy, Rodney Joe
Hoster, Craig William
Hughes, Carl Douglas
Jaques, Frank Hesketh
Jones, Kent Leonard
Jones, Stephen
Kenney, John Arthur
Kline, David Adam
Lambird, Mona Salyer
Lester, Andrew William
Lloyd, James Robert (Jim)
Luthey, Graydon Dean, Jr.
Mash, Jerry L.
Matthies, Mary Constance T.
McCarty, Jack De
McElroy, Bert Colyar
Mirabile, Thomas Keith
Moss, Raymond Gene, II
Nelon, Robert Dale
Norman, John Wayne
Paul, William George
Rodgers, Ricardo Juan (Rick)
Rogers, William Britton
Stamper, Joe Allen
Thompson, Lee Bennett
Thurman, Andrew Edward
Tompkins, Raymond Edgar
Tuttle, Roger Lewis
Verity, George Luther
Wagner, John Leo
Wallace, Thomas Andrew
Walsh, Lawrence Edward
Warren, Loyde Hugh
White, Brinda Kaye
Williams, Betty Outhier
Williams, James William

Oregon

Bailey, Ronald E.
Banks, Roland Fitzgerald, Jr.
Barton, William Arnold
Beckman, Douglas Gary
Bonyhadi, Ernest
Brown, Stuart Melville
Buehler, John Wilson
Bullivant, Rupert Reid
Burnham, Carl von Hoffmann, Jr.
Chadsey, Phillip Duke
Cooney, Thomas Emmett
Day, Frank E.
Deatherage, William Vernon
Eakin, Margaretta Morgan
Eyerman, Linda Kathleen
Fechtel, Edward Ray
Foster, Randolph Courtney
Geil, John Clinton
Goldstein, Bennett Howard
Griffith, Stephen Loyal
Harris, Roger King
Hunt, Lawrence Boyd
Hurd, Paul Gemmill
Kennedy, Jack Leland
Kester, Randall Blair
LaBarre, Jerome Edward
Loomis, Donald Alvin
Lowry, Robert Dudley
Markowitz, David Benjamin
Mechanic, Gene Barry
O'Halloran, Robert Luis
O'Neill, Phoebe Joan
Pickett, Douglas Gene
Reinke, Cecil Eugene
Rice, James Gordon
Rieke, Forrest Neill
Rutzick, Mark Charles
Spier, Richard Gary
Spooner, Ralph Charles
Tilbury, Roger Graydon
Turnbow, William Randolph
Turner, Charles Hamilton
Walters, Stephen Scott
Westwood, James Nicholson

Pennsylvania

Albert, Neil Lawrence
Alderman, Mark Louis
Armstrong, Stephen Wales
Baker, Frank Adams, III
Baker, Sidney
Bala, Gary Ganesh
Basinski, Anthony Joseph
Beachler, Edwin Harry, III
Becker, John Francis
Beemer, John Barry
Best, Franklin L., Jr.
Binder, David Franklin
Black, Alexander
Blenko, Walter J(ohn), Jr.
Bogus, Carl Thomas
Borish, Arnold Peter
Bosick, Joseph John, Jr.
Brenner, Thomas Edward
Bricklin, Louis E.
Brogan, James Martin
Brown, Richard P., Jr.
Brown, William Hill, III
Buell, Eugene F(ranklin)
Burns, Michael William
Camen, Toby Paul
Carter, Daniel Paul
Chadwick, H. Beatty
Chanin, Bernard
Cheever, George Martin
Cimini, Joseph Fedele
Cohen, Robert (Avram)
Connors, Eugene Kenneth
Cooper, Thomas Louis
Corcoran, Andrew Patrick, Jr.
Cramer, Harold
Crane, Maida Rosenfeld
Creato, Anthony Edmund
Creedon, Michael Patrick
Crowley, Thomas Michael
Damsgaard, Kell Marsh
D'Angelo, Christopher Scott
D'Angelo, George A.
Dattilo, James Anthony
Davis, Donald Marc
DeMay, John Andrew
DeWald, John Edward
Durant, Marc
Eagan, Charlene Ann
Edelstein, Stanley Barton
Egler, Frederick Norton
Ehrenwerth, Charlene Reidbord
Einhorn, Edgar Robert
Elliott, Richard Howard
Faucher, John Dennis
Feese, Brett Owen
Feinour, John Stephen
Ferrario, Raymond William
Fiebach, H. Robert
Forney, Susan Jane
Fox, Reeder Rodman
Frank, Frederick Newman
Frank, Mark Stephen
Friedman, Joseph
Galanter, Robert Allen
Garcia, Rudolph
Geiger, William David
Gelso, Charles Patric
Georgiades, Peter Nicholas
German, Edward Cecil
Ginsburg, Bruce Martin
Godwin, Robert Anthony
Gondelman, Harold
Goodman, Marguerite Ruth
Gordon, Robert Jay
Gowen, Thomas Leo, Jr.
Granoff, Gail Patricia
Grant, M. Duncan
Grosh, Susan Ellen
Gurevitz, Mark Stuart
Gutnick, H. Yale
Hangley, William Thomas
Hauben, Ronald Bruce
Heim, Robert Charles
Helmreich, Martha Schaff
Hemphill, Meredith, Jr.
Hershey, Dale
Hochberg, Robert Boaz
Jacob, Mark Craig
Jellinek, Miles Andrew
Johanson, Thomas Jonathan
Jones, Craig Ward
Jones, Ronald Richard
Kairys, David Marc
Kalis, Peter John
Kanner, Allan
Kaplan, Ronald Ira
Kauffman, Bruce William
Keller, David Scott
Kelly, Robert Edward, Jr.
Kenrick, Charles William

Kenworthy, Thomas Bausman
Kessler, Alan Craig
King, Dominic Benson
Klayman, Barry Martin
Kohn, Harold Elias
Kole, Janet Stephanie
Kramer, Gilda Lea
Kusturiss, Dennis John
LaPorte, RocLyne Emile
Lawless, Joseph Francis, Jr.
Leddy, John Henry
Ledwith, John Francis
Levin, Arnold
Lewis, Alvin Bower, Jr.
Lewis, Christopher Alan
Lieberman, George Eric
Lillie, Charisse Ranielle
Lincicome, Brian Leslie
Litman, Roslyn Margolis
Long, Stephen Michael
Lowery, William Herbert
Luchak, Frank Alexander
Madva, Stephen Alan
Manning, James Hamington, Jr.
Mannino, Edward Francis
Mattern, Patricia Ann
Mattioni, John
McAneny, Eileen S.
McBride, James Francis
McCabe, James J.
McComb, John Paul
McConomy, James Herbert
McDonald, James Daniel, Jr.
McDowell, Michael David
McGinley, John Regis, Jr.
Mc Gough, Walter Thomas
McGurk, Eugene David, Jr.
McKeever, John Eugene
McKenna, J. Frank, III
McLane, John Thomas
McNew, Robert Bruce
Messer, Howard Francis
Meyer, Martin Jay
Meyers, Jeffrey
Middleton, Stephanie Adele
Milbourne, Walter Robertson
Milone, Francis Michael
Monteverde, Tom Peter
Morris, Neil Alan
Moser, Melvin Lavalle, Jr.
Mulligan, John Thomas
Mullinix, Edward Wingate
Mulvihill, David Brian
Munsing, Peter Nicholas
Musto, Joseph J.
Mustokoff, Michael Mark
Myers, Robert Earl
Nalle, Horace Disston, Jr.
Nowak, Darlene M.
Ober, Russell John, Jr.
O'Connor, Edward Gearing
Opalinski, Christopher Richard
Orloski, Richard J.
Parry, William DeWitt
Pedri, Charles Raymond
Perer, Alan Harvey
Perer, Diane Wilson
Perlstein, Paul Mark
Peterson, Neil Raymond
Petock, Michael F(rances)
Plowman, Jack Wesley
Pokotilow, Manny D.
Posy, David Howard
Poul, Franklin
Prewitt, David Edward
Rainone, Michael Carmine
Reed, Lowell Andrew, Jr.
Reich, Abraham Charles
Reif, Eric Peter
Reiter, Joseph Henry
Renz, William Tomlinson
Restivo, James John, Jr.
Richman, Stephen Ian
Robb, John Anthony, Jr.
Rome, Edwin Phillips
Rosenberg, H. N.
Rosenblum, Glenn Fredrick
Ross, Alan Harold
Rovner, David Patrick Ryan
Rubendall, Charles Wesley, II
Rutter, Thomas Bell
Saltzman, Joan
Samson, Peter
Scher, Howard Dennis
Schmidt, Edward Craig
Schmidt, Gordon Williams
Schmidt, Harold Robert
Schwabenland, Edward John
Schwartz, Jeffrey Byron
Schwartzman, James Charles
Senker, Richard C.
Shaffer, Charles Alan
Shepherd, Carol Nelson
Sherman, Carl Leon
Sherry, John Sebastian
Shertz, Perry Jack
Shestack, Jerome Joseph
Shields, Francis Edward
Shoop, Roger Thomas
Siedzikowski, Henry Francis
Silberblatt, Jay Ned
Silver, Stuart Robert
Simpson, Robert Edward, Jr.
Sisk, Paul Douglas
Skelly, Joseph Gordon
Smith, John Francis, III
Smith, Templeton, Jr.
Smolinsky, Sidney Joseph
Snite, Albert John, Jr.
Solano, Carl Anthony
Sonnenfeld, Marc Jay
Spiegel, Robert Joseph
Squires, Mark Elliott
Stiller, Jennifer Anne
Straub, J(ames) Kurt
Strazzella, James Anthony
Stroyd, Arthur Heister
Suojanen, Wayne William
Swartz, Lee Carter
Swensen, Jan Clovis
Tarlow, Marc Gary
Teklits, Joseph Anthony
Thomas, Richard Irwin
Thompson, Beverly Kay
Toll, Seymour I.
Unkovic, Dennis
Van Dusen, Lewis Harlow, Jr.
Voss, James Victor

Ward, William Francis
Washburn, Robert Buchanan
Webb, William Hess
Weil, Jeffrey George
Weinfeld, David M.
Weingarten, Marc Philip
Weinstein, David Haym
Weiss, Philip David
Welsh, Thomas Harry
Weston, John Kerry
Williams, Gerald Joseph
Wilson, Steven (White)
Wingerter, John Raymond
Wise, Sandra Elizabeth
Wolf, Edward Leonard
Yohe, Susan Ann
Youngman, John Crawford
Zeehandelaar, David Nico
Zeiter, William Emmet
Zemaitis, Thomas Edward
Ziegler, Craig E.
Ziff, Lloyd Richard

Rhode Island

Arcaro, Harold Conrad, Jr.
Blish, John Harwood
Cappalli, Richard Anthony
Dickinson, Thomas More
DiSandro, Edmond A.
Fogarty, Edward Michael
Hastings, Edwin Hamilton
Mandell, Mark Steven
McElroy, Michael Robert
Medeiros, Matthew Francis
Parks, Albert Lauriston
Penza, Joseph Fulvio, Jr.
Purcell, James Edward
Southgate, (Christina) Adrienne Graves
Turner, Terrance Neil

South Carolina

Babcock, Keith Moss
Berly, Joel Anderson, III
Breibart, Richard Jerome
Buchanan, Robert Lee, Jr.
Choate, John Lee
Coates, William Alexander
Cooke, Morris Dawes, Jr.
Cothran, James Clardy, Jr.
Darling, Stephen Edward
Dominick, Paul Allen
DuBose, Clarke Wardlaw
Erwin, Sue Carlanne
Esposito, John Vincent
Figg, Robert McCormick, Jr.
Finkel, Gerald Michael
Furr, O(lin) Fayrell, Jr.
Gergel, Richard Mark
Gibbes, William Holman
Gibson, Carroll Allen, Jr.
Grimball, William Heyward
Harvey, William Brantley, III
Holleman, Frank Sharp, III
Irvin, Wilmot Brown
Kahn, Ellis Irvin
Knowlton, Robert Yates
Kosko, George Carter
Laws, James Terry
Licata, Steven Barry
Mc Cullough, Ralph Clayton, II
McKay, John Judson, Jr.
Pritchard, Michael Gregg
Robinson, David Wallace
Sheftman, Howard Stephen
Shoemaker, James Marshall, Jr.
Smiley, Robert Rennslaer, III
Smith, Cody Walker, Jr.
Swagart, Harry Augustus, III
Tapp, Richard N.
Trinkley, Jane Wilroy
Wall, Susan Taylor
White, Daniel Bowman
Williams, Charles Hiram
Winn, Marshall
Wittenberg, Philip
Zelenka, Donald John

South Dakota

Eichstadt, Craig Martin
Gerdes, David Alan
Hogen, Philip Nere
Hoy, Carleton Robert
Hughes, John Robert
Pieplow, Michael Flinn
Prendergast, Terry Neill
Sveen, Jeffrey T.

Tennessee

Allen, Newton Perkins
Armstrong, Walter Preston, Jr.
Arnett, Foster Deaver
Bahner, Thomas Maxfield
Barr, James Victor, III
Bernstein, Bernard Emanuel
Boston, Robert Earl
Bridgesmith, Larry W.
Brothers, Thomas White
Bush, Wendell Earl
Bush, William
Campbell, Paul, III
Carr, Oscar Clark, III
Chambliss, Prince Caesar, Jr.
Charney, Jonathan Isa
Cooper, Gary Allan
Cosner, Charles Kinian, Jr.
Dixon, James Mikel
Dupree, Charles Patrick
Durand, Philip Poyntell
Fine, Thomas Fleming
Garts, James Rufus, Jr.
Gearhiser, Charles Josef
Gill, John Welch, Jr.
Glasgow, James Monroe
Gordon, J. Houston
Gorrell, Frank Cheatham
Hardin, Hal D.
Harris, Tyree Bryson
Headrick, Stirman Russell
Holmes, Hal
Ingraham, Frank Calvin
Jones, John Thomas, Jr.
Jones, Kenneth Ray, Jr.
Kerr, Thomas Draper, Jr.
King, Robert Lewis
Knowles, Emmitt Clifton
Lander, Gary David

Lawless, Thomas William
Lay, Patti Jane
Layman, Earl Robert
Leitner, Gregory Marc
Leitner, Paul R.
Lockaby, Robert Lee, Jr.
Maier, Harold Geistweit
McCormack, Donnell James
McLaren, Michael Glenn
McQuiston, John Ward, II
McWhirter, J(ames) Cecil
Meyer, Michael Alan
Moore, James M(ack), Jr.
Moriarty, Herbert Bernard, Jr.
Newman, Charles Forrest
Noel, Randall Deane
Ogden, Harry Peoples
Patterson, Robert Shepherd
Pickering, William Henry
Price, Walter Lee
Raines, Jim Neal
Riley, Steven Allen
Robinson, Samuel Francis, Jr.
Rogers, Helen Sfikas
Rush, Stephen Kenneth
Sanger, Herbert Shelton, Jr.
Schwarz, Earle Jay
Shockley, Gary Clark
Siciliano, Gerard Michael
Sims, Wilson
Smith, Drayton Beecher, II
Smith, William Holt
Sobieski, Wanda Graham
Speros, Michael Carl
Thomason, John Joseph
Todd, Ben
Veal, Rex R.
Watson, James William
Watson, Robert Harmon, Jr.
Williams, Thomas Ashurst
Wilson, Fred Palmer
Woods, Larry David
Wright, James Charles
Young, Jason Ober, Jr.
Youngblood, Elaine Michele

Texas

Ackerman, John Edward
Adams, Kent Morrison
Addison, Linda Leuchter
Albright, William James
Aldrich, Lovell W(eld)
Alexander, Neil Kenton, Jr.
Allison, Stephen Philip
Amdur, Arthur R.
Arnett, Richard Lynn
Atlas, Morris
Atlas, Scott Jerome
Auld, Bruce
Austin, Page Insley
Baggett, W. Mike
Baker, Thomas Eugene
Ball, Craig Douglas
Ballanfant, Richard Burton
Bayko, Emil Thomas
Beane, Jerry Lynn
Beirne, Martin Douglas
Benckenstein, John Henry
Berg, David Howard
Bernard, Robert Louis
Berndt, Karen Ann
Bingham, Loyd Edward, Jr.
Black, Robert Allen
Blair, Graham Kerin
Bohannon, Paul
Bonesio, Woodrow Michael
Boswell, John Howard
Bowmer, Jim Dewitt
Boyland, Herbert Layton
Branson, Frank Leslie, III
Brinson, Gay Creswell, Jr.
Brister, Scott Andrew
Brown, Karen Kennedy
Brown, Stephen Smiley
Buether, Eric W.
Burch, Voris Reagan
Burkett, Joe Wylie
Bux, William John
Carnes, Lamar
Carrigan, Stephen Paul
Cashion, Shelley Jean
Casterline, Cecil W.
Chappell, David Franklin
Cheavens, Joseph D.
Cherry, David Earl
Chrisman, Perry Oswin
Clark, Ronald Hurley
Conley, Ned Leroy
Constant, Patricia Reed
Craddock, Thomas Wofford
Craig, Robert Mark, III
Cross, Janis Alexander
Crotty, Robert Bell
Cunningham, Tom Alan
Davis, Clarice M.
Davis, Harrel Leon, III
Degenhardt, Harold F.
DeGuerin, Dick
DeHay, John Carlisle, Jr.
DeShazo, Gary Forrest
Donaldson, David Howard, Jr.
Eddins, Gerald Wayne
Eisenbraun, Eric Charles
Elliott, Frank Wallace
Ellis, James Alvis, Jr.
Engel, David Wayne
Engerrand, Kenneth Gabriel
Erben, Randall Harvey
Essmyer, Michael Martin
Estes, Harper
Evans, Roger
Ezzell, James Michael
Falk, Robert Hardy
Fanning, Barry Hedges
Farr, Sidney Lavelle
Fellers, Rhonda Gay
Fenwick, Lynda Beck
Figari, Ernest Emil, Jr.
Finlayson, Dawn Bruner
Fladung, Richard Denis
Flanary, Donald Herbert, Jr.
Flegle, Jim L.
Fleming, George Matthews
Flynn, Rory Christopher
Folse, Parker C(amile), III
Fountain, Kenneth Paul
Freytag, Sharon Nelson
Frisby, Thomas Newton

Frost, Charles Estes, Jr.
Furgeson, William Royal
Garcia, Humberto Sigifredo
Garrison, Pitser Hardeman
Gayle, Gibson, Jr.
Gibson, Michael Morgan
Gilberg, Howard Larry
Glickman, Julius
Gold, Paul Nicholas
Golden, H. Bruce
Gonsoulin, Dewey Jude
Goodfriend, Robert Edward
Graham, Michael Paul
Greer, Raymond White
Guleke, James O., II
Gulley, Jack Haygood
Haggard, Carl Douglas
Halbach, Joseph James, Jr.
Hall, John Hopkins
Hall, William Wendell
Hanen, Andrew Scott
Harmon, Melinda Furche
Harrel, Alan David
Harris, Charles Dick
Harrison, Orrin Lea, III
Harrison, Reese Lenwood, Jr.
Harrison, Richard Wayne
Hart, John Clifton
Hartnett, Thomas Robert, III
Harvey, Mark Wayne
Harvin, David Tarleton
Harvin, William Charles
Hayes, Burgain Garfield
Henderson, John Robert
Hilder, Philip Harlan
Hinshaw, Chester John
Hoffman, Leonard Elbert, Jr.
Holstead, John Burnham
Howie, John Robert
Hudspeth, Chalmers Mac
Huffman, Gregory Scott Combest
Hunsucker, Philip Carl
Hunt, Richard Martin
Hunter, Todd Ames
Hytken, Franklin Harris
Immler, Michael Earl
Ingram, Temple Byrn, Jr.
Irvin, Charles Leslie
Jacobellis, Mike
Jacobo, Paulina Moreno
Jayson, Melinda Gayle
Jenkins, Richard Coleman
Jett, Joseph Craig
Johnson, D. Thomas
Johnson, Philip Wayne
Jones, David Stanley
Jones, Edith Hollan
Jordan, Charles Milton
Jordan, W. Carl
Jung, Peter Michael
Kacal, George Jerome, Jr.
Kaplan, Lee Landa
Kay, Joel Phillip
Keeshin, Scott Avery
Keltner, David E.
Kendall, David Matthew
Kennedy, John Edward
Kent, Don Wayne
King, Ronald Baker
Kinnan, David E.
Kirkman, William Louis
Kizzia, Don Bradley
Knisely, Paul Emil
Krieger, Paul Edward
Lacey, David Morgan
Lake, Simeon Timothy, III
Langley, Earnest Lee
Larimore, Tom L.
Larkin, Lee Marshall
Latino, Anthony Leon
Lawton, Kenneth Wayne
Laycock, Harold Douglas
Leach, Sydney Minturn
Leatherbury, Thomas Shawn
Legendre, John Peter
Legg, Reagan Houston
Lents, Ann
Leon, Jack Paul
Lezar, Tex
Lilienstern, O. Clayton
Lippe, Emil, Jr.
Loewinsohn, Alan Stewart
Lowenberg, Michael
Lynch, Jeffrey Scott
Mack, Theodore
MacNaughton, William Alexander
Maddox, Charles J., Jr.
Mainz, Edward Charles, Jr.
Marbut, Syrian Erasmus
Marshall, Richard Treeger
Matthews, Dan Gus
Matthews, Wilbur Lee
McAtee, David Ray
McCormick, J(oseph) Burke
Mc Elhaney, John Hess
McFall, Donald Beury
McGehee, Jack Edward, Jr.
McGowan, Gary V.
McGowan, Patrick Francis
McNamara, Lawrence John
Mercy, John R.
Merz, Daniel Lee
Micks, D. Fred
Mills, William Michael
Mora, David Baudilio
Morgan, Cecilia Hufstedler
Morgenstern, Jonathan David
Moroney, Linda Lelia Susan
Mow, Robert Henry, Jr.
Moye, Eric Vaughn
Moynihan, John Bignell
Myers, J(oseph) Michael
Nesbitt, Frank Wilbur
Newman, Lawrence Graham
Noel, David Bobbitt, Jr.
Nunnally, Knox Dillon
Ochs, Robert Francis
Oldenettel, Rick Lee
Oldham, Darius Dudley
Ory, Charles Nathan
Palmer, Philip Isham, Jr.
Pannill, William Presley
Parmley, Robert James
Peck, Leonard Warren, Jr.
Perkins, James Allen
Perlmutter, Mark L.
Pettiette, Alison Yvonne
Pew, John Glenn, Jr.

Pfunder, Curtis Clark
Phillips, Thomas Marion
Pickle, George Edward
Pinnell, Gary Ray
Plunkett, Allen Lewin
Poehner, George Richard
Prather, Robert Charles
Prestridge, Pamela Adair
Price, John Aley
Pridavka, Gary Michael
Pulliam, Karen Ann
Rapp, Robert David
Ray, Cread L., Jr.
Ray, Hugh Massey, Jr.
Reasoner, Harry Max
Redden, Joe Winston, Jr.
Rice, Ben Herbert, III
Richman, Marc Hersh
Riney, Thomas Charles
Ringle, Brett Adelbert
Robichaux, James Hall
Rubagumya, George William
Ruhl, John Benjamin
Rusk, L. Giles
Sadler, Paul Lindsey
Sales, James Bohus
Schenkkan, Pieter (Pete) Meade
Schuurman, Willem Gerhard
Schuwerk, Robert Paul
Schwartz, Charles Walter
Schwartz, Leonard Jay
Scuro, Joseph E., Jr.
Secrest, Ronald Dean
Selinger, Jerry Robin
Sessions, William Lewis
Shafer, W. O.
Sheetz, William Dean
Shurn, Peter Joseph, III
Sides, Jack Davis Jr.
Silva, Eugene Joseph
Simmental, David Anthony
Smith, George Duffield, Jr.
Smith, Phillip Nolan, Jr.
Smith, Russell Bryan
Sparkman, Roy T.
Steele, Joseph Robert
Stephens, R(obert) Gary
Stephens, Walter David
Stewart, Joseph Ward
Stinnett, Mark Allan
Stradley, William Jackson
Susman, Morton Lee
Suttle, Stephen Hungate
Sutton, John F., Jr.
Swan, Michael Robert
Sweeney, Gregory Louis
Swindle, Mack Ed
Sydow, Michael David
Tabak, Morris
Taft, Lee McCreary
Tartt, Blake
Thompson, T. Jay
Timaeus, Dana Lee
Toedt, D(ell) C(harles), III
Turley, Windle
Tygrett, Howard Volney, Jr.
Valdes, Richard Albert
Van Fleet, George Allan
Van Gilder, Derek Robert
Van Slyke, Paul Christopher
Vickrey, Jack
Voyles, Robb Lawrence
Wallis, Olney Gray
Walls, Robert Ernest
Warrick, Richard Lloyd
Watson, Robert Francis
Weisfeld, Sheldon
Westmoreland, Kent Ewing
White, Steven Gregory
Whitehurst, William O.
Wicka, Richard Vincent
Wiles, William Dixon, Jr.
Wilkins, Jerry Lynn
Wilson, David Keith
Winn, David Burton
Wise, Robert Kenneth
Woodard, Linda Strite
Woody, Clyde Woodrow
Wortham, Robert John
Worthington, William Albert, III
Wray, Thomas Jefferson
Wright, Charles Alan

Utah

Anderson, Craig W.
Christensen, Patricia Anne Watkins
Dallimore, Suzanne Meredith
Dolowitz, David Sander
Erickson, David Belnap
Gardiner, Lester Raymond, Jr.
Hansen, Royal Ivory
Jensen, Allen Reed
Jensen, Dallin W.
Kaplan, Neil Alan
Lambert, Dale John
Lochhead, Robert Bruce
Mabey, Ralph Rampton
Nelson, Merrill Francom
Shea, Patrick A.
Shields, Jeffrey Weston
Slaughter, David Wayne
Verhaaren, Harold Carl

Vermont

Cassidy, Richard Thomas
Chase, Jonathon B.
Cory, Barbara Ellen
French, Thomas McGuinness
Jarrett, Glenn Alan
Kiel, Edward Rowland
Lang, Richard Arnold, Jr.
Miller, William Bayard, Jr.
Rachlin, Robert David
Saltonstall, Stephen Lee
Terwilliger, George James, III
Williams, Norman Charles

Virginia

Allen, Jeffrey Rodgers
Alper, Joanne Fogel
Anderson, John Foster
Anderson, John Frederick
Armstrong, Henry Jere
Bacon, James Thomas
Baird, Charles Bruce
Baird, Edward Rouzie, Jr.

Beller, Charles Roscoe, III
Beutel, Richard Armstrong
Billingsley, Robert Thaine
Birch, Terrell Colhoun
Booker, James Foster
Booker, Lewis Thomas
Brittigan, Robert Lee
Brooks, Robert Franklin
Brown, Frank Eugene, Jr.
Burnette, Ralph Edwin, Jr.
Byrom, Robert Milton
Cabaniss, Thomas Edward
Carrell, Daniel Allan
Chappell, Milton Leroy
Chappell, Robert Harvey, Jr.
Clinard, Robert Noel
Collins, Philip Reilly
Cranwell, C. Richard
Crigler, B. Waugh
Davis, Douglas Witfield
Davis, Gilbert Kenneth
Donlan, Martin Andrew, Jr.
Economou, Stewart Charles
Emroch, Emanuel
Farnham, James Edward
Finnegan, Edward James
Flannery, John Philip, II
Folk, Thomas Robert
Freyvogel, William Thomas
Georges, Peter John
Gilbert, Oscar Lawrence
Gladstone, Michael Harper
Hajek, Francis Paul
Halbrook, Stephen Porter
Hall, Franklin Perkins
Harrison, John Edwards
Henderson, James Rutledge, IV
Hoffman, Walter Edward
Hulvey, Craig Wallace
Jenkins, Douglas Tucker
Kanovsky, Helen Renee
Kearfott, Joseph Conrad
Kieff, Nelson Richard
Kiser, Jackson L.
Korman, James William
Kotlarchuk, Ihor O. E.
Koutoulakos, Louis
Landin, David Craig
Laughlin, James Harold, Jr.
LeBlanc, Robert Edmond, III
Levit, Jay J(oseph)
Litten, Donald Douglas
Mannix, Charles Raymond
McClard, Jack Edward
McCloskey, Michael Patrick
McElligott, James Patrick, Jr.
McElroy, Howard Chowning
McGavin, John David
Meekins, Samuel Warrenton, Jr.
Metcalfe, James Ashford
Morton, Woolridge Brown, Jr.
Najjoum, Linda Lemmon
Napier, Douglas William
Nicholas, Edward Ernest, III
Patterson, Robert Hobson, Jr.
Pietrovito, Guy Roy
Plaetzer, Ross Frederick
Poole, Albert Harrison
Powell, Lewis Franklin, III
Prince, William Taliaferro
Proffitt, John Stephen, III
Pugh, William Wallace
Pysell, Paul Edward
Quillen, Ford Carter
Roberts, Russell Hill
Robol, Richard Thomas
Rolfe, Robert Martin
Rollinson, Mark
Rudlin, David Alan
Schroeder, James White
Scott, Betsy Sue
Shevlin, Brian Charles
Shields, William Gilbert
Shortridge, Michael L.
Skolrood, Robert Kenneth
Slonaker, Jerry Paul
Tatum, Franklin M., III
Tegenkamp, Gary Elton
Toothman, John William
Trotter, Haynie Seay
Walsh, James Hamilton
Walton, Morgan Lauck
Waters, Charles Richard, II
Wheeler, R(ichard) Kenneth
Whitehead, John W.
Williams, Glen Morgan
Williamson, Thomas W., Jr.
Wilson, Rodger Lee
Winston, Robert Tunstall, Jr.
Wood, John Martin
Woodley, John Paul, Jr.
Woodrum, Clifton A., III
Zerkin, Gerald Thomas
Zucker, David Clark

Washington

Allison, John Robert
Alsdorf, Robert Hermann
Andersen, Charles Matthew
Anderson, David Bowen
Berman, Steve William
Berry, Douglas Clayton
Bishin, William Robert
Brenner, David (Merle)
Budlong, John
Burman, David John
Campbell, Fremont Lee
Cline, Thomas Farrell
Connelly, John Robert, Jr.
Corning, Nicholas F.
Coughenour, John Clare
Cressman, Paul Russell, Jr.
Danelo, Peter Anthony
Day, Stephen Leo
Dillon, Janet Jordan
Dunham, Douglas Spence
Ecton, Douglas Brian
Eubanks, Ronald W.
Gandara, Daniel
Glein, Richard Jeriel
Greenan, Thomas J.
Harris, Thomas V.
Hendricks, Katherine
Hereford, Earle J., Jr.
Hindman, Dennis Michael
Hollingsworth, Jeffrey Alan
Keller, Bradley Scott
Lamp, John Ernest

Leed, Roger Melvin
Leipham, Jay Edward
Lied, Erik Robert
McGarry, Arthur Daniel
McKay, Michael Dennis
Mines, Michael
Mitchell, Robert Bertelson
Nielsen, Ruth
O'Connor, Bruce Edward
Otorowski, Shawn Elizabeth
Rummage, Stephen Michael
Russell, Steven Turner
Sandler, Michael David
Sargeant, Robert Walton
Schwartz, Irwin H.
Scott, Steven George
Smith, James Alexander, Jr.
Squires, William Randolph, III
Tollefson, G. Val
Tomlinson, John Randolph
Utevsky, David
Waitt, Robert Kenneth
Walker, G(lenn) Perrin
Wells, Christopher Brian
Whitson, Lish
Woolston, V.L.
Yalowitz, Kenneth Gregg
Zilly, Thomas Samuel

West Virginia

Artimez, John Edward, Jr.
Bell, Harry Fullerton, Jr.
Berthold, Robert Vernon, Jr.
Bryant, Sanford Benjamin
Cowan, John Joseph
Flaherty, Thomas Vincent
Fusco, Andrew G.
Haviland, James Morrison
Hill, Barry Morton
Hurt, Charles E.
Johnson, David Whitley
Kent, James Albert, Jr.
Lawson, Robert William, Jr.
Lewin, Jeff Lee
MacCallum, James Judson
Peterson, James Charles
Richardson, Randolf Emrys
Schaub, Clarence Robert
Silver, Gray, III
Wilmoth, William David

Wisconsin

Anderson, Michael Steven
Arnold, Bruce George
Atterbury, Lee Richard
Bergen, Thomas Joseph
Burroughs, John Townsend
Busch, John Arthur
Christiansen, Jon Peter
Cole, James Ray
Cook, Daniel John
Croak, Francis R.
Croak, Francis R.
Cross, David R.
De Bruin, David Lee
Decker, John Robert
Fischer, Michael Davin
Gasiorkiewicz, Eugene Anthony
Habush, Robert Lee
Harrington, Arthur John
Hesslink, Robert Melvin, Jr.
Hildebrand, Daniel Walter
Kahn, Charles Frederick, Jr.
Lathrop, Trayton LeMoine
Levit, William Harold, Jr.
Liccione, Stephen John
Melin, Robert Arthur
Mitby, John Chester
Murray, James Thomas, Jr.
Nohr, William Arthur
Owens, Joseph Francis
Peterson, Donald Roy
Politano, Frank Louis
Rasche, William Grether
Robinson, Richard Russell
St. John, Thomas William
Schmitt, Joseph Francis
Schrank, Raymond Edward, II
Sostarich, Mark Edward
Stadtmueller, Joseph Peter
Steuer, Robert Karl
Stevens, Charles Paul
Terschan, Frank Robert
Towers, Lawrence Alan
Walther, David Louis
Whitney, Robert Michael
Will, Trevor Jonathan

Wyoming

Bommer, Timothy J.
Bostwick, Richard Raymond
Botham, Lisa Anne
Burke, E. James
Combs, William Henry, III
Dyekman, Gregory Chris
Hunkins, Raymond Breedlove
Kidd, David Thomas
Kline, Stephen Hibbard
Pickering, Robert Gein
Rideout, Richard Scott
Santini, George
Schuster, Robert Parks
Selig, Joel Louis
Shockey, Gary Lee
Speight, John B.
Stanfield, John Edmiston
Thomson, Rebecca Wunder

TERRITORIES OF THE UNITED STATES

Guam

LaFleur, Gary James
O'Connor, Karl William

Puerto Rico

Ezratty, Harry Aaron
Ruiz-Suria, Fernando
Vallone, Ralph, Jr.

CANADA

Nova Scotia

Dickey, John Horace

Saskatchewan

Elliott, William McBurney

PEOPLES REPUBLIC OF CHINA

Capener, Cole R.

ADDRESS UNPUBLISHED

Adler, Kenneth
Arrowood, Lisa Gayle
Auther, Jeri Lynn Kishiyama
Beattie, Donald Gilbert
Beldock, Myron
Bentley, Anthony Miles
Berger, Lawrence Douglas
Blevins, Jeffrey Alexander
Boyle, Elizabeth Mary Hunt
Braun, Jerome Irwin
Brodsky, David M.
Brooks, Patrick William
Canova, Leo Phillip, Jr.
Carrington, Morris Clifford
Cheek, Louis Eugene
Culver, Robert Winthrop
Davidson, Keith L.
Davis, Jonathan David
De Angelis, Arnold John
Dement, Kenneth Lee
Djokic, Walter Henry
DuPre, John Leacy
Englebrecht, Bruce
Frank, James Stuart
Gallagher, Michael Gerald
Garza, Rudy A.
Goldman, Barbara Lynn
Graham, Keith Everett
Greenberg, Susan Ann
Harnack, Don Steger
Harrison, Roddy L.
Heins, Samuel David
Heise, John Irvin, Jr.
Himeles, Martin Stanley, Jr.
Hirsch, Jeffrey Allan
Holbrook, Donald Benson
Hughes, Linda Renate
Jensen, John Robert
Johnson, Gary William
Kaczynski, Stephen John
Kadish, Lloyd Alan
Kafka, Anne G.
Kahn, Ronald Howard
Kamin, Daniel Tucker
Kamp, Steven Mark
Kemp, Alson Remington, Jr.
Klein, Richard L.
Lerman, Cathy Jackson
Leydig, Carl Frederick
Locke, John Howard
Manget, Frederic Fairfield
Margolis, Emanuel
Markewich, Robert
McCoy, Henry Drewry, II
McInerney, Gary John
McIntyre, Anita Grace
McPherson, James Aubrey
Metzger, Jeffrey Paul
Michaels, David Seth
Michaels, George
Midkiff, Charles Franklin
Moore, Elizabeth Reitz
Neese, Sandra Anne
Nelson, Jay Scott
Newman, Carol L.
O'Donnell, Pierce Henry
O'Mara, William Michael
Quinn, Stacy Smith
Reycraft, George Dewey
Samples, Stephen Shay
Schwartz, S. Bernard
Scott, Thomas Stratton, Jr.
Shaffert, Kurt
Showers, H. Robert, Jr.
Sommers, Louise
Spiller, William, Jr.
Sterling, A(merica) Mary Fackler
Weisman, Paul Howard
Welch, Ernest Wendell
Wilson, Hugh Steven
Zeltonoga, William Leo
Ziker, Barry Gene

CIVIL LITIGATION, STATE

UNITED STATES

Alabama

Bains, Lee Edmundson
Barnard, Hollinger Farmer
Blan, Ollie Lionel, Jr.
Boardman, Mark Seymour
Brown, Earl Terry
Brown, Joseph Morris, Jr.
Browning, Richard Edward
Burns, Peter Francis
Byram, James Asberry, Jr.
Byrne, Bradley Roberts
Colquitt, Joseph Arlington
Conwell, Joseph Thomas
Cook, Walter McQueen
Coplin, William Thomas, Jr.
Crouch, James Michael
Davis, Ronald Lee
Deen, Thomas Jefferson, III
De Ment, Ira
Dinning, Woodford Wyndham, Jr.
Donahue, Timothy Patrick
Downes, Robert Bruce
Embry, Thomas Eric
Fuller, S. Wayne
Fuller, William Sidney
Gillis, Lucian, Jr.
Gray, William Patton, Jr.
Hanson, Frank Oscar, Jr.
Hines, Rodney Alan
Hoff, Timothy
Hollis, Louie Andrew
Howell, Allen Windsor
Hughes, Patrick Paul
Huskey, Dow Thobern
Jackson, Micheal Stewart
Jones, Patrick Allen
Karrh, John Maxwell
King, John Thomas
Kominos, Bill

Kracke, Robert Russell
Lawson, Thomas Seay, Jr.
Lewis, Cyrus Roys
Manley, Richard Shannon
McCorkle, Lucy Virginia
McPhillipps, Julian Lenwood, Jr.
McWhorter, Robert Dale, Jr.
Merrill, Walter James
Miller, Barbara Currie
Mills, William Hayes
Moorer, Mac Mitchell
Moss, Robert William
Newton, Alexander Worthy
Noojin, Ray Oscar, Jr.
Norman, Robert Daniel
Norwood, Dorothy F.
Owens, James Bentley, III
Paschal, Beverly Jo
Patton, Martha Jane
Philips, James Albert
Pittman, Joseph Stafford, Jr.
Potts, Robert Leslie
Powell, Scott Ashley
Quillen, Michael Clay
Rebarchak, James
Redden, Lawrence Drew
Richardson, Schuyler Harris, III
Rogers, Ernest Mabry
Ryan, L(awrence) Thomas, Jr.
Sanderson, William Woodrow, Jr.
Sheehan, Charles Winston, Jr.
Shields, Robert Lloyd, III
Shoulders, Bobby Harris
Smith, Carol Ann
Smith, Charles Lynwood, Jr.
Smith, Robert McDavid
Smith, Rufus Randolph, Jr.
Smith, William Wayne
Stabler, Lewis Vastine, Jr.
Stedham, Brenda Smith
Stephens, (Holman) Harold
Stephens, William Taft
Stewart, Julia Smeds
Sullivan, Carroll Hart
Tatum, Fred Menefee, Jr.
Van Tassel, George Martin, Jr.
Varley, Robert John
Wagner, Charles Stephen
Wells, Huey Thomas, Jr.
Whiteside, David Powers, Jr.
Wilson, Duane Albert
Wilson, Jack
Wood, James Jerry
Woodrow, Randall Mark

Alaska

Anderson, Lloyd Vincent, Jr.
Bankston, William Marcus
Beistline, Ralph Robert
Beiswenger, Allan David
Branson, Albert Harold
Clough, John F., III
Cuadra, Dorothy Elizabeth
De Lisio, Stephen Scott
Dickson, Robert Jay
Feldman, Jeffrey Marc
Hayes, George Nicholas
Hedland, John Sigurd
Maloney, Philip Dennis
McCracken, Sarah Elizabeth
Molloy, Robert Joseph
Moody, Ralph E.
Nave, Thomas George
Offret, Ronald (Alvin)
Pfiffner, Frank Albert
Richmond, Robert Lawrence
Silvey, Charles Delbert, II
Taylor, Kneeland Lamoureux
Therrien, Valerie Monica
Thomas, Michael Tracy
Wagstaff, Robert Hall
Walther, Dale Jay
Weinig, Richard Arthur
Willard, Donna Carol Morris
Yospin, Richard Lawrence

Arizona

Abraham, Andrew
Anderson, Lawrence Ohaco
Bachstein, Harry Samuel
Bakker, Thomas Gordon
Barker, J(ohn) Emery
Barron, Caroline Joan
Barry, Edward Louis
Begam, Robert George
Bowman, C(harles) Alan
Brown, Steven Jay
Cameron, James Duke
Campbell, Carol Nowell
Chickering, John Bradley
Condo, James Robert
Crenshaw, Richard N.
Curtis, David William, Jr.
D'Antonio, Gregory Douglas
Daughton, Donald
Dulberg, Michael Seth
Ehinger, James Oakleaf
Feder, Bruce Stanley
Finson, Lowell Wayne
Fisher, Peter Francis
Forrester, Stephen Cary
Frazelle, Michael Jerome
Gaines, Edwin Metcalf, Jr.
Galbut, Martin Richard
Ganson, Norris Lloyd
Glicksman, Elliott Aaron
Gomez, David Frederick
Goodman, Mark N.
Grant, Merwin Darwin
Gustafson, David Earl
Harrison, Mark I.
Hendricks, Edwin Francis
Hossler, David Joseph
Howard, Robert Campbell, Jr.
Jensen, Robert Arthur
Jenson, Dennis Dion
Kelly, Joseph Sylvester, Jr.
Kennedy, Michael Kevin
Kimble, William Earl
Korn, Gary Clifford
Lagerman, Susan Borden
Lee, Carl Douglas
Lemberg, Frederic Gary
Lesher, Stephen Harrison
Myers, Robert David
Ong, Henry Hop
Ostapuk, David R.

Paige, David Alwin
Parker, Jeffrey Robert
Parker, Myrna Jean
Peck, Deana S.
Peters, Donald Mullen
Placenti, Frank Michael
Polan, David Jay
Pratte, Deborah Miriam
Price, Guy Bradley
Ricker, William Howard
Rusing, Michael John
Ryan, D. Jay
Ryan, Timothy Leo
Sandweg, William Henry, III
Sims, Terrance Lee
Smith, David Burnell
Thorpe, William Lee
Ulrich, Paul Graham
Wall, Donald Arthur
Waterman, David Moore
Wezelman, Janice Anne
Williams, Steven Henry
Winthrop, Lawrence Fredrick
Wirken, Charles William
Wolfe, David K.

Arkansas

Allen, H. William
Baker, Darryl Ellis
Bristow, Bill Wayne
Butt, Thomas Franklin
Cross, Junius Bracy, Jr.
Crow, Carl Arnold, Jr.
Dillahunty, Wilbur Harris
Drummond, Winslow
Dunn, James Melvin
Ellis, George Dawlin
Fleming, Victor Anson
Griffin, Richard Earl
Hall, Betsy
Hamilton, Herman Lynn, Jr.
Hargis, David Michael
Harkey, John Norman
Howard, Steven Gray
Jennings, Alston
Julian, Jim Lee
Karr, Charles
Mayes, S. Hubert, Jr.
Mullen, William David
Nestrud, Charles Robert
Pinson, Jerry D.
Ross, Robert Dwain
Simpson, James Marlon, Jr.
Skinner, Jack Merle
Smith, Michael Glen
Taylor, Hendrix Arthur, Jr.
White, Stephen Alan

California

Adler, Erwin Ellery
Aguirre, Michael Jules
Ajalat, Sol Peter
Albert, Ward Wian
Allan, Walter Robert
Allen, Jeffrey Michael
Amidon, Robert Bruce
Armstrong, Orville A.
Aronson, Craig Douglas
Askew, James Albert
Asmundson, Vigfus Anthony
Atkinson, Sheridan Earle
Axelrad, David M.
Ayoob, Richard Joseph
Bakaly, Charles George, Jr.
Balestracci, Paul Noel
Barbabelata, Robert D.
Barber, Stephan Allen
Barnhorst, Howard Joseph, II
Baron, Frederick David
Barrett, Dennis Christopher
Barrett, Jane H.
Barrett, Robert Matthew
Barza, Harold A.
Baskin, David Green
Bassett, Craig Jay
Belcher, John Arthur
Bell, Frank Ouray, Jr.
Bell, Wayne Steven
Belleville, Philip Frederick
Bender, Charles William
Bennett, James Patrick
Bennett, Lawrence Arthur
Bentley, John Martin
Berger, Harvey Charles
Bergman, Gregory Mark
Bernhard, Herbert Ashley
Berry, Samuel Harper, Jr.
Bigler, Ross Lowell
Bingman, Terrence L.
Bitting, William McClure
Bjork, Robert David, Jr.
Blumberg, John Philip
Bodkin, Henry Grattan, Jr.
Bohn, Robert Herbert
Bolles, Donald Scott
Bonesteel, Michael John
Bonham, Terrence James
Bonney, George William
Booher, Lawrence J., Jr.
Borges, David Joseph
Borowsky, Philip
Bottger, William Carl, Jr.
Boyd, William Sprott
Brenner, Anita Susan
Bressan, Paul Louis
Brick, Ann Veta
Bridges, B. Ried
Broderick, Daniel Thomas, III
Brookman, Anthony Raymond
Brown, Don C.
Brown, Donald Wesley
Brown, John Clark, Jr.
Brown, Lawrence
Brown, Phillip Edward
Brown, Ralph Evan
Burgess, John All
Burns, Bruce William
Busch, Peter Jonathan
Bushnell, Roderick P.
Butler, Felicita Therese
Bysshe, Frederick Herbert, Jr.
Cadwell, David Robert
Callahan, Gary Brent
Callan, Terrence A.
Callison, Russell James
Cameron, Mark Alan
Candland, D. Stuart

Caplan, Morton Lawrence
Caples, Michael Edward
Carlson, Jeffery John
Carrow, Robert Duane
Castello, Raymond Vincent
Cathcart, Patrick Alan
Chilvers, Robert Merritt
Ching, Anthony
Chu, Morgan
Clark, Alan Benjamin
Clark, Charles Edward
Cleary, William Joseph, Jr.
Coats, William Sloan, III
Cobey, Christopher Earle
Coil, Horace Orcutt
Colley, Nathaniel S(extus), Jr.
Connally, Michael W.
Cook, Ronald Walter
Corrales, Manuel, Jr.
Costello, Donald Fredric
Costello, Edward J., Jr.
Cotchett, Joseph Winters
Crosby, William Marshall
Crowe, Daniel Walston
Daar, David
Dalton, Douglas
Daniels, John Peter
Dazé, David Timothy
Deane, George Ingram, III
Delaughter, Jerry L.
Dell'Ergo, Robert James
Demko, Joseph Nicholas, Jr.
Dempsey, Michael Douglas
Derin, Greg David
DeVries, Scott Philip
Dickerson, William Roy
Diedrich, Peter Joseph
Dolan, Peter Brown
Dorit, J Niley
Dorr, Roderick Akin
Dostal, Milan Mathias
Downing, James Christie
Drachman, Frank Emanuel, Jr.
Drexler, Kenneth
Drummond, Donald Francis
Dryden, Robert Eugene
Duggan, Thomas Michael
Dunlavey, Dean Carl
Dunne, Stephen Lewis
Dyer, Charles Arnold
Ebiner, Robert Maurice
Elion, Gary Douglas
Engstrand, Paul David, Jr.
Ericson, Bruce Alan
Evans, John William
Fainsbert, Ann Rubenstein
Fairbank, Robert Harold
Fallman, James Mitchell, Jr.
Farley, Barbara Suzanne
Fenster, Fred A.
Field, Richard Clark
Finch, David Samuel
Fine, Richard Isaac
Finger, John Holden
Fischbach, Donald Richard
Fischer, Dale Susan
FitzGerald, John Edward, III
Fitzgerald, Stephen Patrick
Fitzgerald, William Brendan, Jr.
Flate, Ronald Allen
Fleischli, Jack A.
Freeman, Beth Labson
Freiser, Lawrence M.
Friedman, Lester James
Friedman, Wallace
Fromholz, Haley James
Gafford, George Nelson
Galton, Stephen Harold
Garman, John William
Garrison, Stuart Hugh
Gauntlett, David Allan
Georgallis, Joann
Germann, J. Gary
Getto, Ernest J.
Glaser, Patricia L.
Gnesin, Mark Meredith
Gold, Michael Allan
Goldie, Ray Robert
Goldie, Ron Robert
Golper, John Bruce
Goodwin, James Jeffries
Gordon, Robert Allen
Gordon, Robert P.
Gould, Harold I.
Gowdy, Franklin Brockway
Graham, Robert Lee
Gray, Veronica Meryl
Greenberg, Harold
Greenfield, Larry Stuart
Gregg, Richard
Grier, John Cummings
Groman, Arthur
Grush, Julius Sidney
Guido, Diana Lydia
Guilford, Andrew John
Haims, Arnold Brody
Hale, Candace
Hallisey, Jeremiah Francis
Hanger, Charles Ernest
Hanks, Maja Kristin
Hanley, Daniel E.
Harney, David Moran
Harris, James Michael
Harris, Lee S.
Harris, Richard Eugene Vassau
Harris, Robert Thomas
Harrison, Robert Wayne
Hart, Larry Calvin
Harutunian, Albert Theodore, III
Hasson, Kirke Michael
Hausmann, Edwin David
Hawkins, Carmen Doloras
Heafey, Edwin Austin, Jr.
Heaton, Roger Laurence
Heilbron, David M(ichael)
Heller, Donald Herbert
Heller, Philip
Henderson, Daniel Eli, Jr.
Hendrickson, Ray
Henke, Raymond Lange
Hensley, William Michael
Herbert, James Keller
Herlihy, Thomas Mortimer
Herring, Charles David
Hetland, John Robert
Hicks, James B(radley)
Higgs, Craig DeWitt
Hipshman, Anne
Hite, Randall Lee
Hobbs, Franklin Dean, III
Hodges, Robert W.
Hoefflin, Richard Michael
Hofstadter, Sarah Katherine
Holden, Charles St. George
Holmes, Kenneth Howard
Holzmann, James Charles
Hooser, Eugene Albert
Hopkins, Donald Ray
Horton, Luther William
Howard, John Wayne
Howard, Kenyon B.
Huebner, Kurt Benoit
Igo, Louis Daniel
Ingram, Robert Bruce
Jacobson, Richard Lee
Jaffe, Frohm Filmore
Jaffe, Stephen R.
Jaffee, Arthur Joseph
Jagiello, Barbara Anne
Johnson, Barbara Jean
Johnson, Robert Howard
Johnson, Terry Turner
Johnston, Faber Laine, Jr.
Jones, Thomas Robert
Jordan, Lawrence Whiting, Jr.
Joyce, Stephen Michael
Judson, Philip Livingston
Kaiser, Erik Michael
Kallberg, Kenneth J(oseph)
Kamine, Bernard Samuel
Kaplin, Gale P. Sonnenberg
Kay, William Thomas, Jr.
Kazanjian, Phillip Carl
Keenan, Richard
Kehoe, Dennis Joseph
Keker, John Watkins
Keller, Coby Norman
Kelley, Thomas Joseph
Kerrigan, Thomas Sherman
Khim, Diane
Kimberling, John Farrell
Kimsey, Dale Boyd
Kind, Kenneth Wayne
King, William J.
Kitchen, Jonathan Saville
Klinedinst, John David
Klinger, Marilyn Sydney
Knierim, K. Phillip
Knox, Alan Anthony
Kock, Arlene Dorothy
Kolkey, Daniel Miles
Kotler, Richard Lee
Kraus, James Alan
Kravitz, Jeffrey Stephen
Krell, Bruce Edward
Kuhl, Paul Beach
Kump, Kary Ronald
Kuntz, Charles Powers
Ladar, Jerrold Morton
Ladikos, Costas Angelo
Lageson, Ernest Benjamin
Lampel, Arthur Harry
Lancaster, Michael James
Langer, Simon Hrimes
Lascher, Edward Leonard
Lascher, Wendy Jean Cole
Lawless, William Burns
Lawton, Eric
Lazo, Ignacio Jesus
Lee, Michael G.W.
Lehan, Jonathan Michael
Lenzi, Albert James, Jr.
Levine, Jerome Lester
Levit, Victor Bert
Levit, William Harold
Liccardo, Salvador A.
Link, George Hamilton
Lloyd, William Emmons, Jr.
Lobner, Kneeland Harkness
Loube, Irving
Lucas, Campbell Macgregor
Lundquist, Weyman I.
Luppi, Michael Dennis
Lurvey, Ira Harold
Luther, Charles William
Lynch, Robert Thomas
Lyon, Bruce Arnold
Maddux, Parker Ahrens
Madory, Richard Eugene
Maillian, LeAnne Elizabeth
Malkus, James Alan
Markey, Christian Edward, Jr.
Markowitz, Michael Jay
Matthews, Philip Richard
McCall, Patrick Anthony
McClintock, Gordon Edwin
McCollum, Susan Hill
Mc Donough, John Richard
McEvers, Duff Steven
McGuire, E. James
McGuire, John Francis
McIntosh, Bruce Terence
McMurry, Robert I.
McNally, Susan Fowler
McNichols, Stephen Lucid Robert, Jr.
McPherson, Edwin Francis
Mehlhaff, Robert
Melbye, Richard Brenton
Mendelson, Steven Earle
Merring, Robert Alan
Michaels, Michael Daniel
Miles, Dori Elizabeth
Millar, Richard William, Jr.
Miller, James L.
Miller, Kenneth Michael
Miller, Milton Allen
Miller, Mona Joy Deutsch
Miller, Owens O'Keefe
Miller, Steven Jeffrey
Minich, Mark Andrew
Mobley, Gary Steven
Mocciaro, Perry D.
Mohr, Anthony James
Monaco, Daniel Joseph
Moore, Douglas Matthew, Jr.
Moore, Raymond Robert
Morgan, Robert Hall
Morgan, William Robert
Morrell, Rivers Judson, III
Mosich, Nicholas Joseph
Mosk, Richard Mitchell
Mussman, William Edward
Mussman, William Edward, III
Negron, Dennis
Neumeyer, Richard Albert
Newell, Thomas Peter
Newman, Michael Rodney
Niles, John Gilbert
Nissly, Kenneth L.
Nocas, Andrew James
Noonan, Dennis Charles
Nordin, John Eric, II
Oder, Kenneth William
Oggel, Stephen Peter
Olson, Ronald Leroy
Orlebeke, William Ronald
Ornstil, Michael Gary
Orr, Robert M.
Otto, James Daniel
Paden, Gary Lewis
Pagano, James Lawrence
Palffy, Thomas
Papiano, Neil Leo
Parish, William Henry
Parton, James, III
Partritz, Joan Elizabeth
Pasternak, David Joel
Payne, Robert Warren
Pearlman, Lisa Ann
Peck, Aaron Martin
Pereyra-Suarez, Charles Albert
Perez, Richard Lee
Perluss, Irving Harvey
Pierry, Thomas James
Pilling, George William
Pingel, Steven R.
Pinkerton, Albert Duane, II
Pitre, Frank Mario
Pizzulli, Francis Cosmo Joseph
Player, Theresa Joan
Pleiss, Larry Thomas
Plishner, Michael Jon
Pollock, John Phleger
Pooley, James Henry Anderson
Poppett, Mark Adams
Poster, Jeffrey Charles
Price, Edward Dean
Prozan, Sylvia Simmons
Pulliam, Mark Stephen
Quittman, Peter Francis
Ramsey, Owen Jasper, Jr.
Randall, Mel Scott
Ray, David Lewin
Ream, Christopher
Reed, Brian Edward
Reed, Wallace Calvin
Reed, William James
Regalia, Edmund Louis
Regnier, Richard Adrian
Reith, Daniel I.
Resneck, William Allan
Rice, Randolf James
Richard, Monte Dwight
Riffer, Jeffrey Kent
Rinck, Gary M.
Ritchie, Thomas Brown
Ritter, G. Christopher
Robinson, Archie Stirling
Robinson, William Adams
Robison, William Robert
Roche, Thomas Garrett
Roethe, James Norton
Roseman, Charles Sanford
Rosenberg, Arnold Steven
Rosenthal, Robert Michael
Rosenthal, Steven S.
Ross, Susan Kohn
Roth, Hadden Wing
Rothwell, Thomas Henry
Rubin, Dale Michael
Rudolph, George Cooper
Ruma, Ronald Edward
Rummonds, James Scott
Russell, Thomas Hunter
Ruston, Donald Allen
Rutten, Rand John
Sallus, Marc Leonard
Salomon, Darrell Joseph
Samson, Anthony Donald
Santandrea, Mary Frances
Sayad, Pamela Miriam
Sceper, Duane Harold
Schachter, Alesa Rose
Schack, David Paul
Schieffer, Joseph H.
Schisler, George Milford, Jr.
Schleicher, Estelle Ann
Schmal, Timothy James
Schroeder, John
Schuck, Carl J.
Scoular, Robert Frank
Seal, James Lee
Sears, Douglas Alson
Severaid, Ronald Harold
Shaw, Stanford Eugene
Shea, Michael Murt
Sherman, Dana
Sherwood, Allen Joseph
Sherwood, Arthur Lawrence
Sherwood, Richard Edwin
Shorr, Matthew Sam
Silberberg, Henry J.
Silver, Mark Steven
Silverman, Bruce Stanly
Simon, Bruce Lee
Simone, Martin Massimo
Simonelli, James John
Simonini, David Michael
Simons, Bernard Philip
Sindon, Geoffrey Stuart
Sinnott, Randolph Paul
Sitkin, Peter Edward
Skaggs, Sanford Merle
Slater, Jill Sherry
Smith, Stanley David
Smith, Steven Ira
Snow, Tower Charles, Jr.
Sobel, Erwin
Solis, Carlos
Solish, Jonathan Craig
Sparks, John Edward
Specter, Richard Bruce
Spencer, Gregory Scott
Stanley, Sabrina Ann
Stavig, Alf Rusten
Steer, Reginald David
Stephenson, Michael Murray
Stone, Jean
Stone, Richard James
Stout, Gregory Stansbury
Stratton, Richard James
Strong, George Gordon, Jr.
Sturdevant, Patricia Tenoso
Sugarman, Paul William
Sullivan, William Francis
Taylor, William James
Telleria, Anthony F.
Tepper, R(obert) Bruce, Jr.
Thoren-Peden, Deborah Suzanne
Thurston, Morris Ashcroft
Tiffany, Joseph Raymond, II
Tonsing, Michael John
Traynor, J. Michael
Truett, Harold Joseph, III
Tsenin, Ksenia
Turek, Kenneth Casper
Urwin, Gary Lee
Vandegrift, Lucian B.
Vanderet, Robert Charles
Vaughn, Lesley Miller Mehran
Vineyard, C L
Vosguanian, Rodney Nerses
Walcher, Alan Ernest
Walter, John F.
Walwyn, Stephen John
Ward, Anthony John
Warnlof, John Skinner
Wasserman, Michael Eric
Weatherup, Roy Garfield
Weingarten, Saul Myer
Weir, William John Arnold
Weisberg, Sheila Roseanne
Weiss, Edward Abraham
Weissman, I. Donald
Weissman, Robert Allen
Welch, Thomas Andrew
Wenzel, Lee Bey
Wertz, John R.
Wesierski, Christopher Paul
Wessling, Donald Moore
Weston, Kenneth Frederick
Wheatley, Jeff R.
Whitaker, Leslie Kent
White, Jack Raymond
Wickham, Dennis J.
Wikle, Kenneth Clinton, Jr.
Wiley, Robert Wayne
Willard, Robert Edgar
Willey, Charles Wayne
Williams, Charles Judson
Williams, Lee Dwain
Williams, Michael Edward
Wilson, Clifford Ralph
Wohlfeil, Joel R.
Wolfe, Richard Frederick
Woocher, Fredric Dean
Wood, Weldon Sanford
Woodhead, Frank Womack
Worley, Donald Robert
Wulfsberg, Harold James
Wykowski, Henry George
Wylie, Richard John
Yim, B(urgess) Casey
Young, Bless Stritar
Young, Douglas Rea
Zafis, Andrew James
Zecher, Albert Michael
Zerger, Kirsten Louise
Zimmerman, Bernard
Zuckerman, Alan Randy
Zweig, Michael K.

Colorado

Baker, Bernard Robert
Barnthouse, William Joseph
Bayer, Richard Stewart
Beattie, Steven Mack
Bernstein, Jeremy Marshall
Blakey, Milton Keith
Brady, William John, Jr.
Branney, Joseph John
Brown, Ian Alexander
Browne, C. Willing, III
Bruce, Neil Curtis
Bryans, Richard W.
Campbell, Leonard Martin
Campbell, Richard Bruce
Caplan, Gerald A.
Carleno, Harry Eugene
Carlson, Alan Douglas
Carlson, Robert James
Carney, Deborah Leah Turner
Carney, Thomas T.J.
Casebolt, James Stanton
Chalat, James Harold
Clark, Roger Earl
Cohen, Jeffrey
Cortez, Miles Cogley, Jr.
Damas, Stanislaw Stefan
DeLaney, Herbert Wade, Jr.
de Marino, Thomas John
Demuth, Lael Saunders
Donnelly, Frederick James
Downey, Arthur Harold, Jr.
Downsbrough, Bruce Owen
Duncan, Stephen Mack
Ebert, Darlene Marie
Englander, Paula Tyo
Epstein, Joseph Marc
Erkenbrack, Stephen K.
Featherstone, Bruce Alan
Feder, Harold Abram
Figa, Phillip Sam
Friedberg, Alan Charles
Geil, Karl James
Geisel, Henry Jules
Gentry, Elvin LeRoy
George, Doug
Goldberg, Charles
Goral, Brian Harold
Green, Philip Burton
Gulley, Kenneth Galen
Hagen, Glenn W(illiam)
Halpern, Alexander
Halpern, Joseph W.
Hanley, Robert Francis
Helmer, David Alan
Henderson, John Richard
Hoffman, Daniel Steven
Holst, Dale Lawson
Horowitz, Jay Stanley
Jackson, Richard Brooke
Jamison, Jamey William
Janklow, Donald Emanuel
Johnson, Dale Eliot
Johnson, Philip Edward
Judd, Joel Stanton
Judd, Richard D(onald)
Keller, Alex Stephen
Kiehnhoff, Thomas Nave
Kimmell, Thomas J.
Kobayashi, John M.
Kogovsek, Daniel Charles
Kraft, C. William, III
Kullby, Roy Sigurd
Lapin, James B.
Laugesen, Richard W.
Law, John Manning
LeHouillier, Patric Jaymes
Leiser, Harvey Wayne
Lerman, Eileen R.
Logan, Valentine Weir
Luce, Charles F., Jr.
Maginness, Craig Richard
Magoon, Brian A(lan)
Mark, Denis Hugh
Martin, E. Gregory
Maywhort, William Walter
McBee, Donald Lawrence
McConnell, Michael T.
McGee, Robert Leon, Jr.
McGill, Scott A.
McGrath, John Nicholas, Jr.
McGrath, William Arthur
McLain, William Allen
Merker, Steven Joseph
Meyer, William Dale
Michaels, Jane
Miller, Gale Timothy
Mitchem, Allen P.
Morris, Marc
Netzorg, Gordon Wemple
Nottingham, Edward Willis, Jr.
O'Donnell, Michael Lawrence
Overholser, John W.
Oxman, Stephen Eliot
Purvis, John Anderson
Raymond, Douglas J.
Redder, Thomas Joseph
Rench, Stephen Charles
Richman, Alan Elliott
Rodgers, Ralph Emerson
Rodriquez, Janet Lois
Roth, Robert Charles
Sandman, James Joseph
Sands, Jon F(rederick)
Satter, Raymond Nathan
Sears, Daniel Joseph
Sedlak, Joseph Anthony, III
Serini, John Peter
Setter, David Mark
Skelton, Darrell Jean
Snyder, Paul, Jr.
Spelts, Richard John
Starrs, Elizabeth Anne
Suthers, John William
Taylor, Robert Lynn
Thomasch, Roger Paul
Tisdale, Douglas Michael
Tisdale, Patricia Claire
Tracey, Jay Walter, Jr.
Treece, James Lyle
Vigil, David Charles
Walta, John Gregory
Wedgle, Richard Jay
Welch, Carol Mae
Welton, Charles Ephraim
Weltzer, Louis Albin
Wendt, John Arthur Frederic, Jr.
Wieman, Terry Lynn
Wilson, William Andrew
Wood, David Leslie

Connecticut

Adams, Richard Glen
Adelman, Robert Bardwell
Alcorn, Hugh Meade, Jr.
Alesevich, Walter Charles
Amento, Carl Joseph
Benedict, Peter Behrends
Boesen, John Michael
Boland, John Daniel
Bonee, John Leon, III
Brady, Matthew Joseph
Brennan, Daniel Edward, Jr.
Cacace, Michael Joseph
Casagrande, Daniel Eugene
Clendenen, William Herbert, Jr.
Coles, Kevin Andrew
Comley, Frederick Luquiens
Conaway-Raczka, Nancy
Cutsumpas, Lloyd
Daniels, Douglas Robert
Dowling, Michael Anthony
Drumm, Francis Joseph, Jr.
Dwyer, Gerald Parker
Eberhard, Robert Vincent
Effron, Wayne Douglas
Elliot, Ralph Gregory
Fain, Joel Maurice
Fallon, John Francis
Farrelly, Francis J.
Feldman, Samuel Botwinik
FitzGerald, Edward Browne
Friar, Martha Jane
Green, Raymond Bert
Greenfield, James Robert
Haviland, James Thomas, II
Hayes, Margaret Mary
Heiman, Maxwell
Holth, Fredrik Davidson
Ivey, Scott Ellsworth
Johnson, Allan Richard
Kanaga, Lawrence Wesley
Karazin, Edward Robert, Jr.
Katz, Melvin Seymour
LaFollette, Ernest Carlton
Lombardo, Michael John
Luby, Thomas Stewart
Mason, Margaret Pendleton Pearson
McGrail, Albert James
McKinney, Ivy Thomas
Meehan, Richard Thomas, Jr.
Miano, Frederick Joseph
Morelli, Joseph Christopher
Morris, Jeffrey Lyons
Morrison, Francis Henry
Murphy, William Robert
Murtha, Thomas Michael
Nevas, Leo
Osis, Daiga Guntra
Pavetti, Francis James
Pepe, Louis Robert
Perlman, Bruce Michael
Piazza, Anthony Andrew
Ponzini, John Lino
Reinen, Jeffrey William
Ryan, Atherton Beal
Ryan, John Joseph
Ryan, William Joseph, Jr.

Rybak, Michael Dennis
Sauer, David Allen
Schaefer, Daniel Robert
Schatz, Arthur Herschel
Schatz, Richard Ansell
Seiger, Mark Brian
Shipman, Mark Samuel
Silver, Elaine Terry
Slez, Anthony Francis, Jr.
Slocum, Shaun Michael
Sussman, Mark Richard
Sweeney, William Jones, Jr.
Taalman, Juri E.
Tanski, James Michael
Trebisacci, Raymond Thomas
Ury, Frederic Stephen
Ward, Charles Daniel
Wiechmann, Eric Watt
Wilcox, Jamison Van Voorhees
Williams, Ronald Doherty
Zagorsky, Peter Joseph

Delaware

Bader, John Merwin
Bailey, James Frederick, Jr.
Balick, Steven Jeffrey
Bradley, Paul Anthony
Carpenter, Edmund Nelson, II
Crompton, Charles Sentman, Jr.
Curtin, Christopher James
Davis, James Francis
Green, James Samuel
Hamermesh, Lawrence Abraham
Harrington, Rick Alan
Johnston, William David
Kimmel, Morton Richard
Levine, Norman Edward
Manley, Marshall
Marin, Bayard
Marlin, Jeffrey Stuart
Marvel, Wayne Andrew
Pepperman, Walter Leon, II
Rich, Michael Joseph
Rothschild, Steven James
Semple, James William
Stokes, Richard Francis
Walsh, Joseph Thomas
Willard, John Martin
Wolhar, Robert Charles, Jr.

District of Columbia

Anikeeff, Anthony Hotchkiss
Attridge, Daniel F.
Bellinger, Edgar Thomson
Berry, Mary Frances
Bierbower, Mark Butler
Bolden, Melvin Wilberforce, Jr.
Bono, Gaspare Joseph
Brand, Michael Edward
Burch, John Thomas, Jr.
Burnim, Ira Abraham
Chapman, Dudley Harry
Chierichella, John W.
Cooter, Dale A.
Daniel, Aubrey Marshall, III
Darling, Charles M., IV
DeBerardinis, Robert Andrew, Jr.
Fox, Hamilton Phillips, III
Fryer, Hugh Nevin
Fryman, Virgil Thomas, Jr.
Glowinski, Robert William
Goodson, Robert Wade
Handleman, Aaron L.
Harbottle, Ann Woodley
Hogan, Thomas Francis
Hundt, Reed Eric
Interdonato, Anthony Paul
Jordan, James Francis
Karp, Ronald Alvin
Kelly, Kathryn
Kovacs, William Lawrence
Kramer, Noël Anketell
Kuder, Armin Ulrich
Leonard, Jerris
Liebman, Ronald Stanley
Lister, Charles
McMillan, Richard, Jr.
Medaglia, Mary-Elizabeth
Mitchell, Gerard Ellsworth
Murphy, James Paul
Nace, Barry John
Nelson, William Eugene
Norwind, Edward Lee
O'Toole, Francis J.
Peck, Jeffrey Jay
Pierson, W. DeVier
Pilger, Karl William
Policy, Vincent Mark
Quarles, James Linwood, III
Raul, Alan Charles
Razzano, Frank Charles
Reback, Richard Neal
Rephan, Jack
Rhodes, Richard Randolph
Rider, James Lincoln
Rosenau, Kenneth H.
Rubin, Janet Beth
Sallet, Jonathan Bruce
Shean, Owen Joseph
Sheehan, Richard Jere
Siemer, Deanne C.
Snider, Jerome Guy
Snyder, Allen Roger
Stabbe, Mitchell Howard
Sutherlund, David Arvid
Swartz, Dean Elliot
Szybala, Renee Leslie
Tomar, Richard Thomas
Tompkins, Joseph Buford, Jr.
Utermohlen, William Jerome
Vance, Kenneth Anthony
Wagshal, Jerome Stanley
Walker, Mary L.
Weiss, Harlan Lee
Weld, William Floyd
Weller, Susan Neuberger
Yannucci, Thomas David

Florida

Abbott, Charles Warren
Abrams, Brenda M.
Adkins, Edward Cleland
Aguila, Adolfo Zacarias
Allen, Richard Lewis
Allen, W. Riley
Alpert, Jonathan Louis
Anderson, Bruce Paige
Anderson, R(obert) Bruce
Anthony, Andrew John
Aragon, Rudolph Fermin
Arencibia, Raul A.
Ashby, Kimberly A.
Astigarraga, Jose Ignacio
Aurell, John Karl
Babler, Wayne E.
Baker, Elizabeth Statuta
Balkany, Caron Lee
Barley, John Alvin
Barnett, Richard Allen
Barnhart, Forrest Gregory
Bartlett, Charles John
Bates, Richard Warden
Bemis, Lawrence Perry
Berger, Steven R.
Berns, Bonnie Ava
Bernstein, Howard Mark
Bernstein, Michael Alan
Berry, Gerald Thomas
Betts, James Robert
Biggs, Thomas Sanford, Jr.
Billingsley, Curtis Ashley
Birnbaum, Richard Michael
Black, Leon David, Jr.
Blank, Nelson Douglas
Blank, Ralph John, Jr.
Blumberg, Edward Robert
Booth, Edgar Charles
Bopp, Thomas Roe
Borgognoni, Gregory Paul
Bosse, Richard Edward
Boyles, Kevan Kenneth
Bratten, Thomas Arnold
Briggs, Randy Robert
Brophy, Gilbert Thomas
Brumbaugh, John Moore
Brumer, Michael
Buchman, Kenneth William
Buesing, Karen Meyer
Burnbaum, Michael William
Burton, Richard Jay
Busch, David John
Butler, Paul B.
Cacciatore, S. Sammy, Jr.
Cagney, William Patrick, III
Cain, May Lydia
Cain, William Allen
Callender, John Francis
Campbell, Charles Philip, Jr.
Capp, Alvin
Carstetter, David Wilson
Castillo, Hal Stephen
Catlin, Harold Harvey
Cheffy, Edward Kefgen
Chopin, Susan Gardiner
Chumbris, Stephen Claude
Clark, Ross Townsend
Clarkson, Julian Derieux
Coe, Jack Martin
Cohen, Jeffrey Michael
Cohen, Stephen M(artin)
Coleman, C. Randolph
Conner, Richard Elwood
Cooney, David Francis
Corcoran, C. Timothy, III
Corlett, Edward Stanley, III
Crabtree, Robert Crosby
Cunningham, James Reynolds
Custureri, Richard Domenick
David, Ronald Albert
Davidson, Michael H.
Davis, William Howard
Day, George Everette
Dayhoff, Charles Sidney, III
Deehl, David Lee
Delancett, John Gerald
Del Russo, Alexander D.
Dempsey, Bernard Hayden, Jr.
Denman, James Burton
DeWitt, Sherri Kandel
Diaz, Benito Humberto
Durie, Jack Frederick, Jr.
Eagan, William Leon
Earle, William George
Eaton, Joel Douglas
Eckhart, James Milton
Edelstein, Steven A(llen)
Ehrlich, Raymond
Ervin, Robert Marvin
Escarraz, Enrique, III
Evans, John F.
Falk, Glenn Phillip
Farese, Lawrence Anthony
Feder, Scott Jay
Feldman, Joel Harvey
Ferencik, Robert Elmer, Jr.
Fernandez, William Warren
Ferrell, Milton Morgan, Jr.
Fletcher, Paul Gerald
Fougerousse, Philip
Fox, Gary Devenow
Franklin, Lucille Espey
Freeman, Stephan John
Fridkin, Jeffrey David
Friedman, Jerrell Don
Gabel, George DeSaussure, Jr.
Gaddy, Rodney Edwin
Gaines, Robert Pendleton
Galamaga, Robert John
Garbis, Gary Edward
Garcia-Pedrosa, Jose Ramon
Gassler, Frank Henry
Gelfand, Michael Joseph
Geller, Steven Anthony
Gerlin, William Lance
Gievers, Karen A.
Gilbert, Richard Allen
Glass, Roy Leonard
Glinn, Franklyn Barry
Gluck, Robin Beverly
Godbold, Gene Hamilton
Goldman, Joel L.
Goldsmith, Karen Lee
Goldstein, Harvey M.
Gorman, Robert James
Graham, Andrew Alan
Graham, Donald Lynn
Greenwald, Steven Jeffrey
Greer, Alan Graham
Grilli, Peter John
Haliczer, James Solomon
Hall, Miles Lewis, Jr.
Hamilton, Robert Lowery
Harris, Christy Franklin
Harrison, Teresa Harshman
Hastings, Lawrence Vaeth
Hastings, Michael Lynn
Hasty, Frederick Emerson, III
Hayes, Neil John
Heindl, Phares Matthews
Hern, Joseph George, Jr.
Hester, Christopher Scott
Hickey, John Heyward
Hill, Brian Donovan
Hingston, Robert Allen
Hinkle, Robert Lewis
Hochman, Jeffrey J.
Hodge, Wilson Eugene
Hoey, William Edward
Hogg, Jesse Stephen
Holland, William Meredith
Hood, Charles David, Jr.
Hoofman, Robert Sidney
Hooper, Joel Randall
Hootman, Gregory Wayne
Horan, John Patrick
Horn, Andrew Warren
Ines, Victor Doroteo
Itkin, Perry Steven
Jacobo, Winston Wendle
Jamieson, James Phillips
Jensen, Jack Albert
Jernigan, Anna Michelle
Johnson, Paul Bryan
Johnston, Charles Motley
Joy, Daniel Foster
Kapner, Lewis
Kauffman, Alan Charles
Kearns, John W.
Keating, Gerard F.
Kelly, John Patrick
Kelly, Thomas Paine, Jr.
Kimber, Brian Lee
Korchin, Judith Miriam
Krathen, David Howard
Kray, Fred Martin
Kreutzer, Franklin David
Lance, Miles A.
Lax, Michael H.
Levenstein, Richard Harry
Levin, David Harold
Levine, Curtis Gilbert
Lewis, Neal Randolph
Lewis, William Adams
Liles, Rutledge Richardson
Lloyd, John Stoddard
London, Jack Edward
Losey, Ralph Colby
Lyng, Reginald William
MacDonald, Thomas Cook, Jr.
Makowski, Raymond Edmund
Mann, Kenneth L.
Mansbach, Robert Earl, Jr.
Marcus, Ira
Martin, James Addison, Jr.
Martin, James William
Martin, Michael David
Martin, Serge Gregory
Martinez, Mel R.
Masterson, Bernard Joseph
Mayans, Steven Anthony
McAliley, Thomas Watson
McDonald, Julia Carol
McDonnell, Michael R. N.
McDuffee, Paul Gerard, II
McGee, C(larence) Edward, Jr.
McIntosh, Douglas Malcolm
McKenzie, James Franklin
McKeown, Frank James
McLemore, Michael Kerr
McNally, James Joseph
McQuigg, John Dolph
Mednick, Glenn Myles
Mehrtens, William Osborne, Jr.
Menendez, Manuel, Jr.
Miller, Raymond Vincent, Jr.
Mitchell, Ann Poe
Mitrani, Isaac Jaime
Mollica, Salvatore Dennis
Montante, Philip Joseph, Jr.
Montgomery, David Paul
Montgomery, Robert Morel, Jr.
Moody, James Shelton, Jr.
Moore, Thomas Adair
Moran, James Michael
Motes, Carl Dalton
Muratides, John Nicholas
Murrell, Robert George
Murrell, Sam Edwin, Jr.
Nachwalter, Michael
Nifong, J. Michael
Nimmons, Ralph Wilson, Jr.
Novack, Catherine Gail
Nyce, John Daniel
O'Flarity, James P.
O'Neal, Michael Scott, Sr.
Ormond, Gregg Joseph
Owen, Richard Knowles
Painter, James Morgan
Palahach, Michael
Park, Joseph Rathbone
Parker, Julius Frederick, Jr.
Parrish, Sidney Howard
Pawluc, Sonia M.
Pertnoy, Leonard David
Peters, Robert Timothy
Phillips, Gary Stephen
Pierce, Francis Edmund, III
Podrecca, Adolfo Augusto
Poole, Sharon Alexandra
Pound, Frank R., Jr.
Pulignano, Nicholas Vincent, Jr.
Raiden, Michael E.
Rakusin, Stephen Bruce
Rashkind, Paul Michael
Reid, R(alph) Benjamine
Reiter, Joseph John
Reynolds, Joseph Jay
Richardson, Sally M.
Richardson, Scott Neil
Richeson, Hugh Anthony, Jr.
Rico, JulieAnn
Roberts, B. K.
Rogel, Todd Stephen
Rogers, Harvey D.
Rojas, Jose Ignacio
Rose, Michael I.
Rose, Norman
Ross, Howard Philip
Rumrell, Richard Gary
Rutledge, Gary Ray
Rydberg, Marsha Griffin
Salem, Albert McCall, Jr.
Sasser, Donald Julian
Sax, Spencer Meridith
Scarola, John
Schember, Steven George
Schiff, Louis Howard
Schmidt, Whitney Lawrence
Schneider, Harvey Robert
Scott, Janice Gail
Scott, Thomas Emerson, Jr.
Scremin, Anthony James
Searcy, Christian Deitrich, Sr.
Seelie, Michael Edward
Semento, Lawrence James
Sheffield, Frank Elwyn
Siegel, Paul
Siemon, Joyce Marilyn
Silverman, Scott Jay
Silvernail, Jesse Preston
Siplin, Gary Anthony
Sistare, Susan Powell
Slaydon, Roger James
Smith, Harold Delane
Smith, William Reece, Jr.
Somers, Clifford Louis
Sperry, Martin J.
Stack, Charles Rickman
Stanley, Bruce McLaren
Starr, Ivar Miles
Stein, Craig Edward
Stevens, Harold Sanford
Stewart, Larry S.
Stieglitz, Albert Blackwell
Stinson, Steven Arthur
Strawn, David Updegraff
Stubbs, Sidney Alton
Sutcliffe, Roland Alton, Jr.
Sutton, Michael Ferris
Symons, Robin Suzanne Taylor
Taitz, Steven Carter
Terrell, James Thomas
Terry, T(aylor) Rankin, Jr.
Thiele, Herbert William Albert
Thomas, Wayne Lee
Thornton, John W.
Thornton, Richard Joseph
Tifford, Arthur W.
Tittsworth, Clayton (Magness)
Tobin, Gerald J.
Traitz, James Joseph, Jr.
Trees, Philip Hugh
Trombley, Michael Jerome
Udell, Michael Bennett
Underwood, Edwin Hill
Velasquez, Patti A.
Vento, John Sebastian
Vernis, Frank Carl, Jr.
Waas, George Lee
Wadsworth, Murray Marvin
Walton, Rodney Earl
Warren, Herbert Albert
Wein, Stephen Joshua
Weissenborn, Sheridan Kendall
Weissman, Jeffrey Mark
Welbaum, R. Earl
Wendel, John Fredric
Whigham, Thomas Edmondson
White, Andrew, III
White, Russell Alan
Williams, Stewart Dorian
Wilson, Brenda Coker
Wilson, William Berry
Windham, John Franklin
Wirtz, Gregg Lee
Wiseheart, Malcolm Boyd, Jr.
Wolf, James Paul
Wood, Hugh Lee
Wood, Julian Emory
Wroble, Arthur G.
Young, Terry Cressler
Zacur, Richard Aaron
Zaiser, Kent Ames
Zaretsky, Esther Anne
Zorie, Stephanie Marie

Georgia

Anderson, Peter Joseph
Armstrong, Edwin Alan
Baker, Verlyn Childs
Barr, Robert Laurence, Jr.
Barrett, David Eugene
Baverman, Alan Jerold
Baverman, Elida Blaine
Biggins, Franklin N.
Billington, Barry E.
Blackstock, Jerry Byron
Blank, A(ndrew) Russell
Bobbitt, Phillip Lamar
Boynton, Frederick George
Branch, Thomas Broughton, III
Breeding, Earnie Rowe
Brown, Stephen Phillip
Childs, Julie
Christy, Gary Christopher
Connelly, Lewis Branch Sutton
Cook, Martha Jean
Cooper, Lawrence Allen
Cowart, Richard Merrill
Crockett, David Gideon
Crumbley, R. Alex
Curry, Stephen Euree
Custer, Lawrence Benjamin
Dalziel, Charles Meredith, Jr.
Davis, George Thomas
Davison, John Arthur
Dettmering, William O'Neal, Jr.
Dickert, Neal Workman
Draughon, John Albert
Duffey, William Simon, Jr.
Eckl, William Wray
Edwards, James Garland, II
Elliott, James Sewell
Elmore, Marvin Jerome
Felton, Jule Wimberly, Jr.
Fitzpatrick, Barry Lane
Fitzpatrick, Duross
Fleming, Julian Denver, Jr.
Freed, Gary Stuart
Gannam, Michael Joseph
Gibbs, Stephen Mark
Gleaton, Frederick Neal
Glucksman, Joyce Francine
Gregory, Hardy, Jr.
Gunn, Robert Russell
Hall, Charles Martin
Harvey, Alan Christopher
Hayes, Dewey Norman, Jr.
Henson, Howard Kirk
Ingram, George Conley
Jenkins, Thomas A(llan)
Jones, Donald Richard, III
Kadish, Mark J.
Kalish, Katherine McAulay
Kelley, Jeffrey Wendell
Kidd, Daryl Leslie
Kirkland, June Ann
Knox, Wyckliffe Austin, Jr.
Lachance, James Martin
Lackland, Theodore Howard
Lanier, Robert Simmons, Jr.
Lester, Charles Turner, Jr.
Lewis, H(enry) Worthington
Lokey, Hamilton
Lore, Stephen Melvin
Malone, Thomas William
Mass, Allen Robert
Mayoue, John Charles
Mears, Michael
Menendez, Kenneth Gary
Miles, Dana Brent
Miller, Alfred Montague
Oliver, Bonnie Chessher
Owens, L(awrence) Dale
Pannell, James Loughridge
Patrick, James Duvall, Jr.
Patton, Matthew H.
Perry, Alan Rogers, Jr.
Pinkston, Calder Finney
Polstra, Larry John
Powell, Douglas Richard
Pujadas, Thomas Edward
Purdom, Wayne Miller
Reemsnyder, Ronald David
Reeves, Gene
Reinhart, Richard Paul
Ross, Robert T.
Rutledge, Ivan Cate
Satcher, James Alton, Jr.
Seacrest, Gary Lee
Shinall, Robert Phillip, III
Shulman, Warren Scott
Smith, Malcolm Percy
Stell, John Elwin, Jr.
Stone, Ralph Kenny
Taylor-Hanington, Paula Kay
Thomas, James Joseph, II
Tolley, Edward Donald
Turnipseed, Sara Sadler
Warner, William Millard
Watson, John Howard
Webb, Michael Steven
Wellon, Robert G.
Wheale, Duncan Douglas
Whiteside, Fife Morris
Wood, L. Lin, Jr.
Young, Robert George
Zolke, Scott Bryan

Hawaii

Akiba, Lorraine Hiroko
Ashford, Clinton Rutledge
Barkai, John Lee
Bays, Albert Bernard
Beaman, Andrew Varnum
Brown, Boyce Reid, Jr.
Burke, Edmund
Ching, Gale Lin Fong
Chuck, Walter G(oonsun)
Chung, Steven Kamsein
Clifton, Richard Randall
Crumpton, Charles Whitmarsh
Deaver, Phillip Lester
Devens, Paul
Duffy, James Earl, Jr.
Eggers, William J., III
Freed, Michael Leonard
Frey, Philip Sigmund
Fried, L. Richard, Jr.
Fujiyama, Wallace Sachio
Fukumoto, Leslie Satsuki
Goldsmith, Stephen Ernest
Hall, David Winston
Hastert, Diane Deskins
Iwai, Wilfred Kiyoshi
Kemper, Edward Crawford
Kim, Edward Y.N.
Kuniyuki, Ken Takaharu
Lau, Jeffrey Daniel
Lawson, William Homer
Louie, David Mark
Marx, Robert Phillip
Meaney, Michael Lawrence
Morse, Jack Craig
Mukaida, Wayne Hideo
Murakami, Alan Tomoo
Neeley, Joyce Yount
Portnoy, Jeffrey Steven
Potts, Dennis Walker
Rack, Thomas Paul
Robinson, John Harvey
Sattler, James Michael
Schraff, Paul Albert
Songstad, Steven Booth
Tanaka, Leila Chiyako
Taylor, Carroll Stribling
Turbin, Richard
Van De Car, Diana Lee
Van Pernis, Mark
Wong, James Thomas
Wong, Patricia Uyehara
Wong, Reuben Sun Fai
Yamada, Stephen Kinichi
Yamamoto, Jerel Ikmo

Idaho

Brown, Charles Alan
Christenson, Jeffrey Robert
Clark, Merlyn Wesley
Dryden, William George
Furey, Sherman Francis, Jr.
Helvie, Kirk Randall
Hines, William Joseph
Hurlbutt, Daniel Chater, Jr
Jarzabek, Joseph Edward
Johnson, L. Charles
Judd, Linda
Lawson, Edward Albert
May, James, Jr.
Miller, Patrick Eugene
Parmenter, David N.
Read, Michael John
Risch, James E.
Schlender, E. Lee
Tait, John Reid
Vander Boegh, Douglas Lee
Webb, Lloyd Jackson

Wetherell, Mike

Illinois

Africk, Joel Jay
Ahlenius, William Matheson
Alesia, James H(enry)
Alexander, Richard Elmont
Allen, Thomas D.
Angst, Gerald L.
Anspach, Kenneth Gordon
Apcel, Melissa Anne
Artman, Eric Alan
Artwick, Frederick John
Austin, Daniel William
Baker, Bennett Joel
Baker, James Edward Sproul
Barron, Howard Robert
Bashaw, Steven Bradley
Bashwiner, Steven Lacelle
Bator, Paul Michael
Baugher, Peter V.
Beatty, William Glenn
Beckett, Amy Louise
Bell, Ronald Lee
Bellah, Kenneth David
Bellows, Laurel Gordon
Bergstrom, Robert William
Beth, Kenneth Norman
Blan, Kennith William, Jr.
Bohlen, Christopher Wayne
Boies, Wilber H.
Bollinger, Barry Gilbert
Bone, Maurice Edgar
Botti, Aldo E.
Bracey, Willie Earl
Bradner, James Holland, Jr.
Brainard, H Ogden
Bresnahan, Arthur Stephen
Bridgman, Thomas Francis
Britton, Clarold Lawrence
Brody, Lita Helen
Brown, Robert Howard
Bruno, Thomas Anthony
Burditt, George Miller, Jr.
Burke, Dennis J.
Burke, John Michael
Burke, Thomas Joseph, Jr.
Callahan, Dennis John
Canel, James Harrison
Carey, Richard Peter
Carlson, Stephen Curtis
Carpenter, David William
Carponelli, Stephen Peter
Cheely, Daniel Joseph
Chemers, Robert Marc
Cherney, James Alan
Chester, Mark Vincent
Churchill, Allen Delos
Cicero, Frank, Jr.
Coccia, Michel Andre
Coghill, William Thomas, Jr.
Cohen, Edward A.
Colantoni, Anthony Michael
Coleman, William T(homas)
Conison, Jay
Cook, James Christopher
Cotteleer, Michael Alexander
Coughlin, Terrance J
Courtney, Thomas Frances
Crowley, Wilbert Francis
Cummins, Robert Patrick
Cunningham, William Francis
Danekas, Steven Ernest
Davis, Dean Martin
Davis, Muller
De Jong, David John
Dell, Robert Michael
Demetrio, Thomas A.
Denkewalter, Kim Richard
Denzel, Ken John
DeSanto, James John
DeWolfe, George Fulton
DeWolfe, John Chauncey, Jr.
Didzerekis, Paul Patrick
Ditkowsky, Kenneth K.
Domanskis, Alexander Rimas
Donlevy, John Dearden
Donohue, Richard Harney
Doughty, H. Reed
Driscoll, Patrick Thomas, Jr.
Duff, David Potter
Duncan, Edward Rogers, Jr.
Eaton, J(ames) Timothy
Ebert, Regan Danielle
Edelman, Daniel Amos
Edlund, Curtis Eric
Egan, Kevin James
Eisenberg, Stephen Paul
Elliott, Ivan A.
Elliott, Ivan A., Jr.
Emerson, William Harry
Epstein, Edna Selan
Erlebacher, Arlene Cernik
Erlich, Barry Arnold
Farrug, Eugene Joseph
Feagley, Michael Rowe
Fedota, Mark Clarke
Ferguson, Stanley Lewis
Finch, Ronald Corydon
Forde, Kevin Michael
Fowle, Frank Fuller
Fowler, Don Wall
Francomb, Lonnie Coleman
Franklin, Randy Wayne
Franklin, Richard Mark
Freehling, Paul Edward
Funderburk, Raymond
Fuson, Douglas Finley
Fylstra, Raymond Alan
Gaffney, Terrence John
Gallagher, Thomas Jordan, Jr.
Garvey, Margaret S.
Gavin, William Patrick
Giampietro, Wayne Bruce
Gibbons, William John
Gifford, Geoffrey L.
Gilbert, Daniel Thomas
Gramlich, Charles J.
Greenough, Walter Croan
Greenspan, Jeffrey Dov
Griffith, D. Kendall
Gundlach, Norman Joseph
Hack, Linda
Hall, Joan M.
Hallock, Robert Wayne
Hamblet, Michael Jon
Hammesfahr, Robert Winter
Hantla, George Bradley
Hardgrove, James Alan
Harper, Steven James
Harris, Donald Ray
Harrold, Bernard
Harvey, Morris Lane
Hay, Peter Heinrich
Hayes, Richard Johnson
Heaton, Joseph Edward, Jr.
Hecht, Frank Thomas
Hegarty, Terrence K.
Heitland, Ann Rae
Hepplewhite, David Wilson
Herald, John Patrick
Herr, Michael Joseph
Hess, Frederick J.
Hoff, William Bruce, Jr.
Hoffman, Alan Craig
Hoover, Russell James
Horsley, Jack Everett
Howard, Timothy John
Howlett, Michael Joseph, Jr.
Hulse, Minard Edwin, Jr.
Hultquist, Robert Charles
Hunter, James Galbraith, Jr.
Hupert, Jeffrey David
Hynes, James Patrick
Jackson, Charles C.
Jordan, Horace William
Kaminsky, Richard Alan
Kapnick, Richard Bradshaw
Kasten, Carl E.
Kathrein, Reed Richard
Katz, Harold Ambrose
Kearns, James Cannon
Keay, David Holm
Keeley, George William
Kell, Vette Eugene
Kennelly, John Jerome
Kimball, Franklyn Davis
Knight, William D., Jr.
Kornichuk, Ellen S.
Koval, Joseph Patrick
Kralovec, Charles Vopicka
Krucks, William Norman
Kuster, Larry Donald
Lane, William Edward
Latshaw, K. Michael
Leech, Michael John
Leopold, Valerie Ann
Lewis, James Brooke
Lieberman, Eugene
Lindenmuth, Noel Charles
Linder, Rex Kenneth
Lindstedt, Norman Edward
Lipton, Mark Daniel
List, David Patton
Livingston, Bradford Lee
Logan, Michael James
Long, Robert Jeffrey
Lousberg, Peter Herman
Mancini, Lorenzo Anthony
Marcus, Richard Leon
Marick, Michael Miron
Marmer, Ronald Louis
Marquard, Henry Francis
Martan, Joseph Rudolf
Mason, Henry Lowell, III
Matchett, Hugh Moore
Mateer, Don Metz
Matushek, Edward J., III
McConnell, James Guy
McCullough, John Thomas
McDonald, Thomas Alexander
McGonegle, Timothy J.
McRae, Donald James
Menges, Eugene Clifford
Miller, Barry Alan
Mohr, Terry Richard
Mone, Peter John
Moore, John L.
Moorehead, Timothy Lucas
Moran, Donald J.
Morsch, Thomas Harvey
Mulack, Donald G.
Mulroy, Thomas Robert, Jr.
Munson, James Calfee
Murphy, William Celestin
Mustain, Douglas Dee
Nicklin, Emily
Nogal, Richard John
Norek, Frances Therese
Nowacki, James Nelson
Oakey, James Leo
O'Brien, Patrick W.
O'Conor, Andrew Joseph, IV
Oglesby, Paul Leonard, Jr.
Oldfield, E. Lawrence
Ozmon, Laird Michael
Pace, O(le) B(ly), Jr.
Palmer, Michael Paul
Palmer, Robert Towne
Parente, James Joseph
Patterson, Robert Bruce, Jr.
Patton, Stephen Ray
Pavalon, Eugene I.
Peck, Kerry Reid
Pelton, Russell Meredith, Jr.
Pelz, Joel Thomas
Perona, Paul Dominic, Jr.
Peterson, Donald George
Phebus, Joseph W.
Phipps, John Tom
Platz, George Arthur, III
Plesko, Jeffrey Michael
Podlewski, Joseph Roman, Jr.
Pope, Daniel James
Prillaman, Frederick Charles
Prochnow, Douglas Lee
Pusch, Herbert Barringer
Raney, Donald Raymond
Rank, John Thomas
Rappaport, Earle Samuel, Jr.
Rawles, Edward Hugh
Record, Richard Franklin, Jr.
Redmond, Richard Anthony
Rein, Eric Steven
Rhode, Shari René
Richard, Douglas Wayne
Richards, Alan Edward
Richmond, William Patrick
Richter, Tobin Marais
Righeimer, Frank S., Jr.
Rindal, Ellen Joan, .
Ring, Leonard M.
Roberts, Keith Edward, Sr.
Robins, Lawrence Richard
Rochelle, Victor Cleanthus
Romanyak, James Andrew
Rose, Dennis Edward
Roustan, Yvon D.
Rudd, Donnie
Rundio, Louis Michael, Jr.
Ruud, Glenn F.
Sale, Edwin Wells
Salomon, Richard Adley
Sanchez, Manuel
Schaefer, Nancy
Schiff, Matthew Bart
Schnack, Kent Richard
Schneider, Earl Gary
Schoumacher, Bruce Herbert
Schroeder, Carl Frederick, Jr.
Schuckit, Robert Jay
Schultz, Allen H.
Schwab, Stephen Wayne
Schwartzberg, Hugh Joel
Seiden, Glenn
Serritella, William David
Sheldon, Harvey M.
Sido, Kevin Richard
Sims, Murray William, Jr.
Sneckenberg, William John
Spears, Ronald Dean
Spina, Anthony Ferdinand
Squires, John Henry
Stanley, Justin Armstrong
Starkman, Gary Lee
Stevens, Douglas Robert
Stitt, LeMoine Donaldson
Stone, Victor J.
Strodel, Robert Carl
Strom, Michael A.
Sullivan, Barry
Tanenbaum, Brian Ira
Tarun, Robert Walter
Terc, Joseph Anthony
Theis, William Harold
Torrey, N. Morrison
Torshen, Jerome Harold
Tozer, Forrest Leigh
Travis, Joan Faye Schiller
Victor, Michael Gary
Vincent, Adrian Roger
Waintroob, Andrea Ruth
Walton, Stanley Anthony, III
Ward, Michael W.
Wascher, James Degen
Weging, James Edwin
Weir, William H.
White, Robert Ellsworth
Wilcox, Mark Dean
Wildman, Max Edward
Winget, Walter Winfield
Witwer, Samuel Weiler, Jr.
Woulfe, Margaret Frances
Wuller, Robert George, Jr.
Zamarin, Ronald George

Indiana

Applegate, Karl Edwin
Bach, Steve Crawford
Bate, Charles Thomas
Becher, Paul Eugene
Belknap, Jerry P.
Bennett, Roger William
Berger, Charles Lee
Berger, Sydney L.
Bishop, Reginald B.
Bodkin, Robert Thomas
Bodle, John Frederick
Bond, Richard Ewing
Borns, Clarence
Braatz, David Edward
Britton, Louis Franklin
Brown, Richard Lawrence
Bunger, Len Edward, Jr
Choplin, John Max, II
Cleveland, Peter Devine
Clouse, John Daniel
Cohen, William J.
Collier-Magar, Kenneth Anthony
Conour, William Frederick
Davis, Ann Gouger
Dieterly, Douglas Kevin
Doehrman, Thomas C.
Drummy, William Wallace, III
Dugan, Michael Thomas, II
Dunsmore, E. Edward
Dywan, Jeffery Joseph
Eggleston, Thomas Warren
Elberger, Ronald Edward
Fairchild, Raymond Francis
Flannery, James Lloyd
Frey, Eric Alan
Fuller, Samuel Ashby
Gerde, Carlyle Noyes (Cy)
Greer, Charles Eugene
Hansell, Ronald Stephen
Harrold, Dennis Edward
Haynie, Gilmore Smith, Jr.
Hays, Thomas Clyde
Henthorn, Charles Rex
Heppenheimer, Harry
Hoffman, John Frederick
Hovde, F. Boyd
Hubbell, Calvin Keith
Jones, David L.
Keen, Robert Thomas, Jr.
King, Douglas Bruce
Koch, Edna Mae
Layden, Charles Max
Lee, William Charles
Leeman, William Kelly
Leopold, Robert Bruce
Levy, Joel C.
Levy, Lawrence Alan
Linnemeier, Philip
Lisher, John Leonard
Loftman, Guy Rickard
McNeely, J. Lee
Montross, W. Scott
Moore, James Dalton
Moss, Kirby Glenn
Muller, John
Muntz, Richard Karl
Murphy, Lester F(uller)
Myers, James Woodrow, III
O'Reilly, Michael James
Palmer, Robert Joseph
Pardieck, Roger L.
Pennell, Stephen Richard
Pope, Mark Andrew
Reinke, William John
Rittner, Kathleen Ardell
Roby, Daniel Arthur
Ruman, Saul I.
Sanders, Carlton Edward
Schreckengast, William O.
Sharpnack, John Trent
Shoulders, Patrick Alan
Shreve, Gene Russell
Skolnik, Bradley William
Smith, Theodore Frederick, Jr.
Springer, Steve Edward
Stalmack, Joseph
Steger, Evan Evans
Stein, Eleanor Bankoff
Stommel, R. Robert
Taylor, Brent Douglas
Thompson, Kerry Lewis
Tolbert, Frank Edward
Townsend, Earl Cunningham, Jr.
Van Bokkelen, Joseph Scott
Van Valer, Joe Ned
Waddick, William Anthony
Wellnitz, Craig Otto
Wickland, David Edwin
Wicks, Charles Carter
Williams, Stephen Lee
Witte, Gordon Michael
Wray, Donn Hayes
Yosha, Louis Buddy
Young, Thomas Jordan

Iowa

Baybayan, Ronald Alan
Beisser, Louie Frederick
Belin, David William
Berry, Jan Vance
Blackburn, Milford Gene
Brown, William Ted
Burns, James
Clogg, Richard Bruce
Conlin, Roxanne Barton
Critelli, Lylea May Dodson
Crook, Charles Samuel, III
Davis, James Casey
Davison, George Frederick, Jr.
Ditmars, Lyle William
Doyle, Richard Henry, IV
Eastman, Forest David
Eckhart, Morris Lee Roy
Eidsmoe, Robert Russell
Ellefson, James C.
Farr, Thomas Carey
Fitzgibbons, Ann
Foxhoven, Jerry Ray
Frederici, C. Carleton
Gibb, William Stewart
Gidel, David Dale
Grace, David Joseph
Hammer, David Lindley
Hileman, Richard Glenn, Jr.
Hoffman, James Paul
Hutchison, Robert Alan
Johnson, Robert Steven
Joyce, Joseph Benedict
Karr, Lloyd
Kelly, Edwin Frost
Kersten, Donald Norbert
Klemesrud, Normand Charles
Koehn, William James
Langdon, Richard Garrett
Lathrop, Roger Alan
Lawyer, Verne
Lemanski, David Alan
Liabo, Mark Elliot
Logan, Thomas Joseph
Lounsberry, Harold Claire
Lyford, F. Richard
Malm, Richard Allan
Manly, Charles M., III
McCoy, John Thomas
McKay, Timothy John
McNeil, Jean Anne
Monson, Terry Lewis
Mueller, Barry Scott
Mull, Richard Eugene
Mullins, Michael Royce
Murray, William Michael (Mike)
Noyes, Michael Lance
Quinn, Kirke Craven
Reilly, Michael Gerard
Rhodes, Keith Stewart
Samuelson, Jacqueline K.
Sanders, Doyle Dee
Scism, Robert Bruce
Spies, Leon Fred
Taylor, Wallace L.
Tompkins, Richard Norton, Jr.
Tully, Robert Gerard
Walker, Bruce LeRoy
Walker, E. Ralph
Warbasse, Steven Kenneth
Wharton, John Michael
Wine, Donald Arthur
Wolle, Charles Robert
Zoss, Paul Arthur

Kansas

Adrian, Robert Mac
Badgerow, John Nicholas
Black, John Victor
Boyle, Edward Michael
Concannon, Don Owen
Davis, Charles Leroy
Delhotal, Van Russell
Erickson, George Everett, Jr.
Gard, Spencer Agassiz
Grace, Brian Guiles
Gross, Edmund Samuel
Hamilton, John Richard
Harbur, Nathan Clayton
Hathaway, Gary Ray
Helbert, Michael Clinton
Herrington, Alvin D.
Hodgson, Arthur Clay
Justus, Jo Lynne
Keplinger, (Donald) Bruce
King, Clarence LeRoy, Jr.
Krusor, Mark William
Lasater, Thomas John
Marshall, Herbert A.
Matlack, Don(ald) (Clyde)
Metzger, Alan Glen
Mitchell, Alexander Baldwin
Nelson, Bryan Eugene
Nygaard, Diane Acker
Ochs, Robert Duane
O'Neal, Michael Ralph
Pierce, Ricklin Ray
Rogers, Terry Lee
Ruse, Steven Douglas
Schroer, Gene Eldon
Sears, Ruth Ann
Short, Timothy Allen
Shull, William Edgar, Jr.
Smithyman, Lee Miller
Solon, James Davis
Stanton, Roger D.
Sullivan, Thomas Eugene
Toepfer, Thomas Lyle
Turner, H. Lee
Walton, Herbert Wilson
Woolf, John Paul

Kentucky

Adams, Wesley Price, Jr.
Bailey, Ann Leslie
Barrickman, Uhel Overton
Bensinger, Carl Joseph
Bishop, Robert Whitsitt
Brandon, Douglas Colliver
Brill, David Alan
Brown, Bonnie Maryetta
Budden, Harry Edward, Jr.
Carroll, Thomas Charles
Chauvin, Leonard Stanley, Jr.
Choate, Dennis Jeffrey
Connolly, Robert Michael
Cowan, Frederic Joseph, Jr.
Davis, Russell H.
Dolt, Frederick Corrance
Dowell, Douglas Melvin
Ely, Hiram, III
Ethridge, Larry Clayton
Greene, James S., Jr.
Guier, Lester Bennett
Hanbury, John Iruine
Herren, Thomas Kelly
Ison, Robert Elwood
Kerr, Thomas Robert
King, Nicholas Neal
Masters, Richard L.
Mathison, Harry Lee
Miller, Carl Theodore
Miller, Edward Douglas
Mulloy, William Patrick, II
Nelson, Richard S.
Ogden, Len Willis, Jr.
Parker, William Jerry
Perkinson, Maurice Leon
Pitt, Dorothy Moore
Powell, Karen Ann Pitts
Prather, John Gideon, Jr.
Ratterman, David Burger
Rawdon, Richard McLean, Jr.
Reinhardt, Roxane Tomasi
Ridings, Marcia Milby
Roark, Jimmy Lee
Robinson, William T., III
Rudloff, William J.
Schoenbaechler, Edward Lewis
Seiller, Bill Victor
Sexton, David Andrew
Shuffett, James Avery
Sitlinger, Leroy Edward, Jr.
Smither, J. Michael
Spalding, Michael Fredrick
Stallings, Robert George
Stopher, Robert Estes
Sullivan, Richard Morrissey
Thomas, Patricia Ann
Todd, James Marion
Turley, Robert Joe
Varellas, James John, Jr.
Weldon, C. Michael
Wilborn, Woody Stephen
Wolnitzek, Stephen Dale

Louisiana

Adams, Ellis Paul, Jr.
Alsobrook, Henry Bernis, Jr.
Andersson, W. Paul
Angelle, Robert
Anzelmo, Donald Joseph
Aucoin, Barney R.
Barry, Michael Francis
Baudier, Adelaide
Benson, Lawrence Kern, Jr.
Bezet, Gary Anthony
Blackman, Gordon N., Jr.
Bringle, William Timothy
Brunson, Hugh Ellis
Buckley, Samuel Olliphant, III
Butcher, Bruce Cameron
Capritto, Anthony Joseph
Cavell, Daniel A.
Centola, Lawrence Joseph
Cheatwood, Roy Clifton
Cheramie, Carlton Joseph
Clement, Leslie Joseph, Jr.
Cole, Luther Francis
Connolly, George Charles, Jr.
Daigle, Patrick Keith
Darden, Marshall Taylor
Davis, S. P.
Davis, Sumpter B., III
Dearie, Harold Emmanuel, II
Didriksen, Caleb H., III
Dodd, Lawrence Roe
Dugas, David Roy
Dwyer, Ralph Daniel, Jr.
Eatman, Robert Emerson
Ensenat, Donald Burnham
Flick, Sheila Ann
Gandy, Kim Allison
Garcia, Patricia A.
Gauthier, Wendell Haynes
Gertler, Meyer H.
Giepert, Melvin John
Godofsky, Harvey Joseph
Gouaux, Eugene Godfrey
Granier, Kirk Raymond
Grundmeyer, Douglas Lanaux
Guidry, Hervin A.
Guilliot, Paul Jerome
Hanemann, James, Jr.
Haygood, John Warren
Henican, Caswell Ellis
Herman, Russ Michel
Hoskins, David LeRoy
Johnson, Patrick, Jr.
Jones, Keith Dunn
Kiefer, John B.
Kleinpeter, Robert Loren
Knutzen, Raymond Edward
Kuhn, James E.
Lamonica, P(aul) Raymond
Lane, Steven Jay

Looney, James Holland
Manard, Robert Lynn, III
McCall, Harry
McClelland, James Ray
McGlinchey, Dermot Sheehan
McGovern, Glenn Charles
McManus, Clarence Elburn
McMichael, James David
Milligan, Edward Joseph, Jr.
Ortique, Revius Oliver, Jr.
Ponder, L(eslie) Barbee, M
Porter IV, Thomas Fitzgerald
Provosty, LeDoux Roger, Jr.
Rigby, Kenneth
Riley, Mark Louis
Roddy, Virginia Niehaus
Rosen, William Warren
Ryan, James, III
Saloom, Kaliste Joseph, Jr.
Scott, L. Havard, III
Shields, Lloyd Noble
Showers, Jack Paul
Simmons, Kermit Mixon
Singletary, Alvin D.
Smith, Charles Sterling
Smith, J. Arthur, III
Stockwell, Oliver Perkins
Thibaut, Joseph H. Major
Thomas, Gerard Frances
Thomas, Joseph Winand
Todaro, Laura Jean
Treeby, William David
Tritico, Russell Thomas
Veron, J. Michael
White, Clair Fox
Whitney, John Franklin
Widmann, Harry Thomas
Wilson, Donald Russell
Wright, William Everar, Jr.

Maine

Ballou, John Waldo
Bohan, Thomas Lynch
Burke, Edmund James
Crawford, Linda Sibery
Dyer, Matthew Finis
Hartwell, Jane Barry
Harvey, Charles Albert, Jr.
Hewes, Richard David
Hirshon, Robert Edward
Horton, Andrew Marcus
Hunt, Merrill Roberts
Johnson, Phillip Edward
Lanham, Samuel Wilbur, Jr.
Martin, Joel Clark
Mills, Sumner Peter, III
Moriarty, James Paul
Moss, Logan Vansen
Nichols, David Arthur
Poe, Franklin Andrew
Reef, Norman Sidney
Romanow, Richard Brian
Rundlett, Ellsworth Turner, III
Stone, Alan G.
Washburn, Robert Michael
Willard, William Wells

Maryland

Appel, Thomas Alan
Ayres, Jeffrey Peabody
Badger, Jeffrey Ewen
Barkley, Brian Evan
Berkson, Jacob Benjamin
Berman, Michael David
Bonner, Leonard John
Boone, Harold Thomas
Braun, Stephen John
Bresnahan, Pamela Anne
Burke, Raymond Daniel
Carney, Bradford George Yost
Clarke, William Anthony Lee, III
Comeau, Michael Gerard
Crowe, Thomas Leonard
Digges, Edward S(imms), Jr.
Dorsey, Charles Henry, Jr.
Fick, Nathaniel Crow, Jr.
Field, Samuel Summers, III
Foster, Philip Carey
Fry, Donald Curtis
Golomb, George Edwin
Grattan, S. Amy
Haldeman, George Paul
Hanley, Robert Lee, Jr.
Hansen, Christopher Agnew
Hare, Glenn Patrick
Harwick, Robert Dean, Jr.
Hennegan, John Owen
Henry, Edwin Maurice, Jr.
Hesson, William M., Jr.
Hicks, Cassandra Pauline
Hill, Milton King, Jr.
Howell, Harley Thomas
Hughes, Leo A., Jr.
Joseph, Fredric Robert
Katz, Stanley Herbert
Kayson, David
King, John Frances
Kirchman, Charles Vincent
Kleid, Wallace
Klein, Gerald S.
Kramer, Paul R.
Kuryk, David Neal
Lechter, Kenneth Alan
Little, William Scott
Loker, F(rank) Ford, Jr.
Matty, Robert Jay
Mix, George Warren
Monahan, John Connolly
Moorhead, James Barr
Morrow, Thomas Campbell
Naditch, Ronald Marvin
Nagle, John Joseph, III
O'Brien, Dennis Francis
Olszewski, Kevin Trent
Orman, Leonard Arnold
Pappas, George Frank
Pensinger, John Lynn
Perkins, Roger Allan
Porter, James Harry, Jr.
Powell, Michael Calvin
Price, Charles U.
Proctor, Kenneth Donald
Radding, Andrew
Reid, Richard Ayres
Rensin, Howard M.
Rochlin, Paul R.
Ruppersberger, Charles Albert, III
Santa Maria, Philip Joseph, III
Schatzow, Michael
Schochor, Jonathan
Shannonhouse, Royal Graham, III
Shar, Marcus Z.
Shepard, Adam Hoffman
Shore, Elbert Russell
Smith, Jonathan Scott
Smouse, H(ervey) Russell
Snyder, William Arthur, Jr.
Souder, Susan
Strandberg, Rebecca Newman
Sweeney, Eileen Cecilia
Taylor, Dane Edward
Tyler, Ralph Sargent, III
Uehlinger, Gerard Paul
Van Grack, Steven
Vaughan, James Joseph Michael
Wallace, Sean Daniel
Weltchek, Robert Jay
Whaley, Joseph Randall
Wimbrow, Peter Ayers, III

Massachusetts

Abraham, Nicholas Albert
Andrews, David Joseph
Apjohn, Nelson George
Bailey, Frank Joseph, Jr.
Bennett, Richard Edward
Berliner, L. Jed
Berman, David
Bolton, Warren Robert
Cabral, Bernardo Joseph
Campbell, Richard P.
Carpenter, Robert Brent
Carter, Paul Stanley
Cheek, Jo Frances
Cherny, David Edward
Chyten, Edwin Richard
Cleary, Philip Edward
Cohen, Donna Eden
Costello, Walter Anthony, Jr.
Curley, Robert Ambrose, Jr.
Cusick, Elizabeth Emma
Dahlen, Richard Lester
Davis, Christopher Patrick
Devlin, Paul Anthony
Dillon, James Joseph
Doherty, Joseph Leo, Jr.
Donahue, Michael Christopher
Donahue, Richard King
Doniger, Anthony M.
Estrine, Andrew Bradley
Felter, John Kenneth
Fillon, Richard
Finn, Marvin Ruven
Fitzpatrick, Lawrence Scott
Fox, Francis Haney
Frieden, James Anthony
Friedman, Michael Phillip
Friedmann, Jonathon David
Furman, Mark Steven
Gad, Robert K., III
Garabedian, Charles Bagdasar
Geiger, David R.
Gelb, Richard Mark
Gens, Richard Howard
Gibson, Daniel Peter
Gilmore, John Allen Dehn
Glovsky, Susan G. L.
Gordon, Stephen Jacob
Greco, Michael S.
Griffin, J. Kenneth
Gross, Susan Larky
Halstrom, Frederic Norman
Herrick, Stewart Thurston
Hoefling, Virginia Ann
Houlihan, F(rancis) Robert, Jr.
Howard, Gregory Charles
Howland, Richard Moulton
Hunt, William John
Hutton, Albert Lee, Jr.
Jackson, Donald H(erbert), Jr.
Kaplan, David Richard
Kavanaugh, James Francis, Jr.
Keeton, Robert Ernest
Keough, Paul Gerard
Klyman, Andrew Michael
Knight, Peter Carter
Kociubes, Joseph Leib
Krasnoo, James B.
Kream, Deborah
Krulewich, Leonard M.
Kuzinevich, John Jacob
Lacek, Michael Joseph
Lamson, David Hinkley
Lee, David Harold
Legasey, John Samuel
Licata, Arthur Frank
Long, Christopher Francis
Looney, William Francis, Jr.
Lovins, Nelson Preston
Madan, Anil
Margolis, Jonathan J.
Marnik, Michael Peter
McNamara, Frank Luke, Jr.
Mercer, Richard James
Messing, Arnold Philip
Meyer, Andrew C., Jr.
Michelson, Mark A.
Miles, Harry Lehman
Monahan, Marie Terry
Murray, Robert Fox
Newton, Francis Chandler, Jr.
Owens, Henry Freeman, III
Packenham, Richard Daniel
Perry, Edward Needham
Peterson, Osler Leopold
Pierce, John Robert
Polk, Victor H., Jr.
Rich, Christopher Charles
Rosenthal, Gerald Allen
Savrann, Richard Allen
Schafer, Steven Harris
Schwartz, William
Scott, David Oscar
Segal, Terry Philip
Semerjian, Evan Yervant
Sherman, Elliot Mark
Simonds, Marshall
Starrett, Loyd Milford
Traficanti, Tina Michele
Trimmier, Roscoe, Jr.
Urquhart, Stephen E.
Vincent, Thomas Philip
Waxler, David Harvey
Weidman, Charles Ray
Weinstein, Lewis H.
Weinstein, Seymour
Wexler, Barbara Lynne
Wilson, Paul Dennis
Witt, Carol Ann
Woolf, Jeffrey David
Zandrow, Leonard Florian

Michigan

Alber, Phillip George
Amsden, Ted Thomas
Andreoff, Christopher Andon
Baker, Frederick Milton, Jr.
Battle, Leonard Carroll
Batzer, James Martin
Baxter, Richard Brian
Bereznoff, Gregory Michael
Berry, Steven Craig
Bishop, Lawrence Ray
Blaske, E. Robert
Blum, Irving Ronald
Brady, Edmund Matthew, Jr.
Bransdorfer, Stephen Christie
Bregman, Judy Ellen
Brooks, Keefe Alan
Browning, Charles W.
Buchanan, John Cowan
Buchanan, William D.
Bushnell, George Edward, Jr.
Byrne, Joseph Ahern, Jr.
Campos, David Nelson
Carney, Donald F., Jr.
Caswell, Roger Lee
Centner, Charles William
Christopher, William Garth
Churchill, David James
Clark, Mark Lee
Cloon, William Graham, Jr.
Cooper, David John
Cothorn, John Arthur
Dahm, Peter Franklin
Darling, Robert Howard
Deats, Paul Edwin
Decker, Harold James
Drummond, Donald Francis
Elsman, James Leonard, Jr.
Farrell, John Brendan
Feringa, Scott Douglas
Fillion, Thomas John
Filoramo, John Robert
Fisher, Edward Walter
Foley, Stephen Bernard
Fortino, Alfred J.
Fosmire, Michael Sean
Franklin, Bruce Walter
Geary, James H.
Gilbert, Ronald Rhea
Gillespie, William Tyrone
Gleiss, Henry Weston
Gofrank, Catherine Ann
Googasian, George Ara
Gorland, Scott Lance
Grate, Marshall Warren
Greve, Guy Robert
Gunderson, Michael Arthur
Gustafson, Richard B.
Haisch, Anthony Albert
Haliw, Andrew Jerome, III
Harris, Patricia Skalny
Hausner, John Herman
Hay, Thomas Harold
Hayes, Kenneth Thomas
Heldt, Jeffrey Alan
Hines, Paul William
Holley, Audrey Rodgers
Hood, Harold
Johnson, Donald Edward, Jr.
Jordan, Glenn Erval
Jordan, Michael Jay
Joseph, Raymond
Kaplan, Steven Marc
Kendricks, George Thomas
King, Thomas George
Koernke, Thomas Frederick
Koop, Charles Hubert
Kopit, Jonathan Throne
Kruse, John Alphonse
Latovick, Paula R(ae)
Lebow, Michael Jeffrey
Lehto, Neil John
Lilly, Terence Joseph
Longhofer, Ronald Stephen
Lopatin, Albert
Lubben, Craig Henry
Marcoux, William Joseph
Marvin, David Edward Shreve
Maxwell, Robert Alexander
May, Alan Alfred
McDevitt, Mary Elizabeth
McDonald, Daryl Patrick
McGarry, Alexander Banting
McGlory, Willie Edward
McGraw, Patrick John
Miela, Deborah Lynn
Mies, James Edward
Miller, Sheldon Lee
Moch, Joseph William
Morganroth, Mayer
Mosher, Richard Underhill
Mossner, Eugene Donald
Murray, Gregory Vincent
Nichols, Charles Leonard
Nizio, Frank
Norris, John Hart
Novak, Michael Alan
O'Brien, Darlene Anne
Oltarz-Schwartz, Sara
Ortega, Cynthia Poti
Ortman, William Andrew, Sr.
Palmieri, Angela
Pappas, Edward Harvey
Parish, Tat
Parker, Dona Scott
Parker, Patric Allan
Payton, Donald Lee
Pierson, William George
Plaszczak, Roman Thaddeus
Platzer, Cynthia Siemen
Potter, George Ernest
Provenzano, Vincent
Pylman, Norman Herbert, II
Raniszeski, Lawrence Frank
Rauss, Dennis Michael
Rhodes, Vincent Ard
Ring, Ronald Herman
Robb, Dean Allan
Rosi, Philip Rinaldo
Rowe, Jack Douglas
Roy, William Alan
Saylor, Larry James
Schefman, Leslie Craig
Schloss, Lawrence James
Schroer, J. Michael
Schrot, John Joseph, Jr.
Scott, Rosemary
Secrest, Stephen Frederick
Shillman, Jeffrey Nathaniel
Sills, John Dennis
Smietanka, John Allen
Smith, Arthur Allan
Snyder, George Edward
Soet, Henry David
Souter, Don Vern
Spreitzer, John Richard
Steiner, Sanford Lee
Stella, Daniel Francis
Stevens, Gerald M.
Sumpter, Jerry Lee
Szymanski, Frank S(tanislaus), Jr.
Tallerico, Thomas Joseph
Thurswell, Gerald Elliott
Tickner, Ellen Mindy
Turner, Lester Nathan
Van Allsburg, Jon Aaron
Vander Ark, Steven John
VanderLaan, Robert D.
Van Leuven, Robert Joseph
Vocht, Michelle Elise
Walker, Jonathan Lee
Ward, Paul Anthony
Warren, John Philip, Jr.
Warren, William Gerald
Washington, Valdemar Luther
Webster, Robert Byron
Weinstein, William Joseph
Wienner, S. Thomas
Wilhelm, Thomas Vincent
Williams, James Joseph
Wilson, Martin Bryant
Winsten, I.W.
Wittlinger, Timothy David
Woodworth, James Nelson
Yockey, Kurt David
Young, Rodger Douglas
Zameck, Harvey Jason
Zimmerman, Norman

Minnesota

Allgeyer, David Alan
Balmer, James W.
Bard, Stephen Allan
Beens, Richard Albert
Bennett, Robert
Berg, Nancy Zalusky
Brosnahan, Roger Paul
Bruner, Philip Lane
Brutlag, Michael Lowell
Bujold, Tyrone Patrick
Bulinski, Gregory Paul
Ciresi, Michael Vincent
Colacci, Irving Roger
Collins, Theodore Joseph
Dalager, Jon Karl
Delano, Stephen James
Devney, John Leo
Dosland, Chester Allen
Eisenberg, Jonathan Lee
Ekstrum, B. William
Finch, Frederick Earl
Finzen, Bruce Arthur
Florence, Dorothy M.
Fossum, Lee Leif
Frauenshuh, Ronald Ray, Sr.
Geck, Donna Dunkelberger
Gislason, Daniel Adam
Gordon, John Bennett
Guthmann, John Howard
Hagglund, Clarance Edward
Hanson, Bruce Eugene
Hanson, Kent Bryan
Hanson, Steven Allen
Hottinger, John Creighton
Hull, Daniel Louis
Hunter, Donald Forrest
Johnson, Dennis Robert
Johnson, Donald E.
Johnson, Richard Walter
Jones, Bradley Mitchell
Karan, Bradlee
Keenan, Kevin Patrick
Kempf, Douglas Paul
Keyes, Leonard John
LaChapelle, Arthur William
Lazar, Raymond Michael
Lindberg, Michael Charles
Mansfield, Seymour J.
Marquart, Steven Leonard
Masica, Mark Alexis
Maus, Robert Michael
McKenna, David William
McReynolds, Michael Patrick
Miller, Keith Lloyd
Mills, Anthony Belden
Nelson, Peggy Ann
Nelson, Susan Richard
Nettles, Alan Ross
O'Leary, Daniel Brian
O'Neill, Joseph Thomas
Pagliaccetti, Gary John
Pederson, Steven Marc
Pentelovitch, Willian Zane
Peterson, William George
Radtke, Stephen David
Rasicot, James Frederick
Reite, Charles Douglas
Remele, Lewis Albert, Jr.
Reuter, James William
Rowlette, Roger Lee
Saeks, Allen Irving
Sand, David Byron
Sayers, Randall William
Scherer, Richard Sigmund
Seykora, David Gerard
Shaw, A. Reid
Short, Marianne Dolores
Shroyer, Thomas Jerome
Skaar, Harvey Engaard
Sokol, Michael Bruce
Tanick, Marshall Howard
Theis, Linda Jane
Thibodeau, Thomas Raymond
Timmer, Steven James
Timmons, Peter John
Tourek, Steven Charles
Trojack, John Edward
Wade, James Alan
Wahl, Karla Rae
Wahoske, Michael James
Weiner, Michael Lewis
Willemssen, Mac Ronald
Wine, Mark Philip
Zotaley, Byron L.

Mississippi

Abbott, William W., Jr.
Barton, William Harvey
Brown, William Houston
Bullock, Jim
Chapman, John Wendell
Currie, Edward Jones, Jr.
Denham, Earl Lamar
Dent, George E.
Fondren, Louis
Goodman, William Flournoy, III
Grower, John Marshall
Hannan, Edwin York
Hatcher, John Leslie
Hopkins, Alben Norris
Howell, Joel Walter, III
King, Robert Wilson
Lancaster, William Robert
Martin, George Gilmore
Montjoy, Richard Wilson, II
Morrison, Harvey Lee, Jr.
Olack, Neil Peter
Perry, Lee Nace
Powell, Roy Durward
Pyle, Luther Arnold
Robertshaw, James
Smith, James Edwin, Jr.
Sumners, Lester Furr
Webb, Thomas Lowry
Wise, Joseph Powell

Missouri

Adams, Philip James, Jr.
Aylward, Timothy Michael
Bartlett, Alex
Bay, William Robert
Beckett, Theodore Charles
Berendt, Robert T.
Berrey, Robert Wilson, III
Bevan, Kent Morgan
Blakeslee, Julia Fay
Braun, N. Barrett
Breen, Jean Marie
Bronsky, A.J.
Brown, Paul Sherman
Burns, Mark Gardner
Chassaing, J. Patrick
Claggett, Daniel Elliot
Clarke, Milton Charles
Cole, James Silas, Jr.
Collins, James Slade, II
Conran, Joseph Palmer
Coughlin, Richard Edward
Cronan, John Michael
DeCuyper, Joseph Ysidore
Dempsey, David Gerard
Derque, Joseph Alexander, III
Devine, James Richard
DeWoskin, Alan Ellis
Dickhaner, Raymond Henry
Douglas, Kerry DeLisle
Drakesmith, Frederick William
Fleddermann, Stephen Roy
Fox, Byron Neal
Gamm, Gordon Julius
Gisler, George Louis
Greiman, Gerald Phillip
Grimm, Stanley Arnold
Growe, Gary Alan
Gunn, Michael Peter
Hart, Michael David
Higgins, Stephen Boyd
Horgan, John Joseph
Hubbell, Ernest
Hullverson, James Everett, Jr.
Humphrey, James William, Jr.
Johnson, Harold Gene
Johnson, Mark Eugene
Kennedy, Walter Jeff, Jr.
Kilroy, John Muir
King, William Robert, II
Kohn, Alan Charles
Kortenhof, Joseph Michael
Kranitz, Theodore Mitchell
Kuenzel, Steven Paul
Lolli, Don R(ay)
Lorenz, Jack Chapin
Lysaught, Patrick
Martucci, William Christopher
McCalpin, Francis William
McDonald, William Henry
Mello, Susan H.
Michener, John Athol
Moore, Mitchell Jay
Mueller, Joseph Henry
Murphy, Edward Elias, Jr.
Newman, Charles A.
Nichols, Stephen Wayne
Noel, Edwin Lawrence
Nordyke, Stephen Keith
Oliver, David Field
Oliver, John Leachman
Owens, Dennis James Campbell
Parrish, John Edward
Pierce, Donald Victor Jr.
Popham, Arthur Cobb, Jr.
Proctor, George Edwin, Jr.
Quitmeier, William Michael
Raack, William James
Rabbitt, Daniel Thomas, Jr.
Reed, David Q.
Reeg, Kurtis Bradford
Remley, David Mark
Reynolds, Jerry Lee
Rice, Canice Timothy, Jr.
Ritter, Robert Forcier
Roberts, Patrick Kent
Roskin, Preston Eugene
Rush, Douglas Kevin
Ryder, Bruce David
Sableman, Mark Stephen
Sands, Darry Gene
Schermerhorn, Sandra Leigh
Schult, Thomas Peter
Schwabe, John Bennett, II
Schwartz, Theodore Frank
Scott, Robert Gene
Scott, Stephen Charles
Sestric, Anthony James
Shapiro, Alvin Dale
Sher, Richard Philip

Sherman, Joseph Allen
Sneeringer, Stephen Geddes
Sowers, David Eric
Spalty, Edward
Sparks, Billy Schley
Standridge, Richard E.
Steimel, Norman Clemens, III
Stribling, Gray Carroll, Jr.
Strong, Thomas Gorman
Sugg, Reed Waller
Susman, Robert M.
Tatlow, Gary Arthur
Terando, G.H.
Terry, Jack Chatterson
Thompson, Michael
Toppins, Roger Keith
Tremayne, Eric Flory
Tucker, James Delzell
Turley, J. William
Ver Dught, ElGene Clark
Vering, John Albert
Wade, Daniel Ples
Waldron, Kenneth Lynn
Wallace, Barbara Wendy
Walsh, Thomas Joseph
Weber, Louis Jerry
Webster, William Lawrence
Weedman, Charles Edward, Jr.
Wheeler, James Julian
Wherritt, Alan Francisco
White, David William
Willenbrock, Ronald Christopher
Wirken, James Charles
Wolf, Jerome Thomas
Woody, Donald Eugene

Montana

Alke, John
Bauer, Mark Eugene
Beiswanger, Gary Lee
Best, George Bullock, Jr.
Crowe, Gary Allen
Dalthorp, George Carrol
Graveley, Charles Allan
Harrington, James Patrick
Hopgood, Tom Kolstad
Jardine, John Hawley
Johnson, Margaret Mary Joyce
Lerner, Alan Jay
Matteucci, Sherry Scheel
McKeon, John Carl
Mitchell, Jayne Francis
Morrison, Frank Brenner, Jr.
Morrison, Sharon McDonald
Mouat, William Gavin
Nye, Jerrold Linden
Parker, Mark David
Pedersen, Lance Alden
Sheehy, Edmund Francis, Jr.
Spaeth, Gary Lewis
Thompson, Theodore Kvale
Trieweiler, Terry Nicholas

Nebraska

Atwood, Raymond Percival, Jr.
Bartle, Robert Franklin
Baumann, Larry R(oger)
Bradford, Charles Steven
Busick, Denzel Rex
Colleran, Kevin
Cuypers, Charles James
Dahlk, Thomas Harlan
Domina, David Alan
Dwyer, Robert Vincent, Jr.
Gordon, James Edward
Inserra, John Phillip
Kratz, Paul David
Lee, Dennis Patrick
Pfeiffer, William Edward
Pohren, Edward Francis
Rossiter, Robert Francis, Jr.
Swihart, Fred Jacob
Urbom, Randall Crawford
Walsh, Thomas John
Warin, Edward George
Wence, Gary Fred
Widtfeldt, James Albert
Wilke, John William

Nevada

Barkley, Thierry Vincent
Bell, Robert Cecil
Carter, George Richard
Cavin, Rhonda Lynn
Cornell, Richard Farnham
Dorsey, Robert Knickerbocker
Galliher, Keith Edwin, Jr.
Giordano, Paul Gregory
Guild, Clark Joseph, Jr.
Harding, Samuel Arlon
Hibbs, Loyal Robert
Jimmerson, James Joseph
Kirkman, Robert Akeridge, Jr.
Koch, Jan Paul
Kravitz, Martin Jay
Maglaras, Chris, Jr.
Murphy, Patrick James
Nelson, Jane Wandel
O'Brien, Daniel Louis
Pagni, Albert Frank
Pearson, Niels L.
Perry, Victor Alan
Pinkerton, C(harles) Frederick
Shaffer, Wayne Alan
Smith, Stephanie Marie
Sourwine, Julien Gillen
Terzich, Milos
Wedge, Virgil Henry
Wenzel, Steve Edwin
White, John Aaron, Jr.
Wicker, Walter Chris
Willick, Marshal Shawn
Zive, Gregg William
Zubel, Eric Louis

New Hampshire

Brown, Kenneth Mackinnon
Brown, Stanley Melvin
Conboy, Carol Ann
Damon, Claudia Cords
Danenbarger, W. Wright
Engel, David Chapin
Gagliuso, Richard Caron
Garod, Harvey Jay
Gottesman, David Mark
Griffin, John Francis, Jr.
Hanna, Katherine Merritt
Harkaway, Aaron Abraham
Johnson, Robert Veiling, II
Keefe, William John
Kitchen, John Scott
McNamara, Richard Bedle
Parnell, William Basil
Shaines, Robert Arthur
Thornton, Edward Robert, Jr.
Tober, Stephen Lloyd
Wiebusch, Richard Vernon

New Jersey

Abut, Charles C.
Alexander, Robert Louis
Amadeo, Natial Salvatore
Ascione, Joseph Anthony
Barnes, Timothy Lee
Bergamo, Charles
Biel, Mark
Bielory, Abraham M.
Biribin, Renato Raymond
Brecher, Stuart Gary
Breslin, John Joseph, III
Cerny, Edward Charles, III
Chappell, Thomas Tye
Chiumento, Gary C.
Cino, Vincent Alphonse
Clemen, John Douglas
Cohen, Barry David
Cohn, Albert Linn
Colaguori, Louis Albert
Cole, Larry Michael
Collins, James Francis
Connell, William Terrence
Cooper, Richard Craig
Curran, Catherine Moore
D'Alessandro, Daniel Anthony
DeRose, James Dominic
Deutsch, Dennis Stuart
Dienst, Gerald A.
Doherty, Robert Christopher
Dughi, Louis John, Jr.
Eder, Todd Brandon
Egan, Robert T.
Epstein, Barry David
Estis, Dennis Arnold
Farr, Linus Gilbert
Feinberg, Jack
Ferreri, Vito Richard
Fisch, Joseph
Fischer, Jay David
Flammer, George Herbert
Ford, John R.
Friedman, Richard Lloyd
Garrigle, William Aloysius
Gogo, Gregory
Gordon, Harrison J.
Gordon, Michael
Greco, Joseph Dominic, Jr.
Greenberg, Steven Morey
Haberbusch, Carl Arthur
Halpern, Samuel Joseph
Hansbury, Stephan Charles
Harbeson, Robert G.
Harrison, Charles Maurice
Haskins, Guy Halifax, Jr.
Hersh, Alvin David
Hewit, Russell Lyle
Honig, Emanuel Aaron
Hopkins, Charles Peter, II
Horan, John Donohoe
Hornstine, Louis Fox
Horton, William Harrison
Humick, Thomas Charles Campbell
Jacobs, Andrew Robert
Johnstone, Irvine Blakeley, III
Kallmann, Stanley Walter
Kantowitz, Jeffrey Leon
Kaps, Warren Joseph
Kiel, Paul Edward
Klein, Paul Ira
Klock, John Henry
Knoblauch, Leo N.
Kondracki, Edward Anthony
Korin, Joel Benjamin
Kott, David Russell
Kruttschnitt, Herbert, III
Kuttner, Bernard A.
Landman, Eric Christopher
Lavigne, Lawrence Neil
Lind, Peter Eugene
Livingston, Richard B.
Luthman, David Andrew
Manshel, Max
Maran, Joe
Markwardt, John James
McClear, Nicholas Willard
McDonnell, Richard C.
McDonough, Joseph Richard
McGuire, William B(enedict)
McMahon, Edward Richard
Medvin, Alan York
Miller, Arthur Harold
Milton, Gabriel
Mintz, Jeffry Alan
Molloy, Brian Joseph
Montana, Janice
Moore, Thomas Michael
Moorman, Elliott Duane
Morgenstern, Robert Terence
Morris, Larry Dean
Mulligan, Elinor Patterson
Muscato, Andrew
Naar, Alan S.
Neibart, Ralph
O'Connell, Hans James
O'Leary, Richard Patrick
O'Neill, Joseph Dean
Ozer, Lisa Goldberg
Palma, Nicholas James
Pearlman, Peter Steven
Peck, James Irving, IV
Peckar, Robert S.
Pentony, Kenneth Richard
Platkin, Lawrence Peter
Polansky, Steven Jay
Pollinger, William Joshua
Portelli, Thomas Frank
Porzio, Ralph
Poyourow, Robert Lee
Puffer, Leonard Bruce, Jr.
Rabinowitz, Daniel Lawrence
Reid, Charles Adams, III
Reiken, Samuel N.
Risinger, D. Michael
Robertson, William Withers
Rockwell, Mark Paul
Rodriguez, Ariel Antonio
Rogers, Matthew Stephen
Rosen, Howard Theodore
Rosenhouse, Nathan
Rowe, Paul Andrew
Samay, Z. Lance
Santoli, Joseph Ralph
Schachter, Richard J.
Schenkler, Bernard
Schwartz, David Elving
Schwartz, Edward Richard
Shackleton, Richard James
Silver, Cole Brian
Simon, David Robert
Slavitt, Ben J.
Smith, Hayden, Jr.
Smith, Peter John
Sosland, Karl Z.
Sponzilli, Edward George
Steedle, Roger Craig
Stern, John Jules
Sterns, Joel H.
Strashun, Jeffrey Marc
Strasser, William Ignatius
Sullivan, Eugene John
Teicher, Martin
Telsey, Norman
Tepper, Alan Michael
Tice, Richard Leveridge
Tinari, Anthony Philip
Tomar, William
Trombadore, Raymond Robert
Veenstra, Yves Cornell
Vena, Joseph Anthony
Ventantonio, James Bartholomew
Vinick, Philip Brod
Warnement, Pamela Pearson
Warren, Lisbeth Ann
Warshaw, Michael Thomas
Weichsel, John Louis
Weinstein, Stephen Saul
Weinstein, Steven David
Weiseman, Jac Burton
White, John Lindsey
Williams, Barbara June
Williams, Henry Joseph
Yurasko, Frank Noel

New Mexico

Berardinelli, David Joseph
Branch, James Alexander, Jr.
Branch, Turner Williamson
Caldwell, Paul Raymond
Casey, Patrick Anthony
Crider, Charles Joseph
Curtis, Stephen Paul
Dahl, Jeffrey A(lan)
Ferrara, Anthony Joseph
Gant, Joseph Erwin, III
Gibson, Louise
Graham, David Antony
Greig, William Harold
Hall, Rex Andrew
Hilgendorf, Robert Nelson
Howell, Mark Franklin
Konrad, Alan Karl
Lopez, Martin, III
Martinez, Carlos Guillermo
Matthews, Marian
McClaugherty, Joe L.
McKinnon, Daniel Angus, III
Morrison, Robert Dale
Moughan, Peter Richard, Jr.
Oman, LaFel Earl
Pearlman, David Henry
Salazar, John Paul
Schwarz, Michael Howard
Singleton, Sarah Michael
Smith, Leslie Clark
Sparkia, Alisa A.
Stuckey, Charles Edward
Vazquez, Martha Alicia
Voegler, Douglas Gene
Wentworth, John
Wertheim, Jerry
Wesch, Calvin Walter
Wilson, Kenneth Belton

New York

Abady, Samuel Aaron
Abinanti, Thomas J., .
Abramowitz, Elkan
Abrams, Stuart
Ackman, Milton Roy
Aliano, Richard Anthony
Allora, Ralph Anthony
Alonso, Andrea Maria
Amabile, John Louis
Amsterdam, Mark Lemle
Arber, Howard Bruce
Arnow, Arthur Emanuel
Aswad, Richard Nejm
Ausubel, Marvin Victor
Avery, Patricia I.
Bader, Howard David
Bader, Izaak Walton
Bader-York, Judith
Baker, Lloyd Harvey
Ballow, John Edward
Barber, Janice Ann
Barry, Desmond Thomas, Jr.
Bartlett, Cody Blake
Bauer, George A., III
Baum, Joseph A.
Baum, Joseph Thomas
Beach, Charles Addison
Beatie, Russel Harrison, Jr.
Beckerman, Ray
Beckey, Sylvia Louise
Begos, Walter Anthony
Beha, James Alexius, II
Behrle, Sandra Gale
Belnick, Mark Alan
Bender, Joel Charles
Benedict, James Nelson
Berg, Alan
Bern, Marc Jay
Berney, Lonn E.
Bernstein, Kenneth Alan
Berry, Charles Gordon
Bienstock, Joshua Elliott
Birnbaum, Edward L.
Bizar, Irving
Black, Warren John
Blangiardo, Frank J.
Blinder, Albert Allan
Bloom, Jeffrey Brian
Boes, Lawrence William
Bonacci, Edward Howard, Jr.
Bowen, John Wesley Edward, IV
Bragar, Raymond Aaron
Braid, Frederick Donald
Braun, Jeffrey Louis
Brenner, Mark B.
Brent, Stephen M.
Brock, David George
Brokate, Brian William
Brooks, Russell Edwin
Brown, David Edward
Brown, Jerrold Stanley
Brown, Lawrence Charles
Brown, Paul M.
Brown, Peter Megargee
Brownell, Carlton Kearns
Bschorr, Paul Joseph
Buchwald, Don David
Burgman, Dierdre Ann
Burns, John MacDougal, III
Burns, Richard Owen
Burrows, Kenneth David
Busner, Philip H.
Butler, John Edward
Bykofsky, Seth Darryl
Byrne, Margaret Mary
Cahn, Richard Caleb
Callahan, Joseph Patrick
Capra, Daniel Joseph
Carlen, Leon C.
Carmien, Donald Charles
Carnegie, Christa Lew
Cartier, Rudolph Henri, Jr.
Cashman, Gideon
Castel, P. Kevin
Cavanaugh, Patrick James, Jr.
Cedarbaum, Miriam Goldman
Charen, Steven Craig
Cherundolo, John Charles
Chizmadia, Stephen Mark
Claire, Judith Susan
Clark, Cameron
Clary, Richard Wayland
Clennan, John Francis
Coen, Seth Ezra
Cohen, Bernard Barrie
Cohen, Richard Barton
Cohen, Robert Stephan
Cole, Charles Dewey, Jr.
Connors, James Patrick
Cook, Charlotte Smallwood
Corso, Frank Mitchell
Costikyan, Edward N(azar)
Cox, Marshall
Cunha, Mark Geoffrey
Curnin, Thomas Francis
Curran, Maurice Francis
Currey, Charles Thomas
Curvin, Steven P.
Dallas, William Moffit, Jr.
Daly, William Joseph
Damashek, Philip Michael
Daniels, George Benjamin
Daniels, James Eliot
Dankner, Jay Warren
Davidson, George Allan
Davoli, Joseph Felix
DeAngelus, Ronald Patrick
Deffina, Thomas Victor
Delehanty, John McDonald
Del Gadio, Robert G.
Dell, Michael John
De Luca, Thomas George
DeMarco, Anthony J., Jr.
De Marie, Anthony Joseph
DiBlasi, John Peter
Dickerson, Thomas Arthur
Di Joseph, Steven
DiNardo, Joseph
Dittenhoefer, Marc Mitchell
Dixon, Harry Thomas
Dolin, Lonny H.
Donley, Joseph Francis
Donovan, Richard Edward
Dubbs, Thomas Allan
Dubow, Alan Martin
Dugan, Sean Francis Xavier
Dunham, Dan Steven
Dweck, Jack S.
Dwyer, Robert Jeffrey
Dwyer, Susan Tate
Earle, Victor Montagne, III
Edelson, Gilbert Seymour
Edwinn, Eugene Paul
Ellenberg, Michael Aron
Elsen, Sheldon Howard
Endieveri, Anthony Frank
Engel, Richard Lee
Englert, Dennis M.
Eno, Lawrence Raphael
Evans, John Thomas
Evans, Martin Frederic
Evans, Richard Joseph
Evans, Thomas William
Ezersky, William Martin
Fagen, Leslie Gordon
Fahey, Joseph Edmund
Falls, Raymond Leonard, Jr
Feder, Saul E.
Fein, Eric David
Fensterstock, Blair Courtney
Fern, Frederick Harold
Fialkoff, Jay R.
Finkelstein, Ira Allen
Firth, Peter Alan
Fisch, Edith L.
Fisher, Cheryl Smith
Fiske, Robert Bishop, Jr.
Fitt, Benjamin Jones
Fleming, Peter Emmet, Jr.
Fletcher, Anthony L.
Flower, Edward
Flynn, Michael
Flynn, William Bernard
Forstadt, Joseph Lawrence
Forster, James Francis
Frankel, Sandor
Freyer, Dana Hartman
Friedberg, Harry Jacob
Friedland, Paul Daniel
Friedman, John Maxwell, Jr.
Frucco, John Peter
Frumento, Aegis Joseph
Fryd, Robert
Furgang, Philip
Gaffney, Mark William
Garfinkel, Barry Herbert
Garley, R. Scott
Geiger, Alexander
Geisler, Thomas Milton, Jr.
Genova, Joseph Steven
George, Carolyn Burke
Gerber, Edward F.
Gerber, Robert Evan
Getlan, Norman
Giacomo, Paul Joseph, Jr.
Gilman, Charles Alan
Ginsberg, Jerome Maurice
Gitter, Max
Glanville, Robert Edward
Gold, Joseph
Goldberg, Harold P.
Goldberg, Neil A.
Goldblum, A. Paul
Goldstein, Kenneth B.
Golomb, David Bela
Goodfriend, Mark F.
Gordon, Michael Mackin
Gorman, Gerald Patrick
Gouldin, David Millen
Graham, Jul Eliot
Greenawalt, William Sloan
Greenbaum, Sheldon Marc
Greenberg, Ira George
Greene, Barry Todd
Greene, Bernard Harold
Greenfield, Jay
Greenhill, Ira Judd
Greilsheimer, James Gans
Grill, Steven Eric
Groman, Tod Philip
Grossman, Mark Donald
Gruen, Michael Stephan
Gulino, Frank
Gurfein, Richard Alan
Gussow, John Andrew
Habian, Bruce George
Hagan, Peter
Halpern, Kenneth Jay, N
Halpern, Philip Morgan
Hamm, David Bernard
Harbison, James Wesley, Jr.
Hardin, Adlai S., Jr.
Harris, Allen
Harris, Joel B(ruce)
Harris, Wayne Manley
Hartzell, Andrew Cornelius, Jr.
Hauser, Gregory Francis
Hayes, Michael Augustine, Jr.
Hazen, James Michael
Hellerstein, Alvin Kenneth
Hellman, Charles David
Henderson, Erskine Dale
Herman, William Charles
Herzog, Ronald Steven
Hesselbach, Bruce William
Hill, Peter Waverly
Himes, Jay L(eslie)
Hinman, James Stuart
Hirsch, Jerome Seth
Hite, Hollis Marie
Hoffman, John Flethcer
Hoffman, Mathew
Hoffmann, Malcolm Arthur
Hollyer, A(rthur) Rene
Horey, Edward Madigan
Horkovich, Robert Michael
Horowitz, Louise Schwartz
Howorth, David Bishop
Hritz, George F.
Hurnyak, Christina Kaiser
Hyde, David Rowley
Iannuzzi, John Nicholas
Isquith, Fred Taylor
Issler, Harry
Itzkoff, Norman Jay
Jacob, Edwin J.
Jacobowitz, Harold Saul
Jacobs, Randall Scott David
Jehu, John Paul
Jensen, J. Christopher
Jewell, Robert Hart
Joffe, Robert David
Joseph, Gregory Paul
Kadet, Samuel
Kahn, Alan Edwin
Kamin, Lawrence O.
Kaminer, Peter H.
Kaplan, Eugene Neal
Kaplan, Joel Stuart
Kaplan, Joseph Charles
Kaplan, Lewis A.
Kapur, David Edmund
Karger, Arthur
Katz, Ascher
Kaufman, Rosalind Fuchsberg
Kaufman, Stephen E.
Kaufmann, Jack
Kavaler, Thomas J.
Kaye, Richard Paul
Kelley, Christopher Donald
Kelner, Robert Steven
Kenny, James Michael
Kerson, Paul Eugene
Keyko, David George
King, Margaret Gram
King, Robert Lucien
Kinzler, Thomas Benjamin
Kirschbaum, Myron
Klein, Arnold Spencer
Klinger, Alan Mark
Klingsberg, David
Knigin, Kenneth Sheldon
Koegel, William Fisher
Koevary, A. George
Kolbrener, Peter D.
Komar, Myron
Konove, Ronald L.
Korman, Iris J.
Kostelanetz, Boris
Kraft, Melvin D.
Krause, Charles Frederick
Krieg, Marc Shea
Krieger, Andrew S.
Krinsky, Andrew Neal
Kuh, Richard Henry
Kurland, Paul C.
Kurzweil, Harvey
Kushel, Glenn Elliot
Lack, Robert Joel
Lacy, Robinson Burrell
LaMancuso, John Lory
Land, David Potts
Landau, Sybil Harriet
Landron, Michel J.

Lange, Paul Kruse
Langer, Bruce Alden
Lans, Deborah Eisner
Lantier, James Daniel
Law, Michael R.
Lawton, Jeff
Leader, Robert John
Leaf, Martin Norman
Lee, Brian Edward
Leininger, William Joseph
Lesser, William Melville
Levi, Mark David
Levin, Robert Daniel
Levine, Melvin Charles
Levine, Ronald Jay
Levinson, David Lawrence
Levinson, Paul Howard
Levitt, Daniel Philip
Levy, Alan C(hester)
Levy, George Michael
Levy, Herbert Monte
Levy, Julius
Levy, Robert S.
Lichtenstein, Sarah Carol
Lindley, David Morrison
Lipsman, Richard Marc
Lipton, Robert Steven
Litman, Jack Theodore
Loehr, Gerald Edward
Loscalzo, Anthony Joseph
Lumbard, Eliot Howland
Lunney, J. Robert
Lupert, Leslie Allan
Lustig, David Carl, III
Lyddane, John Lawrence Ashton
Lynch, Margaret Comard
Lynn, Robert Patrick, Jr.
MacCrate, Robert
Malapero, Raymond Joseph, Jr.
Mangone, Louis A.
Mantel, Allan David
Markel, Sheldon Martin
Martirano, John Joseph
Mattar, Lawrence Joseph
Mattiaccio, Richard L.
Matus, Wayne Charles
Maulsby, Allen Farish
Mayesh, Jay Philip
McAmis, Edwin Earl
McBaine, John Neylan
McClaskey, Norman Dean
McCrory, John Brooks
McDonough, Thomas Joseph
McDuffee, Renée Renaud
McGraw, Charlene Evertz
McMahon, Colleen
McShane, Bruce Winthrop
McSherry, William John, Jr.
McSorley, Bernard Thomas
Medina, Standish Forde, Jr.
Meiselman, David J.
Meister, Ronald William
Melbardis, Wolfgang Alexander
Menton, Francis James, Jr.
Meyer, Bernard Stern
Meyer, Martin Arthur
Millane, John Vaughan, Jr.
Miller, Frederick Lloyd
Miller, Steven Scott
Milligram, Steven Irwin
Mirone, Robert C(armelo)
Mirsky, Moshe Z.
Molod, Frederick M.
Moloney, Thomas Joseph
Monaghan, Peter Gerard
Mone, Mathias Edward
Morelli, Ronald Joseph
Morosco, B. Anthony
Morris, Eugene Jerome
Morrison, Peter Henry
Morrissey, James Malcolm
Moxley, Charles Joseph, Jr.
Muccia, Joseph William
Muka, Betty Loraine Oakes
Mullaney, Thomas Joseph
Mullen, Michael Francis
Mulligan, William G(eorge)
Mulvehill, John Henry
Murphy, Robert Anthony, Jr.
Murphy, Samuel Wilson, Jr.
Muskin, Victor Philip
Nardone, Richard
Neff, Michael Alan
Nelson, Norman Roy
Nemser, Earl Harold
Nicholson, Michael
Novotny, F. Douglas
O'Connor, William Matthew
Ohlman, Douglas Ronald
Olick, Arthur Seymour
Oliensis, Sheldon
O'Neill, John Ignatius
Ordman, Howard Francis
O'Reilly, Kevin Thomas
Osterman, Melvin Howard, Jr.
O'Sullivan, Thomas J.
Page, Alfred Emil, Jr.
Palermo, Anthony Robert
Parker, Douglas Martin
Patte, George David, Jr.
Payment, Kenneth Arnold
Pedowitz, Arnold Henry
Pennell, William Brooke
Pepper, Allan Michael
Persons, John Wade
Petito, Bruce Anthony
Petito, Christopher Salvatore
Pfeffer, Milton B.
Phillips, Anthony F.
Piel, Eleanor Jackson
Pietrzak, Alfred Robert
Pikus, David Heller
Pinsky, Michele Dougherty
Piziali, Michael H.
Plastaras, Thomas Edward
Platto, Charles
Plotka, Richard F.
Podell, Albert N.
Polak, Werner L.
Polakas, John
Poss, Stephen Daniel
Powers, John Kieran
Prodsky, Edward
Profeta, Fred Robert, Jr.
Prutzman, Lewis Donald, Jr.
Pugh, David Edward
Pulos, William Whitaker
Purcell, Edward Aloysius, Jr.
Queller, Fred
Quinlan, Guy Christian
Quinn, James W.
Quinn, Yvonne Susan
Raab, Ira Jerry
Raab, Sheldon
Rakoff, Jed Saul
Raylesberg, Alan Ira
Raymond, Dana Merriam
Reed, James Alexander, Jr.
Reibstein, Richard Jay
Reich, Perry Seth
Reiner, John Paul
Rice, Terry August
Rich, Marcia R.
Rifkind, Robert Singer
Rikon, Michael
Ringel, Dean (I.)
Rivera, Walter
Robinson, Edward T., III
Rogers, Sharyn Gail
Rolfe, Ronald Stuart
Rose, Robert Stanter
Rosen, Ted Manus
Rosenberg, Gerald Alan
Rosenblith, Robert Manuel
Rosenzweig, Theodore B.
Rosner, Jonathan Levi
Rothman, Bernard
Rountree, Asa
Rovine, Arthur William
Rovins, Jeffrey Seth
Rubenstein, Martin Jeffrey
Rubin, Joseph
Rubinstein, Aaron
Ruzow, Daniel Arthur
Ryan, Leonard Eames
Safer, Jay Gerald
Saltzman, Barry Neal
Saltzman, Michael I.
Salvan, Sherwood Allen
Salzman, Stanley P.
Samalin, Edwin
Samel, Jeffrey
Samuel, Raphael
Santucci, John J.
Saunders, Paul Christopher
Savit, Joel B.
Scarzafava, John Francis
Schack, Robert J.
Schaefer, Charles Harold
Scheinkman, Alan David
Schiavetti, Anthony Louis
Schlau, Philip
Schleifer, Richard Wayne
Schneider, Kenneth Paul
Schnurman, Alan Joseph
Schuman, Clifford Richard
Schwartz, Marvin
Schwarzer, Franklin John
Seitelman, Mark Elias
Senn, Laurence Vaughn, Jr.
Shaddock, Robert Montgomery
Shalhoub, Michael David
Shanahan, James Patrick
Shanman, James Alan
Shannon, Michael George
Shapiro, Daniel Murry
Shapiro, Hadassah R(uth)
Shapiro, Jerome Gerson
Shatz, Phillip
Shaughnessy, James Michael
Shollenberger, Elizabeth Ann
Siegel-Baum, Judith Ellen
Sieratzki, Steven Solomon
Siffert, John Sand
Silk, Robert Howard
Silverman, Karen Fay
Silverman, Leon
Silverman, Moses
Simon, Michael Scott
Simoson, William Eugene
Slade, Jeffrey Christopher
Sladkus, Harvey Ira
Slote, Edwin Michael
Smiley, Guy Ian
Smith, Brian Joseph
Smith, Briscoe R.
Smith, Jeffrey G.
Smith, Robert Everett
Smith, Robert Sherlock
Smyk, Stephen Douglass
Snider, Donald Stephen
Socol, Melinda
Sola, Anthony Marce
Sonberg, Michael Robert
Sparkes, James Edward
Sparks, Robert W.
Speiser, Stuart Marshall
Spillane, Dennis Kevin
Squire, Sidney
Stachowski, Michael Joseph
Stanisci, Thomas William
Steer, Richard Lane
Steinbrecher, William John
Steinthal, Kenneth L.
Stern, Gerald Daniel
Stern, Peter R.
Stern, Warren Roger
Stevens, Peter Nicholas
Steyer, Roy Henry
Stine, John
Stone, Paula Lenore
Stratton, Walter Love
Straub, Chester John
Struve, Guy Miller
Summit, Stuart A.
Sussman, Alexander R.
Sword, Carl H(arry)
Symmers, William Garth
Tanenbaum, Ted Jay
Tannenbaum, Calvin Michael
Tarnoff, Jerome
Teitelbaum, Steven Usher
Terry, James Joseph, Jr.
Toback, Arthur Malcolm
Toplitz, George Nathan
Towns, Emanuel Alexander
Triebwasser, Jonah Ignatius
Tucker, Robert Henry
Tutrone, Ronald Francis
Twomey, Thomas Aloysius, Jr.
Van setter, George Gerard
Velie, Franklin B.
Viktora, Richard Emil
Vilardo, Lawrence Joseph
Vincent, Oreste
Vitkowsky, Vincent Joseph
Vogel, John Walter
Walinsky, Adam
Walsh, Francis Michael
Walshe, John William Leo
Warden, John L.
Webster, Luther Ira
Weiner, Jack H.
Weiner, Robin Wendy
Weinstock, Leonard
Weisberg, David Charles
Wells, Peter Nathaniel
Wendel, Martin
Wessel, Peter
Whalen, Daniel Aloysius, III
Wiener, Ira Edward
Wilensky, Saul
Wilkens, Jeffrey Martin
Willig, William Paul
Witkin, Eric Douglas
Wittman, Michael Lee
Wolff, Kurt Jakob
Wolin, Debra Ruth
Wollan, Eugene
Wukitsch, David John
Yeager, Dennis Randall
Yelenick, Mary Therese
York, Louis B.
Zauderer, Mark Carl
Zedrosser, Joseph John
Zerin, Steven David
Zimmett, Mark Paul
Zysk, Robert Joseph

North Carolina

Abrams, Douglas Breen
Ayscue, Edwin Osborne, Jr.
Bennett, Harold Kimsey
Blomeley, James Lee, Jr.
Bradshaw, Penni Pearson
Bragg, Ellis Meredith, Jr.
Brisson, Lloyd Clifford, Jr.
Buie, Donald Ray
Cannon, Thomas Roberts
Carroll, Seavy Alexander
Cheshire, Lucius McGehee
Clontz, Stanford Kent
Coenen, Dan Thomas
Cogburn, Max Oliver
Comerford, Walter Thompson, Jr.
Cunningham, George Gray
Curtis, Michael Kent
Davis, Jeffrey J.
Davis, Joslin
Davis, Roy Walton, Jr.
Derrick, Jack Holley
Doss, Marion Kenneth
Durham, Richard Monroe
Enns, Rodrick John
Etringer, Walter James, Jr.
Eve, Robert Michael, Jr.
Farmer, Ryland Lee
Flaherty, David Thomas, Jr.
Gantt, Charles David
Garlitz, Thomas Drake
Gates, James Edward
Gillespie, James Davis
Gitter, Allan Reinhold
Grier, Joseph Williamson, Jr.
Harkey, Henry Averill
Holleman, Carl Partin
Hoof, James Bruce
Huffstetler, Noah Haywood, III
Hunter, Richard Samford, Jr.
Johnson, Bruce Cannon
Johnson, Joseph Davis
Jones, Bonnie Dee Durham
Jones, Paul Lawrence
Jorgensen, Ralph Gubler
Joyner, Gary Kelton
Kapp, Michael Keith
King, Ronnie Patterson
Langson, Seth Harris
Logan, Leonard Gilmore, Jr.
Maxwell, James Beckett
McIver, Robert Gilmour
Michael, Mark A.
Mills, William S.
Mineo, Robert Anthony
Morris, Thomas Hansley
Phillips, Randel Eugene
Plyler, Cranford Oliver, III
Poling, Richard Duane
Pope, Patrick Harris
Porter, Leon Eugene, Jr.
Raper, William Cranford
Reynolds, Mark Floyd, II
Ruppe, Arthur Maxwell
Sasser, Jonathan Drew
Sentelle, David Bryan
Shuping, C(larence) Leroy, Jr.
Smith, Norman Barrett
Starnes, Oscar Edwin, Jr.
Stockton, Ralph Madison, Jr.
Strayhorn, Ralph Nichols, Jr.
Stroud, Joseph E., Jr.
Taylor, Michael William
Thompson, Eugene Cebron, III
Thornburg, Lacy Herman
Tilghman, Carl Lewis
Waldrup, J(ohn) Charles
Walker, James Edward
Wilson, LeVon Edward

North Dakota

Bair, Bruce B.
Herauf, William Anton
Hermes, Pamela Jane
Kelsch, William Charles
Maxson, R. James
McKechnie, William Elliott
Quast, Larry Wayne
Solberg, Wayne O.
Sortland, Paul Allan
Weir, Harlan Patrick
Yuill, William Duane
Zuger, William Peter

Ohio

Adams, John Marshall
Alkire, Richard Charles
Ammer, William
Ashmus, Keith Allen
Ashworth, John Lawrence
Ausnehmer, John Edward
Bacon, Brett Kermit
Baker, Richard Southworth
Beckwith, Karen Lu
Belton, John Thomas
Bennett, Marshall Alton Jr.
Bertrand, Louis Robertson
Binning, J. Boyd
Birne, Kenneth Andrew
Bixenstine, Kim Fenton
Blackburn, Thomas Irven
Boggs, Ralph Stuart
Boles, Edgar Howard, II
Bonaventura, Mark Gabriel
Boone, Timothy J.
Bouscaren, Timothy Lincoln
Bradigan, Brian Jay
Brant, Charles Ensign
Bressler, H.J.
Briggs, Marjorie Crowder
Britain, James Edward
Brown, Seymour R.
Browne, John Patrick
Buchmann, Alan Paul
Buckley, Daniel Jerome
Buckley, Frederick Jean
Budish, Armond David
Bunda, Robert Alan
Burd, Charles Leslie
Burdge, Michael Joseph
Burke, Kim Kenneth
Burns, Donald Andrew
Burth, John Hamrick
Capizzi, Anthony
Carpenter, James Willard
Carroll, James Michael
Carto, David Draffan
Cassidy, William Anthony
Cherpas, Christopher Theodore
Chester, John Jonas
Chockley, Frederick Wilson, Jr.
Cissell, James Charles
Climer, James Alan
Cline, Richard Allen
Comstock, David Cooper
Covatta, Anthony Gallo, Jr.
Crist, Paul Grant
Cvetanovich, Danny Lee
Dailey, Coleen Hall
Davis, Bradley Mark
Davis, Charles Joseph
Davis, Robert Lawrence
Dean, J. Thomas
DeLong, Deborah
Donovan, James
Dornette, W(illiam) Stuart
Dublikar, Ralph F(rank)
Duff, Gerald Patrick
Edwards, John Wesley, II
Evans, Stanley Robert
Eynon, Ernest Alfred, II
Fain, Mike
Farrell, Clifford Michael
Ferguson, Gerald Paul
Ferruccio, Samuel Joseph, Jr.
Fisher, John Edwin
Friedman, Jerome
Gambol, Robert Alan
Gertner, Michael Harvey
Gippin, Robert Malcolm
Gold, Gerald Seymour
Grabow, Raymond John
Gray, Alvin L.
Greene, Gordon Christopher
Greer, David Carr
Gross, Seymour
Grove, Jack Frederick
Guehl, Robert Lee
Guttman, Rubin
Hagel, Thomas Leo
Halleck, Michael Johnston
Hamilton, Richard Abbott
Hanna, Martin Shad
Hardy, William Robinson
Harshman, Michael Stuart
Hart, Douglas Edward
Hawley, William Lee
Heaton, Gerald Lee
Heck, Grace Fern
Herbert, David Lee
Hermanies, John Hans
Hermann, Philip J.
Hermann, Thomas George
Herrold, Russell Phillips, Jr.
Hershey, Adrian Vernon
Hiller, Robert Stanford
Hoefle, H. Frederick
Hoffheimer, Daniel Joseph
Hoover, Earl Reese
Hutson, Jeffrey Woodward
Jackson, Reginald Sherman, Jr.
James, Larry Holliday
Jenks, Thomas Edward
Jones, Michael Charles
Jordan, Joseph Patrick, Jr.
Kafantaris, George Nicholas
Kampinski, Charles
Kancler, Edward
Kennedy, Charles Allen
Kernen, Will
Kilbane, Thomas Stanton
Kitchen, Charles William
Knapp, A. Michael
Knepper, William Edward
Koenig, Kenneth John
Koenig, Peter Edward
Kondzer, Thomas Allen
Kopit, Alan Stuart
Kostyo, John Francis
Kovich, Don Edmond
Krembs, Peter Joseph
Kulewicz, John Joseph
Lancione, Nelson
Lancione, Richard Lee
Lane, Matthew Jay
Largent, Jeffrey Willard
Lavelle, John Philip
Leach, Russell
Lee, Ronald Bruce
Leksan, Thomas John
Lemire, Jerome Albert
Lewis, James William
Lieberman, Dennis Alan
Long, Thomas Leslie
Madden, Stephan DuPont
Madsen, H(enry) Stephen
Major, Ronald David
Manley, Robert Edward
Marco, Richard Joseph, Jr.
Maxwell, Robert Wallace, II
McCoy, John Joseph
Mc Elhaney, James Willson
McIlvaine, James Ross
McIlvaine, Stephen Brownlee
Mc Neal, Harley John
Meikle, William MacKay
Meily, William Davis
Metz, Jerome Joseph, Jr.
Moore, Kenneth Cameron
Morelli, Arnold
Morris, Earl Franklin
Moss, Judith Dorothy
Murtaugh, John Patrick
Naegele, Jori Bloom
Nelson, Steven Sibley
Nissl, Colleen Kaye
O'Brien, Ronald Joseph
Olivas, Adolf
Paddock, Harold Dewolf
Palmer, Thomas Earl
Perin, Charles Henry, Jr.
Petro, James Michael
Pheils, David R., Jr.
Plakas, Leonidas Evangelos
Potash, M. Steven
Pratt, Gregory Kent
Ray, Frank Allen
Reminger, Richard Thomas
Riley, Paul E.
Roberts, Brian Michael
Rockel, John Edward
Rossi, Michael Dudley
Rossi, William Matthew
Roush, Bradley Craig
Rubin, Robert Samuel
Ruport, Scott Hendricks
Ruppert, James Delano, II
Sanders, James Worthington
Sandrock, Scott Paul
Saul, Irving Isaac
Sawyer, Theodore D(aniel)
Schneider, Karl Herbert
Serraino, Stephen R.
Shaw, Nancy Ann
Shea, Joseph William, III
Silverman, Peter Ray
Sinclair, Virgil Lee, Jr.
Skulina, Thomas Raymond
Smart, Irene Balogh
Sobecki, Thomas Alva
Souers, Loren Eaton, Jr.
Spero, Keith Erwin
Spurgeon, Roberta Kaye
Stancati, Joseph Anthony
Stanton, Elizabeth McCool
Stewart, Lawrence Edward
Stratton, Evelyn Joyce
Strauch, John L.
Stuhldreher, George William
Sulzer, Joseph Paul
Swartzbaugh, Marc L.
Sweebe, Richard Dale
Sydlow, Holly Taft
Tait, Robert Ed
Taylor, Hilary Sheldon
Theado, Thomas Robert
Theis, Donald Eugene
Thomas, James William
Thompson, Stephen David
Thornton, Robert Floyd
Tipping, Harry Anthony
Todd, William Michael
Trester, Joseph Edward
Tucker, Theodore Brush, III
Turoff, Jack Newton
Tyack, George Gary
Ucker, David A.
Utz, Edward Joseph
Vance, Victoria Lynne
Van De Mark, Julie Ann
Walker, Patricia Ann
Wallach, Mark Irwin
Weber, Robert Carl
Weisman, Fred
Werber, Stephen Jay
Whipps, Edward Franklin
White, Arnold S.
White, Daniel Joseph
White, Kenneth James
Whitney, Richard B.
Wieland, Robert Richard
Williamson, Gregory Lopez
Woods, Kay
Wykoff, John Robert
Yontz, Randall Eugene
Zackaroff, Peter Timothy
Zaremba, Thomas S.
Zavatsky, Michael Joseph
Zoll, David Wesley

Oklahoma

Abrahamson, A. Craig
Alexander, Linda Diane (Graham)
Armstrong, Richard Volker
Barnes, Robert Norton
Basham, Marshall Denver
Beech, Johnny Gale
Bergner, William Joseph
Brett, Thomas Rutherford
Brewster, Clark Otto
Carson, Michael Jay
Catron, Gary Wayne
Crawford, B(urnett) Hayden
Davis, Charles Bishop
Dawson, Jack Sterling
Eldridge, Richard Mark
Elias, William Keith
Ellis, Thomas Taylor
Featherly, Henry Frederick
Fellers, James Davison
Fenton, Elliott Clayton
Frieze, H(arold) Delbert
Graves, Herbert Mac
Gray, Linda (Lou)
Green, Gerald Patrick
Gurich, Noma Diane
Haught, Robert Steven
Henneke, David Charles
Hoster, Craig William
Huffman, William Hicks
Jaques, Frank Hesketh
Jones, Kent Leonard
Kaufman, James Mark
Kenney, John Arthur
Lester, Andrew William
Lloyd, James Robert (Jim)
Looney, Robert Dudley
Luthey, Graydon Dean, Jr.
Mantooth, John Albert

Martin, Gary Duncan
McCarty, Jack De
McCollam, M. E.
Miskovsky, George, Sr.
Murphy, Robert Moore
Musser, James William
Norman, John Wayne
Parks, Ed Horace, III
Paul, William George
Peterson, David L.
Purcell, Gary Morgan
Reid, David Paul
Robinson, Patricia Dougherty
Rodgers, Ricardo Juan (Rick)
Rogers, William Britton
Ryals, Kent
Schuller, Stephen Arthur
Shaw, Donald Ray
Spencer, Thomas Lee
Spiegelberg, Frank David
Stamper, Joe Allen
Taylor, Joe Clinton
Taylor, Michael Conrad
Thurman, Andrew Edward
Todd, Robert Allen
Tompkins, Raymond Edgar
Warren, Loyde Hugh
Williams, Betty Outhier

Oregon

Adler, A(rthur) Michael
Bailey, Ronald E.
Banks, Roland Fitzgerald, Jr.
Barrett, Cynthia Louise
Barton, Richard Lee
Barton, William Arnold
Beckman, Douglas Gary
Brown, Anna Jaeger
Brown, Lisa Claire
Brown, Stuart Melville
Buehler, John Wilson
Bullivant, Rupert Reid
Calzaretta, Victor
Carroll, Catherine North
Chadsey, Phillip Duke
Cloran, William Francis
Cooney, Thomas Emmett
Cramer, William Donald
Day, Bartley Fuller
Day, Frank E.
Deatherage, William Vernon
Eakin, Margaretta Morgan
Eichelberger, Stephen
Enfield, Myron Leroy
Engel, Edward Ignatius
Eyerman, Linda Kathleen
Fechtel, Edward Ray
Feibleman, Gilbert Bruce
Foster, Randolph Courtney
Frohnmayer, David Braden
Geil, John Clinton
Glazer, Peter Kendall
Goldstein, Bennett Howard
Greene, Michael Alan
Griffith, Stephen Loyal
Gronso, Wendell E.
Harris, Roger King
Hodges, Charles Edward, Jr.
Honsowetz, Frank William
Hunt, Lawrence Boyd
Johnston, Ronald Allen
Kennedy, Jack Leland
Kester, Randall Blair
Kitchel, Jan Kelly
Kurtz, Louis Laird
LaBarre, Jerome Edward
Langslet, John Loring
Lombard, Herbert William, Jr.
Loomis, Donald Alvin
MacRitchie, Brian John
Mannix, Kevin Leese
Mansfield, William Amos
Marandas, John Steve
Markowitz, David Benjamin
Miller, David Kenneth
Morrison, David Patrick
O'Neill, Phoebe Joan
Pickett, Douglas Gene
Rice, James Gordon
Robertson, Joseph David
Rose, Steven Marc
Sahlstrom, E(lmer) B(ernard)
Savage, John William
Schade, Aloha Lee
Snouffer, William Campbell
Spencer, Jesse Neal
Spier, Richard Gary
Stiles, William Neil
Tankersley, Thomas Channing
Turnbow, William Randolph
Vallerand, Patricia Ann
Walters, Stephen Scott
Westwood, James Nicholson
Williamson, Charles Ready
Wyse, Scott Campbell

Pennsylvania

Adams, John Joseph
Auerbach, Sheryl Lynn
Baker, Frank Adams, III
Baker, Sidney
Bala, Gary Ganesh
Barkman, Jon Albert
Barrett, Bruce Alan
Basinski, Anthony Joseph
Beachler, Edwin Harry, III
Beck, Robert David
Becker, John Francis
Beemer, John Barry
Belden, H. Reginald
Bigman, Anton W.
Binder, David Franklin
Black, Alexander
Bogus, Carl Thomas
Bonner, Eugene Aloysius
Borish, Arnold Peter
Bosick, Joseph John, Jr.
Brady, George Charles, III
Brenner, Thomas Edward
Bricklin, Louis E.
Brogan, James Martin
Brosky, John G.
Brown, Richard P., Jr.
Brown, William Hill, III
Burns, Michael William
Burr, Charles Bentley, II
Camen, Toby Paul

Carter, Daniel Paul
Chanin, Bernard
Cheswick, Phillip Thomas
Cleaver, David Charles
Cohen, Earl S.
Cohen, Robert (Avram)
Connors, Eugene Kenneth
Cooper, Thomas Louis
Cramp, John Franklin
Crane, Maida Rosenfeld
Creato, Anthony Edmund
Creedon, Michael Patrick
Crowley, Thomas Michael
Damsgaard, Kell Marsh
D'Angelo, George A.
Dattilo, James Anthony
Davis, Donald Marc
De Fino, Michael G.
DeMay, John Andrew
Dill, William Allen
DiPiero, Andrew Edward, Jr.
Donahue, John M(ichael)
Douglass, Robert Duncan
Dubin, Stephen Victor
Eagan, Charlene Ann
Ehrenwerth, Charlene Reidbord
Einhorn, Edgar Robert
Elliott, John Michael
Eshelman, David Richard
Evey, Merle Kenton
Faucher, John Dennis
Federline, Robert Louis
Feese, Brett Owen
Feinour, John Stephen
Feldstein, Jay Harris
Fetzner, Michael Alan
Fiebach, H. Robert
Flint, Daniel Waldo Boone
Follows, Jill Marilyn
Forney, Susan Jane
Fox, Reeder Rodman
Frank, Frederick Newman
Frank, Mark Stephen
Friedman, Joseph
Garcia, Rudolph
Gathright, Howard T.
Geiger, William David
German, Edward Cecil
Godwin, Robert Anthony
Gondelman, Harold
Goodman, Marguerite Ruth
Gordesky, Morton
Gordon, Robert Jay
Gounley, Dennis Joseph
Gowen, Thomas Leo, Jr.
Greenberg, James
Grosh, Susan Ellen
Gurevitz, Mark Stuart
Gutshall, Frederick Raym
Hankin, Mitchell Robert
Hauben, Ronald Bruce
Heim, Robert Charles
Helmreich, Martha Schaff
Hemphill, Meredith, Jr.
Herman, Charles Jacob
Herman, Lee Merideth
Hershenson, Gerald Martin
Heslop, John William, Jr.
Holsinger, Candice Doreen
Hovis, Raymond Leader
Jacob, Mark Craig
Jellinek, Miles Andrew
Johanson, Thomas Jonathan
Jones, Craig Ward
Jones, Ronald Richard
Kalis, Peter John
Kaplan, Ronald Ira
Kashkashian, Arsen, Jr.
Kauffman, Bruce William
Keenan, C. Robert, III
Kelly, Robert Edward, Jr.
Kenrick, Charles William
Kenworthy, Thomas Bausman
King, Peter Joseph
Klayman, Barry Martin
Klein, Joel Aaron
Kolansky, Jeffrey Mark
Kole, Janet Stephanie
Kormes, John Winston
Kramer, Gilda Lea
Krawitz, Sidney L.
Kupperman, Louis Brandeis
Kupperman, Louis Brandeis
Kusturiss, Dennis John
LaPorte, RocLyne Emile
Lawless, Joseph Francis, Jr.
Ledwith, John Francis
Lewis, Alvin Bower, Jr.
Lewis, Christopher Alan
Lieberman, George Eric
Lincicome, Brian Leslie
Linshaw, Jack G.
Lisko, Roy Kenneth
Litman, Roslyn Margolis
Lorenzo, Nicholas Francis, Jr.
Lubin, David S.
Luchak, Frank Alexander
MacDonald, Richard Barry
Maleski, Cynthia Maria
Manning, James Hamington, Jr.
Mattioni, John
McAneny, Eileen S.
McBride, James Francis
McCabe, James J.
McCloskey, Stephen Paul
McConomy, James Herbert
McDonald, James Daniel, Jr.
McDowell, Michael David
McGinley, John Regis, Jr.
Mc Gough, Walter Thomas
McGurk, Eugene David, Jr.
McKenna, James L.
McLane, John Thomas
Mermelstein, Jules Joshua
Messer, Howard Francis
Micale, Frank Jude
Milbourne, Walter Robertson
Milone, Francis Michael
Mintzer, Edward Carl, Jr.
Mojock, David Theodore
Monteverde, Tom Peter
Moribondo, Thomas Peter
Moritz, Preston William
Morris, Neil Alan
Moser, Melvin Lavalle, Jr.
Mott, John C.
Mulligan, John Thomas
Mulvey, W. Michael

Mulvihill, David Brian
Munsing, Peter Nicholas
Muraca, Frank John
Musto, Joseph J.
Myers, Robert Earl
Ober, Russell John, Jr.
O'Connor, Edward Gearing
O'Dell, Debbie
Opalinski, Christopher Richard
Orloski, Richard J.
Osterhout, Richard Cadwallader
Parry, William DeWitt
Patterson, Christopher Malone
Pedri, Charles Raymond
Perer, Alan Harvey
Perer, Diane Wilson
Perlstein, Paul Mark
Peterson, Neil Raymond
Petrush, John Joseph
Pfaff, Robert James
Phillips, Dorothy Kay
Plowman, Jack Wesley
Pollins, John William, III
Posy, David Howard
Pribanic, Victor Hunter
Price, William Charles, Jr.
Radcliffe, William M., III
Rainone, Michael Carmine
Reed, Lowell Andrew, Jr.
Reif, Eric Peter
Renz, William Tomlinson
Restivo, James John, Jr.
Robb, John Anthony, Jr.
Roeger, William Coley, Jr.
Rome, Edwin Phillips
Roper, Peter P.
Rosenberg, H. N.
Roskovensky, Vincent Joseph, II
Ross, Alan Harold
Ross, Eunice Latshaw
Rossi, Mary Ann
Rovner, David Patrick Ryan
Rubendall, Charles Wesley, II
Saltzman, Joan
Salus, Herbert Wieder, Jr.
Samson, Peter
Saunders, Robert Leonard
Scheck, Donald Gordon
Scheffler, Stuart Jay
Scher, Howard Dennis
Schermer, Oscar Selig
Schmidt, Harold Robert
Schoener, George Francis, Jr.
Schroeder, William Francis
Schwabenland, Edward John
Schwartz, Jeffrey Byron
Segal, Frederick Leslie
Senker, Richard C.
Serbin, Richard Martin
Shaffer, Charles Alan
Shane, B(enjamin) Jerome
Shelton, Fincourt Braxton
Shepherd, Carol Nelson
Sherman, Carl Leon
Sherry, John Sebastian
Shertz, Perry Jack
Shields, Francis Edward
Shoop, Roger Thomas
Shuster, Morris Myer
Silberblatt, Jay Ned
Silver, Stuart Robert
Simon, David Frederick
Simpson, Robert Edward, Jr.
Skeel, Peter Brooks
Skelly, Joseph Gordon
Smith, John Churchman
Smith, Templeton, Jr.
Smolinsky, Sidney Joseph
Snite, Albert John, Jr.
Solano, Carl Anthony
Sonnenfeld, Marc Jay
Spiegel, Robert Joseph
Squires, Mark Elliott
Stack, Michael J.
Standish, William Lloyd
Straub, J(ames) Kurt
Stroyd, Arthur Heister
Suojanen, Wayne William
Swartz, Lee Carter
Swensen, Jan Clovis
Szczepaniak, Joseph Dennis
Tabas, Allan M.
Tamulonis, Frank Louis, Jr.
Thomas, Richard Irwin
Thompson, John Wilson, Jr.
Van Dusen, Lewis Harlow, Jr.
Voss, James Victor
Ward, William Francis
Weinfeld, David M.
Weingarten, Marc Philip
Weiss, Philip David
Weston, John Kerry
Wilson, Steven (White)
Wingerter, John Raymond
Wolf, Edward Leonard
Wolfe, Steven Edward
Youngman, John Crawford
Youngs, Christopher Jay
Zeehandelaar, David Nico
Ziegler, Craig E.
Zimmerman, LeRoy S.

Rhode Island

Blanding, Sandra Ann
Blish, John Harwood
DiSandro, Edmond A.
Dub, Larry
Fox, Francis Anthony
Mandell, Mark Steven
McGuirl, Susan Elizabeth
Miller, Samuel Aaron
Najarian, Malcolm Askanaz
Parks, Albert Lauriston
Purcell, James Edward
Reilly, John Bernard
Riffkin, Mitchell Sanford
Southgate, (Christina) Adrienne Graves
Turner, Terrance Neil

South Carolina

Albergotti, Samuel Fretwell
Allison, James McWilliams
Babcock, Keith Moss
Bacot, John Paisley, Jr.
Baggett, Stephen Dallas
Barker, Joseph Ransom
Bolt, J. Dennis

Breibart, Richard Jerome
Buchanan, Robert Lee, Jr.
Choate, John Lee
Cooper, Robert Gordon
Cothran, James Clardy, Jr.
Darling, Stephen Edward
DeWitt, Franklin Roosevelt
Dominick, Paul Allen
DuBose, Clarke Wardlaw
Esposito, John Vincent
Furr, O(lin) Fayrell, Jr.
Gibbes, William Holman
Gibson, Carroll Allen, Jr.
Goude, Charles Reuben
Grimball, William Heyward
Harvey, William Brantley, III
Hite, Thomas Erskine, Jr.
Hocker, Donald Bruce
Holleman, Frank Sharp, III
Horne, Terrell Thomas
Hudson, James Patrick
Irvin, Wilmot Brown
Jedziniak, Lee Peter
Johnson, Mordecai Christopher
Jones, Marvin Coleman
Kahn, Ellis Irvin
King, Jimmy R.
Knight, David Webster
Knowlton, Robert Yates
Kuhn, Harold Fred, Jr.
Laws, James Terry
Licata, Steven Barry
Martin, John Randolph
Massey, Raymond David
McKay, John Judson, Jr.
Newby, Fred Bryant
O'Donnell, Robert Harry
Reeves, Phillip Earl
Robinson, David Wallace
Seth, J Cabot
Sheftman, Howard Stephen
Shoemaker, James Marshall, Jr.
Smith, Cody Walker, Jr.
Smith, Jefferson Verne, Jr.
Smith, Sherman N., III
Smith, Walter Henry
Spears, Michael Eugene
Spitz, Hugo Max
Steadman, Richard Anderson, Jr.
Tapp, Richard N.
Wall, Susan Taylor
White, Daniel Bowman
Williams, Charles Hiram
Williams, Karen Johnson
Wittenberg, Philip

South Dakota

Eichstadt, Craig Martin
Hoy, Carleton Robert
Hughes, John Robert
Kennedy, Craig Allen
Nipe, Chris Alan
Pieplow, Michael Flinn
Sabers, Richard Wayne
Sveen, Jeffrey T.
Thompson, Charles Murray
Zimmer, John Herman

Tennessee

Alexander, Dave Almon
Armstrong, Walter Preston, Jr.
Arnett, Foster Deaver
Bahner, Thomas Maxfield
Barr, James Victor, III
Bernstein, Bernard Emanuel
Boston, Robert Earl
Bridgesmith, Larry W.
Brothers, Thomas White
Butler, Edward Franklyn
Campbell, Paul, III
Carr, Oscar Clark, III
Cary, Charles Muse
Catalano, Michael William
Chambliss, Prince Caesar, Jr.
Cook, Bratten Hale, II
Cooper, Gary Allan
Creekmore, David Dickason
Culp, James David
Dixon, James Mikel
Drowota, Frank F., III
Dupree, Charles Patrick
Ehmling, Miles Allen
Faulk, Michael Anthony
Fordham, Benjamin Cleveland
Garts, James Rufus, Jr.
Gearhiser, Charles Josef
Gentry, Gavin Miller
Gill, John Welch, Jr.
Gordon, J. Houston
Gorrell, Frank Cheatham
Grisham, Alvin MacRandle
Grisham, Arthur C., Jr.
Hardin, Hal D.
Harris, Tyree Bryson
Headrick, Stirman Russell
Henry, Arthur Wayne
Holmes, Hal
James, Erich William
Jones, John Thomas, Jr.
Jones, Kenneth Ray, Jr.
Keeton, Robert Taylor, Jr.
Kerr, Thomas Draper, Jr.
Kilcrease, Irvin Hugh, Jr.
King, Robert Lewis
Kirby, James Lynn
Knowles, Emmitt Clifton
Koontz, George Edward
Lander, Gary David
Lawless, Thomas William
Lay, Patti Jane
Layman, Earl Robert
Leitner, Paul R.
Lloyd, William Nelson
Lockaby, Robert Lee, Jr.
Lockett, George Houston
McCaleb, Joe Wallace
McCormack, Donnell James
McKenney, Edward Jerome, Jr.
McLaren, Michael Glenn
McWhirter, J(ames) Cecil
Midgett, James Clayton, Jr.
Moriarty, Herbert Bernard, Jr.
Newman, Charles Forrest
Noel, Randall Deane
Ogden, Harry Peoples
O'Hearn, William Wilson
Patterson, Robert Shepherd

Pearman, Joel Edward
Pickering, William Henry
Price, Walter Lee
Rice, George Lawrence (Larry), III
Riley, Joe Glenard
Robinson, Samuel Francis, Jr.
Rogers, Helen Sfikas
Schwarz, Earle Jay
Sheppeard, Sarah Y.
Shockley, Gary Clark
Siciliano, Gerard Michael
Sims, Wilson
Speros, Michael Carl
Stark, Kelly Shira
Strand, Alfred Benjamin, Jr.
Tarpy, Thomas Lynn
Thomason, John Joseph
Todd, Ben
Veal, Rex R.
Walker, Joseph Hillary, Jr.
Walton, John Wayne
Watson, James William
Watson, Robert Harmon, Jr.
Whitaker, Michael Wright
Williams, Thomas Ashurst
Wilson, Fred Palmer
Winston, Russell Clay
Witcher, Roger Kenneth, Jr.
Wright, James Charles
Yarbrough, Edward Meacham
Young, Jason Ober, Jr.

Texas

Adair, William B. (Ben)
Adams, Ray Harris
Addison, Linda Leuchter
Akers, Brock Cordt
Albach, Henry John, IV
Alberts, Harold
Albright, William James
Aldrich, Lovell W(eld)
Alexander, John William
Alexander, Neil Kenton, Jr.
Allison, Stephen Philip
Ammerman, James Harry, II
Anderson, E. Karl
Anton, Richard Henry
Atlas, Morris
Atlas, Scott Jerome
Auld, Bruce
Austin, Page Insley
Baber, Wilbur H., Jr.
Baggett, W. Mike
Ballanfant, Richard Burton
Barr, John H.
Bashline, James Duane
Baskette, William L., Jr.
Bayko, Emil Thomas
Beachley, Charles Edward, III
Beane, Jerry Lynn
Beirne, Martin Douglas
Bell, Henry Newton, III
Bell, William Woodward
Benckenstein, John Henry
Benton, John Bunyan
Bernard, Robert Louis
Bingham, Loyd Edward, Jr.
Blair, Graham Kerin
Bohannon, Paul
Bonesio, Woodrow Michael
Borchers, Marion Jack
Boswell, John Howard
Bousquet, Thomas Gourrier
Boyland, Herbert Layton
Branson, Frank Leslie, III
Brennan, Diantha Garrett
Briggs, Tom Peery
Brinson, Gay Creswell, Jr.
Brister, Scott Andrew
Brock, Roy C.
Brown, Robert Charles
Buether, Eric W.
Burch, Voris Reagan
Burkett, Joe Wylie
Bux, William John
Cantilo, Patrick Herrera
Carnes, Lamar
Carrigan, Stephen Paul
Casterline, Cecil W.
Chappell, David Franklin
Cheavens, Joseph D.
Cherry, David Earl
Chrisman, Perry Oswin
Clark, Ronald Hurley
Coleman, Bryan Douglas
Conner, George Manion, III
Cook, Eugene Augustus
Craddock, Thomas Wofford
Craig, Robert Lee, Jr.
Craig, Robert Mark, III
Crotty, Robert Bell
Cuba, Benjamin James
Cunningham, Tom Alan
Davis, Clarice M.
Davis, Jimmy Frank
Davis, Michael A.
Dean, Daniel Frank
Degenhardt, Harold F.
DeHay, John Carlisle, Jr.
Delk, Russell Louis
DeShazo, Gary Forrest
Donaldson, David Howard, Jr.
Dowd, Steven Milton
Driscoll, Michael Hardee
Duncan, Ernest Louis, Jr.
Eckhardt, William Rudolf, III
Eddins, Gerald Wayne
Eisenbraun, Eric Charles
Elliott, Frank Wallace
Ellis, James Alvis, Jr.
Erben, Randall Harvey
Estes, Harper
Evans, George Frederick, Jr.
Evans, Roger
Ezell, Michael R.
Ezzell, James Michael
Fanning, Barry Hedges
Farnsworth, T Brooke
Farr, Sidney Lavelle
Feeney, Patrick Joseph
Feldman, H. Larry
Fellers, Rhonda Gay
Fenwick, Lynda Beck
Figari, Ernest Emil, Jr.
Finkelstein, William Berndt
Flanary, Donald Herbert, Jr.
Flegle, Jim L.
Fleming, George Matthews

Folse, Parker C(amile), III
Forbes, Arthur Lee, III
Freytag, Sharon Nelson
Frigerio, Charles Straith
Frost, Charles Estes, Jr.
Furgeson, William Royal
Gandy, Francis I., Jr.
Garrison, Pitser Hardeman
Gayle, Gibson, Jr.
Glickman, Julius
Gold, Paul Nicholas
Golden, H. Bruce
Goodfriend, Robert Edward
Gordon, Norman James
Graham, Michael Paul
Greer, Raymond White
Guleke, James O., II
Gulley, David Wesley
Gulley, Jack Haygood
Hagerman, John David
Haggard, Carl Douglas
Halbach, Joseph James, Jr.
Hall, John Hopkins
Hamilton, Elwin Lomax
Hampton, Charles Edwin
Hanen, Andrew Scott
Hankins, Mitchell Dale
Harmon, Melinda Furche
Harrel, Alan David
Harrison, Orrin Lea, III
Harrison, Reese Lenwood, Jr.
Harrison, Richard Wayne
Hart, John Clifton
Hartnett, Thomas Robert, III
Hartnett, Will Ford
Harvin, David Tarleton
Harvin, William Charles
Hawkins, John Claiborne, Jr.
Hayes, Burgain Garfield
Henderson, John Robert
Hennessey, John William
Hoffman, Leonard Elbert, Jr.
Hohman, A.J., Jr.
Holstead, John Burnham
Holt, Wayland Garth
Howie, John Robert
Huffman, Gregory Scott Combest
Hughes, Karen Gray
Hughes, Nancy Nutto
Hunsucker, Philip Carl
Hunt, Richard Martin
Hunter, Todd Ames
Hytken, Franklin Harris
Ingram, Temple Byrn, Jr.
Irby, Holt
Irvin, Charles Leslie
Jack, Larry A.
Jayson, Melinda Gayle
Jenkins, Richard Coleman
Johnson, D. Thomas
Johnson, Philip Wayne
Johnson, Scott Warren
Jones, David Stanley
Jones, Edith Hollan
Jones, Lindy Don
Jordan, Charles Milton
Jordan, W. Carl
Jung, Peter Michael
Kacal, George Jerome, Jr.
Kaplan, Lee Landa
Keeshin, Scott Avery
Keltner, David E.
Kendall, David Matthew
Kennedy, John Edward
Kent, David Charles
Kerry, Henry Eugene
Kilgore, Gary Lynn
King, Ira Thomas
King, Ronald Baker
Kirkman, William Louis
Kizzia, Don Bradley
Kline, Allen Haber, Jr.
Knisely, Paul Emil
Konopisos, Konstantine A.
Kousz, Carolyn Gertrude
Krebs, Arno W., Jr.
Labay, Eugene Benedict
Lacey, David Morgan
Lake, Simeon Timothy, III
Lamb, Jonathan Howard
Larimore, Tom L.
Larkin, Lee Marshall
Latino, Anthony Leon
Lawton, Kenneth Wayne
Legendre, John Peter
Legg, Reagan Houston
Lezar, Tex
Liebbe, William Howard
Lilienstern, O. Clayton
Lippe, Emil, Jr.
Loewinsohn, Alan Stewart
Lowenberg, Michael
Lynch, Jeffrey Scott
Maddox, Charles J., Jr.
Mainz, Edward Charles, Jr.
Marshall, Richard Treeger
Matthews, Dan Gus
McAtee, David Ray
McConnico, Stephen E.
McCormick, J(oseph) Burke
McDaniel, Myra Atwell
Mc Elhaney, John Hess
McFall, Donald Beury
McGinnis, Robert Campbell
McGowan, Gary V.
McPherson, Nancy Jo Buenzli
McQuarrie, Claude Monroe, III
Mercy, John R.
Merz, Daniel Lee
Meyer, Leonard James
Micks, D. Fred
Miller, Stewart Ransom
Mills, William Michael
Minor, David Michael
Morgan, Cecilia Hufstedler
Morgan, Jack Cochran
Morgenstern, Jonathan David
Moroney, Linda Lelia Susan
Mow, Robert Henry, Jr.
Moye, Eric Vaughn
Mullen, John Clancy
Myers, J(oseph) Michael
Nelson, Jack Odell, Jr.
Nesbitt, Frank Wilbur
Newsom, Daniel Oren
Noel, David Bobbitt, Jr.
Nunnally, Knox Dillon
Oldenettel, Rick Lee

Oldham, Darius Dudley
Orn, Clayton Lincoln
Owen, Frank, III
Pannill, William Presley
Park, J(ames) Walter, IV
Parker, Allan Edward
Parmley, Robert James
Peck, Leonard Warren, Jr.
Perkins, James Allen
Perkins, Lloyd Wesley
Perlmutter, Mark L.
Petry, Herbert Charles, Jr.
Pew, John Glenn, Jr.
Pfunder, Curtis Clark
Phillips, Thomas Marion
Phillips, Travis R.
Plunkett, Allen Lewin
Poehner, George Richard
Porter, Charles Raleigh, Jr.
Powers, William Leonard
Prather, Robert Charles
Prestridge, Pamela Adair
Pridavka, Gary Michael
Rainey, John David
Rapp, Robert David
Ray, Cread L., Jr.
Ray, Donald Arvin
Ray, Hugh Massey, Jr.
Reaser, Vernon Neal, Jr.
Reasoner, Harry Max
Redden, Joe Winston, Jr.
Rentz, Joe Houston
Reynolds, Dixon Jace
Rice, Ben Herbert, III
Richards, Robert William
Richman, Marc Hersh
Riddles, Amis Joe
Riney, Thomas Charles
Ringle, Brett Adelbert
Roberts, Ted Blake
Robichaux, James Hall
Roessler, P. Dee
Rubagumya, George William
Rusk, L. Giles
Sadler, Paul Lindsey
Sales, James Bohus
Sandage, Douglas S.
Schenkkan, Pieter (Pete) Meade
Schwartz, Aaron Robert
Scuro, Joseph E., Jr.
Secrest, Ronald Dean
Selinger, Jerry Robin
Sessions, William Lewis
Shaddock, William Charles
Shafer, W. O.
Shaw, Tex Ronnie
Shirley, Robert Preston
Shurn, Peter Joseph, III
Sides, Jack Davis Jr.
Siegel, Mark Jordan
Slaughter, David Alan
Smith, George Duffield, Jr.
Smith, James Bonner
Smith, Phillip Nolan, Jr.
Smith, Russell Bryan
Smith, Steven Lee
Sparkman, Roy T.
Steele, Joseph Robert
Stephens, R(obert) Gary
Stephens, Walter David
Stewart, Annette
Stewart, Joseph Ward
Stinnett, Mark Allan
Stovall, Thomas J., Jr.
Stradley, William Jackson
Sutherland, Richard Thomas
Suttle, Stephen Hungate
Sutton, John F., Jr.
Swan, Michael Robert
Sweeney, Gregory Louis
Swindle, Mack Ed
Tabak, Morris
Taft, Lee McCreary
Talmadge, Jeffrey David
Tartt, Blake
Terrell, Richard Clark
Thaddeus, Aloysius Peter, Jr.
Thompson, Peter Rule
Thrall, Gordon Fish
Timaeus, Dana Lee
Timmons, Patrick Francis, Jr.
Trimble, Dale Lee
Truitt, Robert Ralph, Jr.
Turley, Windle
Tyson, Roy Knox
Valdes, Richard Albert
Vander Woude, Richard John
Van Fleet, George Allan
Van Gilder, Derek Robert
Vickrey, Jack
Voyles, Robb Lawrence
Walker, Dee Brown
Wallis, Ben Alton, Jr.
Wallis, Olney Gray
Walls, Robert Ernest
Warnock, Curtlon Lee
Warrick, Richard Lloyd
Wendorf, Hulen Dee
Wester, Ruric Herschel, Jr.
Westmoreland, Kent Ewing
White, Steven Gregory
Whitehurst, William O.
Wicka, Richard Vincent
Wiles, William Dixon, Jr.
Wilkerson, James Neill
Wilkins, Jerry Lynn
Wilkinson, Toby Charles
Williams, Nancy Ondrovik
Williams, Walter Waylon
Wilson, Charles Julian
Wilson, David Keith
Wilson, James William
Winn, David Burton
Wise, Robert Kenneth
Worthington, William Albert, III
Wren, James Eric, III
Young, Ardell Moody

Utah

Anderson, Craig W.
Carlile, Craig
Cassity, James Junior
Christensen, Patricia Anne Watkins
Dallimore, Suzanne Meredith
Dolowitz, David Sander
Erickson, David Belnap
Hansen, Royal Ivory
Holm, Floyd W.

Judd, Dennis L.
Kaplan, Neil Alan
Kent, Dale R.
Lyman, Paul D.
McIntosh, James Albert
Nelson, Merrill Francom
Newton, Joseph Steven
Purser, Donald Joseph
Rasmussen, Thomas Val, Jr.
Reeder, F. Robert
Shields, Jeffrey Weston
Slaughter, David Wayne
Sullivan, Kevin Patrick
Verhaaren, Harold Carl
Walsh, John Thomas
Walstad, Paul J.
Westfall, George Michael
Winward, LaMar J.

Vermont

Cassidy, Richard Thomas
Cheney, Kimberly Bunce
Corum, Jesse Maxwell, IV
Cory, Barbara Ellen
Fitzhugh, John Hardy
French, Thomas McGuinness
Greenberg, David Herbert
Holme, John Charles, Jr.
Langrock, Peter Forbes
Leddy, John Thomas
Lisman, Bernard
Massucco, Lawrence Raymond
Mc Carty, William Michael, Jr.
Miller, William Bayard, Jr.
Otterman, Harvey Boyd, Jr.
Plante, Peter Paul
Rachlin, Robert David
Rath, David
Saltonstall, Stephen Lee
Smith, Norman Charles
Stevens, Harold Burr
Storrow, Charles Fiske
Williams, Norman Charles
Wysolmerski, Sigismund John Albert

Virginia

Ackerly, Benjamin Clarkson
Alexander, Bevin Ray, Jr.
Allen, Jeffrey Rodgers
Allen, Wilbur Coleman
Allen, Wilbur Coleman, Jr.
Alper, Joanne Fogel
Anderson, John Foster
Appleton, Randall Eugene
Arnold, William McCauley
Bacon, James Thomas
Bankert, Joseph Edward
Beach, Barbara Purse
Beller, Charles Roscoe, III
Billingsley, Robert Thaine
Blank, Irving Michael
Booker, James Foster
Booker, Lewis Thomas
Bromm, Frederick Whittemore
Brooks, Robert Franklin
Brown, Frank Eugene, Jr.
Burnette, Ralph Edwin, Jr.
Byrom, Robert Milton
Carrington, Frank Gamble, Jr.
Chappell, Robert Harvey, Jr.
Church, Randolph Warner, Jr.
Cranwell, C. Richard
Crigler, B. Waugh
Dansby, Harry Bishop
Davis, Douglas Witfield
Davis, Richard Waters
Economou, Stewart Charles
Emroch, Emanuel
Farnham, James Edward
Finnegan, Edward James
Flannagan, Francis Wills
Fletcher, John Richard
Folk, Thomas Robert
Freyvogel, William Thomas
Gardner, Mark S.
Gilbert, Oscar Lawrence
Gladstone, Michael Harper
Haight, Gregory Dale
Hajek, Francis Paul
Harrison, John Edwards
Hicks, Robert DeHardit
Hogshire, Edward Leigh
Jenkins, Douglas Tucker
Jones, Robert James
Kearfott, Joseph Conrad
Kiser, Jackson L.
Kloeppel, Byron Peter
Koutoulakos, Louis
Krasnow, Jeffrey Harry
LaGow, John Christopher
Lawrence, John Schrumpf
Leffler, Rodney G.
Levit, Jay J(oseph)
Loe, Brian Robert
Martin, Ronald Allen
McClard, Jack Edward
McElroy, Howard Chowning
McFarlane, Walter Alexander
McGavin, John David
McGlothlin, Michael Gordon
McKenry, James Reinhardt
Meekins, Samuel Warrenton, Jr.
Montagna, Anthony Louis, Jr.
Moore, Tyler Moses
Najjoum, Linda Lemmon
Napier, Douglas William
Nicholas, Edward Ernest, III
O'Connell, Kevin Michael
O'Donnell, Hugh David
Palmer, William Ralph
Parks, William Anthony
Patterson, Robert Hobson, Jr.
Payne, Frederick Warren
Pearsall, John Wesley
Pietrovito, Guy Roy
Plaetzer, Ross Frederick
Pochucha, Larry Arthur
Poole, Albert Harrison
Powell, Lewis Franklin, III
Prince, William Taliaferro
Proffitt, John Stephen, III
Pysell, Paul Edward
Roberts, Russell Hill
Saul, Ira Stephen
Scott, Betsy Sue
Shell, Louis Calvin
Shields, William Gilbert

Shortridge, Michael L.
Skinker, Donald Ray
Slenker, Norman Frederick
Slonaker, Jerry Paul
Small, Marc James
Snook, John Lloyd, III
Somerville, Frank Walker
Spero, Morton Bertram
Spirn, Stuart Douglas
Stanback, Clarence Freeman, Jr.
Stone, Steven David
Sweeny, Peter Michael
Tankersley, Glenn Rayburn
Tatum, Franklin M., III
Tegenkamp, Gary Elton
Thomas, Norman Allan
Treakle, James Edward, Jr.
Trotter, Haynie Seay
Walton, Edmund Lewis, Jr.
Warburton, Roy David
Waters, Charles Richard, II
Wheeler, R(ichard) Kenneth
Wilcox, Bruce Andrew
Williamson, Thomas W., Jr.
Wilson, Rodger Lee
Winston, Robert Tunstall, Jr.
Woodrum, Clifton A., III
Wright, Grover Cleveland, Jr.
Youngs, John Curtis

Washington

Adams, Lori Nelson
Addington, Darrel Blair
Allison, John Robert
Andersen, Charles Matthew
Angevine, Earl Francis
Bailey, William Scherer
Berry, Douglas Clayton
Bishin, William Robert
Bor, Daniel
Bradbury, Timothy Dewet
Broihier, Jeffrey T.
Budlong, John
Buzzard, Steven Ray
Campbell, Fremont Lee
Cline, Thomas Farrell
Cornell, Kenneth Lee
Corning, Nicholas F.
Cressman, Paul Russell, Jr.
Cushing, James Robert
Dacca, Franklin Louis
Danelo, Peter Anthony
Davis, James Edward
Dawson, Robert Kevin
Devlin, Greg Martin
Dudley, J. Jeffrey
Dunham, Douglas Spence
Eadie, Richard Douglas
Ecton, Douglas Brian
Eubanks, Ronald W.
Foreman, Dale Melvin
Fritzler, Randal Brandt
Gaddis, Stephen Michael
Gandara, Daniel
Glein, Richard Jeriel
Hendricks, Katherine
Hoff, Valerie Margaret Knecht
Hollingsworth, Jeffrey Alan
Houger, L(eroy) William
Huey, Diane Marie
Johnson, Richard Bruce
Kaiser, Bruce Allen
Keller, Bradley Scott
Lang, Pamela Ann
Leed, Roger Melvin
Leipham, Jay Edward
Lied, Erik Robert
Luce, Kenyon Eldridge
Mahoney, Philip Charles
Manni, Kenneth Allen
Marshall, James Markham
Matthews, Stephen Ross
McDermott, Richard Francis, Jr.
McGarry, Arthur Daniel
McKay, Michael Dennis
Mines, Michael
Mitchell, Robert Bertelson
Moniz, Donna Maria
Moren, Charles Verner
Moses, Gene Ronald
Nichols, Howard Melvin
Nielsen, Ruth
Otorowski, Shawn Elizabeth
Peery, Charles Eugene
Raaen, G(ary) Lee
Reed, Glenn Edward
Ricketts, Michael Edward
Sargeant, Robert Walton
Sayre, Matt Melvin Mathias
Smith, James Alexander, Jr.
Stritmatter, Paul Lester
Swanson, Arthur Dean
Tanksley, Raymond Richard, Jr.
Thurston, Hal
Tomlinson, John Randolph
Tuffley, Francis Douglas
Waitt, Robert Kenneth
Webster, Ronald B.
Whitson, Lish
Younglove, Edward Earl, III
Zilly, Thomas Samuel

West Virginia

Artimez, John Edward, Jr.
Bell, Harry Fullerton, Jr.
Berthold, Robert Vernon, Jr.
Bryant, Sanford Benjamin
Coleman, James Howard, Jr.
Cowan, John Joseph
Davis, Stephen Allen
Flaherty, Thomas Vincent
Ford, Richard Edmond
Frankovitch, Carl Nicholas
Harrington, Travers Rountree, Jr.
Haviland, James Morrison
Hearst, James Henry
Hill, Barry Morton
Hurt, Charles E.
Johnson, David Whitley
Judy, John David, III
Lawson, Robert William, Jr.
Null, Gregory B.
Peterson, James Charles
Powell, James Corbley
Richardson, Randolf Emrys
Sanders, William Henry
Saville, Royce Blair

Silver, Gray, III
Swope, Derek Craig
Wehner, Richard Karl
Wilmoth, William David

Wisconsin

Anderson, Michael Steven
Arnold, Bruce George
Atterbury, Lee Richard
Bergen, Thomas Joseph
Berres, Terrence Robert
Bosshard, John
Brant, Kirby Ensign
Burroughs, John Townsend
Busch, John Arthur
Callahan, Carroll Bernard
Christiansen, Jon Peter
Cole, James Ray
Connolly, L. William
Conrad, Paul Edward
Cook, Daniel John
Cross, David R.
Curry, George Steven
Curtis, George Warren
Decker, John Robert
Domnitz, Merrick Robert
Eckert, Michael Louis
Ehrke, William Warren
Gagliardi, Paul
Gass, James Ric
Gehringer, John G.
Glowacki, Thomas Robert
Grzeca, Michael (Gerard)
Gust, Gerald Norman
Habush, Robert Lee
Hans, Peter E.
Hansher, David Allen
Hartley, Glenn Henry
Hertel, Theodore Bernhard, Jr.
Higgins, John Patrick
Hildebrand, Daniel Walter
Hoag, Jack Carter
Hupy, Michael Frederick
Israel, Scott Michael
Kammer, Robert Arthur, Jr.
Krueger, John William
Lathrop, Trayton LeMoine
Laufenberg, Lynn Raymond
LeBell, Robert
Levit, William Harold, Jr.
Long, J. Richard
Mason, Jon Gerard
Melin, Robert Arthur
Mitby, John Chester
Moser, William R.
Murray, James Thomas, Jr.
Nohr, William Arthur
Owens, Joseph Francis
Pappas, David Christopher
Pernitz, Scott Gregory
Peterson, John Christian
Pettit, Roger Lee
Pollack, Michael Alan
Rainey, Charles James
Rasche, William Grether
Robinson, Richard Russell
St. John, Thomas William
Schmitt, Joseph Francis
Schober, Thomas Leonard
Schrank, Raymond Edward, II
Smith, Charles F., Jr.
Sostarich, Mark Edward
Steuer, Robert Karl
Stoltz, John Robert
Storck, Robert Emil
Suran, Robert Herman
Szymanski, Barry Walter
Tease, Ralph Joseph, Jr.
Tess-Mattner, Kent A.
Te Winkle, William Peter
Thompson, Edward Francis
Towers, Lawrence Alan
Tuerkheimer, Barbara Wolfson
Vollmer, Steven Lyle
Walsh, John
Walther, David Louis
Warshafsky, Ted M.
Weidner, Gary Richard
Whitcomb, Michael Arthur Isaac
Whitney, Robert Michael
Wilcox, Francis John
Will, Trevor Jonathan
Winner, John Dennett

Wyoming

Ahlstrom, Bert Tavelli, Jr.
Bommer, Timothy J.
Bostwick, Richard Raymond
Burke, E. James
Cardine, Godfrey Joseph
Clauss, C. David
Combs, William Henry, III
Dyekman, Gregory Chris
Godfrey, Paul Bard
Hunkins, Raymond Breedlove
Johnson, Robert Henry
Kidd, David Thomas
Kline, Stephen Hibbard
Klus, Charles Robert, Jr.
McLaughlin, Douglas Ray
Rideout, Richard Scott
Santini, George
Schuster, Robert Parks
Shockey, Gary Lee
Speight, John B.
Stanfield, John Edmiston
Tarver, Timothy Stephen
Thomson, Rebecca Wunder
Webster, C. Edward, II
Whynott, Philip Percy
Williams, Houston Garvin

TERRITORIES OF THE UNITED STATES

Guam

Diaz, Ramon Valero

Puerto Rico

Gonzalez-Diaz, Raul E.
Ruiz-Suria, Fernando

CANADA

Saskatchewan

Elliott, William McBurney

ENGLAND

Wiese, Larry Clevenger

ADDRESS UNPUBLISHED

Adams, Thomas Lawrence
Adler, Kenneth
Aldrich, Richard Dennis
Alexander, Carla J.
Aronsohn, Richard Frank
Arrowood, Lisa Gayle
Auther, Jeri Lynn Kishiyama
Baudler, William John
Baumohl, Harry Alan
Beattie, Donald Gilbert
Beger, John David
Beldock, Myron
Berger, Lawrence Douglas
Bernard, Pamela Jenks
Bernheim, Peggy
Blevins, Jeffrey Alexander
Boyle, Elizabeth Mary Hunt
Brodsky, David M.
Bush, Robert G., III
Cancio, Pablo Ramón
Canova, Leo Phillip, Jr.
Carrol, Robert Kelton
Christopher, M. Ronald
Culver, Robert Winthrop
Culver, Sue Ann Ray
Davidson, Keith L.
Davis, Jonathan David
Dement, Kenneth Lee
Djokic, Walter Henry
Fekete, George O.
Ferguson, Marvin Elwood
Fowler, Flora Daun
Garza, Rudy A.
Gee, Delbert Calvin
Glantz, Ronald Paul
Glywasky, Donald Steven
Gonzales, Jeffrey Charles
Graham, Keith Everett
Griffith, James Lewis
Harrison, Roddy L.
Heins, Samuel David
Hirsch, Jeffrey Allan
Holland, Randy James
Howe, Drayton Ford, Jr.
Hughes, Linda Renate
Hughes, Roy Fredericks
Hurst, Ernest Connor
Jensen, John Robert
Johnson, Gary William
Kadish, Lloyd Alan
Kafka, Anne G.
Kahn, Ronald Howard
Kamp, Steven Mark
Kauger, Yvonne
Kemp, Alson Remington, Jr.
Klein, Richard L.
Labdon, Kenneth Charles
Lapidus, Steven Richard
Lerman, Cathy Jackson
Leventhal, Howard G.
Levinson, Kenneth Lee
Linnehan, Joseph Arthur, Jr.
Locke, John Howard
Markewich, Robert
Martin, James Henry
McInerney, Gary John
Michaels, George
Midkiff, Charles Franklin
Murphy, Thomas Hugh
Nelson, Jay Scott
Newman, Carol L.
Nicolaides, Mary
O'Mara, William Michael
Orlins, Peter Irwin
Panec, William Joseph
Peterson, Laurel J.
Plitt, Steven
Quinn, Joseph Francis
Quinn, Stacy Smith
Reycraft, George Dewey
Robinson, David Howard
Rohrbach, William John, Jr.
Rosenberg, Arthur Harrison
Saliterman, Richard Arlen
Salomon, Barbara
Scott, Thomas Stratton, Jr.
Sheahan, Joseph D.
Siris, Michael John
Sommers, Louise
Spiller, William, Jr.
Sweeney, Robert John
Vida, Glen Joseph
von Dioszeghy, Adam George
Walker, Robert Donald
Weaver, John Hosch
Webster, Daniel Robert
Welch, Ernest Wendell
Wildey, Sharon Ann
Wright, Frances Mina Johnson
Zeltonoga, William Leo
Ziker, Barry Gene

CIVIL RIGHTS

UNITED STATES

Alabama

Davenport, George William
Flowers, Francis Asbury, III
Haycraft, Charles Arthur
Lyles, Harry Arthur
Mandell, Howard Allyn
Morse, George Wray, II
Prestwood, Alvin Tennyson
Still, Edward
Varley, Robert John
Whiteside, David Powers, Jr.

Alaska

Goldberg, Robert M.
Wagstaff, Robert Hall

Arizona

Ching, Anthony Bartholomew
Cowser, Danny Lee
Glicksman, Elliott Aaron
Jacobs-Schwartz, Loretta (Barbara)
Jakubczyk, John Joseph
Wohl, Kenneth Allan

Arkansas

Boe, Myron Timothy
Davis, James Edwin
Hall, John Wesley, Jr.
Lyon, Philip Kirkland
Roachell, Richard Wilson

California

Aaronson, Mark N.
Alexander, George Jonathon
Atkins, Robert Alan
Braafladt, Arnie Rolf
Brisson, Claudia Wisner
Brooks, Roy Lavon
Bryan, Robert Russell
Carter, Glenn Thomas
Cochran-Bond, Walter C.
Donnici, Peter Joseph
Dryovage, Mary Margaret
Grofman, Bernard Norman
Hall, Carlyle Washington, Jr.
Hightower, George Willis
Hipshman, Anne
Kaufman, Albert I.
Kershnar, Harris Edwin
Levy, Leonard Williams
Lynch, James Joseph, Jr.
Mintz, Ronald Steven
Ninnis, William Raymond, Jr.
Schachter, Alesa Rose
Talmo, Ronald Victor
Wallace, Elaine Wendy
Webb, Michael Joseph
Woocher, Fredric Dean

Colorado

Barnes, Thomas Arthur, Jr.
LaFond, Richard Charles
McClung, Merle Steven
Minahan, Daniel F., Jr.
Rudy, Peter Harris
Satter, Raymond Nathan
Smith, Michael Louis
Walta, John Gregory

Connecticut

Cooper, George
Dempsey, Edward Joseph
Gelfman, Mary Hughes Boyce
Margulies, Martin B.
Oleyer, George Richard
Pinsky, Irving Jay
Sheldon, Michael Richard
Simmons, Donald Charles
Slez, Anthony Francis, Jr.
Solecki, Trina Anne

Delaware

Mekler, Arlen B.

District of Columbia

Apperson, Bernard James
Bergman, Carol Amy
Berry, Mary Frances
Bolick, Clint Daniel
Bonventre, Vincent Martin
Brody, David A.
Burnim, Ira Abraham
Christensen, Karen Kay
Covington, Alice Lucille
Crumlish, Joseph Dougherty
Deutsch, David
Dinerstein, Robert David
Donegan, Charles Edward
Fasman, Zachary Dean
Flynn, David Kevin
Foscarinis, Maria
Hill, Rufus Sadler, Jr.
Houseman, Alan William
Keeney, John Christopher, Jr.
Kent, M. Elizabeth
King, James Forrest, Jr.
Kramer, Andrew Michael
Levin, Betsy
Matthews, Steve Allen
Reynolds, William Bradford
Snyder, Allen Roger
Sutherlund, David Arvid
Vanderstar, John
Vogt, Carl William
Wolf, Christopher

Florida

Audlin, David John, Jr.
Barnes, Donald King
Berns, Bonnie Ava
Connor, Terence Gregory
Escarraz, Enrique, III
Grogan, Michael Kevin
Haddad, Fred
Holland, William Meredith
Howie, Bruce Griffith
Jacob, Bruce Robert
Kaimowitz, Gabe Hillel
Nagin, Stephen E.
Rogers, Gordon Dean
Silverman, Scott Jay
Spann, Ronald Thomas
Spriggs, Kent
Stapleton, John Owen
Swan, George Steven
Watson, Robert James
Winter, Steven Lawrence

Georgia

Ashe, Robert Lawrence, Jr.
Canfield, Peter Crane
Emmons, Peter Ribeiro
England, John Melvin
Harness, William Walter
Hogue, L(ouis) Lynn
Martin, Charles Lee
Satcher, James Alton, Jr.
Totenberg, Amy Mil
Weaver, George Marvin

Hawaii

Foley, Daniel Robert
Kim, Edward Y.N.
Van Dyke, Jon Markham
White, Lawrence Richard

Idaho

Davis, James Julian
Madsen, Roger Bryan
McCabe, Thomas James
McLaughlin, Robert Francis
Penland, Paul Stephan
Vander Boegh, Douglas Lee

Illinois

Badel, Julie
Baker, Helen
Barnhill, Charles J., Jr.
Bernstein, Stuart
Beschle, Donald L.
Burns, Robert Patrick
Cipolla, Vincent Charles
Freed, Mayer Goodman
Freerksen, Gregory Nathan
Futterman, Ronald L.
Gagliardo, Joseph M(ichael)
Garnett, Marion Winston
Giampietro, Wayne Bruce
Gilbert, Daniel Thomas
Gutman, Richard Martin
Harris, Daniel Mark
Hecht, Frank Thomas
Hegarty, Terrence K.
Hubbard, Elizabeth Louise
Johnson, Gary Thomas
Lefkow, Michael Francis
Lieb, Roslyn Corenzwit
McClure, Thomas Edward
Miller, Barry Alan
Murray, Lorene Frances
Nagel, Stuart Samuel
Palm, Gary Howard
Radzilowsky, Michael
Rhode, Shari René
Rosemarin, Carey Stephen
Schmidt, Wayne Walter
Schoenfield, Rick Merrill
Schulhofer, Stephen Joseph
Smith, Arthur B(everly), Jr.
Sneckenberg, William John
Steinman, Joan Ellen
Streeter, Benjamin Arrington, III
Theobald, Edward Robert
Weinstein, David L.

Indiana

Bennett, Roger William
Ford, Lee Ellen
Gikas, Rick Christopher
Miller, David Anthony
Stimson, Judith Nemeth

Iowa

Goldman, David Harris

Kansas

Badgerow, John Nicholas
Dillon, Wilburn, Jr.
Nelson, Bryan Eugene
Patterson, Donald
Yarbrough, Marilyn Virginia

Kentucky

Boylan, Michael Lee
Friedman, David Alan
Isaac, Teresa Ann
Leightty, David
Lilly, Nolte Scott Ament
Neuber, Frank William, Jr.
Pitt, Dorothy Moore
Powell, Karen Ann Pitts
Sexton, David Andrew
Walker, Patricia Gail

Louisiana

Colbert, Kathryn Hendon
Dwyer, Ralph Daniel, Jr.
Everett, Stephen Edward
Friedman, Joel William
Huffman, Gerald James, Jr.
Jones, Johnnie Anderson
Lampard, Catherine Ann
Lyons, Laurie Wilkinson
Mitchell, Robert Burdette
Nalls, Clarence Theo
Palmer, Vernon Valentine
Surprenant, Mark Christopher
Thomas, Joseph Winand
Walker, Henry Clay, IV

Maine

Kirchner, Theodore Harry
Levandoski, Dennis

Maryland

Berman, Michael David
Dorsey, Charles Henry, Jr.
Nemetz, Margaret Nottingham
Wimbrow, Peter Ayers, III

Massachusetts

Avery, Michael Aaron
Bartholet, Elizabeth
Bell, Derrick Albert
Chayes, Abram
Culpepper, Miniard
Dimare, Charles Joseph
Donahue, Michael Christopher
Doniger, Anthony M.
Felter, John Kenneth
Field, Martha Amanda
Fillon, Richard
Fischer, Thomas Covell
Golder, Frederick Thomas
Miles, Harry Lehman
O'Connor, James Michael

Michigan

Abraham, Douglas Clark
Alatalo, Richard
Boal, Ellis
Fallon, William Hume
Feikens, John
Fink, Sally Claire
Golden, Joseph Aaron
Goodman, William Harry
Harvey, Barbara
Heldt, Jeffrey Alan
Holman, Charles F(redrick), III
Hwang, Roland
Kara, Paul Mark
Ludolph, Robert Charles
Maxwell, Robert Alexander
O'Brien, Thomas C.
Robb, Dean Allan
Rossen, Jordan
Schneider, Karen Bush
Shakoor, Adam Adib
Simmons, Brent Elliott
Turner, Donald Allen
Williams, D. Lee

Minnesota

Farber, Daniel Alan
Mansfield, Seymour J.
Nesseler, Steven Edward
Nora, Wendy Alison
Rosenbaum, James Michael
Short, Marianne Dolores

Mississippi

Fuselier, Louis Alfred
Mitchell, Cynthia Inis
Will, Joseph Henry Michael

Missouri

Buder, Eugene Hauck
Callahan, Robert John, Jr.
Chackes, Kenneth Michael
Gordon, Michael David
Hipsh, Harlene Janet
Popper, Robert
Schermerhorn, Sandra Leigh
Simon, Roy D., Jr.

Nebraska

Gleason, James Mullaney
Loudon, Timothy Dale

Nevada

Sarnowski, David Francis
Stumpf, Felix Franklin
Zubel, Eric Louis

New Jersey

Beakley, Robert Paul
Graziano, Ronald Anthony
Harris, David B.
Manshel, Max
Raveson, Louis Sheppard
Reitman, Sidney
Weichsel, John Louis
Wolf, John Barton

New Mexico

Caldwell, Paul Raymond
Huffaker, Gregory Dorian, Jr.
Mitchell, Gary Colas
Rothstein, Robert Richard
Schwarz, Michael Howard
Word, Terry Mullins

New York

Adler, Alan Michael
Autin, Diana Marie Therese Katherine
Berkow, Michael
Brewer, Curtis
Carlisle, Jay Charles, II
Chernoff, Carl G.
Clark, Ramsey
Cooke, Bradford
Crain, William Earl
Dershowitz, Nathan Zev
Dorsen, Norman
Eisenberg, Theodore
Erlichster, Joe
Fernandez, Lillian
Fink, Janet Rose
Fink, Rosalind Sue
Flamm, Leonard N(athan)
Fontana, Vincent Robert
Golick, Toby Barbara
Hauhart, Robert Charles
Heath, Joseph John
Henkin, Louis
Herman, Susan N.
Jackson, Ronald James Leonard
Jauvtis, Robert Lloyd
Kennedy, Michael John
Kostelny, Albert Joseph, Jr.
Leonard, Arthur Sherman
Levick, Marsha Lynn
Levitan, Katherine D.
Mahoney, David John
Masliansky, Nechama
Mendez, William, Jr.
Millman, Bruce Russell
Moses, Mary Helen
Nagy, Jill Harriet
Posner, Michael Hoffman
Raff, David
Ratner, Michael D.
Schulz, David Alan
Stevens, Peter Nicholas
Teitelbaum, Steven Usher
Valentine, John William
Watanabe, Roy Noboru
Weinstein, Alan Abraham
Wilson, Leroy, Jr.

North Carolina

Curtis, Michael Kent
Dahl, Tyrus Vance, Jr.
Newby, Paul Martin
Rowe, Thomas Dudley, Jr.
Sasser, Jonathan Drew
Smith, Norman Barrett
Van Noppen, Donnell, III

North Dakota

Lockney, Thomas Michael

Ohio

Berger, Sanford Jason
Besser, Howard Russell
Binning, J. Boyd
Cobau, Charles Duffy, Jr.
Duckett, Douglas Edward
Elam, John William
Gray, Alvin L.
Holzer, Richard Jean
James, Larry Holliday
Kramer, Edward George
Krass, Marc Stern
Kurek, James David
Lewis, John Bruce
Lipton, Andrew S.
McMahon, Michael Sean
Pheils, David R., Jr.
Rossi, Michael Dudley
Sternberg, Richard
Taylor, Hilary Sheldon
Tobias, Paul Henry
Vaughn, Noel Wyandt
Weaver, Susan M.

Oklahoma

Court, Leonard
Day, Ronald Liles
Gray, Linda (Lou)
Jones, Stephen
Lieber, John Howard
Matthies, Mary Constance T.
Rogers, William Britton
Salem, Micheal Charles
Shaw, Donald Ray
Stuart, John Bruce
Vanderburg, Michael Robert
Whitten, Reggie Neil

Oregon

Barilla, Frank (Rocky)
Brown, Anna Jaeger
Overgaard, Mary Ann

Pennsylvania

Beer, Lawrence Ward
Carroll, James Walter, Jr.
Forney, Susan Jane
Granat, Richard Stuart
Kairys, David Marc
Krampf, John Edward
Krzemien, Louis John
Leddy, John Henry
Lillie, Charisse Ranielle
Mermelstein, Jules Joshua
Morris, Neil Alan
Mulvihill, David Brian
Murtagh, John Walter, Jr.
Newberg, Herbert Barkan
Pasek, Jeffrey Ivan
Sisk, Paul Douglas
Smith, John Churchman
Speers, Thomas James
Squires, Mark Elliott
Thompson, Beverly Kay
Williams, Gerald Joseph
Yohe, Susan Ann

Rhode Island

Blanding, Sandra Ann
Mann, Robert Barney
Medeiros, Matthew Francis

South Carolina

Ballard, Wade Edward
Carr, Robert Stuart
Mitchell, Theo Walker
Trinkley, Jane Wilroy

Tennessee

Akers, Charles David
Bates, Albert Kealiinui
Blumstein, James Franklin
Bush, William
Durand, Philip Poyntell
Ferguson, April Rose W.
Hunt, William Walter, III
Jaqua, David Palmer
Lockett, William Alexander
Marty, James Owen
McCoy, Thomas Raymond
Sobieski, Wanda Graham
Watson, Robert Harmon, Jr.
Whitaker, Michael Wright
White, Penny J.

Texas

Baker, Thomas Eugene
Berg, David Howard
Brewer, Lewis Gordon
Brim, Jefferson Kearney, III
Finlayson, Dawn Bruner
Foster, Ben Frank, Jr.
Fryburger, Lawrence Bruce
Greig, Brian Strother
Hall, William Wendell
Harper, Alfred John, II
Hollin, Shelby W.
Holt, Robert Blaine
Johnson, Karen Lee
Laycock, Harold Douglas
Linden, Louis Frederick
Moynihan, John Bignell
Parker, Allan Edward
Peck, Leonard Warren, Jr.
Reamey, Gerald S.
Rendon, Ruben
Schorr, Kenneth L.
Thompson, T. Jay
Wheeler, Susan Lynn
Wray, Thomas Jefferson
Yett, Charles William

Vermont

Chase, Jonathon B.

Virginia

Carrington, Frank Gamble, Jr.
Crouch, Richard Edelin
Flannery, John Philip, II
Garrett, Stacy F., III
Hajek, Francis Paul
Hall, Betty Jean
Henderson, James Rutledge, IV
Hill, Oliver White, Sr.
McConnell, Paul Stewart
Miller, Charles Joseph
Skolrood, Robert Kenneth

Smith, Baker Armstrong
Taubman, Glenn Matthew
Thomas, Norman Allan
Whitehead, John W.
Zeese, Kevin Bruce
Zerkin, Gerald Thomas

Washington

Chellis, Eugene Clifton
Dussault, William L.E.
Halverson, Lowell Klark
Peterson, Jan Eric
Phillips, Brian Reed
Scott, Steven George
Tasker, Michael Kenneth
Wilson, James Barker

Wisconsin

Akavickas, Gary Robert
Dalton, LeRoy LaVerne
English, Dale Lowell
Fribance, Caroline Eleanor
Glynn, Stephen Michael
Graylow, Richard Vernon
Jones, James Edward, Jr.
Jurkovic, Daniel John
Kelly, Walter Francis
Krukowski, Thomas Paul
Olson, Jeffrey Scott
Pappas, David Christopher
Pollack, Michael Alan

Wyoming

Botham, Lisa Anne
Honaker, Richard Henderson
Kline, Stephen Hibbard
Selig, Joel Louis
Zollinger, Thomas Tennant

TERRITORIES OF THE UNITED STATES

Puerto Rico

Roman, David William

ADDRESS UNPUBLISHED

Atwood, Ronald Wayne
Becker, Frank Gregory
Berger, Joel
Frank, James Stuart
Friedrich, Bruce Robert
Margolis, Emanuel
McFarland, Robert Edwin
Michaels, David Seth
Moore, Elizabeth Reitz
Paul, Joel Richard
Schulman, Joanne
Shareef, Michael T.
Weclew, Robert George
Wildey, Sharon Ann

COLLECTIONS. *See* **Commercial, consumer.**

COMMERCIAL FINANCING. *See* **Commercial, contracts.**

COMMERCIAL, CONSUMER

UNITED STATES

Alabama

Bailey, Robert Theodore Russ
Bonner, William Joel, Jr.
Borg, Joseph Philip
Campbell, Maria Bouchelle
Centeno, Douglas Joseph
Chastain, David Jesse
Crespi, Michael Albert
Friedman, Barry Allen
Hardegree, Arthur Lee, III
Howell, William Ashley, III
Kelly, Leon Fred, Jr.
Moore, Gary Alan
Olshan, Gary Steven
Ray, Thomas Morgan
Shepard, Tazewell Taylor, III
Teague, Dewey Wayne
Wise, Steven Lanier

Alaska

Longacre, Roy Lee
Ostrovsky, Jan Samuel
Silvey, Charles Delbert, II
Sneed, Spencer Craig

Arizona

Bachstein, Harry Samuel
Clarke, Marilee Miller
Goodman, Mark N.
Hoog, Patrick Edward
Howard, Robert Campbell, Jr.
Jennings, Marianne Moody
Ryan, D. Jay
Simon, Jack Hunt
Zukowski, Michael Chester

Arkansas

Eaton, Jimmy Don
Hughes, Steven Jay
Strother, Lane H.

California

Abbott, Barry A.
Andrew, John Henry
Bolles, Donald Scott
Buchanan, James Douglas
Chilleri, Gino Amerigo
Freeburger, Thomas Oliver
Germann, J. Gary
King, Franklin Weaver
Krahelski, Michael Anthony
Lee, John Jin
Lewis, Adam Aiken
McCrary, Toni Maree
Michaels, Sheldon
Munn, Ford Dent
Ornstil, Michael Gary
Porter, Verna Louise
Santandrea, Mary Frances
Share, Richard Hudson
Smith, Scott Ormond
Solis, Carlos
Sturdevant, Patricia Tenoso
Tonsing, Michael John
Tumpson, Albert Joseph
Weiss, Edward Abraham

Colorado

Appel, Garry Richard
Briggs, George Scott
Gabriel, Eberhard John
Geisel, Henry Jules
Kiehnhoff, Thomas Nave
Lapin, James B.
Markel, Robert Edwin
Martin, Ronald M.
McBee, Donald Lawrence
Merrick, Glenn Warren
Peck, Kenneth Eldon
Rowe, Russell Paul
Ruda, Jacques Serge
Seifert, Stephen Wayne
Torpy, Richard Donald

Connecticut

Chinitz, Stephen Solomon
Clendenen, William Herbert, Jr.
Peters, Ellen Ash
Stuart, Peter Fred
Yen, Elizabeth Chih-Sheng

Delaware

Blancato, Lydia Cox
Ciconte, Edward Thomas
Wolhar, Robert Charles, Jr.

District of Columbia

Ballen, Robert Gerald
Channon, Patricia Sugrue
Kass, Benny Lee
Muris, Timothy Joseph
Schukoske, Jane Ellen

Florida

Abrams, Lehn Edward
Ashby, Kimberly A.
Bogue, Russell S.
Burns, Katherine Mills
Cohen, Jules Simon
Cohen, Stephen M(artin)
Coleman, C. Randolph
Eggen, Eric Carl
Hartz, Steven Edward Marshall
Hern, Joseph George, Jr.
Hoofman, Robert Sidney
Horn, Andrew Warren
Krinzman, Richard Neil
London, Jack Edward
Morrall, Matthew Earl
Rakusin, Stephen Bruce
Rosenfeld, Alexander M.
Siegel, Edward
Singer, David Harris
Stein, Allan Mark
Swygert, Michael Irven
Trees, Philip Hugh
Wroble, Arthur G.

Georgia

Bobbitt, Phillip Lamar
Brannon, William Earl
Deegan, Nan Marie
Jordan, Hilary Peter
Kessler, Richard Paul, Jr.
Pinkston, Calder Finney

Hawaii

Chung, Harrison Paul
Dang, Marvin S.C.
Dyer, George Lewis, Jr.
Iczkovitz, Leslie Keith
Moon, John Paul
Okinaga, Lawrence Shoji
Rolls, John Marland, Jr.
Shklov, Mark Thomas

Idaho

Fawcett, Charles Winton
Hart, Stephen Strong

Illinois

Bell, Allen Andrew, Jr.
Brown, Bruce Allen
Clamage, Brett D.
Cleaver, William Lehn
Cohen, Allan Richard
Coston, James E.
Curran, Barbara Adell
Edmiston, Charles Nathan
Erschen, Gail Lee
Gieseke, Corinne Joyce
Gossage, Roza
Hoseman, Daniel
Howard, Timothy John
Inman, Arthur James
Kahn, Mitchell Charles
Lasaine, Dorian Barnett
Mayerson, Sandra Elaine
Moore, Kathleen Ann
Oglesby, Paul Leonard, Jr.
Patricoski, Paul Thomas
Rodkey, Frederick Stanley, Jr.
Schwartz, Stuart Randall
Travis, Joan Faye Schiller
Vaughn, Ray W.
Wesley, Howard Barry

Indiana

Abels, Jonathan Berle
Bishop, Reginald B.
Brainard, James C.
Cox, John Coates
Gehring, Ronald Kent
Hammel, John Wingate
Hammer, Howard Martin
Hansell, Ronald Stephen
Jaffe, Jay
Jewell, John J.
Light, Kenneth J.
McNaughton, George Theodore
Meacham, Jerald Samuel
Miller, Peter David
Nicholls, Jeffrey Michael
Nussbaum, Richard Anton, II
Price, Phillip Vincent
Reuben, Lawrence Mark
Sembroski, Robert Edmund
Sheets, Thomas Wade
Starkes, Dale Joseph
Vician, Glenn Steven
Zaharako, Lew Daleure

Iowa

Boresi, Richard L(eo)
Bowman, Michael Allen
Capps, George Hall
Coonrad, Douglas V.
McEnroe, Michael Louis
Mullins, Michael Royce
Phelps, Robert J.
Stoller, Larry Alan
Taylor, Richard Lee

Kansas

Altenhofen, Craig Joseph
Bertholf, Terry Donald
Fursman, Nancy Johanna
Karlin, Calvin Joseph
McPherson, Brock Richard
Walker, Huffman Reed

Kentucky

Aulenbach, W(illiam) Craig
Brammell, William Hartman
Hogg, Stephen Leslie
Ison, Robert Elwood
Kasacavage, Kenneth Stephen
Merkel, Roland Peter
Rhinerson, David Keith

Louisiana

Begoun, Michael Jay
Cavell, Daniel A.
Cheatham, Robin Bryan
Dearie, Harold Emmanuel, II
Dodd, Lawrence Roe
Garcia, Patricia A.
Hartel, Stephen Camille
Kaplan, Edward Alan
Larke, George Joseph, Jr.
Patin, Sidney L.
Puglia, Phyllis Mary
Richards, Marta Alison
Rowley, Horace Perez, III
Rubin, David Samuel
Schewe, Bruce Victor
Sklamba, Stephen Gerard
Thibaut, Joseph H. Major
Vance, Robert Patrick
Willis, Richard Allan
Wolfe, William Milton

Maryland

Calhoun, John L.
Christensen, Gordon Edward
Field, Samuel Summers, III
Goldman, Brian A.
Harwick, Robert Dean, Jr.
Katz, Stanley Herbert
Kochanski, David Majlech
Krensky, Michael Ian
Little, William Scott
Ruppersberger, Charles Albert, III
Taylor, Dane Edward
Wilson, Christian Burhenn

Massachusetts

Belford, Lloyd Earl
Boyd, F. Keats, Jr.
Bryson, David C.
Cullinane, Paul Blake
Garber, Philip Charles
Haldane, Mark Thomas
Kravetz, David Hubert
Kream, Deborah
Krulewich, Leonard M.
Mitchell, John Bruce
Parker, Christopher William
Widett, Irving
Wollman, Steven Lance

Michigan

Boltz, Russ Edward
Cornelius, Ellen Audrey
Flessland, Dennis Michael
Good, Carl Soren
Harms, Steven Alan
Mears, Patrick Edward
Osstyn, Randolph Beier
Riemersma, Jeffrey Kurt
Rochkind, Louis Philipp
Ronquillo, Allan Louis
Scott, Rosemary
Secrest, Stephen Frederick
Thomas, Robert Weston
Travis, Robert Frederick

Minnesota

Brown, John Lewis
Brutlag, Michael Lowell
Dettmann, Marc John
Johnston, Donald Robert
Kantor, David
Leonard, Brian Francis
Maus, Robert Michael
Tennessen, Robert Joseph
Weil, Cass Sargent
Yost, Gerald B.

Mississippi

Martin, George Gilmore
Pate, William August
Rosenblatt, Stephen Woodburn
Steadman, Susan Kirkpatrick
Webb, Thomas Lowry
Wilson, Leonard Henry (L.H.)
Wise, Robert Powell

Missouri

Beard, Charles Richard
Giorza, John C.
Lonardo, Charles Henry
Rund, William Drake

Montana

Graham, William Arthur
Larsen, Dirk Herbert
Matteucci, Sherry Scheel

Nebraska

Ball, Jordan Mitchell
Cada, James Alden
Kassmeier, Randolf Frank
Katskee, Melvin Robert
Lee, Dennis Patrick

Nevada

Dorsey, Robert Knickerbocker
Mushkin, Michael Robert

New Hampshire

Cloutier, Raymond Arthur
Gagliuso, Richard Caron

New Jersey

Brecher, Stuart Gary
Goldberger, Alan Steven
Hubschman, Richard Anthony, Jr.
Karp, Donald Mathew
Knoblauch, Leo N.
Kuller, Jonathan Mark
Leff, David
Manshel, Max
Matlin, David Stuart
Obara, Patricia Evelyn
Orr, Thomas John
Romano, Janet Bocchino
Tepper, Alan Michael

New Mexico

Bartholomew, James Ira
Hilgendorf, Robert Nelson
Moughan, Peter Richard, Jr.
Mulhern, John Joseph
Robinson, Bernard Leo
Schumacher, Rod M.

New York

Ackerman, Neil Harris
Baker, Barton
Beckerman, Ray
Benton, Donald Stewart
Block, Lester H.
Clair, Ira S.
Cohen, Linda Meryl
Curran, John Gerard
Drexler, Mark Andrew
Du Boff, Michael H(arold)
Edwinn, Eugene Paul
Eisenberg, Theodore
Fine, A(rthur) Kenneth
Fishman, James Bart
Friedler, Sydney
Geltzer, Robert Lawrence
Goldberg, Harold P.
Hatt, Donald Gregory
Helldorfer, Bernard George
Heussi, Jonathan A.
Hillman, Robert Andrew
Hull, Thomas J.
Klosk, Ira David
Kriger, Brian Elliott
Marinstein, Elliott F.
Mayka, Stephen P.
McConnell, John Hay
Miller, Robert M.
Mitchell, Richard Austin
Obremski, Charles Peter
O'Connor, William Jennings, Jr.
Peterson, James Richard
Peterson, Linda Sue
Petrone, Louis S.
Rosen, Ted Manus
Rothman, Robert Pierson
Rubin, Joseph
Salzman, Stanley P.
Schechter, Donald Robert
Schleifer, Richard Wayne
Silverberg, Sheldon
Silverman, William Michael
Smith, Brian Joseph
Steves, Edward Mickel
Taverni, Linda Troy
Tidwell, Drew Virgil, III
Tucker, Robert Henry
Zelmanovitz, Menachem Osher

North Carolina

Buckley, Charles Robinson, III
Craven, David Leigh
Ellis, Sharon Barclay
Frassineti, Jordan Joseph
Galloway, Hunter Henderson, III
Glover, Durant Murrell
Haywood, Edmund Burke
King, Thomas Wesley
Robbins, Robert Joseph, Jr.

North Dakota

Zander, Janet Holter

Ohio

Biars, Mark Martin
Burgess, Julia Edith
Campbell, Anita Peli
Cochran, Shirley Ann
Cohen, Arlene Switow
Dockry, Michael Brian
Dulebohn, Diana Gay
Frasier, Ralph Kennedy
Goettemoeller, Duane A.
Gruber, William Michael Ondrey
Haines, Richard McKinney
Hershey, Adrian Vernon
Hoerner, Robert Jack
Johnston, Lorene Gayle
MacKay, John Norman
Petersen, Lee
Piazza, Anthony Michael
Sayler, John Liston
Schuh, Stephen Joseph
Shaw, Elwin Scott
Sully, Ira Bennett
Trotter, Thomas Robert
Yogi, Nolan Kimei

Oklahoma

Dean, Bill Verlin, Jr.
Fitzgerald, Tami Lynn
Gierhart, Douglas Mark
Graves, Herbert Mac
Hammer, Bruce Edward
Lyon, Jim Allen
McCollam, M. E.
McMillian, Roger Lee
Miner, Joseph Brian
Oden, Waldo Talmage, Jr.
Settle, John Marshall
Ungerman, Maynard I.
Vogt, James Wayne
Walke, Geary Lynn

Oregon

Crane, Donald Ray
Eichelberger, Stephen
Greenwood, Myrtle Rae
Johnston, Ronald Allen
Langslet, John Loring

Pennsylvania

Berger, Lawrence Howard
Blank, Mark, Jr.
Feld, Arthur Michael
Greenberg, James
Herman, Lee Merideth
Hershenson, Gerald Martin
Johnson, Rena
Kemp, K(enneth) Lawrence
Marcovsky, Gerald Bennett
Meyers, Jeffrey
Morrissey, Philip Patrick
Page, Clemson North, Jr.
Picker, Millicent Ann
Posner, David S.
Rainone, Michael Carmine
Sanders, Russell Ronald
Siegel, Neil Yahr

Rhode Island

Dub, Larry
Fox, Francis Anthony
Tracy, David J.

South Carolina

Applegate, William Russell
Cooper, Robert Gordon
Johnson, Lawrence Wilbur, Jr.
Scott, Earl Daniel
Simpson, David Eugene
Smith, Thorn McClellan
Steadman, Richard Anderson, Jr.

South Dakota

Johnson, Richard Arlo

Tennessee

Crain, James Michael
Creekmore, David Dickason
Grisham, Arthur C., Jr.
Kavass, Igor Ivar
Lawless, Thomas William
Noel, Randall Deane
Patterson, Robert Shepherd
Wagerman, Howard Louis

Texas

Alderman, Richard Mark
Bell, Henry Newton, III
Borchers, Marion Jack
Boyd, William Clark
Bradie, Peter Richard
Burgchardt, Kathryn Dee
Cambrice, Robert Louis
Charles, Beverly M.M.
Coane, Bruce A.
Ehrle, William Lawrence
Hampton, Charles Edwin
Jennings, Karen Lynn
Jentz, Gaylord Adair
Jones, Russell C.
Kent, David Charles
Kincaid, William H(atton)
Lobert, James Edward
May, David P.
McMillen, Linda Louise
Meyer, Leonard James
Raine, Charles Macon
Steele, Glenn Horace, Jr.
Tutt, John Marion
White, Andrea Walker
White, Sharon Elizabeth
Williams, Johnny Jackson

Utah

Kent, Dale R.
Lewis, Kay Michie
Pleshe, Dorothy Clare
Rasmussen, Thomas Val, Jr.
Wells, Frank Milton

Vermont

Gravel, John Cook
Stevens, Harold Burr

Virginia

Abreu, Luis Alberto
Ackerly, Benjamin Clarkson
Brincefield, James Clifford, Jr.
Hamilton, Jeffrey Scott
Jones, Robert James
Mott, Joseph William Hooge
O'Donnell, Hugh David
Redmond, Robert
Seymour, William Francis, IV
Short, DeRonda Miniard
Trout, Stran Lippincott
Van Landingham, Leander Shelton, Jr.
Walk, Thomas Preston
Walker, Woodrow Wilson

Washington

Carlson, Timothy John
Fitterer, Richard Clarence
Gingerich, Florine Rose
Hames, William Lester

Uhrig, Ira John
Wirt, Alexander Wells

West Virginia

Cline, Michael Robert

Wisconsin

Cook, Joseph Lee
Deffner, Roger L.
Doran, Kenneth John
Flynn, William Frederick
Fons, John Joseph
Gass, David
Glowacki, Thomas Robert
Israel, Scott Michael
Johnson, Craig Robert
Kelly, Mark Daniel
Kenyon, Allen Francis
Mann, Douglas Floyd
Moore, David Charles
Rameker, William John
Smith, Wrede Howard, Jr.
Sturm, William Charles
Vollmer, Steven Lyle

Wyoming

Sachs, Philip David
Thomas, John Arlyn
Woodhouse, Gay Vanderpoel

ADDRESS UNPUBLISHED

Comer, Vivian Adelia
Fisher, Joseph Freiler
Goldman, Matthew Ralph
Hirsch, Jeffrey Allan
Holloway, Jan Charlene
Ivory, Cecil Augustus
Jensen, Gail Kathleen
Katz, Maurice Harry
Mell, Patricia
Palmer, Edwin Kayser
Rhinehart, R(ichard) Scott
Rodenburg, Clifton Glenn
Sherrard, Alexander Conn
Shopsin, (Marc) Moshe
Van Voorhis, Harold L.
Wolfson, Jack Leonard

COMMERCIAL, CONTRACTS

UNITED STATES

Alabama

Borg, Joseph Philip
Bowdre, John Birch, Jr.
Byrne, Bradley Roberts
Coplin, William Thomas, Jr.
Cornelius, Walter Felix
Dinning, Woodford Wyndham, Jr.
Funderburk, Kenneth Leroy
Hinds, Caroline Wells
Howell, William Ashley, III
Kennemer, John Maclin
Knight, Martha Kathryn
Lane, Robert Pitt
Max, Rodney Andrew
Riegert, Robert Adolf
Ryan, L(awrence) Thomas, Jr.
Scott, Romaine Samples, III
Shepard, Tazewell Taylor, III
Sims, Ronald Louis
Stoudenmire, William Ward
Trimmier, Charles Stephen, Jr.
Warren, Manning Gilbert, III
Wilson, Jack

Alaska

Bond, Marc Douglas
Bradbury, John Howard
Longacre, Roy Lee
Molloy, Robert Joseph
Ostrovsky, Jan Samuel
Wilson, Joseph Morris, III

Arizona

Baker, William Dunlap
Bender, Kenneth N.
Charles, Robert Marshall, Jr.
Clarke, Marilee Miller
Cowser, Danny Lee
Dickey, Harrison Gaslin
Epling, Richard Louis
Finson, Lowell Wayne
Furnish, Dale Beck
Henry, John Alfred
Levitan, Roger Stanley
McMorrow, William John
McRae, Hamilton Eugene, III
Meyer, Paul Joseph
Miner, Don Jones
Novak, Peter John
Seidenfeld, Glenn Kenneth, Jr.
Slavin, Francis John, Jr.
Terry, Peter Anthony
Young, Jeanne Catherine

Arkansas

Ball, William Kenneth
Creasman, William Paul
Grace, David Allen
Hargis, David Michael
Hopkins, Randolph Byrd
Jordan, Steven Ben
Lee, John Terry
Leflar, Robert B
Rhoads, George Robert
Scott, Isaac Alexander, Jr.
Strode, Joseph Arlin

California

Adams, Marcia Howe
Adams, William Gillette
Atkins, Thomas Jay
Baigent, Julia Marie
Baumgarten, Ronald Neal
Bedford, Daniel Ross
Berman, Howard Jonathan
Bramley, William Alexander, III
Brisson, Claudia Wisner
Broude, Richard Frederick
Brown, John Clark, Jr.

Brunette, Steven Edward
Bull, Howard Livingston
Burns, Bruce William
Camp, James Carroll
Cecchini, Garrett Lee
Chilleri, Gino Amerigo
Clabaugh, Elmer Eugene, Jr.
Coleman, Richard Michael
Collas, Juan Garduño, Jr.
Cologne, Knox Mason, III
Curotto, Ricky Joseph
Degallegos, Richard
Demirdjian, Jean-Claude
Demko, Joseph Nicholas, Jr.
Diamond, Philip Ernest
DuBose, Guy Steven
Dworkin, Michael Leonard
Engel, George Larry
Ervin, Howard Guy, III
Freed, Kenneth Alan
Fuller, Maurice DeLano, Jr.
Garay, Erica Blythe
Gardiner, Stuart Korson
Gauntlett, David Allan
Gay, Michael Hubert
Glines, Jack Holloway
Goldstein, Richard Jay
Gordon, Robert P.
Guilford, Andrew John
Hagel, James A.
Hansen, Richard King
Hayes, Byron Jackson, Jr.
Hendrickson, Robert Charles
Hieronymus, Edward Whittlesey
Hinman, Harvey DeForest
Hirsch, David L.
Hirsch, Morris Wayne
Holden, Frederick Douglass, Jr.
Huegel, Peter Andrew Vincent
Hughes, William Jeffrey
Johnson, Darrell Bruce
Jordan, Robert Leon
Kane, Margaret McDonald
Kant, Harold Sanford
Katz, Martha Lessman
Katz, Robert Nathan
Kimport, David Lloyd
Kinzler, William Charles
Klinger, Marilyn Sydney
Kornblum, Guy Orville
Kozinski, Alex
Kraw, George Martin
Lawton, Eric
Lazo, Ignacio Jesus
Leslie, Robert Lorne
Liebersbach, Richard William
Lombardi, David Ennis, Jr.
Loo, John
Lund, James Louis
Mack, John Oscar
Marker, Marc Linthacum
McNally, Susan Fowler
Minnick, Malcolm David
Munn, Ford Dent
Nownejad, Cyrus Sirouss
Ocheltree, Richard Lawrence
Olson, Walter Gilbert
Owens, Aletha Riedel
Pahl, Stephen Donald
Peters, Samuel Anthony
Pinkerton, Albert Duane, II
Power, John Bruce
Preble, Laurence George
Reed, Charles Rufus
Restrick, John Knight
Roby, Richard Eric
Rosett, Arthur Irwin
Russell, John Drinker
Ryan, Reade Haines, Jr.
Scheidegger, Kent Stephen
Sherman, Dana
Sherman, Martin Peter
Sherwood, Linda Kathleen
Shultz, John David
Silver, Mark Steven
Smith, Milan Dale, Jr.
Smith, Steven Ira
Snipes, G(eorge) William
Staley, John Fredric
Stenfeldt, Lillian Gerda
Stovitz, Chuck
Sullivan, James Anderson
Teitler, Harold Herman
Toftness, Cecil Gillman
Tormey, James Roland, Jr.
Traynor, J. Michael
Van Der Wal, Jeanne Huber
Walsh, Joseph Richard
Weg, Howard J.
Wein, Joseph Alexander
Weiss, Sherman David
Weissman, Robert Allen
Weltman, Jordan Scott
Wessling, Robert Bruce
Wetmore, Keith Chidester
Wiley, Robert Wayne
Wilka, William Charles
Williams, Michael Edward
Wilson, Clifford Ralph
Wise, Toni Pryor
Wong, Jackson D.

Colorado

Abbott, Keith Eugene
Aronstein, James Karpeles
Aschkinasi, David Jay
Barney, Patrick Earl
Beattie, Steven Mack
Bermant, George Wilson
Blair, Andrew Lane, Jr.
Brown, James Elliott
Chapman, Karen Louise
Cook, Terry Lee
Dauer, Edward Arnold
Dean, James B.
Dixon, Richard Dean
Durfee, Amy Lee McElheny
Erickson, David L.
Fiflis, Ted J.
Gebow, Thomas Eugene
Green, Lawrence Jamalian
Haake, Catharine Ann
Haskins, Thomas Marston
Hillestad, Charles Andrew
Honaker, Jimmie Joe
Joss, W. Bruce
Katz, Michael Jeffery
Kins, Tonya

Knudsen, Curtis Edwin
Levine, Gary H.
Maas, John Edward
Mauro, Richard Frank
McGill, Scott A.
Miers, James William
Montgomery, Robert Cornelius, III
Padilla, James Earl
Payne, Raymond Lee, Jr.
Pluss, Stewart Jay
Reid, John Edward
Rodgers, Frederic Barker
Seifert, Stephen Wayne
Slavin, Howard Leslie
Smith, Michael Alan
Wilkie, Barry Lynn
Zimmerman, Steven Louis

Connecticut

Abate, Ernest Nicholas
Austin, Richard David
Becker-Lewke, Laura Virginia
Cederbaum, Eugene E.
Chinitz, Stephen Solomon
Corthell, Jon Randolph
Crozier, John Huntington
Cuminale, James William
DiPietro, Andrew Michael, Jr.
Duke, Robert Dominick
Ewing, Robert
Feldman, Samuel Botwinik
Fignar, Eugene Michael
Fineberg, David L(eman)
Gates, Signe Sandra
Gold, Steven Michael
Goodridge, George Sidney
Greenspon, Robert Alan
Kalaher, Richard Alan
Lowry, Houston Putnam
Madorin, A. Raymond, Jr.
Mitchell, Thomas Bradford
Paladino, Robert Christopher
Parkin, Jeffrey Robert
Peters, Ellen Ash
Putman, Linda Murray
Rice, Michael Downey
Rome, Donald Lee
Rose, Richard Loomis
Rosenblatt, Edward Milton
Royston, Christopher Michael
Sachs, Jeffrey Michael
Santopietro, Albert Robert
Santoro, Michael Anthony
Scannell, David George
Smiddy, James Dallas
Sobol, Alan J.
Swerdloff, David Alan
Terk, Glenn Thomas
Theodore, Carol N.
Trager, Philip
Travis, Susan Topper
Williams, Michael Peter Anthony
Wolfe, Robert J.
Worley, Robert William, Jr.
Yoskowitz, Irving Benjamin

Delaware

Blancato, Lydia Cox
Bradley, Paul Anthony
Brown, James Wilcox
Carrad, David Clayton
Gallagher, Henry Edmond, Jr.
Hatch, Denison Hurlbut, Jr.
Jacobs, Jack Bernard
Kristol, Daniel Marvin
Morris, Kenneth Donald
O'Toole, John James
Winslow, Helen Littell

District of Columbia

Anthony, David Vincent
Bruemmer, Russell John
Clubb, Bruce Edwin
Crotty, Edward
Day, Gregg Alan
DeWeese, Kathleen Batchelder
Dickinson, Timothy L.
Eccard, Walter Thomas
Efron, Samuel
Eiselt, Erich Raymond
Epstein, David
Feller, Lloyd Harris
Fried, Charles
Golsong, Heribert
Goodwin, Robert Cronin
Guttman, Egon
Harris, Scott Blake
Harrison, Earl David
Herman, Stephen Allen
Himelfarb, Stephen Roy
Hughes, Dennis Michael
Kelly, William Charles, Jr.
Lamb, Kevin Thomas
Lubic, Robert Bennett
Mazo, Mark Elliott
Medalie, Richard James
Melamed, Carol Drescher
Miller, Eugene Paul
Okun, Todd Alan
Parkinson, Kenneth Wells
Pomeroy, Harlan
Portnoy, Ian Karl
Ralston, David Thomas, Jr.
Rhodes, Paula Renette
Roberts, Jared Ingersoll
Rothschild, Donald Phillip
Rowe, Robert Gammell, III
Ruud, Millard Harrington
Saba, Joseph Philip
Schram, Steven H.
Schukoske, Jane Ellen
Schwartz, David Harold
Shafferman, Howard Haswell
Singer, Daniel Morris
Smith, Robert Anthony
Soble, Stephen M.
Splitt, David Alan
Steingold, Stuart Geoffrey
Tether, Ivan Joseph
Vogel, John Henry
Vollmann, Alan Peter
Weiss, Arnold Hans
Williams, Wesley Samuel, Jr.

Florida

Abrams, Lehn Edward

Arencibia, Raul A.
Bagge, Douglas Malcolm
Barley, John Alvin
Bartlett, Charles John
Beall, Kenneth Sutter, Jr.
Burris, Johnny Clark
Campbell, Charles Philip, Jr.
Chesser, David Michael
Christian, Gary Irvin
Cohen, Stephen M(artin)
Dariotis, Terrence Theodore
Dayhoff, Charles Sidney, III
Del Russo, Alexander D.
Douglas, Hubert Gene, II
Doyle, Martin
Feola, Eugene David
Fildes, Richard James
Forman, Robert Steven
Friend, Richard E.
Golden, Donald Alan
Gonzalez-Pita, J. Alberto
Hadlow, Earl Bryce
Harris, Christy Franklin
Harrison, Teresa Harshman
Hayes, Neil John
Hodge, James Edward
Hodge, Wilson Eugene
Hollander, Bruce Lee
Iden, Bruce Franklin
Jamieson, Michael Lawrence
Jensen, Jack Albert
Jernigan, Anna Michelle
Johnston, Shepherd Davis
Jones, John Arthur
Joy, Daniel Foster
Kagan, Edwin Bruce
Kennedy, Marc J.
Leonhardt, Frederick Wayne
Lester, Edgel Celsus
Levenstein, Richard Harry
Lipson, Gary David
Mandell, Craig Jack
Marcus, Jonathan Seth
Martinez-Cid, Ricardo
Maurer, Virginia Gallaher
McHugh, William F.
Mednick, Glenn Myles
Mitchell, Ann Poe
Moreno, M. Cristina
Neiwirth, Ronald George
Ordonez, Luis Enrique
Ormond, Gregg Joseph
Pajon, Eduardo Rodriguez
Patsavos, Evelyn Christou
Pertnoy, Leonard David
Rosenberg, Sheldon
Rosenfeld, Alexander M.
Sanchez, Ernesto
Schwenke, Roger Dean
Simon, James Lowell
Singer, David Harris
Sisco, Thomas Edward, II
Sistare, Susan Powell
Stein, Allan Mark
Stevens, Edwin Dan
Teblum, Gary Ira
Thomas, Wayne Lee
Tripp, Norman Densmore
Waller, Edward Martin, Jr.
Wellbaum, Robert William, Jr.
Whatley, Jacqueline Beltram
Williamson, Julie Ann Stulce
Wolf, James Paul
Wynn, Charles Milton

Georgia

Ahlstrom, Michael Joseph
Beringer, William Ernst
Blumoff, Theodore Yale
Bratton, James Henry, Jr.
Cadle, Jerry Neal
Childs, Julie
Eubanks, Gary Franklin
Geiger, James Norman
Grove, Russell Sinclair, Jr.
Hall, Charles Martin
Herzog, Richard Blum, Jr.
Hishon, Elizabeth Anderson
Jordan, Hilary Peter
Maines, James Allen
Mass, Allen Robert
Miles, Dana Brent
Nesmith-Rosner, Joanna
Pujadas, Thomas Edward
Richards, Pamela Motter
Ross, Robert T.
Schwartz, Arthur Jay
Sharpe, Robert Francis, Jr.
Simmons, Raymond Hedelius, Jr.
Stamps, Thomas Paty
Walker, James Durward, Jr.
Watson, John Howard
Williams, Lyman Neil, Jr.

Hawaii

Barbin, Ryther Lynn
Chang, Donald Mark
Char, Randall Yau Kunn
Dyer, George Lewis, Jr.
Green, Randall Wayne
Matsushige, Cary Shigeru
Neeley, Joyce Yount
Rack, Thomas Paul
Rolls, John Marland, Jr.
Tam, James Kellett
Wong, Danton Sunmun
Woo, Vernon Ying-Tsai

Idaho

Beard, David Benjamin
Hoagland, Samuel Albert

Illinois

Adair, Wendell Hinton, Jr.
Adami, Paul E.
Anderson, J. Trent
Baer, John Richard Frederick
Baird, Douglas Gordon
Barnes, James Garland, Jr.
Bashaw, Steven Bradley
Bennett, Robert William
Blaszak, Michael William
Boblick, Shelby Susan
Brennan, James Joseph
Brock, Charles Marquis
Brown, Bruce Allen

Burns, Kenneth Jones, Jr.
Cleaver, William Lehn
Closen, Michael Lee
Cohen, Allan Richard
Cotteleer, Michael Alexander
Coughlan, Kenneth Lewis
Fawcett, Dwight Winter
Fazio, Peter Victor, Jr.
Feinstein, Fred Ira
Field, Robert Edward
Fishman, Robert Michael
Gabbay, Alan
Gaines, Peter Mathew
Greenblatt, Ray Harris
Gregg, Jon Mann
Henry, Robert John
Hoellen, John James
Hoffman, Thomas Joseph
Hoseman, Daniel
Hull, J(ames) Richard
Jacobs, James Ethan
Jadwin, Ted Richard
Johnson, Douglas Wells
Kahn, Mitchell Charles
Kamin, Kay Hodes
Kaplan, Howard Gordon
Katz, Stuart Charles
Kois, George Stephen
Kravitt, Jason Harris Paperno
Kurz, Thomas Patrick
Lapin, Andrew William
Lapins, Scott Michael
LeBaron, Charles Frederick, Jr.
Lippe, Melvin Karl
Macneil, Ian Roderick
MacPhail, Douglas Francis
Marks, Roger Harris
Marovitz, James Lee
McDunn, Susan Jeanine
McErlean, Charles F., Jr.
McGrath, William Joseph
McWhirter, Bruce J.
Meador, James Lewis
Mills, John Welch
Modlin, Lowell Ronald
Moltz, Marshall Jerome
Mulack, Donald G.
Nekritz, Barry B.
Nyberg, William Arthur
Overton, George Washington
Pallasch, B. Michael
Parson, David
Pell, Wilbur Frank, III
Prather, William Chalmers
Pratt, Robert Windsor
Proczko, Taras Roman
Rabinowitz, Mark Allan
Richards, Alan Edward
Rohrman, Douglass Frederick
Roos, Robert Carl, Jr.
Ross, Robert John
Roti, Thomas David
Sarabia, Antonio Rosas
Schiff, Matthew Bart
Schimberg, A. Bruce
Schreck, Robert A., Jr.
Schwartz, Donald Lee
Schwartz, Stuart Randall
Sconyers, Anthony Booker
Speidel, Richard Eli
Squires, John Henry
Steinberg, Morton M.
Sujack, Edwin Thomas
Tabb, Charles Jordan
Tabis, Bruno Walter, Jr.
Tallant, David, Jr.
Tanenbaum, Brian Ira
Thomas, Frederick Bradley
Valley, Mark R.
Vanneman, Edgar, Jr.
Vaughn, Ray W.
Wartman, Carl Henry
Watts, Dey Wadsworth
Webber, Carl Maddra
Yoon, Hoil
Zaander, Mark Charles

Indiana

Abrams, Jeffrey Alan
Anast, Nick James
Ancel, Jerald Irwin
Ancel, Steven Harlan
Baker, Ronald Lee
Bever, Robert Lynn
Bowman, Carol Ann
Buehler, James Carroll
Byrne, Maurice Andrew, Jr.
Dahling, Gerald Vernon
Densborn, Donald Keith
Eggleston, Thomas Warren
Greeneburg, Thomas Michael
Greer, Charles Eugene
Grund, James Arthur
Hammer, Howard Martin
Hanger, William Joseph
Harman, John Royden
Henderson, Eugene Leroy
Jordan, Denver Christian
Kahlenbeck, Howard, Jr.
Miller, David Anthony
Moore, James Dalton
Motsinger, Carl Daniel
Pope, Mark Andrew
Powlen, David Michael
Pytynia, Thomas Lee
Smith, Bruce Arthur
Tillman, Douglas Leon
Vandivier, Blair Robert
Zaharako, Lew Daleure

Iowa

Dykstra, Daniel D.
Hansell, Edgar Frank
Lam, Eric Wing-sum
Malm, Richard Allan
O'Connor, John Charles
Reasoner, Carroll Jane
Sanders, Doyle Dee
Shostrom, Earl Russell
Stageman, Richard Frederick
Stoller, Larry Alan
Widiss, Alan I.
Wing, Stephen Prentice

Kansas

Aylward, Paul Leon

Bertholf, Terry Donald
Clinkscales, J(ames) Randall
Gillmore, Alver James
Griffin, Ronald Charles
Haddock, Bradley Eugene
Ice, Theodore Branine
Johnson, Kevin Blaine
Lasater, Thomas John
McGee, John Francis
Peters, Geoffrey Wright
Powell, Craig Steven
Snowbarger, Vincent Keith
Speer, Wilson Edward
Stavely, Richard William
Woolf, John Paul

Kentucky

Atherton, Bruce Dwain
Brule, Thomas Raymond
Davis, Russell H.
Dieffenbach, Charles Maxwell
Ethridge, Larry Clayton
Fannin, David Cecil
Feazell, Thomas Lee
Hanbury, John Iruine
Hilliard, William Raymond, Jr.
Hutchinson, Mark Randall
Lester, Roy David
Newberry, James H., Jr.
Perchik, Jerrold R.
Philpott, James Alvin, Jr.
Stipanowich, Thomas Joseph
Van Meter, John David
Weldon, C. Michael

Louisiana

Anderson, Lawrence Robert, Jr.
Burck, Cyril B., Jr.
Capritto, Anthony Joseph
Chastain, Merritt Banning, Jr.
Danner, William B.
Friend, Joseph Ernest
Gruning, David William
Hardy, Ashton Richard
Hoffman, Robert Dean, Jr.
LeClere, David Anthony
Leefe, Richard K.
Lenz, Laurence Henry, Sr.
Madison, James Robinson
Perez, Luis Alberto
Raymond, Charles Michael
Richards, Marta Alison
Sher, Leopold Zangwill
Stuart, Walter Bynum, IV
Vermillion, John Richard
Waechter, Arthur Joseph, Jr.
Wilson, Donald Russell

Maine

Brett, Tybe Ann
Cooper, Michael David
Coward, Thomas Scott
Martin, Joel Clark
Patterson, Dennis Michael

Maryland

Arey, Patrick Kane
Asti, Alison Louise
Axelson, Jeffrey Mark
Baker, William Parr
Blakeslee, Wesley Daniel
Choate, Alan G.
Deerson, Bruce Alan
Gadhia, Lalit Harilal
Klein, Gerald S.
Kuryk, David Neal
Le Brun, Michael David
Maffitt, James Strawbridge
Marlow, William Freeman Coale, Jr.
Phillips, Leo Harold, Jr.
Priest, Gordon Webb, Jr.
Risik, Philip Maurice
Samuelson, Kenneth Lee
Scully, Roger Tehan
Siegel, Harold Aryai
Stalfort, John Arthur
Tanenbaum, Richard Hugh
Vanderlinde, Susan Kay

Massachusetts

Aresty, Jeffrey Michael
Berman, Mark Niles
Blanker, Alan Harlow
Bryson, David C.
Casson, Richard Frederick
Countryman, Vern
Creme, Paul David
Frederick, Samuel Adams
Friedmann, Jonathon David
Garber, Philip Charles
Geogan, Francis Joseph, II
Gleason, Joseph Howard
Gonson, S. Donald
Hall, Susan Medbury
Hemnes, Thomas Michael Sheridan
Hewitt, Emily Clark
Huang, Thomas Weishing
Jackson, Thomas Humphrey
Kream, Deborah
Levin, Charles Robert
Ley, Andrew James
Lyons, Nance
Mason, Paul Eric
McNulty, Thomas Joseph, Jr.
Moschos, Michael Christos
Parsons-Salem, Diane Lora
Polebaum, Mark Neal
Portnoy, Barry Michael
Ritter, Deborah Bradford
Rudolph, James Leonard
Salter, Leonard Melvin
Saltzberg, Edward Charles
Sheils, James Bernard
Simons, Steven J(ay)
Simpson, Russell Gordon
Solk, Gerald
Stokes, James Christopher, Jr.
Van, Peter
Webb, Henley Ross
Wollman, Steven Lance

Michigan

Batchelor, James Wiley
Bauer, Jeffry Mark
Bolton, Robert Saul
Carlin, John Bernard, Jr.
Case, Matthew Alan
Centner, Charles William
Churchill, David James
Davis, Roger Edwin
Ellmann, Douglas Stanley
Fauri, Eric Joseph
Gale, Connie R(uth)
George, Barry Brian
Gordon, Robert Jay
Greenhalgh, Stephen Irving
Haggerty, William Francis
Harms, Steven Alan
Harris, Stephen James
Hemker, Joseph Bernard
Hunter, Larry Dean
Johnson, Clark Cumings
Kanter, Alan Michael
Kerwin, J(ames) Eugene
Koernke, Thomas Frederick
London, Leslie Ann
Lubben, Craig Henry
Marotta, Robert
McCallum, Albert Donald
Nehra, Gerald Peter
Pierce, William James
Porro, James Earle
Robinson, Logan Gilmore
Rochkind, Louis Philipp
Ronquillo, Allan Louis
Sarb, Thomas Patrick
Schroer, J. Michael
Slavin, John Jeremiah
Stasson, Shelley Andrea
Steffel, Vern John, Jr.
Sullivan, Timothy Joseph
Theut, C(larence) Peter
Twitchell, Ervin Eugene
Vogel, Theodore John
Von Drehle, Ramon Arnold
Watson, Daniel Carvin
White, James Justesen
Yared, Paul David

Minnesota

Albers, Fern Beth
Altman, Milton Hubert
Angle, Margaret Susan
Barry, Charles Byron
Beattie, Charles Robert, III
Diracles, James Constantine
Edelman, Hyman
Erickson, Phillip Arthur
Fisher, Michael Bruce
Frecon, Alain Jean-Christian
Gurstel, Norman Keith
Johnston, Donald Robert
Lantz, William Charles
Mortrud, David Lloyd
Nora, Wendy Alison
Oh, Matthew In-Soo
Radtke, Stephen David
Rebane, John T.
Schatz, James Edward
Silverman, Robert J(oseph)
Stroup, Stanley Stephenson
Sullivan, Michael Patrick
Tourek, Steven Charles
Tyra, Kenneth Thomas
Wald, John Roger
Watson, John Slater
Weil, Cass Sargent
Wilcox, Donald Alan
Yost, Gerald B.
Zotaley, Byron L.

Mississippi

Chaney, Mark James, Jr.
Holbrook, Frank Malvin
King, Robert Wilson
Rosenblatt, Stephen Woodburn
Shiyou, Orvis A., Jr.
Steadman, Susan Kirkpatrick
Wiser, Nicholas Van
Young, Ralph Edward, Jr.

Missouri

Ball, Owen Keith, Jr.
Blakeslee, Julia Fay
Bowman, Pasco Middleton, II
Cooper, Corinne
Denneen, John Paul
Doheny, Donald Aloysius
Duesenberg, Richard William
Ellebrecht, Mark Gerard
Fretwell, Norman Elliott
Godiner, Donald Leonard
Goldstein, Steven
Graham, Harold Steven
Halpern, Burton
Harris, Harvey Alan
Hendin, Roy Allen
Knoten, Thomas Patrick
Lander, David Allan
Lee, James Roger
Levings, Theresa Lawrence
Mays, William Gay, II
McCubbin, Garry
Minogue, Thomas John
Noonan, Thomas Joseph
O'Loughlin, John Patrick
Pajda, Thomas Albin
Pollihan, Thomas Henry
Radasky, David Jacob
Reaves, Craig Charles
Ringer, John William
Roser, Michael R.
Schlecht, William Rogers
Standridge, Richard E.
Starnes, James Wright
Summers, Hugh Scott
Sutter, William Franklin
Terando, G.H.
Wallace, Barbara Wendy
Willy, Thomas Ralph
Wilson, Walter William
Wrobley, Ralph Gene

Montana

Graham, William Arthur
Guthals, Joel Eric
Hansen, Max A.
Karell, Allan L.
Majerus, Michael Gerard

Nebraska

Domina, David Alan
Jones, Ida Mae
Kassmeier, Randolf Frank
Katskee, Melvin Robert
Kreifels, Frank Anthony
Lang, James Edward
LaPuzza, Paul James
Loftis, Nancy Lynn
Rager, Kurt Thomas
Urbom, Randall Crawford
Walkley, Robert Earle
Wence, Gary Fred

Nevada

Allf, Nancy L.
Beesley, Bruce Thomas
Haase, M. Craig
Kelesis, George Peter
Kravitz, Martin Jay

New Hampshire

Cloutier, Raymond Arthur
Dahar, Victor William
Doleac, Charles Bartholomew
Gayman, Benjamin Franklin
Haughey, Thomas Malcolm
Marts, Anthony Charles
Platt, Thomas C., III
Potter, Fred Leon
Rakowsky, Connie Lee
Wyatt, Donald L., Jr.

New Jersey

Alexander, Robert Louis
Aspero, Benedict Vincent
Baron, Richard Mark
Bastedo, Wayne Webster
Bergamo, Charles
Berkley, Peter Lee
Bertsche, Copeland Gray
Bongiorno, Andrew William
Boyle, Matthew Anthony
Brecher, Stuart Gary
Campolucci, Roger Louis
Casiello, Nicholas, Jr.
Chaitman, Helen Davis
Cole, Murray L.
Corash, Richard
Curran, Catherine Moore
Deutsch, Dennis Stuart
Diamond, Gloria Beverly
Diktas, Christos James
Dornbusch, Arthur A., II
Epstein, Milton Aaron
Falcon, Raymond Jesus, Jr.
Finestein, Russell Mark
Freis, James Henry
Friedman, Robert Martin
Fries Gardner, Lisa
Gilman, Claudia Jane
Gogo, Gregory
Greenberg, Steven Morey
Harris, Allan Michael
Hayes, Lewis Mifflin, Jr.
Hayward, George John
Hubschman, Richard Anthony, Jr.
Isele, William Paul
Jacobson, Gary Steven
Jacobson, Michael
Kaplan, Howard Mark
Katz, Richard W.
Kennedy, Harold Edward
Kraus, Robert H.
Kutner, Mark David
Lambert, Richard Justin, Jr.
Lerner, Harry
Levavy, Bardin
Lubcke, Kip Charles
Lustbader, Philip Lawrence
Markwardt, John James
Martin, Russell White
Miner, Richard Thomas
Moore, Janet Patricia
Muscato, Andrew
Obara, Patricia Evelyn
Perzley, Alan Harris
Pojanowski, Joseph A., III
Sarakin, Lloyd Bradley
Schechner, David
Schenkler, Bernard
Schwartz, David Elving
Serata, Samuel Jacob
Sheldon, Scott Jeffrey
Sosland, Karl Z.
Staehle, Sandra Johnson
Statmore, Kenneth T.
Stone, Sheldon
Sweeney, Gerald Bingham
Watson, Mark Henry
Wayne, Robert Andrew
Welch, Gerald Thomas
Whelan, Charles Duplessis, III
Wingate, Richard Charles
Zegas, Alan Lee
Zlotnick, Norman Lee

New Mexico

Barnett, Barry Howard
Curtis, Stephen Paul
Grammer, David Allen, Jr.
Jontz, Dennis Eugene
Lopez, Martin, III
Matthews, Marian
Mckim, Lowell E.
Myers, Edward Doran
Rager, R. Russell
Ricco, Edward Robert
Schuler, Alison Kay
Skarda, Lynell Griffith

New York

Ackerman, Kenneth Edward
Ackerman, Neil Harris
Allen, Richard Marlow
Arango, Emilio
Axelrod, Charles Paul
Balaber-Strauss, Barbara
Barney, John Charles
Bass, Fred
Beller, Barry
Beltre, Luis Oscar
Bendes, Barry Jay
Bernstein, Edward Allan
Bernstein, Richard Forbes
Berzow, Harold Steven
Bitsky, Jason Isidore
Blachor, Isaac
Bleich, David Lloyd
Bobroff, Harold
Bohm, Joel Lawrence
Booth, Edgar Hirsch
Borger, John Emory
Brackett, Ronald E.
Brantl, Robert Francis
Brendzel, Michael L.
Brenner, Marshall Leib
Brown, Geraldine Reed
Brown, Lawrence Charles
Bruno, Richard Thomas
Callahan, Nancy Kay
Campanie, Samuel John
Cantor, Louis
Carr, Joseph B.
Cartenuto, David J.
Catanzano, Raymond Augustine
Chazen, Hartley James
Cho, Tai Yong
Clair, Ira S.
Cohen, Arthur Alan
Cohen, Marcy Sharon
Cohen, Robin Ellen
Cohen, Stanley Dale
Collazo, Salvador
Cooke, George Alexander, Jr.
Cooper, Michael Anthony
Cornelison, Albert Otto, Jr.
Costa, John Anthony
Cowen, Edward S.
Cropper, Stephen Wallace
Damashek, Philip Michael
Davidoff, Barry Frederick
De Lachapelle, Philippe
De Natale, Andrew Peter
Derzaw, Richard Lawrence
Dib, Albert
DiSciullo, Alan Michael
Dixon, Bonnie Lynn
Du Boff, Michael H(arold)
Dune, Steve Charles
Evans, George Walton, Jr.
Farnsworth, Edward Allan
Feder, Saul E.
Fernandez, Jose Walfredo
Finkelstein, Saul Haym
Franciscovich, George
Frankfurt, Morton Allen
Ganis, Stephen Lane
Ganz, David L.
Garro, Alejandro Miguel
Gibbs, Lippman Martin
Goebel, William Horn
Goldbrenner, Ronald Steven
Goldstein, Marcia Landweber
Gooch, Anthony Cushing
Green, Michael Aaron
Gross, Jack
Gursky, Steven Richard
Gussow, John Andrew
Hackett, Kevin R.
Hahn, Paul Bernard
Hancock, James H.
Healy, Harold Harris, Jr.
Hecker, Robert J.
Herbst, Todd Leslie
Hesselbach, Bruce William
Hillman, Robert Andrew
Howard, Joel Manning, III
Jaglom, Andre Richard
Jones, Lucian Cox
Kalb, Robert Joseph
Keller, Robin Elizabeth
Kilkenny, John Jude
King, Lawrence Philip
Kinney, Stephen Hoyt, Jr.
Kraver, Richard Matthew
Kullen, Richard Charles, Jr.
Lalla, Thomas Rocco, Jr.
Landa, Howard Martin
Leifer, Max David
Levie, Joseph Henry
Levitsky, Asher Samuel
Ligorio, Mario Eduard
Lobel, Douglas Arthur
Lunde, Asbjorn Rudolph
Lyman, Nathan M.
Maccarini, Anthony George
MacRae, Cameron Farquhar, III
Maloney, Thomas Joseph
Mann, Philip Roy
Mantle, Raymond Allan
Marcus, Eric Peter
Marcus, Myron
Margolin, Eric Mitchell
Marks, Alfred Mitchell
Mayka, Stephen P.
McGahren, Eugene Dewey, Jr.
Medford-Rosow, Traci
Mendales, Richard Ephraim
Meneilly, James Kevin
Menken, David A.
Meyer, Henry Theodore, III
Mindus, Howard Victor
Mirsky, Moshe Z.
Modlin, Howard S.
Moskowitz, Stuart Stanley
Murray, Conal Eugene
Nelson, Joni Lysett
Nemser, Earl Harold
Newman, Lawrence Walker
Nicholson, Michael
Nogee, Jeffrey Laurence
O'Connor, William Jennings, Jr.
Odell, Stuart Irwin
Olschwang, Alan Paul
Oppenheimer, Randolph Carl
Ordman, Howard Francis
O'Rorke, James Francis, Jr.
Pacious, Shaun Francis
Papernik, Joel Ira
Parmet, Donald Jay
Pisar, Samuel
Plum, Stephen Haines, IV
Podell, Albert N.
Polakas, John
Pollack, Stanley P.
Pollan, Stephen Michael
Puleo, Frank Charles
Rago, Daniel Anthony
Rappaport, A. Jack
Reitman, Jeffrey B.
Resnicow, Norman Jakob
Reynolds, Lola Sullivan
Richter, Gary Stephen
Ridloff, Richard
Rinaldi, Frank Robert
Ringer, James Milton
Rose, Michael Edward
Ross, Otho B., III
Ruda, Howard
Ryan, J. Richard
Sager, Jonathan Ward
Samet, Joseph
Samuel, Reuben
Samuels, Janet Lee
Sands, Judith Davies
Schaefer, Charles Harold
Scheibe, Robert Henry
Scheler, Brad Eric
Schnall, Flora
Schober, Gary Michael
Schwartz, Richard Morton
Shadley, Kay Lee
Shapiro, Barry Robert
Sherman, Jeffrey Scott
Siegel, Lewis Wolfe
Sims, Garland Dwight
Siphron, Joseph Rider
Soden, Paul A.
Sovern, Jeff
Spiegel, Jerrold Bruce
Ssekandi, Francis Muzingu
Stengel, Mark Allen
Stevenson, Justin Jason, III
Stillman, Bernard M.
Stratakis, Christ
Strickon, Harvey Alan
Stuart, Alice Melissa
Swanson, David Warren
Sweet, Joseph Church, Jr.
Tabachnik, Douglas T.
Tanenbaum, William Alan
Tannenbaum, Bernard
Taubenfeld, Harry Samuel
Terry, James Joseph, Jr.
Terry, John Hart
Toback, Arthur Malcolm
Trainor, Patricia Helen
Veneruso, James John
Wacker, Daniel James
Wald, Bernard Joseph
Walder, Robert Alan
Walton, Robert Prentiss
Warshavsky, Suzanne May
Webb, Morrison DeSoto
Weil, Peter Henry
Weinstock, Benjamin
Weisman, Barbara
Wertheimer, Sydney Bernard
White, Katherine Patricia
Wilkens, Beth Ela
Williamson, Steven Lloyd
Wise, Aaron Noah
Wittner, Derek A.
Wolff, Kurt Jakob
Wood, Clement Biddle, III
Wood, John Busey
Wukitsch, David John
Yamin, Michael Geoffrey
Zaretsky, Barry Lewis
Zeichner, Mark
Zeller, Paul William
Zimmerman, Jean
Zinman, Robert Marshall
Zuckerman, Mitchell

North Carolina

Burke, Frederick Augustine
Burti, Christopher Louis
Carter, Charles Michael
Conley, David Thomas
Eve, Robert Michael, Jr.
Guterman, James Hans
Jolly, Raymond A., Jr.
Joyner, Gary Kelton
Kirby, Mark Clayton
Schmutz, John Francis
Sharp, Starkey, V
Stevens, John Shorter
Tate, David Kirk
Tyson, John Marsh

North Dakota

Minch, Roger James
Sortland, Paul Allan

Ohio

Ballard, Mary Beth
Barz, Patricia
Baumgart, Richard Alan
Beck, James Hayes
Belville, Barbara Ann
Brown, Seymour R.
Buchenroth, Stephen Richard
Calkins, Benjamin
Carlin, Clair Myron
Cavendish, Thomas Edgar
Coady, Michael Francis
Coler, William Lee
Coombs, Frederick Stanley, III
Cunningham, James Joseph
Davis, Philip Carl
Detec, David Alan
Gherlein, John Harlan
Giles, Homer Wayne
Goss, Colleen Flynn
Greene, Bernard Wilburn
Gurley, Michael Edward
Heintz, Jeffrey Theodore
Hinerman, Philip Lee
Holmes, Robert Allen
Holt, G. Woodrow
Hornbostel, John F., Jr.
Hoyt, Marcia Swigart
Joseph, John James
Kilbane, Thomas Stanton
Klaus, Charles
Kopit, Alan Stuart
Kostyo, John Francis
Loewenthal, Marc Sheldon
MacKay, John Norman
Marx, Dianne Frances
McCracken, Christopher Cornell
Metz, Jerome Joseph, Jr.
Meyer, Charles Mulvihill
Pallam, John James
Peltier, Linda Jeanne
Ragley, Michele Ann Garrick
Richner, Robert Andrew

Rickert, Jeanne Martin
Rieser, John Paul
Savage, Barry Emery
Selak, Robert Allen
Sheward, Richard S.
Snow, David Forrest
Souers, Loren Eaton, Jr.
Stillpass, John Edward
Sully, Ira Bennett
Taft, Frederick Irving
Tobias, Charles Harrison, Jr.
Veltri, Stephen Charles
Waiwood, Michael Francis
Wilbur, Peter Davis
Wirt, William Stephen
Worhatch, S. David
Yogi, Nolan Kimei
Young, Charles Floyd

Oklahoma

Banker, Barbara L.
Bogan, Neil Earnest
Britton, James Edward
Cates, Ronald Dean
Cundiff, James Nelson
Cunningham, M.C., II
Durham, Ronald Dale
Ford, Michael Raye
Forsyth, John Emery
Frieze, H(arold) Delbert
Golden, Thomas Fuller
Moss, Raymond Gene, II
Reis, Robert Richard
Roff, Alan Lee
Schuller, Stephen Arthur
Steinhorn, Irwin Harry
Swinford, John Walker
Turner, Andrew Roland
Vogt, James Wayne
Waldman, Robert Allan
Williams, Bradford J., Jr.
Wyatt, Harry Miller, III

Oregon

Alberty, Steven Charles
Baer, Peter Edward
Bailey, Henry John, III
Bock, Jeffrey William
Brown, Lisa Claire
Brown, Stuart Melville
Deguc, Vincent Anthony
Eakin, Margaretta Morgan
Glasgow, Robert Efrom
Hunt, Lawrence Boyd
Jennings, George Mahlon
Langslet, John Loring
Levine, Howard Michael
Lindley, Mark Robert
MacRitchie, Brian John
McMenamin, Robert William
Muhlheim, Wilson C.
Philpott, Steven Lee
Rasmussen, Richard Robert
Robertson, Douglas Stuart
Stiles, William Neil
Thorndike, Daniel Carl
Wald, Sandra Louise
Wilcox, Robin Bachrach
Wyse, William Walker

Pennsylvania

Aronstein, Martin Joseph
Baldwin, Frank Bruce, III
Bambrick, Joseph Thomas, Jr.
Beam, Robert Charles
Becci, Michael Nelson
Bernard, Bruce William
Bernstein, Robert Steven
Blasier, Peter Cole
Brogan, James Martin
Brown, Donald
Brown, Robert Wayne
Byler, M. Elvin
Cerminaro, Anthony Richard
Checver, George Martin
Conti, Joy Flowers
Corcoran, Andrew Patrick, Jr.
Coyne, Charles Cole
DeYoung, Jonathan Harvey
Finkelstein, Joseph Simon
Fox, Michael David
Gaertner, Gary J.
Galanter, Robert Allen
Goss, Michael Mayer
Greenfield, James Milton
Gruenstein, Debra Lynne
Hammond, Mark Bashline
Hankin, Mitchell Robert
Hender, George Snowden
Herman, Charles Jacob
Hershenson, Gerald Martin
Hershman, Morris Paul
Heubel, William Bernard
Holland, Fred Anthony
Jaffe, Gary
Kaminsky, Ira Samuel
Kiever, Paul Kenneth
Killian, John Doran, III
Klee, John P.
Knapp, George Robert
Lipton, Robert S.
Loomis, Michael Eugene
Lotman, Arline Jolles
Marcovsky, Gerald Bennett
Mazer, Lawrence
McConomy, James Herbert
McKenna, J. Frank, III
McKnight, Henry James
Mooney, Charles W., Jr.
Morgan, David Scott
Nowak, Darlene M.
Pang, Peter Chiusing
Pleet, Jesse Lawn
Preate, Ernest D.
Preate, Robert Anthony
Puhala, James Joseph
Reath, George, Jr.
Reitz, Curtis Randall
Reuben, Allan Herbert
Richards, Robert Byam
Rouge, Cheryl Anne
Ruder, Jay Stanley
Sander, Malvin Gustav
Schorling, William Harrison
Siegel, Marlena
Stephens, Marlin Gerard
Vollmer, Charles Joseph
Weil, Andrew L.
Weir, Walter, Jr.
Welty, John Rider
Woodward, William John, Jr.
Yarmey, Richard Andrew

Rhode Island

Berkelhammer, Robert Bruce
Freedman, Carl Ira
McElroy, Michael Robert
Terry, Brian Stephen
Tobin, Bentley

South Carolina

Bethea, William Lamar, Jr.
Finkel, Gerald Michael
Lawrimore, Eugene Salmon Napier
Newby, Fred Bryant
Scheider, James Pringle, Jr.
Seaman, Robert E., III
Smith, Thorn McClellan
Winn, Marshall

South Dakota

Hughes, John Robert
Taylor, James Danforth

Tennessee

Bird, Agnes Thornton
Bird, Frank Babington
Boswell, George Harvey
Crain, James Michael
Frey, Kelly Leibert
Green, Lynne Knight
Henry, Arthur Wayne
Jett, Edward Stephen
Kavass, Igor Ivar
Kennedy, Richard Carl
McIntosh, James Arthur
Oldfield, Russell Miller
Patrick, Gary Ray
Phillips, John Bomar
Tate, James Solomon, Jr.
Turner, Wesley Dale
Veal, Rex R.
Winston, Russell Clay
Wise, Stephen Rule

Texas

Alderman, Richard Mark
Anders, Milton Howard
Atlas, Morris
Auld, Bruce
Baker, Mark Bruce
Barlow, Donald Eugene
Batson, David Warren
Bennett, Kevin Dane
Bircher, Edgar Allen
Block, Nelson Richard
Boos, Arthur Charles
Boze, Uriele L.
Bradie, Peter Richard
Brundrett, George L(ee), Jr.
Burns, Sandra K.
Bursley, Kathleen A.
Callahan, James Carroll
Carrigan, Stephen Paul
Charles, Beverly M.M.
Chase, Sam J.
Clark, David Keith
Conlon, Michael William
Crook, Charles David
Cunningham, William Allen
Dack, Christopher Edward Hughes
Doke, Marshall J., Jr.
Douglas, James Matthew
Ellinger, Steven
Elliott, Brady Gifford
Estle, Mark David
Ezell, Michael R.
Farley, Jan Edwin
Farnsworth, T Brooke
Feeney, Patrick Joseph
Freeman, Philip Dayne
Goldsmith, Mary Ann
Grant, Patrick Gerard
Green, Ray Eugene
Hagerman, John David
Hoag, Mary Moore
Holbrook, James Mitchell
Hoyt, Mont Powell
Ingram, Temple Byrn, Jr.
Irby, Holt
Jameson, Gene Lanier
Jentz, Gaylord Adair
Jones, John Gornal
Jones, Lindy Don
Kolodey, Fred James
Kosut, Kenneth Paul
Leach, Terry Ray
Liles, John H(enry), Jr.
Lowenberg, Michael
Marks, Gary Lee
Marquardt, Robert Richard
Martin, Richard Kelley
Menges, John Kenneth, Jr.
Miller, John Eddie
Moye, Eric Vaughn
Nadorff, Norman J.
Neal, A. Curtis
Nolan, John Michael
Nolte, Melvin, Jr.
Orleans, Neil Jeffrey
Painton, Russell Elliott
Phillips, Travis R.
Portman, Glenn Arthur
Prather, Robert Charles
Pulliam, Karen Ann
Ray, Donald Arvin
Rendell, Robert Sloat
Riley, Peter James
Robichaux, James Hall
Sandage, Douglas S.
Sanders, John Moncrief
Seeman, Robert Foster
Slaydon, Kathleen Amelia
Sylvester, Jon Howard
Taylor, Mark Edward
Thomas, Sheryl Lynn
True, Roy Joe
Vander Woude, Richard John
Wald, Michael H.
White, David Lawrence
White, Steven Gregory
Whitten, C. G.
Williams, Percy Don
Winship, Peter

Utah

Baron, Roger Frederick
Beckstead, John A.
Carlile, Craig
Cassity, James Junior
Christensen, Krege Bowen
Hunt, George Andrew
Jones, Michael Frank
Kennicott, James W.
Lochhead, Robert Bruce
Lowe, Kathlene Winn
Mabey, Ralph Rampton
Ockey, Ronald J.
Pleshe, Dorothy Clare
Reeder, F. Robert
Ross, Yan Michael
Siegler, Lora Celia

Vermont

Capel, Guy B.
Greenberg, David Herbert
McCamley, John Edward
Nichols, Elaine Kilburn

Virginia

Abreu, Luis Alberto
Ambler, Thomas Wilson
Anderson, John Foster
Arzt, Lee Robert
Bacon, James Thomas
Bankert, Joseph Edward
Brincefield, James Clifford, Jr.
Bromm, Frederick Whittemore
Brown, Frank Eugene, Jr.
Carter, Joseph Carlyle, Jr.
Dutton, Harold Hilbert, Jr.
Faggert, David Young
Fashbaugh, Howard Dilts, Jr.
Friedlander, Jerome Peyser, II
Gary, Stuart Hunter
Glenn, Robert Eastwood
Gregory, John Lunsford, III
Harrison, David George
James, Gus John, II
Kuykendall, Ronald Edward
Levy, Richard
Mandell, Steve Allen
Markovich, Stephen Edward
Massey, James Buckner, III
McGuire, Edward David, Jr.
Morris, Dewey Blanton
Parker, Richard Wilson
Pietrovito, Guy Roy
Robol, Richard Thomas
Sheffield, Walter Jervis
Simon, Alexander Nathan
Smolen, Jason David
Tankersley, Glenn Rayburn
Thomas, William Griffith
Waldo, Joseph Thomas
Walker, Woodrow Wilson
Waxman, Ned Warren
Wilson, Paul Lowell
Wimbush, Frederick Blair

Washington

Abelite, Jahnis John
Andersen, Charles Matthew
Belfiglio, Jeff
Blais, Jan David
Bonesteel, Richard David
Bradbury, Timothy Dewet
Clemons, Alpha Ottis, Jr.
Crandall, Patricia Irene
Crofts, Michael Lynn
Edmondson, Frank Kelley, Jr.
Gay, Carl Lloyd
Gilyeart, Steven Craig
Graham, Stephen Michael
Gustafson, Albert Katsuaki
Hulse, Brian Douglas
Jones, Bradley Tyler
Lundin, John W.
Maulding, Barry Clifford
Megaard, Susan Lynne
Mitchell, John Joseph
Otorowski, Shawn Elizabeth
Packer, Mark Barry
Peterson, Ronald Arthur
Reardon, Mark William
Robinson, Jeffrey Alan
Rockwell, David Hosmer
Sandman, Irvin Willis
Scowcroft, Jerome Chilwell
Spadoni, Peter Anthony
Tune, James Fulcher
Webster, Ronald B.
Whittington, Thomas Lee
Yalowitz, Kenneth Gregg
Zilly, Thomas Samuel

West Virginia

Crim, Joseph Calvin
Davis, Stephen Allen
Kent, James Albert, Jr.
Riley, Arch Wilson, Jr.
Thompson, Stephen Lee

Wisconsin

Boucher, Joseph William
Bush, Edwin Franklin, Jr.
Eustice, Francis Joseph
Fons, John Joseph
Friend, Henry Charles
Howarth, Kim A.
Hurt, Michael Carter
Josten, Roy Joseph
Kelly, Mark Daniel
Lavers, Richard Marshall
Leary, Nancy May
Levine, Herbert
Martin, Quinn William
Moore, David Charles
Olander, Ray Gunnar
Perkins, Randolph M.
Rameker, William John
Simon, Dennis Lee
Skilton, Robert Henry
Steuer, Robert Karl
Suran, Robert Herman
Taus, Armin Kenneth

Wyoming

Girard, Nettabell
Guetz, Burton Walter

TERRITORIES OF THE UNITED STATES

Puerto Rico

Gonzalez-Diaz, Raul E.

AUSTRALIA

Browne, Jeffrey Francis

ENGLAND

Brown, James Scott
Mecz, Jane Beltzer
Morrison, William David
Scott, John Andrew

FRANCE

Conrad, Winthrop Brown, Jr.
MacCrindle, Robert Alexander

HONG KONG

Randt, Clark Thorp, Jr.

MEXICO

Ritch, James Earle, Jr.

PEOPLES REPUBLIC OF CHINA

Capener, Cole R.

SINGAPORE

Siegfried, David Charles

ADDRESS UNPUBLISHED

Bell, Haney Hardy, III
Brodhead, David Crawmer
Elterman, Warren Bart
Familo, Edward Douglas
Godard, Randy Eugene
Graham, Keith Everett
Gulick, Peter VanDyke
Hafner, Thomas Mark
Hamel, Richard Paul
Hefner, Archie
Hemmer, James P.
Hernandez, David N(icholas)
Hildebrand, Charles Frederick
Holloway, Jan Charlene
Kaufmann, Roy Leslie
Kennedy, Nolan Malcom
McKenna, Edward James, Jr.
O'Mara, William Michael
Palmer, Edwin Kayser
Pooley, Beverley John
Rhinehart, R(ichard) Scott
Rohrbach, William John, Jr.
Rosen, Alex L.
Ryan, William J.
Sanger, Scott Howard
Stehlik, Frederick D.
Sullivan, James Washburn
Vida, Glen Joseph

COMPUTER

UNITED STATES

Arizona

Bender, Kenneth N.
Bivens, Donald Wayne
Henderson, David Allen
Korn, Gary Clifford
Price, Charles Steven

Arkansas

Goodner, Donald Scott

California

Adams, Marcia Howe
Anglin, Richard Lee, Jr.
Barnes, John Breasted
Bull, Howard Livingston
Chan, Thomas Tak-Wah
Derber, Robert Raymond
Dettmer, Scott Charles
DiLoreto, Ann Marie
Eisenstat, Albert A.
Fromholz, Haley James
Gay, Michael Hubert
Hiaring, Anne
Jacobson, Richard Lee
Kruger, Gilbert Nelson
Metzger, Robert Streicher
Moskatel, Ira Dennis
Newacheck, David John
Pasahow, Lynn Harold
Perez, Richard Lee
Radcliffe, Mark Flohn
Riter, Bruce Douglas
Schwarzstein, Richard Joseph
Scoular, Robert Frank
Seltzer, Leon Eugene
Star, Ronald H.
Strong, George Gordon, Jr.
Van Praag, Jane Catherine

Colorado

Dorr, Robert Charles
Gebow, Thomas Eugene
Johnson, David William
Linfield, James Clark Taylor
Prichard, Vincent Marvin

Connecticut

Asija, S(atya) Pal
Corthell, Jon Randolph
Lowry, Houston Putnam
McCobb, John Bradford, Jr.
Menchel, Arnold Ira
Smiddy, James Dallas
Smiddy, Linda O'Riordan
Stone, Dennis J.

District of Columbia

Bannon, Brian Anthony
Brooks, Daniel Townley
Burgett, David Wallace
Chabot, Elliot Charles
Davidson, Duncan Mowbray
Doyle, Gerard Francis
Epstein, Gary Marvin
Fennell, William Alfred
Franklin, William Jay
Frieden, Robert M.
Garvey, John Cotton
Greenberger, I. Michael
Grossman, Garry S.
Kaufman, Joshua Jacob
Kenchelian, Mark Levon
Latimer, Allie B.
Mackles, Glenn Frederick
Morgan, William Caswell
Moss, Kathleen Susan
Oakley, Robert Louis
Peters, Frederick Whitten
Polansky, Larry Paul
Riley, Dennis James
Shaffer, Roberta Ivy
Stern, Richard Harvey
Vovakis, Lewis Harry
Westermeier, John Thomas, Jr.
Yoches, Edward Robert
Zwick, Kenneth Lowell

Florida

Bonham-Yeaman, Doria
Gelfand, Michael Joseph
Harris, Charles Edison
Losey, Ralph Colby
Miller, Carla Dorothy
O'Neill, Michael Joseph
Rojas, Jose Ignacio
Roseman, Mark Alan
Rosenblatt, Joel I.

Georgia

Arkin, Robert David
Garland, John Louis, Sr.
Goldman, Joel S.
Maines, James Allen
Marianes, William Byron
Murphy, Charles Conrow, Jr.
Saidman, Gary K.

Hawaii

Iczkovitz, Leslie Keith
Schraff, Paul Albert

Illinois

Bloom, Christopher Arthur
Cannon, Benjamin Winton
Don, Arthur
Gagne, James L.
Greenstein, Martin Richard
Kohlstedt, James August
Markey, James Kevin
Miranti, Richard Frederick
Nagel, Stuart Samuel
Sanders, Michael Leo
Smedinghoff, Thomas J.
Spain, Patrick James
Van Duerm, James
Wilson, Michael B(ruce)

Indiana

Deveau, Francis Joseph
Hammer, Howard Martin
Light, Kenneth J.

Kentucky

Lester, Charles Theodore, Jr.
Snyder, Paul Stewart

Louisiana

Evans, Robert Collin
Harris, Thorne D., III
Lipsich, Jerome K.

Maine

Gemignani, Michael Caesar

Maryland

Falkson, Susan Dory
Patrick, Philip Howard

Massachusetts

Andrews, David Joseph
Ballantyne, Richard L(ee)
Barber, Robert Cushman
Bigelow, Robert P.
Creme, Paul David
Fischer, Mark Alan
Gleason, Joseph Howard
Hadzima, Joseph George, Jr.
Katsh, M. Ethan
Mugler, Molly Scott
Paglierani, Ronald Joseph
Rubenstein-Kursh, Nan
Saltzberg, Edward Charles
Trautman, Donald Theodore
Updegrove, Andrew Scott

Michigan

Callahan, Michael Sean
Hemker, Joseph Bernard
Hitchcock, Stephen Jay
Legg, Michael William
Polley, Vincent Ira

Minnesota

Beha, Ralph Werner
Boyer, David Randall
Brown, John Lewis
Glanzman, Scotty Lynn
Jamar, Steven Dwight
Wine, Mark Philip

Nebraska

O'Connor, James Edward
O'Hara, Michael James

Nevada

Willick, Marshal Shawn

New Hampshire
Coolidge, Daniel Scott

New Jersey
Adler, Jack Philip
Allen, Michael Lewis
Brewer, Andrea Bordiga
Ehrlich, Leslie Sharon
Ernst, Charles Stephen
Katz, Jeffrey Harvey
Lubcke, Kip Charles
MacDonald, Joseph J.
Miner, Richard Thomas
Monti, Renard George
Pace, Thomas
Riley, Robert Henry
Sherman, Lenore Shustak
Zaloom, John B(asil)

New York
Andrew, Leonard DeLessio
Ashley, Daniel Joseph
Berger, C. Jaye
Bierce, William Blaikie
Bohm, Joel Lawrence
Chapuran, Ronald Francis
Clary, Richard Wayland
Davidoff, Barry Frederick
Dwyer, Robert Jeffrey
Epstein, Michael A.
Erim, Ahmet Martin
Farley, William Patrick
Garcia, Maria Elias
Gaylord, Bruce Michael
Haken, Jack Edward
Heines, Molly Kathleen
Hoffman, Paul Shafer
Jaglom, Andre Richard
Jennings, Jeffrey Howells
Kasselman, Stevens Jay
Kinney, Stephen Hoyt, Jr.
Lieberman, Steven Paul
Lyman, Nathan M.
Maidman, Stephen Paul
Matus, Wayne Charles
Moskowitz, Stuart Stanley
Nogee, Jeffrey Laurence
O'Neill, Patrick Joseph
Oppedahl, Carl W.
Relson, Morris
Robertson, Edwin David
Savage, Edward Turney
Schober, Gary Michael
Schwartz, Laurens R.
Spath, Gregg Anthony
Tanenbaum, William Alan
Taylor, Job, III
Trainor, Patricia Helen
Weinstock, Benjamin

North Carolina
Case, Charles Dixon
Conley, David Thomas
Linker, Raymond Otho, Jr.
Olive, Susan Freya

Ohio
Dettinger, Warren Walter
Emmert, Steven Michael
Hermann, Thomas George
Jenkins, Matthew Richard
Johnson, John Richard
Kahrl, Robert Conley
Mullin, Michael Joseph
Nauman, Joseph George
Potash, M. Steven
Purdy, Roger Daniel
Ragley, Michele Ann Garrick
Troxell, James Dane

Oregon
Campbell, William Coolidge
Chapman, Matthew William
Chernoff, Daniel Paregol
Marks, J(ohn) Barrett
Webb, Jere M.

Pennsylvania
Armstrong, Stephen Wales
Brown, Edward George
Cerminaro, Anthony Richard
Doyle, William A.
Ferguson, Sanford Barnett
Fox, Michael David
Grace, Eugene Peter
Hauben, Ronald Bruce
Hunter, Martha Louise
James, Keith Alan
Lipton, Robert S.
McKenna, James L.
Murphy, Joseph Edward
Rosenberg, John Edward
Ross, Murray Louis
Silverman, Arnold Barry
Simkanich, John Joseph
Simon, David Frederick
Starr, Mark Toby
Szczepaniak, Joseph Dennis
Weisburd, Steven I.

Rhode Island
Del Sesto, Ronald W.

Tennessee
Frey, Kelly Leibert
Hunt, William Walter, III

Texas
Dillon, Andrew Joseph
Keys, Jerry Malcom
Maher, Mary Frances
Miller, John Eddie
Mylott, Thomas Raymond, III
Premack, Paul Allen
Scott, Eddie Elmer
Strawn, James Roy
Toedt, D(ell) C(harles), III
Traver, Alfred Ellis, Jr.
Walter, Charles Frank

Virginia
Baird, Charles Bruce

Beutel, Richard Armstrong
Cambridge, Robert Matthew
Chelen, John Cas
DeGolia, James B.
Greigg, Ronald Edwin
Lester, James Lee
MacMurray, Worth Daniels
Roth, Alexander Dunbar
Schwartzstein, Linda Ann

Washington
Batey, Douglas Leo
Carlson, Timothy John
Clemons, Alpha Ottis, Jr.
Crofts, Michael Lynn
Greenburg, G. Scott
Jensen, Sherman Holbrook
Reardon, Mark William
Wells, Christopher Brian

Wisconsin
Frasch, David Edward
Kahn, Charles Frederick, Jr.
Martin, Quinn William
Shupe, Larry Lewis

ADDRESS UNPUBLISHED
Brotman, Stuart Neil
Brunell, Norman Eliot
Herrell, Roger Wayne
Joike, Trevor B.
Kutten, Lawrence Joseph
Moravsik, Robert James
Rosen, Nathan Aaron
Slowiaczek, John Steven

CONDEMNATION

UNITED STATES

Alabama
Little, Joe Hollis, Jr.

Alaska
Hughes, Mary Katherine
Weinig, Richard Arthur

Arizona
Abraham, Andrew
Irvine, Thomas Kenneth
McRae, Hamilton Eugene, III

Arkansas
Julian, Jim Lee
Wilson, Robert Martin, Jr.

California
Bitting, William McClure
Endeman, Ronald Lee
Kehoe, Dennis Joseph
Kovacic, Gary Anton
Kozinski, Alex
McMurry, Robert I.
Mehlhaff, Robert
Scharf, Robert Lee
Schimmenti, John Joseph
Sutherland, Lowell Francis
Vandegrift, Lucian B.
Wylie, Richard John

Colorado
Bryans, Richard W.
Feder, Harold Abram
Glasser, Matthew David
Marsh, William Robert
Tisdale, Patricia Claire

Connecticut
Alcorn, Hugh Meade, Jr.
Fallon, John Francis
Mittelman, Irwin David
Morelli, Joseph Christopher
Snaider, Benson Abram

District of Columbia
Brookshire, James Earl
Bryan, Mildred Gott
Loeb, Dorothy Pearl
Moskof, Howard Richard
Verrill, Charles Owen, Jr.

Florida
Black, Leon David, Jr.
Churuti, Susan Hamilton
Donaldson, Dorothea E.
Earle, William George
Foerster, David Wendel
Harris, Gordon H.
Lloyd, John Stoddard
Norman, Donald Hamilton
Stubbs, Sidney Alton

Georgia
Champion, Forrest Lee, Jr.

Hawaii
Leas, Philip Joseph
Tanaka, Leila Chiyako

Illinois
Powless, Kenneth Barnett
Redmond, Richard Anthony
Righeimer, Frank S., Jr.
Stevens, Douglas Robert

Indiana
Carroll, John Leo
Williams, Bradley Louis

Iowa
Mull, Richard Eugene
Nelson, Robert Charles

Kansas
Aylward, Paul Leon
Hamilton, John Richard

Louisiana
Davidson, Van Michael, Jr.
Gallaspy, John Norman

Maryland
Brown, R. Edwin
Brugger, George Albert
Crocker, Michael Pue
Reid, Richard Ayres

Massachusetts
Huber, Richard Gregory
Meserve, Robert William
O'Connell, Henry Francis

Michigan
Ackerman, Alan Thomas
Burgoyne, Bert
Christopher, William Garth
Gleiss, Henry Weston
Logie, John Hoult
Martin, Walter

Minnesota
Edelman, Hyman
Hillstrom, Robert Arthur

Mississippi
Robertshaw, James

Missouri
Crigler, Susan Gum
Frantze, David W.
Parker, Linda Louise

New Jersey
Honig, Emanuel Aaron

New York
Emanuel, Ira Michael
Flower, Edward
Goldstein, M. Robert
Greilsheimer, James Gans
Grossman, James Stuart
Rikon, Michael
Santemma, Jon Noel
Spivack, Edith Irene
Squire, Sidney
Triebwasser, Jonah Ignatius
Wallace, Herbert Norman

North Carolina
Harkey, Henry Lee
Underwood, Samuel Bobbitt, Jr.
Walker, Daniel Joshua, Jr.

North Dakota
Bair, Bruce B.
Sperry, Floyd Benjamin

Ohio
Ray, Frank Allen

Oklahoma
Hacker, Jerry William
Miskovsky, George, Sr.
Rorschach, Jack L.
Wallace, Thomas Andrew

Pennsylvania
Kelsen, Peter Foster
Krawitz, Sidney L.
Kubacki, Stanley Louis
Mendelson, Leonard (Melvin)

South Carolina
Babcock, Keith Moss

Texas
Ballew, William Virgil, Jr.
Boyd, Roland
Forbes, Arthur Lee, III
Gandy, Francis I., Jr.
Garcia, Humberto Sigifredo
Hartnett, Will Ford
Hays, Larry Weldon
Purnell, Charles Giles
Wallis, Ben Alton, Jr.
Wilson, Charles Julian
Young, Ardell Moody

Virginia
Blankingship, A. Hugo, Jr.
Rolfe, Robert Martin
Stone, Steven David
Trotter, Haynie Seay

Washington
Greenan, Thomas J.

West Virginia
Colan, Owen Richard
Sanders, William Henry

Wisconsin
Callahan, Carroll Bernard

ADDRESS UNPUBLISHED
Weaver, John Hosch

CONSTRUCTION

UNITED STATES

Alabama
Centeno, Douglas Joseph
Childs, Larry Brittain
Hull, Daniel Talmadge
Max, Rodney Andrew
Rogers, Ernest Mabry

Alaska
Bankston, William Marcus

Clark, Julie Ann
De Lisio, Stephen Scott
Dickson, Robert Jay
Parker, Douglas Stuart
Petersen, A. Lee
Pfiffner, Frank Albert
Wade, Hugh Gerald

Arizona
Barker, J(ohn) Emery
Condo, James Robert
Dickey, Harrison Gaslin
Dulberg, Michael Seth
Irvine, Thomas Kenneth
Jacques, Raoul Thomas
Jakubczyk, John Joseph

Arkansas
Cross, Junius Bracy, Jr.
Davis, Steven Ray
Grace, David Allen

California
Abdulaziz, Sam K.
Atkinson, Steven Douglas
Baigent, Julia Marie
Byron, Thomas William
Coombs, William Elmer
Cummins, Neil Joseph, Jr.
Drachman, Frank Emanuel, Jr.
Eisenstat, Albert A.
Fleischli, Jack A.
Gade, Thomas Andrew
Hanley, Thomas Francis, III
Heilbron, David M(ichael)
Hendrickson, Robert Charles
Jagiello, Barbara Anne
Johnson, Drew Martin
Kamine, Bernard Samuel
Kramer, Kenneth Scott
Leslie, Robert Lorne
Liebersbach, Richard William
McGuinn, John Francis
McGuire, John Francis
McLeod, Robert Macfarlan
Miller, Kenneth Michael
Neary, Christopher J.
Negron, Dennis
Richards, Gerald Thomas
Ritchie, Thomas Brown
Robison, William Robert
Ross, Susan Kohn
Ruma, Ronald Edward
Schmal, Timothy James
Schneier, Marc Malvin
Schroeder, John
Sherman, Glenn Terry
Simon, Bruce Lee
Smith, Diane Rapp
Smitter, Ronald Warren
Smolker, Gary Steven
Snipes, G(eorge) William
Vallens, Brent Edward
Wagner, D. William
Walker, Jordan Clyde
Wheatley, Jeff R.
Wilhelm, Robert Oscar
Wolfe, Richard Frederick
Wulfsberg, Harold James

Colorado
Campbell, Richard Bruce
Donnelly, Frederick James
Goorman, Perry Lee
Green, Lawrence Jamalian
Gulley, Kenneth Galen
Jablonski, James Arthur
Keatinge, Cornelia Wyma
McGowan, Rodney Ralph
Michaels, Jane
Richman, Alan Elliott
Rodgers, Ralph Emerson
Sands, Jon F(rederick)
Serini, John Peter
Wells, David Conrad

Connecticut
Brady, Matthew Joseph
Cooney, Bradley Kent
Dowling, Vincent John
Pepe, Louis Robert

District of Columbia
Braude, Herman Martin
Colton, Herbert Spencer
Croessmann, Philip Richard
Field, Charles G.
Ittig, Gerard W.
Keiser, Henry Bruce
Kornblut, Arthur T.
Krump, Gary Joseph
Lifschitz, Judah
Lynham, John Marmaduke
Morant, Blake Dominic
Rephan, Jack
Riley, Dennis James
Stinchfield, John Edward
Ursini, Josephine Lucille
Whitney, John Adair

Florida
Anderson, Bruce Paige
Barley, John Alvin
Burnette, Guy Ellington, Jr.
Burton, Richard Jay
Ferencik, Robert Elmer, Jr.
Fuller, Diana L.
Greenleaf, Walter Franklin
Harris, Gordon H.
Hart, Karl Vance
Hingston, Robert Allen
Horan, John Patrick
Justice, Thomas Hardwick, III
Leib, Patricia Shane
Leiby, Larry Raymond
Levine, Curtis Gilbert
Manne, Robert Jay
Mitchell, Ann Poe
O'Neal, Leslie King
Park, Joseph Rathbone
Rakusin, Stephen Bruce
Richardson, Sally M.
Rico, JulieAnn
Rougeux, Donna Riselli

Sax, Spencer Meridith
Simon, James Lowell
Sutcliffe, Roland Alton, Jr.
White, Andrew, III
Wilson, William Berry

Georgia
Clark, Herman
DuBose, Charles Wilson
Fortune, Philip Lee
Gray, Herbert Harold, III
Griffin, Harry Leigh
Hinchey, John William
Humphries, James Donald, III
Jones, Glower Whitehead
King, Thad Denton
Knox, Wyckliffe Austin, Jr.
Menendez, Kenneth Gary
Neuren, Michael Scott
Oastler, Bert Robert
Pollard, Brenda Krebs
Sours, John Delmar
Stone, Freddie Ray Josh
Sweeney, Neal James
Thompson, Patrick Alan
Wright, Frederick Lewis, II

Hawaii
Deaver, Phillip Lester
Floyd, Shelby Anne
Freed, Michael Leonard
Hakoda, Harvey Nobuo
Iwai, Wilfred Kiyoshi
Iwamoto, Raymond Shigeo
Meyer, William George, III
Mukaida, Wayne Hideo
Robinson, Harlo Lyle
Uyeno, Theodore Yoshi
Wong, James Thomas

Idaho
Banducci, Thomas Anthony
Ebert, Larry Paul
Hanks, Stephen Grant

Illinois
Adami, Paul E.
Brody, Lita Helen
Franz, William Mansur
Fylstra, Raymond Alan
Greenberger, Ernest
Hajek, Robert J.
Nowacki, James Nelson
Prillaman, Frederick Charles
Richardson, William F.
Schoumacher, Bruce Herbert
Sklar, Stanley Paul
Vree, Roger Allen

Indiana
Dutton, Clarence Benjamin
Lowe, Louis Robert, Jr.
Speicher, John Allan
Stalmack, Joseph

Iowa
Gibb, William Stewart
Koehn, William James
Rhodes, Keith Stewart
Strutt, David Stanley

Kansas
Callahan, Michael Thomas
Myers, Jesse Jerome

Kentucky
Connolly, Robert Michael
Ethridge, Larry Clayton
Moore, Charles Dudley, Jr.
Perchik, Jerrold R.
Stipanowich, Thomas Joseph

Louisiana
Andersson, W. Paul
Becnel, Philip Alfred, III
Brian, A(lexis) Morgan, Jr.
Butcher, Bruce Cameron
Cheatwood, Roy Clifton
Danner, William B.
Dearie, Harold Emmanuel, II
Holliday, James Sidney, Jr.
Huffman, Gerald James, Jr.
Kracht, Eric Alan
Lipsich, Jerome K.
Rowley, Horace Perez, III
Seabolt, Charles Frederick
Shields, Lloyd Noble
Wright, William Everar, Jr.

Maryland
Grattan, S. Amy
Pappas, George Frank
Rosenthal, Lawrence Gerald

Massachusetts
Buczkowski, David John
Carpenter, Robert Brent
Carroll, John Thomas
Connolly, Thomas Edward
Covel, Richard Allan
Davidson, Frank Paul
Fraser, Everett MacKay
Glovsky, Susan G. L.
Molineaux, Charles Borromeo, Jr.
Moschos, Michael Christos
Whalen, James Michael
Wollman, Steven Lance
Zito, Frank R.

Michigan
Alber, Phillip George
Gustafson, Richard B.
Oltarz-Schwartz, Sara
Scudi, Morgan John Clift
Twitchell, Ervin Eugene
Wittlinger, Timothy David

Minnesota
Halverson, Steven Thomas
Jamar, Steven Dwight
Lillehaug, David Lee

Maffei, Rocco John
Martin, Kathleen Minder
Mayerle, Thomas Michael
Pentelovitch, Willian Zane
Sand, David Byron
Stephens, Mary Elizabeth Giuliani
Straughn, Robert Oscar, III

Mississippi

Hubbard, Robert Dale
Wise, Robert Powell

Missouri

Biesterfeld, Craig Stewart
Colagiovanni, Joseph Alfred, Jr.
Coughlin, Richard Edward
Hapke, Daniel S., Jr.
Johnson, Leonard James
Lerner, Lawrence
Pierce, Donald Victor Jr.
Rottler, Terry Robert
Stoup, Arthur Harry
Vandever, William Dirk

Montana

Bauer, Mark Eugene

Nebraska

Baumann, Larry R(oger)
Jones, Ronald Lee
Lash, Douglas Steven
Lauritsen, Thomas Christian
Smith, Richard Wendell

Nevada

Hammer, Bill C.
Trachok, Richard M(athew), II

New Hampshire

Danenbarger, W. Wright
Hanna, Katherine Merritt

New Jersey

Baron, Richard Mark
Corash, Richard
Estis, Dennis Arnold
Haberbusch, Carl Arthur
Klock, John Henry
Kronman, Carol Jane
Lind, Peter Eugene
McKenna, Michael Francis
Peckar, Robert S.
Smith, Peter John
Sterling, Harold G.

New Mexico

Fish, Paul Mathew

New York

Beckey, Sylvia Louise
Berger, C. Jaye
Bergman, Bruce Jeffrey
Bernstein, Richard Forbes
Bernstein, Stephen Michael
Brown, Paul M.
Cantor, Louis
Couch, Leslie Franklin
DeBonis, Sharon Couch
De Luca, Thomas George
Dib, Albert
Feinstein, Sheldon
Flynn, William Bernard
Forster, James Francis
Halper, Emanuel Barry
Herbst, Todd Leslie
Howard, Joel Manning, III
Kinney, Stephen Hoyt, Jr.
Leader, Robert John
Lindskog, David Richard
Lipsman, Richard Marc
Marcellino, Stephen Michael
Martirano, John Joseph
Matus, Wayne Charles
Militello, Samuel Philip
Newman, Howard Julian
Osborn, John Emory
Patte, George David, Jr.
Ridloff, Richard
Salup, Stephen
Senn, Laurence Vaughn, Jr.
Stachowski, Michael Joseph
Stutman, Michael David
Weiner, Robin Wendy
Wells, Crosby
Wood, John Busey

North Carolina

McIver, Robert Gilmour
Miller, John Randolph
Tate, David Kirk

North Dakota

Solberg, Wayne O.

Ohio

Brandt, Stephen Dennis
Climer, James Alan
Coady, Michael Francis
Ferguson, Gerald Paul
Hutson, Jeffrey Woodward
Lanza, Shelley Brown
Lee, Ronald Bruce
McAndrews, James Patrick
Nippert, Alfred Kuno, Jr.
O'Brien, William Scott
Ruport, Scott Hendricks
Schatz, William Bonsall
Switzer, Donald Hugh

Oklahoma

King, Michael James

Oregon

Cloran, William Francis
Franzke, Richard Albert
O'Halloran, Robert Luis
Reinke, Cecil Eugene
Schrader, Charles Raymond

Pennsylvania

Adler, Theodore Arthur
Auerbach, Sheryl Lynn
Edelstein, Stanley Barton
Kerrigan, Paul Brendan
Korn, Robert A.
Lackman, James Stephen
Lee, Edward B., III
McCabe, Robert Fource, Jr.
McKenna, J. Frank, III
Moser, Melvin Lavalle, Jr.
Opalinski, Christopher Richard
Puhala, James Joseph
Reitz, Curtis Randall
Ross, James Andrew
Ruck, Andrew Joseph
Shagin, Craig Randall
Simon, David Frederick
Stephens, Marlin Gerard
Stroyd, Arthur Heister

Rhode Island

Tracy, David J.

South Carolina

Hassold, Robert Wilkinson, Jr.

Tennessee

Fordham, Benjamin Cleveland
Oldfield, Russell Miller
Patrick, Gary Ray
Sobieski, Wanda Graham

Texas

Ballew, William Virgil, Jr.
Blair, Graham Kerin
Boles, David LaVelle
Brown, William Alley
Connally, Tom
Dieter, James George
Frisby, Thomas Newton
Greig, Brian Strother
Hainsfurther, A. Michael
Henderson, John Robert
Koppenheffer, Julie B.
McCoy, Reagan Scott
Meyer, Leonard James
Peters, Loren Walter
Rucker, Jerry Don
Smith, Frank Forsythe, Jr.
Van Gilder, Derek Robert
Wexler, Charles W., Jr.
Winchell, Michael George

Utah

Hunt, George Andrew
Larsen, Lynn Beck
Walstad, Paul J.

Virginia

Arnold, William McCauley
Gladstone, Michael Harper
Harrison, John Edwards
Lester, James Lee
Nicholas, Edward Ernest, III
Norris, John Stevens, Jr.
Rucker, William Browning
Schwartz, Arthur Edward
Waldo, Joseph Thomas
Wilson, Douglas Downes

Washington

Addington, Darrel Blair
Bor, Daniel
Cressman, Paul Russell, Jr.
Fitterer, Richard Clarence
Oles, Douglas S.
Petrie, Gregory Steven
Scott, Douglas Walter
Squires, William Randolph, III
Sullivan, Patrick Arthur
Yalowitz, Kenneth Gregg

West Virginia

Schaub, Clarence Robert

Wisconsin

Burroughs, Charles Edward
Decker, John Robert
Smith, Robert John

Wyoming

Hunkins, Raymond Breedlove

FEDERAL REPUBLIC OF GERMANY

Prevost, Richard James

ADDRESS UNPUBLISHED

Diamond, Josef
Gerber, Jack
Kahn, Ronald Howard
Lappen, Timothy
McIntyre, Anita Grace
Murray, Kathleen Anne
Whitehorn, Jo-Ann H.

CONSUMER CREDIT. *See* **Commercial, consumer.**

CONTRACTS. *See* **Commercial, contracts.**

CORPORATE, GENERAL

UNITED STATES

Alabama

Adams, John Edmund
Albright, Carl Wayne, Jr.
Allen, Robert A.
Bell, Thomas Reuben
Bowdre, John Birch, Jr.
Campbell, Maria Bouchelle
Clark, John Foster
Cobia, Paula Ivey
Dacso, Sheryl Tatar
Davis, Mallory Donald, Jr.
Ely, Bruce Peter
Garner, Robert Edward Lee
Hughston, Harold Vaughan, Jr.
Huskey, Dow Thobern
Jones, Patrick Allen
Lacy, Alexander Shelton
Little, Joe Hollis, Jr.
McGowin, Nicholas Stallworth
Meigs, Walter Ralph
Morgan, Wendell Richmond
Patrick, J. Vernon, Jr.
Ritchey, Joseph Thomas
Ruegsegger, Martin Craig
Silver, Irving
Sims, Ronald Louis
Smith, Andrew Lovgren
Smith, John Joseph, Jr.
Smith, John Joseph
Spransy, Joseph William
Stedham, Brenda Smith
Stoudenmire, William Ward
Sullivan, Michael Maurice
Taylor, George Malcolm, III
Trimmier, Charles Stephen, Jr.
Whisonant, Michael Wayne
Woodrow, Randall Mark

Alaska

Davies, Bruce Owen
Erlich, Richard Henry
Fortier, Samuel John
Gardner, Ray Dean, Jr.
Gidcumb, Lance Edward
Goldberg, Robert M.
Longacre, Roy Lee
Maloney, Philip Dennis
Wilson, Joseph Morris, III
Yerbich, Joseph Thomas
Yerbich, Thomas Joseph

Arizona

Basinger, Richard Lee
Bender, Kenneth N.
Berry, Charles Richard
Bluemle, Robert Louis
Burton, Osmond Alexander, Jr.
Case, David Leon
Chanen, Steven Robert
Chauncey, Tom Webster, II
Cocanower, David Lehman
DiMatteo, Philip Stephen
Dunipace, Ian Douglas
Evans, Lawrence Jack, Jr.
Fisher, Peter Francis
Folsom, Victor Clarence
Frazelle, Michael Jerome
Gabaldon, Theresa A.
Hackett, Robert John
Hanshaw, A. Alan
Hay, John Leonard
Hicks, William Albert, III
Hornisher, Michael
Hutchison, Samuel Robert
Jekel, Louis G.
King, Jack A.
Le Clair, Douglas Marvin
Lemon, Leslie Gene
Levitan, Roger Stanley
Lowry, Edward Francis, Jr.
Mangum, John K.
Martori, Joseph Peter
Meyer, Paul Joseph
Miner, Don Jones
Nopar, Alan Scott
O'Connell, Daniel Henry
Patton, Jock
Peters, Daniel Wayne
Pietzsch, Michael Edward
Rainey, William Joel
Rivoir, William Henry, III
Sabin, John Merrill
Seidenfeld, Glenn Kenneth, Jr.
Smith, Kenneth McKay
Stirton, Charles Paul
Tennen, Leslie Irwin
Terry, Peter Anthony
Thompson, Terence William
Tubman, William Charles
Warner, Teddy Fleming
Waterfall, Gordon Garrett
Williams, Quinn Patrick
Williams, Steven Henry

Arkansas

Britt, Henry Middleton
Campbell, George Emerson
Choate, Murray Rickliffe, II
Crow, Carl Arnold, Jr.
Dumeny, Marcel Jacque
Eichenbaum, E. Charles
Fitton, Garvin
Friday, Herschel Hugar
Hill, Rhonda Kenyon
Jordan, Steven Ben
Mayersohn, Arnold Linn, Jr.
Watkins, Jerry West
Wilson, Robert Martin, Jr.

California

Abbott, Barry A.
Adams, Dirk Standley
Adams, William Gillette
Adelson, Benedict James
Allan, Lionel Manning
Anderson, Suellen
Anglin, Richard Lee, Jr.
Anzur, John Andrew
Apfel, Gary
Arthur, Jeanne L.
Asmundson, Vigfus Anthony
Atkins, Thomas Jay
Atkinson, Sheridan Earle
Bagley, Constance Elizabeth
Baker, Robert Kenneth
Balluff, John Joseph
Barash, Anthony Harlan
Barbarowicz, Robert Paul
Basile, Paul Louis, Jr.
Bass, Lewis
Bastiaanse, Gerard C.
Battaglia, Philip Maher
Bauch, Thomas Jay
Baudler, David Evan
Baumgarten, Ronald Neal
Bear, Henry Louis
Beard, Ronald Stratton
Bedford, Daniel Ross
Behrendt, John Thomas
Bell, Wayne Steven
Bernstein, Scot D(avid)
Bex, Richard Elmer
Birney, William Joseph, Jr.
Biscay, Marcel Pierre
Blewett, Robert Noall
Blitz, Stephen Michael
Boelter, Allen Boyd
Boltz, Gerald Edmund
Bond, George Cline
Branson, Harley Kenneth
Brown, Albert Jacob
Brown, J(oan) Devon
Brown, Louis Daniel
Brown, Marc Laurence
Brunette, Steven Edward
Burrill, Janice Hilary
Buzaid, Laurence Edwin
Cahill, Michael Edward
Callender, William Lacey
Camp, James Carroll
Canady, Richard Warren
Carrey, Neil
Castro, Leonard Edward
Cattani, Maryellen Billette
Chan, Thomas Tak-Wah
Ching, Anthony
Chuman, Frank Fujio
Clabaugh, Elmer Eugene, Jr.
Clark, R(ufus) Bradbury
Climan, Richard Elliot
Cohen, Nancy M.
Collas, Juan Garduño, Jr.
Cologne, Knox Mason, III
Crandall, Nelson David, III
Crews, Kenneth Donald
Cross, Sandra Lee
Crowe, John T.
Curotto, Ricky Joseph
Currer, William John, Jr.
Curry, Daniel Arthur
Daniels, James Walter
Darman, Dinah Lea
Daugherty, Richard Bernard
Davey, Gerard Paul
Dazé, David Timothy
Deming, Willis Riley
Dettmer, Scott Charles
Diamond, Philip Ernest
Downer, Michael Josef
Doyle, Morris McKnight
Dran, Robert Joseph
DuBose, Guy Steven
Duncan, John Alexander
Eckardt, Richard William
Edwards, Robin Morse
Elion, Gary Douglas
Epstein, Judith Ann
Eres, Thomas W.
Erickson, Ralph Ernest
Ervin, Howard Guy, III
Ewell, A(ustin) B(ert), Jr.
Fabian, JoAnne Frances
Factor, Max, III
Fein, Ronald Lawrence
Finck, Kevin William
Flate, Ronald Allen
Flattery, Thomas Long
Flick, John Edmond
Fowler, Donald Raymond
Frank, Vincent Antonio
Frankel, James Burton
Freed, Kenneth Alan
Fried, Alexander
Friedman, Wallace
Fuller, Maurice DeLano, Jr.
Gade, Thomas Andrew
Gafford, George Nelson
Gambaro, Ernest Umberto
Garcia, Terry Donato
Gay, Michael Hubert
Gevurtz, Franklin Andrew
Gill, Keith Hubert
Glass, Beverly Elaine
Glenn, Everett Lamar
Gold, Michael Allan
Goldie, Ray Robert
Goldie, Ron Robert
Gooch, Robert Francis
Gould, Harold I.
Gray, Jan Charles
Greenstein, Robert Stanley
Gross, Justin Arthur
Grush, Julius Sidney
Guest, Karl Reed
Gunderson, Robert Vernon, Jr.
Haines, Michael Anthony
Halluin, Albert Price
Hamilton, Jackson Douglas
Handschuh, G. Gregory
Hanley, Thomas Francis, III
Hansen, Richard King
Hanson, Gary A.
Harlan, Nancy Margaret
Harley, Halvor Larson
Harroch, Richard David
Harwood, Dennis Westcott
Hayes, Byron Jackson, Jr.
Heckman, Donald Rex, II
Heidrich, Robert Wesley
Hertzberg, Harold Joel
Higbe, Clifton Melton Harvin
Hinueber, Mark Arthur
Hoffman, Kris
Houck, John Burton
Howard, John Wayne
Howell, Weldon Ulric, Jr.
Huegel, Peter Andrew Vincent
Hughes, William Jeffrey
Hunji, Prem Litta
Jacobs, Leedia Gordeev
Jaffer, David Hussain
Jelin, Beth Maloney
Jensen, Douglas Blaine
Johnson, Drew Martin
Jones, Thomas McReynolds
Kadri, Tariq Rashid
Kamei, Susan Hiroko
Kane, Margaret McDonald
Katayama, Robert Nobuichi
Katz, Jason Lawrence
Katz, Martha Lessman
Katz, Robert Nathan
Keller, Coby Norman
Kelly, Daniel Grady, Jr.
Kennedy, William Irl
Keup, Erwin J.
Kimsey, Dale Boyd
Kirchheimer, Arthur E(dward)
Kirkelie, Gregory Evan
Kitta, John Noah
Klein, Jeffrey S.
Kofford, Cree-L
Krahelski, Michael Anthony
Kraw, George Martin
Kruger, Gilbert Nelson
Lagle, John Franklin
Lee, Paulette Wang
Lemmon, John Vincent
Lentz, Robert Henry
Lerner, William C.
Lerrigo, Frank C.
Lombardi, David Ennis, Jr.
Loo, John
Loring, David Charles
Loube, Irving
Lund, James Louis
Luther, Charles William
Mack, John Oscar
Maillian, LeAnne Elizabeth
Mandel, Martin Louis
Mannerino, John David
Mansour, Nadim Ned
Marsh, Richard Melvin
Marshall, Ellen Ruth
Martin, Joseph, Jr.
May, Lawrence Edward
McBride, Keith Wesley
McChesney, Peter Brooks
Mc Cormack, Francis Xavier
McCroskey, Elizabeth Wear
McDonough, Patrick Joseph
McEvers, Duff Steven
McGee, Francis Parker, II
McGuinn, John Francis
McLain, Christopher
McLane, Frederick Berg
McMillan, M. Sean
Metz, Robert Ernest
Meyer, Donald Robert
Mickelson, Hal M.
Miles, Lawrence William, Jr.
Miller, Jeremy Matthew
Miller, Jules Frederick
Million, Stephen A.
Miyoshi, David Masao
Moore, Julie E.
Morando, Marta Lucile Hope
Moretti, August Joseph
Moskatel, Ira Dennis
Muller, Edward Robert
Murphy, Arthur John, Jr.
Musacchio, Kirk Anthony
Mutek, Michael Wendell
Nelson, David Edward
Nicholas, Carol Lynn
Nichols, Alan Hammond
Nigg, Karl Frederick
Ocheltree, Richard Lawrence
O'Keefe, Patrick Francis
O'Keefe, William Patrick
Oliver, Robert Harold
Olson, James Calvin
Olson, Walter Gilbert
O'Malley, James Terence
Orr, Robert M.
Osborne, Carol Ann
Ostrach, Michael Sherwood
Owens, Aletha Riedel
Pagano, James Lawrence
Passé, James G.
Patterson, Robert Edward
Pearman, Robert Charles
Peluso, Charles John
Perlis, Michael Fredrick
Perry, David Lewis
Peterson, Richard Thomas
Petrie, Bernard
Pierno, Anthony Robert
Pircher, Leo Joseph
Pollard, Henry
Power, John Bruce
Powers, Marcus Eugene
Prewoznik, Jerome Frank
Putnam, Philip Conrad
Radcliffe, Mark Flohn
Radlo, Edward John
Ramirez, William Earl
Randall, Richard Parks
Ratner, David Louis
Ray, Gilbert T.
Ream, Christopher
Reed, Charles Rufus
Restrick, John Knight
Richardson, Douglas Fielding
Richardson, Karen Lerohl
Riter, Bruce Douglas
Roby, Richard Eric
Rosenstein, Robert Bryce
Rowe, Helen Roberta
Russell, John Drinker
Ryan, Joseph
Ryan, Reade Haines, Jr.
Sanders, Gary Wayne
Schechter, Stuart
Scheidegger, Kent Stephen
Schiff, Gunther Hans
Schlinkert, William Joseph
Schmutz, Arthur Walter
Schwarzstein, Richard Joseph
Scott, Kenneth Eugene
Scott, Valerie Weeks
Seavey, William Arthur
Severaid, Ronald Harold
Sewall, William Dana
Shaffer, Richard James
Shannon, Malcolm Lloyd, Jr.
Sharpe, Norah G.
Sheehan, Lawrence James
Sherman, Dana
Sherman, Lawrence M.
Sherman, William Delano
Sherwood, Linda Kathleen
Shorr, Matthew Sam
Shultz, John David
Sickler, Sandra Davis
Silk, Thomas
Silver, Mark Steven
Skaff, Andrew Joseph
Sloan, Sheldon Harold

Small, Harold S.
Small, Marshall Lee
Smith, Ora Everett
Spatz, Alan Brent
Specter, Richard Bruce
Star, Ronald H.
Stauber, Ronald Joseph
Sterrett, James Kelley, II
Stromme, Gary L.
Sutro, John Alfred
Taft, Perry Hazard
Tavrow, Richard Lawrence
Thompson, Jeffrey Dale
Tomberlin, George E., Jr.
Tomich, Lillian
Toms, Robert Lee
Tornstrom, Robert Ernest
Truman, Rolland A.
Turner, John Miller
Twomey, Joseph Gerald
Van Camp, Brian Ralph
van de Bunt, Dirk Wouter
Van Der Wal, Jeanne Huber
Van Praag, Jane Catherine
van Schoonenberg, Robert G.
Walsh, William, IV
Weinman, Glenn Alan
Weinstein, Steven Louis
Weiss, Sherman David
Weissman, Barry Leigh
Welch, John Edward
Weltman, Jordan Scott
Wetmore, Keith Chidester
Whitaker, Leslie Kent
White, Bryan Stanford
Williams, Lawrence Dwight
Williams, Lee Dwain
Willsey, F. Patterson
Winnick, Helene Ann
Wise, Toni Pryor
Witus, David Gordon
Woodhouse, Thomas Edwin
Wrobel, Robert Franklin
Young, Bryant Llewellyn
Yslas, Stephen Daniel
Ziering, William Mark

Colorado

Abbott, Keith Eugene
Arkin, Harry Lee
Aronstein, James Karpeles
Aschkinasi, David Jay
Barney, Patrick Earl
Bermant, George Wilson
Blair, Andrew Lane, Jr.
Bluestein, Louis Allen
Brewer, Marion Alyce
Briggs, George Scott
Bryans, Richard W.
Cahan, Judith E.
Callison, James William
Cleveland, Leslie Click
Cockrell, Richard Carter
Cohen, Jeffrey
Cook, Terry Lee
Cramer, R. Norman, Jr.
Dean, James B.
Demuth, Lael Saunders
Ducker, Bruce
DuVivier, Katharine Keyes
Eckstein, John Alan
Elliott, Darrell Stanley
Elrod, Richard Bryan
Englander, Paula Tyo
Erickson, David L.
Gabriel, Eberhard John
Gaddis, Larry Roy
Gates, Stephen Frye
Goral, Brian Harold
Green, Carol H.
Grissom, Garth Clyde
Gunckel, Stuart Squier
Hampton, Clyde Robert
Hanrahan, Kathleen Susan
Holmes, Charles Everett
Husney, Elliott Ronald
Irwin, R. Robert
Johnson, David Stafford
Katz, Michael Jeffery
Keithley, Roger Lee
Kelly, Eric Damian
King, Dennis William
Kins, Tonya
Kraft, C. William, III
Ledingham, Thomas Max
Lerman, Eileen R.
LeSatz, Stephen, Jr.
Lidstone, Herrick Kenley, Jr.
Linfield, James Clark Taylor
Long, Lawrence Alexander
Lutz, John Shafroth
Mall, Loren L(ee)
Martin, J. Landis
Martin, James Russell
Mauro, Richard Frank
McCallie, Spencer Wyatt
McClung, Merle Steven
McMichael, Donald Earl
Meininger, John Alexander
Meyer, Lee Gordon
Meyer, Lynn Nix
Miers, James William
Miller, David William
Montgomery, Robert Cornelius, III
Nakarado, Gary Lee
O'Connor, Donald John
O'Dorisio, John William, Jr.
Parker, George Earl
Pautsch, Richard Joseph
Peirce, Frederick Fairbanks
Peterson, Brooke Alan
Press, Caren Sue
Ragonetti, Thomas John
Ramsey, John Arthur
Reddien, Charles Henry, Jr.
Rowan, Ronald Thomas
Salcito, Donald
Schoonover, Randall Charles
Scott, Peter Bryan
Shafer, Stephanie Jane
Sherman, Lester Ivan
Shuman, Mark Patrick
Skelton, Darrell Jean
Sloat, Gerald Charles
Smethills, Harold Reginald
Talesnick, Alan Lee
Thorson, David Morris
Timmins, Edward Patrick
Ward, Lester Lowe, Jr.
Wendt, John Arthur Frederic, Jr.
Wiegand, Robert, II
Wilder, Raymond Edward
Wood, David Leslie

Connecticut

Anestis, Robert William
Arturi, Peter A., II
Austin, Richard David
Bamford, David Ellery
Banks, Robert Sherwood
Barnett, Charles E.
Barreca, Christopher Anthony
Becker-Lewke, Laura Virginia
Bell, Robert Collins
Bentley, Peter
Berger, Robert Bertram
Bernstein, Robert Gary
Blumberg, Phillip Irvin
Borod, Donald Lee
Burrasca, Raymond Peter
Cooper, George Wilson
Crimmins, Eileen Marie
Crozier, John Huntington
Cullina, William Michael
Cuminale, James William
Del Negro, John Thomas
Dowling, Victor James
Drost, Marianne
Duke, Robert Dominick
Dzurik, John Gerard
Elliott, Stephen K.
Ewing, Robert
Fanwick, Ernest
Finch, Frank Herschel, Jr.
Finn, Harold Bolton, III
FitzGerald, Edward Browne
Frank, Mark Kennith, III
Fuller, Robert Ferrey
Gates, Signe Sandra
Gildea, Edward Joseph
Gilliam, Charles Phillips
Ginsberg, Larry Floyd
Ginsky, Marvin H.
Gold, Steven Michael
Goodridge, George Sidney
Gorski, Walter J.
Grafstein, Joel M.
Gray, Chester L., Jr.
Greeley, Paul David
Harris, Edward Monroe, Jr.
Hawkins, Barry Curtis
Hennessy, Dean McDonald
Hudnut, Stewart
Hurwich, Robert Allan
Ivey, Scott Ellsworth
Jensen, Frode, III
Kalaher, Richard Alan
Kaye, Joel Michael
Klein, Jonathan Joseph
Koomey, Richard Alan
Lamb, Frederic Davis
Leepson, Peter Lawrence
Lloyd, James Hendrie, III
Macleod, Anthony Michael
Marsching, Ronald Lionel
Mazadoorian, Harry Nicholas
McCarthy, Francis James
McConnell, David Kelso
McGovern, Kevin Michael
McGuire, Eugene Guenard
Middlebrook, Stephen Beach
Milliken, Charles Buckland
Mirsky, Ellis Richard
Mittelman, Irwin David
Morelli, Joseph Christopher
Nelson, Douglas Thomas
Nelson, Geoffrey William
Owen, H. Martyn
Paladino, Robert Christopher
Parkin, Jeffrey Robert
Pastore, Richard Steel
Pedersen, C. Richard
Perlah, Philip Michael
Phifer, Virginia Hudson
Rice, Michael Downey
Rohrer, Dean Cougill
Rondepierre, Edmond Francois
Rubenstein, Mark A.
Russell, Allan David
Sachs, Jeffrey Michael
Sanetti, Stephen Louis
Santopietro, Albert Robert
Santoro, Michael Anthony
Scannell, David George
Schatz, Arthur Herschel
Schlotterbeck, Walter Albert
Schultz, Manuel
Sherer, Frank Audemars, Jr.
Simonelli, Jerry
Siverd, Robert Joseph
Smiddy, James Dallas
Smiddy, Linda O'Riordan
Sparks, William James Ashley
Strone, Michael Jonathan
Stuart, Peter Fred
Swerdloff, David Alan
Trager, Bernard H.
Travis, Susan Topper
Turrentine, James Drake
Vogel, Marilyn Beth
Walk, Donald Willard
Weinstein, Arthur David
Whiston, Richard Michael
Wilkes, Beverly Lake
Wolfe, Harriet Munrett
Wolfe, Robert J.
Wolson, Craig Alan
Yachmetz, Philip Keith
Yamin, Robert Joseph
Yen, Elizabeth Chih-Sheng
Yoskowitz, Irving Benjamin

Delaware

Bailey, James Frederick, Jr.
Balick, Steven Jeffrey
Brown, James Wilcox
Campbell, William Gant
Carpenter, Edmund Nelson, II
Carrad, David Clayton
Carroll, John Hawkins
Crane, John Murdoch
Crompton, Charles Sentman, Jr.
Edelson, Harold Jesse
Gallagher, Henry Edmund, Jr.
Hamermesh, Lawrence Abraham
Holzman, James L(ouis)
Jacobs, Jack Bernard
Johnston, William David
Kuniholm, John Gardner
Lassen, John Kai
Mankin, Hart Tiller
Manley, Marshall
Moran, Joseph Milbert
Morris, Kenneth Donald
O'Toole, John James
Partnoy, Ronald Allen
Peet, John Carlisle, Jr.
Rothschild, Steven James
Sanson, Barbara Elizabeth
Turk, S. Maynard
Twilley, Joshua Marion
Walsh, Joseph Thomas

District of Columbia

Ackerson, Nels J(ohn)
Alprin, Brian Dean
Alvarado, Ricardo Raphael
Anderson, Scott Gale
Baker, Keith Leon
Baller, James
Bayly, John Henry
Bebchick, Leonard Norman
Becker, Brandon
Bell, Olin Nile
Benjamin, Edward A.
Bernstein, Caryl Salomon
Blair, Robert Allen
Bodansky, Robert Lee
Boehm, Steven Bruce
Bokat, Stephen A.
Brand, Joseph Lyon
Brodsky, Arthur James
Brooks, Daniel Townley
Browne, Richard Cullen
Burns, Arnold Irwin
Byington, S. John
Campilongo, Michael
Caron, Wilfred Rene
Chambers, Charles MacKay
Chanin, Michael Henry
Clifford, Clark McAdams
Colton, Herbert Spencer
Coplan, Larry Myles
Corber, Robert Jack
Crotty, Edward
Curran, John Peter
Cutler, Charles Russell
Cutler, John Arthur
Daniel, Royal, III
Delaney, Edward Norman
Duckenfield, Thomas Adams
Duncan, Charles Tignor
Dunnan, Weaver White
Ehrenhaft, Peter David
Eiselt, Erich Raymond
Eisenberg, Meyer
Ellicott, John LeMoyne
Evans, John Kedrich
Fegan, David Albert
Feinerman, James Vincent
Feldman, Roger David
Feller, Lloyd Harris
Ferman, Irving
Finkelstein, Anita Jo
Flax, Samuel Allan
Fleischman, Edward Hirsh
Focht, Theodore Harold
Ford, David R(ucker)
Fread, Joan P.
Freedman, Walter
Freeman, Milton Victor
Futrell, John William
Gell, Carl Leddin
Gerson, Ralph Joseph
Gingold, Dennis Marc
Ginsburg, Charles David
Gittens, James P.
Glasser, Robert
Gleason, Jean Wilbur
Goelzer, Daniel Lee
Goldson, Amy Robertson
Graham, Peter Jeffrey Stuart
Gray, John Walker, Jr.
Gribbon, Daniel McNamara
Grier, Phillip Michael
Guttman, Egon
Habicht, Frank Henry, II
Halpern, James Bladen
Halvorson, Newman Thorbus, Jr.
Harmon, Gail McGreevy
Heller, Jack Isaac
Heller, John Roderick, III
Henderson, Harold Richard
Himelfarb, Stephen Roy
Hobbs, Caswell O., III
Hobelman, Carl Donald
Holtz, Edgar Wolfe
Horn, Lawrence Alan
Howard, Daggett Horton
Huge, Harry
Hunt, David Wallingford
Isbell, David Bradford
Jacobsen, Raymond Alfred, Jr.
Jaskiewicz, Leonard Albert
Johns, Richard Warren
Johns, Warren LeRoi
Kaminer, Stevenson Scott
Kelly, Anastasia Donovan
Kelly, John James
Kempson, Kenneth Earl
Kieve, Loren
Klein, Robert Allan
Kramer, Franklin David
Kriesberg, Simeon M.
Kroener, William Frederick, III
Lamia, Thomas Roger
Landfield, Richard
Lange, William Michael
Laporte, Gerald Joseph Sylvestre
Latham, Weldon Hurd
Law, Alfred John, III
Lew, Ginger
Lide, Vinton DeVane
Lipkin, Gary Dennis
Lipton, Frederick Steven
Long, Charles Thomas
Lyon, Edwin Leon
Maiwurm, James John
Maloney, Barry Charles
Mansbach, Robert Allen
Manthei, Richard Dale
Marans, J. Eugene
Martin, Keith
Martin, Lowell Frank
Marvin, Charles Raymond
Matthews, Steve Allen
Mazo, Mark Elliott
McReynolds, Mary Armilda
Middlekauff, Roger David
Millstein, Leo Lee
Moore, Robert Madison
Morgan, Daniel Louis
Muir, J. Dapray
Murphy, Terence Roche
Nelson, Robert Louis
Newsome, George Marvin
Okun, Todd Alan
Olson, John Frederick
Oser, Ralph Crandall
Palmer, Robert Alan
Parkinson, Kenneth Wells
Parsky, Gerald Lawrence
Patton, James Richard, Jr.
Poe, Luke Harvey, Jr.
Porter, William Glover, Jr.
Potter, Tanya Jean
Price, Joseph Hubbard
Provorny, Frederick Alan
Pursley, Ricky Anthony
Quinn, John Harvey, Jr.
Rath, Francis Steven
Reed, John Grady
Renfro, William Leonard
Robinson, Davis Rowland
Roccograndi, Anthony Joseph
Rosen, Jeffrey J.
Russell, Harold Swift
Russin, Jonathan
Sapir, Michael Lynn
Sayler, Robert Nelson
Schaefer, William Goerman, Jr.
Schropp, James Howard
Scott, Michael
Sczudlo, Raymond Stanley
Sedky, Cherif
Shapiro, Gary Joel
Shaw, David Anthony
Silver, Daniel Ben
Slayton, John Howard
Smith, Brian William
Snyder, John Freeman
Soble, Stephen M.
Sommer, Alphonse Adam, Jr.
Spitz, Robert John
Splitt, David Alan
Spradlin, Thomas Richard
Stanley, William, Jr.
Stinchfield, John Edward
Stranahan, Robert Paul, Jr.
Strother, James French
Swendiman, Alan Robert
Tapley, James Leroy
Taylor, Richard Powell
Teague, Randal Cornell, Sr.
Thaler, Martin S.
Thomas, Ritchie Tucker
Vance, Sheldon Baird
Vogel, John Henry
Walker, Robert Benson
Wall, Christopher Read
Weiss, Jerome Paul
Weiss, Stephen Joel
West, Togo Dennis, Jr.
Westermeier, John Thomas, Jr.
Whitaker, A(lbert) Duncan
White, Peter Allen
Whiting, Richard Matthew
Williams, David Huntington
Williams, Wesley Samuel, Jr.
Williamson, Thomas Samuel, Jr.
Wilson, Craig Alan
Wolf, Maurice
Woody, Robert James
Yoder, John Christian
Yung, Carroll John
Zimmer, Janet Rose

Florida

Adcock, Louie Norman, Jr.
Alonso, Antonio Enrique
Alper, Harvey Martin
Ames, Stuart D.
Andrews, Dean
Ansbacher, Lewis
Arlt, Mary Ann Kokoszyna
Baccus, Tonya Lynn
Bagge, Douglas Malcolm
Bailey, Brant Allan
Barnes, Donald King
Barnett, Charles Dawson
Beall, Kenneth Sutter, Jr.
Benson, John Scott
Bernard, Lawrence Jay
Birnbaum, Richard Michael
Bloomgarden, Paul M.
Braddock, Donald Layton
Bratten, Thomas Arnold
Brett-Major, Lin
Buchman, Paul Sidney
Buck, Thomas Randolph
Burnaman, Phillip R.
Butterworth, Alan Randolph
Cane, Marilyn Blumberg
Capp, Alvin
Carlile, Robert Toy
Carstetter, David Wilson
Chabrow, Penn Benjamin
Champion, Roger Cornelius
Cheffy, Edward Kefgen
Chesser, David Michael
Conner, Timothy James
Cronig, Steven Carlyle
Dady, Robert Edward
Davis, Louis Poisson, Jr.
Day, Karen Spring
del Valle, Ignacio Gonzalez
DeWitt, Sherri Kandel
Doliner, Nathaniel Lee
Douglas, Hubert Gene, II
Dunlap, Charles Leonard
Emerton, Robert Walter, III
Engel, Steven Ira
Falk, Victor S., III
Farrior, J. Rex, Jr.
Feldman, Joel Harvey
Fildes, Richard James
Fishman, Lewis Warren
Forman, Robert Steven
Friedman, Ronald Michael
Friend, Richard E.
Garlick, Michael
Geiger, William Harold
Genauer, Martin Jay
Georges, Richard Martin
Gescheidt, Richard Anthony
Gillen, William Albert
Golden, Donald Alan
Golden, E(dward) Scott
Grimm, William Thomas
Hall, David Wayne
Hall, Frank Dawson
Hall, Miles Lewis, Jr.
Harris, Charles Edison
Harris, Christy Franklin
Hartman, Burton Arthur
Hayes, Mark Stephen
Hedrick, David Warrington
Hendry, Robert Ryon
Henn, Harry George
Herb, Frank Steven
Hickman, Paula Diane
Hollander, Bruce Lee
Holliday, Ronald Sturgis
Hornsby, Cyrus Edward, III
Hume, John
Ines, Victor Doroteo
Itkin, Perry Steven
Jamieson, Michael Lawrence
Kagan, Edwin Bruce
Kennedy, Marc J.
Kievit, Robert Warren
Klein, Marina Shank
Lamont, Robert Sheldon
Landy, Burton Aaron
Lasser, Mark Lawrence
Leone, James Russell
Levitt, Preston Curtis
Lewis, Mark Russell
Lipson, Gary David
Livingston, Edward Michael
Lowndes, John Foy
Lurie, Jeanne Flora
Luskin, Paul Bansech
Mann, Kenneth L.
Markus, Andrew Joshua
Martin, Serge Gregory
Martinez-Cid, Ricardo
Maurer, Virginia Gallaher
Maxwell, Richards DeNyse, Jr.
Meeks, William Herman, III
Merriam, Lauren Evert, III
Mims, William Lovanda
Mofsky, James Steffan
Morales, Nestor
Morrall, Matthew Earl
Mudd, John Philip
Murray, David G.
Napoli, Joseph Anthony
Neiwirth, Ronald George
Novack, Catherine Gail
Oberhausen, Frank Clay, Jr.
O'Brien, Thomas George, III
Olson, Carl Eric
O'Neill, Michael Joseph
Orlin, Karen J.
Painter, James Morgan
Pajon, Eduardo Rodriguez
Passidomo, John Michael
Patsavos, Evelyn Christou
Patton, Arthur Gordon
Paul, Robert
Pearce, Lewis Richard
Perlstein, Mitchell Leslie
Pevsner, Beverly Limmer
Pfenniger, Richard Charles, Jr.
Pierce, John G.
Pippen, Joseph Franklin, Jr.
Poller, Jeri
Prom, Stephen G.
Pulignano, Nicholas Vincent, Jr.
Pumphrey, Gerald Robert
Reid, John James
Reinstein, Joel
Remsen, John Lockwood
Reynolds, Joseph Jay
Richeson, Hugh Anthony, Jr.
Ringel, Fred Morton
Risner, Paul Edward
Roberts, B. K.
Roddenberry, Bonnie Lindquist
Roman, Ronald Peter
Ross, Howard Philip
Royce, Raymond Watson
Ruggles, Rudy Lamont
Rush, Fletcher Grey, Jr.
Sadowski, William Edward
Salem, Richard Joseph
Sanchez, Ernesto
Sanders, Barrett
Schechterman, Lawrence
Schneider, Laz Levkoff
Scott, Janice Gail
Segal, Martin Edward
Sharpe, Leon Edward
Silber, Norman Jules
Singer, David Harris
Stein, Leslie Reicin
Stiefel, Charles Werner
Tannen, Edward Cooper
Thornburg, Frederick Fletcher
Urban, Edmund Theodore
Vogel, Howard Michael
Wallace, Milton Jay
Watts-FitzGerald, Abigail Cory
Wickersham, Ralph Read
Wilder, Fred Jennings
Wilson, Gary Keith
Wynn, Charles Milton
Zamora, Antonio Rafael
Zschau, Julius James

Georgia

Ahlstrom, Michael Joseph
Arkin, Robert David
Baker, Anita Diane
Baker, David S.
Bart, Randall Kerr
Baxter, Harry Stevens
Beringer, William Ernst
Berry, Alonzo Franklin, Jr
Birchfield, J. Kermit, Jr.
Bisbee, David George
Brown, Colin W(egand)
Burt, Barry Wakefield
Callison, James W.
Candler, John Slaughter, II
Carpenter, Raymond Prince
Center, Tony
Clark, Herman

Clarke, Thomas Hal
Davis, Claude-Leonard
Dean, George Ross
DeLoach, Donald Brian
Dowling, Roderick Anthony
Draughon, John Albert
Drescher, Ann Marie
DuBose, Charles Wilson
Durrett, James Frazer, Jr.
Edwards, James Garland, II
Elliott, James Sewell
Eubanks, Gary Franklin
Fiorentino, Carmine
Ganz, Charles David
Garcia, Luis Cesareo
Gartzman, Jeffrey Scott
Gaynes, Bruce Harvey
Giffin, Gordon D.
Gilbert, John Jordan
Graham, Charles Benjamin, Jr.
Grant, Walter Matthews
Greenblatt, Edward Lande
Hall, Charles Martin
Head, William Carl
Hines, John Pridgen
Howell, Arthur
Jeffries, McChesney Hill, Jr.
Johnson, Donald (Don) Wayne
Kelly, James Patrick
Killorin, Edward Wylly
Kolber, Daniel Hackner
Lamberth, J. Michael
Langway, Richard Merritt
Lee, William Clement, III
Marianes, William Byron
Marquis, Harold Lionel
McClain, William Asbury
Meyer, William Lorne
Mirandola, Loretta Jean
Moorhead, William David, III
Neuren, Michael Scott
O'Callaghan, William Lawrence, Jr.
Ortiz, Jay Richard Gentry
Parrish, Benjamin Franklin, Jr.
Pendergast, John Francis, Jr.
Pennington, Brooks Maddox, III
Pryor, Shepherd Green, III
Raines, Stephen Samuel
Saidman, Gary K.
Scavo, James J.
Schwartz, Arthur Jay
Searcy, William Nelson
Sharpe, Robert Francis, Jr.
Shulman, Warren Scott
Sibley, James Malcolm
Simmons, Raymond Hedelius, Jr.
Somers, Fred Leonard, Jr.
Walker, James Durward, Jr.
Wasserman, Michael Gary
Williams, Lyman Neil, Jr.
Wilson, Rhys Thaddeus
Zink, Deborah Burks
Zito, Jeffrey Raymond

Hawaii

Bays, Albert Bernard
Cades, Julius Russell
Case, James Hebard
Char, Randall Yau Kunn
Coates, Bradley Allen
Conrad, John Regis
Cumbs, Charles Wilcox
Dang, Marvin S.C.
Dixon, Steven Bedford
Eggers, William J., III
Fujiyama, Rodney Michio
Grinpas, Robert Mark
Heller, Ronald Ian
Jackson, Bruce George
Kaneshige, Melvin Yoshio
Lee, James Hon Quon
Meyer, William George, III
Moon, John Paul
Moroney, Michael John
Neeley, Joyce Yount
Okinaga, Lawrence Shoji
Oshiro, Sharleen H.
Porter, Michael Pell
Shiraishi, Sherman T.
Shklov, Mark Thomas
Sumida, Gerald Aquinas
Suzuki, Norman Hitoshi

Idaho

Chapman, John Sherwood
Clute, John E
Eisele, R. Joseph
Fawcett, Charles Winton
Fields, James Ralph
Hanks, Stephen Grant
Johnson, L. Charles
McCann, William Vern, Jr.
Park, William Anthony
Risch, James E.
Thomas, Eugene C.

Illinois

Ackman, Richard LeRoy
Adams, John Richard
Addis, Lauane Cleo
Aldrich, Thomas Lawrence
Ambrister, John Charles
Anderson, Geoffrey Allen
Anderson, J. Trent
Axley, Frederick William
Babb, Frank Edward
Bacall, Elliot Stephen
Baird, Russell Miller
Baker, Benjamin Joseph
Banks, Theodore Lee
Barack, Peter Joseph
Barnes, James Garland, Jr.
Bassitt, Janet Louise
Bell, Dennis Arthur
Berens, Mark Harry
Bergonia, Raymond David
Berner, Robert Lee, Jr.
Berry, Richard Morgan
Blank, Gary L.
Bloom, Christopher Arthur
Blount, Michael Eugene
Bockelman, John Richard
Boodell, Thomas Joseph, Jr.
Bose, Thomas Lewnau
Bouma, Robert Edwin
Bowen, Stephen Stewart
Bowman, Phillip Boynton
Bradner, James Holland, Jr.
Braun, William David
Breen, James Joseph
Brennan, Danolda Jean
Brennan, James Joseph
Brennan, Richard Snyder
Brock, Charles Marquis
Bunge, Jonathan Gunn
Burgess, Robert Kyle
Burke, Richard William
Burns, Kenneth Jones, Jr.
Cannon, Benjamin Winton
Carasik, Karen Sue
Carlin, Donald Walter
Cascino, Anthony Elmo, Jr.
Cass, Neil Earl
Chanen, Franklin Allen
Chiles, Stephen Michael
Choo, Yeow Ming
Clay, John Ernest
Clemens, Richard Glenn
Coletta, Ralph John
Collen, Sheldon Orrin
Congalton, Susan Tichenor
Costigan, John Mark
Coston, James E.
Cotteleer, Michael Alexander
Crawford, Sandra Kay
Crawford, William Walsh
Cross, Chester Joseph
Crowley, Wilbert Francis
Davis, Scott Jonathan
Deer, William Henry
Delp, Wilbur Charles, Jr.
Demas, Jean V.
Denkewalter, Kim Richard
Devience, Alex, Jr.
DeVries, James Howard
DeWolfe, John Chauncey, Jr.
Diamant, William
Diller, Theodore Craig
Dodd, Robert Warren
Don, Arthur
Drymalski, Raymond Hibner
Easterbrook, Frank Hoover
Eckols, Thomas Aud
Eisner, Thomas Sultan
Elias, John Samuel
Engling, Robert John
Erickson, Roy Lydeen
Ermentrout, John Curtis
Everett, C. Curtis
Farnell, Alan Stuart
Farrell, Richard James
Fein, Roger G.
Feirich, John Cottrill
Fenton, Marc Ira
Fewell, Terry Glenn
Finke, Robert Forge
Fisher, Patricia Sweeney
Flanagin, Neil
Flood, Vincent Patrick
Fortier, Robert Frederic
Fowler, William Craig
Fox, Shayle Phillip
Francois, William Armand
Fraumann, Willard George
Frick, Robert Hathaway
Frisch, Sidney, Jr.
Frisch, Sidney
Fuerstenberg, James P.
Gabbay, Alan
Gavin, John Neal
Gibson, James Thomas, Jr.
Gilbert, Howard N(orman)
Glass, Stanford Lee
Gonser, Thomas Howard
Goodrich, John Bernard
Grabarek, William Christian
Graham, William B.
Greenberger, Ernest
Greenblatt, Ray Harris
Gregg, Jon Mann
Gritchen, Lyle Steven
Hablutzel, Philip Norman
Hahn, Richard Ferdinand
Hamblet, Michael Jon
Hanson, Fred B.
Harring, Michael Adrian
Harris, Daniel Mark
Hart, David Churchill
Hartigan, John M.
Hartmann, Kenneth
Hayward, Thomas Zander, Jr.
Head, Patrick James
Hegarty, Mary Frances
Heinen, Paul Abelardo
Heinz, William Denby
Helman, Robert Alan
Henning, Joel Frank
Henry, Robert John
Herzel, Leo
Hetke, Richard L.
Hiering, James G.
High, Suzanne Irene
Hill, Philip
Hoagland, Karl King, Jr.
Hoekstra, Kathlyn B.
Hoenicke, Edward Henry
Hoffman, S. David
Hoffman, Thomas Joseph
Hofmann, William Eckhardt
Holleb, Marshall Maynard
Hollins, Mitchell Leslie
Hollis, Everett Loftus
Hook, George Clive, II
Horwitz, John
Hubbard, Elizabeth Louise
Hudetz, Joseph Bernard
Hull, J(ames) Richard
Hultquist, Robert Charles
Huston, Steven Craig
Jacobs, James Ethan
Jacobson, Marian Slutz
Jadwin, Ted Richard
Janich, Daniel Nicholas
Jarrett, Valerie Bowman
Jenkins, Neil Edmund
Jersild, Thomas Nielsen
Jesser, Steven H.
Jock, Paul F., II
Johnson, Gary Thomas
Johnson, Grant Lester
Johnson, Thomas Stuart
Jones, Richard Cyrus
Kahn, Mitchell Charles
Kamin, Kay Hodes
Karaba, Frank Andrew
Keck, Robert Clifton
Keeley, George William
Kirkpatrick, John Everett
Kirsner, Kenneth Stephen
Knight, William D., Jr.
Knox, James Edwin
Kohlstedt, James August
Kois, George Stephen
Kopp, Frederick Philip
Kornichuk, Ellen S.
Kotz, Richard Frederick
Krohn, Frank Ronald
Kurz, Thomas Patrick
Ladd, Jeffrey Raymond
Lane, Marc Jay
Lapelle, William J.
Lapin, Andrew William
Lapin, Harvey I.
Lauderdale, Katherine Sue
Lause, Christopher Allen
LeBaron, Charles Frederick, Jr.
Lederer, William Joseph
Lee, Mark Richard
Leifel, Danny John
Leopold, Mark Freudenthal
Levin, Jack S.
Levin, Michael David
Liebling, Norman Robert
Linde, Maxine Helen
Lippe, Melvin Karl
Liss, Jeffrey Glenn
Lorenz, Hugo Albert
Lowinger, Alexander I
Lutz, Karl Evan
MacPhail, Douglas Francis
Malkin, Cary Jay
Malloy, Kathleen Sharon
Markey, James Kevin
Marks, Roger Harris
Mason, Peter Ian
Mayerson, Sandra Elaine
McConnell, Jack Lewis
McDermott, John Henry
McDermott, Robert B.
McErlean, Charles F., Jr.
McGrath, William Joseph
McMahon, Thomas Michael
McMenamin, John Robert
McWhirter, Bruce J.
Michaels, Richard Edward
Millard, Richard Steven
Miller, Arthur Robert
Miller, John Leed
Miller, Ronald Stuart
Miller, Russell George
Miller, Stanton Bernett
Mills, Andre Micheaux
Mills, John Welch
Mintel, Judith King
Miranti, Richard Frederick
Mitchell, Lee Mark
Modlin, Lowell Ronald
Mollet, Chris John
Morrison, Sidney Eder
Motchan, Brent L.
Murphy, Thomas Lee
Nagelberg, Howard Allen
Nekritz, Barry B.
Nicholson, Thomas Laurence
Nordlund, William Chalmers
Nyberg, William Arthur
Nygren, Karl Francis
O'Brien, Walter Joseph, II
Ogle, Jerry Michael
Orloff, Ronald Leonard
O'Rourke, Daniel
Overgaard, Cordell Jersild
Overton, George Washington
Painter, John Woodward
Pallasch, B. Michael
Palmberg, Earl Laverne
Parkhurst, Beverly Susler
Parson, David
Peake, Darryl Lee
Peck, Kerry Reid
Pell, Wilbur Frank, III
Phelps, Paul Michael
Poper, Michael Charles
Prather, William Chalmers
Presser, Stephen Bruce
Proczko, Taras Roman
Provenzano, William Joseph
Quinlan, William Joseph, Jr.
Rapp, James Anthony
Ratkovich, Cynthia
Rauner, Vincent Joseph
Raymond, David Walker
Redman, Clarence Owen
Reicin, Ronald Ian
Rendleman, Dennis Alan
Reum, James Michael
Reynolds, Daniel
Rhind, James Thomas
Rindal, Ellen Joan, .
Ritchie, William Paul
Rooks, John Newton
Rooney, Michael James
Roos, Robert Carl, Jr.
Roti, Thomas David
Ruder, David Sturtevant
Saltiel, David Michael
Santona, Gloria
Sarabia, Antonio Rosas
Saulsberry, Charles R.
Schaaf, Douglas Allan
Schaffner, Theodore W.
Schramm, Marilyn Jean
Schreck, Robert A., Jr.
Schwartz, Thomas D.
Scott, John Joseph
Scott, Robert Kent
Sebat, John Edward
Seith, Alex Robert
Selfridge, Calvin
Senescu, Stuart
Sernett, Richard Patrick
Seyfarth, Henry Edward
Shank, William O.
Sholem, David Bennett
Siegan, Jerold Nathan
Siegel, Howard Jerome
Sigal, Michael Stephen
Silliman, Richard George
Skadow, Ronald Robert
Smedinghoff, Thomas J.
Smith, Edward Jerome
Snell, Thaddeus Stevens, III
Southern, Robert Allen
Spain, Patrick James
Sprowl, Charles Riggs
Stassen, John Henry
Staubitz, Arthur Frederick
Stein, Carey M.
Steinberg, Morton M.
Stephan, Edmund Anton
Stone, Bertram Allen
Sujack, Edwin Thomas
Sulkes, Carol Fay
Thomas, Frederick Bradley
Thompson, David F.
Thornton, Robert Richard
Trenda, Regis J(ohn)
Tucker, Bowen Hayward
Valley, Mark R.
Vanneman, Edgar, Jr.
Veverka, Donald John
Vieregg, Robert Todd
Wade, Edwin Lee
Walbaum, Robert C.
Wardell, John Watson
Warnock, William Reid
Wartman, Carl Henry
Watts, Dey Wadsworth
Weeks, Robert Walker
Wexler, Warren Marshall
Whalen, Wayne W.
Whitlock, Brian Thomas
Wilkinson, John Bruce
Williams, Robert Jene
Wilson, Roger Goodwin
Winget, Walter Winfield
Wise, Nancy Joan
Wolfe, David Louis
Wolfman, Paul Irwin
Woulfe, Margaret Frances
Wright, Robert Williams
York, John C.
Zaander, Mark Charles
Zabrosky, Alex Walter

Indiana

Abels, Jonathan Berle
Anast, Nick James
Ancel, Sorelle Jean Lewis
Bailey, Patricia Seasor
Bartlett, Rick E.
Blackwell, Henry Barlow, II
Blythe, James David, II
Bodle, John Frederick
Bond, Richard Ewing
Bowen, Willard Gene
Bowman, Carol Ann
Brainard, James C.
Carey, John Leo
Cleveland, Peter Devine
Coons, Stephen Merle
Coukos, Carolyn Cook
Coyne, Lynn Harry
Coz, Thomas Anthony
Croner, Fred B., Jr.
Crump, Francis Jefferson, III
Culp, Charles William
Dennis, Ralph Emerson, Jr.
Dorocke, Lawrence Francis
Drummy, William Wallace, III
Dugan, Michael Thomas, II
Dutton, Clarence Benjamin
Eichhorn, Frederick Foltz, Jr.
Elkin, Paul Stanley
Evans, Daniel Fraley, Jr.
Ferguson, Stephen Luther
Ferguson, Theodore James
FitzGibbon, Daniel Harvey
Gerberding, Miles Carston
Germann, Douglas Dean, Sr.
Grodnik, Charles Hubert
Hackman, Marvin Lawrence
Hamilton, John Anthony
Harman, John Royden
Henderson, Eugene Leroy
Hunter, Jack Duval
Jewell, John J.
Kahlenbeck, Howard, Jr.
Kalsi, Swadesh Singh
Katich, Nick
Kingdon, Victor Scott
Kline, Gary Alan
Leopold, Robert Bruce
Long, Douglas Paul
Lowell, Cym Hawksworth
Maine, Michael Roland
Mallers, George Peter
Mascher, Gilbert Ernsting
Millard, David B.
Murrell, Jack Oliver
Neff, R. Matthew
Oldham, Steve Anthony
Patrick, William Bradshaw
Paul, Stephen Howard
Powlen, David Michael
Pytynia, Thomas Lee
Reinke, William John
Roberts, Patricia Susan
Sanborn, Albert Beckwith, II
Schultess, LeRoy Kenneth
Schwarz, James Harold
Smith, Maxwell Paul
Suedhoff, Carl John, Jr.
Swhier, Robert Dewain, Jr.
Tillman, Douglas Leon
Truitt, Patricia Peyton
Vandivier, Blair Robert
Waddick, William Anthony
Wood, William Jerome
Young, Barbara Ann
Zaharako, Lew Daleure

Iowa

Belin, David William
Brown, Paul Edmondson
Bump, Wilbur Neil
Byers, Donald Charles
Clark, Beverly Ann
Dull, Wilbur Robbins
Ehlers, Michael Gene
Einck, Dean Robert
Farr, Thomas Carey
Fisher, Thomas George
Fox, Terry Roy
Gray, William Oxley
Graziano, Craig Frank
Hansell, Edgar Frank
Hoth, Steven Sergey
Joyce, Joseph Benedict
Kelley, Bruce Gunn
Kersten, Donald Norbert
Klinger, Phillip Dennis
Laird, Morris E.
Lambert, George Robert
Makeig, Thomas Howard
Morf, Darrel Arle
O'Connor, John Charles
Pechacek, Frank Warren, Jr.
Peshkin, Samuel David
Reasoner, Carroll Jane
Ruttenberg, Harold Seymour
Scism, Robert Bruce
Seitzinger, Edward Francis
Seitzinger, Edward Francis
Simpson, Lyle Lee
Starcevic, Joseph Francis
Strutt, David Stanley
Thelen, John Frederick
Thorson, Larry Jonathan
Zenk, Ann Marie

Kansas

Bertholf, Terry Donald
Cranford, Steven Leon
Erickson, George Everett, Jr.
Fursman, Nancy Johanna
Gillmore, Alver James
Haddock, Bradley Eugene
Hageman, John Ashley
Jones, Lloyd Wesley
Leffel, Russell Calvin
Logan, Carl M.
Martin, Alson Robert
Martin, Barry Douglas
Myers, Jesse Jerome
Peters, Geoffrey Wright
Reeves, Jean Brooks
Sears, Ruth Ann
Seed, Thomas Finis
Shull, William Edgar, Jr.
Snyder, Brock Robert
Stover, Kathy Ann
Stull, Gordon Bruce
Toepfer, Thomas Lyle
Weinberg, Gary Scott
Westerhaus, Douglas Bernard
Whitman, Douglas Frank

Kentucky

Aberson, Leslie Donald
Ardery, Joseph Lord Tweedy
Bardenwerper, William Burr
Carroll, Thomas Charles
Carter, Robert Philip
Cocklin, Kim Roland
Coombs, Ronald Lee
Dieffenbach, Charles Maxwell
Feazell, Thomas Lee
Fenton, Thomas Conner
Hallenberg, Robert Lewis
Handmaker, S.A.
Hetman, Nicholas Wayne
La Brie, Lawrence James
Lester, Roy David
Lile, Charles Alan
Miller, Herbert Allan, Jr.
Miller, J. Bruce
Morris, Benjamin Hume
Murphy, Richard Vanderburgh
Newberry, James H., Jr.
Niemi, Bruce Alan
Ockerman, Edwin Foster, Jr.
Pedley, Lawrence Lindsay
Pettyjohn, Shirley Ellis
Philpott, James Alvin, Jr.
Reeves, L. Brian
Schaeffer, Edwin Frank, Jr.
Tannon, Jay Middleton
Van Meter, John David
Vish, Donald H.
Williamson, Charles Gurley, Jr.
Winslow, Donald Arthur

Louisiana

Beckner, Donald Lee
Becnel, Philip Alfred, III
Boyd, Joseph Robert
Bronfin, Fred
Burkett, David Ingram
Campbell, Joseph H(oward), Jr.
Cheramie, Carlton Joseph
Cook, David Sherman
Cutshaw, James Michael
Dodd, Lawrence Roe
Duncan, Nora Kathryn
Fadaol, Robert Frederick
Feldman, Martin L. C.
Gallagher, John M., Jr.
Garrett, David Isaiah, Jr.
Goldblatt, Michael L.
Hardtner, Quintin Theodore, III
Hardy, Ashton Richard
Holliday, James Sidney, Jr.
Hurley, Paul Edward
Jeter, Katherine Leslie Brash
Kracht, Eric Alan
Lenz, Laurence Henry, Sr.
Leonard, Paul Haralson
Little, Michael Frederick
McMillan, Lee Richards, II
Milly, Raymond Anthony
Molony, Michael Janssens, Jr.
Morgan, Louis Linton
Mote, Clyde A
Patin, Sidney L.
Perez, Luis Alberto
Peroni, Robert Joseph
Reso, Jerome John, Jr.
Rinker, Andrew, Jr.
Rives, James Davidson, Jr.
Ryan, Gary Lee
Shinn, Clinton Wesley
Simon, H(uey) Paul
Snyder, Charles Aubrey
Stewart, Melinda Jane
Thibaut, Charest deLauzon, Jr.
Title, Peter Stephen
Vermillion, John Richard
Vickery, Eugene Benton, Jr.
Volk, Jerome Milton, Jr.
Waechter, Arthur Joseph, Jr.
Weiss, Donald Paul
Wright, Paul William

Maine

Broder, James Nelson
Coward, Thomas Scott
Curran, Richard Emery, Jr.
Dench, Bryan Mundy
Fuller, Atherton
Hughes, David Emery
Hunt, Philip Courtney
Keenan, James Francis
Scribner, Fred Clark, Jr.
Slater, Brent R.
Taintor, Frederick Giles
Trevett, Kenneth Parkhurst
Webster, Peter Bridgman
Willihnganz, Paul W.

Maryland

Ahearn, Charles Dennis
Asti, Alison Louise
Astrachan, James Barry
Axelson, Jeffrey Mark
Berndt, Richard Olaf
Boone, Harold Thomas
Bové, Edward Joseph
Bowen, Debra Lynn
Burke, Raymond Daniel
Carmel, Alan Stuart
Chernow, Jeffrey Scott
Choate, Alan G.
Clancy, Joseph Patrick
Clarke, Edward Owen, Jr.
Colton, Sterling Don
Curran, Robert Bruce
Davison, Warren Malcolm
Deerson, Bruce Alan
Duer, Andrew Adgate
Fisher, Jeffrey B.
Foltz, Richard Nelson, III
Freeland, Charles
Fry, Donald Curtis
Gershberg, Richard Louis
Gobbel, Luther Russell
Goldman, Brian A.
Gray, Richard Edward
Greenstein, Ruth Louise
Guttenberg, Aryeh
Harris, Janine Diane
Harrison, James Joshua, Jr.
Hecht, Isaac
Hendricks, John Charles
Hershman, Murray John
Hesson, William M., Jr.
Jackley, Michael Dano
Johnsen, Peter Henry
Kafes, William O.
Katz, Steven Martin
Kaylor, Omer Thomas, Jr.
Klein, Gerald S.
Maffitt, James Strawbridge
Maseritz, Guy B.
McCauley, Richard Gray
Patz, Edward Frank
Phillips, Leo Harold, Jr.
Priest, Gordon Webb, Jr.
Quillen, William Tatem
Smith, David Robinson
Staples, Lyle Newton
Tanenbaum, Richard Hugh
Tilghman, Richard Carmichael, Jr.
Vanderlinde, Susan Kay
Whaley, Joseph Randall
Wildhack, William August, Jr.

Massachusetts

Abbott, William Saunders
Abraham, Nicholas Albert
Arden, John Réal
Ardiff, William B.
Auerbach, Joseph
Bacon, Douglas Arms
Baker, Horace Ross, Jr.
Ballantyne, Richard L(ee)
Bateman, Thomas Robert
Beeby, Kenneth Jack
Bernfeld, Jeffray Alan
Bernhard, Alexander Alfred
Blanker, Alan Harlow
Borenstein, Milton Conrad
Brophey, Alicia Tracy
Burgoyne, John Albert
Burr, Francis Hardon
Casson, Richard Frederick
Chapin, David Chester
Cherwin, Joel Ira
Chyten, Edwin Richard
Coltun, Harry
Cook, Charles Addison
Countryman, Vern
Covel, Richard Allan
Cummins, Kenneth Copeland
Davenport, David Sterling
Davis, Alan Hugh
Dello Iacono, Paul Michael
Dickie, Robert Benjamin
Dwyer, William Edward
Eaton, William Lawrence
Estrine, Andrew Bradley
Ferriter, Maurice Joseph
Fischer, Eric Robert
FitzGibbon, Scott Thomas
Fluker, Brenda Ann
Fortier, Albert Mark, Jr.
Frankenheim, Samuel
Fraser, Everett MacKay
Frederick, Samuel Adams
Gannon, Christopher Richard
Garcia, Adolfo Ramon
Glazer, Donald Wayne
Goldman, Richard Harris
Gonson, S. Donald
Goodman, Louis Allan
Grahame, Orville Francis Booth
Grassia, Thomas C.
Grayson, Edward Davis
Greer, Gordon Bruce
Hadzima, Joseph George, Jr.
Heilman, Carl Edwin
Hodge, Nicholas Sim
Horn, Everett Byron, Jr.
Jordan, Alexander Joseph, Jr.
Joyce, James Joseph, Jr.
Keuthen, Catherine J. Norman
Korb, Kenneth A.
Kovar, Stuart Charles
Krulewich, Helen D.
Lamson, David Hinkley
Lerman, Herbert S.
Lincoln, J(ames) Alden
Lougee, David Louis
Lovins, Nelson Preston
Malley, Robert John
Marullo, Steven Jeffrey
Matthews, James Bernard
May, William Leopold, Jr.
McCready, Leo Stephen
McDaniel, James Alan
Milan, Edwin Ramon
Mills, Michael Francis
Minot, Winthrop Gardner
Molineaux, Charles Borromeo, Jr.
Notopoulos, Alexander Anastasios, Jr.
O'Connell, Charles Francis
O'Connell, Joseph Francis, III
Olshan, Joseph Raymond
Paran, Mark Lloyd
Parsons-Salem, Diane Lora
Pearlstein, Gerald
Penman, Gordon Reese
Phillipes, Peter Michael
Provanzano, Joseph Stephen
Railsback, David Phillips
Redlich, Marc
Repetti, James Randolph
Resnick, Charles H.
Ritter, Deborah Bradford
Rockefeller, Regina Strazzulla
Rosensaft, Lester Jay
Rubens, James I.
Rudolph, James Leonard
Savrann, Richard Allen
Schwartz, Edward Arthur
Serafini, Linda Ann
Silver, Marvin S.
Simpson, Russell Gordon
Snyder, Richard Joseph
Soforenko, Joel Fredrick
Solk, Gerald
Stern, Edward Mayer
Stokes, James Christopher, Jr.
Thibeault, George Walter
Thomas, David Lloyd, Jr.
Tierney, Albert Gerard, III
Updegrove, Andrew Scott
Vagts, Detlev Frederick
Webb, Henley Ross
Weinstein, Seymour
Weiss, Dudley Albert
West, Richard Angus
Whipple, Robert Jenks
White, Barry Bennett
Widett, Irving
Wilcox, Steven Alan
Wolfson, Jeffrey Steven
Wright, Benjamin Tappan

Michigan

Allen, James Lee
Andrews, H(oward) Raymond, Jr.
Austin, Margaret Schilt
Aycock, William Robert
Babcock, Charles Witten
Balagna, Steven David
Borders, Sidney Richard
Bransdorfer, Stephen Christie
Bullard, Rockwood Wilde, III
Bushnell, George Edward, Jr.
Calkins, Stephen
Callahan, Michael Sean
Campbell, Scott Robert
Case, Matthew Alan
Centner, Charles William
Chapman, Conrad Daniel
Clark, John Scott
Cohan, Leon Sumner
Colombo, Frederick J.
Davis, Roger Edwin
Dawda, Edward C.
Dew, Thomas Edward
Dresser, Raymond H., Jr.
Durant, James Robert
Eklund, Robert D.
Elkins, Bettye Swales
Ellmann, Douglas Stanley
Epstein, Robert E.
Fisher, Edward Walter
Flessland, Dennis Michael
Fortino, Alfred J.
Gale, Connie R(uth)
Goldberg, Fredric Norman
Gordon, Edgar George
Gordon, Robert Jay
Grumbine, David Lee
Haines, Michael Curtis
Haliw, Andrew Jerome, III
Hanes, James Henry
Haron, David Lawrence
Harris, Robert James
Harris, Stephen James
Heil, Paul William
Helminski, Francis Joseph
Hindelang, Robert Louis
Holley, Audrey Rodgers
Hunter, Larry Dean
Huss, Allan Michael
Hwang, Roland
Jackson, Mark Andrew
Kamins, John Mark
Kanter, Alan Michael
Kaplow, Robert David
Kienbaum, Karen Smith
Kirk, John MacGregor
Kopack, Laura Reyes
Kuehn, George E.
Lambert, Robert Bradley
Lashbrooke, Elvin Carroll, Jr.
Leavitt, Martin Jack
Legg, Michael William
Lenihan, Robert Joseph, II
Lindemer, Lawrence Boyd
Logie, John Hoult
Mc Callum, Charles Edward
McDonald, Daryl Patrick
McGlynn, Joseph Michael
McKim, Samuel John, III
Meyer, George Herbert
Murphy, Joseph Albert, Jr.
Myers, Rodman Nathaniel
Nehra, Gerald Peter
Nern, Christopher Carl
Nielsen, William Robert
Norris, Lawrence Geoffrey
Nowinski, Thomas Stephen
O'Rourke, Peter Edward
Parker, Patric Allan
Peirce, Kenneth B., Jr.
Pelavin, Michael Allen
Peterson, David Reid
Phillips, Elliott Hunter
Pierce, Richard William
Polley, Vincent Ira
Ponitz, John Allan
Porro, James Earle
Provenzano, Vincent
Raven, Jonathan Ezra
Rewald, Roman
Rich, Edward William
Robinson, Logan Gilmore
Rosi, Philip Rinaldo
Ruwart, David Peter
Schanz, Stephen John
Schloss, Lawrence James
Sharp, John
Shoop, Deborah
Sills, John Dennis
Skipper, Nathan Richard, Jr.
Slavin, John Jeremiah
Smith, Brook McCray
Smith, Stanton Kinnie, Jr.
Sorge, Jay Wootten
Spicer, S(amuel) Gary
Spivak, Peter Beeching
Steinberg, Harvey Laurance
Steingold, Fred Saul
Stoetzer, Gerald Louis
Talcott, Kent Patterson
Tarnacki, Duane L.
Tartt, Tyrone Chris
Thomas, Gerard
Thomas, Michael Eli
Thurber, Cleveland
Twitchell, Ervin Eugene
Ulrich, Gregory Leslie
Valentine, Stephen Kenneth, Jr.
Van Allsburg, Jon Aaron
van Horne, Pieter Hammond
Vilders, Kurt Ronald
Vining, (George) Joseph
Vogel, Theodore John
Von Drehle, Ramon Arnold
Walle, James Paul
Westerman, Susan S.
Williams, J. Bryan
Winchell, William Olin
Winquist, Thomas Richard
Yared, Paul David
Zalecki, Paul Henry
Zameck, Harvey Jason

Minnesota

Albers, Fern Beth
Altman, Milton Hubert
Anderson, James Hurd
Anderson, Laurence Alexis
Angle, Margaret Susan
Barry, Charles Byron
Beha, Ralph Werner
Bernhardson, Ivy Schutz
Bloedel, Philip John
Brooks, William James, III
Burke, Paul Bradford
Davis, Stephen Jeffrey
Dietz, Charlton Henry
Diracles, James Constantine
Dosland, William Buehler
DuFour, R(ichard) W(illiam), Jr.
Dzurak, Steven J.
Engle, Donald Edward
Erickson, Phillip Arthur
Fisher, Michael Bruce
Florence, Dorothy M.
Foarde, Mary Patricia
Frecon, Alain Jean-Christian
Giberson, Francis Eugene
Habicht, James Robert
Hanson, Steven Allen
Hasselquist, Maynard Burton
Hayward, Edward Joseph
Hirl, Patricia Ann
Hitch, Horace
Johnson, Donald E.
Kaplan, Harvey Frederick
Kaplan, Sheldon
Klein, William David
Knapp, John Anthony
Larsen, Karen Marie
Larson, Andrew Robert
LeVander, Bernhard Wilhelm
Lindgren, D(erbin) Kenneth, Jr.
Luis, Juanita Bolland
Lyons, M. Arnold
Maffei, Rocco John
Marousek, Robert Joseph
Marquardt, Merritt Reno
Marrinan, Timothy David
McNally, Pierce Aldrich
Moland, Bruce
Montgomery, John Vincent
Mundt, Daniel Henry
Nordaune, Roselyn Jean
Norton, John William
Nyquist, Dean Allen
Nys, John Nikki
Perlman, Lawrence
Peterson, Ralph Henry
Radmer, Michael John
Radtke, Stephen David
Rebane, John T.
Rossini, Raymond Dominic
Sanner, Royce Norman
Savelkoul, Donald Charles
Sayers, Randall William
Schatz, James Edward
Silver, Melvin Jacob
Skare, Robert Martin
Sullivan, Michael Patrick
Tennessen, Robert Joseph
Tyra, Kenneth Thomas
Vitko, John Peter
Wahl, Karla Rae
Wald, John Roger
Watson, John Slater
Wegener, Richard James
Whitehill, Clifford Lane
Williams, James Edward
Woods, Robert Edward
Yost, Gerald B.
Young, Stephen Bonsal
Yucel, Edgar Kent
Zotaley, Byron L.

Mississippi

Baggett Boozer, Linda Dianne
Bush, Fred Marshall, Jr.
Cavanaugh, Michael Flynn
Corlew, John Gordon
Glover, William Hudson, Jr.
Hafter, Jerome Charles
Lalor, Owen Patrick
Low, John T.C.
Magee, William Eugene
Mingee, James Clyde, III
Painter, William Steene
Russell, Glover Alcorn, Jr.
Snowden, Elton Gregory
Stubblefield, Joseph Stephen
Travis, Jay A., III
Twiford, H. Hunter, III
Wise, Sherwood Willing

Missouri

Akre, Steven Heetland
Allen, Thomas Ernest
Anderson, Christopher James
Appleton, R.O., Jr.
Armstrong, Owen Thomas
Arnold, John Fox
Ball, Owen Keith, Jr.
Banks, Eric Kendall
Barkofske, Francis Lee
Bates, William Hubert (Bert)
Beachy, Robert M.
Beard, Charles Richard
Berg, Julius Harry
Bierman, Norman
Blackwell, Menefee Davis
Bley, Joseph Russell, Jr.
Bowman, Pasco Middleton, II
Braun, N. Barrett
Brouillette, Gary Joseph
Bruening, Richard Patrick
Bryan, Henry C(lark), Jr.
Byers, Ronald Gregory
Christiansen, Steven Allan
Coffin, Richard Keith
Copilevitz, Errol
Craig, Bernard Duffy
Crawford, Howard Allen
Cullen, James D.
Curtis, Thomas Bradford
Deacy, Thomas Edward, Jr.
Denneen, John Paul
Doheny, Donald Aloysius
Drakesmith, Frederick William
Duesenberg, Richard William
Dyer, John Gilbert
Elbert, Charles Steiner
Ellebrecht, Mark Gerard
English, Mark Gregory
Ewing, Lynn Moore, Jr.
Fallon, John Joseph
Fox, Byron Neal
Fretwell, Norman Elliott
Gallop, Donald Philip
Gayer, Katherine L.
Gisler, George Louis
Godiner, Donald Leonard
Gorman, Gerald Warner
Gould, Terry Allen
Graham, Harold Steven
Graham, Robert Clare, III
Gross, Monnye R.
Gulley, William Louis
Haller, Albert John
Halpern, Burton
Hamra, Sam Farris, Jr.
Hancock, S. Lee
Hapke, Daniel S., Jr.
Harris, Harvey Alan
Hass, William Ralph
Higgins, Stephen Boyd
Hoffman, John Raymond
Hoyne, Andrew Thomas
Jenkins, James M(ichael)
Kaveney, Frank John
Knoten, Thomas Patrick
Kohn, Michael Elliott
Kranitz, Theodore Mitchell
Kretsinger, Tom Bark, Jr.
Lange, C. William
Lents, Don Glaude
Long, Michael Evans
Lorenz, Jack Chapin
Lynch, Robert Martin
Malacarne, C. John
Manning, John Patrick, V
Mattern, Keith Edward
Mayfield, Edgar
McCalpin, Francis William
McCandless, Jeffry Scott
Miller, Stephen
Minogue, Thomas John
Minton, Goodridge Venable Morton
Moore, Jean Bante
Morrison, John Stanley
Murphy, Edward Elias, Jr.
Neill, Robert
Noonan, Thomas Joseph
O'Loughlin, John Patrick
Pajda, Thomas Albin
Palmer, Randall Bruce
Peper, Christian Baird
Pickle, Robert Douglas
Pollihan, Thomas Henry
Proost, Robert Lee
Quitmeier, William Michael
Radasky, David Jacob
Reefer, Elizabeth Dross
Rice, Charles Marcus, II
Rice, Guy Garner
Rich, Marvin Lewis
Rund, William Drake
Sands, Darry Gene
Sant, John Talbot
Schnuck, Terry Edward
Schramm, Paul Howard
Seigel, Stephen Paul
Sparks, Stephen Stone
Stanziola, James Alan
Starnes, James Wright
Stevens, Bradford Lee
Suhre, Walter Anthony, Jr.
Sutter, William Franklin
Tatlow, Gary Arthur
Thompson, Edmonstone Field
Thomson, Harry Pleasant, Jr.
Toft, Martin John, III
Tremayne, Bertram William, Jr.
Tremayne, Eric Flory
Tripp, Donald William
Tucker, James Delzell
Van Cleve, William Moore
Vines, Leonard Dean
Walsh, Rodger John
Wiggins, Kip Acker
Willis, Russell Anthony, III
Willy, Thomas Ralph
Wochner, William James
Wrobley, Ralph Gene
Yates, David Floyd

Montana

Bahls, Steven Carl
Beiswanger, Gary Lee
Ogg, Robert Kelley
Robinson, Calvin Stanford
Seelye, Lynn McVeigh

Nebraska

Adams, Joseph
Aitken, Philip Martin
Benak, James Donald
Blazek, George Thomas
Bloomingdale, Arthur Lee, Jr.
Bradford, Charles Steven
Council, Brenda Joyce
Crosby, Robert Berkey
Dolan, James Vincent
Dwyer, Robert Vincent, Jr.
Frazier, Lawrence Alan
Hewitt, James Watt
Hutfless, Frank James
Jahn, Gregory Dean
Jones, Ronald Lee
Kassmeier, Randolf Frank
Lash, Douglas Steven
Lipp, Louis Ellis
Lyons, William Drewry
Lyons, William Harry
Minter, Gregory Byron
Munro, Robert Allan
O'Connor, James Edward
Schneider, Gary Bruce
Schumacher, Paul Maynard
Stern, Arnold Jay
Vosburg, Bruce David
Walkley, Robert Earle
Wegner, James Darwin

Nevada

Ashleman, Ivan Reno, II
Baer, Luke
Brown, Joseph Wentling
Cavin, Rhonda Lynn
Gallagher, Dennis Vincent
Goldstein, Mark Harold
Gubler, John Gray
Jones, Clifford Aaron
Kladney, David
Leverty, Vernon Eugene
Logar, Ronald John
Lowe, Bryan A.
Maglaras, Chris, Jr.
Mushkin, Michael Robert
Pike, George Russell
Richards, Paul A.
Schouweiler, Bart McClain
Wicker, Walter Chris

New Hampshire

Budnitz, Arron Edward
Carbon, Susan Berkson
Chamberlain, Douglas Reginald
Cohen, Steven
Coolidge, Daniel Scott
Cronmiller, Thomas Bernard
Gayman, Benjamin Franklin
Griffin, John Francis, Jr.
Gutin, Irving
Haughey, Thomas Malcolm
Hood, James Calton
Jones, Franklin Charles
Lagos, George Peter
Lopez, Chester Henry, Jr.
Marsh, Norman James, Jr.
Marts, Anthony Charles
Michels, John Rudolf
Platt, Thomas C., III
Potter, Fred Leon
Rakowsky, Connie Lee
Ransmeier, Joseph Sirera
Shaines, Robert Arthur
Snierson, Richard S.
Snow, Robert Brian
Toll, Charles Hansen, Jr.
Wiebusch, Richard Vernon
Wilson, William Harold, Jr.
Wyatt, Donald L., Jr.

New Jersey

Adler, Jack Philip
Alexander, John Donald
Allen, Michael Lewis
Anderson, Ellis B.
Arnold, Kenneth Robert
Aspero, Benedict Vincent
Baldino, John Joseph
Banse, Robert Lee
Bantivoglio, Thomas Nicholas
Bastedo, Wayne Webster
Bello-Monaco, Deborah Ann
Berman, Steven Paul
Bertsche, Copeland Gray
Biaett, Doddridge Hewitt, III
Bittman, Mitchell David
Boardman, Harold Frederick, Jr.
Borteck, Robert D.
Bovaird, Brendan Peter
Boyle, Matthew Anthony
Brewer, Andrea Bordiga
Bullock, Thomas Francis
Cangelosi, Carl J.
Carr, Hubert Franklin
Case, Douglas Manning
Casiello, Nicholas, Jr.
Coben, Carl Gerald
Cohen, Mitchell Robert
Colaguori, Louis Albert
Cole, Larry Michael
Conway, Kevin George
Conway, Richard James, Jr.
Cornish, Jeannette Carter
Croft, John W.
Cuoco, Daniel Anthony
D'Amico, John, Jr.
DeBois, James Adolphus

DeRose, James Dominic
Dilts, Thomas Harold
Donnella, Michael Andre
Dornbusch, Arthur A., II
Dougherty, James Douglas
Drakeman, Donald Lee
Duff, Vaughn W.
Ellenport, Robert Saul
Ernst, Charles Stephen
Falcon, Raymond Jesus, Jr.
Fischer, Jay David
Fitzpatrick, Harold Francis
Flanders, Howard Barrett, Jr.
Fleming, Russell, Jr.
Frazza, George S.
Fredericks, Wesley Charles, Jr.
Friedman, Robert Martin
Fries Gardner, Lisa
Galiardo, John William
Gang, Irving Lloyd
Gerard, Stephen Stanley
Goldberg, Leonard M.
Greenberg, Steven Morey
Greene, Michael Roy
Gruccio-Thorman, Lillian Joan
Guest, Brian Milton
Gutterman, Alan J.
Hackman, Richard Paul
Harris, Allan Michael
Hasl, Hannelore Vera Margarete
Hayward, George John
Hector, Bruce John
Heerwagen, Elwood J., Jr.
Herpst, Robert Dix
Hetsko, Cyril Francis
Holt, Michael Bartholomew
Honig, Emanuel Aaron
Humick, Thomas Charles Campbell
Hutson, Frank Alfred, Jr.
Iannarone, Anthony Joseph
Iatesta, John Michael
Irenas, Joseph Eron
Israels, Michael Jozef
Jacobs, Joseph James
Jeffer, Herman
Jeffers, Albert Brown
Joel, Jack Bowers
Kagan, Irving
Kaps, Warren Joseph
Kassoff, Mitchell Jay
Katz, Richard W.
Kelsky, Richard Brian
Kennedy, Harold Edward
Kent, Thomas Day
Klinghoffer, Steven Harold
Kotok, Lester
Lambert, Richard Justin, Jr.
Lario, Frank M., Jr.
Lavey, Stewart Evan
Lawatsch, Frank Emil, Jr.
Lerner, Harry
Lind, Peter Eugene
Linett, David
Lundy, Audie Lee, Jr.
Lustbader, Philip Lawrence
Lyon, Rexford Lowell
Mahoney, George LeFevre
Martin, Thomas L.
Martini, George henry
Marton, Emery
Masanoff, Michael David
McDonald, James Douglas
Metzger, John Mackay
Miller, Arthur Harold
Milton, Gabriel
Miner, Richard Thomas
Monti, Renard George
Moore, Janet Patricia
Murray, William James
Neibart, Ralph
O'Leary, Richard Patrick
Orbe, Octavius Anthony
Ornitz, Richard Martin
Pace, Thomas
Pearlman, Peter Steven
Perzley, Alan Harris
Pickus, Robert Mark
Porter, John Issac
Reich, Laurence
Riley, Robert Henry
Ritter, Robert Joseph
Rosen, Howard Theodore
Rosenberg, Michael
Rosenhouse, Nathan
Samet, Andrew Benjamin
Schiefelbein, Lester Willis, Jr.
Schuster, Steven Vincent
Shandor, Bohdan Donald
Shea, Edward Emmett
Sherman, Lenore Shustak
Sholk, Steven Howard
Silver, Cole Brian
Simon, Gary Richard
Slifkin, Irving
Staehle, Sandra Johnson
Stalker, Timothy Wayne
Statmore, Kenneth T.
Stone, Sheldon
Storms, Clifford Beekman
Strull, James Richard
Sudol, Walter Edward
Tauber, Frederic J.
Tyler, George Joseph
Ulrich, Robert Gardner
Van Rensselaer, Robert Mickle Miles
Ventantonio, James Bartholomew
Virelli, Louis James, Jr.
Wadler, Arnold L.
Walter, William Eugene
Watson, Mark Henry
Weber, Walter Winfield, Jr.
Welch, Gerald Thomas
Whelan, Charles Duplessis, III
Wilson, Abraham
Wingate, Richard Charles
Wolk, Stuart Rodney
Woller, James Alan
Woodbridge, Richard Carveth
Yoerg, Norman, Jr.
Zaloom, John B(asil)
Zimmer, Richard Alan

New Mexico

Apodaca, Patrick Vincent
Barnett, Barry Howard
Cargo, David Francis
Conner, William Roby
Crider, Charles Joseph
Kennedy, Roderick Thomas
Lopez, Martin, III
Losee, Arthur Jarrell
Martin, Connie Ruth
Paskind, Martin Benjamin
Rager, R. Russell
Robinson, Bernard Leo
Roehl, Jerrald J(oseph)
Schoen, Stevan Jay
Ussery, Albert Travis

New York

Abrams, Alan
Abrams, Stuart
Ahrensfeld, Thomas Frederick
Albans, Gabrielle Victoria
Allen, Richard Marlow
Allison, Richard Clark
Altman, Robert Harry
Amhowitz, Harris J.
Andersen, Richard Esten
Anderson, Arnold Stuart
Andrew, Leonard DeLessio
Angell, Nicholas Biddle
Appel, Alfred
Arango, Emilio
Armstrong, John Kremer
Arouh, Jeffrey Alan
Atkins, Peter Allan
Atkins, Ronald Raymond
Axelrod, Charles Paul
Baker, Bruce J.
Baker, David Remember
Balaber-Strauss, Barbara
Balka, Sigmund Ronell
Ballot, Alissa E.
Banker, Stephen M.
Bankston, Archie Moore, Jr.
Barandes, Robert
Barbanel, Jack A.
Bass, Fred
Baumgardner, John Ellwood, Jr.
Beach, John Arthur
Bean, Bruce Winfield
Beaton, Neal N.
Beattie, Richard Irwin
Beck, Andrew James
Beckstrom, Charles G.
Beekman, William Bedloe
Begley, Louis
Beller, Gary A.
Bender, Alan Ronald
Bender, Joel Charles
Benjamin, Jeffrey
Bennett, Scott Lawrence
Berend, Robert William
Bergstein, Daniel Gerard
Berlin, Alan Daniel
Bernard, Richard Phillip
Berner, Thomas Franklyn
Berzow, Harold Steven
Beshar, Robert Peter
Beuchert, Edward William
Bezikos, Lynne A.
Bialkin, Kenneth J.
Bidwell, James Truman, Jr.
Biegen, Arnold Irwin
Bierce, William Blaikie
Birrell, George Andrew
Bishar, John Joseph, Jr.
Bitsky, Jason Isidore
Black, Louis Engleman
Blackman, Kenneth Robert
Blanc, Roger David
Bloom, Arnold Sanford
Bloomquist, Dennis Howard
Blumberg, Gerald
Bobroff, Harold
Boehner, Leonard Bruce
Bohm, Joel Lawrence
Boone, William Daniel
Borger, John Emory
Bornmann, Carl M(alcolm)
Bowen, John Wesley Edward, IV
Boylan, William Alvin
Bozzo, Paul Peter
Brackett, Ronald E.
Brandrup, Douglas Warren
Brantl, Robert Francis
Braun, Robert Alan
Briggs, Taylor Rastrick
Brock, Mitchell
Bronner, William Roche
Brovitz, Richard Stuart
Brown, Francis Cabell, Jr.
Brown, Geraldine Reed
Brown, G(lenn) William, Jr.
Brown, Meredith M.
Brown, Ralph Sawyer, Jr.
Browning, David Stuart
Bruno, Richard Thomas
Bryan, Barry Richard
Bryan, Thomas Lynn
Bryant, George McEwan
Buckstein, Mark Aaron
Burgman, Dierdre Ann
Burns, John MacDougal, III
Burstein, Neil Alan
Burt, Richard Max
Butler, Samuel Coles
Campbell, Carolyn Clark
Campbell, Woodrow Wilson
Cantor, Samuel C.
Cantwell, Robert
Cape, Billie Jean
Capell, Walter Richard
Carlucci, Joseph Paul
Carr, Joseph B.
Carswell, Robert
Cartenuto, David J.
Cashman, Gideon
Catanzano, Raymond Augustine
Catuzzi, J.P., Jr.
Caywood, Warren Gustave, Jr.
Certilman, Morton Lawrence
Chapin, Edward Whiting
Chapin, Melville
Cherovsky, Erwin Louis
Cho, Tai Yong
Ciovacco, Robert John
Coffee, John Collins, Jr.
Cohen, Arthur Alan
Cohen, Bennett D.
Cohen, Edward Herschel
Cohen, Murray
Cohen, Robin Ellen
Cohen, Stanley Dale
Collins, Wallace Edmund James
Colloff, Margery A.
Condliffe, David Charles
Cook, Barbara Ann
Cooke, George Alexander, Jr.
Cooney, Michael Francis
Cooper, R. John, III
Cooper, Stephen Herbert
Cooperman, Robert N.
Corso, Frank Mitchell
Cotter, James Michael
Cotton, James Alexandre
Cowen, Edward S.
Cox, Melvin Monroe
Cropper, Stephen Wallace
Daitz, Ronald Frederick
Danilek, Donald J.
Davis, Richard Ralph
Daw, Harold John
Dayan, Rodney S.
DeBaets, Timothy Joseph
Deer, James Willis
De Lachapelle, Philippe
de Lasa, José M.
Del Gadio, Robert G.
Derwin, Jordan
Derzaw, Richard Lawrence
Deutsch, Irwin Frederick
Diamant, Aviva F.
DiSciullo, Alan Michael
Dixon, Bonnie Lynn
Dixon, Paul Edward
Donald, Norman Henderson, III
Dorado, Marianne Gaertner
Douglas-Hamilton, Margaret Hambrecht
Doyle, Joseph Anthony
Drebsky, Dennis Jay
Dresner, Byron
Driver, Albert Westcott, Jr.
Dubin, James Michael
Du Boff, Michael H(arold)
Duerbeck, Heidi Barbara
Duffy, Edmund Charles
Duffy, James Henry
Duffy, James P., III
Dune, Steve Charles
Dunham, Wolcott Balestier, Jr.
Dunnington, Walter Grey, Jr.
Eaton, William Mellon
Edmondson, John Richard
Edwinn, Eugene Paul
Ehrlich, Jerrold Ivan
Eisenberg-Mellen, Viviane
Eisert, Edward Gaver
Ekern, George Patrick
Ellis, James Henry
Eltzroth, Carter Weaver
England, William Thomas
Epstein, Melvin
Ercklentz, Enno Wilhelm, Jr.
Erickson, Gail
Erim, Ahmet Martin
Eustis, Albert Anthony
Evans, George Walton, Jr.
Faison, William Franklin, II
Falvey, Patrick Joseph
Farrell, Thomas Dinan
Feder, Robert
Feiman, Ronald Mark
Fein, Eric David
Felcher, Peter L.
Feldman, Jay N.
Fenn, George Karl, Jr.
Fenster, Marvin
Fenster, Robert David
Fernbach, Robert Dennis
Finberg, Alan Robert
Fine, A(rthur) Kenneth
Finkelstein, Allen Lewis
Finkelstein, Bernard
Finkelstein, Saul Haym
Finley, John Jordan
Fisher, Ann Bailen
Fisher, Harold Leonard
Fishman, Fred Norman
Fishman, Mitchell Steven
Fleming, John C.
Fogelman, Martin
Fogg, Blaine Viles
Folger, Oscar David
Forte, Wesley Elbert
Frank, Bernard Alan
Frank, Lloyd
Frankfurt, Morton Allen
Franklin, Blake Timothy
Freda, Frank Anthony
French, John, III
Freund, James Coleman
Fried, Donald David
Friedman, Bart
Friedman, Robert Laurence
Friedman, Stanley Joseph
Fry, Morton Harrison, II
Fullem, L. Robert
Fuller, David Otis, Jr.
Gaetanos, Christ
Gaines, Weaver Henderson, Jr.
Galant, Herbert Lewis
Galef, Steven Allen
Gambro, Michael S.
Ganis, Stephen Lane
Garber, Robert Edward
Gardner, Arnold Burton
Geitz, Michael M(eyer)
Gelatt, Timothy Arthur
Geller, Diane Joyce
Genovese, Thomas L.
Genrich, Willard Adolph
Gerhart, Eugene Clifton
Getlan, Norman
Gettner, Alan Frederick
Gibbs, Lippman Martin
Gilden, Richard Henry
Gill, E. Ann
Gillespie, Alexander Joseph, Jr.
Gillespie, David Arthur
Gillespie, Jane
Ginsberg, Ernest
Ginsberg, Eugene Stanley
Giusti, William Roger
Goetz, Maurice Harold
Goff, Betsy Kagen
Goff, Michael Harper
Gold, Neil D.
Goldberg, Paul Joseph
Goldfarb, Ronald Carl
Goldman, Louis Budwig
Goldman, Roy Lawrence
Goldner, Leonard Howard
Goldschmid, Harvey Jerome
Goldstein, Howard Sheldon
Goodale, James Campbell
Goodman, Edward William
Goodman, Helen Geyh
Gordon, Jeffrey Neil
Gorin, Robert Seymour
Gould, Dirk Samuel
Gowen, George W.
Gracin, Hank
Grames, Conan Paul
Grant, Stephen Allen
Grant, Susan Irene
Green, Jonathan David
Green, Michael Aaron
Greenbaum, Maurice C.
Greenberg, Ronald David
Greene, Herman Fortescue
Grew, Robert Ralph
Grosso, Robert John
Gruen, Michael Stephan
Gunning, Francis Patrick
Gursky, Steven Richard
Gussow, John Andrew
Halperin, Theodore Philip
Halpern, Kenneth Jay, N
Halpern, Ralph Lawrence
Hamel, Rodolphe
Hanft, Noah Jonathan
Hanson, Jean Elizabeth
Hargesheimer, Elbert, III
Hariri, Ronald David
Harkins, Francis Joseph, Jr.
Harrigan, Nancy Stafford
Harris, Wayne Manley
Hart, Robert M.
Haskel, Jules J.
Hatt, Donald Gregory
Hawes, Douglas Wesson
Hawkins, John Donald, Jr.
Hayes, David Michael
Hayes, Norman Robert, Jr.
Head, Christopher Alan
Headrick, Thomas Edward
Healy, Harold Harris, Jr.
Hecht, Charles Joel
Hecker, Robert J.
Heilman, Pamela Davis
Heine, Andrew Noah
Heines, Molly Kathleen
Helldorfer, Bernard George
Heller, Ronald Gary
Henderson, Donald Bernard, Jr.
Hersh, Robert Michael
Hershberg, David Stephen
Hershman, Mendes
Herzeca, Lois Friedman
Hessberg, Albert, II
Hiden, Robert Battaile, Jr.
Higginson, Thomas Lee
Hirsch, Daniel
Hirsch, Melvin L.
Hirshon, Sheldon Ira
Hoblin, Philip J., Jr.
Hoffman, Richard (Melvin)
Holm, Melvin Edward
Hopkins, Thomas Arscott
Horowitz, Harold A.
Howe, Richard Rives
Hoynes, Louis LeNoir, Jr.
Humphreys, Noel Dutton
Hurley, James G.
Immerman, Paul Alan
Iovenko, Michael
Jacobs, Arnold Stephen
Jacobs, Sherry Raphael
Jacobson, Marc
Jagow, Charles Herman
Jakes, Peter H.
Janney, Oliver James
Jarblum, William
Jefferies, Jack P.
Jenkins, Jon Mark
Jibilian, Gerald Arsen
Jinnett, Robert Jefferson
Johnson, Kathryn Gibbons
Johnson, Kenneth Theodore
Johnstone, Jeffrey Marwill
Jones, Jeffrey Russell
Joseph, Stephanie Rudman
Josephson, William Howard
Joye, E. Michael
Kaeser, Clifford Richard
Kahn, David Miller
Kahn, Richard Dreyfus
Kamarck, Martin Alexander
Kamen, Harry Paul
Kane, Alice T.
Kanter, Carl Irwin
Kaplan, Joel Stuart
Kaplan, Mark Norman
Kassebaum, John Philip
Kasselman, Stevens Jay
Katz, Gary M.
Kay, Stanley Lloyd
Kelly, William Wright
Keltner, Thomas Nethery, Jr.
Kessler, Lawrence Bert
Kiernan, Edwin A., Jr.
Klaperman, Joel Simcha
Klatell, Robert Edward
Kleckner, Robert George, Jr.
Klemann, Gilbert Lacy, II
Klosk, Ira David
Koblenz, Michael Robert
Kobrin, Lawrence Alan
Koch, Kenneth Richard
Kocher, Walter William
Koo, Richard
Koplik, Marc Stephen
Kossar, Ronald Steven
Kramaric, Peter Stefan
Kramer, Morris Joseph
Krasnow, Robert Louis
Kraver, Richard Matthew
Kreitman, Lenore Roberts
Kreppel, Milton Mark
Kruteck, Laurence R.
Kullen, Richard Charles, Jr.
Kumble, Steven Jay
Kury, Bernard Edward
Lahey, Edward Vincent, Jr.
Lalla, Thomas Rocco, Jr.
Lampen, Richard Jay
Land, David Potts
Landa, Howard Martin
Landau, Walter Loeber
Lane, Arthur Alan
Langer, Bruce Alden
Larson, Frederick Albin
Lawrence, Linwood Grant, III
Lawton, James Patrick
Leaf, Martin Norman
Lederman, Lawrence
Leitner, Anthony Joseph
Levin, Roger Michael
Levinson, Leslie J.
Levitsky, Asher Samuel
Levitt, Bonnie K.
Levy, Robert S.
Licker, Jeffrey Alan
Lieb, Charles Herman
Lieberman, Steven Paul
Liggio, Carl Donald
Lightstone, Ronald
Ligorio, Mario Eduard
Lilley, Albert Frederick, III
Lippe, Richard Allen
Lipsman, Richard Marc
Lloyd, David Livingstone, Jr.
Lobel, Douglas Arthur
Lovejoy, Allen Fraser
Lunde, Asbjorn Rudolph
Lutzker, Elliot Howard
Lynch, Thomas Halpin
Lyon, Carl Francis, Jr.
Macioce, Frank Michael, Jr.
Mack, Dennis Wayne
Madden, Donald Paul
Madden, John Joseph
Maher, Daniel Francis, Jr.
Mahoney, David John
Maidman, Richard Harvey Mortimer
Maloney, Thomas Joseph
Mangano, Joseph S.
Mannis, Bob Davis
Manshel, Andrew Maximilian
Mantle, Raymond Allan
Margolin, Eric Mitchell
Mark, Jonathan I.
Marks, Ramon Paul
Marks, Theodore Lee
Masinter, Edgar Martin
Massengale, John Edward, 3d
Mattar, Lawrence Joseph
Matteson, William Bleecker
McCabe, David Allen
McCarthy, Robert Emmett
Mc Donald, William J.
McDonald, Willis, IV
McElvein, Thomas I., Jr.
McEnroe, John Patrick
McGahren, Eugene Dewey, Jr.
Mc Goldrick, John Gardiner
McHugh, James Bernard
McKee, Francis John
McLean, David Lyle
McMeen, Elmer Ellsworth, III
McNally, John Joseph
Meader, John Daniel
Meath, Brian Patrick
Meislahn, Harry Post
Melican, James Patrick, Jr.
Meltzer, Roger
Meneilly, James Kevin
Menken, David A.
Merow, John Edward
Merrill, George Vanderneth
Meyer, Henry Theodore, III
Michel, Clifford Lloyd
Mighdoll, Stephen J.
Militello, Samuel Philip
Millard, John Alden
Miller, Frederick Lloyd
Miller, Peter Putnam
Miller, Phebe Condict
Miller, Richard Clark, Jr.
Miller, Sam Scott
Millimet, Erwin
Minahan, Daniel Francis
Mindus, Howard Victor
Missan, Richard Sherman
Mitchell, Robert Everitt
Modell, Michael Steven
Modlin, Howard S.
Mohen, Thomas Patrick
Moomjian, Gary Thomas
Moore, Harold Francis
Moore, Thomas R.
Morgan, Frank Edward, II
Morris, James Malachy
Moskin, Morton
Moskowitz, Stuart Stanley
Mosoff, Serle Ian
Moss, William John
Most, Jack Lawrence
Mur, Raphael
Murphy, Gavin Palmer
Murtagh, James P.
Mushkin, Martin
Myerson, Toby Salter
Nadkarni, Girish Vishwanath
Nash, Paul LeNoir
Neidell, Martin H.
Nelson, Bernard Edward
Newborn, Samuel R(euben)
Newman, Jeffrey K.
Newman, William Arthur
Nguyen, Paul Dung Quoc
Nicholas, Christopher Paul
Nimetz, Matthew
Nimkin, Bernard William
Norton, Gerard Francis, Jr.
Null, Douglas Peter
Nusbaum, Jack Henry
Nyland, W(illiam) Donald
O'Brien, Christopher Edward
Obstler, Harold
O'Connell, John Ryan
O'Flinn, Peter Russell
O'Hara, Robert Sydney, Jr.
Ohlman, Douglas Ronald
O'Keeffe, John Joseph, Jr.
O'Keeffe, John Joseph, Jr.
Olschwang, Alan Paul
Ombres, Teresa
Oppenheimer, Laurence Brian
Oppenheimer, Randolph Carl
Ormsby, David George
Osgood, Robert Mansfield
Pacious, Shaun Francis
Padgett, George Arthur
Panitz, Lawrence Herbert
Papernik, Joel Ira
Parent, Louise Marie
Parmet, Donald Jay

Patel, Pravinchandra J.
Paul, Herbert Morton
Pavia, George M.
Payson, Martin David
Pearlman, Michael Allen
Pergam, Albert Steven
Perkins, George Foster
Perlmuth, William Alan
Perlmutter, Jerome Alan
Peterson, James Richard
Peterson, Linda Sue
Pettibone, Peter John
Picardi, Ferdinand Louis
Pisani, Michael Joseph
Pisar, Samuel
Pollan, Stephen Michael
Pollio, Benedict James
Powers, Elizabeth Whitmel
Prem, F. Herbert, Jr.
Prentice, Eugene Miles, III
Price, Robert
Probstein, Jon Michael
Prodsky, Edward
Puleo, Frank Charles
Pulis, Gregory Milton
Pyle, Robert Milner, Jr.
Rabb, Bruce
Rado, Peter Thomas
Radon, Jenik Richard
Raikes, Charles FitzGerald
Rankin, Clyde Evan, III
Ray, Jeanne Cullinan
Read, Charles Arthur
Reid, Ross
Reilly, Conor Desmond
Reinstein, Paul Michael
Reitman, Jeffry B.
Resnicow, Norman Jakob
Resor, Stanley Rogers
Reynolds, Lola Sullivan
Richards, Arthur V.
Richter, Gary Stephen
Riley, David Edward
Rivette, Francis Robert
Robb, Scott Hall
Robinson, Irwin Jay
Robinson, Kenneth Patrick
Robinson, Lee Harris
Rocklen, Kathy Hellenbrand
Röhm, Eberhard Heinrich
Romney, Richard Bruce
Rosenberg, Priscilla Elliott
Rosenzweig, Charles Leonard
Ross, Gerald Elliott
Ross, Matthew
Ross, Michael Aaron
Rotgin, Philip Norman
Rothman, Henry Isaac
Rothschild, Steven Bruce
Rubenfeld, Stanley Irwin
Rubens, Jane Cora
Rubin, Stephen Wayne
Rudnick, Marvin Jack
Ruegger, Philip Theophil, III
Russell, Edwin Fortune
Ryan, Michael Edmond
Saft, Stuart Mark
Samels, Stephen Cooper
Samuels, Janet Lee
Savage, Edward Turney
Schaefer, David Stuart
Schechter, Daniel Philip
Schirmeister, Charles F.
Schleifer, Richard Wayne
Schneiderman, Irwin
Schober, Gary Michael
Schuman, Clifford Richard
Schuur, Robert George
Schwab, David E., II
Schwartz, Richard Morton
Schwartz, Stephen Jay
Schwed, Peter Gregory
Scofield, Milton N.
Seltzer, Jeffrey Lloyd
Semel, Martin Ira
Serchuk, Ivan
Sexton, David Farrington
Sexton, Richard
Shapiro, Barry Robert
Shapiro, George M.
Shatz, Phillip
Shaw, Arnold H(arold)
Shea, William Alfred
Shelley, Heywood
Sheridan, Peter N.
Sherman, Jeffrey Scott
Sherman, Michael Paul
Shinkle, John Thomas
Shyer, Herbert Paul
Siegel, Edward M.
Siegel, Lewis Wolfe
Siegel, Stanley
Silkenat, James Robert
Siller, Stephen I.
Silverberg, Sheldon
Simonton, Robert Bennet
Skolan-Logue, Amanda Nicole
Slough, John Edward
Smalley, David Vincent
Smith, George Emmett
Smith, Robert Everett
Snow, Charles
Soden, Paul A.
Solberg, Thomas Allan
Solomon, Stephen L.
Spatt, Robert Edward
Spiegel, Jerrold Bruce
Spike, Michele Kahn
Spollen, John W.
Springer, Paul David
Stack, Daniel
Starr, Richard Marc
Steinbach, Harold I.
Steinberg, Howard E.
Stephenson, Alan Clements
Stern, Lewis Arthur
Stewart, Duncan James
Steyer, Roy Henry
Stimmel, Todd Richard
Story, John Harold
Stratakis, Christ
Strom, Milton Gary
Stuart, Alice Melissa
Susser, Stuart J.
Swanson, David Warren
Tabachnik, Douglas T.
Tanner, Douglas Alan
Tanous, James Joseph
Targoff, Michael Bart
Taylor, Gregory Frederick
Taylor, Richard Trelore
Tehan, John Bashir
Tengi, Frank R.
Terner, Linda M. Johnson
Terrell, J. Anthony
Terry, John Hart
Terry, Tai Chang
Thomas, Ronald James
Todman, Terence Alphonso, Jr.
Tondel, Lawrence Chapman
Toomey, Richard Andrew, Jr.
Tormey, Douglas Joseph
Tortoriello, Robert Laurence
Tract, Harold M.
Trainor, Patricia Helen
Traube, Victoria Gilbert
Trott, Dennis Charles
Tursi, Carl Thomas
Tyler, Harold Russell, Jr.
Ughetta, William Casper
Ullman, Leo Solomon
Untermeyer, Salle Podos
Valentine, John William
Vega, Matias Alfonso
Versfelt, David Scott
Vigdor, Justin Leonard
Vogel, Howard Stanley
Wacker, Daniel James
Wald, Bernard Joseph
Waldoks, Phillip Harry
Wallace, Richard Powell
Wanderman, Susan Mae
Wang, George Hansen
Warner, Edward Waide, Jr.
Warren, William Clements
Warshavsky, Suzanne May
Warwick, Kathleen Ann
Webb, Morrison DeSoto
Wein, Bruce J.
Weiner, Earl David
Weir, Peter Frank
Weitzel, William Conrad, Jr.
Welikson, Jeffrey Alan
Wells, Andrew Norman
Wells, Crosby
Wheeler, John William
Whelan, John Kenneth
Whitaker, Benjamin Palmer, Jr.
White, Claude Esley
Wilcox, John Caven
Williamson, Steven Lloyd
Wilson, Leroy, Jr.
Windels, Paul, Jr.
Winikoff, Robert Lee
Wise, Aaron Noah
Wittner, Derek A.
Wood, Clement Biddle, III
Worenklein, Jacob J.
Wrapp, Emilie D.
Yamin, Michael Geoffrey
Zeller, Paul William
Zimmerman, Jean
Zoghby, Guy Anthony
Zuckerman, Mitchell
Zukerman, Michael

North Carolina

Alala, Joseph Basil, Jr.
Alexander, H. Heath
Bambury, Joseph Anthony, Jr.
Barham, Charles Dewey, Jr.
Bost, Deborah Jacobs
Burke, Frederick Augustine
Burns, Byron Bernard, Jr.
Carter, Charles Michael
Craven, David Leigh
Derrick, Jack Holley
Dillard, John Robert
Diosegy, Arlene Jayne
Doss, Marion Kenneth
Dunn, Jackson Thomas, Jr.
Gallant, Wade Miller, Jr.
Ganly, David Milton
Goodrum, Wayne Louis
Griffith, Steve Campbell, Jr.
Hamrick, Claude Meredith
Harkey, Henry Lee
Healy, Joseph Francis, Jr.
Jones, Bonnie Dee Durham
Jones, Henry W., Jr.
Joyner, Walton Kitchin
Koonce, Neil Wright
Lloyd, Robert Blackwell, Jr.
Loughridge, John Halsted, Jr.
Manthei, Gayl Marie
Page, James Wilson
Peirce, Ellen Rust
Perschetz, Arthur Driban
Petree, William Horton
Pope, William Robert
Reagan, Owen Walker, III
Remsburg, F(rank) Raine
Riley, John Frederick
Robinson, Russell Marable, II
Rusher, Derwood H., II
Schmutz, John Francis
Sharp, Starkey, V
Shuping, C(larence) Leroy, Jr.
Simpson, Daniel Reid
Simpson, James Reid, II
Smith, Stephen Jerome
Stevens, John Shorter
Townsend, William Jackson
Vaughan, Donald Ray
Vaughn, Robert Candler, Jr.
Ward, David Livingstone, Jr.
Wilkerson, Leo Carl
Wilson, Charles Michael

North Dakota

Bailly, David Ryan
Maichel, Joseph Raymond

Ohio

Amodio, James Anthony
Ashford, Thomas Steven
Ashworth, John Lawrence
Atkinson, William Edward
Bailey, Daniel Allen
Beck, James Hayes
Bemiller, F. Loyal
Bender, John Timothy
Benedict, Ronald Louis
Biars, Mark Martin
Blackburn, Thomas Irven
Bonsky, Jack Alan
Booth, Robert Alvin
Borowitz, Albert Ira
Branagan, James Joseph
Brandt, Stephen Dennis
Braverman, Herbert Leslie
Bremer, Thomas Francis
Bridgeland, James Ralph, Jr.
Buehler, Thomas Lee
Burlingame, John Hunter
Calkins, Benjamin
Campbell, Paul Barton
Carroll, James Joseph
Cavendish, Thomas Edgar
Chatroo, Arthur Jay
Childs, Alan D.
Christensen, Jon Alexander
Cissell, James Charles
Cobey, John Geoffrey
Comstock, Clyde Nelson
Cooper, Douglas Kenneth
Coquillette, William Hollis
Covatta, Anthony Gallo, Jr.
Crane, Edward Holman
Craver, James B.
Crowe, James Joseph
Davis, Philip Carl
Dean, J. Thomas
De Brier, Donald Paul
DeRousie, Charles Stuart
Detec, David Alan
Dettinger, Warren Walter
Donnem, Roland William
Dunn, George J.
Dye, Sherman
Eilers, John Wagner, Jr.
Ensign, Gregory Moore
Eynon, Ernest Alfred, II
Falsgraf, William Wendell
Farah, Benjamin Frederick
Farrar, Elizabeth Grace Tufrell
Federico, Andrew John
Fiala, David Marcus
Fisher, Fredrick Lee
Fisher, Stanley Morton
Flowers, Michael Edward
Ford, Ashley Lloyd
Fort, Jeffrey Edward
Francoeur, Robert Alfred
Frank, Harvey
Franz, Paul Allen
Frasier, Ralph Kennedy
Freedman, Howard Joel
Frutkin, Harvey Lee
Furber, Philip Craig
Garfunkel, Steven Brooks
Gherlein, Gerald Lee
Giannini, Matthew C.
Giles, Homer Wayne
Gillen, Stephen Earl
Gorman, Joseph Tolle
Goss, Colleen Flynn
Grabow, Raymond John
Greene, Ralph Vernon
Grundstein, Nathan David
Gunning, David Hall
Guttman, Rubin
Haas, Douglas Eric
Haase, William Xavier
Haddox, Jerome B.
Harden, Gary Martin
Harpster, Linda Marie
Hausser, Robert Louis
Hays, Robert D.
Herbert, David Lee
Herold, Karl Guenter
Hill, Jay
Hinerman, Philip Lee
Holland, Patricia Marcus
Holt, G. Woodrow
Hornbostel, John F., Jr.
Hoyt, Marcia Swigart
Inglis, David Stuart
Inzetta, Mark Stephen
Jackson, Robert Howard
Kacir, Barbara Brattin
Katz, Alfred B.
Kenrich, John Lewis
Kern, Keith William
Kessler, Alan
Keyser, George Harold
Kidder, Fred Dockstater
Kingsbury, Dorothea Jane
Kinney, Aldon Monroe, Jr.
Klaus, Charles
Kline, James Edward
Koch, Kenneth Hobson
Korosec, Kenneth David
Krembs, Peter Joseph
Krone, Paul William
Kubiak, Jon Stanley
Lanza, Shelley Brown
LaValley, Richard Gerard
Lawson, Margaret Avril
Lehman, Robert Frank
Leibold, William Joseph
Lenn, Stephen Andrew
Leonard, George Adams
Levine, Judith Dee
Libert, Donald Joseph
Lindberg, Charles David
Linnert, Terrence Gregory
Loewenthal, Marc Sheldon
Lucas, John Michael
Markey, Robert Guy
Martin, Oscar Thaddeus
McBride, Beverly Jean
Mc Connaughey, George Carlton, Jr.
McCoy, John Joseph
McCracken, Christopher Cornell
McCuen, John Francis, Jr.
Mc Henry, Powell
McKee, Thomas Frederick
Meehan, Michael Jan
Meek, Leslie Applegate
Menke, William Charles
Meyers, Karen Diane
Miller, Alan Leigh
Montgomery, Thomas Charles
Nelson, Roger Milton
Nicholson, Brent Bentley
Oestreicher, Michael Robert
Office, James Richard
O'Reilly, Timothy Patrick
Palmer, Mark Joseph
Pearlman, Samuel Segel
Petro, James Michael
Piraino, Thomas Anthony
Plakas, Leonidas Evangelos
Plumly, Daniel Harp
Porter, Robert Carl, Jr.
Postlewaite, Charles Chapman
Ragley, Michele Ann Garrick
Rapp, Gerald Duane
Rasmussen, Frank Morris
Reidenbach, William John
Rickert, Jeanne Martin
Rieser, John Paul
Roj, William Henry
Rooney, George Willard
Rorimer, Louis
Roush, Bradley Craig
Rubin, Robert Samuel
Sager, Sheldon Morris
Sanders, James Worthington
Sandrock, Scott Paul
Sharp, Robert Weimer
Shore, Michael Allan
Shumaker, Roger Lee
Silverman, Peter Ray
Simon, Gilbert Stanley
Smith, Ruth Hunter
Sogg, Wilton Sherman
Spetrino, Russell John
Spies, Howard A.
Sprang, Kenneth Allyn
Steinmanis, Karl Sven
Stevenson, Donald W.
Stillpass, John Edward
Stith, John Stephen
Stratton, Evelyn Joyce
Streicher, James Franklin
Strobel, Martin Jack
Suter, Carol Joan
Taft, Frederick Irving
Taft, Seth Chase
Teeple, Richard Duane
Thompson, Stephen David
Tillery, Dwight
Tobias, Charles Harrison, Jr.
Vance, James
Vorys, Arthur Isaiah
Walker, Kenneth Lynn
Watts, Steven Richard
Wayne, Richard Stuart
Webb, Thomas Irwin, Jr.
Weber, H. Patrick
Westbrook, Gayle Robinson
Westphal, Marjorie Lord
White, Arnold S.
Wieland, Robert Richard
Wietmarschen, Donald Alan
Wilbur, Peter Davis
Wisniewski, Marshall Donald
Worhatch, S. David
Yogi, Nolan Kimei
Yost, William Kent
Young, Charles Floyd
Zellner, Robert John
Zerner, Richard Egon
Zox, Benjamin Louis

Oklahoma

Andrews, John Charles
Arrington, John Leslie, Jr.
Biolchini, Robert Fredrick
Bogan, Neil Earnest
Brown, Michael DeWayne
Bryant, Ira Houston, III
Canon, Jack Arthur
Cundiff, James Nelson
Cunningham, M.C., II
Draughon, Scott Wilson
Estill, John Staples, Jr.
Golden, Thomas Fuller
Heimann, William Emil
Huff, R. Robert
Huffman, Robert Allen, Jr.
Huffman, Robert Allen
Jaques, Frank Hesketh
Jarboe, John Bruce
Kachigian, Mark George
Kenney, Bruce Allen
Kihle, Donald Arthur
Lewis, John Furman
Lyon, Jim Allen
Mash, Jerry L.
Paul, William George
Pray, Donald Eugene
Reis, Robert Richard
Robertson, Mark Alexander
Roff, Alan Lee
Scott, Willard Philip
Sloan, Steven Kent
Spiegelberg, Frank David
Steelman, Jacob DeHart
Steinhorn, Irwin Harry
Steltzlen, Janelle Hicks
Stewart, Robert Desbrow, Jr.
Waldman, Robert Allan
Wallace, John R.
Welch, James Stephen
Williams, Bradford J., Jr.
Williams, James William
Williford, John Lea

Oregon

Arthur, Michael Elbert
Baxendale, James Charles Lewis
Bogdanski, John Andrew, III
Brand, Malcolm Leigh
Bullivant, Rupert Reid
Cegavske, Wallace Duane
Deguc, Vincent Anthony
DuBoff, Leonard David
Feder, Miriam
Fenner, John Benjamin
Fulsher, Allan Arthur
Glasgow, Robert Efrom
Glasgow, William Jacob
Gleaves, Curt B.
Grant, Eugene L.
Gray, Francis Ignacy
Hager, Orval O.
Halle, John Joseph
Hampson, Alfred Aubert
Harris, Roger King
Hurd, Paul Gemmill
Jennings, George Mahlon
Korth, James William
Lindley, Mark Robert
Moore, David Lewis
Nash, Frank Erwin
Newton, Gregory Clark
Nunn, Robert Warne
Ormseth, Milo E.
Potter, William R.
Robertson, Douglas Stuart
Schrader, Charles Raymond
Schweitz, Martha Leach
Tankersley, Thomas Channing
Thompson, Orval Nathan
Wald, Sandra Louise
Webb, Jere M.
Wilcox, Robin Bachrach

Pennsylvania

Aaron, Marcus, II
Albright, Charles Lloyd, Jr.
Alderman, Mark Louis
Allen, Richard Hoopes
Aman, George Matthias, III
Amelio, Laura Lane
Appel, T. Roberts, II
Auerbach, Ernest Sigmund
Baker, Sidney
Baldwin, Frank Bruce, III
Bales, John Foster, III
Barkan, Leonard
Barrett, Karen Moore
Bauer, Edward Greb, Jr.
Becci, Michael Nelson
Beckman, Donald
Beckman, Jill Marie
Berger, Lawrence Howard
Bertsch, Gene Clair
Besser, Amy Helene
Blasier, Peter Cole
Blenko, Don Balman
Blue, Donald Sherwood
Bogutz, Jerome E.
Borden, Randolph Tyson
Boswell, William Douglas
Boswell, William Paret
Bower, Ward Alan
Bradshaw, William Elbert
Brady, George Charles, III
Bressman, Marc Ira
Briscoe, Jack Clayton
Brody, Nancy Louise
Brown, Donald
Brown, Edward George
Brown, Lawrence Raymond, Jr.
Burns, Douglas Foster
Busch, H. Donald
Cameron, John Clifford
Carnecchia, Baldo M., Jr
Chadwick, H. Beatty
Chamberlain, Gerard Alfred
Chamberlain, James Robert
Cherewka, Michael
Clauss, Peter Otto
Connell, Janice Timchak
Conti, Joy Flowers
Coyne, Charles Cole
Cramer, Harold
Cramp, John Franklin
Cross, Milton H.
Curtis, Gregory Dyer
D'Angelo, Christopher Scott
Davies, Norleen O'Sullivan
DeLaurentis, Michael John
Dell, Ernest Robert
Demmler, John Henry
Denby, Peter
DeWald, John Edward
DeYoung, Jonathan Harvey
Diehl, Kristin Knoell
Doerr, John Maxwell
Donohue, Robert John
Dougherty, James Thomas
Douglass, Robert Duncan
Doyle, William A.
Dubin, Stephen Victor
Dunaway, Wayland Fuller, III
Duroni, Charles Eugene
Duval, Robert
Eberly, Russell Albert
Elliott, Richard Howard
Elman, Gerry Jay
Emerson, S. Jonathan
Engler, W. Joseph, Jr.
Esser, Carl Eric
Evey, Merle Kenton
Farley, Andrew Newell
Fenza, William Joseph, Jr.
Ferguson, Sanford Barnett
Fischer, Richard Lawrence
Frank, Bernard
Galie, Lawrence Pius
Garfinkel, Marvin
Gilbert, Bruce Rits
Gilhooly, Edward Foster
Girard-DiCarlo, David Franklin
Goldman, Gary Craig
Goldman, Jerry Stephen
Goss, Michael Mayer
Graf, Bayard Mayhew
Granoff, Gail Patricia
Gray, Kathleen Ann
Gruenstein, Debra Lynne
Harff, Charles Henry
Hartman, Gregory Calvin
Hays, Richard Martin
Hemphill, Meredith, Jr.
Hender, George Snowden
Herchenroether, Peter Young
Hess, Emerson Garfield
Hickel, Gerard Frederick
Hoffstot, Henry Phipps, Jr.
Holloway, Hiliary Hamilton
Hooton, Michael Edward
Horoho, Kenneth Joseph, Jr.
Hunter, James Austen, Jr.
Jaffe, Gary
James, Keith Alan
Jenne, Kirk
Kain, William Henry
Kalogredis, Vasilios J.
Kashkashian, Arsen, Jr.
Kelley, George Lawrence, Jr.
King, Donita McRae
Kirby, Jack Arthur
Klapinsky, Raymond Joseph
Klee, John P.
Knapp, George Robert
Koplin, Bernice Judith
Krasney, Reginald Alan
Kreder, Joseph Casimir
Krefman, Stephen David
Krzyzanowski, Richard Lucien
Kulik, Joseph Michael

Laberee, Peter Walter
Lackman, James Stephen
LaFaver, Jon Fetherolf
Lampl, Sanford Mark
Lane, Maryl A.
LaPorte, RocLyne Emile
Leech, Noyes Elwood
Lehr, William, Jr.
Letwin, Jeffrey William
Lewis, Alvin Bower, Jr.
Linn, Michael Charles
Lipsitz, Robert Joel
Lipson, Barry J.
Litmans, Murray Ian
Loewenstein, Benjamin Steinberg
Ludwig, Charles Fine
Lynch, James Edward
Madeira, David Beckman
Maio, Carl Anthony
Marcovsky, Gerald Bennett
Marsico, Leonard Joseph
McAneny, Eileen S.
McBride, Milford Lawrence, Jr.
McCabe, Lawrence James
McKnight, Henry James
McNitt, David Garver
Meigs, John Forsyth
Mesirov, Leon I.
Michie, Daniel Boorse, Jr.
Middleton, Stephanie Adele
Milkman, Murray
Millinger, Donald Michael
Moores, Edward Harrison
Mundheim, Robert Harry
Ogden, W. Edwin
Orban, Frank Anton, III
Page, Clemson North, Jr.
Parker, James Lee
Pillai, K. G. Jan
Porach, Richard Andrew
Preate, Ernest D.
Pringle, Samuel Wilson, Jr.
Proctor, Charles William, III
Pugliese, Robert F.
Puhala, James Joseph
Quay, Thomas Emery
Reath, George, Jr.
Reed, Robert Alan
Reed, W. Franklin
Reuben, Allan Herbert
Richardson, Joseph Ablett, Jr.
Rosenberg, John Edward
Rosenn, Harold
Ross, James Andrew
Rouge, Cheryl Anne
Sander, Malvin Gustav
Schmuhl, Thomas Roeger
Schoyer, David Kennedy
Schulte, Jeffrey Lewis
Schwartz, James William
Scoratow, Martin Murray
Scudder, Charles Seelye Kellgren
Singer, Paul Meyer
Stack, Michael J.
Stamberg, Louis Mann
Stepanian, Steven Arvid, II
Stephens, Marlin Gerard
Stone, Laura Williams
Subak, John Thomas
Szczepaniak, Joseph Dennis
Tabas, Lawrence Jeffrey
Thiess, Kenneth Charles
Thomas, Robert Allen
Tollen, Allen Harold
Tumola, Thomas Joseph
Turrell, James Joel
Unkovic, Dennis
Vinci, Martin F.P., III
Walker, David Todd
Wallace, Christopher Baird
Walsh, Donald Peter
Walters, Bette Jean
Warren, William Ziegler
Weiner, Richard Norman
Welsh, Thomas Harry
Wiegand, Bruce
Wiener, Howard Alan
Williams, Stuart Alan
Wolff, Deborah H(orowitz)
Woosnam, Richard Edward
Wynstra, Nancy Ann
Yarmey, Richard Andrew
Yohlin, Joseph Michael
Zearfoss, Herbert Keyser
Zeiter, William Emmet
Zimmerman, Dona Hope

Rhode Island

Berkelhammer, Robert Bruce
Cohen, Linda Marks
Davis, Andrew Hambley, Jr.
Del Sesto, Ronald W.
Dowling, Sarah T.
Fogarty, Edward Michael
Freedman, Carl Ira
Hendel, Maurice William
Ialongo, Michael Angelo
Maneckji, Bhikhaji Maneck
Miller, Donald Eugene
Oster, Gerald Arthur
Schoenfeld, Barbara Braun

South Carolina

Barnes, Rudolph Counts
Chapman, Charles Alan
Clement, Robert Lebby, Jr.
Cooke, Morris Dawes, Jr.
DeLoach, Harris E(ugene), Jr.
Devereux, Anthony Quentin
Dunbar, James V., Jr.
Edwards, Harry LaFoy
Finkel, Gerald Michael
Harvey, William Brantley, III
Harvey, William Brantley, Jr.
Haskins, Terry Edward
King, George Savage, Jr.
Lawrimore, Eugene Salmon Napier
Mc Cullough, Ralph Clayton, II
McKnew, Natalma M.
McLawhorn, Richard Edward
Morehouse, Arthur Rogers Grant
Muller, Carl Frederick
Phillips, Joseph Brantley, Jr.
Rasor, Charles Lewis, Jr.
Roberts, Edward Calhoun
Rodgers, Sharon Lynette
Rose, William Shepard, Jr.
Scarminach, Charles Anthony
Scheider, James Pringle, Jr.
Seaman, Robert E., III
Shoemaker, James Marshall, Jr.
Traxler, William Byrd
Winn, Marshall
Winston, Jacqueline Berrier
Wyche, Bradford Wheeler
Wyche, Cyril Thomas

South Dakota

Carlsen, Chris Jeffrey
Rose, Lois Ann

Tennessee

Anderson, Mary Virginia
Armstrong, Walter Preston, Jr.
Aronson, Morton Henry
Bahner, Thomas Maxfield
Barnes, Herschiel Sevier
Beasley, Thomas Tarry, II
Bell, William Hall
Bernstein, Bernard Emanuel
Berry, William Wells
Bird, Agnes Thornton
Boyd, Mary Olert
Burcham, Randall Parks
Cameron, Clarence Arnold
Campbell-Bell, Dorothy Kathryn
Carr, Oscar Clark, III
Chambliss, Prince Caesar, Jr.
Cheek, James Howe, III
Congleton, Joseph Patrick
Cosner, Charles Kinian, Jr.
Crain, James Michael
De Young, Vincent Gerald
Donelson, Lewis Randolph, III
Evans, Thomas Martin
Ezell, Kenneth Pettey, Jr.
Farris, Frank Mitchell, Jr.
Fowler, John Ballard
Freeman, James Atticus, III
Friedman, Robert Michael
Gentry, Gavin Miller
Gordon, Thomas Napier
Heffington, Jack Grisham
Howell, Morton Boyte
Ingraham, Frank Calvin
Jett, Edward Stephen
Jolly, Charles Nelson
Kennedy, Richard Carl
Kirby, James Lynn
Kramer, Russell Arnold
Kramer, Steven Emert
Lawler, Edward James
Lynch, Carole Yard
Masterson, Kenneth Rhodes
McCormack, Donnell James
McQuiston, John Ward, II
Meyer, Michael Alan
Midgett, James Clayton, Jr.
Montgomery, Robert H., Jr.
Norville, Craig Hubert
Oldfield, Russell Miller
Rutledge, Roger Keith
Samuels, Seymour, Jr.
Sanger, Herbert Shelton, Jr.
Shelton, David Cochran
Sims, Wilson
Sisson, Jerry Allan
Soderquist, Larry Dean
Standel, Richard Reynold, Jr.
Stokes, Carl Nicholas
Stringham, Jack Fred, II
Tate, S. Shepherd
Thomas, Robert Paige
Townsend, Edwin Clay
Warren, Richard Fenton, Jr.
Wise, Stephen Rule
Woods, Larry David

Texas

Agnich, Richard John
Ainbinder, Michael Cooper
Allen, Joan Howard
Allender, John Roland
Anderson, Eric Severin
Andrews, Bolivar Coleman, Jr.
Arno, James
Baker, Mark Bruce
Baker, Scott Russell
Barber, Monty Clyde
Barlow, Donald Eugene
Bartholdt, William Edward, Jr.
Bartley, Albert Lea, Jr.
Barton, James Cary
Bateman, Hal Marion
Beard, Jane Ann Varner
Beasley, Norma Lea
Beasley, Rebecca Octavia
Beirne, Martin Douglas
Benson, Larry John
Bernard, Donald Ray
Beuttenmuller, Rudolf William
Biehl, Kathy Anne
Bishop, Bryan Edwards
Bissex, Walter Earl
Blachly, Jack Lee
Blanchette, James Grady, Jr.
Blazier, John Charles
Block, Steven Robert
Boos, Arthur Charles
Boss, Steven Sprague
Branhagen, Darrel Raymond
Bridges, Russell Brian
Bromberg, Alan Robert
Brown, C. Harold
Brown, Michael Lance
Brown, Ronald Lee
Browning, John Raum
Brundrett, George L(ee), Jr.
Bryce, William Delf
Burke, William Temple, Jr.
Burney, Cecil Edward
Burns, Sandra K.
Bursley, Kathleen A.
Busbee, Kline Daniel, Jr.
Carr, Thomas Eldridge
Cassin, William Bourke
Castle, John Raymond, Jr.
Chalk, John Allen
Chase, Sam J.
Cobb, Charles Louis
Cobb, Chester Lee
Cobb, Sam Burton, Jr.
Conlon, Michael William
Cosgrove, Ritamae Gober
Craig, Robert Mark, III
Crook, E(dward) Carter, Jr.
Cross, Janis Alexander
Crowley, James Worthington
Cuba, Benjamin James
Cuellar, Enrique Roberto
Curfiss, Robert C.
Curry, Donald Robert
Dack, Christopher Edward Hughes
Davis, Clarence Clinton, Jr.
Davis, Harrel Leon, III
Davis, Martha Algenita Scott
Davis, Michael A.
de la Garza, Luis Adolfo
DeShazo, Gary Forrest
Dilg, Joseph Carl
Doty, James Robert
Duenser, Ruth Edwards
Durell, Jay Glenn
Dutton, Diana Cheryl
Eckman, David Walter
Elliott, Brady Gifford
Engerrand, Kenneth Gabriel
Engle, William Thomas, Jr.
Ericson, Roger Delwin
Fant, Douglas Vernon
Farley, Jan Edwin
Faye, Stanley Ethan
Feldwisch, David Lewis
Felger, Thomas Robert
Ferguson, Charles Alan
Finch, Michael Paul
Fishman, Edward Marc
Fortado, Michael George
Freeman, Philip Dayne
Freling, Richard Alan
Ginsburg, Marcus
Glazier, Kenneth Charles
Godfrey, Cullen Michael
Golden, Alvin Joseph
Goodman, John Peter
Gosselink, Margaret Lavidge
Greanias, George Constantine
Greenspan, Abraham Alcon
Griffin, Campbell Arthur, Jr.
Guzzetti, William Louis
Hainsfurther, A. Michael
Hallman, Leroy
Hanson, Arnold Philip, Jr.
Harden, Richard Lee
Harrington, Bruce Michael
Harvin, William Charles
Hedrick, John Richard
Heffington, Joseph Robert
Heffron, Jonathon Kenneth
Higgins, Robert Gerard
Hodges, Jot Holiver, Jr.
Hoffman, Joseph Anthony
Howard, Timothy Jon
Hoyt, Mont Powell
Hunt, John Floyd
Hunter, Robert Frederick
Immler, Michael Earl
Jennings, Susan Jane
Johnson, Edward Michael
Johnson, Karen Lee
Johnstone, Debbi Merriman
Jones, John Gornal
Joor, William Eugene, III
Jordan, Bruce
Kaufman, Andrew Michael
Kelly, Francis Thomas
Kelly, William Franklin, Jr.
Kendall, William Theodore
Kerry, Henry Eugene
King, Steve Mason
Kinnan, David E.
Kneipper, Richard Keith
Kolodey, Fred James
Koppenheffer, Julie B.
Kosut, Kenneth Paul
Lacy, John Ford
Langston, Homer Anthony, Jr.
Larimore, Tom L.
Leach, Terry Ray
Legg, Reagan Houston
Lempert, Richard A.
Lionberger, Richard Lee
Looper, Donald Ray
Maher, Mary Frances
Manley, Larry Paul
Marbut, Syrian Erasmus
Marks, Gary Lee
Marlow, Orval Lee, II
Marquardt, Robert Richard
Marsteller, Thomas Franklin, Jr.
Matthews, Wilbur Lee
May, David P.
McClure, Donald John
McElwrath, Michael Rogers
McFarland, Jaclanel Moore
McGreevy, Terrence Gerard
McKnight, Rufus Nicolaus, Jr.
McLane, David Glenn
McNamara, Martin Burr
Meer, Julian Milton
Menges, John Kenneth, Jr.
Miller, Norman Richard
Mills, Marcia Joan
Mitchell, Joe Day
Mittenthal, Freeman Lee
Moehlman, Michael Scott
Moore, Lawrence Jack
Moros, Nicholas Peter
Morris, Rebecca Robinson
Morrison, Jeanne Lunsford
Moss, Joe Albaugh
Moy, Celeste Marie
Murphy, Ewell Edward, Jr.
Nahlen, Dana Gayle
Narisi, Stella Maria
Neal, A. Curtis
Neblett, Stewart Lawrence
Newman, Lawrence Graham
Newsom, Jan Lynn Reimann
Newsom, Neil Edward
Noack, Charles Elroy
Nolan, Jenelle White
Nolen, Roy Lemuel
Oates, Carl Everette
Ochs, Robert Francis
Oldham, Darius Dudley
Omer, Michael Lee
Operhall, Harrie Marie Pollok
Otto, Byron Leonard
Paden, Lyman Rushton
Painton, Russell Elliott
Parker, Dallas Robert
Payne, James Parker
Perry, William Shelbern
Peters, Loren Walter
Pettigrew, Karen Beth
Phillips, Kathleen A.
Phillips, Thomas Marion
Pierson, Grey
Pitner, Joseph A.
Porter, Jeffrey James
Porter, Thomas William, III
Post, Earl Stock
Premack, Paul Allen
Prince, Wayman Lee
Profusek, Robert Alan
Reaser, Vernon Neal, Jr.
Regenbogen, Ellis Arnold
Rendell, Robert Sloat
Rentz, Joe Houston
Rhem, John Fitzhugh, Jr.
Richter, Alfred Grammar, Jr.
Ritchie, Robert Field
Roberts, Thomas Alba
Rodgers, John Hunter
Rowland, Sam E.
Rundel, Kenneth Martin
Sapp, Walter William
Schreiber, Sally Ann
Scott, Richard Waldo
Scuro, Joseph E., Jr.
Seay, George Edward, Jr.
Shaddock, William Charles
Sharp, Christopher Glenn
Shipp, H(amilton) Thomas
Shouse, August Edward
Simmental, David Anthony
Simmons, Stephen Judson
Simpson, Searcy Lee, Jr.
Slugg, Ramsay Hill
Smith, Russell Bryan
Smith, Tad Randolph
Steen, John Thomas, Jr.
Stein, Sheldon Irvin
Stephens, John F., Jr.
Stowe, Charles Robinson Beecher
Strauss, Robert Schwarz
Strohl, Paul E.
Sullenbarger, Daniel James
Sutphen, Robert Louis
Szalkowski, Charles Conrad
Tallis, Alan Louis
Tankersley, Michael Wayne
Thau, William Albert, Jr.
Thomas, Patrick Powers
Thompson, Peter Rule
Timmons, Patrick Francis, Jr.
True, Roy Joe
Tutt, John Marion
Tuttle, Franlin L., Jr.
Tyson, Roy Knox
Unger, Adrienne Penrod
Varner, David Eugene
Vazquez, Gilbert Falcon
Wagner, Michael Duane
Warnock, Curtlon Lee
Watson, Cary Stephen
Watson, Robert Francis
Wells, Peter Boyd
White, David Lawrence
White, Sharon Elizabeth
Whitten, C. G.
Williams, Percy Don
Wilson, James William
Winship, Peter
Wommack, Jr. George Tobin
Woodward, Charles Carroll M.
Wozencraft, Frank McReynolds
Wright, Eugene Box
Yost, William Arthur, III
Young, David Haywood
Zipprich, John L., II

Utah

Ashworth, Brent Ferrin
Baucom, Sidney George
Buffmire, Andrew Wallace
Burgon, Barre Glade
Chancellor, Thomas Harvey
Christensen, Krege Bowen
Curtis, Dale Jay
Edwards, Helen Jex
Frei, Michael Clark
Gardiner, Lester Raymond, Jr.
Gill, Ruland J., Jr.
Groussman, Raymond G.
Headman, Arlan Osmond, Jr.
Jones, Michael Frank
Lauritzen, David Kay
Lewis, Leonard J.
Lowe, Kathlene Winn
Mackey, Randall Aubrey
McCullough, William Andrew
McIntosh, James Albert
Monson, Thomas Lee
Rector, Joel Kirk
Shields, Jeffrey Weston
Siegler, Lora Celia
Vernon, Robert Gerard

Vermont

Capel, Guy B.
Cummings, Charles Rogers
Debevoise, Thomas McElrath
Gravel, John Cook
Guild, Alden
Levy, James Lewis
Marshall, John Henry
Morrow, Emily Rubenstein
Oettinger, Mark David
Prentice, Frederick Sheldon
Smith, Norman Charles
Sullivan, Richard Francis
Winer, Jonathan Herman

Virginia

Babirak, Milton Edward, Jr.
Baird, Edward Rouzie, Jr.
Barron, Myra Hymovich
Bates, Harold Martin
Beach, Barbara Purse
Beck, Joseph James
Belcher, Dennis Irl
Brent, Andrew Jackson
Bridewell, Sherry Hazelwood
Broadbent, Peter Edwin, Jr.
Buford, Robert Pegram
Cambridge, Robert Matthew
Carrell, Daniel Allan
Carter, Joseph Carlyle, Jr.
Chappell, Robert Harvey, Jr.
Chapple, Thomas Leslie
Church, Randolph Warner, Jr.
Crump, Beverley L.
Cutchins, Clifford Armstrong, IV
Daniels, Michael Alan
Davidson, Frank Gassaway, III
Elmore, Edward Whitehead
Fashbaugh, Howard Dilts, Jr.
Freed, Robert Leslie
Galea, John Henry
Gary, Stuart Hunter
Glenn, Robert Eastwood
Goolrick, Robert Mason
Gregory, John Lunsford, III
Hall, Franklin Perkins
Hancock, William Glenn
Harrison, David George
Herge, J. Curtis
Higgins, Mary Celeste
Hoffman, David Gary
Jackson, William Paul, Jr.
James, Gus John, II
Jameson, Paula Ann
Kamp, Arthur Joseph, Jr.
Kay, William Richard, Jr.
Klewans, Samuel N.
Kyle, Penelope W.
Layton, Garland Mason
Litten, Donald Douglas
Lowenstein, Marshall Leigh
MacKinlay, Edgar Harold
MacMurray, Worth Daniels
Mandell, Steve Allen
Mar, Eugene
Markovich, Stephen Edward
Massey, James Buckner, III
McCauley, Cleyburn Lycurgus
McGuire, Edward David, Jr.
McNider, James Small, III
Mezzullo, Louis Albert
Moore, Tyler Moses
Morris, Dewey Blanton
Moshos, Arthur Leon
O'Connell, Kevin Michael
Paturis, E(mmanuel) Michael
Payne, J(oe) Stanley
Pearsall, John Wesley
Philpott, Albert Lee
Pratt, Stephen Michael
Price, Ilene Rosenberg
Procopio, Joseph Guydon
Rau, Lee Arthur
Rawls, Frank Macklin
Redmond, David Dudley
Regan, Michael Patrick
Revoile, Charles Patrick
Rollinson, Mark
Roth, Alexander Dunbar
Sargeant, William Leslie
Schmidt, William Lesnett
Schwartz, Arthur Edward
Schwartz, Philip
Settlage, Steven Paul
Seymour, William Francis, IV
Simon, Alexander Nathan
Smolen, Jason David
Smoots, Carol Anne
Spirn, Stuart Douglas
Spitzli, Donald Hawkes, Jr.
Stegeman, Thomas Albert
Stephens, William Theodore
Talbott, Frank, III
Tansill, Frederick Joseph
Thomson, Paul Rice, Jr.
Tolmie, Donald McEachern
Vandeventer, Braden
Wallman, Steven Mark Harte
Walton, Edmund Lewis, Jr.
Ware, Guilford Dudley
Wartelle, Barbara Louisa
Whitaker, Thomas Patrick
Whitt, Jane Rebecca
Whittemore, F(rank) Case
Wilson, Paul Lowell
Wolcott, Edward Wallace
Woodhouse, Edward James, Jr.
Woodward, Roland Carey
Wooldridge, William Charles
Young, Hubert Howell, Jr.

Washington

Abelite, Jahnis John
Arnold, Nancy Tarbuck
Batey, Douglas Leo
Blais, Jan David
Blom, Daniel Charles
Bridge, Jonathan Joseph
Brooks, Julie Anne
Bruhn, Soren Frederick
Clemons, Alpha Ottis, Jr.
Collette, Kevin J.
Crofts, Michael Lynn
Dowdy, Robert Alan
Duvall, Gary Ross
Eubanks, Ronald W.
Gates, Kenneth W.
Gay, Sandra Bates
Giles, Robert Edward, Jr.
Gilyeart, Steven Craig
Gingerich, Florine Rose
Greenburg, G. Scott
Henderson, Kevin James
Hulse, Brian Douglas
Jensen, Sherman Holbrook
Krueger, James A.
Krueger, Larry Eugene
Langlie, Arthur Sheridan
Lied, Erik Robert
Loftus, Thomas Daniel
Malone, Thomas William
Maulding, Barry Clifford
McCorkle, Linda Ann
McGarry, Arthur Daniel
McInnis, Emmett Emory, Jr.
McLaughlin, Thomas Orville
Medved, Robert Allen
Mozena, Peter Joseph
Munson, Mark Parr
Oles, Laura Treadgold
Oseran, Melville
Palmer, Harvard
Raff, Douglass Alan
Sandman, Irvin Willis
Saracino, Samuel Francis

Spring, Max Edward
Stamper, Randall Lee
Tune, James Fulcher
Walker, G(lenn) Perrin
Wells, Christopher Brian
Wright, Willard Jurey

West Virginia

Barnette, David Allen
Bayley, Thomas Way, Jr.
Bell, Charles D.
Blair, Andrew Lane
Chaney, Michael Thomas
Colburn, James Allan
Fusco, Andrew G.
Halbritter, Marc Alan
Haley, Charles Frederick
Keltner, Robert Earl
Kidner, Edward Franklin
Phillips, John Davisson
Riley, Arch Wilson, Jr.
Ringer, Darrell Wayne
Shepherd, Richard Earnshaw
Stone, Samuel Spencer
Thaxton, Everette Frederick
Wehner, Charles Vincent

Wisconsin

Abbott, William Anthony
Aiken, Jeffrey Paul
Akavickas, Gary Robert
Berry, Roberta Marie
Billick, Brooke Jay
Boucher, Joseph William
Bruce, Peter Wayne
Bush, Edwin Franklin, Jr.
Christiansen, Eric Robert
Collins, Michael John
Connolly, Gerald Edward
Davis, Kenneth Boone, Jr.
Davis, Walter Stewart
Demet, Donal Moffatt
Du Rocher, James Howard
Dye, William Ellsworth
English, Dale Lowell
Ericson, James Donald
Fairbanks, Roberta R(onya)
Falstad, David Bergfeld
FitzSimmons, Richard M.
Fons, John Joseph
Franzoi, Joseph Frank, IV
Frasch, David Edward
Fribance, Caroline Eleanor
Galanis, John William
Gorske, Robert Herman
Hallett, Kenneth Victor
Higgins, John Patrick
Holz, Harry George
Jinkins, Mark Allen
Kiessling, William Edward
Kite, Richard Lloyd
Klos, Jerome John
Kobriger, Richard Roman, Jr.
LaBudde, Roy Christian
Laikin, George Joseph
LaRowe, Myron Edward
Lavers, Richard Marshall
Layden, Donald William, Jr.
Levine, Herbert
Liebmann, Herbert Charles, III
Ludwig, R. Arthur
Martin, Quinn William
Mihal, Thomas Harlan
Minahan, Roger Copp
Muchin, Arden Archie
Newton, Mary S.
Olander, Ray Gunnar
Pellino, Charles Edward, Jr.
Perkins, Randolph M.
Perry, Wilson David
Rotter, Emanuel Norman
Ryan, Thomas Joseph
Sauer, William Jacob
Schmitt, Joseph Francis
Schramm, Bernard Hall
Schroeder, Stuart R.
Sedor, Gilbert D.
Shiely, John Stephen
Sikora, Ted Robert, II
Smith, Wrede Howard, Jr.
Steil, George Kenneth, Sr.
Sweet, Lowell Elwin
Szymanski, Barry Walter
Tease, Ralph Joseph, Jr.
Trebon, Lawrence Alan
Vollmer, Steven Lyle
White, Walter Hiawatha, Jr.
Wiley, Edwin Packard

Wyoming

Case, Irvin Vincent, Jr.
Dray, William Perry
Hathaway, Stanley Knapp
Lowe, Robert Stanley
Sachs, Philip David

TERRITORIES OF THE UNITED STATES

Puerto Rico

Rodriguez-Diaz, Juan E.
Vallone, Ralph, Jr.

AUSTRALIA

Browne, Jeffrey Francis

CANADA

Ontario

Gulden, Simon

Quebec

Pascoe, Christopher John Campbell
Vineberg, Philip Fischel

Saskatchewan

Elliott, William McBurney

ENGLAND

Herzog, Brigitte
Mecz, Jane Beltzer
Morrison, William David
Reiter, Glenn M.
Scott, John Andrew
Wiese, Larry Clevenger
Wohl, James Paul

FRANCE

Conrad, Winthrop Brown, Jr.
Iseman, Joseph Seeman
McGovern, David Talmage
Riggs, John Hutton, Jr.

JAPAN

Dickson, Thomas Page
Shannon, William James

MEXICO

Rogers, John Ellsworth

SAUDI ARABIA

Shea, Gerald MacDonald

SWITZERLAND

Muller, Johannes Joseph

TRINIDAD

Gordon, Kenneth

UNITED ARAB EMIRATES

Stockwell, David Michael

ADDRESS UNPUBLISHED

Armstrong, Robert Elmer
Avery, James Thomas, III
Bagan, Grant Alan
Baird, James Kenneth
Bamberger, Michael Albert
Baris, Jay G.
Bolch, Susan Bass
Boorstein, Beverly Weinger
Breen, James Patrick, Jr.
Breidenbach, Cherie Elizabeth
Brodhead, David Crawmer
Coleman, Robert Lee
Cook, Wayne Ralph
Coplin, Mark David
Crawford, R(obert) George
Culver, Robert Winthrop
Daleiden, Norbert Alfred
Derrick, William Alfred, Jr.
Diamond, Josef
Dickey, Sam S.
Diehl, Deborah Hilda
Eastin, Keith E.
Edwards, Vern Downing
Elterman, Warren Bart
Englebrecht, Bruce
English, Richard D.
Fagan, Peter Thomas
Familo, Edward Douglas
Fine, Robert Paul
Flechner, Stephen E.
Francis, Jerome Leslie
Fried, Samuel
Friedman, Lawrence Andrew
Glober, George Edward, Jr.
Godard, Randy Eugene
Gresham, Wayne Edgar
Griffin, Thomas Patrick
Gulick, Peter VanDyke
Hartwell, Christopher Lynn
Hays, Samuel Spartan
Hecht, Barbara Elizabeth Roberts
Heise, John Irvin, Jr.
Hemmer, James P.
Hildebrand, Charles Frederick
Howitt, Idelle Anne
Hurst, Ernest Connor
Jackson, Louise Anne
Katz, Maurice Harry
Kaufmann, Roy Leslie
Kellerman, Harry Miles
Kirschner, Paul David
Koeller, Robert Marion
Lande, James Avra
Lappen, Timothy
Lungren, John Howard
McCoy, Henry Drewry, II
McInerney, Gary John
McKay, David Lawrence
Mell, Patricia
Mendel, Stephen Frank
Meran, Harry Bruce
Merrill, Abel Jay
Meyerson, Stanley Phillip
Michaels, George
Middleton, Harlow Clester
Moravsik, Robert James
Moylan, James Joseph
Murray, Kathleen Anne
Nash, James Harry
Osimitz, Dennis Victor
Palizzi, Anthony N.
Palmer, Ann Therese Darin
Palmer, Edwin Kayser
Quigley, Leonard Vincent
Rifman, Avrum Katz
Rivera, Oscar R.
Roth, Michael Dundon
Saliterman, Richard Arlen
Sangalis, Gregory Theodore
Schager, Richard Joseph, Jr.
Schiesswohl, Cynthia Rae Schlegel
Schreiber, Eliot Bruce
Schroeder, John Walter
Shambaugh, Stephen Ward
Shughart, Donald Louis
Solkoff, Jerome Ira
Stone, Edward Herman
Stout, George McBride
Stubbs, William Perry, Jr.
Surratt, John Richard
Swift, Aubrey Earl
Tanenbaum, Jay Harvey
Tisdale, Jeffrey Alan
Tolins, Roger Alan
Tomczak, Starr Lyn
Van Antwerp, Rosemary Dirkie
Webster, Daniel Robert
Whitehorn, Jo-Ann H.
Wilkinson, George Albert, Jr.
Williams, Frank J.
Wilson, Hugh Steven
Winston, Harold Ronald
Wise, Philip J.
Wolfson, Jack Leonard
Wright, Frances Mina Johnson

CREDITOR. *See* **Commercial, consumer.**

CRIMINAL

UNITED STATES

Alabama

Alexander, Melton Lee
Bonner, William Joel, Jr.
Colquitt, Joseph Arlington
Conwell, Joseph Thomas
Crespi, Michael Albert
Crownover, Walter Parker
Deen, Thomas Jefferson, III
Downes, Robert Bruce
Granade, Callie Virginia Smith
Heffler, Paul Mark
Hughes, Andy Karl
Karrh, John Maxwell
Kominos, Bill
Lane, Wilford Jones
Luskin, Joseph
Martin, Ludger D.
Morse, George Wray, II
Ott, John Edward
Paschal, Beverly Jo
Pennington, Al
Rebarchak, James
Redden, Lawrence Drew
Smith, Charles Lynwood, Jr.
Stephens, Ferris W.
Tatum, Fred Menefee, Jr.
Whisonant, Michael Wayne
Wood, James Jerry

Alaska

Angstman, Myron Eugene
Beiswenger, Allan David
Bolger, Joel Harold
Branson, Albert Harold
Erlich, Richard Henry
Fabe, Dana Anderson
Feldman, Jeffrey Marc
Johnson, Donald Milby
Jones, Charles Robert
Moody, Ralph E.
Nave, Thomas George
Ostrovsky, Lawrence Zelig
Richard, John Marston, Jr.
Ross, Wayne Anthony
Stockholm, Kendall Ray
Yospin, Richard Lawrence

Arizona

Butler, A(rthur) Bates, III
Corbin, Robert K.
Feder, Bruce Stanley
Florence, Henry John
Freedman, Kenneth David
Gonzales, Richard Joseph
Hirsh, Robert Joel
Klahr, Gary Peter
LaSota, Peter Douglas
Leshner, Stephen I.
Marcus, Paul
Morgan, Eddie Lamont
Parker, Myrna Jean
Rubenstein, Hy David
Smith, David Burnell
Spritzer, Ralph Simon
Verkamp, John

Arkansas

Carpenter, Thomas Milton
Davis, James Edwin
Dudley, Timothy Oliver
Fogleman, John Nelson
Gleghorn, Linda Bon Lipe
Hall, John Wesley, Jr.
Karr, Charles
McClurg, Andrew Jay
Mullen, William David
Perroni, Samuel Arnold
Taylor, Hendrix Arthur, Jr.

California

Abrams, Norman
Albert, Ward Wian
Alexander, Katharine Violet
Amidon, Robert Bruce
Babcock, Barbara Allen
Bancroft, David Phillips
Barrett, Dennis Christopher
Bell, Frank Ouray, Jr.
Berman, David Ira
Bigler, Ross Lowell
Bondoc, Rommel
Bonney, George William
Borden, Mark Stanley
Brenner, Anita Susan
Broome, Thomas Jefferson
Brosnahan, James Jerome
Brown, Lawrence
Bryan, Robert Russell
Buchanan, James Douglas
Burgess, John All
Carrow, Robert Duane
Chaleff, Gerald Lawrence
Chang, Peter Asha, Jr.
Cohen, Steven Elliott
Cohn, Nathan
Coleman, Richard Michael
Combs, Richard Ennis
Dalton, Douglas
Dean, Shari Lavola
Duvall, Paul Hamilton
English, Charles Royal
Fallman, James Mitchell, Jr.
Fisher, Myron R.
Fletcher, R(ufus) Burton, Jr.
Frant, Ronald Mayer
Frazier, Thomas Louis
Goldberg, Charles L.
Green, Kenneth Norton
Greenberg, Harold
Gulartie, Louise Baur
Harley, Robison Dooling, Jr.
Heene, Fred Lewis, Jr.
Heller, Donald Herbert
Heyck, Theodore Daly
Hillberg, Marylou Elin
Hite, Randall Lee
Hoagland, Grant Taylor
Honeychurch, Denis Arthur
Hudson, Dirk Ludwig
Johnson, Richard Wesley
Kadish, Sanford Harold
Kay, William Thomas, Jr.
Keker, John Watkins
Kleier, James Patrick
Kock, Arlene Dorothy
Ladar, Jerrold Morton
Ladikos, Costas Angelo
Lascher, Wendy Jean Cole
Lauchengco, Jose Yujuico, Jr.
Leavitt, Jack
Lehan, Jonathan Michael
Levy, Leonard Williams
Little, Jan Nielsen
Lynch, James Joseph, Jr.
Malkus, James Alan
Markowitz, Michael Jay
McCaslin, Leon
McKechnie, C. Logan
Melton, Barry
Messinger, Sheldon L(eopold)
Miller, Jeremy Matthew
Millstein, David J.
Mintz, Ronald Steven
Mogin, Daniel Jay
Nadler, Jerome Steven
Nasatir, Michael David
Neithercutt, Marcus Gibbs
Nypaver, Stephen, III
Osborne, Michael Claude
Paden, Gary Lewis
Pereyra-Suarez, Charles Albert
Quadri, Fazle Rab
Roberson, Clifford Eugene
Roche, Thomas Garrett
Rogan, Patrick Goode
Rothwell, Thomas Henry
Rozanski, Stanley Howard
Rubin, Dale Michael
Russell, Thomas Hunter
Samson, Anthony Donald
Scharf, Robert Lee
Schleicher, Estelle Ann
Scott, Terrence Verson
Shapiro, Anita Rae
Simonelli, James John
Steinberger, Jeffrey Wayne
Stout, Gregory Stansbury
Streeter, Tom
Talmo, Ronald Victor
Taylor, Lawrence Eric
Telleria, Anthony F.
Vienna, Kevin Richard
Wallin, Paul Jeffrey
Webb, Michael Joseph
Wellins, Sheldon (Shel) Gary
Whittaker, Marion Alma
Wilson, Stephen Victor
Wolf, Lawrence
Wright, Frank Clarence, Jr.
Wykowski, Henry George
Young, Douglas Rea

Colorado

Baker, Bernard Robert
Blakey, Milton Keith
Brega, Charles Franklin
Carlton, Diane Michele
Chestnutt, Ellen Joanne
Edwards, Daniel Walden
Erkenbrack, Stephen K.
Fierst, Bruce Philip
Fritze, James Ronald
Geil, Karl James
Gentry, Elvin LeRoy
Hale, Daniel Cudmore
Hobson, Bernard Edward
Horowitz, Jay Stanley
Janklow, Donald Emanuel
Keller, Alex Stephen
Lutz, John Shafroth
Manley, Douglas Rempet
Mark, Denis Hugh
McBee, Donald Lawrence
McCormick, George Paul, Jr.
McDowell, Karen Ann
Metzger, Karen Susan
Miller, Robert Nolen
Mygatt, Ann Bliss
Nottingham, Edward Willis, Jr.
Palmer, David Gilbert
Redder, Thomas Joseph
Rench, Stephen Charles
Rose, Charles Jon
Ruppert, Mark Richard
Sears, Daniel Joseph
Sedlak, Joseph Anthony, III
Spelts, Richard John
Springer, Jeffrey Alan
Tegtmeier, Richard Lewis
Walta, John Gregory
Wendt, John Arthur Frederic, Jr.
West, Laurie Diane
Westbrook, Jane Elizabeth
Wilson, Edward Miller
Woodard, Duane

Connecticut

Argenta, Craig Jon
Carrano, Frank Anthony
Carta, John James, Jr.
Cocheo, John Frank
Collins, John Albert, III
Dalton, Victoria Clayman
Duke, Steven Barry
Dumont, James Allan
Dwyer, Gerald Parker
Eisenman, Gerard Paul
Endrelunas, Richard Michael
Goldstein, Abraham S.
Hayes, Margaret Mary
Heiman, Maxwell
Klein, Jonathan Joseph
Luby, Thomas Stewart
Lynn, Robert John
McGrail, Albert James
Medzie, Kenneth Stephen
Meehan, Richard Thomas, Jr.
Nevas, Alan Harris
Noonan, Patrick Matthew
Ponzini, John Lino
Ruane, James Joseph
Ryan, John Joseph
Sauer, David Allen
Schatz, Richard Ansell
Sheldon, Michael Richard
Simmons, Donald Charles
Skuret, Daniel D.
Sweeney, William Jones, Jr.
Trebisacci, Raymond Thomas
Wedgwood, Ruth Glushien
Zagorsky, Peter Joseph

Delaware

Brandt, Charles
Curtin, Christopher James
Mekler, Arlen B.
Oberly, Charles Monroe, III
Whitehurst, Charles Elwood, Jr.
Willard, John Martin

District of Columbia

Ambrose, Myles Joseph
Baker, James Jay
Barcella, Ernest Lawrence, Jr.
Beckler, Richard William
Bergman, Carol Amy
Bonner, Walter Joseph
Bonventre, Vincent Martin
Byrne, Edward Mark
Canerday, Jon Jackson
Cates, C. Brad
Chafetz, Marc Edward
Christensen, Karen Kay
Crump, Ronald Cordell
Daniel, Aubrey Marshall, III
Danzig, Richard Jeffrey
DeBerardinis, Robert Andrew, Jr.
DeStein, Beverlee Jean
English, Gregory Bruce
Fox, Hamilton Phillips, III
Fraser, D. Larry
Friedman, Paul Lawrence
Fryman, Virgil Thomas, Jr.
Gardiner, Richard Ernest
Garland, Merrick Brian
Gorelick, Jamie Shona
Greenebaum, Leonard Charles
Halle, Peter Edward
Hamilton, James
Hauptly, Denis James
Horn, Stephen
Janis, N. Richard
Junkin, Timothy Deforest
Kent, M. Elizabeth
King, John Winston
Klawiter, Donald Casimir
Klonoff, Robert Howard
Koller, Benedict Joseph
Larroca, Raymond G.
Leon, Richard John
L'Heureux, Robert Dolor
Lide, Vinton DeVane
Liebman, Ronald Stanley
Long, Clarence Dickinson, III
Martoche, Salvatore Richard
Meese, Edwin, III
Micheel, Richard Arthur
Morrison, Alexia
Mueller, Robert Clare
Muller, Scott William
Murphy, Thomas Patrick
Myren, Richard Albert
Orenberg, Allen Howard
Oyewole, G. Godwin
Peters, Frederick Whitten
Povich, David
Quarles, William Daniel
Richardson, Greg Drexel
Robbins, Ira Paul
Rogovin, Mitchell
Rosenau, Kenneth H.
Ruff, Charles F.C.
Rusch, Jonathan Jay
Sallet, Jonathan Bruce
Sarko, Lynn Lincoln
Seaman, Richard Norman
Shapiro, Benjamin Louis
Shust, Diane Marie
Spaeder, Roger Campbell
Stewart, James Kevin
Stuart, Pamela Bruce
Stuntz, Reid Pendleton Fitzhugh
Sullivan, Eugene Raymond
Sykes, Thomas Dale
Thompson, William Carrington, Jr.
Tompkins, Joseph Buford, Jr.
Trott, Stephen Spangler
Turnage, Fred Douglas
Vance, Kenneth Anthony
Vanlier, Charlene
Weinberg, Robert Lester
Weiner, Robert Neil
Weingarten, Reid H.
Weld, William Floyd
West, Togo Dennis, Jr.
Young, Marlene Annette
Zenoff, Elyce Hope

Florida

Aguila, Adolfo Zacarias
Aguilar, Humberto Juan
Albrechta, Mark Jerome
Arlt, Paul Edward
Audlin, David John, Jr.
Berk, John Steven
Berry, Gerald Thomas
Blackwell, William Leggett
Blake, Stanford
Bombino, Isabel Piñera
Bonner, Mary Catherine
Bratten, Thomas Arnold
Brett-Major, Lin
Brock, Newman Dempsey
Bronis, Stephen J.
Burnbaum, Michael William
Busch, David John
Cagney, William Patrick, III
Cain, May Lydia
Cain, William Allen
Cano, Mario Stephen
Carres, Louis George
Castillo, Hal Stephen

Clark, Ross Townsend
Cohen, Eric Martin
Cohen, Meredith Joseph
Cordell, Martin Lewis
Crespo, Manuel A.
Davidson, Michael H.
Dean, Denis Allen
Dekle, George Robert
Dempsey, Bernard Hayden, Jr.
Denaro, Gregory
de Vlaming, Denis Michael
Dohaney, Joseph George, Jr.
Ellis, Herbert Wayne
Evans, George Michael
Evans, John F.
Ferrell, Milton Morgan, Jr.
Fitzgibbons, John Murray
Fowler, Sandra T.
Gaddy, Rodney Edwin
Gold, I. Randall
Graham, Donald Lynn
Gross, Terence Alan
Gussow, Irving Bernard
Haddad, Fred
Hartz, Steven Edward Marshall
Hernandez, Daniel Mario
Hirschhorn, Joel
Hochman, Jeffrey J.
Howie, Bruce Griffith
Jacob, Bruce Robert
Jamieson, James Phillips
Johnson, Paul Bryan
Jones, John Edward
Jorandby, Richard Leroy
Joseph, Paul R.
Keating, Gerard F.
Koch, Ky Marshall
Kogan, Gerald
Kogan, Stephen Jay
Kohl, Donald Phillip
Kollin, Gary
Korchin, Paul Maury
Kuehne, Benedict P.
LaBoda, Barry Charles
Laeser, Abraham
Lewis, Neal Randolph
Lida, Carl Howard
Link, Robert James
Loewy, Ira N.
Lubet, Marc Leslie
Lyng, Reginald William
Makowski, Raymond Edmund
Maniatty, Philip Ward
McBurney, Charles Walker, Jr.
McDonnell, Michael R. N.
McGee, C(larence) Edward, Jr.
McGovern, Peter John
McNeill, Frederick Wallace
Meade, Russell Arthur
Menendez, Manuel, Jr.
Messing, Howard Robert
Midgley, Douglas Merritt
Miller, Carla Dorothy
Miller, Robert Charles
Mitcham, Bob Anderson
Mitrani, Isaac Jaime
Mollica, Salvatore Dennis
Montante, Philip Joseph, Jr.
Moore, John Henry, II
Moreno, Federico Antonio
Murrell, Robert George
Nimmons, Ralph Wilson, Jr.
Oberhausen, Frank Clay, Jr.
Overby, Jon Jefferson
Palmer, R. Scott
Penland, Samuel Perry, Jr.
Pugh, Irby Gene
Quinon, Jose Manuel
Rachlin, Richard Stanley
Raiden, Michael E.
Rashkind, Paul Michael
Reno, Janet
Richardson, Scott Neil
Rivera, Luis Ernesto
Rodriguez, Jose Gabriel
Rogers, Harvey D.
Rosen, Michael James
Rothman, David Bill
Rougeux, Donna Riselli
Samek, Jeffrey Wayne
Schmidt, Whitney Lawrence
Schneider, Harvey Robert
Schneider, Michael Louis
Schreiber, Alan Hickman
Scott, Thomas Emerson, Jr.
Scremin, Anthony James
Sheaffer, William Jay
Sheffield, Frank Elwyn
Slaughter, Marshall Glenn
Smith, Horace, Jr.
Sprowls, Paul Alan
Stein, Stuart Leonard
Taitz, Steven Carter
Tarkoff, Michael Harris
Thornton, John William, Jr.
Tifford, Arthur W.
Tobin, Gerald J.
Tygart, S. Thompson, Jr.
Van Hook, Claude Ashton, III
Vogel, Howard Michael
Wadsworth, Murray Marvin
Watson, Robert James
Wein, Stephen Joshua
Weisberg, Alan Lerner
Whitcomb, William Grandon
White, Stephen Richard
Williams, Stewart Dorian
Wills, Robert Roy
Winter, Steven Lawrence
Witlin, Barry Ethan
Zeidwig, Howard Michael

Georgia

Barr, Robert Laurence, Jr.
Baverman, Alan Jerold
Biggins, Franklin N.
Bostic, Harris Clemon
Bright, Joseph Converse
Christy, Gary Christopher
Cohen, Darryl Brandt
Connelly, Lewis Branch Sutton
Cooper, Lawrence Allen
Cowen, Martin Lindsey, III
Crumbley, R. Alex
Davis, E. Marcus
Deegan, Nan Marie
Dodd, Roger James
Duttweiler, Larry L.
Earls, Margaret Bernardine Holley
Flowers, William Harold, Jr.
Franzén, Stephen Edwards
Gifford, William David
Gignilliat, William Robert, III
Good, Richard Federick
Gregory, Hardy, Jr.
Halle, Mollie Johnson
Hames, Luther Claude, Jr.
Hanington, Paula Kay
Harrison, Gresham Hughel
Harrison, Samuel Hughel
Henderson, Daniel Lamar
Hubbard, George Morrison, III
Kadish, Mark J.
Lanier, Robert Simmons, Jr.
Mallory, Arthur Eugene, III
Marger, Edwin
Miller, Jack Everett
Mull, Gale W.
Ordover, Abraham Philip
Ossick, John Joseph, Jr.
Parker, Wilmer, III
Pierce, Hinton Rainer
Pilcher, James Brownie
Polstra, Larry John
Ponsoldt, James Farmer
Powell, Richard Lynn
Reeves, Gene
Shapiro, Michael Bruce
Taylor-Hanington, Paula Kay
Thomas, Richard English
Tolley, Edward Donald
Underwood, William Fleming, Jr.
Warner, William Millard
Webb, Michael Steven
Weber, David Victor

Hawaii

Acoba, Simeon Rivera, Jr.
Apo, Jan Kanani
Barkai, John Lee
Berman, Pamela Jill
Ching, Gale Lin Fong
Crebbin, Anthony Micek
Gillin, Malvin James, Jr.
Hall, David Winston
Kuniyuki, Ken Takaharu
Lowenthal, Philip Henry
Moroney, Michael John
Songstad, Steven Booth
Weight, Michael A.
Zola, Michael S.

Idaho

Bengoechea, Shane Orin
Brown, Charles Alan
Ellsworth, Maurice Owens
Gallant, Kenneth Stuart
Hart, Stephen Strong
Hicks, George Gregory
Hoff, Renae
May, James, Jr.
McCabe, Thomas James
Parmenter, David N.

Illinois

Africk, Joel Jay
Alesia, James H(enry)
Allen, Ronald Jay
Bacall, Elliot Stephen
Bailey, Robert Short
Barnett, William A.
Bassitt, Janet Louise
Bauer, Joseph Louis
Bauer, Lawrence Michael
Bauer, William Joseph
Bell, Allen Andrew, Jr.
Bell, Ronald Lee
Benson, James Robert
Bernardi, Donald Delpho
Beu, William Raymond
Boharic, Robert Vincent
Bortman, David
Botti, Aldo E.
Bracey, Willie Earl
Braden, Everette Arnold
Bruno, Thomas Anthony
Burns, Robert Patrick
Carroll, William Kenneth
Cifelli, John Louis
Coulson, William Roy
Cummings, Walter Dillon
Cummins, Robert Patrick
Decker, John Francis
Donlevy, John Dearden
Doughty, H. Reed
Driscoll, Patrick Thomas, Jr.
Ebert, Regan Danielle
Edmiston, Charles Nathan
Ettinger, Joseph Alan
Francomb, Lonnie Coleman
Frederick, Robert George
Gallagher, Thomas Jordan, Jr.
Gekas, Constantine John
Gottfried, Theodore Alexander
Gutof, Richard Stewart
Hamrock, Mark Andrew
Harris, Donald Ray
Harrison, Keith Michaele
Hartman, Marshall J.
Heinz, John Peter
Hermann, Donald Harold James
Herr, Michael Joseph
Hess, Frederick J.
Hicks, James Thomas
Hoover, Russell James
Hoskins, Richard Jerold
Inman, Arthur James
Kenny, Robert Emmett, Jr.
Kerstetter, Wayne Arthur
King, Michael Howard
Komie, Stephen Mark
Koval, Joseph Patrick
Kuczwara, Thomas Paul
Lasaine, Dorian Barnett
Lerner, Jeffrey Michael
Linklater, William Joseph
Logli, Paul Albert
Lyons, Kevin W.
MacCarthy, Terence (F.)
Maganzini, Teresa Aversa
Malvik, John
Mateas, Kenneth Edward
McCullough, John Thomas
Meyer, Stanley Russell
Moore, John L.
Morrissey, George Michael
Mullen, Margaret Jean
Mulroy, Thomas Robert, Jr.
Murer, Michael Anton
Nixon, Lewis Michael
Null, Michael Elliot
Oakey, James Leo
Oglesby, Paul Leonard, Jr.
Patel, Ahmed Adam
Paul, Bernard Arthur
Pearlman, Alan
Pelz, Joel Thomas
Phillips, Michael James
Pope, Daniel James
Reeder, Robert Harry
Richards, Robert Mayo
Ripplinger, George Raymond, Jr.
Roberts, Keith Edward, Sr.
Rodkey, Frederick Stanley, Jr.
Roustan, Yvon D.
Ryan, Frank James
Schmidt, Wayne Walter
Schoenfield, Rick Merrill
Schulhofer, Stephen Joseph
Scully, John Joseph
Seiden, Glenn
Skinner, Samuel Knox
Spears, Larry Jonell
Starkman, Gary Lee
Stone, Howard Lawrence
Stone, Jed
Swain, John Barry
Tarun, Robert Walter
Theis, William Harold
Theobald, Edward Robert
Tobin, Craig Daniel
Troelstrup, John Frederick
Valukas, Anton Ronald

Indiana

Braatz, David Edward
Brown, Elaine Marie Becher
Carpenter, Susan Karen
Clark, Eric Oden
Clouse, John Daniel
Coffman, Anne Blankenburg
Cohen, William J.
Cox, John Coates
Gillenwater, Michael Allen
Grund, James Arthur
Haury, John Carroll
Hubbell, Calvin Keith
Kammen, Richard
Kiefer, J(ames) Richard
Leeman, William Kelly
Lewis, Robert Lee
Lisher, James Richard
Loveall, George Michael
McDowell, Dock, Jr.
McGaughey, Jerry Joseph
McNeely, Mark Wright
Meltzer, Kris
Moody, James T(yne)
Nasser, Woodrow Sam
Nussbaum, Richard Anton, II
O'Reilly, Michael James
Petersen, Howard Edwin
Plouff, Thomas O'Connor
Risacher, Martin Eugene
Saint, Robert Edwards
Sanders, Carlton Edward
Schultess, LeRoy Kenneth
Stein, Eleanor Bankoff
Thompson, Kerry Lewis
Vaidik, Nancy Harris
Van Bokkelen, Joseph Scott
Webster, Dale Philip
Wellnitz, Craig Otto
Witte, Gordon Michael

Iowa

Bowman, Michael Allen
Butler, David Douglas
Critelli, Lylea May Dodson
Fitzgibbons, Ann
Giles, William Jefferson, IV
Mullins, Michael Royce
Norris, James Robert
Rosenberg, Paul Herschel
Sallen, David Urban
Smith, William Sidney
Spies, Leon Fred
Wing, Stephen Prentice

Kansas

Bideau, Edwin Hale, III
Braun, Glenn Robert
Burgess, Benjamin L., Jr.
Carver, Kevin Scott
Gard, Spencer Agassiz
Hecht, Robert D.
Johnson, Kevin Blaine
Kessler, Stephen
Krusor, Mark William
Lowe, Jon Kent
Manning, Donna Kaser
Pierce, Ricklin Ray
Schultz, Richard Allen
Stovall, Carla Jo
Wall, Larry William

Kentucky

Armstrong, David Love
Barr, James Houston, Jr.
Bowles, Jerry Jay
Bradshaw, Alice Linda
Chapuk, Thomas Christopher
Choate, Dennis Jeffrey
DeFalaise, Louis
Hagan, Charles Curtis, Jr.
Isaac, Teresa Ann
Jefferson, Janice Lee Roehler
Jewell, Franklin P.
Jones, William Rex
Megibow, Tod Douglas
Meredith, Ronald Edward
Miller, Edward Douglas
Miller, Scott Mitchell
Ogden, Len Willis, Jr.
Rawdon, Richard McLean, Jr.
Shuffett, James Avery
Taylor, Warren Anthony
Vest, David Gardner
Whalen, Paul Lewellin
Wilborn, Woody Stephen

Louisiana

Adams, Ellis Paul, Jr.
Alarcon, Terry Quentin
Barry, Michael Francis
Bassett, Jeffrey Michael
Beckner, Donald Lee
Brainis, Leon Irving
Brunson, Hugh Ellis
Burns, Premila Irene
Burns, William Glenn
Burt, Earl Daniel, Jr.
Cole, Luther Francis
Davis, Sumpter B., III
Everett, Stephen Edward
Flick, Sheila Ann
Gallagher, Michael Stephen
Granier, Kirk Raymond
Gravel, Camille Francis, Jr.
Grundmeyer, Douglas Lanaux
Hawkins, Cynthia Rayburn
Hingle, Gilmer Paul
Jones, William Roby
Knoll, Jerold Edward
Kuhn, James E.
Kuss, Mark Davis
Looney, James Holland
McClelland, James Ray
McManus, Clarence Elburn
Mickel, Joseph Thomas
Murray, Julian R., Jr.
Ponder, L(eslie) Barbee, M
Pugh, George Willard
Ratcliff, John Garrett
Reed, John Wilson
Riccio, Marie Olympia
Smith, J. Arthur, III
Stokes, Douglas Leon
Tritico, Russell Thomas
Unglesby, Lewis O.
Vitiello, Michael
Walker, Henry Clay, IV
Warshauer, Irving Jay
Willis, Richard Allan
Woodard, Billie Elayne Colombaro
Woodward, William Edward
Wright, Jack, Jr.

Maine

Levandoski, Dennis
Massey, Donald Terhune
Pearson, Clinton Charles
Picavet, Robert Clement
Romanow, Richard Brian
Stone, Alan G.
Tierney, James Edward
Washburn, Robert Michael
Willey, N. Laurence, Jr.

Maryland

Ashin, Jeffery Gordon
Badger, Jeffrey Ewen
Bonner, Leonard John
Braun, Stephen John
Buchanan, Phillip Gerald
Calhoun, John L.
Clarke, William Anthony Lee, III
Cobb, Ty
Creech, Jay Heyward
Crowe, Thomas Leonard
Duckett, Warren Bird, Jr.
Eisenberg, Harvey Ellis
Gallavan, Michael Lee
Hall, Marc Gregory
Hall, William Bryan, Jr.
Joseph, Fredric Robert
Junghans, Paula Marie
Katz, Stanley Herbert
Kelberman, Dale Preston
Kramer, Paul R.
Lavenstein, Terry Stuart
Lazzaro, Robert Wayne
Lulie, Edward, III
Martin, Clifford
Matty, Robert Jay
Miliman, David Jay
Mix, George Warren
Monahan, John Connolly
Morrow, Thomas Campbell
Motz, John Frederick
Mullenbach, Linda Herman
Neil, Benjamin Arthur
Nemetz, Margaret Nottingham
Ohly, D. Christopher
Parsky, Keith Alan
Porter, James Harry, Jr.
Radding, Andrew
Robinson, Stuart Jay
Ruark, Davis Rutherford
Schatzow, Michael
Schneider, James Frederick
Smith, Jonathan Scott
Snyder, Stuart Jay
Thomas, Robert Boyce
Van Grack, Steven
Wallace, Sean Daniel
Warren, Richard Dexter
Willcox, Breckinridge Long
Wood, Judson Rawlings

Massachusetts

Angell, James Edward
Avery, Michael Aaron
Bellotti, Francis Xavier
Bennett, Clarence J.
Berman, David
Carter, Paul Stanley
Cullinane, Paul Blake
Culpepper, Miniard
Cunha, John Henry, Jr.
Deren, Donald David
Dokurno, Anthony David
Donahue, Kathleen Ann
Donahue, Richard King
Espinosa, Jose A., Jr.
Fecteau, Francis Roger
Fillon, Richard
Gens, Richard Howard
Goldfarb, Phyllis
Gordon, Richard Warren
Green, Joseph Benjamin
Harris, Richard Bates
Hurley, Daniel Gerard
Hutton, Albert Lee, Jr.
Katzmann, Gary Stephen
Klyman, Andrew Michael
Krasnoo, James B.
Landy, James Leonard
Levine, Julius Byron
Long, Christopher Francis
Looney, William Francis, Jr.
Lowinger, Lazar
Manfreda, Michael Joseph
Manion, Harry Leo
McMahon, Katherine Ellen
Miles, Judith Ellen
Mycock, Frederick Charles
Nesson, Charles R.
Newton, Francis Chandler, Jr.
Oulton, Donald Paul
Owens, Henry Freeman, III
Parker, Richard Davies
Rosenthal, Martin Richard
Ryan, Marian Teresa
Segal, Jerome A.
Segal, Terry Philip
Small, Daniel I.
Sullivan, William Francis
Tremblay, Michael Jeffrey
Vincent, Thomas Philip
Waxler, David Harvey
Wild, Victor Allyn

Michigan

Andreoff, Christopher Andon
Batzer, James Martin
Boyle, Patricia Jean
Breczinski, Michael Joseph
Bregman, Judy Ellen
Brennan, Joseph Vincent
Brennan, Thomas Emmett, Jr.
Brenneman, Hugh Warren, Jr.
Caswell, Roger Lee
Chambers, David L., III
Cloon, William Graham, Jr.
Cooper, Richard I.
Danko, Stephen Gaspar
Deats, Paul Edwin
Dodge, David A.
Dutka, Robert Joseph
Eklund-Easley, Molly Sue
Fawcett, Kim Robert
Fenn, Bruce Hunter
Fillion, Thomas John
Filoramo, John Robert
Forrest, Robert Edwin
Goethel, Stephen B.
Hausner, John Herman
Hess, Robert Kennedy
Hood, Harold
Jacobs, Wendell Early, Jr.
Johnson, Donald Edward, Jr.
Kalec, Robert Michael
Kaplan, Steven Marc
Kelley, Frank Joseph
Koop, Charles Hubert
Mann, John Raymond, III
McDevitt, Mary Elizabeth
McGarry, Alexander Banting
McGinnis, Thomas Michael
Mengel, Christopher Emile
Morgan, Michael Vincent
Morganroth, Mayer
Mullendore, James Myers
O'Brien, Thomas C.
Oltarz-Schwartz, Sara
Palmieri, Angela
Pasula, Angela Marie
Perkins, Michael Dennis
Platzer, Cynthia Siemen
Reynolds, Frank Harrison
Riemersma, Jeffrey Kurt
Salan, John Francis
Smietanka, John Allen
Spence, Howard Tee Devon
Steeno, David Lawrence
Swain, Dennis Michael
Talpos, John C.
Tushla, Dennis Michael
VanderRoest, James Edward
Wells, Bill Charles
White, James Boyd
Wilhelm, Thomas Vincent
Williams, D. Lee
Zuckerman, Richard Engle

Minnesota

Beens, Richard Albert
Bloedel, Philip John
Cleary, Edward Joseph
Collins, Theodore Joseph
Delano, Stephen James
Holmstrom, Gregory Leonard
Jones, C. Paul
Kief, Paul Allan
LaChapelle, Arthur William
Magnuson, Roger James
Maki, Susan Kay
Murphy, Diana E.
Neff, Fred Leonard
Orwoll, Kimball Gregg
Petersen, Jan Farel
Peterson, Mark Warren
Peterson, William George
Resnick, Phillip Stanley
Sagstuen, Warren Richard
Timmons, Peter John

Mississippi

Clark, Charles
Denham, Earl Lamar
Gay, Joe Thomas
Harper, Gregory Livingston
Harris, David Neil
James, L. C.
Kirksey, William Boyd
Mayer, John William
Mord, Irving Conrad, II
Pittman, Edwin Lloyd
Turner, Bennie L.

Missouri

Anzalone, Frank Anthony
Banks, Eric Kendall
Bradshaw, Thomas Michael
Derque, Joseph Alexander, III
Downey, Joseph W.
Fleming, Robert Laurence
Fox, Byron Neal
Gorla, Michael Joseph
Jones, David Christopher
Kaveney, Frank John
Lonardo, Charles Henry

Lowes, Albert Charles
Mays, William Gay, II
McClellan, Janet Elaine
McConnell, James David
McKune, Ina Ruth
Moore, Mitchell Jay
Narrow, Nancy Hentig
Parker, Linda Louise
Parrish, John Edward
Passanante, Paul Jasper
Popper, Robert
Radasky, David Jacob
Radke, Daniel Lee
Ringer, John William
Summers, Hugh Scott
Vleisides, Gregory William
Wade, Daniel Ples
Webster, William Lawrence
Welch, Robert C.
Wheeler, James Julian
Wyrsch, James Robert
Zerr, Richard Kevin

Montana

Best, George Bullock, Jr.
Birkenbuel, Marcia Lee
Caughlan, Deirdre
Dunbar, Byron Herbert
Greely, Michael Truman
Knuchel, Karl G.
McKeon, John Carl
O'Connor, Teresa McCann
Sheehy, Edmund Francis, Jr.
Smartt, Michael Stewart

Nebraska

Eaton, David Foster
Gallup, J. William
Gutowski, Michael Francis
Lahners, Ronald Dean
Line, William Gunderson
Salerno, Terrence Joseph
Smith, Wilbur Cowan
Spire, Robert M.
Swihart, Fred Jacob
Troia, Anthony Samuel
Warin, Edward George
Wilke, John William

Nevada

Bell, Robert Cecil
Burns, Thomas Martin
Byrne, Barbara
Cornell, Richard Farnham
Flanagan, Norman Patrick
Galliher, Keith Edwin, Jr.
Grad, Neil Elliott Marshall
Lumkes, Deborah Lee
McKay, D. Brian
Pinkerton, C(harles) Frederick
Sarnowski, David Francis
Specchio, Michael Ronald
Stein, Stephen
Wright, Thomas Preston

New Hampshire

Boyle, Gerard Joseph
Catalfo, Alfred (Alfio), Jr.
Evans, Craig Fletcher
Garod, Harvey Jay
McNamara, Richard Bedle
Snow, Robert Brian

New Jersey

Adlerstein, Jo Anne Chernev
Biribin, Renato Raymond
Bottitta, Joseph Anthony
Carluccio, Robert James
Collins, James Francis
D'Alfonso, Mario Joseph
Farr, Linus Gilbert
Ferreri, Vito Richard
Ford, John R.
Friedman, Richard Lloyd
Gernert, Richard Charles
Gilbreth, Peter Nelson
Hiltebrand, Stephen Mark
Hornstine, Louis Fox
Hurley, Lawrence Joseph
Jacobs, Andrew Robert
Jesperson, John Edward
Katz, Jeffrey Harvey
Korin, Joel Benjamin
Kozyra, Barry Alan
Littman, David Bernard
Masucci, Louis M., Jr.
McCracken, Carol Weaver
Menendez, Robert
Mitzner, Michael Jay
Moczula, Boris
Morris, Joseph Dean
Nucciarone, A. Patrick
O'Neill, Joseph Dean
Palma, Nicholas James
Portelli, Joseph Andrew
Rabinowitz, Daniel Lawrence
Raviola, Patrick Richard
Robertson, William Withers
Rogers, Matthew Stephen
Rogoff, Marc Jeffrey
Ronca, James Alexander
Sperber, Mark David
Susswein, Ronald
Telsey, Norman
Tolleris, M(ary) Angela
Trombadore, Raymond Robert
Van Rye, Kenneth
Weichsel, John Louis
Weinstein, Stephen Saul
Weitzman, Donald Martin
Widman, Douglas Jack
Zegas, Alan Lee

New Mexico

Atkins, Spencer Bert
Brockman, Eugene E.
Cargo, David Francis
Dal Santo, Diane
Darnell, Richard Wayne
Ferrara, Anthony Joseph
Gant, Joseph Erwin
Gant, Joseph Erwin, III
Graham, David Antony
Greig, William Harold
Kennedy, Paul John

Kennedy, Roderick Thomas
Koch, Ron
Lutz, William Lan
Manzanares, Dennis
Martin, Connie Ruth
Mitchell, Gary Colas
Paternoster, John Miller
Pederson, Robert David
Rothstein, Robert Richard
Schiff, Steven Harvey
Vazquez, Martha Alicia
Westheimer, Stephen James
Wilson, Kenneth Belton

New York

Abady, Samuel Aaron
Abramowitz, Elkan
Adin, Richard H(enry)
Amsterdam, Mark Lemle
Ardam, David Mitchell
Armani, Frank Henry
Ascher, Richard Alan
Aurnou, Joel Martin
Baird, Bruce Allen
Ballow, John Edward
Barsamian, J(ohn) Albert
Baumgarten, Sidney
Bavero, Ronald Joseph
Beltre, Luis Oscar
Berkow, Michael
Berney, Lonn E.
Bernstein, Kenneth Alan
Blangiardo, Frank J.
Bradshaw, Leslie Arnold
Bramwell, Henry
Brand, Ray Manning
Brandveen, Antonio Isadore
Braun, Robert Alan
Breakstone, Jay L.T.
Brenner, Frank
Brent, Stephen M.
Brownell, Carlton Kearns
Brunetti, John Joseph
Buchwald, Don David
Burger, Lewis Stephen
Burgess, John Richard
Butler, John Edward
Cahn, Richard Caleb
Capetola, Anthony Adam
Capra, Daniel Joseph
Carr, Rokki Knee
Cartier, Rudolph Henri, Jr.
Chamberlain, John
Clarey, Robert Louis
Clark, Ramsey
Clark, Robert Francis
Clayman, Charles Elliott
Clennan, John Francis
Coffee, John Collins, Jr.
Coffin, Mary McCarthy
Collazo, Salvador
Condon, John William, Jr.
Costantino, Mark Americus
Costello, Robert Joseph
Currey, Charles Thomas
Curvin, Steven P.
Daniels, George Benjamin
Daniels, John Hill
DeAngelus, Ronald Patrick
De Lucia, John Joseph
DeMarco, Anthony J., Jr.
Dershowitz, Nathan Zev
Devendorf, Alfred Ervin
Devine, Eugene Peter
DiPrima, Michael Thomas
Dorf, Robert Clay
Dowling, William Francis
Druker, James Owen
Dulin, Thomas N.
Dunn, William David
Eiszner, James Richard, Jr.
Elliott, A. Irene
Elsen, Sheldon Howard
Englert, Dennis M.
Evans, John Thomas
Ezersky, William Martin
Fahey, Joseph Edmund
Feedore, Jeremy Randolph
Fein, Scott Norris
Feldberg, Michael Svetkey
Figueora, Nicholas
Finerty, Margaret Joan
Fiske, Robert Bishop, Jr.
Fleming, Peter Emmet, Jr.
Folks, Robert Logue
Frankel, Sandor
Freedman, Monroe Henry
Friedler, Sydney
Friedman, Jon George
Frost, Jerome Kenneth
Gallet, Jeffry Hershel
Garry, John Thomas, II
Gerber, Edward F.
Getnick, Neil Victor
Gioffre, Anthony Bruno
Glekel, Jeffrey Ives
Gold, Joseph
Goldstein, Howard Warren
Goltzer, George R.
Gorman, Gerald Patrick
Graham, Jul Eliot
Grossman, Mark Donald
Gulotta, Frank Andrew, Jr.
Hagan, Peter
Halberstam, Malvina Guggenheim
Harris, Allen
Heath, Joseph John
Henner, Peter William
Herman, Susan N.
Himelein, Larry M.
Horner, Terry David
Hudson, Paul Stephen
Iannuzzi, John Nicholas
Isaacs, Leonard Bernard
Jacobson, Barry Stephen
Jones, E. Stewart, Jr.
Jordan, David Francis, Jr.
Kamins, Barry Michael
Kaplan, Eugene Neal
Kaufman, Stephen E.
Kelly, Michael Thomas
Kelly, Raymond Aloysius, Jr.
Kennedy, Michael John
Kenney, John Joseph
Kerson, Paul Eugene
King, Robert Lucien
Kirk, Patrick Laine
Kissane, Thomas

Koelzer, George Joseph
Kostelanetz, Boris
Krieg, Marc Shea
Kuh, Richard Henry
La Forge, Gladys Candace
Lake, Barbara Ruth
Lauer, Eliot
Levick, Marsha Lynn
Levine, Alan
Levinson, David Lawrence
Levinson, Paul Howard
Lewis, David L.
Litman, Jack Theodore
Lowe, John Anthony
Lubitz, Howard Arnold
Lunney, J. Robert
Lupert, Leslie Allan
Lyman, Nathan M.
Marcheso, Joseph James
Marrero, Louis John
Masliansky, Nechama
McCloskey, Patrick Lawrence
McDonough, Thomas Joseph
McGeady, Paul Joseph
McGuire, Harold Frederick
McSorley, Bernard Thomas
Meister, Ronald William
Meltzer, Sanford
Mendez, William, Jr.
Merola, Mario
Millane, John Vaughan, Jr.
Morabito, David Robertson, Sr.
Morosco, B. Anthony
Morrison, Peter Henry
Mulhern, Edwin Joseph
Myers, William Edward
Naftalis, Gary Philip
Nardone, Richard
Nebush, Frank John, Jr.
Nissan, Randy S.
Nowicki, Michael Thomas
Obermaier, Otto George
O'Connor, Liam T(homas)
Panzer, Edward S.
Perrin, Gregory J.
Peskin, Stephan Haskel
Piel, Eleanor Jackson
Pilato, Louis Peter
Pittari, Stephen Joseph
Pohorelsky, Viktor Vaclav
Porco, Domenick Joseph
Rakoff, Jed Saul
Ralls, Geoffrey Quentin
Rappaport, A. Jack
Raylesberg, Alan Ira
Reich, Perry Seth
Roseman, Arnold David
Rosner, Jonathan Levi
Ross, Christopher Theodore William
Ryan, Leonard Eames
Saltzman, Michael I.
Salvan, Sherwood Allen
Santangelo, Betty J.
Santucci, John J.
Scharf, Jared J.
Schechter, Donald Robert
Schlinger, Alexander Peter
Schwartz, Martin Weber
Schwartz, Michael Adam
Schwed, Michael J.
Shanahan, James Patrick
Shapiro, Irving
Sherwood, James Cruze
Siffert, John Sand
Silbering, Robert Howard
Silverman, Elliot
Silverman, Karen Fay
Slade, Jeffrey Christopher
Smith, Lisa Margaret
Spillane, Dennis Kevin
Stahr, Thomas James
Stephan, H. Peskin
Summit, Paul Eliot
Suraci, Joseph Anthony
Sussman, Howard S(ivin)
Tabak, Michael L.
Tendy, William Michael, Jr.
Tomao, Peter Joseph
Treanor, John McCormack
Velie, Franklin B.
Vergari, Carl Anthony
Vilardo, Lawrence Joseph
Wales, H.Elliot
Wasserman, Edward Henry
Weil, Gary Ronald
Weinrich, Johnathan Edward
Weinstein, Alan Abraham
Weisfuse, David B.
Wessel, Peter
White, Renee Allyn
Wildes, Leon
Wittman, Michael Lee
Wukitsch, David John
Yagerman, Howard W.

North Carolina

Alexander, Charles Jackson, II
Badger, David Russell
Blomeley, James Lee, Jr.
Bunch, W. Edward
Burleson, Lynn Pierce
Carroll, Seavy Alexander
Carter, John Tilton, Jr.
Conway, Robert George, Jr.
Currin, Samuel Thomas
Eads, Wayne Buchanan
Elliott, Joseph Bryan
Farmer, Ryland Lee
Farver, Harry Craig
Flaherty, David Thomas, Jr.
Gillespie, James Davis
Griffin, Robert Wooten
Hampton, Thurman Bruce
Harkey, Henry Averill
Horowitz, Donald Leonard
Hulse, William Frederick
Hunter, Richard Samford, Jr.
Johnson, Bruce Cannon
Jones, Bonnie Dee Durham
Jones, Michael Morrie
Jones, Paul Lawrence
Joyce, Dennis Robert
King, Ronnie Patterson
Kripner, George Martin
Lefstein, Norman
Morgan, Thomas Jada
Rawls, Eben Turner, III
Sentelle, David Bryan

Shields, Karen Bethea
Smith, Roger Theodore
Stroud, Joseph E., Jr.
Switzer, Robert Earl
Taylor, Vaughan Edward
Thornburg, Lacy Herman
Tilghman, Carl Lewis
Walker, James Edward

North Dakota

Gregg, John Ralph
Kautzmann, Dwight C(larence) H(arry)
Lieb, Arthur Hilary
Lockney, Thomas Michael
Maxson, R. James
McKechnie, William Elliott
Nelson, Carol Susan
Quast, Larry Wayne
Snyder, Robert John
Spaeth, Nicholas John
Webb, Rodney Scott

Ohio

Allen, Nadine Lovelace
Ammer, William
Ausnehmer, John Edward
Beane, Frank Llewellyn
Belton, John Thomas
Binning, J. Boyd
Callahan, John Joseph
Carroll, James Michael
Carto, David Draffan
Cassidy, Paul David
Cissell, James Charles
Cline, Richard Allen
Colby, Richard DeAtlee
Dana, Randall M.
Davis, Bradley Mark
Detling, Glenn Eugene
Faigin, Arnold Jeffrey
Ferruccio, Samuel Joseph, Jr.
Fingerman, Albert Ross
Giannelli, Paul Clark
Gold, Gerald Seymour
Hagel, Thomas Leo
Hall, James Alexander
Hanna, Martin Shad
Hardig, Mark Nelson
Heaton, Gerald Lee
Hennenberg, Michael Chaim
Hoefle, H. Frederick
Hohn, Michael
Jones, Michael Charles
Kennedy, Charles Allen
King, J(oseph) Michael
Kirschner, Leonard
Koenig, Kenneth John
Lacki, Ralph Stephen
Lagos, James Harry
Lantz, Charles Jeffery
Lavelle, John Philip
Lieberman, Dennis Alan
Madden, Stephan DuPont
Mayberry, Alan Reed
McAdams, Sheilah Helen
McIlvaine, Stephen Brownlee
McNew, Robert A.
Meyer, Douglas Oliver
Millhoff, Patricia Ann
Morelli, Arnold
Nichelson, James Lee
O'Brien, Ronald Joseph
Olivas, Adolf
Painter, Mark Philip
Paul, Dennis Edward
Postlewaite, Charles Chapman
Racine, Kathleen Celeste
Rogers, Richard Michael
Rolston, George Drew
Rosen, Gary Mitchell
Ruppert, James Delano, II
Russo, Nancy Margaret
Schaffer, Thomas Alan
Schiff, Scott W.
Schuh, Stephen Joseph
Shaw, Elwin Scott
Sheward, Richard S.
Slagle, James William
Smart, Irene Balogh
Steinhouse, Carl Lewis
Sullivan, Mark Edward
Thompson, Jayne Audrey
Tucker, Theodore Brush, III
Tyack, George Gary
Van De Mark, Julie Ann
Wettlaufer, Karl Frederick
Wolaver, Stephen Arthur
Wood, Wendy Ann
Yontz, Randall Eugene
Zwayer, Ted

Oklahoma

Berry, Dean Clement
Berry, James W. Bill
Berry, James Wilson
Brewster, Clark Otto
Collins, Leon Frederick
Crawford, B(urnett) Hayden
Gordon, Jack Elliott, Jr.
Hughes, Carl Douglas
Jones, Larry Alan
Jones, Stephen
King, Michael James
Kline, David Adam
Miller, Michael John
Miskovsky, George, Sr.
Moore, Roy Dean
Morris, Greg Arthur
Musser, James William
Parks, Ed Horace, III
Peterson, David L.
Price, William Scott
Purcell, Gary Morgan
Reid, Sue Titus
Salem, Micheal Charles
Scott, Lawrence Rowe
Shaw, Donald Ray
Sullivan, Edward Paul
Taylor, Joe Clinton
Tully, Brian Brendan
Turpen, Michael Craig
Warren, Loyde Hugh

Oregon

Barton, Richard Lee
Fennell, Dennis Eugene

Forcum, Richard Eugene
Geil, John Clinton
Hardman, Christopher Ray
Jagger, James Cloyd
Lorenz, Daniel Christopher
Marquis, Joshua Kai
Overgaard, Mary Ann
Rich, Steven Eugene
Rieke, Forrest Neill
Rogers, Jeffrey Langston
Savage, John William
Snouffer, William Campbell
Steele, Kathie Fay
Turner, Charles Hamilton
Wong, Hap Yee

Pennsylvania

Albert, Neil Lawrence
Barrett, Bruce Alan
Beemer, John Barry
Benn, Sara Kitchen
Blakley, Benjamin Spencer, III
Bonner, Eugene Aloysius
Borden, Randolph Tyson
Brosky, John G.
Brysh, Paul John
Carroll, James Walter, Jr.
Cassarino, Joseph Francis
Cimini, Joseph Fedele
Cohen, Anita Marilyn
Cohen, Earl S.
Colville, Robert E
Cooper, Thomas Louis
Coslett, Charles Reynolds
Davis, James Thomas
Donato, Arthur Thomas, Jr.
Durant, Marc
Ellis, Alan
Eshelman, David Richard
Farrell, J. Michael
Feese, Brett Owen
Flower, David Jeffrey
Fogelnest, Robert Craig
Friel, Karen Eileen
Gambescia, Joseph M(ario), Jr.
Garhart, John Paul
Gelso, Charles Patric
Gondelman, Harold
Gordesky, Morton
Gordon, Robert Jay
Grimaud, Gerald C.
Guyton, Odell
Hochberg, Robert Boaz
Jarvis, Kingsley Albright
Jones, David Arthur
Kaplan, Ronald Ira
Keeler, Jean Marie
Keller, David Scott
King, Peter Joseph
Klein, Joel Aaron
Kochems, Robert Gregory
Kubacki, Stanley Louis
LaCheen, Stephen Robert
Lawless, Joseph Francis, Jr.
Lepore, Alphonse Paul
Levenson, Stanton Don
Lisko, Roy Kenneth
Long, Stephen Michael
Love, Mark Steven
Lublin, Mark Aaron
Madva, Stephen Alan
Malloy, Michael Joseph
McEvilly, James Patrick
Mellon, Thomas Edward, Jr.
Mermelstein, Jules Joshua
Mogil, Gary Marc
Mullinix, Edward Wingate
Muraca, Frank John
Mustokoff, Michael Mark
Muth, Michael Raymond
Nemeth, Charles Paul
Newman, George Henry
O'Dell, Debbie
Patterson, Christopher Malone
Pisani, Robert Louis
Platt, William Henry
Pribanic, Victor Hunter
Pyfer, John Frederick, Jr.
Reagle, Jack Evan
Reiff, Jeffrey Marc
Reiter, Joseph Henry
Ristau, Mark Moody
Rosen, Cathryn Jo
Roskovensky, Vincent Joseph, II
Rutter, Thomas Bell
Samuelson, Wayne Paul
Schoener, George Francis, Jr.
Schulz, William Frederick, Jr.
Schwabenland, Edward John
Schwartzman, James Charles
Scianna, Russell William
Scoratow, Martin Murray
Shelton, Fincourt Braxton
Shmukler, Stanford
Skeel, Peter Brooks
Smith, Judy Goldstein
Snite, Albert John, Jr.
Sobota, John Raymond
Spengler, Daniel George
Stack, Michael J.
Strazzella, James Anthony
Swaim, John Joseph
Voluck, Jeffrey M.
Voss, James Victor
Walker, Wallace Lee
Ward, William Francis
Weaver, Cynthia Marie
Wertheimer, Spencer Miles
West, James Joseph
Witherel, Michael Joseph
Wolfe, Steven Edward
Zimmerman, LeRoy S.

Rhode Island

Arcaro, Harold Conrad, Jr.
Davenport, Teresa Joanna
Dickinson, Thomas More
Mann, Robert Barney
Martin, David Luther
McMahon, John Joseph
O'Donnell, William Kenneth
O'Neil, James E.
Parsons, Rymn James
Reilly, John Bernard
Reilly, William F(rancis)
Simmons, Howard Koorken

South Carolina

Armstrong, Robert Sitgreaves
Barker, Joseph Ransom
Bartlett, Stephen Sheppard
Bolt, J. Dennis
Breibart, Richard Jerome
Carr, Robert Stuart
Coates, William Alexander
Condon, Charles Molony
DeWitt, Franklin Roosevelt
Esposito, John Vincent
Harte, John Williams
Hudson, James Patrick
Kauser, Janson Allen
Lake, Robert Campbell, Jr.
Mauldin, John Inglis
McIntyre, Bernard
Medlock, Thomas Travis
Smith, Walter Henry
Spears, Michael Eugene
Vieth, Rick
Watson, Patricia Seets
Wedlock, Eldon Dyment, Jr.
Zelenka, Donald John

South Dakota

Baumann, Christopher John
Hersrud, Leslie Raymond
Hogen, Philip Nere
Johnson, Richard Arlo
Kennedy, Craig Allen
Stickney, Paul Douglas
Wyman, William Alan

Tennessee

Bandy, Thomas Rochelle, III
Barr, James Victor, III
Boyd, Mary Olert
Brothers, Thomas White
Brown, Joe Blackburn
Cody, Walter James Michael
Cohen, William Mark
Culp, James David
Davis, Jimmy Kyle
Dillard, W. Thomas
Dixon, James Mikel
Drowota, Frank F., III
Dupree, Charles Patrick
Durand, Philip Poyntell
Ehmling, Miles Allen
Ellis, Bobby James
Estes, Jerry Nelson
Ewing, William Hickman, Jr.
Ferguson, April Rose W.
Friedman, Robert Michael
Garts, James Rufus, Jr.
Gill, John Welch, Jr.
Gordon, J. Houston
Hardin, Hal D.
Harrell, Limmie Lee, Jr.
Harrington, Penny Nancy
Hayes, David Greene
High, David Erwin
Kiener, John Leslie
King, Robert Lewis
Lloyd, William Nelson
Logan, James Franklin, Jr.
Marty, James Owen
McClarty, John Westley
Oberman, Steven
Purcell, William Paxson, III
Raines, Jim Neal
Ridenour, Ronald H.
Riley, Joe Glenard
Rogers, John T. Milburn
Rutherford, Glen Bibee
Shirley, Raymond Andrew, Jr.
Summers, Gerald (Jerry) Howard
Trant, Douglas Allen
Wagerman, Howard Louis
Whitaker, Michael Wright
White, Penny J.
Yarbrough, Edward Meacham

Texas

Ackerman, John Edward
Alexander, John William
Banales, J(ose) Manuel
Barton, Hugh Mitchell, III
Baskette, William L., Jr.
Beauchamp, Gary Fay
Berchelmann, David Adolph, Jr.
Berg, David Howard
Berg, Thomas Sidney
Brennan, Diantha Garrett
Brown, Karen Kennedy
Carnahan, Robert Narvell
Chapman, Stephen Sperry
Cliff, John William, Jr.
Collins, Kyle Boyd
Connors, Joseph Aloysius, III
Creeden, Carl Francis
Darnell, James Oral
Davis, Jimmy Frank
DeGuerin, Dick
Driscoll, Michael Hardee
Dunn, Richard Clement
Duty, Tony Edgar
Essmyer, Michael Martin
Figueroa, Luis Antonio
Flynn, Rory Christopher
Fohn, Gerald Anthony
Garcia, Humberto Sigifredo
Garcia, Lawrence L.
Gilbert, Steven John
Gulley, David Wesley
Guthrie, Dan Calvin, Jr.
Hammons, Allen James, Jr.
Harvey, Mark Wayne
Hilder, Philip Harlan
Holmes, Clifton Lee, (Scrappy)
Holt, Robert Blaine
Holt, Wayland Garth
Hughes, Nancy Nutto
Jackson, Freddie Newell
Jacobo, Paulina Moreno
James, Jimmy Robert
Jameson, David Alan
Jenkins, Richard Coleman
Jennings, Karen Lynn
Jett, Joseph Craig
Kousz, Carolyn Gertrude
Latino, Anthony Leon
Leon, Jack Paul
Linden, Louis Frederick
Maloney, Frank

Mattox, James Albon
Miller, Charles E.
Minor, David Michael
Morgan, Thomas Sidney
Moseley, Patricia Ann
Mullen, John Clancy
Orsburn, Charles Claude
Perkins, Lloyd Wesley
Porto, Joseph Anthony
Price, Robert Alexander
Reamey, Gerald S.
Reimer, Bill Monroe
Rendon, Ruben
Richman, Marc Hersh
Rickhoff, Thomas Emmet
Roessler, P. Dee
Saul, Roland Dale
Schaffer, Kent Alan
Schlueter, David Arnold
Seidlits, Curtis Lee, Jr.
Shannon, Joe, Jr.
Sheetz, William Dean
Shugart, James Elmer
Simpson, Searcy Lee, Jr.
Sims, Ricky Reece
Stewart, Annette
Thornton, Russell James
Tobias, Andy Monroe
Vick, Phillip Oran
Wald, Michael H.
Wall, Jack Knox
Wallis, Olney Gray
Walsh, Gerry O'Malley
Weisfeld, Sheldon
Wilkinson, Toby Charles
Wilson, David Keith
Woldy, Kristine Carol
Woodard, Linda Strite
Woody, Clyde Woodrow
Wortham, Robert John
Wright, Charles Alan
Yett, Charles William

Utah

Baron, Roger Frederick
Hatch, Sumner Jones
Kaplan, Neil Alan
Kaufman, Steven Michael
McCullough, William Andrew
Mooney, Jerome Henri
Morgan, Bruce Kent
Owens, Robert Franklin
Rasmussen, Thomas Val, Jr.
Rich, Bradley Pope
Russell, Cheryl Anne
Sam, David
Skordas, Gregory G.
Sullivan, Kevin Patrick
Walsh, John Thomas
Walz, Stewart Chaussee
Westfall, George Michael

Vermont

Amestoy, Jeffrey Lee
Corum, Jesse Maxwell, IV
Curtis, David W.
Glinka, Gleb
Langrock, Peter Forbes
Oettinger, Mark David
Saltonstall, Stephen Lee
Terwilliger, George James, III

Virginia

Baird, Thomas Bryan, Jr.
Bangel, Stanley Jerome
Beale, J. Burkhardt
Bedinger, Frank Cleveland, Jr.
Benser, Frank Leroy
Blank, Irving Michael
Boone, David Eason
Brown, Henry Otis
Cabell, Robert Gamble, Jr.
Carrington, Frank Gamble, Jr.
Chute, Alan Dale
Crewe, Trenton Guy, Jr.
Curtis, Jeffrey Hutton
Davis, Gilbert Kenneth
Dodge, Cynthia Ellen
Economou, Stewart Charles
Flannery, John Philip, II
Fletcher, John Richard
Gardner, Mark S.
Garrett, Stacy F., III
Haight, Gregory Dale
Halbrook, Stephen Porter
Hancock, George Louis, Jr.
Hankins, Timothy Howard
Hicks, Robert DeHardit
Hoffman, Walter Edward
Hogshire, Edward Leigh
James, Richard Robert
Kennett, John Holliday, Jr.
Kotlarchuk, Ihor O. E.
Koutoulakos, Louis
Krasnow, Jeffrey Harry
Lawrence, John Schrumpf
Lederer, Fredric Ira
Leffler, Rodney G.
Lindsey, Thomas Leslie, Jr.
Loe, Brian Robert
McCloskey, Michael Patrick
McGlothlin, Michael Gordon
McKenry, James Reinhardt
Meekins, Samuel Warrenton, Jr.
Metcalfe, James Ashford
Morrison, Johnny Edward
Mott, Joseph William Hooge
Payne, Frederick Warren
Phillips, Dennis Leslie
Philpott, Albert Lee
Pochucha, Larry Arthur
Pollard, Overton Price
Robinson, Thomas Hart
Rosenstock, Louis Anthony, III
Savage, Thomas Yates
Schmidt, C. Jeffers, Jr.
Segall, James Arnold
Slonaker, Jerry Paul
Smith, S(ydney) Strother, III
Snook, John Lloyd, III
Spero, Morton Bertram
Treakle, James Edward, Jr.
Tucker, James Letcher
Varoutsos, George Douglas
Warburton, Roy David
Weinman, Ellen Shelton

Whalen, Michael Patrick
Whitehead, John W.
Whitt, Robert Holt, Jr.
Williams, Glen Morgan
Williams, Ronald Wayne, Sr.
Youngs, John Curtis
Zeese, Kevin Bruce
Zerkin, Gerald Thomas

Washington

Berman, Steve William
Connelly, John Robert, Jr.
Cordes, Clifford Frederick, III
Dacca, Franklin Louis
Day, Stephen Leo
Defelice, Dennis Joseph
Devlin, Greg Martin
Dodds, Michael Bruce
Haynes, George Cleve
Heid, Daniel Brian
Kram, Peter
Lamp, John Ernest
Lundin, John W.
Mahoney, Philip Charles
Marler, Dirk Alan
Matthews, Stephen Ross
McBroom, Douglas D.
Mestel, Mark David
Meyers, Anthony James
Nevin, Jack Frederick
Oreskovich, Carl Joseph
Peters, Frank August
Phillips, Brian Reed
Reiman, Scott A.
Schwartz, Irwin H.
Schweda, Peter Steven
Stanfield, Sally Fite
Tanksley, Raymond Richard, Jr.
Wayne, Robert Jonathan

West Virginia

Arrington, Roy David
Brown, Charles Gailey
Bryant, Sanford Benjamin
Bunner, Patricia Andrea
Cline, Michael Robert
Cowan, John Joseph
Cross, David Bert
Gibson, Michael Fielding
Hearst, James Henry
Howley, Loren Blackman
Humphries, Judy Lynn
Judy, John David, III
Keltner, Robert Earl
Powell, James Corbley
Rich, Wayne Adrian, Jr.
Ringer, Darrell Wayne
Swope, Derek Craig
Woods, Jeff Chandler

Wisconsin

Bruno, Gary Robert
Byers, Stephen Michael
Connolly, L. William
Curtis, George Warren
Flatley, Robert Rahr
Foust, C. William
Glynn, Stephen Michael
Hammer, Thomas John
Hoag, Jack Carter
Hupy, Michael Frederick
Johnson, Kenneth Nolan
Kahn, Charles Frederick, Jr.
Kucirek, Joseph Charles
LeBell, Robert
Liccione, Stephen John
Long, J. Richard
Marohl, David William
Mason, Jon Gerard
Montabon, Dennis Gene
Moser, William R.
Pellino, Charles Edward, Jr.
Rogers, James Thomas
Sostarich, Mark Edward
Stadtmueller, Joseph Peter
Stellman, L. Mandy
Van Buren, David Paul
Wilson, Oscar, Jr.

Wyoming

Botham, Lisa Anne
Gillum, Forrest Earl
Honaker, Richard Henderson
Miller, Linda Suzanne
Rideout, Richard Scott
Spence, Gerald Leonard
Statkus, Jerome Francis
Zollinger, Thomas Tennant

TERRITORIES OF THE UNITED STATES

American Samoa

Faalevao, Aviata Fano

Guam

O'Connor, Karl William

Puerto Rico

Lopez-Romo, Daniel Francisco
Roman, David William

ADDRESS UNPUBLISHED

Adelman, Michael Schwartz
Allison, Howard Mervyn
Beger, John David
Beldock, Myron
Berger, Joel
Bernheim, Peggy
Bono, Anthony Salvatore Emanuel
Brodsky, David M.
Byrnes, John Robert
Cacciatore, Ronald Keith
Canova, Leo Phillip, Jr.
Chirra, Joseph
Christopher, M. Ronald
Damaska, Mirjan Radovan
Doherty, John L.
Dorrier, Lindsay Gordon, Jr.
Ecker, James Marshall

Ferguson, Marvin Elwood
Fitzgerald, John Elmer
Garrigues, Gayle Lynne
Garza, Graciano Jaime
Gianotti, Ernest F.
Gregory, Rick Dean
Gribbs, Paula Rewald
Guste, William Joseph, Jr.
Hanes, Leigh B., Jr.
Harrison, Roddy L.
Himeles, Martin Stanley, Jr.
Jensen, John Robert
Kamin, Daniel Tucker
Leventhal, Howard G.
Lewis, Peter
Margolis, Emanuel
McDonald, Tom
McPherson, James Aubrey
Michaels, David Seth
Narus, Edward R.
Nash, Melvin Samuel
O'Donnell, Pierce Henry
Reardon, Michael Edward
Rossi, Alan David
Showers, H. Robert, Jr.
Thomas, Johnny Wesley
Thornbury, William Mitchell
Vida, Glen Joseph
Weinberg, Martin Gety
Weinstein, Arthur Gary
Wilson, Hugh Steven
Winstein, Stewart Robert

DEBTOR-CREDITOR. *See* Commercial, consumer.

DIVORCE. *See* Family.

EDUCATION, LEGAL

UNITED STATES

Alabama

Davis, Penelope Ann
Ellison, W(illie) James
Luskin, Joseph
Morse, George Wray, II
Nelson, Leonard John, III
Weeks, Arthur Andrew
Wood, Randal Lee

Alaska

Gorsuch, Norman Clifford
Stockholm, Kendall Ray

Arizona

Ascher, Mark Louis
Folsom, Victor Clarence
Fortman, Marvin
Hufford, Carl Benson
Jennings, Marianne Moody
Marcus, Paul
Matheson, Alan Adams
Sabin, John Merrill
Starr, Isidore
Vosburgh, John Addison

Arkansas

Arnold, Morris Sheppard
Gitelman, Morton
Looney, Jake Wayne
Malone, David Roy
Roachell, Richard Wilson
Wright, Robert Ross, III

California

Abel, Richard L.
Abrams, Norman
Alexander, George Jonathon
Anderson, Alison Grey
Asimow, Michael R.
Aynes, James Paul, Jr.
Barnes, Thomas G.
Barnett, Stephen R.
Barnett, Wayne G.
Bartosic, Florian
Bauman, John Andrew
Benton, Andrew Keith
Bettwy, Samuel William
Biederman, Donald Ellis
Binder, David A.
Bomberger, Russell Branson
Cappelletti, Mauro
Choper, Jesse Herbert
Cole, Robert H.
Coons, John E.
Costello, Edward J., Jr.
Dukeminier, Jesse
Eisenberg, Melvin A.
Ellickson, Robert Chester
Ely, John Hart
Eule, Julian N.
Feller, David E.
Foote, Caleb
Franklin, Marc A.
Gafford, George Nelson
Gevurtz, Franklin Andrew
Gould, William Benjamin
Green, Kenneth Norton
Grey, Thomas C.
Gunther, Gerald
Hamilton, Mary Jane
Hanson, Gary A.
Herbert, James Keller
Heyman, Ira Michael
House, Calvin Richard
Ingram, Jeffrey Charles
Johnson, Darrell Bruce
Johnson-Champ, Debra Sue
Jones, Edgar Allan, Jr.
Kaplan, John
Karst, Kenneth Leslie
Klein, William A.
Krell, Bruce Edward
Lawless, William Burns
Letwin, Leon
Levine, David Israel
Lewis, Gerald Jorgensen
Mann, J. Keith

Mc Govern, William Montgomery, Jr.
Mellinkoff, David
Merryman, John Henry
Messinger, Sheldon L(eopold)
Mishkin, Paul J.
Montgomery, John Warwick
Morris, Herbert
Neithercutt, Marcus Gibbs
Parks, George Brooks
Peters, Samuel Anthony
Player, Theresa Joan
Polinsky, A. Mitchell
Prager, Susan Westerberg
Prozan, Sylvia Simmons
Rabin, Robert L.
Ratner, David Louis
Ritter, G. Christopher
Roberson, Clifford Eugene
Rose, I. Nelson
Rosenhan, David L.
Rosett, Arthur Irwin
Rubinfeld, Daniel L.
Russell, John Drinker
Salomon, Darrell Joseph
Sato, Sho
Scheiber, Harry N.
Schmal, Timothy James
Shapiro, Martin
Shelley, Susanne Mary
Sher, Byron D.
Shire, Harold Raymond
Skolnick, Jerome H.
Stolz, Preble
Sullivan, Lawrence A.
Sun, Cossette Tsung-hung Wu
Sweet, Justin
Tachna, Ruth C.
Trompeta, Jesus Iglesias
Vetter, Jan
Wald, Michael S.
Warren, William David
Weisberg, Sheila Roseanne
Williams, Jerry John

Colorado

Blackstone, Sandra Lee
Caplan, Gerald A.
Chestnutt, Ellen Joanne
Hoffman, Daniel S.
Meyer, Christopher Hawkins

Connecticut

Ackerman, Bruce Arnold
Blumberg, Phillip Irvin
Burt, Robert Amsterdam
Clark, Elias
Deutsch, Jan C.
Fiss, Owen M.
Gewirtz, Paul D.
Goldstein, Abraham S.
Hansmann, Henry Baethke
Holder, Angela Roddey
Klevorick, Alvin K.
Kronman, Anthony Townsend
Lipson, Leon
Margulies, Martin B.
Marmor, Theodore Richard
Mashaw, Jerry L.
Reisman, William M.
Rose-Ackerman, Susan
Schatzki, George
Smiddy, Linda O'Riordan
Taub, Sheila Kurzrock
Tilson, John Quillin
Wedgwood, Ruth Glushien
Wilcox, Jamison Van Voorhees
Winter, Ralph Karl
Yandle, Stephen Thomas

Delaware

Munneke, Gary Arthur
Nachmias, Carolyn Sharenow
Ott, William Griffith

District of Columbia

Aaronson, David Ernest
Barron, Jerome Aure
Becker, Fred Reinhardt, Jr.
Berry, Mary Frances
Berwick, Philip Cregar
Bloch, Susan Low
Brown, James Milton
Chambers, Charles MacKay
Dinerstein, Robert David
Donegan, Charles Edward
Everett, Robinson Oscar
Ferman, Irving
Green, Paul Andrew
Leon, Richard John
Levin, Betsy
McGuire, Patricia A.
McNeill, John Henderson
Mullenix, Linda Susan
Murphy, Marcia Gaughan
Myren, Richard Albert
Noone, Michael F., Jr.
Oakley, Robert Louis
Provost, James H(arrison)
Renfro, William Leonard
Robbins, Ira Paul
Rubenstein, Richard Edward
Rubin, Kenneth Allen
Sargentich, Thomas Oliver
Simon, Samuel Alan
Smith, George Patrick, II
Stern, Samuel Alan
Vaughn, Robert Gene
Zenoff, Elyce Hope
Zimmerly, James Gregory

Florida

Anderson, Terence James
Armstrong, Suzanne Rae
Bonham-Yeaman, Doria
Burris, Johnny Clark
Coletta, Raymond Robert
Efron, Muriel Cohen
Henn, Harry George
Jacob, Bruce Robert
Joseph, Paul R.
McGovern, Peter John
McHugh, William F.
Messing, Howard Robert
Mofsky, James Steffan
Montante, Philip Joseph, Jr.

Moreno, Fernando
Oliva, Robert Rogelio
Sarkis, Frederick Derr
Stern, Duke Nordlinger
Swan, George Steven
Swygert, Michael Irven
White, Stephen Richard
Winter, Steven Lawrence
Wolfe, Bardie Clinton, Jr.

Georgia

Beaird, James Ralph
Blumoff, Theodore Yale
Buergenthal, Thomas
Fischer, David Jon
Garland, John Louis, Sr.
Hogue, L(ouis) Lynn
Marvin, Charles Arthur
Ordover, Abraham Philip
Voynich, John Joseph

Hawaii

Barkai, John Lee
Bloede, Victor Carl

Idaho

Gallant, Kenneth Stuart
Vincenti, Sheldon Arnold

Illinois

Ashman, Allan
Atkinson, Jeff John Frederick
Bator, Paul Michael
Beckstrom, John H.
Bennett, Robert William
Beschle, Donald L.
Blum, Walter J.
Clark, Natalie Loder
Closen, Michael Lee
Collens, Lewis Morton
Connelly, P. Kevin
Cosgrave, Carmel M.
Decker, John Francis
Draznin, Anne L.
Elwin, James William, Jr.
Epstein, Richard A.
Geraghty, Thomas F.
Goldberg, Stephen B.
Gordon, Irving A.
Grossman, George Stefan
Hablutzel, Nancy Zimmerman
Hablutzel, Philip Norman
Haddad, James Brian
Harrison, Keith Michaele
Hartman, Marshall J.
Heinz, John Peter
Henning, Joel Frank
Howlett, Michael Joseph, Jr.
Hutchinson, Dennis James
Kearley, Timothy G.
Kindt, John Warren
Kurland, Philip B.
Landes, William M.
Liljequist, Jon Leon
Lucas, Jo Desha
MacPhail, Douglas Francis
Merrill, Thomas Wendell
Morris, Norval
Nagel, Stuart S.
Netsch, Dawn Clark
Palm, Gary Howard
Parente, James Joseph
Postlewaite, Philip Frederick
Presser, Stephen Bruce
Rahl, James Andrew
Ream, Davidson
Reeder, Robert Harry
Reese, Harry Browne
Rodenberg, George William, Jr.
Rooney, Michael James
Rose, Carol Marguerite
Rosenblum, Victor Gregory
Rubinowitz, Leonard S.
Schaeffer, Shirley Ann
Scheller, Arthur Martin, Jr.
Shapo, Helene S.
Shapo, Marshall Schambelan
Smith, Len Young
Speidel, Richard Eli
Steinman, Joan Ellen
Stone, Geoffrey R.
Stone, Victor J.
Victor, Michael Gary
Waltz, Jon Richard

Indiana

Ehrlich, Thomas
Hewitt, John David
Palmer, Judith Grace
Pellicciotti, Joseph Michael
Persyn, Mary Geraldine
Risacher, Martin Eugene
Scaletta, Phillip Jasper
Shreve, Gene Russell
White, James Patrick
Woodard, Harold Raymond

Iowa

Shane, Peter Milo
Widiss, Alan I.

Kansas

Davis, Michael James
Griffin, Ronald Charles
Killough, Howard Patrick, Jr.
Schanck, Peter Carr

Kentucky

Eades, Ronald Wayne
Isaac, Teresa Ann
Jones, William Rex
Levy, Charlotte Lois
McMahon, Martin James, Jr.
Neuber, Frank William, Jr.
Schneider, Frederick Richard
Vish, Donald H.

Louisiana

Burns, Premila Irene
Gruning, David William
Knutzen, Raymond Edward
Lamonica, P(aul) Raymond
Palmer, Vernon Valentine

Rudolph, Richard
Uddo, Basile Joseph
Vitiello, Michael

Maine

Webster, Peter Bridgman

Maryland

Bernard, Hugh Y(ancey), Jr.
Cox, Irvin Edmond
Duckett, Warren Bird, Jr.
Evelius, John Charles
Gray, Oscar Shalom
Levin, Marshall Abbott
McLain, Susan Lynn
Ruark, Davis Rutherford
Shannonhouse, Royal Graham, III

Massachusetts

Andrews, William Dorey
Bell, Derrick Albert
Bellow, Gary
Clark, Robert Charles
Cleary, Philip Edward
Coquillette, Daniel Robert
Dershowitz, Alan Morton
Donahue, Charles, Jr.
Fischer, Thomas Covell
Freeman, Florence Eleanor
Frug, Gerald E.
Garabedian, Charles Bagdasar
Goldfarb, Phyllis
Herwitz, David Richard
Huber, Richard Gregory
Jones, Michael Earl
Kalodner, Howard Isaiah
Katsh, M. Ethan
Kindregan, Charles Peter
Kravetz, David Hubert
Liebman, Lance Malcolm
Mansfield, John H.
Miles, Judith Ellen
Miller, Arthur Raphael
Nicholson, Francis Joseph
O'Connor, James Michael
Oldman, Oliver
Parker, Richard Davies
Pepyne, Edward Walter
Perlin, Marc Gerald
Platt, Rutherford Hayes, Jr.
Ryan, James Frederick
Salacuse, Jeswald William
Sander, Frank Ernest Arnold
Saradjian, Martin Luther
Sargentich, Lewis D.
Scott, Hal S.
Shapiro, David Louis
Solk, Gerald
Spencer, Patti S.
Steelman, David Carl
Steiner, Henry J.
Stewart, Richard Burleson
Taylor, John Anthony
von Mehren, Arthur Taylor
Weinstein, Lewis H.
Wolfman, Bernard

Michigan

Allen, Layman Edward
Anderson, Austin Gothard
Calkins, Stephen
Cameron, John Gray, Jr.
Cooper, Edward Hayes
Cunningham, Roger A.
Estep, Samuel D.
Fitzgerald, John Warner
Gray, Whitmore
Green, Thomas Andrew
Haggerty, William Francis
Holman, Charles F(redrick), III
Krier, James Edward
Lashbrooke, Elvin Carroll, Jr.
Lempert, Richard Owen
Palincsar, John Ernest
Pierce, William James
Regan, Donald H.
Sandalow, Terrance
Solomon, Mark Raymond
Soper, E. Phillip
Steeno, David Lawrence
Steiner, Peter Otto
Victor, Richard Steven
Watson, Andrew Samuel
Westen, Peter
White, James Boyd

Minnesota

Johnson, Michael Almer
Radmer, Michael John
Rasicot, James Frederick

Mississippi

Fenton, Howard Nathan, III
Southwick, Leslie Harburd
West, Carol Catherine

Missouri

Chackes, Kenneth Michael
Devine, James Richard
Dye, David Alan
Mahaffey, George H.
McClellan, Janet Elaine
Popper, Robert
Reams, Bernard Dinsmore, Jr.
Simon, Roy D., Jr.
Wyrsch, James Robert

Montana

Bahls, Steven Carl
Mudd, John O.

Nebraska

Shkolnick, Rodney

Nevada

Stumpf, Felix Franklin

New Jersey

Boskey, James Bernard
Flammer, George Herbert
Garth, Leonard I.
Kerman, Lewis H.

Lynch, Joseph Martin
Marotta, James Steven
Mullins, Margaret-Ann Frances
Raveson, Louis Sheppard
Risinger, D. Michael
Schmoll, Harry F., Jr.
Simmons, Peter
Warmington, Robert Anthony

New Mexico

Branch, James Alexander, Jr.

New York

Amhowitz, Harris J.
Barsamian, J(ohn) Albert
Baum, Joseph Thomas
Bavero, Ronald Joseph
Belsky, Martin Henry
Berger, Curtis Jay
Bergman, Bruce Jeffrey
Bermann, George Alan
Birnbaum, Sheila L.
Brooks, George Andrew
Calamari, Joseph August
Carlisle, Jay Charles, II
Christensen, Craig Wane
Clermont, Kevin Michael
Cramton, Roger Conant
Curtiss, Willis David
Dorsen, Norman
Edgar, Harold S. H.
Eustice, James Samuel
Evan, Charles
Fink, Norman Stiles
Garro, Alejandro Miguel
Glasser, Israel Leo
Grad, Frank Paul
Graham, Arnold Harold
Graham, Jul Eliot
Greenberg, Ronald David
Hagmeir, Thomas Edmiston
Hammond, Jane Laura
Hazard, John Newbold
Henkin, Louis
Hilts, Earl T.
Hoover, James Lloyd
Hutter, Robert Grant
Jensen, J. Christopher
Jordan, Daniel Patrick, Jr.
Katz, Stanley Nider
Kernochan, John Marshall
Kissane, Thomas
Korn, Harold Leon
Kurland, Paul C.
Leonard, Arthur Sherman
Liuzzo, Anthony L.
Loffman, Leslie Howard
Mc Kay, Robert Budge
Meltzer, Sanford
Moses, Mary Helen
Murphy, Gavin Palmer
Nebush, Frank John, Jr.
Northrop, Cynthia Ellen
Olsson, Harry Rudolph, Jr.
Parker, Kellis E.
Patte, George David, Jr.
Pogrebin, Bertrand B.
Price, Monroe Edwin
Robbins, Sara Ellen
Roberts, E. F.
Robinson, Nicholas Adams
Roseman, Arnold David
Rosenberg, Maurice
Rosenfeld, Michel
Rosenthal, Albert Joseph
Rossi, Faust F.
Schachter, Oscar
Scheinkman, Alan David
Schwarcz, Steven Lance
Schwartzman, Jack
Seidel, Selvyn
Shapiro, Irving
Siegel, Stanley
Simson, Gary Joseph
Sinnott, John Patrick
Stone, Kathleen Gale
Stone, Richard B.
Strauss, Peter L(ester)
Teclaff, Ludwik Andrzej
Thoron, Gray
Triffin, Nicholas
Ward, Ettie
White, Renee Allyn
Wiacek, Bruce Edward
Wright, Douglas Rich
Zaretsky, Barry Lewis

North Carolina

Christie, George Custis
Cone, Lorynn Adderholdt
Cox, James D.
Dellinger, Walter Estes, III
Demott, Deborah Ann
Foster, Charles Allen
Gann, Pamela Brooks
Garland, James Boyce
Havighurst, Clark Canfield
Hutchins, Terry Richard
Lefstein, Norman
Loeb, Ben Fohl, Jr.
Luney, Percy Robert, Jr.
Mann, Richard Allan
Orth, John Victor
Paschal, Joel Francis
Robertson, Horace Bascomb, Jr.
Rowe, Thomas Dudley, Jr.
Schmalbeck, Richard Louis
Shimm, Melvin G.
Sparks, Bertel Milas
Switzer, Robert Harold
Walker, George Kontz
Wilson, LeVon Edward

North Dakota

Spain, Larry Robert
Vickrey, Barry Roland

Ohio

Besser, Howard Russell
Blackburn, John D(avid)
Browne, John Patrick
Cook, Robert Nevin
Davis, Frederick Benjamin
Durham, James Geoffrey
George, Joyce Jackson

Gerhart, Peter Milton
Giannelli, Paul Clark
Goostree, Robert Edward
Greenbaum, Arthur Franklin
Hagel, Thomas Leo
Hanson, Eugene Nelson
Lobenhofer, Louis Fred
Lynn, Arthur Dellert, Jr.
Mann, Richard Lynn
Mc Elhaney, James Willson
Meyers, Karen Diane
Peltier, Linda Jeanne
Purdy, Roger Daniel
Riley, Paul E.
Sites, Richard Loren
Smith, Timothy Daly
Sogg, Wilton Sherman
Sprang, Kenneth Allyn
Tillery, Dwight
Veltri, Stephen Charles
Watts, Barbara Gayle
Werber, Stephen Jay

Oklahoma

Tuttle, Roger Lewis

Oregon

Barilla, Frank (Rocky)
Funk, William F.
Griffith, Stephen Loyal

Pennsylvania

Aronstein, Martin Joseph
Bainbridge, John Seaman
Beer, Lawrence Ward
Benn, Sara Kitchen
Carter, Daniel Paul
Cimini, Joseph Fedele
Fineman, S. David
Follows, Jill Marilyn
Friedrichs, David O.
Gerstenhaber, Murray
Goodman, Frank I.
Gorman, Robert A.
Granat, Richard Stuart
Haddon, Phoebe Anniese
Hudiak, David Michael
Jones, David Arthur
Kalis, Peter John
Lally-Green, Maureen Ellen
Laub, George Cooley
Leech, Noyes Elwood
Madeira, David Beckman
Meisel, Alan
Mooney, Charles W., Jr.
Murphy, John Francis
Nasri, William Zaki
Pierce, George Carter
Rosen, Cathryn Jo
Rosenblum, Glenn Fredrick
Sloane, William Martin
Strazzella, James Anthony
Summers, Clyde Wilson
Wecht, Cyril Harrison
White, Thomas Owen
Woodward, William John, Jr.
Zanolli, Steve (William)
Zimmer, Bruce Irwin
Zimmerman, Dona Hope

Rhode Island

Davenport, Teresa Joanna
Terry, Brian Stephen

South Carolina

Dunbar, James V., Jr.
Haimbaugh, George Dow, Jr.
Lightsey, Harry McKinley, Jr.
Watson, Patricia Seets
Wedlock, Eldon Dyment, Jr.

South Dakota

LaFave, LeAnn Larson

Tennessee

Bennett, Horace Michael
Blumstein, James Franklin
Coffman, Claude T.
Covington, Robert Newman
Hookanson, Kathryn
Kavass, Igor Ivar
Langevoort, Donald Carl
Levinson, L(eslie) Harold
Soderquist, Larry Dean
Wade, John Webster

Texas

Allison, John Robert
Baker, Thomas Eugene
Ball, Craig Douglas
Borgeson, Earl Charles
Boyd, Roland
Brown, William Alley
Castaño, Sylvia Elizabeth
Caudill, David Stanley
Christianson, James Milton
Douglas, James Matthew
Figari, Ernest Emil, Jr.
Gaines, Sanford Ervin
Getman, Julius Gerson
Jentz, Gaylord Adair
Johnson, Vincent Robert
Jones, Albert Pearson
Knauss, Robert Lynn
Laycock, Harold Douglas
Miller, Jack Burleson
Muster, Douglas Frederick
Palmer, Randall Parham, III
Parkin-Speer, Diane
Pratt, John Edward
Reamey, Gerald S.
Roberts, Bonita Koehler
Schlueter, David Arnold
Schuwerk, Robert Paul
Stovall, Thomas J., Jr.
Stowe, Charles Robinson Beecher
Sutton, John F., Jr.
Sylvester, Jon Howard
Traver, Alfred Ellis, Jr.
Wendorf, Hulen Dee
Wright, Charles Alan

Utah

Fleming, J. Clifton, Jr.
Hawkins, Carl S.
McConkie, Oscar Walter

Vermont

Bischoff, Ralph Frederic
Chase, Jonathon B.
Doria, Anthony Notarnicola
Rath, David

Virginia

Aronin, Louis
Gawalt, Gerard W(ilfred)
Jensen, Walter Edward, Jr.
Lederer, Fredric Ira
Mannix, Charles Raymond
Mulligan, Jennifer
Murphy, Nina Rebecca
Shepherd, Robert Edward, Jr.
Smail, Laurence Mitchell
Spong, William Belser, Jr.
Theberge, Norman Bartlett
Williams, Marcus Doyle

Washington

Bailey, William Scherer
Cross, Harry Maybury
Murray, James Michael
Newcity, Michael Albert
Peterson, Ronald Arthur
Pilat, Michael Joseph
Steele, Anita (Margaret Anne Martin)

West Virginia

Lewin, Jeff Lee
Selinger, Carl M.

Wisconsin

Baldwin, Gordon Brewster
Davis, Kenneth Boone, Jr.
Foster, George William, Jr.
Gass, James Ric
Jones, James Edward, Jr.
Kircher, John Joseph
Moser, William R.
Raushenbush, Walter Brandeis
Schacherl, Anne Washechek
Shapiro, Robyn Sue
Van Buren, David Paul
Wetzel, Volker Knoppke

Wyoming

Gillum, Forrest Earl
Maxfield, Peter C.
Selig, Joel Louis

TERRITORIES OF THE UNITED STATES

Puerto Rico

Cuprill, Charles

ENGLAND

Wohl, James Paul

ADDRESS UNPUBLISHED

Bernard, Pamela Jenks
Damaska, Mirjan Radovan
Dratler, Jay, Jr.
Eovaldi, Thomas L.
Flamm, Martin Benjamin
Lichter-Heath, Laurie Jean
Lungren, John Howard
Marks, Leon
McFarland, Anne Southworth
Pendergrass, John Ambrose
Pooley, Beverley John
Simon, Richard Hege
Tancredi, Laurence Richard

EMINENT DOMAIN. See Condemnation.

ENERGY, FERC PRACTICE

UNITED STATES

Alabama

Lacy, Alexander Shelton

California

Gardiner, Stuart Korson
Hanzlik, Rayburn DeMara
McLennan, Robert Bruce
Minich, Mark Andrew
Norris, Cynthia Ann

Colorado

Hawley, Robert Cross
Ramsey, John Arthur

Connecticut

Golden, Lawrence James

District of Columbia

Bachman, Kenneth Leroy, Jr.
Baller, James
Bardin, David J.
Batla, Raymond John, Jr.
Baynard, Ernest Cornish, III
Bell, James Frederick
Berger, Melvin Gerald
Berner, Frederic George, Jr.
Betts, Kirk Howard
Boland, Christopher Thomas, II
Brown, Thomas Philip, III
Bruder, George Frederick
Calderwood, James Albert
Chabot, Philip Louis, Jr.
Darling, Charles M., IV
Drennan, D. Jane
Elrod, Eugene Richard
Fels, Nicholas Wolff
Fishman, Charles Louis

Gallagher, Walter Edward
Gibson, Joseph Lee
Gilliam, Carroll Lewis
Grammer, Elisa Joan
Grenier, Edward Joseph, Jr.
Griff, Marvin T.
Herman, Stephen Allen
Hoecker, James John
Hollis, Sheila Slocum
Howard, Glen Scott
Hughes, John David
Jones, Keith Alden
Journey, Drexel Dahlke
Kalish, Steven Joseph
Kilcarr, Andrew Joseph
Kissel, Peter Charles
Lange, William Michael
Lichtenberg, J(oan) Cathy
Lobel, Martin
Loeffler, Robert Hugh
Mapes, William Rodgers, Jr.
Matt, Peter Kent
McBride, Michael Flynn
McDiarmid, Robert Campbell
McKinney, James DeVaine, Jr.
Miller, John T., Jr.
Miller, Richard William, Jr.
Moler, Elizabeth Anne
Moore, Margaret Ann
Nordlinger, Douglas Edward
Norton, Floyd Ligon, IV
O'Neill, Brian Dennis
Pedersen, Norman A.
Petrash, Jeffrey Michael
Pierson, W. DeVier
Quint, Arnold Harris
Rexinger, Allan Robert
Shibley, Raymond Nadeem
Simons, Morton Leonard
Spiegel, George
Stuntz, Linda Gillespie
Sweeney, Kevin Michael
Swiger, Michael Andre
Wagner, Curtis Lee, Jr.
Walker, Mary Ann
Wallace, Arch Lee

Florida

Lester, Paul Arthur
Zambo, Richard Alan

Georgia

Strassner, Kenneth Allen

Illinois

Adair, Wendell Hinton, Jr.
Emerson, William Harry
Fazio, Peter Victor, Jr.

Iowa

Low, Susan A.
Smith, William Herbert, Jr

Kansas

Lefebvre, David Marshall

Kentucky

Cocklin, Kim Roland
Hetman, Nicholas Wayne

Louisiana

Burlingame, James Montgomery
Hargrove, Robert Clyde
Keithley, Bradford Gene
Wilhelm, Jack Morton
Wright, Paul William

Maryland

Kimball, Sherman Paul
Wolfe, J. Thomas

Michigan

Balagna, Steven David
Pestle, John William

Missouri

Bates, William Hubert (Bert)
Hackmann, Frank H(enry)

Nebraska

Dessonville, Loren Edward

New Hampshire

Cronmiller, Thomas Bernard

New Mexico

Tully, Richard T. C.

New York

Bader, Albert Xavier, Jr.
Bergen, G. S. Peter
Bernstein, Robert Bruce
Hall, Robert Turnbull, III
Hope, Theodore Sherwood, Jr.
Jibilian, Gerald Arsen
Poth, Harry Augustus, Jr.
Russell, Edwin Fortune

North Carolina

Lansche, John Elmer

North Dakota

Sandstrom, Dale Vernon

Ohio

Battaglia, Timothy Joseph
Ruxin, Paul Theodore
Van Heyde, G. James

Oklahoma

Cates, Jennifer Ann
Dowd, William Timothy
Legg, William Jefferson
Towery, Curtis Kent
Williamson, Walter Bland

Oregon

Baxendale, James Charles Lewis

Glick, Richard Myron
Larson, John Francis

Pennsylvania

Hall, Walter Randall, II
Klodowski, Amy Martha Auslander
Linn, Michael Charles
Pompo, Vincent Matthew
Weston, R. Timothy
Wiegand, Bruce
Yarmey, Richard Andrew

Texas

Andrews, Bolivar Coleman, Jr.
Armour, James Lott
Berndt, Karen Ann
Boss, Steven Sprague
Cassin, William Bourke
Conine, Gary Bainard
Cross, Janis Alexander
Greenspan, Abraham Alcon
Jackson, Randall Calvin
Kennedy, John Edward
May, Henry S., Jr.
McNamara, Martin Burr
Orn, Clayton Lincoln
Pannill, William Presley
Pierce, Richard James, Jr.
Soliz, Joseph Guy
Stevens, Jeron Lynn
Strohl, Paul E.
Vickrey, Jack
Webb, Robert Allen

Utah

Edwards, Helen Jex

Virginia

Gary, Richard David
Hulvey, Craig Wallace
Nassikas, John Nicholas
Smoots, Carol Anne

Washington

Campbell, Robert Hedgcock
Redman, Eric

ADDRESS UNPUBLISHED

Clark, Anja Maria
George, Fredric Joel

ENERGY, NUCLEAR POWER

UNITED STATES

California

McGuinn, John Francis
Restrick, John Knight
Shollenberger, Lewis Winnbert, Jr.

District of Columbia

Burns, Stephen Gilbert
Cutchin, James McKenney, IV
Fishman, Charles Louis
Frye, John H., III
Jones, Bradley Wayne
Klucsik, John Francis
Kraemer, Jay R.
McBride, Michael Flynn
Olmstead, William J.
Patton, Thomas Earl
Rader, Robert Michael
Swiger, Michael Andre
Trosten, Leonard Morse
Williams, Stephen Fain

Florida

Rubinstein, Louis Baruch

Georgia

Fleming, Julian Denver, Jr.

Illinois

Haubold, Samuel Allen
Hoff, William Bruce, Jr.
Nyeste, James Thomas
Rooney, Matthew A.

Kansas

Mingle, John Orville

Louisiana

Burlingame, James Montgomery

Maryland

Doub, William Offutt
Wolfe, J. Thomas

Massachusetts

Casson, Richard Frederick
Dignan, Thomas Gregory, Jr.
Meyer, Michael Broeker

Michigan

Melia, James Patrick
Pestle, John William
Scudi, Morgan John Clift

Minnesota

Miranda, Thom Bernard

Missouri

Young, Mary Garr

Nebraska

McClure, John Campbell

New Jersey

Cino, Vincent Alphonse

New Mexico

Lopez, Owen Michael

New York

Bergen, G. S. Peter
Cassan, Vito J.
Earley, Anthony Francis, Jr.
Eldridge, Douglas Alan
England, William Thomas
Hayes, Gerald Joseph
Kirschbaum, Myron
Pikus, David Heller

North Carolina

Carrow, Harvey Hill, Jr.
Roach, Edgar Mayo, Jr.

Ohio

Goldberg, Steven Charles
Migden-Ostrander, Janine Lee

Pennsylvania

Gerjuoy, Edward
Hall, Walter Randall, II
Hickel, Gerard Frederick
Stivison, David Vaughn

South Carolina

Bergholz, Warren Ernest, Jr.

Tennessee

Bates, Albert Kealiinui

Texas

McRae, Hamilton Eugene, Jr.
Soliz, Joseph Guy
Tartt, Blake
Webb, Robert Allen

Virginia

Freeman, George Clemon, Jr.
Reveley, Walter Taylor, III
Rolfe, Robert Martin

ADDRESS UNPUBLISHED

Buffington, John Victor

ENERGY, OIL AND GAS LEASING

UNITED STATES

Alabama

Ely, Bruce Peter
Lyons, George Sage
Otts, Lee MacMillan

Alaska

Gardner, Ray Dean, Jr.
Linxwiler, James David
Sedwick, John Weeter

Arkansas

Spencer, James Victor, III
Thrailkill, Daniel B.
Unger, John William, Jr.
Wright, Susan Webber
Wynne, William Joseph

California

Bond, George Cline
Burden, James Ewers
Day, James McAdam, Jr.
Hieronymus, Edward Whittlesey
Hinman, Harvey DeForest
Holden, Charles St. George
Kostant, Ralph Bennett
Krueger, Robert Blair
Loring, David Charles
Norris, Cynthia Ann
Shannon, Malcolm Lloyd, Jr.
Shortz, Richard Alan
Tornstrom, Robert Ernest
Yarema, Geoffrey Steven

Colorado

Abbott, Keith Eugene
Barnthouse, William Joseph
Blackstone, Sandra Lee
Boigon, Howard Lawrence
Elliott, Darrell Stanley
Gates, Stephen Frye
Hampton, Clyde Robert
Hawley, Robert Cross
Holmes, Charles Everett
Hook, Mary Julia
Irwin, R. Robert
Kaup, Daniel John
Kimmell, Thomas J.
Lavenhar, Jeffrey Drew
LeSatz, Stephen, Jr.
Mandell-Rice, Bonnie Starr
Martz, Clyde Ollen
McMichael, Donald Earl
Nakarado, Gary Lee
Olson, Ronald Keith
Pautsch, Richard Joseph
Rossi, Ronald Gregory
Sullivan, Stephen Joseph
Sumners, William Glenn, Jr.
Thompson, Stephen Michael
Tippit, John Harlow
Tucker, William E.
Wilkie, Barry Lynn

District of Columbia

Batla, Raymond John, Jr.
Casson, Joseph Edward
Craft, Winfred Owens, Jr.
Habicht, Frank Henry, II
Quarles, Steven Princeton
Whitfield, Milton Bailey
Williams, Stephen Fain

Florida

Blackwell, William Leggett
Ozark, Damian Michael

Georgia

Grove, Russell Sinclair, Jr.

Illinois

Cascino, Anthony Elmo, Jr.
Dieker, James William
Frick, Robert Hathaway
Gavin, William Patrick
Helmholz, R. H.
Jersild, Thomas Nielsen
Mason, Peter Ian
Morris, James W.
Stout, James Dudley

Indiana

Bach, Steve Crawford

Kansas

Black, John Victor
Concannon, Don Owen
DeLaTorre, Phillip Eugene
Hathaway, Gary Ray
Lowe, Roy Goins
McPherson, Brock Richard
Nordling, Bernard Erick
Stull, Gordon Bruce
Toland, Stanley E.

Kentucky

Hetman, Nicholas Wayne
Hogg, Stephen Leslie
Hutchinson, Mark Randall
Kasacavage, Kenneth Stephen
Massengale, Roger Lee
Mathison, Harry Lee
Pedley, Lawrence Lindsay
Thomas, Patricia Ann
Vish, Donald H.

Louisiana

Arceneaux, M. Thomas
Burlingame, James Montgomery
Daigle, Patrick Keith
Darden, Marshall Taylor
Duncan, Nora Kathryn
Ellison, David McQuown, Jr.
Ewin, Gordon Overton
Garrett, David Isaiah, Jr.
Hall, Luther Egbert, Jr.
Hargrove, Joseph Leonard, Jr.
Herbert, John Campbell
Johnson, Joseph Clayton, Jr.
Mansfield, James Norman, III
McAdams, Don Randall, Jr.
Morgan, Louis Linton
Mote, Clyde A
Rives, James Davidson, Jr.
St. John, James Berry, Jr.
Smith, Duncan McLaurin, Jr.
Stewart, Melinda Jane
Stockwell, Oliver Perkins
Story, Clement, III
Taylor, John McKowen
Vermillion, John Richard
Weiss, Donald Paul
Wilhelm, Jack Morton
Wilson, Donald Russell
Wolfe, William Milton

Michigan

Deems, Nyal David
Haines, Michael Curtis
Koop, Charles Hubert
McCallum, Albert Donald
Norris, John Hart
Peterson, David Reid
Rosi, Philip Rinaldo
Storey, Scott Alfred

Mississippi

Grower, John Marshall
Hughes, Byron William
Kirkland, Thomas Lee, Jr.
Montjoy, Richard Wilson, II
Polk, Ross B.
Presson, William Russell
Southwick, Leslie Harburd
Thompson, James Grant, III
Ueltschey, Watts Casper

Missouri

Doan, Kirk Hugh
Tockman, Gerald

Nebraska

McCarthy, Patrick James

New Jersey

Croft, John W.

New Mexico

Cox, Lewis Calvin
Gose, Richard Vernie
Hunker, George Henry, Jr.
Lopez, Owen Michael
Losee, Arthur Jarrell
Reagan, Gary Don
Tully, Richard T. C.

New York

Asante, Samuel Kwadwo Boaten
Edgerton, Lynne Todd
Elicker, Gordon Leonard
Fenster, Robert David
Heyer, John Henry, II
Kent, James Ewart
Laurita, Alan John
Militello, Samuel Philip
Miller, Peter Putnam
Stack, Daniel
Svenson, Charles Oscar
Vock, Robert Daniel

North Dakota

Gregg, John Ralph
Kingstad, Timothy Lorens
Wilkes, Richard Clarence

Ohio

Battaglia, Timothy Joseph
Flowers, Michael Edward
Fort, Jeffrey Edward
Lemire, Jerome Albert
Walker, Patricia Ann

Oklahoma

Barnes, Robert Norton
Beech, Johnny Gale
Bell, William Henry
Bryant, Ira Houston, III
Canon, Jack Arthur
Cates, Jennifer Ann
Catron, Gary Wayne
Dale, Douglas Don
Davis, Charles Bishop
Dean, Bill Verlin, Jr.
Decker, Michael Lynn
Dowd, Pamela J. Cuplin
Drake, David Allen
Durham, Ronald Dale
Elias, William Keith
Elsener, G. Dale
Enis, Thomas Joseph
Estill, John Staples, Jr.
Fitzgerald, Tami Lynn
Forsyth, John Emery
Hammer, Bruce Edward
Huff, R. Robert
Huffman, William Hicks
Jones, Kent Leonard
Kallstrom, James David
Kenney, Bruce Allen
Kihle, Donald Arthur
Legg, William Jefferson
Lewis, John Furman
Lyon, Jim Allen
Martin, Gary Duncan
Michalak, William Steven
Mitchell, Alice Schaffer
Murphy, Robert Moore
Musser, R. Clark
Nesbitt, Charles Rudolph
Scribner, Beverly Kinnear
Specht, Randolph Stephen
Spiegelberg, Frank David
Stewart, Robert Desbrow, Jr.
Taylor, Kenneth David
Thompson, Lee Bennett
Towery, Curtis Kent
Tully, Brian Brendan
Turner, Andrew Roland
Verity, George Luther
Williamson, Walter Bland
Williford, John Lea
Young, John Mark

Pennsylvania

Bogutz, Jerome E.
Boswell, William Paret
Duke, Charles Jeffrey
Linn, Michael Charles
Thomas, Robert Allen
Wallace, Christopher Baird
Walsh, Donald Peter
Wiegand, Bruce

South Dakota

Bennett, Donn
Graslie, Thomas Eric

Tennessee

McCoy, Thomas Raymond

Texas

Albright, William James
Anders, Milton Howard
Anderson, Doris Ehlinger
Armour, James Lott
Baber, Wilbur H., Jr.
Barlow, Donald Eugene
Batson, David Warren
Berger, Howard Charles
Betow, Joel Thomas
Blachly, Jack Lee
Black, William Earl
Boze, Uriele L.
Brown, Michael Lance
Brundrett, George L(ee), Jr.
Carnes, Lamar
Carroll, James Vincent, III
Chappell, Clovis Gillham, Jr.
Clark, Pat English
Cline, Lee Williamson
Cobb, Sam Burton, Jr.
Coffield, Conrad Eugene
Collins, Kyle Boyd
Conine, Gary Bainard
Cosgrove, Ritamae Gober
Crump, Thomas Richard
Curry, Donald Robert
Duenser, Ruth Edwards
Edmonds, Thomas Leon
Fant, Douglas Vernon
Farnsworth, T Brooke
Feldwisch, David Lewis
Flynn, Rory Christopher
Fort, D. Stephen
Fountain, Kenneth Paul
Gandy, Dean Murray
Glass, John D., Jr.
Glazier, Kenneth Charles
Godfrey, Cullen Michael
Graham, Seldon Bain, Jr.
Harrison, Clarence Buford, Jr.
Head, Hayden Wilson
Hinton, Quincy Thomas, Jr.
Hoag, Mary Moore
Hunter, Emmett Marshall
Irvin, Charles Leslie
Kawaguchi, Meredith Ferguson
Kendall, William Theodore
King, C. Glyn
Kinnan, David E.
Kirk, John Robert, Jr.
Kittler, Leslie Howard
Labay, Eugene Benedict
LaGrone, William Taylor
Langston, Homer Anthony, Jr.
LaSalle, Lowell LeRoy
Leaverton, Mark Kane
Lionberger, Richard Lee
Lynch, Thomas Wimp
MacNaughton, William Alexander
Masters, Claude Bivin
McCall, David Blair
McCoy, Reagan Scott
McElwrath, Michael Rogers
McGinnis, Robert Campbell
McGreevy, Terrence Gerard
McKay, Robert Connally
McNamara, Martin Burr

McNeil, Buck W.
McPhail, Robert Wilson
Mittenthal, Freeman Lee
Moore, Lawrence Jack
Morrison, Jeanne Lunsford
Morton, Thomas Edward, Jr.
Moss, Joe Albaugh
Muzzy, Gray Howard
Nesbitt, Frank Wilbur
Nolan, Jenelle White
Omer, Michael Lee
Orn, Clayton Lincoln
Patman, Philip Franklin
Patterson, Donald Ross
Pennebaker, Susan McClimans
Perry, William Shelbern
Pierce, Richard James, Jr.
Pope, David Bruce
Pope, Joseph Ronald
Porter, Charles Raleigh, Jr.
Purvis, Daniel Burford
Ray, Cread L., Jr.
Reaser, Vernon Neal, Jr.
Reed, Harry Lowe
Rice, Ben Herbert, III
Rochelle, Williams Jennings, Jr.
Rowan, Justin Michael
Rowland, Sam E.
Schmidt, Michael Bruce
Scott, John Roland
Sealy, Tom
Seaman, Stephen Henry
Shirley, Robert Preston
Smart, James Hudson
Smith, James Bonner
Smith, William Randolph
Soliz, Joseph Guy
Steele, Richard Parks
Stoltz, Michael Rae
Strawn, James Roy
Strohl, Paul E.
Sullenbarger, Daniel James
Taylor, Thomas Alan
Thomas, Patrick Powers
Thompson, Peter Rule
Timmons, Patrick Francis, Jr.
Townes, Edgar Eggleston, Jr.
Wallace, William Farrier, Jr.
Warford, Tommy Gene
Warnock, Curtlon Lee
Watson, Cary Stephen
Weaver, Jacqueline Lang
Wheat, Thomas Allen
Whitten, C. G.
Whitworth, H. Philip, Jr.
Wilkins, Jerry Lynn
Woodward, Marion Kenneth

Utah
Buffmire, Andrew Wallace
Gill, Ruland J., Jr.
Groussman, Raymond G.
Lewis, Leonard J.
Melich, Mitchell
Monson, Thomas Lee
Pruitt, Robert Grady, Jr.
Stirba, Anne Melinda Morr
Vernon, Robert Gerard

Virginia
Goolrick, Robert Mason
Grant, Charles Randall, Jr.
Kleiler, James Robert
Wright, Blandin James

West Virginia
Crim, Joseph Calvin
Grottendieck, William Joseph, III
Reed, James Wilson

Wyoming
Durham, Harry Blaine, III
Klus, Charles Robert, Jr.
Riggs, Dan Britt
Webster, C. Edward, II
Williams, Houston Garvin

CANADA

Nova Scotia
Dickey, John Horace

ENGLAND
Wiese, Larry Clevenger

ADDRESS UNPUBLISHED
Campbell, John Timothy
Hurst, Ernest Connor
Ice, Clarence Frederick
Learned, James Roy
Lungren, John Howard
McKay, David Lawrence
Quigley, Leonard Vincent
Rutland, John Dudley
Safi, Deborah Cavazos
Shambaugh, Stephen Ward
Swift, Aubrey Earl
Wright, Frances Mina Johnson

ENTERTAINMENT

UNITED STATES

Alabama
Mandell, Howard Allyn

California
Biederman, Donald Ellis
Boelter, Allen Boyd
Bower, Paul George
Branca, John Gregory
Brown, Marc Laurence
Cochran, Adam
Coleman, Richard Michael
Demoff, Marvin Alan
Denman, Alexandra
Diamond, Stanley Jay
Dougherty, F. Jay
Glenn, Everett Lamar
Greenfield, Larry Stuart
Greenstein, Robert Stanley
Greenwood, Steven Matlin
Howard, John Wayne
Jelin, Beth Maloney
Joyce, Stephen Michael
Kant, Harold Sanford
Klein, Alan Richard
Kotler, Richard Lee
Kuklin, Jeffrey Peter
Levine, Jerome Lester
Lowy, Steven Robert
Lurvey, Ira Harold
Matter, Bruce E.
McKechnie, C. Logan
McPherson, Edwin Francis
Nuanes, John Gilbert
Overton, John Blair
Palazzo, Robert P.
Pizzulli, Francis Cosmo Joseph
Ramer, Bruce M.
Roberts, Virgil Patrick
Schiff, Gunther Hans
Schreiber, James Phillip
Schwartz, Alan Uriel
Seltzer, Leon Eugene
Shaw, William Albert
Steinberger, Jeffrey Wayne
Streicker, Richard Daniel
Thompson, Larry Angelo
van de Bunt, Dirk Wouter
Wallenstein, Raymond
Winnick, Helene Ann

Colorado
Elliott, Darrell Stanley

Connecticut
Lupica, Joseph Richard
Russ, Lawrence
Sahl, John Patrick

District of Columbia
Cooper, Patricia Jacqueline
Czarra, Edgar F., Jr.
Davidson, Tom William
Gittens, James P.
Goldson, Amy Robertson
Kaufman, Joshua Jacob
May, Randolph Joseph
Violante, Joseph Anthony

Florida
Bellak, Richard Charles
Falk, Victor S., III
Hest, Bruce Henry
Lax, Michael H.
Sisco, Thomas Edward, II
Witlin, Barry Ethan

Georgia
Cohen, Darryl Brandt
Gignilliat, William Robert, III
Lewis, H(enry) Worthington
Phillips, Charles Patrick
Price, Terry
Zolke, Scott Bryan

Illinois
Bassitt, Janet Louise
Besson, Paul Smith
Ephraim, Donald Morley
Fifer, Samuel
Fritz Cohn, Loreli
Goldstein, Richard M.
Hoekstra, Kathlyn B.
Juettner, Paul Gerard
Kopp, Frederick Philip
Lauderdale, Katherine Sue
Maher, David Willard
Saltiel, David Michael
Saunders, Lonna Jeanne

Indiana
Elberger, Ronald Edward
McKeon, Thomas Joseph

Kentucky
Bardenwerper, William Burr

Louisiana
Miller, Patrick Lynn
Pierce, James Winston, Jr.
Price, Lionel Franklin

Maryland
Astrachan, James Barry
Parsky, Keith Alan

Massachusetts
Bernfeld, Jeffrey Alan
Fischer, Mark Alan
Lang, Scott Wesley
Margolis, Jonathan J.
Pittas, Sydelle
Segal, Robert Mandal
Wolfson, Jeffrey Steven

Michigan
Anderson, Thomas Ernest
Keller, Gerald Douglas
Lloyd, Leona Loretta
Malone, Daniel Patrick
Novak, Michael Alan
Shakoor, Adam Adib
Spicer, S(amuel) Gary
Spivak, Peter Beeching

Minnesota
Bard, Stephen Allan

Missouri
Scott, Robert Gene
Wallace, Robert E.

Nebraska
Ellis, Ronnie Gene
Vacanti, Alfred Charles, Jr.

Nevada
Tratos, Mark George

New Jersey
Jacobs, Joseph James
Marotta, James Steven

New Mexico
Hanna, Robert Cecil
Kennedy, Roderick Thomas

New York
Angel, Dennis
Barandes, Robert
Breglio, John F.
Brown, Ronald Wellington
Cole, Richard Charles
Condliffe, David Charles
Conway, Andrew Wayne
Cooke, George Alexander, Jr.
Cowan, Philip Matthew
Curtis, Frank R.
Daly, Joan Chilton
DeBaets, Timothy Joseph
Dowling, William Francis
Dunn, William David
Eisenberg-Mellen, Viviane
Farrell, Thomas Dinan
Feiman, Ronald Mark
Felcher, Peter L.
Fierstein, Ronald Karl
Fischel, Shelley Duckstein
Franciscovich, George
Franklin, Leonard
Fry, Morton Harrison, II
Fuhrer, Arthur K.
Gilman, Andrew D.
Goff, Betsy Kagen
Green, Jonathan David
Green, Richard George
Grill, Steven Eric
Grossberg, David
Haims, Bruce David
Hathaway, Gerald Thomas
Jacobson, Jeffrey Eli
Jacobson, Marc
Janney, Oliver James
Johnston, Harry Melville, III
Kaminsky, Arthur Charles
Kessler, Lawrence Bert
Kruteck, Laurence R.
Lanchner, Bertrand Martin
Langenthal, Stephen Roger
Lightstone, Ronald
Litwin, Burton Lawrence
Logigian, John Douglas
Manshel, Andrew Maximilian
Marames, William Etheme
Marks, Alfred Mitchell
McSherry, William John, Jr.
Messing, Harold
Miller-Wachtel, Ellen
Moyer, Jay Edward
Nearing, Vivienne W.
Newborn, Samuel R(euben)
Newman, Jeffrey K.
Papernik, Joel Ira
Plotkin, Loren H.
Polakas, John
Price, Todd Alan
Probstein, Jon Michael
Pulis, Gregory Milton
Reis, Muriel Henle
Robb, Scott Hall
Rose, John T., II
Rose, Michael Edward
Rosini, Neil Justin
Rudoff, Surie
Schiffman, Daniel
Schiffman, Steven Mitchell
Schwartz, Laurens R.
Silberman, John Alan
Stengel, Mark Allen
Stevens, Lee
Thall, Peter Morgan
Traube, Victoria Gilbert

Ohio
Downing, George
Troxell, James Dane

Oregon
Redden, Michael Aloysius

Pennsylvania
Busch, H. Donald
Farrell, J. Michael
Gribok, Stephan Paul
Gutnick, H. Yale
Kaufman, Phyllis Cynthia
Millinger, Donald Michael
Reiff, Jeffrey Marc
Wertheimer, Spencer Miles

Tennessee
Campbell-Bell, Dorothy Kathryn
Kramer, Steven Emert
Rush, Stephen Kenneth
Smith, Drayton Beecher, II

Texas
Black, William Earl
Jacobs, Gregory R.
Moy, Celeste Marie
Regenbogen, Ellis Arnold
Rundel, Kenneth Martin
Simon, Hinda Bookstaber

Utah
Mooney, Jerome Henri
Shea, Patrick A.

Virginia
Broadbent, Peter Edwin, Jr.

CANADA

Ontario
Roberts, Richard Jack

ADDRESS UNPUBLISHED
Brotman, Stuart Neil
Carrol, Robert Kelton
Graff, Debra Jo
Kantrowitz, Susan Lee
Markewich, Robert
McKenna, Edward James, Jr.
Meyerson, Stanley Phillip
Wise, Philip J.

ENVIRONMENTAL

UNITED STATES

Alabama
Knight, Martha Kathryn
Pierce, Donald Fay

Alaska
Clough, John F., III
Linxwiler, James David
McCann, Richard Eugene
McCracken, Sarah Elizabeth
Mertz, Douglas Kemp
Tangen, Jon Paul

Arizona
Verkamp, John
Wolf, G. Van Velsor, Jr.

Arkansas
Nestrud, Charles Robert

California
Anglin, Richard Lee, Jr.
Benton, Andrew Keith
Bold, Frederick, Jr.
Bull, Howard Livingston
Collins, James Ignatius
Crump, Gerald Franklin
Cummings, John Patrick
Darman, Dinah Lea
DeVries, Scott Philip
Duggan, Thomas Michael
Fisher, Barry Alan
Garay, Erica Blythe
Giannotti, David Allen
Gissberg, John Gustav
Gralnek, Donald D.
Hall, Carlyle Washington, Jr.
Hoffman, John Douglas
Joyce, James Donald
Khim, Diane
Kirlin, Anne Marget
Kovacic, Gary Anton
Krueger, Robert Blair
Lathrop, Mitchell Lee
Lerner, William C.
Lundquist, Weyman I.
MacDougall, William Roderick
Matthews, Philip Richard
McDevitt, Ray Edward
McMurry, Robert I.
Nadler, Jerome Steven
Norris, Cynthia Ann
Otto, James Daniel
Parker, Jeffrey Lionel
Peterson, Paul Ames
Quadri, Fazle Rab
Rossmann, Antonio
Sax, Joseph Lawrence
Scheiber, Harry N.
Simmons, Robert Michael
Smith, Diane Rapp
Squarcy, Charlotte Van Horne
Wagner, D. William
Williams, Richard D.
Woocher, Fredric Dean
Yarema, Geoffrey Steven

Colorado
Campbell, Brian Thomas
Carr, James Francis
Cope, Joseph Adams
Deutsch, Harvey Elliot
Dominick, David DeWitt
Fognani, John Dennis
Foster, Tad Stevenson
Freeman, Deborah Lynn
Gablehouse, Timothy Reuben
Grant, Patrick Alexander
Hampton, Clyde Robert
Hook, Mary Julia
Johnson, Ruth Brammer
Martz, Clyde Ollen
McClain, Vaughn Leon
Meyer, Christopher Hawkins
Micsak, Robert William
Patrick, Kevin Land
Paulson, Christopher Robert
Smith, Thomas Fenton
Vranesh, George
White, Charles B.
White, Michael Douglas

Connecticut
Buck, Gurdon Hall
Dumont, James Allan
Eberhart, Harry Simon
Elliott, Edwin Donald, Jr.
Fisher, Clyde Olin, Jr.
Goodridge, George Sidney
Pavetti, Francis James
Rose-Ackerman, Susan
Schroth, Peter W(illiam)
Smith, Cornelius C., Jr.
Sussman, Mark Richard

Delaware
Boggs, James Caleb
Devine, Donn
Reichert, Robert Joseph

District of Columbia
Adams, John Jillson
Alushin, Michael Stephen
Anderson, David Lawrence
Baller, James
Bardin, David J.
Barnard, Robert C.
Bassman, Robert Stuart
Baur, Donald Christian
Baynard, Ernest Cornish, III
Bear, Dinah
Bell, Robert Brooks
Bergerbest, Nathan Steven
Bowen, Brooks Jefferson
Brookshire, James Earl
Browne, Richard Cullen
Bruce, E(stel) Edward
Campilongo, Michael
Cannon, Daniel Willard
Carr, Lawrence Edward, Jr.
Cates, C. Brad
Cerar, Jeffrey O'Dell
Cooper, Iver Peter
Craft, Winfred Owens, Jr.
Cudlipp, Katherine Yeamans
Cutler, Eliot Raphael
De Simone, Daniel V.
DeWeese, Kathleen Batchelder
Disheroon, Fred Russell
Emmett, Robert Addis, III
Ewing, Ky Pepper, Jr.
Faron, Robert Steven
Feldman, Roger David
Fenster, Herbert Lawrence
Frank, William Harris
Frye, John H., III
Futrell, John William
Garrett, Theodore Louis
Gibbs, Jeffrey Neil
Grammer, Elisa Joan
Habicht, Frank Henry, II
Harrison, Donald
Herbolsheimer, Robert Tilton
Hinds, Richard De Courcy
Hollingsworth, Joe Gregory
Howard, Jeffrey Hjalmar
Hundt, Reed Eric
Hutt, Peter Barton
Jones, Theodore Lawrence
Joseph, Daniel Mordecai
Kirsch, Laurence Stephen
Klucsik, John Francis
Koller, Benedict Joseph
Kovacs, William Lawrence
Kraemer, Jay R.
Lettow, Charles Frederick
Lewis, William Henry, Jr.
Lichtenstein, Elissa Charlene
Litvin, David Anthony
Loeb, Dorothy Pearl
Machlin, Marc David
Macleod, John Amend
Martin, Lowell Frank
Mathews, Craig
McGuirl, Marlene Dana Callis
Meserve, Richard Andrew
Meyers, Erik Jon
Olmstead, William J.
Provorny, Frederick Alan
Quarles, Steven Princeton
Ramsey, Stephen Douglas
Rathmell, Anne Elizabeth
Roberts, Jared Ingersoll
Robertson, Joseph Martin
Rogers, Edward Lee
Rosenthal, Steven Siegmund
Rubin, Kenneth Allen
Rummel, Edgar Ferrand
Russell, Harold Swift
Schaefer, William Goerman, Jr.
Schiffbauer, William G.
Shea, Francis Michael
Sherk, George William
Silverglade, Bruce A.
Smith, George Patrick, II
Taylor, Robert Stanley
Tether, Ivan Joseph
Thode, Anna Catharine
Tinney, Richard Townsend, Jr.
Topol, Allan Jerry
Ughetta, Valerie Jeanne
Vlcek, Jan Benes
Walker, Mary L.
Walker, Vern Robert
Wallace, Wilton Lawrence
Weissman, William R.

Florida
Benson, John Scott
Brightman, Richard Stephen
Canter, Bram D. E.
Chumbris, Stephen Claude
Dee, David Scott
Denker, Randall Elizabeth
Dye, Dewey Albert, Jr.
Fleming, Joseph Z.
Gussow, Irving Bernard
Hastings, Michael Lynn
Kuersteiner, Jonathan Daniel Boone
Martin, Michael David
Mintz, Joel Alan
Ozark, Damian Michael
Pritchard, Teresa Noreen
Pugh, Irby Gene
Risner, Paul Edward
Schwenke, Roger Dean
Spriggs, Kent
Steele, Robert Michael
Zaiser, Kent Ames

Georgia
Baker, David S.
Casto, Keith Michael
Clark, Herman
Denham, Vernon Robert, Jr.
Fortune, Philip Lee
Kessler, Kathleen
Ortiz, Jay Richard Gentry
Strassner, Kenneth Allen
Turnipseed, Sara Sadler

Hawaii
Van Dyke, Jon Markham

Idaho
Ellsworth, Maurice Owens
Gasser, Emmett Clark
Russell, Robie George

Illinois
Angst, Gerald L.
Anspach, Kenneth Gordon
Bleiweiss, Shell J.

Bosselman, Fred Paul
Boyle, Patrick Otto
Currie, David Park
Eaton, Larry Ralph
Ettinger, Albert Franklin
Flood, Vincent Patrick
Freeborn, Michael D.
Gladden, James Walter, Jr.
Grabarek, William Christian
Hammesfahr, Robert Winter
Kindt, John Warren
Levine, Laurence Harvey
Lieberman, Eugene
Lockwood, Gary Lee
Lown, Carolyn Ann
Matushek, Edward J., III
McMahon, Thomas Michael
Merrill, Thomas Wendell
Mitchell, Neil Ralph
Olian, Robert Martin
Perona, Paul Dominic, Jr.
Podlewski, Joseph Roman, Jr.
Pope, Michael Arthur
Prillaman, Frederick Charles
Radler, Warren S.
Ropiequet, John L.
Rose, Carol Marguerite
Rosemarin, Carey Stephen
Rundio, Louis Michael, Jr.
Rupert, Donald William
Schink, James Harvey
Sechen, Glenn Charles
Sheldon, Harvey M.
Stone, Bertram Allen
Valauskas, Charles C.
Winter, Frank Louis
Wulfers, John Manning

Indiana

Beckwith, Lewis Daniel
Blomquist, Robert Frank
Deveau, Francis Joseph
McDermott, Renée R(assler)
Weeks, Walter William
Williams, Bradley Louis

Iowa

Clark, Beverly Ann
Zenk, Ann Marie

Kansas

Haddock, Bradley Eugene
Lefebvre, David Marshall

Kentucky

Feather, Mark Randolph
Foley, Margaret Sweeney

Louisiana

Buckley, Samuel Olliphant, III
Goldberg, Charles
Raymond, Charles Michael
Rudolph, Richard
St. John, James Berry, Jr.
Shinn, Clinton Wesley
Stetter, Roger Alan
Surprenant, Mark Christopher

Maine

Brett, Tybe Ann
Neagle, Christopher Scott

Maryland

Blake, Francis Stanton
Keplinger, Helen Bunten
McComas, Albert Laun
Powell, Michael Calvin
Sack, Sylvan Hanan
White, Pamela Janice
Wolfe, J. Thomas

Massachusetts

Atkinson, James Peter
Covel, Richard Allan
Davis, Christopher Patrick
Dignan, Thomas Gregory, Jr.
Gould, Kenneth B.
Hoover, David Carlson
Kovar, Stuart Charles
Lepore, Ralph Thomas, III
Lewis, Sanford Jay
Murphy, Kathryn Cochrane
Murray, Robert Fox
Platt, Rutherford Hayes, Jr.
Rikleen, Lauren Stiller
Saradjian, Martin Luther
Thornton, Michael Paul
Vance, Verne Widney, Jr.

Michigan

Balagna, Steven David
Burgoyne, Bert
Charla, Leonard Francis
Dudley, Dennis Michael
Gootee, Jane Marie
Kopack, Laura Reyes
Krier, James Edward
Mann, John Raymond, III
Messmer, Kirk Daniel
Miller, Sheldon Lee
O'Rourke, Peter Edward
Palincsar, John Ernest
Petersen, O. Keith
Polito, Joseph Michael
Simmons, Brent Elliott
Tickner, Ellen Mindy
Walle, James Paul
Zimmerman, Norman

Minnesota

Anderson, Thomas Willman
Cattanach, Robert Edward, Jr.
Christensen, Donn Douglas
Farber, Daniel Alan
Gordon, John Bennett
Hillstrom, Robert Arthur
Jensen, Patricia Ann
Keppel, William James
Meier, Carl Carsten
O'Neill, Joseph Thomas
Straughn, Robert Oscar, III

Mississippi

Baggett Boozer, Linda Dianne
Will, Joseph Henry Michael

Missouri

Clegg, Karen Kohler
Gilhousen, Brent James
Hackmann, Frank H(enry)
Nassif, Joseph Gerard
Noel, Edwin Lawrence
Proctor, George Edwin, Jr.
Taylor, David Afton
Willman, Philip Louis
Wuestner, Linda Douglas

Montana

Thorson, John Eric

Nebraska

Aiken, J. David
Eaton, David Foster

New Hampshire

Baldwin, Carolyn Whitmore
Coolidge, Daniel Scott
Peltonen, John Ernest
Smith, Gregory Hayes

New Jersey

Alexander, John Donald
Arnold, Kenneth Robert
Balikov, Henry R.
Bullock, Thomas Francis
Cino, Vincent Alphonse
Cohen, Lawrence Gene
Conway, Richard James, Jr.
English, Jerry Fitzgerald
Farr, Linus Gilbert
Fitzpatrick, Harold Francis
Gelman, Jon Leonard
Goldfarb, William
Gordon, Michael
Guest, Brian Milton
Harris, David B.
Hector, Bruce John
Heerwagen, Elwood J., Jr.
Hewit, Russell Lyle
Hill, Henry Albert
Horan, John Donohoe
Irenas, Joseph Eron
Kantowitz, Jeffrey Leon
Kent, Thomas Day
Kienz, Glenn Charles
Klock, John Henry
Kondracki, Edward Anthony
Lubcke, Kip Charles
Maraziti, Joseph James, Jr.
McKinney, John Adams, Jr.
Munoz, Robert F.
Nucciarone, A. Patrick
Pane, Michael Anthony, IV
Pantel, Glenn Steven
Ronca, James Alexander
Roth, Kenneth David
Scagnelli, John Mark
Seeley, James J.
Shea, Edward Emmett
Spinrad, Max
Stewart, James
Taldone, Nicholas John
Thomason, Charles Lee
Tinari, Anthony Philip
Tyler, George Joseph

New Mexico

Huffaker, Gregory Dorian, Jr.
Kehl, Randall Herman

New York

Bearak, Corey B(ecker)
Beattie, Richard Irwin
Bergen, G. S. Peter
Billauer, Barbara Pfeffer
Brickwedde, Richard James
Bronner, William Roche
Carmien, Donald Charles
Chamberlain, John
Davidoff, Barry Frederick
Devendorf, Alfred Ervin
Dib, Albert
Edgerton, Lynne Todd
Feder, Robert
Fein, Scott Norris
Freeman, David John
French, John, III
Gerrard, Michael Burr
Goldman, Jerry Alan
Gordon, Michael Mackin
Grad, Frank Paul
Greenberg, Joshua F.
Henner, Peter William
Heyer, John Henry, II
Hill, Janet Wadsworth
Hoffman, Marvin
Horowitz, Steven Gary
Hunziker, Robert McKee
Kelley, Christopher Donald
Killeen, Henry Walter
Lebowitz, Jack Richard
Lee, Henry
Lester, Howard
Marcus, Norman
Matias, Thomas Redmond
Newcombe, George Michael
Oppenheimer, Laurence Brian
O'Rorke, James Francis, Jr.
Rivet, Diana Wittmer
Roberts, E. F.
Robinson, Nicholas Adams
Rosenthal, Albert Joseph
Rudnick, Marvin Jack
Ruzow, Daniel Arthur
Samansky, J. Leonard
Schachner, Mark J.
Silverberg, Steven Mark
Smith, Janet Diane
Snider, Donald Stephen
Stutman, Michael David
Susser, Stuart J.
Walsh, John Bronson
Weir, John Keeley
Willig, William Paul
Wilson, Clifford H.
Zedrosser, Joseph John
Zeisel, Laura

North Carolina

Carmichael, Carson, III
Carrow, Harvey Hill, Jr.
Case, Charles Dixon
Clodfelter, Daniel Gary
Hirsch, Alan Seth
Lansche, John Elmer
Schwenn, William Lee

North Dakota

Kopacz, Stanley William, Jr.

Ohio

Aukland, Duncan Dayton
Beckwith, Karen Lu
Buchanan, J. Vincent Marino
Burke, Kim Kenneth
Burke, Timothy Michael
Casper, Paul William, Jr.
Cook, Robert Nevin
Crane, Edward Holman
Donohoe, James D.
Edwards, John White
Ensign, Gregory Moore
Falsgraf, William Wendell
Fort, Jeffrey Edward
Goldberg, Steven Charles
Hardy, Michael Lynn
Hinerman, Philip Lee
Janke, Ronald Robert
Klaus, Charles
Lemire, Jerome Albert
McMahon, Michael Sean
Migden-Ostrander, Janine Lee
Moore, Kenneth Cameron
O'Reilly, James Thomas
Pallam, John James
Rennick, Kyme Elizabeth Wall
Schatz, William Bonsall
Schmitz, Thomas Mathias
Wang, Charleston Cheng-Kung
Ziegler, Edward Howard, Jr.

Oklahoma

Cundiff, James Nelson
Dowd, William Timothy
Reis, Robert Richard

Oregon

Adler, A(rthur) Michael
Feder, Miriam
Funk, William F.
Glick, Richard Myron
Huffman, James Lloyd
Larson, John Francis
Reinke, Cecil Eugene

Pennsylvania

Anderson, Margret Elizabeth
Bertsch, Gene Clair
Bradshaw, William Elbert
Crane, Maida Rosenfeld
Engler, W. Joseph, Jr.
Everett, Carl Bell
Gerjuoy, Edward
Grimaud, Gerald C.
Hickel, Gerard Frederick
Kanner, Allan
Klayman, Barry Martin
Kury, Franklin Leo
MacGregor, David Bruce
Madva, Stephen Alan
McKenna, James L.
Mulligan, John Thomas
Mustokoff, Michael Mark
Pompo, Vincent Matthew
Preate, Robert Anthony
Rubin, Scott Jeffrey
Simmons, Bryan J.
Weston, R. Timothy
Williams, Gerald Joseph

Rhode Island

Miller, Samuel Aaron
O'Neil, James E.

South Carolina

Bergholz, Warren Ernest, Jr.
Harleston, John
Schweitzer, Eric Campbell
Smoak, Lewis Tyson
Wyche, Bradford Wheeler
Wyche, Madison Baker, III

South Dakota

Wyman, William Alan

Tennessee

Baker, Josiah Carr Eggleston
Bates, Albert Kealiinui
Dadds, Harry Leon, II
Gray, John Carter Stewart
McCaleb, Joe Wallace
Moriarty, Herbert Bernard, Jr.
Penny, William Lewis
Williams, Eddie Erwin, III

Texas

Arizaga, Lavora Spradlin
Bader, Gregory Vincent
Ballanfant, Richard Burton
Bayko, Emil Thomas
Bohannon, Paul
Branhagen, Darrel Raymond
Dinkins, Carol Eggert
Dutton, Diana Cheryl
Ellis, Donald Lee
Evans, James A.
Feldcamp, Larry Bernard
Gaines, Sanford Ervin
Gibson, Michael Morgan
Gilberg, Howard Larry
Keys, Jerry Malcom
Lake, Simeon Timothy, III
Parker, Emily Ann
Pickle, George Edward
Pope, David Bruce
Reed, Harry Lowe
Ruhl, John Benjamin
Santire, Stanley Paul
Secrest, Ronald Dean
Sutphen, Robert Louis
Tanner, Sheryl Malick
Thomas, Patrick Powers
Weaver, Jacqueline Lang
Wheat, Josiah
Whitworth, H. Philip, Jr.
Williams, Charles Michael

Utah

Allred, Steven Wesley
Dragoo, Denise Ann

Vermont

Faignant, John Paul
O'Donnell, Robert John
Storrow, Charles Fiske

Virginia

Baird, Edward Rouzie, Jr.
Freeman, George Clemon, Jr.
Gasch, Manning
Grant, Charles Randall, Jr.
Gresham, Timothy Ward
Kelly, Lawrence Edward
' ight, Alfred Robert
Merrill, Richard Austin
Middleton, J. Howard, Jr.
Parker, Richard Wilson
Powell, Lewis Franklin, III
Reveley, Walter Taylor, III
Rosbe, William Louis
Rudlin, David Alan
Talarek, Walter Glenn
Theberge, Norman Bartlett

Washington

Belfiglio, Jeff
Chellis, Eugene Clifton
Coogan, Patrick Donlan
Crane, Stephen Joel
Defelice, Dennis Joseph
Haggard, Joel Edward
Hill, (George) Richard
Kuhrau, Edward W.
Leed, Roger Melvin
Maulding, Barry Clifford
Medved, Robert Allen
Packer, Mark Barry
Pilat, Michael Joseph
Serka, Philip Angelo
Weinman, Richard Stephen
Wilkinson, Jane Rae
Youngs, Linda Miller

West Virginia

Bunner, William Keck
Flannery, David Michael

Wisconsin

Croak, Francis R.
Harrington, Arthur John
Long, Theodore James
Rankin, Gene Raymond
Smith, Robert John

Wyoming

Godfrey, Paul Bard

ADDRESS UNPUBLISHED

Bolch, Susan Bass
Casella, Peter F(iore)
Eastin, Keith E.
Francis, Jerome Leslie
Kemp, Alson Remington, Jr.
Lichter-Heath, Laurie Jean
Lippes, Richard James
Mattson, James Stewart
O'Donnell, Pierce Henry
Pendergrass, John Ambrose
Reynolds, H. Gerald
Stephens, Henry L., Jr.
Woodruff, Charles Norman
Ziker, Barry Gene

ESTATE PLANNING. *See also* Probate; Taxation, estate.

UNITED STATES

Alabama

Blackburn, John Gilmer
Bowdre, John Birch, Jr.
Bryant, Thomas Earle, Jr.
Foster, Arthur Key, Jr.
Fox, John Charles
Holberg, Ralph Gans, Jr.
Little, Joe Hollis, Jr.
Mathews, Melinda McEachern
Shanks, William Ennis, Jr.
Smith, Robert McDavid
Webster, Bruce Charles

Alaska

Davis, Trigg Thomas

Arizona

Ascher, Mark Louis
Ehmann, Anthony Valentine
Isaak, Gotthilf Eugene
Larson, Ronald Frederick
May, Robert A.
O'Connell, Daniel Henry
Olsen, Alfred Jon
Smith, Kenneth McKay
Waterfall, Gordon Garrett

Arkansas

Hamilton, Herman Lynn, Jr.
Jackson, Blaine Albert
Looney, Jake Wayne
Mackey, Benjamin Franklin, Jr.
Stockburger, Jean Dawson
Strother, Lane H.
Stroud, John Fred, Jr.

California

Adams, Robert Morford, Jr.
Alvarez, Edna R. S.
Barton, Babette B.
Blewett, Robert Noall
Blumenfeld, Eli
Bohlmann, Daniel Robert
Brown, Lorne James
Calleton, Theodore Edward
Carter, Glenn Thomas
Copenbarger, Lloyd Gaylord
Degallegos, Richard
Dell'Ergo, Robert James
Finch, Nathan C.
Fried, Alexander
Gleim, Michael Alan
Greene, Richard Lawrence
Guest, Karl Reed
Guggenhime, Richard Johnson
Halstead, Harry Moore
Hanley, Daniel E.
Hart, Lynn Patricia
Heene, Fred Lewis, Jr.
Hertzberg, Harold Joel
Hunter, William Carlton
Igo, Louis Daniel
Kearn, Orene Levenson
Lemmon, John Vincent
Lindgren, Arne Sigfrid
Maggard, Sarah Elizabeth
McGinty, Brian Donald
Merrill, Byron Robert
Merritt, Valerie Jorgensen
Mitchell, Michael Charles
Myers, Philip Eric
Nigg, Karl Frederick
O'Keefe, William Patrick
Oliver, Robert Harold
Osborne, Carol Ann
Rae, Matthew Sanderson, Jr.
Rand, Richard Malcolm
Sceper, Duane Harold
Schechter, Stuart
Showley, Lon Duane
Sickler, Sandra Davis
Slabach, Stephen Hall
Stark, Franklin Culver
Stephens, George Edward, Jr.
Stinehart, William, Jr.
Sullivan, James Anderson
Sutro, John Alfred
Thatcher, Dickinson
Thomas, Howard Berkeley
Tutoli, Michele Ann
Voegelin, Harold Stanley
Ward, Diane Korosy
Williams, Lawrence Dwight
ZoBell, Karl

Colorado

Alberts, Celia Anne
Brant, John Getty
Buchanan, James William, III
Elrod, Richard Bryan
Fevurly, Keith Robert
Greenberg, Morton Paul
Griffith, Mary Cornwall
Guyton, Samuel Percy
Kraemer, Sandy Frederick
Levine, Gary H.
McMichael, Donald Earl
Owen, James Churchill
Sherman, Lester Ivan
Smith, Sheldon Harold

Connecticut

Abate, Ernest Nicholas
Abery-Wetstone, Holly Ann
Anderson, Henry Brackenridge
Bell, Mary-Katherine
Elliott, Stephen K.
Fisher, Everett
Gregory, Julian Arthur, Jr.
Phelps, Robert Frederick, Jr.
Schiff, Alan Lewis

Delaware

Shearin, Kathryn Kay

District of Columbia

Blazek, Doris Defibaugh
Damico, Nicholas Peter
Determan, Sara-Ann
Eagan, R(oderick) Russell
Faley, R(ichard) Scott
Grindle, John, Jr.
Kellison, James Bruce
Lynham, John Marmaduke
McGuire, Patricia A.
Medalie, Richard James
Reiner, Samuel Theodore
Sachs, Sidney Stanley
Vance, Sheldon Baird
Ward, Nicholas Donnell

Florida

Chambliss, Linda Christine
Click, David Forrest
Doliner, Nathaniel Lee
Dressler, Robert A.
Edwards, William Thomas, Jr.
Farrior, J. Rex, Jr.
Gaylord, Harry Eugene
Haile, John Sanders
Hall, Miles Lewis, Jr.
Hess, George Franklin, II
Kahn Levenberg, Corinne Beth
Koren, Edward Franz
Lambertus, Christine Lundt
Lefkowitz, Ivan Martin
Martin, Michael David
Peck, Bernard Sidney
Price, Pamela Odell
Pyle, Frank LeForest, Sr.
Reinstein, Joel
Salem, Albert McCall, Jr.
Stewart, Thomas Wilson
Trombley, Michael Jerome
Waite, Blakeley Robinson
Warwick, Charles Henry, III
Weidemeyer, Carleton Lloyd
Wilson, George Allen
Wood, William McBrayer
Wutt, Robert Anthony

Georgia

Austin, Thomas Nelson

Bart, Randall Kerr
Bloodworth, A(lbert) W(illiam) Franklin
Childs, Julie
DeLoach, Donald Brian
Durrett, James Frazer, Jr.
Hasson, James Keith, Jr.
Head, Hugh Garland, III
Jones, Donald Richard, III
Radford, Mary Frances
Searcy, William Nelson
Voynich, John Joseph
White, Benjamin Taylor
Wright, Harry Ralph, Jr.

Hawaii

Bodden, Thomas Andrew
Goo, Colin Kim Keong
Hastings, Robert William, II
Miyasaki, Shuichi

Idaho

Bickel, Dwight Franklin
Blaser, Stephen Jeffery
Chapman, John Sherwood
Olson, Gerald W.

Illinois

Armstrong, Edwin Richard
Ashley, James Wheeler
Beer, Betty Louise
Berning, Larry D.
Bogert, George Taylor
Breen, James Joseph
Burke, Richard William
Carr, Walter Stanley
Chiles, Stephen Michael
Colombik, Richard Michael
Davidson, Lawrence Ira
Ephraim, Donald Morley
Ermentrout, John Curtis
Felsenthal, Steven Altus
Fort, Lyman Rankin
Friedman, Roselyn L.
Gary, Susan Nannette
Gerek, William Michael
Gertz, Theodore Gerson
Gillies, Donald Allastair
Gingiss, Randall Jon
Glass, Stanford Lee
Goodman, Bruce Dennis
Graver, Nancy J.
Hoffman, John Harry
Holleb, Marshall Maynard
Johnson, Thomas Stuart
Juhl, Loren Earl
Liss, Jeffrey Glenn
Marshall, John David
McDonough, John Michael
Milligan, Francis Joseph, Jr.
Nathan, Kenneth Sawyer, Sr.
Nitikman, Franklin W.
Nortell, Bruce
O'Flaherty, Paul Benedict
Pape, Glenn Michael
Rikli, Donald Carl
Schaffer, George John
Schreiber, Ronald
Schuyler, Daniel Merrick
Sebat, John Edward
Stanhaus, James Steven
Swaney, Thomas Edward
Thomas, James Gladwyn
Thomson, William Hills
Tracy, William Francis, II
Trio, Edward Alan
Trost, Eileen Bannon
Ward, Philip Henry, Jr.
Weber, Alban
Witt, Alan Michael
Wrigley, Julie Ann

Indiana

Adams, Robert Wendell
Baker, Ronald Lee
Baker, Ronald Lee
Culp, Charles William
Dennis, Ralph Emerson, Jr.
Gerde, Carlyle Noyes (Cy)
Manterfield, Eric Alan
Mazur, Lawrence Joseph
Pantzer, Kurt Friedrich, Jr.

Iowa

Campbell, Bruce Irving
Galer, Benjamin Anderson
Harl, Neil Eugene
Morf, Darrel Arle
Morrison, Edmund Dunham, Jr.
Pechacek, Frank Warren, Jr.
Simpson, Lyle Lee

Kansas

Aylward, Paul Leon
Buechel, William Benjamin
Martin, Barry Douglas
Stallard, Wayne Minor
Toland, Clyde William

Kentucky

Aberson, Leslie Donald
Hallenberg, Robert Lewis
Reeves, L. Brian
Spalding, Wallace Hugh, Jr.

Louisiana

Hardtner, Quintin Theodore, III
Hill, William James, III
Mayoral, Paul G.
Powell, David Wayne
Reso, Jerome John, Jr.
Simon, H(uey) Paul
Snyder, Charles Aubrey
Tarcza, Robert Emmet
Wedig, Harold Harvey

Maine

Dench, Bryan Mundy
Hunt, Philip Courtney
LeBlanc, Richard Philip
Perkins, James Blenn, Jr.
Scribner, Fred Clark, Jr.

Maryland

Calimafde, Paula Annette
Gingell, Robert Arthur
Hecht, Isaac
O'Brien, Joseph Edward, Jr.
Respess, James Walter
Staples, Lyle Newton

Massachusetts

Ames, James Barr
Auchter, John Richard
Borenstein, Milton Conrad
Fitzpatrick, Lawrence Scott
Guimond, Robert Wilfrid
Keegan, John Robert
Li, Winifred I.
Pratt, Harold Irving
Puzo, Michael John
Riley, Michael Hylan
Roche, John Jefferson
Schwartz, William
Silver, Marvin S.
Spencer, Patti S.
Weiss, Dudley Albert
Westfall, David

Michigan

Bennett, Thompson
Carney, Donald F., Jr.
Chapekis, Nicholas Peter
Chapman, Conrad Daniel
Clark, John Scott
Clink, Stephen Henry
Colombo, Frederick J.
Currier, Timothy Jordan
Eklund, Robert D.
Fortino, Alfred J.
Hemker, Joseph Bernard
Irish, Michael William
Jackson, Mark Andrew
Laughter, Ron D.
Norris, John Hart
Nowinski, Thomas Stephen
Panek, Michael John
Reynolds, Frank Harrison
Richardson, Robert Woodrow
Riecker, John E(rnest)
Skora, Susan Sundman
Solomon, Mark Raymond
Tarnacki, Duane L.
van Horne, Pieter Hammond
Waggoner, Lawrence William
Westerman, Susan S.
Winquist, Thomas Richard

Minnesota

Altman, Milton Hubert
Anderson, James Hurd
Brand, Steve Aaron
Burns, Richard Ramsey
DuFour, R(ichard) W(illiam), Jr.
Hitch, Horace
Lindgren, D(erbin) Kenneth, Jr.
Mooty, David Nelson
Peterson, Ralph Henry
Reister, Raymond Alex
Rossini, Raymond Dominic
Stein, Robert Allen

Mississippi

Fountain, Richard Maurice
Jones, Barry Kent
Painter, William Steene
Stubblefield, Joseph Stephen
Travis, Jay A., III

Missouri

Anderson, Christopher James
Baer, David, Jr.
Beachy, Robert M.
Cupples, Stephen Elliot
Gross, Monnye R.
McClannahan, Cindy Ann
McKee, Barnet M.
Moffitt, William A., Jr.
Peper, Christian Baird
Polster, Carl Conrad
Reaves, Craig Charles
Redd, Charles Appleton
Rice, Charles Marcus, II
Stevens, Bradford Lee
Van Cleve, William Moore
Willis, Russell Anthony, III

Montana

Moog, Mary Ann Pimley

Nebraska

Blazek, George Thomas
Borghoff, John Joseph
DeRoin, Jan Elizabeth
Stern, Arnold Jay

Nevada

Gubler, John Gray
Lowe, Bryan A.
Maher, O. Kent
Schouweiler, Bart McClain
Wedge, Virgil Henry

New Hampshire

Brouillard, Philip André
Cohen, Steven
Donovan, Robert Bickford
Lopez, Chester Henry, Jr.
Morse, Richard Allen

New Jersey

Beidler, Marsha Wolf
Cappuccio, Ronald Joseph
Clapp, Alfred C.
Clinch, H(enri) Carleton
Fasolo, William Alexander
Fogel, Richard
Forkin, Thomas S.
Herr, Philip Michael
Lambert, Samuel Waldron, III
Olszak, Daniel Dominic
Rose, Edith Sprung
Slutsky, Kenneth Joel
Vandervoort, Peter

New Mexico

McKinnon, Daniel Angus, III
Messinger, J. Henry
Rosenberg, Myer (Mike)
Tully, Richard T. C.

New York

Allora, Ralph Anthony
Ashton, Robert
Backus, Bradley
Baldwin, Robert Frederick, Jr.
Bennett, James Davison
Black, Howard
Black, James Isaac, III
Bockstein, Herbert
Boehner, Leonard Bruce
Brandrup, Douglas Warren
Brovitz, Richard Stuart
Bush, Julian S.
Cardozo, Benjamin Mordecai
Case, Edward Haile
Christ, Donald C.
Clark, Carolyn Cochran
Cowles, Frederick Oliver
Danziger, Joel Bernard
Dean, William Tucker
Dolan, James Francis
Duckworth, R(oy) Demarest, III
Early, John Collins
Eisenberg, Ronald Alan
Engel, Ralph Manuel
Evans, Douglas Hayward
Feitelson, Robert Joel
Finch, Edward Ridley, Jr.
Fink, Norman Stiles
Finkelstein, Bernard
Gelb, Judith Anne
Gelberg, Frederick
Gerhart, Eugene Clifton
Greenbaum, Maurice C.
Guth, Paul C.
Hawkins, Eliot Dexter
Heming, Charles E.
Hendrickson, Robert Augustus
Herzog, Jacob Hawley
Hochberg, Ronald Mark
Hull, Philip Glasgow
Hurley, James G.
Ingraham, Frederic Beach
Jacoby, James Joseph
Kramer, William Joseph
Levine, Samuel Milton
Lingelbach, Albert Lane
Mahon, Arthur J.
Manning, Jerome Alan
Martin, Malcolm Elliot
McGrath, Thomas J.
Meaders, Paul Le Sourd
Moore, Thomas R.
Neuwirth, Gloria S.
O'Connor, Michael E.
Paul, Herbert Morton
Pollio, Benedict James
Prye, Steven Marvell
Ralli, Constantine Pandia
Rappaport, A. Jack
Reese, William Willis
Robinson, Barbara Paul
Rotgin, Philip Norman
Schlesinger, Edward Samuel
Sederbaum, Arthur David
Setterberg, Patricia Ann
Solberg, Thomas Allan
Steyer, Hume Richmond
Sweeney, Deidre Ann
Thompson, Lawrence Bigelow
Twomey, Thomas Aloysius, Jr.
Ufford, Charles Wilbur, Jr.
Vick, Paul Ashton
Wadsworth, James Marshall
Waldorf, Geraldine Polack
Wallace, Richard Powell
Warren, William Clements
Watson, Richard A.
Zack, David
Zuckerman, Paul Herbert

North Carolina

Alala, Joseph Basil, Jr.
Garland, James Boyce
Ingle, John D.
Lavelle, Brian Francis David
McGirt, Sherri Lynn
Orsbon, Richard Anthony
Silverstein, Carol Kauffman
Underwood, Samuel Bobbitt, Jr.
Weick, Paul Alfred, II

North Dakota

Bailly, David Ryan
Crockett, Richard Boyd
Sperry, Floyd Benjamin

Ohio

Amodio, James Anthony
Anthony, Thomas Dale
Bank, Malvin E.
Barrett, David Carroll
Brenneman, Fleet B.
Brucken, Robert Matthew
Buechner, Robert William
Eilers, John Wagner, Jr.
Francoeur, Robert Alfred
Furber, Philip Craig
Gariepy, Stephen Henry
Geneva, Louis Brion
Goettemoeller, Duane A.
Goldsmith, James Arthur
Goulder, Diane Kessler
Gray, Meryl Benjamin
Hartsel, Norman Clyde
Healy, Mary Jacqueline
Hinton, Virgil Otterbein
Hobson, Henry Wise, Jr.
Hohn, Michael
Holtz, Gregory Theodore
Kern, Keith William
Lobenhofer, Louis Fred
Nelson, Robert Bruce
Pillari, Thomas
Shapiro, Fred David
Suter, Carol Joan
Warrington, John Wesley
Yager, John Warren

Oklahoma

Davis, Jesse Dunbar
Draughon, Scott Wilson
Pray, Donald Eugene
Robinson, Adelbert Carl
Ross, William Jarboe
Stewart, Murray Baker
Taliaferro, Bruce Owen

Oregon

Bolliger, Ralph Wendell
Boly, Jeffrey Elwyn
Hager, Orval O.
Kantor, Stephen Edward
Nash, Frank Erwin
Thompson, Orval Nathan

Pennsylvania

Abramowitz, Robert Leslie
Bookman, Mark
Brand, Ronald Alvah
Briscoe, Jack Clayton
Cancelli, Dante Antonio
Carroll, Donald R.
Curtis, Gregory Dyer
Frank, Bernard
Gathright, Howard T.
Haber, Richard Jerome
Herchenroether, Henry Carl, Jr.
Hetherington, John Joseph
Heywood, Barbara Lorentson
Hoffstot, Henry Phipps, Jr.
Horoho, Kenneth Joseph, Jr.
Kabala, Edward John
Kaufman, David J.
Kutz, Robert H.
Laub, George Cooley
Lees, Steven Thomas
Lentz, Edward James
Madeira, David Beckman
Mauger, Lee Fillmen
Meigs, John Forsyth
Pilling, Janet Kavanaugh
Plotnick, Charles Keith
Rabinowitz, Samuel Nathan
Sproull, Frederick Anthony Raymond
Straus, Joseph Pennington
Taulane, John Baptist, Jr.
Van Dusen, Lewis Harlow, Jr.
Wagner, Joseph Hagel
Weisz, Frank Barry
Wood, William Philler
Yates, Alfred Glenn, Jr.

Rhode Island

Hastings, Edwin Hamilton
Lincoln, Michael David

South Carolina

Beasley, Frederick Alexander
Beckett, Alice Talbird
Brunson, Nolen Landford
Clement, Robert Lebby, Jr.
Edwards, Harry LaFoy
Handel, Richard Craig
Lynch, John Timothy
Rasor, Charles Lewis, Jr.
Todd, Albert Creswell, III
Traxler, William Byrd

Tennessee

Bird, Frank Babington
Donelson, Lewis Randolph, III
Farris, Frank Mitchell, Jr.
Galvin, Charles O'Neill
Green, Lynne Knight
Holbrook, Dan W.
Marquis, Robert Stillwell
Stokes, Carl Nicholas
Tate, S. Shepherd
Walker, Joseph Hillary, Jr.
Watson, James William
Wilkinson, Robert Warren

Texas

Allen, Michael Douglas
Berry, Thomas Eugene
Carpenter, Gordon Russell
Chrisman, Perry Oswin
Conkel, Robert Dale
Dougherty, John Chrysostom, III
Eastland, S. Stacy
Edmonds, Thomas Leon
French, Colin Val
Geffen, Arthur Harold
Goldberg, William Jeffrey
Henkel, Kathryn G.
Hudspeth, Chalmers Mac
Jack, Larry A.
Jackson, Randall Calvin
Jansen, Donald Orville
Jennings, Susan Jane
Johanson, Stanley Morris
Koenig, Rodney Curtis
Leshin, Richard Lee
Martin, Paul E(dward)
Moy, Celeste Marie
Olson, George Albert
Oppenheimer, Jesse Halff
Pinnell, Gary Ray
Premack, Paul Allen
Prince, Wayman Lee
Remy, William Emmett
Smith, Edward Vance, III
Ward, Gary Ardus
Wilkes, John Michael
Wilson, Donald L.
Wright, Wallace Mathias

Utah

Jeppson, Joseph Gaddis

Vermont

Morrow, Emily Rubenstein

Virginia

Bates, Harold Martin
Conway, William Augustine
Cooper, Charles Neilson
Davidson, Frank Gassaway, III
Frith, Douglas Kyle
Horsley, Waller Holladay
Knighton, Alton Lefleur, Jr.

Massey, Arthur Blanton
McClure, Roger John
Mezzullo, Louis Albert
Pollard, Overton Price
Simmonds, James Henry
Ward, Joe Henry, Jr.

Washington

Arnold, Nancy Tarbuck
Cunningham, Janis Ann
Malone, Thomas William
McLaughlin, Thomas Orville
Olver, Michael Lynn
Panchot, Dudley Bradford

West Virginia

Bayley, Thomas Way, Jr.
Reed, James Wilson
Stone, Samuel Spencer

Wisconsin

Bennett, David H.
Kabaker, Richard Zohn
LaBudde, Roy Christian
Mihal, Thomas Harlan
Orth, Charles Adam, Jr.
Rasmussen, Carl John
Roberson, Linda
Thuermer, Richard Joseph
Trebon, Lawrence Alan

Wyoming

Patrick, H. Hunter

ADDRESS UNPUBLISHED

Armstrong, Robert Elmer
Bergman, Arlie Walter
Corcoran, Sheila Margaret
Dickey, Sam S.
Dimon, John E.
Dunn, Thomas Tinsley
Edwards, Daniel Paul
Eisen, Edwin Roy
Feingold, Victor
Gamble, E. James
Gorochow, Vera Zina
Howe, Drayton Ford, Jr.
Howitt, Idelle Anne
James, Joyce Marie
Katz, Maurice Harry
Merrill, Abel Jay
Meyerson, Stanley Phillip
Niehaus, Susan Patricia
Rosen, Alex L.
Salomon, Barbara
Shughart, Donald Louis
Solkoff, Jerome Ira
Stone, Edward Herman
Worley, L. Glenn

ETHICS. See Jurisprudence.

FAMILY AND MATRIMONIAL

UNITED STATES

Alabama

Bains, Lee Edmundson
Black, Claire Alexander
Cotton, Gregory Dale
Davis, Penelope Ann
Deen, Thomas Jefferson, III
Dinning, Woodford Wyndham, Jr.
Downes, Robert Bruce
Friedman, Barry Allen
Frierson, Sarah Stewart
Hamm, Coleman Durden, Jr.
Higgins, Ronald Clarence
Hughes, Patrick Paul
Lane, Wilford Jones
Martin, Ludger D.
Means, Tyrone Carlton
Paschal, Beverly Jo
Patton, Martha Jane
Sapp, Ernestine S.
Tatum, Fred Menefee, Jr.
Tucker, Billie Anne
Waddell, John Emory
Wise, Steven Lanier

Alaska

Branson, Albert Harold
Davies, Bruce Owen
Johnson, Donald Milby
Ross, Wayne Anthony
Therrien, Valerie Monica

Arizona

Bachstein, Harry Samuel
Bellah, C. Richard
Butler, A(rthur) Bates, III
Cantor, Alena
Freedman, Kenneth David
Friedlander, Susan Oliver
Hossler, David Joseph
Howard, Robert Campbell, Jr.
Howard, Shari Irene
Hyams, Harold
Jensen, Robert Arthur
Jenson, Dennis Dion
Kjos, Victoria Ann
Larson, Ronald Frederick
Mallin, Robert Harold
Ong, Henry Hop
Ostapuk, David R.
Parker, Myrna Jean
Paupore, Jeffrey George
Pratte, Deborah Miriam
Stanford, Kenneth Charles
Sternberg, Melvin
Traynor, William Patrick
Wolfe, David K.

Arkansas

Bailey, Frank Henry
Butt, Thomas Franklin
Carpenter, Charles L.
Gant, Horace Zed
Goodner, Donald Scott

Hobbs, Richard White
Hughes, Steven Jay
Lineberger, John Ralph
Talley-Morris, Neva Bennett
Thomas, Albert, Jr.
Young, Robert Earl

California

August, Ann
Balliet, Susan Jackson
Batchelor, James Kent
Berman, Howard Jonathan
Borell, Karen Lorraine
Borges, David Joseph
Briggs, Steven Ernest
Broome, Thomas Jefferson
Brown, Lawrence
Brown, Ralph Evan
Chamberlin, C. Rick
Childs, Marjorie M.
Cleary, William Joseph, Jr.
DeRonde, John Allen, Jr.
Diamond, Ann Landy
Drexler, Kenneth
Fainsbert, Ann Rubenstein
Farr, G(ardner) Neil
Fischer, Dale Susan
Flanagan, James Henry, Jr.
Fleischli, Jack A.
Fletcher, R(ufus) Burton, Jr.
Gough, Aidan Richard
Greenberg, Harold
Gutierrez, Max, Jr.
Halsey, Patricia Frederick
Hamilton, Mary Jane
Hearsch, Janis Camille Brown
Hendrickson, Ray
Hoagland, Grant Taylor
Hoefflin, Richard Michael
Horwin, Leonard
Jacobs, Paul Elliot
Jaffe, Frohm Filmore
Johnson, Barbara Jean
Kaufman, Albert I.
Kay, Herma Hill
Kelly, John Michael
Kock, Arlene Dorothy
Kotler, Richard Lee
Kraus, James Alan
Ladikos, Costas Angelo
Lampel, Arthur Harry
Lane, Robert K.
Lurvey, Ira Harold
Lynch, Robert Berger
Mac Gowan, Mary Eugenia
Markey, Christian Edward, Jr.
Marmon, David Glenn
McCall, Patrick Anthony
McCallum, Barbara Eiland
McCroskey, Elizabeth Wear
Mc Elwain, Lester Stafford
McFarland, Carol Anne
McKechnie, C. Logan
Moore, Julie E.
Nigg, Karl Frederick
Ofner, William Bernard
O'Shields, June Cruce
Perri, Audrey Ann
Philo, DuWayne Allen
Pilling, George William
Ponomareff, Guyla Woodward
Prozan, Sylvia Simmons
Ragetté-Blaine, Dorothea Constance
Reith, Daniel I.
Richmond, Diana
Riffer, Jeffrey Kent
Roberts, Jayne Kelly
Schreiber, James Phillip
Seheult, Malcolm McDonald Richardson
Shapiro, Anita Rae
Shaw, Stanford Eugene
Silveria, Linda Lorraine
Silverman, Bruce Stanly
Simonelli, James John
Sindon, Geoffrey Stuart
Spence, Kristi Cotton
Staley, John Fredric
Stephenson, Michael Murray
Stotter, Lawrence Henry
Susi, Mart Sven
Taylor, Howard Harper
Teitler, Harold Herman
Weingarten, Saul Myer
Wellins, Sheldon (Shel) Gary
Weston, Kenneth Frederick
Wooley, Kenneth Virgil
Wright, Frank Clarence, Jr.
Zinn, Henry Jackson

Colorado

Adkins, Marilyn Biggs
Bernstein, Jeremy Marshall
Billings, Bruce Arthur
Bisgard, Eileen Bernice Reid
Boyle, John Edward
Brega, Charles Franklin
Bugdanowitz, Robert
Carleno, Harry Eugene
Carlton, Diane Michele
Chestnutt, Ellen Joanne
Cox, Mary Jane Truesdell
Cronan, Kathleen Michele
Donlon, William James, Jr.
Evans, Paul Vernon
Feiger, Lynn Diamond
Gardner, Dale Ray
Geil, Karl James
Geisel, Henry Jules
George, Doug
Gunn, Rebecca Louise
Johnson, Dale Eliot
Joss, W. Bruce
LaCroix, Thomas Russell
Lerman, Eileen R.
Livingston, John L.
Lohman, Richard Verne
Malone, Thomas Paul
Manley, Douglas Rempet
McCormick, George Paul, Jr.
McDowell, Karen Ann
McGee, Robert Leon, Jr.
McGuane, Frank L., Jr.
Metzger, Karen Susan
Mygatt, Ann Bliss
Oxman, Stephen Eliot
Robinson, Wayne E.
Rodriquez, Janet Lois

Rose, Charles Jon
Schenkein, Pamela Ephraim
Taylor, Robert Lynn
Wedgle, Richard Jay
West, Laurie Diane

Connecticut

Abery-Wetstone, Holly Ann
Argenta, Craig Jon
Berman, John Arthur
Bracken, Nanette Beattie
Carrano, Frank Anthony
Carta, John James, Jr.
Coan, Richard Morton
Cutsumpas, Lloyd
Daniels, Douglas Robert
Densen-Gerber, Judianne
Effron, Wayne Douglas
Fricke, Richard John
Gerlt, Wayne Christopher
Gersten, Sandra Joan Pessin
Greenfield, James Robert
Harper, Monica Lafferty
Johnson, Allan Richard
Karazin, Edward Robert, Jr.
Katz, Jay
Kiefer, Louis
Lang, Edward Gerald
MacKenzie, Roderick John, Jr.
Meehan, Richard Thomas, Jr.
Nevas, Leo
Nicola, Robert James
Osis, Daiga Guntra
Piazza, Anthony Andrew
Ross, Michael Frederick
Rubenstein, Mark A.
Sheiman, Stuart Melvyn
Silver, Elaine Terry
Sorokin, Ethel Silver
Telker, Ellen Melinda
Widing, Carol Scharfe
Wolfson, Susan Wartur
Wynn, Mary Ellen

Delaware

Levine, Norman Edward
Mekler, Arlen B.
Ridgely, Henry Johnson
Willard, John Martin

District of Columbia

Ain, Sanford King
Cook, Frank Robert, Jr.
Doyle, Joyce Ann
Feldman, Clarice Rochelle
King, John Winston
Knab, Karen Markle
Kuder, Armin Ulrich
Lerman, Lisa Gabrielle
Murawski, Roberta Lee
Oyewole, G. Godwin
Rider, James Lincoln
Rosenau, Kenneth H.
Rubenstein, Herbert R.
Sachs, Sidney Stanley
Snyder, John Freeman
Statland, Edward Morris
West, Togo Dennis, Jr.
Young, Marlene Annette

Florida

Abrams, Brenda M.
Asencio, Diego Carlos
Atlas, Allan Jay
Baccus, Tonya Lynn
Baker, Elizabeth Statuta
Berns, Bonnie Ava
Birnbaum, Richard Michael
Bombino, Isabel Piñera
Boyles, Kevan Kenneth
Boynton, Gary John
Brock, Newman Dempsey
Brophy, Gilbert Thomas
Buchman, Kenneth William
Cano, Mario Stephen
Carbo, Michael James
Chopin, Susan Gardiner
Clark, Ross Townsend
Cohen, Meredith Joseph
Custureri, Richard Domenick
Day, George Everette
Dayhoff, Charles Sidney, III
Eggen, Eric Carl
Finkelstein, Joseph Judah
Fletcher, Paul Gerald
Fowler, Sandra T.
Franklin, Lucille Espey
Fromberg, Malcolm Hubert
Gilbert, Ronald Bart
Glick, Brian Jay
Gluck, Robin Beverly
Goldman, Joel L.
Harris, Warren Louis
Hastings, Michael Lynn
Hern, Joseph George, Jr.
Hernandez, Daniel Mario
Kapner, Lewis
Kimber, Brian Lee
Koch, Ky Marshall
Kutner, Maurice Jay
LaBoda, Barry Charles
Lancaster, Kenneth G.
Levin, David Harold
Luskin, Paul Bansech
Lyng, Reginald William
McCormick, John Hoyle
McCoy, Francis Tyrone
McGovern, Peter John
McMakin, J. Gary
Miller, Robert Charles
Milstein, Richard Craig
Nyce, John Daniel
Oberhausen, Frank Clay, Jr.
O'Flarity, James P.
Penland, Samuel Perry, Jr.
Poole, Sharon Alexandra
Quiat, Bette Ellen
Rexrode, David Stephen
Rose, Michael I.
Rosinek, Jeffrey
Rowan, Beverly Adele
Samole, Myron Michael
Sasser, Donald Julian
Schneider, Harvey Robert
Schnell, Ronald Hans
Semento, Lawrence James

Sessums, Stephen Walker
Shaffer, Sanford Joel
Sharett, Alan Richard
Sheffield, Frank Elwyn
Siegel, Edward
Siegel, Paul
Silver, Roger Allen
Silvernail, Jesse Preston
Slaughter, Marshall Glenn
Smith, Horace, Jr.
Strawn, David Updegraff
Tobin, Gerald J.
Tombrink, Richard, Jr.
Udell, Michael Bennett
Walsh, Michael Raymond
Watson, Roberta Casper
Wilson, Brenda Coker
Young, Terry Cressler
Zacur, Richard Aaron
Zorie, Stephanie Marie

Georgia

Barrett, David Eugene
Bassler, Harry Warren
Bostic, Harris Clemon
Breeding, Earnie Rowe
Brinson, Benjamin Pierce
Callner, Bruce Warren
Cook, Martha Jean
Cooper, Lawrence Allen
Cowen, Martin Lindsey, III
Crumbley, R. Alex
Custer, Lawrence Benjamin
Dally, Rebecca Polston
Davis, E. Marcus
Dean, George Ross
Dodd, Roger James
Duttweiler, Larry L.
Edlin, Shiel Graham
Emmons, Peter Ribeiro
Fitzpatrick, Duross
Flowers, William Harold, Jr.
Fox, Patrick Joseph
Freed, Gary Stuart
Hames, Luther Claude, Jr.
Hanington, Paula Kay
Harrison, Samuel Hughel
Harvey, Alan Christopher
Hibbert, David Wilson
Hubbard, George Morrison, III
Kalish, Katherine McAulay
Kidd, Daryl Leslie
Lanier, Robert Simmons, Jr.
Lee, Carol Elizabeth
Liston, Paul Sperry
Mahan, John Ernest
Manis, Stephanie Brodie
Mull, Gale W.
Phillips, Charles Patrick
Polstra, Larry John
Porter, Mary Helen (Howard)
Shapiro, Michael Bruce
Shulman, Warren Scott
Steger, Susan St. John
Stone, Brian
Taylor-Hanington, Paula Kay
Wellon, Robert G.
Zachary, William Edmund

Hawaii

Aduja, Peter Aquino
Barbin, Ryther Lynn
Berman, Pamela Jill
Coates, Bradley Allen
Darrah, William Charles
Gillin, Malvin James, Jr.
Iwai, Wilfred Kiyoshi
Kitagawa, Audrey Emiko
Rice, V(irgil) Thomas
Sabath, Kenneth Michael
Simms, Sandra Arlene
Wong, Michael Jung-Yen

Idaho

Christenson, Jeffrey Robert
Hart, Stephen Strong
Hicks, George Gregory
Hoff, Renae
Smyser, (Charles Arvil) Skip
Thompson, Frances Hoene
Wetherell, Mike

Illinois

Armstrong, Edwin Richard
Atkinson, Jeff John Frederick
Auerbach, Marshall Jay
Beal, Bruce Curtis
Beneke, William Scott
Biestek, John Paul
Bracey, Willie Earl
Braden, Everette Arnold
Bruno, Thomas Anthony
Church, Glenn J.
Citrin, Phillip Marshall
Clark, Natalie Loder
Conway, Martin Eugene, Jr.
DaRosa, Ronald Anthony
Davis, Muller
Didzerekis, Paul Patrick
Dodd, Robert Warren
Doughty, H. Reed
DuCanto, Joseph Nunzio
Dunn, Melvin Edward
Ealy, F. Ronald
Edmiston, Charles Nathan
Feinstein, Paul Louis
Field, Harold Gregory
Franklin, Randy Wayne
Frederick, Robert George
Gabe, Caryl Jacobs
Glenn, Cleta Mae
Goldstein, Richard M.
Gordon, Barry L.
Gossage, Roza
Grant, Louis Z.
Greenberg, Lorraine M.
Gutof, Richard Stewart
Hamrock, Mark Andrew
Harvey, Morris Lane
Hubbard, Elizabeth Louise
Hunter, Eugenia C.
Inman, Arthur James
Keay, David Holm
Keith, John Ray
Komie, Stephen Mark
Kurowski, John Joseph

Lasaine, Dorian Barnett
Leving, Jeffery Mark
Lindstedt, Norman Edward
Lousberg, Peter Herman
Mateas, Kenneth Edward
McClow, Thomas Alan
McCullough, John Thomas
Meyer, Stanley Russell
Miller, Geoffrey Charles
Minton, Michael Harry
Mohr, Terry Richard
Moore, John L.
Moore, Kathleen Ann
Moorman, Helen Louise
Murer, Michael Anton
Murphy, Sandra Robison
Murphy, William Celestin
Narusis, Regina GytéFirant
Nye, Sandra Gayle
Paul, Bernard Arthur
Pearlman, Alan
Phipps, John Tom
Poper, Michael Charles
Rappaport, Earle Samuel, Jr.
Reardon, Timothy Joseph
Robb, Elizabeth Ann
Roberts, Keith Edward, Sr.
Robertson, David Haswell, Jr.
Ruud, Glenn F.
Ryan, Frank James
Schiller, Donald Charles
Schlott, Mary Camille
Sfasciotti, Mary L.
Sims, E. Jane
Spears, Larry Jonell
Stanfield, James Caleb
Stitt, LeMoine Donaldson
Swain, John Barry
Szewczyk, Stephen Michael
Tungate, Susan Sumner
Veverka, Donald John
Walker, Daniel, Jr.
Webster, John Clyde

Indiana

Baker, Ronald Lee
Baker, Ronald Lee
Bamberth, Hugo Arnold
Barden, Kenneth Eugene
Bennett, Maxine Taylor
Blythe, James David, II
Brown, Elaine Marie Becher
Clouse, John Daniel
Coffman, Anne Blankenburg
Cox, John Coates
Davis, Ann Gouger
Ford, Lee Ellen
Grodnik, Charles Hubert
Hanger, William Joseph
Harrold, Dennis Edward
Haury, John Carroll
Johnson, Shelli Wright
Leopold, Robert Bruce
Lewis, Robert Lee
Lindsey, Roger Leighton
Loveall, George Michael
Mascher, Gilbert Ernsting
McNeely, Mark Wright
Meltzer, Kris
Petersen, Howard Edwin
Sembroski, Robert Edmund
Sheets, Thomas Wade
Stimson, Judith Nemeth
Tourkow, Joshua Isaac
Walmer, James L.
Wicks, Charles Carter
Woods, Joseph Reid
Young, Randy William

Iowa

Baybayan, Ronald Alan
Beisser, Louie Frederick
Boresi, Richard L(eo)
Burns, James
Butler, David Douglas
Critelli, Lylea May Dodson
Danielson, Cynthia Howard
Danilson, David Ray
Eckhart, Morris Lee Roy
Fitzgibbons, Ann
Giles, William Jefferson, IV
Giles, William Jefferson, III
Grace, David Joseph
Gray, William Oxley
Harding, Marc Steven
Larson, David Christopher
Manly, Charles M., III
Ouderkirk, Mason James
Visser, Kevin James

Kansas

Braun, Glenn Robert
Elrod, Linda Diane Henry
Gastl, Eugene Francis
Hejtmanek, Danton Charles
Hess, Jerry John
Kreamer, Scott Harrison
Krusor, Mark William
Lowe, Jon Kent
Manning, Donna Kaser
Marquardt, Christel Elisabeth
Walker, Huffman Reed
Walters, Amy Ottinger
Walton, Herbert Wilson

Kentucky

Bailey, Ann Leslie
Bowles, Jerry Jay
Bradshaw, Alice Linda
Bratton, Robert Milton
Brown, Bonnie Maryetta
Budden, Harry Edward, Jr.
Dunlap, Tavner Branham
Guier, Lester Bennett
Jefferson, Janice Lee Roehler
Megibow, Tod Douglas
Niemi, Bruce Alan
O'Daniel, Jean Elizabeth
Seiller, Bill Victor
Smither, J. Michael
Walker, Patricia Gail
Whalen, Paul Lewellin

Louisiana

Arceneaux, James Shaw

Barranger, Garic Kenneth
Bernheim, Sadye Kern
Brainis, Leon Irving
Cavell, Daniel A.
Clement, Leslie Joseph, Jr.
Facussé, Albert Shucry
Gallagher, Michael Stephen
Gandy, Kim Allison
Hauver, Terence Lee
Herring, Charles Evans, Jr.
Kiefer, John B.
Kuss, Mark Davis
Lane, Steven Jay
Larke, George Joseph, Jr.
Marx, Paula Jeannette
McKay, Dan Boies, Jr.
McManus, Clarence Elburn
Milly, Lawrence Arthur
Morris, Frank Lowry
Pitts, Birdia Marie Greer
Poirrier, Michael Joseph
Reed, Bruce Gilbert
Rigby, Kenneth
Ross, Bobbie Jean
Smith, Christopher Michael
Spencer, Philip Polmer
Stracener, Carol Elizabeth
Taylor, John McKowen
Todaro, Laura Jean
Trombatore, Janet Moulton
Weisler, Faye Leslie
White, Trudy Melita
Woodard, Billie Elayne Colombaro
Wright, Jack, Jr.

Maine

Dyer, Matthew Finis
Hirshon, Robert Edward
Laney, William R.
Massey, Donald Terhune
Reef, Norman Sidney
Romanow, Richard Brian

Maryland

Barkley, Brian Evan
Brooks, Sheila Durant
Cohen, Hyman K.
Dunn, John Benjamin
Ferris, William Michael
Fisher, Jeffrey B.
Hackett, Sylvia Lavada
Hall, William Bryan, Jr.
Haskins, Patrick Dean
Henry, Edwin Maurice, Jr.
Hicks, Cassandra Pauline
Kleid, Wallace
Lazzaro, Robert Wayne
Lewis, Leah H.
Mitnick, Harold
Mix, George Warren
Naditch, Ronald Marvin
Ogletree, Anne Meve Callahan
Olszewski, Kevin Trent
Papkin, Rachel Friedberg
Perkins, Roger Allan
Petraitis, Karel Colette
Protokowicz, Stanley Edward, Jr.
Putzel, Constance Kellner
Santa Maria, Philip Joseph, III
Scott, Charles Lurman
Shore, Elbert Russell
Simons, David Warren
Williams, Kathryn Diggs
Ziegler, Arnold Gerard

Massachusetts

Burstein, Merwyn Jerome
Cherny, David Edward
Cohen, Donna Eden
Cullinane, Paul Blake
Cusick, Elizabeth Emma
Fidnick, Linda Susan
Field, Martha Amanda
Haldane, Mark Thomas
Kaplan, David Richard
Kindregan, Charles Peter
Lee, David Harold
Legasey, John Samuel
Lipman, Stephen I.
Manion, Harry Leo
McGinnis, Andrew Mosher
Monahan, Marie Terry
Packenham, Richard Daniel
Pearson, Paul David
Perera, Lawrence Thacher
Robbins, Lynda Jean
Sander, Frank Ernest Arnold
Sherman, Elliot Mark
Snyder, Marie Elizabeth
Takas, Marianne Heath
Tremblay, Michael Jeffrey
Vincent, Thomas Philip
Westfall, David
Whitbeck, James Allis
Witt, Carol Ann
Zito, Frank R.

Michigan

Austin, Margaret Schilt
Barnhart, Katherine Louise
Barton, Judith Marie
Bos, John Earl
Centers, Louise Claudena
Chambers, David L., III
Chartrand, Douglas Arthur
Chin, Sherry (Lynn)
Colombo, Frederick J.
Cooper, Richard I.
Cox, Joseph King
Dilley, Thomas Robert
Dobry, Stanley Thomas
Eklund-Easley, Molly Sue
Fenn, Bruce Hunter
Ferrier, Jon Todd
Filoramo, John Robert
Fink, Sally Claire
Freilich, Diane M.
Greve, Guy Robert
Harper, Linda Walker
Hausner, John Herman
Jacobs, Wendell Early, Jr.
Keller, Gerald Douglas
Landers, Diann Jeanette
Larky, Sheldon Glen
Lehto, Neil John
Lemcool, Michael James

Lint, Louis Raymond
Marin, Paul Martin
McGarry, Alexander Banting
Morganroth, Fred
Mullendore, James Myers
Prather, Kenneth Earl
Schrot, John Joseph, Jr.
Seglund, Bruce Richard
Shulaw, Richard Allen
Smith, Terry J.
Snyder, George Edward
Spivak, Peter Beeching
Talpos, John C.
Thomas, Robert Weston
Travis, Robert Frederick
Vanderkloot, William Robert
Victor, Richard Steven
Virtue, Maxine Boord
Williams, D. Lee
Zameck, Harvey Jason

Minnesota

Aaron, Allen Harold
Baker, Gail Dyer
Bard, Stephen Allan
Berg, Nancy Zalusky
Cafarella, Joan Marie Coursolle
Delano, Stephen James
Edelman, Hyman
Ferguson, Elizabeth Norton
Gislason, Daniel Adam
Gorlin, Cathy Ellen
Gurstel, Norman Keith
Hanson, Steven Allen
Higgs, David Corey
Koch, Scott James
Kubes, Eugene Leonard
Lazar, Raymond Michael
Leighninger, Sally Heinz
Masica, Mark Alexis
Murrin, John Owen
Nesseler, Steven Edward
Nordaune, Roselyn Jean
Nyquist, Dean Allen
Olup, Linda Ann
Skaar, Harvey Engaard
Younger, Judith Tess

Mississippi

Fant, Lester Glenn
Harper, Gregory Livingston
Harris, David Neil
James, L. C.
Kirksey, William Boyd
Meek, Walter Buchanan
Odom, Elizabeth Ann
Reeves, John Raymond
Shaw, Susan Boyce
Taylor, Ronald Louis
Thompson, James Grant, III

Missouri

Albano, Michael Santo John
Bayer, Elmer Valentine
Berrey, Robert Wilson, III
Blanke, Richard B.
Bryan, Henry C(lark), Jr.
Calvin, Edward Eugene
Crites, Richard Don
Cruse, Fredrich James
Dixon, Scott William
Fleddermann, Stephen Roy
Gifford, Wayne Daniel
Gunn, Michael Peter
Hessel, Mildred Reda
Kaplan, Chester B.
Keller, Elizabeth Ann
Koffman, Robert Lawrence
Kranitz, Theodore Mitchell
Kruger, Mark Howard
Lange, C. William
Lonardo, Charles Henry
McConnell, James David
Moore, Mitchell Jay
Radke, Daniel Lee
Russell, William Oliver
Schramm, Paul Howard
Steimel, Norman Clemens, III
Swann, Elizabeth Walker
Terry, Jack Chatterson
Thayer, Charlotte P.
Turcotte, John Arthur, Jr.
Ver Dught, ElGene Clark
Walsh, Thomas Joseph
Wells, David Lee
Wight, Les D., II
Willis, Wayne George
Zerr, Richard Kevin

Montana

Bauer, Mark Eugene
Birkenbuel, Marcia Lee
Caughlan, Deirdre
Graveley, Charles Allan
Smartt, Michael Stewart

Nebraska

Ball, Jordan Mitchell
Dorwart, Charles Edward
Ellis, John Patrick
Gordon, James Edward
Jones, Ida Mae
Line, William Gunderson
Rowland, Richard Arthur
Smith, Wilbur Cowan
Troia, Anthony Samuel

Nevada

Burns, Thomas Martin
Carter, George Richard
Claassen, Sharon Elaine
Cornell, Richard Farnham
Golden, Michael Patrick
Grad, Neil Elliott Marshall
Logar, Ronald John
Lumkes, Deborah Lee
Puccinelli, Leo J.
Sumpter, Rodney Evert

New Hampshire

Drucker, Leonard Murray
King, Michael Paul

New Jersey

Abrams, Robert Allen
Abut, Charles C.
Altman, Jane R.
Amadeo, Natial Salvatore
Baker, Max Allen
Biel, Mark
Boardman, Michael Neil
Borelli, B. Michael
Boskey, James Bernard
Brown, James B., Jr.
Cheifetz, Cary Bennet
Cohen, Diane Berkowitz
Cohn, Albert Linn
Diamond, Gloria Beverly
Domzalski, Kenneth Stanley
Forkin, Thomas S.
Friend, Israel
Golden, Daniel Lewis
Gourvitz, Elliot Howard
Graziano, Ronald Anthony
Grosman, Alan M.
Hansbury, Stephan Charles
Hiltebrand, Stephen Mark
Hoffman, Bernard H.
Johnstone, Irvine Blakeley, III
Kantor, Lawrence Dorn
Kaplan, Howard Mark
Kaplan, Steven Samuel
Kearns, William John, Jr.
Kleinberg, Robert Samuel
Kozyra, Barry Alan
Kraus, Robert H.
Lihotz, Marie Elaine
Littman, David Bernard
Markus, Allan Lewis
Masucci, Louis M., Jr.
McCracken, Carol Weaver
McDonnell, Richard C.
Menendez, Robert
Mulligan, Elinor Patterson
Osofsky, Herman
Paley, Phillip Lewis
Pizzi, Frank Anthony, Jr.
Rinsky, Joel Charles
Robinson, Sandra Ann
Rochkind, Mark Howard
Rodriguez, Ariel Antonio
Rogoff, Marc Jeffrey
Rose, Edith Sprung
Roth, Jeffrey Stuart
Rowe, Paul Andrew
Savage, Harold Michael
Schoenewolf, Walter Wayne
Schreiber, William Mark
Sikora, Frederick Joseph
Slavitt, Ben J.
Smith, Seymour Alan
Trenner, Kathryn
Weitzman, Donald Martin
White, Ivan Vance, Jr.
Wildstein, David M.
Wood, Leonard James
Wszolek, Dennis Francis
Yudes, James Peyton
Zurav, David Bernard

New Mexico

Brockman, Eugene E.
Cargo, David Francis
Conway, Susan Marie
Diamond, Jeffrey Brian
Dutton, Dominic Edward
Ferrara, Anthony Joseph
Gant, Joseph Erwin, III
Gant, Joseph Erwin
Henderson, William Nelson
Mckim, Lowell E.
McKinnon, Daniel Angus, III
Vigil, Carol Jean

New York

Abramowitz, Alton Lee
Abrams, Stuart
Abramson, Joel Eliot
Alter, Eleanor Breitel
Arber, Howard Bruce
Ardam, David Mitchell
Arenstein, Robert David
Aris, Joram Jehudah
Ascher, Richard Alan
Avner, Judith I.
Bader-York, Judith
Bavero, Ronald Joseph
Bender, Joel Charles
Birmingham, Richard Francis
Black, Warren John
Bloom, Robert Avrum
Bodnar, Peter O.
Booth, Mitchell B.
Bradshaw, Leslie Arnold
Brenner, Frank
Brettschneider, Rita Roberta
Brezinsky, Helene
Brown, Harvey R.
Burger, Lewis Stephen
Burgess, John Richard
Burke, Carol Elizabeth
Burrows, Kenneth David
Burstein, Beatrice S.
Capell, Walter Richard
Capetola, Anthony Adam
Cartier, Rudolph Henri, Jr.
Casey, Kathleen Heirich
Chamberlain, John
Clark, Robert Francis
Coffin, Mary McCarthy
Cohen, Robert Stephan
Daly, William Joseph
DaSilva, Willard H.
Dikman, Michael
Dorf, Robert Clay
Drexler, Mark Andrew
Eckelman, Paul John
Eiche, Jay S.
Elliott, A. Irene
Enochs, Elizabeth M.
Farr, Charles Sims
Felder, Raoul Lionel
Feldman, Warren Bruce
Finkelstein, Allen Lewis
Friedberg, Harry Jacob
Frost, Jerome Kenneth
Frucco, John Peter
Gallet, Jeffry Hershel
Ghandhi, Madonna Stahl
Ginsberg, Jerome Maurice
Glavin, John Joseph
Goldman, Joel J.
Goldman, Marshall Stanley
Goldstein, Howard Sheldon
Goldstein, Kenneth B.
Goodfriend, Mark F.
Greenbaum, Sheldon Marc
Gulotta, Frank Andrew, Jr.
Hargesheimer, Elbert, III
Heath, Joseph John
Herman, William Charles
Heussi, Jonathan A.
Higginson, James Jackson
Hill, Janet Wadsworth
Hinman, James Stuart
Horey, Edward Madigan
Isaacs, Leonard Bernard
Issler, Harry
Jewell, Robert Hart
Kahn, David Miller
Kaplan, Joel Stuart
Kapur, David Edmund
Kaye, Richard Paul
Knigin, Kenneth Sheldon
Kurzman, Robert Graham
La Forge, Gladys Candace
Lake, Barbara Ruth
LaMancuso, John Lory
Lamutis, Donald Franklin
Landau, Sybil Harriet
Leben, Jeffrey Michael
Leininger, William Joseph
Leiser, Burton Myron
Leventhal, A. Linda
Levine, David Ethan
Levine, Steven Jon
Levinson, David Lawrence
Levitan, Katherine D.
Levy, Alan C(hester)
Lipman, Howard Stewart
Lotwin, Stanford Gerald
Lustgarten, Ira Howard
Mahon, Arthur J.
Mahoney, David John
Maissel, Raina Eve
Malach, Herbert John
Mantel, Allan David
Markel, Sheldon Martin
Marrero, Louis John
Masliansky, Nechama
McCaffrey, Carlyn Sundberg
McPhillips, Joseph William
Meltzer, Sanford
Meyer, Bernard Stern
Mulhern, Edwin Joseph
Mulligan, William G(eorge)
Neff, Michael Alan
O'Connor, Liam T(homas)
O'Neil, John Joseph
Paganuzzi, Oden Stephen, Jr.
Parisi, Frank Nicholas
Pilato, Louis Peter
Plotka, Richard F.
Porco, Domenick Joseph
Pugh, David Edward
Rich, Marcia R.
Riebesehl, E. Allan
Ritter, Ann L.
Rivera, Juan
Roman, David John
Rosen, Martin Jay
Rothman, Bernard
Runfola, Ross Thomas
Samalin, Edwin
Samuel, Reuben
Satz, Perry
Schack, Robert J.
Schechter, Donald Robert
Scheinkman, Alan David
Schwartz, Sydney James
Shapiro, Hadassah R(uth)
Shatz, Phillip
Shaughnessy, James Michael
Sheresky, Norman M.
Siegel-Baum, Judith Ellen
Silk, Robert Howard
Sladkus, Harvey Ira
Sokolow, Lloyd Bruce
Stachowski, Michael Joseph
Stahr, Thomas James
Stein, Leslie E.
Stone, Henry
Stone, Kathleen Gale
Targoff, Cheri Kamen
Tarnoff, Jerome
Taub, Eli Irwin
Tepper, Eric Alan
Thompson, Katherine Genevieve
Tucker, Robert Henry
Vick, Paul Ashton
Wallman, Lester
Weinreb, Michael Leonard
Wels, Richard Hoffman
Wildes, Leon
Yablon, Babette
Yagerman, Howard W.
Zabel, William David
Zeitlan, Marilyn L.
Zerin, Steven David
Zimmerman, Golda
Zionts, Harriette Abrams

North Carolina

Alexander, Charles Jackson, II
Bragg, Ellis Meredith, Jr.
Burleson, Lynn Pierce
Calhoun, Marilyn Jean
Cannon, Thomas Roberts
Carroll, Seavy Alexander
Carter, John Tilton, Jr.
Cunningham, George Gray
Davis, Joslin
Dixon, Phillip Ray
Ellis, Sharon Barclay
Farver, Harry Craig
Gantt, Charles David
Harris, Richard Foster, III
Hemphill, Kathryn Glenn
Hopkins, Grover Prevatte
Hulse, William Frederick
Randolph, Clyde Clifton, Jr.
Reppy, William Arneill, Jr.
Riddle, Robert Edward
Schwenn, William Lee
Shields, Karen Bethea
Smith, Roger Theodore
Thompson, Eugene Cebron, III
Townsend, William Jackson

North Dakota

Kautzmann, Dwight C(larence) H(arry)
Nelson, Carol Susan
Quast, Larry Wayne
Spain, Larry Robert

Ohio

Ammer, William
Bamburowski, Thomas Joseph
Bebout, Bradley Carey
Berger, Sanford Jason
Braverman, Herbert Leslie
Bressler, H.J.
Cade, Daniel Steven
Capizzi, Anthony
Cohen, Arlene Switow
Conroy, John Thomas
Cooper, Linda Dawn
Cusack, Mary Jo
Dailey, Coleen Hall
Derivan, Hubert Thomas
Dulebohn, Diana Gay
Fine, Michael William
Fingerman, Albert Ross
Fox, Mary Ellen
Gambol, Robert Alan
Gerlach, Franklin Theodore
Gertner, Michael Harvey
Giannini, Matthew C.
Hall, James Alexander
Hardig, Mark Nelson
Heier, David Scott
Hill, Jay
Hill, Stephen A.
Horowitz, Ilana
Jacobs, Ann Elizabeth
Jones, Michael Charles
Kamine, Charles Stephen
Kanak, Joseph Robert
Kazdin, Margaret Ellen
Kennedy, Charles Allen
King, J(oseph) Michael
Klingenberg, Donald Herbert
Lagos, James Harry
Lantz, Charles Jeffery
Lukey, Paul Emeran
Machan, Mitchell Alan
McIlvaine, James Ross
Meily, William Davis
Moore, Lloyd Evans
O'Brien, William Scott
O'Connor, John Paul
Paul, Dennis Edward
Piazza, Anthony Michael
Postlewaite, Charles Chapman
Preston, Kevin Mark
Reed, Tyrone Edward
Sayler, John Liston
Sinclair, Virgil Lee, Jr.
Skotynsky, Walter John
Sowald, Heather Gay
Spero, Keith Erwin
Sternberg, David J.
Stocker, Thomas Edwin
Thomas, James William
Thompson, Jayne Audrey
Tucker, Theodore Brush, III
Tyack, George Gary
Vaughn, Noel Wyandt
Weaver, Susan M.
Wells, Lesley Brooks
Wettlaufer, Karl Frederick
Whipps, Edward Franklin
Wilson, Laura Jane
Wolaver, Stephen Arthur
Wood, Wendy Ann

Oklahoma

Basham, Marshall Denver
Corbitt, Sharon L.
Dale, Douglas Don
Ellis, Thomas Taylor
Galaska, Michael Francis
Hester, Jon Lee
Hood, William Wayne, Jr.
Johnson, H. Allen
Krepps, Ethel Constance
Moore, Roy Dean
Murphy, Robert Moore
Nolen, Lynn Dean
Parks, Ed Horace, III
Ryals, Kent
Shoemake, Bransford Hunt
Sullivan, Edward Paul
Ungerman, Maynard I.
Walke, Geary Lynn
Williams, Thomas Arthur

Oregon

Carroll, Catherine North
Crane, Donald Ray
Enfield, Myron Leroy
Feibleman, Gilbert Bruce
Forcum, Richard Eugene
Glasgow, Robert Efrom
Glazer, Peter Kendall
Honsowetz, Frank William
Jagger, James Cloyd
Johnston, Ronald Allen
Kronenberg, Debra Ann
Lombard, Herbert William, Jr.
Menashe, Albert Alan
Raines, Keith R.
Ringle, Philip Hamilton, Jr.
Sahlstrom, E(lmer) B(ernard)
Schade, Aloha Lee
Spencer, Jesse Neal
Spiegel, Laurence Harold
Trubo, Herbert Alan
Vallerand, Patricia Ann

Pennsylvania

Adams, John Joseph
Beck, Robert David
Bigman, Anton W.
Blakley, Benjamin Spencer, III
Blume, Karolyn Vreeland
Blumstein, Edward
Brosky, John G.
Cassarino, Joseph Francis
Ceraul, David James
Chomas, James Louis, Jr.
Cohen, Anita Marilyn
Cohen, Earl S.
Corse, Chester Clinton, Jr.
Coslett, Charles Reynolds
DeYoung, Jonathan Harvey
Doherty, Mary Cushing
Eshelman, David Richard
Farber, Howard
Favero, James Anthony
Feder, Robert David
Ferri, Karen Lynn
Fingerman, Michael Elliott
Foley, Joseph Llewellyn
Frank, Frederick Newman
Gold-Bikin, Lynne Z.
Graf, Bayard Mayhew
Grosh, Susan Ellen
Hartman, John Ives, Jr.
Herbruck, John Henry
Hess, Lawrence Eugene, Jr.
Horoho, Kenneth Joseph, Jr.
Houpt, Robert Campbell
Isabella, Mary Margaret
John, Robert McClintock
Jones, David Arthur
Kaminsky, Ira Samuel
Kennedy, James Edward
King, Peter Joseph
Klein, Joel Aaron
Kochems, Robert Gregory
Kormes, John Winston
Kotler, Helen Rose
Krouse, Gwin M.
Krug, Howard Barry
Krug, Rob Alan
Kulik, Joseph Michael
Leibel, Shelley Joy
Lepore, Alphonse Paul
Loewenstein, Benjamin Steinberg
Long, Christine Mathews
Lublin, Mark Aaron
Ludwig, Edmund V.
MacDonald, Richard Barry
Malady, Eugene Joseph
Markham, Rosemary
Mazer, Lawrence
Menaker, Bonnie Douglass
Meyer, Martin Jay
Moritz, Preston William
Moses, Carl Michael
Muth, Michael Raymond
O'Dell, Debbie
Osterhout, Richard Cadwallader
Peluso, Gino Francis
Perer, Diane Wilson
Perlman, Richard Brian
Phillips, Dorothy Kay
Pholeric, Karen Joy
Pyfer, John Frederick, Jr.
Rathgeber, Joanne Weil
Reagle, Jack Evan
Roeger, William Coley, Jr.
Rosenn, Harold
Rounick, Jack Abraham
Schauffler, Harvey Elliott, Jr.
Scheck, Donald Gordon
Scianna, Russell William
Shane, B(enjamin) Jerome
Siegel, Arthur Bernard
Smith, Sharon Louise
Sobota, John Raymond
Spry, Donald Francis, II
Standish, William Lloyd
Steadman, James Robert
Susmarski, Ronald James
Tesone, Robert Joseph
Van Horn, Carol Lynn
Vinci, Martin F.P., III
Whitling, Terrance LeRoy
Wrigley, Albert Blakemore
Zimmerman, D(onald) Patrick

Rhode Island

Driscoll, Robert George
Hendel, Maurice William
Lipsey, Howard Irwin
Loffredo, Pasco Frank
Lombardi, Valentino Dennis
McGuirl, Susan Elizabeth
O'Donnell, William Kenneth
Oster, Robert Daniel
Riffkin, Mitchell Sanford
Simmons, Howard Koorken

South Carolina

Abernathy, Harry Hoyle, Jr.
Allison, James McWilliams
Applegate, William Russell
Bailey, Nancy Hawkins
Elliott, John Dewey
Goode, Kenneth George
Goude, Charles Reuben
Harte, John Williams
Hite, Thomas Erskine, Jr.
Hocker, Donald Bruce
Kauser, Janson Allen
Knight, David Webster
Martin, John Randolph
McIntyre, Bernard
Metcalfe, Walter Geoffrey
Scott, Earl Daniel
Sheftman, Howard Stephen
Shemwell, Arthur Luther, Jr.
Simmons, Charles Bedford, Jr.
Smith, Jefferson Verne, Jr.
Tapp, Richard N.
Vieth, Rick

South Dakota

Allred, Forrest Carlson
Baumann, Christopher John
Burns, Mary Elizabeth
Johnson, Richard Arlo
LaFave, LeAnn Larson
Rabuck, Steven Kent
Stickney, Paul Douglas

Tennessee

Boyd, Mary Olert
Ellis, Bobby James
Grisham, Alvin MacRandle
Kirkpatrick, Scott Lucillious
Koontz, George Edward
Merkel, Albert Benton
Ogden, Harry Peoples
Purcell, William Paxson, III
Rice, George Lawrence (Larry), III
Ridenour, Ronald H.
Sheppeard, Sarah Y.
Sproles, Donald Ray

Stark, Kelly Shira
Wagerman, Howard Louis
Wiltshire, Ashley Turman, Jr.
Winston, Russell Clay
Witcher, Roger Kenneth, Jr.

Texas

Adair, William B. (Ben)
Adams, Ray Harris
Albach, Henry John, IV
Anton, Richard Henry
Armstrong, John Douglas
Barr, John H.
Beachley, Charles Edward, III
Bell, Henry Newton, III
Berchelmann, David Adolph, Jr.
Berenson, William Keith
Bousquet, Thomas Gourrier
Calvert, Nadia Rae Venable
Chae, Don Baird
Cliff, John William, Jr.
Conner, George Manion, III
Conner, Warren Wesley
Cook, Eugene Augustus
Crosby, Philip
Cunningham, William Allen
Dean, Daniel Frank
DeGuerin, Dick
Figueroa, Luis Antonio
Fohn, Gerald Anthony
Fouts, Louis Milner, III
Gagnon, Stewart Walter
Garcia, Lawrence L.
Gilbert, Steven John
Godwin, Elva Cockrell
Green, Ray Eugene
Hammons, Allen James, Jr.
Hinson, Hillord Hensley
Hughes, Karen Gray
Jack, Larry A.
Jameson, David Alan
Jennings, Karen Lynn
Jett, Joseph Craig
Kerry, Henry Eugene
Koons, William Conrad
Krause, Sarraine Sieger
Kvinta, Charles J.
Leon, Jack Paul
McFarland, Jaclanel Moore
McMillen, Linda Louise
Milligan, Michael Roy
Morgan, Jack Cochran
Moseley, Patricia Ann
Mullen, John Clancy
Murray, Frederick Franklin
Newsom, Daniel Oren
Odiorne, James Thomas
Porter, James Eduardo
Price, Robert Alexander
Rasor, Reba Graham
Rduch, Evita Joanne
Reinhard, Henry Corben, Jr.
Rentz, Joe Houston
Reynolds, Dixon Jace
Roessler, P. Dee
Rowan, Justin Michael
Sanders, Thelma E.
Schonberger, Arne Carl
Schwab, Elmo
Seidlits, Curtis Lee, Jr.
Shannon, Joe, Jr.
Shepherd, James Edward
Somers, Constance Reynolds
Stewart, Annette
Sutherland, Richard Thomas
Sweitzer, Harry Averil
Thornton, Russell James
Thrall, Gordon Fish
Trusch, Norma Levine
Vick, Phillip Oran
Wald, Michael H.
Wall, Jack Knox
Walsh, Gerry O'Malley
Wilkerson, James Neill
Wilkinson, Toby Charles
Williams, Nancy Ondrovik
Woldy, Kristine Carol
Woody, Clyde Woodrow

Utah

Dolowitz, David Sander
Hillyard, Lyle William
Kaufman, Steven Michael
Lyman, Paul D.
McCullough, William Andrew
Russell, Cheryl Anne
Winward, LaMar J.

Vermont

Cheney, Kimberly Bunce
Corum, Jesse Maxwell, IV
Cummings, Charles Rogers
Mc Carty, William Michael, Jr.
Oettinger, Mark David
Wright, Richard Jay
Wysolmerski, Sigismund John Albert

Virginia

Alan, Sondra Kirschner
Alper, Joanne Fogel
Cassell, Richard Emmett
Crouch, Richard Edelin
Dodge, Cynthia Ellen
Etherington, William Fisher
Hankins, Timothy Howard
Henderson, James Rutledge, IV
Hicks, Robert DeHardit
Holland, William Louis
Kennedy, Joe Jack, Jr.
Korman, James William
Kuykendall, Ronald Edward
Malone, William Grady
McKenry, James Reinhardt
Miller, William Frederick
Montagna, Anthony Louis, Jr.
Mott, Joseph William Hooge
Mulligan, Jennifer
Peyton, Gordon Pickett
Pochucha, Larry Arthur
Rosenstock, Louis Anthony, III
Savage, Thomas Yates
Schmidt, William Lesnett
Schwartz, Philip
Segall, James Arnold
Shepherd, Robert Edward, Jr.
Short, DeRonda Miniard
Small, Marc James
Smolen, Jason David
Spero, Morton Bertram
Steffen, Joseph John, Jr.
Trompeter, Philip
Tucker, James Letcher
Varoutsos, George Douglas
Walk, Thomas Preston
Weimer, Peter Dwight
Weinman, Ellen Shelton
Williams, Ronald Wayne, Sr.
Wright, Grover Cleveland, Jr.

Washington

Abelite, Jahnis John
Althauser, Thomas Charles
Anderson, Wolfgang R.
Bartheld, Richard Henry
Burke, Thomas Gerald
Cordes, Clifford Frederick, III
Cross, Harry Maybury
Gaddis, Stephen Michael
Gavilanes, Diego P.
Halverson, Lowell Klark
Hoff, Valerie Margaret Knecht
Kram, Peter
Manni, Kenneth Allen
Mashita, Lloyd Isao
Mathieu, Richard Louis
Pinckney, Ronald Robert
Price, Clark Alan
Robinson, Jeffrey Alan
Uhrig, Ira John
Whittington, Thomas Lee

West Virginia

Arrington, Roy David
Harrington, Travers Rountree, Jr.
Howley, Loren Blackman
Jackson-Gillison, Helen Lucille
Kwass, Sidney J.
Wehner, Richard Karl

Wisconsin

Bohren, Michael Oscar
Castro, Robert C.
Collins, Michael John
Eberhardt, Daniel Hugo
Frank, Katherine Marie
Grundahl, John Alvin
Hoag, Jack Carter
Hurt, Michael Carter
Jinkins, Mark Allen
Jursik, Patricia Dolores
Kaestner, Richard Darwin
Karp, David Barry
Kucirek, Joseph Charles
Loeb, Leonard L.
Mason, Jon Gerard
Melchert, Lori Layne McLario
Meldman, Clifford Kay
Neubecker, Edward Frederick
Owens, Joseph Francis
Pappas, David Christopher
Penegor, Robert Joseph
Roberson, Linda
Rotter, Emanuel Norman
Simon, Dennis Lee
Splitt, Cody
Stellman, L. Mandy
Stoltz, John Robert
Swartwout, Willis Brewster, III
Tess-Mattner, Kent A.
Te Winkle, William Peter
Walther, David Louis
Weidner, Gary Richard
Wild, Norman Richard
Wilson, Oscar, Jr.

Wyoming

Alburn, Cary Rudolph, III
Clauss, C. David
Hjelmstad, William David
Norman, Cherie Shelton
Thomas, John Arlyn

TERRITORIES OF THE UNITED STATES

Guam

Diaz, Ramon Valero

ADDRESS UNPUBLISHED

Adler, Kenneth
Alexander, Carla J.
Alexander, John Nickolas, Jr.
Baumohl, Harry Alan
Bello-Truland, Rosemarie
Bono, Anthony Salvatore Emanuel
Brown, Manny S.
Bush, Robert G., III
Cowan, Robert Charles, Jr.
Ecker, James Marshall
Fowler, Flora Daun
Garza, Graciano Jaime
Graff, Debra Jo
Gribbs, Paula Rewald
Groner, Beverly Anne
Hanig, Lynn
Kellerman, Harry Miles
Labdon, Kenneth Charles
Leaf, Frederick Peter
Leventhal, Howard G.
Lewis, Peter
Marshall, Kathryn Sue
Mittelstadt, Russell James
Palmer, Rudolph Martin, Jr.
Robinson, David Howard
Rutland, John Dudley
Salomon, Barbara
Schulman, Joanne
Shapiro, Marge Diana
Sheetz, Ralph Albert
Slowiaczek, John Steven
Van Voorhis, Harold L.
Wildey, Sharon Ann
Winstein, Stewart Robert

GENERAL PRACTICE

UNITED STATES

Alabama

Adams, John Edmund
Alidor, Gary Paul, Sr.
Black, Claire Alexander
Bonner, William Joel, Jr.
Bryant, Thomas Earle, Jr.
Chastain, David Jesse
Cicio, Anthony Lee
Coplin, William Thomas, Jr.
Cornelius, Walter Felix
Fuller, S. Wayne
Gleissner, John Dewar
Heffler, Paul Mark
Hellums, Clarence Theo
Hicks, Deborah Ann Whitmore
Hughes, Andy Karl
Hull, Daniel Talmadge
Jackson, John Hollis, Jr.
Kracke, Robert Russell
Lane, Robert Pitt
Lewis, Christine Whitesell
Lewis, Cyrus Roys
Lyons, George Sage
Manley, Richard Shannon
McWhorter, Robert Dale, Jr.
Miller, Barbara Currie
Mills, William Hayes
Monroe, Cecil Barlow
Moorer, Mac Mitchell
Munsey, Stanley Edward
Owings, William Donovan
Patton, Martha Jane
Pittman, Joseph Stafford, Jr.
Potter, Ernest Luther
Potts, Robert Leslie
Putnam, Terry Michael
Ryan, L(awrence) Thomas, Jr.
Sanderson, William Woodrow, Jr.
Sessions, Jefferson Beauregard, III
Sledge, James Scott
South, Mark Omega
Stedham, Brenda Smith
Teague, Dewey Wayne
Timberlake, H. Kenan
Tucker, Billie Anne
Wise, Steven Lanier

Alaska

Clark, Julie Ann
Cuadra, Dorothy Elizabeth
Erlich, Richard Henry
Nave, Thomas George
Rice, Julian Casavant
Taylor, Kneeland Lamoureux
Winner, Russell Lee

Arizona

Arana, Kimberly Ann
Barron, Caroline Joan
Beggs, Harry Mark
Bellah, C. Richard
Burton, Osmond Alexander, Jr.
Butler, A(rthur) Bates, III
Cantor, Alena
Evans, Lawrence Jack, Jr.
Freedman, Kenneth David
Frost, Smith Gibbons
Glicksman, Elliott Aaron
Gonzales, Richard Joseph
Hornisher, Michael
Mallin, Robert Harold
Murphy, R. Anthony
Stoddard, Charles Warner, III
Udall, Calvin Hunt

Arkansas

Ball, William Kenneth
Boyce, Edward Wayne, Jr.
Brady, Lawrence Joseph
Britt, Henry Middleton
Carpenter, Charles L.
Crow, Carl Arnold, Jr.
Davis, James Edwin
Deacon, John C.
Dunn, James Melvin
Epley, Lewis Everett, Jr.
Finley, John Cyrus, Jr.
Finley, John Cyrus, III
Fogleman, John Nelson
Gant, Horace Zed
Griffin, Richard Earl
Howard, Steven Gray
Hughes, Steven Jay
Hughes, Thomas Morgan, III
Karr, Charles
Ledbetter, Thomas Dale
Leslie, Robert Bruce
Mackey, Benjamin Franklin, Jr.
Mullen, William David
Pearson, Charles Thomas, Jr.
Pinson, Jerry D.
Ross, Robert Dwain
Spencer, James Victor, III
Strode, Joseph Arlin
Strother, Lane H.
Thomas, Albert, Jr.
Thrailkill, Daniel B.
Wynne, William Joseph
Young, Robert Earl

California

Ajalat, Sol Peter
Allen, Albert Herman
Arnold, Kenneth James
Atkinson, Sheridan Earle
Auser, Wallace Van Cortlandt, III
Balliet, Susan Jackson
Barrett, Jane H.
Belli, Melvin Mouron
Blum, Melanie Rae
Boelter, Allen Boyd
Bolles, Donald Scott
Borell, Karen Lorraine
Borowsky, Philip
Braafladt, Arnie Rolf
Bray, Absalom Francis, Jr.
Brown, J(oan) Devon
Buchanan, James Douglas
Burton, Randall James
Caswell, Paulette Reva
Cohn, Nathan
Crosby, William Marshall
Crowe, John T.
Currer, William John, Jr.
Davies, Paul Lewis, Jr.
Dostal, Milan Mathias
Drexler, Kenneth
Ellwanger, J. David
Enersen, Burnham
Ervin, Howard Guy, III
Finch, Nathan C.
Fitzgerald, Stephen Patrick
Fluharty, Jesse Ernest
Frazier, Thomas Louis
Gambaro, Ernest Umberto
Gilbert, Richard Lee
Gould, Harold I.
Groman, Arthur
Guest, Karl Reed
Haas, Richard
Hagel, James A.
Halsey, Patricia Frederick
Harrow, Barry Richard
Heyck, Theodore Daly
Hopkins, Donald Ray
Horwin, Leonard
Howard, Kenyon B.
Jaffe, Frohm Filmore
Jorgensen, Erik Holger
Joyce, Stephen Michael
Keller, Coby Norman
King, Franklin Weaver
Kraft, Henry R.
Kraus, James Alan
Lee, Michael G.W.
Lehan, Jonathan Michael
Loomis, John Elmer
Luppi, Michael Dennis
Lynch, Robert Berger
Lyon, Bruce Arnold
McCaslin, Leon
McFarland, Carol Anne
McGuire, E. James
McReynolds, Stephen Paul
Miller, Mary Jane
Neary, Christopher J.
Noe, Ralph Henderson, Jr.
Orlebeke, William Ronald
Peluso, Charles John
Peters, Samuel Anthony
Peterson, Richard Thomas
Petrie, Bernard
Philo, DuWayne Allen
Pilling, George William
Pinkerton, Albert Duane, II
Price, William Furlow
Resich, John James
Richards, Gerald Thomas
Rodgers, Thomas Paul
Rosenthal, Steven S.
Rowland, Gilford Glenn
Rutten, Rand John
Shaw, John LeRoy, Jr.
Shaw, Stanford Eugene
Sherwood, Allen Joseph
Smith, Maxine Steward
Spuehler, Donald Roy
Stagner, Robert Dean
Stavig, Alf Rusten
Steiner, Philip
Stevenson, Noel C.
Stokes, John Reynolds
Tachna, Ruth C.
Tobin, Harold William
Tomberlin, George E., Jr.
Tomich, Lillian
Vena, David Henry
Vineyard, C L
Weingarten, Saul Myer
Weissman, Barry Leigh
Wertz, John R.
Wooley, Kenneth Virgil
Yamakawa, David Kiyoshi, Jr.

Colorado

Anderson, Adele Konkel
Billings, Bruce Arthur
Bluestein, Louis Allen
Briggs, George Scott
Callison, James William
Clark, Roger Earl
Cleveland, Leslie Click
Cook, Kenneth Totman
Cronan, Kathleen Michele
Donley, Jerry Alan
Fried, Joseph
Fritze, James Ronald
Gentry, Elvin LeRoy
Gill, Anne Whalen
Griff, Harry
Hagen, Glenn W(illiam)
Helmer, David Alan
Hopp, Walter James
Inman, Robert Dale
LaCroix, Thomas Russell
Manley, Douglas Rempet
McGrath, John Nicholas, Jr.
McGrath, William Arthur
Metzger, Karen Susan
Mitchem, Allen P.
Overholser, John W.
Oxman, Stephen Eliot
Peterson, Brooke Alan
Redder, Thomas Joseph
Rodriquez, Janet Lois
Ruda, Jacques Serge
Savage, John William, Jr.
Slaninger, Frank Paul
Thorson, David Morris
Tippit, John Harlow
Warren, Bruce Willard
Weltzer, Louis Albin
Wilson, Edward Miller

Connecticut

Alcorn, Hugh Meade, Jr.
Amento, Carl Joseph
Benedict, Peter Behrends
Bentley, Peter
Berman, John Arthur
Boland, John Daniel
Bracken, Nanette Beattie
Brennan, Daniel Edward, Jr.
Cacace, Michael Joseph
Capecelatro, Mark John
Cederbaum, Eugene E.
Cocco, Leonard M.
Conaway-Raczka, Nancy
Daniels, Douglas Robert
De Barbieri, Roy Louis
Dupont, Ralph Paul
Eberhard, Robert Vincent
Ecklund, John Edwin
Finch, Frank Herschel, Jr.
Freccia, Vincent John, III
Fricke, Richard John
Galligan, Matthew G.
Gerlt, Wayne Christopher
Ginsberg, Larry Floyd
Goldfarb, Alexander A.
Greene, Thurston
Greenfield, James Robert
Hershatter, Richard Lawrence
Hollander, William Victor
Madorin, A. Raymond, Jr.
Medvecky, Thomas Edward
Medzie, Kenneth Stephen
Miano, Frederick Joseph
Micci, Eugene D.
Morelli, Carmen
Nielsen, Anita Spector
Pastore, Richard Steel
Ribicoff, Irving S.
Rout, Robert Howard
Ryan, Atherton Beal
Ryan, William Joseph, Jr.
Rybak, Michael Dennis
Scannell, David George
Stuart, Peter Fred
Taalman, Juri E.
Terk, Glenn Thomas
Vetere, Robert Louis
Weinstein, Arthur David
Wolfson, Susan Wartur
Yamin, Robert Joseph
Zagorsky, Peter Joseph

Delaware

Bader, John Merwin
Moore, James Everett, Jr.
Munneke, Gary Arthur
Rich, Michael Joseph
Ridgely, Henry Johnson
Stokes, Richard Francis
Uebler, E(rnest) Alan

District of Columbia

Allen, Nicholas Eugene
Andersen, Daniel Johannes
Anderson, Scott Gale
Bergerbest, Nathan Steven
Bierbower, Mark Butler
Buechner, Jack W.
Burch, John Thomas, Jr.
Burns, Arnold Irwin
Campbell, Frank Andrew Scott
Close, David Palmer
Cohen, Wallace M.
Cohrssen, John Joseph
Cook, Frank Robert, Jr.
Cutler, Charles Russell
Dell, Donald Lundy
Gibson, Reginald Walker
Gillmarten, Mary Del Rey
Goldson, Amy Robertson
Greenebaum, Leonard Charles
Hakola, David Brown
Heller, Jack Isaac
Huge, Harry
Interdonato, Anthony Paul
Johns, Warren LeRoi
Kass, Benny Lee
Kaufman, Joshua Jacob
Kent, M. Elizabeth
King, Rufus
Kirk, Dennis Dean
Latimer, Allie B.
Leva, Marx
Lillard, John Franklin, III
Lyon, Richard Kirshbaum
Murawski, Roberta Lee
Murry, Harold David, Jr.
Orenberg, Allen Howard
Pilger, Karl William
Poe, Luke Harvey, Jr.
Richards, Suzanne V.
Riggs, Douglas A.
Rubenstein, Herbert R.
Sachs, Sidney Stanley
Schmidt, Dale Russell
Scullen, James Roche
Spencer, Samuel
Stewart, Eugene Lawrence
Swartz, Christian LeFevre
Tesoro, George Alfred
Wagner, Curtis Lee, Jr.
Wald, Robert Lewis
Weinstein, Les
Wolf, William B., Jr.

Florida

Aguila, Adolfo Zacarias
Albrechta, Mark Jerome
Alonso, Antonio Enrique
Alper, Harvey Martin
Anderson, Bruce Paige
Armstrong, Timothy Joseph
Breed, E(rnest) Mark, III
Brooks, Roy Howard, Jr.
Brophy, Gilbert Thomas
Cain, May Lydia
Cain, William Allen
Carbo, Michael James
Conner, Timothy James
Crum, James Merrill
Dariotis, Terrence Theodore
Davidson, Michael H.
Edwards, Claude Reynolds
Edwards, William Thomas, Jr.
Ervin, Robert Marvin
Fernandez, William Warren
Fougerousse, Philip
Fowler, Sandra T.
Freeman, Stephan John
Friedman, Jerrell Don
Getman, Willard Etheridge
Gilbert, Richard Allen
Gillen, William Albert
Gurney, James Thomas
Gussow, Irving Bernard
Hall, Frank Dawson
Harris, Gordon H.
Iden, Bruce Franklin

Jensen, Jack Albert
Kearns, John W.
Kent, Frederick Heber
Lewis, William Adams
Lyman, Curtis Lee, Jr.
Martin, James William
McDuffee, Paul Gerard, II
McNeill, Frederick Wallace
Merting, John Webster
Middleton, Elwyn Linton
Milne, Jack Fagerland
Milstein, Richard Craig
Murrell, Sam Edwin, Jr.
Norman, Donald Hamilton
Nutzhorn, Carl Robbins
Olson, Carl Eric
Patton, Arthur Gordon
Pawluc, Sonia M.
Pugh, Irby Gene
Pumphrey, Gerald Robert
Rogers, Harvey D.
Rogovin, Lawrence H.
Rosenberg, Sheldon
Rosinek, Jeffrey
Rothblatt, Emma Alden
Salem, Albert McCall, Jr.
Sasser, Donald Julian
Schiff, Louis Howard
Schneider, Michael Louis
Schnell, Ronald Hans
Semento, Lawrence James
Shaffer, Sanford Joel
Sharpe, Leon Edward
Siemon, Joyce Marilyn
Silber, Norman Jules
Sill, Lauren Ann
Silver, Roger Allen
Sistare, Susan Powell
Spencer, W(alter) Thomas
Starr, Ivar Miles
Stein, Stuart Leonard
Stepp, Kenneth Stephenson
Strickland, Delphene Coverston
Tombrink, Richard, Jr.
Waas, George Lee
Warren, Herbert Albert
Weidemeyer, Carleton Lloyd
Wilson, Brenda Coker
Wilson, Gary Keith
Wood, Hugh Lee
Zaretsky, Esther Anne

Georgia

Ahlstrom, Michael Joseph
Armstrong, Edwin Alan
Bentley, Fred Douglas, Sr.
Bird, Francis Marion
Brannon, William Earl
Brinson, Benjamin Pierce
Brown, Stephen Phillip
Cadenhead, Alfred Paul
Center, Tony
Chapman, Barry Ryan
Claxton, Edward Burton, III
Cook, Martha Jean
Cork, Robert Lander
Custer, Lawrence Benjamin
Eckl, William Wray
Elliott, James Sewell
England, John Melvin
Fiorentino, Carmine
Fischer, David Jon
Fitzpatrick, Barry Lane
Fitzpatrick, Duross
Gaiser, Richard Edward
Gannam, Michael Joseph
Geiger, James Norman
Gibbs, Stephen Mark
Graham, Charles Benjamin, Jr.
Griffeth, Ronald Clyde
Harris, Earl Douglas
Harrison, Gresham Hughel
Harvey, Alan Christopher
Ingram, George Conley
Kelly, James Patrick
Kidd, Daryl Leslie
Lee, Carol Elizabeth
Lee Hing, Anthony Courtney
Lester, Charles Turner, Jr.
Lester, James Luther
Liston, Paul Sperry
McCracken, Eugene Luke
Miller, Jack Everett
Mull, Gale W.
Nash, Thomas Acton, Jr.
Ossick, John Joseph, Jr.
Patrick, James Duvall, Jr.
Patrick, Robert Winton, Jr.
Porter, Mary Helen (Howard)
Pryor, Shepherd Green, III
Pujadas, Thomas Edward
Roberts, James Isaac, Sr.
Shapiro, Michael Bruce
Stamps, Thomas Paty
Steger, Susan St. John
Stone, Ralph Kenny
Weber, David Victor
Zachary, William Edmond, Jr.
Zachary, William Edmund

Hawaii

Cades, Julius Russell
Chong, Clayton Elliott
Chuck, Walter G(oonsun)
Esaki, Amy Itsumi
Hakoda, Harvey Nobuo
Howell, Alan Peter
Olson, John Louis
Uyeno, Theodore Yoshi
Yamamoto, Jerel Ikmo
Zola, Michael S.

Idaho

Bengoechea, Shane Orin
Blaser, Stephen Jeffery
Furey, Sherman Francis, Jr.
Hicks, George Gregory
Hogue, Terry Glynn
Judd, Linda
McLaughlin, Robert Francis
Rigby, Ray Wendell
Smyser, (Charles Arvil) Skip
Sorensen, Murray Jim
Tait, John Reid
Thompson, Frances Hoene

Illinois

Adami, Paul E.
Alexander, Ellen Jo
Andrin, Albert Antal
Atkinson, Jeff John Frederick
Bacall, Elliot Stephen
Baer, John Richard Frederick
Beer, Betty Louise
Bell, Allen Andrew, Jr.
Belsheim, Harold Gulbrand, II
Bernstein, Charles Bernard
Besson, Paul Smith
Black, August Bernard
Boucek, George Washington
Bowman, Phillip Boynton
Boyle, Patrick Otto
Brainard, H Ogden
Canganelli, Michael Antonio
Casey, Robert Fitzgerald
Choate, Edward L.
Ciaccio, Karin McLaughlin
Cifelli, John Louis
Cohen, Stephen Bruce
Collen, Sheldon Orrin
Coston, James E.
Cromley, Jon Lowell
Deer, William Henry
Denzel, Ken John
Ditkowsky, Kenneth K.
Dodd, Robert Warren
Dorf, Michael Charles
Duff, David Potter
Edlund, Curtis Eric
Elliott, Ivan A.
Elman, William
Erschen, Gail Lee
Finch, Ronald Corydon
Fisher, Edward Joseph
Fleischli, Franz K., III
Fleming, Milo Joseph
Folgate, Homer Emmett, Jr.
Franklin, Randy Wayne
Franz, William Mansur
Frederick, Robert George
Gevers, Marcia Bonita
Ginsberg, Lewis Robbins
Glenn, Cleta Mae
Golko, Andrew Albin
Gordon, Theodora
Graf, Carl Norval, Jr.
Hantla, George Bradley
Harrold, Bernard
Heinz, William Denby
Henke, Robert John
Henning, Joel Frank
Herr, Michael Joseph
High, Suzanne Irene
Howe, Scott William
Hunter, Eugenia C.
Huntoon, Harry Karl
Immke, Keith Henry
Johnson, Preston King
Johnson, Thomas Stuart
Jordan, Horace William
Juergensmeyer, John Eli
Kaminski, Stanley Ronald
Keeley, George William
Kell, Vette Eugene
Keryczynskyj, Leo Ihor
Kois, George Stephen
Kopp, Frederick Philip
Kuta, Jeffrey Theodore
Landmeier, Allen Lee
Laski, James Emil
Lerner, Jeffrey Michael
Lewis, William Theodore, Jr.
Logan, Michael James
Lynn, Richard C.
Lyons, Kevin W.
Maganzini, Paul John
Malmgren, James H(oward)
Manion, Paul Thomas
Matchett, Hugh Moore
McCarthy, John Francis
Meersman, Robert Francis
Miller, Geoffrey Charles
Miller, Ralph William, Jr.
Minow, Newton Norman
Mittelman, Robert Hirsch
Moorman, Helen Louise
Morrison, Sidney Eder
Murphy, Matthew M.
Murphy, Thomas Lee
Murray, David Eugene
Mustain, Douglas Dee
Nagel, Stuart Samuel
Narko, Medard Martin
Narusis, Regina GytéFirant
Nekritz, Barry B.
Nissen, William Forbes
Nortell, Bruce
Oakey, James Leo
Oldfield, E. Lawrence
Palmberg, Earl Laverne
Parham, James Robert
Patricoski, Paul Thomas
Paul, Bernard Arthur
Perona, Paul Dominic, Jr.
Polzin, John Theodore
Rapp, James Anthony
Rehberger, Robert Lee
Reicin, Ronald Ian
Richard, Douglas Wayne
Romano, Henry Schuberth, Jr.
Rooks, John Newton
Saladino, Joseph Charles
Saunders, George Lawton, Jr.
Schuyler, Daniel Merrick
Serritella, James Anthony
Shapiro, Paul Stuart
Smith, Len Young
Spina, Anthony Ferdinand
Stanfield, James Caleb
Stanley, Justin Armstrong
Stout, James Dudley
Swanson, Lenard Charles
Thies, Richard Leon
Thomas, William Harrold
Thompson, David F.
Tognarelli, Richard Lee
Tom, Ping
Tonozzi, Thomas Albert
Tungate, James Lester
Veverka, Donald John
Walker, Daniel, Jr.
Ward, Jack Donald
Wright, Robert Williams
Wuller, Robert George, Jr.
Zimmerman, Austin Manlove

Indiana

Applegate, Karl Edwin
Austgen, David Michael
Aylsworth, Robert Reed
Bamberth, Hugo Arnold
Bartlett, Rick E.
Bate, Charles Thomas
Bishop, Reginald B.
Bitzegaio, Harold James
Braatz, David Edward
Britton, Louis Franklin
Bunger, Len Edward, Jr
Calhoun, John Henry, Jr
Carroll, John Leo
Cohen, William J.
Davis, Ann Gouger
Dunsmore, E. Edward
Ferguson, Stephen Luther
Fleece, Steven Michael
Ford, Lee Ellen
Frey, Eric Alan
Gleason, Charles Sappington
Glick, Cynthia Susan
Henthorn, Charles Rex
Hoffman, John Frederick
Jackson, Andrew Dudley
Justice, Robert Scott
Laszynski, Robert Steven
Lebamoff, Ivan Argire
Levy, Lawrence Alan
Lewis, Daniel Edwin
Lindsey, Roger Leighton
Lisher, James Richard
Loftman, Guy Rickard
Longer, William John
McNabney, Ronald Ladd
McNaughton, George Theodore
Meltzer, Kris
Modesitt, Fritzy Dal
Muntz, Richard Karl
Murphy, Sharon Funcheon
Nasser, Woodrow Sam
Nesbitt, John Robert
Pantzer, Kurt Friedrich, Jr.
Pellicciotti, Joseph Michael
Reuben, Lawrence Mark
Sanders, Carlton Edward
Saunders, David Livingston
Sheets, Thomas Wade
Skolnik, Bradley William
Smith, Bruce Arthur
Specter, Melvin H.
Tourkow, Joshua Isaac
Truitt, Patricia Peyton
Waddick, William Anthony
Walmer, James L.
Webster, Dale Philip
Wernle, Robert Frederick
Wickland, David Edwin
Woods, Joseph Reid

Iowa

Bappe, Daniel Eugene
Baybayan, Ronald Alan
Berkland, Roger Alan
Brown, William Ted
Burns, James
Caldwell, Gilbert Raymond, III
Clogg, Richard Bruce
Coonrad, Douglas V.
Danilson, David Ray
Frey, A. John, Jr.
Gidel, David Dale
Hileman, Richard Glenn, Jr.
Hinton, Charles Franklin
Hoth, Steven Sergey
Howe, Jay Edwin
Joyce, Joseph Benedict
Kelley, Bruce Gunn
Klemesrud, Normand Charles
Langdon, Herschel Garrett
Larson, David Christopher
Manly, Charles M., III
Manly, Charles M.
McEnroe, Michael Louis
Mueller, Barry Scott
Ouderkirk, Mason James
Palmer, Bruce Alexander
Peterson, Richard William
Phelps, Robert J.
Poffenberger, Richard Lee
Rosenberg, Paul Herschel
Sallen, David Urban
Swaim, R(obert) Kurt
Swanson, Mark Douglas
Thorson, Larry Jonathan
Tompkins, Richard Norton, Jr.
Vance, Michael Charles
White, William Richard
Wieck, Paul Hans, II

Kansas

Aadalen, David Kevin
Altenhofen, Craig Joseph
Arabia, Paul
Clinkscales, J(ames) Randall
Condray, Scott Robert
Conner, Fred L.
Depew, Harry Luther
Dillon, Wilburn, Jr.
Emler, Jay Scott
Goering, Alan Clyde
Grillot, Timothy Joseph
Hankins, Gale William
Haviland, Camilla Klein
Hodgson, Arthur Clay
Howland, Gary Marvin
Jordan, Harold Nathan
Kessler, Stephen
Knappenberger, Don J.
Manning, Donna Kaser
Metcalf, William Evans
Neustrom, Patrik William
Nordling, Bernard Erick
Powell, Craig Steven
Seed, Thomas Finis
Sevart, Daniel Joseph
Smith, Glee Sidney, Jr.
Snyder, Brock Robert
Solbach, John Martin, III
Toepfer, Thomas Lyle
Westerhaus, Douglas Bernard

Kentucky

Adams, James G., Jr.
Bailey, Ann Leslie
Brammell, William Hartman
Bucalos, Dean Walter
Budden, Harry Edward, Jr.
Carey, Marcus Stephen
Carter, Robert Philip
Fenton, Thomas Conner
Foley, Margaret Sweeney
Greene, James S., Jr.
Gregory, Gary Hugh
Gregory, William David
Guier, Lester Bennett
Johns, Harold Mac
Kerr, Thomas Robert
Kirven, Gerald
Meagher, Virginia Murnane
Merkel, Roland Peter
Nelson, Richard S.
Perkinson, Maurice Leon
Prather, John Gideon, Jr.
Prather, John Gideon
Secrest, James Seaton, Sr.
Snyder, Paul Stewart
Thomas, Patricia Ann
Vimont, Richard Elgin
Walker, Henry Lawson, II
Wehr, William James
Welsh, Alfred John
White, Paul Stephen
Wilborn, Woody Stephen
Wilson, George Simpson, III

Louisiana

Avery, Darrell Robert
Baudier, Adelaide
Benson, Lawrence Kern, Jr.
Bernheim, Sadye Kern
Blackman, Gordon N., Jr.
Bossier, Larry Sherman
Clement, Leslie Joseph, Jr.
Coleman, James Julian
Cook, David Sherman
Facussé, Albert Shucry
Gouaux, Eugene Godfrey
Harris, Thorne D., III
Hartel, Stephen Camille
Hauver, Terence Lee
Herring, Charles Evans, Jr.
Hetherwick, Gilbert Lewis
Hickman, Paula Hazelrig
Hingle, Gilmer Paul
Jackson, Thomas Haller, Jr.
Jones, William Roby
Kaplan, Edward Alan
Kleinpeter, Robert Loren
Knoll, Jerold Edward
Lain, Clyde, II
LaVergne, Luke Aldon
Marx, Paula Jeannette
McAdams, Don Randall, Jr.
McCall, Harry
McDonald, John Franklin, III
McKay, Dan Boies, Jr.
Mickel, Joseph Thomas
Miller, Patrick Lynn
Milligan, Edward Joseph, Jr.
Patin, Sidney L.
Pierce, James Winston, Jr.
Pitts, Birdia Marie Greer
Porter IV, Thomas Fitzgerald
Prestridge, Rogers Meredith
Pucheu, John Henri
Puglia, Phyllis Mary
Riddick, Winston Wade, Sr.
Riley, Mark Louis
Rives, James Davidson, Jr.
Robinson, Michael
Rosen, William Warren
Rosenberg, Samuel Irving
Singletary, Alvin D.
Smith, Christopher Michael
Smith, Duncan McLaurin, Jr.
Stracener, Carol Elizabeth
Thibaut, Charest deLauzon, Jr.
Weinmann, John Giffen
White, Trudy Melita
Wolfe, William Milton
Woodley, John Paul
Woodward, Madison Truman, Jr.

Maine

Fletcher, David James
Humpert, Samuel Jay
Moriarty, James Paul
Rundlett, Ellsworth Turner, III
Scribner, Fred Clark, Jr.
Slater, Brent R.
Smith, Jeffrey Allen

Maryland

Baker, William Parr
Bald, LeRoy
Berkson, Jacob Benjamin
Boyer, Elroy George
Braun, Stephen John
Brill, Lawrence Joel
Brown, R. Edwin
Buchanan, Phillip Gerald
Carney, Bradford George Yost
Christensen, Gordon Edward
Cohen, Hyman K.
Dorsey, Charles Henry, Jr.
Dulany, William Bevard
Elliott, J. Victor
Epstein, Philip Edward
Ferris, William Michael
Foltz, Richard Nelson, III
Foster, Philip Carey
Fry, Donald Curtis
Furrer, David Eugene
Gallavan, Michael Lee
Gohn, Jack Lawrence Benoit
Hall, William Bryan, Jr.
Haskins, Patrick Dean
Kandel, Nelson Robert
Kleid, Wallace
Krensky, Michael Ian
Laws, Jean Sadowsky
Lechter, Kenneth Alan
Lewis, Leah H.
Masters, Kenneth Halls
Mathias, Joseph Marshall
Mitnick, Harold
Mowell, George Mitchell
Naditch, Ronald Marvin
Neil, Benjamin Arthur
Nolan, Paul William
Olszewski, Kevin Trent
Pairo, Preston Abercrombie, Jr.
Porter, James Harry, Jr.
Price, Charles U.
Price, Howard Jack, Jr.
Proctor, Kenneth Donald
Protokowicz, Stanley Edward, Jr.
Rasin, Alexander Parks, III
Redden, Roger Duffey
Robinson, Stuart Jay
Salim, Abdullah (Reginald Armistice Hawkins), Jr.
Sheble, Walter Franklin
Simons, David Warren
Staples, Lyle Newton
Sweeney, Eileen Cecilia
Terrell, Herbert Arthur
Thomas, David Michael
Whaley, Joseph Randall
Wood, Judson Rawlings
Ziegler, Arnold Gerard

Massachusetts

Arden, John Réal
Belford, Lloyd Earl
Boyd, F. Keats, Jr.
Bridge, Winston Jay
Buczkowski, David John
Burns, Thomas David
Chyten, Edwin Richard
Cleary, Philip Edward
Coquillette, Daniel Robert
Dwyer, William Edward
Ely, John P.
Epstein, Stanley Murray
Espinosa, Jose A., Jr.
Fidnick, Linda Susan
Friedman, Michael Phillip
Garabedian, Charles Bagdasar
Gargiulo, Andrea Weiner
Hoffman, Robert Joseph
Houlihan, F(rancis) Robert, Jr.
Howland, Richard Moulton
Hurley, Daniel Gerard
Jones, Michael Earl
Kaloosdian, Robert Aram
Keough, Paul Gerard
Kravetz, David Hubert
Lipman, Stephen I.
Lowinger, Lazar
Manfreda, Michael Joseph
Marr, David Erskine
Mastrangelo, Richard Edward
Mc Cormack, Edward Joseph, Jr.
McGinnis, Andrew Mosher
Mills, Michael Francis
Murray, Elizabeth Ann
O'Connor, James Michael
Pepyne, Edward Walter
Perera, Lawrence Thacher
Peterson, Osler Leopold
Petrucelly, Jeffrey Paul
Pierce, John Robert
Politi, Stephen Michael
Provanzano, Joseph Stephen
Redlich, Marc
Scott, David Oscar
Sherman, Elliot Mark
Simpson, Russell Gordon
Stern, Edward Mayer
Sullivan, William Francis
Weidman, Charles Ray
Whitbeck, James Allis
Wolfson, Jeffrey Steven

Michigan

Alatalo, Richard
Archer, Dennis Wayne
Ashmall, Roy Alfred
Barr, John Monte
Breczinski, Michael Joseph
Burns, Marshall Shelby, Jr.
Byington, Robert Lee
Caswell, Roger Lee
Chin, Sherry (Lynn)
Churchill, David James
Clark, Mark Lee
Cline, Daniel James
Cooper, Richard I.
Cox, Joseph King
Crehan, Joseph Edward
Danko, Stephen Gaspar
Davis, Henry Barnard, Jr.
Dimmers, Albert Worthington
Dutka, Robert Joseph
Eklund-Easley, Molly Sue
Fink, Sally Claire
Flessland, Dennis Michael
Garcia, Joseph Antonio
Harper, Linda Walker
Hirschhorn, Austin
Holley, Audrey Rodgers
Jacobs, Wendell Early, Jr.
Johnson, Donald Edward, Jr.
LaBre, William Luke
Ladd, Thomas A.
Larky, Sheldon Glen
Lemcool, Michael James
Marcoux, William Joseph
Marin, Paul Martin
Marshall, J. Stephen
Massie, Joel Lee
McLain, Dennis O.
Mengel, Christopher Emile
Meyer, Philip Gilbert
North, Thomas Brian
O'Brien, Darlene Anne
Perlos, Alexander Charles
Peterson, David Reid
Purcell, Paul M.
Raniszeski, Lawrence Frank
Reynolds, Frank Harrison
Ring, Ronald Herman
Roy, William Alan
Sefcovic, Henry John
Seglund, Bruce Richard
Slavin, John Jeremiah
Smith, Arthur Allan
Smith, Brook McCray
Spelman, John Henry
Stevens, Gerald M.
Swain, Dennis Michael
Szymanski, Frank S(tanislaus), Jr.
Thomas, Robert Weston

Turner, Lester Nathan
Ulrich, Gregory Leslie
Urick, Walter Aleksy
Valentine, Stephen Kenneth, Jr.
VanderRoest, James Edward
Webster, Robert Byron
Wilson, Martin Bryant
Winchell, William Olin
Woodworth, James Nelson

Minnesota

Baker, Gail Dyer
Coller, Julius Anthony, II
Collins, Theodore Joseph
Dalager, Jon Karl
Donohue, Peter Salk
Ekstrum, B. William
Engwall, Gregory Bond
Feinberg, Sidney S.
Grannis, Vance Burns
Higgs, David Corey
Hillstrom, Robert Arthur
Hoke, George Peabody
Holmstrom, Gregory Leonard
Hulstrand, George Eugene
Johnson, Joseph Bernard
Kaplan, Sheldon
Kempf, Douglas Paul
Kief, Paul Allan
Larsen, Karen Marie
Larson, Andrew Robert
Loper, Stewart Collins
Maus, Robert Michael
Mundt, Daniel Henry
Neff, Fred Leonard
Oh, Matthew In-Soo
Orwoll, Kimball Gregg
Palmer, John Marshall
Peterson, Steven A.
Rippe, John Henry
Solum, Gregory Randal
Timmons, Mary Sarazin
Trojack, John Edward

Mississippi

Barber, Frank David
Chaney, Mark James, Jr.
Clayton, Hugh Newton
Corlew, John Gordon
Crook, Robert Lacey
Gay, Joe Thomas
Goldman, Thomas Laverne
Goodman, Herbert Raymond
Griffin, Joseph Ruble
Hubbard, Robert Dale
Hurlbert, Clyde Osborne
Mayer, John William
McKibben, Dale Harbour
Meek, Walter Buchanan
Mord, Irving Conrad, II
Netterville, Robert Lavelle
Odom, Elizabeth Ann
Pate, William August
Peresich, Stephen G.
Pritchard, Thomas Alexander
Pyle, Luther Arnold
Reeves, John Raymond
Rood, Ralph Edward
Smith, James Edwin, Jr.
Sumners, Lester Furr
Twiford, H. Hunter, III
Waddle, Robert Glen
Yoste, Charles Todd
Young, Ralph Edward, Jr.

Missouri

Allen, Thomas Ernest
Anton, Donald C.
Banton, Stephen Chandler
Barkofske, Francis Lee
Barvick, William Michael
Bayer, Elmer Valentine
Blanke, Richard B.
Brenner, Daniel Leon
Buder, Eugene Hauck
Coffin, Richard Keith
Copilevitz, Errol
Craig, Bernard Duffy
Cruse, Fredrich James
DeCuyper, Joseph Ysidore
DeWoskin, Alan Ellis
Dixon, Scott William
Duesenberg, Richard William
Dye, David Alan
Fleischaker, Jack
Gartner, Richard Anthony
Gifford, Wayne Daniel
Giorza, John C.
Gisler, George Louis
Goffstein, John Howard
Greiman, Gerald Phillip
Haller, Albert John
Hamra, Sam Farris, Jr.
Hessel, Mildred Reda
Hipsh, Harlene Janet
Jennings, William Hathaway, II
Johnson, Harold Gene
Klamen, Marvin
Kretsinger, Tom Bark, Jr.
Kruger, Mark Howard
Kuenzel, Steven Paul
Lange, C. William
McConnell, James David
McGannon, Robert Eugene
McManaman, Kenneth Charles
Mello, Susan H.
Moffitt, William A., Jr.
Oliver, David Field
Pierce, Donald Victor Jr.
Pletz, John Stephen
Raack, William James
Radke, Daniel Lee
Rice, James Briggs, Jr.
Ring, Lucile Wiley
Rottler, Terry Robert
Russell, William Oliver
Shapiro, Alvin Dale
Sparks, Billy Schley
Steimel, Norman Clemens, III
Swann, Elizabeth Walker
Terry, Jack Chatterson
Thomson, Harry Pleasant, Jr.
Toft, Martin John, III
Toppins, Roger Keith
Tremayne, Bertram William, Jr.
Ver Dught, ElGene Clark

Vines, Leonard Dean
Wade, Daniel Ples
Waldron, Kenneth Lynn
Walsh, Thomas Joseph
Wells, David Lee
Wheeler, James Julian
White, Jerusha Lynn
Wight, Les D., II
Willenbrock, Ronald Christopher
Willis, Wayne George
Willy, Thomas Ralph
Zahnd, Lloyd Glen

Montana

Conover, Richard Corrill
Crowe, Gary Allen
Dunbar, Byron Herbert
Gilbert, Robert Bruce
Hansen, Max A.
Hartelius, Channing Julius
Haxby, Leonard James
Hopgood, Tom Kolstad
Kaze, James Michael
Kottas, Leo Joseph, Sr.
Larsen, Dirk Herbert
Majerus, Michael Gerard
Mouat, William Gavin
Olsen, Arnold
Seiffert, Terry L.
Sheehy, Edmund Francis, Jr.
Spaeth, Gary Lewis

Nebraska

Aitken, Philip Martin
Atwood, Raymond Percival, Jr.
Baldwin, Michael Wendel
Bixby, Joseph Nathan
Bloomingdale, Arthur Lee, Jr.
Crosby, Robert Berkey
Dorwart, Charles Edward
Ellis, John Patrick
Ellis, Ronnie Gene
Glidden, Richard Mark
Gutowski, Michael Francis
Haggart, Virgil James, Jr.
Hill, Denise Ann
Klein, Michael Clarence
Lahners, Ronald Dean
LaPuzza, Paul James
Line, William Gunderson
Papik, James Elvin
Schumacher, Paul Maynard
Smith, Wilbur Cowan
Stern, Arnold Jay
Urbom, David Ward
Vacanti, Alfred Charles, Jr.
Whitney, Charles Leroy

Nevada

Bell, Robert Cecil
Brown, Joseph Wentling
Garcia, Eva
Grad, Neil Elliott Marshall
Guild, Clark Joseph, Jr.
Horton, Thomas David
Maher, O. Kent
Sourwine, Julien Gillen
Specchio, Michael Ronald

New Hampshire

Arnold, Wynn Edmund
Boyle, Gerard Joseph
Brouillard, Philip André
Brown, Stanley Melvin
Bruno, Kevin Robert
Bruzga, Paul Wheeler
Catalfo, Alfred (Alfio), Jr.
Dahar, Victor William
Donovan, Robert Bickford
Drucker, Leonard Murray
Genz, Mary Keohan
Harkaway, Aaron Abraham
Johnson, Robert Veiling, II
Keefe, William John
Smith, Gregory Hayes
Snierson, Richard S.
Tober, Stephen Lloyd

New Jersey

Aisenstock, Barry Alan
Baker, Max Allen
Bastedo, Wayne Webster
Bate, David Soule
Beakley, Robert Paul
Boardman, Michael Neil
Bookbinder, Ronald Eric
Borelli, B. Michael
Breslin, John Joseph, III
Brown, Harold Jensen
Carluccio, Robert James
Carroll, Michael Dennis
Chiumento, Gary C.
Cipollone, Anthony Dominic
Cohen, Diane Berkowitz
Connolly, Joseph Thomas
D'Alessandro, Daniel Anthony
D'Alfonso, Mario Joseph
Davidson, Robert Lee, III
DeBois, James Adolphus
DeMaio, Andrew John
Diktas, Christos James
Doherty, Robert Christopher
Downs, Thomas Edward, IV
Ferreri, Vito Richard
Fisch, Joseph
Fischer, Jay David
FitzPatrick, Francis James
Flammer, George Herbert
Gimmy, Daniel Patrick
Golden, Daniel Lewis
Hall, Raymond Percival, III
Harrison, Charles Maurice
Hayward, George John
Hersh, Alvin David
Holt, Michael Bartholomew
Hornstine, Louis Fox
Howell, Brian Graham
Johnson, Elizabeth Diane Long
Katz, Jeffrey Harvey
Kearns, William John, Jr.
Kelsky, Richard Brian
Kienz, Glenn Charles
Kleinberg, Robert Samuel
Kotok, Lester
Landman, Eric Christopher

Lario, Frank M., Jr.
Levin, Susan Bass
Littman, David Bernard
Livingston, Richard B.
Loigman, Larry Scott
Manco, Dominick Michael
Markus, Allan Lewis
McDonnell, Richard C.
McGinn, Howard Anthony
Metzger, John Mackay
Mitzner, Michael Jay
Morrison, John Dittgen
Mulligan, Elinor Patterson
Needell, Russell Lawrence
Oliver, Raymond A.
Orr, Thomas John
Osofsky, Herman
Paley, Phillip Lewis
Pandolfe, John Thomas, Jr.
Paterson, Keith Edward
Peck, James Irving, IV
Pizzi, Frank Anthony, Jr.
Portelli, Joseph Andrew
Portelli, Thomas Frank
Robinson, Sandra Ann
Rose, Edith Sprung
Roth, Jeffrey Stuart
Sachs, William
Samay, Z. Lance
Schoenewolf, Walter Wayne
Seeley, James J.
Slade, George Kemble, Jr.
Stickel, Frederick George, III
Strashun, Jeffrey Marc
Strong, John Van Rensselaer
Sudol, Walter Edward
Sweeney, Gerald Bingham
Talafous, Joseph John
Tauber, Frederic J.
Tompkins, William Finley
Trenner, Kathryn
Warshaw, Michael Thomas
Weitzman, Donald Martin
Williams, Barbara June
Wilson, Abraham
Yurasko, Frank Noel

New Mexico

Addis, Richard Barton
Atkinson, William Wilder
Bassett, John Walden, Jr.
Branch, Turner Williamson
Chavez, Rudolph Ben
Gose, Richard Vernie
Manzanares, Dennis
Paskind, Martin Benjamin
Skarda, Lynell Griffith
Skinner, Robert Stanley
Smith, Leslie Clark
Templeman, James Edwin
Vigil, Carol Jean
Wesch, Calvin Walter

New York

Abdella, H. James
Aliano, Richard Anthony
Allora, Ralph Anthony
Altieri, Peter Louis
Anderson, Eugene Robert
Andreoli, Peter Donald
Aris, Joram Jehudah
Armani, Frank Henry
Arning, John Fredrick
Arouh, Jeffrey Alan
Aswad, Richard Nejm
Aurnou, Joel Martin
Bader-York, Judith
Barney, John Charles
Bartlett, Cody Blake
Baumgarten, Sidney
Bekritsky, Bruce Robert
Berg, Gale Diane
Beshar, Robert Peter
Black, Warren John
Block, Lester H.
Bloom, Arnold Sanford
Blum, Maurice Henry
Bolan, Thomas Anthony
Boxer, Harold S.
Boylan, William Alvin
Bramwell, Henry
Brandrup, Douglas Warren
Breakstone, Jay L.T.
Brenner, Frank
Brenner, Mark B.
Brenner, Marshall Leib
Brinton, Bradford Hickman
Brown, Harvey R.
Brown, Peter Megargee
Burger, Lewis Stephen
Busner, Philip H.
Bykofsky, Seth Darryl
Campanie, Samuel John
Campbell, Carolyn Clark
Capetola, Anthony Adam
Caplicki, Dennis P.
Cavanaugh, Patrick James, Jr.
Chapin, Edward Whiting
Chapin, Melville
Chazen, Hartley James
Claire, Judith Susan
Clark, Ramsey
Cohen, Bernard Barrie
Conway, Andrew Wayne
Costikyan, Edward N(azar)
Curran, John Gerard
De Lucia, John Joseph
Deutsch, Irwin Frederick
Devine, Eugene Peter
Dittenhoefer, Marc Mitchell
Duncombe, Raynor Bailey
Early, John Collins
Eckelman, Paul John
Evans, Richard Joseph
Feder, Saul E.
Fernbach, Robert Dennis
Figueora, Nicholas
Fisher, Harold Leonard
Fisher, Kenneth Knight
Fishman, James Bart
Fix, Meyer
Galef, Steven Allen
Galvin, Madeline Sheila
Garley, R. Scott
Garry, John Thomas, II
Getnick, Neil Victor
Ghandhi, Madonna Stahl

Gilman, Andrew D.
Ginsberg, Eugene Stanley
Glavin, A. Rita Chandellier
Glavin, James Henry, III
Gold, David Marcus
Goldfarb, Ronald Carl
Goldstein, Alvin
Greene, Barry Todd
Greenhill, Ira Judd
Griffith, Emlyn Irving
Grossberg, David
Grosso, Robert John
Guglielmino, Rosario Joseph
Gulotta, Frank Andrew, Jr.
Handelman, Walter Joseph
Hargesheimer, Elbert, III
Harris, Isaac Ron
Harvey, Jonathan Paul
Haslinger, John Edward
Heming, Charles E.
Henry, James R.
Hicks, John Stanton
Hill, Peter Waverly
Hinman, James Stuart
Hoffman, Marvin
Holden, Stephen, III
Hollyer, A(rthur) Rene
Horowitz, Louise Schwartz
Howley, John
Hull, Thomas J.
Hunziker, Robert McKee
Jacobs, Sherry Raphael
Jacobson, Marc
Jones, Lawrence Tunnicliffe
Jordon, Deborah Elizabeth
Junkerman, William Joseph
Katz, Ascher
Kelley, Christopher Donald
Kirk, Patrick Laine
Klemann, Gilbert Lacy, II
Kornstein, Michael Allen
Kossar, Ronald Steven
Krainin, Harold L.
Kreppel, Milton Mark
Kreutzer, S. Stanley
Krieger, Andrew S.
Landron, Michel J.
Lane, Arthur Alan
Leader, Robert John
Leamer, Robert Eldon
Leiser, Burton Myron
Leventhal, A. Linda
Levine, Ronald Jay
Levine, Samuel Milton
Levine, Steven Jon
Levitan, Katherine D.
Levy, Alan C(hester)
Levy, Robert S.
Lewis, Murray F.
Lieb, Charles Herman
Lincoln, Franklin Benjamin, Jr.
Lipman, Howard Stewart
Lira, David M.
Loehr, Gerald Edward
Lovallo, Timothy Robin
Lubitz, Howard Arnold
Luria, Remy
Madigan, Kathryn Grant
Mahar, Thomas Daniel, Jr.
Maissel, Raina Eve
Malapero, Raymond Joseph, Jr.
Marks, Theodore Lee
Martin, Alan Jay
Mathers, Allen Stanley
Mathewson, George Atterbury
McGill, Gilbert William
McPhillips, Joseph William
Meiselman, David J.
Merrill, George Vanderneth
Miranda, Neal Joseph
Missan, Richard Sherman
Morosco, B. Anthony
Morris, James Malachy
Mullen, Michael Francis
Munson, Nancy Kay
Myers, William Edward
Nagy, Jill Harriet
Natiss, Gary Mitchell
Neff, Michael Alan
Nesbitt, John Benedict
Ng, Peter Joseph
Null, Douglas Peter
Osterman, Melvin Howard, Jr.
Palermo, Anthony Robert
Parmet, Donald Jay
Perrin, Gregory J.
Petito, Bruce Anthony
Platt, Harold Kirby
Plotkin, Loren H.
Raab, Ira Jerry
Reichel, Aaron Israel
Reynolds, Lola Sullivan
Rivera, Walter
Rivette, Francis Robert
Roegner, Harold Edward
Rolfe, Ronald Stuart
Roseman, Arnold David
Ross, Gerald Elliott
Ross, Matthew H.
Rubin, Joseph
Ryan, J. Richard
Sanna, Richard Jeffrey
Scarzafava, Nettie Jean
Schiffman, Daniel
Schoeneck, Charles A., Jr.
Schuman, Clifford Richard
Schwartz, Sydney James
Schwartzman, Jack
Selkirk, Alexander MacDonald, Jr.
Sexton, Richard
Seymour, Whitney North, Jr.
Shelley, Heywood
Sherman, Michael Paul
Sinsheimer, Alan J.
Somer, Stanley Jerome
Sotir, Richard Louis, Jr.
Stasack, Stephen Andrew
Steinhaus, Richard Zeke
Stern, Peter R.
Stevenson, Jocke Shelby
Steves, Edward Mickel
Stillman, Bernard M.
Stone, Kathleen Gale
Stroud, Alan Neil
Strougo, Robert
Sullivan, Mortimer Allen, Jr.
Sussman, Howard S(ivin)
Takashima, Hideo

Taub, Eli Irwin
Thompson, Katherine Genevieve
Tishler, Nicholas Eugene
Twining, Rollin Laverne
Vogel, John Walter
Walinsky, Adam
Wallace, Herbert Norman
Walshe, John William Leo
Watson, Richard A.
Weil, Gilbert Harry
Weinmann, Richard Adrian
Weinstein, Alan Abraham
Weisberg, David Charles
Weston, Stephen Burns
Wiacek, Bruce Edward
Williams, Frank John, Jr.
Williams, Henry Ward, Jr.
Wittman, Michael Lee
Wolff, Jesse David
Yablon, Babette
Zeichner, Mark
Zimmerman, Aaron Mark
Zionts, Harriette Abrams
Zwack, Henry Francis
Zysk, Robert Joseph

North Carolina

Blanton, Mary Rutherford
Bragg, Ellis Meredith, Jr.
Brooks, Dexter
Buckley, Charles Robinson, III
Buie, Donald Ray
Bunch, W. Edward
Cheshire, Lucius McGehee
Cogburn, Max Oliver
Cross, James Estes, Jr.
Dixon, Phillip Ray
Elliott, Joseph Bryan
Ellis, Sharon Barclay
Farmer, Ryland Lee
Flaherty, David Thomas, Jr.
Graham, William Thomas
Grier, Joseph Williamson, Jr.
Griffin, Robert Wooten
Harkey, Henry Lee
Haywood, Edmund Burke
Hemphill, Kathryn Glenn
Holleman, Carl Partin
Hunter, Pamela Anne
Hutchins, Terry Richard
Hyde, Clarence Edwin
Johnson, Bruce Cannon
Jones, Michael Morrie
Jordan, V. Thomas
King, Thomas Wesley
Leonard, Charles Jerome, Jr.
Logan, Leonard Gilmore, Jr.
Love, Walter Bennett, Jr.
Mason, James Walter, Jr.
McIntyre, Douglas Carmichael, II
Morris, Thomas Hansley
Pope, Patrick Harris
Pope, William Robert
Post, Edward Neal
Prevatte, Elias Jesse
Riddle, Robert Edward
Shepard, Paul Cooper
Shuping, C(larence) Leroy, Jr.
Snyder, Vernon Gilbert, III
Stroud, Joseph E., Jr.
Taylor, Michael William
Ward, David Livingstone, Jr.
Williamson, Carlton Forrest
Wright, Luke Williams

North Dakota

Herauf, William Anton
Nelson, David Wayne
Solberg, Wayne O.
Spain, Larry Robert
Tebelius, Mark Alan
Widdel, John Earl, Jr.
Zander, Janet Holter

Ohio

Amodio, James Anthony
Angel-Shaffer, Arlene Beth
Aukland, Duncan Dayton
Bamburowski, Thomas Joseph
Bebout, Bradley Carey
Bell, Napoleon Arthur
Bemiller, F. Loyal
Bindley, Richard Stephen
Blair, James F.
Boulger, William Charles
Boyko, Christopher Allan
Bramley, Jeffrey Lee
Bronson, Barbara June
Browne, William Bitner
Cade, Daniel Steven
Chester, John Jonas
Cline, Richard Allen
Cobau, Charles Duffy, Jr.
Coen, George Weber
Cooper, Linda Dawn
Creech, Herbert
De Brier, Donald Paul
Derivan, Hubert Thomas
DiLeone, Peter, Jr.
Dockry, Michael Brian
Donovan, James
Duckett, Douglas Edward
Dulebohn, Diana Gay
Evans, Stanley Robert
Fadel, William Isaac
Farah, Benjamin Frederick
Fazio, John Cesare
Fingerman, Albert Ross
Fox, Mary Ellen
Gerhardt, Richard Lee
Gertner, Michael Harvey
Gibson, Rankin MacDougal
Gillen, Stephen Earl
Goldfarb, Bernard Sanford
Guehl, Robert Lee
Halleck, Michael Johnston
Hartman, George Edward
Heck, Grace Fern
Heier, David Scott
Hill, Stephen A.
Hoefle, H. Frederick
Hoffheimer, Daniel Joseph
Hoopingarner, John Martin
Huth, Lester Charles
Johnston, Lorene Gayle
Kamine, Charles Stephen

Kanak, Joseph Robert
Keiser, J. Alan
Kemp, Barrett George
Kernen, Will
Kirschner, Leonard
Kitchen, James Denny
Klingenberg, Donald Herbert
Kondzer, Thomas Allen
Korosec, Kenneth David
Kostyo, John Francis
Lacki, Ralph Stephen
Lane, James Edward
Leach, Russell
Leb, Arthur S.
Lee, William Johnson
Mathews, S. Paul
Mawer, William Thomas
Meikle, William MacKay
Meyer, Douglas Oliver
Mowry, Kathy Suzanne
Muttalib, Kalam
Neff, Robert Clark
Orosz, Richard Thomas
Perry, George Williamson
Petersen, Lee
Pratt, Gregory Kent
Reno, Ottie Wayne
Robe, Edward Scott
Rogers, Richard Michael
Rolston, George Drew
Rorick, Alan Green
Schrader, Alfred Eugene
Severs, Eric Robertson
Shifrin, Debra Sue
Skotynsky, Walter John
Slagle, James William
Smith, Edward (Ted) Lewis, Jr.
Snoderly, John Allen Shelby
Sternberg, Richard
Suter, Carol Joan
Thorndyke, Gordon William
Thornton, Robert Floyd
Todt, Daniel Thomas
Turoff, Jack Newton
Utrecht, James David
Vaughn, Noel Wyandt
Weaver, Susan M.
Wilson, Laura Jane
Young, Charles Floyd
Zackaroff, Peter Timothy
Zychowicz, Ralph Charles

Oklahoma

Angel, Arthur Ronald
Armstrong, Richard Volker
Ashton, Mark Alfred
Baker, Thomas Edward
Berry, James W. Bill
Brooks, Rex Dwain
Burch, Melvin Earl
Chesnut, Charles Caldwell
Cornish, Richard Pool
Cowdery, Allen Craig
Davis, Frank Wayne
Davis, Jesse Dunbar
Fellers, James Davison
Forsyth, John Emery
Gabbard, (James) Douglas, II
Galaska, Michael Francis
Gierhart, Douglas Mark
Gordon, Jack Elliott, Jr.
Hammer, Bruce Edward
Hampton, Robert Joseph
Johnson, H. Allen
Martin, Gary Duncan
Martin, Michael Rex
Mitchell, Alice Schaffer
Musser, William Wesley, Jr.
Nolen, Lynn Dean
Rife, Gary Alan
Ross, William Jarboe
Ryals, Kent
Scott, Lawrence Rowe
Settle, John Marshall
Stamper, Joe Allen
Sullivan, Edward Paul
Walke, Geary Lynn
Wallace, John R.
Wyatt, Harry Miller, III
Young, John Mark

Oregon

Baer, Peter Edward
Bechtold, Paula Miller
Benedetto, William Ralph
Bloom, Stephen
Clark, David Lewis
Crane, Donald Ray
Cummins, Elliott Bird
Harms, Edward Clair, Jr.
Kennedy, Jack Leland
Lombard, Benjamin (Kip), Jr.
Mansfield, William Amos
Marandas, John Steve
Martin, William Charles
Moore, David Lewis
Nash, Frank Erwin
Raines, Keith R.
Rose, Steven Marc
Schmerer, Susan Ann
Williamson, Charles Ready
Wyse, Scott Campbell

Pennsylvania

Anderson, Toni-Renee
Aronson, Mark Berne
Ashcraft, John Marion, III
Barkman, Jon Albert
Barrett, Bruce Alan
Bauer, Edward Greb, Jr.
Beckman, Allen Joel
Blakley, Benjamin Spencer, III
Blank, Mark, Jr.
Blume, Karolyn Vreeland
Bogutz, Jerome E.
Boswell, William Douglas
Brady, George Charles, III
Cancelli, Dante Antonio
Cassarino, Joseph Francis
Cheswick, Phillip Thomas
Coldren, Ira Burdette, Jr.
Davis, John Phillips, Jr.
De Fino, Michael G.
DeMarco, James Joseph
Dillon, Charles Edward
DiPietro, Melanie
Dissen, Richard William
Donohue, Robert John
Douglass, Robert Duncan
Esposito, Robert S.
Favero, James Anthony
Federline, Robert Louis
Ferrario, Raymond William
Ferri, Karen Lynn
Fineman, S. David
Flower, David Jeffrey
Foley, Joseph Llewellyn
Friel, Karen Eileen
Furst, Stephen W.
Gaertner, Gary J.
Girard-DiCarlo, David Franklin
Godwin, Robert Anthony
Gowa, Andrew J.
Gross, Malcolm Joseph
Gutshall, Frederick Raym
Hackman, Karen Lee
Hamilton, Perrin C.
Hauger, Harold Keith
Helmreich, Martha Schaff
Herbruck, John Henry
Herchenroether, Peter Young
Hess, Lawrence Eugene, Jr.
Hetherington, John Joseph
Hoffmeyer, William Frederick
Holsinger, Candice Doreen
Honeyman, Robert Wayne
Hudiak, David Michael
Ingram, Niki Teresa
Jack, James Ernest
Jacob, Mark Craig
Jarvis, Kingsley Albright
John, Robert McClintock
Jones, Anna Belle
Kelley, Dennis Scott Clark
Kessler, Steven Fisher
Killian, John Doran, III
Krouse, Gwin M.
Krug, Rob Alan
Kulik, Joseph Michael
Kusturiss, Dennis John
Leete, John Bruce
Linshaw, Jack G.
Litman, Roslyn Margolis
Locke, Ronald Jackson
Lubin, David S.
Lynch, James Edward
MacDonald, Richard Barry
Makowski, Thomas Anthony
Maleski, Cynthia Maria
Mardinly, Peter Alan
McCabe, Robert Fource, Jr.
McEvilly, James Patrick
McLaughlin, John Sherman
Mellon, Thomas Edward, Jr.
Mintzer, Edward Carl, Jr.
Morrissey, Philip Patrick
Moses, Carl Michael
Mott, John C.
Mulvihill, Mead James, Jr.
Murtagh, John Walter, Jr.
Osterhout, Richard Cadwallader
Peluso, Gino Francis
Perlman, Richard Brian
Pholeric, Karen Joy
Price, William Charles, Jr.
Proctor, Charles William, III
Pyfer, John Frederick, Jr.
Reagle, Jack Evan
Roof, Vernon Donald
Rose, Andrew James Evans
Rosenn, Harold
Roskovensky, Vincent Joseph, II
Salus, Herbert Wieder, Jr.
Sanders, Russell Ronald
Scianna, Russell William
Sebastian, Winifred Moran
Shay, Michael Patrick
Siegel, Neil Yahr
Silberblatt, Jay Ned
Sloane, William Martin
Smith, Sharon Louise
Spengler, Daniel George
Sproull, Frederick Anthony Raymond
Tabas, Allan M.
Tesone, Robert Joseph
Thomas, Robert Allen
Tollen, Allen Harold
Uhl, Simon Krebs
Van Horn, Carol Lynn
Weary, Thomas Squires
Witherel, Michael Joseph
Wolkin, Paul Alexander

Rhode Island

Abilheira, Richard B.
Carr, Mary Jo
Keough, Joseph Aloysios
Martin, David Luther
McElroy, Michael Robert
Oster, Robert Daniel
Penza, Joseph Fulvio, Jr.
Reilly, John Bernard
Terry, Brian Stephen

South Carolina

Abernathy, Harry Hoyle, Jr.
Beasley, Frederick Alexander
Boensch, Arthur Cranwell
Brunson, Nolen Landford
DeLoach, Harris E(ugene), Jr.
Figg, Robert McCormick, Jr.
Gibbes, William Holman
Goude, Charles Reuben
Harvey, James Martin, Jr.
Harvey, William Brantley, Jr.
Hocker, Donald Bruce
Johnson, Darrell Thomas, Jr.
Johnson, Mordecai Christopher
King, Jimmy R.
Mitchell, Theo Walker
Morehouse, Arthur Rogers Grant
Scarminach, Charles Anthony
Seth, J Cabot
Shemwell, Arthur Luther, Jr.
Smith, Cody Walker, Jr.
Smith, Sherman N., III
Steadman, Richard Anderson, Jr.
Wheless, Albert Eugene

South Dakota

Bettmann, Frank Adam, Jr.
Graslie, Thomas Eric
Kemnitz, Ralph A.
Kennedy, Craig Allen
McCann, William Robert
Nipe, Chris Alan
Rabuck, Steven Kent
Stickney, Paul Douglas
Taylor, James Danforth
Thompson, Charles Murray

Tennessee

Alexander, Dave Almon
Allen, Newton Perkins
Beasley, Thomas Tarry, II
Butler, Edward Franklyn
Camp, Randy Coleman
Cary, Charles Muse
Cox, Stephen Jeffrey
Creekmore, David Dickason
Culp, James David
Drowota, Frank F., III
Elliott, Sam Davis
Epps, James Haws, III
Faulk, Michael Anthony
Frazier, Steven Carl
Glasgow, James Monroe
Grisham, Alvin MacRandle
Harrell, Limmie Lee, Jr.
Hicks, Ross Hamilton
Higgins, Kenneth Dyke
Holmes, Hal
Kilcrease, Irvin Hugh, Jr.
Kizer, John Fuqua
Lanier, James Olanda
Lee, Sharon Gail
Lloyd, William Nelson
Lockaby, Robert Lee, Jr.
Lockett, George Houston
Manire, James McDonnell
McClarty, John Westley
Meredith, Jennings Bryan
Merkel, Albert Benton
Newman, Charles Forrest
Pearman, Joel Edward
Ragan, Charles Oliver, Jr.
Roach, Jon Gilbert
Rogers, John T. Milburn
Rutledge, Roger Keith
Samuels, Seymour, Jr.
Schlechty, John L.
Strand, Alfred Benjamin, Jr.
Swanson, Charles Walter
Walker, Joseph Hillary, Jr.
Wilkinson, Robert Warren
Wise, Stephen Rule
Woods, Larry David

Texas

Adair, William B. (Ben)
Alberts, Harold
Arizaga, Lavora Spradlin
Banales, J(ose) Manuel
Beachley, Charles Edward, III
Beauchamp, Gary Fay
Bell, William Woodward
Berchelmann, David Adolph, Jr.
Berenson, William Keith
Biehl, Kathy Anne
Bonilla, Tony
Bowmer, Jim Dewitt
Boyd, William Clark
Bradie, Peter Richard
Brown, C. Harold
Bryce, William Delf
Burke, William Temple, Jr.
Burroughs, Richard Ray
Burrows, Jon Hanes
Callahan, James Carroll
Chae, Don Baird
Chapman, Stephen Sperry
Clark, Edward Aubrey
Cliff, John William, Jr.
Coffield, Conrad Eugene
Crosby, Philip
Cuellar, Enrique Roberto
Curione, Charles
Dean, Daniel Frank
DeBusk, Edith M.
Duty, Tony Edgar
Eckman, David Walter
Ellinger, Steven
Ellis, David Dale
Engle, William Thomas, Jr.
Fitzpatrick, Sandra Marlene
Forbes, Arthur Lee, III
Fouts, Louis Milner, III
Garrison, Pitser Hardeman
Gayle, Gibson, Jr.
Godwin, Elva Cockrell
Goldsmith, Mary Ann
Guleke, James O., II
Gulley, Jack Haygood
Hammons, Allen James, Jr.
Harvey, Leigh Kathryn
Haskett, Martin Carlaton
Hawkins, John Claiborne, Jr.
Head, Hayden Wilson
Heffington, Joseph Robert
Hennessey, John William
Hodges, Jot Holiver, Jr.
Hollin, Shelby W.
Hullum, Billy Don
Hunter, Robert Frederick
Irby, Holt
Jackson, Randall Calvin
Jeffers, Ronald Thomas
Johnson, Scott Warren
Jones, Scranton
Kelly, Joseph Patrick
Kemp, William Franklin
Kincaid, Eugene D., III
Kincaid, William H(atton)
King, Gerald Lee
Konopisos, Konstantine A.
Kousz, Carolyn Gertrude
Lamb, Jonathan Howard
Langley, Earnest Lee
LaSalle, Lowell LeRoy
Levin, Harvey Phillip
Line, Judson Edward
Loomis, Richard Foster
Mallory, Harold Darlington
Masquelette, Philip Edward
McMillen, Linda Louise
Mercer, Edwin Wayne
Mercy, John R.
Mittenthal, Freeman Lee
Morgan, Cecilia Hufstedler
Morgan, Jack Cochran
Moursund, Albert Wadel, III
Mueller, Mark Christopher
Newsom, Daniel Oren
Olson, George Albert
Oppenheimer, Jesse Halff
Owen, Frank, III
Park, J(ames) Walter, IV
Pennebaker, Susan McClimans
Potter, C. Burtt
Purnell, Charles Giles
Rduch, Evita Joanne
Reinhard, Henry Corben, Jr.
Richards, Robert William
Ringle, Brett Adelbert
Saul, Roland Dale
Schwab, Elmo
Seaman, Stephen Henry
Shepherd, James Edward
Shugart, James Elmer
Sims, Ricky Reece
Sloman, Marvin Sherk
Smith, Steven Lee
Tate, Milton York, Jr.
Wagner, Leslie
Wall, Jack Knox
Walsh, Gerry O'Malley
Watson, Cary Stephen
Weathersby, Earl Eugene
Westbrook, Joel Whitsitt, III
Wester, Ruric Herschel, Jr.
Wilkerson, James Neill
Williams, Lon Rayburn, Jr.
Williams, Percy Don
Witherspoon, James Winfred
Wood, James Allen
Young, David Haywood

Utah

Bunderson, Jon J.
Harding, Ray Murray, Jr.
Holm, Floyd W.
Judd, Dennis L.
Lewis, Leonard J.
Mangan, George Edward
McConkie, Oscar Walter
Melich, Mitchell
Russell, Cheryl Anne
Sam, David
Wells, Frank Milton
Wilkinson, Homer Fawcett
Winward, LaMar J.

Vermont

Fitzhugh, John Hardy
Greenberg, David Herbert
Holme, John Charles, Jr.
Kissell, Tony Fred
Langrock, Peter Forbes
Leddy, John Thomas
Levy, James Lewis
Marsh, Pamela Alison
Massucco, Lawrence Raymond
O'Donnell, Robert John
Otterman, Harvey Boyd, Jr.
Stevens, Harold Burr
Sullivan, Richard Francis

Virginia

Alan, Sondra Kirschner
Ames, Edward Almer, III
Anderson, John Frederick
Arey, Stephen Edward
Armstrong, Henry Jere
Arzt, Lee Robert
Bedinger, Frank Cleveland, Jr.
Blankingship, A. Hugo, Jr.
Brent, Andrew Jackson
Brittigan, Robert Lee
Chappell, Milton Leroy
Chute, Alan Dale
Clark, Bruce Arlington, Jr.
Crump, Beverley L.
Dansby, Harry Bishop
Dodge, Cynthia Ellen
Eason, Carl Edward, Jr.
Edmunds, Felix Elmer
Edwards, James Edwin
Friedlander, Jerome Peyser, II
Gardner, Mark S.
Goforth, William Clements
Greenbacker, John Everett
Hartshorn, Roland DeWitt
Hill, Oliver White, Sr.
Holland, William Louis
Kennedy, Joe Jack, Jr.
Kuykendall, Ronald Edward
Macfarlane, Robert Bruce
Massey, Arthur Blanton
McFarlane, Walter Alexander
McGlothlin, Michael Gordon
McGowan, Kevin Murray
Miller, William Frederick
Montagna, Anthony Louis, Jr.
Morrison, Johnny Edward
Mullins, Roger Wayne
Nassikas, John Nicholas
Pearsall, John Wesley
Rawls, Frank Macklin
Redmond, Robert
Revercomb, Horace Austin, Jr.
Robinson, Thomas Hart
Schmidt, C. Jeffers, Jr.
Schmidt, William Lesnett
Segall, James Arnold
Skinker, Donald Ray
Small, Marc James
Spirn, Stuart Douglas
Spitzli, Donald Hawkes, Jr.
Tillar, Darrel Long
Treakle, James Edward, Jr.
Walker, Woodrow Wilson
Ware, Guilford Dudley
Weinman, Ellen Shelton
Whitaker, Steven King
Whitt, Robert Holt, Jr.
Williams, Glen Morgan
Woodhouse, Edward James, Jr.
Woodrum, Clifton A., III
Young, Hubert Howell, Jr.

Washington

Angevine, Earl Francis
Armstrong, Grant
Backstein, Robert Joseph
Barline, John
Burman, David John
Buzzard, Steven Ray
Devlin, Greg Martin
Dillon, Janet Jordan
Dunham, Douglas Spence
Ellis, James Reed
Fine, Eleanor Rose
Glein, Richard Jeriel
Gross, Richard Arthur
Haynes, George Cleve
Hoff, Valerie Margaret Knecht
Huey, Diane Marie
Johnson, Richard Bruce
Krueger, Larry Eugene
Mahoney, Timothy William
Mashita, Lloyd Isao
McGavick, Donald Hugh
Murray, James Michael
Phillabaum, Stephen Day
Pinckney, Ronald Robert
Raaen, G(ary) Lee
Roubicek, Christopher John
Sayre, Matt Melvin Mathias
Serka, Philip Angelo
Sessions, G. P.
Wagoner, David Everett
Walker, G(lenn) Perrin
Westland, John Alden
Wilson, James Barker
Wirt, Alexander Wells

West Virginia

Ansel, William Henry, Jr.
Bayley, Thomas Way, Jr.
Bell, Charles D.
Bunner, William Keck
Colburn, James Allan
Coleman, James Howard, Jr.
Cross, David Bert
Hearst, James Henry
Howley, Loren Blackman
Humphries, Judy Lynn
Judy, John David, III
Kennedy, David Tinsley
Kent, James Albert, Jr.
Markey, E. Lowell
Powell, James Corbley
Richmond, William Frederick, Jr.
Riley, Arch Wilson, Jr.
Saville, Royce Blair
Thaxton, Everette Frederick
Watson, William E.
Wehner, Charles Vincent
Wehner, Richard Karl

Wisconsin

Bauman, Susan Joan Mayer
Bennett, David H.
Bohren, Michael Oscar
Bolger, T(homas) Michael
Byers, Stephen Michael
Cook, Joseph Lee
Deffner, Roger L.
Drengler, William Allan John
Flatley, Robert Rahr
Gass, David
Giese, Heiner
Glowacki, Thomas Robert
Halferty, James Burkhardt
Hartley, Glenn Henry
Hertel, Theodore Bernhard, Jr.
Hurt, Michael Carter
Jennings, David Vincent, Jr.
Jinkins, Mark Allen
Josten, Roy Joseph
Kelly, John Martin
Kiessling, William Edward
Kobriger, Richard Roman, Jr.
Lathrop, Trayton LeMoine
Liebmann, Herbert Charles, III
Mitby, John Chester
Neubecker, Edward Frederick
Nohr, William Arthur
Orth, Charles Adam, Jr.
Rice, Zelotes Sylvester
Russell, David Brent
Sedor, Gilbert D.
Stoltz, John Robert
Thompson, Edward Francis
Wild, Norman Richard
Winton, Ward William

Wyoming

Ahlstrom, Bert Tavelli, Jr.
Alburn, Cary Rudolph, III
Allison, James Stanley
Case, Irvin Vincent, Jr.
Girard, Nettabell
Hathaway, Stanley Knapp
Hjelmstad, William David
Johnson, Robert Henry
Patrick, H. Hunter
Sachs, Philip David
Statkus, Jerome Francis
Tarver, Timothy Stephen

TERRITORIES OF THE UNITED STATES

American Samoa

Faalevao, Aviata Fano

CANADA

Nova Scotia

Dickey, John Horace

SWITZERLAND

Muller, Johannes Joseph

ADDRESS UNPUBLISHED

Ackerman, Robert A(rthur)
Alexander, Carla J.
Allison, Howard Mervyn
Baumohl, Harry Alan
Bohrer, Nancy King
Boorstein, Beverly Weinger
Brock, John Tabor
Christopher, M. Ronald
Cook, Wayne Ralph
Easterling, Charles Armo
Ecker, James Marshall
Fitzgerald, John Elmer
Fowler, Flora Daun

Garza, Graciano Jaime
Gerber, Jack
Gleason, Gerald Wayne
Hanig, Lynn
Hebl, Thomas Lee, Sr.
Ice, Clarence Frederick
Lambert, Arthur Gorman
Leleiko, Steven Henry
Levinson, Kenneth Lee
Lordi, Katherine M.
McCormick, David Arthur
Mollinger, Judith Ellen
Montee-Charest, Karen Ann
Montgomery, Kenneth Floyd
Moravsik, Robert James
Newman, Alan Harvey
Nix, Marie Louise Guste
Olsen, Kenneth Allen
Panec, William Joseph
Pitrof, Eugene Edward
Porricelli, Gerald Joseph
Regenstreif, Herbert
Rifman, Avrum Katz
Saliterman, Richard Arlen
Schiesswohl, Cynthia Rae Schlegel
Shapiro, Marge Diana
Sheetz, Ralph Albert
Sherrard, Alexander Conn
Stout, George McBride
Sullivan, James Washburn
Sweeney, Robert John
Welch, Ernest Wendell
West, George F(erdinand), Jr.
Whittington, Marvin Edward
Wilkinson, George Albert, Jr.
Winslow, Julian Dallas
Winstein, Stewart Robert
Winston, Harold Ronald
Yorra, Myron Seth

GOVERNMENT CONTRACTS AND CLAIMS

UNITED STATES

Alabama

Durnya, Louis Richard
Forbus, Sharon Ann
Howell, William Ashley, III
Miller, Barbara Currie

Alaska

McGee, Jack Brian

Arizona

Bartos, John Bury
Cassidy, Frank Joseph
McMorrow, William John
Schurr, M. Randolph

Arkansas

Carpenter, Thomas Milton

California

Aynes, James Paul, Jr.
Bagley, William Thompson
Bailey, Craig Bernard
Bancroft, David Phillips
Delaughter, Jerry L.
Diedrich, Peter Joseph
Fowler, Donald Raymond
Glazer, Jack Henry
Hagberg, Chris Eric
Hagberg, Viola Wilgus
Hirsch, David L.
Kamine, Bernard Samuel
Katayama, Robert Nobuichi
Kuelbs, John Thomas
Lemmon, John Vincent
Leslie, Robert Lorne
McLeod, Robert Macfarlan
Metzger, Robert Streicher
Miller, Jules Frederick
Mutek, Michael Wendell
Neary, Christopher J.
Owens, Aletha Riedel
Rawlings, Suzanne Corinne
Richards, Gerald Thomas
Richardson, Karen Lerohl
Schneier, Marc Malvin
Shelley, Susanne Mary
Sherrer, Charles William
Simmons, Robert Michael
Smith, Diane Rapp
Smith, Robert Catlett
Stanley, Sabrina Ann
Thornton, D. Whitney, II
Twomey, Joseph Gerald
Walcher, Alan Ernest
Waldsmith, Mary Louise
Wallace, Elaine Wendy
Wehde, Albert Edward
Wilhelm, Robert Oscar

Colorado

Davis, Wanda Rose
Dixon, Richard Dean
Glasser, Matthew David
Green, Lawrence Jamalian
Reardon, Gerard Vincent
Wells, David Conrad

Connecticut

Battersby, Gregory John
Cooney, Bradley Kent
Crimmins, Eileen Marie
Solecki, Trina Anne

Delaware

Brown, James Wilcox
Crane, John Murdoch

District of Columbia

Alvarado, Ricardo Raphael
Anthony, David Vincent
Baker, Keith Leon
Bannon, Brian Anthony
Bennett, Marion Tinsley
Berkin, Jeffrey Jack
Bowman, Michael Floyd
Boyce, Katharine Randolph
Braude, Herman Martin
Brodhead, William McNulty
Brookshire, James Earl
Buck, David Patrick
Burch, John Thomas, Jr.
Burgett, David Wallace
Burrow, Rhea Morgan
Chierichella, John W.
Clarkson, Stephen Batchelder
Cohen, Jay Loring
Crumlish, Joseph Dougherty
Dameron, Del Stiltner
Danzig, Richard Jeffrey
Day, Gregg Alan
Dempsey, David B.
Denniston, John Baker
Doyle, Gerard Francis
Duerk, William Adam
Dunnan, Weaver White
Duvall, Richard Osgood
Dyer, Michael Joseph
Feldman, Richard David
Fenster, Herbert Lawrence
Fitzhugh, David Michael
Frame, Nancy Davis
French, E. LaVon
Gallagher, Shawn Thomas
Garrett, Henry Lawrence, III
Golub, Martin Joseph
Gray, John Walker, Jr.
Greenberger, I. Michael
Grossman, Garry S.
Herz, Charles Henry
Hidalgo, Edward
Hodgson, Morgan Day
Hoppel, Robert Gerald, Jr.
Ittig, Gerard W.
Johnson, David Raymond
Johnson, Richard Tenney
Keiser, Henry Bruce
Kramer, Kenneth Stephen
Krivit, Daniel Henry
Krump, Gary Joseph
Latham, Weldon Hurd
Latimer, Allie B.
Leva, Marx
Levin, Edward M., Jr.
L'Heureux, Robert Dolor
Lifschitz, Judah
Long, Clarence Dickinson, III
Longstreth, Robert Christy
Lovitky, Jeffrey Aeryae
Merrigan, William Joseph
Morant, Blake Dominic
Newberger, Stuart Henry
Oliver, Dale Hugh
Oliver, Robert Spencer
Oser, Ralph Crandall
Pohl, Mark Ronald
Preston, Charles George
Preston, Colleen Ann
Principi, Elizabeth Ahlering
Rader, Robert Michael
Regalado, Eloisa
Riley, Dennis James
Roberts, James Harold, III
Schwartz, David
Seaman, Richard Norman
Seidman, Paul Joseph
Seto, Robert Mahealani Ming
Shafferman, Howard Haswell
Silver, Harry R.
Simchak, Matthew Stephen
Spriggs, William James
Sullivan, Eugene Raymond
Swartz, Christian LeFevre
Tomaszczuk, Alexander Daniel
Townsend, Diane Kathleen
Ursini, Josephine Lucille
Wallace, Wilton Lawrence
Whitney, John Adair
Williams, Thomas Scott
Wittig, Raymond Shaffer
Worthy, K(enneth) Martin
Yellott Jr., John Bosley
Younger, Alexander
Yuspeh, Alan Ralph
Zagami, Anthony James

Florida

Ferencik, Robert Elmer, Jr.
Kollin, Gary
Leiby, Larry Raymond
O'Neill, Michael Joseph
Parker, Whilden Sessions
Rico, JulieAnn
Ruggles, Rudy Lamont
Sarkis, Frederick Derr
Wind, Carol Marlene

Georgia

Baxter, Harry Stevens
Gaiser, Richard Edward
Halle, Mollie Johnson
Jones, Glower Whitehead
Pollard, Brenda Krebs
Sours, John Delmar
Sweeney, Neal James
Wright, Frederick Lewis, II

Hawaii

Bloede, Victor Carl

Illinois

Beckett, Amy Louise
Dodegge, Thomas Roland
Fuerstenberg, James P.
Gerdy, Harry
Palmberg, Earl Laverne
Polk, Lee Thomas
Renner, Michael John
Speidel, Richard Eli
Willmeth, Roger Earl
Zimmermann, John Joseph

Indiana

Kalsi, Swadesh Singh
Murrell, Jack Oliver
Palmer, Judith Grace
Robisch, Robert Karl

Kansas

Callahan, Michael Thomas
Myers, Jesse Jerome
Winkler, Dana John

Kentucky

Edelen, Francis Hennessy, Jr.
Moore, Charles Dudley, Jr.
Ratterman, David Burger
Stipanowich, Thomas Joseph

Louisiana

Brian, A(lexis) Morgan, Jr.
Davidson, Van Michael, Jr.
Guillot, Elaine Wolfe

Maine

Pearson, Clinton Charles

Maryland

Falkson, Susan Dory
Geldon, Fred Wolman
Gobbel, Luther Russell
Hanley, David Burris
Jayson, Lester Samuel
Kimball, Sherman Paul
Nystrom, Harold Charles
Paul, Carl Frederick
Risik, Philip Maurice
Siegel, Harold Aryai
Smith, David Robinson
Willcox, Breckinridge Long

Massachusetts

Brophey, Alicia Tracy
Erlich, Jacob Nathan
Gleason, Joseph Howard
Haar, Charles Monroe
Loftin, Melinda Jayne
McCready, Leo Stephen
Oulton, Donald Paul
Siegel, Julian Lee

Michigan

Blaske, Thomas Hugh
Lobenherz, William Ernest
Marks, Andrew James
Simmons, Brent Elliott

Minnesota

Bruner, Philip Lane
Halverson, Steven Thomas
Maffei, Rocco John
Marquardt, Merritt Reno
Stephens, Mary Elizabeth Giuliani

Missouri

Clegg, Karen Kohler
Crigler, Susan Gum
Ferry, Joseph Dean
Lerner, Lawrence
Minton, Goodridge Venable Morton
Pletz, John Stephen

Nebraska

Smith, Richard Wendell

New Hampshire

Marsh, Norman James, Jr.
McGonagle, Shirlee Ann

New Jersey

Baron, Richard Mark
Brown, Garrett E., Jr.
Campolucci, Roger Louis
Ehrlich, Leslie Sharon
Greene, Michael Roy
Hackman, Richard Paul
Hoens, Charles Henry, Jr.
Martin, Russell White
McKenna, Michael Francis
Protigal, Stanley Nathan
Schiefelbein, Lester Willis, Jr.
Statmore, Kenneth T.

New Mexico

Jontz, Dennis Eugene
Kehl, Randall Herman

New York

Blinder, Albert Allan
Calamari, Joseph August
Cantor, Louis
Cape, Billie Jean
Cohen, Linda Meryl
Eiche, Jay S.
Flynn, William Bernard
Forster, James Francis
Gotimer, Harry Albert
Head, Christopher Alan
Hilts, Earl T.
Koster, Eric David
McGahren, Eugene Dewey, Jr.
Meader, John Daniel
Mur, Raphael
Nicholson, Michael
Parker, Douglas Martin
Samuel, Raphael
Silverberg, Steven Mark
Stroud, Alan Neil
Toplitz, George Nathan
Wells, Peter Nathaniel

North Carolina

Cramer, Mark Clifton
Flowers, Kent Gordon, Jr.

North Dakota

Hand, James S.
Kopacz, Stanley William, Jr.

Ohio

Batt, Nick
Cochran, Shirley Ann
Coler, William Lee
Gurley, Michael Edward
Mullin, Michael Joseph
Rennick, Kyme Elizabeth Wall
Schatz, William Bonsall
Seal, Thomas David
Zychowicz, Ralph Charles

Oklahoma

Vanderburg, Michael Robert

Oregon

Westwood, James Nicholson

Pennsylvania

Adler, Theodore Arthur
Edelstein, Stanley Barton
Feld, Arthur Michael
Freeman, Antoinette Rosefeldt
Glantz, Douglas Gene
Heubel, William Bernard
Lackman, James Stephen
Moores, Edward Harrison
Reiter, Joseph Henry
Ruck, Andrew Joseph
West, James Joseph

South Carolina

Bergholz, Warren Ernest, Jr.
Lake, Robert Campbell, Jr.

Tennessee

Bennett, Andy Dwane
Dadds, Harry Leon, II
Dillard, W. Thomas
Sanger, Herbert Shelton, Jr.

Texas

Crowley, James Worthington
Davis, Harold Clayton, Jr.
Doke, Marshall J., Jr.
Dunn, Richard Clement
Foster, Ben Frank, Jr.
Johnson, Scott Warren
Miller, John Eddie
Rucker, Jerry Don
Weiner, Marcia Myra
Wheeler, Susan Lynn
Winchell, Michael George

Utah

Bigler, Glade S.
Larsen, Lynn Beck
Morgan, Bruce Kent
Wilkinson, David Lawrence

Virginia

Cambridge, Robert Matthew
DeGolia, James B.
Gales, Robert Robinson
Goforth, William Clements
Kovacic, William Evan
Lane, John
Lester, James Lee
Markovich, Stephen Edward
Phillips, Dennis Leslie
Revoile, Charles Patrick
Sargeant, William Leslie
Schroeder, James White
Schwartz, Arthur Edward
Smail, Laurence Mitchell
Wentink, Michael James
Williams, Marcus Doyle
Wilson, Douglas Downes
Zucker, David Clark

Washington

Edmondson, Frank Kelley, Jr.
Oles, Douglas S.
Phillips, Catherine
Reardon, Mark William

Wisconsin

Jambois, Robert James
Liccione, Stephen John
Smith, Robert John
Wilcox, Jean Evelyn

CANADA

Quebec

Pascoe, Christopher John Campbell

FEDERAL REPUBLIC OF GERMANY

Prevost, Richard James

ADDRESS UNPUBLISHED

Crandell, John Smith
Fagan, Peter Thomas
George, Fredric Joel
Gusman, Robert Carl
Lande, James Avra
Metzger, Jeffrey Paul
Milbrath, Dennis Henry
Shareef, Michael T.
Stehlik, Frederick D.

GOVERNMENT, LOCAL

UNITED STATES

Alabama

Adams, John Edmund
Johnson, Joseph H., Jr.
Martin, Arthur Lee, Jr.
Smith, Carol Jean
Wagner, Charles Stephen
Wyatt, Charles Herbert, Jr.
Yates, Lawden Henry

Alaska

Bolger, Joel Harold
Hedland, John Sigurd
Hughes, Mary Katherine

Arizona

Baker, William Dunlap
George, Maureen Rose
Meister, Frederick William
Ong, Henry Hop
Schurr, M. Randolph
Stoddard, Charles Warner, III

Arkansas

Campbell, George Emerson
Clark, John Steven

California

Abt, Evet Sue Loewen
Amerikaner, Steven Albert
Aynes, James Paul, Jr.
Busch, Peter Jonathan
Clark, Dwight William
Cobey, James Alexander
Cook, Ronald Walter
Crump, Gerald Franklin
Freeman, Beth Labson
Hall, Carlyle Washington, Jr.
Harris, Robert Thomas
Heisinger, James Gordon, Jr.
Holmes, Dallas Scott
Jensen, Dennis Lowell
Jensen, Douglas Blaine
Johnston, Faber Laine, Jr.
Kirlin, Anne Marget
Lehman, Edward George
MacDougall, William Roderick
McDevitt, Ray Edward
Noe, Ralph Henderson, Jr.
O'Hearn, Barbara Ann
Papiano, Neil Leo
Perry, Matilda Toni
Rawlings, Suzanne Corinne
Roth, Hadden Wing
Sato, Sho
Skaggs, Sanford Merle
Snyder, Arthur Kress
Taft, Perry Hazard
Tepper, R(obert) Bruce, Jr.
Williams, Charles Judson
Zafis, Andrew James

Colorado

Billings, Bruce Arthur
Brady, William John, Jr.
Craig, Benjamin Lawrence
Dominick, David DeWitt
Foster, Tad Stevenson
Fritze, James Ronald
Glasser, Matthew David
Halpern, Alexander
Kelly, Eric Damian
Kiehnhoff, Thomas Nave
Patrick, Kevin Land
Ramirez, David Eugene
Robinson, Julia Ormes
Sayre, Charles Michael
Sayre, John Marshall
Smith, Michael Louis
Smith, Thomas Fenton
Sonntag, Richard Arthur
Strenski, Robert Francis
Tisdale, Patricia Claire

Connecticut

Bingham, Lisa Blomgren
Boland, John Daniel
Eberhart, Harry Simon
Goldfarb, Alexander A.
Greenblatt, Morton Harold
Hershatter, Richard Lawrence
Killian, Robert Kenneth, Jr.
MacKenzie, Roderick John, Jr.
Morrison, Francis Henry
Owen, H. Martyn
Solecki, Trina Anne

Delaware

Devine, Donn
Sheridan, John Robert

District of Columbia

Breitenberg, John Francis
Chabot, Elliot Charles
Cutler, Eliot Raphael
Duncan, Charles Tignor
Glasgow, Norman M.
Levin, Edward M., Jr.
McNeal, John Edward
Michaels, Gary David
Schwartz, David Harold

Florida

Allen, Jospeh Bernard
Anderson, R(obert) Bruce
Bartolone, Frank Salvatore
Bernstein, Howard Mark
Book, Ronald Lee
Buchman, Kenneth William
Buchman, Paul Sidney
Cardwell, David Earl
Clements, Allen, Jr.
Dekle, George Robert
Dressler, Robert A.
Franklin, Lucille Espey
Garcia-Pedrosa, Jose Ramon
Glickman, Ronnie Carl
Gougelman, Paul Reina
Gray, J. Charles
Grogan, Michael Kevin
Hamilton, Robert Lowery
Hootman, Gregory Wayne
Hurtgen, Peter Joseph
Lewis, William Adams
Lloyd, John Stoddard
McCormick, John Hoyle
McCurdy, Robert Clark
McWilliams, John Lawrence, III
Napoli, Joseph Anthony
Passidomo, John Michael
Rogers, Gordon Dean
Rydberg, Marsha Griffin
Sechen, Robert Nicholas
Thiele, Herbert William Albert

Georgia

Dillard, George Douglas
Fitzpatrick, Barry Lane
Graham, Charles Benjamin, Jr.
Mears, Michael
Stone, Hugh William
Young, Robert George

Hawaii

Callies, David Lee
Meaney, Michael Lawrence
Simms, Sandra Arlene
Takayama, Ken Hideshi

Idaho
Bengoechea, Shane Orin
Litteneker, Edwin Lee
Russell, Robie George

Illinois
Alexander, Ellen Jo
Beckett, Amy Louise
Benson, James Robert
Bernardi, Donald Delpho
Beth, Kenneth Norman
Burkey, Lee Melville
Callis, Felix L.
Clem, Gary Smith
Coppinger, John Bampfield
Cummings, Walter Dillon
Davis, Chester R., Jr.
Fisher, Edward Joseph
Fleming, Milo Joseph
Folgate, Homer Emmett, Jr.
Gagliardo, Joseph M(ichael)
Gagne, James L.
Garofalo, John Richard
Greenspan, Jeffrey Dov
Haines, Martha Mahan
Juergensmeyer, John Eli
Kaminski, Stanley Ronald
Kelty, Thomas Walsh
Klaff, Ramsay Laing
Kuehn, Angelika Maria
Landmeier, Allen Lee
Leifel, Danny John
Logli, Paul Albert
Long, Robert Jeffrey
Malmgren, James H(oward)
Miller, John Leed
Narko, Medard Martin
Narusis, Regina GytéFirant
Netsch, Dawn Clark
Poper, Michael Charles
Powless, Kenneth Barnett
Radzilowsky, Michael
Rapp, James Anthony
Roddewig, Richard John
Schmidt, Wayne Walter
Spina, Anthony Ferdinand
Stitt, LeMoine Donaldson
Swanson, Warren Lloyd
Warnock, William Reid
Zimmermann, John Joseph

Indiana
Austgen, David Michael
Barden, Kenneth Eugene
Brown, Richard Lawrence
Campbell, Edward Adolph
Gerde, Carlyle Noyes (Cy)
Greeneburg, Thomas Michael
McNaughton, George Theodore
Saunders, David Livingston
Walmer, James L.
White, James Patrick

Iowa
Luchtel, Keith Edward
Nowadzky, Roger Alan
Ouderkirk, Mason James
Walker, Bruce LeRoy
White, Harold Wayne

Kansas
Bush, Granville McCutcheon, III
Gaar, Norman Edward
Harris, Phillip Lloyd
Hess, Jerry John
Lang, Joe Allen
Stovall, Carla Jo
Tittsworth, David Gregory
Winkler, Dana John

Kentucky
Bardenwerper, William Burr
Edelen, Francis Hennessy, Jr.
Knopf, William Lee
Leightty, David
Lilly, Nolte Scott Ament
Miller, J. Bruce

Louisiana
Alarcon, Terry Quentin
Beck, William Harold, Jr.
Cicet, Donald James
Guillot, Elaine Wolfe
Marcello, David Anthony
Todaro, Laura Jean
Villavaso, Stephen Donald
Wooderson, James Michael

Maine
Cooper, Michael David

Maryland
Armold, Judith Ann
Comeau, Michael Gerard
Duckett, Warren Bird, Jr.
Hopkins, Samuel
Perkins, Roger Allan
Porro, Alfred Anthony, Jr.
Rhodes, Thurman Haywood
Tierney, Philip James

Massachusetts
Bernard, Michael Mark
Dello Iacono, Paul Michael
Fellows, John White
Freeman, Florence Eleanor
Gargiulo, Andrea Weiner
Marullo, Steven Jeffrey
Mastrangelo, Richard Edward
Michelman, Frank I.
Moschos, Demitrios Mina
O'Connell, Henry Francis
Platt, Rutherford Hayes, Jr.
Ryan, James Frederick
Sears, John Winthrop
Starrett, Loyd Milford

Michigan
Austin, Margaret Schilt
Barr, John Monte
Bruin, Linda Lou
Bultje, Ronald Alan
Cinabro, Robert Henry
Clark, Mark Lee
Connelly, Thomas Joseph
Cox, Joseph King
Danko, Stephen Gaspar
Graham, W(illiam) Thomas, III
King, Thomas George
Latovick, Paula R(ae)
Lehto, Neil John
Massie, Joel Lee
Nora, John Joseph
Platzer, Cynthia Siemen
Richardson, Robert Woodrow
Salan, John Francis
Schultz, Stephen Otto
Smith, Terry J.
Smith, Wayne Richard
Spelman, John Henry
Swain, Dennis Michael
Thurswell, Gerald Elliott
Travis, Robert Frederick
Virtue, Maxine Boord

Minnesota
Anderson, Thomas Willman
Deans, Thomas Seymour
Donohue, Peter Salk
Frauenshuh, Ronald Ray, Sr.
Holmstrom, Gregory Leonard
Pagliaccetti, Gary John
Petersen, Jan Farel
Skare, Robert Martin

Mississippi
Crook, Robert Lacey
Gay, Joe Thomas
Golden, Wilson
Goldman, Thomas Laverne
Griffith, Benjamin Elmo
Mord, Irving Conrad, II
Shepard, Robert Payne
Taylor, Ronald Louis
Taylor, Zachary, III

Missouri
Biesterfeld, Craig Stewart
Blunt, Ronald L.
Burch, David Ryan
Cipolla, Thomas Alphonse
Crigler, Susan Gum
Ferry, Joseph Dean
Gilmore, Webb Reilly
Lashley, Curtis Dale
Sands, Darry Gene
Terando, G.H.
Weber, William Randolph

Nebraska
Bixby, Joseph Nathan
Burns, Steven Dwight
Cuypers, Charles James
Glidden, Richard Mark
Rice, John Edward
Schumacher, Paul Maynard

Nevada
Curran, Bill
White, John Aaron, Jr.
Wright, Thomas Preston

New Jersey
Bardack, Paul Roitman
Bate, David Soule
Biel, Mark
Bookbinder, Ronald Eric
Cox, William Martin
Dilts, Thomas Harold
Doherty, Robert Christopher
Domzalski, Kenneth Stanley
Downs, Thomas Edward, IV
Estis, Dennis Arnold
Fasolo, William Alexander
Hurley, Lawrence Joseph
Jacobson, Michael
Kearns, William John, Jr.
Kleinberg, Robert Samuel
Kondracki, Edward Anthony
Loigman, Larry Scott
Luthman, David Andrew
Manco, Dominick Michael
Maraziti, Joseph James, Jr.
McGinn, Howard Anthony
Munoz, Robert F.
Paley, Phillip Lewis
Pane, Michael Anthony, IV
Pojanowski, Joseph A., III
Rogers, Matthew Stephen
Schechner, David
Schuster, Steven Vincent
Shackleton, Richard James
Stickel, Frederick George, III
Wilson, Martin S., Jr.
Wilson, William Edward
Yurasko, Frank Noel
Zlotnick, Norman Lee
Zurav, David Bernard

New York
Baumgarten, Sidney
Bernstein, Stephen Michael
Costa, John Anthony
Curran, Maurice Francis
Curtiss, Willis David
Davison, Irwin Stuart
Duncombe, Raynor Bailey
Emanuel, Ira Michael
Falvey, Patrick Joseph
Fishberg, Gerard
Gerrard, Michael Burr
Goldman, Jerry Alan
Gulino, Frank
Hofrichter, Lawrence S.
Jordon, Deborah Elizabeth
Josephson, William Howard
Kabak, Bernard Joshua
Kalb, Robert Joseph
Lippe, Richard Allen
Lyon, Carl Francis, Jr.
Marcus, Norman
McCarthy, William Joseph
Miller, Richard Clark, Jr.
Millman, Bruce Russell
Nesbitt, John Benedict
Nguyen, Paul Dung Quoc
Nowicki, Michael Thomas
Picardi, Ferdinand Louis
Rice, Terry August
Rose, Robert Stanter
Savitt, Susan Schenkel
Sotir, Richard Louis, Jr.
Stamato, Philomena
Suraci, Joseph Anthony
Taubenfeld, Harry Samuel
Trotta, Frank Paul
Wilson, Clifford H.

North Carolina
Blomeley, James Lee, Jr.
Buckley, Charles Robinson, III
Burti, Christopher Louis
Higgins, Danny Glenn
Prevatte, Elias Jesse
Walker, Daniel Joshua, Jr.
Wilson, LeVon Edward
Wolfe, John George, III

Ohio
Batt, Nick
Bindley, Richard Stephen
Burke, Timothy Michael
Climer, James Alan
Goostree, Robert Edward
Gruber, William Michael Ondrey
Heier, David Scott
Holzer, Richard Jean
Largent, Jeffrey Willard
Leach, Russell
Lipton, Andrew S.
McAdams, Sheilah Helen
McClain, William Andrew
Neff, Robert Clark
Petrey, Katherine Gossick
Rosen, Gary Mitchell
Rossi, William Matthew
Schrader, Alfred Eugene
Severs, Eric Robertson
Slagle, James William
Sydlow, Holly Taft
Taylor, Edward McKinley, Jr.
Trotter, Thomas Robert
Wallach, Mark Irwin
Ziegler, Edward Howard, Jr.
Zychowicz, Ralph Charles

Oklahoma
Cates, Ronald Dean
Lester, Andrew William
McMillian, Roger Lee
Tully, Brian Brendan
Vanderburg, Michael Robert

Oregon
Bechtold, Paula Miller
Clark, David Lewis
Harms, Edward Clair, Jr.
Launer, Jeannette Maureen
Rogers, Jeffrey Langston
Thorndike, Daniel Carl

Pennsylvania
Aman, George Matthias, III
Ashcraft, John Marion, III
Ceraul, David James
Coslett, Charles Reynolds
Dillon, Charles Edward
Fernsler, John Paul
Gelso, Charles Patric
Gray, Kathleen Ann
Haber, Richard Jerome
Hackman, Karen Lee
Henry, Ronald George
Hovis, Raymond Leader
Kessler, Alan Craig
Knupp, Robert Louis
Kramer, Gilda Lea
LaFaver, Jon Fetherolf
Leete, John Bruce
Love, Mark Steven
Mulvihill, Mead James, Jr.
Muraca, Frank John
Schroeder, William Francis
Siegel, Arthur Bernard
Smith, Templeton, Jr.
Stevens, Paul Lawrence
Tesone, Robert Joseph
Tucker, Jeffrey Thornt
Turrell, James Joel
Witherel, Michael Joseph
Yanity, Gerald Joseph
Youngs, Christopher Jay

Rhode Island
Abilheira, Richard B.
Carr, Mary Jo
Driscoll, Robert George
Harrop, R(obert) Daniel

South Carolina
Bell, Robert Morrall
Eltzroth, Clyde Alfred, Jr.

Tennessee
Cook, Bratten Hale, II
Cramer, William Mitchell
Epps, James Haws, III
Howell, Morton Boyte
Lander, Gary David
Meyer, Stephen Leonard
Swanson, Charles Walter
Walton, John Wayne

Texas
Abercrombie, Thomas Vernon
Armstrong, John Douglas
Balough, Richard Charles
Bell, William Woodward
Berger, Howard Charles
Clark, Ronald Hurley
Cortez, Hernan Glenn
Dunn, Richard Clement
Erben, Randall Harvey
Fletcher, Riley Eugene
Greanias, George Constantine
Hardy, Harvey Louchard
Jones, Russell C.
Kraus, Nancy Jane
Landers, Gary Clinton
McCreary, Frank E., III
Morris, Rebecca Robinson
Morris, Robert Smith
Purnell, Charles Giles
Schwartz, Aaron Robert
Thornton, Russell James
Williams, Nancy Ondrovik

Utah
Allred, Steven Wesley
Anderson, Craig W.
Ashworth, Brent Ferrin
Gallian, Russell Joseph
Judd, Dennis L.
Morgan, Bruce Kent
Newton, Joseph Steven

Vermont
Facey, John Abbott, III
Plante, Peter Paul

Virginia
Arey, Stephen Edward
Arnold, William McCauley
Barron, Myra Hymovich
Beach, Barbara Purse
Benser, Frank Leroy
Campbell, Thomas Douglas
Finnegan, Edward James
Litten, Donald Douglas
Middleton, J. Howard, Jr.
Napier, Douglas William
Roettger, Clyde Edward, Jr.
Rucker, William Browning
Schmidt, C. Jeffers, Jr.
Sheffield, Walter Jervis
Steinhilber, August William
Thomas, Norman Allan

Washington
Addington, Darrel Blair
Defelice, Dennis Joseph
Dohn, George Thomas
Ellis, James Reed
Heid, Daniel Brian
Koegen, Roy Jerome
Weinman, Richard Stephen
Youngs, Linda Miller

West Virginia
Harrington, Travers Rountree, Jr.

Wisconsin
Clark, James Francis
De Bruin, David Lee
Dietrich, Dean Richard
Dietz, Richard Joseph
Drengler, William Allan John
Dye, William Ellsworth
Jambois, Robert James
Kaiser, John Atwood
Kraft, Warren P(aul)
Krueger, William Frederick
Kwiatkowski, Thomas Eugene
LaRowe, Myron Edward
Mukamal, Stuart Sassoon
Rankin, Gene Raymond
Whitcomb, Michael Arthur Isaac

Wyoming
Patrick, H. Hunter
Smith, Thomas Shore

UNITED ARAB EMIRATES
Stockwell, David Michael

ADDRESS UNPUBLISHED
Brock, John Tabor
George, Fredric Joel
Gleason, Gerald Wayne
Glywasky, Donald Steven
Kuss, Herbert Patrick
Middleton, Harlow Clester
Quinn, Joseph Francis
Sheahan, Joseph D.
Stough, Charles Daniel
Williams, Frank J.

HEALTH

UNITED STATES

Alabama
Chambers, K.W. Michael
Dacso, Sheryl Tatar
Martin, Arthur Lee, Jr.
McCorkle, Lucy Virginia
Morgan, Wendell Richmond
Pierce, Donald Fay

Arizona
Cohn, Janice Marie
Hanshaw, A. Alan
Meister, Frederick William

Arkansas
Leflar, Robert B

California
Adams, Cary Meredith
Finney, Joseph Claude Jeans
Frank, Vincent Antonio
Gough, Aidan Richard
Harris, Michael Gene
Mancino, Douglas Michael
Manley, Michael Alexander
Memel, Sherwin Leonard
Mobley, Gary Steven
Nichols, Alan Hammond
Nocas, Andrew James
Ostrach, Michael Sherwood
Powers, Marcus Eugene
Sanders, Gary Wayne
Stone, Jean
Thompson, Jeffrey Dale
Tomberlin, George E., Jr.

Colorado
Grissom, Garth Clyde
Scott, Paul Edward
Shanaberger, Carol Jean

Connecticut
Densen-Gerber, Judianne
Graham, Kenneth Albert
Hefferan, Harry Howard, Jr.
Holder, Angela Roddey
Katz, Jay
Mandell, David E.
Maniatis, Charlynn Carol
Marmor, Theodore Richard
Menchel, Arnold Ira
Schwartz, Kove Jerome
Smith, Cornelius C., Jr.
Taub, Sheila Kurzrock
Tilson, John Quillin
Yamin, Robert Joseph

District of Columbia
Bachrach, Eve Elizabeth
Bersoff, Donald Neil
Boudreaux, Andree Anita
Byington, S. John
Campbell, W(illiam) Douglas
Casson, Joseph Edward
Cohrssen, John Joseph
Cole, Michael Frederick
Cook, Michael Harry
Deleon, Patrick Henry
Downey, Richard Morgan
Duerk, William Adam
Dyer, Michael Joseph
Edwards, Charles Henry, III
Evans, John Kedrich
Ford, David R(ucker)
Gibbs, Jeffrey Neil
Houseman, Alan William
Johns, Richard Warren
Johns, Warren LeRoi
Kelly, Kathryn
Kingham, Richard Frank
Krump, Gary Joseph
Manthei, Richard Dale
Middlekauff, Roger David
Monaco, Grace Powers
Novak, Nina
Onek, Joseph Nathan
Pollard, Michael Ross
Postol, Lawrence Philip
Powers, Galen Dean
Principi, Elizabeth Ahlering
Rexinger, Allan Robert
Roccograndi, Anthony Joseph
Rosenfield, Harry Nathan
Scheer, Peter Edward
Schweitzer, Sandra Lynn
Scott, Michael
Stromberg, Clifford Douglas
Tenney, Paul Anthony
Thompson, Richard Leon
Ughetta, Valerie Jeanne
Verville, Richard Emery
Wheeler, Anne Marie
Williamson, Thomas Samuel, Jr.
Zimmerly, James Gregory

Florida
Billingsley, Curtis Ashley
Book, Ronald Lee
Davis, Gary Scott
Fishman, Lewis Warren
Goldsmith, Karen Lee
Haliczer, James Solomon
Hart, Deborah Diane
Hasty, Frederick Emerson, III
Hood, Charles David, Jr.
Kibler, Rhoda Smith
Martin, James Addison, Jr.
Mathews, Byron B., Jr.
McCurdy, Robert Clark
Mudd, John Philip
Prom, Stephen G.
Thornton, John W.
Watson, Roberta Casper

Georgia
Allen, Hunter Smith, Jr.
Hasson, James Keith, Jr.
Kelly, James Patrick
Menkin, Lita Sue
Sensenig, Lana Smith

Hawaii
D'Olier, H(enry) Mitchell
Iwamoto, Raymond Shigeo

Idaho
Hoagland, Samuel Albert

Illinois
Allen, Henry Sermones, Jr.
Arkin, Henry Russell
Baffes, Thomas Gus
Berry, Richard Morgan
Bierig, Jack R.
Bleiweiss, Shell J.
Brent, Nancy Jean
Dechene, James Charles
DeWolfe, George Fulton
Dilling, Kirkpatrick Wallwick
Egan, Kevin James
Franks, Herbert Hoover
Gilbert, Howard N(orman)
Gorey, Thomas Michael
Gutstein, Solomon
Hermann, Donald Harold James
Hicks, James Thomas
Jesser, Steven H.
Kamensky, Marvin
Ladd, Jeffrey Raymond
McVisk, William Kilburn
Mollet, Chris John
Morse, Saul Julian
Murer, Michael Anton
Norden, Dennis Arthur
Nye, Sandra Gayle
Nygren, Karl Francis
Plesko, Jeffrey Michael
Polk, Lee Thomas
Potter, Richard Clifford
Rankin, James Winton

Ropiequet, John L.
Rovner, Jack Alan
Rymer, Terrie Adrienne
Schuyler, Daniel Merrick
Shannon, Peter Michael, Jr.
Shapo, Marshall Schambelan
Stone, Howard Lawrence
Thomas, William Harrold
Victor, Michael Gary
Wilson, Roger Goodwin
Wohlreich, Jack Jay

Indiana
Abbott, Jacquelyn Meng
McDermott, Renée R(assler)
Sanborn, Albert Beckwith, II
Trigg, Donald Clark

Iowa
Bump, Wilbur Neil
Eastman, Forest David
Graziano, Craig Frank
Klemesrud, Normand Charles
McNeil, Jean Anne
Rhodes, Ann Marie

Kansas
Adams, Stephen Thornton
Bell, Thomas Lee
Hay, Charles Richard
Snowbarger, Vincent Keith
Wing, David Leslie

Kentucky
Brown, Bonnie Maryetta
Fink, Joseph Leslie, III
Philipps, Kurt A.
Schoenbaechler, Edward Lewis

Louisiana
Fraiche, Donna DiMartino
Trostorff, Danielle Lombardo

Maine
Crawford, Linda Sibery
Douglas, Wayne Rodger
Trevett, Kenneth Parkhurst

Maryland
Berndt, Richard Olaf
DeVries, Donald Lawson, Jr.
Duer, Andrew Adgate
Rheinstein, Peter Howard
Roth, Robert Lloyd
Sfekas, Stephen James
Tilghman, Richard Carmichael, Jr.

Massachusetts
Beal, John Arthur
Fein, Sherman Edward
Gens, Richard Howard
Gibbs, Richard Frederic
Portnoy, Barry Michael
Rockefeller, Regina Strazzulla
Snyder, Marie Elizabeth
White, Barry Bennett

Michigan
Andersen, David Charles
Drutchas, Gregory G.
Durant, James Robert
Elkins, Bettye Swales
Harris, Robert James
Helminski, Francis Joseph
Jacobs, Seth Alan
Jordan, Michael Jay
Logie, John Hoult
Ludolph, Robert Charles
Mc Callum, Charles Edward
Muraski, Anthony Augustus
Murphy, Joseph Albert, Jr.
Raven, Jonathan Ezra
Rhodes, Vincent Ard
Schanz, Stephen John
Steinberg, Harvey Laurance
Swift, Theodore Wells

Minnesota
Broeker, John Milton
Dettmann, Marc John
Flynn Peterson, Kathleen A.
Foarde, Mary Patricia
Giberson, Francis Eugene
Grindal, Harald Theodore
Hanson, Bruce Eugene
Johnson, Michael Almer
Kress, Marjorie Mae
LeVander, Bernhard Wilhelm
Martin, Mary Kay
Nesseler, Steven Edward

Missouri
Allen, Thomas Ernest
Arneson, James H.
Beachy, Robert M.
Bierman, Norman
Colagiovanni, Joseph Alfred, Jr.
Curtis, Thomas Bradford
Fallon, John Joseph
Lehr, Sharon Ruth
Newman, Charles A.
O'Donnell, Thomas Patrick
Shank, Suzanne
Weber, William Randolph

Montana
McKeon, John Carl

Nebraska
Buntain, David Robert
Holdenried, John Richard
Jahn, Gregory Dean

Nevada
Ashleman, Ivan Reno, II

New Hampshire
Parnell, William Basil

New Jersey
Balikov, Henry R.
Barnes, Timothy Lee
Beidler, John Nathan
Brennan, Mary Kathryn Gonya
Eichler, Burton Lawrence
Gilman, Claudia Jane
Isele, William Paul
Manzo, Peter Thomas
Martini, George henry
Porzio, Ralph
Strasser, William Ignatius

New Mexico
Ricco, Edward Robert
Schumacher, Rod M.

New York
Beach, John Arthur
Beattie, Richard Irwin
Begos, Walter Anthony
Billauer, Barbara Pfeffer
Buldrini, George James
Carroll, Joseph J.
Conroy, Robert J.
Davison, Irwin Stuart
de Lasa, José M.
Devendorf, Alfred Ervin
Ehrlich, Jerrold Ivan
Fischer, Richard Samuel
Fisher, Kenneth Knight
Glass, Joel
Goldman, Roy Lawrence
Golick, Toby Barbara
Jacobson, Barry Stephen
Jacobson, Jerold Dennis
Leamer, Robert Eldon
Leben, Jeffrey Michael
McKee, Francis John
Melbardis, Wolfgang Alexander
Meneilly, James Kevin
Moy, Donald Richard
Northrop, Cynthia Ellen
Piver, Susan M.
Robb, Scott Hall
Sands, Judith Davies
Scher, Stanley Jules
Sokolow, Lloyd Bruce
Watson, Richard A.
White, Claude Esley
Wolf, Susan M.

North Carolina
Diosegy, Arlene Jayne
Etringer, Walter James, Jr.
Huffstetler, Noah Haywood, III
Manthei, Gayl Marie
Porter, Leon Eugene, Jr.
Silverstein, Carol Kauffman
Waldrup, J(ohn) Charles

Ohio
Allen, Richard Lee, Jr.
Buckley, Daniel Jerome
Dennis, William Robert
DeRousie, Charles Stuart
Fisher, Fredrick Lee
Harpster, Linda Marie
Jones, Edgar Wagstaff
Katz, Susan Stanton
Konrad, Bruce Joseph
Lee, William Johnson
Meehan, Michael Jan
Office, James Richard
Perin, Charles Henry, Jr.
Russo, Nancy Margaret
Sites, Richard Loren
Speros, James Mandamadiotis
Todd, William Michael
Vance, Victoria Lynne
Weller, Charles David
Witherell, Dennis Patrick
Zouhary, Kathleen Maher
Zox, Benjamin Louis

Oklahoma
Brown, Michael DeWayne
Thurman, Andrew Edward

Oregon
Brown, Gene L.
Kane, Henry Smith
Lowry, Robert Dudley
Marks, J(ohn) Barrett
Rogers, Jeffrey Langston

Pennsylvania
Aaron, Marcus, II
Bales, John Foster, III
Beautyman, Michael John
Beckman, Allen Joel
Black, Frederick Evan
Brier, Bonnie Susan
Brodbeck, Charles Richard
Brown, Judith Renzi
Burr, Charles Bentley, II
Cameron, John Clifford
Cramer, Harold
DiPietro, Melanie
Esser, Carl Eric
Flanagan, Joseph Patrick, Jr.
Friedman, Joseph
Garber, Marc Ricky
Gilbert, Bruce Rits
Holleran, Kevin Joseph
Hough, Thomas Henry Michael
Kalogredis, Vasilios J.
Keeler, Jean Marie
Klimon, Ellen Louise
Kolansky, Jeffrey Mark
Lowery, William Herbert
MacGregor, David Bruce
Maleski, Cynthia Maria
McComb, John Paul
Meisel, Alan
Minno, Frances Patricia Fraher
Rhodes, Kenneth Anthony, Jr.
Schulz, William Frederick, Jr.
Schwartz, Jeffrey Byron
Springer, Eric Winston
Stiller, Jennifer Anne
Tabas, Allan M.
Tupitza, Thomas Anton
Voss, Donald Henry

Wilkinson, James Allan
Wynstra, Nancy Ann
Yanity, Gerald Joseph

Rhode Island
Roszkowski, Joseph John
Schoenfeld, Barbara Braun
Southgate, (Christina) Adrienne Graves

South Carolina
Pollard, William Albert

South Dakota
Gerdes, David Alan

Tennessee
Anderson, Mary Virginia
Bennett, Horace Michael
Blumstein, James Franklin
Bush, William
Gentry, Gavin Miller
Jolly, Charles Nelson
Penny, William Lewis

Texas
Barton, Hugh Mitchell, III
Beard, Jane Ann Varner
Bissex, Walter Earl
Cambrice, Robert Louis
Clements, Jamie Hager
Davis, Harold Clayton, Jr.
Farley, Jan Edwin
Fryburger, Lawrence Bruce
Gosselink, Margaret Lavidge
Hedrick, John Richard
Holmquest, Donald Lee
James, Ann Nixon
Johnstone, Debbi Merriman
King, Daniel Dwade
King, Steve Mason
Newsom, Jan Lynn Reimann
Reinhard, Henry Corben, Jr.
Ricciardelli, Thomas Patrick
Smith, James Bonner
Toth, Robert Stephen
Waugh (Zucker), Karin Welles
Wren, James Eric, III
Yett, Charles William
Young, David Haywood
Zipprich, John L., II

Utah
Conard, Jane Reister

Virginia
Bussewitz, Roy Jon
Cutchins, Clifford Armstrong, IV
Donlan, Martin Andrew, Jr.
Indest, George Felix, III
Merrill, Richard Austin
Pope, Robert Dean
Regirer, Walter Wlodzimierz
Walsh, James Hamilton

Washington
Fine, Eleanor Rose
McCorkle, Linda Ann
Moniz, Donna Maria
Petrie, Gregory Steven
Stamper, Randall Lee
Waldman, Bart

West Virginia
Brushwood, David Benson
Frankovitch, Carl Nicholas
Humphries, Judy Lynn

Wisconsin
Baldwin, Janice Murphy
Berry, Roberta Marie
Biehl, Michael M.
Bolger, T(homas) Michael
Burroughs, Charles Edward
Busch, John Arthur
Katayama, Alyce Coyne
LaRowe, Myron Edward
Lund, John Richard
Shapiro, Robyn Sue
Vliet, Daniel George
White, Walter Hiawatha, Jr.

TERRITORIES OF THE UNITED STATES

Guam
LaFleur, Gary James

ADDRESS UNPUBLISHED
Cazalas, Mary Rebecca Williams
Flamm, Martin Benjamin
Gire, Michael Kent
Goldman, Barbara Lynn
Holland, Randy James
Levine, Samuel
Reynolds, H. Gerald
Roth, Michael Dundon
Shopsin, (Marc) Moshe
Tancredi, Laurence Richard
Trilling, Helen Regina

HISTORY, LEGAL

UNITED STATES

Alabama
Langum, David John

Arizona
Starr, Isidore

Arkansas
Gitelman, Morton

California
Bakken, Gordon Morris
Combs, Richard Ennis

Gunther, Gerald
Hamilton, Mary Jane
Hicks, James B(radley)
Levy, Leonard Williams
McGinty, Brian Donald
Mc Govern, William Montgomery, Jr.
Messinger, Sheldon L(eopold)
Parker, Charles Edward
Perkins, Steven Curtis
Scheiber, Harry N.

Connecticut
Ecklund, John Edwin
Goetsch, Charles Carnahan

Delaware
Ott, William Griffith

District of Columbia
Beach, Chester Paul, Jr.
Bloch, Susan Low
Brick, Barrett Lee
Caplan, Russell L.
Danzig, Richard Jeffrey
Fortenberry, Joseph Edwin
Gallagher, Walter Edward
Littlefield, Roy Everett, III
Lotkin, Ralph Louis
Rummel, Edgar Ferrand
Shaffer, Roberta Ivy

Florida
McCoy, Francis Tyrone

Georgia
Blumoff, Theodore Yale
Harrison, Samuel Hughel
Hogue, L(ouis) Lynn

Hawaii
Cades, Julius Russell

Idaho
Gallant, Kenneth Stuart

Illinois
Bender, Paul Edward
Cargerman, Alan William
Currie, David Park
Hall, Reed Stanley
Helmholz, R. H.
Hutchinson, Dennis James
Kearley, Timothy G.
Kimball, Spencer Levan
Kurland, Philip B.
Langbein, John Harriss
Macneil, Ian Roderick
Peck, Robert Stephen
Presser, Stephen Bruce
Solomon, Rayman Louis
Walker, Sue Sheridan
Young, Rowland Lee

Indiana
Funk, David Albert
Hewitt, John David

Kentucky
Bratton, Robert Milton

Louisiana
Palmer, Vernon Valentine

Maryland
Belz, Herman Julius
Bernard, Hugh Y(ancey), Jr.
Levin, Marshall Abbott
McDermitt, Edward Vincent
Respess, James Walter
Schneider, James Frederick

Massachusetts
Silverman, Robert Alan
Steelman, David Carl

Michigan
Fawcett, Kim Robert
Helminski, Francis Joseph
Kaplan, Steven Marc

Missouri
Berrey, Robert Wilson, III

New Jersey
Brandon, Mark Edward
Ronca, James Alexander

New York
Austin, John DeLong
Farnum, Henry Merritt
Gold, David Marcus
Grech, Anthony Paul
Hoover, James Lloyd
Jordan, Daniel Patrick, Jr.
Katz, Stanley Nider
Marke, Julius Jay
Osgood, Russell King
Purcell, Edward Aloysius, Jr.
Robbins, Sara Ellen
Tishler, Nicholas Eugene
Triffin, Nicholas
Wasserman, Edward Henry
Wishingrad, Jay Marc

North Carolina
Orth, John Victor

Ohio
Goostree, Robert Edward
Hitchcock, J. Gareth
Lehman, Robert Frank
Riley, Paul E.
Veltri, Stephen Charles

Oklahoma
Opala, Marian P(eter)

Oregon
Snouffer, William Campbell

Pennsylvania
Carroll, Mark Thomas
Haskins, George Lee
Kubacki, Stanley Louis
Mayer, Ann Elizabeth
Roper, Peter P.
Stivison, David Vaughn

Tennessee
Ely, James Wallace, Jr.

Texas
Baade, Hans Wolfgang
Hood, Lawrence E.
Parkin-Speer, Diane
Winship, Peter

Virginia
Gawalt, Gerard W(ilfred)
McConnell, Paul Stewart
Wiswall, Frank Lawrence, Jr.

Washington
Haynes, George Cleve
Henderson, Dan Fenno
Newcity, Michael Albert

West Virginia
Walkup, Homer Allen

ADDRESS UNPUBLISHED
Casper, Gerhard
Montee-Charest, Karen Ann
Rifman, Avrum Katz

IMMIGRATION, NATURALIZATION, AND CUSTOMS

UNITED STATES

Alaska
Bell, Keith Whitman

Arizona
Bartos, John Bury
Castro, Raul Hector
Lipson, Ann Louise
O'Leary, Thomas Michael
Vosburgh, John Addison

California
Appleman, Jeff Thome
Audett, Theophilus Bernard
Bettwy, Samuel William
Bonaparte, Ronald H.
Chuman, Frank Fujio
Gotcher, James Ronald
Klein, Alan Richard
Lee, Michael G.W.
Loewy, Peter Henry
Lublinski, Michael
Shostak, Stanley Richard
Simone, Martin Massimo
Snaid, Leon Jeffrey
Tan, William Lew
Trompeta, Jesus Iglesias
Vela, William Paul
Werner, Robert George
Wong, Jackson D.
Yelnick, Marc M(aurice)

Colorado
Heiserman, Robert Gifford
Radosevich, George Edward

District of Columbia
Ambrose, Myles Joseph
Blatchford, Joseph Hoffer
Carliner, David
Chang, Sam Hsien-Cheng
Danziger, Martin Breitel
Denniston, John Baker
Einhorn, Bruce Jeffrey
Engel, Tala
Feldman, Clarice Rochelle
Gannascoli, Rudolph Lance
Gordon, Charles
Hoffman, Michael Harris
Houlihan, David Paul
Inman, Maurice Cushing, Jr.
LaFrance, Ann Juliette
Lehman, Leonard
Robinson, Sara Moore
Schmidt, Paul Wickham
Stewart, Eugene Lawrence
Stewart, Terence Patrick
Walker, Robert Benson
Yale-Loehr, Stephen William
Yambrusic, Edward Slavko

Florida
Barker, Charles Thomas
Bracete, Juan Manuel
Campion, Edward
Cano, Mario Stephen
Day, Karen Spring
Kuehne, Benedict P.
Rose, Michael I.
Sandler, Gilbert Lee
Shaffer, Sanford Joel

Georgia
Bird, Terry Cornelius

Hawaii
Aduja, Peter Aquino

Illinois
Bates, R. Edward
Boecker, Sylvia Jean
Clamage, Brett D.
Cooper, Scott Francis

Harrison, Keith Michaele
Keryczynskyj, Leo Ihor
Moorman, Helen Louise
Paprocki, Thomas John
Sfasciotti, Mary L.
Spiegel, Robert Ira
Stack, Paul Francis

Indiana

Allen, Kenneth James

Iowa

Ruttenberg, Harold Seymour

Kansas

Metcalf, William Evans

Louisiana

Lampard, Catherine Ann

Maryland

Brodhurst, Albert Edward
Chaplin, Peggy Fannon
Gadhia, Lalit Harilal
Johnson, Laurence Fleming
Pisani, Robert Joseph
Salim, Abdullah (Reginald Armistice Hawkins), Jr.

Massachusetts

Huang, Thomas Weishing
Hurley, Daniel Gerard
Landy, James Leonard
Pearlstein, Gerald
Yee, Kenneth M.P.

Michigan

Dobkin, Donald Sidney
Kramer, LeRoy, III
Pierce, Richard William
Rewald, Roman

Minnesota

Hayward, Edward Joseph
Ingber, Jerome Burton
Oh, Matthew In-Soo

Mississippi

Will, Joseph Henry Michael

Missouri

Blume, Lawrence Dayton
Golbert, Albert Sidney

Nebraska

Minter, Gregory Byron
Pfeiffer, William Edward

Nevada

Garcia, Eva
Schutt, William Eldon

New Jersey

Blanco, Franklin Augusto
Bongiorno, Andrew William
Gilbert, Paul Nelson
Preiser, Godfrey Krause, Jr.
St. Landau, Norman

New Mexico

Ferreira, Beatriz Valadez

New York

Abrams, Franklin Stephen
Beltre, Luis Oscar
Bernstein, Edward Allan
Brent, Stephen M.
Costantino, Mark Americus
Cowles, Frederick Oliver
Donohue, John Patrick
Einhorn, Joseph Harold
Grunblatt, David Michael
Hagan, Peter
Irwin, Richard Frank
Juceam, Robert E.
Klipstein, Robert Alan
Nagy, Jill Harriet
Patel, Pravinchandra J.
Posner, Michael Hoffman
Pryor, William Bernard
Ritter, Ann L.
Rivera, Juan
Samansky, J. Leonard
Slatus, Robert Earl
Takashima, Hideo
Wildes, Leon

Ohio

Carro, Jorge Luis
Elam, John William
Emmert, Steven Michael
Zavatsky, Michael Joseph

Oklahoma

Mirabile, Thomas Keith

Oregon

Barilla, Frank (Rocky)
Bovarnick, Paul Simon
Marandas, John Steve
Nafziger, James Albert Richmond
Ryan, Tomas Finnegan

Pennsylvania

Janos, Joseph John, III
Klasko, Herbert Ronald
Newman, George Henry
Scoratow, Martin Murray

Rhode Island

Rego, Alfred R., Jr.
Saha, Sunil Kumar

Tennessee

Rutledge, Roger Keith

Texas

Amdur, Arthur R.
Chae, Don Baird
Coane, Bruce A.
Foster, Charles Crawford
Lamb, Jonathan Howard
McDonald, Laurier Bernard
Patterson, Donald Ross
Rendon, Josefina Muniz
Williamson, Peter David

Virginia

Armstrong, Henry Jere
Biddle, Eric Harbeson, Jr.
Foster, Judith Christine
Robie, William Randolph

Washington

Gavilanes, Diego P.
King, William Kimble, Jr.

Wisconsin

Katayama, Alyce Coyne

Wyoming

Whynott, Philip Percy

ADDRESS UNPUBLISHED

English, Richard D.
Gonzales, Jeffrey Charles
Greenberg, Susan Ann
Scher, Mark Waclaw
Schwartz, S. Bernard
Shopsin, (Marc) Moshe

INSURANCE. *See also* Personal injury.

UNITED STATES

Alabama

Blan, Ollie Lionel, Jr.
Boardman, Mark Seymour
Brown, Joseph Morris, Jr.
Carter, Gordon Thomas
Crouch, James Michael
Davis, Ronald Lee
Donahue, Timothy Patrick
Ferguson, Harold Laverne, Jr.
Gillis, Lucian, Jr.
Gleissner, John Dewar
Jackson, Micheal Stewart
Kracke, Robert Russell
Merrill, Walter James
Moss, Robert William
Owens, James Bentley, III
Pittman, Craig Sorrell
Porter, James Wallace, II
Porterfield, Jack Berry, Jr.
Putnam, Terry Michael
Richardson, Schuyler Harris, III
Sheehan, Charles Winston, Jr.
Smith, Carol Ann
Somerville, William Glassell, Jr.
Stephens, (Holman) Harold
Sullivan, Carroll Hart
Wilson, Duane Albert
Wright, David Scott

Alaska

Conway, John Martin
Petersen, A. Lee
Tangen, Jon Paul
Thomas, Michael Tracy
Walther, Dale Jay

Arizona

Anderson, Lawrence Ohaco
Bowman, C(harles) Alan
Campbell, Carol Nowell
Crenshaw, Richard N.
Ehinger, James Oakleaf
Frazelle, Michael Jerome
Gaines, Edwin Metcalf, Jr.
Gustafson, David Earl
Hay, John Leonard
Kaminsky, Larry Michael
Kimble, William Earl
King, Jack A.
Lesher, Stephen Harrison
Micheaels, John Allan
Paige, David Alwin
Ricker, William Howard
Sandweg, William Henry, III
Wisniewski, Robert Edward

Arkansas

Hopkins, Randolph Byrd
Mayes, S. Hubert, Jr.
McKenzie, Horace Houston
Zukowski, Mark Daniel

California

Armstrong, Orville A.
Aronson, Craig Douglas
Aycock, Felix Alfred
Bailey, Patrick Joseph
Bakeman, Willard Patrick, III
Balestracci, Paul Noel
Bandy, Jack D.
Barbarowicz, Robert Paul
Barber, Stephan Allen
Bass, Lewis
Belcher, John Arthur
Bennett, Lawrence Arthur
Berger, Harvey Charles
Bex, Richard Elmer
Bingman, Terrence L.
Black, Donald Bruce
Blum, Melanie Rae
Blumberg, John Philip
Bodkin, Henry Grattan, Jr.
Bohlmann, Daniel Robert
Bonesteel, Michael John
Bonham, Terrence James
Buzaid, Laurence Edwin
Byron, Thomas William
Callahan, Gary Brent
Callison, Russell James
Candland, D. Stuart
Carlson, Jeffery John
Coil, Horace Orcutt
Connally, Michael W.
Daar, David
Deane, George Ingram, III
Demos, Jeffrey Charles
Denniston, Thomas Robert
DeVries, Scott Philip
Dodge, Richard Edgar
Dolan, Peter Brown
Dryden, Robert Eugene
Dworkin, Michael Leonard
Einhorn, Lawrence Martin
Faile, Wendell Wayne
Field, Richard Clark
Fink, Robert Stanley
Fischbach, Donald Richard
Fisher, Myron R.
Fitzgerald, Stephen Patrick
Galton, Stephen Harold
Garman, John William
Garrison, Stuart Hugh
Gnesin, Mark Meredith
Graham, Robert Lee
Grier, John Cummings
Guido, Diana Lydia
Haims, Arnold Brody
Hamilton, Phillip Douglas
Harrison, Robert Wayne
Hart, Larry Calvin
Hawkins, Carmen Doloras
Heaton, Roger Laurence
Henderson, Daniel Eli, Jr.
Herlihy, Thomas Mortimer
Herring, Charles David
Heywood, Robert Gilmour
Hodges, Robert W.
Hooser, Eugene Albert
Horton, Luther William
Huebner, Kurt Benoit
Ingram, Jeffrey Charles
Jedeikin, Joseph
Johnson, Robert Howard
Kaiser, Erik Michael
Katz, Jason Lawrence
Kelley, Thomas Joseph
Kind, Kenneth Wayne
King, William J.
Klinger, Marilyn Sydney
Knox, Alan Anthony
Kornblum, Guy Orville
Kravitz, Jeffrey Stephen
Kroger, Catharine Elisabeth
Kuhl, Paul Beach
Kuntz, Charles Powers
Langan, Keith Edward
Lathrop, Mitchell Lee
Lenzi, Albert James, Jr.
Levit, Victor Bert
Levy, David
Levy, Steven R.
LiMandri, Charles Salvatore
Lynch, Robert Thomas
Madory, Richard Eugene
Matthews, Philip Richard
McClintock, Gordon Edwin
McDonough, Patrick Joseph
McGuire, John Francis
Meadows, John Frederick
Melbye, Richard Brenton
Miles, Dori Elizabeth
Miles, Lawrence William, Jr.
Miller, Milton Allen
Miller, Owens O'Keefe
Moore, Douglas Matthew, Jr.
Moore, Raymond Robert
Morrell, Rivers Judson, III
Mosich, Nicholas Joseph
Muhlbach, Robert Arthur
Mullen, Thomas Moore
Murphy, Stephen Michael
Nelson, Paul Douglas
Neumeyer, Richard Albert
Newman, Michael Rodney
Niles, John Gilbert
Nisson, Timothy James
O'Keefe, Patrick Francis
Ornstil, Michael Gary
Otto, James Daniel
Parton, James, III
Pitre, Frank Mario
Pollak, Jeffrey Saul
Poppett, Mark Adams
Poster, Jeffrey Charles
Randall, Mel Scott
Reed, Brian Edward
Reed, Wallace Calvin
Richard, Monte Dwight
Riggs, Charles Earle
Robertson, James Allen
Robinson, Archie Stirling
Robinson, William Adams
Roseman, Charles Sanford
Rozanski, Stanley Howard
Rudolph, George Cooper
Ruma, Ronald Edward
Sceper, Duane Harold
Schack, David Paul
Schroeder, John
Schulner, Lawrence Mayer
Sears, Douglas Alson
Shea, Michael Murt
Simonini, David Michael
Smith, Stanley David
Smitter, Ronald Warren
Sobel, Erwin
Squarcy, Charlotte Van Horne
Staring, Graydon Shaw
Steiner, Philip
Stewart, Helen Margery
Sutherland, Lowell Francis
Thon, William Marvin
Urwin, Gary Lee
Veatch, Wayne Otis, Sr.
Vineyard, C L
Walker, Walter Herbert, III
Walwyn, Stephen John
Wasserman, Michael Eric
Weatherup, Roy Garfield
Weissman, I. Donald
Wesierski, Christopher Paul
Wikle, Kenneth Clinton, Jr.
Wilka, William Charles
Williams, Richard D.
Wood, Weldon Sanford
Woodhead, Frank Womack
Woolls, Paul
Zimmermann, John Frederick
Zuckerman, Alan Randy

Colorado

Aspinwall, David Charles
Brewer, Marion Alyce
Carlson, Robert James
Casebolt, James Stanton
Cooper, Paul Douglas
Donley, Jerry Alan
Downey, Arthur Harold, Jr.
Gulley, Kenneth Galen
Jamison, Jamey William
Laugesen, Richard W.
Law, John Manning
Long, Lawrence Alexander
McCallie, Spencer Wyatt
McConnell, Michael T.
McGee, Robert Leon, Jr.
Miller, David William
O'Donnell, Michael Lawrence
Pack, Stuart Harris
Rector, Leo Daniel
St. Clair, Scott Andrew
Setter, David Mark
Treece, James Lyle
Vanatta, Dean R.
Welch, Carol Mae
Wieman, Terry Lynn

Connecticut

Alesevich, Walter Charles
Blazzard, Norse Novar
Coles, Kevin Andrew
Dyer, Charles Herbert
Gorski, Walter J.
Hasenauer, Judith Anne
Maniatis, Charlynn Carol
Mazadoorian, Harry Nicholas
Middlebrook, Stephen Beach
Mirsky, Ellis Richard
Morris, Jeffrey Lyons
Muhlanger, Gilda Oliver
Orth, Paul William
Rondepierre, Edmond Francois
Slocum, Shaun Michael
Whiston, Richard Michael

Delaware

Curtin, Christopher James
Del Pesco, Susan Marie Carr
Hudson, George Naylor
Kimmel, Morton Richard
Semple, James William

District of Columbia

Abelson, Michael Allen
Becker, Ralph Elihu
Bellamy, Frederick Robert
Bellinger, Edgar Thomson
Boehm, Steven Bruce
Brodsky, Arthur James
Carr, Lawrence Edward, Jr.
Curran, John Peter
Dickinson, Timothy L.
Dolin, Mitchell F.
Faron, Robert Steven
Farrell, George Edwin
Feldman, Michael Harris
Frank, William Harris
Glowinski, Robert William
Goodson, Robert Wade
Hubschman, Henry Allan
Jones, Theodore Lawrence
Kay, Kenneth Robert
Kornblut, Arthur T.
Lynham, John Marmaduke
Medaglia, Mary-Elizabeth
Monaco, Grace Powers
Pruitt, Jana Lee
Raim, David Matthew
Rhodes, Richard Randolph
Sapir, Michael Lynn
Sayler, Robert Nelson
Schweitzer, Sandra Lynn
Shean, Owen Joseph
Skinner, William Polk
Smith, Walter Joseph, Jr.
Stabbe, Mitchell Howard
Thode, Anna Catharine
Weiss, Harlan Lee
Whalen, Thomas J.

Florida

Abbott, Charles Warren
Anthony, Andrew John
Atkinson, John Bond
Barr, Harry E.
Bates, Richard Warden
Berger, Steven R.
Berman, Richard Bruce
Bernstein, Howard Mark
Bopp, Thomas Roe
Burnette, Guy Ellington, Jr.
Butler, Paul B.
Catlin, Harold Harvey
Chidnese, Patrick N.
Cooney, David Francis
Cordell, Martin Lewis
Corlett, Edward Stanley, III
Crabtree, Robert Crosby
David, Ronald Albert
Davis, Barry Lee
Durie, Jack Frederick, Jr.
Echsner, Stephen Herre
Eckhart, James Milton
Edelstein, Steven A(llen)
Emerton, Robert Walter, III
Falk, Glenn Phillip
Farrell, Patrick Joseph, Jr.
Fishman, Lewis Warren
Freeman, Stephan John
Geiger, William Harold
Georges, Richard Martin
Gillen, William Albert
Glick, Brian Jay
Graham, Andrew Alan
Greenleaf, Walter Franklin
Greenwald, Steven Jeffrey
Gross, Terence Alan
Hayes, Neil John
Hickey, John Heyward
Hoey, William Edward
Hood, Charles David, Jr.
Katz, Allan Jack
Kelly, John Patrick
Kray, Fred Martin
Kreutzer, Franklin David
Lax, Michael H.
Liles, Rutledge Richardson
Mang, Douglas A.
Mansbach, Robert Earl, Jr.
Marshall, Valerie Ann
McKenzie, James Franklin
McNally, James Joseph
Merlin, William Firman, Jr.
Moseley, James Francis
O'Neal, Leslie King
Ordonez, Luis Enrique
Parker, Julius Frederick, Jr.
Pierce, Francis Edmund, III
Podrecca, Adolfo Augusto
Pomeroy, Gregg Joseph
Ramsey, Bruce Mitchell
Rivera, Luis Ernesto
Rogel, Todd Stephen
Rose, Norman
Sadowski, William Edward
Siplin, Gary Anthony
Skolnick, S. Harold
Slaydon, Roger James
Smith, James Hibbert
Somers, Clifford Louis
Spellacy, John Frederick
Spencer, W(alter) Thomas
Sperry, Martin J.
Stern, Duke Nordlinger
Stevens, Harold Sanford
Stinson, Steven Arthur
Sutcliffe, Roland Alton, Jr.
Sutton, Michael Ferris
Symons, Robin Suzanne Taylor
Traitz, James Joseph, Jr.
Tygart, S. Thompson, Jr.
Urban, Edmund Theodore
Vernis, Frank Carl, Jr.
Welbaum, R. Earl
West, Harold
Whigham, Thomas Edmondson
Wirtz, Gregg Lee
Wood, Julian Emory
Zook, David Lloyd

Georgia

Allen, Hunter Smith, Jr.
Bassler, Harry Warren
Claxton, Edward Burton, III
Davis, George Thomas
Davison, John Arthur
Eckl, William Wray
Forbes, Morton Gerald
Gadrix, Edward Wallace, Jr.
Garcia, Luis Cesareo
Griffeth, Ronald Clyde
Gunn, Robert Russell
Hayes, Dewey Norman
Henson, Howard Kirk
Hinchey, John William
Hines, John Pridgen
Johnson, Daniel Patrick
Killorin, Edward Wylly
McCracken, Eugene Luke
Mirandola, Loretta Jean
Nash, Thomas Acton, Jr.
Oliver, Bonnie Chessher
Patton, Matthew H.
Reemsnyder, Ronald David
Reinhardt, Daniel Sargent
Roberson, Lynn Marie
Seacrest, Gary Lee
Smith, Malcolm Percy
Stell, John Elwin, Jr.
Wood, L. Lin, Jr.
Zito, Jeffrey Raymond

Hawaii

Krueger, James
Louie, David Mark
Portnoy, Jeffrey Steven
Turk, David L.
Williams, Allen Kenneth
Wilson, Virgil James, III
Wong, Wayson Wai Sun

Idaho

Banducci, Thomas Anthony
Dale, Candy Wagahoff
Davis, James Julian
Dryden, William George
Gasser, Emmett Clark
Helvie, Kirk Randall
Kerrick, David Ellsworth
Miller, Patrick Eugene
Nye, W. Marcus W.
Penland, Paul Stephan
Stoker, Robin Jeffrey
Thomas, Eugene C.
Vaughn, David Brent

Illinois

Beatty, William Glenn
Bellah, Kenneth David
Bernstein, John Thomas
Blume, Paul Chiappe
Bollinger, Barry Gilbert
Bose, Thomas Lewnau
Bragg, Michael Ellis
Brennan, Danolda Jean
Bresnahan, Arthur Stephen
Cass, Robert Michael
Chemers, Robert Marc
Churchill, Allen Delos
Coghill, William Thomas, Jr.
Cohen, Edward A.
Cosgrave, Carmel M.
Cunningham, William Francis
Danekas, Steven Ernest
Davis, Dean Martin
Devience, Alex, Jr.
Duncan, Edward Rogers, Jr.
Eckols, Thomas Aud
Eisenberg, Stephen Paul
Engling, Robert John
Essig, William John
Fortier, Robert Frederic
Fowler, Don Wall
Garley, Barry Ernest
Garofalo, John Richard
Gavin, John Neal
Gilford, Steven Ross
Goldstein, Candice
Gorman, James Edward

Gramlich, Charles J.
Griffith, D. Kendall
Hammesfahr, Robert Winter
Hayes, Richard Johnson
Heaton, Joseph Edward, Jr.
Hook, George Clive, II
Hoyne, Scott William
Jesser, Steven H.
Johnson, Richard Fred
Jones, Dwain Leon
Jordan, Horace William
Kearns, James Cannon
Kelty, Thomas Walsh
Kimball, Spencer Levan
Kralovec, Charles Vopicka
Liebling, Norman Robert
Linder, Rex Kenneth
Lockwood, Gary Lee
Lorenz, Hugo Albert
Malloy, Kathleen Sharon
Mancini, Lorenzo Anthony
Marick, Michael Miron
Marquard, Henry Francis
Martan, Joseph Rudolf
Matushek, Edward J., III
Mazewski, Aloysius Alex
McCabe, Charles Kevin
McCarthy, Kitty Monaghan
McConnell, James Guy
McDonald, Thomas Alexander
McVisk, William Kilburn
Miller, Kenneth Charles
Mintel, Judith King
Mittelman, Robert Hirsch
Modlin, Lowell Ronald
Mueller, Richard Edward
Mulcahy, Daniel Joseph, Jr.
Murphy, Matthew M.
Nebel, Mary Beth
Norek, Frances Therese
Nutter, Franklin Winston
Nyeste, James Thomas
O'Conor, Andrew Joseph, IV
Palmer, Robert Towne
Peterson, Donald George
Pope, Michael Arthur
Prochnow, Douglas Lee
Richard, Douglas Wayne
Richardson, William F.
Robison, Charles Bennett
Rochelle, Victor Cleanthus
Rohrman, Douglass Frederick
Rose, Dennis Edward
Roth, Ronald Anthony
Russell, Tomas Morgan
Sanchez, Manuel
Scantlebury, Hilary Thomas
Schiff, Matthew Bart
Schuckit, Robert Jay
Seith, Alex Robert
Sido, Kevin Richard
Sims, Murray William, Jr.
Smith, John Gelston
Swanson, Lenard Charles
Torshen, Jerome Harold
Vincent, Adrian Roger
Walsh, Christopher G., Jr.
Wanca, Brian John
Weinstein, David L.
Weir, William H.
Welbel, Michael Gary
Wilcox, Mark Dean
Wilson, Roger Goodwin
Wolfman, Paul Irwin
Wulfers, John Manning

Indiana

Bever, Robert Lynn
Borns, Clarence
Buehler, James Carroll
Dieterly, Douglas Kevin
Eckert, Stephen Paul
Emerson, Andrew Craig
Gleason, Charles Sappington
Hammel, John Wingate
Haynie, Gilmore Smith, Jr.
Hays, Thomas Clyde
Jennings, Charles Thomas
Jones, David L.
Kingdon, Victor Scott
Koch, Edna Mae
Linnemeier, Philip
Lisher, John Leonard
McKeon, Thomas Joseph
McNeely, J. Lee
Morgan, Darwin Edward
Murphy, Lester F(uller)
Palmer, Robert Joseph
Roberts, Patricia Susan
Schreckengast, William O.
Springer, Steve Edward
Wood, William Jerome
Yoder, Thomas Woodrow

Iowa

Blackburn, Milford Gene
Brown, Paul Edmondson
Capps, George Hall
Cutler, Charles Edward
Dahl, Harry Waldemar
Duckworth, Marvin E.
Dull, Wilbur Robbins
Graziano, Craig Frank
Hamilton, James R.
Hammer, David Lindley
Henderson, Thomas
Hoffmann, Michael Richard
Kelley, Bruce Gunn
Lambert, George Robert
Langdon, Herschel Garrett
Leitner, David Larry
McCoy, John Thomas
McKay, Timothy John
Narber, Gregg Ross
Peddicord, Roland Dale
Rinden, Gerry Mundt
Seitzinger, Edward Francis
Stefani, Randall H.
Thelen, John Frederick
Wharton, John Michael
Widiss, Alan I.

Kansas

Adrian, Robert Mac
Bideau, Edwin Hale, III
Carroll, Timothy Wayne
Cornish, Lebbeus M.
Grace, Brian Guiles
King, Clarence LeRoy, Jr.
Marshall, Herbert A.
Metzger, Alan Glen
Parker, William Lawrence, Jr.
Patterson, Donald
Peters, Geoffrey Wright
Ruse, Steven Douglas
Solon, James Davis
Stavely, Richard William
Turner, H. Lee
Williams, Ronald Paul

Kentucky

Adams, Wesley Price, Jr.
Barrickman, Uhel Overton
Brandon, Douglas Colliver
Coombs, Ronald Lee
Hanbury, John Iruine
Kerrick, Thomas Neal
Massengale, Roger Lee
Penick, Michael Preston
Philipps, Kurt A.
Reinhardt, Roxane Tomasi
Ridings, Marcia Milby
Roark, Jimmy Lee
Rudloff, William J.
Simpson, Ronald Vincent
Sitlinger, Leroy Edward, Jr.
Stopher, Robert Estes
Wilson, George Simpson, III
Winslow, Donald Arthur
Wolnitzek, Stephen Dale

Louisiana

Andersson, W. Paul
Angelle, Robert
Aucoin, Barney R.
Boyd, Joseph Robert
Brian, A(lexis) Morgan, Jr.
Cook, David Sherman
Denhollem, James Scott
Dugas, David Roy
Fadaol, Robert Frederick
Furman, Michael Joseph
Gallagher, John M., Jr.
Griffith, Steven Franklin, Sr.
Holmes, James Richard
Hurley, Grady Schell
Johnson, Ronald Adams
Jones, Keith Dunn
Kleinpeter, Robert Loren
Lenz, Laurence Henry, Sr.
Lombard, Michael Albert
Metrailer, Ann Marie
Moliere, Donna Renee
Olinde, John Francis
Payne, Roy Steven
Perlman, Jerald Lee
Roddy, Virginia Niehaus
St. Pe, Philippi Pierre
Salas, Camilo Kossy, III
Sanders, Mike Charles
Schoemann, Rudolph Robert
Siegel, Robert Irwin
Sklamba, Stephen Gerard
Smith, Brian David
Smith, Charles Sterling
Stiel, David Harold, III
Story, Clement, III
Swift, John Goulding
Treadaway, Randell Edward
Tschirn, Darryl Jude
Vickery, Eugene Benton, Jr.
Volk, Jerome Milton, Jr.
Wooderson, James Michael

Maine

Brett, Tybe Ann
Douglas, Wayne Rodger
Hughes, David Emery
Kirchner, Theodore Harry
Lanham, Samuel Wilbur, Jr.
Willard, William Wells
Willihnganz, Paul W.

Maryland

Bartlett, James Wilson, III
Bonner, Leonard John
Clancy, Joseph Patrick
Crocker, Michael Pue
DeVries, Donald Lawson, Jr.
Dodson, Wilmer Byrd
Elliott, J. Victor
Furrer, David Eugene
Godey, Laurence Ringgold
Goss, Thomas Marks
Gray, Oscar Shalom
Haldeman, George Paul
Hansen, Christopher Agnew
Hill, Milton King, Jr.
Mann, Michael Bond
McComas, Albert Laun
Miles, Gerard Frances
Nagle, John Joseph, III
Nolan, Paul William
O'Brien, Dennis Francis
Vanderlinde, Susan Kay
Ward, John Thomas

Massachusetts

Adler, Sidney W.
Baker, Horace Ross, Jr.
Buczkowski, David John
Burgoyne, John Albert
Burns, Thomas David
Devlin, Paul Anthony
Fecteau, Francis Roger
Finn, John Joseph
Fluker, Brenda Ann
Gibbs, Richard Frederic
Grahame, Orville Francis Booth
Griffin, J. Kenneth
Gross, Susan Larky
Gulko, Paul Michael
Haas, William Lambert
Halstrom, Frederic Norman
Hartigan, Michael David
Hoefling, Virginia Ann
Horn, Everett Byron, Jr.
Hunt, William John
Keeton, Robert Ernest
King, Kernan Francis
Korb, Kenneth A.
Lepore, Ralph Thomas, III
Licata, Arthur Frank
Madan, Anil
Meehan, James Francis
Milan, Edwin Ramon
Murphy, Philip Dever
O'Connell, Joseph Francis, III
Olshan, Joseph Raymond
Towner, Frank Schwable, Jr.
Urquhart, Stephen E.
Wolfe, Robert Shenker

Michigan

Baker, Frederick Milton, Jr.
Bell, John Wright
Brander, Reynolds A., Jr.
Brennan, Joseph Vincent
Brenton, Michael Scott
Buchanan, William D.
Byrne, Joseph Ahern, Jr.
Campos, David Nelson
Caretti, Richard Louis
Cooper, David John
Cotter, Dennis Blair
Drutchas, Gregory G.
Farrell, John Brendan
Fisher, Edward Walter
Gilbert, Ronald Rhea
Goethel, Stephen B.
Gofrank, Catherine Ann
Gunderson, Michael Arthur
Hart, Clifford Harvey
Hayes, Kenneth Thomas
Hitchcock, Stephen Jay
Kerwin, J(ames) Eugene
Knecht, Timothy Harry
Kritselis, William Nicholas
Kruse, John Alphonse
Lucow, Milton
Marin, Paul Martin
Marotta, Robert
Marshall, J. Stephen
McGraw, Patrick John
Mundell, John Andrew, Jr.
Padilla, Gerald Vincent
Payton, Donald Lee
Pierson, William George
Potter, George Ernest
Purcell, Paul M.
Rinkel, Michael Joseph
Schloss, Lawrence James
Shoop, Deborah
Shulaw, Richard Allen
Sinas, George Thomas
Souter, Don Vern
Storey, Scott Alfred
Sullivan, Timothy Joseph
Teicher, Mark L.
Vander Ark, Steven John
Zanot, Craig Allen

Minnesota

Balmer, James W.
Bassford, Charles Addison
Bulinski, Gregory Paul
Cattanach, Robert Edward, Jr.
Degnan, John Michael
Fitch, Raymond William
Geck, Donna Dunkelberger
Guthmann, John Howard
Hektner, Candice Elaine
Hoke, George Peabody
Hottinger, John Creighton
Hull, Daniel Louis
Hunter, Donald Forrest
Johnson, Dennis Robert
Jones, Bradley Mitchell
Keenan, Kevin Patrick
Kirsch, Steven Jay
Kress, Marjorie Mae
Lapham, Mark William
Lichtor, David T.
Lillehaug, David Lee
Lindberg, Michael Charles
Luis, Juanita Bolland
Maclin, Alan Hall
Marquart, Steven Leonard
Miranda, Thom Bernard
Pagliaccetti, Gary John
Pederson, Steven Marc
Remele, Lewis Albert, Jr.
Rowlette, Roger Lee
Sanner, Royce Norman
Scherer, Richard Sigmund
Willemssen, Mac Ronald

Mississippi

Bullock, Jim
Bush, Fred Marshall, Jr.
Cavanaugh, Michael Flynn
Chaffin, William Michael
Clayton, Hugh Newton
Currie, Edward Jones, Jr.
Dent, George E.
Dornan, Donald C., Jr.
Dukes, James Otis
Hannan, Edwin York
Harlow, Eugene Marchant
Harral, John Menteith
Kirkland, Thomas Lee, Jr.
Morrison, Harvey Lee, Jr.
Peresich, Stephen G.
Rood, Ralph Edward
Shepard, Robert Payne
Welch, Walter Scott, III
Whitfield, William Ernest

Missouri

Arneson, James H.
Bevan, Kent Morgan
Brown, Paul Sherman
Burns, Mark Gardner
Deacy, Thomas Edward, Jr.
Ewing, Lynn Moore, Jr.
Gulley, William Louis
Horgan, John Joseph
King, William Robert, II
Lerner, Lawrence
Levings, Theresa Lawrence
Lowes, Albert Charles
Malacarne, C. John
McManaman, Kenneth Charles
Michener, John Athol
Monaco, Nicholas M.
Mueller, Joseph Henry
Myers, Ronald Lynn
Noonan, Thomas Joseph
Passanante, Paul Jasper
Popham, Arthur Cobb, Jr.
Riner, James William
Roberts, Patrick Kent
Schumaier, Steven George
Scott, Stephen Charles
Shank, Suzanne
Stockman, Harry Michael
Weedman, Charles Edward, Jr.
Willenbrock, Ronald Christopher
Willman, Philip Louis

Montana

Clarke, Dennis Person
Dalthorp, George Carrol
Jones, James Leonard
Murphy, Gregory G.
Sommerfeld, Donald Drovdal
Thompson, Theodore Kvale

Nebraska

Anderson, Robert Louis
Atwood, Raymond Percival, Jr.
Bloomingdale, Arthur Lee, Jr.
Busick, Denzel Rex
Davlin, Michael Charles
Frazier, Lawrence Alan
Fuller, Diana Clare
Gleason, James Mullaney
Kay, Stephen William
Krutter, Forrest Nathan
Lyons, William Drewry
O'Connor, James Edward
Walsh, Thomas John

Nevada

Badger, Raymond Louis, Jr.
Barkley, Thierry Vincent
Harding, Samuel Arlon
Hibbs, Loyal Robert
Hoppe, Craig Allen
Leverty, Vernon Eugene
Murphy, Patrick James
Pagni, Albert Frank
Pearson, Niels L.
Perry, Robert Harry
Perry, Victor Alan
Shaffer, Wayne Alan
Springmeyer, Don

New Hampshire

Gagliuso, Richard Caron
Lagos, George Peter
Peltonen, John Ernest
Potter, Fred Leon

New Jersey

Bello-Monaco, Deborah Ann
Biaett, Doddridge Hewitt, III
Carr, Hubert Franklin
Cernigliaro, Michael J.
Cerny, Edward Charles, III
Chappell, Thomas Tye
Cohen, Barry David
Connell, William Terrence
D'Amico, John, Jr.
Eittreim, Richard MacNutt
Facher, Irwin Lee
Flinn, Thomas D.
Garrigle, William Aloysius
Gernert, Richard Charles
Gilbreth, Peter Nelson
Goldberger, Alan Steven
Harbeson, Robert G.
Hoens, Charles Henry, Jr.
Hopkins, Charles Peter, II
Jordan, Richard Allen
Kallmann, Stanley Walter
Kiel, Paul Edward
Kott, David Russell
Kruttschnitt, Herbert, III
Manzo, Peter Thomas
McGuire, William B(enedict)
Monti, Renard George
Moore, Janet Patricia
Moorman, Elliott Duane
Morris, Larry Dean
Murray, William James
Needell, Russell Lawrence
O'Brien, John Graham
Ornitz, Richard Martin
Polansky, Steven Jay
Pollinger, William Joshua
Poyourow, Robert Lee
Reid, Charles Adams, III
Rizzo, Paul Robert
Schwartz, Edward Richard
Stalker, Timothy Wayne
Steedle, Roger Craig
Sullivan, Robert Joseph
Twaddell, Miles Edmiston
Weinstein, Stephen Saul
White, John Lindsey
Widman, Douglas Jack
Wszolek, Dennis Francis
Zarnowski, James David

New Mexico

Dutton, Dominic Edward
Hone, Jay R.
Mckim, Lowell E.
Pelton, Gregory Vern
Roehl, Jerrald J(oseph)
Stoker, Arlon L., Jr.
Stuckey, Charles Edward
Templeman, James Edwin

New York

Alcorn, Wendell Bertram, Jr.
Ausubel, Marvin Victor
Barber, Janice Ann
Barrett, James P.
Barry, Desmond Thomas, Jr.
Bennett, James Martin
Bizzell, Kinchen Carey
Bonacci, Edward Howard, Jr.
Brand, Ray Manning
Brock, David George
Brody, Neil
Burke, Thomas Edmund
Byrne, Margaret Mary
Calhoun, Monica Dodd
Calkins, Steven Potter
Cayea, Donald Joseph
Chizmadia, Stephen Mark
Coakley, Charles
Coen, Seth Ezra
Cole, Richard Charles
Colmant, Andrew Robert
Connors, James Patrick
Cooney, Michael Francis
Dalton, Kenneth M.
De Marie, Anthony Joseph
DeMarie, Joseph
Devers, Peter Dix
Di Joseph, Steven
Donat, Walter Kennedy
Dugan, Sean Francis Xavier
Dunham, Wolcott Balestier, Jr.
Ehrlich, Jerrold Ivan
Eisenberg, Bertram William
Ellenberg, Michael Aron
Endieveri, Anthony Frank
Fenn, George Karl, Jr.
Fine, A(rthur) Kenneth
Firth, Peter Alan
Fix, Meyer
Fogelman, Martin
Foley, Patrick Joseph
Fontana, Vincent Robert
Freedman, Warren
Gabay, Donald David
Gaines, Weaver Henderson, Jr.
Garbarini, Chas. J.
Gebo, Stephen Wallace
Geitz, Michael M(eyer)
Geller, Diane Joyce
Gerhart, Eugene Clifton
Glass, Joel
Goldberg, Neil A.
Gordon, Burton
Gotimer, Harry Albert
Greenhill, Ira Judd
Groman, Tod Philip
Gurfein, Richard Alan
Hagelin, Michael Thomas
Hamm, David Bernard
Hausen, Stanley Sherman
Hayes, Gerald Joseph
Hayes, Michael Augustine, Jr.
Hellerstein, Alvin Kenneth
Henderson, Donald Bernard, Jr.
Hersh, Robert Michael
Hershman, Mendes
Hirsch, Daniel
Hite, Hollis Marie
Huber, Melvyn Jay
Immerman, Paul Alan
Iovenko, Michael
Jacobowitz, Harold Saul
Jagow, Charles Herman
Joye, E. Michael
Kastellec, Philip Richard
Kempler, Cecelia
Killarney, John Paul
Kroll, Sol
Kushel, Glenn Elliot
Lee, Brian Edward
Lee, Henry
Lesser, William Melville
Luchsinger, John Francis, Jr.
Lyddane, John Lawrence Ashton
Lynch, Margaret Comard
Maher, Daniel Francis, Jr.
Mandel, Richard Gordon
Marcellino, Stephen Michael
Martin, Alan Jay
Martowski, David William
McCabe, Stephen M.
McCormick, Hugh Thomas
McShane, Bruce Winthrop
Milligram, Steven Irwin
Molod, Frederick M.
Morelli, Ronald Joseph
Morris, John E.
Mulvehill, John Henry
Murphy, Daniel Hayes, II
Newman, Howard Julian
Nicholas, Christopher Paul
O'Flinn, Peter Russell
O'Gara, James Vincent
Oliveri, Paul Francis
Page, Alfred Emil, Jr.
Petrone, Louis S.
Pfeffer, Milton B.
Pisani, Michael Joseph
Platto, Charles
Pottle, Willard Marsh, Jr.
Reed, James Alexander, Jr.
Rogers, Sharyn Gail
Rosow, Malcolm Bertram
Rovins, Jeffrey Seth
Sager, Jonathan Ward
Samel, Jeffrey
Scher, Stanley Jules
Schiavetti, Anthony Louis
Schlau, Philip
Schmidt, Charles Edward
Schnurman, Alan Joseph
Seitelman, Mark Elias
Sequeira, Manuel Alexandre, Jr.
Shaddock, Robert Montgomery
Shalhoub, Michael David
Shanman, James Alan
Shapiro, Daniel Murry
Sheehan, Kenneth Edward
Short, Skip
Smyk, Stephen Douglass
Sola, Anthony Marce
Stanisci, Thomas William
Stine, John
Sullivan, Mortimer Allen, Jr.
Tanenbaum, Ted Jay
Tarangelo, Richard Michael
Tract, Harold M.
Trevett, Thomas Neil
Tucker, Stephen
Vitkowsky, Vincent Joseph
Warshauer, Irene Conrad
Whalen, Daniel Aloysius, III
Whiteman, Robert Gordon
Will, Alfred Joseph
Williamson, Walter
Wilson, Thomas William
Wolf, Lewis Isidore
Wolgel, Harold Horace
Wollan, Eugene
Yeager, Dennis Randall

North Carolina

Bambury, Joseph Anthony, Jr.

Comerford, Walter Thompson, Jr.
Dahl, Tyrus Vance, Jr.
Davis, Roy Walton, Jr.
Diosegy, Arlene Jayne
Garlitz, Thomas Drake
Gitter, Allan Reinhold
Hoof, James Bruce
Langson, Seth Harris
Morris, Thomas Hansley
Osborn, Malcolm Everett
Perschetz, Arthur Driban
Starnes, Oscar Edwin, Jr.

North Dakota

Gilbertson, Joel Warren
Hermes, Pamela Jane
Yuill, William Duane

Ohio

Allen, Richard Lee, Jr.
Benedict, Ronald Louis
Bennett, Marshall Alton Jr.
Blackburn, Thomas Irven
Bradigan, Brian Jay
Brant, Charles Ensign
Briggs, Marjorie Crowder
Buckley, Daniel Jerome
Buckley, Frederick Jean
Bunda, Robert Alan
Carpenter, James Craig
Carpenter, James Willard
Comstock, David Cooper
Cruikshank, David Earl
Dublikar, Ralph F(rank)
Duff, Gerald Patrick
Fisher, John Edwin
Garfunkel, Steven Brooks
Greene, Gordon Christopher
Gurley, Michael Edward
Haddox, Jerome B.
Hawley, William Lee
Herbert, David Lee
Hermann, Philip J.
Hiller, Robert Stanford
Hogan, Robert B.
Jenks, Thomas Edward
Jones, Edgar Wagstaff
Katz, Susan Stanton
Knepper, William Edward
Lancione, Robert Michael
Lane, James Edward
Lee, Ronald Bruce
Lewis, James William
Maher, Edward Joseph
Marx, Dianne Frances
Meyer, Douglas Oliver
Meyers, Karen Diane
Montgomery, Thomas Charles
Morris, Earl Franklin
Nelson, Roger Milton
Perin, Charles Henry, Jr.
Reidenbach, William John
Russo, Nancy Margaret
Schoeni, Kenneth Roger
Seeley, Glenn J.
Serraino, Stephen R.
Shepard, Darrell Royce
Sweebe, Richard Dale
Switzer, Donald Hugh
Theis, Donald Eugene
Utz, Edward Joseph
Vance, Victoria Lynne
Vorys, Arthur Isaiah
Weller, Charles David
Whitney, Richard B.
Williamson, Gregory Lopez
Wolfe, John Leslie

Oklahoma

Bergner, William Joseph
Corley, E. Terrill
Dawson, Jack Sterling
Green, Gerald Patrick
Gurich, Noma Diane
Haskins, Walter Dewey
Heggy, Rodney Joe
Kaufman, James Mark
Lieber, John Howard
Morris, Greg Arthur
Stuart, John Bruce
Taylor, Michael Conrad
Walker, Ronald Lynn
Whitten, Reggie Neil

Oregon

Bailey, Ronald E.
Beckman, Douglas Gary
Bowerman, Donald Bradley
Brenneman, Delbert Jay
Brown, Anna Jaeger
Brown, Lisa Claire
Buehler, John Wilson
Burnham, Carl von Hoffmann, Jr.
Cooney, Thomas Emmett
Cummins, Elliott Bird
Day, Frank E.
Deatherage, William Vernon
Engel, Edward Ignatius
Hodges, Charles Edward, Jr.
Kitchel, Jan Kelly
Kurtz, Louis Laird
Lowry, Robert Dudley
Mannix, Kevin Leese
Markowitz, David Benjamin
Martin, William Charles
McMenamin, Robert William
Miller, David Kenneth
Morrison, David Patrick
Robertson, Joseph David
Spier, Richard Gary
Spooner, Ralph Charles

Pennsylvania

Baker, Frank Adams, III
Bala, Gary Ganesh
Belden, H. Reginald
Benson, Stuart Wells, III
Best, Franklin L., Jr.
Black, Frederick Evan
Booz, Nina Robin
Bosick, Joseph John, Jr.
Brenner, Thomas Edward
Bressman, Marc Ira
Bricklin, Louis E.
Brown, Lawrence Raymond, Jr.
Browne, Michael L.
Corse, Chester Clinton, Jr.
Cramp, John Franklin
Davis, Donald Marc
Devlin, John Gerard
DeWald, John Edward
DiPiero, Andrew Edward, Jr.
Donahue, John M(ichael)
Duke, Charles Jeffrey
Feinour, John Stephen
Feldmann, Louis George
Gale, Randall Glenn
Garcia, Rudolph
Geiger, William David
Gilhooly, Edward Foster
Ginsburg, Bruce Martin
Hafer, Joseph Page
Herman, Charles Jacob
Heslop, John William, Jr.
Jellinek, Miles Andrew
Kapetan, Alex Nick
Kennedy, James Edward
King, Donita McRae
Klazmer, Gary Michael
Klimon, Ellen Louise
Kolansky, Jeffrey Mark
Ledwith, John Francis
Lowery, William Herbert
Ludwig, Charles Fine
Maio, Carl Anthony
Mattern, Patricia Ann
McCabe, James J.
McCloskey, Stephen Paul
Milbourne, Walter Robertson
Mojock, David Theodore
Musto, Joseph J.
Nauman, Spencer Gilbert, Jr.
Ober, Russell John, Jr.
Pfaff, Robert James
Pleet, Jesse Lawn
Pollins, John William, III
Radcliffe, William M., III
Reed, Lowell Andrew, Jr.
Restivo, James John, Jr.
Robb, John Anthony, Jr.
Rosenblum, Glenn Fredrick
Scheffler, Stuart Jay
Segal, Frederick Leslie
Shay, Michael Patrick
Sherry, John Sebastian
Simpson, Robert Edward, Jr.
Skeel, Peter Brooks
Stahl, Stanley Paul
Stewart, Allen Warren
Wagner, Thomas Joseph
Wolke, Milton Spencer, Jr.
Zearfoss, Herbert Keyser
Zeehandelaar, David Nico

Rhode Island

Goodwin, Hyman S.

South Carolina

Baggett, Stephen Dallas
Bailey, Nancy Hawkins
Boyd, Stanley Jeffrey, Jr.
Chapman, Charles Alan
Cooke, Morris Dawes, Jr.
Gibson, Carroll Allen, Jr.
Henry, Angela Louise
Jedziniak, Lee Peter
Jones, Hartwell Kelley, Jr.
Jones, Marvin Coleman
Lynch, John Timothy
Oswald, Billy Robertson
Painter, Samuel Franklin
Reeves, Phillip Earl
Rodgers, Paul Baxter, III
Smith, Barney Oveyette, Jr.
Wall, Susan Taylor
White, Daniel Bowman
Wittenberg, Philip

South Dakota

Gerdes, David Alan
Pieplow, Michael Flinn
Thompson, Charles Murray

Tennessee

Baker, Josiah Carr Eggleston
Buchignani, Leo Joseph
Campbell, Paul, III
Cooper, Gary Allan
Ehmling, Miles Allen
Fleissner, Phillip Anton
Freeman, James Atticus, III
Gerrish, Jeffrey C.
James, Erich William
Kirby, James Lynn
Kirkpatrick, Scott Lucillious
Lay, Patti Jane
Leitner, Gregory Marc
Marcus, Harry Richard
McIntosh, James Arthur
McLaren, Michael Glenn
McWhirter, J(ames) Cecil
Midgett, James Clayton, Jr.
Montgomery, Joseph Tucker
Schlechty, John L.
Shelton, David Cochran
Taylor, Jerry Francis
Thomason, John Joseph
Williams, Thomas Ashurst
Wilson, Fred Palmer
Young, Jason Ober, Jr.

Texas

Adams, Kent Morrison
Akers, Brock Cordt
Altman, William Kean
Baker, Scott Russell
Barnett, George David
Bashline, James Duane
Bingham, Loyd Edward, Jr.
Boyland, Herbert Layton
Brock, Roy C.
Brown, James Earle
Brown, Robert Charles
Browning, John Raum
Cambrice, Robert Louis
Cantilo, Patrick Herrera
Carnahan, Robert Narvell
Coleman, Bryan Douglas
Connally, Tom
Darnell, James Oral
Davis, Clarice M.
Dimitry, Theodore George
Eckhardt, William Rudolf, III
Evans, George Frederick, Jr.
Fanning, Barry Hedges
Ferguson, Charles Alan
Flanary, Donald Herbert, Jr.
Geiger, Richard Stuart
Greer, Raymond White
Hankins, Mitchell Dale
Hart, John Clifton
Henry, Peter York
Hughes, Karen Gray
Hunsucker, Philip Carl
Jennings, Susan Jane
Jordan, Bruce
Kacal, George Jerome, Jr.
Kent, Don Wayne
King, Daniel Dwade
King, Ira Thomas
Kirkman, William Louis
Krebs, Arno W., Jr.
Masters, Claude Bivin
McColloch, Murray Michael
McCormick, J(oseph) Burke
McHugh, Margaret Colleen
McQuarrie, Claude Monroe, III
Merz, Daniel Lee
Mills, William Michael
Nelson, Jack Odell, Jr.
Newsom, Jan Lynn Reimann
Owen, Frank, III
Payne, James Parker
Plunkett, Allen Lewin
Pollan, Thomas Miller
Powers, William Leonard
Prince, Wayman Lee
Raschke, Fred David
Riddles, Amis Joe
Ridgeway, Henry Dorman
Roan, Forrest Calvin, Jr.
Roark, John Olen
Roberts, Ted Blake
Rothermel, John Fisher, III
Shannon, Joe, Jr.
Smith, George Duffield, Jr.
Stewart, Joseph Ward
Thompson, Jay Alan
Toth, Robert Stephen
Trimble, Dale Lee
Warrick, Richard Lloyd

Utah

Hansen, Royal Ivory
Purser, Donald Joseph
Slaughter, David Wayne

Vermont

Faignant, John Paul
Guild, Alden
Kiel, Edward Rowland
Rachlin, Robert David

Virginia

Alexander, Bevin Ray, Jr.
Allen, Wilbur Coleman
Anderson, John Frederick
Baird, Thomas Bryan, Jr.
Beck, Joseph James
Blank, Irving Michael
Bozarth, Robert Stephen
Burgess, Jack Thompson
Burnette, Ralph Edwin, Jr.
Campbell, George Wendal, Jr.
Davis, Richard Waters
Evans, Susan Ann
Farnham, James Edward
Flannagan, Francis Wills
Hamilton, Jeffrey Scott
Hancock, William Glenn
Jenkins, Douglas Tucker
Macrae, Howard Taft, Jr.
McElroy, Howard Chowning
McGavin, John David
Norris, John Stevens, Jr.
Purcell, William Riker
Schwartz, Steven Gary
Shevlin, Brian Charles
Slenker, Norman Frederick
Somerville, Frank Walker
Tegenkamp, Gary Elton
Woodrum, Milton Lanier

Washington

Adams, Lori Nelson
Baker, James Edyrn
Blom, Daniel Charles
Bor, Daniel
Campbell, Fremont Lee
Cushing, James Robert
Davis, James Edward
Dawson, Robert Kevin
Dohn, George Thomas
Foreman, Dale Melvin
Harris, Thomas V.
Hindman, Dennis Michael
Houger, L(eroy) William
Kaiser, Bruce Allen
Keating, Robert Clark
Lang, Pamela Ann
Loftus, Thomas Daniel
Mathieu, Richard Louis
McCoy, Brian Lloyd
McDermott, Richard Francis, Jr.
McMahon, Michael Joseph
Meyers, Bruce France
Mines, Michael
Moses, Gene Ronald
Nichols, Howard Melvin
Peery, Charles Eugene
Pence, Christopher Cyrus
Reed, Glenn Edward
Ricketts, Michael Edward
Sargeant, Robert Walton
Stritmatter, Paul Lester
Swanson, Arthur Dean
Tasker, Michael Kenneth
Thurston, Hal
Tuffley, Francis Douglas
Waitt, Robert Kenneth
Woolston, V.L.
Ziontz, Martin Lowell

West Virginia

Bell, Charles D.
Bell, Harry Fullerton, Jr.
Hayhurst, Richard Allen
Hurt, Charles E.
Jackson-Gillison, Helen Lucille
MacCallum, James Judson
Miller, Jack Lee
Richmond, William Frederick, Jr.
Silver, Gray, III
Watson, William E.
Weaver, William Carroll
Williams, Jacques Ralph André

Wisconsin

Berres, Terrence Robert
Berry, Roberta Marie
Bruce, Peter Wayne
Curry, George Steven
Domnitz, Merrick Robert
Eckert, Michael Louis
Ehrke, William Warren
Evans, William James
Grzeca, Michael (Gerard)
Haarmann, Bruce Donald
Hans, Peter E.
Higgins, John Patrick
Kammer, Robert Arthur, Jr.
Kircher, John Joseph
Krueger, John William
Penegor, Robert Joseph
Perez, David William
Pernitz, Scott Gregory
Perry, Wilson David
Peterson, Donald Roy
Peterson, John Christian
Schober, Thomas Leonard
Skilton, Robert Henry
Terschan, Frank Robert
Te Winkle, William Peter
Walsh, John
Winner, John Dennett

Wyoming

Harrison, Frederick Joseph
Riggs, Dan Britt
Rolich, Frank Alvin

FEDERAL REPUBLIC OF GERMANY

Pfennigstorf, Werner

FRANCE

MacCrindle, Robert Alexander

ADDRESS UNPUBLISHED

Aldrich, Richard Dennis
Beger, John David
Brooks, Patrick William
Carrington, Morris Clifford
Cheek, Louis Eugene
Crawford, Muriel Laura
Fekete, George O.
Friedrich, Bruce Robert
Gee, Delbert Calvin
Gregory, Rick Dean
Griffith, James Lewis
Henningsen, David Sean
Hughes, Roy Fredericks
Johnson, Gary William
Linnehan, Joseph Arthur, Jr.
Martin, Terence Alan
Nelson, Jay Scott
Plattner, Richard Serber
Plitt, Steven
Puttock, John Lawrence
Samples, Stephen Shay
Spiller, William, Jr.
Stetler, Nevin

INTERNATIONAL, PRIVATE

UNITED STATES

Alabama

Riegert, Robert Adolf
Sullivan, Michael Maurice
Trimmier, Charles Stephen, Jr.

Arizona

Castro, Raul Hector
Folsom, Victor Clarence
Furnish, Dale Beck
Grant, Merwin Darwin
Meek, Marcellus Robert
Tennen, Leslie Irwin

Arkansas

Dumeny, Marcel Jacque
Watkins, Jerry West

California

Adams, William Gillette
Allan, Lionel Manning
Armour, George Porter
Balkin, Jeffrey Gilbert
Barrett, Robert Matthew
Barton, John Hays
Basile, Paul Louis, Jr.
Bastiaanse, Gerard C.
Bazyler, Michael J.
Beard, Ronald Stratton
Behrendt, John Thomas
Blaustein, Frances Jan
Bond, George Cline
Branson, Harley Kenneth
Burke, Robert Bertram
Burrill, Janice Hilary
Cahill, Michael Edward
Castro, Leonard Edward
Cathcart, Patrick Alan
Chan, Thomas Tak-Wah
Childs, Marjorie M.
Collas, Juan Garduño, Jr.
Cummings, John Patrick
Demirdjian, Jean-Claude
Doan, Xuyen Van
Erickson, Ralph Ernest
Fields, Henry Michael
Finck, Kevin William
Flynn, John Allen
Foley, Martin James
Gambaro, Ernest Umberto
Gibson, Thomas Harris, III
Gilbert, Robert Wolfe
Glad, Edward Newman
Grossman, Richard Alan
Hamilton, Jackson Douglas
Heng, Donald James, Jr.
Hinman, Harvey DeForest
Houck, John Burton
Hughes, William Jeffrey
Kant, Harold Sanford
Katayama, Robert Nobuichi
Kimport, David Lloyd
Kolkey, Daniel Miles
Kraw, George Martin
Krueger, Robert Blair
Langer, Simon Hrimes
Leventhal, Frederic Daniel
Loring, David Charles
Lund, James Louis
Mallory, Frank Linus
Mansour, Nadim Ned
McEvers, Duff Steven
McLeod, Robert Macfarlan
McMillan, M. Sean
Meyer, Donald Robert
Millard, Neal Steven
Miyoshi, David Masao
Myers, Philip Eric
Nelson, David Edward
Nelson, Paul Douglas
Nownejad, Cyrus Sirouss
Offer, Stuart Jay
Olson, James Calvin
Patterson, Robert Edward
Radlo, Edward John
Ramirez, William Earl
Randall, Richard Parks
Rinck, Gary M.
Robertson, David Govan
Rosett, Arthur Irwin
Schlesinger, Rudolf Berthold
Schwarzstein, Richard Joseph
Seavey, William Arthur
Shaney, Kevin Robert
Sherman, Martin Peter
Shorr, Matthew Sam
Smith, Ora Everett
Snaid, Leon Jeffrey
Stagner, Robert Dean
Toms, Robert Lee
Tornstrom, Robert Ernest
van Schoonenberg, Robert G.
Walsh, Joseph Richard
Wehde, Albert Edward
Weiss, Sherman David
Weissman, Barry Leigh
Welch, John Edward
Welch, Thomas Andrew
Woodhouse, Thomas Edwin
Worley, Donald Robert
Young, Bryant Llewellyn

Colorado

Arkin, Harry Lee
Del Piccolo, Silvana Pannella
McClain, Vaughn Leon
Radosevich, George Edward
Rich, Robert Stephen
Sumners, William Glenn, Jr.
Tippit, John Harlow

Connecticut

Bell, Robert Collins
Borod, Donald Lee
Burrasca, Raymond Peter
Cooper, George Wilson
Eisner, Lawrence Brand
Fuller, Robert Ferrey
Gray, Chester L., Jr.
Greeley, Paul David
Greenspon, Robert Alan
Kalaher, Richard Alan
Koh, Harold Hongju
Marsching, Ronald Lionel
McCobb, John Bradford, Jr.
McConnell, David Kelso
McGovern, Kevin Michael
Nelson, Douglas Thomas
Pastore, Richard Steel
Perlah, Philip Michael
Putman, Linda Murray
Schroth, Peter W(illiam)
Sherer, Frank Audemars, Jr.
Theodore, Carol N.
Turrentine, James Drake
Walk, Donald Willard
Whiston, Richard Michael
Yachmetz, Philip Keith

Delaware

Kuniholm, John Gardner

District of Columbia

Abrams, Elliott
Ackerson, Nels J(ohn)
Angarola, Robert Thomas
Anikeeff, Anthony Hotchkiss
Atwood, James R.
Baker, David Harris
Baker, Keith Leon
Barr, Michael Blanton
Bebchick, Leonard Norman
Becker, Ralph Elihu
Benjamin, Edward A.
Besozzi, Paul Charles
Bishop, Wayne Staton
Blair, Robert Allen
Blatchford, Joseph Hoffer
Bodansky, Robert Lee
Brand, Joseph Lyon
Branson, David John
Brenner, Edgar H.
Broches, Aron
Brower, Charles Nelson
Burt, Jeffrey Amsterdam
Calabrese, Michael Raphael
Cameron, Duncan Hume
Carey, Sarah Collins
Carter, Barry Edward
Clagett, Brice McAdoo
Clark, Donald Otis
Cobbs, Louise Bertram
Crotty, Edward
Cutler, John Arthur
Daniel, Royal, III
deKieffer, Donald Eulette

Dempsey, David B.
Dickinson, Timothy L.
Dinan, Donald Robert
Dunn, Christopher Allan
Efron, Samuel
Ehrenhaft, Peter David
Eiselt, Erich Raymond
Ellicott, John LeMoyne
Epstein, David
Epstein, Gary Marvin
Fegan, David Albert
Feinerman, James Vincent
Feldman, Mark B.
Fennell, William Alfred
Finch, John Marshall
Finton, Timothy Christopher
Fishman, Charles Louis
Flowe, Benjamin Hugh, Jr.
Gerson, Ralph Joseph
Golsong, Heribert
Golub, Martin Joseph
Goodwin, Robert Cronin
Gray, John Walker, Jr.
Green, Carl Jay
Harris, Scott Blake
Harrison, Donald
Harrison, Earl David
Heller, Jack Isaac
Heller, John Roderick, III
Hemmendinger, Noel
Heron, Julian Briscoe, Jr.
Hidalgo, Edward
Hoffman, Joseph Bowytz
Hoffman, Michael Harris
Hollis, Sheila Slocum
Houlihan, David Paul
Jaffe, Robert A.
Johnson, David Raymond
Johnson, Oliver Thomas, Jr.
Jones, Aidan Drexel
Juster, Kenneth Ian
Kaplan, Sheldon Zachary
Kenchelian, Mark Levon
Kharasch, Robert Nelson
Koffler, Warren William
Kraemer, Jay R.
Kramer, Franklin David
Kramer, William David
Kriesberg, Simeon M.
Kroener, William Frederick, III
Kurrelmeyer, Louis Hayner
Lamia, Thomas Roger
Lamm, Carolyn Beth
Landfield, Richard
Larroca, Raymond G.
Lebow, Edward Michael
Lehman, Leonard
Leonard, Will Ernest, Jr.
Levy, Steven Abraham
Lippo, Tom A.
Lipstein, Robert A.
Lubic, Robert Bennett
Lucas, Steven Mitchell
Maloof, Farahe Paul
Marans, J. Eugene
Marshall, Sylvan Mitchell
Mathews, Craig
McGivern, Thomas Michael
McGuirl, Marlene Dana Callis
Meany, Bernard Anthony
Mendelsohn, Martin
Merthan, Lawrence Casper
Miller, Eugene Paul
Millman, Richard Martin
Millstein, Leo Lee
Moore, Robert Madison
Muir, J. Dapray
Murphy, Terence Roche
Nealer, Kevin Glenn
Newsome, George Marvin
Norberg, Charles Robert
Olson, John Frederick
O'Neill, Lawrence Daniel
Oser, Ralph Crandall
Palmeter, N. David
Parsky, Gerald Lawrence
Patrick, Robert John, Jr.
Pearce, Cary Jack
Pietrowski, Robert Frank, Jr.
Poe, Luke Harvey, Jr.
Portnoy, Ian Karl
Powell, Robert Dominick
Price, Joseph Hubbard
Rath, Francis Steven
Raul, Alan Charles
Reed, John Grady
Reichler, Paul Stuart
Rhodes, Paula Renette
Richman, Sheldon Barnett
Roach, Patrick Joseph
Robinson, Davis Rowland
Rose, Jonathan Chapman
Rosenblatt, Peter Ronald
Ruggeri, Robert Edward
Russell, Harold Swift
Russin, Jonathan
Saba, Joseph Philip
Schneebaum, Steven Marc
Sczudlo, Raymond Stanley
Sedky, Cherif
Shepherd, John Michael
Shihata, Ibrahim Fahmy Ibrahim
Silver, Daniel Ben
Smith, Walter Joseph, Jr.
Soble, Stephen M.
Spak, Walter Joseph
Spina, George Charles
Spradlin, Thomas Richard
Steingold, Stuart Geoffrey
Stevenson, John Reese
Stewart, David Pentland
Stewart, Terence Patrick
Stovall, James Truman, III
Tanaka, Akihiko
Tasker, Joseph
Tendler, Paul Marc
Thomas, Ritchie Tucker
Timberg, Sigmund
Tomaszczuk, Alexander Daniel
Vance, Sheldon Baird
Verrill, Charles Owen, Jr.
Vidal-Cordero, David
Vogel, John Henry
Vollmer, Andrew N.
Wall, Christopher Read
Wegener, Mark Douglas
Wegner, Harold Claus
Weiss, Arnold Hans
Westin, David Lawrence
White, Peter Allen
Wilson, Craig Alan
Winter, Audrey Stacey
Wolf, Maurice
Wolff, Alan William
Yale-Loehr, Stephen William
Young, John Hardin
Young, William Fielding

Florida

Aguilar, Humberto Juan
Arensberg, Cornelius Wright
Barnard, George Smith
Barnett, Charles Dawson
Butterworth, Alan Randolph
Doyle, Martin
Epley, Marion Jay
Gonzalez-Pita, J. Alberto
Hendry, Robert Ryon
Justice, Thomas Hardwick, III
Landy, Burton Aaron
Markus, Andrew Joshua
Moreno, Fernando
Olson, Carl Eric
Paul, Robert
Petrey, Roderick Norman
Rappaport, Richard Warren
Rougeux, Donna Riselli
Sacasas, Rene
Sandler, Gilbert Lee
Vento, John Sebastian
Vogel, Howard Michael
Zamora, Antonio Rafael

Georgia

Barr, Robert Laurence, Jr.
Branch, Thomas Broughton, III
Dailey, Michael Alan
Doyle, Michael Anthony
Flynt, John James, Jr.
Henderson, Daniel Lamar
Hipple, Robert John
Marger, Edwin
Marquis, Harold Lionel
Saidman, Gary K.
Wilcox, Everett Hammock, Jr.
Wilson, Rhys Thaddeus
Zoukis, Stephen James

Hawaii

Green, Randall Wayne
Hakoda, Harvey Nobuo
Robinson, Harlo Lyle
Shklov, Mark Thomas
Sumida, Gerald Aquinas

Illinois

Abbott, Kenneth Wayne
Allen, John Trevett, Jr.
Baisley, Joan Ann
Baker, Donald
Banks, Theodore Lee
Barack, Peter Joseph
Barnes, James Garland, Jr.
Baugher, Peter V.
Belmore, F. Martin
Bentley, Peter John Hilton
Berens, Mark Harry
Berner, Robert Lee, Jr.
Boodell, Thomas Joseph, Jr.
Braun, William David
Brennan, James Joseph
Cannon, Benjamin Winton
Choo, Yeow Ming
Cicero, Frank, Jr.
Clemens, Richard Glenn
Cunningham, Robert James
DeVries, James Howard
Evanoff, Michael Blaine
Farrell, Richard James
Fowler, William Craig
Franklin, Richard Mark
Gaffney, Terrence John
Golko, Andrew Albin
Greenstein, Martin Richard
Hay, Peter Heinrich
Henry, Frederick Edward
Hetke, Richard L.
Horwitz, John
Hunt, Lawrence Halley, Jr.
Jacobs, James Ethan
Kathrein, Reed Richard
Klotsche, John Chester
Kuehn, Angelika Maria
Lorentzen, John Carol
Michaels, Richard Edward
Mitchell, Neil Ralph
Morrow, John Ellsworth
Nicholson, Thomas Laurence
North, Kenneth Earl
Pallasch, B. Michael
Pattishall, Beverly Wyckliffe
Ritchie, William Paul
Rodenberg, George William, Jr.
Rosso, David John
Saltoun, Andre M.
Sarabia, Antonio Rosas
Seith, Alex Robert
Staubitz, Arthur Frederick
Valauskas, Charles C.
Wade, Edwin Lee
Wardell, John Watson
Webber, Carl Maddra
Witz, Allen Barry
Wood, Diane Pamela
Yoon, Hoil

Indiana

Barden, Kenneth Eugene
Blackwell, Henry Barlow, II
Funk, David Albert
Henderson, Eugene Leroy
Kalsi, Swadesh Singh
Levy, Ron Karl
Richardson, Andrew James
Russell, David Williams

Iowa

Devine, Michael Buxton
Hoth, Steven Sergey
Peshkin, Samuel David

Kansas

Griffin, Ronald Charles

Kentucky

Moremen, John S.

Louisiana

Danner, William B.
Fowler, George J., III
Holmes, James Richard
Osakwe, Christopher
Salas, Camilo Kossy, III

Maine

Curtis, Kenneth M.

Maryland

Carmel, Alan Stuart
Chaplin, Peggy Fannon
Gray, Richard Edward
Marlow, William Freeman Coale, Jr.
Ohly, D. Christopher
Papkin, Robert David
Paul, Carl Frederick
Phillips, Leo Harold, Jr.
Rosenthal, Lawrence Gerald

Massachusetts

Aresty, Jeffrey Michael
Bernhard, Alexander Alfred
Bigelow, Robert P.
Chayes, Abram
Davidson, Frank Paul
Davis, Alan Hugh
Gannon, Christopher Richard
Garcia, Adolfo Ramon
Gonson, S. Donald
Greer, Gordon Bruce
Huang, Thomas Weishing
Korff, Ira A.
Lynch, John Gregory, Jr.
Mason, Paul Eric
May, William Leopold, Jr.
Molineaux, Charles Borromeo, Jr.
Nicholson, Francis Joseph
Rose, Leonard
Salacuse, Jeswald William
Snyder, Frederick Edward
Stokes, James Christopher, Jr.
Thibeault, George Walter
Towner, Frank Schwable, Jr.
Trautman, Donald Theodore
Vagts, Detlev Frederick
von Mehren, Arthur Taylor

Michigan

Birnbaum, Roy Bennett
Dobranski, Bernard
Elsman, James Leonard, Jr.
Heil, Paul William
Hindelang, Robert Louis
Jackson, John Howard
Mitchell, James Albee
Muraski, Anthony Augustus
Polley, Vincent Ira
Porro, James Earle
Robinson, Logan Gilmore
Stella, Daniel Francis
Talcott, Kent Patterson
Theut, C(larence) Peter
Thierstein, Emma Joan
Von Drehle, Ramon Arnold

Minnesota

Angle, Margaret Susan
Barry, Charles Byron
Beha, Ralph Werner
Boyer, David Randall
Frecon, Alain Jean-Christian
Halbach, Patrice Haley
Hasselquist, Maynard Burton
Hayward, Edward Joseph
Marousek, Robert Joseph
Perlman, Lawrence
Sippel, William Leroy
Swanson, Steven Richard
Timmer, Steven James
Whitehill, Clifford Lane
Williams, James Edward
Young, Stephen Bonsal
Yucel, Edgar Kent

Mississippi

Fenton, Howard Nathan, III
Mingee, James Clyde, III

Missouri

Blume, Lawrence Dayton
Carlson, Mary Susan
Craig, Bernard Duffy
Hapke, Daniel S., Jr.
Knoten, Thomas Patrick
Lee, James Roger
Lents, Don Glaude
Wilson, Walter William
Wrobley, Ralph Gene

Nevada

Jones, Clifford Aaron
Schutt, William Eldon

New Hampshire

Marsh, Norman James, Jr.

New Jersey

Adams, William Tennant
Biribauer, Richard Frank
Case, Douglas Manning
Cohen, Lawrence Gene
Donnella, Michael Andre
English, Jerry Fitzgerald
Fredericks, Wesley Charles, Jr.
Gilman, Claudia Jane
Gimmy, Daniel Patrick
Goekjian, Samuel Vahram
Hasl, Hannelore Vera Margarete
Herpst, Robert Dix
Kagan, Irving
Kennedy, Harold Edward
Lundy, Audie Lee, Jr.
McDonald, James Douglas
Ornitz, Richard Martin
Rosen, Norman Edward
Shandor, Bohdan Donald
Shea, Edward Emmett
Staehle, Sandra Johnson
Storms, Clifford Beekman
Sudol, Walter Edward
Talafous, Joseph John
Yoerg, Norman, Jr.

New Mexico

Ferreira, Beatriz Valadez
Hanna, Robert Cecil
Schoen, Stevan Jay
Schuler, Alison Kay

New York

Aksen, Gerald
Allen, Ronald Roger, Jr.
Allison, Richard Clark
Andersen, Richard Esten
Angell, Nicholas Biddle
Angulo, Manuel Rafael
Appel, Alfred
Armstrong, John Kremer
Asante, Samuel Kwadwo Boaten
Ashley, Daniel Joseph
Baker, David Remember
Barbanel, Jack A.
Barcelo, John James, III
Barist, Jeffrey
Beach, Charles Addison
Beaton, Neal N.
Begley, Louis
Beller, Barry
Bennett, James Martin
Berlin, Alan Daniel
Bermann, George Alan
Bernard, Richard Phillip
Bidwell, James Truman, Jr.
Bierce, William Blaikie
Blanchard, Kimberly Staggers
Blum, Maurice Henry
Bolan, Thomas Anthony
Boulanger, Carol Seabrook
Breckenridge, James Richard
Brendzel, Michael L.
Broady, Tolly Rupert
Brock, Mitchell
Brown, Francis Cabell, Jr.
Brown, G(lenn) William, Jr.
Brown, Ronald Wellington
Browning, David Stuart
Bryan, Barry Richard
Burkard, Peter Hubert
Burke, Thomas Edmund
Burrell, Lizabeth Lorie
Burt, Richard Max
Busch, Benjamin
Butler, Samuel Coles
Campanie, Samuel John
Cantwell, Robert
Carswell, Robert
Cashel, Thomas William
Cassan, Vito J.
Catuzzi, J.P., Jr.
Chamberlin, Michael Meade
Cho, Tai Yong
Clark, Cameron
Cooper, Stephen Herbert
Cowles, Frederick Oliver
Cox, Melvin Monroe
Critchlow, Charles Howard
Davidow, Joel
Davidson, Robert Bruce
Davis, Richard Joel
Daw, Harold John
Decker, Frank Norton, Jr.
DeKoven, Ronald
De Lachapelle, Philippe
de Lasa, José M.
De Vivo, Edward Charles
Dixon, Bonnie Lynn
Donohue, John Patrick
Duerbeck, Heidi Barbara
Duffy, Edmund Charles
Duffy, James Henry
Duffy, James P., III
Dunham, Corydon Bushnell
Dunn, M(orris) Douglas
Eaton, William Mellon
Edelman, Paul Sterling
Ekern, George Patrick
Elicker, Gordon Leonard
Eltzroth, Carter Weaver
Epstein, Melvin
Ercklentz, Enno Wilhelm, Jr.
Evan, Charles
Fagan, John Ernest
Farnsworth, Edward Allan
Farnum, Henry Merritt
Fernandez, Jose Walfredo
Fernandez, Lillian
Fersko, Raymond Stuart
Flowers, William Ellwood
Franklin, Blake Timothy
Friedland, Paul Daniel
Friedman, Jon George
Friedman, Victor Stanley
Fuller, David Otis, Jr.
Futterman, Stanley Norman
Galef, Steven Allen
Ganz, David L.
Garro, Alejandro Miguel
Gelatt, Timothy Arthur
Gettner, Alan Frederick
Gewirtz, Elliot
Gillespie, Alexander Joseph, Jr.
Gillespie, Jane
Goldhirsch, Lawrence Bertram
Goldman, Louis Budwig
Gooch, Anthony Cushing
Gorin, Robert Seymour
Gracin, Hank
Grames, Conan Paul
Grant, Stephen Allen
Guth, Paul C.
Hamel, Rodolphe
Hancock, James H.
Harkins, Francis Joseph, Jr.
Harris, Joel B(ruce)
Hauser, Gregory Francis
Hauser, Rita Eleanore Abrams
Hayes, Gerald Joseph
Healy, Harold Harris, Jr.
Hendrickson, Robert Augustus
Hill, Alfred
Hirsch, Daniel
Hoffman, John Ernest, Jr.
Hoffman, Richard (Melvin)
Hopkins, Thomas Arscott
Howe, Richard Rives
Hritz, George F.
Irwin, Richard Frank
Jackson, William Eldred
Jagow, Charles Herman
Jefferies, Jack P.
Jinnett, Robert Jefferson
Kaminer, Peter H.
Kessler, Jeffrey L.
Kies, David M.
Kimball, John Devereux
Koplik, Marc Stephen
Kramaric, Peter Stefan
Kreitman, Lenore Roberts
Kuhn, Perla M.
Lackert, Clark William
Landau, Walter Loeber
Leaf, Martin Norman
Levitt, Daniel Philip
Ligelis, Gregory John
Lincoln, Franklin Benjamin, Jr.
Lindskog, David Richard
Lovejoy, Allen Fraser
Lunde, Asbjorn Rudolph
Luria, Remy
Mack, Dennis Wayne
MacRae, Cameron Farquhar, III
Malloy, Michael Patrick
Marks, Ramon Paul
Martowski, David William
Massengale, John Edward, 3d
Matteson, William Bleecker
Mattiaccio, Richard L.
Maxeiner, James Randolph
McConnell, John Hay
McHugh, James Bernard
McLaughlin, Joseph Thomas
McLean, Sheila Avrin
Medford-Rosow, Traci
Mendales, Richard Ephraim
Menken, David A.
Merow, John Edward
Michel, Clifford Lloyd
Miller, Peter Putnam
Morgan, Frank Edward, II
Mosoff, Serle Ian
Muskin, Victor Philip
Myerson, Toby Salter
Nadkarni, Girish Vishwanath
Nelson, Joni Lysett
Newcomb, Danforth
Newman, Lawrence Walker
Nimetz, Matthew
Nixon, Elliott Bodley
Nogee, Jeffrey Laurence
Norton, Gerard Francis, Jr.
O'Brien, Timothy James
Odell, Stuart Irwin
Offner, Eric Delmonte
Oliver, Milton McKinnon
Olschwang, Alan Paul
Osborn, Donald Robert
O'Sullivan, Thomas J.
Panitz, Lawrence Herbert
Pavia, George M.
Pearlman, Michael Allen
Peet, Charles D., Jr.
Pennell, William Brooke
Pergam, Albert Steven
Perlmuth, William Alan
Pettibone, Peter John
Piliero, Robert Donald
Prem, F. Herbert, Jr.
Prentice, Eugene Miles, III
Prounis, Theodore Othon
Rabb, Bruce
Radon, Jenik Richard
Rago, Daniel Anthony
Rankin, Clyde Evan, III
Read, Charles Arthur
Resnicow, Norman Jakob
Richter, Gary Stephen
Robinson, Nicholas Adams
Röhm, Eberhard Heinrich
Rosenberg, Maurice
Rosensaft, Menachem Zwi
Rosenzweig, Charles Leonard
Rovine, Arthur William
Sands, Judith Davies
Saviano, Edward Steven
Schiffman, Steven Mitchell
Schuit, Steven Reiner
Schwartz, Stephen Jay
Scofield, Milton N.
Seader, Paul Alan
Seidel, Selvyn
Seltzer, Jeffrey Lloyd
Shapiro, George M.
Short, Skip
Shoss, Cynthia Renee
Silkenat, James Robert
Siller, Stephen I.
Siphron, Joseph Rider
Slote, Edwin Michael
Solmonson, Steven Jay
Sorensen, Theodore Chaikin
Steinthal, Kenneth L.
Stevenson, Justin Jason, III
Steyer, Hume Richmond
Swanson, David Warren
Terry, Tai Chang
Thomas, Ronald James
Todman, Terence Alphonso, Jr.
Toomey, Richard Andrew, Jr.
Townsend, John Michael
Tursi, Carl Thomas
Ullman, Leo Solomon
Vega, Matias Alfonso
Vock, Robert Daniel
Wacker, Daniel James
Wald, Bernard Joseph
Waldoks, Phillip Harry
Weiner, Earl David
Whiteman, Robert Gordon
Williamson, Steven Lloyd
Wise, Aaron Noah
Woolley, Edward Alexander
Wragg, Laishley Palmer, Jr.
Yamin, Michael Geoffrey
Zimmett, Mark Paul

North Carolina

Burke, Frederick Augustine
Conley, David Thomas

Eads, Wayne Buchanan
Frassineti, Jordan Joseph
Gann, Pamela Brooks
Ross, John Bowen, Jr.
Walker, George Kontz

Ohio

Bridgeland, James Ralph, Jr.
Coquillette, William Hollis
De Brier, Donald Paul
Dettinger, Warren Walter
Gunning, David Hall
Hadji, Serge Basil
Herold, Karl Guenter
Jacobs, Leslie William
Masek, Raymond John
Oestreicher, Michael Robert
Roj, William Henry
Schollenberger, David Kennon
Seeley, Glenn J.
Stith, John Stephen
Walker, Kenneth Lynn
Wilbur, Peter Davis

Oklahoma

Hitchcock, Bion Earl
Roff, Alan Lee
Scott, Willard Philip
Sloan, Steven Kent
Steelman, Jacob DeHart
Williford, John Lea

Oregon

Campbell, William Coolidge
Feder, Miriam
Halle, John Joseph
Nafziger, James Albert Richmond
Nunn, Robert Warne
Nye, Daniel Alan
Schweitz, Martha Leach
Wyse, William Walker

Pennsylvania

Auerbach, Ernest Sigmund
Baldwin, Frank Bruce, III
Brand, Ronald Alvah
Brawner, Gerald Theodore
Brown, Richard P., Jr.
Burns, Douglas Foster
Cerminaro, Anthony Richard
Cook, Cameron H.
Curtis, Gregory Dyer
Dilks, Park Bankert, Jr.
Duval, Robert
Ellis, Alan
Fogelnest, Robert Craig
Gilhooly, Edward Foster
Goldberg, Stanley Zelig
Hershey, Dale
Heubel, William Bernard
Honnold, John Otis, Jr.
Hooton, Michael Edward
Janos, Joseph John, III
Jenne, Kirk
Jones, David Mattern
King, Dominic Benson
Krzyzanowski, Richard Lucien
Lipson, Barry J.
Litmans, Murray Ian
Maio, Carl Anthony
McCabe, Lawrence James
McKnight, Henry James
Mirabello, Francis Joseph
Mooney, Charles W., Jr.
Murphy, John Francis
Orban, Frank Anton, III
Pang, Peter Chiusing
Pisani, Robert Louis
Rhodes, Kenneth Anthony, Jr.
Sander, Malvin Gustav
Scudder, Charles Seelye Kellgren
Simmons, Bryan J.
Sosnov, Steven Robert
Unkovic, Dennis
Walters, Bette Jean
Weary, Thomas Squires
Whiteside, William Anthony, Jr.

Rhode Island

Maneckji, Bhikhaji Maneck

South Carolina

Dibble, Charles Lemmon

Tennessee

Bell, William Hall
Charney, Jonathan Isa
Folmar, Oliver Wiley
Maier, Harold Geistweit

Texas

Amdur, Arthur R.
Armour, James Lott
Baade, Hans Wolfgang
Baker, Mark Bruce
Beacroft, Percival Thomas
Bernard, Donald Ray
Brown, Stephen Smiley
Burleson, Karen Tripp
Burns, Sandra K.
Busbee, Kline Daniel, Jr.
Casseb, Robert Michael
Cuellar, Enrique Roberto
Dack, Christopher Edward Hughes
Dilg, Joseph Carl
Dimitry, Theodore George
Doke, Marshall J., Jr.
Elliott, Frank Wallace
Estes, Carl L., II
Fant, Douglas Vernon
Feldwisch, David Lewis
Freling, Richard Alan
Godfrey, Cullen Michael
Grant, Patrick Gerard
Hinshaw, Chester John
Hoyt, Mont Powell
Hunter, Robert Frederick
Jordan, Bruce
Kosut, Kenneth Paul
Larson, Mark Edward, Jr.
Levine, Harold
Lionberger, Richard Lee
Looper, Donald Ray
Marlow, Orval Lee, II

Masters, Claude Bivin
McClure, Donald John
Mercer, Edwin Wayne
Moore, Lawrence Jack
Murphy, Ewell Edward, Jr.
Murray, Frederick Franklin
Nadorff, Norman J.
Nahlen, Dana Gayle
Newman, Lawrence Graham
Omer, Michael Lee
Pierson, Grey
Porter, Thomas William, III
Powers, Timothy Eugene
Rendell, Robert Sloat
Rubagumya, George William
Rucker, Jerry Don
Salch, Steven Charles
Santire, Stanley Paul
Sapp, Walter William
Silva, Eugene Joseph
Steele, Richard Parks
Stephens, John F., Jr.
Sullenbarger, Daniel James
Sylvester, Jon Howard
Vazquez, Gilbert Falcon
Wexler, Charles W., Jr.
Woodward, Charles Carroll M.
Yost, William Arthur, III
Zahn, Donald Jack

Utah

Ashworth, Brent Ferrin
Chancellor, Thomas Harvey
Joslin, Gary James

Vermont

Doria, Anthony Notarnicola

Virginia

Biddle, Eric Harbeson, Jr.
Briney, Roger Albert
Calkins, Gary Nathan
Daniels, Michael Alan
DeGolia, James B.
English, William deShay
Foster, Judith Christine
Gales, Robert Robinson
Higgins, Mary Celeste
Kieff, Nelson Richard
Kondracki, Edward John
MacKinlay, Edgar Harold
Mannix, Charles Raymond
McClard, Jack Edward
Procopio, Joseph Guydon
Revoile, Charles Patrick
Robol, Richard Thomas
Rosenberg, Peter David
Sargeant, William Leslie
Schroeder, James White
Schwartz, Philip
Wright, Blandin James
Zaphiriou, George Aristotle

Washington

Friend, David Lee
Gibbs, Nancy Patricia
Greenburg, G. Scott
King, William Kimble, Jr.
Newcity, Michael Albert
Sandler, Michael David
Scowcroft, Jerome Chilwell
Simburg, Melvyn Jay

Wisconsin

Akavickas, Gary Robert
Lavers, Richard Marshall
Levit, William Harold, Jr.
Politano, Frank Louis
Ryan, Thomas Joseph
Schroeder, Stuart R.
White, Walter Hiawatha, Jr.
Wiley, Edwin Packard

Wyoming

Whynott, Philip Percy

TERRITORIES OF THE UNITED STATES

Guam

LaFleur, Gary James

Puerto Rico

Flax-Davidson, Ron Hunter

BELGIUM

Tattersall, William James

ENGLAND

Brown, James Scott
Herzog, Brigitte
Jackman, Robert L.
Morrison, William David

FEDERAL REPUBLIC OF GERMANY

Pfennigstorf, Werner

FRANCE

Cochran, John M., III
Iseman, Joseph Seeman
McGovern, David Talmage
Riggs, John Hutton, Jr.

HONG KONG

Randt, Clark Thorp, Jr.

JAPAN

Dickson, Thomas Page
Shannon, William James

MEXICO

Ritch, James Earle, Jr.
Rogers, John Ellsworth

PEOPLES REPUBLIC OF CHINA

Capener, Cole R.

SAUDI ARABIA

Chang, Leo
Shea, Gerald MacDonald

SINGAPORE

Siegfried, David Charles

SWITZERLAND

Goldstein, E. Ernest
Muller, Johannes Joseph
Ulmer, Nicolas Courtland

THAILAND

Enos, Priscilla Beth

UNITED ARAB EMIRATES

Stockwell, David Michael

ADDRESS UNPUBLISHED

Ackerman, Robert A(rthur)
Bateman, David Alfred
Bell, Haney Hardy, III
Branscomb, Anne Wells (Mrs. Lewis McAdory Branscomb)
Brunell, Norman Eliot
Campbell, John Timothy
Cunningham, Alice Welt
Damaska, Mirjan Radovan
Derrick, William Alfred, Jr.
Ellis, Neil Richard
Elterman, Warren Bart
Gianotti, Ernest F.
Godard, Randy Eugene
Hafner, Thomas Mark
Hays, Samuel Spartan
Hecht, Barbara Elizabeth Roberts
Hildebrand, Charles Frederick
Israel, Nancy Diane
Kasper, Horst Manfred
Kling, Edward Lewis
Lande, James Avra
Lobl, Herbert Max
Marx, Gary Samuel
McCoy, Henry Drewry, II
Mendel, Stephen Frank
Meran, Harry Bruce
Paul, Joel Richard
Puttock, John Lawrence
Quigley, Leonard Vincent
Schager, Richard Joseph, Jr.
Scher, Mark Waclaw
Schreiber, Eliot Bruce
Silberman, Curt C.

INTERNATIONAL, PUBLIC

UNITED STATES

Alabama

Warren, Manning Gilbert, III

Arizona

Castro, Raul Hector
Lipson, Ann Louise
Parker, Jeffrey Robert
Vosburgh, John Addison

California

Barton, John Hays
Bazyler, Michael J.
Bettwy, Samuel William
Doan, Xuyen Van
Ely, Northcutt
Glazer, Jack Henry
Gleim, Michael Alan
Lehman, Edward George
Montgomery, John Warwick
Mosk, Richard Mitchell
Mutek, Michael Wendell
Perkins, Steven Curtis
Riesenfeld, Stefan Albrecht
Shostak, Stanley Richard
Simone, Martin Massimo

Colorado

Rossi, Ronald Gregory
Smith, Milton Lovett

Connecticut

Koh, Harold Hongju
Wedgwood, Ruth Glushien

District of Columbia

Abrams, Elliott
Anthony, David Vincent
Apperson, Bernard James
Atwood, James R.
Bannon, Brian Anthony
Bastek, John Anthony
Baur, Donald Christian
Becker, Ralph Elihu
Blatchford, Joseph Hoffer
Bowen, Brooks Jefferson
Brand, Joseph Lyon
Branson, David John
Broches, Aron
Brower, Charles Nelson
Buck, David Patrick
Burns, Arnold Irwin
Byrne, Edward Mark
Calabrese, Michael Raphael
Cameron, Duncan Hume
Carter, Barry Edward
Clagett, Brice McAdoo
Clark, Donald Otis
Clubb, Bruce Edwin
Cobbs, Louise Bertram
Cullen, Thomas Francis, Jr.
Dean, Robert Scott
deKieffer, Donald Eulette
Dembling, Paul Gerald
Denniston, John Baker
Dunn, Christopher Allan
Efron, Samuel
Einhorn, Bruce Jeffrey
Feinerman, James Vincent
Feldman, Mark B.
Fisher, Bart Steven
Frame, Nancy Davis

Frieden, Robert M.
Garrett, Henry Lawrence, III
Gaughan, John Anthony
Goans, Judy Winegar
Golsong, Heribert
Golub, Martin Joseph
Graham, Peter Jeffrey Stuart
Green, Carl Jay
Heller, John Roderick, III
Hemmendinger, Noel
Hill, Robert Charles
Hinds, Richard De Courcy
Johnson, Oliver Thomas, Jr.
Jones, Bradley Wayne
Kammerer, Kelly Christian
Kaplan, Richard Alan
Kaplan, Sheldon Zachary
Kenchelian, Mark Levon
Kriesberg, Simeon M.
Leonard, Will Ernest, Jr.
Lew, Ginger
Mathews, Craig
McGivern, Thomas Michael
McNeill, John Henderson
Mendelsohn, Martin
Nealer, Kevin Glenn
Norberg, Charles Robert
Oliver, Robert Spencer
Oman, Ralph
O'Sullivan, James Paul
Pietrowski, Robert Frank, Jr.
Regalado, Eloisa
Reichler, Paul Stuart
Reifsnyder, Daniel Alan
Rhodes, Paula Renette
Rivera, Henry Michael
Robinson, Davis Rowland
Rogers, David H.
Rosenblatt, Peter Ronald
Schneebaum, Steven Marc
Scocozza, Matthew Vincent
Shihata, Ibrahim Fahmy Ibrahim
Spak, Walter Joseph
Stevenson, John Reese
Stewart, David Pentland
Stovall, James Truman, III
Stuart, Pamela Bruce
Tanaka, Akihiko
Thaler, Martin S.
Thompson, Paul Barker
Turner, Robert Foster
Van Orman, Chandler L.
Wallach, Evan Jonathan
Weingarten, Reid H.
Weisgall, Jonathan Michael
Weiss, Arnold Hans
Winslow, John Franklin
Wolf, Maurice
Wolff, Alan William
Yale-Loehr, Stephen William
Yambrusic, Edward Slavko
Younger, Alexander

Florida

Arensberg, Cornelius Wright
Barnett, Bernard Harry
Davis, Louis Poisson, Jr.
Dunlap, Charles Leonard
Moreno, Fernando
O'Neal, Leslie King
Swan, George Steven

Georgia

Bird, Terry Cornelius
Flynt, John James, Jr.
Huszagh, Fredrick Wickett
Marger, Edwin
Marvin, Charles Arthur

Hawaii

Burgess, Hayden Fern
Van Dyke, Jon Markham

Illinois

Abbott, Kenneth Wayne
Boyle, Francis Anthony
Branding, Frederick H.
D'Amato, Anthony
Gottlieb, Gidon Alain Guy
Kindt, John Warren
LaRue, Paul Hubert
Lynch, John Peter
Uchtmann, Donald Louis
Wilkinson, John Bruce

Indiana

Dugan, Michael Thomas, II
Ehrlich, Thomas

Kansas

Metcalf, William Evans

Louisiana

Halliburton, John Robert

Maryland

Pisani, Robert Joseph
Price, James Lee
Ryan, David Charles
Sheble, Walter Franklin

Massachusetts

Bateman, Thomas Robert
Davidson, Frank Paul
Fisher, Roger Dummer
Korff, Ira A.
Merritt, Thomas Butler
Nicholson, Francis Joseph
Oulton, Donald Paul
Ryan, Allan Andrew, Jr.
Salacuse, Jeswald William
Snyder, Frederick Edward
Vagts, Detlev Frederick

Michigan

Jackson, John Howard

Minnesota

Swanson, Steven Richard

Missouri

Carlson, Mary Susan
Golbert, Albert Sidney

Nevada

Trachok, Richard M(athew), II

New Jersey

Corbett, Peter Gerald
Greene, Michael Roy
Hasl, Hannelore Vera Margarete
Lewis, Albert Michael
Ritter, Robert Joseph

New York

Angulo, Manuel Rafael
Arango, Emilio
Asante, Samuel Kwadwo Boaten
Barcelo, John James, III
Blake, Harlan Morse
Busch, Benjamin
Debo, Vincent Joseph
Dubbs, Thomas Allan
Erlichster, Joe
Evan, Charles
Finch, Edward Ridley, Jr.
Frank, Lloyd
Gardner, Richard Newton
Gewirtz, Elliot
Halberstam, Malvina Guggenheim
Hauser, Rita Eleanore Abrams
Lincoln, Franklin Benjamin, Jr.
Lombardi, Joseph Edward
Luria, Remy
Malloy, Michael Patrick
McLean, Sheila Avrin
Posner, Michael Hoffman
Ratner, Michael D.
Riddle, David Andrew
Rosenbaum, Eli M.
Satrom, Robert Charles
Schuit, Steven Reiner
Silkenat, James Robert
Sloan, F(rank) Blaine
Sorensen, Theodore Chaikin
Ssekandi, Francis Muzingu
Teclaff, Ludwik Andrzej
Todman, Terence Alphonso, Jr.
Watson, James Lopez

North Carolina

Kane, Terry Richard
Luney, Percy Robert, Jr.
Robertson, Horace Bascomb, Jr.
Walker, George Kontz

Ohio

Carro, Jorge Luis
Christenson, Gordon A.
Hadji, Serge Basil
Schmitz, Thomas Mathias

Oregon

Nafziger, James Albert Richmond
Schweitz, Martha Leach

Pennsylvania

Auerbach, Ernest Sigmund
Ellis, Alan
Fox, James Robert
Krzyzanowski, Richard Lucien
Leech, Noyes Elwood
Murphy, John Francis
Pisani, Robert Louis

South Carolina

Haimbaugh, George Dow, Jr.

South Dakota

Reed, Walter Dudley

Tennessee

Bell, William Hall
Charney, Jonathan Isa
Maier, Harold Geistweit

Texas

Baade, Hans Wolfgang
Barber, Monty Clyde
Busbee, Kline Daniel, Jr.
Goodman, John Peter
Greenspan, Abraham Alcon
Jacobs, Gregory R.
Mercer, Edwin Wayne
Miller, Norman Richard
Strauss, Robert Schwarz

Utah

Butler, Geoffrey John Butler

Vermont

Doria, Anthony Notarnicola
French, Thomas McGuinness

Virginia

Angulo, Charles Bonin
Biddle, Eric Harbeson, Jr.
Brittigan, Robert Lee
Curtis, Jeffrey Hutton
Downey, William Gerald, Jr.
Higgins, Mary Celeste
Indest, George Felix, III
Klewans, Samuel N.
Lewis, Walter Laughn
Walkup, Charlotte Lloyd
Wiswall, Frank Lawrence, Jr.
Zaphiriou, George Aristotle

Washington

King, William Kimble, Jr.
Meyers, Anthony James

Wisconsin

Baldwin, Gordon Brewster
Wetzel, Volker Knoppke

TERRITORIES OF THE UNITED STATES

Guam
Troutman, Charles Henry, III

Puerto Rico
Roman, David William

SWITZERLAND
Ulmer, Nicolas Courtland

ADDRESS UNPUBLISHED
Avery, Bruce Edward
Branscomb, Anne Wells (Mrs. Lewis McAdory Branscomb)
English, Richard D.
Israel, Nancy Diane
Lichtenstein, Natalie G.
Metzger, Jeffrey Paul
Paul, Joel Richard
Schager, Richard Joseph, Jr.
Taylor, Daniel Edwin

JUDICIAL ADMINISTRATION. See also Jurisprudence.

UNITED STATES

Alabama
Acker, William Marsh, Jr.
Blankenship, Jeri Burnette
Cox, Emmett Ripley
Hancock, James Hughes
McKelvey Wright, Anne Farrell
Monk, Samuel Holt, II
Monroe, Cecil Barlow
Nation, Horace Hendrix, III
Norwood, Dorothy F.
Propst, Robert Bruce
Shores, Janie Ledlow
Taylor, Samuel Wayne
Torbert, Clement Clay, Jr.

Alaska
Compton, Allen T.
Greenstein, Marla Nan
Holland, H. Russel
Moody, Ralph E.

Arizona
Babbitt, David Berkeley
Broomfield, Robert Cameron
Browning, William Docker
Carroll, Earl Hamblin
Marquez, Alfredo C.
Reinstein, Ronald S.
Strand, Roger Gordon

Arkansas
Newbern, William David
Tedder, Cecil A.
Waters, H. Franklin

California
Alarcon, Arthur Lawrence
Brewster, Rudi Milton
Chotiner, Kenneth Lee
Clark, Dwight William
Conti, Samuel
Coyle, Robert Everett
Files, Gordon Louis
Gilbert, Richard Lee
Gilliam, Earl Ben
Hupp, Harry L.
Ideman, James M.
Irving, J. Lawrence
Jamin, Noah Ned
Keep, Judith N.
Kenyon, David V.
Lewis, Gerald Jorgensen
Lynch, Eugene F.
Malkus, James Alan
Mc Laughlin, Joseph Mailey
Moore, Henry Trumbull, Jr.
Nelson, Dorothy Wright (Mrs. James F. Nelson)
Patel, Marilyn Hall
Rafeedie, Edward
Rymer, Pamela Ann
Schwarzer, William W
Stotler, Alicemarie H.
Vega, Benjamin Urbizo

Colorado
Kirshbaum, Howard M.
Matsch, Richard P.
Ogburn, Robert Wilson
Ramirez, David Eugene

Connecticut
Burke, Christopher Mark
Cabranes, José Alberto
Coffey, Robert Dennis
Dalton, Victoria Clayman
Dannehy, Joseph F.
Drumm, Francis Joseph, Jr.
Healey, Arthur H.
Horwitch, Daniel B.

Delaware
Christie, Andrew Dobbie
DiSabatino, Arthur Frank
Walsh, Joseph Thomas

District of Columbia
Archer, Glenn LeRoy, Jr.
Burchill, William Roberts, Jr.
Chabot, Herbert L.
Channon, Patricia Sugrue
Doyle, Joyce Ann
Gardner, William Courtleigh
Greene, Harold H.
Hauptly, Denis James
Jacobs, Julian I.
Katzmann, Robert Allen
King, Rufus Gunn, III
Knab, Karen Markle
Lawrence, Glenn Robert
Lydon, Thomas J.
Parker, Barrington Daniels

Parker, Edna G.
Polansky, Larry Paul
Powell, Lewis Franklin, Jr.
Ramsey, Robert Lee
Sarko, Lynn Lincoln
Steadman, John Montague
Stewart, James Kevin
Wertheim, Ronald P.
Wiese, John Paul

Florida
Aronovitz, Sidney M.
Bracete, Juan Manuel
Carbo, Michael James
DeFoor, James Allison, II
Kehoe, James W.
King, James Lawrence
Moore, John Henry, II
Moreno, Federico Antonio
Paul, Maurice M.
Raiden, Michael E.
Rosinek, Jeffrey
Sharp, George Kendall
Shaw, Leander Jerry, Jr.
Silver, Roger Allen
Vinson, Roger

Georgia
Alverson, Luther
Bell, Richard
Forrester, J. Owen
Martin, Faye Sanders
Purdom, Wayne Miller
Shoob, Marvin H.
Stow, Elizabeth Glenn
Vining, Robert Luke, Jr.

Hawaii
Hayashi, Yoshimi
Moroney, Michael John
Nakamura, Edward H.

Idaho
Burnett, Donald Lee, Jr.
Hurlbutt, Daniel Chater, Jr
Ryan, Harold L.
Shepard, Allan Guy

Illinois
Braden, Everette Arnold
Bua, Nicholas John
Cargerman, Alan William
Conway, Martin Eugene, Jr.
Garnett, Marion Winston
Grady, John F.
Howlett, Michael Joseph, Jr.
Manikas, Peter Michael
Marcus, Richard Leon
Nordberg, John Albert
Plunkett, Paul Edward
Provenzale, Maryellen Kirby
Richards, Robert Mayo
Schulhofer, Stephen Joseph
Shadur, Milton I.
Timberlake, George William
Williams, George Howard
Wilson, James Donehoo

Indiana
Brown, Elaine Marie Becher
Campbell, Edward Adolph
Capshaw, Tom Dean
Drury, Ronald Eugene
Fleece, Steven Michael
Kern, Raymond Lex
Petersen, Howard Edwin
Pivarnik, Alfred J.
Richert, John Louis
Witte, Gordon Michael

Iowa
Van Metre, Peter
Wolle, Charles Robert

Kansas
Crow, Sam Alfred
Lockett, Tyler C.
Miller, Robert Haskins
Walker, Richard Bruce

Kentucky
Apperson, Jeffrey Allen
Choate, Dennis Jeffrey
Johnstone, Edward H.
Knopf, William Lee
Miller, Carl Theodore
O'Daniel, Jean Elizabeth
Wintersheimer, Donald Carl

Louisiana
Collins, Robert Frederick
Duhe, John M., Jr.
McNamara, A. J.
Ragland, Alwine Mulhearn
Steen, Wesley Wilson

Maine
Glassman, Caroline Duby
Roberts, David Glendenning

Maryland
Carr, William Orville
Corderman, John Printz
Hargrove, John R.
Levitz, Dana Mark
Murray, Herbert Frazier
Platt, Steven Irving
Steinberg, Marvin Bernard

Massachusetts
Adomeit, Peter Loring
Dacey, Kathleen Ryan
Flannery, J(ohn) Harold
Lynch, Neil L(awrence)
McNeil, Alexander Mallory
Melican, John Joseph
Miles, Judith Ellen
Nelson, David S.
O'Connor, Francis Patrick
Skinner, Walter Jay
Steelman, David Carl

Woodlock, Douglas Preston

Michigan
Basso, Ronald Matthew
Batzer, James Martin
Brennan, Thomas Emmett, Jr.
Cavanagh, Michael F.
Danhof, Robert John
Deats, Paul Edwin
Dunn, Richard Devere
Fitzgerald, John Warner
Jordan, Glenn Erval
Newblatt, Stewart Albert
Resteiner, Harold Edward
Riley, Dorothy Comstock
Root, Lawrence Charles
Supina, Gerald Joseph
Ulrich, Gregory Leslie

Minnesota
Amdahl, Douglas Kenneth
Olson, Lynn Cloonan
Wahl, Rosalie E.

Mississippi
Biggers, Neal Brooks, Jr.
Coleman, William Franklin
Fant, Lester Glenn
Jolly, E. Grady
Lee, Roy Noble
Robertson, James L.
Sullivan, Michael D.

Missouri
Bartlett, D. Brook
Billings, William Howard
Deutsch, James Bernard
Grimm, Stanley Arnold
Koffman, Robert Lawrence
Mauer, William F.
Roberts, Ross T.

Montana
Larsen, Dirk Herbert
Sheehy, John C.
Turnage, Jean A.
Weber, Fred J.

Nebraska
Beam, C. Arlen
Krivosha, Norman
Murphy, John Paul
Shanahan, Thomas M.
White, C. Thomas

Nevada
Reed, Edward Cornelius, Jr.
Steffen, Thomas Lee
Young, C. Clifton

New Hampshire
Batchelder, William F.
Souter, David Hackett

New Jersey
Barry, Maryanne Trump
Brotman, Stanley Seymour
Garibaldi, Marie Louise
Gerry, John Francis
O'Hern, Daniel Joseph
Stein, Gary
Warmington, Robert Anthony

New Mexico
Alarid, Albert Joseph
Conway, Susan Marie
Dal Santo, Diane
Kaufman, Bruce Eric
Stowers, Harry E., Jr.
Walters, Mary Coon

New York
Alexander, Fritz W., II
Altimari, Frank X.
Berg, Gale Diane
Brind, David Hutchison
Duffy, Kevin Thomas
Keenan, John Fontaine
Kenny, Philip William
Lamutis, Donald Franklin
Lombardi, Joseph Edward
Miner, Roger Jeffrey
Ralls, Geoffrey Quentin
Scarzafava, Nettie Jean
Stark, Thomas Michael

North Carolina
Boyle, Terrence W.
Bullock, Frank William, Jr.
Frye, Henry E.
Martin, Harry Corpening
Potter, Robert Daniel
Stevens, Henry Leonidas, III

North Dakota
Eckert, Robert Laird
Erickstad, Ralph John
Erickstad, Ralph John
Medd, Joel Douglas
Meschke, Herbert L.

Ohio
Battisti, Frank Joseph
Bell, Samuel H.
Contie, Leroy John, Jr.
Damiani, Louis Carmen
Douglas, Andrew
Dowd, David D., Jr.
Eckstein, Steven Douglas
Fain, Mike
George, Joyce Jackson
Hottle, Darrell Rizer
Kinneary, Joseph Peter
Manos, John M.
Maurer, John William
Merz, Michael
Paddock, Harold Dewolf
Painter, Mark Philip
Parish, Dennis MacDonald
Ringland, Robert Paul

Rogers, Richard Michael
Stacey, James Allen
Walters, Sumner Junior
Wells, Lesley Brooks
White, George W.

Oklahoma
Basham, Marshall Denver
Gabbard, (James) Douglas, II
Hansen, Carol M.
Hodges, Ralph B.
Purcell, Gary Morgan
Wagner, John Leo
Wilson, Alma D.

Oregon
Clark, David Lewis
Crookham, Charles Sewell
Frye, Helen Jackson
Jones, Robert Edward
O'Scannlain, Diarmuid Fionntain
Roth, Phillip Joseph
Valentine, Eric Woodson

Pennsylvania
Bechtle, Louis Charles
Cahn, Edward N.
Caldwell, William W.
Cassimatis, Emanuel Andrew
Cohill, Maurice Blanchard, Jr.
Fullam, John P.
Gambescia, Joseph M(ario), Jr.
Giles, James T.
Keller, John William
McDermott, James T.
Mencer, Glenn Everell
Olszewski, Peter Paul
Schaeffer, Forrest Grim, Jr.
Shaulis, Norman Albert
Sisk, Paul Douglas
Weis, Joseph Francis, Jr.
Zappala, Stephen A.

Rhode Island
Svengalis, Kendall Frayne

South Carolina
Bartlett, Stephen Sheppard
Blatt, Solomon, Jr.
Hamilton, Clyde H.
Pyle, Charles Victor, Jr.
Thomy, George Albert

South Dakota
Hersrud, Leslie Raymond
Morgan, Robert Edward
Neiles, Joseph
Sabers, Richard Wayne

Tennessee
Estes, Jerry Nelson
Hull, Thomas Gray
Jarvis, James Howard
Kilcrease, Irvin Hugh, Jr.
Meredith, Jennings Bryan
Riley, Joe Glenard

Texas
Black, Norman William
Garcia, Sylvia R.
Gibson, Hugh
Gulley, David Wesley
Harkey, Paul
Haskett, Martin Carlaton
Hassell, Morris William
Hawkins, John Claiborne, Jr.
Hecht, Nathan Lincoln
Hill, John, Jr.
Hoffman, Leonard Elbert, Jr.
Holt, Wayland Garth
Hughes, William Augustus, Jr.
Judice, C(harles) Raymond
Kazen, George Philip
Keltner, David E.
McDonald, Gabrielle Anne Kirk
Palmer, Randall Parham, III
Parker, Robert M.
Prado, Edward Charles
Rendon, Josefina Muniz
Richter, Martin Edward
Sondock, Ruby Kless
Sterling, Ross N.
Stovall, Thomas J., Jr.
Williams, Jerre Stockton

Utah
Butler, Geoffrey John Butler
Sam, David

Vermont
Allen, Frederick W.
Peck, Louis Provost

Virginia
Doumar, Robert G.
Feidler, Robert Ernest
Pearson, Henry Clyde
Robertson, William Shore
Robie, William Randolph
Thomas, John Charles

Washington
Adams, Mark Harris
Andersen, James A.
Bryan, Robert J.
Durham, Barbara
Goodloe, William Cassius, III
Luce, Kenyon Eldridge
Mullins, George Holland
Pearson, Vernon R.
Tanksley, Raymond Richard, Jr.
Webster, Walter Earnest, Jr.

West Virginia
Brotherton, W. T., Jr.
Hallanan, Elizabeth V.

Wisconsin
Callow, William Grant
Long, J. Richard

Montabon, Dennis Gene
Shabaz, John C.
Van Buren, David Paul
Wetzel, Volker Knoppke

Wyoming
Cardine, Godfrey Joseph
Gillum, Forrest Earl

TERRITORIES OF THE UNITED STATES

Guam
Weeks, Janet Healy

Puerto Rico
Gierbolini-Ortiz, Gilberto
Pieras, Jaime, Jr.
Torruella, Juan R.

Virgin Islands
O'Brien, David Vincent

ADDRESS UNPUBLISHED
Brown, Gary Ross
Davidson, Glen Harris
Fillner, Russell Kenneth
Gianotti, Ernest F.
Kauger, Yvonne

JURISPRUDENCE. See also Judicial administration.

UNITED STATES

Alabama
Adams, Oscar William, Jr.
Beatty, Samuel Alston
Clemon, U. W.
Embry, Thomas Eric
Faulkner, James Hardin
Guin, Junius Foy, Jr.
Hand, William Brevard
Hoff, Timothy
Johnson, Frank Minis, Jr.
Maddox, Alva Hugh
Nelson, Leonard John, III
Nesbit, Phyllis Schneider
Pointer, Sam Clyde, Jr.
Smith, Charles Lynwood, Jr.
Vance, Robert Smith

Alaska
Fitzgerald, James Martin
Greenstein, Marla Nan

Arizona
Bilby, Richard Mansfield
Cameron, James Duke
Hardy, Charles Leach
Hays, Jack D.H.
Meek, Marcellus Robert
Schroeder, Mary Murphy
Sims, Terrance Lee
Tang, Thomas

Arkansas
Arnold, Richard Sheppard
Dudley, Robert Hamilton
Fleming, Victor Anson
Hays, Steele
Hickman, Darrell David
Overton, William Ray
Purtle, John Ingram
Roy, Elsijane Trimble
Taylor, Hendrix Arthur, Jr.
Woods, Henry

California
Alexander, Richard
Bigler, Ross Lowell
Broussard, Allen E.
Byrne, William Matthew, Jr.
Champlin, Philip Alden
Dixon, William Cornelius
Ferguson, Warren John
Files, Gordon Louis
Freiser, Lawrence M.
Goodwin, Alfred Theodore
Henderson, Thelton Eugene
Ingram, William Austin
Kadish, Sanford Harold
Karlton, Lawrence K.
Marshall, Consuelo Bland
Miller, Jeremy Matthew
Montgomery, John Warwick
Nonet, Philippe
Norris, William Albert
Ofner, William Bernard
Ogg, Wilson Reid
Poole, Cecil F.
Pregerson, Harry
Ramirez, Raul Anthony
Schwartz, Milton Lewis
Seheult, Malcolm McDonald Richardson
Shire, Harold Raymond
Takasugi, Robert Mitsuhiro
Teitler, Harold Herman
Vega, Benjamin Urbizo
Vukasin, J. P., Jr.
Wallace, J. Clifford
Williams, Spencer M.

Colorado
Baker, Bernard Robert
Carrigan, Jim Richard
Dauer, Edward Arnold
Dubofsky, Jean Eberhart
Finesilver, Sherman Glenn
Ogburn, Robert Wilson
Reardon, Gerard Vincent
Rovira, Luis Dario

Connecticut
Bieluch, William Charles
Calabresi, Guido
Daly, T(homas) F(rancis) Gilroy
Ecklund, John Edwin

Hazard, Geoffrey Cornell, Jr.
Katz, Jay
Newman, Jon O.
Reisman, William M.

Delaware

Mankin, Hart Tiller
Munneke, Gary Arthur
Stapleton, Walter King

District of Columbia

Bennett, Marion Tinsley
Blackmun, Harry Andrew
Bolick, Clint Daniel
Bonventre, Vincent Martin
Brennan, William Joseph, Jr.
Buffon, Charles Edward
Caplan, Russell L.
Cohen, Mary Ann
Davis, Oscar Hirsh
Drennan, Joseph Peter
Ferman, Irving
Gesell, Gerhard Alden
Goffe, William Arthur
Jacobs, Julian I.
Johnson, Norma Holloway
Lotkin, Ralph Louis
Marshall, Thurgood
Mullenix, Linda Susan
Nies, Helen Wilson
Nims, Arthur Lee, III
Oberdorfer, Louis F.
O'Brien, Timothy Andrew
O'Connor, Sandra Day
Penn, John Garrett
Rehnquist, William Hubbs
Robinson, Aubrey Eugene, Jr.
Rubenstein, Richard Edward
Sargentich, Thomas Oliver
Sofaer, Abraham David
Sterrett, Samuel Black
Stevens, John Paul
Wald, Patricia McGowan
White, Byron R.
Wright, James Skelly
Yannello, Judith Ann
Yock, Robert John

Florida

Anderson, Terence James
Audlin, David John, Jr.
Black, Susan Harrell
Carrere, Charles Scott
Castagna, William John
Clark, Harold Robinson
Davis, Edward Bertrand
Hastings, Alcee Lamar
Hatchett, Joseph Woodrow
Herin, William Abner
Hoeveler, William M.
Kogan, Gerald
Messing, Howard Robert
Paine, James Carriger
Paul, Jeremy Ralph
Pritchard, Teresa Noreen
Roney, Paul H.
Spellman, Eugene Paul
Swygert, Michael Irven
Tjoflat, Gerald Bard

Georgia

Bentley, Fred Douglas, Sr.
Bowen, Dudley Hollingsworth, Jr.
Clark, Thomas Alonzo
Evans, Orinda D.
Hall, Robert Howell
Hames, Luther Claude, Jr.
Jackson, Joe David
Mayoue, John Charles
O'Kelley, William Clark
Pope, Iree Rose Williams
Tidwell, George Ernest
Voynich, John Joseph
Welch, Denise Majette
Weltner, Charles Longstreet

Hawaii

Acoba, Simeon Rivera, Jr.

Idaho

Anderson, J. Blaine
Bakes, Robert Eldon
Donaldson, Charles Russell

Illinois

Allen, Richard Blose
Allen, Ronald Jay
Baker, Harold Albert
Beatty, William Louis
Boharic, Robert Vincent
Burns, Robert Patrick
Burrows, Cecil J.
Cargerman, Alan William
Carroll, William Kenneth
Clark, William George
Cudahy, Richard D.
D'Amato, Anthony
Easterbrook, Frank Hoover
Flaum, Joel Martin
Getzendanner, Susan
Gold, George Myron
Goldstein, Candice
Gottlieb, Gidon Alain Guy
Hart, William Thomas
Hartman, Marshall J.
Hermann, Donald Harold James
Kocoras, Charles Petros
Leighton, George Neves
Levi, Edward Hirsch
Malvik, John
Manikas, Peter Michael
Mc Garr, Frank J.
Moran, James Byron
Palmer, Michael Paul
Pell, Wilbur Frank, Jr.
Rissman, Emanuel A.
Simon, Seymour
Williams, George Howard
Young, Rowland Lee

Indiana

Ehrlich, Thomas
Fleece, Steven Michael
Funk, David Albert

Givan, Richard Martin
Kanne, Michael Stephen
Noland, James Ellsworth
Risacher, Martin Eugene
Speicher, John Allan

Iowa

Goldman, David Harris
Mc Giverin, Arthur A.
Schultz, Louis William

Kansas

Holmes, Richard Winn
Logan, James Kenneth
Macnish, James Martin, Jr.
Meeks, Cordell David, Jr.
O'Connor, Earl Eugene
Renner, Clarence E.
Rogers, Richard Dean
Saffels, Dale Emerson
Schultz, Richard Allen
Walker, Richard Bruce

Kentucky

Ballantine, Thomas Austin, Jr.
Bertelsman, William Odis
Garvey, Kevin Lee
Levy, Charlotte Lois
Lively, Pierce
Martin, Boyce Ficklen, Jr.
Shadoan, William Lewis
Siler, Eugene Edward, Jr.
Unthank, G. Wix
Whitmer, Leslie Gay

Louisiana

Brunson, Hugh Ellis
Carr, Patrick E.
Cole, Luther Francis
Dixon, John Allen, Jr.
Flick, Sheila Ann
Gallagher, Michael Stephen
Grundmeyer, Douglas Lanaux
Hoskins, David LeRoy
Lemmon, Harry Thomas
Politz, Henry Anthony
Polozola, Frank Joseph
Ratcliff, John Garrett
Rubin, Alvin Benjamin
Sear, Morey Leonard
Stagg, Tom
Uddo, Basile Joseph
Veron, Earl Ernest
Wicker, Veronica DiCarlo

Maine

Patterson, Dennis Michael

Maryland

Harvey, Alexander, II
Kaufman, Frank Albert
Levin, Marshall Abbott
McDermitt, Edward Vincent
Miller, James Rogers, Jr.
Ramsey, Norman Park
Rodowsky, Lawrence Francis
Skoler, Daniel Lawrence
Thomas, Robert Boyce
Young, Joseph H.

Massachusetts

Breyer, Stephen Gerald
Coquillette, Daniel Robert
Donohue, Michael J.
FitzGibbon, Scott Thomas
Garrity, W. Arthur, Jr.
Goldfarb, Phyllis
Liacos, Paul Julian
Mc Naught, John J.
Merritt, Thomas Butler
Michelman, Frank I.
Nolan, Joseph Richard
Sargentich, Lewis D.
Skinner, Walter Jay
Tauro, Joseph Louis
Zobel, Rya W.

Michigan

Brenneman, Hugh Warren, Jr.
DeMascio, Robert Edward
Dobranski, Bernard
Enslen, Richard Alan
Feikens, John
Gibson, Benjamin F.
Gillespie, William Tyrone
Guy, Ralph B., Jr.
Hillman, Douglas Woodruff
Hood, Harold
Kennedy, Cornelia Groefsema
LaBre, William Luke
Miles, Wendell A.
Palmieri, Angela
Pratt, Philip
Ryan, James Leo
Taylor, Anna Diggs
Vining, (George) Joseph
White, James Boyd

Minnesota

Farber, Daniel Alan
MacLaughlin, Harry Hunter
Murphy, Diana E.
Renner, Robert George
Todd, John Joseph
Yetka, Lawrence Robert
Young, Stephen Bonsal

Mississippi

Clark, Charles
Fant, Lester Glenn
Senter, Lyonel Thomas, Jr.

Missouri

Cahill, Clyde S.
Devine, James Richard
Filippine, Edward L.
Gaertner, Gary M.
Gibson, Floyd Robert
Hungate, William Leonard
McClure, Lawrence Ray
McMillian, Theodore
Owens, Dennis James Campbell

Sachs, Howard F(rederic)
Wright, Scott Olin

Montana

Harrison, John Conway
Hatfield, Paul Gerhart

Nebraska

Boslaugh, Leslie
Hastings, William Charles
Reagan, Ronald Evan
Urbom, Warren Keith

Nevada

Gunderson, Elmer Millard
Mowbray, John Code
Springer, Charles Edward

New Hampshire

Bownes, Hugh Henry
Brock, David Allen
Loughlin, Martin Francis

New Jersey

Brandon, Mark Edward
Garth, Leonard I.
Handler, Alan B.
Kravarik, Martin Edward
Lacey, Frederick Bernard
Pollock, Stewart Glasson
Serata, Samuel Jacob
Wilentz, Robert N.
Wszolek, Dennis Francis

New Mexico

Burciaga, Juan Guerrero
Conway, Susan Marie
Dal Santo, Diane
Sosa, Dan, Jr.

New York

Baird, Bruce Allen
Brandveen, Antonio Isadore
Brieant, Charles La Monte, Jr.
Burstein, Beatrice S.
Cooper, Irving Ben
Cramton, Roger Conant
Dunham, Dan Steven
Eno, Lawrence Raphael
Feinberg, Robert Julian
Feinberg, Wilfred
Freedman, Monroe Henry
Gardner, Romaine Luverne
Goettel, Gerard Louis
Griesa, Thomas Poole
Haight, Charles Sherman, Jr.
Hazard, John Newbold
Kaufman, Irving Robert
Leiser, Burton Myron
Leisure, Peter Keeton
Leval, Pierre Nelson
Lowe, Mary Johnson
Lyons, David Barry
McCurn, Neal Peters
Miller, Wesley A. Looney
Nickerson, Eugene H.
Platt, Thomas Collier
Re, Edward D.
Rosenfeld, Michel
Sand, Leonard B.
Schwartzman, Jack
Sifton, Charles Proctor
Ssekandi, Francis Muzingu
Sweet, Robert Workman
Teclaff, Ludwik Andrzej
Telesca, Michael Anthony
Wachtler, Sol
Ward, Robert Joseph
Wolf, Susan M.

North Carolina

Britt, W. Earl
Christie, George Custis
Erwin, Richard C.
Horowitz, Donald Leonard
Martin, Harry Corpening
Martin, John Charles
Meyer, Louis B.
Phillips, James Dickson, Jr.
Ward, Hiram Hamilton

North Dakota

Lockney, Thomas Michael
Vickrey, Barry Roland

Ohio

Aldrich, Ann
Balester, Vivian Shelton
Bierce, James Malcolm
Black, Robert L., Jr.
Brown, Clifford F.
Christenson, Gordon A.
Damiani, Louis Carmen
Evans, Stanley Robert
Fain, Mike
George, Joyce Jackson
Grundstein, Nathan David
Hanson, Eugene Nelson
Holschuh, John David
Krupansky, Robert Bazil
Lambros, Thomas Demetrios
Lantz, Charles Jeffery
McMahon, William Robert
Menke, William Charles
Merz, Michael
Moss, Judith Dorothy
Painter, Mark Philip
Purdy, Roger Daniel
Souers, Loren Eaton, Jr.
Stacey, James Allen
Sweeney, Asher William
Wells, Lesley Brooks

Oklahoma

Collins, Leon Frederick
Cook, Harold Dale
Daugherty, Frederick Alvin
Decker, Michael Lynn
Ellison, James Oliver
Gabbard, (James) Douglas, II
Opala, Marian P(eter)
Russell, David L.

Seymour, Stephanie Kulp
Thompson, Ralph Gordon
West, Lee Roy

Oregon

Crookham, Charles Sewell
Huffman, James Lloyd
Lent, Berkeley
Linde, Hans Arthur
Peterson, Edwin J.
Riemer, George Arthur
Skopil, Otto Richard, Jr.
Sullivan, Edward Joseph

Pennsylvania

Becker, Edward Roy
Brody, Anita Blumstein
Crowley, Thomas Michael
Curran, William James, III
Flaherty, John P.
Friedrichs, David O.
Gambescia, Joseph M(ario), Jr.
Granat, Richard Stuart
Ludwig, Edmund V.
McGlynn, Joseph Leo, Jr.
Rambo, Sylvia H.
Roper, Peter P.
Schaeffer, Forrest Grim, Jr.
Shapiro, Norma Sondra Levy
Sloviter, Dolores Korman
Van Antwerpen, Franklin Stuart
Walker, Wallace Lee
Weiner, Charles R.
Ziegler, Donald Emil

Rhode Island

Weisberger, Joseph Robert

South Carolina

Anderson, George Ross, Jr.
Bristow, Walter James, Jr.
Chapman, Robert Foster
Gregory, George Tillman, Jr.
Harwell, David Walker
Hawkins, Falcon Black
Houck, Charles Weston
Russell, Donald Stuart
Wells, Robert Steven

South Dakota

Heege, Robert Charles
Wollman, Roger Leland

Tennessee

Cooper, Robert Elbert
Dillard, W. Thomas
Ferguson, April Rose W.
Harbison, William James
Hunt, William Walter, III
McCoy, Thomas Raymond
Merritt, Gilbert Stroud
Wellford, Harry Walker

Texas

Belew, David Owen, Jr.
Brown, Karen Kennedy
Caudill, David Stanley
DeAnda, James
Estes, Joe Ewing
Higginbotham, Patrick Errol
Hudspeth, Harry Lee
Jackson, Freddie Newell
Johnson, Sam D.
Parkin-Speer, Diane
Porter, Robert William
Reavley, Thomas Morrow
Richter, Martin Edward
Robinson, Mary Lou
Schuwerk, Robert Paul
Schwab, Elmo
Sessions, William Steele
Singleton, John Virgil, Jr.
Thornberry, William Homer
Vela, Filemon B.
Walker, Dee Brown
Zipp, Ronald Duane

Utah

Durham, Christine Meaders
Stewart, Isaac Daniel, Jr.
Winder, David Kent

Vermont

Coffrin, Albert Wheeler
Oakes, James L.

Virginia

Carrico, Harry Lee
Clarke, J. Calvitt, Jr.
Cochran, George Moffett
Compton, Asbury Christian
Halbrook, Stephen Porter
Harthun, Luther Arthur
Jamison, John Ambler
Merhige, Robert Reynold, Jr.
Michael, James Harry, Jr.
Poff, Richard Harding
Revercomb, Horace Austin, Jr.
Russell, Charles Stevens
Skolrood, Robert Kenneth
Stephenson, Roscoe Bolar, Jr.
Widener, Hiram Emory, Jr.

Washington

Callow, Keith McLean
Dimmick, Carolyn Reaber
Dolliver, James Morgan
Dore, Fred Hudson
Fletcher, Hon. Betty B.
Gaddis, Stephen Michael
Quackenbush, Justin Lowe
Rothstein, Barbara Jacobs
Voorhees, Donald Shirley

West Virginia

Copenhaver, John Thomas, Jr.
Maxwell, Robert Earl
Mc Graw, Darrell Vivian, Jr.
McHugh, Thomas Edward
Neely, Richard
Sprouse, James Marshall

Wisconsin

Abrahamson, Shirley Schlanger
Evans, Terence Thomas
Jurkovic, Daniel John
Marohl, David William
Rasmussen, Carl John
Shapiro, Robyn Sue
Warren, Robert Willis

Wyoming

Brimmer, Clarence Addison
Senkewicz, Mary E.

TERRITORIES OF THE UNITED STATES

Guam

Duenas, Cristobal Camacho

Northern Mariana Islands

Laureta, Alfred

ADDRESS UNPUBLISHED

Bernheim, Peggy
Christensen, Albert Sherman
Cook, Wayne Ralph
Cyr, Conrad Keefe
Kauger, Yvonne
Lambert, Arthur Gorman
Meskill, Thomas J.
Newman, Theodore R., Jr.
Reinhardt, Stephen Roy
Ryan, Thomas Timothy, Jr.
Saxon, John David
Shaw, John Malach
Simmons, Paul Allen
Staker, Robert Jackson
Yorra, Myron Seth

JUVENILE

UNITED STATES

Alabama

Heffler, Paul Mark
Higgins, Ronald Clarence

Arizona

Bellah, C. Richard
Klahr, Gary Peter
LaSota, Peter Douglas
Lipson, Ann Louise
Starr, Isidore
Traynor, William Patrick

California

Alexander, Katharine Violet
Chaleff, Gerald Lawrence
English, Charles Royal
Freeman, Beth Labson
Gilbert, Richard Lee
Gough, Aidan Richard
Green, Kenneth Norton
Harley, Robison Dooling, Jr.
Hillberg, Marylou Elin
Johnson, Barbara Jean
Mac Gowan, Mary Eugenia
Melton, Barry
Mones, Paul Alan
Neithercutt, Marcus Gibbs
Seheult, Malcolm McDonald Richardson
Shapiro, Anita Rae
Wallin, Paul Jeffrey
Whittaker, Marion Alma
Wolf, Lawrence

Colorado

Bisgard, Eileen Bernice Reid
Green, Philip Burton
Lohman, Richard Verne
Malone, Thomas Paul
McCotter, James Rawson
Rodgers, Frederic Barker
Warren, Bruce Willard
West, Laurie Diane

Connecticut

Cocco, Leonard M.
Mandell, David E.
Oleyer, George Richard
Telker, Ellen Melinda

District of Columbia

Koller, Benedict Joseph
Myren, Richard Albert
Shust, Diane Marie
Stewart, James Kevin

Florida

McBurney, Charles Walker, Jr.
Mollica, Salvatore Dennis
Nichols, Cynthia Leigh
Reno, Janet
Samek, Jeffrey Wayne
Sheaffer, William Jay
Slaughter, Marshall Glenn
Stapleton, John Owen
Van Hook, Claude Ashton, III
Wind, Carol Marlene

Georgia

Dally, Rebecca Polston
Hanington, Paula Kay
Hubbard, George Morrison, III
Porter, Mary Helen (Howard)
Steger, Susan St. John

Hawaii

Aduja, Peter Aquino
Apo, Jan Kanani
Wong, Michael Jung-Yen

Illinois

Baker, Helen
Bauer, Lawrence Michael
Bernardi, Donald Delpho
Francomb, Lonnie Coleman

Hablutzel, Nancy Zimmerman
Maganzini, Teresa Aversa
Robb, Elizabeth Ann
Tucker, Bowen Hayward

Indiana

Carpenter, Susan Karen
Drury, Ronald Eugene
Gillenwater, Michael Allen
Saunders, David Livingston
Sembroski, Robert Edmund
Walker, Ross Paul

Iowa

Lawyer, Vivian Jury
Neuhaus, Mary Lynn
Sallen, David Urban

Kentucky

Adams, James G., Jr.
Jewell, Franklin P.
Lester, Charles Theodore, Jr.
O'Daniel, Jean Elizabeth

Louisiana

Cicet, Donald James
Dinwiddie, Bruce Wayland
Saloom, Kaliste Joseph, Jr.
White, Trudy Melita

Maine

Tepler, Sheldon Joel

Maryland

Nemetz, Margaret Nottingham

Massachusetts

Green, Joseph Benjamin
Takas, Marianne Heath

Michigan

Fenn, Bruce Hunter
Lloyd, Leona Loretta
Salan, John Francis
Supina, Gerald Joseph

Minnesota

Berg, Nancy Zalusky
Maki, Susan Kay

Missouri

Narrow, Nancy Hentig
Parrish, John Edward
Ringer, John William

Montana

Birkenbuel, Marcia Lee

Nebraska

Dorwart, Charles Edward
Frank, Julie Ann

Nevada

Specchio, Michael Ronald

New Hampshire

Drucker, Leonard Murray
Harkaway, Aaron Abraham
O'Neill, Martha Emma

New Jersey

McCracken, Carol Weaver

New Mexico

Hone, Jay R.
Pederson, Robert David

New York

Autin, Diana Marie Therese Katherine
Burstein, Beatrice S.
Clark, Robert Francis
Fink, Janet Rose
Gallet, Jeffry Hershel
Jacobson, Barry Stephen
Levick, Marsha Lynn
Malach, Herbert John
Rich, Marcia R.
Schack, Robert J.

North Carolina

Burleson, Lynn Pierce
Flowers, Kent Gordon, Jr.
Shields, Karen Bethea

Ohio

Conroy, John Thomas
Eckstein, Steven Douglas
Friedman, Jerome
Giannelli, Paul Clark
O'Connor, John Paul
Parish, Dennis MacDonald
Reno, Ottie Wayne
Robison, Joseph Albert
Sowald, Heather Gay
Wilson, Laura Jane

Oklahoma

Krepps, Ethel Constance
Miller, Michael John
Taylor, Joe Clinton

Oregon

Schmerer, Susan'Ann
Trubo, Herbert Alan
Vallerand, Patricia Ann

Pennsylvania

Benn, Sara Kitchen
Cassimatis, Emanuel Andrew
Cohen, Anita Marilyn
Gross, Malcolm Joseph
Kochems, Robert Gregory
Ludwig, Edmund V.
Smith, Sharon Louise
Weaver, Cynthia Marie

Rhode Island

McMahon, John Joseph
O'Neil, James E.

South Carolina

Elliott, John Dewey
Watson, Patricia Seets

Tennessee

Kiener, John Leslie
Meredith, Jennings Bryan
Purcell, William Paxson, III

Texas

Baskette, William L., Jr.
Davis, Jimmy Frank
Fohn, Gerald Anthony
Morgan, Thomas Sidney
Moseley, Patricia Ann
Reimer, Bill Monroe
Rickhoff, Thomas Emmet
Vick, Phillip Oran
Woldy, Kristine Carol

Virginia

Shepherd, Robert Edward, Jr.
Trompeter, Philip

Washington

Burke, Thomas Gerald

Wisconsin

Bruno, Gary Robert
Castro, Robert C.
Grundahl, John Alvin
Melchert, Lori Layne McLario
Stellman, L. Mandy

Wyoming

Alburn, Cary Rudolph, III

TERRITORIES OF THE UNITED STATES

Guam

Diaz, Ramon Valero

ADDRESS UNPUBLISHED

Ferguson, Marvin Elwood
Garrigues, Gayle Lynne
McDonald, Tom
McFarland, Anne Southworth

LABOR. *See also* **Workers' compensation; Pension.**

UNITED STATES

Alabama

Cobia, Paula Ivey
Davenport, George William
Davis, Donald William
Goldstein, Debra Holly
Haycraft, Charles Arthur
King, John Thomas
Lyles, Harry Arthur
Meigs, Walter Ralph
Spotswood, Robert Keeling
Spransy, Joseph William
Tidwell, William C., III
Whiteside, David Powers, Jr.
Wyatt, Charles Herbert, Jr.

Alaska

Brown, Fred Grant
Goldberg, Robert M.
Maloney, Philip Dennis
Parker, Douglas Stuart

Arizona

Gomez, David Frederick
Guttell, Steven Michael
Jacobs-Schwartz, Loretta (Barbara)
Laws-Coats, Laurie Ann
McMorrow, William John
Murphy, R. Anthony
Wohl, Kenneth Allan

Arkansas

Boe, Myron Timothy
Creasman, William Paul
Hill, Rhonda Kenyon
Lyon, Philip Kirkland
Stodola, Mark Allen

California

Adell, Hirsch
Ahrens, Frederick
Atkins, Robert Alan
Atkinson, Steven Douglas
Aycock, Felix Alfred
Bakaly, Charles George, Jr.
Bakken, Gordon Morris
Bartosic, Florian
Bottger, William Carl, Jr.
Bressan, Paul Louis
Brickner, Jed Walter
Brunette, Steven Edward
Bushnell, Roderick P.
Caples, Michael Edward
Carella, Eugene John
Carr, Willard Zeller, Jr.
Cesinger, John Robert
Cobey, Christopher Earle
Cochran-Bond, Walter C.
Diedrich, William Lawler
Drachman, Frank Emanuel, Jr.
Dryovage, Mary Margaret
Feller, David E.
Finch, David Samuel
Florence, Kenneth James
Gelhaus, Robert Joseph
Gentile, Joseph F.
Gilbert, Robert Wolfe
Golper, John Bruce
Gross, Justin Arthur
Hagberg, Chris Eric

Harutunian, Albert Theodore, III
Highberger, William Foster
Hightower, George Willis
Hipshman, Anne
Holmes, Dallas Scott
Hon, Donald Allen
Hudson, Carolyn Anne
Huebner, Ted Raymond
Kaplin, Gale P. Sonnenberg
Kay, Herma Hill
Kerrigan, Thomas Sherman
Kershnar, Harris Edwin
Klein, Alfred
Kruse, Scott August
LaRocco, John Bernard
Latham, Joseph Al, Jr.
Leff, Irwin
Lehman, Edward George
Le Prohn, Robert
Libbin, Anne E.
McDaniel, David Jamison
Mendelsohn, Susan Rae
Mickelson, Hal M.
Moss, Herbert Allen
Nelson, Luella Eline
Nissly, Kenneth L.
Novotny, Ronald Wayne
Nussbaum, Peter David
Oder, Kenneth William
Oliver, Anthony Thomas, Jr.
O'Shields, June Cruce
Pahl, Stephen Donald
Pingel, Steven R.
Pulliam, Mark Stephen
Rice, Randolf James
Roberson, Clifford Eugene
Rosenberg, Arnold Steven
Rowland, Gilford Glenn
Rudy, Mark Stuart
Scheer, Robert J.
Schnapp, Roger Herbert
Shelley, Susanne Mary
Sherrer, Charles William
Silbergeld, Arthur F.
Skol, Armand George
Solo, Gail Dianne
Stagner, Robert Dean
Stanley, Sabrina Ann
Tallent, Stephen Edison
Thoren-Peden, Deborah Suzanne
Wallace, Elaine Wendy
Werner, Robert George
Whitmore, Sharp
Wilcox, Maurice Kirby C.
Williams, Jerry John
Young, Bless Stritar
Yslas, Stephen Daniel
Zerger, Kirsten Louise

Colorado

Carr, James Francis
Craig, Benjamin Lawrence
Damas, Stanislaw Stefan
Ebert, Darlene Marie
Feiger, Lynn Diamond
Goorman, Perry Lee
Green, Carol H.
Hautzinger, James Edward
Jablonski, James Arthur
LaFond, Richard Charles
LeSatz, Stephen, Jr.
Marquess, Lawrence Wade
Merker, Steven Joseph
Minahan, Daniel F., Jr.
Morris, Marc
Olsen, Theodore Alan
Rowe, Russell Paul
Rudy, Peter Harris
Ruppert, Mark Richard
Schaecher, Susan Marie
Smith, Michael Louis

Connecticut

Barreca, Christopher Anthony
Bingham, Lisa Blomgren
Brady, Robert Lindsay
Brennan, Daniel Edward, Jr.
Coffey, Robert Dennis
Cullina, William Michael
Czajkowski, Frank Henry
Day, John Baldwin
Dempsey, Edward Joseph
Engstrom, Mark William
Finley, Lucinda Margaret
Gelfman, Mary Hughes Boyce
Gilliam, Charles Phillips
Goetsch, Charles Carnahan
Hershatter, Richard Lawrence
Hollander, William Victor
Horner, Stephen Pullar
Koomey, Richard Alan
LaFollette, Ernest Carlton
McGrail, Albert James
McKinney, Ivy Thomas
Orth, Paul William
Phifer, Virginia Hudson
Rosenberg, Burton Stuart
Scheer, Alan I.
Sobol, Alan J.
Travis, Susan Topper
Weinberger, Steven
Zakarian, Albert
Zolot, Norman

Delaware

Goldlust, Perry Felix

District of Columbia

Axelrod, Jonathan Gans
Beckler, Richard William
Bishop, Wayne Staton
Bokat, Stephen A.
Bolick, Clint Daniel
Boudreaux, Andree Anita
Broida, Peter Barry
Buck, David Patrick
Burrow, Rhea Morgan
Calhoun, Carol Victoria
Casey, Bernard Joseph
Cerar, Jeffrey O'Dell
Cohen, Laurence Joel
Covington, Alice Lucille
Curtin, William Joseph
Daugherty, Michael Dennis
Devaney, Dennis Martin
Di Tullio, Donna Marie

Donegan, Charles Edward
Doyle, Joyce Ann
Dozier, Daniel Preston
Edwards, Charles Henry, III
Elisburg, Donald Earl
Ellis, Mark Gregory
Etters, Ronald Milton
Evans-Harrell, Valerie Dianne
Farmer, Guy
Fasman, Zachary Dean
Fay, Raymond Charles
Fenton, John Henry
Fleischer, Sarah Perry
Frazier, Henry Bowen, III
Fried, Charles
Gannascoli, Rudolph Lance
Gold, Laurence Stephen
Goldberg, Avrum M.
Goldsmith, Willis Jay
Griffin, L. Robert
Groner, Isaac Nathan
Halpern, Linda Ann
Heenan, Michael Terence
Heifetz, Alan William
Henderson, Harold Richard
Hennemuth, Jeffrey Alan
Henschel, George Lipman
Heylman, Paul Monroe
Highsaw, James Leonard, Jr.
Hodgson, Morgan Day
Horne, Michael Stewart
Hyde, Patrick Alan
Kerrine, Theodore Michael
Kilberg, William Jeffrey
Kiley, Edward John
King, James Forrest, Jr.
Kinsey, Carrol Hughes, Jr.
Kirschner, Richard
Kramer, Andrew Michael
Krivit, Daniel Henry
Lipkin, Gary Dennis
Lubic, Robert Bennett
Mackiewicz, Edward Robert
McCann, Joseph Leo
McNamara, Roger Thomas
Morris, Frank Charles, Jr.
Murphy, Thomas Patrick
Newberger, Stuart Henry
Palmer, Robert Alan
Panaro, Gerard Paul
Preston, Charles George
Quigley, Thomas J.
Railton, William Scott
Ramsey, Robert Lee
Reback, Joyce Ellen
Rothschild, Donald Phillip
Sauntry, Susan Schaefer
Scheige, Steven Sheldon
Schwarzbart, Robert Morton
Siegel, Allen George
Skinner, William Polk
Taylor, Carl Larsen
Tenney, Paul Anthony
Treacy, Vincent Edward
Vogt, Carl William
Weisberg, Stuart Elliot
Wilder, Roland Percival, Jr.

Florida

Bartlett, Michael John
Chandler, John Brandon, Jr.
Coffman, Daniel Ray, Jr.
Connor, Terence Gregory
Fleming, Joseph Z.
Grogan, Michael Kevin
Hamilton, Robert Lowery
Hogg, Jesse Stephen
Hurtgen, Peter Joseph
Lane, Robin R.
Langley, Dorothy Ann
LeWinter, William Jacob
McHugh, William F.
Rogers, Gordon Dean
Rubinstein, Louis Baruch
Schwedock, Peter Saul
Sharett, Alan Richard
Smith, Harold Delane
Stapleton, John Owen
Stein, Leslie Reicin
Tannen, Edward Cooper
Thiele, Herbert William Albert
Thornburg, Frederick Fletcher
Wich, Donald Anthony, Jr.

Georgia

Adair, Thomas Scarborough
Artis, Gregory Dwight
Ashe, Robert Lawrence, Jr.
Branch, John Ellison
Brewer, Edward Cage, III
Davis, Claude-Leonard
Eastwood, Myles Eric
Foulke, Edwin Gerhart, Jr.
Glucksman, Joyce Francine
Harness, William Walter
Humphries, James Donald, III
Kalish, Katherine McAulay
Langford, James Tafford
Linder, Harvey Ronald
Mirandola, Loretta Jean
Newman, Stuart
Owens, L(awrence) Dale
Price, Terry
Riggs, Gregory Lynn
Rutledge, Ivan Cate
Slawsky, Norman Joel
Smith, George Maynard
Sours, John Delmar
Totenberg, Amy Mil
Wilson, Brent Lawrence
Wymer, John Francis, III

Hawaii

Chang, Donald Mark
Chun-Hoon, Lowell Koon Ying
Freed, Michael Leonard
Fujimoto, Wesley Minoru
Knorek, John Lee

Idaho

Dale, Candy Wagahoff
Greenfield, John Frederic
Madsen, Roger Bryan
Mauk, William Lloyd

Illinois

Adelman, Steven Herbert
Allison, Thomas D., Jr.
Ardito, Laurie Ann
Badel, Julie
Barron, Howard Robert
Beal, Bruce Curtis
Bernstein, Stuart
Besson, Paul Smith
Brennan, Danolda Jean
Brown, Robert Howard
Burkey, Lee Melville
Callis, Felix L.
Carey, Richard Peter
Carton, Laurence Alfred
Clem, Gary Smith
Coffee, Richard Jerome, II
Cohen, Seymour
Coleman, William T(homas)
Connelly, P. Kevin
Cook, James Christopher
Cotton, Eugene
Curran, Mark Cooney
Dombrow, Anthony Eric
Draznin, Anne L.
Fedota, Mark Clarke
Finnegan, Thomas Joseph
Fleps, John Joseph
Fox, Shayle Phillip
Freeborn, Michael D.
Freed, Mayer Goodman
Freerksen, Gregory Nathan
Fuerstenberg, James P.
Gagliardo, Joseph M(ichael)
Galatz, Henry Francis
Garvey, Margaret S.
Gerdy, Harry
Gladden, James Walter, Jr.
Gleeson, Paul Francis
Goslawski, Leonard Stephen
Goulet, Lionel Joseph
Grabemann, Karl W.
Greenfield, Michael C.
Hoffman, Robert B.
Horsley, George William
Jackson, Charles C.
Kaminsky, Richard Alan
Katz, Harold Ambrose
Kipperman, Lawrence I.
Krucks, William Norman
Laner, Richard Warren
Leech, Michael John
Lefkow, Michael Francis
Lieb, Roslyn Corenzwit
Livingston, Bradford Lee
Lowinger, Alexander I
Lynch, James Daniel
Lynn, Richard C.
Lythcott, Stephen Xavier
Mansfield, Karen Lee
Meltzer, Bernard David
Mills, Andre Micheaux
Moorehead, Timothy Lucas
Motchan, Brent L.
Murray, David Eugene
Murray, Lorene Frances
Naylor, George LeRoy
Nelson, Mark Douglas
Nichols, Robert Hastings
Parham, James Robert
Proczko, Taras Roman
Provenzano, William Joseph
Pusch, Herbert Barringer
Radzilowsky, Michael
Reardon, Timothy Joseph
Redman, Clarence Owen
Rutkoff, Alan Stuart
Schur, Jerome
Schwab, Stephen Wayne
Schwartzman, Mark Lee
Serwer, Alan Michael
Seyfarth, Henry Edward
Shaw, Lee Charles
Smith, Arthur B(everly), Jr.
Sulkes, Carol Fay
Theobald, Edward Robert
Thies, David Charles
Torrey, N. Morrison
Trenda, Regis J(ohn)
Waintroob, Andrea Ruth
Wolf, Charles Benno

Indiana

Beckwith, Lewis Daniel
Clark, Eric Oden
Coz, Thomas Anthony
Craft, Alice May
Draper, Monette Elaine
Gikas, Rick Christopher
Highfield, Robert Edward
Levy, Joel C.
Lewis, Daniel Edwin
Maine, Michael Roland
McNeely, J. Lee
Murrell, Jack Oliver
Oldham, Steve Anthony
Peterson, Clyde L.
Rubright, Charles Russell
Scaletta, Phillip Jasper
Schmitt, John Francis
Scism, Daniel Reed
Stommel, R. Robert
Walker, Ross Paul
Zazas, George John

Iowa

Goldman, David Harris
Visser, Kevin James
Wilson, Robert Foster
Wolle, Charles Robert

Kansas

Bukaty, Steve A.J.
Cranford, Steven Leon
Howland, Gary Marvin
Marquardt, Christel Elisabeth
Parker, William Lawrence, Jr.
Sanborn, Richard John Jay
Wing, David Leslie

Kentucky

Boylan, Michael Lee
Brill, David Alan
Chambers, Dorothy J.
Cleary, Richard Simon
Fenton, Thomas Conner

Fitch, Howard Mercer
Leightty, David
Lile, Charles Alan
Lohoff, Randy Keith
Miller, Scott Mitchell
Perchik, Jerrold R.

Louisiana

Angelico, Dennis Michael
Boyd, Joseph Robert
Colbert, Kathryn Hendon
Friedman, Joel William
Gardner, Jerry Louis, Jr.
Garrett, David Isaiah, Jr.
Goldberg, Charles
Guidry, Gregory
Hearn, Sharon Sklamba
Hillyer, Haywood Hansell, III
Huffman, Gerald James, Jr.
Jones, Johnnie Anderson
Malone, Ernest Roland, Jr.
Mitchell, Robert Burdette
Molony, Michael Janssens, Jr.
Payne, Roy Steven
Plaeger, Frederick Joseph, II
Ratcliff, John Garrett

Maine

Payne, Clare Hudson
Priest, Charles Randall
Taintor, Frederick Giles
Watson, Thomas Riley

Maryland

Ayres, Jeffrey Peabody
Buchsbaum, Norman Robert
Carey, Jana Howard
Davison, Warren Malcolm
Dubé, Lawrence Edward, Jr.
Duer, Andrew Adgate
Fries, Jay Robert
Hare, Glenn Patrick
Kruchko, John Gregory
Levinson, Daniel Ronald
Masterson, Richard Arthur
Nystrom, Harold Charles
Papkin, Robert David
St. Rose, Edwina Losey
Spitzberg, Irving Joseph, Jr.
Strandberg, Rebecca Newman
White, Pamela Janice

Massachusetts

Adomeit, Peter Loring
Cook, Charles Addison
Eisenberg, Andrew Lewis
Felper, David Michael
Golder, Frederick Thomas
Krasnow, Willard
Lang, Scott Wesley
Loftin, Melinda Jayne
Menard, Arthur Patrick
Moschos, Demitrios Mina
Perry, Edward Needham
Segal, Robert Mandal
Sinrich, Diane Wingard
Straus, William Marc
Weiler, Paul Cronin
Westfall, David

Michigan

Adams, Michael Ross
Boal, Ellis
Bultje, Ronald Alan
Burns, Marshall Shelby, Jr.
Busch, Gary M(itchell)
Cohen, Norton Jacob
Dahm, Peter Franklin
Dobranski, Bernard
Dobry, Stanley Thomas
Drenth, Thomas Lee
Ellmann, William Marshall
Entenman, John Alfred
Fallon, William Hume
Freeberg, Edward Ronald
Geary, James H.
Golden, Joseph Aaron
Grate, Marshall Warren
Haisch, Anthony Albert
Hanes, James Henry
Harvey, Barbara
Heinen, Mark Lee
Henry, Forrest Alfred
Howlett, Robert Glasgow
Kara, Paul Mark
Kienbaum, Karen Smith
Kurtz, James P.
Ladd, Thomas A.
Ludolph, Robert Charles
Mamat, Frank Trustick
McGlory, Willie Edward
Mosher, Richard Underhill
Muraski, Anthony Augustus
Murg, Gary Earl
Murray, Gregory Vincent
Nielsen, William Robert
Nora, John Joseph
Page, Leonard Ronald
Parish, Tat
Petersen, O. Keith
Price, Russell Eugene
Raniszeski, Lawrence Frank
Rauss, Dennis Michael
Rossen, Jordan
St. Antoine, Theodore Joseph
Schneider, Karen Bush
Schultz, Stephen Otto
Sefcovic, Henry John
Smith, Edward Michael
Spence, Howard Tee Devon
Swift, Theodore Wells
Vocht, Michelle Elise
Walle, James Paul
White, James Alfred

Minnesota

Bleck, Michael John
Broeker, John Milton
Finch, Frederick Earl
Koskinen, David John
Latz, Robert
Oates, Kathleen Marie
Petersen, Jan Farel
Seykora, David Gerard
Sovereign, Kenneth Lester

Wegener, Richard James

Mississippi

Fuselier, Louis Alfred
Glover, William Hudson, Jr.
Nicholas, Samuel John, Jr.
Ott, Emile Cutrer

Missouri

Atwood, Hollye Stolz
Bioff, Allan Lewis
Cain, Kenneth Jefferson
Cipolla, Thomas Alphonse
Clark, Charles Edward
Clegg, Karen Kohler
Delaney, Michael Francis
Elbert, Charles Steiner
Elliott, Clifton Langsdale
Fritz, Tobias Bodwell
Goffstein, John Howard
Gordon, Michael David
Jolley, William A.
Kennedy, Walter Jeff, Jr.
Kuelthau, Paul Stauffer
Levin, Morris Jacob
Martucci, William Christopher
Mattern, Keith Edward
Mello, Susan H.
Reichman, Fred Marshall
See, Andrew Bruce
Shaffer, Herman Morris
Sowers, David Eric
Tockman, Gerald
Vering, John Albert
Welch, David William
Wellford, Robin Sonneland
Whipple, Clyde David
Willard, James Robert
Yates, David Floyd
Zobrist, Karl

Montana

Matovich, Carey E.

Nebraska

Buntain, David Robert
Burns, Steven Dwight
Harding, William Alan
Holdenried, John Richard
Jensen, Sam
Kratz, Paul David
Lauritsen, Thomas Christian
Lipp, Louis Ellis
Loudon, Timothy Dale
Miller, Roger James
O'Connor, Robert Edward, Jr.
Rossiter, Robert Francis, Jr.
Zalewski, James Conrad

Nevada

Kladney, David
Nelson, Jane Wandel

New Hampshire

Conboy, Carol Ann
Hall, Alan

New Jersey

Aisenstock, Barry Alan
Blumrosen, Alfred William
Blumrosen, Ruth Gerber
Bovaird, Brendan Peter
Coben, Carl Gerald
Cole, Larry Michael
Cooper, Richard Craig
Cornish, Jeannette Carter
Ellenport, Robert Saul
Falkin, Jeffrey Curtis
Finn, Jerry Martin
Gerard, Stephen Stanley
Greenbaum, William I.
Hurley, Lawrence Joseph
Maurer, Henry Stephen, Jr.
Obara, Patricia Evelyn
Portelli, Thomas Frank
Preiser, Godfrey Krause, Jr.
Reitman, Sidney
Saffer, Judith M.
Scagnelli, John Mark
Seham, Martin Charles
Sponzilli, Edward George
Suflas, Steven William
Taldone, Nicholas John
Weiner, Paul I.
Wolf, John Barton
Wolk, Stuart Rodney

New York

Abinanti, Thomas J., .
Agatstein, David Joseph
Alexander, Christine Ann
Ames, Marc L.
Ashe, Bernard Flemming
Autin, Diana Marie Therese Katherine
Bader, Albert Xavier, Jr.
Barsamian, J(ohn) Albert
Beckstrom, Charles G.
Benjamin, Jeffrey
Berg, Alan
Bienstock, Joshua Elliott
Braid, Frederick Donald
Bress, Joseph Michael
Brizel, Michael Alan
Brossman, Mark Edward
Brunetti, John Joseph
Burns, Richard Owen
Burstein, Neil Alan
Canoni, John David
Cape, Billie Jean
Carey, Joseph Patrick
Chernoff, Carl G.
Clifton, Henry, Jr.
Coakley, Charles
Collins, John Francis
Derwin, Jordan
Devine, Eugene Peter
Doren, Robert Alan
Drake, E. Thayer
England, William Thomas
Estreicher, Samuel
Ferguson, Tracy Heiman
Fernandez, Lillian
Fink, Rosalind Sue
Fischel, Shelley Duckstein

Fishberg, Gerard
Flamm, Leonard N(athan)
Futterman, Stanley Norman
Gale, Peter L.
Garcia, Maria Elias
Goetz, Maurice Harold
Greenspan, Richard Mathew
Hanft, Noah Jonathan
Harren, Kevin Hugh
Hathaway, Gerald Thomas
Henner, Peter William
Hilts, Earl T.
Hofrichter, Lawrence S.
Hoynes, Louis LeNoir, Jr.
Isaacs, Robert Charles
Jacobs, Roger Bruce
Jacobs, Sherry Raphael
Jacobson, Jerold Dennis
Jauvtis, Robert Lloyd
Kandel, William Lloyd
Katz, Charles R.
Katz, Michael Albert
Kostelny, Albert Joseph, Jr.
Krieg, Marc Shea
LaMancuso, John Lory
Lee, Christopher Peter
Leonard, Arthur Sherman
Levin, Roger Michael
Levine, Marilyn Markovich
Maglaras, Nicholas George
Mahar, Thomas Daniel, Jr.
Maidman, Stephen Paul
Margolin, Eric Mitchell
Mathers, Allen Stanley
Maurer, Ira Mark
Mc Kay, Robert Budge
Meath, Brian Patrick
Meyer, Sidney L.
Miller, Lee Edward
Millman, Bruce Russell
Minahan, Daniel Francis
Minuse, Catherine Jean
Moerdler, Charles Gerard
Mortensen, Philip Stephen
Moses, Mary Helen
Nolan, Terrance Joseph, Jr.
Novick, Mindy
O'Dwyer, Brian
Odza, Randall M.
Oppenheimer, Laurence Brian
Oppenheimer, Randolph Carl
Osterman, Melvin Howard, Jr.
Paul, James William
Pedowitz, Arnold Henry
Perlmutter, Jerome Alan
Pogrebin, Bertrand B.
Pohorelsky, Viktor Vaclav
Raff, David
Rains, Harry Hano
Reibstein, Richard Jay
Roberts, Allen B.
Rose, John T., II
Rothermel, Joan Ebert
Saltzman, Barry Neal
Salup, Stephen
Samansky, J. Leonard
Savitt, Susan Schenkel
Schwartz, Martin Weber
Schwarz, Carl Alfred, Jr.
Slough, John Edward
Soyster, Margaret Blair
Spelfogel, Evan J.
Steer, Richard Lane
Swirsky, Steven Mitchell
Taussig, Eric Alfred
Tocci, Dominick P.
Tuchman, Morris
Watanabe, Roy Noboru
Weinmann, Richard Adrian
Weir, John Keeley
Wiacek, Bruce Edward
Witkin, Eric Douglas
Wolin, Debra Ruth
Wood, Teri Wilford
Zelman, Andrew Ernest
Zimmerman, Sandra L.

North Carolina

Bradshaw, Penni Pearson
Cone, Lorynn Adderholdt
Foster, Charles Allen
Horowitz, Donald Leonard
Peirce, Ellen Rust
Reynolds, Mark Floyd, II
Sheahan, Robert Emmett
Valois, Robert Arthur
Van Hoy, Philip Marshall
Van Noppen, Donnell, III

North Dakota

Kautzmann, Dwight C(larence) H(arry)

Ohio

Allotta, Joseph John
Allport, William Wilkens
Ashmus, Keith Allen
Belkin, Jeffrey A.
Besser, Howard Russell
Blackburn, John D(avid)
Bloch, Marc Joel
Buehler, Thomas Lee
Burdge, Michael Joseph
Cade, Daniel Steven
DeLong, Deborah
Dennis, William Robert
DiLeone, Peter, Jr.
Duckett, Douglas Edward
Duvin, Robert Phillip
Elam, John William
Ensign, Gregory Moore
Fadel, William Isaac
Feheley, Lawrence Francis
Finn, Chester Evans
Garvey, Mary Anne
Gary, Robert Dale
Geer, Thomas Lee
George, Donald Elias
Gibson, Rankin MacDougal
Goldfarb, Bernard Sanford
Haas, Douglas Eric
Hays, Robert D.
Holmes, Robert Allen
Holzer, Richard Jean
Hoyt, Marcia Swigart
Jacobs, Gregory Alexander
Kadela, David Anthony

Kafantaris, George Nicholas
Katz, Alfred B.
Koenig, Kenneth John
Konrad, Bruce Joseph
Krass, Marc Stern
Kurek, James David
Leb, Arthur S.
Levering, Robert Bruce
Lewis, John Bruce
Mason, Ronald Lee
Maurer, John William
Maxwell, Robert Wallace, II
McMenamin, Michael Terrence
Millisor, Kenneth Ray
Minamyer, William Eric
Morelli, Arnold
Morgan, Dennis Richard
O'Reilly, James Thomas
Pallam, John James
Palmer, Mark Joseph
Phalen, Thomas Francis, Jr.
Plumly, Daniel Harp
Rooney, George Willard
Rosenfeld, Robert Thomas
Rossi, William Matthew
Ruf, H(arold) William, Jr.
Seeley, Glenn J.
Shaw, Nancy Ann
Smoot, Thurlow Ted
Somrak, David Joseph
Sprang, Kenneth Allyn
Stanton, Elizabeth McCool
Steinmanis, Karl Sven
Sternberg, David J.
Strimbu, Victor, Jr.
Strozdas, Jerome Mark
Swigert, James Mack
Tell, A. Charles
Tipping, Harry Anthony
Tobias, Paul Henry
Wang, Charleston Cheng-Kung
Westbrook, Gayle Robinson

Oklahoma

Angel, Steven Michael
Berry, Dean Clement
Cates, Ronald Dean
Court, Leonard
Draughon, Scott Wilson
Lambird, Mona Salyer
Lawter, J. Mike
Matthies, Mary Constance T.
Petrikin, James Ronald
Ungerman, Maynard I.
Williams, Bradford J., Jr.

Oregon

Imperati, Samuel J(ohn)
Launer, Jeannette Maureen
Lindsay, Dennis John
Mechanic, Gene Barry
Overgaard, Mary Ann
Potter, William R.
Tedesco, Michael J.

Pennsylvania

Abrams, Nancy
Baccini, Laurance Ellis
Bertsch, Gene Clair
Brown, James Benton
Brown, William Hill, III
Candris, Laura A.
Connors, Eugene Kenneth
Creo, Robert Angelo
Decker, Kurt Hans
Dichter, Mark S.
Dissen, Richard William
Dougherty, Brian James
Duff, James Clair
Ehrenwerth, Charlene Reidbord
Flannery, Harry Audley
Freeman, Antoinette Rosefeldt
Fritton, Karl Andrew
Gilbert, Bruce Rits
Girard-DiCarlo, David Franklin
Goldman, Gary Craig
Goldstein, Neal
Hill, John Howard
Hough, Thomas Henry Michael
Janos, Joseph John, III
Kane, Jonathan A.
King, Donita McRae
Kotler, Helen Rose
Krampf, John Edward
Krzemien, Louis John
Leddy, John Henry
Lipsitz, Robert Joel
McDowell, Michael David
McFadden, Joseph R., Jr.
Mesirov, Leon I.
Middleton, Stephanie Adele
Mills, Kathleen Anne Merry
Milone, Francis Michael
Murtagh, John Walter, Jr.
Olson, Stephen M(ichael)
O'Reilly, Timothy Patrick
Orkin, Neal
Orsatti, Ernest Benjamin
Pasek, Jeffrey Ivan
Reagan, Harry E., III
Ross, James Andrew
Saltman, Stuart Ivan
Sampath, Elizabeth Margaret Deborah
Satinsky, Barnett
Scheinholtz, Leonard Louis
Schmidt, Gordon Williams
Schmidt, Lynne Dianne
Smith, John Francis, III
Steiner, Julius Michael
Stevens, Paul Lawrence
Summers, Clyde Wilson
Tarlow, Marc Gary
Teklits, Joseph Anthony
Thomas, Richard Irwin
Thompson, Beverly Kay
Tucker, Jeffrey Thornt
Vadnais, Alfred William
Voluck, Philip Ritter
Walters, Bette Jean
Whiteside, William Anthony, Jr.
Williams, Stuart Alan

Rhode Island

Najarian, Malcolm Askanaz
Parks, Albert Lauriston
Pendergast, John Joseph, III

Saha, Sunil Kumar
Turner, Terrance Neil

South Carolina

Ballard, Wade Edward
Erwin, Sue Carlanne
Gergel, Richard Mark
Haynsworth, Knox Livingston, Jr.
Mitchell, Theo Walker
Rodgers, Sharon Lynette
Schweitzer, Eric Campbell
Smoak, Lewis Tyson
Suggs, Fred Wilson, Jr.
Thompson, Robert Thomas
Wyche, Madison Baker, III

Tennessee

Blair, Allen Stuart
Boston, Robert Earl
Brakebusch, Margaret Guill
Bridgesmith, Larry W.
Bush, Wendell Earl
Covington, Robert Newman
Faulk, Michael Anthony
Fine, Thomas Fleming
Fleissner, Phillip Anton
Grubb, Kitty Goldsmith
Hardin, Patrick Henry
Jaqua, David Palmer
Kramer, Steven Emert
Leitner, Gregory Marc
McKenney, Edward Jerome, Jr.
Parker, Richard Ralph
Phillips, John Bomar
Pickering, William Henry
Schlechty, John L.
Speros, Michael Carl
Summers, Gerald (Jerry) Howard
Thomas, Robert Paige
Weatherspoon, Floyd Douglas

Texas

Abney, Joe L.
Allison, John Robert
Bader, Gregory Vincent
Bambace, Robert Shelly
Benckenstein, John Henry
Benton, John Bunyan
Boles, David LaVelle
Brewer, Lewis Gordon
Brown, Stephen Smiley
Brown, William Alley
Bruckner, William H.
Burch, Voris Reagan
Bux, William John
Carroll, James Vincent, III
Coane, Bruce A.
Eubank, Christina
Evans, James A.
Finlayson, Dawn Bruner
Foster, Ben Frank, Jr.
Fryburger, Lawrence Bruce
Gonsoulin, Dewey Jude
Goodstein, Barnett Maurice
Greig, Brian Strother
Hall, William Wendell
Harper, Alfred John, II
Hollin, Shelby W.
Holt, Robert Blaine
Immler, Michael Earl
Johnson, Karen Lee
Jones, David Stanley
Jordan, W. Carl
Loeffler, James Joseph
McHugh, Margaret Colleen
McNamara, Lawrence John
Miller, Thomas Raymond
Moynihan, John Bignell
Noack, Charles Elroy
Ory, Charles Nathan
Putman, (James) Michael
Riggs, Arthur Jordy
Roberts, Bonita Koehler
Schorr, Kenneth L.
Schwartz, Leonard Jay
Seay, George Edward
Sutphen, Robert Louis
Swan, Michael Robert
Tabak, Morris
Taylor, Robert Love
Thompson, T. Jay
Valanty, Burton John
Wagner, Leslie
Wagner, Michael Duane
Wheeler, Susan Lynn
Wheelock, Eugene Thomas
Williams, Charles Michael
Williams, Lon Rayburn, Jr.
Wolf, Michael Jay
Wray, Thomas Jefferson

Utah

Burgon, Barre Glade
Butler, Geoffrey John Butler
Lowe, Kathlene Winn

Virginia

Aronin, Louis
Chappell, Milton Leroy
Etherington, William Fisher
Flannagan, Francis Wills
Hancock, George Louis, Jr.
Hogshire, Edward Leigh
Kacoyanis, Dennis Charles
Lanphear, Martha Jean
Levit, Jay J(oseph)
McElligott, James Patrick, Jr.
Miller, Charles Joseph
O'Connor, Raymond Vincent, Jr.
Serumgard, John R.
Smith, Baker Armstrong
Smith, S(ydney) Strother, III
Taubman, Glenn Matthew
Thomson, Paul Rice, Jr.
Tillar, Darrel Long
Wentink, Michael James
Wilson, Douglas Downes
Woodley, John Paul, Jr.

Washington

Condon, David Bruce
Eadie, Richard Douglas
Harmon, E(verett) Glenn
Heid, Daniel Brian
Hollingsworth, Jeffrey Alan

Lemly, Thomas Adger
Lurie, Donna Ellen
Marshall, James Markham
Matthews, Stephen Ross
McMahon, Michael Joseph
Ogden, Warren Cox
Ransom, Clark Taylor
Rosen, Jon Howard
Rummage, Stephen Michael
Sessions, G. P.
Silvernale, Lawrence Duggan
Squires, William Randolph, III
Waldman, Bart
Wilkinson, Jane Rae
Younglove, Edward Earl, III

West Virginia

Crandall, Grant Fotheringham
Dissen, James Hardiman
Frankovitch, Carl Nicholas
Haley, Charles Frederick
Hamrick, Karen Susan
Haviland, James Morrison
Schaub, Clarence Robert
Williams, Jacques Ralph André

Wisconsin

Bauman, Susan Joan Mayer
Bush, Edwin Franklin, Jr.
Dalton, LeRoy LaVerne
Dau-Schmidt, Kenneth Glenn
Davis, Walter Stewart
Dietrich, Dean Richard
Dietz, Richard Joseph
Du Rocher, James Howard
Fairbanks, Roberta R(onya)
FitzSimmons, Richard M.
Fribance, Caroline Eleanor
Graylow, Richard Vernon
Hesslink, Robert Melvin, Jr.
Hlavin, Joseph Raymond, Jr.
Jones, James Edward, Jr.
Kelly, Walter Francis
Krukowski, Thomas Paul
Kwiatkowski, Thomas Eugene
Muchin, Arden Archie
Mukamal, Stuart Sassoon
Patzke, John Charles
Pettit, Roger Lee
Previant, David
Rice, Zelotes Sylvester
Rogers, James Thomas
Stevens, Charles Paul
Vliet, Daniel George
Wilcox, Jean Evelyn

Wyoming

Miller, Linda Suzanne

TERRITORIES OF THE UNITED STATES

Guam

O'Connor, Karl William

BELGIUM

Tattersall, William James

CANADA

Ontario

Roberts, Richard Jack

ENGLAND

Jackman, Robert L.

ADDRESS UNPUBLISHED

Alexander, James Patrick
Asher, Lester
Atwood, Ronald Wayne
Blevins, Jeffrey Alexander
Carrol, Robert Kelton
Crawford, Muriel Laura
Donlon, William James
Feingold, Victor
Frank, James Stuart
Gallagher, Michael Gerald
Greenberg, Susan Ann
Helms, David Alonzo
Hughes, Linda Renate
Leleiko, Steven Henry
Marx, Gary Samuel
McFarland, Robert Edwin
Milbrath, Dennis Henry
Mollinger, Judith Ellen
Neese, Sandra Anne
Newman, Alan Harvey
Richman, Stephen Charles
Rodenburg, Clifton Glenn
Sullivan, James Washburn
Torkildson, Raymond Maynard
White, Richard Clarence

LANDLORD-TENANT. *See also* Commercial.

UNITED STATES

Alabama

Chastain, David Jesse
Knight, Martha Kathryn
Olshan, Gary Steven
Ray, Thomas Morgan

Alaska

Bond, Marc Douglas

Arizona

Blum, Paul J.
Hoog, Patrick Edward
Slavin, Francis John, Jr.
Wood, Nicholas Joseph
Zukowski, Michael Chester

California

Daniels, James Walter
Gulartie, Louise Baur
Hoffman, Kris
Hotchkiss, Nancy
Jedeikin, Joseph
Kramer, Kenneth Scott
McCollum, Susan Hill
Melton, Barry
Munn, Ford Dent
Murphy, Stephen Michael
Porter, Verna Louise
Rodgers, Thomas Paul
Rosenthal, Steven S.
Schieffer, Joseph H.
Sherrell, John Bradford
Sloan, Sheldon Harold
Tsenin, Ksenia
Walker, Jordan Clyde
Warne, William Raymond
Willsey, F. Patterson

Colorado

Donlon, William James, Jr.
Fried, Joseph
Hillestad, Charles Andrew
Peirce, Frederick Fairbanks
Smith, Michael Alan

Connecticut

Boesen, John Michael
Mark, Henry Allen
Rosenblatt, Edward Milton

Delaware

Kristol, Daniel Marvin

District of Columbia

Aluise, Timothy John
Blumenthal, Carol
Brand, Michael Edward
Hyde, Patrick Alan
Loewinger, Kenneth Jeffery

Florida

Allen, Richard Lewis
Feola, Eugene David
Layman, David Michael
Mandell, Craig Jack
Miller, Robert Charles
Poller, Jeri
Wiseheart, Malcolm Boyd, Jr.

Georgia

Burt, Barry Wakefield
Hishon, Elizabeth Anderson

Hawaii

Lockwood, John Allen
Wong, Alfred Mun Kong

Illinois

Bernstein, Charles Bernard
Boblick, Shelby Susan
Bone, Maurice Edgar
Feinstein, Fred Ira
Kawitt, Alan
Marovitz, James Lee
Martin, Wayne Mallott
Reichelderfer, Frank A.
Ritchie, Albert
Vree, Roger Allen
Winter, Frank Louis

Indiana

Abrams, Jeffrey Alan
Dorocke, Lawrence Francis
Hackman, Marvin Lawrence
Speicher, John Allan
Stein, Eleanor Bankoff

Louisiana

Mmahat, John Anthony
Ross, Bobbie Jean
Sher, Leopold Zangwill

Maryland

Loewy, Steven A.
Wilson, Christian Burhenn

Massachusetts

Carroll, John Thomas
Cohen, Donna Eden
Gould, Kenneth B.
Hewitt, Emily Clark
Lerman, Herbert S.
Ley, Andrew James
Matthews, James Bernard
Sawyer, Robert Kendal, Jr.
Snyder, Richard Joseph
Tierney, Albert Gerard, III
Urban, Lee Donald
Whalen, James Michael

Michigan

Brennan, Thomas Emmett, Jr.
Deems, Nyal David
Knecht, Timothy Harry
Lambert, Robert Bradley
Ortega, Cynthia Poti

Minnesota

Hamel, Mark Edwin
Lantz, William Charles
Mayerle, Thomas Michael

Missouri

Byers, Ronald Gregory
Frantze, David W.
Long, Michael Evans

Montana

Seiffert, Terry L.

New Jersey

Berkley, Peter Lee
Klinghoffer, Steven Harold
Meiser, Kenneth Edward

New York

Adler, Edward Andrew Koeppel
Baum, Peter Alan
Brandveen, Antonio Isadore
DiSciullo, Alan Michael
Fenster, Marvin
Fishman, James Bart
Genrich, Willard Adolph
Goldstein, Kenneth B.
Hackett, Kevin R.
Katz, Gary M.
Korman, Iris J.
Landau, Sybil Harriet
Levine, Melvin Charles
Malone, Georgia Joan
Michaelson, Melvin
Modell, Michael Steven
Morris, Eugene Jerome
Paroff, Philip Steven
Petito, Bruce Anthony
Rahm, David Alan
Rosenberg, Gary Marc
Sanseverino, Raymond Anthony
Schnall, Flora
Shollenberger, Elizabeth Ann
Sieratzki, Steven Solomon
Simon, Michael Scott
Smith, Vincent Milton
Somer, Stanley Jerome
Towns, Emanuel Alexander
Treiman, David Michael
Uram, Gerald Robert
Vernon, Darryl Mitchell
Weisman, Barbara
York, Louis B.
Young, Sidney David

North Carolina

Tate, David Kirk
Tyson, John Marsh

Ohio

Ballard, Mary Beth
Barz, Patricia
Galip, Ronald George
Gleisser, Marcus David
Joseph, John James
Kramer, Edward George
McAndrews, James Patrick
Muttalib, Kalam

Oklahoma

McMillian, Roger Lee

Oregon

Grant, Eugene L.

Pennsylvania

Doerr, John Maxwell
Goldman, Gary Craig
Gounley, Dennis Joseph
Kiever, Paul Kenneth
Lushis, John Francis, Jr.
Ruder, Jay Stanley
Taulane, John Baptist, Jr.
Zimmerman, D(onald) Patrick

Rhode Island

Saha, Sunil Kumar

South Carolina

Simpson, David Eugene

Tennessee

Kerr, Thomas Draper, Jr.
Okrasinski, Mary Ann
Trent, J(ohn) Thomas, Jr.

Texas

Bennett, Kevin Dane
Clark, David Keith
Davis, Martha Algenita Scott
DeBusk, Edith M.
Fisher, J(ohn) Robert
Fishman, Edward Marc
Halpin, Steven Edward
Liles, John H(enry), Jr.
Lippman, Kyle David
Miller, Stewart Ransom
Riley, Peter James
Roberts, Harry Morris, Jr.
Sagehorn, Thomas John
Shouse, August Edward
Smith, Frank Forsythe, Jr.
Weiner, Marcia Myra

Utah

Frei, Michael Clark

Virginia

Ambler, Thomas Wilson
Connelly, Sharon Rudolph
Settlage, Steven Paul

Wisconsin

Jennings, David Vincent, Jr.
Rainey, Charles James
Raushenbush, Walter Brandeis

ENGLAND

Baker, Paul Vivian

ADDRESS UNPUBLISHED

Assael, Michael
Bentley, Anthony Miles
Breen, James Patrick, Jr.
Ivory, Cecil Augustus
Rivera, Oscar R.
Shareef, Michael T.

LEGAL PHILOSOPHY. *See* Jurisprudence.

LEGISLATIVE

UNITED STATES

Alabama

Davis, Penelope Ann
Lewis, Christine Whitesell
Stephens, Ferris W.

Alaska

Gorsuch, Norman Clifford
Greenstein, Marla Nan
McGee, Jack Brian

Arizona

George, Maureen Rose
Lewis, Orme
Verkamp, John
Wolf, G. Van Velsor, Jr.

Arkansas

Malone, David Roy
Stodola, Mark Allen

California

Andrew, John Henry
Bagley, William Thompson
Bohrer, Robert A.
Cobey, James Alexander
Feeney, Andrea Charlton
Hallisey, Jeremiah Francis
Hanzlik, Rayburn DeMara
Holmes, Dallas Scott
Hunji, Prem Litta
Jensen, Dennis Lowell
Joyce, James Donald
Kinzler, William Charles
Manley, Michael Alexander
McCallum, Barbara Eiland
McDonough, Patrick Joseph
Memel, Sherwin Leonard
Mispagel, Mark Francis
Priest, Maurice Abner, Jr.
Quadri, Fazle Rab
Rowland, Gilford Glenn
Schnapp, Roger Herbert
Sun, Cossette Tsung-hung Wu
Switzer, Robert Joseph
Taft, Perry Hazard
Tallent, Stephen Edison
Tingle, James O'Malley

Colorado

Adkins, Marilyn Biggs
Amaral, Mary Ellen
Brewer, Marion Alyce
Davis, Wanda Rose
Eberhardt, Robert Schuler, Jr.
Loewi, Andrew William
McLain, William Allen
Pulley, Lewis Carl
Smethills, Harold Reginald

Connecticut

Densen-Gerber, Judianne
McConnell, David Kelso
Sorokin, Ethel Silver

Delaware

Boggs, James Caleb
Campbell, William Gant
Hudson, George Naylor
Mankin, Hart Tiller
Marlin, Jeffrey Stuart
Moran, Joseph Milbert
Reichert, Robert Joseph
Sheridan, John Robert

District of Columbia

Aluise, Timothy John
Alvarado, Ricardo Raphael
Anderson, Scott Gale
Apperson, Bernard James
Babbitt, Edward Joseph
Bachrach, Eve Elizabeth
Baker, James Jay
Baran, Jan Witold
Barnes, Mark James
Becker, Fred Reinhardt, Jr.
Bergerbest, Nathan Steven
Bergman, Carol Amy
Bernhard, Berl
Besozzi, Paul Charles
Bonvillian, William Boone
Bowen, Brooks Jefferson
Boyce, Katharine Randolph
Breitenberg, John Francis
Brinkmann, Robert Joseph
Brodhead, William McNulty
Brody, David A.
Brooten, Kenneth Edward, Jr.
Buechner, Jack W.
Butner, Blain Byerly
Campbell, W(illiam) Douglas
Carey, Sarah Collins
Caron, Wilfred Rene
Chabot, Elliot Charles
Chabot, Philip Louis, Jr.
Chip, William Waddington
Columbus, R. Timothy
Condrell, William Kenneth
Coursen, Christopher Dennison
Craft, Winfred Owens, Jr.
Cutler, John Arthur
Dalrymple, Donald Wylie
Daniel, Royal, III
Daugherty, Michael Dennis
Davis, Smith Wormley
Davis, Timothy Scott
Delaney, Edward Norman
De Simone, Daniel V.
Dickson, Peter Dean
Dill, John Christopher
Dinan, Donald Robert
Downey, Richard Morgan
Dozier, Daniel Preston
Dyer, Michael Joseph
Edwards, Charles Henry, III
Elisburg, Donald Earl
Ell, Douglas William
Engman, Patricia Hanahan
Evans, Donald Charles, Jr.
Finch, John Marshall
FitzSimon, Jean Kathleen
Fleming, Mack Gerald
French, E. LaVon
Gallagher, Walter Edward
Gardiner, Richard Ernest
Garrett, Henry Lawrence, III
Gaskin, Lillian Bernice
Gellhorn, Ernest Albert Eugene
Gerson, Ralph Joseph
Geske, Alvin Jay
Glosser, Jeffrey Mark
Goans, Judy Winegar
Hamilton, James
Hanford, Timothy Lloyd
Herbolsheimer, Robert Tilton
Heron, Julian Briscoe, Jr.
Hill, Robert Charles
Hobson, James Richmond
Hoecker, James John
Howard, Glen Scott
Huberman, Richard Lee
Humphries, Derrick Anthony
Ifshin, David Michael
Ingersoll, William Boley
Jaskiewicz, Leonard Albert
Jolly, Thomas R.
Jones, Erika Ziebarth
Jones, Theodore Lawrence
Kaplan, Sheldon Zachary
Kaswell, Stuart Joel
Katzmann, Robert Allen
Kautter, David John
Kay, Kenneth Robert
Kelly, William Charles, Jr.
Kirby, Peter Mangan
Knab, Karen Markle
Lacovara, Philip Allen
Lane, Bruce Stuart
Laporte, Gerald Joseph Sylvestre
Lassman, Malcolm
Leva, Marx
Levinson, Peter Joseph
Littlefield, Roy Everett, III
Litvin, David Anthony
Lobel, Martin
Lockhart, Robert Earl
Lopatin, Alan G.
Lotkin, Ralph Louis
Lutzker, Arnold Paul
Mallory, Charles King, III
Maloof, Farahe Paul
Martin, Keith
Marvin, Charles Raymond
McCann, Joseph Leo
McNeal, John Edward
Mendelsohn, Martin
Merrigan, William Joseph
Micek, Terrance Dean
Moler, Elizabeth Anne
Muckenfuss, Cantwell Faulkner, III
Nateman, Gary M.
Nealer, Kevin Glenn
Neidich, George Arthur
Nelson, Stephen Dale
Newman, William Bernard, Jr.
Novak, Nina
Oliver, Robert Spencer
Oman, Ralph
Palmer, Robert Alan
Panaro, Gerard Paul
Pate, Michael Lynn
Payne, Nell
Peck, Jeffrey Jay
Pehrson, Gordon Oscar, Jr.
Platt, Leslie A.
Preston, Colleen Ann
Pruitt, Jana Lee
Rainbolt, John Vernon, II
Raines, Lisa Joy
Renfro, William Leonard
Rexinger, Allan Robert
Richardson, Greg Drexel
Ris, William Krakow, Jr.
Rosenfield, Harry Nathan
Rouvelas, Emanuel Larry
Rowe, James Henry, III
Rubenstein, Herbert R.
Ruggeri, Robert Edward
Ruud, Millard Harrington
Sackler, Arthur Brian
Sagett, Jan Jeffrey
Schiffbauer, William G.
Schmidt, Paul Wickham
Schmidt, Richard Marten, Jr.
Schutzer, George Jeffrey
Shapiro, Benjamin Louis
Shapiro, Gary Joel
Sharp, Stephen Alan
Siegel, Gerald William
Simon, Samuel Alan
Spiegel, Robert Alan
Sterrett, Malcolm McCurdy Burdett
Stuntz, Linda Gillespie
Teague, Randal Cornell, Sr.
Tendler, Paul Marc
Thompson, Richard Leon
Tongour, Michael Alexander
Turner, Robert Foster
Ufholz, Philip John
Van Etten, Laura
Vanlier, Charlene
Vary, George Folk
Vaughn, Robert Gene
Verville, Richard Emery
Vlcek, Jan Benes
Wallace, Arch Lee
Wallace, Wilton Lawrence
Waz, Joseph Walter, Jr.
Weisberg, Stuart Elliot
Weisgall, Jonathan Michael
Wewer, William
Williams, Yvonne LaVerne
Winkler, Andrea Joanne
Wittig, Raymond Shaffer
Wolff, Alan William
Yuspeh, Alan Ralph
Zagami, Anthony James

Florida

Glickman, Ronnie Carl
Hart, Deborah Diane

Hochman, Jeffrey J.
Kerns, David Vincent
Kibler, Rhoda Smith
Kollin, Gary
Roess, Martin John
Rutledge, Gary Ray
Strickland, Delphene Coverston

Georgia

Dunn, Wesley Brankley
Huszagh, Fredrick Wickett
Menkin, Lita Sue

Hawaii

Chang, Donald Mark
Foley, Daniel Robert
Suzuki, Norman Hitoshi
Takayama, Ken Hideshi

Idaho

Fields, James Ralph
Stoker, Robin Jeffrey

Illinois

Artman, Eric Alan
Baker, Bruce Jay
Barr, John Robert
Bernstein, John Thomas
Berry, Richard Morgan
Blume, Paul Chiappe
Bragg, Michael Ellis
Cherry, Barbara Ann
Crane, Charlotte
Dodegge, Thomas Roland
Dorf, Michael Charles
Fortier, Robert Frederic
Gekas, Constantine John
Gieseke, Corinne Joyce
Goodrich, John Bernard
Guthman, Jack
Hollis, Everett Loftus
Lynn, Richard C.
Manikas, Peter Michael
Mazewski, Aloysius Alex
Miller, John Leed
Morse, Saul Julian
Nutter, Franklin Winston
Salomon, Richard Adley
Sanders, Michael Leo
Thompson, William Scott
Walner, Robert Joel
Weber, Alban

Indiana

Allen, David James
Miller, David Anthony

Iowa

Brown, Paul Edmondson
Byers, Donald Charles
Lambert, George Robert
Luchtel, Keith Edward
Nowadzky, Roger Alan

Kansas

Bell, Thomas Lee
McCullough, George Elwood
O'Neal, Michael Ralph
Schanck, Peter Carr
Schultz, Richard Allen
Snowbarger, Vincent Keith
Solbach, John Martin, III

Kentucky

Apperson, Jeffrey Allen
Miller, Herbert Allan, Jr.

Louisiana

Adams, Ellis Paul, Jr.
Alarcon, Terry Quentin
Cutshaw, James Michael
Gandy, Kim Allison
Gravel, Camille Francis, Jr.
Marcello, David Anthony

Maine

Broder, James Nelson
Hughes, David Emery
Perkins, Donald W.
Vickerson, William Leo

Maryland

Brill, Lawrence Joel
Doub, William Offutt
Roth, Robert Lloyd
Schwartz, Joseph Anthony, III
Sheble, Walter Franklin
Spitzberg, Irving Joseph, Jr.

Massachusetts

Bellotti, Francis Xavier
Coltun, Harry
Kanin, Dennis Roy
Mastrangelo, Richard Edward
Sears, John Winthrop
Sinrich, Diane Wingard

Michigan

Barton, Judith Marie
Bruin, Linda Lou
Garcia, Joseph Antonio
Holman, Charles F(redrick), III
Lobenherz, William Ernest
Marks, Andrew James
Nielsen, William Robert
Pierce, William James
Stasson, Shelley Andrea

Minnesota

Deans, Thomas Seymour
Fisher, Michael Bruce
Grindal, Harald Theodore
Halverson, Steven Thomas
Jensen, Patricia Ann
Knapp, John Anthony
Koch, Scott James
Latz, Robert
Martin, Mary Kay
Miranda, Thom Bernard
O'Neill, Joseph Thomas

Mississippi

Barber, Frank David
Crook, Robert Lacey
Golden, Wilson
Wilson, Leonard Henry (L.H.)

Missouri

Banton, Stephen Chandler
Bates, William Hubert (Bert)
Christiansen, Steven Allan
Curtis, Thomas Bradford
Gallop, Donald Philip
Hart, Michael David
Krukiel, Charles Edward
McNeill, Paul Spurgeon, Jr.
Schnuck, Terry Edward

Montana

Spaeth, Gary Lewis
Towe, Thomas Edward

Nebraska

Adams, Joseph
Buntain, David Robert
Crosby, Robert Berkey
Davlin, Michael Charles
Frazier, Lawrence Alan
Fuller, Diana Clare
Mueller, William Jeffrey

Nevada

Faiss, Robert Dean

New Hampshire

Lagos, George Peter

New Jersey

Balikov, Henry R.
Blumrosen, Alfred William
D'Amico, John, Jr.
Holt, Jason
Marotta, James Steven
Maurer, Henry Stephen, Jr.
Moczula, Boris
Monaco, Mario Anthony
Pane, Michael Anthony, IV
Protigal, Stanley Nathan
Schuster, Steven Vincent
Sterns, Joel H.
Sullivan, Robert Joseph
Susswein, Ronald
Zarnowski, James David

New Mexico

Carpenter, Richard Norris
Cox, Lewis Calvin

New York

Albans, Gabrielle Victoria
Alexander, Christine Ann
Bearak, Corey B(ecker)
Boone, William Daniel
Bress, Joseph Michael
Burke, Carol Elizabeth
Burke, Thomas Edmund
Certilman, Morton Lawrence
Curtiss, Willis David
Derwin, Jordan
Evans, George Walton, Jr.
Fink, Janet Rose
Fioramonti, Frank Robert
Foley, Patrick Joseph
Ganz, David L.
Geltzer, Robert Lawrence
Givens, Richard Ayres
Grad, Frank Paul
Green, Jeffrey Steven
Holm, Melvin Edward
Hudson, Paul Stephen
Josephson, William Howard
Joye, E. Michael
Kernochan, John Marshall
Lewis, David L.
Lundy, Daniel Francis
McGeady, Paul Joseph
Miller, Sam Scott
Rogers, Thomas Sydney
Sack, Edward J.
Schiffman, Steven Mitchell
Schoeneck, Charles A., Jr.
Seader, Paul Alan
Steinhaus, Richard Zeke
Suraci, Joseph Anthony
Tannenbaum, Bernard
Tocci, Dominick P.
Trotta, Frank Paul
Underberg, Neil
Wasserman, Edward Henry
Weinrich, Johnathan Edward
Weprin, Barry Alan
Yagerman, Howard W.
Zwack, Henry Francis

North Carolina

Carmichael, Carson, III
Cohen, Gerry Farmer
Cramer, Mark Clifton
Dunn, Jackson Thomas, Jr.
Hirsch, Alan Seth
Jones, Henry W., Jr.
Vaughan, Donald Ray
Wilson, Samuel Alexander, III
Yow, Cicero Preston

North Dakota

Hand, James S.
Vickrey, Barry Roland

Ohio

Carpenter, James Craig
Casper, Paul William, Jr.
Damiani, Louis Carmen
Edwards, John White
Fazio, John Cesare
James, Larry Holliday
Kessler, Alan
Lehman, Robert Frank
Long, Thomas Leslie
Masek, Raymond John
McLaren, Richard Wellington, Jr.
Montgomery, Thomas Charles
Morgan, Dennis Richard
Smith, Edward (Ted) Lewis, Jr.

Oklahoma

Brown, Michael DeWayne
Olson, Rebecca J. McGee

Oregon

Lombard, Benjamin (Kip), Jr.
Williamson, Charles Ready

Pennsylvania

Beren, Daniel Edward
Henry, Ronald George
Lotman, Arline Jolles
Murren, Philip Joseph
Oplinger, Jon Carl
Swaim, John Joseph
Wagner, Thomas Joseph
Zeiter, William Emmet
Zimmer, Bruce Irwin

South Carolina

Carter, Samuel Hebard
Chapman, Charles Alan
McLawhorn, Richard Edward
Medlock, Thomas Travis
Rouse, LeGrand A., II
Spencer, Mary Elizabeth

Tennessee

Akers, Charles David
Bennett, Andy Dwane
Bruce, William Roland
Davis, Jimmy Kyle
Gorrell, Frank Cheatham
Harrington, Penny Nancy
Lanier, James Olanda
Ramsaur, Allan Fields

Texas

Armstrong, John Douglas
Barlow, W. P., Jr.
Bridges, Russell Brian
Calhoun, Frank Wayne
Forbes, Thomas Allen
Geiger, Richard Stuart
Greanias, George Constantine
Hargis, James Richard
Hathcox, VaLinda
Hilder, Philip Harlan
Judice, C(harles) Raymond
McColloch, Murray Michael
Randolph, Robert Raymond
Rhem, John Fitzhugh, Jr.
Ricciardelli, Thomas Patrick
Roberts, Ted Blake
Schwartz, Aaron Robert
Steimel, Walter Earl, Jr.
Temple, Larry Eugene
Thompson, Jay Alan
White, Mark Wells, Jr.

Utah

Allred, Steven Wesley
McConkie, Oscar Walter
Riggs, Robin L.

Virginia

Bussewitz, Roy Jon
Campbell, Thomas Douglas
Collins, Philip Reilly
Donovan, William Jeremiah
English, William deShay
Feldman, Richard Jay
Gawalt, Gerard W(ilfred)
Jackson, William Paul, Jr.
James, Richard Robert
LaGow, John Christopher
Laughlin, James Harold, Jr.
Light, Alfred Robert
McFarlane, Walter Alexander
Morrison, James Lawrence
Morrison, Johnny Edward
Payne, J(oe) Stanley
Peters, David Frankman
Quillen, Ford Carter
Rasmus, John Charles
Steinhilber, August William
Stephens, William Theodore
Stone, Steven David
Talarek, Walter Glenn
Talbott, Frank, III
Thomas, William Griffith

Washington

Brooks, Julie Anne
McGavick, Donald Hugh
Pelandini, William Albert
Phillips, Catherine
Welsh, John Beresford, Jr.

Wisconsin

Dau-Schmidt, Kenneth Glenn
Drengler, William Allan John
Vaughan, Michael Richard
Whitcomb, Michael Arthur Isaac

TERRITORIES OF THE UNITED STATES

Guam

Troutman, Charles Henry, III

BELGIUM

Tattersall, William James

ADDRESS UNPUBLISHED

Fainter, John Wells, Jr.
Fossum, Donna L.
Gusman, Robert Carl
Ketcham, Robert Conrad
Lichter-Heath, Laurie Jean
Ryan, William J.
Saxon, John David
Williams, Frank J.

LIBEL

UNITED STATES

Alabama

Barnard, Hollinger Farmer

Arizona

Bodney, David Jeremy
Chauncey, Tom Webster, II

California

Battaglia, Philip Maher
Brosnahan, James Jerome
Chu, Morgan
Epstein, Judith Ann
Hinueber, Mark Arthur
Jedeikin, Joseph
Klein, Jeffrey S.
Newell, Thomas Peter
Reuben, Timothy D.
Tiffany, Joseph Raymond, II
van de Bunt, Dirk Wouter
Vanderet, Robert Charles
Zimmerman, Bernard

Colorado

Cooper, Paul Douglas
Green, Carol H.

Connecticut

Elliot, Ralph Gregory
Neigher, Alan

Delaware

Green, James Samuel

District of Columbia

Gorelick, Jamie Shona
Horne, Michael Stewart
Isbell, David Bradford
Kieve, Loren
Kirtley, Jane Elizabeth
Melamed, Carol Drescher
Onek, Joseph Nathan
Pickering, John Harold
Schmidt, Richard Marten, Jr.
Szybala, Renee Leslie
Wallach, Evan Jonathan

Florida

Abrell, Joseph Kindred
Barnett, Richard Allen
Campbell, Charles Philip, Jr.
Hayes, Mark Stephen

Georgia

Canfield, Peter Crane
Denham, Vernon Robert, Jr.
Forbes, Morton Gerald
Merdek, Andrew Austin

Hawaii

Portnoy, Jeffrey Steven

Idaho

Brown, Charles Alan

Illinois

Carponelli, Stephen Peter
Fifer, Samuel
Gilford, Steven Ross
Hefter, Daniel S.
Kohn, Shalom L.
Nicklin, Emily
O'Brien, Patrick W.
Saunders, Lonna Jeanne
Zamarin, Ronald George

Indiana

Sharpnack, John Trent

Louisiana

Weinmann, John Giffen

Maine

Vickerson, William Leo

Maryland

Howell, Harley Thomas

Massachusetts

Fox, Francis Haney
Goldman, Robert Huron
Kociubes, Joseph Leib
Lewis, Anthony
Zandrow, Leonard Florian

Michigan

Brooks, Keefe Alan
Lebow, Michael Jeffrey
Winsten, I.W.

Minnesota

Hirl, Patricia Ann
Magnuson, Roger James
Tanick, Marshall Howard

Mississippi

Henegan, John Clark
Welch, Walter Scott, III

Missouri

Mahaffey, George H.
Sableman, Mark Stephen

Nevada

Faiss, Robert Dean
Galane, Morton Robert

New Jersey

Eittreim, Richard MacNutt
MacDonald, Joseph J.

New Mexico

Rothstein, Robert Richard

New York

Abelman, Arthur F.
Barron, Francis Patrick
Cayea, Donald Joseph
Curtis, Frank R.
Dunham, Corydon Bushnell
Farley, William Patrick
Finberg, Alan Robert
Fuller, David Otis, Jr.
Gold, Stuart Walter
Goodale, James Campbell
Green, Richard George
Hall, Christopher Patrick
Johnston, Harry Melville, III
Kennedy, Michael John
Kessler, Lawrence Bert
Killarney, John Paul
Killeen, Henry Walter
Klinger, Alan Mark
Koeltl, John George
Kurnit, Richard Alan
Larkin, Leo Paul, Jr.
Lester, Howard
McCrory, John Brooks
Messing, Harold
Nearing, Vivienne W.
Reis, Muriel Henle
Rembar, Charles (Isaiah)
Ringel, Dean (I.)
Robertson, Edwin David
Rosini, Neil Justin
Schulz, David Alan
Soyster, Margaret Blair
Sugarman, Robert Gary

North Carolina

Ayscue, Edwin Osborne, Jr.
Lange, David

Ohio

Coombs, Frederick Stanley, III
Downing, George
Finn, Chester Evans
McMenamin, Michael Terrence
Smith, Timothy Daly

Oklahoma

Kachigian, Mark George
Nelon, Robert Dale

Oregon

Bonyhadi, Ernest
Van Valkenburg, Edgar Walter

Pennsylvania

Beasley, James Edwin
Carroll, Mark Thomas
Grant, M. Duncan
Gross, Malcolm Joseph
Kohn, Harold Elias
McComb, John Paul
Mc Gough, Walter Thomas
Reif, Eric Peter
Solano, Carl Anthony
Toll, Seymour I.

South Carolina

Figg, Robert McCormick, Jr.
Haimbaugh, George Dow, Jr.

Tennessee

Headrick, Stirman Russell
Phillips, John Bomar
Rush, Stephen Kenneth
Wade, John Webster

Texas

Black, Robert Allen
Donaldson, David Howard, Jr.
Johnson, Vincent Robert
Leatherbury, Thomas Shawn
Mc Elhaney, John Hess
Waldman, Steve

Utah

Lambert, Dale John
Shea, Patrick A.

Virginia

Allen, Wilbur Coleman, Jr.
Rudlin, David Alan
Wartelle, Barbara Louisa

Washington

Dudley, J. Jeffrey
Harmon, E(verett) Glenn
Mitchell, Robert Bertelson
Utevsky, David

West Virginia

Bunner, Patricia Andrea

ADDRESS UNPUBLISHED

Bamberger, Michael Albert
Fuson, Harold Wesley, Jr.
Kamp, Steven Mark
Rhinehart, R(ichard) Scott
Sommers, Louise

LIBRARIANSHIP, LEGAL

UNITED STATES

Alabama

Younger, William Carl

Arizona

Schneider, Elizabeth Kelley

California

Crews, Kenneth Donald
DiLoreto, Ann Marie
Iamele, Richard Thomas

Jacobstein, J(oseph) Myron
Johnson-Champ, Debra Sue
Perkins, Steven Curtis
Stromme, Gary L.
Sun, Cossette Tsung-hung Wu

Connecticut
Plotnick, Robert Nathan
Stone, Dennis J.

District of Columbia
Berwick, Philip Cregar
Gehringer, Michael Edward
Gehringer, Susanne Elkins
McGuirl, Marlene Dana Callis
Oakley, Robert Louis
Pursley, Ricky Anthony

Florida
Efron, Muriel Cohen
Koenig, Sherman
Painter, Conrad Lee
Pritchard, Teresa Noreen
Sheng, Jack Tse-liang
Wolfe, Bardie Clinton, Jr.

Georgia
Garland, John Louis, Sr.

Illinois
Andrus, Kay LeGrand
Grossman, George Stefan

Indiana
Persyn, Mary Geraldine

Kansas
Schanck, Peter Carr

Kentucky
Levy, Charlotte Lois

Maryland
Bernard, Hugh Y(ancey), Jr.
Cox, Irvin Edmond

Michigan
Virtue, Maxine Boord

Mississippi
West, Carol Catherine

Missouri
Burch, David Ryan
Reams, Bernard Dinsmore, Jr.

New York
Cole, Charles Dewey, Jr.
Ellenberger, Jack Stuart
Goldman, Martha Ann
Grech, Anthony Paul
Hoover, James Lloyd
Jordan, Daniel Patrick, Jr.
Lauer, Judy Anne
Marke, Julius Jay
Robbins, Sara Ellen
Triffin, Nicholas
Tschinkel, Andrew Joseph, Jr.
Williams, David Wesley

Ohio
Balester, Vivian Shelton
Johnson, John Richard
Suhre, Carol Ann

Oregon
Spiegel, Laurence Harold

Pennsylvania
Fox, James Robert

Rhode Island
Svengalis, Kendall Frayne

South Carolina
Cross, Joseph Russell, Jr.

Texas
Borgeson, Earl Charles
Castaño, Sylvia Elizabeth
Hood, Lawrence E.
Riemann, Frederick Aloysius
Roberts, Bonita Koehler

Virginia
Calhoun, Clayne Marsh
Wiltse, James Burdick

Washington
Murray, James Michael
Steele, Anita (Margaret Anne Martin)

Wisconsin
Marohl, David William
Wren, Jill Robinson

ADDRESS UNPUBLISHED
McFarland, Anne Southworth
Pooley, Beverley John
Rosen, Nathan Aaron

MALPRACTICE. See Personal Injury.

MILITARY

UNITED STATES

Alabama
Forbus, Sharon Ann
Hughes, Andy Karl

Alaska
Jones, Charles Robert

Arizona
O'Leary, Thomas Michael

Arkansas
Carpenter, Charles L.

California
Crump, Gerald Franklin
Fox, Richard Paul
Frazier, Thomas Louis
Glazer, Jack Henry
Harley, Robison Dooling, Jr.
Igo, Louis Daniel
Moriarity, John L.
Nypaver, Stephen, III
Shollenberger, Lewis Winnbert, Jr.
Vienna, Kevin Richard
Waldsmith, Mary Louise
Zinn, Henry Jackson

Colorado
Duncan, Stephen Mack
Ruppert, Mark Richard

Connecticut
Klein, Jonathan Joseph

Delaware
Crane, John Murdoch

District of Columbia
Andersen, Daniel Johannes
Bastek, John Anthony
Beach, Chester Paul, Jr.
Becker, Fred Reinhardt, Jr.
Bowman, Michael Floyd
Byrne, Edward Mark
Casey, Geraldine Holland
Daus, Donald George
Fleming, Mack Gerald
Goldsmith, Alan Evans
Kaplan, Richard Alan
Long, Clarence Dickinson, III
McNamara, Roger Thomas
Metcalfe, Robert Davis, III
Mueller, Robert Clare
Noone, Michael F., Jr.
Norris, Robert Wheeler
Rathmell, Anne Elizabeth
Thomas, William Brinker
Thompson, Paul Barker
Thompson, William Carrington, Jr.
Wims, Michael David

Florida
Arensberg, Cornelius Wright
Atkinson, John Bond
Langley, Dorothy Ann
Rivera, Luis Ernesto
Wood, Hugh Lee

Hawaii
Crebbin, Anthony Micek
Meaney, Michael Lawrence
Sabath, Kenneth Michael

Idaho
Burnett, Donald Lee, Jr.

Illinois
Casey, Robert Fitzgerald
Hayes, David John Arthur, Jr.
Parente, James Joseph
Renner, Michael John
Richards, Robert Mayo

Indiana
Kern, Raymond Lex

Kansas
Jacobson, Susan Curtis

Kentucky
Barr, James Houston, Jr.

Louisiana
Buchler, Peter Robert
Hawkins, Cynthia Rayburn

Maine
Pearson, Clinton Charles

Maryland
Brodhurst, Albert Edward
Gnocchi-Franco, Claudio
Thomas, Robert Boyce

Massachusetts
Calabro, Michael James
Dokurno, Anthony David
Gordon, Richard Warren
Loftin, Melinda Jayne

Michigan
Battle, Leonard Carroll

Mississippi
Mayer, John William

Missouri
Zobrist, Karl

Nebraska
Eaton, David Foster

New Jersey
Walsh, Robert Anthony

New Mexico
Kehl, Randall Herman

New York
Arnow, Arthur Emanuel
Eiche, Jay S.
Feedore, Jeremy Randolph
Issler, Harry
Kasold, Bruce Edward
Katz, Michael Albert
Kruteck, Laurence R.
Quinn, James Francis
Riddle, David Andrew
Seidl, James Peter
Stroud, Alan Neil
Treanor, John McCormack
Wright, Douglas Rich
Wysocki, Henry Victor

North Carolina
Conway, Robert George, Jr.
Hampton, Thurman Bruce
Kane, Terry Richard
Kripner, George Martin
Switzer, Robert Earl
Taylor, Vaughan Edward

Ohio
Griffith, Stephen Murray, Jr.
Minamyer, William Eric
Racine, Kathleen Celeste
Seal, Thomas David

Oklahoma
Gray, Linda (Lou)

Oregon
Cloran, William Francis
Crookham, Charles Sewell

Pennsylvania
Kenworthy, Thomas Bausman
Samuelson, Wayne Paul

Rhode Island
Davenport, Teresa Joanna
McMahon, John Joseph
Parsons, Rymn James

South Carolina
Powell, Osborne Eugene, Jr.

South Dakota
Reed, Walter Dudley

Texas
Berg, Thomas Sidney
Brewer, Lewis Gordon
Davis, Harold Clayton, Jr.
Engel, David Wayne
Haskett, Martin Carlaton
Reimer, Bill Monroe
Rickhoff, Thomas Emmet
Schlueter, David Arnold
Simpson, Searcy Lee, Jr.
Westbrook, Joel Whitsitt, III
Woodard, Linda Strite

Utah
Gill, Ruland J., Jr.

Virginia
Allen, Jeffrey Rodgers
Chute, Alan Dale
Crouch, Richard Edelin
Curtis, Jeffrey Hutton
Downey, William Gerald, Jr.
Flynn, Thomas Edward
Folk, Thomas Robert
Hancock, George Louis, Jr.
James, Richard Robert
Lederer, Fredric Ira
Lewis, Walter Laughn
McCloskey, Michael Patrick
O'Connor, Raymond Vincent, Jr.
Phillips, Dennis Leslie
Wentink, Michael James
Wilcox, Bruce Andrew
Woodley, John Paul, Jr.
Zucker, David Clark

Washington
Bridge, Jonathan Joseph
Meyers, Bruce France
Nevin, Jack Frederick
Price, Clark Alan

West Virginia
Rich, Wayne Adrian, Jr.
Walkup, Homer Allen
Woods, Jeff Chandler

Wisconsin
Conrad, Paul Edward

ADDRESS UNPUBLISHED
Avery, Bruce Edward
De La Garza, Roberto Eduardo
Gallagher, Michael Gerald
Kaczynski, Stephen John
Marshall, Kathryn Sue
Taylor, Daniel Edwin
Thomas, Johnny Wesley

MUNICIPAL BONDS

UNITED STATES

Alabama
Caldwell, Carol Gray
Clark, John Foster
Foster, Arthur Key, Jr.
Haskell, Wyatt Rushton
Johnson, Joseph H., Jr.
Martin, Arthur Lee, Jr.

Arizona
Hicks, William Albert, III
Thompson, Terence William

Arkansas
Gliege, John Gerhardt

California
Burke, Robert Bertram
Israel, Perry Elemore
Klafter, Cary Ira
Lava, Leslie Michele
Leventhal, Frederic Daniel
Perry, Matilda Toni
Richardson, Douglas Fielding
Ryan, Joseph
Sobel, Larry D.

Colorado
Eckstein, John Alan
Faxon, Thomas Baker
Sayre, Charles Michael
Sonntag, Richard Arthur

Connecticut
Lloyd, James Hendrie, III

Delaware
Nachmias, Carolyn Sharenow

District of Columbia
Bucholtz, Harold Ronald
Carroll, Raoul Lord
Journey, Drexel Dahlke
Lynn, James Bruce
Simpkins, Mary Nell
Vidal-Cordero, David

Florida
Cardwell, David Earl
Genauer, Martin Jay
Katz, Allan Jack
Lester, Paul Arthur
Napoli, Joseph Anthony
Prom, Stephen G.
Roberts, B. K.

Georgia
Meyer, William Lorne
Pannell, James Loughridge
Wadsworth, Joel Stuart

Idaho
Fawcett, Charles Winton

Illinois
Baker, Benjamin Joseph
Kite, Steven B.
Ladd, Jeffrey Raymond
Mumford, Manly Whitman
Myers, Lonn William
Pratt, Robert Windsor
Quinlan, William Joseph, Jr.
Reynolds, Daniel
Saulsberry, Charles R.
Whalen, Wayne W.

Indiana
Paul, Stephen Howard
Swhier, Robert Dewain, Jr.

Kansas
Curfman, Lawrence Everett
Gaar, Norman Edward
Harris, Phillip Lloyd
Tittsworth, David Gregory

Louisiana
Dwyer, Stephen Irwin
Judell, Harold Benn
Rinker, Andrew, Jr.

Maryland
Arey, Patrick Kane
Clarke, Edward Owen, Jr.
Gorman, Joyce Johanna
Olander, Christopher Dean
Pollak, Mark
Redden, Roger Duffey
Stalfort, John Arthur

Massachusetts
Matthews, Roger Hardin
Notopoulos, Alexander Anastasios, Jr.
Simons, Steven J(ay)
Wilcox, Steven Alan

Minnesota
Deans, Thomas Seymour
Jarboe, Mark Alan

Mississippi
Bush, Fred Marshall, Jr.
Golden, Wilson
Taylor, Zachary, III

Missouri
Arnold, John Fox
Blunt, Ronald L.
Gilmore, Webb Reilly
Johnson, William Ashton
Sparks, Stephen Stone
Yates, Carl Eugene

Nebraska
Christensen, Curtis Lee

Nevada
Jost, Richard Frederic, III

New Jersey
Banks, Cecil James
Fitzpatrick, Harold Francis
Israels, Michael Jozef
Jaffe, Sheldon E.
Scally, John Joseph, Jr.
Vanderbilt, Arthur T., II
Walsh, Gary Eugene
Weinstein, Steven David

New York
Bach, Thomas Handford
Bar-Levav, Doron Mordecai
Barton, Anthony Blackshaw
Bond, Kenneth Walter
Buchbinder, Darrell Bruce
Carroll, Joseph J.
Eisert, Edward Gaver
Ganzi, Victor Frederick
Gibbons, Robert John
Gill, E. Ann
Green, Jeffrey Steven
Haroldson, Jeffrey David
Hofrichter, Lawrence S.
Kabak, Bernard Joshua
Kastellec, Philip Richard
Kilkenny, John Jude
Lloyd, David Livingstone, Jr.
Mc Goldrick, John Gardiner
Miller, Arthur Madden
Peaslee, Maurice Keenan
Picardi, Ferdinand Louis
Reese, William Willis
Rivet, Diana Wittmer
Rooney, Paul C., Jr.
Ruggiero, Thomas W.
Weprin, Barry Alan
Wilkens, Beth Ela
Zucker, Howard

North Carolina
Guterman, James Hans
Yow, Cicero Preston

Ohio
Anderson, John MacKenzie
Batt, Nick
Federico, Andrew John
Fisher, Roberta Lane
Gambol, Robert Alan
Greene, Bernard Wilburn
Petrey, Katherine Gossick
Ptaszek, Edward Gerald, Jr.
Selak, Robert Allen
Trotter, Thomas Robert
Webb, Thomas Irwin, Jr.
Zisser, Steven Lawrence

Oklahoma
Brandenburg, Robert Fairchild, Jr.
Fagin, George J.
Spencer, Thomas Lee

Pennsylvania
Aman, George Matthias, III
Blue, Donald Sherwood
Brawner, Gerald Theodore
Brodbeck, Charles Richard
Carnecchia, Baldo M., Jr
Demmler, John Henry
Gray, Kathleen Ann
Henry, Ronald George
Hovis, Raymond Leader
Lotman, Arline Jolles
Lynch, Victor K.
Strauss, Edward Kenneth
Tupitza, Thomas Anton
Wilkinson, James Allan

South Carolina
Foster, John Witherspoon

Tennessee
Buchanan, Alexander Blackman
Congleton, Joseph Patrick
Doggrell, Henry Patton
Ezell, Kenneth Pettey, Jr.
Meyer, Stephen Leonard
Roach, Jon Gilbert
Trent, J(ohn) Thomas, Jr.

Texas
Anderson, Eric Severin
Caldwell, James Wiley
Cowling, David Edward
Groves, Mary Lynett
Horton, Paul Bradfield
Kobdish, George Charles
McCreary, Frank E., III
Ording, Michael K.
Randolph, Robert Raymond
Stone, Michael K.
Vazquez, Gilbert Falcon

Utah
Riggs, Robin L.

Virginia
Knighton, Alton Lefleur, Jr.
Moore, Tyler Moses
Moorstein, Mark Alan
Pope, Robert Dean
Shimer, Charles Purinton

Washington
Campbell, Robert Hedgcock
Gottlieb, Daniel Seth
Koegen, Roy Jerome

Wisconsin
Flynn, William Frederick
Groethe, Reed
Taus, Armin Kenneth

TRINIDAD AND TOBAGO
Gordon, Kenneth

ADDRESS UNPUBLISHED
Diehl, Deborah Hilda
Fainter, John Wells, Jr.
Howell, Donald Lee
Pitcher, Griffith Fontaine
Wittebort, Robert John, Jr.

OIL AND GAS. See Energy.

PATENT

UNITED STATES

Alaska
Anderson, Lloyd Vincent, Jr.

Arizona
Barbee, Joe E.
Lieb, John Stevens
Mueller, Foorman Lloyd
Phillips, James Harold

California
Alleman, Rodger Neal
Ansell, Edward Orin
Bailey, Craig Bernard
Cochran, Adam
Flattery, Thomas Long
Gallagher, Thomas Allen
Green, William Porter
Greenstein, Neil David
Hale, Charles Russell
Halluin, Albert Price
Hamann, H. Fredrick
Hasak, Janet Elinore
Heslin, James Mitchell
Higgins, Willis Edward
Israelsen, Ned Alma
Jaffer, David Hussain
Jessup, Warren T.
Klein, Henry
Lippman, Peter Ira
Lyon, R. Douglas
Nownejad, Cyrus Sirouss
Passé, James G.
Pavitt, William Hesser, Jr.
Radlo, Edward John
Riter, Bruce Douglas
Roush, George Edgar
Slehofer, Richard Donald
Smegal, Thomas Frank, Jr.
Smith, Robert Catlett
Stevens, Henry Patrick
Streeter, Tom
Tachner, Leonard
Tinsley, Walton Eugene
Weissenberger, Harry George
Wylie, Paul Richter, Jr.

Colorado
Carson, William Scott
Dixon, Richard Dean
Dorr, Robert Charles
Meyer, Lee Gordon
Spangler, Edwin Leroy

Connecticut
Asija, S(atya) Pal
Battersby, Gregory John
Benson, Gregg Carl
Carten, Francis Noel
Cifelli, Armand
Crozier, John Huntington
De Lio, Anthony Peter
Fanwick, Ernest
Fitzgerald, Thomas Raymond
Fournier, Arthur Edmond, Jr.
Fuller, Robert Ferrey
Greeley, Paul David
Green, Clarence Arthur
Kastriner, Lawrence George
Kelmachter, Barry Lee
Kramer, Barry
Ktorides, Stanley
Manbeck, Harry Frederick, Jr.
Perman, Martey Robert
Razzano, Pasquale Angelo
Smith, Spencer Thomas
Soltow, William Donald, Jr.
Sommer, Evelyn Morrison
Thompson, Frank J(oseph)
Walk, Donald Willard
Webster, Stuart Arthur
Weinstein, Paul

Delaware
Frank, George Andrew
Hunter, Frederick Douglas
Huntley, Donald Wayne
Paintin, Francis Arthur
Shoaf, Charles Jefferson
Staves, Marion Cole
Uebler, E(rnest) Alan
Whitney, Douglas E., Sr.
Wolfson, Herbert Milton

District of Columbia
Aisenberg, Irwin Morton
Berman, Stanford Warner
Breneman, William Dudley
Cooper, Iver Peter
Daus, Donald George
DeGrandi, Joseph A.
De Simone, Daniel V.
Garvey, John Cotton
Goans, Judy Winegar
Goodman, Alfred Nelson
Hefter, Laurence Roy
Holman, John Clarke
Hoscheit, Dale Herbert
McCann, Clifton Everett
McKie, Edward Foss
Meany, Bernard Anthony
Miller, Jack Richard
Mobille, George Thomas
Moss, Kathleen Susan
Mossinghoff, Gerald Joseph
Payne, Kenneth Eugene
Potenza, Joseph Michael
Price, Donald Douglas
Railton, William Scott
Repper, George Robert
Rommel, John Marshall
Rubin, Burton Jay
Seto, Robert Mahealani Ming
Spencer, George Henry
Stern, Richard Harvey
Sturtevant, Brereton

Swartz, Christian LeFevre
Wegner, Harold Claus
Wildensteiner, Otto Melvin
Yoches, Edward Robert

Florida
Dominik, Jack Edward
Kerns, David Vincent
Lanham, Charles Warren
Livingston, Edward Michael
Malloy, John Cyril
Monacelli, Walter Joseph
Rosenblatt, Joel I.
Saliwanchik, Roman
Sanchelima, Jesus
Zambo, Richard Alan

Georgia
Goldman, Joel S.
Harris, Earl Douglas
Herrick, William Duncan
Hopkins, George Mathews Marks
Lee, William Clement, III
Middleton, James Boland

Illinois
Altman, Louis
Amend, James Michael
Berenzweig, Jack Charles
Berghoff, Paul Henry
Birmingham, William Joseph
Boehnen, Daniel A.
Brand, Robert Joseph
Brezina, David Charles
Cherry, Daniel Ronald
Coffee, James Frederick
Edgell, George Paul
Flattery, Paul Charles
Gerstman, George Henry
Gilkes, Arthur Gwyer
Gottschalk, Robert
Grabarek, William Christian
Haight, Edward Allen
Harmon, Robert Lon
Henke, Robert John
Hill, Philip
Hoffman, Richard Bruce
Jacover, Jerold Alan
Jager, Melvin Francis
Johnston, A. Sidney
Juettner, Paul Gerard
Katz, Avrum Sidney
Kozak, John W.
Krupka, Robert George
Lee, William Marshall
Liljequist, Jon Leon
Lindgren, Thomas Bernard
Lucas, John Kenneth
Muir, Robert Eugene
Osann, Edward William, Jr.
Paniaguas, John Steven
Parad, Boris
Rauner, Vincent Joseph
Roper, Harry Joseph
Ropski, Gary Melchior
Scott, Theodore R.
Sheppard, Berton Scott
Smith, Herman Eugene
Snyder, Eugene I.
Szczepanski, Slawomir Zbigniew Steven
Thompson, William Scott
Valauskas, Charles C.
Vittum, Daniel Weeks, Jr.
Walters, Gomer Winston
Ward, Robert Morton
Welsh, Donald LeRoy
Willian, Clyde Franklin
Wood, James Clarence

Indiana
Calhoun, John Henry, Jr.
Campbell, Edward Adolph
Dahling, Gerald Vernon
Emhardt, Charles David
Hansell, Ronald Stephen
Harrison, Nancy Jane
Jeffers, Albert Lavern
Kinney, Richard Gordon
Levy, Ron Karl
Nesbitt, John Robert
Richardson, Andrew James
Whitaker, Leroy
Woodard, Harold Raymond
Zlatos, Steve Edward

Kansas
Mingle, John Orville

Kentucky
Fitch, Howard Mercer
Fletcher, Robert Wesley
Reed, John Squires, II

Louisiana
Leonard, Paul Haralson

Maine
Bohan, Thomas Lynch
Hulbert, William Rowsell, Jr.

Maryland
Brady, Rupert Joseph
Sherer, Ronald Brian
Troffkin, Howard Julian

Massachusetts
Asher, Robert Michael
Ballantyne, Richard L(ee)
Channing, Stacey Lisa
Danner, Douglas
Erlich, Jacob Nathan
Foster, Scott Raymond
Fraser, Everett MacKay
Hieken, Charles
Isaacs, Alvin
Linek, Ernest Vincent
Martin, Terrence
McCarter, Lowell Harold
Neuner, George William
Paglierani, Ronald Joseph
Payne, Leslie Julian
Russell, Robert Bernard
Schiller, Robert James

Siegel, Julian Lee
Wolf, David

Michigan
Anderson, Thomas Ernest
Farris, Robert Lee
Gifford, Ernest Irving
Harrington, Donald Joseph
Mitchell, James Albee
Norris, Lawrence Geoffrey
Rader, Ralph Terrance
Thierstein, Emma Joan

Minnesota
Arrett, Oliver Ford
Brink, Richard Edward
Friederichs, Norman Paul
Lange, Frederick Emil
Seaburg, Jean
Vidas, Scott Quinn

Missouri
Gilster, Peter Stuart
Krukiel, Charles Edward
Lucchesi, Lionel Louis
Meyer, Scott John
Moore, McPherson Dorsett
Nutter, Thomas Edward
Roedel, John Kennedy, Jr.

Montana
Conover, Richard Corrill

Nevada
Quirk, Edward John

New Hampshire
Weins, Michael James

New Jersey
Berman, Steven Paul
Bittman, Mitchell David
Cipollone, Anthony Dominic
Einhorn, Harold
Gerb, Bernard
Grindle, Robert Paul
Kassenoff, Melvyn Mark
Michaelson, Peter Lee
Monaco, Mario Anthony
Protigal, Stanley Nathan
Raines, Stephen
Rohm, Benita Jill
Rosen, Norman Edward
Thomason, Charles Lee
Virelli, Louis James, Jr.
Walsh, Robert Anthony
Welch, Gerald Thomas
Wilson, Abraham
Woodbridge, Richard Carveth

New Mexico
Smith, Donald Perry

New York
Alice, Ronald William
Bader, Izaak Walton
Baechtold, Robert Louis
Bazerman, Steven Howard
Beck, Thomas Henry
Berry, Rynn
Bosses, Stevan J.
Calvaruso, Joseph A.
Carr, Francis Thomas
Chapuran, Ronald Francis
Cole, Harold Edwin
Conner, William Curtis
Cooper, John Nicholas
Costantino, Mark Americus
Creel, Thomas Leonard
Decker, Frank Norton, Jr.
Dowling, Thomas Patrick
Dunne, Gerard Francis
Eberle, William Frederic
Evans, Barry Leonard
Farnum, Henry Merritt
Feldman, Stephen E.
Felfe, Peter Franz
Fiddler, Robert William
Finnegan, George Bernard, Jr.
Fitzpatrick, Joseph Mark
Foster, David Lee
Frommer, William S.
Furgang, Philip
Gibson, Thomas Martin
Goodman, Edward William
Haffner, Alfred Loveland, Jr.
Haken, Jack Edward
Hamburg, Charles Bruce
Helfgott, Samson
Hepner, Charles Edward
Huettner, Richard Alfred
Jacobson, Allan Jeffrey
Jordan, Frank J.
Kalow, David Arthur
Kane, David Schilling
Katona, Gabriel Paul
Kelton, John Tremain
Kidd, John Edward
Kunstadt, Robert M.
Lee, Jerome G.
Lipsitz, Randy
Martone, Patricia Ann
Medford-Rosow, Traci
Meiklejohn, Paul Thomas
Mosoff, Serle Ian
O'Donnell, Paul Eugene, Jr.
Oliver, Milton McKinnon
Oppedahl, Carl W.
Pegram, John Braxton
Pelton, Russell Gilbert
Pfeffer, David H.
Plottel, Roland
Ralabate, James J(oseph)
Raymond, Dana Merriam
Reilly, John Albert
Relson, Morris
Robinson, Kenneth Patrick
Rogers, Laurence Steven
Rubenstein, Allen Ira
Scheck, Frank Foetisch
Shear, Stephen Barrett
Sherman, Charles Israel
Simon, Morton Sonny

Sinnott, John Patrick
Smith, Robert Blakeman
Spath, Gregg Anthony
Sullivan, Joseph Charles
Sutton, Paul J.
Sweeney, John Francis
Sweet, Joseph Church, Jr.
Thomashower, William Jay
White, John Patrick
Whitney, George Ward
Wingate, C(harles) Douglas
Woglom, Eric Cooke
Zivin, Norman H.

North Carolina
Bell, Paul Buckner
Hurewitz, David Lewis
Linker, Raymond Otho, Jr.
MacCord, Howard Arthur, Jr.
Olive, Susan Freya
Pinckney, Francis Morris
Ross, John Bowen, Jr.
Shefte, Dalbert Uhrig
Vestal, Tommy Ray

Ohio
Baranowksi, Edwin Michael
Bobak, Donald John
Brinkman, Herbert Charles
Cooper, Hal Dean
Donohoe, James D.
Ely, Albert Love, Jr.
Fraser, Donald Ross
Hoerner, Robert Jack
Jenkins, Matthew Richard
Jones, John Frank
Kahrl, Robert Conley
Karch, George Frederick, Jr
Kreek, Louis Francis, Jr.
Maky, Walter
McCoy, William Charles, Jr.
Nauman, Joseph George
Phillips, Patrick Paul
Sajovec, Frank Michael, Jr.
Schmitz, Thomas Mathias
Schramm, Frederic Bernard
Sessler, Albert Louis, Jr.
Slough, J(osephine) Helen
Utz, Edward Joseph
Wieland, Robert Richard
Zellner, Robert John

Oklahoma
Fish, John Mancil, Jr.
Hitchcock, Bion Earl
Robbins, Archie Lew
Williams, James William

Oregon
Chernoff, Daniel Paregol
Gray, Francis Ignacy
Smith, Kim Ridgely

Pennsylvania
Alstadt, Lynn Jeffery
Beam, Robert Charles
Beck, Paul Augustine
Blenko, Walter J(ohn), Jr.
Buell, Eugene F(ranklin)
Caldwell, John Warwick
Child, John Sowden, Jr.
Chovanes, Eugene
Dorfman, John Charles
Driks, Jordan Joseph
Elliott, William Homer, Jr.
Elman, Gerry Jay
Glantz, Douglas Gene
Gribok, Stephan Paul
Hauger, Harold Keith
Krefman, Stephen David
Lavorgna, Gregory Joseph
Lee, Edward B., III
Lipton, Robert S.
Lovercheck, Charles Lester
Lushis, John Francis, Jr.
Nadel, Alan Steven
Petock, Michael F(rances)
Pokotilow, Manny D.
Ruano, William J.
Seidel, Arthur Harris
Silverman, Arnold Barry
Simkanich, John Joseph
Simmons, Bryan J.
Starr, Mark Toby
Urey, David Stauffer
Warren, William Ziegler
Washburn, Robert Buchanan
Webb, William Hess
Weisburd, Steven I.

Rhode Island
Skenyon, John Michael

South Carolina
Skord, Jennifer Lynne

Tennessee
Good, Adrian J.
Lackey, Harrington Ashton

Texas
Agnich, Richard John
Arno, James
Boos, Arthur Charles
Brookhart, Walter Ray
Burleson, Karen Tripp
Conley, Ned Leroy
Curfiss, Robert C.
Dieter, James George
Dillon, Andrew Joseph
Duncan, John Milton
Falk, Robert Hardy
Feldcamp, Larry Bernard
Felger, Thomas Robert
Fladung, Richard Denis
Greenberg, Howard Ralph
Hodgins, Daniel Stephen
Hunt, John Floyd
Kaplan, Lee Landa
Keys, Jerry Malcom
Kirk, John Robert, Jr.
Krieger, Paul Edward
Lacy, John Ford

Leach, Sydney Minturn
Levine, Harold
Livingston, Ann Chambliss
Marsteller, Thomas Franklin, Jr.
Moore, Stanley Ray
Muster, Douglas Frederick
Petersen, Gale Roy
Peterson, Gale Roy
Rosenthal, Alan David
Schuurman, Willem Gerhard
Scott, Eddie Elmer
Shurn, Peter Joseph, III
Toedt, D(ell) C(harles), III
Traver, Alfred Ellis, Jr.
Van Slyke, Paul Christopher
Walter, Charles Frank
Wheelock, Eugene Thomas
Woodward, Charles Carroll M.
Zahrt, William Dietrich, II

Utah
Cornaby, Kay Sterling
Jensen, Allen Reed
Madson, Craig James
Thorpe, Calvin E.

Virginia
Adams, Robert Walker
Bent, Stephen Andrew
Birch, Terrell Colhoun
Calvetti, Frederick F.
Dutton, Harold Hilbert, Jr.
Georges, Peter John
Greigg, Ronald Edwin
Hugin, Adolph Charles
Joynt, John Howard
Kondracki, Edward John
Laughlin, James Harold, Jr.
LeBlanc, Robert Edmond, III
Mar, Eugene
McDonald, Alan Thomas
Morton, Woolridge Brown, Jr.
Rosenberg, Peter David
Schwaab, Richard Lewis
Shapiro, Nelson Hirsh
Stanback, Clarence Freeman, Jr.
Van Landingham, Leander Shelton, Jr.
Weinrieb, Steven William
Wendel, Charles Allen

Washington
Coogan, Patrick Donlan
Leggett, James Francois
O'Connor, Bruce Edward

Wisconsin
Long, Theodore James
Shupe, Larry Lewis
Swartwout, Willis Brewster, III

ISRAEL
Luzzatto, Edgar

LUXEMBOURG
Dennemeyer, John James

REPUBLIC OF KOREA
Sabo, William Denes

SWITZERLAND
Goldstein, E. Ernest

ADDRESS UNPUBLISHED
Adams, Thomas Lawrence
Brunell, Norman Eliot
Casella, Peter F(iore)
De Angelis, Arnold John
Dolgorukov, D. Edward
DuPre, John Leacy
Ertman, Willis Marion
Glober, George Edward, Jr.
Hays, Robert Alexander
Herrell, Roger Wayne
Joike, Trevor B.
Kasper, Horst Manfred
Kegan, Esther Oswianza
Leydig, Carl Frederick
McCarthy, J. Thomas
Mento, Mary Ann
Nicolaides, Mary
Peters, R. Jonathan
Pollock, E. Kears
Richardson, Robert Owen
Shaffert, Kurt
Woronoff, David Smulyan

PENSION, PROFIT-SHARING, AND EMPLOYEE BENEFITS

UNITED STATES

Alabama
Fox, John Charles
Hughes, James Donald
Shanks, William Ennis, Jr.
Stephens, William Taft

Arizona
Daum, Bryan Edwin
DiMatteo, Philip Stephen
Ehmann, Anthony Valentine
Pietzsch, Michael Edward
Pingree, Bruce Douglas
Rainey, William Joel
Turner, Daniel Charles

Arkansas
Nisbet, Alexander Wyckliff, Jr.

California
Anzur, John Andrew
Balliet, Susan Jackson
Bex, Richard Elmer
Brickner, Jed Walter
Carella, Eugene John
Carrey, Neil
Cesinger, John Robert

Dean, Ronald Glenn
Diehl, Joseph Burnett
Dostart, Paul Joseph
Ferchland, William Thomas
Gibson, Virginia Lee
Gilbert, Robert Wolfe
Glass, Beverly Elaine
Gordon, David Eliot
Goulding, J(ohn) Michael
Gross, Justin Arthur
Hasson, Kirke Michael
Highberger, William Foster
Homer, Barry Wayne
Hurabiell, John Philip, Sr.
Klein, Alfred
Levy, David
Lipsig, Ethan
Ludwig, Ronald L.
Marshall, Ellen Ruth
Niehans, Daniel
Offer, Stuart Jay
Orth, Beverly Jean
Romero, Frederick Armand
Ross, Bruce Shields
Sacks, Barry Howard
Scott, David Ernest
Scott, Valerie Weeks
Smiley, Stanley Robert
Spuehler, Donald Roy
Whitaker, Leslie Kent

Colorado

Elrod, Richard Bryan
Hill, Robert Dean
Marquess, Lawrence Wade
Smith, Sheldon Harold

Connecticut

Cullina, William Michael
Czajkowski, Frank Henry
Koomey, Richard Alan
Milliken, Charles Buckland
Rosenberg, Burton Stuart
Strone, Michael Jonathan

Delaware

Hatch, Denison Hurlbut, Jr.
Hindmarch, Thomas Michael
Hyman, Jerry Allan
Popper, Richard J.A.

District of Columbia

Alexander, Donald Crichton
Bason, George Francis, Jr.
Bostick, George Hale
Brodsky, Arthur James
Calhoun, Carol Victoria
Chip, William Waddington
Cummings, Frank
Curran, John Peter
Damico, Nicholas Peter
Deutsch, David
Ell, Douglas William
Faley, R(ichard) Scott
Fay, Raymond Charles
Green, Paul Andrew
Guarini, Frank J.
Hennessy, Ellen Anne
Heylman, Paul Monroe
Hoopes, Terence James
Hyde, Patrick Alan
Kilberg, William Jeffrey
Kusma, Kyllikki
Mackiewicz, Edward Robert
McCann, Joseph Leo
Miller, Evan
Morgan, Daniel Louis
Oppenheimer, Jerry L.
Pohl, Mark Ronald
Quintiere, Gary G.
Roach, Arvid Edward, II
Rothenberg, Steven Alan
Roy, James Robert
Smith, Arthur Lee
Smith, Willard Mark
Taylor, Carl Larsen
Treacy, Vincent Edward
Ufholz, Philip John
Wallach, Evan Jonathan
Wolf, Mark Charles

Florida

Arlt, Mary Ann Kokoszyna
Champion, Roger Cornelius
Hest, Bruce Henry
Lefkowitz, Ivan Martin
Watson, Roberta Casper

Georgia

Gerstein, Joe Willie
Hayes, Dewey Norman
Hill, John Earll
Johnson, Lester Benjamin, III
Lamon, Harry Vincent, Jr.
Langford, James Tafford
Linder, Harvey Ronald
Martin, Charles Lee
Price, Terry
Quinlan, James William
Radford, Mary Frances
Slawsky, Norman Joel

Hawaii

Knorek, John Lee
Tam, James Kellett

Idaho

Erickson, Robert Stanley

Illinois

Adams, John Richard
Allison, Thomas D., Jr.
Barnes, Karen Kay
Bates, R. Edward
Chandler, Kent, Jr.
Cohen, Seymour
Cotton, Eugene
Daley, Susan Jean
Davidson, Lawrence Ira
Dombrow, Anthony Eric
Fellows, Jerry Kenneth
Ferencz, Robert Arnold
Freeman, Richard Lyons
Gerek, William Michael
Gertz, Theodore Gerson
Goslawski, Leonard Stephen
Grayck, Marcus Daniel
Greenfield, Michael C.
Hoffman, John Harry
Hudetz, Joseph Bernard
Kamensky, Marvin
Kelly, Peter McClorey, II
Krueger, Herbert William
Lewis, William Theodore, Jr.
Lynch, James Daniel
Margolin, Stephen M.
McErlean, Charles F., Jr.
Meadors, Gayle Marleen
Moline, Gary L.
Murphy, Thomas Lee
Pape, Glenn Michael
Peake, Darryl Lee
Polk, Lee Thomas
Provenzano, William Joseph
Rombs, Vincent Joseph
Sachs, Irving Joseph
Schlott, Mary Camille
Schwartzman, Mark Lee
Scogland, William Lee
Serwer, Alan Michael
Shaw, Lee Charles
Thompson, David F.
Thomson, William Hills
Trio, Edward Alan
Wise, William Jerrard
Wolf, Charles Benno
Wolfe, David Louis
Zoll, Jeffery Mark

Indiana

Abbott, Jacquelyn Meng
Adinamis, George Peter
Capshaw, Tom Dean
Coukos, Carolyn Cook
Coz, Thomas Anthony
Culp, Charles William
Greeneburg, Thomas Michael
Highfield, Robert Edward
Peterson, Clyde L.
Price, Phillip Vincent
Roberts, Patricia Susan
Sheridan, John Kress, II
Urda, Richard Bernard, Jr.

Iowa

Berry, Jan Vance
Einck, Dean Robert
Narber, Gregg Ross
Petersen, Jack Martin
Ruttenberg, Harold Seymour
Smith, Kim LeRoy

Kansas

Hankins, Gale William
Hay, Charles Richard
Karlin, Calvin Joseph
Martin, Alson Robert
Parker, William Lawrence, Jr.
Stavely, Richard William
Winkler, Dana John

Kentucky

Gilman, Sheldon G.
Hallenberg, Robert Lewis
Jackson, James Ronald
Voyles, James Robert

Louisiana

Angelico, Dennis Michael
Bayard, Alton Ernest, III
Buchler, Peter Robert
Charboneau, Brian Paige
Hearn, Sharon Sklamba
Malone, Ernest Roland, Jr.
Powell, David Wayne

Maine

Hunt, Philip Courtney

Maryland

Adkins, Edward James
Batoff, Steven Irving
Bové, Edward Joseph
Calimafde, Paula Annette
Cashour, Mary Catherine
Curran, Robert Bruce
Dubé, Lawrence Edward, Jr.
Gonya, Donald Alan
Grubbs, Donald Shaw, Jr.
Jenkins, Robert Rowe
Miliman, David Jay
Morris, David Michael
Ziegler, William Joseph

Massachusetts

Dreyer, Harold Emil
Felper, David Michael
Haas, William Lambert
Keegan, John Robert
Kovar, Stuart Charles
Lynch, John Gregory, Jr.
Matthews, Roger Hardin
Straus, William Marc
Walker, Paul Howard
Wright, Benjamin Tappan

Michigan

Bultje, Ronald Alan
Freeberg, Edward Ronald
Hirschman, Sherman Joseph
Hitchcock, Stephen Jay
Kinney, Gregory Hoppes
McKendry, John H., Jr.
Meyers, Arthur S., Jr.
Nora, John Joseph
Page, Leonard Ronald
Panek, Michael John
Phillips, Elliott Hunter
Taunt, Charles Joseph

Minnesota

Bernhardson, Ivy Schutz
Burns, Richard Ramsey
Chester, Stephanie Ann
D'Aquila, Thomas Carl
Dzurak, Steven J.
Ellingsworth, Patrick James
Hitch, Horace
Martin, Judith Moran
Meier, Carl Carsten
Norton, John William
Sovereign, Kenneth Lester
Vanhove, Lorri Kay

Mississippi

Garrity, Thomas Anthony, Jr.
Jones, Barry Kent
Russell, Glover Alcorn, Jr.
Shaw, Susan Boyce

Missouri

Armstrong, Owen Thomas
Cooper, Richard Alan
Crowe, Robert Alan
Dyer, John Gilbert
Goffstein, John Howard
Kuhlmann, Fred Mark
Matthews, James Michael
Morrison, John Stanley
Shaffer, Herman Morris
Thompson, Michel Allen
Tripp, Donald William
Voelpel, Mark Steven
Wellford, Robin Sonneland
Yates, David Floyd

Nebraska

Dwyer, Robert Vincent, Jr.
Jahn, Gregory Dean
Zalewski, James Conrad

Nevada

Greene, Addison Kent
Morris, Trude McMahan

New Hampshire

Chamberlain, Douglas Reginald

New Jersey

Biaett, Doddridge Hewitt, III
Cuttler, H. Karen
Day, Edward Francis, Jr.
Fogel, Richard
Gerard, Stephen Stanley
Gramm, JoAnn Leigh
Halpern, Samuel Joseph
Herr, Philip Michael
Kaplan, Steven Samuel
Mach, Joseph David
Nelson, Warren Owen
O'Carroll, Anita Louise
Reich, Laurence
Rockwell, Mark Paul
Taldone, Nicholas John
Yellin, Stanley Jay

New Mexico

Diamond, Jeffrey Brian

New York

Backus, Bradley
Bagge, Michael Charles
Beckstrom, Charles G.
Black, Howard
Brossman, Mark Edward
Byrne, Margaret Mary
Calhoun, Monica Dodd
Canoni, John David
Carlson, David Bret
Clifton, Henry, Jr.
Curtis, Susan Grace
Danziger, Joel Bernard
Dell, Michael John
Donat, Walter Kennedy
Dreyspool, Anthony Alan
Fields, Robert Meddin
Fischer, Richard Samuel
Fogelgaren, Eric Israel
Friedman, Harvey
Fuller, Robert L(eander)
Golick, Toby Barbara
Greenspan, Richard Mathew
Halliday, Lana
Heffernan, Michele Olga
Hirsh, Leonard Steven
Hochberg, Ronald Mark
Huber, Melvyn Jay
Ivanick, Carol W. Trencher
Jain, Lalit K.
Katz, Charles R.
Kimball, Jesse Dudley Baldwin
Kravitz, William N.
Kroll, Arthur Herbert
Lawton, James Patrick
Lee, Christopher Peter
Leifer, Max David
Levitt, Bonnie K.
Machlowitz, David Steven
Maglaras, Nicholas George
Mamorsky, Jeffrey Dean
Mandel, Richard Gordon
Martin, Peter William
Mathers, Allen Stanley
Meyer, Sidney L.
Miller, Lee Edward
Moore, Donald Francis
Morris, Richard Paul
Nolan, Terrance Joseph, Jr.
O'Dwyer, Brian
Probert, Mark Stanley
Ray, Jeanne Cullinan
Robinson, Lee Harris
Rose, Elihu Isaac
Rotgin, Philip Norman
Rothermel, Joan Ebert
Rover, Edward Frank
Russo, Anthony Joseph, Jr.
Schwarz, Carl Alfred, Jr.
Simonton, Robert Bennet
Stokes, Robert Jerome
Story, John Harold
Sussman, Daniel Leonard
Taussig, Eric Alfred
Tormey, Douglas Joseph
Twietmeyer, Don Henry
Wagner, Michael G.
White, Cheryl Denney
Winger, Ralph O.
Wood, Teri Wilford
Zimmerman, Sandra L.

North Carolina

Daniel, James Edward
Gunter, Michael Donwell
Hunter, Pamela Anne
Kersh, John Danzey, Jr.
McGirt, Sherri Lynn
Page, James Wilson
Silverstein, Carol Kauffman
Webb, W(illiam) Y(oung) Alex
Wilson, Thomas Johnston

North Dakota

Bailly, David Ryan

Ohio

Allotta, Joseph John
Belville, Barbara Ann
Bremer, Thomas Francis
Buechner, Robert William
Cornell, John Robert
Frutkin, Harvey Lee
Geer, Thomas Lee
Geneva, Louis Brion
Goldsmith, James Arthur
Goodin, Eileen Sue
Goulder, Diane Kessler
Haase, William Xavier
Hays, Robert D.
Leavitt, Jeffrey Stuart
Levin, Debbe Ann
Linnert, Terrence Gregory
Manring, Daniel Lee
McCormick, Shawn Charles
Meek, Leslie Applegate
Ruf, H(arold) William, Jr.
Shelley, John Fletcher
Sites, Richard Loren
Stark, Michael Lee
Wainblat, Neal Bruce
Walker, Patricia Ann
Zoll, David Wesley

Oklahoma

Blair, Clifford Jennings, II
Chapman, Russell Dale
Petrikin, James Ronald
Stewart, Murray Baker
Swimley, Gary Wallace

Oregon

Hittle, David William
Mechanic, Gene Barry
Muhlheim, Wilson C.
Stuart, Michael George
Zalutsky, Morton Herman

Pennsylvania

Abraham, James Esber
Abramowitz, Norbert Leslie
Abrams, Nancy
Bildersee, Robert Alan
Boocock, Stephen William
Burke, Linda Beerbower
Candris, Laura A.
Carroll, Donald R.
Clauss, Peter Otto
Dougherty, Brian James
Elliott, Homer Lee
Freedman, Barbara Widman
Gallagher, John Paul
Garber, Marc Ricky
Geeseman, Robert George
Hetherington, John Joseph
Heywood, Barbara Lorentson
Johnston, Henry Richard, III
Kabala, Edward John
Kalogredis, Vasilios J.
Kephart, James William
Krampf, John Edward
Kutz, Robert H.
Lind, Deborah Celia
Louis, Robert Henry
Lynch, James Edward
Mansori, Zubair S.
Mills, Kathleen Anne Merry
O'Reilly, Timothy Patrick
Preate, Robert Anthony
Reagan, Harry E., III
Reed, Robert Alan
Salus, Herbert Wieder, Jr.
Scheinholtz, Leonard Louis
Schmidt, Lynne Dianne
Thomas, Lowell Shumway, Jr.
Welty, John Rider
Whiteside, William Anthony, Jr.
Zearfoss, Herbert Keyser

South Carolina

Carr, Robert Stuart
Gilchrist, Dennis Clinton
Hutton, Susan Pawlias
Jordan, Michael Lee McAdams
Lynch, John Timothy
McChesney, Paul Townsend
Pollard, William Albert
Rodgers, Sharon Lynette

South Dakota

Rose, Lois Ann

Tennessee

Butts, Samuel Arthur, III
Dadds, Harry Leon, II
De Young, Vincent Gerald
Jett, Edward Stephen
Little, Hampton Stennis, Jr.
Marquis, Robert Stillwell

Texas

Adams, Harold Gene
Bader, Gregory Vincent
Barber, Monty Clyde
Benton, John Bunyan
Bumpas, Stuart Maryman
Bush, Edward Philip
Conkel, Robert Dale
Cowart, T(homas) David
Croom, Sam Gaston, Jr.
Fenner, Suzan Ellen
Guest, Floyd Emory, Jr.
Harkey, Paul
Ice, Noel Carlysle
Kay, Joel Phillip
Klancnik, James Michael
Lawson, Gary B.
Mark, Richard Steve
McLane, David Glenn
Milner, Christy Elizabeth
O'Brien, Claudine Michele Niedzielski
Page, Jack Randall
Riggs, Arthur Jordy
Seeman, Robert Foster
Seymour-Harris, Barbara Laverne
Smith, Frank Tupper
Spooner, Arthur Elmon, Jr.
Suhre, Karen Kay
Tracy, J. David
Wendorf, Hulen Dee

Utah

Babcock, Bruce Edward
Curtis, Dale Jay
Lauritzen, David Kay

Vermont

Winer, Jonathan Herman

Virginia

Davidson, Frank Gassaway, III
Goode, David Ronald
Knighton, Alton Lefleur, Jr.
Regan, Michael Patrick
Sarosdy, Jane Graffeo
Scott, Betsy Sue
Whitaker, Thomas Patrick

Washington

Belfiglio, Jeff
Birmingham, Richard Joseph
Marten, Judd Robert
Petrie, Gregory Steven
Powers, Mark Gregory
Ray, Rodney Bruce

West Virginia

Kidner, Edward Franklin
Shepherd, Richard Earnshaw
Simmons, Alan Russell

Wisconsin

Bauman, Susan Joan Mayer
Berman, Ronald Charles
Newton, Mary S.
Shiely, John Stephen
Smith, Wrede Howard, Jr.
Stevens, Charles Paul

ADDRESS UNPUBLISHED

Crandell, John Smith
Crawford, Muriel Laura
Daleiden, Norbert Alfred
Feingold, Victor
Fine, Robert Paul
Howitt, Idelle Anne
Jackson, Louise Anne
Leeds, Mindy Robin
Lewellyn, Bruce
Marks, Leon
Mattingly, William Earl
Palmer, Ann Therese Darin
Rutland, John Dudley
Saboughi, Joseph M.
Schroeder, John Walter
Sklar, Steven J.

PERSONAL INJURY. *See also* Insurance.

UNITED STATES

Alabama

Alexander, Melton Lee
Black, Claire Alexander
Blan, Ollie Lionel, Jr.
Brown, Joseph Morris, Jr.
Browning, Richard Edward
Carr, Davis
Cicio, Anthony Lee
Cotton, Gregory Dale
Crespi, Michael Albert
Crownover, Walter Parker
Dacso, Sheryl Tatar
Davis, Ronald Lee
De Ment, Ira
Ferguson, Harold Laverne, Jr.
Fuller, S. Wayne
Fuller, William Sidney
Funderburk, Kenneth Leroy
Gray, William Patton, Jr.
Hamm, Coleman Durden, Jr.
Hanson, Frank Oscar, Jr.
Harris, Benjamin Harte, Jr.
Hicks, Deborah Ann Whitmore
Hines, Rodney Alan
Hollis, Louie Andrew
Howell, Allen Windsor
Hughes, Patrick Paul
Kelly, Leon Fred, Jr.
Kennemer, John Maclin
Kominos, Bill
Lane, Wilford Jones
Lattof, Mitchell George, Jr.
Lewis, Cyrus Roys
Mandell, Howard Allyn
Manley, Richard Shannon
Martin, Ludger D.
McCorkle, Lucy Virginia
Means, Tyrone Carlton
Monroe, Cecil Barlow
Moore, Gary Alan
Mountain, C(linton) Delaine
Munsey, Stanley Edward
Newton, Alexander Worthy
Norman, Robert Daniel
Pennington, Al
Pittman, Joseph Stafford, Jr.
Porterfield, Jack Berry, Jr.
Powell, Scott Ashley
Quillen, Michael Clay
Rebarchak, James
Smith, Rufus Randolph, Jr.
Smith, William Wayne
South, Mark Omega
Sullivan, Carroll Hart

Taylor, Ted
Timberlake, H. Kenan
Tucker, Billie Anne
Van Tassel, George Martin, Jr.
Waddell, John Emory
Wright, David Scott

Alaska

Anderson, Lloyd Vincent, Jr.
Angstman, Myron Eugene
Beistline, Ralph Robert
Bendell, James Michael
Brown, Fred Grant
Clark, Julie Ann
Gidcumb, Lance Edward
Hayes, George Nicholas
Johnson, Donald Milby
Molloy, Robert Joseph
Offret, Ronald (Alvin)
Porter, James (Lamar)
Rice, Julian Casavant
Ross, Wayne Anthony
Sedwick, John Weeter
Silvey, Charles Delbert, II
Taylor, Kneeland Lamoureux
Wagstaff, Robert Hall
Walther, Dale Jay
Weinig, Richard Arthur
Winner, Russell Lee

Arizona

Anderson, Lawrence Ohaco
Bakker, Thomas Gordon
Barry, Edward Louis
Begam, Robert George
Bowman, C(harles) Alan
Brock, Warren Richard
Campbell, Carol Nowell
Clark, Richard Edward
Condo, James Robert
Dulberg, Michael Seth
Feder, Bruce Stanley
Finson, Lowell Wayne
Fisher, Peter Francis
Friedlander, Susan Oliver
Frost, Smith Gibbons
Gaines, Edwin Metcalf, Jr.
Ganson, Norris Lloyd
Gonzales, Richard Joseph
Grand, Richard D.
Gustafson, David Earl
Haralson, Dale
Hendricks, Edwin Francis
Hossler, David Joseph
Hyams, Harold
Jakubczyk, John Joseph
Jensen, Robert Arthur
Jenson, Dennis Dion
Kelly, Joseph Sylvester, Jr.
Kennedy, Michael Kevin
Kjos, Victoria Ann
Klahr, Gary Peter
LaSota, Peter Douglas
Lee, Carl Douglas
Lesher, Stephen Harrison
Leshner, Stephen I.
Mallin, Robert Harold
Micheaels, John Allan
Murphy, R. Anthony
Myers, Robert David
Novak, Peter John
O'Steen, Van
Ricker, William Howard
Rivera, Armando
Rubenstein, Hy David
Rusing, Michael John
Ryan, Timothy Leo
Sandweg, William Henry, III
Simon, Jack Hunt
Smith, David Burnell
Stanford, Kenneth Charles
Stephan, Robert Joseph, Jr.
Thorpe, William Lee
Van Wagner, Albert Edwin, Jr.
Wall, Donald Arthur
Waterman, David Moore
Wezelman, Janice Anne
Winthrop, Lawrence Fredrick
Wisniewski, Robert Edward

Arkansas

Bailey, Frank Henry
Bristow, Bill Wayne
Davis, Steven Ray
Drummond, Winslow
Dudley, Timothy Oliver
Ellis, George Dawlin
Eubanks, Gary Leroy
Fergus, William Lee
Fogleman, John Nelson
Hamilton, Herman Lynn, Jr.
Harkey, John Norman
Hobbs, Richard White
Hughes, Thomas Morgan, III
Julian, Jim Lee
Leslie, Robert Bruce
McKenzie, Horace Houston
Pearson, Charles Thomas, Jr.
Perroni, Samuel Arnold
Pinson, Jerry D.
Ralls, Rawleigh Hazen, III
Skinner, Jack Merle
Spencer, Frederick S.
Spinks, Hugh Franklin, Jr.
Thrailkill, Daniel B.
Walters, William Peter
Wright, John Homer
Zukowski, Mark Daniel

California

Albert, Ward Wian
Alexander, Richard
Askew, James Albert
Atkins, Robert Alan
August, Ann
Bakeman, Willard Patrick, III
Bandy, Jack D.
Barbabelata, Robert D.
Barber, Stephan Allen
Baskin, David Green
Bass, Lewis
Bennion, David Jacobsen
Bentley, John Martin
Berger, Harvey Charles
Berman, David Ira
Biscay, Marcel Pierre
Bisetti, Richard L.
Bjork, Robert David, Jr.
Blum, Melanie Rae
Blumberg, John Philip
Bohn, Robert Herbert
Bonham, Terrence James
Bonney, George William
Braafladt, Arnie Rolf
Bridges, B. Ried
Brisson, Claudia Wisner
Broderick, Daniel Thomas, III
Brookman, Anthony Raymond
Broome, Thomas Jefferson
Brown, Don C.
Brown, Phillip Edward
Burns, Bruce William
Burton, Randall James
Byron, Thomas William
Bysshe, Frederick Herbert, Jr.
Cadwell, David Robert
Callahan, Gary Brent
Callison, Russell James
Caplan, Morton Lawrence
Carlson, Jeffery John
Carr, James Patrick
Castello, Raymond Vincent
Chang, Peter Asha, Jr.
Ching, Anthony
Ciambella, Cory Joseph
Cleary, William Joseph, Jr.
Cohen, Steven Elliott
Cohn, Nathan
Coil, Horace Orcutt
Colley, Nathaniel S(extus), Jr.
Corrales, Manuel, Jr.
Costello, Donald Fredric
Cox, Stephen Troyce
Crosby, William Marshall
Darling, Scott Edward
Dean, Ronald Glenn
Deane, George Ingram, III
de Kirby, Vaughan Ransone
Delaughter, Jerry L.
Demos, Jeffrey Charles
DeRonde, John Allen, Jr.
Doan, Xuyen Van
Dodge, Richard Edgar
Dorit, J Niley
Dorr, Roderick Akin
Dryden, Robert Eugene
Duggan, Thomas Michael
Ebiner, Robert Maurice
Einhorn, Lawrence Martin
Engel, R. Jay
Evans, John William
Faile, Wendell Wayne
Finger, John Holden
Fink, Robert Stanley
Fischbach, Donald Richard
Fisher, Myron R.
Flanagan, James Henry, Jr.
Flanders, Gilbert Lee
Fletcher, R(ufus) Burton, Jr.
Friedman, Bruce A.
Friedman, Lester James
Friedman, Morton Lee
Friedman, Wallace
Garman, John William
Garrison, Stuart Hugh
Georgallis, Joann
Germann, J. Gary
Glaser, Patricia L.
Gnesin, Mark Meredith
Goethals, Richard Bernard, Jr.
Goodwin, James Jeffries
Graham, Robert Lee
Greenstein, Robert Stanley
Gregg, Richard
Grier, John Cummings
Guido, Diana Lydia
Haims, Arnold Brody
Hamilton, Phillip Douglas
Hanks, Maja Kristin
Harris, Lee S.
Harris, Michael Gene
Harrison, Robert Wayne
Hassan, Allen C.
Heaton, Roger Laurence
Henderson, Daniel Eli, Jr.
Hendrickson, Ray
Henke, Raymond Lange
Heywood, Robert Gilmour
Higgs, Craig DeWitt
Hoagland, Grant Taylor
Hodges, Robert W.
Hoey, James Douglas, III
Holzmann, James Charles
Hooser, Eugene Albert
Hopkins, Donald Ray
Horton, Luther William
Hovland, Carl Michael
Ingram, Jeffrey Charles
Ingram, Robert Bruce
Jagiello, Barbara Anne
Johnson, Richard Wesley
Johnson-Champ, Debra Sue
Jones, Thomas Robert
Kaufman, Albert I.
Kay, William Thomas, Jr.
Kazanjian, Phillip Carl
Kehoe, Dennis Joseph
King, Franklin Weaver
King, William J.
Kirkpatrick, Richard Charles
Kitta, John Noah
Klein, Alan Richard
Kleinberg, Joel Williams Harris
Koep, Richard Michael
Kornblum, Guy Orville
Krell, Bruce Edward
Kroger, Catharine Elisabeth
Kuhl, Paul Beach
Kump, Kary Ronald
Kuntz, Charles Powers
Lageson, Ernest Benjamin
Lampel, Arthur Harry
Lancaster, Michael James
Lauchengco, Jose Yujuico, Jr.
Lawton, Eric
Lenzi, Albert James, Jr.
Levine, David Israel
Levy, Peter Ludwig
Levy, Steven R.
Liccardo, Salvador A.
LiMandri, Charles Salvatore
Lloyd, William Emmons, Jr.
Lynch, Robert Thomas
Madory, Richard Eugene
Mannerino, John David
Markowitz, Michael Jay
McCall, Patrick Anthony
McCaslin, Leon
McCollum, Susan Hill
Mc Elwain, Lester Stafford
McIntosh, Bruce Terence
Mehlhaff, Robert
Mendelson, Steven Earle
Michaels, Michael Daniel
Miles, Dori Elizabeth
Miller, Thomas Eugene
Millstein, David J.
Monaco, Daniel Joseph
Moore, Raymond Robert
Morgan, William Robert
Moriarity, John L.
Morrell, Rivers Judson, III
Muhlbach, Robert Arthur
Mullen, Thomas Moore
Murphy, Stephen Michael
Negron, Dennis
Ninnis, William Raymond, Jr.
Nissenberg, Merel Grey
Nisson, Timothy James
Noe, Ralph Henderson, Jr.
O'Shields, June Cruce
Paden, Gary Lewis
Palitz, Murray
Parton, James, III
Peters, Louis Donald
Pierry, Thomas James
Pitre, Frank Mario
Pleiss, Larry Thomas
Pollak, Jeffrey Saul
Poppett, Mark Adams
Priest, Maurice Abner, Jr.
Rabin, Robert L.
Ragetté-Blaine, Dorothea Constance
Ramsey, Owen Jasper, Jr.
Randall, Mel Scott
Reed, Brian Edward
Reed, Wallace Calvin
Regnier, Richard Adrian
Reith, Daniel I.
Resich, John James
Resneck, William Allan
Roberts, Jayne Kelly
Robertson, James Allen
Robinson, Archie Stirling
Rogan, Patrick Goode
Roseman, Charles Sanford
Rosenthal, Kenneth Wolfgang
Rozanski, Stanley Howard
Rubin, Dale Michael
Rummonds, James Scott
Russell, Thomas Hunter
Ruston, Donald Allen
Rutten, Rand John
Sadler, Bruce Phillip
Saroyan, Suren Michael
Sayad, Pamela Miriam
Schulner, Lawrence Mayer
Sears, Douglas Alson
Shaw, William Albert
Shea, Michael Murt
Silveria, Linda Lorraine
Silverman, Milton Joseph, Sr.
Simonini, David Michael
Smith, Stanley David
Smitter, Ronald Warren
Sobel, Erwin
Solish, Jonathan Craig
Solo, Gail Dianne
Spriggs, Everett Lee
Squarcy, Charlotte Van Horne
Steinberger, Jeffrey Wayne
Stephenson, Michael Murray
Stewart, Helen Margery
Stolpman, Thomas Gerard
Stone, Jean
Sussman, Mitchell Reed
Sutherland, Lowell Francis
Telleria, Anthony F.
Thon, William Marvin
Tobin, Harold William
Truett, Harold Joseph, III
Truman, Rolland A.
Tsenin, Ksenia
Turek, Kenneth Casper
Vandegrift, Lucian B.
Veatch, Wayne Otis, Sr.
Walker, Walter Herbert, III
Walwyn, Stephen John
Ward, Anthony John
Warnlof, John Skinner
Wasserman, Michael Eric
Weatherup, Roy Garfield
Weinberg, Steven Jay
Weisberg, Sheila Roseanne
Weissman, I. Donald
Wellins, Sheldon (Shel) Gary
Wentworth, Theodore Sumner
Wenzel, Lee Bey
Werner, Robert George
Wesierski, Christopher Paul
Wohlfeil, Joel R.
Wolfe, Richard Frederick
Woodhead, Frank Womack
Worthington, Leonard A.
Wright, Frank Clarence, Jr.
Wylie, Richard John
Yim, B(urgess) Casey
Zimmermann, John Frederick

Colorado

Adkins, Marilyn Biggs
Aspinwall, David Charles
Barnes, Thomas Arthur, Jr.
Bogue, Jeffrey A.
Brady, William John, Jr.
Branney, Joseph John
Brega, Charles Franklin
Brown, Ian Alexander
Browne, C. Willing, III
Carlson, Alan Douglas
Carlton, Diane Michele
Carney, Deborah Leah Turner
Carney, Thomas T.J.
Casebolt, James Stanton
Chalat, James Harold
Clay, Aaron Richard
Cook, Kenneth Totman
Cooper, Paul Douglas
DeLaney, Herbert Wade, Jr.
de Marino, Thomas John
Donlon, William James, Jr.
Downsbrough, Bruce Owen
Eberhardt, Robert Schuler, Jr.
Eckelberger, Jerrie Francis
Epstein, Joseph Marc
Evans, Paul Vernon
Falcone, Richard Edward
Feiger, Lynn Diamond
Fierst, Bruce Philip
Friedberg, Alan Charles
Gessling, James Place
Hale, Daniel Cudmore
Heldman, Victoria C.
Hoffman, Daniel Steven
Holst, Dale Lawson
Jackson, Richard Brooke
Jamison, Jamey William
Janklow, Donald Emanuel
Jersin, Edward Anthony
Judd, Joel Stanton
Laugesen, Richard W.
LeHouillier, Patric Jaymes
Leiser, Harvey Wayne
Livingston, John L.
Logan, Valentine Weir
Martin, E. Gregory
McConaty, Brian Gilmour
McCormick, George Paul, Jr.
Meyer, William Dale
Moss, Victor
Noall, L. Scott
Olson, Ronald Keith
Pack, Stuart Harris
Parker, George Earl
Petrucci, Stephen Gerard
Purvis, John Anderson
Raymond, Douglas J.
Rector, Leo Daniel
Rench, Stephen Charles
Richman, Alan Elliott
St. Clair, Scott Andrew
Scott, Paul Edward
Sedlak, Joseph Anthony, III
Shanaberger, Carol Jean
Slaninger, Frank Paul
Sloat, Gerald Charles
Snyder, Paul, Jr.
Springer, Jeffrey Alan
Taylor, Robert Lynn
Tegtmeier, Richard Lewis
Vanatta, Dean R.
Vigil, David Charles
Vogel, Lawrence Mark
Welton, Charles Ephraim
Weltzer, Louis Albin
Wieman, Terry Lynn
Wilcox, Martha Anne

Connecticut

Adelman, Robert Bardwell
Amento, Carl Joseph
Asselin, John Thomas
Bartolini, James Daniel
Benedict, Peter Behrends
Calabresi, Guido
Carrano, Frank Anthony
Carta, John James, Jr.
Casagrande, Daniel Eugene
Cocco, Leonard M.
Collins, John Albert, III
Crimmins, Eileen Marie
De Barbieri, Roy Louis
Dupont, Ralph Paul
Dzurik, John Gerard
Effron, Wayne Douglas
Endrelunas, Richard Michael
Fain, Joel Maurice
Finley, Lucinda Margaret
FitzGerald, Edward Browne
Friar, Martha Jane
Goldfarb, Alexander A.
Halloran, Robert Bartley
Harper, Monica Lafferty
Hayes, Margaret Mary
Holth, Fredrik Davidson
Johnson, Allan Richard
Karazin, Edward Robert, Jr.
Lamb, Frederic Davis
Lynn, Robert John
MacKenzie, Roderick John, Jr.
Maniatis, Charlynn Carol
Miano, Frederick Joseph
Morelli, Carmen
Nicola, Robert James
Nielsen, Anita Spector
Noonan, Patrick Matthew
O'Connor, James Michael
Osis, Daiga Guntra
Piazza, Anthony Andrew
Pinsky, Irving Jay
Ross, Michael Frederick
Royston, Christopher Michael
Sauer, David Allen
Schatz, Arthur Herschel
Schatz, Richard Ansell
Schwartz, Kove Jerome
Sheiman, Stuart Melvyn
Skuret, Daniel D.
Slocum, Shaun Michael
Snaider, Benson Abram
Sorokin, Ethel Silver
Sweeney, William Jones, Jr.
Taalman, Juri E.
Trebisacci, Raymond Thomas
Williams, Ronald Doherty
Zakarian, Albert

Delaware

Bader, John Merwin
Bradley, Paul Anthony
Brandt, Charles
Ciconte, Edward Thomas
Del Pesco, Susan Marie Carr
Harrington, Rick Alan
Herrmann, Philip Eric
Kimmel, Morton Richard
Levine, Norman Edward
Marin, Bayard
Marlin, Jeffrey Stuart
Marvel, Wayne Andrew
Morris, Kenneth Donald
Partnoy, Ronald Allen
Ridgely, Henry Johnson
Semple, James William
Stokes, Richard Francis
Suddard, Oliver Vincent
Whitehurst, Charles Elwood, Jr.
Wolhar, Robert Charles, Jr.

District of Columbia

Abelson, Michael Allen
Bolden, Melvin Wilberforce, Jr.
Brown, Thomas Philip, III
Dembrow, Dana Lee
Dombroff, Mark Andrew
Drennan, Joseph Peter
Farley, John Joseph, III
Farrell, George Edwin
Feldman, Michael Harris
Fise, Thomas Francis
Fitzpatrick, John Michael
Frank, William Harris
Himelfarb, Stephen Roy
Janis, N. Richard
Junkin, Timothy Deforest
Karp, Ronald Alvin
Kelly, Kathryn
King, John Winston
Kornblut, Arthur T.
Lenhart, James Thomas
Longstreth, Robert Christy
Lyon, Richard Kirshbaum
Madden, Jerome Anthony
Micheel, Richard Arthur
Mitchell, Gerard Ellsworth
Nace, Barry John
Nelson, William Eugene
Norwind, Edward Lee
Principi, Elizabeth Ahlering
Rhodes, Richard Randolph
Rubin, Janet Beth
Scullen, James Roche
Statland, Edward Morris
Swartz, Dean Elliot
Tate, Thomas Harrison
Ughetta, Valerie Jeanne
Walker, Vern Robert
Zimmerly, James Gregory

Florida

Abbott, Charles Warren
Abramson, Harvey Stanley
Allen, W. Riley
Anderson, Carol McMillan
Anthony, Andrew John
Asencio, Diego Carlos
Atkinson, John Bond
Balkany, Caron Lee
Barnett, Richard Allen
Barnhart, Forrest Gregory
Barr, Harry E.
Bates, Richard Warden
Berger, C. William
Berger, Steven R.
Berman, Richard Bruce
Bernstein, Michael Alan
Berry, Gerald Thomas
Biggs, Thomas Sanford, Jr.
Blumberg, Edward Robert
Bombino, Isabel Piñera
Bopp, Thomas Roe
Bosse, Richard Edward
Boyles, Kevan Kenneth
Boynton, Gary John
Briggs, Randy Robert
Brock, Newman Dempsey
Bronis, Stephen J.
Brumbaugh, John Moore
Brumer, Michael
Burnette, Guy Ellington, Jr.
Busch, David John
Cacciatore, S. Sammy, Jr.
Callender, John Francis
Carpenter, Darrell Franklin
Castillo, Hal Stephen
Catlin, Harold Harvey
Chidnese, Patrick N.
Chopin, Susan Gardiner
Cohen, Jeffrey Michael
Cole, Robert Allen
Cooney, David Francis
Cordell, Martin Lewis
Corlett, Edward Stanley, III
Crespo, Manuel A.
Cunningham, James Reynolds
Custureri, Richard Domenick
David, Ronald Albert
Davis, Barry Lee
Davis, William Howard
Deehl, David Lee
Denker, Randall Elizabeth
Denman, James Burton
Diaz, Benito Humberto
Donaldson, Dorothea E.
Durie, Jack Frederick, Jr.
Eaton, Joel Douglas
Echsner, Stephen Herre
Eckhart, James Milton
Edwards, William Thomas, Jr.
Ehrlich, Raymond
Emerton, Robert Walter, III
Epperson, Joel Rodman
Evans, George Michael
Ezzo, Ralph Patrick
Falk, Glenn Phillip
Farrell, Patrick Joseph, Jr.
Feder, Scott Jay
Fernandez, William Warren
Finkelstein, Joseph Judah
Fox, Gary Devenow
Fromberg, Malcolm Hubert
Galamaga, Robert John
Gassler, Frank Henry
Geller, Steven Anthony
Gievers, Karen A.
Gilbert, Ronald Bart
Glass, Roy Leonard
Glick, Brian Jay
Glinn, Franklyn Barry
Gluck, Robin Beverly
Goldstein, Harvey M.
Graham, Andrew Alan
Greenwald, Steven Jeffrey
Grilli, Peter John
Gross, Terence Alan
Haliczer, James Solomon
Harris, Warren Louis
Hasty, Frederick Emerson, III
Heindl, Phares Matthews
Hernandez, Daniel Mario
Hickman, Paula Diane
Hill, Brian Donovan
Hooper, Joel Randall
Horn, Andrew Warren
Itkin, Perry Steven
Jamieson, James Phillips

Johnston, Charles Motley
Jones, John Edward
Joseph, Paul R.
Joyner, Arthenia Lee
Keating, Gerard F.
Kelly, Thomas Paine, Jr.
Koenig, Sherman
Kohl, Donald Phillip
Krathen, David Howard
Kray, Fred Martin
Lance, Miles A.
Lane, Robin R.
Levin, David Harold
Levin, Frederic Gerson
Liles, Rutledge Richardson
Lipcon, Charles R.
London, Jack Edward
Mansbach, Robert Earl, Jr.
Martinez, Mel R.
Masterson, Bernard Joseph
McAliley, Thomas Watson
McCurdy, Robert Clark
McDonnell, Michael R. N.
McDuffee, Paul Gerard, II
McGee, C(larence) Edward, Jr.
McGill, Gerald Allen
McIntosh, Douglas Malcolm
McKenzie, James Franklin
McKeown, Frank James
McMakin, J. Gary
McNally, James Joseph
Mehrtens, William Osborne, Jr.
Merlin, William Firman, Jr.
Merting, John Webster
Miller, Carla Dorothy
Miller, Raymond Vincent, Jr.
Montgomery, David Paul
Montgomery, Robert Morel, Jr.
Moody, James Shelton, Jr.
Moore, Thomas Adair
Murrell, Robert George
Nichols, Cynthia Leigh
O'Neal, Michael Scott, Sr.
Palahach, Michael
Park, Joseph Rathbone
Parrish, Sidney Howard
Peck, Bernard Sidney
Penland, Samuel Perry, Jr.
Phillips, Gary Stephen
Podrecca, Adolfo Augusto
Pomeroy, Gregg Joseph
Pound, Frank R., Jr.
Ramsey, Bruce Mitchell
Reiter, Joseph John
Rexrode, David Stephen
Richardson, Scott Neil
Richeson, Hugh Anthony, Jr.
Roach, Richard R., Jr.
Rodriguez, Jose Gabriel
Rogel, Todd Stephen
Rojas, Jose Ignacio
Rose, Norman
Schember, Steven George
Schiff, Louis Howard
Schnell, Ronald Hans
Schwartz, Bruce S.
Schwedock, Peter Saul
Scremin, Anthony James
Searcy, Christian Deitrich, Sr.
Seelie, Michael Edward
Shea, J. Michael
Sheaffer, William Jay
Shields, William Henry
Siegel, Paul
Silverman, Scott Jay
Slaydon, Roger James
Smith, James Hibbert
Somers, Clifford Louis
Spellacy, John Frederick
Spencer, W(alter) Thomas
Sperry, Martin J.
Stack, Charles Rickman
Stanley, Bruce McLaren
Stein, Stuart Leonard
Stepp, Kenneth Stephenson
Stern, Duke Nordlinger
Stevens, Harold Sanford
Stewart, Larry S.
Stieglitz, Albert Blackwell
Stinson, Steven Arthur
Sutton, Michael Ferris
Symons, Robin Suzanne Taylor
Telepas, George Peter
Terrell, James Thomas
Terry, T(aylor) Rankin, Jr.
Tombrink, Richard, Jr.
Traitz, James Joseph, Jr.
Tygart, S. Thompson, Jr.
Valle, Laurence Francis
Vernis, Frank Carl, Jr.
Watson, Robert James
West, Harold
Whigham, Thomas Edmondson
Whitcomb, William Grandon
Wich, Donald Anthony, Jr.
Williams, Stewart Dorian
Wiltshire, William Harrison Flick
Wirtz, Gregg Lee
Wood, Julian Emory
Yerrid, C. Steven
Young, Terry Cressler
Zaretsky, Esther Anne
Zorie, Stephanie Marie

Georgia

Allen, Hunter Smith, Jr.
Armstrong, Edwin Alan
Baker, Verlyn Childs
Bassler, Harry Warren
Baverman, Elida Blaine
Billington, Barry E.
Blackstock, Jerry Byron
Blank, A(ndrew) Russell
Bostic, Harris Clemon
Breeding, Earnie Rowe
Bright, Joseph Converse
Brown, Stephen Phillip
Curry, Stephen Euree
Davis, E. Marcus
Davison, John Arthur
Dean, George Ross
Deegan, Nan Marie
Dettmering, William O'Neal, Jr.
Dickert, Neal Workman
Dodd, Roger James
Duttweiler, Larry L.
England, John Melvin
Felton, Jule Wimberly, Jr.
Finnell, Robert Kirtley
Fiorentino, Carmine
Flowers, William Harold, Jr.
Fox, Patrick Joseph
Frey, Monroe Lynn, III
Gifford, William David
Gleaton, Frederick Neal
Griffeth, Ronald Clyde
Hayes, Dewey Norman
Head, Hugh Garland, Jr.
Henderson, Daniel Lamar
Hibbert, David Wilson
Jenkins, Thomas A(llan)
Johnson, Donald (Don) Wayne
Johnson, Lester Benjamin, III
Kellogg, Edward Herbert, Jr.
Kessler, Kathleen
Lachance, James Martin
Lokey, Hamilton
Lore, Stephen Melvin
Mahan, John Ernest
Malone, Thomas William
McCracken, Eugene Luke
Miller, Alfred Montague
Miller, Jack Everett
Nesmith-Rosner, Joanna
Oliver, Bonnie Chessher
Patrick, James Duvall, Jr.
Perry, Alan Rogers, Jr.
Pilcher, James Brownie
Powell, Douglas Richard
Powell, Richard Lynn
Reinhardt, Daniel Sargent
Roberson, Lynn Marie
Roberts, James Isaac, Sr.
Savell, Edward Lupo
Shinall, Robert Phillip, III
Thomas, Richard English
Thrash, Thomas Woodrow
Underwood, William Fleming, Jr.
Weaver, George Marvin
Wellon, Robert G.
Wood, L. Lin, Jr.
Zachary, William Edmund

Hawaii

Acoba, Simeon Rivera, Jr.
Apo, Jan Kanani
Berman, Pamela Jill
Burke, Edmund
Chun-Hoon, Lowell Koon Ying
Cohn, Lawrence William
Crumpton, Charles Whitmarsh
Duffy, James Earl, Jr.
Fong, Valerie (Wai Hin)
Frey, Philip Sigmund
Fried, L. Richard, Jr.
Fritz, Collin Martin
Fukumoto, Leslie Satsuki
Gillin, Malvin James, Jr.
Goldsmith, Stephen Ernest
Grinpas, Robert Mark
Hastert, Diane Deskins
Howell, Alan Peter
Krueger, James
Kuniyuki, Ken Takaharu
Louie, David Mark
Lowenthal, Philip Henry
Marx, Robert Phillip
Morse, Jack Craig
Mukaida, Wayne Hideo
Potts, Dennis Walker
Robinson, John Harvey
Sabath, Kenneth Michael
Songstad, Steven Booth
Turbin, Richard
Turk, David L.
Van De Car, Diana Lee
Van Pernis, Mark
White, Lawrence Richard
Williams, Allen Kenneth
Wilson, Virgil James, III
Wong, James Thomas
Wong, Michael Jung-Yen
Wong, Wayson Wai Sun
Yamada, Stephen Kinichi
Yano, Francis Hisao

Idaho

Dale, Candy Wagahoff
Gasser, Emmett Clark
Greenfield, John Frederic
Hines, William Joseph
Hoagland, Samuel Albert
Jarzabek, Joseph Edward
Kerrick, David Ellsworth
Luker, Lynn Michael
Mauk, William Lloyd
May, James, Jr.
McCabe, Thomas James
McLaughlin, Robert Francis
Nye, W. Marcus W.
Park, William Anthony
Parmenter, David N.
Schlender, E. Lee
Smyser, (Charles Arvil) Skip
Sorensen, Murray Jim
Stoker, Robin Jeffrey
Webb, Lloyd Jackson
Wetherell, Mike

Illinois

Ackman, Richard LeRoy
Ahern, Gregory Emmett
Baker, Bennett Joel
Bauer, Joseph Louis
Beatty, William Glenn
Berman, Michael Howard
Biestek, John Paul
Blan, Kennith William, Jr.
Blank, Gary L.
Bohlen, Christopher Wayne
Bollinger, Barry Gilbert
Bone, Maurice Edgar
Brand, Robert Joseph
Brent, Nancy Jean
Burke, Dennis J.
Burke, John Michael
Burke, Thomas Joseph, Jr.
Callahan, Dennis John
Callis, Felix L.
Canel, James Harrison
Cheely, Daniel Joseph
Church, Glenn J.
Cifelli, John Louis
Cipolla, Vincent Charles
Coccia, Michel Andre
Cohen, Stephen Bruce
Colantoni, Anthony Michael
Cosgrave, Carmel M.
Costello, James Paul
Coughlin, Terrance J
Cunningham, William Francis
Curran, Mark Cooney
Davis, Dean Martin
De Jong, David John
DeSanto, James John
Donohue, Richard Harney
Driscoll, Patrick Thomas, Jr.
Duncan, Edward Rogers, Jr.
Ebert, Regan Danielle
Elman, William
Erlebacher, Arlene Cernik
Erschen, Gail Lee
Ettinger, Joseph Alan
Fahey, Robert Francis
Farrug, Eugene Joseph
Fedota, Mark Clarke
Finnegan, Thomas Joseph
Fleischli, Franz K., III
Freerksen, Gregory Nathan
Garofalo, John Richard
Gifford, Geoffrey L.
Glenn, Cleta Mae
Goldenhersh, Murray Jacob
Goldstein, Candice
Gordon, Barry L.
Gordon, Theodora
Gorman, James Edward
Gossage, Roza
Gramlich, Charles J.
Greenberg, Lorraine M.
Grossgold, Nathan
Gutof, Richard Stewart
Hamrock, Mark Andrew
Harvey, Morris Lane
Heaton, Joseph Edward, Jr.
Hegarty, Terrence K.
Heiligenstein, Christian Erica
Hepplewhite, David Wilson
Herald, John Patrick
Hoffman, Alan Craig
Horsley, George William
Horwitz, Clifford Wolf
Horwitz, Mitchell Wolf
Hultquist, Robert Charles
Hynes, James Patrick
Johnson, Richard Fred
Johnson, William Vincent
Johnston, A. Sidney
Juergensmeyer, John Eli
Kasten, Carl E.
Kawitt, Alan
Kearns, James Cannon
Kell, Vette Eugene
Kennelly, John Jerome
Kimball, Spencer Levan
Kralovec, Charles Vopicka
Kurowski, John Joseph
Kuster, Larry Donald
Laski, James Emil
Lederer, William Joseph
Leigh, Gary Dean
Leopold, Valerie Ann
Lewis, James Brooke
Lewis, William Theodore, Jr.
Lindenmuth, Noel Charles
Lipton, Mark Daniel
Logan, Michael James
Loggans, Susan Elizabeth
Long, Robert Jeffrey
Lyons, Kevin W.
Malvik, John
Mancini, Lorenzo Anthony
Manion, Paul Thomas
Marquard, Henry Francis
Martan, Joseph Rudolf
Mateer, Don Metz
McCabe, Charles Kevin
McCarthy, Kitty Monaghan
McCarthy, Timothy Michael
McClure, Thomas Edward
McVisk, William Kilburn
Menges, Eugene Clifford
Meyer, Stanley Russell
Miller, Kenneth Charles
Mone, Peter John
Moore, Kathleen Ann
Mueller, Richard Edward
Murphy, William Celestin
Narko, Medard Martin
Nixon, Lewis Michael
O'Conor, Andrew Joseph, IV
Ozmon, Laird Michael
Pace, O(le) B(ly), Jr.
Parad, Boris
Patterson, Robert Bruce, Jr.
Pavalon, Eugene I.
Pearlman, Alan
Phebus, Joseph W.
Phipps, John Tom
Pope, Michael Arthur
Prochnow, Douglas Lee
Raney, Donald Raymond
Rank, John Thomas
Rawles, Edward Hugh
Rehberger, Robert Lee
Richmond, William Patrick
Ring, Leonard M.
Ripplinger, George Raymond, Jr.
Robertson, David Haswell, Jr.
Rochelle, Victor Cleanthus
Rose, Dennis Edward
Ross, Robert John
Roth, Ronald Anthony
Ruud, Glenn F.
Ryan, Frank James
Sanchez, Manuel
Scantlebury, Hilary Thomas
Schneider, Earl Gary
Schoenfield, Rick Merrill
Schroeder, Carl Frederick, Jr.
Scudder, Theodore Townsend, III
Serritella, William David
Shapiro, Donald Allan
Shapo, Marshall Schambelan
Sims, Murray William, Jr.
Snyder, Dean Edward
Soltis, Robert Alan
Spears, Ronald Dean
Strodel, Robert Carl
Strom, Michael A.
Swain, John Barry
Swanson, Lenard Charles
Terc, Joseph Anthony
Tobin, Craig Daniel
Tognarelli, Richard Lee
Tungate, Susan Sumner
Vincent, Adrian Roger
Walker, Daniel, Jr.
Walston, Beth Elaine
Walton, Stanley Anthony, III
Ward, Jack Donald
Webster, John Clyde
Weir, William H.
Weisman, Larry Edward
Wesley, Howard Barry
Wilcox, Mark Dean
Williams, Michael Stephen
Williamson, Nile Jay
Wilson, Edward Churchill
Wohlreich, Jack Jay

Indiana

Allen, Kenneth James
Applegate, Karl Edwin
Bamberth, Hugo Arnold
Bate, Charles Thomas
Becher, Paul Eugene
Bennett, Maxine Taylor
Berger, Charles Lee
Berger, Sydney L.
Bodkin, Robert Thomas
Borns, Clarence
Buehler, James Carroll
Choplin, John Max, II
Clark, Eric Oden
Cline, Lance Douglas
Coffman, Anne Blankenburg
Doehrman, Thomas C.
Dywan, Jeffery Joseph
Eckert, Stephen Paul
Fairchild, Raymond Francis
Gray, George Clyde
Grodnik, Charles Hubert
Hamilton, John Anthony
Hammel, John Wingate
Harrold, Dennis Edward
Haury, John Carroll
Hays, Thomas Clyde
Henthorn, Charles Rex
Hovde, F. Boyd
Hubbell, Calvin Keith
Jennings, Charles Thomas
Johnson, Shelli Wright
Jordan, Denver Christian
Justice, Robert Scott
Katich, Nick
Keen, Robert Thomas, Jr.
King, Douglas Bruce
Koch, Edna Mae
Layden, Charles Max
Lebamoff, Ivan Argire
Levy, Lawrence Alan
Lewis, Robert Lee
Lindsey, Roger Leighton
Lisher, John Leonard
Loveall, George Michael
McDowell, Dock, Jr.
Meacham, Jerald Samuel
Modesitt, Fritzy Dal
Montross, W. Scott
Moss, Kirby Glenn
Muller, John
Murphy, Sharon Funcheon
Myers, James Woodrow, III
Nasser, Woodrow Sam
O'Reilly, Michael James
Pardieck, Roger L.
Pennell, Stephen Richard
Roby, Daniel Arthur
Ruman, Saul I.
Saint, Robert Edwards
Scaletta, Phillip Jasper
Schmitt, John Francis
Schreckengast, William O.
Sharpnack, John Trent
Shoulders, Patrick Alan
Smith, Theodore Frederick, Jr.
Springer, Steve Edward
Starkes, Dale Joseph
Stimson, Judith Nemeth
Townsend, Earl Cunningham, Jr.
Wellnitz, Craig Otto
Wicks, Charles Carter
Woods, Joseph Reid
Yosha, Louis Buddy
Young, Randy William
Young, Thomas Jordan

Iowa

Beisser, Louie Frederick
Brown, William Ted
Butler, David Douglas
Clogg, Richard Bruce
Conlin, Roxanne Barton
Coonrad, Douglas V.
Crook, Charles Samuel, III
Cutler, Charles Edward
Ditmars, Lyle William
Doyle, Richard Henry, IV
Duckworth, Marvin E.
Eastman, Forest David
Eckhart, Morris Lee Roy
Ellefson, James C.
Foxhoven, Jerry Ray
Frey, A. John, Jr.
Giles, William Jefferson, III
Giles, William Jefferson, IV
Grove, Lad
Hamilton, James R.
Harding, Marc Steven
Henderson, Thomas
Hoffman, James Paul
Hoffmann, Michael Richard
Hood, James Michael
Johnson, John Paul
Langdon, Richard Garrett
Larson, David Christopher
Lathrop, Roger Alan
Lawyer, Verne
Leitner, David Larry
Liabo, Mark Elliot
Logan, Thomas Joseph
Manly, Charles M.
McCoy, John Thomas
McKay, Timothy John
Mueller, Barry Scott
Mull, Richard Eugene
Murray, William Michael (Mike)
Nelson, Robert Charles
Norris, James Robert
Peddicord, Roland Dale
Poffenberger, Richard Lee
Reilly, Michael Gerard
Rhodes, Ann Marie
Rinden, Gerry Mundt
Spies, Leon Fred
Stefani, Randall H.
Swanson, Mark Douglas
Taylor, Wallace L.
Tompkins, Richard Norton, Jr.
Tully, Robert Gerard
Walker, Bruce LeRoy
Warbasse, Steven Kenneth
White, Harold Wayne
Wilson, Robert Foster
Wing, Stephen Prentice

Kansas

Adrian, Robert Mac
Arnhold, Thomas Dean
Barnett, James Monroe
Boyle, Edward Michael
Carroll, Timothy Wayne
Dillon, Wilburn, Jr.
Fisher, Randall Eugene
Gross, Edmund Samuel
Hejtmanek, Danton Charles
Herrington, Alvin D.
Hodgson, Arthur Clay
Jacobson, Susan Curtis
Keplinger, (Donald) Bruce
Kessler, Stephen
King, Clarence LeRoy, Jr.
Kreamer, Scott Harrison
Matlack, Don(ald) (Clyde)
Neustrom, Patrik William
Nygaard, Diane Acker
Ochs, Robert Duane
O'Neal, Michael Ralph
Rogers, Terry Lee
Schroer, Gene Eldon
Sevart, Daniel Joseph
Short, Timothy Allen
Smithyman, Lee Miller
Snyder, Brock Robert
Sullivan, Thomas Eugene
Walker, Huffman Reed
Wall, Larry William
Williams, Ronald Paul
Yarbrough, Marilyn Virginia

Kentucky

Bowles, Jerry Jay
Bucalos, Dean Walter
Carey, Marcus Stephen
Connolly, Robert Michael
Eades, Ronald Wayne
Emmons, Alison Lobb
Feather, Mark Randolph
Gregory, Gary Hugh
Hagan, Charles Curtis, Jr.
Herren, Thomas Kelly
Ison, Robert Elwood
Johns, Harold Mac
Kerrick, Thomas Neal
King, Nicholas Neal
Massengale, Roger Lee
Meagher, Virginia Murnane
Megibow, Tod Douglas
Miller, Edward Douglas
Parker, William Jerry
Pettyjohn, Shirley Ellis
Prather, John Gideon, Jr.
Rawdon, Richard McLean, Jr.
Reinhardt, Roxane Tomasi
Ridings, Marcia Milby
Riggs, Roger D.
Robinson, William T., III
Rose, Charles Alexander
Simpson, Ronald Vincent
Sitlinger, Leroy Edward, Jr.
Smither, J. Michael
Sullivan, Richard Morrissey
Turley, Robert Joe
Varellas, James John, Jr.
Varellas, Sandra Motte
Wehr, William James
Weiner, Neil Steven
Welsh, Alfred John
Whalen, Paul Lewellin
Wolnitzek, Stephen Dale

Louisiana

Alsobrook, Henry Bernis, Jr.
Arceneaux, James Shaw
Ates, J. Robert
Aucoin, Barney R.
Bains, David Paul
Barranger, Garic Kenneth
Bassett, Jeffrey Michael
Begoun, Michael Jay
Bengtson, Karl Wayne
Booksh, Robert William, Jr.
Bossier, Larry Sherman
Brainis, Leon Irving
Bringle, William Timothy
Broussard, Richard C.
Bryan, Trevor George
Burt, Earl Daniel, Jr.
Centola, Lawrence Joseph
Chapman, Alex David, Jr.
Colvin, Charles Bruce
Connolly, George Charles, Jr.
David, Robert Jefferson
Davis, S. P.
Davis, Sumpter B., III
Denhollem, James Scott
Denton, Roger Marius
Didriksen, Caleb H., III
Dinwiddie, Bruce Wayland
Facussé, Albert Shucry
Fuhrer, Leonard
Furman, Michael Joseph
Gallagher, John M., Jr.
Gauthier, Wendell Haynes
Giepert, Melvin John
Granier, Kirk Raymond
Gravel, Camille Francis, Jr.
Griffith, Steven Franklin, Sr.
Guilliot, Paul Jerome
Halliburton, John Robert
Herman, Russ Michel
Herring, Charles Evans, Jr.
Hurley, Grady Schell
Johnson, James McDade

Jones, Keith Dunn
Kaplan, Edward Alan
Knoll, Jerold Edward
Kracht, Eric Alan
Kuss, Mark Davis
Lane, Charles Ray
Lane, Steven Jay
Leger, Walter John, Jr.
Lestelle, Andrea Sucherman
Levy, Adolph J.
Lirette, Danny Joseph
Lombard, Michael Albert
Lyons, Laurie Wilkinson
Manard, Robert Lynn, III
McClelland, James Ray
McGovern, Glenn Charles
Mickel, Joseph Thomas
Milly, Lawrence Arthur
Milly, Raymond Anthony
Moliere, Donna Renee
Morris, Frank Lowry
Murray, Julian R., Jr.
Nalls, Clarence Theo
Nungesser, Nancy Ann
Olinde, John Francis
Perlman, Jerald Lee
Pierce, James Winston, Jr.
Pitts, Birdia Marie Greer
Poirrier, Michael Joseph
Porter IV, Thomas Fitzgerald
Prestridge, Rogers Meredith
Price, Lionel Franklin
Pucheu, John Henri
Reed, Bruce Gilbert
Riccio, Marie Olympia
Rigby, Kenneth
St. Pe, Philippi Pierre
Sanders, Mike Charles
Schoemann, Rudolph Robert
Scott, L. Havard, III
Showers, Jack Paul
Smith, Brian David
Smith, Christopher Michael
Stout, A(rthur) Wendel, III
Swift, John Goulding
Thomas, Joseph Winand
Treadaway, Randell Edward
Trombatore, Janet Moulton
Tschirn, Darryl Jude
Uddo, Basile Joseph
Veron, J. Michael
Vitiello, Michael
Walker, Henry Clay, IV
Warshauer, Irving Jay
Webb, Daniel Andrew
Weisler, Faye Leslie
Widmann, Harry Thomas
Windmeyer, Joseph Edwin
Woodard, Billie Elayne Colombaro
Wright, Bob Forrest
Wright, Jack, Jr.
Wysocki, James Anthony

Maine

Ballou, John Waldo
Burke, Edmund James
Burns, Jeffrey Robert
Crawford, Linda Sibery
Dyer, Matthew Finis
Hunt, Merrill Roberts
Kirchner, Theodore Harry
Laney, William R.
Levandoski, Dennis
Mills, Sumner Peter, III
Moriarty, James Paul
Moss, Logan Vansen
Picavet, Robert Clement
Priest, Charles Randall
Reef, Norman Sidney
Rundlett, Ellsworth Turner, III
Smith, Jeffrey Allen
Tepler, Sheldon Joel
Vickerson, William Leo
Watson, Thomas Riley
Willard, William Wells
Willey, N. Laurence, Jr.

Maryland

Appel, Thomas Alan
Ashin, Jeffery Gordon
Badger, Jeffrey Ewen
Bekman, Paul D.
Berkson, Jacob Benjamin
Blakeslee, Wesley Daniel
Bresnahan, Pamela Anne
Brill, Lawrence Joel
Brooks, Sheila Durant
Calhoun, John L.
Clancy, Joseph Patrick
Cohen, Hyman K.
DeVries, Donald Lawson, Jr.
Elliott, J. Victor
Evelius, John Charles
Fick, Nathaniel Crow, Jr.
Freeman, Martin Henry
Gallavan, Michael Lee
Goldscheider, Sidney
Haldeman, George Paul
Hanley, Robert Lee, Jr.
Hennegan, John Owen
Henry, Edwin Maurice, Jr.
Hicks, Cassandra Pauline
Hughes, Leo A., Jr.
Jayson, Lester Samuel
Jenkins, Robert Rowe
Katz, Barry Edward
Kayson, David
King, John Frances
Klein, Robert Dale
Krensky, Michael Ian
Kuryk, David Neal
Lazzaro, Robert Wayne
Lechter, Kenneth Alan
Loker, F(rank) Ford, Jr.
Mann, Michael Bond
Martin, Clifford
Matty, Robert Jay
Miles, Gerard Frances
Miliman, David Jay
Miller, Max Dunham, Jr.
Monahan, John Connolly
Nagle, John Joseph, III
O'Brien, Dennis Francis
Orman, Leonard Arnold
Petraitis, Karel Colette
Protokowicz, Stanley Edward, Jr.
Rheinstein, Peter Howard
Robinson, Stuart Jay
Rochlin, Paul R.
Ruppersberger, Charles Albert, III
Sack, Sylvan Hanan
Salim, Abdullah (Reginald Armistice Hawkins), Jr.
Santa Maria, Philip Joseph, III
Schochor, Jonathan
Scott, Charles Lurman
Scott, Doris Petersen
Shar, Marcus Z.
Shepard, Adam Hoffman
Siegel, Harold Aryai
Simons, David Warren
Smith, Jonathan Scott
Snyder, Stuart Jay
Uehlinger, Gerard Paul
Van Grack, Steven
Vaughan, James Joseph Michael
Weiss, Irwin E.
Weltchek, Robert Jay
Williams, Kathryn Diggs
Wood, Judson Rawlings
Wright, Jefferson Vaughan
Ziegler, Arnold Gerard

Massachusetts

Adler, Sidney W.
Angell, James Edward
Avery, Michael Aaron
Beal, John Arthur
Bennett, Clarence J.
Bolton, Warren Robert
Burnstein, Daniel
Burstein, Merwyn Jerome
Cabral, Bernardo Joseph
Calabro, Michael James
Campbell, Richard P.
Carter, Paul Stanley
Connolly, Thomas Edward
Culpepper, Miniard
Cunha, John Henry, Jr.
Curley, Robert Ambrose, Jr.
Cusick, Elizabeth Emma
Czerwonka, Joseph John
Dimare, Charles Joseph
Doherty, Joseph Leo, Jr.
Espinosa, Jose A., Jr.
Fecteau, Francis Roger
Fein, Sherman Edward
Finn, John Joseph
Finn, Marvin Ruven
Frieden, James Anthony
Friedman, Michael Phillip
Furman, Mark Steven
Gelb, Richard Mark
Gibbs, Richard Frederic
Goodman, Henry A.
Gordon, Stephen Jacob
Guimond, Robert Wilfrid
Haldane, Mark Thomas
Halstrom, Frederic Norman
Harris, Richard Bates
Herrick, Stewart Thurston
Howard, Gregory Charles
Howland, Richard Moulton
Hutton, Albert Lee, Jr.
Jackson, Donald H(erbert), Jr.
Kaplan, David Richard
Keough, Paul Gerard
Kindregan, Charles Peter
Landy, James Leonard
Lang, Scott Wesley
Lewis, Sanford Jay
Licata, Arthur Frank
Lipman, Stephen I.
Lowinger, Lazar
Marnik, Michael Peter
Marr, David Erskine
Meehan, James Francis
Meyer, Andrew C., Jr.
Miles, Harry Lehman
Mills, Michael Francis
Murray, Robert Fox
Peterson, Osler Leopold
Petrucelly, Jeffrey Paul
Provanzano, Joseph Stephen
Savrann, Richard Allen
Schafer, Steven Harris
Segal, Jerome A.
Soforenko, Joel Fredrick
Sullivan, William Francis
Traficanti, Tina Michele
Urquhart, Stephen E.
Wolfe, Robert Shenker
Woolf, Jeffrey David
Zandrow, Leonard Florian

Michigan

Abraham, Douglas Clark
Alexander, Kerry Duane
Andersen, David Charles
Babcock, Charles Witten
Barr, Charles Joseph Gore
Battle, Leonard Carroll
Bell, John Wright
Bennett, Thompson
Bereznoff, Gregory Michael
Berry, Steven Craig
Bishop, Lawrence Ray
Blaske, E. Robert
Blaske, Thomas Hugh
Blum, Irving Ronald
Borders, Sidney Richard
Brady, Edmund Matthew, Jr.
Brander, Reynolds A., Jr.
Breczinski, Michael Joseph
Brennan, Joseph Vincent
Brenton, Michael Scott
Buchanan, John Cowan
Busch, Gary M(itchell)
Campos, David Nelson
Caretti, Richard Louis
Carson, Robert William
Centers, Louise Claudena
Chapekis, Nicholas Peter
Chartrand, Douglas Arthur
Connelly, Thomas Joseph
Cooper, David John
Cooper, David Joseph
Cotter, Dennis Blair
Crehan, Joseph Edward
Darling, Robert Howard
Decker, Harold James
Dilley, Thomas Robert
Dimmers, Albert Worthington
Dudley, Dennis Michael
Elsman, James Leonard, Jr.
Fagan, Thomas James
Farrell, John Brendan
Feringa, Scott Douglas
Foley, Stephen Bernard
Fosmire, Michael Sean
Franklin, Bruce Walter
Freilich, Diane M.
Gilbert, Ronald Rhea
Goethel, Stephen B.
Gofrank, Catherine Ann
Goodman, William Harry
Googasian, George Ara
Graham, W(illiam) Thomas, III
Greve, Guy Robert
Grumbine, David Lee
Gunderson, Michael Arthur
Haines, John Alden
Hall, Terrence Lyon
Haron, David Lawrence
Harris, Patricia Skalny
Hart, Clifford Harvey
Hay, Thomas Harold
Hayes, Kenneth Thomas
Hines, Paul William
Jackson, Mark Andrew
Johnson, Sheila Mary
Joseph, Raymond
Keller, Gerald Douglas
King, Thomas George
Knecht, Timothy Harry
Kritselis, William Nicholas
Kruse, John Alphonse
Larky, Sheldon Glen
Leib, Jeffrey M.
Lopatin, Albert
Lucow, Milton
Malone, Daniel Patrick
Marshall, J. Stephen
Martin, Walter
McDevitt, Mary Elizabeth
McDonald, Daryl Patrick
McGinnis, Thomas Michael
McGraw, Patrick John
McLain, Dennis O.
Mengel, Christopher Emile
Meyer, Philip Gilbert
Mies, James Edward
Moch, Joseph William
Moher, Thomas Gerald
Mossner, Eugene Donald
Mullendore, James Myers
Mundell, John Andrew, Jr.
Nichols, Charles Leonard
Nizio, Frank
O'Brien, Darlene Anne
O'Brien, Thomas C.
Ornstein, Alexander Thomas
Padilla, Gerald Vincent
Payton, Donald Lee
Perlos, Alexander Charles
Phillips, Dwight Wilburn
Pierson, William George
Plaszczak, Roman Thaddeus
Ponitz, John Allan
Potter, George Ernest
Prather, Kenneth Earl
Provenzano, Vincent
Purcell, Paul M.
Pylman, Norman Herbert, II
Resteiner, Harold Edward
Rhodes, Vincent Ard
Ring, Ronald Herman
Rinkel, Michael Joseph
Rowe, Jack Douglas
Schefman, Leslie Craig
Schrot, John Joseph, Jr.
Sefcovic, Henry John
Shillman, Jeffrey Nathaniel
Shulaw, Richard Allen
Sinas, George Thomas
Smith, Edward Michael
Smith, Mark Richard
Soet, Henry David
Steiner, Sanford Lee
Stevens, Gerald M.
Storey, Scott Alfred
Sullivan, Timothy Joseph
Sumpter, Jerry Lee
Talpos, John C.
Teicher, Mark L.
Thurswell, Gerald Elliott
Turner, Donald Allen
Tushla, Dennis Michael
Vanderkloot, William Robert
Van Leuven, Robert Joseph
Victor, Richard Steven
Walker, Jonathan Lee
Washington, Valdemar Luther
Weinstein, William Joseph
Whitelaw, Brian William
Wienner, S. Thomas
Wilson, Martin Bryant
Yockey, Kurt David
Zanot, Craig Allen
Zimmerman, Norman

Minnesota

Aaron, Allen Harold
Abrams, Richard Brill
Bailey, Timothy Gordon
Bassford, Charles Addison
Bennett, Robert
Brosnahan, Roger Paul
Bujold, Tyrone Patrick
Ciresi, Michael Vincent
Cleary, Edward Joseph
Dalager, Jon Karl
Daly, Leo Michael
Degnan, John Michael
Eustis, Warren Penhall
Finzen, Bruce Arthur
Fitch, Raymond William
Flynn Peterson, Kathleen A.
Geck, Donna Dunkelberger
Gordon, Corey Lee
Guthmann, John Howard
Hagglund, Clarance Edward
Hektner, Candice Elaine
Higgs, David Corey
Hottinger, John Creighton
Hull, Daniel Louis
Johnson, Dennis Robert
Johnson, Richard Walter
Johnson, Robert R.
Kirsch, Steven Jay
Lichtor, David T.
Lyons, M. Arnold
McCarten, Paul Vincent
McKenna, David William
McReynolds, Michael Patrick
Miller, Keith Lloyd
Mills, Anthony Belden
Murrin, John Owen
Nelson, Susan Richard
Nettles, Alan Ross
O'Leary, Daniel Brian
Orwoll, Kimball Gregg
Pederson, Steven Marc
Peterson, William George
Rasicot, James Frederick
Savelkoul, Donald Charles
Scherer, Richard Sigmund
Seaburg, Jean
Silver, Melvin Jacob
Sokol, Michael Bruce
Stephens, Mary Elizabeth Giuliani
Stoneking, Gary Edwin
Theis, Linda Jane
Thibodeau, Thomas Raymond
Timmons, Peter John
Wade, James Alan
Weiner, Michael Lewis
Zalasky, Jeff M.

Mississippi

Barton, William Harvey
Breland, Norman Leroy
Byrd, Isaac Kenith, Jr.
Chaney, Mark James, Jr.
Chapman, John Wendell
Cook, William Leslie, Jr.
Dukes, James Otis
Ferrell, Wayne Edward, Jr.
Fondren, Louis
Griffith, Benjamin Elmo
Harper, Gregory Livingston
Harris, David Neil
Hatcher, John Leslie
Howell, Joel Walter, III
Hubbard, Robert Dale
James, L. C.
Kirksey, William Boyd
Lancaster, William Robert
Mitchell, Cynthia Inis
Netterville, Robert Lavelle
Pate, William August
Peresich, Stephen G.
Pritchard, Thomas Alexander
Reeves, John Raymond
Taylor, Ronald Louis
Turner, Bennie L.
Welch, Walter Scott, III
Whitfield, William Ernest
Yoste, Charles Todd

Missouri

Adams, Philip James, Jr.
Anton, Donald C.
Arneson, James H.
Aylward, Timothy Michael
Beezley, Theodore
Berendt, Robert T.
Blanke, Richard B.
Bradshaw, Thomas Michael
Breckenridge, Bryan Craig
Brenner, Daniel Leon
Bronsky, A.J.
Burns, Mark Gardner
Callahan, Robert John, Jr.
Chassaing, J. Patrick
Collins, James Slade, II
Crepeau, Dewey Lee
Crites, Richard Don
Cronan, John Michael
Dickhaner, Raymond Henry
Dixon, Scott William
Drakesmith, Frederick William
Fleddermann, Stephen Roy
Fleming, Robert Laurence
Gartner, Richard Anthony
Gifford, Wayne Daniel
Gorla, Michael Joseph
Growe, Gary Alan
Hessel, Mildred Reda
Hubbell, Ernest
Hullverson, James Everett, Jr.
Johnson, Harold Gene
Johnson, Leonard James
Kaplan, Chester B.
Kaveney, Frank John
Kilroy, John Muir
King, William Robert, II
Kuenzel, Steven Paul
Levings, Theresa Lawrence
Lowes, Albert Charles
McDonald, William Henry
McKay, John Edward
Myers, Ronald Lynn
Nassif, Joseph Gerard
Nichols, Stephen Wayne
Nordyke, Stephen Keith
Passanante, Paul Jasper
Quitmeier, William Michael
Rabbitt, Daniel Thomas, Jr.
Reed, David Q.
Reeg, Kurtis Bradford
Remley, David Mark
Reynolds, Jerry Lee
Rice, Canice Timothy, Jr.
Rice, James Briggs, Jr.
Ringkamp, Stephen H.
Ritter, Robert Forcier
Roskin, Preston Eugene
Ryan, Hugh Harvey
Ryder, Bruce David
Schult, Thomas Peter
Schumaier, Steven George
Schwabe, John Bennett, II
Scott, Stephen Charles
Seigel, Stephen Paul
Shank, Suzanne
Sherman, Joseph Allen
Stierberger, Edward Albert
Stockman, Harry Michael
Stoup, Arthur Harry
Strong, Thomas Gorman
Sugg, Reed Waller
Summers, Hugh Scott
Susman, Robert M.
Toft, Martin John, III
Turcotte, John Arthur, Jr.
Turley, J. William
Vandever, William Dirk
Vleisides, Gregory William
Waldron, Kenneth Lynn
Wells, David Lee
Weston, Theodora White
Whipple, Clyde David
White, David William
Willman, Philip Louis
Wirken, James Charles
Woodbury, Marie Spencer
Woody, Donald Eugene
Zerr, Richard Kevin

Montana

Clarke, Dennis Person
Crowe, Gary Allen
Goldstein, Mort
Harrington, James Patrick
Hartelius, Channing Julius
Haxby, Leonard James
Johnson, Margaret Mary Joyce
Jones, James Leonard
Knuchel, Karl G.
Lerner, Alan Jay
Luck, Bradley James
Majerus, Michael Gerard
Morales, Julio K.
Parker, Mark David
Sommerfeld, Donald Drovdal
Trieweiler, Terry Nicholas

Nebraska

Anderson, Robert Louis
Cada, James Alden
Ellis, John Patrick
Friedman, Herbert Jerome
Gleason, James Mullaney
Gordon, James Edward
Inserra, John Phillip
Kay, Stephen William
Klein, Michael Clarence
Lahners, Ronald Dean
Mueller, William Jeffrey
Munro, Robert Allan
O'Connor, Robert Edward, Jr.
Perlman, Harvey Stuart
Pohren, Edward Francis
Rager, Kurt Thomas
Salerno, Terrence Joseph
Snowden, James Arthur
Swihart, Fred Jacob
Troia, Anthony Samuel
Vacanti, Alfred Charles, Jr.
Wilke, John William

Nevada

Badger, Raymond Louis, Jr.
Galliher, Keith Edwin, Jr.
Garcia, Eva
Hammer, Bill C.
Harding, Samuel Arlon
Horton, Thomas David
Kladney, David
Koch, Jan Paul
Kravitz, Martin Jay
Lohse, William Kurt
Maglaras, Chris, Jr.
O'Brien, Daniel Louis
Pagni, Albert Frank
Perry, Robert Harry
Perry, Victor Alan
Puccinelli, Leo J.
Risman, Marc Dale
Shaffer, Wayne Alan
Springmeyer, Don
Sumpter, Rodney Evert
Terzich, Milos
Wenzel, Steve Edwin
Wright, Thomas Preston

New Hampshire

Catalfo, Alfred (Alfio), Jr.
Dahar, Victor William
Damon, Claudia Cords
Doleac, Charles Bartholomew
Engel, David Chapin
Evans, Craig Fletcher
Garod, Harvey Jay
Mertens, Edward Joseph, II
Parnell, William Basil
Peltonen, John Ernest
Snow, Robert Brian
Thornton, Edward Robert, Jr.
Tober, Stephen Lloyd
Walker, George William
Wilder, Joyce Ann

New Jersey

Amadeo, Natial Salvatore
Baker, Max Allen
Baldino, John Joseph
Barnes, Timothy Lee
Beidler, John Nathan
Bielory, Abraham M.
Borelli, B. Michael
Bottitta, Joseph Anthony
Breslin, John Joseph, III
Bright, Francis Edward
Brown, James B., Jr.
Carluccio, Robert James
Carroll, Michael Dennis
Cernigliaro, Michael J.
Chappell, Thomas Tye
Clemen, John Douglas
Clinch, H(enri) Carleton
Cohen, Barry David
Cohn, Albert Linn
Collins, James Francis
Connolly, Joseph Thomas
D'Alfonso, Mario Joseph
DeRose, James Dominic
Dienst, Gerald A.
Eder, Todd Brandon
Epstein, Barry David
Facher, Irwin Lee
Feinberg, Jack
Finn, Jerry Martin
FitzPatrick, Francis James
Flinn, Thomas D.
Gelman, Jon Leonard
Gernert, Richard Charles
Gilbreth, Peter Nelson
Gogo, Gregory
Gordon, Harrison J.
Graham, Paul Eugene
Graziano, Ronald Anthony
Griffiths, David

Haidri, Amirali Yusufali
Harbeson, Robert G.
Harris, Brian Craig
Hersh, Alvin David
Hiltebrand, Stephen Mark
Hopkins, Charles Peter, II
Howell, Brian Graham
Johnstone, Irvine Blakeley, III
Jordan, Richard Allen
Kantor, Lawrence Dorn
Kaplan, Howard Mark
Kiel, Paul Edward
Klein, Paul Ira
Kotok, Lester
Kruttschnitt, Herbert, III
Kuttner, Bernard A.
Landman, Eric Christopher
Lavigne, Lawrence Neil
Lieberman, Marvin Samuel
Livingston, Richard B.
Luthman, David Andrew
Maran, Joe
Masucci, Louis M., Jr.
Matlin, David Stuart
Medvin, Alan York
Milstein, Edward Philip
Mintz, Jeffry Alan
Mitzner, Michael Jay
Moorman, Elliott Duane
Morris, Joseph Dean
Morris, Larry Dean
Needell, Russell Lawrence
Norman, Victor Conrad
O'Brien, John Graham
O'Connell, Hans James
Oliver, Roseann Sellani
O'Neill, Joseph Dean
Osofsky, Herman
Palma, Nicholas James
Peck, James Irving, IV
Pentony, Kenneth Richard
Polansky, Steven Jay
Pollinger, William Joshua
Portelli, Joseph Andrew
Porter, John Issac
Puffer, Leonard Bruce, Jr.
Rinsky, Joel Charles
Rizzo, Paul Robert
Rodriguez, Ariel Antonio
Rogoff, Marc Jeffrey
Romano, Janet Bocchino
Roth, Jeffrey Stuart
Sachs, William
Salibello, Salvatore Joseph
Santoli, Joseph Ralph
Schwartz, Edward Richard
Spinrad, Max
Stewart, James
Strashun, Jeffrey Marc
Strong, John Van Rensselaer
Teicher, Martin
Tepper, Alan Michael
Thomas, Brian Sean
Tice, Richard Leveridge
Tinari, Anthony Philip
Tolleris, M(ary) Angela
Tomar, William
Van Rye, Kenneth
Vazquez, Peter Joseph
Velazquez, Hector Radames
Vinick, Philip Brod
Warren, Lisbeth Ann
Weiseman, Jac Burton
Whelan, Charles Duplessis, III
White, Ivan Vance, Jr.
Widman, Douglas Jack
Williams, Henry Joseph
Wolfson, William Steven
Wood, Leonard James

New Mexico

Bartholomew, James Ira
Berardinelli, David Joseph
Branch, Margaret Moses
Casey, Patrick Anthony
Chavez, Rudolph Ben
Darnell, Richard Wayne
Diamond, Jeffrey Brian
Ferreira, Beatriz Valadez
Gibson, Louise
Graham, David Antony
Greig, William Harold
Hone, Jay R.
McClaugherty, Joe L.
Mitchell, Gary Colas
Moughan, Peter Richard, Jr.
Oman, LaFel Earl
Pearlman, David Henry
Pelton, Gregory Vern
Rosenberg, Myer (Mike)
Sherman, Frederick Hood
Smith, Paul Ray
Sparkia, Alisa A.
Stoker, Arlon L., Jr.
Vazquez, Martha Alicia
Voegler, Douglas Gene
Waldman, Robert Irwin
Wentworth, John
Wilson, Kenneth Belton
Word, Terry Mullins

New York

Alcorn, Wendell Bertram, Jr.
Aliano, Richard Anthony
Alonso, Andrea Maria
Ames, Marc L.
Ardam, David Mitchell
Aris, Joram Jehudah
Armani, Frank Henry
Ascher, Richard Alan
Ballow, John Edward
Barber, Janice Ann
Barrett, James P.
Baum, Joseph A.
Begos, Walter Anthony
Bekritsky, Bruce Robert
Beltz, Paul William
Bern, Marc Jay
Bernstein, Kenneth Alan
Billauer, Barbara Pfeffer
Birmingham, Richard Francis
Birnbaum, Edward L.
Block, Martin
Bloom, Jeffrey Brian
Bloom, Robert Avrum
Bonacci, Edward Howard, Jr.
Brand, Ray Manning

Brearton, James Joseph
Brock, David George
Brody, Neil
Brown, David Edward
Brown, Harvey R.
Brown, Jerrold Stanley
Burns, Richard Owen
Butler, John Edward
Bykofsky, Seth Darryl
Cardali, Richard James
Carlen, Leon C.
Cherundolo, John Charles
Claire, Judith Susan
Coen, Seth Ezra
Collins, John Francis
Connors, James Patrick
Conroy, Robert J.
Cook, Charlotte Smallwood
Cooke, Bradford
Corso, Frank Mitchell
Crain, William Earl
Crowley, Dennis Daniel
Dalton, Kenneth M.
Daly, William Joseph
Damashek, Philip Michael
Dankner, Jay Warren
Davoli, Joseph Felix
De Lucia, John Joseph
De Marie, Anthony Joseph
DeMarie, Joseph
DiBlasi, John Peter
Di Joseph, Steven
DiPrima, Michael Thomas
Dittenhoefer, Marc Mitchell
Dolin, Lonny H.
Dorf, Robert Clay
Dugan, Sean Francis Xavier
Dulin, Thomas N.
Dweck, Jack S.
Eckelman, Paul John
Edelman, Paul Sterling
Endieveri, Anthony Frank
Engel, Richard Lee
Englert, Dennis M.
Evans, John Thomas
Ezersky, William Martin
Feedore, Jeremy Randolph
Fein, Eric David
Feldman, Warren Bruce
Fern, Frederick Harold
Firth, Peter Alan
Fisher, Bertram Dore
Flynn, Michael
Fogelgaren, Eric Israel
Fontana, Vincent Robert
Frost, Jerome Kenneth
Frucco, John Peter
Gale, Peter L.
Garbarini, Chas. J.
Garry, John Thomas, II
Gebo, Stephen Wallace
Geiger, Alexander
George, Carolyn Burke
Gingold, Irving
Ginsberg, Jerome Maurice
Ginsberg, Robert Michael
Glass, Joel
Glauberman, Melvin L.
Gold, Joseph
Goldberg, Neil A.
Goldblum, A. Paul
Goldhirsch, Lawrence Bertram
Golomb, David Bela
Goodfriend, Mark F.
Gordon, Burton
Gouldin, David Millen
Groman, Tod Philip
Grossman, Mark Donald
Gunn, Alan
Gurfein, Richard Alan
Habian, Bruce George
Hagelin, Michael Thomas
Harvey, Jonathan Paul
Hauhart, Robert Charles
Hausen, Stanley Sherman
Hayes, Michael Augustine, Jr.
Hill, Alfred
Hite, Hollis Marie
Hurnyak, Christina Kaiser
Isaacs, Leonard Bernard
Jackson, Ronald James Leonard
Jacobowitz, Harold Saul
Jewell, Robert Hart
Jones, E. Stewart, Jr.
Kasold, Bruce Edward
Katz, Ascher
Kaufman, Rosalind Fuchsberg
Kelly, Raymond Aloysius, Jr.
Kelner, Robert Steven
Kerson, Paul Eugene
Killarney, John Paul
Kolbrener, Peter D.
Komar, Myron
Koob, Charles Edward
Krause, Charles Frederick
Kreppel, Milton Mark
Kushel, Glenn Elliot
Lamutis, Donald Franklin
Law, Michael R.
Lawton, Jeff
Leben, Jeffrey Michael
Lee, Brian Edward
Lee, Henry
Leifer, Max David
Leininger, William Joseph
Lesser, William Melville
Levi, Mark David
Levine, David Ethan
Levine, Steven Jon
Levy, George Michael
Lewis, Murray F.
Lipman, Howard Stewart
Loehr, Gerald Edward
Loscalzo, Anthony Joseph
Lubitz, Howard Arnold
Lustig, David Carl, III
Lyddane, John Lawrence Ashton
Lynch, Margaret Comard
Lysaght, James Ignatius
Malapero, Raymond Joseph, Jr.
Mannis, Bob Davis
Markel, Sheldon Martin
Maurer, Ira Mark
McCabe, Stephen M.
McCrory, John Brooks
McDonough, Thomas Joseph
McDuffee, Renée Renaud
McGraw, Charlene Evertz

Meiselman, David J.
Melbardis, Wolfgang Alexander
Melican, James Patrick, Jr.
Melley, Steven Michael
Meyer, Martin Arthur
Millane, John Vaughan, Jr.
Milligram, Steven Irwin
Minniti, Joseph A.
Molod, Frederick M.
Monaghan, Peter Gerard
Morelli, Ronald Joseph
Morris, John E.
Morris, Richard Paul
Muka, Betty Loraine Oakes
Mulhern, Edwin Joseph
Mulvehill, John Henry
Mur, Raphael
Murphy, Robert Anthony, Jr.
Nardone, Richard
Natiss, Gary Mitchell
Nissan, Randy S.
Nolan, Kenneth Paul
O'Gara, James Vincent
Oliveri, Paul Francis
Orr, Dennis Patrick
Paganuzzi, Oden Stephen, Jr.
Persons, John Wade
Peskin, Stephan Haskel
Petrone, Louis S.
Pittoni, Luke M.
Plastaras, Thomas Edward
Plotka, Richard F.
Porco, Domenick Joseph
Pottle, Willard Marsh, Jr.
Probert, Mark Stanley
Profeta, Fred Robert, Jr.
Pulos, William Whitaker
Queller, Fred
Raab, Ira Jerry
Rassner, Alan Carl
Rice, Terry August
Rinaldi, Keith Stephen
Ritter, Ann L.
Rivette, Francis Robert
Rogers, Sharyn Gail
Rose, Robert Stanter
Rosenzweig, Theodore B.
Ross, Christopher Theodore William
Rubenstein, Martin Jeffrey
Samel, Jeffrey
Sanna, Richard Jeffrey
Savit, Joel B.
Sawyer, James
Scarzafava, John Francis
Scher, Stanley Jules
Schiavetti, Anthony Louis
Schnurman, Alan Joseph
Schwartz, Stephen Jay
Seitelman, Mark Elias
Selkirk, Alexander MacDonald, Jr.
Sequeira, Manuel Alexandre, Jr.
Shaddock, Robert Montgomery
Shalhoub, Michael David
Shapiro, Daniel Murry
Silk, Robert Howard
Simoson, William Eugene
Smiley, Guy Ian
Sola, Anthony Marce
Sparks, Robert W.
Speiser, Stuart Marshall
Stahr, Thomas James
Stanisci, Thomas William
Steinbrecher, William John
Stengel, Mark Allen
Stephan, H. Peskin
Stevens, Peter Nicholas
Steves, Edward Mickel
Stone, Paula Lenore
Stutman, Michael David
Sword, Carl H(arry)
Tanenbaum, Ted Jay
Tannenbaum, Calvin Michael
Tarangelo, Richard Michael
Taub, Eli Irwin
Tendy, William Michael, Jr.
Tocci, Dominick P.
Tutrone, Ronald Francis
Viktora, Richard Emil
Vincent, Oreste
Vogel, John Walter
Weinreb, Michael Leonard
Weinstock, Leonard
Weisberg, David Charles
Wendel, Martin
Whiteman, Robert Gordon
Wilensky, Saul
Wilkens, Jeffrey Martin
Williamson, Walter
Willig, William Paul
Willinger, Warren Jay
Wolf, Lewis Isidore
Yablon, Babette
Yankowitz, Jack Alan
Zimmerman, Aaron Mark

North Carolina

Abrams, Douglas Breen
Alexander, Charles Jackson, II
Bennett, Harold Kimsey
Brooks, Dexter
Buie, Donald Ray
Bunch, W. Edward
Calhoun, Marilyn Jean
Christie, George Custis
Clontz, Stanford Kent
Curtis, Michael Kent
Davis, Joslin
Durham, Richard Monroe
Eve, Robert Michael, Jr.
Gantt, Charles David
Gates, James Edward
Gillespie, James Davis
Harkey, Henry Averill
Harris, Richard Foster, III
Hoof, James Bruce
Hopkins, Grover Prevatte
Hubbard, Thomas Edwin (Tim)
Hulse, William Frederick
Hunter, Richard Samford, Jr.
Ingle, John D.
Jones, Michael Morrie
Jordan, V. Thomas
Joyce, Dennis Robert
King, Ronnie Patterson
Koonce, Neil Wright
Langson, Seth Harris
Markham, Charles Buchanan
Maxwell, James Beckett

McIntyre, Douglas Carmichael, II
Morgan, Thomas Jada
Peirce, Ellen Rust
Poling, Richard Duane
Pope, Patrick Harris
Randolph, Clyde Clifton, Jr.
Raper, William Cranford
Robbins, Robert Joseph, Jr.
Robertson, Horace Bascomb, Jr.
Ruppe, Arthur Maxwell
Shepard, Paul Cooper
Smith, Roger Theodore
Snyder, Vernon Gilbert, III
Stockton, Ralph Madison, Jr.
Taylor, Michael William
Thompson, Eugene Cebron, III
Townsend, William Jackson
Waldrup, J(ohn) Charles
Wilson, Charles Michael

North Dakota

Bucklin, Leonard Herbert
Gilbertson, Joel Warren
Herauf, William Anton
Hermes, Pamela Jane
McKechnie, William Elliott
Snyder, Robert John
Sperry, Floyd Benjamin
Weir, Harlan Patrick
Zuger, William Peter

Ohio

Adams, John Marshall
Alkire, Richard Charles
Allen, Richard Lee, Jr.
Anderson, Dale Kenneth
Ausnehmer, John Edward
Bacon, Brett Kermit
Baxter, Randolph
Bebout, Bradley Carey
Beery, Fred Jerome
Bell, Napoleon Arthur
Belton, John Thomas
Belville, Barbara Ann
Bertrand, Louis Robertson
Birne, Kenneth Andrew
Blair, James F.
Boone, Timothy J.
Boulger, William Charles
Brandt, Stephen Dennis
Bressler, H.J.
Britain, James Edward
Browne, John Patrick
Burd, Charles Leslie
Burdge, Michael Joseph
Capizzi, Anthony
Carlin, Clair Myron
Carpenter, James Craig
Carroll, James Michael
Carto, David Draffan
Cherpas, Christopher Theodore
Chesley, Stanley Morris
Cohen, Arlene Switow
Colby, Richard DeAtlee
Cooper, Linda Dawn
Creech, Herbert
Davis, Bradley Mark
Davis, Charles Joseph
Davis, Frederick Benjamin
Davis, Robert Lawrence
Derivan, Hubert Thomas
Detling, Glenn Eugene
Dockry, Michael Brian
Dublikar, Ralph F(rank)
Farrell, Clifford Michael
Fellmeth, Scott Eugene
Ferruccio, Samuel Joseph, Jr.
Ford, Seabury Hurd
Friedman, Jerome
Gary, Robert Dale
Gehrig, Michael Ford
George, Donald Elias
Gerlach, Franklin Theodore
Giannini, Matthew C.
Gray, Alvin L.
Greene, Gordon Christopher
Greer, David Carr
Gross, Seymour
Guehl, Robert Lee
Gustaferro, Barbara Jean
Guttman, Rubin
Halleck, Michael Johnston
Hamilton, Richard Abbott
Hanna, Martin Shad
Hanson, Eugene Nelson
Hardig, Mark Nelson
Harpster, Linda Marie
Harris, Jerald David
Harrison, William K.
Harshman, Michael Stuart
Hawley, William Lee
Heaton, Gerald Lee
Hershey, Adrian Vernon
Hill, Jay
Hiller, Robert Stanford
Hochman, James Bertram
Hohn, Michael
Huhn, Richard M.
Jacobs, Ann Elizabeth
Jenks, Thomas Edward
Jordan, Joseph Patrick, Jr.
Kafantaris, George Nicholas
Kampinski, Charles
Katz, Alfred B.
Kazdin, Margaret Ellen
King, J(oseph) Michael
Klingenberg, Donald Herbert
Koenig, Peter Edward
Kovich, Don Edmond
Lacki, Ralph Stephen
Lagos, James Harry
Lancione, Nelson
Lancione, Richard Lee
Lancione, Robert Michael
Lane, James Edward
Lane, Matthew Jay
Largent, Jeffrey Willard
Lavelle, John Philip
Leksan, Thomas John
Levin, Arnold Sampson
Lipton, Andrew S.
Lowe, James Allison
Machan, Mitchell Alan
Madden, Stephan DuPont
Maher, Edward Joseph
Major, Ronald David
Marco, Richard Joseph, Jr.

McIlvaine, James Ross
McLaughlin, Patrick Michael
Mc Neal, Harley John
Meehan, Michael Jan
Meily, William Davis
Millhoff, Patricia Ann
Moore, Lloyd Evans
Naegele, Jori Bloom
Namanworth, Eli
Nelson, Roger Milton
Nelson, Steven Sibley
Olivas, Adolf
O'Reilly, Timothy Patrick
Paleudis, John George
Paul, Dennis Edward
Piazza, Anthony Michael
Plakas, Leonidas Evangelos
Potash, M. Steven
Pratt, Gregory Kent
Preston, Kevin Mark
Ray, Frank Allen
Reed, Tyrone Edward
Reminger, Richard Thomas
Roberts, Brian Michael
Rockel, John Edward
Ruppert, James Delano, II
Sawyer, Theodore D(aniel)
Scanlon, Lawrence Joseph
Schaffer, Thomas Alan
Schiff, Scott W.
Schoeni, Kenneth Roger
Schrader, Alfred Eugene
Schuh, Stephen Joseph
Shaw, Elwin Scott
Shea, Joseph William, III
Shepard, Darrell Royce
Sinclair, Virgil Lee, Jr.
Sindell, David Irwin
Smart, Irene Balogh
Spero, Keith Erwin
Spurgeon, Roberta Kaye
Sternberg, David J.
Sternberg, Richard
Stewart, Lawrence Edward
Stratton, Evelyn Joyce
Sullivan, Mark Edward
Sulzer, Joseph Paul
Switzer, Donald Hugh
Tait, Robert Ed
Taylor, Hilary Sheldon
Theado, Thomas Robert
Thomas, James William
Thompson, Harold Lee
Thornton, Robert Floyd
Tobias, Paul Henry
Trester, Joseph Edward
Turoff, Jack Newton
Ucker, David A.
Utrecht, James David
Van De Mark, Julie Ann
Wang, Charleston Cheng-Kung
Weisman, Fred
Weisman, Harry Jed
Wettlaufer, Karl Frederick
White, Daniel Joseph
White, Kenneth James
Williamson, Gregory Lopez
Wisniewski, Marshall Donald
Wykoff, John Robert
Yontz, Randall Eugene
Zackaroff, Peter Timothy
Zoll, David Wesley

Oklahoma

Alexander, Linda Diane (Graham)
Angel, Arthur Ronald
Armstrong, Richard Volker
Ashton, Mark Alfred
Berry, James W. Bill
Berry, James Wilson
Brooks, Rex Dwain
Chesnut, Charles Caldwell
Corley, E. Terrill
Day, Ronald Liles
Eldridge, Richard Mark
Ellis, Thomas Taylor
Fenton, Elliott Clayton
Green, Gerald Patrick
Hampton, Robert Joseph
Haskins, Walter Dewey
Heggy, Rodney Joe
Henneke, David Charles
Hughes, Carl Douglas
Kaufman, James Mark
King, Michael James
Lieber, John Howard
Lloyd, James Robert (Jim)
McCarty, Jack De
Moore, Roy Dean
Morris, Greg Arthur
Musser, James William
Norman, John Wayne
Northcutt, Clarence Dewey
Reid, David Paul
Robinson, Randall Philip
Rodgers, Ricardo Juan (Rick)
Salem, Micheal Charles
Shoemake, Bransford Hunt
Stuart, John Bruce
Taylor, Michael Conrad
Todd, Robert Allen
Tompkins, Raymond Edgar
Wagner, John Leo
Walker, Ronald Lynn
Wallace, Thomas Andrew
Welch, James Stephen
Whitten, Reggie Neil
Williams, Thomas Arthur
Wyatt, Harry Miller, III

Oregon

Adler, A(rthur) Michael
Banks, Roland Fitzgerald, Jr.
Barton, Richard Lee
Barton, William Arnold
Bovarnick, Paul Simon
Burnham, Carl von Hoffmann, Jr.
Calzaretta, Victor
Day, Bartley Fuller
Eyerman, Linda Kathleen
Feibleman, Gilbert Bruce
Gangle, Sandra Smith
Glazer, Peter Kendall
Greene, Michael Alan
Hittle, David William
Hodges, Charles Edward, Jr.
Honsowetz, Frank William

Imperati, Samuel J(ohn)
Jagger, James Cloyd
Kitchel, Jan Kelly
Kurtz, Louis Laird
Lombard, Herbert William, Jr.
Loomis, Donald Alvin
Lorenz, Daniel Christopher
Mansfield, William Amos
Morrison, David Patrick
Rice, James Gordon
Richardson, Dennis Michael
Rieke, Forrest Neill
Ringle, Philip Hamilton, Jr.
Ryan, Tomas Finnegan
Sahlstrom, E(lmer) B(ernard)
Savage, John William
Schade, Aloha Lee
Schuster, Philip Frederick, II
Spooner, Ralph Charles
Steele, Kathie Fay
Velure, Lyle Carl
Wong, Hap Yee

Pennsylvania

Adams, John Joseph
Albert, Neil Lawrence
Aronson, Mark Berne
Barkman, Jon Albert
Barson, Stephen Paul
Beachler, Edwin Harry, III
Beasley, James Edwin
Beck, Robert David
Beckman, Allen Joel
Bell, Paul Anthony, II
Benson, Stuart Wells, III
Bernard, Bruce William
Bigman, Anton W.
Binder, David Franklin
Black, Frederick Evan
Blumstein, Edward
Bonner, Eugene Aloysius
Borden, Randolph Tyson
Bowen, Gerald L.
Brown, Judith Renzi
Buccino, Ernest John, Jr.
Burns, Michael William
Burr, Charles Bentley, II
Carroll, James Walter, Jr.
Cheswick, Phillip Thomas
Cohen, Robert (Avram)
Corcoran, Andrew Patrick, Jr.
Corse, Chester Clinton, Jr.
Creato, Anthony Edmund
Creedon, Michael Patrick
D'Angelo, George A.
Dattilo, James Anthony
Davis, James Thomas
De Fino, Michael G.
DeMarco, James Joseph
DeMay, John Andrew
DiPiero, Andrew Edward, Jr.
Donahue, John M(ichael)
Duke, Charles Jeffrey
Eagen, Frank P.
Egler, Frederick Norton
Einhorn, Edgar Robert
Farber, Howard
Farrell, J. Michael
Federline, Robert Louis
Feldstein, Jay Harris
Ferrario, Raymond William
Flint, Daniel Waldo Boone
Flower, David Jeffrey
Follows, Jill Marilyn
Frank, Mark Stephen
Gale, Randall Glenn
Garhart, John Paul
Georgiades, Peter Nicholas
Ginsburg, Bruce Martin
Gold, Stephen Howard
Gordesky, Morton
Gowen, Thomas Leo, Jr.
Greenberg, James
Grimaud, Gerald C.
Haddon, Phoebe Anniese
Hafer, Joseph Page
Hannon, Gregory John
Herbruck, John Henry
Heslop, John William, Jr.
Hunter, Keith Alan
Ingram, Niki Teresa
Jarvis, Kingsley Albright
Jones, Ronald Richard
Kane, John Joseph
Kanner, Allan
Kanter, Seymour
Kapetan, Alex Nick
Keeler, Jean Marie
Keller, David Scott
Kennedy, James Edward
Kerrigan, Paul Brendan
Kessler, Steven Fisher
Klimon, Ellen Louise
Kormes, John Winston
Kotler, Helen Rose
Krug, Howard Barry
Krzemien, Louis John
Kulp, Dolores Rocco
Leete, John Bruce
Lincicome, Brian Leslie
Lisko, Roy Kenneth
Long, Stephen Michael
Lorenzo, Nicholas Francis, Jr.
Love, Mark Steven
Lubin, David S.
Lublin, Mark Aaron
Malady, Eugene Joseph
Malloy, Michael Joseph
Martin, Charles Howard
McBride, James Francis
McCloskey, Stephen Paul
McDonald, James Daniel, Jr.
McEvilly, James Patrick
McFadden, Joseph R., Jr.
McLane, John Thomas
Mellon, Thomas Edward, Jr.
Mendel, M. Mark
Messer, Howard Francis
Meyers, Jerry Ivan
Micale, Frank Jude
Mintzer, Edward Carl, Jr.
Mojock, David Theodore
Moribondo, Thomas Peter
Moritz, Preston William
Moses, Carl Michael
Mulvey, W. Michael
Munsing, Peter Nicholas
Myers, Robert Earl

Orban, Frank Anton, III
Parry, William DeWitt
Patterson, Christopher Malone
Pedri, Charles Raymond
Perer, Alan Harvey
Perlstein, Paul Mark
Perry, Sherryl R.
Peterson, Neil Raymond
Petrush, John Joseph
Pfaff, Robert James
Pleet, Jesse Lawn
Pollins, John William, III
Porach, Richard Andrew
Prewitt, David Edward
Pribanic, Victor Hunter
Price, William Charles, Jr.
Radcliffe, William M., III
Rathgeber, Joanne Weil
Rayman, Robert Craig
Reiff, Jeffrey Marc
Richman, Stephen Ian
Roeger, William Coley, Jr.
Ross, Alan Harold
Rossi, Mary Ann
Rubendall, Charles Wesley, II
Rutter, Thomas Bell
Saltzman, Joan
Samson, Peter
Saunders, Robert Leonard
Schauffler, Harvey Elliott, Jr.
Scheffler, Stuart Jay
Schermer, Oscar Selig
Schmidt, Edward Craig
Schoener, George Francis, Jr.
Schwartzman, James Charles
Seacrist, Geoffrey Lynn
Segal, Frederick Leslie
Senker, Richard C.
Serbin, Richard Martin
Shaffer, Charles Alan
Shane, B(enjamin) Jerome
Shelton, Fincourt Braxton
Shepherd, Carol Nelson
Shertz, Perry Jack
Shields, Francis Edward
Shoop, Roger Thomas
Shuster, Morris Myer
Silver, Stuart Robert
Smith, John Churchman
Smolinsky, Sidney Joseph
Specter, Howard Alan
Sproull, Frederick Anthony Raymond
Stahl, Stanley Paul
Stopford, Jeffrey Morgan
Strader, James David
Suojanen, Wayne William
Swaim, John Joseph
Swartz, Lee Carter
Swensen, Jan Clovis
Tamulonis, Frank Louis, Jr.
Thompson, John Wilson, Jr.
Tollen, Allen Harold
Tomlinson, Herbert Weston
Vinci, Martin F.P., III
Voluck, Jeffrey M.
Weaver, Cynthia Marie
Wecht, Cyril Harrison
Weinfeld, David M.
Weingarten, Marc Philip
Wertheimer, Spencer Miles
Weston, John Kerry
Whitling, Terrance LeRoy
Wilson, Steven (White)
Wingerter, John Raymond
Wolf, Edward Leonard
Wolfe, Steven Edward
Wynstra, Nancy Ann
Yates, Alfred Glenn, Jr.
Zeglen, John Michael
Zimmerman, D(onald) Patrick

Rhode Island

Blanding, Sandra Ann
Brady, Robert Michael
Cappalli, Richard Anthony
DiSandro, Edmond A.
Fox, Francis Anthony
Goodwin, Hyman S.
Ialongo, Michael Angelo
Lipsey, Howard Irwin
Loffredo, Pasco Frank
Mandell, Mark Steven
McGuirl, Susan Elizabeth
Miller, Samuel Aaron
Najarian, Malcolm Askanaz
O'Donnell, William Kenneth
Penza, Joseph Fulvio, Jr.
Purcell, James Edward
Riffkin, Mitchell Sanford
Simmons, Howard Koorken

South Carolina

Applegate, William Russell
Bacot, John Paisley, Jr.
Bailey, Nancy Hawkins
Barker, Joseph Ransom
Bell, Robert Morrall
Berly, Joel Anderson, III
Bolt, J. Dennis
Boyd, Stanley Jeffrey, Jr.
Choate, John Lee
Christian, Warren Harold, Jr.
Coates, William Alexander
Cooper, Robert Gordon
Cothran, James Clardy, Jr.
Elliott, John Dewey
Eltzroth, Clyde Alfred, Jr.
Furr, O(lin) Fayrell, Jr.
Gergel, Richard Mark
Goode, Kenneth George
Harte, John Williams
Harvey, James Martin, Jr.
Haskins, Terry Edward
Henry, Angela Louise
Hudson, James Patrick
Irvin, Wilmot Brown
Johnson, Darrell Thomas, Jr.
Johnson, Mordecai Christopher
Jones, Hartwell Kelley, Jr.
Kahn, Ellis Irvin
King, Jimmy R.
Knight, David Webster
Kuhn, Harold Fred, Jr.
Mauldin, John Inglis
McChesney, Paul Townsend
McIntyre, Bernard
McKay, John Judson, Jr.

Metcalfe, Walter Geoffrey
Oswald, Billy Robertson
Reeves, Phillip Earl
Rodgers, Paul Baxter, III
Seth, J Cabot
Simmons, Charles Bedford, Jr.
Smiley, Robert Rennslaer, III
Smith, Barney Oveyette, Jr.
Smith, Jefferson Verne, Jr.
Smith, Walter Henry
Spears, Michael Eugene
Spitz, Hugo Max
Vieth, Rick
Wheless, Albert Eugene
Williams, Charles Hiram
Williams, Karen Johnson

South Dakota

Allred, Forrest Carlson
Baumann, Christopher John
Bettmann, Frank Adam, Jr.
Hoy, Carleton Robert
Nipe, Chris Alan
Sabers, Richard Wayne
Wyman, William Alan

Tennessee

Arnett, Foster Deaver
Baker, Josiah Carr Eggleston
Bandy, Thomas Rochelle, III
Bennett, Horace Michael
Boswell, George Harvey
Buchignani, Leo Joseph
Cameron, Clarence Arnold
Catalano, Michael William
Cook, Bratten Hale, II
Cramer, William Mitchell
Davis, Jimmy Kyle
Day, John Arthur
Elliott, Sam Davis
Ellis, Bobby James
Folmar, Oliver Wiley
Fordham, Benjamin Cleveland
Freeman, James Atticus, III
Friedman, Robert Michael
Glasgow, James Monroe
Goldin, Arnold B.
Harrell, Limmie Lee, Jr.
Harris, Tyree Bryson
High, David Erwin
Ingraham, Frank Calvin
Keeton, Robert Taylor, Jr.
Kirkpatrick, Scott Lucillious
Kizer, John Fuqua
Knowles, Emmitt Clifton
Lanier, James Olanda
Layman, Earl Robert
Lee, Sharon Gail
Leitner, Paul R.
Lockett, William Alexander
Logan, James Franklin, Jr.
Long, Michael Sidney
Marcus, Harry Richard
McCaleb, Joe Wallace
McClarty, John Westley
McKenney, Edward Jerome, Jr.
Montgomery, Joseph Tucker
Moore, James M(ack), Jr.
Oberman, Steven
O'Hearn, William Wilson
Parker, Mary Ann
Pearman, Joel Edward
Ragan, Charles Oliver, Jr.
Rice, George Lawrence (Larry), III
Ridenour, Ronald H.
Riley, Steven Allen
Robinson, Samuel Francis, Jr.
Rogers, Helen Sfikas
Rogers, John T. Milburn
Rutherford, Glen Bibee
Shirley, Raymond Andrew, Jr.
Shockley, Gary Clark
Smith, William Holt
Sproles, Donald Ray
Summers, Gerald (Jerry) Howard
Swanson, Charles Walter
Taylor, Jerry Francis
Townsend, Edwin Clay
Wade, John Webster
White, Penny J.
Wright, James Charles

Texas

Abney, Joe L.
Adams, Kent Morrison
Adams, Ray Harris
Akers, Brock Cordt
Albach, Henry John, IV
Aldrich, Lovell W(eld)
Alexander, John William
Altman, William Kean
Ammerman, James Harry, II
Arango, Ana
Arthur, Harry Cornelius
Ball, Craig Douglas
Banales, J(ose) Manuel
Bashline, James Duane
Beaman, Glen Edward
Beauchamp, Gary Fay
Black, Robert Allen
Boswell, John Howard
Boyd, Roland
Branson, Frank Leslie, III
Brennan, Diantha Garrett
Briggs, Tom Peery
Brister, Scott Andrew
Brock, Roy C.
Brown, James Earle
Brown, Robert Charles
Byrd, Linward Tonnett
Carnahan, Robert Narvell
Chalk, John Allen
Chapman, Stephen Sperry
Chappell, David Franklin
Coleman, Bryan Douglas
Cortez, Hernan Glenn
Craig, Robert Lee, Jr.
Darnell, James Oral
Davis, John Whittaker
Delk, Russell Louis
Demarest, Sylvia M.
Dorsey, Clarence W.
Dryden, Woodson E.
Eddins, Gerald Wayne
Ellis, Donald Lee
Engel, David Wayne

Essmyer, Michael Martin
Evans, George Frederick, Jr.
Evans, James A.
Ezzell, James Michael
Feeney, Patrick Joseph
Feldman, H. Larry
Felton, Dale Wiley
Fisher, Philip Wayne
Fleming, George Matthews
Fox, Jacqueline R.
Frigerio, Charles Straith
Gandy, Francis I., Jr.
Garcia, Lawrence L.
Gilbert, Steven John
Gold, Paul Nicholas
Gonsoulin, Dewey Jude
Gordon, Norman James
Haggard, Carl Douglas
Hanen, Andrew Scott
Hankins, Mitchell Dale
Harrel, Alan David
Henry, Peter York
Hohman, A.J., Jr.
Holmes, Clifton Lee, (Scrappy)
Howie, John Robert
Jacobellis, Mike
Johnson, D. Thomas
Johnson, Philip Wayne
Johnson, Vincent Robert
Jones, Albert Pearson
Junell, Robert Alan
Kelly, Joseph Patrick
Kent, David Charles
Kent, Don Wayne
Kilgore, Gary Lynn
King, Daniel Dwade
King, Gerald Lee
Kizzia, Don Bradley
Kline, Allen Haber, Jr.
Knisely, Paul Emil
Krebs, Arno W., Jr.
Latham, B. Mills
Lawton, Kenneth Wayne
Lewis, Kenneth Wayne
Liebbe, William Howard
Loewinsohn, Alan Stewart
Lynch, Jeffrey Scott
Malouf, Stephen Ferris
Marshall, Richard Treeger
McAninch, Edwin Lee
McConnico, Stephen E.
McFall, Donald Beury
McFarland, Jaclanel Moore
McGehee, Jack Edward, Jr.
McHugh, Margaret Colleen
McPherson, Nancy Jo Buenzli
McQuarrie, Claude Monroe, III
Micks, D. Fred
Milligan, Michael Roy
Minor, David Michael
Misko, Fred M., Jr.
Moore, Robert Allen
Mow, Robert Henry, Jr.
Muster, Douglas Frederick
Myers, J(oseph) Michael
Nunnally, Knox Dillon
Oldenettel, Rick Lee
Orsburn, Charles Claude
Palmer, Randall Parham, III
Pena, Richard
Perlmutter, Mark L.
Petry, Herbert Charles, Jr.
Pettiette, Alison Yvonne
Pluymen, Bert W.
Porter, James Eduardo
Porto, Joseph Anthony
Powers, William Leonard
Putman, (James) Michael
Raine, Charles Macon
Rapp, Robert David
Raschke, Fred David
Rduch, Evita Joanne
Redden, Joe Winston, Jr.
Rendon, Ruben
Richards, Robert William
Riddles, Amis Joe
Ridgeway, Henry Dorman
Riney, Thomas Charles
Roark, John Olen
Rusk, L. Giles
Sadler, Paul Lindsey
Sales, James Bohus
Schechter, Arthur Louis
Schonberger, Arne Carl
Shafer, W. O.
Shaw, Tex Ronnie
Shepherd, James Edward
Shirley, Robert Preston
Siegel, Mark Jordan
Simmental, David Anthony
Slaughter, David Alan
Somers, Constance Reynolds
Steele, Joseph Robert
Stephens, R(obert) Gary
Stephens, Walter David
Stewart, Mark Steven
Stinnett, Mark Allan
Stradley, William Jackson
Suttle, Stephen Hungate
Sydow, Michael David
Taft, Lee McCreary
Terrell, Richard Clark
Thaddeus, Aloysius Peter, Jr.
Tillman, Massie Monroe
Toth, Robert Stephen
Trimble, Dale Lee
Turley, Windle
Vickery, Glenn
Volk, Michael Douglas
Waldman, Steve
Wheat, Thomas Allen
Whitehurst, William O.
Wicka, Richard Vincent
Wilder, William Keith
Wiles, William Dixon, Jr.
Wilk, David I.
Williams, Walter Waylon
Wills, Don Paul
Witherspoon, James Winfred
Wortham, Robert John
Worthington, William Albert, III

Utah

Belnap, Michael Gary
Bigler, Glade S.
Harding, Ray Murray, Jr.
Hatch, Sumner Jones
Hillyard, Lyle William

Holm, Floyd W.
Kaufman, Steven Michael
Lambert, Dale John
Lyman, Paul D.
Purser, Donald Joseph
Sullivan, Kevin Patrick
Walsh, John Thomas
West, David Clay
Westfall, George Michael
Wilkinson, Homer Fawcett

Vermont

Babb, Guy Lee
Cassidy, Richard Thomas
Cory, Barbara Ellen
Faignant, John Paul
Kiel, Edward Rowland
Levy, James Lewis
Lisman, Bernard
Massucco, Lawrence Raymond
McCamley, John Edward
Mc Carty, William Michael, Jr.
Rath, David
Wright, Richard Jay
Wysolmerski, Sigismund John Albert

Virginia

Allen, Wilbur Coleman, Jr.
Allen, Wilbur Coleman
Appleton, Randall Eugene
Baird, Charles Bruce
Bangel, Herbert K.
Bangel, Stanley Jerome
Beale, J. Burkhardt
Beller, Charles Roscoe, III
Bent, Stephen Andrew
Booker, James Foster
Brown, Henry Otis
Burgess, Jack Thompson
Byrom, Robert Milton
Campbell, George Wendal, Jr.
Cassell, Richard Emmett
Chandler, Lawrence Bradford, Jr.
Cranwell, C. Richard
Crewe, Trenton Guy, Jr.
Crigler, B. Waugh
Dansby, Harry Bishop
Davis, Douglas Witfield
Davis, Gilbert Kenneth
Davis, Richard Waters
Emroch, Emanuel
Evans, Susan Ann
Fletcher, John Richard
Friedlander, Jerome Peyser, II
Frith, Douglas Kyle
Gilbert, Oscar Lawrence
Haight, Gregory Dale
Hamilton, Jeffrey Scott
Hammer, Donald Gordon
Hankins, Timothy Howard
Harris, John Paul, III
Hartshorn, Roland DeWitt
Hovis, Robert Houston, III
Kennedy, Joe Jack, Jr.
Kloeppel, Byron Peter
Korman, James William
Krasnow, Jeffrey Harry
Landin, David Craig
Lawrence, John Schrumpf
Leffler, Rodney G.
Malone, William Grady
Martin, Ronald Allen
Marzloff, George Ernest
Moody, Willard James, Sr.
Najjoum, Linda Lemmon
Norris, John Stevens, Jr.
O'Donnell, Hugh David
Palmer, William Ralph
Parks, William Anthony
Philpott, Albert Lee
Prince, William Taliaferro
Proffitt, John Stephen, III
Pysell, Paul Edward
Quillen, Ford Carter
Rawls, Frank Macklin
Redmond, Robert
Robinson, Thomas Hart
Rosenstock, Louis Anthony, III
Saul, Ira Stephen
Schwartz, Steven Gary
Shell, Louis Calvin
Shevlin, Brian Charles
Shields, William Gilbert
Short, DeRonda Miniard
Shortridge, Michael L.
Skinker, Donald Ray
Slenker, Norman Frederick
Smith, S(ydney) Strother, III
Snook, John Lloyd, III
Somerville, Frank Walker
Stanback, Clarence Freeman, Jr.
Sweeny, Peter Michael
Tillar, Darrel Long
Varoutsos, George Douglas
Warburton, Roy David
Wheeler, R(ichard) Kenneth
Whitaker, Steven King
Whitlock, Willie Walker
Whitt, Robert Holt, Jr.
Whittemore, F(rank) Case
Williams, Ronald Wayne, Sr.
Williamson, Thomas W., Jr.
Wilson, Rodger Lee
Winston, Robert Tunstall, Jr.
Woodrum, Milton Lanier
Youngs, John Curtis

Washington

Adams, Lori Nelson
Althauser, Thomas Charles
Anderson, David Bowen
Angevine, Earl Francis
Armstrong, Grant
Bailey, William Scherer
Baker, James Edyrn
Barnett, Hollis H.
Bartheld, Richard Henry
Broihier, Jeffrey T.
Burke, Thomas Gerald
Buzzard, Steven Ray
Chambers, Thomas Jefferson
Cline, Thomas Farrell
Condon, David Bruce
Connelly, John Robert, Jr.
Cordes, Clifford Frederick, III
Cornell, Kenneth Lee

Corning, Nicholas F.
Cushing, James Robert
Dacca, Franklin Louis
Davis, James Edward
Davis, Susan Rae
Dawson, Edward A.
Dawson, Robert Kevin
Dohn, George Thomas
Ecton, Douglas Brian
Fine, Eleanor Rose
Fitterer, Richard Clarence
Gavilanes, Diego P.
Hames, William Lester
Harris, Thomas V.
Hindman, Dennis Michael
Houger, L(eroy) William
Jackson, David William
Johnson, Richard Bruce
Kaiser, Bruce Allen
Keating, Robert Clark
Kram, Peter
Krueger, Larry Eugene
Lamp, John Ernest
Lang, Pamela Ann
Leggett, James Francois
Leipham, Jay Edward
Loftus, Thomas Daniel
Ludolph, Marla Rose
Mahoney, Philip Charles
Mahoney, Timothy William
Manni, Kenneth Allen
Marler, Dirk Alan
McBroom, Douglas D.
McCoy, Brian Lloyd
McDermott, Richard Francis, Jr.
McGavick, Donald Hugh
McMahon, Michael Joseph
Meyers, Anthony James
Meyers, Bruce France
Moren, Charles Verner
Mozena, Peter Joseph
Nevin, Jack Frederick
Nichols, Howard Melvin
Nielsen, Ruth
Olver, Michael Lynn
Oreskovich, Carl Joseph
Peery, Charles Eugene
Pelandini, William Albert
Pence, Christopher Cyrus
Peters, Frank August
Peterson, Jan Eric
Phillips, Brian Reed
Pinckney, Ronald Robert
Raaen, G(ary) Lee
Ray, Rodney Bruce
Reed, Glenn Edward
Ryan, James Francis
Schweda, Peter Steven
Scott, Douglas Walter
Scott, Steven George
Sharpe, Christopher Grant
Shogan, Alexander Joe, Jr.
Silvernale, Lawrence Duggan
Stamper, Randall Lee
Stritmatter, Paul Lester
Swanson, Arthur Dean
Tasker, Michael Kenneth
Thurston, Hal
Tuffley, Francis Douglas
Uhrig, Ira John
Wayne, Robert Jonathan
Webster, Ronald B.
Westland, John Alden
Whitson, Lish
Wirt, Alexander Wells
Ziontz, Martin Lowell

West Virginia

Artimez, John Edward, Jr.
Berthold, Robert Vernon, Jr.
Brushwood, David Benson
Cline, Michael Robert
Colburn, James Allan
Cross, David Bert
Flaherty, Thomas Vincent
Gibson, Michael Fielding
Hatfield, Harry Maxwell
Hill, Barry Morton
Jackson-Gillison, Helen Lucille
Johnson, David Whitley
Keltner, Robert Earl
MacCallum, James Judson
Null, Gregory B.
Peterson, James Charles
Ringer, Darrell Wayne
Sanders, William Henry
Swope, Derek Craig
Thaxton, Everette Frederick
Watson, William E.
Weaver, William Carroll

Wisconsin

Atterbury, Lee Richard
Bennett, David H.
Berres, Terrence Robert
Bohren, Michael Oscar
Brant, Kirby Ensign
Callahan, Carroll Bernard
Castro, Robert C.
Christiansen, Jon Peter
Cole, James Ray
Cook, Daniel John
Curry, George Steven
Curtis, George Warren
Domnitz, Merrick Robert
Eckert, Michael Louis
Ehrke, William Warren
Evans, William James
Gagliardi, Paul
Gaines, Irving David
Gasiorkiewicz, Eugene Anthony
Gass, James Ric
Grzeca, Michael (Gerard)
Gust, Gerald Norman
Habush, Robert Lee
Hans, Peter E.
Hansher, David Allen
Hartley, Glenn Henry
Howarth, Kim A.
Kaiser, John Atwood
Kammer, Robert Arthur, Jr.
Karp, David Barry
Kelly, Walter Francis
Kircher, John Joseph
Krueger, John William
Kucirek, Joseph Charles
Laufenberg, Lynn Raymond
LeBell, Robert
McCusker, William LaValle
Melchert, Lori Layne McLario
Montabon, Dennis Gene
Neubecker, Edward Frederick
Penegor, Robert Joseph
Pernitz, Scott Gregory
Peterson, Donald Roy
Peterson, John Christian
Pettit, Roger Lee
Pollack, Michael Alan
Rasche, William Grether
Rogers, James Thomas
Schrank, Raymond Edward, II
Sedor, Gilbert D.
Smith, Charles F., Jr.
Storck, Robert Emil
Stutt, John Barry
Terschan, Frank Robert
Tess-Mattner, Kent A.
Thompson, Edward Francis
Walsh, John
Warshafsky, Ted M.
Weidner, Gary Richard
Whitney, Robert Michael
Wilcox, Francis John
Winner, John Dennett

Wyoming

Ahlstrom, Bert Tavelli, Jr.
Bommer, Timothy J.
Bostwick, Richard Raymond
Burke, E. James
Clauss, C. David
Combs, William Henry, III
Guetz, Burton Walter
Harrison, Frederick Joseph
Honaker, Richard Henderson
Johnson, Robert Henry
McLaughlin, Douglas Ray
Miller, Linda Suzanne
Pickering, Robert Gein
Riggs, Dan Britt
Rolich, Frank Alvin
Santini, George
Shockey, Gary Lee
Speight, John B.
Spence, Gerald Leonard
Stanfield, John Edmiston
Statkus, Jerome Francis
Thomas, John Arlyn
Zollinger, Thomas Tennant

TERRITORIES OF THE UNITED STATES

American Samoa

Faalevao, Aviata Fano

CANADA

Quebec

Pascoe, Christopher John Campbell

FEDERAL REPUBLIC OF GERMANY

Pfennigstorf, Werner

ADDRESS UNPUBLISHED

Ackerman, Robert A(rthur)
Adelman, Michael Schwartz
Aldrich, Richard Dennis
Alexander, John Nickolas, Jr.
Arrowood, Lisa Gayle
Auther, Jeri Lynn Kishiyama
Avery, Bruce Edward
Bateman, David Alfred
Beattie, Donald Gilbert
Becker, Frank Gregory
Boyle, Elizabeth Mary Hunt
Brooks, Patrick William
Cancio, Pablo Ramón
Cheek, Louis Eugene
Chirra, Joseph
Corcoran, Sheila Margaret
Cowan, Robert Charles, Jr.
Davidson, Keith L.
De Angelis, Arnold John
Djokic, Walter Henry
Doherty, John L.
Fekete, George O.
Fitzgerald, John Elmer
Friedrich, Bruce Robert
Garza, Rudy A.
Gee, Delbert Calvin
Godfrey, Thomas Grant
Gonzales, Jeffrey Charles
Gregory, Rick Dean
Griffith, James Lewis
Henningsen, David Sean
Hughes, Roy Fredericks
Joike, Trevor B.
Kaczynski, Stephen John
Kellerman, Harry Miles
Kirschner, Paul David
Labdon, Kenneth Charles
Leaf, Frederick Peter
Lerman, Cathy Jackson
Lewis, Peter
Lippes, Richard James
Locke, John Howard
Martin, James Henry
Martin, Terence Alan
Mittelstadt, Russell James
Nash, Melvin Samuel
Orlins, Peter Irwin
Palmer, Rudolph Martin, Jr.
Peterson, Laurel J.
Plattner, Richard Serber
Plitt, Steven
Porricelli, Gerald Joseph
Puttock, John Lawrence
Quinn, Joseph Francis
Quinn, Stacy Smith
Robinson, David Howard
Roether, Robert Henry, II
Rosenberg, Arthur Harrison
Samples, Stephen Shay
Scott, Thomas Stratton, Jr.
Sheahan, Joseph D.
Showers, H. Robert, Jr.
Sweeney, Robert John
Tanenbaum, Jay Harvey
Thomas, Johnny Wesley
von Dioszeghy, Adam George
Walker, Robert Donald
Zeltonoga, William Leo

PROBATE. *See also* **Estate planning; Taxation, estate.**

UNITED STATES

Alabama

Bell, Thomas Reuben
Bryant, Thomas Earle, Jr.
Cicio, Anthony Lee
Foster, Arthur Key, Jr.
Frierson, Sarah Stewart
Harris, John Clinton, Jr.
Hinds, Caroline Wells
Holberg, Ralph Gans, Jr.
Holland, Lyman Faith, Jr.
Hughes, James Donald
Hughston, Harold Vaughan, Jr.
Irons, William Lee
Kennemer, John Maclin
King, John Thomas
Leatherbury, Gregory Luce, Jr.
Mathews, Melinda McEachern
McGowin, Nicholas Stallworth
McKinley, Edmon Howard
Merrill, Walter James
Price, Walter Jasper, Jr.
Schiff, Gary Steven
Silver, Irving
Smith, Andrew Lovgren
Smith, Hardy Bolton
Smith, John Joseph, Jr.
Smith, John Joseph
Stoudenmire, William Ward
Waddell, John Emory

Alaska

Davis, Trigg Thomas
Lowe, Robert Charles

Arizona

Basinger, Richard Lee
Baughn, Alfred Fairhurst
Brock, Warren Richard
Cantor, Alena
Clark, Richard Edward
Cocanower, David Lehman
DiMatteo, Philip Stephen
Fortman, Marvin
Friedlander, Susan Oliver
Frost, Smith Gibbons
Ganson, Norris Lloyd
Hutchison, Samuel Robert
Jennings, Marianne Moody
Larson, Ronald Frederick
Levitan, Roger Stanley
Lowry, Edward Francis, Jr.
Mangum, John K.
Martori, Joseph Peter
May, Robert A.
Olsen, Alfred Jon
Paupore, Jeffrey George
Rubenstein, Hy David
Stirton, Charles Paul
Swartz, Melvin Jay
Turner, Daniel Charles

Arkansas

Ball, William Kenneth
Britt, Henry Middleton
Butt, Thomas Franklin
Cooper, Rick William
Epley, Lewis Everett, Jr.
Fergus, William Lee
Finley, John Cyrus, Jr.
Finley, John Cyrus, III
Fitton, Garvin
Gant, Horace Zed
Hobbs, Richard White
Jackson, Blaine Albert
Jordan, Steven Ben
Lineberger, John Ralph
McKenzie, Horace Houston
Spencer, James Victor, III
Stockburger, Jean Dawson
Stroud, John Fred, Jr.
Talley-Morris, Neva Bennett
Wright, John Homer
Wright, Robert Ross, III

California

Adams, Robert Morford, Jr.
Allen, Albert Herman
Alvarez, Edna R. S.
Arthur, Jeanne L.
Asmundson, Vigfus Anthony
August, Ann
Auser, Wallace Van Cortlandt, III
Ballsun, Kathryn Ann
Barnes, John Breasted
Bassett, Craig Jay
Bear, Henry Louis
Biscay, Marcel Pierre
Blewett, Robert Noall
Bold, Frederick, Jr.
Borges, David Joseph
Bray, Absalom Francis, Jr.
Brooks, Claudia Marie
Brown, Lorne James
Brown, Louis Daniel
Brown, Ralph Evan
Burton, Randall James
Butler, Felicita Therese
Caillat, Charles Victor
Calleton, Theodore Edward
Castello, Raymond Vincent
Childs, Marjorie M.
Coffill, William Charles
Cohan, John Robert
Copenbarger, Lloyd Gaylord
Crowe, Daniel Walston
Curtiss, Thomas, Jr.
Dell'Ergo, Robert James
Dukeminier, Jesse
Duncan, John Alexander
Ebiner, Robert Maurice
Eskin, Barry Sanford
Factor, Max, III
Farley, Barbara Suzanne
Faust, Leland Howard
Finch, Nathan C.
Flanagan, James Henry, Jr.
Frankel, James Burton
Freeburger, Thomas Oliver
Fried, Alexander
Gill, Keith Hubert
Glines, Jack Holloway
Gooch, Robert Francis
Grim, Douglas Paul
Guggenhime, Richard Johnson
Gutierrez, Max, Jr.
Halbach, Edward Christian, Jr.
Halstead, Harry Moore
Harrow, Barry Richard
Hart, Lynn Patricia
Hawkins, Carmen Doloras
Hawkins, Richard Michael
Heckman, Donald Rex, II
Heene, Fred Lewis, Jr.
Higbe, Clifton Melton Harvin
Hunter, William Carlton
Hurabiell, John Philip, Sr.
Jackson, Pamela Curulewski
Jacobs, Leedia Gordeev
Jordan, Paul S.
Jorgensen, Erik Holger
Kearn, Orene Levenson
Knecht, James Herbert
Landay, Andrew Herbert
Lerrigo, Frank C.
Levin, Marvin Eugene
Lindgren, Arne Sigfrid
Loomis, John Elmer
Lynch, Robert Berger
Maciel, Ronald John
Maggard, Sarah Elizabeth
Maillian, LeAnne Elizabeth
Mallory, Frank Linus
Marshall, Arthur K.
McCallum, Barbara Eiland
McCroskey, Elizabeth Wear
McDaniel, David Jamison
Mc Elwain, Lester Stafford
McFarland, Carol Anne
McGee, Francis Parker, II
Mc Govern, William Montgomery, Jr.
Merrill, Byron Robert
Merritt, Valerie Jorgensen
Miller, Mary Jane
Miller, Michael Patiky
Mitchell, Michael Charles
Moore, Julie E.
Morgan, Robert Hall
Ofner, William Bernard
Osborne, Carol Ann
Palitz, Murray
Partritz, Joan Elizabeth
Payne, Margaret Anne
Peluso, Charles John
Petty, Keith
Pollock, John Phleger
Ponomareff, Guyla Woodward
Quittman, Peter Francis
Rabin, Jane Hurwitz
Rae, Matthew Sanderson, Jr.
Ragetté-Blaine, Dorothea Constance
Rai, Shambhu K.
Rand, Richard Malcolm
Resich, John James
Rodgers, Thomas Paul
Rosenstein, Robert Bryce
Rosky, Burton Seymour
Ross, Bruce Shields
Sallus, Marc Leonard
Schechter, Stuart
Shaw, John LeRoy, Jr.
Sherr, Morris Max
Sherwood, Allen Joseph
Showley, Lon Duane
Sickler, Sandra Davis
Sikora, Warren
Silveria, Linda Lorraine
Sindon, Geoffrey Stuart
Sires, Bruce David
Small, Harold S.
Smiley, Stanley Robert
Smith, Maxine Steward
Stark, Franklin Culver
Stavig, Alf Rusten
Stephens, George Edward, Jr.
Stinehart, William, Jr.
Sullivan, James Anderson
Taylor, Howard Harper
Thatcher, Dickinson
Thomas, William Scott
Tobin, Harold William
Toftness, Cecil Gillman
Tomich, Lillian
Trover, Ellen Lloyd
Vallens, Brent Edward
Voegelin, Harold Stanley
Vosguanian, Rodney Nerses
Wade, Milam Lee Roy
Wallenstein, Raymond
Walsh, William, IV
Ward, Anthony John
Ward, Diane Korosy
Weagant, Lance Maxwell
Willey, Charles Wayne
Williams, Lawrence Dwight
Worthington, Leonard A.

Colorado

Arkin, Harry Lee
Boyle, John Edward
Brant, John Getty
Bruce, Neil Curtis
Buchanan, James William, III
Carleno, Harry Eugene
Cockrell, Richard Carter
Cronan, Kathleen Michele
Donley, Jerry Alan
Earnhart, Mark Warren
Eberhardt, Robert Schuler, Jr.
Fairlamb, Millard Schuyler
Fevurly, Keith Robert
Flanders, Laurence Burdette, Jr.
Gaddis, Larry Roy
Gast, Richard Shaeffer
Griffith, Mary Cornwall
Guyton, Samuel Percy
Hill, Robert Dean
Honaker, Jimmie Joe
Hopp, Walter James
Jersin, Edward Anthony
Joss, W. Bruce
Kaup, Daniel John
King, Dennis William
Kogovsek, Daniel Charles
Kraemer, Sandy Frederick
Logan, Valentine Weir
Long, Lawrence Alexander
McGowan, Rodney Ralph
Moss, Victor
Payne, Raymond Lee, Jr.
Perkins, Eugene Oral
Quiat, Gerald M.
Reid, John Edward
Robinson, Julia Ormes
Robinson, Wayne E.
Schenkein, Pamela Ephraim
Scott, Peter Bryan
Stauffer, Scott William
Thompson, Stephen Michael
Ward, Lester Lowe, Jr.
Wilder, Raymond Edward
Wilson, Edward Miller

Connecticut

Altermatt, Paul Barry
Anderson, Henry Brackenridge
Ayres, Steven Edward
Bell, Mary-Katherine
Bentley, Peter
Berger, Robert Bertram
Berman, John Arthur
Bonee, John Leon, III
Capecelatro, Mark John
Coates, Charles Elting, III
Comley, Frederick Luquiens
Conaway-Raczka, Nancy
Dupont, Ralph Paul
Elliott, Stephen K.
Ewing, Robert
Farrelly, Francis J.
Fisher, Everett
Galligan, Matthew G.
Gersten, Sandra Joan Pessin
Green, Marshall Munro
Green, Raymond Bert
Greene, Thurston
Gregory, Julian Arthur, Jr.
Kaye, Joel Michael
Lang, Edward Gerald
Leepson, Peter Lawrence
Mandell, David E.
Medvecky, Thomas Edward
Mittelman, Irwin David
Morelli, Carmen
Nielsen, Anita Spector
Phelps, Robert Frederick, Jr.
Reinen, Jeffrey William
Ross, Michael Frederick
Rout, Robert Howard
Silver, Elaine Terry
Telker, Ellen Melinda
Valentine, Garrison Norton
Vetere, Robert Louis
Webster, Stuart Arthur
Weinstein, Arthur David
Williams, Michael Peter Anthony
Worley, Robert William, Jr.

Delaware

Lassen, John Kai
Popper, Richard J.A.

District of Columbia

Allen, Nicholas Eugene
Andersen, Daniel Johannes
Bellinger, Edgar Thomson
Blazek, Doris Defibaugh
Blumenthal, Carol
Cannon, Daniel Willard
Close, David Palmer
Cohen, Wallace M.
Cushing, Robert Hunter
Determan, Sara-Ann
Duckenfield, Thomas Adams
Freedman, Walter
Harris, James Alan
Hogan, Thomas Francis
Kellison, James Bruce
Lynn, James Bruce
Lyon, Richard Kirshbaum
McGuire, Patricia A.
Murphy, Marcia Gaughan
Quinn, John Harvey, Jr.
Robinson, Sara Moore
Snyder, John Freeman
Spencer, Samuel
Stanley, William, Jr.
Swendiman, Alan Robert
Vance, Kenneth Anthony
Ward, Nicholas Donnell
Whitney, John Adair

Florida

Adcock, Louie Norman, Jr.
Ade, James L.
Aguilar, Humberto Juan
Ansbacher, Lewis
Bailey, Brant Allan
Beall, Kenneth Sutter, Jr.
Berlin, Mark A.
Bernard, Lawrence Jay
Blank, Ralph John, Jr.
Bloomgarden, Paul M.
Boyd, Joseph Arthur, Jr.
Braden, Dana Danielle
Breed, E(rnest) Mark, III
Brooks, Roy Howard, Jr.
Buchman, Paul Sidney
Burns, Katherine Mills
Campion, Eileen
Carlile, Robert Toy
Chabrow, Penn Benjamin
Chambliss, Linda Christine
Clark, Harold Robinson
Click, David Forrest
Coletta, Raymond Robert
Conner, Richard Elwood
Constant, Joseph
Cron, Jennifer Lynne
Crum, James Merrill
Dando, David Frederick
Dressler, Robert A.
Ellwanger, Thomas John
Emmanuel, Michel George
Farrior, J. Rex, Jr.
Friedman, Jerrell Don
Friedman, Ronald Michael
Gardner, Russell Menese
Gaylord, Harry Eugene
Geller, Steven Anthony
Greenleaf, Walter Franklin

Gurney, James Thomas
Hedrick, David Warrington
Hess, George Franklin, II
Hest, Bruce Henry
Holcomb, Lyle Donald, Jr.
Jones, John Arthur
Joyner, Arthenia Lee
Kievit, Robert Warren
Kimber, Brian Lee
Koren, Edward Franz
Krause, Andrew James
Lambertus, Christine Lundt
Lancaster, Kenneth G.
Lang, Joseph Hagedorn
Levitt, Preston Curtis
Lewis, Mark Russell
Lopacki, Edward Joseph, Jr.
Matthias, Robert Charles
Maxwell, Richards DeNyse, Jr.
McCollum, James Fountain
McEwan, Oswald Beverley
Meade, Russell Arthur
Meeks, William Herman, III
Merriam, Lauren Evert, III
Middleton, Elwyn Linton
Milstein, Richard Craig
Morales, Nestor
Nichols, Cynthia Leigh
Nordahl, Norris George
Norman, Donald Hamilton
Patterson, George Anthony
Pearce, Lewis Richard
Peck, Bernard Sidney
Peters, Robert Timothy
Pippen, Joseph Franklin, Jr.
Price, Pamela Odell
Pyle, Frank LeForest, Sr.
Rexrode, David Stephen
Ringel, Fred Morton
Roddenberry, Bonnie Lindquist
Roman, Ronald Peter
Rosenberg, Sheldon
Rowan, Beverly Adele
Rush, Fletcher Grey, Jr.
Schorner, James Alan
Segal, Martin Edward
Sill, Lauren Ann
Skolnick, S. Harold
Stepp, Kenneth Stephenson
Stevens, Edwin Dan
Stewart, Thomas Wilson
Sulzberger, Eugene William
Tittsworth, Clayton (Magness)
Waite, Blakeley Robinson
Warwick, Charles Henry, III
Watson, Keith
Wellbaum, Robert William, Jr.
Wilder, Fred Jennings
Wilson, George Allen
Wood, William McBrayer
Wutt, Robert Anthony
Zook, David Lloyd
Zschau, Julius James

Georgia

Bloodworth, A(lbert) W(illiam) Franklin
Cadle, Jerry Neal
Candler, John Slaughter, II
Champion, Forrest Lee, Jr.
Cork, Robert Lander
Cowart, Richard Merrill
Cowen, Martin Lindsey, III
Edee, James Philip
Ellis, Edward Prioleau
Gannam, Michael Joseph
Gaynes, Bruce Harvey
Gerstein, Joe Willie
Head, Hugh Garland, Jr.
Head, Hugh Garland, III
Howell, Arthur
Johnson, Walter Frank, Jr.
Lamon, Harry Vincent, Jr.
McLemore, Gilbert Carmichael, Jr.
Moorhead, William David, III
Nesmith-Rosner, Joanna
Radford, Mary Frances
Richards, Pamela Motter
Sibley, James Malcolm
Stone, Hugh William
Trotter, William Perry
White, Benjamin Taylor
Wright, Harry Ralph, Jr.

Hawaii

Ashford, Clinton Rutledge
Bodden, Thomas Andrew
Coates, Bradley Allen
Conrad, John Regis
Dixon, Steven Bedford
Goo, Colin Kim Keong
Hastings, Robert William, II
Howell, Alan Peter
Jackson, Bruce George
Lockwood, John Allen
Peters, Ronald Lloyd
Robinson, John Harvey
Shiraishi, Sherman T.
Suzuki, Norman Hitoshi
Taylor, Carroll Stribling
Yamamoto, Jerel Ikmo
Yano, Francis Hisao

Idaho

Erickson, Robert Stanley
Furey, Sherman Francis, Jr.
Judd, Linda
McCann, William Vern, Jr.
Olson, Gerald W.
Thompson, Frances Hoene

Illinois

Adams, John Richard
Addis, Lauane Cleo
Armstrong, Edwin Richard
Ashley, James Wheeler
Austin, Daniel William
Beer, Betty Louise
Beneke, William Scott
Berning, Larry D.
Bernstein, Charles Bernard
Bixby, Frank Lyman
Bockelman, John Richard
Bogert, George Taylor
Boucek, George Washington
Brainard, H Ogden
Carr, Walter Stanley

Carter, Melanie Sue
Cass, Neil Earl
Choate, Edward L.
Coletta, Ralph John
Conway, Martin Eugene, Jr.
Coppinger, John Bampfield
Coughlin, Terrance J
Cromley, Jon Lowell
Cross, Chester Joseph
Cummings, Walter Dillon
Dees, Richard Lee
DeWolfe, George Fulton
Diamant, William
Didzerekis, Paul Patrick
Dieker, James William
Diller, Theodore Craig
Elliott, Ivan A.
Elliott, Ivan A., Jr.
Ellwood, Scott
Elmore, Elbert Francis
Finnegan, Thomas Joseph
Flack, Charles Haynes
Fleming, Milo Joseph
Folgate, Homer Emmett, Jr.
Fort, Lyman Rankin
Freeman, Richard Lyons
Friedman, Roselyn L.
Frisch, Sidney
Funderburk, Raymond
Gary, Susan Nannette
Gerek, William Michael
Gibson, James Thomas, Jr.
Gingiss, Randall Jon
Gold, George Myron
Goldstein, Richard M.
Goodman, Bruce Dennis
Gordon, Theodora
Gutstein, Solomon
Hahn, Richard Ferdinand
Hanson, Fred B.
Hartzell, Franklin MacVeagh
Hayes, David John Arthur, Jr.
Hegarty, Mary Frances
Heisler, Quentin George, Jr.
Herting, Claireen LaVern
High, Suzanne Irene
Hoellen, John James
Hoffman, John Harry
Hoffman, Thomas Joseph
Hofmann, William Eckhardt
Horsley, George William
Howard, Robert Henry
Huntoon, Harry Karl
Johnson, Preston King
Jones, Richard Cyrus
Juhl, Loren Earl
Kaplan, Howard Gordon
Kasten, Carl E.
Kennedy, John Foran
Kenny, Robert Emmett, Jr.
Kirkpatrick, John Everett
Kohlstedt, James August
Koval, Joseph Patrick
Langbein, John Harriss
Lawless, John Martin
Lesar, Hiram Henry
Levy, Katherine Judith
Mamer, Stuart Mies
Marmet, Gottlieb John
Marshall, John David
Mazewski, Aloysius Alex
McCarthy, John Francis
McClow, Thomas Alan
McDonough, John Michael
McRae, Donald James
Miller, Russell George
Miller, Stanton Bernett
Milligan, Francis Joseph, Jr.
Moline, Gary L.
Nathan, Kenneth Sawyer, Sr.
Naylor, George LeRoy
Newlin, Charles Fremont
Nitikman, Franklin W.
O'Brien, Walter Joseph, II
O'Flaherty, Paul Benedict
Pace, O(le) B(ly), Jr.
Peck, Kerry Reid
Plesko, Jeffrey Michael
Polzin, John Theodore
Rehberger, Robert Lee
Reilly, Sheila Ann
Rikli, Donald Carl
Robinson, Robert George
Rodkey, Frederick Stanley, Jr.
Romano, Henry Schuberth, Jr.
Ross, Robert John
Rosso, Christine Hehmeyer
Sale, Edwin Wells
Schaffer, George John
Scheller, Arthur Martin, Jr.
Schreiber, Ronald
Schwartzberg, Hugh Joel
Selfridge, Calvin
Shapiro, Paul Stuart
Shayne, David
Sims, E. Jane
Sprowl, Charles Riggs
Stanfield, James Caleb
Stanhaus, James Steven
Stone, Bertram Allen
Strasburger, Joseph Julius
Swaney, Thomas Edward
Tabb, Charles Jordan
Thomas, James Gladwyn
Thomas, William Harrold
Thomson, William Hills
Tognarelli, Richard Lee
Tracy, William Francis, II
Trost, Eileen Bannon
Tungate, James Lester
Tungate, Susan Sumner
Van Duerm, James
Walbaum, Robert C.
Ward, Philip Henry, Jr.
Wardell, John Watson
Weber, Alban
Wexler, Warren Marshall
White, Robert Ellsworth
Wrigley, Julie Ann

Indiana

Adams, Robert Wendell
Adinamis, George Peter
Bach, Steve Crawford
Bailey, Patricia Seasor
Bartlett, Rick E.
Bennett, Maxine Taylor
Blythe, James David, II

Bowen, Willard Gene
Brames, Arnold Henry
Bunger, Len Edward, Jr.
Carroll, John Leo
Coukos, Carolyn Cook
Coyne, Lynn Harry
Crump, Francis Jefferson, III
Dennis, Ralph Emerson, Jr.
Draper, Monette Elaine
Dutton, Clarence Benjamin
Eggleston, Thomas Warren
Ferguson, Theodore James
Fuller, Samuel Ashby
Gehring, Ronald Kent
Gelber, Linda Cecile
Gerberding, Miles Carston
Germann, Douglas Dean, Sr.
Gordon, Daniel R.
Grund, James Arthur
Guy, John Martin
Hamilton, John Anthony
Harman, John Royden
Heppenheimer, Harry
Hughes, John Newell
Johnson, G. Weldon
Justice, Robert Scott
Laszynski, Robert Steven
Lewis, Daniel Edwin
Lisher, James Richard
Long, Douglas Paul
Longer, William John
Lowe, Louis Robert, Jr.
Mallers, George Peter
Manterfield, Eric Alan
Mascher, Gilbert Ernsting
McDowell, Dock, Jr.
Muntz, Richard Karl
Murphy, Sharon Funcheon
Nesbitt, John Robert
Pantzer, Kurt Friedrich, Jr.
Patrick, William Bradshaw
Schemahorn, Clyde E.
Smith, Maxwell Paul
Suedhoff, Carl John, Jr.
Tolbert, Frank Edward
Truitt, Patricia Peyton
Wood, William Jerome
Young, Barbara Ann
Young, Randy William

Iowa

Bappe, Daniel Eugene
Berkland, Roger Alan
Butler, Wallace Webb
Clem, Robert Charles
Dull, Wilbur Robbins
Dykstra, Daniel D.
Einck, Dean Robert
Gidel, David Dale
Klinger, Phillip Dennis
Laird, Morris E.
Lenihan, Thomas Parker
Lounsberry, Harold Claire
Manly, Charles M.
Morf, Darrel Arle
Morrison, Edmund Dunham, Jr.
Nelson, Robert Charles
O'Connor, John Charles
Palmer, Bruce Alexander
Peterson, Richard William
Phelps, Robert J.
Simpson, Lyle Lee
Vanorsdel, Robert Alan

Kansas

Aadalen, David Kevin
Black, John Victor
Brewer, Dana
Buechel, William Benjamin
Bush, Granville McCutcheon, III
Condray, Scott Robert
Conner, Fred L.
Curfman, Lawrence Everett
DeLaTorre, Phillip Eugene
Depew, Harry Luther
Gastl, Eugene Francis
Gillmore, Alver James
Hejtmanek, Danton Charles
Hess, Jerry John
Horttor, Donald J.
Ice, Theodore Branine
Jones, Lloyd Wesley
Jordan, Harold Nathan
Karlin, Calvin Joseph
Knappenberger, Don J.
Lowe, Roy Goins
Martin, Barry Douglas
Mikkelsen, Charles R.
Nordling, Bernard Erick
Peckham, Charles Allen
Pierce, Ricklin Ray
Seed, Thomas Finis
Smith, Glee Sidney, Jr.
Springer, Byron Eugene
Toland, Clyde William
Toland, Stanley E.
Walters, Amy Ottinger

Kentucky

Adams, James G., Jr.
Bensinger, Carl Joseph
Carroll, Thomas Charles
Chauvin, Leonard Stanley, Jr.
Coombs, Ronald Lee
Dieffenbach, Charles Maxwell
Emmons, Alison Lobb
Gilman, Sheldon G.
Hagan, Charles Curtis, Jr.
Irtz, Frederick G., II
Jackson, James Ronald
Lester, Charles Theodore, Jr.
Lester, Roy David
Logan, James Ashlin
Merkel, Roland Peter
Niemi, Bruce Alan
Noe, Randolph
Pettyjohn, Shirley Ellis
Prather, John Gideon
Reeves, L. Brian
Rhinerson, David Keith
Schneider, Frederick Richard
Schoenbaechler, Edward Lewis
Spalding, Wallace Hugh, Jr.
Varellas, Sandra Motte
Voyles, James Robert
Walker, Patricia Gail

Weiner, Neil Steven
Williamson, Charles Gurley, Jr.
Wilson, George Simpson, III

Louisiana

Arceneaux, James Shaw
Baudier, Adelaide
Bayard, Alton Ernest, III
Benjamin, Edward Bernard, Jr.
Bringle, William Timothy
Bronfin, Fred
Burkett, David Ingram
Campbell, Joseph H(oward), Jr.
Coleman, James Julian
Connolly, George Charles, Jr.
Denhollem, James Scott
Denton, Roger Marius
Duncan, Nora Kathryn
Ellison, David McQuown, Jr.
Ewin, Gordon Overton
Fadaol, Robert Frederick
Fenderson, Faun Louise
Gallaspy, John Norman
Giepert, Melvin John
Gouaux, Eugene Godfrey
Gruning, David William
Hardtner, Quintin Theodore, III
Hickman, Paula Hazelrig
Hill, William James, III
Johnson, Delos Rozelus, Jr.
King, C. A., II
Lilley, Roy Stuart
Losavio, Peter Joseph
Mansfield, James Norman, III
Marx, Paula Jeannette
Mayoral, Paul G.
McAdams, Don Randall, Jr.
McDonald, John Franklin, III
Morris, Frank Lowry
Nalls, Clarence Theo
Prestridge, Rogers Meredith
Pucheu, John Henri
Puglia, Phyllis Mary
Rinker, Andrew, Jr.
Rosenberg, Samuel Irving
Shinn, Clinton Wesley
Simmons, Kermit Mixon
Singletary, Alvin D.
Smith, Duncan McLaurin, Jr.
Spencer, Philip Polmer
Stokes, Douglas Leon
Stone, Saul
Stracener, Carol Elizabeth
Tarcza, Robert Emmet
Thomas, Gerard Frances
Tramonte, James Albert
Vickery, Eugene Benton, Jr.
Wedig, Harold Harvey
Weiss, Donald Paul
Woodward, Madison Truman, Jr.
Woodward, William Edward

Maine

Cowan, Caspar Frank
Currie, Michael Robert
Fletcher, David James
Fuller, Atherton
Hewes, Richard David
LeBlanc, Richard Philip
Nichols, David Arthur
Perkins, James Blenn, Jr.
Poe, Franklin Andrew
Walker, Frank Briggs

Maryland

Bald, LeRoy
Boyer, Elroy George
Conkling, Daniel Charles
Dulany, William Bevard
Dunn, John Benjamin
Evelius, John Charles
Field, Samuel Summers, III
Fisher, Jeffrey B.
Gingell, Robert Arthur
Gnocchi-Franco, Claudio
Hackett, Sylvia Lavada
Hanley, David Burris
Hecht, Isaac
Hennegan, John Owen
Jones, Alexander Gray
Katz, Steven Martin
Kaylor, Omer Thomas, Jr.
Kirchman, Charles Vincent
Lawler, Theresa Anne
Lewis, Leah H.
Michaelson, Benjamin, Jr.
Morris, David Michael
O'Brien, Joseph Edward, Jr.
Ogletree, Anne Meve Callahan
Petraitis, Karel Colette
Price, Charles U.
Rachanow, Gerald Marvin
Rasin, Alexander Parks, III
Rome, Morton Eugene
Scott, Charles Lurman
Scott, Doris Petersen
Snyder, William Arthur, Jr.
Stone, James Dorsey
Williams, Kathryn Diggs

Massachusetts

Ames, James Barr
Ardiff, William B.
Auchter, John Richard
Boyd, F. Keats, Jr.
Bridge, Winston Jay
Burgoyne, John Albert
Burstein, Merwyn Jerome
Cherny, David Edward
Coltun, Harry
Dreyer, Harold Emil
Dwyer, William Edward
Eaton, William Lawrence
Ely, John P.
Fellows, John White
Fortier, Albert Mark, Jr.
Freeman, Florence Eleanor
Geogan, Francis Joseph, II
Goldman, Richard Harris
Jackson, Donald H(erbert), Jr.
Kaloosdian, Robert Aram
Keshian, Richard
Korff, Ira A.
Lee, David Harold
Levin, Charles Robert
Levine, Julius Byron

Li, Winifred I.
Lynch, John Gregory, Jr.
McNulty, Thomas Joseph, Jr.
Mitchell, John Bruce
Monahan, Marie Terry
Pearson, Paul David
Perera, Lawrence Thacher
Pierce, John Robert
Pratt, Harold Irving
Puzo, Michael John
Riley, Michael Hylan
Robbins, Lynda Jean
Roche, John Jefferson
Sears, John Winthrop
Segal, Jerome A.
Snyder, Marie Elizabeth
Sykes, Peter M'Cready
Taylor, John Anthony
Weiss, Dudley Albert
Wexler, Barbara Lynne
Whipple, Robert Jenks

Michigan

Bennett, Thompson
Bos, John Earl
Brown, (Robert) Wendell
Byington, Robert Lee
Carney, Donald F., Jr.
Chapekis, Nicholas Peter
Chartrand, Douglas Arthur
Clark, John Scott
Clink, Stephen Henry
Cotner, Roger Garner
Currier, Timothy Jordan
Davis, Henry Barnard, Jr.
Dettloff, Richard Ward
Devlin, Eugene Joseph
Dimmers, Albert Worthington
Dresser, Raymond H., Jr.
Dufendach, Carl William
Dutka, Robert Joseph
Eklund, Robert D.
Ellmann, William Marshall
Fagan, Thomas James
Feldman, Michael Sanford
George, Barry Brian
Graham, W(illiam) Thomas, III
Haines, John Alden
Harper, Linda Walker
Irish, Michael William
Jordan, Glenn Erval
Joslyn, Robert Bruce
Kendricks, George Thomas
Ladd, Thomas A.
Leib, Jeffrey M.
Lloyd, Leona Loretta
Martin, Walter
May, Alan Alfred
McGinnis, Thomas Michael
McGlynn, Joseph Michael
Olson, M(elvin) Richard
Ortman, William Andrew, Sr.
Pelavin, Michael Allen
Pierce, Robert Barth
Resteiner, Harold Edward
Rewald, Roman
Riecker, John E(rnest)
Rolf, Ramon Frederick, Jr.
Ruwart, David Peter
Schoder, Wendell Louis
Scott, Rosemary
Skora, Susan Sundman
Smith, Wayne Richard
Supina, Gerald Joseph
Szymanski, Frank S(tanislaus), Jr.
Thomas, Michael Eli
Thurber, Cleveland
Tushla, Dennis Michael
Urick, Walter Aleksy
VanderRoest, James Edward
Waggoner, Lawrence William
Warren, John Philip, Jr.
Westerman, Susan S.
Williams, James Joseph
Winchell, William Olin
Winkelman, Roger Edward

Minnesota

Brand, Steve Aaron
Burke, John Barrett, Jr.
Cafarella, Joan Marie Coursolle
Christensen, Donn Douglas
Coller, Julius Anthony, II
Donohue, Peter Salk
Dosland, William Buehler
DuFour, R(ichard) W(illiam), Jr.
Engwall, Gregory Bond
Ferguson, Elizabeth Norton
Fossum, Lee Leif
Hoke, George Peabody
Hulstrand, George Eugene
Johnson, Joseph Bernard
LaChapelle, Arthur William
LeVander, Bernhard Wilhelm
Lyons, M. Arnold
Martin, Judith Moran
Masica, Mark Alexis
Mennell, Robert L.
Mooty, David Nelson
Nordaune, Roselyn Jean
Peterson, Ralph Henry
Peterson, Steven A.
Reister, Raymond Alex
Rippe, John Henry
Sayers, Randall William
Seymour, McNeil Vernam, Jr.
Silver, Melvin Jacob
Stein, Robert Allen
Swanson, Steven Richard
Trojack, John Edward
Vanhove, Lorri Kay
Vitko, John Peter
Wilcox, Donald Alan
Younger, Judith Tess

Mississippi

Dossett, James Kearney, Jr.
Edwards, Arthur Martin, III
Goodman, Herbert Raymond
Low, John T.C.
Magee, William Eugene
Martin, George Gilmore
Presson, William Russell
Shepard, Robert Payne
Shiyou, Orvis A., Jr.
Stubblefield, Joseph Stephen

Thomas, James Talbert, IV
Ueltschey, Watts Casper

Missouri

Baer, David, Jr.
Berg, Julius Harry
Blackwell, Menefee Davis
Breckenridge, Bryan Craig
Brenner, Daniel Leon
Brouillette, Gary Joseph
Bryan, Henry C(lark), Jr.
Buder, Eugene Hauck
Byers, Ronald Gregory
Callahan, Robert John, Jr.
Calvin, Edward Eugene
Clarke, Milton Charles
Crawford, Howard Allen
Cupples, Stephen Elliot
Doheny, Donald Aloysius
Douglas, Kerry DeLisle
Fleischaker, Jack
Giorza, John C.
Gorman, Gerald Warner
Greenley, Beverly Jane
Gunn, Michael Peter
Haller, Albert John
Hass, William Ralph
Ingram, Kevin Roney
Jennings, William Hathaway, II
Keller, Elizabeth Ann
Kincaid, Arthur Roy
Knight, Herman Elvin, Jr.
Koffman, Robert Lawrence
McClure, Lawrence Ray
McKee, Barnet M.
Moffitt, William A., Jr.
Murphy, Edward Elias, Jr.
Neill, Robert
Polster, Carl Conrad
Preuss, Ronald Stephen
Raack, William James
Redd, Charles Appleton
Russell, William Oliver
Stierberger, Edward Albert
Thompson, Edmonstone Field
Tindel, John Curtis
Tremayne, Bertram William, Jr.
Tripp, Donald William
Walker, Walter Ladare
Weber, Louis Jerry
Wherritt, Alan Francisco
Woods, Richard Dale
Zahnd, Lloyd Glen

Montana

Dostal, John Anthony
George, Alexander Andrew
Gilbert, Robert Bruce
Goldstein, Mort
Goldstein, Mort
Hansen, Max A.
Haxby, Leonard James
Jardine, John Hawley
Kaze, James Michael
Kottas, Leo Joseph, Sr.
Kronmiller, Bert Wilson
Morales, Julio K.
Robinson, Calvin Stanford

Nebraska

Aitken, Philip Martin
Blazek, George Thomas
Borghoff, John Joseph
DeRoin, Jan Elizabeth
Gaines, Tyler Belt
Gewacke, John Clifford
Glidden, Richard Mark
Haggart, Virgil James, Jr.
Jelkin, John Lamoine
Lipp, Louis Ellis
Munro, Robert Allan
Rager, Kurt Thomas
Rowland, Richard Arthur
Schneider, Gary Bruce
Smith, Richard Wendell
Stogsdill, Daniel Ray
Urbom, David Ward
Whitney, Charles Leroy
Widtfeldt, James Albert

Nevada

Dorsey, Robert Knickerbocker
Greene, Addison Kent
Gubler, John Gray
Hibbs, Loyal Robert
Jones, Clifford Aaron
Logar, Ronald John
Lowe, Bryan A.
Maher, O. Kent
Morris, Trude McMahan
Puccinelli, Leo J.
Schouweiler, Bart McClain

New Hampshire

Bruno, Kevin Robert
Budnitz, Arron Edward
DeHart, Barbara Boudreau
Donovan, Robert Bickford
King, Michael Paul
Kitchen, John Scott
Morse, Richard Allen
O'Neill, Martha Emma
Plaut, Nathan Michael
Ransmeier, Joseph Sirera
Toll, Charles Hansen, Jr.
Treat, William Wardwell
Walker, George William
Wilder, Joyce Ann
Wyatt, Donald L., Jr.

New Jersey

Aspero, Benedict Vincent
Bantivoglio, Thomas Nicholas
Bate, David Soule
Beidler, Marsha Wolf
Biribin, Renato Raymond
Blumberg, Leonard Richard
Borteck, Robert D.
Brown, Harold Jensen
Clapp, Alfred C.
Cole, Murray L.
Cuttler, H. Karen
Day, Edward Francis, Jr.
DeMaio, Andrew John
Domzalski, Kenneth Stanley
Dougherty, Maureen Patricia
Epstein, Milton Aaron
FitzPatrick, Francis James
French, Bruce Hartung
Friend, Israel
Gang, Irving Lloyd
Gavin, Louis Brooks
Goldberg, Leonard M.
Gorrin, Eugene
Gramm, JoAnn Leigh
Gruccio-Thorman, Lillian Joan
Gutterman, Alan J.
Hayes, Lewis Mifflin, Jr.
Hock, Frederick Wyeth
Hoffman, Bernard H.
Jeffer, Herman
Kamens, Harold
Kantor, Lawrence Dorn
Kerman, Lewis H.
Kronman, Carol Jane
Kutner, Mark David
Lambert, Samuel Waldron, III
Lario, Frank M., Jr.
Levavy, Bardin
Levin, Susan Bass
Liebman, Emmanuel
Lyon, Rexford Lowell
Marshall, Anthony Parr
Morgenstern, Robert Terence
Morrison, John Dittgen
Neibart, Ralph
Norman, Victor Conrad
Orbe, Octavius Anthony
Paterson, Keith Edward
Pfaltz, Hugo Menzel, Jr.
Rochkind, Mark Howard
Rosenhouse, Nathan
Sachs, William
Schoenewolf, Walter Wayne
Sholk, Steven Howard
Smith, Seymour Alan
Stickel, Frederick George, III
Strong, John Van Rensselaer
Strull, James Richard
Talafous, Joseph John
Vandervoort, Peter
Van Rye, Kenneth
Williams, Henry Joseph
Wurms, Marcel Ronald
Yellin, Stanley Jay

New Mexico

Atkinson, William Wilder
Brockman, Eugene E.
Conner, William Roby
Grammer, David Allen, Jr.
Henderson, William Nelson
Losee, Arthur Jarrell
Morrison, Robert Dale
Mulhern, John Joseph
Rosenberg, Myer (Mike)
Schaefer, Patrick Mark
Schoen, Stevan Jay
Westerfield, Frank Orlen, Jr.

New York

Abdella, H. James
Atkins, Ronald Raymond
Baker, Barton
Barbeosch, William Peter
Beha, James Alexius, II
Bell, Jonathan Robert
Bennett, James Davison
Bernstein, Jacob
Berry, Charles Gordon
Birmingham, Richard Francis
Black, James Isaac, III
Bloom, Robert Avrum
Blumberg, Gerald
Bobroff, Harold
Bockstein, Herbert
Bolan, Thomas Anthony
Booth, Mitchell B.
Boxer, Harold S.
Bozorth, Squire Newland
Brearton, James Joseph
Brind, David Hutchison
Brownell, Carlton Kearns
Bryant, George McEwan
Bucci, Earl Michael
Bush, Julian S.
Buttenwieser, Lawrence Benjamin
Callahan, Joseph Patrick
Caplicki, Dennis P.
Cardozo, Benjamin Mordecai
Carlucci, Joseph Paul
Carruba, Salvatore John
Case, Edward Haile
Chapin, Melville
Christ, Donald C.
Christensen, Henry, III
Clarey, Robert Louis
Clark, Carolyn Cochran
Cohen, Bernard Barrie
Collazo, Salvador
Cook, Charlotte Smallwood
Cowan, Philip Matthew
Cranney, Marilyn Kanrek
Crowley, Dennis Daniel
Daly, Michael Francis
Daniels, John Hill
Danilek, Donald J.
Dean, William Tucker
DiNardo, Joseph
Dolan, James Francis
Dubow, Alan Martin
Duckworth, R(oy) Demarest, III
Duetsch, John Edwin
Dutcher, B(enjamin) Andrew
Early, John Collins
Einhorn, Joseph Harold
Eisenberg, Ronald Alan
Engel, Ralph Manuel
English, Harry Gordon
Enochs, Elizabeth M.
Epstein, Hyman David
Evans, Douglas Hayward
Farr, Charles Sims
Feitelson, Robert Joel
Finch, Edward Ridley, Jr.
Finkelstein, Bernard
Fisch, Edith L.
Fishman, Felix Arthur
Flood, Kevin Patrick
Frank, Bernard Alan
Fried, Donald David
Galella, Joseph Peter
Galvin, Madeline Sheila
Gelb, Judith Anne
Genzlinger, Dorothea
Gioffre, Anthony Bruno
Gioffre, Bruno Joseph
Glauberman, Melvin L.
Glavin, John Joseph
Goodman, Mortimer
Gowen, George W.
Graham, Arnold Harold
Greene, Bernard Harold
Griffith, Emlyn Irving
Guglielmino, Rosario Joseph
Hagmeir, Thomas Edmiston
Halperin, Theodore Philip
Handelman, Walter Joseph
Harrington, Charles Frederick
Harris, Wayne Manley
Haskel, Jules J.
Haslinger, John Edward
Hawkins, Eliot Dexter
Henry, James R.
Herzog, Jacob Hawley
Hessberg, Albert, II
Hesterberg, Gregory Xavier
Higginson, James Jackson
Hill, Janet Wadsworth
Holden, Stephen, III
Horey, Edward Madigan
Huber, Melvyn Jay
Hull, Philip Glasgow
Hutter, Robert Grant
Ingraham, Frederic Beach
Iselin, Josephine Lea
Jacoby, James Joseph
Jadd, Robert Ira
Jeffers, Fred Hards
Johnson, Kenneth Theodore
Jones, Lawrence Tunnicliffe
Kahn, Alan Edwin
Kasselman, Stevens Jay
Katsoris, Constantine Nicholas
Klipstein, Robert Alan
Komar, Myron
Krainin, Harold L.
Kramer, William Joseph
Kress, Ralph Herbert
Kroll, Arthur Herbert
Kurzman, Robert Graham
Larson, Frederick Albin
Laux, Russell Frederick
Lee, Robert Edward, Jr.
Levitan, David M(aurice)
Lewis, Murray F.
Lingelbach, Albert Lane
Lore, Martin Maxwell
Lovallo, Timothy Robin
Lusky, Louis
Lustgarten, Ira Howard
Maccarini, Anthony George
Madigan, Kathryn Grant
Mahar, Thomas Daniel, Jr.
Mahon, Arthur J.
Malm, Eric S.
Manning, Jerome Alan
Marcheso, Joseph James
Mariani, Michael Matthew
Marinstein, Elliott F.
Martin, Malcolm Elliot
Mayo, John Tyler
McCaffrey, Carlyn Sundberg
McElvein, Thomas I., Jr.
McGrath, Thomas J.
Meaders, Paul Le Sourd
Meadow, Claire Samuelson
Meli, Salvatore Andrew
Meyer, Martin Arthur
Milberg, Lawrence
Minniti, Joseph A.
Moore, Donald Francis
Morris, James Malachy
Mullen, Michael Francis
Munson, Nancy Kay
Nesbitt, John Benedict
Neuwirth, Gloria S.
Ng, Peter Joseph
Nyland, W(illiam) Donald
O'Connor, Michael E.
O'Grady, John Joseph, III
O'Neil, John Joseph
Osborn, Donald Robert
Paganuzzi, Oden Stephen, Jr.
Parisi, Frank Nicholas
Parry, William Henry
Paul, Herbert Morton
Peckham, Eugene Eliot
Perkins, George Foster
Pfeffer, Milton B.
Piedmont, Richard Stuart
Platt, Harold Kirby
Prye, Steven Marvell
Rado, Peter Thomas
Ralli, Constantine Pandia
Reese, William Willis
Rinaldi, Keith Stephen
Robinson, Barbara Paul
Robinson, Edward T., III
Rosenberg, Jerome Roy
Russo, Anthony Joseph, Jr.
Sawyer, James
Schlesinger, Edward Samuel
Schwab, David E., II
Sederbaum, Arthur David
Seidler, B(ernard) Alan
Severs, Charles A., III
Shaw, Arnold H(arold)
Shea, James William
Siegel-Baum, Judith Ellen
Sigall, Michael William
Sills, Nancy Mintz
Slote, Edwin Michael
Squire, Sidney
Stack, Joanne Tunney
Stasack, Stephen Andrew
Steiner, Bruce Darrell
Stevenson, Jocke Shelby
Steyer, Hume Richmond
Stone, Henry
Sweeney, Deidre Ann
Targoff, Cheri Kamen
Thompson, Lawrence Bigelow
Tooker, Robert Luce
Trevett, Thomas Neil
Tweedy, William Elwyn
Twietmeyer, Don Henry
Twining, Rollin Laverne
Ufford, Charles Wilbur, Jr.
Valente, Peter Charles
Vincent, Oreste
Volkmann, Alfred Armistead
Wadsworth, James Marshall
Waldorf, Geraldine Polack
Wallace, Richard Powell
Webster, Luther Ira
Wehringer, Cameron Kingsley
Wels, Richard Hoffman
Wertheimer, Sydney Bernard
Weston, Stephen Burns
Whalen, Daniel Aloysius, III
Wheeler, John William
Whitaker, Benjamin Palmer, Jr.
Wilkie, Robert Arthur
Williams, Frank John, Jr.
Witkin, Susan Peckett
Wolff, Jesse David
Yanas, John Joseph
Zabel, William David
Zankel, Jeffrey Alan
Zerin, Steven David

North Carolina

Bata, Rudolph Andrew, Jr.
Beddow, John Warren
Cross, James Estes, Jr.
Cunningham, George Gray
Dixon, Phillip Ray
Glover, Durant Murrell
Harris, Richard Foster, III
Hemphill, Kathryn Glenn
Hester, Worth Hutchinson
Holleman, Carl Partin
Ingle, John D.
Johnson, Joseph Davis
Joyner, Walton Kitchin
Kersh, John Danzey, Jr.
Lavelle, Brian Francis David
Lloyd, Robert Blackwell, Jr.
Love, Walter Bennett, Jr.
Orsbon, Richard Anthony
Page, James Wilson
Petree, William Horton
Plyler, Cranford Oliver, III
Prevatte, Elias Jesse
Reagan, Owen Walker, III
Riley, John Frederick
Sharp, Starkey, V
Shepard, Paul Cooper
Simpson, James Reid, II
Smith, Stephen Jerome
Vaughn, Robert Candler, Jr.
Walker, Daniel Joshua, Jr.
Webb, W(illiam) Y(oung) Alex
Weick, Paul Alfred, II
Wilson, Thomas Johnston
Yow, Cicero Preston

North Dakota

Bair, Bruce B.
Burgum, Bradley Joseph
Kelsch, William Charles
Maxson, R. James
Price, Robert Quentin
Tebelius, Mark Alan
Widdel, John Earl, Jr.
Wilkes, Richard Clarence
Zander, Janet Holter

Ohio

Adams, Harold Francis
Bamburowski, Thomas Joseph
Beery, Fred Jerome
Bemiller, F. Loyal
Bindley, Richard Stephen
Blair, James F.
Boggs, Ralph Stuart
Booth, Robert Alvin
Boulger, William Charles
Boyko, Christopher Allan
Braverman, Herbert Leslie
Bremer, Thomas Francis
Brenneman, Fleet B.
Bronson, Barbara June
Browne, William Bitner
Brucken, Robert Matthew
Bruestle, Eric George
Buckley, Frederick Jean
Cairns, James Donald
Coady, Michael Francis
Coen, George Weber
Conroy, John Thomas
Cusack, Mary Jo
Davis, Robert Lawrence
Dean, J. Thomas
Detling, Glenn Eugene
Driggs, Charles Mulford
Eckstein, Steven Douglas
Edmiston, Robert Gray
Eilers, John Wagner, Jr.
Falsgraf, William Wendell
Farah, Benjamin Frederick
Fellmeth, Scott Eugene
Fiala, David Marcus
Fisher, Fredrick Lee
Ford, Seabury Hurd
Gariepy, Stephen Henry
Goldsmith, James Arthur
Grabow, Raymond John
Gray, Meryl Benjamin
Greene, Ralph Vernon
Gross, Seymour
Hartsel, Norman Clyde
Hausser, Robert Louis
Healy, Mary Jacqueline
Heck, Grace Fern
Hill, Stephen A.
Hinton, Virgil Otterbein
Holtz, Gregory Theodore
Hoopingarner, John Martin
Hoover, Earl Reese
Izor, David E.
John, Sidney Charles
Johnson, Keith Karleton
Jones, Edgar Wagstaff
Kamine, Charles Stephen
Kanak, Joseph Robert
Kazdin, Margaret Ellen
Keyser, George Harold
Kinney, Aldon Monroe, Jr.
Kitchen, James Denny
Kondzer, Thomas Allen
Korosec, Kenneth David
Krone, Paul William
Lancione, Bernard Gabe
Lancione, Richard Lee
Lang, Francis Harover
LaValley, Richard Gerard
Levin, Arnold Sampson
Lynn, Arthur Dellert, Jr.
Machan, Mitchell Alan
Maher, Edward Joseph
Mantonya, John Butcher
Martin, Oscar Thaddeus
Mathews, S. Paul
Mawer, William Thomas
McIlvaine, Stephen Brownlee
Meikle, William MacKay
Menninger, Henry Edward, Jr.
Moss, Judith Dorothy
Mowry, Kathy Suzanne
Neff, Robert Clark
Nelson, Robert Bruce
Nichelson, James Lee
Nicholson, Brent Bentley
Nippert, Alfred Kuno, Jr.
Parish, Dennis MacDonald
Petersilge, Robert
Pillari, Thomas
Porter, Robert Carl, Jr.
Preston, Kevin Mark
Rabin, Mary Ann
Reno, Ottie Wayne
Richner, Robert Andrew
Robe, Edward Scott
Robison, Joseph Albert
Rorick, Alan Green
Severs, Eric Robertson
Shapiro, Fred David
Sharp, Robert Weimer
Shelley, John Fletcher
Shore, Michael Allan
Shumaker, Roger Lee
Smith, Timothy Daly
Sowald, Heather Gay
Stark, Michael Lee
Stocker, Thomas Edwin
Sulzer, Joseph Paul
Taylor, Edward McKinley, Jr.
Tobias, Charles Harrison, Jr.
Warrington, John Wesley
Weber, H. Patrick
Weisman, Harry Jed
Westphal, Marjorie Lord
Wiersma, David Charles
Wolaver, Stephen Arthur
Wood, Wendy Ann
Yager, John Warren
Yost, William Kent
Zerner, Richard Egon
Zwayer, Ted

Oklahoma

Baker, Thomas Edward
Bell, William Henry
Blair, Clifford Jennings, II
Burch, Melvin Earl
Chapman, Russell Dale
Chesnut, Charles Caldwell
Conner, Leslie Lynn, Jr.
Cornish, Richard Pool
Cowdery, Allen Craig
Dale, Douglas Don
Davis, Frank Wayne
Dowd, Pamela J. Cuplin
Drake, David Allen
Elsener, G. Dale
Galaska, Michael Francis
Gierhart, Douglas Mark
Hampton, Robert Joseph
Huff, R. Robert
Kells, Richard B.
Mantooth, John Albert
Miner, Joseph Brian
Mitchell, Alice Schaffer
Musser, William Wesley, Jr.
Nolen, Lynn Dean
Northcutt, Clarence Dewey
Oden, Waldo Talmage, Jr.
Plater, Frederick Oliver
Rorschach, Jack L.
Ross, William Jarboe
Shoemake, Bransford Hunt
Sparks, John O.
Steltzlen, Janelle Hicks
Sullivan, Lovell Wayne
Thompson, Lee Bennett
Towery, Curtis Kent
Wallace, John R.
Williams, Thomas Arthur

Oregon

Barrett, Cynthia Louise
Bass, Shirley Ann
Bauer, Henry Leland
Bechtold, Paula Miller
Brand, Malcolm Leigh
Brown, Gene L.
Cegavske, Wallace Duane
Cramer, William Donald
Cummins, Elliott Bird
Cyr, Steven Miles
Enfield, Myron Leroy
Engel, Edward Ignatius
Fenner, John Benjamin
Gangle, Sandra Smith
Hager, Orval O.
Harms, Edward Clair, Jr.
Kantor, Stephen Edward
Korth, James William
Lombard, Benjamin (Kip), Jr.
Martin, William Charles
Rich, Steven Eugene
Ryan, Tomas Finnegan
Schuster, Philip Frederick, II
Thompson, Orval Nathan

Pennsylvania

Anderson, Toni-Renee
Appel, T. Roberts, II
Armstrong, Jack Gilliland
Bell, Paul Anthony, II
Best, Franklin L., Jr.
Bookman, Mark
Booz, Nina Robin
Boswell, William Douglas
Bowen, Gerald L.
Brand, Ronald Alvah
Briscoe, Jack Clayton
Broeker, Bernard Dreher
Byler, M. Elvin
Cancelmo, William Weinert

Cherewka, Michael
Chomas, James Louis, Jr.
Coldren, Ira Burdette, Jr.
D'Angelo, Christopher Scott
Davis, James Thomas
Davis, John Phillips, Jr.
Denby, Peter
Diehl, Kristin Knoell
Dill, William Allen
Dillon, Charles Edward
Donohue, Robert John
Dunaway, Wayland Fuller, III
Eagen, Frank P.
Elliott, Richard Howard
Emerson, S. Jonathan
Esposito, Robert S.
Evey, Merle Kenton
Farber, Howard
Favero, James Anthony
Ferri, Karen Lynn
Flint, Daniel Waldo Boone
Foley, Joseph Llewellyn
Gallagher, John Paul
Goldman, Jerry Stephen
Graf, Bayard Mayhew
Greenfield, James Milton
Gutshall, Frederick Raym
Hammond, Mark Bashline
Hartman, John Ives, Jr.
Haskins, George Lee
Heller, Richard Martin
Herchenroether, Henry Carl, Jr.
Herchenroether, Peter Young
Herman, Lee Merideth
Hess, Emerson Garfield
Hess, Lawrence Eugene, Jr.
Hoffstot, Henry Phipps, Jr.
Holleran, Kevin Joseph
Hollinshead, Earl Darnell, Jr.
Honeyman, Robert Wayne
Isabella, Mary Margaret
Jack, James Ernest
John, Robert McClintock
Johnston, Henry Richard, III
Jones, David Mattern
Jones, Edward White, II
Kabala, Edward John
Kain, William Henry
Kaufman, David J.
Kelley, Dennis Scott Clark
Kephart, James William
Kessler, Steven Fisher
Kirby, Jack Arthur
Kline, Sidney DeLong, Jr.
Knupp, Robert Louis
Koplin, Bernice Judith
Krasney, Reginald Alan
Kreder, Joseph Casimir
Krug, Howard Barry
LaFaver, Jon Fetherolf
Lally-Green, Maureen Ellen
Ledebur, Linas Vockroth, Jr.
Lee, Edward B., III
Lees, Steven Thomas
Lentz, Edward James
Loewenstein, Benjamin Steinberg
Long, Christine Mathews
Louis, Robert Henry
Lucey, John David, Jr.
Makowski, Thomas Anthony
Mardinly, Peter Alan
Mauger, Lee Fillmen
McBride, Milford Lawrence, Jr.
McLaughlin, John Sherman
Meigs, John Forsyth
Michie, Daniel Boorse, Jr.
Minno, Frances Patricia Fraher
Mirabello, Francis Joseph
Mulvihill, Mead James, Jr.
Nauman, Spencer Gilbert, Jr.
Nicholson, Bruce Allen
Nofer, George Hancock
Orloski, Richard J.
Phillips, Larry Edward
Plotnick, Charles Keith
Rabinowitz, Samuel Nathan
Rhodes, Kenneth Anthony, Jr.
Richards, Robert Byam
Rosenberg, H. N.
Ross, Eunice Latshaw
Schauffler, Harvey Elliott, Jr.
Schermer, Oscar Selig
Soll, Arthur Martin
Stamberg, Louis Mann
Steadman, James Robert
Straus, Joseph Pennington
Susmarski, Ronald James
Taulane, John Baptist, Jr.
Temple, L. Peter
Tomlinson, Herbert Weston
Voss, Donald Henry
Wagner, Joseph Hagel
Weil, Andrew L.
Welsh, Thomas Harry
Wiener, Howard Alan
Wiley, Jan M.
Wolff, Deborah H(orowitz)
Wood, William Philler
Wrigley, Albert Blakemore
Yanity, Gerald Joseph
Yates, Alfred Glenn, Jr.
Yohlin, Joseph Michael
Youngman, John Crawford
Zeglen, John Michael

Rhode Island

Abedon, Herbert Joseph
Brady, Robert Michael
Cappalli, Richard Anthony
Carr, Mary Jo
Davis, Andrew Hambley, Jr.
Del Sesto, Ronald W.
Harrop, R(obert) Daniel
Hastings, Edwin Hamilton
Hendel, Maurice William
Oster, Gerald Arthur
Rego, Alfred R., Jr.
Roszkowski, Joseph John
Tobin, Bentley
Worrell, Lee Anthony

South Carolina

Beckett, Alice Talbird
Gilchrist, Dennis Clinton
Jordan, Michael Lee McAdams
Leverette, Sarah Elizabeth
Massey, Raymond David
O'Donnell, Robert Harry
Rasor, Charles Lewis, Jr.
Rose, William Shepard, Jr.
Smith, Sherman N., III
Thomy, George Albert
Todd, Albert Creswell, III
Wyche, Cyril Thomas

South Dakota

Bennett, Donn
Burns, Mary Elizabeth
Graslie, Thomas Eric
Gustafson, Lawrence Raymond
Kemnitz, Ralph A.
Rose, Lois Ann
Zimmer, John Herman

Tennessee

Allen, Newton Perkins
Barnes, Herschiel Sevier
Beasley, Thomas Tarry, II
Berry, William Wells
Bird, Agnes Thornton
Bland, James Theodore Jr.
Bostick, Charles Dent
Buchignani, Leo Joseph
Evans, Thomas Martin
Frazier, Steven Carl
Gordon, Thomas Napier
Holbrook, Dan W.
Jordan, James D(ee)
Kiener, John Leslie
Lawler, Edward James
Lynch, Carole Yard
Marquis, Robert Stillwell
Montgomery, Robert H., Jr.
Price, Walter Lee
Roach, Jon Gilbert
Sheppeard, Sarah Y.
Sisson, Jerry Allan
Skefos, Harry J(erry)
Smith, Drayton Beecher, II
Stark, Kelly Shira
Stokes, Carl Nicholas
Tate, S. Shepherd
Townsend, Edwin Clay
Walton, John Wayne
Witcher, Roger Kenneth, Jr.

Texas

Alberts, Harold
Allen, Michael Douglas
Arizaga, Lavora Spradlin
Baber, Wilbur H., Jr.
Barnhill, Robert Edwin, III
Barr, John H.
Beard, Jane Ann Varner
Berry, Thomas Eugene
Betow, Joel Thomas
Biehl, Kathy Anne
Blanchette, James Grady, Jr.
Blazier, John Charles
Boone, Taylor Scott
Bowmer, Jim Dewitt
Briggs, Tom Peery
Brown, C. Harold
Brown, Michael Lance
Bryce, William Delf
Burrows, Jon Hanes
Callahan, James Carroll
Calvert, Nadia Rae Venable
Carpenter, Gordon Russell
Carr, Thomas Eldridge
Cline, Lee Williamson
Cobb, Charles Louis
Collins, Kyle Boyd
Conner, Warren Wesley
Cox, Sanford Curtis, Jr.
Crook, Charles David
Crook, E(dward) Carter, Jr.
Crosby, Philip
Davis, John Whittaker
Dougherty, John Chrysostom, III
Durell, Jay Glenn
Duty, Tony Edgar
Eastland, S. Stacy
Emery, Herschell Gene
Engelhardt, John Hugo
Eubank, J. Thomas
Fitzpatrick, Sandra Marlene
Fluke, Randall Lynn
Fort, D. Stephen
French, Colin Val
Godwin, Elva Cockrell
Golden, Alvin Joseph
Gregg, Tom Will, Jr.
Guest, Floyd Emory, Jr.
Hamilton, Elwin Lomax
Hardy, Harvey Louchard
Hartnett, Will Ford
Hayers, Paul Hugh
Henkel, Kathryn G.
Ice, Noel Carlysle
Jansen, Donald Orville
Johanson, Stanley Morris
Jones, Scranton
Joynton, Stanley Forrest
Kemp, William Franklin
Kendrick, Herbert Spencer, Jr.
Kincaid, William H(atton)
King, Gerald Lee
King, Steve Mason
Koenig, Rodney Curtis
Kvinta, Charles J.
Laney, Daniel Milton
LaSalle, Lowell LeRoy
Leach, Terry Ray
Leshin, Richard Lee
Line, Judson Edward
Mallory, Harold Darlington
Marbut, Syrian Erasmus
Martin, Paul E(dward)
McElwrath, Michael Rogers
McKnight, Rufus Nicolaus, Jr.
McNamara, John Bolivar, Jr.
McNeil, Buck W.
McRae, Hamilton Eugene, Jr.
Moncure, John Lewis
Morrison, Walton Stephen
Nolte, Melvin, Jr.
Operhall, Harrie Marie Pollok
Owens, Rodney Joe
Perkins, Lloyd Wesley
Petry, Herbert Charles, Jr.
Post, Earl Stock
Ratliff, William D., III
Remy, William Emmett
Ritchie, Robert Field
Ross, James Ulric
Sealy, Tom
Seaman, Stephen Henry
Seay, George Edward
Seay, George Edward, Jr.
Smart, James Hudson
Smith, Edward Vance, III
Stoltz, Michael Rae
Taylor, Robert Love
Thrall, Gordon Fish
Topper, Robert Carlton
Townes, Edgar Eggleston, Jr.
Tracy, J. David
Tygrett, Howard Volney, Jr.
Walker, Dee Brown
Wallis, Ben Alton, Jr.
Ward, Gary Ardus
Warford, Tommy Gene
Weekley, Frederick Clay, Jr.
Wells, Peter Boyd
Wharton, Thomas H(eard), Jr.
Wilkes, John Michael
Wilson, Donald L.
Woodward, Marion Kenneth
Wright, Eugene Box
Wright, Wallace Mathias
Young, Ardell Moody

Utah

Anderson, Reese C.
Baron, Roger Frederick
Belnap, Michael Gary
Curtis, Dale Jay
Hatch, Sumner Jones
Hillyard, Lyle William
Jeppson, Joseph Gaddis
Joslin, Gary James
Kennicott, James W.
Mangan, George Edward
Verhaaren, Harold Carl
West, David Clay

Vermont

Cummings, Charles Rogers
Debevoise, Thomas McElrath
Gravel, John Cook
Kissell, Tony Fred
Lisman, Bernard
Morrow, Emily Rubenstein
Otterman, Harvey Boyd, Jr.
Plante, Peter Paul
Sincerbeaux, Robert Abbott

Virginia

Acker, Alan Scott
Alan, Sondra Kirschner
Ames, Edward Almer, III
Belcher, Dennis Irl
Blair, Richard Eugene
Clark, Lynne Nuber
Collins, Philip Reilly
Cooper, Charles Neilson
Edmunds, Felix Elmer
Greenbacker, John Everett
Hammer, Donald Gordon
Hartshorn, Roland DeWitt
Herge, J. Curtis
Hill, Oliver White, Sr.
Lewis, Gordon
Lowenstein, Marshall Leigh
Mackall, Henry Clinton
Malone, William Grady
Massey, James Buckner, III
Musselman, Robert Metcalfe
Parks, Kenneth F.
Peyton, Gordon Pickett
Ritchie, John
Roberts, Russell Hill
Seymour, William Francis, IV
Sheffield, Walter Jervis
Simmonds, James Henry
Spainhour, Tremaine Howard
Tansill, Frederick Joseph
Walton, Edmund Lewis, Jr.
Whitlock, Willie Walker
Wolcott, Edward Wallace
Woodward, Roland Carey

Washington

Armstrong, Grant
Barline, John
Barnett, Hollis H.
Bradbury, Timothy Dewet
Cunningham, Janis Ann
Dussault, William L.E.
Gates, Kenneth W.
Gay, Carl Lloyd
Gay, Sandra Bates
Gross, Richard Arthur
Huey, Diane Marie
Krueger, James A.
Langlie, Arthur Sheridan
Luce, Kenyon Eldridge
Marler, Dirk Alan
McInnis, Emmett Emory, Jr.
Olver, Michael Lynn
Oseran, Melville
Palmer, Harvard
Panchot, Dudley Bradford
Parsons, James Bowne
Peters, Frank August
Price, Clark Alan
Roubicek, Christopher John
Sayre, Matt Melvin Mathias
Shogan, Alexander Joe, Jr.
Spring, Max Edward
Walker, Francis Joseph
Westland, John Alden
Wright, Willard Jurey

West Virginia

Coleman, James Howard, Jr.
Ford, Richard Edmond
Kagler, Robert Wayne
Kwass, Sidney J.
Lunsford, David H.
Phillips, John Davisson
Reed, James Wilson
Simmons, Alan Russell

Wisconsin

Bergen, Thomas Joseph
Bosshard, John
Byers, Stephen Michael
Clark, James Francis
Cook, Joseph Lee
Daniel, Marvin Valerius
Demet, Donal Moffatt
Du Rocher, James Howard
Eberhardt, Daniel Hugo
Everard, Gerald Wilfred
Flatley, Robert Rahr
Friend, Henry Charles
Herbers, John A.
Jursik, Patricia Dolores
Kabaker, Richard Zohn
Kaestner, Richard Darwin
Karp, David Barry
Kenyon, Allen Francis
Kiessling, William Edward
Klos, Jerome John
Krueger, William Frederick
Laikin, George Joseph
Liebmann, Herbert Charles, III
Ludwig, R. Arthur
Lund, John Richard
Mihal, Thomas Harlan
Minahan, Roger Copp
Newton, Mary S.
Orth, Charles Adam, Jr.
Rasmussen, Carl John
Rice, Zelotes Sylvester
Roberson, Linda
Rotter, Emanuel Norman
Sauer, William Jacob
Schacherl, Anne Washechek
Splitt, Cody
Steil, George Kenneth, Sr.
Storck, Robert Emil
Sweet, Lowell Elwin
Thuermer, Richard Joseph
Tollers, Jeffery Barnet
Wilcox, Francis John
Wilcox, Jean Evelyn
Wilson, Oscar, Jr.

Wyoming

Allison, James Stanley
Case, Irvin Vincent, Jr.
Dray, William Perry
Durham, Harry Blaine, III
Hjelmstad, William David
Smith, Thomas Shore
Tarver, Timothy Stephen
Williams, Houston Garvin

ENGLAND

Baker, Paul Vivian

FRANCE

Iseman, Joseph Seeman

ADDRESS UNPUBLISHED

Ansley, Shepard Bryan
Baudler, William John
Beck, Robert Edward
Bergman, Arlie Walter
Bono, Anthony Salvatore Emanuel
Breidenbach, Cherie Elizabeth
Brock, John Tabor
Brown, Gary Ross
Cancio, Pablo Ramón
Corcoran, Sheila Margaret
Cox, James Darrell
De La Garza, Roberto Eduardo
Dunn, Thomas Tinsley
Easterling, Charles Armo
Edwards, Vern Downing
Fine, Robert Paul
Fink, Monroe
Gamble, E. James
Gleason, Gerald Wayne
Godfrey, Thomas Grant
Gorochow, Vera Zina
Gribbs, Paula Rewald
Hamel, Richard Paul
Hebl, Thomas Lee, Sr.
Hefner, Archie
Hernandez, David N(icholas)
Holland, Randy James
Ice, Clarence Frederick
James, Joyce Marie
Kirschner, Paul David
Lambert, Arthur Gorman
Martin, James Henry
Merrill, Abel Jay
Nicolaides, Mary
Niehaus, Susan Patricia
Panec, William Joseph
Regenstreif, Herbert
Sanger, Scott Howard
Sheetz, Ralph Albert
Simon, Richard Hege
Stetler, Nevin
Stone, Edward Herman
Stough, Charles Daniel
Stubbs, William Perry, Jr.
Surratt, John Richard
von Dioszeghy, Adam George
Weclew, Robert George
Winston, Harold Ronald
Yorra, Myron Seth

PROPERTY DAMAGE. *See* **Personal injury.**

PROPERTY, REAL

UNITED STATES

Alabama

Albright, Carl Wayne, Jr.
Alidor, Gary Paul, Sr.
Bailey, Robert Theodore Russ
Cornelius, Walter Felix
Davis, Mallory Donald, Jr.
Funderburk, Kenneth Leroy
Gray, William Patton, Jr.
Hardegree, Arthur Lee, III
Harris, Benjamin Harte, Jr.
Harris, John Clinton, Jr.
Hellums, Clarence Theo
Hicks, Deborah Ann Whitmore
Hinds, Caroline Wells
Holland, Lyman Faith, Jr.
Hughston, Harold Vaughan, Jr.
Irons, William Lee
Kloess, Lawrence H., Jr.
Lane, Robert Pitt
Leatherbury, Gregory Luce, Jr.
McGowin, Nicholas Stallworth
McKinley, Edmon Howard
Moore, Gary Alan
Olshan, Gary Steven
Otts, Lee MacMillan
Philips, James Albert
Pittman, Craig Sorrell
Price, Walter Jasper, Jr.
Scott, Romaine Samples, III
Smith, Andrew Lovgren
Smith, Hardy Bolton
Smith, John Joseph
South, Mark Omega
Wilson, Jack

Alaska

Beiswenger, Allan David
Bolger, Joel Harold
Gidcumb, Lance Edward
McCann, Richard Eugene
Winner, Russell Lee

Arizona

Alexander, David Cleon, III
Baker, William Dunlap
Barker, J(ohn) Emery
Basinger, Richard Lee
Baughn, Alfred Fairhurst
Berry, Charles Richard
Blum, Paul J.
Brueckner, Kurt Malcolm
Burton, Osmond Alexander, Jr.
Case, David Leon
Cassidy, Frank Joseph
Chauncey, Tom Webster, II
Cole, George Thomas
Curtis, David William, Jr.
D'Antonio, Gregory Douglas
George, Maureen Rose
Goodman, Mark N.
Hanshaw, A. Alan
Henry, John Alfred
Herman, Steven Roger
Hornisher, Michael
Hutchison, Samuel Robert
Irvine, Thomas Kenneth
Isaak, Gotthilf Eugene
Jacques, Raoul Thomas
Jekel, Louis G.
Kaminsky, Larry Michael
Lagerman, Susan Borden
Lee, Richard H(arlo)
Lewis, Orme
Lowry, Edward Francis, Jr.
Mangum, John K.
May, Bruce Barnett
McRae, Hamilton Eugene, III
Miner, Don Jones
Ostapuk, David R.
Peters, Daniel Wayne
Polan, David Jay
Price, Guy Bradley
Sabin, John Merrill
Simon, Jack Hunt
Slavin, Francis John, Jr.
Smith, Kenneth McKay
Stanley, Brian Keith
Stirton, Charles Paul
Stoddard, Charles Warner, III
Terry, Peter Anthony
Titus, Jon Alan
Warner, Teddy Fleming
Williams, Quinn Patrick
Wood, Nicholas Joseph
Young, Jeanne Catherine

Arkansas

Brady, Lawrence Joseph
Choate, Murray Rickliffe, II
Cross, Junius Bracy, Jr.
Dumeny, Marcel Jacque
Epley, Lewis Everett, Jr.
Fergus, William Lee
Finley, John Cyrus, Jr.
Finley, John Cyrus, III
Fitton, Garvin
Gitelman, Morton
Goodner, Donald Scott
Howard, Steven Gray
Jackson, Blaine Albert
Ledbetter, Thomas Dale
Leslie, Robert Bruce
Looney, Jake Wayne
Mayersohn, Arnold Linn, Jr.
Pearson, Charles Thomas, Jr.
Rhoads, George Robert
Stodola, Mark Allen
Stroud, John Fred, Jr.
Walters, William Peter
Warner, Cecil Randolph, Jr.
White, Stephen Alan
Wilson, Robert Martin, Jr.
Wright, Robert Ross, III
Wright, Susan Webber
Young, Robert Earl

California

Abdulaziz, Sam K.
Abt, Evet Sue Loewen
Adelson, Benedict James
Allen, Albert Herman
Allen, Jeffrey Michael
Appel, Martin Sherman
Atkins, Thomas Jay
Auser, Wallace Van Cortlandt, III
Baigent, Julia Marie
Balluff, John Joseph
Barash, Anthony Harlan
Barbarowicz, Robert Paul
Barnhorst, Howard Joseph, II
Bassett, Craig Jay
Battaglia, Philip Maher
Baumgarten, Ronald Neal
Beasley, Oscar Homer
Bell, Wayne Steven
Benton, Andrew Keith
Berman, Howard Jonathan
Birney, William Joseph, Jr.
Blitz, Stephen Michael

Bohlmann, Daniel Robert
Bohrer, Robert A.
Bramley, William Alexander, III
Brown, Louis Daniel
Burden, James Ewers
Callender, William Lacey
Cameron, Mark Alan
Camp, James Carroll
Cheatham, Robert William
Clabaugh, Elmer Eugene, Jr.
Clark, Charles Edward
Cook, Ronald Walter
Crowe, Daniel Walston
Cummins, Neil Joseph, Jr.
Curotto, Ricky Joseph
Curtiss, Thomas, Jr.
Daniels, James Walter
Darling, Scott Edward
Daugherty, Richard Bernard
Day, James McAdam, Jr.
Degallegos, Richard
DeRonde, John Allen, Jr.
Diamond, Philip Ernest
Diehl, Joseph Burnett
DuBose, Guy Steven
Dukeminier, Jesse
Eckardt, Richard William
Edwards, Robin Morse
Ellickson, Robert Chester
Ellsworth, David G.
Enersen, Burnham
Eres, Thomas W.
Evans, John William
Ewell, A(ustin) B(ert), Jr.
Fabian, JoAnne Frances
Factor, Max, III
Fainsbert, Ann Rubenstein
FitzGerald, John Edward, III
Flate, Ronald Allen
Frankel, James Burton
Fraser, Bruce William
Freeburger, Thomas Oliver
Freed, Kenneth Alan
Fuller, Maurice DeLano, Jr.
Funk, Jonathan A.
Gade, Thomas Andrew
Georgallis, Joann
Glenn, Everett Lamar
Goldie, Ray Robert
Goldie, Ron Robert
Gooch, Robert Francis
Gralnek, Donald D.
Greenberg, Maxwell Elfred
Greenwood, Steven Matlin
Grim, Douglas Paul
Grush, Julius Sidney
Hagel, James A.
Haines, Michael Anthony
Hanley, Thomas Francis, III
Hanna, John Paul
Hannon, Timothy Patrick
Harlan, Nancy Margaret
Harris, Lee S.
Harroch, Richard David
Harrow, Barry Richard
Harwood, Dennis Westcott
Hausmann, Edwin David
Hayes, Byron Jackson, Jr.
Heisinger, James Gordon, Jr.
Herring, Charles David
Hetland, John Robert
Hieronymus, Edward Whittlesey
Higbe, Clifton Melton Harvin
Hightower, George Willis
Hobbs, Franklin Dean, III
Hoefflin, Richard Michael
Hoffman, John Douglas
Hoffman, Kris
Holden, Charles St. George
Horodas, Eric David
Horwin, Leonard
Hotchkiss, Nancy
Hurabiell, John Philip, Sr.
Jackson, Pamela Curulewski
Jensen, Douglas Blaine
Johnson, Darrell Bruce
Johnson, Drew Martin
Johnston, Faber Laine, Jr.
Jones, Thomas McReynolds
Jordan, Paul S.
Jorgensen, Erik Holger
Kamei, Susan Hiroko
Kane, Margaret McDonald
Katz, Martha Lessman
Kelley, Thomas Joseph
Kennedy, William Irl
Kimport, David Lloyd
Kimsey, Dale Boyd
Kind, Kenneth Wayne
Kinney, James Howard
Kirkelie, Gregory Evan
Kirkman, Reymond Fauche, III
Kirlin, Anne Marget
Kitta, John Noah
Knierim, K. Phillip
Knox, Alan Anthony
Kostant, Ralph Bennett
Kramer, Kenneth Scott
Lagle, John Franklin
Lancaster, Michael James
Lane, Robert K.
Lee, John Jin
Lee, Paulette Wang
Levin, Marvin Eugene
Liebersbach, Richard William
Lightner, Merrie Turner
Loomis, John Elmer
Loube, Irving
Luther, Charles William
Lyon, Bruce Arnold
Mack, John Oscar
Mandel, Martin Louis
Mansour, Nadim Ned
Marsh, Richard Melvin
Matter, Bruce E.
May, Lawrence Edward
McBride, Keith Wesley
McClintock, Gordon Edwin
McDevitt, Ray Edward
McGinty, Brian Donald
McIntosh, Bruce Terence
McNally, Susan Fowler
McNichols, Stephen Lucid Robert, Jr.
Mebane, Julie Shaffer
Miles, Jerold Lane
Miles, Lawrence William, Jr.
Millard, Neal Steven
Miller, Harry Daniel
Miller, Kenneth Michael
Miller, Mary Jane
Miyoshi, David Masao
Mohr, Anthony James
Moore, Jacqueline Ursula
Mosich, Nicholas Joseph
Musacchio, Kirk Anthony
Nemir, Donald Philip
Nesbitt, Mark Thomas
Norris, Janet Clare
Ogg, Wilson Reid
O'Keefe, William Patrick
O'Malley, James Terence
Orr, Robert M.
Pagano, James Lawrence
Pahl, Stephen Donald
Parker, Charles Edward
Parks, George Brooks
Pearman, Robert Charles
Peterson, Paul Ames
Peterson, Richard Thomas
Petty, Keith
Pircher, Leo Joseph
Pollard, Henry
Porter, Verna Louise
Preble, Laurence George
Rabin, Jane Hurwitz
Rai, Shambhu K.
Ray, David Lewin
Reed, Charles Rufus
Regalia, Edmund Louis
Riesenfeld, Stefan Albrecht
Riggs, Charles Earle
Riley, Kirk Holden
Ritchie, Thomas Brown
Roberts, Jayne Kelly
Robison, William Robert
Roby, Richard Eric
Roth, Hadden Wing
Sax, Joseph Lawrence
Schiff, Gunther Hans
Schumacher, Stephen Joseph
Scott, David Ernest
Severaid, Ronald Harold
Shannon, Malcolm Lloyd, Jr.
Shaw, John LeRoy, Jr.
Shaw, William Albert
Sheppard, Thomas Richard
Sherman, Glenn Terry
Sherman, Lawrence M.
Sherrell, John Bradford
Siegan, Bernard Herbert
Sikora, Warren
Sitkin, Peter Edward
Skaggs, Sanford Merle
Sloan, Sheldon Harold
Small, Harold S.
Smith, Milan Dale, Jr.
Smolker, Gary Steven
Snyder, Arthur Kress
Staley, John Fredric
Stauber, Ronald Joseph
Stegall, Daniel Richard
Stenfeldt, Lillian Gerda
Stevenson, Noel C.
Stipanov, Kenneth Jerome
Stovitz, Chuck
Stratton, Richard James
Sullivan, Maureen
Sussman, Mitchell Reed
Suter, Bernard Reynold
Tan, William Lew
Tepper, R(obert) Bruce, Jr.
Tormey, James Roland, Jr.
Turek, Kenneth Casper
Turner, John Miller
Van Atta, David Murray
Vaughn, Lesley Miller Mehran
Vena, David Henry
Vosguanian, Rodney Nerses
Wagner, D. William
Waks, Stephen Harvey
Walker, Jordan Clyde
Wallenstein, Raymond
Walsh, William, IV
Walters, Judy Harue
Warne, William Raymond
Warnlof, John Skinner
Weiner, Edward A.
Weiss, Edward Abraham
Wessling, Robert Bruce
Willard, Robert Edgar
Willey, Charles Wayne
Willsey, F. Patterson
Wise, Toni Pryor
Wooley, Kenneth Virgil
Worley, Donald Robert
Yancey, David Wallace
Yarema, Geoffrey Steven
Young, Bryant Llewellyn
Zecher, Albert Michael
ZoBell, Karl

Colorado

Alberts, Celia Anne
Aspinwall, David Charles
Barad, Edward Nelson
Barney, Patrick Earl
Benjamin, James Gilbert
Bluestein, Louis Allen
Boyle, John Edward
Breggin, Janis Ann
Brown, James Elliott
Bruce, Neil Curtis
Cahan, Judith E.
Carlson, Alan Douglas
Chapman, Karen Louise
Clark, Roger Earl
Clay, Aaron Richard
Cockrell, Richard Carter
Cope, Joseph Adams
Cortez, Miles Cogley, Jr.
Craig, Benjamin Lawrence
Deutsch, Harvey Elliot
Dowdle, Patrick Dennis
Durfee, Amy Lee McElheny
DuVivier, Katharine Keyes
Eckelberger, Jerrie Francis
Erickson, David L.
Fairlamb, Millard Schuyler
Fognani, John Dennis
Freeman, Deborah Lynn
Fried, Joseph
Gaddis, Larry Roy
Gallegos, Larry Duayne
Gast, Richard Shaeffer
Gessling, James Place
Goral, Brian Harold
Grant, Patrick Alexander
Hagen, Glenn W(illiam)
Hanrahan, Kathleen Susan
Helmer, David Alan
Henderson, John Richard
Hillestad, Charles Andrew
Honaker, Jimmie Joe
Hopp, Walter James
Hybl, William Joseph
Irwin, R. Robert
Jacobs, Ronald Hedstrom
Jersin, Edward Anthony
Johnson, Philip Edward
Judd, Richard D(onald)
Katz, Michael Jeffery
Kaup, Daniel John
Keatinge, Cornelia Wyma
Kelly, Eric Damian
Kins, Tonya
Knudsen, Curtis Edwin
Kraemer, Sandy Frederick
Kumli, Karl Fredrick, III
LaCroix, Thomas Russell
Lavenhar, Jeffrey Drew
Levine, Gary H.
Levine, Kent Jay
Mall, Loren L(ee)
Martin, James Russell
Martz, Clyde Ollen
McClain, Vaughn Leon
McClung, Merle Steven
McGill, Scott A.
McGowan, Rodney Ralph
McGrath, John Nicholas, Jr.
McGrath, William Arthur
Meininger, John Alexander
Micsak, Robert William
Mitchem, Allen P.
Montgomery, Robert Cornelius, III
O'Dorisio, John William, Jr.
Overholser, John W.
Patrick, Kevin Land
Paulson, Christopher Robert
Pautsch, Richard Joseph
Payne, Raymond Lee, Jr.
Peck, Kenneth Eldon
Peirce, Frederick Fairbanks
Perkins, Eugene Oral
Peterson, Brooke Alan
Pluss, Stewart Jay
Quail, Beverly Jo
Quiat, Gerald M.
Ragonetti, Thomas John
Reid, John Edward
Robinson, Julia Ormes
Rodgers, Frederic Barker
Ruda, Jacques Serge
Savage, John William, Jr.
Sayre, Charles Michael
Sayre, John Marshall
Schenkein, Pamela Ephraim
Schoonover, Randall Charles
Shafer, Stephanie Jane
Sherman, Lester Ivan
Slaninger, Frank Paul
Slavin, Howard Leslie
Sloat, Gerald Charles
Smith, Michael Alan
Sonntag, Richard Arthur
Thorson, David Morris
Timmins, Edward Patrick
Tisdale, Douglas Michael
Torpy, Richard Donald
Tracey, Jay Walter, Jr.
Vogel, Lawrence Mark
Warren, Bruce Willard
White, Charles B.
White, Michael Douglas
Wilder, Raymond Edward
Wood, David Leslie

Connecticut

Abate, Ernest Nicholas
Adams, Richard Glen
Amschler, James Ralph
Anderson, Henry Brackenridge
Argenta, Craig Jon
Ayres, Steven Edward
Berger, Robert Bertram
Bernstein, Robert Gary
Bracken, Nanette Beattie
Buck, Gurdon Hall
Cacace, Michael Joseph
Capecelatro, Mark John
Cederbaum, Eugene E.
Coan, Richard Morton
Coates, Charles Elting, III
Cuminale, James William
De Barbieri, Roy Louis
Dowling, Michael Anthony
Dowling, Victor James
Dzurik, John Gerard
Eberhard, Robert Vincent
Eberhart, Harry Simon
Fallon, John Francis
Farrelly, Francis J.
Fignar, Eugene Michael
Finch, Frank Herschel, Jr.
Frank, Mark Kennith, III
Freccia, Vincent John, III
Fricke, Richard John
Galligan, Matthew G.
Gerlt, Wayne Christopher
Gersten, Sandra Joan Pessin
Ginsberg, Larry Floyd
Greene, Thurston
Hawkins, Barry Curtis
Hefferan, Harry Howard, Jr.
Herbst, Peter Caldwell
Ivey, Scott Ellsworth
Kaye, Joel Michael
Killian, Robert Kenneth, Jr.
Leepson, Peter Lawrence
Lloyd, James Hendrie, III
Macleod, Anthony Michael
Madorin, A. Raymond, Jr.
Mark, Henry Allen
Medvecky, Thomas Edward
Mitchell, Thomas Bradford
Murtha, Thomas Michael
Nevas, Leo
Nicola, Robert James
O'Connor, James Michael
Pavetti, Francis James
Perlman, Bruce Michael
Reinen, Jeffrey William
Rome, Lewis B.
Rosenblatt, Edward Milton
Rout, Robert Howard
Rubenstein, Mark A.
Ryan, Atherton Beal
Ryan, John Joseph
Ryan, William Joseph, Jr.
Rybak, Michael Dennis
Sachs, Jeffrey Michael
Santopietro, Albert Robert
Schwartz, Lawrence B.
Skuret, Daniel D.
Snaider, Benson Abram
Strone, Michael Jonathan
Terk, Glenn Thomas
Theodore, Carol N.
Trager, Philip
Ury, Frederic Stephen
Valentine, Garrison Norton
Vetere, Robert Louis
Webster, Stuart Arthur
Williams, Michael Peter Anthony
Wolfe, Robert J.
Wolfson, Susan Wartur

Delaware

Amick, Steven Hammond
Devine, Donn
Kristol, Daniel Marvin
Moore, James Everett, Jr.

District of Columbia

Ain, Sanford King
Aluise, Timothy John
Bardwell, Stanford O., Jr.
Bernstein, Caryl Salomon
Bernstein, Edwin S.
Blinkoff, James Bladen
Bodansky, Robert Lee
Bonvillian, William Boone
Brand, Michael Edward
Breitenberg, John Francis
Brown, Donald Arthur
Brown, James Milton
Brown, Thomas Philip, III
Bryan, Mildred Gott
Buechner, Jack W.
Carmel, Frank Joseph
Cates, C. Brad
Chamblin, Spencer Diehl
Colton, Herbert Spencer
Cook, Frank Robert, Jr.
Cushing, Robert Hunter
Cutler, Eliot Raphael
Duerk, William Adam
Edson, Charles Louis
Field, Charles G.
Ford, David R(ucker)
Fread, Joan P.
Gibson, Joseph Lee
Gillmarten, Mary Del Rey
Glasgow, Norman M.
Hakola, David Brown
Harrison, Earl David
Howard, Daggett Horton
Howard, Glen Scott
Ingersoll, William Boley
Interdonato, Anthony Paul
Kass, Benny Lee
Kelly, William Charles, Jr.
Klein, Robert Allan
Landfield, Richard
Lane, Bruce Stuart
Loeb, Dorothy Pearl
Loewinger, Kenneth Jeffery
Maloof, Farahe Paul
Marvin, Charles Raymond
Moskof, Howard Richard
Murphy, Brian Paul
Murphy, Lynda Marie
Murphy, Marcia Gaughan
Nichols, Henry Eliot
Platt, Leslie A.
Policy, Vincent Mark
Portnoy, Ian Karl
Ralston, David Thomas, Jr.
Rathmell, Anne Elizabeth
Reifsnyder, Daniel Alan
Rider, James Lincoln
Roberts, Jared Ingersoll
Robinson, Sara Moore
Rosenberg, Ruth Helen Borsuk
Rummel, Edgar Ferrand
Schwartz, David Harold
Shanks, Hershel
Singer, Daniel Morris
Smith, George Patrick, II
Smith, Robert Anthony
Spiegel, Robert Alan
Stanley, William, Jr.
Stinchfield, John Edward
Teitelbaum, Steven Alan
Utermohlen, William Jerome
Van Etten, Laura
Violante, Joseph Anthony
Walker, Lynda Kay
Wegner, Brent Allen
Weissbard, Samuel Held
Wolf, William B., Jr.
Young, Marlene Annette
Zax, Leonard A.

Florida

Adams, Daniel Lee
Adcock, Louie Norman, Jr.
Allen, Jospeh Bernard
Alonso, Antonio Enrique
Ames, Stuart D.
Andersen, Michael Page
Andrews, Dean
Ansbacher, Lewis
Baccus, Tonya Lynn
Bamberg, Jonathan Baker
Barish, George
Barker, Charles Thomas
Benson, John Scott
Berley, David Richard
Bernard, Lawrence Jay
Bernstein, Zayle Abraham
Blank, Ralph John, Jr.
Bloomgarden, Paul M.
Breed, E(rnest) Mark, III
Brightman, Richard Stephen
Buck, Thomas Randolph
Capp, Alvin
Carlile, Robert Toy
Chesser, David Michael
Christian, Gary Irvin
Clements, Allen, Jr.
Click, David Forrest
Coletta, Raymond Robert
Conner, Richard Elwood
Conner, Timothy James
Constant, Joseph
Cronig, Steven Carlyle
Crum, James Merrill
Currier, Barry Arthur
Dady, Robert Edward
Dariotis, Terrence Theodore
Day, Karen Spring
Dee, David Scott
del Valle, Ignacio Gonzalez
Dicks, Jack William
Dye, Dewey Albert, Jr.
Eagan, William Leon
Engel, Steven Ira
Feldman, Joel Harvey
Feola, Eugene David
Fildes, Richard James
Fletcher, Paul Gerald
Forman, Robert Steven
Fougerousse, Philip
Friend, Richard E.
Fry, Stephen
Gardner, Russell Menese
Garlick, Michael
Gelfand, Michael Joseph
Genauer, Martin Jay
Georges, Richard Martin
Gescheidt, Richard Anthony
Godbold, Gene Hamilton
Goldberg, Alan Joel
Golden, Donald Alan
Golden, E(dward) Scott
Gorman, Robert James
Gougelman, Paul Reina
Grant, Karleen Ann
Gray, J. Charles
Grimm, William Thomas
Haile, John Sanders
Hall, David Wayne
Hall, Frank Dawson
Hartman, Burton Arthur
Hedrick, David Warrington
Hendry, Robert Ryon
Hickman, Paula Diane
Hodge, James Edward
Hoffman, Stuart Kenneth
Holcomb, Lyle Donald, Jr.
Hollander, Bruce Lee
Hume, John
Iden, Bruce Franklin
Jernigan, Anna Michelle
Johnston, Shepherd Davis
Julin, Joseph Richard
Kennedy, Wallace Walton
Kievit, Robert Warren
Kittleson, Henry Marshall
Krinzman, Richard Neil
Lancaster, Kenneth G.
Lang, Joseph Hagedorn
Layman, David Michael
Leib, Patricia Shane
Leone, James Russell
Leonhardt, Frederick Wayne
Lester, Edgel Celsus
Lester, Paul Arthur
Levine, Curtis Gilbert
Lewis, Mark Russell
Lopacki, Edward Joseph, Jr.
Losey, Ralph Colby
Lowndes, John Foy
Mandell, Craig Jack
Mann, Kenneth L.
Marcus, Jonathan Seth
Markus, Andrew Joshua
Martin, James William
Martinez-Cid, Ricardo
Matthias, Robert Charles
McCollum, James Fountain
McEwan, Oswald Beverley
Mednick, Glenn Myles
Meeks, William Herman, III
Merriam, Lauren Evert, III
Middleton, Elwyn Linton
Mims, William Lovanda
Montgomery, David Paul
Morales, Nestor
Moreno, M. Cristina
Mudd, John Philip
Murray, David G.
Nordahl, Norris George
Nyce, John Daniel
Ozark, Damian Michael
Painter, James Morgan
Passidomo, John Michael
Patterson, George Anthony
Patton, Arthur Gordon
Paul, Jeremy Ralph
Pearce, Lewis Richard
Perlstein, Mitchell Leslie
Peters, Robert Timothy
Pierce, John G.
Pippen, Joseph Franklin, Jr.
Poller, Jeri
Pumphrey, Gerald Robert
Pyle, Frank LeForest, Sr.
Remsen, John Lockwood
Reynolds, Joseph Jay
Risner, Paul Edward
Roddenberry, Bonnie Lindquist
Rogovin, Lawrence H.
Rowan, Beverly Adele
Royce, Raymond Watson
Rush, Fletcher Grey, Jr.
Sacasas, Rene
Samole, Myron Michael
Sanders, Barrett
Schwenke, Roger Dean
Segal, Martin Edward
Shea, J. Michael
Siegel, Edward
Siemon, Joyce Marilyn
Silber, Norman Jules
Sill, Lauren Ann
Sisco, Thomas Edward, II
Soble, James Barry
Solomon, Douglas Paul
Spann, Ronald Thomas
Sprouls, Joseph Walter
Starr, Ivar Miles
Steele, Robert Michael
Stevens, Edwin Dan
Stewart, Thomas Wilson
Tannenbaum, Herbert Walter
Tripp, Norman Densmore

Urban, Edmund Theodore
Wallace, Milton Jay
Warren, Jeffrey Wayne
Watson, Keith
Weaver, Ronald L.
Wellbaum, Robert William, Jr.
Whatley, Jacqueline Beltram
White, Russell Alan
Wilder, Fred Jennings
Williamson, Julie Ann Stulce
Wilson, Gary Keith
Wiseheart, Malcolm Boyd, Jr.
Wolf, James Paul
Wutt, Robert Anthony
Zacur, Richard Aaron
Zamora, Antonio Rafael
Zook, David Lloyd
Zschau, Julius James

Georgia

Baker, Anita Diane
Barrett, David Eugene
Bassett, William Randall
Berry, Alonzo Franklin, Jr
Bobbitt, Phillip Lamar
Brading, Stanley Gatewood, Jr.
Brannon, William Earl
Brinson, Benjamin Pierce
Burt, Barry Wakefield
Cadle, Jerry Neal
Chapman, Barry Ryan
Clarke, Thomas Hal
Cork, Robert Lander
Cowart, Richard Merrill
Crean, John Anthony
Dally, Rebecca Polston
Dawkins, William J(ames)
Dillard, George Douglas
Dunn, Wesley Brankley
Edwards, James Garland, II
Gadrix, Edward Wallace, Jr.
Geiger, James Norman
Gilbert, John Jordan
Gold, Ronald Theodore
Gray, Herbert Harold, III
Grove, Russell Sinclair, Jr.
Harris, Earl Douglas
Head, William Carl
Hishon, Elizabeth Anderson
Johnson, Walter Frank, Jr.
King, Thad Denton
Lester, James Luther
Lower, Robert Cassel
Mahan, John Ernest
McLemore, Gilbert Carmichael, Jr.
Neuren, Michael Scott
O'Callaghan, William Lawrence, Jr.
Pinkston, Calder Finney
Pryor, Shepherd Green, III
Robillard, Walter George
Scavo, James J.
Simmons, Raymond Hedelius, Jr.
Sinowski, Thomas Charles
Somers, Fred Leonard, Jr.
Stell, John Elwin, Jr.
Stone, Freddie Ray Josh
Stone, Hugh William
Trotter, William Perry
Volentine, Richard J., Jr.
Wadsworth, Joel Stuart
Wasserman, Michael Gary
Weber, David Victor
Zoukis, Stephen James

Hawaii

Akiba, Lorraine Hiroko
Ashford, Clinton Rutledge
Bays, Albert Bernard
Bodden, Thomas Andrew
Brown, Boyce Reid, Jr.
Callies, David Lee
Cumbs, Charles Wilcox
Dang, Marvin S.C.
Devens, Paul
Dixon, Steven Bedford
Dodd, William Horace
Floyd, Shelby Anne
Fujiyama, Rodney Michio
Gelber, Don Jeffrey
Grinpas, Robert Mark
Iwamoto, Raymond Shigeo
Jackson, Bruce George
Kaneshige, Melvin Yoshio
Leas, Philip Joseph
Lockwood, John Allen
Matsushige, Cary Shigeru
Meyer, William George, III
Peters, Ronald Lloyd
Rack, Thomas Paul
Rolls, John Marland, Jr.
Sattler, James Michael
Shiraishi, Sherman T.
Tam, James Kellett
Taylor, Carroll Stribling
Uyeno, Theodore Yoshi
Van De Car, Diana Lee
Van Pernis, Mark
Wong, Alfred Mun Kong
Wong, Danton Sunmun
Wong, Reuben Sun Fai
Woo, Vernon Ying-Tsai
Yano, Francis Hisao

Idaho

Bickel, Dwight Franklin
Clark, Merlyn Wesley
Ebert, Larry Paul
Eisele, R. Joseph
Hines, William Joseph
Kerrick, David Ellsworth
Lawson, Edward Albert
McCann, William Vern, Jr.
Read, Michael John
Vander Boegh, Douglas Lee

Illinois

Ahlenius, William Matheson
Antonio, Douglas John
Austin, Daniel William
Bashaw, Steven Bradley
Belsheim, Harold Gulbrand, II
Bender, Paul Edward
Beneke, William Scott
Beth, Kenneth Norman
Biestek, John Paul
Blank, Gary L.
Boblick, Shelby Susan
Bockelman, John Richard
Boucek, George Washington
Brody, Lita Helen
Brown, Bruce Allen
Carter, Melanie Sue
Casey, Robert Fitzgerald
Choate, Edward L.
Cleaver, William Lehn
Cohen, Stephen Bruce
Coletta, Ralph John
Collen, John Olaf
Colombik, Richard Michael
Coppinger, John Bampfield
Courtney, Thomas Frances
Cromley, Jon Lowell
Davis, Chester R., Jr.
Demas, Jean V.
Denkewalter, Kim Richard
Diamant, William
Dieker, James William
Domanskis, Alexander Rimas
Duker, Ann
Eisner, Thomas Sultan
Elmore, Elbert Francis
Feinstein, Fred Ira
Feirich, John Cottrill
Felsenthal, Steven Altus
Field, Robert Edward
Fisher, Ned Lawrence
Flack, Charles Haynes
Fowler, William Craig
Franz, William Mansur
Freeman, Richard Lyons
Frisch, Sidney
Frisch, Sidney, Jr.
Funderburk, Raymond
Gerdy, Harry
Gerson, Jerome Howard
Gevers, Marcia Bonita
Gilbert, Howard N(orman)
Golko, Andrew Albin
Goodman, Bruce Dennis
Gralen, Donald John
Greenberger, Ernest
Guthman, Jack
Gutstein, Solomon
Hack, Linda
Hajek, Robert J.
Hartmann, Kenneth
Haynie, Howard Edward
Hayward, Thomas Zander, Jr.
Hegarty, Mary Frances
Helmholz, R. H.
Hennessey, Gilbert Hall, Jr.
Hochman, James Alan
Hoellen, John James
Hofmann, William Eckhardt
Holleb, Marshall Maynard
Hulse, Minard Edwin, Jr.
Hunter, Eugenia C.
Huntoon, Harry Karl
Jacobson, Kenneth Mark
Jadwin, Ted Richard
Jarrett, Valerie Bowman
Johnson, Preston King
Jones, Richard Cyrus
Kanter, Burton Wallace
Katz, Stuart Charles
Keay, David Holm
Kennedy, John Foran
Kenny, Robert Emmett, Jr.
Keryczynskyj, Leo Ihor
Kohn, Richard Fredrick
Kuehn, Angelika Maria
Kurowski, John Joseph
Kuta, Jeffrey Theodore
Landmeier, Allen Lee
Lane, William Edward
Lapelle, William J.
Lapin, Andrew William
Lapins, Scott Michael
Lawless, John Martin
Lederer, William Joseph
Lesar, Hiram Henry
Levy, Richard Herbert
Lippe, Melvin Karl
Liss, Jeffrey Glenn
Malmgren, James H(oward)
Mamer, Stuart Mies
Marovitz, James Lee
Martin, Wayne Mallott
Matanky, Robert William
McCarthy, John Francis
McClow, Thomas Alan
McMahon, Thomas Michael
Millard, Richard Steven
Miller, Geoffrey Charles
Miller, Ronald Stuart
Miller, Russell George
Mittelman, Robert Hirsch
Mohr, Terry Richard
Moltz, Marshall Jerome
Morris, James W.
Morrison, Sidney Eder
Motchan, Brent L.
Murray, John Charles
Nagelberg, Howard Allen
Naylor, George LeRoy
Nissen, William Forbes
Norden, Dennis Arthur
O'Brien, Walter Joseph, II
Ogle, Jerry Michael
Overton, George Washington
Powless, Kenneth Barnett
Ratkovich, Cynthia
Reichelderfer, Frank A.
Reicin, Ronald Ian
Resnick, Donald Ira
Richter, Tobin Marais
Rikli, Donald Carl
Rindal, Ellen Joan, .
Ritchie, Albert
Robb, Elizabeth Ann
Robertson, David Haswell, Jr.
Robinson, Robert George
Roddewig, Richard John
Romano, Henry Schuberth, Jr.
Rooney, Michael James
Rose, Carol Marguerite
Saltiel, David Michael
Sanders, Michael Leo
Sawyier, Michael Tod
Scheller, Arthur Martin, Jr.
Schwartzberg, Hugh Joel
Selfridge, Calvin
Shapiro, Paul Stuart
Sholem, David Bennett
Siegel, Howard Jerome
Sims, E. Jane
Sklar, Stanley Paul
Snyderman, Perry James
Spain, Patrick James
Stanley, Justin Armstrong
Steinberg, Morton M.
Swanson, Warren Lloyd
Tabis, Bruno Walter, Jr.
Uchtmann, Donald Louis
Vanneman, Edgar, Jr.
Vaughn, Ray W.
Vree, Roger Allen
Walner, Robert Joel
Wanca, Brian John
Ward, Philip Henry, Jr.
Warnock, William Reid
Webber, Carl Maddra
Wexler, Warren Marshall
Winter, Frank Louis
York, John C.
Zimmermann, John Joseph

Indiana

Abrams, Jeffrey Alan
Bowen, Willard Gene
Bowman, Carol Ann
Brainard, James C.
Brames, Arnold Henry
Britton, Louis Franklin
Byrne, Maurice Andrew, Jr.
Calhoun, John Henry, Jr.
Coons, Stephen Merle
Coyne, Lynn Harry
Crump, Francis Jefferson, III
Densborn, Donald Keith
Dorocke, Lawrence Francis
Elkin, Paul Stanley
Ferguson, Theodore James
Flannery, James Lloyd
Gehring, Ronald Kent
Hackman, Marvin Lawrence
Hanger, William Joseph
Jewell, John J.
Kennedy, Sheila Suess
Laszynski, Robert Steven
Light, Kenneth J.
Longer, William John
Nussbaum, Richard Anton, II
Oldham, Steve Anthony
Russell, David Williams
Schwarz, James Harold
Thompson, Kerry Lewis
Vandivier, Blair Robert
Van Valer, Joe Ned
Vician, Glenn Steven
Whitehill, Charles Allen
Wickland, David Edwin

Iowa

Bappe, Daniel Eugene
Boresi, Richard L(eo)
Butler, Wallace Webb
Capps, George Hall
Dykstra, Daniel D.
Frey, A. John, Jr.
Galer, Benjamin Anderson
Grove, Lad
Johnson, Robert Steven
Klinger, Phillip Dennis
Laird, Morris E.
Lenihan, Thomas Parker
Lounsberry, Harold Claire
Monson, Terry Lewis
Shostrom, Earl Russell
Stoller, Larry Alan
Swanson, Mark Douglas
Taylor, Richard Lee
Zenk, Ann Marie

Kansas

Aadalen, David Kevin
Adams, Stephen Thornton
Brewer, Dana
Bush, Granville McCutcheon, III
Condray, Scott Robert
Conner, Fred L.
Davis, Michael James
DeLaTorre, Phillip Eugene
Elrod, Linda Diane Henry
Guy, James Matheus
Hageman, John Ashley
Hankins, Gale William
Harbur, Nathan Clayton
Haviland, Camilla Klein
Helbert, Michael Clinton
Ice, Theodore Branine
Johntz, John Hoffman, Jr.
Knappenberger, Don J.
Leffel, Russell Calvin
Lowe, Roy Goins
McGee, John Francis
Speer, Wilson Edward
Springer, Byron Eugene
Stallard, Wayne Minor
Stull, Gordon Bruce
Toland, Stanley E.
Weinberg, Gary Scott
Willard, James Stuart

Kentucky

Aberson, Leslie Donald
Bensinger, Carl Joseph
Brammell, William Hartman
Carter, Robert Philip
Fannin, David Cecil
Foley, Margaret Sweeney
Goldberg, James S.
Hilliard, William Raymond, Jr.
Hutchinson, Mark Randall
Johns, Harold Mac
Kasacavage, Kenneth Stephen
Kerr, Thomas Robert
Meagher, Virginia Murnane
Mulloy, William Patrick, II
Murphy, Richard Vanderburgh
Noe, Randolph
Ockerman, Edwin Foster, Jr.
Rhinerson, David Keith
Todd, James Marion
Vice, Robert Bruce

Louisiana

Arceneaux, M. Thomas
Bronfin, Fred
Burck, Cyril B., Jr.
Burkett, David Ingram
Capritto, Anthony Joseph
Chastain, Merritt Banning, Jr.
Coleman, James Julian
Didriksen, Caleb H., III
Dwyer, Stephen Irwin
Ewin, Gordon Overton
Gallaspy, John Norman
Griffith, Steven Franklin, Sr.
Guillot, Elaine Wolfe
Hall, Luther Egbert, Jr.
Hartel, Stephen Camille
Henican, Caswell Ellis
Hill, William James, III
Hingle, Gilmer Paul
Hoffman, Robert Dean, Jr.
Johnson, Delos Rozelus, Jr.
Kiefer, John B.
LeClere, David Anthony
Lilley, Roy Stuart
Madison, James Robinson
Mansfield, James Norman, III
Mayoral, Paul G.
McDonald, John Franklin, III
McKay, Dan Boies, Jr.
Miller, Patrick Lynn
Mmahat, John Anthony
Poirrier, Michael Joseph
Riddick, Winston Wade, Sr.
Sher, Leopold Zangwill
Spencer, Philip Polmer
Stiel, David Harold, III
Stokes, Douglas Leon
Stone, Saul
Taylor, John McKowen
Thibaut, Charest deLauzon, Jr.
Thibaut, Joseph H. Major
Title, Peter Stephen
Villavaso, Stephen Donald
Waechter, Arthur Joseph, Jr.
Woods, Gerald Marion Irwin
Woodward, William Edward

Maine

Broder, James Nelson
Burns, Jeffrey Robert
Cooper, Michael David
Cowan, Caspar Frank
Coward, Thomas Scott
Fletcher, David James
Fuller, Atherton
Gordan, Vicki Jolene Tripp
Humpert, Samuel Jay
Martin, Joel Clark
Massey, Donald Terhune
Mills, Paul Harland
Neagle, Christopher Scott
Perkins, James Blenn, Jr.
Poe, Franklin Andrew
Slater, Brent R.
Walker, Frank Briggs
Washburn, Robert Michael

Maryland

Bald, LeRoy
Berghel, Victoria Smouse
Berndt, Richard Olaf
Boyer, Elroy George
Brown, R. Edwin
Brugger, George Albert
Carney, Bradford George Yost
Christensen, Gordon Edward
Colton, Sterling Don
Curzan, Myron Paul
Gershberg, Richard Louis
Gingell, Robert Arthur
Goldman, Brian A.
Gorman, Joyce Johanna
Haas, John Howard
Harrison, James Joshua, Jr.
Hesson, William M., Jr.
Jones, Alexander Gray
Kaylor, Omer Thomas, Jr.
Kochanski, David Majlech
Le Brun, Michael David
Loewy, Steven A.
Maffitt, James Strawbridge
Marlow, William Freeman Coale, Jr.
Maseritz, Guy B.
Mathias, Joseph Marshall
McCauley, Richard Gray
Michaelson, Benjamin, Jr.
Miller, Max Dunham, Jr.
O'Brien, Joseph Edward, Jr.
Ogletree, Anne Meve Callahan
Pairo, Preston Abercrombie, Jr.
Pollak, Mark
Porro, Alfred Anthony, Jr.
Price, Howard Jack, Jr.
Rasin, Alexander Parks, III
Rhodes, Thurman Haywood
Samuelson, Kenneth Lee
Scott, Doris Petersen
Scully, Roger Tehan
Shannonhouse, Royal Graham, III
Tanenbaum, Richard Hugh
Tierney, Philip James
Weinberg, Robert Leonard
Wilson, Christian Burhenn
Winston, Roger Dean

Massachusetts

Abbott, William Saunders
Abraham, Nicholas Albert
Angell, James Edward
Arden, John Réal
Aresty, Jeffrey Michael
Atkinson, James Peter
Auchter, John Richard
Bacon, Douglas Arms
Barber, Robert Cushman
Berman, Michael Dexter
Bernard, Michael Mark
Blanker, Alan Harlow
Bolton, Warren Robert
Bridge, Winston Jay
Carroll, John Thomas
Cherwin, Joel Ira
Czerwonka, Joseph John
Dello Iacono, Paul Michael
Dineen, John K.
Dreyer, Harold Emil
Eaton, William Lawrence
Ely, John P.
Fellows, John White
Fidnick, Linda Susan
Fine, Phil David
Galvin, Robert J.
Geogan, Francis Joseph, II
Goldman, Richard Harris
Goodman, Henry A.
Gould, Kenneth B.
Grassia, Thomas C.
Greenman, Karl
Guimond, Robert Wilfrid
Haar, Charles Monroe
Hall, Susan Medbury
Heilman, Carl Edwin
Hewitt, Emily Clark
Hoffman, Robert Joseph
Huber, Richard Gregory
Jordan, Alexander Joseph, Jr.
Kaloosdian, Robert Aram
Kanin, Dennis Roy
Keshian, Richard
Korb, Kenneth A.
Krulewich, Helen D.
Larson, Allen Robert
Latham, Oliver Bradley
Lerman, Herbert S.
Levin, Charles Robert
Ley, Andrew James
Lindsay, Stephen Prout
Loria, Martin Alan
Marnik, Michael Peter
Matthews, James Bernard
Mc Cormack, Edward Joseph, Jr.
McCready, Leo Stephen
McGinnis, Andrew Mosher
McNamara, Frank Luke, Jr.
McNulty, Thomas Joseph, Jr.
Michelman, Frank I.
Milan, Edwin Ramon
Mitchell, John Bruce
Moschos, Michael Christos
Murphy, Kathryn Cochrane
Murray, Elizabeth Ann
Norstrand, Hans Peter
O'Connell, Charles Francis
Parsons-Salem, Diane Lora
Pearlstein, Gerald
Pearson, Paul David
Penman, Gordon Reese
Rabinowitz, Alan James
Ritter, Deborah Bradford
Rosensaft, Lester Jay
Rubenstein-Kursh, Nan
Rudolph, James Leonard
Saradjian, Martin Luther
Sawyer, Robert Kendal, Jr.
Schepps, Victoria Hayward
Snyder, Richard Joseph
Soforenko, Joel Fredrick
Stern, Edward Mayer
Sykes, Peter M'Cready
Taylor, John Anthony
Thomas, David Lloyd, Jr.
Tierney, Albert Gerard, III
Urban, Lee Donald
Van, Peter
Weinstein, Lewis H.
Whalen, James Michael
Whitbeck, James Allis
White, Barry Bennett
Wild, Victor Allyn
Yee, Kenneth M.P.

Michigan

Abraham, Douglas Clark
Barrows, Ronald Thomas
Barton, Judith Marie
Batchelor, James Wiley
Bauer, Jeffry Mark
Bolton, Robert Saul
Borders, Sidney Richard
Bos, John Earl
Brown, (Robert) Wendell
Burgoyne, Bert
Callahan, Michael Sean
Cameron, John Gray, Jr.
Chin, Sherry (Lynn)
Cline, Daniel James
Connelly, Thomas Joseph
Cornelius, Ellen Audrey
Davis, Henry Barnard, Jr.
Dawda, Edward C.
Deems, Nyal David
Dettloff, Richard Ward
Devlin, Eugene Joseph
Durant, James Robert
Epstein, Robert E.
Feldman, Michael Sanford
Fitzgerald, John Warner
George, Barry Brian
Good, Carl Soren
Gordon, Robert Jay
Greenhalgh, Stephen Irving
Haines, John Alden
Hanes, James Henry
Haron, David Lawrence
Harris, Robert James
Kaplow, Robert David
Kendricks, George Thomas
Kopack, Laura Reyes
Krier, James Edward
Lambert, Robert Bradley
Laughter, Ron D.
Leib, Jeffrey M.
Lemcool, Michael James
Lenihan, Robert Joseph, II
Lint, Louis Raymond
London, Leslie Ann
McCallum, Albert Donald
McGlynn, Joseph Michael
Merigan, Gary Douglas
Morganroth, Fred
O'Rourke, Peter Edward
Ortega, Cynthia Poti
Ortman, William Andrew, Sr.
Parker, Patric Allan
Polito, Joseph Michael
Rabidoux, Mark Kenneth
Richardson, Robert Woodrow
St. Antoine, Theodore Joseph
Schanz, Stephen John
Seglund, Bruce Richard
Shakoor, Adam Adib
Smith, Brook McCray
Smith, Terry J.
Smith, Wayne Richard
Steffel, Vern John, Jr.
Steingold, Fred Saul
Tobin, Bruce Howard

Urick, Walter Aleksy
Van Allsburg, Jon Aaron
Vilders, Kurt Ronald
Ward, Paul Anthony
Watson, Daniel Carvin

Minnesota

Anderson, James Hurd
Anderson, Laurence Alexis
Anderson, Thomas Willman
Brown, John Lewis
Brutlag, Michael Lowell
Burke, John Barrett, Jr.
Cafarella, Joan Marie Coursolle
Christensen, Donn Douglas
Cleary, Edward Joseph
Coller, Julius Anthony, II
Dosland, William Buehler
Ekstrum, B. William
Engwall, Gregory Bond
Foarde, Mary Patricia
Fossum, Lee Leif
Hamel, Mark Edwin
Heckt, Paul Norman
Horn, Charles Lilley
Hulstrand, George Eugene
Kantor, David
Keate, Kenneth Earl
Kempf, Douglas Paul
Koch, Scott James
Lantz, William Charles
Larsen, Karen Marie
Larson, Andrew Robert
Leighninger, Sally Heinz
Martin, Kathleen Minder
Mayerle, Thomas Michael
Mortrud, David Lloyd
Mozer, Michael Theodore
Nyquist, Dean Allen
Peterson, Steven A.
Rippe, John Henry
Rossini, Raymond Dominic
Seymour, McNeil Vernam, Jr.
Silverman, Robert J(oseph)
Skare, Robert Martin
Stein, Robert Allen
Straughn, Robert Oscar, III
Tyra, Kenneth Thomas
Vitko, John Peter
Wald, John Roger
Watson, John Slater
Wilcox, Donald Alan
Younger, Judith Tess

Mississippi

Cavanaugh, Michael Flynn
Chaffin, William Michael
Glover, William Hudson, Jr.
Goldman, Thomas Laverne
Harlow, Eugene Marchant
Hughes, Byron William
Odom, Elizabeth Ann
Perry, Lee Nace
Polk, Ross B.
Powell, Roy Durward
Snowden, Elton Gregory
Thomas, James Talbert, IV
Thompson, James Grant, III
Twiford, H. Hunter, III
Ueltschey, Watts Casper
Wright, Michael Eugene

Missouri

Berg, Julius Harry
Biesterfeld, Craig Stewart
Bodker, Stuart Eliot
Burch, David Ryan
Calvin, Edward Eugene
Coffin, Richard Keith
Coughlin, Richard Edward
Cullen, James D.
Dempsey, David Gerard
Douglas, Kerry DeLisle
Dyer, John Gilbert
Elbert, Charles Steiner
Feder, Gary Harold
Fleischaker, Jack
Frantze, David W.
Gould, Terry Allen
Graham, Harold Steven
Graham, Robert Clare, III
Hamra, Sam Farris, Jr.
Harris, Harvey Alan
Hass, William Ralph
Hazelwood, Keith William
Hetlage, Robert Owen
Howes, Brian Thomas
Hoyne, Andrew Thomas
Jenkins, James M(ichael)
Keller, Elizabeth Ann
Klamen, Marvin
Knight, Herman Elvin, Jr.
Lander, David Allan
Levin, Morris Jacob
Levine, Bernard Benton
Long, Michael Evans
Manning, John Patrick, V
Mays, William Gay, II
McCandless, Jeffry Scott
Pletz, John Stephen
Pollihan, Thomas Henry
Rice, Charles Marcus, II
Riner, James William
Rottler, Terry Robert
Seigel, Stephen Paul
Sestric, Anthony James
Sobol, Lawrence Raymond
Soshnik, Robert Mark
Sparks, Stephen Stone
Sterling, Edward Emanuel
Stevens, Bradford Lee
Sutter, William Franklin
Tindel, John Curtis
Tucker, James Delzell
Walker, Walter Ladare
Weber, William Randolph
Weisenfels, John Robert
Whitman, Dale Alan
Wight, Les D., II
Woods, Richard Dale
Zahnd, Lloyd Glen

Montana

Beiswanger, Gary Lee
George, Alexander Andrew
Graveley, Charles Allan
Hartelius, Channing Julius
Karell, Allan L.
Kottas, Leo Joseph, Sr.
Parker, Mark David
Pedersen, Lance Alden
Schaplow, Terry Frederick

Nebraska

Ball, Jordan Mitchell
Ellis, Ronnie Gene
Jelkin, John Lamoine
Kreifels, Frank Anthony
Lang, James Edward
LaPuzza, Paul James
Lash, Douglas Steven
Loftis, Nancy Lynn
McClure, John Campbell
Papik, James Elvin
Pfeiffer, William Edward
Rice, John Edward
Rowland, Richard Arthur
Slattery, David Edmund
Urbom, David Ward
Walkley, Robert Earle
Whitney, Charles Leroy
Widtfeldt, James Albert

Nevada

Goldstein, Mark Harold
Haase, M. Craig
Hammer, Bill C.
Pike, George Russell
Terzich, Milos
Zive, Gregg William

New Hampshire

Baldwin, Carolyn Whitmore
Boyle, Gerard Joseph
Brouillard, Philip André
Brown, Kenneth Mackinnon
Bruno, Kevin Robert
Carbon, Susan Berkson
Evans, Craig Fletcher
Gayman, Benjamin Franklin
Gottesman, David Mark
Griffin, John Francis, Jr.
Haughey, Thomas Malcolm
Jones, Franklin Charles
Keefe, William John
King, Michael Paul
Michels, John Rudolf
O'Neill, Martha Emma
Thornton, Edward Robert, Jr.
Walker, George William
Wilder, Joyce Ann

New Jersey

Alexander, John Donald
Arnold, Kenneth Robert
Babineau, Anne Serzan
Baldino, John Joseph
Banks, Cecil James
Bergamo, Charles
Berkley, Peter Lee
Bertsche, Copeland Gray
Bielory, Abraham M.
Blumberg, Leonard Richard
Boardman, Michael Neil
Bookbinder, Ronald Eric
Bottitta, Joseph Anthony
Brown, Harold Jensen
Brown, James B., Jr.
Bullock, Thomas Francis
Cappuccio, Ronald Joseph
Carroll, Michael Dennis
Clinch, H(enri) Carleton
Cohen, Mitchell Robert
Cole, Murray L.
Connolly, Joseph Thomas
Conway, Richard James, Jr.
Cornish, Jeannette Carter
D'Alessandro, Daniel Anthony
Day, Edward Francis, Jr.
Dienst, Gerald A.
Diktas, Christos James
Dilts, Thomas Harold
Dowd, Dennis Owen
Downs, Thomas Edward, IV
Eichler, Burton Lawrence
Epstein, Milton Aaron
Ernst, Charles Stephen
Facher, Irwin Lee
Falcon, Raymond Jesus, Jr.
Feinberg, Jack
Fenichel, Saul Michael
Finestein, Russell Mark
Fisch, Joseph
Flanders, Howard Barrett, Jr.
Fogel, Richard
French, Bruce Hartung
Gang, Irving Lloyd
Gavin, Louis Brooks
Greco, Joseph Dominic, Jr.
Griffiths, David
Gruccio-Thorman, Lillian Joan
Guest, Brian Milton
Gutterman, Alan J.
Hansbury, Stephan Charles
Heerwagen, Elwood J., Jr.
Hill, Henry Albert
Hoffman, Bernard H.
Holt, Michael Bartholomew
Hubschman, Richard Anthony, Jr.
Irenas, Joseph Eron
Jacobson, Michael
Jaffe, Sheldon E.
Jeffers, Albert Brown
Kaps, Warren Joseph
Karp, Donald Mathew
Kassoff, Mitchell Jay
Kerman, Lewis H.
Klinghoffer, Steven Harold
Kraus, Robert H.
Kuller, Jonathan Mark
Kutner, Mark David
Levin, Susan Bass
Lieb, L. Robert
Linett, David
Lyon, Rexford Lowell
Mahoney, George LeFevre
Manco, Dominick Michael
Markus, Allan Lewis
Markwardt, John James
Martin, Thomas L.
Masanoff, Michael David
Matlin, David Stuart
Meiser, Kenneth Edward
Menendez, Robert
Moore, Kevin John
Morgenstern, Robert Terence
Morris, Joseph Dean
Morrison, John Dittgen
Munoz, Robert F.
Norman, Victor Conrad
O'Carroll, Anita Louise
Olszak, Daniel Dominic
Orbe, Octavius Anthony
Pandolfe, John Thomas, Jr.
Pantel, Glenn Steven
Paterson, Keith Edward
Perzley, Alan Harris
Pojanowski, Joseph A., III
Pozycki, Harry Steven, Jr.
Reiken, Samuel N.
Rinsky, Joel Charles
Rizzo, Paul Robert
Rochkind, Mark Howard
Romano, Janet Bocchino
Roth, Kenneth David
Schechner, David
Seeley, James J.
Serata, Samuel Jacob
Slavitt, Ben J.
Smith, Seymour Alan
Sosland, Karl Z.
Stanger, Douglas Scott
Sterling, Harold G.
Stone, Sheldon
Strasser, William Ignatius
Strull, James Richard
Tobin, Irving
Trenner, Kathryn
Trombadore, Raymond Robert
Van Rensselaer, Robert Mickle Miles
Velazquez, Hector Radames
Vena, Joseph Anthony
Warshaw, Michael Thomas
Wayne, Robert Andrew
White, Ivan Vance, Jr.
Wilson, Martin S., Jr.
Wilson, William Edward
Wolfson, William Steven
Woller, James Alan
Wolloch, Richard David
Wood, Leonard James
Zurav, David Bernard

New Mexico

Atkinson, William Wilder
Branch, Margaret Moses
Burton, John Paul
Conner, William Roby
Dutton, Dominic Edward
Gose, Richard Vernie
Grammer, David Allen, Jr.
Hanna, Robert Cecil
Jontz, Dennis Eugene
Lopez, Owen Michael
Madrid, Patricia Ann
Martin, Connie Ruth
Monroe, Jerald Jacob
Morrison, Robert Dale
Mulhern, John Joseph
Rager, R. Russell
Reagan, Gary Don
Salazar, John Paul
Skinner, Robert Stanley
Smith, Paul Ray
Ussery, Albert Travis

New York

Abelman, Arthur F.
Abinanti, Thomas J., .
Abramson, Joel Eliot
Adler, Edward Andrew Koeppel
Alden, Steven Michael
April, Rand Scott
Arber, Howard Bruce
Arnow, Arthur Emanuel
Arouh, Jeffrey Alan
Ash, David Charles
Baker, Barton
Barbeosch, William Peter
Barney, John Charles
Barton, Anthony Blackshaw
Baum, Joseph A.
Baum, Peter Alan
Belfer, Andrew Benjamin
Bender, Alan Ronald
Bendes, Barry Jay
Bennett, Scott Lawrence
Benton, Donald Stewart
Berger, C. Jaye
Berger, Curtis Jay
Bergman, Bruce Jeffrey
Berner, Thomas Franklyn
Bernstein, Edward Allan
Bernstein, Jacob
Bernstein, Stephen Michael
Beuchert, Edward William
Blachor, Isaac
Black, Howard
Black, James Isaac, III
Blinder, Albert Allan
Bloom, Robert Thomas
Bloomquist, Dennis Howard
Blum, Maurice Henry
Blumberg, Gerald
Bond, Kenneth Walter
Borger, John Emory
Boxer, Harold S.
Bozzo, Paul Peter
Bragar, Raymond Aaron
Braun, Robert Alan
Brenner, Marshall Leib
Brind, David Hutchison
Broadwin, Joseph Louis
Broady, Tolly Rupert
Brovitz, Richard Stuart
Bryant, George McEwan
Caplicki, Dennis P.
Carlucci, Joseph Paul
Carr, Joseph B.
Case, Edward Haile
Catanzano, Raymond Augustine
Certilman, Morton Lawrence
Ciovacco, Robert John
Clair, Ira S.
Coffin, Mary McCarthy
Cohen, Stanley Dale
Cole, Harold Edwin
Cook, Barbara Ann
Cooperman, Robert N.
Costa, John Anthony
Crowley, Dennis Daniel
Daniels, John Hill
Danilek, Donald J.
DaSilva, Willard H.
Davoli, Joseph Felix
Dean, William Tucker
Devers, Peter Dix
Dietze, John Leslie
Donat, Walter Kennedy
Dresner, Byron
Drexler, Mark Andrew
Dubow, Alan Martin
Duckworth, R(oy) Demarest, III
Duetsch, John Edwin
Duncombe, Raynor Bailey
Einhorn, Joseph Harold
Eisenberg, Bertram William
Eldridge, Douglas Alan
Elliott, A. Irene
Emanuel, Ira Michael
English, Harry Gordon
Enochs, Elizabeth M.
Epstein, Hyman David
Erlichster, Joe
Falvey, Patrick Joseph
Feder, Robert
Feitelson, Robert Joel
Feldman, Edward Steven
Fenster, Marvin
Fenster, Robert David
Finkelstein, Allen Lewis
Fisher, Harold Leonard
Fisher, Kenneth Knight
Flood, Kevin Patrick
Flower, Edward
Frank, Bernard Alan
Frankfurt, Morton Allen
Freda, Frank Anthony
Fried, Donald David
Gaetanos, Christ
Galella, Joseph Peter
Galvin, Madeline Sheila
Ganzi, Victor Frederick
Genrich, Willard Adolph
George, Carolyn Burke
Ghandhi, Madonna Stahl
Gioffre, Anthony Bruno
Gioffre, Bruno Joseph
Glauberman, Melvin L.
Glavin, John Joseph
Goebel, William Horn
Golden, Christopher Anthony
Goldfarb, Ronald Carl
Goldman, Jerry Alan
Goldstein, Charles Arthur
Goldstein, Howard Sheldon
Goodman, Mortimer
Green, Jonathan David
Grew, Robert Ralph
Griffith, Emlyn Irving
Grossman, James Stuart
Gruenberger, Peter
Guglielmino, Rosario Joseph
Gursky, Steven Richard
Guttlein, Jorge de Jesus
Hackett, Kevin R.
Hallinan, Robert Edward
Halper, Emanuel Barry
Halperin, Theodore Philip
Halprin, Henry S.
Hancock, James H.
Handlin, Joseph Jason
Harris, Isaac Ron
Harvey, Jonathan Paul
Haskel, Jules J.
Haslinger, John Edward
Hayes, Norman Robert, Jr.
Headrick, Thomas Edward
Hecker, Robert J.
Heine, Andrew Noah
Henry, James R.
Herbst, Todd Leslie
Hershcopf, Gerald Thea
Hershman, Mendes
Hesselbach, Bruce William
Hesterberg, Gregory Xavier
Heussi, Jonathan A.
Hirsch, Melvin L.
Holden, Stephen, III
Holm, Melvin Edward
Holtzschue, Karl Bressem
Horowitz, Steven Gary
Howard, Joel Manning, III
Hull, Thomas J.
Hutter, Robert Grant
Hyman, Montague Allan
Ingram, Samuel William, Jr.
Jadd, Robert Ira
Jarblum, William
Jawin, Paul Gregory
Jeffers, Fred Hards
Jinnett, Robert Jefferson
Jones, Lawrence Tunnicliffe
Kahn, David Miller
Kalb, Robert Joseph
Kamarck, Martin Alexander
Kapur, David Edmund
Katz, Gary M.
Katzenstein, Charles Bernard
Kelly, William Wright
Keltner, Thomas Nethery, Jr.
Kent, James Ewart
Kobrin, Lawrence Alan
Konove, Ronald L.
Korda, Peter J.
Kornstein, Michael Allen
Kossar, Ronald Steven
Koster, Eric David
Kowaloff, Steven David
Krasnow, Robert Louis
Kress, Ralph Herbert
Krieger, Andrew S.
Krinsky, Andrew Neal
Kuklin, Anthony Bennett
Kumble, Steven Jay
Lake, Barbara Ruth
Larson, Frederick Albin
Lascher, Alan Alfred
Laurita, Alan John
Laux, Russell Frederick
Lee, Robert Edward, Jr.
Leffler, Bruce Steven
Lesk, Ann Berger
Leventhal, A. Linda
Levin, Jeffrey Kenneth
Levin, Robert Daniel
Levine, David Ethan
Levine, Melvin Charles
Levine, Samuel Milton
Levinson, Leslie J.
Levitt, Bonnie K.
Levy, Mark Allan
Licker, Jeffrey Alan
Ligorio, Mario Eduard
Lobel, Douglas Arthur
Maccarini, Anthony George
Maher, Daniel Francis, Jr.
Maidman, Richard Harvey Mortimer
Malone, Georgia Joan
Mandel, Newton W.
Marcheso, Joseph James
Marcus, Kenneth Ben
Marcus, Myron
Marcus, Norman
Marks, Theodore Lee
Martin, Peter William
Mayo, John Tyler
McDuffee, Renée Renaud
McPhillips, Joseph William
Meadow, Claire Samuelson
Meli, Salvatore Andrew
Meyer, Bernard Stern
Michaelson, Melvin
Mighdoll, Stephen J.
Miller, Richard Clark, Jr.
Minniti, Joseph A.
Miranda, Neal Joseph
Missan, Richard Sherman
Modell, Michael Steven
Moerdler, Charles Gerard
Moerdler, Jeffrey Alan
Monroe, Kendyl Kurth
Montgomerie, Bruce Mitchell
Morris, Eugene Jerome
Morris, Richard Paul
Morrissey, James Malcolm
Munson, Nancy Kay
Munzer, Stephen Ira
Myers, William Edward
Neveloff, Jay A.
Newman, Jeffrey K.
Ng, Peter Joseph
Nguyen, Paul Dung Quoc
Nussbaum, Paul Allan
Obremski, Charles Peter
Olmstead, Clarence Walter, Jr.
O'Rorke, James Francis, Jr.
Paley, Pierce
Parisi, Frank Nicholas
Parry, William Henry
Patel, Pravinchandra J.
Pedowitz, Arnold Henry
Perkins, George Foster
Piedmont, Richard Stuart
Pike, Laurence Bruce
Pilato, Louis Peter
Pinover, Eugene Alfred
Platt, Harold Kirby
Plotkin, Loren H.
Plump, Leslie Z.
Prounis, Theodore Othon
Rahm, David Alan
Rahm, Susan Berkman
Reed, Lloyd H.
Richards, David Alan
Ridloff, Richard
Rikon, Michael
Rivera, Juan
Rivet, Diana Wittmer
Roberts, E. F.
Robinson, Edward T., III
Robinson, Irwin Jay
Röhm, Eberhard Heinrich
Roman, David John
Root, Stuart Dowling
Rose, John T., II
Rosenberg, Gary Marc
Rubock, Daniel Benjamin
Saft, Stuart Mark
Saiman, Martin S.
Salup, Stephen
Samalin, Edwin
Samuel, Reuben
Sanna, Richard Jeffrey
Sanseverino, Raymond Anthony
Sarter, Alvin Jay
Schaefer, Charles Harold
Schwartz, Richard Morton
Schwartz, Sydney James
Seidler, B(ernard) Alan
Semel, Martin Ira
Shapiro, Ivan
Shaughnessy, James Michael
Shelley, Heywood
Sieratzki, Steven Solomon
Sigall, Michael William
Silverberg, Steven Mark
Simon, Michael Scott
Siskind, Donald H.
Smith, Vincent Milton
Snider, Donald Stephen
Sokolow, Lloyd Bruce
Solomon, Stephen L.
Soloway, Louis
Somer, Stanley Jerome
Sotir, Richard Louis, Jr.
Sparkes, James Edward
Spike, Michele Kahn
Spivack, Edith Irene
Steinbach, Harold I.
Stevenson, Jocke Shelby
Stillman, Bernard M.
Strauss, Gary Joseph
Strougo, Robert
Tabachnik, Douglas T.
Tannenbaum, Bernard
Targoff, Cheri Kamen
Taubenfeld, Harry Samuel
Taylor, Brian Lawrence
Tepper, Eric Alan
Tooker, Robert Luce
Towns, Emanuel Alexander
Treiman, David Michael
Trevett, Thomas Neil
Triebwasser, Jonah Ignatius
Tweedy, William Elwyn
Twining, Rollin Laverne
Twomey, Thomas Aloysius, Jr.
Underberg, Neil
Uram, Gerald Robert
Veneruso, James John
Vernon, Darryl Mitchell
Viener, John David
Vigdor, Justin Leonard
Volkmann, Alfred Armistead

Walder, Robert Alan
Wallace, Herbert Norman
Walton, Robert Prentiss
Webster, Luther Ira
Weinreb, Michael Leonard
Weinstock, Benjamin
Weir, Peter Frank
Weprin, Barry Alan
Weston, Stephen Burns
Whitaker, Benjamin Palmer, Jr.
Wilson, Clifford H.
Winikoff, Robert Lee
Wood, John Busey
Yanas, John Joseph
Young, Sidney David
Zimmerman, Golda
Zinman, Robert Marshall
Zionts, Harriette Abrams
Zipfinger, Frank Peter
Zukerman, Michael
Zwack, Henry Francis
Zysk, Robert Joseph

North Carolina

Adams, Alfred Gray
Bata, Rudolph Andrew, Jr.
Beddow, John Warren
Burti, Christopher Louis
Calhoun, Marilyn Jean
Carter, John Tilton, Jr.
Cramer, Mark Clifton
Cross, James Estes, Jr.
Dillard, John Robert
Durham, Richard Monroe
Etringer, Walter James, Jr.
Galloway, Hunter Henderson, III
Garland, James Boyce
Glover, Durant Murrell
Griffin, Robert Wooten
Haywood, Edmund Burke
Hester, Worth Hutchinson
Hyde, Clarence Edwin
Johnson, Joseph Davis
Johnson, Robert Keith
Jolly, Raymond A., Jr.
Jordan, V. Thomas
Joyner, Gary Kelton
King, Thomas Wesley
Kirby, Mark Clayton
Logan, Leonard Gilmore, Jr.
Loughridge, John Halsted, Jr.
Love, Walter Bennett, Jr.
McIntyre, Douglas Carmichael, II
Morgan, Thomas Jada
Newby, Paul Martin
Orth, John Victor
Parker, Daniel Louis
Plyler, Cranford Oliver, III
Pope, William Robert
Post, Edward Neal
Price, Christie Speir
Reagan, Owen Walker, III
Reeves, Michael C.
Riley, John Frederick
Robbins, Robert Joseph, Jr.
Snyder, Vernon Gilbert, III
Tyson, John Marsh
Wilson, Thomas Johnston

North Dakota

Burgum, Bradley Joseph
Crockett, Richard Boyd
Gregg, John Ralph
Kingstad, Timothy Lorens
Price, Robert Quentin
Widdel, John Earl, Jr.

Ohio

Acomb, James Richard, II
Adams, Harold Francis
Allen, Nadine Lovelace
Anthony, Thomas Dale
Ballard, Mary Beth
Barz, Patricia
Beery, Fred Jerome
Branagan, James Joseph
Brenneman, Fleet B.
Bronson, Barbara June
Brown, Eric Steven
Brown, Seymour R.
Buchenroth, Stephen Richard
Burd, Charles Leslie
Burke, Timothy Michael
Campbell, Anita Peli
Carpenter, James Willard
Carroll, James Joseph
Cobey, John Geoffrey
Colby, Richard DeAtlee
Cook, Robert Nevin
Cooper, Douglas Kenneth
Coscarelli, Dianne Smith
Covatta, Anthony Gallo, Jr.
Crane, Edward Holman
Csank, Paul Lewis
Cunningham, James Joseph
Dailey, Coleen Hall
Davis, Philip Carl
Dixon, Carl Franklin
Donnem, Roland William
Edmiston, Robert Gray
Fellmeth, Scott Eugene
Fine, Michael William
Ford, Seabury Hurd
Freedman, Howard Joel
Galip, Ronald George
Gherlein, John Harlan
Gleisser, Marcus David
Goettemoeller, Duane A.
Greene, Bernard Wilburn
Griffith, Stephen Murray, Jr.
Grove, Jack Frederick
Hausser, Robert Louis
Heintz, Jeffrey Theodore
Herrold, Russell Phillips, Jr.
Hinton, Virgil Otterbein
Hoopingarner, John Martin
Inzetta, Mark Stephen
Izor, David E.
Jackson, Robert Howard
John, Sidney Charles
Joseph, John James
Kernen, Will
Keyser, George Harold
Kinney, Aldon Monroe, Jr.
Koenig, Peter Edward
Krone, Paul William
Lancione, Bernard Gabe
Lang, Francis Harover
Lanza, Shelley Brown
Levin, Arnold Sampson
Levine, Judith Dee
Loewenthal, Marc Sheldon
MacKay, John Norman
Manley, Robert Edward
Mann, Richard Lynn
Mantonya, John Butcher
Mathews, S. Paul
McAndrews, James Patrick
Menninger, Henry Edward, Jr.
Meyer, Charles Mulvihill
Muttalib, Kalam
Nichelson, James Lee
Palmer, Mark Joseph
Pearlman, Samuel Segel
Richner, Robert Andrew
Robe, Edward Scott
Robison, Joseph Albert
Rolston, George Drew
Rorick, Alan Green
Ruport, Scott Hendricks
Schneider, Karl Herbert
Selak, Robert Allen
Sheward, Richard S.
Skotynsky, Walter John
Smith, Ruth Hunter
Sogg, Wilton Sherman
Spies, Howard A.
Stocker, Thomas Edwin
Streicher, James Franklin
Sullivan, Mark Edward
Sully, Ira Bennett
Taft, Frederick Irving
Taylor, Edward McKinley, Jr.
Thompson, Harold Lee
Waiwood, Michael Francis
Walker, Charles Henri
Westbrook, Gayle Robinson
White, Arnold S.
Wiersma, David Charles
Wirt, William Stephen
Wisniewski, Marshall Donald
Yost, William Kent
Ziegler, Edward Howard, Jr.
Zox, Benjamin Louis

Oklahoma

Bogan, Neil Earnest
Bryant, Ira Houston, III
Burch, Melvin Earl
Casey, Patrick Jon
Conner, Leslie Lynn, Jr.
Davis, Frank Wayne
Davis, Jesse Dunbar
Dowd, Pamela J. Cuplin
Durham, Ronald Dale
Elsener, G. Dale
Enis, Thomas Joseph
Fischer, John Frederick
Frieze, H(arold) Delbert
Golden, Thomas Fuller
Huffman, Robert Allen, Jr.
Kallstrom, James David
Legg, William Jefferson
Mantooth, John Albert
Musser, William Wesley, Jr.
Oden, Waldo Talmage, Jr.
Pringle, Lynn Allan
Robinson, Adelbert Carl
Rorschach, Jack L.
Schuller, Stephen Arthur
Scribner, Beverly Kinnear
Settle, John Marshall
Specht, Randolph Stephen
Steltzlen, Janelle Hicks
Sullivan, Lovell Wayne
Todd, Robert Allen
Willey, Benjamin Tucker, Jr.

Oregon

Alberty, Steven Charles
Arthur, Michael Elbert
Barrett, Cynthia Louise
Bauer, Henry Leland
Bock, Jeffrey William
Bolliger, Ralph Wendell
Brand, Malcolm Leigh
Byczynski, Edward Frank
Cegavske, Wallace Duane
Chevis, Cheryl Ann
Cramer, William Donald
Eichelberger, Stephen
Feuerstein, Howard M.
Forcum, Richard Eugene
Grant, Eugene L.
Greenwood, Myrtle Rae
Jennings, George Mahlon
Korth, James William
Launer, Jeannette Maureen
MacRitchie, Brian John
Nunn, Robert Warne
Philpott, Steven Lee
Potter, William R.
Rich, Steven Eugene
Rose, Steven Marc
Schuster, Philip Frederick, II
Steele, Kathie Fay
Stiles, William Neil
Tankersley, Thomas Channing
Thorndike, Daniel Carl
Wyse, Scott Campbell
Wyse, William Walker

Pennsylvania

Alderman, Mark Louis
Appel, T. Roberts, II
Aranson, Michael J.
Aronson, Mark Berne
Bell, Paul Anthony, II
Berson, Norman Scott
Besser, Amy Helene
Black, Alexander
Blume, Karolyn Vreeland
Bowen, Gerald L.
Brawner, Gerald Theodore
Brodbeck, Charles Richard
Brody, Nancy Louise
Brown, Robert Wayne
Byler, M. Elvin
Ceraul, David James
Cherken, Harry Sarkis, Jr.
Chomas, James Louis, Jr.
Connell, Janice Timchak
Cook, Cameron H.
Cross, Milton H.
Davies, Norleen O'Sullivan
Dean, Morris Jonathan
Doerr, John Maxwell
Dubin, Stephen Victor
Dunaway, Wayland Fuller, III
Ehrenwerth, David Harry
Esposito, Robert S.
Ferguson, Sanford Barnett
Fernsler, John Paul
Fetzner, Michael Alan
Finkelstein, Joseph Simon
Galanter, Robert Allen
Garfinkel, Marvin
Gathright, Howard T.
Glantz, Douglas Gene
Goss, Michael Mayer
Gounley, Dennis Joseph
Gowa, Andrew J.
Haber, Richard Jerome
Hackman, Karen Lee
Hankin, Mitchell Robert
Heller, Richard Martin
Hershman, Morris Paul
Hess, Emerson Garfield
Hoffmeyer, William Frederick
Holland, Fred Anthony
Hollinshead, Earl Darnell, Jr.
Houpt, Robert Campbell
Howard, Barry
Hunter, Martha Louise
Jack, James Ernest
Jacobson, Miriam Nechamah
Jaffe, Gary
Jaffe, Paul Lawrence
Kashkashian, Arsen, Jr.
Keenan, C. Robert, III
Keene, John Clark
Kelsen, Peter Foster
Kemp, K(enneth) Lawrence
Kiever, Paul Kenneth
Klee, John P.
Kline, Sidney DeLong, Jr.
Korn, Robert A.
Krug, Rob Alan
Kupperman, Louis Brandeis
Kury, Franklin Leo
Lepore, Alphonse Paul
Letwin, Jeffrey William
Linshaw, Jack G.
Lipsitz, Robert Joel
Loomis, Michael Eugene
Lord, G(eoffrey) Craig
Lushis, John Francis, Jr.
Makowski, Thomas Anthony
Markham, Rosemary
Mauger, Lee Fillmen
Mazer, Lawrence
McBride, Milford Lawrence, Jr.
Mendelson, Leonard (Melvin)
Mesirov, Leon I.
Messina, Joseph F., Jr.
Michie, Daniel Boorse, Jr.
Minney, Michael Jay
Mott, John C.
Nicholson, Bruce Allen
Noel, Simon
Panzer, Mitchell Emanuel
Pholeric, Karen Joy
Pompo, Vincent Matthew
Posner, David S.
Posy, David Howard
Pringle, Samuel Wilson, Jr.
Proctor, Charles William, III
Rayman, Robert Craig
Reed, W. Franklin
Richards, Robert Byam
Rogers, Thomas Charles
Rosenberg, John Edward
Rossi, Mary Ann
Rouge, Cheryl Anne
Ruder, Jay Stanley
Scheck, Donald Gordon
Seacrist, Geoffrey Lynn
Shagin, Craig Randall
Siegel, Arthur Bernard
Sobota, John Raymond
Speers, Thomas James
Steadman, James Robert
Stepanian, Steven Arvid, II
Susmarski, Ronald James
Temple, L. Peter
Wagner, Joseph Hagel
Weil, Andrew L.
Weiner, Richard Norman
Weiss, Philip David
Whitling, Terrance LeRoy
Wiley, Jan M.
Wilkinson, James Allan
Wolff, Deborah H(orowitz)
Wrigley, Albert Blakemore
Zeglen, John Michael

Rhode Island

Abedon, Herbert Joseph
Abilheira, Richard B.
Berkelhammer, Robert Bruce
Brady, Robert Michael
Driscoll, Robert George
Dub, Larry
Freedman, Carl Ira
Harrop, R(obert) Daniel
Ialongo, Michael Angelo
Loffredo, Pasco Frank
Lombardi, Valentino Dennis
Miller, Donald Eugene
Rego, Alfred R., Jr.
Roszkowski, Joseph John
Tobin, Bentley
Tracy, David J.
Wiley, H. Seymour

South Carolina

Abernathy, Harry Hoyle, Jr.
Albergotti, Samuel Fretwell
Allison, James McWilliams
Bacot, John Paisley, Jr.
Barnes, Rudolph Counts
Beasley, Frederick Alexander
Beckett, Alice Talbird
Bethea, William Lamar, Jr.
Brunson, Nolen Landford
Buchanan, Robert Lee, Jr.
Devereux, Anthony Quentin
Dunbar, James V., Jr.
Edwards, Harry LaFoy
Goode, Kenneth George
Haskins, Terry Edward
Hite, Thomas Erskine, Jr.
Lawrimore, Eugene Salmon Napier
Laws, James Terry
Martin, John Randolph
Morehouse, Arthur Rogers Grant
Newby, Fred Bryant
O'Donnell, Robert Harry
Scarminach, Charles Anthony
Scheider, James Pringle, Jr.
Scott, Earl Daniel
Scott, Ronald Charles
Shemwell, Arthur Luther, Jr.
Simpson, David Eugene
Thomy, George Albert
Wheless, Albert Eugene
Williams, Karen Johnson

South Dakota

Allred, Forrest Carlson
Bettmann, Frank Adam, Jr.
Burns, Mary Elizabeth
Carlsen, Chris Jeffrey
Fosheim, Jon
Gustafson, Lawrence Raymond
Kemnitz, Ralph A.
Prendergast, Terry Neill

Tennessee

Barnes, Herschiel Sevier
Bostick, Charles Dent
Bruce, William Roland
Buchanan, Alexander Blackman
Camp, Randy Coleman
Campbell-Bell, Dorothy Kathryn
Cary, Charles Muse
De Young, Vincent Gerald
Doggrell, Henry Patton
Ely, James Wallace, Jr.
Ezell, Kenneth Pettey, Jr.
Fowler, John Ballard
Frazier, Steven Carl
Frey, Kelly Leibert
Gordon, Thomas Napier
Jordan, James D(ee)
Lockett, George Houston
Meyer, Stephen Leonard
Montgomery, Robert H., Jr.
Norville, Craig Hubert
Okrasinski, Mary Ann
Sisson, Jerry Allan
Skefos, Harry J(erry)
Tate, James Solomon, Jr.
Thomas, Robert Paige
Trent, J(ohn) Thomas, Jr.
Turner, Wesley Dale
Warren, Richard Fenton, Jr.

Texas

Adams, Harold Gene
Ainbinder, Michael Cooper
Albers, Rick M.
Allen, Michael Douglas
Anderson, Doris Ehlinger
Arnett, Richard Lynn
Barnett, George David
Barton, James Cary
Beacroft, Percival Thomas
Beasley, Norma Lea
Bennett, Kevin Dane
Benson, Larry John
Berger, Howard Charles
Berry, John Fredrick
Betow, Joel Thomas
Beuttenmuller, Rudolf William
Blazier, John Charles
Borchers, Marion Jack
Bousquet, Thomas Gourrier
Boyd, William Clark
Burney, Cecil Edward
Burney, Frank Burleson
Burrows, Jon Hanes
Caldwell, James Wiley
Casseb, Robert Michael
Castle, John Raymond, Jr.
Caudill, David Stanley
Chaney, William Calvin
Chappell, Clovis Gillham, Jr.
Clark, David Keith
Clark, Pat English
Cline, Lee Williamson
Conine, Gary Bainard
Cox, Sanford Curtis, Jr.
Craft, George Sullivan
Crook, Charles David
Crook, E(dward) Carter, Jr.
Crump, Thomas Richard
Cuba, Benjamin James
Cunningham, William Allen
Curione, Charles
Davidson, Charles E.
Davis, John Whittaker
Davis, Michael A.
DeBusk, Edith M.
Doty, James Robert
Dowd, Steven Milton
Duncan, Ernest Louis, Jr.
Duncan, John Milton
Durell, Jay Glenn
Eckman, David Walter
Elliott, Brady Gifford
Engelhardt, John Hugo
Engle, William Thomas, Jr.
Estle, Mark David
Falls, Craig Thomas
Faye, Stanley Ethan
Fenwick, Lynda Beck
Figueroa, Luis Antonio
Fisher, J(ohn) Robert
Fishman, Edward Marc
Fluke, Randall Lynn
Fouts, Louis Milner, III
Ginsburg, Marcus
Goldberg, Charles Ned
Golden, Alvin Joseph
Goldsmith, Mary Ann
Goodstein, Barnett Maurice
Gorman, Joseph Thomas, Jr.
Grant, Patrick Gerard
Green, Ray Eugene
Gregg, Tom Will, Jr.
Halpin, Steven Edward
Hamilton, Elwin Lomax
Hardin, George Timothy
Hargis, James Richard
Hayers, Paul Hugh
Hays, Larry Weldon
Head, Hayden Wilson
Hendricks, Randal Arlan
Hennessey, John William
Higgins, Robert Gerard
Hodges, Jot Holiver, Jr.
Holbrook, James Mitchell
Holmes, Ronald Loyd
Hudspeth, Chalmers Mac
Hunter, Emmett Marshall
Jackson, Freddie Newell
Jacobs, Gregory R.
Jacobus, Charles Joseph
Jeffers, William A., Jr.
Jones, John Gornal
Kaufman, Andrew Michael
Kivelson, Nancy Lynn
Kolodey, Fred James
Koppenheffer, Julie B.
Kraus, Nancy Jane
Kvinta, Charles J.
Labay, Eugene Benedict
Laney, Daniel Milton
Langston, Homer Anthony, Jr.
Ledlie, Douglas Edward
Liles, John H(enry), Jr.
Line, Judson Edward
Lippman, Kyle David
Longacre, Kenneth Wyatt
Mainz, Edward Charles, Jr.
Marlow, Orval Lee, II
Martin, Richard Kelley
McCoy, Reagan Scott
McKay, Robert Connally
McKnight, Rufus Nicolaus, Jr.
McNamara, John Bolivar, Jr.
McPhail, Robert Wilson
McRae, Hamilton Eugene, Jr.
Melamed, Richard
Miller, Stewart Ransom
Millet, John Porath
Moncure, John Lewis
Moroney, Linda Lelia Susan
Morrison, Walton Stephen
Mueller, Mark Christopher
Muzzy, Gray Howard
Nahlen, Dana Gayle
Newsom, Neil Edward
Nolan, Jenelle White
Nolan, John Michael
Nolte, Melvin, Jr.
Oates, Carl Everette
Odiorne, James Thomas
Oppenheimer, Jesse Halff
Ording, Michael K.
Otto, Byron Leonard
Park, J(ames) Walter, IV
Perry, William Shelbern
Peters, Loren Walter
Pettigrew, Karen Beth
Phillips, Kathleen A.
Phillips, Travis R.
Pierson, Grey
Pope, Joseph Ronald
Porter, Jeffrey James
Portman, Glenn Arthur
Randolph, Robert Raymond
Ratliff, William D., III
Ray, Donald Arvin
Reynolds, Dixon Jace
Riddle, Michael Lee
Riley, Peter James
Roberts, Harry Morris, Jr.
Rodgers, John Hunter
Rothermel, John Fisher, III
Rowan, Justin Michael
Rowan, Michael John
Sagehorn, Thomas John
Sandler, Lewis Herbsman
Schmidt, John Aldin
Seay, George Edward, Jr.
Shaddock, William Charles
Sharp, Christopher Glenn
Shipp, H(amilton) Thomas
Shouse, August Edward
Silver, Louis Edgar
Sims, Ricky Reece
Smart, James Hudson
Smith, Frank Forsythe, Jr.
Steele, Glenn Horace, Jr.
Stevens, Michael Dean
Stoffer, James Myron, Jr.
Tallis, Alan Louis
Taylor, Joseph William
Taylor, Robert Love
Taylor, Thomas Alan
Thau, William Albert, Jr.
Thomas, Sheryl Lynn
Topper, Robert Carlton
Townes, Edgar Eggleston, Jr.
Turner, Bruce Edward
Warford, Tommy Gene
Weiner, Marcia Myra
Weisbrod, Marcy Helfand
Wester, Ruric Herschel, Jr.
Wheat, Thomas Allen
White, Sharon Elizabeth
Wilson, Reid Carroll
Winchell, Michael George
Winick, Mitchel Lane
Wommack, Jr. George Tobin
Wright, Eugene Box
Yost, William Arthur, III
Young, Jess Wollett

Utah

Belnap, Michael Gary
Bigler, Glade S.
Burgon, Barre Glade
Cornaby, Kay Sterling
Frei, Michael Clark
Gallian, Russell Joseph
Headman, Arlan Osmond, Jr.
Hunt, George Andrew
Jones, Michael Frank
Kennicott, James W.
Lewis, Kay Michie
McIntosh, James Albert
Monson, Thomas Lee
Mooney, Jerome Henri
Moore, Larry G.
Pruitt, Robert Grady, Jr.
West, David Clay
Wilkinson, Homer Fawcett

Vermont

Babb, Guy Lee
Facey, John Abbott, III
Fitzhugh, John Hardy
Holme, John Charles, Jr.
Kissell, Tony Fred
Lang, Richard Arnold, Jr.
McCamley, John Edward
Miller, William Bayard, Jr.
Nichols, Elaine Kilburn
Smith, Norman Charles
Wright, Richard Jay

Virginia

Ambler, Thomas Wilson
Ames, Edward Almer, III
Arzt, Lee Robert
Baird, Thomas Bryan, Jr.
Bankert, Joseph Edward
Barron, Myra Hymovich
Beck, Joseph James
Bedinger, Frank Cleveland, Jr.
Benser, Frank Leroy
Blankingship, A. Hugo, Jr.
Bozarth, Robert Stephen
Brincefield, James Clifford, Jr.
Crewe, Trenton Guy, Jr.
Crump, Beverley L.
Eason, Carl Edward, Jr.
Edmunds, Felix Elmer
Faggert, David Young
Freed, Robert Leslie
Freyvogel, William Thomas
Frith, Douglas Kyle
Gary, Stuart Hunter
Glenn, Robert Eastwood
Gregory, John Lunsford, III
Hammer, Donald Gordon
Hancock, William Glenn
Jianos, Jean Terese
Jones, Robert James
Kamp, Arthur Joseph, Jr.
Kennett, John Holliday, Jr.
Kovacic, William Evan
Kyle, Penelope W.
Land, Charles Edwards
Layton, Garland Mason
Lewis, Gordon
Loe, Brian Robert
Lowenstein, Marshall Leigh
Mackall, Henry Clinton
Martin, Ronald Allen
Marzloff, George Ernest
McClure, Roger John
McGuire, Edward David, Jr.
Middleton, J. Howard, Jr.
Milchak, Michael Edward
Miller, William Frederick
Moorstein, Mark Alan
Moshos, Arthur Leon
Parker, Richard Wilson
Payne, Frederick Warren
Pratt, Stephen Michael
Purcell, William Riker
Redmond, David Dudley
Rucker, William Browning
Saul, Ira Stephen
Savage, Thomas Yates
Settlage, Steven Paul
Simon, Alexander Nathan
Stegeman, Thomas Albert
Tankersley, Glenn Rayburn
Thomas, William Griffith
Waldo, Joseph Thomas
Walk, Thomas Preston
Weimer, Peter Dwight
Whitaker, Steven King
Whitlock, Willie Walker
Wilcox, Bruce Andrew
Wilson, Paul Lowell
Wolcott, Edward Wallace
Woodhouse, Edward James, Jr.
Young, Hubert Howell, Jr.

Washington

Althauser, Thomas Charles
Arnold, Nancy Tarbuck
Backstein, Robert Joseph
Barnett, Hollis H.
Bonesteel, Richard David
Broihier, Jeffrey T.
Brooks, Julie Anne
Collette, Kevin J.
Cornell, Kenneth Lee
Crane, Stephen Joel
Cross, Harry Maybury
Fritzler, Randal Brandt
Gay, Carl Lloyd
Gross, Richard Arthur
Haggard, Joel Edward
Henderson, Kevin James
Hill, (George) Richard
Jones, Bradley Tyler
Kuhrau, Edward W.
Leen, David Arthur
Leggett, James Francois
Lundin, John W.
Mashita, Lloyd Isao
Mozena, Peter Joseph
Munson, Mark Parr
Oseran, Melville
Packer, Mark Barry
Palmer, Harvard
Panchot, Dudley Bradford
Petrie, John Thomas
Phillabaum, Stephen Day
Raff, Douglass Alan
Robinson, Jeffrey Alan
Rockwell, David Hosmer
Roubicek, Christopher John
Ryan, James Francis
Schweda, Peter Steven
Scott, Douglas Walter
Serka, Philip Angelo
Sessions, G. P.
Simburg, Melvyn Jay
Spring, Max Edward
Weinman, Richard Stephen
Whittington, Thomas Lee
Youngs, Linda Miller

West Virginia

Arrington, Roy David
Bunner, William Keck
Colan, Owen Richard
Crim, Joseph Calvin
Davis, Stephen Allen
Ford, Richard Edmond
Kagler, Robert Wayne
Kwass, Sidney J.
Null, Gregory B.
Saville, Royce Blair
Thompson, Stephen Lee
Wehner, Charles Vincent

Wisconsin

Abbott, William Anthony
Aiken, Jeffrey Paul
Biehl, Michael M.
Collins, Michael John
Connolly, Gerald Edward
Conrad, Paul Edward
Daniel, Marvin Valerius
Deffner, Roger L.
Eberhardt, Daniel Hugo
Eustice, Francis Joseph
Friend, Henry Charles
Gaines, Irving David
Gavin, Connie Kay
Gehringer, John G.
Giese, Heiner
Greenberg, Martin Jay
Grundahl, John Alvin
Haarmann, Bruce Donald
Hertel, Theodore Bernhard, Jr.
Jennings, David Vincent, Jr.
Johnson, Craig Robert
Josten, Roy Joseph
Jursik, Patricia Dolores
Kenyon, Allen Francis
Kite, Richard Lloyd
Krueger, William Frederick
Leary, Nancy May
Levine, Herbert
Lund, John Richard
Perkins, Randolph M.
Rainey, Charles James
Rankin, Gene Raymond
Raushenbush, Walter Brandeis
Sauer, William Jacob
Simon, Dennis Lee
Splitt, Cody
Stutt, John Barry
Suran, Robert Herman
Sweet, Lowell Elwin
Szymanski, Barry Walter
Taus, Armin Kenneth
Tease, Ralph Joseph, Jr.

Wyoming

Durham, Harry Blaine, III
Harrison, Frederick Joseph
Kidd, David Thomas
Klus, Charles Robert, Jr.
Smith, Thomas Shore
Webster, C. Edward, II

TERRITORIES OF THE UNITED STATES

Puerto Rico

Gonzalez-Diaz, Raul E.
Ruiz-Suria, Fernando

ENGLAND

Baker, Paul Vivian
Wohl, James Paul

TRINIDAD AND TOBAGO

Gordon, Kenneth

ADDRESS UNPUBLISHED

Alexander, John Nickolas, Jr.
Ansley, Shepard Bryan
Assael, Michael
Bateman, David Alfred
Beck, Robert Edward
Boorstein, Beverly Weinger
Breen, James Patrick, Jr.
Brown, Gary Ross
Buffington, John Victor
Cazalas, Mary Rebecca Williams
Crawford, R(obert) George
De La Garza, Roberto Eduardo
Diamond, Josef
Dimon, John E.
Edwards, Daniel Paul
Eisen, Edwin Roy
Familo, Edward Douglas
Francis, Jerome Leslie
Glantz, Ronald Paul
Goldstein, Paul
Griffin, Thomas Patrick
Gulick, Peter VanDyke
Hamel, Richard Paul
Hanes, Leigh B., Jr.
Hebl, Thomas Lee, Sr.
Hecht, Barbara Elizabeth Roberts
Hefner, Archie
Helms, David Alonzo
Hernandez, David N(icholas)
Higginbotham, John Taylor
Holloway, Jan Charlene
Kaplan, Susan Robin
Kaufmann, Roy Leslie
Kennedy, Nolan Malcom
Klein, Judah B.
Lapidus, Steven Richard
Lappen, Timothy
Leaf, Frederick Peter
Learned, James Roy
Levinson, Kenneth Lee
Levitt (Topol), Robin April
McCarthy, Vincent Paul
McKenna, Edward James, Jr.
Middleton, Harlow Clester
Mittelstadt, Russell James
Murphy, Thomas Hugh
Newman, Alan Harvey
Olsen, Kenneth Allen
Pistillo, Bernadino Joseph, Jr.
Poliakoff, Gary A.
Porricelli, Gerald Joseph
Regenstreif, Herbert
Rivera, Oscar R.
Roberts, Larry F.
Rohrbach, William John, Jr.
Sanger, Scott Howard
Solkoff, Jerome Ira
Stehlik, Frederick D.
Stough, Charles Daniel
Vaughan, Herbert Wiley
Weclew, Robert George
Whitehorn, Jo-Ann H.
Winslow, Julian Dallas
Wise, Philip J.
Wittebort, Robert John, Jr.
Woodruff, Charles Norman

REAL ESTATE DEVELOPMENT. *See* **Property, real.**

SALES OF GOODS. *See* **Commercial, contracts.**

SECURITIES

UNITED STATES

Alabama

Caldwell, Carol Gray
Carter, Gordon Thomas
Childs, Larry Brittain
Garner, Robert Edward Lee
Johnson, Joseph H., Jr.
Patrick, J. Vernon, Jr.
Ritchey, Joseph Thomas
Taylor, George Malcolm, III
Warren, Manning Gilbert, III

Alaska

Bankston, William Marcus
Bradbury, John Howard

Arizona

Berry, Charles Richard
Bivens, Donald Wayne
Bluemle, Robert Louis
Brown, Steven Jay
Brueckner, Kurt Malcolm
Chanen, Steven Robert
Cocanower, David Lehman
Curtis, David William, Jr.
Dunipace, Ian Douglas
Gabaldon, Theresa A.
Hackett, Robert John
Herman, Steven Roger
Hicks, William Albert, III
Lagerman, Susan Borden
Patton, Jock
Phillips, Steven William
Placenti, Frank Michael
Price, Charles Steven
Rainey, William Joel
Thompson, Terence William
Titus, Jon Alan
Tubman, William Charles
Williams, Quinn Patrick

Arkansas

Mayersohn, Arnold Linn, Jr.

California

Aguirre, Michael Jules
Allan, Lionel Manning
Anzur, John Andrew
Apfel, Gary
Armour, George Porter
Bagley, Constance Elizabeth
Barnes, John Breasted
Baudler, David Evan
Beard, Ronald Stratton
Benninghoff, Charles Franklyn, III
Bernstein, Scot D(avid)
Black, Donald Bruce
Brown, Albert Jacob
Cahill, Michael Edward
Cheatham, Robert William
Chong, Debra Ann
Climan, Richard Elliot
Crandall, Nelson David, III
Curry, Daniel Arthur
Davey, Gerard Paul
Dettmer, Scott Charles
Edwards, Robin Morse
Fairbank, Robert Harold
Fields, Henry Michael
Finck, Kevin William
Fink, Scott Alan
Frank, Vincent Antonio
Fredericks, Dale E.
Garcia, Terry Donato
Gill, Margaret Gaskins
Glass, Beverly Elaine
Gunderson, Robert Vernon, Jr.
Harley, Halvor Larson
Harroch, Richard David
Howell, Weldon Ulric, Jr.
Huegel, Peter Andrew Vincent
Jacobs, Leedia Gordeev
Jelin, Beth Maloney
Johnson, Terry Turner
Kelly, Daniel Grady, Jr.
Kirchheimer, Arthur E(dward)
Klafter, Cary Ira
Lagle, John Franklin
Lerner, William C.
Loo, John
Marshall, Douglas Anton
May, Lawrence Edward
McBride, Keith Wesley
McGinley, Nancy Elizabeth
McLane, Frederick Berg
Metz, Robert Ernest
Million, Stephen A.
Mogin, Daniel Jay
Morando, Marta Lucile Hope
Moretti, August Joseph
Murphy, Arthur John, Jr.
Nicholas, Carol Lynn
Olson, Walter Gilbert
Ostrach, Michael Sherwood
Pierno, Anthony Robert
Pollard, Henry
Power, John Bruce
Prewoznik, Jerome Frank
Ream, Christopher
Robertson, David Govan
Ryan, Joseph
Schisler, George Milford, Jr.
Scott, Kenneth Eugene
Scott, Valerie Weeks
Shaeffer, Henry Warren
Sheehan, Lawrence James
Sherman, Lawrence M.
Sherman, William Delano
Sherwood, Linda Kathleen
Shortz, Richard Alan
Snow, Tower Charles, Jr.
Sparks, Thomas E., Jr.
Spatz, Alan Brent
Star, Ronald H.
Sterrett, James Kelley, II
Sullivan, Patrick James
Suter, Bernard Reynold
Van Camp, Brian Ralph
van Schoonenberg, Robert G.
Ward, Diane A.
Welch, John Edward
White, Bryan Stanford
Woodhouse, Thomas Edwin
Ziering, William Mark

Colorado

Bermant, George Wilson
Blair, Andrew Lane, Jr.
Cook, Terry Lee
Dean, James B.
Eckstein, John Alan
Feigin, Philip Alan
Fiflis, Ted J.
Gallegos, Larry Duayne
Gates, Stephen Frye
Gessling, James Place
Grissom, Garth Clyde
Husney, Elliott Ronald
Johnson, David Stafford
Keatinge, Robert Reed
Keithley, Roger Lee
Lavenhar, Jeffrey Drew
Lidstone, Herrick Kenley, Jr.
Linfield, James Clark Taylor
Martin, J. Landis
Mauro, Richard Frank
Miers, James William
Netzorg, Gordon Wemple
Rossi, Ronald Gregory
Salcito, Donald
Schoonover, Randall Charles
Schumacher, Barry Lee
Shuman, Mark Patrick
Talesnick, Alan Lee
Thevenet, Susan Marie
Wiegand, Robert, II

Connecticut

Bamford, David Ellery
Bernstein, Robert Gary
Blazzard, Norse Novar
Burrasca, Raymond Peter
Drost, Marianne
Duke, Robert Dominick
Gildea, Edward Joseph
Hasenauer, Judith Anne
Hurwich, Robert Allan
Jensen, Frode, III
McGovern, Kevin Michael
McGuire, Eugene Guenard
Nelson, Douglas Thomas
Perlah, Philip Michael
Wilkes, Beverly Lake
Wolfe, Harriet Munrett
Wolson, Craig Alan

Delaware

Carrad, David Clayton
Edelson, Harold Jesse

District of Columbia

Atwood, Charles Starr
Ballen, Robert Gerald
Becker, Brandon
Bell, Olin Nile
Bellamy, Frederick Robert
Benjamin, Edward A.
Bergmann, Larry Edward
Boehm, Steven Bruce
Carroll, Thomas Phillip
Chafetz, Marc Edward
Coplan, Larry Myles
Day, Gregg Alan
Eccard, Walter Thomas
Eisenberg, Meyer
Evans, John Kedrich
Feller, Lloyd Harris
Finch, John Marshall
Finkelstein, Anita Jo
Fleischer, James Sidney
Fleischman, Edward Hirsh
Focht, Theodore Harold
Freeman, Milton Victor
Gilberg, David Jay
Goelzer, Daniel Lee
Graham, Peter Jeffrey Stuart
Grundfest, Joseph Alexander
Guttman, Egon
Halpern, James Bladen
Howell, Wesley Grant, Jr.
Hubschman, Henry Allan
Hunt, David Wallingford
Kaswell, Stuart Joel
Komoroske, John H.
Laporte, Gerald Joseph Sylvestre
Lawton, Bettina Mary
Lenhart, James Thomas
Levenson, Alan Bradley
Long, Charles Thomas
Lucas, Steven Mitchell
Lyon, Edwin Leon
Maiwurm, James John
Maloney, Barry Charles
Marinaccio, Charles Lindbergh
Markham, Jerry Wayne
Matthews, Steve Allen
Mazo, Mark Elliott
McNeily, Curtlan Roger
Morrison, Alexia
Muir, J. Dapray
Muller, Scott William
Murphy, Richard Patrick
Olson, John Frederick
Oyewole, G. Godwin
Quarles, James Linwood, III
Raimi, Burton Louis
Rainbolt, John Vernon, II
Razzano, Frank Charles
Sapir, Michael Lynn
Schropp, James Howard
Sheehan, Richard Jere
Siegel, Gerald William
Slayton, John Howard
Smith, Arthur Lee
Smith, Willard Mark
Strother, James French
Vidal-Cordero, David
Vollmer, Andrew N.
Wallison, Frieda K.
Wegner, Brent Allen
Weiss, Jerome Paul
Weiss, Stephen Joel
Zimmer, Janet Rose

Florida

Andersen, Michael Page
Barker, Charles Thomas
Cane, Marilyn Blumberg
Dicks, Jack William
Doyle, Martin
Golden, E(dward) Scott
Harris, Charles Edison
Hornsby, Cyrus Edward, III
Jamieson, Michael Lawrence
Kagan, Edwin Bruce
Kiefner, John Robert, Jr.
Klein, Marina Shank
Leone, James Russell
Lipson, Gary David
Martin, Serge Gregory
Morrall, Matthew Earl
O'Brien, Thomas George, III
Orlin, Karen J.
Patsavos, Evelyn Christou
Perlstein, Mitchell Leslie
Pfenniger, Richard Charles, Jr.
Pierce, John G.
Pulignano, Nicholas Vincent, Jr.
Schechterman, Lawrence
Schneider, Laz Levkoff
Singer, Stuart H.
Spector, Brian F.
Watts-FitzGerald, Abigail Cory

Georgia

Anderson, Peter Joseph
Arkin, Robert David
Bassett, William Randall
Birchfield, J. Kermit, Jr.
Brading, Stanley Gatewood, Jr.
Brewer, Edward Cage, III
Brown, Colin W(egand)
Dalziel, Charles Meredith, Jr.
Davidson, Joseph Q., Jr.
Ganz, Charles David
Hipple, Robert John
Jeffries, McChesney Hill, Jr.
Kolber, Daniel Hackner
Meyer, William Lorne
Parrish, Benjamin Franklin, Jr.
Prince, David Cannon
Schwartz, Arthur Jay
Sharpe, Robert Francis, Jr.
Sinowski, Thomas Charles
Somers, Fred Leonard, Jr.
Williams, Lyman Neil, Jr.

Hawaii

Case, James Hebard
Conrad, John Regis
O'Malley, Michael John
Porter, Michael Pell
Robinson, Harlo Lyle

Idaho

Hanks, Stephen Grant

Illinois

Addis, Lauane Cleo
Anderson, Geoffrey Allen
Axley, Frederick William
Babb, Frank Edward
Baker, Benjamin Joseph
Barack, Peter Joseph
Bashwiner, Steven Lacelle
Bell, Dennis Arthur
Bellows, Laurel Gordon
Bergonia, Raymond David
Blount, Michael Eugene
Bodenstein, Ira
Bortman, David
Boyd, David Parker
Bramnik, Robert Paul
Brennan, James Joseph
Burgess, Robert Kyle
Carasik, Karen Sue
Clemens, Richard Glenn
Crawford, Sandra Kay
Davis, Scott Jonathan
Demas, Jean V.
Don, Arthur
Elias, John Samuel
Emerson, Carter Whitney
Engling, Robert John
Everett, C. Curtis
Fahner, Tyrone Clarence
Farnell, Alan Stuart
Fein, Roger G.
Filler, Ronald Howard
Fisher, Patricia Sweeney
Flanagin, Neil
Francois, William Armand
Fraumann, Willard George
Gagne, James L.
George, John Martin, Jr.
Golden, Bruce Paul
Goodrich, John Bernard
Gregg, Jon Mann
Gritchen, Lyle Steven
Hanson, Kenneth Hamilton
Harring, Michael Adrian
Helman, Robert Alan
Henry, Robert John
Herzel, Leo
Hoekstra, Kathlyn B.
Hollins, Mitchell Leslie
Hook, George Clive, II
Huston, Steven Craig
Jock, Paul F., II
Johnson, Gary Thomas
Kanner, Steven Alan

Kimball, Franklyn Davis
Kirsner, Kenneth Stephen
Kotz, Richard Frederick
Kravitt, Jason Harris Paperno
Krieger, Frederic Michael
Kurz, Thomas Patrick
Lause, Christopher Allen
Levin, Michael David
Markey, James Kevin
Marmer, Ronald Louis
Martin, Wayne Mallott
Mason, Peter Ian
McDermott, John Henry
McGrath, William Joseph
McWhirter, Bruce J.
Millard, Richard Steven
Miller, Ronald Stuart
Miranti, Richard Frederick
Nordlund, William Chalmers
Nyberg, William Arthur
Ogle, Jerry Michael
O'Rourke, Daniel
Pell, Wilbur Frank, III
Phelps, Paul Michael
Quinlan, William Joseph, Jr.
Reum, James Michael
Rooney, Matthew A.
Rosenfield, Andrew M.
Ruder, David Sturtevant
Santona, Gloria
Sawyier, Michael Tod
Schaeffer, Shirley Ann
Schaffner, Theodore W.
Schreck, Robert A., Jr.
Schuman, William Paul
Scott, John Joseph
Shank, William O.
Siegan, Jerold Nathan
Sigal, Michael Stephen
Silliman, Richard George
Southern, Robert Allen
Thornton, Robert Richard
Uhlenhop, Paul Buscher
Vieregg, Robert Todd
Walner, Robert Joel
Wartman, Carl Henry
Watts, Dey Wadsworth
Witz, Allen Barry
York, John C.
Zaander, Mark Charles
Zabrosky, Alex Walter

Indiana

Bailey, Patricia Seasor
Coons, Stephen Merle
Densborn, Donald Keith
Eichhorn, Frederick Foltz, Jr.
Kahlenbeck, Howard, Jr.
Lowe, Louis Robert, Jr.
Millard, David B.
Neff, R. Matthew
Russell, David Williams
Saint, Robert Edwards
Swhier, Robert Dewain, Jr.
Welch, William F.

Kansas

Cranford, Steven Leon
Gaar, Norman Edward
Haag, Gerald Dean
Hageman, John Ashley

Kentucky

Pedley, Lawrence Lindsay
Philpott, James Alvin, Jr.
Van Meter, John David
Vice, Robert Bruce

Louisiana

Buchler, Peter Robert
Goldblatt, Michael L.
Losavio, Peter Joseph
McMillan, Lee Richards, II
Whitney, John Franklin

Maryland

Arey, Patrick Kane
Asti, Alison Louise
Chernow, Jeffrey Scott
Haas, John Howard
Kafes, William O.
Maseritz, Guy B.
Olander, Christopher Dean
Priest, Gordon Webb, Jr.
Rittenhouse, Susan Merrick
Tilghman, Richard Carmichael, Jr.
Wildhack, William August, Jr.

Massachusetts

Bateman, Thomas Robert
Berman, Michael Dexter
Bernfeld, Jeffrey Alan
Boxer, Jeffrey Victor
Chapin, David Chester
Dickie, Robert Benjamin
Fischer, Eric Robert
FitzGibbon, Scott Thomas
Frederick, Samuel Adams
Garcia, Adolfo Ramon
Glazer, Donald Wayne
Goodman, Louis Allan
Hadzima, Joseph George, Jr.
Hodge, Nicholas Sim
Jordan, Alexander Joseph, Jr.
Loring, Arthur
Lougee, David Louis
Malley, Robert John
Minot, Winthrop Gardner
Notopoulos, Alexander Anastasios, Jr.
Paran, Mark Lloyd
Penman, Gordon Reese
Rubens, James I.
Thibeault, George Walter
Updegrove, Andrew Scott
West, Richard Angus

Michigan

Avant, Grady, Jr.
Bauer, Jeffry Mark
Campbell, Scott Robert
Case, Matthew Alan
Dufendach, Carl William
Gale, Connie R(uth)
Goldberg, Fredric Norman
Greenhalgh, Stephen Irving
Hunter, Larry Dean
Kamins, John Mark
Kanter, Alan Michael
Marotta, Robert
Mc Callum, Charles Edward
Sharp, John
Sorge, Jay Wootten
Stoetzer, Gerald Louis
Williams, J. Bryan
Yared, Paul David

Minnesota

Albers, Fern Beth
Beattie, Charles Robert, III
Bernhardson, Ivy Schutz
Bleck, Michael John
Brooks, William James, III
Burke, Paul Bradford
Diracles, James Constantine
Giberson, Francis Eugene
Mortrud, David Lloyd
Mozer, Michael Theodore
Norton, John William
Ozzello, Jan Lorraine
Palmer, Deborah Jean
Radmer, Michael John
Sanner, Royce Norman
Woods, Robert Edward

Mississippi

Lalor, Owen Patrick
Low, John T.C.

Missouri

Arnold, John Fox
Ball, Owen Keith, Jr.
Bley, Joseph Russell, Jr.
Blunt, Ronald L.
Bruening, Richard Patrick
Clear, John Michael
Denneen, John Paul
Doan, Kirk Hugh
Gatewood, Diane Ridley
Gilmore, Webb Reilly
Gould, Terry Allen
Hancock, S. Lee
Johnson, William Ashton
Lents, Don Glaude
Lynch, Robert Martin
Monaco, Nicholas M.
Peper, Christian Baird
Proost, Robert Lee
Rich, Marvin Lewis
Sher, Richard Philip
Sneeringer, Stephen Geddes
Sobol, Lawrence Raymond
Stanziola, James Alan

Montana

Bahls, Steven Carl
Ogg, Robert Kelley
Seelye, Lynn McVeigh

Nebraska

Dahlk, Thomas Harlan
Dessonville, Loren Edward
Kreifels, Frank Anthony
Minter, Gregory Byron
Slattery, David Edmund
Vosburg, Bruce David

New Hampshire

Gutin, Irving

New Jersey

Allen, Michael Lewis
Duff, Vaughn W.
Flanders, Howard Barrett, Jr.
Fries Gardner, Lisa
Harris, Micalyn Shafer
Lavey, Stewart Evan
Lawatsch, Frank Emil, Jr.
Sherman, Lenore Shustak
Vanderbilt, Arthur T., II
Walsh, Gary Eugene

New Mexico

Apodaca, Patrick Vincent
Barnett, Barry Howard
Schuler, Alison Kay

New York

Abelle, Patsy Caples
Abramson, Joel Eliot
Ackman, Milton Roy
Altman, Robert Harry
Angland, Joseph
Appel, Alfred
Arenson, Gregory K.
Armstrong, James Sinclair
Atkins, Peter Allan
Avery, Patricia I.
Axelrod, Charles Paul
Axinn, Stephen Mack
Bader, Izaak Walton
Baker, Bruce J.
Banker, Stephen M.
Barandes, Robert
Barbanel, Jack A.
Bar-Levav, Doron Mordecai
Barton, Anthony Blackshaw
Bass, Fred
Bauer, George A., III
Bean, Bruce Winfield
Beck, Andrew James
Beekman, William Bedloe
Belnick, Mark Alan
Bender, Alan Ronald
Bendes, Barry Jay
Benedict, James Nelson
Benedict, Thane, III
Bennett, Scott Lawrence
Bergstein, Daniel Gerard
Bernard, Richard Phillip
Bernstein, Paul Murray
Beyda, Daniel
Biegen, Arnold Irwin
Bitsky, Jason Isidore
Bizar, Irving
Blackman, Kenneth Robert
Blanc, Roger David
Bloom, Arnold Sanford
Boehner, Leonard Bruce
Borgese, John A.
Bornmann, Carl M(alcolm)
Brackett, Ronald E.
Brantl, Robert Francis
Brown, Geraldine Reed
Brown, G(lenn) William, Jr.
Brown, Meredith M.
Bryan, Barry Richard
Buckstein, Mark Aaron
Butler, Samuel Coles
Butowsky, David Martin
Campbell, Woodrow Wilson
Cantwell, Robert
Caywood, Warren Gustave, Jr.
Cherovsky, Erwin Louis
Ciovacco, Robert John
Cirillo, Richard Allan
Cohen, Arthur Alan
Cohen, Edward Herschel
Cohen, Murray
Cohen, Robin Ellen
Collins, Wallace Edmund James
Condliffe, David Charles
Cook, Barbara Ann
Cooper, Michael Anthony
Cooper, Stephen Herbert
Costello, Robert Joseph
Cotter, James Michael
Cotton, James Alexendre
Cranney, Marilyn Kanrek
Cropper, Stephen Wallace
Daitz, Ronald Frederick
Daw, Harold John
Dayan, Rodney S.
Deer, James Willis
Deutsch, Irwin Frederick
Diamant, Aviva F.
Donley, Joseph Francis
Dorado, Marianne Gaertner
Douglas-Hamilton, Margaret Hambrecht
Dubin, James Michael
Duerbeck, Heidi Barbara
Duffy, Edmund Charles
Dunham, Wolcott Balestier, Jr.
Dunn, M(orris) Douglas
Edel, Martin David
Eilen, Howard Scott
Eisert, Edward Gaver
Ellis, James Henry
Eltzroth, Carter Weaver
Epstein, Melvin
Ercklentz, Enno Wilhelm, Jr.
Erickson, Gail
Feiman, Ronald Mark
Feldman, Jay N.
Fenn, George Karl, Jr.
Fensterstock, Blair Courtney
Finberg, Alan Robert
Finkelstein, Saul Haym
Fisher, Ann Bailen
Fishman, Mitchell Steven
Flatley, Daniel Kevin
Fleischer, Arthur, Jr.
Fogelman, Martin
Fogg, Blaine Viles
Folger, Oscar David
Frank, Lloyd
Freund, James Coleman
Friedman, Bart
Friedman, John Maxwell, Jr.
Friedman, Robert Laurence
Friedman, Stanley Joseph
Frumento, Aegis Joseph
Fullem, L. Robert
Gambro, Michael S.
Ganis, Stephen Lane
Gardner, Romaine Luverne
Garfinkel, Barry Herbert
Gettner, Alan Frederick
Giacomo, Paul Joseph, Jr.
Gibbons, Robert John
Gilden, Richard Henry
Gillespie, Jane
Gilman, Charles Alan
Goff, Michael Harper
Gold, Neil D.
Goldberg, Joel Henry
Goldman, Louis Budwig
Goldman, Roy Lawrence
Goldner, Leonard Howard
Gracin, Hank
Grant, Stephen Allen
Grant, Susan Irene
Green, Michael Aaron
Hall, Christopher Patrick
Handwerker, Kevin
Hanson, Jean Elizabeth
Haroldson, Jeffrey David
Hart, Robert M.
Hawes, Douglas Wesson
Hawkins, John Donald, Jr.
Head, Christopher Alan
Hecht, Charles Joel
Heine, Andrew Noah
Heines, Molly Kathleen
Heller, Richard Stewart
Heller, Ronald Gary
Henderson, Erskine Dale
Herlihy, Edward D.
Hersh, Robert Michael
Hershberg, David Stephen
Hershcopf, Gerald Thea
Herzeca, Lois Friedman
Hiden, Robert Battaile, Jr.
Hirsch, Jerome Seth
Hoff, Jonathan M(orind)
Hoffman, Mathew
Hoffman, Richard (Melvin)
Horowitz, Harold A.
Howe, Richard Rives
Humphreys, Noel Dutton
Hurley, Geoffrey Kevin
Immerman, Paul Alan
Isquith, Fred Taylor
Jackson, Ronald James Leonard
Jackson, Thomas Gene
Jacobs, Arnold Stephen
Jakes, Peter H.
Jarblum, William
Jawin, Paul Gregory
Jones, Jeffrey Russell
Joseph, Stephanie Rudman
Kadet, Samuel
Kahn, Richard Dreyfus
Kaplan, Mark Norman
Katz, Robert James
Kavaler, Thomas J.
Keltner, Thomas Nethery, Jr.
Kenney, John Joseph
Kies, David M.
Kilkenny, John Jude
Klaperman, Joel Simcha
Klatell, Robert Edward
Koblenz, Michael Robert
Koch, Kenneth Richard
Koo, Richard
Kramer, Morris Joseph
Krane, Steven Charles
Kreitman, Lenore Roberts
Lampen, Richard Jay
Landau, Walter Loeber
Laughlin, James Patrick
Lawrence, Linwood Grant, III
Leitner, Anthony Joseph
Levinson, Leslie J.
Levitsky, Asher Samuel
Levy, Julius
Lewis, Grant Stephen
Liggio, Carl Donald
Lilley, Albert Frederick, III
Lloyd, David Livingstone, Jr.
Lowe, John Anthony
Lutzker, Elliot Howard
Macioce, Frank Michael, Jr.
Madden, John Joseph
Malawsky, Donald N.
Maloney, Thomas Joseph
Mangano, Joseph S.
Mark, Jonathan I.
Marlatt, Jerry Ronald
Martin, Allan A.
Masinter, Edgar Martin
McCabe, David Allen
McDonald, Willis, IV
McEnroe, John Patrick
Mc Goldrick, John Gardiner
McHugh, James Bernard
McKinney, James Bernard, Jr.
McLean, David Lyle
McMeen, Elmer Ellsworth, III
McNally, John Joseph
McNeill, Walter Giles
Meiklejohn, Donald Stuart
Meislahn, Harry Post
Meltzer, Roger
Merow, John Edward
Meyer, Henry Theodore, III
Michel, Clifford Lloyd
Miller, Frederick Lloyd
Miller, Phebe Condict
Miller, Richard Allan
Millimet, Erwin
Mirvis, Theodore Neal
Mitchell, Robert Everitt
Modlin, Howard S.
Monroe, Kendyl Kurth
Moomjian, Gary Thomas
Moore, Harold Francis
Morgan, Frank Edward, II
Morris, Edward William, Jr.
Morrissey, James Malcolm
Moskin, Morton
Most, Jack Lawrence
Moxley, Charles Joseph, Jr.
Muccia, Joseph William
Mullaney, Thomas Joseph
Murray, Conal Eugene
Mushkin, Martin
Nash, Paul LeNoir
Neidell, Martin H.
Nemser, Earl Harold
Newcombe, George Michael
Newman, William Arthur
Nicholas, Christopher Paul
Nimetz, Matthew
Nimkin, Bernard William
Nusbaum, Jack Henry
Obermaier, Otto George
O'Brien, Christopher Edward
O'Connell, John Ryan
O'Flinn, Peter Russell
Ohlman, Douglas Ronald
Ormsby, David George
Orr, Dennis Patrick
Osgood, Robert Mansfield
Parent, Louise Marie
Perlmuth, William Alan
Peterson, Linda Sue
Pettibone, Peter John
Pietrzak, Alfred Robert
Pinzler, William Michael
Pisani, Michael Joseph
Presant, Sanford Calvin
Pulis, Gregory Milton
Pyle, Robert Milner, Jr.
Raisler, Kenneth Mark
Ray, Jeanne Cullinan
Reilly, Conor Desmond
Reinstein, Paul Michael
Reinthaler, Richard Walter
Riley, David Edward
Ringer, James Milton
Rocklen, Kathy Hellenbrand
Romney, Richard Bruce
Ross, Matthew
Rothman, Henry Isaac
Rothschild, Steven Bruce
Rubin, Stephen Wayne
Rubinstein, Aaron
Russo, Anthony Joseph, Jr.
Ryan, James Vincent
Sacks, Ira Stephen
Samels, Stephen Cooper
Samuels, Janet Lee
Santangelo, Betty J.
Satrom, Robert Charles
Savage, Edward Turney
Schaefer, David Stuart
Schneiderman, Irwin
Schulman, Steven Gary
Schuur, Robert George
Scofield, Milton N.
Segall, Mark Edward
Seltzer, Jeffrey Lloyd
Sexton, David Farrington
Shapiro, Barry Robert
Sherman, Jeffrey Scott
Sherman, Michael Paul
Siller, Stephen I.
Sinsheimer, Alan J.
Siphron, Joseph Rider
Skolan-Logue, Amanda Nicole
Smith, Jeffrey G.
Snow, Charles
Spatt, Robert Edward
Spiegel, Jerrold Bruce
Starr, Richard Marc
Steinberg, Howard E.
Stengel, James Lamont
Stephenson, Alan Clements
Stern, Lewis Arthur
Stern, Warren Roger
Stewart, Duncan James
Stimmel, Todd Richard
Stine, John
Strom, Milton Gary
Strougo, Robert
Sussman, Alexander R.
Swanson, Richard Paul
Szwalbenest, Benedykt Jan
Tanner, Douglas Alan
Tanous, James Joseph
Taylor, Gregory Frederick
Tehan, John Bashir
Terrell, J. Anthony
Tondel, Lawrence Chapman
Tormey, Douglas Joseph
Tortoriello, Robert Laurence
Tursi, Carl Thomas
Untermeyer, Salle Podos
Urowsky, Richard J.
Versfelt, David Scott
Viener, John David
Vigdor, Justin Leonard
Vogel, Howard Stanley
Walder, Robert Alan
Waldoks, Phillip Harry
Wang, George Hansen
Ward, Ettie
Warner, Edward Waide, Jr.
Warwick, Kathleen Ann
Welikson, Jeffrey Alan
Wells, Andrew Norman
Whelan, John Kenneth
Wilcox, John Caven
Winikoff, Robert Lee
Wishingrad, Jay Marc
Wittner, Derek A.
Wolfe, Richard Barry Michael
Wrapp, Emilie D.
Young, Michael Richard
Zeller, Paul William
Zipfinger, Frank Peter
Zucker, Howard
Zuckerman, Mitchell

North Carolina

Alexander, H. Heath
Carter, Charles Michael
Davis, Jeffrey J.
Gallant, Wade Miller, Jr.
Miller, John Randolph
Parker, Daniel Louis
Robinson, Russell Marable, II
Wilkerson, Leo Carl

North Dakota

Alleva, Patti Ann

Ohio

Ashford, Thomas Steven
Atkinson, William Edward
Bailey, Daniel Allen
Benedict, Ronald Louis
Bouscaren, Timothy Lincoln
Branagan, James Joseph
Burlingame, John Hunter
Calkins, Benjamin
Campbell, Paul Barton
Cooper, Douglas Kenneth
Craver, James B.
Csank, Paul Lewis
Donnem, Roland William
Farrar, Elizabeth Grace Turrell
Faruki, Charles Joseph
Federico, Andrew John
Flowers, Michael Edward
Frank, Harvey
Freedman, Howard Joel
Goss, Colleen Flynn
Haas, Douglas Eric
Holland, Patricia Marcus
Holt, G. Woodrow
Inglis, David Stuart
Kubiak, Jon Stanley
Lawson, Margaret Avril
Leibold, William Joseph
Lenn, Stephen Andrew
Linnert, Terrence Gregory
Markey, Robert Guy
McCracken, Christopher Cornell
McKee, Thomas Frederick
Piraino, Thomas Anthony
Plumly, Daniel Harp
Rasmussen, Frank Morris
Rorimer, Louis
Spies, Howard A.
Stith, John Stephen
Watts, Steven Richard
Webb, Thomas Irwin, Jr.

Oklahoma

Biolchini, Robert Fredrick
Derrick, Gary Wayne
Kihle, Donald Arthur
Luthey, Graydon Dean, Jr.
Mash, Jerry L.
Mirabile, Thomas Keith
Morgan, William Borden
Robertson, Mark Alexander
Steinhorn, Irwin Harry
Sullivan, Lovell Wayne
Waldman, Robert Allan
Walker, Ronald Lynn
Welch, James Stephen

Oregon

Bock, Jeffrey William
Burt, Robert Gene
DuBoff, Leonard David
Fulsher, Allan Arthur
Gleaves, Curt B.
Halle, John Joseph
Newton, Gregory Clark
O'Halloran, Robert Luis

Pennsylvania

Amelio, Laura Lane
Bales, John Foster, III
Barrett, Karen Moore

Basinski, Anthony Joseph
Beckman, Donald
Berger, David
Blasier, Peter Cole
Blue, Donald Sherwood
Chadwick, H. Beatty
Chamberlain, Gerard Alfred
Connell, Janice Timchak
Davies, Norleen O'Sullivan
Demers, Timothy Francis
Diehl, Kristin Knoell
Dougherty, James Thomas
Ehrenwerth, David Harry
German, Edward Cecil
Grace, Eugene Peter
Hangley, William Thomas
Harff, Charles Henry
Hooton, Michael Edward
Kelley, George Lawrence, Jr.
Kelvin, Jeffrey Barnett
Klapinsky, Raymond Joseph
Lane, Maryl A.
Letwin, Jeffrey William
Litmans, Murray Ian
McCabe, Lawrence James
McGonigle, John William
McNew, Robert Bruce
McNitt, David Garver
Nalle, Horace Disston, Jr.
Pillai, K. G. Jan
Poul, Franklin
Reed, Robert Alan
Reich, Abraham Charles
Reuben, Allan Herbert
Ross, Murray Louis
Schulte, Jeffrey Lewis
Schwartz, James William
Scudder, Charles Seelye Kellgren
Specter, Howard Alan
Stone, Laura Williams
Strauss, Edward Kenneth
Tarlow, Marc Gary
Thiess, Kenneth Charles
Weil, Jeffrey George
Weiner, Richard Norman
Weinstein, David Haym

Rhode Island

Abedon, Herbert Joseph
Cohen, Linda Marks

South Carolina

Dominick, Paul Allen
Foster, John Witherspoon
King, George Savage, Jr.
Roberts, Edward Calhoun
Seaman, Robert E., III
Swagart, Harry Augustus, III
Winston, Jacqueline Berrier

Tennessee

Buchanan, Alexander Blackman
Cheek, James Howe, III
Doggrell, Henry Patton
Langevoort, Donald Carl
Lynch, Carole Yard
Meyer, Michael Alan
Norville, Craig Hubert
Soderquist, Larry Dean
Warren, Richard Fenton, Jr.

Texas

Anderson, Eric Severin
Baker, Scott Russell
Bartholdt, William Edward, Jr.
Bateman, Hal Marion
Bishop, Bryan Edwards
Bissex, Walter Earl
Blachly, Jack Lee
Block, Steven Robert
Bromberg, Alan Robert
Brown, Ronald Lee
Cobb, Chester Lee
Conlon, Michael William
de la Garza, Luis Adolfo
Faye, Stanley Ethan
Finch, Michael Paul
Fortado, Michael George
Gabert, Nori Lauren
Glazier, Kenneth Charles
Griffin, Campbell Arthur, Jr.
Guzzetti, William Louis
Hainsfurther, A. Michael
Harden, Richard Lee
Hoffman, Joseph Anthony
Howard, Timothy Jon
Johnson, Edward Michael
Joor, William Eugene, III
Kelly, Francis Thomas
Kelly, William Franklin, Jr.
Kneipper, Richard Keith
Larson, Mark Edward, Jr.
Manley, Larry Paul
McLane, David Glenn
Meer, Julian Milton
Menges, John Kenneth, Jr.
Miller, Norman Richard
Moehlman, Michael Scott
Morris, Rebecca Robinson
Nolen, Roy Lemuel
Ording, Michael K.
Painton, Russell Elliott
Parker, Dallas Robert
Porter, Thomas William, III
Price, John Aley
Profusek, Robert Alan
Regenbogen, Ellis Arnold
Reser, Don Clayton
Roberts, Thomas Alba
Rowland, Sam E.
Sandler, Lewis Herbsman
Sapp, Walter William
Schmidt, John Aldin
Schreiber, Sally Ann
Schwartz, Charles Walter
Scott, Richard Waldo
Slugg, Ramsay Hill
Smith, Tad Randolph
Stein, Sheldon Irvin
Stowe, Charles Robinson Beecher
Sweeney, Gregory Louis
Szalkowski, Charles Conrad
Tankersley, Michael Wayne
Tygrett, Howard Volney, Jr.
Unger, Adrienne Penrod
Wagner, Michael Duane
Watson, Robert Francis
Zahn, Donald Jack

Utah

Buffmire, Andrew Wallace
Christensen, Krege Bowen
Headman, Arlan Osmond, Jr.
Mackey, Randall Aubrey
Ockey, Ronald J.
Siegler, Lora Celia

Vermont

Guild, Alden
Prentice, Frederick Sheldon

Virginia

Buford, Robert Pegram
Conway, William Augustine
Cutchins, Clifford Armstrong, IV
Fisher, Catherine Ambrosiano
Harrison, David George
Macrae, Howard Taft, Jr.
O'Connell, Kevin Michael
Pope, Robert Dean
Procopio, Joseph Guydon
Tatum, Franklin M., III
Wallman, Steven Mark Harte
Whitt, Jane Rebecca

Washington

Alsdorf, Robert Hermann
Batey, Douglas Leo
Berman, Steve William
Brenner, David (Merle)
Duvall, Gary Ross
Gay, Sandra Bates
Graham, Stephen Michael
Koegen, Roy Jerome
McLaughlin, Thomas Orville
Oles, Laura Treadgold
Oreskovich, Carl Joseph
Parsons, James Bowne
Rummage, Stephen Michael
Smith, James Alexander, Jr.
Spadoni, Peter Anthony

Wisconsin

Aiken, Jeffrey Paul
Billick, Brooke Jay
Christiansen, Eric Robert
Davis, Kenneth Boone, Jr.
Hallett, Kenneth Victor
Holz, Harry George
Layden, Donald William, Jr.
Sikora, Ted Robert, II

Wyoming

Woodhouse, Gay Vanderpoel

AUSTRALIA

Browne, Jeffrey Francis

ENGLAND

Reiter, Glenn M.
Scott, John Andrew

FRANCE

Conrad, Winthrop Brown, Jr.

ADDRESS UNPUBLISHED

Avery, James Thomas, III
Bagan, Grant Alan
Baird, James Kenneth
Baris, Jay G.
Braun, Jerome Irwin
Brodhead, David Crawmer
Edwards, Daniel Paul
Fried, Samuel
Griffin, Thomas Patrick
Heath, Charles Dickinson
Koeller, Robert Marion
Maher, John A.
Morimoto, Mary A.
Moylan, James Joseph
Osimitz, Dennis Victor
Schroeder, John Walter
Tomczak, Starr Lyn
Van Antwerp, Rosemary Dirkie
Wittebort, Robert John, Jr.

SOCIAL SECURITY. *See* Pension.

TAXATION, CORPORATE

UNITED STATES

Alabama

Allen, Robert A.
Blackburn, John Gilmer
Ely, Bruce Peter
Garth, Thomas Fearn
Hughes, James Donald
Leatherbury, Gregory Luce, Jr.
Lucas, Patrick Hewell
Poole, William Stitt, Jr.
Proctor, David Ray
Schiff, Gary Steven
Shanks, William Ennis, Jr.

Alaska

Clough, John F., III
Yerbich, Joseph Thomas
Yerbich, Thomas Joseph

Arizona

Brown, Steven Jay
Case, David Leon
Cohn, Jeffrey Brooks
Daum, Bryan Edwin
DeBerry, Dennis Charles
Derdenger, Patrick
Ehmann, Anthony Valentine
Henry, John Alfred
Le Clair, Douglas Marvin
Martori, Joseph Peter
Meek, Marcellus Robert
Meyer, Paul Joseph
Olsen, Alfred Jon
Phillips, Steven William
Pietzsch, Michael Edward
Pingree, Bruce Douglas
Simonson, Michael
Spitzer, Marc Lee
Turner, Daniel Charles
Waterfall, Gordon Garrett
Wood, Nicholas Joseph

Arkansas

Eichenbaum, E. Charles
Nisbet, Alexander Wyckliff, Jr.
Watkins, Jerry West

California

Adelson, Benedict James
Appel, Martin Sherman
Arkin, Michael Barry
Balkin, Jeffrey Gilbert
Barton, Babette B.
Basile, Paul Louis, Jr.
Benninghoff, Charles Franklyn, III
Berry, Samuel Harper, Jr.
Blaustein, Frances Jan
Blumenfeld, Eli
Boatwright, David Croft
Bost, Thomas Glen
Brickner, Jed Walter
Brookes, Valentine
Canady, Richard Warren
Chatzky, Michael Gary
Claremon, Glenda Ruth
Crawford, Roy Edgington
Derber, Robert Raymond
Dostart, Paul Joseph
Doti, Frank John
Eres, Thomas W.
Foster, David Scott
Gibson, Thomas Harris, III
Gordon, David Eliot
Greenberg, Maxwell Elfred
Greenberg, Myron Silver
Greene, Richard Lawrence
Grim, Douglas Paul
Hamilton, Jackson Douglas
Hawkins, Karen L(ee)
Heckman, Donald Rex, II
Hogan, Claude Hollis
Homer, Barry Wayne
Irwin, Philip Donnan
Israel, Perry Elemore
Kirkelie, Gregory Evan
Kleier, James Patrick
Klott, David Lee
Knecht, James Herbert
Kohl, Glen Arlen
LaCasse, James Phillip
Levy, David
Lipton, Alvin E(lliot)
Livsey, Robert Callister
London, Barry Joseph
Maciel, Ronald John
Maeder, Gary William
Maier, Thomas Andrew
Mancino, Douglas Michael
McNulty, John Kent
Michel, Trudi Louise
Moskatel, Ira Dennis
Offer, Stuart Jay
Orth, Beverly Jean
Palazzo, Robert P.
Petty, Keith
Pircher, Leo Joseph
Putnam, Philip Conrad
Ramirez, William Earl
Richman, Frederick Alexander
Riley, Kirk Holden
Romero, Frederick Armand
Rosky, Burton Seymour
Sacks, Barry Howard
Schlinkert, William Joseph
Schumacher, Stephen Joseph
Shaney, Kevin Robert
Sheppard, Thomas Richard
Shimoff, Paul Martin
Silk, Thomas
Sires, Bruce David
Smiley, Stanley Robert
Sobel, Larry D.
Spiegel, Hart Hunter
Stegall, Daniel Richard
Steinberg, Elliot Gershom
Thorpe, Geoffrey Lawton
Weagant, Lance Maxwell
Wood, Robert Warren

Colorado

Alberts, Celia Anne
Callison, James William
Earnhart, Mark Warren
Gehres, James
Greenberg, Morton Paul
Hill, Robert Dean
Hodson, Thane Raymond
Keatinge, Robert Reed
Keely, George Clayton
Nakarado, Gary Lee
O'Connor, Donald John
Pottick, Frances Jean
Rich, Robert Stephen
Ruppert, John Lawrence
Schumacher, Barry Lee
Scott, Peter Bryan
Smith, Sheldon Harold
Stauffer, Scott William
Waggoner, Michael James
Wiegand, Robert, II

Connecticut

Allan, John Malcolm, Jr.
Anestis, Robert William
Bellamy, William Murray, Jr.
Blazzard, Norse Novar
Del Negro, John Thomas
Grodd, Leslie Eric
LaFollette, Ernest Carlton
Lyon, James Burroughs
Marsching, Ronald Lionel
Milliken, Charles Buckland
Schiff, Alan Lewis
Schwartz, Lawrence B.
Sheiman, Ronald Lee
Simonelli, Jerry
Weinshank, Arthur Charles

Delaware

Grossman, Jerome Kent
Hatch, Denison Hurlbut, Jr.
Hindmarch, Thomas Michael
Lassen, John Kai
Olson, Mark Douglas
Popper, Richard J.A.

District of Columbia

Aiken, Jeffrey Howard
Alexander, Donald Crichton
Barth, Roger Vincent
Bassett, Joel Eric
Birnkrant, Henry Joseph
Bostick, George Hale
Brown, Hank
Bucholtz, Harold Ronald
Calhoun, Carol Victoria
Chabot, Herbert L.
Chanin, Michael Henry
Chip, William Waddington
Clark, Donald Otis
Cohen, Sheldon Stanley
Cohen, Wallace M.
Condrell, William Kenneth
Cook, Harry Clayton, Jr.
Damico, Nicholas Peter
Delaney, Edward Norman
Doyle, Austin Joseph, Jr.
Duncan, Robert Michael
Dunnan, Weaver White
Ell, Douglas William
Evans, Donald Charles, Jr.
Faley, R(ichard) Scott
Fegan, David Coyle
Frazier, Henry Bowen, III
Freeland, T. Paul
Gerber, Joel
Gibson, Reginald Walker
Gideon, Kenneth Wayne
Gillmarten, Mary Del Rey
Griswold, Erwin Nathaniel
Guarini, Frank J.
Halvorson, Newman Thorbus, Jr.
Hanford, Timothy Lloyd
Hardee, David Wyatt
Harmon, Gail McGreevy
Harris, Don Victor, Jr.
Harris, James Alan
Herz, Charles Henry
Hopkins, Bruce Richard
Jacobson, David Edward
Jenner, Gregory Franklin
Johnson, James Walker
Kahn, Edwin Leonard
Kautter, David John
Kempson, Kenneth Earl
Knudson, Scott Gregory
Kurtz, Jerome
Kusma, Kyllikki
Lane, Bruce Stuart
Leedy, William H.
Libin, Jerome B.
Mackles, Glenn Frederick
Martin, Keith
May, Gregory Evers
May, Richard Edward
McNeily, Curtlan Roger
Mentz, J. Roger
Metcalfe, Robert Davis, III
Meyers, Erik Jon
Miller, Jack Richard
Morgan, Daniel Louis
Morris, William
Neidich, George Arthur
Nolan, John Stephan
O'Hara, James Thomas
Oppenheimer, Jerry L.
Oyler, Gregory Kenneth
Parr, Carolyn Miller
Pate, Joan Seitz
Patrick, Robert John, Jr.
Paul, William McCann
Pehrson, Gordon Oscar, Jr.
Pierce, Kevin Michael
Pomeroy, Harlan
Quiggle, James Williams
Rainbolt, John Vernon, II
Rosen, Jeffrey J.
Roy, James Robert
Sampson, Michael Paul
Schiffbauer, William G.
Schram, Steven H.
Schutzer, George Jeffrey
Shields, Perry
Silverstein, Leonard Lewis
Simpkins, Mary Nell
Simpson, Charles Reagan
Slayton, John Howard
Stanley, Keith Eugene
Swift, Stephen Jensen
Teague, Randal Cornell, Sr.
Toth, Claire E.
Ufholz, Philip John
Van Etten, Laura
Walker, Lynda Kay
Warden, Robert Allison
Wegner, Brent Allen
Weinman, Howard Mark
Weiss, Jerome Paul
Worthy, K(enneth) Martin
Zapruder, Henry G.

Florida

Ade, James L.
Arlt, Mary Ann Kokoszyna
Bailey, Brant Allan
Barnett, Bernard Harry
Barnett, Charles Dawson
Bernstein, Zayle Abraham
Braden, Dana Danielle
Butterworth, Alan Randolph
Chabrow, Penn Benjamin
Champion, Roger Cornelius
Doliner, Nathaniel Lee
Dunlap, Charles Leonard
Emmanuel, Michel George
Falk, Victor S., III
Gachet, Thomas McInnis
Hagendorf, Stanley
Haile, John Sanders
Hull, David John
Lamont, Robert Sheldon
Lasser, Mark Lawrence
Lefkowitz, Ivan Martin
Margolis, John Gilbert
Oliva, Robert Rogelio
Reid, John James
Reinstein, Joel
Rubenstein, Robert Mayer
Ruffner, Charles Louis
Stankee, Glen Allen
Teblum, Gary Ira
Weisberg, Alan Lerner
Whitesman, Guy Edward

Georgia

Bell, Mildred Bailey
Berry, Alonzo Franklin, Jr
Brading, Stanley Gatewood, Jr.
Carpenter, Raymond Prince
Cheney, Huddie Lee, III
Cooney, William J.
Davidson, Joseph Q., Jr.
Ganz, Charles David
Gartzman, Jeffrey Scott
Gerstein, Joe Willie
Gold, Ronald Theodore
Hasson, James Keith, Jr.
Hines, John Pridgen
Hipple, Robert John
Lamon, Harry Vincent, Jr.
Nickerson, Mark William
O'Callaghan, William Lawrence, Jr.
Quinlan, James William
Sensenig, Lana Smith
Sinowski, Thomas Charles
Wasserman, Michael Gary

Hawaii

D'Olier, H(enry) Mitchell
Epstein, Roger Harris
Heller, Ronald Ian
Lee, James Hon Quon
Miyasaki, Shuichi
Shea, Michael Alan

Idaho

Erickson, Robert Stanley

Illinois

Antonio, Douglas John
Baker, Donald
Baker, Keith Brian
Belmore, F. Martin
Berens, Mark Harry
Bergonia, Raymond David
Bloom, Christopher Arthur
Bowen, Stephen Stewart
Bower, Glen L.
Bryan, Arthur Eldridge, Jr.
Cagney, Joseph Bert
Chanen, Franklin Allen
Clamage, Brett D.
Crane, Charlotte
Cunningham, Robert James
Drymalski, Raymond Hibner
Ehrlich, Jeff Paschal
Elias, John Samuel
Ellwood, Scott
Emmett, James Robert
Evanoff, Michael Blaine
Felsenthal, Steven Altus
Ferencz, Robert Arnold
Fields, Howard M.
Foster, Lloyd Bennett
Garrison, Ray Harlan
Gillies, Donald Allastair
Grayck, Marcus Daniel
Henry, Frederick Edward
Hudetz, Joseph Bernard
Janich, Daniel Nicholas
Janis, Richard Alan
Kanter, Burton Wallace
Kaplan, Howard Gordon
Klotsche, John Chester
Knight, Bernard John, Jr.
Lane, Marc Jay
Lapin, Harvey I.
Lapins, Scott Michael
Levin, Jack S.
Levun, Charles R(alph)
Levy, Katherine Judith
Lifschultz, Phillip
Lindgren, Thomas Bernard
Lorentzen, John Carol
Lowinger, Alexander I
Malone, James Laurence, III
Malone, James Laurence, III
Margolin, Stephen M.
Marmet, Gottlieb John
McDermott, Robert B.
McKenzie, Robert E.
Michalak, Edward Francis
Miller, Arthur Robert
Minnick, Craig Alan
Mollet, Chris John
Myers, Lonn William
Peake, Darryl Lee
Ras, Robert A.
Rombs, Vincent Joseph
Saltoun, Andre M.
Schaaf, Douglas Allan
Schneider, Daniel Max
Scogland, William Lee
Smith, Edward Jerome
Van Duerm, James
Wise, William Jerrard
Witt, Alan Michael
Wolfe, David Louis
Zoll, Jeffery Mark

Indiana

Adinamis, George Peter
Carey, John Leo
FitzGibbon, Daniel Harvey
Gerberding, Miles Carston
Hendrickson, Thomas Atherton
Hinkle, Donald Earl
Jegen, Lawrence A., III
Johnson, G. Weldon
Keber, Kenneth James
Long, Douglas Paul
Lowell, Cym Hawksworth
Ponder, Lester McConnico
Sanborn, Albert Beckwith, II
Schwarz, James Harold
Urda, Richard Bernard, Jr.
Whitehill, Charles Allen

Iowa

Narber, Gregg Ross

Peshkin, Samuel David
Smith, William Sidney
Stark, Maurice Edmund
Strutt, David Stanley
Vanorsdel, Robert Alan

Kansas

Logan, Carl M.
Martin, Alson Robert

Kentucky

Ardery, Joseph Lord Tweedy
Decker, Jennifer Henson
Gilman, Sheldon G.
McMahon, Martin James, Jr.
Romaine, Douglas Patteson
Ryan, Donald Kevin
Winslow, Donald Arthur
Yonts, Stewarts H.

Louisiana

Benjamin, Edward Bernard, Jr.
Blackman, John Calhoun, IV
Ellett, John Spears, II
Hurley, Paul Edward
King, C. A., II
Losavio, Peter Joseph
Peroni, Robert Joseph
Powell, David Wayne
Reso, Jerome John, Jr.
Simon, H(uey) Paul
Stone, Saul
Tramonte, James Albert
Trostorff, Alex P.

Maine

Curran, Richard Emery, Jr.
Currie, Michael Robert
Sang, Peter Bennett

Maryland

Adkins, Edward James
Astrachan, James Barry
Bowen, Debra Lynn
Calimafde, Paula Annette
Choate, Alan G.
Colton, Sterling Don
Curran, Robert Bruce
De Jong, David Samuel
Freeland, Charles
Grange, George Robert, II
Guttenberg, Aryeh
Hershman, Murray John
Jackley, Michael Dano
Robbins, Vernon Earl
Scully, Roger Tehan
Turney, Kenneth Wayne

Massachusetts

Bergen, Kenneth William
Berman, Michael Dexter
Bernhard, Alexander Alfred
Cutler, Arnold R.
Davenport, David Sterling
Elfman, Eric Michael
Gabovitch, Steven Alan
Gabovitch, William
Hartigan, Michael David
Lappin, Robert Sidney
Lougee, David Louis
Matthews, Roger Hardin
May, William Leopold, Jr.
Murphy, Philip Dever
Niswander, Frank Clyde
Oldman, Oliver
Pabian, Jay Michael
Repetti, James Randolph
Repetti, Susan Leonard
Richer, Alan Brian
Sullivan, Charles William
Walker, Paul Howard
Warren, Alvin Clifford, Jr.
Wolfman, Bernard
Yee, Kenneth M.P.

Michigan

Chapman, Conrad Daniel
Dew, Thomas Edward
Dill, Everett Charles
Dresser, Raymond H., Jr.
Feldman, Michael Sanford
Gornick, Alan Lewis
Hindelang, Robert Louis
Hirschman, Sherman Joseph
Kahn, Douglas Allen
Kirk, John MacGregor
Lashbrooke, Elvin Carroll, Jr.
London, Leslie Ann
McKendry, John H., Jr.
Meyer, George Herbert
Newman, Bruce Allen
Ruwart, David Peter
Smoliar, Burton Bruce
Solomon, Mark Raymond
Spicer, S(amuel) Gary
Talcott, Kent Patterson
Tobin, Bruce Howard
Vogel, Theodore John
Winquist, Thomas Richard
Zalecki, Paul Henry

Minnesota

Dzurak, Steven J.
Ellingsworth, Patrick James
Geis, Jerome Arthur
Halbach, Patrice Haley
Hasselquist, Maynard Burton
Kaplan, Harvey Frederick
Kaplan, Sheldon
Klein, William David
Lindgren, D(erbin) Kenneth, Jr.
Ozzello, Jan Lorraine
Whitehill, Clifford Lane

Mississippi

Dossett, James Kearney, Jr.
Edwards, Arthur Martin, III
Fountain, Richard Maurice
Ludlam, Warren VanGilder, Jr.
Painter, William Steene
Russell, Glover Alcorn, Jr.
Thomas, James Talbert, IV

Missouri

Akre, Steven Heetland
Baier, David Donald
Barrie, John Paul
Evans, William Ellis
Goldstein, Michael Gerald
Gorman, Gerald Warner
Greenley, Beverly Jane
Hancock, S. Lee
Hoyne, Andrew Thomas
Knight, Herman Elvin, Jr.
Kohn, Michael Elliott
Kuhlmann, Fred Mark
Levine, Bernard Benton
Lowenhaupt, Charles Abraham
Lynch, Robert Martin
Matthews, James Michael
McClannahan, Cindy Ann
McGannon, Robert Eugene
McNeill, Paul Spurgeon, Jr.
Meives, Joseph Richard
Morrison, John Stanley
Preuss, Ronald Stephen
Rich, Marvin Lewis
Voelpel, Mark Steven

Montana

Dostal, John Anthony
George, Alexander Andrew
Seelye, Lynn McVeigh

Nebraska

Brockman, Terry James
Drozda, Robert Lee
Gaines, Tyler Belt
Gewacke, John Clifford
Greene, Richard Francis
Lyons, William Harry
Wegner, James Darwin

Nevada

Mushkin, Michael Robert
Sully, William Leslie, Jr.
Williams, David Roy

New Hampshire

Chamberlain, Douglas Reginald
Cohen, Steven

New Jersey

Ascione, Joseph Anthony
Bantivoglio, Thomas Nicholas
Bearg, Martin Lee
Beidler, Marsha Wolf
Cappuccio, Ronald Joseph
Conway, Kevin George
Davidoff, E. Martin
Dougherty, Maureen Patricia
Fenichel, Saul Michael
Flaster, Richard Joel
Fusco, Claude Eugene, Jr.
Gorrin, Eugene
Hinshaw, David Love
Kamens, Harold
Liebman, Emmanuel
Mach, Joseph David
Mann, Donald J.
Masanoff, Michael David
Massler, Howard Arnold
Neary, Gerald Clarke
Olszak, Daniel Dominic
Pesin, Edward
Reich, Laurence
Ritter, Robert Joseph
Rosen, Arthur R.
Sholk, Steven Howard
Slutsky, Kenneth Joel
Soderman, Kenneth John
Tobin, Irving
Wurms, Marcel Ronald

New Mexico

Robinson, Bernard Leo
Westerfield, Frank Orlen, Jr.

New York

Agranoff, Gerald Neal
Aidinoff, M(erton) Bernard
Alexander, Mary R.
Amdur, Martin Bennett
Andersen, Richard Esten
Andresen, Malcolm
Baldwin, Robert Frederick, Jr.
Beck, Jan Scott
Beerbower, Cynthia Gibson
Benedict, Thane, III
Berlin, Alan Daniel
Black, Louis Engleman
Blanchard, Kimberly Staggers
Bloomquist, Dennis Howard
Bobrow, Alvan Lee
Boulanger, Carol Seabrook
Brecher, Howard Arthur
Brenner, Jonathan Scott
Bronstein, Richard J.
Burt, Richard Max
Calhoun, Monica Dodd
Campbell, Carolyn Clark
Carlson, David Bret
Carruba, Salvatore John
Chazen, Hartley James
Cliff, Walter Conway
Cohen, Benjamin Jack
Cohen, Bennett D.
Collinson, Dale Stanley
Cooperman, Robert N.
Crowley, Richard Allerton
Dantzler, John William, Jr.
Danziger, Joel Bernard
Davis, Hal Scott
Debo, Vincent Joseph
Dougherty, Thomas Paul, Jr.
Duffy, James P., III
Einstein, Steven Henry
Eustice, James Samuel
Evans, David Lee
Faber, Peter Lewis
Fagan, John Ernest
Feder, Arthur A.
Feeney, David Wesley
Ferguson, Milton Carr, Jr.
Flanagan, Deborah Mary
Flowers, William Ellwood
Friedman, Harvey

Frisch, Robert Emile
Fuller, Robert L(eander)
Gaetanos, Christ
Gamboni, Ciro Anthony
Ganzi, Victor Frederick
Gardner, Arnold Burton
Garfunkel, Alan J.
Gelberg, Frederick
Geoghegan, Patricia
Gillespie, David Arthur
Goldberg, Paul Joseph
Gorin, Robert Seymour
Greenberg, Ronald David
Gunn, Alan
Haims, Bruce David
Halliday, Lana
Handler, Harold Robert
Heitner, Kenneth Howard
Hellawell, Robert
Henderson, Donald Bernard, Jr.
Henderson, Gordon Desmond
Hirschfeld, Michael
Hope, Theodore Sherwood, Jr.
Hunziker, Frederick John, Jr.
Irwin, Richard Frank
Jain, Lalit K.
Jassy, Everett Lewis
Johnstone, Jeffrey Marwill
Kagan, Robert Alexander
Kail, Kenneth Stoner
Kalish, Arthur
Karls, John Spencer
Kimball, Jesse Dudley Baldwin
Koch, Edward Richard
Koff, Howard Michael
Koffey, Richard Stephan
Kroll, Arthur Herbert
Land, Stephen Britton
Lawton, James Patrick
Levitan, James A.
Levy, Mark Allan
Lewis, James Berton
Lipsky, Burton G.
Lisch, Howard
Loffman, Leslie Howard
Lore, Martin Maxwell
Lundy, Daniel Francis
Macchia, Vincent Michael
Mack, Dennis Wayne
MacLean, Babcock
Mandel, Newton W.
McCormick, Hugh Thomas
Meyer, Irwin Stephan
Miller, Elliot I.
Montgomerie, Bruce Mitchell
Moore, Thomas R.
Morgen, Richard Burton
Murtagh, James P.
Nelson, Bernard Edward
Newman, Scott David
Nicholls, Richard H.
O'Brien, Kevin J.
Odell, Stuart Irwin
Oleske, Michael Matthew
O'Neill, Patrick Joseph
Osborn, Donald Robert
Osgood, Russell King
Pollio, Benedict James
Poretsky, Joel A.
Preiskel, Robert Howard
Presant, Sanford Calvin
Prounis, Theodore Othon
Rado, Peter Thomas
Rappaport, Charles Owen
Richardson, John Carroll
Roberts, Sidney I.
Rooney, Paul C., Jr.
Rose, Elihu Isaac
Rosenbaum, Martin Michael
Rosow, Stuart L.
Rothenberg, Peter Jay
Rothman, Howard Joel
Rover, Edward Frank
Rubenfeld, Stanley Irwin
Saviano, Edward Steven
Schapiro, Ruth Goldman
Sheehan, Kenneth Edward
Shorter, James Russell, Jr.
Shoss, Cynthia Renee
Siegel, Stanley
Silvers, Eileen S.
Small, Jonathan Andrew
Steiner, Bruce Darrell
Story, John Harold
Strizever, William J(ay)
Sussman, Daniel Leonard
Tengi, Frank R.
Ullman, Leo Solomon
Vogel, Howard Stanley
Warren, William Clements
Wein, Bruce J.
White, Cheryl Denney
Whoriskey, Robert Donald
Winger, Ralph O.
Wittenstein, Arthur
Zack, David
Zuckerman, Paul Herbert
Zychick, Joel David

North Carolina

Alala, Joseph Basil, Jr.
Alexander, H. Heath
Bost, Deborah Jacobs
Branan, Carolyn Benner
Etheridge, Donald McGee, Jr.
Gann, Pamela Brooks
Gunter, Michael Donwell
Johnston, David Graham
Kersh, John Danzey, Jr.
McGirt, Sherri Lynn
Osborn, Malcolm Everett
Schmalbeck, Richard Louis
Schwab, Carol Ann
Simpson, Steven Drexell

North Dakota

Larson, Mark Vincent

Ohio

Aley, Charles R.
Alfred, Stephen Jay
Anthony, Thomas Dale
Chatroo, Arthur Jay
Cornell, John Robert
Dye, Sherman
Frutkin, Harvey Lee

Geer, Thomas Lee
Geneva, Louis Brion
Giles, Homer Wayne
Goulder, Diane Kessler
Harden, Gary Martin
Hobson, Henry Wise, Jr.
Hogan, Robert B.
Hughes, Kenneth Russell
Kerester, Charles John
Kern, Keith William
Kidder, Fred Dockstater
Kline, James Edward
LaValley, Richard Gerard
Levin, Debbe Ann
Liegl, Joseph Leslie
Lobenhofer, Louis Fred
McCormick, Shawn Charles
Meek, Leslie Applegate
Menke, William Charles
Nechemias, Stephen Murray
Perris, Terrence George
Porter, Robert Carl, Jr.
Ptaszek, Edward Gerald, Jr.
Sager, Sheldon Morris
Schiraldi, Richard John
Stark, Michael Lee
Stevenson, Donald W.
Walk, Steven Marc
Wanner, Kathleen Ann
Wasserman, David S.
Wietmarschen, Donald Alan
Wilson, Robert M.
Zerner, Richard Egon

Oklahoma

Burget, Mark Edward
Casey, Patrick Jon
Chapman, Russell Dale
Cogdell, Joe Bennett, Jr.
Eagleton, Edward John
Ford, Michael Raye
Forman, Jonathan Barry
Henshaw, Sigrid Marguerite
Plater, Frederick Oliver
Shannonhouse, Joseph Granberry, IV
Stewart, Murray Baker

Oregon

Alberty, Steven Charles
Bogdanski, John Andrew, III
Boly, Jeffrey Elwyn
Burt, Robert Gene
Chevis, Cheryl Ann
Cyr, Steven Miles
Glasgow, William Jacob
Greenwood, Clarence Henry
Hanna, Joseph John, Jr.
Kuntz, Joel Dubois
Nicholes, Steven Atwater
Redden, Michael Aloysius
Stuart, Michael George
Zalutsky, Morton Herman

Pennsylvania

Abraham, James Esber
Bambrick, Joseph Thomas, Jr.
Bildersee, Robert Alan
Blum, Jeffrey Stuart
Boocock, Stephen William
Bowen, Thomas Allan
Brier, Bonnie Susan
Brown, Lawrence Raymond, Jr.
Burke, Linda Beerbower
Cancelli, Dante Antonio
Cherewka, Michael
Clauss, Peter Otto
Cross, Milton H.
DeLaurentis, Michael John
Dell, Ernest Robert
Ellenbogen Handelsman, Joan
Elliott, Homer Lee
Flannery, Harry Audley
Freedman, Barbara Widman
Geeseman, Robert George
Goldman, Jerry Stephen
Gutman, Harry Largman
Hartman, Gregory Calvin
Kelvin, Jeffrey Barnett
Ketter, David Lee
Knapp, George Robert
Krasney, Reginald Alan
Kutz, Robert H.
Louis, Robert Henry
Mansori, Zubair S.
Mardinly, Peter Alan
McNitt, David Garver
Nauman, Spencer Gilbert, Jr.
Nemeth, Charles Paul
Newman, John Andrew
Noel, Simon
Odell, Herbert
Phillips, Larry Edward
Pilling, Janet Kavanaugh
Prosperi, Louis Anthony
Rosoff, William A.
Tammany, Donald Timothy
Thomas, Lowell Shumway, Jr.
Tumola, Thomas Joseph
Wecht, Alan Charles
Whitman, Jules I.
Woosnam, Richard Edward

Rhode Island

Cotter, William Henry, III
Davis, Andrew Hambley, Jr.
Dowling, Sarah T.
Lincoln, Michael David
Olsen, Hans Peter
Salter, Lester Herbert

South Carolina

Dobson, Robert Albertus, III
Gilchrist, Dennis Clinton
Handel, Richard Craig
Horne, Terrell Thomas
Hutton, Susan Pawlias
Rose, William Shepard, Jr.
Winston, Jacqueline Berrier
Wyche, Cyril Thomas

Tennessee

Berry, William Wells
Bland, James Theodore Jr.
Cook, August Joseph
Grubb, Kitty Goldsmith

Leckrone, James David
Little, Hampton Stennis, Jr.
Skefos, Harry J(erry)

Texas

Alford, Margaret Suzanne
Allender, John Roland
Attermeier, Fredric Joseph
Barnhill, Robert Edwin, III
Batson, David Warren
Berry, Buford Preston
Blackshear, A.T., Jr.
Blair, William Henry
Bumpas, Stuart Maryman
Bush, Edward Philip
Cashion, Shelley Jean
Collie, Marvin Key
Copley, Edward Alvin
Covington, Earl Gene
Cowling, David Edward
Davis, Clarence Clinton, Jr.
Eggleston, Robert Dale
Emery, Herschell Gene
Estes, Carl L., II
Freling, Richard Alan
Futterer, Edward Philip
Gardner, Bruce Elwyn
Geffen, Arthur Harold
Goodman, John Peter
Guest, Floyd Emory, Jr.
Guzzetti, William Louis
Hedrick, John Richard
Henkel, Kathryn G.
Jeffers, Ronald Thomas
Jewell, George Hiram
Jones, Lawrence Ray, Jr.
Kendrick, Herbert Spencer, Jr.
Larson, Mark Edward, Jr.
Lawson, Gary B.
Ledlie, Douglas Edward
Lofgren, Norman Arthur
Looper, Donald Ray
Marinis, Thomas Paul, Jr.
Mark, Richard Steve
Mitchell, Joe Day
Morgan, Timi Sue
Murray, Frederick Franklin
Overton, Shana L.
Page, Jack Randall
Parker, Emily Ann
Peck, David Hill
Rhem, John Fitzhugh, Jr.
Ross, James Ulric
Salch, Steven Charles
Seymour-Harris, Barbara Laverne
Sinak, David Louis
Smith, David Oliver
Smith, Frank Tupper
Spooner, Arthur Elmon, Jr.
Stone, Michael K.
Stukenberg, Michael Wesley
Suhre, Karen Kay
Tiller, Edward Allan
Tracy, J. David
Tuttle, Franlin L., Jr.
Vetter, James George, Jr.
Wagner, Jon Mark
Wallace, Anderson, Jr.
Watson, Robert Allan
Wells, Peter Boyd
Williams, Johnny Jackson
Wilson, Claude Raymond, Jr.
Zahn, Donald Jack

Utah

Babcock, Bruce Edward
Howard, Mark Hale
Lauritzen, David Kay

Vermont

Errecart, Joyce Hier

Virginia

Babirak, Milton Edward, Jr.
Bates, Harold Martin
Bishop, Alfred Chilton, Jr.
Bowling, David Joseph
Clark, Lynne Nuber
Facer, Eric Fouts
Fashbaugh, Howard Dilts, Jr.
Frantz, Thomas Richard
Freed, Robert Leslie
Goode, David Ronald
Hahn, Michael James
Hambrick, Jackson Reid
Hoffman, David Gary
James, Gus John, II
Klewans, Samuel N.
Macrae, Howard Taft, Jr.
McCauley, Cleyburn Lycurgus
McNider, James Small, III
Mezzullo, Louis Albert
Morrison, James Lawrence
Paturis, E(mmanuel) Michael
Philipps, Joseph Timothy
Rightnour, Donald
Sarosdy, Jane Graffeo
Schwartzstein, Linda Ann
Serumgard, John R.
Shimer, Charles Purinton
Spainhour, Tremaine Howard
Tansill, Frederick Joseph
Ward, Joe Henry, Jr.
Wright, Blandin James

Washington

Barline, John
Edwards, Bruce Neil
Evered, Donna R.
Gates, Kenneth W.
Giles, Robert Edward, Jr.
Kovacevich, Robert Eugene
Krueger, James A.
Malone, Thomas William
Marten, Judd Robert
Medved, Robert Allen
Megaard, Susan Lynne
Munson, Mark Parr
O'Donnell, John James
Parsons, James Bowne
Saracino, Samuel Francis
Spadoni, Peter Anthony

West Virginia

Rife, O(scar) Jennings

Wisconsin
Abbott, William Anthony
Berman, Ronald Charles
Boucher, Joseph William
Case, Karen Ann
Connolly, Gerald Edward
Franzoi, Joseph Frank, IV
Laikin, George Joseph
Meldman, Robert Edward
Minahan, Roger Copp
Peters, James Henry
Schroeder, Stuart R.
Shiely, John Stephen
Trebon, Lawrence Alan
Wojahn, Dennis Gilbert

TERRITORIES OF THE UNITED STATES

Puerto Rico
Rodriguez-Diaz, Juan E.

CANADA

Quebec
Vineberg, Philip Fischel

ADDRESS UNPUBLISHED
Armstrong, Robert Elmer
Bishins, Larry V.
Cohen, Robert Yale, II
Coplin, Mark David
Cox, James Darrell
Crawford, R(obert) George
Cunningham, Alice Welt
Daleiden, Norbert Alfred
Derrick, William Alfred, Jr.
Edwards, Vern Downing
Fried, Samuel
Friedman, Lawrence Andrew
Harnack, Don Steger
Hartwell, Christopher Lynn
Hays, Samuel Spartan
Heath, Charles Dickinson
Helprin, Lisa Kennedy
Howe, Drayton Ford, Jr.
Jackson, Louise Anne
Kennedy, Nolan Malcom
Lerner, Deborah Mae
Lobl, Herbert Max
Marks, Leon
Palmer, Ann Therese Darin
Pistillo, Bernadino Joseph, Jr.
Sabounghi, Joseph M.
Shughart, Donald Louis
Sklar, Steven J.
Stetler, Nevin
Stoyanoff, David Joseph
Tolins, Roger Alan
Worley, L. Glenn

TAXATION, ESTATE. *See also* **Estate planning; Probate.**

UNITED STATES

Alabama
Blackburn, John Gilmer
Booker, R. Michael
Garth, Thomas Fearn
Mathews, Melinda McEachern
Poole, William Stitt, Jr.
Schiff, Gary Steven
Smith, John Joseph, Jr.

Alaska
Davis, Trigg Thomas
Lowe, Robert Charles

Arizona
Cohn, Jeffrey Brooks
DeBerry, Dennis Charles
Isaak, Gotthilf Eugene
Simonson, Michael
Swartz, Melvin Jay

Arkansas
Eichenbaum, E. Charles
Warner, Cecil Randolph, Jr.

California
Alvarez, Edna R. S.
Arkin, Michael Barry
Blumenfeld, Eli
Brown, Lorne James
Calleton, Theodore Edward
Chatzky, Michael Gary
Cohan, John Robert
Coombs, William Elmer
Darling, Scott Edward
Derber, Robert Raymond
Duncan, John Alexander
Faust, Leland Howard
Glines, Jack Holloway
Greenberg, Myron Silver
Gutierrez, Max, Jr.
Halstead, Harry Moore
Hart, Lynn Patricia
Hawkins, Richard Michael
Hunter, William Carlton
Kearn, Orene Levenson
Knecht, James Herbert
Landay, Andrew Herbert
Levin, Marvin Eugene
London, Barry Joseph
Merrill, Byron Robert
Merritt, Valerie Jorgensen
Michel, Trudi Louise
Miller, Michael Patiky
Mitchell, Michael Charles
Payne, Margaret Anne
Rae, Matthew Sanderson, Jr.
Rand, Richard Malcolm
Rosky, Burton Seymour
Ross, Bruce Shields
Sherr, Morris Max
Shimoff, Paul Martin
Stark, Franklin Culver
Steinberg, Elliot Gershom

Stephens, George Edward, Jr.
Stinehart, William, Jr.
Thatcher, Dickinson
Thomas, Howard Berkeley
Trover, Ellen Lloyd
Voegelin, Harold Stanley
Wade, Milam Lee Roy
Weagant, Lance Maxwell
ZoBell, Karl

Colorado
Brant, John Getty
Buchanan, James William, III
Fevurly, Keith Robert
Flanders, Laurence Burdette, Jr.
Gehres, James
Keely, George Clayton
King, Dennis William
Pottick, Frances Jean
Thompson, Stephen Michael

Connecticut
Ayres, Steven Edward
Bell, Mary-Katherine
Calabresi, Guido
Fisher, Everett
Gregory, Julian Arthur, Jr.
Grodd, Leslie Eric
Sheiman, Ronald Lee
Weinshank, Arthur Charles

Delaware
Grossman, Jerome Kent
Hyman, Jerry Allan
Shearin, Kathryn Kay

District of Columbia
Bassett, Joel Eric
Birnkrant, Henry Joseph
Blazek, Doris Defibaugh
Brown, Hank
Bucholtz, Harold Ronald
Chabot, Herbert L.
Cohen, Sheldon Stanley
Condrell, William Kenneth
Determan, Sara-Ann
Gerber, Joel
Griswold, Erwin Nathaniel
Harris, Don Victor, Jr.
Hoopes, Terence James
Jenner, Gregory Franklin
Kahn, Edwin Leonard
Kellison, James Bruce
Kurtz, Jerome
Merthan, Lawrence Casper
Morris, William
Nolan, John Stephan
Norris, Robert Wheeler
Parr, Carolyn Miller
Pate, Joan Seitz
Quiggle, James Williams
Reiner, Samuel Theodore
Sampson, Michael Paul
Shields, Perry
Silverstein, Leonard Lewis
Simpson, Charles Reagan
Warden, Robert Allison
Wolf, Mark Charles

Florida
Barnard, George Smith
Berlin, Mark A.
Braddock, Donald Layton
Braden, Dana Danielle
Burton, Clayton B., Sr.
Chambliss, Linda Christine
Chopin, L. Frank
Cron, Jennifer Lynne
Dando, David Frederick
Ellwanger, Thomas John
Emmanuel, Michel George
Gardner, Russell Menese
Gescheidt, Richard Anthony
Hagendorf, Stanley
Hull, David John
Kahn Levenberg, Corinne Beth
Koren, Edward Franz
Krause, Andrew James
Maxwell, Richards DeNyse, Jr.
Patterson, George Anthony
Price, Pamela Odell
Schorner, James Alan
Warwick, Charles Henry, III
Whitesman, Guy Edward
Wilson, George Allen
Wood, William McBrayer

Georgia
Bell, Mildred Bailey
Bloodworth, A(lbert) W(illiam) Franklin
Candler, John Slaughter, II
Cheney, Huddie Lee, III
Edee, James Philip
Ellis, Edward Prioleau
Moorhead, William David, III
Nickerson, Mark William
Wright, Harry Ralph, Jr.

Hawaii
Epstein, Roger Harris
Goo, Colin Kim Keong
Hastings, Robert William, II
Lee, James Hon Quon
Miyasaki, Shuichi

Idaho
Baker, Susan Elaine Neher

Illinois
Baker, Keith Brian
Beal, Bruce Curtis
Cagney, Joseph Bert
Carr, Walter Stanley
Chiles, Stephen Michael
Cross, Chester Joseph
Dees, Richard Lee
Elliott, Ivan A., Jr.
Flack, Charles Haynes
Friedman, Roselyn L.
Gibson, James Thomas, Jr.
Gingiss, Randall Jon
Gold, George Myron
Graver, Nancy J.

Hartzell, Franklin MacVeagh
Heisler, Quentin George, Jr.
Herting, Claireen LaVern
Juhl, Loren Earl
Kanter, Burton Wallace
Kennedy, John Foran
Kirkpatrick, John Everett
Levun, Charles R(alph)
Mamer, Stuart Mies
Marshall, John David
McDonough, John Michael
Minnick, Craig Alan
Nitikman, Franklin W.
Nortell, Bruce
O'Flaherty, Paul Benedict
Rooks, John Newton
Schaffer, George John
Schneider, Daniel Max
Schreiber, Ronald
Shayne, David
Sprowl, Charles Riggs
Strasburger, Joseph Julius
Swaney, Thomas Edward
Szewczyk, Stephen Michael
Thomas, James Gladwyn
Tracy, William Francis, II
Trost, Eileen Bannon
Uchtmann, Donald Louis
Whitlock, Brian Thomas
Witt, Alan Michael

Indiana
Adams, Robert Wendell
Draper, Monette Elaine
Jegen, Lawrence A., III
Johnson, G. Weldon
Keber, Kenneth James
Lowell, Cym Hawksworth
Manterfield, Eric Alan
Patrick, William Bradshaw
Ponder, Lester McConnico
Schemahorn, Clyde E.
Young, Barbara Ann

Iowa
Bowman, Michael Allen
Campbell, Bruce Irving
Gray, William Oxley
Harl, Neil Eugene
Poffenberger, Richard Lee
Smith, Kim LeRoy
Stark, Maurice Edmund

Kansas
Brewer, Dana
Buechel, William Benjamin
Horttor, Donald J.
Mikkelsen, Charles R.
Peckham, Charles Allen
Smith, Glee Sidney, Jr.
Springer, Byron Eugene
Stallard, Wayne Minor
Toland, Clyde William

Kentucky
Bagby, William Rardin
Decker, Jennifer Henson
Irtz, Frederick G., II
Jackson, James Ronald
Logan, James Ashlin
Noe, Randolph
Prather, John Gideon
Romaine, Douglas Patteson
Ryan, Donald Kevin
Schneider, Frederick Richard
Voyles, James Robert
Williamson, Charles Gurley, Jr.

Louisiana
Bayard, Alton Ernest, III
Benjamin, Edward Bernard, Jr.
Blackman, John Calhoun, IV
Ellett, John Spears, II
Hurley, Paul Edward
King, C. A., II
Tarcza, Robert Emmet
Wedig, Harold Harvey

Maine
Curran, Richard Emery, Jr.
Dench, Bryan Mundy
LeBlanc, Richard Philip
Sang, Peter Bennett

Maryland
Carmel, Alan Stuart
De Jong, David Samuel
Morris, David Michael
Robbins, Vernon Earl
Snyder, William Arthur, Jr.
Stone, James Dorsey

Massachusetts
Ames, James Barr
Bergen, Kenneth William
Cutler, Arnold R.
Gabovitch, Steven Alan
Hartigan, Michael David
Lappin, Robert Sidney
Li, Winifred I.
Long, Christopher Francis
O'Connell, Charles Francis
Pabian, Jay Michael
Pratt, Harold Irving
Puzo, Michael John
Repetti, Susan Leonard
Richer, Alan Brian
Riley, Michael Hylan
Roche, John Jefferson
Silver, Marvin S.
Spencer, Patti S.
Sullivan, Charles William
Walker, Paul Howard
Warren, Alvin Clifford, Jr.

Michigan
Brown, (Robert) Wendell
Clink, Stephen Henry
Dew, Thomas Edward
Dufendach, Carl William
Gornick, Alan Lewis
Irish, Michael William
Joslyn, Robert Bruce

Kahn, Douglas Allen
Kinney, Gregory Hoppes
Kirk, John MacGregor
Olson, M(elvin) Richard
Pierce, Robert Barth
Riecker, John E(rnest)
Tobin, Bruce Howard
Waggoner, Lawrence William

Minnesota
Brand, Steve Aaron
Johnson, Joseph Bernard
Mennell, Robert L.
Mooty, David Nelson
Reister, Raymond Alex

Mississippi
Dossett, James Kearney, Jr.
Fountain, Richard Maurice
Jones, Barry Kent
Ludlam, Warren VanGilder, Jr.
Travis, Jay A., III

Missouri
Crawford, Howard Allen
Dickhaner, Raymond Henry
Greenley, Beverly Jane
Katzenstein, Lawrence P.
Kincaid, Arthur Roy
Lowenhaupt, Charles Abraham
McClannahan, Cindy Ann
McKee, Barnet M.
Reaves, Craig Charles
Redd, Charles Appleton
Willis, Russell Anthony, III
Woods, Richard Dale

Montana
Dostal, John Anthony
Moog, Mary Ann Pimley

Nebraska
Borghoff, John Joseph
DeRoin, Jan Elizabeth
Greene, Richard Francis
Schneider, Gary Bruce

Nevada
Morris, Trude McMahan
Sully, William Leslie, Jr.
Williams, David Roy

New Hampshire
DeHart, Barbara Boudreau
Morse, Richard Allen

New Jersey
Ascione, Joseph Anthony
Bearg, Martin Lee
Borteck, Robert D.
Cuttler, H. Karen
DeMaio, Andrew John
Dougherty, Maureen Patricia
Flaster, Richard Joel
French, Bruce Hartung
Gavin, Louis Brooks
Greco, Joseph Dominic, Jr.
Israels, Michael Jozef
Lihotz, Marie Elaine
Marshall, Anthony Parr
Massler, Howard Arnold
Pesin, Edward
Pfaltz, Hugo Menzel, Jr.
Slutsky, Kenneth Joel
Soderman, Kenneth John
Vandervoort, Peter

New Mexico
Anderson, Charles Edward

New York
Ashton, Robert
Atkins, Ronald Raymond
Backus, Bradley
Baldwin, Robert Frederick, Jr.
Barbeosch, William Peter
Becker, John Ernest, Jr.
Bennett, James Davison
Berger, Curtis Jay
Bloom, Robert Thomas
Booth, Mitchell B.
Boulanger, Carol Seabrook
Bozorth, Squire Newland
Brush, Louis Frederick
Bucci, Earl Michael
Bush, Julian S.
Cardozo, Benjamin Mordecai
Carruba, Salvatore John
Christensen, Henry, III
Clark, Carolyn Cochran
Daly, Michael Francis
Dolan, James Francis
Duetsch, John Edwin
Dutcher, B(enjamin) Andrew
Einstein, Steven Henry
Eisenberg, Ronald Alan
Engel, Ralph Manuel
Evans, David Lee
Evans, Douglas Hayward
Feder, Arthur A.
Ferguson, Milton Carr, Jr.
Flood, Kevin Patrick
Gelb, Judith Anne
Gelberg, Frederick
Goldberg, Paul Joseph
Graham, Arnold Harold
Greene, Bernard Harold
Guttlein, Jorge de Jesus
Harrington, Charles Frederick
Hawkins, Eliot Dexter
Hendrickson, Robert Augustus
Herzog, Jacob Hawley
Hessberg, Albert, II
Hesterberg, Gregory Xavier
Hochberg, Ronald Mark
Hull, Philip Glasgow
Hurley, James G.
Ingraham, Frederic Beach
Jacoby, James Joseph
Jadd, Robert Ira
Katsoris, Constantine Nicholas
Klipstein, Robert Alan
Koff, Howard Michael

Kramer, William Joseph
Kurzman, Robert Graham
Laux, Russell Frederick
Levitan, David M(aurice)
Levitan, James A.
Lewis, James Berton
Lingelbach, Albert Lane
Lipsky, Burton G.
Lore, Martin Maxwell
Lustgarten, Ira Howard
Macchia, Vincent Michael
Manning, Jerome Alan
Mariani, Michael Matthew
McGrath, Thomas J.
Meyer, Irwin Stephan
Morgen, Richard Burton
Neuwirth, Gloria S.
Newman, Scott David
Nyland, W(illiam) Donald
O'Connor, Liam T(homas)
O'Connor, Michael E.
Peckham, Eugene Eliot
Prye, Steven Marvell
Ralli, Constantine Pandia
Rheinstein, Thomas Philipp
Robinson, Barbara Paul
Roman, David John
Rosenbaum, Martin Michael
Rover, Edward Frank
Schapiro, Ruth Goldman
Schlesinger, Edward Samuel
Sederbaum, Arthur David
Setterberg, Patricia Ann
Severs, Charles A., III
Sills, Nancy Mintz
Solberg, Thomas Allan
Sweeney, Deidre Ann
Thompson, Lawrence Bigelow
Tweedy, William Elwyn
Ufford, Charles Wilbur, Jr.
Wadsworth, James Marshall
Waldorf, Geraldine Polack
Wels, Richard Hoffman
Wilkie, Robert Arthur
Witkin, Susan Peckett
Zabel, William David
Zack, David
Zankel, Jeffrey Alan
Zuckerman, Paul Herbert

North Carolina
Branan, Carolyn Benner
Etheridge, Donald McGee, Jr.
Johnston, David Graham
Orsbon, Richard Anthony
Schwab, Carol Ann
Simpson, Steven Drexell
Smith, Stephen Jerome
Vaughn, Robert Candler, Jr.
Weick, Paul Alfred, II

North Dakota
Larson, Mark Vincent
Wilkes, Richard Clarence

Ohio
Bank, Malvin E.
Brucken, Robert Matthew
Driggs, Charles Mulford
Gariepy, Stephen Henry
Gray, Meryl Benjamin
Greene, Ralph Vernon
Hartsel, Norman Clyde
Healy, Mary Jacqueline
Hobson, Henry Wise, Jr.
Hughes, Kenneth Russell
Johnson, Keith Karleton
Levin, Debbe Ann
Martin, Oscar Thaddeus
Mawer, William Thomas
Nelson, Robert Bruce
Pillari, Thomas
Schiraldi, Richard John
Shapiro, Fred David
Shelley, John Fletcher
Shumaker, Roger Lee
Walk, Steven Marc
Wilson, Robert M.
Yager, John Warren
Zisser, Steven Lawrence

Oklahoma
Blair, Clifford Jennings, II
Cogdell, Joe Bennett, Jr.
Henshaw, Sigrid Marguerite
Kells, Richard B.

Oregon
Bass, Shirley Ann
Cyr, Steven Miles
Greenwood, Clarence Henry
Hanna, Joseph John, Jr.
Kantor, Stephen Edward
Nicholes, Steven Atwater
Stuart, Michael George
Zalutsky, Morton Herman

Pennsylvania
Armstrong, Jack Gilliland
Bookman, Mark
Cancelmo, William Weinert
Ellenbogen Handelsman, Joan
Emerson, S. Jonathan
Gutman, Harry Largman
Hartman, Gregory Calvin
Herchenroether, Henry Carl, Jr.
Jones, Edward White, II
Kaufman, David J.
Kelvin, Jeffrey Barnett
Ketter, David Lee
Kirby, Jack Arthur
Kreder, Joseph Casimir
Lally-Green, Maureen Ellen
Ledebur, Linas Vockroth, Jr.
Lentz, Edward James
Lucey, John David, Jr.
Messina, Joseph F., Jr.
Minno, Frances Patricia Fraher
Odell, Herbert
Pilling, Janet Kavanaugh
Plotnick, Charles Keith
Rabinowitz, Samuel Nathan
Ross, Eunice Latshaw
Straus, Joseph Pennington
Temple, L. Peter

Weisz, Frank Barry
Wiener, Howard Alan
Wood, William Philler
Yohlin, Joseph Michael

Rhode Island

Salter, Lester Herbert
Worrell, Lee Anthony

South Carolina

Dobson, Robert Albertus, III
Horne, Terrell Thomas
Jordan, Michael Lee McAdams
Massey, Raymond David
Todd, Albert Creswell, III
Traxler, William Byrd

South Dakota

Kolker, Richard Lee

Tennessee

Bland, James Theodore Jr.
Cook, August Joseph
Galvin, Charles O'Neill
Holbrook, Dan W.
Jordan, James D(ee)
Lawler, Edward James
Little, Hampton Stennis, Jr.
Wilkinson, Robert Warren

Texas

Berry, Thomas Eugene
Blanchette, James Grady, Jr.
Boone, Taylor Scott
Christianson, James Milton
Collie, Marvin Key
Copley, Edward Alvin
Covington, Earl Gene
Dougherty, John Chrysostom, III
Eastland, S. Stacy
Edmonds, Thomas Leon
Emery, Herschell Gene
Eubank, J. Thomas
French, Colin Val
Gardner, Bruce Elwyn
Goldberg, William Jeffrey
Ice, Noel Carlysle
Jansen, Donald Orville
Johanson, Stanley Morris
Joynton, Stanley Forrest
Kendrick, Herbert Spencer, Jr.
Koenig, Rodney Curtis
Martin, Paul E(dward)
Milner, Christy Elizabeth
Moncure, John Lewis
Morrison, Walton Stephen
O'Brien, Claudine Michele Niedzielski
Owens, Rodney Joe
Ritchie, Robert Field
Smith, Edward Vance, III
Smith, Frank Tupper
Stukenberg, Michael Wesley
Turner, Bruce Edward
Vetter, James George, Jr.
Wagner, Jon Mark
Wallace, Anderson, Jr.
Ward, Gary Ardus
Watson, Robert Allan
Wharton, Thomas H(eard), Jr.
Wilkes, John Michael
Wilson, Claude Raymond, Jr.
Wilson, Donald L.
Wright, Wallace Mathias

Utah

Howard, Mark Hale
Jeppson, Joseph Gaddis

Vermont

Errecart, Joyce Hier
Sincerbeaux, Robert Abbott

Virginia

Acker, Alan Scott
Belcher, Dennis Irl
Cooper, Charles Neilson
Frantz, Thomas Richard
Hambrick, Jackson Reid
Horsley, Waller Holladay
Parks, Kenneth F.
Paturis, E(mmanuel) Michael
Shimer, Charles Purinton
Spainhour, Tremaine Howard
Woodward, Roland Carey

Washington

Edwards, Bruce Neil
Marten, Judd Robert
McInnis, Emmett Emory, Jr.
O'Donnell, John James
Ruen, Lowell Vernon
Wright, Willard Jurey

West Virginia

Rife, O(scar) Jennings

Wisconsin

Demet, Donal Moffatt
Franzoi, Joseph Frank, IV
Herbers, John A.
Kabaker, Richard Zohn
Meldman, Robert Edward
Muchin, Arden Archie
Tollers, Jeffery Barnet
Wojahn, Dennis Gilbert

Wyoming

Dray, William Perry

ADDRESS UNPUBLISHED

Bergman, Arlie Walter
Bishins, Larry V.
Cohen, Robert Yale, II
Cox, James Darrell
Eisen, Edwin Roy
Fink, Monroe
Gamble, E. James
Gorochow, Vera Zina
James, Joyce Marie
Leeds, Mindy Robin
Lerner, Deborah Mae
Sabounghi, Joseph M.
Stubbs, William Perry, Jr.
Surratt, John Richard

TAXATION, PERSONAL INCOME

UNITED STATES

Alabama

Alexander, Melton Lee
Fox, John Charles
Garth, Thomas Fearn
Lucas, Patrick Hewell
Poole, William Stitt, Jr.
Proctor, David Ray
Ritchey, Joseph Thomas
Smith, Hardy Bolton
Webster, Bruce Charles

Alaska

Offret, Ronald (Alvin)

Arizona

Ascher, Mark Louis
Cohn, Jeffrey Brooks
Daum, Bryan Edwin
DeBerry, Dennis Charles
Derdenger, Patrick
Phillips, Steven William
Pingree, Bruce Douglas
Simonson, Michael
Spitzer, Marc Lee
Youney, John William

California

Appel, Martin Sherman
Arkin, Michael Barry
Barton, Babette B.
Blaustein, Frances Jan
Boatwright, David Croft
Bost, Thomas Glen
Brookes, Valentine
Carrey, Neil
Chatzky, Michael Gary
Claremon, Glenda Ruth
Cohan, John Robert
Crawford, Roy Edgington
Doti, Frank John
Faust, Leland Howard
Foster, David Scott
Gill, Keith Hubert
Gleim, Michael Alan
Gordon, David Eliot
Greenberg, Myron Silver
Greene, Richard Lawrence
Harris, Michael Gene
Hawkins, Richard Michael
Heng, Donald James, Jr.
Hogan, Claude Hollis
Howell, Weldon Ulric, Jr.
Israel, Perry Elemore
Lipton, Alvin E(lliot)
Livsey, Robert Callister
London, Barry Joseph
Maeder, Gary William
Maier, Thomas Andrew
Mandel, Martin Louis
McNulty, John Kent
Michel, Trudi Louise
Miller, Michael Patiky
Newacheck, David John
Orth, Beverly Jean
Palazzo, Robert P.
Richman, Frederick Alexander
Riley, Kirk Holden
Rosenstein, Robert Bryce
Schumacher, Stephen Joseph
Sheppard, Thomas Richard
Sherr, Morris Max
Shimoff, Paul Martin
Sikora, Warren
Sires, Bruce David
Stegall, Daniel Richard
Steinberg, Elliot Gershom
Stewart, Helen Margery
Thomas, Howard Berkeley
Thomas, William Scott
Trompeta, Jesus Iglesias
Tutoli, Michele Ann
Vallens, Brent Edward
Van Atta, David Murray
Wade, Milam Lee Roy
Waks, Stephen Harvey
Wood, Robert Warren

Colorado

Earnhart, Mark Warren
Gehres, James
Greenberg, Morton Paul
Gunn, Rebecca Louise
Guyton, Samuel Percy
Hodson, Thane Raymond
Keatinge, Robert Reed
Pottick, Frances Jean
Ruppert, John Lawrence
Schumacher, Barry Lee
Stauffer, Scott William
Waggoner, Michael James

Connecticut

Abery-Wetstone, Holly Ann
Cooper, George
Dowling, Victor James
Grodd, Leslie Eric
Lyon, James Burroughs
Perlman, Bruce Michael
Phelps, Robert Frederick, Jr.
Schiff, Alan Lewis
Sheiman, Ronald Lee
Simonelli, Jerry
Weinshank, Arthur Charles

Delaware

Grossman, Jerome Kent
Hyman, Jerry Allan
Nachmias, Carolyn Sharenow
Olson, Mark Douglas

District of Columbia

Aiken, Jeffrey Howard
Alexander, Donald Crichton
Barth, Roger Vincent
Bassett, Joel Eric
Birnkrant, Henry Joseph
Bradley, George Havis
Brown, Hank
Cohen, Sheldon Stanley
Dickieson, David H.
Duncan, Robert Michael
Evans, Donald Charles, Jr.
Fegan, David Coyle
Fise, Thomas Francis
Frazier, Henry Bowen, III
Gannascoli, Rudolph Lance
Gerber, Joel
Geske, Alvin Jay
Gideon, Kenneth Wayne
Harris, Don Victor, Jr.
Harris, James Alan
Hoffman, Joseph Bowytz
Hoopes, Terence James
Hopkins, Bruce Richard
Jacobson, David Edward
Jenner, Gregory Franklin
Johnson, James Walker
Kahn, Edwin Leonard
Kautter, David John
Klein, Robert Allan
Kuder, Armin Ulrich
Kurtz, Jerome
Kusma, Kyllikki
Leon, Richard John
Libin, Jerome B.
Mackles, Glenn Frederick
McNeily, Curtlan Roger
Mentz, J. Roger
Nolan, David Brian
Nolan, John Stephan
Oyler, Gregory Kenneth
Parr, Carolyn Miller
Pate, Joan Seitz
Paul, William McCann
Pierce, Kevin Michael
Quiggle, James Williams
Reiner, Samuel Theodore
Rogovin, Mitchell
Roy, James Robert
Sampson, Michael Paul
Schmidt, Dale Russell
Schram, Steven H.
Schutzer, George Jeffrey
Shields, Perry
Silverstein, Leonard Lewis
Simpkins, Mary Nell
Simpson, Charles Reagan
Spencer, Samuel
Sykes, Thomas Dale
Toth, Claire E.
Walker, Lynda Kay
Warden, Robert Allison
Worthy, K(enneth) Martin

Florida

Barnard, George Smith
Berlin, Mark A.
Bernstein, Zayle Abraham
Chopin, L. Frank
Currier, Barry Arthur
Davis, Louis Poisson, Jr.
Ellwanger, Thomas John
Friedman, Ronald Michael
Hagendorf, Stanley
Hess, George Franklin, II
Hull, David John
Kahn Levenberg, Corinne Beth
Klein, Herman Fred
Lamont, Robert Sheldon
Levitt, Preston Curtis
Margolis, John Gilbert
Matthias, Robert Charles
Ruffner, Charles Louis
Schorner, James Alan
Terry, T(aylor) Rankin, Jr.
Whitesman, Guy Edward

Georgia

Austin, Thomas Nelson
Bell, Mildred Bailey
Cheney, Huddie Lee, III
Davidson, Joseph Q., Jr.
Durrett, James Frazer, Jr.
Ellis, Edward Prioleau
Gartzman, Jeffrey Scott
Gaynes, Bruce Harvey
Gold, Ronald Theodore
Nickerson, Mark William
Parker, Wilmer, III
Quinlan, James William
Wadsworth, Joel Stuart
White, Benjamin Taylor
Wilson, Rhys Thaddeus

Hawaii

Epstein, Roger Harris
Shea, Michael Alan

Idaho

Bickel, Dwight Franklin

Illinois

Baffes, Thomas Gus
Baker, Keith Brian
Berning, Larry D.
Bowen, Stephen Stewart
Bower, Glen L.
Brown, Steven Spencer
Bryan, Arthur Eldridge, Jr.
Cagney, Joseph Bert
Cass, Neil Earl
Chandler, Kent, Jr.
Chanen, Franklin Allen
Colombik, Richard Michael
Crane, Charlotte
Ehrlich, Jeff Paschal
Ellwood, Scott
Ephraim, Donald Morley
Fellows, Jerry Kenneth
Fields, Howard M.
Fort, Lyman Rankin
Foster, Lloyd Bennett
Glass, Stanford Lee
Graver, Nancy J.
Kamensky, Marvin
Lane, Marc Jay
Lawless, John Martin
Lesar, Hiram Henry
Levun, Charles R(alph)
Levy, Katherine Judith
Lifschultz, Phillip
Marmet, Gottlieb John
McKenzie, Robert E.
Michalak, Edward Francis
Miller, Arthur Robert
Minnick, Craig Alan
Myers, Lonn William
Pape, Glenn Michael
Robinson, Robert George
Roddewig, Richard John
Rombs, Vincent Joseph
Schaaf, Douglas Allan
Schneider, Daniel Max
Shayne, David
Smith, Edward Jerome
Stanhaus, James Steven
Stone, Howard Lawrence
Szewczyk, Stephen Michael
Trio, Edward Alan
Whitlock, Brian Thomas
Wise, William Jerrard
Zoll, Jeffery Mark

Indiana

Germann, Douglas Dean, Sr.
Heppenheimer, Harry
Keber, Kenneth James
Mazur, Lawrence Joseph
Ponder, Lester McConnico
Schemahorn, Clyde E.
Whitehill, Charles Allen

Iowa

Berkland, Roger Alan
Campbell, Bruce Irving
Galer, Benjamin Anderson
Palmer, Bruce Alexander
Smith, Kim LeRoy
Stark, Maurice Edmund
Thorson, Larry Jonathan
Vanorsdel, Robert Alan

Kansas

Jordan, Harold Nathan
Mikkelsen, Charles R.
Peckham, Charles Allen
Stover, Kathy Ann
Walters, Amy Ottinger

Kentucky

Bagby, William Rardin
Decker, Jennifer Henson
Dunlap, Tavner Branham
Irtz, Frederick G., II
McMahon, Martin James, Jr.
Romaine, Douglas Patteson
Ryan, Donald Kevin
Vice, Robert Bruce
Yonts, Stewarts H.

Louisiana

Blackman, John Calhoun, IV
Campbell, Joseph H(oward), Jr.
Ellett, John Spears, II
Hoffman, Robert Dean, Jr.
Leonard, Paul Haralson
Peroni, Robert Joseph
Tramonte, James Albert
Trostorff, Alex P.

Maine

Cowan, Caspar Frank
Currie, Michael Robert
Sang, Peter Bennett

Maryland

Adkins, Edward James
Batoff, Steven Irving
Bowen, Debra Lynn
Conkling, Daniel Charles
De Jong, David Samuel
Freeland, Charles
Guttenberg, Aryeh
Haas, John Howard
Hanley, David Burris
Hendricks, John Charles
Hershman, Murray John
Junghans, Paula Marie
Katz, Barry Edward
Price, James Lee
Rachanow, Gerald Marvin
Robbins, Vernon Earl

Massachusetts

Ardiff, William B.
Cutler, Arnold R.
Elfman, Eric Michael
Gabovitch, Steven Alan
Haas, William Lambert
Keegan, John Robert
Niswander, Frank Clyde
Pabian, Jay Michael
Railsback, David Phillips
Repetti, Susan Leonard
Richer, Alan Brian
Sullivan, Charles William
Warren, Alvin Clifford, Jr.
Whipple, Robert Jenks
Wolfman, Bernard

Michigan

Cotner, Roger Garner
Cwirko, Claris Kaye
Ferrier, Jon Todd
Forrest, Robert Edwin
Gornick, Alan Lewis
Hirschman, Sherman Joseph
Joslyn, Robert Bruce
Kahn, Douglas Allen
Kaplow, Robert David
Laughter, Ron D.
McKendry, John H., Jr.
Nowinski, Thomas Stephen
Pelavin, Michael Allen
Pierce, Robert Barth
Rolf, Ramon Frederick, Jr.

Minnesota

Brooks, William James, III
D'Aquila, Thomas Carl
Geis, Jerome Arthur
Keate, Kenneth Earl
Klein, William David
Martin, Judith Moran
Mennell, Robert L.
Ozzello, Jan Lorraine
Vanhove, Lorri Kay

Missouri

Anderson, Christopher James
Baier, David Donald
Barrie, John Paul
Brouillette, Gary Joseph
Cupples, Stephen Elliot
Evans, William Ellis
Goldstein, Michael Gerald
Gross, Monnye R.
Jones, David Christopher
Katzenstein, Lawrence P.
Kincaid, Arthur Roy
Kohn, Michael Elliott
Lowenhaupt, Charles Abraham
Meives, Joseph Richard
Preuss, Ronald Stephen

Montana

Gilbert, Robert Bruce
Moog, Mary Ann Pimley

Nebraska

Bixby, Joseph Nathan
Brockman, Terry James
Drozda, Robert Lee
Greene, Richard Francis
Jelkin, John Lamoine
Lyons, William Harry
Slattery, David Edmund
Wegner, James Darwin

Nevada

Greene, Addison Kent
Kelesis, George Peter
Sully, William Leslie, Jr.
Williams, David Roy

New Hampshire

Budnitz, Arron Edward
DeHart, Barbara Boudreau

New Jersey

Adlerstein, Jo Anne Chernev
Bearg, Martin Lee
Davidoff, E. Martin
Fenichel, Saul Michael
Flaster, Richard Joel
Forkin, Thomas S.
Fusco, Claude Eugene, Jr.
Gorrin, Eugene
Hinshaw, David Love
Kamens, Harold
Liebman, Emmanuel
Mann, Donald J.
Marshall, Anthony Parr
Massler, Howard Arnold
Neary, Gerald Clarke
Pesin, Edward
Soderman, Kenneth John
Tobin, Irving
Wurms, Marcel Ronald
Yellin, Stanley Jay

New Mexico

Anderson, Charles Edward
Messinger, J. Henry
Westerfield, Frank Orlen, Jr.

New York

Agranoff, Gerald Neal
Amdur, Martin Bennett
Becker, John Ernest, Jr.
Black, Louis Engleman
Blanchard, Kimberly Staggers
Brearton, James Joseph
Breckenridge, James Richard
Bronstein, Richard J.
Brush, Louis Frederick
Carlson, David Bret
Christensen, Henry, III
Cohen, Bennett D.
Cranney, Marilyn Kanrek
Crowley, Richard Allerton
Daly, Michael Francis
Dougherty, Thomas Paul, Jr.
Druker, James Owen
Dutcher, B(enjamin) Andrew
Einstein, Steven Henry
English, Harry Gordon
Epstein, Hyman David
Feder, Arthur A.
Fink, Norman Stiles
Fischer, Richard Samuel
Flanagan, Deborah Mary
Friedman, Harvey
Frisch, Robert Emile
Garfunkel, Alan J.
Greenspan, Leon Joseph
Gunn, Alan
Haims, Bruce David
Handler, Harold Robert
Heffernan, Michele Olga
Heitner, Kenneth Howard
Hellawell, Robert
Henderson, Gordon Desmond
Hirschfeld, Michael
Hirsh, Leonard Steven
Jain, Lalit K.
Jassy, Everett Lewis
Johnstone, Jeffrey Marwill
Kagan, Robert Alexander
Kahn, Alan Edwin
Kail, Kenneth Stoner
Kalish, Arthur
Katsoris, Constantine Nicholas
Kimball, Jesse Dudley Baldwin
Koch, Edward Richard
Koff, Howard Michael
Landzberg, Alan Jeffrey
Levitan, James A.
Levy, Mark Allan
Lewis, James Berton
Lipsky, Burton G.
Lisch, Howard
Loffman, Leslie Howard
Lynch, Thomas Halpin
Macchia, Vincent Michael

MacLean, Babcock
Meaders, Paul Le Sourd
Meyer, Irwin Stephan
Miller, Arthur Madden
Miller, Elliot I.
Mills, Edward Warren
Newman, Scott David
Nicholls, Richard H.
O'Brien, Kevin J.
Peckham, Eugene Eliot
Poretsky, Joel A.
Presant, Sanford Calvin
Reichel, Aaron Israel
Riebesehl, E. Allan
Rinaldi, Keith Stephen
Roberts, Sidney I.
Rooney, Paul C., Jr.
Rose, Elihu Isaac
Rosenbaum, Martin Michael
Rosenberg, Jerome Roy
Rosow, Stuart L.
Rothenberg, Peter Jay
Rothman, Howard Joel
Rubenfeld, Stanley Irwin
Saviano, Edward Steven
Schapiro, Ruth Goldman
Scharf, Jared J.
Setterberg, Patricia Ann
Severs, Charles A., III
Shea, James William
Sherwood, James Cruze
Shorter, James Russell, Jr.
Shoss, Cynthia Renee
Sills, Nancy Mintz
Silverman, Elliot
Silvers, Eileen S.
Small, Jonathan Andrew
Stack, Joanne Tunney
Steiner, Bruce Darrell
Strizever, William J(ay)
Tengi, Frank R.
Twietmeyer, Don Henry
Wein, Bruce J.
Whoriskey, Robert Donald
Wilkie, Robert Arthur
Winger, Ralph O.
Witkin, Susan Peckett
Wittenstein, Arthur
Zankel, Jeffrey Alan
Zychick, Joel David

North Carolina
Beddow, John Warren
Bost, Deborah Jacobs
Branan, Carolyn Benner
Cohen, Gerry Farmer
Etheridge, Donald McGee, Jr.
Johnston, David Graham
Lloyd, Robert Blackwell, Jr.
Osborn, Malcolm Everett
Petree, William Horton
Schmalbeck, Richard Louis
Schwab, Carol Ann
Webb, W(illiam) Y(oung) Alex

North Dakota
Burgum, Bradley Joseph
Larson, Mark Vincent
Nelson, Carol Susan

Ohio
Aley, Charles R.
Bank, Malvin E.
Bender, John Timothy
Buechner, Robert William
Carroll, James Joseph
Cornell, John Robert
Dye, Sherman
Fiala, David Marcus
Hughes, Kenneth Russell
Kerester, Charles John
Leavitt, Jeffrey Stuart
Liegl, Joseph Leslie
Lynn, Arthur Dellert, Jr.
Nechemias, Stephen Murray
Nicholson, Brent Bentley
Office, James Richard
Perris, Terrence George
Ptaszek, Edward Gerald, Jr.
Sager, Sheldon Morris
Schiraldi, Richard John
Stevenson, Donald W.
Troxell, James Dane
Walk, Steven Marc
Wanner, Kathleen Ann
Weber, H. Patrick
Westphal, Marjorie Lord
Wietmarschen, Donald Alan
Wilson, Robert M.
Zisser, Steven Lawrence

Oklahoma
Casey, Patrick Jon
Forman, Jonathan Barry
Henshaw, Sigrid Marguerite
Kells, Richard B.
Plater, Frederick Oliver
Shannonhouse, Joseph Granberry, IV
Taliaferro, Bruce Owen

Oregon
Bass, Shirley Ann
Bogdanski, John Andrew, III
Boly, Jeffrey Elwyn
Burt, Robert Gene
Byczynski, Edward Frank
Greenwood, Clarence Henry
Hanna, Joseph John, Jr.
Kuntz, Joel Dubois
Moore, David Lewis
Nicholes, Steven Atwater
Redden, Michael Aloysius

Pennsylvania
Abraham, James Esber
Armstrong, Jack Gilliland
Blum, Jeffrey Stuart
Brier, Bonnie Susan
Cancelmo, William Weinert
Carroll, Donald R.
DeLaurentis, Michael John
Ehrenwerth, David Harry
Ellenbogen Handelsman, Joan
Elliott, Homer Lee
Gallagher, John Paul

Geeseman, Robert George
Gerstenhaber, Murray
Gutman, Harry Largman
Heywood, Barbara Lorentson
Johnston, Henry Richard, III
Kelley, Dennis Scott Clark
Kephart, James William
Ketter, David Lee
Koplin, Bernice Judith
Long, Christine Mathews
Messina, Joseph F., Jr.
Mirabello, Francis Joseph
Newman, John Andrew
Noel, Simon
Odell, Herbert
Phillips, Larry Edward
Prosperi, Louis Anthony
Rosoff, William A.
Tammany, Donald Timothy
Thomas, Lowell Shumway, Jr.
Wecht, Alan Charles
Whitman, Jules I.
Woosnam, Richard Edward

Rhode Island
Cotter, William Henry, III
Lincoln, Michael David
Olsen, Hans Peter
Salter, Lester Herbert
Worrell, Lee Anthony

South Carolina
Dobson, Robert Albertus, III
Handel, Richard Craig
Hutton, Susan Pawlias
Scott, Ronald Charles

South Dakota
Bennett, Donn
Gustafson, Lawrence Raymond
Kolker, Richard Lee

Tennessee
Cook, August Joseph
Green, Lynne Knight
Grubb, Kitty Goldsmith

Texas
Abercrombie, Thomas Vernon
Attermeier, Fredric Joseph
Barnhill, Robert Edwin, III
Berry, Buford Preston
Blackshear, A.T., Jr.
Blair, William Henry
Boone, Taylor Scott
Bush, Edward Philip
Cashion, Shelley Jean
Christianson, James Milton
Collie, Marvin Key
Conkel, Robert Dale
Copley, Edward Alvin
Covington, Earl Gene
Cowling, David Edward
Davis, Clarence Clinton, Jr.
Estes, Carl L., II
Eubank, J. Thomas
Fellers, Rhonda Gay
Futterer, Edward Philip
Gardner, Bruce Elwyn
Geffen, Arthur Harold
Gibson, Michael Morgan
Goldberg, William Jeffrey
Hayers, Paul Hugh
Hendricks, Randal Arlan
Jeffers, Ronald Thomas
Jewell, George Hiram
Jones, Lawrence Ray, Jr.
Joynton, Stanley Forrest
Laney, Daniel Milton
Lawson, Gary B.
Marinis, Thomas Paul, Jr.
Mark, Richard Steve
Mitchell, Joe Day
Mora, David Baudilio
Morgan, Timi Sue
O'Brien, Claudine Michele Niedzielski
Operhall, Harrie Marie Pollok
Owens, Rodney Joe
Page, Jack Randall
Peck, David Hill
Post, Earl Stock
Ross, James Ulric
Schmidt, John Aldin
Sinak, David Louis
Slugg, Ramsay Hill
Spooner, Arthur Elmon, Jr.
Stone, Michael K.
Stukenberg, Michael Wesley
Suhre, Karen Kay
Tiller, Edward Allan
Tuttle, Franlin L., Jr.
Vetter, James George, Jr.
Wagner, Jon Mark
Wallace, Anderson, Jr.
Watson, Robert Allan
Williams, Johnny Jackson
Wilson, Claude Raymond, Jr.

Utah
Anderson, Reese C.
Babcock, Bruce Edward
Chancellor, Thomas Harvey
Howard, Mark Hale
Joslin, Gary James
Walz, Stewart Chaussee

Vermont
Errecart, Joyce Hier

Virginia
Bishop, Alfred Chilton, Jr.
Calhoun, Clayne Marsh
Clark, Lynne Nuber
Connelly, Sharon Rudolph
Conway, William Augustine
Frantz, Thomas Richard
Hambrick, Jackson Reid
Hoffman, David Gary
McClure, Roger John
Murphy, Nina Rebecca
Musselman, Robert Metcalfe
Parks, Kenneth F.
Philipps, Joseph Timothy
Rightnour, Donald

Sarosdy, Jane Graffeo
Schwartzstein, Linda Ann
Ward, Joe Henry, Jr.

Washington
Birmingham, Richard Joseph
Edwards, Bruce Neil
Evered, Donna R.
Giles, Robert Edward, Jr.
Kovacevich, Robert Eugene
Mahoney, Timothy William
Megaard, Susan Lynne
Ruen, Lowell Vernon

West Virginia
Kidner, Edward Franklin
Rife, O(scar) Jennings

Wisconsin
Berman, Ronald Charles
Case, Karen Ann
Daniel, Marvin Valerius
Greenberg, Martin Jay
Herbers, John A.
Kite, Richard Lloyd
LaBudde, Roy Christian
Meldman, Robert Edward
Thuermer, Richard Joseph
Tollers, Jeffery Barnet
Wojahn, Dennis Gilbert

ADDRESS UNPUBLISHED
Assael, Michael
Baird, James Kenneth
Bishins, Larry V.
Breidenbach, Cherie Elizabeth
Coplin, Mark David
Cunningham, Alice Welt
Hartwell, Christopher Lynn
Leeds, Mindy Robin
Lerner, Deborah Mae
Niehaus, Susan Patricia
Pistillo, Bernadino Joseph, Jr.
Sklar, Steven J.
Stoyanoff, David Joseph
Weisman, Paul Howard
Worley, L. Glenn

TAXATION, STATE AND LOCAL

UNITED STATES

Alabama
Lucas, Patrick Hewell
Proctor, David Ray
Webster, Bruce Charles

Alaska
Wilson, Joseph Morris, III

Arizona
Derdenger, Patrick
Le Clair, Douglas Marvin
O'Connell, Daniel Henry

California
Ayoob, Richard Joseph
Balkin, Jeffrey Gilbert
Boatwright, David Croft
Bost, Thomas Glen
Brookes, Valentine
Coombs, William Elmer
Crawford, Roy Edgington
Doti, Frank John
Hogan, Claude Hollis
Kleier, James Patrick
Maeder, Gary William
Maier, Thomas Andrew
McGee, Francis Parker, II
Newacheck, David John
Papiano, Neil Leo
Polley, Terry Lee
Putnam, Philip Conrad
Richman, Frederick Alexander
Schlinkert, William Joseph
Spiegel, Hart Hunter
Thomas, William Scott
White, Jack Raymond
Wood, Robert Warren

Colorado
McCray, Sandra Broomfield
O'Connor, Donald John
Ruppert, John Lawrence
Strenski, Robert Francis

Connecticut
Allan, John Malcolm, Jr.
Del Negro, John Thomas
Lyon, James Burroughs

Delaware
Hindmarch, Thomas Michael
Olson, Mark Douglas

District of Columbia
Hanford, Timothy Lloyd
Mentz, J. Roger
Murphy, Lynda Marie
Oyler, Gregory Kenneth
Walker, Jean Ann

Florida
Barnes, Donald King
Churuti, Susan Hamilton
Currier, Barry Arthur
Margolis, John Gilbert
McWilliams, John Lawrence, III
Phipps, Benjamin Kimball, II
Ringel, Fred Morton
Ruffner, Charles Louis

Georgia
Bart, Randall Kerr
Carpenter, Raymond Prince
Mears, Michael
Richards, Pamela Motter

Hawaii
D'Olier, H(enry) Mitchell
Eggers, William J., III
Heller, Ronald Ian
O'Malley, Michael John
Shea, Michael Alan

Illinois
Barr, John Robert
Bower, Glen L.
Bryan, Arthur Eldridge, Jr.
Chester, Mark Vincent
Emmett, James Robert
Foster, Lloyd Bennett
Garrison, Ray Harlan
Hulse, Minard Edwin, Jr.
Janis, Richard Alan
Kaminski, Stanley Ronald
Kart, Eugene
Lorentzen, John Carol
Nathan, Kenneth Sawyer, Sr.
O'Keefe, Kevin Michael
Parham, James Robert

Indiana
Cracraft, Bruce Noel
Fisher, Thomas Graham
Jegen, Lawrence A., III
Paul, Stephen Howard

Kansas
Bonebrake, Carol Buchele
Horttor, Donald J.
Tittsworth, David Gregory

Kentucky
Ardery, Joseph Lord Tweedy
Bagby, William Rardin
Dowell, Douglas Melvin
Masters, Richard L.
Yonts, Stewarts H.

Louisiana
Snyder, Charles Aubrey
Trostorff, Alex P.
Wooderson, James Michael

Maryland
Bové, Edward Joseph
Conkling, Daniel Charles
Proctor, Kenneth Donald
Roth, Robert Lloyd
Turney, Kenneth Wayne

Massachusetts
Davenport, David Sterling
Lappin, Robert Sidney
Oldman, Oliver
Politi, Stephen Michael
Ryan, James Frederick
Semerjian, Evan Yervant

Michigan
Basso, Ronald Matthew
Cinabro, Robert Henry
Cotner, Roger Garner
Cwirko, Claris Kaye
McKim, Samuel John, III

Minnesota
Ellingsworth, Patrick James
Geis, Jerome Arthur
Stepan, M(argaret) Jean

Mississippi
Edwards, Arthur Martin, III
Ludlam, Warren VanGilder, Jr.
Robertshaw, James

Missouri
Akre, Steven Heetland
Armstrong, Owen Thomas
Barrie, John Paul
Deutsch, James Bernard
Evans, William Ellis
Fleming, Robert Laurence
Howes, Brian Thomas
Matthews, James Michael
McNeill, Paul Spurgeon, Jr.
Voelpel, Mark Steven
Ward, Robert Alan
Weston, Theodora White

Montana
Hopgood, Tom Kolstad

Nebraska
Brockman, Terry James
Drozda, Robert Lee

New Jersey
Davidoff, E. Martin
Hall, Raymond Percival, III
Hinshaw, David Love
Mann, Donald J.
Metzger, John Mackay
Neary, Gerald Clarke
Rosen, Arthur R.
Small, Joseph Chauncey
Stanger, Douglas Scott

New Mexico
Anderson, Charles Edward

New York
Agranoff, Gerald Neal
Andresen, Malcolm
Bobrow, Alvan Lee
Bond, Kenneth Walter
Brecher, Howard Arthur
Bronstein, Richard J.
Brush, Louis Frederick
Crowley, Richard Allerton
Evans, David Lee
Faber, Peter Lewis
Flanagan, Deborah Mary
Frisch, Robert Emile
Fuller, Robert L(eander)
Garfunkel, Alan J.

Goldstein, M. Robert
Hunziker, Frederick John, Jr.
Hyman, Montague Allan
Koch, Edward Richard
Lisch, Howard
Morgen, Richard Burton
Peaslee, Maurice Keenan
Rosenberg, Jerome Roy
Rothman, Howard Joel
Santemma, Jon Noel
Schumacher, Harry Richard
Schwarzer, Franklin John
Shea, James William
Small, Jonathan Andrew
Spillane, Dennis Kevin
Whoriskey, Robert Donald
Young, Sidney David
Zipfinger, Frank Peter
Zucker, Howard

North Carolina
Cohen, Gerry Farmer

Ohio
Aley, Charles R.
Furber, Philip Craig
Hogan, Robert B.
Nechemias, Stephen Murray
Sharp, Robert Weimer
Wanner, Kathleen Ann

Oklahoma
Eagleton, Edward John
Forman, Jonathan Barry

Oregon
Chevis, Cheryl Ann
Girard, Leonard Arthur
Kuntz, Joel Dubois
Ormseth, Milo E.

Pennsylvania
Blum, Jeffrey Stuart
Boocock, Stephen William
Gornish, Gerald
Hunter, Keith Alan
Mendelson, Leonard (Melvin)
Prosperi, Louis Anthony
Summers, Clyde Wilson
Tumola, Thomas Joseph
Wecht, Alan Charles

Rhode Island
Arcaro, Harold Conrad, Jr.
Olsen, Hans Peter

South Dakota
Fosheim, Jon

Texas
Allender, John Roland
Attermeier, Fredric Joseph
Blair, William Henry
Futterer, Edward Philip
Greene, John Joseph
Harrison, Richard Wayne
Hathcox, VaLinda
Hays, Larry Weldon
Heffington, Joseph Robert
McDaniel, Myra Atwell
Meyer, Cathy Lynn
Milner, Christy Elizabeth
Morgan, Timi Sue
Seymour-Harris, Barbara Laverne
Sinak, David Louis
Smith, David Oliver
Wilson, Charles Julian

Utah
Riggs, Robin L.
Walz, Mary Beth

Virginia
Bowling, David Joseph
Facer, Eric Fouts
Goode, David Ronald
Greenbacker, John Everett
Horsley, Waller Holladay
McNider, James Small, III
Murphy, Nina Rebecca
Philipps, Joseph Timothy
Rightnour, Donald

Washington
Dempsey, Thomas Lawrence
Evered, Donna R.
Kilbane, Thomas Martin, Jr.
Kovacevich, Robert Eugene
O'Donnell, John James
Ruen, Lowell Vernon
Saracino, Samuel Francis

West Virginia
Lawson, Robert William, Jr.

Wisconsin
Baldwin, Janice Murphy
Case, Karen Ann
Johnson, Craig Robert

ADDRESS UNPUBLISHED
Drabkin, Murray
Fink, Monroe
Harnack, Don Steger
Stoyanoff, David Joseph
Weaver, John Hosch

TRADEMARK AND COPYRIGHT

UNITED STATES

Alabama
Sullivan, Michael Maurice

Arizona
Barbee, Joe E.
Lieb, John Stevens

Mueller, Foorman Lloyd
Phillips, James Harold

California

Alleman, Rodger Neal
Ansell, Edward Orin
Bailey, Craig Bernard
Cochran, Adam
Crews, Kenneth Donald
Daggett, Robert Sherman
Denman, Alexandra
Derin, Greg David
Dougherty, F. Jay
Finney, Joseph Claude Jeans
Flattery, Thomas Long
Fleming, John Gunther
Green, William Porter
Greenstein, Neil David
Grossman, Richard Alan
Hale, Charles Russell
Halluin, Albert Price
Hamann, H. Fredrick
Hasak, Janet Elinore
Heslin, James Mitchell
Hiaring, Anne
Higgins, Willis Edward
House, Calvin Richard
Israelsen, Ned Alma
Jaffer, David Hussain
Jessup, Warren T.
Kahane, Dennis Spencer
Keup, Erwin J.
Kinzler, William Charles
Klein, Henry
Klein, Jeffrey S.
Libott, Robert Yale
Lippman, Peter Ira
Lowy, Steven Robert
Lublinski, Michael
Lyon, R. Douglas
Matter, Bruce E.
Mebane, Julie Shaffer
Nuanes, John Gilbert
Overton, John Blair
Passé, James G.
Pavitt, William Hesser, Jr.
Radcliffe, Mark Flohn
Reuben, Timothy D.
Roush, George Edgar
Seltzer, Leon Eugene
Slater, Jill Sherry
Slehofer, Richard Donald
Smegal, Thomas Frank, Jr.
Smith, Robert Catlett
Stevens, Henry Patrick
Switzer, Robert Joseph
Tachner, Leonard
Thomas, Joseph Edward
Tinsley, Walton Eugene
Weissenberger, Harry George
Winnick, Helene Ann
Wylie, Paul Richter, Jr.

Colorado

Carson, William Scott
Devine, Sharon Jean
Dorr, Robert Charles
Luce, Charles F., Jr.
Meyer, Lynn Nix
Spangler, Edwin Leroy

Connecticut

Arturi, Peter A., II
Asija, S(atya) Pal
Battersby, Gregory John
Carten, Francis Noel
Cifelli, Armand
Cooper, George Wilson
De Lio, Anthony Peter
Fitzgerald, Thomas Raymond
Green, Clarence Arthur
Kelmachter, Barry Lee
Kramer, Barry
Manbeck, Harry Frederick, Jr.
Razzano, Pasquale Angelo
Russ, Lawrence
Sahl, John Patrick
Smith, Spencer Thomas
Soltow, William Donald, Jr.
Thompson, Frank J(oseph)
Turrentine, James Drake
Weinstein, Paul

Delaware

Staves, Marion Cole
Uebler, E(rnest) Alan
Whitney, Douglas E., Sr.
Winslow, Helen Littell

District of Columbia

Aisenberg, Irwin Morton
Berman, Stanford Warner
Blumenthal, Carol
Breneman, William Dudley
Brody, David A.
Browne, Richard Cullen
Cooper, Alan Samuel
Cooper, Iver Peter
Cotter, Frank James
Davidson, Tom William
DeGrandi, Joseph A.
Garvey, John Cotton
Gastfreund, Irving
Goodman, Alfred Nelson
Hefter, Laurence Roy
Holman, John Clarke
Hoscheit, Dale Herbert
Hughes, Dennis Michael
Kintner, Earl Wilson
Kurtz, James Louis
Levin, Lon Carl
Lippo, Tom A.
Lipstein, Robert A.
Lutzker, Arnold Paul
McCann, Clifton Everett
McKie, Edward Foss
Meany, Bernard Anthony
Melamed, Carol Drescher
Midlen, John Holbrook, Jr.
Miller, Jack Richard
Morgan, William Caswell
Moss, Kathleen Susan
Mossinghoff, Gerald Joseph
Oman, Ralph
Orenberg, Allen Howard
Payne, Kenneth Eugene
Potenza, Joseph Michael
Repper, George Robert
Rommel, John Marshall
Rubin, Burton Jay
Rubin, Stephen
Seto, Robert Mahealani Ming
Shapiro, Gary Joel
Sheldon, Jeffrey Lee
Spencer, George Henry
Stern, Richard Harvey
Straser, Richard Alan
Thompson, Richard Leon
Timberg, Sigmund
Waz, Joseph Walter, Jr.
Wegner, Harold Claus
Weller, Susan Neuberger
Yambrusic, Edward Slavko
Yoches, Edward Robert

Florida

Bellak, Richard Charles
Blank, Nelson Douglas
Chandler, John Brandon, Jr.
Dominik, Jack Edward
Henn, Harry George
Livingston, Edward Michael
Malloy, John Cyril
Monacelli, Walter Joseph
Rosenblatt, Joel I.
Saliwanchik, Roman
Sanchelima, Jesus
Simon, James Lowell
Singer, Stuart H.
Spector, Brian F.

Georgia

Cooney, William J.
Dailey, Michael Alan
Gignilliat, William Robert, III
Goldman, Joel S.
Hopkins, George Mathews Marks
Marianes, William Byron
Middleton, James Boland

Illinois

Alexander, Richard Elmont
Altman, Louis
Amend, James Michael
Baird, Russell Miller
Berenzweig, Jack Charles
Berghoff, Paul Henry
Birmingham, William Joseph
Boehnen, Daniel A.
Brand, Robert Joseph
Brezina, David Charles
Cherry, Daniel Ronald
Edgell, George Paul
Fewell, Terry Glenn
Fifer, Samuel
Flattery, Paul Charles
Gerstman, George Henry
Gibbons, William John
Gilkes, Arthur Gwyer
Gottschalk, Robert
Greenstein, Martin Richard
Haight, Edward Allen
Henke, Robert John
Hilliard, David Craig
Hoffman, Richard Bruce
Horwitz, John
Huston, Steven Craig
Jacover, Jerold Alan
Jager, Melvin Francis
Johnston, A. Sidney
Juettner, Paul Gerard
Katz, Avrum Sidney
Krupka, Robert George
Liljequist, Jon Leon
Lindgren, Thomas Bernard
Lucas, John Kenneth
Maher, David Willard
Marks, Roger Harris
Morsch, Thomas Harvey
Osann, Edward William, Jr.
Paniaguas, John Steven
Parad, Boris
Pattishall, Beverly Wyckliffe
Polzin, John Theodore
Rauner, Vincent Joseph
Robins, Lawrence Richard
Roper, Harry Joseph
Ropski, Gary Melchior
Schramm, Marilyn Jean
Scott, Theodore R.
Scudder, Theodore Townsend, III
Sheppard, Berton Scott
Smedinghoff, Thomas J.
Thompson, William Scott
Valley, Mark R.
Van Hagey, William
Vittum, Daniel Weeks, Jr.
Walters, Gomer Winston
Ward, Robert Morton
Welsh, Donald LeRoy
Wood, James Clarence

Indiana

Emhardt, Charles David
Harrison, Nancy Jane
Jeffers, Albert Lavern
Kinney, Richard Gordon
Richardson, Andrew James
Zlatos, Steve Edward

Iowa

Hinton, Charles Franklin

Kansas

Killough, Howard Patrick, Jr.
Mingle, John Orville

Maine

Burke, Edmund James
Hulbert, William Rowsell, Jr.

Maryland

Brady, Rupert Joseph
McLain, Susan Lynn
Parsky, Keith Alan
Sherer, Ronald Brian
Skoler, Daniel Lawrence

Massachusetts

Asher, Robert Michael
Beeby, Kenneth Jack
Channing, Stacey Lisa
Danner, Douglas
Erlich, Jacob Nathan
Hemnes, Thomas Michael Sheridan
Hieken, Charles
Isaacs, Alvin
Lacek, Michael Joseph
Linek, Ernest Vincent
Martin, Terrence
Mason, Paul Eric
McCarter, Lowell Harold
Neuner, George William
Paglierani, Ronald Joseph
Rubenstein-Kursh, Nan
Russell, Robert Bernard
Schiller, Robert James
Vance, Verne Widney, Jr.
Wild, Victor Allyn
Wolf, David

Michigan

Anderson, Thomas Ernest
Bullard, Rockwood Wilde, III
Farris, Robert Lee
Gifford, Ernest Irving
Harrington, Donald Joseph
Meyer, George Herbert
Mitchell, James Albee
Rader, Ralph Terrance
Tartt, Tyrone Chris
Thierstein, Emma Joan

Minnesota

Arrett, Oliver Ford
Boyer, David Randall
Friederichs, Norman Paul
Lange, Frederick Emil
Marousek, Robert Joseph
Mays, Charles Andrew
Schatz, James Edward
Vidas, Scott Quinn

Mississippi

Mingee, James Clyde, III

Missouri

Baier, David Donald
Forsman, Alpheus Edwin
Gilster, Peter Stuart
Kaufman, Lisa Nadine
Krukiel, Charles Edward
Lucchesi, Lionel Louis
Moore, McPherson Dorsett
Nutter, Thomas Edward
Perotti, Rose Norma
Pickle, Robert Douglas
Roedel, John Kennedy, Jr.
Scott, Robert Gene
Woods, Curtis E(ugene)

Montana

Conover, Richard Corrill

Nebraska

Jensen, Sam
Perlman, Harvey Stuart
Vosburg, Bruce David

Nevada

Quirk, Edward John
Tratos, Mark George
Willick, Marshal Shawn

New Hampshire

Weins, Michael James

New Jersey

Biribauer, Richard Frank
Bittman, Mitchell David
Brewer, Andrea Bordiga
Cipollone, Anthony Dominic
Gerb, Bernard
Grindle, Robert Paul
Haidri, Amirali Yusufali
Levavy, Bardin
MacDonald, Joseph J.
Mahoney, George LeFevre
Martin, Russell White
Michaelson, Peter Lee
Raines, Stephen
Riley, Robert Henry
Rohm, Benita Jill
Saffer, Judith M.
St. Landau, Norman
Scagnelli, John Mark
Virelli, Louis James, Jr.
Walsh, Robert Anthony
Whitmer, Frederick Lee
Woodbridge, Richard Carveth

New Mexico

Smith, Donald Perry

New York

Abelman, Arthur F.
Alice, Ronald William
Angel, Dennis
Armstrong, John Kremer
Ash, Karen Artz
Baechtold, Robert Louis
Bazerman, Steven Howard
Beaton, Neal N.
Beekman, William Bedloe
Berry, Rynn
Bosses, Stevan J.
Brokate, Brian William
Burke, Carol Elizabeth
Burstein, Neil Alan
Calvaruso, Joseph A.
Carr, Francis Thomas
Chapuran, Ronald Francis
Cole, Harold Edwin
Conner, William Curtis
Cooper, John Nicholas
Cowan, Philip Matthew
Creel, Thomas Leonard
Curtis, Frank R.
DeBaets, Timothy Joseph
Decker, Frank Norton, Jr.
Dickerson, Thomas Arthur
Dowling, Thomas Patrick
Dunne, Gerard Francis
Eberle, William Frederic
Eisenberg-Mellen, Viviane
Epstein, Michael A.
Evans, Barry Leonard
Feldman, Stephen E.
Felfe, Peter Franz
Fiddler, Robert William
Fierstein, Ronald Karl
Finnegan, George Bernard, Jr.
Fitzpatrick, Joseph Mark
Fletcher, Anthony L.
Frommer, William S.
Gallantz, George Gerald
Gibson, Thomas Martin
Goldbrenner, Ronald Steven
Goldstein, Margaret Frenkel
Goodman, Edward William
Green, Richard George
Haffner, Alfred Loveland, Jr.
Hamburg, Charles Bruce
Handler, Milton
Hanft, Noah Jonathan
Harab, Elliot Peter
Hepner, Charles Edward
Hoffman, Paul Shafer
Huettner, Richard Alfred
Iselin, Josephine Lea
Jacobson, Allan Jeffrey
Jacobson, Jeffrey Eli
Jefferies, Jack P.
Johnston, Harry Melville, III
Jordan, Frank J.
Kalow, David Arthur
Kane, David Schilling
Katona, Gabriel Paul
Kernochan, John Marshall
Kidd, John Edward
Kuhn, Perla M.
Kunstadt, Robert M.
Kurnit, Richard Alan
Lackert, Clark William
Landron, Michel J.
Lankenau, John Clausen
Lee, Jerome G.
Lieb, Charles Herman
Lipsitz, Randy
Litwin, Burton Lawrence
Manshel, Andrew Maximilian
Mantle, Raymond Allan
Marames, William Etheme
Marke, Julius Jay
Marks, Alfred Mitchell
Martone, Patricia Ann
McCarthy, Catherine Frances
Meadway, Jay Kenneth
Meiklejohn, Paul Thomas
Messing, Harold
Newborn, Samuel R(euben)
O'Donnell, Paul Eugene, Jr.
Offner, Eric Delmonte
Oliver, Milton McKinnon
Olsson, Harry Rudolph, Jr.
Pegram, John Braxton
Pelton, Russell Gilbert
Penney, Freeland N.F.T. Christian
Pfeffer, David H.
Plottel, Roland
Price, Robert
Ralabate, James J(oseph)
Reid, Ross
Reilly, John Albert
Reiner, John Paul
Relson, Morris
Rembar, Charles (Isaiah)
Rich, R(obert) Bruce
Robinowitz, Stuart
Rogers, Laurence Steven
Rosini, Neil Justin
Ross, Otho B., III
Rubenstein, Allen Ira
Rudnick, Marvin Jack
Rudoff, Surie
Ryan, J. Richard
Scheck, Frank Foetisch
Schwartz, Laurens R.
Selkirk, Alexander MacDonald, Jr.
Shadley, Kay Lee
Shear, Stephen Barrett
Sherman, Charles Israel
Simon, Morton Sonny
Simoson, William Eugene
Sinnott, John Patrick
Slough, John Edward
Smith, John Stuart
Smith, Robert Blakeman
Socol, Melinda
Spath, Gregg Anthony
Steuer, Richard Marc
Sugarman, Robert Gary
Sullivan, Joseph Charles
Sutton, Paul J.
Sweeney, John Francis
Swire, James Bennett
Taffet, Richard S.
Warshavsky, Suzanne May
Wehringer, Cameron Kingsley
White, John Patrick
Whitney, George Ward
Wingate, C(harles) Douglas
Woglom, Eric Cooke
Zissu, Roger Lloyd
Zivin, Norman H.

North Carolina

Bell, Paul Buckner
Lange, David
Linker, Raymond Otho, Jr.
MacCord, Howard Arthur, Jr.
Olive, Susan Freya
Shefte, Dalbert Uhrig
Vestal, Tommy Ray

Ohio

Andorka, Frank Henry
Baranowksi, Edwin Michael
Bobak, Donald John
Brinkman, Herbert Charles
Cooper, Hal Dean
Downing, George
Ely, Albert Love, Jr.
Emmert, Steven Michael
Fraser, Donald Ross
Gerhart, Peter Milton
Hadji, Serge Basil
Jenkins, Matthew Richard
Jones, John Frank
Kingsbury, Dorothea Jane
Maky, Walter
McCoy, William Charles, Jr.
Nauman, Joseph George
Phillips, Patrick Paul
Sajovec, Frank Michael, Jr.
Schramm, Frederic Bernard
Seal, Thomas David
Slough, J(osephine) Helen
Zellner, Robert John

Oklahoma

Fish, John Mancil, Jr.
Kachigian, Mark George

Oregon

Chernoff, Daniel Paregol
Day, Bartley Fuller
Foster, Randolph Courtney
Gleaves, Curt B.
Gray, Francis Ignacy
Lindley, Mark Robert
Smith, Kim Ridgely
Van Valkenburg, Edgar Walter

Pennsylvania

Alstadt, Lynn Jeffery
Beam, Robert Charles
Beck, Paul Augustine
Blenko, Walter J(ohn), Jr.
Buell, Eugene F(ranklin)
Caldwell, John Warwick
Child, John Sowden, Jr.
Chovanes, Eugene
Dorfman, John Charles
Doyle, William A.
Elliott, William Homer, Jr.
Gribok, Stephan Paul
Hauger, Harold Keith
Kole, Janet Stephanie
Krefman, Stephen David
Lavorgna, Gregory Joseph
Lovercheck, Charles Lester
Millinger, Donald Michael
Nadel, Alan Steven
Nasri, William Zaki
Petock, Michael F(rances)
Pokotilow, Manny D.
Ruano, William J.
Seidel, Arthur Harris
Silverman, Arnold Barry
Simkanich, John Joseph
Starr, Mark Toby
Urey, David Stauffer
Warren, William Ziegler
Washburn, Robert Buchanan
Webb, William Hess
Weisburd, Steven I.

Rhode Island

Skenyon, John Michael

South Carolina

Day, Richard Earl

South Dakota

Kolker, Richard Lee

Tennessee

Good, Adrian J.
Lackey, Harrington Ashton
Marlow, H(obson) McKinley, Jr.

Texas

Brookhart, Walter Ray
Bursley, Kathleen A.
Conley, Ned Leroy
Curfiss, Robert C.
Dillon, Andrew Joseph
Falk, Robert Hardy
Felger, Thomas Robert
Fladung, Richard Denis
Greenberg, Howard Ralph
Hunt, John Floyd
Kirk, John Robert, Jr.
Krieger, Paul Edward
Lacy, John Ford
Leach, Sydney Minturn
Levine, Harold
Livingston, Ann Chambliss
Maher, Mary Frances
Marsteller, Thomas Franklin, Jr.
McGowan, Patrick Francis
Moore, Stanley Ray
Petersen, Gale Roy
Peterson, Gale Roy
Pitner, Joseph A.
Rosenthal, Alan David
Rundel, Kenneth Martin
Scott, Eddie Elmer
Selinger, Jerry Robin
Simmons, Stephen Judson
Swindle, Mack Ed
Tanner, Sheryl Malick
Valdes, Richard Albert
Van Slyke, Paul Christopher
Walter, Charles Frank
Zahrt, William Dietrich, II

Utah

Cornaby, Kay Sterling
Jensen, Allen Reed
Madson, Craig James
Thorpe, Calvin E.

Virginia

Adams, Robert Walker
Bent, Stephen Andrew
Birch, Terrell Colhoun
Calvetti, Frederick F.
Dutton, Harold Hilbert, Jr.
Georges, Peter John
Greigg, Ronald Edwin
Hugin, Adolph Charles
Jameson, Paula Ann
Joynt, John Howard
Kondracki, Edward John
LeBlanc, Robert Edmond, III
McDonald, Alan Thomas
Morton, Woolridge Brown, Jr.
Regan, Michael Patrick

Rosenberg, Peter David
Schwaab, Richard Lewis
Shapiro, Nelson Hirsh
Spitzli, Donald Hawkes, Jr.
Steinhilber, August William
Van Landingham, Leander Shelton, Jr.
Weinrieb, Steven William

Washington

Coogan, Patrick Donlan
Harmon, E(verett) Glenn
Jensen, Sherman Holbrook
O'Connor, Bruce Edward

Wisconsin

Long, Theodore James
Politano, Frank Louis
Shupe, Larry Lewis
Swartwout, Willis Brewster, III

ISRAEL

Luzzatto, Edgar

LUXEMBOURG

Dennemeyer, John James

REPUBLIC OF KOREA

Sabo, William Denes

ADDRESS UNPUBLISHED

Adams, Thomas Lawrence
Casella, Peter F(iore)
Dolgorukov, D. Edward
Dratler, Jay, Jr.
DuPre, John Leacy
Gerber, Jack
Goldstein, Paul
Graff, Debra Jo
Herrell, Roger Wayne
Kamin, Daniel Tucker
Kasper, Horst Manfred
Kegan, Esther Oswianza
Leydig, Carl Frederick
McCarthy, J. Thomas
Mendel, Stephen Frank
Peters, R. Jonathan
Pollock, E. Kears
Richardson, Robert Owen
Woronoff, David Smulyan

TRIAL. See Civil Litigation; Criminal.

TRUSTS. See Probate.

UTILITIES, PUBLIC

UNITED STATES

Alabama

Lacy, Alexander Shelton
Ruegsegger, Martin Craig

Arkansas

Friday, Herschel Hugar

California

Clark, R(ufus) Bradbury
Daugherty, Richard Bernard
Dungan, Malcolm Thon
Feeney, Andrea Charlton
Firestone, Charles Morton
Gardiner, Stuart Korson
Hackmann, Kathy Alene
McLennan, Robert Bruce
Michaels, Sheldon
Roethe, James Norton
Sharpe, Norah G.
Skaff, Andrew Joseph
Stromme, Gary L.
Zimmermann, John Frederick

Colorado

Campbell, Leonard Martin
Conway, John Joseph
DeMuth, Alan Cornelius
Hjelmfelt, David Charles
Ledingham, Thomas Max
McCotter, James Rawson
Meiklejohn, Alvin J., Jr.
Rowe, Russell Paul
Walker, John Sumpter, Jr.

Connecticut

Golden, Lawrence James
Rohrer, Dean Cougill
Vogel, Marilyn Beth

Delaware

Edelson, Harold Jesse
Twilley, Joshua Marion

District of Columbia

Bader, Michael Haley
Betts, Kirk Howard
Brecher, Mitchell Fredrick
Bruder, George Frederick
Curtin, William Joseph
DeMuth, Christopher Clay
Drennan, D. Jane
Duckenfield, Thomas Adams
Elrod, Eugene Richard
Griff, Marvin T.
Gross, David Andrew
Hobson, James Richmond
Hoecker, James John
Hughes, John David
Jacobson, David Edward
Kirby, Peter Mangan
Levy, Steven Abraham
Machlin, Marc David
Mallory, Charles King, III
Manly, Marc Edward
Mathis, John Prentiss
May, Randolph Joseph

Miller, Richard William, Jr.
Moler, Elizabeth Anne
Norton, Floyd Ligon, IV
O'Neill, Brian Dennis
Petrash, Jeffrey Michael
Polsky, Howard David
Porter, William Glover, Jr.
Quint, Arnold Harris
Rivera, Henry Michael
Sagett, Jan Jeffrey
Shibley, Raymond Nadeem
Simons, Morton Leonard
Sternstein, Alan Barry
Sugrue, Thomas Joseph

Florida

Ade, James L.
Anderson, R(obert) Bruce

Georgia

Artis, Gregory Dwight
Baxter, Harry Stevens
Drescher, Ann Marie
Langstaff, James Pope
Strassner, Kenneth Allen
Trotter, William Perry

Hawaii

Case, James Hebard

Illinois

Arlow, Allan Joseph
Cherry, Barbara Ann
Delp, Wilbur Charles, Jr.
Fazio, Peter Victor, Jr.
Helman, Robert Alan
Kelty, Thomas Walsh
Lee, Mark Richard
Merrill, Thomas Wendell
Orloff, Ronald Leonard
Perlberg, Jules Martin
Renner, Michael John
Weging, James Edwin
Willmeth, Roger Earl
Wilson, Michael B(ruce)

Indiana

Allen, David James
Belknap, Jerry P.
Collier-Magar, Kenneth Anthony
Cracraft, Bruce Noel
Eichhorn, Frederick Foltz, Jr.
Ferguson, Stephen Luther
Welch, William F.
Yoder, Thomas Woodrow

Iowa

Fox, Terry Roy
Johnson, Robert Steven
Smith, William Herbert, Jr

Kansas

Dimmitt, Lawrence Andrew
Mudrick, David Phillip

Kentucky

Chambers, Dorothy J.
Dozier, Rush Watkins, Jr.
Emmons, Alison Lobb
Lile, Charles Alan

Louisiana

Burns, William Glenn
Keithley, Bradford Gene
LeClere, David Anthony
Wilhelm, Jack Morton

Maine

Hartwell, Jane Barry
Stone, Alan G.

Maryland

Doub, William Offutt
Foltz, Richard Nelson, III
Freeman, Martin Henry
Rettberg, Charles Clayland, Jr.

Massachusetts

Cook, Charles Addison
Keuthen, Catherine J. Norman
Kuzinevich, John Jacob
Meyer, Michael Broeker
Rabinowitz, Alan James
Rich, Christopher Charles

Michigan

Burgess, Kenneth John
Cohan, Leon Sumner
Fagan, Thomas James
Haines, Michael Curtis
Latovick, Paula R(ae)
Lindemer, Lawrence Boyd
Marvin, David Edward Shreve
McLain, Dennis O.
Melia, James Patrick
Nern, Christopher Carl
Palincsar, John Ernest
Pestle, John William
Sullivan, Alfred A.

Minnesota

Timmons, Mary Sarazin

Mississippi

Smith, Stanley Quinten
Wise, Joseph Powell
Wise, Sherwood Willing

Missouri

Barvick, William Michael
Brooks, Douglas Michael
English, Mark Gregory
Gardner, Paul Hendricks
Godiner, Donald Leonard
Hoffman, John Raymond
Mayfield, Edgar
Palmer, Randall Bruce
Young, Mary Garr

Montana

Alke, John
Kaze, James Michael

Nebraska

Dessonville, Loren Edward
Dolan, James Vincent
McClure, John Campbell
O'Hara, Michael James

Nevada

Pearson, Niels L.

New Hampshire

Arnold, Wynn Edmund
Hood, James Calton
Ransmeier, Joseph Sirera
Toll, Charles Hansen, Jr.
Wilson, William Harold, Jr.

New Jersey

Babineau, Anne Serzan
Bright, Francis Edward
Donnella, Michael Andre
Ehrlich, Leslie Sharon
Fleming, Russell, Jr.
Gleit, Ernest Aaron
Golin, Margery S.
Hutson, Frank Alfred, Jr.
Hyland, William Francis
Lewis, Albert Michael
Manzo, Peter Thomas
Rosen, Howard Theodore
Seham, Martin Charles
Weber, Walter Winfield, Jr.

New Mexico

Carpenter, Richard Norris
Cox, Lewis Calvin

New York

Allen, Leon Arthur, Jr.
Bankston, Archie Moore, Jr.
Brecher, Howard Arthur
Cassan, Vito J.
Cotter, James Michael
Davis, Steven H.
Dunn, M(orris) Douglas
Earley, Anthony Francis, Jr.
Gibbons, Robert John
Glanville, Robert Edward
Hawes, Douglas Wesson
Hunziker, Frederick John, Jr.
Joseph, Leonard
Lebowitz, Jack Richard
Lilley, Albert Frederick, III
Lyon, Carl Francis, Jr.
Matias, Thomas Redmond
McMeen, Elmer Ellsworth, III
Meath, Brian Patrick
Poth, Harry Augustus, Jr.
Powers, Elizabeth Whitmel
Read, Charles Arthur
Russell, Edwin Fortune
Schuur, Robert George
Stuart, John M.
Terry, John Hart
Wagner, Richard Hopkins
White, Katherine Patricia
Worenklein, Jacob J.

North Carolina

Carrow, Harvey Hill, Jr.
Goodrum, Wayne Louis
Jolly, Raymond A., Jr.
Roach, Edgar Mayo, Jr.

North Dakota

Maichel, Joseph Raymond
Sandstrom, Dale Vernon

Ohio

Battaglia, Timothy Joseph
Buchmann, Alan Paul
Gruber, William Michael Ondrey
Kessler, Alan
Leibold, William Joseph
Mc Connaughey, George Carlton, Jr.
McLaren, Richard Wellington, Jr.
Migden-Ostrander, Janine Lee
Ruxin, Paul Theodore
Sanders, James Worthington
Schermer, Marsha Rockey
Spetrino, Russell John
Tell, A. Charles
Van Heyde, G. James

Oklahoma

Arrington, John Leslie, Jr.
Estill, John Staples, Jr.
Huffman, Robert Allen
Huffman, Robert Allen, Jr.
Stewart, Robert Desbrow, Jr.

Oregon

Girard, Leonard Arthur
Larson, John Francis
Walters, Stephen Scott

Pennsylvania

Amelio, Laura Lane
Bauer, Edward Greb, Jr.
Beckman, Jill Marie
Boswell, William Paret
Browne, Michael L.
Demmler, John Henry
Galie, Lawrence Pius
Gornish, Gerald
Hall, Walter Randall, II
Haskins, George Lee
Kain, William Henry
Klodowski, Amy Martha Auslander
MacGregor, David Bruce
Mendel, M. Mark
Milkman, Murray
Ogden, W. Edwin
Oplinger, Jon Carl
Reed, W. Franklin
Rubin, Scott Jeffrey
Sampath, Elizabeth Margaret Deborah
Satinsky, Barnett

Stewart, Allen Warren
Stivison, David Vaughn

South Carolina

Fusco, Arthur Geiger
Roberts, Edward Calhoun

Tennessee

Cherry, Mack Henry
Whiteaker, Raymond Combs

Texas

Ballew, William Virgil, Jr.
Balough, Richard Charles
Beard, Glenda Rainwater
Cortez, Hernan Glenn
Gordon, Norman James
Gregg, Tom Will, Jr.
Harden, Richard Lee
Kawaguchi, Meredith Ferguson
Morton, Thomas Edward, Jr.
Richter, Alfred Grammar, Jr.
Roan, Forrest Calvin, Jr.
Steimel, Walter Earl, Jr.
Tyson, Roy Knox
Webb, Robert Allen
Wexler, Charles W., Jr.

Utah

Edwards, Helen Jex
Groussman, Raymond G.
Mangan, George Edward
Reeder, F. Robert
Stirba, Anne Melinda Morr

Vermont

Debevoise, Thomas McElrath
Marshall, John Henry
Storrow, Charles Fiske
Winer, Jonathan Herman
Zamore, Peter Hokanson

Virginia

Fisher, Catherine Ambrosiano
Gary, Richard David
Hahn, Michael James
Williams, Marcus Doyle

Washington

Campbell, Robert Hedgcock
Dempsey, Thomas Lawrence
Dudley, J. Jeffrey
Redman, Eric

West Virginia

Halbritter, Marc Alan

Wisconsin

Gorske, Robert Herman
Riordan, Ray Joseph, Jr.

Wyoming

Godfrey, Paul Bard

ADDRESS UNPUBLISHED

Buffington, John Victor
Diehl, Deborah Hilda
Heath, Charles Dickinson
McCormick, David Arthur
O'Leary, Marilyn C.
Rubinkowski, Conrad Sigmund

WATER. See Property, real.

WILLS. See Probate.

WORKERS' COMPENSATION. See also Labor; Personal injury.

UNITED STATES

Alabama

Booker, R. Michael
Donahue, Timothy Patrick
Ferguson, Harold Laverne, Jr.
Harris, Benjamin Harte, Jr.
Hines, Rodney Alan
Lattof, Mitchell George, Jr.
Porterfield, Jack Berry, Jr.
Smith, William Wayne
Wright, David Scott

Alaska

Beistline, Ralph Robert
Bendell, James Michael
Brown, Fred Grant

Arizona

Chickering, John Bradley
Crossman, Harlan Jay
Rivera, Armando
Waterman, David Moore
Wisniewski, Robert Edward

Arkansas

Davis, Steven Ray
Rhoads, George Robert
Roe, Ramona Jeraldean
Spencer, Frederick S.

California

Aycock, Felix Alfred
Bandy, Jack D.
Bartosic, Florian
Beauzay, Victor H(ilton)
Ciambella, Cory Joseph
Faile, Wendell Wayne
Fallman, James Mitchell, Jr.
Fedirko, Robert John
Ferchland, William Thomas
Fluharty, Jesse Ernest
Friedman, Lester James
Hassan, Allen C.

Heywood, Robert Gilmour
Leff, Irwin
Levy, Steven R.
Mendelson, Steven Earle
Miller, Owens O'Keefe
Ninnis, William Raymond, Jr.
O'Brien, Daniel Paul
Palitz, Murray
Partritz, Joan Elizabeth
Resneck, William Allan
Riordan, John
Robertson, James Allen
Sadler, Bruce Phillip
Scharf, Robert Lee

Colorado

Barnes, Thomas Arthur, Jr.
de Marino, Thomas John
Falcone, Richard Edward
Felter, Edwin Lester, Jr.
Gandy, H. Conway
Goorman, Perry Lee
Noall, L. Scott
Vogel, Lawrence Mark

Connecticut

Asselin, John Thomas
Collins, John Albert, III
Czajkowski, Frank Henry
Greenblatt, Morton Harold
Halloran, Robert Bartley
Pinsky, Irving Jay
Sheiman, Stuart Melvyn

Delaware

Ciconte, Edward Thomas
Herrmann, Philip Eric
Hudson, George Naylor
Suddard, Oliver Vincent

District of Columbia

Elisburg, Donald Earl
Evans-Harrell, Valerie Dianne
Fenton, John Henry
Jordan, James Francis
Lawrence, Glenn Robert
Postol, Lawrence Philip
Siegel, Allen George

Florida

Abramson, Harvey Stanley
Alpert, Jonathan Louis
Barish, George
Berman, Richard Bruce
Boynton, Gary John
Brumer, Michael
Chidnese, Patrick N.
Donaldson, Dorothea E.
Finkelstein, Joseph Judah
Fleischmann, Pamela
Gladson, Guy Allen, Jr.
Glinn, Franklyn Barry
Harris, Warren Louis
Heindl, Phares Matthews
Marshall, Valerie Ann
McDonald, Julia Carol
McQuigg, John Dolph
Moore, Thomas Adair
Owen, Richard Knowles
Roach, Richard R., Jr.
Schwedock, Peter Saul
Smith, James Hibbert
Valle, Laurence Francis

Georgia

Baker, Verlyn Childs
Baverman, Elida Blaine
Finnell, Robert Kirtley
Fox, Patrick Joseph
Frey, Monroe Lynn, III
Hayes, Dewey Norman, Jr.
Henson, Howard Kirk
Hibbert, David Wilson
Johnson, Lester Benjamin, III
Linder, Harvey Ronald
Marcus, Steven Ezra
Pilcher, James Brownie
Roberts, James Isaac, Sr.
Shinall, Robert Phillip, III
Thomas, Richard English
Underwood, William Fleming, Jr.

Hawaii

Chun-Hoon, Lowell Koon Ying
Cumbs, Charles Wilcox
Fujimoto, Wesley Minoru
Furuya, Laurie E.
Goldsmith, Stephen Ernest
Turbin, Richard

Idaho

Greenfield, John Frederic
Jarzabek, Joseph Edward
Luker, Lynn Michael
Mauk, William Lloyd
Penland, Paul Stephan
Tait, John Reid
Thomas, Eugene C.

Illinois

Ackman, Richard LeRoy
Ahern, Gregory Emmett
Ardito, Laurie Ann
Callahan, Dennis John
Church, Glenn J.
Donlevy, John Dearden
Elman, William
Fahey, Robert Francis
Fisher, Edward Joseph
Franks, Herbert Hoover
Goldenhersh, Murray Jacob
Goulet, Lionel Joseph
Heiligenstein, Christian Erica
Hoffman, Alan Craig
Horwitz, Mitchell Wolf
Hynes, James Patrick
Krucks, William Norman
Kuster, Larry Donald
Laski, James Emil
Latshaw, K. Michael
Lindenmuth, Noel Charles
Manion, Paul Thomas
McCarthy, Kitty Monaghan

Miller, Ralph William, Jr.
Mills, Andre Micheaux
Murray, David Eugene
Picha, George John
Ripplinger, George Raymond, Jr.
Schur, Jerome
Schwartzman, Mark Lee
Soltis, Robert Alan
Webster, John Clyde
Wesley, Howard Barry

Indiana

Allen, Kenneth James
Eckert, Stephen Paul
Highfield, Robert Edward
Schmitt, John Francis
Walker, Ross Paul

Iowa

Berry, Jan Vance
Cutler, Charles Edward
Dahl, Harry Waldemar
Ditmars, Lyle William
Duckworth, Marvin E.
Hamilton, James R.
Henderson, Thomas
Hoffman, James Paul
Hoffmann, Michael Richard
Hood, James Michael
Lemanski, David Alan
Lenihan, Thomas Parker
Monson, Terry Lewis
Murray, William Michael (Mike)
Norris, James Robert
Reilly, Michael Gerard
Wilson, Robert Foster

Kansas

Arnhold, Thomas Dean
Bideau, Edwin Hale, III
Carroll, Timothy Wayne
Carver, Kevin Scott
Fisher, Randall Eugene
Gastl, Eugene Francis
Helbert, Michael Clinton
Howland, Gary Marvin
McCullough, George Elwood
McPherson, Brock Richard
Mitchell, Alexander Baldwin
Neustrom, Patrik William
Short, Timothy Allen

Kentucky

Eades, Ronald Wayne
Jefferson, Janice Lee Roehler
Penick, Michael Preston
Reverman, Philip John, Jr.
Riggs, Roger D.
Simpson, Ronald Vincent
Wehr, William James
Weiner, Neil Steven
Welsh, Alfred John

Louisiana

Chapman, Alex David, Jr.
Ellison, David McQuown, Jr.
Fuhrer, Leonard
Gardner, Jerry Louis, Jr.
Lane, Charles Ray
Madison, Vivian L.
Malone, Ernest Roland, Jr.
Milly, Lawrence Arthur
Riley, Mark Louis
Thomas, Gerard Frances

Maine

Burns, Jeffrey Robert
Hewes, Richard David
Laney, William R.
Mills, Sumner Peter, III
Picavet, Robert Clement
Priest, Charles Randall
Tepler, Sheldon Joel
Watson, Thomas Riley
Willey, N. Laurence, Jr.

Maryland

Ashin, Jeffery Gordon
Bekman, Paul D.
Dunn, John Benjamin
Goldscheider, Sidney
Mann, Michael Bond
Martin, Clifford
Miller, Max Dunham, Jr.
Rochlin, Paul R.
Vaughan, James Joseph Michael
Weiss, Irwin E.

Massachusetts

Bennett, Clarence J.
Cabral, Bernardo Joseph
Driscoll, Kathleen Elizabeth
Fein, Sherman Edward
Felper, David Michael
Finn, Marvin Ruven
Harris, Richard Bates
Weiler, Paul Cronin

Michigan

Brenton, Michael Scott
Busch, Gary M(itchell)
Byrne, Joseph Ahern, Jr.
Carson, Robert William
Cohen, Norton Jacob
Cooper, David Joseph
Dilley, Thomas Robert
Dudley, Dennis Michael
Foley, Stephen Bernard
Hall, Jacqueline Yvonne
Kopit, Jonathan Throne
May, Alan Alfred
Moher, Thomas Gerald
Ornstein, Alexander Thomas
Perlos, Alexander Charles
Phillips, Dwight Wilburn
Rettig, James Melvin
Rinkel, Michael Joseph
Smith, Edward Michael
Smith, Mark Richard
Zanot, Craig Allen

Minnesota

Abrams, Richard Brill

Fitch, Raymond William
Hektner, Candice Elaine
Johnson, Robert R.
Miller, Keith Lloyd
O'Leary, Daniel Brian
Sokol, Michael Bruce
Sovereign, Kenneth Lester
Zalasky, Jeff M.

Mississippi

Cook, William Leslie, Jr.
Garmon, Ollie Lorance, III
Harlow, Eugene Marchant
Pritchard, Thomas Alexander

Missouri

Banton, Stephen Chandler
Bayer, Elmer Valentine
Beezley, Theodore
Bronsky, A.J.
Cain, Kenneth Jefferson
Clark, Charles Edward
Crepeau, Dewey Lee
Crites, Richard Don
Gallen, James M.
Gartner, Richard Anthony
Gorla, Michael Joseph
Humphrey, James William, Jr.
Kaplan, Chester B.
Levin, Morris Jacob
McKay, John Edward
McManaman, Kenneth Charles
Nordyke, Stephen Keith
Rice, James Briggs, Jr.
Riner, James William
Roskin, Preston Eugene
Ryan, Hugh Harvey
Schwabe, John Bennett, II
Stockman, Harry Michael
Susman, Robert M.
Swann, Elizabeth Walker
Tutt, Louise Thompson
Whipple, Clyde David
White, David William

Montana

Harrington, James Patrick
Knuchel, Karl G.
Lerner, Alan Jay
Luck, Bradley James
Morales, Julio K.
Sommerfeld, Donald Drovdal

Nebraska

Klein, Michael Clarence
O'Connor, Robert Edward, Jr.
Salerno, Terrence Joseph

Nevada

Badger, Raymond Louis, Jr.
Sarnowski, David Francis

New Hampshire

Brown, Kenneth Mackinnon
Doleac, Charles Bartholomew

New Jersey

Boskey, James Bernard
Diamond, Gloria Beverly
Epstein, Barry David
Fannon, Stephen Thomas
Finn, Jerry Martin
Gelman, Jon Leonard
Haidri, Amirali Yusufali
Jordan, Richard Allen
Lashman, Shelley Bortin
Lieberman, Marvin Samuel
O'Brien, John Graham
O'Carroll, Anita Louise
Preiser, Godfrey Krause, Jr.
Sullivan, Robert Joseph
Weiseman, Jac Burton
Zarnowski, James David

New Mexico

Branch, Margaret Moses
Darnell, Richard Wayne
Martinez, Carlos Guillermo
Pearlman, David Henry
Pelton, Gregory Vern
Sherman, Frederick Hood
Sparkia, Alisa A.
Stoker, Arlon L., Jr.
Waldman, Robert Irwin
Word, Terry Mullins

New York

Cardali, Richard James
Chernoff, Carl G.
Coakley, Charles
Collins, John Francis
Douchkess, George
Fogelgaren, Eric Israel
Gebo, Stephen Wallace
Hill, Peter Waverly
Loscalzo, Anthony Joseph
Probert, Mark Stanley
Schwartz, Martin Weber
Tannenbaum, Calvin Michael
Wagner, Michael G.
Wolfe, Richard Barry Michael
Zimmerman, Aaron Mark

North Carolina

Brisson, Lloyd Clifford, Jr.
Clontz, Stanford Kent
Doss, Marion Kenneth
Hunter, Pamela Anne
Markham, Charles Buchanan
Ruppe, Arthur Maxwell

Ohio

Baker, Richard Southworth
Bell, Napoleon Arthur
Birne, Kenneth Andrew
Bruestle, Eric George
Buonpane, Guerin
Cusack, Mary Jo
Davis, Charles Joseph
Duber, Michael Joseph
Gerlach, Franklin Theodore
Goodin, Eileen Sue

Harris, Jerald David
Hermanies, John Hans
Herrold, Russell Phillips, Jr.
Hochman, James Bertram
Kadela, David Anthony
Konrad, Bruce Joseph
Lancione, Bernard Gabe
Lancione, Robert Michael
Major, Ronald David
Paleudis, John George
Rabold, C(harles) Steven
Roberts, Brian Michael
Ruf, H(arold) William, Jr.
Shepard, Darrell Royce
Somrak, David Joseph
Tait, Robert Ed
Trester, Joseph Edward
Wilson, Harrison Benjamin, III

Oklahoma

Brooks, Rex Dwain
Featherly, Henry Frederick
Lawter, J. Mike
Link, Antony Cole
Petrikin, James Ronald
Reid, David Paul
Robinson, Randall Philip
Taliaferro, Bruce Owen
Taylor, Kenneth David
Tuttle, Roger Lewis

Oregon

Bovarnick, Paul Simon
Brenneman, Delbert Jay
Calzaretta, Victor
Hittle, David William
Imperati, Samuel J(ohn)
Kronenberg, Debra Ann
Lorenz, Daniel Christopher
Mannix, Kevin Leese
Ringle, Philip Hamilton, Jr.
Robertson, Joseph David
Velure, Lyle Carl

Pennsylvania

Becker, John Francis
Belden, H. Reginald
Benson, Stuart Wells, III
Bernard, Bruce William
Bond, Thomas Richard
Conley, Martha Richards
DeMarco, James Joseph
Dill, William Allen
Eagen, Frank P.
Egler, Frederick Norton
Fetzner, Michael Alan
Flannery, Harry Audley
Gale, Randall Glenn
Hafer, Joseph Page
Ingram, Niki Teresa
Kane, John Joseph
Keenan, C. Robert, III
Lorenzo, Nicholas Francis, Jr.
Malloy, Michael Joseph
Martin, Charles Howard
Mattern, Patricia Ann
McFadden, Joseph R., Jr.
Meyer, Martin Jay
Moribondo, Thomas Peter
Mulvey, W. Michael
Orsatti, Ernest Benjamin
Petrush, John Joseph
Richman, Stephen Ian
Rovner, David Patrick Ryan
Saunders, Robert Leonard
Seacrist, Geoffrey Lynn
Shay, Michael Patrick
Sidebottom, William Jeffrey
Strader, James David
Tamulonis, Frank Louis, Jr.
Wecht, Cyril Harrison
Youngs, Christopher Jay

Rhode Island

Lipsey, Howard Irwin

South Carolina

Baggett, Stephen Dallas
Bell, Robert Morrall
Christian, Warren Harold, Jr.
Darling, Stephen Edward
DeWitt, Franklin Roosevelt
Eltzroth, Clyde Alfred, Jr.
Haynsworth, Knox Livingston, Jr.
Johnson, Darrell Thomas, Jr.
Kuhn, Harold Fred, Jr.
Leverette, Sarah Elizabeth
Mauldin, John Inglis
McChesney, Paul Townsend
Metcalfe, Walter Geoffrey
Oswald, Billy Robertson
Painter, Samuel Franklin
Rodgers, Paul Baxter, III
Spitz, Hugo Max
Wyche, Madison Baker, III

Tennessee

Cameron, Clarence Arnold
Covington, Robert Newman
Cramer, William Mitchell
Fleissner, Phillip Anton
Goldin, Arnold B.
James, Erich William
Keeton, Robert Taylor, Jr.
Lee, Sharon Gail
Lockett, William Alexander
Marcus, Harry Richard
Moore, James M(ack), Jr.
Parker, Mary Ann
Rutherford, Glen Bibee
Shirley, Raymond Andrew, Jr.
Smith, William Holt
Sproles, Donald Ray
Youngblood, Elaine Michele

Texas

Abney, Joe L.
Altman, William Kean
Ammerman, James Harry, II
Arthur, Harry Cornelius
Brown, James Earle
Byrd, Linward Tonnett
Chase, Sam J.
Craig, Robert Lee, Jr.

Delk, Russell Louis
Ellis, Donald Lee
Feldman, H. Larry
Felton, Dale Wiley
Fox, Jacqueline R.
Frigerio, Charles Straith
Henry, Peter York
Holmes, Clifton Lee, (Scrappy)
Jacobellis, Mike
Jones, Albert Pearson
Junell, Robert Alan
Kilgore, Gary Lynn
Latham, B. Mills
Lewis, Kenneth Wayne
McAninch, Edwin Lee
McPherson, Nancy Jo Buenzli
Moore, Robert Allen
Orsburn, Charles Claude
Pena, Richard
Perkins, James Allen
Pluymen, Bert W.
Porter, James Eduardo
Price, Robert Alexander
Putman, (James) Michael
Raine, Charles Macon
Rainey, John David
Raschke, Fred David
Ridgeway, Henry Dorman
Roark, John Olen
Shaw, Tex Ronnie
Siegel, Mark Jordan
Slaughter, David Alan
Somers, Constance Reynolds
Stewart, Mark Steven
Terrell, Richard Clark
Thaddeus, Aloysius Peter, Jr.
Wilder, William Keith
Wilk, David I.
Williams, Charles Michael
Williams, Walter Waylon
Wills, Don Paul

Virginia

Alexander, Bevin Ray, Jr.
Burgess, Jack Thompson
Cassell, Richard Emmett
Evans, Susan Ann
Gresham, Timothy Ward
Moody, Willard James, Sr.
O'Connor, Raymond Vincent, Jr.
Parks, William Anthony
Steffen, Joseph John, Jr.
Sweeny, Peter Michael
Woodrum, Milton Lanier

Washington

Condon, David Bruce
Ludolph, Marla Rose
Phillabaum, Stephen Day
Ransom, Clark Taylor
Ray, Rodney Bruce
Russell, Steven Turner
Sharpe, Christopher Grant

West Virginia

Crandall, Grant Fotheringham
Gibson, Michael Fielding
Hamrick, Karen Susan
Richmond, William Frederick, Jr.
Weaver, William Carroll
Williams, Jacques Ralph André
Woods, Jeff Chandler

Wisconsin

Dau-Schmidt, Kenneth Glenn
Dietrich, Dean Richard
Gagliardi, Paul
Gasiorkiewicz, Eugene Anthony
Graylow, Richard Vernon
Gust, Gerald Norman
Kaiser, John Atwood
Krukowski, Thomas Paul
Laufenberg, Lynn Raymond
McCusker, William LaValle
Smith, Charles F., Jr.
Towers, Lawrence Alan
Vliet, Daniel George

Wyoming

Allison, James Stanley

ADDRESS UNPUBLISHED

Adelman, Michael Schwartz
Atwood, Ronald Wayne
Brown, Manny S.
Bush, Robert G., III
Cowan, Robert Charles, Jr.
Easterling, Charles Armo
Glywasky, Donald Steven
Kafka, Anne G.
Winslow, Julian Dallas

OTHER

UNITED STATES

Alabama

Flowers, Francis Asbury, III *Appellate practice*
Graddick, Charles Allen
Langum, David John *Evidence*
Luskin, Joseph
Norwood, Dorothy F. *Appellate practice*
Putnam, Terry Michael *College & University Law*
Sapp, Ernestine S. *Tort*
Still, Edward *Elections and voting*
Turner, William Howard *Aviation*
Yates, Lawden Henry *General practice, Firearms expert*
Yen, David Shu-fang *Poverty law*

Alaska

Bond, Marc Douglas *Natural resources*
Fortier, Samuel John *Alaska native law*
Mertz, Douglas Kemp *Indian law*
Petersen, A. Lee *Federal and state civil litigation*
Tangen, Jon Paul *Mining and minerals*

Arizona

Abraham, Andrew *Zoning*
Alexander, David Cleon, III *Tax controversy work, Federal income taxation*
Bodney, David Jeremy *Media law*
Clark, Richard Edward *Commercial and mediation*
Hay, John Leonard *Franchising*
Herman, Steven Roger *Taxation-- partnerships.*
Nopar, Alan Scott *Mergers and acquisitions, Franchise law*
Polan, David Jay *Communications*
Schneider, Elizabeth Kelley *Law office administration, Professional responsibility*
Schurr, M. Randolph *Land use and planning*
Spitzer, Marc Lee *Tax litigation*
Swartz, Melvin Jay *Legal Problems of Aging*
Tennen, Leslie Irwin *Aerospace and aviation*
Ulrich, Paul Graham *Appellate practice*
Van Wagner, Albert Edwin, Jr. *Product liability, Medical malpractice*
Wolf, G. Van Velsor, Jr. *Zoning*
Youney, John William *Business and tax planning*

Arkansas

Boe, Myron Timothy *Employment discrimination*
Choate, Murray Rickliffe, II *Inter/intra- state sale of real property litigation*
Gliege, John Gerhardt *Land use and planning law*
Hall, John Wesley, Jr. *Federal Constl. litigation*
Hill, Rhonda Kenyon *State Government/ consumer protection*
Ledbetter, Thomas Dale *Civil Litigation*
Mackey, Benjamin Franklin, Jr. *Foundation law*
Nestrud, Charles Robert *Hospital law*

California

Aaronson, Mark N. *Poverty Law*
Adams, Robert Morford, Jr. *Non-Profit organizations*
Anderson, Suellen *Voluntary legal services*
Armour, George Porter *Energy, oil and gas*
Armstrong, Robert Weaver
Ballentine, Kathryn E. *Equine Law*
Barrett, Robert Matthew *Mass product liability litigation*
Bennett, Bruce Scott *Insolvency and out of court financial workouts*
Benninghoff, Charles Franklyn, III *Venture capital*
Bennion, David Jacobsen *Products liability, Civil litigation*
Bice, Scott Haas
Bold, Frederick, Jr. *Water rights*
Bomberger, Russell Branson *Aviation*
Booher, Lawrence J., Jr. *Contracts commercial*
Caswell, Paulette Reva *Legal services pro bono*
Cobey, James Alexander *Water law*
Coleman, Thomas Young *Contracts financing*
Copenbarger, Lloyd Gaylord *Non-profit corporations*
Cummings, John Patrick *Customs and trade practice*
Cummins, Neil Joseph, Jr. *Malpractice defense; engineers and surveyors*
Davey, Gerard Paul *Franchising*
Demirdjian, Jean-Claude *Aviation safety, accidents*
Demoff, Marvin Alan *Sports*
Dempsey, Michael Douglas *Surety bonds*
Dickerson, William Roy *Professional negligence*
DiLoreto, Ann Marie *Litigation Support*
Dostart, Paul Joseph *International trade and U.S. customs service*
Downer, Michael Josef *General taxation*
Dworkin, Michael Leonard *Aviation*
Ellwanger, J. David *Bar executive*
Ely, John Hart
Ely, Northcutt *Natural resources*
Eskin, Barry Sanford *Conservatorships, guardianships*
Eule, Julian N. *Constitutional law*
Fedirko, Robert John *Social security*
Fine, Timothy Herbert *Franchising*
Fink, Scott Alan *Accountant liability*
Finney, Joseph Claude *Jeans Computer*
Firestone, Charles Morton *Communications/Telecommunications*
Fisher, Barry Alan *Constitutional*
FitzGerald, John Edward, III *Business law*
Fleming, John Gunther *Comparative, Torts*
Foley, Martin James *High technology, Lenders liability*
Fox, Richard Paul *Veterans, Federal employees*
Gentile, Joseph F. *Arbitration*
Gibson, Virginia Lee *Fiduciary services and institutional funds*
Glad, Edward Newman *Import and export law, and customs*
Grofman, Bernard Norman *Law and social science*
Gunderson, Robert Vernon, Jr. *Venture capital and emerging companies*
Gunther, Gerald *Constitutional law*
Hamann, H. Fredrick
Handschuh, G. Gregory *Intellectual property law*
Hanson, Gary A. *College and university law*
Hanzlik, Rayburn DeMara *Attorney recruiting*
Harris, Robert Lewis *Corportate free speech-first amendment*
Hassan, Allen C. *Professional negligence*
Hawkins, Karen L(ee) *Tax litigation, Taxation partnership*
Hearsch, Janis Camille Brown *Mediation business and family law*
Hoffman, John Douglas *Civil litigation*

Hudson, Dirk Ludwig *State appellate litigation, Federal appellate litigation*
Jackson, Michele Chickerella *Unfair trade practices*
Jaffee, Arthur Joseph *Medical-Legal Matters, Products Liability Litigation*
Jensen, Dennis Lowell *Election*
Johnson, Richard Wesley *Trial attorney*
Kahane, Dennis Spencer *Communications*
Kay, Herma Hill *Conflicts*
Keup, Erwin J. *Franchise law*
Kilbourne, George William *Toxic tort litigation*
Klott, David Lee *Nonprofit corporate law*
Kofford, Cree-L *Business*
Kojima, Robin Dale *Legal publishing*
Kostant, Ralph Bennett *Energy, geothermal*
Kovacic, Gary Anton *Zoning and land use regulation*
Lane, Robert K. *State and federal civil litigation*
LaRocco, John Bernard *Arbitration*
Lascher, Edward Leonard *Civil and criminal appeals*
Lehat, Steven Bruce *International trade*
Lindley, F(rancis) Haynes, Jr. *estate management*
Lipton, Alvin E(lliot) *International taxation*
Lobner, Kneeland Harkness *General Corporate and Construction*
Lucas, Campbell Macgregor *Appellate judiciary*
Ludwig, Ronald L. *Corporate Finance*
Lynch, James Joseph, Jr. *Constitutional law*
Maciel, Ronald John *Tax planning or individual taxation*
Marsh, Richard Melvin *Title Insurance*
McCarthy, John Charles *Insurance bad faith, Wrongful discharge, Commercial bad faith*
McNichols, Stephen Lucid Robert, Jr. *General business*
McNulty, John Kent *International taxation*
Metz, Robert Ernest *Intellectual property*
Miller, James L. *Product Liability Litigation*
Miller, Thomas Eugene *Legal writing*
Miller, William Napier Cripps *Water law*
Mintz, Ronald Steven *Police abuse and official corruption*
Mishkin, Paul J. *Constitutional law*
Mispagel, Mark Francis *Airport & Air Transportation Development*
Monaco, Daniel Joseph *Product and malpractice.*
Mones, Paul Alan *Intra-family homicide, emphasis on parricide with relation to child abuse*
Moomjian, Cary Avedis, Jr. *Contract drilling activities*
Neiman, Tanya Marie *Legal services to the poor, Bar association and legal services program administration*
Nelson, Paul Douglas *Sports injury*
Nesbitt, Mark Thomas *Mining-land acquistion and management*
Nissenberg, Merel Grey *Medical malpractice*
O'Hearn, Barbara Ann *Housing*
O'Malley, James Terence *Broadcasting*
Pasternak, David Joel *Receiverships*
Patterson, Robert Edward *High technology business*
Payne, Robert Warren *Trade secrets litigation*
Perluss, Irving Harvey *arbitration; private judging*
Pierno, Anthony Robert *Franchising*
Pongracz, Ann Cecilia *Telecommunications*
Prager, Susan Westerberg *Marital property law*
Priest, Maurice Abner, Jr. *Mobile home law*
Rai, Shambhu K. *Business law*
Randall, Richard Parks *Mergers and acquisitions*
Ray, David Lewin *Receivership law*
Riordan, John *Social security disabilities claims*
Robinson, William Adams *Arbitration*
Rose, I. Nelson *Gambling law*
Rosenhan, David L. *Constitutional*
Ross, Susan Kohn *Customs and international trade law*
Rossmann, Antonio *Natural Resources*
Salzberg, Arthur Jonathan *Commodities*
Schlesinger, Rudolf Berthold *Comparative*
Sewall, William Dana *Leasing*
Sherman, Glenn Terry *Franchising*
Sherrell, John Bradford *Secured financing*
Shire, Harold Raymond *Japanese*
Siegan, Bernard Herbert *Constitutional*
Slabach, Stephen Hall *General business*
Sloane, Owen Jay *Entertainment*
Solish, Jonathan Craig *Franchise law*
Spuehler, Donald Roy *Exempt organizations*
Stanwyck, Steven Jay *Corporate finance, Commercial, Criminal and civil litigation*
Staring, Graydon Shaw *General Appellate*
Stevenson, Noel C. *Legal writing*
Stovitz, Chuck *Space law*
Switzer, Robert Joseph *Legal writing*
Tingle, James O'Malley *Intellectual property licensing*
Truett, Harold Joseph, III *Aviation and space*
Tutoli, Michele Ann *Financial consulting*
Van Camp, Brian Ralph *Franchising*
Van de Kamp, John Kalar
Van Praag, Jane Catherine *High technology*
von Kalinowski, Julian Onesime
Ward, Diane A. *Corporate finance*
Welch, Walter Andrew, Jr. *Aviation accident law*
Williams, Jerry John *Labor arbitration and third party despute resolution*
Wolf, Lawrence *Alternative sentencing specialist*
Woolls, Paul *Reinsurance litigation and arbitration*
Yancey, David Wallace *Mortgage law*
Zumbrun, Ronald Arthur *Public interest law*

Colorado

Arnold, Harry H., III *Education and schools*
Aronstein, James Karpeles *Mining and Public Lands*
Beattie, Steven Mack *Educational law*
Boigon, Howard Lawrence *Energy*
Campbell, Leonard Martin *Municipal law*
Carson, William Scott *Franchising*
Clay, Aaron Richard *Water and natural resources law*
Conway, John Joseph *Transportation*
Cope, Joseph Adams *Water rights*
Damas, Stanislaw Stefan *School law*
Dominick, David DeWitt *Water rights law*
Dowdle, Patrick Dennis *Civil litigation*
DuVivier, Katharine Keyes *Natural resources*
Echohawk, John Ernest *Indian law*
Eckelberger, Jerrie Francis *Civil litigation*
Evans, Paul Vernon *Mining and minerals*
Gablehouse, Timothy Reuben *Biotechnology*
Gardner, Dale Ray *Child support enforcement*
Gebow, Thomas Eugene *Architect and engineering malpractice*
Gill, Anne Whalen *Legal publishing*
Goldberg, Charles *Matters peculiar to the Roman Catholic Church*
Grant, Patrick Alexander *Transportation*
Halpern, Joseph W. *Communications*
Heldman, Victoria C. *Aviation*
Henderson, John Richard *Mine and minerals*
Hook, Mary Julia *Mining and Minerals*
Hope, Mary *Legal publishing*
Jacobs, Ronald Hedstrom *Savings and Loan*
Johnson, Ruth Brammer *Oil and gas exploration and production*
Keatinge, Cornelia Wyma *Historic preservation law*
Leaming-Elmer, Judy *Indian law*
Loewi, Andrew William *Land use and planning*
Mall, Loren L(ee) *Natural resources*
Mandell-Rice, Bonnie Starr *Public lands law, Mining and natural resources*
Marsh, William Robert *Mineral law*
McCallie, Spencer Wyatt *Engineering contracts and services*
Meininger, John Alexander *Farmer and rancher debtor representation*
Meyer, Lee Gordon *Licensing*
Micsak, Robert William *Mining*
Nunn, Leslie Edgar *Agricultural law*
Ogburn, Robert Wilson *Water law*
Outerbridge, Cheryl *Mining & Minerals*
Petrucci, Stephen Gerard *Medical legal affairs, Sports law*
Press, Caren Sue *Communications*
Prichard, Vincent Marvin *Computer-assisted Legal Research*
Pulley, Lewis Carl *Communications*
Radosevich, George Edward *National, international water policy law*
Ragonetti, Thomas John *Land use and planning*
Ramirez, David Eugene *Business licensing*
Rose, Charles Jon *Municipal prosecution*
Roth, Robert Charles *Oil and gas*
Rowan, Ronald Thomas *Sports and entertainment*
St. Clair, Scott Andrew *Automobile law*
Sanford, Kendall Thaine *Transportation*
Savage, John William, Jr. *Water law and oil shale claims patent litigation*
Shafer, Stephanie Jane *Commercial*
Shanaberger, Carol Jean *Pre-hospital care and emergency medical services liabilty*
Smith, Milton Lovett *Space law*
Starrs, Elizabeth Anne *Malpractice defense*
Sullivan, Stephen Joseph *Oil and gas exploration geology*
Sumners, William Glenn, Jr. *Reinsurance risk management*
Turner, Charles Carre
Ullstrom, L. Berwyn *Aviation law*
Vogels, David Sellers, Jr. *Legal administration*
Vranesh, George *Mining and minerals*
Weinshienk, Zita Leeson *Judiciary*
White, Michael Douglas *Water*
Wilcox, Martha Anne *Professional disciplinary defense*

Connecticut

Allan, John Malcolm, Jr. *International taxation*
Austin, Richard David *Financing*
Bassick, Edgar Webb, III
Bell, Robert Collins *Indian*
Bingham, Lisa Blomgren *Edn. law (school bds.)*
Black, Charles Lund, Jr.
DiPietro, Andrew Michael, Jr. *Chapter 11 commercial*
Finn, Harold Bolton, III
Fisher, Clyde Olin, Jr. *Land use and planning*
Gates, Signe Sandra *Mergers and acquisitions*
Gentile, Michael Anthony *Office of the Reporter of Judicial Decisions*
Gitlin, Richard Alan *Corp fin*
Hazard, Geoffrey Cornell, Jr. *Civil Procedure, Legal ethics*
Holder, Angela Roddey *Medical*
Hollander, William Victor *Product Liability*
Kramer, Barry *Unfair Competition*
Ktorides, Stanley *Technology creation and transfer*
Loh, Robert Daniel, Jr. *Corporate secretary, investor relations*
Sahl, John Patrick *Sports*
Sanetti, Stephen Louis *Product liability*
Sommer, Evelyn Morrison *Intellectual property law*
Sparks, William James Ashley *Product Liability*
Trager, Philip *Art*
Valentine, Garrison Norton *Land use and zoning*
Weinstein, Paul *Unfair competition*

Delaware

Brandt, Charles *Plantiff's personal injury and criminal defense*
Davis, James Francis *Product liability*
Herrmann, Philip Eric *Lobbying*
Holzman, James L(ouis)
Ott, William Griffith *Business law*
Paintin, Francis Arthur *International trade commission practice*
Shearin, Kathryn Kay *Legal humor*
Whitehurst, Charles Elwood, Jr. *Toxic tort*

District of Columbia

Ackerson, Nels J(ohn) *Civil litigation international*
Aisenberg, Irwin Morton *Unfair Competition*
Allen, Nicholas Eugene *Copyright*
Andrews, Dale Carter *Maritime law, Aviation*
Angarola, Robert Thomas *Food and drug*
Atwood, Charles Starr *Hotels and motels*
Bardin, David J. *Energy*
Bardwell, Stanford O., Jr. *Civil litigation*
Barr, Michael Blanton *Communications*
Barron, Jerome Aure *Communications*
Beers, Donald Osborne *Food and drug*
Bellamy, Frederick Robert *Investment companies*
Berman, Stanford Warner *Unfair competition*
Bernstein, Marc Alan *Transportation*
Blake, Jonathan Dewey *Communications*
Blattner, Jeffrey Hirsh
Boyce, Katharine Randolph *Federal election law*
Braden, Efrem Mark *Election law*
Brecher, Mitchell Fredrick *Communications*
Brinkmann, Robert Joseph *Communications and media law*
Broches, Aron *International arbitration*
Brooten, Kenneth Edward, Jr. *Medical malpractice—personal counsel for physicians*
Brown, James Milton *Land use and zoning*
Burleson, William Anderson *Legal services in aid*
Butner, Blain Byerly *Higher education*
Casey, Bernard Joseph *Product liability*
Christensen, Karen Kay *Communications*
Clubb, Bruce Edwin *International trade*
Cobbs, Louise Bertram *Aviation*
Cole, Michael Frederick *Food and drug*
Coursen, Christopher Dennison *Communications*
Cox, C. Christopher
Cummings, Frank *Insurance, Labor*
Danziger, Martin Breitel *legal audit*
Davidson, Duncan Mowbray *Venture capital*
Dembling, Paul Gerald
DeStein, Beverlee Jean *Public Education legal*
Dinerstein, Robert David *Lawyer skills-interviewing, counseling and negotiation*
Disenhaus, Helen Elizabeth *Communications*
Di Tullio, Donna Marie *labor arbitration and mediation*
Dombroff, Mark Andrew *Aviation, Products liability*
Doyle, Austin Joseph, Jr. *White collar and tax fraud defense*
Dubuc, Carroll Edward *Aviation*
Edwards, Mary Frances *Legal association executive*
Eisenberg, Meyer *Financial services*
Elikann, Peter Todd *Reporting television news*
Ellis, Emory Nelson, Jr. *Transportation*
Ellis, Mark Gregory *Mining or natural resources*
Evans, Robert David *Legal assn. exec.*
Feldman, Roger David *Energy*
Fels, Nicholas Wolff *Communications*
Fenster, Herbert Lawrence *Product liability*
Finton, Timothy Christopher *international communications*
Fisher, Bart Steven *International trade*
Flowe, Benjamin Hugh, Jr. *Commercial financing*
Forrest, Herbert Emerson *Communications*
Foscarinis, Maria *Poverty law*
Franklin, William Jay *Communications*
Fraser, D. Larry *Aviation*
Fried, Charles *Constitution*
Gastfreund, Irving *Communications*
Gilberg, David Jay *Commodities*
Glasgow, Norman M. *Land use, historic preservation*
Glazier, Jonathan Hemenway *International tax, International trade*
Glowinski, Robert William *Fire protection law*
Grindle, John, Jr. *Probate and taxation*
Gross, David Andrew *Communications and Telecommunications*
Guarini, Frank J. *International trade*
Halpern, Linda Ann *Medical malpractice*
Hammer, Sandra Neiman *Food and drug*
Handleman, Aaron L. *Insurance litigation--defense legal malpractice suits*
Hess, Michael Anthony *Election law reapportionment and redistricting law*
Hoffman, Joseph Bowytz *Equine law*
Holtz, Edgar Wolfe *Communications*
Horn, Lawrence Alan *Business start-up, acquisition and development*
Howard, Daggett Horton *Arbitration*
Howell, Wesley Grant, Jr. *General communications litigation*
Humphries, Derrick Anthony *Telecommunications*
Ittig, Gerard W. *Surety law*
Johnson, Richard Tenney *Aviation*
Joseph, Robert George *Law related services*
Kalish, Steven Joseph *Transportation*
Kaplan, Richard Alan
Katzen, Sally *Communications*
Kay, Kenneth Robert *Technology*
Keeney, John Christopher, Jr. *Election law*
Kinsey, Carrol Hughes, Jr. *Federal personnel law*
Kirk, Alan Goodrich, II
Kirtley, Jane Elizabeth *First Amendment-News Media Law*
Klonoff, Robert Howard *Appellate litigation*
Knauer, Leon Thomas *Telecommunications, International private*
Korth, Fred
Kurrelmeyer, Louis Hayner *Aviation*
LaFrance, Ann Juliette *Telecommunications, postal*
Leonard, Jerris *Elections*
Levin, Betsy *Education law*
Levin, Lon Carl *Space commercialization*
Levine, Henry David *Telecommunications*
Levy, Steven Abraham *Telecommunications*
Lipkin, Gary Dennis *Election, campaign and political finance law*
Litvin, David Anthony *Oil and gas*
Loftus, Carroll Michael *Energy, coal*
Lyon, Edwin Leon *Commodities*
Macleay, Donald *Transportation*
Madole, Donald Wilson *Aviation*
Maloney, Barry Charles *Franchise law*
Markham, Jerry Wayne *Commodities*
Mathers, Peter Robert *Food and Drug*
McAvoy, John Joseph *Trade*
McGivern, Thomas Michael *Commodities law*
McGrew, Thomas James *Advertising*
Means, Thomas Cornell *Mining and natural resources*
Meyers, Erik Jon *Non-profit exempt organization corporate*
Micek, Terrance Dean *Intoxicating liquors*
Midlen, John Holbrook, Jr. *Communications*
Millhauser, Marguerite Sue *Alternative dispute resolution, Negotiation*
Millstein, Leo Lee *Communications*
Nateman, Gary M. *Restaurant and bar*
Neal, Anne deHayden
Nelson, Robert Louis *Law firm management*
O'Brien, Timothy Andrew *Supreme court constitutional law*
Owen, Roberts Bishop *International*
Podberesky, Samuel *Aviation*
Polsky, Howard David *Telecommunications*
Potenza, Joseph Michael *Litigation*
Potter, Tanya Jean *International trade*
Powell, Ramon Jesse
Powell, Robert Dominick *Air*
Raim, David Matthew *Reinsurance arbitration*
Ramsey, Robert Lee *Aviation*
Reback, Joyce Ellen *Education law*
Reeder, Joe Robert
Reidl, Paul William *Mine safety and health*
Rill, James Franklin
Roper, Robert St. John *Communications*
Rosenblatt, Peter Ronald *Government relations*
Rouvelas, Emanuel Larry *Transportation law*
Russin, Jonathan *Latin America transactions*
Salzman, Richard Stephen
Scheer, Peter Edward *National security*
Schildhause, Sol *Telecommunications, Cable TV and Broadcast*
Shaffer, Roberta Ivy *Comparative law*
Shafferman, Howard Haswell *Telecommunications*
Sharp, Stephen Alan *Communications*
Shaw, David Anthony *Entrepreneural*
Sherk, George William *Water Law*
Shihata, Ibrahim Fahmy Ibrahim *Development finance*
Silverglade, Bruce A. *Food and drug*
Simon, Samuel Alan *Communications*
Smith, Robert Anthony *Franchising*
Stevenson, John Reese *International arbitration*
Strother, James French *Accountants liability*
Tansill, Frederick Riker
Tate, Thomas Harrison *Drug product liability, Birth defect product liability litigation*
Thode, Anna Catharine *Professional liability*
Trosten, Leonard Morse *Transportation*
Turner, Robert Foster *National security law*
Vanlier, Charlene *Judicial administration, Telecommunications*
Vary, George Folk *International trade*
Vlcek, Jan Benes *Oil and gas general*
Walker, Mary Ann *Energy, alternate energy practice*
Walker, Vern Robert *Scientific evidence (administrative and court proceedings)*
Wallison, Frieda K. *Public finance*
Ward, Nicholas Donnell *Art*
Waz, Joseph Walter, Jr. *Communications*
Weinstein, Les *Food and drug law*
Wewer, William *Non-profit organizations*
Wiley, Richard Emerson *Communications*
Yung, Carroll John *Communications*
Zagami, Anthony James *Federal government in general*
Zeidman, Philip Fisher *Franchising*
Zenoff, Elyce Hope *Mental health*
Zwick, Kenneth Lowell *Automated litigation support*

Florida

Abrell, Joseph Kindred *Communications*
Andersen, Michael Page *Legal counsel for comprehensive investment department*
Asencio, Diego Carlos *Wrongful death*
Atlas, Allan Jay *Commercial litigation*
Austin, Robert Eugene, Jr. *Trial practice*
Bagge, Douglas Malcolm *High technology and venture capital*
Bartolone, Frank Salvatore *Growth mamgement, land use planning and zoning*
Berger, C. William *Aviation*
Berley, David Richard *Commercial*
Betts, James Robert *Commercial collections*
Braddock, Donald Layton *Civil litigation*
Bronis, Stephen J. *national security cases*
Burton, Clayton B., Sr. *General business, Living trusts*
Canter, Bram D. E. *Land use and planning*
Cassel, Marwin Shepard
Chopin, L. Frank *International taxation*
Coe, Jack Martin *Appellate*
Cooper, Margaret Leslie *Commercial state and federal litigation*
DeFoor, James Allison, II *Technology and the courts*
Delancett, John Gerald *Criminal tax law*
Denman, James Burton *Aviation*
Edwards, Claude Reynolds *Civil trial judge*
Efron, Muriel Cohen *Paralegal management and training.*
Epperson, Joel Rodman *Trial practice*
Escarraz, Enrique, III *College and university law*
Farrell, Patrick Joseph, Jr. *Products liability and professional malpractice*
Gougelman, Paul Reina *Land use and planning*
Hayes, Mark Stephen *Communications*
Herron, Janet D. *Disability benefits*
Ines, Victor Doroteo *Advertising Law*
Irvin, Robert Julian
Jacobo, Winston Wendle *Agricultural reorganization consultant*
Jones, John Edward *Products liability*
Kaimowitz, Gabe Hillel *Poverty law*
Kerr, Ann Loughridge
Klein, Larry A. *Appellate practice*
Lambertus, Christine Lundt *Trust & guardianship administration*
Leib, Patricia Shane *Condominium*
Leibowitz, Matthew Leon *Communications*
Lipnack, Martin I.
McNeill, Frederick Wallace *Air*
Melton, Howell Webster
Mitchell, George Oles
Morgan, Rebecca C. *Legal problems of the elderly*
Motes, Carl Dalton *Professional liability*
Nutzhorn, Carl Robbins *Constitutional*
Oliva, Robert Rogelio *International taxation*
Phipps, Benjamin Kimball, II *Federal taxation*
Ramsey, Bruce Mitchell *Products liability*
Rashkind, Paul Michael
Reid, R(alph) Benjamine *Product liability*
Roman, Ronald Peter *Franchise Law*
Ross, Howard Philip *Commercial*
Rubio, Herman Frank
Samole, Myron Michael *Negligence*
Sanchez, Ernesto *International franchising, trademark licensing*
Sanders, Edwin Perry Bartley
Sax, Spencer Meridith *Condominium*
Schechterman, Lawrence *Taxation*
Scott, Thomas Emerson, Jr. *Product liability*
Sechen, Robert Nicholas *Development and land use*
Solomon, Douglas Paul *Franchising*
Spann, Ronald Thomas *Arbitration and mediation*
Stankee, Glen Allen *Federal and state tax litigation (civil & criminal)*
Thornburg, Frederick Fletcher *Taxation*
Thornton, Richard Joseph *Aviation and insurance law*
Tittsworth, Clayton (Magness) *Corps Relations, Domestic Relations*
Velasquez, Patti A. *Real estate tax appeals*
Warren, Jeffrey Wayne *Commercial collections*
Wendel, John Fredric *Sports law*
White, Stephen Richard *Prosecution management*
Wich, Donald Anthony, Jr. *Constitutional*
Witlin, Barry Ethan *Sports*

Georgia

Brown, Colin W(egand) *Mergers and acquisitions*
Center, Tony *Sports law*
Champion, Forrest Lee, Jr. *General civil practice*
Davis, Claude-Leonard *University counsel*
DeLoach, Donald Brian *Tax litigation*
Dillard, George Douglas *Land use and planning law*
Earls, Margaret Bernardine Holley *Mediation and Arbitration*
Eastwood, Myles Eric *Personal bankruptcy and injury*
Fischer, David Jon *Aviation*
Garcia, Luis Cesareo *Legal insurance and services*
Giffin, Gordon D. *Election law*
Johnson, Donald (Don) Wayne *State and federal civil litigation*
Jones, Donald Richard, III *Sales of business*
Lower, Robert Cassel *Commodities*
McClain, William Asbury *Corporate Finance*
Pendergast, John Francis, Jr. *Professional athlete representation*
Phillips, Charles Patrick *Mediation*
Pollard, Brenda Krebs *Surety*
Riggs, Gregory Lynn *Aviation*
Robillard, Walter George *Boundary law--riparian*
Savell, Edward Lupo *Business torts*
Smith, Jeffrey Michael *Legal malpractice litigation, Accounting malpractice litigation, Directors and officers malpractice litigation*
Stone, Brian *Legal services and aid*
Webb, Michael Steven *Legal publishing*
Welch, Denise Majette *Drafting appellate court opinions*
Zito, Jeffrey Raymond *Aviation*

Hawaii

Bloede, Victor Carl *Geothermal*

Callies, David Lee *Land use and planning*
Foley, Daniel Robert *Constitutional law*
Hart, Brook *Federal criminal litigation, State criminal litigation*
Murakami, Alan Tomoo *Public interest, native Hawaiian rights*
O'Malley, Michael John *Personal income taxation*
Turk, David L. *Aviation litigation*
Weight, Michael A. *Professional responsibility*
Woo, Vernon Ying-Tsai *Civil litigation*

Idaho

Fields, James Ralph *International-Private Arbitration*
Park, William Anthony *General civil practice*

Illinois

Alexander, Ellen Jo *Arbitrator, mediator*
Antonio, Douglas John *Partnership taxation*
Arlow, Allan Joseph *Communications*
Baker, Helen *Rights of Handicapped; Family Rights*
Bell, Dennis Arthur *Commodities*
Bennett, Robert William *Constitutional*
Bentley, Peter John Hilton *English and British commonwealth*
Bernthal, David Gary
Beu, William Raymond *Social security disability*
Bramnik, Robert Paul *Futures regulation-financial services*
Branding, Frederick H. *Food and drug*
Brent, Nancy Jean *Representation of health professionals*
Carasik, Karen Sue *Commodities*
Closen, Michael Lee *Agency and partnership*
Coffee, Richard Jerome, II *Higher education law*
Costello, John William
Danne, William Herbert, Jr. *Legal publishing*
Davis, Chester R., Jr. *Land use and planning*
Dees, Richard Lee *Agriculture*
Denzel, Ken John *Sports law*
Dorf, Michael Charles *Cultural planning*
Draznin, Anne L. *Arbitration and mediation*
Duff, David Potter *Airline litigation*
Early, Bert Hylton *legal search consultant*
Eaton, J(ames) Timothy *Defense of pharmaceutical companies in products liability actions*
Emerson, Carter Whitney *Acquisitions, Venture capital*
Everett, C. Curtis *Municipal bonds*
Fields, Howard M. *Personal Financial Planning*
Filler, Ronald Howard *Commodities*
Finman, Terry Jeanette
Flood, Vincent Patrick *Takeover defense*
Franklin, Frederick Russell *Legal association executive*
Gabe, Caryl Jacobs *Paternity*
Galatz, Henry Francis *Public education law*
Garley, Barry Ernest *Aviation*
Gary, Susan Nannette *Charitable and not for profit organizations*
George, John Martin, Jr. *Accountants liability*
Godfrey, Richard Cartier *Litigation relating to the oil industry*
Gottlieb, Paul Mitchel *Commodities*
Goulet, Lionel Joseph *Labor arbitrator and mediator*
Greenspan, Jeffrey Dov *Land use and planning*
Gutman, Richard Martin *Political surveillance*
Hablutzel, Nancy Zimmerman *Disability law*
Hack, Linda *Alternate dispute resolution*
Hall, Reed Stanley *Consumer credit*
Harvitt, Adrianne Stanley *Commodities*
Hayes, David John Arthur, Jr. *Legal association executive*
Heinz, John Peter
Herman, Stephen Charles *Transportation*
Hochman, James Alan *Civil litigation*
Horsley, Jack Everett *Medical*
Hoyne, Scott William *Commercial, corporate*
Hutchinson, Dennis James *Constitutional*
Keith, John Ray *Election law*
Klaus, Roger Dean *Legal and Tax Publishing*
Kozak, John W. *Licensing*
Langbein, John Harriss *Employee benefits*
Lapin, Harvey I. *Cemetery law*
Lee, William Marshall *Trademark*
Lerner, Jeffrey Michael *Civil litigation*
Levi, Edward Hirsch
Macneil, Ian Roderick *Arbitration*
Malkin, Cary Jay *Leasing*
Matanky, Robert William *Real estate securities*
McCabe, Charles Kevin *Aviation*
McLaughlin, T. Mark *Franchise law*
Miller, Kenneth Charles *Aviation*
Minow, Newton Norman *Communications*
Mlsna, Kathryn Kimura *Marketing, advertising (not trademarks)*
Morris, James W. *Mining and minerals*
Muir, Robert Eugene *Licensing*
Munson, James Calfee *Utilities*
Nissen, William John *Commodity futures law and litigation*
North, Kenneth Earl *Federal white collar criminal*
Ntephe, Azike A.
Null, Michael Elliot *Constitutional*
Nye, Sandra Gayle *Mental Health*
Paniaguas, John Steven *Unfair competition*
Paprocki, Thomas John *Counsel, religious organization, Nonprofit legal clinic*
Parkhurst, Beverly Susler *Travel law*
Pavela, D. Jean *Lawyer referral, Bar association administration*
Peck, Robert Stephen *Constitutional Law, First Amendment Law*

Pelton, Russell Meredith, Jr. *Association representation*
Pepper, Joyce M. *Trade practices*
Phelps, Paul Michael *Corporate secretary*
Phillips, Michael James *Legal advisor to county government*
Pitt, George *Municipal Bonds*
Polaski, Anne Spencer *Commodity futures law*
Raymond, David Walker *Trade Regulation*
Ream, Davidson *Legal publishing, Lawyers' associations*
Reeder, Robert Harry
Rendleman, Dennis Alan *Legal ethics professional responsibility, Association law and activities*
Reynolds, Daniel *Legal Ethics*
Rohrman, Douglass Frederick *Food and drug*
Rosenfield, Andrew M. *Regulated industries*
Rudd, Donnie *Condominium law*
Rupert, Donald William
Rutkoff, Alan Stuart *Professional liability--accountants, lawyers*
Santona, Gloria *Financial law*
Scott, John Joseph *Mutual funds*
Senescu, Stuart *Aviation*
Shannon, Peter Michael, Jr. *Ecclesiastical law*
Sholem, David Bennett *Communications*
Snyder, Dean Edward *Food and drug*
Szczepanski, Slawomir Zbigniew Steven *Licensing of intellectual property*
Thompson, Earl G(eorge) *International tax*
Townsend, Donald Joseph *Franchise law*
Troelstrup, John Frederick *Commodity futures/securities*
Van Hagey, William *Franchising*
Ward, Michael W. *Telecommunications*
Willmeth, Roger Earl *Telecommunications*
Wilson, Edward Churchill *Aviation*
Wilson, Michael B(ruce) *Telecommunications*
Witz, Allen Barry *Communications*
Wrigley, Julie Ann *Equine law*
Wulfers, John Manning *Reinsurance*

Indiana

Blomquist, Robert Frank *Torts*
Kingdon, Victor Scott *Arts and cultural affairs*
McKeon, Thomas Joseph *Communications*
Pellicciotti, Joseph Michael *Legal research and writing*
Weeks, Walter William *Natural Area property and tax law*
Wray, Donn Hayes *Automotive retail defense*

Iowa

Dunn, Susan M. *Librarianship support staff*
Frederici, C. Carleton *Class actions*
Harl, Neil Eugene *Agricultural law*
McEnroe, Michael Louis *Agricultural*
Shane, Peter Milo *Constitutional*
Steinger, Charles Stanford
Walker, E. Ralph *Product liability litigation*

Kansas

Barnett, James Monroe *Medical malpractice*
Gard, Spencer Agassiz *Consultant on evidence*
Jacobson, Susan Curtis *Medical malpractice*
Sanborn, Richard John Jay *Municpal corporations*
Weinberg, Gary Scott *Principal of corporation*

Kentucky

Aulenbach, W(illiam) Craig *Communications*
Brule, Thomas Raymond *Franchise law*
DeFalaise, Louis *Law enforcement*
Fink, Joseph Leslie, III *Pharmacy law, Food and drug*
Hilliard, William Raymond, Jr. *Equine law*
Huddleston, Joseph Russell
Miller, J. Bruce *Sports*
Newberry, James H., Jr. *Equine*
Ockerman, Edwin Foster, Jr. *Equine law*
Reverman, Philip John, Jr. *Federal black lung law*
Riggs, Roger D. *Medical negligence*
Tannon, Jay Middleton *Mergers and acquisitions, Alternative dispute resolution*
Todd, James Marion *Collections*
Walker, Henry Lawson, II *Aviation*

Louisiana

Beer, Peter Hill
Benson, Lawrence Kern, Jr. *Federal criminal prosecution*
Bryan, Trevor George *Medical malpractice, Home*
David, Robert Jefferson *Federal and state civil litigation*
DeMahy, Paul Joseph
Denegre, Stanhope Bayne-Jones *Commercial litigation*
Furman, Michael Joseph *Product liability defense*
Gertler, Meyer H. *Product liability*
Lampard, Catherine Ann *Constitutional law*
Levy, Adolph J. *Legal consulting, motion practice*
Madison, Vivian L. *Products liability*
Matheny, Tom Harrell *Mental health*
Moliere, Donna Renee *Errors and omissions*
Osakwe, Christopher *Soviet*
Pugh, George Willard *Comparative, Evidence criminal justice law*
Rosenberg, Samuel Irving *School litigation*
Saloom, Kaliste Joseph, Jr. *Traffic Laws*
Surprenant, Mark Christopher *Products liability law*

Villavaso, Stephen Donald *Zoning land use*
Williamson, Harold Edward *Criminal justice education*

Maine

Hart, Ronald Alton
Nichols, David Arthur *Evidence*
Perkins, Donald W. *Natural Resources, administrative*
Tureen, Thomas Norton *Indian affairs law, Indian financial transaction*

Maryland

Ahearn, Charles Dennis *Space commercialization*
Anderson, Lee Berger *Constitutional*
Appel, Thomas Alan *Product liability*
Armold, Judith Ann *Land use and planning*
Axelson, Jeffrey Mark *Condominium homeowner association*
Blakeslee, Wesley Daniel
Brodhurst, Albert Edward *Contracts law*
Chernow, Jeffrey Scott *Franchise law*
Clarke, Edward Owen, Jr. *Tax exempt financing and Local government*
Curzan, Myron Paul *Communications*
Fick, Nathaniel Crow, Jr. *Product liability*
Gohn, Jack Lawrence Benoit *Transportation, Litigation*
Goss, Thomas Marks *Products liability, Civil litigation, federal and state*
Grange, George Robert, II *Nonprofit, communications.*
Gray, Oscar Shalom *Torts*
Heller, Robert Henry, Jr. *Judiciary*
Hendricks, John Charles *Estate planning and administration*
Hitchcock, Paul Richard *Transportation*
Klein, Robert Dale *Product Liability*
Laws, Jean Sadowsky *Legal rights of the elderly*
McDermitt, Edward Vincent *Constitutional law*
Mowell, George Mitchell *Land use and planning law*
Munday, Melvin Wayne *Trial practice*
Respess, James Walter *General litigation and corporate*
Ryan, David Charles *Intelligence Law*
Sack, Sylvan Hanan *Toxic chemical exposure torts*
Simpson, Robert Edward
Souder, Susan *Tax litigation*
Spitzberg, Irving Joseph, Jr. *Education and Schools*
Terrell, Herbert Arthur *Litigation support and appellate work*
Tobias, Jeffrey *Communications*
Todd, Casey Ira *Business law as it relates to the seafood industry*
Ward, Richard Alvord
Wilson, Thomas Matthew, III *Franchise Litigation*
Winston, Roger Dean *Community Association Development*
Wright, Jefferson Vaughan *Corporate and commercial litigation*

Massachusetts

Adler, Sidney W. *Professional liability litigation*
Apjohn, Nelson George *Products liabiltiy*
Bartholet, Elizabeth *Employment discrimination*
Beal, John Arthur *Inter-professional relationship dilemmas*
Bernard, Michael Mark
Bigelow, Robert P. *copyright*
Burns, Thomas David *Medical*
Burnstein, Daniel *Non-Profit orgns, Freedom of information*
Carter, T. Barton *Communications law*
Cherwin, Joel Ira *Finance*
Deren, Donald David *Constitutional*
Fine, Phil David *Corporate finance*
Fischer, Mark Alan *Copyright and trademark*
Fisher, Roger Dummer *Negotiation and Conflict Resolution*
Gad, Robert K., III *Nuclear power plant licensing*
Goodman, Henry A. *Litigation*
Green, Joseph Benjamin *Missing Children*
Heilman, Carl Edwin *Private Financing*
Hoover, David Carlson *Wildlife management*
Howard, Gregory Charles *Real estate*
Katsh, M. Ethan *Communications*
Katzmann, Gary Stephen *Federal prosecution*
Lepore, Ralph Thomas, III *Aviation*
Lewis, Sanford Jay *Negotiation and alternative dispute resolution*
Lyons, Nance *Employment disputes*
Malone, Sue Urwyler
Marr, David Erskine *Family*
Nesson, Charles R. *Constitutional*
Parker, Richard Davies *Constitutional*
Sander, Frank Ernest Arnold *Dispute resolution*
Sawyer, Robert Kendal, Jr. *Franchising*
Simpson, Russell Avington *Law firm management*
Snyder, Frederick Edward *Comparative*
Takas, Marianne Heath *Writing, legal*
Urban, Lee Donald *Historic preservation*
Zito, Frank R. *Fidelity and surety bond investigations*

Michigan

Allen, Layman Edward *Logic of legal writing*
Anderson, Austin Gothard *Law firm management*
Babcock, Charles Witten *Product liability litigation*
Barrows, Ronald Thomas *Investments*
Bereznoff, Gregory Michael *Employment Litigation-Wrongful Discharge*
Bruin, Linda Lou *Education and schools*
Caretti, Richard Louis *Product liability defense*
Carlin, John Bernard, Jr. *Retaurants and liquor licenses*

Centers, Louise Claudena *Forensic evaluation*
Charla, Leonard Francis *Art Law*
Cotter, Dennis Blair *Product liability construction*
Currier, Timothy Jordan *School law*
Danhof, Robert John *Appellate court judge*
Ellmann, William Marshall *Civil litigation*
Fawcett, Kim Robert *Constitutional law*
Freilich, Diane M. *Medical malpractice*
Friedman, Bernard Alvin
Gleiss, Henry Weston *Malpractice*
Golden, Joseph Aaron *Wrongful discharge*
Haggerty, William Francis *Reporter of judicial decisions*
Hall, Terrence Lyon *Social security disability appeals*
Heil, Paul William *Pension, securities and finance*
Kamins, John Mark *Municipal Bonds*
Kennedy, Kael Behan *Associations and cooperatives*
Legg, Michael William *Law firm management*
Lempert, Richard Owen *Evidence, law and social science*
Marks, Andrew James *Non-profit organizations*
Messmer, Kirk Daniel *Election law*
Perry, James B.
Phillips, Elliott Hunter *Non-profit organizations*
Pierce, Richard William *Intellectual property transfers*
Regan, Donald H. *Constitutional*
Rich, Edward William *Financial law*
St. Antoine, Theodore Joseph *Contracts*
Sandalow, Terrance *Constitutional*
Sarb, Thomas Patrick *corporate reorganization*
Skipper, Nathan Richard, Jr. *Other*
Smith, Mark Richard *Liquor liability*
Sorge, Jay Wootten *Non-profit organizations*
Steeno, David Lawrence *Legal aspects of private security industry, police civil liability*
Steiner, Peter Otto *Economics and law*
Tarnacki, Duane L. *Tax exempt organizations*
Thomas, Michael Eli *Church - state*
Thurber, Cleveland, Jr.
Vanderkloot, William Robert *Commercial litigation, corporate & business practice*
White, James Alfred *Agricultural*

Minnesota

Aaron, Allen Harold *Business litigation*
Burns, Richard Ramsey *Broadcast law*
Degnan, John Michael *Federal and state civil litigation*
Dettmann, Marc John *Licensing*
Erickson, Phillip Arthur *Diverse practice*
Halva, Allen Keith *Editing law books*
Hanson, Kent Bryan *Product liability litigation*
Jarboe, Mark Alan *Indian law*
Johnson, Michael Almer *Dental Contract and Business Law*
Koskinen, David John *Employment*
Leighninger, Sally Heinz *Small business*
Magnuson, Paul A.
Martin, Kathleen Minder *Lending, secured transactions*
McNally, Pierce Aldrich *Corporate finance*
Montgomery, John Vincent *Federal communications commission*
Mozer, Michael Theodore *Development of marketing programs for lenders*
Murrin, John Owen *Small business*
Nadler, Richard Gregory *Consumer law*
Neff, Fred Leonard *Law firm management*
Odahowski, David Anthony *Exempt organizations, private foundations*
Palmer, John Marshall *Commercial litigation*
Rebane, John T. *Mergers and acquisitions*
Reuter, James William *Technological litigation*
Sand, David Byron
Singer, Norman Bruce *Continuing legal education, Law office administration*
Somsen, Henry Northrop
Yucel, Edgar Kent *Intellectual property licensing*
Zalasky, Jeff M. *Employment law*

Mississippi

Ferrell, Wayne Edward, Jr. *Aviation*
Fuselier, Louis Alfred *Defense*
Garrity, Thomas Anthony, Jr. *Natural resources*
Magee, William Eugene *General, federal, state and local taxation*
McKibben, Dale Harbour *Oil and gas law*
Southwick, Leslie Harburd *Public education*
Taylor, Zachary, III *Finance*

Missouri

Anton, Donald C. *Business*
Bartimus, James Russell
Becker, William Henry
Beezley, Theodore *Product liabilty*
Bierman, Norman *Hospital and physician's malpractice defense*
Bodker, Stuart Eliot *Commodities*
Bradshaw, Thomas Michael *Business litigation*
Breen, Jean Marie *Employment law*
Clark, Charles Edward *Arbitration*
Cooper, Corinne *Alternative dispute resolution arbitration*
Copilevitz, Errol *Constitutional*
Crepeau, Dewey Lee *Social security disability*
Crowe, Robert Alan *Arbitration, Mediation*
Dement, Sandra Helene *Prepaid legal service plans*
Gamm, Gordon Julius *Consumer employee fraud litigation*
Golbert, Albert Sidney *Taxation international*

Goldstein, Michael Gerald *Municipal Bonds*
Hackmann, Frank H(enry) *Utility rate intervention*
Holt, Ivan Lee, Jr. *Trial judge, Industrial*
Hulston, John Kenton
Jennings, William Hathaway, II *handicapped law, mental health law*
Katzenstein, Lawrence P. *Charitable and deferred giving*
Kretsinger, Tom Bark, Jr. *Motor carrier law*
Kuhlmann, Fred Mark *Acquisitions, divestitures*
Lashley, Curtis Dale *State government*
Lolli, Don R(ay) *Commodities*
McClellan, Janet Elaine
Miller, Stephen *Employee termination*
Nassif, Joseph Gerard *Toxic tort law*
Reddis, Frances Elaine *U.S. Government/ Dept. Health and Human Services*
Schramm, Paul Howard *General civil trial and appellate practice, federal and state*
See, Andrew Bruce *Product liability litigation*
Spalty, Edward *Franchising*
Stevens, Joseph Edward, Jr. *U.S. district judge*
Vines, Leonard Dean *Franchise law*
Walker, Walter Ladare *Transportation*
Wallace, Robert E. *Sports law*
Weber, Louis Jerry *School law*
Weisenfels, John Robert *Taxation of partnerships*
Wiggins, Kip Acker *Venture capital, Mergers and acquisitions*
Wuestner, Linda Douglas *Product liability litigation, Litigation*

Montana

Dunbar, Byron Herbert
Thorson, John Eric *Water law*

Nebraska

Aiken, J. David *Natural resources*
Burns, Steven Dwight *Business*
Colleran, Kevin *Litigation state agencies*
Frank, Julie Ann *Social security disability*
Hewitt, James Watt
Jones, Ronald Lee *Preventive Corporate*
O'Hara, Michael James *Franchising law and economics*
Scudder, Earl H., Jr.
Snowden, James Arthur *Medical malpractice defense*

Nevada

Claassen, Sharon Elaine *Indian law*
Crowell, William Jefferson
Gallagher, Dennis Vincent *Gaming*
Gourley, Robert Vaughn *Water law, natural resource law*
Haase, M. Craig *Mining and minerals*
Hill, Earl McColl *Public land and natural resources, Aviation*
Hoppe, Craig Allen *Alternative dispute resolution--arbitration and mediation*
Horton, Thomas David *Mining*
Risman, Marc Dale *Sports and entertainment law, Airline and travel industry law*
Tratos, Mark George *Art Law*

New Hampshire

Baldwin, Carolyn Whitmore *Planning and zoning*
DeHart, James Louis *Professional responsibility*
Platt, Thomas C., III *Mergers and acquisitions*

New Jersey

Aisenstock, Barry Alan *Education and civil service law*
Bardack, Paul Roitman *Venture capital, Economic development*
Bello-Monaco, Deborah Ann *Reinsurance*
Bennington, Alfred Joseph, Jr.
Bentley, Antoinette Cozell
Berman, Steven Paul *licensing*
Boyle, Matthew Anthony *Aviation*
Brandon, Mark Edward *Constitutional Interpretation*
Case, Douglas Manning *Mergers and acquisitions*
Chobot, John Charles *Commercial, Secured transactions*
Cox, William Martin *Land Use and planning*
Davidson, Robert Lee, III ,
Deutsch, Dennis Stuart *Computer and high technology law*
Dowd, Dennis Owen *Equine law*
Drakeman, Donald Lee *Constitutional--church state*
Egan, Robert T. *Franchise litigation*
Flinn, Thomas D. *Legal malpractice defense*
Freis, James Henry *Municipal Bonds*
Goldberg, Leonard M. *Taxation*
Goldberger, Alan Steven *Sports law*
Gonnella, Louis Gregory
Graham, Paul Eugene *Product liability*
Hall, Raymond Percival, III *Poverty and law*
Harris, Brian Craig *Product liability*
Herpst, Robert Dix *Mergers and acquisitions*
Herr, Philip Michael *Taxation-estate, gift, trust, personal and corporate*
Holt, Jason *Municipal law*
Iannarone, Anthony Joseph *Food and drug, Law office administration*
Joel, Jack Bowers *Product liability*
Kantowitz, Jeffrey Leon *Land use and planning*
Kaplan, Steven Samuel *Group and prepaid legal services*
Kassoff, Mitchell Jay *Franchising*
Kienz, Glenn Charles *Land use and planning*
Lechner, Alfred James, Jr.
Loigman, Larry Scott *Law enforcement matters*
Lustbader, Philip Lawrence *Franchising*

Meiser, Kenneth Edward *Land use and planning*
Moczula, Boris *Appellate*
Molloy, Brian Joseph *Gambling law*
Mullins, Margaret-Ann Frances *Criminal appellate practice*
Murray, William James *Government relations*
Nelson, Warren Owen *Executive compensation*
Oliver, Roseann Sellani *Plaintiff medical malpractice*
Pace, Thomas *Commercial law*
Percell, Marion *Appellate-federal criminal appeals*
Pickus, Robert Mark *Casino*
Salibello, Salvatore Joseph *Aviation tort litigation*
Shandor, Bohdan Donald *Mergers and acquisitions*
Sperber, Mark David *Appellate practice*
Vena, Joseph Anthony *Land use and planning*
Warmington, Robert Anthony *Legal placement*
Warnement, Pamela Pearson *Products liability*
Wilson, William Edward *Adminstrv. law, horse racing*
Wolf, John Barton *College and university law*
Zaloom, John B(asil) *Intellectual property*

New Mexico

Addis, Richard Barton *Mining Law*
Carpenter, Richard Norris *Natural resources*
Manzanares, Dennis *Aviation*
Sherman, Frederick Hood *Social security*
Vigil, Carol Jean *Indian law*

New York

Abrams, Robert *Law Enforcement Administration*
Adin, Richard H(enry) *Legal writing, Medical*
Aksen, Gerald *International arbitration*
Alexander, Mary R. *International taxation*
Altman, Robert Harry *Mergers and acquisitions*
Amdursky, Robert Sidney *Municipal Bonds*
Ames, Marc L. *Disability matters*
Angulo, Manuel Rafael *Latin American law*
Armstrong, James Sinclair *Landmarks preservation*
Augello, William Joseph *Transportation*
Barr, Thomas Delbert
Beck, Jan Scott *Mergers, acquisitions and divestitures*
Bekritsky, Bruce Robert *Civil litigation*
Bell, Jonathan Robert *Tax exempt organizations*
Belsky, Martin Henry *Public Interest Research*
Beltz, Paul William *Product liability*
Benedict, Thane, III
Bergstein, Daniel Gerard *Venture capital*
Bernstein, Jacob *Land Use and planning*
Bernstein, Paul Murray *Litigation*
Blake, Harlan Morse *Constitutional law*
Bobrow, Alvan Lee *International taxation*
Bonomi, John Gurnee *Atty. and Jud. disciplinary law, Med. disciplinary law*
Boone, William Daniel *Public affairs*
Borgese, John A. *Commodities*
Bozorth, Squire Newland *Education*
Breakstone, Jay L.T. *Federal and state civil litigation*
Breglio, John F. *Copyright*
Brewer, Curtis *Disability law*
Buckstein, Mark Aaron *Commodities*
Carey, Joseph Patrick *Employment law*
Carmien, Donald Charles *Transportation*
Carr, Rokki Knee
Carter, James Hal, Jr. *International commercial arbitration*
Catuzzi, J.P., Jr. *Mergers and acquisitions*
Cohen, Linda Meryl *Investment banking*
Collins, Wayne Dale *Constitutional law*
Condon, John William, Jr. *Taxation - personal and corporate*
Conroy, Robert J. *Medical legal affairs*
Contino, Richard Martin
Conway, Andrew Wayne *contracts*
Cooke, Bradford *Federal and state civil litigation*
Cramton, Roger Conant *Professional responsibility*
Davidson, Robert Bruce *Commercial arbitration*
Davis, Evan Anderson
DeBonis, Sharon Couch *Suretyship*
Deffina, Thomas Victor *Fidelity/Surety bond claims*
Devers, Peter Dix *Investment*
De Vivo, Edward Charles *Aviation*
Dickerson, Thomas Pasquali
Dixon, Harry Thomas *Insurance company defense*
Drebsky, Dennis Jay *Corporate litigation*
Edelson, Gilbert Seymour *Art law*
Eilen, Howard Scott *Commodities Regulation and Litigation*
Enberg, Henry Winfield *Legal Writing*
Feldman, Edward Steven *Cooperatives and condominiums*
Feldman, Jay N. *Mergers and acquisitions*
Feldman, Warren Bruce *Prepaid Legal Services*
Ferguson, Whitworth, III *Business law*
Fernbach, Robert Dennis *Public service and not for profit organizations*
Fersko, Raymond Stuart *Aviation*
Feuerstein, Donald Martin
Fink, Robert Steven *Litigation, Taxation, White collar criminal defense*
Franck, Thomas Martin
Franklin, Justin Duke, Jr. *Communications*
Freedman, Warren *Product liability, Transnational and international law*
Freeman, Robert John *Government information and privacy*
Freund, Fred A. *Employment discrimination*
Freund, James Coleman *Mergers and acquisitions*
Fry, Morton Harrison, II *Communications*
Galant, Herbert Lewis *Finance*
Gale, Peter L. *Civil service*
Gardner, Richard Newton *International Trade*
Gardner, Romaine Luverne *Commodities*
Gaylord, Bruce Michael *Telecommunications*
Gibson, Thomas Martin *Copyright*
Gingold, Irving *Products liability*
Giuliani, Rudolph W.
Goff, Betsy Kagen *Sports*
Goldblum, A. Paul *Professional Responsibility*
Golden, Marc Alan
Goodman, Mortimer *Consultant securities arbitration*
Gould, Dirk Samuel *Communication litigation*
Gowen, George W. *Sports*
Greenbaum, Maurice C. *Literary and copyright*
Greenman, Frederick Francis *Civil Ligitation*
Grossberg, David *Advertising*
Grossman, James Stuart
Guth, Paul C. *Mergers and acquisitions*
Handelman, Walter Joseph *Church and ecclesiastical*
Hanson, Jean Elizabeth *Mergers and acquisitions*
Hawkins, John Donald, Jr. *Leverage lease financing*
Hazard, John Newbold *Soviet Law*
Hegarty, William Edward *Civil litigation*
Heller, Fred Ira *Video documentary production for litigation*
Hemingway, Alfred Henry, Jr. *Patent and trademark*
Henkin, Louis *Human rights*
Hiden, Robert Battaile, Jr. *Mergers and acquisitions*
Hirschfeld, Michael *International and real estate taxation*
Hoff, Jonathan M(orind) *Corporate commercial litigation, Mergers and acquisitions*
Horowitz, Steven Gary *Public law*
Itzkoff, Norman Jay *Photographic art law*
Jacobs, Randall Scott David *Letters of credit*
Jawin, Paul Gregory *Syndications*
Jehu, John Paul *School district law*
Johnson, Kathryn Gibbons *Mergers and acquisitions*
Jordon, Deborah Elizabeth *Satellite and telecommunications law*
Junkerman, William Joseph *Aviation*
Kabak, Bernard Joshua *Land use and planning*
Kahn, Richard Dreyfus *Philanthropic organizations*
Kaminsky, Arthur Charles *Sports*
Kaplan, Mark Norman
Kassebaum, John Philip *Art*
Keen, Andrew Nick *Product liability, Aviation litigation*
Kies, David M. *Mergers and acquisitions*
Klein, Paul E.
Koblenz, Michael Robert *Commodities*
Koo, Richard *Mergers and acquisitions*
Koplik, Marc Stephen *Alternative energy*
Kowaloff, Steven David *Land use and planning*
Kraft, Melvin D. *Commercial and real estate arbitration, domestic and international*
Krainin, Harold L. *Trade Association*
Krasnow, Robert Louis *Real property taxes, assessment proceedings, abatements and exemptions*
Kress, Ralph Herbert *General litigation*
Kuhn, Perla M. *Foreign trade*
Kurnit, Richard Alan *Advertising*
Lanchner, Bertrand Martin *Communications*
Landzberg, Alan Jeffrey *Taxation, magazines, cable TV and other media, Taxation, patents, copyrights and other intellectual property*
Lankenau, John Clausen *Federal and state civil litigation, Publishing*
LeFevre, Eugene de Daugherty *Lawbook publishing*
Levin, Jack K. *Legal publishing*
Levine, Marilyn Markovich *Labor arbitration - mediation*
Levine, Sanford Harold *Education and schools*
Levitan, David M(aurice) *Constitutional*
Liuzzo, Anthony L. *Law and economics*
Longstreth, Bevis
Lusky, Louis *Constitutional law*
Madden, Murdaugh Stuart, Jr. *Evidence, Products liability, Torts*
Malach, Herbert John *Child Custody*
Mankes, Karen Marcoux *Agricultural*
Mannis, Bob Davis *Mergers and acquisitions*
Mayesh, Jay Philip *Product liability*
Mayo, John Tyler *General business*
McEnroe, John Patrick *Sports law*
McNeill, Walter Giles *Mortgage finance*
Milberg, Lawrence *Class actions*
Miller, Richard Steven *Corporate reorganizations*
Miller, Wesley A. Looney *Professional responsibility*
Mogil, Bernard Marc
Monroe, Kendyl Kurth *Corporate taxation, Corporate general*
Morris, Edward William, Jr. *Arbitration*
Mudge, George Alfred *Country debt restructure*
Muller, Frederick Arthur *legal editing and publishing*
Murray, William Peter *Federal apellate litigation, State appellate litigation, Water rights*
Myerson, Harvey Daniel *Securities and antitrust*
Nash, Paul LeNoir *Mergers and acquisitions*
Nates, Jerome Harvey *Legal publishing*
Newman, Howard Julian *Professional liability litigation*
Newman, William Arthur *Mergers and acquisitions*
Nierenberg, Gerard Irwin *Negotiation training*
Nowicki, Michael Thomas *Prosecution*
Ombres, Teresa *promotion marketing*
O'Neill, Patrick Joseph *Communications*
Osgood, Russell King *Constitutional law*
Owen, Joseph G.
Parent, Louise Marie *Mergers and acquisitions*
Parker, Kellis E. *Constitutional*
Plum, Stephen Haines, IV *Commercial litigation*
Potter, Hamilton Fish, Jr. *Commercial financing*
Pottle, Willard Marsh, Jr. *State and federal civil litigation*
Price, Monroe Edwin *Indian*
Price, Richard Lee
Primps, William G. *Litigation, Product liability litigation*
Probstein, Jon Michael *Civil litigation*
Rains, Harry Hano *Labor Arbitrator*
Redpath, John S(loneker), Jr. *Communications*
Reese, Willis Livingston Mesier *Legal*
Reichel, Aaron Israel *Freedom of information act (government disclosure)*
Reis, Muriel Henle *Communications, contract litigation*
Robinson, Herbert *Conflict of interest in business, Fidelity bond litigation*
Rogers, Thomas Sydney *Communications*
Rosdeitcher, Sidney S. *Civil litigation*
Rosenbaum, Eli M. *Prosecution of Nazi war criminals*
Rosenberg, Gerald Alan *Real estate valuation and taxation*
Rosenthal, Albert Joseph *Constitutional*
Rosenzweig, Theodore B. *Medical malpractice*
Ross, Christopher Theodore William *Aviation negligence*
Ross, Matthew *Accountants' Liability*
Ross, Michael Aaron *Energy financing*
Rothschild, Steven Bruce *Venture capital*
Rubin, Stephen Wayne *Mergers and acquisitions*
Sager, Jonathan Ward *Individual life insurance operations in a mutual company*
Santemma, Jon Noel *Federal practice*
Schecter, Sandra Jan *Project finance, Public finance*
Scheler, Brad Eric *Corporate finance and business reorganizations*
Schor, Edward Neil *Broadcasting and cable*
Schwab, David E., II *Transportation*
Schwarzer, Franklin John *Real property assessment reduction*
Sheridan, Peter N. *product liability*
Sherman, Charles Israel *Licensing*
Sigall, Michael William *Immigration and naturalization*
Silberman, John Alan *Advertising*
Simson, Gary Joseph
Sinsheimer, Alan J. *Mergers and aquisitions*
Sklar, Stanley Lawrence
Sloan, F(rank) Blaine *Water Law*
Smit, Hans
Solmonson, Steven Jay *Commodities*
Sommers, Elizabeth Boone *Appellate and trial court research, drafting and case management*
Spatt, Robert Edward *Mergers and acquisitions*
Spike, Michele Kahn *Art*
Sprizzo, John Emilio *Judge*
Stack, Joanne Tunney *Explaining law in plain english to general public*
Storette, Ronald Frank *Immigration and naturalization, Consular law*
Strauss, Peter L(ester) *Constitutional*
Swire, James Bennett *Food and drug*
Tabak, Michael L. *Litigation*
Tepper, Eric Alan *Vehicle and traffic*
Terrell, J. Anthony *Project and municipal finance*
Thoron, Gray *Legal ethics and professional discipline*
Tishler, Nicholas Eugene *Appellate civil, criminal, state and fed. cts.*
Tondel, Lawrence Chapman *Partnership Law*
Trope, Jack Frederick *Indian law*
Tucker, Stephen *Space law*
Vernon, Darryl Mitchell *Animal rights*
Viener, John David *Corporations, Taxation*
Walsh, John Bronson *Lobbying*
Warshauer, Irene Conrad *Product liability*
Wehringer, Cameron Kingsley *Space*
Weil, Gilbert Harry *Trade regulation*
Weinstock, David S(tanley) *Food, drug and cosmetic law, Federal practice*
Weir, John Keeley *Aviation*
Williamson, Walter *Civil litigation*
Willinger, Warren Jay *Products liability, Medical malpractice*
Windman, Joel A. *Trade Regulation*
Wolf, Lewis Isidore *Appeals*
Woolley, Edward Alexander *Containers*
York, Louis B. *Welfare*
Young, Michael Richard *Mergers and acquisitions*
Zimmerman, Golda *Adoptions*

North Carolina

Brooks, Dexter *Civil litigation*
Burns, Byron Bernard, Jr. *Venture capital*
Carrington, Paul DeWitt
Ganly, David Milton *Pension, profit-sharing, and employee benefits*
Glass, Fred Stephen *Medical*
Hubbard, Thomas Edwin (Tim) *Food and Drug*
Hurewitz, David Lewis *Intellectual property licensing*
Jorgensen, Ralph Gubler *Tax litigation*
Luney, Percy Robert, Jr. *Natural resources law*
Mineo, Robert Anthony *Aviation*
Parker, Daniel Louis *Investment banking*
Reppy, William Arneill, Jr.
Ross, John Bowen, Jr. *Technology transfer*
Schmutz, John Francis *Franchising*
Shefte, Dalbert Uhrig *Unfair competition*
Simpson, Steven Drexell *Exempt organizations*
Wilson, Samuel Alexander, III *Judicial and recruitment; commutations and pardons; extraditions*

North Dakota

Alleva, Patti Ann *Federal courts, Intellectual property*
Bucklin, Leonard Herbert *Products liability litigation*
Crockett, Richard Boyd *Higher education law*
Kingstad, Timothy Lorens *Land use and planning*
Minch, Roger James *Agricultural law*
Snyder, Robert John *State and federal civil litigation*

Ohio

Andorka, Frank Henry *Character merchandise licensing*
Angel-Shaffer, Arlene Beth *Social security disability*
Bailey, Daniel Allen *Director and officer liability*
Barrett, David Carroll *Agricultural*
Berger, Sanford Jason *Constitutional*
Booth, Robert Alvin *Legal Publishing*
Brown, Eric Steven *Small business consulting and litigation, Education and schools*
Buchenroth, Stephen Richard *Franchise law.*
Budish, Armond David *Consumer law*
Carro, Jorge Luis *Legal ethics*
Cassidy, William Anthony *Child pornography*
Chatroo, Arthur Jay *High technology venture capital*
Christenson, Gordon A. *Constitutional*
Comstock, Clyde Nelson *Mining and minerals*
Conner, William Herbert *Tax-exempt financing*
Edmiston, Robert Gray *Equine law*
Faigin, Arnold Jeffrey *Sports*
Fazio, John Cesare *Legal publishing*
Galip, Ronald George *Shopping centers*
Garner, James Parent *Sports*
Gleisser, Marcus David *Investments*
Goldberg, Steven Charles *Transportation*
Gustaferro, Barbara Jean *State and federal civil litigation, Plantiff and defense*
Haase, William Xavier *Mergers, acquisitions & leveraged buyouts*
Huhn, Richard M. *Federal Employers' Liability Act (railroad)*
Kancler, Edward *Zoning litigation*
Leb, Arthur S. *Education and schools*
Lewis, James William *Arson and insurance fraud defense law*
Lucas, John Michael *Transportation*
McMahon, Michael Sean *Election and campaign finance law*
Millhoff, Patricia Ann *Mental health*
Namanworth, Eli *toxic tort litigation, state and federal*
Nelson, David Aldrich
Nippert, Alfred Kuno, Jr. *Transportation*
Paddock, Harold Dewolf *Alternative dispute resolution*
Palmer, Thomas Earl *Coal Industry*
Roscoe, George Dennis *Social security*
Rosen, Gary Mitchell *Mental health*
Scanlon, Lawrence Joseph *Professional negligence*
Schoeni, Kenneth Roger *Sports law*
Skulina, Thomas Raymond *Railroad*
Streicher, James Franklin *Partnership*
Strozdas, Jerome Mark *Agriculture*
Stuhldreher, George William *Professional liability defense*
Todt, Daniel Thomas *International finance*
Ucker, David A. *Medical-legal*
Waiwood, Michael Francis *Civil litigation*
Wayne, Richard Stuart *Litigation securities and complex commercial transaction, General buy-sells, organizations and reorganizations*
Wilson, Harrison Benjamin, III *Product liability*
Wolfe, John Leslie *Civil litigation*
Zwayer, Ted *Municipal law*

Oklahoma

Andrews, John Charles
Baker, Thomas Edward *Oil and gas law*
Beauchamp, James Harry
Bell, William Henry *Tax exempt organizations*
Britton, James Edward *Franchise law*
Burget, Mark Edward *Taxation partnership*
Cogdell, Joe Bennett, Jr. *Tax litigation*
Day, Ronald Liles *Education law*
Fish, John Mancil, Jr. *Licensing and Technology Transfer*
Fulton, Robert Edward *Public administration.*
Gordon, Jack Elliott, Jr. *Civil litigation*
Hansen, Carol M. *Poverty law*
Hitchcock, Bion Earl *Intellectual property*
Krepps, Ethel Constance *Indian law*
Miller, Michael John *Mental health*
Rife, Gary Alan *Professional responsibility, lawyer discipline*
Sparks, John O. *Oil and gas*
Swimley, Gary Wallace *Unemployment benefits*
Willey, Benjamin Tucker, Jr. *Oil and gas, Civil litigation*
Young, John Mark *Tort litigation*

Oregon

Baer, Peter Edward *Mining*
Bowerman, Donald Bradley *Medical legal malpractice, Aviation business litigation*
Brown, Gene L. *General mining law*
DuBoff, Leonard David *Art law*
Fenner, John Benjamin *Charitable foundations*
Frohnmayer, David Braden *State government*
Gangle, Sandra Smith *Arbitration*
Glasgow, William Jacob *Leveraged leasing*
Greene, Michael Alan *Legal malpractice*
Horrigan, Elizabeth Brander *Bond and debt services for national bank*
Huffman, James Lloyd *Constitutional*
Kester, Randall Blair *Insurance and Railroad and transportation law*
Kronenberg, Debra Ann *Social Security*
McMenamin, Robert William *General corporate and Clergy malpractice*
Miller, David Kenneth *Medical malpractice defense*
Raines, Keith R. *Public interest law*
Spiegel, Laurence Harold *Adoption*
Sullivan, Edward Joseph *Planning and zoning*
Tilbury, Roger Graydon *Trial appellate negligence*

Pennsylvania

Alstadt, Lynn Jeffery *Trade regulation*
Anderson, Margret Elizabeth *product liability, food and drug*
Anderson, Toni-Renee *Legal research*
Ashcraft, John Marion, III *Legal research*
Auten, David Charles
Beasley, James Edwin
Beer, Lawrence Ward *Japanese*
Berger, David *Class actions, commercial litigation, mass torts, toxic torts litigation*
Bower, Ward Alan *Law office management and marketing*
Bromfield, Wayne Allan
Browne, Michael L. *Transportaion*
Camen, Toby Paul *Aviation*
Candris, Laura A. *Employment law and contracts, wrongful discharge*
Carson, Timothy Joseph
Cook, Cameron H. *Custom import and export*
Dorfman, John Charles *Unfair competition*
Duroni, Charles Eugene *General counsel*
Eagan, Charlene Ann *Food and drug*
Elliott, John Michael *Constitutional law*
Feldmann, Louis George *Industrial development*
Flanagan, Joseph Patrick, Jr. *Public finance*
Fox, James Robert *Air and space law*
Freedman, Barbara Widman *Partnership taxation*
Garfinkel, Marvin *Franchising*
Georgiades, Peter Nicholas *Civil litigation with cultic groups and orgns.*
Gerstenhaber, Murray *Statistical questions in law*
Guyton, Odell *Crime victim's rights.*
Haddon, Phoebe Anniese *Constituional law*
Hamilton, Perrin C. *Constitutional law*
Hunter, Martha Louise *Voting rights and apportionment*
Kelsen, Peter Foster *Land use and planning*
Kulp, Dolores Rocco *Federal employer's liability*
Laub, George Cooley *College law*
Lieberman, George Eric *Railroad*
Manning, James Hamington, Jr. *Premise security litigation*
Marsico, Leonard Joseph *Commercial litigation*
Mayer, Ann Elizabeth *Islamic law, Middle Eastern Law*
McKeever, John Eugene *Postal law*
Meisel, Alan *Mental health*
Minney, Michael Jay *Criminal sentencing*
Moores, Edward Harrison *Litigation*
Mundheim, Robert Harry *Securities*
Murdoch, David Armor *Creditors rights*
Murren, Philip Joseph *Constitutional law, Nonprofit organizations*
Muth, Michael Raymond *Senior citizen advocacy*
Newberg, Herbert Barkan *Class actions*
Newman, John Andrew *Tax policy development*
Perry, Sherryl R. *Products liability, Preventive law, insurance law*
Pilgrim, Gail Louise *Food and drug*
Prewitt, David Edward *Aviation litigation*
Quay, Thomas Emery *Food and drug*
Rathgeber, Joanne Weil *State and federal civil litigation*
Reitz, Curtis Randall *Professional responsibility*
Schulte, Jeffrey Lewis *Resource recovery*
Shestack, Jerome Joseph *Communications*
Siedzikowski, Henry Francis *Franchising and distribution*
Smith, John Francis, III *Business negotiations*
Spry, Donald Francis, II *Education and schools*
Stepanian, Steven Arvid, II *Corporate finance*
Stevens, Paul Lawrence *Education law*
Straub, J(ames) Kurt *Products liability defense*
Strauss, Edward Kenneth *International finance*
Tabas, Lawrence Jeffrey *Public election law*
Urey, David Stauffer *Licensing, technology transfer*
Weisz, Frank Barry *Life Insurance/estate and business planning*
Wiley, Jan M. *Corporations*
Wise, Sandra Elizabeth *Constitutional law, Nonprofit organizations*
Wolke, Milton Spencer, Jr. *Financial*
Wolkin, Paul Alexander *Continuing legal education*
Yares, Howard Scott *Delivery of legal services*
Zimmerman, Dona Hope *Bar review program*

Rhode Island

Dickinson, Thomas More *Appellate practice*
Isaacs, Michael Burton *Communications*
Keough, Joseph Aloysios

Lombardi, Valentino Dennis *Medicare Part B and OCHAMPUS Hearing Officer*
Wiley, H. Seymour *Advising Developers*

South Carolina

Boyd, Stanley Jeffrey, Jr. *Education for summary court judges*
McLawhorn, Richard Edward *executive*
Pritchard, Michael Gregg *Management civil legal services program*
Smiley, Robert Rennslaer, III *Aviation*
Wedlock, Eldon Dyment, Jr. *Constitutional*
Wells, Robert Steven *Professional responsibility*

South Dakota

Carlsen, Chris Jeffrey *Sports law*
Fosheim, Jon *Constitutional*
Reed, Walter Dudley *Professional responsibility and legal education*

Tennessee

Anderson, Stephen Guy
Aronson, Morton Henry *franchising*
Bennett, Andy Dwane *Tennessee constitutional law*
Bird, Frank Babington *Bond issues*
Burcham, Randall Parks *State and federal litigation, Real estate and probate*
Carnall, George Hursey, II *Franchising*
Catalano, Michael William *Legislative reapportionment*
Congleton, Joseph Patrick *Coal*
Howell, Morton Boyte *Litigation*
Ramsaur, Allan Fields *Public benefits*
Wiltshire, Ashley Turman, Jr. *Legal services/legal aid*
Yarbrough, Edward Meacham *Domestic relations litigation*

Texas

Alford, Margaret Suzanne *Exempt organizations*
Allen, Joan Howard *Education law*
Anderson, Doris Ehlinger
Arnett, Richard Lynn *Commercial litigation*
Blair, John Houston *Oil and gas law*
Boss, Steven Sprague *Energy, oil and gas contracts*
Branhagen, Darrel Raymond *Government contracts*
Brookhart, Walter Ray *Trade secret and unfair competition*
Browning, John Raum *Aviation*
Bumpas, Stuart Maryman *Non-profit organizations*
Burleson, Karen Tripp *Contracts and general corporate consulting*
Butler, Gary Frank
Byrd, Linward Tonnett *Aviation*
Carmody, James Albert *Business litigation*
Carr, Thomas Eldridge *School law*
Cunningham, G. Kevin *Oil and gas*
Cunyus, George Marvin *Oil and gas exploration and production*
Duenser, Ruth Edwards *Election law*
Eiland, Gary Wayne
Ellinger, Steven *Sports*
Ellis, David Dale
Falls, Craig Thomas *Financial institutions*
Fitzpatrick, Sandra Marlene *Family*
Fluke, Randall Lynn *Criminal prosecution*
Forbes, Thomas Allen *Public finance*
Goodstein, Barnett Maurice *Arbitration*

Gorman, Joseph Thomas, Jr. *Representation of savings and loans associations*
Greenberg, Howard Ralph *Technology licensing*
Hendricks, Randal Arlan *Sports*
Hodgins, Daniel Stephen *Biotechnology*
Holmes, Marian McGrath
Howard, Timothy Jon *Corporate finance and structuring joint ventures*
Johnson, Edward Michael *Investment banking*
Junell, Robert Alan *Products liability*
Kelly, Joseph Patrick *Federal and State civil litigation*
Kemp, William Franklin *Home health services*
Kincaid, Eugene D., III *Mining and minerals*
Kivelson, Nancy Lynn *Real property finance--conventional and equity, Tax exempt financing*
Law, Thomas Hart
Ledlie, Douglas Edward *Taxation, partnerships*
Levin, Harvey Phillip *Occupational disease consultant*
Loeffler, James Joseph *Management labor law*
Lofgren, Norman Arthur *Taxation of Natural Resources*
Manning, B. Herbert *Governmental assistance and financing elderly housing*
McAninch, Edwin Lee *Wrongful death*
McNamara, Lawrence John *Trade secret litigation*
Parker, Allan Edward *Litigation and school law*
Pettiette, Alison Yvonne *Products liability*
Phillips, Kathleen A. *Energy, minerals, precious metals*
Porter, Jeffrey James *Mergers and acquisitions, secured transactions*
Roberts, Harry Morris, Jr. *Purchase and development*
Roberts, Thomas Alba *Mergers and acquisitions*
Robinett, Mark Webster *School law*
Sagehorn, Thomas John *Franchise law*
Sanders, Thelma E. *Civil rights*
Schulman, Michael Robert *Municipal and public finance*
Simmons, Stephen Judson *Franchising*
Simon, Hinda Bookstaber *Art, Exempt organizations*
Sing, William Bender
Sutherland, Richard Thomas *Consumer protection and deceptive trade practices*
Taylor, Joseph William *Oil and gas*
Tiller, Edward Allan *Tax, international*
Wagner, Leslie *Law placement*
Waugh (Zucker), Karin Welles *Medical bioethics*
Westbrook, Joel Whitsitt, III *Litigation*
Winick, Mitchel Lane *Mergers and acquisitions, Management consulting*
Zipprich, John L., II *Religious congregations*

Utah

Abbott, Charles Favour, Jr. *Marketing law*
Dragoo, Denise Ann *Mining and minerals*
Frederick, Joel Dennis
Jensen, Dallin W. *Natural resources*
Madson, Craig James *Franchise law*
Murphy, Michael R.
Nelson, Merrill Francom *Education, hospital and church law*
Pruitt, Robert Grady, Jr. *Mining and minerals*

Ross, Yan Michael *Mergers and acquisitions*
Thorpe, Calvin E. *Unfair competition*
Wilkinson, David Lawrence

Vermont

Marsh, Pamela Alison *Mental health*
Ochmanski, Charles James *Legal association executive*
O'Donnell, Robert John *Mediation*

Virginia

Appleton, Randall Eugene *Federal employer's liability act*
Bozarth, Robert Stephen *Land titles*
Bridewell, Sherry Hazelwood *Utility law*
Broadbent, Peter Edwin, Jr. *Communications*
Burrus, Robert Lewis, Jr. *Corporate finance and taxation*
Bybee, Jay Scott *Constitutional law*
Calkins, Gary Nathan *Air*
Campbell, George Wendal, Jr. *Corporate and Business law*
Clinard, Robert Noel *Franchise law*
Connelly, Sharon Rudolph *Export control law*
Feldman, Richard Jay *Political consulting*
Goolrick, Robert Mason *Business finance*
Helvin, Stephen Holland
Jameson, Paula Ann *Communications*
Kelly, Lawrence Edward *Land use and planning*
Kieff, Nelson Richard *Constitutional law*
Kleiler, James Robert *Natural resources law, public land law*
Landin, David Craig *Industry wide litigation*
Lanphear, Martha Jean *Personnel law*
Massey, Arthur Blanton *Personal financial management law*
McCann, John Anthony *Advocacy*
Moorstein, Mark Alan *Real estate finance*
Moshos, Arthur Leon *Negligence*
Price, Ilene Rosenberg *Telecommunications*
Pugh, William Wallace *Transportation*
Ranier, Norman B.
Regirer, Walter Wlodzimierz
Rouland, Jay Thomas *Legal association executive*
Simmonds, James Henry *Contracts*
Smith, James Randolph, Jr.
Steffen, Joseph John, Jr. *Education law*
Taubman, Glenn Matthew *Constitutional Law*
Theberge, Norman Bartlett *Law, science and resource management*
Thomson, Paul Rice, Jr. *Coal and energy*
Trompeter, Philip *Mental Health*
Trout, Stran Lippincott *Government management*
Walkup, Charlotte Lloyd *International trade*
Weckstein, Clifford Robert
Wellons, William Lindley
Whittemore, F(rank) Case *Energy, coal*
Wimbish, Robert Allan *Transportation, Railroad-commerce law*

Washington

Chellis, Eugene Clifton *Civil litigation*
Collette, Kevin J. *Computer*
Cullitan, Reginald Kenneth *General assistant to Chief Judge Robert J. McNichols*

Cunningham, Janis Ann *Adoptions*
Dawson, Edward A. *Toxic tort, Professional negligence litigation*
Day, Stephen Leo *Transportation*
Dillon, Janet Jordan *Indian law*
Dowdy, Robert Alan *Transportation*
Dussault, William L.E. *Disability and mental health law*
Duvall, Gary Ross *Franchising*
Fritzler, Randal Brandt *Arbitration and alternative dispute resolution methods*
Gardner, Alan Joel *Federal and state regulatory*
Gilyeart, Steven Craig *Equipment leasing*
Gustafson, Albert Katsuaki *International*
Haggard, Joel Edward *Land use*
Henderson, Kevin James *Franchising*
Hill, (George) Richard *Zoning*
Krutch, Richard Francis *Aviation*
Ludolph, Marla Rose *Social security disability*
McCoy, Brian Lloyd *State and federal civil litigation*
Moses, Gene Ronald *Insurance defense litigation*
Pence, Christopher Cyrus *Professional negligence*
Riddell, Richard Harry
Ryan, James Francis *Land use and planning*
Sill, Peter Lewis
Silvernale, Lawrence Duggan *Railroad law*
Tollefson, G. Val *Aviation*
Woolston, V.L. *Products liability litigation*

West Virginia

Blair, Andrew Lane *Church law*
Chaney, Michael Thomas *energy, coal, oil and gas*
Kennedy, David Tinsley *Arbitration*
Lewin, Jeff Lee *Law and economics*
Rich, Wayne Adrian, Jr. *Government attorney*
Stone, Samuel Spencer *Arbitration*

Wisconsin

Baldwin, Janice Murphy *Marital property*
Burroughs, John Townsend *Medical malpractice*
De Bruin, David Lee *Scientific and technical litigation*
Gaines, Irving David *Civil litigation*
Gronowski, Joseph Edward *Fidelity and surety*
Haarmann, Bruce Donald *Commercial collections*
Hansher, David Allen *Transportation*
Jurkovic, Daniel John
Kwiatkowski, Thomas Eugene *School law*
Mann, Douglas Floyd *State court receiverships*
Melin, Robert Arthur *Charitable organizations*
Nedwek, Thomas Wayne
Noelke, Paul
Pellino, Charles Edward, Jr. *Federal tax litigation*
Schober, Thomas Leonard *Transportation rail*
Tuerkheimer, Barbara Wolfson *Consumer protection*
Wren, Christopher Gove *Criminal law, appellate*

Wyoming

Lowe, Robert Stanley *Oil and gas*
Spence, Gerald Leonard *Product liability*

FRANCE

Cochran, John M., III *International commercial arbitration, Common market, antitrust*
MacCrindle, Robert Alexander *Arbitration*

LUXEMBOURG

Dennemeyer, John James *Patent and trademark software development*

REPUBLIC OF KOREA

Sabo, William Denes *Technology related law*

SWITZERLAND

Ulmer, Nicolas Courtland *International commercial arbitration*

THAILAND

Enos, Priscilla Beth *Professional development*

ADDRESS UNPUBLISHED

Alexander, James Patrick *Litigation*
Bamberger, Michael Albert *Publishing*
Branscomb, Anne Wells (Mrs. Lewis McAdory Branscomb) *Communications*
Brotman, Stuart Neil *Communications*
Casper, Gerhard *Constitutional*
Eovaldi, Thomas L. *Consumer protection*
Flechner, Stephen E.
Garrigues, Gayle Lynne *Indian law*
Glantz, Ronald Paul *Negotiations*
Kadish, Lloyd Alan *Commodities and Trading*
Kegan, Esther Oswianza *Food, Drug and Medical Devices*
Klein, Judah B. *Title Insurance*
Koeller, Robert Marion *Venture Capital*
Lackmann, Ernest Albin
Leleiko, Steven Henry *Non-Profit Organizations*
Magness, Michael Kenneth *Management consultant to legal profession*
Manget, Frederic Fairfield *National security matters*
Mell, Patricia *Alternative dispute resolution*
Morimoto, Mary A. *Business*
Moylan, James Joseph
Norton, Jane Marie *Legal editing & writing*
Olsen, Kenneth Allen *Transportation*
Palmer, Rudolph Martin, Jr. *Father's rights in abortion*
Randall, Roger Darrel
Richardson, Robert Owen *Patent Arbitration*
Rosenberg, Arthur Harrison *Aviation litigation*
Ryan, William J. *Pharmaceutical drug and medical devices*
Schiesswohl, Cynthia Rae Schlegel *Church law*
Schulman, Joanne *Poverty law*
Siris, Michael John *Transportation*
Stephens, Henry L., Jr. *Mining and minerals*
Tanenbaum, Jay Harvey *Commercial litigation*
Weiss, Alvin
Woodruff, Charles Norman *Water rights*
Woronoff, David Smulyan *Unfair Competition*